American Men & Women of Science

1998-99 • 20th Edition

The 20th edition of *AMERICAN MEN & WOMEN OF SCIENCE* was
prepared by the R.R. Bowker Database Publishing Group in
collaboration with the Publication Systems Department.

Senior Staff of the Database Publishing Group includes:

Senior Vice President & Chief Operating Officer, R.R. Bowker
Neal Goff

Publisher
Nan Hudes

Vice President, Database Publishing
Leigh Yuster-Freeman

Editorial:
Director: *Owen O'Donnell*
Managing Editor: *Karen Hallard*
Senior Editor: *Alison J. Butkiewicz*
Associate Editors: *Angela Krakow*
　　　　　　　　　Elizabeth McCarthy

Research:
Director: *Judy Redel*
Senior Managing Editor: *Tanya Hurst*
Senior Editor: *Beverly Heath*

Tampa Division:
Director: *Valerie Harris*
Production Manager: *Debra Wilson*
Associate Coordinator: *Jennifer Rodgers*

American Men & Women of Science

1998-99 • 20th Edition

A Biographical Directory of Today's Leaders in Physical, Biological and Related Sciences.

Volume 4 • J-L

R.R. BOWKER
A Unit of Reed Elsevier Business Information
New Providence, New Jersey

Published by R.R. Bowker, A Unit of Reed Elsevier Business Information

Copyright© 1998 by Reed Elsevier Inc. All rights reserved. Except as permitted under the Copyright Act of 1976, no part of *American Men and Women of Science* may be reproduced or transmitted in any form or by any means stored in any information storage and retrieval system, without prior written permission of R.R. Bowker, 121 Chanlon Road, New Providence, New Jersey, 07974.

International Standard Book Number
    Set: 0-8352-3748-6
    Volume 1: 0-8352-3749-4
    Volume 2: 0-8352-3775-3
    Volume 3: 0-8352-3776-1
    Volume 4: 0-8352-3778-8
    Volume 5: 0-8352-3779-6
    Volume 6: 0-8352-3781-8
    Volume 7: 0-8352-3782-6
    Volume 8: 0-8352-3783-4

International Standard Serial Number: 0192-8570
Library of Congress Catalog Card Number: 6-7326
Printed and bound in the United States of America.

R.R. Bowker has used its best efforts in collecting and preparing material for inclusion in this publication but does not warrant that the information herein is complete or accurate, and does not assume, and hereby disclaims, any liability to any person for any loss or damage caused by errors or omissions in *American Men and Women of Science*, whether such errors or omissions result from negligence, accident or any other cause.

8 Volume Set

ISBN 0-8352-3748-6

9 780835 237482

Contents

Advisory Committee vi

Preface vii

Major Honors & Awards ix

Statistics xi

Sample Entry xvii

Abbreviations xviii

Biographies 1

Advisory Committee

Dr. Charles Henderson Dickens
Former Executive Secretary, Federal Coordinating Council for Science, Engineering & Technology
Office of Science & Technology Policy

Dr. Oscar Nicolas Garcia
NCR Distinguished Professor & Chair, Department of Computer Science & Engineering
Wright State University

Dr. Michael J. Jackson
Executive Director
Federation of American Societies for Experimental Biology

Dr. Shirley Mahaley Malcom
Head, Directorate for Education and Human Resources Programs
American Association for the Advancement of Science

Ms. Beverly Fearn Porter
Assistant to the Executive Director for Society Relations
American Institute of Physics

Dr. William Eldon Splinter
Former Vice Chancellor for Research
University of Nebraska-Lincoln

Dr. Dael Lee Wolfle
Professor Emeritus, Graduate School of Public Affairs
University of Washington

Dr. Ahmed H. Zewail
Linus Pauling Professor of Chemistry & Physics
California Institute of Technology

Preface

American Men and Women of Science remains without peer as a chronicle of North American and Canadian scientific endeavor and achievement. The present work is the twentieth edition since it was first compiled as *American Men of Science* by J. McKeen Cattell in 1906. In its ninety-two year history, *American Men and Women of Science* has profiled the careers of over 300,000 scientists and engineers. Since the first edition, the number of American scientists and the fields they pursue has grown immensely. This edition alone lists full biographies for 119,618 engineers and scientists, 4184 of which are listed for the first time. Although the book has grown, our stated purpose is the same as when Dr. Cattell first undertook the task of producing a biographical directory of active American scientists. It was his intention to record educational, personal and career data which would make "a contribution to the organization of science in America" and "make men [and women] of science acquainted with one another and with one another's work." It is our hope that this edition will fulfill these goals.

The biographies of engineers and scientists constitute seven of the eight volumes and provide birthdate, birthplace, field of specialty, education, honorary degrees, current position, professional and concurrent experience, awards, memberships, research information and addresses for each entrant when applicable. The eighth volume, the discipline index, organizes biographees by field of activity. This index, adapted from the National Science Foundation's Taxonomy of Degree and Employment Specialties, classifies entrants by 192 subject specialties listed in the table of contents of Volume 8. The index lists scientists and engineers by state within each subject specialty, allowing the user to easily locate a scientist in a given area. Also included are statistical information and charts showing the distribution of *AMWS* listees by age and discipline and and annotated listing of the recipients of the Nobel Prizes, the Craaford Prize, the Charles Stark Draper Prize, the National Medals of Science and Technology, the Fields Medal and the Alan T. Waterman Award since the last edition.

While the scientific fields covered by *American Men and Women of Science* are comprehensive, no attempt has been made to include all American scientists. Entrants are meant to be limited to those who have made significant contributions in their field. The names of new entrants were submitted for consideration at the editors' request by current entrants and by leaders of academic, government and private research programs and associations. Those included met the following criteria:

1. Distinguished achievement, by reason of experience, training or accomplishment, including contributions to literature, coupled with continuing activity in scientific work;

or

2. Research activity of high quality in science as evidenced by publication in reputable scientific journals; or, for those whose work cannot be published due to governmental or industrial security, research activity of high quality in science as evidenced by the judgement of the individual's peers;

or

3. Attainment of a position of substantial responsibility requiring scientific training and experience.

This edition profiles living scientists in the physical and biological fields, as well as public health scientists, engineers, mathematicians, statisticians, and computer scientists. The information is collected by means of direct communication whenever possible. All entrants receive forms for corroboration and updating. New entrants receive questionaires and verification proofs before publication. The information submitted by entrants is included as completely as possible within the boundaries of editorial and space restrictions. If an entrant does not return the form and his or her current location can be verified in secondary sources, the full entry is repeated. References to the previous edition are given for those who do not return forms and cannot be located, but who are presumed to be still active in science or engineering. Entrants known to be deceased are noted as such and a reference to the previous edition is given. Scientists and engineers who are not citizens of the United States or Canada are included if a significant portion of their work was performed in North America.

The information in *American Men & Women of Science* is available on magnetic tape. For information, contact Bowker Electronic Publishing (888-BOWKER-2). *American Men and Women of Science* is also available for online searching through Lexis®-Nexis® (800-227-4908) and through DIALOG, a service of Knight-Ridder Information, Inc. (800-334-2564). The online products allow fielded as well as key word searches of all elements of a record, including field of interest, experience, and location. An ERL-compliant CD-ROM is available through SilverPlatter Information (800-343-0064). Mailing lists are available through Reed Elsevier Business Information Lists (John Panza, Account Manager, Bowker Files, 245 W 17th St, New York, NY, 10011; 212-337-7164).

A project as large as publishing *American Men and Women of Science* involves the efforts of a great many people. The editors take this opportunity to thank the twentieth edition advisory committee for their guidance, encouragement and support. Appreciation is also expressed to the many scientific societies who provided their membership lists for the purpose of locating former entrants whose addresses had changed, and to the tens of thousands of scientists across the country who took time to provide us with biographical information. We also wish to thank Donna Brinkmann and Carol Carr of Reed Technology & Information Services, Inc. for their assistance in the successful production of this directory.

Comments, suggestions and nominations for the twenty-first edition are encouraged and should be directed to The Editors, *American Men and Women of Science*, R.R. Bowker, 121 Chanlon Road, New Providence, New Jersey, 07974.

Karen Hallard
Managing Editor

Major Honors & Awards

Nobel Prizes
Nobel Foundation, Royal Swedish Academy of Sciences & Nobel Assembly of the Karolinska

The Nobel Prizes were established in 1900 (and first awarded in 1901) to recognize those people who "have conferred the greatest benefit on mankind."

1995 Recipients

Chemistry:
   Paul Josef Crutzen, Mario Jose Molina & Frank Sherwood Rowland
Awarded "for their work in atmospheric chemistry, particularly concerning the formation and decomposition of ozone."

Physics:
   Martin Lewis Perl
   Frederick Reines
Awarded to Perl "for the discovery of the tau lepton" and to Reines "for the detection of the nutrino."

Physiology or Medicine:
   Edward B. Lewis, Christiane Nusslein-Volhard & Eric F. Wieschaus
Awarded "for their discoveries concerning the genetic control of early embryonic development."

1996 Recipients

Chemistry:
   Robert Floyd Curl, Harold Walter Kroto & Richard Errett Smalley
Awarded "for their discovery of fullerenes, carbon atoms bound in the form of a ball."

Physics:
   David Morris Lee, Douglas Dean Osheroff & Robert Coleman Richardson
Awarded "for their discovery of superfluidity in helium-3."

Physiology or Medicine:
   Peter Charles Doherty & Rolf Martin Zinkernagel
Awarded "for their discoveries of how the immune system recognizes virus-infected cells."

1997 Recipients

Chemistry:
   Paul Delos Boyer, Jens Christian Skou & John Ernest Walker
Awarded to Boyer & Walker "for their elucidation of the enzymatic mechanism underlying the synthesis of adenosine triphosphate (ATP)" and to Skou "for the first discovery of an ion-transporting enzyme, NA^+, K^+-ATPase."

Physics:
   Claude Nessin Cohen-Tannoudji, Steven Chu & William Daniel Phillips
Awarded "for their development of methods to cool and trap atoms with laser light."

Physiology or Medicine:
Stanley Ben Prusiner
Awarded to Prusiner for his discovery of prions, a new genre of infectious agents.

Crafoord Prize
Royal Swedish Academy of Sciences

The Crafoord Prize was introduced in 1982 to award scientists in disciplines not covered by the Nobel Prize, namely mathematics, astronomy, geosciences and biosciences.

1995 Recipients

Willi Dansgaard & Nicholas John Shackleton
Awarded "for their fundamental work on developing and applying isotope geological analysis methods for the study of climatic variations during the Quaternary period."

1996 Recipient

Robert McRedie May
Awarded to May "for his pioneering ecological research concerning theoretical analysis of the dynamics of populations, communities and ecosystems."

1997 Recipients

Fred Hoyle & Edwin Ernest Salpeter
Awarded "for their pioneering contributions involving the study of nuclear reactions in stars and stars' development."

Charles Stark Draper Prize
National Academy of Engineering

The Draper Prize, awarded biennially, was introduced in 1989 to recognize engineering achievement.

1995 Recipients

John Robinson Pierce & Harold A. Rosen
Awarded for developing communications satellite technology.

1997 Recipients
Vladimir Haensel
Awarded to Haensel for inventing "Platforming" — platinum reforming to convert petroleum into high-performance fuels.

National Medal of Science
National Science Foundation

The National Medals of Science were established by the United States Congress in 1959 and have been awarded by the President of the United States since 1962. The National Science Foundation's selection criteria are based on the "total impact of an individual's work on the present state of physical, biological, mathematical, engineering, behavioral, or social sciences."

1995 Recipients

Thomas Robert Cech
Hans Georg Dehmelt
Peter Goldreich
Hermann A(nton) Haus
Isabella Lugoski Karle
Louis Nirenberg
Alexander Rich
Roger N. Shepard

1996 Recipients

Wallace Broecker
Norman Ralph Davidson
James L(oton) Flanagan
Richard M. Karp
Chandra Kumar Naranbhai Patel
Ruth Patrick
Paul Anthony Samuelson
Stephen Smale

1997 Recipients

William K. Estes
Darleane Christian Hoffman
Harold Sledge Johnston
Marshall N. Rosenbluth
Martin Schwarzschild (deceased)
James Dewey Watson
Robert A. Weinberg
George West Wetherill
Shing-Tung Yau

Fields Medal
International Mathematical Union

The Fields Medals were established in 1936 by Canadian mathematician John Fields to acknowledge outstanding research by young mathematicians. The medals are awarded every four years at the International Congress of Mathematicians.

1994 Recipients

Jean Bourgain
Pierre Louis Lions
Jean-Christophe Yoccoz
Efim Isaakovich Zelmanof

Awarded to Bourgain for his insights into the geometry of infinite dimensional spaces. Awarded to Lions for advances in non-linear partial differential equations. Awarded to Yoccoz for analyzing the end results of complicated sequences of circle maps. Awarded to Zelmanov for solving the unrestricted Burnside problem.

National Medal of Technology
U.S. Department of Commerce

The National Medals of Technology were created as part of the 1980 Stevenson-Wydler Technology Innovation Act and were first awarded in 1985. They are bestowed by the President of the United States to recognize individuals and companies for their development or commercialization of technology or for their contributions to the establishment of a technologically-trained workforce.

1995 Recipients

Praveen Chaudhari
Jerome John Cuomo
Richard Joseph Gambino
Edward R. McCracken
Sam B. Williams
Alejandro Zaffaroni
Procter & Gamble Company
3M

1996 Recipients

Charles Huron Kaman
Stephanie Louise Kwolek
James C. Morgan
Peter Henry Rose
Johnson & Johnson

1997 Recipients

Norman R. Augustine
Vinton Gray Cerf
Ray Milton Dolby
Robert Elliot Kahn
Robert Steven Ledley

Alan T. Waterman Award
National Science Foundation & National Science Board

Established by the United States Congress in 1975, the Waterman Award is given annually to an outstanding researcher, aged 35 or younger, in any field of science or engineering supported by the National Science Foundation.

1995 Recipient

Matthew P.A. Fisher
Awarded to Fisher "for his pioneering contributions to the theory of disordered superconductors."

1996 Recipient

Robert Mebane Waymouth
Awarded to Waymouth for discovering new ways to make polymers.

1997 Recipient

Eric Allin Cornell
Awarded to Cornell for creation of Bose-Einstein condensate (BEC).

Statistics

Statistical distribution of entrants in *American Men & Women of Science* with U.S. mailing addresses is illustrated on the following five pages. The regional scheme for geographical analysis is diagrammed in the map below. A table enumerating the geographic distribution can be found on page xvi, following the charts. The statistics are compiled by tallying all occurrences of a major index subject. Each scientist may choose to be indexed under as many as four categories; thus, the total number of subject references is greater than the number of entrants in *AMWS*.

All Disciplines

	Number	Percent
Northeast	56,006	34%
Southeast	41,313	25%
North Central	19,699	12%
South Central	12,169	7%
Mountain	11,675	7%
Pacific	25,703	15%
TOTAL	**166,565**	**100%**

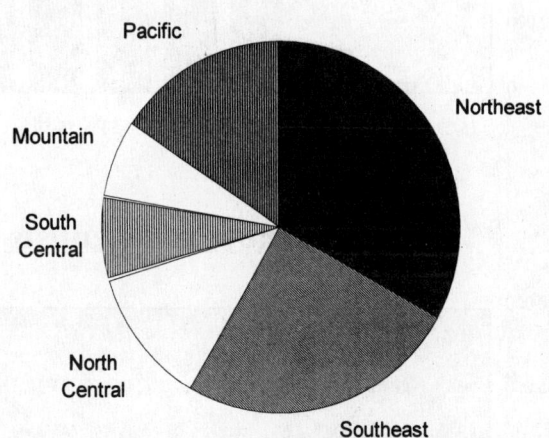

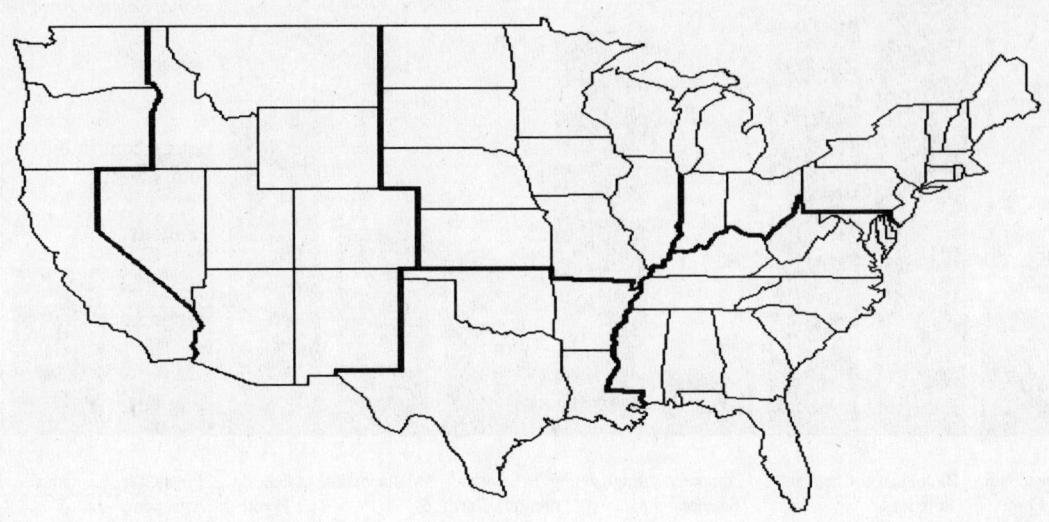

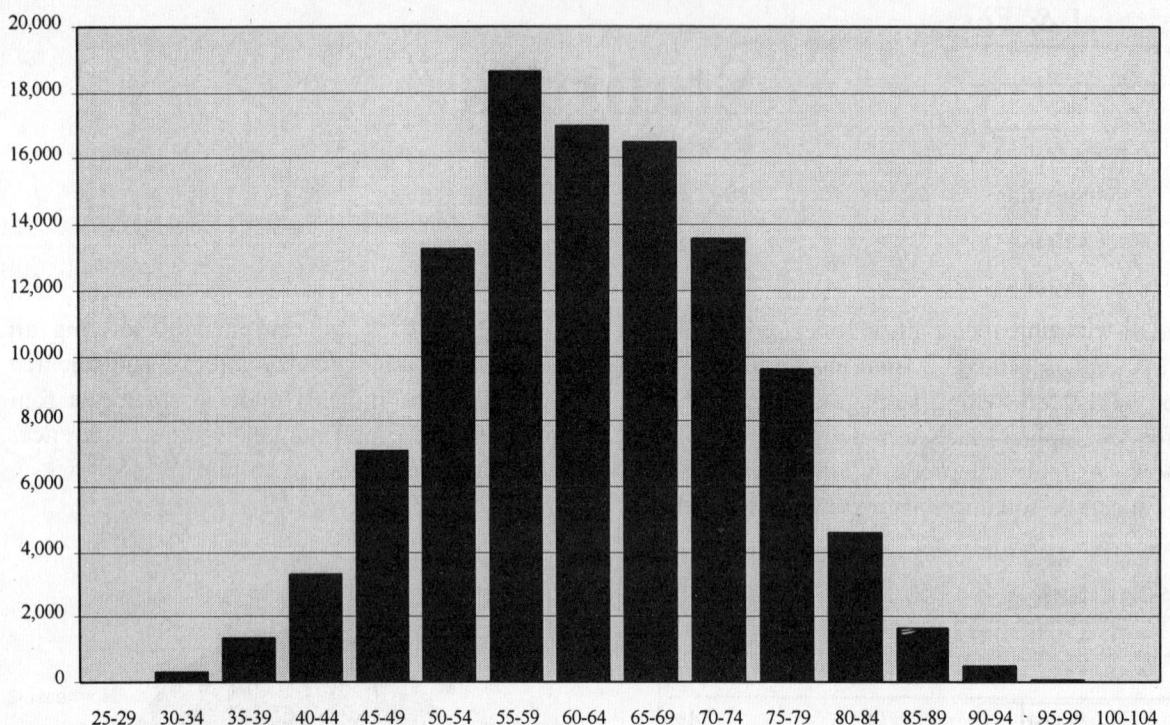
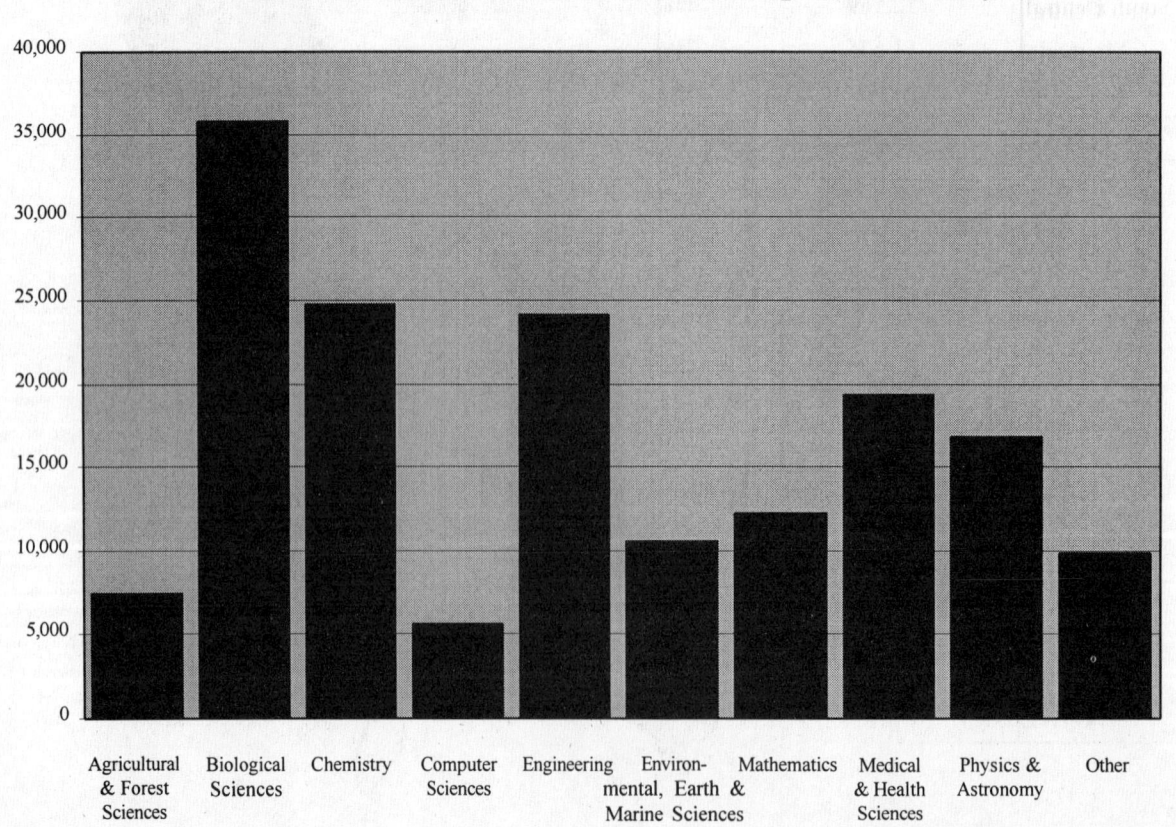

xii

Agricultural & Forest Sciences

	Number	Percent
Northeast	1,585	21%
Southeast	2,053	27%
North Central	1,171	16%
South Central	635	8%
Mountain	739	10%
Pacific	1,305	17%
TOTAL	**7,488**	**100%**

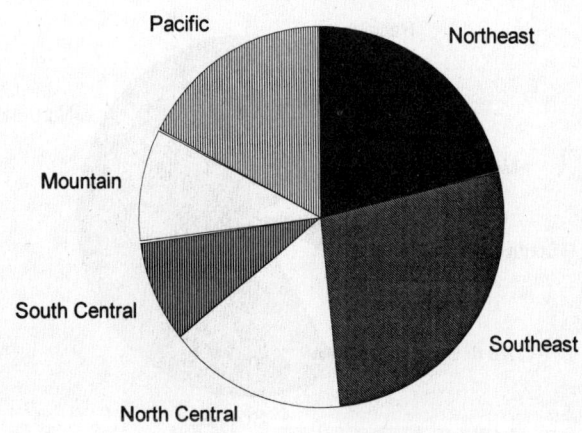

Biological Sciences

	Number	Percent
Northeast	11,671	33%
Southeast	9,045	25%
North Central	4,918	14%
South Central	2,741	8%
Mountain	2,125	6%
Pacific	5,277	15%
TOTAL	**35,777**	**100%**

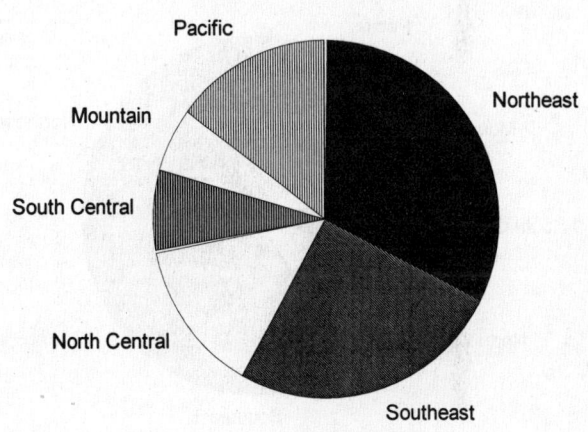

Chemistry

	Number	Percent
Northeast	9,296	38%
Southeast	6,196	25%
North Central	2,964	12%
South Central	1,724	7%
Mountain	1,381	6%
Pacific	3,139	13%
TOTAL	**24,700**	**100%**

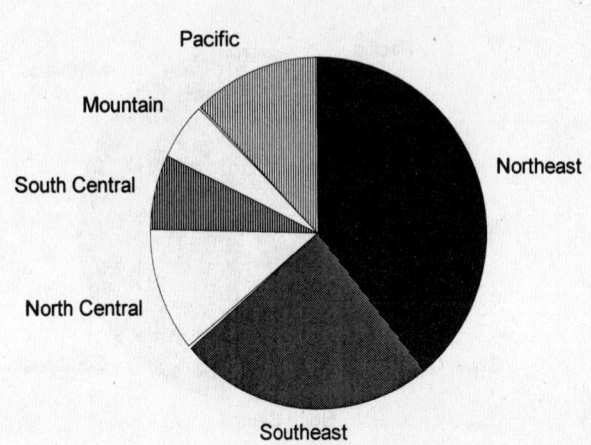

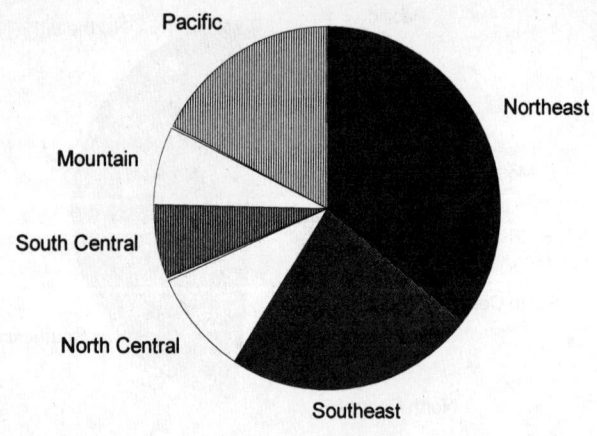

Computer Sciences

	Number	Percent
Northeast	1,983	35%
Southeast	1,278	23%
North Central	556	10%
South Central	378	7%
Mountain	423	7%
Pacific	1,034	18%
TOTAL	**5,652**	**100%**

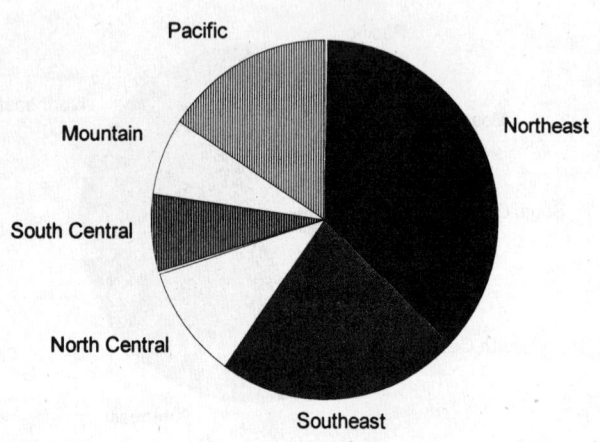

Engineering

	Number	Percent
Northeast	8,780	36%
Southeast	5,487	23%
North Central	2,501	10%
South Central	1,742	7%
Mountain	1,760	7%
Pacific	3,883	16%
TOTAL	**24,153**	**100%**

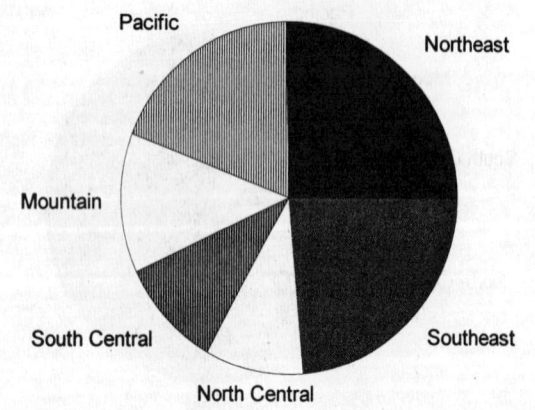

Environmental, Earth & Marine Sciences

	Number	Percent
Northeast	2,654	25%
Southeast	2,507	24%
North Central	984	9%
South Central	1,008	10%
Mountain	1,365	13%
Pacific	2,008	19%
TOTAL	**10,526**	**100%**

Mathematics

	Number	Percent
Northeast	4,292	35%
Southeast	2,865	23%
North Central	1,552	13%
South Central	933	8%
Mountain	760	6%
Pacific	1,901	15%
TOTAL	**12,303**	**100%**

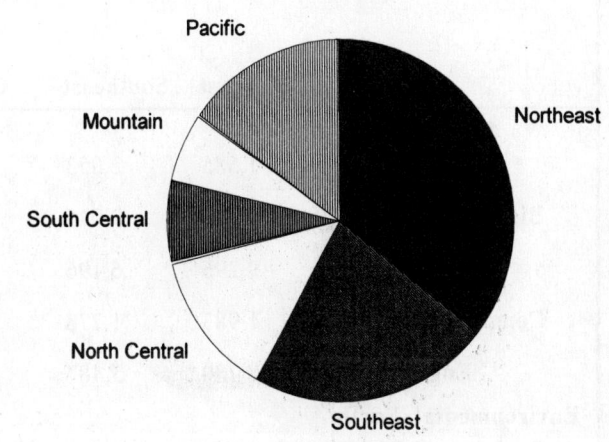

Medical & Health Sciences

	Number	Percent
Northeast	6,883	36%
Southeast	5,139	27%
North Central	2,471	13%
South Central	1,494	8%
Mountain	804	4%
Pacific	2,501	13%
TOTAL	**19,292**	**100%**

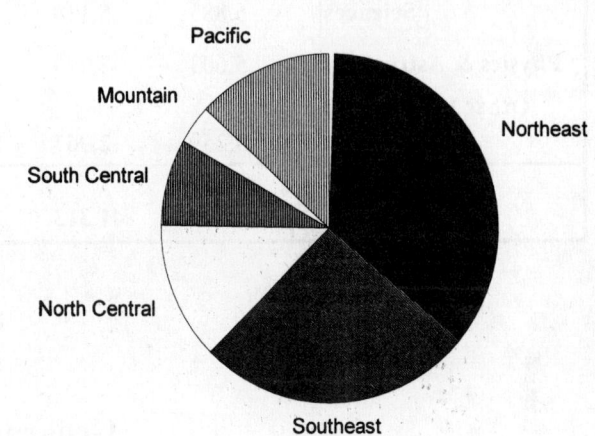

Physics & Astronomy

	Number	Percent
Northeast	5,603	33%
Southeast	3,776	22%
North Central	1,545	9%
South Central	904	5%
Mountain	1,674	10%
Pacific	3,307	20%
TOTAL	**16,809**	**100%**

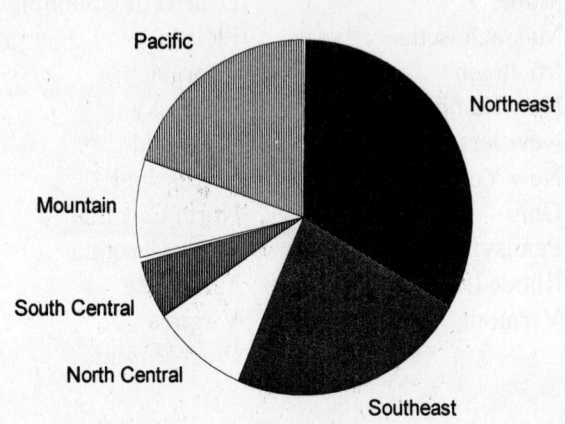

Geographic Distribution of Scientists by Discipline

	Northeast	Southeast	North Central	South Central	Mountain	Pacific	TOTAL
Agricultural & Forest Sciences	1,585	2,053	1,171	635	739	1,305	**7,488**
Biological Sciences	11,671	9,045	4,918	2,741	2,125	5,277	**35,777**
Chemistry	9,296	6,196	2,964	1,724	1,381	3,139	**24,700**
Computer Sciences	1,983	1,278	556	378	423	1,034	**5,652**
Engineering	8,780	5,487	2,501	1,742	1,760	3,883	**24,153**
Environmental, Earth & Marine Sciences	2,654	2,507	984	1,008	1,365	2,008	**10,526**
Mathematics	4,292	2,865	1,552	933	760	1,901	**12,303**
Medical & Health Sciences	6,883	5,139	2,471	1,494	804	2,501	**19,292**
Physics & Astronomy	5,603	3,776	1,545	904	1,674	3,307	**16,809**
Other Professional Fields	3,259	2,967	1,037	610	644	1,348	**9,865**
TOTAL	**56,006**	**41,313**	**19,699**	**12,169**	**11,675**	**25,703**	**166,565**

Geographic Definitions

Northeast
Connecticut
Indiana
Maine
Massachusetts
Michigan
New Hampshire
New Jersey
New York
Ohio
Pennsylvania
Rhode Island
Vermont

Southeast
Alabama
Delaware
District of Columbia
Florida
Georgia
Kentucky
Maryland
Mississippi
North Carolina
South Carolina
Tennessee
Virginia
West Virginia

North Central
Illinois
Iowa
Kansas
Minnesota
Missouri
Nebraska
North Dakota
South Dakota
Wisconsin

South Central
Arkansas
Louisiana
Texas
Oklahoma

Mountain
Arizona
Colorado
Idaho
Montana
Nevada
New Mexico
Utah
Wyoming

Pacific
Alaska
California
Hawaii
Oregon
Washington

Sample Entry

American Men & Women of Science (AMWS) is an extremely useful reference tool. The book is most often used in two ways: to find more information about a particular scientist and to locate a scientist in a specific field.

To locate information about an individual, the biographical section is most helpful. It encompasses the first seven volumes and lists scientists and engineers alphabetically by last name. The fictitious biographical listing shown below illustrates every type of information an entry may include.

The Discipline Index, volume 8, can be used to easily find a scientist in a specific subject specialty. This index is first classified by area of study; within each specialty entrants are divided further by state of residence.

REED, SAMANTHA J(EAN), OCEANOGRAPHY, MARINE BIOLOGY. *Current Pos:* SR ASSOC OCEANOGRAPHER, DEPT NAVY, 86- *Personal Data:* b Brooklyn, NY, Nov 9, 42; m 67, James A. Mayer; c Steven C & Lillian M. *Educ:* Univ Notre Dame, BS, 63, MS, 65, Fla State Univ, PhD(oceanog), 70. *Hon Degrees:* DSc, Univ Calif, Davis, 79. *Honors & Awards:* Henry Bryant Bigelow Medal, Oceanog, 92; *Prof Exp:* Asst prof oceanog, 71-73, assoc prof oceanog & biol, Harvard Univ, 73-75. *Concurrent Pos:* Consult, New England Aquarium, 74-78; vis lect, Wash Univ, 77. *Mem:* AAAS, Am Soc Naval Engrs, Sigma Xi, Oceanog Soc (vpres 82-83). *Res:* Ocean pollution prevention, water treatment and analysis, ecology of marine plankton and sponges, author of 13 publications. *Mailing Address:* 121 102 Smithfield Way, Boca Raton, FL 33431. *Fax:* 407-555-5939; *E-Mail:* sreed@usnavy.mil.fla

Labels: Name, Birthdate, Children's Name(s), Honors & Awards, Concurrent Experience, Memberships, E-Mail Address, Field of Specialty, Current Position, Marriage/Spouse data, Education, Honorary Degrees, Professional Experience, Research and Publications, Mailing Address, Fax Number

Abbreviations

AAAS—American Association for the Advancement of Science
abnorm—abnormal
abstr—abstract
acad—academic, academy
acct—account, accountant, accounting
acoust—acoustic(s), acoustical
ACTH—adrenocorticotrophic hormone
actg—acting
activ—activities, activity
addn—addition(s), additional
Add—Address
adj—adjunct, adjutant
adjust—adjustment
Adm—Admiral
admin—administration, administrative
adminr—administrator(s)
admis—admission(s)
adv—adviser(s), advisory
advan—advance(d), advancement
advert—advertisement, advertising
AEC—Atomic Energy Commission
aerodyn—aerodynamic
aeronaut—aeronautic(s), aeronautical
aerophys—aerophysical, aerophysics
aesthet—aesthetic
AFB—Air Force Base
affil—affiliate(s), affiliation
agr—agricultural, agriculture
agron—agronomic, agronomical, agronomy
agrost—agrostologic, agrostological, agrostology
agt—agent
AID—Agency for International Development
Ala—Alabama
allergol—allergological, allergology
alt—alternate
Alta—Alberta
Am—America, American
AMA—American Medical Association
anal—analysis, analytic, analytical
analog—analogue
anat—anatomic, anatomical, anatomy
anesthesiol—anesthesiology
angiol—angiology
Ann—Annal(s)
ann—annual
anthrop—anthropological, anthropology
anthropom—anthropometric, anthropometrical, anthropometry

antiq—antiquary, antiquities, antiquity
antiqn—antiquarian
apicult—apicultural, apiculture
APO—Army Post Office
app—appoint, appointed
appl—applied
appln—application
approx—approximate(ly)
Apr—April
apt—apartment(s)
aquacult—aquaculture
arbit—arbitration
arch—archives
archaeol—archaeological, archaeology
archit—architectural, architecture
Arg—Argentina, Argentine
Ariz—Arizona
Ark—Arkansas
artil—artillery
asn—association
assoc(s)—associate(s), associated
asst(s)—assistant(s), assistantship(s)
assyriol—Assyriology
astrodyn—astrodynamics
astron—astronomical, astronomy
astronaut—astronautical, astronautics
astronr—astronomer
astrophys—astrophysical, astrophysics
attend—attendant, attending
atty—attorney
audiol—audiology
Aug—August
auth—author
AV—audiovisual
Ave—Avenue
avicult—avicultural, aviculture

b—born
bact—bacterial, bacteriologic, bacteriological, bacteriology
BC—British Colombia
bd—board
behav—behavior(al)
Belg—Belgian, Belgium
Bibl—Biblical
bibliog—bibliographic, bibliographical, bibliography
bibliogr—bibliographer
biochem—biochemical, biochemistry
biog—biographical, biography
biol—biological, biology
biomed—biomedical, biomedicine

biomet—biometric(s), biometrical, biometry
biophys—biophysical, biophysics
bk(s)—book(s)
bldg—building
Blvd—Boulevard
Bor—Borough
bot—botanical, botany
br—branch(es)
Brig—Brigadier
Brit—Britain, British
Bro(s)—Brother(s)
byrol—byrology
bull—Bulletin
bur—bureau
bus—business
BWI—British West Indies

c—children
Calif—California
Can—Canada, Canadian
cand—candidate
Capt—Captain
cardiol—cardiology
cardiovasc—cardiovascular
cartog—cartographic, cartographical, cartography
cartogr—cartographer
Cath—Catholic
CEngr—Corp of Engineers
cent—central
Cent Am—Central American
cert—certificate(s), certification, certified
chap—chapter
chem—chemical(s), chemistry
chemother—chemotherapy
chg—change
chmn—chairman
citricult—citriculture
class—classical
climat—climatological, climatology
clin(s)—clinic(s), clinical
cmndg—commanding
Co—County
Co—Companies, Company
co-auth—co-author
co-dir—co-director
co-ed—co-editor
co-educ—co-education, co-educational
col(s)—college(s), collegiate, colonel
collab—collaboration, collaborative
collabr—collaborator

ABBREVIATIONS

Colo—Colorado
com—commerce, commercial
Comdr—Commander
commun—communicable, communication(s)
comn(s)—commission(s), commissioned
comndg—commanding
comnr—commissioner
comp—comparitive
compos—composition
comput—computation, computer(s), computing
comt(s)—committee(s)
conchol—conchology
conf—conference
cong—congress, congressional
Conn—Connecticut
conserv—conservation, conservatory
consol—consolidated, consolidation
const—constitution, constitutional
construct—construction, constructive
consult(s)—consult, consultant(s), consultantship(s), consultation, consulting
contemp—contemporary
contrib—contribute, contributing, contribution(s)
contribr—contributor
conv—convention
coop—cooperating, cooperation, cooperative
coord—coordinate(d), coordinating, coordination
coordr—coordinator
corp—corporate, corporation(s)
corresp—correspondence, correspondent, corresponding
coun—council, counsel, counseling
counr—councilor, counselor
criminol—criminological, criminology
cryog—cryogenic(s)
crystallog—crystallographic, crystallographical, crystallography
crystallogr—crystallographer
Ct—Court
Ctr—Center
cult—cultural, culture
cur—curator
curric—curriculum
cybernet—cybernetic(s)
cytol—cytological, cytology
Czech—Czechoslovakia, Czech Republic

DC—District of Columbia
Dec—December
Del—Delaware
deleg—delegate, delegation
delinq—delinquency, delinquent
dem—democrat(s), democratic
demog—demographic, demography
demogr—demographer
demonstr—demontrator
dendrol—dendrologic, dendrological, dendrology
dent—dental, dentistry
dep—deputy
dept—department
dermat—dermatologic, dermatological, dermatology

develop—developed, developing, development, developmental
diag—diagnosis, diagnostic
dialectol—dialectological, dialectology
dict—dictionaries, dictionary
Dig—Digest
dipl—diploma, diplomate
dir(s)—director(s), directories, directory
dis—disease(s), disorders
Diss Abst—Dissertation Abstracts
dist—district
distrib—distributed, distribution, distributive
distribr—distributor(s)
div—division, divisional, divorced
DNA—deoxyribonucleic acid
doc—document(s), documentary, documentation
Dom—Dominion
Dr—Drive

E—East
ecol—ecological, ecology
econ(s)—economic(s), economical, economy
economet—econometric(s)
ECT—electroconvulsive or electroshock therapy
ed—edition(s), editor(s), editorial
ed bd—editorial board
educ—education, educational
educr—educator(s)
EEG—electroencephalogram, electroencephalographic, electroencephalography
Egyptol—Egyptology
EKG—electrocardiogram
elec—electric, electrical, electricity
electrochem—electrochemical, electrochemistry
electroph—electrophysical, electrophysics
elem—elementary
embryol—embryologic, embryological, embryology
emer—emeriti, emeritus
employ—employment
encour—encouragement
encycl—encyclopedia
endocrinol—endocrinologic, endocrinology
eng—engineering
Eng—England, English
engr(s)—engineer(s)
enol—enology
Ens—Ensign
entom—entomological, entomology
environ—environment(s), environmental
enzym—enzymology
epidemiol—epidemiologic, epidemiological, epidemiology
equip—equipment
ERDA—Energy Research & Development Administration
ESEA—Elementary & Secondary Education Act
espec—especially
estab—established, establishment(s)
ethnog—ethnographic, ethnographical, ethnography
ethnogr—ethnographer

ethnol—ethnologic, ethnological, ethnology
Europ—European
eval—evaluation
Evangel—Evangelical
eve—evening
exam—examination(s), examining
examr—examiner
except—exceptional
exec(s)—executive(s)
exeg—exegeses, exegesis, exegetic, exegetical
exhib(s)—exhibition(s), exhibit(s)
exp—experiment, experimental
exped(s)—expedition(s)
explor—exploration(s), exploratory
expos—exposition
exten—extension

fac—faculty
facil—facilities, facility
Feb—February
fed—federal
fedn—federation
fel(s)—fellow(s), fellowship(s)
fermentol—fermentology
fertil—fertility, fertilization
Fla—Florida
floricult—floricultural, floriculture
found—foundation
FPO—Fleet Post Office
Fr—French
Ft—Fort

Ga—Georgia
gastroenterol—gastroenterological, gastroenterology
gen—general
geneal—genealogical, genealogy
geod—geodesy, geodetic
geog—geographic, geographical, geography
geogr—geographer
geol—geologic, geological, geology
geom—geometric, geometrical, geometry
geomorphol—geomorphologic, geomorphology
geophys—geophysical, geophysics
Ger—German, Germanic, Germany
geriat—geriatric
geront—gerontological, gerontology
Ges—Gesellschaft
glaciol—glaciology
gov—governing, governor(s)
govt—government, governmental
grad—graduate(d)
Gt Brit—Great Britain
guid—guidance
gym—gymnasium
gynec—gynecologic, gynecological, gynecology

handbk(s)—handbook(s)
helminth—helminthology
hemat—hematologic, hematological, hematology
herpet—herpetologic, herpetological, herpetology
HEW—Department of Health, Education & Welfare

ABBREVIATIONS

Hisp—Hispanic, Hispania
hist—historic, historical, history
histol—histological, histology
HM—Her Majesty
hochsch—hochschule
homeop—homeopathic, homeopathy
hon(s)—honor(s), honorable, honorary
hort—horticultural, horticulture
hosp(s)—hospital(s), hospitalization
hq—headquarters
HumRRO—Human Resources Research Office
husb—husbandry
Hwy—Highway
hydraul—hydraulic(s)
hydrodyn—hydrodynamic(s)
hydrol—hydrologic, hydrological, hydrologics
hyg—hygiene, hygienic(s)
hypn—hypnosis

ichthyol—ichthyological, ichthyology
Ill—Illinois
illum—illuminating, illumination
illus—illustrate, illustrated, illustration
illusr—illustrator
immunol—immunologic, immunological, immunology
Imp—Imperial
improv—improvement
Inc—Incorporated
in-chg—in charge
incl—include(s), including
Ind—Indiana
indust(s)—industrial, industries, industry
Inf—Infantry
info—information
inorg—inorganic
ins—insurance
inst(s)—institute(s), institution(s)
instnl—institutional(ized)
instr(s)—instruct, instruction, instructor(s)
instrnl—instructional
int—international
intel—intellligence
introd—introduction
invert—invertebrate
invest(s)—investigation(s)
investr—investigator
irrig—irrigation
Ital—Italian

J—Journal
Jan—January
Jct—Junction
jour—journal, journalism
jr—junior
jurisp—jurisprudence
juv—juvenile

Kans—Kansas
Ky—Kentucky

La—Louisiana
lab(s)—laboratories, laboratory
lang—language(s)
laryngol—larygological, laryngology
lect—lecture(s)

lectr—lecturer(s)
legis—legislation, legislative, legislature
lett—letter(s)
lib—liberal
libr—libraries, library
librn—librarian
lic—license(d)
limnol—limnological, limnology
ling—linguistic(s), linguistical
lit—literary, literature
lithol—lithologic, lithological, lithology
Lt—Lieutenant
Ltd—Limited
m—married
mach—machine(s), machinery
mag—magazine(s)
maj—major
malacol—malacology
mammal—mammalogy
Man—Manitoba
Mar—March
Mariol—Mariology
Mass—Massachusetts
mat—material(s)
mat med—materia medica
math—mathematic(s), mathematical
Md—Maryland
mech—mechanic(s), mechanical
med—medical, medicinal, medicine
Mediter—Mediterranean
Mem—Memorial
mem—member(s), membership(s)
ment—mental(ly)
metab—metabolic, metabolism
metall—metallurgic, metallurgical, metallurgy
metallog—metallographic, metallography
metallogr—metallographer
metaphys—metaphysical, metaphysics
meteorol—meteorological, meteorology
metrol—metrological, metrology
metrop—metropolitan
Mex—Mexican, Mexico
mfg—manufacturing
mfr—manufacturer
mgr—manager
mgt—management
Mich—Michigan
microbiol—microbiological, microbiology
micros—microscopic, microscopical, microscopy
mid—middle
mil—military
mineral—mineralogical, mineralogy
Minn—Minnesota
Miss—Mississippi
mkt—market, marketing
Mo—Missouri
mod—modern
monogr—monograph
Mont—Montana
morphol—morphological, morphology
Mt—Mount
mult—multiple
munic—municipal, municipalities
mus—museum(s)
musicol—musicological, musicology
mycol—mycologic, mycology

N—North
NASA—National Aeronautics & Space Administration
nat—national, naturalized
NATO—North Atlantic Treaty Organization
navig—navigation(al)
NB—New Brunswick
NC—North Carolina
NDak—North Dakota
NDEA—National Defense Education Act
Nebr—Nebraska
nematol—nematological, nematology
nerv—nervous
Neth—Netherlands
neurol—neurological, neurology
neuropath—neuropathological, neuropathology
neuropsychiat—neuropsychiatric, neuropsychiatry
neurosurg—neurosurgical, neurosurgery
Nev—Nevada
New Eng—New England
New York—New York City
Nfld—Newfoundland
NH—New Hampshire
NIH—National Institute of Health
NIMH—National Institute of Mental Health
NJ—New Jersey
NMex—New Mexico
No—Number
nonres—nonresident
norm—normal
Norweg—Norwegian
Nov—November
NS—Nova Scotia
NSF—National Science Foundation
NSW—New South Wales
numis—numismatic(s)
nutrit—nutrition, nutritional
NY—New York State
NZ—New Zealand

observ—observatories, observatory
obstet—obstetric(s), obstetrical
occas—occasional(ly)
occup—occupation, occupational
oceanog—oceanographic, oceanographical, oceanography
oceanogr—oceanographer
Oct—October
odontol—odontology
OEEC—Organization for European Economic Cooperation
off—office, official
Okla—Oklahoma
olericult—olericulture
oncol—oncologic, oncology
Ont—Ontario
oper(s)—operation(s), operational, operative
ophthal—ophthalmologic, ophthalmological, ophthalmology
optom—optometric, optometrical, optometry
ord—ordnance
Ore—Oregon
org—organic

ABBREVIATIONS

orgn—organization(s), organizational
orient—oriental
ornith—ornithological, ornithology
orthod—orthodontia, orthodontic(s)
orthop—orthopedic(s)
osteop—osteopathic, osteopathy
otol—otological, otology
otolaryngol—otolaryngological, otolaryngology
otorhinol—otorhinologic, otorhinology

Pa—Pennsylvania
Pac—Pacific
paleobot—paleobotanical, paleobotany
paleont—paleontology
Pan-Am—Pan-American
parasitol—parasitology
partic—participant, participating
path—pathologic, pathological, pathology
pedag—pedagogic(s), pedagogical, pedagogy
pediat—pediatric(s)
PEI—Prince Edward Islands
penol—penological, penology
periodont—periodontal, periodontic(s)
petrog—petrographic, petrographical, petrography
petrogr—petrographer
petrol—petroleum, petrologic, petrological, petrology
pharm—pharmacy
pharmaceut—pharmaceutic(s), pharmaceutical(s)
pharmacog—pharmacognosy
pharamacol—pharmacologic, pharmacological, pharmacology
phenomenol—phenomenologic(al), phenomenology
philol—philological, philology
philos—philosophic, philosophical, philosophy
photog—photographic, photography
photogeog—photogeographic, photogeography
photogr—photographer(s)
photogram—photogrammetric, photogrammetry
photom—photometric, photometrical, photometry
phycol—phycology
phys—physical
physiog—physiographic, physiographical, physiography
physiol—physiological, phsysiology
Pkwy—Parkway
Pl—Place
polit—political, politics
polytech—polytechnic(s)
pomol—pomological, pomology
pontif—pontifical
pop—population
Port—Portugal, Portuguese
Pos—Position
postgrad—postgraduate
PQ—Province of Quebec
PR—Puerto Rico
pract—practice
practr—practitioner
prehist—prehistoric, prehistory

prep—preparation, preparative, preparatory
pres—president
Presby—Presbyterian
preserv—preservation
prev—prevention, preventive
prin—principal
prob(s)—problem(s)
proc—proceedings
proctol—proctologic, proctological, proctology
prod—product(s), production, productive
prof—professional, professor, professorial
Prof Exp—Professional Experience
prog(s)—program(s), programmed, programming
proj—project(s), projection(al), projective
prom—promotion
protozool—protozoology
Prov—Province, Provincial
psychiat—psychiatric, psychiatry
psychoanal—psychoanalysis, psychoanalytic, psychoanalytical
psychol—psychological, psychology
psychomet—psychometric(s)
psychopath—psychopathologic, psychopathology
psychophys—psychophysical, psychophysics
psychophysiol—psychophysiological, psychophysiology
psychosom—psychosomatic(s)
psychother—psychoterapeutic(s), psychotherapy
Pt—Point
pub—public
publ—publication(s), publish(ed), publisher, publishing
pvt—private

Qm—Quartermaster
Qm Gen—Quartermaster General
qual—qualitative, quality
quant—quantitative
quart—quarterly
Que—Quebec

radiol—radiological, radiology
RAF—Royal Air Force
RAFVR—Royal Air Force Volunteer Reserve
RAMC—Royal Army Medical Corps
RAMCR—Royal Army Medical Corps Reserve
RAOC—Royal Army Ordnance Corps
RASC—Royal Army Service Corps
RASCR—Royal Army Service Corps Reserve
RCAF—Royal Canadian Air Force
RCAFR—Royal Canadian Air Force Reserve
RCAFVR—Royal Canadian Air Force Volunteer Reserve
RCAMC—Royal Canadian Army Medical Corps
RCAMCR—Royal Canadian Army Medical Corps Reserve
RCASC—Royal Canadian Army Service Corps

RCASCR—Royal Canadian Army Service Corps Reserve
RCEME—Royal Canadian Electrical & Mechanical Engineers
RCN—Royal Canadian Navy
RCNR—Royal Canadian Naval Reserve
RCNVR—Royal Canadian Naval Volunteer Reserve
Rd—Road
RD—Rural Delivery
rec—record(s), recording
redevelop—redevelopment
ref—reference(s)
refrig—refrigeration
regist—register(ed), registration
registr—registrar
regt—regiment(al)
rehab—rehabilitation
rel(s)—relation(s), relative
relig—religion, religious
REME—Royal Electrical & Mechanical Engineers
rep—represent, representative
Repub—Republic
req—requirements
res—research, reserve
rev—review, revised, revision
RFD—Rural Free Delivery
rhet—rhetoric, rhetorical
RI—Rhode Island
Rm—Room
RM—Royal Marines
RN—Royal Navy
RNA—ribonucleic acid
RNR—Royal Naval Reserve
RNVR—Royal Naval Volunteer Reserve
roentgenol—roentgenologic, roentgenological, roentgenology
RR—Railroad, Rural Route
Rte—Route
Russ—Russian
rwy—railway

S—South
SAfrica—South Africa
SAm—South America, South American
sanit—sanitary, sanitation
Sask—Saskatchewan
SC—South Carolina
Scand—Scandinavia(n)
sch(s)—school(s)
scholar—scholarship
sci—science(s), scientific
SDak—South Dakota
SEATO—Southeast Asia Treaty Organization
sec—secondary
sect—section
secy—secretary
seismog—seismograph, seismographic, seismography
seismogr—seismographer
seismol—seismological, seismology
sem—seminar, seminary
Sen—Senator, Senatorial
Sept—September
ser—serial, series
serol—serologic, serological, serology
serv—service(s), serving

ABBREVIATIONS

silvicult—silvicultural, silviculture
soc(s)—societies, society
soc sci—social science
sociol—sociologic, sociological, sociology
Span—Spanish
spec—special
specif—specification(s)
spectrog—spectrograph, spectrographic, spectrography
spectrogr—spectrographer
spectrophotom—spectrophotometer, spectrophotometric, spectrophotometry
spectros—spectroscopic, spectroscopy
speleol—speleological, speleology
Sq—Square
sr—senior
St—Saint, Street(s)
sta(s)—station(s)
stand—standard(s), standardization
statist—statistical, statistics
Ste—Sainte
steril—sterility
stomatol—stomatology
stratig—stratigraphic, stratigraphy
stratigr—stratigrapher
struct—structural, structure(s)
stud—student(ship)
subcomt—subcommittee
subj—subject
subsid—subsidiary
substa—substation
super—superior
suppl—supplement(s), supplemental, supplementary
supt—superintendent
supv—supervising, supervision
supvr—supervisor
supvry—supervisory
surg—surgery, surgical
surv—survey, surveying
survr—surveyor
Swed—Swedish
Switz—Switzerland
symp—symposia, symposium(s)
syphil—syphilology
syst(s)—system(s), systematic(s), systematical

taxon—taxonomic, taxonomy
tech—technical, technique(s)
technol—technologic(al), technology
tel—telegraph(y), telephone

temp—temporary
Tenn—Tennessee
Terr—Terrace
Tex—Texas
textbk(s)—textbook(s)
text ed—text edition
theol—theological, theology
theoret—theoretic(al)
ther—therapy
therapeut—therapeutic(s)
thermodyn—thermodynamic(s)
topog—topographic, topographical, topography
topogr—topographer
toxicol—toxicologic, toxicological, toxicology
trans—transaction(s)
transl—translated, translation(s)
translr—translator(s)
transp—transport, transportation
treas—treasurer, treasury
treat—treatment
trop—tropical
tuberc—tuberculosis
TV—television
Twp—Township

UAR—United Arab Republic
UK—United Kingdom
UN—United Nations
undergrad—undergraduate
unemploy—unemployment
UNESCO—United Nations Educational Scientific & Cultural Organization
UNICEF—United Nations International Childrens Fund
univ(s)—universities, university
UNRRA—United Nations Relief & Rehabilitation Administration
UNRWA—United Nations Relief & Works Agency
urol—urologic, urological, urology
US—United States
USAAF—US Army Air Force
USAAFR—US Army Air Force Reserve
USAF—US Air Force
USAFR—US Air Force Reserve
USAID—US Agency for International Development
USAR—US Army Reserve
USCG—US Coast Guard
USCGR—US Coast Guard Reserve

USDA—US Department of Agriculture
USMC—US Marine Corps
USMCR—US Marine Corps Reserve
USN—US Navy
USNAF—US Naval Air Force
USNAFR—US Naval Air Force Reserve
USNR—US Naval Reserve
USPHS—US Public Health Service
USPHSR—US Public Health Service Reserve
USSR—Union of Soviet Socialist Republics

Va—Virginia
var—various
veg—vegetable(s), vegetation
vent—ventilating, ventilation
vert—vertebrate
Vet—Veteran(s)
vet—veterinarian, veterinary
VI—Virgin Islands
vinicult—viniculture
virol—virological, virology
vis—visiting
voc—vocational
vocab—vocabulary
vol(s)—voluntary, volunteer(s), volume(s)
vpres—vice president
vs—versus
Vt—Vermont

W—West
Wash—Washington
WHO—World Health Organization
WI—West Indies
wid—widow, widowed, widower
Wis—Wisconsin
WVa—West Virginia
Wyo—Wyoming

Yearbk(s)—Yearbook(s)
YMCA—Young Men's Christian Association
YMHA—Young Men's Hebrew Association
Yr(s)—Year(s)
YT—Yukon Territory
YWCA—Young Women's Christian Association
YWHA—Young Women's Hebrew Association

zool—zoological, zoology

AMERICAN MEN & WOMEN OF SCIENCE

J

JA, WILLIAM YIN, ANALYTICAL CHEMISTRY. *Current Pos:* RES ASSOC, RICHMOND RES CTR, STAUFFER CHEM CO, 66- *Personal Data:* b Mar 5, 36; US citizen. *Educ:* Univ Calif, Berkeley, BS, 60. *Prof Exp:* Chemist, Qual Assurance Tech Agency, US Army Chem Corps, 60-62; analytical chemist, Hyman (Julius) Labs, Inc, 62-64; analytical chemist, Philadelphia Quartz Co, Calif, 64-66. *Mem:* Am Chem Soc; Am Soc Testing & Mat; Assoc Official Anal Chem. *Res:* Analytical methods development; trace analysis; separations and purification techniques, especially preparation of high-purity pesticide standards and metabolites by large-scale, high-speed column chromatography. *Mailing Add:* 145 Windward Ct ValleJo CA 94591-6938

JAANUS, SIRET DESIREE, PHARMACOLOGY, OCULAR PHARMACOLOGY. *Current Pos:* VIS PROF & CHAIRPERSON, DEPT BIOL SCIS, STATE UNIV NY COL OPTOM, 94- *Personal Data:* b Tallinn, Estonia; US citizen; m 73, Jaak Jurison. *Educ:* City Col New York, BS, 60; Hunter Col, MA, 66; State Univ NY Downstate Med Ctr, PhD(pharmacol), 70. *Honors & Awards:* Paul Yarwood Award, 79. *Prof Exp:* Res asst pharmacol, Albert Einstein Col Med, 60-64; res asst, State Univ Downstate Med Ctr, 64-66, NIH fel pharmacol, 66-70, path, 70-71; asst prof basic sci, State Univ NY Col Optom, 71-72, chmn dept, 72-73; chairperson, Dept Basic & Visual Sci, Southern Calif Col Optom, 78-81, prof basic sci, 73-93. *Concurrent Pos:* Consult; assoc ed, Clin Ocular Pharmacol, 84, 89 & 95; vis prof, Pa Col optom, 91-94. *Mem:* Am Optom Asn; Am Soc Pharmacol & Exp Therapeut; Am Acad Optom; Asn Res Vision & Opthal. *Res:* Autonomic and endocrine pharmacology. *Mailing Add:* 65 Central Park W New York NY 10023. *Fax:* 212-780-5176; *E-Mail:* sjaanus@sunyopt.edu

JABALPURWALA, KAIZER E, INORGANIC CHEMISTRY, PHYSICAL CHEMISTRY. *Current Pos:* TECH DIR, JABALPUR INDUST, INC, 83- *Personal Data:* b Surat, India; m 60, Sharifa Ahmadi; c Sheila & Inez. *Educ:* Univ Bombay, BSc, 54, MSc, 56, PhD(coord chem), 60. *Honors & Awards:* Gold Medalist, Univ Bombay, 61. *Prof Exp:* Res asst phys chem, Inst Sci, Univ Bombay, 58-61; res assoc inorg chem, Boston Univ, 61-64; chief chemist, Zinc Oxide Co Can Ltd, Hudson Bay Mining & Smelting Co, Montreal, 64-68, tech dir, 68-74; tech mgr, Zochem Ltd, 74; partner, G H Chem Ltd, 74-83. *Mem:* Am Chem Soc; Brit Chem Soc; Sigma Xi; Chem Inst Can. *Res:* Light scattering by colloid systems; solution stabilities of complex ions; electrophotography related to photoconductivity of zinc oxide; technology of zinc oxide; zinc dust. *Mailing Add:* 350 L'Esperance St St Lambert PQ J4P 1Y5 Can. *Fax:* 514-671-1197

JABARIN, SALEH ABD EL KARIM, POLYMER CHEMISTRY. *Current Pos:* SR SCIENTIST, OWENS-ILLINOIS TECH CTR, 71- *Personal Data:* b Haifa, Israel, Feb 7, 39; m 69; c 1. *Educ:* Dartmouth Col, BA, 66; Polytech Inst Brooklyn, MS, 68; Univ Mass, PhD(polymer sci & eng), 71. *Mem:* Am Chem Soc; Soc Plastics Engrs. *Res:* Studies of thermal, mechanical and optical properties of polymers and polymer crystallization using light scattering, x-ray diffraction, infra-red dichroism and birefringence; molecular orientation and solution characterization. *Mailing Add:* 2115 Old Planke Rd Holland OH 43528-9562

JABBOUR, J T, PEDIATRIC NEUROLOGY. *Current Pos:* CONSULT, 85- *Personal Data:* b Tiptonville, Tenn, Aug 5, 27; m 57, Helen Block; c 5. *Educ:* Univ Tenn, Martin, BS, 48; Univ Tenn, Memphis, MD, 51; Am Bd Pediat, dipl, 60. *Prof Exp:* Rotating intern, Baylor Univ Hosp, Dallas, 52-53; gen pract, Tenn, 53-56; resident, Col Med, Univ Tenn, Memphis, 56-58, res assoc pediat, 57; co-dir pediat neurol & seizure clin, Sch Med, Univ Okla, 59-61, asst prof pediat & neurol & assoc dir clin study, Ctr Birth Defects, 61-65; asst prof, Univ Tenn, Memphis, 65-67, prof pediat & neurol & head child div child neurol, 67-75. *Concurrent Pos:* Fel neurol, Univ Minn, Minneapolis, 58-61; consult, Oklahoma City Speech & Hearing Ctr, 61-65; consult, Oklahoma City Children's Ctr, 61-65; chief pediat neurol, Child Develop Ctr, Med Units, Univ Tenn, Memphis, 65-68; consult, Ment Retardation Br, Bur Chronic Dis, USPHS, 66-69. *Mem:* AMA; Am Acad Pediat; Am Acad Neurol; Am Acad Cerebral Palsy; Child Neurol Soc. *Res:* Subacute sclerosing panencephalitis; behavioral neurology. *Mailing Add:* 777 Washington Ave No P-320 Memphis TN 38105-4566. *Fax:* 901-572-5090

JABBOUR, KAHTAN NICOLAS, ENGINEERING. *Current Pos:* sr mech engr, 73-80, SR PROJ MGR, US NUCLEAR REGULATORY COMN, 80- *Personal Data:* b Safita, Syria, Aug 26, 34. *Educ:* Damascus Univ, cert math, 53 & 54; Sch Advan Eng, Beirut, BS, 57; Purdue Univ, MS, 60, PhD(struct), 62. *Prof Exp:* Field engr, Arabian Am Oil Co, Saudi Arabia, 57-58; design engr, El-Ghab Proj, Syria, 58-59; asst prof eng, Kans State Univ, 62-63; assoc prof eng sci, Tenn Technol Univ, 63-67; staff engr, Fairchild Hiller Corp, 67-69; aerospace engr, Goddard Space Flight Ctr, NASA, 69-73. *Concurrent Pos:* NSF res grant, 65-66. *Mem:* Am Soc Eng Educ. *Res:* Structural mechanics and engineering; perforated plates. *Mailing Add:* 109 Lucas Lane Bethesda MD 20814

JABBOUR, KAMAL, HIGH SPEED COMPUTER NETWORKS, COMPUTER APPLICATION TO POWER SYSTEMS. *Current Pos:* Asst prof elec eng, 82-88, chmn, Dept Elec & Comput Eng, 90-93, ASSOC PROF ELEC ENG, SYRACUSE UNIV, 88- *Personal Data:* b Chemlan, Lebanon, Aug 10, 57; m, Marla Bennett; c Randa, Marc & Paula. *Educ:* Am Univ Beirut, Bachelor Eng, 79; Univ Salford, UK, PhD(elec eng), 82. *Concurrent Pos:* Prin investr, Niagara Mohawk Power Corp, 85-90 & Int Bus Mach, 88-91. *Mem:* Sr mem Inst Elec & Electronics Engrs. *Res:* Modeling and performance evaluation of high-speed computer networks and in the application of artificial intelligence to power systems. *Mailing Add:* ECE Dept 121 Link Hall Syracuse Univ Syracuse NY 13244-1240. *E-Mail:* jabbour@cat.syr.edu

JABBUR, RAMZI JIBRAIL, INDUSTRIAL CHEMISTRY, ECONOMETRICS STRATEGIC PLANNING. *Current Pos:* MGT CONSULT, 78- *Personal Data:* b Beirut, Lebanon, Mar 9, 37; US citizen; div; c James R. *Educ:* Am Univ Beirut, BS, 58; Stanford Univ, MS, 60, PhD(high energy physics), 63. *Prof Exp:* Rockefeller Found fel, 57-58, Stanford Univ fel, 58-60; res assoc physics, Columbia Univ, 63-65; res physicist, Argonne Nat Lab, 65-67; asst prof physics, Univ Grad Prog, City Univ NY, 67-71; assoc dir, Mgt Sci Dept, BBDO Inc, 71-74; mgr corp strategic planning, W R Grace & Co, 74-78. *Concurrent Pos:* Dir, UBAF Arab Am Bank, 75-78. *Mem:* Am Phys Soc; NY Acad Sci; Inst Mgt Sci. *Res:* Management of major petrochemical projects; operations research and applications to managerial decisions; econometric statistical and dynamic models; strategic corp planning; investments, acquisitions and divestments. *Mailing Add:* 1380 Riverside Dr Apt 5H New York NY 10033

JABINE, THOMAS BOYD, APPLIED STATISTICS. *Current Pos:* STATIST CONSULT, 80- *Personal Data:* b Brooklyn, NY, Jan 26, 25; m 50, Marian Smith; c Thomas P, William T, Ann B & Leslie N. *Educ:* Mass Inst Technol, BS & MS, 49. *Prof Exp:* Var pos, US Census Bur, 49-68, chief statist res div, 69-73; chief math statistician, Social Security Admin, 73-79; statist policy expert, Energy Info Admin, US Dept Energy, 79-80. *Concurrent Pos:* Constituent mem, Inter-Am Statist Inst. *Mem:* Fel Am Statist Asn; Int Statist Inst. *Res:* Survey methodology; sampling; quality control. *Mailing Add:* 3231 Worthington St NW Washington DC 20015-2362. *E-Mail:* tjabine@nas.edu

JABLON, SEYMOUR, BIOSTATISTICS, EPIDEMIOLOGY. *Current Pos:* RETIRED. *Personal Data:* b New York, NY, June 2, 18; m 41; c 2. *Educ:* City Col New York, BS, 39; Columbia Univ, MA, 40. *Honors & Awards:* Order of Sacred Treasure, Govt of Japan, 87. *Prof Exp:* Prof assoc, Med Follow-up Agency, Nat Res Coun, 48-60; chief dept statist, Atomic Bomb Casualty Comn, 60-63; assoc dir, Med Follow-up Agency, Nat Res Coun, 63-68; chief dept statist, Atomic Bomb Casualty Comn, 68-71; assoc dir, 71-75, dir med

1

follow-up agency, Nat Res Coun, 75-87; expert, Radiation Epidemiol Br, Nat Cancer Inst, 87-93. *Concurrent Pos:* Mem, Nat Comn Radiation Protection, 74-87. *Mem:* Fel Am Statist Asn; Am Epidemiol Soc; Radiation Res Soc; Biomet Soc; Health Physics Soc; fel AAAS. *Res:* Late effects of radiation; epidemiology of cancer. *Mailing Add:* 6813 Persimmon Tree Rd Bethesda MD 20817

JABLONER, HAROLD, POLYMER CHEMISTRY, ORGANIC CHEMISTRY. *Current Pos:* sr res chemist, 68-71, res scientist, 71-78, RES ASSOC, HERCULES INC, 78- *Personal Data:* b New York, NY, Oct 25, 37; m 61; c 3. *Educ:* City Col New York, BS, 57; Polytech Inst Brooklyn, PhD(chem), 63. *Prof Exp:* Res chemist, Hercules Powder Co, 63-68. *Concurrent Pos:* Adj prof, Drexel Univ, 78- *Mem:* Am Chem Soc. *Res:* Solution properties and synthesis of macromolecules; hydrocarbon oxidation kinetics and mechanisms; thermally stable polymers; food; taste perception; polymer taste perception; solution properties of polymers; paper and synthetic pulp. *Mailing Add:* 16 Annes Way Landenberg PA 19350-1035

JABLONSKI, DANIEL GARY, ELECTRONICS. *Current Pos:* PHYSICIST, JOHNS HOPKINS UNIV APPL PHYSICS LAB, 91- *Personal Data:* b Washington, DC, Nov 15, 54; m 82; c 2. *Educ:* Mass Inst Technol, BS, 76, MS, 77; Cambridge Univ, PhD(physics), 82. *Prof Exp:* Res physicist, Naval Surface Weapons Ctr, 81-86; res staff mem, Supercomput Res Ctr, 86-91. *Concurrent Pos:* Adj prof, Capitol Inst Technol, 85- *Mem:* Am Phys Soc; Inst Elec & Electronics Engrs. *Res:* Microwave properties of superconducting devices; properties of materials at millimeter wavelengths; phase-locked loops; supercomputing; theory of computation; microwave systems, electronic seniors; satellite navigation. *Mailing Add:* 12220 Somersworth Dr Silver Spring MD 20902. *E-Mail:* dan.jablonski@jhuapl.edu

JABLONSKI, DAVID, PALEONTOLOGY. *Current Pos:* assoc prof, Dept Geophys Sci, 85-89, PROF PALEOBIOL, UNIV CHICAGO, 89- *Personal Data:* b New York, NY, June 23, 53. *Educ:* Columbia Univ, BA, 74; Yale Univ, MS, 76, PhD(geol), 79. *Honors & Awards:* Paleont Soc Schuchert Award, 88. *Prof Exp:* Asst res geol, Univ Calif, Santa Barbara, 79-80, Miller res fel paleobiol, Dept Paleont, Berkeley, 80-82; asst prof evolutionary biol, Dept Ecol & Evolutionary Biol, Univ Ariz, 82-85. *Concurrent Pos:* Assoc ed, Paleobiol, 83-85 & 86-88, Evolution, 84-86; assoc ed, Conserv Biol, 86-95, Am Rev Ecol Syst, 89-94 & Geol, 91-93; hon res fel, Nat Hist Mus, London, 93- *Mem:* Paleont Soc; Soc Study Evolution; Int Paleont Union; Soc Syst Biol; Am Soc Naturalists. *Res:* Evolutionary patterns and processes above the species level, in living and fossil organisms; marine inverts, particularly mollusks. *Mailing Add:* Dept Geophys Sci Univ Chicago Chicago IL 60637

JABLONSKI, FRANK EDWARD, ELECTROOPTICS. *Current Pos:* RETIRED. *Personal Data:* b Brooklyn, NY, Feb 2, 15; m 49, Dorothy E Condor; c Timothy, Michael & Daniel. *Educ:* Fordham Univ, BS, 36; NY Univ, MS, 40; Harvard Univ, MS, 46. *Prof Exp:* Physicist bur ord, US Dept Navy, 40-43, active duty, US Navy, 43-46 physicist influence devices, US Naval Ord Lab, 46-57, ord engr, Spec Projs Off, 57-58; physicist, Nat Security Agency, 58-59; physicist, Goddard Space Flight Ctr & NASA Hq, 59-61, physicist off long range plans & progs, 61-63; tech adv, Chief Naval Opers, 63-73, consult physicist, 73-87. *Concurrent Pos:* Mem, Polaris Re-entry Body Coord Comt, 57-58; res adv comt control, guid & navig, NASA, 59-60. *Mem:* Fel AAAS; Am Phys Soc; Wilderness Soc. *Res:* Degaussing of ships; proximity exploders and fuzes; warheads for missiles; communications; space electronics; sonar; infrared; lasers. *Mailing Add:* 9916 Julliard Dr Bethesda MD 20817

JABLONSKI, WERNER LOUIS, ORGANIC CHEMISTRY. *Current Pos:* RETIRED. *Personal Data:* b Frankfurt, Ger, May 6, 24; m 54; c 5. *Educ:* Univ Toronto, BA & MA, 49; McGill Univ, PhD(org chem), 53. *Prof Exp:* Chemist, Can Indust Ltd, 49-50; chemist, Dow Chem Co, 50-69 & US Plywood Champion Papers, Inc, 69-71; chemist, Foster Grant, Inc, 71-85. *Mem:* Soc Plastics Engrs; Am Chem Soc; Sigma Xi. *Res:* Polymers. *Mailing Add:* 404 Woodberry Dr Chesapeake VA 23320

JACCARINO, VINCENT, SOLID STATE PHYSICS. *Current Pos:* chmn dept, 69-72, PROF PHYSICS, UNIV CALIF, SANTA BARBARA, 66-, DIR, QUANTUM INST, 85- *Personal Data:* b Brooklyn, NY, May 12, 24; m 65; c 2. *Educ:* Brooklyn Col, BS, 48; Mass Inst Technol, PhD(physics), 52. *Prof Exp:* Res assoc, Mass Inst Technol, 52-54; mem tech staff, Bell Tel Labs, 54-63, head solid state phys res dept, 63-66. *Concurrent Pos:* Guggenheim Found fel, 73-74, Lady Davis fel, 79, Yamada Found fel, Japan, 80; chmn, Int Conf Magnetism, 85-; USA chmn, magnetism sect, Int Union Pure & Appl Physics, 91. *Mem:* Fel Am Phys Soc. *Res:* Magnetic resonance in solids; magnetism; superionic conductors; critical phenomena. *Mailing Add:* 1115 Arbolado Rd Santa Barbara CA 93103

JACCHIA, LUIGI GIUSEPPE, astronomy, for more information see previous edition

JACH, JOSEPH, PHYSICAL CHEMISTRY. *Current Pos:* RETIRED. *Personal Data:* b SAfrica, Dec 15, 29; m 64; c 2. *Educ:* Univ Cape Town, BSc, 50, MSc, 52; Oxford Univ, PhD, 55. *Prof Exp:* Lectr chem, Univ Cape Town, 53; res assoc, Brookhaven Nat Lab, 56-63; assoc prof eng, State Univ NY, Stony Brook, 63-91. *Concurrent Pos:* At Lawrance Radiation Lab, Calif, 69-70. *Res:* Solid state chemistry, particularly thermal decomposition of solids and Szillard-Challmers reactions and chemical reactivity at defect sites in solids. *Mailing Add:* 46 Bay Rd Patchogue NY 11772

JACHE, ALBERT WILLIAM, INORGANIC CHEMISTRY, FLOURINE CHEMISTRY. *Current Pos:* chmn, Dept Chem, Marquette Univ, 67-72, prof, 67-90, dean, Grad Sch, 72-77, assoc acad vpres health sci, 74-77, assoc vpres acad affairs, 77-85, EMER PROF CHEM, MARQUETTE UNIV, 90- *Personal Data:* b Manchester, NH, Nov 5, 24; m 48, Lucy Haaslein; c Ann Gail (Smiley), Ellen (Hoium), Philip W & Heidi (Houtl). *Educ:* Univ NH, BS, 48, MS, 50; Univ Wash, PhD(chem), 52. *Honors & Awards:* Outstanding Serv, Div Flourine, Am Chem Soc. *Prof Exp:* Sr chemist, Air Reduction Co, Inc, 52-53; res assoc physics, Duke Univ, 53-55; from asst prof to assoc prof chem, Agr & Mech Col Tex, 55-61; assoc res dir, Ozark Mahoning Co, 61-64; sr res assoc, Olin Mathieson Chem Corp, 64-67, sect mgr, 65-67. *Concurrent Pos:* Consult, Olin Corp, 67-75, Allied Chem Corp, 77-78; chmn, Div Flourine Chem, Am Chem Soc, 82; scientist in residence, Argonne Nat Lab, 85-86. *Mem:* Fel AAAS; Am Chem Soc; NY Acad Sci; Sigma Xi; fel Am Inst Chem. *Res:* Fluorine chemistry; halogens; nonaqueous solvent systems; environmental problems. *Mailing Add:* 301 Ohio St Marietta OH 45750. *Fax:* 740-376-9107; *E-Mail:* jack.@frognet.net

JACHENS, ROBERT C, MINING GEOPHYSICS. *Current Pos:* res geophysicist, 75-85, chief, 85-88, REG CRUSTEL STRUCT ANALYST, CRUSTEL DYNAMICS SECT, US GEOL SURV OFF MINERAL RESOURCES & GEOPHYS BR, 88- *Personal Data:* b San Francisco, Calif, June 4, 39. *Educ:* Santa Fe State Univ, BS, 62; Columbia Univ, MS, 68, PhD(geophys), 71. *Prof Exp:* Res assoc, Lamont Doherty, Geol Observ, Columbia Univ, 72-75. *Mem:* Fel Geol Soc Am; AAAS; Am Geophys Union. *Res:* Solid earth geophysics & tectonics; mining geophysics. *Mailing Add:* 10488 Bonney Dr Cupertino CA 95014

JACHIMOWICZ, FELEK, PHOTOCHEMISTRY, POLYMER CHEMISTRY. *Current Pos:* SR RES CHEMIST, RES DIV, W R GRACE & CO, 78- *Personal Data:* b Poznan, Poland, July 2, 47; nat US; m 71; c 2. *Educ:* Univ Basel, Switz, dipl, 71, PhD(phys org chem), 75. *Prof Exp:* Fel phys org chem, Col Environ Sci & Forestry, State Univ NY, 78. *Mem:* Am Chem Soc. *Res:* Physical organic chemistry; synthetic chemistry; homogeneous catalysis; synthetic chemistry; radical ions chemistry; analytical chemistry; spectroscopy; polymer chemistry. *Mailing Add:* 36 Cypress St Brookline MA 02146

JACHOWSKI, RICHARD LEO, MANAGEMENT RESEARCH SUPPORTING WILDLIFE CONSERVATION, SCIENTIFIC ADVICE SUPPORTING ECOSYSTEM MANAGEMENT. *Current Pos:* chief, Br Migratory Bird Res, 85-96, CHIEF RES, PATUXENT WILDLIFE RES CTR, US GEOL SURV, 96- *Personal Data:* b Washington, DC, Jan 18, 44; m 74, Martha Herrin; c David. *Educ:* Univ Md, BS, 65, PhD(zool), 70; Univ Miami, MSc, 67. *Honors & Awards:* Resolution Appreciation, Am Asn Zool Parks & Aquariums, 85; Governors Salute to Excellence, State of Md, 94. *Prof Exp:* Mgr, Smithsonian Inst-Peace Corps Environ Prog, Smithsonian Inst, 71-72; gen biologist, Fed Wildlife Permit Off, US Fish & Wildlife Serv, 76-80, chief, Off Sci Authority, 80-85. *Concurrent Pos:* Chief, Off Mgt Authority, US Fish & Wildlife Serv, 87; mem mgt bd, Black Duck Joint Venture, 91-97; spec asst to regional dir, Nat Biol Surv, 93-94; co-chair, Res Working Group, Partners in Flight, 95-96. *Res:* Leadership of a research program that is linked with management in natural resource conservation through the development of partnerships and other working relationships among institutions. *Mailing Add:* 11410 American Holly Dr Laurel MD 20708-4015. *Fax:* 301-497-5624; *E-Mail:* richard__jachowski@nbs.gov

JACK, HULAN E, JR, PHYSICS. *Current Pos:* ASST PROF PHYSICS, KANS STATE UNIV, 71- *Personal Data:* b New York, NY, May 6, 35; m; c 4. *Educ:* NY Univ, BS, 60, MS, 64, PhD(physics), 71. *Prof Exp:* Instr physics, NY Inst Technol, 61-66 & Eng Sch, Pratt Inst, 66-68; lectr, Wash Sq Col, NY Univ, 68-70; instr, Finch Col, 70-71. *Mem:* AAAS; Am Asn Physics Teachers; Am Phys Soc; Asn Comput Mach. *Res:* Solid state and atomic physics. *Mailing Add:* 9832 57th Ave Apt 8D Flushing NY 11368

JACK, JOHN JAMES, ANALYTICAL CHEMISTRY, PLASTICS MARKETING & PROCESSING. *Current Pos:* Res chemist & tech mgt plastics mkt, Polymer Prod Dept, 70-93, mgr, nylon prod progs, Dupont eng polymers, 93-97, BUS CONSULT EI DUPONT DE NEMOURS & CO, INC, 97- *Personal Data:* b Trenton, NJ, Jan 11, 43; m 67; c 2. *Educ:* Princeton Univ, AB, 65; Mass Inst Technol, PhD(anal chem), 71. *Res:* Development of instrumental methods of analysis, especially spectroscopic, and application to industrial analytical problems; automation of laboratory testing and efficient use of newly developing mini- and micro-computers. *Mailing Add:* Du Pont Chestnut Run Plaza-715 Wilmington DE 19880-0715

JACK, ROBERT CECIL MILTON, BIOCHEMISTRY. *Current Pos:* RETIRED. *Personal Data:* b St Vincent, WI, Oct 10, 29; m 59; c Valerie & Marcy. *Educ:* McGill Univ, BSc, 56; Columbia Univ, PhD(plant biochem), 64. *Prof Exp:* Chemist, Cent Exp Sta, WI, 58-60; asst biochemist, Boyce Thompson Inst, 64-66, assoc biochemist, 67; assoc prof, St John's Univ, 67-76, prof biol, arts & sci, 76-90, chmn, Dept Biol, 77-80. *Mem:* Am Chem Soc; Am Soc Biochem Molecular Biol; AAAS; NY Acad Sci. *Res:* Lipid chemistry and metabolism; lipids; biological membranes; biomed applications of computers. *Mailing Add:* 97 Mohican Park Ave Dobbs Ferry NY 10522-2308

JACK, THOMAS RICHARD, PETROLEUM MICROBIOLOGY, INORGANIC CHEMISTRY. *Current Pos:* res scientist, NOVACOR Res & Technol Corp, 81-83, group leader, 83-87, mgr appl sci, Div Nova Corp, 87-92, RES SUPVR, NOVACOR RES & TECHNOL CORP, DIV NOVACOR CHEM, 92- *Personal Data:* b Toronto, Ont, Mar 4, 47; c 1. *Educ:* Univ

Toronto, BSc, 69, PhD(chem), 75. *Prof Exp:* Fel bioeng, Fac Eng Sci, Univ Western Ont, 75-76; vis asst prof chem, Scarborough Col, Univ Toronto, 76-77, asst prof, 77-79; petrol microbiologist, BC Res, 80-81. *Concurrent Pos:* Fel, Nat Res Coun Can, 75; indust assoc, Arctic Inst NAm, Univ Calgary, 81-83; chmn, Biominet Steering Comt. *Mem:* fel Chem Inst Can; Am Soc Microbiol; Am Chem Soc. *Res:* Interface between inorganic chemistry and microbiology; biotechnology and inorganic chemistry in energy production; environmental research spanning air, water and soil; concerns related to petrochemical operations. *Mailing Add:* NOVA Res & Technol Group 2928 16th St NE Calgary AB T2E 7K7 Can

JACKANICZ, THEODORE MICHAEL, REPRODUCTIVE ENDOCRINOLOGY. *Current Pos:* staff scientist 70-74, SCIENTIST REPRODUCTION, POP COUN, NY, 74- *Personal Data:* b Chicago, Ill, Oct 6, 38; div; c 1. *Educ:* Northwestern Univ, BA, 59; Mich State Univ, PhD(biochem), 65. *Prof Exp:* Res fel endocrinol, Harvard Med Sch & Karolinska Inst, Sweden, 65-68; proj specialist pop, Ford Found, 69-70. *Concurrent Pos:* NIH fel, Harvard Med Sch, 65-67 & Karolinska Inst, 67-68. *Mem:* Sigma Xi; AAAS; NY Acad Sci. *Res:* Reproductive endocrinology and contraceptive development. *Mailing Add:* CBR York Ave & 66th St New York NY 10021

JACKEL, LAWRENCE DAVID, MACHINE LEARNING, KNOWLEDGE DISCOVERY. *Current Pos:* mem tech staff exp solid state physics, AT&T Bell Labs, 75-84, head, Device Struct Res Dept, 84-90, head, Adaptive Systs Res Dept, 90-95, ADAPTIVE INFO SERV RES, AT&T LABS, 95- *Personal Data:* b New York, NY, June 16, 48; m 69; c 2. *Educ:* Brandeis Univ, BA, 69; Cornell Univ, MA, 72, PhD(exp physics), 76. *Honors & Awards:* Paul Rappaport Award, Inst Elec & Electronics Engrs Electron Device Soc, 85. *Prof Exp:* Res asst, Sch Appl & Eng Physics, Cornell Univ, 71-75, res assoc, 75. *Mem:* Am Phys Soc; fel Inst Elec & Electronics Engrs. *Res:* Machine learning methods are applied to problems in pattern recognition and knowledge discovery. *Mailing Add:* 4G308 AT&T Labs Holmdel NJ 07733. *E-Mail:* ldj@research.att.com

JACKEL, SIMON SAMUEL, FOOD SCIENCE & CHEMISTRY, FOOD PRODUCT DEVELOPMENT & IMPROVEMENT. *Current Pos:* RETIRED. *Personal Data:* b New York, NY, Nov 11, 17; m 54, Betty Carlson; c Phyliss (deceased) & Glenn E. *Educ:* City Col NY, BS, 38; Columbia Univ, AM, 47, PhD(biochem), 50. *Honors & Awards:* Charles N Frey Award, Am Asn Cereal Chemists, 81. *Prof Exp:* Anal chemist, Plymouth Labs, 38-41; instr instrumentation, Air Corps Tech Training Sch, Ill, 41-43; instr chem & instrumentation, Army Air Forces Eng Officers Sch, Yale Univ, 43-44; res chemist analytical chem, Fleischmann Labs, 44-47; asst biochem, Columbia Univ, 47-50; head, Yeast Dept, Fleischmann Labs, 50-54, head, Fermentation Div, 54-59; vpres & dir res, Vico Prod Co, 59-61; dir, Res & Develop Lab, Qual Bakers Am Coop Inc, 61-76, vpres & dir res & develop, 76-84; chmn bd, Plymouth Tech Serv Assocs, 84. *Concurrent Pos:* Am Bakers Asn tech liaison comt, USDA, 70-86, chmn, 75-86; USPHS res grant, 47-50; pres, Plymouth Tech Serv, 66-; tech ed, Bakery Prod & Mkt Mag, 68-84; mem sci adv comt, Am Inst Baking, 70-92; mem indust adv comt, NDak State Univ, 72-86; chmn, Tech Info Serv, Am Soc Bakery Engrs, 80-; columnist, Cereal Foods World, 83- *Mem:* AAAS; Am Chem Soc; hon fel Am Asn Cereal Chemists; Inst Food Technologists; fel Am Inst Chemists. *Res:* Fermentation; yeast metabolism; baking technology; nutrition; research management; new product development; regulatory affairs compliance; ingredient applications to food manufacturing; enzyme technology; foods; biochemistry. *Mailing Add:* 684 Hidden Lake Dr Tarpon Springs FL 34689. *Fax:* 813-785-6372

JACKELS, CHARLES FREDERICK, QUANTUM CHEMISTRY. *Current Pos:* from asst prof to assoc prof, 77-90, PROF CHEM, WAKE FOREST UNIV, 90- *Personal Data:* b St Paul, Minn, Nov 3, 46; m 70; c 1. *Educ:* Univ Minn, Minneapolis, BChem, 68; Univ Wash, PhD(chem), 75. *Prof Exp:* Fel theoret chem, Battelle Mem Inst, 75-77. *Mem:* Am Chem Soc. *Res:* Ab initio quantum chemical investigations of small molecules; potential energy surface calculations using self-consistent-field and configuration-interaction methods; applications to atmospheric chemistry. *Mailing Add:* Dept Chem Wake Forest Univ 2240 Reynolda Rd Winston-Salem NC 27106-5193

JACKELS, SUSAN CAROL, INORGANIC CHEMISTRY, BIO-INORGANIC CHEMISTRY. *Current Pos:* asst prof, 77-83, ASSOC PROF CHEM, WAKE FOREST UNIV, 83- *Personal Data:* b Wichita, Kans, July 12, 46; m 70. *Educ:* Carleton Col, BA, 68; Univ Wash, PhD(inorg chem), 73. *Prof Exp:* Res biochem, Univ Wash, 73-75 & inorg chem, Ohio State Univ, 75-77. *Concurrent Pos:* Sabbatical leave, Mass Gen Hosp, Harvard Univ, 85-86. *Mem:* Am Chem Soc; Sigma Xi. *Res:* Design, synthesis and study of transition metal complexes relevant to biological systems; macrocyclic complexes; electrochemistry of transition metal complexes. *Mailing Add:* Dept Chem Seattle Univ Broadway & Madison Seattle WA 98122-4460

JACKISCH, PHILIP FREDERICK, ORGANIC CHEMISTRY. *Current Pos:* RES CHEMIST, RES LABS, ETHYL CORP, MICH & LA, 64- *Personal Data:* b Oshkosh, Wis, June 25, 35; m 60; c 1. *Educ:* Univ Wis, BS, 57; Univ Mich, PhD(chem), 65. *Concurrent Pos:* Sci consult to wine industry, 70-81; Sci consult to wine indust, 70-81; tech ed, Am Wine Soc J, 73-81. *Mem:* Am Chem Soc. *Res:* Gasoline additives; lubricant additives; computer applications; enology; viticulture; sensory evaluation of foods; drugs, polymers; flame retardants. *Mailing Add:* 3653 Lake La Berge Circle Baton Rouge LA 70816

JACKIW, ROMAN WLADIMIR, THEORETICAL PHYSICS, HIGH ENERGY PHYSICS. *Current Pos:* from asst prof to assoc prof, 69-77, JERROLD ZACHARIAS PROF PHYSICS, MASS INST TECHNOL, 77- *Personal Data:* b Lublinec, Poland, Nov 8, 39; US citizen; M 81, So Young PI; c 3. *Educ:* Swarthmore Col, AB, 61; Cornell Univ, PhD(physics), 66. *Honors & Awards:* D Heineman Math Phys Prize, Am Phys Soc & Am Inst Physics. *Prof Exp:* Soc Fels jr fel physics, Harvard Univ, 66-69. *Concurrent Pos:* A P Sloan Found res fel, 69-71; consult, Los Alamos Nat Lab, 74-84; J S Guggenheim Mem Found fel, 77-78; vis prof, Rockefeller Univ, 77-78, Univ Calif, Los Angeles & Santa Barbara, 80, Columbia Univ, 89-90; group leader, Inst Theoret Physics, Univ Calif, Santa Barbara, 80. *Mem:* Am Phys Soc; Am Acad Arts & Sci. *Res:* Theoretical and mathematical physics with specialization to particle, condensed matter and gravitational physics. *Mailing Add:* Ctr Theoret Physics Mass Inst Technol 6-320 77 Massachusetts Ave Cambridge MA 02139-4307. *Fax:* 617-253-8674; *E-Mail:* jackiw@mitlns.mit.edu

JACKLET, JON WILLIS, NEUROPHYSIOLOGY, ANIMAL BEHAVIOR. *Current Pos:* from asst prof to assoc prof, 68-80, chmn, Dept Biol Sci, 85-91, PROF BIOL SCI, STATE UNIV NY ALBANY, 81- *Personal Data:* b Springfield Gardens, NY, Apr 16, 35; m 62; c 3. *Educ:* Univ Ore, BS, 62, MA, 64, PhD(biol), 66. *Prof Exp:* USPHS res fel neurophysiol, Calif Inst Technol, 67-68. *Concurrent Pos:* Vis scientist, Alta Heritage Found, 92. *Mem:* Soc Neurosci; Am Physiol Soc; fel AAAS. *Res:* Neurophysiology of behavior; plasticity and specificity of neural organization; cellular and molecular aspects of circadian rhythms. *Mailing Add:* Dept Biol Sci State Univ NY Albany NY 12222. *Fax:* 518-442-4767; *E-Mail:* jwj74@aibnyvms

JACKMAN, DONALD COE, INORGANIC CHEMISTRY, ANALYTICAL CHEMISTRY. *Current Pos:* From asst prof to assoc prof inorg & anal chem, 66-80, PROF CHEM, PFEIFFER COL, 80-, CHAIR, DEPT CHEM & PHYSICS, 90- *Personal Data:* b Cleveland, Tenn, Nov 29, 40; m 65, 81, Jane Lloyd; c 3. *Educ:* Maryville Col, BS, 62; Univ Tenn, Knoxville, PhD(inorg chem), 66. *Concurrent Pos:* NSF res grant, 71; Celanese grant, 85-86; Dept Energy grant, 87 & 88. *Mem:* Am Chem Soc; Int Union Pure & Appl Chem. *Res:* Electron exchange mechanisms in Cobalt-III and Chromium-II systems; immobilized liquid membrane; ruthenium polypyridyls. *Mailing Add:* Dept Chem Pfeiffer Univ Misenheimer NC 28109. *E-Mail:* djackman@jfh.pfeiffer.edu

JACKMAN, LLOYD MILES, ORGANIC CHEMISTRY. *Current Pos:* PROF CHEM, PA STATE UNIV, UNIVERSITY PARK, 67- *Personal Data:* b Goolwa, SAustralia, Apr 1, 26; m 50; c 3. *Educ:* Univ Adelaide, BSc, 45, Hons, 46, MSc, 48, PhD(chem), 51. *Prof Exp:* Beit fel, Univ London, 51-52; asst lectr chem, Imp Col, Univ London, 52-53, lectr, 53-61, reader org chem, Univ, 61-62; prof, Univ Melbourne, 62-67. *Concurrent Pos:* Royal Commonwealth Soc bursary, 60; consult, Monsanto Co, UK & Australia, 60-67, Esso Res & Eng Co, 67-70 & Smith, Kline & French Labs, 67-; vis prof, Iowa State Univ, 62 & Univ Tenn, 65; NSF sr foreign fel, 65; Guggenheim Found fel, 73; Humboldt fel, 77-78; Wilsmore fel, 88. *Mem:* Am Chem Soc; The Chem Soc; fel Royal Australian Chem Inst; fel AAAS. *Res:* Applications of nuclear magnetic resonance spectroscopy in organic chemistry; structures and mechanisms of reactions of organic compounds with lithium. *Mailing Add:* 152 Davey Lab Pa State Univ University Park PA 16802

JACKMAN, THOMAS EDWARD, INTERFACE SCIENCE, ION-SOLID INTERACTIONS. *Current Pos:* res off, 86-94, actg dir technol, 93-94, DIR MAT TECHNOL, NAT RES COUN, 94- *Personal Data:* b Thamesville, Ont, Mar 16, 51; m 77; c 2. *Educ:* Univ Guelph, BSc, 72, MSc, 74, PhD(physics), 79. *Prof Exp:* Guest scientist, Max Planck Inst, Stuttgart, 74-75; vis fel, Chalk River Nuclear Labs, Ont, 80, res officer, 80-86. *Concurrent Pos:* Res asst, Dept Physics, Univ Guelph, Ont, 76-; resident vis, Bell Labs, Murray Hill, NJ, 77-78; secy & treas, Surf Sci Div, Chem Inst Can & Can Asn Physicists, 87-90; adj prof eng physics, MacMaster Univ, 88-; mem, Grant Selection Comt, Nat Sci & Eng Res Coun Can, 90- *Mem:* Chem Inst Can; Can Asn Physicists; Boehmische Phys Soc; Sigma Xi. *Res:* Fundamental interactions between MeV ion beams and solids and their application in material science; the growth and characterization of two-dimensional, multilayer semiconductor structures. *Mailing Add:* Microstruct Sci Inst Nat Res Coun Can Ottawa ON K1A 0R6 Can

JACKNOW, JOEL, PHYSICAL CHEMISTRY, GENERAL ENGINEERING. *Current Pos:* PROG ANALYST & MGR, ENG PROG MGT, RES & DEVELOP SERV, FED AVIATION ADMIN, 89- *Personal Data:* b New York, NY, Dec 15, 37. *Educ:* City Col New York, BChE, 59; Univ Utah, PhD(phys chem), 63. *Prof Exp:* Res chemist, Fundamental Res Sect, Texaco Inc, 63-65; res assoc & fel chem, Polytech Inst Brooklyn, 65-66; res assoc med sch, Tufts Univ, 66-67; sr physiologist, Bioelectronics Br, Instrumentation Lab, NASA Electronics Res Ctr, 67-68; sr staff mem, Int Res & Technol, 68-71; phys sci adminr, Environ Protection Agency, Off Planning & Eval, 71-74; sr prog mgr, Environ Qual Systs Inc, 74-75; environ & energy consult, 75-79; proj mgr & sr scientist, Habitat Resources Prog, US Fish & Wildlife Serv, 79-86. *Mem:* Am Chem Soc; Wildlife Soc; Asn Sci Technol & Innovation; Technol Transfer Soc. *Res:* Sources of water pollution; economic and technical analysis of environmental alternatives; research and progammatic strategic guidance; resource allocation; environmental contaminant impacts on fish and wildlife; airport safety and aviation weather development. *Mailing Add:* 8110 Timber Valley Ct Dunn Loring VA 22027

JACKO, MICHAEL GEORGE, TRIBOLOGY, CHEMISTRY. *Current Pos:* CONSULT, 97- *Personal Data:* b Windsor, Ont, Oct 11, 38; m 63, Mary Boldizer. *Educ:* Assumption Univ, BSc, 61; Univ Windsor, PhD(phys chem), 64. *Prof Exp:* Phys chemist, Imp Oil Res Dept, Sarnia, Ont, 64-66; phys chemist, Bendix Res Lab, 66-79, sr prin chemist, Bendix Advan Technol Ctr, 79-80, prin chemist, Bendix Mat Ctr, 81-82; mem staff, Allied Automotive Tech Ctr, 83-92, mem staff, Allied Signal Braking Systs, 93-96, Allied Signal Friction Mat, 96-97. *Concurrent Pos:* Res assoc chem, Univ Windsor, 73-74. *Mem:* Am Chem Soc; Soc Automotive Engrs; fel Am Chem Inst. *Res:* Gas kinetics; radical reactions; gas chromatography; petroleum products; polymers; thermal analysis; friction materials; functional fluids; brake wear debris studies; brake interace reactions; new friction materials; tribology; light weight brakes for automotive. *Mailing Add:* 23721 Merrill Ave Southfield MI 48075-3496

JACKOBS, JOHN JOSEPH, PHYSICAL CHEMISTRY, X-RAY CRYSTALLOGRAPHY. *Current Pos:* SR PROJ MGR, CARS INFO SYSTS CORP, 88- *Personal Data:* b Hibbing, Minn, Mar 25, 39; m 65; c 3. *Educ:* Wis State Univ, Superior, BA, 61; Iowa State Univ, MS, 64; Ariz State Univ, PhD(phys chem), 67. *Prof Exp:* Res asst chem, Case Western Reserve Univ, 67-69; asst prof physics, Heidelberg Col, 69-75; registr & dir, Comput Ctr, Coe Col, 75-87; programmer/analyst, Info Systs, Inc, 87-88. *Mem:* AAAS; Am Crystallog Asn; Sigma Xi. *Res:* X-ray diffraction studies of organic and small biological molecules. *Mailing Add:* 7733 Westwind Dr Cincinnati OH 45242-5027

JACKOBS, JOSEPH ALDEN, AGRONOMY. *Current Pos:* RETIRED. *Personal Data:* b Shell Lake, Wis, Oct 23, 17; m 40; c 3. *Educ:* Univ Wis, BS, 40, MS, 43, PhD(agron), 47. *Prof Exp:* Asst agronomist, Irrig Exp Sta, State Col Wash, 46-51; assoc prof agron, Univ Ill, Urbana, 51-55, prof crop prod. *Concurrent Pos:* Grass & fodder specialist, Int Coop Admin, India, 58-60, crop prod agronomist, US AID, 67-69, Int Soybean Agronomist, 79-86. *Mem:* Fel AAAS; fel Am Soc Agron; Sigma Xi. *Res:* Alfalfa management, cutting treatments; legume, grass and fertility interactions; seed rotting in sweetclover caused by Pythium; genetic shifts in forage species when grown outside region of adaptation; establishment of forage species; soybean production in the tropics; grassland ecology. *Mailing Add:* 101 W Windsor Rd Urbana IL 61801

JACKOVITZ, JOHN FRANKLIN, PHYSICAL INORGANIC CHEMISTRY. *Current Pos:* sr scientist, 67-73, sr res scientist, 73-76, ADV SCIENTIST, WESTINGHOUSE RES & DEVELOP LABS, 76- *Personal Data:* b Greensburg, Pa, Nov 9, 39; m 64; c 3. *Educ:* St Vincent Col, BSc, 61; Univ Notre Dame, PhD(chem), 65. *Prof Exp:* NSF vis scholar chem, Northwestern Univ, 66-67. *Concurrent Pos:* Res assoc, Univ Pittsburgh, 67-73. *Mem:* Soc Appl Spectros (pres, 81); Am Chem Soc; Electrochem Soc; Coblentz Soc; Sigma Xi; Soc Electroanal Chem. *Res:* Chelate chemistry, infrared and Raman spectra and force fields of inorganic molecules; uranium chemistry; electrod rxns. *Mailing Add:* 1340 Knollwood Dr Monroeville PA 15146-4449. *Fax:* 412-256-1948

JACKOWSKI, SUZANNE, CELL PHYSIOLOGY. *Current Pos:* res asst, Dept Biochem, St Judes Children's Res Hosp, 80-81, res assoc, 81-85, asst mem, 85-90, ASSOC MEM, DEPT BIOCHEM, ST JUDES CHILDREN'S RES HOSP, MEMPHIS, TENN, 90- *Personal Data:* b Lackawanna, NY, Jan 8, 51. *Educ:* Canisius Col, BA, 72; Univ Tenn, PhD(cell physiol), 77. *Prof Exp:* Fel, Dept Physiol, Univ Conn, Health Ctr, Farmington, 77-70; res assoc, Dept Microbiol, Univ Ill, Urbana, 79. *Concurrent Pos:* Prin investr, Am Cancer Soc, 80-81 & 84-85, Am Heart Asn, 85-88, NIH, 81-; comt mem, Horng-Mo Lee, Dept Biochem, Univ Tenn, 89-91, Zhiwei Shen, Dept Biochem, Dalhousie Univ, Halifax, Nova Scotia, Can, 94; adj asst prof, Dept Biochem, Univ Tenn, Memphis, 89-91, adj assoc prof, 91-; mem, physiol chem study sect, NIH, 92- *Mem:* Am Soc Biochem & Molecular Biol; Am Soc Microbiol; AAAS. *Res:* Regulation of phospholipid and fatty acids biosynthesis; coordination of membrane biogenesis with the cell cycle; lipid-mediated signal transduction; control of intracellular coenzyme A content; author of 44 publications. *Mailing Add:* Dept Biochem St Jude Children's Res Hosp 332 N Lauderdale Memphis TN 38105-2729

JACKS, THOMAS JEROME, BIOCHEMISTRY, PLANT PHYSIOLOGY. *Current Pos:* Nat Acad Sci res fel biochem, 65-67, RES LEADER, SOUTHERN REGIONAL RES CTR, USDA, 67- *Personal Data:* b Chicago, Ill, Jan 24, 38. *Educ:* Western Reserve Univ, BS, 60, PhD, 65. *Concurrent Pos:* Res staff, Tulane Univ, 74-; assoc ed, Am Oil Chemist's Soc, 75- *Mem:* Am Oil Chemist's Soc; Electron Micros Soc Am; Am Chem Soc; Am Soc Plant Physiol; AAAS. *Res:* Protein chemistry; enzymology; electron microscopy; oxygen radical chemistry. *Mailing Add:* PO Box 19687 Southern Regional Res Ctr New Orleans LA 70179. *Fax:* 504-286-4419; *E-Mail:* tjacks@nola.srrc.usda.gov

JACKS, THOMAS MAURO, MEDICAL MICROBIOLOGY. *Current Pos:* SR RES FEL, MERCK RES LABS, RAHWAY, NJ, 76- *Personal Data:* b Harrisburg, Pa, Mar 13, 41; m 69, Lynne Gorss; c 2. *Educ:* Duquesne Univ, BS, 64; Pa State Univ, MS, 66, PhD(microbiol), 68. *Prof Exp:* Asst prof biol, State Univ NY Col New Paltz, 68-69; sr res microbiologist, Vet Microbiol Sect, Norwich Pharmacol Co, 69-76. *Concurrent Pos:* Instr, State Univ NY Agr & Tech Col Morrisville, 69-70 & 74-75; mem, NJ State Bd Vet Med Examrs, 84- *Mem:* NY Acad Sci; Am Soc Microbiol; Infectious Dis Soc Am. *Res:* Escherichia coli pathogenicity in man and animals; bovine antibodies against Escherichia coli; salmonellosis in cattle and swine; swine dysentery; pneumonic pasteurellosis in cattle and swine; endocrinology-tropic hormone secretion. *Mailing Add:* 842 Wallberg Ave Westfield NJ 07090. *Fax:* 732-594-1298; *E-Mail:* tom_jacks@merck.com

JACKSON, ALBERT S(MITH), COMPUTER SCIENCE, CONTROL SYSTEMS. *Current Pos:* APPLN ENG MGR, MOTOROLA, INC, 75- *Personal Data:* b Sylvia, Kans, Feb 2, 27; m 78, Elaine S Spontak; c Linda, Jill, Terri, Steve & Craig. *Educ:* Calif Inst Technol, BS, 51, MS, 52; Cornell Univ, PhD(elec eng), 56. *Prof Exp:* Engr, Bell Tel Labs, 52; instr, Cornell Univ, 52-55, asst prof, 56-59; mgr, Data Processing & Controls Dept, Thompson-Ramo-Wooldridge Prod Co, 59-61; pres, Control Technol, Inc, 61-65; chief scientist, Milgo Electronics Corp, 65-70; pres, Opto Logic Corp, 70-75. *Concurrent Pos:* Consult, Gen Elec Co, 53-59, Gen Dynamics/Convair, 56-58 & Naval Res Lab, 57-59; chmn prof group Human Factors in Electronics, Inst Elec & Electronics Engrs, 63-64, educ coordr Region 6 & corresp mem Educ Activ Bd, 84-85; lectr, Univ Calif, Irving, 65- & Univ Calif, Los Angeles, 78-80. *Mem:* Inst Elec & Electronics Engrs. *Res:* Analog and digital computers; feedback control system theory; application of computers to control systems; human factors research; concurrent computer architecture; computer simulation, microprocessor-based system design. *Mailing Add:* Motorola Semiconductor 101 Pacific 300 Irvine CA 92718

JACKSON, ANDREW, TRIBOLOGY. *Current Pos:* Res engr, Mobil Res & Develop Corp, 74-76, sr res engr, 76-80, assoc, 80-84, res assoc, 84-88, sr res assoc, Cent Res Lab, Princeton, NJ, 88-93, SCIENTIST, PAULSBORO RES LAB, MOBIL RES & DEVELOP CORP, PAULSBORO, NJ, 93- *Personal Data:* b Preston, Eng, Dec 5, 48; m 81; c Robert, David & Lily. *Educ:* Imperial Col, London Univ, BSc, 70, PhD(mech eng), 74. *Honors & Awards:* Hunt Award, Am Soc Lubrication Engrs, 77, Hodson Award, 82, Bisson Award, 93. *Concurrent Pos:* Dir, Soc Tribologists & Lubrication Engrs, 87. *Mem:* Soc Tribologists & Lubrication Engrs, (treas, 92, secy, 93, vpres, 94, pres, 95); Am Soc Mech Engrs; Inst Mech Engrs. *Res:* Lubrication science (tribology); elastohydrodynamic lubrication; traction; rolling contact fatigue; internal combustion engine lubrication; synthetic lubricants. *Mailing Add:* 4 Walking Purchase Dr Pennington NJ 08534-2917. *Fax:* 609-224-3669; *E-Mail:* axjackson@pau.mobil.com

JACKSON, ANDREW C, BIOMEDICAL ENGINEERING. *Current Pos:* assoc prof, 83-91, chmn ad interim, 89-92, PROF BIOMED ENG, COL ENG, BOSTON UNIV, 91- *Personal Data:* b Loma Linda, Calif, Aug 10, 40. *Educ:* Univ Nev, Reno, BS, 63, MS, 66; Univ Miss, PhD(mech eng), 72. *Prof Exp:* Res assoc physiol, Harvard Sch Pub Health, 72-76; asst prof pediat, Harvard Med Sch & Children's Hosp, 76-79; from asst prof to assoc prof, Calif Primate Res Ctr, Sch Vet Med & Sch Med, Univ Calif, Davis, 79-83. *Concurrent Pos:* Vis prof, Univ Cape Town, Africa, 89 & Lab de Genie Medical, Inst Physique Appl, Lausanne, Switz, 91. *Mem:* Am Physiol Soc; Bio Med Eng Soc. *Mailing Add:* Dept Biomed Eng Boston Univ 44 Cummington St Boston MA 02215

JACKSON, ANDREW D, JR, THEORETICAL NUCLEAR PHYSICS. *Current Pos:* from asst prof to assoc prof, 68-76, PROF PHYSICS, STATE UNIV NY STONY BROOK, 76- *Personal Data:* b Orange, NJ, Dec 20, 41; m 66. *Educ:* Princeton Univ, AB, 63, MA, 65, PhD(physics), 67. *Prof Exp:* Res assoc physics, Princeton Univ, 67; NATO res fel, Univ Sussex, 67-68. *Concurrent Pos:* Alfred P Sloan Found fel, 71-72. *Mem:* Am Phys Soc. *Res:* Nucleon-nucleon interaction and nuclear structure calculations. *Mailing Add:* Dept Physics State Univ NY Stony Brook NY 11794

JACKSON, ANDREW OTIS, PLANT VIROLOGY. *Current Pos:* asst prof, 73-77, ASSOC PROF PLANT VIROL, PURDUE UNIV, 77- *Personal Data:* b Enterprise, Ala, Apr 14, 41. *Educ:* Okla State Univ, BS, 64, MS, 67; Univ Man, PhD(plant path), 70. *Prof Exp:* Fel plant virol, Dept Agr Biochem, Univ Ariz & Dept Plant Path, Univ Nebr, 70-73. *Mem:* Am Phytopathological Soc; AAAS; Sigma Xi; Soc Gen Microbiol. *Mailing Add:* 111 Kashland Hall Berkeley CA 94720-3102

JACKSON, ANNE LOUISE, IMMUNOLOGY. *Current Pos:* RETIRED. *Personal Data:* b Watertown, NY. *Educ:* Cornell Univ, BS, 56; Univ Mich, MS, 57, PhD(microbiol), 63. *Prof Exp:* Res assoc biochem, Univ Mich, 61-63; asst prof microbiol, Sch Med & Dent, Georgetown Univ, 63-68; dir tech serv, Meloy Labs, 68-74; dir res immunol, Kent Labs, 74-77; mem staff, Dept Microbiol, Univ BC, 77-80; mgr tech serv, Becton Dickinson Monoclonal Ctr, 80- *Concurrent Pos:* Guest worker, Lab Immunol, Nat Inst Allergy & Infectious Dis, NIH, 63-65; asst guest prof, Univ BC, 75- *Mem:* Am Asn Immunol; Fedn Am Socs Exp Biol; Can Asn Immunol; Am Fedn Clin Res. *Res:* Production and development of immunologic tests for in vitro diagnostics. *Mailing Add:* 3613 NW 199th St Ridgefield WA 98642

JACKSON, BENITA MARIE, PREVENTIVE MEDICINE, EPIDEMIOLOGY. *Current Pos:* clin asst prof, 92-93, asst prof, 93-95, MED DIR EPIDEMIOL, MED CTR, OHIO STATE UNIV, 95-, CLIN ASST PROF EPIDEMIOL, SCH PUB HEALTH, 95- *Personal Data:* b Englewood, NJ, Aug 14, 56; m 93, Lewis R Smoot Jr; c Lewis R Smoot III. *Educ:* Mt Holyoke Col, AB, 78; Howard Univ, MD, 82; Emory Univ, MPH, 89. *Prof Exp:* Epidemic intel officer, Ctrs Dis Control, 90-92. *Mem:* Nat Med Asn; Soc Health Care Epidemiol; Practrs Infection Control. *Res:* Applied epidemiology; nosocomial infections; health care policy. *Mailing Add:* Ohio State Univ Med Ctr Epidemiol 410 W Tenth Ave Columbus OH 43210

JACKSON, BENJAMIN A, TOXICOLOGY. *Current Pos:* PVT CONSULT, 92- *Personal Data:* b Hillburn, NY, July 8, 29; m 55, Gloria Smith; c Benita M, Jolie A, Pamela S & Benjamin A Jr. *Educ:* NY State Col Teachers, Albany, BA, 50; Rensselaer Polytech Inst, MS, 51; NY Univ, PhD(biol), 57; Fairleigh Dickinson Univ, MBA, 78, Acad Toxicol Sci, dipl, 84, cert gen toxicol. *Prof Exp:* Res biologist, Am Cyanamid Co, 51-67; electron microscopist, Toxicol

Dept, Sterling-Winthrop Res Inst, 67-69; sr res toxicologist, Reproductive Safety Eval Group Toxicol Res, Lederle Labs, Am Cyanamid Co, 69-75, mgr teratology & mutagenicity, Toxicol Sect, 75-78; supvr petitions reviewers, Ctr Food Safety & Appl Nutrit Food & Drug Admin, 78-80, chief, Color & Cosmetic Eval Br, Bur Foods, 80-85, dir path, Ctr Food Safety & Appl Nutrit, 85-90, prog mgr, Risk Assessment Res & Policy Develop, 87-90; sr sci adv, Environ Corp, 90-92. *Concurrent Pos:* Res assoc, Cornell Med Col, 64-65; adj asst prof pharmacol & toxicol, Howard Univ, 80-85. *Mem:* Soc Toxicol; fel Acad Toxicol Sci. *Res:* Experimental liver tumors; short term effects of drugs; mitotic activity; drug toxicity; quantitation of morphological changes; electron microscopy; teratology; mutagenicity; correlation between mutagenicity and carcinogenic potential of drugs; regulatory toxicology; color additive toxicology; cosmetic ingredients safety evaluation; mutagenicity testing, submitting pathology data; risk assessment. *Mailing Add:* Jackson Assoc 3116 Birchtree Lane Silver Spring MD 20906. *Fax:* 301-871-6821

JACKSON, BENJAMIN T, SURGERY, FETAL PHYSIOLOGY. *Current Pos:* PROF SURG, SCH MED, BROWN UNIV, 80- *Personal Data:* b Jacksonville, Fla, Apr 28, 29; m 53, Jean Davis; c Benjamin Jr, Leigh, Kimberly & Jillian. *Educ:* Duke Univ, MD, 54. *Prof Exp:* Intern med, Duke Univ Hosp, 54-55; asst resident surg, Univ Minn Hosps, 57-58; resident, Med Col Va, 58-62, instr, 63-64; from asst prof to prof surg, Sch Med, Boston Univ, 64-80. *Concurrent Pos:* USPHS res fel, Med Col Va, 58-62; advan res fel, Am Heart Asn, 61-63, estab investr, 63-68; asst chief surg serv, Boston Vet Admin Hosp, 74-80; chief surg serv, Providence Vet Admin Med Ctr, 80. *Mem:* Soc Gynec Invest; Am Fedn Clin Res; Am Soc Exp Path; Soc Univ Surg; Am Col Surg; Am Physiol Soc. *Res:* Fetal cardiovascular and endocrine physiology; pathophysiology of congenital cardiovascular anomalies; fetal hormonal responses in diabetic pregnancy. *Mailing Add:* 11 October Lane Weston MA 02193

JACKSON, BERNARD VERNON, SOLAR PHYSICS, INTERPLANETARY MEDIUM PHYSICS. *Current Pos:* asst res physicist, 79-87, assoc res physicist astrophys, 88-93, RES PHYSICIST, DEPT ELEC ENG & COMPUT SCI, UNIV CALIF, SAN DIEGO, 93- *Personal Data:* b Peoria, Ill, Nov 7, 42; m 90; c 2. *Educ:* Univ Ill, Urbana, BS, 64; Ind Univ, Bloomington, MS, 67, PhD(astrophys),70. *Honors & Awards:* Glacier named in honor, Jackson Glacier. *Prof Exp:* Res asst, Ind Univ, Bloomington, 64-70; geophysicist, Univ Calif, Los Angeles, 70-73; sci programmer astrophys, Arecibo Observ, Cornell Univ, 73-75; res fel skylab, High Altitude Observ, Nat Ctr Atmospheric Res, Boulder, Colo, 75-77; res assoc astrophys, Commonwealth Sci & Indust Res Orgn, Sydney, Australia, 77-79. *Concurrent Pos:* Vis prof, Nagoya Univ, Japan, 95 & Max Planck Inst Astron, Ger, 96. *Mem:* Am Astron Soc; Am Geophys Union; Int Astron Union. *Res:* Solar and interplanetary physics; solar wind and its interaction with other material as this plasma flows outward from the sun. *Mailing Add:* CASS 424 Univ Calif San Diego La Jolla CA 92093-0424

JACKSON, BETTINA B CARTER, BIOCHEMISTRY, BACTERIOLOGY. *Current Pos:* RETIRED. *Personal Data:* b Woburn, Mass, Sept 4, 10; m 51, Daniel F; c Bettina C (de Weeger), Anthony A Carter & Lawrence Q Carter. *Educ:* Univ Mich, AB, 29, MS, 45; Univ Pittsburgh, PhD(biochem & immunol), 51. *Honors & Awards:* Gerber Award Biochem, 56. *Prof Exp:* Chief blood grouping lab & res immunol, Inst Path, Pittsburgh, 44-53; lectr epidemiol, Duquesne Univ, 46; asst prof microbiol, State Univ NY Col Med, 53-55; asst prof biol, Western Mich Univ, 55-59, assoc prof, 59; assoc prof, Univ Louisville, 59-63, res assoc med sch, 59-63; assoc prof microbiol, Syracuse Univ, 63-69, prof, 70; prof biol, Cazenovia Col NY, 70-73, chmn sci & math, 70-73. *Concurrent Pos:* Distinguished lectr, Miners Mem Hosp, WVa, 58. *Mem:* Sigma Xi; Am Chem Soc; NY Acad Sci; Am Inst Biol Sci; AAAS. *Res:* Use of various types of blood components in therapeutics similar to employment of Rh factor in relation to erythroblastosis fetalis. *Mailing Add:* 3323 Guilford Ct Naples FL 33962

JACKSON, BILL GRINNELL, BETA-LACTAM ANTIBIOTICS, BIOCATALYTIC ORGANIC CHEMISTRY. *Current Pos:* PRES, BETA-EVAR INC, 93- *Personal Data:* b 1931; m 54, Beverly Dunnette; c William B & Brenda J. *Educ:* Iowa State Univ, BS, 53, PhD(org chem), 57. *Prof Exp:* Sr org chemist, Eli Lilly & Co, 59-64, res scientist, 64-70, sr res scientist, 70-88, res adv, 88-93. *Concurrent Pos:* Adj fac chem, Ind Purdue Univ, 60-91. *Mem:* Am Chem Soc; Am Soc Microbiol. *Res:* Methods for synthesis of beta lactam antibiotics with emphasis on biocatalytic processes and processes which provide single enantiomers as product. *Mailing Add:* 4230 Lincoln Rd Indianapolis IN 46208. *Fax:* 317-328-9692; *E-Mail:* bjackbeuar@worldnet.att.net

JACKSON, C(HARLES) IAN, SCIENCE POLICY. *Current Pos:* DIR, CHREOD LTD, OTTAWA, 93- *Personal Data:* b Keighley, Eng, Feb 11, 35; Can & UK citizen; div; c Janet (Louise). *Educ:* Univ London, BA, 56; McGill Univ, MSc, 59, PhD(geog), 61. *Honors & Awards:* Darton Prize, Royal Meteorol Soc, 62; Evan Durbin Prize, Inst Econ Affairs, 66. *Prof Exp:* Lectr geog, London Sch Econ & Polit Sci, 59-69; head, Econ Geog Sect, Can Dept Energy, Mines & Resources, 69-71; dir priorities & planning, Can Ministry State Urban Affairs, 71-75; exec dir, Can Habitat & Energy Secretariat, 75, tech officer, 75-78; sr econ affairs officer, UN Econ Comn Europe, 78-81; exec dir, Sigma Xi, 81-87. *Concurrent Pos:* Dir, Chreod Ltd, (Ohawa, Can), 91-; assoc fel, Timothy Dwight Col, Yale Univ, 94- *Mem:* Hakluyt Soc; Champlain Soc. *Res:* Environmental protection; energy use; history of discovery; global warming. *Mailing Add:* 29 N Lake Dr Hamden CT 06517

JACKSON, CARL WAYNE, EXPERIMENTAL HEMATOLOGY, RADIATION BIOLOGY. *Current Pos:* postdoctoral fel hemat, St Jude Children's Hosp, 71-73, res assoc, 73-75, asst mem, 76-80, assoc mem, 81-87, MEM, ST JUDE CHILDREN'S RES HOSP, 87- *Personal Data:* b Carbondale, Ill, Nov 27, 42; m 63, Ernestine A Williams. *Educ:* Southern Ill Univ, BA, 63; Univ Tenn, Knoxville, PhD(radiation biol), 71. *Prof Exp:* Biol lab specialist physiol, Oak Ridge Nat Lab, 63-71. *Mem:* Am Soc Hemat; Int Soc Exp Hemat; Int Soc Thrombosis & Haemostasis. *Res:* Hemopoiesis; thrombopoiesis; cell kinetics; cell regulation and differentiation; radiation hematology; megakaryocyte differentiation; megakaryocytopoieses; animal models of defective platelet production; identification of megakaryocyte precursors. *Mailing Add:* St Jude Children's Res Hosp 332 N Lauderdale Memphis TN 38101. *Fax:* 901-495-2176; *E-Mail:* carl.jackson@stjude.org

JACKSON, CARLTON DARNELL, BIOCHEMISTRY, ONCOLOGY. *Current Pos:* ASSOC PROF BIOCHEM & INTERDISCIPLINARY TOXICOL, MED SCH, UNIV ARK, LITTLE ROCK, 72- *Personal Data:* b Wiggins, Miss, Dec 1, 38; div; c Martin & Janet. *Educ:* Miss Col, BS, 61; Univ Tenn, MS, 63, PhD(biochem), 67. *Prof Exp:* Res trainee biochem, St Jude Children's Res Hosp, 64-67; USPHS fel, Univ Miami, 67-69; asst prof biochem, Univ Tenn, 69-72; res chemist carcinogenesis, Nat Ctr Toxicol Res, Food & Drug Admin, 72-75, chief, Div Carcinogenic Res, 76-79. *Concurrent Pos:* Res biochemist carcinogenesis, Vet Admin Hosp, Memphis, 69-72; pharmacologist, Off Sci Intel, Nat Ctr Toxicol Res, Food & Drug Admin, Div Molecular Biol, 81-84, Div Comp Toxicol, 84-88, Div Nutrit Toxicol, 88- *Mem:* Am Asn Cancer Res; Sigma Xi. *Res:* Mechanisms of chemical carcinogenesis; molecular mechanism of hormone action; protein and nucleic acid synthesis; molecular biology of cell division and differentiation; nutrition and cancer. *Mailing Add:* Nat Ctr Toxicol Res Food & Drug Admin Jefferson AR 72079

JACKSON, CARMAULT B, JR, INTERNAL MEDICINE, HEMATOLOGY. *Current Pos:* CONSULT, 86- *Personal Data:* b Newton, Mass, Apr 19, 24; m 47; c 3. *Educ:* Bucknell Univ, BS, 48; Univ Pa, MD, 52. *Prof Exp:* Mem, Proj Mercury, NASA Space Task Group, 58-61; pvt prac internal med, San Antonio, Tex, 61-76; assoc dir extramural progs, Univ Tex Syst, 77-79; exec vpres & adminr, Metrop Med Ctr, San Antonio, Tex, 79-83; med adv, Baptist Med Ctr, San Antonio, Tex, 83-86. *Concurrent Pos:* Mem bd, Tex Inst Med Assessment, 76-80, pres, 80-81. *Mem:* Inst Med Nat Acad Sci; Am Cancer Soc. *Res:* Cancer control information and technology dissemination. *Mailing Add:* Med Adv Serv 16902 Hidden Timber Wood San Antonio TX 78248-1417

JACKSON, CRAIG MERTON, BIOCHEMISTRY, MEDICAL DEVICES & DIAGNOSTICS. *Current Pos:* INDEPENDENT CONSULT, 96- *Personal Data:* b Staples, Minn, Dec 2, 41; m 95, Beth A Dambeck; c Brian A. *Educ:* Wash State Univ, BS, 63; Univ Wash, PhD(biochem), 67. *Prof Exp:* Res assoc, Col Med, Univ Ariz, 67; Am Cancer Soc fel chem physics, Unilever Res Lab, Port Sunlight, Eng, 67-69; from asst prof to prof chem, Sch Med, Wash Univ, 69-83; sci dir, Southeast Mich Region, Am Red Cross, 83-92; pres, Reagents Appls Inc, San Diego, 93-95. *Concurrent Pos:* Res grants, Nat Heart, Lung & Blood Inst, res reviewer, Am Heart Asn, 71-74, estab investr, 74-79, chmn, Int Comt Thrombosis, 82-84; mem coun thrombosis, Am Heart Asn, 71-; vis prof, Kyushi Univ, Japan, 82; Am Red Cross estab investr, 83-92; adj prof biochem, Sch Med, Wayne State Univ, 84-; mem adv comt, Div Blood Dis & Resources, Nat Heart, Lung & Blood Inst, 87-89, chmn, 89-90. *Mem:* Fel AAAS; Int Soc Thrombosis & Hemostasis; Am Asn Clin Chem; Am Chem Soc; Am Heart Asn; Sigma Xi; Am Soc Qual Control. *Res:* Protein chemistry and enzymology of blood coagulation, lipid-protein interactions in blood coagulation; physical chemistry of lipids; plasma proteins; invitro diagnostics. *Mailing Add:* 13024 Caminito Mar Villa Del Mar CA 92014-3608. *E-Mail:* craigmj561@aol.com

JACKSON, CRAWFORD GARDNER, JR, VERTEBRATE BIOLOGY, PALEONTOLOGY. *Current Pos:* RETIRED. *Personal Data:* b Birmingham, Ala, Jan 5, 31; div; c Crawford III. *Educ:* Emory Univ, AB, 52; Univ Fla, MS, 59, PhD(biol), 64; Nat Univ, MA, 85. *Prof Exp:* Instr biol, Armstrong Col, 52-53; asst prof, Univ Sala, 65-67; from assoc prof to prof, Col Women, Miss State Univ, 67-74; managing ed, Ecol Monogr, 74-78; cur & actg dir, San Diego Natural Hist Mus, 78-80; prof, Dept Natural Sci, Nat Univ, 80-92. *Concurrent Pos:* Vis lectr, San Diego State Col, 70-71; ed-in-chief, Herpetologica, 73-79; adj prof biol, San Diego State Univ, 74-79; res assoc, Smithsonian Inst, 74- & San Diego Natural Hist Mus, 75-; lectr, Sch Med & Continuing Educ, Univ Calif, San Diego, 77-83. *Mem:* Sigma Xi. *Res:* Ecology, morphology, ethology, pathobiology of amphibians and reptiles; paleobiology of reptiles. *Mailing Add:* PO Box 2044 Port Angeles WA 98362-0276

JACKSON, CURTIS M(AITLAND), SHAPE-MEMORY ALLOYS, ALLOY DEVELOPMENT AND PRODUCTION. *Current Pos:* Prin metallurgist, Alloy Develop Div, Battelle Mem Inst, 54-61, proj leader, Specialty Alloys Div, 61-67, assoc chief, 67-77, ASSOC MGR PHYS & APPL METALL, COLUMBUS LABS, BATTELLE MEM INST, 77- *Personal Data:* b New York, NY, Apr 20, 33; m 57; c David C & Carol (Adams). *Educ:* NY Univ, BMetE, 54; Ohio State Univ, MS, 59, PhD(metall), 66. *Honors & Awards:* IR-100 Award, Indust Res Mag, 76; Mordica Mem Award, Wire Asn Int, 77, J Edward Donnellan Award, 78; Meritous Technical Paper Award, 81. *Concurrent Pos:* Chmn, N Cent US region, Am Inst Mining, Metall & Petrol Engrs, 65-66; dir, Wire J, 73-78 & Wire Found, 74-86. *Mem:* Am Inst Mining, Metall & Petrol Engrs; Am Soc Metals; Am Vacuum Soc; Wire Asn Int (second vpres, 73-74, first vpres, 74-76, pres, 76-77); Sigma Xi. *Res:* Physical metallurgy; alloy development; nucleation and growth of thin films; technical economics; shape-memory alloys; metal failure analysis; electrical and electronic alloys; melting, casting and mechanical working of metals; wire technology. *Mailing Add:* 5088 Dalmeny Ct Columbus OH 43220-2693

JACKSON, CURTIS RUKES, RESEARCH MANAGEMENT, FOREIGN AGRICULTURAL DEVELOPMENT. *Current Pos:* RETIRED. *Personal Data:* b Kansas City, Mo, July 25, 27; m 51, Sarah J Saffold; c 6. *Educ:* Univ Miami, BS, 49; Fla State Univ, MS, 51; Univ Fla, PhD(plant path). 58. *Honors & Awards:* Res Award, Nat Peanut Coun. *Prof Exp:* Assoc dir, Agr Exp Sta, Univ Ga, 73-83; dir, Int Coop, Icrisat, India & Niger, 83-86; dir, Off Res & Univ Rels Aid, Washington, 86-92. *Concurrent Pos:* Consult foreign agr develop proj, Indust & Govt, 70- *Res:* Diseases of peanuts; vegetables and ornamental plants; soil microbiology; tropical agricultural development. *Mailing Add:* Rte 1 Box 1189 Clayton GA 30525

JACKSON, DALE LATHAM, ZOOLOGY. *Current Pos:* from asst prof to assoc prof, 61-69, DEPT HEAD, UNIV AKRON, 68-, PROF BIOL, 69- *Personal Data:* b Eng, May 20, 32; m 59; c 1. *Educ:* Univ Durham, BSc, 55, PhD(entom), 59. *Prof Exp:* Asst prof zool, Univ Guelph, 59-61. *Mem:* Entom Soc Can; fel Royal Entom Soc; Soc Syst Zool; Sigma Xi. *Res:* Host relationships and taxonomy of proctotrupoidea experimental taxonomy. *Mailing Add:* 555 Royal Ave Akron OH 44303

JACKSON, DANIEL FRANCIS, LIMNOLOGY. *Current Pos:* MEM STAFF, JACKSON & JACKSON ASSOC, 78- *Personal Data:* b Pittsburgh, Pa, June 11, 25; m 51, Bettina Bush. *Educ:* Univ Pittsburgh, BS, 49, MS, 50; State Univ NY, PhD(water resources), 57. *Prof Exp:* Lectr biol, Univ Pittsburgh, 49-51; asst prof, Col of Steubenville, 51-52; hydrologist, US Army Corps Engrs, Pa, 52-53; asst col forestry, State Univ NY, 53-55; asst prof, Western Mich Univ, 55-59; from asst prof to assoc prof, Univ Louisville, 59-63; prof limnol, Syracuse Univ, 63-73; dir & prof environ & urban systs, Sch Technol, Fla Int Univ, 73-78. *Concurrent Pos:* Dir, C C Adams Ctr, 55-59; dir, Drinking Water Qual Res Ctr, Fla Int Univ, 76-78; dir & prof, Inst Environ Studies, La State Univ, Baton Rouge, 82-86. *Mem:* Am Soc Limnol & Oceanog; Ecol Soc Am; Am Micros Soc; Am Fisheries Soc; Int Asn Theoret & Appl Limnol; Soc Nat Sci. *Res:* Limnology, primary productivity; environmental planning, plankton; pollution, environmental toxicology; biotechnology. *Mailing Add:* 3323 Guilford Court Naples FL 33962

JACKSON, DARRYL DEAN, CHEMICAL INSTRUMENTATION. *Current Pos:* STAFF MEM, LOS ALAMOS NAT LAB, 56- *Personal Data:* b Lexington, Okla, 1932; m 59; c 2. *Educ:* Univ Okla, BS, 55, MS, 56; Univ NMex, PhD(radiochem), 68. *Mem:* AAAS; Am Inst Chemists; Am Chem Soc; Sigma Xi. *Res:* Structure of optically active inorganic complexes; chemistry of solutions of carrier-free iodine-131; radiochemistry of transuranium elements and fission products; development of automated instruments for chemical analysis. *Mailing Add:* Box 1663 MS G740 Los Alamos NM 87544-0010

JACKSON, DAVID ARCHER, molecular biology, virology, for more information see previous edition

JACKSON, DAVID DIETHER, GEOPHYSICS. *Current Pos:* Assoc prof, 69-80, PROF GEOPHYS, UNIV CALIF, LOS ANGELES, 80- *Personal Data:* b San Francisco, Calif, Sept 18, 43; m 68, Kathleen J Sloan; c 2. *Educ:* Calif Inst Technol, BS, 65; Mass Inst Technol, PhD(geophys), 69. *Concurrent Pos:* Mem, US Nat Comt Seismol, Panel Crustal Movement Measurements & Comt Geodesy/Seismol, 78-81; sr resident res associateship, Nat Acad Sci/ Nat Res Coun, 81; mem, Calif Earthquake Prediction Eval Coun, 84-; secy, Seismol Sect, Am Geophys Union, 92-93, pres-elect, 93-94. *Mem:* AAAS; fel Am Geophys Union; Seismol Soc Am; Seismol Soc Japan. *Res:* Seismology; solid earth geophysics; geophysical inverse problems; applications of solid state physics to geophysics; earthquake prediction and control. *Mailing Add:* Dept Earth & Space Sci Univ Calif 405 Hilgard Ave Los Angeles CA 90024-1301. *Fax:* 310-825-2779; *E-Mail:* djackson@cyclop.ess.ucla.edu

JACKSON, DAVID PHILLIP, MATHEMATICAL PHYSICS. *Current Pos:* asst sci officer, Atomic Energy Can Ltd, 68-70, assoc, 70-80, sr res officer, 81-85, mgr fusion progs, 85-86, DIR NAT FUSION PROG, ATOMIC ENERGY CAN LTD, 86- *Personal Data:* b Toronto, Ont, Oct 2, 40; m 75, Susan J Bell; c Scott P & Timothy D. *Educ:* Univ Toronto, BSc, 62, MA, 64, MASc, 66, PhD(eng physics), 68; Univ Ottawa, dipl, 85. *Prof Exp:* Mathematician, IBM, Toronto, 62-63; res asst, Inst Aerospace Studies, Toronto, 65-68. *Concurrent Pos:* Vis scientist, Max-Planck Inst Plasma Physics, 75-76; assoc prof eng physics, McMaster Univ, 78-81; mem, Inst Mat Res, 79-, mem staff, Inst Energy Studies, 80-, prof, 81-; vis prof, Bell Labs, Murray Hill, 81-87; mem, Int Energy Agency, Fusion Power Coord Comt, 86-; chmn, Int Atomic Energy Agency, Int Fusion Res Coun, 93- *Mem:* Chem Inst Can. *Res:* Mathematical modeling of particle-surface and particle-solid interactions; the wall problem in fusion reactors. *Mailing Add:* Dept Eng Physics McMasters Univ 1280 Main St Chalk River ON L8S 4L7 Can. *Fax:* 613-584-4243

JACKSON, DONALD CARGILL, PHYSIOLOGY. *Current Pos:* assoc prof, 73-79, PROF MED SCI, BROWN UNIV, 79- *Personal Data:* b Philadelphia, Pa, May 4, 37; m 66; c 2. *Educ:* Geneva Col, BS, 59; Univ Pa, PhD(physiol), 63. *Prof Exp:* Res asst physiol, John B Pierce Lab, Conn, 61-63; res asst, Duke Univ, 63-65; res fel physiol, Sch Med, Univ Pa, 65-68, asst prof, 68-73. *Concurrent Pos:* Pa Plan scholar, 68-71. *Mem:* AAAS; Am Soc Zool; Am Physiol Soc. *Res:* Acid-base physiology in reptiles. *Mailing Add:* Div Biomed Sci Brown Univ Box G Providence RI 02912-0001

JACKSON, DURWARD P, DATABASE MANAGEMENT. *Current Pos:* PROF COMPUT INFO SYSTS, CALIF STATE UNIV, LOS ANGELES, 81- *Personal Data:* b Hartsville, SC, Apr 12, 40; m 84, Alice Renfroe. *Educ:* Univ Ariz, BS, 64; Univ Utah, MEA, 69; Golden Gate Univ, MBA, 78; Claremont Grad Sch, PhD(exec mgt), 83. *Prof Exp:* Consult, Touche Ross & Co, 69-71; owner & consult, Dataphase Inc, 71-75; data adminr, Air Force Flight Test Ctr, 76-81. *Concurrent Pos:* Consult, 81-; dir, Ctr Info Resource Mgt, 84-87. *Mem:* Asn Comput Mach; Data Processing Mgt Asn; Soc Info Mgt. *Res:* Techniques for enterprise-wide information management; integrated information structures. *Mailing Add:* Dept Info Systs Calif State Univ Los Angeles CA 90032. *Fax:* 213-243-5209; *E-Mail:* djackso2@calstatela.edu, djackso2@gnet.com

JACKSON, EARL GRAVES, PHYSICAL CHEMISTRY. *Current Pos:* RETIRED. *Personal Data:* b Springfield, Mass, Mar 27, 20; m 43; c 3. *Educ:* Am Int Col, BS, 42; Clark Univ, AM, 43; Rutgers Univ, PhD(chem), 51. *Prof Exp:* Chemist, Merck & Co, 46-48; lubricants specialist, Gen Elec Co, 51-55, supvr bearings, lubrication & seals develop, 55-60; sr phys chemist, Nat Res Corp, Cambridge, 60-62 & United Shoe Mach Corp, 62-69; dir chem physics lab, Res Div, USM Corp, Mass, 69-73, head adhesives sect, Lexington Res Lab, 73-79, mgr admin, Kendall Co, 80-83. *Concurrent Pos:* Mem subcomt lubrication & wear, Nat Adv Comt Aeronaut, 56-58. *Res:* Physical chemistry of polymeric soaps; properties and mechanisms of lubricating greases; high temperature lubrication and fatigue; structural sealants; shoe technology; pressure sensitive adhesives and tapes. *Mailing Add:* 201 Willow Oak Lane Hendersonville NC 28791

JACKSON, EARL ROGERS, FOOD CHEMISTRY. *Current Pos:* chemist, Heekin Can Co, 58-64, asst res dir, 64-77, vpres res, 78-90, DIR RES, HEEKIN CAN, INC, 78-, SR VPRES RES, 90- *Personal Data:* b Madison, Ind, Aug 6, 30; m 51; c Deborah. *Educ:* Hanover Col, AB, 52. *Prof Exp:* Chemist, Am Can Co, 52-57. *Mem:* Inst Food Technologists; Soc Soft Drink Technologists; Am Soc Testing & Mat. *Mailing Add:* 6220 Neuvelle Lane Cincinnati OH 45243

JACKSON, EDGAR B, JR, COMMUNITY MEDICINE & HEALTH. *Current Pos:* sr instr med, Case Western Res Univ, 70-71, asst prof, 71-77, asst clin prof, 77-83, assoc clin prof, 83-86, CLIN PROF MED, CASE WESTERN RES UNIV, 86- *Personal Data:* b Rison, Ark, May 30, 35; m 57, Thelma; c Gary, David, Michael & Laura. *Educ:* Western Res Univ, BA, 62, MD, 66. *Prof Exp:* US Army, 59-61; intern, Cleveland Metrop Gen Hosp, 66-67, resident, 67-70. *Concurrent Pos:* Chief resident med, Cleveland Metrop Gen Hosp, 69-70; Carnegie Common Wealth Clin scholar, 70-72; asst dean, Case Western Res Univ, 71-74, asst prof community med, 74-79, commmunity health, 77-88. *Mem:* Inst Med-Nat Acad Sci; Am Sickle Cell Anemia Asn Inc; Am Pub Health Asn. *Res:* Contributed numerous articles to professional journals. *Mailing Add:* Univ Hosp Cleveland 11100 Euclid Ave Cleveland OH 44106

JACKSON, EDWIN ATLEE, PHYSICS. *Current Pos:* asst prof, 61-63, assoc prof physics & mech eng, 63-77, PROF PHYSICS, UNIV ILL, URBANA, 77- *Personal Data:* b Lyons, NY, Apr 18, 31; m 54; c 2. *Educ:* Syracuse Univ, BS, 53, MS, 55, PhD(physics), 58. *Honors & Awards:* Fel, Am Phys Soc. *Prof Exp:* Asst, Syracuse Univ, 54-57; asst & instr, Brandeis Univ, 57-58; Nat Acad Sci res assoc, Air Res & Develop Command, Air Force Cambridge Res Ctr, Mass, 58-59; staff mem, Proj Matterhorn, Princeton Univ, 59-61. *Concurrent Pos:* Vis sr physicist, Found Fundamental Res Matter, Inst Plasma-Physics, Netherlands, 67-68; vis mem staff, Los Alamos Sci Lab, 71; mem adv bd, Physica D: Nonlinear Phenomena, 80-; vis prof, Chalmers Univ, Sweden, 84, JIFT vis prof, Nagoya Univ, Japan, 84. *Mem:* Am Phys Soc. *Res:* Nonlinear dynamics; plasma physics; kinetic theory of gases. *Mailing Add:* Dept Physics Loomis Lab Univ Ill 1110 W Green St Urbana IL 61801

JACKSON, EDWIN KERRY, CARDIOVASCULAR & RENAL. *Current Pos:* PROF PHARMACOL & MED, UNIV PITTSBURGH SCH MED, 91- *Personal Data:* b Oct 21, 52; m 73, Donna; c Ethan & Travis. *Educ:* Univ Tex, Dallas, PhD(pharmacol), 79. *Honors & Awards:* Glaxo Cardiovasc Discovery Award. *Prof Exp:* from assoc prof to prof pharmacol, Sch Med, Vanderbilt Univ, 79-91. *Concurrent Pos:* Estab investr, Am Heart Asn. *Mem:* Am Soc Hypertension; Am Fedn Clin Res; Fedn Am Soc Exp Biol; Am Heart Asn. *Res:* Cardiovascular pharmacology. *Mailing Add:* Ctr Clin Pharmacol Univ Pittsburgh Med Ctr 623 Scaife Hall 200 Lothrop St Pittsburgh PA 15213-2582. *Fax:* 412-648-7107; *E-Mail:* jackson@druginfonet.pharm_epid.pitt.edu

JACKSON, EDWIN L, ELECTRICAL ENGINEERING. *Current Pos:* RETIRED. *Personal Data:* b Albany, Tex, Jan 21, 30; m 53, Ruby R Corn; c Elisabeth, Elaine & Gene. *Educ:* Univ Okla, BSEE, 52. *Prof Exp:* Sr design engr, Gen Dynamics, 56-62; prog mgr, E Syst, 63-68; vpres, Forney Eng Co, 72-83; sr vpres & gen mgr, Dallas Corp, 83-88; staff, Div Static Power, Varo Inc, 62-63 & 68-72, vpres & gen mgr, Div Elec Systs, 89- *Res:* Engineering; electronic systems. *Mailing Add:* 6010 Troon Circle Garland TX 75044

JACKSON, ELIZABETH BURGER, BIOLOGY, CHEMISTRY. *Current Pos:* Prof natural sci, 40-80, EMER PROF NATURAL SCI, LONGWOOD COL, 80- *Personal Data:* b Clay, WVa, Oct 20, 14; m 62. *Educ:* Col William & Mary, BS, 34, MA, 35; Univ Va, DEd, 60. *Concurrent Pos:* Res grant, Univ Ctr, Univ Va, 58-59. *Mem:* AAAS; Nat Sci Teachers Asn; Sigma Xi. *Res:* Science education through commercial television; science for elementary schools. *Mailing Add:* c/o Brookview Lodge 2005 Cobb St Farmville VA 23901

JACKSON, ERNEST BAKER, AGRONOMY, BOTANY. *Current Pos:* RETIRED. *Personal Data:* b Bicknell, Utah, Mar 31, 14; m 43, Elva Ellett; c Ernest L, David E, JoAnn (Kalama), Anita (Shields), Mary A (Curl), Barbara (Broby), Donna (Rohbock) & Jeri L (Taylor). *Educ:* Brigham Young Univ, BSc, 46; Univ Nebr, MSc, 54, PhD(agron), 56. *Prof Exp:* Pub sch teacher, Utah, 35-42, prin, 47-51; soils technologist, Bur Reclamation, Colo, 46-47; Filing Asst, Univ Nebr, 52-55, asst agronomist, 55-58; from asst agronomist to assoc agronomist, Univ Ariz, 58-71, prof agron & agronomist, Agr Exp Sta, 71-76, prof plant sci & res scientist, 76-83. *Mem:* Am Soc Agron. *Res:* Forage crops, cotton and small grains; salinity management. *Mailing Add:* 1355 Gateway Yuma AZ 85364

JACKSON, ETHEL NOLAND, MOLECULAR BIOLOGY, RECOMBINANT DNA METHODOLOGY. *Current Pos:* res suprv life sci, 87-90, RES MGR, CENT RES & DEVELOP DEPT, E I DU PONT DE NEMOURS & CO, 90- *Personal Data:* b Geneva, NY, Apr 27, 44; m 66, David A; c Holly (Bunting). *Educ:* Harvard Univ, BA, 66; Stanford Univ, PhD(biol sci), 73. *Prof Exp:* Fel biochem genetics, Dept Human Genetics, Sch Med, Univ Ala, 41-42; prof asst, Detroit Pub Libr, 42-46; chief, Libr Sect, Cent Air Doc Off, Army-Navy-Air Force, 46-49; chief, Res Info Div, Off Qm Gen, US Dept Army, 49; chief, Div Res Info, Nat Adv Comt Aeronaut, 49-56; head, Libr Dept, Gen Motors Res Labs, 56-65; dir info retrieval & libr serv, IBM Corp, 65-71. *Concurrent Pos:* Chief, Wright Field Ref Libr, 46-49; US mem doc comt, Adv Group Aeronaut Res & Develop, NATO, Paris, 52-57; mem, Kresge-Hooker Sci Libr Assocs, Wayne State Univ, 57-65, pres, 64-65; vis lectr, Simmons Col, 65; mem exec bd, US Nat Comt Int Fedn Doc, 65-70, chmn, 70-72; vpres, Eng Index, Inc, 68-69, pres, 69-73, secy, 75-77; vis lectr, Kans State Teachers Col, 70; Lincoln lectr, Bus Sch, Ariz State Univ, 70; proj leader, Centralized Processing Med Libr Res Proj, 71-72; ed, Spec Librarianship, New Reader, 80; founder mem, Facul Sem Brit Studies, Univ Tex, Austin, 88- *Mem:* Am Inst Aeronaut & Astronaut; Spec Libr Asn (pres, 61-62); Am Soc Info Sci; Am Rec Mgt Asn. *Res:* Analysis and use of scientific literature by and for physical scientists; application of conventional and nonconventional information retrieval procedures to scientific information problems; industrial information systems; indexing and abstracting of physical science literature; records management systems; information center management. *Mailing Add:* Univ Tex Grad Sch Libr Info Sci Austin TX 78712-1276. *Fax:* 512-471-3971

JACKSON, FRANCIS CHARLES, MEDICINE. *Current Pos:* chmn dept surg, 75-80, assoc dean clin educ, 80-82, PROF SURG, SCH MED, TEX TECH UNIV,75- *Personal Data:* b Rutherford, NJ, Sept 2, 17; m 49; c 4. *Educ:* Yale Univ, AB, 39; Univ Va, MD, 43. *Honors & Awards:* Billings Gold Medal, AMA, 66; Stitt Award, Asn Mil Surgeons US, 68; Distinguished Serv Citation, US Dept Defense, 69; Physician's Recognition Award, AMA, 70, 73, 76, 79. *Prof Exp:* Intern surg, NY Hosp, Cornell Med Ctr, 44, asst resident surgeon, 44-45 & 47-49; asst anat, Med Col, Cornell Univ, 46, instr surg, 50; chief surgeon & consult, Arabian-Am Oil Co, 51; asst chief surgeon, Vet Admin Ctr, Maine, 52; from asst prof to prof surg, Sch Med, Univ Pittsburgh, 53-70; dir emergency & disaster med serv staff, Vet Admin Cent Off, 72-75; interim med dir, South Plains Emergency Med Serv Syst, 79-87. *Concurrent Pos:* Asst, Med Col, Cornell Univ, 45-49; chief resident surgeon, NY Hosp, Cornell Med Ctr, 50; chief surgeon, Vet Admin Hosp, 52-70; consult staff, Presby Univ Hosp, Pittsburgh, 59-70; mem ad hoc adv group emergency health serv, Bur Health Serv, USPHS, 67-75; chief surv teams, USPHS, 68-69; mem review comn, Vet Admin Res & Educ Trainee Progs, 68-70; consult & mem med surv team, Westinghouse Corp Proj New Generation Mil Hosps, 69-70; consult, Off Emergency Planning, 69-71; co-med dir & consult, Ctr Western Pa Health Res & Develop, Carnegie-Mellon Univ, 69-72; clin prof surg, Sch Med, Georgetown Univ, 70-75; mem surg adv group, Food & Drug Admin, 71-76; mem & vchmn comt emergency med serv, Nat Acad Sci-Nat Res Coun; mem, President's Comn Study Med Aspects of Los Angeles Earthquake, 71; clin prof surg, Sch Med, George Washington Univ, 71-75; mem ad hoc comt emergency med serv commun, Off Telecommun Policy, 73-74; mem interdept comt emergency med serv, Dept Health, Educ & Welfare, 73-75; chief surgeon, Lubbock Gen Hosp, 75-80. *Mem:* Fel Am Col Surg; Am Med Asn; Soc Surg Alimentary Tract; Soc Surg Chmn; Am Surg Asn. *Res:* Portal hypertension; cirrhosis; esophageal varices; vascular surgery; schistosomiasis; chemotherapy as an adjuvant to surgery in the control of cancer; percutaneous splenoportography; spleen pressure; portal hemodynamics in Wilson's and other diseases; emergency medical services; trauma; telecommunications; disaster medical care; mass casualty care. *Mailing Add:* Off of the Dean Tex Tech Univ Sch Med Lubbock TX 79430

JACKSON, FRANCIS J, PHYSICS, UNDERWATER ACOUSTICS. *Current Pos:* sr vpres, BBN Labs, Inc, 84-88, SR VPRES, BBN SYSTS & TECHNOL CORP, 88- *Personal Data:* b Providence, RI, May 23, 32; m 56, 83, Nancy M McMahon; c 3. *Educ:* Providence Col, BS, 54; Brown Univ, ScM, 57, PhD(physics), 60. *Prof Exp:* Res assoc physics, Brown Univ, 59-60; sr scientist, Bolt Beranek & Newman, Inc, 60-70, vpres, Phys Sci Div, 70-75, vpres, Underwater Technol Div, 75-77, corp vpres, 77-84. *Concurrent Pos:* Adj prof, Cath Univ Am, 68-74. *Mem:* Acoust Soc Am; Inst Elec & Electronics Engrs. *Res:* Nonlinear acoustics; underwater acoustics and sonar; underwater sound propagation; array theory and design. *Mailing Add:* Bolt Beranek & Newman Inc 70 Fawcett St Cambridge MA 02138

JACKSON, GARY LESLIE, PLASMA PHYSICS, ELECTROMAGNETICS. *Current Pos:* PRIN SCIENTIST, GEN ATOMICS CO, 77- *Personal Data:* b Minneapolis, Minn, Jan 5, 45; m 70, Melissa McCarthy; c Shannon, Jeff & Courtney. *Educ:* Univ Idaho, BS, 67; Calif State Univ, Northridge, MS, 72; Univ Ariz, PhD, 77. *Mem:* Am Phys Soc; Am Vacuum Soc; Elec Automobile Asn. *Res:* Fusion plasmas; plasma/wall interactions; electric vehicle. *Mailing Add:* 13-411 Gen Atomics PO Box 85608 San Diego CA 92186. *E-Mail:* jackson@gav.gat.com

JACKSON, GARY LOUCKS, NEUROENDOCRINOLOGY, REPRODUCTIVE PHYSIOLOGY. *Current Pos:* NIH fel, 67-68, assoc prof, 68-77, PROF ENDOCRINOL, UNIV ILL, URBANA, 77- *Personal Data:* b Skidmore, Mo, Nov 4, 38; m 70, Dixie Smith; c Andrea. *Educ:* Univ Mo, BS, 60, AM, 63; Univ Ill, Urbana, PhD(animal sci), 67. *Concurrent Pos:* NIH reprod biol study sect, 83-87; vis prof, Univ Bristol, 85; mem, Animal Reproduction Panel, USDA, 89-91; panel mgr, animal reproduction panel, USDA, 93. *Mem:* Soc Study Reproduction; Endocrine Soc; Brit Soc Study Fertil; Neurosci Soc. *Res:* Hypothalamic control of gonadotropin and prolactin secretion; biosynthesis of luteinizing hormone; biological rhythms. *Mailing Add:* Dept Vet Physiol & Pharmacol Univ Ill Col Vet Med Urbana IL 61801. *Fax:* 217-333-4628; *E-Mail:* g-jackson@uiuc.edu

JACKSON, GEORGE FREDERICK, III, PHYSICAL CHEMISTRY, ANALYTICAL CHEMISTRY. *Current Pos:* assoc prof, 73-80, PROF CHEM, UNIV TAMPA, 80-, DIV CHMN, 82- *Personal Data:* b Brooklyn, NY, May 16, 43; m 66; c 2. *Educ:* MacMurray Col, BA, 65; Northwestern Univ, PhD(chem), 69. *Prof Exp:* Asst prof chem, Lake Forest Col, 69-73. *Mem:* AAAS; Am Chem Soc. *Res:* Studies of atomic inversion; involving arsenic and phosphorus atoms; properties of the allenic bond; use of NMR shift reagents for determination of molecular structures. *Mailing Add:* Div Sci & Math Univ Tampa 401 W Kennedy Blvd Tampa FL 33606

JACKSON, GEORGE G, internal medicine, microbiology, for more information see previous edition

JACKSON, GEORGE JOHN, FOOD MICROBIOLOGY, PARASITOLOGY. *Current Pos:* head lab parasitol, US Food & Drug Admin, 72-80, chief food & cosmetics, Microbiol Br, 80-87, chief, Food Microbiol Methods Develop Br, 88-92, spec asst to dir, 92-94, ACTG DIR, OFF SPEC RES SKILLS, CTR FOOD SAFETY & APPL NUTRIT, US FOOD & DRUG ADMIN, 94- *Personal Data:* b Vienna, Austria, Dec 10, 31; nat US. *Educ:* Univ Chicago, AB, 51, MS, 54, PhD, 58. *Prof Exp:* Fel, La State Univ, 58; res assoc & instr, Univ Chicago, 58-59; USPHS res fel & guest investr, Rockefeller Inst, 59-63; fac mem, Rockefeller Univ, 63-72. *Concurrent Pos:* Consult, Pathway Labs, 58-59, guest researcher, Amazon Res Inst, Manaus, Brazil, 63; adj prof, Rockefeller Univ & Lehigh Univ, 72-76; ed, Exp Parasitol, 76-87; US deleg, Food Hyg Comt of Codex Alimentarius Comn of WHO/Food & Agr Orgn of UN, 80-88; mem, microbiol adv comt, Calif State Univ, Riverside, 85-93; FDA Food microbiol liaison with int orgn, 87-; sect ed, J Asn Off Anal Chem Int, 93-95. *Mem:* Am Soc Parasitologists; Soc Protozoologists; Am Soc Trop Med & Hyg; Asn Off Anal Chem; Helminthol Soc. *Res:* Immunity; invertebrate physiology; axenic culture; food borne parasites; anisakiasis. *Mailing Add:* HFS-500 US Food & Drug Admin 200 C St SW Washington DC 20204. *Fax:* 202-401-7740

JACKSON, GEORGE RICHARD, CHEMISTRY. *Current Pos:* CONSULT, 78- *Personal Data:* b Chagrin Falls, Ohio, Sept 27, 20; m 43; c 3. *Educ:* Baldwin-Wallace Col, BS, 42; Johns Hopkins Univ, MA, 43, PhD(org chem), 48. *Prof Exp:* From instr to asst prof chem, Western Reserve Univ, 47-53; dir res, H C Fisher Co, 53-55; pres, Cliffdale Prod Corp, 55-57, Top-Scor Prod Inc, 57-61 & SuCrest Corp, 61-69; pres, Southern Shortenings, 69-77. *Mem:* Am Chem Soc; Am Oil Chem Soc; Am Asn Cereal Chem; Inst Food Technol. *Res:* Food chemistry; fats and oils; analytical chemistry. *Mailing Add:* 2828 N Atlantic Ave Apt 1903 Daytona Beach FL 32118

JACKSON, GILCHRIST LEWIS, SURGICAL ONCOLOGY, HEAD & NECK SURGERY. *Current Pos:* HEAD, NECK SURGEON & SURG ONCOLOGIST, KELSEY-SEYBOLD MED GROUP, 81-, MED DIR, KELSEY-SEYBOLD FOUND CANCER PREV CTR, 88- *Personal Data:* b Dayton, Ohio, Sept 30, 48; m 70, Katina Ballantyne; c Marina, Alex, Scott & George. *Educ:* Vanderbilt Univ, BA, 70; Univ Louisville, Sch Med, MD, 74. *Honors & Awards:* A J Miller Award, 74; Sword of Hope Award, Am Cancer Soc, 83-85, 87. *Prof Exp:* Internship, Parkland Mem Hosp, 74-75; residency, Gen Surg, Univ Tex, 75-79, fel, Surg Oncol, Med Dept Anderson Hosp, 79-80. *Concurrent Pos:* Surgeon, St Luke's Episcopal Hosp, Houston, Methodist Hosp, Houston, Tex Childrens Hosp, Houston, Vet Admin Hosp, Houston & Ben Taub Hosp, Harris Co Hosp Dist, 81-; med dir, Joe & Jessie Crump Ctr Clin Cancer Res & Educ, Kelsey Seybold Found, 83-, Kelsey-Seybold Cancer Prog, 86-93; clin asst surgeon, Univ Tex Med Sch,

84-; clin asst prof surg, Baylor Col Med, 85-; adj asst surgeon, M D Anderson Cancer Ctr, Univ Tex, 85-; cancer prog liason, Physician/Am Col Surgeons Comn Cancer, St Luke's Episcopal Hosp, 89-, Cancer Res Comt, 92-, Cancer Prev Comt, 92- *Mem:* Am Col Surgeons; Soc Surg Oncol; Soc Head & Neck Surgeons; Int Soc Surg; Am Soc Head & Neck Surg. *Res:* Cancer prevention-control; chemotherapy, chemoprevention trials; comparison of diagnostic-survival outcomes; breast cancer; diagnostic accuracy, needle biopsy-thyroid; localizing scans-parathyroid. *Mailing Add:* 6624 Fannin No 1700 Houston TX 77030-2329. *Fax:* 713-790-0482

JACKSON, GRANT D, SOIL & SOIL SCIENCE, AGRONOMY. *Current Pos:* exten specialist cropping systs, 77-79, AGRONOMIST CROP, MONT STATE UNIV, 84- *Personal Data:* b Perryton, Tex, Apr 3, 45; m 65; c 2. *Educ:* Okla Panhandle State Col, BS, 68; Mont State Univ, MS, 70, PhD(crop & soil sci), 74. *Prof Exp:* Soil scientist, US Dept Agr, 74-77; agronomist crop & soil sci, Univ Wyo, 77-84. *Mem:* Am Soc Agron; Soil Sci Soc Am. *Res:* Development of zero-till technology for dry land and irrigating cropping system; nutrient management for irrigated and dry land cropping systems. *Mailing Add:* Mont Res Ctr Mont State Univ PO Box 1474 Conrad MT 59425

JACKSON, HAROLD, FOOD SCIENCE. *Current Pos:* RETIRED. *Personal Data:* b Preston, Lancashire, Eng, Aug 10, 37; m 61; c 3. *Educ:* Univ Nottingham, BSc, 59, MSc, 61; Univ Alta, PhD(dairy sci), 63. *Prof Exp:* Asst prof dairy & food microbiol, Univ Alta, 63-69, assoc prof food sci, 69-74, prof food sci & chmn dept, 74-82, prof food sci, 82-97. *Mem:* Am Soc Microbiol; Inst Food Technologists; Can Inst Food Sci & Technol; Brit Soc Appl Bact; Int Asn Milk Food & Environ Sanitarians. *Res:* Food microbiology; effects of environmental stress on microbial growth and activity; food-borne pathogens. *Mailing Add:* Dept Food Sci Univ Alta Edmonton AB T6G 2P5 Can

JACKSON, HAROLD E, JR, NUCLEAR PHYSICS, PARTICLE PHYSICS. *Current Pos:* Physicist, 59-81, res proj dir, 81-84, SR PHYSICIST, ARGONNE NAT LAB, 85-, ASSOC DIV DIR, 95- *Personal Data:* b Pittsburgh, Pa, Jan 5, 33; m 58, Sally Moseley; c Mark, Matthew & Kimberly. *Educ:* Princeton Univ, AB, 54; Cornell Univ, PhD(physics), 60. *Concurrent Pos:* Mem nuclear cross sect adv comt, AEC, 67-, secy, 71-73; chmn, US Nuclear Data Comt, 74-75; mem, nuclear data comt, Nuclear Energy Agency, 74-77; mem bd dirs, Los Alamos Meson Physics Fac Users Group, 79-80, chmn, 81-82; mem nat adv bd, Southeastern Univ Res Asn, 83-90; chmn, Continuous Electron Beam Accelerator Facil Users Group, 88-89; assoc ed, Phys Rev C, 91-93; co-mgr, Hall C Prog, Continuous Electron Beam Accelerator Facil, 92- *Mem:* Fel Am Phys Soc; AAAS. *Res:* High energy physics; lepton scattering; nuclear physics; study of nuclear structure with deep inelastic scattering; photonuclear interactions; medium energy physics; pion interactions with complex nuclei. *Mailing Add:* Physics Div Argonne Nat Lab Argonne IL 60439

JACKSON, HAROLD LEONARD, POLYMER CHEMISTRY, FLUORINE CHEMISTRY. *Current Pos:* CONSULT CHEMIST, 95- *Personal Data:* b Wichita, Kans, Mar 13, 23; m 52, Shirley Alvarado; c Sara, Ann, Davis & Thomas. *Educ:* Munic Univ Wichita, AB, 43, MS, 46; Univ Ill, PhD(chem), 49. *Prof Exp:* Res chemist, Cent Res Dept, E I DuPont de Nemours & Co, 49-59, Org Chem Dept, 59-65, res assoc, Org Chem Dept, 66-77, res assoc, Petrolchem Dept, 78-90, res fel, DuPont Chem, 90-92, consult chemist, 93-95. *Concurrent Pos:* Vis prof, Univ Kans, 62-63. *Mem:* AAAS; Am Chem Soc; Fedn Socs Coating Technol. *Res:* Organic solvents; polymer solvency; polymer characterization; fluorocarbon solvents and polymers; organic synthesis; paint removers; cleaning solvents. *Mailing Add:* 102 Stratton Dr Canterbury Hills Hockessin DE 19707

JACKSON, HAROLD WOODWORTH, ANALYTICAL CHEMISTRY. *Current Pos:* group leader chromatog & instrumental anal, 69-75, sr group leader, Kraftco Corp, 75-78, SR GROUP LEADER, BASIC FLAVOR CHEM RES & DEVELOP DIV, KRAFT, INC, 78- *Personal Data:* b Lawrence, Mass, Mar 14, 28; m 50; c 4. *Educ:* Univ NH, BS, 49; Univ Conn, MS, 51, PhD(biochem, dairy technol), 54. *Prof Exp:* Instr dairy technol, Univ Conn, 52-53; prod leader cheese, Kraft Foods Res Lab, 54-55, res chemist, 55-59, group leader chromatog, 59-60; group leader chromatog & infrared spectros, Res & Develop Div, Fundamental Chem Sect, Nat Dairy Prod Corp, 60-69. *Mem:* Am Oil Chemist's Soc; Am Chem Soc. *Res:* Isolation and identification of natural flavor compounds; analytical methodology on fatty acid derivatives; gas chromatography; nuclear magnetic resonance; basic flavor chemistry; mass spectrometry. *Mailing Add:* 56 Sunny Shore Dr Ormond Beach FL 32176-3716

JACKSON, HERBERT LEWIS, NUCLEAR PHYSICS. *Current Pos:* RETIRED. *Personal Data:* b Sawyer, Kans, May 9, 21; m 46; c 2. *Educ:* Univ Wis, PhD(physics), 52. *Prof Exp:* Asst, Phys Inst, Univ Basel, 52-54; asst prof physics, Univ Nebr, 54-60; from asst prof to assoc prof, Univ Iowa, 60-68, prof radiol, 68- *Mem:* Am Phys Soc; Health Physics Soc; Am Asn Physicists in Med; Sigma Xi. *Res:* Scattering of protons and neutrons from light elements; radiological physics. *Mailing Add:* PO Box 1700 Iowa City IA 52244

JACKSON, IVOR MICHAEL DAVID, NEUROENDOCRINOLOGY, COMPARATIVE ENDOCRINOLOGY. *Current Pos:* PROF MED, BROWN UNIV, 84-; DIR, DIV ENDOCRINOL, RI HOSP, 84- *Personal Data:* b Glasgow, Scotland, Apr 17, 36; US citizen; m 72, Barbara Weiss; c Heather Rochelle & Amanda Ruth. *Educ:* Univ Glasgow Med Sch, MB, ChB, 60; FACP; FRCP, 96. *Hon Degrees:* MA, Brown Univ, 85. *Prof Exp:* Res fel neuroendocrinol, Univ Conn, 71-72; res fel endocrinol, Tufts Univ, 72-73, from asst prof med to prof, Sch Med, 73-84. *Concurrent Pos:* Prin investr, Diabetes, Digestive & Kidney Dis, Nat Inst Arthritis, 78-81 & 81-; mem, Spec Rev Comt, NIH, 81, Salk Inst Biol Studies, La Jolla, 84; co-organizer & co-chmn, Fedn Am Soc Exp Biol, 80, Workshop Hormone Stand, NIH, 82, Int Conf, NY Acad Sci, Md, 87; vis prof med, Univ Toronto, Can, 84, Univ Ottowa, 86, Venezuelan Soc Endocrinol, Univ Caracas, 88; Spinoza prof, Univ Amsterdam, Neth, 96. *Mem:* Endocrine Soc; fel Am Col Physicians; Am Thyroid Asn; Soc for Neurosci; Am Soc Clin Invest; Asn Am Physicians; hon mem Endocrin Soc China. *Res:* To determine the physiologic, cellular and molecular mechanisms regulating the biosynthesis and post-translational processing of proTRH, a 255 amino acid polyprotein which contains 5 copies of a thyrotrophin releasing hormone (TRH) progenitor sequence flanked by paired basic residues and the secretion of TRH in the various regions of the neuroendocrine system where TRH and its prohormone occur. *Mailing Add:* Div Endocrinol Dept Med Brown Univ RI Hosp 593 Eddy St Providence RI 02903-0001

JACKSON, JAMES EDWARD, MULTIVARIATE ANALYSIS, QUALITY CONTROL. *Current Pos:* PVT CONSULT, 85- *Personal Data:* b Rochester, NY, Jan 12, 25; m 47, Suzanne Montgomery; c James, Janice & Judith. *Educ:* Univ Rochester, AB, 47; Univ NC, MA, 49; Va Polytech Inst, PhD, 60. *Honors & Awards:* Brumbaugh Award, Am Soc Qual Control, 78. *Prof Exp:* Statistician, Eastman Kodak Co, 48-57; asst process engr, Hercules Powder Co, 57-58; asst prof, Va Polytech Inst, 58-59; statistician, Kodak Park, Eastman Kodak Co, 59-85. *Mem:* Psychomet Soc; fel Am Soc Qual Control; fel Am Statist Asn. *Res:* Development of statistical methods, particularly multivariate analysis; quality control. *Mailing Add:* 16 Kettering Dr Rochester NY 14612

JACKSON, JAMES EDWARD, PHYSICAL ORGANIC CHEMISTRY. *Current Pos:* asst prof, 88-94, ASSOC PROF CHEM, MICH STATE UNIV, 94- *Personal Data:* b Boston, Mass, June 14, 55; m 87, Evelyn M Parker; c Kelvin C Parker. *Educ:* Princeton Univ, PhD(chem), 87. *Prof Exp:* Fel, Ohio State Univ, 86-88. *Mem:* Am Chem Soc; AAAS; InterAm Photochem Soc; Mat Res Soc; Sigma Xi. *Res:* Organic reactive intermediates and reaction mechanisms, as well as approaches to synthesis and characterization of organic-based magnetic and conductive materials. *Mailing Add:* Dept Chem Mich State Univ East Lansing MI 48824. *Fax:* 517-353-1793; *E-Mail:* jackson@cemvax.cem.msu.edu

JACKSON, JAMES FREDRICK, NUCLEAR ANALYSIS, NUCLEAR REACTOR SAFETY. *Current Pos:* reactor safety group leader, Los Alamos Nat Lab, 76-80, energy div leader, 80-84, assoc dir eng sci, 84-86, DEP DIR, LOS ALAMOS NAT LAB, 86- *Personal Data:* b Aug 15, 39; m 60, Joan Borger; c James D, Bret A, Tracy L & Wendy L. *Educ:* Univ Utah, BS, 61; Mass Inst Technol, MS, 62; Univ Calif, Los Angeles, PhD(eng), 69. *Honors & Awards:* EO Lawrence Award, Dept Energy, 83. *Prof Exp:* Res engr, Atomics Int, 62-66, Argonne Nat Lab, 69-74; assoc prof eng, Brigham Young Univ, 74-76. *Mem:* Nat Acad Eng; Am Nuclear Soc. *Res:* Developed and applied advanced computer codes for nuclear reactor safety analysis; performed analysis and evaluation of advanced nuclear reactor systems. *Mailing Add:* 1090 Los Pueblos Los Alamos NM 87544. *E-Mail:* jackson_james_f@lanl.gov

JACKSON, JAMES OLIVER, MEDICAL MICROBIOLOGY, IMMUNOLOGY & APPLIED MICROBIOLOGY. *Current Pos:* from asst prof to assoc prof, 72-80, coordr microbiol sect, Biol Sci Dept, 84-92, PROF MICROBIOL, CALIF STATE POLYTECH UNIV, POMONA, 80- *Personal Data:* b New Iberia, La, July 16, 39; m 64, Geraldine Moncriffe; c Jamie R. *Educ:* Univ Southwestern La, BS, 66, MS, 67; Univ Kans, PhD(microbiol), 70. *Prof Exp:* Asst prof microbiol, Southern Univ, 70-72. *Concurrent Pos:* Ad hoc consult, NIH, 70-95. *Mem:* Am Soc Microbiol; Sigma Xi. *Res:* Metabolic changes in experimental Listeria monocytogenes infections; extracellular proteins produced by Listeria monocytogenes; pathogenic mechanisms of Chromobacterium violecium; microorganisms associated with sea mammals. *Mailing Add:* Dept Biol Sci Calif State Polytech Univ Pomona CA 91768

JACKSON, JASPER ANDREW, JR, EXPERIMENTAL PHYSICS. *Current Pos:* RETIRED. *Personal Data:* b Washington, DC, Jan 26, 23; m 61, Betty Southgate; c Paul S. *Educ:* Univ Okla, BS, 48, MS, 50, PhD(physics), 55. *Prof Exp:* Asst, Univ Okla, 49-51; mem staff, Los Alamos Sci Lab, 51-52; sr nuclear engr, Convair Div, Gen Dynamics Corp, 55; mem staff, Los Alamos Nat Lab, 56-86. *Mem:* Fel AAAS; Soc Prof Well Log Analysts; Soc Magnetics Resonance Med. *Res:* Nuclear magnetic resonance; infrared and Raman spectroscopy; dynamic nuclear polarization; mass spectrometry; nuclear magnetic resonance well logging. *Mailing Add:* 1600 Conestoga Dr SE Albuquerque NM 87123. *E-Mail:* jajbsj@swcp.com

JACKSON, JEREMY BRADFORD COOK, marine ecology, paleobiology, for more information see previous edition

JACKSON, JEROME ALAN, ORNITHOLOGY, ECOLOGY. *Current Pos:* From asst prof to assoc prof, 70-79, PROF ZOOL, MISS STATE UNIV, 79- *Personal Data:* b Ft Benning, Ga, Feb 4, 43; m 65, 84, Bette J Schardien; c Jerome A Jr, Paul C, Ann C, Peter M, S Brent & Matthew C. *Educ:* Iowa State Univ, BS, 65; Univ Kans, PhD(zool), 70. *Honors & Awards:* Recognition for Contributions to Bird Conserv, Prov Assembly of Popular Power, Havana, Cuba, 87. *Concurrent Pos:* Ed, Wilson Bull, 74-78, The Mississippi Kite, 76-, Inland Bird Banding, 78-81, J Field Ornithol, 80-85 & N Am Bird Bander,

81-83; regional ed, Am Birds, 78-90; pres, Eco-Inventory Studies, Inc, 78-; leader endangered species recovery team, US Fish & Wildlife Serv, 75-82. *Mem:* Fel Am Ornith Union; Wilson Ornith Soc (treas, 73-74, vpres, 79-, pres, 83-85); Sigma Xi; fel AAAS; Am Soc Mammalogists; Herpetologists League; Asn Field Ornithologists; fel Explorer's Club. *Res:* Population dynamics and adaptation in hole-nesting birds; biology and ecology of endangered species; behavior of rat snakes, Elaphe. *Mailing Add:* Dept Biol Sci Miss State Univ Mississippi State MS 39762. *Fax:* 601-325-7939

JACKSON, JO-ANNE ALICE, PHYSICAL CHEMISTRY. *Current Pos:* specialist, chem & mat export licensing, Int Trade Admin, 81-86, PHYS SCI FOREIGN TECH ANALYST, BUR EXPORT ADMIN, US DEPT COM, WASHINGTON, DC, 86- *Personal Data:* b Washington, DC, July 30, 51. *Educ:* Am Univ, BS, 73, PhD(phys chem), 77. *Prof Exp:* Teaching asst gen, quant anal & phys chem, Lab Nursing Gen Chem, Am Univ, 73-75; chemist, Nat Bur Stand, 74-81. *Mem:* Am Chem Soc; Soc Appl Spectros; Fedn Orgs Prof Women. *Mailing Add:* 14711 Myer Terr Rockville MD 20853

JACKSON, JOHN DAVID, THEORETICAL PHYSICS. *Current Pos:* group leader theoret physics, Berkeley Lab, Univ Calif, Berkeley, 74-78, chmn dept, 78-81, assoc dir & head physics div, Lawrence Berkeley Labs, 82-84, dep dir, SSC Cent Design Group, 85-87, prof, 67-92, EMER PROF PHYSICS, UNIV CALIF, BERKELEY, 93- *Personal Data:* b London, Ont, Jan 19, 25; nat US; m 49, M Barbara Cook; c Ian, Nan, Maureen & Mark. *Educ:* Univ Western Ont, BSc, 46; Mass Inst Technol, PhD(physics), 49. *Hon Degrees:* DSc, Univ Western Ont, 89. *Prof Exp:* Res assoc physics, Mass Inst Technol, 49; from asst prof to assoc prof math, McGill Univ, 50-56; from assoc prof to prof physics, Univ Ill, 57-67; head, Theoret Sect, Fermi Nat Accelerator Lab, 72-73. *Concurrent Pos:* Guggenheim fel, Princeton Univ, 56-57; consult, Argonne Nat Lab, 62-65, 75-78; Ford Found fel, Europ Orgn Nuclear Res, 63-64; assoc ed, Rev of Modern Physics, 68-72; vis fel, Clare Hall, Cambridge Univ, 70; consult, Stanford Linear Accelerator Ctr, 71-73 & Nat Accelerator Lab, 71-75; mem vis comt, Dept Physics, Mass Inst Technol, 73-76; ed, Annual Rev Nuclear & Particle Sci, 77-93; chmn, Vis Comt for Fermilab, Univs Res Asn, 80-82; sr vis res fel, Jesus Col, Oxford, 88-89; sci assoc, Europ Orgn Nuclear Res, 76-77, 81, 84 & 88; mem, Prog Adv Comt, SSC Lab, 90-92. *Mem:* Nat Acad Sci; fel AAAS; Fel Am Phys Soc; Am Acad Arts & Sci. *Res:* Theoretical physics of fundamental particles. *Mailing Add:* Dept Physics Univ Calif Berkeley CA 94720. *Fax:* 510-486-6808; *E-Mail:* jdj@.lbl.gov

JACKSON, JOHN ELWIN, JR, FLUID-STRUCTURE INTERACTION, ANALYSIS OF METAL FLOW DURING FORMING. *Current Pos:* DEPT HEAD, AEROSPACE ENG, UNIV ALA, TUSCALOOSA, 91- *Personal Data:* b Tuscaloosa, Ala, Oct 11, 48; m 71; c 3. *Educ:* Univ Ala, BS, 71, MS, 73, PhD(eng mech), 77. *Prof Exp:* Mech engr, Tenn Valley Authority, 76-78; from asst prof to assoc prof eng mech, Clemson Univ, 78-91. *Concurrent Pos:* Consult, finite element anal. *Mem:* Am Soc Mech Engrs; Am Acad Mech; Sigma Xi; Am Soc Metals. *Res:* Fluid-structure interaction including fluids in reactor containment vessels and underwater explosions on structures; improved design for nuclear power plant cable-tray hangers; finite element analysis of railroad track-structures; finite element analysis of nonlinear systems; finite element analysis of metal forming process. *Mailing Add:* 1301 Mallard Circle Tuscaloosa AL 35405

JACKSON, JOHN ERIC, CHEMICAL ENGINEERING. *Current Pos:* RETIRED. *Personal Data:* b Cincinnati, Ohio, July 25, 37; m 60; c 1. *Educ:* Purdue Univ, BS, 58; Univ Mich, MSE, 59. *Prof Exp:* Res engr, Speedway Labs, Union Carbide Corp, 59-63, group leader welding & lasers, 63-66, supvr, 66-68, dir technol, Union Carbide Coating Serv Corp, 68-93. *Mem:* Am Inst Chem Engrs; Am Welding Soc. *Res:* Directing development of high performance materials for aircraft, nuclear, petroleum and related energy industries; wear and corrosion prevention; thermal barriers; composites; fossil fuel production and utilization; oil and gas extraction. *Mailing Add:* 60 Carnary Brownsburg IN 46112

JACKSON, JOHN FENWICK, INTERNAL MEDICINE, GENETICS. *Current Pos:* from asst prof to assoc prof internal med & from assoc prof to prof prev med, Univ Miss, 64-92, prof internal med, 80, chmn, 81, EMER PROF INTERNAL MED & PREV MED, SCH MED, UNIV MISS, 92- *Personal Data:* b Kosciusko, Miss, Nov 19, 28; m 54; c 3. *Educ:* Univ Miss, BA, 50; Tulane Univ, MD, 53; Am Bd Internal Med, dipl, 65; Am Bd Med Genetics, Clin Genetics, Clin Cytogenetics, dipl, 82. *Prof Exp:* Intern, Philadelphia Gen Hosp, 53-54; gen pract, Minter City, Miss, 54-56; resident res physician internal med, Med Ctr, Univ Miss, 58-60, chief resident physician, 60; from instr to asst prof internal med, Tulane Univ, 61-64. *Concurrent Pos:* Res fel cancer, Univ Miss, 60-61; trainee, Inst Med Genetics, Univ Uppsala, 62-63; vis physician, Charity Hosp La, New Orleans, 63-64; attend physician, Univ Miss Hosp, Jackson, 64-; consult, Vet Admin Hosp, Jackson, 64-; vis investr, Pop Genetics Lab, Univ Hawaii, 70-71. *Mem:* Am Fedn Clin; Sigma Xi; Am Soc Hemat; Soc Human Genetics. *Res:* Hematology; medical genetics; cytogenetic investigations in human disease; human linkage studies. *Mailing Add:* 2024 Southwood Rd Jackson MS 39211-6031

JACKSON, JOHN MATHEWS, FOOD SCIENCE. *Current Pos:* CONSULT, 73- *Personal Data:* b Chicago, Ill, July 9, 08; m 31; c 7. *Educ:* Univ Chicago, BS, 29, PhD(chem), 32. *Prof Exp:* Chemist, Thermal Eng Group, Am Can Co, Ill, 32-37, supvr, 38-41, asst chief packaging res, 42-49, asst mgr res, Pac Div, 49-51, mgr, Res Div Lab, 52-55, Ill, 55-57, sect mgr, 57-63; dir res, Green Giant Co, 63-67, dir packaging res, 68-73. *Concurrent Pos:* Mem, Comt Foods, Subcomt Radiation Sterilization, Nat Res Coun, 55-57; pres, Res & Develop Assocs Food & Container Inst, 62-63; mem, Sci Res Comt, Nat Canners Asn, 65-72; mem, Comt Microbiol Food, Adv Bd Mil Personnel Supplies, Nat Acad Sci, 65-68, Container Comt, 68-71; consult, Process Rev Comt, Bur Foods, Food & Drug Admin, 74- *Mem:* Am Chem Soc; fel Inst Food Technologists (pres, 62-63). *Res:* Decomposition of organic compounds in electrical discharges; heat penetration in canned foods; sterilization of canned foods; packaging of frozen foods; aerosol packaging. *Mailing Add:* PO Box 87 Lakeside MI 49116

JACKSON, JOHN STERLING, economic system modeling, for more information see previous edition

JACKSON, JULIUS, INORGANIC CHEMISTRY. *Current Pos:* CONSULT PIGMENTS, 80- *Personal Data:* b New York, NY, Apr 20, 16; m 41, Helen Nalidow; c Steven A. *Educ:* Polytech Inst Brooklyn, BS, 37, MS, 39, PhD(inorg chem), 41. *Prof Exp:* Res chemist, Otto H Henry, Brooklyn, 41-42; chemist-metallurgist, Nat Prod Refining Co, NJ, 42-44; res chemist, E I du Pont de Nemours & Co, Inc, 44-65, sr res chemist, 65-66, res assoc, 66-80. *Concurrent Pos:* Eve instr, Polytech Inst Brooklyn, 42-47 & Brooklyn Col, 47. *Mem:* Am Chem Soc. *Res:* Inorganic chemistry; metallurgy of chromium alloys; nonaqueous solvents; chromium chemicals; selenium oxycholoro compounds of pyridine and related compounds; inorganic pigments; phthalocyanine pigments; quinacridone pigments; flame retardants; light stabilizers. *Mailing Add:* 224 Charles St Westfield NJ 07090-4027

JACKSON, KENNETH ARTHUR, CRYSTAL GROWTH THIN FILMS & PHASE TRANSFORMATIONS, MICRO ELECTRONIC PACKAGING MATERIALS. *Current Pos:* PROF MAT SCI & ENG, UNIV ARIZ, 89- *Personal Data:* Stacy (Pendell) & Meredith. *Educ:* Univ Toronto, BSc, 52, MSc, 53; Harvard Univ, PhD(appl physics), 56. *Honors & Awards:* Matthewson Gold Metal, Minerals, Metals & Mat Soc, Am Inst Mining, Metall & Petrol Engrs, 66; Crystal Growth Award, Am Asn Crystal Growth, 93. *Prof Exp:* Asst prof appl physics, Harvard Univ, 58-62; mem tech staff, AT&T Bell Labs, 62-66, dept head, 67-89. *Concurrent Pos:* Consult, Panel Mat Processing in Space, NASA, 74 & 82; lectr & consult, Chinese Univ Develop Prog, Nat Acad Sci, 85. *Mem:* Mat Res Soc (vpres, 76-77, pres, 78); Am Asn Crystal Growth (pres, 70-76); fel Metall Soc; fel Phys Soc; fel AAAS. *Res:* Crystal growth phenomena, surface and interface structures, modelling of kinetic processes of phase transformations, interface instabilities, computer modelling of crystal growth and thin film deposition process, optical materials, integrated surface waveguide structures, microelectric packaging materials. *Mailing Add:* Univ Ariz 4715 E Ft Lowell Rd Tucson AZ 85712

JACKSON, KENNETH LEE, PHYSIOLOGY. *Current Pos:* from asst prof to prof environ health, Univ Wash, 63-91, head div, 76-91, CHMN, RADIOL SCI GROUP, UNIV WASH, 67-, EMER PROF, ENVIRON HEALTH, 91- *Personal Data:* b Berkeley, Calif, Jan 6, 26; m 48; c 4. *Educ:* Univ Calif, Berkeley, AB, 49, PhD(physiol), 54. *Prof Exp:* Res asst physiol, Donner Lab, Univ Calif, Berkeley, 49-51; res physiologist, Off Naval Res Unit One, 51-53; sr investr, Biochem Br, US Naval Radiol Defense Lab, 54-60; head radiobiol group, Bioastronaut Sect, Boeing Co, 60-63. *Concurrent Pos:* Consult, Fred Hutchinson Cancer Res Ctr, 80-, DOE Pac Northwest Lab, 85-87; vis scientist, Inst Exp Gerontol, TNO, Rijswijk, Netherlands, 77. *Mem:* AAAS; Am Physiol Soc; Radiation Res Soc; Health Physics Soc; Sigma Xi. *Res:* Biochemical and physiological mechanisms in mammalian radiation biology; cell and intestinal physiology. *Mailing Add:* Dept Environ Health Univ Wash SB-75 Seattle WA 98195

JACKSON, KENNETH RONALD, NUMERICAL ANALYSIS & SCIENTIFIC COMPUTING, ORDINARY DIFFERENTIAL EDUCATION & LINEAR ALGEBRA. *Current Pos:* from asst prof to assoc prof, 81-92, assoc chair, 87-89, PROF COMPUT SCI, UNIV TORONTO, 92- *Personal Data:* b Montreal, Que, Mar 3, 51; m 83, Ivana Zivic; c G Frederick & Katherine Alexandra. *Educ:* Univ Toronto, BSc, 73, MSc, 74, PhD(comput sci), 78. *Prof Exp:* Gibbs instr comput sci, Yale Univ, 78-81. *Concurrent Pos:* Chmn, Comt Human Rights, Soc Indust & Appl Math, 85-94. *Mem:* Soc Indust & Appl Math; Can Appl Math Soc. *Res:* Numerical analysis; mathematical software; scientific computing; numerical solution of ordinary differential equations and numerical linear algebra. *Mailing Add:* Comput Sci Dept Univ Toronto Toronto ON M5S 3G4 Can. *Fax:* 416-978-1931; *E-Mail:* krj@cs.toronto.edu

JACKSON, KENNETH WILLIAM, ANALYTICAL ATOMIC SPECTROMETRY. *Current Pos:* res scientist, 72-77, RES SCIENTIST NY DEPT HEALTH, 87-; PROF ENVIRON & ANALYTICAL CHEM, STATE UNIV NY, ALBANY, 87- *Personal Data:* b Shipley, Yorkshire, Eng, Feb 11, 44; m 71, Pauline Robinson; c Paul J. *Educ:* Royal Soc Chem, UK, GRSC, 68; Univ London, MSc & DIC, 70, PhD(anal chem), 72. *Prof Exp:* From lectr to sr lectr anal chem, Sheffield City Polytech, UK, 77-84; prof, Univ Sask, 84-87. *Mem:* Fel Royal Soc Chem UK; Soc Appl Spectros. *Res:* Electrothermal atomic absorption spectrometry with emphasis on mechanisms of atomization from slurry samples; chemistry and physics of the action of modifiers. *Mailing Add:* Wadsworth Ctr NY Dept Health PO Box 509 Albany NY 12201-0509. *Fax:* 518-474-6184; *E-Mail:* jackson@wadsworth.org

JACKSON, KERN CHANDLER, GEOLOGY. *Current Pos:* from asst prof to prof geol, 52-84, chmn dept, 55-59, EMER PROF GEOL, UNIV ARK, 84- *Personal Data:* b Kansas City, Mo, Oct 13, 20; m 70; c 4. *Educ:* Mich Technol Univ, BS, 47, MS, 50; Univ Wis, PhD(geol), 51. *Prof Exp:* From instr to asst prof geol, Univ Maine, 50-52. *Mem:* AAAS; Am Mineral Soc; Geol Soc Am. *Res:* Petrology and petrography; petrography of Arkansas syenites and lamprophyres. *Mailing Add:* 235 Baxter Lane Fayetteville AR 72701

JACKSON, LAIRD GRAY, MEDICAL GENETICS. *Current Pos:* instr med, Jefferson Med Col, 62-64, from asst prof to assoc prof med, 64-69, assoc prof, 69-78, PROF MED, PEDIAT, OBSTET & GYNEC, JEFFERSON MED COL, 78-, DIR DIV MED GENETICS, 69- *Personal Data:* b Seattle, Wash, Oct 10, 30; m 56, Marie Barr; c 3. *Educ:* Pomona Col, BA, 51; Univ Cincinnati, MD, 55. *Prof Exp:* Capt USAF, Sch Aviation Med, Gunter AFB, Ala, 56-69. *Concurrent Pos:* NIH fel, 61-62; Leukemia Soc fel, 63-65, scholar, 65-; Nat Cancer Inst res grants, 64-66 & 65-68; Nat Found res grant, 64-66. *Mem:* Am Fedn Clin Res; Tissue Cult Asn; Am Soc Human Genetics; Am Asn Cancer Res; Am Col Med Genetics. *Res:* Efficacy and safety of prenatal diagnoses. *Mailing Add:* Dept Med Div Med Genetics Thomas Jefferson Univ 1100 Walnut St Philadelphia PA 19107-5563. *Fax:* 215-955-7560

JACKSON, LARRY LAVERN, VETERINARY ANESTHESIOLOGY. *Current Pos:* instr, 68-71, assoc prof, 71-, PROF VET MED, IOWA STATE UNIV, 71- *Personal Data:* b Charlotte, Mich, June 2, 42; m 63; c 2. *Educ:* Mich State Univ, BS, 64, DVM, 66; Iowa State Univ, MS, 71. *Prof Exp:* Vet, Miller Animal Clin, Lansing, Mich, 66-68. *Mem:* Am Vet Med Asn; Am Soc Vet Anesthesiol. *Res:* Cardio-pulmonary function of the equine and bovine species while under the influence of various anesthetic agents. *Mailing Add:* 631 X Ave Ames IA 50010

JACKSON, LARRY LEE, BIOCHEMISTRY. *Current Pos:* From asst prof to assoc prof, 65-75, PROF CHEM, MONT STATE UNIV, 75- *Personal Data:* b Livingston, Mont, Oct 8, 40; m 62; c 4. *Educ:* Mont State Univ, BS, 62; NDak State Univ, PhD(biochem), 65. *Mem:* Int Soc Chem Ecol. *Res:* Lipid chemistry and biochemistry; surface lipids of insects and plants; hydrocarbon biosynthesis; microbial cell wall chemistry; insect pheromone biochemistry; insect sterols. *Mailing Add:* Dept Chem & Biochem Mont State Univ Bozeman MT 59717-0001

JACKSON, LARRY LYNN, POLYMER CHARACTERIZATION. *Current Pos:* RES MGR, DOW CHEM CO, 69- *Personal Data:* b Defiance, Ohio, Aug 21, 40; m 62; c 3. *Educ:* Va Mil Inst, BS, 62; Ohio State Univ, PhD(org chem), 67. *Honors & Awards:* John C Vaaler, Chem Processing Mag, 72 & 78; IR-100, Indust Res Mag, 76. *Mem:* Am Chem Soc; Sigma Xi. *Res:* New product and process research with emphasis on advanced analytical instrumentation and technology. *Mailing Add:* 1776 Peers Lane Auburn MI 48611-9524

JACKSON, LELAND BROOKS, DIGITAL SIGNAL PROCESSING, DIGITAL FILTERS. *Current Pos:* assoc prof, 74-79, PROF ELEC ENG, UNIV RI, 79- *Personal Data:* b Atlanta, Ga, July 23, 40; m 68, Diana Norton; c Anita N. *Educ:* Mass Inst Technol, SB & SM, 63; Stevens Inst Technol, ScD, 70. *Honors & Awards:* Tech Achievement Award, Acoust Speech & Signal Processing Soc. *Prof Exp:* Res eng radar, Sylvania Electronic Systs, 64-66; mem tech staff digital filters, Bell Tel Labs, 66-70; vpres eng, Rockland Systs Corp, 70-74. *Concurrent Pos:* Res grants, NSF & Air Force Off Sci Res, 76, Off Naval Res, 77 & NSF, 83-88. *Mem:* Fel Inst Elec & Electronics Engrs. *Res:* Optimum synthesis of digital filter structures; estimation of signal parameters and its application to speech analysis instrumentation and bioengineering. *Mailing Add:* Dept Elec Eng Kelley Hall Univ RI Kingston RI 02881. *E-Mail:* jackson@ele.uri.edu

JACKSON, LIONEL ERIC, QUATERNARY GEOLOGY, ENVIRONMENTAL GEOLOGY. *Current Pos:* GEOLOGIST, GEOL SURV CAN, 77- *Personal Data:* b San Mateo, Calif, Jan 20, 47; Can citizen; m 69, Carol N Thompson; c Lisa C. *Educ:* San Francisco State Univ, AB, 68; Stanford Univ, MS, 73; Univ Calgary, PhD(geol), 77. *Honors & Awards:* Serv Award, Can Asn Petrol Geologists; Thomas Roy Award, Can Geotech Soc. *Prof Exp:* Geologist, Hudson Bay Oil & Gas Ltd, 69-70; hydrologist, US Geol Surv, 71-73. *Concurrent Pos:* Consult, Calif Dept Transp, 79; instr, Univ Calgary, 81; adj prof, Simon Fraser Univ, 86-, dir Inst Quart Res, 89, 91-93. *Mem:* Fel Geol Asn Can; Am Quaternary Asn; Can Soc Petrol Geologists. *Res:* Quaternary geology and paleo-ecology of western interior plains and Rocky Mountain Foothills; natural hazards in northern Montana regions; quaternary geology of Yukon Territory. *Mailing Add:* 972 Porter St Coquitlam BC V3J 5C2 Can

JACKSON, LLOYD K, MATHEMATICS. *Current Pos:* From asst prof to prof, 50-84, EMER PROF MATH, UNIV NEBR, LINCOLN, 84- *Personal Data:* b Fairbury, Nebr, Aug 25, 22; m 43; c 1. *Educ:* Univ Nebr, AB, 43, MA, 48; Univ Calif, Los Angeles, PhD, 50. *Mem:* Am Math Soc; Math Asn Am; Sigma Xi. *Res:* Partial differential equations; function theory. *Mailing Add:* 4301 Normal Blvd Apt 39 Lincoln NE 68506-5533

JACKSON, M(ELBOURNE) L(ESLIE), ENVIRONMENTAL ENGINEERING. *Current Pos:* prof chem eng & head dept, 53-65, dean, Grad Sch, 65-70, res prof chem eng, 71-80, dean eng, 73, 78-80 & 83, EMER PROF, UNIV IDAHO, 80- *Personal Data:* b Wisdom, Mont, Sept 27, 15; m 44; c 4. *Educ:* Mont State Col, BS, 41; Univ Minn, PhD(chem eng), 48. *Hon Degrees:* Dr, Montana State Univ, 80. *Prof Exp:* Instr chem eng, Mont State Col, 42-44 & Univ Minn, 44-48; asst prof, Univ Colo, 48-50; head process develop br, US Naval Ord Test Sta, Calif, 50-53. *Concurrent Pos:* Consult, indust firms, 53-; E L Phillips intern, univ admin, Pa State Univ, 63-64. *Mem:* Fel Am Inst Chem Engrs; Am Chem Soc. *Res:* Bioreactors for fermentation and waste water treatment. *Mailing Add:* Dept Chem Eng Univ Idaho Moscow ID 83843

JACKSON, MARGARET E, INORGANIC CHEMISTRY, PHYSICAL CHEMISTRY. *Current Pos:* asst prof chem, 65-77, ASSOC PROF CHEM, UNIV SALA, 77- *Personal Data:* b Zanesville, Ohio, Sept 2, 28. *Educ:* Muskingum Col, BS, 50; Auburn Univ, MS, 58, PhD(phys chem), 64. *Prof Exp:* Chemist, Dow Chem Co, Mich, 51-52, Atlantic Supply Co, Md, 53 & Calverton Chem Co, Md, 53-56; asst chem, Auburn Univ, 56-62, instr, 62-64; asst prof, Delta State Col, 64-65. *Mem:* Am Chem Soc; The Chem Soc. *Res:* The preparation and properties of organo-niobium compounds; determination of stability constants for metal diketo chelates and other coordination compounds. *Mailing Add:* 113 Vanderbilt Dr Mobile AL 36608

JACKSON, MARION LEROY, SOIL SCIENCE, TRACE ELEMENTS. *Current Pos:* from assoc prof to prof soils, Univ Wis-Madison, 46-74, chmn, Phys Sci Div, 52-55, Franklin Hiram King prof, 74-90, EMER FRANKLIN HIRAM KING PROF SOILS, UNIV WIS-MADISON, 90- *Personal Data:* b Reynolds, Nebr, Nov 30, 14; m 37; c 4. *Educ:* Univ Nebr, BS, 36, MS, 37; Univ Wis, PhD(soil chem), 39. *Hon Degrees:* DSc, Univ Nebr, 74. *Honors & Awards:* Soil Sci Achievement Award, Am Soc Agron, 58; Career Award, Soil Sci Soc Am, 83. *Prof Exp:* Land classification aide, Resettlement Admin, USDA, Nebr, 36-37; Alumni Res Found & univ fel, Univ Wis, 39-41, from instr to asst prof soils, 41-45; assoc prof agron, Exp Sta, Purdue Univ, 45-46. *Concurrent Pos:* Vis prof, Cornell Univ, 59, Univ Calif, 60, Univ Nebr, 61, Va Polytech Inst, 62, Can Dept Agr, 64, Univ Thesaloniki, 66, Univ Tex, 67, Kyushu Univ, 69, Ohio Univ, 71 & distinguished vis prof, Univ Wash, 73; mem, Panel Radioactive Wastes, Nat Res Coun, 76-77. *Mem:* Nat Acad Sci; Clay Minerals Soc (vpres, 65, pres, 66); fel Soil Sci Soc Am (vpres, 67, pres, 68); fel Am Soc Agron; fel Am Mineral Soc; fel AAAS. *Res:* Crystal chemistry of soil colloids responsible for soil acidity; cation exchange, phosphate fixation and other chemical reactions; electron microscopy of soil minerals; world distribution of radioactive elements in global dust; soil influence on trace elements in the food chain and human health. *Mailing Add:* 309 Ozark Trail Madison WI 53705

JACKSON, MARION T, PLANT ECOLOGY. *Current Pos:* From asst prof to assoc prof, 64-71, PROF LIFE SCI, IND STATE UNIV, TERRE HAUTE, 71- *Personal Data:* b Versailles, Ind, Aug 19, 33; m 63, Jaleh Jorjani; c Arshia & Grousha. *Educ:* Purdue Univ, BS, 61, PhD(plant ecol), 64. *Honors & Awards:* Oak Leaf Award, The Nature Conservancy; James Mason Environ Serv Award, Audubon Soc. *Concurrent Pos:* Pres, Nature Conservancy, Ind Chap, 76-82; pres, Wabash Valley Audubon Soc, 96-97. *Mem:* AAAS; Sigma Xi; Ecol Soc Am; Natural Areas Asn. *Res:* Forest ecology of Midwest; flowering phenology; biotic inventories of natural areas and national parks; ecological life histories; regional plant geography; long-term ecological research of old-growth forests. *Mailing Add:* Dept Life Sci Ind State Univ Terre Haute IN 47809. *Fax:* 812-237-4480

JACKSON, MARTIN PATRICK ARDEN, SEDIMENTARY TECTONICS, TECTONIC MODELING. *Current Pos:* res sci assoc, 80-81, res scientist, 81-87, SR RES SCIENTIST, BUR ECON GEOL, UNIV TEX, AUSTIN, 87-, DIR, APPL GEODYNAMICS LAB, 88- *Personal Data:* b Salisbury, Rhodesia, May 14, 47; Irish citizen; m 69, Josephine Vincent; c Britt & Kirsty. *Educ:* Univ London, BSc, 68, BSc, 69; Univ Cape Town, PhD(geol), 76. *Honors & Awards:* Sproule Award, Am Asn Petrol Geologists, 85, Matson Award, 90. *Prof Exp:* Proj geologist, Cominco, SAfrica, 70-72; res assoc, Precambrian Res Unit, Univ Cape Town, 72-76; lectr, Geol Dept, Univ Natal, 76-79. *Concurrent Pos:* Prin investr, Dept Energy, Tex Bur Econ Geol, 80-84; vis scientist, Univ Uppsala, Sweden, 84; lectr, Am Asn Petrol Geologists Sch Struct Geol, 84-85; assoc ed, Am & Asn Petrol Geologists Bull, 85-90 & Geol Soc Am Bull, 89-; mem, Int Union Geol Sci Comn Tectonics, 87-; external PhD exam, Univ Uppsala; distinguished lectr, Am Asn Petrol Geologists, 91-92, co- convenor, Hedberg Int Res Conf, 93; guest ed, Marine Petrol Geol, 92. *Mem:* Fel Geol Soc Am; Am Asn Petrol Geologists. *Res:* Diapirism and halokinesis; geodynamic modeling; petroleum structural traps; syndepositional deformation; geology of central Iran; structural analysis of Precambrian genesises and greenstone belts; metamorphic petrology and geochemistry; crustal evolution of Southern Africa; tectonic evolution of sedimentary basins; Phanerozoic tectonics of West Africa; tectonics of Triton; strain analysis. *Mailing Add:* Bur Econ Geol Univ Tex Austin Univ Station Box X Austin TX 78713-7508. *Fax:* 512-471-0140; *E-Mail:* jacksona@begv.beg.utexas.edu

JACKSON, MARVIN ALEXANDER, MEDICINE, PATHOLOGY. *Current Pos:* from asst prof to assoc prof, 57-68, PROF PATH, COL MED, HOWARD UNIV, 68-, CHMN DEPT, 60- *Personal Data:* b Dawson, Ga, Oct 28, 27; m 57; c 2. *Educ:* Morehouse Col, BS, 47; Meharry Med Col, MD, 51; Univ Mich, MA, 56. *Prof Exp:* Intern, US Naval Hosp, St Albans, NY, 51-52, mem staff, 52-53; asst resident, Univ Mich Hosp, 53-54, teaching asst path, 54-55, instr, 55-56. *Concurrent Pos:* Resident, Hosp Joint Dis, New York, 56-57; attend physician, Howard Univ Hosp, 57; consult physician, Vet Admin Hosp, Washington, DC, 60 & NIH, 68. *Mem:* Fel Col Am Path; Am Asn Anatomists; Am Asn Path & Bact; Int Acad Path; Tissue Cult Asn; Sigma Xi. *Mailing Add:* Dept Path Howard Univ Col Med 520 W St NW Washington DC 20059. *Fax:* 202-865-4098

JACKSON, MATTHEW PAUL, BACTERIAL PATHOGENESIS, MICROBIAL TOXINS. *Current Pos:* ASST PROF MICROBIOL, SCH MED, WAYNE STATE UNIV, 89- *Personal Data:* b Kansas City, Mo, July 17, 59. *Educ:* Univ Mo, BS, 80, MS, 82; Kans State Univ, PhD(microbiol), 85. *Prof Exp:* Fel microbiol, Uniformed Serv Univ Health Sci, 85-89. *Mem:* Am Soc Microbiol; AAAS. *Res:* Genetic regulation and structure-function analyses of bacterial toxins; pathogenic mechanisms of diarrheagenic Escherichia coli with emphasis on the Shiga toxin family of cytotoxins. *Mailing Add:* Dept Immunol & Microbiol Med Sch Wayne State Univ 540 E Canfield Detroit MI 48201-1928

JACKSON, MEL CLINTON, protein purification, enzymology, for more information see previous edition

JACKSON, MELVIN ROBERT, METALLURGY, MATERIALS SCIENCE. *Current Pos:* METALLURGIST, CORP RES & DEVELOP, GEN ELEC CO, 72- *Personal Data:* b Norwood, Pa, Nov 21, 43; m 68; c 1. *Educ:* Lehigh Univ, BS, 65, MS, 67, PhD(metall & mat sci), 71. *Prof Exp:* Metallurgist, Paul D Merios Res Labs, Int Nickel, 71-72. *Mem:* Am Inst Mining, Metall & Petrol Engrs; Sigma Xi. *Res:* Phase equilibria of high temperature metal and metal-ceramic systems, metallurgical coatings, tool materials. *Mailing Add:* 2208 Niskayuna Dr Schenectady NY 12309-4012

JACKSON, MEYER B, NEUROSCIENCE, DEVELOPMENTAL NEUROBIOLOGY. *Current Pos:* PROF PHYSIOL & NEWUROSCI, MED SCH, UNIV WIS, 90- *Personal Data:* b Iowa City, Iowa, Mar 24, 51; m 80; c 1. *Educ:* Brandeis Univ, BA, 73; Yale Univ, PhD(molecular biophys & biochem), 77. *Prof Exp:* NIH fel, 78-81; asst prof, Univ Calif, Los Angeles, 81-87, assoc prof biol, 87-90. *Mem:* Biophys Soc; Soc Neurosci. *Res:* Physical and chemical factors involved in synaptic transmission and excitability. *Mailing Add:* Dept Physiol SMI-129 Univ Wis Med Sch 1300 University Ave Madison WI 53706-1532. *Fax:* 608-265-5512

JACKSON, MICHAEL J, EPITHELIAL PHYSIOLOGY, MEMBRANE TRANSPORT. *Current Pos:* EXEC DIR, FEDN AM SOC EXP BIOL, 90- *Personal Data:* b Walton, Eng, Apr 12, 38; m 60, Beryl Ann Tidy. *Educ:* Univ London, BSc, 63; Univ Sheffield, PhD(physiol), 66. *Prof Exp:* Asst exp officer biochem, Vet Lab, Ministry Agr, Eng, 57-63; res asst physiol, Univ Sheffield, 63-65, from asst lectr to lectr, 65-67; from asst prof to prof physiol, George Washington Univ, 67-90, assoc dean Res & Sponsor Prog, Med Ctr, 85-89, dean res, 89-90. *Concurrent Pos:* USPHS Res Career Develop Award, 72-77; guest worker, Sect Gastroenterol, Nat Inst Arthritis, Metab & Digestive Dis, 75-76; consult, Vet Admin Merit Rev Bd Basic Sci, 78-80; assoc ed, Am J Physiol, Gastrointestinal & Liver Physics, 79-85. *Mem:* Brit Physiol Soc; Coun Eng Sci Soc Execs; Am Physiol Soc. *Mailing Add:* Exec Off Fedn Am Soc Exp Biol 9650 Rockville Pike Bethesda MD 20814-3998. *Fax:* 301-530-7049; *E-Mail:* mjackson@execofc.faseb.org

JACKSON, NOEL, PLANT PATHOLOGY. *Current Pos:* from asst prof to assoc prof, 65-75, PROF PLANT PATH, UNIV RI, 75-, PROF ENTOM, 77- *Personal Data:* b Northallerton, Eng, Dec 25, 31; m 56; c 2. *Educ:* Univ Durham, BSc, 53, Hons, 54, PhD, 61. *Prof Exp:* Biologist, Sports Turf Res Inst, Eng, 58-65. *Mem:* Brit Asn Appl Biol; Am Phytopath Soc; Trans Brit Mycol Soc; Brit Soc Plant Path; Int Turfgrass Soc. *Res:* Diseases of turf grasses and ornamentals. *Mailing Add:* Dept Plant Path-Entom 234 Woodward Hall Univ RI Kingston RI 02881

JACKSON, PETER RICHARD, PARASITOLOGY. *Current Pos:* SCI REV OFFICER, NAT INST ALLERGY & INFECTIOUS DIS, NIH, 90- *Personal Data:* b New York, NY, Dec 9, 48; m 76. *Educ:* Seton Hall Univ, BA, 70; Univ Tex, Austin, MA, 73; Rice Univ, PhD(biol), 76. *Prof Exp:* NIH assoc parasitol dept biol, Rice Univ, 76 & dept zool, Univ Mass, 76-78; Nat Res Coun assoc immunol, Walter Reed Army Inst Res, 78-87; res mgr, Am Inst Biol Sci, Washington, DC, 87-90. *Mem:* Am Soc Parasitologists; Soc Protozoologists; AAAS; Am Inst Biol Sci; Am Soc Zoologist; Sigma Xi. *Res:* Immunology of parasitic infections; biochemistry and physiology of parasites, especially parasitic protozoa. *Mailing Add:* 16609 Lescot Terr Rockville MD 20853

JACKSON, PRINCE A, JR, PHYSICS, MATHEMATICS. *Current Pos:* RETIRED. *Personal Data:* b Savannah, Ga, Mar 17, 25; m 50; c 4. *Educ:* Savannah State Col, BS, 49; NY Univ, MS, 50; Boston Col, PhD(sci, ed), 66. *Prof Exp:* Instr high sch, Ga, 50-55; instr physics, Savannah State Col, 55-61, asst prof math & physics, 61-64, assoc prof phys sci, 66-69, prof math & physics, 71-80, pres, 71-80. *Concurrent Pos:* Chmn div natural sci, Savannah State Col, 69-71. *Mem:* AAAS; Nat Sci Teachers Asn; Nat Inst Sci. *Res:* Improvement of science and mathematics education at all levels of instruction; differential equations of mathematical physics; pedagogical interrelationship between science and mathematics; philosophy of science. *Mailing Add:* Dept Math & Physics Savannah State Col PO Box 20345 Savannah GA 31404

JACKSON, RAY DEAN, SOIL PHYSICS. *Current Pos:* RETIRED. *Personal Data:* b Shoshone, Idaho, Sept 28, 29; m 52, 68; c 7. *Educ:* Utah State Univ, BS, 56; Iowa State Univ, MS, 57; Colo State Univ, PhD(soil sci), 60. *Honors & Awards:* Superior Serv Unit Award, USDA, 63. *Prof Exp:* Soil scientist soil physics, Soil & Water Conserv Res Div, Agr Res Serv, USDA, 57-60, soil scientist, US Water Conserv Lab, 60-62, physicist, US Water Conserv Lab, 62-92. *Concurrent Pos:* Orgn Econ Coop & Develop Sci fel, Eng, 64; adj prof soil & water sci, Univ Ariz, Tuscon. *Mem:* Fel AAAS; fel Soil Sci Soc Am; fel Am Soc Agron; Am Geophys Union. *Res:* Heat, water and water vapor transfer in soils; remote sensing of soil water and crop stress; agricultural remote sensing. *Mailing Add:* 710 E La Jolla Dr Tempe AZ 85282

JACKSON, RAY WELDON, PHYSICS, SCIENCE POLICY. *Current Pos:* RETIRED. *Personal Data:* b Toronto, Ont, Nov 11, 21; m 51, Ruth Comfort; c Suzanne, Martha, Kathren & Fraser. *Educ:* Univ Toronto, BASc, 44; McGill Univ, PhD(physics), 50. *Prof Exp:* Res asst physics, McGill Univ, 50-51; Am Coun Learned Soc fel, Yale Univ, 51-52, asst, 52-54; sr engr physics res, Sprague Elec Co, 54-56; assoc labs dir, RCA Victor Co, Ltd, 56-65; sci adv to sci secretariat, Privy Coun Off, Ottawa, 66-69; sci adv, Sci Coun Can, 69-86. *Concurrent Pos:* Vis prof, McMaster Univ, 64-65 & Carleton Univ, 78-80. *Mem:* sr mem Inst Elec & Electronics Engrs; Can Asn Physicists. *Res:* Semiconductor physics; electronic circuitry; nuclear detectors; philosophy of science and technology; appropriate technology for development. *Mailing Add:* 208 Clemow Ottawa ON K1S 2B4 Can

JACKSON, RAYMOND CARL, CYTOGENETICS. *Current Pos:* prof, 71-90, PAUL WHITFIELD HORN PROF BIOL, TEX TECH UNIV, 90- *Personal Data:* b Medora, Ind, May 7, 28; m 47, T June Snyder; c Jeffrey W & Rebecca J. *Educ:* Ind Univ, AB, 52, AM, 53; Purdue Univ, PhD, 55. *Honors & Awards:* Cert Merit for Res, Am Bot Soc. *Prof Exp:* Asst, Purdue Univ, 53-55; from instr to asst prof biol, Univ NMex, 55-58; from asst prof to prof bot, Univ Kans, 58-71. *Mem:* AAAS; Bot Soc Am; Am Soc Plant Taxon; Genetics Soc Am; Genetics Soc Can. *Res:* Evolutionary mechanisms in Haplopappus and Machaeranthera; cytogenetics of Haplopappus gracilis; genetics and cytogenetics of diploid species of Triticum; evolution and genetics of polyploids. *Mailing Add:* Dept Biol Sci Tex Tech Univ Lubbock TX 79409. *Fax:* 806-742-2963

JACKSON, RICHARD H F, PRECISION ENGINEERING, MECHANICAL METROLOGY. *Current Pos:* prog mgr, Mfg Technol Ctr Prog, 88-89, DEP DIR, CTR MFG ENG, NAT INST STANDARDS & TECHNOL, 89- *Personal Data:* b Jan 29, 47; US citizen; m 81; c 2. *Educ:* Johns Hopkins Univ, BA, 69; Southern Methodist Univ, MS, 70; George Wash Univ, DSc(opers res), 83. *Prof Exp:* Res asst, Computer Sci & Opers Res Ctr, Southern Methodist Univ, 69-70; opers res analyst, Appl Math Div, Nat Bur Standards, Wash, DC, 71-75, math consult, Boulder, Colo, 75-78, proj leader & sr mathematician, Ctr Appl Mat, Gaithersburg, 78-86, prog analyst, Nat Eng Lab, 86-87 & Off Dir, 87-88. *Concurrent Pos:* Assoc prof, Opers Res Dept, George Wash Univ, Wash, DC; mem & chmn, numerous comts, Opers Res Soc Am, Math Prog Soc & Soc Indust & Appl Math. *Mem:* Opers Res Soc Am; Math Prog Soc; Soc Indust & Appl Math. *Res:* Author of numerous mathematical publications. *Mailing Add:* 8625 Stableview Ct Gaithersburg MD 20882

JACKSON, RICHARD J, PUBLIC HEALTH & EPIDEMIOLOGY. *Current Pos:* DIR, NAT CTR ENVIRON HEALTH, CTR DIS CONTROL & PREV, DEPT HEALTH & HUMAN SERVS, 94- *Educ:* Univ Calif, San Francisco, MD; Univ Calif, Berkeley, MPH. *Concurrent Pos:* Chmn, Comt Environ Hazards, Am Acad Pediat; mem, Comt Environ Hazards, Nat Acad Sci. *Res:* Acute and chronic health effects of environmental and infectious exposures. *Mailing Add:* Nat Ctr Environ Health 4770 Buford Hwy NE F-29 Atlanta GA 30341-3724

JACKSON, RICHARD LEE, BIOCHEMISTRY, PROTEIN CHEMISTRY. *Current Pos:* VPRES DISCOVERY RES, WYETH-AYERST RES, PRINCETON, NJ, 93- *Personal Data:* b Springfield, Ill, Dec 30, 39. *Educ:* Univ Ill, BS, 63, PhD(microbiol), 67. *Prof Exp:* Res assoc protein chem, Biol Dept, Brookhaven Nat Lab, 67-69; Nat Heart & Lung Inst jr staff fel, 69-70; Nat Inst Arthritis & Metab Dis sr staff fel, 70-71; asst prof exp med, Baylor Col Med, 71-73, assoc prof exp med & cell biol, 73-77; prof pharmacol & cell biophys, Univ Cincinnati Col Med, 77- 92, head Div Lipoprotein Res, 80-86. *Concurrent Pos:* Estab investr, Am Heart Asn, 72-77, mem, Coun Arteriosclerosis; vis prof, Hadassah Univ Hosp, Jerusalem, Israel, 74, Biochem Lab, State Univ, Utrecht Neth, 78, 80-81, 83-86, Chiba Univ, Japan, 80 & 82, Nat Cardiovasc Ctr Res Inst, Japan, 84, Rockefeller Univ, NY, 85; dir macromolecular biochem, Merrell Dow Res Inst, Cincinnati, Ohio, 85-90, dir, biochem sci, 86-90, dir res sci & actg dir cell biol, 90, managing dir res sci & actg dir metab & inflammatory dis, 90-91, vpres res sci, 92; assoc ed, J Lipid Res, 88-92. *Mem:* AAAS; Am Soc Biochem & Molecular Biol; Am Fedn Clin Res; Am Heart Asn; Am Soc Pharmacol & Exp Therapeut. *Res:* Structure and metabolism of plasma lipoproteins and apolipoproteins; protein-glycosaminoglycan-lipid interaction; structure, mechanism of action and regulation of expression of lipoprotein lipase and hepatic triglyceride lipase; diet, high density lipoproteins and lipid metabolism; cellular mechanisms of atherosclerosis, ischemic heart disease and diabetes; oxygen radicals and disease; regulation of IL-1 expression; drugs affecting lipid metabolism, ischemic heart disease and diabetes. *Mailing Add:* Discovery Res Wyeth-Ayerst Res CN8000 Princeton NJ 08543

JACKSON, RICHARD THOMAS, PHYSIOLOGY. *Current Pos:* instr ophthal & physiol, 63-71, assoc prof, 71-76, dir, Otolaryngol Lab, 67-, PROF SURG, EMORY UNIV, 76- *Personal Data:* b Detroit, Mich, Jan 19, 30; m 55; c 2. *Educ:* Univ Detroit, BS, 52, MS, 54; Fla State Univ, PhD(physiol), 60. *Honors & Awards:* Hon Award, Am Acad Otolaryngol. *Prof Exp:* Asst physiol, Fla State Univ, 54-57, instr, 57-59; from asst prof to assoc prof, Loyola Univ, La, 59-63; res assoc, Lab Ophthal Res, 63-67. *Concurrent Pos:* Consult, Comt Drugs, Am Acad Otolaryngol; consult, Yerkes Regional Primate Ctr, 82-; vis prof, Kagoshima Sch Med, Japan, 85; consult, Va Med Ctr, equilibrium tests, 88- *Mem:* Asn Res Otolaryngol; Am Acad Otolaryngol. *Res:* Nasal and eustachian tube physiology; control of blood flow to the nose and ear; clinical and animal testing of drugs that effect blood flow; equilibrium testing, antivertigo drugs. *Mailing Add:* Dept Surg 441 WMB Emory Univ 1440 Clifton Rd NE Atlanta GA 30307-1053

JACKSON, RICHARD W, AMINO ACIDS, PROTEINS. *Current Pos:* RETIRED. *Educ:* Univ Ill, PhD(biochem), 25. *Prof Exp:* Chief fermentation div, US Dept Agr, Northern Regional Res Lab, 47-66. *Mailing Add:* 1319 N Institute Pl Peoria IL 61606-1024

JACKSON, ROBERT BRUCE, JR, MATHEMATICS. *Current Pos:* from asst prof to prof, 56-83, chmn dept, 78-83, VAIL PROF MATH, DAVIDSON COL, 83- *Personal Data:* b Drakes Branch, Va, June 5, 29. *Educ:* Davidson Col, BS, 50; Duke Univ, PhD(math), 67. *Prof Exp:* Teacher math, Battle Ground Acad, 50-51; asst, Duke Univ, 53-56. *Mem:* Math Asn Am. *Res:* Probability. *Mailing Add:* 568 TNRB Brigham Young Univ Provo UT 84602

JACKSON, ROBERT W, MICROBIOLOGY, IMMUNOLOGY. *Current Pos:* EXEC ASSOC DEAN, SCH MED, SOUTHERN ILL UNIV, 74- *Educ:* Purdue Univ, PhD(immunol), 63. *Mailing Add:* Microbiol & Immunol Dept Southern Ill Univ Med PO Box 19230 Springfield IL 62794-9230

JACKSON, RONALD SPENCER, VITICULTURE, ENOLOGY. *Current Pos:* PROF BOT & MICROBIOL, BRANDON UNIV, 72- *Personal Data:* m 75, Suzanne Ouellet. *Educ:* Queens Univ, BSc, 64, MSc, 67; Univ Toronto, PhD(plant path), 70. *Prof Exp:* Teacher, RH King High Sch, 64-65; postdoctorate, Queen's Univ, 70-72. *Concurrent Pos:* Vis prof, Cornell Univ, 79-80. *Mem:* Am Soc Enol & Viticult; Am Phytopath Soc. *Res:* Science of wine, including commercial grape growing, wine production, wine sensory evaluation and influences of wine on health. *Mailing Add:* 270 18th St Brandon MB R7A 6A9 Can. *Fax:* 204-728-7346; *E-Mail:* jackson@brandonu.ca

JACKSON, ROSCOE GEORGE, II, SEDIMENTOLOGY, FLUID DYNAMICS. *Current Pos:* GEOLOGIST & PROJ COORDR, JACKSON BROS CO, 81- *Personal Data:* b Eureka, Kans, May 14, 48. *Educ:* Univ Kans, BS, 70; Univ Ill, Urbana-Champaign, MS, 73, PhD(geol), 75. *Prof Exp:* Instr, Northwestern Univ, Evanston, 74-75, asst prof geol, 75-80; mem fac, Dept Geol Sci, Univ Mich, Ann Arbor, 80-81. *Mem:* Geol Soc Am; Int Asn Sedimentologists; Soc Econ Paleontologists & Mineralogists. *Res:* Ancient and modern alluvial sediments; mathematical models and mechanics of bedforms, sediment transport and fluid flow in modern sedimentary environments; flow structures of geophysical turbulent boundary layers; petroleum geology. *Mailing Add:* 603 N Elm St Eureka KS 67045

JACKSON, ROY, TWO-PHASE FLOW. *Current Pos:* PROF CHEM ENG, PRINCETON UNIV, 82- *Personal Data:* b Manchester, Eng, Oct 6, 31; m 57, Susan Birch; c Fiona & Andrew. *Educ:* Cambridge Univ, BA, 54, MA, 58; Univ Edinburgh, DSc(chem eng), 68. *Honors & Awards:* Alpha Chi Sigma Award, Am Inst Chem Engr, 80, Thomas Baron Award, 93. *Prof Exp:* Tech officer, Imp Chem Industs Ltd, 55-61; lectr chem eng, Univ Edinburgh, 61-64, reader, 64-68; prof, Rice Univ, 68-77; prof, Univ Houston, 77-82. *Concurrent Pos:* Consult, Shell Oil Co, 69-; assoc ed, J Fluid Mech. *Mem:* Am Inst Chem Engrs. *Res:* Chemical reaction engineering; fluid-particle systems; granular materials. *Mailing Add:* Dept Chem Eng Princeton Univ Princeton NJ 08544. *Fax:* 609-258-0211; *E-Mail:* rjackson@princeton.edu

JACKSON, ROY JOSEPH, PHOTOCHEMISTRY. *Current Pos:* RES CHEMIST, SHELL DEVELOP CO, 75- *Personal Data:* b Cotton Port, La, Feb 8, 44. *Educ:* Southern Univ, Baton Rouge, BS, 65, MS, 69; Univ Calif, San Diego, PhD(chem), 75. *Prof Exp:* Instr chem, Southern Univ, Baton Rouge, 69-70. *Mem:* Am Chem Soc. *Res:* Norish type II photoelimination, photocylization reactions, especially new aryl-alkyl systems; photocure of resins; development of new photocure systems. *Mailing Add:* 12707 Havant Circle Houston TX 77077

JACKSON, SHARON WESLEY, GENETICS, ENVIRONMENTAL SCIENCES. *Current Pos:* co-dir, 76-89, PRES, LAND INST, 89- *Personal Data:* b Topeka, Kans, June 15, 36; m 57; c 3. *Educ:* Kans Wesleyan Univ, BA, 58; Univ Kans, MA, 60; NC State Univ, PhD(genetics), 67. *Prof Exp:* Teacher high sch, Kans, 60-62; instr biol, Kans Wesleyan Univ, 62-64, from asst prof to assoc prof, 67-71; prof environ studies & chmn dept, Sacramento State Col, 71, dir, Environ Studies Ctr, 74-76. *Mem:* AAAS; Int Asn Plant Taxon; Sigma Xi. *Res:* Development of perennial grain crops. *Mailing Add:* Theland Inst 2440 E Waterwell Rd Salina KS 67401

JACKSON, SHIRLEY ANN, THEORETICAL SOLID STATE PHYSICS. *Current Pos:* CHMN, NUCLEAR REGULATORY COMN, 95- *Personal Data:* b Washington, DC, Aug 5, 46; m, Morris A Washington; c Alan. *Educ:* Mass Inst Technol, SB, 68, PhD(physics), 73. *Hon Degrees:* Several honorary degrees. *Prof Exp:* Res assoc theoret physics, Fermi Nat Accelerator Lab, 73-74; vis sci assoc, Europ Orgn Nuclear Res, 74-75; res assoc theoret physics, Fermi Nat Accelerator Lab, 75-76; mem tech staff, Bell Tel Labs, 76-91; prof physics, Rutgers Univ, 91-95. *Concurrent Pos:* Adv study fel, Ford Found, 71-73; fel, Martin Marietta Corp, 72-73; grant, Ford Found, 74-75; mem bd trustees, MIT Corp, 75-85 & Lincoln Univ, 80-; mem, Comt Educ & Employ Women Sci & Eng, Nat Acad Sci, 81-82. *Mem:* Fel Am Phys Soc; AAAS; NY Acad Sci; Sigma Xi; Nat Inst Sci; fel Am Acad Arts & Sci. *Res:* Landau theories of charge density waves in one and two dimensions; transport properties of random systems; correlation effects in electron-hole plasmas; channeling in metals and semiconductors. theory; two dimensional yang-mills gauge theories; neutrino reactions. *Mailing Add:* Off Pub Affairs US Nuclear Regulatory Comn Washington DC 20555

JACKSON, STEPHEN THOMAS, PLANT ECOLOGY, PALEOECOLOGY. *Current Pos:* ASST PROF BIOL, NORTHERN ARIZ UNIV, 90- *Personal Data:* b E St Louis, Ill, May 28, 55; m 87, Anne M Bowen. *Educ:* Southern Ill Univ, Carbondale, BA, 77, MS, 78; Ind Univ, Bloomington, PhD(ecol & evolutionary biol), 83. *Prof Exp:* Vis asst prof biol, Ind Univ, 83-84 & Idaho State Univ, 84-85; NSF fel environ biol, Brown Univ, 86-88, res assoc geol sci, 88-90. *Concurrent Pos:* Chair, Paleoecol Sect, Ecol Soc Am, 92-93. *Mem:* Ecol Soc Am; Am Quaternary Asn; AAAS; Soc Wetland Scientists; Sigma Xi. *Res:* Vegetation-sensing properties of paleoecological data (pollen and plant macrofossils), and applying paleoecological data toward understanding ecological and climatic dynamics. *Mailing Add:* Dept Biol Sci Northern Ariz Univ Box 5640 Flagstaff AZ 86011-0001. *Fax:* 520-523-7500; *E-Mail:* jackson@nauvax.ucc.nau.edu

JACKSON, THOMAS A J, ENVIRONMENTAL SAMPLE CONTROL. *Current Pos:* SR RES SCIENTIST, NJ DEPT ENVIRON PROTECTION, 84- *Personal Data:* b Sumter, SC, Dec 26, 42. *Educ:* Seton Hall Univ, BS, 72; Fairleigh Dickinson Univ, MS, 77. *Prof Exp:* Chemist, Sherwin-Williams Co, 73-75 & Ethican Inc, 75-79; mgr, anal chem, Boyle-Midway, Inc, 79-84. *Mem:* Fel Am Inst Chemists; Am Chem Soc. *Res:* Gel chromatography and high performance liquid chromatography methods development for environmental samples; environmental sample clean up and computer applications in gel chromatography and high performance liquid chromatography. *Mailing Add:* 11 Anita Dr Piscataway NJ 08854-2430

JACKSON, THOMAS EDWIN, MEDICINAL CHEMISTRY, PATENT LAW. *Current Pos:* res chemist med chem, Biomed Res, ICI-Americas, Inc, 75-85, PATENT LIAISON, AGENT & ATTY, ICI AMERICAS/ ZENNECA INC, 85- *Personal Data:* b Amarillo, Tex, May 7, 44; m 69. *Educ:* Rice Univ, BA, 66; Mass Inst Technol, PhD(org chem), 71; Widener Law Sch, JD, 90. *Prof Exp:* Fel org chem, Univ SC, 71-73; sr scientist med chem, Sandoz Inc, 73-75. *Mem:* Am Chem Soc; Sigma Xi. *Res:* Biochemical consideration in drug design; selectivity in organic synthesis; heterocyclic chemistry. *Mailing Add:* Eli Lilly & Co Lilly Corp Ctr Indianapolis IN 46285

JACKSON, THOMAS GERALD, ORGANIC CHEMISTRY. *Current Pos:* PROF CHEM, UNIV S ALA, 65- *Personal Data:* b Mt Sterling, Ala, Dec 26, 36; m 67. *Educ:* Univ Southern Miss, BS, 59, MS, 61; Univ Tenn, Knoxville, PhD(org chem), 65. *Prof Exp:* Asst org chem, Univ Southern Miss, 59-61. *Concurrent Pos:* Consult, Res Prod, Inc, Ala, 71- *Mem:* Am Chem Soc; Sigma Xi; Royal Soc Chem; Nat Asn Prev Health Prog Advisors. *Res:* Synthesis of organic compounds of potential medicinal interest; metalation studies of nitrogen containing heterocycles; investigations of compounds containing the nitrogen-silicon bond. *Mailing Add:* Dept Chem Rm 223 Univ S Ala Mobile AL 36688

JACKSON, TOGWELL ALEXANDER, BIOGEOCHEMISTRY OF AQUATIC ENVIRONMENTS, LIMNOLOGY. *Current Pos:* res scientist biogeochem, Freshwater Inst, Winnipeg, 72-86, Nat Hydrol Res Inst, 86-90 & NAT WATER RES INST, 90- *Personal Data:* b New York, NY, Nov 1, 39; Can & US citizen; m 67, Chung Ja Choi; c Bertrand & Alexander. *Educ:* Columbia Univ, BA, 61; Univ Wis, MSc, 63; Univ Mo, Columbia, PhD(geol), 69. *Prof Exp:* A P Green fel clay mineral, Univ Mo, 66-68; fel org geochem, Woods Hole Oceanog Inst, Dept Chem, NSF, 68-69; res assoc soil microbiol, Yale Univ Sch Forestry, 69-70; res assoc org geochem, Univ Calif, Santa Barbara, Dept Geol Sci, 70-72. *Concurrent Pos:* Adj prof soil sci, Univ Man, 77-80, conducted grad-level reading course, 81-82; external examiner, PhD student, Univ Sask, 84. *Mem:* Sigma Xi; Rawson Acad Aquatic Sci. *Res:* Humic matter in recent lakes and streams, and its ecological role; paleobiological significance of organic matter in ancient, especially pre-Cambrian, sediments; biogeochemistry of various toxic heavy metals, especially mercury, including methyl mercury in freshwater environments; forms speciation and bio-availability of metals; biochemical weathering of rocks; clay-organic interactions; freshwater environments polluted with various heavy metas from mines and smelters or with mercury; microbial ecology and biogeochemistry in sediments; biogeochemistry and related aspects of ecology; microbiol transformations of metals; microbiol ecology (effects of metal species, clay humic matter). *Mailing Add:* Nat Water Res Inst PO Box 5050 Burlington ON L7R 4A6 Can. *Fax:* 905-336-6430; *E-Mail:* t.a.jackson@cciw.ca

JACKSON, WARREN, JR, ELECTRICAL ENGINEERING. *Current Pos:* RETIRED. *Personal Data:* b Oak Park, Ill, May 8, 22; m 47, Sarah F Goodwin; c John B & Peter G. *Educ:* Purdue Univ, BS, 47; Case Inst Technol, MS, 54. *Prof Exp:* Radio engr, Police Dept, River Forest, Ill, 41-42 & Purdue Univ, 46-47; elec engr, Chem & Physics Res Div, Standard Oil Co, Ohio, 47-54, sr tech specialist, Process Eng Div, 54-61, sr proj leader, Mgt Sci Unit, 61-70, instrumentation supvr, res & develop, 70-74, sr process control specialist, res & develop lab, 74-82, sr res specialist, Alaska Iceberg Studies, res lab, 82-85. *Mem:* Inst Elec & Electronics Engrs; hon mem Soc Comput Simulation. *Res:* On line digital computer process control; electronic instrumentation for petroleum research; electronic computers; analog computer simulation of physical and business systems; iceberg drift in Alaskan waters. *Mailing Add:* 4871 Westbourne Rd Cleveland OH 44124-2361

JACKSON, WILLIAM ADDISON, PLANT NUTRITION, SOIL FERTILITY. *Current Pos:* from asst prof to prof, 58-72, William Neal Reynolds prof soil sci, 72-93, alumni distinguished grad prof, 84-93, EMER PROF SOIL SCI, NC STATE UNIV, 93- *Personal Data:* b Castile, NY, Apr 24, 26; m 64. *Educ:* Cornell Univ, BS, 50; Purdue Univ, MS, 52; NC State Univ, PhD(soil sci), 57. *Honors & Awards:* Co-recipient, Campbell Award, Am Inst Biol Sci, 64. *Prof Exp:* Res instr soil sci, NC State Univ, 52-57; Ford Found fel plant nutrit, Univ Mich, 57-58. *Concurrent Pos:* Mem comt post-doctoral fel eval, Div Biol & Agr, Nat Acad Sci-Nat Res Coun, 65-68; vis prof, Univ Ill, Urbana, 70-71. *Mem:* Soil Sci Soc Am; Crop Sci Soc Am; Am Soc Agron; Am Soc Plant Pathologists; Japan Soc Soil Sci & Plant Nutrit; fel Australian Inst Biol Sci; fel Royal Irish Acad. *Res:* Absorption, assimilation and distribution of nitrogen by higher plants; effects of nitrogen assimilation on photosynthesis, respiration and mineral accumulation. *Mailing Add:* 3611 Swann Dr Raleigh NC 27612

JACKSON, WILLIAM BRUCE, ANIMAL ECOLOGY. *Current Pos:* asst prof, Bowling Green State Univ, 57-64, asst dean, Col Lib Arts, 64-69, asst dean grad sch, 69-70, dir, Environ Studies Ctr, 70-80, prof biol, 64-81, distinguished univ prof, 81-84, dir, Ctr Environ Res & Serv, 80-84, EMER

PROF, BOWLING GREEN STATE UNIV, 85- *Personal Data:* b Milwaukee, Wis, Sept 10, 26; m 52, Shirley Slentz; c Beth, Mark & Craig. *Educ:* Univ Wis, BA, 48, MA, 49; Johns Hopkins Univ, ScD(hyg & vert ecol), 52. *Honors & Awards:* Envioron Qual Award, US Environ Protection Agency, Region V, 75. *Prof Exp:* Asst zool, Univ Wis, 47-49; asst vert ecol, Johns Hopkins Univ, 49-52; res assoc animal behav, Am Mus Natural Hist, 52; sr asst scientist ecol, USPHS, 52-55; biologist, Pac Sci Bd, 55-57. *Concurrent Pos:* Collabr, US Fish & Wildlife Serv & Nat Pest Control Asn, 64-; consult, WHO & Food & Agr Orgn, UN, 69- & Ford Found, 75; consult ed, J Environ Educ, 73-77; chmn, Exec Comt, Ohio Biol Surv, 70-84; adj prof community med, Med Col Ohio, Toledo, 74-80; chmn, subcomt E 35.17 vert pesticides, Am Soc Testing & Mgt; pres, Bio Cenotics Inc, 85-; consult, 85- *Mem:* Fel AAAS; Animal Behav Soc; Am Inst Biol Sci; Am Ornithologists' Union; Ecol Soc Am; Sigma Xi; Am Soc Mammal. *Res:* Effects of insecticides on vertebrate populations; microclimatic factors in army ant behavior; ecology of small mammals and of arthropod disease vectors; economic and environmental biology; rodent and bird control methods; studies of anticoagulant resistance; environmental assessment. *Mailing Add:* Dept Biol Sci Bowling Green State Univ Bowling Green OH 43403-0001. Fax: 419-372-2024

JACKSON, WILLIAM DAVID, ELECTRICAL POWER SYSTEMS, MAGNETOHYDRODYNAMICS. *Current Pos:* PRES, HMJ CORP, 82- *Personal Data:* b Edinburgh, Scotland, May 20, 27; div; c 2. *Educ:* Glasgow Univ, BSc, 47, PhD(elec eng), 60. *Honors & Awards:* Energy Res & Develop Admin Spec Achievement Award, 76; SERI Award, 78. *Prof Exp:* Asst, Royal Col Sci & Technol, Glasgow Univ, 47-51; asst lectr elec eng, Col Sci & Technol, Univ Manchester Inst Sci & Technol, 51-54, lectr, 54-58; from asst prof to assoc prof, Mass Inst Technol, 58-66; prof, Univ Ill, Chicago Circle, 66-67; prin res scientist, Avco-Everett Res Lab, 67-72; prof elec eng, Univ Tenn Space Inst, 72-73; mgr thermal-mech energy conversion & storage, Elec Power Res Inst, Palo Alto, 73-74; mgr, MHD Prog, Off Coal Res & Energy Res & Develop Admin, Washington, DC, 74-75, dir, MHD Div, 75-77; dir, Div Tech Anal & Spec Projs, Dept Energy, Washington, DC, 77-79; pres, Energy Consult Inc, 79-84. *Concurrent Pos:* Vis lectr, Mass Inst Technol, 55-57, lectr, 68-72; Fulbright travel scholar, UK, 55-57; consult var industs & labs, 60-; vis prof, Tech Univ Berlin, 66, George Washington Univ, 86-87; mem int liaison group on magnetohydrodyn, 66-, chmn, 68-73, secy, 84-; mem, US Steering Comt Eng Aspects Magnetohydrodyn, 67-, prog chmn, 68-69, chmn, 69-70, secy, 71-; mem, US-Ger Natural Resources Panel Magnetohydrodyn Power, 70-72; mem, Task Force Tech Aspects, Comt Conserv Energy, Nat Power Surv, Fed Power Comn, 73; chmn, Steering Comt, US-USSR Coop Prog on Magnetohydrodyn Power Generation, 73-79; prof lectr, George Washington Univ, 79-86, 87-92, adj prof, 92-; mem, Energy Resources Operating Bd, Am Soc Mech Engrs, 81-83; mem, Energy Develop Sub Comt, Inst Elec & Electronic Engrs, pres, 72-, chmn, 88-, Power Generation Comt, pres, 86-; prog chair, Intersoc Energy Conversion Eng Conf, 89- *Mem:* Fel Inst Elec & Electronics Engrs; Am Phys Soc; assoc fel Am Inst Aeronaut & Astronaut; fel Brit Inst Elec Engrs; fel Am Soc Mech Engrs. *Res:* Electrical power systems; magnetohydrodynamic power generation; analysis of energy systems, especially electrical aspects; development of technology base and engineering design data for first of a kind technologies; engineering of magnetohydrodynamic power systems; power electronics. *Mailing Add:* 10400 Connecticut Ave Kensington MD 20895

JACKSON, WILLIAM F, VASCULAR SMOOTH MUSCLE, LOCAL CONTROL OF BLOOD FLOW. *Current Pos:* assoc prof, 89-94, PROF, WESTERN MICH UNIV, 94- *Personal Data:* b Detroit, Mich, Nov 18, 52; m 76; c 3. *Educ:* Mich State Univ, PhD(physiol), 79. *Prof Exp:* From asst prof to assoc prof physiol, Med Col Ga, 83-89. *Mem:* Am Physiol Soc; Microcirculatory Soc Inc; Am Soc Zoologists; AAAS; Am Heart Asn. *Res:* Regulation of blood flow in the microcirculation; cardiovascular physiology. *Mailing Add:* Dept Biol Sci Western Mich Univ 5380 McCracken Hall Kalamazoo MI 49008-3899

JACKSON, WILLIAM G(ORDON), CHEMISTRY. *Current Pos:* RETIRED. *Personal Data:* b Iron Mountain, Mich, Apr 22, 19; m 43, Kathleen L Swingley; c Lee W & Elizabeth A (Gray). *Educ:* Univ Mich, BS, 42; Univ Ill, MS, 43, PhD(org chem), 45. *Prof Exp:* Asst chem, Univ Ill, 42-43, spec asst, Nat Defense Res Comt Proj, 43-45; res chemist, Upjohn Co, 46-59; pres, Burdick & Jackson Labs, 59-77, consult, 78-84. *Mem:* Am Chem Soc; Sigma Xi. *Res:* Antibiotics, vitamin B12; natural product fractionation and structure; chromatography; countercurrent distribution; organic synthesis; laboratory automation apparatus; high-purity solvents. *Mailing Add:* 3840 Mariner's Way No 515 Cortez FL 34215

JACKSON, WILLIAM JAMES, NEUROPSYCHOLOGY. *Current Pos:* asst prof, 71-77, ASSOC PROF PHYSIOL, MED COL GA, 77- *Personal Data:* b Houston, Tex, Aug 1, 40. *Educ:* Univ Tex, El Paso, BA, 62; Tex Tech Col, PhD(psychol), 66. *Prof Exp:* Nat Acad Sci-Nat Res Coun fel psychol, Aeromed Res Lab, Holloman AFB, NMex, 66-68; res asst prof, Univ Houston, 68-69 & Univ S Fla, 69-71. *Mem:* Soc Neurosci. *Res:* Neural substrate of learning and motivation; neuropsycho-pharmacology. *Mailing Add:* Dept Physiol & Endocrinol Med Col Ga 1120 15th St Augusta GA 30901-3181

JACKSON, WILLIAM MORGAN, PHOTOCHEMISTRY, CHEMICAL PHYSICS. *Current Pos:* assoc dean, Col Lett & Sci, 90-93, PROF CHEM, UNIV CALIF, DAVIS, 85- *Personal Data:* b Birmingham, Ala, Sept 24, 36; m 59; c Eric & Cheryl. *Educ:* Morehouse Col, BS, 56; Cath Univ Am, PhD(phys chem), 61. *Honors & Awards:* Guggenheim Fel, 89; Miller Fel, 88. *Prof Exp:* Chemist res, Nat Bur Stand, 60-61; res scientist, Martin-Marietta Corp, 61-63; assoc, Nat Bur Stand, 63-64; asst, Goddard Space Flight Ctr, NASA, 64-67, sr chemist, 67-69; vis assoc prof physics, Univ Pittsburgh, 69-70; sr chemist, Goddard Space Flight Ctr, NASA, 70-74; prof, Howard Univ, 74-85. *Concurrent Pos:* Mem, US comt, Int Comn Optics, 75-77, Int Astron Union Comn on Comets. *Mem:* AAAS; Am Chem Soc; Am Phys Soc; Int Astron Union; Optical Soc Am; Sigma Xi. *Res:* Chemical kinetics; photochemistry; molecular beams; astrochemistry; mass spectroscopy; application of tunable lasers to problems in photochemistry and chemical kinetics; photochemistry of comets. *Mailing Add:* Dept Chem Rm 214 Univ Calif Davis CA 95616-5224. *Fax:* 530-752-8995; *E-Mail:* wmjackson@ucdavis.edu

JACKSON, WILLIAM MORRISON, INORGANIC CHEMISTRY, PHYSICAL CHEMISTRY. *Current Pos:* RETIRED. *Personal Data:* b Colbert Co, Ala, Aug 2, 26; m 54; c 2. *Educ:* Univ Ala, BS, 50; Univ Tenn, MS, 52 & 60, PhD(chem), 53; Am Bd Health Physics, cert, 80. *Prof Exp:* Chemist, Goodyear Atomic Corp, 53-55 & Union Carbide Corp, Oak Ridge Nat Lab, 55-61; group leader, Diamond Alkali Co, Ohio, 61-66; sr scientist, Oak Ridge Assoc Univs, Tenn, 66-68; tech mgr, Am Nuclear Corp, 68-70; syst chemist, ALA Power Co, 70-74, environ & health physics coordr, 74-83; sr proj mgr, Inst Nuclear Powers Opers, 83-89. *Concurrent Pos:* Tech Consult, Tiztek Corp, 91- *Mem:* Am Chem Soc; Health Physics Soc. *Res:* Radiochemistry; health physics. *Mailing Add:* 459 Bonner Rd Carrollton GA 30117

JACKSON, WILLIAM ROY, JR, NUCLEAR PHYSICS. *Current Pos:* Asst prof, 67-71, ASSOC PROF PHYSICS, SOUTHWEST TEX STATE UNIV, 71- *Personal Data:* b Port Lavaca, Tex, Nov 26, 36. *Educ:* Columbia Univ, BA, 59; Rice Univ, MA, 65, PhD(physics), 67. *Mem:* Am Phys Soc. *Res:* Low energy experimental nuclear physics; reaction mechanisms. *Mailing Add:* Dept Physics & Astron Southwest Tex State Univ San Marcos TX 78666-4602

JACKSON, WILLIAM THOMAS, PLANT PHYSIOLOGY. *Current Pos:* CONSULT, 90- *Personal Data:* b Stockdale, Ohio, May 10, 23; m 49; c 3. *Educ:* Ohio State Univ, BS, 47; Duke Univ, PhD(bot), 53. *Prof Exp:* Instr biol, WVa Univ, 49-50; asst bot & plant physiol, Duke Univ, 50-53; from instr to asst prof bot, Yale Univ, 53-59; from asst prof to prof biol, Dartmouth, 59-90. *Concurrent Pos:* Mem fel panel, NIH, 63-66. *Mem:* Am Soc Plant Physiol; Bot Soc Am. *Res:* Mitosis and other events of cell cycle. *Mailing Add:* 1370 Mendovia Ave Coral Gables FL 33146

JACKSON, WINSTON JEROME, JR, POLYMER CHEMISTRY. *Current Pos:* RETIRED. *Personal Data:* b Asheville, NC, Feb 4, 26; m 52, Louisa Black; c Ann & Blane. *Educ:* Va Polytech Inst, BS, 49; Duke Univ, PhD(org chem), 52. *Prof Exp:* From res chemist to sr res chemist, Eastman Kodak Co, 52-57, res assoc, 58-72, sr res assoc, 73-80, res fel, Eastman Chemicals Div, 80-91. *Mem:* Am Chem Soc. *Res:* Organic synthesis; preparation, characterization and evaluation of new polymers and discovery of polymer-forming reactions; liquid crystalline polymers. *Mailing Add:* 4408 Greenspring Circle Kingsport TN 37664

JACO, CHARLES M, JR, INDUSTRIAL & MANUFACTURING ENGINEERING, PRODUCT RESEARCH & DEVELOPMENT. *Current Pos:* PARTNER, JCI CONSULTS, 76-, MANAGING PARTNER, 85- *Personal Data:* b Montgomery Co, Miss, Jan 28, 24; m 46, Jennie E Cox; c Charles E. *Educ:* US Mil Acad, BS, 46; Univ Del, MChE, 57. *Prof Exp:* Proj & contract officer, Redstone Arsenal, 50-54; mem staff, Ord Off JTF Seven, Marshall Islands, 54-56; mil attache, US Embassy, Switz, 62-65; mgr corp develop, Res & Develop Div, Dravo Corp, 66-71; plant mgr, Midland Ross Corp, 71-72; pres, chief exec officer & gen mgr, Georgetown Ferreduction, 72-74; pres & chief oper officer, Midrex Corp, 74-76. *Concurrent Pos:* Adj prof, Ballistic Res Lab Br, Univ Md, 60; mil attache & tech adv to ambassador, US Embassy, Switz, 63-65; cert mgt consult. *Mem:* Am Mgt Asn; Inst Mgt Consults; Am Inst Chem Eng; Asn Iron & Steel Engrs; Defense Preparedness Asn. *Res:* Management of corporate organizations, including role of research, development and engineering; role of research, development and engineering to corporate growth and development; systems and multi-discipline engineering; co-author of two textbooks; process engineering; general management consultant to over 600 companies including research, development and organizations. *Mailing Add:* 122 Pine Grove Circle Clover SC 29710. *Fax:* 803-831-2979

JACO, WILLIAM HOWARD, TOPOLOGY. *Current Pos:* prof, 82-93, head dept, 82-87, GRACE B KERR PROF MATH, OKLA STATE UNIV, 93- *Personal Data:* b Grafton, WVa, July 14, 40; m 78, Linda Kanewske; c William, Brent, John & Andrew. *Educ:* Fairmont State Univ, BA, 62; Pa State Univ, MA, 64; Univ Wis, PhD(math), 68. *Prof Exp:* Proj mathematician underwater activities, Ord Res Lab, 61-64; instr math, Univ Mich, 68-70; from asst prof to prof math, Rice Univ, 70-82. *Concurrent Pos:* NSF fel math, Inst Advan Study, 71-72, 78-79, Math Sci Res Inst, 84-85; exec dir, Am Math Soc, 88-95. *Mem:* Am Math Soc; hon mem Math Asn Am; Nat Coun Teachers Math; AAAS. *Res:* Geometric topology with particular interest in classical three-manifold topology; classification problems for three-manifolds and geometric structures, algorithms and decision problems. *Mailing Add:* Dept Math Okla State Univ Stillwater OK 74078. *Fax:* 405-744-8275; *E-Mail:* jaco@math.okstate.edu

JACOB, CHAIM O, IMMUNOGENETICS. *Current Pos:* SR STAFF SCIENTIST, IMMUNOGENETICS, SYNTEX RES, 90- *Personal Data:* b Carei, Romania, Sept 24, 51; Israeli citizen. *Educ:* Univ Tel-Aviv, Israel, MD, 76; Weizmann Inst Sci, Rehovot, Israel, PhD(immunol), 85. *Honors &*

Awards: J F Kennedy Mem Prize, Pvt Int Orgn, 85; Res Presidential Award, Reticulo Endothelial Soc, 87. *Prof Exp:* Res fel immunogenetics, Stanford Univ Sch Med, 85-90. *Mem:* Am Asn Immunologists. *Res:* Immunogenetics basis of autoimmune diseases; genetic basis of lymphokine production and the interactions between cytokines and major histocompatibility complex genes; author of 45 publications. *Mailing Add:* Univ S Calif Sch Med 2011 Zone/Ave HHR #711 Los Angeles CA 90033

JACOB, DANIEL JAMES, ATMOSPHERIC CHEMISTRY, ENVIRONMENTAL ENGINEERING. *Current Pos:* Res fel, Harvard Univ, 85-87, asst prof, 87-91, assoc prof, 91-94, GORDON MCKAY PROF, ATMOSPHERIC/ENVIRON ENG, HARVARD UNIV, 94- *Personal Data:* b East Patchogue, NY, June 14, 58; m 90, Janice F Foley; c Eric Oscar & Richard Alex. *Educ:* Advan Sch Physics & Indust Chem, Paris, chem eng, 80; Calif Inst Technol, MS, 82, PhD, 85. *Honors & Awards:* Presidential Young Investr Award, NSF, 87; James B Macelwane Young Investr Medal, Am Geophys Union, 94. *Concurrent Pos:* Sci & eng fel, Packard Found, 89; assoc ed, Atmospheric Environ, 92- *Mem:* Fel Am Geophys Union. *Mailing Add:* Harvard Univ Pierce Hall 29 Oxford St Cambridge MA 02138

JACOB, FIELDEN EMMITT, ANALYTICAL CHEMISTRY, PHYSICAL CHEMISTRY. *Current Pos:* assoc prof, 47-75, prof, 75-80, EMER PROF CHEM, DRAKE UNIV, 80- *Personal Data:* b Columbia, Mo, July 20, 10; m 37; c 3. *Educ:* Univ Mo, AB, 32, BS & MA, 35, PhD(chem), 39. *Prof Exp:* Instr chem, Univ Mo, 39-42; asst prof, Mont Sch Mines, 42-45; assoc prof, Kans State Teachers Col, Emporia, 45-47. *Mem:* Am Asn Univ Profs; Am Chem Soc. *Res:* Colorimetric analysis; carotinoid pigments of egg yolks from hens on various diets; spectrophotometry; stability constants. *Mailing Add:* 1520 48th St Des Moines IA 50311

JACOB, FRANCOIS, CELLULAR GENETICS. *Current Pos:* Asst, 50-56, head, Dept Cellular Genetics, 60-92, pres, 82-88, EMER PROF, PASTEUR INST, 92-, EMER PROF CELLULAR GENETICS, COL FRANCE, 92- *Personal Data:* b Nancy, France, June 17, 20; wid; c Pierre, Laurent, Odile & Henri. *Educ:* Fac Med, Paris, MD, 47; Fac Sci, Paris, DSc, 54. *Hon Degrees:* DSc, Univ Chicago, 65. *Honors & Awards:* Nobel Prize in Physiol & Med, 65; Charles Leopold Mayer Prize, 62. *Concurrent Pos:* prof cellular genetics, Col France, 64-92. *Mem:* Nat Acad Sci; foreign mem Royal Danish Acad Sci & Lett; Am Acad Arts & Sci; Am Philos Soc; Royal Acad Med Belg; Acad Sci Hungary. *Res:* Genetics of bacterial cells and viruses; mechanisms of information transfer (messenger RNA) and genetic basis of regulatory circuits; early stages of the mouse embryo. *Mailing Add:* Pasteur Inst 25 Rue du Dr Roux Paris Cedex 15 75724 France

JACOB, GARY STEVEN, SOLID STATE NUCLEAR MAGNETIC RESONANCE, GLYCOBIOLOGY. *Current Pos:* MONSANTO FEL & HEAD GLYCOSCI, MONSANTO CO, 90- *Personal Data:* b St Louis, Mo, Mar 18, 47; m 75; c 2. *Educ:* Univ Mo-St Louis, BS, 69; Univ Wis-Madison, PhD(biochem), 76. *Prof Exp:* Fel biophysics, Thomas J Watson Res Ctr, IBM Corp, 76-79; res specialist, Monsanto Co, St Louis, 79-86; res mgr, Oxford Proj, GD Searle, 86-90. *Mem:* AAAS; Am Chem Soc; Sigma Xi; Am Soc Biochem & Molecular Biol. *Res:* Solid-state N-15 and C-13 nuclear magnetic resonance studies of bacterial metabolism, with emphasis on bacteria capable of degrading herbicides; cell-wall crosslinking in bacteria and nitrogen fixation; glycobiology; antivirals. *Mailing Add:* Dept Glycobiol GD Searle 800 N Lindbergh Blvd St Louis MO 63167-0001. *Fax:* 314-694-8949

JACOB, GEORGE KORATHU, PARALLEL CIRCUIT SIMULATION, PARALLEL COMPILERS. *Current Pos:* Software develop, Columbus, Ohio, Berkeley, Calif, 87-89, software develop, 89-92, SOFTWARE ENG MGR, FRANZ, INC, COLUMBUS, OHIO, 92- *Personal Data:* b Calcutta, India, Aug 19, 59; m 89; c 1. *Educ:* Indian Inst Technol, Kharagpur, BTech, 81; Pa State Univ, MS, 83; Univ Calif, Berkeley, PhD(elec eng & computer sci), 87. *Res:* Parallel processing applications, especially circuit simulation; compilers and programming environments for parallel processes. *Mailing Add:* Franz Inc 1995 University Ave Berkeley CA 94704

JACOB, HARRY S, INTERNAL MEDICINE, HEMATOLOGY. *Current Pos:* assoc prof, 68-70, PROF MED & CHIEF SECT HEMAT, MED SCH, UNIV MINN, MINNEAPOLIS, 70- *Personal Data:* b San Francisco, Calif, Apr 6, 33; m 54; c 3. *Educ:* Reed Col, BA, 54; Harvard Univ, MD, 58. *Honors & Awards:* Conrad Elvehjem Mem Award, 71; Hickam lectr, 93. *Prof Exp:* Intern med, Boston City Hosp, 58-59, resident, 59-60; NIH fels hemat, Thorndike Mem Lab, Harvard Univ, 60-63, tutor med sci, Harvard Med Sch, 63-65; asst prof med, Sch Med, Tufts Univ, 65-68. *Concurrent Pos:* NIH res grants, 65-; prof, Royal Postgrad Med Sch London, 66; prof, Med Sch, Univ Chicago, 71; prof med, Univ Man, 71; vice chmn Dept Med, Med Sch, Univ Minn, Minneapolis, 70, ed- in-chief, Journal Lab & Clin Med, 91- *Mem:* Am Soc Clin Invest; Am Fedn Clin Res; Am Soc Hemat (pres elect, 97); Int Soc Hemat; Asn Am Physicians; fel AAAS. *Res:* Red cell metabolism; hemoglobin function-structure relationships; granulocyte function; reticuloendothelial physiology; endothelial physiology. *Mailing Add:* Dept Med Univ Minn Med Ctr Minneapolis MN 55455-0132

JACOB, HENRY GEORGE, JR, MATHEMATICS. *Current Pos:* prof, 62-87, EMER PROF MATH, UNIV MASS, AMHERST, 87- *Personal Data:* b New Haven, Conn, June 11, 22; m 44; c 3. *Educ:* Yale Univ, BE, 43, ME, 47, PhD(math), 53. *Prof Exp:* Asst instr calculus, Yale Univ, 50-53; from asst prof to assoc prof math, La State Univ, 53-62. *Concurrent Pos:* asst prof math, Johns Hopkins Univ, 56-57. *Mem:* Am Math Soc; Math Asn Am. *Mailing Add:* 51 Butterfield Terr Amherst MA 01002-1707

JACOB, HORACE S, poultry science, physiological genetics; deceased, see previous edition for last biography

JACOB, JONAH HYE, LASER PHYSICS, PLASMA PHYSICS. *Current Pos:* PRES, SCI RES LAB, 83- *Personal Data:* b Calcutta, India, May 15, 43; US citizen; m 77; c 2. *Educ:* London Univ, BSc, 64; Yale Univ, PhD(plasma physics), 70. *Prof Exp:* Res assoc plasma physics, Yale Univ, 70-71; prin res scientist laser & plasma physics, Avco-Everett Res Lab, 71-82. *Mem:* Am Phys Soc; AAAS. *Res:* High power lasers; discharge physics; atomic physics; environmental physics. *Mailing Add:* 15 Ward St Somerville MA 02143

JACOB, KLAUS H, SEISMOLOGY, TECTONICS. *Current Pos:* Res assoc, 68-83, SR SCIENTIST SEISMOL & TECTONICS, LAMONT-DOHERTY GEOL OBSERV, COLUMBIA UNIV, 83- *Personal Data:* Stuttgart, Ger, Aug 20, 36. *Educ:* Univ Frankfurt, PhD(gophys), 68. *Concurrent Pos:* Assoc ed, Geophys Res Lett, Am Geophys Union, 83- *Mem:* Am Geophys Union; Seismol Soc Am; Am Geol Inst; Ger Geophys Soc. *Res:* Geophysics of active plate margins (subduction and continental collision zones) based on earthquake information; seismic and volcanic hazards; microearthquake studies in Alaska, Himalaya and Central America; earthquake prediction; earthquake engineering. *Mailing Add:* PO Box 729 Valley Cottage NY 10989

JACOB, LEONARD STEVEN, CLINICAL INVESTIGATION. *Current Pos:* exec vpres, Pharmaceut Div, 89-91, exec vpres res & develop, 91-92, EXEC VPRES & CHIEF OPER OFFICER, MAGAININ PHARMACEUT, INC, 92- *Personal Data:* b Philadelphia, Pa, Mar 18, 49; m 69; c 2. *Educ:* Philadelphia Col Pharm & Sci, BS, 70; Temple Univ, PhD(pharmacol), 75; Med Col Pa, MD, 78. *Prof Exp:* Group dir clin invest, Smith-Kline Beckman, 83-84, vpres clin res & develop NAm, 84-86, vpres clin res & develop worldwide, Smith Kline & French, Labs, 86-88. *Concurrent Pos:* Fel, Dept Pharmacol, Hahnemann Med Col, 70-71 & Temple Univ Sch Med, 73-75; house staff anesthesiol, Hosp Univ Pa, 78- *Mem:* AMA; AAAS; Sigma Xi; fel Am Col Clin Pharmacol; Pharmaceut Mfrs Asn. *Res:* Linking molecular biology to clinical trial design; pharmaceutical agents. *Mailing Add:* 3901 City Ave Philadelphia PA 19131

JACOB, MARY, NUTRITIONAL STATUS ASSESSMENT OF ELDERLY, NUTRIENT REQUIREMENT OF ELDERLY. *Current Pos:* PROF HUMAN NUTRIT, CALIF STATE UNIV, LONG BEACH, 80- *Personal Data:* b Kerala, India, May 28, 33; US citizen. *Educ:* Univ Madras, India, BS, 53, MS, 58; Univ London, MS, 63; Univ Ill, Urbana, PhD(nutrit biochem), 69. *Prof Exp:* Asst res nutritionist, Univ Calif, Los Angeles, 69-76; lectr nutrit, Western Australia Inst Technol, Perth, 76-77; asst prof, Ariz State Univ, Tempe, 77-80. *Concurrent Pos:* Res asst, Univ Bombay, India, 58-61; vis asst prof, Ariz State Univ, Tempe, 77-78; vis res fel, Dept Pediat, Med Col Va, Richmond, 79-90. *Mem:* Am Soc Nutrit Sci; Sigma Xi; Geront Soc Am; Am Col Nutrit; Inst Food Technol; NY Acad Sci. *Res:* Calcium, zinc metabolism and interdependence of these on vitamin D status; changes in body composition with age with main focus on elderly; effect of calorie restriction on lean body mass. *Mailing Add:* Dept Family & Consumer Sci Calif State Univ 1250 Bellflower Blvd Long Beach CA 90840-0501. *Fax:* 562-985-4414

JACOB, PAUL B(ERNARD), JR, ELECTRICAL ENGINEERING. *Current Pos:* RETIRED. *Personal Data:* b Columbus, Miss, June 9, 22; m 46; c 2. *Educ:* Miss State Col, BS, 44; Northwestern Univ, MS, 48. *Prof Exp:* Jr engr, Tenn Eastman Corp, 44-46; from instr to prof elec eng prof, Miss State Univ, 46-88, assoc head dept, 61-88. *Mem:* Am Soc Eng Educ; Inst Elec & Electronics Engrs; Power Eng Soc. *Res:* High voltage engineering; electric power system analysis. *Mailing Add:* Dept Elec Eng Miss State Univ PO Drawer Ee Mississippi State MS 39762

JACOB, PEYTON, III, DRUG METABOLISM, ORGANIC SYNTHESIS. *Current Pos:* NIH fel, 75-78, ASST RES CHEMIST, DIV CLIN PHARMACOL, SCH MED, UNIV CALIF, SAN FRANCISCO & SAN FRANCISCO GEN HOSP MED CTR, 78- *Personal Data:* b Ann Arbor, Mich, Sept 23, 47. *Educ:* Univ Calif, BS, 69; Purdue Univ, PhD(chem), 75. *Mem:* Am Chem Soc; Sigma Xi. *Res:* Tobacco alkaloid metabolites; development of new analytical methodology for drugs and their metabolites in biologic fluids. *Mailing Add:* 3787 Highland Rd Lafayette CA 94549-3530

JACOB, RICHARD JOHN, THEORETICAL PHYSICS. *Current Pos:* From asst prof to assoc prof, 63-78, chmn dept, 85-90, PROF PHYSICS, ARIZ STATE UNIV, 78- *Personal Data:* b Salt Lake City, Utah, Oct 9, 37; m 59; c 4. *Educ:* Univ Utah, BS, 58, PhD(physics), 63. *Concurrent Pos:* Vis prof, Univ Karlsruhe, 70-71, Univ Kaiserlautern, 73, 78-79. *Mem:* Am Phys Soc; Am Asn Physics Teachers; Sigma Xi. *Res:* Theoretical elementary particle physics. *Mailing Add:* Dept Physics Ariz State Univ Box 871504 Tempe AZ 85287-1504

JACOB, RICHARD L, THEORETICAL PHYSICS, QUANTUM THEORY. *Current Pos:* assoc prof, 68-82, acad comp coordr, 72-90, PROF PHYSICS, CORNELL COL, 82- *Personal Data:* b Ripon, Wis, July 6, 32; m 67, Donna Miller; c Martha. *Educ:* Stanford Univ, BS, 55; Univ Wis, MS, 56, PhD(physics), 59. *Prof Exp:* Res assoc, Univ Wis, 59-60; asst prof physics, Tufts Univ, 60-65; assoc prof, Claremont Men's Col, 65-68. *Mem:* Am Phys Soc; Am Asn Physics Teachers. *Res:* Elementary particle physics; relativistic quantum mechanics; philosophy of physics. *Mailing Add:* Dept Physics Cornell Col Mt Vernon IA 52314. *Fax:* 319-895-4492; *E-Mail:* jacob@cornell_iowa.edu

JACOB, ROBERT ALLEN, ANALYTICAL CHEMISTRY, CLINICAL CHEMISTRY. *Current Pos:* Res chemist, Human Nutrit Lab, 75-79, sr chemist, Midwest Res Inst, Kemo, 79-81, RES CHEMIST, BOSTON, 81-, AT NUTRIT RES CTR, USDA, SAN FRANCISCO. *Personal Data:* b Chicago, Ill, Dec 16, 42; m 71. *Educ:* Ill Col, BA, 65; Southern Ill Univ, MA, 67, PhD, 70. *Mem:* Am Chem Soc; Am Asn Clin Chem; Sigma Xi. *Res:* Trace metal analysis and metabolism; analytical chemistry of nutrients; clinical lab methods for assessing nutritional status; clinical chemistry. *Mailing Add:* USDA Human Nutrit Res Ctr PO Box 29997 Presidio San Francisco CA 94129-0602. *Fax:* 415-556-1432

JACOB, ROBERT J(OSEPH) K(ASSEL), HUMAN-COMPUTER INTERACTION. *Current Pos:* ASST PROF, DEPT ELEC ENG & COMPUT SCI, TUFTS UNIV, 94- *Personal Data:* b Brooklyn, NY, Nov 11, 50; m 73, Kathryn Allamong; c Charlotte & Anne. *Educ:* Johns Hopkins Univ, BA, 72, MS, 74, PhD(elec eng), 76. *Prof Exp:* Res asst & instr, Johns Hopkins Univ, 72-76; comput scientist, Human Comput Interaction Lab, Naval Res Lab, Washington, DC, 77-94. *Concurrent Pos:* Prof lectr, George Washington Univ, 78-94; mem, Var Prog Comts, Asn Comput Mach, 87-, vchair, Spec Interest Group Human-Comput Interaction, 90-93; group leader, Input/Output Devices, George Washington Univ/NSF Workshop, 91. *Mem:* Sigma Xi; Asn Comput Mach; Inst Elec & Electronics Engrs; Human Factors Soc; Am Asn Artificial Intel; AAAS. *Res:* Human-computer interaction; eye movement-based interaction; formal specification of user-computer interfaces; visualization of multi-dimensional data; author of numerous publications on human-computer interaction; user interface software, non-wimp interfaces, virnac environments. *Mailing Add:* 30 Valleyfield St Lexington MA 02173. *E-Mail:* jacob@eecs.tufts.edu

JACOB, SAMSON T, RIBONUCLEIC ACID ENZYMOLOGY, GENE TRANSCRIPTION. *Current Pos:* PROF & CHMN, DEPT PHARMACOL & MOLECULAR BIOL, CHICAGO MED SCH, 89- *Educ:* Agra Univ, India, PhD(biochem), 64. *Prof Exp:* Prof pharmacol, Col Med, Pa State Univ, 72-89. *Res:* Gene expression. *Mailing Add:* Dept Pharmacol & Molecular Biol Chicago Med Sch 3333 Green Bay Rd North Chicago IL 60064-3095. *Fax:* 847-578-3255

JACOB, STANLEY W, MEDICINE, SURGERY. *Current Pos:* asst prof, 59-65, ASSOC PROF SURG, MED SCH, UNIV ORE, 65-, GERLINGER ASSOC PROF, 81- *Personal Data:* b Philadelphia, Pa, Jan 7, 24; m 64; c 2. *Educ:* Ohio State Univ, BA, 45, MD, 48. *Prof Exp:* Instr surg, Harvard Med Sch, 57-59. *Mem:* Am Col Surg; Soc Univ Surg; NY Acad Sci. *Res:* Preservation and transplantation of tissues; biologic applications of dimethyl sulfoxide. *Mailing Add:* Ore Health Sci Univ 3181 SW Sam Jackson Park Rd Portland OR 97201-3011

JACOB, THEODORE AUGUST, ORGANIC CHEMISTRY, BIOCHEMISTRY. *Current Pos:* sr chemist, 49-57, group leader natural prod develop, 57-69, mgr animal drug metab, 69-76, sect dir, 76-80, DIR ANIMAL DRUG METAB & RADIOCHEM, MERCK, SHARP & DOHME RES LABS, 80- *Personal Data:* b Braddock, Pa, Aug 22, 19; m 44; c 3. *Educ:* Col Wooster, BA, 41; Rensselaer Polytech Inst, MS, 43; Purdue Univ, PhD(org chem), 49. *Prof Exp:* Asst res chemist, Rensselaer Polytech Inst, 41-43; org chemist, Standard Oil Co, NJ, 43-46; asst, Purdue Univ, 46-48. *Mem:* Am Chem Soc. *Res:* Isolation, purification and identification of biologically active products from plant, animal and fermentation sources; preparation and isolation of synthetic peptides, steroids and nucleotides; isolation and identification of drug metabolites. *Mailing Add:* 828 St Marks Ave Westfield NJ 07090-2025

JACOB, WILLIS HARVEY, INSTRUCTIONAL TECHNOLOGY, ACADEMIC ADVISEMENT. *Current Pos:* ASSOC PROF BIOL/ANAT, SOUTHERN UNIV & A&M COL, 91- *Personal Data:* b Lake Charles, La, June 6, 43. *Educ:* Southern Univ, BS, 65; Univ Kans, PhD(biochem & physiol), 71. *Prof Exp:* Asst prof biol, Southern Univ & A&M Col, 70-71; chief, Basic Sci Br, Med & Surg Div, US Army Acad Health Sci, 71-77; physiologist clin invest, Madigan Army Med Ctr, 78-81, chief physiol serv, 81-83; prod mgr, Directorate Prod Mgt, US Army Med Res & Develop Command, 83-85; staff physiologist, Pharmaceut Syst, US Army Med Develop Activ, 85-88; chief, Anat & Physiol Br, Acad Health Sci, 88-91. *Concurrent Pos:* Asst prof health sci, Baylor Univ, 75-76, assoc prof, 76-77. *Mem:* Sigma Xi; Nat Inst Sci. *Res:* Development of multimedia-based instructional materials in anatomy, physiology and general biology. *Mailing Add:* PO Box 73001 Baton Rouge LA 70874. *E-Mail:* wjacob@subrum.subr.edu

JACOBER, WILLIAM JOHN, CHEMISTRY, PHYSICS. *Current Pos:* RETIRED. *Personal Data:* b Newark, NJ, Feb 13, 17; m 42, Catherine E Burrow; c Theresa, Mary, Margaret & William Jr. *Educ:* Union Col, NY, BS, 38; Brown Univ, PhD(chem), 42. *Prof Exp:* Res chemist, NY, E I DuPont de Nemours, 42-53, engr, 53-54, sr engr, 54-74, staff engr, 74-84; consult, 84-94. *Mem:* Am Chem Soc; Sigma Xi. *Res:* Cellophane softeners and coatings; Mylar and other packaging films; separation of hydrogen isotopes; tritium control technology. *Mailing Add:* 1022 Hitchcock Dr Aiken SC 29803

JACOBI, ANTHONY MARK, THERMAL FLUID SCIENCES, HEAT TRANSFER. *Current Pos:* ASST PROF MECH ENG, UNIV ILL, URBANA, CHAMPAIGN, 92- *Personal Data:* b Louisville, KY, Jan 12, 60; m 81, Cindy Bline; c Benjamin, Christopher & Mary. *Educ:* Purdue Univ, BS, 84, PhD(mech eng), 89; Univ Cent Fla, MS, 86. *Prof Exp:* Sr engr, Harris Corp, 84-86; res asst, Purdue Univ, 86-89; asst prof mech eng, Johns Hopkins Univ, 89-92. *Mem:* Am Soc Mech Engrs; Am Soc Heating Refrig & Air Conditioning Engrs; Am Soc Elec Eng. *Res:* Experimental heat and mass transfer with an emphasis on phase change; connection in complex flows and thermal system modeling; applications in heat exchangers, HVAC/R, petro-chemical processing, alternative refrigerants and computer modeling. *Mailing Add:* 1618 Golf Dr Mahomet IL 61853. *Fax:* 217-244-6534

JACOBI, GEORGE (THOMAS), ELECTRONICS ENGINEERING. *Current Pos:* CONSULT, 90- *Personal Data:* b Mannheim, Ger, May 19, 22; nat US; m 55; c 1. *Educ:* Ohio State Univ, BEE, 47, MSc, 48. *Honors & Awards:* Wiener Medal, Am Soc Cybernetics, 68. *Prof Exp:* Asst, Betatron Lab, Ohio State Univ, 48; engr, Res Lab, Gen Elec Co, NY, 48-50, mgr analog comput eng, Gen Eng Lab, 50-55, electronic recording mach acct systs lab, Comput Dept, Calif, 56-57, mgr spec comput eng, 57-59; dir comput & mgt sci res, ITT Res Inst, 59-77; dir bldg automotive syst, Johnson Controls, Inc, 77-84, vpres technol, 84-90. *Mem:* Sr mem Inst Elec & Electronics Engrs; Asn Comput Mach; NY Acad Sci; Sigma Xi. *Res:* Computer logic and storage devices; system theory; electronic component technology; engineering management. *Mailing Add:* 2375 N Wahl Ave Milwaukee WI 53211-4513

JACOBI, PETER ALAN, SYNTHETIC ORGANIC CHEMISTRY. *Current Pos:* ASST PROF CHEM, WESLEYAN UNIV, 75- *Personal Data:* b Abington, Pa, Sept 14, 45; m 75. *Educ:* Univ NH, BS, 67; Princeton Univ, MS, 70, PhD(chem), 73. *Concurrent Pos:* Corp appointee, Harvard Univ, 73-75; consult, Anderson Oil Co, 76- *Mem:* Am Chem Soc; Royal Soc Chem; Sigma Xi. *Res:* Mechanistic organic chemistry; chemistry of natural products. *Mailing Add:* Chem Dept Wesleyan Univ Middletown CT 06457

JACOBI, W(ILLIAM) M(ALLETT), TECHNICAL MANAGEMENT. *Current Pos:* CONSULT, 91- *Personal Data:* b Elizabeth, NJ, Apr 27, 30; m 62; c 4. *Educ:* Syracuse Univ, BChE, 51; Univ Del, MChE, 53, PhD(chem eng), 55. *Prof Exp:* Supvry engr nuclear design, Bettis Atomic Power Div, Westinghouse Elec Corp, 55-61; consult, Nuclear Utilities Serv, Inc, 61-63; mgr adv reactor design, Westinghouse Astronuclear Lab, 63-66, mgr design & anal, systs & tech eng, 66-68, mgr mark 48 design eng, Weapons Dept, 68-70, eng mgr, Fast Flux Test Facil, Westinghouse Advan Reactors Div, 70-73; proj mgr, Clinch River Breeder Reactor Plant, systs eng mgr, Westinghouse Pressurized Water Reactor Systs Div, 78-79, gen mgr, Westinghouse Nuclear Technol Div, 79-80, gen mgr, Westinghouse Nuclear Fuel Div, 81-84, vpres, Westinghouse Adv Power Systs, 84-86, pres, Westinghouse Hanford Co, 87-88, vpres, Westinghouse Govt Opers, 89-91. *Mem:* Am Nuclear Soc. *Res:* Reactor physics; fluid flow and mechanical design. *Mailing Add:* 119 Mt Vernon Dr Monroeville PA 15146. *Fax:* 412-856-4655; *E-Mail:* jacobib@wcsmail.com

JACOBOWITZ, DAVID, PHARMACOLOGY, BIOCHEMISTRY. *Current Pos:* HEAD, HISTOPHARMACOL SECT, LAB CLIN SCI, NIH, 71- *Personal Data:* b Brooklyn, NY, July 15, 31; m 57; c 2. *Educ:* City Col New York, BS, 53; Ohio State Univ, MS, 58, PhD(pharmacol), 62. *Prof Exp:* NIH fel pharmacol, Sch Med, Univ Pa, 62-63, instr, 63-65, assoc, 65-67, from asst prof to assoc prof, 67-71. *Concurrent Pos:* Pa Plan scholar, Sch Med, Univ Pa, 63-65; USPHS career develop award, 66; Lady Davis vis prof, Hebrew Univ Jerusalem, Israel, 81. *Mem:* Neurochem Soc; Am Soc Pharmacol & Exp Therapeut; Neurosci Soc; Am Col Neuropsychopharmacol & Psychoneuroendocrinol; Am Asn Anat. *Res:* Endocrine pharmacology; effect of stress on pituitary and hypothalamic metabolism and adrenocorticotropic hormone synthesis; cellular pharmacology; localization and mechanism of action of the autonomic neurotransmitters; histochemistry of catecholamines and acetylcholinesterase; immunohistochemistry of peptides; localization of neuromodulatory and neurotransmitter pathways in the brain; two-dimensional electrophoresis of brain proteins; insituhybridization histochemistry; calcium binding proteins, fetal brain development. *Mailing Add:* Lab Clin Sci NIMH Bldg 10 Rm 3D-48 Bethesda MD 20892. *Fax:* 301-402-2312; *E-Mail:* dwj@helix.nih.gov

JACOBOWITZ, ELLEN SUE, MUSEUM & TEMPLE ADMINISTRATION. *Current Pos:* ADMINR, TEMPLE EMANU-EL, 95- *Personal Data:* b Detroit, Mich, Feb 21, 48. *Educ:* Univ Mich, BA, 69, MA, 70. *Prof Exp:* Cur, Philadelphia Mus Art, 72-90; adminr, Cranbrook Inst Sci, 91-94. *Mailing Add:* Temple Emanuel 14450 W 10 Mile Rd Oak Park MI 48237

JACOBOWITZ, RONALD, ALGEBRAIC NUMBER THEORY, BIOSTATISTICS EDUCATION. *Current Pos:* PROF MATH, ARIZ STATE UNIV, 70- *Personal Data:* b New York, NY, Oct 18, 34; m 60; c 3. *Educ:* City Col New York, BA, 55; Univ Chicago, SM, 56; Princeton Univ, PhD(math), 60. *Prof Exp:* Instr math, Mass Inst Technol, 60-62; asst prof, Univ Ariz, 62-66; assoc prof, Univ Kans, 66-70. *Concurrent Pos:* Vis statistician, NIH, 79-80. *Mem:* Math Asn Am; Am Statist Asn. *Res:* Algebra; biomedical statistics; theory of quadratic forms. *Mailing Add:* Dept Math Ariz State Univ Tempe AZ 85287-0002

JACOBS, ABIGAIL CONWAY, BIOCHEMISTRY, TOXICOLOGY. *Current Pos:* toxicologist, Div Antiviral Drug Prods, 91-95, TEAM LEADER/TOXICOLOGIST, DIV DERM & DENT DRUGS, US FOOD & DRUG ADMIN, 95- *Personal Data:* b St Louis, Mo, Nov 11, 42; m 69, Verne; c 2. *Educ:* Univ Mich, Ann Arbor, BS, 64; Univ Calif, Berkeley, PhD(biochem), 68. *Prof Exp:* Fel immunochem, Am Cancer Soc, 68-70; res assoc biochem, Weizmann Inst Sci & Rehovot, Israel, 70-71; Queen's Univ, Belfast, 71-72; sr tech writer & researcher chem carcinogenesis, Tracor Jitco, 79-82; assoc proj mgr & sr scientist, Carltech Assocs, 82-89; sr biochemist,

Technol Resources, Inc, 89-91. *Concurrent Pos:* Res assoc, Nuffield Found, 71-72. *Mem:* Sigma Xi; Am Chem Soc; NY Acad Sci; AAAS; Soc Toxicol. *Res:* Carcinogenicity and phototoxicology of drugs. *Mailing Add:* 9621 McAlpine Rd Silver Spring MD 20901. *E-Mail:* jacobsa@cder.fda.gov

JACOBS, ALAN M(ARTIN), RADIATION ENGINEERING, STATISTICAL MECHANICS. *Current Pos:* prof & chmn nuclear eng sci, 80-82, PROF, UNIV FLA, 83- *Personal Data:* b New York, NY, Nov 14, 32; m 55, 78, Sharon Auerbach; c Fred, Heidi (Gearhart), Aaron & Seth. *Educ:* Cornell Univ, BEngPhys, 55; Pa State Univ, MS, 58, PhD(physics), 63. *Prof Exp:* Res assoc, Pa State Univ, University Park, 55-63, assoc prof nuclear eng, 63-68, prof, 68-80. *Concurrent Pos:* Consult, Allis-Chalmers Mfg Co, 56-59, Westinghouse Astronuclear Lab, 61-62, Millitron, Inc & HRB-Singer, Inc, 63-, Combustion Eng Inc, 75- & Future-Tech Corp, 86- *Mem:* Sigma Xi; Am Soc Nondestructive Testing. *Res:* Many body problems, especially radiation transport and plasma physics; radiography; image analysis & enhancement. *Mailing Add:* Nuclear & Radiol Eng Dept Univ Fla Gainesville FL 32611-8300. *Fax:* 904-392-3380; *E-Mail:* ajsjajsj@msn.com

JACOBS, ALAN MARTIN, GEOLOGY. *Current Pos:* LECTR, CIVIL ENG DEPT, CARNEGIE-MELLON UNIV, 87- *Personal Data:* b New York, NY, Feb 17, 42; m 68; c 2. *Educ:* City Col New York, BS, 63; Ind Univ, MA, 65, PhD(geol), 67. *Honors & Awards:* Cert Merit, Am Inst Prof Geologists, 84. *Prof Exp:* Teaching asst, Ind Univ, 63-64, teaching assoc, 64; asst geologist, Ill State Geol Surv, 67-74; from asst proj geologist to sr proj geologist, STS D'Appolonia Ltd, 74-85; mfr rep, Westinghouse Elec Corp, 81-88; pres, geoprobe, Alan M Jacobs, Inc, 81-; geosci mgr, IT Corp, 88- *Mem:* Geol Soc Am; Am Inst Prof Geologists; Explorers Club. *Res:* Engineering geology; glacial and quaternary geology; geomorphology; geologic factors in site selection; seismicity; age-dating; environmental geology; borehole camera surveys; hazardous waste chemicals management. *Mailing Add:* 323 Lime Oak Dr Pittsburgh PA 15235

JACOBS, ALLAN EDWARD, THEORETICAL SOLID STATE PHYSICS. *Current Pos:* from asst prof to assoc prof, 69-83, PROF PHYSICS, UNIV TORONTO, 83- *Personal Data:* b Toronto, Ont, Aug 7, 38; m 62. *Educ:* Univ Toronto, BASc, 60; Univ Waterloo, MSc, 62; Univ Ill, Urbana, PhD(physics), 68. *Prof Exp:* Res asst phys metall, Univ Toronto, 60-61; Nat Res Coun Can fel, Univ Hamburg, 68-69. *Concurrent Pos:* Nat Res Coun Can res grants, 69- *Mem:* Am Phys Soc; Can Asn Physicists. *Res:* Theory of inhomogeneous superconductors; superfluid helium; incommensurate systems; spin glasses; disordered. *Mailing Add:* Dept of Physics Univ Toronto 60 St George St Toronto ON M5S 1A7 Can

JACOBS, ALLEN LEON, PHARMACEUTICAL CHEMISTRY. *Current Pos:* RETIRED. *Personal Data:* b New York, NY, May 22, 31; m 54; c 3. *Educ:* Columbia Univ, BS, 52, MS, 54, PhD(pharmaceut chem), 62. *Prof Exp:* Instr chem, Col Pharmacol, Columbia Univ, 60-62; res analyst chemist, Sandoz Pharmaceut Inc, 62-63, mgr analytical res, 63-94. *Mem:* Am Chem Soc; Am Pharmaceut Asn; Sigma Xi. *Res:* Plant biochemistry; analytical chemistry. *Mailing Add:* 5 Alcor Rd Randolph NJ 07869

JACOBS, BARBARA B, ENDOCRINOLOGY, IMMUNOLOGY. *Current Pos:* CONSULT, 84- *Personal Data:* b Cambridge, Mass, July 23, 29; c 2. *Educ:* Mich State Univ, BS, 50, MS, 52; Ind Univ, PhD(zool), 56; Univ Hawaii, MPH, 86. *Prof Exp:* Res assoc cancer res, Med Ctr, Ind Univ, 56; Am Cancer Soc-NSF fel, Med Ctr, Univ Colo, 56-58; USPHS fel, State Univ NY Downstate Med Ctr, 58-59; sr res scientist, Roswell Park Mem Inst, 59-63; assoc res scientist, 63-70, dir immunol, Am Med Ctr Denver, 70-77; from assoc prof to prof, Life Sci Ctr, Nova Univ, 78-80; clin prof, Sch Pub Health, Univ Hawaii, 87-88. *Concurrent Pos:* Lect consult, State Univ NY Buffalo, 63; adj assoc prof, Sch Med, Univ Colo, 76-78. *Mem:* Am Pub Health Asn. *Res:* Endocrine and hormonally influenced neoplasms; growth of tumors in allogeneic hosts following passage in vitro; tumor-host immunologic interactions; epidemiology of goiter and malaria. *Mailing Add:* 3470 S Poplar St Apt 108 Denver CO 80224-2930

JACOBS, BARRY LEONARD, NEUROSCIENCE, NEUROPHYSIOLOGY. *Current Pos:* PROF NEUROSCI, DEPT PSYCHOL, PRINCETON UNIV, 72- *Educ:* Univ Calif, Los Angeles, PhD(psychol & neurosci), 71. *Mailing Add:* Green Hall Princeton Univ Green Hall Princeton NJ 08544-1099

JACOBS, CARL HENRY, ORTHOPEDICS, BIOMATERIALS. *Current Pos:* DIR MFG ENG OPERS, COLLAGEN PROD DIV, DATASCOPE CORP, 93- *Personal Data:* b Lewisburg, Pa, Jan 29, 48; m 70, Anita Isaacson; c Eliezer & Abraham. *Educ:* Univ Vt, BS, 70, MS, 73, PhD(mech eng), 74. *Prof Exp:* Asst prof, Sch Mech Eng, Ga Inst Technol, 74-79; group leader, Res & Develop, Howmedica Corp, Pfizer, Inc, 79-83; dir res labs & qual assurance, Zimmer Orthop Implant Div, Bristol-Myers, Inc, 83-89; vpres mfg, Orthomet Corp, 89-91; dir qual assurance, Osteonics Div, Stryker Corp, 91-93. *Concurrent Pos:* Clin asst prof, Dept Clin Rehab Med, Emory Univ, 77-79. *Mem:* Sigma Xi; Am Soc Mech Engrs; Soc Mfg Engrs; Orthop Res Soc; NY Acad Sci; Soc Biomat. *Res:* Development and design of orthopedic implants; arterial implants. *Mailing Add:* 1504 Jefferson St Teaneck NJ 07666. *Fax:* 201-307-5577

JACOBS, CHARLES WARREN, CELL DIVISION, CYTOSKELETON. *Current Pos:* PROF BIOL, HENRY FORD COMMUNITY COL, 94- *Personal Data:* b Gainesville, Fla, Nov 2, 54; m 77; c 2. *Educ:* Univ Miami, Fla, BS, 76; Univ Tex, Austin, PhD(microbiol), 83. *Prof Exp:* Fel cell biol, Univ Mich, 83-87 & Ohio State Univ, 87-89; asst prof biol, Albion Col, 89-94. *Concurrent Pos:* Instr phys sci; Eastern Mich Univ, 89. *Res:* Regulation of microtubules during the cell cycle; analyzing mutants of and molecular cloning the beta-tubulin gene of ustilago maydis. *Mailing Add:* Dept Biol Henry Ford Community Ctr Dearborn MI 48128

JACOBS, DAVID R, JR, CARDIOVASCULAR EPIDEMIOLOGY, BIOSTATISTICS. *Current Pos:* from asst prof to assoc prof biostatist, Lab Physiol Hyg, 74-81, assoc prof, 82-88, PROF, DIV EPIDEMIOL, SCH PUB HEALTH, UNIV MINN, MINNEAPOLIS, 88- *Personal Data:* b Brooklyn, NY, Apr 16, 45; m 93, Susan Koehner; c Stephen, Theodore, Adam J, Jennifer, Christopher & Patrick. *Educ:* Hofstra Univ, BA, 66; Johns Hopkins Univ, PhD(math statist), 71. *Prof Exp:* Asst prof, Towson State Col, 70-71; asst prof biostatist, Dept Social & Prev Med, Univ Md, 71-74. *Concurrent Pos:* Fel, Coun Epidemiol, Am Heart Asn; Res Career Develop Award, 77-82; consult epidemiol & biostatist. *Mem:* Am Statist Asn; Soc Epidemiol Res; Am Heart Asn; Am Epidemiol Soc. *Res:* Cardiovascular epidemiology, including intervention methodologies for lowering the risk factors and relevant statistical techniques; epidemiology of cardiovascular risk in young adults; relationship of cholesterol to noncardiovascular diseases. *Mailing Add:* Div Epidemiol Sch Pub Health Univ Minn Suite 300 1300 S Second St Minneapolis MN 55454. *Fax:* 612-624-0315; *E-Mail:* jacobs@epivax.epi.umn.edu

JACOBS, DIANE MARGARET, IMMUNOLOGY. *Current Pos:* PROF MICROBIOL & VPRES RES & GRAD STUDIES, UNIV CENT FLA, 94- *Personal Data:* b Port-of-Spain, Trinidad, Mar 24, 40; US citizen; m 85, Michael K Shelley. *Educ:* Radcliffe Col, AB, 61; Harvard Univ, PhD(bact), 67. *Prof Exp:* Instr immunol, Hadassah Med Sch, Hebrew Univ, Jerusalem, 67-68, lectr, 68-71; New York Cancer Res Inst fel, Dept Biol, Univ Calif, San Diego, 71-73, instr biol, 73-74; sr res assoc, Salk Inst Biol Sci, 74-76; from assoc prof to prof microbiol, State Univ NY, Buffalo, 80-89; assoc vchancellor res & dean Grad Sch, E Carolina Univ, 89-94. *Concurrent Pos:* Prin investr on res grants from NIH, 74-86 & Am Cancer Inst, 77-80; consult, Hoffman-LaRoche, 75-76 & 78-79; mem cause & prev sci rev comt, Nat Cancer Inst, 77-81; mem, Spec Sci Rev Comt, NIH, 87. *Mem:* AAAS; NY Acad Sci; Am Asn Immunologists; Am Soc Microbiol; Int Endotoxin Soc; Asn Women Sci. *Res:* Immunomodulatory agents of bacterial origin, particularly lipopolysaccharide; mechanism of triggering lymphocytes; nature of interaction with lymphocytes; lymphocyte membrane determinants interacting with lipopolysaccharide; structural requirements for lipopolysaccharide biological activity. *Mailing Add:* Univ Cent Fla 4000 Central Florida Blvd Orlando FL 32816-0150. *Fax:* 407-823-3299; *E-Mail:* djacobs@adm.ucf.edu

JACOBS, DONALD THOMAS, PHASE TRANSITIONS, CRITICAL PHENOMENA. *Current Pos:* From asst prof to assoc prof, 76-87, PROF PHYSICS, COL WOOSTER, 87- *Personal Data:* b Detroit, Mich, Sept 16, 49; c 2. *Educ:* Univ SFla, BA, 71, MA, 72; Univ Colo, PhD(physics), 76. *Concurrent Pos:* Vis scientist, Univ Md, 79; consult, The Col Wooster, 81-82. *Mem:* Am Phys Soc; Sigma Xi. *Res:* Experimental investigations of critical phenomena in binary fluid mixtures are conducted; coexistence curves, heat capacity, turbidity, dielectric constant, impurity and electric field effects are measured on various near-critical mixtures. *Mailing Add:* Physics Dept The Col Wooster Wooster OH 44691

JACOBS, ELLIOTT WARREN, APPLIED MATHEMATICS. *Current Pos:* ASST PROF MATH, EMBRY-RIDDLE AERONAUT UNIV, 78- *Personal Data:* b Brooklyn, NY, Feb 10, 50; m 71. *Educ:* State Univ New York, Stony Brook, BS, 71; Adelphi Univ, MS, 73, PhD(math), 76. *Prof Exp:* Asst prof math, Muskingum Col, 76-77 & Mt Union Col, 77-78. *Mem:* Am Math Soc; Math Asn Am. *Res:* Differential equations; nonstandard analysis. *Mailing Add:* Div Embry-Riddle Aeronaut Daytona Beach FL 32114-3900

JACOBS, EMMETT S, AIR POLLUTION. *Current Pos:* RETIRED. *Personal Data:* b Selma, NC, Mar 17, 26; m 52; c 2. *Educ:* Univ NC, BS, 50; Lehigh Univ, MS, 55, PhD(anal chem), 58. *Prof Exp:* Chemist, Nitrogen Div, Allied Chem Corp, 50-52; instr anal chem, Lehigh Univ, 52-55; res chemist anal, Jackson Lab, Petrochem Dept, E I du Pont de Nemours & Co, Inc, 58-66, res supvr anal res, 66-69, supvr automotive emission studies, petrol Lab, 69-71, supvr anal & environ studies, 71-74, div head, Emissions & Eng Test Div, Petrol Lab, 74-78, div head, petrol additives & environ & mgr antiknocks tech serv, Petrol Lab, Petrochem Dept, 78-85. *Mem:* Am Chem Soc; Am Soc Testing & Mat. *Res:* Analytical chemistry, especially gas chromatography, electrochemistry, x-ray and infrared spectroscopy; atmospheric chemistry and analysis of automotive emissions; gasoline quality and volume demand; gasoline blinding; lead in gasoline environmental issues. *Mailing Add:* 33 Paxon Dr Wilmington DE 19803

JACOBS, FRANCIS ALBIN, BIOCHEMISTRY, NUTRITION. *Current Pos:* from asst prof to prof, 54-87, EMER PROF BIOCHEM, SCH MED, UNIV NDAK, 87- *Personal Data:* b Minneapolis, Minn, Feb 23, 18; m 53; c 5. *Educ:* Regis Col, BS, 39; St Louis Univ, PhD(biochem), 49. *Prof Exp:* Asst chem, Univ Denver, 39-41; chemist, Shattuck Chem Co, 41; biochemist, Off Sci Res & Develop, 42-45; Nat Cancer Inst fel chemotherapeut, 49 & 50; from instr to asst prof biochem, Sch Med, Univ Pittsburgh, 51-54. *Concurrent Pos:* Dir res participation for teacher training prog, Univ NDak, 59-63; mem adv comt sci & math, Dept Pub Instr, NDak, 59-80; mem rev & eval comt, NSF,

60-80. *Mem:* Fel AAAS; Am Soc Biochem & Molecular Biol; Am Chem Soc; Soc Exp Biol & Med; Am Inst Nutrit; Sigma Xi. *Res:* Antibiotics and antitumor agents from microorganisms; gastroenterology, intestinal transport of amino acids and lipids; audiovisual aids for teaching biochemistry and nutrition; trace metal nutrition and bioavailability of zinc and copper. *Mailing Add:* 1525 Robertson Ct Grand Forks ND 58201

JACOBS, GEORGE JOSEPH, SPACE BIOLOGY, FISH & WILDLIFE SCIENCE. *Current Pos:* CONSULT LIFE SCI, 79- *Personal Data:* b New York, NY, Aug 30, 17; m 47, Joan Fischer; c Tamara, Douglas B & Jeremy. *Educ:* Univ Miss, AB, 40; WVa Univ, MSc, 46; George Washington Univ, PhD(zool), 55. *Honors & Awards:* Apollo Achievement Award, NASA, 69, Group Achievement Award, 72, 76 & 77. *Prof Exp:* Biologist oceanog, US Navy Hydrographic Off, 49-50, biologist hematol, Naval Med Res Inst, 50-56; res biologist, Atomic Bomb Casualty Comn, Nat Acad Sci-Nat Res Coun, Japan, 56-59; space biologist, NASA, 59-62, chief phys biol, 62-71, chief ecol, 71-79. *Concurrent Pos:* Collabr, Brookhaven Nat Lab, 55; managing ed, J Am Soc Ichthyologists & Herpetologists, 66-72; exec-secy, NASA-USSR Comn Found Space Biol & Med, 67-72; hon res assoc, Smithsonian Inst, 71-85; herpetol ed, J Am Soc Ichthyol & Herpetol, 78-82; consult, Am Physiol Soc, 80-86. *Mem:* AAAS; Am Soc Ichthyologists & Herpetologists; Biophys Soc; Am Physiol Soc; Am Soc Gravitational & Space Biol; Sigma Xi. *Res:* Space biology; herpetology; environmental quality; ecology; remote sensing; comparative animal physiology. *Mailing Add:* RD 2 Box 635 Montgomery PA 17752

JACOBS, GERALD DANIEL, PHYSICAL CHEMISTRY, SPECTROSCOPY. *Current Pos:* assoc prof, 64-70, head dept, 70-89, PROF CHEM, NORTHERN MICH UNIV, 70- *Personal Data:* b Perrysburg, Ohio, Jan 19, 35; m 58; c 2. *Educ:* Bowling Green State Univ, BA, 57; Mich State Univ, PhD(microwave spectros), 61. *Prof Exp:* Res chemist, Chem Div, Union Carbide Corp, 63-64. *Mem:* Am Chem Soc. *Res:* Microwave spectroscopy as applied to molecular structure determinations; determination of crystal structure by x-ray diffraction; physical chemistry of clathrates. *Mailing Add:* Dept of Chem Northern Mich Univ 1401 Presque Isle Ave Marquette MI 49855-5301

JACOBS, H KURT, CORONARY BLOOD FLOW, POSITIVE END EXPIRATORY PRESSURE. *Current Pos:* PROF SURG & PHYSIOL, LOYOLA UNIV MED CTR, 73- *Personal Data:* b Sept 8, 43; m; c 2. *Educ:* St Norbert Col, BS, 65; Univ Mich, MS, 68; Univ Mo, PhD(physiol), 73. *Concurrent Pos:* Res physiologist & dir, Hines Vet Admin Hosp. *Mem:* Am Physiol Soc; Am Asn Lab Animal Sci. *Res:* Cardiopulmonary interactions. *Mailing Add:* Dept Surg & Physiol Sch Med Loyola Univ Hines VA Hosp 2160 S First Ave Maywood IL 60153. *Fax:* 708-216-2319

JACOBS, HAROLD ROBERT, MECHANICAL ENGINEERING, THERMAL SCIENCES. *Current Pos:* from asst prof to assoc prof mech eng, 67-74, chmn dept civil eng, 78-79, PROF MECH ENG, UNIV UTAH, 74-, ASSOC DEAN RES, COL ENG, 81- *Personal Data:* b Portland, Ore, Nov 19, 36; m 61; c 3. *Educ:* Univ Portland, BS, 58; Wash State Univ, MSME, 61; Ohio State Univ, PhD(mech eng), 65. *Prof Exp:* Res & develop engr, Gen Elec Co, 58-59 & Boeing Co, 61-62; mem tech staff, Aerospace Corp, 65-68. *Mem:* Assoc fel Am Inst Aeronaut & Astronaut; Am Soc Mech Engrs; Sigma Xi. *Res:* Heat transfer; fluid mechanics; geothermal energy; oil shale processing; direct contact processing; condensers; thermal stresses; fracture. *Mailing Add:* Univ Pa East Stroudsburg PA 18301-9988

JACOBS, HARRY LEWIS, PSYCHOPHYSIOLOGY, NUTRITION. *Current Pos:* RETIRED. *Personal Data:* b Philadelphia, Pa, Apr 10, 25; m 50; c 4. *Educ:* Univ Del, BA, 50, MA, 51; Cornell Univ, PhD, 55. *Prof Exp:* Asst prof psychol, Bucknell Univ, 54-60; NIMH spec res fel physiol, Sch Med, Univ Rochester, 59-61, assoc prof psychol, Univ Ill, 61-67; assoc dir behav sci div, US Army Natick Labs, 66-68. *Concurrent Pos:* Vis lectr nutrit & food sci, Mass Inst Technol, 66-67; assoc prof physiol, Clark Univ, 66-69, prof, 70-76; affil scientist, Worcester Found Exp Biol, 71- *Mem:* AAAS; fel Am Psychol Asn; Am Physiol Soc; Am Inst Nutrit; Am Inst Biol Sci. *Res:* Appetite, hunger and food habits. *Mailing Add:* 63 Moore Rd Behav Sci Div Natick Labs Wayland MA 01778-1430

JACOBS, HARVEY, PHYSICAL CHEMISTRY, ORGANIC CHEMISTRY. *Current Pos:* ANALYTICAL CHEMIST, THE GLIDDEN CO, 72- *Personal Data:* b Cleveland, Ohio, Aug 10, 28; m 53; c 3. *Educ:* Ohio State Univ, BS, 50; Temple Univ, MA, 54, PhD(chem), 56. *Prof Exp:* Res chemist, Anal Lab, Rohm & Haas Co, 56-71; toxicologist, Philadelphia Med Exam Off, 71-72. *Mem:* Am Chem Soc; Soc Appl Spectros. *Res:* Gas chromatography; nuclear magnetic resonance; mass spectrometry. *Mailing Add:* 1481 Blackmore Rd Cleveland Heights OH 44118-1314

JACOBS, HYDE SPENCER, AGRONOMY. *Current Pos:* from asst prof to assoc prof, Kans State Univ, 57-66, dir, Kans Water Resources Res Inst, 64-74, prof soils, 66-80, dir, Kans Evapotranspiration Lab, 68-79, head dept agron, 71-80, asst dir exten & dir agr progs, 81-87, asst to dean of agr, 87-95, dir, Kans Water Resource Res Inst, 88-95, EMER PROF, KANS STATE UNIV, 95- *Personal Data:* b Declo, Idaho, May 15, 26; m 50; c 5. *Educ:* Univ Idaho, BS, 52, MS, 54; Mich State Univ, PhD(soil chem), 57. *Prof Exp:* Instr soils, Mich State Univ, 53-57. *Concurrent Pos:* Consult, Earth Sci Curric Proj, Am Geol Inst, 64-65; NSF fel, Utah State Univ, 68-69; assoc ed, J Agron Educ, 70-74. *Mem:* Fel Am Soc Agron; Soil Sci Soc Am. *Res:* Agronomy, soils; irrigation; water resources. *Mailing Add:* 1520 Nichols Hall Manhattan KS 66503

JACOBS, IRA, TELECOMMUNICATIONS, FIBER OPTICS. *Current Pos:* PROF ELEC ENG, VA TECH, 87- *Personal Data:* b Brooklyn, NY, Jan 3, 31; m 56, Irene Schuman; c Phillip, Mona & Nancy. *Educ:* City Col New York, BS, 50; Purdue Univ, MS, 52, PhD(physics), 55. *Prof Exp:* Summer physicist, Signal Corps Eng Labs, 52; mem tech staff, Mil Res Div, Bell Labs, 55-60, supvr, 60-62, head electromagnetic res dept, 62-66, head mil commun res dept, 66-67, dir, Digital Transmission Lab, 71-76, Wideband Transmission Facil Lab, 76-85 & Transmission Technol Lab, Transmission Div, 85-87. *Mem:* Fel Inst Elec & Electronics Engrs; Optical Soc Am. *Res:* Study of radar and military communications systems; analysis of transmission systems performance; development and evaluation of pulse code modulation transmission systems; research and development of fiber optic communication technology and systems. *Mailing Add:* Dept Elec Eng Virginia Tech Blacksburg VA 24061-0111. *Fax:* 540-231-3362; *E-Mail:* ijacobs@vt.edu

JACOBS, IRWIN MARK, COMMUNICATION THEORY, COMPUTER SCIENCES. *Current Pos:* pres, 85-91, CHMN & CHIEF EXEC OFFICER, QUALCOMM INC, 91- *Personal Data:* b New Bedford, Mass, Oct 18, 33; m 54; c 4. *Educ:* Cornell Univ, BEE, 56; Mass Inst Technol, MS, 57, ScD(elec eng), 59. *Honors & Awards:* Biann Award Outstanding Contrib Aerospace Commun, Inst Aeronaut & Astronaut, 80; First Ann Excellence Award, Am Electronics Asn, 89; Nat Medal Technol, 94. *Prof Exp:* Res asst elec eng, Mass Inst Technol, 58-59, from asst prof to assoc prof, 59-66; from assoc prof to prof info & comput sci, Univ Calif, San Diego, 66-72; pres, Linkabit Corp, 68-85. *Concurrent Pos:* Consult, Appl Res Lab, Sylvania Elec Prod, Inc, 59-, Lincoln Lab, Mass Inst Technol, 61-62, Indust Teaching, Minneapolis-Honeywell, Inc, 63 & Bolt Beranek & Newman, Inc, 65; NASA resident res fel, Jet Propulsion Lab, 64-65; chmn, Sci Adv Group, Defense Commun Agency & Eng Adv Coun, Univ Calif; mem gov bd, Inst Elec & Electronics Engrs Commun Soc. *Mem:* Nat Acad Eng; fel Inst Elec & Electronics Engrs; Asn Comput Mach; Sigma Xi. *Res:* Information theory, coding theory and applications to digital communications; satellite multiple access, microprogrammed communications systems and packet switching; author of numerous technical publications. *Mailing Add:* Qualcomm Inc 6455 Lusk Blvd San Diego CA 92121. *Fax:* 619-658-2500; *E-Mail:* ijacobs@qualcomm.com

JACOBS, ISRAEL S(AMSON), SOLID STATE PHYSICS. *Current Pos:* CONSULT, 94- *Personal Data:* b Buffalo, NY, July 20, 25; m 50, Judith Booth; c 2. *Educ:* Univ Mich, BS, 47; Univ Chicago, SM, 51, PhD(physics), 53. *Prof Exp:* Asst physics, Univ Chicago, 49-50; physicist, Gen Elec Res & Develop Ctr, 54-94. *Concurrent Pos:* Mem adv comt, Conf Magnetism & Magnetic Mat, 59-94, prog chmn, 61, pub chmn, 62-64, steering comt, 68-71; mem organizing comt, Int Cong Magnetism, 62-67 & 79-85, exec chmn, 66-67; res, High Magnetic Field Lab, Univ Grenoble, 65-66, Mass Inst Technol, 83-84, Solid State Chem Lab, Univ Bordeaux, 89; consult, US Energy Res & Develop Admin, 77, Nat Res Coun, 78 & 84 & 86; Coolidge fel, Gen Elec, 82; mem comt educ, Am Phys Soc, 79-82, comt opportunities, 80-87, 82-84, panel pub affairs, 87-89 & 92-94, chmn, 93; distinguished lectr, Inst Elec & Electronics Engrs-Magnetics Soc, 82-83. *Mem:* Fel Am Phys Soc; fel Inst Elec & Electronics Engrs; Magnetics Soc; fel AAAS. *Res:* Magnetism and magnetic materials; high magnetic field phenomena; antiferromagnetism; low-dimensional magnetic model systems; industrial applications of magnetics research; microwave properties of composites. *Mailing Add:* Gen Elec Res Develop Ctr PO Box 8 Schenectady NY 12301. *Fax:* 518-387-5299; *E-Mail:* isjacobs@crd.ge.com

JACOBS, J(AMES) H(ARRISON), METALLURGICAL ENGINEERING. *Current Pos:* mgr chem eng develop, Tech Dept, Union Carbide Metals Co Div, 51-63, tech mgr nickel-cadmium battery develop, Consumer Prod Div, 63-72, TECH MGR CARBON/ZINC BATTERIES, BATTERY PROD DIV, UNION CARBIDE CORP, 72- *Personal Data:* b St Charles, Mo, Apr 13, 16; m 42; c 2. *Educ:* Pa State Univ, BS, 36; Univ Mo, BS, 39, MS, 40. *Prof Exp:* Chemist, Western Elec Co, Ill, 36-39; metallurgist, US Bur Mines, 41-51. *Mem:* Electrochem Soc; Am Inst Mining, Metall & Petrol Engrs. *Res:* Hydrometallurgy and electrometallurgy of non-ferrous metals. *Mailing Add:* Math Scis Dept, Cas-154 Bay Village OH 44140

JACOBS, JACQUELINE E, ENVIRONMENTAL BIOLOGY. *Current Pos:* CONSULT, 83- *Personal Data:* b Wilkinsburg, Pa, June 17, 23; m 47; c 3. *Educ:* Coker Col, AB, 44; Univ SC, MS, 61, PhD(biol), 68. *Hon Degrees:* LHD, Coker Col, 86. *Honors & Awards:* SC Conserv Educ of Year Award, SC Wildlife Fedn; Conserv Award of Year, SC, Woodmen of the World, 75; F Bartow Culp Award Distinguished Serv, SC Wildlife Fedn, 75; Distinguished Serv Award, Nat Wildlife Fedn, 82. *Prof Exp:* Teacher, Moultrie High, Mt Pleasant, SC, 57-58 & Dreher High Sch, Columbia, 58-64; asst, Univ SC, 64-68; instr specialist, Instr TV, SC State Dept Educ, 68-71; instr, Spring Valley High Sch, 71-73; exec dir, SC Wildlife Fedn, 74-83. *Concurrent Pos:* Bd trustees, Coker Col, 71-77; fel botany, W Gordon Belser, Univ SC, 64-65; grant, Belle W Baruch Found, Univ SC, 67-68; mem bd trustees, Coker Col, SC, 71-77; mem, Wildlife Adv Comt, Col Agr Sci, Clemson Univ, 76-82; mem, Harry Hampton Mem Wildlife Fund bd dir, 83-88; life mem, bd, SC Wildlife Fedn. *Mem:* The Wildlife Soc; Sigma Xi; Bot Soc Am. *Res:* Freshwater algae of South Carolina; a curriculum guide for life science on educational TV. *Mailing Add:* Five Northlake Rd Columbia SC 29223

JACOBS, JEROME BARRY, CANCER BIOLOGY, DIAGNOSTIC ELECTRON MICROSCOPY. *Current Pos:* ASST CHIEF, DEPT LAB MED, ST VINCENT HOSP, 71- *Personal Data:* b Worcester, Mass, Dec 15, 42; m; c 3. *Educ:* Univ Vt, BS, 65, MS, 67; Clark Univ, PhD(cell biol), 71. *Concurrent Pos:* Prof cell biol, Clark Univ; prof life sci, Worcester Polytech

Inst; assoc prof path, Univ Mass Med Sch. *Mem:* Int Acad Path; Am Asn Pathologists; Am Soc Clin Pathologists; Am Soc Cell Biol; AAAS; Am Asn Cancer Res; Sigma Xi. *Res:* Renal diseases; bladder cancer. *Mailing Add:* 48 Stark Rd Worcester MA 01602

JACOBS, JOHN ALLEN, ANIMAL SCIENCE. *Current Pos:* asst prof, 70-74, ASSOC PROF ANIMAL SCI, UNIV IDAHO, 74- *Personal Data:* b Cumberland, Ky, Aug 8, 39; m 64; c 2. *Educ:* Univ Ky, BS, 63, MS, 65; Univ Wyo, PhD(animal sci), 70. *Prof Exp:* Supt beef, Stadler Packing Co, Columbus, 65-67; instr animal sci, Univ Wyo, 68-69. *Mem:* Am Soc Animal Sci; Am Meat Sci Asn. *Res:* Physiology and biochemistry of domestic animals as related to meat quality and quantity. *Mailing Add:* Dept Animal Sci Calif State Univ 2415 E San Ramon Fresno CA 93740-8033

JACOBS, JOHN EDWARD, BIOMEDICAL ENGINEERING, ELECTRICAL ENGINEERING. *Current Pos:* prof elec eng, Northwestern Univ, 60-69, exec dir, Biomed Eng Ctr, Walter P Murphy prof, 69-90, EMER WALTER P MURPHY PROF ELEC ENG SCI, NORTHWESTERN UNIV, 90- *Personal Data:* b Kansas City, Mo, June 15, 20; m 46; c 6. *Educ:* Northwestern Univ, BS, 47, MS, 48, PhD(elec eng), 50. *Hon Degrees:* ScD, Univ Strathclyde, 71. *Honors & Awards:* Coffin Award, Gen Elec Co, 53; Silver Medal, Am Soc Nondestructive Testing, 68. *Prof Exp:* Supvry res engr, X-Ray Dept, Gen Elec Co, 50-53, mgr, Adv Develop Lab, 53-59, elec engr, Res Lab, 59-60. *Concurrent Pos:* Lectr grad sch, Northwestern Univ, 52-58; McKay vis prof, Univ Calif, 57-58; adj prof, Rensselaer Polytech Inst, 59-60; pres, Biomed Eng Resource Corp, 69-71; mem, Automated Clin Lab Comt, Nat Inst Gen Med Sci, NIH, 70-74, mem, Biomed Training Comt Consult Radiol Sect, Army Res Off; chmn, Manpower Comt, President's Adv Coun Mgt Improv, 71-73; consult, Fed Coun Sci & Technol, 71-77. *Mem:* Nat Acad Eng; Biomed Eng Soc (treas, 68-72); Instrument Soc Am. *Res:* Photoconduction electron optics; biomedicine; transducers. *Mailing Add:* 631 Milburn Evanston IL 60201

JACOBS, JOSEPH DONOVAN, CIVIL ENGINEERING. *Current Pos:* RETIRED. *Personal Data:* b Motley, Minn, Dec 24, 08; m 37; c 1. *Educ:* Univ Minn, BSCE, 34. *Prof Exp:* Civil engr & construct supvr, Walsh Construct Co, New York & San Francisco, 34-54; chief engr, Kaiser-Walsh-Perini-Raymond, Australia, 54-55; sr officer, Jacobs Assocs, 55-78. *Concurrent Pos:* Chmn, US Nat Comt Tunneling Technol, Nat Acad Sci, 77. *Mem:* Nat Acad Eng; fel Am Soc Civil Engrs; Am Inst Mining, Metal & Petrol Engrs; Nat Soc Prof Engrs. *Mailing Add:* 35 Bevmar Lane Alamo CA 94507

JACOBS, JOSEPH JOHN, CHEMICAL ENGINEERING. *Current Pos:* pres, Jacobs Eng Co, 55-74, chief exec officer, 74-92, CHMN BD, JACOBS ENG GROUP INC, 74- *Personal Data:* b New York, NY, June 13, 16; m 42; c 3. *Educ:* Polytech Inst Brooklyn, BChE, 37, MChE, 39, DChE, 42. *Hon Degrees:* DSc, Polytech Univ. *Honors & Awards:* Hoover Medal, 83; Distinguished Career Award, Am Inst Chem Engrs, 90. *Prof Exp:* Res chem engr, Autoxygen, Inc, New York, 39-42; sr chem engr, Merck & Co, Rahway, NJ, 42-44; vpres & tech dir, Chemurgic Corp, Calif, 44-47; consult chem engr, 47-55. *Concurrent Pos:* Chmn bd trustees, Polytech Univ, 74-84 & 92-94; mem bd dir, Inst Contemp Studies, Digital Gene Techol; mem bd trustees, Harvey Mudd Col. *Mem:* Nat Acad Eng; Am Chem Soc; fel Am Inst Chem Engrs; AAAS; fel Inst Advan Eng; fel Am Inst Chemists. *Res:* Distillation; extraction; chlorination; plant design; unit processes; concentration of lactic acid; dehydration of caustic soda; continuous saponification; improved lubricating composition; deterioration of lubricating oils; economic surveys; published numerous articles and granted several patents. *Mailing Add:* Jacobs Eng Group Inc 251 S Lake Ave Pasadena CA 91101. *Fax:* 626-578-6990

JACOBS, JUDITH E, MATH EDUCATION. *Current Pos:* DIR, CTR EDUC & EQUITY IN MATH, SCI & TECHNOL, PROF MATH, CALIF STATE UNIV POMONA. *Personal Data:* b Newark, NJ, June 16, 43. *Educ:* City Univ New York, BA, 63, MA, 67; NY Univ, PhD(math), 73. *Honors & Awards:* Dora Helen Skipek Award, Int Women Math Educ, 84. *Mem:* AAAS; Math Asn Am; Nat Coun Teachers Math. *Res:* Math Education. *Mailing Add:* 1603 Aspen Village Way West Covina CA 91791-3103

JACOBS, KENNETH CHARLES, PHYSICS & ASTRONOMY, PHILOSOPHY OF SCIENCE. *Current Pos:* assoc prof & chair, Physics Dept, 84-94, sabbatical researcher, 90-91, PROF & CHAIR, PHYSICS DEPT, HOLLINS COL, ROANOKE, VA, 94- *Personal Data:* b McAllen, Tex, Sept 17, 42; m 68, Frances Elinor Allred. *Educ:* Mass Inst Technol, BS, 64; Calif Inst Technol, PhD(physics), 69. *Prof Exp:* Postdoctoral fel cosmology res, Physics Dept, Univ Md, College Park, 68-70; asst prof astron, Astron Dept, Univ Va, Charlottesville, 70-76; vis researcher astrophysics, Max Planck Inst, Munich, WGer, 77; mem tech staff econ, Bell Tel Labs, Murray Hill, NJ, 77-79, oper anal, AT&T Bell Labs, Whippany, NJ, 79-84. *Concurrent Pos:* Res aide, Lampf Accelerator, Los Alamos, NMex, 65; vis prof, Max Planck Inst, Munich, WGer, 72, Inst Astron, Cambridge Univ, Eng, 74-75, Kapteyn Lab, Univ Groningen, Neth, 75. *Mem:* Am Astron Soc; Int Astron Union; Sigma Xi; fel Royal Astron Soc. *Res:* Cosmological models; quantum cosmology; relativistic astrophysics; radio galaxies/quasars; tachyon theory; solar neutrino problem; celestial mechanics of Jovian Galilean moons; philosophy of science (mathematics); author of three textbooks. *Mailing Add:* Dept Physics Hollins Col Box 9661 Roanoke VA 24020

JACOBS, LAURENCE ALAN, THEORETICAL PHYSICS, ELEMENTARY PARTICLE PHYSICS. *Current Pos:* MEM STAFF, THINKING MACHINES, 90- *Personal Data:* b Mexico City, Mex, Dec 17, 49; div; c 2. *Educ:* Nat Univ Mex, BS, 72; Mass Inst Technol, PhD(physics), 76. *Honors & Awards:* Gunnar Kallen Award, 75. *Prof Exp:* Res assoc physics, Mass Inst Technol, 76-77; res assoc, Brookhaven Nat Lab, 77-79; asst prof physics, Nat Univ Mex, 79-81; asst prof, Inst Theoret Physics, Univ Calif, Santa Barbara, 81-83; mem staff, Bell Labs, 83-85; mem staff, Mass Inst Technol, 85- *Concurrent Pos:* Sci adv physics, Nat Sci & Technol, Mex. *Mem:* Am Phys Soc; Soc Mex Physics; Acad Invert Sci; NY Acad Sci. *Res:* Theoretical physics, field theory; mathematical physics; statistical mechanics; condensed-matter physics. *Mailing Add:* Ctr Theo Phys/6-403 MIT/77 Massachusetts Ave Cambridge MA 02139

JACOBS, LAURENCE STANTON, GENERAL ENDOCRINOLOGY, NEUROENDOCRINOLOGY. *Current Pos:* assoc prof, Univ Rochester Med Ctr, 77-82, dir, Clin Res Ctr, 77-91, actg head gastroenterol, 83-88, PROF MED, UNIV ROCHESTER MED CTR, 82-, ASSOC DEAN STUDENT AFFAIRS, UNIV ROCHESTER SCH MED & DENT, 90- *Personal Data:* b Boston, Mass, Mar 24, 40; m 63; c 2. *Educ:* Harvard Univ, AB, 60; Univ Rochester, MD, 65. *Prof Exp:* Res asst, Res Inst Med & Chem, 60-61; intern & resident internal med, Wash Univ & Barnes Hosp, 65-67, fel endocrinol, 67-68 & 70-72, instr med, 71-72 & asst prof, 72-77; lieutenant comdr & med officer lab med, Ctrs Dis Control, USPHS, 68-70. *Concurrent Pos:* Asst physician & consult clin chem, Barnes Hosp, St Louis, 71-77; sr assoc physician, Strong Mem Hosp, Rochester, NY, 77-82, sr physician, 82-; chmn, merit rev bd endocrinol, Vet Admin, 83-86; mem, Biomed Sci Study Sect, NIH, 87-91; pres, Asn Clin Res Ctr Prog Dirs, 87-89. *Mem:* AAAS; Am Soc Clin Invest; Endocrine Soc; Am Soc Biol Chemists; Int Soc Neuroendocrinol; Am Diabetes Asn; Am Fed Clin Res; Central Soc Clin Res. *Res:* Hypothalamic control and molecular mechanisms of secretion of growth hormone and prolactin; structure, composition and enzymatic activities of isolated adenohypophysial secretory granules. *Mailing Add:* Dept Med Endocrin Assoc Dean's Off Univ Rochester Sch Med & Dent 601 Elmwood Ave Box 693 Rochester NY 14642-8693. *Fax:* 716-256-2789

JACOBS, LOIS JEAN, MEDICINE, GENETICS. *Current Pos:* PVT PRACT, 90- *Personal Data:* b Portage, Wis, Mar 10, 47. *Educ:* Univ Wis-Madison, BS, 69, PhD(genetics), 77, MD, 87. *Prof Exp:* Res assoc genetics, Inst Med Res, 77-80; asst scientist, Dept Med Genetics, 81-83, first yr resident, Med Sch, Wis-Madison, 87-88; second yr resident, Bay State Med Ctr, Affil Tufts Univ Med Sch, 88-90. *Mem:* Environ Mutagen Soc; AMA. *Res:* Somatic cell genetics, specifically mutagenesis and carcinogenesis in diploid human cells. *Mailing Add:* 456 Madison Ave Omro WI 54963

JACOBS, LOUIS JOHN, FLUID MIXING TECHNOLOGY, PHASE SEPARATION TECHNOLOGY. *Current Pos:* dir eng develop, Res & Develop Div, 89-91, DIR TECHNOL & ENG, KOCH INDUSTS INC, 91- *Personal Data:* b Chicago, Ill, Mar 27, 43; m 65, Phyllis Clark; c Julie A & Matthew L. *Educ:* Univ Wis-Madison, BS, 65; Washington Univ, St Louis, Mo, MS, 69. *Prof Exp:* Engr, Monsanto Co, 65-77, eng supt, 77-79, bus develop mgr, 79-80, mgr technol risk anal, Monsanto Co, 80-82; dir, Corp Eng Div, A E Staley Mfg Co, 82-88, vpres starch opers, 88-89. *Concurrent Pos:* Chmn, Mixing Comt, Am Inst Chem Engrs, 75-76, St Louis Sect, 77; affil prof, Wash Univ, St Louis, 78-79. *Mem:* Am Inst Chem Engrs. *Res:* Author of various publications. *Mailing Add:* 8955 Boxthorn Ct Wichita KS 67226

JACOBS, LOYD DONALD, ACOUSTICS. *Current Pos:* RETIRED. *Personal Data:* b Wolcott, Ind, Nov 22, 32; m 56; c Paul, John (deceased) & Ann. *Educ:* Emporia State Univ, BA, 54; Univ Nebr, MS, 58. *Prof Exp:* Engr, Boeing Co, Wichita, Kans, 57-62, sr engr, Seattle, Wash, 62-73, group engr, 74-82, prin engr, 82-89, sr prin engr, 90-94. *Mem:* Acoust Soc Am; Sigma Xi. *Res:* Control and reduction of aircraft noise; response of aircraft structure to noise; noise radiation from surfaces immersed in airflow. *Mailing Add:* 2004 128th Ave SE Bellevue WA 98005

JACOBS, MARC QUILLEN, MATHEMATICS. *Current Pos:* assoc prof, 71-74, PROF MATH, UNIV MO-COLUMBIA, 74- *Personal Data:* b Chandler, Okla, June 28, 38. *Educ:* Univ Okla, BS, 60, MA, 63, PhD(math), 66. *Prof Exp:* Jr mathematician, Int Bus Mach Corp, 60-61; instr math, Univ Okla, 65-66; res asst prof appl math, Brown Univ, 66-67; asst prof math, Rice Univ, 67-68 & appl math, Brown Univ, 68-71. *Mem:* Am Math Soc; Math Asn Am; Soc Indust & Appl Math; Sigma Xi. *Res:* Optimal control theory. *Mailing Add:* 206 Phillip Lane Leonardtown MD 20650

JACOBS, MARK, PLANT DEVELOPMENT, CELL RECEPTOR PROTEINS. *Current Pos:* From asst prof to assoc prof, Swarthmore Col, 81-89, chmn, 87-88 & 88-90, assoc provost, 93-96, PROF BIOL, SWARTHMORE COL, 89- *Personal Data:* b Princeton, NJ, May 19, 50; m 73, Candace Clarke; c Jeffrey, Robinson & Patrick. *Educ:* Harvard Univ, BA, 71; Stanford Univ, PhD(biol), 76. *Concurrent Pos:* NATO fel, Freiburg Univ, Ger, 76-77; Guggenheim fel, Cambridge Univ, Eng, 86-87; NAm ed, Plant Physiol & Biochem, 90- *Mem:* Am Soc Plant Physiologists (treas, 91-); Sigma Xi. *Res:* Biochemical mode of action of the plant growth regulators; hormonal control of plant development. *Mailing Add:* Dept Biol Swarthmore Col Swarthmore PA 19081. *Fax:* 610-328-8663; *E-Mail:* mjacobs1@cc.swarthmore.edu

JACOBS, MARTIN JOHN, MEDICINAL CHEMISTRY, PHARMACEUTICAL & ORGANIC CHEMISTRY. *Current Pos:* Res chemist, Int Minerals & Chem Corp, 75-82, sr res scientist, 82-92, mgr, 92-93, VIS PROF CHEM, INT MINERALS & CHEM CORP, 94- *Personal Data:* b Chicago, Ill, June 28, 44; m 66, Gail L Burchett; c 5. *Educ:* Ill Inst Technol, BS, 69; Colo State Univ, PhD(org chem), 75. *Prof Exp:* Chmn, Wabash Valley Sect, Am Chem Soc, 93. *Concurrent Pos:* Bd dirs, Ind State Univ Chapter Sigma Xi. *Mem:* Am Chem Soc; Sigma Xi; Am Asn Pharm Soc; AAAS. *Res:* Synthesis of compounds as products for use in pharmaceutical application; industrial intermediates and process chemistry; preformulation of new pharmaceutical agents. *Mailing Add:* Dept Chem Lifesci Rose Hulman Inst Technol 5500 E Wabash Ave Terre Haute IN 47803. *Fax:* 812-877-3198

JACOBS, MARY ELIZABETH, LIFE SCIENCES. *Current Pos:* staff, 78-89, DIR, DIV LIFE SCI, CTR DEVICES & RADIOL HEALTH, FOOD & DRUG ADMIN, 89- *Personal Data:* b Chicago, Ill, Aug 2, 42. *Educ:* Trinity Col, BA, 64; Univ Ill, Urbana, MS, 66, PhD(biophysics), 69. *Prof Exp:* Postdoctoral fel, Univ Iowa, 69 & Ind Univ, 70-74; res asst prof, George Washington Univ Med Sch, 74-77. *Concurrent Pos:* Grass fel, Marine Biol Lab, Woods Hole, 72. *Mem:* AAAS; Asn Res Vision & Opthal; Biophys Soc; Asn Women Sci. *Res:* Risk assessment; ocular properties. *Mailing Add:* Food & Drug Admin HFZ-110 5600 Fishers Lane Rockville MD 20857

JACOBS, MARYCE MERCEDES, TOXICOLOGY, CARCINOGENESIS. *Current Pos:* VPRES RES, AM INST CANCER RES, 88- *Personal Data:* b El Paso, Tex, June 15, 44. *Educ:* NMex State Univ, BS, 66; Univ Calif, Los Angeles, PhD(biochem), 70. *Prof Exp:* Res assoc, Univ Colo Med Ctr, 70-71; res assoc, M D Anderson Hosp & Tumor Inst, Univ Tex, 71-72, asst prof & asst biochemist, 72-77, co-chmn biochem, Grad Sch Biomed Sci, Houston, 73-75; from asst prof to assoc prof, Eppley Inst Res Cancer, Univ Nebr, 77-83, indust contract coordr, 79-83; biochem toxicologist, Metrek Div, Mitre Corp, 83-88. *Concurrent Pos:* Consult, Nat Large Bowel Cancer Cadre, Nat Cancer Inst, 78-82; opponent, Univ Oulu, Finland, 80. *Mem:* Am Asn Cancer Res; NY Acad Sci; Sigma Xi; Soc Toxicol; Am Acad Clin Toxicol. *Res:* Inhibition of chemical carcinogenesis; dietary selenium inhibition of tumor induction by 1, 2-Dimethylhydrazine and other carcinogens in animals; determination of the mechanisms of inhibition in in-vivo and in-vitro systems. *Mailing Add:* 1800 Old Meadow Rd Unit 801 McLean VA 22102-1813

JACOBS, MERLE EMMOR, ZOOLOGY, INSECT BIOCHEMISTRY. *Current Pos:* RES PROF ZOOL, GOSHEN COL, 64- *Personal Data:* b Hollsopple, Pa, Nov 30, 18; m 59, Elizabeth Beyeler. *Educ:* Goshen Col, AB, 49; Univ Ind, PhD(zool), 53. *Honors & Awards:* Lalor Award, Sigma Xi. *Prof Exp:* Instr zool, Goshen Col, 53-54 & Duke Univ, 54-57; asst prof biol, Bethany Col, WVa, 57-62; prof biol, EM Col, Va, 62-64. *Concurrent Pos:* Grant, NIH, 59-85; Eigenmann fel, Ind Univ. *Mem:* Sigma Xi; Am Men Sci; AAAS. *Res:* Behavior and biochemical genetics; melanistic polymorphism, Darwinian sexual selection revision; Drosophila genetics. *Mailing Add:* Dept Biol Goshen Col Goshen IN 46526. *Fax:* 219-535-7234; *E-Mail:* merleej@goshen.edu

JACOBS, MICHAEL MOISES, INFARED PHYSICS, ELECTRO-OPTIC SPACE SYSTEMS & SPACE SYSTEMS ENGINEERING. *Current Pos:* PHYSICIST, SPACE SYSTS ANALYST & SYSTS DIR, SURVEILLANCE SYSTS ENG, AEROSPACE CORP, EL SEGUNDO, CALIF, 80- *Personal Data:* b Miami, Fla, June 21, 50; m 80, Gloria R Benis; c Nicole, Amber & Michael. *Educ:* Univ Miami, BS, 72, MS, 73, PhD(physics), 75. *Prof Exp:* Res physicist laser optics, Sci Applns Inc, Atlanta, Ga, 76; physicist & mem tech staff electro-optics, Satellite Systs Div, Rockwell Int, Seal Beach, Calif, 77-80. *Concurrent Pos:* Instr physics, Orange Coast Col, 76-79. *Mem:* Am Inst Physics; Optical Soc Am. *Res:* Electro-optic infrared & laser physics; acousto-optics; radiative transfer; atmospheric and oceanic optics; systems engineering; infrared focal plane device physics; space sensor mission planning/requirements; surveillance systems; simulations and modeling. *Mailing Add:* 2350 E El Segundo Blvd Aerospace Corp El Segundo CA 90245-4691

JACOBS, MORTON HOWARD, ANALYTICAL CHEMISTRY, TECHNICAL MANAGEMENT. *Current Pos:* RETIRED. *Personal Data:* b Newark, NJ, June 28, 24; m 70, Helen Raschkover; c Paul. *Educ:* Univ Pa, BA, 46. *Prof Exp:* Biochemist, Univ Hosp, Univ Mich, 50-52; chemist, Control Lab, Int Flavors & Fragrances, Inc, 53-58, Res Dept, 58-60, proj leader spectroscopy, Instrumentation & Anal Res Dept, 60-, sr proj chemist, Chromatography & Spectros Res Dept, 78-, Spec Projs, 90- *Mem:* Am Chem Soc; Int Soc Magnetic Resonance; Soc Appl Spectros. *Res:* Application of chromatographic and spectroscopic techniques; magnetic resonance to structure elucidation of flavor and aroma chemicals, both natural and synthetic. *Mailing Add:* 97 Cotswold Circle Ocean NJ 07712

JACOBS, MYRON SAMUEL, PATHOLOGY, ANATOMY. *Current Pos:* asst anat, 51-54, from assoc prof to prof path, 73-87, EMER PROF PATH, COL DENT, NY UNIV, 87- *Personal Data:* b Jersey City, NJ, May 17, 22; m 59, Miriam Klebaner; c Louise S & Suzanne S. *Educ:* Univ Pa, BA, 45; NY Univ, MS, 51, PhD, 55. *Prof Exp:* Lectr histol & embryol, Queen's Univ, Ont, 54-56; instr histol, embryol & neuroanat, NY Med Col, 56-57, from asst prof to assoc prof anat, 57-65, dir cetacean brain lab, 62-65, vis prof histol & neurosci, 81-85; res assoc comp path, Osborn Lab Marine Sci, NY Aquarium, 66-72. *Concurrent Pos:* Adj assoc prof, Neural Sci & Gross Anat, Cornell Univ Med Col, 67-73. *Mem:* Am Asn Anat; Soc Neurosci; NY Acad Sci; Sigma Xi. *Res:* Skin grafts and thermal changes in transplantation, rat; alloxan diabetes, hamster; cetacean nervous system. *Mailing Add:* 4422 Langtry Dr Glen Arm MD 21057

JACOBS, NICHOLAS JOSEPH, BACTERIOLOGY. *Current Pos:* from instr to assoc prof, 64-80, PROF MICROBIOL, DARTMOUTH MED SCH, 80- *Personal Data:* b Oakland, Calif, Mar 29, 33; m 59; c 1. *Educ:* Univ Ill, BS, 55; Cornell Univ, PhD, 60. *Hon Degrees:* MA, Dartmouth Col, 85. *Prof Exp:* Res assoc, Univ Ill, 59-61; from asst bacteriologist to assoc bacteriologist, Am Meat Inst Found, 61-64. *Mem:* AAAS; Am Soc Microbiol; Sigma Xi. *Res:* Bacterial physiology; pathogenic bacteriology; heme synthesis in bacteria, plants, and animals. *Mailing Add:* Dept Microbiol & Physiol Dartmouth Med Sch Hanover NH 03755-3842

JACOBS, PATRICIA ANN, GENETICS. *Current Pos:* PROF ANAT, SCH MED, UNIV HAWAII, 73- *Personal Data:* b London, Eng, Oct 8, 34. *Educ:* Univ St Andrews, BSc, 56, DSc(cytogenetics), 66. *Prof Exp:* Scientist, Med Res Coun, 57-72. *Mem:* Genetics Soc Gt Brit; Am Soc Human Genetics. *Res:* Human cytogenetics. *Mailing Add:* Emory Univ Med 2040 Ridgewood Dr NE Atlanta GA 30322

JACOBS, PATRICIA ANNE, OPERATIONS RESEARCH. *Current Pos:* assoc prof, 78-86, PROF OPERS RES, NAVAL POSTGRAD SCH, 86- *Personal Data:* b Chicago, Ill. *Educ:* Northwestern Univ, BS, 69, MS, 71, PhD(appl math), 73. *Prof Exp:* Asst prof opers res, Stanford Univ, 72-78. *Concurrent Pos:* Assoc ed, Mgt Sci, 81- & Naval Res Logistics, 82-92. *Mem:* Int Statist Inst; Inst Math Statist; Royal Statist Soc; AAAS. *Res:* Stochastic processes and their applications; stochastic modeling and statistical analysis in operations research and related fields. *Mailing Add:* Naval Postgrad Sch 1411 Cunningham Rd Glascow 320 Code OR/JC Monterey CA 93943

JACOBS, PATRICK W M, SOLID STATE CHEMISTRY & CHEMICAL PHYSICS, COMPUTER SIMULATION. *Current Pos:* from asst lectr to sr lectr phys chem, Univ Western Ont, 50-64, reader, 64-65, sr prof, 65-89, EMER PROF PHYS CHEM, UNIV WESTERN ONT, 89- *Personal Data:* b Durban, SAfrica, Sept 15, 23; m 50, 81; c Richard, Laura & Robert. *Educ:* Univ Natal, BSc, 41, MSc, 43; Univ London, PhD(phys chem), 51, DSc(phys Chem), 63. *Honors & Awards:* Solid State Chem Medal, Royal Soc Chem, 83. *Prof Exp:* Lectr chem, Rhodes Univ, SAfrica, 46-48; Beit fel, Imp Col, London, 48-50. *Concurrent Pos:* Overseas fel, Churchill Col, Cambridge, Eng, 73-74; vis fel, Wolfson Col, Oxford, Eng, 82. *Mem:* Fel Royal Soc Chem; Can Inst Chem; Can Asn Physicists. *Res:* Decomposition of solids; optical and electrical properties of solids; computer simulation of condensed matter. *Mailing Add:* Dept Chem Univ Western Ont London ON N6A 5B7 Can. *Fax:* 519-661-3022; *E-Mail:* pjacobs@uwo.ca

JACOBS, PETER MARTIN, ULTRARELATIVISTIC HEAVY ION COLLISIONS, NUCLEAR EQUATION OF STATE. *Current Pos:* researcher, 88-90, staff scientist, 90-92, DIV FEL NUCLEAR SCI DIV, LAWRENCE BERKELEY LAB, 92- *Personal Data:* b Hamilton, Ont, Nov 7, 57; m 91, Karen L Pliskin; c Eliana S. *Educ:* Univ Toronto, BSc, 79; Yale Univ, MPhil, 82; Weizmann Inst Sci, PhD(physics), 87. *Prof Exp:* Researcher, Univ Calif, San Francisco, 87-88. *Mem:* Am Phys Soc. *Res:* Very high energy collisions of heavy nuclei to elucidate the properties of nuclear matter at high temperatures and densities, including possible phase transitions. *Mailing Add:* 4401 Terrabella Way MS-50D One Cyclotron Rd Oakland CA 94619. *Fax:* 510-486-4818; *E-Mail:* pmjacobs@lbl.gov

JACOBS, RALPH R, QUANTUM ELECTRONICS, ENGINEERING PHYSICS. *Current Pos:* DIR, NEW TECHNOL INITIATIVES, LAWRENCE LIVERMORE NAT LAB, 90- *Personal Data:* b Niagara Falls, NY, Dec 31, 42; div; c Aleda A & Liana L. *Educ:* NY Univ, BS, 64; Yale Univ, MS, 65, PhM, 67, PhD(physics), 69. *Prof Exp:* Lab instr physics, Yale Univ, 67-69; mem tech staff, GTE Labs, Inc, Bayside, NY, 69-72; sr physicist & proj mgr, laser-prog, Lawrence Livermore Lab, Univ Calif, 72-80; mgr res & advan develop, Spectra-Physics, 80-85, eng mgr, 85-89, dir, Corp Tech Develop, 89-90. *Concurrent Pos:* Mem bd govs, Lasers & Electro-optics Soc, Inst Elec & Electronics Engrs. *Mem:* Sigma Xi; fel Am Phys Soc; fel Optical Soc Am; fel Inst Elec & Electronics Engrs Lasers & Electro-Optic Soc. *Res:* Basic and applied aspects of atomic, molecular and laser physics in gaseous, liquid and solid state media; quantum electronics; laser spectroscopy-linear and nonlinear (ultraviolet, visible, infrared); low and high pressure gas discharges; high resolution microwave spectroscopy; rotational, vibrational, and electronic relaxation in molecules; new laser research and development various laser applications including areas of laser medicine, laser materials processing, laser metrology; heightened skills in management of technologists and strategic planning that emphasizes optimization of research and development, engineering, marketing, and manufacturing considerations for major program and commercial success. *Mailing Add:* Lawrence Livermore Nat Lab PO Box 808 L-466 Livermore CA 94551

JACOBS, RICHARD L, ORTHOPEDIC SURGERY, BIOCHEMISTRY. *Current Pos:* PROF ORTHOP SURG & HEAD DIV, ALBANY MED CTR, 74- *Personal Data:* b Elsberry, Mo, Dec 29, 30; m 54; c 3. *Educ:* State Univ Iowa, BA, 52, MD, 56, MS, 61. *Prof Exp:* Arthritis & Rheumatism Found fel, State Univ Iowa, 59-62, resident orthop surg, 62-65; from asst prof to prof orthop, Univ Ill Med Ctr, 66-74. *Concurrent Pos:* Orthop Res & Educ Found res fel orthop, Mass Gen Hosp-Harvard Univ, 61-62; consult, Ill Div Serv Crippled Children, 65-74, Dixon State Sch, 66-74 & US Vet Admin Hosps, 68- *Mem:* AAAS; AMA; Am Chem Soc; Am Inst Chem; Am Acad Orthop Surg; Sigma Xi; Am Orthop Asn. *Res:* Vitamin metabolism; collagen chemistry; immunology. *Mailing Add:* 47 New Scotland Ave Albany Med Col Albany NY 12208-3412

JACOBS, RICHARD LEE, ORGANIC CHEMISTRY. *Current Pos:* RETIRED. *Personal Data:* b Perrysburg, Ohio, Aug 4, 31; m 56; c 4. *Educ:* Bowling Green State Univ, BA, 53; Mich State Univ, MS, 55, PhD(org chem), 59. *Prof Exp:* Asst, Mich State Univ, 53-59; res chemist, Koppers Co, Inc, Pa, 59-62; sr chemist, Maumee Chem Co, 62-66; dir lab, Sherwin Williams Chems, 66-82; tech & legal mgr, Prin Bus Enterprises, 82-88. *Concurrent Pos:* assoc chair, Chem Dept, Bowling Green State Univ, 88-95. *Mem:* Am Chem Soc; Soc Heterocyclic Chemists; Sigma Xi; fel Am Inst Chemists. *Res:* Organic sulfur compounds, especially thiacyclopropanes and thiophene; nitriles preparation and reactions; alkylation and reaction mechanisms of aromatics; nitrogen heterocycles. *Mailing Add:* 558 Clover Lane Perrysburg OH 43551

JACOBS, RICHARD M, ORTHODONTICS, ANATOMY. *Current Pos:* asst dean col dent, Univ Iowa, 66-67, actg head dept oral biol & curric coordr, 66-71, assoc dean col, 67-71, PROF ORTHOD, COL DENT, UNIV IOWA, 66- *Personal Data:* b Wloclawek, Poland, Oct 31, 24; US citizen; m 50, Federbusch; c Steven K. *Educ:* Maximilian Univ, Dr med dent, 48; NY Univ, DDS, 52; Univ Calif, Berkeley, MPH, 61; Med Col Va, PhD(anat), 64; Univ Ill, MS(orthod), 65. *Prof Exp:* Resident dent, NY State Dept Ment Hyg, 52-53; dentist, Nev State Dept Pub Health, 59-60; Nat Inst Dent Res fel, Med Col Va, 61-63 & Univ Ill, 63-65; assoc prof orthod & head dept, Fac Dent, Univ KC, 65-66. *Concurrent Pos:* Chmn, Grad Educ Sect, Am Asn Dent Schs, 73-76. *Mem:* Fel Am Pub Health Asn; Am Asn Anat; Am Asn Orthod; fel Sigma Xi; Am Educ Res Asn; Asn Study Higher Educ. *Res:* Effects of spontaneous muscular activity on fetal development; relation between knowledge and diagnostic reasoning; cost effectiveness of professional education; organizational behavior and control in formal organizations; profiling providers of orthodontic services in general practice. *Mailing Add:* Col Dent Univ Iowa Iowa City IA 52242

JACOBS, ROBERT SAUL, MARINE PHARMACOLOGY, NEUROPHARMACOLOGY. *Current Pos:* PROF PHARMACOL, UNIV CALIF, SANTA BARBARA, 74- *Educ:* Loyola Univ, PhD(pharmacol), 71. *Mailing Add:* Dept Biol Sci Univ Calif Santa Barbara CA 93106-0001. *Fax:* 805-893-4724

JACOBS, ROSS D, BIOCHEMISTRY. *Current Pos:* RETIRED. *Personal Data:* b Montreal, Que, Feb 27, 25; m 53; c 4. *Educ:* McGill Univ, BSc, 48, MSc, 52, PhD, 54. *Prof Exp:* Res biochemist, Ayerst Labs, Inc, 54-55, asst to dir pharmaceut develop labs, 55-57; res assoc med, Univ Southern Calif, 57-58; asst prof obstet & gynec, Col Med, State Univ NY Upstate Med Ctr, 58-64, asst prof biochem, 58-87. *Concurrent Pos:* Dir labs, Calif Found Med Res, 57-58. *Mem:* Biochem Soc; Endocrine Soc. *Res:* Biosynthesis and metabolism of steroid hormones; gonadotropins. *Mailing Add:* PO Box 184 Henderson Harbor NY 13651

JACOBS, S LAWRENCE, CLINICAL CHEMISTRY, ANALYTICAL TOXICOLOGY. *Current Pos:* RETIRED. *Personal Data:* b New York, NY, Nov 27, 29; m 53, Charlotte Bell; c 3. *Educ:* Rensselaer Polytech Inst, BS, 51; Univ Ill, MS, 52, PhD(chem), 55. *Prof Exp:* Asst chem, Univ Ill, 52-55; res chemist, Northern Regional Lab, USDA, 55; chief spec projs div, Los Angeles Br Lab, Bio Sci Labs, 56-65, dir dept chem, 66-67, qual assurance officer, 68-71, asst to dir, 71-75, mgr prof rels & corp accounts, 76-77, dir, Dept Clin & Indust Toxicol, 78-81, dir, 81-84; dir, Pacific Toxicol Labs, 85-86. *Mem:* Am Chem Soc; Am Asn Clin Chem; Sigma Xi. *Res:* Clinical chemistry; adrenal hormones; bile pigments; enzymes; lipids; quality assurance; analytical toxicology. *Mailing Add:* 16055 Miami Way Pacific Palisades CA 90272-4232

JACOBS, SHEILA J, IMMUNOCHEMISTRY. *Current Pos:* sr scientist, 82-84, prin scientist, 84-85, SECT LEADER, SCHERING-PLOUGH RES INST, 85- *Personal Data:* b New York, NY, Oct 10, 39; m 85, Robert Carey; c Marcy (Little) & Sharon. *Educ:* Carnegie Inst Technol, BS, 61; Long Island Univ, MS, 64; Columbia Univ, PhD(microbiol), 68. *Prof Exp:* Instr microbiol & immunol, Downstate Med Ctr, State Univ NY, 68-71; res assoc prof med microbiol, NY Med Col, 76-81; assoc prof microbiol, Wagner Col, 81-82. *Concurrent Pos:* Adj prof microbiol, Rutgers Univ, 81. *Mem:* Sigma Xi; AAAS; Am Chem Soc; Int Soc Interferon & Cytokine Res. *Res:* Developing immunoassays for and investigating the structure and immunogenicity of cytokines and interferon alfa, interleukin-4, interleukin-10, as well as a humanized monoclonal anti-interleukin-5 antibody and an adenovirus vector containing P53. *Mailing Add:* Schering-Plough Res Inst 2015 Galloping Hill Rd Kenilworth NJ 07033. *E-Mail:* sheila.jacobs@spcorp.com

JACOBS, SIGMUND JAMES, PHYSICS, FLUID DYNAMICS. *Current Pos:* sr scientist Explosives Div, 75-80, CONSULT DETONATION PHYSICS, NAVAL SURFACE WEAPONS CTR, WHITE OAK LAB, 80- *Personal Data:* b Minneapolis, Minn, Mar 25, 12; m 44. *Educ:* Univ Minn, BChE, 33, MS, 52; Univ Amsterdam, PhD(physics), 53. *Honors & Awards:* Meritorious Civilian Serv Award, US Navy, 51, 60; DuPont Medal, Soc Motion Picture & TV Eng, 64. *Prof Exp:* Res assoc, Carnegie Inst Technol, 42-45; res assoc physics, Woods Hole Oceanog Inst, 46; res physicist, Naval Ord Lab, 46-50, chief detonation div, 50-57, sr scientist explosives res dept, 57-75. *Mem:* Am Phys Soc; Am Chem Soc; Soc Motion Picture & TV Eng; Combustion Inst. *Res:* Deflagration of propellants and explosives; detonation of solid explosives; high pressure instrumentation; rapid expansion of gases; shock wave phenomena; electronic and photographic instrumentation; equation of fluid and solid states at high pressure. *Mailing Add:* 1208 Ruppert Rd Silver Spring MD 20903-1023

JACOBS, STANLEY J, GEOPHYSICS, FLUID MECHANICS. *Current Pos:* from asst prof to assoc prof, 64-74, PROF OCEANOG, UNIV MICH, ANN ARBOR, 74- *Personal Data:* b Milwaukee, Wis, Feb 11, 36; m 65; c 2. *Educ:* Northwestern Univ, BS, 59; Harvard Univ, AM, 60, PhD(appl math), 63. *Prof Exp:* Res fel atmospheric sci, Harvard Univ, 63-64. *Mem:* Am Meteorol Soc. *Res:* Geophysical fluid mechanics. *Mailing Add:* 1705 Hermitage Rd Ann Arbor MI 48104

JACOBS, STANLEY S, ANTARCTIC OCEANOGRAPHY. *Current Pos:* from grad res asst to sr res asst, Columbia Univ, 62-72, res staff assoc, 72-73, sr staff assoc phys oceanog, 74-94, RES SCIENTIST, LAMONT-DOHERTY GEOL OBSERV, COLUMBIA UNIV, 94- *Personal Data:* b Rochester, NH, Apr 19, 40; m 79; c 2. *Educ:* Mass Inst Technol, BS, 62. *Prof Exp:* Res asst marine geophysics, Woods Hole Oceanog Inst, 61-62. *Concurrent Pos:* Chief scientist oceanog res, NSF, Columbia Univ & US Coast Guard ships, 64-84; mem, Comt Polar Res & Panel Antarctic Oceanog, Nat Acad Sci-Nat Res Coun, 71 & 84; prin investr, NSF, NASA, Nat Oceanic & Atmospheric Admin & Dept Energy, 74- *Mem:* Am Geophys Union. *Res:* Interactions between southern oceans and the Antarctic ice shelves; analyses of satellite sea ice observations; icebergs, mass balance of polar ice sheets, sea level rise. *Mailing Add:* Lamont-Doherty Earth Observ Columbia Univ Palisades NY 10964. *Fax:* 914-365-8157; *E-Mail:* sjacobs@lamont-columbia.edu

JACOBS, STEPHEN FRANK, OPTICS. *Current Pos:* EMER PROF OPTICAL SCI, UNIV ARIZ, 65- *Personal Data:* b New York, NY, Oct 1, 28; m 63, Kathleen Mitchell; c Henry, Tom & Jane. *Educ:* Antioch Col, BS, 51; Johns Hopkins Univ, PhD(physics), 56. *Prof Exp:* Engr, Perkin-Elmer Corp, 56-60; sr physicist, TRG, Inc, 60-65. *Mem:* Optical Soc Am; Am Phys Soc. *Res:* Dimensional stability of materials. *Mailing Add:* Optical Sci Univ Ariz Tucson AZ 85721. *Fax:* 520-621-4558; *E-Mail:* stephen.jacobs@Opt_sci.arizona.edu

JACOBS, THEODORE ALAN, CHEMICAL PHYSICS. *Current Pos:* RETIRED. *Personal Data:* b Atlanta, Ga, Oct 19, 27; m 61; c 1. *Educ:* Emory Univ, AB, 50; Univ Southern Calif, MSME, 54; Calif Inst Tech, PhD(chem physics), 60. *Prof Exp:* Designer, Douglas Aircraft Co, 51-52; res engr, G O Noville & Assocs, 53-55; res assoc & lectr mech eng, Univ Southern Calif, 55-57; sr res engr eng sci, Rocketdyne Div, NAm Aviation, Inc, 57-58; sr res fel, Calif Inst Tech, 60-61; head chem kinetics sect, Aerospace Corp, 61-67, head aerophys dept, 67-71; sr scientist & dir high energy laser technol, TRW, Inc, 71-76; supt, Optical Sci Div, Naval Res Lab, 76-78, dep asst secy navy, res eng & systs, 78-85. *Concurrent Pos:* Consult, Gen Appl Sci Labs, 58-60, Plasmadyne Corp, 60-61 & Vickers Div, Sperry Rand Corp, 61-62; pvt consult, 85- *Mem:* Fel Am Phys Soc; fel Optical Soc Am; Am Chem Soc; Am Defense Preparedness Asn; Sigma Xi. *Res:* High temperature chemical kinetics; chemical lasers; high energy lasers. *Mailing Add:* 4915 Loosestrife Ct Annandale VA 22003

JACOBS, THOMAS LLOYD, organic chemistry, polymer chemistry; deceased, see previous edition for last biography

JACOBS, VERNE LOUIS, ATOMIC PHYSICS. *Current Pos:* res physicist, Plasma Physics Div, 77-85, res physicist, E O Hulburt Ctr Space Res, 85-88, RES PHYSICIST, CONDENSED MATTER & RADIATION SCI DIV, NAVAL RES LAB, 88- *Personal Data:* b Los Angeles, Calif, Aug 30, 41; m 69, Abigail Conway; c Naomi S & Aviva R. *Educ:* Mass Inst Technol, BS, 64; Univ Calif, Berkeley, PhD(physics), 68. *Prof Exp:* Res fel appl math, Weizmann Inst Sci, 68-71; res fel atomic physics, Queen's Univ, Belfast, 71-72; Nat Res Coun assoc space physics, Goddard Space Flight Ctr, NASA, 72-74; scientist plasma physics, Sci Applns, Inc, 74-77. *Mem:* Fel Am Phys Soc. *Res:* Atomic radiation processes in plasmas. *Mailing Add:* Condensed Matter & Radiation Sci Div Naval Res Lab Washington DC 20375

JACOBS, VIRGIL LEON, neuroscience; deceased, see previous edition for last biography

JACOBS, WILLIAM DONALD, ANALYTICAL CHEMISTRY. *Current Pos:* assoc prof & chmn dept, 68-78, PROF CHEM, STILLMAN COL, 78-, CHMN, DIV MATH & SCI, 81- *Personal Data:* b Birmingham, Ala, Apr 18, 28; m 63; c 3. *Educ:* Col Charleston, BS, 51; Clemson Col, MS, 54; Univ Va, PhD(chem), 58. *Prof Exp:* Instr chem, Clemson Col, 52-54; instr chem, Gordon Mil Col, 54-55 & Univ Va, 57-58; asst prof, Univ Ga, 58-65; assoc prof, WGa Col, 65-68. *Mem:* Am Chem Soc. *Res:* Spectrophotometric trace analysis; analytical chemistry of the platinum group elements. *Mailing Add:* 3033 Pine Haven Dr Gainesville GA 30506-4230

JACOBS, WILLIAM PAUL, PLANT DEVELOPMENT. *Current Pos:* mem fac, 48-89, EMER PROF BIOL, PRINCETON UNIV, 89- *Personal Data:* b Boston, Mass, May 25, 19; m 49; c 2. *Educ:* Harvard Univ, AB, 42, MA, 45, PhD(biol), 46. *Honors & Awards:* Morrison Award, NY Acad Sci, 51; Dimond Prize, Bot Soc Am, 75. *Prof Exp:* Fel histogenesis in vascular plants, Harvard Univ, 46-47, mem, Soc Fels, 47-48. *Concurrent Pos:* Sheldon traveling fel, 45-46; Lalor fel, 50-51; sr fel, NSF, 56-57, sci fac fel, 62; vis prof, Univ Calif, Berkeley, 52, Zool Sta, Napoli, 57, Univ Oxford, 62, Univ Lausanne, 67, Univ Colo, 72, Univ Bristol, 80; mem adv panel, develop biol, NSF, 56, plant biol in space, NASA, 76-78 & US-Soviet space flights, 78; mem comt innovation in lab instr, Biol Sci Curriculum Study, Am Inst Biol Sci, 59-64; Guggenheim fel, 67. *Mem:* Soc Develop Biol (secy, 58-60, pres, 60-61); Am Soc Plant Physiol; Bot Soc Am; Int Soc Plant Morphologists; Int

Plant Growth Substances Asn; Int Phycol Soc. *Res:* Internal factors controlling cell and organ differentiation and longevity; hormone transport and polarity; gravitational effects on giant coenocytes. *Mailing Add:* Dept Biol Princeton Univ Washington Rd Princeton NJ 08544

JACOBS, WILLIAM WESCOTT, INTERMEDIATE ENERGY NUCLEAR PHYSICS. *Current Pos:* res assoc, 76-79, ASSOC RES SCIENTIST INTERMEDIATE ENERGY NUCLEAR PHYSICS, CYCLOTRON FACIL, IND UNIV, 79- *Personal Data:* b Madison, Wis, Sept 8, 43; m 77; c 2. *Educ:* Reed Col, Portland, BA, 65; Univ Wash, MS, 67, PhD(physics), 74. *Prof Exp:* Res assoc nuclear & atomic physics, Univ NC, Chapel Hill, 74-76. *Mem:* Am Phys Soc; AAAS; Am Fedn Scientists. *Res:* Intermediate-energy nuclear physics; polarization effects in nuclear reactions and scattering; nuclear astrophysics; heavy-ion x-ray production; tests of fundamental symmetries. *Mailing Add:* NSCL Ind Univ Bloomington IN 47405

JACOBS, WILLIAM WOOD, JR, ANIMAL BEHAVIOR, ETHOLOGY. *Current Pos:* BIOLOGIST RODENTICIDES, US ENVIRON PROTECTION AGENCY, 78- *Personal Data:* b Harrisburg, Pa, May 23, 47; m 69; c 3. *Educ:* Pa State Univ, BS, 69; Univ Chicago, MS, 71, PhD(biopsychol), 73. *Prof Exp:* Biologist rodenticides, US Environ Protection Agency, 74-75; fel olfaction & taste, Monell Chem Senses Ctr, 75-78. *Concurrent Pos:* Fel, US Nat Inst Neurol Dis & Stroke, 75-78. *Res:* Investigations of taste, food selection, social and individual behavior of small mammals; use of containers in closed system transfer of pesticides; development of protective bait stations for rodenticides; vertebrate pesticides. *Mailing Add:* 7505C Regist Div US Environ Protection Agency Washington DC 20460

JACOBSEN, BARRY JAMES, plant pathology, administration, for more information see previous edition

JACOBSEN, CHRIS J, X-RAY OPTICS. *Current Pos:* researcher, 89-91, ASSOC PROF PHYSICS, STATE UNIV NY, STONY BROOK, 91- *Personal Data:* b Redwing, Minn, Oct 3, 60; m 82; c 2. *Educ:* St Olaf Col, BA, 83; State Univ NY, Stony Brook, PhD(physics), 88. *Prof Exp:* Postdoctoral physics, Ctr X-Ray Optics, Lawrence Berkeley Lab, 88-89. *Concurrent Pos:* Mem, Biophys Prog, State Univ NY, Stony Brook, 91- *Mem:* Optical Soc Am; Am Phys Soc. *Res:* X-ray microscopy using holography and zone plates; biological applications of x-ray microscopy; image processing; x-ray lithography; coherent x-ray sources. *Mailing Add:* Dept Physics State Univ NY-Stony Brook Stony Brook NY 11794-3800

JACOBSEN, DONALD WELDON, BIOCHEMISTRY, CHEMISTRY. *Current Pos:* PROF STAFF, CLEVELAND CLIN FOUND, 84- *Personal Data:* b Portland, Ore, Apr 26, 39; m 62, Margaret L Cunningham; c Mark W & Gregg T. *Educ:* Univ Pa, BA, 61; Ore State Univ, MS, 64, PhD(biochem, cell biol), 67. *Prof Exp:* NIH fel biochem, 67-71, assoc biochem, Scripps Clin & Res Found, 71-84. *Concurrent Pos:* Dernham fel, Am Cancer Soc, Calif, 72; mem, Ad Hoc Adv Comt Food Hypersensitivity, Food & Drug Admin, 85-87; dir, Biochem Core Lab, Cleveland Clin, 87-92; adj prof, Cleveland State Univ, 88-; chmn-elect, Cleveland Sect, Am Chem Soc, 91, chmn, 92. *Mem:* AAAS; Am Chem Soc; Biophys Soc; Am Soc Microbiol; Am Soc Biochem & Molecular Biol; Am Soc Hemat; Am Fedn Clin Res; Protein Soc. *Res:* Function of cobalamin-binding proteins; receptor-mediated transport of cobalamin-binding proteins; mechanisms of enzyme action, especially ribonucleotide reductase, methionine synthase and other vitamin B12-dependent enzymes; cobalamin and cobinamide chemistry; sulfur biochemistry of homocysteine as related to vascular disease; pathogenesis and prevention of sulfite hypersensitivity; homocysteine and cardiovascular disease, pathogenesis and prevention. *Mailing Add:* Cleveland Clin Found Dept Cell Biol FF4 9500 Euclid Ave Cleveland OH 44195-5139. *Fax:* 216-445-5480; *E-Mail:* jacobsd@ccsmtp.ccf.org

JACOBSEN, EDWARD HASTINGS, PHYSICS, ELECTRON OPTICS. *Current Pos:* PROF PHYSICS, UNIV ROCHESTER, 62- *Personal Data:* b Elizabeth, NJ, Jan 2, 26; wid. *Educ:* Mass Inst Technol, BS, 50, PhD(physics), 54. *Prof Exp:* Fulbright fel, Col France, 54-55; res physicist, Res Lab, Gen Elec Co, 55-61; Brit Dept Sci & Indust Res fel, Nottingham, 61. *Concurrent Pos:* Vis scientist, Molecular Biol Lab, Harvard Med Sch, 65; vis prof, Mass Inst Technol, 67-68, vis scientist, Res Lab Electronics, 70-72; NIH, career develop fel, Biol Dept, Columbia Univ, 79. *Mem:* Am Phys Soc; Sigma Xi. *Res:* Magnetic resonance; x-ray and neutron diffraction; microwave ultrasonics; statistical mechanics; semiconductors; plasma physics; biophysics; machine computation. *Mailing Add:* 770 Massachusetts Ave PO Box 391533 Cambridge MA 02139

JACOBSEN, ERIC N, CHEMISTRY. *Current Pos:* PROF CHEM, HARVARD UNIV. *Honors & Awards:* Arthur C Cope Award, Am Chem Soc, 94. *Mailing Add:* Dept Chem Harvard Univ Cambridge MA 02138

JACOBSEN, FRED MARIUS, COMPUTER SCIENCE, APPLIED STATISTICS. *Current Pos:* CONSULT, 83- *Personal Data:* b Brooklyn, NY, May 19, 25; m 49, Maude Battle; c Frederick. *Educ:* Polytech Inst Brooklyn, BChE, 44; Iowa State Univ, PhD(chem eng), 54. *Prof Exp:* Minor shift foreman, US Army, Carbide & Carbon Chem Corp, 45; staff mem phys chem, Los Alamos Sci Lab, 46-50; asst chem engr, Inst Atomic Res, 51-54; chem engr statist, Am Oil Co, 55-56; group leader comput, 57-60, tech comput supvr, 61-69; dir comput serv, Standard Oil Co, Ind, 70-73, res supvr comput, Amoco Corp, 74-83,. *Concurrent Pos:* Consult, 83- *Mem:* Fel AAAS; Asn Comput Mach; Am Inst Chem Engrs; Am Phys Soc; Inst Math Statist; Am Chem Soc. *Res:* Scientific computing; engineering statistics; applied mathematics; systems design. *Mailing Add:* 828 Hawthorn Dr Naperville IL 60540-7425

JACOBSEN, FREDERICK MARIUS, PSYCHOPHARMACOLOGY, BIOLOGICAL PSYCHIATRY. *Current Pos:* asst clin prof psychiat, 85-91, ASSOC CLIN PROF PSYCHIAT & BEH SCI, GEORGE WASHINGTON UNIV SCH MED, 91-; GUEST RESEARCHER, LAB CLIN SCI, NIMH, 88-; ASSOC CLIN PROF PSYCHIAT, GEORGETOWN UNIV SCH MED, 91- *Personal Data:* b Ames, Iowa, Jan 19, 54; m 83, Lillian Comas-Diaz. *Educ:* Cornell Univ, AB, 76; Univ Ill, MPH, 78, MD, 80; Am Bd Psychiat & Neurol, cert. 85. *Prof Exp:* Fel, Yale Univ Sch Med, 80-84, chief resident psychiat, 73-84; clin assoc, NIMH, 84-87, med officer, 87-88. *Concurrent Pos:* Med dir, Transcult Mental Health Inst, 86-; med adv, Depressive & Manic Depressive Asn, 87-; consult, VOCA Corp, 87- *Mem:* Soc Biol Sci; AAAS; Math Asn Am; Am Psychiat Asn; AMA; NY Acad Sci; Soc Biol Psychiat; Am Sleep Dis Asn; Am Soc Clin Psychopharmacol. *Res:* Biological psychiatry; physiological bases of depression and manic-depressive illness; neuropsychiatric diagnosis; public health; manifestations of illness from a cultural perspective; psychopharmacology of mood and sleep disorders. *Mailing Add:* 1301 20th St NW Suite 711 Washington DC 20036. *Fax:* 202-659-9303

JACOBSEN, JEFFREY SCOTT, AGRONOMY. *Honors & Awards:* Ciba-Geigy Agron, Am Soc Agron, 94. *Mailing Add:* Plant Soil & Environ Sci Dept Mont State Univ Bozeman MT 59717

JACOBSEN, NADINE KLECHA, PHYSIOLOGICAL ECOLOGY. *Current Pos:* ASSOC PROF WILDLIFE BIOL, UNIV CALIF, DAVIS, 74- *Personal Data:* b Milwaukee, Wis, Dec 13, 41; m 67. *Educ:* Drake Univ, BA, 64; Ore State Univ, MS, 66; Cornell Univ, PhD(wildlife ecol), 73. *Prof Exp:* Instr biol, Blue Mountain Community Col, 66-67; res assoc, Dept Radiation Biol, Cornell Univ, 68-69, fel, Dept Natural Resources, 73-74. *Mem:* Sigma Xi; Am Soc Mammal; Wildlife Soc; Am Soc Animal Scientists; Ecol Soc Am. *Res:* Ecological energetics of wildlife, particularly deer, over the annual cycle and between birth and weaning of young; how energy and nutrient metabolism are affected by environmental, behavioral and physiological states. *Mailing Add:* Wildlife Fish & Conserv Biol Univ Calif Davis CA 95616

JACOBSEN, NEIL SOREN, ACADEMIC ADMINISTRATION. *Current Pos:* RETIRED. *Personal Data:* b Waterloo, Iowa, June 13, 30; m 54, Ruth A Stewart; c Teresa, Dennis & Linda. *Educ:* Univ Iowa, BA, 52; Univ Denver, MS, 56; Okla State Univ, PhD(physiol), 65. *Prof Exp:* Teacher high schs, Calif, 57-62; NIH fel, Univ Mass, 64-66; asst prof, NDak State Univ, 66-71, dir student acad affairs, 69-72, actg vpres acad affairs, 79-80, assoc prof zool, 71-86, dean univ studies, 72-86, assoc vpres acad affairs, 81-86. *Res:* Lipid metabolism of intestinal parasites; effect of pesticides on the cardiovascular system. *Mailing Add:* 5283 A Beach Dr SE St Petersburg FL 33705

JACOBSEN, RICHARD T, MECHANICAL ENGINEERING, THERMODYNAMICS. *Current Pos:* From instr to prof eng, Univ Idaho, 64-80, assoc dir, Ctr Appl Thermodyn Studies, prof mech eng & chmn dept, 80-85, assoc dean eng, 85-90, DIR, CTR APPL THERMODYN STUDIES, UNIV IDAHO, 86-, DEAN ENG, 90- *Personal Data:* b Pocatello, Idaho, Nov 12, 41; m 73, Bonnie L Stewart; c Richard T, Eric E, Jay M, Erik D Lustig & Pamela S (Moats). *Educ:* Univ Idaho, BS, 63, MS, 65; Wash State Univ, PhD(eng sci), 72. *Concurrent Pos:* Mem correlating functions working panel, Int Union Pure & Appl Chem, 73-86; guest worker, Thermophysics Div, Nat Bur Stand, 79 & 86. *Mem:* Sigma Xi; fel Am Soc Mech Engrs; Soc Automotive Engrs; Am Soc Heating Refrig & Air Conditioning Engrs; Nat Soc Prof Engrs; Am Soc Eng Educ. *Res:* Thermodynamics; thermodynamic properties of fluids and fluid mixtures; thermodynamic system analysis; development of computer programs, tables and charts for engineering applications including envirnmentally-safe alternative refrigerants. *Mailing Add:* 1224 Tamarack St Moscow ID 83843-9438. *Fax:* 208-885-6448; *E-Mail:* deaneng@iduil.csrv.uidaho.edu

JACOBSEN, STEIN BJORNAR, GEOCHEMISTRY. *Current Pos:* asst prof, 81-83, assoc prof, 84-, PROF GEOCHEM, HARVARD UNIV. *Personal Data:* b Baerum, Norway, Feb 12, 50. *Educ:* Univ Oslo, Norway, BS, 75, MS, 75; Calif Inst Technol, PhD(geochem), 80. *Prof Exp:* Fel geochem, Calif Inst Technol, 80-81. *Mem:* Am Geophys Union; Geol Soc Am; Am Chem Soc; Meteoritical Soc. *Res:* Neodymium, strontium and lead isotope studies of mantle structure and differentiation, crustal evolution and chronology; petrological and geochemical studies of granulite and eclogite facies rocks, ophiolites, orogenic peridotites and chondritic meteorites. *Mailing Add:* Dept Earth & Planetary Sci Harvard Univ 20 Oxford St Cambridge MA 02138. *Fax:* 617-496-0434; *E-Mail:* jacobsen@neodymium.harvard.edu

JACOBSEN, STEPHEN C, ENGINEERING. *Current Pos:* PROF, DEPT MECH ENG, UNIV UTAH, 73-, RES PROF, DEPT BIOENG, 73- & DEPT SURG, 73-, DIR, CTR ENG DESIGN, 73-; CHMN & CHIEF EXEC OFFICER, SARCOS INC, 83- *Educ:* Univ Utah, BS, 67, MS, 70; Mass Inst Technol, PhD(mech eng), 73. *Honors & Awards:* Lawrence Poole Prize Fac Med, Univ Edinburgh, Scotland, 82; Becton Dickinson Award, Asn Advan Med Instrumentation, 85; Leonardo da Vinci Design Award, Am Soc Mech Eng, 87. *Concurrent Pos:* Adj prof, Dept Comput Sci, Univ Utah, 73-; mem, bd dir, IOMED Inc, 73-; chmn bd dir, Sarcos Orgn, 83- *Mem:* Nat Acad Eng; Inst Med-Nat Acad Sci; Am Inst Med & Biol Eng. *Mailing Add:* 3176 Merrill Eng Bldg Univ Utah Salt Lake City UT 84112

JACOBSEN, TERRY DALE, PLANT SYSTEMATICS. *Current Pos:* asst to dir & res scientist, 79-81, asst dir & sr res scientist, Hunt Inst Bot Doc, 81-93, PRIN RES SCIENTIST, CARNEGIE MELLON UNIV, 93- *Personal Data:* b Nampa, Idaho, Aug 17, 50; m 79. *Educ:* Col Idaho, BS, 73; Wash State Univ, MS, 75, PhD(bot), 78. *Prof Exp:* Lectr, Biol Prog, Wash State Univ, 77-78, instr bot, 78-79. *Concurrent Pos:* Adj res scientist, Carnegie Mus Natural Hist, 79-; ed, Bull Hunt Inst Bot Doc, 81-; adj assoc prof biol, Carnegie-Mellon Univ, 84-93, prof biol, 93-. *Res:* Cytotaxonomy, anatomy and numerical analysis of the genus Allium L in North America. *Mailing Add:* Hunt Inst Bot Doc Carnegie-Mellon Univ 5000 Forbes Ave Pittsburgh PA 15213

JACOBS-LORENA, MARCELO, MOLECULAR BIOLOGY, EMBRYOLOGY. *Current Pos:* asst prof, 77-83, ASSOC PROF DEVELOP GENETICS, CASE WESTERN RESERVE UNIV, 83- *Personal Data:* b Sao Paulo, Brazil, May 5, 42; m 70; c 1. *Educ:* Sao Paulo Univ, BS, 64; Osaka Univ, MS, 67; Mass Inst Technol, PhD(biol), 72. *Prof Exp:* Fel biol, Univ Geneva, 72-77. *Concurrent Pos:* Fel, Europ Molecular Biol Orgn, 72-74; asst prof, Am Cancer Soc Inst grant, 77-78, NIH, 78-83, 85-90 & NSF, 83-86. *Mem:* Soc Develop Biol; Soc Cell Biol. *Res:* Drosophilia oogenesis and embryogenesis, Drosophila development and control of gene expression. *Mailing Add:* Dept Genetics Case Western Reserve Univ 10900 Euclid Ave Cleveland OH 44106-4955

JACOBSOHN, GERT MAX, BIOCHEMISTRY. *Current Pos:* from asst prof to assoc prof, 62-77, PROF BIOL CHEM, ALLEGHENY UNIV, 77- *Personal Data:* b Berlin, Ger, Aug 1, 29; nat US; m 59, Myra Kramer; c Hannah G, Jamie A, Diane R & Alyse P. *Educ:* Ill Col, AB, 52; Purdue Univ, MS, 55, PhD(biochem), 57. *Prof Exp:* Fel, Col Physicians & Surgeons, Columbia Univ, 57-60; asst mem endocrinol, Albert Einstein Med Ctr, 60-61. *Concurrent Pos:* Coun mem, Pan Am Soc Pigment Cell Res. *Mem:* AAAS; fel Am Cancer Soc; Endocrine Soc; Am Soc Biochem & Molecular Biol. *Res:* Metabolic control of blood enzymes; membrane transfer phenomena; steroid interconversion and function in plants; regulation of steroid, methods of steroid assay and instrumentation; metabolism of catechol estrogens; melanin formation; tyrosinase. *Mailing Add:* Dept Biochem Allegheny Univ Philadelphia PA 19102. *E-Mail:* jacobsohng@allegheny.edu

JACOBSOHN, MYRA K, MEMBRANE BIOCHEMISTRY, BIOCHEMISTRY OF MELANIN. *Current Pos:* lectr, 74-76, from asst prof to assoc prof, 76-90, RES ASSOC, ALLEGHENY UNIV, 85-; PROF BIOL, BEAVER COL, 90- *Personal Data:* b New York, NY, Feb 13, 39; c 4. *Educ:* Columbia Univ, BA, 60; Univ Pa, MS, 62; Bryn Mawr Col, PhD(biol), 75. *Honors & Awards:* Lindback Award, 82. *Prof Exp:* Res assoc, Hahnemann Med Col, 71-74, fel biochem, 74-76. *Mem:* AAAS; Pan-Am Soc Pigment Cell Res; Am Soc Biochem & Molecular Biol. *Res:* Enzymes; membrane structure; melanin synthesis; lipid-enzyme interactions. *Mailing Add:* Dept Biol Beaver Col Glenside PA 19038. *Fax:* 215-572-0240

JACOBSON, ABRAM ROBERT, PHYSICS. *Current Pos:* staff mem, 53, assoc, 55, PARTNER, MUESER RUTLEDGE CONSULT ENGRS, 73- *Honors & Awards:* Kapp Mem Lect, Am Soc Civil Engrs, 74 & 82; Crom Lectr, Univ Fla, 78; Haley Mem Lect, Soc Civil Engrs, 85. *Prof Exp:* US Army Corps Engrs, 44-45; eng asst, Harvard Univ, 48-49; staff mem, Earth Dams Sect, US Bur Reclamation, 50-53. *Concurrent Pos:* In charge geotech studies, Reconstruct E Front, US Capitol Bldg, 55-60, US Navy Dry Dock 6, 56-60, landslide study, Pac Palisades, Los Angeles, 58-60, underpinning, House Rep Wing, 62-64, NY Waterfront Redevelop, 65-68 & Wash Metro Subway, 66-, Interceptor Sewer, Charleston, SC, 66-70, Nat Gallery Art Add, 70-72, Terminals Develop, Port Corp, 70-74, Battery Park City Develop, NY, 70-76, Locks C&E, Tenn & Tombigbee, 72-78, Dry Dock 4, 79-81, Nuclear Plant, Power Block Underpinning, Midland, Mich, 80-84, S Quadrangle Develop, Smithsonian Inst, 84-86, Little River Dam, Durham, NC, 82-88, Baldwin Bridge Replacement, 86-89, Schoharie Creek Bridge Failure Study, 87, US Navy Homefort Pier, Staten Island, 86-88, Conrail Tunnel Rehab, WPt, 85-88, Park Ave Tunnel Rehab, & NY Rock Slope Stabil, Westchester County, 88. *Mem:* Am Soc Civil Engrs. *Res:* Author of 30 publications. *Mailing Add:* MS D466 LANL PO Box 1663 Los Alamos NM 87545

JACOBSON, ADA LEAH, PHYSICAL CHEMISTRY, BIOCHEMISTRY. *Current Pos:* from instr to assoc prof chem, 60-86, ASSOC PROF BIOCHEM, UNIV CALGARY, 86- *Personal Data:* b Boston, Mass, Oct 8, 33; m 58. *Educ:* Mass Inst Technol, BS, 54; Yale Univ, PhD(chem), 57. *Prof Exp:* Chemist, Shell Develop Co, Calif, 57-58; instr phys chem, Albertus Magnus Col, 58-59; instr biochem, Dartmouth Med Sch, 59-60. *Concurrent Pos:* Fel phys org chem, Yale Univ, 58-59; sr fel, Can Heart Found, 65- *Mem:* Am Chem Soc; Can Biochem Soc; Sigma Xi; Biophys Soc. *Res:* Physical chemistry of proteins, solutions and polymers. *Mailing Add:* 312 Superior Ave SW Calgary AB T3C 2J2 Can

JACOBSON, ALBERT H(ERMAN), JR, INDUSTRIAL ENGINEERING, SYSTEMS ENGINEERING. *Current Pos:* prof eng, 62-69, COFOUNDER & COORDR CYBERNETIC SYSTS GRAD PROG, SAN JOSE STATE UNIV, 67-, PROF INDUST & SYSTS ENG, 69- *Personal Data:* b St Paul, Minn, Oct 27, 17; m 60, Elaine Swanson; c Keith & Paul. *Educ:* Yale Univ, BS, 39; Mass Inst Technol, SM, 52; Univ Rochester, MS, 54; Stanford Univ, PhD(mgt eng), 76. *Prof Exp:* Personnel asst, Yale Univ, 39-40; indust engr, Radio Corp Am, NJ, 40-43; chief engr & dir qual control, Bur Ord, Navy Ord Div, Eastman Kodak Co, 46-57, from staff engr to mgr field opers, Space Satellite Prog, Apparatus Div, 57-59; assoc dean, Col Eng & Archit, Pa State Univ, 59-61; pres & gen mgr, Knapic Electro-Physics Co, Calif, 61-62. *Concurrent Pos:* Alfred P Sloan fel, Mass Inst Technol, 51-52; consult numerous indust firms, 63-; NSF sci fac fel, Stanford Univ, 65-66. *Mem:* AAAS; Am Soc Eng Educ; Am Inst Indust Engrs; Am Prod & Inventory Control Soc; Sigma Xi. *Res:* Infrared; guided missiles; satellites; engineering management; management development; cybernetic systems; transportation systems; information systems. *Mailing Add:* 1864 Lime Trees Lane Mountain View CA 94040

JACOBSON, ALEXANDER DONALD, ARTIFICIAL INTELLIGENCE TECHNOLOGY, ELECTRICAL ENGINEERING. *Current Pos:* PRES & CHIEF EXEC OFFICER, TRIVIDA, 96- *Personal Data:* b New York, NY, Dec 1, 33; m 71, Rebecca M Davies; c Juliet A & David C. *Educ:* Univ Calif, Los Angeles, BS, 55, MS, 58; Calif Inst Technol, PhD(electro-magnetic theory), 64. *Honors & Awards:* Rank Prize, 86. *Prof Exp:* Mem tech staff optics res, Hughes Res Labs Div, Hughes Aircraft Co, 55-68, head, Unconventional Imaging Sect, 68- 72, assoc mgr, Explor Studies Dept, 72-76, prog mgr liquid crystal displays progs, Indust Prod Div, 76-77; consult, 77-79; co-founder, chmn & chief exec officer, Inference Corp, 79-95; pres & chief exec officer, Limbex Corp, 95-96. *Res:* Laser technology; electromagnetic theory; x-ray diffraction studies of crystals; display technology; computer systems; telecommunications; artificial intelligence computer software products; applications of artificial intelligence technology to the development of expert systems for industrial, commercial and military applications; development of computer software products that contain artificial intelligence technology for such purposes; electro-optic device technology. *Mailing Add:* Trivida 3524 Hayden Ave Culver City CA 90232

JACOBSON, ALLAN JOSEPH, INTERCALATION CHEMISTRY, SOLID STATE CHEMISTRY. *Current Pos:* RETIRED. *Personal Data:* b Newcastle, Eng, May 28, 44; m 68; c 1. *Educ:* Oxford Univ, BA, 65, MA, 69, DPhil, 69. *Prof Exp:* Lectr chem, Oxford Univ, 70-76; sr staff chemist, Exxon Res & Eng Co, Exxon Corp, 76-80, res assoc, 80-91. *Mem:* Chem Soc; Am Chem Soc; Electrochem Soc; Mat Res Soc. *Res:* Synthetic and structural solid state inorganic chemistry; neutron x-ray and electron diffraction; intercalation chemistry. *Mailing Add:* Univ Houston Houston TX 77204-5641

JACOBSON, ALLAN STANLEY (BUD), COMPUTER GRAPHICS, GAMMA RAY ASTRONOMY. *Current Pos:* mem tech staff, Jet Propulsion Lab, 69-73, tech group supvr, 73-86, asst sect mgr sci visualization & comput graphics, 88-90, SR RES SCIENTIST, JET PROPULSION LAB, 81- *Personal Data:* b Chattanooga, Tenn, June 18, 32; m 86. *Educ:* Univ Calif Los Angeles, AB, 62; Univ Calif San Diego, MS, 64 & PhD(physics), 68. *Honors & Awards:* Bruno Rossi Prize, Am Astron Soc, 86. *Prof Exp:* Res asst, Univ Calif San Diego, 62-68, asst res physicist, 68-69. *Concurrent Pos:* Prin investr, NASA, 70-; guest lectr, Calif Inst Technol, 80-82; consult, Ashton-Tate, 85-89; mem, Comput Soc, Inst Elec & Electronic Engrs. *Mem:* Fel Am Phys Soc; Am Astron Soc; Asn Comput Mach; Inst Elec & Electronics Engrs; Inst Elec & Electronics Engrs Computer Sci. *Res:* Gamma-ray astronomy; computer-aided science visualization; visual science data analysis. *Mailing Add:* Jet Propulsion Lab 4800 Oak Grove Dr 183-501 Pasadena CA 91109. *Fax:* 818-354-0966; *E-Mail:* budj@apex.jpl.nasa.gov

JACOBSON, ALLEN F, MANUFACTURING ADMINISTRATION. *Current Pos:* RETIRED. *Personal Data:* b Omaha, Nebr, Oct 7, 26. *Educ:* Iowa State Univ, Ames, BS, 47. *Honors & Awards:* Mgr Of The Yr, AMA, 94. *Prof Exp:* Prod engr, Tape Lab, 3M, 47-50, tech asst to plant mgr, Hutchinson, 50-53, Bristol, 53-55, tape prod supt, Bristol, 55- 59, plant mgr, St Paul Tape Prod, 59-61, combined Tape & AC&S Opers, Bristol, 61-63, tape prod mgr, Tape & Allied Prod Group, 63, mfg mgr, 63-68, gen mgr, Indust Tape Div, 68-70, div vpres, 70-72, exec vpres & gen mgr, 3M Can Ltd, 73-75, vpres, Europ Opers, 75, Tape & Allied Prod Group, 75-81, exec vpres, Indust & Consumer Sector, 75-84, pres, US Opers, 84-86, chmn bd & chief exec officer, 86-91, emer chmn bd & emer chief exec officer, 91. *Concurrent Pos:* Dir, Mobil Corp, NY, Northern States Power Co, Minneapolis, Minn, US West, Inc, Englewood, Colo, Valmont Industs, Inc, Valley, Nebr, Potlatch Corp, San Francisco, Calif, Sara Lee Corp, Chicago, Ill, Minn Bus Partnership, Minneapolis; mem bd dirs, Am Qual Found, Chamber Com US & Nat Legal Ctr Pub Interest; chmn, US Coun Int Bus, Emergency Comt Am Trade; mem, Bus Can, Washington, DC, Bus Roundtable, US-USSR Trade & Econ Coun, Inc & Bus Coun Sustainable Develop. *Mem:* Nat Acad Eng; hon mem Soc Mfg Engrs. *Mailing Add:* 3050 Minneapolis World Trade Ctr 30 E Seventh St St Paul MN 55101-4901. *Fax:* 612-223-5107

JACOBSON, ANN BEATRICE, MOLECULAR BIOLOGY. *Current Pos:* lectr, 76-80, res asst prof, 80-86, RES ASSOC PROF, DEPT MICROBIOL, STATE UNIV NY, STONY BROOK, 86- *Personal Data:* b New York, NY, July 24, 38. *Educ:* Univ Chicago, BS, 58, PhD(bot), 62; Purdue Univ, MS, 61. *Prof Exp:* Res assoc plant biochem, Univ Chicago, 63-67; biologist, Biol Div, Oak Ridge Nat Lab, 67-71; vis scientist, Max Planck Inst Biochem, Munich, 71-75; Europ Molecular Biol Orgn Fel, Dept Molecular Biol, Univ Geneva, Switz, 75-76. *Mem:* AAAS; Am Soc Biochem & Molecular Biol. *Res:* RNA folding, computer modeling and electron microscopy. *Mailing Add:* Dept Microbiol State Univ NY Stony Brook NY 11794-5222. *Fax:* 516-632-8891; *E-Mail:* jacobson@abj.b10.sunsb.edu

JACOBSON, ANTONE GARDNER, DEVELOPMENTAL BIOLOGY. *Current Pos:* From instr to assoc prof, 57-68, PROF ZOOL, UNIV TEX, AUSTIN, 68- *Personal Data:* b Salt Lake City, Utah, May 22, 29; m 63, Jacqueline James; c Lauren & Eric. *Educ:* Harvard Univ, AB, 51; Stanford Univ, PhD(exp embryol, biol), 55. *Mem:* Am Asn Anatomists; Am Soc Zool; Soc Develop Biol; Int Soc Develop Biol. *Res:* Embryonic induction, morphogenesis and development of the nervous system in embryos; segmentation of the mesoderm; pattern formation. *Mailing Add:* Dept Zool Univ Tex Austin TX 78712-1064. *Fax:* 512-471-9651; *E-Mail:* antone@mail.utexas.edu

JACOBSON, ARNOLD P, RADIATION BIOLOGY. *Current Pos:* Asst prof environ health, 65-79, assoc prof, 71-79, PROF ENVIRON & INDUST HEALTH, SCH PUB HEALTH, UNIV MICH, ANN ARBOR, 79- *Personal Data:* b Rawlins, Wyo, July 21, 32; m 65. *Educ:* Univ Wyo, BS, 58, MS, 60; Univ Mich, MPH, 62, PhD(radiation biol), 66. *Honors & Awards:* Marie Curie Gold Medal Award, Health Physics Soc. *Concurrent Pos:* Assoc res scientist, Inst Environ & Indust Health, 74-80. *Mem:* Am Radon Asn; Health Physics Soc. *Res:* Indoor radon risk, mitigation and measurement; low dose effects of radiations. *Mailing Add:* 7 Redwing Lane Carbondale CO 81623

JACOBSON, ARTHUR E, MEDICINAL CHEMISTRY. *Current Pos:* RES CHEMIST, NAT INST ARTHRITIS, METAB & DIGESTIVE DIS, NIH, 62-, DEP CHIEF, NAT INST DIABETES & DIGESTIVE & KIDNEY DIS, 91- *Personal Data:* b New York, NY, May 2, 28; m 64, Linda Perry; c Jay & Laura. *Educ:* Fordham Univ, BS, 49; Rutgers Univ, MS(pharm chem), 52, MS(chem), 54, PhD(org & phys chem), 60. *Honors & Awards:* J Michael Morrison Award, 90. *Prof Exp:* Nat Insts Health, US Pub Health Serv fel & org chemist, Albert Einstein Col Med, 59-62. *Concurrent Pos:* Instr spectros, Found Adv Ed in Sci, Inc, 64-88 mem, Comt Probs Drug Dependence, 74-81; mem, Col Probs Drug Dependence, 74-81, chmn, drug testing prog, 77-90; adj prof pharmacol & toxicol, Med Col Va, Va Commonwealth Univ, 84-93; biol coordr, Drug Eval Comt, 91- *Mem:* AAAS; Am Chem Soc. *Res:* Synthesis of alkaloids and heterocycles; computer-assisted molecular modelling; spectroscopy; synthesis of affinity ligands for and characterization of, opioid and phencyclidine receptors. *Mailing Add:* Nat Inst Diabetes & Digestive & Kidney Dis Bldg 8 Rm B1-22 Bethesda MD 20892. *E-Mail:* aej@helix.mih.gov

JACOBSON, BARUCH S, BIOPHYSICS. *Current Pos:* RETIRED. *Personal Data:* b New York, NY, Nov 23, 25; m 51; c 4. *Educ:* Columbia Univ, AB, 51; Univ Calif, PhD(biophys), 56. *Prof Exp:* NSF fel, Donner Lab, Univ Calif, 56-58, biophysicist, 58; from instr to asst prof zool, Univ Tex, 58-61; asst prof radiol, Univ Minn, Minneapolis, 61-68; assoc prof physics, Cent Mich Univ, 68-87. *Concurrent Pos:* Vis res prof, Inst Ecol, Univ Calif, Davis, 75; res fel, Battelle Pac Northwest Labs, Richland, Wash, 82-83; fac res fels, Battelle Pac Northwest Labs, Richland, Wash, 85, 86 & 87. *Mem:* AAAS; Biophys Soc; Radiation Res Soc; Sigma Xi. *Res:* Cellular radiobiology; effects of ionizing radiation on cell reproduction; metabolic reversal of radiation damage; ultraviolet photobiology; environmental systems analysis. *Mailing Add:* Dept Pharm Washington State Univ 100 Sprout Rd Richmond WA 99352

JACOBSON, BERNARD, MATHEMATICS. *Current Pos:* assoc prof, 63-69, PROF MATH, FRANKLIN & MARSHALL COL, 69- *Personal Data:* b Cleveland, Ohio, Apr 7, 28; m 56; c 2. *Educ:* Western Reserve Univ, BS, 51; Mich State Univ, MS, 52, PhD(math), 56. *Prof Exp:* From asst prof to assoc prof math, Franklin & Marshall Col, 56-61; assoc dir comt on undergrad prog in math, Math Asn Am, 62-63. *Mem:* Am Math Soc; Math Asn Am. *Res:* Number theory. *Mailing Add:* Franklin & Marshall Col PO Box 3003 Lancaster PA 17604-3003

JACOBSON, BERTIL, HUMAN IMPRINTING. *Current Pos:* RETIRED. *Personal Data:* b Stockholm, Sweden, Jan 21, 23; div; c Cecilia & Magnus. *Educ:* Karolinska Inst, MD, 50. *Prof Exp:* Asst prof med electronics, Karolinska Inst, 57-60, prof med eng, 60-89. *Res:* Human imprinting; perinatal origin of self-destructive adult behavior. *Mailing Add:* Vastra Myrskaren 41 S-74691 Balsta Sweden. *Fax:* 46-171-51212

JACOBSON, BRUCE SHELL, BIOLOGICAL CHEMISTRY. *Current Pos:* PROF BIOCHEM, UNIV MASS, AMHERST, 86- *Personal Data:* b Los Angeles, Calif, Jan 11, 40. *Educ:* Calif State Col, Los Angeles, BA, 62, MA, 64; Univ Calif, Los Angeles, PhD(plant biochem), 70. *Prof Exp:* Res biologist, Univ Calif, Riverside, 70-71; res biochemist, Univ Calif, Davis, 71-73; res assoc, Harvard Univ, 73-77; from asst prof to assoc prof biochem, 77-86. *Concurrent Pos:* Estab investr, Am Heart Asn; NIH predoctoral fel, Univ Calif, Los Angeles; NIH postdoctoral fel, Harvard Univ; fel Maria Moor Cabot, Harvard Univ. *Mem:* Am Soc Biol Chem; Am Soc Cell Biologists. *Res:* Molecular and cellular biology of biological membranes; interaction of plasma membrane receptors with the extracellular matrix and the cytoskeleton; transcellular polarity of the plasma membrane in vascular endothelial cells; protein targeting the apical and basolateral plasma membrane domains during endo-lexocytosis, transcytosis, membrane protein synthesis and cell movement. *Mailing Add:* Dept Biochem & Molecular Biol Univ Mass Amherst MA 01003

JACOBSON, ELAINE LOUISE, BIOCHEMISTRY & NUTRITION. *Current Pos:* PROF, DEPT CLIN SCI & MARKEY CANCER CTR, UNIV KY, 92- *Personal Data:* b Miller, Kans, Mar 29, 45; m 67. *Educ:* Kans State Univ, BS, 67, PhD(biochem), 71. *Prof Exp:* Res fel biochem, Mayo Clin, Found & Grad Sch Med, 72-73; res assoc biochem, Dept Chem, NTex State Univ, 74-77; asst prof biol, Tex Woman's Univ, 77-81, assoc prof, 81-85; assoc prof med & biochem, Univ NTex Health Sci Ctr, Ft Worth, 85-91, prof, 91-92. *Concurrent Pos:* NIH fel, Mayo Clin, Found & Grad Sch Med, 72-73; Extramanal Assoc, 79-80. *Mem:* Am Soc Biochem & Molecular Biol; Am Asn Cancer Res; Am Soc Nutrit Sci; Am Col Nutrit; Int Soc Cancer Prev; Women Cancer Res. *Res:* Regulation of poly (adenosine diphosphate ribose) synthesis with a particular interest in events following DNA damage by carcinogens; niacin status and cancer prevention; poly (adenosine disphosphate ribose) metabolism as a target for design of anti-cancer therapies. *Mailing Add:* A323 ASTECC Bldg Univ Ky Lexington KY 40506-0286. *E-Mail:* ejacob@pop.uky.edu

JACOBSON, ELIZABETH D, HEALTH SCIENCES. *Current Pos:* Res geneticist, 75-82, chief, Optical Radiation Br, 82-85, dir, Off Sci & Technol, 85-90, DEP DIR SCI, CTR DEVICES & RADIOL HEALTH, FOOD & DRUG ADMIN, 90- *Educ:* State Univ NY, Binghamton, BA, 70; Georgetown Univ, PhD(biol), 75. *Honors & Awards:* Arthur S Flemming Award, 84. *Mem:* Am Soc Photobiol; Environ Mutagen Soc; AAAS. *Res:* Development of programs to assure the safety and effectiveness of medical devices; reduce population exposure to radiation emitted from medical and consumer products. *Mailing Add:* Ctr Devices & Radiol Health Food & Drug Admin 9200 Corporate Blvd Rockville MD 20850

JACOBSON, EUGENE DONALD, PHYSIOLOGY. *Current Pos:* dean, 88-90, PROF MED & PHYSIOL, SCH MED, UNIV COLO, 90-, ACTG HEAD GASTROENTEROL, 94- *Personal Data:* b Bridgeport, Conn, Feb 19, 30; m 73, Laura K Osborn; c Laura E, Susan R, Morrid D, Daniel F & Miriam L. *Educ:* Wesleyan Univ, BA, 51; Univ Vt, MD, 55; State Univ NY, MS, 60. *Hon Degrees:* Dr, Jagellonian Univ, 96. *Prof Exp:* Intern, State Univ NY, 55-56, resident internal med, 57-60; assoc prof physiol, Sch Med, Univ Calif, Los Angeles, 64-66; prof & chmn dept, Sch Med, Univ Okla, 66-71; prof physiol & chmn dept, Univ Tex Med Sch, Houston, 71-77; vdean, Col Med, Univ Cincinnati, 77-85; dean, Sch Med, Univ Kans, 85-88. *Concurrent Pos:* NIH spec fel, Univ Calif, Los Angeles, 64-66, NIH res career develop award, 66; consult, Gen Med Study Sect, NIH, 68-72, Vet Admin, 69-71 & Upjohn Co, Mich, 70-88; prof physiol, Baylor Col Med, 72-77; chairperson, Nat Comn Digestive Diseases, 77-79; mem, Nat Digestive Dis Adv Bd, NIH, 85-87. *Mem:* Am Physiol Soc; AMA; Am Soc Clin Invest; fel Am Col Physicians; Am Gastroenterol Asn (pres, 89-90); Asn Am Physicians. *Res:* Splanchnic circulation; gastrointestinal physiology. *Mailing Add:* 2000 E 12th Ave Box 27 Denver CO 80206

JACOBSON, FLORENCE DORFMAN, mathematics; deceased, see previous edition for last biography

JACOBSON, FRANK HENRY, PHYSIOLOGY. *Current Pos:* RETIRED. *Personal Data:* b Providence, RI, Sept 11, 15; m 40, Bessie Levy; c Deborah M. *Educ:* Emory Univ, BA, 42; Univ Rochester, PhD(physiol), 51. *Prof Exp:* From instr to asst prof physiol, Jefferson Med Col, 51-59; physiologist, Aerospace Med Res Dept, US Naval Develop Ctr, 59-70, Appl Physiol Lab, Aircraft Crew Systs Directorate, 70-81. *Mem:* Am Physiol Soc; Aerospace Med Asn. *Res:* Temperature regulation of mammals; hypothalamus; acceleration; mechanism and pharmacology of cerebral concussion, sleep, arousal and affective illness. *Mailing Add:* 1035 Gravel Hill Rd Southampton PA 18966

JACOBSON, GAIL M, BIOCHEMISTRY. *Current Pos:* RETIRED. *Personal Data:* b Bartlesville, Okla, Feb 6, 38; m 63; c 3. *Educ:* Mt Holyoke Col, BA, 60, MA, 62; Cornell Univ, PhD(biochem), 66. *Prof Exp:* Res fel biochem, Calif Inst Technol, 66-68; asst mem, Okla Med Res Found, 68-76; lectr, Dept Chem, Calif Polytech State Univ, 76-95. *Concurrent Pos:* Vis asst prof nutrit, Univ Okla, 68-75. *Mem:* Sigma Xi. *Res:* Enzymology; enzyme kinetics; coenzyme B12; enzymes; methylation of ribosomal RNA. *Mailing Add:* 156 Broad St San Luis Obispo CA 93405

JACOBSON, GUNNARD KENNETH, FERMENTATION. *Current Pos:* scientist, Universal Foods Corp, 77-82, sr scientist, molecular biol, 82-88, proj scientist, 88-91, MGR, UNIVERSAL FOODS CORP, 91- *Personal Data:* b Phoenix, Ariz, Feb 19, 47; m 71, Claudia Hale. *Educ:* Univ Ariz, BS, 69; Ore State Univ, PhD(microbiol), 73. *Prof Exp:* Fel, Univ Chicago, 72-75; res assoc, Argonne Nat Lab, 75-77. *Mem:* Am Soc Microbiol; AAAS; Genetics Soc Am; Sigma Xi. *Res:* Genetics and molecular biology of industrial microorganisms-new strain construction and improvement by classical genetics and recombinant DNA technology. *Mailing Add:* Molecular Biol Universal Foods Corp 6143 N 60th St Milwaukee WI 53218

JACOBSON, HAROLD, PHYSICAL CHEMISTRY, PHYSICAL PHARMACY. *Current Pos:* sr res scientist pharmaceut & biophys, Squibb Inst Med Res, 63-76, dept head methods develop & testing standards, 76-87, TECH DIR REGULATORY AFFAIRS, BRISTOL-MYERS SQUIBB, 87- *Personal Data:* b New York, NY, Jan 15, 29; m 52; c 3. *Educ:* City Col NY, BS, 50; Polytech Inst Brooklyn, PhD(phys chem), 59. *Prof Exp:* Chemist pharmaceut, Robin Pharmacal Co, 50-51; analyst, Nat Bur Standards, 51-54; sr res chemist electrochem devices, Nat Cash Register Co, 59-62; mem tech staff, Bell Tel Labs, 62-63. *Concurrent Pos:* Adj prof, Middlesex Community Col, 67-70 & Fairleigh Dickinson Univ, 82-83. *Mem:* Am Pharmaceut Asn; Am Chem Soc; NY Acad Sci. *Res:* Ion-exchange membranes; electrochemistry; solution chemistry; differential thermal analysis; ion-specific electrodes; drug dissolution; particle size and surface area measurements; particulate contamination of parenterals; x-ray diffraction; crystal polymorphism; high performance liquid chromatography. *Mailing Add:* 36 Clearview Rd East Brunswick NJ 08816-4268

JACOBSON, HAROLD GORDON, RADIOLOGY. *Current Pos:* RADIOLOGIST-IN-CHIEF, MOTEFIORE HOSP & MED CTR, 55-; PROF RADIOL, ALBERT EINSTEIN COL MED, 64- *Personal Data:* b Cincinnati, Ohio, Oct 12, 12; m 42; c 2. *Educ:* Univ Cincinnati, BS, 34, BM, 36, MD, 37. *Honors & Awards:* Crookshank lectr, London, Eng, 74; Holmes lectr, Boston, 74. *Prof Exp:* Asst radiol, Sch Med, Univ Tex, 41-42; instr, Sch Med, Yale Univ, 42; assoc to chief radiol serv & assoc radiologist, Vet Admin Hosp, Bronx, 46-50, chief radiol serv, 50-52; from asst clin prof to clin prof radiol, Col Med, NY Univ, 52-59, prof clin radiol, 59-64. *Concurrent Pos:* Dir dept radiol, Hosp Spec Surg, 53-54; consult, Vet Admin Hosp, Bronx, 57-; vis prof, Col Med, Univ Cincinnati, 59; chmn comt on affairs, Am Inst Radiol, Am Col Radiol, 71, co-chmn comt diag coding index & thesaurus, 73-; consult, Nat Bd Med Examiners, 75-; vis prof radiol, Inst Orthop, Univ London, Eng, 75- *Mem:* Radiol Soc NAm (1st vpres, 64-65, pres, 66-67); Am Roentgen Ray Soc; Int Skeletal Soc (pres, 74-75); AMA; Am Col Radiol. *Res:* Bone and joint radiology; neuroradiology; radiology of skeletal disorders. *Mailing Add:* 111 E 210th St Bronx NY 10467-2401

JACOBSON, HAROLD KARAN, POLITICAL SCIENCE. *Current Pos:* from assoc prof to prof, 61-84, chmn dept, 72-77, JESSE SIDDAL REEVES PROF POLIT SCI, UNIV MICH, 84- *Personal Data:* b Detroit, Mich, June 28, 29; m 51, Merelyn Jean Lindbloom; c Harold Knute, Eric Alfred, Kristoffer Olaf & Nils Karl. *Educ:* Univ Mich, AB, 50; Yale Univ, MA, 52, PhD, 55. *Honors & Awards:* Inst Sci Coop Award, AAAS, 95. *Prof Exp:* Asst prof, Univ Houston, 55-57. *Concurrent Pos:* World Affairs Ctr fel, 59-60; vis prof, Grad Inst Int Studies, Univ Geneva, 65-66, 70-71 & 77-78; vis res scholar, Europ Ctr Carnegie Endowment Int Peace, Geneva, 70-71; res scientist, Univ Mich, 77-, dir, Ctr Polit Studies, 86-96, interim assoc vpres int acad affairs, 90-92, actg dir, Inst Social Res, 92-93 & 94-95; mem, US Nat Comn, UNESCO, 80-85; Woodrow Wilson fel, 84; Ctr Advan Studies in Behav Sci fel, 88-89; Ctr Int Climate & Environ Res fel, Oslo, 96. *Mem:* AAAS; Am Polit Sci Asn; fel Am Acad Arts & Sci; Int Studies Asn; Int Polit Sci Asn. *Res:* International institutions and politics; environmental issues. *Mailing Add:* 2174 Delaware Dr Ann Arbor MI 48103-6017. *Fax:* 313-764-3341; *E-Mail:* hkj@umich.edu

JACOBSON, HARRY C, PHYSICS. *Current Pos:* PROF, DEPT PHYSICS & ASTRON, UNIV TENN, KNOXVILLE, 64-, PROF PHYSICS & ASTRON, 82- *Personal Data:* b Bozeman, Mont, July 13, 31; m 64, Marilyn Quinn; c Kara C (Dallmam), Stephen C, Paula C & Aubrie C. *Educ:* Col Holy Cross, BS, 53; Yale Univ, MS, 61; PhD(physics), 65. *Prof Exp:* Physicist, Nuclear Div, Combustion Eng Inc, 56-60. *Mem:* Am Phys Soc. *Res:* Theory of atomic and molecular structure; theory of spectral line shapes. *Mailing Add:* Dept Physics & Astron Univ Tenn Knoxville TN 37996-1200

JACOBSON, HARRY R, MEDICINE. *Current Pos:* STAFF PHYSICIAN/ NEPHROLOGIST, VET ADMIN HOSP, NASHVILLE, 85- *Personal Data:* b June 21, 47; US citizen; m. *Educ:* Univ Ill, Champaign, BS, 69; Univ Ill, Chicago, MD, 72; Am Bd Internal Med, cert, 75. *Prof Exp:* Internship med, Johns Hopkins Hosp, Baltimore, Md, 72-73, med residency, 73-74; chief, Renal Sect, US Army Surg Res Ctr, Brooke Army Med Ctr, San Antonio, Tex, 76-78; nephrology fel, Univ Tex Health Sci Ctr, Dallas, 74-76, from asst prof to assoc prof internal med, 78-85; prof med & dir, div nephrology, dept med, Med Ctr, Vanderbilt Univ, Nashville, Tenn, 85- *Concurrent Pos:* NIH res career develop award, 78-83; assoc ed, News Physiol Sci, 88- & Kidney Int, 90-; mem, Nat Kidney & Urol Dis Adv Bd, NIH, 90- *Mem:* Am Fedn Clin Res; Am Soc Nephrology; Int Soc Nephrology; Am Physiol Soc; Am Soc Clin Invest; Asn Am Physicians. *Res:* Author of numerous publications. *Mailing Add:* Renal Div Vanderbilt Univ Sch Med Nashville TN 37232-0001

JACOBSON, HERBERT (IRVING), REPRODUCTIVE ENDOCRINOLOGY, BIOCHEMISTRY. *Current Pos:* assoc prof obstet & gynec, 64-73, RES PROF & CHIEF SECT REPROD STUDIES, DEPT OBSTET & GYNEC, ALBANY MED COL, 73-, RES PROF BIOCHEM, 75- *Personal Data:* b Chicago, Ill, Mar 17, 23; m 53; c 3. *Educ:* Univ Chicago, SB, 48, SM, 49, PhD(chem), 57. *Honors & Awards:* US Sr Scientist Award, Fed Repub Ger & Alexander von Humboldt Found, 75. *Prof Exp:* Res assoc & instr, Univ Chicago, 52-57, res assoc & asst prof, 57-59, asst prof, Ben May Lab Cancer Res, 59-64. *Concurrent Pos:* Res partic, Chem Div, Oak Ridge Nat Lab, 61; USPHS spec fel, Max Planck Inst Biochem, Munich, 62-63; Nat Inst Arthritis & Metabolic Dis res career develop award, 66-70; vis prof, Max Planck Inst Cell Biol, 75-76. *Mem:* Endocrine Soc; Soc Exp Biol & Med; NY Acad Sci; Soc Study Reprod. *Res:* Steroid biochemistry; mechanism of hormone action; regulation of hormone receptor synthesis; control processes in mammalian reproduction; response mechanisms in hormone-dependent cancer. *Mailing Add:* Dept Obstet & Gynec Albany Med Col Albany NY 12208

JACOBSON, HOMER, INFORMATION & BIOPOLYMER THEORY. *Current Pos:* from instr to prof, 50-86, EMER PROF CHEM, BROOKLYN COL, 86- *Personal Data:* b Cleveland, Ohio, Nov 27, 22; m 57; c William, Guy, Ethan & Lisbeth. *Educ:* Calif Inst Technol, BS, 41; Columbia Univ, AM, 42, PhD(chem), 48. *Prof Exp:* Res scientist, Manhattan Proj, NY, 44-46; assoc chemist, Brookhaven Nat Lab, 47-49; instr chem, Hunter Col, 49-50. *Concurrent Pos:* Guggenheim fel, Calif Inst Technol, 59-60; NIH spec fel, 60-61. *Res:* Chemical mutagenesis in bacterial viruses; virus growth in continuous culture; steady-state kinetics; information theory in biological systems; configurational entropy of superhelices and catenanes. *Mailing Add:* 140 Carrollyn Dr Tarrytown NY 10591

JACOBSON, HOWARD NEWMAN, PHYSIOLOGY. *Current Pos:* DIR, INST NUTRIT, UNIV NC, CHAPEL HILL, 79- *Personal Data:* b St Paul, Minn, Aug 13, 23; m 61. *Educ:* Northwestern Univ, BS, 47, BM, 50, MD, 51. *Prof Exp:* Intern med, Presby Hosp, Chicago, 50-51, resident obstet & gynec, 51-52; Asn Aid Crippled Children fel, 52-55; resident, Boston Lying-in-Hosp & Free Hosp for Women, 55-57; obstetrician-physiologist, PR Proj, Nat Inst Neurol Dis & Blindness, 58-60; asst obstet & gynec, Harvard Med Sch, 60-61, instr, 61-64, assoc, 64-65; actg assoc prof obstet & gynec, Sch Med & lectr pub health, Sch Pub Health, Univ Calif, San Francisco, 65-67, assoc coord allied health professions, 67-69; assoc prof obstet & gynec, Boston Hosp for Women & dir Macy prog, Harvard Med Sch, 69-74; prof community med, Rutgers Med Sch, Col Med & Dent NJ, 74-79. *Concurrent Pos:* Res fel physiol, Harvard Med Sch, 52-54; mem adv panel maternal & child health, Children's Bur, 64-; NIH res career develop award, 64-65; mem food & nutrit bd, Nat Res Coun, 70-; chmn comt on maternal nutrit, Nat Acad Sci-Nat Res Coun, 71- *Mem:* Am Soc Clin Nutrit; assoc Am Physiol Soc. *Res:* Fetal physiology and responses of fetuses to asphyxia and hypoxia; autonomic nervous system in reproduction; maternity services, with emphasis on maternal nutrition; health manpower needs, nutrition monitoring. *Mailing Add:* Dept Community & Family Health Univ SFla 13201 Bruce B Downs Blvd Tampa FL 33612

JACOBSON, HOWARD W, RESEARCH CHEMISTRY. *Current Pos:* RES SCIENTIST, DUPONT CO INC. *Honors & Awards:* Creative Invention Award, Am Chem Soc, 94. *Mailing Add:* DuPont 211 Jackson Lab-Chamber Works Deepwater NJ 08023

JACOBSON, IRA DAVID, FLIGHT MECHANICS, FLUID MECHANICS. *Current Pos:* VPRES ACADEMICS, EMBRY RIDDLE AERONAUT UNIV, 93- *Personal Data:* b New York, NY, May 28, 42; m 64, Judy; c 2. *Educ:* New York Univ, BS, 63; Univ VA, MS, 67, PhD(aerospace eng), 70. *Honors & Awards:* Atwood Award, Am Inst Aeronaut & Astronaut/Am Soc Eng Educr. *Prof Exp:* Aerospace engr, NASA, 63-67; res scientist & lectr, Univ Va, 70-73, from asst prof to prof aerospace eng, 73-92, dir, Ctr Comput Aided Eng, 83-92, dir comput & commun, 91-92. *Concurrent Pos:* Dir, Inst Comput Aided Eng, Ctr Innovative Technol. *Mem:* Am Inst Aeronaut & Astronaut; Am Soc Eng Educr; Sigma Xi; Soc Mfg Engrs. *Res:* Flight mechanics, especially stability and control; fluid mechanics, especially the magnus effect; vehicle systems, especially vehicle ride quality; computer aided design and manufacturing. *Mailing Add:* Vpres Academics Embry Riddle Aeronaut Univ Spruance Hall Rm 221 6005 Clyde Morris Blvd Daytona Beach FL 32114-3966

JACOBSON, IRVEN ALLAN, JR, PHYSICAL CHEMISTRY, CHEMICAL KINETICS. *Current Pos:* RETIRED. *Personal Data:* b Denver, Colo, Apr 19, 28; m 64; c 1. *Educ:* Univ Colo, BA, 50. *Prof Exp:* Chemist, Laramie Energy Res Ctr, Bur Mines, US Dept Interior, 50-60, res chemist, 60-75, res chemist & proj leader, Laramie Energy Technol Ctr, US Dept Energy, 75-78, Chemical Engr 78-83. *Mem:* Fel AAAS; Am Chem Soc; Sigma Xi. *Res:* Directing research on the kinetics of oil shale thermal gasification and low temperature oxidation. *Mailing Add:* 2626 Park Ave Laramie WY 82070

JACOBSON, JAY STANLEY, PLANT PHYSIOLOGY, AIR POLLUTION. *Current Pos:* RETIRED. *Personal Data:* b New York, NY, Oct 5, 34; m 71; c 1. *Educ:* Cornell Univ, BS, 55; Columbia Univ, MA, 57, PhD(plant biochem), 60. *Prof Exp:* Assoc plant biochemist, Boyce Thompson Inst, 60-70, plant physiologist, 70-96. *Concurrent Pos:* Adj prof, Dept Natural Resources, Cornell Univ; consult, USDA & Environ Protection Agency. *Mem:* Am Soc Plant Physiol; Am Inst Biol Sci; Air Pollution Control Asn. *Res:* Effects of air pollutants and acid rain on growth, development, yield and quality of agricultural crops and forest trees. *Mailing Add:* Boyce Thompson Inst Tower Rd Ithaca NY 14853-1801

JACOBSON, JERRY I, JACOBSON RESONANCE, BIOELECTROMAGNETICS. *Current Pos:* PRES, INST THEORET PHYSICS, ALZHEIMERS RES FOUND, 85- *Personal Data:* b Brooklyn, NY, Jan 25, 46; m 75, Debra M Deiso; c Solomon, Jacqueline & Faith. *Educ:* Brooklyn Col, BA, 66; Temple Univ, DDS-DMD, 70; City Univ NY, PhD(physics), 83. *Concurrent Pos:* Pres, Perspectivism Found, 80-; lectr, Int Confs, 86- *Mem:* Bioelectromagnetics Soc; Am Phys Soc; Europ Bioelectromagnetics Soc. *Res:* Discovered a physico-mathematical apparatus called Jacobson Resonance which enables the scientist to establish magnetic field parameters by which to mechanically vibrate masses in a biological system to therein recrystallize critical molecules; reorder structures of ions in the plasma of a fusion test reactor. *Mailing Add:* 2006 Mainsail Circle Jupiter FL 33477

JACOBSON, JIMMY JOE, GEOPHYSICS, EARTH SCIENCES. *Current Pos:* CONSULT GEOPHYS, 83- *Personal Data:* b Lonepine, Wyo, Feb 11, 37; m 73; c 3. *Educ:* Univ Wyo, BS, 59; Colo Sch Mines, MSc, 64, DSc(geophys), 69. *Prof Exp:* From jr to sr geophysicist, Deco Electronics, 60-65; sr geophysicist, Westinghouse Geores Labs, 65-67; asst prof physics & geophys, Mont Col Mineral Sci & Technol, 70-74; mgr field opers, Geonomics, Inc, 74-77; sr res scientist geophys, Pac Northwest Div, Battelle Mem Inst, 77-80; MCR Geothermal, Denver, 80-83. *Concurrent Pos:* Geophysicist, Group Seven, Inc, 69-73. *Mem:* Sigma Xi. *Res:* Exploration of the earth and earth materials utilizing electrical and other geophysical tools. *Mailing Add:* 11009 W 65th Way Arvada CO 80004

JACOBSON, JOAN, AUDIOLOGY, SPEECH PATHOLOGY. *Current Pos:* RETIRED. *Personal Data:* b Hull, Iowa, Apr 26, 24; div. *Educ:* Morningside Col, BA, 44; Syracuse Univ, MA, 48, PhD(speech corrections), 58. *Prof Exp:* Instr speech path, Syracuse Univ, 46-51; therapist, Brookline Pub Schs, Mass, 51-57; res asst speech path, Syracuse Univ, 57-58; asst prof speech path & audiol & audiologist, Eastern Ill Univ, 58-62; from assoc prof to prof speech sci, path & audiol, St Cloud State Univ, 62-93. *Concurrent Pos:* Therapist, Mass Gen Hosp, Boston, 51-57; mem prof adv comt, Minn Soc Crippled Children & Adults, 63- & Minn Easter Seal Soc, 64-; mem, Gov Adv Comt Serv Hearing Impaired, 64-66 & Model Presch Ctr Hearing-Impaired Children & Families, 69-72. *Mem:* Am Speech Lang Hearing Asn; Am Cleft Palate Asn; Am Acad Rehab Audiol. *Res:* Lip reading; cleft palate. *Mailing Add:* 412 1/2 7 Ave S St Cloud MN 56301

JACOBSON, JOHN OBERT, MECHANICAL ENGINEERING. *Current Pos:* CONSULT ENGR, JACOBSON ENGRS, 78- *Personal Data:* b Alexandria, Minn, Oct 23, 39; c 1. *Educ:* Wash State Univ, BS, 62; Univ Wash, MS, 65, PhD(bioeng), 72. *Prof Exp:* Safety engr, Boeing Co, 62-63; eng supvr, Lockheed Shipbuilding Co, 65-66; res scientist, Va Mason Med Ctr, 71-74 & Flow Res Inc, 74-75; res consult, Appl Physics Lab, 74; consult engr, Westinghouse Hausford, Olympic Engr, 76-78; asst prof, Cogswell Col, 79-82; assoc prof mech eng, Seattle Univ, 83-85. *Concurrent Pos:* Consult engr, Engineered Indust Systs, Inc, 66-86; comt mem, Nat Asn Fire Protection, 81-; rev comt mem, NIH, 86- *Mem:* Am Soc Mech Engrs; Human Factors Soc. *Res:* Ultrasonic imaging for medical diagnostics; laser development for military applications; material development for ultra high pressure applications; design and development of ultra high gravity centrifuge. *Mailing Add:* 5220 Roosevelt Way NE Seattle WA 98105

JACOBSON, KARL BRUCE, DNA DIAGNOSTICS. *Current Pos:* biochemist Biol Div, 58-93, PROF BIOMED SCI, HEALTH SCI RES DIV, OAKRIDGE NAT LAB, UNIV TENN, 93- *Personal Data:* b Manning, Iowa, Mar 5, 28; m 51, Phyllis Greenler; c Deborah, Paul, Steven & Dan. *Educ:* St Bonaventure Col, BS, 48; Johns Hopkins Univ, PhD(biol), 56. *Prof Exp:* Am Cancer Soc fel chem, Calif Inst Technol, 56-58. *Mem:* AAAS; Am Soc Biol Chem; Am Chem Soc; Human Genome Orgn. *Res:* New technologies for DNA sequencing; development and differentiation in terms of biochemical changes; relationship of structure of transfer RNA to its function; biochemical genetics in Drosophila; mechanism of toxicity of cadmium and other metals. *Mailing Add:* Health Scis Res Div PO Box 2009 Oak Ridge TN 37831-6123. *E-Mail:* bru@ornl.gov

JACOBSON, KEITH HAZEN, PHARMACOLOGY, TOXICOLOGY. *Current Pos:* RETIRED. *Personal Data:* b Yankton, SDak, Nov 4, 18. *Educ:* Univ SDak, BA, 40, MA, 41; NY Univ, BS, 44; Univ Cincinnati, PhD(phys biochem), 49. *Prof Exp:* Chemist, Rustless Iron & Steel Corp, 41-43; biochemist, staff supv & coordr res, Res & Eng Div, US Army Chem Ctr, 49-51, indust toxicol res, Med Labs, Chem Corps, 51-56, coordr, Mil Chem Prog, 56-63, med res dir, Chem Warfare Labs, 57- 63, asst to dir, 57-63; supvr res pharmacol, Div Pharmacol, Food & Drug Admin, DC, 63-64; chief lab invests, Div Toxicol Eval, 64-68, chief toxicol res, Div Pharmacol & Toxicol, 68-69; assoc prof med, Lab Environ Med, Sch Med, Tulane Univ, 69-72; chief criteria develop br, Nat Inst Occup Safety & Health, 72-74, sr scientist, div criteria doc & stand develop, 74-81. *Concurrent Pos:* Consult toxicol & environ health, 81- *Mem:* Am Chem Soc; Am Indust Hyg Asn; AAAS; Am Acad Indust Hyg. *Res:* Occupational toxicology; pesticide and food additive toxicology. *Mailing Add:* 740 Beall Ave Rockville MD 20850-2107

JACOBSON, KENNETH ALAN, RECEPTOR PHARMACOLOGY, MEDICINAL CHEMISTRY. *Current Pos:* sr staff fel, 83-88, RES CHEMIST, NAT INST DIABETES, DIGESTIVE & KIDNEY DIS, NIH, BETHESDA, MD, 88- *Personal Data:* b Euclid, Ohio, July 18, 53; m 78, Arlette Cadoche; c Gabriel, Dorit & Mihal. *Educ:* Reed Col, BA, 76; Univ Calif, San Diego, MS, 78, PhD(chem), 81. *Honors & Awards:* Giuliana Fassina Award, Purine Club, 96. *Prof Exp:* Bantrell res fel, Dept Org Chem, Weizmann Inst Sci, Rehovot, Israel, 81-83. *Concurrent Pos:* Instr, Found Advan Educ Sci, Bethesda, Md, 84-85; scientific adv bd, Res Biochem, Inc, Natick, Mass, 90-91. *Mem:* Am Chem Soc; Soc Neurosci; Am Soc Pharmaceut & Exp Therapeut. *Res:* Developing novel ligands for neurotransmitter receptors; chemistry and pharmacology of purines; muscarinic acetylcholine receptors; neurochemistry and imaging. *Mailing Add:* Lab Bioorg Chem Nat Inst Diabetes Digestive & Kidney Dis NIH Bldg 8A Rm B1A-17 Bethesda MD 20892-0810. *Fax:* 301-480-8422; *E-Mail:* kajacobs@helix.nih.gov

JACOBSON, KENNETH ALLAN, MEMBRANE BIOPHYSICS, CELL MOTILITY. *Current Pos:* assoc prof anat & core mem, Cancer Res Ctr, 80-87, PROF CELL BIOL & ANAT, UNIV NC, CHAPEL HILL, 87- *Personal Data:* b Milwaukee, Wis, Oct 29, 41; m 66, Judith A Ruder; c Jill, Joy & Julie. *Educ:* Univ Wis-Madison, BS, 64, MS, 66; State Univ NY, Buffalo, PhD(biophys), 72. *Hon Degrees:* MD, Univ Linkoping, Linkoping, Sweden, 93. *Prof Exp:* Physicist, Dow Corning Corp, 66-69; mem, Ctr Theoret Biol, State Univ NY, Buffalo, 72-80, asst prof biophys, 76-80, chmn, Grad Group Biomembranes, 77-80; pres, Fluorescence Unltd Consults, 83-90. *Concurrent Pos:* Sr cancer res scientist, Roswell Park Mem Inst, 72-80; prin investr grants, NIH, 74- & Am Cancer Soc, 83-; estab investr, Am Heart Asn, 77-82; ed, Cell Physiol Sect, Am J Physiol, 80-84, Comments in Molecular & Cell Biophys, 86-; guest prof, Dept Physics, Tech Univ, Munich, Ger, 93- *Mem:* Am Soc Cell Biol; Biophys Soc; AAAS. *Res:* Development of fluorescence microscopy; use of digital image processing to measure the distribution of single classes of molecules in single, living cells; lateral diffusion in membranes; cell locomotion; nanovid microscopy and single particle tracking. *Mailing Add:* Dept Cell Biol & Anat Univ NC CB7090 108 Taylor Hall Chapel Hill NC 27599-9090

JACOBSON, LARRY A, NUCLEAR PHYSICS, GEOPHYSICS. *Current Pos:* mgr nuclear res sect, 88-95, MGR RES, HALLIBURTON ENERGY SERV INC, 96- *Personal Data:* b Madison, Wis, Oct 29, 40; m 65, Adrienne Coakley. *Educ:* Univ Wis-Madison, BS, 63, MS, 64, PhD(physics), 69. *Prof Exp:* Develop proj physicist, Schlumberger Ltd, 69-74, sect mgr, Pulsed Neutron Sect, 74-76, dept mgr elec eng, 76-79, mgr sensor physics, 80-81, mgr nuclear logging, Schlumberger Well Serv Co, 81-84; mgr nuclear res group, Austin Res Ctr, Gearhart Industs, Inc, 84-88. *Concurrent Pos:* Distinguished vis prof, Elec Eng Dept, Univ Houston, 80. *Mem:* AAAS; Am Phys Soc; Soc Prof Well Log Analysts; Soc Petrol Eng; Sigma Xi. *Res:* Negative ion source development; heavy ion nuclear elastic scattering; nuclear techniques in mineral and petroleum exploration and evaluation; data processing of nuclear data; computer simulations of nuclear processes; awarded 6 US patents. *Mailing Add:* 1610 Windsong Dr Richmond TX 77469

JACOBSON, LEWIS A, MOLECULAR BIOLOGY, BIOCHEMISTRY. *Current Pos:* From asst prof biophys to assoc prof biophys & microbiol, 67-76, ASSOC PROF BIOL SCI, UNIV PITTSBURGH, 76- *Personal Data:* b Brooklyn, NY, Oct 10, 42; m 67; c 2. *Educ:* Amherst Col, AB, 63; Univ Ill, MS, 65, PhD(biochem), 67. *Concurrent Pos:* Vpres, Tutorials Group Inc. *Mem:* AAAS; Am Soc Microbiol; Am Soc Biochem & Molecular Biol. *Res:* Regulation of gene expression in bacteria, biochemistry and genetics of lysosomal proteases; neural control of muscle proteolysis. *Mailing Add:* Dept Biol Sci 304 Langley Hall Univ Pittsburgh Pittsburgh PA 15260. *Fax:* 412-624-4759; *E-Mail:* ljac@vms.cis.pitt.edu

JACOBSON, LOUIS, PLANT PHYSIOLOGY. *Current Pos:* Analyst, Div Plant Nutrit, 38-42, radiochemist, Radiation Lab, 42-46, from asst prof & asst plant biochemist to assoc prof nutrit & assoc plant biochemist, 45-58, PROF PLANT NUTRIT & PLANT PHYSIOLOGIST EXP STA, DEPT SOILS & PLANT NUTRIT, UNIV CALIF, BERKELEY, 58- *Personal Data:* b Chicago, Ill, Nov 21, 15; m 38; c 3. *Educ:* Univ Calif, Los Angeles, AB, 36; Univ Calif, PhD(plant physiol), 43. *Mem:* Am Chem Soc; Am Soc Plant Physiol; Bot Soc Am. *Res:* Absorption and accumulation of ions by plants; inorganic nutrition of plants; plant physiology. *Mailing Add:* 150 Poplar St Berkeley CA 94708-1326

JACOBSON, MARCUS, ENGINEERING MECHANICS. *Current Pos:* RETIRED. *Personal Data:* b Houston, Tex, May 2, 30; m 65. *Educ:* Rice Univ, BA, 51, BSME, 52, MSME, 54; Univ Calif, Los Angeles, PhD(eng), 65. *Prof Exp:* Asst prof mech eng, Rice Univ, 52-62; design engr, Douglas Aircraft Co, 62; sr dynamics engr, Lockheed-Calif Co, 63-64; eng specialist struct dynamics, Aircraft Div, Northrop Corp, 64-95. *Mem:* Am Inst Aeronaut & Astronaut. *Res:* Structural dynamics. *Mailing Add:* 5337 S Holt Ave Los Angeles CA 90056

JACOBSON, MARCUS, PHYSIOLOGY, BIOPHYSICS. *Current Pos:* chmn, Dept Anat, 77-89, PROF, DEPT NEUROBIOL & ANAT, SCH MED, UNIV UTAH, SALT LAKE CITY, 89- *Personal Data:* b Cape Town, SAfrica, Apr 2, 30; US citizen; m 60; c 3. *Educ:* Univ Cape Town, BSc, 51, MB, ChB, 56; Univ Edinburgh, PhD(physiol), 60. *Prof Exp:* Intern med, Groote Schuur Hosp, Cape Town, 56-57; lectr physiol, Med Sch, Univ Edinburgh, 60-65; guest investr biophys, Naval Med Res Inst, Bethesda, 65-66; from assoc prof to prof, Johns Hopkins Univ, 67-73; prof physiol, Sch Med, Univ Miami, 73-77. *Concurrent Pos:* Assoc ed, Brain Res, 71-74, J Neurosci Res, 74- & Exp Neurol, 81- *Mem:* Brit Physiol Soc; Am Physiol Soc; Soc Neurosci. *Res:* Development and growth of the nervous system. *Mailing Add:* Dept Neurobiol & Anat Univ Utah Sch Med 50 N Medical Dr Salt Lake City UT 84132-0001

JACOBSON, MARTIN, PHYTOCHEMISTRY, PESTICIDES. *Current Pos:* RETIRED. *Personal Data:* b New York, NY, Nov 11, 19; m 42; c Barbara. *Educ:* City Univ NY, BS 40. *Honors & Awards:* Bronze Medals, Int Cong Pesticide Chem, 74; Hillebrand Prize, Wash Sect, Am Chem Soc, 64. *Prof Exp:* Lab aide chem, NIH, 41-42; res chemist, USDA, 42-86. *Concurrent Pos:* Res fel, Wash Acad Sci, 66; vis prof, dept chem, Univ Idaho, 71; agr consult, 86- *Mem:* Am Chem Soc; Entom Soc Am; AAAS. *Res:* Isolation, identification and synthesis of insect toxicants, repellents and attractants from plants and animals. *Mailing Add:* 1131 University Blvd W No 616 Silver Spring MD 20902-3308

JACOBSON, MARTIN MICHAEL, BIOCHEMICAL PHARMACOLOGY. *Current Pos:* biochemist, Hoffmann- Laroche Inc, 70-73; sr scientist, 74, coordr exp therapeut, 74-78, res planning mgr exp therapeut, 78-80, asst dir exp therapeut, 80-81, asst dir res planning & develop, 81-83, asst dir pharm res & develop, 83-84, asst dir res qual assurance, 84-85, DIR RES PLANNING, SCI & FINANCIAL ADMIN, HOFFMANN-LAROCHE INC, 85- *Personal Data:* b New York, NY, Nov 24, 34; m 65. *Educ:* City Col New York, BS, 57; Long Island Univ, MS, 68. *Prof Exp:* Res technician, Rockefeller Inst Med Res, 57-58; res biochemist, Wellcome Res Labs, Burroughs Wellcome & Co, 59-70. *Mem:* Am Soc Pharmacol & Exp Therapeut; NY Acad Sci; AAAS; Am Pharmaceut Asn; Acad Pharmaceut Sci; Sigma Xi; Drug Info Asn. *Res:* Biochemical, pharmacologic and toxicologic effects and metabolism of drugs, carcinogens and steroids; involvement of the various disciplines in drug development. *Mailing Add:* Preclin Res & Develop Hoffmann LaRoche Inc Bldg 76 5th Floor 340 Kingsland St Nutley NJ 07110-1199. *Fax:* 973-235-6253

JACOBSON, MARVIN, oral pathology, periodontics; deceased, see previous edition for last biography

JACOBSON, MELVIN JOSEPH, APPLIED MATHEMATICS, WAVE PROPAGATION. *Current Pos:* from asst prof to prof, 56-90, res consult, 91-95, EMER PROF MATH, RENSSELAER POLYTECH INST, 91- *Personal Data:* b Providence, RI, Nov 25, 28; c Deborah L (Karczewski) & Donald B. *Educ:* Brown Univ, AB, 50; Carnegie Inst Technol, MS, 52, PhD(math), 54. *Prof Exp:* Res mathematician, United Aircraft Corp, 52; res assoc, Carnegie Inst Technol, 52-53, instr math, 53-54; mem tech staff, Bell Tel Labs, Inc, 54-56. *Concurrent Pos:* Prin investr, US Navy, Army, NASA & Indust, 57-90; vis prof, Inst Marine Sci, Univ Miami, 63-64, adj prof, 69-72; consult indust, 65- *Mem:* Fel Acoust Soc Am; Soc Indust & Appl Math; Am Asn Univ Profs; Sigma Xi. *Res:* Theories of underwater acoustics, including ocean environmental effects; mathematical studies of electromagnetic wave propagation in the atmosphere; low frequency atmospheric acoustics. *Mailing Add:* 4705 Chandlers Forde Sarasota FL 34235

JACOBSON, MICHAEL F, SCIENCE POLICY, MOLECULAR BIOLOGY. *Current Pos:* EXEC DIR, CTR SCI PUBLIC INTEREST, 71- *Personal Data:* b Chicago, Ill, July 29, 43; m 89; c Sonya. *Educ:* Univ Chicago, BA, 65; Mass Inst Technol, PhD(microbiol), 69. *Honors & Awards:* Harvey W Wiley Medal & Comnr's Spec Citation, US Food & Drug Admin. *Prof Exp:* Res assoc, Salk Inst Biol Studies, 70-71. *Concurrent Pos:* Tech consult, Ctr Study Responsive Law, 70-71; dir, Ctr Sci Pub Interest, 71, Nat Coalition Dis Prev & Environ Health, 79-82; co-founder, Ctr Study Commercialism, 90. *Res:* Impact of dietary and environmental factors on human health. *Mailing Add:* Ctr Sci Pub Interest 1875 Connecticut Ave NW Suite 300 Washington DC 20009-5728

JACOBSON, MICHAEL RAY, OPTICAL MEASUREMENTS, THIN FILM DEPOSITION. *Current Pos:* Res specialist, 77-86, assoc res scientist, Optical Sci Ctr, 86-90, ASSOC RES PROF OPTICAL SCI, OPTICAL SCI & MAT SCI & ENG DEPT, UNIV ARIZ, 90-; ASSOC, OPTICAL DATA ASSOCS. *Personal Data:* b Pittsburgh, Pa, Jan 11, 50; m 73, Simone Jacobs; c Tivon, Shira & Natan. *Educ:* Harvard Col, AB, 71; Cornell Univ, MS, 75, PhD(astron), 77. *Concurrent Pos:* Consult, Energy Conversion Devices, 80-81 & Dow Chem, 89-; instr short course, Int Soc Optical Eng, 84-; vis fac, Battelle Northwest Pac Lab, 90-; consult, Sci Appln Int Corp, 91- *Mem:* Optical Soc Am; Am Vacuum Soc; Int Soc Optical Eng; Am Meteorol Soc. *Res:* Optical materials, their deposition, characterization, and availability in thin film form; solar energy conversion materials; space applications; polymer films. *Mailing Add:* Optical Data Asn 5237 E Seventh St Tucson AZ 85711

JACOBSON, MURRAY M, CHEMICAL ENGINEERING, MATERIALS ENGINEERING. *Current Pos:* PRES, JACON INDUSTS, 75- *Personal Data:* b Boston, Mass, Jan 2, 15; m 62, Madelyn Marder; c Marc, Paul & Richard. *Educ:* Tufts Univ, BS, 35. *Prof Exp:* Chemist, Whiting Labs, Mass, 36-39; chief corrosion & lubrication sect, Watertown Arsenal Labs, 40-46, chem engr, 46-49, chief, Surface Chem Sect, 49-54, Phys Chem Br, 54-56, Chem Metall Lab, 56-59 & Mat Sci Lab, 59-64; dep chief, Mat Eng Div, Army Mat Res Agency, 64-66, chief prototypes lab, Army Mat & Mech Res Ctr, 66-69, chief mat test div, 69-74. *Concurrent Pos:* Army liaison mem, Subgroup on Greases, Coord Res Coun, War Adv Comt & Adv Comt on Corrosion, Ord Dept, 42-45; liaison mem subpanel on chromium, Panel on Refractory Metals, Mat Adv Bd, 49 & Comt Coatings, 68-69. *Mem:* Am Chem Soc; Nat Asn Corrosion Engrs; Am Soc Metals. *Res:* Research management; corrosion; erosion; oxidation; wear; lubrication; protective coatings and treatments; antigalling coatings; titanium surface metallurgy. *Mailing Add:* Jacon Industs PO Box 231 Boston MA 02146-0002

JACOBSON, MYRON J, TRAUMA SURGERY, THORACIC SURGERY. *Current Pos:* CLIN ASSOC PROF, STATE UNIV NY, STONY BROOK, 74-; CHIEF THORACIC SURG, NPORT VET ADMIN MED CTR, 74- *Personal Data:* b New York, NY, June 19, 32; c Barry, Michael & Daniel. *Educ:* McGill Univ, BS, 54; Univ Chicago, MD, 58. *Prof Exp:* Instr surg, Univ Chicago, 64-66; assoc prof, Chicago Med Sch, 66-70. *Concurrent Pos:* Vis prof surg, Ben Gerner Univ, 84; police surgeon, NY Police Dept, 93- *Mem:* Am Col Surgeons; Am Col Chest Physicians; Soc Thoracic Surgeons; Sigma Xi. *Res:* Risk factors in patients undergoing lung resection; lung cancer. *Mailing Add:* 653 Howard Ave West Hempstead NY 11552

JACOBSON, MYRON KENNETH, BIOCHEMISTRY. *Current Pos:* asst prof, 74-80, ASSOC PROF CHEM & BASIC HEALTH SCI, NTEX STATE UNIV, 80-; FAC MEM, COL PHARM, UNIV KY. *Personal Data:* b Richland Center, Wis, Sept 20, 43; m 67. *Educ:* Univ Wis-Platteville, BS, 65; Kans State Univ, PhD(biochem), 70. *Prof Exp:* NIH fel biochem, Univ Utah, 70-72; from res assoc to res assoc biochem, Mayo Clin & Found, 73-74. *Mem:* AAAS; Am Soc Biol Chemists. *Res:* Nicotinamide nucleotide metabolism, chemical carcinogenesis and DNA repair mechanisms. *Mailing Add:* Div Med Chem & Pharm Univ Ky Lexington KY 40536-0082. *Fax:* 606-257-6445

JACOBSON, NATHAN, MATHEMATICS. *Current Pos:* from assoc prof to prof, 47-67, Henry Ford II prof, 67-81, EMER PROF MATH, YALE UNIV, 81- *Personal Data:* b Warsaw, Poland, Sept 8, 10; US citizen; m 42; c 2. *Educ:* Univ Ala, AB, 30; Princeton Univ, PhD(math), 34. *Hon Degrees:* DSc, Univ Chicago, 72. *Prof Exp:* Asst math, Inst Advan Study, Princeton Univ, 33-34, Procter fel, 34-35; lectr, Bryn Mawr Col, 35-36; Nat Res Found fel, Univ Chicago, 36-37; from instr to asst prof, Univ NC, 37-40, assoc prof, 41-42, assoc ground sch instr, USN preflight sch, 42-43; assoc prof, Johns Hopkins Univ, 43-47. *Concurrent Pos:* Vis assoc prof, Johns Hopkins Univ, 40-41; ed, Bull Am Math Soc, 48-53; Guggenheim fel, 51-52; Fulbright res grant, Univ Paris, 51-52; vis prof, Univ Chicago, 64, Univ Tokyo, 65, Tata Inst Fundamental Res, India, 70, Univ Rome, 71, Hebrew Univ Jerusalem, 71, Rehovoth, 71, Australian Nat Univ, 78, ETH Zurich, 81, Nanjing Univ, 83, Taiwan Nat Univ, 83 & Wesleyan Univ, 88; vpres, IMU, 72-74. *Mem:* Nat Acad Sci; Am Math Soc (vpres, 57-58, pres, 71-73); Fr Math Soc; Math Soc Japan; Am Acad Arts & Sci; hon mem London Math Soc. *Res:* Topological algebra; structure theory of rings; non-associative algebra, especially Lie and Jordan algebras; Galois theory. *Mailing Add:* Dept Math Yale Univ PO Box 2155 Yale Sta New Haven CT 06520

JACOBSON, NORMAN LEONARD, ANIMAL NUTRITION. *Current Pos:* RETIRED. *Personal Data:* b Eau Claire, Wis, Sept 11, 18; m 43, Gertrude Neff; c Gary & Judy. *Educ:* Univ Wis, BS, 40; Iowa State Univ, MS, 41, PhD(nutrit), 47. *Honors & Awards:* Am Feed Mfgrs Award, 55; Borden Award, 60; Morrison Award, Am Soc Animal Sci, 70. *Prof Exp:* From asst prof to prof animal & dairy sci, Iowa State Univ, 47-53, distinguished prof agr, 63-, assoc dean, Grad Col, 73-88, assoc vpres res, 79-88, assoc provost res, 88-89, dean grad col, 88-89, interim chair, Dept Food Sci & Human Nutrit, 90-92. *Concurrent Pos:* Moorman travel fel nutrit, 66. *Mem:* Fel AAAS; Am Dairy Sci Asn (vpres, 71, pres, 72); fel Am Inst Nutrit; fel Am Soc Animal Sci; Sigma Xi. *Res:* Animal nutrition, particularly nutrition and physiology of the ruminant; relation of diet to coronary heart disease and artheroscleroses. *Mailing Add:* 313 Kildee Hall Iowa State Univ Ames IA 50011-3150

JACOBSON, RALPH ALLEN, MOLECULAR BIOLOGY, BIOCHEMISTRY. *Current Pos:* from asst prof to assoc prof, 75-83, PROF BIOCHEM, CALIF POLYTECH STATE UNIV, 83- *Personal Data:* b Jersey City, NJ, June 3, 40; m 63, Gail; c 3. *Educ:* Montclair State Col, BA, 62; Cornell Univ, PhD(biochem), 66. *Prof Exp:* NIH res fel biol, Calif Inst Technol, 66-68; asst prof biochem, Univ Okla, 68-75. *Concurrent Pos:* Vis scientist, W Alton Jones Cell Sci Ctr, NY, 83-84 & Molecular Biotechnol, Univ Wash, Seattle, 94. *Mem:* AAAS; Sigma Xi; Am Chem Soc. *Res:* Molecular biology & biotechnology recombinant DNA. *Mailing Add:* Dept Chem Calif Polytech State Univ San Luis Obispo CA 93407-0001

JACOBSON, RAYMOND E, ELECTRONICS, COMPUTER SCIENCE. *Current Pos:* RETIRED. *Personal Data:* b St Paul, Minn, May 25, 22; m 59, 86; c Michael D, Karl R & Christopher E. *Educ:* Yale Univ, BE, 44; Harvard Univ, MBA, 48; Oxford Univ, BA, 50, MA, 54. *Prof Exp:* Asst to gen mgr, PRD Electronics Inc, 50-55; prod sales mgr, Curtiss Wright Corp, 55-57; from div sales mgr to dir mkt, TRW Comput Co, 57-60; vpres opers, Electro-Sci Investors, Inc, 60-63; pres, Maxson Electronics, 63-64; mgmt consult, 64-67; chmn & pres, Anderson Jacobson, Inc, 67-88, France, 74-88, UK, 75-85, Can, 75-85, Ger, 78-83; chmn CKR Corp, 88-93. *Concurrent Pos:* Chmn, Staco, Inc & Gen Electronic Controls, 60-63 & Whitehall Electronics, Inc, 61-63; dir, Tamar Electronics, Inc, & Rawco Instruments, Inc, 60-63; Micro-Radionics, Inc, 65-67. *Mem:* Am Electronics Asn; Asn Am Rhodes Scholars; Sigma Xi. *Res:* Acoustic data couplers; specialized feature modems; high speed modems; dot matrix thermal printers; dot matrix needle printers; ink jet printers; cathode ray tube terminals. *Mailing Add:* 1247 Montcourse Lane San Jose CA 95131-2420

JACOBSON, RICHARD MARTIN, SYNTHETIC ORGANIC CHEMISTRY. *Current Pos:* sr res chemist, 80-84, RES FEL, ROHM & HAAS RES LAB, 84- *Personal Data:* b New York, NY, Dec 23, 47; m 75. *Educ:* Case Western Res Univ, BS, 69; Columbia Univ, PhD(org chem), 73. *Prof Exp:* Asst prof chem, Ind Univ, Bloomington, 75-80. *Mem:* Am Chem Soc. *Res:* Design and synthesis of agricultural chemicals. *Mailing Add:* Rohm & Haas Co 727 Norristown Rd Spring House PA 19477

JACOBSON, ROBERT ANDREW, PHYSICAL CHEMISTRY, CRYSTALLOGRAPHY. *Current Pos:* assoc prof, 64-69, PROF CHEM, IOWA STATE UNIV, 69- *Personal Data:* b Waterbury, Conn, Feb 16, 32; m 62, Margaret McMahon; c Robert & Cheryl. *Educ:* Univ Conn, BA, 54; Univ Minn, PhD(phys chem), 59. *Prof Exp:* From instr to asst prof chem, Princeton Univ, 59-64. *Concurrent Pos:* Chemist, Ames Lab, 64-69, sr chemist, 69- *Mem:* Am Chem Soc; Am Crystallog Asn. *Res:* Molecular structure of solids; x-ray and neutron diffraction. *Mailing Add:* Dept Chem Iowa State Univ Ames IA 50011. *Fax:* 515-294-5233; *E-Mail:* raj@vaxld.ameslab.gov

JACOBSON, ROBERT LEROY, CHEMICAL ENGINEERING. *Current Pos:* REFORMING PROCESS CONSULT, 89- *Personal Data:* b Miles City, Mont, Mar 11, 32; m 53, Marie E Larson; c Robert Richard (deceased), Kim (Allen), Charles Leroy & Art Eric. *Educ:* Mont State Univ, BS, 54, PhD(chem eng), 58. *Prof Exp:* res engr petrol process develop, Chevron Res Co, 58-72, sr eng assoc, 72-77, group leader process develop, 77-84, group leader process res explor, Chevron Res Co, Stand Oil Co, Calif, 84-89. *Mem:* Am Inst Chem Engrs; Am Chem Soc; Catalysis Soc. *Res:* Petroleum process research and development; exploratory research. *Mailing Add:* 2951 Cascade Lane Valley Springs CA 95252-9260

JACOBSON, STANLEY, NEUROANATOMY. *Current Pos:* asst prof, 67-70, assoc prof, 70-80, PROF ANAT, SCH MED, TUFTS UNIV, 80- *Personal Data:* b Chicago, Ill, Aug 24, 37; m 60; c 1. *Educ:* Univ Ill, BS, 59; Northwestern Univ, MS, 61, PhD(anat), 63. *Prof Exp:* Biologist, NIH, 63-65; biologist, Vet Admin Res Hosp, Chicago, 65-67. *Concurrent Pos:* Lectr, Sch Med, George Washington Univ, 64-65; assoc, Med Sch, Northwestern Univ, 65-67. *Mem:* AAAS; Am Asn Anatomists. *Res:* Structure of central nervous system in normal and diseased animals; connections between cerebral cortex and thalamus; degeneration of nerve fibers. *Mailing Add:* Dept Anat Tufts Univ Sch Med 136 Harrison Ave Boston MA 02111-1800

JACOBSON, STEPHEN ERNEST, ORGANIC FLUORINE CHEMISTRY, CATALYSIS OF HYDROGENATION. *Current Pos:* res assoc, 87-93, SR RES ASSOC, E I DU PONT DE NEMOURS & CO, 94- *Personal Data:* b State Center, Iowa, Apr 6, 45; m 75, Lydia Bubba. *Educ:* Iowa State Univ, BS, 67; Ohio State Univ, MS, 70, PhD(inorg chem), 72. *Prof Exp:* Res chemist inorg & catalysis, Allied-Signal Corp, 75-80; res assoc, Halcon Res, 80-86. *Concurrent Pos:* Fel, Univ Waterloo, 72-74, Univ Ala, 74-75. *Mem:* Am Chem Soc; NAm Catalysis Soc. *Res:* Process chemical research and development; new product research; organic synthesis; catalysis research. *Mailing Add:* Two Buchak Circle Princeton Junction NJ 08550. *Fax:* 609-540-4302

JACOBSON, STEPHEN RICHARD, geology, paleontology, for more information see previous edition

JACOBSON, STUART LEE, CARDIAC PHYSIOLOGY, CARDIAC CELL CULTURE. *Current Pos:* RETIRED. *Personal Data:* b Chicago, Ill, Apr 29, 34; m 59; c 2. *Educ:* Cornell Univ, BCE, 57; Univ Minn, Minneapolis, MS, 63, PhD(biophys), 68. *Prof Exp:* Proj engr, Aeromed Lab, Wright Air Develop Ctr, USAF, 57-59; from asst prof to assoc prof biol, Carleton Univ, 68-97. *Mem:* Int Soc Heart Res; Biophys Soc; Soc Gen Physiologists. *Res:* Engineering of systems for maintaining life in sealed environments; instrumentation for ecological studies; sensory physiology; electrophysiology, culture and electrophysiology of myocardial cells. *Mailing Add:* Dept Biol Carleton Univ Ottawa ON K1S 5B6 Can

JACOBSON, WILLARD JAMES, SCIENCE EDUCATION, ENVIRONMENTAL SCIENCE. *Current Pos:* co-dir, Population Educ Proj, 72-80, chmn, Dept Sci Educ, 65-73, dir, Citizens & Sci Educ Study, PROF NATURAL SCI, TEACHERS COL, COLUMBIA UNIV, 52- *Personal Data:* b Northfield, Wis, May 22, 22; m 46; c 3. *Educ:* Univ Wis, River Falls, BS, 46; Columbia Univ, AM, 48, EdD, 52. *Honors & Awards:* Robert Carleton Award, Nat Sci Teachers Asn. *Prof Exp:* Teacher pub schs, Wis, 46-47. *Concurrent Pos:* Fulbright lectr, Univ London, 60; consult, Royal Afghan Ministry Educ, 54-56, Am Sch Guatemala, 58, 61 & 64, UNESCO, 65, 84, Nat Coun Sci Educ India, 69, Nat Textbook Comn Brazil, 71 & Ministry Educ, Jamaica, 79-80; chmn, Educ Adv Comt, NY Acad Sci, 75-78, mem bd govs, 78-80; nat res coordr, Second Int Sci Study, 82- *Mem:* Fel AAAS (vpres, 68-69); Nat Asn Res Sci Teaching (pres, 68-69); fel NY Acad Sci; Asn Educ Teachers Sci (pres, 62-63). *Res:* Science for children and early adolescents; population education; science education survey. *Mailing Add:* 290 Kings Town Apt 391 Duxbury MA 02332

JACOBSON-KRAM, DAVID, TOXICOLOGY. *Current Pos:* vpres, Genetic Toxicol Div, 88-90, VPRES TOXICOL GROUP, MICROBOL ASSOCS INC, 90- *Educ:* Univ Conn, BA, 71, PhD(develop biol), 76. *Prof Exp:* Staff fel, Nat Inst Aging, NIH, 76-79, sr staff fel, 79; biologist, Toxic Effects Br, Off Toxic Substances, US Environ Protection Agency, 79-83, geneticist, Reproductive Effects Assessment Group, Off Health & Environ Assessment, Off Res & Develop, 83-88, actg br chief, Genetic & Molecular Toxicol Assessment Br, 88; from res asst prof to res assoc prof, Dept Radiol, George Washington Univ, Sch Med, 79-84; assoc prof oncol, Dept Radiobiol, Johns Hopkins Univ, Oncol Ctr, 84-90. *Concurrent Pos:* Ed, Cell Biol & Toxicol, 86-88; vis assoc prof, Johns Hopkins Univ, Oncol Ctr, 90- *Mem:* AAAS; Am Col Toxicol; Radiation Res Soc; Teratology Soc; Genetic Toxicol Asn; Environ Mutagen Soc; Soc Toxicol. *Res:* Cell biology; toxicology. *Mailing Add:* Microbiol Assocs Inc 9900 Blackwell Rd Rockville MD 20850

JACOBUS, DAVID PENMAN, MEDICINE, RADIOBIOLOGY. *Current Pos:* OWNER, JACOBUS PHARMACEUT CO, INC, 78- *Personal Data:* b Boston, Mass, Feb 26, 27; m 56; c 5. *Educ:* Harvard Univ, BA, 49; Univ Pa, MD, 53. *Prof Exp:* Resident & researcher, Hosp Univ Pa, 53-57; chief dept radiobiol, Div Nuclear Med, Walter Reed Army Inst Res, 59-63, chief dept med chem, 63-65, dir, Div Med Chem, 65-69; vpres basic res, Merck Sharp & Dohme Res Labs, vpres, 74-78. *Concurrent Pos:* Mem revision comt, US Pharmacopeia, 70-; trustee, Cold Spring Harbor Lab, 70-; consult, St Luke's Hosp Ctr, New York, 71-; chmn Nat Cancer Inst Comt on Info Handling, 78- *Mem:* Am Chem Soc; Am Soc Info Sci; Asn Comput Mach; NY Acad Sci. *Res:* Information handling. *Mailing Add:* 37 Cleveland Lane Box 5290 Princeton NJ 08540

JACOBUS, OTHA JOHN, ORGANIC CHEMISTRY. *Current Pos:* VPRES, C H & A CORP, 89- *Personal Data:* b Phoenix, Ariz, Dec 23, 39; m 62; c 2. *Educ:* Southwestern at Memphis, BS, 62; Univ Tenn, Knoxville, PhD(org chem), 65. *Prof Exp:* NIH fel org chem, Princeton Univ, 66-67, instr, 67-69; from asst prof to prof org chem, Clemson Univ, 74-76; prof org chem, Tulane Univ, 78-89, chmn dept, 80-89. *Mem:* Am Chem Soc. *Res:* Stereochemistry; NMR spectroscopy; reaction mechanisms. *Mailing Add:* 2218 Northpark Dr Kingwood TX 77339

JACOBUS, WILLIAM EDWARD, BIOCHEMISTRY. *Current Pos:* asst prof med & physiol chem, 77-82, ASSOC PROF MED, BIOL & CHEM, JOHNS HOPKINS SCH MED, 82- *Personal Data:* b Cleveland, Ohio, Nov 30, 42; m 66. *Educ:* Ohio Wesleyan Univ, BA, 64; Ohio State Univ, PhD(bchem), 69. *Prof Exp:* Fel biochem, Sch Med, Johns Hopkins Univ, 70-73, Heart Asn Md res fel & NIH res grant, Myocardial Infarction Res Unit, 71-73; asst prof zool, Univ Calif, Davis, 73-77. *Concurrent Pos:* Nat Heart & Lung Inst res grant, 74-77. *Mem:* AAAS; Am Chem Soc; Am Physiol Soc; Sigma Xi; Biophys Soc; Am Soc Biol Chem; Soc Magnetic Res Med; Int Soc Heart Res. *Res:* Mitochondrial oxidative phosphorylation and ion transport; mitochondrial compartmentation and enzymology; metabolic regulation; cardiac bioenergetics; tissue nuclear magnetic resonance. *Mailing Add:* 4550 Eddington Ct Toledo OH 43615-1605

JACOBY, ALEXANDER ROBB, MATHEMATICS. *Current Pos:* PROF MATH, UNIV NH, 61- *Personal Data:* b St Louis, Mo, Oct 8, 22; m 45. *Educ:* Univ Chicago, SB, 41, SM, 42, PhD(math), 46. *Prof Exp:* Asst math, Univ Chicago, 43-45, instr, 45-47; asst prof, Univ Miami, 47-49 & Rutgers Univ, 49-57; with Gen Elec Corp, 57-61. *Res:* Topology and algebra. *Mailing Add:* Dept Math Univ NH Durham NH 03824

JACOBY, HENRY I, GASTROINTESTINAL PHARMACOLOGY, RENAL PHARMACOLOGY. *Current Pos:* group leader, McNeil Labs Pharmaceut, 72-77, prin scientist, 78-79, res fel gen pharmacol, 79-87, RES FEL GEN PHARM, RW JOHNSON PHARMACEUT RES INST, 88- *Personal Data:* b Scranton, Pa, Aug 26, 36; m 67; c 2. *Educ:* Philadelphia Col Pharm & Sci, BSc, 58; Univ Mich, PhD(pharmacol), 63. *Honors & Awards:* Philip B Hoffman Res Award, Johnson & Johnson, 79. *Prof Exp:* Res pharmacologist, Res Lab, Merck Sharpe & Dohme, 63-72. *Mem:* Am Gastroent Asn; Am Soc Pharmacol & Exp Therapeut. *Res:* Neurokinin and opioid receptors; gastrointestinal pharmacology especially drug effecting motility; intestinal secretion. *Mailing Add:* 4119 Ocean Ave Brigantine NJ 08203-3373

JACOBY, JAY, ANESTHESIOLOGY. *Current Pos:* CLIN PROF, OHIO STATE UNIV, 88- *Personal Data:* b New York, NY, Dec 12, 17; m 42; c 3. *Educ:* Univ Minn, BS, 39, MB, 41, MD, 42; Univ Chicago, PhD(anesthesiol), 47; Am Bd Anesthesiol, dipl. *Prof Exp:* Res assoc & instr anesthesia, Univ Chicago, 46-47; assoc prof surg & dir anesthesia, Ohio State Univ, 47-53, prof, 53-59; prof & chmn dept, Med Sch, Marquette Univ, 59-65; prof, Jefferson Med Col, 65-84, emer prof anesthesiol & chmn dept, 84-88. *Mem:* Am Soc Anesthesiol; Am Col Anesthesiol; Int Anesthesia Res Soc; AMA; Asn Univ Anesthetists. *Res:* Anesthetic and analgesic drugs; gas therapy. *Mailing Add:* 155 W Main St No 1206 Columbus OH 43215-5062

JACOBY, JEAN, PHYSIOLOGY OF THE EYE MUSCLE. *Current Pos:* Res scientist, Med Ctr, 85-88, ASST PROF NEUROSCI, NY UNIV, 88-, ASST PROF OPHTHAL, 88- *Personal Data:* b New York, NY, Mar 8, 51. *Educ:* Univ Chicago, BS, 72; Univ Ore, PhD(neurosci), 79. *Mem:* AAAS; Biophys Soc; Soc Neurosci; Asn Res Vision & Ophthal. *Mailing Add:* Dept Ophthal NY Univ Med Ctr 550 First Ave New York NY 10016-6402. *Fax:* 212-263-7602

JACOBY, LAWRENCE JOHN, ORGANIC CHEMISTRY, ANALYTICAL CHEMISTRY. *Current Pos:* QUAL ASSURANCE COORDR, COLUMBIA ANALYTIC SERV INC, KELSO, WASH, 90- *Personal Data:* b Portland, Ore, May 19, 43; m 84; c 2. *Educ:* Ore State Univ, BS, 65; Colo State Univ, PhD(org chem), 69. *Prof Exp:* Asst prof org chem, Portland State Univ, 69-71; asst prof chem, Chemeketa Community Col, 71-76; anal chemist, Teledyne Wah Chang, Albany, 76-86; lab mgr, CH2M Hill, Corvallis, Ore, 86-88, client serv mgr, CH2M Hill, Redding, Calif, 88-90. *Mem:* Am Chem Soc; Asn Official Anal Chemists. *Res:* Valence tautomerism induced by electron transfer. *Mailing Add:* 104 Hackett Rd Longview WA 98632-9611

JACOBY, ROBERT OTTINGER, COMPARATIVE PATHOLOGY. *Current Pos:* From asst prof to assoc prof, 71-87, CHMN, SECT COMPARATIVE MED & DIR, DIV ANIMAL CARE, YALE SCH MED, 78-, PROF COMPARATIVE MED. *Personal Data:* b New York, NY, June 20, 39. *Educ:* Cornell Univ, DVM, 63; Ohio State Univ, MSc, 68, PhD(path), 69. *Honors & Awards:* Res Award, Am Asn Lab Animal Sci, 87; Griffin Award, Am Asn Lab Animal Sci, 93. *Prof Exp:* Asst prof path, Ohio State Univ, 69; NIH fel, Univ Chicago, 69-71. *Mem:* AAAS; Am Col Vet Pathologists; Am Vet Med Asn; Sigma Xi; Am Soc Investigative Pathologists; Am Soc Virol. *Res:* Pathogenesis of infectious diseases; diseases of laboratory animals; animal models of human disease. *Mailing Add:* PO Box 208016 Yale Univ New Haven CT 06520. *Fax:* 203-785-7499

JACOBY, RONALD LEE, MEDICINAL CHEMISTRY, COMPUTER-ASSISTED INSTRUCTION. *Current Pos:* From asst prof to assoc prof, 70-80, PROF MED CHEM, FERRIS STATE COL, 80- *Personal Data:* b Muskegon, Mich, Jan 30, 43; m 66; c 3. *Educ:* Ferris State Col, BSPharm, 66; Univ Conn, PhD(med chem), 71. *Res:* Computer-assisted instruction. *Mailing Add:* Sch Pharm Ferris State Univ 901 S State St Big Rapids MI 49307-2251

JACOBY, RUSSELL STEPHEN, METAMORPHIC PETROLOGY, URANIUM GEOLOGY. *Current Pos:* asst prof, 71-73, ASSOC PROF GEOL, ST LAWRENCE UNIV, 73- *Personal Data:* b Lehighton, Pa, June 23, 39; m 59; c 3. *Educ:* Syracuse Univ, BS, 61, MS, 64; Queen's Univ, PhD(geol), 68. *Prof Exp:* Asst prof geol, Cent Mo State Univ, 68-71. *Mem:* Geol Soc Am; Geol Asn Can; Sigma Xi. *Res:* Structural geology and metamorphic petrology of precambrian metamorphic shield areas; uranium exploration. *Mailing Add:* 67 State St Canton NY 13617

JACOLEV, LEON, chemical engineering; deceased, see previous edition for last biography

JACOT, A DEAN, SMART STRUCTURES, POINTING CONTROL. *Current Pos:* TECH FEL, BOEING CORP, 92- *Personal Data:* b Tacoma, Wash, Apr 7, 36; m, Amie; c Christine, Bruce & Colleen. *Educ:* Univ Wash, BSME, 68, MSME, 70. *Honors & Awards:* Eng Tech Achievement Award, Am Inst Aeronaut & Astronaut, 97. *Mem:* Assoc fel Am Inst Aeronaut & Astronaut; Int Soc Optical Eng. *Res:* Applying smart structures to spacecraft and aircraft; applying vibration isolation to spacecraft. *Mailing Add:* Boeing Defense & Space PO Box 3999 MS 82-24 Seattle WA 98124-2499. *E-Mail:* dean.jacot@boeing.com

JACOVIDES, LINOS J, ELECTRICAL ENGINEERING. *Current Pos:* Sr res engr, Defense Res Labs, Gen Motors Corp, 65-67, sr res engr, Res Labs, Warren, Mich, 67-75, dept res engr & asst dept head, Elec Eng Dept, 85-87, prin res engr, Elec Eng Dept, 87-88, HEAD, ELEC & ELECTRONIC RES DEPT, GEN MOTORS, RES & DEVELOP CTR, 88- *Personal Data:* b Paphos, Cyprus, May 10, 40; US citizen; m, Kathleen McNamee; c James, Michael, Christina & Julia. *Educ:* Glasgow Univ, BSc, 61, MSc, 63; Univ

London, PhD, 65. *Mem:* Fel Inst Elec & Electronics Engrs; Brit Inst Elec Engrs; Soc Automotive Engrs. *Res:* Electromagnetics and electromagnetic energy conversion; high performance electric drive systems; automotive electrical systems; electric vehicles and locomotive electric drives; electromechanical devices; automotive powertrain and chassis control systems. *Mailing Add:* EL Dept Bldg 1-6 30500 Mound Rd Warren MI 48090-9055. *Fax:* 810-986-0886; *E-Mail:* ljacovid@cmsa.gmr.com

JACOX, ADA K, MEDICINE. *Current Pos:* ASSOC DEAN RES, COL NURSING, WAYNE STATE UNIV, 96- *Educ:* Columbia Univ, BS; Wayne State Univ, MS; Case Western Reserve Univ, PhD. *Honors & Awards:* Shirley Titus Award, Am Nurses Asn, 88. *Prof Exp:* Staff nurse, Kalamazoo State Hosp, Mich, 56-57; pvt duty nurse pediat & neurol, Columbia-Presby Hosp, NY, 58-59; staff nurse acute & chronic pediat, Children's Hosp Mich, Detroit, 59-60; assoc dir nursing & dir nursing educ, Plymouth State Home & Training Sch, Northville, Mich, 61-62, dir nursing, 62-64; psychiat nurse, Johnson County Mental Health Ctr, Kans City, 68-69; from assoc prof to prof, Col Nursing, Univ Iowa, 69-76; assoc dean res & doctoral prog & prof nursing, Sch Nursing, Univ Colo, 76-79; prof nursing, Sch Nursing, Univ Md, 80-90, dir, Ctr Nursing & Health Serv Res, 80-90; prof independance found chair & health policy, Sch Nursing, Johns Hopkins Univ, 90-95. *Concurrent Pos:* Asst prof, Dept Nursing Educ, Univ Kans, 68-69; res consult, Ment Health Inst, Mt Pleasant, Iowa, 70-71, Iowa Vet Home, Marshalltown, 72-76, Vet Admin Hosp, Iowa City, 74-76 & Clin Ctr, NIH, 75-79; Carver fel, Univ Iowa, 72; prin investr, HEW, 72-79; actg dean advan studies, Grad Col, Univ Iowa, 75-76. *Mem:* Inst Med-Nat Acad Sci; fel Am Acad Nurses; Am Nurses Asn; Am Nurses Found (pres, 82-85). *Res:* Author of 6 books and over 20 journal articles. *Mailing Add:* Col Nursing Wayne State Univ 5557 Cass Ave Detroit MI 48202

JACOX, MARILYN ESTHER, MOLECULAR SPECTROSCOPY, PHOTOCHEMISTRY. *Current Pos:* phys chemist, 62-95, EMER SCIENTIST, NAT INST STANDARDS & TECHNOL, 96- *Personal Data:* b Utica, NY, Apr 26, 29. *Educ:* Syracuse Univ, BA, 51; Cornell Univ, PhD, 56. *Hon Degrees:* ScD, Syracuse Univ, 93. *Honors & Awards:* Outstanding Alumnus Award, Utica Col, 63; Award Phys Sci, Washington Acad Sci, 68; Gold Medal Award for Distinguished Serv, US Dept Com, 70; Federal Woman's Award, Fed Woman's Award Bd of Trustees, 73; Samuel Wesley Stratton Award, Nat Bur Stand, 73; Ellis R Lippincott Award, Coblentz Soc, 89; Hilebrand Prize, Chem Soc Wash, 90; WISE Lifetime Achievement Award, Interagency Comt Women Sci & Eng, 91. *Prof Exp:* Res assoc phys chem, Univ NC, 56-58; fel spectros of solids, Mellon Inst Sci Res, 58-62. *Concurrent Pos:* Chief, Photochem Sect, Nat Bur Stand, 73-74, chief, Environ Chem Processes Sect, 74-78. *Mem:* Fel Am Phys Soc; Am Chem Soc; Int-Am Photochem Soc; fel AAAS; Sigma Xi. *Res:* Chemistry of free radicals and molecular ions; molecular spectroscopy. *Mailing Add:* Nat Inst Stand & Technol Gaithersburg MD 20899. *E-Mail:* marilyn.jacox@nist.gov

JACOX, RALPH FRANKLIN, internal medicine; deceased, see previous edition for last biography

JACQUES, FELIX ANTHONY, BIOLOGY. *Current Pos:* asst prof, 62-64, ASSOC PROF PHYSIOL, ST BONAVENTURE UNIV, 64- *Personal Data:* b Kansas City, Kans, July 17, 24. *Educ:* Univ Iowa, BA, 50, MS, 53; St Louis Univ, PhD(biol), 60. *Prof Exp:* Instr biol, Langston Univ, 53-55; lectr zool, Southern Ill Univ, 59-61; asst prof physiol & evolution, Webster Col, 61-62. *Concurrent Pos:* Nat Heart Inst fel, 60-62, res grant, 65-68. *Mem:* AAAS; Am Soc Zool; assoc Am Physiol Soc; Am Inst Biol Sci; Sigma Xi. *Res:* Comparative and environmental physiology; environmental effects on blood and other tissues. *Mailing Add:* Dept Biol St Bonaventure Univ St Bonaventure NY 14778-9999. *Fax:* 716-375-2389

JACQUET, HERVE, NUMBER THEORY. *Current Pos:* PROF MATH, COLUMBIA UNIV, 74- *Personal Data:* b France, Aug 4, 39; m 69; c 1. *Educ:* Univ Paris, Licence, 61, PhD(math), 67. *Honors & Awards:* Prix Petit d'Ormoy, Acad Sci, Paris, 79. *Prof Exp:* Researcher, Nat Ctr Sci Res, France, 63-65; assoc prof math, Univ Md, 69-70; prof math, Grad Sch City Univ New York, 70-74. *Concurrent Pos:* Mem, Inst Advan Studies, 67-69. *Mem:* Am Math Soc. *Res:* Automorphic L-functions. *Mailing Add:* Columbia Univ 2990 Broadway New York NY 10027-0029

JACQUET, YASUKO F, BEHAVIORAL NEUROPHARMACOLOGY, OPIATE NEUROPHARMACOLOGY. *Current Pos:* RETIRED. *Personal Data:* b San Francisco, Calif; c 1. *Educ:* Tsuda Col, Tokyo, Japan, dipl, 51; State Univ Iowa, Iowa City, BA, 53; Ind Univ, Bloomington, PhD(exp psychol), 62. *Prof Exp:* Postdoctoral fel, Sch Med, Yale Univ, 62-64; staff fel, NIMH, Bethesda, Md, 64-65; vis scientist, Nat Inst Med Res, London, UK, 77, Uppsala Univ, Sweden, 79, Mass Gen Hosp, Boston, 82 & Columbia Univ Med Ctr, New York, 83-85; res scientist, NY State Dept Ment Hyg, NY, 66-93. *Mem:* Am Soc Pharmacol & Exp Therapeut; Soc Neurosci; Europ Behav Pharmacol Soc; Am Pain Soc; Int Narcotics Res Conf; Asn Res Nervous & Ment Dis. *Res:* Central nervous system sites involved in opiate effects; physiological actions of endogenous opiate peptides; neurotransmitters mediating opiate effects. *Mailing Add:* 200 California Rd No 22 Bronxville NY 10708-4427

JACQUEZ, JOHN ALFRED, COMPARTMENTAL ANALYSIS, EPIDEMIOLOGICAL MODELING. *Current Pos:* from assoc prof to prof physiol, Med Sch, Univ Mich, 62-90, from assoc prof to prof biostatist, Sch Pub Health, 62-90, actg chmn physiol, Med Sch, 85-87, EMER PROF PHYSIOL & BIOSTATIST, UNIV MICH, 90- *Personal Data:* b Pfastatt, Alsace, France, June 26, 22; US citizen; m 48, Marianne R Reibel; c Albert R, Nicholas P, Geoffrey M & Phillip F. *Educ:* Cornell Univ, MD, 47. *Prof Exp:* Res fel, Sloan-Kettering Inst, 47-50, from asst to assoc prof chemother, 50-60, assoc mem, 60-62; from instr to assoc prof biol, Sloan-Kettering Div, Cornell Univ, 52-63. *Concurrent Pos:* Vis investr path & bact, Rockefeller Inst, 47-48; consult, Rand Corp, 59-64; mem sci adv comt, Ore Regional Primate Res Ctr, 65-68; mem comput res study sect, NIH, 66-70, chmn, 68-70, mem chem & biol info handling rev comt, 75-79 & biotech res adv comt, 77-79; assoc ed, Math Biosci, 67-75, ed, 75-95. *Mem:* Am Physiol Soc; Biophys Soc; Soc Indust & Appl Math; Soc Math Biol (pres, 85-87); Sigma Xi. *Res:* Active transport; structure and function of membranes; mathematical modeling of physiological systems; compartmental systems; logical and probabilistic structure of the diagnostic process; respiratory physiology; epidemiological modeling. *Mailing Add:* 490 Huntington Dr Ann Arbor MI 48104. *Fax:* 313-936-8813; *E-Mail:* jacquez@umich.edu

JACQUIN, ARNAUD ERIC, IMAGE & VIDEO CODING, FRACTAL CODING. *Current Pos:* MEM TECH STAFF SIGNAL PROCESSING RES, SIGNAL PROCESSING DEPT, AT&T BELL LABS, MURRAY HILL, NJ, 90- *Personal Data:* b Reims, France, Feb 18, 64. *Educ:* Ecole Superieure d'Electricite, EngrESE, 86; Ga Inst Tech, MS, 87, PhD(math), 89. *Honors & Awards:* Sr Award, Signal Processing Soc, Inst Elec & Electronics Engrs, 93. *Mem:* Inst Elec & Electronics Engrs. *Res:* Image processing; image and video coding. *Mailing Add:* AT&T Bell Labs Rm 2D-337 600 Mountain Ave Murray Hill NJ 07974. *Fax:* 908-582-7308; *E-Mail:* arnaud@research.att.com

JACQUOT, RAYMOND G, MECHANICAL ENGINEERING, ELECTRICAL ENGINEERING. *Current Pos:* from asst prof to assoc prof, 69-77, PROF ELEC ENG, UNIV WYO, 77- *Personal Data:* b Casper, Wyo, Nov 16, 38; div; c 1. *Educ:* Univ Wyo, BS, 60, MS, 62; Purdue Univ, PhD(mech eng), 69. *Prof Exp:* Supply instr mech eng, Univ Wyo, 60-62, instr, 62-64; instr, Purdue Univ, 64-65. *Concurrent Pos:* Vis prof elec & comput eng, Univ Calif, Davis, 84. *Mem:* Am Soc Mech Engrs; Am Soc Eng Educ; Inst Elec & Electronics Engrs. *Res:* Vibration of elastic systems; simulation of large scale systems by digital computer; digital control and signal processing; nonlinear system analysis; digital filtering. *Mailing Add:* Dept Elec Eng Univ Wyo Laramie WY 82071

JADHAV, A L, PHARMACOLOGY. *Current Pos:* ASST DEAN RES & GRAD EDUC, TEX SOUTHERN UNIV, 91- *Mem:* Fedn Am Socs Exp Biol. *Res:* Pharmacology. *Mailing Add:* Tex Southern Univ Col Pharm & Health Sci 3100 Cleburne Houston TX 77004-4598. *Fax:* 713-639-1889

JADUS, MARTIN ROBERT, CYTOKINES, HEMATOLOGY. *Current Pos:* HEALTH RES SPECIALIST, VET ADMIN MED CTR, 90- *Personal Data:* b Girardville, Pa, Jan 10, 53; m, Yolanda Yong Chan. *Educ:* Univ Del, BA(biol), 75, BA(chem), 76; Fla Inst Technol, MS, 78; Univ Fla, PhD(med sci), 83. *Prof Exp:* Vis asst prof, Univ SFla, 85-86; res scientist, Bio Therapeut Inc, 86-88; sr scientist, Marrow Tech Inc, 88-90. *Concurrent Pos:* Lectr chem, Fla Inst Tech, 77-78; res scholar, Univ Southern Calif, 83-85; asst res, Univ Calif, Irvine, 90-; adj prof chem & biochem, Calif State Univ, Long Beach, 96- *Mem:* AAAS; Am Asn Immunol; Soc Biol Ther; Am Asn Hematologists; Soc Leukocyte Biol; Int Soc Hemat. *Res:* Immune regulation by cytokines and possible roles in the disease process; molecular biology of macrophage colony stimulating factor stimulating natural suppressor cells; Rosai-Dorfman disease and psoriasis. *Mailing Add:* 3473 Bellflower Blvd Long Beach CA 90808

JADUSZLIWER, BERNARDO, ELECTRON SCATTERING, ATOMIC FREQUENCY STANDARDS. *Current Pos:* mem tech staff, 85-87, res scientist, 87-93, mgr, Atomic Clocks Sect, 93-96, DIR, LASERS & OPTICAL PHYSICS DEPT, AEROSPACE CORP, 96- *Personal Data:* b Buenos Aires, Argentina, Oct 17, 43; m 68; c 1. *Educ:* Univ Buenos Aires, Lic en physics, 68; Univ Toronto, MSc, 70, PhD(physics), 73. *Prof Exp:* Fel physics, Univ Toronto, 73-74; assoc res scientist, NY Univ, 74-78, from asst res prof to assoc res prof physics, 81-85. *Concurrent Pos:* Tech adv, Physics Today Buyers Guide, 83-93; adj assoc prof, Univ Southern Calif, 85- *Mem:* Am Phys Soc; Inst Elec & Electronics Engrs. *Res:* Low energy electron positron scattering on ground and excited state atoms and molecules; measurement of atomic and molecular polarizabilities; atom photon interaction; atomic frequency standards; fiber optic sensor systems. *Mailing Add:* Aerospace Corp M2-253 PO Box 92957 Los Angeles CA 90009. *E-Mail:* jaduszliwer@aero.org

JADVAR, HOSSEIN, BIOMEDICAL ENGINEERING, ONCOLOGY. *Current Pos:* AT PRITZKER INST IIT. *Personal Data:* b Tehran, Iran, Apr 6, 61. *Educ:* Iowa State Univ, BS, 82; Univ Wis, MS, 84; Univ Mich, Ann Arbor, MS, 86, PhD, 88; Univ Chicago, MD, 93. *Prof Exp:* Sr res engr, Arzco Med Electronics Inc, 88-89; sr res assoc, Pritzker Inst, Ill Inst Technol, 89-92; resident, Univ Calif, San Francisco, 93-94. *Mem:* AMA; Inst Elec & Electronics Engrs; Asn Advan Med Instrumentation; Biomed Eng Soc; Sigma Xi. *Res:* Esophageal catheters; method and apparatus for detection of posterior ischemia; granted several patents. *Mailing Add:* Stanford Univ Med Ctr Stanford CA 94305

JAECKER, JOHN ALVIN, CATALYSIS. *Current Pos:* Sr chemist, 73-84, RES ADV, ATLANTIC RICHFIELD CO, 84- *Personal Data:* b Troy, NY, Feb 21, 45; m 68; c 2. *Educ:* Hope Col, BA, 68; Purdue Univ, MA & PhD(inorg chem), 73. *Concurrent Pos:* Purchasing agent. *Mem:* Am Chem Soc; Catalysis Soc; Am Soc Testing & Mat. *Res:* Analytical chemistry of petroleum catalysts and products; studies of catalysts. *Mailing Add:* 1248 N Valle Vista Dr Fullerton CA 92631-1942

JAECKS, DUANE H, ATOMIC PHYSICS, TIME RESOLVED SPECTROSCOPY. *Current Pos:* From asst prof to assoc prof, 66-74, PROF PHYSICS, UNIV NEBR-LINCOLN, 74- *Personal Data:* b Wausau, Wis, Sept 24, 35; m 59; c 3. *Educ:* Univ Wis, BS, 58; Miami Univ, MA, 60; Univ Wash, Seattle, PhD(physics), 64. *Mem:* Fel Am Phys Soc. *Res:* Basic atomic collisions research. *Mailing Add:* Dept Physics Univ Nebr Lincoln NE 68588

JAEGER, CHARLES WAYNE, DYES & INKS FOR COLOR PRINTERS. *Current Pos:* chemist III, Tektronix, Inc, 80-81; sr res scientist IV, 81-83, mgr, Ink Jet Technol Group, 84-85, bus develop & spec proj mgr, Color Printing & Imaging Div, 85-86, PRIN SCIENTIST, COLOR PRINTING & IMAGING DIV, TEKTRONIX, INC, 83- *Personal Data:* b Kissimmee, Fla, Sept 8, 43; m 65, Carol Bryant; c Jennifer & Sara. *Educ:* Fla State Univ, BS, 66; Purdue Univ, PhD(org chem), 71. *Prof Exp:* Res fel org chem, Ga Inst Technol, 71-73; res chemist, Dyes & Chem Div, Crompton & Knowles Corp, 73-80. *Concurrent Pos:* Gen chmn, Soc Photog Scientists & Engrs Fifth Int Cong Adv Non-Impact Printing Technol; mem bd dirs, Soc Imaging Sci & Technol, 94- *Mem:* Am Chem Soc; Am Asn Textile Chem & Colorists; Soc Info Display; fel Soc Imaging Sci & Technol. *Res:* Research, development and manufacture of specialty phase change and aqueous inks for color ink-jet printers; evaluation of dyes for special color applications; computer simulation and evaluation of experimental dyes. *Mailing Add:* Tektronix Inc 26600 SW Pkwy Wilsonville OR 97070. *Fax:* 503-682-1183; *E-Mail:* wayne.jaeger@tek.com

JAEGER, DAVID ALLEN, ORGANIC CHEMISTRY. *Current Pos:* from asst prof to assoc prof, 71-82, PROF CHEM, UNIV WYO, 82- *Personal Data:* b San Diego, Calif, June 3, 44; m 68; c 1. *Educ:* Stanford Univ, BS, 65; Univ Calif, Los Angeles, PhD(org chem), 70. *Prof Exp:* NSF fel chem, Stanford Univ, 70-71. *Mem:* Am Chem Soc. *Res:* Chemistry; micellar catalysis; surfactant chemistry. *Mailing Add:* Dept Chem Univ Wyo Box 3838 Laramie WY 82071-3838

JAEGER, HEINRICH MARTIN, PHYSICS. *Current Pos:* asst prof, 91-96, ASSOC PROF PHYSICS, UNIV CHICAGO, 96- *Personal Data:* b Flensburg, Ger, May 15, 57. *Educ:* Univ Minn, MS, 82, PhD(physics), 87. *Prof Exp:* Sr researcher, Ctr Submicrotech, Neth, 89-91. *Concurrent Pos:* David & Lucile Packard fel, 91; Alfred P Sloan fel, 92; Cottrell scholar, Res Corp, 94. *Mem:* Am Phys Soc; Mat Res Soc. *Res:* Experimental condensed matter physics; superconductivity; mesoscopic structures; granular materials. *Mailing Add:* James Frank Inst Univ Chicago 5640 S Ellis Ave Chicago IL 60637

JAEGER, HERBERT KARL, ORGANIC CHEMISTRY. *Current Pos:* RETIRED. *Personal Data:* b Harpolingen-Saeckingen, Ger, June 29, 31; m 59; c 1. *Educ:* Univ Basel, PhD(org chem), 58. *Prof Exp:* Res fel chem, Univ Basel, 58-59 & Univ Calif, Los Angeles, 60-61; res assoc, Upjohn Co, 61-65, sect head, 65-70, res mgr org chem, 70-78, group mgr, 78-85, dir, fine chem prod, 85-90. *Mem:* Am Chem Soc. *Res:* Isolation and chemistry of cardiac glycosides; microbial production and chemistry of carotenoids; process research and development of steroidal and other chemical products. *Mailing Add:* 4901 Gulf Shore Blvd N No 203 Naples FL 34103

JAEGER, JAMES J, CARDIOVASCULAR PHYSIOLOGY, PULMONARY PHYSIOLOGY. *Current Pos:* Proj mgr, Walter Reed Army Inst Res, 73-85, CHIEF PHYSIOL BR, US ARMY MED RES INST CHEM DEFENSE, 85- *Educ:* Rutgers Univ, PhD(physiol), 73. *Mailing Add:* Univ Md Baltimore 714 W Lombard St Baltimore MD 21201-1010

JAEGER, KLAUS BRUNO, TECHNICAL MANAGEMENT. *Current Pos:* mgr, 85, PHYSICIST, LOCKHEED CO, 82- *Personal Data:* b Lubeck, Ger, May 8, 38; US citizen; m 69; c 1. *Educ:* Syracuse Univ, BS, 65, MS, 68, PhD(physics), 70. *Prof Exp:* Fel exp high energy physics, Argonne Nat Lab, 70-71; asst physicist, 71-75, physicist, 75-80; physicist, Brookhaven Nat Lab, 80-81. *Concurrent Pos:* Assoc group leader, Bubble Chamber, Argonne Nat Lab, 71-77, proj mgr 12ft solenoid magnet, 77-80, dep group leader for measuring & testing superconducting magnets, 80-81, metrologist, 82-85. *Mem:* Am Phys Soc; Am Inst Physics. *Res:* Design and implementation of new particle detection techniques such as solenoidal magnets with shower counters; inclusive hadron physics at high and medium energies; colliding electron positron beams; design and implementation of measuring techniques for superconducting dipole and quadrapole magnets; primary standards development. *Mailing Add:* 13685 Calle Tacuba Saratoga CA 95070

JAEGER, LESLIE GORDON, CIVIL ENGINEERING. *Current Pos:* spec asst to pres, 80-85, VPRES, TECH UNIV, NS, 86- *Personal Data:* b Southport, Eng, Jan 28, 26; m 48, 81, Kathleen Grant; c Valerie Ann & Hilary Frances. *Educ:* Cambridge Univ, BA, 46, MA, 50; London Univ, PhD, 55, DSc, 86. *Honors & Awards:* A B Sanderson Award, Can Soc Civil Eng, 83; Gzowski Medal, Eng Inst Can, 85. *Prof Exp:* Mem fac, Univ Col Khartoum, 52-56; univ lectr, Cambridge Univ, 56-62; prof civil eng & appl mech, McGill Univ, 62-64 & 66-70; Regius prof eng, Univ Edinburgh, 64-66; dean, Col Eng, Univ NB, 70-75, actg vpres, 72-73; acad vpres, Acadia Univ, 75-80. *Concurrent Pos:* Nat Res Coun Can res grantee, 62- *Mem:* Fel Eng Soc Can; fel Can Soc Civil Eng. *Res:* Author of numerous publications and research papers. *Mailing Add:* PO Box 1000 Halifax NS B3J 2X4 Can

JAEGER, MARC JULES, RESPIRATORY PHYSIOLOGY, SEPARATION OF GASES. *Current Pos:* PROF PHYSIOL & DENT, COL MED, UNIV FLA, 70- *Personal Data:* b Berne, Switz, Apr 4, 29; m 60, 73, Ina C Burlinghaur; c 2. *Educ:* Univ Berne, Baccalaureat, 48, MD, 54. *Prof Exp:* Res assoc med, Univ Berne, 57-61; res assoc physiol, Col Med, Univ Fla, 61-63; res asst med, Univ Berne, 63-65; asst prof physiol, Univ Fribourg, 65-70. *Concurrent Pos:* Vis prof, Yale Univ, 68, Dept Med, McGill Univ, Montreal, 80-81; Fogarty fel. *Mem:* Swiss Med Asn; Swiss Asn Physiol & Pharmacol; Swiss Soc Advan Sci; Int Union Physiol Sci; Sigma Xi. *Res:* Mechanics of breathing; fluid dynamics; mechanical and analog computer modelling; environmental physiology, especially diving, smoking and air pollution; diffusion of gases; separation of gases and isotopes; granted 5 US patents. *Mailing Add:* Univ Fl Col Med Box 100274 Gainesville FL 32610

JAEGER, RALPH R, INORGANIC CHEMISTRY. *Current Pos:* SR RES CHEMIST, MOUND LAB, MONSANTO RES CORP, 67- *Personal Data:* b Cincinnati, Ohio, Jan 30, 40. *Educ:* Univ Cincinnati, BS, 62; Purdue Univ, PhD(inorg chem), 67. *Mem:* Am Chem Soc; Am Inst Chemists. *Res:* Chemical vapor deposition of refractory metals; high temperature chemistry of plutonium; fuel forms containing plutonium. *Mailing Add:* 5092 Benner Rd Miamisburg OH 45342-4202

JAEGER, RICHARD CHARLES, MICROELECTRONICS, INTEGRATED CIRCUIT DESIGN. *Current Pos:* assoc prof, 79-82, alumni prof, 83-88, DISTINGUISHED UNIV PROF, AUBURN UNIV, 90- *Personal Data:* b New York, NY, Sept 2, 44; m 64, Joan C Hill; c Peter & Stephanie. *Educ:* Univ Fla, BS, 66, ME, 66, PhD(elec eng), 69. *Honors & Awards:* Outstanding Contrib Award, Computer Soc, Inst Elec & Electronics Engrs, Golden Core. *Prof Exp:* Staff eng, IBM Corp, 69-72, adv eng, 72-74, res staff mem, 74-76, adv eng, 76-79. *Concurrent Pos:* Prog comt mem, Int Solid-State Circuits conf, 78-92, chair, 93; mem, gov bd, comput soc, Inst Elec & Electronics Engrs, 85-86, secy, Solid State Circuits Coun, 85-87, vpres, 87-89, pres, 90-91; dir, Ala Microelectronics Sci & Technol Ctr, 84-; ed, Solid-State Circuits, Inst Elec & Electronics Engrs, 95- *Mem:* Fel Inst Elec & Electronics Engrs. *Res:* Microelectronic circuit, device and process design; electronic packaging and cooling; low temperature semiconductor electronics. *Mailing Add:* 711 Jennifer Dr Auburn AL 36830-7116. *E-Mail:* jaeger@eng.auburn.edu

JAEGER, ROBERT GORDON, POPULATION ECOLOGY. *Current Pos:* from asst prof to assoc prof, 81-86, PROF BIOL, UNIV SOUTHWESTERN LA, 86- *Personal Data:* b Baltimore, Md, Dec 16, 37; m 64. *Educ:* Univ Md, BS, 60, PhD(ecol), 69; Univ Calif, Berkeley, MA, 63. *Honors & Awards:* Stoye Award, Am Soc Ichthyol & Herpet, 69. *Prof Exp:* Fac res asst ecol, Univ Md, 69-70, instr zool, 70-71; res assoc zool, Univ Wis, Madison, 71-74; asst prof zool, State Univ NY, Albany, 74-80, adj asst prof, 80-81. *Concurrent Pos:* Ed, J Herpetologica, 82- *Mem:* Ecol Soc Am; Animal Behav Soc; Soc Study Evolution; Am Inst Biol Sci; Am Soc Ichthyol & Herpet; Sigma Xi. *Res:* Competitive exclusion and environmental pressures in the distributions of salamander species; comparative phototactic responses of anuran species in relation to their natural habitats. *Mailing Add:* Dept Biol Univ Southwestern La Lafayette LA 70504-2451

JAEGER, RUDOLPH JOHN, BIOCHEMISTRY. *Current Pos:* assoc prof, 79-83, RES PROF ENVIRON MED, SCH MED, NY UNIV, 85- *Personal Data:* b Weehawken, NJ, Jan 17, 44; m 66, 87; c 3. *Educ:* Renesselaer Polytech Inst, BS, 66; Johns Hopkins Univ, PhD(biochem toxicol), 71. *Honors & Awards:* Leslie Silverman Award, Am Indust Hyg Asn, 80. *Prof Exp:* Res assoc toxicol, Harvard Sch Pub Health, 71-73, asst prof, 73-78, assoc prof, 78-79. *Concurrent Pos:* Toxicol consult, Polaroid Corp, 77-, Southern Calif Edison, 84-87, Esselte Letraset Mfg, 85-, Goodwin, Proctor & Hoar, 87-, Womble, Carlyle, Sandridge & Rice, 88-90, Lockheed Aeronaut Systs, 87-89, Sidley & Austin, 89-, Polymerics Inc, 89-; tech support & prod eval, AT&T Bell Labs, 83-85; hazard commun training progs, Bell Commun Res, 88-89; mem, Toxicol Info Prog Comt, NAS, 90- *Mem:* Soc Toxicol; AAAS; NY Acad Sci; Am Indust Hygiene Asn; Sigma Xi; Am Soc Testing Mat; Am Chem Soc; Am Col Toxicol; Am Asn Path; Am Acad Clin Toxicol. *Res:* Inhalation toxicology of plastics monomers, pulmonary toxicology of combustion products. *Mailing Add:* Environ Med NY Univ Med Ctr 263 Center Ave Westwood NJ 07675-1701. *Fax:* 201-666-8119

JAEGER, WOLFGANG, SPECTROSCOPY & CHEMISTRY, VAN DER WAALS COMPLEXES. *Current Pos:* ASST PROF, DEPT CHEM, UNIV ALTA, 95- *Personal Data:* b Husum, Ger, Dec 23, 57. *Educ:* Christian Albrecuts Univ, dipl, 85, PhD(chem), 89. *Prof Exp:* Postdoctoral fel & res assoc, Univ BC, 89-95. *Mem:* Am Chem Soc. *Res:* Molecular beam techniques and pulsed excitation; emission spectroscopic methods for study of weak intermolecular interactions; many-body non-additive interactions. *Mailing Add:* Dept Chem Univ Alta Edmonton AB T6G 2G2 Can

JAEHNING, JUDITH A, BIOCHEMISTRY. *Current Pos:* asst prof, 85-88, ASST PROF BIOL, IND UNIV, 88- *Personal Data:* b Yakima, Wash, Oct 14, 50. *Educ:* Univ Wash, Seattle, BS, 72; Washington Univ, St Louis, PhD(biol chem), 77. *Prof Exp:* Fel biochem, Univ Calif, Berkeley, 77-78 & Stanford Univ, 78-80; asst prof biochem, Univ Ill, Urbana, 81-85. *Mem:* Am Soc Microbiologists; Am Soc Biochem & Molecular Biol; Genetics Soc Am. *Res:* Regulation and mechanisms of eukaryotic transcription; nuclear and mitochondrial RNA polymerase; saccharomyces cerevisiae. *Mailing Add:* Dept Biochem Biophys & Genetics Univ Colo Health Sci Ctr 4200 E Ninth Ave B121 Denver CO 80262

JAENIKE, JOHN ROBERT, medicine, for more information see previous edition

JAENISCH, RUDOLF, RETROVIRUSES, MAMMALIAN DEVELOPMENT. *Current Pos:* PROF, WHITEHEAD INST & DEPT BIOL, MASS INST TECHNOL, 84- *Personal Data:* Ger citizen. *Educ:* Univ Munich, MD, 67. *Prof Exp:* Postdoc fel, Max-Planck Inst, 67-69, Princeton Univ, 70-72; asst prof, Salk Inst, San Diego, 73-77; prof, Henrich-Pette Inst, Hamburg, Ger, 77-84. *Res:* Control of mammalian development using retroviruses and transgenic technology; generation of insertional mutations which affect mouse development; interaction of retroviruses with embryos. *Mailing Add:* 111 Seaver St Brookline MA 02146

JAESCHKE, WALTER HENRY, pathology, for more information see previous edition

JAFEK, BRUCE WILLIAM, HEAD & NECK SURGERY, NASAL & SINUS DISEASES. *Current Pos:* PROF OTOLARYNGOL & CHMN NECK-HEAD SURG, UNIV COLO, 76- *Personal Data:* b Chicago, Ill, Mar 4, 41; m 62, Mary B Kirkpatrick; c Lynette, Robert, Timothy, Britta, Kayla & Kristen. *Educ:* Coe Col, Iowa, BS, 62; Univ Calif, Los Angeles, MD, 66. *Honors & Awards:* Fowler Award, Triologic Soc, 83. *Prof Exp:* Intern gen surg, New Haven Hosp, 66-67; resident gen surg, Univ Calif, Los Angeles, 67-68, res otolaryngol, head & neck surg, 68-71; instr otolaryngol, Johns Hopkins Univ, 71-73; asst prof otolaryngol, Univ Pa, 73-76. *Mem:* Am Acad Facial Plastic Surg; Am Acad Otolaryngol-Head & Neck Surg; Am Col Surgeons; Asn Acad Dir Otolaryngol; Soc Univ Otolaryngologists; Triological Soc. *Res:* Chemosensation of the head and neck region; processing of biopsies from dysfunctional patients to correlate ultrastructural changes. *Mailing Add:* Dept Otolaryngol Box B-205 Univ Colo Health Sci Ctr Denver CO 80262. *Fax:* 303-315-8787; *E-Mail:* bruce.jafek@uchsc.edu

JAFFA, ROBERT E, MATHEMATICS. *Current Pos:* AT DEPT MATH, CALIF STATE UNIV. *Personal Data:* b Berkeley, Calif, Nov 11, 35. *Educ:* Univ Calif, BA, 57, MA, 60, PhD(math), 64. *Prof Exp:* Res mathematician, Univ Calif, 64-65; from asst prof to assoc prof, 65-76, prof math, Sacramento State Univ, 76- *Mem:* Am Math Soc. *Res:* Abstract algebra; functional analysis. *Mailing Add:* Dept Math Calif State Univ 6000 J St Sacramento CA 95819

JAFFE, ANNETTE BRONKESH, PHYSICAL ORGANIC CHEMISTRY, PHYSICAL CHEMISTRY. *Current Pos:* PRIN SCIENTIST, IMAGING PRODS, APPLE COMPUT, INC, SANTA CLARA, 90- *Personal Data:* b Munich, Ger, July 25, 46; US citizen; m 70; c Matthew & Elizabeth. *Educ:* Douglass Col, Rutgers Univ, BA, 68; Yale Univ, MPhil, 70, PhD(chem), 72. *Prof Exp:* Mem res staff, Res Labs, IBM Corp, 74-90. *Mem:* Am Chem Soc; sr mem Soc Photog Scientists & Engrs; Soc Imaging Sci & Technol. *Res:* Solid state chemistry; electro-organic chemistry in aprotic solvents; reaction mechanisms; ink chemistry; electrophotography; toner electrification; color science; non-impact printing. *Mailing Add:* 328 S 17th St San Jose CA 95112

JAFFE, ARTHUR MICHAEL, MATHEMATICAL PHYSICS. *Current Pos:* from asst prof to prof math physics, 67-85, LANDON T CLAY PROF MATH & THEORET SCI, HARVARD UNIV, 85- *Personal Data:* b New York, NY, Dec 22, 37; m 92, Sarah R Warren; c Margaret. *Educ:* Princeton Univ, AB, 59, PhD(physics), 65; Cambridge Univ, BA, 61. *Hon Degrees:* MA, Harvard Univ, 70. *Honors & Awards:* NY Acad Sci award, 79; Dannie Heineman Prize, Am Inst Physics & Phys Soc, 80. *Prof Exp:* Res assoc physics, Princeton Univ, 65-66; actg asst prof math, Stanford Univ, 66-67; visitor natural sci, Inst Advan Study, 67. *Concurrent Pos:* Nat Acad Sci-Nat Res Coun, Air Force Off Sci Res fel, 65-67; res assoc, Stanford Linear Accelerator Ctr, 66-67; Alfred P Sloan Found fel, 68-70; John S Guggenheim Found fel, 77 & 92; ed, Comn Math Physics, 75-79, chief ed, 79-; ed, Progress in Physics, 80-83, Selecta Mathematica Sovietica, 81- *Mem:* Am Math Soc; Am Phys Soc; NY Acad Sci; AAAS; Am Acad Arts Sci; Int Asn Math Physics (pres, 91-). *Res:* Mathematics and theoretical physics. *Mailing Add:* Dept Math & Theoret Sci Harvard Univ 1 Oxford St Cambridge MA 02138-2901

JAFFE, BERNARD MORDECAI, physics, optics; deceased, see previous edition for last biography

JAFFE, DONALD, MATERIALS SCIENCE, ELECTRONICS ENGINEERING. *Current Pos:* DEPT DIR, MICROELECTRONICS PACKAGING, LEHIGH UNIV, 90- *Personal Data:* b New York, NY, May 17, 31; m 53; c 5. *Educ:* Mass Inst Technol, BS, 52, MS, 53; Carnegie-Mellon Univ, PhD(metall eng), 63. *Prof Exp:* Engr, Gen Elec Co, 53-58 & Westinghouse Elec Co, 58-65; mem tech staff magnetic mat, AT&T Bell Labs, 65-68 supvr thin film mat, 68-72, supvr encapsulation mat, 72-77, supvr integrated circuit technol, 77-81, head, Film Technol Dept, 81-84 & Film Circuits Design & Technol Dept, 84-87, head, Analytical Technol Dept, 87-89. *Concurrent Pos:* Instr eve sch, Carnegie-Mellon Univ. *Mem:* Inst Elec & Electronics Engrs; Int Soc Hybrid Microelectronics; Am Vacuum Soc. *Res:* Technical management involving structure, properties, design and assembly techniques relative to materials and components used for microelectronics applications. *Mailing Add:* 962 Donald Dr Emmaus PA 18049

JAFFE, EDWARD E, ORGANIC CHEMISTRY. *Current Pos:* distinguished res fel, Ciba-Geigy Corp, 84-87, dir res, 87-88, vpres res, 88-95, CONSULT, CIBA-GEIGY CORP, 95- *Personal Data:* b Poland, Sept 22, 28; nat US; m 54, Ann Swirski; c 3. *Educ:* City Col NY, BS, 52; NY Univ, MS, 54, PhD(org chem), 57. *Honors & Awards:* Armin J Bruning Award, Fedn Socs Coatings Technol. *Prof Exp:* Tech asst res, Mt Sinai Hosp, NY, 51-54; from res chemist to sr res chemist, E I du Pont de Nemours & Co, 57-65, res assoc, 65-73, res supvr, 73-75, tech supt, 75-78, res mgr, 78-80, res fel, 80-84. *Mem:* Am Chem Soc; Sigma Xi. *Res:* Heterocyclic chemistry and the characterization of colored organic compounds; varied organic syntheses in the fields of organophosphorus chemistry, pigments, polymers; organic microchemistry; holder of over 100 United States and International patents. *Mailing Add:* 6 Penny Lane Ct Wilmington DE 19803

JAFFE, EILEEN KAREN, ENZYMOLOGY & INORGANIC BIOCHEMISTRY, MAGNETIC RESONANCE. *Current Pos:* MEM, INST CANCER RES, FOX CHASE CANCER CTR, 91-; ADJ ASSOC PROF, SCH DENT MED, UNIV PA, 91- *Personal Data:* b New York, NY, May 7, 54; m 83; c 1. *Educ:* State Univ NY Col Cortland, BS, 75; Univ Pa, PhD(biochem), 79. *Prof Exp:* NIH res fel chem, Harvard Univ, 79-81; asst prof, Haverford Col, 81-83; res asst prof biochem, Jefferson Med Col, Thomas Jefferson Univ, 83-84; res asst prof biochem, Sch Dent Med, Univ Pa, 84-90, res assoc prof, 90-91. *Concurrent Pos:* NIH prin investr, Haverford Col, Jefferson Med Col, Univ Pa & Inst Cancer Res, 81- *Mem:* Am Chem Soc; AAAS; Sigma Xi; Am Asn Women Sci; Am Soc Biochem & Molecular Biol. *Res:* The chemical mechanisms of enzyme catalyzed reactions; the role of metal ions; the binding of metals to adenosinetriphosphate; the roles of zinc and magnesium in the porphobilinogen synthase catalyzed reaction; protein structure. *Mailing Add:* Inst Cancer Res Fox Chase Cancer Ctr 7701 Burholme Ave Philadelphia PA 19111. *E-Mail:* ek__jaffe@fccc.edu

JAFFE, ELAINE SARKIN, HEMATOPATHOLOGY, IMMUNOPATHOLOGY. *Current Pos:* CLIN PROF PATH, SCH MED HEALTH SCI, GEORGE WASHINGTON UNIV, 85- *Personal Data:* b Brooklyn, NY, Aug 27, 43; m 67, Michael E; c Gregory & Caleb. *Educ:* Cornell Univ, AB, 65; Univ Pa, MD, 69; Am Bd Path, cert, 74. *Honors & Awards:* Pritzker Mem lectr, Acad Med, Toronto, Can, 89; W M Barriss McAllister Mem lectr, Yale Univ, 93. *Prof Exp:* Resident, Lab Path, Nat Cancer Inst, NIH, Bethesda, Md, 70-72, fel hematopath, 72-74, sr investr, 74-80, chief, Hematopath Sect, 80-, dep chief, 82- *Concurrent Pos:* Chief, Path Anat Br, Lab Path, Nat Cancer Inst, NIH, 82-; co-chair, Expert Panel Cytochem, ICSH; mem sci comt, Histiocyte Soc, 87-91; mem women's comt, Am Asn Pathologists, 90- *Mem:* Am Soc Hemat (vpres, 92-94, pres, 94-96); US-Can Int Acad Path (vpres, 96-97, pres elect, 97-); Am Asn Pathologists; Soc Hematopath (pres, 94-96); Histiocyte Soc; fel AAAS; Int Retrovirus Asn. *Res:* Analysis of human malignant lymphomas and leukemia to determine relationship to normal immune system and their role as models of the normal immune system; immunologic characterization of lymphomas with delineation of new clinicopathologic entities. *Mailing Add:* Lab Path Nat Cancer Inst NIH Bldg 10 Rm 2N202 Bethesda MD 20892

JAFFE, ERIC ALLEN, HEMATOLOGY, ONCOLOGY. *Current Pos:* from instr to asst prof, 71-77, assoc prof, 77-82, PROF MED, CORNELL UNIV MED COL, 82- *Personal Data:* b New York, NY, Apr 7, 42; m 71; c 2. *Educ:* Downstate Med Ctr, State Univ NY, MD, 66. *Honors & Awards:* Passano Found Young Scientist Award, 77. *Prof Exp:* Intern internal med, Kings County Hosp, Brooklyn, 66-67; resident, 67-68; resident, New York Hosp, 68-69; guest investr, Rockefeller Univ, 69; sr resident, New York Hosp, 70, fel hemat, 70-72. *Concurrent Pos:* Res fel, Nat Hemophilia Found, 74-76; career scientist, Health Res Coun City New York, 74-75, Irma T Hirschl Career Scientist Award, 76-81 & NIH Res Career Develop Award, 76-81. *Mem:* Asn Am Physicians; Am Soc Clin Invest; Am Soc Cell Biol; Am Soc Hematology; Am Asn Pathologists. *Res:* Role of endothelial cells in coagulation and the relationship of enothelial cells to platelets, white cells, and atherosclerosis. *Mailing Add:* Dept Med Interfaith Med Ctr 555 Prospect Pl Brooklyn NY 11238-0001. *Fax:* 718-935-7323

JAFFE, ERNST RICHARD, MEDICINE, HEMATOLOGY. *Current Pos:* from instr to prof med, Albert Einstein Col Med, 56-84, head, Div Hemat, 70-82, actg dean, 72-74 & 83-84, sr assoc dean, 74-91, assoc dean fac, 76-83, EMER SR ASSOC DEAN, ALBERT EINSTEIN COL MED, 91-, EMER DISTINGUISHED UNIV PROF MED, 92- *Personal Data:* b Chicago, Ill, Jan 4, 25; m 50, Anne J Sylvestre; c Stephanie A (Green) & Richard S. *Educ:* Univ Chicago, BS, 45, MD & MS, 48; Am Bd Internal Med, dipl & Cert hemat. *Hon Degrees:* LHD, Yeshiva Univ, 87. *Honors & Awards:* Charles R Drew Award, Am Red Cross, 90. *Prof Exp:* Asst path, Univ Chicago, 46 & 47-48, asst physiol, 47; intern, Med Serv, Presby Hosp, NY, 48-49, asst resident, 49-51 & 53-55. *Concurrent Pos:* Clin asst vis physician, Med Serv, Bronx Munic Hosp Ctr, 55-56, from asst vis physician to assoc vis physician, 55-63, attend physician, 63-; Nat Found Infantile Paralysis fel, 55-57; career scientist, Health Res Coun, NY, 61-71; assoc vis physician, Lincoln Hosp, NY, 61-73; co-ed, Sem in Hemat, 68-; study Sect, NIH Hemat, 72-79, chmn, 79-81; adv coun Nat Diabetes, Digestive & Kidney Dis, NIH 84-87; Nat Bd Govs, Am Red Cross, 84-90, chmn, Blood Serv Comt, 88-90; pres, Henry M & Lillian Stratton Found, 92-96. *Mem:* Am Soc Hemat (pres, 83); Am Fedn Clin Res; Am Physiol Soc; Asn Am Physicians; Soc Exp Biol & Med (pres, 93-95); Am Soc Clin Invest. *Res:* Internal medicine and hematology; metabolism of the mammalian erythrocyte and hereditary enzyme deficiencies with hemolysis or methemoglobinemia. *Mailing Add:* Nine Orchard Pl Tenafly NJ 07670. *Fax:* 201-567-1031; *E-Mail:* ejaffe@mem.pol.com

JAFFE, FRED, ORGANIC CHEMISTRY, ORGANOPHOSPHORUS CHEMISTRY. *Current Pos:* sect head, 89-96, SCIENTIST, AKZO NOBEL CENTRAL RES, 97- *Personal Data:* b Cleveland, Ohio, Apr 5, 30; m 60, Barbara Mae Meyerson; c Beth, Lynn & David. *Educ:* Western Reserve Univ, BS, 52; Cornell Univ, PhD, 57. *Prof Exp:* Sloan fel, Cornell Univ, 57-58; res chemist, Washington Res Ctr, W R Grace & Co, Md, 58-63, sr res chemist, 63-65, coordr oxidation chem, 64-65; res chemist, Miami Valley Labs, Procter

& Gamble Co, 65-68; sr res chemist, Eastern Res Ctr, Stauffer Chem Co, 68-75, res assoc, 75-88. *Concurrent Pos:* Mem, Global Mat Safety Data Sheets Comm & New Idea Generation & Improvement Comt. *Mem:* AAAS; Am Chem Soc; Royal Soc Chem; Soc Plastics Engrs; NY Acad Sci. *Res:* Synthesis, stabilization and modification of formaldehyde polymers and copolymers; synthesis of para-bridged benzenes, liquid phase autoxidation, oxidation of decalin; hydroperoxides; carbanion oxidations; organometallic alkali chemistry; phosphorus and silicon; lubricant and hydraulic fluid base stocks and additives; flame retardants; plasticigers polymer additives, process development, organs phosphorus chemistry; granted 8 US patents. *Mailing Add:* Akzo Nobel Cent Res 2 Livingstone Ave Dobbs Ferry NY 10522-3401

JAFFE, HAROLD, NUCLEAR SCIENCE. *Current Pos:* dep dir, Off Int Tech Coop, 76-81, dir, Off Int Res & Develop Policy, 81-94, SPEC ASST INT PROG, OFF ENERGY RES, DEPT ENERGY, 94- *Personal Data:* b Chicago, Ill, May 8, 30; m 51; c 3. *Educ:* Univ Ill, BS, 51, PhD(nuclear chem), 54. *Prof Exp:* Asst res chemist, Union Oil Co, 54-55; sr chemist, Tracerlab, Inc, 55-56; prin nuclear chemist, Aerojet-Gen Nucleonics Div, Aerojet-Gen Corp, 56-57, prog mgr gas-cooled reactor exp, 57-59, mgr fuel develop dept, 60-62, asst mgr nuclear tech div, 62-64, mgr appl sci div, 64-66, asst to vpres, Nuclear Div, 66-69; mgr San Ramon Plant & asst to pres, 69-70; chief isotope power systs proj br, Space Nuclear Systs Div, US Atomic Energy Comn, 70-72, mgr Isotope Flight Systs, 72-75; tech asst to asst admin nuclear energy, Energy Res & Develop Agency, 75-76. *Concurrent Pos:* Asst prof, John F Kennedy Univ, 66-70; mem bd dirs, Idaho Nuclear Corp, 68-70. *Mem:* AAAS; Am Nuclear Soc; Am Chem Soc; fel Am Inst Chemists. *Mailing Add:* 10702 Great Arbor Dr Potomac MD 20854

JAFFE, HOWARD WILLIAM, GEOLOGY. *Current Pos:* from assoc prof to prof, 65-90, EMER PROF GEOL, UNIV MASS, AMHERST, 90-; ADJ PROF, UNIV VT, 91- *Personal Data:* b New York, NY, Feb 16, 19; m 50, Elizabeth Boudreau; c Andrew W, Stephen A & Marina L. *Educ:* Brooklyn Col, BA, 42; Univ Geneve, DSc, 72. *Prof Exp:* Sr engr aid, US Geol Surv, 42-44; petrographer, US Bur Mines, 44-51; geologist, US Geol Surv, 51-58; res sect leader mineral & geochem, Union Carbide Nuclear Co Div, Union Carbide Corp, 58-65. *Concurrent Pos:* Vis prof, Univ Geneva, 71-72, 78-79 & 85-86. *Mem:* Fel Am Mineral Soc; fel Geol Soc Am; Geochem Soc; Am Geophys Union; Mineral Soc Gt Brit & Ireland; Sigma Xi. *Res:* Optical properties and crystal chemistry of rockforming minerals; petrography of igneous and metamorphic rocks; physical and chemical mineralogy of ores; geochronology; geochemistry of minor elements; Precambrian geology of the Hudson highlands and Adirondacks in New York. *Mailing Add:* RR 1 540 Range Rd Underhill VT 05489

JAFFE, ISRAELI AARON, INTERNAL MEDICINE. *Current Pos:* CLIN ASSOC INSTR MED, COLUMBIA UNIV, 57-, PROF CLIN MED, COL PHYSICIANS & SURGEONS, 78- *Personal Data:* b New York, NY, Dec 21, 27; m 52, Judith Snyder; c Naomi, Audrey & Caroline. *Educ:* NY Univ, BS, 46; Columbia Univ, MD, 50; Am Bd Internal Med, dipl. *Prof Exp:* Clin assoc, NIH, 53-55. *Concurrent Pos:* Asst prof instr med, NY Med Col, 60-63, prof instr med & dir rheumatic dis serv, 63-78. *Mem:* Am Col Physicians; AMA; Am Col Rheumat. *Res:* Rheumatic diseases and penicillamine treatment of rheumatoid arthritis. *Mailing Add:* 16 E 60th St New York NY 10021

JAFFE, JAMES MARK, PHARMACEUTICS. *Current Pos:* EXEC DIR PHARM DEPT, SANDOZ, 93- *Personal Data:* b New York, NY, Apr 11, 43; m 64; c 2. *Educ:* Univ Pittsburgh, BS, 68, BA, 69, MS, 70, PhD(pharmaceut), 72. *Prof Exp:* asst pharmaceut, Sch Pharm, Univ Pittsburgh, 68-70, from instr to asst prof pharmaceut, 70-75, assoc prof, 75-80. *Concurrent Pos:* Reviewer, J Pharmaceut Sci, 74- & Am J Hosp Pharm. *Mem:* Am Pharmaceut Asn; Acad Pharmaceut Sci; Sigma Xi. *Res:* Physiological and formulation factors that influence the absorption and excretion of drugs. *Mailing Add:* 66 W Main St Mendham NJ 07945

JAFFE, JEROME HERBERT, PSYCHOPHARMACOLOGY, ADDICTION. *Current Pos:* DIR, OFF EVAL, SCI ANALYSIS & SYNTHESIS, CTR SUBSTANCE ABUSE TREATMENT, SUBSTANCE ABUSE & MENT HEALTH SERV ADMIN, 92- *Personal Data:* b Philadelphia, Pa, July 6, 33; m 58; c 3. *Educ:* Temple Univ, AB, 54, MA, 56, MD, 58. *Prof Exp:* Fel pharmacol, Albert Einstein Col Med, 61-64, asst prof, 64-66, instr psychiat, 64-66; from asst prof to assoc prof psychiat, Univ Chicago, 68-73; prof psychiat, Col Physicians & Surgeons, Columbia Univ, 73-92. *Concurrent Pos:* NIMH res career develop award, 64-71; NIH grant, 65-71; consult, NIMH, NY State Narcotics Control Comn & Ill Narcotics Adv Coun, 66-; dir, Ill Drug Abuse Progs, 67-71; dir, Spec Action Off Drug Abuse Prev, 71-73; consult, WHO, 71-; consult to Pres for narcotics & dangerous drugs, 71-73. *Mem:* AAAS; fel Am Col Neuropsychopharmacol; AMA; Am Psychiat Asn. *Res:* Compulsive drug use; mechanisms of tolerance and physical dependence to narcotics and other drugs; treatment of drug dependence; social aspects of drug abuse. *Mailing Add:* Ctr Substance Abuse Treat Substance Abuse & Ment Health Serv Admin 5600 Fishers Lane Rockville MD 20857

JAFFE, JONAH, PHARMACY, TECHNICAL MANAGEMENT. *Current Pos:* RETIRED. *Personal Data:* b New York, NY, Oct 5, 29; m 51; c 2. *Educ:* Columbia Univ, BS, 53; Univ Md, MS, 55, PhD(pharmaceut chem), 56. *Prof Exp:* Sr res chemist, E R Squibb, 56-62; dir, res & develop, Organon, US, 62-63, dir, res, develop & prod, 63-65; tech dir, Whitehall Labs Div, Am Home Prod, 65-70, asst vpres, 70-76; vpres res & develop, Johnson & Johnson, 76-85, vpres sci affairs, 85-88; vpres, Res & Develop Labs, McNeil Consumer Prod Co, 88- *Mem:* Am Pharmaceut Asn; Sigma Xi; AAAS; NY Acad Sci. *Res:* Management of research and development; quality control; medical research and regulatory affairs; manufacture of proprietary and ethical drugs and toiletries. *Mailing Add:* 4 Partridge Ct Cherry Hill NJ 08003

JAFFE, JULIAN JOSEPH, PHARMACOLOGY. *Current Pos:* RETIRED. *Personal Data:* b New York, NY, Feb 17, 26; m 53; c 4. *Educ:* Univ Conn, BA, 49; Harvard Univ, MA, 51, PhD(biol), 55. *Prof Exp:* Instr biol, Brown Univ, 54-55, USPHS fel, 55-56; asst, Harvard Univ, 56-61; from instr to asst prof pharmacol, Sch Med, Yale Univ, 56-61; from assoc prof to prof pharmacol, Col Med, Univ Vt, 61-89. *Concurrent Pos:* Wellcome res travel grants, Oxford Univ, 58 & Nuffield Inst Comp Med, London, 67, guest worker, Nuffield Inst Comp Med, 67-68; mem, Panel Parasitic Dis, US-Japan Coop Med Sci Prog, 71-76 & Trop Med Parasitol Study Sect, 77-81; mem spec working group filariasis, WHO, 77, 80, 83 & 85. *Mem:* Am Soc Pharmacol & Exp Therapeut; Am Soc Parasitol; Am Soc Trop Med & Hyg; AAAS; Am Asn Univ Prof. *Res:* Biochemical pharmacology; biochemistry of parasites. *Mailing Add:* 21 Ivy Lane Burlington VT 05401

JAFFE, LAURINDA A, PHYSIOLOGY OF FERTILIZATION. *Current Pos:* asst prof, 81-86, ASSOC PROF PHYSIOL, UNIV CONN, 86- *Personal Data:* b Pasadena, Calif, Jan 9, 52. *Educ:* Purdue Univ, BS, 73; Univ Calif, Los Angeles, PhD(biol), 77. *Prof Exp:* NIH fel electrophysiol fertil, Marine Biol Lab, Woods Hole, Mass, 78-79; NSF fel electrophysiol fertil, Univ Calif, San Diego, 79-81. *Concurrent Pos:* Instr embryol, Marine Biol Lab, Woods Hole, 83-87; vis fac, Univ Wash, 85 & 88; assoc ed, Develop Biol, 85- *Mem:* Am Soc Cell Biol; Biophys Soc; Soc Develop Biol. *Res:* Physiology of fertilization. *Mailing Add:* Dept Physiol Univ Conn Health Ctr 263 Farmington Ave Farmington CT 06030-1515. *Fax:* 860-679-1269, 203-679-2518

JAFFE, LEONARD, NUCLEAR SAFETY. *Current Pos:* PRES, EARTH SATELLITE, 95- *Personal Data:* b Feb 1, 26; m 49, Elaine J Michael; c Ronald H & Norman D. *Honors & Awards:* Inst Elec & Electronics Engrs Award, 67; Am Inst Aeronaut & Astronaut, 78; Lloyd V Berkener Space Ulitization Award, Am Acad Sci; William Pecora Award, Dept Comn & NASA, 81. *Prof Exp:* Aeronaut Res Scientist, Lewis Res Lab, Nat Adv Comt Aeronaut, 48-51, Instruments Res Div, 51-57, chief, Data Systs Br, 57-59; chief, Commun Satellite Prog, Hq, NASA, 59-61, dir, Comm Systs, 61-63, dir, Commun & Navigation Prog, 63-66, dir, Space Appln Prog, 66-69, dep assoc, Admin Space & Sci Appln, 69-71, Space Appln, 71-77, dep assoc, Admin Space and Terrestrial Appln, Hq, 77-78, specialist to chief eng, 78-81; head, Tech Assessment Task Force, President's Comn Accident at Three Mile Island, 79; vpres systs group, prog mgt & prod assurance, Comput Sci Corp, 81-82, pres, Systs Div, 82-84, vpres, Systs Group, Prog Mgt & Prod Assurance, 84-95. *Concurrent Pos:* Chmn, NASA Space Appln Adv Comt, 86- *Mem:* Fel Inst Elec & Electronics Engrs; fel Am Inst Aeronaut & Astronaut; fel Am Astronaut Soc; Int Acad Astronaut; Int Astronaut Fedn (pres, 74-76). *Res:* Development of communications satellite systems. *Mailing Add:* 418 Sisson Ct Silver Spring MD 20902

JAFFE, LEONARD DAVID, PLANETARY EXPLORATION SOLAR ENERGY. *Current Pos:* mgr, Mat Res Sect, Jet Propulsion Lab, Calif Inst Technol, 54-64, res specialist, Space Sci Div, 64, proj scientist Surveyor proj, 65- 68, mem tech staff, Space Sci & Energy Conversion Divs, 68-81, Syst Engr Solar Thermal Power Systs, 81-84, proj syst engr space nuclear power proj, 85-88, SCI PAYLOAD ENGR, CRAF CASSINI PROJ JET PROPULSION LAB CALIF INST TECHNOL, 89- *Personal Data:* b New York, NY, June 25, 19; m 45, Esther Karol; c Harold, Walter, Lisa (Ruiz), & Miriam (Barer). *Educ:* Mass Inst Technol, SB, 39, SM, 40; Harvard Univ, ScD(phys metall), 47. *Prof Exp:* Metallurgist, Watertown Arsenal, 40-42, metallurgist & supvr res on phase transformation in steel, 42-46, chief phys metall sect, 46-54. *Mem:* AAAS; Am Geophys Union; Am Inst Aeronaut & Astronaut; Am Astron Soc; Am Inst Mining, Metall & Petrol Eng. *Res:* Solar thermal energy conversion; planetary exploration; properties of the lunar surface. *Mailing Add:* M/S 301-485 Jet Propulsion Lab Calif Inst Technol 4800 Oak Grove Dr Pasadena CA 91109. *E-Mail:* ljaffe@jpl.nasa.gov

JAFFE, LIONEL F, DEVELOPMENTAL PHYSIOLOGY, BIOPHYSICS. *Current Pos:* SR SCIENTIST, MARINE BIOL LAB, WOODS HOLE, MASS, 82-; ADJ PROF BOT, UNIV MASS AMHERST, 90- *Personal Data:* b New York, NY, Dec 28, 27; m 49, Miriam E Walther; c Laurinda, Amanda & David. *Educ:* Harvard Univ, SB, 48; Calif Inst Technol, PhD(embryol), 54. *Prof Exp:* Fel, Nat Res Coun, Hopkins Marine Sta, Stanford Univ, 53-54, NSF, 54-55; fel marine biol, Scripps Inst, Calif, 55-56; asst prof biol, Brandeis Univ, 56-60; from asst prof to assoc prof, Univ Pa, 60-67; prof biol, Purdue Univ, 67-84; dir, Nat Vibrating Probe Facil, 82-93. *Mem:* Biophys Soc; Am Soc Cell Biol; Dev Biol Soc; Soc Gen Physiol. *Res:* Development and nature of morphogenetic polarity; cellular tropisms; bioelectric and ionic aspects of development; calcium waves and gradients. *Mailing Add:* Marine Biol Lab Woods Hole MA 02543. *Fax:* 508-540-6902; *E-Mail:* ljaffe@mbl.edu

JAFFE, MARVIN RICHARD, TEACHING CHEMISTRY FOR HEALTH SCIENCES, CONSUMER SCIENCES. *Current Pos:* from asst prof to assoc prof, 71-84, PROF, SCI DEPT, MANHATTAN COMMUNITY COL, 85- *Personal Data:* b New York, NY, May 23, 38. *Educ:* Brooklyn Col, BS, 60, MA, 65; Fordham Univ, PhD(anal chem), 70. *Prof Exp:* Qual control chemist, Schrafft's, NY, 60-62, prod develop chemist, 62-63, supvr prod develop, 63-65; instr chem, Bronx Community Col, 65-68; res asst, Fordham Univ, 68-70; guest jr res assoc, Brookhaven Nat Lab, 69-70. *Mem:* Sigma Xi; Nat Sci Teachers Asn; Am Chem Soc. *Res:* Consumer science; science education of non-scientists; kinetics and mechanisms of beta-diketones. *Mailing Add:* Dept Sci Manhattan Community Col 199 Chambers St New York NY 10007

JAFFE, MICHAEL, POLYMER PHYSICS, PHYSICAL CHEMISTRY. *Current Pos:* res supvr, Celanese Res Co, 81-82, res mgr, 82-88, SR RES ASSOC & RES FEL, HOECHST CELANESE RES DIV, 88- *Personal Data:* b New York, NY, May 10, 42; m; c 2. *Educ:* Cornell Univ, BA, 63; Rensselaer

Polytech Inst, PhD(chem), 67. *Prof Exp:* Res chemist to sr res chemist, Celanese Res Co, 67-73, res assoc, 73-74, res supvr, 74-78; group leader, Res & Develop Lab, Fiber Industs, Inc, 78-80. *Mem:* Am Chem Soc; Am Phys Soc; fel NAm Thermal Anal Soc; fel AAAS. *Res:* Morphology of crystalline high polymers; transition behavior of polymers; structure-property relationships of polymers and related materials. *Mailing Add:* 215 Wyoming Ave Maplewood NJ 07040

JAFFE, MIRIAM WALTHER, ASTRONOMY. *Current Pos:* RETIRED. *Personal Data:* b Clinton, Ind, Feb 6, 22; m 49, Lionel F; c Laurinda A, Amanda J & David B. *Educ:* Ind Univ, AB, 43; Univ Va, MA, 45; Radcliffe Col & Harvard Univ, PhD(astron), 48. *Prof Exp:* Instr astron, Wellesley Col, 48-49 & Univ Southern Calif, 49-51; asst prof astron, Haverford Col, 65-66; asst prof astron, Purdue Univ, 68-85. *Mem:* Am Astron Soc. *Res:* Photographic photometry; classification of stellar spectra. *Mailing Add:* 59 Cumloden Dr Falmouth MA 02540-1609

JAFFE, MORDECAI J, PLANT PHYSIOLOGY. *Current Pos:* BABCOCK PROF BOTANY, WAKE FOREST UNIV, 80- *Personal Data:* b New York, NY, July 7, 33; m 61, Amy C Cooke; c Jennie (Lane), Ben & Sam. *Educ:* City Col New York, BS, 58; Cornell Univ, PhD(veg physiol), 64. *Prof Exp:* Lectr & res assoc biol, Yale Univ, 64-67; from asst prof to prof, plant physiol, Ohio Univ, 67-80. *Concurrent Pos:* NSF res grant, 67-74 & 75-86; vis prof, Hebrew Univ, Jerusalem, 75, Lady Davis vis prof, 84; NASA res grant, 77-84; Bard res grant, 80-83; vis scientist, Boyce Thompson Inst Cornell Univ, 80; permanent vis prof, Hebrew Univ, Jerusalem, 84- *Mem:* AAAS; Am Soc Plant Physiologists; Soc Develop Biol; Phytochem Soc NAm; Japanese Soc Plant Physiol. *Res:* Sensory physiology and biochemistry; rapid movements in plants; biochemistry of touch mediated processes in plants; physiology of stress in plants; flowering mechanisms in plants. *Mailing Add:* Biol Dept Wake Forest Univ Winston-Salem NC 27109. *Fax:* 910-759-6008; *E-Mail:* jaffemj@wfu.edu

JAFFE, MORRY, EXPERIMENTAL PHYSICS, APPLICATION DEVELOPMENT. *Current Pos:* CONSULT, AGS, 90-; ASST COMNR, NY CITY DEPT RECORDS & INFO SERVS, 94- *Personal Data:* b New York, NY, Oct 10, 40; m 90, Lou Bronusa. *Educ:* City Col New York, BS, 62; Boston Univ, MA, 64; City Univ New York, PhD(physics), 71. *Honors & Awards:* Cert Appreciation, US Environ Protection Agency, 78. *Prof Exp:* Asst, Boston Univ, 62-64; lectr, 64-65, res asst, City Col New York, 65-69 & 70-71; lab asst, New York Dept Air Resources, 73-78; Data processing consult, Group 88, New York, 84-90. *Res:* Database administration. *Mailing Add:* 65 Park Terr E New York NY 10034

JAFFE, PHILIP MONLANE, INORGANIC CHEMISTRY. *Current Pos:* PROF CHEM, OAKTON COMMUNITY COL, 70- *Personal Data:* b Bronx, NY, Aug 14, 27; m 50; c 3. *Educ:* City Col New York, BS, 48; Polytech Inst Brooklyn, MS, 53, PhD, 62. *Prof Exp:* Chemist, City Chem Corp, NY, 48-51; res chemist, Westinghouse Elec Co, 53-63; sr staff scientist, Aerospace Res Ctr, Gen Precision, Inc, 63-66; sr res chemist, Zenith Radio Corp, 66-72. *Concurrent Pos:* Dean, Div Sci Allied Health, 85-91. *Mem:* Fel AAAS; Am Chem Soc; fel Am Inst Chem; fel Sigma Xi. *Res:* Inorganic phosphors and preparations; semiconductors; photoconductors; technical and educational writing. *Mailing Add:* 9818 Maynard Terr Niles IL 60618

JAFFE, RANDAL CRAIG, ENDOCRINOLOGY, BIOCHEMISTRY. *Current Pos:* from asst prof to assoc prof, 75-92, PROF PHYSIOL, MED CTR, UNIV ILL, 92- *Personal Data:* b St Louis, Mo, Dec 18, 47; m 70, Rose-Lynn Pfefferman; c Tod, Aron & Tracy. *Educ:* Univ Southern Calif, BS, 68; Univ Calif, Davis, PhD, 72. *Prof Exp:* Fel endocrinol, Sch Med, Vanderbilt Univ, 72-73; fel cell biol, Baylor Col Med, 73-75. *Concurrent Pos:* NIH fel, 74-75; vis fel med, Mass Gen Hosp, 85-86; vis assoc prof med & physiol, Harvard Univ, 85-86. *Mem:* AAAS; Endocrine Soc; Am Soc Biol Chem; Soc Study Reproduction. *Res:* Mechanism of hormone action; comparative endocrinology; hormonal control of development. *Mailing Add:* Dept Physiol MC 901 Univ Ill 901 S Wolcott Chicago IL 60612-7342. *E-Mail:* v25169@uicvm

JAFFE, ROBERT B, ENDOCRINOLOGY, OBSTETRICS & GYNECOLOGY. *Current Pos:* chmn dept, 73-96, PROF OBSTET, GYNEC & REPROD SCI, DIR, REPROD ENDOCRINOL CTR, UNIV CALIF, SAN FRANCISCO, 73- *Personal Data:* b Detroit, Mich, Feb 18, 33; m 54; c 2. *Educ:* Univ Mich, MD, 57; Univ Colo, MS, 66; Am Bd Obstet & Gynec, dipl, 67 & reproductive endocrin cert. *Prof Exp:* Lab asst biochem, Univ Mich, 53-54; rotating intern, Univ Colo, 57-58, resident obstet & gynec, 59-63; from asst prof to prof obstet & gynec, Med Ctr, Univ Mich, Ann Arbor, 64-73. *Concurrent Pos:* USPHS postdoctoral fel endocrinol, Dept Internal Med, Med Ctr, Univ Colo, 58-59; NIH postdoctoral fel reprod endocrinol, Hormone Lab, Karolinska Sjukhuset, Sweden, 63-64; Josiah Macy, Jr Found fac fel, 66-69 & 80-81; chmn, Div Endocrinol & Fertil, Am Col Obstetricians & Gynecologists; mem, Human Embryol & Develop Study Sect, NIH, Sci Adv Bd, Nat Inst Child Health & Human Develop Coun, Reprod Biol Study Sect, NIH, Med Adv Bd, Nat Pituitary Agency, Steering Comt, Perinatal Res Soc, Sci Adv Bd, Prog Appl Res Fertil Regulation & Biomed Comt, Projs Pop Action; vis prof, Univ Mich, Univ Mo, Cornell Univ, Univ Wash, Univ Ore, Yale Univ, Univ Wis, Univ Va & Wash Univ; Fred Gellert chair reprod med & biol, 90. *Mem:* Inst Med-Nat Acad Sci; Endocrine Soc; Am Fedn Clin Res; Soc Gynec Invest (pres); fel Am Col Obstet & Gynec; Am Gynec Soc; Asn Am Physicians; Sigma Xi. *Res:* Endocrinology; gynecology; author of numerous technical publications. *Mailing Add:* Dept Obstet Gynec & Reproduction Sci Med Sch Univ Calif San Francisco CA 94143. *Fax:* 415-520-7866; *E-Mail:* robert.jaffe@quickmail.ucsf.edu

JAFFE, ROBERT LOREN, QUANTUM CHROMODYNAMICS, THEORY OF PARTICLES AND FIELDS. *Current Pos:* Res assoc, 72-74, from asst prof to assoc prof, 74-83, PROF PHYSICS, MASS INST TECHNOL, 83-, *PROF & CHMN FAC*, 93- *Personal Data:* b Bath, Maine, May 23, 46. *Educ:* Princeton Univ, AB, 68; Stanford Univ, MS, 71, PhD(physics), 72. *Concurrent Pos:* Sloan fel, 75-77; vis scientist, Stanford Linear Accelerator Ctr, 76; sr vis fel, Dept Theoret Physics, St Catherine's Col, Oxford, 79; sci assoc, Europ Coun Nuclear Res, 79; vis lectr, Beijing Univ, China, 81; consult, Los Alamos Nat Lab, 85- *Mem:* Fel Am Phys Soc; fel AAAS. *Mailing Add:* Dept Physics 6-311 Mass Inst Technol 77 Massachusetts Ave Cambridge MA 02139. *Fax:* 617-253-8674; *E-Mail:* jaffe@mitlns.mit.edu

JAFFE, RUSSELL M, IMMUNOLOGY. *Current Pos:* dir, Princeton Bio Ctr, 83-92, FEL, HEALTH STUDIES COL, 79-, DIR, SERAMMUNE PHYS LAB, 83- *Personal Data:* b Albany, NY, Jan 1, 47. *Educ:* Boston Univ, BA, MD & PhD(biochem & med sci), 72. *Honors & Awards:* J D Lang Jr Investr Award, USPHS, 75; Norman E Clarke Sr lectr, Am Col Advan Med, 92. *Prof Exp:* Intern, Univ Hosp, Boston Univ Med Col, 72-73; resident, Clin Ctr, NIH, 73-75, sr staff physician, 75-79, collab investr, Nat Heart Lung & Blood Inst & LEA, 76-79. *Concurrent Pos:* Assoc ed, The New Physician, 71-72, sr assoc ed, 72-73. *Mem:* AAAS; NY Acad Sci; Am Asn Clin Chemists; fel Am Col Nutrit; fel Am In-Vitro Allergy/Immunol Soc; Am Prev Med Asn; Am Pub Health Asn; fel Am Soc Clin Pathologists; Am Soc Microbiol; Int Col Appl Nutrit; Royal Soc Med. *Res:* Connective tissue; biology of mental function; coagulation; atherosclerosis; clinical biochemistry; biochemical immunology. *Mailing Add:* 1890 Preston White Dr Suite 120 Reston VA 20191

JAFFE, SIGMUND, PHYSICAL CHEMISTRY, CHEMICAL KINETICS OF STRATOSPHERE. *Current Pos:* from asst prof to prof, 58-86, chair, Dept Chem, 59-64, EMER PROF CHEM, CALIF STATE UNIV, LOS ANGELES, 86- *Personal Data:* b New Haven, Conn, Mar 1, 21; m 46, Elaine H Leventhal; c Matthew L & Paul J. *Educ:* Wesleyan Univ, AB, 49; Iowa State Univ, PhD(chem), 53. *Prof Exp:* Asst phys chem, Ames Lab, AEC, 49-53; sr engr, Air Reduction Res Lab, 53-58. *Concurrent Pos:* NIH fel, Weizmann Inst, 64-65; res grant, Environ Protection Agency-US Pub Health, 66; res fel, Weizmann Inst Sci, 71-72; res scientist, Jet Propulsion Lab, Calif, 72-; vis prof, Queen Mary Col, Univ London, 78-79. *Mem:* Am Chem Soc; Sigma Xi. *Res:* Chemical kinetics; photo-chemical reactions of stratosphere and atmosphere including the reactions of Cl, Br NO_2 O_3; electrochimistry of rare earth salts; ion cyclotron mass spectrometry studies of ion-molecule reactions; discharge-flow, resonance absorption studies of H and D with Co_2 and BR_2; oscillator strengths of transitions in atomic N. *Mailing Add:* 14107 Village 14 Camarillo CA 93012

JAFFE, SOL SAMSON, TEACHING OF MATH & SCIENCE. *Current Pos:* INSTR MATH & SCI, BLOOMFIELD COL, 87- *Personal Data:* b Ft Wayne, Ind, Feb 7, 20; m 52, Frances Diamond; c David & Susan. *Educ:* Drew Univ, AB, 41; Stevens Inst Technol, MS, 45. *Prof Exp:* Chemist, Fidelity Chem Prod Corp Div, Maas & Waldstein Co, NJ, 42-46; res labs, Thomas A Edison Inc, 46-51, res chemist, 51-57, Thomas A Edison Res Labs Div, McGraw Edison Co, 57-64; sr res chemist, Res & Develop Lab, Alkaline Battery Div, Gulton Industs, 64-65; chief chemist, Bright Star Industs, 65-70; formulating chemist, Nitine, Inc, 70-72; electrochem engr, Mallory Battery Co Div, P R Mallory & Co, Inc, 72-79; sect head electrochem eng, Battery Technol Co Div, Duracell Int Inc, 79-83, staff scientist, Duracell Prod Technol, 83-87. *Mem:* Electrochem Soc. *Res:* Leclanche, air-zinc, mercury-zinc, divalent silver-zinc, alkaline and fuel cells; nickel-iron, nickel-cadmium, silver-cadmium and lead-acid storage batteries; hermetically sealed cells; charge control electrodes; state-of-charge indicators; electrochemical devices; metal finishing; electroless plating. *Mailing Add:* Seven Nance Rd West Orange NJ 07052

JAFFE, WERNER G, NUTRITION, BIOCHEMISTRY. *Current Pos:* DIR POSTGRAD COURSE NUTRIT PLANNING, 74- *Personal Data:* b Frankfurt, Ger, Oct 27, 14; m 46; c 6. *Educ:* Univ Zurich, PhD(chem), 39; Cent Univ Venezuela, DrSc(biochem), 50. *Hon Degrees:* Hon Prof, Cent Univ & Univ Simon Boliver. *Honors & Awards:* Nat Sci Award, Ministry of Educ, 58; Gold Medal Sci Res, Cent Univ Venezuela, 60; Nat Sci Award of Venezuela, 78. *Prof Exp:* Asst prof org chem, Sch Pharm, 47-50, assoc prof biochem, Sch Sci, 50-58, prof biochem, Sch Sci Cent, Univ Venezuela, 58-; res assoc, Nat Nutrit Inst, 50- *Concurrent Pos:* Ed, Arch Latinoamerican Nutrit. *Mem:* AAAS; Venezuelan Asn Advan Sci (pres, 56); Venezuelan Chem Soc (pres, 53); cor mem Peruvian Chem Soc; cor mem Mex Chem Soc; Am Chem Soc. *Res:* Enzymology; toxicology; lectins, enzyme inhibition; toxic food constituents. *Mailing Add:* 5TA Avenida No 211-1811 Los Palos Grandes Caracas 1062 Venezuela

JAFFE, WILLIAM J(ULIAN), INDUSTRIAL ENGINEERING. *Current Pos:* instr math, NJ Inst Technol, 46, from instr to asst prof indust eng, 46-50, from asst exec assoc to exec assoc, 49-60, from assoc prof to prof eng, 50-73, distinguished prof, 73-75, EMER DISTINGUISHED PROF ENG, NJ INST TECHNOL, 75- *Personal Data:* b Passaic, NJ, Mar 22, 10. *Educ:* NY Univ, BS, 30, Engr ScD(eng), 53; Columbia Univ, MA, 31, MS, 41. *Honors & Awards:* Centennial Medal, Am Soc Mech Engrs, Dedication Medal. *Prof Exp:* Naval architect, Philadelphia Navy Yard, US Dept Navy, 41-45. *Concurrent Pos:* Adj assoc prof, Col Eng, NY Univ, 53-54; mem, Inst Bus Admin & Mgt, Japan, Comn on Manpower, Israel & Clark Bd Int Mgt, Comt Int Orgn Sci, Bd Stand Rev, Am Nat Stand Inst, Stand Bd, Am Soc Mech Engrs. *Mem:* Fel AAAS; fel Am Soc Mech Engrs; fel Inst Indust Engrs; fel Soc Advan Mgt; fel NY Acad Med; Am Math Soc. *Res:* Industrial and management engineering. *Mailing Add:* 1175 York Ave Apt 9E New York NY 10021

JAFFEE, OSCAR CHARLES, EXPERIMENTAL EMBRYOLOGY. *Current Pos:* RETIRED. *Personal Data:* b New York, NY, Sept 26, 16; m 62, Danguole Bartnikas; c 1. *Educ:* NY Univ, BA, 46, MS, 48, Ind Univ, PhD(zool), 52. *Prof Exp:* Instr anat, Sch Med, Univ Ark, 52-56; embryologist, Chronic Dis Res Inst, State Univ NY Buffalo, 58-60, asst assoc prof biol, 60-66,; from assoc prof to prof biol, Univ Dayton, 66-89. *Concurrent Pos:* Mem staff, Mt Desert Island Biol Lab; mem, Am Heart Asn Coun; vis prof, dept anat & embryol, Hadassah Med Sch, Hebrew Univ Jerusalem, Israel, 85, vis prof, Zool Dept, 87. *Mem:* Am Asn Anat; Teratology Soc; Int Soc Stereology; Int Soc Biorheol. *Res:* Cardiovascular embryology; teratology; physiology of the embryonic heart. *Mailing Add:* 1218 N Barcelona St Pensacola FL 32501

JAFFEY, ARTHUR HAROLD, NUCLEAR CHEMISTRY. *Current Pos:* res assoc, 46-50, GROUP LEADER & SR CHEMIST, ARGONNE NAT LAB, 50- *Personal Data:* b Chicago, Ill, Dec 25, 14; m 45; c 2. *Educ:* Univ Chicago, BS, 36, PhD(phys chem), 41. *Prof Exp:* Instr chem lab, Univ Chicago, 37-40, res assoc detection poisonous gases, Off Sci Res & Develop Proj, 41-42 & Metall Lab, Manhattan Dist, 42-46. *Concurrent Pos:* Jr chemist, Rock Island Arsenal, US War Dept, Ill, 41; res assoc, Off Sci Res & Develop, Columbia Univ, 42. *Mem:* Am Phys Soc; Sigma Xi. *Res:* Measurement of disintegration properties of radioactive isotopes; measurement of thermal neutron reactions with heavy elements; statistical analysis of nuclear measurement data; development of superconducting heavy ion linear accelerator. *Mailing Add:* 5550 S Shore Dr No 1315 Chicago IL 60637

JAFVERT, CHAD TIMOTHY, ENVIRONMENTAL CHEMISTRY & MASS TRANSFER IN ENVIRONMENTAL SYSTEMS, SURFACTANT PHYSICAL CHEMISTRY. *Current Pos:* asst prof, 91-95, ASSOC PROF, SCH CIVIL ENG, PURDUE UNIV, 95-, AREA HEAD, ENVIRON & HYDRAUL ENG, 96- *Personal Data:* b Nevada, Iowa, Dec 2, 56; m 81, Mary Beth Chamberlain; c Benjamin Aaron & Paul David. *Educ:* Iowa State Univ, BS, 79; Univ Iowa, MS, 82, PhD(civil & environ eng), 85. *Prof Exp:* Res assoc, Nat Res Coun, 85-86; res environ engr, Environ Res Lab, US Environ Protection Agency, Ga, 86-91. *Concurrent Pos:* Prin investr, Soil & Water Conserv Comn, Ind, 92-93, US Environ Protection Agency, 92, Purdue Res Found, 92-94 & 94-95, NSF, 93-96 & Construct Eng Res Lab, US Army, 94. *Mem:* Am Chem Soc; Soc Environ Toxicol & Chem; Sigma Xi; Asn Environ Eng Profs; Int Asn Water Pollution Res & Control; Water Environ Fedn; Int Asn Water Qual. *Res:* Phase distribution and mass transfer of organic chemicals in natural and designed environmental systems; remediation of contaminated soils and sediments; applicaton of surfactants in pollution control. *Mailing Add:* Sch Civil Eng Purdue Univ West Lafayette IN 47907-1284

JAGADEESH, GOWRA G, AUTONOMIC CARDIOVASCULAR, DRUG RECEPTOR-EFFECTOR COUPLING. *Current Pos:* PHARMACOLOGIST, CARDIO-RENAL DIV, FOOD & DRUG ADMN, ROCKVILLE, MD 90-; ADJ SCIENTIST, NAT INST CHILD HEALTH HUMAN DEVELOP, NIH, BETHESDA, MD, 93- *Personal Data:* b Karnataka, India, Sept 18, 49; m 78, G Jayashree Burji; c Shilpa & Neetal. *Educ:* Bangalore Univ, India, BPharm, 70; All-India Inst Med Sci, New Delhi, India, MS, 71; Banaras Hindu Univ, India, PhD(pharmacol), 80. *Prof Exp:* Dept physiol, Univ Sask, Can, 82-85. *Concurrent Pos:* Res officer, Inst Hist Med & Med Res, NDelhi, India, 75; from asst prof to assoc prof pharmacol, Banaras Hindu Univ, IT, Varanasi, India, 75-86; vis res assoc, Northeastern Univ Col Pharm, Boston, 86-89, staff sci, 89-90. *Mem:* Soc Exp Biol & Med. *Res:* G-protein-coupled adrenergic and muscarinic receptors in liver, vascular and cardiac tissues; modulation by protein kinase c; signal transduction; structure-function study of angiotensin at-1 receptor in cos cells; regulatory review of new drug applications. *Mailing Add:* 8700 Cathedral Way Gaithersburg MD 20879

JAGANNATHAN, KANNAN, THEORETICAL HIGH ENERGY PHYSICS. *Current Pos:* asst prof, 81-87, ASSOC PROF PHYSICS, AMHERST COL, 87- *Personal Data:* b Madras, India, Nov 4, 54. *Educ:* Univ Madras, India, BSc, 73; Indian Inst Technol, Madras, MSc, 75; Univ Rochester, PhD(physics), 81. *Prof Exp:* Res assoc physics, Univ Rochester, 80-81. *Mem:* Am Phys Soc; Am Asn Physics Teachers; Am Math Asn. *Res:* Theoretical high energy physics; elementary particle physics; foundations of quantum mechanics. *Mailing Add:* Dept Physics Amherst Col Amherst MA 01002

JAGANNATHAN, SINGANALLUR N, NUTRITIONAL BIOCHEMISTRY, BIOCHEMICAL PATHOLOGY. *Current Pos:* asst prof path & biochem, 74-77, ASSOC PROF PATH & BIOCHEM, DEPT PATH, SCH MED, WVA UNIV, MORGANTOWN, 77-, ASSOC PROF NUTRIT, SCH DENT, 79- *Personal Data:* b Coonoor, India, Mar 10, 34; m 68; c 2. *Educ:* Univ Bombay, BSc, 54, MSc, 59, PhD(biochem), 62. *Prof Exp:* Res asst to sr res officer, Indian Coun Med Res, Nat Inst Nutrit, 56-70; res scientist, lipid, lipoprotein & biochem, Col Med, Univ Iowa, 70-74. *Concurrent Pos:* Nat Res Coun Can fel nutrit biochem, Queen's Univ, Kingston, Ont, 62-64; Brit Coun fel, 64; fel, Coun Arteriosclerosis, Am Heart Asn, 72. *Mem:* Am Inst Nutrit; Am Soc Clin Nutrit; fel Am Heart Asn. *Res:* Lipid and proteoglycans in relation to human atherosclerosis; platelet function; human nutrition; iron metabolism. *Mailing Add:* Dept Path & Biochem WVa Univ Health Sci Ctr Morgantown WV 26506-9203. Fax: 304-293-6249

JAGEL, KENNETH I(RWIN), JR, CHEMICAL ENGINEERING. *Current Pos:* PRES, TRAILTREE ASSOCS, 89- *Personal Data:* b Jamaica, NY, Feb 2, 27; m 51; c 2. *Educ:* Columbia Univ, BSc, 51, MSc, 53, DEngSc, 61. *Prof Exp:* Asst chem eng, Columbia Univ, 51-53, res asst, 55-57; res engr, Socony Mobil Oil Co, Inc, 57-59, sr res engr, 59-65, group leader, Mobil Res & Develop Corp, 65-68, eng assoc, 68-71; mgr mfg, Engelhard Minerals & Chem Corp, 71-72, mgr process eng & develop, 72-73, dir prod assurance, 73-81, dir qual & mfg serv, Engelhard Corp, 81-82, dir prod develop, 82-85, exec engr, 85-89. *Mem:* AAAS; fel Am Inst Chem; Am Chem Soc; Am Inst Chem Engrs; Am Soc Testing & Mat. *Res:* Catalyst manufacture; auto-exhaust emission control catalysts; cracking catalysts; oil shale retorting processes; distillation equipment. *Mailing Add:* Trailtree Assoc Box 112 Stanton NJ 08885

JAGENDORF, ANDRE TRIDON, PLANT PHYSIOLOGY, BIOCHEMISTRY. *Current Pos:* prof plant physiol, 66-96, Liberty Hyde Bailey prof, 81-96, LIBERTY HYDE BAILEY EMER PROF, CORNELL UNIV, 97- *Personal Data:* b New York, NY, Oct 21, 26; m 52, Jean Whitenack; c Suzanne, Judith & Daniel. *Educ:* Cornell Univ, AB, 48; Yale Univ, PhD(plant sci), 51. *Honors & Awards:* Kettering Res Award, Am Soc Plant Physiologists, 63, Kettering Award in Photosyn, 78, Charles Reid Barnes Award, 89- *Prof Exp:* Res assoc bot, Univ Calif, Los Angeles, 51-53; from asst prof to prof biol, Johns Hopkins Univ, 53-66, with McCollum-Pratt Inst, 53-66. *Concurrent Pos:* Merck fel, 51-53, Weizmann fel, 62. *Mem:* Nat Acad Sci; Am Soc Photobiol; Am Soc Cell Biol; Am Soc Plant Physiol (pres, 67-68); fel AAAS; Am Acad Arts & Sci. *Res:* Photosynthetic phosphorylation; biochemistry; chloroplast biogenesis; chloroplast DNA repair and recombination enzymes. *Mailing Add:* Plant Biol Sect Plant Sci Bldg Cornell Univ Ithaca NY 14853. Fax: 607-255-5407; E-Mail: atj1@cornell.edu

JAGERMAN, DAVID LEWIS, MATHEMATICS, ELECTRICAL ENGINEERING. *Current Pos:* CONSULT MATH, NEC CCRL, 89- *Personal Data:* b Aug 27, 23; m 51; c 3. *Educ:* Cooper Union Univ, BEE, 49; NY Univ, MS, 54, PhD(math), 62. *Prof Exp:* Sr engr analog comput, Reeves Instrument Corp, NY, 51-55; staff scientist math guided missiles, Stavid Eng, NJ, 55-57 & 57-59; design specialist trajectories, Gen Dynamics/Convair, Calif, 57; staff mem math control systs, Syst Develop Corp, NJ, 59-64; mem tech staff, AT&T Bell Labs, 63-86, distinguished mem tech staff, 86-89. *Concurrent Pos:* Assoc prof math, Fairleigh Dickinson Univ, 59-66; prof, Stevens Inst Technol, 67-72. *Mem:* Am Math Soc; sr mem Inst Elec & Electronics Engrs. *Res:* Diophantine analysis and numerical quadrature theory with application to the mathematical properties of pseudo-random numbers; information theory; telephone traffic theory. *Mailing Add:* NEC USA 4 Independence Way Princeton NJ 08540

JAGGARD, DWIGHT LINCOLN, ELECTROMAGNETISM, OPTICS. *Current Pos:* from asst prof to assoc prof, Dept Elec Eng, 80-88, PROF, MOORE SCH ELEC ENG, UNIV PA, 88-, ASSOC DEAN GRAD EDUC & RES, SCH ENG & APPL SCI, 92- *Personal Data:* b Oceanside, NY, Apr 14, 48; m 68; c 2. *Educ:* Univ Wis-Madison, BSEE, 71, MSEE, 72; Calif Inst Technol, PhD(elec eng & appl physics), 76. *Hon Degrees:* MA, Univ Pa, 82. *Prof Exp:* Res asst geophys & elec eng, Univ Wis-Madison, 68-72; engr imaging radar & DFB lasers, Jet Propulsion Lab, Calif Inst Technol, 73-76, postdoctoral res fel, 76-78; asst prof optics & electromagnetics, Dept Elec Eng, Univ Utah, 78-80. *Concurrent Pos:* Consult, Jet Propulsion Lab, 76-78, Environ Studies Lab, 78-81, Naval Res Lab, 82-85, Sohio, 85, IDA, 89, Johns Hopkins Appl Physics Lab, 91; forensic consult, 83-; dir, ExMSE Grad Prog, Technol & Leadership, Univ PA, 88-90, R&B Enterprises, 91-95, Rohm & Haas, 91 & Ethicon Inc, 92; co-founder & pres, Main Line Waves, Inc, 88-; ed, J Electromagnetic Wave Appln, 91-95. *Mem:* Fel Inst Elec & Electronics Engrs; Int Union Radio Sci; fel Optics Soc Am; Sigma Xi. *Res:* Electromagnetic chirality, fractal electrodynamics; inverse scattering and remote sensing; imaging and classification; light scattering from aerosols; wave interactions with knots and knotted media; chaos and fractals; imaging. *Mailing Add:* 829 Malin Rd Newtown Square PA 19073-3515. Fax: 215-573-2245; E-Mail: jaggard@pender.ee.upenn.edu

JAGGER, JOHN, RADIATION BIOLOGY, PHOTOBIOLOGY. *Current Pos:* RETIRED. *Personal Data:* b New Haven, Conn, Feb 22, 24; m 56, Mary E Gaulden; c Thomas & Yvonne. *Educ:* Yale Univ, BS, 49, MS, 53, PhD(biophys), 54. *Honors & Awards:* Lifetime Achievement Award, Am Soc Photobiol, 91. *Prof Exp:* Asst, Mem Hosp, NY, 50-51 & Yale Univ, 53-54; Nat Found Infantile Paralysis fel, Radium Inst, France, 54-56; biophysicist, Biol Div, Oak Ridge Nat Lab, 56-65; from assoc prof to prof biol, Southwest Ctr Advan Studies, 65-69; prof biol, Univ Tex, Dallas, 69-81, prof gen studies & biol, 81-86, sr lectr biol, 91-94. *Concurrent Pos:* Lectr, Univ Tenn, 61-65; vis prof, Pa State Univ, 63 & Univ Kyoto, Japan, 79; consult, Aerojet Med & Biol Systs, 71-73; ed, Photochem & Photobiol, 73-75; mem, US Nat Comt Photobiol, Nat Res Coun, 75-80, pres, 78-80; consult, Pure Pulse Technol, 93- *Mem:* Fel AAAS; Health Physics Soc; Am Soc Photobiol (pres, 83-84). *Res:* Effects of radiations on large molecules and cells; effects of ultraviolet on bacteria; photoprotection; effects of near ultraviolet on cell growth and membrane function; social impact of science. *Mailing Add:* 7532 Mason Dells Dr Dallas TX 75230-3246

JAGIELLO, GEORGIANA MARY, GENETICS. *Current Pos:* PROF OBSTET, GYNEC & HUMAN GENETICS, COL PHYSICIANS & SURGEONS, COLUMBIA UNIV, 70- *Personal Data:* b Boston, Mass, Aug 2, 27; m 57. *Educ:* Boston Univ, AB, 49; Tufts Univ, MD, 55. *Prof Exp:* Exchange fel surg, St Bartholomew's Hosp, London, 54; intern med, Res & Educ Hosps, Univ Ill, 55-56; resident, New Eng Med Ctr, Boston, 56-57; fel endocrinol, Scripps Clin, La Jolla, 57-58; res fel, New Eng Med Ctr, Boston, 58-60; USPHS res fel cytogenetics, Guy's Hosp, London, 60-61; asst prof, Sch Med, Univ Ill, Chicago Circle, 61-66; sr lectr cytogenetics, Guy's Hosp, London, 66-69; res prof pediat, Sch Med, Univ Ill, Chicago Circle, 69-70. *Concurrent Pos:* Mem, Inst Advan Study, Univ Ill, 64; NIH career develop award, 65; consult, Guy's Hosp, London, 66-69. *Mem:* Endocrine Soc; Teratology Soc; Environ Mutagen Soc; Am Soc Cell Biol; Soc Study Reproduction. *Res:* Mammalian meiosis; reproductive endocrinology. *Mailing Add:* Univ Col Physicians & Surgeons 630 W 168th St New York NY 10032-8702. *Fax:* 212-305-3869

JAGLAN, PREM S, HIGH-PERFORMANCE LIQUID CHROMATOGRAPHY, GAS-LIQUID CHROMATOGRAPHY. *Current Pos:* SR RES SCIENTIST IV BIOCHEM, UPJOHN CO, 69- *Personal Data:* b India, Sept 17, 29; US citizen; m 51, Mohinder; c Vikramjit S, Samarjit S & Amarjit S. *Educ:* Univ Calif, Riverside, PhD(toxicol), 69. *Mem:* Am Chem Soc; Int Soc Study Xenobiotics. *Res:* Separation science and identification of metabolites using chemical and instrumental methods. *Mailing Add:* 2713 Texel Dr Kalamazoo MI 49001. *Fax:* 616-385-7721

JAGOE, CHARLES HENRY, ENVIRONMENTAL TOXICOLOGY, AQUATIC TOXICOLOGY. *Current Pos:* ASST RES ECOLOGIST, SAVANNAH RIVER ECOL LAB, UNIV GA, 90- *Personal Data:* b Bethpage, NY, Sept 7, 56; m 86, Rosemary Herer; c Rebekah & William. *Educ:* Clarkson Univ, BS, 78; Univ Maine, MS, 83, PhD(zool), 88. *Prof Exp:* Teaching asst biol, Univ Maine, 78-80, res assoc, Dept Zool, 83-86, res asst, 86-88; biol technician fisheries, Nat Fisheries Contaminant Res Ctr, US Fish & Wildlife Serv, Field Sta Orono, 80-82; assoc, Div Pinelands Res, Ctr Coastal & Environ Studies, Rutgers Univ, 88-90. *Concurrent Pos:* Adj asst prof, Dept Pharmacol & Toxicol, Col Pharm, Univ Ga, 92-, Inst Ecol, 93- *Mem:* Am Fisheries Soc; Soc Environ Toxicol & Chem. *Res:* Effects of pollutants, especially metals and radioactive substances on organisms; aquatic toxicology, physiological, morphological and behavioral responses of fish and amphibians to pollutants; genetic toxicology; biogeochemistry of mercury and radio-nuclides. *Mailing Add:* Savannah River Ecol Lab PO Drawer E Aiken SC 29802. *Fax:* 803-725-3309; *E-Mail:* jagoe@srel.edu

JAHANMIR, SAID, TRIBOLOGY, CERAMIC MACHINING. *Current Pos:* GROUP LEADER & DIV SCIENTIST, CERAMICS DIV, NAT INST STAND & TECHNOL, 87- *Personal Data:* b Tehran, Iran, Mar 18, 50; US citizen; m, Feri Moaveni; c Sam & Farid. *Educ:* Univ Wash, BS, 71; Mass Inst Technol, SM, 73, PhD(mech eng), 77. *Honors & Awards:* Dedicated Serv Award, Am Soc Mech Engrs, 95; Int Award, Soc Tribologists & Lubrication Engrs, 97. *Prof Exp:* Lectr, Dept Mech Eng, Univ Calif, Berkeley, 77-78; asst prof, Dept Mech Eng, Cornell Univ, 78-80; sr staff engr, Exxon Res & Eng Co, 80-85; prog dir, NSF, 85-87. *Concurrent Pos:* Adj prof, Dept Mech Eng, Univ Med, 87-97; chair, Versailles Proj Advan Mat & Stands, 90-93, Int Wear Stand Comn; ed, Mach Sci & Technol J, 97- *Mem:* Fel Am Soc Mech Eng; fel Soc Tribologists & Lubrication Engrs. *Res:* Machining, tribology and mechanical behavior of advanced materials; machinery of ceramics, mechanics of interfaces, mechanisms of wear, boundary lubrication and mechanical property testing. *Mailing Add:* Nat Inst Stand & Technol Gaithersburg MD 20899

JAHAN-PARWAR, BEHRUS, NEUROBIOLOGY. *Current Pos:* SR SCIENTIST NEUROBIOL, WORCESTER FOUND EXP BIOL, 73-; ADJ PROF, ALBANY MED CTR. *Personal Data:* b Ghoochan, Iran, May 26, 38, nat US; m 66; c 2. *Educ:* Univ Gottingen, MD, 64, DMSc(physiol), 65. *Prof Exp:* Res assoc neurophysiol, Dept Physiol, Univ Gottingen, 64-66; asst res neurophysiologist, Ment Health Res Inst, Univ Mich, 66-68; from asst prof to assoc prof physiol, Dept Biol, Clark Univ, 68-73. *Concurrent Pos:* Prin investr, NIH grants, 69-73, 74-77, 75-83 & 78-81 & NIH res career develop award, 70-73; Grass Found grant, 75-78; NSF grant, 78-82. *Mem:* Soc Neurosci; Am Physiol Soc; Am Soc Zoologist; Europ Chemoreception Res Orgn. *Res:* The elucidation of the principles of neuronal organization underlying processing of sensory information and generation and modification of behavior; neural mechanisms of chemoreception, learning and rhythmic behaviors such as feeding and locomotion. *Mailing Add:* 43 Carstead Dr Slingerlands NY 12159

JAHIEL, RENE, HEALTH SERVICES RESEARCH, MICROBIOLOGY. *Current Pos:* CONSULT, HEALTH SERV RES, 89- *Personal Data:* b France, Mar 29, 28; nat US; m 55; c 3. *Educ:* NY Univ, BA, 46; State Univ NY, MD, 50; Columbia Univ, PhD(microbiol), 57. *Prof Exp:* Intern, Montefiore Hosp, NY, 50-51; res, Mt Sinai Hosp, 51-52, fel, 52-55; asst prof microbiol, Sch Med, Univ Colo, 57-59; asst prof path, Columbia Univ, 59-61; asst prof pub health, Med Col, Cornell Univ, 61-67; from res assoc prof prev med to res prof prev med, NY Univ, 67-76, res prof med, 76-88. *Concurrent Pos:* Exp immunologist, Nat Jewish Hosp, Denver, Colo, 57-59; asst attend pathologist, Mt Sinai Hosp, NY, 59-61; career scientist, Health Res Coun NY, 62-66; prin investr, USPHS grants on several health res serv, 68-82; physician, Asn Children Retarded Mental Develop, 88- *Mem:* NY Acad Sci; Soc Social Study Sci; Tissue Cult Asn; Am Pub Health Asn; Asn Health Serv Res. *Res:* Immunopathology; autoantibodies; tissue culture virology; tissue culture; interferon; community medicine; sociology of knowledge; health serv res. *Mailing Add:* 60 E Eighth St 19 F New York NY 10003

JAHN, EDWIN CORNELIUS, ORGANIC CHEMISTRY. *Current Pos:* EXEC SECY, EMPIRE STATE PAPER RES ASSOCS, INC, 70- *Personal Data:* b Oneonta, NY, Sept 6, 02; m 27, 70; c 2. *Educ:* NY State Col Forestry, BS, 25, MS, 26; McGill Univ, PhD(org chem), 29. *Hon Degrees:* DSc, Syracuse Univ, 72. *Honors & Awards:* Tech Asn Pulp & Paper Indust Award, 70. *Prof Exp:* Asst, NY State Col Forestry, 25-26 & McGill Univ, 26-29; fel, Am-Scand Found, 29-30; from assoc prof to prof forestry, Univ Idaho, 30-38; prof forest chem, State Univ NY Col Environ Sci & Forestry, 38-72, dir res, 49-52, assoc dean phys sci, 52-66, exec dean, 66-67, dean, 67-69. *Concurrent Pos:* Consult, USDA, Sweden, 43-44; sr econ analyst, US Dept Com, 45-46; tech attache to US State Dept for Sweden, Finland, Norway & Denmark, 45-46; mem wood chem comt, Food & Agr Orgn, UN, 47-64. *Mem:* Am Chem Soc; fel Soc Am Foresters; fel Tech Asn Pulp & Paper Indust; AAAS. *Res:* Cellulose, wood and polymer chemistry. *Mailing Add:* 109 Hillcrest Rd Syracuse NY 13224-1945

JAHN, ERNESTO, animal science, ruminant nutrition, for more information see previous edition

JAHN, J RUSSELL, ANIMAL SCIENCE. *Current Pos:* RETIRED. *Personal Data:* b Spirit Lake, Iowa, Dec 2, 26; m 50; c 3. *Educ:* SDak State Univ, BS, 59, MS, 60, PhD(animal sci), 63. *Prof Exp:* Assoc prof, Univ Wis-Platteville, 62-66, prof animal sci & head, Dept Agr Sci, 66-88. *Mem:* Am Soc Animal Sci. *Res:* Artificial insemination of beef cattle. *Mailing Add:* 16864 255th Ave Spirit Lake IA 51360

JAHN, LAURENCE R, MIGRATORY BIRDS, AQUATIC AREAS. *Current Pos:* RETIRED. *Personal Data:* b Jefferson, Wis, June 24, 26; m 47, Helen Faville; c Katharine M (Cook) & Richard A. *Educ:* Univ Wis-Madison, BS, 49, MS, 58, PhD(wildlife ecol & zool), 65. *Honors & Awards:* Outstanding Civilian Serv Medal, Dept Army, 85; Aldo Leopold Mem Award, Wildlife Soc, 89; Barbara Swain Award of Honor, Natural Resources Coun Am, 91. *Prof Exp:* Biologist migratory bird populations & habitats, Wis Dept Natural Resources, 49-59; vpres res mgt & res, Wildlife Mgt Inst, 59-87, pres, 87-91, chmn bd, 90-91. *Concurrent Pos:* Assoc mem, Int Asn of Fish & Wildlife Agencies, 59; chmn, Nat Watershed Cong, 74-90; mem, adv comt marine fisheries, US Dept Com, 82-84, adv comt wildlife, Dept State, 72-77 & adv comt fish, wildlife & parks, US Dept Interior, 75-79; chmn, chief of engrs environ adv bd, US Dept Army, 83-85; chmn, Nat Resources Coun Am, 83-85; mem, US Implementations Bd, NAm Waterfowl Mgt Plan, 88-91, chmn, 90-91. *Mem:* Fel AAAS; Wildlife Soc (pres, 79-80); Am Fisheries Soc; Am Water Resources Asn; Soil & Water Conserv Soc Am; Am Inst Biol Sci; Am Wildlife Found (secy, 78-91). *Res:* Wildlife populations and habitats, particularly projects designed to provide information for strengthening management programs, especially guidelines for avoiding and minimizing adverse impacts on wildlife as development proceeds. *Mailing Add:* 2435 Riviera Dr Vienna VA 22181. *Fax:* 703-255-1767

JAHN, LAWRENCE A, AQUATIC BIOLOGY, FISHERIES MANAGEMENT. *Current Pos:* From asst prof to assoc prof, 68-81, PROF BIOL SCI, WESTERN ILL UNIV, 81- *Personal Data:* b Cudahy, Wis, Dec 2, 41; m 66, Mary Jane Andrus; c Nicholas & Christopher. *Educ:* Univ Wis, BS, 63; Mont State Univ, MS, 66, PhD(zool), 68. *Concurrent Pos:* Dir, Inst Environ Mgt, 88- *Mem:* Am Fisheries Soc; Am Soc Ichthyol & Herpet. *Res:* Fish management, ecology and life histories; aquarium management. *Mailing Add:* Dept Biol Sci Western Ill Univ Macomb IL 61455. *Fax:* 309-298-2270; *E-Mail:* la_jahn@WIV.edu

JAHN, REINHARD, MECHANISMS OF NEURO-TRANSMITTER RELEASE. *Current Pos:* ASSOC PROF PHARMACOL & CELL BIOL, YALE UNIV, 91-; ASSOC INVESTR, HOWARD HUGHES MED INST, 91- *Personal Data:* b Leverkusen, Ger. *Educ:* Univ Gottingen, Ger, PhD, 81. *Honors & Awards:* Max-Planck Res Prize, Max-Plank Inst, 90. *Prof Exp:* Fel, Univ Gottingen, Ger, 81-83; fel, Rockefeller Univ, 83-85, asst prof microbiol, 85-86; group leader, Max-Planck Inst Psychol, 86-91. *Mem:* Am Soc Cell Biol; Am Soc Neuro Sci; Am Soc Biochem & Molecular Biol. *Mailing Add:* Dept Pharmacol & Assoc Invest Howard Hughes Med Inst BCMM2504 Yale Univ Sch Med PO Box 9812 New Haven CT 06536-0812. *Fax:* 207-737-1763

JAHN, ROBERT G(EORGE), ENGINEERING PHYSICS, HUMAN & MACHINE ANOMALIES. *Current Pos:* from asst prof to assoc prof, Princeton Univ, 62-67, dean, Sch Eng & Appl, 71-86, dir grad studies, Dept Aerospace & Mech Sci, 88-90, PROF AEROSPACE SCI, PRINCETON UNIV, 67- *Personal Data:* b Kearny, NJ, Apr 1, 30; m 53, Catherine Seibert; c Eric G, Jill E, Nina M & Dawn A. *Educ:* Princeton Univ, BS, 51, MA, 53, PhD(physics), 55. *Hon Degrees:* DSc, Andhra Univ, Vishakhapatnam, India, 86. *Honors & Awards:* Curtis W McGraw Res Award, Am Soc Eng Educ, 69. *Prof Exp:* Asst prof physics. Lehigh Univ, 55-58; asst prof jet propulsion, Calif Inst Technol, 58-61. *Concurrent Pos:* Mem res & technol adv subcomt electrophys, NASA, 68-71, mem res & technol adv comt space propulsion & power, 71-72, mem res & technol adv coun comt space propulsion & power, 76-77, mem nat adv coun space systs & technol adv comt, 78-; mem bd trustees, Assoc Univs Inc, Washington, DC, 71-74, trustee rep, 74-86, chmn bd, 77-79, mem nominating comt, 78-79; mem bd dirs, John E Fetzer Inst, 83-94, vchmn, 83, nominating comt, 83-94; mem, Soc Sci Explor, 83-, vpres & counr, 84-, prog comt, 91-; mem bd dirs, Hercules Inc, 85-, technol comt, 87-, strategic comt, 87-, compensation comt, 87-, nominating comt, 88-; mem bd dirs, Roy F Weston Inc, 88-, Audit & Compensation Comt, 88-92. *Mem:* Am Inst Aeronaut & Astronaut; Am Phys Soc; Am Inst Phys; Soc Sci Expl; Am Soc Psychol Res. *Res:* Plasma propulsion; high temperature gasdynamics and fluid mechanics; shock tubes; plasmajets; ionization phenomena; electromagnetic wave propagation in ionized gases; engineering anomalies and human/machine interactions. *Mailing Add:* D-334 EQ SEAS Princeton Univ Princeton NJ 08544-5263. *Fax:* 609-258-1993; *E-Mail:* rgjahn@princeton.edu

JAHNCKE, CATHERINE LEE, PHYSICS. *Current Pos:* ASST PROF PHYSICS, ST LAWRENCE UNIV, 95- *Personal Data:* b New Orleans, La, Nov 3, 64. *Educ:* Auburn Univ, BS, 88; NC State Univ, PhD(physics), 96. *Mem:* Am Phys Soc. *Res:* Optical investigation of materials with sub wavelength resolution using near-field optical microscopy/spectroscopy. *Mailing Add:* Dept Physics St Lawrence Univ Canton NY 13617. *Fax:* 315-229-7421

JAHNGEN, EDWIN GEORG EMIL, JR, ORGANIC CHEMISTRY, BIORGANIC CHEMISTRY. *Current Pos:* AT DEPT CHEM, UNIV LOWELL. *Personal Data:* b Pittsburgh, Pa, Jan 8, 46. *Educ:* Bates Col, BSc, 68; Univ Vt, PhD(chem), 74. *Prof Exp:* Chemist, Water Improv Comn, Maine, 67-68; chemist org synthesis, Polaroid Corp, 68-70; res assoc nat prod, Univ BC, 74-76; groupleader, New Eng Nuclear Corp, 76-78; asst prof org chem, Wilkes Col, 78- *Concurrent Pos:* NIH fel, Nat Res Coun, Univ BC, 74-76; consult, Med Sch, Univ Conn, 78- *Mem:* Am Chem Soc; Sigma Xi. *Res:* Studies of bio-organic systems; synthesis and modification of exogenous; endogenous drugs and hormones. *Mailing Add:* Dept Chem Univ Lowell Lowell MA 01854-2882. *Fax:* 978-458-9571

JAHNS, HANS O(TTO), PETROLEUM ENGINEERING, ARCTIC ENGINEERING. *Current Pos:* RETIRED. *Personal Data:* b Kamen, Ger, Sept 4, 31; m 59; c 5. *Educ:* Clausthal Tech Univ, dipl, 55, dipl, 56, Dr(Ing), 61. *Prof Exp:* Res asst petrol eng, Inst Drilling & Petrol Prod, Clausthal Tech Univ, 56-59; reservoir engr, Reservoir Lab, Wintershall AG, Ger, 59-62; res engr prod res, Jersey Prod Res Co, Stand Oil Co NJ, Okla, 62-65, res engr, 65-68, res assoc, 68-73, res adv, 73-77, sr res adv, 77-80, res scientist, 80-82, sr res scientist, Exxon Prod Res Co, 82- *Concurrent Pos:* Mem, Permafrost Comt, Nat Res Coun, 75-80, mem, Polar Res Bd, 76-84; mem adv bd, Geophys Inst, Univ Alaska, 78-87; mem, Polar Adv Comt, NSF, 85-87. *Mem:* Soc Petrol Engrs; AAAS; Am Petrol Inst. *Res:* Petroleum reservoir description; oceanography; arctic research; arctic engineering; sea ice mechanics; expert system, production geophysics; oil spill cleanup technology. *Mailing Add:* 8840 Larston St Houston TX 77055

JAHNS, MONROE FRANK, PHYSICS. *Current Pos:* RETIRED. *Personal Data:* b Seguin, Tex, May 16, 28; m 54; c 2. *Educ:* Tex A&M Univ, BS, 49; Univ Tex, Austin, MA, 64, PhD(physics), 66. *Prof Exp:* Instr physics, Unit Tex, Austin, 65-66; asst prof, Sam Houston State Col, 66-67; advan sr fel med physics, Univ Tex M D Anderson Hosp & Tumor Inst, Houston, 67-68, assoc physicist & assoc prof biophysics, 68-88. *Mem:* Am Phys Soc; Soc Nuclear Med; Am Asn Physicists Med. *Mailing Add:* 6319 Vanderbilt St Houston TX 77005

JAHODA, FRANZ C, PLASMA DIAGNOSTICS, FIBER OPTIC SENSORS. *Current Pos:* RETIRED. *Personal Data:* b Vienna, Austria, Sept 16, 30; nat US; m 55; c 2. *Educ:* Swarthmore Col, BA, 51; Cornell Univ, PhD, 57. *Prof Exp:* Mem staff, Los Alamos Nat Lab, 57-91, group leader, 74-91. *Concurrent Pos:* Mem staff, Culham Lab, Abingdon, Eng, 64-65; mem staff, Inst voor Plasmafysica, Jutphaas, Neth, 72-73. *Mem:* Optical Soc Am; Inst Elec & Electronics Engrs. *Res:* Plasma physics; spectroscopy; lasers; optical diagnostics. *Mailing Add:* 819 Bishops Lodge Rd Santa Fe NM 87501

JAHODA, GERALD, INFORMATION SCIENCE. *Current Pos:* RETIRED. *Personal Data:* b Vienna, Austria, Oct 22, 25; US citizen; m 52. *Educ:* NY Univ, AB, 47; Columbia Univ, MS, 52, DLS, 60. *Prof Exp:* Instr & chem librn, Univ Wis, 52-53; group leader, Colgate-Palmolive Co, 53-57; sect head, Esso Res & Eng Co, 57-63; prof info sci & librarianship, Fla State Univ, 63-92. *Concurrent Pos:* Instr, Polytech Inst Brooklyn, 53-54 & Rutgers Univ, 61-62; Air Force Sci Res grant, 65-66; mem, Sci Inst Pub Info; US Off Educ grant, 74-; NSF grant, Exxon Educ Found, 81-82; Am Coun Blind. *Mem:* Am Libr Asn; Am Soc Info Sci. *Res:* Information needs of scientists; organization of the literature of science and technology; information service for the blind. *Mailing Add:* 2012 Forest Glen Ct Tallahassee FL 32303

JAHODA, JOHN C, ECOLOGY, MAMMALOGY. *Current Pos:* from asst prof to assoc prof, 70-81, PROF BIOL, BRIDGEWATER STATE COL, 81- *Personal Data:* b Dalhart, Tex, Feb 9, 44. *Educ:* Univ Conn, BA, 66; Okla State Univ, PhD(zool), 69. *Prof Exp:* Asst prof biol, State Univ NY Col Geneseo, 69-70. *Concurrent Pos:* Consult, Raytheon Serv Co, 70-; mem, Corp Bermuda Biosta Res. *Mem:* Am Soc Mammal; Ecol Soc Am; Sigma Xi. *Res:* Ecology and ethology of mammals; salt marsh ecology; pollution of salt marshes. *Mailing Add:* Dept Biol Sci Bridgewater State Col Bridgewater MA 02325

JAICKS, FREDERICK G, ENGINEERING. *Current Pos:* RETIRED. *Prof Exp:* Chmn, Inland Steel, Chicago. *Mem:* Nat Acad Eng. *Mailing Add:* Meadow Lane Lakeside MI 49116

JAIN, ANANT VIR, TOXICOLOGY. *Current Pos:* anal chemist, Univ Ga, 74-81, assoc anal toxicologist, 81-90, sr anal toxicologist, 90-91, HEAD, TOXICOL SECT, UNIV GA, 97- *Personal Data:* b Sardhana, India, March 15, 40; US citizen; m 71; c 2. *Educ:* Agra Univ, India, BS, 59, MS, 62; Purdue Univ, PhD(chem), 72. *Honors & Awards:* First Place Cert, Am Oil Chemists' Soc, 81. *Prof Exp:* Lectr chem, DAV Col, India, 62-64; res asst, Purdue Univ, 64-66, chem analyst, 66-72, res assoc, 72-74. *Concurrent Pos:* Pres, Southeast Regional Sect Assoc, Off Analytical Chemists, 86-87; mem, AOAC Comt, Regional Sect, 85-90; mem, Comt Prof Develop, 96- *Mem:* Am Chem Soc; Am Asn Vet Lab Diagnosticians; Am Acad Vet & Comp Toxicol; Asn Off Anal Chem Int. *Res:* Analytical methods for the detection of poisons, drugs,and metals from biological and agricultural materials; analytical chemistry of poisons; mycotoxin decontamination; diagnostic laboratory service; methods validation. *Mailing Add:* Diag Asst Lab Col Vet Med Univ Ga Athens GA 30601. *Fax:* 706-542-5977; *E-Mail:* jain.a@adl300.vet.uga.edu

JAIN, ANIL KUMAR, ELECTRICAL ENGINEERING. *Current Pos:* actg assoc prof, 78-79, PROF ELEC ENG, UNIV CALIF, DAVIS, 79- *Personal Data:* b India, Jan 21, 46. *Educ:* Indian Inst Technol, Kharagpur, BTech Hons, 67; Univ Rochester, MS, 69, PhD(elec eng), 71. *Honors & Awards:* Image Coding Achievement Award, Int Picture Coding Symp, Tokyo, 77; Donald G Fink Prize Award, Inst Elec & Electronics Engrs, 83. *Prof Exp:* Fel, Univ Southern Calif, 70-71, asst prof, 71-74; assoc prof elec eng, State Univ NY, Buffalo, 74-78. *Concurrent Pos:* Proj dir, NASA res grant, 75-76, Naval Undersea Ctr, San Diego, 76-77, Army Res Off grant, 76-78, Naval Ocean Syst Ctr grant, San Diego, 78-79, Army Res Off, 78-85, Off Naval Res, 82-84 & Univ Micro Projs, 82-86; topical ed, J Optical Soc Am. *Mem:* Sr mem Inst Elec & Electronics Engrs; Optical Soc Am. *Res:* Digital image processing; signal processing; pattern recognition; communication theory; systems theory; computer applications; real time systems. *Mailing Add:* Mich State Univ Comput Sci East Lansing MI 48824

JAIN, ANRUDH KUMAR, POPULATION STUDIES, PUBLIC HEALTH & EPIDEMIOLOGY. *Current Pos:* asst dir biostatist, Pop Coun, 73-76, assoc, 76-79, dep dir, Progs Div, 81-94, SR ASSOC, DEMOGRAPHIC IMPACTS DEVELOP PROG, POP COUN, 80-, DIR PROG, 94- *Personal Data:* b India, Oct 23, 41; m 71, Usha; c Anupma & Aparna. *Educ:* Agra Univ, BSc, 58; Delhi Univ, MA, 60; Univ Mich, Ann Arbor, MA, 65, PhD(sociol), 68. *Prof Exp:* Res assoc pop studies & asst prof sociol, Univ Mich, Ann Arbor, 68-70; prog assoc family planning, Ford Found, India, 70-71; staff assoc, Pop Coun, India, 71-73. *Concurrent Pos:* Vis scholar, Univ Mich, 79-80. *Mem:* Int Union Sci Study Pop; Pop Asn Am; Indian Asn Study Pop. *Res:* Consequences of population growth and determinants of fertility, fecundability, lactation and postpartum amenorrhea; assessing quality of family planning and health services. *Mailing Add:* Pop Coun 1 Dag Hammarskjold Plaza New York NY 10017. *Fax:* 212-755-6052

JAIN, ARIDAMAN KUMAR, APPLIED STATISTICS. *Current Pos:* mem tech staff, Bell Labs, 67-83, distinguished mem tech staff, 84-86, dist mgr, 87-91, DISTINGUISHED MEM TECH STAFF, BELL COMMUN RES, 92- *Personal Data:* b Delhi, India, Apr 14, 38; m 63, Nirmal Jain; c Anjali & Arvind. *Educ:* Delhi Univ, BSc, 57; Purdue Univ, PhD(statist & indust eng), 68. *Prof Exp:* Statistician, SQC Units Indian Statist Inst, Baroda & Bombay, 60-61; statistician, Tata Oil Mills, Bombay, 61-63. *Concurrent Pos:* Adj prof, NJ Inst Technol, 93, Monmouth Col, 93- *Mem:* Am Statist Asn; Oper Res Soc Am; Am Soc Qual Control; Inst Elec & Electronics Engrs. *Res:* Data analysis; design of experiments; statistical modelling; monte-carlo simulation; survey sampling; quality assurance. *Mailing Add:* 15 Emory Dr 331 Newman Springs Redd Rm NVC 2X2 11 Red Bank NJ 07701

JAIN, ATUL, OCEANOGRAPHY, ELECTRONICS ENGINEERING. *Current Pos:* SR SCIENTIST, HUGHES ELECTRONICS, 81- *Personal Data:* b Dehradun, India, Mar 26, 50, US citizen; m 87, Mamta; c Rahul & Priti. *Educ:* Calif Inst Technol, BS & MS, 70, PhD(elec eng/physics), 74. *Prof Exp:* Res fel, Calif Inst Technol, 73-75; mem tech staff, Jet Propulsion Lab, 75-81. *Concurrent Pos:* Consult, Jet Propulsion Lab, 73-74. *Res:* Pioneering undersanding of coherent speckle noise; invention and development of the inverse synthetic aperture radar and associated super-resolution imaging techniques; theoretical understanding of imaging of ocean waves with the synthetic aperture radar; airport surveillance radar systems; low observable systems; antennas, RCS and antenna pattern measurements; optics. *Mailing Add:* PO Box 45863 Los Angeles CA 90045-0863. *Fax:* 310-607-1015; *E-Mail:* 0026093@ccmail.emis.hac.com

JAIN, DULI CHANDRA, MOLECULAR SPECTROSCOPY, DATABASE SYSTEMS. *Current Pos:* lectr, 68-70, from asst prof to assoc prof, 71-85, PROF PHYSICS, YORK COL, NY, 86- *Personal Data:* b Mungaoli, India, Feb 11, 29; m 51, Sunita Jain; c Avanindra & Ahamindra. *Educ:* Banaras Hindu Univ, BS, 49; Univ Calcutta, MS, 51, DPhil(phys), 63; City Univ New York, MS, 74. *Prof Exp:* Lectr physics, Holkar Sci Col, India, 54-60, asst prof, 60-62; res fel, Saha Inst Nuclear Physics, India, 62-64; asst res scientist chem, NY Univ, 64-68. *Concurrent Pos:* Adj assoc prof comput sci, Queens Col, 78-; vis prof admin comput systs, Hofstra Univ, Hempstead, NY, 80-81. *Mem:* Am Phys Soc; Sigma Xi. *Res:* Intensity distribution in molecular band systems; potential energy curves and vibrational wave functions of diatomic molecules; programming systems for computers; quantum chemical study of molecular complexes. *Mailing Add:* York Col City Univ NY 94-20 Guy R Brewer Blvd Jamaica NY 11451. *E-Mail:* jain@ycvax.york.cuny.edu

JAIN, FAQUIR C, CONDENSED MATTER PHYSICS. *Current Pos:* From asst prof to assoc prof, 73-87, dept head, Elec & Systs Eng, 86-90, PROF, UNIV CONN, 87-, PROG DIR, 93- *Personal Data:* b India, Mar 23, 46. *Educ:* Agra Univ, BS, 62, MS, 63; Roorkee Univ, BSEE, 65; Indian Inst Technol, MSEE, 68; Univ Conn, PhD, 73. *Prof Exp:* Res scientist, NSF, 89-92. *Mem:* Am Phys Soc; sr mem Inst Elec & Electronics Engrs; Sigma Xi; Optical Soc Am; Nat Asn Corrosion Engrs; Int Soc Hybrid Microelectonics; Int Soc Optical Eng. *Res:* Electrical and optical processes in semi-conductors and their device applications. *Mailing Add:* Dept Elec Eng U-157 Univ Conn Storrs CT 06269

JAIN, HIMANSHU, ELECTRONIC CERAMIC MATERIALS, INORGANIC GLASSES. *Current Pos:* from asst prof to assoc prof ceramics, 85-93, PROF MAT SCI & ENG, LEHIGH UNIV, 93- *Personal Data:* b Mainpuri, India, Jan 20, 55; m 90, Sweety Agrawal; c Isha H. *Educ:* Kanpur Univ, BS, 70; Banaras Univ, MS, 72; Indian Inst Technol, Kanpur, MTech, 74; Columbia Univ, Eng, ScD(metall & mat sci), 79. *Prof Exp:* Appointee, Argonne Nat Lab, Ill, 80-82; assoc metallurgist nuclear waste, Brookhaven Nat Lab, Upton, NY, 82-85. *Concurrent Pos:* Vis scientist, Inst Physics, Univ

Dortmund, Ger, 84 & Advan Ctr Mat Sci, Indian Inst Technol, 85; guest lectr, Krumb Sch Mines, Columbia Univ, 85; consult, Mass Inst Technol Sch Chem Eng Pract, Brookhaven Nat Lab, Upton, NY, 85; Humboldt fel, Ger, 91; vis prof, Univ Dortmund, Ger & Nat Hellenic Res Ctr, Athens, Greece, 91-92. *Mem:* Am Ceramic Soc; Am Inst Mining Metall & Petrol Engrs; Ceramic Educ Coun. *Res:* Electrical relaxation, conductivity and dielectric properties of amorphous and crystalline ceramics; surface conduction and diffusion; effect of radiation on transport properties; diffusion and nuclear spin relaxation in glasses; corrosion in nuclear waste environment; sintering of ceramics; physical and chemical structure of glasses. *Mailing Add:* 2018 Chester Rd Bethlehem PA 18017. *Fax:* 610-758-4244; *E-Mail:* hj00@lehigh.edu

JAIN, KAILASH CHANDRA, FABRICATION METHODS, MICROSTRUCTURES. *Current Pos:* STAFF RES ENGR ELECTRONICS, GEN MOTORS RES LABS, WARREN, MICH, 79- *Personal Data:* b Indore, Jan 1, 43; US citizen; m 69; c 3. *Educ:* Banaras Hindu Univ, India, BEng, 64; State Univ NY, Stony Brook, MS, 69, PhD(mat sci), 72; Hofstra Univ, NY, MBA, 78. *Prof Exp:* Sci officer, Alloy Dept, AEC India, 64-66; teaching asst & lab instr variety, Dept Mat Sci, State Univ NY, Stony Brook, 66-72, res, Dept Earth & Space Sci, 72-73; sr process engr integrated circuits mfg, Gen Instrument Corp, NY, 73-76; device engr integrated circuits mfg, RCA Corp, West Palm Beach, Fla, 77-79. *Concurrent Pos:* Consult, 70-76; recruiter, Electronics Dept, Gen Motors Res Lab, 80-86. *Mem:* Sr mem Inst Elec & Electronics Engrs. *Res:* Develop new materials and processes to realize novel sensors, power devices, and integrated circuits; propose improved fabrication methods and device structures; develop processes to improve current product; net shape metal parts; granted seven patents. *Mailing Add:* 1939 Spiceway Dr Troy MI 48098

JAIN, MAHAVIR, EXPERIMENTAL NUCLEAR PHYSICS. *Current Pos:* MEM STAFF, LOS ALAMOS NAT LAB, 78- *Personal Data:* b Barther, India, Jan 1, 41; US citizen; m 66. *Educ:* Agra Univ, BSc, 57; Univ Delhi, MSc, 59; Univ Md, College Park, PhD(physics), 69. *Honors & Awards:* Res Publ Award, Naval Res Lab, 75. *Prof Exp:* Fel nuclear physics, Univ Man, 69-71; res assoc nuclear physics, Tex A&M Univ, 71-78. *Concurrent Pos:* Guest scientist, Los Alamos Sci Lab, 74-78. *Mem:* Am Phys Soc. *Res:* Direct interactions, especially quasi-free scattering from nucleons and clusters; excited states, breakup and polarization in three nucleon systems, neutron-proton scattering; polarization and pion production at LAMPF energies and transport calculations; diagnostics and simulations. *Mailing Add:* 1368 35th St Los Alamos NM 87544

JAIN, MAHENDRA KUMAR, BIOPHYSICS, NEUROSCIENCES. *Current Pos:* from asst prof to assoc prof, 73-81, PROF BIOCHEM, UNIV DEL, 81- *Personal Data:* b Ujjain, India, Oct 12, 38; m 74; c 1. *Educ:* Vikram Univ, India, MSc, 59; Weizmann Inst Sci, PhD(chem), 67. *Prof Exp:* Lectr chem, Educ Dept, Govt Madhya Pradesh, India, 59-64 & Punjabi Univ, 64-65; res assoc biochem, Ind Univ, Bloomington, 67-73. *Mem:* Biophys Soc; Fed Am Soc Exp Biol. *Res:* Membrane structure and function; mode of action of phospholipases on bilayers; reconstitution; effect of drugs on the phase properties of membrane; inhibitors of phospholipase. *Mailing Add:* Dept Chem Univ Del Newark DE 19716-0001. *Fax:* 302-831-2968

JAIN, MAHENDRA KUMAR, MATHEMATICAL ANALYSIS. *Current Pos:* assoc prof, 75-83, PROF MATH, UNIV TENN, MARTIN, 83- *Personal Data:* b Muzaffarnagar, India, Jan 4, 29; m 49, Chandra; c Sushil, Anil, Dave & Parker. *Educ:* Univ Lucknow, BS, 48, MS, 51, PhD(math), 55. *Prof Exp:* Lectr math, M J Inter Col Asara, 51-52; Vidyant Col, Univ Lucknow, 52-55; H D Jain Col, Magadh Univ, 55-59; res instr, WVa Univ, 67-69, asst prof, 69-70. *Concurrent Pos:* Asst prof, Bihar Inst Technol, Sindri, 59-72; Agency Int Develop fel, Univ Wis, 63-64. *Mem:* Am Math Soc. *Res:* Complex variables; integral transforms. *Mailing Add:* 2101 Meadowbrook Dr Martin TN 38237

JAIN, NARESH C, TOXICOLOGY, ANALYTICAL CHEMISTRY. *Current Pos:* assoc prof pharmacol & toxicol, 71-78, assoc prof community med & pub health, 72-78, PROF PHARMACOL & TOXICOL & PROF COMMUNITY MED & PUB HEALTH, SCH MED, UNIV SOUTHERN CALIF, 78-; DIR TOXICOL, NAT TOXICOL LABS, 87- *Personal Data:* b Meerut, India, Dec 30, 32; m 87, Plomp. *Educ:* Univ Lucknow, BS, 51, MS, 54; Univ Calif, Berkeley, PhD(criminol/toxicol), 65. *Prof Exp:* Sci officer toxicol, Govt Brit Guiana, 59-62; res toxicologist, Univ Calif, Berkeley, 63-66; assoc dir toxicol, Sch Med, Ind Univ, 66-71. *Concurrent Pos:* Mem clin toxicol devices panel, Food & Drug Admin, 75-; consult, USN, 83-, USAF, 85- *Mem:* Soc Toxicol; Am Acad Forensic Sci; Int Asn Toxicol; Soc Forensic Toxicologists. *Res:* Toxicology both clinical and forensic; application of instrumentation in the detection of drugs from biological fluids; drug metabolism; interaction of drugs, marijuana and alcohol; laboratory services to drug abuse and overdose patients; environmental monitoring of toxic wastes, herbicides, and pesticides; expert witness in toxicology; interpretation of alcohol & drug levels for impairment; environmental toxicology. *Mailing Add:* Nat Toxicol Labs 5451 Rockledge Dr Buena Park CA 90621. *Fax:* 714-521-3896

JAIN, NEMICHAND B, INDUSTRIAL PHARMACY, PHYSICAL PHARMACY. *Current Pos:* res investr, E R Squibb & Sons, 80-82, lab supvr, 82-85, RES GROUP LEADER & SECT HEAD, BRISTOL-MYERS SQUIBB CO, 85- *Personal Data:* b Akola, India, July 1, 51; m 78; c 2. *Educ:* Nagpur Univ, India, BSc, 71; Univ Bombay, India, Bsc, 74; Univ Kans, MS, 76, PhD(pharmaceut), 78. *Prof Exp:* Res asst, Univ Kans, 74-78; res pharmacist, Wyeth Labs, subsid Am Home Prod Corp, 78-80. *Mem:* Am Pharmaceut Asn; Acad Pharmaceut Sci; Controlled Release Soc; AAAS. *Res:* Development of pharmaceutical dosage forms; controlled drug delivery; in-vitro-in-vivo evaluation of dosage forms; drug stability degradation mechanisms; physio-chemical evaluation of drug entities. *Mailing Add:* PO Box 191 New Brunswick NJ 08903

JAIN, PIYARE LAL, PHYSICS, RELATIVISTIC HEAVY ION INTERACTION. *Current Pos:* from instr to assoc prof, 54-67, PROF PHYSICS, STATE UNIV NY BUFFALO, 67- *Personal Data:* b Punjab, India, Dec 11, 21; US citizen; m 66, Sulakshna K Dhawan; c Navin K & Atul. *Educ:* Punjab Univ, India, BA, 44, MA, 48; Mich State Univ, PhD(physics), 54. *Prof Exp:* Asst physics, Mich State Univ, 51-53; res assoc chem, Univ Minn, 53-54. *Concurrent Pos:* Res assoc, Univ Chicago, 59-60; mem staff, Lawrence Radiation Lab, Univ Calif, 61-62; vis prof, Bristol Univ, 61-62; Fulbright vis prof, Rajasthan Univ, India, 65-66; sci adv, Am Embassy AID, New Delhi, India, 66. *Mem:* Fel Am Phys Soc. *Res:* Solid state, electron and nuclear magnetic resonance; nuclear physics; cosmic radiation and high energy physics; radiation physics; heavy ion physics. *Mailing Add:* Dept Physics State Univ NY Buffalo NY 14260. *Fax:* 716-645-2507; *E-Mail:* phyjain@ubums.cc.buffalo.edu

JAIN, RAKESH KUMAR, TUMOR PHYSIOLOGY, MICROCIRCULATION. *Current Pos:* PROF, DIV HEALTH SCI & TECHNOL, MASS INST TECHNOL, 91- *Personal Data:* b Lalitpur, India, Dec 18, 50. *Educ:* Indian Inst Technol, Kanpur, BTech, 72; Univ Del, Newark, MChE, 74, PhD(chem eng), 75. *Honors & Awards:* Int Inst Microcirculation Res Award, 84. *Prof Exp:* Asst prof chem & biomed engr, Columbia Univ, 76-78; from asst prof to prof chem & biomed eng, Carnegie Mellon Univ, 78-91; Andrew Work Cook prof tumor biol, Harvard Med Sch, 91-; dir, Edwin L Steele Lab Tumor Bio, Mass Gen Hosp, 91- *Concurrent Pos:* Adj prof neurosurg, Univ Pittsburgh Sch Med, 78-80; consult, Pathophysiol Lab, Nat Cancer Inst, 76-84 & Hybritech, 87-; vis prof, dept chem eng, Mass Inst Technol, 83, dept bioeng, Univ Calif, San Diego & dept radiol, Stanford Univ Med Sch, 84-; chair, Nat Prog Comt Life Sci, Am Inst Chem Engrs, 81-84, mem comt, Am Microcirculation Soc, 86-88 & meeting prog comt, Biomed Eng Soc, 86-89; co-chair, Conf Thermal Characteristics Tumors, NY Acad Sci, 79-; assoc mem, Ctr Fluorescence Res Biol, 85-; mem, Pittsburg Cancer Inst, 86-; mem bd dirs, Int Inst Microcirculation, 87-; John Simon Guggenheim Mem Found fel, 83-84; NIH res career develop award, 80-85. *Mem:* Am Asn Cancer Res; AAAS; Am Inst Chem Engrs; Am Microcirculation Soc; Biomed Eng Soc; Int Inst Microcirculation; NY Acad Sci. *Res:* Develop a quantitative understanding of physiological events in the tumor microcirculation to improve cancer detection and treatment; transport of molecules in tumors; blood flow and microcirculatory hemodynamics in tumors; physiological studies in tissues isolated tumors; heat transfer and temperature distribution in tumors; rheology of malignant and non-malignant cells; interaction of cells with vasculature. *Mailing Add:* Dept Radiation Oncol Harvard Med Sch Mass Gen Hosp Boston MA 02114. *Fax:* 617-726-4172

JAIN, RAKESH KUMAR, synthetic antigens, synthetic acceptors for glycosyltransferases, for more information see previous edition

JAIN, RAVINDER KUMAR, ENVIRONMENTAL ENGINEERING, INTELLIGENT SYSTEMS. *Current Pos:* ASSOC DEAN RES & INT ENG, UNIV CINCINNATI. *Personal Data:* b Punjab, India, Oct 12, 35; US citizen. *Educ:* Calif State Univ, Sacramento, BS, 61, MS, 68; Tex Tech Univ, PhD(civil eng), 71; Harvard Univ, MPA, 80. *Honors & Awards:* Sustained Super Performance Awards, US Army Corps Engr, 72, 73 & 74; Res & Develop Award, US Army, 76, Commendations for Exemplary Performance & Except Mgt Res Prog, 82-90. *Prof Exp:* Civil engr design, Spink Eng Corp, 61-64; assoc engr water resources, Calif Dept Water Resources, 64-68; civil engr, Develop & Resources Corp, 68-69; chief Environ Div Environ Res, US Army Corps Engrs, Construct Eng Res Lab, 71-89; dir, Army Environ Policy Inst, 90- *Concurrent Pos:* Adj prof, Univ Ill, Urbana-Champaign, 75-; exec & prof develop fel, Harvard Univ, 79-80; res affil, Mass Inst Technol, 84-; Churchill Col fel, Cambridge Univ, Eng, 86. *Mem:* Fel Am Soc Civil Engrs; Soc Am Mil Engrs. *Res:* Environmental impact analysis, environ quality management related to solid waste, air, water, noise pollution and hazardous waste; management of research and development organizations; environmental policy development; computer systems and artificial intelligence; author/co-author six books. *Mailing Add:* 11263 Snider Rd Cincinnati OH 45249

JAIN, SUBODH K, POPULATION BIOLOGY, ECONOMIC BOTANY. *Current Pos:* RETIRED. *Personal Data:* b Nanauta, India, Dec 11, 34; m 57, Saroj Singhal; c Sudhanshu, Vinoo & Sarita. *Educ:* Univ Delhi, BSc, 54; Indian Agr Res Inst, New Delhi, IARI, 56; Univ Calif, Davis, PhD(genetics), 60. *Honors & Awards:* Central govt India Prize, 54. *Prof Exp:* Pool off genetics, Coun Sci & Indust Res, New Delhi, 61-63; asst res geneticists, Univ Calif, Davis, 63-67, assoc biologist, 67-72, prof biol, 72-94. *Concurrent Pos:* NSF res grant, 69-71, 76-78 & 79-82, SOHIO grant, 81-85, SLOAN grant, 87; Guggenheim Found fel & sr fel, Coun Sci & Indust Res Orgn, Australia, 71-72; Indo-US fel, 78-79; Fulbright fel, 78 & 95; consult & vis prof, Hyderabad, India, 79, 82, Mendoza, Argentina, 82, Piracicaba, Brazil, 83, Plant Breeding Inst, Wageningen, 84 & Turkey, 93; assoc ed, Evolution, 81-83; mem, Nat Acad Sci Panel Amaranth, 82-85, Orgn Int Symp in pop biol, 78, 83, 86, 87, 88. *Mem:* Soc Study Evolution; Am Soc Naturalists; Bot Soc Am; Am Inst Biol Sci. *Res:* Population genetics; plant breeding; plant evolution; dynamics of grassland communities; genetics and ecology of avena, bromus, trifolium species; analysis of life histories and relative fitnesses; genetic resources in crop breeding; development of new crops; conservation of rare and endangered plants. *Mailing Add:* Dept of Agronomy & Range Sci Univ of Calif Davis CA 95616

JAIN, SURENDER K, RING THEORY, LINEAR ALGEBRA. *Current Pos:* PROF MATH, OHIO UNIV, 69- *Personal Data:* b Amritsar, India, Nov 16, 38; m 63; c 2. *Educ:* Panjab Univ, India, BA Hons, 57, MA, 59; Univ Delhi, India, PhD(ring theory), 63. *Prof Exp:* Res mathematician & lectr, Univ Calif, Riverside, 63-65; reader math, Univ Delhi, India, 65-69. *Concurrent Pos:* Vis prof, Univ Frankfurt, Univ Chicago, McMaster Univ, Can, Kuwait Univ, Riyad Univ, Saudi Arabia, Ohio State Univ, NC State Univ & Univ Calif, Santa Barbara, 63-90. *Mem:* Am Math Soc; Math Asn Am; Soc Indust & Appl Math. *Res:* Noncommutative ring theory and applied linear algebra; author of 60 research publications and 6 books. *Mailing Add:* Three Ransom Rd Ohio Univ Athens OH 45701-2979

JAIN, SUSHIL C, PRODUCTIVITY IMPROVEMENT, QUALITY CONTROL. *Current Pos:* MGR, QUAL ASSURANCE, AM FUJI SEAL, 96- *Personal Data:* b Lucknow, India, June 14, 39; US citizen; m 69, Usha; c Rachna & Mohit. *Educ:* St John's Col, Agra, India, BS, 57; Indian Inst Technol, Kharagpur, BSEE, 61; Purdue Univ, Ind, MSIE, 64. *Prof Exp:* Elec engr, Gwalior Rayons, India, 61-63; indust engr, Ford Motor Co, 64-65 & Safran Printing Co, 66-68; sr indust engr, Edwards Bros, Inc, 71-73; staff engr, Alco Gravure, Inc, 73-78; mgr indust eng, Unified Data Prod, 79-81; dir indust eng, Universal Folding Box Inc, 81-89; process engr, Sealed Air Corp, 90-92; dir, qual assurance, Tekkote Corp, 93-94; dir qual, Mebane Packaging Group, 95-96. *Concurrent Pos:* Pres, Jain Consult, 89. *Mem:* Sr mem Inst Indust Engrs; sr mem Am Soc Qual Control. *Mailing Add:* 60 Winthrop Rd Hillsdale NJ 07642

JAIN, SUSHIL KUMAR, HEMATOLOGY, NUTRITION. *Current Pos:* from instr to asst prof, 81-91, PROF PEDIAT, BIOCHEM & PHYSIOL, LA STATE UNIV MED CTR, SHREVEPORT, CHIEF, SECT PEDIAT RES, 87- *Personal Data:* b Nabha, Punjab, India, Mar 31, 50; m 80; c 2. *Educ:* Punjab Univ, Chandigarh, BS, 70; Postgrad Inst Med Educ & Res, Chandigarh, MS, 72, PhD(biochem), 76. *Honors & Awards:* Founder's Award & Ross Award, Southern Soc Pediat Res; Beecham Award. *Prof Exp:* Tutor biochem, Postgrad Inst Med & Res, 76-77; fel pharmacol & nutrit, Univ Southern Calif, Los Angeles, 77-79; fel hemat, Sch Med, Univ Calif, San Francisco, 79-81. *Concurrent Pos:* Prin investr, NIH res grant, 85-88, Nat Am Diabetes Asn, 87- *Mem:* NY Acad Sci; Am Soc Biol Chemists; Am Soc Hemat; Soc Pediat Res; Am Inst Nutrit; Am Fed Clin Res. *Res:* Mechanisms of reduced red blood cell life span in sickle cell disease, newborn red cells, copper deficiency, iron deficiency; red cell aging, membrane lipid peroxidation; hyperlipidemia and lecithin-cholesterol acyltranferase deficiency; diabetes. *Mailing Add:* Dept Pediat La State Univ Med Ctr 1501 Kings Hwy Shreveport LA 71130. *Fax:* 318-675-6059

JAIN, VIJAY KUMAR, ELECTRICAL ENGINEERING. *Current Pos:* PROF ELEC ENG, UNIV SFLA, 80- *Personal Data:* b Gwalior, India, Nov 15, 37; m 57; c 3. *Educ:* Univ Rajasthan, BE, 56; Univ Roorkee, ME dipl, 57; Mich State Univ, PhD(elec eng), 64. *Prof Exp:* Asst prof elec eng, Birla Eng Col, India, 57-61; asst prof, Mich State Univ, 64; asst prof, Birla Inst Technol & Sci, India, 65-66, assoc prof, 66-68; assoc prof, Univ SFla, 68-74, prof, 74-79; prof, Ga Inst Technol, 79-80. *Concurrent Pos:* Consult, Honeywell, Sperry, Vet Admin Hosp & A C Nielsen; prof, Bell Lab, 82-84. *Mem:* Inst Elec & Electronics Engrs. *Res:* Communication electronics; computer networking; digital signal-processing; pattern recognition; speech signals analysis; very-large-scale integration and microprocessors; system identification. *Mailing Add:* Dept Elec Eng Univ SFla Tampa FL 33620

JAIN, VINOD KUMAR, POLYMER TRIBOLOGY, MACHINE DESIGN. *Current Pos:* from instr to assoc prof, 79-89, PROF MECH ENG DEPT, UNIV DAYTON, 89- *Personal Data:* US citizen; m 67; c 2. *Educ:* Univ Roorkee, India, BE, 64, ME, 70; Iowa State Univ, PhD(mech eng), 80. *Prof Exp:* Lectr, Mech Eng Dept, Univ Roorkee, India, 64-75. *Mem:* Am Soc Mech Engrs. *Res:* Friction and wear of polymers; characterization of surface topography; fatigue of polymeric composites; lubrication technology; metal processing sciences; forging. *Mailing Add:* 1045 Hyde Park Dr Dayton OH 45429

JAINCHILL, JEROME, ENVIRONMENT, BIOCHEMISTRY. *Current Pos:* SCI EDUC, NEW YORK BD EDUC, 81- *Personal Data:* b New York, NY, Jan 27, 32; m 64, Robert Cohen; c Charles, Melissa & Susan. *Educ:* NY Univ, BA, 53, MS, 60, PhD(genetics), 63. *Prof Exp:* Res assoc radiobiol, Sloan-Kettering Inst, NY, 63-65; res assoc biochem carcinogens, Dept Environ Med, NY Univ Med Ctr, 65-67; res biochemist, Endo Labs, 67-77, Cornell Univ, 77-80 & North Star Res, 80-81. *Concurrent Pos:* Mem, Long Island Environ Comt, Am Chem Soc. *Mem:* AAAS; NY Acad Sci; Am Chem Soc. *Res:* Biochemistry of carcinogenic agents on DNA; drug metabolism; pharmacokinetics; retrovirus; murine leukemia. *Mailing Add:* 2362 Garfield St North Bellmore NY 11710

JAISINGHANI, RAJAN A, RESEARCH & DEVELOPMENT FOR PRODUCT & BUSINESS DEVELOPMENT. *Current Pos:* PRES, PROD DEVELOP ASSISTANCE, INC, 90- *Personal Data:* b Karachi, Pakistan, Jan 21, 45; c 2. *Educ:* Banaras Hindu Univ, India, BS, 69; Univ Wis, MS, 73. *Prof Exp:* Engr, Fiebing Chem Co, 71-73; res asst, Univ Wis, 71-73; mgr res, Nelson Indust, 74-82; mgr res & develop, Am Filtrona Corp, 82-90. *Mem:* Am Inst Chem Eng; Soc Automotive Eng; Am Asn Aerosol Res; Int Asn Colloid Scientists; Am Chem Soc; Am Inst Chem Engrs; Filtration Soc; Int Asn Colloid Scientists. *Res:* Air and liquid filtration; colloid and aerosols; electrically simulated filtration; capillarity and other surface phenomena; fluid flow coalescence; research management and planning. *Mailing Add:* Prod Develop Assistance Inc 13511 E Boundary Rd Suites D & E Midlothian VA 23112. *Fax:* 804-744-0677

JAKAB, GEORGE JOSEPH, PULMONARY IMMUNOLOGY, DISEASES & TOXICOLOGY. *Current Pos:* assoc prof, 77-86, PROF, SCH HYG & PUB HEALTH, JOHNS HOPKINS UNIV, 86-, ASSOC DEPT CHMN, 90- *Personal Data:* b Budapest, Hungary, April 7, 39; m 63; c 2. *Educ:* Univ Wis-Madison, BS, 65, MS, 67, PhD(med microbiol), 70. *Prof Exp:* Fel, Univ Vt, 70-72, res assoc, 72-77. *Concurrent Pos:* Res career develop award, Nat Heart, Lung & Blood Inst, 77. *Mem:* Infectious Dis Soc Am; Am Thoracic Soc; Reticuloendothelial Soc; Am Soc Microbiol; Soc Toxicol. *Res:* Pulmonary defense mechanisms against infectious agents; interaction of infectious agents and environmental contaminants in the genesis and exacerbation of acute and chronic lung disease. *Mailing Add:* 5706 Oakshire Rd Baltimore MD 21209

JAKACKY, JOHN M, JR, ATOM MOLECULE COLLISION, ACOUSTIC. *Current Pos:* Analyst, 84-87, SR ANALYST, SONALYSTS INC, 87- *Personal Data:* b Hartford, Conn, July 22, 56. *Educ:* Univ Conn, BS, 78, MS, 79, PhD(physics), 84. *Mem:* Am Phys Soc. *Mailing Add:* 185 Pruitt Pl Oakdale CT 06370

JAKEN, SUSAN, BIOLOGICAL CHEMISTRY. *Current Pos:* SR SCIENTIST, W ALTON JONES CELL SCI CTR, INC, LAKE PLACID, NY, 86- *Personal Data:* b Painesville, Ohio, Oct 23, 50. *Educ:* Bowling Green Univ, BS, 72; Univ Mich, MS, 74, PhD(biochem), 77. *Prof Exp:* Res fel med, Mass Gen Hosp & Harvard Med Sch, 77-79, interdisciplinary prog health, Harvard Sch Pub Health, 79-81; instr, Johns Hopkins Univ, 81-85; cancer expert, Lab Cellular Carcinogenesis & Tumor Promotion, Nat Cancer Inst, 83-85; sr staff fel, Div Virol, Ctr Drugs & Biol, Food & Drug Admin, 85-86. *Concurrent Pos:* Prin investr, NIH, 7-79. *Mem:* Am Soc Cell Biol; Am Asn Cancer Res. *Res:* Biological Chemistry; author of 68 publications. *Mailing Add:* W Alton Jones Cell Sci Ctr 10 Old Barn Rd Lake Placid NY 12946. *Fax:* 518-522-1849

JAKES, KAREN SORKIN, MOLECULAR BIOLOGY. *Current Pos:* Asst res genetics, 71-75, RES ASSOC GENETICS, ROCKEFELLER UNIV, 76- *Personal Data:* b Washington, DC, June 18, 47; m 70; c 2. *Educ:* Brown Univ, BSc, 69; Yale Univ, PhD(molecular biophys & biochem), 74. *Mem:* AAAS. *Res:* Mechanism of action and synthesis of colicin E3 and its immunity protein; export of colicins E1, E2 and E3; replication of bacteriophage fluid. *Mailing Add:* Dept Physiol & Biophys Albert Einstein Col Med 1300 Morris Park Ave Bronx NY 10461. *Fax:* 718-430-8819

JAKES, W(ILLIAM) C(HESTER), ELECTRICAL ENGINEERING. *Current Pos:* RETIRED. *Personal Data:* b Milwaukee, Wis, May 15, 22; m 48, Mary Bristle; c 2. *Educ:* Northwestern Univ, BS, 44, MS, 47, PhD(elec eng), 49. *Hon Degrees:* PhD, Iowa Wesleyan Univ, 61. *Honors & Awards:* Co-winner, Alexander Graham Bell Medal, Inst Elec & Electronics Engrs, 87. *Prof Exp:* Mem tech staff, Bell Tel Labs, 49-62, head mobile radio res, 62-71, dir radio transmission lab, 71-84, dir Transmission Terminals & Radio Lab, 84-87. *Concurrent Pos:* Mem sci adv bd, Voice of Am, 60-62. *Mem:* Fel Inst Elec & Electronics Engrs. *Res:* Microwave propagation and antennas; satellite communication; microwave transmission systems development. *Mailing Add:* 58 Wildrose Dr Andover MA 01810

JAKLEVIC, JOSEPH MICHAEL, PHYSICS, ENVIRONMENTAL SCIENCES. *Current Pos:* fel, 67-69, staff scientist eng, 69-78, SR STAFF SCIENTIST, DEPT INST SCI, LAWRENCE BERKELEY LAB, 78- *Personal Data:* b Kansas City, Kans, Jan 16, 41; m 66; c 2. *Educ:* Rockhurst Col, AB, 62; Univ Notre Dame, PhD(physics), 66. *Prof Exp:* Fel nuclear physics, Univ Notre Dame, 66-67. *Mem:* Am Phys Soc; Mat Res Soc; Air Pollution Control Asn; Mat Res Soc. *Res:* Application of nuclear and atomic physics principles and techniques to problems of environmental sampling and analysis; x-ray and atomic physics techniques. *Mailing Add:* Lawrence Berkeley Lab Cyclotron Rd No 1 Berkeley CA 94720

JAKLEVIC, ROBERT C, EXPERIMENTAL PHYSICS, CONDENSED MATTER. *Current Pos:* staff scientist solid state physics, 62-80, PRIN SCIENTIST, FORD SCI LABS, 80- *Personal Data:* b Kansas City, Kans, July 27, 34; m 62; c 2. *Educ:* Rockhurst Col, BS, 56; Univ Notre Dame, PhD(physics), 60. *Honors & Awards:* Tech Achievement Award, Ford Motor Co, 90. *Prof Exp:* Fel, Univ Notre Dame, 61-62. *Mem:* Fel Am Phys Soc; Sigma Xi; Am Chem Soc. *Res:* Superconductivity; Josephson tunneling; normal metal tunneling; photoelectric effect in metals; thin film technology; tunneling in semiconductors; organic conductors; surface science; scanning tunneling spectroscopy; nanoscale devices. *Mailing Add:* 28988 Augusta Farmington MI 48331-4812

JAKOB, FREDI, ANALYTICAL CHEMISTRY. *Current Pos:* from asst prof to assoc prof, 61-69, chmn dept, 65-68, PROF CHEM, CALIF STATE UNIV, SACRAMENTO, 69- *Personal Data:* b Horstein, Ger, Jan 11, 34; US citizen; m 57; c 4. *Educ:* City Col NY, BS, 55; Rutgers Univ, PhD(anal chem), 61. *Prof Exp:* Instr chem, Rutgers Univ, 60-61. *Concurrent Pos:* NSF grants, 61-; consult, St Bd Equalization, 62-78 & consult chemist, Anal Assocs Inc; vis assoc prof, Univ Wis, Madison, 68-69; vis prof, Victoria Univ, Wellington, NZ, 71, Univ Wollongong, Australia, 82. *Mem:* Am Chem Soc. *Res:* Theory and application of separation methods and chemical instrumentation; laboratory applications of computers. *Mailing Add:* Dept Chem Calif State Univ 6000 J St Sacramento CA 95819-2605

JAKOB, KARL MICHAEL, NUCLEIC ACIDS BIOLOGY, CELL BIOLOGY. *Current Pos:* res assoc plant genetics, 53-68, sr scientist, 69-78, ASSOC PROF, WEIZMANN INST SCI, ISRAEL, 79- *Personal Data:* b Berlin, Ger, Nov 5, 21; nat US; m 54; c 2. *Educ:* Univ Ill, BS, 43, MS, 48; Univ Calif, PhD(cytogenetics, bot), 52. *Prof Exp:* Plant breeder, Marshall Farm Serv, Ill, 43-45; asst bot & cytol, Univ Ill & Univ Calif, 47-51. *Concurrent Pos:* Vis sr lectr, Univ Bar Ilan, Israel, 62-72; vis investr, Biol Div, Oak Ridge Nat Lab, 63-64. *Mem:* Int Soc Plant & Molecular Biol. *Res:* Biochemistry of the cell division cycle of eukaryotes; plant RNA metabolism; use of antisense RNA probes to locate transcriptional activity by insitu hybridization; molecular biology of chromatin during DNA replication in vivo. *Mailing Add:* Dept Plant Genetics Weizmann Inst Sci Rehovot 76100 Israel

JAKOBIEC, FREDERICK ALBERT, OPHTHALMOLOGY, PATHOLOGY. *Current Pos:* CHMN, MANHATTAN EYE, EAR, & THROAT HOSP, 80- *Educ:* Harvard Univ, MD. *Res:* Tumor surgery. *Mailing Add:* 243 Charles St Boston MA 02114-3004

JAKOBSEN, ROBERT JOHN, VIBRATIONAL SPECTROSCOPY, ESPECIALLY AS PERTAINS TO BIOLOGICAL MOLECULES. *Current Pos:* PRES, IR-ACTS, 88- *Personal Data:* b Chicago, Ill, Jan 29, 29; m 52, Jayne Mailloux. *Educ:* Col of Emporia, BS, 51. *Honors & Awards:* Coblentz Soc Williams-Wright Award, 84; Rappaport Mem Award, Ohio Valley Sect, Soc Appl Spectros, 90. *Prof Exp:* Asst phys chem, Kans State Univ, 51-55 & Univ Kans, 55-56; prin chemist, Battelle Columbus Labs, 56-64, sr chemist, 64-76, res leader, 76-86; tech dir, Mattson Inst Spectros Res, 86-88. *Concurrent Pos:* Adj prof chem, Kans State Univ, 88- *Mem:* Soc Appl Spectros; Coblentz Soc; Sigma Xi; NY Acad Sci. *Res:* Molecular spectroscopy, mainly infrared and Raman; application of molecular spectroscopy to structure, especially the structure of proteins and other biological molecules. *Mailing Add:* 326 Walhalla Rd Columbus OH 43202

JAKOBSON, MARK JOHN, NUCLEAR PHYSICS. *Current Pos:* from asst prof to assoc prof, 53-58, chmn dept astron & physics, 68-73, PROF PHYSICS, UNIV MONT, 58- *Personal Data:* b Carlyle, Mont, May 4, 23; m 45; c 2. *Educ:* Univ Mont, AB, 44, MA, 47; Univ Calif, PhD(physics), 51. *Prof Exp:* Asst physics, Univ Calif, 47-49, physicist, Radiation Lab, 50-52; instr physics, Univ Wash, 52-53. *Mem:* Fel Am Phys Soc. *Res:* Photonuclear reactions; accelerator design; pion interactions. *Mailing Add:* 3000 Queen St Missoula MT 59801

JAKOBSSON, ERIC GUNNAR, SR, BIOPHYSICS, PHYSIOLOGY. *Current Pos:* res assoc, 71-72, asst prof, 72-78, ASSOC PROF PHYSIOL & BIOPHYS, UNIV ILL, URBANA, 78-, ASSOC PROF BIOENG, 81-, PROF PHYSIOL, BIOPHYS, BIOENG, 91-, SR RES SCIENTIST, NAT CTR SUPERCOMPUT APPLNS, 91- *Personal Data:* b New York, NY, Nov 18, 38; m 63, Naomi Dick; c 6. *Educ:* Columbia Univ, BA, 59, BS, 60; Dartmouth Col, PhD(physics), 69. *Prof Exp:* Process engr cryog, Air Prod & Chem, 60-62; develop engr, Malaker Corp, 62-65; fel, Case Western Reserve Univ, 69-71. *Concurrent Pos:* Fel, NSF, 70-71; vis assoc prof physiol, Duke Univ, 79. *Mem:* Biophys Soc; AAAS; fel Am Phys Soc. *Res:* Osmoregulation of animal cells; rhythmic and repetitive electrical activity in nerve physics of biological membranes; epithelial transport. *Mailing Add:* Nat Ctr Supercomput Applns Univ Ill 4039 Beckman Urbana IL 61801. *Fax:* 217-244-2909; *E-Mail:* jake@ncsa.uiuc.edu

JAKOBY, WILLIAM BERNARD, BIOCHEMISTRY, ENZYMOLOGY. *Current Pos:* sr investr, Nat Inst Arthritis, Metab & Digestive Dis, 55-68, CHIEF SECT ENZYMES & INTERMEDIARY METAB, NAT INST DIABETES & DIGESTIVE & KIDNEY DIS, 68-, CHIEF, LAB BIOCHEM & METAB, 84- *Personal Data:* b Breslau, Ger, Nov 17, 28; nat US; c Michael & Robert. *Educ:* Brooklyn Col, BS, 50; Yale Univ, PhD(microbiol), 54. *Prof Exp:* Fel pharmacol, NY Univ-Bellevue Med Ctr, 53-54, fel biochem, 54-55. *Concurrent Pos:* Mem bd dirs, Found Advan Educ in Sci, 68-87; consult, Molecular Biol Panel, NSF, 70-73 & 76; mem, Enzyme Comn, Int Union Biochem, 69-71, Comn Biochem Nomenclature, 74-80; ed in chief, Anal Biochem, 86-; assoc ed Hepatol, 80-85 & Protein Expression & Purification, 90-92. *Mem:* Am Soc Biol Chemists. *Res:* Enzymology; detoxication. *Mailing Add:* NIH Bldg 10 Rm 9N119 Bethesda MD 20892. *E-Mail:* wbjakoby@helix.nih.gov

JAKOI, EMMA RAFF, CELL BIOLOGY, MOLECULAR BIOLOGY. *Current Pos:* ASSOC PROF, DEPT NEUROL, MED COL VA, 89- *Personal Data:* b Cornwall, Ont, May 10, 46; US citizen; m 71. *Educ:* Wash State Univ, BS, 68; Duke Univ, PhD(physiol, pharmacol), 73. *Prof Exp:* Asst prof anat, Med Ctr, Duke Univ, 77-89. *Concurrent Pos:* Res assoc anat, Med Ctr, Duke Univ, 73-74; USPHS instnl res fel, 74-75, USPHS fel, 75-77. *Mem:* Am Soc Cell Biol; Biophys Soc; Sigma Xi. *Res:* Biochemical and morphological studies of ligatin, a membrane bound baseplate for cell surface proteins involved in intercellular adhesion during development of embryonic chick neural retina and in degradation of glycoproteins and glycolipids in suckling rat ileal epithelial cells. *Mailing Add:* Med Col Va Box 599 MCV Sta Richmond VA 23298-0001. *Fax:* 804-371-6373

JAKOWSKA, SOPHIE, PATHOBIOLOGY, ENVIRONMENTAL ETHICS & ECO-SPIRITUALITY. *Current Pos:* RETIRED. *Personal Data:* b Warsaw, Poland, Feb 12, 22; nat US; m 41, Constantine L Jeannopoulos; c Peter, John & Marie-Helene. *Educ:* Lycee Warsaw, Poland, cert, 39; Univ Rome, cert, 42; Fordham Univ, MS, 45, PhD(biol), 47. *Honors & Awards:* Tree Learning Award, Int Union Conserv of Nature & Natural Resources, 88; Liga Ochrony Przyrody gold medal, League Protection Nature, 89. *Prof Exp:* Instr bact, Col Mt St Vincent, 46; asst, Chemother Div, Sloan-Kettering Inst Cancer Res, 47-48; from asst prof to assoc prof, Col Mt St Vincent, 48-58; asst to vpres med affairs, Nat Cystic Fibrosis Res Found, 61-62; head, Dept Path, Food & Drug Res Labs, Inc, 64-67; tech adv & res coordr biol, Santo Domingo Univ, 67-68; spec proj dir, Nat Cystic Fibrosis Res Found, 68-69; biologist, Food & Drug Admin, 69-71; prof biol sci, Col Staten Island, City Univ NY, 70-75. *Concurrent Pos:* Collabr, NY Aquarium, NY Zool Soc, 48-59, res assoc exp biol, Dept Marine Biochem & Ecol, 59-62; collabr, Brookhaven Nat Lab, 52-62; vis prof, Grad Sh, St Louis Univ, 57; res assoc, Dept Labs, Beth Israel Hosp, 59- & Inst Crippled & Disabled, 62; NSF biol teacher inst lectr, Iona Col, 63-; consult, Inst Marine Biol, Santo Domingo Univ, 63-, res coordr & hon prof fac sci, 68-; consult, Animal Med Ctr, 64-68; pvt consult, 66-; consult, Span Dept, Grolier, Inc, NY, 68-75; reviewer proposals & projs, Comn Educ, Int Union Conserv Nature; sci consult, 77-; mem, Int Union Conserv Nature & Natural Resources Working Group on Ehtics, 84-, liaison, World Coun Churches, 88, sr adv bd mem, Global Harmony Found, 89-; mem, Patronato Parque Nac Mirador Norte, 96- *Mem:* Fel AAAS; Am Micros Soc; Soc Protozool; Am Soc Ichthyologists & Herpetologists; Am Inst Biol Sci; fel NY Acad Sci; Sigma Xi. *Res:* Plant and animal cytology; comparative pathology and hematology; experimental biology; parasitology; radiobiology; biochemical ecology; mucous secretions; conservation and religious environmental education; writing books for children and new readers in Spanish on conservation and environmental education, e.g., on crocodiles, parrots, etc; author of numerous scientific papers and books; continuing work and education of environmental conservation with religious motivation. *Mailing Add:* Arz Merino 154 Z-1 Santo Domingo Dominican Republic. *Fax:* 809-687-3948

JAKUBIEC, ROBERT JOSEPH, ANALYTICAL CHEMISTRY. *Current Pos:* CONSULT, 91-, PROF, ROOSEVELT UNIV, CHICAGO, 95- *Personal Data:* b Detroit, Mich, June 19, 41; m 64; c 2. *Educ:* Univ Detroit, BS, 63; Wayne State Univ, PhD(anal chem), 68. *Prof Exp:* Chemist, US Food & Drug Admin, 63-65; sr chemist, Corn Prod Co, 68-69; sr chemist, Armak Co, Div Akzona, 69-70, sect mgr anal chem, 70-76; vpres & lab dir, Enviro-Test/Perry Chicago Dairy Labs, Inc, 76-91. *Concurrent Pos:* Guest lectr, Northwestern Univ & Roosevelt Univ, 71-; instr, Chicago Gas Chromatog Sch, 73-; vis prof, Northeastern Univ, Chicago. *Mem:* Am Chem Soc; Am Oil Chem Soc; Am Soc Testing & Mat; Water Pollution Control Fedn; Am Asn Cereal Chemists; Asn Off Anal Chemists. *Res:* General analytical methods development; gas chromatography; thin layer chromatography; atomic absorption spectroscopy; ultraviolet and visible spectroscopy; residue analysis; general instrumentation; high pressure liquid chromatography; ion chromatography. *Mailing Add:* 155 N Harbor Dr 3103 Chicago IL 60601. *Fax:* 312-861-9184

JAKUBOWSKI, GERALD S, ENGINEERING EDUCATION ADMINISTRATION, LASER DOPPLER VELOCIMETRY. *Current Pos:* DEAN, COL SCI & ENG, LOYOLA MARYMOUNT UNIV, 90- *Personal Data:* b Toledo, Ohio, Nov 22, 49; m 72; c 2. *Educ:* Univ Toledo, BSME, 74, MSME, 76, PhD(eng sci), 78. *Honors & Awards:* Ralph R Teetor Award, Soc Automotive Engrs, 85. *Prof Exp:* Grad & admin asst, Col Eng, Univ Toledo, 74-78, from asst prof to assoc prof mech eng, 78-86, asst dean eng, 86-88; assoc dean eng, Memphis State Univ, 88-89, interim dean, 89-90. *Concurrent Pos:* Fel, NASA-Lewis Res Ctr, 84-85; chair, New Eng Educ Comt, Am Soc Eng Educ, 85-86; mem, Student Activ Comt, Soc Automotive Engrs, 86-, eng educ bd, 90- *Mem:* Am Soc Eng Educ; Soc Automotive Engrs; Am Soc Mech Engrs; Am Inst Aeronaut & Astronaut. *Res:* Thermodynamics; fluid mechanics; heat transfer and energy; pump cavitation; ice melting; laser Doppler velocimetry. *Mailing Add:* Loyola Marymount Univ Col Sci & Eng Los Angeles CA 90045

JAKUBOWSKI, HIERONIM ZBIGNIEW, PROTEIN SYNTHESIS REGULATION & ACCURACY, MOLECULAR MECHANISMS OF CELLULAR DEFENSES AGAINST STRESS. *Current Pos:* adj asst prof, 84-91, ADJ ASSOC PROF MICROBIOL & MOLECULAR GENETICS, NJ MED SCH, NEWARK, 91- *Personal Data:* b Szczecinek, Poland, Sept 30, 46; m; c 2. *Educ:* Poznan Univ, MSc, 69; Agr Univ, Poznan, PhD(biochem), 74; Inst Biochem & Biophysics, Warsaw, DrHabil, 78. *Honors & Awards:* J Parnas Award, Polish Biochem Soc, 84. *Prof Exp:* Res asst biochem, Akademia Rolniczaiw Poznaniu, 69-73, sr res asst, 73-75, adj, 75-78, adj habil, 79-87. *Concurrent Pos:* Vis scientist, Univ NMex, Albuquerque, 75-76, Imp Col, London, Eng, 80 & Hanover Med Sch, Ger, 82; dep chmn, Dept Biochem, Agr Univ Poznan, 81. *Mem:* Am Soc Microbiol; Polish Inst Arts & Sci Am. *Res:* Mechanisms which maintain high degree of accuracy in the transmission and flow of information from gene to finished protein product; molecular mechanisms of cellular defenses against stress. *Mailing Add:* 9 Galloway Ct West Orange NJ 07052

JAKUS, KARL, MECHANICAL ENGINEERING, CERAMICS ENGINEERING. *Current Pos:* from asst prof to assoc prof, 70-83, PROF MECH ENG, UNIV MASS, AMHERST, 84- *Personal Data:* b Gyor, Hungary, Mar 21, 38; US citizen; m; c 2. *Educ:* Univ Wis-Madison, BS, 63; Univ Calif, Berkeley, MS, 65, PhD(aerosci), 68. *Honors & Awards:* F H Norton Award, Am Ceramic Soc, 93. *Prof Exp:* Asst prof mech eng, Johns Hopkins Univ, 68-70. *Concurrent Pos:* Consult govt labs & indust; assoc ed, J Am Ceramic Soc. *Mem:* Am Ceramics Soc. *Res:* Mechanical behavior of ceramics. *Mailing Add:* Dept Mech Eng Rm 322 Eng Shop Univ Mass Amherst MA 01003

JAKUS, MARIE A, biology; deceased, see previous edition for last biography

JAKWAY, JACQUELINE SINKS, ANATOMY. *Current Pos:* ASST PROF ANAT, STATE UNIV NY DOWNSTATE MED CTR, 67- *Personal Data:* b San Juan, PR, Dec 13, 28; div. *Educ:* Park Col, AB, 50; Univ Kans, PhD(anat), 58. *Prof Exp:* Asst histochem, Sch Med, Univ Kans, 50-52, asst anat, Univ, 52-57; asst animal path & hyg, Col Agr, Univ Nebr, 58, res assoc animal husb, 59, res assoc animal path & hyg, 59-61; from instr to asst prof anat, Sch Dent, Univ Southern Calif, 61-67. *Concurrent Pos:* Nat Cancer Inst fel, 59-61. *Mem:* Fel AAAS; NY Acad Sci; Soc Neurosci. *Res:* Comparative neuroanatomy; animal behavior. *Mailing Add:* 270 Lenox Rd Apt 612 Brooklyn NY 11226-2157

JALAL, SYED M, CLINICAL CYTOGENETICS. *Current Pos:* CO-DIR, CYTOGENETICS LAB; CONSULT, MED GENETICS DEPT, DEPT LAB MED & PATH, ASSOC PROF MAYO MED SCH, 90- *Personal Data:* b Ranchi, India, Dec 2, 38; nat US; m 66, Nikhat; c Shadeen. *Educ:* Univ Bihar, BSc, 59; Univ Wis, MS, 62, PhD(cytogenetics), 65; Am Bd Med Genetics, dipl, 85. *Prof Exp:* From asst prof to assoc prof, Univ N Dak, 64-77, prof biol, 77-88; human cytogenetics consult, 80-88; dir, cytogenetics lab, Genetic Screening & Coun Serv, Tex, 87-90. *Concurrent Pos:* Vis prof, Univ Tex Cancer Ctr, Houston, 74, 79; adj prof biol, Univ N Tex, 88-90; lab dir, NY Dept Health, 91. *Mem:* AMA; fel, Am Col Med Genetics; Am Soc Human Genetics; Sigma Xi. *Res:* Neonatal human cytogenetics; high resolution banded chromosome analysis; utility of fluorescent DNA probes for congenital and hematologic disorders. *Mailing Add:* Mayo Found 970 Hilton Bldg 200 First St SW Rochester MN 55905. *Fax:* 507-284-0043

JALAN, VINOD MOTILAL, electrochemistry, catalysis; deceased, see previous edition for last biography

JALBERT, JEFFREY SCOTT, NUCLEAR PHYSICS. *Current Pos:* PRES, JCC CONSULT, INC, 84- *Personal Data:* b Bridgeport, Conn, Jan 9, 40; m 66; c 2. *Educ:* Fairfield Univ, BS, 61; Va Polytech Inst, PhD(physics), 67. *Prof Exp:* Asst prof physics, Hollins Col, 66-67; assoc prof, Denison, 67-75, dir, Comput Ctr, 76-84, prof physics, 75-86. *Mem:* Am Phys Soc; Am Math Soc; Sigma Xi. *Res:* Siting of power plants. *Mailing Add:* 600 Newark Rd PO Box 381 Granville OH 43023

JALIFE, JOSE, CARDIAC ELECTROPHYSIOLOGY, ARRHYTHMIAS. *Current Pos:* from asst prof to prof, 80-81, PROF & CHMN PHARMACOL, HEALTH SCI CTR, STATE UNIV NY, SYRACUSE, 88- *Personal Data:* b Mex City, Mex, Mar 7, 47; m 71. *Educ:* Nat Univ Mex, BA, 65, MD, 72. *Hon Degrees:* Dr, Univ Buenos Aires, Arg, 85. *Honors & Awards:* Young Investr Award, Am Col Cardiol, 79; Dr Harold Lamport Award, Am Physiol Soc, 80; Develop Achievement Award, Am Heart Assn. *Prof Exp:* Fel pharmacol, Inst Cardiol, Mex, 68-70, instr, Univ Mex, 72-73; fel pharmacol, Upstate Med Ctr, State Univ NY, Syracuse, 73-75 & cardiac elec, Masonic Med Res Lab, Utica, 75-77. *Concurrent Pos:* Res scientist cardiac elec, Masonic Med Res Lab, Utica, NY, 77-81; estab investr, Am Heart Asn, 82-87; fel, Cardiovasc Sect, Am Physiol Soc, 85; fac exchange scholar, State Univ NY, 87-; pres, res award, Health Sci Ctr, State Univ NY, 90. *Mem:* Am Physiol Soc; Cardiovasc Sec Am Physiol Soc; NY Acad Sci; AAAS; Electrophysiol Soc; Am Heart Asn; Biophys Soc; hon mem Arg Soc Cardiol. *Res:* Theoretical and experimental work related to three major areas of experimental cardiology; cellular mechanism of cardiac arrhythmias; mechanism of pacemaker synchronization in heart cells; nervous control of heart rate and atrioventricular conduction. *Mailing Add:* Health Sci Ctr State Univ NY 766 Irving Ave Syracuse NY 13210. *Fax:* 315-464-8000

JALIL, MAZHAR, ACAROLOGY, BACTERIOLOGY. *Current Pos:* ENTOMOLOGIST & MICROBIOLOGIST, OHIO DEPT HEALTH, 69- *Personal Data:* b India, Nov 2, 38; US citizen; m 70, Betty A Lunsford; c Tariq, Khalid & Aisha. *Educ:* Univ Agra, BSc, 52, MSc, 54; Univ Nottingham, MSc, 63; Univ Waterloo, PhD(biol), 67; Am Registry Prof Entomologist cert, 71. *Prof Exp:* Farm supt, R A K Agr Inst, Sehore, India, 55-56; teacher & lectr agr, Govt Col, Sehore, 56-60; instr zool, Univ Nottingham, 62-64; instr biol, Univ Waterloo, 64-67; res assoc acarology, Univ Ky, 67-69. *Concurrent Pos:* Lord Belper fel, 62-63, teaching fel, 64-67, Ontario Grad fel, 65-67; consult, UN Develop Prog, NIH, Govt Pakistan, 80-81; mem, Columbus Comn Ethics & Values, 88-91; bd trustees, Islamic Ctr, Columbus, Ohio, 88-93; chmn, Sci Adv Comt, City Hall, Columbus, Ohio, 90-91. *Mem:* Acarological Soc Am; Entom Soc Am; Royal Agr Soc Eng. *Res:* Bionomics and ecology of oribatid mites; genetic control of mites and insects; biology, ecology and reproductive physiology of mosquitoes; diagnosis of streptococcal infection; proficiency testing program for clinical labs. *Mailing Add:* Ohio Dept Health PO Box 2568 Columbus OH 43216-2568. *Fax:* 614-752-9863

JALLOUL, LOUAY M A, ELECTRICAL ENGINEERING. *Current Pos:* sr engr, 94-96, STAFF ENGR, MOTOROLA INC, 96- *Personal Data:* b Beirut, Lebanon, Oct 24, 64. *Educ:* Okla Univ, BS, 85; Ohio State Univ, MS, 88; Rutgers Univ, PhD(elec eng), 93. *Prof Exp:* Teaching assoc elec eng, Okla Univ, 85-86; res assoc, Electro Sci Lab, Ohio State Univ, 86-88, Wireless Info Network Lab, Rutgers Univ, 89-93. *Mem:* Inst Elec & Electronics Engrs. *Res:* Wireless communications with emphasis on modulation and coding; spread spectrum systems and fading channel characterization; invented and applied new methods of demodulation for multi-user code division multiple access systems; designed new modems for high speed data over wireless links. *Mailing Add:* 5600 N Beach St No 226 Ft Worth TX 76137. *Fax:* 817-245-6148; *E-Mail:* ljalloul@ftw.mot.com

JALUFKA, NELSON WAYNE, ATOMIC PHYSICS, PLASMA PHYSICS. *Current Pos:* RES SCIENTIST ATOMIC & PLASMA PHYSICS, LANGLEY RES CTR, NASA, 62- *Personal Data:* b Austwell, Tex, Dec 2, 32; m 62; c 2. *Educ:* Lamar Univ, BS, 62; Col William & Mary, MA, 67; Univ Colo, Boulder, PhD(physics), 72. *Mem:* Am Phys Soc. *Res:* Nuclear pumped lasers, experimental; solar pumped lasers, experimental; basic atomic processes in plasmas. *Mailing Add:* 505 Brokenbridge Rd Yorktown VA 23692

JALURIA, YOGESH, NATURAL CONNECTION FLOWS & HEAT TRANSFER. *Current Pos:* from asst prof to assoc prof, 80-85, PROF MECH ENG, RUTGERS UNIV, 85- *Personal Data:* b Nabha, Punjab, India, Sept 8, 49; m 75, Anuradha Malhotra; c Pratik, Aseem & Ankur. *Educ:* Indian Inst Technol, Delhi, BS, 70; Cornell Univ, MS, 72, PhD(mech eng), 74. *Honors & Awards:* Young Scientist Medal, Indian Nat Sci Acad, 79; Cert Recognition, Nat Inst Stand & Technol, 82. *Prof Exp:* Asst & fel, Cornell Univ, 70-74; mem res staff thermal eng, Bell Tel Syst, Princeton, NJ, 74-76; asst prof mech eng, Indian Inst Technol, Kanpur, 76-80. *Concurrent Pos:* Consult, Steel Authority India, Ltd, 79-80, SRI Int & other co, 82-; prin investr, NSF, 82- & Dept Com, 83- *Mem:* Fel Am Soc Mech Engrs; Combustion Inst; Am Phys Soc. *Res:* Natural convection flows, cooling of electronic equipment, enclosure fires, environmental heat transfer, solar ponds, and numerical simulation of manufacturing processes; computational heat transfer and thermal stratification; heat transfer; fire; computer methods; manufacturing processes; combustion and fire modeling. *Mailing Add:* 55 Overhill Rd East Brunswick NJ 08816. *Fax:* 732-932-5313; *E-Mail:* jaluria@jove.rutgers.edu

JAMASBI, ROUDABEH J, CLINICAL MICROBIOLOGY, CANCER IMMUNOLOGY. *Current Pos:* asst prof microbiol & immunol, 81-83, ASSOC PROF CLIN MICROBIOL & TUMOR IMMUNOL, BOWLING GREEN STATE UNIV, 84- *Personal Data:* US citizen. *Educ:* Univ Tehran, BS, 66; Antaeus Res Inst, MT, 69; Univ Ark, MS, 70, PhD(microbiol & immunol), 74. *Prof Exp:* Investr, Oak Ridge Nat Lab; cancer immunologist, Oak Ridge Nat Lab, 78-80; prog dir immunol, Antaeus Res Inst, 80-81. *Concurrent Pos:* Assoc mem, Antaeus Res Inst, 81-; vis investr, Oak Ridge Nat Lab, 82- *Mem:* Am Asn Cancer Res; Am Soc Microbiol; Am Acad Microbiol; Am Asn Immunologists; Am Soc Clin Pathologists; Am Asn Blood Bank. *Res:* Immunological characterization of respiratory and digestive tract carcinomas; production of monoclonal antibodies; demonstration of cellular heterogeneity; isolation and characterization of radiation and drug resistance phenotypes. *Mailing Add:* 647 Flanders Ave Bowling Green OH 43402

JAMBOR, PAUL EMIL, RINGS & MODULES. *Current Pos:* assoc prof, 81-87, PROF MATH, UNIV NC, 88- *Personal Data:* b Olomouc, Czechoslovakia, March 29, 37. *Educ:* Inst Advan Technol, Prague, Dipl Ing, 62; Columbia Univ, MA, 70; Charles Univ, Prague, PhD(math), 73. *Prof Exp:* Assoc prof math, Charles Univ, Prague, 71-76; vis position, Math Inst, Tubingen, 76-77; lectr, Univ Mich, 77-80. *Concurrent Pos:* Assoc ed, Math Rev, 77-80. *Mem:* Am Math Soc; Math Asn Am. *Res:* Homological properties and structure theory of associative unitary rings; rings with no superdecomposable modules. *Mailing Add:* 407 Wexford Pl New Bern NC 28562

JAMDAR, SUBHASH C, LIPID BIOCHEMISTRY. *Current Pos:* RES SCIENTIST & DIR ANALYTICAL LAB, DEPT ANESTHESIA, COLUMBIA-PRESBY MED CTR, 88- *Personal Data:* b Nagpur, India, Apr 11, 37. *Educ:* Govt Col Sci, India, BS, 58; Nagpur Univ, India, MS, 60, PhD(biochem), 66. *Prof Exp:* Res assoc, Dept Med, Univ NC, Chapel Hill, 71-74; res asst prof, Dept Biochem & Anesthesiol, Med Col Va, 74-79; res assoc prof, Med Res Inst, Fla Inst Technol, 79-88. *Mem:* Am Soc Biochem; Biol & Molecular Biol Soc. *Mailing Add:* Dept Anesthesiol Columbia-Presby Med Ctr P&S Box 46 New York NY 10032. *Fax:* 212-305-6991

JAMERSON, FRANK EDWARD, PHYSICS. *Current Pos:* PRES, ELEC BATTERY BICYCLE CO, 93-; PRES, JAMERSON & ASSOC, 93- *Personal Data:* b Lowell, Mass, Nov 5, 27; m 50; c 5. *Educ:* Mass Inst Technol, BS, 48; Univ Notre Dame, PhD(physics), 52. *Prof Exp:* Physicist atomics br, US Naval Res Lab, Washington, DC, 51-52, head neutron physics sect reactors br, 54-57; sr scientist atomic power div, Westinghouse Elec Corp, 53; sr res physicist, Nuclear Power Eng Dept, Gen Motors Corp, 57-61 & Physics Dept, 61-63, supvry res physicist & supv phys electronics group, Physics Dept 63-69, head, Physics Dept, 69-85, head, Electrochem Dept, 85-87, mgr, div & staff contracts, 87-93; asst prof mgr, US Advan Battery Consorium, Elec Vehicle Platform, Gen Motors Eng Staff, 91-93. *Concurrent Pos:* Mem Nat Acad Sci-Nat Bur Standards eval panel, Off Air & Water Measurement, 71-72, chmn, 73-77; mem Nat Acad Sci-Nat Bur Standards eval panel, Inst Mat Res, 74-78 & panel Nat Measurement Lab, 78-80; chmn comt corp assoc, Am Inst Physics, 79-81, chmn comt pub policy, 85-88; mem, comt educ, Am Phys Soc, 83-85 & Nat Mat Adv Bd, 89-92. *Mem:* AAAS; fel Am Phys Soc; Soc Automotive Engrs; Sigma Xi. *Res:* Plasma physics; nuclear reactor physics; energy conversion; research management solid state physics; surface physics; chemical physics; electro optical physics; metal physics; electrochemistry; electric propulsion advanced batteries. *Mailing Add:* 6590 Ridgewood Dr Naples FL 34108-8262. *Fax:* 941-566-2106

JAMES, ALTON EVERETTE, JR, RADIOLOGY, NUCLEAR MEDICINE. *Current Pos:* SR PROF OFFICER, INST MED, NAT ACAD SCI, 93- *Personal Data:* b Oxford, NC, Aug 22, 38; m 60; c 3. *Educ:* Univ NC, AB, 59; Duke Univ, MD, 63; Johns Hopkins Univ, MS, 71; Am Bd Radiol, dipl, 69; Am Bd Nuclear Med, cert, 72, Vanderbilt Law Sch, 77-79; Harvard Bus Sch, 79. *Honors & Awards:* Gold Medal, Soc Nuclear Med; Silver Medal,

Am Roentgen Ray Soc; Bronze Medal, Soc Nuclear Med. *Prof Exp:* Intern med, Univ Fla, 63-64; resident radiol, Mass Gen Hosp, 66-68; chief res & fel, Harvard Med Sch, 68-69; from asst prof to assoc prof radiol sci, Med Sch, Johns Hopkins Univ, 69-75, dir res radiol, 73-75; prof & chmn dept, radiol & radiol sci, Vanderbilt Univ, 75-93, prof med admin & lectr legal med, 79-93, sr res assoc, Inst Pub Policy, 80-93, prof biomed eng, 81-93. *Concurrent Pos:* Nat Acad Sci-Nat Res Coun James Picker fel, Sch Hyg & Pub Health, Johns Hopkins Univ, 69-71; consult, Walter Reed Army Hosp, 73-75, Armed Forces Radiobiol Res Inst, 73-, Nat Zool Park, Smithsonian Inst, 73-, Nat Naval Med Ctr, 74-75 & Nuffield Inst Comp Zool, London, 74; hon res fel, Univ Col, London, 74. *Mem:* AAAS; Am Soc Clin Invest; Radiol Soc NAm: Soc Chmn Acad Radiol Depts; Am Roentgen Ray Soc; Am Inst Ultrasound Med (treas, 78-81); Sigma Xi; fel Royal Soc Med. *Res:* Cerebrospinal fluid physiology; avian respiration; computerized axial tomography; ultrasonography; medical jurisprudence; paleoradiology; nuclear magnetic resonance; positron emission tomography; evaluation of authenticity of paintings; xerography; medical jurisprudence; author or coauthor of 18 texts over 500 publications. *Mailing Add:* St James Pl Box 789 Robersonville NC 27871

JAMES, BELA MICHAEL, BIOLOGICAL OCEANOGRAPHY, FATE & EFFECTS OF OIL SPILLS. *Current Pos:* SCIENTIST, SHELL OIL CO, 91- *Personal Data:* b Wichita Falls, Tex, Jan 20, 40; m 68; c 2. *Educ:* Tarleton State Col, BS, 63; Tex A&M Univ, MS, 66, PhD(oceanog), 72. *Prof Exp:* Res asst oceanog, Tex A&M Univ, 68-70, res scientist, 70-73; exec vpres & chief researcher, Tereco Corp, 73-83; sr scientist & off mgr, Continental Shelf Assocs, 83-91. *Res:* Marine ecology; taxonomy and ecology of euphausiacean crustaceans and palaeotaxodont mollusks; deep-sea oceanography; water quality and pollution control; oil spill contigency planning; fate and effect of oil. *Mailing Add:* 15131 Morning Pine Lane Houston TX 77068

JAMES, BRIAN ROBERT, HOMOGENEOUS CATALYSIS, BIOINORGANIC CHEMISTRY. *Current Pos:* from asst prof to assoc prof, 64-74, PROF INORG CHEM, UNIV BC, 74- *Personal Data:* b Birmingham, Eng, Apr 21, 36; m 62, M Jane Thompson; c Jennifer, Peter, Sarah & Andrew. *Educ:* Oxford Univ, BA, 57, MA, DPhil(chem), 60. *Honors & Awards:* Noranda Award, Chem Inst Can, 75, Can Catal Award, 90, EWR Steacie Award, 97; Award in Chem of Noble Metals & Compounds, Royal Soc Chem 96. *Prof Exp:* Fel inorg reaction mechanisms, Univ BC, 60-62; sr sci officer, UK Atomic Energy Auth, 62-64. *Concurrent Pos:* Mem, Nat Res Coun Chem Grants Selection Comt, 74-77; ed, Catalysis by Metal Complexes, 75- & Can J Chem, 78-88; vis prof, Univ Pisa, 79, Univ Venice, 83, Univ Amsterdam, 90, Australian Nat Univ, 91; Killam fel, Can Coun, 93; bd dirs, Org Reaction Catalysis Soc. *Mem:* Fel Chem Soc; fel Chem Inst Can; NY Acad Sci; Am Chem Soc; fel Japan Soc Prom Sci. *Res:* Synthesis, homogeneous catalytic properties of, and mechanistic studies on, coordination compounds, organometallics, and bioinorganic model systems; author of one book, several book chapters and 275 publications in journals. *Mailing Add:* Dept Chem Univ BC Vancouver BC V6T 1Z1 Can. *Fax:* 604-822-2847; *E-Mail:* brj@chem.ubc.ca

JAMES, CHARLES FRANKLIN, JR, INDUSTRIAL ENGINEERING. *Current Pos:* DEAN, COL ENG & APPL SCI, UNIV WIS, MILWAUKEE, 84- *Personal Data:* b Des Arc, Mo, July 16, 31; m 74, Mollie Keeler; c Thomas E & Matthew J. *Educ:* Purdue Univ, BSc, 58, MSc, 60, PhD(indust eng), 63. *Honors & Awards:* Silver Medal, Tech Univ Budapest. *Prof Exp:* Sr indust engr, McDonnell Aircraft Co, 63; asst prof indust eng, Univ RI, 63-66; assoc prof, Univ Mass, 66-67; prof indust eng & chmn dept, Univ RI, 67-83. *Concurrent Pos:* Labor arbitrator, Am Arbit Asn & Fed Mediation & Conciliation Serv; indust consult, US & foreign indust & govt agencies, 65-90; US Dept Transp res grant, 72-82; vis fac mem, Massey Univ, NZ, 79; C Paul Stocker distinguished vis prof eng, Ohio Univ, 82-83; mem, Accreditation Processes Comt, Am Soc Eng Educ, 86 & NSF Panel Eval Grad Fel Applications, Nat Res Coun. *Mem:* Am Inst Indust Engrs; Am Soc Mech Engrs; Soc Mfg Engrs; Am Foundrymen's Soc; Am Soc Eng Educ; Am Arbit Soc; Nat Soc Prof Engrs; Sigma Xi. *Res:* Materials processing; robotics; highway safety. *Mailing Add:* MSOE 1025 N Broadway Milwaukee WI 53202-3109

JAMES, CHARLES WILLIAM, SYSTEMATIC BOTANY. *Current Pos:* from asst prof to assoc prof bot, 57-70, asst to dean, 63-70, PROF BOT & ASSOC DEAN COL ARTS & SCI, UNIV GA, 70- *Personal Data:* b Dade City, Fla, Aug 13, 29; m 60; c 3. *Educ:* Univ Fla, BS, 50, MS, 52; Duke Univ, PhD(bot), 55. *Prof Exp:* Instr bot, Univ Tenn, 55-56; res botanist herbarium, Harvard Univ, 56-57. *Mem:* Am Soc Plant Taxon; Int Asn Plant Taxon. *Res:* Taxonomy of seed plants primarily of the southeastern United States. *Mailing Add:* 1175 Whit Davis Rd Athens GA 30605

JAMES, CHRISTOPHER ROBERT, PLASMA PHYSICS, ELECTROMAGNETICS. *Current Pos:* RETIRED. *Personal Data:* b Vancouver, BC, Nov 15, 35; m 56; c 5. *Educ:* Univ BC, BASc, 60, MASc, 61, PhD(elec Eng), 64. *Prof Exp:* Nat Res Coun-NATO fel, Oxford Univ, 64-65; from asst prof to prof plasmas, Univ Alta, 65-96, chmn dept, 74-87, vpres res, 87-96. *Concurrent Pos:* Nat Res Coun grant, 65-81; mem, Dept External Affairs Negotiating Team, 78-, bd examiners, Asn Prof Engrs, Geologists & Geophysicists Alta, 74-; dir negotiated develop grant, Nat Res Coun, 71-75. *Mem:* Can Asn Physicists; Eng Inst Can; Am Phys Soc; AAAS. *Res:* Nonlinear laser heating of plasmas; laser-plasma interaction studies. *Mailing Add:* VPres Res Univ Alta 238 Civil Elec Bldg Edmonton AB T6G 2J9 Can

JAMES, DAVID EUGENE, ORGANIC CHEMISTRY. *Current Pos:* RES ASSOC, AMOCO CHEM CO, 75- *Personal Data:* b Washington, Iowa, June 19, 45; m 77; c 2. *Educ:* Cornell Col, BA, 67; Univ Iowa, PhD(org chem), 75. *Prof Exp:* Instr chem, Linn Mar Community Sch Dist, 67-71. *Concurrent Pos:* Bd dirs, Sci & Technol Interactive Ctr. *Mem:* Sigma Xi; Am Chem Soc; AAAS. *Res:* Liquid chromatographic separations of industrially important compounds; photochemistry of aromatic hydrocarbons; homogeneous catalysis using transition metals; oxidation of aromatic hydrocarbons; condensation polymerization. *Mailing Add:* 1133 Woodland Hills Rd Batavia IL 60510. *Fax:* 630-961-6223; *E-Mail:* dejames@amoco.com

JAMES, DAVID EVAN, SEISMOLOGY. *Current Pos:* Fel geophys, 66-68, assoc staff mem, 68-70, STAFF MEM GEOPHYS, DEPT TERRESTRIAL MAGNETISM, CARNEGIE INST, 70- *Personal Data:* b Bellingham, Wash, Dec 14, 39; m 77; c Kaitlin & Kristen. *Educ:* Stanford Univ, BS, 62, MS, 63, PhD(geophysics), 67. *Concurrent Pos:* Ed, US Nat Report to the Int Union Geodesy & Geophysics, 79-83; assoc ed, J Geophys Res, 94- *Mem:* Am Geophys Union; Seismol Soc Am; Soc Explor Geophys. *Res:* Seismic studies of continental lithosphere and subduction zones; evolution of central Andean volcanic arc; isotope and trace element geochemistry of igneous rocks of volcanic arcs; precise hypocenter determinations; paleomagnetism. *Mailing Add:* Dept Terrestrial Magnetism 5241 Broad Branch Rd NW Washington DC 20015. *Fax:* 202-364-8726; *E-Mail:* james@dtm.ciw.edu

JAMES, DAVID F, FLUID MECHANICS, BIOMEDICAL ENGINEERING. *Current Pos:* Asst prof, 67-71, assoc prof, 71-79, PROF MECH ENG, UNIV TORONTO, 79- *Personal Data:* b Belleville, Ont, July 9, 39. *Educ:* Queen's Univ, Ont, BSc, 62; Calif Inst Technol, MS, 63, PhD(mech eng), 67; Univ Cambridge, MA, 74. *Res:* Flow of dilute polymer solutions; rheology of non-Newtonian fluids; fluid mechanics of physiological systems. *Mailing Add:* 210 Caledonia Rd Toronto ON M5J 3G8 Can

JAMES, DAVID RANDOLPH, BIOLOGICAL & RADIATION PHYSICS. *Current Pos:* RES STAFF MEM, HEALTH & SAFETY RES DIV, OAK RIDGE NAT LAB, 76- *Personal Data:* b Atlanta, Ga, June 13, 48. *Educ:* Ga Inst Technol, BS, 70, MS, 71, PhD(physics), 75. *Prof Exp:* Res asst, Ga Inst Technol, 70-75; res fel, Univ Tenn, Knoxville, 75-76. *Mem:* Am Phys Soc; Sigma Xi. *Res:* Approximately 34 open literature publications. *Mailing Add:* Oak Ridge Nat Lab PO Box 30098 Knoxville TN 37930

JAMES, DAVID WINSTON, AGRONOMY. *Current Pos:* assoc prof soils & biometerol, Utah State Univ, 69-75, prof, 75-94, EMER PROF, 94- *Personal Data:* b Logan, Utah, Apr 10, 29; m 52; c 6. *Educ:* Utah State Univ, BS, 56, MS, 57; Ore State Univ, PhD(soil chem), 62. *Honors & Awards:* Sigma Xi. *Prof Exp:* Instr soil chem, Ore State Univ, 60-62; from asst soil scientist to assoc soil scientist, Wash State Univ, 62-69. *Concurrent Pos:* Tech adv, On-Farm Water Mgt Res in Develop Countries, Latin Am, USAID contract & Utah State Univ, 75-; res dir, Agr Res & Develop Prog, Utah State Univ, Bolivia, 77-80; tech adv & prog leader irrigated agr, Bangladesh, India, Nepal, Peru, Egypt, Dominican Repub, & Ecuador. *Mem:* Am Soc Agron; Soil Sci Soc Am; Soil Conserv Soc Am. *Res:* Chemistry of plant nutrients in soils and the interactions between plant nutrients, soil moisture and other factors of plant growth; modeling of crop yield responses to soil fertility and soil moisture. *Mailing Add:* Dept Plants Soils & Biometeorol Utah State Univ Logan UT 84321-4830

JAMES, DEAN B, PHYSICAL INORGANIC & NUCLEAR POWER CHEMISTRY. *Current Pos:* SR CHEMIST, ULTRAPURE WATER TECH, 88- *Personal Data:* b Ames, Iowa, June 14, 34; m 60, Ethel Bortle; c Katherine & Karen. *Educ:* Iowa State Univ, BS, 56, PhD, 60. *Prof Exp:* Res asst, Ames Lab, Atomic Energy Comn, 52-60; staff mem, Los Alamos Sci Lab, 60-66; group leader rare-earth res, Mich Chem Corp, 66-68; fel scientist res & develop, Nuclear Mat & Equip Corp, Atlantic Richfield Co, Apollo, 68-71; prin engr, Nuclear Energy Group, Gen Elec Co, 72-75, mgr, Safeguards Audits, 75-85, advan tech, 85-88; sr chemist, Advan Process Tech, Inc, 85-88. *Res:* Ion exchange; waste treatment; process development; technical management; nuclear materials safeguards systems; nuclear power chemistry. *Mailing Add:* 20518 Deerpark Ct Saratoga CA 95070

JAMES, DONALD GORDON, MATHEMATICS. *Current Pos:* from asst prof to assoc prof, 66-76, PROF MATH, PA STATE UNIV, 76- *Personal Data:* b Auckland, NZ, Mar 18, 38; m 67, Ingrid F Sander; c Michael A. *Educ:* New Zealand Univ, BSc, 59, MSc, 60; Mass Inst Technol, PhD(math), 63. *Prof Exp:* Lectr math, Univ Auckland, 64-65. *Concurrent Pos:* Fel Alexander von Humboldt Stiftung, Ger, 69-70. *Mem:* Am Math Soc; London Math Soc. *Res:* Algebra and number theory, particularly quadratic and hermitian forms, orthogonal and unitary groups. *Mailing Add:* Dept Math Pa State Univ University Park PA 16802. *E-Mail:* james@math.psu.edu

JAMES, DOUGLAS GARFIELD LIMBREY, CHEMISTRY. *Current Pos:* RETIRED. *Personal Data:* b London, Eng, Oct 31, 24; m 59; c 3. *Educ:* Cambridge Univ, BA, 48, MA & PhD(chem), 55. *Prof Exp:* Lectr chem, Univ St Andrews, 54-59; from asst prof to assoc prof chem, Univ BC, prof, 68-90; consult. *Concurrent Pos:* Vis fel chem, Aberdeen Univ, 65-66. *Mem:* Fel Chem Inst Can; fel Royal Soc Chem. *Res:* Chemical kinetics; addition of free radicals to unsaturated molecules. *Mailing Add:* 391 Roland Rd Salt Spring Island BC V8K 1V1 Can

JAMES, EDWARD, JR, PHYSICAL CHEMISTRY, EXPLOSIVES. *Current Pos:* CONSULT, 80- *Personal Data:* b El Paso, Tex, July 14, 17; m 40; c 1. *Educ:* Univ Mich, BS, 37. *Prof Exp:* Chemist, Sherwin Williams Co, 37-46; chemist, Los Alamos Sci Labs, 46-49, sect leader, 49-60; sect leader, Lawrence Livermore Nat Lab, Univ Calif, 60-63, asst div leader, 63-80. *Concurrent Pos:* Mem, Sci Adv Bd, USAF, 85. *Mem:* Am Chem Soc; AAAS. *Res:* Resin bonded pigments for textiles; emulsion paints; polyester resins; plastic bonded explosives; explosives, polymer synthesis and manufacture; detonation hydrodynamics. *Mailing Add:* 1085 Peary Ct Livermore CA 94550-5611

JAMES, FRANCES CREWS, ECOLOGY. *Current Pos:* assoc prof, 77-84, PROF, DEPT BIOL SCI, FLA STATE UNIV, TALLAHASSEE, 84- *Personal Data:* b Philadelphia, Pa, Sept 29, 30; c 3. *Educ:* Mt Holyoke Col, AB, 52; La State Univ, MS, 56; Univ Ark, PhD(zool), 70. *Honors & Awards:* E P Edwards Prize, Wilson Ornith Soc. *Prof Exp:* Instr zool & bot, Univ Ark, 60-70, res assoc, Mus, 71-73; asst prog dir, Ecol Prog, NSF, 73-76, assoc prog dir, 76-77. *Concurrent Pos:* Res assoc, Smithsonian Inst, 75- *Mem:* Ecol Soc Am; Am Ornithologists Union (pres, 84-86); Soc Syst Zool; AAAS; Cooper Ornith Soc. *Res:* Geographic variation in vertebrates; analysis of avian communities; habitat selection in birds; thermal behavioral ecology of lizards; avian systematics; allometry. *Mailing Add:* Dept Biol Sci Fla State Univ Tallahassee FL 32306-2043

JAMES, FRANKLIN WARD, ANALYTICAL CHEMISTRY. *Current Pos:* prof chem, Mercer Univ, 61-70, chmn dept, 61-80, Fuller E Callaway prof, 70-88, EMER CALLAWAY PROF CHEM, MERCER UNIV, 88- *Personal Data:* b Montrose, Miss, Sept 2, 22; m 58, Jewell Slocum; c Craig & Nancy. *Educ:* Miss Col, BS, 47; Univ NC, PhD(chem), 52. *Prof Exp:* From assoc prof to prof chem, Millsaps Col, 51-58; sr chemist, Res & Tech Dept, Texaco, Inc, 58-61. *Mem:* Am Chem Soc. *Res:* Standard electrode potentials of electrodes in aqueous glycerol solutions. *Mailing Add:* 4179 Vallie Dr Macon GA 31204-4758

JAMES, GARTH A, ENDODONTICS. *Current Pos:* RETIRED. *Personal Data:* b Malad City, Idaho, Aug 1, 26; m 47; c 7. *Educ:* Utah State Univ, BS, 48, MS, 51; Univ Nebr, DDS, 60. *Prof Exp:* Teacher pub sch, Idaho, 47-49; res technician, Naval Biol Lab, Univ Calif, 52; instr bact & pub health, Utah State Agr Col & bacteriologist, Exp Sta, 52-56; res assoc bact, Col Dent, Univ Nebr-Lincoln, 56-60, from assoc prof to prof endodontics, 60-88, chmn dept, 70-88. *Concurrent Pos:* Dir bact, St Elizabeth Hosp, 56-60. *Mem:* Am Dent Asn; Am Asn Endodont; Am Soc Microbiol; fel Am Col Dentists; fel Int Col Dentists. *Mailing Add:* 1150 Mountain Ridge Rd Provo UT 84604

JAMES, GEORGE ELLERT, ELECTRONICS ENGINEERING. *Current Pos:* RETIRED. *Personal Data:* b Douglas, Alaska, Apr 26, 17; m 53, Joan Leamy. *Educ:* Univ Wash, BS, 40; George Washington Univ, MS, 62, DSc(eng sci), 69. *Prof Exp:* Electronic develop engr, Gen Elec Co, 40-45; chief engr, Gen Commun Co, 46-47; asst proj engr, Hughes Aircraft Co, 47-48; chief engr, Lab for Electronics, Inc, 48-56; dir, Boston Div, Ramo-Wooldridge Corp, 56-57; tech staff mem, Inst Defense Anal, 58-70; vpres, Adcole Corp, 70-71; consult scientist, Missile Systs Div, Bedford Lab, Raytheon Co, 71-72; vpres, Adcole Corp, 72-90. *Mem:* Sr mem Inst Elec & Electronics Engrs. *Res:* Electromagnetic field theory; electronic circuit design; radar and control systems; applied mathematics; operations analysis; computer software development. *Mailing Add:* 14 Temple St Apt 3B Framingham MA 01701

JAMES, GEORGE WATSON, III, MEDICINE. *Current Pos:* from asst prof to assoc prof, 49-65, chmn, Div Hemat, 57-83, PROF MED, MED COL VA 65- *Personal Data:* b Richmond, Va, July 3, 18; m 43; c 3. *Educ:* Washington & Lee Univ, AB, 40; Med Col Va, MD, 43. *Prof Exp:* USPHS fel, 48-49. *Concurrent Pos:* Markle scholar, Med Col Va, 49-54; consult, McGurie Vet Admin Hosp, 48-, Keecoughtan Vet Hosp 52-80. *Mem:* AAAS; Am Soc Clin Invest; Am Fedn Clin Res; Am Clin & Climat Asn; Am Soc Clin Nutrit. *Res:* Clinical investigations; bile pigment metabolism; red cell survival with N-15 label; leukemia and lymphoma chemotherapy; hematology. *Mailing Add:* Dept Med Med Col Va Commonwealth Univ Richmond VA 23298. *Fax:* 804-371-8079

JAMES, GORDON THOMAS, PROTEIN CHEMISTRY, CELL CULTURE. *Current Pos:* ANALYTICAL CHEMIST, NAT JEWISH HOSP, DENVER, 89- *Personal Data:* b Ft Scott, Kans, Mar 7, 40. *Educ:* Univ Calif, Riverside, PhD(biochem), 71. *Prof Exp:* Asst prof biochem, Dept Surg, Health Sci Ctr, Univ Colo, 76-86; sr biochemist, Electropore Co, Boulder, Co, 86-89. *Mem:* Am Soc Biochem & Molecular Biol. *Res:* Protein chemistry; pharmacokinetics of tuberculosis drugs. *Mailing Add:* 3036 S Cherry Way Denver CO 80222-6744

JAMES, HAROLD LEE, MOLECULAR BIOLOGY & BIOCHEMISTRY, GENERAL PHYSIOLOGY. *Current Pos:* ASSOC PROF BIOCHEM, HEALTH CTR, UNIV TEX-TYLER, 83- *Personal Data:* b Taylorsville, NC, Oct 31, 39; m 65; c 1. *Educ:* ETenn State Univ, BS, 62; Univ Tenn, Memphis, PhD(biochem), 68. *Prof Exp:* Res technician, Med Units, Univ Tenn, 62-63, res instr biochem, 68; res instr med & biochem, Sch Med, Temple Univ, 68-70; res scientist, Blood Res Lab, Am Nat Red Cross, 70-72; asst prof biochem, Univ Tenn Ctr for Health Sci, 72-75; res asst prof med, Sch Med, Pulmonary Div, Temple Univ, 76-80, res assoc prof med, Sch Med, Pulmonary Div, 80-83. *Concurrent Pos:* Res assoc, Lab Hemat, St Jude Children's Res Hosp, 72-75. *Mem:* Sigma Xi; Am Physiol Soc; Int Soc Thrombosis & Haemostasis; Am Heart Asn. *Res:* Biochemistry and physiology of plasma and platelet fibrinogens; mechanism of interaction of alpha-1-antitrypsin with elastase; lung physiology of alpha-1-antitrypsin; animal models of emphysema; molecular biology of genetic variants of factors VIII and X; structure-function conclates of factors VIII and X; molecular. *Mailing Add:* Dept Biochem Tex Health Sci Ctr PO Box 2003 Tyler TX 75710-2003. *Fax:* 908-877-7558

JAMES, HAROLD LLOYD, MINERALOGY-PETROLOGY. *Current Pos:* Field asst, 38-40, from geologist to chief geologist, 40-71, RES GEOLOGIST, US GEOL SURV, 71- *Personal Data:* b Nanaimo, BC, June 11, 12; US citizen; m 36; c 4. *Educ:* State Col Wash, BS, 38; Princeton Univ, PhD(geol), 45. *Honors & Awards:* Distinguished Serv Award, US Dept Int, 66; Penrose Medal, Soc Econ Geologists, 76. *Concurrent Pos:* Instr, Princeton Univ, 42; vis lectr, Northwestern Univ, Ill, 53-54; prof, Univ Minn, 61-65. *Mem:* Nat Acad Sci; fel Geol Soc Am; Soc Econ Geol; Geochem Soc; Mineral Soc Am; Geol Asn Can. *Res:* Iron formations and iron ores; Precambrian history and time classification; Precambrian geology of southwestern Montana; geology of the Lake Superior region. *Mailing Add:* 1320 Lakeway Dr No 121 Bellingham WA 98226-2005

JAMES, HELEN JANE, ANALYTICAL CHEMISTRY. *Current Pos:* asst prof, 71-75, assoc prof chem, 75-80, PROF CHEM, WEBER STATE COL, 80- *Personal Data:* b Nebraska City, Nebr, June 15, 43. *Educ:* Univ Nebr, BS, 65, PhD(anal chem), 70. *Prof Exp:* Fel, Univ Ariz, 70-71. *Mem:* Sigma Xi; Am Chem Soc. *Res:* Development and application of ion selective electrodes; the use of coated wire electrodes containing liquid membranes. *Mailing Add:* Dept Chem Weber State Col Ogden UT 84408-2503

JAMES, HERBERT I, PHYSICAL CHEMISTRY. *Current Pos:* REAL ESTATE AGENT. *Personal Data:* b St Thomas, VI, Mar 30, 33; US citizen; m 62; c 2. *Educ:* Hampton Inst, BS, 55; Clark Univ, MA, 58, PhD(chem), 65. *Honors & Awards:* Commendation Award, President of US. *Prof Exp:* Teacher, Elec Storage Battery Co, 65-76; scientist, US, 76-84. *Concurrent Pos:* Scientist, Xerox Res Ctr, mgr affirmative action, Webster Res Ctr, Xerox, mgr personnel. *Mem:* Electrochem Soc. *Res:* Diffusion and sedimentation studies of macromolecules; nuclear and radiochemistry; bioelectrochemistry. *Mailing Add:* 49 Cumberland Dr Mississauga ON L5G 3N1 Can

JAMES, HUGO A, PARASITOLOGY, HELMINTHOLOGY. *Current Pos:* CONSULT, 90- *Personal Data:* b Bridgeport, Conn, May 24, 30. *Educ:* Univ Bridgeport, BA, 57, MS, 58; Univ Va, MA, 61; Iowa State Univ, PhD(parasitol), 68. *Prof Exp:* from instr to assoc prof, Univ Bridgeport, 58-73, prof biol, 73-85, chmn biol & dir, Div Biol & Health Technol, 85-90. *Concurrent Pos:* NSF res grant, Univ Va, 69. *Mem:* Am Soc Parasitol; Am Micros Soc (treas, 79-81). *Res:* Host-parasite interrelationships of helminths, specifically the Cestoda; zoonotic associations, particularly aspects of taxonomy, morphology, pathology and evolution. *Mailing Add:* Seven Franklin St Trumbull CT 06611

JAMES, JACK N, MISSILE & SPACE PROJECT ENGINEERING. *Current Pos:* RETIRED. *Personal Data:* b Dallas, Tex, Nov 22, 20; m 44, Ruth F Shockley; c Jeffrey D, Jeremy R, Jack F & Susan E. *Educ:* Southern Methodist Univ, BS, 42; Union Col, MS, 49. *Honors & Awards:* Pub Serv Award, NASA, 63; Hill Award, Am Inst Aeronaut & Astronaut, 63; Except Sci Achievement Medal, NASA, 65; Stuart Ballantine Medal, Franklin Inst, 67. *Prof Exp:* Test engr, Gen Elec Co, 42-43 & 46-49; res engr, Radio Corp Am, 49-50; res engr, Jet Propulsion Lab, 50-54, eng group supvr, 54-56, sect mgr, 56-58, div mgr, 58-60, dep prog mgr, 60-61, proj mgr, 61-65, dep asst lab dir, Lunar & Planetary Projs, 65-67, asst lab dir, Tech Divs, 67-76, asst lab dir, Tech & Space Prog Develp, Jet Propulsion Lab, 76-80, asst lab dir, Defense & Civil Progs; Calif Inst Technol, Set Propulsion Orgn. *Mem:* assoc fel Am Inst Aeronaut & Astronaut; fel Inst Elec & Electronics Engrs. *Res:* Management of Mariner II to Venus and Mariner IV to Mars projects; guidance systems for Corporal and Sergeant missiles. *Mailing Add:* 1345 El Vago St LaCanada Flintridge CA 91011

JAMES, JEFFREY, ANALYTICAL CHEMISTRY, INORGANIC CHEMISTRY. *Current Pos:* From asst prof to assoc prof, 72-84, PROF, SAVANNAH STATE COL, 84- *Personal Data:* b Savannah, Ga, Aug 27, 44. *Educ:* Savannah State Col, BS, 66; Tuskegee Inst, MS, 70; Howard Univ, PhD(inorg chem), 73. *Concurrent Pos:* Res chemist, Agronne Nat Lab, 65, 69 & 83, Eli Lily & Co, 69, Savannah River Lab, 75 & 80, Lawrence Livermore Lab, 78. *Mem:* Am Chem Soc; AAAS. *Res:* Kinetic study of metalloporphyrins and oxidation of dithionite by manganese; hematoporphyrins in basic solution; characterization of mercury; electrodes; solubility products and thermodynamic functions for the Lanthanon fluride-water system. *Mailing Add:* Savannah State Col PO Box 20443 Savannah GA 31404-9716

JAMES, JESSE, BIOCHEMISTRY. *Current Pos:* Assoc prof, 65-73, chmn dept, 73-76, PROF CHEM, KNOXVILLE COL, 73- *Personal Data:* b Haynesville, La, Jan 26, 37; m 59; c 5. *Educ:* Tex Southern Univ, BSc, 61, MSc, 62; Univ Tex, PhD(biochem), 65. *Concurrent Pos:* Consult, Union Carbide Corp, Tenn, 66-70; res chemist, Nat Bur Stand, 70- *Res:* Kinetics and mechanisms of enzyme-catalyzed reactions; standardization of reference materials for clinical chemistry. *Mailing Add:* Math & Sci Knoxville Col 901 Col St NW Knoxville TN 37921-4724

JAMES, JOHN CARY, ORGANIC CHEMISTRY. *Current Pos:* chief, Res Anal & Eval Br, 71-84, asst dir spec projs, Div Res Grants, 84-95, DEPT DIR, DIV EXTRAMURAL OUTREACH & INFO RESOURCES, NIH, 96- *Personal Data:* b Ceredo, WVa, May 8, 26; m 58, Geraldine Fantini; c Lisa. *Educ:* WVa Wesleyan Col, BS, 49; Univ Del, PhD(org chem), 60. *Prof Exp:* Teacher, Callao High Sch, Peru, 50-53; sr res chemist, Boston Labs, Monsanto Res Corp, 59-66; sr chemist, Northrop Carolina, Inc, 66-67; exec secy, Med Chem Fel Rev Comt, Div Res Grants, NIH, 67-70, chief, Sci Eval Sect, Res Anal & Eval Br, 70-71. *Mem:* AAAS. *Res:* Synthesis of anti-oxidants; research on jet fuels; antiradiation drug research; high temperature explosives; health sciences administration; research analysis and information science; electronic communications; peer review appeals. *Mailing Add:* 4874 Chevy Chase Dr Chevy Chase MD 20815. *E-Mail:* jqj@cu.nih.gov

JAMES, KAREN K(ANKE), IMMUNOLOGY. *Current Pos:* CONSULT IMMUNOL, 93- *Personal Data:* b Vinton, Iowa, June 2, 44; m 64; c 3. *Educ:* Ohio State Univ, BS, 67, MS, 72; Rush Med Univ, PhD(immunol), 80. *Prof Exp:* Med technologist, Riverside Methodist Hosp, 67-71; supv clin immunol, Ohio State Univ Hosp, 73-76; instr, Rush Presby St Luke's Med Ctr, 76-80, dir immunol, 80-82, asst prof immunol, Rush Univ 80-87; clin asst prof med lab sci, Univ Ill, Chicago, 77-87; assoc dir labs, Cent Dupage Hosp, 82-93; assoc prof path, Loyola Univ Med Ctr, Chicago, 86- *Concurrent Pos:* Clin instr allied med professions, Ohio State Univ, 73-77; chmn, immunol comt, Bd Registry, 77-85; consult, Smith Kline Biosci Labs, 84-86; acting ed, Lab Med, 85-86; chmn, lab mgt comt, Bd Registry, 86- *Mem:* Am Soc Clin Path; Am Asn Immunol. *Res:* Biologic response modifying properties of C-reactive protein; natural killer cells; cellular immunology. *Mailing Add:* 1584 Hill Rd Vilas NC 28692

JAMES, KRISTIN BOWMAN, INORGANIC CHEMISTRY. *Current Pos:* Asst prof, 75-81, assoc prof, 81-87, PROF CHEM, UNIV KANS, 87- *Personal Data:* b Philadelphia, Pa, June 4, 46; m 76. *Educ:* Temple Univ, BA, 68, PhD(chem), 74. *Mem:* Am Chem Soc; Am Crystallographer's Asn. *Res:* Structure reactivity aspects of transition metal complexes particularly with macrocyclic ligand systems. *Mailing Add:* Dept Chem Univ Kans Lawrence KS 66045-0501

JAMES, L(AURENCE) ALLAN, GLACIAL & QUATERNOMY FLUVIAL GEOMORPHOLOGY, MODELING WATER & SEDIMENT YIELDS IN WATERSHEDS. *Current Pos:* asst prof, 88-94, ASSOC PROF PHYS GEOG, GEOG DEPT, UNIV SC, 94- *Personal Data:* b Glendale, Calif, Mar 18, 49. *Educ:* Univ Calif, Berkeley, BA, 78; Univ Wis-Madison, MS, 81, MS, 83, PhD(geog & geol), 88. *Prof Exp:* Lectr phys geog, Geog Dept, Univ Wis-Madison, 86, Univ Oregon, 87, Univ Ga, 87-88. *Concurrent Pos:* Prin investr, res & prod scholarship, Univ SC, 89, NSF, 89-90 & SE Regional Climate Ctr, 90-91; Nat Res Coun Com Am River, 94-96; chair, Geomorphol Spec Group, Asn, Am Geographics, 95-96. *Mem:* Asn Am Geogr; Geol Soc Am; Am Geophys Union; Am Water Resources Asn; Am Quaternary Asn; Int Asn Geomorphologists. *Res:* Water and sediment yields from fluvial systems; historical anthropogenic sedimentation; modeling watershed processes with digital geographic information techniques; monitoring hydraulic gold mining sediment in the northern Sierra Nevada of California; quaternary glacial mapping in Sierra Nevada, Calif. *Mailing Add:* Geog Dept Univ SC Columbia SC 29208. *Fax:* 803-758-6040; *E-Mail:* ajames@mccoy.geog.scarolina.edu

JAMES, LARRY GEORGE, AGRICULTURAL ENGINEERING, IRRIGATION ENGINEERING. *Current Pos:* from asst prof to assoc prof, Agr Eng, Wash State Univ, 77-88, prof & chair, 88-91, interim assoc dean & dir coop ext, 91-93, ASSOC DEAN & DIR ACAD PROGS, AGR ENG, WASH STATE UNIV, 93- *Personal Data:* b Bellingham, Wash, May 1, 47; m 68, Elaine R Jolly; c Gregory A, Jeffrey L, Elizabeth I & Carolyn N. *Educ:* Wash State Univ, BS, 70; Univ Minn, PhD(agr eng), 75. *Prof Exp:* Asst prof agr eng, Cornell Univ, 75-77. *Mem:* Am Soc Agr Engrs; Am Soc Engr Educ; Am Soc Civil Eng. *Res:* Plant water requirements; energy requirements for irrigation; sprinkler irrigation; infiltration; water resources management. *Mailing Add:* Col Agr & Home Econs Wash State Univ Pullman WA 99164-6243. *Fax:* 509-335-1065

JAMES, LAURENCE BERESFORD, GEOLOGY. *Current Pos:* CONSULT GEOLOGIST, 76- *Personal Data:* b Hollywood, Calif, Aug 20, 16; m 39, Cormellia Venter; c Catherine (DeMauro), Benjamin W, Stephen M & Laurence A. *Educ:* Stanford Univ, AB, 40. *Prof Exp:* Mining geologist, Consol Coppermines Corp, Nev, 40-41; mining engr, Anaconda Copper Co, Mont, 41; eng geologist, Calif State Dept Water Resources, 46-56, chief eng geologist, 56-76. *Concurrent Pos:* Mem, nat comt rock mech, Nat Acad Sci, 67; consult geologist, United Nations, 69-73; mem, US Comt Large Dams; consult, US Army Corps Engrs, US Bur Reclamation & World Bank. *Mem:* Fel Geol Soc Am; Seismol Soc Am; fel Am Soc Civil Eng; Asn Eng Geol; Soc Am Mil Engrs. *Res:* Engineering and groundwater geology. *Mailing Add:* 120 Grey Canyon Dr Folsom CA 95630

JAMES, LAYLIN KNOX, JR, SURFACE CHEMISTRY. *Current Pos:* from asst prof to assoc prof, Lafayette Col, 59-77, actg dept head, 70-71, dept head, 79-85, prof chem, 77-90, EMER PROF CHEM, LAFAYETTE COL, 90- *Personal Data:* b Pittsburgh, Pa, Sept 17, 27; m 52; c 4. *Educ:* Univ Mich, BS, 50, MS, 52; Univ Ill, PhD(chem), 58. *Prof Exp:* Chemist, Shell Chem Co, div Shell Oil Co, 52-54; asst, Univ Ill, 54-56 & Wash State Univ, 57-58; res chemist, Procter & Gamble Co, 58-59. *Concurrent Pos:* Chemist, US Naval Res Lab, 63; guest prof, Hohenheim Univ, Stuttgart, WGer, 82. *Mem:* AAAS; Am Chem Soc. *Res:* Surface chemistry of proteins and lipoproteins. *Mailing Add:* 18 E Santa Belia Green Valley AZ 85614-1537

JAMES, LEE MORTON, FORESTRY. *Current Pos:* assoc prof, 51-58, chmn dept, 66-78, PROF FORESTRY, 58-, EMER PROF, MICH STATE UNIV. *Personal Data:* b New York, NY, Dec 14, 16; m 46. *Educ:* Pa State Col, BS, 37; Univ Mich, MF, 43, PhD(forest econ), 45. *Prof Exp:* Instr forestry, Pa State Col, 37-38; unit supvr, New Eng Forest Emergency Proj, US Forest Serv, 38-40, forester, Appalachian Forest Exp Sta, 40-41 & 43-46, forest economist in charge unit resource analysis, Div Forest Econ, Southern Forest Exp Sta, 46-51. *Concurrent Pos:* Consult, Resources for the Future, Inc, Forest Indust Coun, US Dept Interior, US Dept Com, Pub Land Law Rev Comt & President's Coun Environ Qual. *Mem:* Soc Am Foresters. *Res:* Forest resource and forest industry analysis; timber products marketing; forest policy. *Mailing Add:* Dept Forestry 126 Natural Resources Bldg Mich State Univ East Lansing MI 48824

JAMES, MARGARET OLIVE, BIOCHEMISTRY, TOXICOLOGY. *Current Pos:* PROF MED CHEM, UNIV FLA, 80-, DEPT CHAIR MED CHEM, 91- *Personal Data:* b Haverfordwest, UK, July 9, 48; m, David I Kramer; c Nathaniel & Kathleen. *Educ:* Univ London, BSc, 69, PhD(org chem), 72, DSc, 93. *Prof Exp:* Fel, Nat Inst Environ Health Sci, 72-75, res assoc, 75-78, sr staff fel, 78-80. *Concurrent Pos:* Mem, Nat Environ Health Sci Rev Coomt, 91-95, Toxics Adv Comt, Coastal Ocean Prog, NOAA, 92-; prog dir, Superfund Basic Res Prog. *Mem:* Int Soc Study Xenobiotics; Am Soc Pharmacol & Exp Ther; Am Chem Soc; Soc Toxicol; Am Asn Pharmaceut Sci; AAAS. *Res:* In vivo and in vitro studies of xenobiotic metabolism in aquatic and mammalian species; enzymes which alter the toxicity of a xenobiotic. *Mailing Add:* Univ Fla PO Box 100485 Gainesville FL 32610-0485

JAMES, MARLYNN REES, PHYSICAL CHEMISTRY. *Current Pos:* PROF CHEM, UNIV NORTHERN COLO, 66- *Personal Data:* b Spanish Fork, Utah, Nov 20, 33; m 61, Jane; c Leslie J, Richard, Bruce, Mark, Karen & Jackie. *Educ:* Brigham Young Univ, BS, 58, MS, 61; Univ Utah, PhD(theoret gas chromatography), 65. *Prof Exp:* Res asst chem, Purdue Univ, 64-66. *Mem:* Am Chem Soc; Nat Sci Supvrs Asn; Nat Sci Teachers Asn; Nat Asn Res Sci Teaching. *Res:* Chemical education and curriculum development involving computers. *Mailing Add:* Dept Chem Univ Northern Colo Greeley CO 80639-5579. *Fax:* 970-351-1269

JAMES, MARY FRANCES, medical education, clinical laboratory science; deceased, see previous edition for last biography

JAMES, MICHAEL G, BIOCHEMISTRY, CRYSTALLOGRAPHY. *Current Pos:* fel, 67-68, from asst prof to assoc prof, 68-78, PROF, DEPT BIOCHEM, UNIV ALTA, 78-, UNIV PROF, 93- *Personal Data:* b Vancouver, BC, May 16, 40. *Educ:* Univ Man, BC, 62, MS, 63; Oxford Univ, PhD(chem crystallog), 66. *Honors & Awards:* Ayerst Award, Can Biochem Soc, 79; G Malcolm Brown Award, 92; Joseph F Foster lectr, Purdue Univ, 94. *Prof Exp:* Fel, Dept Chem, Crystallog, Oxford Univ, 66-67. *Concurrent Pos:* Mem, MRC group protein struct & function, Dept Biochem, Univ Alta, 74-; sr res fel, Weizmann Inst Sci, Israel, 75-76; Pfizer travelling fel, Clin Res Inst Montreal, 77; lectr, Biochem Sem, Purdue Univ, 80. *Mem:* Can Biochem Soc; Am Chem Soc; Fedn Am Soc Exp Biol; Am Crystallog Asn; fel Royal Soc Can. *Mailing Add:* Dept Biochem Univ Alta Edmonton AB T6G 2H7 Can

JAMES, MICHAEL ROYSTON, MATERIALS SCIENCE. *Current Pos:* mem tech staff, 78-86, mgr tech staff, 86-94, DIR MAT SCI, ROCKWELL INT SCI CTR, 94- *Personal Data:* b London, Eng, Sept 11, 50; US citizen; m 72, Rita Riemersma; c LeAnn, Ryan & Jeremy. *Educ:* Tulane Univ, BS, 72; Northwestern Univ, PhD(mat Sci), 77. *Prof Exp:* Fel, Lab Metal Physics, State Univ Groningen, Neth, 77-78; consult, Am Anal Corp, 78. *Mem:* Soc Exp Mech; Metall Soc; Am Soc Metals. *Res:* Nondestructive testing and component life prediction especially with residual stress measurement and its influence on metal fatigue; microstructural phenomena influencing microcrack initiation; mechanics of microelectronic packaging. *Mailing Add:* 419 Thunderhead St Thousand Oaks CA 91360. *Fax:* 805-373-4719; *E-Mail:* mrjames@scimail.risc.rockwell.com

JAMES, ODETTE BRICMONT, LUNAR PETROLOGY, IGNEOUS PETROLOGY. *Current Pos:* GEOLOGIST, US GEOL SURV, 67- *Personal Data:* b San Jose, Calif, Feb 7, 42; m 80, David P Stewart; c Jeffrey B. *Educ:* Stanford Univ, BS, 63, PhD(geol), 67. *Concurrent Pos:* Mem, Lunar Sample Anal Planning Team, NASA, 72-74, 80-82, chmn, 81-82, prin investr, 75-; mem, Lunar Planet Geosci Review Panel, 85-87; vchair, Planet Geol Div, Geol Soc Am. *Mem:* Fel Mineral Soc Am (treas, 81-84); fel Geol Soc Am; Am Geophys Union; Meteoritical Soc. *Res:* Petrology of lunar highland rocks; lunar highland breccias; igneous petrology; shock metamorphism. *Mailing Add:* 10715 Midsummer Dr Reston VA 20191. *Fax:* 703-648-6789

JAMES, PHILIP BENJAMIN, PLANETARY ATMOSPHERES. *Current Pos:* CHMN DEPT PHYSICS & ASTRON, UNIV TOLEDO, 90- *Personal Data:* b Kansas City, Mo, Mar 18, 40; m 65, Sharon Check; c Eric, Kevin & Kirsten. *Educ:* Carnegie-Mellon Univ, BS, 61; Univ Wis-Madison, MS, 63, PhD(physics), 66. *Prof Exp:* Off Naval Res res assoc physics, Univ Ill, Urbana, 66-68; from asst prof to prof physics, Univ Mo, St Louis, 68-90. *Concurrent Pos:* Nat Res Coun assoc, Jet Propulsion Lab, Calif Inst Technol, 77-78; mem, Viking Mars Proj, 77-78, Mars Observer Camera Team, 92-; ed, Am J Physics, 82-83; adj scientist, Lowell Observ, 84-; prin investr, Hubble Space Telescope Observing Prog; partic scientist, Mars Global Surv; co-investr, MARCI camera Mars '98 orbiter. *Mem:* Am Geophys Union; Am Astron Soc; fel Am Phys Soc. *Res:* Studies relevant to meteorology of and condensate cycles on Mars, includes analyses of spacecraft data, astronomical observations, and modeling; chemical physics. *Mailing Add:* Dept Physics & Astron Univ Toledo Toledo OH 43606. *Fax:* 419-530-2723; *E-Mail:* pbj@physics.vtoledo.edu

JAMES, PHILIP NICKERSON, DATA PROCESSING. *Current Pos:* FAC MEM, COL BUS ADMIN, CALIF STATE UNIV, LONG BEACH, 88-, PRES, STRATEGIC MGT SERV, 88- *Personal Data:* b Boston, Mass, Aug 16, 32; m 54; c 2. *Educ:* Mass Inst Technol, SB, 54; Univ Ill, PhD(org chem), 57. *Prof Exp:* Instr chem, Univ Calif, Berkeley, 57-58, asst prof, 58-59; res chemist, Lederle Labs, Am Cyanamid Co, 59-60, col rels rep, 60-62; photog chemist, Systs Res Div, Technicolor Corp, 62-63, proj leader, 63, sr res chemist, 63-66, staff asst to dir, 64-66; asst vchancellor grad studies & res, Univ Calif, San Diego, 66-69, exec asst to chancellor, 69-74; dir, Univ Southern Calif, Idyllwild Campus, 74-77; dir admin & planning, Deluxe Gen Inc, 20th Century-Fox, 77-78; dir mgt systs, Teledyne Systs Co, 78-79; sr res engr, Electronics Div, Northrop Corp, 79-80, dir strategy planning data processing, 80-84; dir, Info Inst & vpres, Int Acad, 84-85; chief, Strategic Info Systs Planning Div, Data Processing Dept, Los Angeles Co, 85-88. *Mem:* Am Chem Soc; Fedn Am Scientists; AAAS; Sigma Xi; Asn Comput Mach; Soc Info Mgt. *Res:* Biologically interesting compounds; structure; synthesis; chemical mechanisms; photographic chemistry; computer assisted solutions to synthetic problems; higher education; information management; information technology and society. *Mailing Add:* 11400 Edenberg Ave Northridge CA 91326-2110

JAMES, RALPH BOYD, CONDENSED MATTER PHYSICS. *Current Pos:* sr mem tech staff, 84-95, DISTINGUISHED MEM TECH STAFF, SANDIA NAT LABS, 95- *Personal Data:* b Nashville, Tenn, Nov 1, 53; c 1. *Educ:* Univ Tenn, BS, 76; Ga Inst Technol, MS, 77, Calif Inst Technol, MS, 78, PhD(appl physics), 80. *Prof Exp:* Res fel, Calif Inst Technol, 80-81; Eugene P Wigner fel, Oak Ridge Nat Lab, 81-84. *Concurrent Pos:* Chmn, Soc Phot-Optical Instr Engrs Working Group Penetrating Radiation, 96- *Mem:* Am Phys Soc; Inst Elec & Electronics Engrs; Sigma Xi; Mat Res Soc; Am Vacuum Soc; Soc Photo-Optical Instrumentation Engrs. *Res:* Semiconductor physics and non-linear optics. *Mailing Add:* 5420 Lenore Ave Livermore CA 94550. *Fax:* 510-294-3231

JAMES, RALPH L, MATHEMATICS, NUMERICAL ANALYSIS. *Current Pos:* asst prof, 70-74, ASSOC PROF MATH, CALIF STATE COL, STANISLAUS, 74- *Personal Data:* b Portland, Ore, Apr 12, 41; m 69; c 2. *Educ:* Univ Wash, BS, 63; Ore State Univ, MS, 65, PhD, 70. *Prof Exp:* Vis asst prof math, Col of Idaho, 65-68. *Mem:* Am Math Soc. *Res:* Functional analysis; ordered topological vector spaces; positive operators; approximation theory. *Mailing Add:* Dept Math Calif Univ Stanislaus Turlock CA 95382

JAMES, RICHARD STEPHEN, GEOCHEMISTRY, PETROLOGY. *Current Pos:* asst prof geol, 70-80, ASSOC PROF GEOL, 80-, PROF GEOL, LAURENTIN UNIV. *Personal Data:* b Hamilton, Ont, Feb 20, 40; m 64; c 2. *Educ:* McMaster Univ, BSc, 62, MSc, 64; Victoria Univ Manchester, PhD(geol), 67. *Prof Exp:* Fel, Univ Toronto, 67-69, lectr geol, 69-70. *Mem:* Mineral Soc Am; Mineral Asn Can; Mineral Soc Gt Brit & Ireland. *Res:* Igneous and metamorphic petrology, application of experimental phase equilibria data to natural systems. *Mailing Add:* Dept Earth Sci Laurentian Univ Ramsey Lake Rd Sudbury ON P3E 2C6 Can

JAMES, ROBERT CLARKE, MATHEMATICAL ANALYSIS. *Current Pos:* prof, 68-81, EMER PROF MATH, CLAREMONT GRAD SCH, 81- *Personal Data:* b Bloomington, Ind, July 30, 18; m 45, Edith M Peterson; c Judith M (Grounds), Linda (Anooshian), David V & Robert G. *Educ:* Univ Calif, Los Angeles, BA, 40; Calif Inst Technol, PhD(math), 47. *Hon Degrees:* DSc, Kent State Univ, 87. *Prof Exp:* Benjamin Pierce instr math, Harvard Univ, 46-47; from instr to asst prof, Univ Calif, 47-51; assoc prof, Haverford Col, 51-57; prof & chmn dept, Harvey Mudd Col, 57-67; prof, State Univ NY Albany, 67-68. *Concurrent Pos:* Mem, Inst Advan Study, Princeton Univ, 62-63, Jerusalem, 76-77 & Mittag-Leffler Inst, Sweden, 78-79. *Mem:* Am Math Soc; Math Asn Am; AAAS; Fedn Am Scientists. *Res:* Normed vector spaces. *Mailing Add:* 14385 Clear Creek Pl Grass Valley CA 95949-8765

JAMES, RODERICK VIVIAN, INFORMATION SCIENCE & SYSTEMS. *Current Pos:* Mgr software develop proj, Texaco EPTD, 85-90, chief, Moscow Comput Ctr, Texaco Europe Res Inc., 90-92, asst to gen mgr, Texaco Angola, 92-94, RES CONSULT, TEXACO EPTD, 94- *Personal Data:* b Port of Spain, Trinidad, Oct 17, 46, US citizen; m, Marcia G McConney; c Rhoda M. *Educ:* Univ Mo, Columbia, PhD(elec eng), 75. *Mem:* Inst Elec & Electronics Engrs. *Res:* Protection of intellectual property. *Mailing Add:* 11234 Sharpcrest Houston TX 77072

JAMES, RONALD VALDEMAR, SOIL CHEMISTRY. *Current Pos:* RES CHEMIST, US GEOL SURV, 68- *Personal Data:* b Oakland, Calif, Apr 27, 43; m 64; c 2. *Educ:* Univ Calif, Davis, BS, 64; Univ Colo, Boulder, MS, 67, PhD(inorg chem), 69. *Mem:* Am Chem Soc; AAAS; Am Geophys Union. *Res:* Chemistry and transport of solutes in the unsaturated zone and ground water; mathematical modeling; fate of pollutants in environmental waters; kinetics and mechanisms of inorganic reactions; ion exchange. *Mailing Add:* 595 Morey Dr Menlo Park CA 94025

JAMES, SHERMAN ATHONIA, BEHAVIORAL STRESS, PSYCHOPHYSIOLOGY. *Current Pos:* acad dean, Sch Pub Health, 93-97, PROF EPIDEMIOL, UNIV MICH, ANN ARBOR, 89- *Personal Data:* b Hartsville, SC, Oct 25, 43; m 65, 90, Vera Lucia Moura; c Alex & Scott. *Educ:* Talladega Col, AB, 64; Wash Univ, St Louis, PhD(psychol), 73. *Prof Exp:* From asst prof to prof epidemiol, Univ NC, Chapel Hill, 73-89. *Concurrent Pos:* Consult, NIMH, 79-83 & NIH, 85-; vis prof, Dept Prev Med, Fed Univ Bahia, Salvador, Brazil, 86-; fel coun epidemiol, Am Heart Asn. *Mem:* Fel Acad Behav Med Res; fel Am Epidemiol Soc; Am Heart Asn; Soc Behav Med; Am Col Epidemiol; Am Pub Health Asn. *Res:* Psychosocial factors and cardiovascular disease risk in Black populations. *Mailing Add:* Dept Epidemiol Sch Pub Health Univ Mich Ann Arbor MI 48109

JAMES, STANLEY D, ELECTROCHEMISTRY. *Current Pos:* CHEMIST, DEPT NAVY. *Personal Data:* b Cardiff, UK, Aug 25, 32; m 61; c 2. *Educ:* Univ Wales, BSc, 53, PhD(phys chem), 59. *Prof Exp:* Vis scientist phys chem, NIH, 59-60; res fel phys & inorg chem, Univ Melbourne, 61-63; asst chemist electrochem, Brookhaven Nat Lab, 63-65, assoc chemist, 65-67; chemist, Electrochem Br, US Naval Surface Weapons Ctr, 67- *Mem:* Electrochem Soc; Inst Elec & Electronics Engrs. *Res:* Ion exchange membranes; electrokinetics; electrode kinetics; fused salt electrochemistry. *Mailing Add:* Carderock Div Naval Surface Warfare Ctr 9500 MacArthur Blvd West Bethesda MD 20817-5700

JAMES, STEPHANIE LYNN, IMMUNOPARASITOLOGY. *Current Pos:* parasitol prog officer, 87-90, CHIEF, PARASITOL & TROP DIS BR, NAT INST ALLERGY & INFECTIOUS DIS, NIH, 91- *Personal Data:* b Little Rock, Ark; m 82; c 2. *Educ:* Hendrix Col, BA, 72; Vanderbilt Univ, PhD(microbiol), 76. *Prof Exp:* Res fel, dept med, Harvard Med Sch, 77-79 & Lab Parasitic Dis, NIH, Nat Inst Allergy & Infectious Dis, 79-83; from asst res prof to assoc res prof med & microbiol, George Washington Univ, 83-87. *Concurrent Pos:* Vis lectr, Univ de Sao Paulo, Brasil, 82; prin investr, NIH, NSF, WHO & Clark Found grants, 81-88; assoc ed, J Immunol, 85-88; sr investr, Biomed Res Inst, 88; travel award, Am Asn Immunologists, 80 & 83. *Mem:* Am Soc Trop Med Hyg; Am Asn Immunologists. *Res:* Parasite immunology, particularly in schistosomiasis, concentrating on the areas of immunopathology and vaccine production; elucidation of the roles of eosinophils and macrophages as effector cells of protective immunity which led to development of experimental vaccine based on cell-mediated immune mechanisms. *Mailing Add:* Nat Inst Allergy & Infectious Dis Solar Bldg Rm 3A-02 6003 Executive Blvd Bethesda MD 20892-7630

JAMES, STEPHEN P, EXPERIMENTAL BIOLOGY. *Current Pos:* HEAD, DIV GASTROENTEROL, UNIV MD, 91- *Personal Data:* b Columbus, Ohio, May 25, 47; m; c 2. *Educ:* Cornell Univ, BA, 69; Johns Hopkins Univ, MD, 73; Am Bd Internal Med, dipl, 76, dipl gastroenterol, 79. *Prof Exp:* Intern, Dept Med, Johns Hopkins Hosp, Baltimore, Md, 73-74, asst resident, 74-75, resident, 75-76; fel, Gastroenterol Div, Univ Md, Baltimore, 76-77; clin assoc, Liver Dis Sect, Nat Inst Arthritis, Diabetes, Digestive & Kidney Dis, NIH, Bethesda, 77-80, expert, Immunophysiol Sect, Metabol Br, Div Cancer Biol & Diag, Nat Cancer Inst, 80-82, sr clin investr, Mucosal Immunity Sect, Lab Clin Invest, Nat Inst Allergy & Infectious Dis, 82-91. *Concurrent Pos:* Chmn clin res comt, Nat Inst Allergy & Infectious Dis, 88-89; assoc ed, J Immunol, 88-; mem grants rev comt, Crohn's & Colitis Found Am, 88- *Mem:* Am Col Physicians; Am Fedn Clin Res; Am Asn Study Liver Dis; Am Immunologists; Am Gastroenterol Asn; Soc Mucosal Immunol; AAAS; Int Asn Study Liver. *Res:* Regulatory functions of CD4 T cells; role of T cells in host defense and disease at mucosal surfaces; inflammatory bowel disease; gastrointestinal disease in immunodeficient patients; immune mechanisms in chronic liver disease; primary biliary cirrhosis. *Mailing Add:* Dept Med Div Gastroenterol Rm N3W62 Univ Md 22 S Greene St Baltimore MD 21201. *Fax:* 410-328-8315

JAMES, TED RALPH, ecology, vertebrate zoology; deceased, see previous edition for last biography

JAMES, THOMAS LARRY, BIOPHYSICAL CHEMISTRY. *Current Pos:* from asst prof to assoc prof phys chem, 80-83, PROF PHARM CHEM, CHEM, RADIOL, UNIV CALIF, SAN FRANCISCO, 83- *Personal Data:* b North Platte, Nebr, Sept 8, 44; m 91, Olga Schmidlin; c Marc & Tristan. *Educ:* Univ NMex, BS, 65; Univ Wis-Madison, PhD(anal chem), 69. *Prof Exp:* NIH trainee biochem, Univ Wis-Madison, 65-66, NIH fel anal chem, 66-69; res chemist, Tech Ctr, Celanese Chem Co, 69-71; NIH fel biophys, Johnson Res Found, Univ Pa, 71-73. *Mem:* Am Chem Soc; Int Soc Magnetic Resonance; Soc Magnetic Resonance Med; Am Biophys Soc. *Res:* Nuclear magnetic resonance applications to biochemical and biological systems; nucleic acids; proteins. *Mailing Add:* Sch Pharm Rm S-926 Dept Pharmaceut Chem Univ Calif San Francisco CA 94143-0446. *E-Mail:* james@picasso.ucsf.edu

JAMES, THOMAS NAUM, CARDIOVASCULAR DISEASES. *Current Pos:* STAFF, UNIV TEX MED BR, UNIV TEX, GALVESTON, 88- *Personal Data:* b Amory, Miss, Oct 24, 25; m 48; c 3. *Educ:* Tulane Univ, BS, 46, MD, 49; Am Bd Internal Med, dipl, 57, cert cardiovasc dis, 60; Am Col Chest Physicians, dipl. *Prof Exp:* Intern & resident med & cardiol, Henry Ford Hosp, 49-53; cardiologist, Ochsner Clin, New Orleans, La, 55-59; chmn sect cardiovasc res, Henry Ford Hosp, 59-68; sr scientist & dir res, Cardiovasc Res & Training Ctr, 68-70, prof path, 68-73, dir cardiovasc res & training ctr, 70-77, prof med, Med Ctr, Univ Ala, Birmingham, 68-88, chmn, Dept Med, 73-88, Mary Gertrude Waters prof cardiol, 77-88. *Concurrent Pos:* From instr to asst prof, Tulane Univ, 55-59; vis physician, Charity Hosp, New Orleans, 55-59; secy, Cardiac Electrophysiol Group, 64-65, pres, 65-66. *Mem:* Am

Heart Asn; fel Am Col Physicians; fel Am Col Cardiol (vpres, 70-71); fel Am Col Chest Physicians; Soc Exp Biol & Med; Sigma Xi. *Res:* Anatomy, pathology, physiology and pharmacology of the heart, particularly coronary arteries and conduction system. *Mailing Add:* Off Pres AZ9 Univ Tex Med Br 301 University Ave Galveston TX 77550-0129

JAMES, THOMAS RAY, MATHEMATICS. *Current Pos:* ASST PROF MATH, OTTERBEIN COL, 79- *Personal Data:* b Dayton, Ohio, Mar 23, 46; m 68; c 1. *Educ:* Otterbein Col, BA, 68; Ohio Univ, MS, 71, PhD(math), 74. *Prof Exp:* Teaching asst, Ohio Univ, 70-74; instr math & physics, Sewickley Acad, 74-75; asst prof math, Lake Erie Col, 75-79. *Mem:* Am Math Soc; Asn Comput Mach; Math Asn Am; Inst Elec & Electronics Engrs. *Res:* Point set topology. *Mailing Add:* Dept Math Otterbein Col Westerville OH 43081

JAMES, THOMAS WILLIAM, zoology; deceased, see previous edition for last biography

JAMES, V(IRGIL) EUGENE, CHEMICAL ENGINEERING. *Current Pos:* RETIRED. *Personal Data:* b Braxton Co, WVa, May 6, 29; m 55, Patricia A Santoro; c Cynthia L. *Educ:* WVa Univ, BS, 51, MS, 56, PhD(chem eng), 58. *Prof Exp:* Chem engr, Nitrogen Div, Allied Chem & Dye Corp, Va, 53-54; chem engr, Bur Mines, US Dept Interior, WVa, 54-58; res engr, Film Dept, Yerkes Res Lab, E I du Pont de Nemours & Co, Inc, 58-61, res supvr, 61-65, process supvr, 65-67, sr supvr, Textile Fibers Dept, 67-83. *Mem:* AAAS; Am Inst Chem Engrs. *Res:* Film forming and polymer research; coal gasification research; synthetic fibers. *Mailing Add:* 214 Masters Ct Chattanooga TN 37343

JAMES, WILLIAM JOSEPH, SOLID STATE CHEMISTRY & ELECTROCHEMISTRY, CRYSTALLOGRAPHY. *Current Pos:* from assoc prof to prof, Univ Mo, Rolla, 53-84, dir grad ctr mat res, 64-75, assoc dir, 75-76, dir, 82-83, EMER PROF CHEM, UNIV MO, ROLLA, 84-; DIR, CTR ENVIRON SCI & TECHNOL, 93- *Personal Data:* b Providence, RI, Sept 17, 22; m 42, Arlene R Carll; c Varie L (Lynch) & Candice L (Metcalf). *Educ:* Tufts Univ, BS, 49; Iowa State Univ, MS, 52, PhD(chem), 53. *Honors & Awards:* Thomas Jefferson Award, 89. *Prof Exp:* Asst physics, Pa State Univ, 52-53. *Concurrent Pos:* Fulbright res fel, Neel Lab Magnetism, Grenoble, France, 61-62; sr investr Grad Ctr Mat Res, 64-; pres & founder, Mead Technol Inc, Rolla, Mo, 76-; bd dir, Brewer Sci, 81-; vpres & bd dir, Filterteck Inc, 82-; pres, Incubator Technol Inc, Rolla, Mo, 84-86; bd dir, APR Inc, Redwood, Ca, 87-90; pres, Mead Environ Assocs, 94- *Mem:* Electrochem Soc; fel Am Inst Chemists; Am Chem Soc; Am Crystallog Asn; Mat Res Soc. *Res:* Lattice imperfections; magnetic and crystal structure determinations by x-ray and neutron diffraction; electrochemical kinetics and corrosion science; plasma-enhanced chemical vapor deposition of thin films. *Mailing Add:* Grad Ctr Mat Res Univ Mo Rolla MO 65401. *Fax:* 573-341-2071; *E-Mail:* wjames@umr.edu

JAMESON, A KEITH, PHYSICAL CHEMISTRY. *Current Pos:* asst prof, 68-73, assoc prof chem, 73-80, PROF CHEM, LOYOLA UNIV CHICAGO, 80- *Personal Data:* b Provo, Utah, June 11, 33; m 63; c 2. *Educ:* Brigham Young Univ, BS, 56, BSE & MS, 57; Univ Ill, Urbana, PhD(phys chem), 63. *Prof Exp:* Res chemist, Esso Res & Eng Co, 62-65; vis assoc prof chem, Ateneo de Manila Univ, 65-67; vis asst prof, Univ Ill, Urbana, 67-68. *Mem:* Am Chem Soc; Am Phys Soc. *Res:* Nuclear magnetic resonance; intermolecular interactions and spectroscopic observables; energy and environmental chemistry. *Mailing Add:* Dept of Chem Loyola Univ Chicago IL 60626

JAMESON, ANTONY, AEROSPACE ENGINEERING. *Current Pos:* prof mech & aerospace eng, 80-82, dir prog in appl & computational math, 86-88, JAMES S MCDONNELL DISTINGUISHED UNIV PROF AEROSPACE ENG, PRINCETON UNIV, 82- *Personal Data:* b Gillingham, Eng, 1934. *Educ:* Cambridge Univ, BA & MA, 58, PhD, 63. *Honors & Awards:* Except Sci Achievement Medal, NASA, 80; Gold Medal, Brit Royal Aerospace Soc, 88; W R Sears Distinguished Lectr, Cornell Univ, 92; Fluid Dynamics Award, Am Inst Aeronaut & Astronaut, 93; Spirit St Louis Medal, Am Soc Mech Engrs, 95. *Prof Exp:* Res fel, Trinity Hall, Cambridge, 60-63; economist, Trades Union Cong, London, 64-65; chief mathematician, Missile Div, Hawker Siddeley Dynamics, 65-66; staff engr, Grumman Aerospace Corp, 66-72; sr res sci, Courant Inst Math Sci, NY Univ, 72-74; prof comput sci, 74-80. *Concurrent Pos:* Hon prof, Northwestern Polytech Univ, Xian, China, 86. *Mem:* Nat Acad Eng; fel Am Inst Aeronaut & Astronaut. *Res:* Published numerous articles. *Mailing Add:* Aerospace Eng 128 Broadmead St Princeton NJ 08540-7216

JAMESON, CHARLES WILLIAM, ORGANIC CHEMISTRY, CHEMICAL CARCINOGENESIS. *Current Pos:* expert chem, 79-80, prog leader chem, Nat Toxicol Prog, 80-90, SR CHEMIST, OFF OF DIR, NIEHS, 90- *Personal Data:* b LaPlata, Md, Feb 3, 48; m 69; c 1. *Educ:* Mt St Mary's Col, BS, 70; Univ Md, PhD(org chem), 76. *Prof Exp:* Fac grad asst, Univ Md, 75-76; chemist bioassay, Tracor Jitco Inc, Tracor, Inc, 76-78, sr chemist, 78-79. *Concurrent Pos:* Sr chemist Bioassay Prog & consult, Chem Selection Group, Nat Cancer Inst, 76-80; mem, WHO task group Environ Health Criteria Partially Halogenated Chlorofluorocarbons. *Res:* Structure activity relationships; toxicokinetics; leukemia. *Mailing Add:* NIEHS PO Box 12233 Research Triangle Park NC 27709-2233

JAMESON, DAVID LEE, EVOLUTION. *Current Pos:* SR RES FEL, CALIF ACAD SCI, 87- *Personal Data:* b Ranger, Tex, June 3, 27; m 49, Marianne Mayo; c Roy A, David L, Robert C & Carol L. *Educ:* Southern Methodist Univ, BS, 48; Univ Tex, MA, 49, PhD(zool), 52. *Prof Exp:* Asst prof biol, Pacific Univ, 52-53; from instr to asst prof, Univ Ore, 53-57; from asst prof to prof zool, San Diego State Col, 57-67; prof biol, Univ Houston, 67-90, assoc dean grad sch, 71-72, dean, 72-74, dir coastal ctr, 72-76. *Concurrent Pos:* Managing ed, Copeia, Am Soc Ichthyologists & Herpetologists; Nat Acad Sci Exchange scholar, Bulgarian Acad Sci, 77 & USSR Acad Sci, 78. *Mem:* Am Soc Mammal; Ecol Soc Am; Soc Study Evolution (secy, 68-73); Am Soc Ichthyologists & Herpetologists; Am Inst Biol Sci; Genetics Soc Am. *Res:* Genetics; amphibians; population genetics; mitochondrial DNA evolution. *Mailing Add:* Osher Lab Molecular Syst Cal Acad Sci Golden Gate Park San Francisco CA 94118. *E-Mail:* djameson@cas.calacademy.org

JAMESON, DAVID M, BIOPHYSICS. *Current Pos:* assoc prof, 89-93, PROF BIOCHEM & BIOPHYS, UNIV HAWAII, 93- *Personal Data:* b Cleveland, Ohio, Apr 15, 48. *Educ:* Ohio State Univ, BS, 71; Univ Ill, MS, 74, PhD(biochem), 78. *Prof Exp:* Asst prof biochem & biophys, Univ Tex, Dallas, 83-89. *Mailing Add:* Dept Biochem & Biophys 2538 The Mall Univ Hawaii Snyder 401 Honolulu HI 96822-2233

JAMESON, DOROTHEA, NEUROSCIENCE. *Current Pos:* res assoc, Univ Pa, 62-68, res prof, 68-72, res prof psychol, 72-74, univ prof psychol & visual sci, 75-91, EMER UNIV PROF PSYCHOL & VISUAL SCI & MEM, INST NEUROL SCI, UNIV PA, 91- *Personal Data:* b Newton, Mass, Nov 16, 20; m 48, Leo M Hurvich. *Educ:* Wellesley Col, BA, 42. *Hon Degrees:* MA, Univ Pa, 72; DSc, State Univ NY, 89. *Honors & Awards:* Warren Medal, Soc Exp Psychologists, 71; Distinguished Sci Contrib Award, Am Psychol Asn, 72; Godlove Award for Res in Color Vision, Inter-Soc Color Coun, 73; Tillyer Medal, Optical Soc Am, 82; Judd Medal, Asn Int de la Couleur, 85; Holmholtz Award, Cognitive Neurosci Asn, 87. *Prof Exp:* Res asst, Harvard Univ, 41-47; res psychologist, Eastman Kodak Co, 47-57; res scientist, NY Univ, 57-62. *Concurrent Pos:* Prin investr res grant, NIH & NSF, 57-; mem, Nat Acad Sci-Nat Res Coun Vision Comt, 70-72 & 76-; vis prof, Univ Rochester, 74-75 & Columbia Univ, 74-76; mem, Visual Sci B Study Sect, NIH, 75-78 & Comn Human Resources, Nat Acad Sci-Nat Res Coun, 77-80; fel, Ctr Adv Study Behav Sci, 81-82, nat adv eye coun, NIH, 85-89. *Mem:* Nat Acad Sci; fel Am Acad Arts & Sci; Soc Neurosci; fel Optical Soc Am; Asn Res Vision & Ophthal; Sigma Xi; Int Res Group Color Vision Deficiencies; Int Brain Res Org; fel Am Psychol Soc. *Res:* Visual mechanisms; human perception. *Mailing Add:* Dept Psychol Univ Pa 3815 Walnut St Philadelphia PA 19104-6196. *E-Mail:* jameson@cattell.psych.upenn.edu

JAMESON, EVERETT WILLIAMS, JR, VERTEBRATE ZOOLOGY, MEDICAL ENTOMOLOGY. *Current Pos:* from instr to prof zool, Univ Calif, 44-88, from asst zoologist to assoc zoologist, Exp Sta, 48-65, vchmn dept, 69-74, EMER PROF ZOOL, UNIV CALIF, DAVIS, 88- *Personal Data:* b Buffalo, NY, May 2, 21; m 69, Sumiko Minazawa; c 5. *Educ:* Cornell Univ, BS, 43, PhD(vert zool), 48; Univ Kans, MA, 46. *Prof Exp:* Field observer, Hastings Reservation, Calif, 42; lab asst zool, Univ Kans, 45-46 & Cornell Univ, 46-48. *Concurrent Pos:* Guggenheim fel, 58-59. *Mem:* Am Soc Mammalogists; assoc Am Soc Ichthyologists & Herpetologists. *Res:* Population investigations of small mammals; food habits of vertebrates; fat and reproductive cycles of reptiles; oxygen consumption of reptiles; ecological, zoogeographic and taxonomic investigations of fleas and mites in North America and the Far East. *Mailing Add:* Dept Evolution & Ecol Univ Calif Davis CA 95616

JAMESON, JAMES LARRY, GLYCOPROTEIN HORMONES, ENDOCRINOLOGY. *Current Pos:* Resident internal med, 81-83, fel endocrinol, 83-85, INSTR MED, LAB MOLECULAR ENDOCRINOL, MASS GEN HOSP, HARVARD MED SCH, 85- *Personal Data:* b Ft Benning, Ga, June 21, 54; m 84. *Educ:* Univ NC, BS, 76, MD, 81, PhD(biochem), 81. *Mem:* AMA. *Res:* Regulation of glycoprotein hormone gene expression in eukaryotic cell line sand pituitary tumors. *Mailing Add:* Endo Metals & Mole Med Northwestern Univ 303 E Chicago ve Tary 15 Chicago IL 60611. *Fax:* 617-726-5072

JAMESON, PATRICIA MADOLINE, MICROBIOLOGY, VIROLOGY. *Current Pos:* REF LIBRN, APPL SCI & TECHNOL, UNIV WIS, MILWAUKEE, 91- *Personal Data:* b Rhinelander, Wis, Mar 17, 39. *Educ:* Carroll Col, Wis, BS, 61; Ind Univ, MS, 63, PhD(microbiol), 65; Univ Wis, Milwaukee, MLIS, 88. *Prof Exp:* Microbiologist viruses, US Army Biol Labs, Ft Detrick, 65-69; from instr to assoc prof microbiol, Med Col Wis, 69-89; asst prof, Booth Libr, Eastern Ill Univ, 89-91. *Mem:* AAAS; Sigma Xi. *Res:* Arboviruses; comparison of neuraminidases of neurotropic and nonneurotropic influenza virus strains, especially with respect to substrate specificity; interferon, especially standards, assay and inducers; feline leukemia virus. *Mailing Add:* 4075 Glenway St Milwaukee WI 53222-1150. *Fax:* 414-229-6791; *E-Mail:* pjameson@csd4.csd.uwm.edu

JAMESON, ROBERT A, PARTICLE ACCELERATOR PHYSICS & ENGINEERING. *Current Pos:* From asst group leader to assoc group leader, Los Alamos Nat Lab, 63-71, group leader, Accelerator Systs, Group MP-9, MP-Div, Lampf, 72-80, from dep div leader to div leader, Accelerator Technol Div, 78-87, STAFF MEM, LOS ALAMOS NAT LAB, 88- *Personal Data:* b Schenectady, NY, May 3, 37; m 59; c 2. *Educ:* Univ Nebr, BS, 58; Univ Colo, MS, 62, PhD(elec eng), 65; Univ NMex, MMgt, 77. *Concurrent Pos:* Vis prof, Ministry Educ, Japan, 88-89. *Mem:* Fel Am Phys Soc. *Res:* Application of automatic control theory to high power microwave systems; systems analysis and development of particle accelerator control and rf-accelerator systems; particle accelerator beam dynamics; electrical engineering. *Mailing Add:* AT-DO MS H811 Los Alamos Nat Lab PO Box 1663 Los Alamos NM 87545

JAMESON, WILLIAM J, JR, NUMERICAL MATHEMATICS, SYSTEMS ANALYSIS. *Current Pos:* ELEC ENG DEPT, MONT STATE UNIV, 87- *Personal Data:* b Billings, Mont, June 8, 30; m 53; c 2. *Educ:* Univ Mont, BA, 52; Univ Tex, MA, 54; Iowa State Univ, PhD(math), 62. *Prof Exp:* Physicist, Lockheed Missiles & Space Co, 58-59; fel & teaching asst appl math, Iowa State Univ, 59-62; mathematician, Collins Radio Co, Spectra Assocs, Inc, 62-72, vpres, 72-85; dir telecommunications, State Mich, 85-87. *Concurrent Pos:* Part-time asst prof math, Iowa State Univ, 62-67, assoc prof, 65-72, 80-81; corresp consult, Nat Acad Sci-Nat Acad Eng Comt Sci & Tech Commun, 67-69; mem, Comn Nat Info Syst Math, 68-70; mem, Pub Info Comt, Fedn Info Processing Socs, 69-72; chmn, Math Sect, Res Div, Am Defense Preparedness Asn, 69-78; mem, Comt on Commun & Info Policy, Inst Elec & Electronics Engrs, 85-88. *Mem:* Soc Indust & Appl Math (secy, 64-69, vpres, 69-74); Inst Elec & Electronics Engrs. *Res:* Numerical analysis and computation telecommunications; systems analysis. *Mailing Add:* 1404 S Bozeman Ave Bozeman MT 59715-5646

JAMIESON, ALEXANDER MACRAE, CHEMICAL PHYSICS, POLYMER SCIENCE. *Current Pos:* From res assoc to sr res assoc, 72-74, from asst prof to assoc prof, 74-82, PROF MOLECULAR SCI, DEPT MACROMOLECULAR SCI, CASE WESTERN RESERVE UNIV, 82- *Personal Data:* b Glasgow, Scotland, Sept 19, 44; m 71; c 3. *Educ:* Univ Glasgow, BS, 66; Oxford Univ, PhD(chem physics), 69. *Mem:* Am Phys Soc; Am Chem Soc; Soc Rheology. *Res:* Physical characterization of polymer materials; hydrodynamic properties of macromolecules; rheological properties of polymer solutions; structure and function of polysaccharides and proteoglycans; quasielastic laser light scattering. *Mailing Add:* 1525 Burlington Rd Cleveland OH 44118

JAMIESON, DEREK MAITLAND, OPERATIONS RESEARCH, STATISTICS. *Current Pos:* RETIRED. *Personal Data:* b Dundee, Scotland, Nov 27, 30; Can citizen; m 55, 83, Janet Morris. *Educ:* St Andrews Univ, BSc, 51, Hons, 53. *Prof Exp:* Statistician, Can Industs, Ltd, 53-57; sci off math & statist, Defence Res Bd Can, 57-60; mem tech staff, Mitre Corp, 60-65; chief, Indust Models Div, Nat Energy Bd, 65-66; planning exec, Simpac Div, Treas Bd, 66-68; dir, Inst Anal & Planning, Univ Guelph, 68-, adj prof math, 82- *Concurrent Pos:* Res dir, Comn Future Develop Univs Ont, 84. *Mem:* Fel AAAS; Inst Mgt Sci; Can Opers Res Soc; fel Royal Statist Soc; Opers Res Soc Am. *Res:* Computer aided analysis and study of large systems. *Mailing Add:* RR2 Puslinch ON N0B 2J0 Can. *Fax:* 519-767-1693; *E-Mail:* jamieson@exec.admin.uoguelph.ca

JAMIESON, GLEN STEWART, FISHERIES MANAGEMENT, INVERTEBRATE ECOLOGY. *Current Pos:* res scientist, Fisheries Res Br, Halifax, 77-81, res scientist, 81-82, HEAD SHELLFISH, FISHERIES RES BR, FISHERIES & OCEANS, NINAIMO, CAN, 82-, RES SCIENTIST. *Personal Data:* b Montreal, Que. *Educ:* McGill Univ, BSc, 67; Univ BC, MSc, 70, PhD(zool), 73. *Prof Exp:* Fel, Dalhousie Univ, 74-75; sr marine biologist, Appl Marine Res Ltd, Halifax, 75-77. *Concurrent Pos:* Head herring, Fisheries Res Br, Nanaimo, 82-84. *Res:* Fisheries management, emphasizing invertebrates; spatial and temporal distributions; stock assessment methodology; predator-prey interactions. *Mailing Add:* Pac Biol Sta Fisheries & Oceans Can Nanaimo BC V9R 5K6 Can

JAMIESON, GRAHAM ARCHIBALD, BIOCHEMISTRY, THROMBOSIS. *Current Pos:* res biochemist, Am Nat Red Cross, 61-64, asst dir res, 65-69, res dir, 69-84, SR SCIENTIST, AM NAT RED CROSS, 84- *Personal Data:* b Wellington, NZ, Aug 14, 29; m 60, Barbara Maclachlan; c Brian. *Educ:* Univ Otago, NZ, MSc, 51; Univ London, PhD(org chem), 54, DSc(biochem), 72. *Honors & Awards:* Winzler Mem Lectr, Univ Fla, 75; Shirley Johnson Lectr, Int Soc Thrombosis Haemostasis, 97. *Prof Exp:* Res assoc org chem, Royal Inst Technol, Sweden, 55-56 & Med Col, Cornell Univ, 56-57; vis scientist, NIH, 57-61. *Concurrent Pos:* Sir George Grey scholar, Univ Otago, NZ, 50, John Edmond fel, 51; adj prof, Sch Med & Dent, Georgetown Univ, 74-; mem exec comt, Thrombosis Coun, Am Heart Asn; mem, Blood Res Study Sect, NIH; mem adv comt, Res Blood Prod & Preserv, Letterman Army Inst Res; ed, Thrombosis & Haemostasis Int J Haematol, Am Soc Biol Chemists; vis prof, Univ Sao Paulo, Brazil, 92 & Imov, Barcelona, Spain, 93. *Mem:* AAAS; Am Soc Biol Chem; Int Soc Thrombosis & Haemostasis; Am Chem Soc. *Res:* Platelet receptor function and membrane biochemistry. *Mailing Add:* Platelet Biol Lab Am Nat Red Cross Rockville MD 20855. *Fax:* 301-738-0794; *E-Mail:* jamieson@usa.redcross.org

JAMIESON, J(OHN) A(NTHONY), INFRARED PHYSICS & ENGINEERING. *Current Pos:* CHIEF SCIENTIST, VANGUARD RES INC, 96- *Personal Data:* b Barnet, Eng, Mar 16, 29; nat US; m 56, Barbara Armstrong; c Gordon, Sava & Douglas. *Educ:* Univ London, BSc, 52; Stanford Univ, MS, 55, PhD(elec eng), 57. *Honors & Awards:* Space Systs Award, Am Inst Aeronaut & Astronauts, 92. *Prof Exp:* Head detector systs anal, Avionics Div, Aerojet-Gen Corp, 56-59; sr scientist, Aeronutronic Div, Ford Motor Co, 59-62; mgr res, Astrionics Div, Aerojet-Gen Corp, 62-66, mgr electronic systs div, 66-70; asst dir & chief, Optics Div, US Army Advan Ballistic Missile Defense Agency, 70-73; pres, Jamieson Sci & Eng Inc, 73-96. *Mem:* Optical Soc Am; sr mem Inst Elec & Electronics Engrs; fel Int Soc Optical Eng. *Res:* Applied infrared physics; noise analysis; systems engineering. *Mailing Add:* 10400 Eaton Pl Suite 450 Fairfax VA 22030-2201. *Fax:* 301-654-6773; *E-Mail:* jamiesonse@aol.com

JAMIESON, JAMES C, GLYCOPROTEIN BIOSYNTHESIS. *Current Pos:* Prof chem, 78-94, DEAN SCI, 94- *Personal Data:* b Aberdeen, Scotland, May 15, 39. *Educ:* Aberdeen Univ, Scotland, PhD(biochem), 67. *Mem:* Am Asn Biol Syst; Can Biochem Soc; Chem Inst Can; Royal Inst Chem; Soc Complex Carbohydrates. *Mailing Add:* Dept Chem Univ Man Winnipeg MB R3T 2N2 Can

JAMIESON, JAMES DOUGLAS, CELL BIOLOGY. *Current Pos:* assoc prof, 73-75, PROF CELL BIOL, YALE UNIV MED SCH, 75-, CHMN DEPT. *Personal Data:* b Armstrong, BC, Jan 22, 34; m 64; c 2. *Educ:* Univ BC, MD, 60; Rockefeller Univ, PhD(cell biol), 66. *Prof Exp:* Res assoc cell biol, Rockefeller Univ, 66-67, from asst prof to assoc prof, 67-73. *Mem:* Am Soc Cell Biol; Am Soc Biol Chemists. *Res:* Intracellular transport of secretory proteins; membrane formation and function; cell-hormone interactions; immunocytochemistry; pathophysiology of vascular smooth muscle; cytodifferentiation of glandular epithelia. *Mailing Add:* Sect Cell Biol Yale Univ Med Sch 333 Cedar St Rm C218 PO Box 208002 New Haven CT 06510-8002

JAMIESON, JOHN ANTHONY, AERONAUTICS. *Current Pos:* PRES, JAMIESON SCI & ENG INC, 73- *Personal Data:* b London, Eng, Mar 16, 29; m 56, Barbara Armstrong; c John Gordon, Sara Felicity & John Douglas. *Educ:* Univ London, BS, 52; Stanford Univ, PhD, 57. *Honors & Awards:* Space Systs Award, Am Inst Aeronaut & Astronaut, 92; Thomas B Dowd Mem Award, 95. *Prof Exp:* From scientist to mgr, Electrooptics Div, Aerojet-Gen Corp, 57-69; asst dir, US Army Advan Ballistic Missile Defense Agency, 70-73. *Concurrent Pos:* Chmn, Sci & Eng Support Group, Strategic Defense Initiative Orgn, Washington, 85-; mem sci adv bd, USAF, 90-94; bd dirs, Optelecom Inc & Space Comput Corp. *Res:* Published book and numerous articles. *Mailing Add:* Jamieson Sci & Eng Inc 10400 Eaton Pl Suite 450 Fairfax VA 22030-2208

JAMIESON, LEAH H, PARALLEL PROCESSING, SPEECH PROCESSING. *Current Pos:* From asst prof to assoc prof, 76-86, PROF ELEC ENG, PURDUE UNIV, 86- *Personal Data:* b Trenton, NJ, Aug 27, 49. *Educ:* Mass Inst Technol, SB, 72; Princeton Univ, MA & MSE, 74, PhD(elec eng & comput sci), 77. *Concurrent Pos:* Assoc ed, J Parallel & Distrib Comput, 85-92. *Mem:* Fel Inst Elec & Electronics Engrs; Asn Comput Mach. *Res:* Computer analysis and recognition of speech; design of parallel processing algorithms for digital speech, signal and image processing; software tools for parallel signal processing applications. *Mailing Add:* Sch Elec Eng Purdue Univ R85 Elec Eng West Lafayette IN 47907

JAMIESON, NORMAN CLARK, ORGANIC CHEMISTRY. *Current Pos:* sr chemist, Mallinckrodt, Inc, 70-77, res assoc, 77-80, dir res & develop, Sci Prod Div, 80-86, asst dir corp analyst res, 86-92, ASSOC DIR RES & DEVELOP SERV, MALLINCKRODT, INC, 92- *Personal Data:* b Edinburgh, Scotland, Nov 21, 35; US citizen; m 64, Wilma Cuddihy; c Anne. *Educ:* Univ Edinburgh, BSc, 58; Univ Alta, MSc, 61; Univ Adelaide, PhD(org chem), 66. *Prof Exp:* Fel org chem, Rensselaer Polytech Inst, 66-67; sr res scientist, Merck & Co, Inc, 67-70. *Mem:* Am Chem Soc. *Res:* Photochemistry; carbohydrates; analytical chemistry. *Mailing Add:* Mallinckrodt Inc PO Box 5439 St Louis MO 63147-0339. *Fax:* 314-539-1198

JAMIESON, WILLIAM DAVID, ANALYTICAL MASS SPECTROMETRY, QUALITY ASSURANCE. *Current Pos:* RETIRED. *Personal Data:* b Toronto, Ont, Aug 6, 29; m 51; c 1. *Educ:* Dalhousie Univ, BSc & dipl chem eng, 50, MSc, 51; Cambridge Univ, PhD(phys chem), 54. *Honors & Awards:* Caledon Award, 91. *Prof Exp:* Prin res officer, Atlantic Res Lab, Nat Res Coun Can, 54-90, asst to dir, 64-75, head marine anal chem, 75-90; sr scientist, Fenwick Labs Ltd, 90- *Concurrent Pos:* Coordr, Atlantic Prov Interuniv Comt Sci, 63-65; head clean-up technol coord, Oper Oil, 70; mgr, Marine Anal Chem Stand Prog, 79-90; chair, Group Experts Stand & Ref Mat, Int Oceanog Comn, 87-, Stand Comt, Can Asn Environ Anal Chem, 89- *Mem:* Fel Chem Inst Can; Am Soc Mass Spectrometry; Spectros Soc Can; Marine Technol Soc; Can Soc Mass Spectrometry. *Res:* Mass spectrometry; instrumentation development; analytical chemistry; kinetics of gas phase ion reactions; oil pollution clean-up technology; marine analytical chemistry; development of analytical chemistry reference materials and standards; quality assurance in analytical chemistry. *Mailing Add:* 30 Colindale Halifax NS B3P 2A4 Can

JAMISON, DEAN T, ECONOMICS OF EDUCATION, INTERNATIONAL HEALTH ECONOMICS & POLICY. *Current Pos:* PROF, SCH PUB HEALTH & GRAD SCH EDUC, UNIV CALIF, LOS ANGELES, 88- *Personal Data:* b Oct 10, 43; m 77, Kin Bing Wu; c Julian C, Eliot A & Leslie S. *Educ:* Stanford Univ, AB, 66, MS, 67; Harvard Univ, PhD(econ), 70. *Prof Exp:* Asst prof, Stanford Univ, 69-73; economist & div chief, World Bank, 76-88, dir, 92-93. *Concurrent Pos:* Dir, Ctr Pac Riim Studies, 93-; econ adv, Human Develop Dept, World Bank, 95- *Mem:* Inst Med-Nat Acad Sci. *Res:* Theory and applications of cost-benefit and cost-effectiveness analysis in health and education. *Mailing Add:* Ctr Pac RIM Studies Univ Calif 11292 Bunche Hall 405 Hilgard Ave Los Angeles CA 90095-1487

JAMISON, HOMER CLAUDE, EPIDEMIOLOGY, DENTISTRY. *Current Pos:* RETIRED. *Personal Data:* b Marion, NC, Apr 14, 21; c 3. *Educ:* Western Carolina Teachers Col, AB, 42; Emory Univ, DDS, 50; Univ Mich, MPH, 57, DrPH(epidemiol), 61; Am Bd Dent Pub Health, dipl. *Prof Exp:* Pub health dentist, NC State Bd Health, 51-54; dent officer, Mecklenburg Health Dept, 54-56; pub health dentist, Mich Dept Health, 57-58; from asst prof to prof dent, Med Ctr, Univ Ala, Birmingham, 60-68, dir grad prog, 62-63, dir comput res lab, 63-64; prof dent, Sch Dent, Univ Mo-Kansas City, 68-72; prof, Sch Dent, Univ Ala, Birmingham, 72-86, emer prof, 86. *Concurrent Pos:* Consult, Div Radiol Health, USPHS, 64-66; mem bd dirs, Jefferson Co Anti-Tuberc Asn, 64-68. *Mem:* Fel Am Pub Health Asn; Am Dent Asn; Biomet Soc; Am Statist Asn. *Res:* Clinical studies of potential prophylactic and therapeutic agents; applications and uses of computers in health research; patterns and trends in oral health and diseases. *Mailing Add:* 3586 Rockhill Rd Birmingham AL 35223-1402

JAMISON, JOEL DEXTER, ORGANIC CHEMISTRY. *Current Pos:* RETIRED. *Personal Data:* b Roanoke, Va, Nov 22, 32; m 59; c 3. *Educ:* Col William & Mary, BS, 55; Northwestern Univ, PhD(org chem), 60. *Prof Exp:* Res chemist, Hurcules Inc, 60-72, res scientist, 72-79, mgr, Tech Div, 79-94. *Mem:* Am Chem Soc. *Res:* Molecular structure elucidation; synthesis and investigation of condensation reactions in strong acid; synthesis of biologically active organic compounds for screening as pesticides; synthesis of lubrication base stocks. *Mailing Add:* PO Box 1655 Hockessin DE 19707-5655

JAMISON, KING W, JR, MATHEMATICS. *Current Pos:* from asst prof to assoc prof, 62-72, PROF MATH, MIDDLE TENN STATE UNIV, 72- *Personal Data:* b Meridian, Miss, Aug 8, 31; m 53; c 4. *Educ:* Union Univ, Tenn, BS, 52; George Peabody Col, MA, 53, PhD(math educ), 62. *Prof Exp:* Lectr math, Vanderbilt Univ, 61-62. *Res:* Mathematics education, especially the relationship of mathematical symbols to English words; variable base abacus as a visual aid. *Mailing Add:* Dept Math Middle Tenn State Univ Box 163 Murfreesboro TN 37132

JAMISON, RICHARD MELVIN, CLINICAL VIROLOGY. *Current Pos:* assoc prof, 70-78, dir, Diag Virol Lab, 79-85, PROF MICROBIOL & IMMUNOL, LA STATE UNIV, SHREVEPORT, 78-, PROF PEDIAT, 87- *Personal Data:* b Rayne, La, Oct 28, 38; div; c Richard W, Diane E & Bonnie A. *Educ:* Univ Southwestern La, BS, 58; Baylor Univ, MS, 62, PhD(virol), 66; Am Bd Med Microbiol, dipl, 76. *Prof Exp:* Res assoc biol div, Oak Ridge Nat Lab, 65-67; asst prof path, Univ Colo, Denver, 67-70. *Concurrent Pos:* Vis prof microbiol, Fac Med, Al Fetah Univ, Tripoli, Libya, 81-82; trustee, Am Bd Med Microbiol, 86-89, 91-97. *Mem:* Am Soc Microbiol; Sigma Xi; fel Am Acad Microbiol. *Res:* Replication of picornaviruses; rapid diagnosis of viral infections. *Mailing Add:* Dept Pediat La State Univ Sch Med 1501 Kings Hwy Shreveport LA 71130

JAMISON, ROBERT EDWARD, COMBINATORIAL GEOMETRY, GRAPH ALGORITHMS. *Current Pos:* assoc prof, 79-83, PROF MATH SCI, CLEMSON UNIV, 83- *Personal Data:* b Tampa, Fla, Dec 21, 48; m 78; c 2. *Educ:* Clemson Univ, BS, 70; Univ Wash, MS, 73, PhD(math), 74. *Prof Exp:* Asst prof, La State Univ, 74-79. *Concurrent Pos:* Vis asst, Inst Appl Math, Univ Bonn, 75-76; Alexander von Humboldt fel, Univ Erlangen, 76-77; vis prof, Tech Univ Darmstadt, 79; Humboldt fel, Univ Freiburg, 84; vis prof, Univ Berne, 86 & Cornell Univ, 93-94. *Mem:* Math Asn Am. *Res:* Combinatorial problems of a geometric nature, especially those arising from ordered sets, graphs, and free structures. *Mailing Add:* Math Sci Dept Clemson Univ Clemson SC 29634-1907. *E-Mail:* rejam@clemson.edu

JAMISON, RONALD D, MATHEMATICS. *Current Pos:* PROF MATH, BRIGHAM YOUNG UNIV, 63- *Personal Data:* b 1931. *Educ:* Univ Utah, PhD(math), 65. *Mem:* Am Math Soc. *Res:* Differential equations & applied math. *Mailing Add:* Bringham Young Univ 290 Talmage Math Bldg Provo UT 84602-1044

JAMISON, WILLIAM H, MATHEMATICS. *Current Pos:* assoc prof, 62-68, PROF MATH & CHMN DIV NATURAL SCI & MATH, ROCKY MOUNTAIN COL, 68- *Personal Data:* b Burlington, Iowa, May 4, 32; m 62. *Educ:* Mont State Col, BS, 59, MS, 61. *Prof Exp:* Instr math, Mont State Col, 59-62. *Mem:* Math Asn Am; Am Math Soc; Am Asn Physics Teachers. *Res:* Boolean algebra; logic; fossil fuel utilization. *Mailing Add:* Dept Phys & Math Rocky Mountain Col Billings MT 59102

JAMMALAMADAKA, SREENIVASA RAO, DIRECTIONAL DATA ANALYSIS. *Current Pos:* from asst prof to assoc prof, 76-83, PROF PROBABILITY & STATIST, UNIV CALIF, SANTA BARBARA, 83- *Personal Data:* b Munipalle, India, Dec 7, nat US; m 72, Vijaya; c Arvind & Aruna. *Educ:* Indian Statist Inst, Calcutta, BS, 64, MS, 65, PhD(statist), 69. *Prof Exp:* Res scholar statist, Indian Statist Inst, 65-69; vis asst prof probability & statist, Ind Univ, 69-70, asst prof, 70-75. *Concurrent Pos:* Vis prof, Univ Wis-Madison, 75-76 & Univ Leeds, 76; dir, Statist Consult Ctr, Univ Calif, Santa Barbara, 80- *Mem:* Fel Am Statist Asn; fel Inst Math Statist; Royal Statist Soc; fel Int Statist Inst; fel Inst Combinatorics & Applications. *Res:* Nonparametric statistical methods; inference based on sample spacings; large sample theory; efficiencies of test procedures; statistics of directional data. *Mailing Add:* Dept Statist & Appl Probability Univ Calif Santa Barbara CA 93106. *Fax:* 805-893-2334; *E-Mail:* rao@pstat.ucsb.edu

JAMMU, K S, PHYSICS. *Current Pos:* assoc prof, 69-80, PROF PHYSICS, UNIV PRINCE EDWARD ISLAND, 82- *Personal Data:* b India, Jan 1, 35; m 59; c 2. *Educ:* Aligarh Muslim Univ, India, MSc, 57; Univ Toronto, MA, 60, PhD(physics), 65. *Prof Exp:* Lectr physics, Khalsa Col, Amritsar, India, 57-59; asst prof, Mem Univ, 65-67; from asst prof to assoc prof, St Dunstan's Univ, 67-69. *Mem:* Am Asn Physics Teachers; Can Asn Physicists. *Res:* Molecular physics; spectroscopy. *Mailing Add:* Dept of Physics Univ of Prince Edward Island Charlottetown PE C1A 4P3 Can

JAMNBACK, HUGO ANDREW, JR, MEDICAL ENTOMOLOGY. *Current Pos:* RETIRED. *Personal Data:* b Fitchburg, Mass, Sept 18, 26; m 53; c 3. *Educ:* Boston Univ, BA, 48; Univ Mass, MS, 51, PhD, 53; London Sch Hyg & Trop Med, Dipl, 66. *Prof Exp:* Scientist entom, NY State Mus & Sci Serv, 53-59, sr scientist, 59-67, assoc scientist, 67-71, dir, NY State Sci Serv, 71-81. *Concurrent Pos:* Consult, WHO, 67-; sr res assoc, Col Environ Sci & Forestry, Syracuse Univ, 73- *Mem:* Entom Soc Am; Am Mosquito Control Asn. *Res:* Taxonomy, biology and control of biting flies. *Mailing Add:* 103 Heritage Rd Apt 8 Guilderland NY 12084-9658

JAMPEL, ROBERT STEVEN, OPHTHALMOLOGY. *Current Pos:* PROF OPHTHAL & CHMN DEPT & DIR, KRESGE EYE INST, WAYNE STATE UNIV, 70- *Personal Data:* b New York, NY, Nov 3, 26; m 52; c 4. *Educ:* Columbia Univ, AB, 47, MD, 50; Univ Mich, MS, 57, PhD(anat), 58. *Prof Exp:* Clin instr ophthal, Univ Mich, 56-57, instr neurol, 57-58; asst prof, State Univ NY, Downstate Med Ctr, 58-62; assoc ophthal, Columbia Univ, 62-70. *Concurrent Pos:* Chief, Dept Ophthal, Hutzel Hosp & Detroit Med Ctr, 88. *Mem:* Asn Res Vision & Ophthal; Am Acad Ophthal & Otolaryngol; Am Acad Neurol. *Res:* Physiology of the ocular muscles. *Mailing Add:* 4717 St Antoine Detroit MI 48201-1423

JAMPLIS, ROBERT W, MEDICAL FOUNDATION EXECUTIVE. *Current Pos:* CHIEF THORACIC SURG, PALO ALTO MED CLIN, 54-; CLIN PROF SURG, MED SCH, STANFORD UNIV, 58- *Personal Data:* b Chicago, Ill, Apr 1, 20; m; c 2. *Educ:* Univ Chicago, BS, 41, MD, 44; Univ Minn, MS, 51; Am Bd Surg, dipl, 52; Am Bd Thoracic Surg, dipl, 53. *Honors & Awards:* Nat Div Award, Am Cancer Soc, 79; Russel V Lee Award Lectureship, 82 & Yater Award, 85, Am Group Pract Asn. *Prof Exp:* Fel thoracic surg, Mayo Clin, 47-52. *Concurrent Pos:* Pres & chief exec officer, Palo Alto Med Found; exec dir, Palo Alto Clin, 66-82; nat bd dir, Am Can Soc. *Mem:* Nat Acad Sci; Sigma Xi; Am Asn Thoracic Surg; Am Col Chest Physicians; Am Col Surgeons; Soc Thoracic Surgeons. *Mailing Add:* Palo Alto Med Found 300 Homer Ave Palo Alto CA 94301

JAMPOLSKY, ARTHUR, OPHTHALMOLOGY, STRABISMUS & BINOCULAR VISION. *Current Pos:* Chief strabismus clin, 50-60, DIR, SMITH-KETTLEWELL EYE RES INST, CALIF PAC MED CTR, 60- *Personal Data:* b Bismarck, NDak, Apr 24, 19, m 57, c 3. *Educ:* Univ Calif, AB, 40; Stanford Univ, MD, 44; Am Bd Ophthal, dipl, 50. *Honors & Awards:* Mildred Weisenfeld Award, Asn Res Vision & Ophthal. *Concurrent Pos:* Mem comt on vision, Armed Forces-Nat Res Coun, 58-, exec coun, comt on vision, 60-64; vis sci study sect, NIH, 67-71, chmn, 70-71; regional consult ophthal, Oak Knoll Naval Hosp, Oakland & Travis AFB; consult, Letterman Gen Hosp, San Francisco & Calif State Bd Health; spec consult, Nat Inst Neurol Dis & Blindness. *Mem:* Am Optom Asn; Am Acad Ophthal; Am Ophthal Soc; Am Asn Ophthal; fel Am Col Surg. *Res:* Binocular vision; strabismus; physiological optics. *Mailing Add:* Smith-Kettlewell Eye Res Inst 2232 Webster St San Francisco CA 94115-1821

JAMRICH, JOHN XAVIER, ACADEMIC ADMINISTRATION, STATISTICS. *Current Pos:* CONSULT, 83- *Personal Data:* b Muskegon Heights, Mich, June 12, 20; m 44, June A Hrupka; c June A, Marna M & Barbara S. *Educ:* Univ Chicago, BS, 43; Marquette Univ, MS, 48; Northwestern Univ, PhD(admin), 51. *Hon Degrees:* LLD, Northern Mich Univ, 68, Grand Valley State Col, 85. *Prof Exp:* Instr math, Marquette Univ, 46-48; asst inst, Univ Wis, 48-49; asst dean men, Northwestern Univ, 49-51; dean students, Coe Col, 51-55; dean fac, Doane Col, 55-57; prof & dir, Ctr Study Higher Educ, Mich State Univ, 57-63, assoc dean, Col Educ, 63-68; pres, Northern Mich Univ, 68-83. *Concurrent Pos:* From asst dir to assoc dir, Legis Surv Higher Educ, Mich, 57-61; dir, Surv Higher Educ Grand Rapids, 59, Saginaw Valley, 62 & Study of Capital Outlay Needs, Ohio's State Insts Higher Educ, 62-63; accreditation examr & consult, NCent Asn Cols & Sec Schs, 62-; consult, Ford Found, Univ Nigeria, 64, State Bd Regents Ohio, 65, Study of Capital Outlay Needs, Va State Comn Higher Educ, 65 & Facil Study, SC Comn Hihgher Educ, 66. *Mem:* AAAS; Am Math Soc; Am Educ Res Asn. *Res:* Educational statistics in connection with administration of the university; meteorology. *Mailing Add:* 523 Governor's Green Dr Venice FL 34293

JAMSHIDI, MOHAMMAD MO, ROBOTICS, COMPUTER-AIDED DESIGN. *Current Pos:* PROF ELEC ENG, UNIV NMEX, 80-, DIR, COMPUTER AIDED DESIGN LAB, 84-, AT&T PROF MFG ENG, 89- *Personal Data:* b Shiraz, Iran, May 10, 44; US citizen; m 74; c 2. *Educ:* Ore State Univ, BSEE, 67; Univ Ill, Urbana-Champaign, MS, 69, PhD(elec eng), 71. *Honors & Awards:* Centennial Medal, Inst Elec & Electronics Engrs. *Prof Exp:* Res assoc, Univ Ill, 70-71; from asst prof to assoc prof, Dept Elec Eng, Pahlavi Univ, Iran, 71-75, prof, 77-79; scientist, Int Bus Mach Res Ctr, Yorktown Heights, 75-77. *Concurrent Pos:* Ed, Inst Elec & Electronics Engrs Control Systs Mag, 80-84, Am Soc Mech Engrs Ser Robotics & Mfg, 86- & Int J Computers & Elec Eng, 89-; adv engr, Info Prod Div, Int Bus Mach, 82-83; consult, USAF Phillips Lab, 84-, Oak Ridge Nat Lab, 88- & Los Alamos Nat Lab, 90-; hon prof, Nanjing Aeronaut Inst, People's Repub China, 86; vis prof, George Washington Univ & Nat Inst Standards & Technol, 87-88 & Univ Va, 88. *Mem:* Fel Inst Elec & Electronics Engrs; Inst Elec & Electronics Engrs Control Systs Soc; Soc Photo-Optical Instrumentation Engrs; Am Soc Mech Engrs. *Res:* Intelligent control systems including fuzzy logic, neural network, and expert systems; robotics control; adaptive control of nuclear reactors; computer-aided design of control systems. *Mailing Add:* Dept Elec & Comput Eng Sch Eng Univ NMex Albuquerque NM 87131

JAN, GEORGE C, OPTICS, MEDICAL LASERS. *Current Pos:* Regulation officer, Regulation & Stand, Food Drug Admin, 74-79, regulatory officer, 79-81, chief, VV Radiation Sect, 81-84, sr reviewer, Div Ophthal, 84-91, BR CHIEF, GEN SURG DEVICES BR, FOOD & DRUG ADMIN, 91- *Personal Data:* b Canton, China, Aug 20, 34; m 63, May Young; c Brend. *Educ:* Taiwan Normal Univ, BA, 59; Govt Ind Univ, MA, 64; Georgetown Univ, PhD(phys), 74. *Mailing Add:* Off Device Eval Food & Drug Admin 9200 Corporate Blvd Rockville MD 20850

JAN, KUNG-MING, CARDIOLOGY, CARDIOVASCULAR PHYSIOLOGY. *Current Pos:* ASSOC PROF PHYSIOL & MED, COL PHYSICIANS & SURGEONS, COLUMBIA UNIV, 68-; ASSOC ATTEND PHYSICIAN, PRESBY HOSP, 78- *Personal Data:* b Jan 14, 43; m 75, Connie Mark; c Rex, Stephen & Thomas. *Educ:* Nat Taiwan Univ, Taipei, MD, 67; Columbia Univ, PhD(physiol), 71. *Mem:* Am Col Cardiol. *Res:* Blood rheology; cardiovascular physiology; cell cell interaction; endothelial cell physiology. *Mailing Add:* Dept Med Columbia Presby Allen Pavilion 5141 Broadway New York NY 10034-1159. *Fax:* 718-601-6102

JAN, KWAN-HWA, IMAGING PROCESSING, SPEECH & DIGITAL SIGNAL PROCESSING. *Current Pos:* sr syst programmer, Dept Elec Eng & Comput Sci, 84-91, consult, 91-92, RES SCIENTIST, NORTHWESTERN UNIV, BIRL INDUST RES LAB, 92- *Personal Data:* b Yung Ching, Chung Hua, Taiwan, Jan 23, 56; US citizen; m; Lih-Jih; c Oliver C. *Educ:* Nat Cheng Kung Univ, Taiwan, Bachelor Sci, 78; Northwestern Univ, MS, 83, PhD(elec eng), 91. *Prof Exp:* Electronics programmer, Hq Chinese Marine Corps, Taiwan, China, 79-80; res engr, Sampo Electronic Co, Taipei, Taiwan, 80-81. *Mem:* Inst Elec & Electronics Engrs; Acoustics Speech & Signals Processing Soc. *Res:* Applying image processing, digital signal processing and pattern recognition techniques to solve industrial inspection and automation problems. *Mailing Add:* 212 E Ohio St Chicago IL 60611. *Fax:* 847-491-7105; *E-Mail:* jan@eecs.nwu.edu

JAN, LILY YEH, PHYSIOLOGY, BIOCHEMISTRY. *Current Pos:* asst prof physiol, 79-83, assoc prof, 83-85, PROF PHYSIOL & BIOCHEM, UNIV CALIF, SAN FRANCISCO, 85-; INVESTR, HOWARD HUGHES MED INST, 84- *Personal Data:* b China, Jan 20, 47; US citizen. *Educ:* Nat Taiwan Univ, 68; Calif Inst Technol, MSc, 70, PhD(biophysics & physics), 74. *Honors & Awards:* W Alden Spencer Award & Lectr, Columbia Univ, 88. *Prof Exp:* Res fel, Calif Inst Technol, 74-77, Dept Neurobiol, Harvard Med Sch, 77-79. *Concurrent Pos:* Alfred P Sloan res fel, 77-79; Klingenstein fel, 83-86; Javits neurosci investr award, Nat Inst Neurol & Commun Dis & Stroke, 88-; fac lectr, Univ Calif, San Francisco, 95. *Mem:* Nat Acad Sci. *Mailing Add:* Howard Hughes Med Inst Univ Calif Third & Parnassus Ave San Francisco CA 94143-0724

JAN, YUH NUNG, BIOCHEMISTRY, PHYSIOLOGY. *Current Pos:* from asst prof to assoc prof, 79-85, PROF PHYSIOL & BIOCHEM, UNIV CALIF, SAN FRANCISCO, 85-; INVESTR, HOWARD HUGHES MED INST, 84- *Personal Data:* b Shanghai, China, Dec 20, 46; m 71, Lily Yeh. *Educ:* Nat Taiwan Univ, BS, 67; Calif Inst Technol, MS, 70, PhD(biophys & physics), 74. *Honors & Awards:* W Alden Spencer Lectr, Columbia Univ, 88. *Prof Exp:* Postdoctoral res fel, Calif Inst Technol, 74-77 & Dept Neurobiol, Harvard Med Sch, 77-79. *Concurrent Pos:* Fel, Scottish Rite Schizophrenia Res Prog, 74-76 & Muscular Dystrophy Asn, 76-78; McKnight scholar, 78. *Mem:* Nat Acad Sci; Genetics Soc Am; Soc Chinese Bioscientists Am; Am Soc Cell Biol; Soc Neurosci; Soc Develop Biol 6. *Res:* Function and development of the nervous system; cell fate specification; ion channels; neuronal morphogenesis. *Mailing Add:* Univ Calif San Francisco CA 94143

JANABI-SHARIFI, FARROKH, ROBOTICS & AUTOMATION, COMPUTER INTEGRATED MANUFACTURING. *Current Pos:* ASST PROF MECH ENG, RYERSON POLYTECHNIC UNIV, 97- *Personal Data:* b Tabriz, Iran, Feb 6, 59; Can citizen. *Educ:* Mid & Tech Univ, BASc, 87; Univ Toronto, MASc, 90; Univ Waterloo, PhD(elec eng), 95. *Prof Exp:* Nat Sci & Eng Res Coun postdoctoral fel, McGill Univ, 95-97. *Concurrent Pos:* Lectr artificial intel, McGill Univ, 96-97, adj prof elec & comput eng, 97- *Mem:* Soc Mfg Engrs; Robotics Int Asn; Inst Elec & Electronics Engrs Robotics & Automation Soc; Inst Elec & Electronics Engrs Systs, Man & Cybernetics Soc; Inst Elec & Electronics Engrs Control Systs Soc. *Res:* Development of an intelligent supervisory control system for visual-serving robotic manipulators, automatic grasp, path and visual feature planners have been designed and integrated; initiation and development of an adaptive velocity estimator for discrete-time position information to be used in haptic interfaces; development of smart vibration generator for fixtureless assembly and experimentation; author of numerous publications. *Mailing Add:* Dept Mech Eng Ryerson Polytechnic Univ Toronto ON M5B 2K3 Can. *E-Mail:* fsharifi@acs.ryerson.ca, sharifi@cim.mcgill.ca

JANAK, JAMES FRANCIS, ELECTRICAL ENGINEERING, PHYSICS. *Current Pos:* MEM RES STAFF THEORET PHYSICS, THOMAS J WATSON RES CTR, IBM CORP, 65- *Personal Data:* b Yonkers, NY, Dec 5, 38; m 65; c 2. *Educ:* Mass Inst Technol, SB, 60, SM, 62, ScD(elec eng), 64. *Prof Exp:* Instr elec eng, Mass Inst Technol, 62-64, asst prof, 64-65. *Concurrent Pos:* Ford Found fel, 64-65; adj assoc prof math, Pace Univ, 78-83, adj prof physics, 83- *Mem:* Am Phys Soc. *Res:* Solid state physics. *Mailing Add:* T J Watson Res Ctr IBM Corp Box 218 Yorktown Heights NY 10598

JANAKIDEVI, K, GROWTH CONTROL MECHANISMS, GENE REGULATION. *Current Pos:* ASSOC PROF MOLECULAR PATH, ALBANY MED SCH, 70- *Educ:* Ofmania Univ, India, PhD(protozool), 57. *Mailing Add:* 40 Marion Ave Albany NY 12203

JANATA, JIRI, ELECTROANALYTICAL, SOLID STATE DEVICES. *Current Pos:* PROF BIOENG, UNIV UTAH, 76- *Personal Data:* b Podebrady, Czech, July 12, 39; Brit citizen; m 62; c 2. *Educ:* Charles Univ, Pargue, MSc, 61, PhD(anal chem), 65. *Prof Exp:* Res fel, Univ Mich, 66-68; sr chemist, Imperial Chem Indust, 68-76. *Concurrent Pos:* Prin investr, NSF, NIH & Dept Defense, 76-; consult, Johnson & Johnson, 79-; adj prof, Dept Chem, Univ Utah, 80- *Mem:* Royal Soc Chem; Electrochem Soc; Am Chem Soc. *Res:* Electroanalytical chemistry: solid state chemically inactive devices and in flow through electrochemical detectors. *Mailing Add:* Battelle Pac NW Labs Molecular Sci Res Ctr K2-20 Richland WA 99352

JANATOVA, JARMILA, BIOCHEMISTRY. *Current Pos:* res instr, 79-81, res asst prof, 81-85, RES ASSOC PROF, DEPT PATH, UNIV UTAH, 85-, ADJ ASSOC PROF, DEPT BIOENG, 89- *Personal Data:* b Pisek, Czech, Jan 9, 29; US citizen; m 62; c 2. *Educ:* Charles Univ, MSc, 61; Czech Acad Sci, PhD(biochem), 65. *Prof Exp:* Res scientist, Inst Org Chem & Biochem, Czech Acad Sci, 65; sr lectr, Dept Phys Chem, Charles Univ, Prague, Czech, 65-66; post doctoral res assoc, Biophysics Div, Inst Sci & Technol, Univ MIch, 66-67; post doctoral res assoc, Dept Biol, Univ Utah, 73-75, 76-77 & 77-79; sr exp officer, Dept Biochem, Univ Liverpool, Eng, 75-76. *Concurrent Pos:* Sr lectr, Charles Univ, 65-66; postdoctoral res assoc, Univ Mich, 66-67, dept biol, Univ Utah, 73-75, dept mat sci & eng, 76-77, dept pathol, 77-79; sr acad vis, MRC Immunochem Unit, Dept Biochem, Univ Oxford, 86-87; acad mem, Ctr Biopolymers, Univ Utah, 86- *Mem:* Sigma Xi; AAAS; Am Chem Soc; Am Soc Biochem & Molecular Biol; Am Asn Immunol; NY Acad Sci. *Res:* Biochemistry of complement proteins; protein chemistry structure/function of proteins from the complement system; isolation and characterization of proteins; biocompatibility of biomedical polymers. *Mailing Add:* Sch Med Dept Biochem Univ Utah 2480 MEB Salt Lake City UT 84112. *Fax:* 801-585-5151

JANAUER, GILBERT E, PHYSICAL ANALYTICAL CHEMISTRY. *Current Pos:* from asst prof to assoc prof, 64-80, PROF CHEM, STATE UNIV NY, BINGHAMTON, 69- *Personal Data:* b Vienna, Austria, Feb 26, 31; m 58; c 1. *Educ:* Univ Vienna, PhD(chem), 62. *Prof Exp:* Jr chemist, Oemvag, Austria, 58-60; res asst, Anal Inst, Univ Vienna, 60-61, instr anal chem, 61-62; res assoc chem, Clarkson Tech, 63-64. *Concurrent Pos:* Speaker, Gordon Res Conf Ion Exchange, 69, 75, 77 & vchmn, 79; vis prof, Graz Inst Technol, Austria, 71-72; NSF fac adv, 73 & 76. *Mem:* AAAS; Am Chem Soc; Sigma Xi. *Res:* Ion exhange equilibria and kinetics in aqueous and aqueous-organic solvents; separation methods; trace preconcentration and analysis; reactive ion exchange; chemical disinfection. *Mailing Add:* 1524 Drexel Dr Vestal NY 13850-4013

JANCA, FRANK CHARLES, GENETICS, DROSOPHILA MUTAGENESIS. *Current Pos:* vis res scientist, 88-90, ADJ ASST PROF, WESTERN MICH UNIV, 90-; PROF SCI, GLEN OAKS COMMUN COL. *Personal Data:* b Chicago, Ill, Oct 27, 46. *Educ:* Western Mich Univ, BA, 68; MA, 72; La State Univ, PhD(zool), 78. *Prof Exp:* Fel genetics, Univ Alta, 78-81; res assoc reproductive toxicol, SDak State Univ, 83-86. *Mem:* Genetics Soc Am; Environ Mutagen Soc; Sigma Xi. *Res:* Mutagen testing and mutagenesis; bacteria; maize; Drosophila and mammalian systems; reproductive toxicology using mouse and rat testes as test system and flow cytometry as research tool. *Mailing Add:* 38660 76th Ave Rt 1 Decatur MI 49045-9189

JANCARIK, JIRI, PLASMA PHYSICS. *Current Pos:* PHYSICIST, LAWRENCE LIVERMORE NAT LAB, UNIV CALIF, LIVERMORE, 81- *Personal Data:* b Brno, Czech, Oct 9, 41; m 63; c 2. *Educ:* Charles Univ, Prague, RNDr(exp physics), 63; Czech Acad Sci, CSc(plasma physics), 68. *Prof Exp:* Fel electron beam & plasma physics, Inst Plasma Physics, Czech Acad Sci, 63-68; res officer plasma turbulence, Culham Lab, UK Atomic Energy Authority, 68-72; res assoc beam-plasma interactions, Eng Dept, Univ Oxford, 69-72; res scientist, Fusion Res Ctr, Univ Tex, Austin, 72-81. *Mem:* Am Phys Soc. *Res:* Plasma heating and containment for thermonuclear applications; study of plasma waves; turbulence using x-ray, magnetic and electromagnetic diagnostics; computer simulation of relativistic beams, plasma turbulence; collective ion accelerators; laser isotope separation. *Mailing Add:* 1954 Woodbury Ct Walnut Creek CA 94596

JANDA, JOHN MICHAEL, INFECTIOUS DISEASES, MICROBIOL PATHOGENICITY & VIRULENCE. *Current Pos:* res microbiologist, 86-90, RES SCIENTIST, MICROBIOL DIS LAB, 90- *Personal Data:* b Burbank, Calif, Nov 4, 49; m 79, Claudia B Kissling; c Michael Jr, Matthew & Jennifer. *Educ:* Loyola Univ, BS, 71; Calif State Univ, Los Angeles, MS, 75; Univ Calif, Los Angeles, PhD(microbiol & immunol), 79. *Honors & Awards:* Aeromonas Jandaei named in honor, 91. *Prof Exp:* Fel, Dept Microbiol, Mt Sinai Hosp, 79-81, asst dir/prof, 81-84, assoc dir/prof, 84-86. *Concurrent Pos:* Mem, subcomt Facultatively Anaerobic Gram-Negative Rods, Am Soc Microbiol, 87-90. *Mem:* Am Soc Microbiol. *Res:* Microbiol pathogenesis; clinical microbiology; diagnostic microbiology; Aeromonas pathogenesis and taxonomy; cellular replication and invasion by enteric bacteria; Vibrio infections; toxigenic bacteria. *Mailing Add:* 106 Amethyst Ct Hercules CA 94547. *Fax:* 510-540-2374

JANDA, KENNETH CARL, MOLECULAR SPECTROSCOPY, SURFACE CHEMISTRY. *Current Pos:* PROF, DEPT CHEM, UNIV CALIF, IRVINE, 92- *Personal Data:* b Denver, Colo, Nov 28, 50; m 71; c 2. *Educ:* Hope Col, AB, 73; Harvard Univ, AM, 75, PhD(phys chem), 77. *Prof Exp:* Fel, Univ Chicago, 77-78; res instr physics, A A Noyes, 78-80; asst prof, Calif Inst Technol, 80-85; prof, Dept Chem, Univ Pittsburgh, 86-92. *Concurrent Pos:* A P Sloan fel, 81-84; Dreyfus fel, 83-85; Fulbright fel, 85. *Mem:* Am Chem Soc; Am Phys Soc. *Res:* Spectroscopy of weakly bound molecules in molecular beams and on solid surfaces; dynamics of energy transfer from strong to weak bonds; dynamics of molecular processes on surfaces, applications of lasers in physical chemistry. *Mailing Add:* Dept Chem Univ Calif Irvine CA 92717-0001

JANDA, KIM D, CHEMISTRY. *Current Pos:* Fel, Dept Molecular Biol, 85-86, adj asst mem, 87-88, asst mem, prof, 89-90, assoc mem, 91-92, PROF, DEPT MOLECULAR BIOL & CHEM, SCRIPPS RES INST, 89-, ASSOC MEM, 93- *Personal Data:* b Cleveland, Ohio, Aug 23, 58; c Nikole. *Educ:* Univ SFla, BS, 80; Univ Ariz, MS, 83, PhD, 84. *Concurrent Pos:* First Award, NIH, 90-95; Alfred P Sloan fel, 93-95. *Mem:* Am Chem Soc; fel Am Inst Chemists. *Res:* Design of antigenic structures to be used for the induction of catalytic antibodies; design of novel transition state-multisubstrate analogues for enzyme inhibitor studies; synthesis of these complex molecules; kinetic studies on these catalytic antibodies and enzymes; matrix immobilized catalytic antibodies in organic synthesis; catalytic antibodies in nonaqueous solvents; probing the evolution of catalytic antibodies via site directed mutagenesis; antibodies-catalytic antibodies as biosensors; immunopharmacotherapy for the treatment of cocaine abuse; novel synthetic methodologies for obtaining encoded combinatorial peptide-peptidomimic libraries. *Mailing Add:* Scripps Res Inst Mail Drop MB-20 Rm MB34 La Jolla CA 92037

JANDACEK, RONALD JAMES, LIPID NUTRITION, FAT DIGESTION & ABSORPTION. *Current Pos:* RES CHEMIST, MIAMI VALLEY LABS, PROCTER & GAMBLE, CINCINNATI, OHIO, 68- *Personal Data:* b Chattanooga, Tenn, Dec 26, 42. *Educ:* Rice Univ, BA, 64; Univ Tex, PhD(chem), 68. *Mem:* Am Chem Soc; Am Oil Chemists Soc; Am Inst Nutrit. *Res:* Physical and biological properties of lipids, including phase behavior, digestion and intestinal absorption. *Mailing Add:* Procter & Gamble Miami Valley Labs PO Box 398707 Cincinnati OH 45239-8707

JANDHYALA, BHAGAVAN S, PHARMACOLOGY. *Current Pos:* PROF PHARMACOL, UNIV HOUSTON, 73- *Mem:* Fedn Am Socs Exp Biol. *Res:* Pharmacoloogy. *Mailing Add:* Univ Houston Col Pharm 4800 Calhoun Blvd Houston TX 77204-5515. *Fax:* 713-743-1232

JANDL, JAMES HARRIMAN, MEDICINE. *Current Pos:* Res fel med, Harvard Med Sch, 52-55, instr med, 55-57, assoc, 57-59, from asst prof to assoc prof, 59-68, dir, Harvard Med Unit, 68-70, George Richards Minot Prof Med, Harvard Med Sch, Boston City Hosp, 68-, HEAD, DEPT HEMAT, HARVARD MED SCH, 73- *Personal Data:* b Racine, Wis, Oct 30, 27; m 50; c 5. *Educ:* Franklin & Marshall Col, BS, 45; Harvard Med Sch, MD, 49. *Mem:* Am Soc Clin Invest; Am Fedn Clin Res; Asn Am Physicians; Am Clin & Climat Asn; Am Soc Hemat. *Res:* Hematology; mechanisms of the anemias, especially the hemolytic anemias; immune hematology; functions of the reticuloendothelial system. *Mailing Add:* Harvard Med Sch 25 Shattuck St Boston MA 02115

JANDORF, BERNARD JOSEPH, BIOCHEMISTRY, TOXICOLOGY. *Current Pos:* RETIRED. *Personal Data:* b Berlin, Ger, May 19, 15; nat US, 44; m 46, Lottie Kaufman; c Evelyn J (Woldman). *Educ:* Cambridge Univ, BA, 38; Harvard Univ, AM, 40, PhD(biochem), 42. *Prof Exp:* Asst, Lilly Res Labs, Woods Hole, 41; Commonwealth Fund sr fel, Thorndike Mem Lab, Boston City Hosp, 42-44; res biochemist, Chem Corps, Med Labs, US Army Chem Ctr, Md, 44-49, chief, Enzyme Chem Br, 49-56, Biochem Res Div, Chem Warfare Labs, 56-62; dep dir res directorate weapons systs, Edgewood Arsenal, 62-65, chief, Chem Res Div, 65-74, sr scientist, Frederick Cancer Res Ctr, 75-89. *Concurrent Pos:* Fel, Harvard Univ, 42-44; lectr, Sch Hyg & Pub Health, Johns Hopkins Univ, 46-49; assoc prof, Univ Md, 59-62. *Mem:* AAAS; Am Chem Soc; Am Soc Biol Chem:. *Res:* Biological oxidations in mammalian tissues; intermediary carbohydrate metabolism; enzyme isolations; action of toxic agents on enzymes. *Mailing Add:* North Oaks Apt 400 725 Mt Wilson Lane Baltimore MD 21208-1122

JANE, JOHN ANTHONY, NEUROSURGERY. *Current Pos:* PROF NEUROSURG, SCH MED, UNIV VA, 69-, CHMN DEPT, 80- *Personal Data:* b Chicago, Ill, Sept 21, 31; m 60; c 4. *Educ:* Univ Chicago, BA, 51, MD, 56, PhD(biol, psychol), 67. *Honors & Awards:* Herbert Olivecrona Lectr. *Prof Exp:* From instr to assoc prof neurosurg, Sch Med, Case Western Reserve, 65-69. *Mem:* Am Asn Anat; Am Physiol Soc. *Res:* Head injury; neuroplasticity; craniofferial surgery. *Mailing Add:* Dept Neurosurg Sch Med Univ Va PO Box 212 Charlottesville VA 22908-0001

JANECKE, JOACHIM WILHELM, NUCLEAR PHYSICS, NUCLEAR STRUCTURE. *Current Pos:* assoc prof, 65-69, PROF PHYSICS, UNIV MICH, ANN ARBOR, 69- *Personal Data:* b Heidelberg, Ger, Feb 5, 29; m 54, Christa Hawner; c Susanne & Roger. *Educ:* Univ Heidelberg, Dipl Physics, 52, Dr rer nat(physics), 55. *Prof Exp:* Res asst, Max Planck Inst Nuclear Res, 55-60; res assoc, Univ Mich, 60-62, Nuclear Res Ctr, Karlsruhe, Ger, 62-65. *Concurrent Pos:* Vis prof, MPI Heidelberg, KVI Groningen, Tel-Aviv Univ, 72, 79, 80, 86 & 88 & Osaka Univ, 93, 94 & 95; fel, Japan Soc Prom Sci, 93. *Mem:* Fel Am Phys Soc; Sigma Xi. *Res:* Nuclear physics; nuclear astrophysics; nuclear reactions; accelerators; nuclear structure and masses; cosmo-chronology. *Mailing Add:* Dept Physics Univ Mich Ann Arbor MI 48109-1120

JANES, DONALD LUCIAN, SOLID STATE CHEMISTRY. *Current Pos:* Sr chemist, Cent Res Lab, 3M Co, 65-71, res specialist, 71-73, supvr, Magnetic Audio-Video Prod Div, 73-79, mgr, 79-81, mgr, Info Storage Lab, 81-85, lab mgr, Appl Res Lab, 85-90, DIR, CORP ANALYSIS LAB, 3M CO, 90- *Personal Data:* b Fresno, Calif, July 1, 39. *Educ:* Grinnell Col, AB, 61; Purdue Univ, PhD(inorg chem), 66. *Mem:* Am Chem Soc. *Res:* Preparation and properties of magnetic materials. *Mailing Add:* 7337 Pinehurst Rd St Paul MN 55115

JANES, DONALD WALLACE, BACTERIOLOGY, BIOLOGY. *Current Pos:* RETIRED. *Personal Data:* b Kansas City, Mo, June 12, 29; m 53, Janina Z Piorkowska; c Todd A, Jeffrey W, Scott Lee D & Nancy M. *Educ:* Baker Univ, AB, 51; Univ Kans, MA, 56; Kans State Univ, PhD(zool), 62. *Prof Exp:* Instr biol, Washburn Univ, 57-60; asst prof, Parsons Col, 61-62; from asst prof to prof biol, Univ SColo, 62-93, assoc vpres acad affairs & dean grad sch, 68-78. *Concurrent Pos:* Fulbright fel, 56-57; intern Acad Admin, Am Coun Educ, 68; consult & examr, NCent Asn Cols & Sec Schs, 72-93. *Mem:* AAAS; Am Soc Zoologists; Am Soc Microbiol; Am Soc Mammal; Sigma Xi. *Res:* Problems of vertebrate distribution and histology; reproduction; vertebrate fauna of Colorado; chemistry and biosynthesis of bacterial pigments, particularly pigments of Serratia marcescens. *Mailing Add:* PO Box 191 Breckenridge CO 80424

JANES, GEORGE SARGENT, physics; deceased, see previous edition for last biography

JANEWAY, CHARLES ALDERSON, JR, IMMUNE RECOGNITION, IMMUNOGENICITY. *Current Pos:* from asst prof to assoc prof, 77-83, PROF PATH & BIOL, SCH MED, YALE UNIV, 83-, PROF IMMUNOBIOL, 88- *Personal Data:* b Boston, Mass, Feb 5, 43; m 77; c 3. *Educ:* Harvard Col, BA, 63; Harvard Univ, MD, 69. *Hon Degrees:* Dr, Univ Cracow, Poland, 91. *Prof Exp:* Res assoc, NIH, 70-75; Moseley fel, Univ Uppsala, 75-77. *Concurrent Pos:* Investr, Howard Hughes Med Inst, 77-; lectr biol, Yale Univ, 79-; mem, Immunobiol Study Sect, NIH, 81-85, 88-92. *Mem:* AAAS; Am Asn Immunologists; Am Soc Microbiol. *Res:* Molecular basis of specific immune recognition and the genes that control it, focusing primarily on T cells that activate all immune responses. *Mailing Add:* Dept Immunobiol Sch Med Yale Univ LH 416 310 Cedar St New Haven CT 06510. *Fax:* 203-737-1765; *E-Mail:* charles.janeway@quickmail.yale.edu

JANEWAY, RICHARD, MEDICINE, NEUROLOGY. *Current Pos:* from instr to assoc prof neurol, Bowman Gray Sch Med, Wake Forest Univ, 66-71, actg chmn, Dept Neurol, 69-70, prog dir, Cerebral Vascular Res Ctr, 69-71, dean, 71-85, vpres health affairs, 83-90, exec dean, 85-94, PROF NEUROL, BOWMAN GRAY SCH MED, WAKE FORESTT UNIV, 71-, EXEC VPRES HEALTH AFFAIRS, 90- *Personal Data:* b Los Angeles, Calif, Feb 12, 33; m 55, Katherine E Pillsbury; c Susan, David & Elizabeth. *Educ:* Colgate Univ, AB, 54; Univ Pa, MD, 58. *Prof Exp:* Intern, Hosp Univ Pa, 58-59; resident neurol, NC Baptist Hosp, 63-66. *Concurrent Pos:* Prog admin, Cerebral Vascular Res Ctr, 66-69; mem spec task force, Joint Coun Subcomt, Cerebrovascular Dis, 68; coun cerebrovascular dis, Am Heart Asn, 69; mem, Spec Procedures & Equip Study Group, Joint Comt Stroke Facil, 70; mem, Nat Adv Coun Regional Med Prog, HEW; consult, US-Egypt Collab Prog Stroke; Markle scholar, 68-73; mem, Coun Deans, As Am Med Col, 71-, chmn, 82-85, Exec Coun, 77-86. *Mem:* Inst Med-Nat Acad Sci; fel Am Heart Asn; fel Am Col Physicians; Soc Med Adminr; Am Neurol Asn; AAAS; Sigma Xi; Am Med Asn; Am Clin & Climat Asn. *Res:* Neurology; cerebrovascular disease; health care economics; health care organization. *Mailing Add:* Bowman Gray Sch Med Wake Forest Univ Winston-Salem NC 27157

JANG, SEI JOO, RELAXOR MATERIALS, OPTICS. *Current Pos:* ASSOC PROF SOLID STATE SCI, PA STATE UNIV, 87- *Personal Data:* b Andong, Korea, Dec 30, 47; m 83; c 2. *Educ:* Sogang Univ, BS, 73; Boston Col, MS, 76; Pa State Univ, PhD(solid state sci), 79. *Prof Exp:* Serv engr med equip, Siemens Elec Eng Co, 73-74; teaching asst physics, Boston Col, 74-76; res asst mat, Pa State Univ, 76-79; sr res staff optics, AT&T Eng Res Ctr, 79-83; res assoc elec mat, Mat Res Labs, 83-87. *Concurrent Pos:* Secy, JBS Consult Inc, 84-; pres, Matronix Inc, 85-; sr res assoc, Mat Res Lab, Pa State Univ, 87- *Mem:* Am Ceramic Soc; Nat Inst Ceramic Engrs; Optical Soc Am. *Res:* Relaxor materials; microwave measurements and materials; optics and electro-optics materials; electrostrictive abd piezoelectric materials for actuator, transducers and motors. *Mailing Add:* 220 Camelot Lane State College PA 16803

JANGAARD, NORMAN OLAF, BIOCHEMISTRY. *Current Pos:* VPRES RES & DEVELOP, KELCO, MERCK & CO, SAN DIEGO, 92- *Personal Data:* b Seattle, Wash, Oct 11, 41; m 63; c 2. *Educ:* San Diego State Univ, BS, 62; Univ Calif, Los Angeles, PhD(biochem), 66; Univ Denver, JD, 76. *Prof Exp:* Lab technician, Scripps Inst Oceanog, Univ Calif, San Diego; biochemist, Pfizer, Inc, 66-68 & Shell Develop Co, 68-72; dir res, Adolph Coors Co, 72-74, dir qual assurance, 74-78, vpres qual assurance & res & develop, 78-80, vpres eng & res & develop, 80-81, vpres qual assurance, regulatory affairs res & develop, 81-83, vpres prod, 83-84; pres, Coors Biotech Inc, 85-92. *Mem:* Am Soc Brewing Chemists; Am Chem Soc; Inst Food Technologists; Am Asn Cereal Chemists; Master Brewer's Asn Am. *Res:* Fermentation and yeast physiology; microbiological control; brewing and malting technology; packaging materials; breeding and growing of hops, barley and rice; waste treatment technology; vitamin production; food ingredient technology. *Mailing Add:* Nutra Sweet Kelco Co 8355 Aero Dr San Diego CA 92123-1718

JANGHORBANI, MORTEZA, STABLE ISOTOPES, NEUTRON ACTIVATION. *Current Pos:* ASSOC PROF PATH, MALLORY INST PATH, BOSTON UNIV SCH MED. *Personal Data:* b Isfahan, Iran, Sept 29, 43; US citizen; m 69; c 1. *Educ:* Am Univ Beirut, Lebanon, BS, 66; Oregon State Univ, MS, 68, PhD(chem), 72. *Prof Exp:* Assoc vis asst prof chem, Univ Ky, 72-73; res chemist, Univ Marburg, Ger, 73-75; group leader, Environ Trace Substances Res Ctr, Univ Mo, 75-77; prin res scientist, Mass Inst Technol, 77- *Mem:* Am Chem Soc; AAAS. *Res:* Trace element research in relation to biology and human nutrition; analytical chemistry of trace elements. *Mailing Add:* Bio Chem Anal Corp 2201 W Campbell Park Dr Chicago IL 60612-3501. *Fax:* 312-243-7283

JANICK, JULES, PLANT BREEDING, TISSUE CULTURE. *Current Pos:* From instr to prof, 54-88, DISTINGUISHED PROF HORT, PURDUE UNIV, 88-, DIR, CTR NEW CROPS & PLANT PROD, 90- *Personal Data:* b New York, NY, Mar 16, 31; m 52; c Peter J & Robin (Weinherger). *Educ:* Cornell Univ, BS, 51; Purdue Univ, MS, 52, PhD(plant genetics & breeding), 54. *Hon Degrees:* DS, Univ Bologna, Italy, Tech Univ Lisbon. *Honors & Awards:* Paul Howe Shepard Award, Am Pomol Soc, 60 & 70, Wilder Medal, 96; Marion W Meadows Award, Am Soc Hort Sci, 71, Wilson Papenoe Award, 80, Kenneth Post Award, 81, Stark Award, 78 & 82, N F Childers Award, 82. *Concurrent Pos:* Hon res assoc bot, Univ Col, Univ London, 63 & 85, Univ Pisa, 85; horticulturist, Agr Univ Minas Gerais, 63-65; vis colleague, Univ Hawaii, 69; consult, World Bank, Indonesia, 73, Portugal, 83, 86, 87 & 96, Morocco, 88, China, 88, Italy, 89 & 90, Equador, 90. *Mem:* Am Pomol Soc; fel Am Soc Hort Sci (pres, 86-87); fel Portuguese Hort Asn; fel AAAS; Sigma Xi; Int Soc Hort Sci. *Res:* Genetics and breeding of horticultural crops; tissue culture; new crops. *Mailing Add:* Dept Hort Purdue Univ West Lafayette IN 47907-1165. *Fax:* 765-494-0391; *E-Mail:* jjanick@hort.purdue.edu

JANICKI, BERNARD WILLIAM, IMMUNOLOGY, MICROBIOLOGY. *Current Pos:* chief, Immunol Br, 74-77, Immunol & Biochem Br, 78-83, HEALTH SCI ADMINR, NAT INST ALLERGY & INFECTIOUS DIS, 74-, DEP DIR, IMMUNOL, ALLERGIC & IMMUNOL DIS PROG, 83- *Personal Data:* b Wilmington, Del, Oct 14, 31; m 54; c 5. *Educ:* Univ Del, BA, 53, MA, 55; George Washington Univ, PhD(microbiol), 60. *Prof Exp:* Microbiologist, Tuberc Res Lab, Vet Admin Hosp, DC, 55-60, chief, 60-63, chief microbiol res lab, 63-72, chief pulmonary immunol res lab, 72-74; *Concurrent Pos:* Lectr microbiol, Univ Md, 69-79; consult, Nat Inst Allergy & Infectious Dis, 69-75; mem US tuberc panel, US-Japan Coop Med Sci Prog, 69-75; spec lectr med, George Washington Univ, 74-79. *Mem:* Am Soc Microbiol; Soc Exp Biol & Med; NY Acad Sci; Am Asn Immunol; Am Thoracic Soc. *Res:* Immunity and hypersensitivity in infectious diseases. *Mailing Add:* Dana-Farber Cancer Inst 44 Binney St Rm 1830 Boston MA 02115-6084. *Fax:* 617-632-4452

JANICKI, CASIMIR A, ANALYTICAL CHEMISTRY, COMPUTER VALIDATION. *Current Pos:* PHARMACEUT CONSULT, 93- *Personal Data:* b Milwaukee, Wis, Sept 20, 34; m 59, Toni Chendorain; c 2. *Educ:* LaSalle Col, BA, 56; Marquette Univ, MS, 58; Loyola Univ, PhD(anal chem), 64. *Prof Exp:* Anal chemist, Smith, Kline & Fr Labs, 57-60; sr anal chemist, McNeil Pharmaceut, Spring House, Pa, 63-66, group leader, 66-74, sect head, McNeil Labs, Ft Washington, 74-80, sect head, 74-81, tech dir anal qual control, 82-93. *Mem:* Am Asn Pharm Sci. *Res:* Pharmaceutical analytical chemistry, including thin layer, chromatography, ultra violet visible and infrared spectrometry, separation techniques including high performance liquid and gas liquid chromatography; kinetics and drug stability; robotics in pharmaceutical analysis, laboratory computers, validation of computer systems in GMP area; FTIR in QC analysis. *Mailing Add:* 2888 Hickory Hill Dr Norristown PA 19403

JANICZEK, PAUL MICHAEL, ASTRONOMY, NAVIGATION. *Current Pos:* astronr, 67-84, ed, Navig, 78-85, chief ephemerides div, 84-90, DIV ASTRON APPLNS DEPT, US NAVAL OBSERV, 90- *Personal Data:* b Hazleton, Pa, Oct 5, 37. *Educ:* King's Col, BA, 60; Georgetown Univ, MA, 65, PhD(astron), 70. *Prof Exp:* Supvr qual control, Lansdale Div, Philco Corp, 60-61; programmer analyst sci satellites, Fed Syst Div, IBM Corp, 61-66. *Concurrent Pos:* Instr, Maryland Col Art & Design, 81-83. *Mem:* Am Astron Soc; AAAS; Inst Navigation; Sigma Xi; Int Astron Union. *Res:* Dynamical astronomy; celestial navigation. *Mailing Add:* US Naval Observ 3450 Massachusetts Ave NW Washington DC 20392-5420

JANIK, BOREK, CLINICAL CHEMISTRY, FILTRATION. *Current Pos:* OWNER, MOREX, CHELSEA, MICH, 91-; MGR, ASIA PAC AREA, CELMAN SCI, 92- *Personal Data:* b Brno, Czech, Oct 29, 33; m 65, Alice; c Peter & Dasha. *Educ:* Purkyne Univ, Brno, MS, 56; Czech Acad Sci, Brno, PhD(chem, biophys), 64; Purkyne Univ, RNDr, 66. *Prof Exp:* Res assoc org chem, Lachema, Pure Chem Corp, Czech, 56-60; fel, Inst Biophys, Czech Acad Sci, Brno, 60-64, res scientist electrochem & biophys, 64-66 & 67-68; fel chem, Univ Mich, Ann Arbor, 66-67, res assoc electrochem, 68-69; sr res scientist phys biochem, Molec Biol, Miles Lab, Inc, 69-74, mem staff & mgr res & develop, Res Prod Div, 75-78, mgr res & develop, Ames Div, 78-79; dir clin res & develop, Gelman Sci, 79-82, dir lab prod develop, 82-85, dir lab technol, 85-90; dir tech affairs, Biopore, Caan, France, 90-91. *Mem:* Electrophoresic Soc; Am Asn Clin Chem. *Res:* Test and instrument programs in clinical chemistry and biotechnology (proteins, nucleic acids, immunochemistry, enzymology and hematology) utilizing separation technologies; binding and transfer of nucleic acids and proteins to binding membranes; author of over 70 technical publications; interdisciplinary applications of micro-filtration. *Mailing Add:* 13805 Waterloo Rd Chelsea MI 48118. *Fax:* 313-474-2441

JANIK, GERALD S, ENVIRONMENTAL SCIENCES, ANALYTICAL CHEMISTRY. *Current Pos:* engr, 73-76, res engr, 76-81, RES DIR, NY STATE ELEC & GAS CORP, 81- *Personal Data:* b Niagara Falls, NY, July 2, 40; m 67; c 3. *Educ:* Niagara Univ, BS, 61; Purdue Univ, MS, 64; Tex A&M Univ, PhD(phy chem), 66. *Prof Exp:* Sr engr, Bell Aerospace Co, 66-72. *Concurrent Pos:* Fossil Fuel Comn, Empire State Elec Energy Res Corp, 76-; reviewer, NY State Energy Res & Develop Authority, 81-; task force, 86-88, div comt, Elec Power Res Inst, 91-94. *Res:* Energy production and pollution control measures. *Mailing Add:* 817 Catalina Blvd Endicott NY 13760

JANIS, ALLEN I(RA), GENERAL RELATIVITY. *Current Pos:* From instr to prof, 57-92, assoc dir, Philos Sci Ctr, 75-92, EMER PROF PHYSICS, UNIV PITTSBURGH, 93-, EMER FEL, PHILOS SCI CTR, 93- *Personal Data:* b Chicago, Ill, Sept 11, 30; m 53, Phyllis Meyer; c Stuart & Wynne. *Educ:* Northwestern Univ, BS, 51; Syracuse Univ, PhD(physics), 57. *Concurrent Pos:* Sr res assoc, Philos Sci Ctr, Univ Pittsburgh, 67-75. *Mem:* AAAS; fel Am Phys Soc; Am Asn Physics Teachers; Philos Sci Asn. *Res:* Gravitational theory; philosophy of physics. *Mailing Add:* Dept Physics Univ Pittsburgh Pittsburgh PA 15260. *E-Mail:* aij@vms.cis.pitt.edu

JANIS, CHRISTINE MARIE, MAMMALIAN PALEOBIOLOGY & SYSTEMATICS. *Current Pos:* asst prof, 83-89, ASSOC PROF BIOL, DIV BIOL & MED, BROWN UNIV, 89- *Personal Data:* b London, Eng, Oct 18, 50; m 91, J John Sepkoski Jr. *Educ:* Univ Cambridge, UK, BA, 73; Harvard Univ, PhD(biol), 79. *Honors & Awards:* G G Simpson Prize in Paleont, 85. *Prof Exp:* Res fel, Newnham Col, Univ Cambridge, UK, 79-83. *Concurrent Pos:* Officer, Harvard Univ, 84-; res assoc, Field Mus, Chicago, 95- *Mem:* Soc Vert Paleont; Paleont Soc; Am Soc Mammalogists; Am Soc Zoologists; Int Soc Cryptozool. *Res:* Paleoecology and patterns of evolutionary diversification in ungulates, hoofed mammals, in relation to environmental change; combining data from living and fossil taxa. *Mailing Add:* Div Biol & Med Brown Univ Providence RI 02912

JANIS, F TIMOTHY, TECHNOLOGY TRANSFER, THEORETICAL CHEMISTRY. *Current Pos:* dir, 91-93, PRES, ARAC, INC, 93- *Personal Data:* b Chicago, Ill, Apr 11, 40; m 62, Kathryn Dickey; c Mark, Paul & Melissa. *Educ:* Wichita State Univ, BS, 62, MS, 63; Ill Inst Technol, PhD(chem), 68. *Prof Exp:* Res assoc chem, Argonne Nat Lab, 66-68; instr chem & data processing, Col DuPage, 68-69; from asst prof to assoc prof chem, Ill Benedictine Col, 69-74; assoc prof & asst acad dean/registr, Franklin Col, 74-77; admin mgr, Indianapolis Ctr Advan Res, 77-78, actg dir, Indust Liaison Off, 78-80, dir, Bus Develop Div, 80-83, dir prog develop, 83-84, technol transfer, 84-90; founder & pres, J-Tech & Assocs, 90-93. *Concurrent Pos:* Fel, Argonne Nat Lab, 68, consult, 68- *Mem:* Am Chem Soc; Technol Transfer Soc. *Res:* Technology transfer methodology, systems, policy and brokering; ab-initio caculations on molecules. *Mailing Add:* ARAC Inc 23 North Main St Suite C Franklin IN 46131. *Fax:* 317-262-5044

JANIS, RONALD ALLEN, NEW DRUG DISCOVERY & DEVELOPMENT, CALCIUM CHANNEL MODULATORS. *Current Pos:* prin res scientist, Miles Inst Preclin Pharmacol, 84, prin staff scientist, 80-92, PRIN STAFF SCIENTIST, BAYER CORP, 84- *Personal Data:* b Sask, Can, Oct 11, 43; m 68; c Mary A & Joseph W. *Educ:* Univ BC, BSP, 66, MSP, 68; State Univ NY Buffalo, PhD(biochem pharmacol), 72. *Prof Exp:* Fel pharmacol, Univ Alta, 72-74; asst prof physiol, Northwestern Univ, 74-80, assoc prof, 80; assoc prof med, Univ Conn Health Ctr, 81-89, assoc clin prof, 89-91. *Mem:* Am Soc Pharmacol & Exp Therapeut; Biophys Soc; Soc Neurosci. *Res:* Drug discovery and development; mechanisms of action of drugs acting on calcium and potassium channels and development of such drugs; ligand binding studies. *Mailing Add:* Bayer Corp 400 Morgan Lane West Haven CT 06516-4175. *Fax:* 203-937-5467

JANISCHEWSKYJ, WASYL, ELECTRICAL ENGINEERING. *Current Pos:* lectr elec eng, Univ Toronto, 59-62, from asst prof to assoc prof, 62-70, asst head Elec Eng Dept, 65-70, assoc dean fac, Appl Sci & Eng, 78-82, prof, 70-90, EMER PROF ELEC ENG, UNIV TORONTO, 90- *Personal Data:* b Prague, Czech, Jan 21, 25; Can citizen; m 51, Emilia Miszczuk; c Roxoilana & Marko. *Educ:* Univ Toronto, BASc, 52, MASc, 54. *Prof Exp:* Demonstr elec eng, Univ Toronto, 52-54, instr, 54-55; elec engr, Aluminum Labs, Ltd, 55-59. *Concurrent Pos:* Nat Res Coun Can res grant, 61-; consult, Elec Eng Consociates, 68- *Mem:* Fel Inst Elec & Electronics Engrs; Can Elec Asn. *Res:* Distribution of mechanical stress in composite transmission-line conductors; extra high voltage transmission of electric power; radio interference caused by high voltage corona; fault behavior of complex electric power systems; methods of testing underground cable; lightning studies; microgap discharges; television interference. *Mailing Add:* Dept Elec & Comput Eng Univ Toronto Toronto ON M5S 1A1 Can. *Fax:* 416-971-2325

JANKE, MARY KIRK, DRIVER ASSESSMENT OF AGE-RELATED FRAILTY. *Current Pos:* res analyst I/II, Dept Motor Vehicles, 76-81, opers res specialist II, 81-85, res prog specialist II, 85-89, res mgr II, 89-93, RES SCIENTIST III, DEPT MOTOR VEHICLES, 93- *Educ:* Univ Chicago, BS; Calif State Univ, Sacramento, MA; Univ Calif, Berkeley, PhD(exp psychol). *Prof Exp:* Asst prof psychol, Calif State Univ, Sacramento, 68; psychologist, Stockton State Hosp, 69-74. *Res:* Assessment system for drivers with dementia or age-related frailty; author of several publications in professional journals. *Mailing Add:* Res & Develop Br Calif Dept Motor Vehicles PO Box 932382 F-126 Sacramento CA 94232-3820

JANKE, NORMAN CHARLES, ENVIRONMENTAL GEOLOGY, MINING-PETROGRAPHY. *Current Pos:* instr geol & math, Calif State Univ, 56-60, from asst prof to prof, 60-83, head dept, 68-74, EMER PROF GEOL, CALIF STATE UNIV, SACRAMENTO, 83-, CONSULT GEOLOGIST, NORMAN JANKE ASSOC. *Personal Data:* b Milwaukee, Wis, Sept 5, 23; m 52, Mary Kirk; c Garth. *Educ:* Univ Chicago, MS, 52; Univ Calif, Los Angeles, PhD(geol), 63. *Prof Exp:* Consult geologist, Geo-Sci Inc, Tex, 53; instr geol, Fresno State Col, 55. *Concurrent Pos:* Trustee bd mem, Moss Landing Marine Lab, 67-71; consult mining, eng & forensic geol, fault & seismic risk, petrography. *Mem:* NY Acad Sci; Sigma Xi; Asn Eng Geologists; Soc Econ Paleont & Mineral; Am Mil Eng; Am Soc Appl Technol; Am Soc Testing Mat; Soc Explosive Engrs; Soc Mining Engrs Scientists & Engrs. *Res:* Slumping and land sliding mechanisms; effects of shape upon settling velocity and sieving; photogrammetric uses of ordinary camera equipment; particle size and shape analysis, sieving and settling methods; swelling clays genesis and effects. *Mailing Add:* 2670 Fair Oaks Blvd Sacramento CA 95864. *E-Mail:* sac69915@saclink.csus.edu

JANKE, RHONDA RAE, AGRONOMY. *Current Pos:* Agron coordr, 86-92, RES DIR, RODALE INST, 92- *Personal Data:* b Junction City, Kans, Apr 20, 58. *Educ:* Kans State Univ, BS, 80; Cornell Univ, MS, 84, PhD(agron), 87. *Concurrent Pos:* Adj asst prof, Pa State Univ, University Park, 88-; regional rep, New World Agr Group. *Mem:* Am Soc Agron; Weed Sci Soc Am; Brit Ecol Soc; Inst Alernative Agr; Sigma Xi. *Res:* Agronomy. *Mailing Add:* Crystal Ridge Rd Kutztown PA 19530-9749

JANKE, ROBERT A, PLANT ECOLOGY, PHYSICS. *Current Pos:* from instr to assoc prof physics, 44-62, assoc prof, 62-84, EMER PROF BIOL, MICH TECHNOL UNIV, 84- *Personal Data:* b Detroit, Mich, Aug 19, 22; m 44, Nadine Key; c David, Daniel, Steven & Janet. *Educ:* Univ Mich, AB, 44, MS, 52; Mich Technol Univ, BS, 48; Univ Colo, PhD(ecol), 68. *Prof Exp:* Teacher pub sch, 44. *Concurrent Pos:* NSF sci fac fel, 63-65. *Mem:* AAAS; Ecol Soc Am; Sigma Xi; Bot Soc Am; George Wright Soc. *Res:* Fire ecology; boreal forest ecology; vascular flora inventory of Isle Royale National Park; physical ecology. *Mailing Add:* Dept Biol Mich Technol Univ Houghton MI 49931

JANKE, WILFRED EDWIN, SOIL SCIENCE. *Current Pos:* RES SPECIALIST, CAMPOTEX, 91- *Personal Data:* b Morris, Man, Dec 24, 32; m 58; c 4. *Educ:* Univ Man, BSA, 55, MSc, 57; Univ Wis-Madison, PhD(soils, geol), 62. *Prof Exp:* Pedologist, Soil Surv Div, Can Dept Agr, 57-59, res scientist, Res Sta, 62-63; dir, Soil Testing Lab, Univ Man, 63-66; res agronomist & mkt coordr, fertilizer mkt div, Sherritt Gordon Mines Ltd, 66-78; fertilize prod mgr, Federated Cooperatives Ltd, 78-81, mkt res sr analyst, Potash Corp, Saskatoon, 81-83; res & develop specialist, BASF Can, Inc, 83-88; agronomist, CIDA Agr Can, 88-91. *Mem:* Am Soc Agron; Can Soc Soil Sci; Agr Inst Can; Int Soc Soil Sci. *Res:* Soil fertility, nutrient requirements of various crops under various soil and climatic conditions; fertilizer research, development of new fertilizer products, determining agronomic uses and effectiveness; evaluation of pesticide products. *Mailing Add:* 14 DeGeer Crescent Saskatoon SK S7H 4P7 Can

JANKOWSKI, CHRISTOPHER K, ORGANIC CHEMISTRY. *Current Pos:* from asst prof to assoc prof, 69-78, dean, Fac Res & Grad Students, 88-95, PROF ORG CHEM, UNIV MONCTON, 78- *Personal Data:* b Warsaw, Poland, July 31, 40; m 65, Iwona Kuczewska; c Agnes. *Educ:* Univ Warsaw, MSc, 63; Univ Montreal, PhD(chem), 68; Univ Paris, Doct Etat(phys), 85. *Prof Exp:* Asst org chem, Univ Warsaw, 63-64; fel, Univ Montreal, 67-68, asst prof, 68-69. *Concurrent Pos:* Res fel chem, Syntex, SA, Mex, 75; res fel, Nuclear Res Ctr, Saclay, France, 75-79; adj prof, Univ Nacional Autonome, Mex, 88-, Univ NB, Can, 90-95, Univ de Paris VI, France, 89- *Mem:* Fel Chem Inst Can; Fr-Can Asn Advan Sci. *Res:* Synthesis of organic compounds with physiological activity; organic application of mass spectrometry and nuclear magnetic resonance; natural products; alkaloids, carbohydrates. *Mailing Add:* Univ Moncton Moncton NB E1A 3E9 Can. *Fax:* 506-858-4086; *E-Mail:* jankowc@umoncton.ca

JANKOWSKI, CONRAD M, ENVIRONMENTAL CHEMISTRY, HIGH TEMPERATURE REACTION. *Current Pos:* asst prof anal chem, 60-63, assoc prof anal chem & chem oceanog, 63-91, EMER PROF ANALYTICAL CHEM & CHEM OCEANOG, NORTHEASTERN UNIV, 91- *Personal Data:* b Chicago, Ill, Feb 25, 28; m 53, Harris. *Educ:* Mich State Univ, BS, 51, MS, 53; State Univ Iowa, PhD(anal chem), 60. *Prof Exp:* Chief anal chemist, Rayovac Corp, 53-55; group leader instrumentation res, Cent Sci Co, 55-58. *Concurrent Pos:* Indust consult; vis prof, Trent Polytechnic Nottingham, Eng. *Mem:* AAAS; Am Chem Soc; fel Royal Soc Chem; fel Am Inst Chemists. *Res:* Electroanalytical chemistry; high temperature reactions; chemical instrumentation; air and water pollution measurements. *Mailing Add:* PO Box 305 West Hyannisport MA 02672

JANKOWSKI, FRANCIS JAMES, DESIGN ENGINEERING, NUCLEAR ENGINEERING. *Current Pos:* RETIRED. *Personal Data:* b Amsterdam, NY, Nov 22, 22; m 46; c 1. *Educ:* Union Col, NY, BScCE, 43; Univ Cincinnati, MSE, 47, ScD(physics), 49. *Prof Exp:* Res engr nuclear, Battelle Mem Inst, 49-50; adv scientist, Westinghouse Elec Corp, 50-55; consult, Battelle Mem Inst, 55-59; prof nuclear & mech, Rutgers Univ, 59-69; chmn dept eng, 69-74, prof systs eng, Wright State Univ, 69-84. *Concurrent Pos:* Consult, Englehard Industs, NJ, 59-62, United Nuclear Corp, 59-65, Picatinny Arsenal, US Army, 64-69, Westinghouse Elec Corp, 60- & US Dept Energy, 73-78; sabbatical leave, Foreign Technol Div, US Air Force, 79-80. *Mem:* Sigma Xi; Am Nuclear Soc; Am Phys Soc; Am Soc Eng Educ. *Res:* Principles and methodologies of engineering design process, with emphasis on incorporating human factors variables, life cycle costs, and systems approach. *Mailing Add:* 5800 Mahogany Pl NE Albuquerque NM 87111-6226

JANKOWSKI, STANLEY JOHN, ANALYTICAL CHEMISTRY. *Current Pos:* sr res chemist, Atlas Chem Indust Inc, 66-70, res supvr, 70-81, RES SPECIALIST, ICI AMERICAS INC, 81- *Personal Data:* b Detroit, Mich, Dec 19, 28; m 54; c 4. *Educ:* Washington & Jefferson Col, BA, 53; Univ Pittsburgh, PhD(anal chem), 60. *Prof Exp:* Supvr, Neville Chem Co, 58-60; anal chemist, Celanese Corp Am, 60-62, sr anal chemist, 62-66. *Mem:* Am Chem Soc; Am Indust Hyg Asn. *Res:* Instrumental methods of analysis; chromatographic methods of analysis; drugs; organic chemicals; industrial hygiene analysis. *Mailing Add:* 28 Amarante St Laguna Niguel CA 92677-8929

JANKUS, VYTAUTAS ZACHARY, NUCLEAR SCIENCE. *Current Pos:* RETIRED. *Personal Data:* b Girvalakis, Lithuania, Sept 6, 19; US citizen; wid; c 1. *Educ:* Univ Vilnius, Lithuania, dipl, 43; Stanford Univ, PhD(physics), 56. *Prof Exp:* Instr physics, Seattle Univ, 48-51; asst, Stanford Univ, 51-55; assoc physicist, Mat Sci Div, Argonne Nat Lab, 55-75, sr physicist, 75-81. *Mem:* Am Asn Physics Teachers; Am Phys Soc; Sigma Xi. *Res:* Electron scattering; neutron thermalization; reactor safety; performance. fuel element. *Mailing Add:* 801 McCarthy Rd Lemont IL 60439-4044

JANNA, WILLIAM SIED, SPRAY RESEARCH. *Current Pos:* chmn, 87-91, PROF, DEPT MECH ENG, MEMPHIS STATE UNIV, 87- *Personal Data:* b Toledo, Ohio, Mar 23, 49; m 75; c 1. *Educ:* Univ Toledo, BSME, 71, MSME, 73, PhD(transport phenomena), 76. *Prof Exp:* From asst prof to assoc prof mech eng, Univ New Orleans, 76-87, chmn dept, 78-83. *Mem:* Am Soc Mech Engrs; Am Soc Eng Educ. *Res:* Windmill economics; droplet sizes of airless sprays; heat transfer from high pressure sprays; heat transfer from fluid flow in a tube to a cooled isothermal wall; economics of pipeline sizing. *Mailing Add:* 3126 Autumn Gold Lane Memphis TN 38119-9136

JANNASCH, HOLGER WINDEKILDE, MICROBIOLOGY. *Current Pos:* asst prof, 61-63, PVT DOCENT, UNIV GOETTINGEN, 63-; SR SCIENTIST, WOODS HOLE OCEANOG INST, 63- *Personal Data:* b Holzminden, Ger, May 23, 27; m 56, Friederun Goldschmidt; c Hans. *Educ:* Univ Gottingen, PhD(microbiol), 55. *Honors & Awards:* Henry Bryant Bigelow Medal Oceanog, 80; Fisher Award in Environ & Appl Microbiol, 82; Becton-Dickinson Award, 84; Cody Award in Ocean Sci, Scripps Inst Oceanog, 92. *Prof Exp:* Asst scientist microbiol, Max Planck Soc, 56-60. *Concurrent Pos:* Fel, Scripps Inst Oceanog, Univ Calif, San Diego, 57-58, Univ Wis, 58-59; mem, Marine Microbiol Panel, Off Naval Res, 65-70; dir microbiol ecol course & mem corp, Marine Biol Lab, Woods Hole, Mass, 71-80; mem, Comt Environ Microbiol, Am Soc Microbiol, 71-73 & 79-81; mem, Panel Water Criteria, Nat Acad Sci & NSF, 75-78; trustee, Marine Biol Lab, Woods Hole, 80-88; mem panel, Comt Probs Environ & Global Sulfur Transformations, 84-; mem panel, Comt Ocean Res & Hydrothermal Emanations Plate Boundaries, 87-; mem, Space Sci Bd, Comt Planetary Biol & Chem Evolution, Nat Res Coun, 87-; hon mem, Woods Hole Oceanog Inst, 89- *Mem:* Nat Acad Sci; Am Soc Microbiol; Am Soc Limnol & Oceanog; Int Asn Theoret & Appl Limnol; fel AAAS; Gottingen Acad Sci; Am Acad Arts & Sci; Am Chem Soc; Am Acad Microbiol. *Res:* Physiology and ecology of freshwater and marine bacteria; deep sea microbiology; growth of microorganisms at extreme temperatures and pressures; deep sea hydrothermal vents; author or co-author of 140 scientific publications in microbiology. *Mailing Add:* Woods Hole Oceanog Inst Woods Hole MA 02543

JANNETT, FREDERICK JOSEPH, JR, MAMMALOGY. *Current Pos:* HEAD & CUR, DEPT BIOL, SCI MUS MINN, ST PAUL, 82- *Personal Data:* b Newark, NJ, Mar 6, 46; m 72. *Educ:* Cornell Univ, BS, 67, PhD(ecol & evolutionary biol), 77; Tulane Univ, MS, 69. *Honors & Awards:* A B Howell Award, Am Soc Mammalogists, 77. *Prof Exp:* Vis fel, Cornell Univ, 77-78, fel, 78-81, lectr mammal, 81. *Concurrent Pos:* Exchange scientist, Acad Sci, USSR, 84, vis scientist, 88; assoc, Bell Mus Natural Hist, Univ Minn, Minneapolis, 85-93; adj assoc prof fisheries, wildlife & conserv biol, Univ Minn, St Paul, 95- *Res:* Variation, social dynamics and demography of microtine rodents; strategies for inventorying and monitoring small mammals; effects of prairie management and clearcutting on mammals; mammals and diseases. *Mailing Add:* Sci Mus Minn 30 E Tenth St St Paul MN 55101. *Fax:* 612-221-4777; *E-Mail:* fjannett@vm1.spcs.umn.edu

JANNETTA, PETER JOSEPH, SURGERY. *Current Pos:* PROF NEUROL SURG & CHMN DEPT, SCH MED, UNIV PITTSBURGH, 71- *Personal Data:* b Philadelphia, Pa, Apr 5, 32; m 54; c 6. *Educ:* Univ Pa, AB, 53, MD, 57; Am Bd Surg, dipl, 64; Am Bd Neurol Surg, dipl, 69. *Prof Exp:* From asst instr to instr surg, Sch Med, Univ Pa, 58-63, instr pharmacol, 60-63; assoc surg & neurosurg, Univ Calif, Los Angeles, 63-66; assoc prof surg & chmn div neurosurg, Med Ctr, La State Univ, 66-71. *Concurrent Pos:* NIH training grant, Univ Pa, 60-63, res grants, Med Ctr, La State Univ, 67-70; develop training grant, 68-71. *Mem:* Fel Am Col Surg; Soc Neurol Surgeons; Am Asn Neurol Surgeons; Cong Neurol Surgeons; Neurosurg Soc Am. *Res:* Pheochromocytoma; catechol amine determinations; single unit recording in the vestibular system; mesoscopic central nervous system anatomy and pathology; trigeminal nerve function; trigeminal neuralgia; cranial nerve dysfunction syndromes-etiology and treatment; spinal cord injury. *Mailing Add:* Dept Neurol Surg Univ Pittsburgh Sch Med Suite B-400 PUH Pittsburgh PA 15213

JANNEY, CLINTON DALES, RADIOLOGICAL PHYSICS. *Current Pos:* RETIRED. *Personal Data:* b Dover, NJ, Mar 10, 20; m 43. *Educ:* Univ Ill, BS, 41; Univ Calif, PhD(physics), 45. *Prof Exp:* Physicist, Manhattan Proj, Univ Calif, 42-46 & 47; from asst prof to assoc prof physiol & med physics, Col Med, Univ Iowa, 47-53; sr physicist, Southwest Res Inst, 53-54; assoc cancer res scientist physics, Roswell Park Mem Inst, 54-59; assoc prof, Univ Vt, 59-70, prof radiol physics, 70-82. *Concurrent Pos:* Am Cancer Soc fel, Nat Res Coun, 46-47. *Mem:* AAAS; Radiol Soc NAm; Am Asn Physicists in Med; Am Phys Soc; Biophys Soc; Sigma Xi. *Res:* Medical radiologic physics. *Mailing Add:* 51 Oak St Hyannis MA 02601

JANNEY, DONALD HERBERT, PHYSICS. *Current Pos:* RETIRED. *Personal Data:* b Kansas City, Mo, Nov 26, 31; m 88, Elizabeth Farnum; c Dawn & Lauren. *Educ:* Univ Ill, BS, 52; Stanford Univ, MS, 53, PhD(appl physics), 57. *Prof Exp:* Asst, Los Alamos Sci Lab, 52; asst, Microwave Lab, Stanford Univ, 53-56; staff mem, Los Alamos Nat Lab, 56-65, alt group leader, 65-74, group leader, 74-81, staff mem, 81-94. *Mem:* AAAS; Am Phys Soc; sr mem Inst Elec & Electronics Engrs; Sigma Xi. *Res:* Gamma ray measurements; flash radiography; image processing; image analysis; non-destructive evaluation; intelligence analyst. *Mailing Add:* 229 Barranca Rd Los Alamos NM 87544-2409. *E-Mail:* janney@compuserve.com

JANNEY, GARETH MAYNARD, OPTICS. *Current Pos:* RETIRED. *Personal Data:* b Toledo, Ohio, Feb 19, 34; m 60, Carol Pauley; c 1. *Educ:* Columbia Univ, AB, 55; Georgetown Univ, MS, 62, PhD(physics), 65. *Prof Exp:* Physicist, US Army Night Vision Lab, US Army Electronics Command, 65-69; from mem tech staff lasers to sr staff physicist, Hughes Aircraft Co, 69-75; asst dept mgr lasers, Hughes Res Labs, 75-79, proj mgr, Space Sensors Div, 79-84, Chief Scientist, Space & Strategic Eng Div, 84-89. *Mem:* Am Optical Soc; Inst Elec & Electronics Engrs. *Res:* Diatomic molecular spectroscopy, gas laser research, laser mode control and diffractionoptics for high energy lasers, tunable electro-optical infrared filters. *Mailing Add:* 1446 NW First St Bend OR 97701

JANOS, DAVID PAUL, TROPICAL PLANT ECOLOGY, MYCORRHIZAE. *Current Pos:* asst prof, 79-84, ASSOC PROF BIOL, UNIV MIAMI, 84- *Personal Data:* b Chicago, Ill, Nov 24, 47. *Educ:* Carleton Col, BA, 69; Univ Mich, Ann Arbor, MS, 71, PhD(bot), 75. *Prof Exp:* Herbarium asst trop bot, Field Mus Natural Hist, 70; fel, Smithsonian Trop Res Inst, 76-79. *Concurrent Pos:* Field sta mgr, Orgn Trop Studies, Inc, 75; mem, Nat Acad Sci-Nat Res Coun Comt Selected Biol Probs Humid Trop, 80-81; counr, Asn Trop Biol, 92-93. *Mem:* Mycol Soc Am; Asn Trop Biol; Sigma Xi; Ecol Soc Am; Orgn Trop Studies (secy, 82-83); Int Soc Trop Foresters. *Res:* Evolutionary ecology of mutualistic associations, and the influences of mutualistic root associations on plant community composition and dynamics, especially those of vesicular-arbuscular mycorrhizae in the tropics. *Mailing Add:* Dept Biol Univ Miami PO Box 248106 Miami FL 33124-8106. *Fax:* 305-284-3039; *E-Mail:* djanos@umiami.ir.miami.edu

JANOS, LUDVIK, MATHEMATICS. *Current Pos:* FAC, DEPT MATH, KENT STATE UNIV. *Personal Data:* b Brno, Czech, Oct 3, 22. *Educ:* Charles Univ, Prague, Dr rer nat(math), 50. *Prof Exp:* Mathematician, Res Inst, Prague, 50-63; vis assoc prof math, George Washington Univ, 63-65; assoc prof, Dalhousie Univ, 65-66; vis assoc prof, Univ Fla, 66-69, assoc prof, 69-74; vis prof, Univ Mont, Missoula, 74-75; assoc prof math, Wash State Univ, 75-77; assoc ed, Math Rev, Univ Mich, 77-80; res prof, Univ Md, 80-86; assoc prof math, Calif State Univ, Long Beach, 86-; fac mem, Univ Karlovy. *Mem:* Am Math Soc. *Res:* Functional analysis applied to the theory of differential equations; theory of fixed points; general topology; mathematical statistics; algebraic topology applied to digital geometry and pattern recognition; mathematical logic; algebraic topology applied to dynamical systems; Ergodic theory; partial differential theory; dimension theory. *Mailing Add:* Dept Math Kent State Univ Kent OH 44242-0001

JANOS, WILLIAM AUGUSTUS, PHYSICS, INFORMATION SCIENCE, ELECTROMAGNETIC MATERIALS. *Current Pos:* CONSULT, ELECTROMAGNETIC MATERIALS, 92- *Personal Data:* b Easton, Pa, Nov 9, 26; m 59, Charlene Kieth. *Educ:* Rutgers Univ, BS, 51; Univ Calif, Berkeley, MA, 54, PhD(physics), 58. *Prof Exp:* Res physicist, Convair Astronaut Div, Gen Dynamics Corp, 58-60; staff physicist, Res Div & Advan Develop Lab, Raytheon Co, 60-63; sr tech specialist, NAm Space & Info Systs Div, 63-66; prin scientist, Philco-Ford Aeronutronic Appl Res Lab, 66-67; sr staff physicist, Missile Syst Div Labs, Raytheon Co, 67; sr scientist, Technic Serv Corp, 67-74; sr staff engr, McDonnell Douglas Astronautics Co, 74-78; prin electronics engr, Interstate Electronics Corp, 78-84; staff consult, Aerojet Gen Corp, 84-; staff specialist, Rockwell Int, 84-92. *Concurrent Pos:* USAEC del, Int Conf Controlled Thermonuclear Fusion, 61; US del, Plasma Physics Symp, Int Union Pure & Appl Chem, USSR, 81. *Mem:* Sigma Xi; Am Phys Soc; Inst Elec & Electronics Engrs; Am Asn Advan Sci. *Res:* Statistical physics and electromagnetics of Boltzmann and Fokker-Planck equations; Wiener-Hopf integral equations of statistical communications and information theory; systems analysis; phenomenology hydrodynamics; analytical modeling of physical systems, sensors and signal processing; mathematical physics; statistical optics. *Mailing Add:* 8381 Snowbird Dr Huntington Beach CA 92646

JANOVY, JOHN, JR, ZOOLOGY. *Current Pos:* assoc prof, 66-74, PROF ZOOL, 74-, ASST DEAN ARTS & SCI, DEPT LIFE SCI, UNIV NEBR, LINCOLN, 66- *Personal Data:* b Houma, La, Dec 27, 37; m 61; c 3. *Educ:* Univ Okla, BS, 59, MS, 62, PhD(zool), 65. *Prof Exp:* Trainee, Rutgers Univ, 65-66. *Mem:* Am Soc Trop Med & Hyg; Am Soc Parasitol. *Res:* Epidemiology of parasitic protozoa; comparative metabolism and evolution and of parasitic flagellates. *Mailing Add:* Sch Biol Sci 345 Manter Univ Nebr PO Box 880118 Lincoln NE 68588-0118

JANOWITZ, GERALD S(AUL), FLUID MECHANICS. *Current Pos:* assoc prof oceanog, 75-80, PROF MARINE SCI, NC STATE UNIV, 80- *Personal Data:* b Bronx, NY, Apr 5, 43; m 68, Barbara Kantrowitz; c David. *Educ:* Polytech Inst Brooklyn, BS, 63; Johns Hopkins Univ, MS, 65, PhD(mech), 67. *Prof Exp:* Fel mech, Johns Hopkins Univ, 67-68; asst prof fluid mech, Case Western Res Univ, 68-75. *Mem:* Am Geophys Union. *Res:* Geophysical fluid mechanics; motion of bodies through stratified fluids; flows in lakes, ocean basins, and the coastal boundary layers. *Mailing Add:* 116 Buckden Pl Cary NC 27511. *Fax:* 919-515-7802

JANOWITZ, HENRY DAVID, GASTROENTEROLOGY. *Current Pos:* asst gastroenterol, Mt Sinai Sch Med, 50-54, chief Gastro-Intestinal Clin, 56-62, dir NIH Training Prog Gastroenterol, 59-75, head, Div Gastroenterol, 56-83, EMER PROF, MT SINAI SCH MED, 83- *Personal Data:* b Paterson, NJ, Mar 23, 15; m 42; c Anna & Mary. *Educ:* Columbia Univ, AB, 35, MD, 39, Univ Ill, MS, 49. *Honors & Awards:* Friedenwald Metal, Am Gastroenterol Asn, 84, Master Gastroenterol, 94; Lifetime Clin Achievement Award, Am Col Gastroenterol, 94. *Prof Exp:* Intern, Mt Sinai Hosp, 39-41, fel path, 46, resident med, 47-48, asst physiol, Univ Ill, 48-49. *Concurrent Pos:* Hon lectr, Guy's Hosp, London, Eng, 56; McArthur lectr, Univ Edinburgh, 56; ed, Am J Digestive Dis, 56-65; asst clin prof med, Columbia Univ, 62-66; ed sect alimentary canal, Handbook Physiol, 65; Comfort Mem lectr, Mayo Found, 65; mem, Am Bd Gastroenterol, 65, chmn gastroenterol res group steering comt, 65; mem prog proj comt, Nat Inst Arthritis & Metab Dis, 65, chmn, 70; clin prof, Mt Sinai Sch Med, 66-85; consult, Bronx Vet Admin Hosp, Horton Hosp, Middletown, NY & Englewood Hosp, NJ; pvt pract. *Mem:* Am Physiol Soc; Soc Exp Biol & Med; Am Soc Clin Investrs; Am Gastroenterol Asn (pres, 72); Asn Am Physicians; hon mem Brit Gastroenterol Soc; hon fel Royal Soc Med. *Res:* Clinical investigation in gastroenterology, especially of the natural history and therapy of inflammatory bowel disease. *Mailing Add:* Div Gastroenterol Mt Sinai Sch Med 11 E 100th St New York NY 10029

JANOWITZ, MELVIN FIVA, ALGEBRA, CLUSTER ANALYSIS. *Current Pos:* assoc prof, 67-70, asst dean, Natural Sci & Math, 79-83, PROF MATH, UNIV MASS, AMHERST, 70- *Personal Data:* b Minneapolis, Minn, May 8, 29; m; c 3. *Educ:* Univ Minn, BA, 50; Wayne State Univ, PhD(math), 63. *Prof Exp:* Asst prof math, Univ NMex, 63-66; assoc prof, Western Mich Univ, 66-67. *Mem:* Am Math Soc; Math Asn Am; Classification Soc. *Res:* Lattice theory; mathematical models for ordinal cluster analysis; ordinal models for semiorders, internal orders and social choice functions; connections between percentile based cluster techniques and probabilistic metric spheres. *Mailing Add:* Dept Math & Statist Univ Mass Leder le Grand Res Ctr Box 34515 Amherst MA 01003-0113

JANOWSKI, GREGG MICHAEL, MATERIALS CHARACTERIZATION, COMPOSITE MATERIALS. *Current Pos:* asst prof, 90-96, ASSOC PROF MAT & MECH ENG, UNIV ALA, BIRMINGHAM, 96- *Personal Data:* b Bay City, Mich, Jan 23, 61; m 88, Karen Banasiak. *Educ:* Mich Technol Univ, BS, 83, MS, 85, PhD(metall eng), 88. *Prof Exp:* Nat Res Coun assoc, Metall Div, Nat Inst Stand & Technol, 88-90. *Mem:* Am Soc Mat Int; Am Inst Mining & Metals Engrs. *Res:* Structure, property and processing relationships in metals and composite materials; electron microscopy; powder processing; aluminum alloys. *Mailing Add:* Univ Ala Birmingham AL 35294-4461

JANOWSKY, DAVID STEFFAN, PSYCHOPHARMACOLOGY. *Current Pos:* chief, Vet Admin Liaison Serv, 73-74, assoc prof, 73-76, PROF, DEPT PSYCHIAT, SCH MED, UNIV CALIF, SAN DIEGO, 76- *Personal Data:* b San Diego, Calif, June 24, 39; m 62; c 4. *Educ:* Univ Calif, San Francisco, BS, 61, MD, 64. *Prof Exp:* Asst prof, Dept Psychiat, Sch Med, Univ Calif, Los Angeles, 69-70; head physician, Crisis Clin, Psychiat Emergency Serv, Dept Psychiat, Harbor Gen Hosp, Calif, 69-70; asst prof pharmacol, Sch Med, Vanderbilt Univ, 70-73, asst prof psychiat, 70-72, assoc prof, 72-73. *Concurrent Pos:* Chief psychiat serv, Univ Hosp, Univ Calif, San Diego, 74-78, prin investr, Ment Health Clin Res Ctr, NIMH, Univ Calif, San Diego; prof & chair, Dept Psychiat, Univ NC Chapel Hill, 86-94, prof, 94-96. *Mem:* Am Col Neuropsychopharmacol; Am Psychiat Asn; Psychiat Res Soc; Soc Neurosci; Col Int Neuropsychopharmacol. *Res:* Effects of adrenergic-cholinergic balance in the affective disorders, using cholinesterase inhibitors and psychostimulant challenges as investigative probes, and correlating these results with pre-clinical animal models. *Mailing Add:* Psychiat Dept CB No 7175 Med Sch Bldg A/U NC Chapel Hill NC 27599. *Fax:* 919-966-0259

JANS, JAMES PATRICK, MATHEMATICS. *Current Pos:* asst prof, 57-64, PROF MATH, UNIV WASH, 64- *Personal Data:* b Detroit, Mich, Apr 6, 27; m 50; c 2. *Educ:* Univ Mich, AB, 49, MA, 50, PhD(math), 55. *Prof Exp:* Jr instr math, Univ Mich, 53-54; instr, Yale Univ, 54-56; asst prof, Ohio State Univ, 56-57. *Mem:* Am Math Soc. *Res:* Algebra; structure of rings; homological and topological algebra. *Mailing Add:* Dept Math Univ Wash Seattle WA 98195-0001

JANSEN, BERNARD JOSEPH, MATHEMATICS, SOFTWARE. *Current Pos:* RETIRED. *Personal Data:* b Rockville, Minn, Aug 10, 27; m 55, S Kathryn Knight; c Kathryn, Bernard Jr, Stephen & David. *Educ:* St John's Univ, Minn, BA, 50; St Louis Univ, MA, 52. *Prof Exp:* Instr math, St John's Univ, Minn, 54-56; comput analyst prog, Unisys, 55-66, mgr Titan III software, 66-69, avionics software, 69-75, systs & software, Int Systs Div, 76-77, planning, control & change proposals, Int Telecommun Div, 77-82, underseas proj mgr, 82-85, mgr syst scheduling & planning, Comput Systs Div, Unisys Defense Systs, 85-88. *Concurrent Pos:* Mem adv panel, Spaceborne Digital Comput Systs, NASA, 68-80; instr math, Univ Wis, River Falls, 90. *Mem:* Math Asn Am; Sigma Xi. *Res:* Technical management of application of computers to systems and software in the underseas, avionics, aerospace, command and control and telecommunications fields. *Mailing Add:* 848 Ivy Lane Eagan MN 55123-2425

JANSEN, FRANK, THIN FILM TECHNOLOGY, ELECTRONIC FABRICATION PROCESSES. *Current Pos:* DIR TECHNOL, BOC COATING TECHNOL, 94- *Personal Data:* b Emmeloord, Neth, Feb 9, 46; m 73; c 3. *Educ:* Tech Univ Delft, ingenieur, 73; Case Western Res Univ, PhD(physics), 77. *Prof Exp:* Tech specialist, Webster Res Ctr, Xerox Corp, 77-80, proj mgr & mem res staff, 80-86, prin scientist, 86-90; mgr, Thin Film

Technologies, BOC Group, 90-92, mgr, Tech Found Group, 92-94. *Concurrent Pos:* Lectr, Am Vacuum Soc, 88-; chmn, Thin Film Div, Am Vacuum Soc, 89, prog chmn, 90. *Mem:* Am Vacuum Soc. *Res:* Management of thin film and vacuum technology; development of industrial coating processes for glass and plastic. *Mailing Add:* BOC Coating Technol 4020 Pike Lane Concord CA 94524. *Fax:* 510-674-9419; *E-Mail:* frank.jansen@us.bocct.boc.com

JANSEN, GEORGE, JR, CHEMICAL ENGINEERING. *Current Pos:* ANALYSIS ENGR, BATTELLE MEM INST, 81- *Personal Data:* b Aloha, Ore, Nov 15, 34; m 56; c 4. *Educ:* Ore State Univ, BS & BA, 55; Mass Inst Technol, SM, 57, ScD(chem eng), 59. *Prof Exp:* Chem engr, Hanford Labs, Gen Elec Co, Wash, 59-62, sr engr, 62-65; sr develop engr, Battelle-Northwest, 65-68, res assoc, 68-75; sr engr, Exxon Nuclear Co, Inc, 75-81. *Mem:* AAAS; Am Chem Soc; Am Inst Chem Engrs; Am Nuclear Soc. *Res:* Ion exchange; heat transfer; process development in nuclear fuel processing; solvent extraction; radioactive waste disposal; risk analysis; centrifuge enrichment. *Mailing Add:* 18365 SW Sandra Lane Beaverton OR 97006

JANSEN, GEORGE JAMES, MINERALOGY. *Current Pos:* PRIN, ROCKY MOUNTAIN CONSULT PETROG, 78- *Personal Data:* b Canton, Ohio, Apr 22, 25; m 53, 71, Marjorie Molloy; c George & Kenneth. *Educ:* Univ Notre Dame, BS, 51; Bryn Mawr Col, MA, 52. *Prof Exp:* Hydrol field asst, US Geol Surv, 51, geologist, 52-57; prin geologist, Battelle Mem Inst, 57; supvr mineral & metallog, Res Ctr, Repub Steel Corp, Ohio, 57-69; mineralogist, Climax Molybdenum Club, 69-76; mineralogist, Com Test & Eng Co, 76-78. *Mem:* Soc Econ Geologists. *Res:* Mineralogy of base metals; quantitative metallography; reflected light optics; coal petrography. *Mailing Add:* 12870 W 15th Dr Golden CO 80401

JANSEN, GUSTAV RICHARD, NUTRITION. *Current Pos:* prof & dept head, 69-90, EMER PROF FOOD SCI & NUTRIT, COLO STATE UNIV, 90- *Personal Data:* b Staten Island, NY, May 19, 30; m 53; c 4. *Educ:* Cornell Univ, BA, 50, PhD(biochem), 58. *Honors & Awards:* Cert of Merit, USDA, 83; Babcock-Hart Award, Inst Food Technologists, 85. *Prof Exp:* Jr & assoc chemist, Am Cyanamid Co, 53-54; asst biochem, Cornell Univ, 54-58; res chemist, E I du Pont de Nemours & Co, 58-62; res fel, Merck Inst Therapeut Res, 62-69. *Concurrent Pos:* Prog mgr, USDA, competition grants prog human nutrit, 81-82; mem, exec comt, Inst Food Technol, 89-91, Human Nutrit Bd Sci Counselors, USDA, 86-92, comt mil nutrit res, Inst Med, Nat Acad Sci. *Mem:* Am Inst Nutrit; Am Soc Biochem & Molecular Biol; AAAS; fel Inst Food Technologists; Sigma Xi. *Res:* Protein nutrition; processed weaning foods; nutrition during lactation; nutrition education. *Mailing Add:* 1804 Seminole Dr Ft Collins CO 80525

JANSEN, HENRICUS CORNELIS, RANGE MANAGEMENT. *Current Pos:* from asst prof to assoc prof, 76-86, PROF RANGE MGT, CALIF STATE UNIV, CHICO, 86- *Personal Data:* b Bergen op Zoom, Holland, Aug 3, 42; US citizen; m 77. *Educ:* Univ Calif, Berkeley, BS, 69, PhD(natural res sci & range mgt), 74. *Prof Exp:* Res forester range mgt, Pac Southwest Forest & Range Exp Sta, US Forest Serv, 72-76. *Concurrent Pos:* Consult range conservationist, Soil Conserv Serv, 79 & Bur Land Mgt, 81; botanist, Fish & Wildlife Serv, 80; range mgt expert, UN Food & Agr Orgn, 84-85. *Mem:* Soc Range Mgt; AAAS. *Res:* Computerized planning method including documentation for the management of federal grazing lands; grazing management of arid lands in North Africa. *Mailing Add:* Dept Agr Calif State Univ First & Normal Sts Chico CA 95929

JANSEN, IVAN JOHN, agronomy, soil science; deceased, see previous edition for last biography

JANSEN, MICHAEL, QUANTUM ELECTRONICS, SEMICONDUCTOR LASERS. *Current Pos:* VPRES RES & DEVELOP, APT, 95- *Personal Data:* b Bucharest, Romania, Jan 27, 56; m 84; c 2. *Educ:* Univ Calif Los Angeles, BS, 78, MS, 79, PhD(quantum electronics), 84. *Prof Exp:* Teaching asst & assoc optics, quantum electronics & electronics, UCLA, 80-83, res assoc, 83-84; sr scientist, Space & Technol Group, Advan Technol Div, Res Ctr, TRW, 84- *Concurrent Pos:* Consult, Monosolar Industs, 80-81; lectr, Elec Eng Dept, Univ Calif Los Angeles, 85-86. *Mem:* Inst Elec & Electronics Engrs. *Res:* Design, development, and characterization of diode lasers and integrated optics; development of monolithic two-dimensional, coherent and incoherent surface-emitting arrays; monolithic components for optical integration; large optical cavity and evanescently-coupled and diffraction-coupled laser arrays; unstable resonators, amplifiers, and LEDs. *Mailing Add:* Coherent Inc 5100 Patrick Henry Dr Santa Clara CA 95054

JANSEN, ROBERT BRUCE, CIVIL ENGINEERING, ENGINEERING OF DAMS. *Current Pos:* CONSULT CIVIL ENG, 80- *Personal Data:* b Spokane, Wash, Dec 14, 22; m 43, Barbara M Courtney. *Educ:* Univ Denver, BSCE, 49; Univ SCalif, MSCE, 55. *Prof Exp:* Chief, Calif Div Dam Safety, 65-68; chief oper, Calif Dept Water Resources, 68-71, dept dir, 71-75, chief design & cons, 75-77; asst comnr, US Bus Reclamation, 77-80. *Concurrent Pos:* mem, US Comt Large Dams, chmn, 79-81; mem Water Sci & Technol Bd, Nat Acad Eng, 82-84; chmn, Nat Comt Safety Dams, Nat Res Coun, 81-83. *Mem:* Nat Acad Eng; Am Soc Civil Engrs. *Res:* Response of dams to earthquake, flood and leakage; methods of dam rehabilitation. *Mailing Add:* 509 Briar Rd Bellingham WA 98225

JANSEN, ROBERT WERNER, RADAR SCATTERING, OCEAN PHYSICS. *Current Pos:* RES PHYSICIST, NAVAL RES LAB, 91- *Educ:* Mankato State Univ, BS, 81; Ariz State Univ, PhD(theoret solid state physics), 87. *Prof Exp:* Res assoc, Nat Res Coun, 87-89; res scientist, Dynamics Technol Inc, 89-91. *Mem:* Sigma Xi; Am Phys Soc. *Res:* Predictions of defect formation, migration and energetics in semiconductors; wave propagation in the ocean and radar scattering from the ocean waves. *Mailing Add:* 700 Seventh St SW No 408 Washington DC 20024. *E-Mail:* jansen@imsy1.nrl.navy.mil

JANSING, JO ANN, ANALYTICAL CHEMISTRY. *Current Pos:* from asst prof to assoc prof, Ind Univ Southeast, 70-81, chair, Div Natural Sci, 79-86, PROF CHEM, IND UNIV SOUTHEAST, 81-, COORDR CHEM, 76-79, 89- *Personal Data:* b Louisville, Ky, Mar 23, 38. *Educ:* Ursuline Col, Ky, BA, 65; Fordham Univ, MS, 67, PhD(anal & phys chem), 70. *Prof Exp:* Teacher high sch, Ky, 62-65; instr chem, Mt St Agnes Col, 69-70. *Mem:* Am Chem Soc; Sigma Xi. *Res:* X-ray crystallographic structure studies of organic molecules. *Mailing Add:* Ind Univ SE 4201 Grantline Rd New Albany IN 47150

JANSKI, ALVIN MICHAEL, BIOCHEMISTRY. *Current Pos:* DIR LIFE SCI, PITMAN-MOORE INC, 86- *Personal Data:* b Braham, Minn, May 27, 49; m 71; c 2. *Educ:* St Cloud State Univ, Minn, BA, 71; NDak State Univ, PhD(biochem), 75. *Prof Exp:* Res assoc, Dept Biochem & Biophys, Iowa State Univ, 75-78, NIH fel, 78; sr staff fel, Lab Metab, Nat Inst Alcohol Abuse & Alcoholism, 78-81; mgr, Biochem Res Sect, Int Minerals & Chem Corp, 81-86. *Concurrent Pos:* Prin investr, Int Minerals & Chem Corp, Northbrook, Ill, 81- *Mem:* Am Soc Biol Chemists; NY Acad Sci; Am Chem Soc; AAAS; Endocrine Soc. *Res:* Protein vaccines by recombinant DNA technology; metabolic pathways through intracellular compartmentation of metabolites and enzymes and hormone-depedent phosphorylation of enzymes; in vitro study of growth. *Mailing Add:* 14473 Brittanius Dr 675 McDonnell Blvd Chesterfield MO 63017-8035

JANSON, BLAIR F, PLANT PATHOLOGY. *Current Pos:* Asst exten plant pathologist, Ohio State Univ, 46, asst instr bot, 47-50, exten plant pathologist, 50-80, prof plant path, 62-80, EMER PROF PLANT PATH, OHIO STATE UNIV, 80- *Personal Data:* b East Trumbull, Ohio, Jan 6, 18; m 44; c 3. *Educ:* Ohio State Univ, BS, 40, MS, 47, PhD, 50. *Mem:* Am Phytopath Soc. *Res:* Ornamental, fruit, cereal and forage crop diseases. *Mailing Add:* 266 Canyon Dr Columbus OH 43214

JANSONS, VILMA KARINA, MICROBIOLOGY. *Current Pos:* asst prof microbiol, 72-77, ASSOC PROF MICROBIOL, NJ MED SCH, UNIV MED & DENT NJ, 77- *Personal Data:* b Riga, Latvia; US citizen. *Educ:* Brooklyn Col, BA, 61; Rutgers Univ, New Brunswick, PhD(microbiol), 67. *Prof Exp:* Lectr biol, Princeton Univ, 68-70, mem res staff biochem sci, 70-72. *Mem:* AAAS; Am Soc Microbiol; Am Soc Cell Biol. *Res:* Surface properties of normal and malignant cells; biochemistry of morphogenesis. *Mailing Add:* Dept Microbiol & Molecular Genetics NJ Med Sch 185 S Orange Ave Newark NJ 07103-2714

JANSSEN, FRANK WALTER, DRUG METABOLISM. *Current Pos:* RETIRED. *Personal Data:* b St Paul, Minn, Sept 10, 26; m 52; c 2. *Educ:* Col St Thomas, BS, 50; Iowa State Univ, MS, 52. *Prof Exp:* Asst scientist biochem, Hormel Inst, Univ Minn, 52-61; res scientist protein chem, Wyeth Labs, Inc, 61-66, sr res scientist & group leader drug metab, 66-78, supvr, Pharmacokinetic Eval Unit, 78-85, mgr, Drug Disposition Sect, 85-96. *Mem:* Sigma Xi. *Res:* Drug disposition; biotransformation and pharmacokinetics of drugs. *Mailing Add:* 309 Westbrook Dr Westchester PA 19382

JANSSEN, JERRY FREDERICK, ORGANIC CHEMISTRY. *Current Pos:* SR PATENT ATTY, ABBOTT LABS, 89-; PATENT COUN, ELI LILLY & CO. *Personal Data:* b Mason City, Iowa, Mar 22, 36; m 84, Carol J Leybourn; c Susan E & Eric P. *Educ:* Iowa State Teachers Col, BA, 57, MA, 59; Mich State Univ, PhD(chem), 67; JD, Suffolk Univ, 83. *Prof Exp:* Instr sci & math, Mason City Jr Col, Iowa, 59-61; asst prof chem, Antioch Col, 66-69; from asst prof to assoc prof, Eisenhower Col, 69-74; sr environ engr, GTE Sylvania, Inc, Seneca Falls, NY, 74-77, chem patent agent, GTE Serv Corp, 77-83; sr patent atty, Parke-Davis/Warner-Lambert, 83-88 & BASF, 88-89. *Concurrent Pos:* Consult, Vernay Labs, Ohio, 68-69; Sylvania Elec Prod, Inc, NY, 69-70 & Inst Chem Washtenaw Comm Col, 85-87. *Mem:* Am Chem Soc; fel Am Inst Chem; Am Bar Asn; Am Intellectual Property Law Asn. *Res:* Organic reaction mechanisms; molecular photochemistry; rearrangement reactions of aromatic compounds. *Mailing Add:* Eli Lilly & Co DC1111 Lilly Corp Ctr Indianapolis IN 46285

JANSSEN, MICHAEL ALLEN, RADIO ASTRONOMY, PLANETARY SCIENCES. *Current Pos:* Nat Res Coun resident res assoc planetary radio astron, 72-74, sr scientist, 74-76, MEM TECH STAFF, JET PROPULSION LAB, CALIF INST TECHNOL, 76-, ASST DIV MGR-DIV 32, 97- *Personal Data:* b Boise, Idaho, Sept 30, 37; m; c 2. *Educ:* Univ Calif, AB, 63, PhD(atmospheric & space sci), 72. *Prof Exp:* Physicist, Lawrence Radiation Lab, 63-67. *Concurrent Pos:* Prin investr, Microwave Atmospheric Exp, Venus Orbiting Imaging Radar Mission, partic scientist, cosmic background explorer. *Mem:* Int Union Radio Sci; Am Astron Soc; Am Geophys Union; Int Astron Union. *Res:* Development of radio interferometric techniques at millimeter wavelengths; investigation of the atmospheres of Venus and the outer planets by microwave techniques; spacecraft microwave radiometry; cosmic microwave background; microwave remote sensing. *Mailing Add:* MS 169-506 Jet Propulsion Lab 4800 Oak Grove Dr Pasadena CA 91109-8099

JANSSEN, PAUL ADRIAAN JAN, PHARMACY, PSYCHIATRY. *Current Pos:* pres & dir res, 58-91, HON CHMN & BD DIR, JANSSEN PHARMACEUT NV, BELG, 91-; CHMN, JANSSEN RES FOUND WORLDWIDE, 87- *Personal Data:* b Turnhout, Belg, Sept 12, 26; m 57, Dora Arts; c Graziella, Herwig, Yasmine, Pablo & Maroussia. *Educ:* Fac Notre Dame de la Paix, BSc, 45; State Univ Ghent, Belg, MD, 51. *Hon Degrees:* Numerous from foreign univs, 78-96. *Honors & Awards:* Carl Wilhelm Scheele Prize, Pharmaceut Soc Sweden, 65; Adriaan Stevens Prize, Flemish Chem Soc, 78; Award in Med Chem, Am Chem Soc, 84, Carothers Award, 90; Quinquennial Prize Pharmaceut & Therapeut Sci, Belg Royal Acad Med, 84; Chauncey D Leake Award, Univ Calif, San Francisco, 86; Baggesgaard Lectr, Copenhagen, 86; Discoverer's Award, Pharmaceut Mfrs Asn, 87; Eleventh Ann E M Papper Lectr, Univ Columbia, 88; Rovenstine Lectr, NY State Soc Anaesthesiologists, 88; Bernard H Eliasberg Medal, Mt Sinai Sch Med, 88; Dirk van Os Medal, Groningen Univ Fund Found, 89; Jacob Henle Medal, Georg-August Univ, Ger, 90; Golden Jaroslav Heyrovsky Medal, Czech Acad Sci, 90; Distinguished Serv Award, Am Col Clin Pharmacol, 90; Pioneer in Sci Award, Nat Alliance Ment Ill, 95; Pharmaceut Discoverer's Award, Nat Alliance Res Schizophrenia & Depression, 96. *Prof Exp:* Asst, Inst Pharmacol & Therapeut, State Univ Ghent, Belg, 50-56, Inst Pharmacol, Univ Cologne, Ger, 51-52; researcher, NV Produkten Richter, Belg, 53-57. *Concurrent Pos:* Lectr psychiat, Univ Liege, Belg, 66; prof med chem, Liege Notre Dame de la Paix, Namur, Belg, 73-74; vchmn, Johnson & Johnson Int, 79-91; pres, Collegium Int Neuro-Psychopharm, 80-82; vis prof med sci, King's Col, Univ London, 82-83; mem, Belg Nat Coun Mgt Sci, 84-87 & Flemish Coun Mgt Sci, 84-; vis prof, Sch Pharmaceut Sci, 87-88; vis prof, Inst Pharmacol Sci, Cath Univ Louvain, 87-88, extraordinary prof, 88-91; hon prof, Peking Union Med Col, China, 90, Chinese PLA Gen Hosp, 92, Stanford Univ, 93; consult prof dermat, Stanford Univ, 94-96. *Mem:* Hon fel Royal Acad Med Ireland; hon fel Col Med SAfrica; fel Royal Soc Med London; Am Chem Soc; Europ Soc Study Drug Toxicity; fel AAAS; Am Col Neuropsychopharmacol; corresp mem Royal Soc Sci Liege; hon mem NAm Clin Dermat Soc; NY Acad Sci; Col Int Med Psychosomaticae; Belg Col Neuropsychopharm & Biol Psychiat; Belg Royal Acad Med. *Res:* Author of over 828 scientific publications and granted over 100 patents as inventor of several drugs. *Mailing Add:* Janssen Pharmaceut Turnhoutseweg 30 Beerse B2340 Belgium

JANSSEN, RICHARD WILLIAM, PHARMACEUTICAL CHEMISTRY, QUALITY ASSURANCE. *Current Pos:* sect head, E R Squibb, 87-90, SR RES INVESTR, BRISTOL MEYERS SQUIBB, 90- *Personal Data:* b Weehawken, NJ, June 22, 40; m 68, Patricia Ware; c William & Jonathan. *Educ:* Ferris State Col, BS, 62; Rutgers Univ, MS, 66, PhD(pharmaceut chem), 69. *Prof Exp:* Sr anal chemist, Smith, Kline & French Labs, 69-71; sr res scientist, Lescarden Ltd, 71-75; group leader, William H Rorer Inc, 75-87. *Mem:* Am Pharmaceut Asn; Am Chem Soc. *Res:* Research and development documentation; GMP review quality assurance; pharmaceutics research and development. *Mailing Add:* Bristol-Myers Squibb Pharmaceut Res Inst One Squibb Dr Box 191 New Brunswick NJ 08903-0191

JANSSEN, ROBERT (JAMES) J, VIROLOGY, IMMUNOLOGY. *Current Pos:* asst prof, 61-67, assoc prof, 67-80, PROF MICROBIOL & MED TECHNOL, UNIV ARIZ, 80- *Personal Data:* b Geneva, Ill, Feb 28, 31; m 57; c 2. *Educ:* Cornell Col, BA, 53; State Univ Iowa, MS, 55, PhD(bact), 57. *Prof Exp:* Med bacteriologist virol, Biol Labs, US Army Chem Corps, Md, 57-61. *Mem:* Sigma Xi; Am Soc Microbiol. *Res:* Smallpox, influenza, enteroviruses, arborviruses; combined infections with two or more microbial agents; aerobiology studies with viral agents; serological techniques; effects of certain drugs on viral infections. *Mailing Add:* Dept Microbiol Immunol Univ Ariz Tucson AZ 85721

JANSSENS, THOMAS J, TEACHING MATHEMATICS & ASTRONOMY. *Current Pos:* ASST PROF MATH & ASTRON, CALIF LUTHERAN UNIV, 89- *Personal Data:* b Los Angeles, Calif, Oct 23, 31; m 85, Sadie M Williams; c Denise, Andrea, David & Karen. *Educ:* Calif Inst Technol, BS, 53; Stanford Univ, MS, 61, PhD(physics), 64. *Prof Exp:* Asst prof physics, Loyola Col, Montreal, Can, 64-65; mem tech staff, Aerospace Corp, 65-89. *Concurrent Pos:* Prin investr, Proj Sunwatch, 67; lectr physics, Calif State Univ, Long Beach, 68-89; spec lectr, Soc Photo-optic Instrument Engrs, 88-89. *Mem:* Fel NSF; Astron Soc Pac. *Res:* Optical and radio emissions from solar flares; track initiation of space objects from angles-only data from 2 or 3 optical sensors. *Mailing Add:* 1321 Hendrix Ave Thousand Oaks CA 91360

JANSSON, BIRGER, BIOMATHEMATICS, EPIDEMIOLOGY. *Current Pos:* biomathematician, Nat Large Bowel Cancer Proj, 73-84, prof, 73-93, EMER PROF BIOMATH, UNIV TEX M D ANDERSON CANCER CTR, 94- *Personal Data:* b Stockholm, Sweden, Sept 4, 21; m 54, Gunhild Brunk; c Jenny, Pehr, Erik & Gustav. *Educ:* Univ Stockholm, FilKand, 46, FilLic, 65, FilDr(math statist), 66. *Hon Degrees:* Docent, Univ Stockholm, 67. *Prof Exp:* Head res math sci, Res Inst Nat Defense, Stockholm, Sweden, 48-73. *Concurrent Pos:* Consult mathematician, Swed Money Lottery, Stockholm, 66-73; consult biomath, Tumor Biol, Karolinska Inst, 66-73; Eleanor Roosevelt fel, Int Union Against Cancer, 70; vis assoc prof, Univ Tex, Houston, 70-71; assoc ed, Math Biosci, 74-87; adj prof, Rice Univ, 74-; pres, Texas Swed Cult Found, 81-; vchmn, Swed Coun Am, 87- *Mem:* AAAS; Soc Environ Geochem & Health; Int Soc Prev Oncol; Am Soc Prev Oncol; European Inst Ecol & Cancer. *Res:* Cancer, epidemiology and prevention, especially cancer of the colon, rectum, stomach and breast; mathematical models of the cell cycle and their use for finding rational protocols for cancer treatment. *Mailing Add:* 8211 S Braeswood Blvd Houston TX 77071. *Fax:* 713-792-4262

JANSSON, CARL RICHARD ERLAND, PROCESS DEVELOPMENT WATER & WASTEWATER, HAZARDOUS WASTES. *Current Pos:* PRES & SR ENVIRON SCIENTIST, JANSSON CONSULT SERV, INC, 83- *Personal Data:* b Canwood, Sask, Apr 17, 35; m, Erline Danaida Arndt. *Educ:* Univ Sask, BE, 60; Univ Waterloo, MASc, 70; Univ Wash, PhD(environ eng & sci), 89. *Prof Exp:* Agr engr, Alta Agr, 60-61; field rep, MacMilan Bloedel Ltd, 61-63; engr, Edinburgh, Scotland Trade & Com, Can, 64-65; instr technol, Sask Tech Inst, 65-69; environ engr, H A Simons, Int, Ltd, 70, Environ Can, 70-72; waste treat engr, Assoc Eng, 72-73; sr environ engr, Keith Consult Engrs, 73-82. *Mem:* Am Waterworks Asn; Water Environ Fedn; Am Chem Soc. *Res:* Utilization of persistant chlorine residuals to inactivate giardia lamblia consitive agent of giardiasis; development of advanced oxidation processes for destruction of taste and odor compounds in water and destruction of inorganic, organic toxic and hazardous materials in aqueous solutions. *Mailing Add:* Jansson Consult Serv 2323 Lorne St Regina SK S4P 2N1 Can. *Fax:* 306-359-3068

JANSSON, PETER ALLAN, OPTICAL PHYSICS, DIGITAL IMAGE PROCESSING. *Current Pos:* res physicist, E I DuPont de Nemours & Co, Inc, 68-71, sr res physicist, 71-76, res assoc, 76-80, sr res assoc, 80-90, RES FEL, DIGITAL IMAGE PROCESSING GROUP, EXP STA, E I DUPONT DE NEMOURS & CO, INC, 80- *Personal Data:* b Teaneck, NJ, May 20, 42; c 2. *Educ:* Stevens Inst Technol, BS, 64; Fla State Univ, PhD(physics), 68. *Prof Exp:* Instr & res asst, Infrared physics, Fla State Univ, 67-68. *Mem:* Int Neural Network Soc; fel Optical Soc Am; Soc Photog Instrumentation Engrs; Sigma Xi. *Res:* Optics; digital image processing and analysis; optical information processing; molecular spectroscopy; super resolving method of deconvolution; artificial neural networks. *Mailing Add:* Rm 213 Bldg 357 DuPont Exp Sta Wilmington DE 19898

JANSSON, RICHARD KEITH, INTEGRATED PEST MANAGEMENT & BIORATIONAL PEST CONTROL, DISCOVERY OF NOVEL BIORATIONAL PESTICIDES. *Current Pos:* SR RES FEL, MERCK & CO, 93- *Personal Data:* b New York, NY, July 8, 57; m 79, Carolyn V Helmich; c Keith H, Kari L & Kate E. *Educ:* Moravian Col, BS, 80; Pa State Univ, MS, 82, PhD(entom), 85. *Prof Exp:* Grad res & teaching asst, Pa State Univ, 81-85; res fel, Rutgers Univ, 85-86; asst prof entom, Univ Fla, 86-91, assoc prof, 91-93. *Concurrent Pos:* Adj assoc prof, Univ PR, 91-93, Rutgers Univ, 94- *Mem:* Entom Soc Am. *Res:* Discovery of novel biorational compounds for use in agricultural crop protection and development of resistance monitoring and management programs; development of biorational methods for managing temperate and tropical insect pests on vegetable crops. *Mailing Add:* Merck Res Labs PO Box 450 Hillsborough Rd Three Bridges NJ 08887. *Fax:* 908-369-8811

JANTZ, O K, ENTOMOLOGY, CROP PROTECTION. *Current Pos:* RETIRED. *Personal Data:* b Newton, Kans, June 16, 34; m 57, C June Whitney; c Tamara, Jodi & Preston. *Educ:* Kans State Univ, BS, 57, MS, 62; Ore State Univ, PhD(entom), 65. *Prof Exp:* Lab asst entom, Kans State Univ, 52-53; field aide, Agr Mkt Serv, USDA, Kans, 53-55, biol aide, 55-57, entomologist, 57; res asst entom, Kans State Univ, 60-63; res asst, Ore State Univ, 63-65; entomologist, Agr Res Serv, USDA, Mich, 65-67; regional tech specialist, Dow Chem, Mich, 67-68, mgr, Field Res Sta, Miss, 68-71, develop specialist, 71-73; mgr res & develop agr & spec prods, Dow Chem Pac Ltd, Hong Kong, 73-77, mgr, Tech Serv & Develop Plant Prod, Agr Prod Dept, 77-81 dir, agr prod develop & regist, 77-84, bus mgr agr herbicide, 84, dir res & develop, NAm Agr Prod, Dow Chem USA, 85-89, global dir res & develop opers, 89-91, Global Prod Develop Engr Insecticides, Dow Elanco, 92- *Concurrent Pos:* Mem bd dirs, Entom Soc Am Found. *Mem:* Entom Soc Am; Weed Sci Soc Am; Sigma Xi. *Res:* Field development of agricultural chemicals; forest insects; stored grain pests; field crop insects. *Mailing Add:* 230 Crestwood E Prescott AZ 86303-5355. *Fax:* 317-337-4966

JANUARY, LEWIS EDWARD, CARDIOLOGY. *Current Pos:* Jr intern, Univ Hosp, Univ Iowa, 37-38, from asst resident to resident internal med, 38-41, asst physician, 41-42, assoc chmn dept med, 73-80, from asst prof to prof, 46-80, EMER PROF MED, COL MED, UNIV IOWA, 80- *Personal Data:* b Haswell, Colo, Nov 14, 10; m 41; c 2. *Educ:* Colo Col, BA, 33; Univ Colo, MD, 37. *Hon Degrees:* DSc, Colo Col, 66. *Honors & Awards:* Honor Achievement Award, Angiol Res Found, 65; Distinguished Serv Citation, Coun Clin Cardiol, Am Heart Asn, 67, Gold Heart Award, Am Heart Asn, 69; Distinguished Serv Citation, Int-Soc Comn Heart Dis Resources, 71; Silver & Gold Award, Univ Colo, 71; Helen B Taussig Award, 72; Int Achievement Award, Am Heart Asn, 77, Citation Distinguished Serv to Int Cardiol, 78; Angel Award, Int soc Performing Arts Adminr Found, 90. *Concurrent Pos:* Chmn coun clin cardiol, Am Heart Asn, 61-63, fel coun clin cardiol; vchmn sect cardiovascular dis, AMA, 70-73; mem, Int-Soc Comn Heart Dis Resources; vis prof, Ain Shams Univ, Cairo, Egypt, 72; mem bd dirs, Joffrey Ballet, 74-; mem exec comt, Int Soc & Fedn Cardiol, 76-78. *Mem:* Am Heart Asn (vpres, 63-65, pres, 66-67); fel Am Col Cardiol; Asn Univ Cardiol; Inter-Am Soc Cardiol; Int Cardiol Fedn (vpres, 70-76). *Res:* Diabetes insipidus; mercurial diuretics; electrocardiography; hypertension; heart diseases. *Mailing Add:* 701 Oaknoll Dr Apt 508 Iowa City IA 52246

JANUS, ALAN ROBERT, SOLID STATE SCIENCE. *Current Pos:* PROJ MGR, NORTHROP, 84- *Personal Data:* b Utica, NY, Dec 27, 37; m 59, 70. *Educ:* Utica Col, BA, 59; Syracuse Univ, PhD(inorg chem), 64. *Prof Exp:* Lab technician qual control, Utica Drop Forge & Tool Co, 56-59; res chemist organometallic, Solvay Process Div, Allied Chem Corp, 60; sr chemist thin films, Sprague Elec Co, Mass, 63-66, assoc prog mgr ceramic develop, 66-68; asst prof, Roanoke Col, 68-70; mgr thin film eng, Electronic Mat Div, Bell & Howell Res Labs, 70-71, dir eng, 71-74; sr scientist, Hughes Aircraft, Calif 74-80 ; proj mgr, TRW, 80-84. *Concurrent Pos:* Res technician, Metals Div,

Kelsey Hayes Co, 58-59; consult, Am Safety Razor Div, Philip Morris Co, 68-70, Electron Tube Div, Int Tel & Tel, 68-70, Bell & Howell, 73-74, Nat Micrometrics, 74- & Optifilm, 75-; dir res, Bourne, 77-80. *Mem:* Am Vacuum Soc. *Res:* Thin film preparation and evaluation; magnetic susceptibilities; organometallic compound preparation and evaluation; coordination chemistry; chrome photoplates; III-IV compounds; ferrites; microanalytical services; surface acoustic wave device development; microwave hybrid device development. *Mailing Add:* 3625 W Hidden Lane Palos Verdes Peninsula CA 90274

JANUSEK, LINDA WITEK, NEONATAL SEPSIS, IMMUNE-ENDOCRINE INTERACTIONS. *Current Pos:* Asst prof, 78-84, assoc prof physiol & nursing, 84-93, ASSOC PROF MATERNAL CHILD HEALTH NURSING, LOYOLA UNIV, CHICAGO, 84- *Personal Data:* b La Salle, Ill, Jan 11, 52; m 75, Alan; c Alex, Marissa & Michael. *Educ:* Bradley Univ, BS, 74; Univ Ill, PhD(physiol), 78. *Honors & Awards:* Young Investr Award, Circulatory Shock Soc, 80. *Mem:* Am Physiol Soc; Circulatory Shock Soc; Fedn Am Soc Exp Biol. *Res:* Metabolic and hormonal responses of the neonate (rat model) to a septic insult; endocrine-immune interactions in the neonate-human. *Mailing Add:* Sch Nursing Loyola Univ Lake Shore Campus 6525 N Sheridan Rd Chicago IL 60626-5311

JANUSZ, GERALD JOSEPH, MATHEMATICS. *Current Pos:* PROF MATH, UNIV ILL, URBANA, 73- *Personal Data:* b Aug 20, 40; US citizen; m 61; c 2. *Educ:* Marquette Univ, BS, 62; Univ Wis, MS, 63; Univ Ore, PhD(math), 65. *Prof Exp:* Mem, Inst Advan Study, 65-66; instr math, Univ Chicago, 66-68; from asst prof to assoc prof, 68-73. *Concurrent Pos:* Exec ed, J Math Rev, 90- *Mem:* Am Math Soc; Math Asn Am. *Res:* Representations of finite groups; finite dimensional algebras. *Mailing Add:* Dept Math Univ Ill 1409 W Green St Urbana IL 61801

JANUSZ, MICHAEL JOHN, INFLAMMATION IMMUNOBIOLOGY. *Current Pos:* SR RES IMMUNOBIOLOGIST, MARION MERRELL DOW RES INST, 89- *Personal Data:* b Pawtucket, RI, Feb 18, 54; m 85. *Educ:* RI Col, BA, 76; Smith Col, AM, 79; Univ NC, PhD(microbiol & immunol), 85. *Prof Exp:* Postdoctoral fel immunol, Brigham & Women's Hosp & Harvard Med Sch, 85-88, instr & res immunobiologist, 88-89. *Mem:* Am Asn Immunologists. *Res:* Role of proteinases in connective tissue matrix turnover; immunobiology of inflammatory diseases. *Mailing Add:* Marion Merrell Dow Res Inst 2110 E Galbraith Rd Cincinnati OH 45215

JANUTOLO, DELANO BLAKE, PLANT PATHOLOGY, MYCOLOGY. *Current Pos:* PROF BIOL & DEAN, SCH SCI & HUMANITIES, ANDERSON UNIV, 77- *Personal Data:* b Bluefield, WVa, July 7, 52; c 2. *Educ:* WVa Univ, BS, 73; Va Polytech Inst & State Univ, PhD(plant path), 77. *Mem:* Am Phytopath Soc; Sigma Xi. *Res:* Evaluation and testing of fungicides; systemic fungicides. *Mailing Add:* Dept Biol Anderson Univ 1100 E Fifth St Anderson IN 46012-3462

JANZ, GEORGE JOHN, PHYSICAL CHEMISTRY. *Current Pos:* from asst prof to assoc prof, 50-53, chmn dept chem, 62-72, prof, 53-80, WM WEIGHTMAN WALKER PROF CHEM, RENSSELAER POLYTECH INST, 80-, DIR, MOLTEN SALTS DATA CTR, 68- *Personal Data:* b Russia, Aug 24, 17; nat US; m 51; c 4. *Educ:* Univ Man, BSc, 40; Univ Toronto, MA, 41, PhD(chem), 43; Univ London, DSc, 54. *Prof Exp:* Res chemist, Can Indust Ltd, 43-46; hon res assoc, Univ Col, London, 46-49; asst prof chem, Pa State Col, 49-50. *Concurrent Pos:* Vis prof, Rockefeller Univ, 72-73. *Mem:* Am Chem Soc; Royal Soc Chem; Electrochem Soc; Faraday Soc; NY Acad Sci. *Res:* Electrochemistry; physical properties ties and spectroscopy of inorganic compounds in the molten state; aqueous and nonaqueous electrolytes; electrolysis of molten salts; thermodynamics and reaction energies of cyanogen-like compounds. *Mailing Add:* 401 Winter St Troy NY 12180

JANZEN, ALEXANDER FRANK, INORGANIC CHEMISTRY, ORGANOMETALLIC CHEMISTRY. *Current Pos:* from asst prof to assoc prof, 67-78, PROF CHEM, UNIV MAN, 78- *Personal Data:* b Einlage, Ukraine, Apr 19, 40; Can citizen; m 67, Frieda Chaly; c Mark, Sonya & Michael. *Educ:* McMaster Univ, BSc, 63; Western Ont Univ, PhD(chem), 66. *Prof Exp:* Fel chem, Univ London, 66-67. *Concurrent Pos:* Vis scientist, Max Planck Inst Exp Med, Ger, 73. *Mem:* Am Chem Soc. *Res:* Synthesis of inorganic fluorine compounds and study of dynamic properties and reaction mechanisms. *Mailing Add:* Dept Chem Univ Man Winnipeg MB R3T 2N2 Can. *Fax:* 204-275-0905; *E-Mail:* ajanzen@cc.umanitoba.ca

JANZEN, DANIEL HUNT, ECOLOGY, EVOLUTION. *Current Pos:* PROF BIOL, UNIV PA, 76- *Personal Data:* b Milwaukee, Wis, Jan 18, 39; c 2. *Educ:* Univ Calif, Berkeley, PhD(entom), 65. *Honors & Awards:* Gleason Award, Am Bot Soc, 75; Crawford Prize, Royal Swed Acad Sci, 84. *Prof Exp:* Asst prof biol, Univ Kans, 65-68; from assoc prof to assoc prof, Univ Chicago, 68-72; from assoc prof to prof, Univ Mich, 72-76. *Concurrent Pos:* Adv, Orgn Trop Studies, Costa Rica & Costa Rican Nat Park Serv. *Mem:* Nat Acad Sci; Ecol Soc Am; Am Soc Naturalists; Brit Ecol Soc; Asn Trop Biol; Soc Study Evolution. *Res:* Interactions of plants and animals, with emphasis on tropical field systems. *Mailing Add:* Dept Biol Univ Pa 34th & Spruce Philadelphia PA 19104

JANZEN, EDWARD GEORGE, PHYSICAL ORGANIC CHEMISTRY. *Current Pos:* prof & chmn, Dept Chem, 76-86, PROF & DIR MAGNETIC RESONANCE IMAGING, UNIV GUELPH, 86- *Personal Data:* b Manitoba, Man, May 23, 32; m 52, Helen S Dyck; c Charles G & Beth E. *Educ:* Univ Man, BSc, 57, MSc, 60; Iowa State Univ, PhD(org chem), 63. *Honors & Awards:* Fulmer Award, Iowa State Univ; Syntex Award, Can Soc Chem-Chem Inst Can. *Prof Exp:* Fel, Dept Chem, Iowa State Univ, 63-64; from asst prof to prof spectros, Univ Ga, 64-75. *Concurrent Pos:* Vis prof & scientist, Okla Med Res Found, 81 & IBM Instruments, Inc, San Jose, 82. *Mem:* Fel Can Inst Chem; Electron Paramagnetic Resonance Soc; Soc Free Radical Res; Sigma Xi; Am Chem Soc; Oxygen Soc; Am Soc Mass Spectros; Am Soc Biochem & Molecular Biol. *Res:* Physical organic, biochemical and biomedical topics in electron spin resonance spectroscopy; spin trapping techniques, development and practice; magnetic resonance imaging and in vivo magnetic resonance spectroscopy. *Mailing Add:* Dept Clin Studies & Biomed Sci-Ont Vet Col Univ Guelph Guelph ON N1G 2W1 Can

JANZEN, HELMUT HENRY, SOILS & SOILS SCIENCE, ENVIRONMENTAL SCIENCES. *Current Pos:* RES SCIENTIST SOIL BIOCHEM, AGR CAN ALTA, 84- *Personal Data:* m 78, Sandra F Bartel; c Kristina, David & Robert. *Educ:* Univ Sask, BSc, 80, PhD(soil sci), 84. *Honors & Awards:* b Coaldale, Alta, Aug 4, 56. *Concurrent Pos:* Mem sci steering comt, Greenhouse Gas Prog Agr Can, 92- *Mem:* Soil Sci Soc Am. *Res:* Investigation of nutrient cycling (carbon, nitrogen and sulfur) in prairie agroecosystems; greenhouse gas emissions; organic matter dynamics; nitrogen volatilization; litter decomposition; elemental sulfur oxidation. *Mailing Add:* PO Box 3000 Main Lethbridge AB T1J 4B1 Can. *Fax:* 403-382-3156; *E-Mail:* janzen@abrsle.agr.ca

JANZEN, JAY, PHYSICAL CHEMISTRY. *Current Pos:* sr res chemist, 68-86, RES ASSOC, PHILLIPS PETROL CO, 86- *Personal Data:* b Chickasha, Okla, Mar 24, 40; m 86, Charlene Byers; c Paul C & Carla M. *Educ:* Univ Kans, BS, 62; Iowa State Univ, PhD(phys chem), 68. *Mem:* Am Chem Soc; Sigma Xi; Soc Rheology. *Res:* Reinforcement of elastopolymers; polyolefin rheology and property-performance relationships; statistical morphology of particulate materials and composite media; random geometry. *Mailing Add:* 2727 Evergreen Dr Bartlesville OK 74006-4705

JANZOW, EDWARD F(RANK), NUCLEAR ENGINEERING, MECHANICAL ENGINEERING. *Current Pos:* PRES, FRONTIER TECHNOL CORP, 85 - *Personal Data:* b St Louis, Mo, Mar 19, 41; m 67, Treva L Barbre; c Lee A. *Educ:* Washington Univ, BS, 63; Univ Mo, MS, 64; Univ Ill, Urbana, PhD(nuclear eng), 70; Univ Dayton, MBA, 81. *Prof Exp:* NASA traineeship, Univ Mo, Columbia, 63-64; NSF traineeship, Univ Ill, Urbana, 64-68, asst, Off Water Resources, 68-69; nuclear eng prog, 69-70; sr res engr, Monsanto Res Corp, 71-72, engr group leader, 72-75, supvr design & develop eng, 75-76, mgr eng design & develop, 76-79, mgr eng & qual assurance, 79-81, mgr opers, 81-84. *Concurrent Pos:* Mem comt, Sealed Radioactive Sources, Am Nat Standard Inst, 74 - *Mem:* Am Nuclear Soc; Am Soc Testing & Mat. *Res:* Nuclear radiation sources especially Cf-252 neutron sources; research, development and design of such sources and techniques, apparatus and facilities for fabrication; development and design of radioisotope shipping containers and shielding. *Mailing Add:* 2671 Crone Rd Beavercreek OH 45434. *Fax:* 937-376-5692

JAOUNI, KATHERINE COOK, MICROBIOLOGY. *Current Pos:* RETIRED. *Personal Data:* b Alexandria, Va, Nov 8, 28; m 64, Taysir M; c Taysir M Jr. *Educ:* Col William & Mary, BS, 49; George Washington Univ, MS, 52, PhD(microbiol), 57. *Prof Exp:* Bacteriologist, Alexandria Health Dept, 49-52; parasitologist, Trop Dis Lab, Nat Inst Allergy & Infectious Dis, 52-57, virologist, Infectious Dis Lab, 57-78, res microbiologist, 78-94. *Concurrent Pos:* Researcher, Pasteur Inst & St Vincent de Paul Hosp, France, 59-61 & Max Planck Inst, Tuebingen, Ger, 61-62; pres, Grad Women Sci, Inc, 81-82. *Mem:* Am Soc Trop Med & Hyg; Am Soc Microbiol; Sigma Xi; AAAS; Grad Women Sci. *Res:* Tissue culture of protozoa and mode of action of drugs against toxoplasma; characterization and antigenic analysis of respiratory viruses; oncogenic virology; viruses of protozoa; mode of action of drugs against protozoa and viruses; science administration. *Mailing Add:* 515 Bradford Dr Rockville MD 20850

JAOUNI, TAYSIR M, ORGANIC CHEMISTRY. *Current Pos:* RES CHEMIST, LAB CHEM, NAT HEART & LUNG INST, 63- *Personal Data:* b Jerusalem, Palestine, Aug 29, 24; US citizen; m 64; c 1. *Educ:* Univ Calif, Berkeley, BA, 50, MA, 51, BSc, 60; Univ Colo, MSc, 63. *Prof Exp:* Asst chem, Univ Colo, 60-63. *Res:* Synthesis of diribonucleoside phosphates; RNA codewords and protein synthesis; GC/MS. *Mailing Add:* 515 Bradford Dr Rockville MD 20850

JAPAR, STEVEN MARTIN, ATMOSPHERIC CHEMISTRY & PHYSICS. *Current Pos:* sr res scientist, 73-80, prin res scientist assoc, Res Lab, 81-90, STAFF SCIENTIST & SUPVR ATMOSPHERIC CHEM GROUP FORD MOTOR CO, 91- *Personal Data:* b New York, NY, Nov 11, 44; m 84, Teresa Martusiewicz; c 2. *Educ:* City Col New York, BS, 65; Case Inst Technol, PhD(phys chem), 69. *Honors & Awards:* Arch T Colwell Award, Soc of Automotive Engrs, 81. *Prof Exp:* Fel, Div Physics, Nat Res Coun Can, 69-71; fel, Chem Dept, Univ Calif, Riverside, 71-72; instr, Chem Dept, Drexel Univ, 72-73. *Concurrent Pos:* Instr, Natural Sci Dept, Univ Mich, Dearborn, 75-76. *Mem:* Am Chem Soc; Air & Waste Mgt Asn; Sigma Xi. *Res:* Photochemistry, spectroscopy and chemical kinetics of species important in atmospheric chemistry; Chemistry and physics of gas phase aerosols generated from combustion sources. *Mailing Add:* 4518 Whisper Way Troy MI 48098. *Fax:* 313-594-2923

JAPIKSE, DAVID, MECHANICAL ENGINEERING, MANUFACTURING. *Current Pos:* PRES, CONCEPTS ETI, INC, 80- *Educ:* Case Inst Technol, BS, 65; Purdue Univ, MSc, 68, PhD(eng sci), 69. *Honors & Awards:* James Harry Potter Gold Medal, Am Soc Mech Engrs, 92. *Prof Exp:* Staff mem, Pratt & Whitney, Creare, Inc. *Concurrent Pos:* Lectr numerous foreign countries; mem, Turbomach Comt, Div Fluids Eng, Am Soc Mech Engrs, 73- *Mem:* Am Inst Aeronaut & Astronaut; Am Soc Mech Engrs; Soc Automotive Engrs; Sigma Xi. *Res:* Fundamental modeling of turbomachinery processes, especially meanline performance codes; derivation and publishing of two-zone modeling equations suitable for any developing flow; introduction of the TEIS model to describe the thermodynamic state change typical of any bladed row. *Mailing Add:* Concepts ETI Inc Billings Farm Rd White River Jct Norwich VT 05001

JAQUES, LOUIS BARKER, PHYSIOLOGY, PHARMACOLOGY. *Current Pos:* prof physiol & pharmacol & head dept, 46-71, Lindsay res prof, 71-79, EMER PROF, COL MED, RES ASSOC COL DENT, UNIV SASKATOON, 79- *Personal Data:* b Toronto, Ont, July 10, 11; m 37; c 1. *Educ:* Univ Toronto, BA, 33, MA, 35, PhD(physiol), 41; Univ Sask, DSc, 74. *Prof Exp:* Asst physiol, Univ Toronto, 34-42, lectr & res assoc, 43-44, asst prof, 44-46. *Concurrent Pos:* Claude Bernard vis prof, Univ Montreal, 48; mem, Int Conf Thrombosis & Embolism, Univ Basel, 54; mem adv comt, Med Div, Nat Res Coun Can, 52-55 & 59-61, mem Int comt nomenclature of blood clotting factors, 54-66, chmn subcomt hemostasis, 62-65; chmn, Can Nat Comt, Int Union Physiol Sci, 62-64; mem Can nat comt, Int Coun Sci Unions, 63-64. *Mem:* Am Physiol Soc; Am Soc Pharmacol & Exp Therapeut; fel NY Acad Sci; fel Royal Soc Can; Pharmacol Soc Can. *Res:* Pharmacology of blood coagulation; anticoagulants; hemorrhage and thrombosis. *Mailing Add:* Dept Oral Biol Col Dent Univ Sask 682 University Dr Saskatoon SK S7N 0W0 Can

JAQUES, ROBERT PAUL, INSECT PATHOLOGY. *Current Pos:* RETIRED. *Personal Data:* b Caledonia, Ont, Jan 1, 31; m 54; c 3. *Educ:* Univ Toronto, BSA, 52, MSA, 54; Cornell Univ, PhD(insect ecol), 60. *Prof Exp:* Res scientist, Can Dept Agr, Kentville, NS, 54-67, res scientist insect path, Res Sta, Harrow, ON, 67-91, res emer scientist. *Concurrent Pos:* Res assoc biol, Acadia Univ, 62-65, assoc prof, 65-67; assoc fac, Univ Guelph, 76-84. *Mem:* Entom Soc Can; Soc Invert Path; Entom Soc Am. *Res:* Factors affecting development of disease in populations of insects; persistence of insect viruses in the environment; microbial control of insects. *Mailing Add:* 166 Augustine Dr Kingsville ON N9Y 1C5 Can

JAQUITH, RICHARD HERBERT, INORGANIC CHEMISTRY. *Current Pos:* from asst prof to assoc prof, 54-65, PROF CHEM, UNIV MD, COLLEGE PARK, 65-, ASST VCHANCELLOR ACAD AFFAIRS, 73- *Personal Data:* b Newton, Mass, Mar 31, 19; m 42; c 5. *Educ:* Univ Mass BS, 40, MS, 42; Mich State Univ, PhD(inorg chem), 55. *Prof Exp:* Instr chem, Univ Conn, 42-44 & 46-47; asst prof, Colby Col, 47-54. *Mem:* Sigma Xi. *Res:* Nonaqueous inorganic solvents; rare earth compounds. *Mailing Add:* 5807 Cherrywood Terr No 201 Greenbelt MD 20770

JARAMILLO, JORGE, PHARMACOLOGY. *Current Pos:* coordr pharmacol, 84-88, DIR PHARMACOL, BIO-MEGA INC, 88- *Personal Data:* b Chinchina, Colombia, Jan 7, 34; m 61; c 4. *Educ:* Univ Caldas, MD, 58; Tulane Univ, MS, 62, PhD(pharmacol), 66. *Prof Exp:* Instr, Tulane Univ, 66-67; asst prof, Univ Conn, 67-68; sr pharmacologist, 68-70, res assoc pharmacol, Ayerst Res Labs, 70-77, sr res assoc, 77-84. *Mem:* Pharmacol Soc Can; Soc Toxicol Can; Am Soc Pharmacol Exp Therapeut. *Res:* Cardiovascular. *Mailing Add:* Dept Pharmacol Bio-Mega Inc 2100 Cunard St Laval Montreal PQ H7S 2G5 Can. *Fax:* 514-682-8434

JARBOE, CHARLES HARRY, TOXICOKINETICS. *Current Pos:* asst, AEC, Univ Louisville, 56, res asst prof org chem, 56-58, res assoc pharmacol, Sch Med, 58-62, assoc prof, Health Sci Ctr, 62-72, prof pharmacol & dir, Therapeut & Toxicol Lab, 72-89, EMER PROF PHARMACOL, SCH MED, UNIV LOUISVILLE, 89- *Personal Data:* b Louisville, Ky, Oct 3, 28; div; c Jamisene L, Charles H, Richard J, Herman H, Nancy H & Elizabeth A. *Educ:* Univ Louisville, BSc, 51, PhD(chem), 56. *Prof Exp:* Chemist, E I du Pont de Nemours & Co, 51-53. *Concurrent Pos:* Consult, Brown & Williamson Tobacco Corp, 57-58, chief scientist, 58-61, consult, 62-64; spec fel, Nat Heart Inst, 61-62; asst dean planning & proj coordr, Univ Louisville, 65-67, actg chmn dept pharmacol, 68; vis scientist, Sci Div, Abbott Labs, 70-71; consult, Am Horse Shows Asn, 73; vis prof, Med Col Va, Va Commonwealth Univ, 74; Ky Med Assistance Prog Formulary Subcomt & Pest Control Adv Bd, Ky Environ Qual Comn, 78-; vis prof, Med Sch, Auckland Univ, 79, Univ Utah, 80, King Faisal Univ Col Med, Saudi Arabia, 82-84 & US Naval Regional Med Ctr, Portsmouth, Va, 82. *Mem:* Am Chem Soc; The Chem Soc; Am Acad Clin Toxicol; Am Soc Pharmacol & Exp Therapeut; NY Acad Sci; Am Col Clin Pharmacol. *Res:* Kinetic aspects of drug action; human pharmacokinetics; human toxicokinetics. *Mailing Add:* Dept Pharmacol & Toxicol Sch Med Univ Louisville Louisville KY 40292. *Fax:* 502-852-7868

JARBOE, JERRY K(ENT), ANALYTICAL METHODOLOGY, FOOD ANALYSIS. *Current Pos:* Res chemist food sci, US Army Natick Res Develop & Eng Ctr, 62-78, group leader anal chem, 78-88, sect chief anal chem & biochem, 88-91, br chief biohazards assessment & control br, 91-93, CHIEF, ADVAN FOODS BR, US ARMY NATICK RES DEVELOP & ENG CTR, 93- *Personal Data:* b Indianapolis, Ind, Sept 28, 40; m 77, Sharon Craddock; c Linda & Sean. *Educ:* Marion Col, BS, 62; Northeastern Univ, MS, 70. *Mem:* Am Chem Soc; Inst Food Technologists; Sigma Xi. *Res:* Separation and analysis of foods; food preservation technologies; methodologies for measuring protection against chemical warfare agents. *Mailing Add:* 9 Simpson Dr Framingham MA 01701

JARBOE, THOMAS RICHARD, PLASMA PHYSICS. *Current Pos:* PROF, UNIV WASH, 89- *Personal Data:* b Paxton, Ill, Aug 23, 45; m 70; c 5. *Educ:* Univ Ill, BS, 67; Univ Calif, Berkeley, PhD(plasma physics), 75. *Prof Exp:* Physicist optics, Naval Weapons Ctr, China Lake, Calif, 68; physicist fusion res, Los Alamos Nat Lab, 74-80, group leader, 80-89. *Mem:* Fel Am Phys Soc. *Res:* Relaxation processes during the interaction of plasma and magnetic field in toroidal geometry; goal is to understand helicity conservation during plasma relaxation processes to understand relaxation in general. *Mailing Add:* 6508 NE 192nd Pl Seattle WA 98155

JARCHO, LEONARD WALLENSTEIN, MEDICINE. *Current Pos:* from asst prof med to prof neurol, 53-86, chmn neurol div, Sch Med, 59-65, chmn , 65-81, neurologist-in-chief, Med Ctr, 65-81, EMER PROF, SCH MED, UTAH UNIV, 86- *Personal Data:* b New York, NY, Aug 12, 16; m 56; c 2. *Educ:* Harvard Univ, AB, 36; Columbia Univ, MA, 37, MD, 41. *Prof Exp:* Instr physiol, Col Physicians & Surgeons, Columbia Univ, 41; Denison fel, Johns Hopkins Univ, 46-47, asst med, 48-51, instr, 51-52. *Concurrent Pos:* Archbold fel med, Johns Hopkins Univ, 48-50, asst physician, Outpatient Dept, 48-52, Nat Found Infantile Paralysis fel, 50-52; asst chief med, Vet Admin Hosp, Salt Lake City, Utah, 53-57, chief med serv, 57, neurol serv, 59; spec clin trainee, NIH, Nat Hosp, London, 58 & Mass Gen Hosp, Boston, 58-59; neurologist-in-chief, Salt Lake County Gen Hosp, 59-65. *Mem:* Am Physiol Soc; Am Neurol Asn; Am Asn Res Nerv & Ment Dis; Am Acad Neurol; Am Fedn Clin Res; Sigma Xi. *Res:* Neurophysiology; neuromuscular disease. *Mailing Add:* Dept Neurol Univ Utah Sch Med 50 N Med Dr Salt Lake City UT 84108

JARCHO, SAUL, HISTORY OF MEDICINE, MEDICAL CARTOGRAPHY. *Current Pos:* MED HISTORIAN, 38- *Personal Data:* b New York, NY, Oct 25, 06; m 48, Irma Seijo; c Thomas & Andrew. *Educ:* Harvard Univ, BA, 25; Columbia Univ, MA, 26, MD, 30. *Honors & Awards:* William Welch Medal, Am Asn History Med, 63; Jacobi Medal, Mt Sinai Hosp, NY, 70; NY Acad Med Medal, 79; Urdang Medal, Am Inst Hist Pharm, 95. *Prof Exp:* Consult, Nat Lib Med, 46-88. *Concurrent Pos:* Consult to Surgeon Gen Army; consult to armed forces, Soc Med; ed, Bull NY Acad Med, 67-77; ed, Trans & Studies, Col Physicians Philadelphia, 79-83. *Mem:* AMA; fel Am Col Physicians; Am Asn Path & Bact; Am Pub Health Asn; Am Asn Hist Med; Am Asn Advan Sci; NY Acad Sci; NY Acad Med; Am Soc Trop Med; Am Soc Parasitologists. *Res:* Cardiology; paleopathology; history of medicine; pathology; medical cartography. *Mailing Add:* 11 W 69th St New York NY 10023

JARDETZKY, OLEG, MOLECULAR BIOLOGY, PHARMACOLOGY. *Current Pos:* actg chmn, 73-74, PROF PHARMACOL, SCH MED, STANFORD UNIV, 69-, DIR, MAGNETIC RESONANCE LAB, 75- *Personal Data:* b Belgrade, Yugoslavia, Feb 11, 29; nat US; m 52, 65, Erika; c Alexander, Theodore & Paul. *Educ:* Macalester Col, BA, 50; Univ Minn, MD, 54, PhD(chem physiol), 56. *Hon Degrees:* DSc, Macalester Col, 74; LLD, Calif Western Univ, 78; MD, Karl-Franzens Univ, 94. *Honors & Awards:* Henry T Kaiser Award, 73; Alexander von Humboldt Award, 77; Linus Pauling lectr, 84; Merian lectr, Mich State Univ, 84. *Prof Exp:* Res asst physiol, Univ Minn, 50-54; Nat Res Coun fel chem, Calif Inst Technol, 56-57, Am Heart Asn fel, Univ Minn; assoc pharmacol, Harvard Med Sch, 57-59, asst prof, 59-66; dir, Dept Biophys & Pharmacol, Merck Sharp & Dohme Res Labs, NJ, 66-68, exec dir basic med sci, Merck Inst Therapeut Res, 68-69. *Concurrent Pos:* Irvine McQuarrie scholar award, 54; consult, Mass Gen Hosp, 61-67; vis prof, State Univ NY, Buffalo, 63, Albany, 70; consult coun drugs, AMA, 64; Japan Chem Soc lectr, Univ Tokyo, 65; vis scientist, Cambridge Univ, 65-66; Chem Students Asn lectr, Univ Amsterdam, 66; basic sci lectr, Med Ctr, Univ Calif, San Francisco, 68; USSR Acad Sci lectr, 70; vis fel, Merton Col, Oxford, 76; vis prof, MPI, Heidelberg, 77 & Univ Calif, Riverside, 82; lectr, Fr Ministry foreign affairs, 79; chmn, Nat Comn, 10th Int Conf Magnetic Resonance Biol Syst, Stanford Univ, 82; vis lectr, Weismann Inst, Israel, 84 & USSR Acad Sci, 84 & 91; plenary lectr, 58th Ann Meeting Japanese Biochem Soc, 85; co-dir, Int Sch Struct Biol & Magnetic Resonance, 93, 95 & 97. *Mem:* Fel AAAS; Am Chem Soc; Sigma Xi; Biophys Soc; Int Soc Magnetic Resonance; Soc Magnetic Resonance Med; Am Soc Biochem & Molecular Biol; Protein Soc. *Res:* Molecular mechanisms of protein function; biological applications of nuclear magnetic resonance. *Mailing Add:* Stanford Magnetic Resonance Lab Stanford Univ Stanford CA 94305-5055. *Fax:* 650-723-2253; *E-Mail:* jardetzky@camis.stanford.edu

JARDIN, STEPHEN CHARLES, PLASMA PHYSICS. *Current Pos:* fel, Princeton Plasma Physics Lab, 76-78, res staff, 78-81, res physicist, 81-86, PRIN RES PHYSICIST, PRINCETON PLASMA PHYSICS LAB, 86-, DEP HEAD, 91-; PROF, DEPT ASTROPHYS SCI, PRINCETON UNIV, 86- *Personal Data:* b Oakland, Calif, Aug 28, 47. *Educ:* Univ Calif, Berkeley, BS, 70; Mass Inst Technol, MS(nuclear eng) & MS(physics), 73; Princeton Univ, PhD(astrophys), 76. *Prof Exp:* Sci comput programmer, Sandia Corp, 67-69; physicist, Physics Int Co, 70-72. *Concurrent Pos:* Assoc prof, Dept Astrophys Sci, Princeton Univ, 84-86; consult, EGG Idaho. *Mem:* Fel Am Phys Soc. *Res:* Theoretical and computational research of magnetohydrodynamics equilibrium, stability and transport of Tokamaks and other magnetically confined plasma configurations; granted four US patents. *Mailing Add:* Plasma Physics Lab Princeton Univ PO Box 451 Princeton NJ 08543

JARDINE, D(ONALD) A(NDREW), COMPUTER SCIENCE. *Current Pos:* RETIRED. *Personal Data:* b Kingston, Ont, July 23, 30; div; c 2. *Educ:* Queen's Univ Ont, BSc, 52, MSc, 54; Univ Del, PhD, 57. *Prof Exp:* Res engr, Du Pont Can Ltd, 56-68, res assoc, 68-70; assoc prof comput sci, Queen's Univ Ont, 70-73, head dept, 73-78, prof, 73- *Concurrent Pos:* Pres, Common Comput Users Group, 66-68. *Mem:* Asn Comput Mach. *Res:* Data base management systems; data description languages. *Mailing Add:* Dept Comput Sci Queens Univ Kingston ON K7L 3N6 Can

JARDINE, IAN, MASS SPECTROMETRY. *Current Pos:* dir anal biochem, 88-91, DIR MKT, FINNEGAN MAT, 92- *Personal Data:* b Glasgow, Scotland, Sept 17, 48. *Educ:* Univ Glasgow, BSc, 70, PhD(chem), 73. *Prof Exp:* Fel pharmacol, Med Sch, Johns Hopkins Univ, 73-76; asst prof med chem & pharmacog, Sch Pharm & Pharmacol Sci, Purdue Univ, West Lafayette, 76-79; from assoc prof to prof pharmacol, Mayo Med Sch, 79-88; consult pharmacol, Mayo Clin, 79-88. *Mem:* Am Chem Soc; Am Soc Mass Spectrometry; AAAS. *Res:* Development of mass spectrometric methods for biochemical and pharmacological analysis. *Mailing Add:* Finnegan Mat 355 River Oaks Pkwy San Jose CA 95134-1991

JARDINE, JOHN MCNAIR, ATOMIC ENERGY, MATHEMATICAL STATISTICS. *Current Pos:* RETIRED. *Personal Data:* b Moncton, NB, June 25, 19; m 45; c 2. *Educ:* Mt Allison Univ, BSc, 40; McGill Univ, MSc, 48. *Honors & Awards:* Can Forces Decoration, Can Govt, 60. *Prof Exp:* Res chemist, Refining Div, Eldorado Mining & Refining Ltd, 48-51, chief analyst, 51-53, chief chemist, 53-62, supt, Metall Lab, Res & Develop Div, 62-69, res supt, Eldorado Nuclear Ltd, 69-72; scientific adv mining, Atomic Energy Control Bd, Can, 72-81. *Mem:* Fel Chem Inst Can; Can Soc Chem Eng. *Res:* Analytical chemistry in the Canadian uranium industry; solvent extraction of uranium and thorium; separation of copper, cobalt and nickel by solvent extraction; development of process for production of hafnium free zirconium metal from zircon sands; transportation of radioactive materials; uranium mining and milling. *Mailing Add:* 467 Broadview Ave Ottawa ON K2A 2L2 Can

JARED, ALVA HARDEN, WOOD TECHNOLOGY, DRAFTING & DESIGN. *Current Pos:* RETIRED. *Personal Data:* b Roseville, Ill, Jan 15, 34; m 55; c 2. *Educ:* Western Ill State Col, BS, 55; Ball State Teachers Col, MAE, 56; Ariz State Univ, EdD(indust educ), 68. *Prof Exp:* Res asst, Ariz State Univ, 65-66; prof indust educ, Univ Wis-Platteville, 56- *Concurrent Pos:* Consult energy mgt & construct. *Mem:* Int Technol Educ Asn; Nat Asn Indust Technol; Int Coun Indust Teacher Educators. *Res:* Technology management; supervision and training of workers; construction management; energy management; technology education; author of several publications. *Mailing Add:* 945 St James Circle Platteville WI 53818

JAREM, JOHN, ELECTRICAL ENGINEERING. *Current Pos:* RETIRED. *Personal Data:* b Jarembina, Czech, July 4, 21; US citizen; c 4. *Educ:* Polytech Inst Brooklyn, BEE, 47, MEE, 50; Univ Pa, MS, 57, PhD(plasma physics), 60. *Prof Exp:* Electronic res engr, Tele-Register Corp, NY, 47; asst prof elec eng & math, US Naval Postgrad Sch, 48-51; math specialist, Lockheed Aircraft Corp, Calif, 51-54; mem systs eng tech staff, Radio Corp Am, NJ, 54-59, engr, 59-62; sr staff mem, Inst Defense Anal, 62-63; staff engr dir & systs engr, Radio Corp Am, 63-64; head, Dept Elec Eng, Drexel Univ, 64-68, prof, 64-90. *Concurrent Pos:* Consult, Radio Corp Am, 64-65, Inst Defense Analysis, 64- & Aero Chem, 66- *Mem:* Sr mem Inst Elec & Electronics Engrs; Am Phys Soc. *Res:* Systems engineering; applied mathematics; plasma physics. *Mailing Add:* Univ Ala 4701 University Dr Huntsville AL 35899

JARETT, LEONARD, CLINICAL PATHOLOGY, BIOCHEMISTRY. *Current Pos:* PROF & CHMN DEPT PATH & LAB MED, SCH MED, UNIV PA, 80- *Personal Data:* b Lubbock, Tex, Aug 25, 36; m 62; c 3. *Educ:* Rice Univ, BA, 58; Wash Univ, MD, 62. *Hon Degrees:* MA, Univ Pa, 82. *Honors & Awards:* David Rumbough Award, Juv Diabetes Found, 80; Cotlove Award, Acad Clin Lab Physicians & Scientists, 85. *Prof Exp:* Intern path, Barnes Hosp, St Louis, Mo, 62-63, resident, 63-64; res assoc, Sect Cellular Physiol, Lab Biochem, Nat Heart Inst, 64-66; from instr path to assoc prof path & med, Wash Univ, 66-75, head div lab med, 69-75, prof path & med, Sch Med, 75-80. *Concurrent Pos:* Dir labs & head div lab med, Barnes Hosp, 69-80; mem sci adv bd, St Jude Children's Res Hosp, 80-83 & metab study sect, 83-87; mem adv bd, Juv Diabetes Found, 81-84. *Mem:* Endocrine Soc; Acad Clin Lab Physicians & Scientists; Am Soc Biol Chemists; Am Fedn Clin Res; fel Am Soc Clin Path; Am Asn Physicians; Am Soc Clin Invest. *Res:* Biochemical and ultrastructural techniques in the study of signal transduction by insulin. *Mailing Add:* Dept Path & Lab Med Hosp Univ Pa 3400 Spruce St 6 Gates Philadelphia PA 19104-4283. *Fax:* 215-662-4063

JARGIELLO, PATRICIA, molecular genetics, for more information see previous edition

JARGON, JERRY ROBERT, PETROLEUM ENGINEERING, CHEMICAL ENGINEERING. *Current Pos:* assoc engr, Marathon Oil Co, 63-66, engr, 66-72, adv engr prod res, 72-77, sr engr petrol technol, 77-80, adv sr engr, 80-85, sr staff engr, 85-87, sr tech consult, 87-88, MGR, RESERVOIR MGT DEPT, MARATHON OIL CO, 88- *Personal Data:* b Beckemeyer, Ill, Aug 2, 39; m 63; c 3. *Educ:* Univ Ill, BS, 63; Univ Denver, MS, 67. *Prof Exp:* Assoc engr res, Chicago Bridge & Iron Co, 62. *Concurrent Pos:* Lectr continuing educ courses, Soc Petrol Engrs, 73-74, prog comt, Rocky Mt Region, 74-75, formation evalu comt, Nat Meeting, 75, mem, Monogr Rev Comt Gas Well Performance, 77-80; tech ed, J Petrol Tech, 85-86; ed, Gaswell Testing, 85-; eng adv bd, Univ Denver, 89- *Mem:* Soc Petrol Engrs; assoc Inst Mech Engrs; Opers Res Soc Am. *Res:* Reservoir modeling and engineering; pressure transient testing in wells; multiphase flow in wells and pipelines. *Mailing Add:* 1695 S Fillmore St Denver CO 80210

JARIWALA, SHARAD LALLUBHAI, FERMENTATION, BIOTECHNOLOGY. *Current Pos:* sr scientist, Fermentation Res & Develop, 70-75, head fermentation prod prod, 75-76, mgr, 77-79, group mgr, 80-83, dir, 83-84, VPRES FERMENTATION OPER, UPJOHN CO, 84- *Personal Data:* b Bombay, India, Oct 15, 40; m 69; c 2. *Educ:* Univ Bombay, BSChE, 62; Johns Hopkins Univ, PhD(chem eng), 66. *Prof Exp:* Res engr, Tenneco Chem, Inc, 66-70. *Mem:* Am Inst Chem Engrs; Am Chem Soc. *Res:* Developing new technology for the separation and recovery of antibiotics from fermentation broths; separations technology; reaction engineering in fixed and fluidized beds; liquid phase oxidations. *Mailing Add:* BIO Pharmic Int Inc 512 Barberry Portage MI 49002

JARIWALLA, RAXIT JAYANTILAL, VIROLOGY, CARCINOGENESIS. *Current Pos:* PRIN RES INVESTR, CALIF INST MED RES, 96- *Personal Data:* b Bombay, India, Nov 18, 49; US citizen; m 90, Sonal Divanji; c Neil R & Nisha R. *Educ:* Bombay Univ, BSc, 71; Med Col Wis, MS, 74, PhD(microbiol), 76. *Prof Exp:* Fel, Div Biophys, Sch Hyg & Pub Health, Johns Hopkins Univ, 76-79, instr, Div Biophys, 79-82; res scientist, Linus Pauling Inst Sci Med, 82-84, sr scientist, 84-96, head, Viral Carcinogenesis & Immunol Prog, 86-92, head, Virol Prog, 92-96. *Concurrent Pos:* Guest lectr, virol course, Dept Med Microbiol, Stanford Univ, 85-86; prin investr, NCI sponsored res grant, Linus Pauling Inst Sci Med, 86-; co-organizer, XVI Int Herpesvirus Workshop, Asilomar, Calif, 91; consult, Div AIDS Treatment Res Initiative, 94-96; tech coordr, James Flood Sci & Technol Sch, 96- *Mem:* Am Soc Microbiol; AAAS; Am Soc Virol. *Res:* HIV suppression and immunomodulation by micronutrients; control of cell proliferation tumor growth and inflammation by biological/dietary antioxidants; role of reactive oxygen radicals in cellular growth control and apoptosis. *Mailing Add:* 19120 Vineyard Lane Saratoga CA 95070. *E-Mail:* ganesh5@ix.netcom.com

JARKE, FRANK HENRY, PHYSICAL CHEMISTRY, ANALYTICAL CHEMISTRY. *Current Pos:* lab dir, 93-95, DIR, SUPPORT SVCS, MOSTARDI-PLATT ASSOC, INC, 95- *Personal Data:* b Bloomington, Ill, Mar 28, 46; m 71, Lynn M Hytry. *Educ:* Southern Ill Univ, BA, 69; Ill Inst Technol, MS, 74. *Prof Exp:* Asst chemist to assoc chemist, ITT Res Inst, 69-78, res chemist odor sci, 78-81; mgr anal serv, chem waste mgt, Riverdale, Ill, 81-83; asst mgr, Environ Waste Mgt, EML Waste Mgt, Oak Brook, Ill, 83-87, mgr, Qual Prog, Geneva, 87-93. *Mem:* Am Chem Soc; AAAS; Soc Appl Spectros; Am Soc Heating, Refrig & Air-Conditioning Engrs; NY Acad Sci. *Res:* Fundamental and applied research of odors and air pollution; development and use of both subjective and objective methods using humans as detectors. *Mailing Add:* 503 Carlsbad Trail Roselle IL 60172

JARMAKANI, JAY M, PEDIATRIC CARDIOLOGY. *Current Pos:* assoc prof, 73-78, DIR CARDIOPULMONARY LAB & PROF PEDIAT, MED CTR, UNIV CALIF, LOS ANGELES, 78- *Personal Data:* US citizen. *Educ:* Damascus Univ, BCP, 56, MD, 62. *Prof Exp:* Pediat resident, Buffalo Children's Hosp & Children's Hosp Philadelphia, 63-65; fel pediat cardiol, Children's Hosp Pittsburgh, 65-66; fel, Med Ctr, Duke Univ, 66-68, asst prof pediat, 68-73. *Mem:* Soc Pediat Res; fel Am Col Cardiol; Am Heart Asn; Am Physiol Soc; Int Soc Heart Res. *Res:* Developmental myocardial function with emphasis on congenital heart disease and the effect of hypoxia on cardiac cell function. *Mailing Add:* Dept Pediat Univ Calif Med Ctr Rm B2-441 10833 Le Conte Ave Los Angeles CA 90095-1398. *Fax:* 310-825-9524

JARMIE, NELSON, NUCLEAR PHYSICS, TAXANOMIC MYCOLOGY. *Current Pos:* MEM STAFF, LOS ALAMOS NAT LAB, 53- *Personal Data:* b Santa Monica, Calif, Mar 24, 28; m 52, 89; c 2. *Educ:* Calif Inst Technol, BS, 48; Univ Calif, PhD(physics), 53. *Honors & Awards:* Distinguished Performance Award, 85, Los Alamos Nat Lab. *Prof Exp:* Res physicist, Radiation Lab, Univ Calif, 50-53; prof physics, Los Alamos Grad Ctr, Univ NMex, 57-75. *Concurrent Pos:* Vis asst prof, Univ Calif, 59-60; partic, Vis Scientist Prog, 65-85; consult, Nat Park Serv, 92- *Mem:* Fel AAAS; fel Am Phys Soc; Am Asn Physics Teachers; Asn Appl Psychophysiol & Biofeedback; Mycol Soc Am; NAm Mycol Asn. *Res:* Light-nuclei energy levels; 3-body breakup, nucleon-nuclear scattering, astrophysical reactions; kinematic codes, straggling calculations and infrared laser diagnostics; fundamental properties of antimatter and gravitational acceleration of anti-protons; nuclear physics, particle physics and astrophysics; taxomomic mycology; taxonomic mycology. *Mailing Add:* Los Alamos Nat Lab Mail Stop D449 PO Box 1663 Los Alamos NM 87545

JARNAGIN, KURT, STRUCTURE FUNCTION STUDIES ON G-PROTEIN COUPLED RECEPTORS, MECHANISM OF RECEPTOR SIGNAL TRANSDUCTION. *Current Pos:* staff researcher I, Syntex Discovery Res, 86-88, staff researcher II, 88-90, res sect leader, 90-95, DEPT HEAD, SYNTEX DISCOVERY RES, 95- *Personal Data:* b New Haven, Conn, Mar 9, 56; m 78, Alisha Stephens; c Karen & Helen. *Educ:* NC State Univ, BS, 78; Univ Wis-Madison, PhD(biochem), 84. *Honors & Awards:* E K Frey-E Werle Prom Prize, 93. *Prof Exp:* Res assoc, Univ Calif, San Francisco, 84-86. *Concurrent Pos:* Fel, Nat Juv Diabetes Found, 85-86. *Mem:* Protein Soc; Am Chem Soc. *Res:* Mediators and mechanisms by which inflammation and pain begins and perpetuates; acute inflammation and pain, such as that occurring post injury and chronic inflammatory disease, such as arthritis and asthma; molecular biology of inflammatory receptors and intra cellular signal transduction molecules. *Mailing Add:* Roche Biosci 3401 Hillview Ave Palo Alto CA 94304. *Fax:* 650-354-7554; *E-Mail:* kurt.jarnagin@roche.com

JARNAGIN, RICHARD CALVIN, PHYSICAL CHEMISTRY. *Current Pos:* from instr to assoc prof, 58-68, PROF CHEM, UNIV NC, CHAPEL HILL, 68- *Personal Data:* b Dallas, Tex, Aug 26, 30; m 52; c 2. *Educ:* Southern Methodist Univ, BS, 52; Yale Univ, PhD, 58. *Prof Exp:* Res chemist, Wright Air Develop Ctr, US Air Force, 53-55. *Concurrent Pos:* Guggenheim fel, 67-68 & NSF fel, Sandia Nat Labs, 78-79. *Mem:* Am Chem Soc; fel Am Phys Soc. *Res:* Electrical and optical properties of molecular systems; photo conduction in organic solids and liquids; kinetics of excited molecular states; catalytic properties of solid oxides and stabilization of oxide films. *Mailing Add:* Dept Chem CB 3290 Univ NC Chapel Hill NC 27599

JAROLMEN, HOWARD, MEDICAL MICROBIOLOGY, GENETICS. *Personal Data:* b New York, NY, Oct 19, 37; m 80, Josephine Tuzeo; c David & Amy. *Educ:* Alfred Univ, BA, 58; Hahnemann Med Col, MS, 60, PhD(microbiol), 64. *Prof Exp:* NIH fel genetics, Cornell Univ, 64-67; res bacteriologist, Am Cyanamid Co, 67-70; group leader bact chemother, 70-74, head, Dept Microbiol & Chemother, 74-76, group leader, 76-80, prin res microbiologist, Fermentation Process Res & Develop Dept, Lederle Labs Div, 80-96. *Mem:* Am Soc Microbiol; Soc Indust Microbiol. *Res:* In vitro and vivo studies of transferable resistance amongst the Enterobacteriaceae; veterinary microbiology; prophylaxis and therapy of experimental infections; bacterial mutagenicity testing; antibiotic discoveries, discovery of antimycobacterials and antiparasitics; strain and media improvement for antibiotic-producing cultures. *Mailing Add:* 41 Pleasant Ave Saddle River NJ 07458

JARON, DOV, BIOMEDICAL ENGINEERING. *Current Pos:* PROF & DIR BIOMED ENG & SCI INST, DREXEL UNIV, 80- *Personal Data:* b Tel-Aviv, Israel, Oct 29, 35; US citizen; m 79; c 2. *Educ:* Univ Denver, BS, 61; Univ Pa, PhD(biomed eng), 67. *Prof Exp:* Sr res assoc, Maimonides Med Ctr, 67-70; dir surg res lab, Sinai Hosp, Detroit, 70-73; from assoc prof to prof biomed eng, Univ RI, 73-80. *Concurrent Pos:* Consult circulatory syst devices panel, Food & Drug Admin, 76-79; chmn, Sixth Ann New Eng Bioeng Conf, 78. *Mem:* Biomed Eng Soc; AAAS; NY Acad Sci; fel Inst Elec & Electronics Engrs; Am Soc Artificial Internal Organs; Eng Med & Biol Soc (vpres, 84-85, pres, 86-87); Int Soc Artificial Organs. *Res:* Cardiovascular dynamics; control and optimization of assisted circulation; cardiovascular modeling and assessment of function; biomedical instrumentation; computer applications to health care. *Mailing Add:* Biomed Eng Sci Inst Drexel Univ 32nd & Chestnut Sts Philadelphia PA 19104

JAROS, STANLEY E(DWARD), CHEMICAL ENGINEERING. *Current Pos:* RETIRED. *Personal Data:* b Syracuse, NY, Mar 23, 19; m 42, 59, Margaret H Steere; c William M, Stanley E Jr, Elaine (Seawell), Diana (King), Lori (Griggs) & John Steere. *Educ:* Syracuse Univ, BChE, 40, MChE, 42. *Prof Exp:* Chem engr, Exxon Res & Eng Co, 42-55, asst dir, Chem Develop Div, 55-57, dir, 57-61, assoc dir, Process Eng Div, 61-65, res coordr, Chem Planning Staff, 65-66, res coordr, New Projs Develop, 66-72, res coordr, Corp Res Feasibility Unit, 72-78; consult, 78-82. *Mem:* Am Chem Soc; Am Inst Chem Engrs. *Res:* Translating research results to commercial projects in the process industries. *Mailing Add:* 1199 Monticello Rd Lafayette CA 94549

JAROWSKI, CHARLES I, PHARMACEUTICAL CHEMISTRY. *Current Pos:* RETIRED. *Personal Data:* b Baltimore, Md, July 29, 17; m 45; c 3. *Educ:* Univ Md, BS, 38, PhD(pharmaceut chem), 43. *Prof Exp:* Fel, Univ Ill, 42-44; res chemist, Wyeth Inc, Pa, 44-46; chief chemist, Vick Chem Co, NY, 46-48; res chemist, Chas Pfizer & Co, Inc, 48-50, mgr pharmaceut res & develop, 50-60, dir, 60-69; from assoc prof to prof pharmaceut, St Johns Univ, 69-88, chmn, Dept Allied Health & Indust Sci, 78-88. *Mem:* Am Pharmaceut Asn. *Res:* Synthesis of antibacterial agents, antioxidants, and medicinals; antioxidant for food and drug industry; germicidal steam aerosolic compounds; antibiotic derivatives; drug detoxification; scientific nutrition; drug delivery systems. *Mailing Add:* 67 Harbor Lane Massapequa Park NY 11762

JARRELL, JOSEPH ANDY, INSTRUMENTATION, BIOPHYSICS. *Current Pos:* DIR, WATERS CHROMATOGRAPHY, DIV MILLTORE, 86- *Personal Data:* b Bad Kissengr, Ger, Mar 5, 50. *Educ:* Mass Inst Technol, BS, 71, PhD(physics), 79. *Prof Exp:* Res assoc, Mass Inst Technol, 78-85. *Mem:* Am Phys Soc; Am Vacuum Soc. *Mailing Add:* 11 Hyde Ave Newton Highlands MA 02161

JARRELL, WESLEY MICHAEL, PLANT-SOIL RELATIONSHIPS, ECOSYSTEM SCIENCE. *Current Pos:* assoc prof, 88-91, PROF ECOSYST SCI, ORE GRAD INST SCI & TECHNOL, 91-, DEPT HEAD, 92- *Personal Data:* b Forest Grove, Ore, May 23, 48; m 72, Linda Illig; c Benjamin & Emily. *Educ:* Stanford Univ, AB, 70; Ore State Univ, MS, 74, PhD(soil sci), 77. *Honors & Awards:* Alex B Laurie Award, Am Soc Hort Sci, 79. *Prof Exp:* From asst prof to assoc prof soil & plant relationships, Univ Calif, Riverside, 76-88, dir, Dry Lands Res Inst, 85-88. *Concurrent Pos:* Consult, Allergan Pharmaceut, 80-85, Benchmark, 84 & Jardinier, 87- *Mem:* Soil Sci Soc Am; Am Soc Agron; Am Soc Hort Sci; Ecol Soc Am; AAAS. *Res:* Relationships between soil conditions and plant growth, water quality and air quality; restoration of disturbed landscapes to stable ecosystems; nutrient and hydrologic cycles, particularly the interactions between hydrology and elemental transport. *Mailing Add:* Oreg Grad Inst Environ Sci Eng PO Box 91000 Portland OR 97219. *Fax:* 503-690-1273; *E-Mail:* wjarrell@ese.ogi.edu

JARRET, RONALD MARCEL, PHYSICAL ORGANIC. *Current Pos:* Asst prof, 86-92, ASSOC PROF ORG CHEM, COL HOLY CROSS, 92- *Personal Data:* b Woonsocket, RI, Dec 22, 60; m 82, Elizabeth; c 3. *Educ:* RI Col, BA, 82, BS, 82; Yale Univ, PhD(chem), 87. *Concurrent Pos:* Prin investr, NSF grants, 88-94. *Mem:* Am Chem Soc. *Res:* Generate novel carbocations and use spectroscopic methods for structure identification. *Mailing Add:* Dept Chem Holy Cross Col Worcester MA 01610. *Fax:* 508-793-3030

JARRETT, HARRY WELLINGTON, III, PLANT BIOCHEMISTRY, PROTEIN CHEMISTRY. *Current Pos:* ASSOC PROF BIOCHEM, UNIV TENN, MEMPHIS, 89- *Personal Data:* b Charleston, SC, June 19, 50; m 77, Karen Mears; c Harry IV, Alexander & Patience. *Educ:* Univ SC, BS, 72; Univ NC, PhD(biochem), 76. *Prof Exp:* fel biochem, Mayo Clin, 76-77; fel chem, Univ Calif, San Diego, 77-80; asst biochemist biochem, Univ Ga, 80-82; from asst prof to assoc prof biol, Ind Univ-Purdue Univ, Indianapolis, 82-89. *Mem:* Am Soc Biochem & Molecular Biol; AAAS. *Res:* Calmodulin and Ca2-dependent metabolic regulation are main areas; development of new supports for affinity, ion exchange, gel filtration and DNA high pressure liquid chromatography. *Mailing Add:* Dept Biochem Univ Tenn 858 Madison Ave Memphis TN 38163-0002. *Fax:* 901-448-7360

JARRETT, HOWARD STARKE, JR, SOLID STATE PHYSICS. *Current Pos:* RETIRED. *Personal Data:* b Charleston, WVa, Oct 24, 27; m 51; c 4. *Educ:* Rensselaer Polytech Inst, BS, 47, MS, 48; Mass Inst Technol, PhD(physics), 51. *Prof Exp:* Res physicist, Cent Res Dept, E I du Pont de Nemours & Co, Inc, 51-55 & 80-90, res suprv, 55-80. *Concurrent Pos:* Prog co-chmn, Conf Magnetism & Magnetic Mat, 65, conf chmn, 69, chmn adv comn, 70. *Mem:* Fel Am Phys Soc. *Mailing Add:* 805 Sycamore Lane Wilmington DE 19807

JARRETT, JEFFREY E, MANAGEMENT SCIENCE. *Current Pos:* chmn, Dept Mgt Sci, 83-89, PROF MGT SCI/STATIST, UNIV RI, 71- *Personal Data:* b Bronx, NY, Dec 13, 40; m 64, Ruth Kurnow; c Michael, Debra & Daniel. *Educ:* Univ BBA, 62; NY Univ, MBA, 63, PhD(statist/opers res), 67. *Prof Exp:* Statistician, Columbia Rec Div, Cent Bur Statist, 62-63; instr statist/opers res, Univ Scranton, 65-66; prof statist/qual control, Wayne State Univ, 66-71; res analyst, Social Security Admin, 74-75, Overseas Progs, Boston Univ, 77-78. *Concurrent Pos:* Sears Found fed fac fel, Div Health Ins, Social Sec Admin, 74-75; consult, Abt Assocs, 79, RI Dept Health, 83, RI Pub Utilities Comn, 84, Tex Instrument, New Eng Tel, 88, Fed Paperboard, 86 & Eastern Utilities, 87; prof, Ohio Savings & Loan Acad, 81-91; mem, Prog Community Pharm Mgt, W M S Apple Found, 91; outstanding res scholar, URICBA, 91-92. *Mem:* Am Statist Asn; Decision Sci Inst; Int Inst Forecasters; Am Asn Univ Prof. *Res:* Applying statistics to business decision making, forecasting, quality control, and other managerial problems. *Mailing Add:* 133 Terre Mar Dr North Kingstown RI 02852. *Fax:* 401-792-4312; *E-Mail:* jeffi@uriacc.uri.edu

JARRETT, NOEL, METALLURGICAL PROCESS ENGINEERING. *Current Pos:* RETIRED. *Personal Data:* b Long Eaton, Eng, Nov 17, 21; nat US; m 49, Violet Dipner; c Robert, Kenneth, James & Thomas. *Educ:* Univ Pittsburgh, BS, 48; Univ Mich, MS, 51. *Prof Exp:* Sales engr indust oil sales, Freedom-Valvoline Oil Co, 49-50; res engr smelting, Aluminum Co Am, 51-55, sect head chem eng, 55-59, asst chief process metall div, 60-69, mgr, 69-73, dir smelting res & develop, 73-81, tech dir chem engr res & develop, Alcoa Labs, 81-87. *Concurrent Pos:* Mem, numerous Nat Res Coun & Nat Mat Adv Bd comts, 81-90; consult, Noel Jarrett Assoc, 87-; Krumb lectr, Am Inst Mining, Metall & Petrol Engrs, 87- *Mem:* Nat Acad Eng; Am Inst Chem Engrs; Mat Soc; fel Am Soc Metals. *Res:* Electrochemical cell development; optimization of Hall-Heroult Process; coker reactor and cell development of Alcoa Smelting Process; pollution control by scrubbing of chlorine from furnace effluent; high purity Al via crystallization; materials science engineering. *Mailing Add:* 149 Jefferson Ave Lower Burrell PA 15068-3127

JARRETT, STEVEN MICHAEL, PHYSICS. *Current Pos:* ENG PROJ MGR, SPECTRA PHYSICS, 75- *Personal Data:* b New York, NY, Mar 17, 36; m 61; c 4. *Educ:* City Col New York, BS, 56; Univ Mich, MS, 58, PhD(physics), 63. *Prof Exp:* Res assoc physics, Univ Mich, 62-63; sr scientist, TRG, Inc, Control Data Corp, NY, 63-66; sr res, Coherent Radiation Labs, Calif, 66-71; pres, Quantum Systs Corp, 71-75. *Mem:* Am Phys Soc; Optical Soc Am. *Res:* Lasers, especially gas, solid state and dye lasers; optics; spectroscopy. *Mailing Add:* 474 Los Ninos Way Los Altos CA 94022

JARROLL, EDWARD LEE, JR, BIOLOGY, PARASITOLOGY. *Current Pos:* PROF BIOL & CHAIR BIOL, NORTHEASTERN UNIV, 96- *Personal Data:* b Huntington, WVa, Jan 4, 48; m 75; c Christopher David. *Educ:* WVa Univ, AB, 69, MS, 71, PhD(biol), 77. *Prof Exp:* From instr to asst prof biol, Salem Col, 73-77; microbiologist, WVa Dept Health, 77; fel microbiol, Health Sci Ctr, Univ Oregon, 77-80; sr res assoc, Cornell Univ, 80-82; asst prof biol, West Chester Univ, 84; from asst prof to prof, Cleveland State Univ, 85-96, chair, 92-96. *Mem:* Am Soc Trop Med & Hyg; Am Soc Parasitologists; AAAS; Sigma Xi; Am Soc Cell Biol; Am Soc Microbiol; Soc Protozoologists. *Res:* Giardia and Trichomonas culture; physiology, immunology, and epidemiology; efficacy of disinfectants on Giardia cyst viability; encaptment pathways forming novel enzymes and a polysacharide. *Mailing Add:* 414 Mugar Hall Northeastern Univ 360 Huntington Ave Boston MA 02115. *Fax:* 617-373-3724; *E-Mail:* gjarroll@lynx.neu.edu

JARUZELSKI, JOHN JANUSZ, INDUSTRIAL ORGANIC CHEMISTRY & MANUFACTURING LUBRICATING OILS COMPONENTS. *Current Pos:* RETIRED. *Personal Data:* b Poland, Oct 4, 26; nat US; wid; c 2. *Educ:* Alliance Col, BS, 51; Pa State Univ, PhD(chem), 54. *Prof Exp:* Res chemist, Pittsburgh Plate Glass Co, 54-56; fel, Mellon Inst, 56-59; res chemist prod develop div, US Steel Corp, 59-60; sr chemist, Esso Res & Eng Co, 60-74, sr staff chemist & res assoc paramins, Technol Div, Exxon Chem Co, 74-93. *Mem:* Am Chem Soc. *Res:* Substitution reactions of aromatic hydrocarbons, especially chloroalkylations; esterification and polyesterification of alcohols and phenols; epoxydation and epoxy resins; thermosetting resins and reinforced plastics; chemistry of lubricating oils additives and antiwear chemicals; antioxidants. *Mailing Add:* 475 Channing Ave Westfield NJ 07090

JARVI, ESA TERO, PHARMACEUTICAL CHEMISTRY, ORGANIC CHEMISTRY. *Current Pos:* SR RES CHEMIST, MERRELL-DOW PHARMACEUT, 82-; SR RES CHEMIST, MALLINCKRODT INC. *Personal Data:* b Turku, Finland, May 12, 54; US citizen; m 83; c 1. *Educ:* Ohio State Univ, BS, 75; Univ Wis-Madison, PhD(org chem), 80. *Mem:* Am Chem Soc. *Res:* Synthesis of new potential drugs; enzyme inhibitors. *Mailing Add:* 1703 Warmington Ct Ballwin MO 63021-5873

JARVIK, JONATHAN WALLACE, ORGANELLE MORPHOGENESIS. *Current Pos:* asst prof, 78-83, ASSOC PROF BIOL SCI, CARNEGIE-MELLON UNIV, 84- *Personal Data:* b Charleston, SC, Mar 18, 45; m; c 3. *Educ:* Columbia Col, BA, 67; Mass Inst Technol, PhD(biol), 75. *Prof Exp:* Helen Hay Whitney fel, Yale Univ, 75-78. *Mem:* Genetics Soc Am; Am Soc Microbiol; Am Soc Cell Biol; Soc Protozoologists. *Res:* Genetic biochemical and ultrastructural analysis of eucaryotic flagellar morphogenesis. *Mailing Add:* Dept Biol Sci Carnegie-Mellon Univ 4400 Fifth Ave Pittsburgh PA 15213-2683

JARVIK, LISSY F, HUMAN GENETICS, GERIATRIC PSYCHIATRY. *Current Pos:* PROF PSYCHIAT, UNIV CALIF, LOS ANGELES, 72-; CHIEF SECT NEUROPSYCHOGERIAT, 83- *Personal Data:* b The Hague, Neth; nat US; m 54; c 2. *Educ:* Hunter Col, AB, 46; Columbia Univ, MA, 47, PhD(phychol), 50; Western Res Univ, MD, 54; Am Bd Pediat, dipl. *Honors & Awards:* Jack Weinberg Award Geriat Psychiat, Am Psychiat Asn, 86; Robert W Kleemeier Award Outstanding Res Aging, Geront Soc Am, 86; Edward B Allen Award, Am Geriat Soc, 86; Irving S Wright Award Distinction, Am Fedn Aging Res, 88; Founder's Award, Am Asn Geriat Psychiat, 90. *Prof Exp:* Asst psychiat, Columbia Univ, 46-48; res assoc, 48-50; asst, Western Res Univ, Sch Med, 53; intern, Mt Sinai Hosp, New York, 54-55; sr res scientist med genetics, Radiation Safety Officer, NY State Psychiat Inst, 55-62, assoc res scientist & assoc attend psychiatrist, 63-72. *Concurrent Pos:* Resident pediat, Columbia-Presby Med Ctr, 55-56, from asst clin prof to assoc clin prof psychiat, Columbia Univ, 62-72; NSF traveling fel, Int Cong Human Genetics, Denmark, 56; fel, Vanderbilt Clin, 57-58; res psychiatrist, NY State Psychiat Inst, 69-72; vis assoc prof, Univ Calif, Los Angeles, 70-71; chief psychogenetics unit, Vet Admin Hosp Brentwood, Los Angeles, 70-; mem joint psychotomimetic adv comt, Nat Inst Ment Health-Food & Drug Admin, 70-72; tech comt res & develop, White House Conf Aging, 71-73; bd dir & med & sci adv coun, Alzheimer's Dis & Rel Disords Asn, 80-; vis McCleod prof, Univ Adelaide, SAustralia, 81; testimony, Joint House Subcom hearings, alzheimer's Dis, 83; vis lectr geriat & geront, Am Asn Med Col, 83-84; distinguished physician, Vet Admin, 87-; Nat Sci Adv Coun, Am Fed Aging Res, 86-; co-ed, Alzheimer Dis & Assoc Disorders, Int J, 87, mem, Nat Adv Mental Health Coun, 84-87, action comt, White House conf aging, 86, Nat Inst Mental Health, Dept Health & Human SErv coun, Alzheimer's Dis, Workshop, epidemiol, 87; Brookdale Nat Fel, med adv bd, 87-; scientist comt, Merck fel clin geriat pharmacol, Am Fed Aging Res, 87-89; bd mem, Am Aging Asn, 91-; found fel, Ctr Advan Study Behav Sci, Stanford, 88-89. *Mem:* Fel Am Psychol Asn; Am Soc Human Genetics; Soc Study Social Biol; Am Psychopath Asn; Am Psychiat Asn; Am Asn Geriat Psychiat; Am Geriat Soc; Geront Soc Am; Behav Genetics Asn; Int Asn Geront; World Psychiat Asn. *Res:* Normal pathological mental changes with aging, particularly dementia of the Alzheimer type and depression; geriatric psychopathology; drug treatment and psychotherapy; basic biological mechanisms in Alzheimer's disease, especially microtubules; family studies. *Mailing Add:* 760 Westwood Plaza Los Angeles CA 90024-1759

JARVIK, MURRAY ELIAS, PHARMACOLOGY. *Current Pos:* PROF PSYCHIAT & PHARMACOL, UNIV CALIF, LOS ANGELES, 72- *Personal Data:* b New York, NY, June 1, 23; m 54; c 2. *Educ:* City Col New York, BS, 44; Univ Calif, Los Angeles, MA, 45; Univ Calif, Berkeley, MD, 51, PhD, 52. *Honors & Awards:* Career Develop Scientist Award, NIMH, 71. *Prof Exp:* Res technician phys chem, Rockefeller Inst, 43-44; asst exp psychol, Univ Calif, Los Angeles, 44-45; res assoc comp physiol psychol, Yerkes Labs, Fla, 51-53; lectr physiol psychol, Columbia Univ, 53-56; vis asst prof, Univ Calif, 55; res assoc psychopharmacol, Long Island Biol Asn, NY, 55-56; from asst prof to prof pharmacol, Albert Einstein Col Med, 56-72, prof psychiat, 69-72. *Concurrent Pos:* Res assoc, Mt Sinai Hosp, NY, 53-55; adj asst prof physiol psychol, Grad Div, NY Univ, 57; managing ed, Psychopharmacologia, 65; mem psychopharmacology study sect, NIMH, 65-70; adv comt abuse of stimulant & depressant drugs, Bur Drug Abuse Control, Food & Drug Admin, 66-68; investr, VA Med Res, 71; chief, Psychopharmacol Unit, Vet Admin Hosp, West Los Angeles, 72- *Mem:* Am Soc Pharmacol & Exp Therapeut; fel Am Psychol Asn; fel NY Acad Sci; Am Col Neuropsychopharmacol; Int Brain Res Orgn; fel, CASBS Ctr Advon Study Behav Sci. *Res:* Effects of drugs upon learning and retention; neurophysiological basis of learning; localization of drug effects in the central nervous system; psychopharmacology; primate behavior; techniques for chronic implantation of arterial catheters; smoking behavior nicotine addiction. *Mailing Add:* Vet Admin Hosp Brentwood 691-B151D Willshire & Sawtelle Blvds Los Angeles CA 90073. *E-Mail:* mjarvik@ucla.edu

JARVINEN, RICHARD DALVIN, MATHEMATICS. *Current Pos:* PROF MATH & STATIST, WINONA STATE UNIV, 90- *Personal Data:* b Virginia, Minn, Dec 5, 38; m 61; c 2. *Educ:* St John's Univ, Minn, BA, 60; Vanderbilt Univ, MAT, 61; Syracuse Univ, PhD(math), 71. *Prof Exp:* Analyst missile simulations, Remington Rand Univac, 61-62; asst prof math, Carleton Col, 67-72; from assoc prof to prof math & statist, St Mary's Col, 72-90. *Concurrent Pos:* Researcher math & statist, St Mary's Col, 75- *Mem:* Math Asn Am; Sigma Xi. *Res:* Bases in topological linear spaces; applications of undergraduate mathematics; computer generated movies and slides for learning mathematics. *Mailing Add:* Dept Math & Statistics 308 Gildemeister Hall Winona MN 55987

JARVIS, BRUCE B, ORGANIC CHEMISTRY. *Current Pos:* from asst prof to assoc prof, 67-79, PROF CHEM, UNIV MD, COLLEGE PARK, 79-, CHMN, DEPT CHEM & BIOCHEM, 93- *Personal Data:* b Van Wert, Ohio, Sept 30, 42; m 63; c 3. *Educ:* Ohio Wesleyan Univ, BA, 63; Univ Colo, PhD(chem), 66. *Prof Exp:* Instr chem, Northwestern Univ, 66-67. *Mem:* Fel AAAS; Am Chem Soc; Sigma Xi; Am Soc Pharmacog; Int Soc Toxinology. *Res:* Natural product chemistry; nucleophilic displacements; sulfur chemistry and molecular rearrangements; mycotoxins. *Mailing Add:* Dept Chem Univ Md College Park MD 20742-0001. *Fax:* 301-314-9121; *E-Mail:* bj6@umail.umd.edu

JARVIS, CHRISTINE WOODRUFF, TEXTILE SCIENCE, PHYSICAL CHEMISTRY. *Current Pos:* Res assoc textiles, Clemson Univ, 76, instr chem, 76-78, from asst prof to prof textiles, 78-89, J E SIRRINE PROF TEXTILES, CLEMSON UNIV, 89- *Personal Data:* b Raleigh, NC, June 19, 49; m 71; c 1. *Educ:* Univ NC, Chapel Hill, 71; Mass Inst Technol, PhD(phys chem), 76. *Concurrent Pos:* Res assoc, Nat Bur Standards, 85. *Mem:* Am Chem Soc; Am Asn Textile Technologists; Sigma Xi; Am Asn Textile Chemists & Colorists; Tech Asn Pulp & Paper Indust. *Res:* Fiber physics; nonwovens; chemical kinetics of polymer flammability; cotton dust analysis; apparel manufacturing. *Mailing Add:* PO Box 430 Six Mile SC 29682-0430

JARVIS, FLOYD ELDRIDGE, JR, GENETICS. *Current Pos:* RETIRED. *Personal Data:* b Richmond, Va, Aug 15, 21; m 53; c 1. *Educ:* Univ Richmond, AB, 47; Va Polytech Inst, PhD(biol), 56. *Prof Exp:* From assoc prof to prof biol, Radford Univ, 55-87. *Mem:* Entom Soc Am. *Res:* Inheritance of insecticidal resistance; residual effectiveness of insecticide formulations. *Mailing Add:* 103 Dogwood Lane Radford VA 24141

JARVIS, JACK REYNOLDS, MEDICINE. *Current Pos:* ASST PROF PSYCHIAT, SCH MED, EMORY UNIV, 61- *Personal Data:* b Menomonie, Wis, Oct 31, 15; m 45; c 2. *Educ:* Birmingham-South Col, BS, 34; Vanderbilt Univ, MD, 38; Am Bd Psychiat & Neurol, dipl, 45. *Prof Exp:* Assoc prof psychiat, Med Col Ala, 48-61. *Concurrent Pos:* Chief psychiat serv, Vet Admin Hosp, Birmingham, Ala, 55-61; area chief psychiat, Vet Admin Ga, 61-65; staff physician, Regional Off, Vet Admin, 65-; staff physician, Vet Admin Hosp, 66- *Mem:* Am Psychiat Asn. *Res:* Psychiatry. *Mailing Add:* Vet Admin Hosp Clairmont Rd Decatur GA 30033

JARVIS, JAMES GORDON, ELECTROPHOTOGRAPHY. *Current Pos:* RETIRED. *Personal Data:* b Aultsville, Ont, July 13, 24; nat US; m 47, Helen Nelson; c 2. *Educ:* Queen's Univ, Can, BSc, 45; Univ Rochester, MS, 54. *Prof Exp:* Instr, Queen's Univ, Can, 45-46; res assoc, Photomat Div, Eastman Kodak Co, 46-69, sr lab head, Res Labs, 69-84. *Mem:* Optical Soc Am; Soc Photog Sci & Eng. *Res:* Colorimetry; physiological optics; solid state physics; electrophotography. *Mailing Add:* 846 Dewitt Rd Webster NY 14580

JARVIS, JOHN FREDERICK, PHYSICS. *Current Pos:* ASST PROF COMPUT SCI, UNIV SC, AIKEN, 91- *Personal Data:* b Montreal, Can, June 22, 41; US citizen; m 63; c 5. *Educ:* Univ Fla, BS, 62; Duke Univ, PhD(physics), 67. *Prof Exp:* Res assoc physics, Duke Univ, 67-68; mem tech staff syst res, AT&T Bell Labs, 68-82, head, Robotics Systs Res Dept, 82-90. *Concurrent Pos:* Vis lectr, Princeton Univ, 78-79; vis astronr, KH Peak Nat Observ, 79-81; adj prof, EE Stevens Inst Technol, 91. *Mem:* Inst Elec & Electronics Engrs; AAAS; Am Astron Soc. *Res:* Computer graphics, computer vision, automated inspection, pattern recognition; robotics; astronomy. *Mailing Add:* Dept Math Comput Sci & Eng Univ SC 171 University Pkwy Aiken SC 29801

JARVIS, JOHN J, TRANSPORTATION & DISTRIBUTION, LOGISTICS. *Current Pos:* from assoc prof to prof indust & systs eng, 68-91, DIR, SCH INDUST & SYSTS ENG, GA INST TECHNOL, 91- *Personal Data:* b Donnelson, Tenn, Aug 7, 41; m 63. *Educ:* Univ Ala, BSIE, 63, MSIE, 65; Johns Hopkins Univ, PhD(opers res), 68. *Prof Exp:* Numerical analyst, NASA, 63; res asst, Univ Ala, 63-65; res assoc, Johns Hopkins Univ, 65-68. *Concurrent Pos:* Consult, Southern Rwy Syst, 69-75, Comput Aided Planning & Scheduling, Inc, 78-, Environ Protection Agency, 78-, Sohio, 82, Coca Cola, 84-85 & Sears, 84-85. *Mem:* Opers Res Soc Am; Inst Mgt Sci; Soc Indust & Appl Math; Am Inst Indust Engrs. *Res:* Modeling and methodology in operations research and network theory-analysis; transportation, distribution and logistics systems analysis. *Mailing Add:* Sch Indust & Systs Eng Ga Tech Atlanta GA 30332-0205

JARVIS, LACTANCE AUBREY, ORGANIC POLYMER CHEMISTRY. *Current Pos:* CONSULT, 82- *Personal Data:* b Homer, Mich, Sept 7, 21; m 43; c 2. *Educ:* Mich State Univ, BS, 43. *Prof Exp:* Chem engr, Firestone Rubber & Tire Co, 43-49; chemist rubber & plastics, Wyandotte Chem Corp, 49-55; chem engr, Whirlpool Corp, 55-60; dir res, Modern Plastics Corp, Mich, 60-66; mgr mat res, Clark Equip Co, 66-82. *Mem:* Am Chem Soc; Soc Plastics Engrs; Sigma Xi. *Res:* Development and application of plastic materials and processes. *Mailing Add:* PO Box 64 Buchanan MI 49107

JARVIS, NELDON LYNN, SURFACE & COLLOID CHEMISTRY, CHEMICAL MICROSENSOR TECHNOL. *Current Pos:* VPRES, MICROSENSOR SYSTS, INC, 88- *Personal Data:* b Salt Lake City, Utah, Nov 16, 35; m 57, Magdalena G Abraham; c Hilary, Lori, Neldon L, Suzanne, Mary L, Virginia & Owen C. *Educ:* Brigham Young Univ, BS, 52; Kans State Univ, PhD(agron), 58. *Prof Exp:* Nat Acad Sci-Nat Res Coun res assoc, US Naval Res Lab, 57-59, phys chemist, 59-69, head, Surface Chem Br, Chem Div, 69-84; chief scientist, Res Directorate, US Army Chem Res Develop & Eng Ctr, 84-86, head, Chem Div, 86-88. *Concurrent Pos:* Lectr, Am Univ, 64 & 69- *Mem:* Sigma Xi; Am Chem Soc; Soc Lubrication Engrs. *Res:* Adsorption-desorption phenomena at solid-liquid and liquid-air interfaces; wetting and spreading phenomena; tribology; lubricant development, analysis and condition monitoring; surface analysis; chemical microsensor development a. *Mailing Add:* 120 S Union Ave Havre de Grace MD 21078-3112

JARVIS, RICHARD S, hydrology, for more information see previous edition

JARVIS, ROGER GEORGE, ENVIRONMENTAL SCIENCES. *Current Pos:* RETIRED. *Personal Data:* b Hugglescote, Eng, Apr 26, 28; Can citizen; m 54, Ruth A Wilson; c Alan R & Hugh W. *Educ:* Oxford Univ, BA, 49, MA & DPhil(physics), 53. *Prof Exp:* Fel nuclear physics, Nat Res Coun, Chalk River, 53-54; res fel, Imp Chem Indust, Univ Liverpool, 55; mem, Atomic Power Div, Gen Elec Co, Eng, 56; sr res off, waste mgt technol, Atomic Energy Can, Ltd, 56-89. *Mem:* Can Appl Math Soc; Math Asn Am. *Res:* Operations research, mainly in nuclear energy; risk analysis; mathematical modeling. *Mailing Add:* 38 Park Dale Box 1570 Deep River ON K0J 1P0 Can

JARVIS, SIMON MICHAEL, MEMBRANE TRANSPORT. *Current Pos:* lectr, 86-92, SR LECTR BIOCHEM, DEPT BIOSCI, UNIV KENT, CANTERBURY, 92- *Personal Data:* b London, Eng; m 80, Barbara Coubon; c Amanda & Mark. *Educ:* Univ Nottingham, UK, BSc, 77; Cambridge Univ, UK, PhD(physiol), 81. *Prof Exp:* Res fel cancer res, Cancer Res Unit, Univ Alta, Edmonton, Can, 80-82, from asst prof to assoc prof physiol, 82-86. *Mem:* Am Physiol Soc; Biochem Soc; Physiol Soc; Brit Soc Parasitol. *Res:* Nucleoside and nucleobase transport in mammalian cells and parasitic protozoa; facilitated-diffusion and sodium-dependent systems; comparison of sugar and nucleoside carriers; dopamine uptake by the central nervous system; physiological actions of adenosine. *Mailing Add:* Dept Biosci Univ Kent Canterbury Kent CT2 7NJ England

JARVIS, WILLIAM R, EPIDEMIOLOGY, PEDIATRIC INFECTIOUS DISEASE. *Current Pos:* asst prof, 85-96; CHIEF, INVEST & PREVENT BR, HOSP INFECTIONS PROG, CTR DIS CONTROL, 87-, ACTG DIR, 96- *Personal Data:* b Oakland, Calif, June 2, 48; m 82, Janine M Jason; c Ashley A & Danielle K. *Educ:* Univ Calif, Davis, BS, 70; Univ Tex, Houston, MD, 74. *Honors & Awards:* Charles C Shepard Award, 93. *Prof Exp:* Asst chief, Nat Nosocomial Infections Study, 81-86. *Concurrent Pos:* US Pub Health Serv Award, US Govt, 85-94. *Mem:* Infectious Dis Soc; Soc Hosp Epidemol Am; Am Soc Microbiol; Am Acad Pediat; Soc Pediat Res. *Res:* Hospital epidemiology. *Mailing Add:* 827 W Ponce de Leon Ave Decatur GA 30030

JARVIS, WILLIAM ROBERT, PLANT PATHOLOGY, MYCOLOGY. *Current Pos:* head, Plant Path Sect, 74-92, sr phytopathologist, 92-94, EMER PHYTOPATHOLOGIST CAN DEPT AGR, 94- *Personal Data:* b Olney, Eng, Nov 15, 27; m 52, Josephine Hayes; c Sarah. *Educ:* Univ Sheffield, BSc, 51; Univ London, PhD(plant Path), 53, DIC, 53, cBiol, 85. *Honors & Awards:* Bailey Award, Can Phytopath Soc, 85. *Prof Exp:* Prin sci officer, Scottish Hort Res Inst, 53-74; asst specialist, Univ Calif, 63-64; scientist, Dept Sci & Indust Res, New Zealand, 69-70. *Concurrent Pos:* Assoc ed, Can J Plant Path, sr ed, Plant Dis; chmn, Biol Control Comt chmn Publ Comt & Can Pythopath Soc, 85-; ed, Hort Res. *Mem:* Am Phytopath Soc; Brit Fedn Plant Pathologists; Brit Mycol Soc; Can Phytopathol Soc. *Res:* Biology of botrytis species; powdery mildews; biological control; diseases of field and greenhouse vegetables, small berry fruits and ornamental bulb crops; intelligent systems; managing diseases in greenhouse crops. *Mailing Add:* Agr Can Res Sta Harrow ON N0R 1G0 Can. *Fax:* 519-738-2929

JARVIS, WILLIAM TYLER, PUBLIC HEALTH. *Current Pos:* from asst prof to prof prev & community dent, 73-82, prof pub health sci & chmn dept, 82-86, ASSOC PROF PREV MED, LOMA LINDA UNIV, 86- , PROF DEPT PUB HEALTH & PREV MED, 89- *Personal Data:* b Takoma Park, Md, Oct 19, 35; m 62; c 2. *Educ:* Univ Minn, Duluth, BS, 61; Kent State Univ, Ohio, MA, 68; Univ Ore, PhD(health educ), 73. *Prof Exp:* Instr, Parkersburg Jr Acad, WVa, 61-62; Mt Vernon Acad, Ohio, 62-68; asst prof health & phys educ, Loma Linda Univ, Calif, 68-71; fel health educ, Univ Ore, 71-73. *Concurrent Pos:* Ed newslett, Nat Coun Against Health Fraud, 78-; mem bd sci adv, Am Coun Sci & Health, 78-; mem nat comt unproven methods cancer mgt, Am Cancer Soc, 86- *Mem:* Nat Coun Against Health Fraud (pres, 77-); Am Pub Health Asn; Am Asn Health Phys Educ & Recreation; Am Cancer Soc. *Res:* Consumer health education; health fraud, misinformation and quackery. *Mailing Add:* 25015 Tulip Loma Linda CA 92354

JARZEN, DAVID MACARTHUR, PALYNOLOGY, PALEOBOTANY. *Current Pos:* SR BIOL SCIENTIST, COLLECTIONS MGR, FLA MUS NAT HISTORY, 97- *Personal Data:* b Cleveland, Ohio, Oct 19, 41; m 62, Susan A Klein; c Thomas D & Robert J. *Educ:* Kent State Univ, BS, 67, MA, 69; Univ Toronto, PhD(geol), 73. *Prof Exp:* Palynologist & cur fossil plants, Nat Mus Can, 73-89, res scientist, Can Mus Nature, 89-97. *Concurrent Pos:* Vis scholar, Univ Queensland, Brisbane, Australia, 87-88; hon mem, St John's Col, Univ Queensland, Brisbane, Australia; photographer, Nature Art & Photography. *Mem:* Can Asn Palynologists (pres, 80); Am Asn Stratig Palynologists; Asn Trop Biol; Int Asn Angiosperm Paleobot; Int Fedn Palynology Soc (secy/treas, 84-88, vpres, 92-96); Palynology & Paleobot Asn Australasia. *Res:* Palynological investigations of terminal Cretaceous and lower Tertiary floras, to discover the paleoenvironmental setting based on the botanical affinities of the fossil pollen and spores; cretaceous spore pollen floras from Australasian (Gondwanan) sediments with an emphasis on evolutionary trends. *Mailing Add:* Fla Mus Nat Hist Univ Fla PO Box 117800 Gainsville FL 32611-7800. *E-Mail:* dmj@flmnh.ufl.edu

JARZYNSKI, JACEK, PHYSICS. *Current Pos:* RES PHYSICIST, NAVAL RES LAB, 71- *Personal Data:* b Warsaw, Poland, Mar 28, 35; US citizen. *Educ:* Imp Col, Univ London, BS, 57, PhD(physics), 61. *Prof Exp:* Fel phys acoustics, Cath Univ Am, 61-62; tech officer optics, Imp Chem Industs, Ltd, Gt Brit, 63; assoc prof physics, Am Univ, 63-71. *Concurrent Pos:* Consult, Naval Ord Lab, 67-70. *Mem:* Acoust Soc Am; Am Phys Soc; Sigma Xi. *Res:* Parametric underwater acoustic arrays and sound propagation; development of ultrasonic methods for study of materials; measurement of thermodynamic properties of metals and alloys and comparison with pseudopotential theory. *Mailing Add:* Sch Mech Eng Ga Inst Technol Atlanta GA 30332-0001

JASANOFF, SHEILA SEN, LAW & SCIENCE, ENVIRONMENTAL POLICY. *Current Pos:* sr res assoc sci policy & law, Prog Sci, Technol & Soc, Cornell Univ, 78-84, assoc prof, 84-89, dir, 88-91, PROF SCI POLICY & LAW, PROG SCI, TECHNOL & SOC, CORNELL UNIV, 90-, CHAIR, DEPT SCI & TECHNOL STUDIES, 91- *Personal Data:* b Calcutta, India, Feb 15, 44; US citizen; m 68, Jay H; c Alan & Maya. *Educ:* Harvard Col, AB, 64, PhD(ling), 73, JD, 76; Univ Bonn, WGer, MA, 66. *Honors & Awards:* Distinguished Achievement Award, Soc Risk Anal, 92. *Prof Exp:* Assoc, Bracken, Selig & Baram, 76-78. *Concurrent Pos:* Consult, Orgn Econ Coop & Develop, 80-89 & Off Technol Assessment, 83-87; mem, Nat Conf Lawyers & Scientists, AAAS & Am Bar Asn, 85-91, Comt Govt-Indust Collab Biomed Res, Inst Med, 88-89 & Adv Comt, NSF, 90-92; contrib ed, Sci, Technol & Human Values, 88-91; vis prof, Yale Univ, 90-91, JFK Sch, Harvard Univ, 96; adj prof, Boston Univ Sch Law, 93; vis scholar, Wolfson Col, Oxford, 96; bd dir, AAAS, 96- *Mem:* Fel AAAS; Soc Social Studies Sci; Sigma Xi. *Res:* Comparative studies of US and European health, safety and environmental regulations; US science policy; law, science and technology; risk management of chemicals and biotechnology. *Mailing Add:* Dept Sci & Technol Studies Cornell Univ 632 Clark Hall Ithaca NY 14853. *Fax:* 607-255-6044; *E-Mail:* ssj2@cornell.edu

JASELSKIS, BRUNO, ANALYTICAL CHEMISTRY, INORGANIC CHEMISTRY. *Current Pos:* from asst prof to assoc prof, 62-69, PROF CHEM, LOYOLA UNIV CHICAGO, 69- *Personal Data:* b Suraitciai, Lithuania, Mar 9, 24; nat US; m 55; c 6. *Educ:* Union Univ, NY, BS, 52; Iowa State Univ, MS, 54, PhD, 55. *Prof Exp:* Instr chem, Univ Mich, 56-59, asst prof, 59-62. *Mem:* Am Chem Soc; AAAS; Sigma Xi. *Res:* Complex ions and their application to analytical problems; solution chemistry of Xenon compounds: determination of micro amounts of various substances. *Mailing Add:* Dept Chem Loyola Univ Chicago IL 60626

JASHNANI, INDRU, CHEMICAL ENGINEERING. *Current Pos:* SR STAFF ENGR, MARTIN MARIETTA CORP, 77-; PRES, ENG & COMPUTER SERV, INC, 90- *Personal Data:* b Ghotki, Pakistan, Nov 2, 44. *Educ:* Indian Inst Technol, Bombay, BTech, 67; Univ Cincinnati, PhD(chem eng), 71. *Prof Exp:* Fel chem & nuclear eng, Univ Cincinnati, 71-72; sr engr, APT, Inc, 72-74; staff mem, Arthur D Little, Inc, 74-77. *Mem:* Am Inst Chem Engrs; Am Chem Soc; Air Pollution Control Asn. *Res:* Environmental control, air, water and solid, for process industries and utility boilers. *Mailing Add:* 5575 Sterredd Pl Suite 250 Columbia MD 21044

JASIN, HUGO E, INTERNAL MEDICINE, IMMUNOLOGY. *Current Pos:* PROF INTERNAL MED & DIR DIV RHEUMATOLOGY CLIN IMMUNOL, UNIV ARK MED SCI, 91- *Personal Data:* b Buenos Aires, Arg, Jan 22, 33; US citizen; m 66; c 3. *Educ:* Univ Buenos Aires, MD, 56. *Prof Exp:* Fel internal med, Univ Tex Southwestern Med Sch, 59-62 & 64-65; Nuffield fel, Med Res Coun Rheumatism Res Unit, Eng, 62-64; from instr to assoc prof, Univ Tex Southwestern Med Sch, 65-78, prof internal med, 78-91. *Concurrent Pos:* Arthritis Found fel, 70-72; USPHS career develop award, 73-77; mem, Gen Med Study Sect, USPHS, 74-78. *Mem:* Fel Am Col Physicians; Am Asn Immunologists; Am Rheumatism Asn; Am Soc Clin Invest; Am Asn Physicians. *Res:* Immunological mechanisms in rheumatic diseases and chronic inflammation. *Mailing Add:* Univ Ark 4301 W Markham Little Rock AR 72205. *Fax:* 501-686-8188; *E-Mail:* hjasin@medlan.uams.edu

JASINSKI, DONALD ROBERT, CLINICAL PHARMACOLOGY. *Current Pos:* staff physician, 65-67, chief opiate unit, 67-68, chief clin pharmacol sect, 69-77, DIR, ADDICTION RES CTR, NAT INST DRUG ABUSE, 77- *Personal Data:* b Chicago, Ill, Aug 27, 38; m 64; c 4. *Educ:* Loyola Univ, Ill, 56-59; Univ Ill, MD, 63. *Prof Exp:* Intern, Res & Educ Hosps, Univ Ill, Chicago, 63-64; fel neuropharmacol, 64-65. *Concurrent Pos:* Assoc mem grad fac, Dept Pharmacol, Col Med, Univ Ky; clin asst prof pharmacol, Univ Ill; clin prof pharmacol & toxicol & mem grad fac, Univ Louisville, Ky. *Mem:* AAAS; Am Soc Clin Pharmacol & Therapeut; Am Soc Pharmacol & Exp Therapeut; Soc Neurosci; Int Brain Res Orgn; Sigma Xi. *Res:* Neuropharmacology; Psychopharmacology. *Mailing Add:* Ctr Chem Dependence MFL Bldg Johns Hopkins Bayview Med Ctr 4940 Eastern Ave Baltimore MD 21224-2780. *Fax:* 410-550-1912

JASINSKI, JERRY PETER, X-RAY CRYSTALLOGRAPHY, BIOCHEMISTRY. *Current Pos:* from asst prof to assoc prof, 78-89, coordr phys sci, 81-83, PROF CHEM, KEENE STATE COL, NH, 89-, DIR, NEW ENG MOLECULAR STRUCT CTR, 90- *Personal Data:* b Newport, NH, July 28, 40; m 66, Jacquelin A Sargeant; c Jana L, John M & Jennifer A. *Educ:* Univ NH, BA, 64, MST, 68; Worcester Polytech Inst, MNS, 68; Univ Wyo, PhD(chem), 74. *Prof Exp:* Teacher, high schs, NY, NH & Vt, 64-70 & 75-78; teaching & res assoc chem, Univ Wyo, 70-73; assoc Western Univs fel, Los Alamos Sci Lab, 73-74; res assoc, Univ Va, 74-75. *Concurrent Pos:* Consult, US Army Mat & Mech Res Ctr, Watertown, Mass, 83-96. *Mem:* Sigma Xi; Am Chem Soc; Am Inst Chemists; Am Crystallog Asn. *Res:* Experimental and theoretical molecular electronic spectroscopy; solid state and coordination chemistry; x-ray crystallography; bioinorganic chemistry; industrial chemistry; chemical design and molecular mechanics modelling; luminescence and laser spectroscopy. *Mailing Add:* 12 Orchard Lane Springfield VT 05156. *Fax:* 603-358-2257; *E-Mail:* jjasinski@keene.edu

JASKOSKI, BENEDICT JACOB, PARASITOLOGY. *Current Pos:* from assoc prof to prof, 54-86, EMER PROF BIOL, LOYOLA UNIV, CHICAGO, 86- *Personal Data:* b Velva, NDak, July 25, 15; m 56; c 1. *Educ:* Jamestown Col, AB, 39; Univ Notre Dame, MS, 42, PhD(zool), 50. *Hon Degrees:* DSc, Ill Col Podiatry, 64. *Prof Exp:* Prin pub sch, NDak, 39-40; asst instr biol, Univ Notre Dame, 49-50; asst prof, Creighton Univ, 50-54. *Concurrent Pos:* Fel trop med, La State Univ, 61; assoc, Am Univ Beirut, 66; USPHS res award; Am Cancer Soc inst grant partic. *Mem:* Fel AAAS; Am Soc Parasitologists; Am Soc Zoologists; Am Micros Soc; fel Am Pub Health Asn. *Res:* Parasites of captive animals; nematode parasites; biochemistry and physiology of parasitic nematodes; human parasitology; culture of metazoan parasites. *Mailing Add:* Dept Biol Damen Hall Eighth Fl Rm 835 Loyola Univ 6525 N Sheraton Rd Chicago IL 60626

JASMIN, GAETAN, PATHOLOGY. *Current Pos:* From asst prof exp path to assoc prof path, 56-67, chmn dept, 70-82, PROF PATH, UNIV MONTREAL,. *Personal Data:* b Montreal, Que, Nov 24, 24; m 52; c 3. *Educ:* St Laurent Col, BA, 45; Univ Montreal, MD, 51, PhD(exp med), 56; CSPQ, 68; FRCP(C), 78. *Concurrent Pos:* Med res assoc, Nat Res Coun Can, 58-70; ed, Revue Canadienne de Biologie, 60-70, Methods & Achievements in Exp Path, 66- *Mem:* Soc Exp Biol & Med; Am Physiol Soc; Histochem Soc; Can Soc Clin Invest; Int Acad Path. *Res:* Endocrinology; muscle diseases and cancer. *Mailing Add:* Dept Path Fac Med Univ Montreal CP 6128 Sta A Montreal PQ H3C 3J7 Can. *Fax:* 514-343-5755

JASNOW, DAVID MICHAEL, CONDENSED MATTER THEORY. *Current Pos:* From asst prof to assoc prof, 71-82, PROF PHYSICS, UNIV PITTSBURGH, 82- *Personal Data:* b New York, NY, Apr 27, 43; m 64, Carol H; c Stephanie & Laine. *Educ:* Cornell Univ, BA, 64; Univ Ill Urbana-Champaign, MS, 65, PhD(physics), 69. *Concurrent Pos:* Prin investr, NSF, 74-; div assoc ed, Phys Rev Lett, 88- *Mem:* Fel Am Phys Soc. *Res:* Theoretical research in statistical physics; phase transitions and critical phenomena; kinetics of phase transitions; equilibruim and non-equilibrium properties of interfaces; polymer statistical mechanics. *Mailing Add:* Dept Physics & Astron Univ Pittsburgh Pittsburgh PA 15260

JASNY, GEORGE R, CHEMICAL & NUCLEAR CHEMICAL ENGINEERING. *Current Pos:* RETIRED. *Personal Data:* b Katowice, Poland, June 6, 24; US citizen; m 51, Gloria Jones; c Elizabeth P & Thomas P. *Educ:* Univ Wash, Seattle, BS, 49; Mass Inst Technol, ScM, 52. *Honors & Awards:* Robert E Wilson Award, Am Inst Chem Engrs, 95. *Prof Exp:* Engr, Y-12 plant, Union Carbide Corp, 50-56, eng dept head, 56-62, tech div head, 62-65, chief engr, 65-71, dir eng, 71-80, vpres eng & comput sci, Nuclear Div, 80-84; vpres eng & comput sci, Martin Marietta Energy Systs, 84-89, vpres tech opers, 89. *Mem:* Nat Acad Eng; Sci Res Soc NAm; fel Am Inst Chem Engrs; Am Soc Eng Mgt. *Res:* Solvent extractions; enriched uranium scrap processing; plant design; quality control; uranium enrichment. *Mailing Add:* 106 Dixie Lane Oak Ridge TN 37830

JASON, ANDREW JOHN, MOLECULAR PHYSICS, SURFACE PHYSICS. *Current Pos:* asst prof, 68-73, ASSOC PROF PHYSICS, UNIV ALA, 73- *Personal Data:* b Detroit, Mich, Jan 27, 38; m 62; c 1. *Educ:* Mass Inst Technol, SB, 59; Univ Chicago, MS, 60, PhD(physics), 67. *Prof Exp:* Res assoc physics, Univ Chicago, 67-68. *Mem:* AAAS; Am Phys Soc. *Res:* Field ionization; atomic physics; high field studies of atoms and molecules; kinetics of evaporation; ion optics; mass spectrometry; optical properties of surfaces. *Mailing Add:* 300 Rim Rd Los Alamos NM 87544

JASON, EMIL FRED, CHEMISTRY. *Current Pos:* PROF CHEM & ASST VPRES, SOUTHERN ILL UNIV, 71- *Personal Data:* b Edwardsville, Ill, Aug 7, 27; m 55; c 2. *Educ:* Lincoln Univ, Mo, BS, 49; Washington Univ, St Louis, MA, 55, PhD(chem), 57. *Prof Exp:* Teacher pub sch, Ethiopia, 49-51; fel, Wash Univ, St Louis, 57-58; asst proj chemist, Stand Oil Co, Ind, 58-60, proj chemist, 60; asst prof chem, Lincoln Univ, Mo, 60-71. *Mem:* Am Chem Soc. *Res:* Organic syntheses; oxidation; free radical reactions. *Mailing Add:* 8543 Goshen Rd Edwardsville IL 62025-9808

JASON, MARK EDWARD, PHYSICAL ORGANIC, REACTION MECHANISMS. *Current Pos:* ASSOC FEL, MONSANTO, 83- *Personal Data:* b Grand Rapids, Mich, Oct 18, 49; m 73, Janet M Westerman; c Elisabeth M & Amanda M. *Educ:* Univ Mich, BS, 71; Yale Univ, PhD(chem), 76. *Prof Exp:* Assoc, Northwestern Univ, 76, 76, NSF assoc, 76-77; asst prof org chem, Amherst Col, 77-83. *Concurrent Pos:* Vis prof, Cornell Univ, 81. *Mem:* Am Chem Soc. *Res:* Physical organic chemistry; chemistry of small ring compounds; chelation chemistry. *Mailing Add:* Monsanto 800 N Lindbergh Blvd T3W St Louis MO 63167-0002. *Fax:* 314-694-4575; *E-Mail:* mejaso@ccmail.monsanto.com

JASPER, DONALD EDWARD, VETERINARY MEDICINE, CLINICAL PATHOLOGY. *Current Pos:* RETIRED. *Personal Data:* b La Grande, Ore, Dec 30, 18; m 43, Elizabeth Ann Miller; c Donald R & Jean E (Edwards). *Educ:* State Col Wash, BS, 40, DVM, 42; Iowa State Col, MS, 44; Univ Minn, PhD(vet med), 47. *Honors & Awards:* Borden Award, 67. *Prof Exp:* Asst clinician, Iowa State Col, 42-44; from asst prof to assoc prof, Univ Calif, Davis, 47-54, prof clin path, Sch Vet Med, 54-89. *Concurrent Pos:* Dean sch vet med & asst dir exp sta, Univ Calif, Davis, 54-62; sr NIH fel, 68; Fulbright Hays sr res scholar, 75; Fulbright Hays distinguished prof, NZ, 78. *Mem:* US Animal Health Asn; Am Vet Med Asn; Am Soc Microbiol. *Res:* Bovine mastitis; mycoplasma infections; discovered and named Mycoplasma californicum. *Mailing Add:* 1826 Alameda Ave Davis CA 95616

JASPER, DONALD K, BIOLOGY. *Current Pos:* asst prof, 69-75, assoc prof cell biol, 75-95, assoc dean grad studies, 86-88, res prof, 95-96, EMER PROF RES, ILL INST TECHNOL, 96- *Personal Data:* b Miami, Fla. *Educ:* Howard Univ, BS, 52; Univ York, PhD(cell ultrastruct & physiol), 69. *Prof Exp:* Electron microscopist, Rockefeller Inst Med Res, 56-60; res asst cytol, Columbia Univ, 60-66; res fel cell biol, Univ York, 66-69. *Concurrent Pos:* Fac res fel, Argonne Nat Lab, 81-86. *Mem:* AAAS; Am Soc Cell Biol; Am Inst Biol Sci; Electron Micros Soc Am; Fedn Am Soc Exp Biol. *Res:* Cellular ultrastructure as related to function, especially as mucosal epithelial and muscle cell structure and function. *Mailing Add:* Dept Biol Ill Inst Technol Chicago IL 60616

JASPER, HERBERT HENRY, NEUROPHYSIOLOGY. *Current Pos:* res prof neurophysiol, Labs Neurol Sci, 65-76, & dir med res coun group neurol sci, Dept Physiol, 67-76, EMER PROF NEUROPHYSIOL, UNIV MONTREAL, 76- *Personal Data:* b La Grande, Ore, July 27, 06; nat Can; m 40, 83, Mary L McDougall; c Stephen & Joan. *Educ:* Reed Col, BA, 27; Univ Ore, MA, 29; Univ Iowa, PhD(psychol), 31; Univ Paris, Dr es Sc(physiol), 35; McGill Univ, MDCM, 43. *Hon Degrees:* Dr, Univ Bordeaux, 49, Univ Aix-Marseille, 60, McGill Univ, 71, Univ Western Ont, 77 & Queens Univ, 79 & Mem Univ, 83. *Honors & Awards:* Officer Order Can, 72; Ralph Gerard Prize, Soc Neurosci, 81; Karl Lashley Prize, Am Philos Soc, 82; McLaughlin Medal, Royal Soc Can, 85; Milken Family Med Found Prize, Am Epilepsy Soc, 93; Albert Einstein Prize, World Cult Coun, 95. *Prof Exp:* Instr psychol, Univ Ore, 27-29; instr, Univ Iowa, 29-31; asst prof, Brown Univ, 33-38; asst prof neurol & neurosurg, McGill Univ, 38-46; prof exp neurol & dir, Neurophysiol & EEG Labs, Montreal Neurol Inst, 46-64. *Concurrent Pos:* First pres, Int Fedn Socs EEG & Clin Neurophysiol, 47-49; founding ed-in-chief & publ Int J EEG & Clin Neurophysiol, 49-62; founding hon exec secy, Int Brain Res Orgn; hon consult neurosci, Univ Montreal & McGill Univ, 75- *Mem:* Am Physiol Soc; Am Neurol Asn; Am EEG Soc (pres, 46-48); fel Royal Soc Can; Int Brain Res Orgn (exec secy, 61-63, hon exec secy, 71-72). *Res:* Brain research; behavioral sciences; neurology; electrical activity of the brain in man and experimental animals in relation to neuro chemistry; states of consciousness; epilepsy; sensori-motor functions and mechanisms of learning and memory; neuroscience. *Mailing Add:* 4501 Sherbrooke W No 1F Westmount PQ H3Z 1E7 Can

JASPER, MARTIN THEOPHILUS, MECHANICAL & CHEMICAL ENGINEERING. *Current Pos:* from instr to assoc prof, 60-75, PROF MECH ENG, MISS STATE UNIV, 75- *Personal Data:* b Hazlehurst, Miss, Mar 19, 34; m 63; c 5. *Educ:* Miss State Univ, BS, 55, MS, 62; Univ Ala, PhD(mech eng), 67. *Prof Exp:* Engr, Am Cast Iron Pipe Co, 55-56; plant metallurgist, Vickers, Inc, 57-59; design engr, Missile Div, Chrysler Corp, 59-60. *Mem:* Am Soc Eng Educ; Am Soc Mech Engrs; Soc Mfg Engrs; NY Acad Sci. *Res:* Parametric analysis, modeling and optimization of thermal and hydrodynamic systems. *Mailing Add:* Box No 77 Mathiston MS 39752

JASPER, ROBERT LAWRENCE, ENDOCRINOLOGY, TOXICOLOGY. *Current Pos:* pharmacologist-in-chg, Pharm Lab, Agr Res Serv, USDA, Md, 62-64, asst chief staff officer pharmacol, Pesticides Regulation Div, 64-67, pharmacologist-in-chg, Pharm Lab, 67-70, head safety & biol sect, Chem & Biol Invest Br, Tech Serv Div, Off Pesticides Progs, 70-73, ASST BR CHIEF, CHEM & BIOL INVEST BR, TECH SERV DIV, OFF PESTICIDES PROGS, ENVIRON PROTECTION AGENCY, 73- *Personal Data:* b Windsor, Ky, Apr 24, 18; m 44, 62; c 1. *Educ:* Berea Col, AB, 49; Univ Ky, MS, 50; Purdue Univ, PhD, 55. *Prof Exp:* Instr physiol, Univ Ky, 50-51; sect chief environ physiol, Army Med Res Lab, Ky, 54-58; co-dir endocrinol, Endocrine Consult Lab, 58-62. *Mem:* Am Inst Chemists; Am Chem Soc; Am Soc Zoologists; Am Asn Lab Animal Sci; NY Acad Sci. *Res:* Effect of low environmental temperature on fat metabolism; tissue and steroid metabolism; development and clinical application of hormone assays; pesticides toxicology. *Mailing Add:* 1731 Maple Ave Hanover MD 21076

JASPER, SAMUEL JACOB, MATHEMATICS. *Current Pos:* from asst prof to assoc prof, 54-67, PROF MATH, OHIO UNIV, 67- *Personal Data:* b Lancaster, Ohio, Nov 1, 21; m 44; c 3. *Educ:* Univ Ohio, BA, 43; Ohio State Univ, MA, 46; Univ Ky, PhD(math), 48. *Prof Exp:* Instr math, Univ Ohio, 43-44; asst prof, Kent State Univ, 48-51 & ETenn State Col, 51-54. *Concurrent Pos:* Asst dean col arts & sci, Ohio Univ, 58-63, dir hon col, 63-66, chmn, Dept Math, 67-68. *Mem:* Math Asn Am. *Res:* Differential geometry; homogeneous functions; calculus of variations. *Mailing Add:* 7399 Village Dr Mason OH 45040

JASPERSE, CRAIG PETER, ORGANOLANTHANIDES, RADICALS. *Current Pos:* ASST PROF ORG CHEM, UNIV NDAK, 89- *Personal Data:* b Sheboygan, Wis, Feb 2, 60; m 91. *Educ:* Calvin Col, BS, 82; Univ Wis-Madison, PhD(org chem), 87. *Prof Exp:* Postdoctoral, Univ Pittsburgh, 87-89. *Mem:* Am Chem Soc. *Res:* Organic chemistry, synthesis; ketyl radical anions, preparation and rearrangements; mechanism and application of SMI2 as a one-electron reducing agent; preparation and rearrangements of alkoxy radicals. *Mailing Add:* Chem Dept Moorhead State Univ Moorhead MN 56563

JASPERSE, JOHN R, PLASMA PHYSICS, SPACE PHYSICS. *Current Pos:* RES PHYSICIST, AIR FORCE GEOPHYS LAB, 65- *Personal Data:* b Seattle, Wash, May 8, 35; m 58; c 2. *Educ:* Harvard Univ, BA, 57; Northeastern Univ, MS, 63, PhD(physics), 66. *Honors & Awards:* Marcus D O'Day Mem Award; Guenter Loeser Mem Award. *Prof Exp:* Res physicist, Arthur D Little, Inc, 59-65. *Concurrent Pos:* Lectr, Northeastern Univ, 68-71; vis scientist, Mass Inst Technol, 79- *Mem:* Am Geophys Union; Sigma Xi; Am Phys Soc. *Res:* Quantum theory of atoms and molecules; scattering theory; three-body problem; electromagnetic theory; plasma theory; space physics. *Mailing Add:* 198 Conant Rd Weston MA 02193

JASPERSON, STEPHEN NEWELL, SOLID STATE PHYSICS. *Current Pos:* asst prof, 70-74, ASSOC PROF PHYSICS, WORCESTER POLYTECH INST, 74-, DEPT HEAD, 84- *Personal Data:* b Wisconsin Rapids, Wis, May 10, 41; m 65; c 2. *Educ:* Univ Wis, BS, 63; Princeton Univ, MA, 65, PhD(physics), 68. *Prof Exp:* Res assoc physics, Princeton Univ, 67-68 & Univ Ill, 68-70. *Concurrent Pos:* Res scientist, Physics Br, Naval Weapons Ctr, 71-78; vis scientist, Nat Magnet Lab, Mass Inst Technol, 82-86. *Mem:* AAAS; Am Phys Soc. *Res:* Optical properties of metals and semiconductors; modulation spectroscopy techniques such as electroreflectance, polarization modulation and magnetoreflectance. *Mailing Add:* Dept Physics Worcester Polytech Inst 100 Institute Rd Worcester MA 01609

JASS, HERMAN EARL, BIOCHEMISTRY, PHARMACOLOGY. *Current Pos:* TECH MGT CONSULT, 76- *Personal Data:* b Chicago, Ill, Mar 30, 18; m 47, Alaine Pabich; c Daniel K & Diane C. *Educ:* Univ Ill, BS, 39; Northwestern Univ, MS, 50, PhD(chem), 53. *Honors & Awards:* Cibs Sci Award, Cosmetic Toiletry & Fragrance Asn, 78. *Prof Exp:* Org chemist, Gas Res Dept, People's Gas Co, Ill, 40-41; chief biochemist, Helene Curtis Indust, Inc, 42-51; group leader biochem, Armour & Co, 53-55; assoc res dir, Revlon, Inc, 55-64; vpres res, Carter Prod Div, Carter-Wallace, Inc, 64-76. *Concurrent Pos:* Guest lectr, Columbia Col Pharm, 64 & 65. *Mem:* AAAS; Am Chem Soc; Soc Cosmetic Chem; Dermal Clin Eval Soc; Am Soc Consult Pharmacists; Regulatory & Prof Soc. *Res:* Proprietary drugs and toiletries; biochemistry and physiology of the skin; regulation and safety of cosmetics & drugs. *Mailing Add:* 29 Platz Dr Skillman NJ 08558

JASSBY, DANIEL LEWIS, CONTROLLED NUCLEAR FUSION. *Current Pos:* res staff, 73-76, res physicist, 76-80, PRIN RES PHYSICIST, PRINCETON PLASMA PHYSICS LAB, 80- *Personal Data:* b Montreal, Que, Jan 27, 42; US citizen. *Educ:* McGill Univ, BSc, 62; Univ BC, MS, 64; Princeton Univ, PhD(plasma physics), 70. *Prof Exp:* Asst prof elec sci, Univ Calif, Los Angeles, 70-73. *Mem:* Fel Am Phys Soc; Inst Elec & Electronics Engrs. *Res:* Production, measurement and application of fusion neutrons; heating of toroidal plasmas; design of magnetic confinement fusion devices. *Mailing Add:* Princeton Plasma Physics Lab PO Box 451 Princeton NJ 08543

JASTAK, J THEODORE, ORAL & MAXILLOFACIAL SURGERY, DENTAL ANESTHESIOLOGY. *Current Pos:* assoc prof, 69-80, PROF ORAL SURG, SCH DENT, ORE HEALTH SCI UNIV, 80-, CHMN HOSP DENT, 80- *Personal Data:* b Astoria, NY, Dec 1, 36; m 62; c 3. *Educ:* Seton Hall Univ, DDS, 62; Univ Rochester, PhD(path), 67. *Prof Exp:* Resident oral maxillofacial surg, Henry Ford Hosp, Detroit, 67-69. *Concurrent Pos:* Vis asst prof, Dent Sch, Univ Detroit, 68-69. *Mem:* AAAS; Am Col Oral Maxillofacial Surg; Am Dent Soc Anesthesiol; Int Asn Dent Res. *Res:* Anesthesia and pain control for dental outpatients. *Mailing Add:* Surg Oral Surg Ore Health Sci Univ Sch Med 3181 SW Sam Jackson Portland OR 97201-3011

JASTROW, ROBERT, ASTRONOMY & PLANETARY SCIENCE. *Current Pos:* RETIRED. *Personal Data:* b New York, NY, Sept 7, 25. *Educ:* Columbia Univ, BA, 44, MA, 45, PhD(physics), 48. *Hon Degrees:* DSc, Manhattan Col, 80. *Honors & Awards:* Arthur S Fleming Award, 65. *Prof Exp:* Fel, Univ Leiden, 48-49; mem, Inst Advan Study, Princeton Univ, 49-50, 53; mem fac, Univ Calif, Berkeley, 50-53; asst prof physics, Yale Univ, 53-54; consult nuclear physics, US Naval Res Lab, 54-58; head, Theoret Div, Goddard Space Flight Ctr, NASA, 58-61, dir, Inst Space Studies, 61-81; prof physics & earth sci, Dartmouth Col, 74-92; dir, Mt Wilson Inst, 92-96. *Concurrent Pos:* Chmn, Lunar Explor Comt, NASA, 59-60, mem comt, 60-62; adj prof, Columbia Univ, 61- & Dartmouth Col, 74-; ed, J Atmospheric Sci, Am Meteorol Soc, 62-74. *Mem:* Fel AAAS; fel Am Geophys Union; fel Am Phys Soc; Am Astron Soc; Am Meteorol Soc. *Res:* Physics of atmosphere, the moon and terrestrial planets. *Mailing Add:* Mount Wilson Inst 740 Holladay Rd Pasadena CA 91106. *Fax:* 310-470-8046

JASWAL, SITARAM SINGH, PHYSICS, MATHEMATICS. *Current Pos:* from asst prof to assoc prof, 66-74, PROF PHYSICS, UNIV NEBR, LINCOLN, 74- *Personal Data:* b Bham, India, Sept 15, 37. *Educ:* Univ Panjab, India, BSc, 58, MSc, 59; Mich State Univ, PhD(physics), 64. *Prof Exp:* Asst geophys, Oil & Natural Gas Comn, India, 59-60; asst physics, Univ Alta, 60-61 & Mich State Univ, 61-64; fel, Univ Pa, 64-66. *Concurrent Pos:* Vis scientist, Max Planck Inst Solid State Res, 74-75; Fulbright fel, Tech Univ Vienna, Austria, 86-87. *Mem:* Fel Am Phys Soc. *Res:* Electronic structure and properties of metallic glasses and magnetic materials. *Mailing Add:* Behlen Lab Physics Univ Nebr Lincoln NE 68588

JASZBERENYI, JOSEPH C, chemistry of antibiotics, heterocyclic chemistry, for more information see previous edition

JASZCZAK, RONALD JACK, MEDICAL PHYSICS, IMAGE PROCESSING PHYSICS. *Current Pos:* assoc prof, Dept Radiol, 79-89, ASSOC PROF BIOMED ENG, DUKE UNIV, 86-, PROF, DEPT RADIOL, 89- *Personal Data:* b Chicago Heights, Ill, Aug 23, 42; m 67; c 2. *Educ:* Univ Fla, BS, 64, PhD(physics), 68. *Prof Exp:* Postdoctoral fel, US AEC, Oak Ridge Nat Lab, 68-69; staff physicist, 69-71; prin res scientist, Nuclear Chicago Corp, Searle Diagnostics Inc, 71-73; sr prin res scientist, 73-77, res group leader, 77-79, chief scientist, 77-79. *Concurrent Pos:* NIH res fel, 80-82; prin investr, Nat Cancer Inst, 83- & Dept Energy, 89-; assoc ed, Inst Elec & Electronics Engrs Trans Med Imaging, 86- & J Nuclear Med Technol, 88- *Mem:* AAAS; Am Phys Soc; Inst Elec & Electronics Engrs; Am Asn Physicists Med; Soc Photo-Optical Instrumentation Engrs; Sigma Xi. *Res:* Nuclear medicine instrumentation; imaging systems for single photon emission computed tomography; nuclear radiation detectors; image reconstruction and restoration; Monte Carlo modeling; quantitative application of medical imaging. *Mailing Add:* Duke Univ Med Ctr Nuclear Med Sec PO Box 3949 Durham NC 27710

JATLOW, J(ACOB) L(AWRENCE), ELECTRONICS, COMMUNICATIONS ENGINEERING. *Current Pos:* RETIRED. *Personal Data:* b Poland, Apr 7, 03; nat US; m 51; c 1. *Educ:* Rensselaer Polytech Inst, EE, 24. *Honors & Awards:* Region 1 Award, Inst Elec & Electronics Engrs, 83. *Prof Exp:* Develop engr, Conner Crouse Corp, 24-32; asst chief engr, F A D Andrea Radio Corp, 32-35; develop engr, Photo Positive Corp, 35-40; chief engr photochem res, Repub Eng Prod, Inc, 40-42; chief engr, Wire Transmission Div, Defense Commun Div, Int Tel & Tel, Inc, 42-54, assoc dir, Radio Transmission Lab, 54-60, dir, Systs Eng Lab, 60-64, tech dir commun div, 64-77. *Concurrent Pos:* Consult, ITT, 77-85. *Mem:* Fel Inst Elec & Electronics Engrs; fel AAAS; NY Acad Sci. *Res:* Communications systems engineering; wire and radio transmission; switching systems; command and control systems; communication and electronic equipment; development of alternating current operated radio sets and power supplies; development of photographic emulsions and photoprocesses. *Mailing Add:* 166 E 61st St Apt 12-J New York NY 10021

JAUCHEM, JAMES ROBERT, CARDIOVASCULAR PHYSIOLOGY, RADIOFREQUENCY RADIATION BIOEFFECTS. *Current Pos:* RES PHYSIOLOGIST, RADIOFREQUENCY RADIATION DIV, OCCUP & ENVIRON HEALTH DIRECTORATE, ARMSTRONG LAB, USAF, 87- *Personal Data:* b Washington, DC, Mar 22, 51; m 90, Wendy Friedman. *Educ:* Heidelberg Col, BS, 73; Baylor Col Med, PhD(physiol), 78. *Honors & Awards:* Award Excellence, Soc Tech Commun, 86. *Prof Exp:* Res assoc, Microcirculatory Systs Res Group, Univ Miss, 77-79; fel, Dept Path, Health Sci Ctr, Univ Tex, San Antonio, 80-81; res scientist, Life Sci Div, Technol Inc, 81-84; Nat Res Coun, sr res assoc, Med Sci Div, Johnson Space Ctr, NASA, 84-85; res physiologist, Crew Tech Div, Sch Aerospace Med, USAF, 85-86; prin sci ed, Dept Info & Defense Progs, Tracor Inc, 86-87. *Concurrent Pos:* Consult, Northrop Corp, 86. *Mem:* Am Physiol Soc; Soc Exp Biol & Med; Aerospace Med Asn; Bioelectromagnetics Soc. *Res:* Physiological effects of radiofrequency radiation; thermoregulation; cardiovascular pharmacology; circulatory shock; electromagnetic field bioeffects. *Mailing Add:* USAF Armstrong Lab-OERB Bldg 1182 8308 Hawks Rd Brooks AFB TX 78235. *E-Mail:* jauchem@rfr.brooks.af.mil

JAUHAR, PREM P, GENETICS, PLANT BREEDING. *Current Pos:* PROF CYTOGENETICS, USDA, NDAK, 91- *Personal Data:* b India, Sept 15, 39. *Educ:* Agra Univ, India, BS, 57, MS, 59; Indian Agr Res Inst, New Delhi, PhD, 65. *Prof Exp:* Asst cytogeneticist, Indian Agr Res Inst, 63-70, asst prof genetics, 70-72 & 75-76; sr sci officer cytology, Univ Col Wales, Welsh Plant Breeding Sta, UK, 72-75; res assoc agron, Univ Ky, 76-78; res geneticist bot & plant sci, Univ Calif, Riverside, 78-81; cytogeneticist, Div Cytogenetics & Cytol, City Hope Nat Med Ctr, Duarte, Calif, 81-82, US Agr Res Develop Corp, Riverside, Calif, 82-84. *Concurrent Pos:* Vis scientist, Welsh Plant Breeding Sta, UK, 72-75; post grad fac, Indian Agr Res Inst, New Delhi, 60-70; Genetics Soc Am travel award, 78. *Mem:* Genetics Soc Am; Crop Sci Soc Am; Am Genetic Asn; Indian Soc Genetics & Plant Breeding. *Res:* Regulatory mechanism that controls chromosome pairing in the polyploid species of Festuca; breeding work on Panicum and Pennisetum; tropical and temperate herbage crops; polyploidy and mutation breeding techniques. *Mailing Add:* 801 Hackberry Dr Fargo ND 58104

JAUMARD, BRIGITTE, COMBINATORIAL OPTIMIZATION, MATHMATICAL PROGRAMMING. *Current Pos:* researcher, 87-90, PROF OPERS RES, POLYTECH INST MONTREAL, 90- *Personal Data:* b Lyon, France, Apr 4, 59; c 2. *Educ:* Univ Paris VI, France, DEA, 84, THab, 90; Int Paris, France, PhD(comput sci), 86. *Prof Exp:* Res engr, CNET, France, 83-85; researcher & postdoctoral, Rutgers Univ, 85-87. *Concurrent Pos:* Women prof sci, NSF, 90-91; vis prof, Princeton Univ, 90-91, Fribourg Univ, Switz, 95-96. *Mem:* Inst Oper Res & Mgt Sci; Soc Indust & Appl Math. *Res:* Operations research; theoretical work and practical work; frequency assignment in cellular network. *Mailing Add:* Polytech Inst Montreal Succursale Centre-Ville CP6079 Montreal PQ H3C 3A7 Can. *Fax:* 514-340-5665; *E-Mail:* brigitt@crt.umontreal.ca

JAUMOT, FRANK EDWARD, JR, SOLID STATE PHYSICS. *Current Pos:* PRES, JAUMOT CONSULT, INC, 84- *Personal Data:* b Charleston, WVa, Aug 3, 23; m 47, Jean Hite; c Cherie J (Kizer) & Frank E III. *Educ:* Western Md Col, BS, 47, DSc, 66; Univ Pa, PhD(physics), 51. *Hon Degrees:* DSc, Western Md Col, 66. *Prof Exp:* Instr physics, Univ Pa, 51-52; chief physics, Metals Sect, Labs Res & Develop, Franklin Inst, 52-56; dir res & eng semiconductors, Delco Radio Div, Gen Motors Corp, 56-70, dir res & eng, 70-79, dir advan eng, Delco Electronics Div, 79-83, dir, Automotive Elec Bus Unit, 83-84. *Concurrent Pos:* Instr asst, Univ Pa, 52-54, vis asst prof, 54-56. *Mem:* Am Phys Soc; Am Inst Aeronaut & Astronaut; Inst Elec & Electronics Engrs; Soc Auto Engrs; Am Asn Physics Teachers; Sigma Xi. *Res:* Order-disorder phenomena and other cooperative phenomena; diffusion in metals; thermoelectricity; semiconductors. *Mailing Add:* 7549 Mahalo Hui Dr Diamond Head MS 39525-3836

JAUSSI, AUGUST WILHELM, PHYSIOLOGY. *Current Pos:* RETIRED. *Personal Data:* b Paris, Idaho, Aug 26, 25; m 55; c 6. *Educ:* Univ Idaho, BS, 53; Brigham Young Univ, MS, 55; Okla State Univ, PhD, 60. *Prof Exp:* From instr to asst prof physiol, Okla State Univ, 56-62; from asst prof to assoc prof, Brigham Young Univ, 62-72, prof physiol, 72-77, prof zool, 77-90. *Res:* Environmental effects on physiological activity. *Mailing Add:* 284 East 400 South Orem UT 84058

JAVAID, JAVAID IQBAL, biochemistry, psychopharmacology, for more information see previous edition

JAVAN, ALI, PHYSICS. *Current Pos:* from assoc prof to prof, 62-78, Francis Wright prof, 78-96, EMER PROF PHYSICS, MASS INST TECHNOL, 96-; FOUNDER & CHIEF SCIENTIST, LASER SCI, INC, 81- *Personal Data:* b Tehran, Iran, Dec 27, 26; nat US; m 62; c 2. *Educ:* Columbia Univ, PhD(physics), 54. *Honors & Awards:* Stuart Ballentine Medal, 62; Hertz Found Award, 66; Sepas Medal, Govt Iran, 71; Frederic Ives Medal, Optical Soc Am, 75. *Prof Exp:* Res assoc physics, Columbia Univ, 54-59; mem tech staff, Bell Tel Labs, Inc, 59-62. *Concurrent Pos:* Sr US Scientist Award, Humboldt Found, 80. *Mem:* Fel Nat Acad Sci; fel Am Phys Soc; fel Optical Soc Am; Sigma Xi; fel Am Acad Arts & Sci; Soc Found Third World Acad Sci. *Res:* Atomic spectroscopy and physics of quantum electronics. *Mailing Add:* Dept Physics Mass Inst Technol Bldg 6 Rm 104 Cambridge MA 02139

JAVEL, ERIC, neurophysiology, for more information see previous edition

JAVICK, RICHARD ANTHONY, ANALYTICAL CHEMISTRY, ENVIRONMENTAL CHEMISTRY. *Current Pos:* from sr res chemist to sr res asst, 80-92, SR RES ASSOC, CHEM RES & DEVELOP CTR, FMC CORP, 92- *Personal Data:* b Plains, Pa, Aug 29, 32; m 61; c 10. *Educ:* King's Col, Pa, BS, 54; Pa State Univ, PhD(chem), 58. *Prof Exp:* Res chemist, E I du Pont de Nemours & Co, Del, 58-59; asst prof chem, King's Col, Pa, 59-61 & State assoc prof, 62-69; res assoc, Pa Univ, 61-62. *Concurrent Pos:* Chmn dept chem, King's Col, Pa, 67-69. *Mem:* Am Chem Soc; Chem Mfg Asn; Int Org Legal Metrol. *Res:* Application of instrumental methods to analytical investigations; electrochemical kinetics; polymer chemistry, synthesis and applications thereof; applications of analytical methods to wastewater analysis; air monitoring for pesticides and pesticide/herbicide residue analysis. *Mailing Add:* 10 Wycombe Way Princeton Junction NJ 08550

JAVID, MANUCHER J, NEUROSURGERY. *Current Pos:* from instr to assoc prof, 53-62, chmn dept, 63-95, PROF NEUROL SURG, SCH MED, UNIV WIS-MADISON, 62- *Personal Data:* b Tehran, Iran, Jan 11, 22; nat US; m 51, Lida E Fabbri; c Roxane (Pfeiffer), Daria D, Jeffrey J & Claudia M. *Educ:* Univ Ill, MD, 46; Am Bd Neurol Surg, dipl, 55. *Prof Exp:* Intern, Augustana Hosp, Ill, 46-47, resident gen surg, 47-48, resident neurosurg, 48-49; resident, New Eng Ctr Hosp, 50 & Mass Gen Hosp, 51-53. *Concurrent Pos:* Fel neurosurg, Lahey Clin, Mass, 49; fel neuropath, Ill Neuropsychiat Inst, 49; res fel, Mass Gen Hosp, 50; teaching fel, Harvard Med Sch, 52. *Mem:* AAAS; AMA; fel Am Col Surg; Am Asn Neurol Surg; Soc Neurol Surgeons; Int Intradiscal Ther Soc (pres, 91-92). *Res:* Intracranial pressure, cerebrovascular diseases, intracranial neoplasms and chemonucleolysis; introduced the use of osmotic agent, urea for the reduction of intracranial and intraocular pressure, cerebrovascular diseases, intracranial neoplasms and chemonucleolysis. *Mailing Add:* Dept Neurosurg Univ Wis Med Ctr Madison WI 53792

JAVIDI, BAHRAM, OPTICAL COMPUTING & PROCESSING, SIGNAL & IMAGE PROCESSING. *Current Pos:* PROF ELEC ENG, UNIV CONN, 88- *Personal Data:* b Tehran, Iran, Feb 14, 59; US citizen; m, Bethany Drews. *Educ:* George Washington Univ, BS, 80; Pa State Univ, MS, 82, PhD(elec eng), 86. *Prof Exp:* Prof elec eng, Mich State Univ, 86-88. *Concurrent Pos:* Prin investr, Inst Elec & Electronics Engrs & Eng Found, 87-88, USAF, 88-89, USAF & US Army, 89-91, NSF presidential young investr, 90-95; ed, spec issue J Optical Eng, 88, guest ed, 89 & 92; conf chmn, Prog Nonlinear Optical Processing, Inst Elec & Electronics Engrs, Lasers & Electro-optics Soc, 91; consult, US Army & USAF, 90-; reviewer & panelist, Nat Res Coun, 90; pres young investr, NSF, 90. *Mem:* Optical Soc Am; Optical Eng Soc; Inst Elec & Electronics Engrs; fel Int Soc Optical Eng. *Res:* optical image processing; pattern recognition; neural networks; associative processing; nonlinear signal processing; holography; applications of spatial light modulators to information processing; communication systems. *Mailing Add:* Elec & Systs Eng Dept U-157 Univ Conn 260 Glenbrook Rd Storrs CT 06269-2157

JAVITT, NORMAN B, MEDICINE, PHYSIOLOGY. *Current Pos:* PROF MED & PEDIAT & DIR DIV HEPATIC DIS, NY UNIV MED CTR, 83- *Personal Data:* b New York, NY, Mar 9, 28; m 55, Suzanne Markovits; c Jonathan, Daniel, Joel & Gail. *Educ:* Syracuse Univ, AB, 47; Univ NC, PhD(physiol), 51; Duke Univ, MD, 54; Am Bd Internal Med, dipl, 62. *Prof Exp:* Intern med, Mt Sinai Hosp, New York, 54-55, asst resident, 57-58; Am Heart Asn adv fel, Col Physicians & Surgeons, Columbia Univ, 58-59; chief resident med, Mt Sinai Hosp, 60, res assoc, 61-62; from instr to asst prof, Sch Med, NY Univ, 62-68; assoc prof, Cornell Univ, 68-72, prof med, 72-84, at Med Col, 73-83, chief, Div Gastroenterol, NY Hosp Med Ctr, 73-79, chief, Div Hepatic Dis, 79-83. *Concurrent Pos:* USPHS spec fel, Mt Sinai Hosp, 61-62; career investr, Health Res Coun City NY, 62-68. *Mem:* Am Fedn Clin Res; fel Am Col Physicians; Am Soc Clin Invest; Am Gastroenterol Asn; Am Asn Study Liver Dis; Am Pediat Soc. *Res:* Biochemical and physiological investigations related to human liver disease; development of the intrahepatic and extrahepatic pathways of bile acid synthesis. *Mailing Add:* Dept Med NY Univ Med Ctr 550 First Ave New York NY 10016. *Fax:* 212-263-8282; *E-Mail:* javitt@is.nyu.edu

JAWA, MANJIT S, APPLIED MATHEMATICS, CONTINUUM MECHANICS. *Current Pos:* PROF MATH, FAYETTEVILLE STATE UNIV, 71- *Personal Data:* b Patiala, India, Aug 5, 34; m 64; c 2. *Educ:* Indian Inst Technol, PhD(appl math), 67. *Prof Exp:* Res asst statist, Panjab Govt, India, 56-58; res fel math, Panjab Univ Cols, India, 58-63 & Indian Inst Technol, 66-67; asst prof appl math & eng mech, Univ Mo-Rolla, 67-70; assoc prof, Hartwick Col, 70-71. *Res:* Exact numerical analysis of fluid dynamics, heat transfer and magnetohydrodynamics problems on digital computers. *Mailing Add:* Dept Math Fayetteville State Univ Fayetteville NC 28301

JAWAD, MAAN HAMID, STRUCTURAL ENGINEERING, ENGINEERING MECHANICS. *Current Pos:* design engr, 68-70, staff consult, 70-77, mgr eng design, 77-87, ASST CHIEF ENG, NOOTER CORP, 87- *Personal Data:* b Baghdad, Iraq, Dec 2, 43; US citizen; m 68; c 2. *Educ:* Al-Hikma Univ, BSc, 64; Univ Kans, MS, 65; Iowa State Univ, PhD(struct eng), 68. *Prof Exp:* Bridge engr, Iowa State Hwy Comn, 67-68. *Mem:* Am Soc Civil Engrs; Am Soc Mech Engrs. *Res:* Pressure vessels area, mainly layered vessels, expansion joints, and high pressure gaskets. *Mailing Add:* 3007 Crossview Est St Louis MO 63129

JAWED, INAM, PHYSICAL & CEMENT CHEMISTRY, MATERIALS SCIENCE. *Current Pos:* PROG MGR, STRATEGIC HWY RES PROG, NAT RES COUN, 87- *Personal Data:* b Sagar, India, Sept 27, 47; US citizen; m 82, Nafeesa Shaikh; c Aysha & Sarah. *Educ:* Karachi Univ, BS, 66, MS, 68; Oxford Univ, PhD(chem), 71, Tokyo Inst Technol, dipl. *Prof Exp:* Asst prof phys chem, Peshawar Univ, 72-74; vis prof inorg chem, Tokyo Inst Technol, 74-76; res scientist, Martin Marietta Labs, 76-78, sr scientist, 78-80, head, Anal Chem Dept, 80-83, mgr, res & eng, 83-87. *Concurrent Pos:* Brit Coun fel, 68; Unesco fel, 74. *Mem:* Am Chem Soc; fel Am Ceramic Soc; Am Concrete Inst; Am Soc Testing & Mat. *Res:* Materials science of cements, concrete, ceramics, and composite materials; technical management; kinetics of formation and hydration of silicates, aluminates, and ferrites; processing and properties of structural and electronic ceramics and composite materials. *Mailing Add:* Transp Res Bd 2101 Constitution Ave N W Washington DC 20418. *Fax:* 202-334-2003

JAWEED, MAZHER, EXERCISE, NERVE REGENERATION. *Current Pos:* CLIN ASSOC PROF, BAYLOR COL, 93- *Educ:* Osmania Univ, BS, 62; WVa Univ, MS, 66; Thomas Jefferson Univ, PhD(pharmacol), 88. *Prof Exp:* Biochemist rehab med, Thomas Jefferson Univ, 70-72, res assoc, 72-78, res asst, 78-82, res asst prof pharmacol, 79-93, res assoc prof rehab med, 82-93. *Concurrent Pos:* Ed, J Archives Phys Med & Rehab, 88-; prin investr, Nat Inst Disability & Rehab, 88-; mem, Am Cong Rehab Med. *Mem:* AAAS; NY Acad Sci; Sigma Xi. *Res:* Nerve and muscle interactions as affected by drugs; evaluations of effects by electrophysiological, histochemical and immunological procedures. *Mailing Add:* 16302 Harvest Summer Ct Houston TX 77059

JAWETZ, ERNEST, MICROBIOLOGY, MEDICINE. *Current Pos:* from asst prof to assoc prof bact, 48-53, chmn dept microbiol, 62-78, PROF MICROBIOL & MED & LECTR PEDIAT, SCH MED, UNIV CALIF, 54- *Personal Data:* b Vienna, Austria, June 9, 16; nat US; m 54; c 4. *Educ:* Univ Vienna, 37; Univ NH, MA, 40; Univ Calif, PhD(microbiol), 42; Stanford Univ, MD, 46. *Honors & Awards:* Florey Mem lectr, Adelaide, 81. *Prof Exp:* Lectr bact, Univ Calif, 42-44; sr asst surgeon, NIH, 46-48. *Concurrent Pos:* Almroth Wright lectr, London, 52 & 58; vis prof, Univ Shiraz, Iran, 77. *Mem:* Am Soc Clin Invest; Am Soc Microbiol; Soc Exp Biol & Med; Am Asn Immunol; Am Acad Microbiol. *Res:* Clinical bacteriology; antibiotics; chemotherapy; infectious diseases; virology. *Mailing Add:* Dept Microbiol & Med Univ Calif Med Ctr San Francisco CA 94143

JAWOROWSKI, ANDRZEJ EDWARD, SOLID STATE PHYSICS. *Current Pos:* PRES, MICRONETICS, DAYTON, 90- *Personal Data:* b Lublin, Poland, Dec 28, 42; m 65; Bozena Natecz; c Peter A. *Educ:* Univ Warsaw, MSc, 66, PhD(physics), 74. *Honors & Awards:* Prize of Ministry Sci, Schs Acad Rank & Technol, Warsaw, Poland, 75. *Prof Exp:* Instr physics, Univ Warsaw, 66-68, lectr physics, 68-74, asst prof physics, 74-78; sr res assoc, State Univ NY-Albany, 78-83; assoc prof physics, semiconductor group leader, Wright State Univ, Dayton, Ohio, 83-89. *Concurrent Pos:* Res assoc, Radiation Physics Lab, Solid State Div, Inst Nuclear Res, Swierk, 67-74; prog head, Inst Physics, Polish Acad Sci, Warsaw, 76-77; consult, Mobil Solar Energy Co, Waltham, 80-85, Univ Energy Systs, Dayton, 85-88; rev, NSF, 87- *Mem:* Europ Phys Soc; Am Phys Soc; Polish Phys Soc; Electrochem Soc; Mat Res Soc. *Res:* Physics of electronic materials; defects in semiconductors; radiation effects and damage; deep levels spectroscopy; hydrogen in solids; real-time measurements; chaos and complexity. *Mailing Add:* Micronetics PO Box 31467 Dayton OH 45437

JAWOROWSKI, JAN W, TOPOLOGY. *Current Pos:* PROF MATH, IND UNIV, 65- *Personal Data:* b Augustow, Poland, Mar 2, 28; m 54; c 1. *Educ:* Univ Warsaw, Magister, 52; Polish Acad Sci, PhD(math), 55. *Prof Exp:* Asst math, Univ Warsaw, 50-52, from adj to docent, 52-63; extraordinary prof, Math Inst, Polish Acad Sci, 63-64; assoc prof, Cornell Univ, 64-65. *Concurrent Pos:* Fel, Polish Acad Sci, 57-58; NSF grant, Inst Advan Study, 60-61. *Mem:* Am Math Soc; Polish Math Soc. *Res:* Algebraic and geometric topology. *Mailing Add:* Ind Univ Bloomington IN 47405-5701

JAWORSKI, CASIMIR A, SOIL SCIENCE, AGRONOMY. *Current Pos:* SOIL SCIENTIST, S ATLANTIC AREA, AGR RES SERV, USDA, 62- *Personal Data:* b South Bend, Ind, Aug 1, 30; m 93, Margie Smith; c Joye M (Waller) & Jill M. *Educ:* Purdue Univ, BSc, 52, MSc, 57; Rutgers Univ, PhD(soil sci), 62. *Prof Exp:* Resident hall counr, Purdue Univ, 54-56, res asst agron, 55-57, fac adv resident halls, 56-57; res fel soil, Rutgers Univ, 57-60. *Mem:* Am Soc Hort Sci; Int Soc Hort Sci; Am Inst Biol Sci; Sigma Xi; Am Soc Agron; Soil Sci Soc Am. *Res:* Develop edible (canola) and industrial rapeseed cultural pract; Develop rapeseed harvesting systems; screen cruciferae; germplasm and accessions for adaptation to southeast US. *Mailing Add:* 2417 Emory Dr Tifton GA 31794

JAWORSKI, ERNEST GEORGE, BIOLOGICAL CHEMISTRY, MOLECULAR BIOLOGY. *Current Pos:* res biochemist, Monsanto Co, 52-54, res group leader, 54-60, scientist, 60-62, sr scientist, 62-70, DISTINGUISHED SCI FEL, MONSANTO CO, 70- *Personal Data:* b Minneapolis, Minn, Jan 10, 26; m 50; c 3. *Educ:* Univ Minn, BChem, 48; Ore State Col, MS, 50, PhD(biochem), 52. *Honors & Awards:* David Rivette Mem Lectr, Commonwealth Sci & Indust Res, Australia. *Prof Exp:* Asst chem, Ore State Col, 48-49, asst biochem, 49-52. *Concurrent Pos:* Mem, Frasch Found Awards Comt, Am Chem Soc, 69-; chmn, Gordon Conf Plant Cell & Tissue Culture, 73-75, trustee, Gordon Res Conf, Inc, 75-81; mem ed bd, J Am Soc Plant Physiologists, 73-83; mem panel, Int Cell Res Orgn UNESCO, 77-; chmn bd trustees, Gordon Res Conf Inc, 78-79; Nat Res Coun, 85- *Mem:* Fel AAAS; Am Chem Soc; Sigma Xi; Am Soc Plant Physiologists; Weed Sci Soc Am. *Res:* Plant growth regulation, hormones and metabolism; plant chemotherapeutic investigations; mechanism of action of herbicides; radioisotope techniques; biosynthesis of chitin; plant cell and tissue culture; plant organogenesis; cell biology; molecular biology; genetic engineering, biotechnology. *Mailing Add:* 11 Clerbrook Lane St Louis MO 63124-1202

JAWORSKI, JAN GUY, BIOCHEMISTRY. *Current Pos:* ASST PROF CHEM, MIAMI UNIV, 74- *Personal Data:* b Woonsocket, RI, Dec 7, 46; m 69; c 2. *Educ:* Col of the Holy Cross, BA, 68; Purdue Univ, PhD(biochem), 72. *Prof Exp:* Res biochemist, Dept Biochem & Biophys, Univ Calif, Davis, 72-74. *Mem:* AAAS; Sigma Xi. *Res:* Metabolism of prostaglandins, long chain fatty acids and lipids. *Mailing Add:* Dept Chem Miami Univ Oxford OH 45056. *Fax:* 513-529-4221

JAY, JAMES MONROE, BACTERIOLOGY, MICROBIAL ECOLOGY. *Current Pos:* RETIRED. *Personal Data:* b Ben Hill Co, Ga, Sept 12, 27; m 59, Patsie Phelps; c Mark E, Alicia D & Byron R. *Educ:* Paine Col, AB, 50; Ohio State Univ, MSc, 53, PhD(bact), 56. *Honors & Awards:* Probus Award, 69. *Prof Exp:* Asst, Ohio State Univ, 53-55, Agr Exp Sta, 55-56, res assoc, 56-57; from asst prof to prof bact, Southern Univ, 57-61; from asst prof to prof biol sci, Wayne State Univ, 61-94; adj prof biol sci, Univ Nev, Las Vegas, 94. *Concurrent Pos:* Mem, Govt Univ Indust Res Round Table, Nat Acad Sci, 84-87, coun, Int Exchange of Scholars (Fulbright Prog), 85-88, Nat Adv Comt Microbiol Criteriia Foods, US Dept Agr, 87-91; distinguished fac fel, 87; chmn, Food Microbiol Div, Am Soc Microbiologists, Food Microbiol Div, Inst Food Technologists, 90-91, mem expert panel, 91- *Mem:* AAAS; Am Soc Microbiol; Inst Food Technologists; Soc Appl Bact; Sigma Xi; Int Asn Milk, Food & Environ Sanitarians. *Res:* Biochemistry and rapid techniques for measuring meat spoilage; rapid determination of microorganisms in foods; microbial ecology; limulus lysate test; lipopolysaccharides in foods; selective culture media for listeria; periplasmic binding proteins. *Mailing Add:* 2208 Lucerne Dr Henderson NV 89014. *Fax:* 702-895-3956

JAYACHANDRAN, TOKE, STATISTICS, MATHEMATICS. *Current Pos:* asst prof math, 67-70, ASSOC PROF MATH, NAVAL POSTGRAD SCH, 70- *Personal Data:* b Madras, India; US citizen. *Educ:* V R Col, Nellore, India, BA, 51; Univ Wyo, MS, 62; Case Inst Technol, PhD(math statist), 67. *Prof Exp:* Res asst statist, Univ Wyo, 61-62; grad asst math, Case Inst Technol, 62-67. *Concurrent Pos:* Consult, Litton Sci Support Labs, Ft Ord, 68-72, BDM Corp, 72-75 & Sci Appln Inc, Monterey, 78-; opers analyst, Off Naval Res, Arlington, 75-77. *Mem:* Sigma Xi; Am Statist Asn; Am Math Soc. *Res:* Design of experiments, prediction intervals, reliability and life testing. *Mailing Add:* 24503 Rimrock Canyon Rd Salinas CA 93908

JAYADEV, T S, ELECTRICAL ENGINEERING, PHYSICS. *Current Pos:* PRES, SIERRA RES, 92- *Personal Data:* b Bangalore, India; US citizen. *Educ:* Univ Mysore, BSE, 58; Ill Inst Technol, MS, 62; Univ Notre Dame, PhD(elec eng), 68. *Prof Exp:* Asst prof elec eng, Karnatak Univ, India, 62-64, prof, 64-65; from asst prof to assoc prof, Univ Wis-Milwaukee, 68-76, prof elec eng, 76-78, mem lab surface studies, 68-78; mgr, Thermoelec, Energy Conversion Devices, 80-82; sr scientist, Lockheed Palo Alto Res Lab, 82-92. *Concurrent Pos:* Sr to prin scientist, Solar Energy Res Inst, 78- *Mem:* Inst Elec & Electronics Engrs; Am Phys Soc; Am Vacuum Soc; Int Solar Energy Soc. *Res:* Infrared and visible sensors; sensor signal processing; solar, wind, geothermal energy conversion systems; solid state energy conversion; electromechanical conversion systems; electrical properties of thin films; thin film devices; device physics; surface physics. *Mailing Add:* Lockheed Palo Alto Res Lab 0/9543B/202 3251 Hanover St Palo Alto CA 94304

JAYANT, NIKIL, ELECTRICAL COMMUNICATIONS ENGINEERING. *Current Pos:* Mgr, Signal Processing Res Dept & Adv Audio Technol Dept, DIR MULTIMEDIA COMM RES LAB, LUCENT TECHNOL, BELL LABS INNOVATIONS. *Educ:* Indian Inst Sci, PhD(elec commun eng), 70. *Honors & Awards:* Browder J Thompson Mem Prize Award, Inst Elec & Electronics Engrs, 74. *Mem:* Nat Acad Eng; fel Int Elec & Electronics Engrs. *Res:* Creation and commercialization of technologies for audiovisual communication and multimedia information systems; published over 100 articles; granted 20 US patents. *Mailing Add:* Lucent Technol-Bell Labs Innovation 700 Mountain Ave Rm 20-540 Murray Hill NJ 07974. *Fax:* 908-582-2498

JAYANT, NUGGEHALLY S, COMMUNICATIONS SCIENCE, SPEECH PROCESSING. *Current Pos:* mem tech staff speech & acoust res, 68-86, HEAD, SIGNAL PROCESSING RES DEPT, BEL TEL LABS, 86- *Personal Data:* b Bangalore, India, Jan 9, 46. *Educ:* Univ Mysore, BSc, 62; Indian Inst Sci, Bangalore, BE, 65, PhD(elec commun), 70. *Prof Exp:* Res assoc commun, Stanford Univ, 67-68. *Concurrent Pos:* Fel Coun Sci & Indust Res, India, 66-67; vis scientist, Indian Inst Sci, Bangalore, 72, 75; vis prof, Univ Calif, 83. *Mem:* Fel Inst Elec & Electronics Engrs. *Res:* Speech communication and information systems; image processing. *Mailing Add:* 135 Preston Dr Gillette NJ 07933

JAYANTY, R K M, ANALYTICAL METHODS DEVELOPMENT & EVALUATION, ATMOSPHERIC CHEMISTRY. *Current Pos:* sr chemist, 78-86, MGR, RES TRIANGLE INST, 86- *Personal Data:* b June 29, 46; m 78, Lakshmi; c Nagendra & Phanindra. *Educ:* Andhra Univ, BS, 64, MS, 66; Pa State Univ, MEng, 75; Univ Bradford, PhD(chem), 72. *Honors & Awards:* Frank A Chambers Award, Air & Waste Mgt Asn, 91. *Prof Exp:* Scientist, Regional Res Lab, 66-69; res assoc, Pa State Univ, 73-76; sr scientist, TRC Res Corp New Eng, 76-78. *Concurrent Pos:* Chmn, Ambient Measurement Comt, Air & Waste Mgt Asn, 83-; adj prof, NC State Univ, 86-; UN vis fel, Coun Sci & Indust Res, India, 90; mem, Sci Adv Bd, State of NC, 90-92. *Mem:* Am Chem Soc; fel Air & Waste Mgt Asn; fel Am Inst Chemists. *Res:* Develop and evaluate sampling and analytical methods for toxic pollutant emissions from ambient, source and hazardous waste atmospheres. *Mailing Add:* 19 Falling Water Dr Durham NC 27713. *Fax:* 919-541-7215; *E-Mail:* vkmj@vti.org

JAYARAM, BEBY, purification characterization of proteins, identification of nucleotide binding domain peptides, for more information see previous edition

JAYARAM, HIREMAGALUR N, EXPERIMENTAL ONCOLOGY. *Current Pos:* PROF BIOCHEM/MOLECULAR BIOL & EXP ONCOL, IND UNIV SCH MED, 85- *Personal Data:* b India. *Educ:* LM Col Pharm, Hmadabad, India, BS, 62; Andhra Univ, Wallier, India, MS, 64; Indian Inst Sci, Bangalore, India, PhD(biochem/pharmacol), 70. *Prof Exp:* Sr investr pharmacol, Nat Cancer Inst, 75-85. *Concurrent Pos:* Fogarty int fel, Nat Cancer Inst, 72-74. *Mem:* Am Soc Biochem & Molecular Biol; Soc Toxicol; Sigma Xi; Am Soc Cancer Res. *Mailing Add:* Lab Exp Oncol Ind Univ Sch Med 702 Barnhill Dr Indianapolis IN 46202-5200. *Fax:* 317-274-3939

JAYARAMAN, AIYASAMI, HIGH PRESSURE PHYSICS. *Current Pos:* SR RES SCIENTIST, UNIV HAWAII, HAWAII INST GEOPHYS, HONOLULU, 92- *Personal Data:* b Madras, India, Dec 5, 26; m 45, Kamala; c Geetha M & Chiltra N. *Educ:* Univ Madras, BSc, 46, MSc, 54, PhD(solid state physics), 60. *Honors & Awards:* Krishan Gold Medal, Int Geog Union, 69; Alexander von Humboldt US Sr Scientist Award, 79; Raman Centenary Medal, 88. *Prof Exp:* Res asst physics, Raman Res Inst, India, 49-54, asst prof, 54-60; asst res geophysicist, Inst Geophys, Univ Calif, Los Angeles, 60-63; mem tech staff, Bell Labs, NJ, 63-83, distinguished mem tech staff, AT&T Bell Labs, 83-90. *Concurrent Pos:* Guggenheim fel, 70-71; vis prof, Indian Inst Sci, Bangalore, 70-71; vis scientist, Nat Aeronaut Lab, India, 70-71; vis prof, Max Planck Inst, 79-80 & JNC Indian Inst Sci, 91-92. *Mem:* Fel Am Phys Soc; fel Indian Acad Sci (treas, 56-60); Sigma Xi; hon fel Mat Res Soc India. *Res:* Optical, x-ray crystallography and luminescence; phase transitions in solids at high pressures; transport properties in semiconductors, magnetic and superconducting properties of metals and alloys. *Mailing Add:* Univ Hawaii Hawaii Inst Geophys 2525 Correa Rd Honolulu HI 96822. *Fax:* 808-956-3188; *E-Mail:* raman@siest.hawaii.edu

JAYARAMAN, H, ORGANIC CHEMISTRY. *Current Pos:* info scientist, Phillips Petrol Co, 73-80, sr info scientist, 80-86, supvr, Tech Planning & Intelligence Div, Res & Develop, 86-91, TECH MGR RES & DEVELOP, PHILLIPS PETROL CO, OKLA, 91- *Personal Data:* b Gudiattam, India, Dec 21, 36; US citizen; m 69, Padma Sastri; c Mythri. *Educ:* Univ Madras, BSc, 56, MA, 58, PhD(chem), 63. *Prof Exp:* Lectr, Madras Christian Col, India, 57-65; Fulbright-Hays res fel, Univ Kans, 65-66; res assoc, Pa State Univ, 66-68; Pool off, Madras Christian Col, India, 69-70; res assoc, Univ Kans, 70-72 & Univ Pa, 72-73. *Concurrent Pos:* Fulbright postdoctoral fel, 65-68; chmn, Petrol Abstr Indus Adv Coun, 92- *Mem:* Am Chem Soc. *Res:* Computerized retrieval and dissemination of technical information; writing on topics of value to technology planning and administrative divisions of corporations. *Mailing Add:* 134 PLB Phillips Petrol Co Bartlesville OK 74004. *Fax:* 918-662-2171; *E-Mail:* slamj@ppco.com

JAYARAMAN, NARAYANAN, CREEP-FATIGUE-ENVIRONMENT. *Current Pos:* fel, Univ Cincinnati, 79-80, vis asst prof, 80-81, asst prof, 81-85, ASSOC PROF METAL, UNIV CINCINNATI, 85- *Personal Data:* b Tamilnadu, India, June 30, 48; m 77. *Educ:* Indian Inst Sci, Bangalore, India, BE, 70, ME, 72, PhD(metal), 79. *Prof Exp:* Res fel metal, Indian Inst Sci, 72-77; scientist, Nat Aeronaut Lab, India, 77-79. *Mem:* Am Soc Metals; Metal Soc; AAAS; Sigma Xi. *Res:* Fracture and fatigue behavior of ni-base superalloys in relationship with their microstructures; stress generation due to oxidation of metals and alloys; life prediction models for high temperature materials. *Mailing Add:* Rm 498 Dept Mat Sci & Metall Eng 497 Rhodes Hall ML 0012 PO Box 21002 Cincinnati OH 45221-0012

JAYAS, DIGVIR SINGH, GRAIN DRYING & STORAGE, MODELING OF BIOLOGICAL SYSTEMS. *Current Pos:* from asst prof to assoc prof, 85-93, PROF BIOSYSTS ENG, UNIV MAN, 93- *Personal Data:* b Mant, Uttar Pradesh, India, Jan 10, 58; Can citizen; m 82, Manju Rajput; c Rajat, Ravi & Rahul. *Educ:* G B Pant Univ, Pantnagar, BTech, 80; Univ Man, Winnipeg, MSc, 82; Univ Sask, Saskatoon, PhD(agr eng), 87. *Honors & Awards:* Young Scientist Award, Appl Zoologists Res Asn, 92; Eng Young Researcher Award, Am Soc Agr Engrs, 94; Young Agr Engr, Can Soc Agr Eng, 95. *Prof Exp:* Pool scientist agr eng, G B Pant Univ, 82; res assoc, Univ Sask, 82-85. *Concurrent Pos:* Assoc ed, Can Agr Eng, Appl Eng Agr & Trans Am Soc Agr Engrs. *Mem:* Am Soc Agr Engrs; Can Soc Agr Eng; Can Inst Food Sci & Technol; Inst Food Technologists; Asian Asn Agr Engrs; Asn Prof Engrs. *Res:* Physical and thermal properties of agricultural products; mathematic modelling of biological systems in relation to biotic and abiotic variables; controlled-atmosphere storage of agricultural products; instrumentation; sterilization of canned foods; digital image processing; food preservation; thermal processing. *Mailing Add:* Dept Biosysts Eng Univ Man Winnipeg MB R3T 5V6 Can. *Fax:* 204-275-0233; *E-Mail:* jayas@cc.umanitoba.ca

JAYASURIYA, SUHADA, ROBUST CONTROL & ACTIVE CONTROL OF VIBRATIONS, DYNAMICS. *Current Pos:* from assoc prof to prof, 87-94, MEINHARD H KOTZEBUE PROF MECH ENG, TEX A&M UNIV, 94- *Personal Data:* b Colombo, Sri Lanka, Dec 20, 53; US citizen; m 79; c 2. *Educ:* Univ Sri Lanka, BSc, 77; Wayne State Univ, MS, 80, PhD(mech eng), 82. *Honors & Awards:* Gustus E Larson Mem Award, 97. *Prof Exp:* Asst lectr mech eng, Univ Sri Lanka, 78-79; asst prof, Mich State Univ, 83-87. *Concurrent Pos:* Vis prof mech eng, Univ Calif, Berkeley, 91-92; fac fel, NASA, 95; distinguished fac fel, USN, 96 & 97. *Mem:* Fel Am Soc Mech Engrs; Inst Elec & Electronics Engrs; Soc Indust & Appl Math; NY Acad Sci; Am Soc Eng Educ. *Res:* Robust control; control of uncertain nonlinear systems; mode localization; vibrations; dynamics; electro-magnetic actuators; frequency domain design; active noise control; smart structures; reconfigurable controls. *Mailing Add:* Dept Mech Eng Tex A&M Univ College Station TX 77843. *Fax:* 409-862-3989; *E-Mail:* sjayasuriya@mengr.tamu.edu

JAYASWAL, RADHESHYAM K, MOLECULAR BIOLOGY, MICROBIOLOGY. *Current Pos:* ASST PROF MICROBIOL GENETICS, DEPT BIOL SCI, ILL STATE UNIV, NORMAL, 88- *Personal Data:* b Ramganj, India, July 6, 49; m 77; c 2. *Educ:* Bombay Univ, India, BSc, 73, MSc, 80; Purdue Univ, PhD(molecular genetics), 85; Bhabha Inst, India, dipl anal methods, 74. *Prof Exp:* Sci asst molecular biol, Tata Inst Fundamental Res, Bombay, 74-80; res asst molecular biol, Dept Hort, Purdue Univ, 80-85, res assoc, Dept Biol, 85-88. *Concurrent Pos:* NIH award, 90-92; Am Heart Asn Award, Am Heart Asn-IA, 91-93. *Mem:* Am Soc Microbiol; Am Phytopath Soc; Am Heart Asn. *Res:* Investigate the possibility of using pseudomonas cepacia as a biocontrol agent after genetic manipulations of antifungal genes; gene cloning, sequencing, and promoter modifications to enhance production of antifungal compound and field testing to determine the efficacy of genetically modified strains. *Mailing Add:* Biol Sci Ill State Univ Campus Box 4120 Normal IL 61790-0001

JAYAWEERA, KOLF, CLOUD PHYSICS. *Current Pos:* DEAN, SCH NATURAL SCI & MATH, CALIF STATE UNIV, 90- *Personal Data:* b Kalutara, Ceylon, Dec 2, 38; m 65; c 3. *Educ:* Univ Ceylon, BS, 60; Univ London, PhD(physics), 65, Imp Col, Univ London, DIC(cloud physics), 65. *Prof Exp:* Asst lectr physics, Univ Ceylon, 60-62, lectr, 65-67; scientist, Commonwealth Sci & Indust Res Orgn res fel, Sydney, 67-70; from asst prof to prof geophys, Univ Alaska, 70-90, dean, Col Natural Sci, 85-90. *Concurrent Pos:* Res grants, NSF, Geophys Inst, Univ Alaska, 71-84, Nat Oceanog & Atmospheric Admin, 73-75 & Off Naval Res, 72-75; prog assoc meteorol, NSF, 78-79 & Air Force Off Sci Res, 79-84. *Mem:* AAAS; fel Royal Meteorol Soc; Am Meteorol Soc; Am Geophys Union. *Res:* Nucleation, growth and aerodynamics of ice crystals in clouds; weather modification; satellite meteorology and sea ice; atmosphere turbulence. *Mailing Add:* Sch Natural Sci & Math Calif State Univ PO Box 6850 Fullerton CA 92834-6850

JAYCOX, ELBERT RALPH, ENTOMOLOGY, APICULTURE. *Current Pos:* RETIRED. *Personal Data:* b Miami, Ariz, Oct 13, 23; m 47, Barbara Gravink; c Susan, John, Julia & Holly. *Educ:* Univ Calif, BS, 49, MS, 51, PhD(entom, apicult), 56. *Honors & Awards:* Outstanding Serv Beekeeping, Western Apicult Soc. *Prof Exp:* Supvr apiary inspection, Calif Dept Agr, 53-58; entomologist apicult, wild bee pollination invests, USDA, Utah State Univ, 58-63; assoc prof hort, Univ Ill, Urbana, 63-69, prof hort & entom, 69-80, prof entom, 80-81. *Concurrent Pos:* Vis prof, Univ Bern, Switz, 73-74; assoc ed, J Apicult Res; adj prof entom, NMex State Univ, 81- *Mem:* Sigma Xi; Entom Soc Am; Int Bee Res Asn. *Res:* Honey bee diseases and parasites; pesticides and bees; bee behavior and biology; pollination; taxonomy of Anthidium. *Mailing Add:* 6100 Shadow Hills Rd Las Cruces NM 88012-9547

JAYE, MURRAY JOSEPH, FOOD SCIENCE, MICROBIOLOGY. *Current Pos:* TECH DIR, FAIRMONT FOODS CO, 80- *Personal Data:* b New York, NY, Aug 17, 37; m 60; c 2. *Educ:* Univ Ga, BS, 59; Univ Ill, Urbana, MS, 61, PhD(food sci), 64. *Prof Exp:* Res scientist, Hercules Inc, 64-67; sr scientist, Frito-Lay Inc, 67-68, sect mgr, 69-70, prin scientist, 71-73, mgr corp develop, 74-75; mgr new food prod, Clorox Co, 75- *Mem:* Am Chem Soc; Inst Food Technologists; Am Mgt Asn. *Res:* New food products research; flavor chemistry and utilization; starch and hydrocolloid chemistry and utilization; food systems development; research administration. *Mailing Add:* 2517 Via Verde Walnut Creek CA 94598-3443

JAYE, SEYMOUR, ENGINEERING PHYSICS, NUCLEAR ENGINEERING. *Current Pos:* SR ADV, RCG HAGLER BAILEY INC, 89- *Personal Data:* b Chicago, Ill, Oct 1, 31; m 58; c 3. *Educ:* Univ Ill, BS, 54, MS, 55. *Prof Exp:* Asst radiant heating, Univ Ill, 54-55; assoc physicist nuclear reactor design, Oak Ridge Nat Lab, 55, physicist, 56-60; group leader nuclear design & reactor physics, high temperature gas-cooled reactor, Gen Atomic Div, Gen Dynamics Corp, 60-66, mgr off high temperature gas-cooled reactor planning & asst dept chmn nuclear anal & reactor physics, 66-70, mgr nuclear fuel mkt, Gulf Gen Atomic, 70-71; mgr fuel studies, S M Stoller Corp, 71-73, dir, vpres & gen mgr, 74-82, pres, 83-85, chief exec officer & chmn, 85-89. *Concurrent Pos:* Lectr, Univ Tenn, 60. *Mem:* Am Nuclear Soc. *Res:* Nuclear design of power reactors; nuclear reactor fuel; reactor physics. *Mailing Add:* 439 S 80th St Boulder CO 80303

JAYME, DAVID WOODWARD, SERUM-FREE NUTRIENT OPTIMIZATION FOR HIGH DENSITY BIOPRODUCTION, SERUM-FREE MEDIA FOR CELL & GENE THERAPY APPLICATIONS. *Current Pos:* SCI DIR, INDUST CELL CULTURE APPL, 95- *Personal Data:* b Paterson, NJ, Dec 30, 50; m 73, Donna L Engstrum; c Lara, Stephen, Kent, Adam, Bethany & Nathan. *Educ:* Brigham Young Univ, BS, 74, MS, 75; Univ Mich, PhD(biol chem), 79. *Prof Exp:* Fel human genetics, Sch Med, Yale Univ, 79-81; res asst prof pharmacol, Med Col Va, Va Commonwealth Univ, 81-83; mgr, Life Technologies Inc, 83-88, dir, 88-92, tech dir cell cult res & develop, 92-95. *Mem:* NY Acad Sci; Am Soc Cell Biol; Tissue Cult Asn; Am Chem Soc; AAAS. *Res:* Serum-free nutrient optimization for research and biotechnology applications of cultured mammalian and invertebrate cells; cultivation of human and other mammalian cells for in vitro toxicology, cellular therapy, and other biomedical applications. *Mailing Add:* 3175 Staley Rd Grand Island NY 14072. *Fax:* 716-774-6811; *E-Mail:* djayme@lifetech.com

JAYNE, JACK EDGAR, CHEMISTRY. *Current Pos:* RETIRED. *Personal Data:* b Spokane, Wash, Dec 18, 25; m 47, Doris Guthrie; c Nancy, Thomas, Brian & Claudia. *Educ:* Univ Wis, BS, 47, MS, 48; Lawrence Univ, MS, 50, PhD, 53. *Prof Exp:* Sr res scientist, Kimberly-Clark Corp, 52-74; corp environ dir, Green Bay Packaging, Inc, 74-88. *Mem:* Tech Asn Pulp & Paper Indust. *Res:* Environmental research on effluents and emissions from pulp and paper manufacture. *Mailing Add:* N4218 Gonnering Ct Kaukauna WI 54130-7258

JAYNE, JERROLD CLARENCE, ANALYTICAL CHEMISTRY, INORGANIC CHEMISTRY. *Current Pos:* From asst prof to assoc prof, 63-74, PROF CHEM, SAN FRANCISCO STATE UNIV, 75- *Personal Data:* b Stevens Point, Wis, Feb 8, 31; m 60; c 2. *Educ:* Univ Wis, BS, 52, PhD(anal chem), 63. *Concurrent Pos:* Partic, Water Chem Prog, Univ Wis, 70-72. *Mem:* Am Chem Soc; Sigma Xi. *Res:* Coordination chemistry; water chemistry. *Mailing Add:* 2351 Evergreen Dr San Bruno CA 94066-1831

JAYNE, THEODORE D, SURFACE SCIENCES, PHYSICAL CHEMISTRY. *Current Pos:* TECH DIR, T JAYNE CO, 69- *Personal Data:* b Painesville, Ohio, Dec 3, 29; m 59; c 3. *Educ:* Univ Chicago, AB, 50. *Prof Exp:* Head, Mat & Instrument Sect, Rand Develop Corp, 50-64; lab dir, Gen Tech Serv Inc, 64-72. *Concurrent Pos:* Chief metallurgist, Rand Develop Corp, 50-64; prin investr, Gen Tech Serv Inc, 65-72 & T Jayne Co, 69-; consult, T Jayne Co, 69-, tech dir, 84- *Res:* Materials; instrumental techniques, light, x-ray, electron, stm microscopies, inertial sensors, stress sensors; vacuum techniques; metrology; instrument design; industrial processes; system design. *Mailing Add:* 10234 Johnnycake Ridge Rd Painesville OH 44077-2055

JAYNES, EDWIN THOMPSON, THEORETICAL PHYSICS. *Current Pos:* from assoc prof to prof, 60-75, WAYMAN CROW PROF PHYSICS, WASHINGTON UNIV, 75- *Personal Data:* b Waterloo, Iowa, July 5, 22. *Educ:* Univ Iowa, BA, 42; Princeton Univ, MA, 48, PhD(physics), 50. *Prof Exp:* Proj engr, Sperry Gyroscope Co, 42-44; actg asst prof, Stanford Univ, 50-55, assoc prof physics, 55-60. *Concurrent Pos:* Vis fel, St John's Col, Cambridge, Eng, 83-84. *Mem:* AAAS; Am Phys Soc; Am Asn Physics Teachers. *Res:* Electromagnetic theory; statistical mechanics. *Mailing Add:* Washington Univ Campus Box 1105 One Brooking Dr St Louis MO 63130

JAYNES, HUGH OLIVER, FOOD SCIENCE. *Current Pos:* assoc prof, 70-79, PROF FOOD TECHNOL & SCI, UNIV TENN, KNOXVILLE, 79-, DEPT HEAD, 85- *Personal Data:* b Greeneville, Tenn, Aug 14, 31; m 53; c 2. *Educ:* Univ Tenn, BS, 53, MS, 54; Univ Ill, PhD(food sci), 70. *Prof Exp:* Bacteriologist, Res & Develop Ctr, Pet, Inc, 56-63, sect leader chem, 63-67; res fel food sci, Univ Ill, 67-70. *Concurrent Pos:* Vis prof, Univ Alexandria, Egypt, 80, coordr, Int Agr Progs, 82-85. *Mem:* Inst Food Technologists; Am Dairy Sci Asn; Sigma Xi. *Res:* Applied research in food color, food chemistry and food product development. *Mailing Add:* 8221 Corteland Dr Knoxville TN 37909

JAYNES, JOHN ALVA, FOOD SCIENCE. *Current Pos:* Proj leader food res, Borden Inc, 60-63, assoc dir res, 63-67, prod mgr, Canned Milk Prod, 67-73, pres beverage prod, 73-75, vpres foods div, 75-76, pres refrigerated prod, 77-79, vpres, 80-81, VPRES OPERS GROCERY PROD, BORDEN INC, 81- *Personal Data:* b Bonham, Tex, Sept 27, 29; m 55; c 2. *Educ:* Sam Houston State Teachers Col, BS, 51; Tex Tech Col, BS, 56, MS, 57; Mich State Univ, PhD(dairy), 60. *Mem:* Am Dairy Sci Asn. *Res:* Canned sterile milk and milk based drinks. *Mailing Add:* 2776 W Dublin Grandville Rd Columbus OH 43235

JAYNES, RICHARD ANDRUS, PLANT BREEDING. *Current Pos:* CONSULT, 84- *Personal Data:* b New Iberia, La, May 27, 35; m 59, Sarah Humphrey; c Burton, Linda B & B Scott. *Educ:* Wesleyan Univ, BA, 57; Yale Univ, MS, 59, PhD(bot), 61. *Honors & Awards:* Edgar T Wherry Award, Am Rock Garden Soc, 91. *Prof Exp:* From asst geneticist to geneticist, Conn Agr Exp Sta, 61-80, horticulturist, 80-84. *Concurrent Pos:* Owner, Broken Arrow Nursery. *Mem:* Am Soc Hort Sci; fel Int Plant Propagators Soc. *Res:* Development of hybrid chestnut trees resistant to the chestnut blight fungus; biological control of the chestnut blight fungus; breeding improved woody ornamentals, especially laurel (Kalmia); vegetative propagation of woody plants. *Mailing Add:* 13 Broken Arrow Rd Hamden CT 06518. *Fax:* 203-287-1035

JAZWINSKI, S MICHAL, GENETICS OF AGING, CELL CYCLE CONTROL. *Current Pos:* assoc prof, 84-90, PROF BIOCHEM & MOLECULAR BIOL, LA STATE UNIV MED CTR, 90-, CO-DIR, CTR ON AGING, 92- *Personal Data:* b Detroit, Mich, June 8, 47; m 70, Barbara M Gebicka; c Michal M & Peter M. *Educ:* Warsaw Univ, Poland, MS, 70; Stanford Univ, Calif, PhD(biochem), 75. *Prof Exp:* Helen Hay Whitney fel, Rockefeller Univ, 75-78, asst prof, 77-84. *Concurrent Pos:* Mem, Molecular

Cytology Study Sect, NIH, 91-95; vpres, KROL Found, 95-; chair-elect, Eukaryotic Biol Div, Am Soc Microbiol, 97. *Mem:* Am Soc Biochem & Molecular Biol; Am Soc Microbiol; Genetics Soc Am; Harvey Soc; Sigma Xi; fel Geront Soc Am. *Res:* Genetics of aging; cloned a set of genes that are differentially expressed during the yeast life span; identified eight longevity assurance genes in this organism. *Mailing Add:* Dept Biochem & Molecular Biol La State Univ Med Ctr 1901 Perdido St New Orleans LA 70112-1393

JEAN, GEORGE NOEL, ORGANIC CHEMISTRY. *Current Pos:* patent chemist, Patent Dept, Legal Div, Chas Pfizer & Co, Inc, 56-71, patent chemist, 71-76, SR PATENT CHEMIST, PATENT DEPT, LEGAL DIV, PFIZER INC, 76- *Personal Data:* b New York, NY, Aug 2, 29. *Educ:* Fordham Univ, BS, 49, MS, 51, PhD(chem), 57. *Prof Exp:* Dye chemist, J P Stevens & Co, Inc, NY, 48; asst phys sci, Med Labs, Army Chem Ctr, Md, 53-55; asst chem, Fordham Univ, 55-56. *Mem:* AAAS; Am Chem Soc; Am Inst Chemists. *Res:* Synthesis and stereochemistry of biaromatic heterocycles; analytical detection of mercaptans; dye chemistry; chemical pharmaceutical patents. *Mailing Add:* 6739 Ingram St Forest Hills NY 11375

JEAN-BAPTISTE, EMILE, MEDICINE, PHYSIOLOGY. *Current Pos:* Res assoc metab & endocrinol, 76-80, asst prof, Lab Cell Biochem & Pharmacol, 80-85, intern/resident internal med, 83-84, ADJ FAC, LAB CELL BIOCHEM & PHARMACOL, ROCKEFELLER UNIV, 85-, & LAB BACT & IMMUNOL, 89-; DIR CLIN RES, DIRECT ACCESS DIAG, JOHNSON & JOHNSON, 94-; EXEC DIR MED AFFAIRS, EUROPE, 94- *Personal Data:* b Port-au-Prince, Haiti, Mar 15, 47; m 68; c 2. *Educ:* Fordham Univ, BS, 71, MS, 72, PhD(physiol), 76; Med Col, Cornell Univ, MD, 83. *Concurrent Pos:* Adj asst prof, Col New Rochelle, 75-76; consult-tranlr, Fr ed, The Med Lett, 77-87; fel, Rockefeller Univ, 76-80, NIH, 78-80; asst prof, City Univ NY, 75-80, prof, 87-; pres & founder, Haitian Biomed Found, 86-; med epidemiologist, New York City Health Dept, 89-93; prof, Hofstra Univ, 89-92; Brooklyn Borough Commnr, NY City Health Dept, 90-93; assoc med dir, AIDS Inst, NY State Health Dept, 93-94. *Mem:* Am Soc Zoologists; Sigma Xi; AAAS; NY Acad Sci; Am Soc Pharmacol & Exp Therapeut; AMA; Am Acad Pain Mgt; Nat Coun Int Health. *Res:* Hormonal regulation of lipolysis in adipose tissue; steroidogenesis in adrenal cortex; magnesium flux in plasma membranes; ACTH and glucagon analogs, endorphins, enkephelins, naloxone, luteinizing-hormone releasing hormone and their mechanism of action through the cyclic adenosine monophosphate system; endocrine pharmacology; biochemistry; public health; endocrinology; pharmacology. *Mailing Add:* 1015 Kings Pkwy Baldwin NY 11510

JEANES, JACK KENNETH, CHEMISTRY. *Current Pos:* PRES & CHIEF EXEC OFF, INDUST RI CHEM LAB, INC, 69- *Personal Data:* b McKinney, Tex, July 2, 23; m 47; c 4. *Educ:* NTex State Col, BS, 47, MS, 48; Oak Ridge Inst Nuclear Studies, cert, 52; Univ Tex, Austin, PhD(biophys), 57. *Prof Exp:* Assoc prof chem, Southwestern State Col, Okla, 48-51; res assoc, Tex Res Found, 51-54; res asst biophys, Southwestern Med Sch, Univ Tex, 54-56, from instr to asst prof, 56-60; assoc prof chem & chem dept, Univ Dallas, 60-69. *Concurrent Pos:* Chem consult, 57-; NIH grant geront, 57-60. *Mem:* Am Chem Soc. *Res:* Biophysics; organic chemistry. *Mailing Add:* 1003 Sierra Pl Richardson TX 75080-4928

JEANLOZ, RAYMOND, MINERAL & MATERIALS PHYSICS, PLANETARY INTERIORS & HIGH PRESSURE RESEARCH. *Current Pos:* from asst prof to assoc prof, 82-85, PROF GEOL & GEOPHYS, UNIV CALIF, BERKELEY, 85- *Personal Data:* b Winchester, Mass, Aug 18, 52. *Educ:* Amherst Col, BA, 75; Calif Inst Technol, PhD(geol & geophys), 79. *Honors & Awards:* J B Macelwane Award, Am Geophys Union, 84; First Birch Lectr, 88; Presidential Young Investr Award, 84; Mineral Soc Am Award, 88; MacArthur Found Award, 88; Eyring Lectr, Ariz State Univ, 89; Hudnall Lectr, Univ Chicago, 90; Abelson Lectr, Carnegie Inst, Wash, 94; Segre Lectr, Tel Aviv Univ, 95. *Prof Exp:* Asst prof, Harvard Univ, 79-81. *Concurrent Pos:* Mem, Mat Res Lab, Harvard Univ, 79-81; A P Sloan Found fel, 81-85; assoc fac, Lawrence Berkeley Lab, 84-; Fairchild scholar, Calif Inst Technol, 88; Miller res prof, Berkeley, Calif, 92. *Mem:* Fel AAAS; fel Am Geophys Union; Geol Soc Am; Mineral Soc Am; Mat Res Soc; fel Am Acad Arts & Sci. *Res:* Experimental and theoretical study of minerals and other materials at high pressures, with particular application to the state of planetary interiors. *Mailing Add:* Dept Geol & Geophys Univ Calif Berkeley CA 94720-4767. *Fax:* 510-643-9980; *E-Mail:* jeanloz@uclink.berkeley.edu

JEANLOZ, ROGER WILLIAM, BIOCHEMISTRY, SYNTHETIC ORGANIC & NATURAL PRODUCTS. *Current Pos:* res assoc, Harvard Med Sch, 51-57, assoc org chem, Dept Med, 57-60, from asst prof to assoc prof, 60-69, EMER PROF BIOL CHEM, HARVARD MED SCH, 69-; BIOCHEMIST, MASS GEN HOSP, 61-; HON BIOCHEMIST, SHRIVER CTR, 92- *Personal Data:* b Berne, Switz, Nov 3, 17; nat US; m 45, Dorothea A H von Passavant; c Patrick M (deceased), Claude A, Raymond F, Danielle R & Sylvie A. *Educ:* Univ Geneva, ChE, 41, PhD(org chem), 43. *Hon Degrees:* AM, Harvard Univ, 61; DSc, Univ Paris, 80. *Honors & Awards:* Fr Soc Biol Chem Medal, 60; Liege Univ Medal, 64; Hudson Prize, Am Chem Soc, 73; Alexander von Humboldt Sr Scientist Award, 83. *Prof Exp:* Instr chem, Univ Geneva, 41-44; assoc, Univ Montreal, 47; sr mem & head, Biochem Lab, Worcester Found Exp Biol, 49-51; assoc biochemist, Mass Gen Hosp, 51-61. *Concurrent Pos:* Swiss Found fel, Univ Basel, 43-45; NIH sr res fel, 48; lectr, Swiss-Am Found Sci Exchange, 53-54; NSF sr fel, 59-60; guest prof, Univ Cologne, 59-60, Univ Freiburg, 60, Univ Tokyo & Univ Kyoto, 75, Univ Geneva, 76, Univ Saar, 83, Univ Kiel, 84; tutor, Harvard Univ, 61; mem, Study Sect Physiol Chem, NIH, 64-68 & 69-70; Nat Acad Sci & Acad Sci USSR exchange fel, 70; mem physiol chem B res study comn, Am Heart Asn, 72-75; lectr, Grenoble, 72 & Lille, 73; Guggenheim Found fel, 76-77. *Mem:* Am Chem Soc; Am Soc Biol Chemists; Royal Soc Chem; Swiss Chem Soc; Biochem Soc; fel AAAS. *Res:* Chemistry of carbohydrates; amino sugars; mucopolysaccharides; glycolipids; glycoproteins; bacterial cell walls; deoxysugars; ribose derivatives; glycogen; steroids; metabolism of corticosteroids. *Mailing Add:* Shriver Ctr Waltham MA 02254. *Fax:* 617-893-4018

JEANMAIRE, ROBERT L, SCIENCE EDUCATION. *Current Pos:* RETIRED. *Personal Data:* b Rockford, Ill, Feb 28, 20; m 58; c 3. *Educ:* Univ Ill, BS, 50, MS, 52; Rensselaer Polytech Inst, MS, 65. *Prof Exp:* Teacher, Melvin Sibley High Sch, 50-52, W Sr High Sch, 52-60 & Auburn High Sch, 60-64; instr physics & math, San Joaquin Delta Col, 64-65; from assoc prof to prof physics, Carthage Col, 65-92. *Concurrent Pos:* Writer and teacher oper jet engine control, Woodward Governor Co, 57-58. *Mem:* Am Asn Physics Teachers. *Res:* Teaching general physics using a computer. *Mailing Add:* 3725 Sherrie Lane Racine WI 53405

JEANNE, ROBERT LAWRENCE, BEHAVIOR OF SOCIAL INSECTS. *Current Pos:* PROF ENTOM, UNIV WIS, 76- *Personal Data:* b New York, NY, Jan 14, 42; m 76, Louise Bluhm; c Thomas L & James M. *Educ:* Denison Univ, BS, 64; Harvard Univ, MA, 68, PhD(biol), 71. *Prof Exp:* Instr biol, Univ Va, 70-71; asst prof biol, Boston Univ, 71-76. *Concurrent Pos:* Assoc ed, Insectes Sociaux, 86-; John Simon Guggenheim Mem fel, 86-87. *Mem:* Animal Behav Soc; Entom Soc Am; Int Union Study Soc Insects. *Res:* Behavior and evolution of tropical and temperate social wasps (Vespidae), with emphasis on communication, defense, nest architecture, colony size and cycle, and the rules governing colony integration and specialization. *Mailing Add:* Dept Entom Univ Wis Madison WI 53706. *Fax:* 608-262-3322; *E-Mail:* jeanne@macc.wisc.edu

JEARLD, AMBROSE, JR, FISHERIES BIOLOGY, FISHERIES RESEARCH. *Current Pos:* SUPVRY RES FISHERY BIOLOGIST, NORTHEAST FISHERIES CTR, WOODS HOLE LAB, US DEPT OF COM, 78- *Personal Data:* b Annapolis, Md, Mar 6, 44; m 76; c 1. *Educ:* Univ Md, Eastern Shore, BS, 65; Okla State Univ, MS, 70, PhD(zool), 75. *Prof Exp:* Chemist, Publickers Indust Inc, 65-67; biol asst med res, US Army Edgewood Arsenal, 69-71; asst prof biol & anat, Lincoln Univ, 75-77; asst prof animal behav & ecol, Howard Univ, 77-78. *Concurrent Pos:* Fel, Nat Sci, Okla State Univ, 73; fac mem, Sandy Hook Lab, Dept Com, 77-78; mem, Annapolis Environ Comn, 77-78. *Mem:* Sigma Xi; Animal Behav Soc; Am Fisheries Soc; Int Asn Fish Ethologists. *Res:* Animal behavior with emphasis on behavioral ecology in an aquatic environment; aging and growth problems and their influence on conservation and management of fishery resources in the northeast Atlantic. *Mailing Add:* 135 Tanglewood Dr East Falmouth MA 02536-5130

JEBE, EMIL H, APPLIED STATISTICS, DESIGN OF EXPERIMENTS. *Current Pos:* res mathematician & consult statistician, 73-79, emer statistician, 79-89, EMER MEM TECH STAFF, ENVIRON RES INST MICH, 89- *Personal Data:* b Clutier, Iowa, Feb 26, 09; wid. *Educ:* Iowa State Univ, BS, 38, MS, 41; NC State Univ, PhD(exp statist), 50. *Prof Exp:* Agr statistician, USDA, 38-40 & 46-49, supvr, USDA-Works Progress Admin & agr statistician, Pilot Res Surv, 40-41; assoc prof statist, Iowa State Univ, 49-59; res mathematician, Infrared & Optics Div, Willow Run Labs, Univ Mich, Ann Arbor, 59-72. *Concurrent Pos:* Consult statistician, 74-; chmn, Scio Twp Planning Comt, 70-74, Zoning Bd Appeals, E-11, Am Soc Testing & Mat, 80-84, Am Statist Asn Youden Award Comt. *Mem:* Fel Am Statist Asn; Int Biomet Soc; Int Asn Statist Phys Sci & Eng Sect; Int Asn Survey Statist; hon fel Am Soc Testing & Mat; NY Acad Sci; sr mem Am Soc Qual Control. *Res:* Application of sampling theory to the design and analysis of sample surveys and experiments; computer programming of least squares and ANOVA; systems analysis and operations research; property assessment analyses; author of over seventy publications. *Mailing Add:* Sunrise Terr Unit 4B 601 Taylor St Traer IA 50675

JEBSEN, ROBERT H, PHYSICAL MEDICINE & REHABILITATION. *Current Pos:* prof phys med & rehab & dir, 68-74, CLIN PROF PHYS MED & REHAB, UNIV CINCINNATI, 74- *Personal Data:* b New York, NY, Sept 5, 31; m 51; c 3. *Educ:* Brooklyn Col, BA, 53; State Univ NY, Downstate Med Ctr, MD, 56; Ohio State Univ, MMS, 60. *Prof Exp:* Intern, Harrisburg Hosp, Pa, 56-57; resident phys & rehab med, Ohio State Univ, Hosp, 57-60; chief phys med & rehab serv, Carswell AFB Hosp, Fort Worth, Tex, 60-62; dir, Rehab Ctr & Muscular Dystrophy Clin, St Luke's Hosp, Cedar Rapids, Iowa, 62-63; from asst prof to assoc prof phys med & rehab, Univ Wash, 63-68. *Concurrent Pos:* Attend physician, Iowa City Vet Admin Hosp, 62-63; consult, Knoxville Vet Admin Hosp, Iowa, 62-63. *Mem:* Am Acad Phys Med & Rehab; Am Asn Electromyog & Electrodiag (pres, 74-75); Am Cong Rehab Med; Asn Acad Physiatrists. *Res:* Neuromuscular electrodiagnosis; orthotics; objective measurements of physical function. *Mailing Add:* 703 Irene Kerrville TX 78028-5000

JECH, THOMAS J, LOGIC, TOPOLOGY. *Current Pos:* PROF MATH, PA STATE UNIV, 74- *Personal Data:* b Prague, Czech, Jan 29, 44; US citizen; m 65, Paula; c Pavel & Susanna. *Educ:* Charles Univ, Prague, PhD(math), 66. *Prof Exp:* Jr fel math, Univ Bristol, 68-69; assoc prof math, State Univ NY, Buffalo, 69-74. *Concurrent Pos:* Vis assoc prof, Univ Calif, Los Angeles, 70-71 & Princeton Univ, 72; vis prof, Stanford Univ, 74, Univ Calif, Los Angeles, 81, Univ Hawaii, 84 & Calif Inst Technol, 91; ed, Proceedings Am Math Soc, 80-; guest prof, Beijing Normal Univ, 85-; Fulbright prof, Hebrew Univ, 89. *Mem:* Inst Advan Study; Am Math Soc; Asn Symbolic Logic. *Res:* Set theory. *Mailing Add:* Math Dept Pa State Univ University Park PA 16802. *E-Mail:* jech@math.psu.edu

JECK, RICHARD KAHR, CLOUD PHYSICS, AVIATION METEOROLOGY. *Current Pos:* RES METEROLOGIST, FED AVIATION ADMIN TECH CTR, 90- *Personal Data:* b Iola, Kans, Oct 6, 38; m 63; c 2. *Educ:* Rockhurst Col, Kansas City, BA, 60; St Louis Univ, MS, 63, PhD(physics), 68. *Prof Exp:* Fel, Nat Acad Sci, Nat Res Coun, US Naval Res Lab, 68-70; res & develop physicist, Bruker Physik, Ger, 70-71; staff scientist, Smithsonian Radiation Biol Lab, 71-73; res physicist, US Naval Res Lab, 73-90. *Concurrent Pos:* Res assoc prof, US Naval Acad, Annapolis, Md, 80-81. *Mem:* Am Meteorol Soc; Am Inst Aeronaut & Astronaut. *Res:* Airborne measurments of cloud characteristics related to aircraft icing; shipboard, airborne, and island based measurements of particulate aerosol size distributions in the maritime environment. *Mailing Add:* 339 N Quail Dr Marmora NJ 08223

JEDRUCH, JACEK, NUCLEAR REACTOR DEVELOPMENT. *Current Pos:* prin engr, Nuclear Eng Dept, 85-90, SR PRIN ENGR, APPL PHYSICS DEPT, EBASCO SERV, INC, 90- *Personal Data:* b Warsaw, Poland, Feb 22, 27; US citizen; m 72, Eva C Hoffman. *Educ:* Northeastern Univ, BS, 56; Mass Inst Technol, MS, 58; Pa State Univ, PhD(nuclear eng), 66. *Prof Exp:* Eng trainee, H B Smith Co, 53-56; res asst, Columbia Nat Co, 57; assoc scientist, Atomic Power Dept, Westinghouse Elec Co, 57-62, sr scientist, Advan Reactor Div, 66-69, fel scientist, Astronuclear Lab, 69-72, Advan Energy Syst Dept, 72-74, Fusion Power Syst Dept, 74-80 & Nuclear Fuels Div, 80-82. *Concurrent Pos:* Mem stand comt, Am Nuclear Soc, 69-81; freelance tech writer, 82-84; consult comput methods, 85; adj assoc prof, Appl Physics & Nuclear Eng Dept, Columbia Univ, NY, 89. *Mem:* Am Soc Mech Engrs; Am Nuclear Soc. *Res:* Development and design of nuclear power sources for electric power generation, space and surface propulsion; fission and fusion technology, safety, economics of fuel cycle of water, gas and liquid metal cooled reactors; development of computing methods for the above; development of nuclear analysis methods. *Mailing Add:* 21 Nassau Dr Summit NJ 07901. *Fax:* 212-839-3304

JEDYNAK, LEO, ELECTRICAL ENGINEERING. *Current Pos:* VPRES OPERS RES & DEVELOP, CUE PAGING CORP, 88- *Personal Data:* b Flint, Mich, Sept 15, 28; m 54; c 4. *Educ:* Mich State Univ, BSc, 54; Mass Inst Technol, MSc, 56, ScD(elec eng), 62. *Prof Exp:* Prog engr, Gen Elec Co, 54; res asst elec eng, Mass Inst Technol, 54-56; instr, Mich State Univ, 56-57; teaching asst, Mass Inst Technol, 57-58, instr, 58-62; from asst prof to assoc prof, Univ Wis-Madison, 62-76, prof elec eng, 76-80; sr vpres corp res & develop, Oak Indust Inc, 80-88. *Concurrent Pos:* Dir corp res, Oak Electro/netics Corp, 69-71, sci & eng consult, 71-; mem bd dirs, Oak Industs Inc, 70- *Mem:* AAAS; Inst Elec & Electronics Engrs; Sigma Xi. *Res:* Insulation of high voltages in high vacuum; electric switches, contacts and relays; real time applications of microcomputer systems. *Mailing Add:* 25931 Serenata Dr Mission Viejo CA 92691-5729

JEE, WEBSTER SHEW SHUN, ANATOMY. *Current Pos:* asst anat, Univ Utah, 52-58, actg bone group leader, Radiol Div, 56-58, instr, 59-60, asst res prof, 60-61, assoc prof, 63-67, dir training Prog Mineralized Tissues, 64-74, actg chmn anat, 73-77, actg dir Div Radiobiol, 73-79, BONE GROUP LEADER RADIOBIOL DIV, 58-, PROF ANAT, COL MED, UNIV UTAH, 67- *Personal Data:* b Oakland, Calif, June 25, 25; wid; c Kenneth W. *Educ:* Univ Calif, BA, 49, MA, 51; Univ Utah, PhD(anat), 59. *Honors & Awards:* Highest Achievement Award, Int Cong Bone Moyhometry, 92. *Prof Exp:* Asst zool, Univ Calif, 49-51. *Concurrent Pos:* Spec consult, Int Atomic Energy Agency, 60 & 64, Proctor & Gamble, 75-78, Upjohn Co, 78-87, Colgate-Palmolive, 79-81, Monsanto, 83-90, Eli Lilly, 84-86 & Sch Dent, China Med Col, Tarchung, Repub of China; mem staff, Radiol Health Res Activ, 63-; mem training comt, Nat Inst Dent Res, 66-70, chmn, 68-70; mem sci comt 33, Nat Coun Radiation Protection & Measurements, 69-86; assoc ed, Anat Rec, 69-; consult ed var jour, 70-; assoc ed, Calcified Tissue Res, 77-78; mem, Comt Animal Models for Res on Aging, Nat Res Coun, 78-81; mem peer rev comt musculoskeletal physiol, Am Inst Biol Sci & NASA, 78-89; hon prof, Guangdong Med Col Zhanggeang, China, 93; consult, Sehering Plough Inc. *Mem:* Radiation Res Soc; Am Asn Anat; Int Asn Dent Res; Geront Soc; Am Soc Bone & Mineral Res; Am Soc Gravitational & Space Biol; Int Chinese Hard Tissue Soc (pres, 97). *Res:* Physiology and metabolism of bone and teeth; radiation biology; hard tissue biology; osteoporosis and osteoarthritis research in animal models. *Mailing Add:* Div Radiobiol Bldg 586 Univ Utah Sch Med Salt Lake City UT 84112. *Fax:* 801-581-7008; *E-Mail:* yanfei@msscc.med.utah.edu

JEEJEEBHOY, KHURSHEED NOWROJEE, GASTROENTEROLOGY, EXERCISE PHYSIOLOGY. *Current Pos:* from asst prof to assoc prof, 68-75, PROF GASTROENTEROL, UNIV TORONTO, 75- *Personal Data:* b Rangoon, Burma, Aug 26, 35; Can citizen; m 61; c 3. *Educ:* Madras, India, MB & BS, 59; FRCP, 61; London Univ, PhD(clin gastrointestinal res) 63; FRCP(E), 66; FRCP(C), 69; FRCP, 75. *Prof Exp:* Tutor gastroenterol, Postgrad Med Sch London, 61-63; staff radiation, Bhabbha Atomic Res Ctr, Bombay, 63, in-chg, 63-65; head radiation, Radiation Med Ctr, Bombay, 65-67. *Concurrent Pos:* Prin investr, three grants, Med Res Coun Can, 68-; spec lectr, Dept Nutrit, Univ Toronto, 74-76, hon lectr, Dept Nutrit & Food Sci, 76-79; prof, Dept Nutrit & Food Sci, Univ Toronto, 79-81, Dept Nutrit Sci, 81-, Dept Physiol, 84-; vis prof, Santa Clara Valley Med Ctr, Stanford Univ, 91. *Mem:* Am Soc Clin Invest; Am Soc Clin Nutrit; Am Gastroenterol Asn; Can Asn Gastroenterol; Can Soc Clin Invest; Nutrit Soc Can; Am Asn Physicians. *Res:* Nutritional support of patients with gastrointestinal disease; effect of nutrition on muscle performance; interaction of nutrition and sepsis; long term support of patients with a short bowel. *Mailing Add:* St Michaels Hosp Rm 372 30 Bond St Toronto ON M5B 1W8 Can. *Fax:* 416-864-5882

JEEVANANDAM, MALAYAPPA, SURGICAL NUTRITION. *Current Pos:* DIR RES, TRAUMA CTR, ST JOSEPH'S HOSP, PHOENIX, AZ, 86- *Personal Data:* b Tirumangalam, India, June 14, 31; m 59, Chellam; c 2. *Educ:* Columbia Univ, PhD(chem), 65. *Prof Exp:* Res assoc, Col Physicians & Surgeons, Columbia Univ, 71-81; assoc lab mem, Sloan-Kettering Cancer Ctr, 81-86. *Mem:* Inst Nutrit; Am Soc Clin Nutritionists; NY Acad Sci; AAAS. *Res:* Nutrition of cancer; metabolism and nutrition of trauma victims. *Mailing Add:* Dir Res Trauma Ctr St Josephs Hosp & Med Ctr 350 W Thomas Rd Phoenix AZ 85013

JEFCOATE, COLIN R, PHARMACOLOGY. *Current Pos:* res assoc, Dept Biochem, 72-73, from asst prof to assoc prof, Dept Pharmacol, Med Sch, 73-82, PROF, DEPT PHARMACOL, MED SCH, UNIV WIS-MADISON, 82-, DIR, ENVIRON TOXICOL CTR, 83- *Personal Data:* b Chesham, Bucks, Eng, Sept 28, 42. *Educ:* Oxford Univ, Eng, BS, 63, PhD(chem), 66. *Prof Exp:* NATO fel, Basel Univ, Switz, 66-67; NIH & NATO fel, Cornell Univ, Ithaca, 67-69; MRC fel, Edinburgh Univ, Scotland, 69-72. *Concurrent Pos:* Mem, NATO Sci Comt Conf on Catalysis, Italy, 72; mem, four study sects, NIH, 76- *Res:* Author of numerous publications. *Mailing Add:* Dept Pharmacol Univ Wis Med Sch 1300 University Ave Madison WI 53706-1532

JEFFAY, HENRY, BIOCHEMISTRY. *Current Pos:* RETIRED. *Personal Data:* b Brooklyn, NY, Feb 9, 27; m 57, Ana Idalia Fmuniz; c Susan, Randall, Kevin, Jason & Stefanie. *Educ:* Univ Wis, BS, 48, MS, 49, PhD(biochem), 53. *Prof Exp:* Instr biochem, Sch Med, Univ PR, 53-55; res assoc, Univ Ill, 55-56, from asst prof to assoc prof, 56-68, asst dean fac affairs, 70-72, assoc dean basic sci, 72-74, dean, 76-79, prof biochem, 68-96. *Concurrent Pos:* Consult, Vet Admin Hosp, Chicago & Norwegian Am Hosp; consult, Roosevelt Mem Hosp, dir med educ; dir basic sci, Rockford Sch Med, Univ Ill, 74-76, actg dean basic sci, 76-79. *Mem:* AAAS; Am Chem Soc; Am Soc Biol Chemists; Int Asn Dent Res. *Res:* Protein metabolism; metabolism of oral tissue; obesity. *Mailing Add:* 4313 N Placita de Suzane Tucson AZ 85718

JEFFCOAT, MARJORIE K, PERIODONTOLOGY, RADIOLOGY. *Current Pos:* prof, 88-91, CHMN, DEPT PERIODONT, UNIV ALA, BIRMINGHAM, 88-, ROSEN PROF, 91- *Personal Data:* b Boston, Mass, June 14, 51; m 73. *Educ:* Mass Inst Technol, SB, 72; Harvard Sch Dent Med, DMD, 76, cert periodont, 78. *Honors & Awards:* Young Investr Award, Int Asn Dent Res, 86; Clin Research Award, Am Acad Periodont, 92. *Prof Exp:* Res fel periodont, Harvard Sch Dent Med, 75-78, from instr to assoc prof, 78-88. *Concurrent Pos:* Consult, Children's Hosp Med Ctr, 81 & Birmingham Vet Admin Hosp. *Mem:* Am Dent Asn; Am Acad Periodont; Int Asn Dent Res; Inst Elec & Electronics Engrs; Eng Med Biol Soc; Am Asn Dent Res. *Res:* Bone resorption and diagnosis periodontal disease utilizing the following approaches, digital radiography, bone scanning, radiolabeled microsphere measurements of blood flow, studies of chemotherapeutic agents for treatment of periodontal disease, studies of the effects of local factors on periodontal disease. *Mailing Add:* Sch Dent Univ Ala Birmingham UAB Station Birmingham AL 35294

JEFFERIES, JOHN TREVOR, ASTROPHYSICS. *Current Pos:* dir, 83-87, astronr, 87-92, EMER ASTRONR, NAT OPTICAL ASTRON OBSERV, 92- *Personal Data:* b Kellerberrin, Western Australia, Apr 2, 25; m 49, Charmian Candy; c Stephen R, Helen C & Trevor R. *Educ:* Western Australia Univ, BSc, 46, DSc(physics), 61; Cambridge Univ, MA, 49. *Prof Exp:* Res off solar physics, Commonwealth Sci & Indust Res Orgn, NSW, 49-56, prin res off astrophys, 59-60; res assoc, Harvard Col Observ, 56-57, res staff, High Altitude Observ, Colo, 57-58 & Sacramento Peak Observ, 58-59; consult to dir, Nat Bur Stand, Colo, 60-62; fel, Joint Inst Lab Astrophys, 62-64; prof astrophys, Univ Hawaii, 64-83, dir, Inst Astron, 67-83. *Concurrent Pos:* Adj prof, Univ Colo, 61-64; res assoc, High Altitude Observ, 61-64; prof, Col France, 70 & 77; Guggenheim fel, 70-71. *Mem:* Am Astron Soc. *Res:* Solar physics; radiative transfer; spectral line information; analysis of stellar spectra. *Mailing Add:* Nat Solar Observ 950 N Cherry Tucson AZ 85719. *E-Mail:* jtj@noao.edu

JEFFERIES, MICHAEL JOHN, TECHNICAL MANAGEMENT. *Current Pos:* RETIRED. *Personal Data:* b London, Eng, Feb 2, 41; m 69, Mary Ann Cenci; c Kevin & Carlyn. *Educ:* Univ Nottingham, BSc, 63, PhD(elec eng), 67. *Prof Exp:* Elec engr, Gen Elec Co, 67-76, managerial res & develop positions, 76-80, res & develop mgr, Eng Physics Labs, Corp Res & Develop, 80-87, gen mgr technol, Gen Elec Motor Bus, 87-90; mem fac, Purdue Univ, 90-93; vpres corp technol & mfg, Carrier Corp, 93-95. *Mem:* Fel Inst Elec & Electronics Engrs; Brit Inst Elec Engrs; Inst Elec Engrs UK. *Res:* Power systems: computer-aided design/computer-aided manufacturing, computers, controls, engineering analysis. *Mailing Add:* 4315 Hepatica Hill Rd Manlius NY 13104

JEFFERIES, STEVEN, SYNTHETIC BIOPOLYMERS. *Current Pos:* clin res dentist, 86-89. DIR CLIN RES, LD CAULK DIV, DENTSPLY INT INC, MILFORD, DEL, 90- *Personal Data:* b Abington, Pa, Sept 27, 51; m 73. *Educ:* Johns Hopkins Univ, BA, 73; Rutgers, MS, 77, Univ Md Dent Sch, DDS(dent), 80. *Prof Exp:* Res asst, environ health, Dept Environ Health, Johns Hopkins Sch Hygiene & Health, 73-75; res intern, chem biochem eng, Dept Chem & Biochem Eng, Rutgers Univ, 75-77; resident gen dent, USPHS Hosp, New Orleans, 80-81; staff dentist, Municipal Health Servs Prog, Albert Witzke Med Ctr, 81-83; gen dent, Steven R Jefferies, DDS, Pa, 83-86. *Concurrent Pos:* Consult, Johns Hopkins Sch Med, 77-78, Stacogen Corp, 86-; ed, Caulk Dent Educ Bull, 86- *Mem:* Am Asn Dent Res; Int Asn Dent Res; AAAS; Am Dent Asn. *Res:* Natural and synthetic biopolmers, controlled drug release technology, applied connective tissue research, clinical applications of collagen-based biomaterials, wound healing. *Mailing Add:* 3692 Wingfield Lane York PA 17402

JEFFERS, THOMAS KIRK, PARASITOLOGY, POULTRY SCIENCE. *Current Pos:* sr parasitologist, 74-83, head, 83-86, DIR ANIMAL SCI DISCOVERY RES, LILLY RES LABS, 86- *Personal Data:* b Syracuse, NY, Apr 30, 41; m 69; c 2. *Educ:* Cornell Univ, BS, 63; Univ Wis, PhD(zool & poultry sci), 69. *Honors & Awards:* P P Levine Award, Am Asn Avian Pathologists, 74. *Prof Exp:* Geneticist, Animal Res Inst, Can Dept Agr, 68-69; dept head parasitol, Hess & Clark Div, Rhodia, Inc, 69-74. *Mem:* Am Soc Parasitologists; Soc Protozoologists; Sigma Xi; Am Asn Avian Pathologists; Poultry Sci Asn; World's Poultry Sci Asn. *Res:* Avian coccidiosis; anticoccidial chemotherapy; intraspecific variation in the coccidia; anticoccidial drug resistance; host response to coccidia. *Mailing Add:* Eli Lilly Res Labs PO Box 708 Greenfield IN 46140

JEFFERS, WILLIAM ALLEN, JR, LOW TEMPERATURE PHYSICS. *Current Pos:* asst prof, 66-76, dean col, 78-87, ASSOC PROF PHYSICS, LAFAYETTE COL, 76- *Personal Data:* b Philadelphia, Pa, May 4, 36; m 58; c 3. *Educ:* Amherst Col, AB, 57; Mass Inst Technol, PhD(physics), 62. *Prof Exp:* Sr physicist, Battelle Mem Inst, 62-66. *Concurrent Pos:* Dean studies, Lafayette Col, 72-75. *Mem:* Am Phys Soc; Am Asn Physics Teachers; Sigma Xi. *Res:* Ultrasonic absorption in liquid helium; superconductivity; transport properties in metals. *Mailing Add:* 10 McIntosh Dr Easton PA 18045-5831

JEFFERSON, CAROL ANNETTE, PLANT ECOLOGY. *Current Pos:* asst prof, 76-81, ASSOC PROF BIOL, WINONA STATE UNIV, 81- *Personal Data:* b Minneapolis, Minn, July 4, 48; m 75; c 2. *Educ:* St Olaf Col, BA, 70; Ore State Univ, PhD(bot), 74. *Prof Exp:* Asst prof biol, Eckerd Col, 74-76. *Mem:* AAAS; Ecol Soc Am. *Res:* Great Lakes sand vegetation; driftless area-relict communities; flood plain vegetation; wetland ecotones. *Mailing Add:* Biol Dept Winona State Univ PO Box 5838 Winona MN 55987-0838

JEFFERSON, DAVID KENOSS, COMPUTER SCIENCE. *Current Pos:* CHIEF INFO SYSTS ENG DIV, NAT INST STAND & TECHNOL, 87- *Personal Data:* b Pasadena, Calif, Dec 21, 38; m 67; c 2. *Educ:* Calif Inst Technol, BS, 60; Columbia Univ, AM, 62; Univ Mich, PhD(comput sci), 69. *Prof Exp:* Vis prof comput sci, Naval Postgrad Sch, 72-73; mathematician, Naval Weapons Lab, 60-72, res mathematician, 73-75; proj leader info syst design, David W Taylor Naval Ship Res & Develop Ctr, 75-82; mgr, Database Archit Group, Nat Bur Stand, 82-87. *Concurrent Pos:* Lectr, Univ Md, 77-82. *Mem:* Sigma Xi; Asn Comput Mach; Inst Elec & Electronics Engrs; Sr Exec Serv. *Res:* Standards and guides for data dictionary systems, database languages, data interchange, graphics, data administration, database design, hypertext, object-oriented databases and knowledge-based systems; development and administration of conformance tests and procedures. *Mailing Add:* 8121 Langport Terr Gaithersburg MD 20877-1135

JEFFERSON, DONALD EARL, SCIENCE POLICY, PHYSICAL OCEANOGRAPHY. *Current Pos:* RETIRED. *Personal Data:* b Homeland, Fla, Sept 27, 27; m 51; c 2. *Educ:* Morehouse Col, BS, 48; Howard Univ, MS, 50. *Prof Exp:* Instr physics, Va Union Univ, 49-51; physicist, US Naval Ord Lab, 51-52, elec engr, 54-72, elec engr, Naval Surface Weapon Ctr, 72-81, sci adv to commander second fleet, Naval Assistance Prog, 81-82, Naval Surface Weapon Ctr, 83-85. *Concurrent Pos:* Vpres eng, Copycomposer Corp, 69-71. *Mem:* Am Defense Preparedness Asn. *Res:* Review of naval operational systems for modification or replacement as needed; design and modification of instrumentation for measuring ocean currents; statistical analysis and prediction of system and environment interactions; underwater acoustics. *Mailing Add:* 13321 Bea Kay Dr Silver Spring MD 20904

JEFFERSON, EDWARD G, RESEARCH ADMINISTRATION. *Current Pos:* RETIRED. *Personal Data:* b London, Eng, July 15, 21; m 53; c 3. *Educ:* Univ London, PhD. *Honors & Awards:* Warren K Lewis Lectr, Mass Inst Technol; Chem Indust Medal, Soc Chem Indust. *Prof Exp:* Supvr, Du Pont, 51-60, mgr res, Plastics Dept, 60-64, asst dir, 64-66, dir, Flurocarbons Div, 66-69, asst gen mgr, Plastics Dept, 69-70, asst gen mgr, Explosives Dept, 70-72, asst gen mgr, Polymer Intermediates Dept, 72, vpres & gen mgr, Film Dept, 72-73, dir, sr vpres & mem exec comt, 73-80, pres & chief oper officer, 80-81, chmn & chief exec off, 81-86. *Concurrent Pos:* Mem bd dirs, Du Pont Co, 86-; dir, Chem Banking Corp & Am Tel & Tel Co; mem, President's Export Coun & US Coun Int Bus. *Mem:* Nat Acad Eng; Am Philos Soc; Am Acad Arts & Sci; Am Inst Chem Engrs; Am Chem Soc. *Mailing Add:* 1007 Market St Wilmington DE 19898. *Fax:* 302-773-4244

JEFFERSON, JAMES WALTER, PSYCHOPHARMACOLOGY. *Current Pos:* resident psychiat, Univ Wis-Madison, 71-74, from asst prof to assoc prof, 74-81, prof, 81-92, CLIN PROF PSYCHIAT, UNIV WIS- MADISON, 92-; DISTINGUISHED SR SCIENTIST, DEAN FOUND, 92- *Personal Data:* b Mineola, NY, Aug 14, 37; m 65; c 3. *Educ:* Bucknell Univ, BS, 58; Univ Wis, MD, 64. *Prof Exp:* Intern, St Lukes Hosp, NY, 64-65; resident internal med, Univ Wis, 65-67; fel, Univ Chicago, 67-68. *Concurrent Pos:* Staff psychiatrist, Vet Admin Hosp, Wis, 74-81; co-dir, Lithium Info Ctr, Madison, 74-; dir, Ctr Affective Disorders, Madison, 84-92. *Mem:* Am Psychiat Asn; Am Psychopath Asn; Int Neuropsychopharmacologium Soc; Am Soc Clin Psychoparmacol. *Res:* Clinical psychopharmacology; complitation and dissertation of information through interactive computer programs in psychiatry; neuropsychiatric aspects of medical disorders. *Mailing Add:* Dean Found 2711 Allen Blvd Middleton WI 53562. *Fax:* 608-827-2399

JEFFERSON, LEONARD SHELTON, PHYSIOLOGY. *Current Pos:* from instr to assoc prof, 67-75, prof & chmn, 88-96, PROF PHYSIOL, COL MED, PA STATE UNIV, 75-, ASSOC DEAN RES & GRAD STUDIES, 91-, EVAN PUGH PROF & CHMN, 96- *Personal Data:* b Maysville, Ky, Jan 14, 39. *Educ:* Eastern Ky Univ, BS, 61; Vanderbilt Univ, PhD(physiol), 66. *Honors & Awards:* Lilly Award, Am Diabetes Asn, 79. *Prof Exp:* Vis scientist, Cambridge Univ, 66-67; res assoc physiol, Col Med, Vanderbilt Univ, 67. *Concurrent Pos:* USPHS fel, 66-67. *Mem:* Am Soc Biol Chemists; Biochem Soc; Am Physiol Soc; Am Diabetes Asn. *Res:* Regulation of skeletal muscle and hepatic carbohydrate and protein metabolism by hormones and other factors, especially mechanism of action of insulin and growth hormone. *Mailing Add:* Milton S Hershey Med Ctr Pa State Univ PO Box 850 Hershey PA 17033. *Fax:* 717-531-7667

JEFFERSON, MARGARET CORREAN, GENETICS. *Current Pos:* Asst prof, 77-81, assoc prof biol, 81-85, PROF BIOL, CALIF STATE UNIV, LOS ANGELES, 85- *Personal Data:* b Eau Claire, Wis, Aug 22, 47. *Educ:* Univ Dubuque, BS, 69; Univ Colo, MA, 71; Univ Ariz, PhD(genetics), 77. *Concurrent Pos:* Consult, Compton Sickle Cell Educ & Detection Ctr, 77-; prin invester biomed res support grants, NIH, 77- & res apprenticeships minority high sch students, NSF, 81-82. *Mem:* AAAS; Am Genetics Asn; Genetics Soc Am; Soc Study Evolution. *Res:* Ecological and behavioral genetics of desert-adapted Drosophila; specifically, pheromonal regulation of reproductive strategies in desert-adapted Drosophila; genetics of learning behavior; cytogenetics of Cycads; eye pigmentation systems. *Mailing Add:* Dept of Biol Calif State Univ 5151 State Univ Dr Los Angeles CA 90032-8000

JEFFERSON, ROLAND NEWTON, ENTOMOLOGY. *Current Pos:* RETIRED. *Personal Data:* b Washington, DC, Nov 7, 11; m 46; c 3. *Educ:* Va Polytech Inst, BS, 34, MS, 36; Iowa State Col, PhD(entom), 42. *Prof Exp:* Asst entomologist, Va Exp Sta, 36-39; instr entom, Va Polytech Inst, 39-40; asst entomologist, Va Exp Sta, 41-42; from asst prof & asst entomologist to prof & entomologist, Exp Sta, Univ Calif, Los Angeles, 46-60; prof entom, Univ Calif, Riverside, 60-76, emer prof entom & entomologist, Exp Sta, 76-77. *Mem:* Entom Soc Am. *Res:* Insect morphology; insects affecting floricultural crops. *Mailing Add:* 5499 Grassy Trail Dr Riverside CA 92504

JEFFERSON, THOMAS BRADLEY, MECHANICAL ENGINEERING. *Current Pos:* dean, Sch Eng & Technol, 69-78, PROF MECH ENG, SOUTHERN ILL UNIV, 78- *Personal Data:* b Urich, Mo, Nov 25, 24; m 46; c 3. *Educ:* Kans State Col, BS, 49; Univ Nebr, MS, 50; Purdue Univ, PhD, 55. *Prof Exp:* Instr mech eng, Univ Nebr, 49-52; from instr to asst prof, Purdue Univ, 52-58; prof & head dept, Univ Ark, Fayetteville, 58-68, assoc dean eng, 68-69. *Concurrent Pos:* Consult, Allison Div, Gen Motors Corp, 56-57; Martin Marietta Aerospace, Denver, 58-68. *Mem:* Am Soc Mech Engrs; Am Soc Eng Educ. *Res:* Heat transfer. *Mailing Add:* 901 S Glenview Carbondale IL 62901

JEFFERSON, THOMAS HUTTON, JR, MASS STORAGE, OPERATING SYSTEMS. *Current Pos:* DISTINGUISHED MEM TECH STAFF, SANDIA LABS, LIVERMORE, 69- *Personal Data:* b Mineola, NY, June 6, 41. *Educ:* Rensselaer Polytech Inst, BS, 63; NC State Univ, MAM, 65; Univ Colo, Boulder, PhD(appl math), 69. *Res:* Computer software libraries; computer mass storag; nonlinear parameter determination. *Mailing Add:* Distributed Comput MS 9011 Sandia Nat Labs Livermore CA 94551-0969

JEFFERTS, KEITH BARTLETT, ATOMIC PHYSICS, FISHERIES MANAGEMENT. *Current Pos:* PRES, NORTHWEST MARINE TECHNOL, 72- *Personal Data:* b Raymond, Wash, May 10, 31; m 53; c 4. *Educ:* Univ Wash, PhD(physics), 62. *Prof Exp:* Mem tech staff physics, Bell Tel Labs, 63-75. *Mem:* Am Phys Soc. *Res:* Structure of simple molecules; molecular astrophysics; application of physical techniques to problems of fishery management. *Mailing Add:* PO Box 427 Shaw Island WA 98286

JEFFERY, DUANE ELDRO, GENETICS. *Current Pos:* Asst prof, 69-77, ASSOC PROF ZOOL, BRIGHAM YOUNG UNIV, 77- *Personal Data:* b Delta, Utah, Sept 28, 37; m 61; c 3. *Educ:* Utah State Univ, BS, 62, MS, 63; Univ Calif, Berkeley, MA, 66, PhD(zool, genetics), 72. *Concurrent Pos:* Vis colleague genetics, Univ Hawaii, 74-75. *Mem:* Soc Study Evolution; Genetics Soc Am; Am Soc Human Genetics; AAAS. *Res:* Developmental and evolutionary genetics in Drosophila populations; human transmission genetics; cytogenetics. *Mailing Add:* Dept of Zool Brigham Young Univ 575 Widb Provo UT 84602-1049

JEFFERY, GEOFFREY MARRON, MALARIOLOGY. *Current Pos:* RETIRED. *Personal Data:* b Dundee, NY, May 13, 19; m 41; c 4. *Educ:* Hobart Col, BA, 40; Syracuse Univ, MA, 42; Johns Hopkins Univ, ScD(parasitol), 44; Yale Univ, MPH, 61. *Honors & Awards:* Ashford Medal, Am Soc Trop Med & Hyg, 59. *Prof Exp:* Biol aide, Tenn Valley Authority, Wilson Dam, Alta, 44; asst sanitarian, USPHS, 44-45, asst sanitarian, Commun Dis Ctr, Ga, 45-46; from asst sanitarian to sr asst scientist, Sch Trop Med, PR, 46-47; from sr asst scientist to scientist, Malaria Res Lab, Lab Trop Dis, NIH, Ga, 48-54, from scientist to sr scientist, SC, 54-60, sci dir, 60-63, asst chief, Lab Parasite Chemother, Nat Inst Allergy & Infectious Dis, 63-66, actg chief, 66, chief, 67-68; chief, Cent Am Res Sta, Ctr Dis Control, 69-74, asst dir, 74-75, dir, Vector Biol & Control Div, Bur Trop Dis, 75-81, asst dir, Div Parasitic Dis, Bur Trop Dis, 81-85. *Concurrent Pos:* Asst prof, Univ Bridgeport, 47-48; mem expert panel malaria, WHO, 63-; scientific group on chemother of malaria, Geneva, 67, parasitol of malaria, Teheran, 68 & Cent Am Malaria Assessment Mission, AID, 64; assoc mem comn malaria, Armed Forces Epidemiol Bd, 65-69, mem, 69-73; deleg, Int Cong Trop Med & Malaria, Lisbon, 58, Rio de Janeiro, 63, Teheran, 68, Int Cong Parasitol, Rome, 64, Wash, 70 & Latin Am Cong Parasitol, 73. *Mem:* AAAS; Am Soc Parasitol; Am Soc Trop Med & Hyg (secy-treas, 61-67, vpres, 71 & pres, 75);

Am Mosquito Control Asn; Royal Soc Trop Med & Hyg. *Res:* Malarias of man and lower animals; chemotherapy of malaria and parasitic infections; epidemiology of malaria and intestinal parasites; biology of human malarias; immunology and pathology of malaria; diagnosis of parasitic infections; drug resistant strains of malaria parasites; methodology of malaria eradication and control. *Mailing Add:* 1093 Blackshear Dr Decatur GA 30033

JEFFERY, LARRY S, WEED SCIENCE, WEED BIOLOGY. *Current Pos:* ASSOC PROF WEED SCI, UNIV TENN, 69- *Personal Data:* b Delta, Utah, June 21, 36; m 59; c 7. *Educ:* Utah State Univ, BS, 62; NDak State Univ, PhD(plant sci), 66. *Prof Exp:* Asst prof weed sci, Univ Nebr Lincoln & Bogota, Colombia, 66-69. *Concurrent Pos:* Consult, Univ Wis & EMBRAPA-Ministry Agr Brazil, Lordrina, 76. *Mem:* Weed Sci Soc Am; Coun Agr Sci & Technol; Int Weed Sci Soc. *Res:* Weed control in economic crops; development of weed control systems in corn, soybeans, grain sorghum, tobacco, alfalfa, small grains and pastures. *Mailing Add:* Agron Brigham Young Univ 269 Widb Provo UT 84602

JEFFERY, LAWRENCE R, SYSTEMS DESIGN, SYSTEMS SCIENCE. *Current Pos:* RETIRED. *Personal Data:* b Memphis, Tenn, June 30, 27; m 48; c 5. *Educ:* Univ Chicago, MS, 53. *Prof Exp:* Instr electronic eng & math, Am TV Inst, Ill, 46-51; engr, Raytheon Mfg Co, Mass, 53-54; staff mem command & control systs, Lincoln Lab, Mass Inst Technol, 54-58, sect leader, 58; assoc dept head, Mitre Corp, Mass, 59-61, dept head, 61-63, assoc tech dir, 63-73, tech dir commun, 73-86. *Mem:* Sr mem Inst Elec & Electronics Engrs. *Res:* Design and evaluation of computer-based command; control and communication systems; military operations research; digital computer engineering. *Mailing Add:* 16 Sherwood Dr Hollis NH 03049

JEFFERY, RONDO NELDEN, SOLID STATE PHYSICS, ELECTRONICS PHYSICS. *Current Pos:* vis assoc prof, Weber State Col, 80-83, assoc prof, 83-86, PROF, WEBER STATE UNIV, 86-; MEM TECH STAFF, TRW, 86- *Personal Data:* b Provo, Utah, Apr 16, 40; m 65, Janet Franson; c Ann, Laura, Sue, Ruth, Janalee, Elizabeth & Julia. *Educ:* Brigham Young Univ, BS, 63, MS, 65; Univ Ill-Urbana, PhD(physics), 70. *Prof Exp:* Res assoc physics, Rensselaer Polytech Inst, 70-73; asst prof, Wayne State Univ, 73-80. *Concurrent Pos:* Asst prof, Cottrell res grant, Res Corp, 75-78 & NSF res grant, 78-81 & CSIP grant, 87-89. *Mem:* Am Phys Soc; Am Asn Physics Teachers; Sigma Xi. *Res:* High pressure effects in solids; properties of point defects such as vacancies under high-pressure, high-temperature conditions using diffusion and positron annihilation techniques; developing microcomputer based physics laboratory experiments and electronics; physic education material. *Mailing Add:* Dept Physics Weber State Univ Ogden UT 84408-2508. *Fax:* 801-626-7445; *E-Mail:* rjeffery@weber.edu

JEFFERY, WILLIAM RICHARD, DEVELOPMENTAL BIOLOGY, CELL BIOLOGY. *Current Pos:* PROF ZOOL, UNIV CALIF, DAVIS, 90- *Personal Data:* b Chicago, Ill, June 9, 44. *Educ:* Univ Ill, BS, 67; Univ Iowa, PhD(zool), 71. *Prof Exp:* Res asst biol, Univ Ill, 65-66; NIH fel zool, Univ Iowa, 67-71; Am Cancer Soc fel oncol, Univ Wis, 71-72; res assoc biochem, Sch Med, Tufts Univ, 72-74; asst prof biophys, Univ Houston, 74-77; from asst prof to prof zool, Univ Tex, 77-90. *Concurrent Pos:* Corp mem, Marine Biol Lab, Woods Hole 75-, instr, 80-82, dir embryol, 83- *Mem:* AAAS; Am Soc Cell Biol; Asn Develop Biol. *Res:* Molecular and cellular mechanisms of cell development and differentiation. *Mailing Add:* Bodega Marine Lab Univ Calif PO Box 247 Bodega Bay CA 94923-0247. *Fax:* 707-875-2089

JEFFERYS, WILLIAM H, III, ASTRONOMY. *Current Pos:* from asst prof to assoc prof, 65-79, PROF ASTRON, UNIV TEX, AUSTIN, 79-, HARLAN J SMITH CENTENNIAL PROF ASTRON, 85- *Personal Data:* b New Bedford, Mass, July 8, 40. *Educ:* Wesleyan Univ, BA, 62; Yale Univ, MS, 64, PhD(astron), 65. *Prof Exp:* Instr astron, Wesleyan Univ, 64-65. *Concurrent Pos:* Alfred P Sloan fel, 65-67. *Mem:* AAAS; Am Astron Soc; Royal Astron Soc; Int Astron Union. *Res:* Astrometry; celestial mechanics; dynamical astronomy. *Mailing Add:* Dept of Astron Univ of Tex Austin TX 78712

JEFFORDS, RUSSELL MACGREGOR, GEOLOGY. *Current Pos:* TECH ASSOC, HOUSTON MUS NATURAL HIST, 70- *Personal Data:* b Shinglehouse, Pa, May 11, 18; wid; c Morton. *Educ:* Syracuse Univ, AB, 39; Univ Kans, MA, 41, PhD(geol), 46. *Prof Exp:* Asst geologist, Kans Geol Surv, 39-42; geologist, US Geol Surv, 42-54 & Humble Oil & Refining Co, 54-64; res adv, Exxon Prod Res Co, 64-79. *Concurrent Pos:* Instr, Brown Univ, 46-47; asst prof, Univ Tex, 47-48; assoc ed, Paleont Inst, Univ Kans, 69-; consult, 79- *Mem:* Soc Tech Commun; Geol Soc Am; Paleont Soc; Soc Econ Paleontologists & Mineralogists; Am Asn Petrol Geologists. *Res:* Stratigraphic paleontology; ground-water hydrology and geochemistry; Paleozoic corals; crinoids; chitinozoans; editing. *Mailing Add:* 8002 Beverly Hill St Houston TX 77063

JEFFREY, GEORGE ALAN, CRYSTALLOGRAPHY. *Current Pos:* prof chem & physics, 53-64, prof crystallog, 65-85, chmn dept, 69-85, EMER PROF CRYSTALLOG, UNIV PITTSBURGH, 85- *Personal Data:* b Cardiff, Eng, July 29, 15; nat US; m 42; c 2. *Educ:* Univ Birmingham, BSc, 36, PhD(chem), 39, DSc, 53. *Honors & Awards:* Hudson Award, Am Chem Soc, 80. *Prof Exp:* X-ray crystallographer, Brit Rubber Producers Res Asn, 39-45; lectr inorg & phys chem, Univ Leeds, 45-53. *Concurrent Pos:* Vis prof crystallog, Univ Pittsburgh, 50-51; mem exec comt gov bd, Am Inst Physics, 71- Award, Am Chem Soc, 78. *Mem:* Am Chem Soc; Am Crystallog Asn (treas, 54-58, pres, 63); The Chem Soc; Brit Inst Physics & Phys Soc. *Res:* Structure of hydrates and carbohydrates; biochemical crystallography; hydrogen bonding; molecular distortions in crystals. *Mailing Add:* 5500 Elgin St Pittsburgh PA 15206

JEFFREY, JOHN J, BIOLOGICAL CHEMISTRY, ENDOCRINOLOGY. *Current Pos:* From instr to assoc prof, 67-81, PROF MED, SCH MED, WASHINGTON UNIV, 81- *Personal Data:* b Worcester, Mass, May 3, 37; m 72. *Educ:* Col of the Holy Cross, BS, 58; Georgetown Univ, PhD(chem), 65. *Res:* Enzymatic mechanisms of collagen degradation; hormonal regulation of mammalian collagenase activity. *Mailing Add:* Albany Med Col 47 New Scotland Ave Albany NY 12208-3479. *Fax:* 518-262-5975

JEFFREY, KENNETH ROBERT, NUCLEAR MAGNETIC RESONANCE, X-RAY & NEUTRON DIFFRACTION. *Current Pos:* From asst prof to assoc prof, 69-81, PROF PHYSICS, UNIV GUELPH, 81-, CHAIR PHYSICS, 93- *Personal Data:* b Toronto, Ont, May 7, 41; m 67, Francis Ann Ogryzlo; c 2. *Educ:* Univ Toronto, BSc, 64, MA, 66, PhD(physics), 69. *Mem:* Can Asn Physicists; Biophys Soc. *Res:* Nuclear magnetic resonance studies of translational and reorientational motion and phase transitions in solids; biophysical techniques (nuclear magnetic resonance, x-ray and neutron diffraction, calorimetry), applied to model and biological membranes. *Mailing Add:* Dept Physics Univ Guelph Guelph ON N1G 2W1 Can

JEFFRIES, CARSON DUNNING, solid state physics; deceased, see previous edition for last biography

JEFFRIES, CHARLES DEAN, MICROBIOLOGY, MEDICAL MYCOLOGY. *Current Pos:* from instr to assoc prof, Wayne State Univ, 58-70, from actg dep chmn to assoc chmn dept, 70-75, prof immunol & microbiol, 70-96, asst dean curric affairs & dir grad progs, 75-80, ASSOC DERMAT, SCH MED, WAYNE STATE UNIV, 68-, PROF BIOL SCI, COL SCI, 90-, EMER PROF, 96-; PROF & DEPT CHAIR MICROBIOL & IMMUNOL, SCH MED, ROSS UNIV, 96-, INTERIM DEAN BASIC SCI, 97- *Personal Data:* b Rome, Ga, Apr 9, 29; m 53, Virginia M Alford. *Educ:* NGa Col, BS, 50; Univ Tenn, MS, 55, PhD(bact), 58. *Prof Exp:* Technician, Div Labs, State Dept Pub Health, Ga, 50-51; Med Serv Corps, US Army, 51-53. *Concurrent Pos:* Fulbright lectr, Cairo Univ, 65-66; mem bd exam basic sci, State Mich, 67-72, vpres, 71-72; guest res, Mycol Div, Ctr Dis Control, US Pub Health Serv, Atlanta, Ga, 80-81; microbiologist consult, Vet Admin Med Ctr, Allen Park, Mich, 89-92. *Mem:* Fel Am Acad Microbiol; Am Soc Microbiol; Soc Exp Biol & Med; Int Soc Human & Animal Mycol. *Res:* Bacterial identification; medical mycology. *Mailing Add:* Ross Univ Sch Med Box 266 Roseau Dominica. *Fax:* 767-445-5383; *E-Mail:* cjeffries@webdom.rossmed.edu.dm

JEFFRIES, GRAHAM HARRY, INTERNAL MEDICINE, GASTROENTEROLOGY. *Current Pos:* PROF MED & CHMN DEPT, COL MED, MILTON S HERSHEY MED CTR, PA STATE UNIV, 69- *Personal Data:* b Barmera, S Australia, May 31, 29; m 55; c 4. *Educ:* Univ NZ, BMedSc, 49, MB, ChB, 53; Oxford Univ, DPhil(physiol), 55. *Prof Exp:* Assoc prof med, Med Col, Cornell Univ, 64-69. *Mem:* Am Fedn Clin Res; Am Gastroenterol Asn; Am Soc Clin Invest; fel Am Col Physicians. *Res:* Gastric secretion; vitamin B-12 metabolism; intestinal absorption; liver disease. *Mailing Add:* Med Gastroenterol Pa State Univ Col Med PO Box 850 Hershey PA 17033-0850

JEFFRIES, HARRY PERRY, ZOOLOGY. *Current Pos:* from asst prof to assoc prof, 59-73, PROF BIOL OCEANOG, UNIV RI, 73- *Personal Data:* b Newark, NJ, Apr 15, 29; m 63; c 5. *Educ:* Univ RI, BS, 51, MS, 55; Rutgers Univ, PhD(zool), 59. *Prof Exp:* Asst biol oceanog, Univ RI, 51-55; pharmacologist, Ciba Pharmaceut Prod, Inc, NJ, 55-56; asst, Rutgers Univ, 56-59. *Concurrent Pos:* Grants, Dept Energy, Nat Oceanog & Atmospheric Admin; Environ Protection Agency Sea Grant, Am Petroleum Inst; pres, Estuarine Res Fedn, 73-75, Nat Sci Found, Off Naval Res. *Mem:* Fel AAAS; Am Soc Limnol & Oceanog; Sigma Xi. *Res:* Comparative ecology of estuarine habitats; biological fertility of inshore marine areas and characterization of community structure; chemical homeostasis of marine organisms in relation to environmental stress; biochemical systematics. *Mailing Add:* 289 Yawgoo Pond Rd West Kingston RI 02892

JEFFRIES, JAY B, MOLECULAR PHYSICS. *Current Pos:* CHEM PHYSICIST, SRI INT, 83- *Personal Data:* b June 3, 47; US citizen. *Educ:* Univ Iowa, BA, 69; Univ Colo, PhD(physics), 80. *Prof Exp:* Assoc prof res, Univ Pittsburgh, 80-83. *Concurrent Pos:* Topical ed, J Appl Optics. *Mem:* Am Phys Soc; Am Chem Soc; Combustion Inst; Mat Res Soc; fel Optical Soc Am. *Res:* Laser-based diagnostic measurements of reacting flows and plasmas with ultimate goal of understanding the fundamental chemical mechanism of the process. *Mailing Add:* Molecular Physics Lab SRI Int 333 Ravenswood Ave Menlo Park CA 94025. *Fax:* 650-859-6196; *E-Mail:* jeffries@mplvax.sri.com

JEFFRIES, NEAL POWELL, MECHANICAL ENGINEERING. *Current Pos:* exec dir, 78-85, PRES, CTR MFG TECH, 85- *Personal Data:* b Indianapolis, Ind, Aug 25, 35; m 58; c 2. *Educ:* Purdue Univ, BS, 57; Mass Inst Technol, MS, 58; Univ Cincinnati, PhD(mech eng), 69. *Prof Exp:* Res asst heat transfer, Stanford Univ, 61-63; engr, Gen Elec Co, Ohio, 63-65, proj mgr heat transfer, 65-67; res assoc mech eng, Univ Cincinnati, 67-69, asst prof, 69-74; mgr Educ Mech Eng Dept, Struct Dynamic Res Corp, 74-78. *Concurrent Pos:* Lectr, Gen Elec Co, 63-74; consult, Struct Dynamics Res Corp, 68-74, Honeywell Res Lab & Am Laundry Mfg, 69-70, Vortex Corp, 70-, & Avco Electronics, 71-; US Navy grant, 70-71. *Mem:* Am Soc Mech Engrs; Soc Mfg Engrs; Am Soc Eng Educ; Robotics Int; Comput & Automated Syst Asn. *Res:* Heat transfer; fluid flow; thermodynamics; boiling phenomena; heat pipe; manufacturing engineering. *Mailing Add:* 9376 Hunters Creek Dr Cincinnati OH 45242

JEFFRIES, QUENTIN RAY, CHEMICAL ENGINEERING. *Current Pos:* prin chem engr, 56-59, tech develop engr, 59-65, CHEM ENGR RES, ENG DEPT, INT MINERALS CORP, 65-; AT CORN SOLVENTS CORP. *Personal Data:* b Terre Haute, Ind, Feb 28, 20; m 51; c 2. *Educ:* Rose Polytech Inst, BS, 41; Univ Mich, MS, 47; Univ Ill, PhD(chem eng), 53. *Prof Exp:* Asst chem engr, Commercial Solvents Corp, 48-49, shift supvr, Penicillin Plant, 49-51; prin chem engr, Battelle Mem Inst, 53-56. *Mem:* Am Chem Soc; Sigma Xi. *Res:* Gaseous diffusion. *Mailing Add:* 11 Allendale Terre Haute IN 47802

JEFFRIES, ROBERT ALAN, OPTICAL PHYSICS. *Current Pos:* CONSULT, 89- *Personal Data:* b Indianapolis, Ind, Nov 11, 33; m 54; c 2. *Educ:* Univ Okla, BS, 54, MS, 61, PhD(ionization kinetics), 65. *Prof Exp:* Proj engr, Pontiac Motor Div, Gen Motors Corp, 54-55; from staff mem to off dir, Los Alamos Nat Lab, 57-89. *Concurrent Pos:* Delegation, Nuclear Testing Talks, Geneva, 86-90; mem, US-Soviet Bilateral Consultative Comn. *Mem:* Am Phys Soc; Sigma Xi. *Res:* Ionization kinetics; shock hydrodynamics; laser produced plasmas; electro optical instrumentation; arms control and verification technology. *Mailing Add:* 160 La Cueva Los Alamos NM 87544

JEFFRIES, THOMAS WILLIAM, BIOCHEMISTRY. *Current Pos:* ASSOC PROF DEPT BACT, UNIV WIS, 87- *Personal Data:* b New Orleans, La, Oct 31, 47; m 74; c 3. *Educ:* Calif State Univ, Long Beach, BS, 69, MS, 72; Rutgers Univ, PhD(microbiol), 75. *Prof Exp:* Asst microbiol, Calif State Univ, Long Beach, 69-71; res intern, Rutgers Univ, 72-75; staff mem microbiol, Lawrence Livermore Lab, Univ Calif, 75-77; res assoc chem eng & appl chem, Columbia Univ, 77-79; microbiologist, forest prod lab, USDA, 79- *Concurrent Pos:* USDA career develop award, 87. *Mem:* Am Soc Microbiol; Soc Indust Microbiol; AAAS; Am Chem Soc; Tech Pulp & Paper Indust. *Res:* Applied microbial ecology; polysaccharide biochemistry; biochemical engineering; biochemistry; biotechnology; enzymology; microbial photosynthesis; biofuels; environmental toxicology; lignin biodegradation; pentose fermentation; yeasts; fermentation, metabolic regulation. *Mailing Add:* Forest Products Lab USDA Forest Serv USDA Forest Service 1 Gifford Pinchot Dr Madison WI 53705-2398

JEFFRIES, WILLIAM BOWMAN, INVERTEBRATE ZOOLOGY. *Current Pos:* from asst prof to prof, 59-81, chmn dept, 65-68, 74-77, 83-86 & 89-90, CHARLES A DANA PROF BIOL, DICKINSON COL, 81- *Personal Data:* b Chicago, Ill, Mar 5, 26; m 88, Joanne Rice; c Robert B, Linda C & Arthur C. *Educ:* Univ Pittsburgh, BS, 49; Univ NC, MA, 52, PhD(zool), 55. *Prof Exp:* Nat Cancer Inst fel, Ind Univ, 55-56; from instr to asst prof microanat, Med Col Ga, 56-59. *Concurrent Pos:* NIH spec res fel, Vet Admin Hosp, Miami, 68-69; res assoc biochem, Sch Med, Univ Miami, 68-69; res assoc, Dept Zool, Field Mus Natural Hist, 77- *Mem:* AAAS; Am Soc Zool; Soc Protozool; Sigma Xi; Am Asn Univ Prof; Crustacean Soc. *Res:* Physiology; parasitology; protozoology; biology of the barnacle genus Octolasmis. *Mailing Add:* Dept Biol Dickinson Col Carlisle PA 17013

JEFFS, GEORGE W, SPACE & COMMUNICATION TECHNOLOGY. *Current Pos:* RETIRED. *Personal Data:* b Stockton, Calif, Mar 9, 25; m; c 3. *Educ:* Univ Wash, BS & MS. *Hon Degrees:* DEE, West Coast Univ, 84. *Honors & Awards:* Presidential Medal of Freedom, 70; Golden Knight of Mgt Award, Nat Mgt Asn, 80; Astronaut Engr Award, Nat Space Club, 82; Von Karman Lectr, Am Inst Aeronaut & Astronaut, 83; Elmer Sperry Award, 86; Leadership Award, Aerospace Elec Soc, 93. *Prof Exp:* Mem, Aerophys Lab, sect chief advan eng, sect chief systs eng, mgr corp tech develop & planning, vpres & prog mgr, Paraglider Prog, corp exec dir eng, Rockwell Int, 47-66; asst prog mgr & chief prog engr, Apollo CSM Progs, 66-69, vpres & prog mgr, 69-73, pres, Space Div, 74-76; corp officer, Rockwell Int, 76-78, pres, NAm Aerospace Opers, 78-86, pres & ctr dir, Strategic Defense Ctr, 86-91, dir vpres strategic defense & technol, 88-91. *Concurrent Pos:* Mem, Adv Panel Ballistic Missile Defense, Cong Off Technol Assessment; US deleg, Prog Indust & Tech Coop Aerospace, China, 84; Jimmy Doolittle educ fel, 89; consult, 91- *Mem:* Nat Acad Eng; fel Am Inst Aeronaut & Astronaut; fel Am Astronaut Soc; fel Inst Advan Eng. *Res:* Advanced space engines; major launch vehicle propulsion engines; solid rockets. *Mailing Add:* 1126 Corsica Dr Pacific Palisades CA 90272

JEFFS, PETER W, ORGANIC CHEMISTRY. *Current Pos:* from asst prof to assoc prof, 64-71, PROF ORG CHEM, DUKE UNIV, 71- *Personal Data:* b Luton, Eng, Jan 9, 33; m 57; c 3. *Educ:* Univ Natal, PhD(chem), 61. *Prof Exp:* Res asst, Akers Res Labs, Imp Chem Indust, Eng, 50-57; lectr org chem, Univ Natal, 60-61. *Mem:* Am Chem Soc; fel The Chem Soc; assoc Royal Inst Chem. *Res:* Chemistry of alkaloids, terpenes and mould metabolites; alkaloid biosynthesis; application of nuclear magnetic resonance to structure determination. *Mailing Add:* Glaxo Inc Five Moore Dr Research Triangle Park NC 27701-4613

JEFIMENKO, OLEG D, ELECTROMAGNETIC THEORY, ELECTROSTATICS. *Current Pos:* from assoc prof, 56-67, PROF PHYSICS, WVA UNIV, 67- *Personal Data:* b USSR, Oct 14, 22; m 45. *Educ:* Univ Göttingen, Ger, Vordiplom, 49; Lewis & Clark Col, BA, 52; Univ Ore, MA, 54, PhD(physics), 56. *Prof Exp:* Asst physics, Univ Ore, 52-55. *Mem:* Am Phys Soc; Am Asn Physics Teachers; Electrostatic Soc Am. *Res:* Electromagnetic theory; cosmical electrodynamics; electrostatics; electrets; atomic physics. *Mailing Add:* 17 Lakeview Manor Morgantown WV 26505

JEGASOTHY, BRIAN V, DERMATOLOGY. *Current Pos:* PROF, DEPT DERMAT, UNIV PA, 82-, ACTG CHMN, 86- *Personal Data:* b Colombo, Sri Lanka, Mar 3, 43. *Educ:* Univ Sri Lanka, MD, 67. *Mem:* Am Acad Dermat; Soc Invest Dermat; Am Fedn Clin Res. *Mailing Add:* Dept Dermat Univ Pittsburgh Sch Med Ctr 190 Lothrop St Pittsburgh PA 15213. *Fax:* 412-648-8117

JEGLA, DOROTHY ELDREDGE, DEVELOPMENTAL BIOLOGY, PLANT BIOLOGY. *Current Pos:* Asst prof, 72-87, ASSOC PROF BIOL, KENYON COL, 87- *Personal Data:* b Brooklyn, NY, Sept 19, 39; m 65; c 2. *Educ:* Mt Holyoke Col, AB, 61; Yale Univ, MS, 64, PhD(biol), 85. *Concurrent Pos:* Plant tissue cult facil, Comprehensive Sch Improv Proj, NSF, 87; vis assoc prof biol, Rennsalaer Polytech Inst, 88. *Mem:* AAAS; Bot Soc Am; Int Soc Plant Molecular Biologists. *Res:* Organization and regulation of apical meristem development in the sunflower, Helianthus annus, by clonal analysis, grafting and sterile culture techniques. *Mailing Add:* Dept Biol Kenyon Col Gambier OH 43022-9623

JEGLA, THOMAS CYRIL, MOLECULAR ENDOCRINOLOGY, INVERTEBRATE PHYSIOLOGY. *Current Pos:* from asst prof to assoc prof, Kenyon Col, 66-85, chmn dept, 76-79 & 84-87, prof, 85-97, EMER PROF, KENYON COL, 97- *Personal Data:* b St Johns, Mich, July 5, 35; m 65; c John & Tim. *Educ:* Mich State Univ, BS, 58; Univ Ill, MS, 60, PhD(zool), 64. *Hon Degrees:* DSc, Kenyon Col, 97. *Honors & Awards:* Tomsich Res Award. *Prof Exp:* Asst prof biol, Univ Minn, 63-64 & Yale Univ, 64-66. *Concurrent Pos:* NSF res grants, 70, 73 & 85-; vis assoc prof, Yale Univ, 81-83; vis prof, Univ Bonn, 81, 83 & 84; NIH res grant, 85; vis res prof, Univ WFla, 88, Univ Iowa, 94-95. *Mem:* AAAS; Am Soc Zool. *Res:* Molting physiology of arthropods; invertebrate biology; comparative endocrinology; biochemistry of steroid and peptide hormones. *Mailing Add:* Dept Biol Kenyon Col Gambier OH 43022

JEGLUM, JOHN KARL, FOREST ECOLOGY, SILVICULTURE. *Current Pos:* PROF FOREST PEATLAND SCI, DEPT FOREST ECOL, SWEDISH UNIV AGR SCI, 94- *Personal Data:* b Medford, Wis, Dec 9, 38; m 64, Susan Rogers; c Karl & John. *Educ:* Univ Wis, BS, 60, MS, 62; Univ Sask, PhD(plant ecol), 68. *Prof Exp:* Asst prof bot, Eastern Ill Univ, 65-66; res scientist forestry ecol, Can Forestry Serv, 68-94. *Concurrent Pos:* Vis researcher, Dept Peatland Forestry, Univ Helsinki, 84-85. *Mem:* Int Peat Soc UK. *Res:* Wetland classification and ecology; boreal vegetational ecology; autecology of black spruce; regeneration silviculture; strip cutting in black spruce; environmental impacts of harvesting; peatland forestry. *Mailing Add:* Dept Forest Ecol Swedish Univ Agr Sci S-90183 Uppsala Sweden. *E-Mail:* john.jeglum@sek.slu.se

JEHN, LAWRENCE ANDREW, COMPUTER SCIENCE, COMPUTER MODELING. *Current Pos:* Instr, Univ Dayton, 46-47, from asst prof to assoc prof math, 50-63, res mathematician, Res Inst, 63-68, assoc prof comput sci, 68-74, prof, 74-88, chmn, 82-86, EMER PROF COMPUT SCI, UNIV DAYTON, 88- *Personal Data:* b Dayton, Ohio, Aug 7, 21; m 44, Betty L James; c David, Judith, James, Paul, Joseph, Ann M, Mary C, Theresa & John. *Educ:* Dayton Univ, BS, 43; Univ Mich, ScM, 49, ABD, 50. *Concurrent Pos:* Consult, Univ Dayton, 51-56 & 57-63, assoc prof comput sci & mech eng, 68-74; res assoc, Univ Mich, 56-57; regist prof engr, State Ohio, 68 & State Colo, 92; chmn, Asn Comput Mach, Comput Sci Conf, 79 & 86, Nat Educ Comput Conf, Comput Sci Comt, 86-88; consult engr, Jehn Water Consults & Jehn & Assocs. *Mem:* Asn Comput Mach. *Res:* Computer science education; numerical analysis and simulation; computer modelling. *Mailing Add:* 6014 Aqua Pl Dayton OH 45459-2902. *Fax:* 937-229-4000; *E-Mail:* jehn@dayton.bitnet; jehn@udavxb.oca.udayton.edu

JEKEL, EUGENE CARL, INORGANIC CHEMISTRY. *Current Pos:* From instr to assoc prof Hope Col, 55-69, chmn dept, 67-70 & 73-76, PROF CHEM, HOPE COL, 69-, CHIEF HEALTH PROFESSIONS ADV, 77- *Personal Data:* b Holland, Mich, Dec 19, 30; m 60; c 2. *Educ:* Hope Col, AB, 52; Purdue Univ, MS, 55, PhD(inorg chem), 64. *Concurrent Pos:* Vis prof, Univ Calif, Berkeley, 70-71. *Mem:* Asn Am Med Cols; Nat Sci Teachers Asn; Am Chem Soc; Sigma Xi. *Res:* Thermodynamics of aqueous solutions at high temperature. *Mailing Add:* 156 W 12th St Holland MI 49423-3215

JEKEL, JAMES FRANKLIN, EPIDEMIOLOGY, PUBLIC HEALTH. *Current Pos:* asst prof, 67-71, assoc prof pub health, 71-80, PROF EPIDEMIOL & PUB HEALTH, YALE UNIV, 80-, CEA WINSLOW PROF PUBLIC HEALTH, 82- *Personal Data:* b St Louis, Mo, Oct 14, 34; m 58, Janice M Clark; c Clifford, Mark, Linda & Timothy. *Educ:* Wesleyan Univ, AB, 56; Wash Univ, MD, 60; Yale Univ, MPH, 65. *Prof Exp:* Res asst pub health, St Louis Co Health Dept, 58; epidemiologist, Ctrs Dis Control, 62-67. *Concurrent Pos:* Fulbright fel, 85-86. *Mem:* Am Pub Health Asn; fel Am Col Prev Med; fel Am Sci Affiliation. *Res:* Program evaluation, especially health programs for teenage mothers; cocaine abuse; perinatal epidemiology; clinical epidemiology; public health planning and evaluation. *Mailing Add:* Dept Epidemiol & Pub Health 60 College St New Haven CT 06510-3210. *Fax:* 203-785-6287

JEKELI, CHRISTOPHER, GEODESY. *Current Pos:* ASSOC PROF GEODESIST SCI & SURV, OHIO STATE UNIV, 93- *Personal Data:* b Marburg, WGermany, Dec 21, 53; m 84. *Educ:* McGill Univ, BA, 76; Ohio State Univ, MSc, 78, PhD(geod), 81. *Honors & Awards:* Weikko A Herskanen Award, Ohio State Univ, 80. *Prof Exp:* Res assoc geod, Ohio State Univ, 77-81; geodesist, Air Force Geophys Lab, 81-93. *Mem:* Am Geophys Union. *Res:* Physical geodesy: methods to analyze and improve knowledge of the earth's external gravity field and application of these methods to gravimetric data. *Mailing Add:* 1201 McCleary Ct Columbus OH 43235

JELACHICH, MARY LOU, CELLULAR IMMUNOLOGY. *Current Pos:* Res assoc, Dept Med, 88-91, dir immunol, Dept Surg, 91-93, DIR IMMUNOL RES, EVANSTON HOSP, 93- *Personal Data:* b Munich, Ger. *Educ:* DePauw Univ, BS, 70; Northeastern Univ, MS, 80; Northwestern Univ,

PhD(immunol), 85. *Concurrent Pos:* Mult Sclerosis grant, Mult Sclerosis Soc, 91. *Mem:* Am Asn Immunol. *Mailing Add:* Dir Immunobiol Res Dept WCH Evanston Hosp 2650 N Ridge Ave Evanston IL 60201-1797. Fax: 847-570-1568

JELEN, FREDERIC CHARLES, CHEMICAL ENGINEERING. *Current Pos:* RETIRED. *Personal Data:* b Chelsea, Mass, Jan 17, 10; m 43; c 2. *Educ:* Mass Inst Technol, SB, 31, SM, 32; Harvard Univ, AM, 34, PhD(phys chem), 35. *Honors & Awards:* Diamond Qual Award, Asn Pushing Gravity Res, 85. *Prof Exp:* Chemist phosphates, Monsanto Co, 35-41; engr electrochem, Battelle Mem Inst, 42-43; chief engr silicates, Cowles Chem Co, 43-49; engr corrosion, Allied Chem Co, 49-61; prof chem eng, Lamar Univ, 61-80; prof, McNeese State Univ, 81-83. *Concurrent Pos:* Consult cost eng, 61-, PPG Industs, Inc, 62-75, Int Nickel, 63, Mobil Oil Corp, 63-, Mobil Chem Co, 64-71 & E I du Pont de Nemours & Co, Inc, 75. *Mem:* Fel Am Asn Cost Engrs. *Res:* Cost engineering. *Mailing Add:* Two Hull Circle Austin TX 78746

JELEN, JAROSLAW ANDRZEJ, DOMAIN DECOMPOSITION & PARALLEL COMPUTING, COMPUTATIONAL FLUID DYNAMICS. *Current Pos:* SR RES SCIENTIST, NOVA RES & TECHNOL CO, CALARY, 85- *Personal Data:* b Nowy Targ, Poland, Sept 14, 43; Can citizen; m 71, Alicja Solecka; c Marek. *Educ:* Univ Wroclaw, MSc, 69; Acad Mining & Metall, Krakow, PhD(appl math), 77. *Honors & Awards:* Prize, Polish Ministry Sci, 78. *Prof Exp:* Asst prof numerical anal, Univ Cracow, 79-84. *Mem:* Am Metall Soc; Soc Indust & Appl Math. *Res:* Numerical modelling of fluid flows; development of novel domain decomposition methods and finite difference schemes for solving partial differential equations. *Mailing Add:* 35 Sanderling Hill NW Calgary AB T3K 3B6 Can. *E-Mail:* jelenj@novachem.com

JELINEK, ARTHUR GILBERT, SYNTHETIC ORGANIC CHEMISTRY. *Current Pos:* RETIRED. *Personal Data:* b Milwaukee, Wis, May 6, 17; m 45; c 3. *Educ:* Univ Wis, BS, 40, PhD(org chem), 44. *Prof Exp:* Res & control chemist, Fox River Paper Corp, Wis, 40-41; asst org chem, Univ Wis, 41-44; res chemist, Grasselli Chem Dept, E I du Pont de Nemours & Co Inc, 44-55, sr res chemist, Biochem Dept, 55-79. *Mem:* Emer mem Am Chem Soc. *Res:* Agricultural chemicals. *Mailing Add:* 2500 Lindell Rd Grendon Farm Wilmington DE 19808-4003

JELINEK, CHARLES FRANK, ORGANIC CHEMISTRY. *Current Pos:* CONSULT, 86- *Personal Data:* b Miles City, Mont, Feb 6, 17; m 44; c 2. *Educ:* Mont State Col, BS, 38; Oxford Univ, BSc, 41; Univ Ill, PhD(org chem), 44. *Prof Exp:* Res chemist, Gen Aniline & Film Corp, 46-47, asst to dir res, 47-49, sales engr & asst dir cent sales develop dept, 49-50, sect leader appln res, 50-52, mgr surfactants res, 52-55, mgr process res & develop dept, 55-59, dir dyestuff & chem div, Cent Res Lab, 59-63; sr staff adv, Chem Staff, Esso Res & Eng Co, 63-66; coordr new ventures, Enjay, 66-71; coordr tech opportunities div, Dart Industs, Inc, 71-72; dir div chem technol, Bur Foods, Food & Drug Admin, 79-86, 72-75, dept assoc dir technol, 75-79, dept dir phys sci, 79-86. *Mem:* Am Chem Soc; Asn Off Anal Chemists; Am Inst Chemists; Com Develop Asn. *Res:* Derivatives of acetylene; dyes; pigments; surfactants; polymers; solvents; coatings; chemical contaminants in foods. *Mailing Add:* 20540 Falcons Landing Circle Apt 4307 Sterling VA 20165

JELINEK, FREDERICK, ELECTRONICS ENGINEERING. *Current Pos:* SR MGR CONTINUOUS SPEECH RECOGNITION, T J WATSON RES CTR, IBM CORP, 72- *Personal Data:* b Prague, Czech, Nov 18, 32; nat US; m 61; c 2. *Educ:* Mass Inst Technol, SB, 56, SM, 58, PhD(elec eng), 62. *Prof Exp:* Instr elec eng, Mass Inst Technol, 59-62; from asst prof to prof, Cornell Univ, 62-74. *Concurrent Pos:* Vis lectr, Harvard Univ, 62; NSF grant, 64-66; vis scientist, IBM T J Watson Res Ctr, 68-69; NASA contracts, 66-72. *Mem:* Fel Inst Elec & Electronics Engrs. *Res:* Transmission of information; coding; data compression; speech recognition; information theory. *Mailing Add:* Ctr Language & Speech Processing John Hopkins Univ 320 Boson Hall 3400 N Charles St Baltimore MD 21218

JELINEK, ROBERT V(INCENT), CHEMICAL ENGINEERING. *Current Pos:* RETIRED. *Personal Data:* b New York, NY, Mar 5, 26; m 55; c 3. *Educ:* Columbia Univ, BS, 45, MS, 47, PhD(chem eng), 53. *Prof Exp:* Asst drafting, Columbia Univ, 43-45, instr chem eng, 49-51; chem engr, Develop Div, Standard Oil Develop Co, 51-53; asst prof chem eng, Columbia Univ, 53-54; from asst prof to prof, Syracuse Univ, 54-72, dir summer res prog high sch teachers, 64-69, asst to dean eng, 55-60, fac secy, 62-64, chm eng fac, 64-65; prof & dean, Sch Environ & Resource Eng, State Univ NY, 72-80, prof, Dept Paper Sci & Eng, Col Environ Sci & Forestry, 80-93. *Concurrent Pos:* Assoc, Danforth Found, 56-60; NSF res grant, 59-61; prog dir eng chem, NSF, 71-72. *Mem:* Am Chem Soc; Electrochem Soc; Nat Asn Corrosion Engrs; Am Inst Chem Engrs. *Res:* Reaction kinetics; corrosion; electrochemistry; adsorption; process design and computer simulation. *Mailing Add:* 6332 Ledgewood Dr Jamesville NY 13078-9512

JELINSKI, LYNN W, PROTEIN FOLDING, BIOLOGICAL RECOGNITION. *Current Pos:* DIR, CTR ADVAN TECHNOL, CORNELL UNIV, 91- *Personal Data:* b Arlington, Va, Jan 19, 49. *Educ:* Duke Univ, BS, 71; Univ Hawaii, PhD(chem), 76. *Prof Exp:* Fel chem, Johns Hopkins Univ, 76-77; fel, Nat Inst Health, 77-78, staff fel, biophysics, 78-80; mem tech staff chem, AT&T Bell Lab, 80-84, head polymer chem, 84-85, head biophys, 85-91. *Res:* Nuclear magnetic resonances and imaging; protein folding, biological recognition. *Mailing Add:* 913 Wyckoff Rd Ithaca NY 14850-2130

JELLARD, CHARLES H, MEDICAL BACTERIOLOGY, PUBLIC HEALTH. *Current Pos:* RETIRED. *Personal Data:* b Abergavenny, Wales, Dec 25, 16; m 50; c 4. *Educ:* Oxford Univ, BA & BM, BCh, 42; Univ London, dipl bact, 51; FRCPath, 65; Oxford Univ, DM, 75. *Hon Degrees:* MA, Cambridge Univ, 48. *Prof Exp:* Dir, Pub Health Lab Serv, Plymouth, UK, 53-68; assoc prof bacj & dep dir, Prov Lab Pub Health, Univ Alta, 68-82. *Concurrent Pos:* Hon consult bacteriologist, Plymouth Hosps, UK, 53-68. *Mem:* Path Soc Gt Brit & Ireland; Brit Soc Gen Microbiol. *Res:* Diagnostic medical bacteriology; epidemiology. *Mailing Add:* 12504 Lansdone Dr Edmonton AB T6H 4L5 Can

JELLIFFE, ROGER WOODHAM, CARDIOLOGY, CLINICAL PHARMACOLOGY. *Current Pos:* from instr to assoc prof, 61-76, PROF MED, SCH MED, UNIV SOUTHERN CALIF, 76- *Personal Data:* b Cleveland, Ohio, Feb 18, 29; m 54, Joyce Miller; c Susan, Amy, Elizabeth & Peter. *Educ:* Harvard Col, AB, 50; Columbia Univ, MD, 54; Am Bd Internal Med, dipl, 62; Am Bd Cardiovasc Dis, dipl, 65. *Prof Exp:* Intern med, Univ Hosps, Cleveland, Ohio, 54-55, asst resident, 55-56; Nat Found Infantile Paralysis fel exp med, Sch Med, Western Res Univ, 56-58; staff physician, Vet Admin Hosp, Cleveland, 58-60, resident med, 60-61. *Concurrent Pos:* Los Angeles Co Heart Asn res fel, Sch Med, Univ Southern Calif, 61-63; NIH res grants digitalis & appl pharmacokinetics, 64-; fel coun clin cardiol, Am Heart Asn; chmn Pharmaceut Sect, Am Soc Clin Pharmacol & Therapeut, 95-98. *Mem:* Fel Am Col Physicians; fel Am Heart Asn; Am Soc Clin Pharmacol & Therapeut; fel Am Col Med Informatics; Am Med Informatics Asn. *Res:* Cardiovascular pharmacology; chemical measurements of digitalis glycosides and mathematical descriptions of the kinetics of digitalis, kanamycin, gentamicin, streptomycin, procainamide, lidocaine and other drugs in man; computer assistance for planning, monitoring and adjusting dosage regimens of the above drugs; methods for optimal study and control of pharmacokinetic systems; population pharmacokinetic modeling. *Mailing Add:* Univ Southern Calif CSC 134B 2250 Alcazar St Los Angeles CA 90033. *Fax:* 213-342-1302; *E-Mail:* jelliffe@hsc.usc.edu

JELLINCK, PETER HARRY, BIOCHEMISTRY, ENDOCRINOLOGY. *Current Pos:* head dept, 76-78, PROF BIOCHEM, QUEEN'S UNIV, ONT, 67- *Personal Data:* b Paris, France, Feb 20, 28; m 54, Mary Topham; c Susan, Caroline & Rosemary. *Educ:* Cambridge Univ, BA, 48; Univ London, BSc, 50, MSc, 52, PhD(biochem), 54. *Prof Exp:* Can Nat Res Coun fel biochem, McGill Univ, 55-56; lectr chem, Norwood Tech Col, Eng, 56-57; lectr biochem, St Bartholomew's Hosp Med Col, London, 57-58 & Middlesex Hosp Med Sch, 58-59; from asst prof to prof, Univ BC, 60-67. *Concurrent Pos:* Nat Cancer Inst Can-Med Res Coun Can res grant, 59-; vis prof, Rockefeller Univ, 78-79, 82- *Mem:* Am Asn Cancer Res; Brit Biochem Soc; Can Biochem Soc; Endocrine Soc. *Res:* Estrogen metabolism and action; hormonal carcinogenesis. *Mailing Add:* Dept Biochem Queen's Univ Kingston ON K7L 3N6 Can. *Fax:* 613-545-2497

JELLINEK, MAX, ORGAN TRANSPLANTATION, SHOCK. *Current Pos:* PROF BIOCHEM, ST LOUIS UNIV, 62- *Personal Data:* b 1929; m 65; c 3. *Educ:* St Louis Univ, PhD(biochem), 61. *Mem:* Am Physiol Soc; Am Chem Soc. *Res:* Metabolism of ischimic hypoxic; organs and shock. *Mailing Add:* Dept Surg Sch Med Physiol Chem Lab St Louis Univ 1402 S Grand Blvd St Louis MO 63104. *Fax:* 573-771-1945

JELLINEK, MICHAEL STEVEN, PSYCHIATRY, PEDIATRICS. *Current Pos:* asst pediat, Mass Gen Hosp, 79-81, asst pediatrician, 81-83, dir outpatient psychiat, 84-93, CHIEF, CHILD PEDIAT SERVS, MASS GEN HOSP, 79-; ASSOC PROF PEDIAT PSYCHIAT, HARVARD UNIV, 87- *Personal Data:* b New York, NY, Sept 30, 48; m 70, Barbara A; c David M, Abraham R, Isaiah T & Hanna R. *Educ:* Columbia Col, BA, 70; Albert Einstein Col Med, MD, 73; Am Bd Pediat, dipl psychiat & child psychiat. *Honors & Awards:* Simon Wile Award, Am Acad Child Psychiat, 93. *Prof Exp:* Instr pediat, Montefiore Hosp & Med Ctr, New York, 76-79. *Concurrent Pos:* Asst instr, Columbia Univ, 70; consult, Shriner Burns Inst, Boston, 79-; assoc pediatrician & psychiatrist, Mass Gen Hosp, 84-86, pediatrician, 86-, psychiatrist, 86-, asst gen dir, Ambulatory Servs, 92-, sr vpres, 94-, sr vpres admin, 95- *Mem:* Fel Am Acad Pediat; fel Am Acad Child Psychiat (treas, 91-93); Soc Prof Child Psychiat. *Mailing Add:* 132 Pleasant St Newton MA 02159-1828

JELLING, MURRAY, INVENTION, PATENTS. *Current Pos:* CONSULT CHEMIST, 57- *Personal Data:* b Brooklyn, NY, Jan 7, 18; m 41, Florence; c Jonathan. *Educ:* Brooklyn Col, BS, 37; Polytech Univ, Brooklyn, MS, 41, PhD(chem), 45. *Prof Exp:* Res chemist, Autoxygen, Inc, 38-41; res chemist, Nopco Chem Co, Inc, 41-43; res assoc, polymer, Polytech Univ, 43-45; res dir org chem, Maguire Industs, Inc, 45-47; pres, Cidex Corp, 48-57, Jonelle Indust Prod, 67-72. *Mem:* Am Chem Soc; Sigma Xi; Soc Asphalt Technologists; Asn Asphalt Paving Technologists; Asn Consult Chemists & Chem Engrs; Transp Res Bd. *Res:* Industrial organic chemistry; polymers; textile maintenance (dry-cleaning and laundry) products; bituminous products; granted 30 patents; licensing. *Mailing Add:* 21 Spring Hill Rd Roslyn Heights NY 11577. *Fax:* 516-621-0060

JELLINGER, THOMAS CHRISTIAN, construction engineering, for more information see previous edition

JELLISON, GERALD EARLE, JR, OPTICS. *Current Pos:* SR STAFF SCIENTIST, OAK RIDGE NAT LAB, 78- *Personal Data:* b Bangor, Maine, Mar 27, 46; m 70, Mary Milkovich; c Lisa & Katie. *Educ:* Bowdoin Col, BA, 68; Brown Univ, ScM, 73, PhD(physics), 77. *Prof Exp:* Nat Res Coun fel,

Naval Res Lab, 76-78. *Mem:* Am Phys Soc; Am Optical Soc; Mat Res Soc. *Res:* Physics of semiconductors; measurement of optical properties of materials as a function of doping and temperature; spectroscopic ellipsometry and thin film diagnostics. *Mailing Add:* Solid State Div Bldg 3025 Oak Ridge Nat Lab Oak Ridge TN 37831-6030. *E-Mail:* jellisongejr@ornl.gov

JELLUM, MILTON DELBERT, AGRONOMY, PLANT BREEDING. *Current Pos:* RETIRED. *Personal Data:* b Starbuck, Minn, Oct 26, 34; m 57; c 2. *Educ:* Univ Minn, BS, 56; Univ Ill, MS, 58, PhD(agron), 61. *Prof Exp:* Asst agronomist, Ga Exp Sta, Univ Ga, 60-67, from assoc prof to prof agron, 67-85. *Mem:* AAAS; Am Soc Agron; Crop Sci Soc Am; Am Oil Chem Soc; Am Asn Cereal Chem. *Res:* Environmental and genetic study of oil content and fatty acid composition of corn grain oil; study of yield components of corn and corn breeding. *Mailing Add:* 920 Buck Creek Rd Griffin GA 30224

JEMAL, MOHAMMED, PHARMACOKINETICS, DRUG METABOLISM. *Current Pos:* res investr anal res & develop, Squibb Inst med Res, 78-82, GROUP LEADER BIOANAL RES, BRISTOL-MYERS SQUIBB, 82- *Personal Data:* b Ethiopian citizen; c 1. *Educ:* Haile Sellassie Univ, BS, 70; Purdue Univ, PhD(pharm anal), 76. *Honors & Awards:* Haile Sellassie Medal Award. *Prof Exp:* Post doctoral res, Purdue Univ, 76-77. *Mem:* Am Chem Soc; Am Asn Pharmaceut Scientists. *Res:* Quantification of drugs and metabolites in body fluids for assessment of pharmacokinetics and safety. *Mailing Add:* Bristol-Myers Squibb PO Box 4500 Princeton NJ 08543-4500

JEMIAN, WARTAN A(RMIN), PHYSICAL METALLURGY. *Current Pos:* from assoc prof to prof mech eng, 62-75, chmn, Mat Eng Curric Comt, 63-82, prof mat eng, 75-93, EMER PROF MECH ENG, AUBURN UNIV, 94- *Personal Data:* b Lynn, Mass, Dec 31, 25; m 51; c 4. *Educ:* Univ Md, BS, 50; Rensselaer Polytech Inst, MS, 53, PhD(metall eng), 56. *Prof Exp:* Engr, Semiconductor Dept, Westinghouse Elec Corp, 55-57; sr fel & head power rectifiers fel, Mellon Inst, 57-62; dir res & develop, Rectifier-Capacitor Div, Fansteel Metall Corp, 62. *Concurrent Pos:* Lectr & adj prof, Univ Pittsburgh, 56-62. *Mem:* Am Inst Mining, Metall & Petrol Engrs; Am Soc Metals; Am Soc Eng Educ; Biomat Res Soc; Int Asn Math & Comput Simulation; Sigma Xi. *Res:* Education; structure and properties of composite materials; computer analysis of materials; education in materials science and engineering. *Mailing Add:* Auburn Univ Auburn AL 36849-3501. *Fax:* 334-887-5705; *E-Mail:* jemian@aub.mindspring.com

JEMMERSON, RONALD RENOMER WEAVER, IMMUNOLOGY, BIOCHEMISTRY. *Current Pos:* asst prof, 85-91, ASSOC PROF, DEPT MICROBIOL, UNIV MINN, 91- *Personal Data:* b Baltimore, Md, Mar 7, 51. *Educ:* Western Md Col, BA, 73; Northwestern Univ, PhD(biochem), 78. *Prof Exp:* Res fel, Scripps Clin & Res Found, 78-81; res assoc, La Jolla Cancer Res Found, 81-84 & Scripps Clin & Res Found, 84-85. *Concurrent Pos:* Damon Runyon-Walter Winchell fel, 79-80. *Mem:* AAAS; Am Asn Immunologists; Protein Soc. *Res:* Protein antigenicity; memory B lymphocytes; antibody and B cell repertoires. *Mailing Add:* Univ Minn Med Sch Dept Microbiol Box 196 UMHC 420 Delaware St SE Minneapolis MN 55455. *Fax:* 612-626-0623; *E-Mail:* von@lenti.med.umn.edu

JEMSKI, JOSEPH VICTOR, MEDICAL MICROBIOLOGY. *Current Pos:* RETIRED. *Personal Data:* b Blackstone, Mass, Mar 19, 20; m 43, Mary; c Thomas. *Educ:* Fordham Univ, AB, 42; Univ Pa, PhD(med microbiol), 52. *Honors & Awards:* Barnett L Cohen Award, Am Soc Microbiol. *Prof Exp:* Head bact dept, Maltine Co, 46-49; chief animal path unit, Ralph M Parsons Co, 52-55; chief animal path sect, Chem Corps, 55-59, chief test sphere br, US Army Biol Defense Res Labs, 59-72, sr investr, US Army Res Inst Infectious Dis, 72-83. *Concurrent Pos:* Comn Rickettsial Dis, Armed Forces Epidemiol Bd, 65-71; chmn Biol Safety Comt, Asn Lab Anal Sci, 65-71. *Mem:* Am Soc Microbiol; Am Asn Lab Animal Sci; fel Am Acad Microbiol. *Res:* Experimental aerosol induced diseases in laboratory animals; aerobiology; biological safety; immunogenesis and immunoprophylaxis of respiratory diseases. *Mailing Add:* 7922 Long Meadow Dr Frederick MD 21701

JEN, CHIH KUNG, MICROWAVE PHYSICS. *Current Pos:* RETIRED. *Personal Data:* b Chin Yuan, Shansi, China, Aug 15, 06; nat US; m 37; c 4. *Educ:* Mass Inst Technol, SB, 28; Univ Pa, SM, 29; Harvard Univ, PhD(physics), 31. *Prof Exp:* Asst physics, Harvard Univ, 30-32, instr, 32-33; prof, Shuntung Univ, China, 33-34; prof, Tsing Hua Univ, Peking, China, 34-37, dir, Radio Res Int, 37-45; res lectr physics, Harvard Univ, 46-50; vchmn, Res Ctr, Johns Hopkins Univ, 58-74, William S Parsons vis prof chem physics, 66-67, physicist & prin staff mem, Appl Physics Lab, 50-76, consult, 78-87. *Concurrent Pos:* Fel, China Found, 31-32; hon prof, Tsinghua Univ, Beijing & Univ Sci & Technol, Hefei, People's Repub China, 78. *Mem:* Fel Am Phys Soc; Acad Sinica, Taiwan. *Res:* Ionosphere; quantum mechanics; electron tube phenomena; microwave spectroscopy. *Mailing Add:* 10203 Lariston Ln Silver Spring MD 20903

JEN, JOSEPH JWU-SHAN, FOOD BIOCHEMISTRY, ACADEMIC ADMINISTRATION. *Current Pos:* DEAN, COL AGR, CALIF POLYTECH STATE UNIV, 92- *Personal Data:* b Sichuan, China, May 8, 39; US citizen; m 65, Salina Fond; c Joanne P & Jeffrey J. *Educ:* Nat Taiwan Univ, BS, 60; Wash State Univ, MS, 64; Univ Calif, Berkeley, PhD(comp biochem), 69; Southern Ill Univ, MBA, 86. *Prof Exp:* From asst prof to prof food biochem, Clemson Univ, SC, 69-79; assoc prof, Mich State Univ, East Lansing, 79-80; mgr, food enzyme, Cambell Inst Res & Tech, Camden, NJ, mgr, vegetable biochem, 83-85, dir, biochem, 85-86; chmn, Div Food Sci & Technol, Univ Ga, 86-92. *Concurrent Pos:* Res food technologist, USDA, 75; vis prof, Nat Taiwan Univ, 76; chmn fruit & vegetables prod, Inst Food Technol, 88-89. *Mem:* Inst Food Technol; Am Chem Soc; Chinese Am Foods Soc (pres, 77-78). *Res:* Food enzymology; vegetable texture; pectin chemistry and function; fruit and vegetable shelf-life extension and quality measurements; value added product development; food biotechnology; agriculture. *Mailing Add:* Col Agr Calif Polytech State Univ San Luis Obispo CA 93407. *E-Mail:* jjen@calpoly.edu

JEN, KAI-LIN CATHERINE, OBESITY, TYPE II DIABETES. *Current Pos:* from asst prof to assoc prof, 84-92, PROF NUTRIT, WAYNE STATE UNIV, 92- *Personal Data:* b Taiwan, Repub China, July 18, 49; US citizen; m 78, Paul Jen; c Elizabeth & John. *Educ:* Wayne State Univ, PhD(nutrit), 77. *Prof Exp:* Asst res scientist, Univ Mich, 78-83. *Mem:* Am Inst Nutrit; Am Physiol Soc; NAm Asn Study Obesity; AAAS. *Res:* Regulation of appetite and body weight; animal model of human gestational diabetes; exercise and obesity; lipid metabolism in obesity; type two diabetes and nutrition. *Mailing Add:* Dept Nutrit & Food Sci Wayne State Univ 3003 Sci Hall Detroit MI 48202. *Fax:* 313-577-8616; *E-Mail:* cjen@lifesci.wayne.edu

JEN, PHILIP HUNGSUN, AUDITORY PHYSIOLOGY, NEUROETHOLOGY. *Current Pos:* from asst prof to assoc prof, 75-84, PROF NERVOUS SYST, UNIV MO, COLUMBIA, 84- *Personal Data:* b Hunan, China, Jan 11, 44; US citizen; m 71, Betty Y Lee. *Educ:* Tunghai Univ BS, 67; Washington Univ, MA, 71, PhD(biol), 74. *Prof Exp:* Res assoc, Washington Univ, 74-75. *Concurrent Pos:* Vis prof, J W Goethe Univ, Frankfurt, 79; prin investr, NSF, 78- & NIH, 80-; guest lectr, Inst Acoust, Chinese Acad Sci, 80; NIH res career develop award, 80. *Mem:* Am Soc Zoologists; Acoust Soc Am; Soc Neurosci; AAAS; NY Acad Sci. *Res:* Neuroethological investigation of acoustic signal encoding, processing and control in the auditory system of echo-locating bats. *Mailing Add:* 6120 S River Hills Rd Columbia MO 65203

JEN, SHEN, APPLIED PHYSICS. *Current Pos:* mem tech staff, 84-87, SR MEM TECH STAFF, TEX INSTRUMENTS, 88- *Personal Data:* b Shanghai, China, Dec 8, 47; m 75. *Educ:* Nat Taiwan Univ, BS, 68; Harvard Univ, MS, 70, PhD(appl physics), 75. *Prof Exp:* Res assoc light scattering spectros, Dept Chem, State Univ NY Stony Brook, 75-76; Proj mgr, Xerox Corp, 77-78, mem tech staff, 79-82; mem tech staff, IBM, 82-84. *Mem:* Soc Photog Scientists & Engrs; Inst Elec & Electronics Engrs. *Res:* Light scaterring spectroscopy; physics of liquid ceystals; electro-photography; magnetic storage technology; acoustic surface wave devices; microwave signal processing. *Mailing Add:* 1200 Stratford Dr Richardson TX 75080

JEN, YUN, ORGANIC CHEMISTRY. *Current Pos:* PRES, J J CHEM, INC, 77- *Personal Data:* b China, Oct 5, 27; nat US; m 51; c 2. *Educ:* Shanghai Univ, BS, 48; Carnegie Inst Technol, MS, 49. *Prof Exp:* Res chemist, Am Cyanamid Co, 51-56; mgr eng, Anaheim Plant, Oronite Chem Co Div, Calif Chem Co, Standard Oil Co, Calif, 56-60; res engr, Gen Elec Co, 60-63; dir res & develop, Tenneco Chem Co, 63-75; mem staff, Chem Div, Union Camp Corp, 75-77. *Mem:* Am Chem Soc. *Res:* Polymers; water soluble resins; alkyds; acrylics; polyesters; pulp and paper; naval stores products; ore benefication. *Mailing Add:* 16 Gale Break Circle Savannah GA 31406-5205

JENA, PURUSOTTAM, ATOMIC CLUSTERS, METAL DEFECTS. *Current Pos:* PROF PHYSICS, VA COMMONWEALTH UNIV, 80- *Personal Data:* b Orissa, India, Feb 5, 43; m 69, Tripti Bardhan; c Anupam. *Educ:* Utkal Univ, India, BSc, 64, MSc, 66; Univ Calif, Riverside, PhD(physics), 70. *Prof Exp:* Lectr physics, State Univ NY, Albany, 70-71; fel, Dalhousie Univ, 71-73; res assoc physics, Univ BC, Vancouver, 73-75; vis asst prof physics, Northwestern Univ, 75-77; vis scientist, Argonne Nat Lab, 77-78; assoc prof physics, Mich Inst Technol Univ, 78-80. *Concurrent Pos:* Prog dir, Div Mat Res,NSF, 86-87; prin investr, NSF, 84-, Army Res Office, 85-, Dept Energy, 87-; consult, BDM Corp, 86- *Mem:* Am Phys Soc; Indian Phys Soc; Mat Res Soc. *Res:* Theoretical condensed matter physics; defects in metals; small atomic clusters; electronic structure and properties. *Mailing Add:* Physics Dept Va Commonwealth Univ PO Box 842000 Richmond VA 23284-2000. *Fax:* 804-367-7073; *E-Mail:* jena@gems.vcu.edu

JENCKS, WILLIAM PLATT, BIOCHEMISTRY, ORGANIC CHEMISTRY. *Current Pos:* RETIRED. *Personal Data:* b Bar Harbor, Maine, Aug 15, 27; m 50; c 2. *Educ:* Harvard Univ, MD, 51. *Honors & Awards:* Eli Lilly Co Award, Am Chem Soc, 62; Merck Award, Am Soc Biol Chemists, 93. *Prof Exp:* Intern, Peter Bent Brigham Hosp, 51-52; res fel biochem, Res Lab, Mass Gen Hosp, 52-53; res fel pharmacol, Army Med Serv Grad Sch, Walter Reed Army Med Ctr, 53-55, chief, Dept Pharm, 54-55; res fel biochem, Res Lab, Mass Gen Hosp, 55-56; res fel, Harvard Univ, 56-57; from asst prof to prof biochem, Brandeis Univ, 57-95. *Mem:* Nat Acad Sci; AAAS; Am Soc Biol Chem; Am Chem Soc; Am Acad Arts & Sci; Fel Royal Soc. *Res:* Mechanism and catalysis of carbonyl, acyl, phosphate transfer and other reactions; mechanism of enzyme action; intermolecular forces in aqueous solution; mechanism of coupled vectorial processes. *Mailing Add:* 11 Revere St Lexington MA 02173-4419

JENDEN, DONALD JAMES, PHARMACOLOGY, ANALYTICAL CHEMISTRY. *Current Pos:* actg chmn, Univ Calif, Los Angeles, 56-57, from asst prof to assoc prof, 52-67, prof & chmn, dept pharmacol, 68-89, PROF PHARMACOL & BIOMATH, UNIV CALIF, LOS ANGELES, 67- *Personal Data:* b Horsham, Eng, Sept 1, 26; nat US; m 50; c 3. *Educ:* Univ London, BSc, 47, MB, BS, 50. *Hon Degrees:* Dr, Univ Uppsala, Sweden, 80. *Prof Exp:* Demonstr pharmacol, Univ London, 48-49; lectr pharmacol, Univ Calif, 50-51. *Concurrent Pos:* Mem, Brain Res Inst, Univ Calif, Los Angeles,

61-; NSF sr fel, hon res assoc, Univ Col Univ Col, Univ London, 61-62; Wellcome vis prof, Univ Ala, Birmingham, 84- *Mem:* Soc Neurosci; Am Soc Pharmacol & Exp Therapeut; Am Physiol Soc; Am Soc Med Sch Pharmacol; fel Am Col Neuropsychopharmacol; AAAS; Am Chem Soc, div Med Chem; Am Soc Neurochem; NY Acad Sci; Physiol Soc London; Int Union Pharmacol. *Res:* Chemical and biochemical pharmacology; applications of mass spectrometry and stable isotopes in pharmacology and toxicology; cholinergic mechanisms; mathematical biology. *Mailing Add:* Dept Pharmacol Sch Med Health Sci Univ Calif 10833 Le Conte Ave Los Angeles CA 90024-1735. *Fax:* 310-825-6267

JENDREK, EUGENE FRANCIS, JR, X-RAY POWDER DIFFRACTION. *Current Pos:* ANAL SPECIALIST, EG&G MOUND, 89- *Personal Data:* b Baltimore, Md, June 11, 49; m 73; c 2. *Educ:* Loyola Col, Baltimore, Md, BS, 71; Univ Conn, Storrs, MS, 73; Univ Md, College Park, PhD(chem), 79. *Prof Exp:* Sr analyst, Davison Chem Div, W R Grace & Co, 74-75; res specialist, Monsanto Res Group, 79-89, res chemist. *Mem:* Am Chem Soc; Am Crystallog Soc. *Res:* Powder X-ray diffraction computation; laboratory computer automation and data management. *Mailing Add:* EG&G Mound Appl Technol PO Box 3000 Miamisburg OH 45343-0987

JENDRESEN, MALCOLM DAN, BIOMATERIALS. *Current Pos:* prof biomat sci, 68-93, asst dent res, 72-93, EMER PROF, SCH DENT, UNIV CALIF, SAN FRANCISCO, 93- *Personal Data:* b Janesville, Wis, June 6, 33; m 54; c 1. *Educ:* Marquette Univ, DDS, 61; Univ Lund, Sweden, PhD(surface sci), 80. *Prof Exp:* Instr & res assoc dent mat, Marquette Univ, Wis, 61-64; chief restoration dent, USAF Sch Aerospace Med, 64-68. *Concurrent Pos:* Consult, USAF Sch Aerospace Med, 68-72, Vet Admin Hosp, San Francisco, 68-, WHO, 72-, Nordisk Inst Odontologisk Mat, 78-, Surg Gen, US Army, 79 & Dept Health & Human Serv, Pub Health Serv, Nat Inst Dent Res, NIH; vis prof, Univ Lund, Sweden, 78-79. *Mem:* Fel Int Asn Dent Res; fel Am Col Dentists; fel Int Col Dentists; fel AAAS; fel Sigma Xi. *Res:* General materials with emphasis on adhesion in biological environments; characterization of biofilm and the clinical adhesiveness of intact biological surfaces and subsequent adhesive events. *Mailing Add:* Dept Restorative Dent Box 0758 Univ Calif San Francisco CA 94143-0758

JENEKHE, SAMSON A, SYNTHESIS & PROCESSING OF POLYMERS, PHOTOPHYSICS OF POLYMERS. *Current Pos:* from asst prof to assoc prof, 88-94, PROF CHEM ENG, UNIV ROCHESTER, 94- *Personal Data:* b Okpella, Bendel State, Nigeria, Mar 3, 51; US citizen. *Educ:* Mich Technol Univ, BS, 77; Univ Minn, MS, 80, MA, 81, PhD(chem eng), 85. *Prof Exp:* Sr res scientist, Honeywell Inc, 81-84, prin res scientist, 84-87, proj leader electronic polymers, 85-87. *Concurrent Pos:* Consult, McDonnell Douglas Corp, 90-92. *Mem:* Am Inst Chem Engrs; Am Chem Soc; Mat Res Soc; Am Phys Soc; AAAS. *Res:* Synthesis and processing of electronic, optoelectronic, and photonic polymers; optoelectronic and photonic properties of polymers; photoinduced charge transfer in polymers; photophysics in polymers and macromolecular assemblies; polymer nanocomposites; polymer complexes; polymer-based devices. *Mailing Add:* Dept Chem Eng Univ Rochester Rochester NY 14627-0166. *Fax:* 716-442-6686; *E-Mail:* jenekhe@che.rochester.edu

JENERICK, HOWARD PETER, PHYSIOLOGY. *Current Pos:* RETIRED. *Personal Data:* b Cicero, Ill, May 20, 23; m 47; c 3. *Educ:* Univ Chicago, PhB, 46, SB, 48, PhD(physiol), 51. *Prof Exp:* From instr biol to asst prof gen physiol, Mass Inst Technol, 51-58; exec secy, Res Training Br, Div Gen Med Sci, NIH, 58-60; assoc prof physiol, Emory Univ, 60-64; chief, Spec Res Resources Br, Div Res Facil & Resources, NIH, 64-65, chief, Res Grants Br, 65-67, prog dir biophys sci, 67-72, spec asst to the dir, 72-76; chief off prog anal, Nat Inst Gen Med Sci, NIH, 76-90, dir, Extramural Inventions Off, 90-93. *Mem:* Biophys Soc; Am Physiol Soc. *Res:* Electrophysiology; scientific administration. *Mailing Add:* 5515 Huntington Pkwy Bethesda MD 20814

JENG, DUEN-REN, FLUID MECHANICS. *Current Pos:* from asst prof to assoc prof, 65-77, PROF MECH ENG, UNIV TOLEDO, 77- *Personal Data:* b Taipei, Taiwan, Mar 1, 32; nat US; m 66; c 3. *Educ:* Nat Univ Taiwan, BS, 55; Univ Ill, MS, 60, PhD(mech eng), 65. *Prof Exp:* Asst mech eng, Nat Univ Taiwan, 56-69 & Univ Ill, 60-64; asst prof, Univ Ala, 65-67. *Mem:* Am Soc Mech Engrs; Sigma Xi; Am Inst Aeronaut & Astronaut. *Res:* Metal cutting; thermal contact resistance and transient heat transfer in laminar boundary layer; wind energy; non-newtonian flow; radiation. *Mailing Add:* 5334 Fredelia Dr Toledo OH 43623

JENG, RAYMOND ING-SONG, HYDROLOGY, HYDRAULICS. *Current Pos:* from asst prof to assoc prof, 68-79, PROF CIVIL ENG, CALIF STATE UNIV, LOS ANGELES, 79-, CHMN DEPT, 85- *Personal Data:* b Taipei, Taiwan, Jan 1, 40; m 71. *Educ:* Nat Taiwan Univ, BS, 62; Colo State Univ, MS, 63, PhD(civil eng), 68. *Prof Exp:* Res asst hydrol invest, Colo State Univ, 64-67. *Concurrent Pos:* Consult, Boise Cascade Property Inc, 70 & Los Angeles County Flood Control Dist, 71-78; vis prof, Nat Taiwan Univ, 80-83. *Mem:* Am Soc Civil Engrs; Am Geophys Union; Am Water Works Asn. *Res:* Hydrologic system analysis; statistical and stochastic hydrology. *Mailing Add:* Dept Eng & Technol Rm C-157A 5151 State University Dr Los Angeles CA 90032-8151

JENICEK, JOHN ANDREW, ANESTHESIOLOGY. *Current Pos:* RETIRED. *Personal Data:* b Chicago, Ill, 22; m 47, Alice Wojcikiewicz; c 1. *Educ:* Univ Ill, MD, 46; Am Bd Anesthesiol, cert, 57. *Prof Exp:* Intern, St Mary Nazareth Hosp, Chicago, 46-47; resident anesthesiol, Brooke Army Hosp, 49-51; chief anesthesiol & oper serv, Tripler Army Hosp, 52-54, asst chief, 54-55; asst chief anesthesiol & oper serv, Walter Reed Army Hosp, 55-57; chief anesthesiol & oper serv, Brooke Army Hosp, 57-61; chief anesthesiol & oper serv, Walter Reed Army Hosp, 62-67; from assoc prof to prof anesthesiol, Univ Tex Med Br, Galveston, 67-92. *Concurrent Pos:* Consult anesthesiol, Surgeon Gen, US Army, 62-67. *Mem:* AMA; Am Soc Anesthesiol; fel Am Col Anesthesiol. *Mailing Add:* 2802 Beluche Dr Galveston TX 77551

JENIKE, ANDREW W(ITOLD), MECHANICAL ENGINEERING. *Current Pos:* RETIRED. *Personal Data:* b Warsaw, Poland, Apr 16, 14; nat US; m 43; c 2. *Educ:* Warsaw Tech Univ, Dipl, 39; Univ London, PhD(struct eng), 48. *Hon Degrees:* DTech, Univ Bradford, Eng, 72. *Prof Exp:* Design & develop engr, Poland, Can & US, 39 & 48-51; res prof mech & mining eng & dir bulk solids flow proj, Eng Exp Sta, Univ Utah, 56-62; consult engr, 62-66; pres, Jenike & Johanson Inc, 66-79; consult engr, 80-85. *Concurrent Pos:* Alexander von Humboldt Found sr scientist award, WGer, 76. *Mem:* Am Soc Mech Engrs; Am Inst Mining, Metall & Petrol Engrs; Am Inst Mech Engrs. *Res:* Storage and flow of solids; flowability testing equipment. *Mailing Add:* 3 Newcastle Dr No 2 Nashua NH 03060

JEN-JACOBSON, LINDA, BIOCHEMISTRY, BIOPHYSICS. *Current Pos:* Res assoc biol sci, Univ Pittsburgh, 67-69, lectr, 69-70, res assoc biophys, 70-80, grad fac, 84, RES ASST PROF BIOL SCI, UNIV PITTSBURGH, 81- *Personal Data:* b Kunming, China, Oct 29, 41; US citizen; m 67; c 2. *Educ:* Radcliffe Col, AB, 62; Univ Ill, MS, 65, PhD(biochem), 67. *Res:* Physicochemical determinants of protein conformation; structure-function relationships in proteins; mechanisms of protein-nucleic acid interactions. *Mailing Add:* Dept Biol Sci Univ Pittsburgh 535 Langley Hall Pittsburgh PA 15260. *Fax:* 412-624-4759

JENKIN, HOWARD M, MICROBIOLOGY, LIPID BIOCHEMISTRY. *Current Pos:* RETIRED. *Personal Data:* b New York, NY, May 1, 25; div; c Keith & Donna. *Educ:* Univ Wis, BS, 49; Univ Chicago, PhD(microbiol), 60. *Prof Exp:* Nat Res Coun fel microbiol, Virus-Rickettsiae Div, Biol Labs, Ft Detrick, Md, 60-61; mem staff, Immunol Br, 61-62; res asst prof prev med, Sch Med, Univ Wash, 62-66; from assoc prof to prof microbiol, Med Sch, Univ Minn, Minneapolis, 66-84; from assoc prof to prof, Hormel Inst, Grad Sch, 66-84, head microbiol sect, 66-84. *Concurrent Pos:* Head virol-tissue cult dept, US Naval Med Res Unit 2, Taiwan, 63-66. *Mem:* Am Soc Microbiol; Soc Trop Med & Hyg; Tissue Cult Asn. *Res:* Comparative lipid biochemistry; biology and serology of members of Chlamydia; herpes virus; leptospires; treponema arbovirus rickettsial groups of microorganisms; tumor-lipid membrane studies; schemiar tissue cultures studies; deep sea diving-human, rat lipid studies; immunology testing-protection studies. *Mailing Add:* 520 Palm Springs Blvd Apt 407 Indian Harbor Beach FL 32937

JENKINS, ALFRED MARTIN, ORGANIC CHEMISTRY. *Current Pos:* PROF SCI, GLASSBORO STATE COL, 60- *Personal Data:* b Boston, Mass, July 27, 17. *Educ:* Tufts Univ, BS, 42; Boston Univ, AM, 47; Okla State Univ, PhD(chem), 52. *Prof Exp:* Metallurgist, Watertown Arsenal, 42; res chemist, E I du Pont de Nemours & Co, 52-60. *Mem:* Am Chem Soc. *Res:* Cyclic polymerization of aldehydes. *Mailing Add:* 1212 N Main St Glassboro NJ 08028-1319

JENKINS, ALVIN WILKINS, JR, PLASMA PHYSICS, ASTROPHYSICS. *Current Pos:* assoc prof, 66-70, PROF PHYSICS, NC STATE UNIV, 70-, HEAD DEPT, 76- ACTG CHMN DEPT, 75- *Personal Data:* b Raleigh, NC, Dec 30, 28; m 51; c 2. *Educ:* NC State Col, BEE, 51, MS, 55; Univ Va, PhD, 58. *Prof Exp:* Sr physicist theoret physics, Ord Res Lab, Univ Va, 58-59; res physicist, Univ Res Inst, Denver, 59-61; assoc prof physics, Wichita State Univ, 61-66. *Mem:* Am Phys Soc; Am Geophys Union; Am Astron Soc. *Res:* Atmospheric and magnetospheric physics; plasma physics. *Mailing Add:* 4369 McCorsley Ave Little River SC 29566

JENKINS, CHARLES ROBERT, SANITARY ENGINEERING, AQUATIC BIOLOGY. *Current Pos:* From asst prof to assoc prof sanit eng, 61-77, prof environ eng, 77-80, PROF CIVIL ENG, WVA UNIV, 80- *Personal Data:* b Newton, Ill, Aug 17, 30; m 53; c 4. *Educ:* Eastern Ill State Col, BS, 52; Univ Ill, MS, 59; Okla State Univ, PhD(zool), 64. *Mem:* Am Soc Limnol & Oceanog; Water Pollution Control Fedn; Am Water Works Asn; Sigma Xi. *Res:* Water pollution control; waste treatment. *Mailing Add:* WVa Univ Dept Civil Eng Box 6103 Morgantown WV 26506

JENKINS, DALE WILSON, ECOLOGY, ENVIRONMENTAL SCIENCES. *Current Pos:* ECOL & ENVIRON CONSULT, WHO WORLD HEALTH ORGN, USAID, WORLDBANK, UN DEVELOP PROG, INTER-AM DEVELOP BANK, 78- *Personal Data:* b Wapakoneta, Ohio, June 17, 18; m 42; c 5. *Educ:* Ohio State Univ, BSc, 38, MA, 39, PhD, 47. *Honors & Awards:* Distinguished Serv Award, Ohio State Univ. *Prof Exp:* Ecologist, Soil Conserv Serv, 35; instr, Ohio State Univ, 38-39, Univ Chicago, 39-40, Univ Ill, 40-41 & Univ Minn, 41-42; agr specialist, Foreign Econ Admin, Washington, DC, 42-43; entomologist & chief animal ecol br, Army Med Labs, Md, 46-52, dep chief allied sci div, 54-56, chief entom div, 53-62; chief environ biol prog, NASA Hq, 62-66, assoc dir biosci progs, 66-70; dir ecol prog, Smithsonian Inst, 70-74; dep dir, Ctr Human Ecol & Health, Pan Am Health Orgn, 75-78. *Concurrent Pos:* Lectr, Sch Pub Health & Hyg, Johns Hopkins Univ, 50-; consult, USDA, Alaska, 47, USPHS, 48, Northern Insect Surv, Defence Res Bd Can, 49-50 & USAF, 59-; planning conf partic, Life Sci Prog, NASA, 60 & WHO, Bangkok, 60; mem, Armed Forces Pest Control Bd, 55-64 & Interdept Pest Control Comt, 58-64; chmn bd gov, Inst Lab Animal Resources, Nat Res Coun, 55-60, adv to UNESCO, 57-; US Dept

State deleg, Int Conf Peaceful Uses Atomic Energy, Geneva, 55; Nat Acad Sci-Nat Res Coun deleg, Int Cong Entom, Montreal, 56. *Mem:* Fel AAAS; Ecol Soc Am; Lepidopterists Soc. *Res:* Ecology of plants and animals; radioisotope tracers; laboratory animals; epidemiology; environmental impacts. *Mailing Add:* 3028 Tanglewood Dr Sarasota FL 34239

JENKINS, DAVID A, INTERMEDIATE ENERGY PHYSICS. *Current Pos:* assoc prof, 67-73, PROF PHYSICS, VA TECH, 74- *Personal Data:* b Seattle, Wash, Dec 28, 37. *Educ:* Yale Univ, BE, 59; Univ Calif, Berkeley, MS, 61, PhD(physics), 64. *Prof Exp:* Res asst, Lawrence Berkeley Lab, 67; dir, NSF, 73-74. *Mem:* Sigma Xi; Am Phys Soc. *Res:* Intermediate energy physics; mesonic atoms; pion-nucleon scattering; pion production; photodisintegration of light nuclei. *Mailing Add:* Physics Dept Va Tech Blacksburg VA 24061

JENKINS, DAVID I, SANITARY ENGINEERING. *Current Pos:* Res chemist, 60-61, from asst prof to assoc prof, 63-74, PROF SANIT ENG, UNIV CALIF, BERKELEY, 74-, DIR, SANIT ENG RES LAB, 61- *Personal Data:* b Shropshire, Eng, Oct 4, 35; m 60; c 2. *Educ:* Univ Birmingham, BSc, 57; Univ Durham, PhD(sanit eng), 60. *Concurrent Pos:* Sabbatical leave, Dept Eng & Appl Physics, Harvard Univ, 69-70. *Mem:* Am Chem Soc; Water Pollution Control Fedn; Asn Environ Eng Prof; fel Royal Inst Chem; Brit Inst Water Pollution Control. *Res:* Chemistry and biochemistry of processes and phenomena associated with the control of environment, especially the upgrading of water quality; biological waste treatment processes; activated sludge operation. *Mailing Add:* 11 Yale Circle Berkeley CA 94708

JENKINS, DAVID JOHN ANTHONY, DIABETES, HYPERLIPIDEMIA. *Current Pos:* PROF MED & CLIN NUTRIT , DEPT NUTRIT SCI & DEPT MED, UNIV TORONTO & ST MICHAEL'S HOSP, 80- *Personal Data:* m; c 1. *Educ:* Oxford Univ, Eng, PhD(clin nutrit), 71, MD, 76, DSc, 86. *Honors & Awards:* Borden Award, Can, 83; Goldsmith Award, Am Col Nutrit, 85. *Mem:* Am Inst Nutrit; Am Soc Clin Nutrit. *Mailing Add:* St Michael's Hosp 61 Queen St E Toronto ON M5C 2T2 Can. *Fax:* 416-975-5882

JENKINS, DAVID R(ICHARD), STRUCTURAL MECHANICS, COMPOSITE MATERIALS. *Current Pos:* RETIRED. *Personal Data:* b Lima, Ohio, Oct 24, 24; m 47; c 3. *Educ:* Case Inst Technol, BSc, 48; Ohio State Univ, MSc, 54; Univ Mich, PhD(eng mech), 62. *Prof Exp:* Stress analyst, Airplane Div, Curtiss-Wright Corp, 48, tech asst, Battelle Mem Inst, 48-50, prin mech engr, 50-55, proj leader, 55-58; instr eng mech, Univ Mich, 58-62, asst prof, 62-65; sr res fel, Tech Ctr, Owens-Corning Fiberglas Corp, 65-69; from assoc prof to prof & chmn engr mech & mat sci, Univ Cent Fla, 69-75, prof civil eng & environ sci & actg chmn, 75-76, actg chmn mech eng & aerospace sci, 81-82, chmn civil eng & environ sci, 84-90, prof eng, 76-93. *Concurrent Pos:* Fac res grant, Univ Mich, 65; on sabbatical leave, mat res eng, Nat Bur Stand, Ctr for Bldg Technol, 78-80; sabbatical, Univ Aalborg, Denmark & Polytech, Wales, 90. *Mem:* AAAS; Am Soc Civil Engrs; Soc Exp Mech Engrs; Am Soc Metals; Soc Eng Sci; Am Soc Mech Engrs. *Res:* Structural testing, composite materials; high temperature structural behavior; crack propagation in steel shells; aircraft structural investigations; yielding and strain hardening in metallic materials; composite materials. *Mailing Add:* PO Box 4065 Winter Park FL 32793-4065

JENKINS, EDGAR WILLIAM, HIGH ENERGY PHYSICS. *Current Pos:* RETIRED. *Personal Data:* b Columbus, Ohio, Apr 29, 33; m 59; c 3. *Educ:* Harvard Univ, AB, 55; Columbia Univ, PhD(physics), 62. *Prof Exp:* From asst physicist to assoc physicist, Brookhaven Nat Lab, 60-64; from asst prof to assoc prof, Univ Ariz, 64-71, prof physics, 71. *Mem:* Am Phys Soc; Am Asn Physics Teachers. *Res:* Interactions, properties and decays of elementary particles. *Mailing Add:* 4938 E Glenn St Tucson AZ 85712

JENKINS, EDWARD BEYNON, ASTROPHYSICS. *Current Pos:* Res assoc astrophys, Princeton Univ Observ, 66-67, res staff mem, 67-73, res astronr, 73-79, SR RES ASTRONOMER, PRINCETON UNIV OBSERV, 79- *Personal Data:* b San Francisco, Calif, Mar 20, 39; m 63; Myrna D Stewart; c Brian F & Eric D. *Educ:* Univ Calif, Davis, BA, 62; Cornell Univ, PhD(physics), 66. *Honors & Awards:* Humboldt Sr US Scientist Res Award, 92. *Concurrent Pos:* Prin investr of a sounding rocket res prog, 80-; mem, Comt Space Astron & Astrophys, 86-88; mem, Sci Definition Teams, Space Telescope Imaging Spectrog & Far Ultraviolet Spectros Explorer, 87-; mem, Astrophsics Subcomt, NASA, 92- *Mem:* Am Astron Soc (vpres, 96-); Int Astron Union. *Res:* Rocket and satellite ultraviolet astronomy; interstellar medium; image sensor development. *Mailing Add:* Princeton Univ Observ Princeton NJ 08544-1001. *E-Mail:* ebj@astro.princeton.edu

JENKINS, ELIZABETH ELLEN, CHIRAL PERTURBATION THEORY. *Current Pos:* Postdoctoral researcher, 89-92, asst prof, 92-97, ASSOC PROF PHYSICS, UNIV CALIF, SAN DIEGO, 97- *Personal Data:* b Tuscon, Ariz, Nov 19, 64. *Educ:* Harvard Univ, AB, 85, PhD(physics), 89. *Concurrent Pos:* Sci assoc, Europ Orgn Nuclear Res, 92-93; vis fel, Princeton Univ, 94; Nat Young Investr Award, NSF, 94-; Alfred P Sloan res fel, Sloan Found, 95-97; vis, Univ Valencia, Spain, 96. *Mem:* Am Phys Soc. *Res:* Study of hadrons at low energies using global approximate symmetries, such as flavor and spin flavor symmetries; techniques include chiral pertubation theory and heavy quark effective theory. *Mailing Add:* Physics Dept Univ Calif San Diego La Jolla CA 92093-0407. *E-Mail:* ejenkins@ucsd.edu

JENKINS, FARISH ALSTON, JR, VERTEBRATE PALEONTOLOGY, ANATOMY. *Current Pos:* assoc prof biol & assoc cur vert paleont, 71-74, PROF BIOL, DEPT ORGANISMIC & EVOLUTIONARY BIOL & CUR VERT PALEONT, MUS COMP ZOOL, HARVARD UNIV, 74-, PROF ANAT, HARVARD-MASS INST TECHNOL DIV HEALTH SCI & TECHNOL, HARVARD MED SCH, 82-, ALEXANDER AGASSIZ PROF ZOOL, 89- *Personal Data:* b New York, May 19, 40; m 63; c 2. *Educ:* Princeton Univ, AB, 61; Yale Univ, MSc, 66, PhD(geol), 68; Harvard Univ, MA, 74. *Prof Exp:* From instr to asst prof anat, Col Physicians & Surgeons, Columbia Univ, 68-71. *Res:* Vertebrate anatomy and evolution, especially reptiles and mammals; biomechanics of musculoskeletal system. *Mailing Add:* Mus Comp Zool Labs Harvard Univ Cambridge MA 02138

JENKINS, FLOYD ALBERT, COMPARATIVE ANATOMY, VERTEBRATE PALEONTOLOGY. *Current Pos:* instr, 43-45 & 53-55, from asst prof to prof, 55-87, EMER PROF BIOL, LOYOLA MARYMOUNT UNIV, 87- *Personal Data:* b Los Angeles, Calif, Aug 14, 16. *Educ:* St Louis Univ, AB, 40, MA, 42, MS, 43, PhD, 54; Alma Col, Calif, STL, 49. *Prof Exp:* Lab instr biol, St Louis Univ, 41-43. *Mem:* Paleont Soc; Soc Vert Paleont. *Res:* Evolution of the mammalian tulus; early evolution of mammals. *Mailing Add:* Xavier Hall 7900 Loyola Blvd Los Angeles CA 90045-8427

JENKINS, HOWARD BRYNER, MATHEMATICS. *Current Pos:* RETIRED. *Personal Data:* b Arimo, Idaho, Jan 30, 28; m 51; c 3. *Educ:* Mass Inst Technol, BS, 50; Univ Southern Calif, PhD(math), 58. *Prof Exp:* Lectr math, Univ Southern Calif, 54-57; instr, Calif Inst Technol, 57-58; temp mem, Inst Math Sci, NY Univ, 58-59, res assoc, 59-60; vis asst prof, Stanford Univ, 60-61; asst prof, Univ Minn, Minneapolis, 61-65, assoc prof, 65-, assoc head, Sch Math, 71- *Concurrent Pos:* Vis assoc prof, Stanford Univ, 66-67. *Mem:* Am Math Soc. *Res:* Partial differential equations; variational problems; minimal surfaces. *Mailing Add:* Sch Math 127 Vincent Hall Univ Minn 206 Church St SE Minneapolis MN 55455

JENKINS, HOWARD JONES, PHARMACOLOGY. *Current Pos:* RETIRED. *Personal Data:* b Oak Hill, Ohio, Sept 14, 16; m 51, Ruth Gerwig; c Melinda (Place), David H, Melissa (Soule) & Kelly-Anne (Lin). *Educ:* Ohio State Univ, PhD(pharmacol), 50. *Prof Exp:* Res pharmacologist, Armour Labs, 51-53; from asst prof to prof, Mass Col Pharm & Allied Health Sci, 53-84, dir, Div Pharmacol & Allied Sci, 64-73, emer prof, 84- *Mem:* AAAS; Acad Pharmaceut Sci; Sigma Xi; Am Pharmaceut Asn. *Res:* Cardiovascular pharmacology; autonomic pharmacology; structure-activity relationships involved in antispasmodic and antihistaminic responses; analgetic potentiation; biological assay. *Mailing Add:* 24 Brooks Rd Wayland MA 01778

JENKINS, HUGHES BRANTLEY, JR, THEORETICAL PHYSICS. *Current Pos:* RETIRED. *Personal Data:* b Jacksonville, Fla, Oct 17, 27. *Educ:* Univ Ga, AB, 48, MS, 55; Univ Ky, PhD(physics), 63. *Prof Exp:* Instr math & physics, Univ Ga, 52-55; asst physicist, Oak Ridge Nat Lab, Union Carbide Corp, Tenn, 55-57; asst mathematician, 57-58; intr physics, Univ Ky, 58-62; assoc prof, Ga State Col, 62-68; assoc prof physics & astron, Valdosta State Col, 68-83. *Res:* Statistical mechanics and mathematical physics. *Mailing Add:* 810 Millpond Rd Valdosta GA 31602

JENKINS, J STEVEN, BIOMEDICAL ENGINEERING, SOFTWARE ENGINEERING. *Current Pos:* SOFTWARE ENGR, JET PROPULSION LAB INC, 89- *Personal Data:* b Memphis, Tenn, Mar 22, 56. *Educ:* Millsaps Col, BS, 77; Southern Methodist Univ, MS, 80; Univ Calif, Los Angeles, PhD(elec eng), 87. *Prof Exp:* Res fel, Dept Anesthesiol, Univ Calif, Los Angeles, 87-89. *Mem:* Inst Elec & Electronics Engrs. *Mailing Add:* Jet Propulsion Lab 4800 Oak Grove Dr Pasadena CA 91109

JENKINS, JAMES ALLISTER, MATHEMATICS. *Current Pos:* PROF MATH, WASH UNIV, 59- *Personal Data:* b Toronto, Ont, Sept 23, 23; nat US. *Educ:* Toronto, BA, 44, MA, 45; Harvard Univ, PhD(math), 48. *Prof Exp:* Jewett fel, Harvard Univ, 48-49 & Inst Advan Study & Princeton Univ, 49-50; asst prof math, Johns Hopkins Univ, 50-54; from assoc prof to prof, Univ Notre Dame, 54-59. *Concurrent Pos:* Mem, Inst Advan Study, 57-59, 61-62, 73-74 & 80-81; Fulbright vis prof, Imp Col, Univ London, 62. *Mem:* Am Math Soc; Math Soc France; Ger Math Asn. *Res:* Geometrical and analytical function theories; topological theory functions. *Mailing Add:* Dept Math Wash Univ St Louis MO 63130

JENKINS, JAMES THOMAS, MECHANICS OF GRANULAR MATERIALS. *Current Pos:* from asst prof to assoc prof, 71-83, PROF THEORET MECH, CORNELL UNIV, 83- *Personal Data:* b Chicago, Ill, June 30, 42; m, Katharine Kelly; c Thomas Nelson & Peter Kelly. *Educ:* Northwestern Univ, BS, 64; Johns Hopkins Univ, PhD(mech), 69. *Prof Exp:* Postdoctoral assoc, Univ Paris, 69-70; vis lectr, Strathclyde Univ, 70-71. *Res:* Theoretical modeling of quasi-static stress strain relations for granular aggregates; application of kinetic theory to collisional grain flows; incorporation of the effects of interstitial fluids and gases. *Mailing Add:* Theoret & Appl Mech Cornell Univ Ithaca NY 14853. *Fax:* 607-255-2011; *E-Mail:* jtj2@cornell.edu

JENKINS, JAMES WILLIAM, ORGANIC CHEMISTRY. *Current Pos:* RETIRED. *Personal Data:* b Jamestown, NY, May 5, 21; c 3. *Educ:* Allegheny Col, BS, 44; Univ Buffalo, MS, 48, PhD(chem), 50. *Prof Exp:* Asst prof chem, Lafayette Col, 49-51; res anal chemist, Gen Aniline & Film Corp, 51-52; res anal chemist, Colgate Palmolive Co, 52-54, group leader anal sect,

54-58, sr group leader, 59-60, sect head, 60-63, res mgr, 63-64; dir, Pfizer Inc, 65-69, vpres res & Develop, consumer prod Div, 69-83. *Mem:* Am Chem Soc; Sigma Xi. *Res:* Product development; proprietary pharmaceuticals; toiletries and cosmetics; hair and skin research. *Mailing Add:* 135 Cheeskogili Way Loudon TN 37774-2524

JENKINS, JEFF HARLIN, PLANT PATHOLOGY. *Current Pos:* From asst prof to assoc prof bot, 63-74, PROF BIOL, WESTERN KY UNIV, 74- *Personal Data:* b Gamaliel, Ky, Mar 8, 37; m 59; c 2. *Educ:* Western Ky Col, BS, 59; La State Univ, MS, 61, PhD(plant path), 63. *Mem:* Am Phytopath Soc. *Res:* Taxonomic mycology; fusarium wilt of alfalfa; bacterial leaf spot of bell pepper. *Mailing Add:* Dept of Biol Western Ky Univ 1 Big Red Way St Bowling Green KY 42101-3576

JENKINS, JIMMY RAYMOND, BIOLOGICAL STRUCTURE. *Current Pos:* PRES, EDWARD WATERS COL, FLA, 97- *Personal Data:* b Selma, NC, Mar 18, 43; m 65; c 2. *Educ:* Elizabeth City State Univ, BS, 65; Purdue Univ, MS, 70, PhD(biol educ), 72. *Prof Exp:* Teacher high schs, Md, 65-69; fel biol, Purdue Univ, 69-70, teaching fel & res asst instrnl develop, 70-72; asst prof biol & asst acad dean, Elizabeth City State Univ, 72-74, assoc prof biol & dean, 73-97, vchancellor acad affairs, 77-97. *Concurrent Pos:* Adv coun mem, Albemarle Regional Planning & Develop Comn, 74-; proposal reviewer, NSF, 74; individualized instr, Region 15, Northeastern NC, 75; instrnl consult, Halifax Co Schs, NC, 75-76; mem, Health Manpower Develop Corp. *Mem:* Nat Asn Res Sci Teaching. *Res:* Instructional development and design geared to biology and the facilitation of biological concepts. *Mailing Add:* Off Pres Edward Waters Col 1658 Kings Rd Jacksonville FL 32209-6167

JENKINS, JOE WILEY, non-abelian harmonic analysis, for more information see previous edition

JENKINS, JOHN BRUNER, GENETICS. *Current Pos:* Asst prof, 68-74, assoc prof, 74-80, PROF & CHMN BIOL, SWARTHMORE COL, 80- *Personal Data:* b Springfield, Mass, July 20, 41; m 63. *Educ:* Utah State Univ, BS, 64, MS, 65; Univ Calif, Los Angeles, PhD(zool), 68. *Mem:* AAAS; Genetics Soc Am; Am Genetic Asn. *Res:* Chemical mutagenesis in Drosophila and its relation to genetic fine structure. *Mailing Add:* Dept of Biol Swarthmore Col 500 College Ave Swarthmore PA 19081-1390

JENKINS, JOHNIE NORTON, PLANT GENETICS, AGRONOMY. *Current Pos:* res geneticist, 61-80, DIR CROP SCI RES LAB, AGR RES SERV, USDA, 80- *Personal Data:* b Barton, Ark, Nov 3, 34; m 59; c 2. *Educ:* Univ Ark, BSA, 56; Purdue Univ, MS, 58, PhD(genetics), 60. *Honors & Awards:* Mobay Cotton Res Recognition Award. *Prof Exp:* Res assoc agron, Univ Ill, 60-61. *Concurrent Pos:* Prof crop sci & mem grad fac, Miss State Univ, 64- *Mem:* Am Soc Agron; Crop Sci Soc Am; Entom Soc Am; AAAS. *Res:* Host plant resistance to cotton insects and nematodes; investigations of basic causes of insect and nematode resistance in cotton plants and development of factors which will confer resistance. *Mailing Add:* Miss State Univ PO Box 5367 Mississippi State MS 39762-5367

JENKINS, KENNETH DUNNING, DEVELOPMENTAL BIOLOGY. *Current Pos:* From asst prof to assoc prof biol, 70-80, PROF BIOL, CALIF STATE UNIV, LONG BEACH, 80- *Personal Data:* b New York, NY, Apr 8, 44; c 3. *Educ:* Calif State Univ, Northridge, BA, 66; Univ Calif, Los Angeles, PhD(develop biol), 70. *Concurrent Pos:* Dep assoc vpres acad affairs, Molecular Ecol Inst, 78-80, dir of inst, 82-; mem panel on fate & effects of drilling fluids on the marine environ, Nat Acad Sci, 82-83; sci adv bd, US Environ Protection Agency, 82- *Mem:* AAAS; Soc Develop Biol. *Res:* Molecular ecology; aquatic toxicology. *Mailing Add:* Dept Biol Calif State Univ 3702 Csulb Long Beach CA 90840-0004

JENKINS, KENNETH JAMES WILLIAM, BIOCHEMISTRY, NUTRITION. *Current Pos:* RETIRED. *Personal Data:* b Montreal, Que, Oct 1, 29; m 69, Betty-Anne Harris; c Victoria. *Educ:* McGill Univ, BSc, 51; Univ Sask, MSc, 53; Univ Wis, PhD(biochem), 58. *Honors & Awards:* Borden Award, Can, 74; Medal for Excellence in Nutrit, Can Packers, 84; Merit Award, Can Soc Animal; Order of Can, 89. *Prof Exp:* Head res & develop emergency rations, Defense Res Med Labs, Dept Nat Defense, Can, 53-54; asst biochem, Univ Wis, 54-58; asst prof biochem & nutrit, Ont Agr Col, Guelph, 58-65; res officer, Can Dept Agr, 65-73, head, Trace Mineral Nutrit Sect, Trace Minerals & Pesticide Div, 73-80, prin scientist, Animal Res Ctr, Cent Exp Farm, 80- *Mem:* Can Nutrit Soc; Can Biochem Soc; Can Soc Animal Sci; Am Dairy Sci Asn. *Res:* Nutritional requirements of animals; biochemical role of mineral elements; tocopherol and selenium metabolism; neonatal nutrition and metabolism. *Mailing Add:* 63 Larkin Dr Nepean ON K2J 1B3 Can. *Fax:* 613-943-2353

JENKINS, LAWRENCE E, mechanical engineering; deceased, see previous edition for last biography

JENKINS, LEONARD CECIL, ANESTHESIOLOGY, PHARMACOLOGY. *Current Pos:* clin instr, Univ BC, 59-61, clin asst prof, 61-67, assoc prof, 67-70, assoc prof pharmacol, Fac Med, 68-, prof anesthesia & head dept, 70-91, EMER PROF, UNIV BC, 91-; DIR ANESTHESIA, VANCOUVER GEN HOSP, 70- *Personal Data:* b Vancouver, BC, June 23, 26; m 66. *Educ:* Univ BC, BA, 48; McGill Univ, MD, CM, 52; FRCP(C), 59. *Prof Exp:* McLaughlin travel fel, 58-59. *Concurrent Pos:* Med Res Coun res grant, 66-68. *Mem:* Am Soc Anesthesiol; Can Anesthetists Soc. *Res:* Anesthesia and the central nervous system; mechanisms of anesthesia; shock. *Mailing Add:* Dept Med 7084 Balaclava St Vancouver BC V6N 1M5 Can

JENKINS, LESLIE HUGH, SURFACE PHYSICS. *Current Pos:* mem res staff, 56-73, SECT HEAD, OAK RIDGE NAT LAB, 73- *Personal Data:* b Bryson City, NC, Sept 26, 24; m 51; c 2. *Educ:* Univ NC, BS, 49, PhD(phys chem), 54. *Prof Exp:* Group leader, Va-Carolina Chem Corp, 54-56. *Mem:* AAAS; Am Phys Soc; Sigma Xi. *Res:* Surface physics; secondary electron emission and Auger spectroscopy; low energy electron diffraction; particle-solid interactions at surfaces. *Mailing Add:* 817 Whirlaway Circle Knoxville TN 37923-2146

JENKINS, MAMIE LEAH YOUNG, NUTRITION, BIOCHEMISTRY. *Current Pos:* RES CHEMIST, DIV NUTRIT, FOOD & DRUG ADMIN, BUR FOODS, 67- *Personal Data:* b Washington, DC, July 10, 40; m 73. *Educ:* Howard Univ, BS, 62, MS, 65, PhD(nutrit), 80. *Prof Exp:* Chemist, Agr Res Serv, US Dept Agr, 64-67. *Mem:* Animal Nutrit Res Coun; Am Chem Soc; Am Inst Nutrit. *Res:* Protein quality, amino acid fortification, amino acid derivatives and vitamins; emphasis on the metabolic role of lecithin as a dietary choline source, and its interrelationships with other nutrients. *Mailing Add:* 8301 Muirkirk Rd No 2304 Laurel MD 20708. *Fax:* 301-594-0517

JENKINS, MELVIN EARL, METABOLISM. *Current Pos:* prof chmn dept pediat & child health, 73-86, EMER PROF PEDIAT, COL MED, HOWARD UNIV, 86- *Personal Data:* b Kansas City, Mo, June 24, 23; m 75, Maria Parker; c Janis, Carol & Lore. *Educ:* Univ Kans, AB, 44, MD, 46. *Honors & Awards:* Melvin E Jenkins MD Lectureship Pediat, Howard Univ, 95. *Prof Exp:* From instr to assoc prof pediat, Col Med, Howard Univ, 50-69; prof, Col Med, Univ Nebr Med Ctr, Omaha, 69-73. *Mem:* Am Acad Pediat; Sigma Xi; Am Pediat Soc; Soc for Pediat Res; Endocrin Soc. *Res:* Gonadal function; human growth and development; sickle cell hemoglobin; fetal and newborn physiology; steroid metabolism. *Mailing Add:* 10401 Grosvenor Pl Apt 504 Rockville MD 20852. *E-Mail:* mpark@aol.com

JENKINS, PHILIP WINDER, ORGANIC CHEMISTRY, ENVIRONMENTAL TOXICOLOGY & CHEMISTRY. *Current Pos:* TECH ADV, ENVIRON CAREEERS ORGN, 94- *Personal Data:* b Birmingham, Ala, Nov 7, 33; m 56; c 4. *Educ:* Univ Ill, BS, 55; Mass Inst Technol, PhD(chem), 59. *Prof Exp:* Res chemist, Eastman Kodak Co, 59-61, sr res chemist, 61-65, res assoc, 65-68, lab head, 68-71, res assoc, Emulsion Res Div, Res Labs, 71-74, res assoc, Anal Sci Div, Res Labs, 74-80, tech assoc, Health Safety & Human Factors Lab, Eastman Kodak Co, 78-91. *Mem:* Am Chem Soc; Royal Inst Chem; Soc Environ Toxicol & Chem; Sigma Xi; NY Acad Sci. *Res:* Cyclooctatetraene derivatives; proximity effects in medium ring compounds; gas chromatography; heterocycles; photographic sensitizing dyes; photochemistry; excited state energy processes; environmental fate and effects of chemicals. *Mailing Add:* 49 Dorvid Rd Rochester NY 14617-2103

JENKINS, ROBERT ALLAN, CELL BIOLOGY. *Current Pos:* from asst prof to assoc prof zool, 66-74, PROF ZOOL, UNIV WYO, 74- *Personal Data:* b Logan, Utah, Apr 1, 34; m 56; c 2. *Educ:* Utah State Univ, BS, 57; Syracuse Univ, MS, 61; Iowa State Univ, PhD(cell biol), 64. *Prof Exp:* Teacher, Jr High Sch, Utah, 56-60, instr & assoc cell biol & electron micros, Iowa State Univ, 63-66. *Mem:* AAAS; Am Soc Cell Biol; Soc Protozool. *Res:* Use of electron microscopy, cytochemistry and biochemical techniques for cytological studies of filamentous structures related to morphogenetic processes typical of dividing, regenerating and excysting ciliates. *Mailing Add:* Dept Zool Univ Wyo PO Box 3166 Laramie WY 82071-3166

JENKINS, ROBERT BRIAN, CYTOGENETICS. *Current Pos:* Resident clin path, Mayo Grad Sch Med, 86, fel hematopath/cytogenetics, 87, instr, Lab Med, Mayo Med Sch, 87-89, sr assoc consult, Dept Lab Med & Path, Mayo Clin & Found, 87-90, ASSOC DIR, CYTOGENETICS LAB, MAYO CLIN, 87-, ASST PROF LAB MED, MAYO MED SCH, 89- *Personal Data:* b Oct 23, 55; m; c 2. *Educ:* Northwestern Univ, BA, 77; Univ Chicago, PhD(develop biol), 81, MD, 83. *Concurrent Pos:* Assoc mem, Biochem & Molecular Biol Dept, Mayo Grad Sch, 90- & consult, Dept Lab Med & Path, Mayo Clin & Found, 90- *Mem:* AAAS; AMA; Am Soc Clin Pathologists; Col Am Pathologists; Am Soc Human Genetics; Am Asn Pathologists; Int Acad Path; Sigma Xi. *Mailing Add:* Cytokine Lab Mayo Clin 970 Hilton Bldg 200 First St SW Rochester MN 55905-0001. *Fax:* 507-284-0043

JENKINS, ROBERT EDWARD, ANALOG SUBTHRESHOLD VERY LARGE SCALE INTEGRATION CIRCUIT DESIGN, NEURAL NETWORKS. *Current Pos:* PRIN ENGR, JOHNS HOPKINS APPL PHYSICS LAB, 61- *Personal Data:* b Baltimore, Md, June 2, 38; m 70; c 2. *Educ:* Univ Md, BS, 60, MS, 66. *Concurrent Pos:* Vis scientist, Defense Mapping Agency, Wash, DC, 78-79; vis prof, Johns Hopkins Univ, 84-85, lectr elec eng, 84-91, prog coordr, Sch Continuing Prof Studies, 86-91. *Mem:* Inst Elec & Electronics Engrs. *Res:* Implementation of advanced sensors and neural networks using analog very large scale integration circuits silicon methods for innovative information processing. *Mailing Add:* Johns Hopkins Univ Appl Physics Lab Johns Hopkins Rd Bldg 23 Rm 306 Laurel MD 20723-6399

JENKINS, ROBERT ELLSWORTH, JR, ecological conservation, for more information see previous edition

JENKINS, ROBERT GEORGE, COAL CONVERSION FUNDAMENTALS, MATERIALS CHARACTERIZATION. *Current Pos:* assoc dean res, 88-91, PROF CHEM ENG, COL ENG, UNIV CINCINNATI, 88- *Personal Data:* b Gwent, Wales, Sept 29, 44; m 69, Susan

Buck; c Sara & George. *Educ:* Univ Leeds, Eng, BSc, 67, PhD(fuel sci), 70. *Prof Exp:* Res assoc, Dept Mat Sci, Pa State Univ, 70-73; res fel chem, Imp Col Sci & Technol, Eng, 73-75; sr res assoc, Dept Mat Sci & Eng, Pa State Univ, 75-78, from asst prof to prof fuel sci, 78-88. *Mem:* Fel Inst Energy; Sigma Xi; Am Chem Soc; Combustion Inst; Am Inst Chem Engrs. *Res:* Coal conversion chemistry; modification and characterization of carbons and zeolites as molecular sciences and absorbants; carbons from waste materials, coal characterization. *Mailing Add:* Univ Cincinnati 466 ERC Cincinnati OH 45221-0171. *Fax:* 513-556-2522

JENKINS, ROBERT M, FISH BIOLOGY. *Current Pos:* CONSULT, 89- *Personal Data:* b Kansas City, Mo, June 18, 23; m 56; c 4. *Educ:* Univ Okla, BS, 48, MS, 49. *Prof Exp:* Regional fishery biologist, Okla Game & Fish Dept, 49-50; dir fishery res, Okla Fishery Res Lab, 52-57; asst exec vpres fish conserv, Sport Fishing Inst, 58-62; dir nat reservoir res prog, US Fish & Wildlife Serv, 63-83; sr scientist, Aquatic Ecosystem Analysts, 83-88. *Concurrent Pos:* Mem panel fisheries experts, Food & Agr Orgn, 63- *Mem:* Am Fisheries Soc, (pres, 70-71); fel Am Inst Fish Res Biol. *Res:* Large reservoir fish production nationally as influenced by various environmental parameters. *Mailing Add:* 1223 Viewpoint Dr Fayetteville AR 72701-4188

JENKINS, ROBERT WALLS, JR, RADIOCHEMISTRY, PLANT ECOLOGY. *Current Pos:* res scientist, 65-67, chief radiochem group, 67-76, ASSOC PRIN SCIENTIST, PHILIP MORRIS INC RES CTR, 76- *Personal Data:* b Richmond, Va, June 12, 36; m 58; c 3. *Educ:* Va Mil Inst, BS, 58; Purdue Univ, MS, 61; Calif Western, PhD, 80. *Honors & Awards:* Philip Morris Award Distinguished Achievement Tobacco Sci, 75. *Prof Exp:* Instr chem, Purdue Univ, 58-60; asst prof, Va Mil Inst, 60-61; chief nuclear chem div, Nuclear Defense Lab, 61-63; res scientist, Naval Res Lab, 63-65. *Mem:* Am Chem Soc; Am Nuclear Soc. *Res:* Radioisotopes; biosynthetic production of radiochemicals and their use in experimentation; gas radiochromatography; neutron activation analysis; smoke formation mechanisms; smoke aerosol generation; smoke chemistry; neutron radiography. *Mailing Add:* 105 Gun Club Rd Richmond VA 23221

JENKINS, RONALD LEE, COMPARATIVE ANIMAL PHYSIOLOGIST, CELLULAR BIOLOGY-ENZYMOLOGY. *Current Pos:* ASSOC PROF BIOL & CHAIR DEPT BIOL, SAMFORD UNIV, BIRMINGHAM, 88- *Personal Data:* b Atlanta, Ga, Oct 24, 52; m 78; c 2. *Educ:* Carson-Newman Col, BS, 74; Auburn Univ, MS, 76, PhD(anat-physiol), 80. *Prof Exp:* Asst prof biol, La Col, 79-81; res chemist diabetes, Vet Admin Med Ctr, 81-88; asst prof endocrinol, Univ Ala, Birmingham, 85-88. *Concurrent Pos:* Prin investr, res grants Am Diabetes Asn, 85-88; lectr, Ala Gov Sch, 86-; chmn, curric renewal, Samford Univ, 90-91. *Mem:* Am Physiol Soc; Am Diabetes Asn. *Res:* Metabolic dysfunction of the heart of diabetic animals and humans; changes in isoenzymes and substrate specificities for the enzymes of nucleotide catabolism. *Mailing Add:* Dept Biol Samford Univ 800 Lakeshore Dr Birmingham AL 35229

JENKINS, TERRY LLOYD, MATHEMATICS. *Current Pos:* from asst prof to assoc prof, 66-74, PROF MATH, UNIV WYO, 74- *Personal Data:* b Beresford, SDak, Nov 7, 35; m 57; c 6. *Educ:* Univ SDak, BA, 57; Univ Iowa, MS, 59; Univ Nebr, PhD(math), 66. *Prof Exp:* Instr math, Univ SDak, 59-60; from instr to asst prof, Univ Nebr, 61-66. *Mem:* Am Math Soc; Math Asn Am. *Res:* Ring theory; radicals of rings. *Mailing Add:* Divine Word Col Epworth IA 52045

JENKINS, THOMAS GORDON, SYSTEMS ANALYSIS. *Current Pos:* RES GENETICIST, US MEAT & ANIMAL RES CTR, AGR RES SERV, USDA, 78- *Personal Data:* b Ft Lewis, Wash, Jan 28, 47; m 68; c 2. *Educ:* Univ Ark, BS, 72, MS, 74; Tex A&M Univ, PhD(animal breeding), 77. *Prof Exp:* Res assoc, Tex A&M Univ, 77-78. *Concurrent Pos:* Consult, Wintock Int Livestock Res & Training Ctr, 76. *Mem:* Am Soc Animal Sci. *Res:* Development and validation of the impact of innovative technologies on the efficiency of production of beef cattle and sheep production systems. *Mailing Add:* USDA-ARS Meat Animal Res Ctr PO Box 166 Clay Center NE 68933

JENKINS, THOMAS LLEWELLYN, ASTROPHYSICS. *Current Pos:* from asst prof to assoc prof, 60-68, PROF PHYSICS, CASE WESTERN RESERVE UNIV, 68- *Personal Data:* b Cambridge, Mass, July 16, 27; m 51; c 4. *Educ:* Pomona Col, BA, 50; Cornell Univ, PhD(physics), 56. *Prof Exp:* Physicist, Lawrence Radiation Lab, Univ Calif, 55-60. *Concurrent Pos:* Sci & eng res coun fel, Southampton Univ, UK, 83. *Mem:* AAAS; Am Phys Soc. *Res:* Neutrino induced reactions; low level counting; electron pair production; photoproduction of mesons; shock hydrodynamics; experimental elementary particle physics; gamma ray astronomy. *Mailing Add:* Dept Physics Case Western Reserve Univ Cleveland OH 44106

JENKINS, THOMAS WILLIAM, ANATOMY, NEUROPATHOLOGY. *Current Pos:* RETIRED. *Personal Data:* b Adrian, Mich, Jan 25, 22; m 48, Helen Nye; c Jennifer, T Mark & Lori. *Educ:* Kent State Univ, BS, 47; Mich State Col, MS, 50, PhD(zool, anat), 54. *Prof Exp:* Asst biol, Kent State Univ, 41-43, 46-47; asst zool, Mich State Univ, 48-52, from instr to prof anat & path, 51-88. *Concurrent Pos:* NIH spec fel, Sch Med, Temple Univ, 62-63. *Mem:* Am Asn Anat; Am Asn Vet Anat; Am Acad Neurol; Soc Neurosci; Sigma Xi. *Res:* Functional anatomy of the nervous system. *Mailing Add:* 3307 Stonebrook Loop Bend OR 97701-8231

JENKINS, VERNON KELLY, RADIOLOGICAL HEALTH & RADIOBIOLOGY, EXPERIMENTAL HEMATOLOGY. *Current Pos:* CONSULT, 92- *Personal Data:* b Chattanooga, Tenn, Dec 29, 32; m 54, Barbara Mae Caylor; c 2. *Educ:* Carson-Newman Col, BS, 54; Univ Tenn, Knoxville, MS, 65, PhD(zool), 67. *Prof Exp:* Res assoc, Biol Div, Oak Ridge Nat Lab, 59-65, res scientist, 67-68; NIH fel exp biol, Baylor Col Med, 68-69, asst prof, 69-70; from asst prof to prof, Univ Tex Med Br, Galveston, 70-92. *Mem:* Radiation Res Soc; Am Soc Exp Path; Soc Exp Hemat; Reticuloendothelial Soc; NY Acad Sci. *Res:* Effects of radiation and drugs on hemopoiesis in mammals, including effects on the immune mechanism; studies of the interrelationships among radiation, drugs, immunity, hemopoiesis and the carcinogenic process. *Mailing Add:* 15938 La Avenida Ave Houston TX 77062

JENKINS, WILLIAM KENNETH, ELECTRICAL ENGINEERING. *Current Pos:* from asst prof to assoc prof, 77-83, PROF ELEC ENG, UNIV ILL, URBANA-CHAMPAIGN, 83-, DIR, COORD SCI LAB, 86- *Personal Data:* b Pittsburgh, Pa, Apr 12, 47; m 70, Suzann Heinricher. *Educ:* Lehigh Univ, BSEE, 69; Purdue Univ, MSEE, 71, PhD(elec eng), 74. *Honors & Awards:* Cas Soc Distinguished Serv Award, Inst Elec & Electronics Engrs, 90. *Prof Exp:* Res scientist assoc elec eng, Lockheed Missiles & Space Co, Inc, 74-77. *Concurrent Pos:* Consult, Ill State Water, 78, Siliconix, Inc, 78-80; AT&T Bell Labs, 83-84, Lockheed Missiles & Space Co, 83-85, Air Force Studies Bd, 89-90. *Mem:* Fel Inst Elec & Electronics Engrs (secy & treas, 82-84, pres, 85); Am Soc Eng Educ. *Res:* Circuit and system theory; digital signal processing: digital filters, algorithms and structures; adaptive signal processing; computed imaging. *Mailing Add:* Dept Elec Eng Coord Sci Lab 1308 W Main St Urbana IL 61801

JENKINS, WILLIAM L, VETERINARY PHARMACOLOGY, VETERINARY PHYSIOLOGY. *Current Pos:* DEAN, SCH VET MED, LA STATE UNIV, 88- *Personal Data:* b Johannesburg, SAfrica, Jan 29, 37; m 61; c 4. *Educ:* Univ Pretoria, BVSc, 58, M Med Vet, 68; Univ Mo, PhD(pharmacol), 70. *Prof Exp:* Asst pvt pract, 59-62; lectr vet med, Univ Pretoria, 62-66, sr lectr, 69-71, prof & head physiol & pharmacol, 71-75, prof & head vet physiol & pharmacol, 76-78; res assoc pharmacol, Univ Mo, 66-69; vis prof physiol & pharmacol, Tex A&M Univ, 75-76, prof vet physiol & pharmacol, 78-88. *Concurrent Pos:* Mem, FDA/CVM Adv Comt, 85-88, USP Convention Comt, Vet Med, 87-; mem, Subcomt Radiation Appln, Agr SAfrican Atomic Energy Bd, 75-78. *Mem:* Am Acad Vet Pharmacol & Therapeut; Am Col Vet Toxicologists; Am Soc Vet Physiologists & Pharmacologists; Am Vet Med Assoc. *Res:* Veterinary pharmacology and therapeutics including comparative pharmacokinetics; pathophysiology of stress in cattle and sheep; ruminant physiology and pharmacology. *Mailing Add:* Acad Affairs La State Univ Baton Rouge LA 70803-0001

JENKINS, WILLIAM ROBERT, NEMATOLOGY. *Current Pos:* assoc res specialist, 60-63, res specialist, 63-65, res prof, 65-69, assoc dean, col, 74-77, PROF BIOL & CHMN DEPT, LIVINGSTON COL, RUTGERS UNIV, 69-, DEAN, COL, 77- *Personal Data:* b Hertford, NC, Sept 12, 27; m 51; c 3. *Educ:* Col William & Mary, BS, 50; Univ Va, MS, 52; Univ Md, PhD(hort, plant path), 54. *Prof Exp:* Asst biol, Univ Va, 50-51; asst plant path, Univ Md, 51-54, from instr to asst prof, 54-60. *Mem:* Soc Nematologists. *Res:* Nematodes in relation to water pollution; transmission of human pathogens in nematodes borne by domestic water supplies; nematodes in soil. *Mailing Add:* Nelson BioLabs Rm A19 Bush Campus Rutgers Univ Piscataway NJ 08854-1059

JENKINS, WILLIAM WESLEY, research administration; deceased, see previous edition for last biography

JENKINS, WINBORNE TERRY, BIOLOGICAL CHEMISTRY, ENZYMOLOGY. *Current Pos:* assoc prof, 66-68, PROF CHEM, IND UNIV, BLOOMINGTON, 68- *Personal Data:* b Waupun, Wis, Mar 23, 32; div; c Christopher, Mary & Mark. *Educ:* Cambridge Univ, BA, 53; Mass Inst Technol, PhD(biol), 57. *Prof Exp:* Instr, Mass Inst Technol, 57-58; asst prof, Univ Calif, Berkeley, 60-66. *Concurrent Pos:* Spec res fel, NIH, 61-62, career develop award, 69-74. *Mem:* Am Soc Biochem & Molecular Biol; Protein Soc. *Res:* Intermediary metabolism of amino acids, especially the purification, characterization and general enzymological properties of transaminases; enzymology of calcium and magnesium; F1-ATPases. *Mailing Add:* Dept Chem Ind Univ Bloomington IN 47405. *Fax:* 812-855-8300; *E-Mail:* jenkinsw@indiana.edu

JENKINSON, MARION ANNE, ornithology; deceased, see previous edition for last biography

JENKINSON, STEPHEN G, PULMONARY DISEASE. *Current Pos:* CHIEF, PULMONARY DIS, AUDIE MURPHY VET ADMIN HOSP, 82- *Personal Data:* b Shreveport, La, Dec 9, 47. *Educ:* La State Univ, Shreveport, MD, 73. *Mailing Add:* Audie L Murphy VA Hosp 7400 Merton Minter Blvd San Antonio TX 78284-0001. *Fax:* 210-567-6677

JENKS, JOHN B, PLASTICS. *Current Pos:* VPRES COMPOSITES, OWEN CORNING. *Honors & Awards:* Bacon Person of Yr Award, Soc Plastics Indust, 94. *Mailing Add:* Owens Corning Fiberglass Tower Toledo OH 43659

JENKS, RICHARD D, MATHEMATICS, COMPUTER ALGEBRA SYSTEM LANGUAGE. *Current Pos:* MGR COMPUT ALGEBRA GROUP, MATH SCI DEPT, IBM TJ WATSON RES CTR, 82- *Personal Data:* b Chicago, Ill, Nov 16, 37; m 60; c Douglas, Daniel & Susan. *Educ:* Univ Ill, BS, 60, PhD(math), 66. *Prof Exp:* Res asst, Coordinated Sci Lab, Univ Ill, 60-66; fel math, Brookhaven Nat Lab, 66-68; res staff, IBM Res, 68-82; prof comput scI, NY Univ, 80-84. *Concurrent Pos:* Adj assoc prof math, NY Univ, 69-72; vis lectr comput sci, Yale Univ, 64 & 74; vis prof, Univ Utah, 76; Nat lectr, Asn Comput Mach, 78-80. *Mem:* Asn Comput Mach; Sigma Xi. *Res:* Computer language and system design, translator writing systems, computer algebra, non-numerical computation; study of very high level languages and their compilation; inventor and major implementor of scratchpad and axiom computer algebra languages and systems. *Mailing Add:* IBM Research Ctr Box 218 Yorktown Heights NY 10598. *Fax:* 914-945-3434; *E-Mail:* jenks@watson.ibm.com

JENKS, WILLIAM FURNESS, ECONOMIC GEOLOGY. *Current Pos:* RETIRED. *Personal Data:* b Philadelphia, Pa, June 28, 09; m 35; c 3. *Educ:* Harvard Univ, AB, 32, PhD(struct geol), 36; Univ Wis, MA, 33. *Prof Exp:* Jr geologist, Tex Col, 36-38; geologist, Cerro de Pasco Copper Corp, Peru, 38-45; US Dept State vis prof, Univ San Agustin, Peru, 45-46; from asst prof to assoc prof geol, Univ Rochester, 46-55; head dept & dir univ mus, Univ Cincinnati, 55-68, prof geol, 55-79. *Concurrent Pos:* Lectr, Univ San Agustin, Peru, 43; hon prof, Univ San Agustin, Peru, 46; Fulbright lectr, Univ Tokyo, 62-63; consult geologist, Newburyport, Mass, 79-82; coordr, Merrimack Valley Coun Nuclear Weapons Freeze, 82-85. *Mem:* Fel Geol Soc Am; Soc Econ Geol; Am Asn Petrol Geol; Am Geophys Union. *Res:* Mineral deposits of South America; disseminated copper deposits; tertiary volcanic rocks of western North America; massive concordant sulfide ore deposits. *Mailing Add:* 19 Monroe St Newburyport MA 01950-2243

JENKS, WILLIAM S, PHOTOCHEMISTRY. *Current Pos:* ASST PROF CHEM, UNIV IOWA, 92- *Personal Data:* b Portland, Ore, Jul 30, 64. *Educ:* Univ Calif, Los Angeles, BS, 86; Columbia Univ, PhD(chem), 91. *Honors & Awards:* Career Award, NSF, 95. *Prof Exp:* Postdoctoral fel, Columbia Univ, 91-92. *Concurrent Pos:* Cottrell scholar award, Res Corp, 95. *Mailing Add:* Dept Chem Univ Iowa Ames IA 50011. *Fax:* 515-294-0105; *E-Mail:* wsjenk@iastate.edu

JENNE, EVERETT A, GEOCHEMICAL MODELING, METAL BIOAVAILABILITY. *Current Pos:* RES SCIENTIST ENVIRON GEOCHEM, BATTELLE PAC NW LAB, RICHLAND, 80- *Personal Data:* b Beattie, Kans, Mar 2, 30; m 58, 85; c 3. *Educ:* Univ Nebr, BS, 52, MS, 53; Ore State Univ, PhD, 60. *Prof Exp:* Res fel soil chem & clay mineral, Ore State Soil Dept, 56-60; res fel rheology, Univ Calif, Berkeley, 60-62; soil scientist, US Geol Surv, Colo, 62-68, Calif, 68-79. *Concurrent Pos:* Mem ad hoc comt trace elements & uralithiasis incidence, Nat Acad Sci, 75-76; mem subcomt, 76-81, Geochem Environ Rel Health & Dis Comt, Nat Acad Sci, 81-83. *Mem:* Soil Sci Soc Am; Soc Environ Geochem & Health; Am Geophys Union; AAAS; Am Chem Soc; Mineral Soc Am. *Res:* Trace element geochemistry; trace element analyses and partitioning processes among solute, sediment and biota; adsorption phenomenon; colloid chemistry of metal oxides; mineral-water reactions of fossil and nuclear fuel wastes; bioavailability of trace elements; metal adsorption by oxides and sediments; watershed acidification modeling; water-sediment reactions twenty five to one hundred twenty degrees celsius; aquifer thermal energy storage. *Mailing Add:* 4203 W Kennewick Ave No 34 Kennewick WA 99336-2868

JENNEMANN, VINCENT FRANCIS, COMPUTER SCIENCE, EXPLORATION GEOPHYSICS. *Current Pos:* RETIRED. *Personal Data:* b St Louis, Mo, Nov 27, 21; m 46, Frances Robinson; c Frances (Bohon), Catherine (Audley), Martha, Charles, Mark, Joseph & Mary (Broussard). *Educ:* St Louis Univ, BS, 47, MS, 49; Univ Tulsa, PhD(earth sci), 72. *Prof Exp:* Instr math, St Louis Univ, 46-48; res computer, Seismog Dept, Sun Oil Co, 48-51; instr math, Lamar Col, 49-51; asst, Lamont Geol Observ, Columbia Univ, 51-54; res engr, Amoco Prod Co, Amoco Corp, 54-58, sr res engr, 58-64, sr res scientist, 64-66, comput analyst, 66-74, staff comput analyst, 74-84. *Mem:* Seismol Soc Am; Soc Explor Geophys; Am Geophys Union; Sigma Xi. *Res:* Various aspects of the metric system (SI). *Mailing Add:* 203 Sunset Dr Tulsa OK 74114-1239

JENNER, DAVID CHARLES, ASTRONOMY, COMPUTER SCIENCE. *Current Pos:* CONSULT, 89- *Personal Data:* b Seattle, Wash, Oct 21, 43; m 69; c 2. *Educ:* Univ Wash, BS(physics) & BS(math), 66; Univ Wis-Madison, PhD(astron), 70. *Prof Exp:* Asst prof astron, NMex State Univ, Las Cruces, 70-72; adj asst prof astron, Univ Calif, Los Angeles, 72-78; res assoc, Dept Astron & dir, Manastash Ridge Observ, Univ Wash, 78-89. *Mem:* Am Astron Soc; Int Astron Union. *Res:* Masses of galaxies; stellar populations in galaxies; the nuclei of active galaxies; planetary nebulae; instrumentation and observational techniques; software systems; hardware systems; laboratory data acquisition and instrument control. *Mailing Add:* 3153 NE 84th St Seattle WA 98115

JENNER, EDWARD L, AGRICULTURAL BIOCHEMISTRY. *Current Pos:* RETIRED. *Personal Data:* b Pontiac, Mich, Mar 27, 18; m 42, Dorothy Ragla; c Charles A, Edward W & Margaret A. *Educ:* Lake Forest Col, AB, 39; Univ Mich, MS, 40, PhD(chem), 42. *Prof Exp:* Res chemist, Univ Mich, 41-45; res chemist, Exp Sta, E I DuPont de Nemours & Co, Inc, 45-82. *Concurrent Pos:* Res assoc cell physiol, Univ Calif, 62-63. *Mem:* Am Chem Soc; Sigma Xi; fel AAAS. *Res:* Synthesis of nitramines; acid-catalyzed telomerizations; reactions of hydroxyl and amino radicals, halogen atoms and aliphatic free radicals; catalysis by soluble derivatives of transition metals; oxidative and photosynthetic phosphorylation; biochemistry of phytochrome; ozone damage to vegetation. *Mailing Add:* 107 Lande End Rd Wilmington DE 19807-2519

JENNESS, ROBERT, BIOCHEMISTRY. *Current Pos:* ADJ PROF CHEM, NMEX STATE UNIV, LAS CRUCES, 84- *Personal Data:* b Rochester, NH, Sept 21, 17; m 40, Katherine Ward; c Douglas F, M Ian & David R. *Educ:* Univ NH, BS, 38; Univ Vt, MS, 40; Univ Minn, PhD(agr biochem), 44. *Honors & Awards:* Borden Award, 53. *Prof Exp:* From instr to prof agr biochem, Univ Minn, St Paul, 40-66, prof biochem, 66-84. *Mem:* AAAS; Am Soc Biol Chem; Am Dairy Sci Asn; Am Chem Soc; Am Soc Mammalogists; Sigma Xi. *Res:* Biosynthesis of ascorbate by mammals; chemistry of milk proteins and salts; comparative biochemistry of milks of various species. *Mailing Add:* 1837 Corte del Ranchero Alamogordo NM 88310

JENNESS, STUART EDWARD, GEOLOGY. *Current Pos:* publ supvr, 67-85, ED CONSULT GEOL, CAN JOUR RES, NAT RES COUN CAN, 85- *Personal Data:* b Ottawa, Ont, Aug 22, 25; m 49, 80, Jean M Morgan; c John D & Mary G (Montgomery). *Educ:* Queens Univ, Ont, BSc, 48; Univ Minn, MS, 50; Yale Univ, PhD(geol), 55. *Prof Exp:* Instr geol, Muhlenberg Col, 49-51; geologist, Nfld Geol Surv, 52-53 & Geol Surv Can, 54-67. *Mem:* Fel Geol Soc Am; Geol Asn Can; Arctic Inst NAm; hon mem Asn Earth Sci Ed. *Mailing Add:* 9 2051 Jasmine Crescent Gloucester ON K1J 7W2 Can

JENNETT, JOSEPH CHARLES, CIVIL & ENVIRONMENTAL ENGINEERING. *Current Pos:* provost & vpres acad affairs, 92-95, ACAD DEAN ENG & PROF ENVIRON SYST ENG, CLEMSON UNIV, 81- *Personal Data:* b Dallas, Tex, June 11, 40; m 63; c 2. *Educ:* Southern Methodist Univ, BSCE, 63, MSCE, 66; Univ NMex, PhD(sanit eng), 69; Am Acad Environ Engrs, Dipl, 78. *Prof Exp:* Engr, Southwestern Design Br, US Corp Engrs, 62-63; construct engr, Calif State Dept Water Resources, Orville, 63-64; consult engr, Pitotmeter Assocs, 65-66 & 69; from asst prof to assoc prof civil eng, Univ Mo-Rolla, 69-75; prof civil eng & chmn dept, Syracuse Univ, 75-81. *Concurrent Pos:* Chmn, Task Force on Toxic Trace Substances in Water, 75 & Comt Water Treatment & Water Resources Mgt, 76; mem, Prof Coord Comt, 77-; mem, Environ Eng Div, Res Coun, 78-; ed, E N Am Minerals Environ J, 78; vis res, Appl Geochem Res Group, Imp Col, UK, 77. *Mem:* Am Soc Civil Engrs; Am Acad Environ Engrs, (trustee, 88-91); Am Soc Eng Educ; Water Pollution Control Fedn; Nat Soc Prof Engrs; Am Asn Environ Eng Prof. *Res:* Urban and rural runoff pollutants; drying of digested sludge; industrial waste treatment techniques; effects of heavy metals on aquatic ecosystems and treatment devices; biological operations on domestic and industrial wastes; analysis and treatment of toxic metals and trace organics; urban and rural run-off quality. *Mailing Add:* Tex A&M Univ 5201 University Blvd Loredo TX 78041

JENNEY, ELIZABETH HOLDEN, PHARMACOLOGY. *Current Pos:* PHARMACOLOGIST, BRAIN BIO CTR, 73- *Personal Data:* b Bennington, Vt, Nov 4, 12. *Educ:* Mt Holyoke Col, AB, 34; Univ Ill, MS, 47. *Prof Exp:* Asst pharmacol, Sch Med, Boston Univ, 35-36; med technologist, Rutland Hosp, Vt, 37-41; med technologist, Cooly Dickinson Hosp, Northampton, Mass, 41-43; res assoc, Univ Ill Col Med, 48-54; instr, Sch Med, Emory Univ, 54-60; res scientist, Sect Pharmacol, Bur Res, NJ Neuropsychiat Inst, 60-73. *Mem:* Sigma Xi; Am Soc Pharmacol & Exp Therapeut. *Res:* Neuropharmacology; psychopharmacology; schizophrenia. *Mailing Add:* Pennswood Village J-212 Newtown PA 18940

JENNI, DONALD ALISON, ETHOLOGY. *Current Pos:* assoc prof zool, Univ Mont, 66-71, chmn dept, 72-75 & 85-88, assoc dean biol sci, Col Arts & Sci, 88-91, PROF ZOOL, UNIV MONT, 71- *Personal Data:* b Pueblo, Colo, June 20, 32; m; c 7. *Educ:* Ore State Univ, BS, 53; Utah State Univ, MS, 56; Univ Fla, PhD(zool), 61. *Prof Exp:* Asst prof zool, Univ Fla, 61-62 & Eastern Ill Univ, 62-66. *Concurrent Pos:* NIH fel & res biologist, Univ Leiden, 64-66; vis prof, Cornell Univ, 75, Univ Wash, 79-80, Univ Melbourne & James Cooke Univ, 85; prin investr, NSF, 70-76, 85, 91-93, BLM, 77-80, Campfire, 83. *Mem:* Animal Behav Soc; Am Ornith Union; Wilson Ornith Soc; Asn Trop Biol; Coop Ornith Soc. *Res:* Ethology and behavioral ecology, especially behavioral approach to classic ecological problems; adaptation and evolution of behavioral patterns including social organization in response to ecological pressures; evolution of mateship systems, especially non-monogamous systems; behavioral problems of territoriality. *Mailing Add:* 17 Greenbrier Dr Missoula MT 59802. *Fax:* 406-243-4184

JENNINGS, ALFRED ROY, JR, hydraulic fracturing, formation damage, for more information see previous edition

JENNINGS, ALFRED S(TONEBRAKER), CHEMICAL ENGINEERING. *Current Pos:* RETIRED. *Personal Data:* b St Louis, Mo, Sept 30, 25; m 49; c 4. *Educ:* Washington Univ, St Louis, BS, 48, MS, 49, DSc(chem eng), 51. *Prof Exp:* Chem engr, Savannah River Lab, E I du Pont de Nemours & Co Inc, 51-57, res supvr, 57-68, res mgr, Separations Eng Div, 68-80, sr res assoc, 80-85. *Mem:* Am Chem Soc; Am Inst Chem Engrs. *Res:* Radiochemical separations and solvent extraction process development; isotope separation processes; high-level waste immobilization. *Mailing Add:* 1469 Canterbury Ct SE Aiken SC 29801

JENNINGS, ALLEN LEE, PESTICIDES, TOXIC CHEMICALS. *Current Pos:* dir, Chem & Statist Policy Div, 85-87, RES ASSOC BIOCHEM, US ENVIRONMENTAL PROTECTION AGENCY, 71-, DIR, BIOL & ECON ANALYSIS DIV, 87- *Personal Data:* b Quincy, Ill, July 5, 43; m 67; c 3. *Educ:* Western Ill Univ, BS, 65; Univ Ark, PhD(chem), 70. *Prof Exp:* Res assoc biochem, Iowa State Univ, 70-71. *Mem:* AAAS; Am Chem Soc. *Mailing Add:* 2306 S Dinwiddie St Arlington VA 22206-1039

JENNINGS, BOJAN HAMLIN, ORGANIC CHEMISTRY. *Current Pos:* from instr to assoc prof, 43-62, PROF CHEM, WHEATON COL, MASS, 62-, CHMN DEPT, 68- *Personal Data:* b Waukegan, Ill, Apr 4, 20; m 42; c 3. *Educ:* Bryn Mawr Col, AB, 42; Radcliffe Col, MA, 43, PhD(chem), 55. *Prof Exp:* Res chemist, Dewey & Almy Chem Co, 42-43. *Mem:* Am Chem Soc; NY Acad Sci; Asn Women Sci. *Res:* Steroid chemistry; cancer research; physical organic chemistry; photochemistry. *Mailing Add:* 25 Priscilla Rd White Horse Beach MA 02381

JENNINGS, BURGESS H(ILL), mechanical & environmental engineering; deceased, see previous edition for last biography

JENNINGS, BYRON KENT, THEORETICAL PHYSICS. *Current Pos:* RES SCIENTIST, TRIUMF, 82- *Personal Data:* b Musquodoboit, NS, Can, Mar 29, 51. *Educ:* Mt Allison Univ, BSc, 72; McMaster Univ, MSc, 73 & PhD (physics), 76. *Prof Exp:* Fel physics, State Univ NY, Stony Brook, 76-80; lectr physics, Univ Regensburg, 80; res fel physics, McGill Univ, 80-82. *Concurrent Pos:* Vis prof, Univ Toronto, 86; assoc ed, Can J Physics, 83-89; adj prof, Simon Fruser Univ, 87- *Res:* Study of nucleon structure as it impacts on nuclear properties. *Mailing Add:* TRIUMF 4004 Wesbrook Mall Vancouver BC V6T 2A3 Can. *Fax:* 604-222-1074; *E-Mail:* jennings@triumf.ca

JENNINGS, CARL ANTHONY, ORGANIC CHEMISTRY, CHEMICAL MANUFACTURING MANAGEMENT. *Current Pos:* from asst to vpres, Ind Chem, 77-78, mgr develop chem, 78-80, mgr agr chem mfg, 80-85, DIR MFG & TECHNOL, BASF WYANDOTTE CORP, 85- *Personal Data:* b Harrisburg, Ill, Dec 28, 44; m 65; c 2. *Educ:* Southern Ill Univ, BS, 67, PhD(org chem), 71. *Prof Exp:* Res assoc org chem, Univ Ill, 71-72; from res chemist to mgr, Photog Emulsion Mfg, GAF Corp, 72-77. *Mem:* Am Chem Soc; Am Inst Chem Engrs; Soc Chem Indust. *Res:* Agricultural chemicals; chemical manufacturing management; polyoxyalkylenes and organic oxide chemicals; urethanes; organic synthesis; photographic emulsion theory; organometallics. *Mailing Add:* 59 Nicole Dr Denville NJ 07834-9547

JENNINGS, CHARLES DAVID, OCEANOGRAPHY. *Current Pos:* PROF PHYSICS, WESTERN ORE STATE COL, 78- *Personal Data:* b Newtonia, Mo, May 21, 39; c 2. *Educ:* Northwest Nazarene Col, BA, 61; Ore State Univ, MS, 66, PhD(oceanog), 68. *Prof Exp:* Instr physics, Ore Col Educ, 62-63; instr oceanog, World Campus Afloat, 68, asst prof, 68; oceanog, US Bur Com Fisheries, 68-70; asst prof oceanog, Ore Col Educ, 70-74, assoc prof physics, 74-78. *Mem:* AAAS; Am Soc Limnol & Oceanog. *Res:* Radioactivity and trace elements in the marine environment; circulation of estuaries; marine radioecology. *Mailing Add:* 7762 Sportsman Club Rd NE Bainbridge Island WA 98110

JENNINGS, CHARLES WARREN, ELECTROCHEMISTRY. *Current Pos:* RETIRED. *Personal Data:* b Toledo, Ohio, Dec 3, 18; m 49, Donna H; c Charles J, Mary M (Hoskins) & Anabelle (Muchmone). *Educ:* Univ Toledo, BEng, 40; Univ Calif, MS, 43; Duke Univ, PhD(chem), 51. *Prof Exp:* Res chemist, Dow Chem Co, Calif, 42-43; chemist, Nat Bur Stand, 46-47, res assoc, 47-48; res assoc, Res Proj, Duke Univ, 48-50; assoc prof chem, NC State Col, 50-57; mem staff, Sandia Corp, 57-88. *Res:* Physical properties of electrodeposited metals; electrochemistry of batteries and fused salt systems; chlorination of hydrocarbons; thermal batteries; printed circuit boards; adhesives. *Mailing Add:* 1209 Mesilla NE Albuquerque NM 87110

JENNINGS, DANIEL THOMAS, FOREST ENTOMOLOGY, ARACHNOLOGY. *Current Pos:* RETIRED. *Personal Data:* b Fulton, Ky, July 4, 35; m 55; c 2. *Educ:* Colo State Univ, BS, 60; Univ NMex, MS, 67, PhD(biol), 72. *Prof Exp:* Entomologist, Forest Serv, USDA, 62-65, res entomologist, NC Forest Exp Sta, 65-68, res entomologist, Rocky Mountain Forest & Range Exp Sta, 68-76, prin res entomologist, Northeastern Forest Exp Sta, 76-91. *Concurrent Pos:* Collabr, Environ Qual Inst, Biol Active Natural Prod Lab, 73-; adj Res Serv, Arkansas, 76-77; adj asst prof biol, Univ NMex, 74-77; fac assoc, Univ Maine, 76- *Mem:* Entom Soc Am; Am Entom Soc; Am Arachnological Soc; Brit Arachnological Soc; Entom Soc Can; Sigma Xi. *Res:* Life histories and habits of forest insects, their biological control by natural enemies and pheromones; the arachnid fauna associated with forest trees. *Mailing Add:* PO Box 130 Garland ME 04939-0130

JENNINGS, DAVID PHIPPS, MEDICAL INFORMATICS, VETERINARY MEDICINE. *Current Pos:* PROF PHYSIOL, MISS STATE UNIV, 77- *Personal Data:* b Columbia, Mo, Aug 3, 41; m 64; c 2. *Educ:* Univ Mo, BS, 63, DVM, 65; Okla State Univ, PhD(physiol), 69. *Prof Exp:* NIH trainee, 65-66, fel, 66-68, from asst prof to assoc prof physiol, Okla State Univ, 68-77. *Concurrent Pos:* NIH spec fel anat, Sch Med, Univ Calif, Los Angeles, 71-72; clin neurol trainee, Univ Ga, 78. *Mem:* AAAS; Am Vet Med Asn; Am Asn Vet Anatomists; Am Asn Vet Cols; Am Soc Vet Physiol & Pharmacol. *Res:* Central nervous system mechanisms for control of physiologic systems; medical informatics and computerized medical records. *Mailing Add:* Col Vet Med Box 9825 Mississippi State MS 39762

JENNINGS, DONALD B, MEDICINE, PHYSIOLOGY. *Current Pos:* from asst prof to assoc prof, 64-74, PROF PHYSIOL, QUEEN'S UNIV, ONT, 74- *Personal Data:* b Windsor, Ont, July 20, 32; m 57, Gail E; c Robert D, Elizabeth A, Lisa E & Hugh D. *Educ:* Queen's Univ, Ont, MD, CM, 57, MSc, 60, PhD(physiol), 62. *Prof Exp:* Jr intern, Montreal Gen Hosp, 57-58, jr asst res med, 58-59; res fel med & physiol, Cardiovasc Res Inst, Med Ctr, Univ Calif, San Francisco, 62-64. *Concurrent Pos:* George Christian Hoffman fel path, 62-63; Can Heart Found sr res fel physiol, 64-69; assoc ed, Can J Physiol Pharmacol, 78; fel, Max Planck Inst Exp Med, 81; vis prof, Med Sch, Dartmouth Col, 81 & Univ Calif, San Francisco, 90. *Mem:* Can Physiol Soc (secy, 75-78); Am Physiol Soc; Can Soc Clin Invest. *Res:* Humoral and nervous regulation of cardiovascular, respiratory, metabolic and erythropoietic adjustments to high carbon dioxide and low oxygen environments and anaemic anoxia; interaction of temperature regulation with the cardio-respiratory admustment to acute and chronic hypercapnia and hypoxia; role of unin-angioleases system and vasopression in the central regulation of ventilation; application of the physicochemistry of H plus homeostasis to respiratory control. *Mailing Add:* Dept Physiol Botterell Hall Queen's Univ Kingston ON K7L 3N6 Can. *Fax:* 613-545-6880; *E-Mail:* jennings@qucdn.queensu.ca

JENNINGS, DONALD EDWARD, MOLECULAR SPECTROSCOPY. *Current Pos:* Nat Acad Sci-Nat Res Coun res assoc, 76-77, SPACE SCIENTIST, GODDARD SPACE FLIGHT CTR, NASA, 77- *Personal Data:* b New Rochelle, NY, May 30, 48; m 70. *Educ:* Northern Ariz Univ, BS, 70; Univ Tenn, PhD(physics), 74. *Prof Exp:* Res assoc physics, Univ Tenn, Knoxville, 74-75. *Res:* Molecular spectroscopy; fourier transform, tuneable diode laser, and grating spectroscopy; planetary infrared astronomy; radio astronomy of interstellar molecules. *Mailing Add:* 4617 Clemson Rd College Park MD 20740

JENNINGS, HARLEY YOUNG, JR, CHEMISTRY, COLLOID & SURFACE CHEMISTRY. *Current Pos:* CONSULT, 85- *Personal Data:* b Clio, Mich, Sept 29, 26; m 50, Barbara Perkins; c Jack, Judy & Janice. *Educ:* Univ NC, BS, 48; Univ Mich, MS, 49, PhD(chem), 52. *Honors & Awards:* Lester C Uren Award, 83; John Franklin Carll Award, Soc Petrol Engrs, 91. *Prof Exp:* Res chemist, Parker Pen Co, 50-52; res chemist, Chevron Oil Field Res Co, La Habra, 52-59, group supvr, 59-62, sr res chemist, 62-67, sr res assoc, 67-83, mgr, 83-85. *Mem:* AAAS; Am Chem Soc; Am Inst Mining, Metall & Petrol Engrs; Soc Petrol Engrs. *Res:* Surface energy relationships, contact angle and interfacial tension; capillarity; fluid flow and enhanced recovery of petroleum; colloid and surface chemistry; oil well stimulation and stimulation and damage prevention mechanisms; phase behavior and fluid analysis. *Mailing Add:* 2501 Terraza Pl Fullerton CA 92635. *E-Mail:* harjen1@aol.com

JENNINGS, JESSE DAVID, ANTHROPOLOGY. *Current Pos:* prof, Univ Utah, 49-70, distinguished res prof, 70-75, distinguished prof, 75-86, EMER PROF ANTHROP, UNIV UTAH, 86- *Personal Data:* b Oklahoma City, Okla, July 7, 09; m 35, Jane Noyes Chase; c Jesse David & Herbert Lee. *Educ:* Montezuma Col, BA, 29; Univ Chicago, PhD, 43; Univ Utah, DSc, 80. *Honors & Awards:* Viking Medal Archeol, Wenner Gren Found, 58; Reynolds Lectr, Univ Utah, 62; Leigh Lectr, 75; Distinguished Serv Award, Soc Am Archeol, 82; Alfred Vincent Kidder Award, Am Anthrop Asn, 95. *Prof Exp:* Anthropologist, Nat Park Serv, 37-42 & 45-48. *Concurrent Pos:* Mem, Anthrop-Psychol Div, Nat Acad Sci-Nat Res Coun, 54-56; vis prof anthrop, Northwestern Univ, 60, Univ Minn, 61, Univ Hawaii, 65 & 67-68; lectr, Summer Inst Anthrop, Univ Colo, 61 & Fairmont Col, 62; adj prof, Univ Ore, 80- *Mem:* Nat Acad Sci; AAAS; Soc Am Archeol (pres, 58-59); Am Anthrop Asn; Sigma Xi. *Mailing Add:* 21801 Siletz Hwy Siletz OR 97380-9721

JENNINGS, LAURENCE DUANE, SOLID STATE PHYSICS. *Current Pos:* RETIRED. *Personal Data:* b New Haven, Conn, Nov 14, 29; m 51; c 3. *Educ:* Mass Inst Technol, SB, 50, PhD(physics), 55. *Prof Exp:* Asst prof chem, Iowa State Univ, 55-59; solid state physicist, US Army Mat Tech Lab, 59-88. *Mem:* Am Phys Soc; Am Crystallog Asn; Inst Elec & Electronics Engrs. *Res:* Diffraction; equilibrium properties of solids. *Mailing Add:* 128 Gibbs St Newton MA 02159-1928

JENNINGS, LISA HELEN KYLE, EXPERIMENTAL HEMATOLOGY, PLATELET MEMBRANE BIOCHEMISTRY. *Current Pos:* ASSOC PROF HEMAT & ONCOL, DIV HEMAT & ONCOL, DEPT MED & ASSOC PROF, DEPT BIOCHEM, UNIV TENN, MEMPHIS, 85-, DIR, INVEST RES, HEMAT & ONCOL DIV, 95- *Personal Data:* b Kingsport, Tenn, Apr 1, 55; m 76, David; c 1. *Educ:* Univ Tenn, BA, 76, PhD(biochem), 83; Memphis State Univ, MS, 78. *Prof Exp:* Res fel, dept biochem, St Jude Children's Res Hosp, Memphis, Tenn, 83-84, Leon Journey fel, 84-85. *Concurrent Pos:* Young investr, Am Heart Asn, 85-87, estab investr, 91-96. *Mem:* AAAS; Soc Anal Cytol; Am Soc Hemat; Int Soc Thromb & Haem. *Res:* Structure and function of platelet membrane surface proteins and their role in thrombosis and hemostasis, particularly the mechanism by which platelet surface proteins mediate platelet aggregation and integrin signaling. *Mailing Add:* Dept Med Div Hemat/Oncol Univ Tenn 956 Court Ave Rm H335 Coleman Bldg Memphis TN 38163. *Fax:* 901-448-5854; *E-Mail:* ljennings@utmem1.utmem.edu

JENNINGS, MICHAEL LEON, TRANSPORT PHYSIOLOGY, MEMBRANE BIOCHEMISTRY. *Current Pos:* PROF, DEPT PHYSIOL & BIOPHYS, UNIV TEX MED BR, GALVESTON, 87- *Personal Data:* b Cleveland, Ohio, June 10, 48; m 76. *Educ:* Mass Inst Technol, SB, 70; Harvard Univ, PhD(biophysics), 76. *Prof Exp:* Fel, Max Planck Inst Biophysics, 77-78; asst prof physiol, Col Med, Univ Iowa, 78-87. *Mem:* Biophys Soc; Am Physiol Soc; Sigma Xi. *Res:* Structure and function of biological ion transport proteins, especially the inorganic anion transport protein of the erythrocyte membrane. *Mailing Add:* Dept Physiol & Biophys Univ Ark Med Sci Little Rock AR 72205. *Fax:* 501-686-8167

JENNINGS, PAUL C(HRISTIAN), CIVIL ENGINEERING, APPLIED MECHANICS. *Current Pos:* from asst prof to prof appl mech, Calif Inst Technol, 66-75, exec officer appl mech & eng, 75-79, chmn, Div Eng & Appl Sci, 85-89, vpres & provost, 89-95, actg vpres bus & finance, 95-96, PROF CIVIL ENG & APPL MECH, CALIF INST TECHNOL, 72- *Personal Data:* b Brigham City, Utah, May 21, 36; m 81, Millicent M Sivers; c Kathryn & Margaret. *Educ:* Colo State Univ, BS, 58; Calif Inst Technol, MS, 60, PhD(civil eng), 63. *Honors & Awards:* Walter Huber Res Prize, Am Soc Civil Engrs, 76, Nathan M Newmark Medal. *Prof Exp:* From instr to assoc prof mech, USAF Acad, 63-66. *Concurrent Pos:* Mem, eng panel, Nat Acad Sci Comt on Alaskan Earthquake, 65-; Erskine fel, Univ Canterbury, 70, 85; consult, Exxon Corp, Ertec Western Inc, AC Martin & Assocs & Stand Oil, Calif. *Mem:* Nat Acad Eng; Am Soc Civil Engrs; Seismol Soc Am (pres, 80); Earthquake Eng Res Inst (pres, 81-83); Am Soc Eng Educ; Am Geophys Union; fel AAAS; fel Am Acad Arts & Sci. *Res:* Structural dynamics and engineering seismology, especially response of structures to earthquake motion; earthquake engineering. *Mailing Add:* Mail Code 104-44 Calif Inst Technol Pasadena CA 91125

JENNINGS, PAUL HARRY, PLANT PHYSIOLOGY. *Current Pos:* head dept, 82-91, PROF, DEPT HORT, KANS STATE UNIV, 82- *Personal Data:* b Brockton, Mass, Jan 31, 38; m 60, Bette A Baker; c 3. *Educ:* Univ Mass, Amherst, BVA, 60; NC State Univ, MS, 62, PhD(plant physiol), 65. *Prof Exp:* Asst res plant physiol, Univ Calif, Davis, 67-69; from asst prof to assoc prof plant physiol, Univ Mass, Amherst, 69-82, secy fac senate, 80-82. *Mem:* Am Soc Plant Physiol; fel Am Soc Hort Sci; Sigma Xi. *Res:* Physiology of disease resistance; anabolic and catabolic pathways of carbohydrate metabolism as related to genetic potential, stage development and isozymic differences in plants; effects of low temperatures on germination and growth of crop plants susceptible to chilling injury. *Mailing Add:* Dept Hort Throckmorton Hall Kans State Univ Manhattan KS 66506. *Fax:* 785-532-6949

JENNINGS, PAUL W, organometallic chemistry, complex materials, for more information see previous edition

JENNINGS, RICHARD LOUIS, CIVIL ENGINEERING, APPLIED MECHANICS. *Current Pos:* Asst prof, 63-67, ASSOC PROF CIVIL ENG, UNIV VA, 67- *Personal Data:* b Newark, NJ, July 28, 33; m 56; c 2. *Educ:* Univ Ohio, BS, 56, BSCE, 57; Univ Ill, MS, 58, PhD(civil eng), 64. *Concurrent Pos:* Consult, Babcock & Wilcox Corp, Va. *Mem:* Am Soc Civil Engrs. *Res:* Earthquake and nuclear blast resistant design structures; mechanical vibrations of thin shells; structural design of large steerable radio telescopes; rehabilitation engineering; highway pavement analysis. *Mailing Add:* Dept of Civil Eng Thornton Hall Univ of Va Charlottesville VA 22903

JENNINGS, ROBERT BURGESS, PATHOLOGY, EXPERIMENTAL PATHOLOGY. *Current Pos:* Prof, 75-80, chmn dept, 75-89, JAMES B DUKE PROF PATH, MED SCH, DUKE UNIV, 80- *Personal Data:* b Baltimore, Md, Dec 14, 26; m 52; c Carol L, Mary G, John B, Anne E & James R. *Educ:* Northwestern Univ, BS, 47, MS & BM, 49, MD, 50; Am Bd Path, dipl, 54. *Honors & Awards:* Peter Harris Award, Int Soc Heart Res, 92; Distinguished Achievement Award, Soc CV Patho, 96. *Prof Exp:* Intern, Passavant Mem Hosp, Chicago, Ill, 49-50, resident path, 50-51; from instr to prof, Med Sch, Northwestern Univ, Ill, 53-69, Magerstadt prof path & chmn dept, 69-75. *Concurrent Pos:* Lab officer, US Navy, 51-53; attend physician, Vet Admin Res Hosp, Chicago, Ill, 55-69, consult physician, 69-75; pathologist, Community Hosp, Evanston, Ill, 57-67; Markle scholar, 58-63; vis scientist, Middlesex Hosp Med Sch, London, 61-62; mem path A study sect, USPHS, 60-65, mem, Cardiol Adv Comt, Nat Heart, Lung & Blood Inst, NIH, 78-82; attend physician & chief labs, Passavant Mem Hosp, 69-72; attend staff, Northwestern Mem Hosp, 72-75. *Mem:* Am Asn Pathologists; Soc Exp Biol & Med; Int Soc Heart Res (pres, 78-80); Am Soc Cell Biol; Am Heart Asn; Am Soc Nephrol. *Res:* Cardiovascular and renal disease; cell physiology; cell injury; electron microscopy; biology of experimental myocardial infarction; molecular mechanisms which cause the death of ischemic myocytes. *Mailing Add:* Dept Path Duke Univ Med Ctr Box 3712 Durham NC 27710. *Fax:* 919-684-4352

JENNINGS, VIVAN M, AGRICULTURAL RESEARCH. *Current Pos:* DEP ADMIN AGR, EXTEN SERV, USDA, 85- *Personal Data:* b Columbus Junction, Iowa, May 2, 36. *Educ:* Iowa State Univ, BS, MS, PhD(agron). *Prof Exp:* Prof plant path, weed & weed sci & exten specialist, Integrated Pest Mgt, Weed Control & Agron, Iowa State Univ; assoc dean & assoc dir, Iowa Exten Serv. *Concurrent Pos:* Interim assoc admin, Exten Serv, USDA, 89; interim sr exten adv, Polish Ministry Agr & Food Econ, 90. *Mem:* Am Soc Agron; Crop Sci Soc Am. *Res:* Integrated pest management; pesticide impact assessment; pesticide applicator training; urban gardening; farm safety and farmers with disabilities along with more traditional programs of farm management, marketing, crop and livestock production systems and agricultural engineering. *Mailing Add:* 5309 Dunleigh Ct Burke VA 22015. *E-Mail:* vjennings@esusda.gov

JENNINGS, WALTER GOODRICH, GAS CHROMATOGRAPHY. *Current Pos:* CONSULT, J & W SCI, 75- *Personal Data:* b Sioux, Iowa, Mar 2, 22; m 47; c 3. *Educ:* Univ Calif, BS, 50, MS, 52, PhD(agr chem), 54. *Honors & Awards:* Medal, Univ Bologna, 67; Medal, Fr Asn Agr Chemists, 71; Beckman Award in Gas Chromatog, 90; MJE Golay Award in Capillary Chromatography, 96. *Prof Exp:* Instr dairy indust, Univ Calif, Davis, 54-59, from asst prof to assoc prof food sci, 59-65, from jr chemist to assoc chemist, 54-65, prof food sci & chem exp sta, 65-89. *Concurrent Pos:* NIH sr scientist award, Vienna, Austria, 67-68; spec award sr Am scientist, Alexander von Humboldt Found, 73; consult, several indust firms; ed, J High Resolution Chromatography & Chromatography Commun, J Food Chem & Chemi, Mikrobiologie, Technologie der Lebensmittel; Founder of J & W Sci, Inc, Rancho Cordova, Calif. *Mem:* Am Chem Soc; hon mem Soc Flavor Chemists. *Res:* Isolation and characterization of trace volatiles; flavor chemistry; glass capillary gas chromatography; author of over 300 publications. *Mailing Add:* J & W Sci 91 Blue Ravine Rd Folsom CA 95630. *Fax:* 916-985-1101

JENNINGS, WILLIAM HARNEY, JR, biophysics, for more information see previous edition

JENNISON, DWIGHT RICHARD, SURFACE SCIENCE, ELECTRONIC STRUCTURE. *Current Pos:* mem tech staff, Solid State Theory Div, 77-80, SUPVR, CONDENSED MATTER THEORY DIV 1151, SANDIA NAT LAB, 81- *Personal Data:* b Teaneck, NJ, June 11, 43; m 68, Mary T Axness; c Amy, David & Matthew. *Educ:* Rensselaer Polytech Inst, BS, 65, MS, 73, PhD(physics), 74. *Prof Exp:* Res asst physics, Univ NDak, 69-70; teaching asst, Rensselaer Polytech Inst, 71, NIH trainee, 71-74; res assoc, Dept Physics & Mat Res Lab, Univ Ill, Urbana, 74-75, res asst prof physics, 76, assoc, 74-76. *Concurrent Pos:* Vis scientist, Univ Liverpool, UK, 83, 91, 92 & Tech Univ Munich, Ger, 85. *Mem:* Am Phys Soc; Am Vacuum Soc. *Res:* Electronic structure of solids, surfaces, clusters and molecules; theory of surface spectroscopies and electronically stimulated desorption; theory of high-temperature superconducting compounds. *Mailing Add:* Sandia Nat Labs PO Box 5800 M/S 1413 Albuquerque NM 87185-1413

JENNRICH, ELLEN COUTLEE, ANIMAL BEHAVIOR, ECOLOGY. *Personal Data:* b Kankakee, Ill, Dec 16, 39; m 71, Robert I; c Alison & Tamara. *Educ:* Wayne State Univ, BA, 60, MS, 62; Univ Calif, Los Angeles, PhD(zool), 66; Pac Lutheran Theological Sem, MDiv, 96. *Prof Exp:* Lectr biol, Mt St Mary's Col, 63-64; lectr, Univ Calif, Riverside, 66-68; lectr zool, Univ Calif, Los Angeles, 68-72; substitute teacher sci & biol, Westlake Sch, Los Angeles, 85-90. *Res:* Population biology of starlings; comparative breeding behavior of goldfinches, fluctuations in population size, avian communication, maintenance and agonistic behavior. *Mailing Add:* 3400 Purdue Ave Los Angeles CA 90066

JENNRICH, ROBERT I, STATISTICS. *Current Pos:* asst prof math & asst res statistician, 62-70, assoc prof math & biomath, 70-74, PROF MATH & BIOMATH, UNIV CALIF, LOS ANGELES, 74- *Personal Data:* b Milwaukee, Wis, Feb 11, 32. *Educ:* Univ Wis, BS, 54, MS, 56; Univ Calif, Los Angeles, PhD(math), 60. *Prof Exp:* Asst prof math, Univ Wis, 60-62. *Mem:* Am Statist Asn; Inst Math Statist. *Res:* Computer algorithms for data analysis; non-linear least squares, methods and statistical properties; factor analysis, rotation and maximum likelihood algorithms; analysis of variance, properties of the mixed model; time series analysis. *Mailing Add:* 3400 Purdue Ave Los Angeles CA 90066

JENNY, HANS K, ELECTRONIC & ELECTRICAL ENGINEERING. *Current Pos:* RETIRED. *Personal Data:* b Glarus, Switz, Sept 14, 19; nat US; m 49; c 3. *Educ:* Swiss Fed Inst Technol, MSEE, 43. *Prof Exp:* Asst prof & res engr, Swiss Fed Inst Technol, 43-46. *Mem:* Fel Inst Elec & Electronics Engrs. *Res:* Parametric amplifiers; variable capacitance and tunnel amplifiers; phase shifters; microwave laser modulators and detectors; microwave devices and systems; engineering organizations; technical information, including communications, publications and information systems. *Mailing Add:* 210 Riveredge Dr RD 1 Leola PA 17540

JENNY, NEIL ALLAN, PESTICIDE CHEMISTRY. *Current Pos:* GROUP LEADER PAPER CHEM, WITCO CORP, 93- *Personal Data:* b Milwaukee, Wis, Sept 6, 36; m 60; c 5. *Educ:* Univ Wis, BS, 58; Univ Kans, PhD(med chem), 63. *Prof Exp:* Res chemist, Polymer Div, Morton Chem Co, Ill, Sherex, 63-66, res chemist, Org Div, 66-69, contract mfg coordr, Div Schering Ag, 77-79, supvr anal res, Nor-Am Agr Prod, 69-85, sr res chemist, Berlin, 86-90, prod develop mgr, 90-92. *Mem:* Am Chem Soc; Am Pharmaceut Asn; Tech Asn Pulp & Paper Indust. *Res:* Resistance factors of crops; pesticide residue analytical methods; pesticide metabolism; effect of pesticide residues on environment; retail pharmacy; pesticide formulation; quality control; production and contract manufacturing; residue chemistry; paper chemistry; surfactant chemistry. *Mailing Add:* PO Box 1018 2001 Afton Rd Janesville WI 53545

JENS, WAYNE H(ENRY), MECHANICAL ENGINEERING & NUCLEAR ENGINEERING. *Current Pos:* PRES, JENS & JENS INC, 88- *Personal Data:* b Manitowoc, Wis, Dec 20, 21; m 46; c 4. *Educ:* Univ Wis, BS, 43; Purdue Univ, MS, 48, PhD(mech eng), 49. *Honors & Awards:* Gold Award, Eng Soc of Detroit, 78. *Prof Exp:* Eng designer, NAm Aviation, Inc, 43-44; eng asst heat transfer, Purdue Univ, 46-49; head eng anal group, Argonne Nat Lab, 49-53; proj leader & mgr, Nuclear Develop Corp Am, 53-57; gen mgr, Atomic Power Develop Assocs, Inc, 57-71; mgr eng & construct, Detroit Edison Co, 76-78, asst vpres eng & construct, 78-80, vpres nuclear oper, 80-86. *Concurrent Pos:* Mem bd trustees, Argonne Univ Asn, 77-; mem nuclear power div comn, Elec Power Res Inst, 78-; mem, Nuclear Training Accrediting Bd, Inst Nuclear Power Opers, 85-88. *Mem:* Fel Am Nuclear Soc; Am Soc Mech Engrs. *Res:* Boiling heat transfer; nuclear fuel irradiation stability; reactor design; nuclear operations and training. *Mailing Add:* 1220 Wild Azalea Pt Seneca SC 29678

JENSEN, ADOLPH ROBERT, ANALYTICAL CHEMISTRY. *Current Pos:* from asst prof to prof, 46-83, chmn dept, 56-71, EMER PROF CHEM, BALDWIN-WALLACE COL, 84- *Personal Data:* b Elmhurst, Ill, Apr 14,15; m 50, Nelle Williams; c Robert & Margaret. *Educ:* Wheaton Col, BS, 37; Univ Ill, MS, 40, PhD(anal chem), 42. *Prof Exp:* Asst chem, Wheaton Col, 37-38; asst anal chem, Univ Ill, 38-42; asst chemist & head anal chem sect, Aircraft Engine Res Lab, Nat Adv Comt Aeronaut, 42-46. *Concurrent Pos:* Consult, Stouffer Frozen Foods, Solon, Ohio, 65. *Mem:* AAAS; Am Chem Soc; Sigma Xi. *Res:* Analytical chemistry of foods; analytical chemistry of fuels and lubricants; instrumental methods of analysis. *Mailing Add:* 25527 Butternut Rd North Olmsted OH 44070-4505

JENSEN, ALBERT CHRISTIAN, ECOLOGY, MARINE ENVIRONMENTAL SCIENCE. *Current Pos:* CONSULT, COASTAL ENVIRON, ENVIRON ASSOCS, 77- *Personal Data:* b New York, NY, Jan 26, 24; m; c 4. *Educ:* State Univ NY Syracuse, BS, 51, MS, 54. *Honors & Awards:* George Washington Hon Medal, Freedoms Found, 73; Spec Sci Book Award, NY Acad Sci, 79. *Prof Exp:* Res biologist marine fisheries, US Fish & Wildlife Serv, Woods Hole, Mass, 54-65; managing ed marine sci, Marine Lab, Univ Miami, 65-67; asst dir coastal environ, NY State Dept Environ Conserv, 67-77. *Concurrent Pos:* Adv, Atlantic States Marine Fisheries Comn, Washington, DC, 67-80 & US Deleg to Int Comn Northwest Atlantic Fisheries, 72-75; asst prof, Grad Dept Marine Sci, C W Post Col, 75-77; prof, Cent Fla Community Col, 78- *Mem:* Nat Marine Educrs Asn; Am Inst Fishery Res Biologists; Fla Acad Sci. *Res:* Marine science education; coastal zone management; fisheries management. *Mailing Add:* Environ Assocs PO Box 223 Inglis FL 34449-0223

JENSEN, ARNOLD WILLIAM, ORGANIC CHEMISTRY, POLYMER CHEMISTRY. *Current Pos:* RETIRED. *Personal Data:* b Racine, Wis, Apr 30, 28; m 60, Marianne Shumate; c Mary K. *Educ:* Dana Col, Nebr, BA, 50; Okla State Col, PhD(chem), 58. *Prof Exp:* Res chemist, Dow Chem Co, Tex, 52-53; res assoc, Textile Fibers Dept, E I Du Pont de Nemours & Co, Inc, 58-92. *Mem:* AAAS; Am Chem Soc; Sigma Xi. *Res:* Nuclear magnetic resonance; infrared; synthetic fibers. *Mailing Add:* 213 Camellia Dr Charlottesville VA 22903-4208

JENSEN, ARTHUR SEIGFRIED, ELECTRONIC PHYSICS. *Current Pos:* RETIRED. *Personal Data:* b Trenton, NJ, Dec 24, 17; m 41, Lillian E Reed; c Deane Ellsworth, Alan F & Nancy L. *Educ:* Univ Pa, BS, 38, MS, 39, PhD(physics), 41; Westinghouse Sch Appl Eng Sci, dipl(advan eng technol) 72, dipl(comput sci), 77. *Prof Exp:* Lab asst physics, Univ Pa, 38-39; res physicist, Naval Res Lab, Washington, DC, 41 & RCA Labs, 45-57; mgr spec electron devices, Electronic Tube Div, Appl Res Dept, Westinghouse Elec Corp, 57-65, sr adv physicist, Defense & Electronics Ctr, 65-91, consult physicist, Electronic Systs, 91-94. *Concurrent Pos:* Instr physics, US Naval Acad, 41-46; Regist prof eng, Md, 66; vchmn, Md State Bd Prof Engrs, 79-86. *Mem:* AAAS; Am Phys Soc; Am Asn Physics Teachers; fel Inst Elec & Electronics Engrs; Nat Coun Eng Examrs; Sigma Xi; Soc Photo-Optical Instrumentation Engrs. *Res:* Solid state electro-optical imaging systems; imaging techniques and sensing devices; image quality and information theory; noise and image sensor detection limitations; electron optics and integrated circuits; infrared image sensors and systems; modeling solid state devices and systems; granted 25 US patents. *Mailing Add:* Chapel Gate 1104 Oak Crest Village 8820 Walther Blvd Parkville MD 21234

JENSEN, BETTY KLAINMINC, ENVIRONMENTAL POLICY, RISK COMMUNICATION. *Current Pos:* sr physicist, Pub Serv Elec & Gas Co, 76-79, prin physicist, 79-84, Nuclear & Environ Prog mgr, 84-88, FUELS & ENVIRON SCI MGR, PUB SERV ELEC & GAS CO, 88- *Personal Data:* b Poland, June 20, 49; US citizen; m 71; c 4. *Educ:* Brooklyn Col, BS, 70; Columbia Univ, NY, MS, 73, MPhil, 74, PhD(physics), 76; St Johns Univ, NY, MBA, 81. *Prof Exp:* Instr physics, City Univ NY, 73-76. *Concurrent Pos:* Adv, Elec Power Res Inst & Princeton Plasma Physics Lab, 77-, Mass Inst Technol, 78-89, Gas Cooled Res Assocs, 79-88, Off Technol Assessment, 82-84 & NJ Inst Technol, 89- *Mem:* Air & Waste Mgt Asn; AAAS; Inst Elec & Electronics Engrs; Am Phys Soc; Bioelectromagnetics Soc; Sigma Xi. *Res:* Environmental impact of electric power generation, transmission and distribution; risk communication; commercialization of new technologies. *Mailing Add:* 630 Armstrong Ave Staten Island NY 10308

JENSEN, BRUCE A, MATHEMATICS. *Current Pos:* assoc prof, 66-73, PROF MATH, PORTLAND STATE UNIV, 73-, DEPT CHMN, 86- *Personal Data:* b Spencer, Iowa, Aug 6, 30; m 51; c 2. *Educ:* Dana Col, BA, 52; Univ Wis-Madison, MS, 55; Univ Nebr-Lincoln, PhD(math), 66. *Prof Exp:* Instr math & physics, Dana Col, 55-58, asst prof math, 58-59; from asst prof to assoc prof, Nebr Wesleyan Univ, 59-66. *Mem:* Am Math Soc; Math Asn Am. *Res:* Algebraic semigroups; finiteness conditions on infinite semigroups; extensions of semigroups; decompositions of semigroups. *Mailing Add:* 59715 Kimberly Ct Bend OR 97702

JENSEN, BRUCE DAVID, pharmaceutical research & development, clinical diagnostic research & development, for more information see previous edition

JENSEN, BRUCE L, ORGANIC CHEMISTRY. *Current Pos:* asst prof, 73-78, ASSOC PROF CHEM, UNIV MAINE, ORONO, 78- *Personal Data:* b Three Rivers, Mich, Aug 6, 44; m 65; c 2. *Educ:* Western Mich Univ, BS, 66, PhD(org chem), 70. *Prof Exp:* Nat Cancer Inst fel, Univ Mich, Ann Arbor, 70-72; instr chem, Univ Maine, Orono, 72-73. *Concurrent Pos:* Sabbatical leave, Univ Southern Calif, 83-84. *Mem:* Am Chem Soc. *Res:* Organic synthesis; infrared, nuclear magnetic resonance and mass spectroscopy; heterocycles; natural products; medicinal chemistry; halonium ion chemistry; steroids; antineoplastic drugs; antiarrhythmic drugs. *Mailing Add:* Dept Chem Univ Maine Orono ME 04469

JENSEN, CLAYTON EVERETT, METEOROLOGY, COMPUTER SCIENCE. *Current Pos:* chmn, Blue Ribbon Citizens Task Force Qual Water, 88-90, LAND DEVELOP, CAPE CORAL, FLA, 83- *Personal Data:* b Hartford, Conn, Oct 23, 20; m 77, Judith Barrett; c Robby, David & Marc. *Educ:* Trinity Col, Conn, BS, 44; Mass Inst Technol, SM, 51, PhD(meteorol), 60. *Honors & Awards:* Gold Medal Award, Dept Comm, 72. *Prof Exp:* Chief eval & develop div, Hq, Air Weather Serv, 51-53, detachment comdr & staff weather officer, Air Force Cambridge Res Labs, 56-58, meteorol systs analyst, Strategic Air Command, 60-63; assoc prof math & dir comput ctr, Va Mil Inst, 63-65; chief supporting res group, Off Fed Coord Meteorol, Environ Sci Serv Admin, 65-69, chief fed plans & coord div, 69-71, chief environ monitoring div, Nat Oceanic & Atmospheric Admin, 71-73, dep assoc adminr, 73-75; consult & weather analyst, WINK TV, CBS, Ft Myers, 78-79, US Dept State, 80-84. *Concurrent Pos:* Lectr, Univ Omaha, 60-63; consult, Nat Environ Satellite Ctr, 64-65; chmn, Interdept Comt Appl Meteorol Res, 65-73 & Interdept Comt Meteorol Serv; observer, Interdept Comt Atmospheric Sci, Fed Coun Sci & Technol; fed coordr meteorol, Dept Com, 73-75; govt & acad consult. *Mem:* Am Meteorol Soc; Sigma Xi. *Res:* General circulation of the atmospheres; cloud physics; instrumentation for atmospheric electricity and airborne measurement of liquid water; satellite meteorology; computer education; global environmental research. *Mailing Add:* 4419 SE 20th Pl Cape Coral FL 33904. *Fax:* 941-542-1718; *E-Mail:* clayjensen@col.com

JENSEN, CRAIG LEEBENS, METALLURGY. *Current Pos:* SR SCI ASSOC, ALCOA TECH CO, 81- *Personal Data:* b Rochester, Minn, Dec 8, 50. *Educ:* Univ Minn, BS, 73; Iowa State Univ, PhD(metall), 77. *Prof Exp:* Asst prof mat sci, Univ Minn, 77-81. *Mem:* Am Soc Metals; Am Inst Mining, Metall & Petrol Engrs; Sigma Xi. *Res:* Transport properties of hydrogen in transition metals. *Mailing Add:* 102 Weir Dr Pittsburgh PA 15215

JENSEN, CREIGHTON RANDALL, SOIL PHYSICS. *Current Pos:* DIR, JENSEN INSTRUMENTS, 68- *Personal Data:* b Harlan, Iowa, Dec 27, 29; div. *Educ:* Calif State Polytech Col, BS, 56; Iowa State Univ, MS, 59, PhD(agron), 61. *Prof Exp:* Res asst soil physics, Iowa State Univ, 56-61; soil physicist, Univ Calif, Riverside, 62-63 & 64-67. *Mem:* Int Soc Soil Sci; Am Soc Agron; Soil Sci Soc Am. *Res:* Soil aeration. *Mailing Add:* 2021 S Seventh St Tacoma WA 98405-3014

JENSEN, CYNTHIA G, CELL BIOLOGY. *Current Pos:* sr lectr anat, 72-87, ASSOC PROF ANAT, SCH MED, UNIV AUCKLAND, 88- *Personal Data:* b Wheeling, WVa, Nov 7, 38; m 60, Lawrence C Winston; c Ellen & Kristen. *Educ:* Brown Univ, AB, 60; Univ Minn, PhD(zool), 66. *Prof Exp:* Res assoc biol, Univ Ore, 66-68; asst prof path, Univ Utah, 68-71. *Concurrent Pos:* Vis scientist, NY State Dept Health, Albany, 84-85 & 93. *Mem:* NZ Soc Electron Micros (vpres, 83-85, pres, 85-87); Am Soc Cell Biol; Australia & NZ Soc Cell Biol (NZ secy/treas, 86-, vpres, 90-); Anat Soc Australia N; Asia Pac Orgn Cell Biol (vpres, 94-). *Res:* Ultrastructural studies of cell division; microtubule structure and organization; cells exposed to anti-tumor drugs; neural cytoskeleton; asbestos in living cells. *Mailing Add:* Dept Anat Sch Med Univ Auckland Auckland New Zealand. *Fax:* 649-373-7484; *E-Mail:* cg.jensen@auckland.ac.nz

JENSEN, DAVID, MEDICAL PHYSIOLOGY. *Current Pos:* RETIRED. *Personal Data:* b San Francisco, Calif, Oct 14, 26; m 50, 70, Barbara J Mills; c Anita E & Phillip D. *Educ:* Univ Calif, Berkeley, BA, 48, MA, 50, PhD(physiol), 54. *Prof Exp:* Asst res physiol chemist, Sch Med, Univ Calif, Los Angeles & Vet Admin Hosp, 55-56, Am Heart Asn estab investr & res assoc, Scripps Inst, Univ Calif, 56-57; asst prof physiol, Med Ctr, Univ Colo, Denver, 67-71. *Concurrent Pos:* Los Angeles Co Heart Asn estab investr, Univ Calif, Los Angeles, 55-56, Riverside Co Heart Asn fel, 56-58 & San Diego Co Heart Asn res fel, 58-60; Am Heart Asn advan res fel, Scripps Inst, Univ Calif, 60-62, estab investr, 62-67; elected to Royal Soc Med, London, 70; sci author, 71- *Mem:* AAAS; Soc Gen Physiol; Roy Soc Med, London. *Res:* Basic mechanisms of cardiac automatism using electrophysiological techniques as well as biochemical approach; comparative physiological studies on a variety of species; intrinsic cardiac rate regulation; neuroanatomy; neurophysiology; theoretical explanation of bioenergetics at the quantum level. *Mailing Add:* 121 Arbor Dr Moab UT 84532-3226

JENSEN, DAVID JAMES, ANALYTICAL CHEMISTRY. *Current Pos:* RETIRED. *Personal Data:* b Racine, Wis, May 10, 35; m 56; c 5. *Educ:* Univ Wis-Milwaukee, BS, 58; Purdue Univ, MS, 65, PhD(biochem), 67. *Prof Exp:* Instr chem, Univ Wis-Milwaukee, 57-61; instr anal chem, Purdue Univ, 61-67; res chemist, Dow Chem USA, 67-84, sr lab supvr, 84-93; adj prof, Suginaw Valley State Univ, 93-96, assoc prof, 94-95. *Concurrent Pos:* State chemist, Ind, 61-67. *Mem:* Am Chem Soc; Sigma Xi. *Res:* Studies on pesticide residues; analysis of pesticide formulations and associated analytical methods development; priority pollutants analysis by GC/MS, product analysis, and industrial quality assurance. *Mailing Add:* 2218 Cranbrook Dr Midland MI 48640-3218

JENSEN, DONALD RAY, MATHEMATICAL STATISTICS. *Current Pos:* from asst prof to assoc prof, 65-73, PROF STATIST, VA POLYTECH INST & STATE UNIV, 73- *Personal Data:* b Nashville, Tenn, Apr 25, 32; m 64; c 4. *Educ:* Univ Tenn, BS, 55; Iowa State Univ, MS, 57, PhD(statist, soils), 62. *Prof Exp:* Asst prof statist, Ore State Univ, 62-65. *Concurrent Pos:* NIH career develop award, 67-72. *Mem:* Biomet Soc; Am Statist Asn; Am Inst Math Statist; Soc Indust Appl Math. *Res:* Probability inequalities; multivariate statistical analysis; multivariate distributions; simultaneous statistical inference; large-sample theory. *Mailing Add:* Dept of Statist Va Polytech Inst & State Univ Blacksburg VA 24061-0131

JENSEN, DONALD REED, MAMMALIAN PHYSIOLOGY, HISTOLOGY. *Current Pos:* RETIRED. *Personal Data:* b Pocatello, Idaho, May 4, 31; m 56, Brigitte Becker; c Linda, Donna & David. *Educ:* Idaho State Univ, BS, 53; Univ Wash, BA, 54; Utah State Univ, MS, 61, PhD(physiol), 64. *Prof Exp:* NIH fel, Inst Physiol Chem, Univ Cologne, 64-66; asst prof, Ill State Univ, 66-69, asst to chmn, Dept Biol Sci, 68-78, prof physiol, 69-93. *Mem:* Fel AAAS; Am Soc Zool; Sigma Xi. *Res:* Toxic effect of gossypol on physiological processes. *Mailing Add:* 1303 S Linden St Normal IL 61761

JENSEN, DOUGLAS ANDREW, ELEMENTARY PARTICLE PHYSICS. *Current Pos:* SCIENTIST, FERMI NAT ACCELERATION LAB, 90- *Personal Data:* b Muskegon, Mich, Oct 18, 40; m 65; c 2. *Educ:* Kalamazoo Col, AB, 63; Univ Chicago, MS, 65, PhD(physics), 70. *Prof Exp:* NSF fel, Joseph Henry Labs, Princeton Univ, 70-71, asst prof physics, 71-77; assoc prof physics, Univ Mass, Amherst, 77-90. *Mem:* Am Asn Physics Teachers; Am Phys Soc. *Res:* Elementary particle physics; weak interaction and symmetries; hadron production of strange and charmed particles. *Mailing Add:* 1515 Dunsten Rd Geneva IL 60134

JENSEN, EDWIN HARRY, FORAGE ALFALFA. *Current Pos:* RETIRED. *Personal Data:* b Phillips, Wis, Aug 29, 22; m 47; c 2. *Educ:* Univ Wis, BS, 49, MS, 50, PhD(agron & soil), 52. *Prof Exp:* Soil scientist, Soil Conserv Serv, USDA, 48-49; asst agronomist & asst prof agron, Univ Nev, 52-54; exten agronomist, Univ Minn, 54-56; assoc agronomist & assoc prof agron, Univ Nev, Reno, 56-64, prof agron & agronomist, 64-91. *Concurrent Pos:* Vis prof, People's Repub China, 83, Kyong Hee Univ, Seoul, Korea, 85 & Univ Seregia, Italy, 87. *Mem:* Am Soc Agron; Crop Sci Soc; Sigma Xi. *Res:* Forage crop management; forage quality; water use; alfalfa nodalation. *Mailing Add:* 100 N Arlington No 6J Reno NV 89501

JENSEN, ELWOOD VERNON, ENDOCRINOLOGY. *Current Pos:* Asst prof, Dept Surg, Univ Chicago, 47-51, from asst prof to assoc prof, Dept Biochem, 51-60, from asst prof to prof, Ben May Lab Cancer Res, 51-63, Am Cancer Soc-Charles Hayden Found res prof, Dept Physiol & Ben May Lab Cancer Res, 63-69, dir, Lab, 69-82, prof biophys, 73-82, prof physiol, 77-82, prof biochem & Chas B Huggins distinguished serv prof biol sci, 80-90, EMER PROF BIOL, UNIV CHICAGO, 90-; PROF, INST HORMONE & FERTIL RES, UNIV HAMBURG, 92- *Personal Data:* b Fargo, NDak, Jan 13, 20; m 41, 83, Hiltrud Herberg; c Karen C & Thomas E. *Educ:* Wittenberg Col, AB, 40; Univ Chicago, PhD(org chem), 44. *Hon Degrees:* DSc, Wittenberg Univ, 63, Acadia Univ, 76, Med Col Ohio, 91, MD, Univ Hamburg, 94. *Honors & Awards:* D R Edwards Medal, 70; La Madonnina Prize, 73; GHA Clowes Award, 75; Papanicolaou Award, 75; Prix Roussel, 76; Nat Award, Am Cancer Soc, 76; Amory Prize, 77; Gregory Pincus Mem Award, 78; Gairdner Award, 79; C F Kettering Prize, 80; Lucy Wortham James Award, 80; Nat Acad Clin Biochem Award, 81; Pharmacia Award, 82; Rolf Luft Medal, 83; Hubert Humphrey Award, 83, Renzo Grattavola Medal, 84, Fred Conrad Kuch Award, 84, Axel Munthe Award, 85, von Humboldt Sr Res Prize, 92, Joseph Bolivar DeLee Award, 95. *Concurrent Pos:* Guggenheim fel, Swiss Fed Inst Technol, 46-47; USPHS spec fel, 58; vis prof, Max Planck Inst, Munich, Ger, 58 & Kyoto Univ, 65; res dir, Ludwig Inst Cancer Res, Zurich, Switz, 83-87; scholar-in-residence, Fogarty Int Ctr, NIH, 88 & Med Col, Cornell Univ, 90-91. *Mem:* Nat Acad Sci; Am Acad Arts & Sci; Am Chem Soc; Am Soc Biol Chemists; Endocrine Soc (pres, 80-81); Am Asn Cancer Res; AAAS. *Res:* Steroid hormone receptors; breast cancer; proteins; organophosphorus chemistry; antihormone action. *Mailing Add:* Inst Hormone & Fertil Res Grandweg 64 22529 Hamburg Germany. *Fax:* 4942-5619-0864

JENSEN, EMRON ALFRED, PARASITOLOGY, PROTOZOOLOGY. *Current Pos:* RETIRED. *Personal Data:* b Richfield, Utah, Jan 5, 25; m 49; c 8. *Educ:* Utah State Univ, BS, 50, MS, 61, PhD(zool), 63. *Prof Exp:* Teacher high sch, Idaho, 50-52; technician, Am Cyanamid Co, 52-53; teacher elem sch, Utah, 54-59; lab instr zool, Utah State Univ, 59-63; from asst prof to prof, Weber State Col, 63-83, chmn dept, 70-83. *Res:* Parasite protozoa, particularly trichomonads. *Mailing Add:* 897 E 1700 N Ogden UT 84414-3117

JENSEN, ERIK HUGO, PHARMACEUTICAL QUALITY CONTROL. *Current Pos:* PRES, JENSEN ENTERPRISES, 86- *Personal Data:* b Fredericia, Denmark, June 27, 24; nat US; m 49, Alice Olesen; c Jan, Lisa & Linda. *Educ:* Royal Danish Sch Pharm, BSc, 45, MS, 48, PhD, 54. *Honors & Awards:* W E Upjohn Award, 62. *Prof Exp:* Res assoc, Upjohn Co, 50-56; head pharmaceut res & develop dept, Ferrosan Ltd, Malmo, Sweden, 56-57; res assoc pharm, Upjohn Co, 57-62, sect head qual control, 62-63, mgr, 63-66, asst dir qual control, 66-81, dir, 81-85, exec dir control develop & admin, 85-86. *Mem:* Am Chem Soc; Am Asn Pharmaceut Scientists. *Res:* Controlled release of pharmaceuticals; stability of pharmaceuticals; assays of pharmaceuticals; analytical applications of sodium borohydride; analytical chemistry; quality control procedures. *Mailing Add:* 2125 Crosswind Kalamazoo MI 49008-1734

JENSEN, GARY LEE, experimental nuclear physics; deceased, see previous edition for last biography

JENSEN, GARY RICHARD, DIFFERENTIAL GEOMETRY. *Current Pos:* fel, Washington Univ, St Louis, 69-70, from asst prof to assoc prof, 70-82, chmn dept, 90-95, PROF MATH, WASHINGTON UNIV, ST LOUIS, 83- *Personal Data:* b Miles City, Mont, Mar 19, 41; m 65, Jen Rivenes; c Ragna A, Niels G & Leah. *Educ:* Mass Inst Technol, BS, 63; Univ Calif, Berkeley, PhD(math), 68. *Prof Exp:* Asst prof math, Carnegie-Mellon Univ, 68-69. *Concurrent Pos:* Vis assoc prof math, Univ Calif, Berkeley, 76-77 & Univ Nancy, France, 82-83; vis prof, Math Res Inst, Berkeley, 93. *Mem:* Am Math Soc. *Res:* Differential geometry, especially of submanifolds of homogeneous spaces. *Mailing Add:* Math Dept Box 1146 Washington Univ St Louis MO 63130. *E-Mail:* gary@math.wustl.edu

JENSEN, GORDON D, PEDIATRICS, PSYCHIATRY. *Current Pos:* PROF PSYCHIAT & PEDIAT, SCH MED, UNIV CALIF, DAVIS, 69- *Personal Data:* b Seattle, Wash, Jan 28, 26; m 57; c 3. *Educ:* Yale Univ, MD, 49. *Prof Exp:* Asst prof pediat, Sch Med, Univ Wash, 57-60; res asst prof psychiat, 61-62, asst psychiat, 62-65, from asst prof to assoc prof, 65-69. *Concurrent Pos:* Mem core staff, Regional Primate Res Ctr, Univ Wash, 67-69; sr consult child psychiat, Sacramento Med Ctr, 69-74. *Mem:* Soc Biol Psychiat; Animal Behav Soc; Am Acad Pediat; Am Col Psychiat; Psychiat Res Soc. *Res:* Primate behavior; sexuality; aging. *Mailing Add:* 221 Monterey Ave Capitola CA 95010-3357

JENSEN, GORDON L, CLINICAL NUTRITION, INTERNAL MEDICINE. *Current Pos:* DIR, SECT NUTRIT SUPPORT, GEISINGER MED CTR, 88-, ASSOC, DEPT GASTROENTEROL & NUTRIT, 88-, RES ASSOC CRITICAL CARE MED, 90- *Personal Data:* b Columbia, Mo, May 29, 53. *Educ:* Pa State Univ, BS, 75; Univ NH, MS, 77; Cornell Univ, MD, 84, PhD(nutrit & biochem), 81. *Concurrent Pos:* Clin asst prof med, Jefferson Med Col, 89-; adj assoc prof nutrit, Pa State Univ, 90- *Mem:* Am Soc Clin Nutrit; Am Inst Nutrit; Am Soc Parenteral & Internal Nutrit; Am Col Physicians; Am Geriat Soc; AMA. *Mailing Add:* Dept Gastroenterol & Nutrit Geisinger Med Ctr Danville PA 17822-0001

JENSEN, HANNE MARGRETE, PRECANCER. *Current Pos:* asst prof, 69-79, ASSOC PROF PATH, DEPT PATH, SCH MED, UNIV CALIF, DAVIS, 79- *Personal Data:* b Copenhagen, Denmark, Dec 9, 35; US citizen; div; c 4. *Educ:* Univ Wash, MD, 61; Am Bd Path, cert anatomic & clin path, 68, cert blood banking, 79. *Prof Exp:* Fel exp path, Dept Path, Sch Med, Univ Wash, 65-67. *Concurrent Pos:* Mem Treatment Comt, Breast Cancer Task Force, Nat Cancer Inst, 77-81, prin investr, Contract Breast Cancer Task Force, 78-81. *Mem:* Am Asn Blood Banks; AAAS; Am Soc Clin Pathologists; Int Acad Path. *Res:* Assessment of precancer of breast parenchyma, using assays for angiogenesis factor; assays for breast fluids for angiogenesis factor; prediction of high cancer risk; morphologic studies of precancer of the prostate gland. *Mailing Add:* Dept Path Sch Med Univ Calif Davis CA 95616

JENSEN, HARBO PETER, POLYMER CHEMISTRY. *Current Pos:* govt affairs coordr, Chevron USA, 80-81, foreign staff adv, 81-90, mgr, Chevron Inst Oil Co, Calif, 90-93, VPRES INT TECH SERVS, CHEVRON CORP, 94- *Personal Data:* b Boston, Mass, Mar 27, 48; m 82, Tyna Diane Herring; c Sarah Elizabeth. *Educ:* Northeastern Univ, BA, 71; Mass Inst Technol, PhD(org chem), 74. *Prof Exp:* Polaroid Corp, 67-70; Chevron Res Co, Standard Oil Co Calif, 74-78, proj supvr, Huntington Beach Co, 78-80; pres, Timoc, 75-80. *Concurrent Pos:* Pres & chmn, Cal Bionics, 81- *Mem:* AAAS; Am Chem Soc; Sigma Xi; Contact Lens Mfrs Asn. *Res:* Petroleum science and synthetic fuels; polymer science, especially hydrophilic polymers for soft contact lenses. *Mailing Add:* Chevron Corp 555 Market St San Francisco CA 94105

JENSEN, HAROLD JAMES, NEMATOLOGY. *Current Pos:* RETIRED. *Personal Data:* b Sunnyside, Wash, Sept 16, 21; m 46; c 3. *Educ:* Univ Calif, BS, 47, PhD(nematol), 50. *Prof Exp:* Instr & asst, 50-51, from asst prof to prof bot & nematologist & from asst nematologist to nematologist, Ore State Univ, 51-84. *Concurrent Pos:* Consult, Hawaiian Sugar Planters Asn, 58. *Mem:* Am Phytopath Soc; Soc Nematol (vpres, 70-71, pres, 71-72). *Res:* Identification, symptomatology and pathology of plant diseases caused by nematodes; nematological control techniques, taxonomy, and teaching; relationships of nematodes with other plant pathogens. *Mailing Add:* 23619 Harris Rd Philomath OR 97370

JENSEN, J(OHN) H(ENRY), JR, CHEMICAL ENGINEERING. *Current Pos:* RETIRED. *Personal Data:* b Aurora, Ill, June 17, 16; m 48, Isabel Hora. *Educ:* SDak Sch Mines & Tech, BS, 39; Iowa State Univ, MS, 42, PhD(chem eng), 48. *Prof Exp:* Instr, Iowa State Univ, 40-48; sr chem engr, Tenn Eastman Co, 48-81. *Mem:* Instrument Soc Am. *Res:* Production of acetic anhydride; application of a digital computer to a chemical manufacturing process; process control by analog instruments or by digital computer; analog computing; interactive computer graphics system. *Mailing Add:* 4560 Old Stage Rd Kingsport TN 37664

JENSEN, JAMES LE ROY, nutrition, for more information see previous edition

JENSEN, JAMES LESLIE, biophysical organic chemistry; deceased, see previous edition for last biography

JENSEN, KEITH EDWIN, CANCER. *Current Pos:* RETIRED. *Personal Data:* b Council Grove, Kans, Sept 6, 24; m 43, Betty M Gardner; c Dennis M, Diana K (Marsh), Karen E (Manix) & Michael B. *Educ:* Univ Kans, AB, 48, MA, 49; Jefferson Med Col, PhD, 51. *Prof Exp:* Asst bacteriologist, State Bd Health, Kans, 49; asst instr, Univ Kans, 49; asst, Jefferson Med Col, 49-51; res assoc epidemiol, Univ Mich, 51-55, asst prof, 55-56; dir, Int Influenza Ctr, USPHS, 56-58; mgr, Respiratory Dis Sect, 58-61; asst dir, Biol Res, 61-65; dir virol, Pfizer Inc, 65-68, dir virol & oncol, Med Prod Res & Develop, 68-72, exec dir cancer res, 72-80, sr sci adv, 80-86; pres, Evergreen Cloning Nurseries, 83-93. *Res:* Epidemiology and immunology of mycoplasmal and viral respiratory diseases; viral oncology; interferon inducers; tumor immunology; cancer chemotherapy; chemical carcinogenesis; antimicrobiols; immunotherapeutics; rheumatology; micropropagation of plants. *Mailing Add:* 13844 N Sutherland Wash Way Tucson AZ 85737

JENSEN, KEITH FRANK, FORESTRY. *Current Pos:* ASST DIR, FOREST SERV, USDA, 92- *Personal Data:* b Fontanelle, Iowa, Apr 9, 38; m 60; c 3. *Educ:* Iowa State Univ, BS, 60, PhD(plant physio physiol, silvicult), 63. *Prof Exp:* Plant physiologist, Dis Div, US Forest Serv, 63-92. *Concurrent Pos:* Res fel, Univ Wis, 73-74. *Mem:* Bot Soc Am; Air Pollution Control Asn; Sigma Xi. *Res:* Effect of air pollution and environmental stresses on growth and development of forest trees. *Mailing Add:* USDA Forest Serv 5 Radnor Corp Ctr Suite 200 Radnor PA 19087-4585

JENSEN, KLAVS FLEMMING, SYNTHESIS & PROCESSING OF ADVANCED INORGANIC MATERIALS MATHEMATICAL MODELLING OF MATERIALS PROCESSING SYSTEMS. *Current Pos:* PROF CHEM ENG & MAT SCI, MASS INST TECHNOL, 89- *Personal Data:* b Cambridge, UK, Aug 5, 52; US citizen. *Educ:* Tech Univ Denmark, MSc, 76; Univ Wis-Madison, PhD(chem eng), 80. *Honors & Awards:* Presidential Young Investers Award, NSF, 84; Allan P Colburn Award, Am Inst Chem Engrs, 87, CMA Stine Award. *Prof Exp:* From asst prof to prof chem eng, Univ Minn, Twin Cities, 80-89. *Concurrent Pos:* Fel, Minn Supercomput Inst, 86-89; John Simon Guggenheim fel, 87. *Mem:* Am Inst Chem Engr; Am Chem Soc; Mat Res Soc; Electrochem Soc; AAAS. *Res:* Processing and characterization of advanced inorganic materials, including chemical vapor deposition of semiconductors and metals, laser assisted processing and fabrication of inorganic composites; synthesis and characterization, as well as mathematical models. *Mailing Add:* Mass Inst Technol Rm 66-566 Cambridge MA 02139

JENSEN, LEO STANLEY, ANIMAL NUTRITION. *Current Pos:* prof poultry sci, 73-84, D W Brooks distinguished prof, 84-91, D W BROOKS DISTINGUISHED EMER PROF, UNIV GA, 91- *Personal Data:* b Bellingham, Wash, Feb 28, 25; m 54, Sylvia; c Peter, Eric, Carol & Kristin. *Educ:* Wash State Univ, BS, 49; Cornell Univ, PhD(animal nutrit), 54. *Honors & Awards:* AFMA Award, Poultry Sci Asn, 66; Merck Award, Poultry Sci Asn, 79. *Prof Exp:* Jr poultry scientist, Wash State Univ, 49-51, from asst prof to prof poultry sci, 54-73, chmn grad prog nutrit, 70-73. *Concurrent Pos:* Oak Ridge Inst Nuclear Studies res partic, AEC, Univ Tenn, 64-65. *Mem:* Poultry Sci Asn; Am Inst Nutrit; Soc Exp Biol & Med. *Res:* Vitamins, minerals, fatty acids and unidentified factors in poultry nutrition; nutritional factors affecting abdominal fat accumulation; amino acid requirements and interactions. *Mailing Add:* Dept Poultry Sci Univ Ga Athens GA 30602. *Fax:* 706-542-1827

JENSEN, LYLE HOWARD, BIOPHYSICAL CHEMISTRY. *Current Pos:* actg asst prof, 47-48, Anderson fel x-ray diffraction, 48-49, from instr to assoc prof anat, 49-61, PROF ANAT, UNIV WASH, 61- *Personal Data:* b East Stanwood, Wash, Nov 24, 15; m 40; c 3. *Educ:* Walla Walla Col, BA, 39; Univ Wash, PhD(phys chem), 43. *Prof Exp:* Res assoc, Univ Chicago, 43-44; assoc prof chem, Emmanuel Missionary Col, 44-46; res assoc, Ohio State Univ, 46-47. *Mem:* AAAS; Am Chem Soc; Am Crystallog Asn; Am Asn Anat; Sigma Xi. *Res:* Chemistry of heavy metals; low temperature thermodynamics of gases; molecular structure; x-ray diffraction studies of biologically important molecules. *Mailing Add:* Dept Biol Struct & Biochem SM-20 Univ Wash Seattle WA 98195-0001. *Fax:* 206-543-1524

JENSEN, MARCUS MARTIN, MEDICAL MICROBIOLOGY. *Current Pos:* from assoc prof to prof, 69-94, EMER PROF MICROBIOL, BRIGHAM YOUNG UNIV, 94- *Personal Data:* b Mantua, Utah, May 26, 29; m 90, Mary Davis; c Joni, Mark & Bruce. *Educ:* Utah State Univ, BS, 52, MS, 54; Univ Calif, Los Angeles, PhD(med microbiol), 61. *Hon Degrees:* Dr, Utah State Univ, 91. *Honors & Awards:* George N Raines Award, Am Psychiat Asn, 62. *Prof Exp:* Res virologist, Res Serv, Vet Admin Ctr, 61-63; asst prof med microbiol, Sch Med, Univ Calif, Los Angeles, 63-69. *Concurrent Pos:* Assoc mem, Brain Res Inst, Med Sch, Univ Calif, Los Angeles, 68-69; pres, Robbins Aseptic Air Systs Inc, Calif, 68-69 & Jensen Res Labs, Utah, 69- *Mem:* Am Soc Microbiol; Am Asn Avian Pathologists. *Res:* Natural resistance to infectious diseases, influence of emotional stress on suscepsusceptibility to viral infections; role of viruses in kidney diseases; methods of controlling the airborne spread of microorganisms in hospitals; development of vaccines for turkey diseases. *Mailing Add:* 1276 E 2300 N Brigham Young Univ Provo UT 84604

JENSEN, MARVIN E(LI), AGRICULTURAL ENGINEERING. *Current Pos:* RETIRED. *Personal Data:* b Clay Co, Minn, Dec 23, 26; m 47, Doris A Lundberg; c Connie, Jeffrey & Eric. *Educ:* NDak State Univ, BS, 51, MS, 52; Colo State Univ, PhD, 65. *Hon Degrees:* DSc, NDak State Univ, 88. *Honors & Awards:* Huber Res Prize, Am Soc Civil Engrs, 68, R J Tipton Award, 82; Hancor Soil & Water Eng Award, Am Soc Agr Engrs, 74, John Deere Medal Award, 82; Arid Lands Hydraul Eng Award, Am Soc Civil Engrs, 90. *Prof Exp:* Asst, NDak State Univ, 51-52, instr & asst agr engr, 52-54, asst prof agr eng & asst agr engr, 54-55; agr eng, Agr Res Serv, USDA, 55-59, invests leader irrig, drainage & water storage facil, 59-61, invests leader water mgt, Northwest Br, 61-69, dir, Snake River Conserv Res Ctr, Sci & Educ Admin, 69-79, nat prog leader, Water Mgt, 79-87; dir, Colo Inst Irrig Mgt, 87-92. *Concurrent Pos:* Pres, Int Comn Irrig & Drainage, 84-87. *Mem:* Nat Acad Eng; hon mem Am Soc Civil Engrs; AAAS; Am Soc Agron; Am Soc Agr Engrs (vpres, 83-86). *Res:* Irrigation engineering research; crop water requirement and irrigation scheduling; irrigation management. *Mailing Add:* 1207 Springwood Dr Ft Collins CO 80525

JENSEN, MEAD LEROY, ECONOMIC GEOLOGY. *Current Pos:* PROF GEOL & GEOPHYS, UNIV UTAH, 65- *Personal Data:* b Salt Lake City, Utah, June 11, 25; m 47, Lou D Davis; c Robert, Pamela, Patricia, Janice & Joseph. *Educ:* Univ Utah, BS, 48; Mass Inst Technol, PhD(geol), 51. *Honors & Awards:* Sr Scientist Award, Australian Acad Sci, 62. *Prof Exp:* From instr to assoc prof geol, Yale Univ, 51-64, dir grad studies, 64-65. *Concurrent Pos:* Lectr, Andhra Univ, India, 55; sr scientist, Australian Acad Sci, 57; hon lectr, Sigma Xi, 67. *Mem:* Fel Geol Soc Am; Am Inst Mining, Metall & Petrol Eng; Am Geophys Union; Soc Petrol Eng; Mineral Soc Am. *Res:* Isotopic and economic geology, metallic, nonmetallic and petroleum; exploration geology. *Mailing Add:* 1354 Ambassador Way Salt Lake City UT 84108

JENSEN, NORMAN P, MEDICINAL CHEMISTRY. *Current Pos:* VPRES CHEM, JACOBUS PHARMACEUT, 96- *Personal Data:* b Pontiac, Mich, Dec 12, 38; m 65, Sara L Moeller; c Marshall, Mitchell & Christine. *Educ:* Univ Mich, BS, 61; Mass Inst Technol, PhD(org chem), 65. *Prof Exp:* Res chemist, Socony Mobil, 61; NIH fel org chem, Stanford Univ, 65-66; dir, Merck & Co, 66-83; asst vpres, Wyeth-Ayerst, 83-95. *Concurrent Pos:* Exec Comt, Organic Div, Am Chem Soc, 95- *Mem:* Am Chem Soc; AAAS; Inflamation Res Asn. *Res:* Search for new drugs in the fields of cardiovascular, anti-inflammatory, metabolic and central nervous system diseases. *Mailing Add:* 119 Linwood Circle Princeton NJ 08540

JENSEN, PAUL ALLEN, OPERATIONS RESEARCH, ELECTRICAL ENGINEERING. *Current Pos:* from asst prof to assoc prof, 67-73, PROF MECH ENG, UNIV TEX, AUSTIN, 73- *Personal Data:* b Chicago, Ill, Aug 27, 36; m 63; c 4. *Educ:* Univ Ill, BS, 59; Univ Pittsburgh, MS, 63; Johns Hopkins Univ, PhD(opers res), 67. *Prof Exp:* Engr, Surface Div, Westinghouse Elec Corp, 59-63. *Mem:* Opers Res Soc Am; Inst Mgt Sci; Inst Indust Eng. *Res:* Mathematical optimization theory and application; network flow techniques used for optimization; reliability engineering; transportation systems; water resources. *Mailing Add:* Dept of Mech Eng Univ of Tex Austin TX 78712

JENSEN, PAUL EDWARD T, SYSTEMS ANALYSIS, OPERATIONS RESEARCH. *Current Pos:* SR STAFF ENG SYSTEM, ESL INC, 82- *Personal Data:* b New Orleans, La, Apr 27, 26; m 53; c 3. *Educ:* Tulane Univ, BS, 47, BBA, 49; Golden Gate Univ, MBA, 75. *Prof Exp:* Asst mgr, Atlantic Gulf Sugar Co, Cuba, 52-55; sr engr, Electronic Defense Labs, GTE Prod Corp, 55-59, develop engr, 59-60, supvr tech pub, 60-63, mgr tech pub, 63-64, eng specialist, 64-76, sr eng specialist, 76-82. *Concurrent Pos:* Consult, Asn Continuing Educ, Stanford, Calif, 74-82, Stanford Univ, 77-79 & GTE Prod Corp, 80-82; lectr, Cogswell Col, San Francisco, 79-; lectr, Northwestern Polytech Univ, Fremont, CA, 88- *Mem:* Am Phys Soc; Inst Elec & Electronics Engrs; assoc fel Soc Tech Comm. *Res:* Systems analysis of tactical and strategic communications and electronics systems; electronic warfare vulnerability analysis. *Mailing Add:* 1191 Bruckner Circle Mountain View CA 94040-4562

JENSEN, PETER S, CHILD PSYCHIATRY. *Current Pos:* CHIEF, CHILD ADOLESCENT DIS RES BR, DIV CLIN & TREATMENT RES, NIMH, NIH, 89-, ASSOC DIR CHILDREN'S RES, 97- *Personal Data:* b Logan, Utah, Nov 14, 49; m73, Susie Cornelia. *Educ:* Brigham Young Univ, BS, 74; George Washington Univ, MD, 78. *Honors & Awards:* Joyce Res Award, 82; Reiger McGavin Award, Am Psychiat Asn, 96; Agnes Purcell. *Prof Exp:* Asst chief, Child Adolescent & Family Psychiat Serv, Eisenhower Army Med Ctr, 83-86, chief, 85-88; res psychiatrist, Med Ctr, Walter Reed Army Inst Res, 88-89. *Concurrent Pos:* Dir fel training, Eisenhower Army Med Ctr, 86-88; chair, Task Force Prev Substance Abuse, 87-88; mem, Coun Res, Am Psychiat Asn. *Mem:* Am Pediat Asn; Am Acad Child & Adolescent Psychiat (secy); Soc Biol Psychiat; Int Soc Res Child & Adolescent Psychopath; Sigma Xi; AAAS. *Res:* child & adolescent clinical trials for psychiatric disorders; attention deficit hyperativity disorder; psychiatric epidemiology; diagnosis and classification. *Mailing Add:* Div Clin & Treatment Res NIMH 5600 Fisher's Lane Rm 18C17 Rockville MD 20857. *E-Mail:* pjensen@nih.gov

JENSEN, RANDOLPH A(UGUST), CHEMICAL ENGINEERING, POLLUTION CONTROL. *Current Pos:* PRES, JENSEN CONSULT INC, 79- *Personal Data:* b Cottonwood, Minn, May 25, 19; m 42, Mary Elizabeth Jacobs; c Marilee Dawn (Heydt), Randi Jean (Butler) & Scott Daniel. *Educ:* Univ Minn, BChE, 40; Univ Iowa, MSChE, 46. *Prof Exp:* Res chem engr, Cliffs Dow Chem Co, Mich, 40-42; proj engr, eng exp sta, Pa State Col, 42-43; res assoc, Inst Hydrol Res, Univ Iowa, 43-46; proj engr, US Govt Synthetic Rubber Labs, Ohio, 46-47; res engr, Battelle Mem Inst, 47-51; chem engr, Houston Plant, Rohm & Haas Co Inc, 51-62, chief chem engr, Louisville Plant, 62-71, pollution control mgr, 71-79. *Concurrent Pos:* Mem, Nat Adv Comt Aeronaut, 42-43. *Mem:* Am Inst Chem Engrs. *Res:* Fluid flow low and high velocity gas streams; chemical plant process improvement; air and water pollution control; solid waste disposal; numerous publications on air and water pollution control, electropolishing, heat transfer and crystallization. *Mailing Add:* Jensen Consult Inc PO Box 43079 Louisville KY 40243

JENSEN, REED JERRY, PHYSICAL CHEMISTRY. *Current Pos:* staff mem phys chem, Los Alamos Nat Lab, 69-72, group leader chem lasers, 72-76, alt div leader laser chem, 76-89, dep assoc dir, Chem & Mat, 89-93, STAFF MEM, LOS ALAMOS NAT LAB, 93- *Personal Data:* b Dec 16, 36; m 60, Nancy G Payne; c Grace, Julie, Ellen, Stuart, Grant & Ann. *Educ:* Brigham Young Univ, BA, 60, PhD(phys chem), 65. *Prof Exp:* Fel phys chem, Univ Calif, Berkeley, 65-66; staff mem, Los Alamos Sci Lab, 66-67; asst prof, Brigham Young Univ, 67-69. *Mem:* Am Chem Soc. *Res:* Research in lasers and applications to chemistry; chemical separations with lasers and modern methods; chemical process development for nuclear systems and transmutation processes. *Mailing Add:* 121 La Vista Los Alamos NM 87544-3436. *Fax:* 505-665-4631

JENSEN, RICHARD ALAN, MACHINE DESIGN, MATERIALS TESTING. *Current Pos:* ASSOC PROF ENG, HOFSTRA UNIV, 89- *Personal Data:* m 71, Betty Klainminc; c David J, Sandra R, Andrew M & Penelope J. *Educ:* Cooper Union, BE, 66; Columbia Univ, MS, 67, Eng, 75; St Johns Univ, MBA, 83. *Prof Exp:* Mech engr, Burns & Roe, 73-79, prin engr, 79-89. *Mem:* Am Soc Mech Engrs; Am Phys Soc; AAAS; Am Vacuum Soc; NY Acad Sci; Sigma Xi. *Res:* Nondestructive testing of polyethylene gas piping and in the end use of natural gas. *Mailing Add:* 630 Armstrong Ave Staten Island NY 10308-1939. *Fax:* 516-463-6010

JENSEN, RICHARD ARTHUR, pharmacology, for more information see previous edition

JENSEN, RICHARD DONALD, VETERINARY PATHOLOGY. *Current Pos:* Res fel path, 70-76, DIR TOXICOL & PATH, MERCK INST THERAPEUT RES, MERCK & CO, INC, 77- *Personal Data:* b Hartington, Nebr, Oct 6, 36; m 57; c 4. *Educ:* Iowa State Univ, DVM, 64; Univ Minn, St Paul, PhD(vet path), 70. *Mem:* Am Col Vet Path; Int Acad Path; Am Vet Med Asn. *Res:* Avian mycoplasma infection; toxicologic and pathologic evaluation of potential therapeutic agents. *Mailing Add:* 463 Ferry Rd Doylestown PA 18901

JENSEN, RICHARD ERLING, ANALYTICAL CHEMISTRY, TOXICOLOGY. *Current Pos:* DIR & PRES, FORENSIC ASSOCS, 84-; DIR FORENSIC TOXICOL, MEDTOX LABS. *Personal Data:* b Des Moines, Iowa, Apr 3, 38; m 60; c 2. *Educ:* Iowa State Univ, BS, 60; Univ Iowa, MS, 64, PhD(anal chem), 65. *Prof Exp:* Asst prof anal chem, Mankato State Col, 65-66; from asst prof to assoc prof, Gustavus Adolphus Col, 66-79; supvr, Alcohol Sect, Forensic Sci Lab, State of Minn, 79-80, asst dir, 80-84. *Mem:* Am Chem Soc; Am Acad Sci; Sigma Xi. *Res:* Alcohol and drug analysis for evidential purposes; trace analysis of metals using spectrophotometry, fluorescence and atomic absorption. *Mailing Add:* Forensic Assocs 4690 Ids Ctr Consult Lab Servs Minneapolis MN 55402

JENSEN, RICHARD EUGENE, PHYSICS. *Current Pos:* RETIRED. *Personal Data:* b Unity, Sask, June 30, 27; US citizen; m 63. *Educ:* Univ Sask, BS, 49, MS, 52; Ariz State Univ, PhD(physics), 66. *Prof Exp:* Proj engr physics, Motorola Inc, 56-59 & Nuclear Corp Am, 59-63; res physicist, Naval Surface Weapons Ctr, 67-89; assoc prin engr, Sverdrup Technol, 89-93. *Mem:* Am Phys Soc; Optical Soc Am; Inst Elec & Electronics Engrs. *Res:* Lasers and optical propagation. *Mailing Add:* 7520 N Thornwood Rd Tucson AZ 85741

JENSEN, RICHARD GRANT, BIOCHEMISTRY, METABOLISM IN PLANTS. *Current Pos:* RETIRED. *Personal Data:* b Los Angeles, Calif, Apr 16, 36; m 61, Annette Anderson; c Karl, Jennifer, Byron & Bruce. *Educ:* Brigham Young Univ, BA, 61, PhD(biochem), 65. *Prof Exp:* Chas F Kettering res fel biochem, Chas F Kettering Res Lab, Ohio, 63-65; NIH fel, Lawrence Radiation Lab, Univ Calif, 65-67; from asst prof to assoc prof biochem, Univ Ariz, 67-79, assoc prof plant sci, 76-79, prof biochem & plant sci, 79-97. *Concurrent Pos:* Vis prof, Chem Inst Tech Univ Munich, Freising-Weihens Tephan, WGer, 74-75; vis prof, Bot Inst, Univ Bern, Switz, 75; consult, Agr Div, Monsanto Co, 76; prog dir, Photosynthesis Prog, Competitive Res Grants Off, Sci & Educ Admin, USDA, 81. *Mem:* Am Soc Biol Chemists; Am Soc Plant Physiol; fel AAAS. *Res:* Cell biology and metabolism; photosynthesis; metabolic regulation in plant cells; carbon dioxide fixation; metabolism of plants during salt and water stress, plant cyclitols and polyols. *Mailing Add:* Dept Biochem Univ Ariz Tucson AZ 85721. *Fax:* 520-621-9288

JENSEN, RICHARD HARVEY, ANATOMY, IMMUNOLOGY. *Current Pos:* MEM STAFF PROG PHYS THER, MARQUETTE UNIV, 77- *Personal Data:* b Estherville, Iowa, June 14, 41; m; c 2. *Educ:* Univ Northern Iowa, BA, 63; Univ Iowa, MA, 69, PhD(anat), 73. *Prof Exp:* Instr math & sci, Charles City High Sch, Iowa, 63-66; clin phys therapist, Univ Iowa, 67-68, from teaching asst to instr gross anat, 69-73; grant seed res, Univ Nebr Med Ctr, Omaha, 73-75, asst prof gross anat, 73-77. *Concurrent Pos:* Vis instr gross anat, Univ Miami, 72; consult design & orgn gross anat prog phys ther, Fla Int Univ, 73. *Mem:* Am Phys Ther Asn; Am Asn Anatomists; Am Col Sports Med. *Res:* Hematology, especially stimulation of bone marrow; biomechanics, with emphasis on kinetic and kinematic analysis of extremities. *Mailing Add:* Phys Ther Prog Rm 346 Marquette Univ Walter Schroeder Complex Milwaukee WI 53233

JENSEN, RICHARD JORG, SYSTEMATIC BOTANY. *Current Pos:* PROF BIOL, ST MARYS COL, 79- *Personal Data:* b Erie Co, Ohio, Jan 17, 47; m 70. *Educ:* Austin Peay State Univ, BS, 70, MS, 72; Miami Univ, PhD(bot), 75. *Prof Exp:* Asst prof biol, Wright State Univ, 75-79. *Concurrent Pos:* NSF res grant, 73, 78, 84, & 87; Sigma Xi grant in aid of res, 74; guest assoc prof biol, Univ Notre Dame, 81-; res corp grant, 84; elected fel, Ind Acad Sci, 86; sr res fel, APSU Ctr Field Biol, 86-87; dir, Greene-Nieuwland Herbarium, 89-; Lilly Found grant, 90. *Mem:* Torrey Bot Club; Int Asn Plant Taxon; Bot Soc Am; Sigma Xi; Am Soc Plant Taxonomists; Soc Syst Zool. *Res:* Systematic and taxonomic studies of Quercus, the oaks, emphasizing numerical taxonomic and morphometric approaches. *Mailing Add:* Dept Biol St Marys Col Notre Dame IN 46556

JENSEN, ROBERT ALAN, NEUROBIOLOGY, PSYCHOBIOLOGY. *Current Pos:* asst prof, 81-83, ASSOC PROF, DEPT PSYCHOL, SOUTHERN ILL UNIV, CARBONDALE, 83-, ASSOC DEAN, COL LIBERAL ARTS, 88-, ASSOC PROF, SCH MED, 89- *Personal Data:* b Bainbridge, NY, Sept 25, 40; m 85, Melissa Hall; c Rebecca A. *Educ:* Col Wooster, Ohio, BA, 65; Kent State Univ, MA, 70; Northern Ill Univ, PhD(biopsychol), 76. *Prof Exp:* Instr psychol, Kent State Univ, 68-71; asst res psychobiologist, Univ Calif, Irvine, 76-81. *Concurrent Pos:* Fel, Univ Calif, Irvine, 75-78; managing ed, Behav & Neural Biol, 78-81; consult, G D Searle Co, Skokie, Ill, 83-85; prin investr res grant, R J Reynolds Tobacco Co, Office Naval Res. *Mem:* AAAS; Int Soc Develop Psychobiol; Soc Neurosci; Sigma Xi. *Res:* Neurobiological aspects of memory modulation; role of catecholamine and opioid systems in the modulation of learning and memory; electrophysical correlates of neural plasticity; neurobiological basis of smoking behavior and alcohol consumption. *Mailing Add:* Southern Ill Univ Carbondale IL 62901. *Fax:* 618-453-3253; *E-Mail:* ga3614@siucvmb.bitnet

JENSEN, ROBERT GORDON, MILK LIPIDS. *Current Pos:* from asst prof to prof dairy mfg, 56-70, prof nutrit sci, 70-90, EMER PROF, UNIV CONN, 91- *Personal Data:* b Carthage, Mo, Jan 2, 26; m 47, Helene C Wickstrom; c Gordon L & Jeffrey A. *Educ:* Univ Mo, BS, 50, MS, 51, PhD(dairy bact), 54. *Honors & Awards:* Macy-Gyorgy Award, Int Soc Res Human Milk Lactation. *Prof Exp:* From instr to asst prof dairy bact, Univ Mo, 54-56. *Mem:* Hon fel Int Soc Res Human Milk & Lactation; Am Oil Chem Soc; Am Dairy Sci Asn; Am Inst Nutrit. *Res:* Human milk lipids; bovine milk lipids. *Mailing Add:* Univ Conn Dept Nutrit Sci 186 Chafferville Rd Storrs CT 06268-2637. *Fax:* 860-486-3674

JENSEN, RONALD HARRY, BIOPHYSICAL CHEMISTRY, CYTOCHEMISTRY. *Current Pos:* PROF LAB MED, UNIV CALIF, SAN FRANCISCO, 92- *Personal Data:* b Chicago, Ill, Nov 25, 38; m 58, Judith Miller; c 3. *Educ:* Lawrence Col, BS, 60; Calif Inst Technol, PhD(chem), 64. *Prof Exp:* Res fel biol, Calif Inst Technol, 64-67; res scientist molecular biol, Int Minerals & Chem Corp, 67-69; sr investr microbiol, Smith Kline & French Labs, 70-74; life scientist biol & med, Lawrence Livermore Nat Lab, 75-79,sect leader cytochem, 79-91. *Mem:* Soc Anal Cytol; AAAS; Am Asn Cancer Res. *Res:* Fluorescent probes of cellular structure and the use of flow and image cytometry of stained cells or chromosomes to study mutagenesis and carcinogenesis; molecular genetics of prostate cancer; molecular cytometry. *Mailing Add:* Dept Lab Med Univ Calif PO Box 0808 San Francisco CA 94143-0808. *Fax:* 415-476-8218; *E-Mail:* jensen@cc.ucsf.edu

JENSEN, ROY A, MICROBIOLOGY, BIOCHEMISTRY. *Current Pos:* PROF MICROBIOL & CELL SCI, UNIV FLA, 86- *Personal Data:* b Racine, Wis, Apr 8, 36; m 56; c 5. *Educ:* Ripon Col, BA, 58; Univ Tex M D Anderson Hosp & Tumor Inst, PhD(biochem, genetics), 63. *Prof Exp:* Res instr, Sch Med, Univ Wash, 65; asst prof biol, State Univ NY, Buffalo, 66-68; assoc prof microbiol, Baylor Col Med, 68-73; prof biol, Univ Tex M D Anderson Hosp & Tumor Inst Houston, 73-76; prof biol, State Univ NY, Binghamton, 76-86, dir Ctr Somatic-Cell Genetics & Biochem, 78-86. *Concurrent Pos:* USPHS fel microbiol, Sch Med, Univ Wash, 64-66. *Mem:* Am Soc Microbiol; Tissue Cult Asn. *Res:* Biochemical genetics; gene-enzyme relationships; regulation of gene and enzyme activities; metabolic interlock; plant tissue culture. *Mailing Add:* Dept Microbiol & Cell Sci Univ Fla Gainesville FL 32611

JENSEN, RUE, VETERINARY PATHOLOGY. *Current Pos:* RETIRED. *Personal Data:* b Vermillion, Utah, Oct 24, 11; m 42; c 2. *Educ:* Utah State Univ, BS, 37, MS, 39; Colo State Univ, DVM, 42; Univ Minn, PhD, 53; Kasetsart Univ, Bangkok, DVSc, 65. *Prof Exp:* Instr vet sci, La State Univ, 42-43; from asst prof to prof path, Colo State Univ, 43-48, dir, Diag Lab, 73-77. *Concurrent Pos:* From asst pathologist exp sta to pathologist chief sta, Colo State Univ, 43-57, chief, Animal Dis Sect & dean, Col Vet Med & Biomed Sci, 57-66, dir, Agr Exp Sta, 66-69, vpres res, 66-73; consult, USDA, 57-, Agency Int Develop, Univ Teheran, 62 & Kasetsart Univ, Bangkok, 64; USDA del, USSR, 58; mem, Agr Res Inst; consult pathologist, Monfort Colo Inc, 77- & Univ Wyo, 78- *Mem:* Soc Exp Biol & Med; Am Vet Med Asn; Am Col Vet Path; Int Acad Path; Sigma Xi. *Res:* Necrobacillosis of cattle; vibriosis of sheep; diseases of feedlot cattle; diseases of sheep. *Mailing Add:* 620 Matthews No 103 Ft Collins CO 80524

JENSEN, SUSAN ELAINE, ANTIBIOTICS, STREPTOMYCES. *Current Pos:* sessional lectr & res assoc, 77-81, ALTA HERITAGE FOUND MED RES SCHOLAR MICROBIOL, UNIV ALTA, 81- *Personal Data:* b Edmonton, Alta, Jan 30, 50; m 71. *Educ:* Univ Alta, BSc, 70, PhD(microbiol), 75. *Prof Exp:* Teaching fel, Univ BC, 74-76. *Mem:* Am Soc Microbiol; Can Soc Microbiologists. *Res:* Biosynthesis of beta-lactam antibiotics by Streptomyces; cell-free enzymatic synthesis of unnatural beta-lactam antibiotics; isolation of genes coding for enzymes involved in antibiotic biosynthesis. *Mailing Add:* Dept Biol Sci Rm CW405 Bio Scis Bldg Univ Alta Edmonton AB T6G 2E9 Can

JENSEN, THOMAS E, CELL BIOLOGY. *Current Pos:* assoc prof, 70-72, PROF BIOL, LEHMAN COL, 73- *Personal Data:* b Waverly, Iowa, Sept 21, 32; m 56; c 2. *Educ:* Wartburg Col, BA, 58; SDak State Univ, MA, 62; Iowa State Univ, PhD(cytol), 65. *Prof Exp:* Res assoc, Iowa State Univ, 64-65; asst prof biol, Wayne State Univ, 65-70. *Mem:* AAAS; Electron Micros Soc Am; Am Soc Cell Biol; Bot Soc Am; Sigma Xi. *Res:* Ultrastructure of cells. *Mailing Add:* Dept Biol Sci Lehman Col 250 Bedford Park Blvd W Bronx NY 10468-1589

JENSEN, THORKIL, MICROBIOLOGY. *Current Pos:* RETIRED. *Personal Data:* b Vejle, Denmark, Jan 23, 19; nat US; m 43; c 1. *Educ:* Gustavus Adolphus Col, BA, 41; Univ Minn, MS, 49, PhD(zool), 52. *Prof Exp:* Instr embryol & histol, Vet Sch, Univ Minn, 51-52; from asst prof to assoc prof microbiol, Sch Med, Univ Kans, 52-63, prof, 63- *Concurrent Pos:* China Med

Bd fel, 55; consult, St Mary's Hosp, Kansas City, 53-58, Vet Admin Hosp, Mo, 54-61, Midwest Res Inst, 61-63 & Baptist Mem Hosp, Kansas City, 65- *Mem:* Am Soc Parasitol; Am Trop Med & Hyg; Sigma Xi. *Res:* In vitro culture of some parasitic protozoa and helminths; possible host-parasite relationships between viruses and protozoa and helminths; biochemistry of excystation in acanthamoeba. *Mailing Add:* 7029 Glenwood Overland Park KS 66204

JENSEN, TIMOTHY B(ERG), CHEMICAL ENGINEERING. *Current Pos:* Sr chem engr, 3M Co, 64-68, res supvr, 68-73, res mgr, 73-74, tech mgr, 74-84, RES MGR, 3M Co, 84- *Personal Data:* b Willmar, Minn, Oct 25, 39; m 91, Susan Heaton; c 2. *Educ:* Univ Minn, Minneapolis, BS, 61; Princeton Univ, PhD(chem eng), 65. *Mem:* Am Soc Testing & Mat; Am Inst Chem Engrs. *Res:* Optimal control theory; reactor design; urethane chemistry; oriented polyester; packaging products; environmental concerns. *Mailing Add:* 2221 Newton Ave S Minneapolis MN 55405

JENSEN, TOMMY GERT, PHYSICAL OCEANOGRAPHY, COMPUTATIONAL FLUID DYNAMICS. *Current Pos:* res assoc, 89-96, RES SCIENTIST/LECTR, COLO STATE UNIV, 96- *Personal Data:* b Copenhagen, Denmark, Mar 4, 54; m 89, Louise Marie Mattacchione; c Gianna Majbritt Mattacchione. *Educ:* Univ Aarhus, BSc, 78; Univ Copenhagen, MSc, 81, PhD(phys oceanog), 86; Fla Stae Univ, PhD(geophys fluid dynamics), 89. *Prof Exp:* Asst teacher oceanog, Univ Copenhagen, 79-84, grad fel researcher, 83-85, lectr phys oceanog, 85. *Concurrent Pos:* Lectr equatorial dynamics, Univ Sau Paulo, Brazil, 90, phys oceanog & air sea interaction, Colo State Univ, 90-; prin investr, US Dept Energy, 92-; vis sr scientist, Int Res Ctr Comput Hydrodyn, Danish Hydrographic Inst, Denmark, 94- *Mem:* Am Geophys Union; Oceanog Soc. *Res:* Numerical modelling of the ocean, primarily with respect to climate change; computational fluid dynamics; interaction between the ocean and atmosphere and coastal processes. *Mailing Add:* Dept Atmospheric Sci Colo State Univ Ft Collins CO 80523. *Fax:* 970-491-8428; *E-Mail:* jensen@neptune.atmos.colostate.edu

JENSEN, TORKIL HESSELBERG, PLASMA PHYSICS. *Current Pos:* MEM STAFF PLASMA PHYSICS, GEN ATOMIC CO, 64- *Personal Data:* b Kolding, Denmark, Apr 9, 32; m 56; c 3. *Educ:* Tech Univ Denmark, MS, 56. *Prof Exp:* Staff mem reactor & plasma physics, Danish Atomic Energy Comn, 56-60. *Mem:* Am Phys Soc. *Res:* Experimental plasma physics. *Mailing Add:* Gen Atomics PO Box 85608 3550 Gen Atomics San Diego CA 92186

JENSEN, WILLIAM AUGUST, BOTANY. *Current Pos:* dean, 84-89, PROF, COL BIOL SCIS, OHIO STATE UNIV, 84- *Personal Data:* b Chicago, Ill, Aug 22, 27; m 48, Beverly Bailey; c Scott & Christina. *Educ:* Univ Chicago, PhB, 49, MS, 50, PhD(bot), 53. *Honors & Awards:* NY Bot Garden Award, Bot Res, 60. *Prof Exp:* USPHS fel, Calif Inst Technol, 53-55; NSF fel, Univ Brussels, 55-56; asst prof biol, Univ Va, 56-57; from asst prof to prof, Univ Calif, Berkeley, 57-84, chmn dept, 71-84. *Concurrent Pos:* Prog dir developmental biol, NSF, 73-74. *Mem:* Bot Soc Am (vpres, 75-76, pres, 77-78); Soc Develop Biol (secy, 62-64). *Res:* Botanical histochemistry; botanical cytology; plant embryology. *Mailing Add:* 396 Pebble Creek Dr Dublin OH 43017

JENSEN, WILLIAM PHELPS, CHEMISTRY. *Current Pos:* assoc prof, 67-77, PROF CHEM, SDAK STATE UNIV, 77- *Personal Data:* b Minneapolis, Minn, May 22, 37; m 62; c 3. *Educ:* Univ Minn, BS, 59; Univ Iowa, MS, 62, PhD(inorg chem), 64. *Prof Exp:* Res chemist, Pittsburgh Plate Glass Co, 63-66; vis asst prof, La State Univ, 66-67. *Mem:* Am Chem Soc. *Res:* Chemistry of lanthanide and actinide elements; structure determination of complex compounds by x-ray diffraction. *Mailing Add:* Dept Chem SDak State Univ Brookings SD 57007

JENSH, RONALD PAUL, RADIATION EMBRYOLOGY, BEHAVIORAL TERATOLOGY. *Current Pos:* Instr anat & res assoc radiol, Thomas Jefferson Univ, 66-68, from asst prof to prof anat, 68-94, from asst to assoc prof radiol, 68-91, vchmn anat, 84-94, SECT CHIEF MICROS ANAT, THOMAS JEFFERSON UNIV, 88-, PROF PATH, ANAT & CELLULAR BIOL, 94- *Personal Data:* b New York, NY, June 14, 38; m 62, Ruth E Dobson; c Victoria & Elizabeth. *Educ:* Bucknell Univ, BA, 60, MA, 62; Jefferson Med Col, PhD(anat), 66. *Concurrent Pos:* Investr, NIH grants, Dept Anat & Pediat, Jefferson Med Col, 66-; consult, Ortho Res Found,, 71-85, Food, Drug & Chem Audits Inc, 79-85, Bio/Search Inc, 79-85, Argus Res Labs Inc, 79-, Am Cyanamid Co, Mobil Oil Corp, 87-88; reviewer, J Abnormal Develop, 77-, Bioelectromagnetics, 82-84 & 86, J Am Toxicol, 82-83, Embryology & Human Develop Study Sect, NIH, 83, Sci, AAAS, 84-85, Int J Radiation Biol, 84-85, 87, 90 & 93-94, Lab Animal Sci, 84 & 85, Radiation Res, 85 & 86, Battelle, Pac NW Labs, 85, Growth Develop & Aging, 88 & 90, Neurotoxicol & Teratology, 90, 93 & 94, Neurochem Int, 90 & Lea & Febiger Co, 92. *Mem:* Am Asn Anatomists; Teratology Soc (treas, 89-92); Neurobehav Teratology Soc (pres, 85-86); Sigma Xi; Soc Exp Biol & Med; Am Asn Univ Professors; Int Asn Human Biologists; Radiation Res Soc. *Res:* Teratology; embryology, statistical applications; behavioral toxicology; reproductive biology, developmental biology and radiobiology; author of numerous publications. *Mailing Add:* Dept Path Anat Cell Biol 562JAH Thomas Jefferson Univ Philadelphia PA 19107-6799. *Fax:* 215-923-3808; *E-Mail:* jenshr@jeflin.tju.edu

JENSKI, LAURA JEAN, MHC RESTRICTION, CYTOXIC T-LYMPHOCYTE. *Current Pos:* asst prof, 87-91, ASSOC PROF BIOL, IND UNIV-PURDUE UNIV INDIANAPOLIS, 91- *Personal Data:* b Chicago, Ill, Feb 23, 52; m. *Educ:* Northern Ill Univ, BS, 73, MS, 75; Univ NC, PhD(oncol), 79. *Prof Exp:* Res assoc, Childrens Hosp Res Found, 83-86. *Concurrent Pos:* Grants, var corp & inst, 86-92. *Mem:* Am Asn Immunologists; Am Soc Cell Biol; AAAS; Asn Women in Sci. *Res:* T-lymphocyte activity and regulation; immunological effects of long chain omega-3 fatty acids. *Mailing Add:* Dept Biol Ind Univ-Purdue Univ Indianapolis 723 W Michigan Indianapolis IN 46202-5132. *Fax:* 317-274-2846

JENSON, A BENNETT, IMMUNOPATHOLOGY, IMMUNOVIROLOGY. *Current Pos:* ACTG CHMN, DEPT DENT, MED & GRAD PATH, GEORGETOWN UNIV, 80- *Educ:* Baylor Col Med, MD, 66. *Mailing Add:* Dept Path Georgetown Univ Med Ctr Med Sch 3900 Reservoir Rd NW Washington DC 20007-2187. *Fax:* 202-687-8935

JENSSEN, THOMAS ALAN, ANIMAL BEHAVIOR, ECOLOGY. *Current Pos:* asst prof, 71-77, ASSOC PROF BIOL, VA POLYTECH INST & STATE UNIV, 77- *Personal Data:* b South Bend, Ind, Mar 18, 39; m 62; c 3. *Educ:* Univ Redlands, BS, 62; Southern Ill Univ, MA, 64; Univ Okla, PhD(zool), 69. *Prof Exp:* Nat Inst Ment Health assoc herpet, Harvard Univ, 69-71. *Concurrent Pos:* Res asst, Med Ctr, Univ Okla, 69-70. *Mem:* Am Soc Ichthyol & Herpet; Animal Behav Soc; Int Soc Behav Ecol; Soc Study Amphibians & Reptiles; Sigma Xi. *Res:* Behavior and ecology of various species of anurans and lizards, especially communicative value of anoline lizard displays. *Mailing Add:* Dept Biol Va Polytech Inst Blacksburg VA 24061-0406

JENTOFT, JOYCE EILEEN, STRUCTURE-FUNCTION RELATIONSHIPS, PHYSICAL BIOCHEMISTRY. *Current Pos:* fel phys biochem, Case Western Res Univ, 77, immunol, 78, sr res assoc phys biochem, Dept Pediat, 79-81, asst prof, 81-89, asst provost, 94-96, ASSOC PROF, DEPT BIOCHEM, SCH MED, CASE WESTERN RES UNIV, 89-, PROVOST & DEAN, SCH GRAD STUDIES, 96- *Personal Data:* b Canton, Ohio, Mar 10, 45; m 26, Neil. *Educ:* Capital Univ, BS, 66; Univ Minn, PhD(inorg chem), 71. *Prof Exp:* Fel phys biochem, Univ Minn, 72. *Concurrent Pos:* Instr biochem, Case Western Univ, 79-81. *Mem:* Am Chem Soc; Biophys Soc; Am Soc Biochem & Molecular Biol. *Res:* Structure-function relationships in proteins and enzymes; protein-nucleic acid interactions; molecular virology (retroviruses); biological spectroscopy (fluorescence, CD, NMR). *Mailing Add:* Case Western Res Univ 10900 Euclid Ave Cleveland OH 44106-7004. *Fax:* 216-368-4325; *E-Mail:* jej@po.cwru.edu

JENTOFT, RALPH EUGENE, JR, PHYSICAL CHEMISTRY, ANALYTICAL CHEMISTRY. *Current Pos:* CONSULT, 80- *Personal Data:* b Tacoma, Wash, Nov 30, 18; m 54, Betty L Eshleman; c Elisabeth (Norosky) & Rolf E. *Educ:* Univ Wash, BS, 41, PhD(chem), 52. *Prof Exp:* Chemist, Oceanog Surv Philippines, US Fish & Wildlife Serv, 47-48; res chemist, Chevron Res Co, Stand Oil Co, Calif, 52-60, sr res chemist, 60-64, sr res assoc phys & anal chem, 64-79. *Mem:* AAAS; Am Chem Soc. *Res:* Phase studies and thermodynamic measurements in field of petroleum chemistry; separation and purification; trace analysis for hydrocarbons and petrochemicals; analytical separations; liquid chromatography and supercritical fluid chromatography; quantum chemistry. *Mailing Add:* 11601 Occidental Rd Sebastopol CA 95472-9648

JENZANO, ANTHONY FRANCIS, ASTRONOMY, PHYSICS. *Current Pos:* RETIRED. *Personal Data:* b Philadelphia, Pa, May 20, 19; m 40; c 2. *Prof Exp:* Head technician, Fels Planetarium, Pa, 46-49; head technician, Univ NC, Chapel Hill, 49-51, mgr, 51-60, dir, Morehead Planetarium, 60-81; planetarium counr US & Can, Carl Zeiss Optical Co, 81-86. *Concurrent Pos:* Consult, London Planetarium, Eng, 55-57, Buhl Planetarium, Pa, 59, var proposed planetaria, 63-, Carl Zeiss Optical Co, 65- & Fernbank Sci Ctr, Ga, 66- *Mem:* Assoc Am Astron Soc; Am Asn Mus. *Res:* Initiation and direction of celestial training program for United States Mercury, Gemini, Apollo, Skylab and Apollo-Soyuz astronauts. *Mailing Add:* 37 Oakwood Dr Chapel Hill NC 27514

JEON, KWANG WU, CELL BIOLOGY, MOLECULAR BIOLOGY. *Current Pos:* assoc prof, 70-75, PROF CELLULAR BIOL, UNIV TENN, KNOXVILLE, 76- *Personal Data:* b Korea, Nov 10, 34; m 58, Myong S Nee Kim; c 2. *Educ:* Seoul Nat Univ, BS, 57, MS, 59; Univ London, PhD(cell physiol), 64. *Prof Exp:* Res fel electron microscopy, Middlesex Hosp, Univ London, 64-65; res asst prof cell physiol, State Univ NY, Buffalo, 65-69. *Concurrent Pos:* Ed, Int Rev Cytol, 67- *Mem:* Am Soc Cell Biol; Soc Develop Biol; Soc Protozoologists (pres, 92-93); fel AAAS; Sigma Xi; Int Soc Endocytobiol (pres, 89-95). *Res:* Cell growth and division; nucleocytoplasmic interactions; cell organelle structure and function; symbiosis. *Mailing Add:* Dept Biochem Univ Tenn Knoxville TN 37996-0840. *Fax:* 423-974-3899; *E-Mail:* jeon-k@utkvx.utk.edu

JEONG, TUNG HON, HOLOGRAPHY. *Current Pos:* from asst prof to assoc prof, 63-78, PROF PHYSICS, LAKE FOREST COL, 78-, DIR, CTR PHOTONICS STUDIES; PRES, INTEGRAF. *Personal Data:* b Kwangtung, China, Dec 19, 31; US citizen; m 63, Anna C Wong; c 3. *Educ:* Yale Univ, BS, 57; Univ Minn, PhD(physics), 62. *Honors & Awards:* Robert Millikin Medal, Am Asn Physics Teachers, 76. *Prof Exp:* Res assoc physics, Univ Minn, 62-63. *Concurrent Pos:* Tech consult. *Mem:* Am Asn Physics Teachers; Soc Photo-Optical Instrumentation Engrs; fel Optical Soc Am. *Res:* Precision proton-nuclear elastic scattering; linear proton accelerator injector; H-source for pre-injectors; optics; physics education; lasers and holography; non-destructive testing; laser applications and holography. *Mailing Add:* Dept Physics Lake Fores Col 555 N Sheridan Rd Lake Forest IL 60045. *Fax:* 847-615-0835; *E-Mail:* jeong@lfc.edu

JEPPESEN, RANDOLPH H, PHYSICS & ASTRONOMY. *Current Pos:* From instr to assoc prof, 61-81, chmn dept, 73-81, PROF PHYSICS & ASTRON, UNIV MONT, 81- *Educ:* Univ Mont, BA, 58; Univ Ill, MS, 60; NMex State Univ, PhD (physics), 80. *Concurrent Pos:* IBM res staff mem, Thomas J Watson Res Ctr, 60-61; co-prin investr, AEC grant, Dept Energy, 72-80; AWA fac partic grants, Los Alamos Nat Lab, 81-86, collabr, exps 665 & 770, 87. *Mem:* Am Phys Soc. *Mailing Add:* Dept Phys & Astron Univ Montana 1824 Dexon A Missoula MT 59812

JEPPSON, ROLAND W, CIVIL ENGINEERING, FLUID MECHANICS & HYDRAULICS. *Current Pos:* PROF, DEPT CIVIL & ENVIRON ENG, UTAH STATE UNIV, 94- *Personal Data:* b Brigham City, Utah, Aug 30, 33; m 59, Mary Anna Marcusere; c 9. *Educ:* Utah State Univ, BS, 58, MS, 60; Stanford Univ, PhD(civil eng), 67. *Honors & Awards:* J C Stevens Award, Am Soc Civil Engrs, 68; Horton Award, Am Geophys Union, 76. *Prof Exp:* Res engr, Utah State Univ, 58-60; asst prof civil eng, Humboldt State Col, 60-64; res engr, summers, Utah State Univ, 61-64, head, Dept Civil & Environ Eng, 73-77, assoc prof civil eng, 66-71, prof, 71-94. *Mem:* Am Soc Civil Engrs; Am Soc Eng Educ; Am Geophys Union. *Res:* Numerical solutions to free surface fluid and porous media flow problems; water resource planning and design; pipeline hydraulics; open channel hydraulics. *Mailing Add:* Dept Civil & Environ Eng Utah State Univ Logan UT 84321-4110. *E-Mail:* jeppson@lab.cee.usu.edu

JEPSEN, DONALD WILLIAM, SURFACE PHYSICS, STATISTICAL MECHANICS & SCIENTIFIC COMPUTER PROGRAMMING. *Current Pos:* RETIRED. *Personal Data:* b Lincoln, Nebr, Jan 14, 32; m 75, Judith Hajos; c Stephanie H. *Educ:* Univ Rochester, BS, 53; Univ Wis, MS, 56, PhD(theoret chem), 59. *Prof Exp:* Gen Motors fel, Inst Fluid Dynamics & Appl Math, Univ Md, 59-60; staff mem, IBM Corp Res Ctr, 60-95. *Mem:* Am Phys Soc; Am Chem Soc; Sigma Xi; Inst Elec & Electronics Engrs; Asn Comput Mach. *Res:* Theoretical chemical physics; nonequilibrium properties of large systems; properties of solid surfaces and low energy electron diffraction. *Mailing Add:* 507 Woodland Hills Rd White Plains NY 10603. *E-Mail:* jepsen1@tribeca.ios.com

JEPSON, WILLIAM W, medicine, psychiatry, for more information see previous edition

JEREMIAH, LESTER EARL, MEAT SCIENCES. *Current Pos:* RES SCIENTIST MEAT SCI, CAN DEPT AGR, 75- *Personal Data:* b Walla Walla, Wash, Dec 9, 41; m 66, 93, Suzette Trestiza; c William E, Johanna S & John D. *Educ:* Wash State Univ, BS, 65; Univ Mo, MS, 67; Tex A&M Univ, PhD(meat sci), 71. *Prof Exp:* Meat lab technician, Wash State Univ, 65, exten agent, 67-69; res asst, Univ Mo, 65-67; grad asst meat sci, Tex A&M Univ, 69-71; salesman real estate, David A Gamache Real Este Co, 72-73; co exten dir, Colo State Univ, 73-74; tech writer human nutrit, Agriserv Found, 74-75. *Mem:* Am Soc Animal Sci; Inst Food Technologists; Am Meat Sci Asn; Can Meat Sci Asn. *Res:* Beef and pork tenderness, quality, preservation, retail case-life, and meat handling systems; frozen storage and display of meat; sensory evaluation and consumer acceptance. *Mailing Add:* Agr & Agr Food Can Res Ctr 6000 C & E Trail Lacombe AB T4L 1W1 Can. *Fax:* 403-782-6120

JEREMIAS, CHARLES GEORGE, ORGANIC CHEMISTRY, INORGANIC CHEMISTRY. *Current Pos:* assoc prof & actg head dept, 62-64, PROF CHEM & HEAD DEPT, NEWBERRY COL, 64- *Personal Data:* b Marlborough, Mass, July 8, 20; m 80; c 2. *Educ:* Univ Ga, BS, 42; Tulane Univ, PhD(chem), 49. *Prof Exp:* Chemist, US Rubber Co, 42-45; res chemist, Tenn Eastman Co, 48-60; group leader res, Southern Dyestuff Co, Martin-Marietta Co, 60-62. *Concurrent Pos:* Consult, Delta 2 Finishing Plant, J P Stevens Co, 65-70 & James Flett Orgn, Inc, 77-79. *Mem:* Am Chem Soc; Am Inst Chemists. *Res:* Organic intermediates for synthetic fibers, dyes and insecticides; sulfur dyes and intermediates. *Mailing Add:* 2103 Johnstone St Newberry SC 29108

JERGER, E(DWARD) W, MECHANICAL ENGINEERING. *Current Pos:* assoc prof, Univ Notre Dame, 55-61, prof & head dept, 61-68, assoc dean eng, 68-82, prof, 82-87, EMER PROF MECH ENG, UNIV NOTRE DAME, 87- *Personal Data:* b Milwaukee, Wis, Mar 13, 22; m 82, Elizabeth Cordiner Swirtzer; c Betty A (Murphy) & Barbara L (Smyth). *Educ:* Marquette Univ, BS, 46; Univ Wis, MS, 47; Iowa State Univ, PhD(theoret & appl mech), 51. *Prof Exp:* Dir process eng, Wis Malting Co, 46-48; asst prof mech eng, Iowa State Col, 48-55. *Concurrent Pos:* Consult engr, 60-; educ consult, Dominican Repub, 65-67. *Mem:* Am Soc Mech Engrs; Am Soc Eng Educ; Nat Fire Protection Asn; Int Asn Arson Investr. *Res:* Thermal systems; fire protection engineering; protective construction; product liability. *Mailing Add:* Col Eng Univ Notre Dame Notre Dame IN 46556

JERINA, DONALD M, ORGANIC CHEMISTRY, BIOCHEMISTRY. *Current Pos:* Fel org chem & biochem, Nat Inst Arthrities, Diabetes, Digestive & Kidney Dis, 66-68, sr fel, 69-70, res chemist, 70-73, CHIEF, OXIDATION MECHANISMS SECT, NAT INST ARTHRITIS, DIABETES, DIGESTIVE & KIDNEY DIS, NIH, 73- *Personal Data:* b Chicago, Ill, Jan 17, 40; m 64, Colleen; c Derek & Julianne. *Educ:* Knox Col, Ill, BA, 62; Northwestern Univ, PhD(org chem), 66. *Honors & Awards:* Hillebrand Prize, Am Chem Soc, 79; Brodie Award, Am Soc Pharmacol & Exp Therapeut, 82. *Mem:* AAAS; Am Chem Soc; Am Cancer Soc; Fedn Am Socs Exp Biol; Am Soc Biochem & Molecular Biol. *Res:* Synthesis of peptides and oligonucleotides on polymer supports; enzymes drug metabolism; microsomal hydroxylation; biochemical mechanisms; migration of ring substituents during aryl hydroxylation, particularly the NIH shift; chemistry and biochemistry of arene oxides; chemical carcinogenesis; mutagenesis; DNA adducts. *Mailing Add:* Lab Bioorg Chem Bldg 8A Rm 1A-11 Nat Inst Diabetes & Digestive & Kidney Dis Bethesda MD 20892-0001. *Fax:* 301-402-0008

JERIS, JOHN S(TRATIS), ENVIRONMENTAL ENGINEERING, SCIENCE. *Current Pos:* from asst prof to assoc prof, 62-71, dir environ eng & sci grad prog, 66-78 & 86-94, PROF CIVIL ENG, MANHATTAN COL, 71- *Personal Data:* b Boston, Mass, June 6, 30; m 58; c Joanne & Paul. *Educ:* Mass Inst Technol, BS, 53, MS, 54, ScD(sanit eng), 62. *Honors & Awards:* Kenneth Allen Mem Award, NY Water Pollution Control Asn, 75; Thomas R Camp Medal, Water Pollution Control Fedn, 79, DeLa Salle Medal, 1985. *Prof Exp:* Proj engr, Stearns & Wheler, NY, 56-59; res asst, Mass Inst Technol, 59-62. *Concurrent Pos:* Vpres res & develop, Ecolotrol Inc, 70-; consult, Environ Eng. *Mem:* Sigma Xi; Am Water Works Asn; Water Pollution Control Fedn; Am Soc Civil Engrs; Asn Environ Eng Prof. *Res:* Biological waste treatment; use of biological fluid beds, transport of polychlorinated biphenyl through sediment; anaerobic and aerobic stabilization of sludges. *Mailing Add:* Dept Environ Eng Manhattan Col Bronx NY 10471. *Fax:* 718-862-8018; *E-Mail:* jsjscd@aol.com

JERISON, HARRY JACOB, NEUROBIOLOGY, MEDICAL PSYCHOLOGY. *Current Pos:* prof, 69-92, EMER PROF BIOBEHAV SCI, DEPT PSYCHIAT, SCH MED & PROF, DEPT PSYCHOL, UNIV CALIF, LOS ANGELES, 92- *Personal Data:* b Bialystok, Poland, Oct 13, 25; US citizen; m 50, Irene Landkof; c Jon, Andy & Elizabeth. *Educ:* Univ Chicago, BS, 47, PhD(psychol), 54. *Honors & Awards:* James Arthur lectr, Am Mus Nat Hist, 89. *Prof Exp:* Res psychologist, AeroMed Lab, USAF, 49-57; assoc prof psychol, Antioch Col, 57-64, dir, Behav Res Lab, 57-69, prof psychol, 64-68, prof biol, 68-69. *Concurrent Pos:* Fel, Ctr Advan Study Behav Sci, 67-68; hon res assoc, Dept Vert Paleont, Los Angeles County Mus, 70-; vis scientist, Med Res Coun, Appl Psychol Unit, Cambridge, Eng, 78-79; vis scholar, Rockefeller Found Bellagio Ctr, 83; vis prof anthrop, Univ Florence, Italy, 86-87; acad vis, Oxford Univ, 86; vis prof psychol, Univ Hawaii, 87; vis prof neurobiol, Max-Plank Inst fo Biologica Cybernetics, Tuebingen, Ger, 89. *Mem:* Psychonomic Soc; Am Psychol Asn; Int Soc Evolutionary Biol; Am Soc Naturalists; Soc Vert Paleont. *Res:* Paleoneurology; evolutionary biopsychology; evolution of specialized and generalized behavioral and cognitive capacities in vertebrates, and its relation to allometry and encephalization (brain/body relations) among living and fossil animals; quantitative neuroanatomy. *Mailing Add:* 503 W Rustic Rd Santa Monica CA 90402. *Fax:* 310-454-3325; *E-Mail:* hjerison@ucla.edu

JERISON, MEYER, mathematics; deceased, see previous edition for last biography

JERKOFSKY, MARYANN, VIROLOGY, CELL CULTURE. *Current Pos:* RETIRED. *Personal Data:* b Alameda, Calif, Feb 18, 43. *Educ:* Univ Tex, BA, 65; Baylor Col Med, PhD(virol), 69. *Prof Exp:* Fel microbiol, Col Med, Pa State Univ, 69-72, res assoc, 72-73, instr, 73-74; res asst prof, Sch Med, Univ Miami, 74-75; asst prof, Univ Maine, Orono, 76-81, assoc prof microbiol, 81-95. *Concurrent Pos:* Vis prof, Univ Amsterdam, Neth, 83, Am Univ Les Cayes, Haiti, 88, 90 & Tokyo Univ Fisheries, Japan, 92. *Mem:* Am Soc Microbiol; Sigma Xi; Am Soc Virol; AAAS. *Res:* Herpes viruses in vitro model for Reye's Syndrome; lipid metabolism modifications produced by herpes viruses; interaction between unrelated animal viruses; characterization of tumors produced in fish by herpes viruses. *Mailing Add:* 8164 Sapphire Ave NE North Canton OH 44721

JERMANN, WILLIAM HOWARD, ELECTRICAL ENGINEERING. *Current Pos:* from asst prof to assoc prof, 67-77, PROF, DEPT ELEC ENG, MEMPHIS STATE UNIV, 77- *Personal Data:* b Cleveland, Ohio, June 29, 35; m 63; c 3. *Educ:* Univ Detroit, BEE, 58, MA, 62; Univ Conn, PhD(elec eng), 67. *Prof Exp:* Jr engr, Toledo Edison Co, Ohio, 58; instr elec eng, Univ Detroit, 61-62; asst prof, USCG Acaad, 62-67. *Concurrent Pos:* NSF res grant, 69-70. *Mem:* Am Soc Eng Educ; Simulation Coun. *Res:* Hybrid Monte-Carlo solutions to partial differential equations; development of engineering concepts curriculum project. *Mailing Add:* 4903 Greenway Ave Memphis TN 38117

JERNE, NIELS KAJ, immunology, experimental therapy; deceased, see previous edition for last biography

JERNER, R CRAIG, METALLURGICAL ENGINEERING, MATERIALS SCIENCE. *Current Pos:* PRES, EMTEC CORP, 73- *Personal Data:* b St Louis, Mo, Oct 12, 38; m 92, Jann S Guest; c Michael, Elisabeth, Stephen & Elizabeth A. *Educ:* Washington Univ, St Louis, BS, 61, MS, 62; Univ Denver, PhD(metall), 65. *Prof Exp:* From asst prof to assoc prof metall eng, Univ Okla, 65-76, asst dean grad col, 71-72. *Concurrent Pos:* Consult, var indust co; SW Metall Consult Inc/Emtec Corp, 72-88; assoc staff mem, Transp Safety Inst, US Dept Transp, 73-78; adj prof metall eng, Univ Okla, 76-78. *Mem:* Am Soc Microbiol; Am Soc Testing Mat; Sigma Xi; Soc Mfg Engrs; Nat Asn Corrosion Engrs; Am Welding Soc. *Res:* Application of scanning electron microscopy and energy dispersive x-ray spectroscopy to the analysis of metallic and non-metallic product failures. *Mailing Add:* 7703 Queens Ferry Lane Dallas TX 75248-1720

JERNIGAN, HOWARD MAXWELL, JR, BIOCHEMISTRY. *Current Pos:* from asst prof to assoc prof, 73-90, PROF BIOCHEM, UNIV TENN, MEMPHIS, 90-, PROF, OPHTHAL, 96- *Personal Data:* b Winston-Salem, NC, Apr 13, 43; m 68, Diane Moore; c 1. *Educ:* WVa Univ, Morgantown, BS, 65; Univ NC, Chapel Hill, PhD(biochem), 70. *Prof Exp:* Fel, dept biochem, Univ Fla, 70-73. *Concurrent Pos:* Res assoc, Lab Vision Res, Nat Eye Inst, NIH, 78-80. *Mem:* Am Soc Biochem & Molecular Biol; Am Chem Soc; Sigma Xi; Asn Res Vision & Ophthal. *Res:* Biochemistry of the eye; lens metabolism; cataract; oxidative damages to tissues; membrane transport; amino acids; lipid metabolism. *Mailing Add:* Univ Tenn Coleman Bldg Rm D-222 956 Court Ave Memphis TN 38163

JERNIGAN, ROBERT LEE, PHYSICAL CHEMISTRY, COMPUTER SIMULATIONS. *Current Pos:* sr staff fel chem, 70-75, THEORET CHEMIST, NIH, 75-, DEP LAB CHIEF, 89-, HEAD, SECT MOLECULAR STRUCT, 92- *Personal Data:* b Portales, NMex, May 4, 41; div; c Alexander L. *Educ:* Calif Inst Technol, BS, 63; Stanford Univ, PhD(phys chem), 67. *Honors & Awards:* Merit Award, NIH, 95. *Prof Exp:* NIH fel, Univ Calif, San Diego, 68-70. *Concurrent Pos:* US Israel Binat Found Grants, 92-97; NATO Collab Res Grant, 96-97; Resource Adv Comt, Parallel Processing Resource, Cornell Univ, 93- *Mem:* AAAS; Am Chem Soc; Biophys Soc; Protein Soc. *Res:* Protein, polypeptide and NA conformations; dimensional, electrical and optical properties; conformations of biopolymers; biophysics; residue-residue interactions in proteins; DNA flexibility; protein folding; RNA folding; drug design; protein engineering. *Mailing Add:* MSC 5677, Room B-116, Bldg 12-B Bethesda MD 20892. *Fax:* 301-402-4724; *E-Mail:* jernigan@lmmb.nci.nih.gov

JERNIGAN, ROBERT WAYNE, COMPUTATIONAL STATISTICS. *Current Pos:* From asst prof to assoc prof, 78-86, PROF STATIST, AM UNIV, 86- *Personal Data:* b Jacksonville, Fla, Feb 4, 51; m 73, Rose M Receveur; c Nicholas & Laura. *Educ:* Univ SFla, BA, 73, MA, 75, PhD(math), 78. *Concurrent Pos:* Sr statistician, Statist Policy Br, US Environ Protection Agency, 84-90; dept chair math & statist, Am Univ, 90-93; researcher, Lab Molecular Systs, Smithsonian Inst, 92. *Mem:* Am Statist Asn; Inst Math Statist; AAAS; Math Asn Am; Soc Study Evolution. *Res:* Development and application of probability and statistical theory and computational statistical methods to the study of ecological systems and evolutionary biology. *Mailing Add:* 14805 Clavel St Rockville MD 20853-1543. *E-Mail:* jernigan@american.edu

JERNOW, JANE L, organic chemistry, for more information see previous edition

JEROME, JOSEPH WALTER, SEMICONDUCTOR MODELING, NONLINEAR SYSTEMS. *Current Pos:* from asst prof to assoc prof, 70-76, PROF MATH, NORTHWESTERN UNIV, 76- *Personal Data:* b Philadelphia, Pa, June 7, 39; div; c 2. *Educ:* St Joseph's Col, Pa, BS, 61; Purdue Univ, MS, 63, PhD(math), 66. *Prof Exp:* Asst prof math, Math Res Ctr, Univ Wis-Madison, 66-68; asst prof, Case Western Res Univ, 68-70. *Concurrent Pos:* Vis sr fel, Oxford Univ, 74-75; sr fel, British Sci Coun, 74-75; vis prof, Univ Tex, 78-79; vis mem tech staff, Bell Labs, NJ, 81 & 82-83; vis scholar, Univ Chicago, 85; vis prof, Rush Med Col, 94- *Mem:* Am Math Soc; Soc Indust Appl Math. *Res:* Approximation of nonlinear partial differential equation models; ionic channels. *Mailing Add:* Dept Math Northwestern Univ Evanston IL 60208-2730. *E-Mail:* jwj@math.nwu.edu

JEROME, NORGE WINIFRED, PUBLIC HEALTH, NUTRITIONAL ANTHROPOLOGY. *Current Pos:* asst prof nutrit, Univ Kans Med Ctr, Kansas City, 69-70, asst prof human ecol, 70-72, assoc prof human ecol & community health, Col Health Sci, 72-78, dir, Educ Resources Ctr, Div Learning Resources, 74-77, prof, Dept Community Health, Sch Med, 78-95, dir, Dept Prev Med, Community Nutrit Div, 81-95, EMER PROF PREV MED, UNIV KANS MED CTR, KANSAS CITY, 96-, ASSOC DEAN MINORITY AFFAIRS, 96- *Personal Data:* b Grenada, WI, Nov 3, 30; US citizen. *Educ:* Howard Univ, BS, 60; Univ Wis-Madison, MS, 62, PhD(nutrit, anthrop), 67. *Honors & Awards:* Spotlight Award, US Dept Labor; Higuchi Res Achievement Award. *Prof Exp:* Instr foods & nutrit, Howard Univ, 62-63; res assoc nutrit & anthrop, Univ Wis-Madison, 66-67. *Concurrent Pos:* Mem, Inst Res on Poverty, Univ Wis-Madison, 66-67; mem awards bd, Am Dietetic Asn, 68-71; assoc ed, J Nutrit Educ, 71-77, mem, Nat Adv Coun, 77-; mem nat adv coun, Children's Advert Rev Unit, 74-; mem nat adv coun, Children's TV Workshop, 74-75; chairperson comt nutrit anthrop, 74-77; mem, Food & Nutrit Coun, Am Pub Health Asn, 75-78; mem study panel 12, World Food & Nutrit Study, Nat Acad Sci, 76, Cancer & Nutrit Sci Review Comt, Diet, Nutrit & Cancer Prog, Nat Cancer Inst, NIH, 76-78 & Lipid Metab Adv Comt, Nat Heart, Lung & Blood Inst, NIH, 78-82, man-food systs interaction comt, Nat Res Coun, 80-82; cancer prev & control study sect, 94- *Mem:* Fel Am Anthrop Asn; Am Dietetic Asn; Am Pub Health Asn; Soc Med Anthrop; Am Inst Nutrit; Inst Food Technologists. *Res:* Dietary patterns of population groups; modernization, diet and health; compliance to medical regimen; consumer response to nutritional and health prescriptions; dietary interventions to reduce chronic diseases. *Mailing Add:* Univ Kans Sch Med 3901 Rainbow Blvd Kansas City KS 66160-7313. *Fax:* 913-962-0925; *E-Mail:* njerome@kumc.edu

JERRARD, RICHARD PATTERSON, FIXED POINTS, MULTIPLE-VALUED FUNCTIONS. *Current Pos:* from asst prof to prof, 58-69, dir grad studies, 91-95, EMER PROF MATH, UNIV ILL, URBANA-CHAMPAIGN, 95- *Personal Data:* b Evanston, Ill, July 23, 25; m 51, Margot; c Laura, Leigh & Robert. *Educ:* Univ Wis, BS, 49, MS, 50; Univ Mich, PhD(math), 58. *Prof Exp:* Engr, Gen Elec Co, 50-54; instr math, Univ Mich, 56-57; mathematician, Bell Labs, 57-58. *Concurrent Pos:* Vis fel, Univ Warwick, 65- 66, 77, 85 & 90, Cambridge Univ, 72-73. *Mem:* Am Math Soc; Math Asn Am; Sigma Xi. *Mailing Add:* Univ Ill 1409 W Green Urbana IL 61801. *E-Mail:* jerrard@math.uiuc.edu

JERRELLS, THOMAS RAY, TUMOR IMMUNOLOGY, CELLULAR IMMUNOLOGY. *Current Pos:* PROF CELL BIOL, LA STATE UNIV MED CTR, 91- *Personal Data:* b Wickenburg, Ariz, Feb 28, 44; m 65; c 2. *Educ:* Univ Ariz, BS, 72; Wash State Univ, MS, 74, PhD(microbiol), 76. *Prof Exp:* Tumor immunologist, Litton Bionetics, Inc, 76-78, head, Immunoregulation Sect, 78-80; mem staff, Dept Rickettsial Dis, Walter Reed Army Inst Res, 80-87; assoc prof path, Univ Tex, 87-91. *Mem:* Am Soc Microbiol; Am Med Technologists. *Res:* Defining immunoregulatory cells involved in cell-mediated immune responses and role in the immunodepression associated with tumor burden. *Mailing Add:* Dept Pharm Sci & Toxicol Wash State Univ Col Pharm Pullman WA 99164-6510. *Fax:* 509-335-0152

JERRI, ABDUL J, APPLIED MATHEMATICS. *Current Pos:* asst prof, 67-70, ASSOC PROF MATH, CLARKSON UNIV, 70- *Personal Data:* b Amarah, Iraq, July 20, 32; m; c 3. *Educ:* Univ Baghdad, BSc, 55; Ill Inst Technol, MSc, 60; Ore State Univ, PhD(math), 67. *Prof Exp:* Instr physics, Baquba Teacher Col, Iraq, 56-58; asst physicist, IIT Res Inst, 59-62. *Concurrent Pos:* Head dept, Am Univ Cairo, 72-73, vis assoc prof, 73-74; vis assoc prof, Am Univ Cairo, 86-88; assoc prof, Kuwait Univ, 78-79, 89-90. *Mem:* Am Math Soc; Soc Indust & Appl Math; Pattern Recognition Soc. *Res:* Sampling expansion; integral and discrete transforms; numerical method. *Mailing Add:* Dept Math Clarkson Univ Box 5815 Potsdam NY 13699-5815

JERRY, L MARTIN, CANCER IMMUNOLOGY. *Current Pos:* dir cancer serv, 77-92, DIR WHO, COLLAB CTR CANCER CONTROL, TOM BAKER CANCER CTR, 93-; PROF MED, UNIV CALGARY. *Personal Data:* b Toronto, Ont, Jan 2, 37. *Educ:* Univ Toronto, MD, 61, PhD(immunol), 71. *Mem:* Am Asn Cancer Res; Am Asn Immunol; Am Col Physicians; Can Soc Immunol; Can Oncol Soc. *Res:* Cancer Immunology. *Mailing Add:* Tom Baker Cancer Ctr 1331 29th St NW Calgary AB T2N 4N2 Can. *Fax:* 402-270-4415

JERSEY, GEORGE CARL, VETERINARY PATHOLOGY. *Current Pos:* CONSULT, 80- *Personal Data:* b Highland Park, Mich, Aug 20, 40; m 58; c 2. *Educ:* Eastern Mich Univ, BA, 64; Mich State Univ, BS, 65, DVM, 67, MS, 69, PhD(vet path), 73. *Prof Exp:* Upjohn fel, Dept Path, Mich State Univ, 67-68, instr, 68-70, instr clin path, 70-72; res specialist path, Toxicol Res Lab, Dow Chem Co, 72-80. *Mem:* Am Vet Med Asn. *Res:* Pathological and toxicological evaluation of industrial, agricultural and consumer chemicals; chemical products in laboratory animals to help establish safe production, handling, transportation and use of these materials. *Mailing Add:* 6401 Gillard Rd Spruce MI 48762

JERSILD, RALPH ALVIN, JR, MICROSCOPIC ANATOMY, CELL BIOLOGY. *Current Pos:* From instr to assoc prof, 61-71, PROF ANAT, SCH MED, IND UNIV INDIANAPOLIS, 71- *Personal Data:* b Janesville, Wis, Sept 29, 31; m 53; c 2. *Educ:* St Olaf Col, BA, 53; Univ Ill, MS, 57, PhD(zool), 61. *Mem:* Am Asn Anat; Electron Micros Soc Am; Am Soc Cell Biol. *Res:* Electron microscopy; intestinal lipid absorption and transport; glycoprotein synthesis and transport; golgi apparatus; cell surface. *Mailing Add:* Ind Univ Sch Med 635 Barnhill Dr Indianapolis IN 46223

JERUCHIM, MICHEL CLAUDE, COMPUTER SIMULATION OF COMMUNICATION SYSTEMS, INTERFERENCE ANALYSIS OF COMMUNICATIONS SYSTEMS. *Current Pos:* Commun engr, Space Systs Div, Gen Elec Co, 61-71, sr commun engr, 71-84, SR STAFF CONSULT COMMUN SCI, GE AEROSPACE/LOCKHEED MARTIN, 84- *Personal Data:* b Paris, France, Apr 4, 37; US citizen; m 69; c 2. *Educ:* City Col NY, BEE, 61; Univ Pa, MSEE, 63, PhD(elec eng/commun), 67. *Concurrent Pos:* Secy, Subcomt Comput-Aided Modeling, Anal & Design Commun Systs, Inst Elec & Electronics Engrs Commun Soc, 84-86, vchmn, 86- *Mem:* Fel Inst Elec & Electronics Engrs. *Res:* Analysis and design of communications systems, especially satellite-based systems; developing computer-aided tools such as simulation, for doing the analysis and design. *Mailing Add:* Lockheed Martin Corp PO Box 8048 Bldg D Rm 24D42 Philadelphia PA 19101

JERUSSI, THOMAS P, CENTRAL NERVOUS SYSTEM. *Current Pos:* Researcher pharmacol, Ohmeda PPD, 84-85, sr researcher, 85-87, group leader cent nerv syst, 87-88, SECT MGR CENT NERV SYST, OHMEDA PPD, 88- *Personal Data:* b New York, NY, Mar 24, 40. *Educ:* City Col New York, BS, 62; Hunter Col, MS, 72; Mt Sinai Med Sch, PhD(pharmacol), 74. *Mem:* AAAS; Soc Neurosci; Am Soc Pharmacol & Exp Therapeut. *Mailing Add:* 1 Childs Circle Framingham MA 01701-4866

JERVIS, HERBERT HUNTER, molecular genetics, for more information see previous edition

JERVIS, ROBERT ALFRED, BOTANY, ECOLOGY & ORNITHOLOGY. *Current Pos:* ADJ FAC NATURAL SCI, JOHNSON STATE COL, 83- *Personal Data:* b Wilmington, Del, May 15, 38; m 81, Linda Radtke; c Michael & Rebecca. *Educ:* Dartmouth Col, BA, 60; Rutgers Univ, MS, 62, PhD(ecol), 64. *Prof Exp:* From asst prof to assoc prof biol, Emory & Henry Col, 64-68; prof, Goddard Col, 68-81 & Community Col Vt, 81-84; instr,

Harwood Union High Sch, Moretown, 81-93. *Concurrent Pos:* Dir, Goddard Col non-resident ecol study projs, SE & SW US, 71-72 & NW & Alaska, 76 & Bahamas, 78; dir, Goddard Col, Raptor Rehab Ctr & Summer Prog in Outdoor Col; adj prof biol, Johnson State Col, 83-; adj fac biol, Community Col, Vt. *Mem:* Ecol Soc Am; Am Nature Study Soc; Am Littoral Soc. *Res:* Freshwater marsh vegetation and productivity; vegetation patterns in the south Appalachians; New England ecology; ornithology; travel study programs in ecology. *Mailing Add:* Middlesex Center Rd RD 3 Montpelier VT 05602

JERVIS, ROBERT E, RADIOCHEMISTRY, APPLICATIONS. *Current Pos:* assoc prof, Univ Toronto, 58-67, assoc dean res eng, 74-78, res chmn, 81-85, PROF APPL CHEM, DEPT CHEM ENG, UNIV TORONTO, 66-, EMER PROF, 92- *Personal Data:* b Toronto, Int, May 21, 27; m 50, Frances J McCourt; c Ann K & Peter R. *Educ:* Univ Toronto, BA, 49, MA, 50, PhD(phys chem), 52. *Honors & Awards:* Hevesy Medal; Lewis Medal, Can Nuclear Soc; Ressovsky Medal, Russ Acad Sci. *Prof Exp:* Assoc res officer, Atomic Energy Can, Ltd, Ont, 52-58. *Concurrent Pos:* Vchmn, Can Sci Fairs Coun, 63-65; vis prof, Fac Sci, Univ Tokyo, 65-66, Energy Res Group, Cambridge Univ, 78 & Nat Univ Malaysia, 79; vchmn, Nuclear Safety Comt, Atomic Energy Control Bd, Can Fed Govt, chmn, 88-95. *Mem:* Can Soc Forensic Sci; fel Chem Inst Can; fel Can Nuclear Soc; fel Indiana Acad Forensic Sci; fel Royal Soc Can. *Res:* Radioactivation research, especially application of nuclear detection methods to crime detection and to environmental pollution problems from heavy metals, mercury, arsenic, cadmium and lead; radiochemical studies of nuclear power reactor safety. *Mailing Add:* Dept Chem Eng Univ Toronto Toronto ON M5S 3E5 Can. Fax: 416-978-8605

JESAITIS, ALGIRDAS JOSEPH, CELL BIOLOGY, IMMUNOLOGY. *Current Pos:* res prof, Dept Chem & Biochem, 89-92, PROF & HEAD, DEPT MICROBIOL, MONT STATE UNIV, 92- *Personal Data:* b Fed Repub Ger, Aug 21, 45; US citizen; m 79; c 3. *Educ:* Sch Eng & Sci, NY Univ, BS, 67; Calif Inst Technol, PhD(biophys), 73. *Prof Exp:* Fel, Univ Freiburg, WGer, 73-75; fel, Univ Calif, San Diego, 75-79; fel, Scripps Clin & Res Found, 79-85, asst mem, 85-89. *Mem:* Biophys Soc; AAAS; Am Soc Cell Biol; Protein Soc; Soc Leukocyte Biol; Am Heart Asn. *Res:* Biophysics and cell biology of sensory transduction mechanisms; role of cell membrane processes in inflammation, chemotaxis and mechanisms of host defense; structure of neutrophil cytochrome b and chemotactic receptor. *Mailing Add:* Dept Microbiol Mont State Univ Bozeman MT 59717. Fax: 406-994-4926

JESAITIS, RAYMOND G, PHYSICAL ORGANIC CHEMISTRY. *Current Pos:* from assoc prof to prof chem, 74-84, PROF COMPUT SCI & CHEM, STATE UNIV NY COL TECHNOL, UTICA, 84- *Personal Data:* b Vilnius, Lithuania, Jan 20, 43. *Educ:* Cooper Union, BChE, 63; Cornell Univ, PhD(org chem), 67. *Prof Exp:* Res fel chem, Univ Calif, Berkeley, 67-68; asst prof, State Univ NY, Stony Brook, 68-74. *Mem:* Am Chem Soc; Royal Soc Chem. *Res:* Physical and theoretical organic chemistry, including molecular structure; molecular interactions; ecological systematics. *Mailing Add:* PO Box 3050 State Univ NY Col Technol Utica NY 13504-3050

JESCHOFNIG, PETER, CHEMISTRY. *Current Pos:* anthrop & sci instr, 87-88, assoc prof environ studies & chem, 88-93, PROF, DEPT ENVIRON STUDIES, COLO MOUNTAIN COL, 93- *Personal Data:* b Nov 6, 43; m 78, Linda Pope; c Autumn. *Educ:* WTex State Univ, BSc, 70; Southern Methodist Univ, MH, 73; Western State Col, MA, 88; Colo State Univ, PhD(environ educ), 92. *Prof Exp:* Grad asst, Southern Methodist Univ, 70-73; well site geologist, Oil Serv Co Iran, 74-75; lead offshore geologist, Enserch Explor Inc, Tex, 75-78 & Santa Fe Energy Co, 78-79; int staff geologist, Occidental Explor & Prod, Calif, 79-81, sr int staff geologist, 83-85; chief geologist, Occidental, Tunisia, 81-83, Madagascar, 85-86; independent geol consult, Salida, Colo, 86-88. *Concurrent Pos:* Res asst, Karisoke Res Ctr, Rwanda, 75; instr anthrop, Eastfield Col, 75-76; NSF grantee, Nat Training Ctr, US Geol Surv, 93, State Univ NY, 95; Fulbright prof, Dept Geol & Geophysics, Addis Ababa Univ, Ethiopia, 95-96. *Mem:* Am Water Resources Asn; Nat Sci Teachers Asn. *Res:* Effects of acid-mine drainage on aquatic populations; developing science labs for distance education. *Mailing Add:* Dept Sci Colo Mountain Col 3000 County Rd 114 Glenwood Springs CO 81601. *E-Mail:* pjeschofnig@coloradomtn.edu

JESKA, EDWARD LAWRENCE, IMMUNOPARASITOLOGY. *Current Pos:* from asst prof to prof vet path & vet med, 67-89, chmn, Dept Immunobiol, 75-80, EMER PROF VET PATH, RES INST, IOWA STATE UNIV, 89- *Personal Data:* b Erie, Pa, Aug 6, 23; m 50, Elizabeth E Ahlgren; c 4. *Educ:* Gannon Col, BA, 51; Marquette Univ, MS, 54; Univ Pa, PhD, 66. *Prof Exp:* Chief parasitologist, Pa Dept Health, 55-63; fel, Univ Pa, 65-67, res asst prof parasitol, Sch Vet Med, 67. *Mem:* Emer mem Am Asn Immunologists. *Res:* Characterization of parasitic nematode antigens involved in white cell reactions of vertebrate hosts; macrophage as effector mechanisms of resistance to infection. *Mailing Add:* 501 Theo Wirth Pkwy Golden Valley MN 55422-5340

JESKEY, HAROLD ALFRED, ORGANIC CHEMISTRY. *Current Pos:* RETIRED. *Personal Data:* b St Louis, Mo, Aug 18, 12; m 39, Margaret G Schlichting; c Janet S & Judith J (Watson). *Educ:* St Louis Col Pharm, BS, 33; Wash Univ, BA, 37; Univ Wis, PhD(org chem), 42. *Prof Exp:* Asst chemist, James F Ballard, Inc, 33-35; instr chem, St Louis Col Pharm, 35-38; asst, Univ Wis, 38-41; from instr to asst prof, Univ Tenn, 41-44; from asst prof to assoc prof, Southern Methodist Univ, 45-57, chmn dept, 62-72, prof, 57-79, emer prof chem, 79-; prof biochem, Southwestern Med Sch, Univ Tex, 80-87. *Mem:* Am Chem Soc. *Res:* Organic synthesis; carbonation of phenols. *Mailing Add:* 2929 Fondren Dr Dallas TX 75205

JESMOK, GARY J, inflammation & immunopharmacology, immunopathology, for more information see previous edition

JESPERSEN, JAMES, RADIOPHYSICS, COMMUNICATION THEORY. *Current Pos:* CONSULT THEORET RADIO PROPAGATION STUDIES, NAT BUR STAND, 74- *Personal Data:* b Weldona, Colo, Nov 17, 34; c 3. *Educ:* Colo Univ, BA, 56, MS, 61. *Honors & Awards:* Bronze Plaque, Korean Stand Res Inst, 78. *Prof Exp:* Proj leader radio astron, Cent Radio Propagation Lab, 56-61, group leader satellite ionospheric scintillation studies, 64-66; exchange scientist theory of VLF radio propagation, Radio Res Lab, Slough, Eng, 62-63; consult time broadcast studies, Nat Bur Stand, 67-68, chief time & frequency, Dissemination Res Group, Exp & Theoret Studies Time Dissemination, 69-72; Dept Comm Sci fel & consult tele-commun, 72-73. *Concurrent Pos:* Consult, Inst-Range Instrumentation Group, 73-79, Korean Stand Res Inst, 77-78 & UN Develop Plan, 78-79. *Mem:* Sr mem Inst Elec & Electronics Engrs; Sigma Xi; Inst Navig. *Res:* Radio astronomy; ionospheric physics; radio propagation; communication and information theory; time dissemination and navigation systems; communication aids for the deaf. *Mailing Add:* Four Mile Canyon 87 Camino Bosque Boulder CO 80302-9746

JESPERSEN, NEIL DAVID, ANALYTICAL CHEMISTRY. *Current Pos:* asst prof, 77-80, ASSOC PROF CHEM, ST JOHN'S UNIV, NY, 80- *Personal Data:* b Brooklyn, NY, Mar 5, 46; m 70; c 2. *Educ:* Washington & Lee Univ, BS, 67; Pa State Univ, PhD(chem), 71. *Prof Exp:* Asst prof chem, Univ Tex, Austin, 71-77. *Mem:* Am Chem Soc; AAAS; Sigma Xi. *Res:* Thermometric titrimetry; clinical analysis; environmental mutagens. *Mailing Add:* St John's Univ Grand Central & Utopuia Pkwys Jamaica NY 11439-0001

JESS, EDWARD ORLAND, meteorology; deceased, see previous edition for last biography

JESSE, KENNETH EDWARD, SOLID STATE PHYSICS. *Current Pos:* PROF PHYSICS, ILL STATE UNIV, 67-, RADIATION SAFETY OFFICER, 71- *Personal Data:* b Chicago, Ill, Jan 3, 33; m 59; c 3. *Prof Exp:* Res physicist, Aerospace Res Lab, Wright-Patterson AFB, 66-67. *Mem:* Am Asn Physics Teachers; Sigma Xi. *Res:* Thermoelectrical and electrical properties of nonmetallic materials. *Mailing Add:* 8 Knollcrest Ct Ill State Univ Normal IL 61761

JESSEN, CARL ROGER, RADIOLOGY, GENETICS. *Current Pos:* assoc prof vet clin sci, 74-77, RADIOLOGIST, DEPT CLIN SCI, COL VET MED, UNIV MINN, ST PAUL, 69-, PROF VET CLIN SCI, 77-, ASSOC DEAN VET MED SERV, 78- *Personal Data:* b Fairmont, Minn, Jan 12, 33; m 55; c 3. *Educ:* Univ Minn, BS, 54, DVM, 56, PhD(genetics), 69. *Prof Exp:* Pvt pract, 56-64. *Mem:* Am Vet Med Asn; Am Vet Radiol Soc; Genetics Soc Am. *Res:* Canine hip dysplasia; bone dysplasias in general. *Mailing Add:* 2161 Folwell Ave St Paul MN 55108

JESSEN, NICHOLAS C, SR, NUCLEAR ENGINEERING. *Current Pos:* RETIRED. *Personal Data:* b Ger, Feb 13, 13. *Prof Exp:* Dir technol, Babcock & Wilcox Co, 30-78. *Concurrent Pos:* Instr metall, Univ Akron, 38-42. *Mem:* Fel Am Soc Metals Int; Am Welding Soc. *Res:* Development of welding processes for heavy pressure vessels and tubular products for low and high alloy steels; developed original guidelines for welding of stainless steel. *Mailing Add:* 4307 Village Oaks Lane Atlanta GA 30338

JESSEN, NICHOLAS C, JR, METALLURGICAL ENGINEERING. *Current Pos:* SUPT, MARTIN MARIETTA CORP, 86- *Personal Data:* b Barberton, Ohio, Mar 29, 44. *Educ:* Univ Tenn, BS, 67, MS, 72. *Mem:* Fel Am Soc Metals; Nat Mgt Asn. *Mailing Add:* 12123 N Fox Den Dr Knoxville TN 37922

JESSER, WILLIAM AUGUSTUS, METAL PHYSICS, MATERIALS SCIENCE. *Current Pos:* from asst prof to prof mat sci, 68-89, THOMAS GOODWIN DIGGES CHAIR, UNIV VA, 89-, DEPT CHAIR, 92- *Personal Data:* b Waynesboro, Va, Dec 20, 39; m 62, Barbara Schwab; c William A & Nicole E. *Educ:* Univ Va, BA, 62, MS, 64, PhD(physics), 66. *Honors & Awards:* Alan Talbott Gwathmey Award, 67. *Prof Exp:* Lectr physics, Univ Witwatersrand, 66-68. *Concurrent Pos:* Mem, Ctr Advan Studies, Univ Va, NSF, 68-70; vis prof, Nagoya Univ, Japan, 78, Univ Pretoria, 82, 87, Univ Witwatersrand, 83 & Hunan Univ, Changsha, 90; fel, Japan Soc Prom Sci, 78; co-ed, Low Energy Dislocation Struct, 86, 89 & 95. *Mem:* Am Soc Metals; Electron Micros Soc Am; Am Inst Mining, Metall & Petrol Engrs; Mat Res Soc; Am Asn Crystal Growth; fel Am Soc Metals Int. *Res:* Growth and properties of thin films; transmission electron microscopy and diffraction; surface and interface properties; radiation damage; electronic materials. *Mailing Add:* Dept Mat Sci Thornton Hall Univ Va Charlottesville VA 22901. Fax: 804-982-5660; *E-Mail:* waj@virginia.edu

JESSOP, ALAN MICHAEL, GEOTHERMICS, GEOTHERMAL ENERGY. *Current Pos:* RETIRED. *Personal Data:* b Wellingborough, UK, Feb 4, 34; Brit & Can citizen; m 59; c 3. *Educ:* Univ Nottingham, BSc, 55, PhD(mining), 58. *Prof Exp:* Res officer, Brit Cotton Indust Res Asn, 58-60; Nat Res Coun Can fel geophysics, Univ Western Ont, 60-62; sci officer, Dominion Observ, Dept Energy Mines & Resources, Ottawa, 62-65, res scientist, Earth Phys Br, 65-86; res scientist, Geol Surv Can, Calgary, 86-93. *Concurrent Pos:* Mem, Int Heat Flow Comn, 63-75, secy, 71-75. *Mem:* Am Geophys Union. *Res:* Thermal state, thermal history, and hydrodynamics of sedimentary basins; energy content of deep groundwater; applications to formation and migration of hydrocarbons. *Mailing Add:* 333 Silver Ridge Crescent NW Calgary AB T3B 3T6 Can

JESSOP, NANCY MEYER, ZOOLOGY. *Current Pos:* chmn dept, 83-86, PROF LIFE SCI, PALOMAR COL, 75- *Personal Data:* b Pasadena, Calif, Dec 24, 26; m 47; c 2. *Educ:* Univ Redlands, BA, 45; Univ Ore, MA, 47; Univ Calif, Berkeley, PhD(zool), 53. *Prof Exp:* Asst zool & biol, Univ Ore, 45-46; asst exp zool, Univ Calif, 46-48; teacher, Calif Pub Schs, 53-55; teacher biol, Oceanside-Carlsbad Col, 55-60; from asst prof to prof, US Int Univ, Calif Western Campus, 60-75, chmn dept, 67-73. *Mem:* Am Soc Zoologists; Animal Behavior Soc (secy, 72-75); Western Soc Naturalists. *Res:* Peromyscus genetics; tissue reactions to deep freezing; evolution and ontogeny of behavior; sociobiology. *Mailing Add:* Dept Life Sci Palomar Col 1140 W Mission Rd San Marcos CA 92069

JESSOP, PHILIP GREGORY, HOMOGENEOUS CATALYSIS, SUPERCRITICAL FLUIDS. *Current Pos:* ASST PROF INORG CHEM, UNIV CALIF, 96- *Personal Data:* b Ottawa, Ont, June 26, 63; Brit & Can citizen; m 86, Lorena Crook; c David & Michael. *Educ:* Univ Waterloo, BS, 86; Univ BC, PhD(inorg chem), 91. *Prof Exp:* Postdoctoral fel chem, Univ Toronto, 91-92; researcher, Erato Molecular Catalyst Proj, Res Develop Corp Japan, 93-96. *Mem:* Am Chem Soc; Chem Inst Can. *Res:* Supercritical fluids as environmentally friendly solvents for homogeneous catalysis and synthesis of chiral products; effect of near-criticality on enantio selective reactions; activation of greenhouse gases. *Mailing Add:* Dept Chem Univ Calif Davis CA 95616. *Fax:* 530-752-8995; *E-Mail:* jessop@chem.ucdavis.edu

JESSUP, GORDON L, JR, biostatistics; deceased, see previous edition for last biography

JESTER, GUY EARLSCORT, STRUCTURAL DYNAMICS, SOIL MECHANICS. *Current Pos:* SR CONSULT, BOOKER ASSOCS, 95- *Personal Data:* b Dyersburg, Tenn, Oct 20, 29; m 93, Babette Sale; c Mark A, Robin A (Harrington), Margarete E (Carey) & Guy L. *Educ:* US Mil Acad, BS, 51; Univ Ill, MS, 58, PhD(civil eng), 69. *Honors & Awards:* Pres Citation, Am Soc Civil Engrs, 79, Award Merit, 83. *Prof Exp:* Chief, Eng Br, Corps Engrs, Europ, US Army, 59-61, asst prof civil eng, US Mil Acad, 62-65, dep dir & actg dir, Dept Res & Mgt, Waterways Exp Sta, 65-67, div engr, Viet Nam, 68-69, asst to chief res & develop & chief of info systs, 68-71, dist engr, Corp Engrs, St Louis Dist, 71-73; vpres corp planning & mkt & vpres & dir, J S Albericiconstruct Co Inc, 73-94; pres, Int Constructors Ltd, 91-96. *Concurrent Pos:* Pres, Asn Improvement Miss River, 74-78; vpres & dir, Int Waste Energy Systs. *Mem:* Am Soc Civil Engrs; fel Soc Am Mil Engrs; Sigma Xi. *Res:* Soil-structure interaction; soils; structural design under dynamic loading conditions. *Mailing Add:* 2 Daryl Lane St Louis MO 63124-1241

JESTER, JAMES VINCENT, EXPERIMENTAL PATHOLOGY, OPHTHALMOLOGY. *Current Pos:* Fel ophthal path, Estelle Doheny Eye Found, 78, INSTR, DEPT OPHTHAL & PATH & VIS PROF, DEPT BIOL, UNIV SOUTHERN CALIF, 81- *Personal Data:* b Riverside, Calif, Sept 7, 50; m 77. *Educ:* Univ Southern Calif, BS, 72, PhD(exp path), 78. *Concurrent Pos:* Prin investr, Fight for Sight-Grant-in-Aid, 81-82. *Mem:* Asn Res Vision & Ophthal; AAAS. *Res:* Ophthalmic experimental pathology with specific emphasis on elucidating the pathogenic mechanism involved in corneal and lid margin disease using morphologic and biochemical techniques. *Mailing Add:* Dept Ophthal Univ Tex Southwestern Med Sch 5323 Harry Hines Blvd Dallas TX 75235-7200

JESTER, WILLIAM A, CHEMICAL & NUCLEAR ENGINEERING, NUCLEAR CHEMISTRY. *Current Pos:* From asst prof to assoc prof, 63-86, PROF NUCLEAR ENG, PA STATE UNIV, 86- *Personal Data:* b Philadelphia, Pa, June 16, 34; m 67, Janet F Tucker; c 2. *Educ:* Drexel Inst, BS, 57; Pa State Univ, MS, 61, PhD(chem eng), 65. *Honors & Awards:* Joan Hodes Queneal Palladium Medal, Nat Audubon Soc & Am Asn Eng Soc, 85. *Concurrent Pos:* Consult; mem, Panel Basic Res Requirements Support Comprehensive Test Ban Monitoring, Nat Res Coun; hon exec dir, Nuclear Sci Teachers Asn, 89. *Mem:* Am Nuclear Soc; fel Am Inst Chem; Am Chem Soc; Sigma Xi; Am Soc Eng Educ; Am Nuclear Sci Teachers Asn. *Res:* Development of radio-nuclear techniques for the solution of scientific and engineering problems; the development of radiation monitoring instrumentation and methods for testing such monitors. *Mailing Add:* Radiation Sci & Eng Ctr Pa State Univ University Park PA 16802-1408. *Fax:* 814-863-4840; *E-Mail:* wajnuc@engr.psu.edu

JESWIET, JACOB, MANUFACTURING AUTOMATION. *Current Pos:* asst prof, 82-86, ASSOC PROF MECH ENG, QUEEN'S UNIV, 86- *Personal Data:* b Neth, Feb 24, 46; Can citizen; m 75; c 3. *Educ:* Queen's Univ, BSc, 70, MSc, 74, PhD(mech eng), 81. *Prof Exp:* Design engr, DuPont Can, 70-71; design & maintenance engr, Celanese, 71-73; asst prof eng, Univ NB, 79-82. *Concurrent Pos:* Assoc prof mech eng, Queen's Univ, 86- *Mem:* Sr mem Soc Mfg Engrs; NAm Mfg Res Inst; Am Soc Mech Engrs. *Res:* Friction and temperature at metal forming inter-faces; manufacturing automation, fns and fnc with emphasis upon diagnostic and robotic use. *Mailing Add:* Queen's Univ McLaughlin Hall Kingston ON K7L 3N6 Can

JETER, DAVID YANDELL, CHEMISTRY OF COPPER II. *Current Pos:* From asst prof to assoc prof, 73-93, PROF CHEM, RHODES COL, 93-, CHAIR CHEM, 88- *Personal Data:* b Cooper, Tex, Dec 19, 46; m 68, Brenda Horn; c Andrew. *Educ:* ETex State Univ, BS, 68; Univ NC, Chapel Hill, PhD(inorg chem), 71. *Mem:* Am Chem Soc. *Res:* Structure and characterization of five coordinate complexes of copper (II). *Mailing Add:* Rhodes Col Dept Chem 2000 N Parkway Memphis TN 38112. *E-Mail:* jeter@rhodes.edu

JETER, HEWITT WEBB, ENVIRONMENTAL RADIOCHEMISTRY, GEOPHYSICS. *Current Pos:* Scientist oceanog, 72-74, LAB MGR RADIOCHEM, TELEDYNE ISOTOPES, 74-, SR SCIENTIST GEOPHYS, 78- *Personal Data:* b Cincinnati, Ohio, Sept 9, 41; m 66, Gerrie Hek; c Mark & Paul. *Educ:* Yale Univ, BE, 63; Ore State Univ, PhD(oceanog), 72. *Res:* Mathematical modeling geophysics and oceanography; development of radiochemical procedures. *Mailing Add:* Teledyne Brown Eng Environ Servs 50 Van Buren Ave Westwood NJ 07675. *Fax:* 102-664-5586

JETER, JAMES ROLATER, JR, CELL DIFFERENTIATION, CELL PROLIFERATION. *Current Pos:* asst prof anat, 75-78, ASSOC PROF ANAT, NEUROSCI, CELL BIOL & HISTOL, TULANE UNIV, 78- *Personal Data:* b Ennis, TX, Sept 4, 40; m 63; c 1. *Educ:* Univ Tex, San Antonio, PhD(anat), 73. *Concurrent Pos:* Consult, NIH; ed adv bd, Cell Biol, A Series of Monographs, 85-90; secy & treas, Int Cell Cycle Soc, 84-90, pres elect, 90-92. *Mem:* AAAS; Am Asn Anatomists; Am Asn Cancer Res; Am Heart Asn; Am Soc Cell Biol; Int Cell Cycle Soc; Sigma Xi. *Res:* Role of nuclear proteins & protein phonylation in controlling cell proliferation and differentiation. *Mailing Add:* Med Sch Tulane Univ 1430 Tulane Ave New Orleans LA 70112-2669. *Fax:* 504-584-1687

JETER, RANDALL MARK, MICROBIAL GENETICS. *Current Pos:* asst prof, 85-91, ASSOC PROF BIOL SCI, TEX TECH UNIV, 91- *Personal Data:* b Iowa City, Iowa, Aug 4, 52. *Educ:* Univ Ariz, BS, 74; Univ Okla, MS, 76; Univ Calif, Davis, PhD(microbiol), 82. *Prof Exp:* Fel & res assoc, Univ Utah, 82-85. *Mem:* Am Soc Microbiol; fel AAAS; Genetics Soc Am; Sigma Xi. *Res:* The regulation of gene expression in microorganisms; specific research projects are designed to investigate the synthesis and use of cobalamin (vitamin B12) by the intestinal bacterium salmonella typhimurium. *Mailing Add:* Dept Biol Sci Texas Tech Univ Lubbock TX 79409-3131. *Fax:* 806-742-2963

JETER, WAYBURN STEWART, MEDICAL MICROBIOLOGY, IMMUNOLOGY. *Current Pos:* dir, Med Technol Prog, Univ Ariz, 75-77, head, dept microbiol, 68-83, prof microbiol, 63-92, dir, Lab Cellular Immunol, 76-92, prof pharmacol & texicol, 84-92, EMER PROF PHARMACOL, TOXICOL, MICROBIOL & IMMUNOL, UNIV ARIZ, 92-; PRES, SCI RELS SERV, 88- *Personal Data:* b Cooper, Tex, Feb 16, 26; m 47, Margaret McDonald; c Randall, Monette & Marcus. *Educ:* Univ Okla, BS, 48, MS, 49; Univ Wis, PhD(med microbiol), 50; Am Bd Med Microbiol, dipl. *Prof Exp:* Instr plant sci, Univ Okla, 48; asst med microbiol, Univ Wis, 48-50; instr bact, Col Med, Univ Iowa, 50-51, assoc, 51-52, from asst prof to assoc prof, 52-63. *Mem:* AAAS; Am Soc Microbiol; Soc Exp Biol & Med; Am Asn Immunol; Sigma Xi; Am Acad Microbiol. *Res:* Hypersensitivity; complement; transfer factor; tissue transplantation; pathogenic bacteria. *Mailing Add:* 5140 N Via Sempreverde Tucson AZ 85750-5966. *E-Mail:* wjeter@vms.ccit.arizona.edu

JETT, JAMES HUBERT, FLOW CYTOMETRY. *Current Pos:* Fel, Physics Div, 69-71, mem staff, Exp Pathol Group, 71-86, DEP GROUP LEADER, CELL BIOL GROUP, LIFE SCI DIV, LOS ALAMOS NAT LAB, 86-, DIR, NAT FLOW CYTOMETRY RESOURCE, 92- *Personal Data:* b Washington, DC, Nov 27, 38; m 62, Evangeline Vazela; c Stephen D & Kathleen M. *Educ:* Univ NMex, BS, 60, MS, 61; Univ Colo, PhD(nuclear physics), 69. *Concurrent Pos:* Adj prof, Dept Cell Biol, Univ NMex, Albuquerque, 85- *Mem:* Am Phys Soc; AAAS; Soc Anal Cytology (secy-treas, 85-90). *Res:* Biomedical instrumentation, development, application and data interpretation; interpretation of biological experiments and computer applications. *Mailing Add:* 545 Navajo Los Alamos NM 87544. *E-Mail:* jet@telomree.lanl.gov

JETT, MARTI, SIGNAL TRANSDUCTION, ROLE OF BIOACTIVE LIPIDS IN LETHAL SHOCK. *Current Pos:* sr fel, Nat Res Coun, 81-82, STAFF SCIENTIST, WALTER REED ARMY INST RES, 82- *Personal Data:* b Springfield, Ohio, July 22, 41; m 71, George Tilton; c Claire & Nicholas. *Educ:* Ind Wesleyan Univ, BA, 62; Georgetown Univ, PhD(biochem), 73. *Prof Exp:* Fel biochem, Blood Res Lab, Am Red Cross, 73-75, res scientist, 75-80. *Concurrent Pos:* Adj prof, Cath Univ & Univ Md, 80-; chief, Dept Molecular Path, Walter Reed Army Inst Res, co-dir, Sci & Eng Apprentice Prog. *Mem:* NY Acad Sci; Am Chem Soc; AAAS; Am Tissue Cult Asn; Am Women Sci; Am Soc Cell Biol; Am Soc Microbiol. *Res:* Breast cancer and autoerine growth factors pathways; regulatory mechanisms involved in the generation of bioactive lipids; mechanism for stimulation of cellular growth or cascades of inflammatory mediators by bioactive lipids; involvement of fatty acid binding proteins in regulation of bioactive lipid functions. *Mailing Add:* 3446 Oakwood Terr NW Washington DC 20010. *Fax:* 202-782-4318; *E-Mail:* dr.__marti_jett@wrair__ccmail.army.mil

JETTE, ARCHELLE NORMAN, PHYSICS SURFACES, STRUCTURE DEFECT CENTERS. *Current Pos:* instr, Whiting Sch Eng, 83-90, RES PHYSICIST, APPL PHYSICS LAB, JOHNS HOPKINS UNIV, 65- *Personal Data:* b Portland, Ore, May 15, 34; m 72, Jamie Drago; c Andrea N. *Educ:* Univ Calif, Riverside, AB, 61, MA, 63, PhD(physics), 65. *Prof Exp:* Res assoc fel physics, Columbia Univ, 65. *Concurrent Pos:* Vis prof solid state physics, Cath Univ, Rio de Janeiro, Brazil, 72; vis scientist, Ctr Interdisciplinary Res, Univ Bielefeld, WGer, 80. *Mem:* Am Phys Soc; Am Vacuum Soc. *Res:* Surface structure; defect centers in ionic crystals; atomic and molecular physics. *Mailing Add:* 4021 Arjay Circle Ellicott City MD 21042. *Fax:* 301-953-6904; *E-Mail:* anj@aplcomm.jhvapl.edu

JETTEN, ANTON MARINUS, DIFFERENTIATION, RETINOIDS. *Current Pos:* HEAD, CELL BIOL GROUP & LAB PULMONARY PATH, NAT INST ENVIRON HEALTH SCI, NIH, 82- *Personal Data:* b June 26, 46; m; c 2. *Educ:* Univ Nijmegen, Neth, PhD(biochem), 73. *Mem:* Am Asn Cancer Res; Am Soc Cell Biol. *Res:* Understanding the molecular mechanisms that regulate the proliferation and differentiation of tracheo bronchial epidermal cells. *Mailing Add:* Nat Inst Environ Health Sci NIH PO Box 12233 Research Triangle Park NC 27709-2233. *Fax:* 919-541-4133

JEUTTER, DEAN CURTIS, ELECTRONICS & RADIO FREQUENCY ENGINEERING. *Current Pos:* asst prof biomed eng, 76-83, ASSOC PROF ELEC, COMPUT & BIOMED ENG, MARQUETTE, 83- *Personal Data:* b Bradford, Pa, Dec 27, 44; m 67; c 1. *Educ:* Drexel Univ, BS, 67, MS, 69, PhD(biomed eng), 74. *Honors & Awards:* Earl W Hatz Mem Award, 84. *Prof Exp:* Chief engr, Electronics Div, Ventron Corp, 69-70; res assoc biotelemetry, Dept Biomed Eng, Drexel Univ, 70-74; fel reprod biol, Dept Obstet & Gynec, Univ Pa, 74-76. *Concurrent Pos:* Adj asst prof physiol, Dept Biol, Drexel Univ, 75-76 & Dept Physiol, Med Col Wis, 77-; asst clin prof neurosurg, Med Col Wis, 78-; consult, Symbion Inc, 85-88. *Mem:* Sr mem Inst Elec & Electronics Engrs; Sigma Xi; sr mem Biomed Eng Soc. *Res:* Transcutaneous data and powering; cochlear prostheses; totally implanted artificial heart; sensors; signal processing; regenerative electrical stimulation. *Mailing Add:* 246 Oak St Grafton WI 53024-2604

JEVNING, RON, BIOPHYSICS. *Current Pos:* SR RES FEL BIOL SCI, CALIF STATE UNIV, LONG BEACH, 88- *Personal Data:* b Winnemucca, Nev, Oct 20, 42. *Educ:* Stanford Univ, PhD, 71. *Prof Exp:* Asst prof, Dept Med, Med Ctr, Univ Calif, Irvine, 72-88. *Mem:* Am Physiol Soc; Am Soc Psychophysiol Res; Soc Neurosci; Soc Behav Med; Am Asn Scientists Practicing TM Tech. *Res:* Subjective foundations of science - in particular, as expressed in theory of measurement and theory of probability. *Mailing Add:* 210 W South St Rialto CA 92376

JEWELL, FREDERICK FORBES, SR, HISTOPATHOLOGY, PATHOLOGICAL ANATOMY OF CONIFERS & HARDWOODS. *Current Pos:* assoc prof, 67-69, PROF FOREST PROTECTION, LA TECH UNIV, 69- *Personal Data:* b Oil City, Pa, June 4, 28; m 78, Daphne Cooper; c Fred Jr, Kimberly, Robert, Michael, Heather & Jessica. *Educ:* Mich State Col, BS, 51, MS, 52; Univ WVa, PhD, 55. *Prof Exp:* Asst plant path, Univ WVa, 52-55; prin plant pathologist forest tree dis, Southern Inst Forest Genetics, 55-67. *Mem:* Am Phytopath Soc; Soc Am Foresters. *Res:* Disease resistance in forest trees; rust-resistance in Southern pines; pathological anatomy; needle cast diseases. *Mailing Add:* La Tech Univ Sch Forestry Ruston LA 71270

JEWELL, JACK LEE, DIODE LASERS, MICRO-OPTICS. *Current Pos:* VPRES, PHOTONICS RES, INC, 91- *Personal Data:* b Jacksonville, Fla, Jan 7, 54; m 83; c 1. *Educ:* Univ Fla, BS, 75; Fla Inst Technol, MS, 77; Univ Ariz, MS, 81, PhD(optical sci), 84. *Prof Exp:* Mem tech staff, AT&T Bell Labs, 84-91. *Concurrent Pos:* Distinguished lectr, Inst Elec & Electronics Engrs Lasers & Electro-Optics Soc, 91-92. *Mem:* Optical Soc Am; Am Phys Soc; Soc Photo-Optical Instrumentation Engrs; Inst Elec & Electronics Engrs. *Res:* Vertical-cavity surface-emitting microlasers; decreasing electrical resistance; extending wavelength range; opto-electronic integration with transistors; micro-optic integration. *Mailing Add:* Picolight Inc 4622 Sunshine Canyon Dr Boulder CO 80302

JEWELL, NICHOLAS PATRICK, BIOSTATISTICS, TIME SERIES. *Current Pos:* from asst prof to assoc prof, 81-87, PROF BIOSTATIST, UNIV CALIF, BERKELEY, 87- *Personal Data:* b Paisley, Scotland, Sept 3, 52; m 80. *Educ:* Univ Edinburgh, BSc, 73, PhD(math), 76. *Prof Exp:* Harkness fel, Commonwealth Fund, NY, 76-78; res fel, Univ Edinburgh, UK, 78-79; asst prof statist, Princeton Univ, 79-81. *Mem:* Am Statist Asn; Inst Math Statist (treas, 85-); Biomet Soc. *Res:* Biostatistics; mathematical statistics; functional analysis; function theory. *Mailing Add:* 8 Parkside Dr Oakland CA 94611

JEWELL, PAUL WILLIAM, SURFACE WATER HYDRODYNAMICS, BIOGEOCHEMICAL CYCLES. *Current Pos:* ASSOC PROF GEOL, UNIV UTAH, 89- *Personal Data:* b Ogden, Utah, Dec 15, 52; m 82, Teresa Highland; c Scott. *Educ:* Beloit Col, BS, 78; Univ Utah, MS, 84; Princeton Univ, PhD(geol), 89. *Prof Exp:* Geol asst, Newmont Mining Co, 79; assoc geologist, Univ Utah Res Inst, 80-81. *Concurrent Pos:* Geol consult, Biomyne, Inc, 87-; prin investr, Petrol Res Fund, 90- *Mem:* Geol Soc Am; Geochem Soc; Am Geophys Union; Asn Eng Geologists. *Res:* Surface water hydrodynamics and the role that it plays in the cycles of carbon, nutrients and oxygen in the natural environment. *Mailing Add:* 4223 Sage St Salt Lake City UT 84124-2434. *Fax:* 801-581-7065; *E-Mail:* pwjewell@mines.utah.edu

JEWELL, WILLIAM R, SURGERY. *Current Pos:* assoc prof med, 71-78, PROF MED & CHIEF GEN SURG, UNIV KANS MED CTR, 78- *Personal Data:* b Evanston, Ill, Oct 7, 35; m 60; c 4. *Educ:* Blackburn Col, BA, 57; Univ Ill, BS, 59, MD, 61. *Honors & Awards:* Meade Johnson Sr Res Award Surg, 66, Health Sci Achievement Award, 71. *Prof Exp:* Asst prof surg, Med Ctr, Univ Ky, 68-71. *Concurrent Pos:* Consult, US Vet Admin Hosp, Lexington, Ky, 68- *Res:* Carcinogenesis; protein metabolism in cancer bearing hosts; oncologic immunology; wound healing. *Mailing Add:* Dept Surg Univ Kans Med Ctr 39th & Rainbow Blvd Kansas City KS 66103

JEWELL, WILLIAM S(YLVESTER), OPERATIONS RESEARCH, ACTUARIAL SCIENCE. *Current Pos:* from asst prof to assoc prof indust eng, 61-67, chmn dept, 67-69 & 76-80, PROF INDUST ENG & OPERS RES, UNIV CALIF, BERKELEY, 67- *Personal Data:* b Detroit, Mich, July 2, 32; m 56; c 4. *Educ:* Cornell Univ, BEngPhys, 54; Mass Inst Technol, SM, 55, ScD, 58. *Honors & Awards:* Halmstead Memorial Prize. *Prof Exp:* Asst, Mass Inst Technol, 55-58; assoc dir, Mgt Sci Div, Broadview Res Corp, 58-60. *Concurrent Pos:* Fulbright res scholar, France, 65; bd mem, Teknekron Indust Inc, Berkeley, 68-83; res scholar, Int Inst Appl Systs Anal, 74-75; guest prof, Fed Inst Technol, Switzer, 80-81. *Mem:* Opers Res Soc Am; Inst Mgt Sci; Swiss Actuarial Asn; Sigma Xi; Int Asn Actuaries. *Res:* Operations research; prediction and estimation; reliability; risk theory. *Mailing Add:* 67 Loma Vista Dr Orinda CA 94563

JEWETT, DON L, EVOKED POTENTIALS, SOURCE LOCALIZATION. *Current Pos:* asst prof, Dept Physiol, Univ Calif, San Francisco, 64-72, asst prof, Dept Neurosurg, 66-72, clin instr, Dept Orthop Surg, 72-75, assoc prof, 75-89, prof, 89-91, EMER PROF, DEPT ORTHOP SURG, UNIV CALIF, SAN FRANCISCO, 91-; DIR RES, ABRATECH CORP, 91- *Personal Data:* b Eureka, Calif, Jan 28, 31; m 54; c 2. *Educ:* San Francisco State Col, AB, Univ Calif, Berkeley, 54-56; Univ Calif, San Francisco, MD, 60; Oxford Univ, DPhil(physiol), 63. *Prof Exp:* NIH fel, Yale Univ, 63-64. *Mem:* Am Asn Aerosol Res; Inst Elec & Electronics Engrs; Sigma Xi. *Res:* Central and peripheral nervous system physiology related to clinical conditions; bioengineering; averaged far field potentials. *Mailing Add:* 475 Gate S Rd Suite 255 Sausalito CA 94965. *Fax:* 415-331-4537; *E-Mail:* jewett@ssu.abratech.com

JEWETT, JOHN GIBSON, PHYSICAL ORGANIC CHEMISTRY. *Current Pos:* dean Col Arts & Sci, 77-89, PROF CHEM, UNIV VT, 77- *Personal Data:* b Birmingham, Ala, Jan 21, 37; m 62, Susan Rideout; c Elizabeth & Jennifer. *Educ:* Harvard Univ, AB, 58; Mass Inst Technol, PhD(org chem), 62. *Prof Exp:* Res assoc org chem, Ind Univ, 62-64; from asst prof to prof chem, Ohio Univ, 64-77. *Mem:* AAAS; Am Chem Soc; Sigma Xi. *Res:* Reaction mechanisms; isotope effects; simple displacement reactions; carbonyl addition reactions. *Mailing Add:* Chem Dept Univ Vt Cook Phys Sci Bldg Burlington VT 05405. *Fax:* 802-656-8705; *E-Mail:* j.jewett@uvmvax.uvm.edu

JEWETT, SANDRA LYNNE, BIOCHEMISTRY, BIO-ORGANIC CHEMISTRY. *Current Pos:* from asst prof to assoc prof, 77-88, PROF CHEM, CALIF STATE UNIV, NORTHRIDGE, 88- *Personal Data:* b Lone Pine, Calif, Nov 13, 45. *Educ:* Univ Calif, Santa Barbara, BA, 67, PhD(chem), 71. *Prof Exp:* Res fel biochem, Stanford Univ, 71-73; res fel enzyme immunoassays, Syva Co, Palo Alto, Calif, 74-75; asst prof chem, Williams Col, 75-77. *Concurrent Pos:* NIH fel, 72-73; Jerome Richfield scholar, 93. *Mem:* AAAS; Am Chem Soc; Sigma Xi. *Res:* Studies of erythrocyte superoxide dismutase; chemical studies of active site and intersubunit interactions; formation of and properties of metal deficient enzymes; reaction of copper-zinc dismutase with hydrogen peroxide; iron-catecholamine complexes. *Mailing Add:* Dept of Chem Calif State Univ Northridge CA 91330-0001

JEYAPALAN, KANDIAH, PHOTOGRAMMETRY. *Current Pos:* PROF SURV, GEOD & PHOTOGRAM, IOWA STATE UNIV, 79- *Personal Data:* b Sri Lanka, June 24, 38; m 64, Nalini Silva; c Suriya & Manjula. *Educ:* Univ Ceylon, BSc, 60; Univ London, MSc, 67, PhD(photogram), 72. *Prof Exp:* Asst supt, Surv Dept, Sri Lanka, 61-67; chief photogrammetrist, 67-69; res assoc, Dept Geodetic Sci, Ohio State Univ, 69-72; asst prof surv, geod & photogram, Calif State Univ, Fresno, 72-74, assoc prof, 74-78, prof, 78-79. *Concurrent Pos:* Ceylon Govt scholar, 63; UN fel, UN Educ & Sci Orgn, 66; lectr, Dept Geod Sci, Ohio State Univ, 69-72; admin asst, Highway Dept, Columbus, Ohio, 72; sr lectr, Univ Dar-es-Salaam, Tanzania, 73 & 74; res civil engr, US Geol Surv, 77; vis prof, Naval Postgrad Sch, Montrey, Calif, 87; UN fel, 86. *Mem:* Am Soc Photogram; Am Congress Surv & Mapping; Sigma Xi. *Res:* Photogrammetry: development of analytical plotter, calibration of cameras, analytical triangulation, shortrange photogrammetry and digital terrain model; geodesy: electronic surveying, Doppler surveying and geoposition system; numerical cadastral survey; global positioning system; surveying, land surveying, geographic information system. *Mailing Add:* Dept Civil Eng Univ Iowa Ames IA 50011. *Fax:* 515-294-8216; *E-Mail:* kjp@iastate.edu

JEZAK, EDWARD V, PHYSICS. *Current Pos:* ASSOC PROF MATH, ROYAL MIL COL CAN, 68- *Personal Data:* b Czestochowa, Poland, Mar 29, 34; US citizen; m 62; c 2. *Educ:* Harvard Univ, AB, 57; Univ Minn, PhD(physics), 62. *Prof Exp:* Asst prof physics, Boston Col, 62-68. *Mem:* Am Phys Soc. *Res:* Nuclear theoretical physics; three body problem; molecular dynamics. *Mailing Add:* Dept Math & Comput Sci Royal Mil Col Kingston Kingston ON K7K 5L0 Can

JEZEK, KENNETH CHARLES, GEOPHYSICS. *Current Pos:* ASSOC PROF GEOL & DIR, BYRD POLAR RES CTR, OHIO STATE UNIV, 89- *Personal Data:* b Chicago, Ill, May 17, 51; m 84, Rosanne M Graziano. *Educ:* Univ Ill, BSc, 73; Univ Wis, MSc, 77, PhD(geophys), 80. *Prof Exp:* Observer, Bartol Res Found Cosmic Ray Lab, McMurdo Sta, Antarctica, 73-74; geophysicist, Ross Ice Shelf, Antarctica, 74-75, Devon Island Ice Cap, 75, Camp Century Greenland, 77, Southern Greenland Ice Sheet, 81, East Antarctica, 81-82; field leader, Ross Ice Shelf, 76-77, Dome C East Antarctica, 78-79; fel, Inst Polar Studies, Ohio State Univ, Columbus, 80-81; proj assoc, Geophys & Polar Res Ctr, Univ Wis, 81-83; geophysicist, Cold Regions Res & Eng Lab, US Army, Hanover, NH, 83-85, 87-89; mgr, Polar Oceans & Ice Sheets Prog, NASA, Washington, 85-87; res asst prof, Thayer

Sch Eng, Dartmouth Col, 87-89. *Concurrent Pos:* Grant NSF, 82-84, Off naval Res, 84-89, CRREL, 85-86, NASA, 85-93, ONR, 92; prin investr, Greenland, 82 & 85, Greenland Sea, 88, Greenland Ice Sheet, 91-92; cons, Polar Ice Coring Off, Greenland, 83; assoc ed, J Geophys Res, 91-; mem, Environ Task Force, 92; coordr, Sea Ice Electromagnetic Accelerated Res Initiative, Off Naval Res, 92. *Mem:* Am Geophus Union; Soc Exploration Geophysicists; Int Glaciological Soc; Sigma Xi. *Mailing Add:* 2556 Andover Rd Upper Arlington OH 43221-3202

JEZESKI, JAMES JOHN, FOOD MICROBIOLOGY, FOOD SCIENCE. *Current Pos:* RETIRED. *Personal Data:* b Minneapolis, Minn, June 8, 18; m 43, Mary Bender. *Educ:* Univ Minn, BS, 40, MS, 42, PhD(bact), 47. *Prof Exp:* Asst dairy bact, Univ Minn, St Paul, 41-43, from asst prof to prof, 48-69; prof bot & microbiol, Mont State Univ, 69-73; dir res & develop, Monarch Chem Div, H B Fuller Co, 73-78; mem staff exten food technol, Univ Fla, 78-84. *Mem:* Am Soc Microbiol; Am Dairy Sci Asn; Int Asn Milk, Food & Environ Sanit; Inst Food Technol. *Res:* Role of microorganisms in manufacturing and deterioration of foods; quality assurance and public health safety of foods. *Mailing Add:* 315 Elm St Winona MN 55987-2056

JEZL, JAMES LOUIS, ORGANIC CHEMISTRY, RESEARCH ADMINISTRATION. *Current Pos:* RETIRED. *Personal Data:* b Tobias, Nebr, Dec 12, 18; m; m 84, Rita M; c Barbara, Patricia J, James L Jr, Mary L, Ann & John. *Educ:* Univ Nebr, AB, 41; Pa State Col, MS, 42; Univ Del, PhD(org chem), 49. *Prof Exp:* Supvry chemist, US Rubber Co, 42-43; jr anal chemist, Sun Oil Co, Ohio, 43-45, sr anal chemist, 45-47, develop chemist, Pa, 47-49, res chemist, 49-54, res group leader, 54-58, sect chief, 58-60, mgr res div, Avisun Corp, 60-68, dir res, 68-70; div dir, Naperville Tech Ctr, Amoco Chem Corp, 70-76, mgr explor res, Res & Develop Dept, 76-86. *Mem:* AAAS; Am Chem Soc. *Res:* Petrochemicals; polyolefins; petroleum processing. *Mailing Add:* 35 W 094 Army Trail St Charles IL 60174

JEZOREK, JOHN ROBERT, ANALYTICAL CHEMISTRY, INORGANIC CHEMISTRY. *Current Pos:* from asst prof to assoc prof, 70-81, PROF ANALYTICAL CHEM, UNIV NC, GREENSBORO, 82- *Personal Data:* b Baltimore, Md, June 12, 42; m 67; c 4. *Educ:* Loyola Col, Md, BS, 64; Univ Del, PhD(anal chem), 69. *Prof Exp:* Res assoc, Univ Mich, 69-70, Univ Ariz, 77-78. *Mem:* Am Chem Soc; Sigma Xi. *Res:* Liquid chromatography; design of novel LC stationary phases; surface modification chemistry. *Mailing Add:* Dept of Chem Univ of NC Greensboro NC 27412

JEZYK, PETER FRANKLIN, VETERINARY MEDICINE. *Current Pos:* asst prof, 75-81, ADJ ASSOC PROF MED GENETICS, SCH VET MED, UNIV PA, 81- *Personal Data:* b Ware, Mass, Nov 7, 39; c 2. *Educ:* Univ Mass, BS, 61, PhD(zool), 66; Univ Pa, VMD, 75. *Prof Exp:* NIH fel biol chem & res assoc, Univ Mich, 66-67; asst prof biochem, Med Col Va, 67-71. *Concurrent Pos:* Dir, Metab Screening Lab, Children's Hosp Philadelphia, 76- *Mem:* AAAS; Am Vet Med Asn. *Res:* Metabolic aspects of inherited disease in companion animals. *Mailing Add:* Dept Med Genetics Univ Pa Sch Vet Med 3900 Delancey St Philadelphia PA 19104-6010

JHA, MAHESH CHANDRA, COAL CONVERSION TECHNOLOGY, PROCESS DEVELOPMENT. *Current Pos:* res metallurgist, 73-75, group leader, 75-78, sect supvr, 78-84, mgr contract res & develop, 85-86, MGR ENERGY RES & DEVELOP, AMAX RES & DEVELOP CTR, 87- *Personal Data:* b Bihar, India, March 13, 45; US citizen; m 64; c 2. *Educ:* Bihar Inst Technol, India, BScEng, 65; Mich Tech Univ, MS, 70; Iowa State Univ, Ames, PhD(metall & chem eng), 74. *Honors & Awards:* Extractive Metall Technol Award, Metall Soc, 86. *Prof Exp:* Lectr extractive metall, Bihar Inst Technol, India, 65-66 & Univ Rorkee, India, 66-69; grad res asst, Inst Mineral Res, Mich Tech Univ, 69-70 & Ames Lab, Iowa State Univ, 70-73. *Mem:* Am Inst Mining, Metall & Petrol Engrs; Am Inst Chem Engrs. *Res:* Improving the processes for extraction of non-ferrous metals such as nickel, cobalt, molybdenum, tungsten, gold, silver from low-grade ores; waste streams; coal conversion and utilization tehnology. *Mailing Add:* 7891 Everett Way Arvada CO 80005

JHA, SHACHEENATHA, EXPERIMENTAL NUCLEAR PHYSICS. *Current Pos:* PROF PHYSICS, UNIV CINCINNATI, 69- *Personal Data:* b Darbhanga, Bihar, India, Nov 15, 18; m 55; c 4. *Educ:* Patna Univ, BS, 39, MS, 41; Univ Edinburgh, PhD(nuclear physics), 50. *Prof Exp:* Res scholar physics, Patna Sci Col, 41-44, lectr, 44-46, asst prof, 51; Govt Bihar scholar nuclear physics, Univ Edinburgh, 46-51; res fel physics, Tata Inst Fundamental Res, India, 51-56, fel, 56-61; asst prof, Carnegie Inst Technol, 61-66; assoc prof, Case Western Reserve Univ, 66-69. *Mem:* Fel Am Phys Soc; Am Asn Physics Teachers. *Res:* Nuclear spectroscopy and reaction; Mossbauer effect; molecular spectroscopy. *Mailing Add:* 1163 Beverley Hill Dr Cincinnati OH 45208

JHAMANDAS, KHEM, PHARMACOLOGY. *Current Pos:* asst prof, 70-75, PROF PHARMACOL & TOXICOL, FAC MED, QUEEN'S UNIV, ONT, 75- *Personal Data:* b EAfrica, May 11, 39; m 71. *Educ:* Univ London, BSc, 64; Univ Alta, MSc, 66, PhD(pharmacol), 69. *Prof Exp:* Med Res Coun Can fel pharmacol & therapeut, Univ Man, 69-70. *Concurrent Pos:* Vis scientist, Mayo Clinic & Killam res fel, 80-81, Kyoto Univ, 86, Univ Melbourne, 87. *Mem:* Pharmacol Soc Can; Am Soc Pharmacol & Exp Therapeut; Soc Neurosci. *Res:* Neuropharmacology; action of drugs on transmitter substances in the central nervous system; mechanisms underlying drug dependence on opioids; neuropharmacology of enkephalins, endorphins and neuropeptides; excitotoxins. *Mailing Add:* Dept Pharmacol & Toxicol Queen's Univ Kingston ON K7L 3N6 Can. Fax: 613-545-6412

JHANWAR, SURESH CHANDRA, CYTOGENETICS. *Current Pos:* ASST PROF GENETICS & ASST ATTEND GENETICIST, SLOAN-KETTERING CANCER CTR, 76- *Educ:* Univ Delhi, India, PhD(genetics), 76. *Mailing Add:* Sloan-Kettering Cancer Ctr Box 147 1275 York Ave New York NY 10021-6094. Fax: 212-794-5830

JHIRAD, DAVID JOHN, PHYSICS, SCIENCE POLICY. *Current Pos:* CONSULT, 84- *Personal Data:* b India, May 29, 39; US citizen; m, Anna G Reid; c Dylan, Nicholas & Alexander. *Educ:* Delhi Univ, BSc, 58; Cambridge Univ, BA, 61, MA, 64; Harvard Univ, PhD(appl physics), 72. *Prof Exp:* Asst prof physics, Boston Univ & Univ Mass, 70-75; staff dir energy, Union Concerned Scientists, 75-78; sr res scientist energy, Jet Propulsion Lab, Calif Inst Technol, 78-80; dir, Int Energy Prog, Brookhaven Nat Lab, 80-84. *Concurrent Pos:* Sr Energy Adv, US Agency for Int Develop, 84- *Mem:* Am Phys Soc; AAAS; Int Solar Energy Soc; Scientists Inst Pub Info. *Res:* New power technology, energy technology assessment and policy analysis; energy and global climate change; international power project financing; thermodynamics and statistical mechanics. *Mailing Add:* 3009 Daniel Lane NW Washington DC 20015. Fax: 703-537-4053; E-Mail: djhirad@usaid.gov

JHON, MYUNG S, POLYMER ENGINEERING, TRIBOLOGY. *Current Pos:* from asst prof to assoc prof, 80-88, PROF CHEM ENG, CARNEGIE MELLON UNIV, 88- *Personal Data:* b Korea; US citizen. *Educ:* Seoul Nat Univ, Seoul, Korea, BS, 67; Univ Chicago, PhD(physics), 74. *Prof Exp:* Res asst physics, James Franck Inst, Univ Chicago, 70-74; postdoctoral fel physics, Univ Toronto, 74-76; res specialist chem, Univ Minn, 76-80. *Concurrent Pos:* Vis prof, Magnetics Recording Inst, Int Bus Mach, 85 & Univ Calif, Berkeley, 89; consult, UN Indust Develop Orgn, 86; sr vis prof, Naval Res Lab, Washington, DC, 86; vis scientist, Int Bus Mach Res Div, Almaden Res Ctr, 88. *Mem:* Am Inst Chem Engrs; Am Phys Soc; Am Chem Soc; Sigma Xi; NY Acad Sci. *Res:* Magnetic and magneto-optical recording; polymer and suspension rheology; interfacial dynamics; membrane science and technology; equilibrium and nonequilibrium statistical mechanics; chemical kinetics; fluid mechanics; turbulent drag reduction. *Mailing Add:* 6381 Monitor St Pittsburgh PA 15217

JI, CHUENG RYONG, PARTICLE & NUCLEAR THEORY. *Current Pos:* asst prof nuclear physics, 87-92, ASSOC PROF PHYSICS, NC STATE UNIV, 92- *Personal Data:* b Seoul, Korea, Jan 7, 54; m 83, Mikyoung Lee; c Stephen, Lisa & David. *Educ:* Seoul Nat Univ, BS, 76; Korea Advan Inst Sci & Technol, MS, 78, PhD(physics), 82. *Prof Exp:* Particle & nuclear physics, Stanford Univ, 84-86; res assoc, Brooklyn Col, City Univ New York, 86-87. *Concurrent Pos:* Vis scholar elem particle physics, Stanford Linear Accelerator Ctr, 82-86; theory consult, Continuous Electron Beam Accelerator Facil, 90; prin investr, Dept Energy, 90-; vis prof, Seoul Nat Univ, 93. *Mem:* Am Phys Soc; Sigma Xi. *Res:* Quark and gluon structures of hadron; theory of strong interaction, quantum chromodynamics, based on the light cone formulation; form factors of meson, nucleon and deuteron, non-topological soliton physics. *Mailing Add:* Dept Physics NC State Univ Raleigh NC 27695-8202. Fax: 919-515-2471; E-Mail: ji@ncsu.edu

JI, GUANGDA WINSTON, III-V SEMICONDUCTOR DEVICES RESEARCH & DEVELOPMENT, REACTIVE ION ETCHING AND PLASMA ENHANCED CHEMICAL VAPOR DEPOSITION SPECIALIST. *Current Pos:* RES SCIENTIST, SUNNYBROOK HEALTH SCI CTR, TORONTO, 93- *Personal Data:* b Tianjin, People's Repub China; c 1. *Educ:* Univ Ill Urbana, MS, 81, PhD(physics), 86. *Honors & Awards:* Chinese Award in Sci & Technol, 82. *Prof Exp:* Res assoc elec eng, Coord Sci Lab, Univ Ill, Urbana, 86-88, Ont Laser & Lightwave Res Ctr, 88-91. *Mem:* Am Phys Soc. *Res:* Semiconductor laser; optoelectronic devices; high-speed semiconductor electronic devices; device modeling and optical measurements for superlattice and heterojunction devices in III-V semiconductors; reactive ion etching and plasma enhanced chemical vapor deposition techniques and diagnosis; author of one publication; x-ray medical image processing. *Mailing Add:* 145 St George St Apt 301 Toronto ON M5R 2M1 Can. E-Mail: chi@srcl.sunnybrook.utoronto.ca

JI, INHAE, HORMONES, RECEPTORS. *Current Pos:* res asst biochem, 78-91, RES PROF MOLECULAR BIOL, UNIV WYO, 91- *Personal Data:* b Seoul, Korea, May 17, 38; m 65; c 2. *Educ:* Seoul Nat Univ, BS, 61, MS, 63; Univ Wyo, PhD(biochem), 77. *Prof Exp:* Postdoctoral biochem, Harvard Med Sch, 77-78. *Mem:* Endocrine Soc; Am Soc Cell Biologists. *Mailing Add:* Dept Molecular Biol Univ Wyo Laramie WY 82071-3944

JI, SUNGCHUL, BIOPHYSICS, CELL PHYSIOLOGY. *Current Pos:* AT GRAD PROG TOXICOL, RUTGERS UNIV. *Personal Data:* b Sheenweejoo, Korea, Dec 17, 37; m 67; c 1. *Educ:* Univ Minn, Duluth, BA, 65; State Univ NY Albany, PhD(org chem), 70. *Prof Exp:* Asst prof chem, Mankato State Col, 68-70; NIH trainee & res asst prof, Inst Enzyme Res, Univ Wis-Madison, 70-74; res assoc, Johnson Res Found, Univ Pa, 74-76; res scientist, Max Planck Inst Systs Physiol, 76-; res asst prof, dept pharmacol, Univ NC, 79- *Mem:* Am Chem Soc; AAAS; Sigma Xi. *Res:* Anion radical chemistry; electron transfer reactions in organic solvents; energy-coupling mechanism in mitochondria; nicotinamide-adenine dinucleotide fluorescence photography; micro-light guide tissue photometry; flow-metabolism coupling in the liver; alcohol-induced liver injury; lobular oxygen gradient in the liver. *Mailing Add:* Toxicol Div EOHSI Rutgers Univ Piscataway NJ 08855

JI, TAE H(WA), BIOCHEMISTRY, MOLECULAR BIOLOGY. *Current Pos:* from asst prof to assoc prof, 70-77, PROF BIOCHEM, UNIV WYO, 77- *Personal Data:* b Andong, Korea, Apr 7, 41; US citizen; m 65; c 2. *Educ:* Seoul Nat Univ, BS, 64; Univ Calif, San Diego, PhD(biol), 68. *Honors & Awards:* Burlington Award, 88. *Prof Exp:* Inst Biomed Res fel, AMA, 68-69; fel, Univ Minn, 69-70. *Concurrent Pos:* Vis prof, Harvard Univ, 77-78; Regent fel, Univ Calif, 64, scholar award cancer res, 77; sr fac res award, Am Cancer Soc, 83-88; mem, Physiol Chem Study Sect, NIH, 90-94. *Mem:* Am Soc Biochem & Molecular Biol; Endocrine Soc; Soc Study Reproduction; Protein Soc; Am Soc Microbiol. *Res:* Structure function and gene expression of gonadotropin receptors; photoaffinity labeling. *Mailing Add:* Dept Molecular Biol Univ Wyo Laramie WY 82071-3944. *Fax:* 307-766-5098; *E-Mail:* ji@plains.uwyo.edu

JIA, QUANXI, THIN FILMS, SEMICONDUCTOR & SUPERCONDUCTOR DEVICES. *Current Pos:* postdoctoral fel, 93-96, STAFF MEM, LOS ALAMOS NAT LAB, 96- *Personal Data:* b Henan Province, China, Sept 3, 57; m 85, Xuming Wu; c Yixuan & Richard. *Educ:* Jiaotong Univ, Xian, China, BS, 82, MS, 85; State Univ NY, Buffalo, PhD(elec & comput eng), 91. *Prof Exp:* Teacher, Middle Sch, Mengxian, China, 75-78; res asst, Jiaotong Univ, 82-85, res assoc, 85-87, asst prof, 87-88; res assoc, State Univ NY Buffalo, 91-93. *Concurrent Pos:* Vis assoc prof, Kumamato Univ, Japan, 93. *Mem:* Am Vacuum Soc; Mat Res Soc; Am Ceramic Soc. *Res:* Semiconductors process development; electronic material analysis; thin film growth and device development; patentee in field. *Mailing Add:* Los Alamos Nat Lab MS K763 Los Alamos NM 87545. *Fax:* 505-665-3164; *E-Mail:* qxjia@lanl.gov

JIANG, JACK BAU-CHIEN, ORGANIC CHEMISTRY, MEDICINAL CHEMISTRY. *Current Pos:* VPRES CHEM RES, PRO-NEURON INC, 96- *Personal Data:* b Sze-chuan, China, Nov 15, 47; m 73, Lily Yang-Bai Chen; c Melody & Hanson. *Educ:* Nat Cheng Kung Univ, BS, 70; Mich State Univ, PhD(org chem), 75. *Prof Exp:* Res specialist, Univ Minn, 75-77; res chemist drug synthesis, Am Cyanamid Co, 77-79; scientist, Ortho Pharm Corp, 79-81, sr scientist, 81-84, DuPont Pharmaceuts, 84-87; group leader, Du Pont Pharmaceut, 87-89; dir med chem, Sphinx Pharmaceut Corp, 89-91, vpres chem res, 91-93; vpres chem, Phytera, 93-95. *Concurrent Pos:* Adj asst prof, Col Pharm, Univ NC, Chapel Hill, 91- *Mem:* Am Chem Soc; Am Asn Cancer Res. *Res:* Design and synthesis of medicinal agents; anticancer chemotherapy discovery and development; natural products. *Mailing Add:* 62 Kato Dr Sudbury MA 01776-2448. *Fax:* 978-443-0040

JIANG, NAI-SIANG, BIOCHEMISTRY. *Current Pos:* res assoc, Mayo Found, Mayo Clinic, 66-67, consult, Dept Endocrine Res, 67-70, asst prof biochem, Mayo Grad Sch Med, 67-75, assoc prof biochem & lab med, 75-80, PROF LAB MED, MAYO MED SCH, UNIV MINN, 80-, HEAD SECT CLIN CHEM, 84- *Personal Data:* b Nanking, China, June 6, 31; m 58; c 2. *Educ:* Nat Taiwan Univ, BS, 55; Emory Univ, MS, 59, PhD(biochem), 62. *Prof Exp:* Instr biochem, Emory Univ, 62-66. *Concurrent Pos:* Dir & consult, Endocrine Lab, Dept Lab Med, Mayo Clin & Found, 71- *Mem:* AAAS; Am Chem Soc; Sigma Xi. *Res:* Measurement of hormones in body fluid. *Mailing Add:* 1305 Ridge Ct NE Rochester MN 55906-8570

JIANG, SHAOYI, THERMODYNAMICS & STATISTICAL MECHANICS, COMPUTATIONAL MATERIALS SCIENCE. *Current Pos:* ASST PROF CHEM ENG, KANS STATE UNIV, 97- *Personal Data:* b Aug 17, 64; m, Qiuming Yu; c Allen J. *Educ:* Hua Qiao Univ, China, BS, 85; Nanjing Univ Chem Technol, China, MS, 88; Cornell Univ, PhD(chem eng), 93. *Prof Exp:* Postdoctoral fel, Univ Calif, Berkeley, 93-94; res fel chem, Calif Inst Technol, 94-96. *Concurrent Pos:* Vis scientist, Lawrence Berkeley Lab, 93-94. *Mem:* Am Inst Chem Engrs; Am Chem Soc; AAAS; Mat Res Soc. *Res:* Thermodynamics. statistical mechanics, molecular simulation, abinitio quantum chemistry, parallel computing and experiment (surface proximal probes, absorption and thermophysical properties of fluids) with applications to interfacial phenomena, molecular tribology and advanced materials. *Mailing Add:* Dept Chem Eng Kans State Univ Manhattan KS 66506-5102. *Fax:* 785-532-7372; *E-Mail:* sjiang@pluto.cheme.ksu.edu

JIBSON, RANDALL W, EARTHQUAKE-INDUCED GROUND FAILURE, SEISMIC ENGINEERING. *Current Pos:* Geologist, 83-88, supvry geologist & geomech res coordr, 88-94, GEOLOGIST, US GEOL SURV, 94- *Personal Data:* b San Jose, Calif, Apr 17, 56; m 82, Linda S Watts; c Matthew, Daniel & Karen. *Educ:* San Diego State Univ, BS, 80; Stanford Univ, MS, 83, PhD(geol), 85. *Concurrent Pos:* Res fel, Japan Pub Works Res Inst, 87; mem, Landslide Comt, Am Asn Geologists, 87- *Mem:* Geol Soc Am; Asn Eng Geologists. *Res:* Basic and applied research in the field of geologic hazards, specifically in earthquake effects, ground-failure processes and coastal erosion. *Mailing Add:* US Geol Surv MS 966 Denver Fed Ctr Box 25046 Denver CO 80225. *E-Mail:* jibson@gldvxa.cr.usgs.gov

JICHA, HENRY LOUIS, JR, ECONOMIC GEOLOGY. *Current Pos:* RETIRED. *Personal Data:* b New York, NY, June 25, 28; m 51; c 3. *Educ:* Columbia Univ, BA, 48, MA, 51, PhD(econ geol), 52. *Prof Exp:* Geologist, Mineral Deposits Br, US Geol Surv, Colo, 48-49 & Fla, 49; field asst, NMex Bur Mines & Mineral Resources, 50-51, econ geologist, 51-56; asst prof geol, Colo Sch Mines, 56-58; analyst mining & mineral stocks, Baker, Weeks & Co, 58-61; ed-analyst, Value Line Invest Surv, Metals, Oils, Brewing, 61-62; mgr, New York Invests, Courts & Co, 62-70; sr analyst, Newberger, Loeb & Co, 70-71; mgr res, Jesup & Lamont, 71-73; vpres & sr analyst, Prudential Bache Securities, Inc, New York, 74-83; dir res, Wood Gundy Corp, NY, 83-89. *Concurrent Pos:* Consult, Baumgartner Oil Co, Colo, 57-58. *Mem:* Sigma Xi. *Res:* Uranium deposits in Colorado, phosphate deposits in Florida; lead-zinc deposits in Europe; tertiary volcanics, lead-zinc-silver deposits, Mesa del Oro Quadrangle and manganese deposits in New Mexico. *Mailing Add:* 12 Western Dr Ardsley NY 10502

JILES, CHARLES WILLIAM, ELECTRICAL ENGINEERING. *Current Pos:* PROF ELEC ENG, UNIV TEX, ARLINGTON, 60- *Personal Data:* b Vienna, La, Aug 11, 27; m 50; c 4. *Educ:* La Polytech Inst, BS & BA, 49; Okla State Univ, MS, 50, PhD, 55. *Prof Exp:* Asst physics, La Polytech Inst, 47-49; res instr, Okla State Univ, 50-55; sr aerophysics engr, Convair Div, Gen Dynamics Corp, 55-58, proj aerophysics engr, 58-60, design specialist, 60. *Mem:* Inst Elec & Electronics Engrs; Am Astronaut Soc; Sigma Xi. *Res:* Application of matrix algebra and tensor analysis to electric circuits and machines; network analysis and synthesis; design of automatic control systems. *Mailing Add:* 620 Westview Terr Arlington TX 76013

JILKA, ROBERT LAURENCE, MOLECULAR ENDOCRINOLOGY. *Current Pos:* staff scientist, Calcium Res Lab, Kansas City, 78-, VET ADMIN MED CTR, INDIANAPOLIS; AT DEPT INT MED, UNIV ARK. *Personal Data:* b Salina, Kans, Nov 26, 48. *Educ:* Kans State Univ, BS, 70, MS, 72; St Louis Univ, PhD(biochem), 75. *Prof Exp:* Fel, Roche Inst Molecular Biol, 75-78. *Concurrent Pos:* Adj asst prof, Dept Biochem, Univ Kans Med Ctr, 79- *Mem:* Am Soc Bone & Mineral Res. *Res:* Biochemical changes caused by parathormone, vitamin D and calcitonin on bone in organ culture and partially purified bone cells in tissue culture; both normal and genetically defined osteopetrotic bone is studied. *Mailing Add:* Univ Ark Med Sci 4301 W Markham Slot 587 Little Rock AR 72205

JIM, KAM FOOK, CARDIOVASCULAR PHARMACOLOGY, BIOCHEMICAL PHARMACOLOGY. *Current Pos:* PRIN SCI WRITER CLIN COMMUN, WYETH-AYERST RES, 88- *Personal Data:* b Po On, China, Nov 13, 53; US citizen; m 81, Margaret Liang; c Carol M & Ryan A. *Educ:* NY Univ, BA, 76; State Univ NY, Buffalo, PhD(pharmacol), 81. *Prof Exp:* Postdoctoral fel biochem, Case Western Res Univ, 80-81; res assoc, Cornell Univ Med Col, 81-83; postdoctoral scientist pharmacol, SmithKline & French Lab, SmithKline Beecham Co, 83-86; consult, Med Col Pa, 86-88. *Mem:* Fel Am Col Clin Pharmacol; Am Soc Pharmacol & Exp Therapeut; AAAS. *Res:* Writing responsibilities include clinical trials reports and global regulatory submission documents for cardiovascular and metabolic drugs including angiotensin II antagonists, lipid-lowering agents, and antiarrhythmic and antianginal compounds. *Mailing Add:* 4 Woodly Rd Royersford PA 19468. *Fax:* 610-341-2092

JIMBOW, KOWICHI, DERMATOLOGY, PATHOLOGY. *Current Pos:* PROF & DIR DERMAT & CUTANEOUS SCI, UNIV ALTA, EDMONTON, 87-, PROF PATH, 88- *Personal Data:* b Nagoya City, Japan, June 4, 41; c 5. *Educ:* Sapporo Med Col, MD, 66, PhD(med sci), 74. *Honors & Awards:* Alfred-Marchionini Prize, Int Asn Dermat, 82; Seiji Mem Prize, Japanese Soc Dermat, 84. *Prof Exp:* Instr dermat, Mass Gen Hosp, Boston, 74-75; from asst prof to assoc prof, Sapporo Med Col, Japan, 75-87. *Concurrent Pos:* Vis assoc prof dematopath, Dept Path, Univ Ark, 75-78; counr, Int Soc Pigment Cell Res, 84-87; mem organizing comt, 2nd Int Melanoma Conf, 86-; chmn & organizer, Third Meeting Pan Am Soc Pigment Cell Res, 90- *Mem:* Am Soc Cancer Res; Am Soc Photobiol; Can Dermat Asn; fel Am Acad Dermat. *Mailing Add:* 260G Heritage Med Res Ctr Univ Alberta Edmonton AB T6G 2S2 Can

JIMENEZ, AGNES E, NEUROENDOCRINOLOGY. *Current Pos:* Asst prof, 77-85, ASSOC PROF PHYSIOL, SCH MED, UNIV LOUISVILLE, 85- *Personal Data:* b Farrell, Pa, Oct 21, 43. *Educ:* Univ Louisville, PhD(physiol), 76. *Mem:* Soc Neurosci; Am Physiol Soc; Sigma Xi. *Mailing Add:* Dept Physiol & Biophysics Sch Med Univ Louisville 2301 S Third St Louisville KY 40292-0001

JIMENEZ, SERGIO, BIOCHEMISTRY. *Current Pos:* assoc prof med & rheumatology, Sch Med, 80-85, prof, 85-87, DIR, COLLAGEN RES, DEPT MED, UNIV PA, 73-; PROF MED, BIOCHEM & MOLECULAR BIOL, THOMAS JEFFERSON UNIV. *Personal Data:* b Cuzco, Peru, Feb 21, 42; m. *Educ:* Univ San Marcos, Lima, MD, 64. *Hon Degrees:* MS, Univ Pa. *Concurrent Pos:* NIH Gen Med Study Sect, Arthritis Found Res Comt. *Res:* Biochemistry and molecular biology of inherited and acquired connective tissue diseases. *Mailing Add:* Biochem & Molecular Biol Blue Life Sci Bldg Thomas Jefferson Univ Rm 509 233 S Tenth St Philadelphia PA 19107-5541. *Fax:* 215-923-4649

JIMERSON, GEORGE DAVID, INORGANIC CHEMISTRY, ANALYTICAL CHEMISTRY. *Current Pos:* Asst prof, 75, ASSOC PROF CHEM, ARK STATE UNIV, 75- *Personal Data:* b Little Rock, Ark, May 12, 44; m 65; c 2. *Educ:* Ouachita Baptist Univ, BS, 66; Ind Univ, Bloomington, PhD(chem), 70. *Honors & Awards:* Hon Sci Award, Bausch & Lomb, 62. *Concurrent Pos:* Prin investr res grant, Ark Educ Res & Develop Proj, 71-72; co-prin investr res contract, Ark Highway Dept, 72- *Mem:* Am Chem Soc; Sigma Xi. *Res:* Waste utilization and resource conservation, specifically the development and evaluation of a substitute for petroleum asphalt that can be produced from wood and other cellulosic wastes; preparation and identification of cyano-halo complexes of chromium III. *Mailing Add:* PO Box 0026 State University AR 72467-0026

JIMESON, ROBERT M(ACKAY), JR, FUEL TECHNOLOGY & PETROLEUM ENGINEERING, RESOURCE MANAGEMENT. *Current Pos:* CONSULT, ENERGY FUELS, ENVIRON MGT, INT ACTIV & CHEM ENG, 78- *Personal Data:* b Charleroi, Pa, Jan 29, 21; m 46, Rosemarie Wolny; c Robyn, Shelley, Robert III & Jeffery. *Educ:* Pa State Univ, BS, 42; George Wash Univ, MS, 65. *Honors & Awards:* Sen Jennings Randolph Award, 96. *Prof Exp:* Engr, Glenn L Martin Co, 42-45; res assoc org synthesis, Mellon Inst Indust Res, 45-47; res assoc, Sales Admin, Union

Carbide Corp, 47-49; chem engr, US Bur Mines, US Dept Interior, 49-59, phys sci adminstr, 59-64; phys sci adminstr, USPH Serv, HEW, 64-70; asst adv environ qual, Fed Power Comn, 70-74; staff, Off Technol Assessment, US Cong, 74-76; mgr, Fossil Technol Overview, Dept Energy, 76-78. *Concurrent Pos:* Lectr, McKeesport Ctr, Pa State Univ, 57-59 & George Washington Univ Grad Sch Eng, 77-79; consult, RMJ Assoc. *Mem:* Am Chem Soc; fel Am Inst Chem Engrs (treas, 64-65, pres, 74-75); Nat Soc Prof Engrs. *Res:* Engineering administration; processes for production of natural fuels, synthetic fuels and chemicals; formulation of plans and policies affecting federal programs in fuels, energy prevention and control of air pollution. *Mailing Add:* 1501 Gingerwood Ct Vienna VA 22182-1437. Fax: 703-759-7751

JIN, DOO JUNG, SEISMOLOGY, GROUND WATER. *Current Pos:* PROF ENVIRON TECHNOL/MATH, COLUMBIA BASIN COL, 92- *Personal Data:* b Hadong, Korea, Aug 6, 42; m 73, Bong Ja; c Sungsoo, Sue Young & Hye won. *Educ:* Inha Inst Technol, BS, 63; Stanford Univ, MS, 71; Southern Methodist Univ, PhD(geophys), 79. *Prof Exp:* Geophysicist, Geol Surv Korea, 68, Korean Groundwater Develop Corp, 69 & Advance Oil & Gas Co, 73-74; teaching fel, Southern Methodist Univ, 71-73; mem tech staff, Tex Instruments Inc, 74-76; sr geophysicist, Texaco Houston Res Ctr, 79-85; consult geophysicist, Geoeng Consult, 85-87; sr staff scientist, Rust Grotech Inc, 87-91; consult geoscientist, Geoenviron Consult, 91-92. *Concurrent Pos:* Lectr, Univ Md, 88. *Mem:* Soc Explor Geophysicists; Am Geophys Union; Nat Groundwater Asn; Korean-Am Scientist & Engrs Asn Am. *Res:* Magnetic induced polarization applied to environmental problems; complex seismic signatures; seismic surface wave phase velocity partial derivatives; hormorphic deconvolution; tru temperature determination of geothermal reservoirs; discriminant function for the determination of productive groundwater well sites. *Mailing Add:* 2223 Camas Ave Richland WA 99352. Fax: 509-546-0401; *E-Mail:* djin@ctc.ctc.edu

JIN, RONG-SHENG, PLANETARY MAGNETISM. *Current Pos:* ASSOC PROF SPACE SCI & PHYSICS, FLA INST TECHNOL, 69- *Personal Data:* b Foochow, Fukien, China, Dec 4, 33; US citizen; m 62, Shirley M Dunn; c Craig, Deborah & Laural. *Educ:* Denison Univ, BS, 57; Ohio State Univ, PhD(physics), 65. *Prof Exp:* Instr physics, Denison Univ, 59-60; asst prof, Loyola Univ, Calif, 65-67; assoc scientist, Lockheed Missiles & Space Co, Calif, 67-69. *Mem:* Sigma Xi; Am Asn Physics Teachers; Am Geophys Soc. *Res:* Nuclear and space physics; planetary magnetism; secular variations of the geomagnetic field and the magnetic field reversals. *Mailing Add:* Dept Physics & Space Sci Fla Inst Technol Melbourne FL 32901. Fax: 407-984-8461; *E-Mail:* rsjin@winnie.fit.edu

JIN, SUNGHO, MATERIALS SCIENCE ENGINEERING. *Current Pos:* mem tech staff, 76-81, SUPVR, AT&T BELL LABS, MURRAY HILL, 81- *Personal Data:* b Daejon, Korea, Nov 6, 45; US citizen; m 72; c 2. *Educ:* Seoul Nat Univ, BS, 69; Univ Calif, Berkeley, MS, 72, PhD(phys metall), 74. *Prof Exp:* Res staff, Univ Calif, Berkeley, 74-76. *Mem:* Am Soc Metals; Am Inst Mining, Metall & Petroleum Engrs Metall Soc; Mat Res Soc. *Res:* New alloys and thin films with unique magnetic, mechanical, electrical or thermal properties useful for applications in electronics or telecommunications industry. *Mailing Add:* 145 Skyline Dr Millington NJ 07946

JINDRAK, KAREL, PATHOLOGY. *Current Pos:* CLIN ASST PROF PATH, STATE UNIV NY DOWNSTATE MED CTR, 72-; PATHOLOGIST, METHODIST HOSP, NEW YORK, 71- *Personal Data:* b Merin, Czech, Mar 29, 26; m 51, Kult; c Heda. *Educ:* Charles Univ, Prague, MUC, 47, MUDr, 50; Charles Univ, Hradec Kralove, CSc, 65; Educ Coun Foreign Med Grad, cert, 68; Am Bd Path, APCP, 72. *Honors & Awards:* Slovak Nat Coun Award, 51; Czech Ministry Health Award, 66. *Prof Exp:* Intern med, Gen Hosp, Roznava, Czech, 51; pathologist & asst prof path, Med Fac, Charles Univ, Hradec Kralove, 56-65; pathologist & head dept path, Res Inst Pharm & Biochem, Prague, 66-67; pathologist, Dept Animal Sci, Univ Hawaii, 67-68; res pathologist, Mt Sinai Hosp, New York, 68-71. *Concurrent Pos:* Ministry Health app head dept path, Czech Hosp, Haiphong, Vietnam, 58-60; consult, Med Fac, Charles Univ, Hradec Kralove, 61-64; Czech Ministry Health res grant, 63-65; NIH grant, Univ Hawaii, 66. *Mem:* Am Soc Trop Med & Hyg; Czech Med Soc; Am Asn Pathologists; fel Col Am Path. *Res:* Pathology of infectious and parasitic diseases of man and animals; neuropathology; pathology of chronic drug toxicity; problems related to cerebral nematodiasis; mechanical effect of vocalization on brain and meninges; acquird immunodeficiency syndrome. *Mailing Add:* Dept Path Methodist Hosp 506 Sixth St Brooklyn NY 11215-2394

JING, LIU, COLLOIDAL PHYSICS, MAGNETORHEOLOGICAL FLUIDS. *Current Pos:* asst prof, 92-95, ASSOC, PROF CALIF STATE UNIV, LONG BEACH, 95- *Personal Data:* b Gansu, China, Nov 25, 60. *Educ:* Zhongshan Univ, China, BS, 82; Univ Mich, MS, 84, PhD(laser spectros), 89. *Prof Exp:* Res asst, Univ Mich, 84-89; res fel, Exxon Res & Eng Co, 89-92. *Concurrent Pos:* Prin investr, Am Chem Soc, Petrol Fund & Res Corp, Catrell Award, 93-95, NSF, NATO 94- & NASA-Fluid, 94- *Mem:* Am Phys Soc; Am Optical Soc. *Res:* Field induced structure, dynamics and rheology in magnetorheological fluids; coherent light crystallograph of shear-aligned hard-sphere colloids; sound propagation in hard-sphere colloids; fractal behavior in vycor glass during draining process; four-wave mixing laser spectroscopy studies of sodium vapor. *Mailing Add:* Dept Physics Calif State Univ Long Beach CA 90840. Fax: 562-985-7924; *E-Mail:* jliu@csulb.edu

JINKS-ROBERTSON, SUE, GENETICS, MOLECULAR BIOLOGY. *Current Pos:* asst prof, 87-93, ASSOC PROF BIOL, EMORY UNIV, 93- *Personal Data:* b Panama City, Fla, Jan 22, 55; m, John Allen; c 3. *Educ:* Agnes Scott Col, BA, 77; Univ Wis-Madison, PhD(genetics), 83. *Prof Exp:* Fel, Univ Chicago, 83-86. *Concurrent Pos:* Assoc ed, Genetics, 93- *Mem:* AAAS; Am Soc Microbiol; Genetics Soc Am; Sigma Xi. *Res:* Recombination and mutation in yeast. *Mailing Add:* Dept Biol Emory Univ Atlanta GA 30322. Fax: 404-727-2880; *E-Mail:* jinks@biology.emory.edu

JIRGENSONS, ARNOLD, POLYMER CHEMISTRY. *Current Pos:* CONSULT, 77- *Personal Data:* b Latvia, Dec 2, 06; nat US; m 42. *Educ:* Univ Latvia, Chem Eng, 32. *Prof Exp:* Instr chem, Univ Latvia, 32-44; res chemist, Zellwolle & Kunstseide Ring, Ger, 44-45; res chemist, Boston Blacking Co, Sweden, 47-50, B B Chem Co, Can 50-54, Endicott Johnson Corp, NY, 54-60 & Jersey State Chem Co, NJ, 60-61; res chemist, RA Chem Corp, 61-73, chief tech dir, 73-77. *Mem:* Am Chem Soc. *Res:* Emulsion polymerization; water base coatings; new emulsion polymers for flame retardant textile coatings; new emulsion copolymers capable of self-crosslinking. *Mailing Add:* 13 Courtshire Dr Brick NJ 08723-7137

JIRKA, GERHARD HERMANN, ENVIRONMENTAL FLUID MECHANICS, WATER POLLUTION CONTROL. *Current Pos:* from asst prof to assoc prof, 77-87, PROF CIVIL & ENVIRON ENG, CORNELL UNIV, 87-, DIR, DEFREES HYDRAUL LAB, 84- *Personal Data:* b Kasten, Austria, Sep 14, 44; m 68, Sonia Kull; c Astrid, Andres & Stefan. *Educ:* Univ Bodenkultur, Vienna, Austria, 69, Mass Inst Technol, MS, 71, PhD(civil eng) 73. *Honors & Awards:* Freeman Hydraul Prize, Am Soc Civil Engrs, 81, Huber Res Prize, 83; A T Ippen Award, Int Asn Hydrol Res, 89. *Prof Exp:* Lectr & res engr, Energy Lab Mass Inst Technol, 73-77. *Concurrent Pos:* Vis prof, Inst Hydromech Zurich, 83-84, Inst Hydraul & Hydrol Tech Univ Vienna, 91-92; Chmn, Hydraul Div, Am Soc Civil Eng, 89-90; chmn, Fluid Mech Sect, Int Asn Hydraul Res, 90-; Fulbright Scholar, Us Info Agency. *Mem:* Fel Am Soc Civil Eng; Int Asn Hydraul Res; Am Geophys Union. *Res:* Environmental fluid mechanics, transport phenomena, hydraulic engineering, water quality prediction, waste heat disposal, turbulent mixing. *Mailing Add:* 119 Hollister Hall Cornell Univ Ithaca NY 14853

JIRKOVSKY, IVO, MEDICINAL CHEMISTRY, RESEARCH ADMINISTRATION. *Current Pos:* sr res chemist, Wyeth-Ayerst Res Labs, 68-73, sect head med chem, 73-77, sr res assoc, 77-84, assoc dir, 84-89, DIR CHEM, WYETH-AYERST RES, 89- *Personal Data:* b Prague, Czech, June 26, 35; Can citizen; m 65. *Educ:* Chem Univ, Prague Dipl chem eng, 58; Czech Acad Sci, PhD (org chem), 63. *Prof Exp:* Asst res chemist, Res Inst Pharm & Biochem, Prague, 58-60, assoc res chemist, 63-68. *Concurrent Pos:* Fel, Univ NB, 66-67. *Mem:* Am Chem Soc; fel Chem Inst Can; AAAS. *Res:* Organic syntheses; alkaloids; heterocycles; physical organic chemistry; biochemistry; structure-activity relationships; antihypertensives; psychotherapeutics and cognition enhancers; hypoglycemic drugs; enzyme inhibitors; antiobesity and hypolipidemic agents; immunoregulation; atherosclerosis; bone metabolism; steroidal research. *Mailing Add:* Wyeth-Ayerst Res Bldg 222/2126 Pearl River NY 10965

JIRMANUS, MUNIR N, CRYOGENICS. *Current Pos:* sr appl engr cryogenics, 78-88, TECH DIR, JANIS RES CO, 89- *Personal Data:* b Jerusalem, Apr 23, 44; US citizen; m 68; c 2. *Educ:* Am Univ, Beirut, Lebanon, BSc, 64; Tufts Univ, MSc, 66, PhD(physics), 73. *Prof Exp:* Lectr physics, Tufts Univ, 74-75; asst prof, Am Univ, Lebanon, 75-77. *Mem:* Am Phys Soc; Mat Res Soc; Am Chem Soc. *Res:* Design and testing of cryogenic equipment for low temperature physics research. *Mailing Add:* Janis Res Co PO Box 696 2 Jewel Dr Wilmington MA 01887-0696

JIRSA, JAMES O, EARTHQUAKE ENGINEERING, STRUCTURAL ENGINEERING. *Current Pos:* from assoc prof to prof, Univ Tex, Austin, 72-82, Stanley P Finch prof eng, 82-84, Phil M Ferguson prof, 84-88, dir Ferguson Struct Eng Lab, 85-88, JANET S COCKRELL CENTENNIAL CHAIR ENG, UNIV TEX, AUSTIN, 88-, CHMN, DEPT CIVIL ENG, 96- *Personal Data:* b Lincoln, Nebr, July 30, 38; m 65; c 2. *Educ:* Univ Nebr, BS, 60; Univ Ill, MS, 62, PhD(civil eng), 63. *Honors & Awards:* Raymond C Reese Award, Am Soc Civil Engr, 70 & 91, Walter L Huber Res Prize, 78; Wason Medal, Am Concrete Inst, 77, Raymond C Reese Struct Award, 77 & 79, Alfred E Lindau Award, 86 & 92, Delmar E Bloem Award, 90; A J Boase Award, Reinforced Concrete Res Coun, 93. *Prof Exp:* Asst prof civil eng, Univ Nebr, 64-65; from asst prof to assoc prof, Rice Univ, 65-71. *Concurrent Pos:* Fulbright scholar, Inst Appl Res Reinforced Concrete, France, 63-64, Portland Cement Asn, 65 & H J Degenkolb Assocs, 80; Erskine fel, Canterbury Univ, NZ, 91; bd dir, Am Concrete Inst, 87-90 & Earthquake Eng Res Inst. *Mem:* Nat Acad Eng; Am Soc Civil Engrs; fel Am Concrete Inst; Earthquake Eng Res Inst; Int Asn Bridge & Struct Engrs. *Res:* Reinforced concrete behavior and design of reinforced concrete structures; earthquake engineering; repair and strengthening of structures. *Mailing Add:* Dept Civil Eng ECJ Hall Suite 4-2 Univ Tex Austin TX 78712-1076

JIRTLE, RANDY L, PATHOLOGY. *Current Pos:* assoc radiol, Duke Univ, 77-79, asst prof radiol, 79-80, from asst prof to assoc prof radiol & path, 80-90, PROF RADIOL & PATH, DUKE UNIV, 90-, PROF RADIATION ONCOL & PATH, 90-, DIR, DIV RADIATION & MOLECULAR ONCOL RES, 91-, DIR, BASIC RES LIVER SURG PROG, 92-, MEM INTEGRATED TOXICOL PROG, 92- *Personal Data:* b Kewaunee, Wis, Nov 9, 47. *Educ:* Univ Wis-Madison, BS, 70, MS, 73, PhD(radiation biol), 76. *Prof Exp:* Fel physiol, Univ Wis-Madison, 76-77. *Concurrent Pos:* Vis asst prof human oncol, Univ Wis-Madison, 81; vis res scientist, Ctr Nuclear Study, Rome, 82. *Mem:* Am Asn Cancer Res; Radiation Res; Am Asn Pathologists;

Soc Toxicol; Fedn Am Soc Exp Biol; AAAS. *Res:* Promotion of hepatocellular tumor formation; breast cancer chemo prevention; radiation response of the liver. *Mailing Add:* Dept Radiol Oncol Duke Univ Med Ctr Box 3433 Durham NC 27710-0001. *Fax:* 919-684-5584

JISCHKE, MARTIN C(HARLES), FLUID MECHANICS. *Current Pos:* PRES, IOWA STATE UNIV, AMES, 91- *Personal Data:* b Chicago, Ill, Aug 7, 41; m 70; c Charles & Marian. *Educ:* Ill Inst Technol, BS, 63; Mass Inst Technol, SM, 64, PhD(aeronaut & astronaut), 68. *Honors & Awards:* Ralph R Teetor Award, Soc Automotive Engrs, 70; Centennial Medallion, Am Soc Eng Educ, 93. *Prof Exp:* Asst aeronaut & astronaut, Mass Inst Technol, 66-68; from asst prof to prof aerospace & mech eng, Univ Okla, 68-81, dean eng, 81-86, interim pres, 85; chancellor, Univ Mo, Rolla, 86-91. *Concurrent Pos:* On leave, White House fel, US Dept Transp, 75-76; prin investr, USAF, 77- & US Nuclear Regulatory Comn, 77-; bd dir, Bankers Trust Co, 95 & Kerr-McGee, 93; pres, Comn Twenty-First Century State & Land-Grand Univ, 95. *Mem:* Fel Am Inst Aeronaut & Astronaut; Am Phys Soc; Soc Automotive Engrs; Sigma Xi; fel AAAS; fel Am Soc Mech Engrs; Nat Soc Prof Engrs. *Res:* Viscous flows; aerodynamics; geophysical; fluid dynamics; heat transfer. *Mailing Add:* 117 Beardshear Hall Iowa State Univ Ames IA 50011-2020. *Fax:* 515-294-0565; *E-Mail:* president@iastate.edu

JIVIDEN, GAY MELTON, MANAGEMENT OF MOLECULAR BIOLOGY & GENETIC ENGINEERING, MANAGEMENT OF PLANT BREEDING PROJECTS. *Current Pos:* mgr, 73-83, assoc dir, 83-88, DIR AGR RES, COTTON INC, 88- *Personal Data:* b Charleston, WVa, Nov 18, 35; m, Loretta Harper; c Jon D & Ann M. *Educ:* WVa State Univ, BS, 62; NC State Univ, PhD(plant physiol), 72. *Prof Exp:* Qual control analyst, Nat Lead Corp, 56-58; math & sci teacher, Kanawha Co Schs, Charleston, WVa, 59-61; res technician, Union Carbide Corp, 62-65; asst to dir, Southeastern Plant Environ Lab, NC State Univ, 67-73. *Concurrent Pos:* Adj fac, NC State Univ, 74- *Mem:* Am Soc Plant Physiol; Am Soc Agron & Crop Sci; Am Oil Chemists; Sigma Xi. *Res:* Determine the direction, scope and funding levels of cotton research for a coordinated national effort in the fields of plant physiology, genetics and molecular biology. *Mailing Add:* Cotton Inc PO Box 30067 Raleigh NC 27622-0067. *Fax:* 919-881-9874

JIZBA, ZDENEK VACLAV, EXPLORATION GEOLOGY. *Current Pos:* RETIRED. *Personal Data:* b Prague, Czech, Feb 25, 27; nat US; m 60; c 3. *Educ:* State Col Wash, BS, 49, MS, 50; Univ Wis, PhD, 53. *Prof Exp:* Res geologist, Chevron Res Co, 55-62, sr res geologist, 62-67, sr res assoc, Chevron Oil Field Res Co, Standard Oil Co, Calif, 67-86. *Res:* Mathematical geology; man-machine interaction to solve complex geological problems; computer applications in geology. *Mailing Add:* 1341 Rebecca Dr La Habra CA 90631-2614

JOANNOPOULOS, JOHN DIMITRIS, SURFACES, AMORPHOUS MATERIALS. *Current Pos:* From asst prof to assoc prof, 74-83, PROF PHYSICS, MASS INST TECHNOL, 83- *Personal Data:* b New York, NY, Apr 26, 47. *Educ:* Univ Calif, Berkeley, BA, 68, PhD(physics), 74; Univ Calif, Davis, MA, 70. *Honors & Awards:* Fel, Am Phys Soc, 83. *Concurrent Pos:* Fel, Alfred P Sloan Found, 76-80, John Simon Guggenheim Found, 81-82. *Mem:* Am Phys Soc; Am Vacuum Soc. *Res:* Theoretical condensed matter physics: including properties of crystalline solids, surfaces of solids, defects and amorphous solids. *Mailing Add:* Dept Physics 12-116 Mass Inst Technol Cambridge MA 02139

JOB, ROBERT CHARLES, INORGANIC CHEMISTRY. *Current Pos:* ASST PROF CHEM, COLO STATE UNIV, 75- *Personal Data:* b Honolulu, Hawaii, May 19, 43. *Educ:* Univ Calif, Berkeley, BS, 67; Univ Mich, PhD(inorg chem), 71. *Prof Exp:* Assoc chem, Univ Calif, Santa Barbara, 71-74, res chemist, 74-75. *Mem:* Sigma Xi. *Res:* Inorganic analogs of biological systems; organometallic chemistry of transition metals with Group IV-a prosthetics; asymmetric induction involving optically active transition metal systems; coordination chemistry. *Mailing Add:* 12126 Westmere Dr Houston TX 77077

JOBE, JOHN M, TOPOLOGY. *Current Pos:* from asst prof to assoc prof, 74-77, PROF MATH, OKLA STATE UNIV, 77- *Personal Data:* b Ponca City, Okla, June 9, 33; m 54; c 5. *Educ:* Univ Tulsa, BS, 55; Okla State Univ, MS, 63, PhD(math), 66. *Prof Exp:* Teacher high sch, Okla, 55-62. *Mem:* Math Asn Am; Am Math Soc. *Res:* Point set topology. *Mailing Add:* Dept Math Okla State Univ Stillwater OK 74078

JOBE, LOWELL A(RTHUR), CHEMICAL ENGINEERING, SYSTEMS ENGINEERING. *Current Pos:* RETIRED. *Personal Data:* b Lead, SDak, Aug 28, 14; m 42, 85, Lorraine H Lucier; c Donna (Oltmanns) & David. *Educ:* SDak Sch Mines & Technol, BS, 38; Univ Iowa, MS, 39. *Prof Exp:* Asst metall, Univ Iowa, 38-39; chief chemist & chem engr, Graver Tank & Mfg Co, Inc, 39-47; from asst prof to assoc prof chem eng, Univ Idaho, 47-60; process control engr, Atomic Energy Div, Phillips Petrol Co, 60-66; sr process control engr, Idaho Nuclear Corp, 66-71; sr process control engr, Idaho Chem Prog, Allied Chem Corp, 71-77; mem staff, Exxon Nuclear, 77-80; instr process technol, Eastern Idaho Voc Tech Sch, 80-85. *Mem:* Instrument Soc Am; Am Inst Chem Engrs. *Res:* Automatic process control; industrial water and waste treatment; nuclear engineering. *Mailing Add:* 14469 N 55th E Idaho Falls ID 83401

JOBE, PHILLIP CARL, NEUROPHARMACOLOGY. *Current Pos:* AT COL MED, UNIV ILL. *Personal Data:* b Carlsbad, NMex, Jan 9, 40; m 59; c 2. *Educ:* Univ NMex, BS, 63; Univ Ariz, PhD(pharmacol), 70. *Prof Exp:* Teaching asst, Univ Ariz, 60-63, assoc, 63-67; asst prof pharmacol, Univ Nebr, 69-70; asst prof, Northeast La Univ, 70-74, dir, Drug Abuse Ctr, 71-74; asst prof, 74-75, assoc prof, 75-80, prof pharmacol, therapeut & psychiat, Sch Med, La State Univ, Shreveport, 80- *Concurrent Pos:* Consult neuropharmacol & clin pharmacologist, Vet Admin Hosp, 74- *Mem:* Soc Neurosci; Sigma Xi. *Res:* Role of central nervous system neurotransmitters in the regulation of seizure intensity and susceptibility with special emphasis on the relative importance of discrete catecholaminergic neuron systems. *Mailing Add:* Dept Basic Sci Col Med Univ Ill 1 Illini Dr PO Box 1649 Peoria IL 61656-1649

JOBES, FORREST CROSSETT, JR, PHYSICS. *Current Pos:* MEM RES STAFF, PLASMA PHYSICS, PHYSICS LAB, PRINCETON UNIV, 71- *Personal Data:* b Trenton, NJ, Nov 26, 35; m 58; c 1. *Educ:* Oberlin Col, AB, 57; Yale Univ, MS, 58, PhD(physics), 62. *Prof Exp:* Asst physics, Yale Univ, 57-62; res physicist cent res div lab, Mobil Oil Co, 62-65; sr res physicist, Mobil Oil Corp, 65-71. *Mem:* Am Phys Soc; Sigma Xi. *Res:* Plasma and nuclear physics. *Mailing Add:* PPPL Princeton Univ PO Box 451 Princeton NJ 08543

JOBS, STEVEN P, ELECTRONICS. *Current Pos:* PRES & CHMN, NEXT COMPUT, INC, 85-; CHIEF EXEC OFFICER, PIXAR ANIMATION STUDIOS, 86-, CHMN, 91-, PRES, 95- *Personal Data:* b Feb 24, 55. *Honors & Awards:* Nat Technol Medal, Pres Reagan, 85; Jefferson Award, 87. *Prof Exp:* Co-founder, Apple Comput, 76, chmn, exec vpres & gen mgr, Macintosh Div. *Concurrent Pos:* Bd dirs, Pixar. *Mem:* Nat Acad Sci; Nat Acad Eng. *Res:* Co-designed Apple II; implementation of PostScript and LaserWriting which helped create the desktop publishing industry. *Mailing Add:* Pixar Animation Studios 1001 W Cutting Blvd Richmond CA 94804

JOBSIS, FRANS FREDERIK, PHYSIOLOGY. *Current Pos:* from asst prof to assoc prof, 64-69, PROF PHYSIOL, DUKE UNIV, 69- *Personal Data:* b Batavia, Indonesia, Apr 1, 29; nat US; m 51, Joan Marie Murray; c Catherine T, Gerrit J, William T, Maria M & Paul D. *Educ:* Univ Md, BS, 51; Univ Mich, MS, 53, PhD(zool), 58. *Prof Exp:* Res fel biophys, Johnson Found, Univ Pa, 58-59, res assoc, 61-62, asst prof biophys & physiol, Univ, 62-64; fel biochem, Univ Amsterdam, 59-60; fel, Nobel Inst Neurophysiol, Sweden, 60-61. *Concurrent Pos:* Guggenheim fel, 71-72; hon prof physiol, Semmelweis Med Univ, Budapest, Hungary. *Mem:* Fel AAAS; Am Physiol Soc; Int Soc Transport Oxygen to Tissues. *Res:* Physiology, biochemistry and biophysics of muscle and nervous tissue; comparative physiology; physiology of behavior; near infrared spectroscopy of organs and tissues; non-invasive monitoring of physiologic and pathophysiologic activities in viro; oxygen delivery and utilization in sitis. *Mailing Add:* Dept Cell Biol Duke Univ PO Box 3709 Durham NC 27710. *Fax:* 919-684-3687

JOBST, JOEL EDWARD, NUCLEAR PHYSICS. *Current Pos:* CONSULT, 95- *Personal Data:* b South Milwaukee, Wis, May 13, 36; m 59; c Brian, Kevin & Erin. *Educ:* Marquette Univ, BS, 59; Univ Wis, MS, 61, PhD(physics), 66. *Prof Exp:* Sci specialist, Remote Sensing Lab, EG&G, 66-95. *Concurrent Pos:* Owner, Solar Energy Co. *Mem:* Health Physics Soc; Am Nuclear Soc; Solar Energy Soc. *Res:* Nuclear research; detector technology; operation and development of particle accelerators and neutron generators; airborne remote sensing, including infrared scanner; preparation of terrestrial radiation maps from gamma data recorded on an aerial survey platform; solar energy systems. *Mailing Add:* 3013 Bryant Ave Las Vegas NV 89102. *Fax:* 702-295-8040

JOCHIM, KENNETH ERWIN, PHYSIOLOGY. *Current Pos:* PROF PHYSIOL, UNIV MICH, ANN ARBOR, 63- *Personal Data:* b St Louis, Mo, July 30, 11; m 37; c 2. *Educ:* Univ Chicago, BS, 39, PhD, 41. *Prof Exp:* Res assoc cardiovasc dept, Michael Reese Hosp, Chicago, 31-42; from instr to asst prof physiol, Sch Med, St Louis Univ, 42-46; prof & chmn dept, Univ Kans, 46-61, asst dean, Sch Med, 52-57; sr res scientist biol sci dept, Defense Systs Div, Gen Motors Corp, Mich, 61-63. *Concurrent Pos:* Fulbright res scholar, Univ Munich, 56-57. *Mem:* Soc Exp Biol & Med; Sigma Xi. *Res:* Coronary circulation; electrocardiography; cardiodynamics; peripheral circulatory dynamics. *Mailing Add:* 2066 Chaucer Dr Ann Arbor MI 48103

JOCHLE, WOLFGANG, THERIOGENOLOGY, CLINICAL PHARMACOLOGY. *Current Pos:* PRES, WOLFGANG JOCHLE ASSOCS, INC, CONSULT VET SCIENTISTS & THERIOGENOLOGISTS, 75- *Personal Data:* b Munich, Ger, Oct 5, 27; m 64, Maria Frank. *Educ:* Univ Munich DrVet Med, 52, DrMedVet, 53; Am Col Theriogenologists, dipl, 75. *Prof Exp:* Ger Res Asn fel endocrinol, Vet Fac, Univ Munich, 53-54; univ res scientist, Hormon-Chemie, 54-56; asst animal husb, Vet Fac, Free Univ Berlin, 56-59; vet res scientist, Schering AG, 59-63; res dir vet med, Fecunda AG, Switz, 64-65. *Concurrent Pos:* Dir vet syntex res, Syntex Corp, Mex, 66-68, int vet sect, 73-75; dir vet syntex res, Palo Alto, Ca, 68-73; hon prof, Sch Vet Med, Hannover, Ger, 87. *Mem:* Am Vet Med Asn; Soc Study Reproduction; Am Soc Animal Sci; Soc Theriogenol; NY Acad Sci; Royal Soc Med UK. *Res:* Interaction between environment and reproductive functions in animals; use of hormones as therapeutic and managerial tools in veterinary medicine and animal industry; comparative reproductive neuroendocrinology; endocrinology of parturition; new drug development in the animal health field; animal models for clinical conditions. *Mailing Add:* 10 Old Boonton Rd Denville Township NJ 07834. *Fax:* 973-627-6345

JOCHMAN, RICHARD LEE, MEDICINAL CHEMISTRY, ORGANIC CHEMISTRY. *Current Pos:* From instr to asst prof, 77-85, ASSOC PROF CHEM, COL ST BENEDICT, 85- *Personal Data:* b Appleton, Wis, Jan 10, 48; m 69; c 1. *Educ:* St Norbert Col, BS, 70; Univ Kans, MS, 74, PhD(med chem), 78. *Mem:* AAAS; Am Chem Soc. *Res:* Synthesis of metabolically stable analogs of neuropeptides. *Mailing Add:* Dept Chem Col St Benedict St Joseph MN 56374

JOCHSBERGER, THEODORE, PHYSICAL ORGANIC CHEMISTRY. *Current Pos:* PROF PHARMACEUT, ARNOLD & MARIE SCHWARTZ COL PHARM & HEALTH SCI, LONG ISLAND UNIV, 68- *Personal Data:* b New York, NY, Mar 6, 40; m 84; c 2. *Educ:* Hunter Col, AB, 61, MA, 63; City Univ New York, PhD(phys chem), 69; Brooklyn Col Pharm, BS, 77. *Mem:* NY Acad Sci; Am Chem Soc. *Res:* Kinetics and mechanisms of free radical reactions; polymers and polymerization mechanisms; metal-peroxide catalyzed reactions; biopharmaceutics. *Mailing Add:* 75 Windsor Rd Staten Island NY 10314-4500

JOCKUSCH, CARL GROOS, JR, COMPUTABILITY THEORY. *Current Pos:* from asst prof to assoc prof, 67-75, PROF MATH, UNIV ILL, URBANA-CHAMPAIGN, 75- *Personal Data:* b San Antonio, Tex, July 13, 41; m 64; c 3. *Educ:* Swarthmore Col, BA, 63; Mass Inst Technol, PhD(math), 66. *Prof Exp:* Instr math, Northeastern Univ, 66-67. *Concurrent Pos:* Ed, J Symbolic Logic, 74-75. *Mem:* Am Math Soc; Math Asn Am; Asn Symbolic Logic. *Res:* Computability theory and its connections with other areas of mathematics. *Mailing Add:* Dept Math Univ Ill Urbana-Champaign 1409 W Green St Urbana IL 61801. *E-Mail:* jockusch@math.uiuc.edu

JOCOY, EDWARD HENRY, ELECTRICAL ENGINEERING. *Current Pos:* Electronics engr, 55-64, head radar & electronics sect, 64-65, 71-74, PRIN ENGR, CALSPAN CORP, 74- *Personal Data:* b Buffalo, NY, Oct 24, 33; m 68; c 1. *Educ:* Rensselaer Polytech Inst, BEE, 55; Univ Buffalo, MS, 59; Cornell Univ, PhD(elec eng), 69. *Mem:* Inst Elec & Electronics Engrs; Sigma Xi. *Res:* Radar and communications; analytical and experimental research of radar and communications systems; mathematical modeling; signal processing. *Mailing Add:* 100 Wiltshire Rd Williamsville NY 14221-4943

JODEIT, MAX A, JR, MATHEMATICS. *Current Pos:* ASSOC PROF MATH, UNIV MINN, MINNEAPOLIS, 73- *Personal Data:* b Tulsa, Okla, Apr 14, 37; div; c 3. *Educ:* Rice Univ, BA, 62, MA, 65, PhD(math), 67. *Prof Exp:* Instr math, Univ Chicago, 67-69, vis asst prof, 69-70, asst prof, 70-73. *Mem:* Am Math Soc; Math Asn Am; Soc Indust & Appl Math. *Res:* Mathematical analysis; singular integrals. *Mailing Add:* Sch Math Univ Minn 206 Church St SE 127 Vincent Minneapolis MN 55455-0488

JODRY, RICHARD L, EXPLORATION GEOLOGY. *Current Pos:* PRES, ENERGY & NATURAL RESOURCE CONSULTS, INC, 77- *Personal Data:* b Toledo, Ohio, May 17, 22; m 45, Betty McElraevy; c Ann, Mary, Louis F, Richard M, Patricia, Michael & Thomas. *Educ:* Mich State Univ, BS, 45, MS, 54. *Prof Exp:* Geologist, Magnolia Petrol Co, 45-47 & Ohio Oil Co, 47-50; chief geologist, Rex Oil & Gas Co, 50-55; from res geologist & group supvr to sr res geologist, Billings Res Group, Sun Oil Co, 55-70, chief geologist geothermal energy, 70-77. *Concurrent Pos:* Distinguished lectr, Am Asn Geologists, 70-72; mem, Bd Mineral Resources, Nat Res Coun, Nat Acad Sci, 75-78. *Mem:* Am Asn Petrol Geologists; Geol Soc Am; Soc Econ Paleontologists & Mineralogists; Soc Explor Geophys; Geothermal Resources Coun (vpres, 74-75). *Res:* Deposition of carbonate sediments; formation of carbonate rocks and their petrographic and petrophysical characteristics; unexplored basin evaluation; world hydrocarbon resource evaluation; coal and geothermal exploration and development. *Mailing Add:* 641 Strings Dr San Antonio TX 78216

JOEBSTL, JOHANN ANTON, ENERGY CONVERSION. *Current Pos:* RETIRED. *Personal Data:* b Graz, Austria, July 17, 27; US citizen; m 57, Erika Kibal; c Barbara. *Educ:* Tech Univ, Graz, Austria, dipl eng, 54, DrTechSci, 56. *Prof Exp:* Res chemist, Eng Res & Develop Lab, US Army, 58-68, Mobility Equip Res & Develop Ctr, 68-76, br chief, 76-81, div chief, Electrochem Div, Mobility Equip Res & Develop Command, 81-85, Tech Adv, Belvoir Res & Develop Ctr, 85-88. *Concurrent Pos:* Asst, Tech Univ, 55-75. *Mem:* Am Chem Soc. *Res:* Electrocatalysis; novel electrolytes; advanced fuel conditioning techniques; fundamental investigations in electrochemistry; fuel cells. *Mailing Add:* 6641 Wakefield Dr Alexandria VA 22307

JOEDICKE, INGO BERND, INORGANIC CHEMISTRY. *Current Pos:* SR INORG CHEMIST, GAF CORP, 76- *Personal Data:* b Grossfurra, Germany, May 17, 48; US citizen; m 68; c 2. *Educ:* Univ Wash, BS, 70; Ore State Univ, PhD(inorg chem), 76. *Prof Exp:* Res asst inorg chem, Ore State Univ, 71-76. *Mem:* Am Chem Soc; Sigma Xi. *Res:* Homogeneous catalysis of coordinated phosphorus ester autooxidation; high temperature chemistry of silicates and clays; silicate films and coatings. *Mailing Add:* GAF Chem Corp 34 Charles St Hagerstown MD 21740-3818

JOEL, AMOS EDWARD, JR, ELECTRICAL ENGINEERING. *Current Pos:* RETIRED. *Personal Data:* b Philadelphia, Pa, Mar 12, 18; c 3. *Educ:* Mass Inst Technol, BS, 40, MS, 42. *Honors & Awards:* Outstanding Patent Award, NJ Coun Res & Develop, 72; Alexander Graham Bell Medal, Inst Elec & Electronics Engrs, 76; Columbian Award, City of Genoa, 84; ITU Award, ITU Geneva Switz, 83; Kyoto Prize, 89; Nat Medal Technol, 93. *Prof Exp:* Switching systs develop engr, Bell Tel Labs, Inc, 52-61, head, Electronic Switching Planning Dept, 60-61, dir, Switching Systs Develop Lab, 61-62 & Local Switching Lab, 62-67, switching consult, 67-83. *Mem:* Nat Acad Eng; Asn Comput Mach; fel Inst Elec & Electronics Engrs; AAAS; fel Am Acad Arts & Sci; Sigma Xi. *Res:* Design of automatic telephone switching systems; communication privacy systems; design of research computer systems; relay and transistor switching circuits; design of automatic accounting systems; teaching telephone switching circuit design and system principles; electronic information processing systems. *Mailing Add:* Bell Tel Labs Holmdel NJ 07733

JOEL, CLIFFE DAVID, NERUOSCIENCE. *Current Pos:* chmn dept, 71-73, 84-87, PROF CHEM, LAWRENCE UNIV, 68- *Personal Data:* b Saskatoon, Sask, Aug 10, 32; US citizen; m 94, Emma Campbell Cullinan; c Lisa, Eric & Sara. *Educ:* Pomona Col, AB, 53; Harvard Univ, MA, 55, PhD(biochem), 59. *Prof Exp:* Res fel biol chem, Harvard Med Sch, 59-60, from instr to asst prof, 60-68. *Concurrent Pos:* NIH res fel, 59-60; biochemist, Mass Ment Health Ctr, 63-68; career develop award, Nat Inst Neurol Dis & Stroke, 68; vis scientist, Inst Animal Psychol, Cambridge, Eng, 74-75; fel ophthal, Baylor Col Med, 82-84; vis prof psychol, Colo Col, 91, 92, 93. *Mem:* Am Soc Neurochem. *Res:* Chemistry and metabolism of lipids, especially polyunsaturated fatty acids; neurochemistry; chemistry of the eye; chemical education. *Mailing Add:* Dept Chem Lawrence Univ Appleton WI 54912-0599

JOEL, DARREL DEAN, EXPERIMENTAL PATHOLOGY, IMMUNOLOGY. *Current Pos:* from asst scientist to scientist, 64-79, chmn, Med Dept, 91-96, SR SCIENTIST, BROOKHAVEN NAT LAB, 79- *Personal Data:* b Woodlake, Minn, Apr 26, 33; m 65, Gretchen Lawrence. *Educ:* Univ Minn, BS, 56, DVM, 58, PhD(vet path), 64. *Prof Exp:* Instr vet path, Univ Minn, 58-60, res fel exp path, 60-64. *Concurrent Pos:* Assoc prof, State Univ NY Stony Brook, 72-85, res prof, 85- *Mem:* AAAS; Am Physiol Soc. *Res:* Lymphocyte kinetics and immune responses; experimental pathology; radiation biology and experimental therapy. *Mailing Add:* Med Res Ctr Brookhaven Nat Lab Upton NY 11973

JOERN, ANTHONY, POPULATION BIOLOGY, INSECT ECOLOGY. *Current Pos:* PROF ECOL, UNIV NEBR, 78- *Personal Data:* b Omaha, Neb, Sept 6, 48; m 79. *Educ:* Univ Wis, BS, 70; Univ Tex, PhD(pop biol), 77. *Mem:* Ecol Soc Am; Soc Study Evolution; Entom Soc Am; Orthopterists Soc; Sigma Xi; Asn Study Animal Behav; Brit Ecol Soc. *Res:* Factors responsible for resource use by assemblages of grasshoppers; factors influencing the population dynamics of grasshoppers; the evolution of diet by herbivores. *Mailing Add:* Sch Biol Sci 345 Manter Univ Nebr PO Box 880118 Lincoln NE 68588-0118

JOESTEN, MELVIN D, INORGANIC CHEMISTRY, SCIENCE EDUCATION. *Current Pos:* assoc prof, 66-75, chmn dept, 76-82, PROF CHEM, VANDERBILT UNIV, 75- *Personal Data:* b Rochelle, Ill, Oct 27, 32; m 53, Maribel Hicks; c Jo Ellen & Charles. *Educ:* Northern Ill Univ, BS, 54; Univ Ill, MS, 59, PhD(inorg chem), 62. *Honors & Awards:* Fulbright Lectr, Trinity Col, Dublin, Ireland, 72-73. *Prof Exp:* Teacher, Ill High Sch, 56-58; asst prof chem, Southern Ill Univ, 62-66. *Concurrent Pos:* Vis prof, Univ NC, 82-83. *Mem:* Am Chem Soc; Sigma Xi; Nat Sci Teachers Asn. *Res:* Hydrogen bonding; bioinorganic and coordination chemistry; science education; chemistry education. *Mailing Add:* Dept Chem Vanderbilt Univ Nashville TN 37235. *E-Mail:* joesten@ctrvax.vanderbilt.edu

JOESTEN, RAYMOND, METAMORPHIC PETROLOGY. *Current Pos:* From instr to assoc prof, 71-83, head dept, 83-88, PROF, GEOL & GEOPHYS, UNIV CONN, 88- *Personal Data:* b San Francisco, Calif, Sept 12, 44; m 67; c 2. *Educ:* San Jose State Col, BS, 66; Calif Inst Technol, PhD, 74. *Concurrent Pos:* Vis scholar, Dept Mineral & Petrol, Cambridge Univ, 79; vis assoc prof, dept Earth & Planetary Sci, Johns Hopkins Univ, 87. *Mem:* Fel Geol Soc Am; Mineral Soc Am; Am Geophys Union; Geochem Soc. *Res:* Analysis of mass transport in metamorphic rocks through study of natural systems and modelling using methods of non-equilibrium thermodynamics. *Mailing Add:* Dept Geol & Geophys U-45 Univ Conn 354 Mansfield Rd Storrs CT 06269-2045

JOFFE, ANATOLE, MATHEMATICS. *Current Pos:* from asst prof to assoc prof, 61-73, PROF MATH & DIR, MATH RES CTR, UNIV MONTREAL, 73- *Personal Data:* b Belg, Sept 1, 32; c 2. *Educ:* Univ Brussels, Lic Sc & advan teaching degree agr, 54, Lic Sc, 55; Cornell Univ, PhD(sci math), 59. *Prof Exp:* Asst prof math, McGill Univ, 60-61. *Concurrent Pos:* Mem, Comt Aid Nat Res Coun, 74-77, Comt Basic Sci Coun Univ, 74- *Mem:* Am Math Soc; Inst Math Statist; Math Soc Can. *Res:* Theory of pure and applied probability; Galton-Watson process; some of independent random variables index by a tree and applications to biology. *Mailing Add:* Math Res Ctr Univ Montreal PO Box 6128 Montreal PQ H3C 3J7 Can

JOFFE, FREDERICK M, BIOCHEMISTRY, FOOD & PAPER TECHNOLOGY. *Current Pos:* Basic develop scientist, Foods Div, Procter & Gamble Co, 62-63, process develop group leader, Folger Coffee Co, 63-64, prod res group leader, 64-68, head prod res & prof serv, 68-70, head shampoo prod develop, Procter & Gamble, 70-72, assoc dir toilet goods prod develop, 72-76, assoc dir, 77-95, DIR PAPER PROD DEVELOP, PROCTER & GAMBLE INT, 95- *Personal Data:* b Chicago, Ill, Oct 26, 36; m 59, Ruth Grey; c 4. *Educ:* Mich State Univ, BS, 58, MS, 59; Rutgers Univ, PhD(food sci), 61. *Res:* Kinetics of enzyme activity; autooxidation of lipids; instant coffee processes; extraction; spray and freeze drying; sensory perception effects on food acceptability; products research; process development and packaging management. *Mailing Add:* 368 Oliver Rd Cincinnati OH 45215. *E-Mail:* joffefm@pg.com

JOFFE, JOSEPH, PHYSICAL CHEMISTRY. *Current Pos:* from instr to assoc prof chem eng, Newark Col Eng, 32-40, from prof to distinguished prof chem eng, 40-75, res dir, Res Found, 59-61, chmn dept, 63-75, EMER PROF CHEM ENG, NJ INST TECHNOL, 75- *Personal Data:* b Moscow, Russia, Oct 14, 09; nat US; m 31, Bertha Pashkovsky; c Robert, Paul & Richard. *Educ:* Columbia Univ, AB, 29, BS, 30, MA, 31, PhD(chem), 33. *Honors & Awards:* Cullimore Medal, NJ Inst Technol, 76. *Prof Exp:* Asst physics, Columbia Univ, 31, asst chem, Univ Exten, 32-33. *Concurrent Pos:* Sr asst, Div War Res, S A M Labs, Manhattan Proj, Columbia Univ, 43; develop phys chemist, Fed Tel & Radio Corp, 44; chem engr, Exxon Res & Eng Co (summers), 50-74 & 77. *Mem:* Am Chem Soc; Am Inst Chem Engrs; Am Soc Eng Educ; Sigma Xi. *Res:* Absorption spectroscopy; selenium rectifiers; thermodynamics of gases and gas mixtures; combustion of carbon; flow of gases in pipelines; thermal cracking of hydrocarbons; chemical reaction kinetics; equations of state; vapor-liquid equilibria. *Mailing Add:* 77 Parker Ave Maplewood NJ 07040

JOFFE, STEPHEN N, LASER SURGERY, GASTROENTEROLOGY. *Current Pos:* PROF SURG, UNIV CINCINNATI, 80- *Personal Data:* b Springs, SAfrica, Jan 11, 43; c 2. *Educ:* Univ Witwatersrand, SAfrica, MD, 67. *Concurrent Pos:* Healthcare consult, lasers med & surg. *Res:* Laser surgery and general surgery; gastroenteroloy. *Mailing Add:* Laser Ctr Am 7840 Montgomery Rd Cincinnati OH 45236

JOFFEE, IRVING BRIAN, ORGANIC CHEMISTRY, SURFACE CHEMISTRY. *Current Pos:* res chemist, 75-83, mgr anal res, 83-87, ASSOC DIR, RES & DEVELOP, PALL CORP, 87- *Personal Data:* b Rochester, NY, Sept 9, 46; m 68, Elga Feuer; c Atara, Micha & Danielle. *Educ:* Mass Inst Technol, SB, 68; Brandeis Univ, MA, 71, PhD(org chem), 73. *Prof Exp:* Fel, Hebrew Univ, Israel, 73; sr chemist res & develop, Dead Sea Bromine Co, Ltd, Israel, 74-75. *Mem:* Am Chem Soc; Parenteral Drug Asn. *Res:* Polymer modification; membrane technology; filtration technology; filing and prosecution of patents; product development. *Mailing Add:* 19 Clearview St Huntington NY 11743

JOFFRE, STEPHEN PAUL, LABORATORY MANAGEMENT, SYNTHETIC ORGANIC CHEMISTRY. *Current Pos:* DIR & OWNER, STEPHEN P JOFFRE & ASSOC, 71- *Educ:* NY Univ, BA, 38; Polytech Univ, NY, PhD(chem), 46. *Prof Exp:* Med res chemist, S L Ruskin & Assocs, 38-40; chief chemist, Parenteral Mfg, Loeser Lab Div, Wm S Merrell & Co, 40-44, Develop Control Labs & Mfg, Drug Prod Co, Inc, 44-49; dir org res, Shulton, Inc. 50-63; res dir, Germaine Monteil Cosmetiques, 64-66; mgr, Explor Res & Develop Dept, Max Factor & Co, 66-71. *Mem:* Emer mem Am Chem Soc; fel Am Inst Chemists; fel AAAS; Soc Cosmetic Chemists; Intersci Res Found; NY Acad Sci. *Res:* Process development of new product creation for the cosmetic, pharmaceutical, fragrance and food industries in developing marketable products; granted seven US, Canadian and British patents. *Mailing Add:* 6194 Kilgord Ct Magalia CA 95954. *Fax:* 530-873-2490; *E-Mail:* sjoffre@aol.com

JOFRIET, JAN CORNELIUS, STRUCTURAL ANALYSIS, BULK SOLIDS FLOW. *Current Pos:* prof solid mech & eng design, 73-95, dir, 93-95, EMER PROF, UNIV GUELPH, 96- *Personal Data:* m 57, Marlene Palmieri; c Peter & Eric. *Educ:* Tech Col Amsterdam, dipl, 50; Univ Waterloo, MASc, 69, PhD(civil eng), 72. *Honors & Awards:* Award for Excellence, Can Soc Agr Eng, 85, Maple Leaf Award, 95. *Prof Exp:* Royal engrs, Royal Dutch Army, 50-53; struct designer, Norman Wagner & Assocs, Hamilton, 53-55; struct engr, Gore & Storrie Ltd, Toronto, 55-57, BC Power Comn, 57-59 & Sir William Halcrow & Partners, Eng, 59-60; prin struct engr, James F MacLaren Ltd, Consult Eng, Toronto, 60-68; grad res asst, Dept Civil Eng, Univ Waterloo, 68-73. *Mem:* Fel Can Soc Civil Engrs; fel Can Soc Agr Engrs; Am Soc Agr Engrs. *Res:* Advanced structural analysis; behavior of plant materials; numerical methods of analysis; reinforced concrete use in agricultural structures and corrosion; published numerous papers, technical reports, articles and publications. *Mailing Add:* Sch Eng Univ Guelph Guelph ON N1G 2W1 Can. *E-Mail:* jofriet@net2.eos.uoguelph.ca

JOFTES, DAVID LION, physiology, developmental biology; deceased, see previous edition for last biography

JOH, TONG HYUB, BIOCHEMISTRY, MOLECULAR BIOLOGY. *Current Pos:* PROF NEUROBIOL, CORNELL UNIV MED COL, 72- *Educ:* NY Univ, PhD(biochem), 71. *Mailing Add:* Burke Med Res Inst 785 Mamaronect Ave White Plains NY 10605-2523. *Fax:* 914-948-9541

JOHAL, SARJIT S, BIOCHEMISTRY. *Current Pos:* MGR PROCESS DEVELOP, ECOSCI CORP, 92- *Personal Data:* b Punjab, India, Feb 15, 51. *Educ:* Univ Calif, Los Angeles, BS, 74, MS, 76; Univ Ariz, PhD(biochem), 80. *Prof Exp:* Res fel biochem, Univ Nebr, 80-83; proj leader, Brit Petrol, 83-85, sr proj leader, 85-90; group leader biochem, Enichem, 90-92. *Mem:* Am Chem Soc; Am Soc Biochem & Molecular Biol. *Res:* Biochemistry. *Mailing Add:* Clarient Corp Biotechnol Res Div 128 Spring St Lexington MA 02173

JOHAM, HOWARD ERNEST, PLANT PHYSIOLOGY. *Current Pos:* instr bot, Tex A&M Univ, 46-47, from asst prof to prof plant physiol, 47-75, sect leader, 59-75, prof plant sci & head dept, 74-80, EMER PROF PLANT SCI, TEX A&M UNIV, 80- *Personal Data:* b Los Angeles, Calif, Oct 12, 19; m 42, Myrtle Franze; c Suzanne M (McElwee) & James R. *Educ:* Univ Calif, BA, 41; Agr & Mech Col, Tex, MS, 43; Iowa State Col, PhD(plant physiol), 50. *Honors & Awards:* Distinguished Serv Award, Am Soc Plant Physiologists. *Prof Exp:* Jr plant physiologist, USDA, Calif, 43-44. *Concurrent Pos:* Mem, Nat Cotton Task Force, 70-72. *Mem:* Am Soc Agron; Am Soc Plant Physiol; Scand Soc Plant Physiol. *Res:* Plant nutrition; role of calcium in translocation of carbohydrates; cation interactions in cotton nutrition. *Mailing Add:* 9633 E State Hwy 21 Bryan TX 77808

JOHANNES, ROBERT, PHYSICS. *Current Pos:* RETIRED. *Personal Data:* b Philadelphia, Pa, Jan 16, 27; m 61; c 3. *Educ:* Dickinson Col, BS, 50; Lehigh Univ, MS, 52, PhD(physics), 61. *Prof Exp:* Asst physics, Lehigh Univ, 52-58, res asst, 58-60; proj scientist res lab, Philco Corp, Ford Motor Co, 60-64, res specialist, Appl Res Lab, 64-66; sr scientist, Westinghouse Res Lab, 66-70; sr scientist, Superior Electronics Res Lab, Que, 70-72; res physicist, Calspan Corp, 72-77, prin scientist, 77-94. *Mem:* Am Phys Soc. *Res:* Electro-optics; ferroelectrics; infrared spectroscopy; optical data processing; optical properties; transition metal oxides; lasers; optics; system analysis. *Mailing Add:* 1217 Edgewood Ave Las Cruces NM 88005

JOHANNES, ROBERT EARL, marine ecology, for more information see previous edition

JOHANNES, VIRGIL IVANCICH, DIGITAL TELECOMMUNICATIONS SYSTEMS & HARDWARE, HIGH-SPEED DIGITAL CIRCUITS. *Current Pos:* PRES, VIRGIL I JOHANNES INC, 89- *Personal Data:* b Omaha, Nebr, Feb 7, 30; m 62, Rachelma Del Pizzo; c Laura. *Educ:* City Col New York, BS, 53; Columbia Univ, MS, 54, ScD(eng), 61. *Prof Exp:* Lectr elec eng, City Col New York, 53-58; prof & chmn, Elec Eng Dept, Fairleigh Dickinson Univ, 62-63; dept head, AT&T Bell Labs, 63-89. *Concurrent Pos:* Adj assoc prof, Columbia Univ, 64-68; vchmn, Study Group XVIII, Int Consultative Comt Tel & Tel, 78-93. *Mem:* Fel Inst Elec & Electronics Engrs. *Res:* High speed digital transmission systems on copper, optical fiber and satellite media (system concepts and detailed implementation); international standards for digital telecommunications. *Mailing Add:* 230 Balfoor Dr Winter Park FL 32792. *Fax:* 407-679-0845; *E-Mail:* v.johannes@ieee.org

JOHANNESSEN, CARL L, BIOGEOGRAPHY, CULTURAL GEOGRAPHY & HORTICULTURE. *Current Pos:* prof, 59-, EMER PROF GEOG, UNIV ORE. *Personal Data:* b Santa Ana, Calif, July 28, 24; m Doris Sawhill; c Bruce E. *Educ:* Univ Calif, Berkeley, BA, 50, MA, 53, PhD(geog), 59. *Prof Exp:* Instr geog, Univ Calif, Davis, 59. *Concurrent Pos:* Agr Develop Coun grant, Costa Rica, 65, Guggenheim Found fel, 65-66, Brazil, 79; pres, Neopropagations, Inc, 69-78; mem, Conf Latin Am Geogr, chair, 84-86; grantee, NSF, Univ Ore Found. *Mem:* AAAS; Asn Am Geogr; Am Geog Soc; Soc Econ Bot; Sigma Xi; Soc Ethnobiol. *Res:* Ways in which humans have modified plants and animals in the domestication process and the distributions of domestic and wild biota; Latin America, Himalayas and India and China in pre-Columbian times. *Mailing Add:* Dept Geog Univ Ore Eugene OR 97403

JOHANNESSEN, GEORGE ANDREW, HORTICULTURE, PLANT BREEDING. *Current Pos:* dir, 78-90, EMER DIR, CALIF TOMATO RES INST, 90- *Personal Data:* b Seattle, Wash, Jan 10, 19; m 49, Patricia M Martin; c Neil, Ann, Sue & Kirsten. *Educ:* Rutgers Univ, BS, 41; Purdue Univ, MS, 48; Cornell Univ, PhD(veg crops, plant breeding, physiol), 50. *Prof Exp:* Asst soil technologist, Va Truck Exp Sta, 46; asst hort, Purdue Univ, 46-48; asst hort, NY Exp Sta, Cornell Univ, Geneva, 48-50; assoc prof veg crops & pomol, Cornell Univ, 50-53; western area agronomist, Am Can Co, 53-60; head plant breeding dept, Pineapple Res Inst Hawaii, 60-64; dir raw prod res, Calif Canners & Growers, 64-67; dir, Calif Tomato Res Inst, 68-72; mgr, Calif Processing Tomato Adv Bd, 72-78. *Concurrent Pos:* Affil mem grad fac, Univ Hawaii, 60-64; vis assoc prof, Cornell Univ, 63-64; consult tomato & pineapple prod, Agency Int Develop, Africa, 68; mem gov bd, Agr Res Inst, Washington, DC, 71-73; consult, Food & Agr Orgn, UN, Ivory Coast, Africa, 80. *Mem:* Fel Am Soc Hort Sci; Am Path Soc; Sigma Xi; Inst Food Technologists. *Res:* Vegetable crops; physiology; tomato fruit cracking; histology of tomato fruit skin; fruit and vegetable crop production; post-harvest handling and storage of fruit and vegetable crops; tomato and pineapple breeding; research administration. *Mailing Add:* 333 Hartford Rd Danville CA 94526

JOHANNESSEN, PAUL ROMBERG, SOLID STATE ELECTRONICS. *Current Pos:* PRES, MEGAPULSE, INC, 70-, CHMN BD, 93- *Personal Data:* b Oslo, Norway, Aug 12, 26; nat US; m 50; c 2. *Educ:* Mass Inst Technol, SB & SM, 53, ScD, 58. *Prof Exp:* Res engr, Electronic Systs Lab, Mass Inst Technol, 53-56, res asst & instr, 56-58, asst prof, 58-59; sr scientist, Sylvania Elec Prod Inc, 59-69; vpres, Symbionics, 69-70. *Mem:* Sr mem Inst Elec & Electronics Engrs; Sigma Xi. *Res:* Solid state power sources; automatic controls; nonlinear circuits; electronics. *Mailing Add:* 40 Tyler Rd Lexington MA 02173-2429

JOHANNINGSMEIER, ARTHUR GEORGE, ECOLOGY. *Current Pos:* CHMN SCI DEPT, CUSHING ACAD, 72- *Personal Data:* b Lafayette, Ind, Nov 5, 30; m 56; c Edward & Charles. *Educ:* Purdue Univ, BS, 56, MS, 62, PhD, 66. *Prof Exp:* Teacher, High Sch, Mich, 56-58; instr biol, bot & zool, Purdue Univ, 58-62, teaching asst biol & zool, 62-64; asst prof biol, Boston Univ, 64-71; NSF fac fel, Grasslands IBP, Colo State Univ, 71-72. *Concurrent Pos:* Consult water qual, New Eng Interstate Water Pollution Control Comn, Boston, 75-78. *Mem:* Ecol Soc Am; Am Inst Biol Scientists; Sigma Xi; Am Soc Mammal. *Res:* Food and energy relationships of small mammals in natural communities; development of field methods for the study of small mammal movements and physiology; water quality assessment. *Mailing Add:* Dept Sci Cushing Acad Ashburnham MA 01430. *Fax:* 508-827-6927; *E-Mail:* jmeier@1.mec.mass.edu

JOHANNSEN, CHRISTIAN JAKOB, SOILS & SOIL SCIENCE, REMOTE SENSING. *Current Pos:* exten agronomist, Purdue Univ, 63-65, res asst soil physics, 65-66, res agronomist, Lab Appln Remote Sensing, 66-69, prog leader, 69-72, Agr Data Network, 85-86, dir, Natural Resources Res Inst, 87-93, dir, Environ Sci & Eng Inst, 94-96, DIR, LAB APPLNS REMOTE SENSING, PURDUE UNIV, 86- *Personal Data:* b Randolph, Nebr, July 24, 37; m 59, Joanne Rockwell; c Erik C & Peter J. *Educ:* Univ Nebr, Lincoln, BS, 59, MS, 61; Purdue Univ, PhD(soil physics, agron), 69. *Honors & Awards:* Technol Innovation Award, NASA, 79; Outstanding Serv Award, Am Soc Photogram & Remote Sensing, 92. *Prof Exp:* Area agronomist, Chevron Chem Co, 61-62; exten agronomist, Univ Mo, Columbia, 72-85. *Concurrent Pos:* Vis chief scientist, Space Imaging Inc, 96-97. *Mem:* Fel Am Soc Agron; fel Soil Sci Soc Am; fel Soil Conserv Soc Am (pres, 82-83); Int Soil Sci Soc; Am Soc Photogram; Sigma Xi. *Res:* Developing natural resources data and information; emphasis on remote sensing and geographic information systems for use in land degradation and global change application. *Mailing Add:* Lab Appl Remote Sensing ENTM Hall Purdue Univ West Lafayette IN 47907-1158. *Fax:* 765-494-0535; *E-Mail:* johannsn@ecn.purdue.edu

JOHANNSEN, FREDERICK RICHARD, RISK ASSESSMENT. *Current Pos:* sr toxicologist, Monsanto Co, 73-78, toxicologist specialist, 78-79, group leader, Environ Health Lab, 79-80, toxicol mgr, 79-86, dir toxicol, 86-92, worldwide dir copr toxicol, 92-94, SR CONSULT TOXICOL & TEAM LEADER, MONSANTO CO, 94- *Personal Data:* b St Louis, Mo, Feb 17, 46; c 2. *Educ:* William Jewell Col, AB, 68; Univ Mo, MS, 70, PhD(toxicol), 73; Am Bd Toxicol, dipl, 81. *Prof Exp:* Grad res asst toxicol, Toxicol Lab, Univ Mo, 68-72, res assoc, 72-73. *Concurrent Pos:* Lectr, Am Indust Hyg Asn, 79-; dir, Toxicol Lab Accreditation BRD Inc, 82-88; adj assoc prof toxicol, Sch Pub Health, St Louis Univ, 92- *Mem:* Soc Toxicol; Am Chem Soc; fel Acad Toxicol Sci. *Res:* Toxicology and risk assessment for use in support of environmental and occupational safety. *Mailing Add:* Monsanto Co 800 N Lindbergh Blvd St Louis MO 63167. *E-Mail:* frjoha@ccmail.monsanto.com

JOHANSEN, ELMER L, ELECTRICAL ENGINEERING. *Current Pos:* RES ENGR, ENVIRON RES INST, MICH, 73- *Personal Data:* b Lake Forest, Ill, June 28, 30; m 58; c 4. *Educ:* Harvard Univ, BA, 52; Univ Mich, Ann Arbor, MSEE, 54, PhD(elec eng), 64. *Honors & Awards:* Barry Carleton Award, Inst Elec & Electronics Engrs Group on Aerospace & Electronic Systs, 73. *Prof Exp:* Sr engr, Cook Res Labs, 56-58, res asst radar systs, Univ Mich, Ann Arbor, 58-60, res assoc, 60-63, assoc engr, 63-65, res engr, 65-77, lectr elec eng, 66-70. *Mem:* Inst Elec & Electronics Engrs; Sigma Xi. *Res:* Radar systems; electromagnetic scattering properties of radar targets; radar systems engineering; synthetic aperture radar; radar cross-section measurements; radar propagation; radar data analysis; millimeter-wave radar. *Mailing Add:* 2630 Manchester Rd Ann Arbor MI 48104-6500

JOHANSEN, ERLING, DENTISTRY, ORAL PATHOLOGY. *Current Pos:* PROF & DEAN DENT SCI, SCH DENT MED, TUFTS UNIV, 80- *Personal Data:* b Overhalla, Norway, Apr 8, 23; nat US; m 52; c 3. *Educ:* Tufts Col, DMD, 49; Univ Rochester, PhD, 55. *Hon Degrees:* PhD, Univ Athens, 81. *Prof Exp:* Asst, Tufts Sch, Tufts Col, 46-49; instr histol, Eastman Sch Dent Hyg, 52-64; from asst prof to prof dent res, Sch Med & Dent, Univ Rochester, 55-66, Margaret & Cy Welcher prof, 66-80, chmn dept, 55-80, prof clin dent, 74-80. *Concurrent Pos:* Consult, Nat Inst Dent Res; consult, Bur Environ Health, mem clin fel rev panel & anat & path fel comt, USPHS; lectr, XIVth World Dent Cong, Paris, France, First Pan-Pac Cong Dent Res, Tokyo, Japan & Asian Pac Regional Orgn Cong, Bangkok, Thailand; spec consult, Comt Asn Role & Function, mem comt advan educ, Task Force on Advan Educ & Exec Comt, chmn sect advan educ & vpres, Advan Educ Prog, Am Asn Dent Schs; hon guest prof, Kanagawa Dent Sch, Japan, 69; int lectr & adv, Pan-Am Health Orgn, WHO, Colombia, Peru & Chile, 73; int lectr, Venezuela, 74; ed, J Dent Educ; USPHS grants; consult, King Abdulaziz Univ, Sch Dent, Jeddah, Saudi Arabia; travelling scholar, Int Col Dentists, Asian Pac Countries, 70; hon prof, Yonsei Univ Col Dent, Seoul, Korea, Peruvian Univ, Lima, Peru, 73; merit award, Rochester Acad Med, 80; mem, Coun Dent Res, Am Dent Asn, 83-87, chmn, 86-87. *Mem:* Fel AAAS; Am Dent Asn; Norweg Dent Asn; Int Asn Dent Res; Sigma Xi; Am Asn Dent Schs; fel Am Col Dentists; fel Int Col Dentists; hon mem Korean Dent Asn; hon mem Pedodontic Soc Peru; hon mem Am Acad Dent Sci. *Res:* Experimental dental caries; electron microscopy; mineralized tissues; graduate education. *Mailing Add:* 69 Windsor Rd Needham MA 02192-1440

JOHANSEN, HANS WILLIAM, MARINE PHYCOLOGY. *Current Pos:* asst prof bot, 68-72, assoc prof, 72-81, PROF BIOL, DEPT BIOL, CLARK UNIV, 81- *Personal Data:* b Worcester, Mass, June 11, 32; m 82, Frances L Pedusey; c Eric J. *Educ:* San Jose State Col, BA, 55; San Francisco State Col, MA, 61; Univ Calif, Berkeley, PhD(phycol), 66. *Prof Exp:* Teacher, San Mateo High Sch, 56-60; USPHS fel, 66-68. *Mem:* Phycol Soc Am; Int Phycol Soc; Sigma Xi. *Res:* Systematics, structure, reproduction and morphogenesis of Corallinaceae; ecology of marine benthic algae. *Mailing Add:* Dept Biol Clark Univ Worcester MA 01610

JOHANSEN, JACK T, ENGINEERING. *Current Pos:* SR VPRES SCI & TECHNOL, MILLIPORE CORP, 87- *Personal Data:* b 1943. *Prof Exp:* From sr mgt to pres, Carlbiotech, Copenhagen. *Mailing Add:* Millipore Corp 80 Ashby Rd Bedford MA 01730-2237

JOHANSEN, NILS IVAR, GEOTECHNICAL ENGINEERING, PERMAFROST ENGINEERING. *Current Pos:* PROF & ADV, UNIV SOUTHERN IND, 96- *Personal Data:* b Oslo, Norway, Dec 25, 41. *Educ:* Purdue Univ, BSCE, 66 MSCE, 67; PhD(civil eng & eng geol), 71. *Prof Exp:* Hwy engr, Ind Dept Highways, 67-71; From asst prof to prof eng, Univ Alaska, 71-96, head, Mining Technol, 90-95. *Concurrent Pos:* Consult, Geotech Eng, 73-; vis prof, Univ Mo, Rolla, 81-82; vis assoc prof & acad skills coordr, Univ Southern Ind, 88-89; chair, Eng Sect, Ind Acad Sci, 91 & 94. *Mem:* Am Soc Civil Engrs; Soc Mining Engrs; Sigma Xi; Nat Asn Develop Educ. *Res:* Geotechnical engineering and permafrost engineering; resource development in arctic and subarctic regions; infrastructure related to resource development; engineering education. *Mailing Add:* Univ Southern Ind 8600 Univ Blvd Evansville IN 47712. *Fax:* 812-421-9880; *E-Mail:* johansen.vcs@smtp.usi.edu

JOHANSEN, ROBERT H, HORTICULTURE. *Current Pos:* RETIRED. *Personal Data:* b Grafton, NDak, July 26, 22; m 48; c 4. *Educ:* NDak State Univ, BS, 49, MS, 56; La State Univ, PhD(hort), 64. *Prof Exp:* From asst horticulturist to assoc horticulturist, NDak State Univ, 53-65, horticulturist, 65-92, prof hort & forestry, 73-92. *Res:* Potato breeding. *Mailing Add:* 2001 Eighth St N Fargo ND 58102

JOHANSON, CHRIS ELLYN, psychopharmacology, for more information see previous edition

JOHANSON, CONRAD EARL, PHYSIOLOGY & BIOLOGY OF CHOROID PLEXUS. *Current Pos:* PROF & DIR NEUROSURG LABS, BROWN UNIV, 86- *Personal Data:* b Brockton, Mass, Aug 6, 42. *Educ:* Eastern Nazarene Col, BA, 65; Univ Kans, PhD(physiol), 70. *Prof Exp:* From asst prof to assoc prof pharmacol, Univ Utah, 74-86. *Concurrent Pos:* NIH res career achievement award, 77. *Mem:* Soc Neurosci; Pharmacol Soc; Am Physiol Soc. *Res:* Physiology and biology of choroid plexus. *Mailing Add:* CSF Res Prog Brown Univ 593 Eddy St Providence RI 02902-0001. *Fax:* 401-444-8727

JOHANSON, DONALD CARL, PHYSICAL ANTHROPOLOGY. *Current Pos:* PRES, INST HUMAN ORIGINS, BERKELEY, CALIF, 81- *Personal Data:* b Chicago, Ill, June 28, 43; m 88, Lenora Carey. *Educ:* Univ Ill, BA, 66; Univ Chicago, MA, 70, PhD, 74. *Hon Degrees:* DSc, John Carroll Univ, 79, Col Wooster, 85. *Honors & Awards:* Jared Potter Kirtland Award, Outstanding Sci Achievement, Cleveland Mus Natural His, 79; Prof Achievement Award, Univ Chicago, 80; San Francisco Exploration Award, 86; Int Premio Fregene Award, 87. *Prof Exp:* Mem, Dept Phys Anthrop, Cleveland Mus Natural Hist, 72-81, curator, 74-81. *Concurrent Pos:* Grant, Wenner-Gren Found, NSF, Nat Geog Soc, LSB Leakey Found, Clevelan Found, George Gund Cound, Roush Found; adj prof, Case Western Reserve Univ & Kent State Univ, 78-81; prof anthrop, Stanford Univ, 83-89. *Mem:* Fel AAAS; fel Royal Geog Soc; Am Asn Phys Anthropologists; Int Asn Dent Res; Int Asn Human Biologists; Am Asn Africanist Archaeologissts; Soc Vert Paleont; Soc Study Human Biol; Founders Coun; Asn Int Study Human Paleont; Explorers Club; Nat Ctr Sci Educ. *Res:* Field and laboratory research into human crisis; field work in Ethiopia and Tanzania, searching for fossilized remains of our ancestors. *Mailing Add:* Inst Human Origins 1288 9th St Berkeley CA 94710. *Fax:* 510-845-9453; *E-Mail:* donj@iho.org

JOHANSON, JERRY RAY, MECHANICAL ENGINEERING, APPLIED MECHANICS. *Current Pos:* PRES, J R JOHANSON, INC, 85- *Personal Data:* b Salt Lake City, Utah, Aug 29, 37; m 57, Shepherd & Harlean; c 5. *Educ:* Univ Utah, BS, 59, PhD(mech eng), 62. *Honors & Awards:* Henry Hess Award, Am Soc Mech Engrs, 66; Neal Rice Award, Int Briquetting Asn. *Prof Exp:* Res engr, Appl Res Lab, US Steel Corp, 62-65, sr res engr, 65-66; vpres, Jenike & Johanson, Inc, 72-80, pres, 80-85. *Concurrent Pos:* Lectr, Caledonian Univ, Glasgow, Scotland. *Mem:* Am Soc Mech Engrs; Int Briquetting Asn; Am Soc Chem Engrs. *Res:* Flow of solids; agglomeration of solids; fluid flow in bulk solids; testing bulk solids properties. *Mailing Add:* 712 Fiero Lane No 37 San Luis Obispo CA 93401. *Fax:* 805-549-8282

JOHANSON, L(ENNART) N(OBLE), CHEMICAL ENGINEERING. *Current Pos:* from asst prof to assoc prof, 51-61, PROF CHEM ENG, UNIV WASH, 61- *Personal Data:* b Salt Lake City, Utah, May 3, 21; m 48; c 3. *Educ:* Univ Utah, BS, 42; Univ Wis, MS, 43, PhD(chem eng), 48. *Prof Exp:* Chem engr, US Bur Mines, Utah, 42; assoc process engr, Richfield Oil Corp, Calif, 44-45, process engr, 48-51; instr chem eng, Univ Wis, 47-48. *Concurrent Pos:* Consult. *Mem:* Am Chem Soc; Am Soc Eng Educ; Am Inst Chem Engrs; Tech Asn Pulp & Paper Indust; Sigma Xi. *Res:* Pulp, paper technology; chemical engineering kinetics; reactor design; fluidization; high temperature technology. *Mailing Add:* 9023 45th Ave NE Seattle WA 98115-3844

JOHANSON, LAMAR, PLANT PHYSIOLOGY. *Current Pos:* assoc prof, 67-71, PROF BIOL & HEAD DEPT BIOL SCI, TARLETON STATE UNIV, 71- *Personal Data:* b Kyle, Tex, Oct 31, 35; m 60. *Educ:* Southwest Tex State Col, BS, 57, MA, 58; Tex A&M Univ, PhD(plant physiol), 67. *Prof Exp:* Asst biol, Southwest Tex State Col, 56-58; instr, Tarleton State Univ, 61-63; asst plant physiol, Tex A&M Univ, 63-65. *Mem:* AAAS; Am Soc Plant Physiologists; Scandinavian Soc Plant Physiologists; Am Inst Biol Sci; Am Oil Chemists' Soc; Sigma Xi. *Res:* Nutrition of excised plant tissues and algae, especially calcium and sodium requirements; lateral root formation; biochemistry and physiology of the peanut; mineral nutrition, oil quality and response to irrigation. *Mailing Add:* Arts & Sci Tarleton Sta Stephenville TX 76402-0001

JOHANSON, ROBERT GAIL, THIN FILM DEPOSITION. *Current Pos:* SR STAFF ENGR, SEAGATE RECORDING MEDIA GROUP, 92- *Personal Data:* b San Francisco, Calif, Aug 26, 36; m 64, Joan B Lee; c 5. *Educ:* Reed Col, AB, 60; Univ Vt, PhD(org chem), 69. *Prof Exp:* Chemist, Aerojet-Gen Corp, 61-66; fel org chem, Case Western Res Univ, 69-70; staff mem, Raychem Corp, 70-76; sr mem staff, Signetics Corp, 76-81; mgr head & disk develop, Datapoint Corp, 81-83; consult, Disk Consults, 83-84; mgr appln lab, CPA Inc, 84-88; mgr thin film eng, Akashic Memories Corp, 88-90; dir mfg eng, KMI Magnetics, Inc, 90-92. *Mem:* Am Chem Soc; Sigma Xi; Inst Elec & Electronics Engrs; Am Vacuum Soc. *Res:* Thin film deposition and analysis. *Mailing Add:* 517 Kenilworth Ct Sunnyvale CA 94087

JOHANSON, WALDEMAR GUSTAVE, JR, INTERNAL MEDICINE, PULMONARY DISEASES. *Current Pos:* assoc prof, 74-78, PROF MED, UNIV TEX HEALTH SCI CTR, SAN ANTONIO, 78-, CHIEF, PULMONARY DIS SECT, 74- *Personal Data:* b St Paul, Minn, Sept 9, 37; m 60; c 3. *Educ:* Gustavus Adolphus Col, BS, 59; Univ Minn, Minneapolis, MD, 62. *Prof Exp:* Intern med, Med Ctr, Univ Calif, Los Angeles, 62-63; resident, Minneapolis Vet Admin Hosp & St Paul Ramsey Hosp, 65-67; from instr to assoc prof med, Univ Tex Health Sci Ctr, Dallas, 69-74. *Concurrent Pos:* Nat Inst Arthritis & Infectious Dis fel, Univ Tex Health Sci Ctr, Dallas, 68-71. *Mem:* Am Thoracic Soc; Am Fedn Clin Res. *Res:* Pulmonary disease models; infectious disease of the lungs. *Mailing Add:* Dept Med NJ Med Sch 185 S Orange Ave Newark NJ 07103

JOHANSON, WILLIAM RICHARD, rare-earth magnetism, specific heat measurements, for more information see previous edition

JOHANSSON, KARL RICHARD, MICROBIAL ECOLOGY, MEDICAL MICROBIOLOGY. *Current Pos:* RETIRED. *Personal Data:* b Bay City, Mich, June 28, 20; m 43, Dorothy Heilig; c Sandra, Peter & Steven. *Educ:* Univ Wis, BS, 42, MS, 46, PhD(bact), 48. *Prof Exp:* Anal chemist, Swift & Co, 42; asst bact, Univ Wis, 42-43, asst vet sci, 46, asst bact, 46-48; instr dairy bact, Univ Calif, Davis, 48-49; from asst prof to assoc prof bact & immunol, Univ Minn, 49-59; exec secy, Virol & Rickettsiol Study Sect, Div Res Grants, NIH, 59-61; assoc prof environ health eng, Calif Inst Technol, 61-63; chief res grants br, Nat Inst Neurol Dis & Blindness, NIH, 63-65, exec secy virol study sect, Div Res Grants, 65-69; prof microbiol, Univ Tex Med Sch San Antonio, 69-70; dep dir sci affairs, Wistar Inst, 70-73; prof biol sci, NTex State Univ, 73-86, chmn dept, 73-79. *Concurrent Pos:* Consult, Gen Mills, Inc, 53, Minneapolis-Honeywell, 58-59, Tex Col Osteop Med, 73-86; fac fel, NASA, 83 & 84; vis scholar, Calif Space Inst, Univ Calif, San Diego, 86- *Mem:* AAAS; Am Soc Microbiol; Am Acad Microbiol; Planetary Soc. *Res:* Pathogenesis, including role of surface proteins, in legionella pneumophila; survival of legionellae in the natural environment; biotransformation and cometabolism of humic compounds; space biology; exobiology. *Mailing Add:* 825 Santa Regina Solana Beach CA 92075

JOHANSSON, SONNY L, GENITAL CANCER, UROLOGICAL DISEASES. *Current Pos:* PROF & DIR PATH, UNIV NEBR MED CTR, 85- *Personal Data:* b Falkoping, Sweden, Oct 27, 42. *Educ:* Univ Goteborg, BS, 65, MD, 72, PhD(path), 76. *Prof Exp:* Assoc prof path, Univ Goteborg, 76-85. *Mem:* Am Asn Cancer Res; AMA; Am Asn Path. *Mailing Add:* Dept Path & Microbiol Univ Nebr Med Ctr 42nd & Dewey Omaha NE 68154-3135

JOHANSSON, SUNE, FIRE RETARDANT COATINGS & TREATMENTS, HIGH TEMPERATURE COATINGS. *Current Pos:* TECH DIR, FLAME CONTROL COATINGS, 82- *Personal Data:* b Falkenberg, Sweden, Apr 8, 28; Can citizen; m 53, Anna Bilous; c Rolf. *Educ:* Hogre Tekniska Laroverket, BE, 49. *Prof Exp:* Chemist, Acme Paint & Varnish, 51-55, chief chemist, 55-61; chief chemist, Ocean Chemicals, 61-62, tech dir, 62-78; tech dir, Wood-Tech, 78-82. *Concurrent Pos:* Tech expert, Teltech Resource Network Corp, 89- *Mem:* Am Chem Soc. *Res:* Fire retardant coatings and treatments; high temperature coatings; general chemical coatings. *Mailing Add:* 436 Aberdeen Rd Lewiston NY 14092-1023. *Fax:* 716-285-6303

JOHANSSON, TOGE (TAGE) SIGVARD KJELL, APICULTURE. *Current Pos:* prof, 52-84, chmn dept, 60-63, EMER PROF BIOL, QUEENS COL, NY, 84- *Personal Data:* b Karlstad, Sweden, Aug 8, 19; nat US; m 50, Mildred Pangburn. *Educ:* Beloit Col, BS, 42; Univ Wis, MS, 44, PhD(zool), 47. *Prof Exp:* Asst zool, Univ Wis, 42-47; instr, Grinnell Col, 47-48, Dartmouth Col, 48-50, NY Univ, 50-52. *Concurrent Pos:* Entomologist, Bee Cult Lab, Agr Res Serv, USDA, Ariz, 56-57; vis assoc prof, Dept Environ Biol, Univ Guelph, 71-72. *Mem:* Entom Soc Am; Int Bee Res Asn. *Res:* Entomology; apiculture. *Mailing Add:* 72 Smokey Hollow Rd W East Berne NY 12059-9801

JOHAR, J(OGINDAR) S(INGH), ENVIRONMENTAL CHEMISTRY, FLUORINE CHEMISTRY. *Current Pos:* PROF CHEM, WAYNE STATE COL, 68- *Personal Data:* b Rawalpindi, West Pakistan, Jan 1, 35; m 60, Manjit K Sodhia; c Ravijot, Jasjot & Navjot. *Educ:* Panjab Univ, India, BSc, 57, MSc, 59; Univ Fla, PhD(chem), 66. *Prof Exp:* Lectr chem, Govt Col, Ludhiana, India, 59-62; chmn sci & math div, Cleveland State Community Col, 67-68. *Concurrent Pos:* Fel, Univ Idaho, 66-67. *Mem:* AAAS; Am Chem Soc; Nat Educ Asn. *Res:* Synthesis and study of fluorine compounds containing nitrogen sulfur and phosphorus; volatile products and use of non-aqueous solvents. *Mailing Add:* Head Math-Sci Div Wayne State Col Wayne NE 68787-1486. *Fax:* 402-375-7204

JOHARI, OM, ELECTRON MICROSCOPY, METALLURGY. *Current Pos:* SECY & TREAS, SCANNING MICROS INT, INC, 77- *Personal Data:* b Jodhpur, India, Aug 13, 40; m 67; c 2. *Educ:* Indian Inst Technol, Kharagpur, BTech, 62; Univ Calif, Berkeley, MS, 63, PhD(metall), 65. *Honors & Awards:* Grossman Award, Am Soc Metals, 66. *Prof Exp:* Res asst metall, Univ Calif, Berkeley, 62-65, res fel & lectr, 65; asst prof, Drexel Inst Technol, 65-66; res metallurgist, IIT Res Inst, 66-68, mgr metal physics, 68-77; pres, Johari Assocs Inc, 78-88. *Concurrent Pos:* Consult, Lockheed-Ga Co, 65-66; ed & managing ed, Scanning Electron Micros & Scanning Micros, 68-, Food Microstruct & Food Struct, 81-, Cell & Mat, 91- *Res:* Relationship between structure and properties of materials; applications of scanning and transmission electron microscopy in material sciences and other branches of science and technology; failure analysis of metallic materials. *Mailing Add:* 1034 Alabama Dr Elk Grove Village IL 60007

JOHN, DAVID THOMAS, PARASITOLOGY. *Current Pos:* PROF MICROBIOL PARASITOL & ASSOC DEAN BASIC SCI, COL OSTEOPATH MED, OKLA STATE UNIV, 90- *Personal Data:* b Kano, Nigeria, Apr 25, 41; m 63, Rebecca Anne Bruner; c David Andrew & Sarah Katherine. *Educ:* Asbury Col, AB, 63; Univ NC, Chapel Hill, MSPH, 66, PhD(parasitol), 70. *Prof Exp:* NIH malariology training res assoc, Univ Ga, 70-72; from asst prof to assoc prof microbiol, Med Col, Va Commonwealth Univ, 72-80; from assoc prof to prof, Sch Med, Oral Roberts Univ, 80-90, chair, 83-90. *Mem:* Am Soc Parasitol; Am Soc Trop Med & Hyg; Soc Protozool; Sigma Xi; fel Am Acad Microbiol. *Res:* Opportunistic amebae; environmental isolation and characterization; factors affecting resistance and virulence. *Mailing Add:* Col Osteopath Med Okla State Univ 1111 W 17th St Tulsa OK 74107. *Fax:* 918-561-8414; *E-Mail:* john@okway.okstate.edu

JOHN, E ROY, NEUROPHYSIOLOGY, PSYCHOPHYSIOLOGY. *Current Pos:* RES SCIENTIST, NATHAN S KLINE INST, 87-; PROF PSYCHIAT & DIR, BRAIN RES LABS, NY UNIV. *Personal Data:* b Brownsville, Pa, Aug 14, 24; m; c 6. *Educ:* Univ Chicago, BS, 48, PhD(physiol psychol), 54. *Prof Exp:* Sr res technician radiochem, Argonne Nat Labs, AEC, 46-51; res asst psychol, Univ Chicago, 51-54; res assoc, Comn Behav Sci, 54-56; assoc res anatomist, Univ Calif, Los Angeles, 56-57, assoc res physiologist, 57-58; assoc prof psychol, Univ Rochester, 59-60, prof psychol & dir, Ctr Brain Res, 60-63; prof psychiat & dir brain res labs, New York Med Col, 63-77, prof physiol, 72-77; prof psychiat & dir, Brain Res Labs, New York Univ Med Ctr, 77- *Concurrent Pos:* Res consult chem, C F Pease Co, Chicago, 52-55; City New York Health Res Coun career scientist awards, 64-75; mem, Nat Adv Coun Brain Res; assoc ed, Behav Biol; ed, Brain & Behav Res. *Mem:* Am Physiol Soc; Am Psychopath Soc; Int Brain Res Orgn; Soc Neurosci; Am EEG Soc. *Res:* Mechanisms of learning and memory; automatic computer evaluation of brain activity; assessment of minimal brain dysfunction in children; cognitive deficit in aging. *Mailing Add:* Brain Res Lab NY Univ Med Ctr Belleview 8th Fl 27th St & First Ave New York NY 10016

JOHN, GEORGE, NUCLEAR ENGINEERING, NUCLEAR RADIATION DETECTION. *Current Pos:* Group leader, Nucleonics Br Mat Lab, 53-56, assoc prof nuclear eng & physics, 56-80, prof, 80-92, EMER PROF NUCLEAR ENG, AIR FORCE INST TECHNOL, WRIGHT-PATTERSON AFB, 92- *Personal Data:* b Nov 24, 21; m, Anne Homer; c Mark & Craig. *Educ:* Ohio State Univ, PhD(nuclear chem), 52. *Mem:* Am Chem Soc; Am Asn Physics Teachers; Health Physics Soc; AAAS. *Res:* Nuclear radiation detection; Mossbauer spectrometry applied to materials science. *Mailing Add:* 5371 Barrett Dr Dayton OH 45431-1473. *Fax:* 937-255-2921; *E-Mail:* gjohn@afit.as.mil

JOHN, HUGO HERMAN, EDUCATION & RESEARCH ADMINISTRATION, NATURAL RESOURCE POLICY & DEVELOPMENT. *Current Pos:* dean admin, Col Agr & Natural Resources, Univ Conn, dir admin, Agr Exp Sta & Coop Exten Serv, 84-87, prof, 88-94, EMER PROF NATURAL RESOURCES, UNIV CONN, 94- *Personal Data:* b Natoma, Kans, Feb 13, 29; m 50, Prudence P Shuck; c 3. *Educ:* Univ Minn, BS, 59, MS, 61, PhD(forestry & statist), 64. *Prof Exp:* Instr forestry, Col Forestry, Univ Minn, 62-64, from asst prof to prof res, 65-72, dir & sta statistician, Agr Exp Sta, 67-69; assoc dean & prof admin & res, Col Forestry & Wildlife, Univ Idaho, 72-73; dean & prof admin & res, Sch Natural Resources, Univ Vt, 73-83, dir, Water Resources Res Ctr, 75-77. *Concurrent Pos:* Expert, Food & Agr Orgn, UN, Nicaragua, 64-65, & Columbia, 69-71; chmn, nat prog comm, Soc Am Foresters, 79; sr consult, UNDP, NY, 88- *Mem:* Soc Am Foresters. *Res:* Development of natural resource and agricultural information and the organizational structures and constraints to their development, management and conservation; land use planning and development; agriculture and natural resource development and allocation policy tropical; tropical deforestation causes and affects; agriculture and natural resource development in Third World; environmental evaluation and policy. *Mailing Add:* 501 SE Fourth Ave PO Box 732 Mapleton MN 56065. *Fax:* 860-486-5408; *E-Mail:* h.john@canr1.cag.uconn.edu

JOHN, JAMES EDWARD ALBERT, MECHANICAL ENGINEERING. *Current Pos:* PRES, GEN MOTORS ENG & MGT INST, 91- *Personal Data:* b Montreal, Que, Nov 6, 33; US citizen; m 58; c 4. *Educ:* Princeton Univ, BSE, 55, MSE, 57; Univ Md, PhD(mech eng), 63. *Prof Exp:* Res engr metall div, Air Reduction Co, Inc, NJ, 56-59; from instr to prof mech eng, Univ Md, 59-71; chmn dept, Univ Toledo, 71-77; prof & chmn dept mech eng, Ohio State Univ, 77-83; dean, Col Eng, Univ Mass, Amherst, 83-91. *Concurrent Pos:* Consult Goddard Space Flight Ctr, NASA, 63-68; exec dir, Nat Acad Sci comt motor vehicle emissions, 71-72. *Mem:* Am Soc Mech Engrs; Am Soc Eng Educ; Soc Automotive Engr. *Res:* Space simulation; vacuum; cryogenics; automotive emissions; thermal pollution; fluid dynamics. *Mailing Add:* GMI Eng & Mgt Inst 1700 W Third Ave Flint MI 48504

JOHN, JOSEPH, nuclear science, instrumentation, for more information see previous edition

JOHN, KAVANAKUVHIY V, VITAMIN A GLYCOLIPIDS, TUMOR ANTIGENS. *Current Pos:* DIR RES & DEVELOP, ST JOSEPH'S HOSP, MILWAUKEE, 78- *Educ:* Indian Inst Sci, PhD(biochem), 69. *Res:* DNA probes; flourescent immunoassays; protein electrophoresis; biochemistry of the retinoids. *Mailing Add:* 1075 Vista View Dr Brookfield WI 53005

JOHN, MALIYAKAL EAPPEN, GENETIC ENGINEERING. *Current Pos:* Scientist, 86-92, DIR FIBER TECH, AGRACETUS, 93- *Personal Data:* b Mar 29, 1949; m 75, Manorama Chand; c Benjamin J. *Educ:* Poona Univ, India, PhD, 75. *Mem:* Am Soc Biol Chemist. *Res:* Plant gene expression; identification and characterization of agriculturally useful genes; integration and expression in crop plants; plant transformation. *Mailing Add:* Agracetus Inc 8520 University Green Middleton WI 53562-2508

JOHN, PETER WILLIAM MEREDITH, MATHEMATICAL STATISTICS. *Current Pos:* PROF MATH, UNIV TEX, AUSTIN, 67- *Personal Data:* b Porthcawl, Wales, Aug 20, 23; nat US; m 54; c 2. *Educ:* Oxford Univ, BA, 44, MA, 48, dipl, 49; Univ Okla, PhD(math), 55. *Prof Exp:* Instr math, Univ Okla, 49-52 & 53-55; math master, Casady Sch, Okla, 52-53; asst prof, Univ NMex, 55-57; assoc res statistician, Chevron Res Corp, Stand Oil Calif, 57-58, res statistician, 58-61; from assoc prof to prof, Univ Calif, Davis, 61-67. *Concurrent Pos:* Vis prof, Univ Calif, Berkeley, 58-61; vis prof, Univ Ky, 70-71. *Mem:* Am Statist Asn; Inst Math Statist; Royal Statist Soc; Int Statist Inst. *Res:* Design of experiments; engineering applications of mathematical statistics; quality assurance. *Mailing Add:* Dept Math Univ Tex Austin Austin TX 78711

JOHN, WALTER, ENVIRONMENTAL PHYSICS. *Current Pos:* res scientist, Air & Indust Hyg Lab, 74-92, PRES, PARTICLE SCI, CALIF DEPT HEALTH, 93- *Personal Data:* b Okla, Feb 16, 24; m 54, Carol Salin; c Kenneth, Laura, Claudi & Leslie. *Educ:* Calif Inst Technol, BS, 50; Univ Calif, PhD, 55. *Prof Exp:* Instr physics, Univ Ill, 55-58; physicist, Lawrence Radiation Lab, Univ Calif, 58-71; prof physics & phys sci & chmn dept, Stanislaus State Col, 71-74. *Concurrent Pos:* Vis scholar, Univ Calif, Berkeley, 93-96. *Mem:* Fel Am Phys Soc; Am Asn Aerosol Res; Am Asn Physics Teachers; Sigma Xi; Am Conf Govt Indust Hygienists. *Res:* Experimental nuclear physics, especially nuclear reactions, fission and bent-crystal gamma ray spectroscopy; photonuclear reactions; x-rays; air pollution; aerosol physics; particulate matter in the atmosphere. *Mailing Add:* 195 Grover Lane Walnut Creek CA 94596

JOHNK, CARL T(HEODORE) A(DOLF), ELECTRICAL ENGINEERING. *Current Pos:* assoc prof, 54-65, PROF ELEC ENG, UNIV COLO, BOULDER, 65- *Personal Data:* b Lutterbeck, Ger, Oct 22, 19; US citizen; m 53; c 4. *Educ:* Shurtleff Col, BS, 41; Mo Sch Mines, BS, 42; Univ Ill, MS, 48, PhD(elec eng), 54. *Prof Exp:* Elec engr, Radio Corp Am, NJ, 42; instr elec eng, Univ Mo, Rolla, 42-44, from instr to asst prof, 45-49; res assoc, Univ Ill, 49-54. *Concurrent Pos:* Consult, Denver Res Inst, 59-62 & Ramo-Wooldridge Corp, 60-61. *Mem:* Inst Elec & Electronics Engrs; Am Soc Eng Educ. *Res:* Antenna and array theory; modeling of antennas above lossy surfaces; modeling of very low frequency propagation in earthionosphere waveguide; electromagnetic fields; passive and active network theory. *Mailing Add:* 7367 Windsor Dr Boulder CO 80301

JOHNS, DAVID GARRETT, PHARMACOLOGY, BIOCHEMISTRY. *Current Pos:* head drug metab sect, Lab Chem Pharmacol, 70-75, actg chief lab med chem & biol, 75-78, chief lab med chem & biol, 78-93, EMER SCIENTIST, NAT CANCER INST, 93- *Personal Data:* b Prince Rupert, BC, Oct 18, 29; m 62; c Gerald & Audrey. *Educ:* McGill Univ, BSc, 54, MD, 58, PhD(biochem), 63. *Prof Exp:* Asst prof med, McGill Univ, 62-63; vis fel pharmacol, Sch Med, Yale Univ, 63-65, from asst prof to assoc prof, 65-70. *Mem:* Am Soc Clin Invest; Asn Cancer Res; Am Soc Pharmacol & Exp Therapeut; Int Soc Antiviral Res. *Res:* Mode of action and metabolism of antiviral and cancer chemotherapeutic agents. *Mailing Add:* Nat Cancer Inst Bldg 37 Rm 5B22 NIH Bethesda MD 20892. *Fax:* 301-496-5839; *E-Mail:* johnsd@dc37a.nci.nih.gov

JOHNS, DENNIS MICHAEL, PROCESS RESEARCH & DEVELOPMENT, PILOT PLANT SCALE-UP. *Current Pos:* ENG SPECIALIST, AVCA CORP, 97- *Personal Data:* b Toledo, Ohio, Apr 7, 48; m 72, Martha L Blue; c Daniel & Matthew. *Educ:* Univ Detroit, BS & MS, 71; Purdue Univ, PhD(chem eng), 76. *Prof Exp:* Teaching asst, Purdue Univ, 72-74; sr res engr, Dow Chem, 76-81, proj leader, 81-85, res leader, 85-89, sr scientist, Dow Elanco, 89-96. *Mem:* Am Chem Soc; Am Inst Chem Engrs. *Res:* Granulation and other solids processing systems. *Mailing Add:* AVCA Corp 1684 Woodlands Dr Maumee OH 43537

JOHNS, HAROLD E, physics, biophysics, for more information see previous edition

JOHNS, KENNETH CHARLES, STABILITY TECHNOLOGY TRANSFER & EDUCATORS. *Current Pos:* Dean fac appl sci, 81-85, vice-rector admin, 91-93, DIR INTER COOPERATION, PROF STRUCT ENG, DEPT CIVIL ENG, UNIV SHERBROOKE, 85- *Personal Data:* b Montreal, Que, June 26, 44; wid; c 3. *Educ:* McGill Univ, BEng, 66; London Univ, Eng, PhD(civil eng), 70. *Concurrent Pos:* Sr vis fel, Cranfield Inst Technol, Eng, 73; vis prof civil eng, Univ BC, Vancouver, 80-88; consult, res policy, Quebec Indust Safety Res Inst, 87-88; educ consult, Can Int Develop Agency, Ottawa, Africa Sect, 84-85; consult struct engr spec topics. *Mem:* Am Acad Mech. *Res:* Stability and dynamics of civil engineering and aerospace structures; safety of concrete formwork shoring systems; timber structures, fracture and buckling of commercial lumber; Third World technical and engineering education; industrial saftey research policy. *Mailing Add:* Dept Civil Eng Univ Sherbrooke Sherbrooke PQ J1K 2R1 Can

JOHNS, LEWIS E(DWARD), JR, CHEMICAL ENGINEERING. *Current Pos:* asst prof, 67-76, assoc prof, 76-80, PROF CHEM ENG, UNIV FLA, 80- *Personal Data:* b Pittsburgh, Pa, Dec 13, 35; m 57; c 3. *Educ:* Carnegie Inst Technol, BS, 57, PhD(chem eng), 64. *Prof Exp:* Chem engr, Dow Chem Co, 62-67. *Concurrent Pos:* Instr, Saginaw Valley Col, 64. *Mem:* Am Inst Chem Engrs; Sigma Xi. *Res:* Fluid mechanics; diffusion. *Mailing Add:* Dept of Chem Eng Univ Fl Rm 227 Gainesville FL 32611

JOHNS, MARTIN WESLEY, NUCLEAR PHYSICS. *Current Pos:* RETIRED. *Personal Data:* b Chengtu, West China, Mar 23, 13; nat Can; m 81, Elsie B North; c Robert (deceased), Elizabeth, Kenneth & Kathryn. *Educ:* McMaster Univ, BA, 32, MA, 34; Univ Toronto, PhD, 38. *Hon Degrees:* DSc, Brandon Univ, 75. *Prof Exp:* Prof physics, Brandon Col, 37-46; assoc res physicist, Nat Res Coun Can, 46-47; from asst prof to prof physics, McMaster Univ, 47-81, chmn dept, 61-67 & 70-77. *Concurrent Pos:* Nuffield travel grant, Oxford Univ, 59-60; vis scientist, Atomic Energy Can, 67-68. *Mem:* Am Phys Soc; Am Asn Physics Teachers; fel Royal Soc Can; Can Asn Physicists. *Res:* Atomic spectroscopy; neutron physics; nuclear decay schemes; angular correlation of gamma rays; nuclear structure spectroscopy. *Mailing Add:* 115 Dalewood Cres Hamilton ON L8S 4B8 Can

JOHNS, MICHAEL MARIEB EDWARD, OTOLARYNGOLOGY. *Current Pos:* CHMN BD DIRS & CHIEF EXEC OFFICER, EMORY HEALTHCARE, EMORY UNIV, 96-, PROF, DEPT SURG, SCH MED, 96-, EXEC VPRES HEALTH AFFAIRS, 96- *Personal Data:* b Detroit, Mich, Jan 27, 42; c Christina & Michael. *Educ:* Wayne State Univ, BS, 64; Univ Mich, MD, 69; Am Bd Otolaryngol, dipl. *Prof Exp:* Intern, Univ Hosp, Ann Arbor, 69-70; resident otolaryngol, 71-75; resident gen surg, St Josephs Mercy Hosp, Ann Arbor, 70-71; from asst prof to assoc prof, Univ Va Med Ctr, 77-82, prof, 82-84; prof, Sch Med, Johns Hopkins Univ, 84-96, dean med fac & vpres med, 90-96. *Concurrent Pos:* Mem, Greater Baltimore Com, 91-; prin investr, Robert Wood Johnson Found, 92. *Res:* Otolaryngology; co-author of one publication. *Mailing Add:* Emory Univ 1440 Clifton Rd Suite 400 Atlanta GA 30322. *Fax:* 404-778-3100; *E-Mail:* mmejohns@emory.edu

JOHNS, MILTON VERNON, JR, MATHEMATICAL STATISTICS. *Current Pos:* Res assoc, 56-57, from asst prof to assoc prof, 57-66, PROF STATIST, STANFORD UNIV, 66- *Personal Data:* b Berkeley, Calif, Sept 27, 25; m 54; c 2. *Educ:* Stanford Univ, BA, 49; Columbia Univ, PhD(math, statist), 56. *Mem:* AAAS; Am Math Soc; Math Asn Am; Inst Math Statist; Am Statist Asn; Sigma Xi. *Res:* Statistical decision theory. *Mailing Add:* Sequoia Hall Stanford CA 94305

JOHNS, PHILIP TIMOTHY, ORGANIC CHEMISTRY. *Current Pos:* ASST PROF CHEM, UNIV WIS-WHITEWATER, 76- *Personal Data:* b Bismarck, NDak, July 17, 43; m 73; c 3. *Educ:* Gustavus Adolphus Col, BA, 65; Univ NDak, PhD(biochem), 70. *Prof Exp:* Fla Heart Asn fel biochem, Col Med, Univ Fla, 70-72; asst prof chem, Va Union Univ, 72-76. *Mem:* Am Chem Soc; AAAS. *Res:* Metabolic control; biosynthesis of plasma lipoproteins; enzymology and control of carbohydrate metabolism. *Mailing Add:* Dept Chem Univ Wis Whitewater WI 53190

JOHNS, RICHARD JAMES, MEDICINE. *Current Pos:* asst, Johns Hopkins Univ, 51-53, fel, 53-55, from instr to assoc prof, 55-66, asst dean admis, 62-66, dir, Sub-Dept Biomed Eng, 66-70 & Dept Biomed Eng, 70-91, Massey prof biomed eng, 80-91, PROF MED, JOHNS HOPKINS UNIV, 66-, PRIN PROF STAFF, APPL PHYSICS LAB, 67-, DISTINGUISHED SERV PROF BIOMED ENG, 91- *Personal Data:* b Pendleton, Ore, Aug 19, 25; m 53, Carol Johnson; c 3. *Educ:* Univ Ore, BS, 47; Johns Hopkins Univ, MD, 48; Am Bd Internal Med, dipl. *Honors & Awards:* Centennial Med, Inst Elec & Electronics Engrs, 84, Career Achievement Award, 90. *Prof Exp:* Intern med, Johns Hopkins Hosp, 48-49. *Concurrent Pos:* Asst resident physician, Johns Hopkins Hosp, 51-53, resident physician, 55-56, physician, 56- *Mem:* Inst Med-Nat Acad Sci; Am Soc Clin Invest; Am Clin & Climatol Asn; Biomed Eng Soc; fel Am Col Physicians; Asn Am Physicians; fel AAAS; fel Royal Soc Med; Sigma Xi. *Res:* Biomedical engineering; chemical sensors. *Mailing Add:* Johns Hopkins Univ Sch Med 720 Rutland Ave Rm 124 Baltimore MD 21205-2196

JOHNS, VARNER JAY, JR, INTERNAL MEDICINE, CARDIOLOGY. *Current Pos:* RETIRED. *Personal Data:* b Denver, Colo, Jan 27, 21; m 44, Dorothy Mippach; c Marcia (Hinshaw), Donna (Bennett), Varner Jay Johns III. *Educ:* La Sierra Col, BS, 44; Col Med Evangelists, MD, 45; Am Bd Internal Med, dipl, 51, cert, 74; Am Bd Cardiovasc Dis, dipl, 66. *Prof Exp:* Intern, White Mem Hosp, 44-45, resident internal med, 45-47; resident path, Loma Linda Sanitarium & Hosp, 47-48; instr internal med, Sch Med, Loma Linda Univ, 48-51, sr physician, 48-86, asst clin prof & assoc dean, 51-54, from asst prof to prof med, 54-86, assoc clin prof, 55-56, chief, Med Serv, Univ Hosp, 64-69, assoc dean continuing educ, 75-86, chmn dept med, 56-59 & 80-86; pres, Audio-Digest Found, 86-91. *Concurrent Pos:* Consult, Off Surg Gen, US, 56-67; sr attend physician, Los Angeles County Hosp, 56-64, physician-in-chief internal med, 58-64; vis colleague, Inst Cardiol, London, 62-63; hon vis physician, Nat Heart Hosp, London, 62-63; co-chmn dept med, White Mem Hosp, 78-80. *Mem:* Am Heart Asn; AMA; Western Asn Physicians; fel Am Col Physicians; Int Soc Internal Med; fel Am Col Cardiol. *Res:* Cardiology; hypertension, pheochromocytoma, and dissecting aneurysm of the aorta. *Mailing Add:* 11565 Hillcrest Ct Loma Linda CA 92354

JOHNS, WILLIAM DAVIS, GEOCHEMISTRY. *Current Pos:* PROF GEOL, UNIV MO-COLUMBIA, 70- *Personal Data:* b Waynesburg, Pa, Nov 2, 25; wid; c Sydney, Susan, David & Amy. *Educ:* Col Wooster, AB, 47; Univ Ill, MS, 51, PhD(geol), 52. *Honors & Awards:* Alexander von Humboldt US Sr Scientist Award, 77. *Prof Exp:* Spec asst petrol, Eng Exp Sta, Univ Ill, 49-52, asst geol, 52-55; from asst prof to prof, Wash Univ, 55-70, chmn, Dept Earth Sci, 62-69; vis prof, Univ Vienna, 83-84 & 95-96. *Concurrent Pos:* Fulbright scholar, Univ Gottingen, 59-60, Univ Heidelberg, 68-69, Univ Vienna, 83-84 & Univ Pittsburgh, 90-91. *Mem:* Fel Geol Soc Am; Am Mineral Soc; Mineral Soc Gt Brit & Ireland; Geochem Soc; Clay Minerals Soc. *Res:* Mineralogy of clays; recent sediments; diagenesis; organic geochemistry; burial diagenesis of pelitic sediments and dispersed organic matter; role played by clay mineral matrix in catalyzing organic reactions involved in transformation of dispersed organic matter in shale source rocks into petroleum hydrocarbons. *Mailing Add:* Dept Geol Univ Mo Columbia MO 65211. *Fax:* 573-882-5458; *E-Mail:* geoscwj@showme.missouri.edu

JOHNS, WILLIAM E, COMPUTATIONAL ADHESION SCIENCE. *Current Pos:* ASSOC PROF MAT SCI, MECH & MAT ENG DEPT, WASH STATE UNIV, 78- *Personal Data:* b Detroit, Mich. *Educ:* Mich Tech Univ, BS, 66; Univ Mich, MS, 68; Univ Minn, PhD(wood & mat sci), 72. *Prof Exp:* Res technologist, Am Plywood Asn, Tacoma, 72-74; asst wood researcher, Forest Prod Lab, Univ Calif, Berkeley, 74-78. *Concurrent Pos:* Vis scientist, Food & Agr Orgn, UN, 83 & Swed Forest Prod Lab, 85-86; Alcoa Res Found researcher, 90. *Mem:* Adhesion Soc; Am Chem Soc. *Res:* Adhesion; wood science. *Mailing Add:* Mech & Mat Eng Dept Wash State Univ Pullman WA 99164-2920

JOHNS, WILLIAM FRANCIS, ORGANIC CHEMISTRY, MEDICINAL CHEMISTRY. *Current Pos:* RETIRED. *Personal Data:* b Chicago, Ill, Aug 31, 30; m 50; c 3. *Educ:* Univ Chicago, PhB, 48, MS, 51; Univ Wis, PhD(org chem), 55. *Prof Exp:* Jr res chemist org synthesis, Merck & Co, 51-53; sr res chemist pharmaceut, 55-65, res fel, 65-71, asst dir chem res, 71-73, dir chem res, Searle Labs, G D Searle & Co, 73-82; sr dir med chem, Sterling Winthrop Res Inst, 82-93. *Mem:* Am Chem Soc; AAAS; NY Acad Sci. *Res:* Organic synthesis, especially steroids, antialdosterone agents. *Mailing Add:* 12787 Hunters Ridge Dr Bonita Springs FL 34135

JOHNSEN, EUGENE CARLYLE, MATHEMATICAL SOCIOLOGY, SOCIAL NETWORKS. *Current Pos:* lectr, 63-64, from asst prof to prof, 64-94, EMER PROF MATH, UNIV CALIF, SANTA BARBARA, 94- *Personal Data:* b Minneapolis, Minn, Jan 27, 32; m 57, Marjorie M Wacklin. *Educ:* Univ Minn, BChem, 54; Ohio State Univ, PhD(math), 61. *Prof Exp:* Instr chem & math, Univ Minn, 56-57; instr math, Ohio State Univ, 62; Nat Acad Sci-Nat Res Coun res assoc, Nat Bur Stand, 62-63. *Concurrent Pos:* Air Force Off Sci res grants, 64-73, vis lectr, Univ Mich, 68-69; Fulbright Hays res grant, Univ Tubingen, 69; NSF res grants, 77-78, 88-90 & 93-; gen ed, Discovery, Univ Calif, Santa Barbara, J Undergrad Res; guest ed, Social Networks, 83; vis scholar, Harvard Univ, 84-85; chair, Math Sociol Sect, Am Sociol Asn, 95-97. *Mem:* AAAS; Am Math Soc; Math Asn Am; Soc Indust & Appl Math; Int Network Soc Network Anal; Am Sociol Asn; Am Statist Asn. *Res:* Mathematical models in the social sciences; social network theory; matrix theory; combinatorial designs and matrices; combinatorial algebraic structures. *Mailing Add:* Dept Math Univ Calif Santa Barbara CA 93106. *Fax:* 805-893-2385; *E-Mail:* johnsen@math.ucsb.edu

JOHNSEN, JOHN HERBERT, GEOLOGY. *Current Pos:* from instr to assoc prof, Vassar Col, 51-67, prof geol, 67-88, chmn dept, 63-66, 69-72, 75-78 & 84-88, EMER PROF GEOL, VASSAR COL, 88- *Personal Data:* b Staten Island, NY, Aug 19, 23; m 48, Catherine Brush; c John, Catherine & Cynthia. *Educ:* Syracuse Univ, AB, 47, MSc, 48; Lehigh Univ, PhD(geol), 57. *Prof Exp:* Asst geol, Syracuse Univ, 46-48; mining geologist, NJ Zinc Co, Va, 48-49. *Concurrent Pos:* Vis prof, Sci Camp, Univ Wyo, 53; del, Int Geol Cong Mex, 56 & Australia, 76; eng geologist, NY State Dept Pub Works, 59; vis prof, St Augustine's Col, 60 & State Univ NY Col New Paltz, 60 & 64-65; geol consult, 60-88; assoc dir, Summer Inst Earth Sci, 61, dir, Summer Inst Geol, 62-72; part time geologist-consult, Hudson River Valley Comn, 65, NY State Off Planning Coord, 66-67, Cent New Region Planning & Develop Bd, 69-70; mem, Conf Geol Lake Superior Region, NSF, 63, Conf Geol Southern Can Rockies, 67 & Environ Task Force, 25th Cong Dist, NY, 74-; part time dir, Ecol-Conserv Prog, Vassar Col, 73-80. *Mem:* Emer fel Geol Soc Am; Soc Econ Paleontologists & Mineralogists; Am Geophys Union; Sigma Xi; Nat Asn Geol Teachers; Am Inst Prof Geologists. *Res:* Stratigraphy and petrography of early and middle Paleozoic carbonate rocks of New York; geology of aggregate materials and reclamation and rehabilitation of mined lands. *Mailing Add:* 32 S Tanglewood Spur Sedona AZ 86351-9209

JOHNSEN, KJELL, PHYSICS, ELECTRICAL ENGINEERING. *Current Pos:* RETIRED. *Personal Data:* b Meland, Norway, June 11, 21; m 45, Aase B Jordal; c Arnlaug, Georg K & Ottar. *Educ:* Tech Univ Norway, BSEE, 48, DTech, 54. *Honors & Awards:* Norsk Data Physics Prize, Norweg Phys Soc, 81; Robert R Wilson Prize, Am Phys Soc, 90. *Prof Exp:* Res asst, Chr Michelsen Inst, Norway, 48-52; physicist, CERN, Switz, 52-57, sr scientist 59-86, proj dir, 66-74; prof elec eng, Tech Univ, Norway, 57-59; prof physics, Univ Bergen, Norway, 72-86; tech dir, ISA proj, Brookhaven Nat Lab, NY, 79-82. *Concurrent Pos:* chmn, HERA mach eval comt, Deutsches Elekronen-Synchrotron, Hamburg, Ger, 84-91. *Res:* Author of numerous articles. *Mailing Add:* Chemin du Molard La Rippe CH-1278 Switzerland

JOHNSEN, KURT H, PHYSIOLOGICAL GENETICS. *Current Pos:* PROJ LEADER, CAN FOREST SERV, 90- *Personal Data:* b Huntington, NY Sept 4, 59; m, Lisa McConnell; c Soven & Jenny R. *Educ:* Univ Vt, BS, 85; Va Tech, MS, 87; Univ Ga, PhD(forest genetics & tree physiol), 90. *Prof Exp:* Res scientist, Forestry Can, 90-92. *Mem:* Am Inst Biol Sci; Ecol Soc Am. *Res:* Designed to quantity and partition genetic variation in black spruce morphological and physiological responses to environmental change (elevated carbon dioxide, drought, temperature extremes). *Mailing Add:* Petawawa Nat Forestry Inst Chalk River ON K0J 1P0 Can. *Fax:* 613-589-2275; *E-Mail:* kjohnsen@phfi.forestry.ca

JOHNSEN, PETER BERGHSEY, SENSORY PHYSIOLOGY, FLAVOR CHEMISTRY. *Current Pos:* res physiologist, 86-88, RES LEADER, USDA AGR RES SERV, 88- *Personal Data:* b Madison, Wis, May 23, 50; m 74; c 2. *Educ:* Univ Wis-Madison, BS, 74, MS, 76, PhD(zool), 78. *Honors & Awards:* Outstanding Researcher, Catfish Farmers Am. *Prof Exp:* Postdoctoral fel, Univ Pa, 78-80, from asst mem to assoc mem, Monell Chem Senses Ctr, 80-86. *Concurrent Pos:* Instr, Col Vet Med, Univ Pa, 80-83 & Dept Biol, 84-86; affil prof, Grad Fac, La State Univ, 88-; Olin fel, Olin Found, Oslo, Norway, 83. *Mem:* Inst Food Scientists; Sigma Xi. *Res:* Biochemical process for food flavor formation; chemical identification of flavor compounds and relationship to human perception of taste and smell. *Mailing Add:* USDA-ARS NCAUR 1815 N Univ Dr Peoria IL 61604. *Fax:* 504-286-4419

JOHNSEN, RAINER, PHYSICS. *Current Pos:* Res assoc physics, 66-68, res asst prof, 68-71, RES ASSOC PROF PHYSICS, UNIV PITTSBURGH, 71- *Personal Data:* b Kiel, Ger, Jan 23, 40; m 65; c 2. *Educ:* Univ Kiel, dipl physics, 65, Dr rer nat, 66. *Mem:* Am Phys Soc; AAAS. *Res:* Atomic physics; atomic collisions; physics of upper atmosphere; mass spectroscopy; laser plasma research. *Mailing Add:* Dept Physics & Astron Univ Pittsburgh Pittsburgh PA 15260

JOHNSEN, RICHARD EMANUEL, INSECTICIDE TOXICOLOGY. *Current Pos:* asst prof, 65-70, ASSOC PROF ENTOM, COLO STATE UNIV, 70- *Personal Data:* b Brooklyn, NY, Feb 8, 36; m 57, Esther Freeland; c Kathryn, Rebecca & Christopher. *Educ:* St Olaf Col, BA, 57; Iowa State Univ, MS, 59, PhD(entom), 62. *Prof Exp:* Asst entom, Iowa State Univ, 62. *Concurrent Pos:* Sabbatical & fel, Dept Pharmacol & Toxicol, Vet Col Norway, Oslo, 76-77. *Mem:* AAAS; Am Chem Soc; Entom Soc Am; NY Acad Sci; Sigma Xi. *Res:* Pesticides and related environmental pollutants, their metabolism, distribution and persistance in plants, soils and the physical environment; microbial degradation; analytical methodology for pollutant studies. *Mailing Add:* Dept Entom Colo State Univ Ft Collins CO 80523-0002. *Fax:* 970-491-0564; *E-Mail:* rjohnsen@shep.agsci.colostate.edu

JOHNSEN, ROGER CRAIG, GENETICS. *Current Pos:* Asst prof, 67-73, ASSOC PROF BIOL, ADELPHI UNIV, 73- *Personal Data:* b Warren, Pa, Apr 25, 38; m 65. *Educ:* Ohio Wesleyan Univ, BA, 60; Univ Ore, MS, 63; Brown Univ, PhD(genetics), 68. *Mem:* AAAS; Soc Study Social Biol; Genetics Soc Am; Am Genetics Asn; Sigma Xi; Amer Soc Human Genetics; NY Acad Sci. *Res:* Chromosome behavior and mechanics; effects of structure and gene action on chromosome recovery during gametogenesis; genetic controls on the competitive behavior of reciprocal gametic types; cancer cytogenetics. *Mailing Add:* Dept of Biol Adelphia Univ 1 South St Garden City NY 11530-4213

JOHNSEN, RUSSELL HAROLD, RADIATION CHEMISTRY, ACADEMIC ADMINISTRATION. *Current Pos:* from asst prof to prof, 51-93, dean, Grad Studies, 86-93, EMER PROF CHEM & DEAN, FLA STATE UNIV, 93- *Personal Data:* b Chicago, Ill, Aug 5, 22; m 48, Dorothy Pehta; c Peter B & Margaret A. *Educ:* Univ Chicago, BS, 47; Univ Wis, PhD(chem), 51. *Prof Exp:* Res chemist, Ninol Lab, 46-47. *Concurrent Pos:* Assoc provost, Col Arts & Sci, Fla State Univ, 74-77, assoc dean grad studies, 77-86. *Mem:* Fel AAAS; Am Chem Soc; Am Phys Soc; Radiation Res Soc; Am Soc Mass Spectrometry. *Res:* Kinetics of reactive intermediates, mechanistic studies; free radical reactions in the atmosphere; electron spin resonance studies. *Mailing Add:* 1425 Devil's Dip Tallahassee FL 32308. *Fax:* 850-644-8281; *E-Mail:* johnsen@chem.fsu.edu

JOHNSEN, THOMAS NORMAN, JR, SOIL-PLANT NUTRIENT CYCLING, PLANT SUCCESSION. *Current Pos:* Res scientist range weed control, USDA, 56-72, res leader, 72-78, res scientist range ecol, 78-90, BIOL SCI COLLABR, AGR RES SERV, USDA, 90- *Personal Data:* b Chicago, Ill, July 3, 29; m 56, Ardith Brask; c Paul T & Suzanne L. *Educ:* Univ Ariz, BS, 50, MS, 54; Duke Univ, PhD(bot), 60. *Honors & Awards:* W R Chapling Res Award, Soc Range Mgt, 88. *Concurrent Pos:* Adj prof forestry, NAriz Univ, 58-78; fac assoc, Range Plants & Habitats, Ariz State Univ, 91-92. *Mem:* Soil Sci Soc Am; Ecol Soc Am; Weed Sci Soc Am; Soc Range Mgt; Am Soc Agron; Sigma Xi. *Res:* Evaluation and development of methods to revegete semiarid grazing land; fate of herbicides in plant, soils and water; plant life history; plant population changes and trends; plant competition; development of crimson poppy as a crop. *Mailing Add:* 5854 E North Wilshire Dr Tucson AZ 85711-4532

JOHNSGARD, PAUL AUSTIN, ZOOLOGY. *Current Pos:* from instr to prof, 61-80, FOUND PROF, UNIV NEBR-LINCOLN, 80- *Personal Data:* b Fargo, NDak, June 28, 31; m 56, Lois Lampe; c Jay, Scott, Ann & Karin. *Educ:* NDak State Univ, BS, 53; Wash State Univ, MS, 55; Cornell Univ, PhD(vert zool), 59. *Honors & Awards:* Mari Sandoz Award, 84; Loren Eiseley Award, 87. *Prof Exp:* NSF fel zool, Bristol Univ, 59-60, USPHS fel,

60-61. *Concurrent Pos:* NSF res grants, 63-67 & 68-71; Guggenheim Found fel, 71; mem bd dirs, Int Wild Waterfowl Asn, 72-76. *Mem:* Am Ornith Union; Wilson Ornith Soc; Cooper Ornith Soc. *Res:* Systematics of birds, especially the family Anatidae; comparative behavior of birds; ecology of vertebrates; speciation and isolating mechanisms; sympatry and hybridization in birds. *Mailing Add:* 7341 Holdrege St Lincoln NE 68505

JOHNSON, A(LFRED) BURTRON, JR, CORROSION, NUCLEAR MATERIALS. *Current Pos:* RETIRED. *Personal Data:* b Salt Lake City, Utah, Apr 8, 29; m 54, zelinda, Sherry, Laurie & Julie; c 4. *Educ:* Univ Utah, BS, 54, PhD(fuel technol), 58. *Honors & Awards:* Mishima Award, Am Nuclear Soc. *Prof Exp:* Mem staff, Hanford Labs, Gen Elec Co, 61-65; staff scientist, Battelle Mem Inst, 65-81, sr staff scientist, Pac Northwest Div, 81-92. *Concurrent Pos:* Lectr, Univ Dayton, 60-61, Richland Grad Ctr, 74-; mem staff, Univ Wis, 73; US deleg, Int Atomic Energy Agency Comt, Vienna, Austria; US coord, US/FRG nuclear fuel info exchange. *Mem:* Am Nuclear Soc; Nat Asn Corrosion Engrs; Am Soc Testing & Mat. *Res:* Corrosion in fission and fusion reactors; nuclear plant life extension; corrosion of ancient metals; spent nuclear fuel storage; author or coauthor of over 200 publications and author of one book. *Mailing Add:* Pac Northwest Div MS P810 Battelle Mem Inst Richland WA 99352. *Fax:* 509-372-6421

JOHNSON, A WILLIAM, ORGANIC CHEMISTRY. *Current Pos:* RETIRED. *Personal Data:* b Calgary, Alta, Dec 16, 33; US citizen; m 56, Joan Auger; c Patricia, Nancy, Robert & Katherine. *Educ:* Univ Alta, BSc, 54; Cornell Univ, PhD(chem), 57. *Prof Exp:* Asst chem, Cornell Univ, 55; fel org chem, Mellon Inst, 57-60; from asst prof to assoc prof, Univ NDak, 60-65; assoc prof & chmn dept, Univ Sask, Regina, 65-67; dir res & develop, Univ NDak, 67-75, dean grad sch, 67-88, prof, 67-94. *Concurrent Pos:* Dir, NDak Regional Environ Assessment Prog, 75-77; vis prof, Univ Mass, Amherst, 89 & US Mil Acad, West Point, 94- *Mem:* Fel AAAS; Am Chem Soc; Sigma Xi; fel Chem Inst Can. *Res:* Chemistry of ylids; d-orbital interactions; synthetic organic chemistry; environmental assessment. *Mailing Add:* 9 Tanyard Lane Bella Vista AR 72714. *Fax:* 701-777-2331

JOHNSON, ADRIAN EARL, JR, CHEMICAL ENGINEERING, MATHEMATICS. *Current Pos:* PROF CHEM ENG, LA STATE UNIV, BATON ROUGE, 68- *Personal Data:* b Port Arthur, Tex, Dec 17, 28; m 49; c 3. *Educ:* La State Univ, BS, 48; Mass Inst Technol, SM, 49; Univ Fla, PhD(chem eng), 58. *Prof Exp:* Process engr, Mobil Oil Co, Tex, 49-53; asst prof chem eng, Lamar State Univ, 53-54; instr, Univ Fla, 54-57; appl scientist, Int Bus Mach Corp, La, 57-60; asst dir, Comput Res Ctr & Eng Res Ctr, La State Univ, 60-62; consult & mgr, Mgt Serv Dept, Union Carbide Corp, NY, 62-67; staff consult, Real Time Systs, Inc, 67-68. *Mem:* Am Inst Chem Engrs. *Res:* Computer control of petrochemical processes; optimization and control of distillation columns and methanol plants. *Mailing Add:* 9126 Pine Moss Dr Baton Rouge LA 70817-6931

JOHNSON, ALAN ARTHUR, MATERIALS SCIENCE & ENGINEERING, FAILURE ANALYSIS & ACCIDENT RECONSTRUCTION. *Current Pos:* dean grad sch, 75-76, PROF MAT SCI, UNIV LOUISVILLE, 75- *Personal Data:* b Beckenham, Eng, Aug 18, 30; m 58, 90, Barbara Davidson; c Stephen G, Michael A, David N, Brian P & Susan C. *Educ:* Univ Reading, BSc, 52; Univ Toronto, MA, 54; Univ London Imp Col, dipl & PhD(metal physics), 60. *Prof Exp:* Demonstr physics, Univ Toronto, 52-54; sci officer, Royal Naval Sci Serv, 54-56; res asst metall, Imp Col, Univ London, 56-57, res fel, 57-60, lectr, 60-62; dir res, Mat Res Corp, NY, 63-65; prof phys metall, Polytech Inst Brooklyn, 65-71, head dept phys & eng metall, 67-71; prof mat sci & chmn dept mat sci & eng, Wash State Univ, 71-75. *Concurrent Pos:* Indust consult & expert witness, prod liability personal injury litigations. *Mem:* Fel Inst Physics; fel Am Soc Metals; Sigma Xi; fel Inst Mat; fel AAAS. *Res:* Materials science especially physical metallurgy; failure analysis; accident reconstruction; approximately 100 articles in journals and conference proceedings. *Mailing Add:* Ernst Hall Rm 311 Univ Louisville Louisville KY 40292

JOHNSON, ALAN KIM, BEHAVIORAL BIOLOGY. *Current Pos:* asst prof, 73-77, ASSOC PROF PSYCHOL, UNIV IOWA, 77- *Personal Data:* b Altoona, Pa, Aug 15, 42; m 65; c 1. *Educ:* Pa State Univ, BS, 64; Temple Univ, MA, 66; Univ Pittsburgh, PhD(psychobiol), 70. *Honors & Awards:* Res Scientist Develop Award, NIMH, 75. *Prof Exp:* Fel psychobiol, Inst Neurol Sci, Univ Pa, 70-73. *Concurrent Pos:* NIH fel, 70. *Mem:* Sigma Xi; AAAS; Soc Neurosci. *Res:* Neurobiology and endocrinology of feeding and drinking; physiological bases of motivation and reinforcement. *Mailing Add:* Dept Psychol & Pharmaceut Univ Iowa 11 Seashore Hall E Iowa City IA 52242-1407. *Fax:* 319-335-0191

JOHNSON, ALAN L, OVARIAN FOLLICULAR DIFFERENTIATION & ATRESIA, OVARIAN CANCER. *Current Pos:* PROF PHYSIOL, UNIV NOTRE DAME, 93- *Personal Data:* b Quincy, Mass, Sept 8, 50; m 85, Joanne McGill; c Jennifer A & Kari L. *Educ:* Univ Vt, BA, 72, MS, 75; Cornell Univ, PhD(physiol), 79. *Prof Exp:* Res assoc, Cornell Univ, 79-81; prof physiol, Rutgers Univ, 81-93. *Mem:* Endocrine Soc; Soc Study Reproduction; Soc Study Fertil; AAAS. *Res:* Vertebrate ovarian follicular differentiation and atresia via the actions of gonadotropins, growth factors and protooncogenes; apoptosis in ovarian follicle. *Mailing Add:* Dept Biol Sci Univ Notre Dame Notre Dame IN 46556. *Fax:* 219-631-7413; *E-Mail:* johnson.128@nd.edu

JOHNSON, ALAN T, ENGINEERING. *Current Pos:* ASST PROF, ENG DEPT, UNIV PA. *Concurrent Pos:* Packard fel, David & Lucille Packard Found, 94. *Mailing Add:* Dept Eng Univ Pa Philadelphia PA 19104-6316

JOHNSON, ALBERT LLEWELLYN, II, RESEARCH ADMINISTRATION, INFORMATION SCIENCE & SYSTEMS. *Current Pos:* sr analyst info technol, 91-95, SR ANALYST SCI & TECHNOL, CORNING INC, 95- *Personal Data:* b Pittsburgh, Pa, Aug 29, 60. *Educ:* Carnegie-Mellon Univ, BS, 83, MS, 89. *Prof Exp:* Mem tech staff, Software Eng Inst, 85-91. *Res:* Strategy and economics of industrial research and development; administration and planning. *Mailing Add:* Corning Inc Sullivan Pk SP-FR-02 Corning NY 14831. *E-Mail:* johnsonal@corning.com

JOHNSON, ALBERT SYDNEY, III, HABITAT ECOLOGY & MANAGEMENT. *Current Pos:* assoc dir, Inst Natural Resources & prof, 68-95, EMER PROF FOREST RESOURCES, UNIV GA, 95- *Personal Data:* b Clarkston, Ga, Dec 27, 33; m 59, Nedra P Tyler; c Dorothy (Callaway), Linda (Fleming), Brian T (deceased) & Merry (Maxey). *Educ:* Univ Ga, BS, 59; Auburn Univ, MS, 62, PhD(zool), 69. *Honors & Awards:* C W Watson Award, SE Sect, Asn Fish & Wildlife Agencies, SE Sect, Wildlife Soc & S Div Am Fisheries Soc. *Prof Exp:* Fire control aide, US Forest Serv, 58; res asst wildlife biol, Auburn Univ, 59-62, instr wildlife biol & zool, 63-68; wildlife biologist, Ala State Dept Conserv, 62-63. *Mem:* Wildlife Soc; Am Soc Mammalogists. *Res:* Wildlife habitat biology and management; wildlife foods and habitat relationships; responses to management. *Mailing Add:* D B Warnell Sch Forest Resources Univ Ga Athens GA 30602

JOHNSON, ALBERT W, PLANT ECOLOGY. *Current Pos:* from asst prof to assoc prof, San Diego State Univ, 64-69, dean, Col Sci, 69-77, actg vpres, acad affairs, 77-78, PROF BIOL, SAN DIEGO STATE UNIV, 69-, VPRES, ACAD AFFAIRS, 78- *Personal Data:* b Belvidere, Ill, July 29, 26; m 45, 70; c 5. *Educ:* Colo Agr & Mech Col, BS, 49; Univ Colo, MS, 51, PhD(bot), 56. *Prof Exp:* Instr biol, Univ Colo, 54-55; from instr to assoc prof bot, Univ Alaska, 56-62, NSF fac sci fel, 60-61; jr res botanist, Univ Calif, Los Angeles, 62-64. *Mem:* AAAS; Sigma Xi. *Res:* Arctic and alpine plant ecology and taxonomy; cytogenetics. *Mailing Add:* San Diego State Univ 5500 Campanile Dr San Diego CA 92182

JOHNSON, ALBERT WAYNE, ENTOMOLOGY. *Current Pos:* Assoc prof tobacco insects, 70-80, assoc prof entom, 74-80, PROF TOBACCO INSECTS & ENTOM, PEE DEE RES & EDUC CTR, CLEMSON UNIV, 80- *Personal Data:* b Mullins, SC, July 19, 44; m 65; c 3. *Educ:* Clemson Univ, BS, 66, MS, 68; Auburn Univ, PhD(entom), 71. *Mem:* Entom Soc Am. *Res:* Insecticide screening, economic thresholds, scouting techniques, insect surveys of pests and beneficials, cultural control practices, biological control, host-plant resistance studies and development of insect-resistant varieties; insect control using insecticides and parasites, predators, and pathogens. *Mailing Add:* 104 Mt Olive Church Rd Nichols SC 29581. *Fax:* 803-661-5676

JOHNSON, ALEXANDER LAWRENCE, ORGANIC CHEMISTRY. *Current Pos:* res chemist, Cent Res Dept, 63-81, res assoc, Biochem Dept, 81-82, res suprv, 82-87, sr res suprv, 87-89, RES MGR, MED PROD DEPT, E I DUPONT DE NEMOURS & CO, INC, 90-, RES MGR, DUPONT MERCK PHARMACEUTICAL CO, 90- *Personal Data:* b Gisborne, NZ, Oct 13, 31; nat US; m 61; c 3. *Educ:* Victoria Univ, Wellington, BSc, 54, MSc, 55; Univ Rochester, PhD(org chem), 64. *Honors & Awards:* Eastman Kodak Prize, Univ Rochester, 62. *Prof Exp:* Sec sch teacher chem, Rongotai Col, NZ, 55-60. *Mem:* Am Chem Soc; NZ Inst Chem. *Res:* Elucidation of the structures of natural products; synthetic organic chemistry relating to these and to heterocyclic systems; application of physical methods to the solution of organic chemical problems; medicinal chemistry. *Mailing Add:* 1372 John Adams Dr Lancaster PA 17601

JOHNSON, ALFRED C, MOLECULAR BIOLOGY. *Current Pos:* Am Cancer Soc fel molecular biol, NIH, 85-87, fel, 87-90, sr staff fel, 90-92, RES EXPERT MOLECULAR BIOL, NIH, 92- *Personal Data:* b Marion Junction, Ala, Aug 17, 57. *Educ:* Albany State Col, BS, 79; Univ Tenn, PhD(biomed sci), 85. *Honors & Awards:* Director's Award, NIH, 93. *Mem:* AAAS; Am Soc Biochem & Molecular Biol. *Mailing Add:* Lab Molecular Biol Bldg 37 Rm 2D18 MSC 4255 Nat Cancer Inst NIH 37 Convent Dr Bethesda MD 20906-4255. *Fax:* 301-495-2212

JOHNSON, ALFRED THEODORE, JR, ELECTRICAL ENGINEERING. *Current Pos:* From asst prof to assoc prof, 74-89, PROF ENG, WIDENER UNIV, 90-, CHMN, DEPT ELEC ENG, 90- *Personal Data:* b Philadelphia, Pa, June 24, 41; m 83. *Educ:* Drexel Univ, BSEE, 63; Univ Pa, PhD(elec eng), 69. *Mem:* Inst Elec & Electronics Engrs. *Res:* Approximation problem using analog and digital filters; analog fault analysis; circuit theory. *Mailing Add:* One University Pl Widener Univ Chester PA 19013. *E-Mail:* alfred.t.johnson@widener.edu

JOHNSON, ALICE RUFFIN, pharmacology, immunology, for more information see previous edition

JOHNSON, ALLAN ALEXANDER, INTERNATIONAL NUTRITION, FOOD SCIENCE. *Current Pos:* asst prof, 78-82, ASSOC PROF HUMAN NUTRIT, HOWARD UNIV, 82- *Personal Data:* b Georgetown, Guyana; c 2. *Educ:* McGill Univ, BSc, 72; Cornell Univ, MNS, 74, PhD(int nutrit), 78. *Honors & Awards:* Res Award, Nat Soc Allied Health; Johnetta M Davis Service Award. *Prof Exp:* Res asst, Cornell Univ, 72-78, nutrit sci, 74, biochem, 74-75, ref asst, Albert R Mann Libr, 75-78. *Mem:* Ame Soc Nutrit Sci. *Res:* Iron, folacin and zinc status and the immune response in the elderly; nutrition, food choices, lifestyle and the outcome of pregnancy; barriers, motivators and facilitators of prenatal care utilization. *Mailing Add:* Dept Nutrit Sci Howard Univ 2400 Sixth St NW Washington DC 20059-0009. *Fax:* 301-459-3442

JOHNSON, ALLEN NEILL, PATHOLOGY. *Current Pos:* asst dir, 89-91, DIR, R W JOHNSON PHARMACEUT RES INST, 91- *Personal Data:* b Colfax, Wash, Dec 29, 44; m 71, Julia A Kaiser; c Beverly & Cameron. *Educ:* Wash State Univ, DVM, 69; Univ Wis, PhD(vet sci), 77; Am Col Vet Pathologists, dipl, 78. *Prof Exp:* Res asst, Univ Wis-Madison, 71-74; asst prof vet path, Univ Ga Vet Med Col, 74-76; pathologist, Lederle Labs, 76-78; group leader path, Ortho Pharmaceut Corp, 78-83, res mgr, 83-87, asst dir, 87-89. *Mem:* Am Col Vet Pathologists; Int Acad Path; Am Vet Med Asn; Soc Toxicol Pathologists; Am Soc Vet Clin Pathologists; AAAS. *Res:* Evaluation of tissues from laboratory animals and farm species to determine and resolve pathologic lesions associated with dosing of experimental drugs. *Mailing Add:* 341 Mine Brook Rd Bernardsville NJ 07924-2111

JOHNSON, ALVA WILLIAM, NEMATOLOGY, PLANT PATHOLOGY. *Current Pos:* SUPVRY RES NEMATOLOGIST, COASTAL PLAIN EXP STA, SCI & EDUC ADMIN, US DEPT AGR, 67- *Personal Data:* b Tifton, Ga, Nov 8, 36; m 60, Barbara Sandifer; c Janet Paige. *Educ:* Univ Ga, BSA, 63, MS, 64; NC State Univ, PhD(plant path), 67. *Honors & Awards:* Distinguished Res Award, Sigma Xi, Tifton, 95. *Mem:* Fel Soc Nematologists; Am Phytopath Soc; Orgn Trop Am Nematologists; Sigma Xi. *Res:* Nematode control; population dynamics; nematode-fungus interactions; multiple plant-pest control; nematode resistance in plants; development of integrated pest management systems to manage nematode populations that are effective, economical and environmentally sound. *Mailing Add:* PO Box 748 Tifton GA 31793. *Fax:* 912-386-3437; *E-Mail:* nemweeds@tifton.cpes.peachnet.edu

JOHNSON, ANNE BRADSTREET, NEUROPATHOLOGY, NEUROSCIENCES. *Current Pos:* asst prof, 70-77, ASSOC PROF PATH & NEUROSCI, ALBERT EINSTEIN COL MED, 77- *Personal Data:* b Boston, Mass, Mar 5, 27; m 48, Jack Minkoff; c Ellen & Paul. *Educ:* Cornell Univ, AB, 48, MD, 51. *Honors & Awards:* Moore Award, Am Asn Neuropathologists. *Prof Exp:* Pvt pract internal med, self-employed, Cleveland, 55-57. *Concurrent Pos:* Prin investr, NIH grants, other grants, 68- *Mem:* Am Asn Neuropathologists; Soc Neurosci; Histochem Soc; Am Soc Cell Biol; Int Acad Path; AAAS; NY Acad Sci. *Res:* Abnormal nervous systems including; Alzheimer's disease; genetic leukodystrophies; enzyme histochemistry; immunocytochemistry; using tissue and tissue culture, light and electron microscope approaches; medical sciences. *Mailing Add:* Dept Math K604 Albert Einstein Col Med 1300 Morris Park Ave Bronx NY 10461

JOHNSON, ARLO F, MECHANICAL ENGINEERING. *Current Pos:* RETIRED. *Personal Data:* b Franklin, Idaho, Dec 2, 15; m 47; c 4. *Educ:* Calif Inst Technol, BS & MS, 42; Stanford Univ, PhD, 52. *Prof Exp:* Aerodynamicist, Douglas Aircraft Corp, 42-45; asst prof aeronaut eng, Univ Ill, 46-47; instr, Stanford Univ, 47-48; asst, Stanford Univ, 48-51; from assoc prof to prof mech eng, Univ Utah, 51-63, head dept, 55-57. *Concurrent Pos:* Prof, Bandung Technol Inst, 61-63; aeronaut res engr, Ames Lab, NASA, 57; mem staff, Sandia Corp, 59. *Mem:* Am Soc Eng Educ. *Res:* Boundary layer theory; gas dynamics; applied mechanics. *Mailing Add:* 2070 E 3620 South Salt Lake City UT 84109

JOHNSON, ARMEAD, IMMUNOGENETICS, HISTOCOMPATIBILITY. *Current Pos:* ASST PROF PEDIAT & MICROBIOL, SCH MED, GEORGETOWN UNIV, 80- DIR, TISSUE TYPING LAB, 85- *Personal Data:* b Waco, Tex, Dec 16, 42. *Educ:* Univ Tex, BS, 64; Baylor Col Med, MS, 70, PhD(microbiol & immunol), 71. *Prof Exp:* Assoc, Med Ctr, Duke Univ, 74-75, asst prof, 75-80. *Concurrent Pos:* Consult, Blood Bank, Charity Hosp La, New Orleans, 75-; consult, 80-85. *Mem:* Transplantation Soc; Am Asn Immunologists; Am Soc Histocompatibilty & Immunogenetics; Sigma Xi. *Res:* Serological identification, characterization and genetics of antigens within the human major histocompatibility complex and investigation of their role in the immune response. *Mailing Add:* Dept Pediat Gorman G2041 Georgetown Univ Sch Med 3800 Reservoir Rd NW Washington DC 20007-2197. *Fax:* 202-687-7161

JOHNSON, ARNOLD, VASCULAR INFLAMATION. *Current Pos:* ASST PROF RES PULMONARY PHYSIOL, ALBANY MED COL, 84- *Educ:* Albany Med Col, PhD(physiol), 81. *Mailing Add:* Stratton Vet Admin Med Ctr 151D 113 Holland Ave Albany NY 12208. *Fax:* 518-642-0626

JOHNSON, ARNOLD I(VAN), HYDROLOGY, SOIL MECHANICS. *Current Pos:* PRES & CONSULT WATER & SOIL ENG, A IVAN JOHNSON, INC, DENVER, 79- *Personal Data:* b Madison, Nebr, June 3, 19; m 41, Betty Spencer; c Robert, Bruce & Carmen (Tiel). *Educ:* Univ Nebr, BS, 49, AB, 50. *Honors & Awards:* Award of Merit, Dept Interior, 62, Meritorious Serv Award, 77; Award of Merit, Am Soc Testing & Mat, 82, Frank W Reinhart Award, 83, William T Cavanugh Mem Award, 88; ICKO Iben Award, Am Water Resources Asn, 86; John Wesley Powell Award, US Geol Surv, 92; Royce J Tipton Award, Am Soc Civil Engrs, 92; Finnigan Medal, Am Nat Stands Inst, 93. *Prof Exp:* Supvr mat testing, Omaha Steel Works, Nebr, 40-43; USN, heavy equip oper, Construct Batallion, 44-45, testing engr soils, Nebr Hwy Testing Lab, 46-48; chief hydrol lab, US Geol Surv, Denver, 48-67, staff hydrologist, Rocky Mountain Region, Water Resources Div, 67, chief, Water Res Div Training Ctr, 68-70, asst chief, Off Water Data Coord, Washington, DC, 71-79. *Concurrent Pos:* Consult, UNESCO, Turkey, 65, 79 & UN, 79, 83-85, 90; fac affil, Colo State Univ, 69-70; pres, Int Comn Subsurface Water, 72-75 & Int Comn Remote Sensing & Data Transmission, 79-87; dir, Renewable Natural Resources Found, 73-79; consult, Woodward-Clyde Consults, 79-84; AID consult, Oman, 85, AID, Egypt, 87 & 90, Senegal, 87 & Morocco, 92; tech adv & coordr, ASTM/EPA/USGS/USN, Coop Agreement Develop Ground Water Monitoring Stand, 88-; secy, Hydrol Sect, Am Geophys Union; mem bd dirs, Am Soc Testing & Mat; chmn bd trustees, Inst Stand Res. *Mem:* Am Geophys Union; Int Asn Hydrol Sci (vpres, 75-79, hon pres, 87-); fel Am Soc Civil Engrs; fel Am Soc Testing & Mat; fel Am Water Resources Asn (pres, 72); Nat Soc Prof Engrs. *Res:* Soil moisture; permeability and specific yield of rock and soil materials; land subsidence; waste management; ground water hydrology; artificial recharge. *Mailing Add:* A Ivan Johnson Inc 7474 Upham Ct Arvada CO 80003

JOHNSON, ARNOLD RICHARD, JR, ANALYTICAL CHEMISTRY. *Current Pos:* from assoc prof to prof, 65-86, EMER PROF CHEM & HEAD DEPT, MINOT STATE COL, 86- *Personal Data:* b Allen, Kans, Jan 12, 29; m 53; c 3. *Educ:* Fresno State Col, BS, 51; Ore State Univ, PhD(anal chem), 62. *Prof Exp:* Anal chemist, Lab, Socony Mobil Oil Co, Inc, NJ, 54-56; asst prof anal chem, Univ Wyo, 62-65. *Mem:* Am Chem Soc; Sigma Xi. *Res:* Differential spectrophotometry; combustion methods of analysis; analytical chemistry of hafnium and zirconium; trace analysis; spot tests. *Mailing Add:* 449 E Brandon Dr Bismarck ND 58501

JOHNSON, ARTHUR ALBIN, PARASITOLOGY. *Current Pos:* From asst prof to prof biol, 55-81, Harold & Lucy Cabe distinguished prof, 81-90, EMER PROF, HENDRIX COL, 90- *Personal Data:* b Chicago, Ill, Feb 24, 25; m 51, Martha K Himmel; c David M, Kathryn R, Kristen M, Paul A & Julie M. *Educ:* Univ Minn, AB, 50; Univ Ill, MS, 52, PhD(zool), 55. *Concurrent Pos:* Vis lectr, Univ Ill, 63 & 64; mem, NSF Radiation Biol Inst, Argonne Nat Lab, 65. *Mem:* Fel AAAS; Am Micros Soc; Am Soc Parasitol; Am Inst Biol Sci; Sigma Xi. *Res:* Mermithidae; parasites of grackles. *Mailing Add:* 53 Meadowbrook Dr Conway AR 72032. *E-Mail:* johnson@hendrix.edu

JOHNSON, ARTHUR EDWARD, BIOPHYSICAL CHEMISTRY, CELL BIOLOGY. *Current Pos:* from asst prof to prof, 77-92, GRAYCE B KERR PROF, CHEM & BIOCHEM DEPT, UNIV OKLA, 92- *Personal Data:* b Graceville, Minn, July 4, 42; m 65, Linda L Harker; c Christine, Robert & Edward. *Educ:* Calif Inst Technol, BS, 64; Univ Ore, PhD(biochem), 73. *Prof Exp:* Instr sci, Milton Acad, Mass, 64-69; Helen Hay Whitney res assoc, Chem Dept, Columbia Univ, 74-77. *Concurrent Pos:* Prin investr, NIH, Am Heart Asn, Am Chem Soc & Res Corp grants, 79-; vis prof, Dept Biochem & Biophys, Univ Calif, San Francisco, 84-85; NSF Biochem Grant Proposal Adv Panel, 85-87; adj asst prof, Dept Biochem & Molecular Biol, Univ Okla Health Sci Ctr, 83-87, adj prof, 87-; mem, spec study sects NIH, 84 & 91; consult, Promega Corp, 91- *Mem:* Am Soc Biochem & Molecular Biol; Am Chem Soc; Am Soc Cell Biol. *Res:* Molecular mechanisms of protein secretion, blood coagulation, membrane protein integration, and protein biosynthesis; topography of macromolecular complexes; protein-protein, protein-RNA, and protein-membrane interactions; fluorescence; fluorescence energy transfer; photocrosslinking. *Mailing Add:* Tex A&M Univ Health Sci Ctr 116 Reynolds Med Bldg College Station TX 77843-1114. *Fax:* 405-325-6111; *E-Mail:* aejohnson@chemdept.chem.uoknor.edu

JOHNSON, ARTHUR FRANKLIN, PHYSICS. *Current Pos:* RETIRED. *Personal Data:* b Can, Oct 8, 17; US citizen; m 43, Audrey M Chiverton; c William F, Paul E, David J & Blake C. *Educ:* Univ Alta, BSc, 38; Univ Toronto, MA, 47, PhD(physics), 49. *Prof Exp:* Res physicist tire eng res, US Rubber Co, 49-52 & Honeywell Res Ctr, Minneapolis-Honeywell Regulator Co, 52-55; res supvr, Minn Mining & Mfg Co, 55-64; prof physics, Gustavus Adolphus Col, 64-66; prof physics & chmn dept, Monmouth Col, Ill, 66-78; asst dean, Sch of Eng & Appl Sci, Washington Univ, 78-84. *Concurrent Pos:* Consult, 84- *Mem:* AAAS; Sigma Xi; Am Phys Soc; Am Asn Physics Teachers. *Res:* Magnetism; photoconductivity and electrical properties of solids. *Mailing Add:* N 8151 Island Lake Rd Spooner WI 54801

JOHNSON, ARTHUR GILBERT, MICROBIOLOGY. *Current Pos:* PROF & HEAD, DEPT MED MICROBIOL & IMMUNOL, SCH MED, UNIV MINN, DULUTH, 78- *Personal Data:* b Eveleth, Minn, Feb 1, 26; m 51; c 4. *Educ:* Univ Minn, BA, 50, MSc, 51; Univ Md, PhD(bact), 55. *Prof Exp:* Biochemist, Immunol Div, Walter Reed Army Inst Res, DC, 52-55; from instr to assoc prof, Med Sch, Univ Mich, Ann Arbor, 55-66, prof bact & immunol, 66-78. *Concurrent Pos:* Mem, Nat Inst Dent Res Coun, 72-75; ed, Infection & Immunity, 77-87; mem, Nat Bd Med Examrs, 80-84; mem, bact & mycol study sect, NIH, 83-87, chmn, 85-87. *Mem:* Am Soc Microbiol; Am Asn Immunologists; Int Soc Immunopharmacol; Reticuloendothelial Soc; Am Acad Microbiol; Infectious Dis Soc; Immunocompromised Host Soc; Soc Biol Therapy. *Res:* Antibody formation; mode of action of bacterial endotoxins; host resistance factors; immunological aspects of aging. *Mailing Add:* Dept Med Microbiol & Immunol Sch Med Univ Minn Duluth MN 55812-2487. *Fax:* 218-726-6235

JOHNSON, ARTHUR THOMAS, BIOENGINEERING, BIOLOGICAL ENGINEERING. *Current Pos:* from asst prof to assoc prof agr eng & assoc prof phys educ, 78-86, PROF BIOL RESOURCES ENG & KINESIOLOGY, UNIV MD, 86- *Personal Data:* b East Meadow, NY, Feb 21, 41; m 63; c 4. *Educ:* Cornell Univ, BAE, 64, MS, 67, PhD(bioeng), 69. *Prof Exp:* Res bioengr, US Army, Edgewood Arsenal, Md, 71-75. *Concurrent Pos:* Grant, Nat Inst Occup Safety & Health, HEW, 78-81; pres, Alliance Eng in Med & Biol, 84-88; chmn, Am Soc Eng Educ, Biol Agr Eng Div, 87-88; consult, Nat Bur Stand Energy Related Devices Prog, 78- & Battelle Mem Inst; dir, Am Inst Med & Biol Engrs; dir, Am Soc Agr Engrs, 95-97; chmn, NABEC, 97-98. *Mem:* Am Soc Agr Engrs; sr mem Inst Elec & Electronics Engrs; Am Indust Hyg Asn; Am Conf Govt Indust Hygienists; Alliance Engrs Med & Biol; fel Am Soc Eng Educ; fel Am Inst Med & Biol Engrs; sr mem Biomed Eng Soc; Inst Biol Engrs (pres, 98); Int Soc Respiratory Protection. *Res:* Instrumentation and control; biological process engineering; respiratory stress and modelling; exercise physiology and physiological modelling. *Mailing Add:* Dept Biol Resources Eng Univ Md College Park MD 20742

JOHNSON, B CONNOR, BIOCHEMISTRY, NUTRITION. *Current Pos:* MEM BIOCHEM, OKLA MED RES FOUND, 65-, DISTINGUISHED CAREER SCIENTIST, 82-85 & 87- *Personal Data:* b Regina, Sask, Apr 28, 11; US citizen; m 66, Halina Teller; c Bruce, Peter, Stephen, Lisa, Christina & Margaret. *Educ:* McMaster Univ, BA, 33, MA, 34; Univ Wis-Madison, PhD(biochem), 40. *Honors & Awards:* Am Feed Mfg Asn-Nutrit Coun US Award, 60; Purkyne Medal, Czech Acad Sci, 69; Osborne-Mendel Award, Am Inst Nutrit, 74. *Prof Exp:* From asst prof to prof animal biochem, Univ Ill, 43-65; prof biochem & head dept, Col Med, Univ Okla Health Sci Ctr, 65-82; res scientist, Dept Pediat, Univ SFla, St Petersburg, 85-87. *Concurrent Pos:* Guggenheim Found fel, Nat Inst Res Dairying, Reading, Eng, 55; consult mem, President's Second Atom for Peace Mission to SAm, 56; consult, Cent Res Labs, Armour & Co, Chicago, 57-63; US Dept State consult, Orgn Europ Econ Coop, Paris, 58; consult, Merck & Co, NJ, 60, Agr Res Coun of Fedn Rhodesia & Nyasaland, 62, Nutrit Div, US Army Natick Labs, 63-72 & SE Asian Ministers Educ-Univ Indonesia, 74, Nutrit Inst, USDA, 77; NSF sr fel, Inst Chem Natural Substances, Nat Ctr Sci Res, Paris, 61-62; vis prof, Inst Biol Chem, Univ Strasbourg, 72. *Mem:* Am Soc Biol Chemists; fel Am Inst Nutrit; Am Chem Soc; Brit Biochem Soc; Soc Exp Biol & Med; Soc Endocrinol; AAAS; NY Acad Sci; Int Soc Thrombosis & Haemostasis. *Res:* Nutritional biochemistry; metabolic functions of vitamins A, K, B-12 and E; starvation-refeeding; nutrition and enzyme induction; calorie intake restriction and longevity; nutrition of newborn; biochem function of vitamin B12, vitamin A, vitamin E, Vitamin K; amino acid req of nutrition, nutrition gene expression, calorie restriction and lifespan, synthetic diets for newborns; science, reality & responsibility. *Mailing Add:* Okla Med Res Found 825 NE 13th Oklahoma City OK 73104. *Fax:* 405-271-3980

JOHNSON, B LAMAR, JR, INTERNAL MEDICINE, INFECTIOUS DISEASES. *Current Pos:* Asst prof, 62-69, asst dean, 63-65, PROF MED, UNIV CALIF, SCH MED, LOS ANGELES, 69- *Personal Data:* b Minneapolis, Minn, May 31, 30; m 54; c 4. *Educ:* Denison Univ, BA, 51; Univ Calif, Los Angeles, MD, 55. *Concurrent Pos:* Attend med, Wadsworth Vet Admin Hosp, 63- *Res:* Drug induced nephropathy; endocarditis. *Mailing Add:* Univ Calif Los Angeles CA 90024

JOHNSON, B(ENJAMIN) M(ARTINEAU), CHEMICAL ENGINEERING, MECHANICAL ENGINEERING. *Current Pos:* mgr, Eng Anal Unit, Pac NW Labs, 65-67, mgr, Sodium Fluid Syst Sect, Fast Flux Text Facil, 67-69, mgr, Fluid & Energy Systs, 69-74, sr engr prog mgr, 74-86, mgr, Energy Sci Dept, 86-91, MGR TANK WASTE REMEDIATION TECHNOL DEVELOP, PAC NW LABS, 91- *Personal Data:* b Chiralla, South India, Oct 28, 30; nat US; m 54, Mary Anderson; c Daniel & Judith. *Educ:* Cornell Univ, BChE, 52; Univ Wis, MS, 53, PhD(chem eng), 56. *Prof Exp:* Sr engr, Chem Res & Develop, Hanford Labs, Gen Elec Co, 56-64. *Concurrent Pos:* Coordr chem eng joint ctr grad study, Univ Wash & Wash State Univ, 65-76, affil assoc prof, 65-74, affil prof, 74- ; mem, Coord Comt, US/USSR Coop Prog in Thermal Power Plant Heat Rejection Systs, 75-80. *Mem:* Fel Am Inst Chem Engrs; Sigma Xi; Am Nuclear Soc; fel Am Inst Chemists. *Res:* Heat and mass transfer; fluid mechanics; economic analysis; nuclear reactor technology; project (development, design, construction) management. *Mailing Add:* 2336 Davison Ave Richland WA 99352-1921

JOHNSON, BARRY LEE, RESEARCH ADMINISTRATION, BIOMEDICAL ENGINEERING. *Current Pos:* ASST ADMINR, AGENCY TOXIC SUBSTANCES & DIS REGISTRY, 86- *Personal Data:* b Sanders, Ky, Oct 24, 38; m 60; c 5. *Educ:* Univ Ky, BS, 60; Iowa State Univ, MS, 62, PhD(elec eng), 67. *Prof Exp:* Biomed engr, USPHS, 62-64, 67-74; biomed engr, Nat Inst Occup Safety & Health, 74-78, exec adminr, 78-86. *Concurrent Pos:* Lectr, Univ Cincinnati, 68-69; consult ed, Arch Environ Health, Neurotoxicol, J Indust Health & Toxicol, J Clean Technol & Environ Sci; mem, Permanent Comn Occup Health; mem, Am Conf Govt Indust Hygientists. *Mem:* Sigma Xi; Am Pub Health Asn; Am Col Toxicol. *Res:* Behavioral toxicology; sensory evoked potentials; electroencephalography; mathematical modelling of physiological systems; occupational safety and health; neurotoxicology. *Mailing Add:* US Geol Surv PO Box 818 La Crosse WI 54602-0818

JOHNSON, BARRY W, ELECTRICAL ENGINEERING. *Current Pos:* PROF, DEPT ELEC ENG, UNIV VA, 84-, DIR, CTR SEMICUSTOM INTEGRATED SYSTS. *Educ:* Univ Va, BS, 79, ME, 80, PhD(elec eng), 83. *Honors & Awards:* Frederick Emmons Terman Award, Am Soc Eng Educ, 91. *Prof Exp:* Staff, Harris Corp, Melbourne, Fla. *Concurrent Pos:* Chair, Opers Comt, Inst Elec & Electronics Engrs. *Mem:* Fel Inst Elec & Electronics Engrs Comput Soc (pres, 97); Sigma Xi. *Res:* Fault-tolerant computing; safety-critical systems; dependability modeling; microprocessor-based systems. *Mailing Add:* Elec Eng Dept Thorton Hall Rm E209 Univ Va Charlottesville VA 22903

JOHNSON, BECKY BEARD, PHYSIOLOGY. *Current Pos:* asst prof biol, 74-80, ASSOC PROF BOT, OKLA STATE UNIV, 80- *Personal Data:* b Denver, Colo, May 4, 42; m 62. *Educ:* Okla State Univ, BS, 64; Univ Ill, Urbana, MS, 66, PhD(physiol), 68. *Concurrent Pos:* NIH fel, 69-70. *Mem:* Am Soc Plant Physiologists; Am Tissue Cult Asn; Sigma Xi. *Res:* Plant tissue culture and protoplast fusion for use in plant breeding and genetics. *Mailing Add:* Dept Bot Okla State Univ 318 Life Sci E Stillwater OK 74078-0001

JOHNSON, BEN BUTLER, INTERNAL MEDICINE. *Current Pos:* from asst prof to assoc prof med, 59-90, head, Div Renal Dis, 59-90, CLIN ASSOC PROF MED, SCH MED, UNIV MISS, 90- *Personal Data:* b Brooklyn, NY, May 23, 20; m 62, Barbara A Maltby; c Louis, Charles, Michael, Mary & Margaret. *Educ:* Harvard Univ, AB, 42; Harvard Med Sch, MD, 44; Am Bd Internal Med, dipl & cert nephrology. *Prof Exp:* Intern path, NY Hosp, 44-45; asst, Med Col, Cornell Univ, 46-47; asst resident med, NY Univ Div, Bellevue Hosp, 47-49; from instr to asst prof med, Stanford Univ, 55-59. *Concurrent Pos:* Res fels, Bassett Hosp, Cooperstown, NY, 49-50 & Sch Med, Stanford Univ, 50-53; head diabetes clin, Univ Hosps, Stanford Univ, 56-59, dir, Grad Training Prog Metab Dis, Univ, 55-59. *Mem:* Int Soc Nephrology; Am Soc Nephrology; fel Am Col Physicians; Endocrine Soc; AMA; Sigma Xi. *Res:* Renal disease; aldosterone and edema; metabolic diseases. *Mailing Add:* Dept Med Univ Miss Med Ctr Jackson MS 39216

JOHNSON, BEN S(LEMMONS), JR, nuclear waste management; deceased; see previous edition for last biography

JOHNSON, BERTIL LENNART, genetics; deceased, see previous edition for last biography

JOHNSON, BERTRAND H, OPTICAL ENGINEERING. *Current Pos:* DISTINGUISHED MEM TECH STAFF, AT&T BELL LAB. *Educ:* Rutgers Univ, BSc. *Honors & Awards:* Eng Excellence Award, Optical Soc Am, 92. *Mailing Add:* AT&T Bell Res Lab 600 Mountain Ave Murray Hill NJ 07974-2008

JOHNSON, BOB DUELL, CYTOLOGY, TOXINOLOGY. *Current Pos:* asst prof, 67-74, assoc prof, 74-80, PROF ZOOL, ARK STATE UNIV, 80- *Personal Data:* b Pocahontas, Ark, June 24, 36; c 2. *Educ:* Ark State Univ, BS, 58; Ariz State Univ, MS, 64, PhD(zool), 67. *Prof Exp:* Teacher, Northeast Independent Sch Dist, Tex, 58-62; partic zool, Acad Year Inst, Ariz State Univ, 62-63, res asst toxinol, 63-66, res assoc, 66-67. *Mem:* Int Soc Toxinol; Sigma Xi. *Res:* Effects of toxins on enzyme systems and morphology of cells. *Mailing Add:* State Univ Main Campus PO Box 599 State University AR 72467-0599

JOHNSON, BOBBY RAY, LIPID SCIENCE, FLAVOR CHEMISTRY. *Current Pos:* ASST MGR, CAMPBELL INST RES TECHNOL, CAMPBELL SOUP CO, 76- *Personal Data:* b Oakwood, Okla, Oct 30, 41; m 62; c 2. *Educ:* Okla State Univ, BS, 63, MS, 66, PhD(biochem), 70. *Prof Exp:* Instr chem, Okla Christian Col, 66-67; instr biochem, Okla State Univ, 67-68; USPHS fel, Univ Calif, Davis, 69-70; asst prof food sci, NC State Univ, 70-76. *Mem:* Am Oil Chemists Soc; Inst Food Technol; Am Dairy Sci Asn. *Res:* Fats and oil chemistry; natural antioxidants; dairy science. *Mailing Add:* 129 Kipling Rd Cherry Hill NJ 08003

JOHNSON, BRANN, STRUCTURAL GEOLOGY. *Current Pos:* asst prof geol, 75-80, civil eng, 76-79 & geophysics, 79-80, ASSOC PROF GEOL & GEOPHYSICS, DEPT GEOL & GEOPHYSICS, TEX A&M UNIV, 80- *Personal Data:* b Annapolis, Md, Dec 4, 46; m 88; c 2. *Educ:* Univ Calif, Berkeley, BA, 68; Pa State Univ, MEng, 73, PhD(geol), 75. *Prof Exp:* Geologist, Marine Geol & Hydrol Div, US Geol Surv, 68; asst geol, Dept Geol & Geophysics, Pa State Univ, 68-71; instr geol, Div Geol & Planetary Sci, Calif Tech, 74-75. *Concurrent Pos:* Vis staff scientist, Los Alamos Sci Lab, 76-81; subpanel mem, Nat Res Coun, 79-80; prin investr, Cambridge Labs, US Air Force, 75-77, Los Alamos Sci Lab, 76-78 & Div Basic Energy Res, Dept Energy, 79-; res assoc, Ctr Tectonophysics, Tex A&M Univ, 75- *Mem:* Int Glaciol Soc; Am Geophys Union. *Res:* Crustal geologic processes; development of mathematical models; glacial abrasion cracks; landslide mechanics; thermal cracking of rock; fracture permeability; water and rock interaction; mechanics of geologic discontinuites. *Mailing Add:* 306 Spruce St College Station TX 77840

JOHNSON, BRANT MONTGOMERY, RELATIVISTIC HEAVY-ION PHYSICS. *Current Pos:* res assoc, Brookhaven Nat Lab, 75-77, asst physicist, 77-79, assoc physicist, 79-80, physicist, Physics Dept, 81-84, physicist, Dept Appl Sci, 84-93, PHYSICIST, RELATIVISTIC HEAVY ION COLLIDER PROJ, BROOKHAVEN NAT LAB, 93- *Personal Data:* b Houston, Tex, Aug 25, 49; m 73, Marcia Prosser; c Anna & Austin. *Educ:* Univ Tex, Austin, BS, 71, MA, 74, PhD(physics), 75. *Prof Exp:* Res sci assoc II, Univ Tex, Austin, 71-73, Welch Found Fel, 73-75. *Concurrent Pos:* Vis scientist, Lawrence Berkeley Lab & Oak Ridge Nat Lab, 77 & Triumf Lab, BC, 80; lectr, Brookhaven Semester Prog, Brookhaven Nat Lab, 81; Ger Acad Exchange Serv study visit, Ger Foreign Exchange Serv, Heidelberg, Fed Repub Ger, 84; assoc ed, Phys Rev Letters, 88-, Phys Rev A, 89-; vis prof, Latin Am Sch Physics, 89; prin investr, Atomic Phys Res, Dept Energy, 90-93; NSLS subgroup rep for atom & molecular sci, 91-93; chmn, NSLS workshop atom & molecular sci, BNL, 91; assoc ed, Phys Rev E, 93-; BNL computer security comt, 93-; electronic publishing comt, Am Phys Soc, 93-; liaison, Phenix, 93- *Mem:* Am Phys Soc. *Res:* Atomic, nuclear, elementary particle, plasma and beam physics; aspects of relativistic heavy-ion collisions. *Mailing Add:* RHIC Bldg 510C Brookhaven Nat Lab PO Box 5000 Upton NY 11973-5000. *Fax:* 516-344-3253; *E-Mail:* brant@bnl.gov

JOHNSON, BRIAN JAMES, ANALYTICAL METHODS DEVELOPMENT FOR ATMOSPHERIC SPECIES, BIOGEOCHEMICAL CYCLES. *Current Pos:* asst prof, 88-94, ASSOC PROF CHEM, UNIV, NEV, LAS VEGAS, 94- *Personal Data:* b Caldwell, Idaho, Aug 6, 61; m 92, Linda A Steele. *Educ:* Col Idaho, BS, 82; Univ Ariz, PhD(chem), 87. *Prof Exp:* Res assoc, Univ Ariz, 88; res chemist, Environ Protection Agency, 90. *Mem:* Am Chem Soc; Am Geophys Union. *Res:* Atmospheric chemistry; development and evaluation of new analytical methods and biogeochemical cycles; analytical chemistry, especially ion chromatography. *Mailing Add:* 4500 Arrowroot Ave Las Vegas NV 89110. *Fax:* 702-895-4072; *E-Mail:* bjj@pioneer.nevada.edu

JOHNSON, BRIAN JOHN, BIOCHEMISTRY, EDUCATIONAL ADMINISTRATION. *Current Pos:* ASSOC PROF MICROBIOL, MED SCH, UNIV ALA, BIRMINGHAM, 71-, CO-DIR GRAD PROG, 78- *Personal Data:* b Reading, Eng, Oct 28, 38; m 68. *Educ:* Univ Leeds, BSc, 60; Univ London, PhD(org chem) & dipl, Imp Col, 63; Univ London, DSc, 77; Inst Educ Mgt, Harvard Univ, 81. *Prof Exp:* Res assoc org chem, State Univ NY Buffalo, 63-64; res assoc, St John's Univ, 64-65; res assoc, Mass Inst Technol, 65-66; asst prof chem, Tufts Univ, 66-71. *Mem:* Am Chem Soc. *Res:* Synthesis, structure and biological properties of peptides and proteins; biochemistry of lipid-protein interactions; immunopharmacology; complement; allergy. *Mailing Add:* 3724 Woodvale Rd Birmingham AL 35223-1444

JOHNSON, BRUCE, naval architecture, ocean engineering, for more information see previous edition

JOHNSON, BRUCE FLETCHER, ORGANIC CHEMICALS, NEW CHELATORS. *Current Pos:* STATE MEM, CORP RES & DEVELOP, GEN ELEC CO, 86- *Personal Data:* b Brooklyn, NY, Apr 5, 56; m 84; c 1. *Educ:* Mass Inst Technol, BS, 78; Harvard Univ, MS, 80, PhD(chem), 84. *Prof Exp:* Fel, Dept Chem, Columbia Univ, 84-86. *Res:* Development of efficient synthetic routes leading to organic chemicals; investigation of novel monomers and polymers; synthesis and study of new chelators and binding materials. *Mailing Add:* Bldg K1 Rm 3C27 GE Corp Res & Develop PO Box 8 Schenectady NY 12301-0008

JOHNSON, BRUCE MCDOUGALL, ANALYTICAL CHEMISTRY. *Current Pos:* from res scientist to sr res scientist, 77-83, sr res investr, 83-85, SECT HEAD, ANALYSIS RES DEPT, PFIZER INC, 85- *Personal Data:* b Ottawa, Ill, Sept 24, 43; m 63; c 3. *Educ:* Univ Wis-Madison, BS, 66, MS, 67, PhD(chem), 72. *Prof Exp:* Asst prof clin oncol, Ctr Health Sci, Univ Wis-Madison, 72-75, asst prof human oncol, 75-77. *Mem:* AAAS; Am Chem Soc; Am Soc Mass Spectrometry. *Res:* Metabolism of antineoplastic drugs and carcinogens; analysis of pharmaceuticals; application of gas chromatography and mass spectrometry to biomedical and biological problems. *Mailing Add:* 4145 Westbrook Dr Florence SC 29501

JOHNSON, BRUCE PAUL, HIGH FREQUENCY ELECTRONICS, COMPUTER AIDED DESIGN. *Current Pos:* assoc prof, 74-78, chmn elec eng, 78-83, 95-95, PROF ELEC ENG, UNIV NV, RENO, 78-83 & 91, PROF, 78- *Personal Data:* b Lewiston, Maine, Aug 8, 38; m 61, Marcia Ann Duarte; c Michael, Robyn, Samuel & Rebecca. *Educ:* Bates Col, BS, 60; Univ NH, MS, 63; Univ Mo, Columbia, PhD(physics), 67. *Prof Exp:* Instr physics, Hobart & William Smith Cols, 62-64; advan physicist, Gen Elec Co, 67-70; supvr, Solid State Lamp Proj, 70-74; vpres, res & develop, Caddo Enterprises Inc, 90-92. *Concurrent Pos:* Presidential appointment, US Metric Bd, 78-80 & 80-82; student activ coordr, Region 6, Inst Elec & Electronics Engrs, 91-95. *Mem:* Inst Elec & Electronics Engrs; Am Soc Eng Educ; Sigma Xi. *Res:* Biomedical Instrumentation; solid state electronic materials and devices; electronic computer aided design and manufacturing; high frequency electronic design. *Mailing Add:* 3190 W Seventh Reno NV 89503. *Fax:* 702-784-6627; *E-Mail:* johnson@ee.unr.edu

JOHNSON, BRUCE VIRGIL, PHYSICS. *Current Pos:* Asst res engr, United Technol Res Ctr, 60-63, assoc res engr, 63-66, res engr, 66-68, SUPVR HEAT & MASS TRANSFER TECHNOL, UNITED TECHNOL RES CTR, 68- *Personal Data:* b Nov 24, 35; m 59, Peggy K Gaalaas; c Karen E, Paul L & Eric V. *Educ:* Univ Minn, BS, 58, MS, 60; Univ Conn, MS, 66, PhD(fluid dynamics), 72. *Honors & Awards:* Gas Turbine Award, Am Soc Mech Engrs, 91. *Mem:* Am Soc Mech Engrs; sr mem Am Inst Aeronaut & Astronaut. *Res:* Experimental and analytical studies in fluid mechanics and heat transfer studies relating to gas turbines and convection in rotation turbine blade coolant passages and rotating disc-cavity configurations. *Mailing Add:* 10924 NE 120th St Kirkland WA 98034

JOHNSON, BRYAN HUGH, ENDOCRINE PHYSIOLOGY. *Current Pos:* AT DEPT ANIMAL SCI, KLEBERG CTR, TEX. *Personal Data:* b Hammond, La, Aug 15, 40; m 62; c 2. *Educ:* Southeastern La Univ, BS, 63; La State Univ, MS, 66; Okla State Univ, PhD(reproduction), 69. *Prof Exp:* NIH res fel, Okla State Univ, 60-71; assoc prof endocrine physiol, NC State Univ, 71- *Concurrent Pos:* Biomed res grant, NDak State Univ, 76 & 78. *Mem:* Soc Study Reproduction; Am Soc Animal Sci; Sigma Xi. *Res:* Testicular steroidogenesis; adrenal-testicular interrelationship. *Mailing Add:* Dept Animal Sci Kleberg Ctr College Station TX 77843-2471

JOHNSON, BRYCE VINCENT, INORGANIC CHEMISTRY, ORGANOMETALLIC CHEMISTRY. *Current Pos:* VPRES, FLUORO THERMAL PLASTICS, DYNEON LLC, 96- *Personal Data:* b Minneapolis, Minn, Oct 24, 49; m 71. *Educ:* St Olaf Col, BA, 71; Yale Univ, MS & MPhil, 72, PhD(chem), 75; Univ Chicago, MBA, 86. *Prof Exp:* Asst prof chem, Univ Louisville, 75-79; sr chemist, Amoco Res Ctr, Amoco Chem Corp, 79-86; prod develop specialist, 3M Corp, 86-89, tech mgr, 89-90, bus develop mgr, 91-96. *Mem:* Am Chem Soc; Sigma Xi; Soc Plastics Engrs. *Res:* Organometallic synthesis; transition metal isocyanide complexes; homogeneous catalysis; fluxional systems; polyolefin additives; fluoroplastics and elastomers. *Mailing Add:* Dyneon LLC 220-10E-10 St Paul MN 55144-1000

JOHNSON, BYRON F, CELL BIOLOGY, MICROBIOLOGY. *Current Pos:* ADJ RES PROF, DEPT BIOL, CARLETON UNIV, 90- *Personal Data:* b St Mary's, Pa, July 25, 28; Can citizen; m 52, 67, Hazel Gulka; c 4. *Educ:* Pa State Univ, BS, 50; Univ Calif, Los Angeles, MA, 58, PhD(zool), 60. *Prof Exp:* Nat Cancer Inst fel zool, Univ Edinburgh, 60-62; res officer, Div Biol Sci, Nat Res Coun Can, 62-90. *Concurrent Pos:* Vis scientist, Nat Inst Med Res, London, Eng, 68-69; mem, Int Comn Yeasts, 80-; adv bd, CRC Crit Rev Biotechnol, 81- *Mem:* Am Soc Cell Biol; Am Soc Microbiol; Can Soc Cell Biol; Can Soc Microbiologists. *Res:* Cell cycle; cellular growth and division; growth of cell organelles; biosynthesis of wall polysaccharides; regulation of cell size; temperature effects in biological systems; cytoplasmic genetics; chemostat culture; flocculation; microbial physiology. *Mailing Add:* Dept Biol Carleton Univ 1125 Colonel By Dr Ottawa ON K1S 5B6 Can. *Fax:* 613-520-4497

JOHNSON, C(HARLES) BRUCE, PHYSICS, ELECTRICAL ENGINEERING. *Current Pos:* PRES, JOHNSON SCI GROUP INC, PHOENIX ARIZ, 96- *Personal Data:* b Sioux City, Iowa, Aug 5, 35; m 58, June Graham; c Kimberly J & Kirsten J. *Educ:* Iowa State Univ, BS, 57; Univ Minn, Minneapolis, MSEE, 63, PhD(elec eng), 67. *Prof Exp:* Assoc scientist, Electronics Group, Gen Mills, Inc, 58-61; res asst gaseous electronics, Univ Minn, 61-63, res fel, 63-67; engr, RCA Electronics Components, 67-70; sr staff engr, Bendix Res Labs, 70-74; prin engr, Int Tel & Telegraph Corp, Ft Wayne, 74-77, tech dir, Electro-Optical Prods Div, 78-91 & sr tech staff eng, Aerospace Div, 91; tech dir, new prod develop, litton electron devices, Tempe, Ariz, 91-96. *Mem:* AAAS; Am Phys Soc; fel Inst Elec & Electronics Engrs; Optical Soc Am; Soc Photo-Optical Instrumentation; Am Astron Soc. *Res:* Space-charge-effects in vacuum and gases; charged particle optics; electro-optical image transfer characteristics, especially modulation transfer function studies; high resolution image-intensifier/camera-tube development; charged particle transport in gases; high altitude instrumentation; infrared studies; electrical-optical sensor analysis; photon-counting imaging. *Mailing Add:* 15204 S 21st St Phoenix AZ 85048-9544. *Fax:* 602-759-2826; *E-Mail:* cbjohnson@compuserve.com

JOHNSON, C SCOTT, PHYSICS, BIOPHYSICS. *Current Pos:* sr res scientist, 67-69, HEAD MARINE BIOSCI DIV, NAVAL UNDERSEA CTR, 69- *Personal Data:* b Sullivan, Mo, Feb 4, 32. *Educ:* Univ Mo-Rolla, BS, 54; Wash Univ, PhD(physics), 59. *Prof Exp:* Res assoc physics, Fermi Inst Nuclear Studies, Univ Chicago, 59-63; physicist, Naval Ord Test Sta, 63-67. *Mem:* Am Phys Soc; Acoust Soc Am; Sigma Xi. *Res:* Marine mammal bioacoustics; shark behavioral studies; nuclear physics. *Mailing Add:* 1876 Sefton Pl San Diego CA 92107

JOHNSON, C WALTER, metallurgical engineering, for more information see previous edition

JOHNSON, CAGE SAUL, INTERNAL MEDICINE, HEMATOLOGY. *Current Pos:* resident, 69-71, instr, 71-74, from asst prof to assoc prof, 74-88, PROF HEMAT, UNIV SOUTHERN CALIF, 88- *Personal Data:* b New Orleans, La, Mar 31, 41; m 68, Shirley L O'Neal; c Stephanie & Michelle. *Educ:* Creighton Univ, MD, 65. *Prof Exp:* Intern Univ Cincinnati, 65-66, resident, 66-67. *Concurrent Pos:* Bd dirs, Sickle Cell Self Help Asn, Los Angeles, 82-86; dir, Hemoglobinopathy Lab, Los Angeles, 76-; active, Nat Med Fel Inc, Chicago, 79-; mem bd dirs, Sickle Cell Dis Res Found & dir, Comprehensive Sickle Cell Ctr. *Mem:* Fel NY Acad Sci; Am Col Angiol; Am Soc Hemat; Am Fedn Clin Res; Int Soc Biocheology. *Res:* Hemoglobinopathies: structure and function. *Mailing Add:* Univ Southern Calif 2025 Zonal Ave Los Angeles CA 90033-4526

JOHNSON, CALVIN KEITH, THERMOSETTING RESINS, ORGANIC CHEMISTRY. *Current Pos:* tech dir foundry & indust resins, 93-94, VPRES & TECH DIR, BORDEN CHEMICAL INC, 95- *Personal Data:* b Litchfield, Minn, Dec 15, 37; m 60; c 3. *Educ:* Olivet Nazarene Univ, AB, 59; Mich State Univ, PhD(org chem), 63. *Honors & Awards:* Award of Sci Merit, Am Foundrymens Soc, 96. *Prof Exp:* NIH fel org chem, Columbia Univ, 63-64; res chemist, Minn Mining & Mfg Co, 64-67; group leader polymer res, CPC Int, 67-69; tech dir res, Acme Resin Corp, 69-77, vpres res & develop, 77-85, sr vpres & tech dir, 85-93. *Concurrent Pos:* Pres, Res Dir Asn Chicago; mem, Res Bd, Am Foundry Men's Soc. *Mem:* Am Chem Soc; Am Inst Chem; Soc Petrol Eng; Am Foundrymens Soc. *Res:* Organic photochemistry; synthesis and reactions of small ring compounds; mechanisms of polymer decomposition; latent curing resin systems; phenolic, thermosetting and foundry resins; polymers; molding compounds. *Mailing Add:* Borden Inc 1401 Circle Ave Forest Park IL 60130

JOHNSON, CANDACE SUE, LEUKEMIA RESEARCH. *Current Pos:* ASSOC PROF DEPTS OTOLARYNGOL & PATH, SCH MED, UNIV PITTSBURGH, 89- *Personal Data:* b Columbus, Ohio, Apr 10, 49. *Educ:* Ohio State Univ, PhD(microbiol), 77. *Prof Exp:* Sr scientist, AMC Cancer Res Ctr, Lakewood, Colo, 81-89, lab chief exp hemat, 88-89. *Res:* T-cells; monoclonal antibodies. *Mailing Add:* Dept Otolaryngol Eye & Ear Inst Pittsburgh Sch Med Univ Pittsburgh 203 Lothrop St No 110 Pittsburgh PA 15213-2588. *Fax:* 412-647-8720

JOHNSON, CARL ARNOLD, ORGANIC CHEMISTRY. *Current Pos:* RETIRED. *Personal Data:* b Bend, Ore, Mar 5, 25; m 49; c 2. *Educ:* Reed Col, BA, 50; State Col Wash, MS, 52, PhD(chem), 56. *Prof Exp:* Fel org synthesis, Mellon Inst, 56-59; chief forest prod res, Owens-Ill Co, 59-60, chief org chem res, 60-64, mgr appln res, 64-68, consult coatings & optical mat, 68-69, proj mgr glass fiber reinforcements technol & chem develop, 69-74, sr scientist chem support, 74-75, res assoc chem support, textile opers, Tech Ctr, Owens Corning Fiberglas Co, 75-86. *Concurrent Pos:* Dir, Bd of Dirs, Toastmasters Int, 78-80. *Mem:* Am Chem Soc; Sigma Xi; AAAS. *Res:* Development of new glass fiber size systems. *Mailing Add:* 51 Meredith St Port Ludlow WA 98365

JOHNSON, CARL BOONE, TOXICOLOGY, ENVIRONMENTAL HEALTH. *Current Pos:* sci adminr, 76-81, TOXICOLOGIST, CFSAN, FOOD & DRUG ADMIN, 81- *Personal Data:* b Jacksonville, Fla, Mar 11, 38; m 64; c 1. *Educ:* Fla State Univ, Tallahassee, BS, 59; Am Univ, MS, 67; Georgetown Univ, PhD(biochem), 74. *Prof Exp:* Res chemist, Nat Naval Med Ctr, 63-72; res scientist, Microbiol Assocs, 74-76. *Mem:* AAAS. *Res:* Solubilized and partially purified a glucagon-binding protein from rat liver plasma membranes; uptake of drugs by rat kidney lysosomes. *Mailing Add:* 12800 Teaberry Rd Silver Spring MD 20906

JOHNSON, CARL EDWARD, SEISMICITY, SEISMIC NETWORKS. *Current Pos:* ASSOC PROF, DEPT GEOL, UNIV HAWAII. *Personal Data:* b Marshalltown, Iowa, Nov 27, 46; m 73; c 2. *Educ:* Mass Inst Technol, BS & MS, 72; Calif Inst Technol, PhD(geophysics), 79. *Prof Exp:* Geophysicist, Off Earthquake Studies, US Geol Surv, 79-88. *Concurrent Pos:* Vis res assoc, Seismol Lab, Calif Inst Technol, 79- *Mem:* Seismol Soc; Am Geophys Union. *Res:* Seismicity studies related to earthquake prediction research including the development of real-time data acquisition and earthquake data base systems. *Mailing Add:* Dept Geol Univ Hawaii 200 W Kawili St Hilo HI 96720-4091

JOHNSON, CARL EDWIN, organic chemistry, for more information see previous edition

JOHNSON, CARL EMIL, JR, physical chemistry; deceased, see previous edition for last biography

JOHNSON, CARL ERICK, ORGANIC CHEMISTRY. *Current Pos:* RETIRED. *Personal Data:* b Chicago, Ill, Feb 17, 14; m 41; c 2. *Educ:* Univ Chicago, BS, 38, MS, 49. *Prof Exp:* Chemist, Western Shade Cloth Co, Ill, 38-45; chief org chemist, Nat Aluminate Corp, 45-52, dir inorg res, 52-56, sr technol adv, 56-59; sect head, Cent Res, Nalco Chem Co, 59-60, res mgr, Metal Indust Div, 60-68, res assoc, 68-71, res assoc Miss, 71-74, res mgr, Brookhaven Res Lab, 74-76. *Concurrent Pos:* Consult, 76- *Mem:* AAAS; Am Chem Soc; Nat Asn Corrosion Engrs. *Res:* Water and textile treatment; flotation of minerals; synthesis of organic compounds; measurement of the film pressure of insoluble films; organic chemistry of boiler water treatment; aqueous corrosion; ion exchange; industrial lubrication, especially metal rolling and emulsion technology. *Mailing Add:* 401 McNair St Brookhaven MS 39601-3744

JOHNSON, CARL LYNN, PHARMACOLOGY, BIOCHEMISTRY. *Current Pos:* ASSOC PROF PHARMACOL, COL MED, UNIV CINCINNATI, 77- *Personal Data:* b Beaumont, Tex, Aug 22, 41. *Educ:* Rice Univ, BA, 64; Univ Houston, MS, 68; Baylor Col Med, PhD(pharmacol), 71. *Prof Exp:* Instr, 71-72, assoc, 72-73, asst prof pharmacol, Mt Sinai Sch Med, 73-77. *Res:* Hormone receptors and adenylate cyclase; molecular pharmacology. *Mailing Add:* Dept Pharmacol & Cell Biophys Univ Cincinnati Col Med 231 Bethesda Ave Cincinnati OH 45267-0575. *Fax:* 513-558-2349

JOHNSON, CARL RANDOLPH, ORGANIC CHEMISTRY. *Current Pos:* from asst prof to prof, 62-90, DISTINGUISHED PROF CHEM, WAYNE STATE UNIV, 90-, CHAIR, CHEM 97- *Personal Data:* b Charlottesville, Va, Apr 28, 37; m 66, Mary Cardwell; c Gregory. *Educ:* Med Col Va, BS, 58; Univ Ill, PhD(chem), 62. *Prof Exp:* NSF res fel chem, Harvard Univ, 62. *Concurrent Pos:* Alfred P Sloan fel, 65-68; adv bd, J of Org Chem, 76-81; assoc ed, J Am Chem Soc, 84-89; bd dirs, Organic Syntheses, Inc, 81-; Humboldt sr scientist, 91. *Mem:* Am Chem Soc; Royal Soc Chem. *Res:* Organic sulfur chemistry, especially sulfoxides & sulfoximines; exploratory synthetic chemistry; synthesis of compounds of potential medicinal activity; organometallic chemistry; synthesis of natural products; enzymes in synthesis. *Mailing Add:* Dept of Chem Wayne State Univ Detroit MI 48202. *E-Mail:* crj@chem.wayne.edu

JOHNSON, CARL WILLIAM, PLANT BREEDING. *Current Pos:* PLANT BREEDER, CALIF COOP RICE RES FOUND, 74- *Personal Data:* b Mound Valley, Kans, Feb 11, 42; m 68; c 2. *Educ:* Kans State Univ, BS, 65; NDak State Univ, MS, 67; Univ Nebr, PhD(agron), 74. *Honors & Awards:* Distinguished Rice Res & Educ Award; First McCaughey Mem Inst Vis Scientists Award, Australia. *Mem:* Crop Sci Soc Am; Am Soc Agronomy; Coun Agr Sci & Technol; Sigma Xi. *Res:* Development of rice varieties for the California rice industry. *Mailing Add:* CA Coop Rice Res Found Rice Exp Sta Box 306 Biggs CA 95917

JOHNSON, CARLTON ROBERT, PETROLEUM GEOLOGY, GROUNDWATER GEOLOGY. *Current Pos:* sr res geologist, Esso Prod Res Co, 65-69, res assoc, Exxon Prod Res Co, 69-72, sr res assoc, 72-79, res adv, 79-91, 3D MODELING PETROL RESERVOIR DESCRIPTION RES, EXXON PROD RES CO, 91- *Personal Data:* b Chicago, Ill, Sept 19, 26; m 51; c 2. *Educ:* Monmouth Col, Ill, BA, 49; Univ Iowa, MS, 54, PhD, 56. *Prof Exp:* Geologist, Univ US Geol Surv, 50-56; res geologist, Jersey Prod Res Co, 56-65. *Mem:* Soc Petrol Engrs. *Res:* Computer mapping and modeling programs; geology and performance of oil, gas and water reservoirs; well testing procedures and instrumentation. *Mailing Add:* 620 Fulton Ave N 406 Rockport TX 78382-5722

JOHNSON, CARROLL KENNETH, CRYSTALLOGRAPHY, BIOPHYSICS. *Current Pos:* RETIRED. *Personal Data:* b Greeley, Colo, Sept 18, 29; m 51, Carol J DeBoer; c Cindy, Valerie, Greg, Gary & Amy. *Educ:* Colo State Univ, BS, 55; Mass Inst Technol, PhD(biophys), 59. *Honors & Awards:* Buerger Award, Am Crystallog Asn, 97. *Prof Exp:* Asst biol, Mass Inst Technol, 55-56, asst biophys, 56-59; Am Cancer Soc res fel x-ray crystallog, Inst Cancer Res, Pa, 59-62; sr scientist comput chem, Chem & Anal Sci Div, Oak Ridge Nat Lab, 62-96. *Concurrent Pos:* Vis scientist, Stanford Comput Dept, 75-76, Naval Res Lab, 81. *Mem:* Am Crystallog Asn (pres, 77). *Res:* Neutron diffraction; crystallographic computing; automated graphics for illustrating crystal structures; crystallographic thermal-motion analysis; combinatorial chemistry; expert systems; machine vision engineering; crystallographic topology. *Mailing Add:* 344 East Dr Oak Ridge TN 37830

JOHNSON, CECIL GRAY, INDUSTRIAL & SYSTEMS ENGINEERING. *Current Pos:* prof, 55-91, EMER PROF INDUST & SYSTS ENG, GA INST TECHNOL, 92- *Personal Data:* b Nanafalia, Ala, Feb 26, 22; m 48, Mary Pinckard; c Gray W, Mark C & Celia (McDaniel). *Educ:* Ga Inst Technol, BS, 48 & 49, MS, 57. *Honors & Awards:* Distinguished Serv Award, Am Inst Indust Engrs. *Prof Exp:* Indust engr, Gen Shoe Corp, 49-50 & Am Art Metals Co, 50-55. *Concurrent Pos:* Mgt & systs eng consult, 55-; ed-in-chief, J Am Inst Indust Engrs, 55-65; res assoc, Off Naval Res, Univ Calif, Los Angeles, 59; consult, Delta Air Lines, 60-, HEW, Univ Ga, 69, Days Inns Am, Burch-Lowe, Crown-Zellerbach, Gulf States; partic, Stanford-Ames NASA-ASEE Educ Res Study, 74; prin, Atlanta Assessment Proj, Atlanta Pub Schs, HEW, 76; prin, Prime DOC Commun Syst, Fulton County, Ga, 80; prin, Systs Study Rehab Serv Blind, State Ga, 80-83; mem, 11E Fel Scholar Comt, 85-87; mem, 11E Heritage Task Force, 86-87, chmn, 87-93. *Mem:* Fel Am Inst Indust Engrs (vpres, 65-67); Nat Soc Prof Engrs. *Res:* Human performance and organizational theory; educational systems, especially American universities; analysis and design methodology for complex systems; improving productivity from mental and physical activity, especially among university educated individuals. *Mailing Add:* 3211 Argonne Dr NW Atlanta GA 30305

JOHNSON, CHARLES ANDREW, MATHEMATICS. *Current Pos:* RETIRED. *Personal Data:* b Chicago, Ill, May 8, 15; m 40; c 2. *Educ:* Northern Ill Univ, BEd, 37; Northwestern Univ, MA, 40; Univ Kans, PhD(math), 50. *Prof Exp:* Teacher & prin pub schs, Ill, 38-40, teacher, 40-43; prof math, Univ Mo-Rolla, 46- *Concurrent Pos:* Instr, Univ Kans, 48-50; res assoc, Argonne Nat Lab, 62. *Mem:* Am Soc Eng Educ; Am Math Asn; Sigma Xi. *Res:* Mathematical education. *Mailing Add:* Dept Math 326 Math Comp Sci Bldg Univ Mo Rolla MO 65409-0020

JOHNSON, CHARLES C, JR, ENVIRONMENTAL ENGINEERING. *Current Pos:* RETIRED. *Educ:* Purdue Univ, BS, 47, MS, 57; Am Acad Environ Engrs, dipl. *Honors & Awards:* Walter F Snyder Award, Nat Environ Health Asn & Nat Sanit Found, 77; Award for Except Achievement, US Dept Health & Human Serv, 89; George Warren Fuller Award, Am Water Works Asn, 90. *Prof Exp:* Asst surgeon gen, USPHS, 47-71; assoc exec dir, Am Pub Health Asn, 71-72; vpres, Wash Tech Inst, 72-74 & Malcolm Pirnie, Inc, 74-75; Pres, C C Johnson & Malhotra, PC, 79-91. *Concurrent Pos:* Comnr, Nat Capital Planning Comn, 71-74, Comn Educ Health Admin, 72-74; mem tech adv group, Munic Wastewater Systs, Environ Protection Agency, 73-75; mem, Task Groups on Eng Career Develop, Surgeon Gen; chmn, Nat Drinking Water Adv Coun, 75-81; adj assoc prof, Sch Environ Med, NY Univ, 76; mem, Adv Comt Water Data Pub Use, US Geol Surv, Dept Interior, 79-80; mem, Safe Drinking Water Act Amendments Tech Adv Workgroup, Am Water Works Asn, 89, Strategic Planning Comt, 90-91; mem, Clean Water Act Reauthorization Comt, Water Pollution Control Fedn, 90; mem, Task Comt Int Relations, Am Acad Environ Engrs, 90-91; mem, Comt Hazardous Waste in Hwy Rights of Way, Transp Res Bd, Nat Res Coun, 90-, Comt Rev Environ Protection Agency's Monitoring & Assessment Prog, 91-; mem bd dirs, Water for People, 91-, Nat Sanit Found, 91- *Mem:* Nat Acad Eng; fel Am Pub Health Asn; hon mem Am Water Works Asn; hon mem Nat Environ Health Asn; Water Pollution Control Fedn. *Res:* Administration of environmental programs; implementation of water supply and waste disposal construction programs. *Mailing Add:* 2801 N Mexico Ave NW Washington DC 20902

JOHNSON, CHARLES EDWARD, ATOMIC PHYSICS. *Current Pos:* from asst prof to assoc prof, 73-83, PROF PHYSICS, NC STATE UNIV, 83- *Personal Data:* b Pennington Gap, Va, Nov 19, 40; m 70; c 2. *Educ:* Yale Univ, BS, 62, MS, 65, PhD(physics), 67. *Prof Exp:* Res physicist, Lawrence Radiation Lab, Univ Calif, Berkeley, 67-72. *Mem:* Am Phys Soc. *Res:* Measurement of the fundamental properties of free atoms and molecules using the techniques of optical pumping and atomic beam magnetic resonance. *Mailing Add:* Dept Physics NC State Univ Box 8202 Raleigh NC 27695-8202

JOHNSON, CHARLES F, medicine, electron microscopy, for more information see previous edition

JOHNSON, CHARLES HENRY, MATHEMATICAL STATISTICS. *Current Pos:* PROF MATH & CHMN DEPT, UNIV WIS-STEVENS POINT, 67- *Personal Data:* b Chicago, Ill, June 12, 25; m 48; c 3. *Educ:* Bradley Univ, BA, 49, MS, 50; Okla State Univ, PhD(math), 63. *Prof Exp:* Asst math, Univ Pittsburgh, 50-52; sect chief, Continental Casualty Co, 52-55; from asst prof to assoc prof math & astron, DePauw Univ, 55-67. *Res:* Astronomy. *Mailing Add:* 2755 S County Rd P Stevens Point WI 54481

JOHNSON, CHARLES LESLIE, AEROSPACE. *Current Pos:* AEROSPACE PHYSICIST, NASA-MARSHALL SPACE FLIGHT CTR, HUNTSVILLE, 90- *Personal Data:* b Ashland, Ky, Mar 1, 62; m 88, Carol Elain Peck; c Carl Stuart & Leslie Arlene. *Educ:* Transylvania Univ, BA, 84; Vanderbilt Univ, MS, 86. *Prof Exp:* Res physicist, Gen Res Corp, 86-90. *Concurrent Pos:* Consult, Gen Res Corp, 90-91. *Mem:* Am Inst Aeronaut & Astronaut; Nat Space Soc; World Future Soc; Am Geophys Union. *Res:* Contributed many articles to professional journals. *Mailing Add:* NASA Prog Develop PSOZ Marshall Space Flight Ctr Huntsville AL 35812

JOHNSON, CHARLES MINOR, PHYSICS, SYSTEM ANALYSIS. *Current Pos:* PRIN ENGR, MITRE CORP, 88- *Personal Data:* b Nashville, Tenn, May 31, 23; m 64, Anne Keech; c Jane & Steve. *Educ:* Vanderbilt Univ, BE, 44; Duke Univ, PhD(physics), 51. *Honors & Awards:* Dept Army Medal Exceptional Civilian Serv, 73. *Prof Exp:* Res assoc, Radiation Lab, Johns Hopkins Univ, 51-53, res scientist, 53-56; res mgr, Electronic Commun, Inc, 56-61; res dir, Emerson Res Lab, 60-61; dep safeguard syst mgr, Sci & Technol, Dept Army, 67-73; res mgr, IBM Corp, 61-67, dep dir, World Wide Mil Command & Control Syst Archit Develop, 73-86; prin scientist, Anser, 86-88. *Concurrent Pos:* Consult, Sperry-Rand Corp, 55 & Eng Res & Develop Lab, US Army, 59-; sci adv, Joint Strategic Target Planning Staff, 72-81; consult, Develop & Readiness Command, US Army, 76; external adv, Ga Tech Res Inst, 80-85. *Mem:* Am Phys Soc; Inst Elec & Electronics Engrs. *Res:* Microwave physics, ferrite devices, phased array radars, millimeter wave techniques, microwave spectroscopy; radiation scattering, lasers and optics; semiconductor devices; ballistic missile defense; command and control systems. *Mailing Add:* 11220 Leatherwood Dr Reston VA 20191

JOHNSON, CHARLES NELSON, JR, APPLIED PHYSICS. *Current Pos:* CONSULT PHYSICIST, ENVIRON RES INST MICH, SEARLE CONSORTIUM, 74- *Personal Data:* b Mt Hope, Kans, June 17, 15; m 67, Ruth E Berry; c Janet A (LaMotte), Diana G (Lee) & Charles B Jr. *Educ:* Friends Univ, AB, 38. *Prof Exp:* Jr instr eng physics, Johns Hopkins Univ, 38-41; physicist, Bur Ord, US Dept Navy, Washington, DC & Naval Operating Base, Norfolk, Va, 41-42, physicist, Norfolk Navy Yard, Va, 42-46, sr physicist, Aviation Ord Dept, 46-51, sr physicist, Ballistic Instrumentation Dept, Naval Proving Ground, 51-55; supvry res physicist, US Army Engr Res & Develop Ctr, 55-67, chief detection br, Intrusion, Detection & Sensor Lab, 67-71, chief phys sci group, Countermine-Counter Intrusion Dept, 71-73. *Mem:* Fel AAAS; Am Phys Soc; Sigma Xi. *Res:* Interior and exterior ballistic measurements; weapons systems evaluation and counter-measures; barrier and intrusion detection systems; remote multiband sensor systems; land mines, concealed explosives, letter bombs and booby trap detectors. *Mailing Add:* 3100 N Oxford St Arlington VA 22207-5352

JOHNSON, CHARLES ROBERT, ORNAMENTAL HORTICULTURE. *Current Pos:* DEPT HORT & LANDSCAPE ARCHIT, WASH STATE UNIV, 90- *Personal Data:* b Ft Collins, Colo, June 8, 41; m 64; c 2. *Educ:* Colo State Univ, BS, 64; Ore State Univ, PhD(ornamental plant physiol), 70. *Honors & Awards:* Porter Henegar Res Award, Nurserymen's Asn, 80. *Prof Exp:* Res floricult, K Stormly Hansen Greenhouses, Copenhagen, Denmark, 64-65; res & teaching, Dept Plant Path, Clemson Univ, 70-73; res & teaching ornamental hort, Univ Fla, 73-80, assoc prof, 80-84; prof & head dept, Dept Hort, Univ Ga, 85-90. *Concurrent Pos:* Bd dir, Int Plant Propagators Soc, 80-82. *Mem:* Am Soc Hort Sci; Int Plant Propagators Soc. *Res:* Physiological aspects of plant-soil microbial symbiosis, growth and develpoment, stress physiology and urban horticulture. *Mailing Add:* Dept Hort Wash State Univ 1 SE Stadium Way Pullman WA 99164-0001

JOHNSON, CHARLES ROYAL, ALGEBRA, APPLIED MATHEMATICS. *Current Pos:* PROF MATH, COL WILLIAM & MARY, 87- *Personal Data:* b Elkhart, Ind, Jan 28, 48; m 72; c 2. *Educ:* Northwestern Univ, BA, 69; Calif Inst Technol, PhD(math, econ), 72. *Prof Exp:* Res assoc fel math, Appl Math Div, Nat Bur Standards, 72-74; res prof appl math & econ, Inst For Phys Sci & Technol, Univ Md, College Park, 74 -84; prof math sci, Clemson Univ, 85-87. *Concurrent Pos:* Consult, Appl Math Div, Nat Bur Stand, 74-82; vis staff mem, Los Alamos Sci Lab, 74-; consult, Icase, 82- *Mem:* Am Math Soc; Soc Indust & Appl Math; Math Asn Am; Int Linear Algebra Soc. *Res:* Matrix analysis and applications; combinatorics; mathematical economics; combinatorial matrix analysis, eigenvalues, inequalities and norms. *Mailing Add:* Dept Math Col William & Mary Williamsburg VA 23187

JOHNSON, CHARLES SIDNEY, JR, PHYSICAL CHEMISTRY. *Current Pos:* prof, 67-88, M A SMITH, PROF CHEM, UNIV NC, CHAPEL HILL, 88- *Personal Data:* b Albany, Ga, Mar 7, 36; m 58, Ellen McFarland; c David M & Daniel C. *Educ:* Ga Inst Technol, BS, 58; Mass Inst Technol, PhD(phys chem), 61. *Prof Exp:* Nat Acad Sci-Nat Res Coun fel, 61-62; from asst prof to assoc prof phys chem, Yale Univ, 62-67. *Concurrent Pos:* Sloan Found res fel, 66; ed bd, J Magnetic Resonance, 71-; Guggenheim Found fel, 72. *Mem:* Fel AAAS; fel Am Phys Soc; Am Chem Soc. *Res:* Nuclear magnetic resonance; spin relaxation; chemical rate processes; laser light scattering; electrophoretic nuclear magnetic resonance; diffusion ordered nuclear magnetic resonance. *Mailing Add:* Dept Chem Univ NC Chapel Hill NC 27599-3290. *Fax:* 919-962-2388; *E-Mail:* charles_johnson@unc.edu

JOHNSON, CHARLES WILLIAM, MICROBIOLOGY. *Current Pos:* Instr bact & parasitol, 47-49, from asst prof to assoc prof, 49-59, chmn dept, 59-73, dean div grad studies & res, 66-81, interim dean, Sch Med, 81-82, PROF MICROBIOL, MEHARRY MED COL, 59-, VPRES ACAD AFFAIRS, 81- *Personal Data:* b Ennis, Tex, Jan 25, 22; m 43; c 3. *Educ:* Prairie View State Col, BS, 42; Univ Southern Calif, MS, 47; Meharry Med Col, MD, 53. *Concurrent Pos:* Actg chmn dept microbiol, Meharry Med Col, 53-59; Rockefeller Found fel, 57-59; consult, Hubbard Hosp, 52-54. *Mem:* AAAS; Am Soc Microbiol; Am Acad Allergy; Am Fedn Clin Res; Am Asn Path; Am Asn Clin Immunol & Allergy; Asn Geront Higher Educ. *Res:* Immunology and mycology. *Mailing Add:* VPres Acad Affairs Meharry Med Col 1005 D B Todd Blvd Nashville TN 37208

JOHNSON, CHRIS ALAN, PSYCHOPHYSICS, PHYSIOLOGICAL OPTICS. *Current Pos:* res fel, 77-78, from asst prof to assoc prof, 78-89, PROF OPHTHAL, UNIV CALIF, DAVIS, 89- *Personal Data:* b Roseburg, Ore, Oct 1, 49; m 71, Debra P Johnson; c Kristin & Matthew. *Educ:* Univ Ore, BA, 70; Pa State Univ, MSc, 72, PhD(psychol), 74. *Honors & Awards:* Distinguished Serv Award, 87, Honor Award, Am Acad Ophthal, 88. *Prof Exp:* Res asst psychol, Univ Ore & Pa State Univ, 70-75; res fel ophthal, Univ Fla, 75-77. *Concurrent Pos:* Nat Eye Inst, NIH fels, 75 & 77, academic investr award, 78; Nat Eye Inst grant, 79-94. *Mem:* Asn Res Vision & Ophthal; Optical Soc Am; Int Perimetric Soc; Am Acad Ophthal. *Res:* Visual psychophysics, analysis of the accommodation mechanism, examination of peripheral visual functions and development and adaptation of psychophysical tests to quantitative perimetry and visual field testing; night vision; vision and driving. *Mailing Add:* Dept Ophthal Univ Calif Sch Med Davis CA 95616. *Fax:* 916-734-6992; *E-Mail:* cajohnson@ucdavis.edu

JOHNSON, CHRISTOPHER R, SCIENTIFIC COMPUTING, SCIENTIFIC VISUALIZATION. *Current Pos:* res assoc internal med, Univ Utah, 89-90, res asst prof, 90-92, res asst prof comput sci, 92-93, asst prof, 93-96, ASSOC PROF & CHMN COMPUT SCI, UNIV UTAH, 96- *Personal Data:* b Kansas City, Kans, Jan 17, 61; m, Katnenine Coles. *Educ:* Wright State Univ, BS, 82; Univ Utah, MS, 84, PhD(biophys), 89. *Honors & Awards:* Whitaker Award, 91; First Award, NIH, 92; A C Suhren Jr Lectr, Tulane Univ, 93. *Prof Exp:* Eng physicist, Advan Technol Div, 84-85; asst prof physics, Westminster Col, 85-89. *Concurrent Pos:* Adj asst prof math, Univ Utah, 91-, adj asst prof bioeng, 92-, res asst prof physics, 93-; patent consult, Vanderbilt Univ, 92-93; Nat young investr award, NSF, 94, pres fac fel, 95; res consult, Smith & Nephew Res Ctr, 95-96. *Mem:* Asn Comput Mach; Inst Elec & Electronics Engrs Comput Soc; Soc Math Biol; Soc Indust & Appl Math; Biomed Eng Soc; Am Inst Physics. *Res:* Scientific computing; computational steering, inverse and imaging problems; adaptive methods for partial differential equations; automatic mesh generation, numerical analysis, large scale computational problems in medicine and scientific visualization. *Mailing Add:* 3190 Merrill Eng Bldg Univ Utah Salt Lake City UT 84112-1107. *Fax:* 801-581-5843; *E-Mail:* crj@cs.utah.edu

JOHNSON, CLARENCE DANIEL, SYSTEMATIC ENTOMOLOGY, ECOLOGY. *Current Pos:* asst prof, 66-70, PROF ZOOL, NORTHERN ARIZ UNIV, 70- *Personal Data:* b Exeter, Calif, July 20, 31; m 51, Margaret Elkins; c John, Cheryl, Kirk & Rod. *Educ:* Fresno State Univ, BA, 53; Ariz State Univ, MS, 61; Univ Calif, Berkeley, PhD(entom), 66. *Prof Exp:* High sch teacher, Calif, 56-63. *Concurrent Pos:* Fulbright res award, SAm, 84-85. *Mem:* Soc Study Evolution; Ecol Soc Am; Entom Soc Am; Soc Syst Biol; Asn Trop Biol. *Res:* Systematics, ecology and behavior of the beetle family Bruchidae; insect-plant interactions. *Mailing Add:* Dept Biol Sci Northern Ariz Univ Box 5640 Flagstaff AZ 86011. *Fax:* 520-523-7500; *E-Mail:* johnson@nauvax.ucc.nau.edu

JOHNSON, CLARENCE EUGENE, ENGINEERING, AGRICULTURE. *Current Pos:* PROF AGR ENG, AUBURN UNIV, 79- *Personal Data:* b Elk City, Okla, Nov 1, 41. *Educ:* Okla State Univ, BS, 63; Iowa State Univ, MS, 68, PhD(agr eng), 69. *Prof Exp:* Instr agr eng, Iowa State Univ, 64-69; assoc prof, SDak State Univ, 70-77; agr engr, Columbia Plateaum Conserv Res Ctr, USDA Agr Res Serv, Ore, 77-79. *Mem:* Am Soc Agr Engrs; Nat Soc Prof Engrs; Sigma Xi; Int Soil Tillage Res Orgn. *Res:* Soil dynamics; tillage and traction; harvesting systems; machinery system simulation; similitude. *Mailing Add:* Dept Agr Eng Auburn Univ Auburn AL 36849

JOHNSON, CLARK E, JR, MAGNETIC RECORDING. *Current Pos:* PRES, CARD SYSTS TESTING LABS, 90-; ASSOC DIR, RES PROGS, MIT. *Personal Data:* b Minneapolis, Minn, Aug 3, 30; div; c 7. *Educ:* Univ Minn, Minneapolis, BS, 50, MS, 61. *Prof Exp:* Sr physicist, Cent Res Labs, Minn Mining & Mfg Co, 50-59; pres res & develop, Leyghton-Paige Corp, 59-61; pres, Telostat Corp, 61-63; Micro-Commun Corp, 72-77; vpres, Minnetech Labs, 63-66; vpres eng, Vibrac Corp Div, USM Corp, 67-72; dir, res & develop, Buckeye Int, Inc, 77-80; pres & chmn, Vertmag Systs Corp, 81-85; consult, 85- *Concurrent Pos:* Consult physicist, Graham Magnetics Inc, 68-74; dir & tech adv, Trans Data Syst; finance comt chmn, Magnetics Soc, 75-80, vpres, 81-82, pres, 83-84; dir, Sciencare Corp, 77-84, Magnum Technol, & Megabyte Storage Systs, 87-90; cong sci fel, 88; chmn bd dirs, Appl Info Systs, 89-94 & Rastech, Inc, 89-94; pres, Pandora Technologies, 95-, USA-Nat Host, 94-; dir, Master Commun Group, 96- *Mem:* AAAS; fel Inst Elec & Electronics Engrs. *Res:* Magnetic theory; magnetic recording and recording materials; fine particle magnetic theory; electromagnetic transducers and devices; electro-optic transducers and devices; new techniques for recording information using magnetic properties of materials; perpendicular magnetic recording. *Mailing Add:* PO Box 50116 Minneapolis MN 55405. *Fax:* 612-922-8820; *E-Mail:* clark@rpcp.mit.edu

JOHNSON, CLELAND HOWARD, NUCLEAR PHYSICS. *Current Pos:* RETIRED. *Personal Data:* b Pierpont, SDak, Sept 16, 22; m 44; c 3. *Educ:* Hastings Col, BA, 44; Univ Wis, PhD(physics), 51. *Prof Exp:* Physicist, Oak Ridge Nat Lab, 51-88. *Mem:* Am Phys Soc. *Res:* Experimental nuclear structure physics. *Mailing Add:* Box 310 Rte 1 Ten Mile TN 37880

JOHNSON, CLIFFORD VICTOR, STRING THEORY. *Current Pos:* ASST PROF, DEPT PHYSICS & ASTRON, UNIV KY, 95- *Personal Data:* b London, Eng, Mar 5, 68. *Educ:* Univ London, BSc, 89; Univ Southampton, PhD(physics), 92. *Prof Exp:* Res assoc, Inst Advan Study, Princeton, 92-94; lectr physics, Princeton Univ, 95. *Concurrent Pos:* Res assoc, Inst Theoret Physics, Univ Calif, Santa Barbara, 95-97. *Res:* Origins and mechanisms underlying matter and fundamental interactions at the most basic level; particle physics and quantum gravity; black holes and cosmology; string theory. *Mailing Add:* Dept Physics & Astron Univ Ky Lexington KY 40506-0055. *Fax:* 606-323-2846; *E-Mail:* cvj@pa.uky.edu

JOHNSON, CLIFTON W, CIVIL & AGRICULTURAL ENGINEERING. *Current Pos:* RETIRED. *Personal Data:* b Lewisville, Idaho, Sept 23, 24; m 52; c 6. *Educ:* Utah State Univ, BS, 56, MS, 57. *Prof Exp:* Water distribution engr, State Engrs Off, Utah, 57-60; hydraul engr, Agr Res Serv, 60-88. *Mem:* Am Soc Civil Engrs; Am Soc Agr Engrs. *Res:* Hydrology, erosion and sediment transport; design, construction and operation of water measuring devices; irrigation water diversion and use; sediment transport, measurement and studies of arid lands hydrology. *Mailing Add:* 3907 Whitehead Boise ID 83703

JOHNSON, CONOR DEANE, ACTIVE & PASSIVE VIBRATION SUPPRESSION. *Current Pos:* PRES, CSA ENG INC, 82- *Personal Data:* b Charlottesville, Va, Apr 20, 43; m 66, Laura Rogers; c William & Catherine. *Educ:* Va Polytech Inst, BS, 65; Clemson Univ, MS, 67, PhD(eng mech), 69. *Honors & Awards:* Struct & Mat Award, Am Soc Mech Engrs, 81. *Prof Exp:* Sr struct analyst, Anamet Labs, Dayton, Ohio, 73-75, prin engr, San Carlos, Calif, 75-81, vpres, 81-82. *Concurrent Pos:* Fel, NDEA, 67-68; prog mgr, Aerospace Struct Info & Anal Ctr, 75-82. *Mem:* Am Inst Aeronaut & Astronaut; Am Soc Mech Engrs; Sigma Xi. *Res:* Modal strain energy method for damping analysis using finite element techniques; combined system analysis techniques (integration of finite element techniques, damping analysis, component mode synthesis, other engineer disciplines, experimental data). *Mailing Add:* 3425 Lodge Dr Belmont CA 94002. *Fax:* 650-494-8749

JOHNSON, CORINNE LESSIG, DEVELOPMENT INFORMATION SYSTEMS, SCIENCE EDUCATION SOFTWARE. *Personal Data:* b Wilmington, Del, Oct 29, 38. *Educ:* Wellesley Col, AB, 60; Univ Rochester, MS, 64, PhD(biol), 69. *Prof Exp:* Sci Res Coun res asst & fel biochem, Univ Leicester, 69-70; fel, Albert Einstein Col Med, 70-72; assoc res scientist & instr biochem, Dent Ctr, NY Univ, 72-74, asst prof microbiol, 75; vis asst prof biol, Vassar Col, 75-77; asst prof biol, Carleton Col, 77-78; res assoc microbiol, Sch Med, Boston Univ, 78-79; biol ed & gen mgr, Edutech Inc, 81-83; software specialist, Gibco Labs, 84-85; temp proj dir, educ technol database, Harvard Univ, 85-86, training coordr, 86-91, mgr, admin serv, Develop Comput Serv, 91-96. *Concurrent Pos:* Treas, Alliance Independent Scholars, 80-85; prog chair, New Eng Chap, Asn Women Sci, 90-91. *Mem:* AAAS; Am Soc Microbiol; Asn Women Sci; Asn Comput. *Mailing Add:* 36 Highland Ave No 48 Cambridge MA 02139

JOHNSON, CORWIN MCGILLIVRAY, agronomy; deceased, see previous edition for last biography

JOHNSON, CURTIS ALAN, MATERIAL SCIENCE, CERAMIC SCIENCE. *Current Pos:* STAFF SCIENTIST CERAMICS, GEN ELEC CORP RES & DEVELOP CTR, 73- *Personal Data:* b Johnstown, Pa, Jan 22, 48; m 69, Michele Bush; c Gregory M & Eric D. *Educ:* Pa State Univ, BS, 69, PhD(metall), 74. *Mem:* Am Ceramics Soc; Am Soc Testing & Mats. *Res:* Mechanical and physical properties of metals and ceramics, in particular high temperature structural ceramics; fabrication methods; densification processes and phase transformations of ceramics. *Mailing Add:* Gen Elec Corp Res & Develop Bldg K1 Mb 187 1 Res Ctr Schenectady NY 12309

JOHNSON, CURTIS ALLEN, agricultural engineering, for more information see previous edition

JOHNSON, D(AVID) LYNN, SINTERING, PROCESSING. *Current Pos:* from asst prof to assoc prof, 62-71, PROF MATS SCI & ENG, NORTHWESTERN UNIV, 71- *Personal Data:* b Provo, Utah, Apr 2, 34; m 59; c 5. *Educ:* Univ Utah, BS, 56, PhD(ceramic eng), 62. *Prof Exp:* Mining engr trainee, US Smelting, Ref & Mining Co, 56. *Concurrent Pos:* Consult; Walter P Murphy Prof, 87. *Mem:* fel Am Ceramic Soc; Am Inst Mining, Metall & Petrol Engrs; Mat Res Soc; Am Powder Metall Inst. *Res:* Mechanisms of material transport in the sintering of oxides and metals; impurity effects in sintering; grain boundary diffusion in sintering; plasma and microwave processing of ceramics and ceramic composites; processing of high temperature superconductors. *Mailing Add:* 1231 Gregory Ave Wilmette IL 60091-3340

JOHNSON, DALE A, PHYSICAL CHEMISTRY, INORGANIC CHEMISTRY. *Current Pos:* From asst prof to assoc prof, 63-73, PROF CHEM, UNIV ARK, FAYETTEVILLE, 73- *Personal Data:* b Chicago, Ill, Nov 18, 37; m 60, Evelyn Venables; c Keith & Scott. *Educ:* Univ Ill, BS, 59; Northwestern Univ, PhD(chem), 64. *Mem:* Am Chem Soc. *Res:* Thermal and photochemical reactions of transition metal complexes; reactions of coordinated molecules; spectroscopy of inorganic compounds. *Mailing Add:* Dept Chem Univ Ark Fayetteville AR 72701-1202

JOHNSON, DALE E, TAXONOMY & EVOLUTION OF PLANTS, BIBLIOGRAPHY & HISTORY OF BOTANY. *Current Pos:* ED DIR, TIMBER PRESS INC, 91- *Personal Data:* b Griffith, Ind, Jan 26, 49; m 91, Marie E Meyer. *Educ:* Grinnell Col, AB, 71; Univ Calif, Berkeley, PhD(bot), 78. *Prof Exp:* Hunt fel, Hunt Inst Bot Doc, Carnegie Mellon Univ, 78-79; ed supvr & actg prod mgr, Academic Press Inc, 82-85; cur bot lit, Mo Bot Garden, 85-91. *Concurrent Pos:* Co-editor, Index to Plant Chromosome Numbers, Mo Bot Garden. *Mem:* Am Soc Plant Taxonomists; Int Asn Plant Taxon; Soc Hist Nat Hist; Bot Soc Am. *Res:* History and bibliography of botany; taxonomy and floristics of plants, especially Compositae. *Mailing Add:* Timber Press Inc Haseltine Bldg 133 SW Second Ave Suite 450 Portland OR 97204. *Fax:* 503-227-3070; *E-Mail:* dale@timber-press.com; web: www.timber-press.com

JOHNSON, DALE HOWARD, CONSUMER PRODUCT DEVELOPMENT, COSMETIC CHEMISTRY. *Current Pos:* RETIRED. *Personal Data:* b Los Angeles, Calif, Feb 23, 45; m 77; c 3. *Educ:* Univ Redlands, BS, 66; Northwestern Univ, PhD(org chem), 71. *Prof Exp:* Res chemist toiletries, Alberto-Culver Co, 71-73; sect head, Appln Lab, Armak Indust Chem, Div Akzona Inc, 73-77; mgr prod develop, Helene Curtis Indust Inc, 77-81; sect head oral hyg, Vicks Div Res, Richardson-Vicks Inc, 81-84; bus tech mgr, James River Corp, 85-87; sr group leader, Toiletries, Amway Corp, 88-90; mgr prod develop, Hair Care, Helen Curtis, Inc, 90-97. *Mem:* Am Chem Soc; Soc Cosmetic Chemists; Sigma Xi. *Res:* Development of personal care products including hair, skin, oral hygiene, cleansers, fine fragrances and treatment products; cosmetic, toiletries & over the counter topical drug type product development. *Mailing Add:* 1505 Lark Lane Naperville IL 60565-1342. *E-Mail:* daledoc@eart.link.net

JOHNSON, DALE RICHARD, cadmium transport across neonatal intestine; deceased, see previous edition for last biography

JOHNSON, DALE WALDO, food science, for more information see previous edition

JOHNSON, DALLAS EUGENE, data analysis, linear models; deceased, see previous edition for last biography

JOHNSON, DANIEL LLOYD, BIOGEOGRAPHY, INSECT ECOLOGY. *Current Pos:* RES SCIENTIST, AGR CAN RES STA, ALTA. *Personal Data:* b Yankton, SDak, Sept 30, 53; m, Pamela Martin; c Sam, Eric & Margaret. *Educ:* Univ Sask, BSc, 78; Univ BC, MSc, 80, PhD(plant sci), 83. *Honors & Awards:* C Gordon Hewitt Award in Can Entom, Entom Soc Can, 92; Issac Walton Killam Scholar. *Prof Exp:* Proj monitor, Can Int Develop Agency. *Concurrent Pos:* Adj assoc prof biogeog, Dept Geog, Univ Lethbridge, Alta; Proj mgr, Alberta Res Coun. *Mem:* Entomol Soc Can; Soc Environ Toxical Chem. *Res:* Ecology and control of grasshoppers attacking grassland, cereals and oilseed crops & non-target impacts of insecticides. *Mailing Add:* Agr Can Res Ctr Lethbridge AB T1J 4B1 Can. *Fax:* 403-382-3156; *E-Mail:* johnsondl@em.agr.ca

JOHNSON, DARELL JAMES, STATISTICAL MECHANICS, FLUIDS. *Current Pos:* ASST PROF PHYSICS & MATH, MO WESTERN STATE COL, 90- *Personal Data:* b Brooklyn, NY, Dec 22, 49; m 73; c 3. *Educ:* Univ Calif, Riverside, BS, 71, MS, 72, PhD(math), 73; Mass Inst Technol, PhD(physics), 86. *Prof Exp:* Instr math, Mass Inst Technol, 73-75; asst prof, NMex State Univ, 75-79; asst prof math, Tex Tech Univ, 86-90. *Mem:* Am Phys Soc; Am Math Soc; Soc Indust Appl Math; Am Astron Soc; AAAS. *Res:* Theoretical investigation of a strongly interacting many body model system using predominately numerical simulation experimental techniques. *Mailing Add:* 3015 Felix St Joseph MO 64501

JOHNSON, DAVID, HIGH ENERGY PHYSICS. *Current Pos:* PHYSICIST & UNIV RES ASSOC, FERMI NAT ACCELERATOR LAB, 73- *Personal Data:* b Newark, NJ, Sept 3, 44. *Educ:* Univ Calif, Berkeley, AB, 66; Iowa State Univ, PhD(high energy physics), 72. *Prof Exp:* Res assoc & instr physics, Iowa State Univ, Ames Lab, USAEC, 67-72, assoc & instr physics, 72-73. *Mem:* AAAS; Sigma Xi; Am Phys Soc. *Res:* High energy accelarator design and research; high energy experimental research. *Mailing Add:* Acceleration Div PO Box 500 Fermi Nat Accelerator Lab Batavia IL 60510

JOHNSON, DAVID ALFRED, PHYSICAL CHEMISTRY OF SOLUTIONS, EXPERIMENTAL & THEORETICAL STUDIES OF SOLIDS. *Current Pos:* PROF CHEM, SPRING ARBOR COL, 66- *Personal Data:* b Muskegon, Mich, Mar 13, 38; m 60; c 3. *Educ:* Greenville Col, AB, 60; La State Univ, PhD(chem), 66. *Prof Exp:* Chemist, Pet Milk Res Labs, summer 60; asst prof chem, Greenville Col, 62-64; instr, La State Univ, 64-65. *Concurrent Pos:* Fel, Dept Chem, La State Univ, 70-71; Am Chem Soc-PFR fel, 85 & 86; NASA fel & Nat Aerospace Serv Asn fel, 80-82; fac fel, Argonne Nat Lab, 90. *Mem:* Am Chem Soc; Sigma Xi. *Res:* Physical chemistry of electrolytes; five coordinate complexes of transition metals; thermodynamics of solid state. *Mailing Add:* Dept Chem Spring Arbor Col Spring Arbor MI 49283

JOHNSON, DAVID ANDREW, BIOCHEMISTRY, PROTEOLYTIC ENZYMES & THEIR INHIBITORS. *Current Pos:* from asst prof to assoc prof, 78-90, PROF BIOCHEM, JAMES H QUILLEN COL MED, 90- *Personal Data:* b Memphis, Tenn, May 27, 44; m 67, Judith Alice Moth; c Colin, Nicholas & Susannah. *Educ:* Memphis State Univ, BS, 67, PhD(chem),

73; Univ Ga, 73-76. *Prof Exp:* Asst biochemist, Univ Ga, 76-78. *Concurrent Pos:* Indust consult. *Mem:* AAAS; Am Soc Biochem & Molecular Biol; Sigma Xi; Protein Soc; Thoracic Soc. *Res:* Biochemistry; proteolytic enzymes and their inhibitors; mast cell proteases; human blood proteins. *Mailing Add:* Dept Biochem & Molecular Biol ETenn State Univ Col Med Johnson City TN 37614-0581

JOHNSON, DAVID B, DYNAMICS & CONTROL, FLUID FLOW SIMULATION. *Current Pos:* PROF SOUTHERN METHODIST UNIV, DALLAS, 83- *Personal Data:* b Big Spring, Tex, Jan 11, 40; m 62, Sara J Peters; c Jennifer L, William P & Molly K. *Educ:* Univ Tex, Austin, BSME, 63, MSME, 64; Stanford Univ, PhD(eng mech), 68. *Prof Exp:* Assoc prof mech eng, Southern Methodist Univ, 68-73; assoc prof eng sci & mech, Iowa State Univ, 75-81; exec vpres, J Y Taylor Mfg, 81-82. *Concurrent Pos:* Mem, NAm Die Casting Asn. *Mem:* Am Soc Mech Engrs; Am Soc Eng Educ; Soc Mfg Engrs; Soc Plastics Engrs. *Res:* Dynamics; vibrations; machine control; free surface; fluid flow simulation. *Mailing Add:* 2806 Colleen Dr Garland TX 75043

JOHNSON, DAVID BARTON, BIO-ORGANIC CHEMISTRY, BIO-ANALYTICAL CHEMISTRY. *Current Pos:* RES SCIENTIST II, UPJOHN CO, 80- *Personal Data:* b Providence, RI, June 5, 46; m 70; c 3. *Educ:* Univ RI, BS, 69; Duke Univ, PhD(org chem), 75. *Prof Exp:* NIH fel biochem pharmacol, Med Sch, Duke Univ, 74-76; sr chemist bio-org chem, Midwest Res Inst, 76-80. *Mem:* Am Chem Soc; Sigma Xi. *Res:* Bio-organic chemistry dealing in the synthesis, biosynthesis, analysis, and structural elucidation of xenobiotic metabolites; analysis of metabolites in biological samples; in vitro studies of xenobiotic metabolizing enzymes; radiochemical synthesis. *Mailing Add:* 3099 Maine Ave Perry OH 44081-9566

JOHNSON, DAVID EDSEL, ELECTRICAL ENGINEERING, APPLIED MATHEMATICS. *Current Pos:* RETIRED. *Personal Data:* b Chatham, La, Aug 16, 27; m 59, Frances White; c Stephen, Nancy, Sandra & Katherine. *Educ:* La Tech Univ, BS & BA, 49; Auburn Univ, MS, 52, PhD(math), 68. *Prof Exp:* Draftsman, La Power & Light Co, 49-50; mathematician, Nat Bur Stand, 52; assoc prof math, 54-62, prof elec eng, LA State Univ, 62-83; prof math, Birmingham-Southern Col, 83-94. *Concurrent Pos:* NSF fac fel, Stanford Univ, 61-62. *Mem:* Sigma Xi. *Res:* Electric circuits and systems. *Mailing Add:* Div Sci & Math Birmingham-Southern Col Birmingham AL 35254

JOHNSON, DAVID GREGORY, ENDOCRINOLOGY, CLINICAL PHARMACOLOGY. *Current Pos:* assoc prof, 78-82, PROF, DEPT INTERNAL MED, HEALTH SCI CTR, UNIV ARIZ, 82- *Personal Data:* b Belvidere, Ill, July 11, 40; m 65, Inger Soderlund; c Elisabeth, Lars & Leif. *Educ:* Yale Univ, BA, 62; Dartmouth Med Sch, BMed Sci, 64; Harvard Univ, MD, 67. *Prof Exp:* Resident, Univ Calif, San Francisco, 67-69; res assoc, NIH, 69-71; fel, Univ Wash, 71-73, from asst prof to assoc prof, 73-78. *Concurrent Pos:* Assoc ed, Life Sci, 81- *Mem:* Am Diabetes Asn; Am Soc Pharmacol & Exp Therapeut; Endocrine Soc; Am Fedn Clin Res. *Res:* Experimental and clinical research regarding diabetes, pancreatic endocrine secretion, gastro intestinal hormones and catecholamine physiology; development and testing of drugs, particularly for the treatment of diabetes. *Mailing Add:* Dept Internal Med Univ Ariz Health Sci Ctr 1501 N Campbell Ave Tucson AZ 85724. *Fax:* 520-626-8110; *E-Mail:* djohnson@u.arizona.edu

JOHNSON, DAVID HARLEY, HEAT TRANSFER, FLUID MECHANICS. *Current Pos:* PRIN ENGR, SOLAR ENERGY RES INST, 79-, GROUP MGR, 80- *Personal Data:* b Brooklyn, NY, May 31, 41; m 61; c 2. *Educ:* Purdue Univ, BS, 63, MS, 64; Cornell Univ, PhD(appl physics), 75. *Prof Exp:* Staff mem, Sandia Corp, 64-67; adj instr hydraul, Tompkins-Cortland Community Col, 69-70; teaching asst statist thermodyn, Cornell Univ, 70-72; sr staff physicist, Appl Physics Lab, Johns Hopkins Univ, 73-79, asst group leader, 78-79. *Concurrent Pos:* Consult, Appl Physics Lab, Johns Hopkins Univ, 79-80 & Flow Industs Inc, 81- *Mem:* Am Soc Mech Engrs; Sigma Xi. *Res:* Dynamics of stratified fluids in the ocean and in solar ponds; direct contact heat transfer phenomena important to the design of open-cycle thermal energy conversion power plants and other heat exchangers. *Mailing Add:* 9658 Masterworks Dr Vienna VA 22181-6131

JOHNSON, DAVID LEE, SOFTWARE SYSTEMS. *Current Pos:* eng orgn mgr, 88-90, dept prog mgr, 90-93, PROG MGR, GTE GOVT SYSTS, 93- *Personal Data:* b Benson, Minn, Apr 28, 46; m 76; c 1. *Educ:* Univ Minn, BS, 64; Syracuse Univ, MS, 71; Univ Minn, PhD(math), 76. *Prof Exp:* John Wesley Young res instr, Dartmouth Col, 76-78; Asst prof math, Univ Southern Calif, 78-80 & Univ Ark, 80-81; sr mem tech staff, El Segundo, 81-84; asst dept mgr, Radar Systs Group, 84-85; dept mgr, Hughes Aircraft Co, 85-86; dept software eng mgr, Rockville, 86-87; dept mgr, Nat Ctr Systs Directorate, 87-88. *Concurrent Pos:* mem tech staff, Logicon Inc, 80-81. *Mem:* Am Math Soc; Math Asn Am; Inst Elec & Electronics Engrs. *Res:* Functional analysis dealing with distribution theory; continuous group representations on general locally compact groups. *Mailing Add:* 3303 Lowman N 3303 Lowman Lane Union Bridge MD 21791-9046

JOHNSON, DAVID LINTON, THEORETICAL SOLID STATE PHYSICS. *Current Pos:* res physicist, 79-88, SCI ADV, SCHLUMBERGER DOLL RES CTR, 88- *Personal Data:* b Chicago, Ill, July 9, 45; div, W Kathy Martin; c 2. *Educ:* Univ Notre Dame, BS, 67; Univ Chicago, MS, 69, PhD(physics), 74. *Prof Exp:* Fel physics, Michelson Lab, Naval Weapons Ctr, 72-74; fel, Ames Lab, Iowa State Univ, 74-76; asst prof physics, Northeastern Univ, 76-79. *Concurrent Pos:* Consult, GTE Labs, 79. *Mem:* fel Am Phys Soc; Acoust Soc Am; Soc Exp Geol; Am Geophys Union. *Mailing Add:* Schlumberger Doll Res Ctr Old Quarry Rd Ridgefield CT 06877-4108. *E-Mail:* djohnson@ridgefield.sdr.slb.com

JOHNSON, DAVID M, BOTANY. *Current Pos:* asst prof, 89-94, ASSOC PROF BOT-MICROBIOL, OHIO WELEYAN UNIV, 94- *Personal Data:* b Conway, Ark, Dec 3, 55. *Educ:* Hendricks Col, BA, 78; Univ Mich, MS, 81, PhD(bot), 85. *Prof Exp:* Res asst, NY Bot Garden, 86-89. *Concurrent Pos:* Fulbright scholar, Univ Dares Salaam, Tanzinia, 96. *Mem:* Am Soc Plant Taxonomists (secy, 93); Int Asn Plant Taxonomists; Am Fern Soc. *Mailing Add:* Dept Bot-Microbiol Ohio Wesleyan Univ Delaware OH 43015. *Fax:* 614-368-3999; *E-Mail:* dmjohnson@cc.owu.edu

JOHNSON, DAVID NORSEEN, BEHAVIORAL & DEVELOPMENTAL DRUG ABUSE RESEARCH. *Current Pos:* PHARMACOLOGIST, NAT INST DRUG ABUSE, 90- *Personal Data:* b Bronx, NY, Sept 28, 38; m 60, Carolyn J Svenson; c Lauren D & Brian D. *Educ:* North Park Col, BS, 60; Univ Louisville, MS, 66; Med Col Va, PhD(neuropharmacol), 75. *Prof Exp:* Res assoc neuropharmacol, A H Robbins Res Inst, 66-68, sr res assoc, 68-76, mgr, 76-90. *Concurrent Pos:* Affil adj prof, Dept Psychol, Va Commonwealth Univ, 83-86, assoc res prof, 87-90. *Mem:* Am Soc Pharmacol & Exp Therapeut; Soc Neurosci; Am Chem Soc. *Res:* Aspects of cocaine abuse, including self-administration models, developmental and teratogenic models; gene expression effects. *Mailing Add:* Div Basic Res Nat Inst Drug Abuse 5600 Fishers Lane Rm 10A-19 Rockville MD 20857-0001. *Fax:* 301-594-6043; *E-Mail:* djohnso1@adada.ssw.dhhs.gov

JOHNSON, DAVID RUSSELL, PHYSICAL CHEMISTRY. *Current Pos:* proj liaison leader, Petrochemicals-AED, 85-88, SR RES ASSOC, DU PONT CHEM, FREON RES & DEVELOP, E I DU PONT DE NEMOURS & CO INC, WILMINGTON, DEL, 88- *Personal Data:* b Manaus, Brazil, Oct 23, 45; m 67; c 2. *Educ:* Austin Col, BA, 67; Tex Christian Univ, PhD(chem), 70. *Prof Exp:* Fel radiation chem, Baylor Univ, 70-72 & Univ Fla, 72-73; res chemist textile fibers, E I du Pont de Nemours & Co Inc, Waynesboro, Va, 73-75; res chemist separations chem, 75-78, staff chemist, 78-79; res supvr anal chem, 79-81; res supvr hydrogen technol, Savannah River Lab, 81-82; chief supvr tritium technol, 82-84; tech supt pretrochemicals, Cape Fear Plant, 84-85. *Mem:* Am Chem Soc. *Res:* Plutonium soil migration studies; environmental dose-to-man modelling methods; uranium fuel fabrication methods; chemical separations processes for nuclear fuel recycle and waste management programs; process development for CFC alternatives. *Mailing Add:* 1803 Streamside Dr Friendswood TX 77546

JOHNSON, DAVID SIMONDS, METEOROLOGY. *Current Pos:* RETIRED. *Personal Data:* b Porterville, Calif, June 29, 24; wid. *Educ:* Univ Calif, Los Angeles, AB, 48, MA, 49. *Honors & Awards:* Gold Medal, Dept Com, 65; Except Serv Medal, NASA, 66; Fed Career Serv Award for Sustained Excellence, Nat Civil Serv League, 74; William T Pecora Award, NASA & Dept Interior, 78; US Presidential Meritorious Exec Award, 80; Achievement Award, Am Astronaut Soc, 81, Lovelace Award, 92; Brooks Award, Am Meteorol Soc, 82; Silver Medal, Dept Com, 85; Group Award, Nat Res Coun, 87. *Prof Exp:* Meteorol aid, US Weather Bur, 46-47; asst meteorol, Univ Calif, Los Angeles, 48-52; assoc meteorologist, Pineapple Res Inst, Honolulu, Hawaii, 52-56; chief, Observ Test & Develop Ctr, US Weather Bur, 56-58, asst chief, Meterol Satellite Lab, 58-60, chief, 60-62, from dep dir to dir, Nat Weather Satellite Ctr, 62-65, dir, Nat Environ Satellite Ctr, Environ Sci Serv Admin, 65-70; dir, Nat Environ Satellite Serv, 70-80, asst admin satellites, Nat Oceanic & Atmospheric Admin, 80-82; spec asst to pres, Univ Corp Atmospheric Res, 82-83; pres, Damar Int, Inc, 84-86; study dir, Nat Res Coun, 86-90. *Concurrent Pos:* Consult to secy gen, World Meteorol Orgn, 82-86; vol adv, Nat Weather Serv Modernization Comt, Nat Res Coun, 94- *Mem:* AAAS; fel Am Meteorol Soc (pres, 74); fel Am Geophys Union; Int Acad Astronaut; Sigma Xi; assoc fel Am Inst Aeronaut & Astronaut; fel Am Astronaut Soc. *Res:* Meteorological instruments and observing techniques; environmental satellites. *Mailing Add:* 1133 Lake Heron Dr Apt 3A Annapolis MD 21403. *E-Mail:* dsjohnsn@nas.edu

JOHNSON, DAVID STIFLER, COMPUTER SCIENCE, MATHEMATICS. *Current Pos:* Tech staff, 93-88, head, Math Found Comput Dept, 88-95, DEPT HEAD, AT&T BELL LABS, 95- *Personal Data:* b Washington, DC, Dec 9, 45; m 69. *Educ:* Amherst Col, BA, 67; Mass Inst Technol, SM, 68, PhD(math), 73. *Honors & Awards:* Lanchester Prize, Inst Opers Res & Mgt Sci, 79. *Concurrent Pos:* Vis prof, Comput Sci Dept, Univ Wis, 80-81. *Mem:* Fel Asn Comput Mach; Soc Indust & Appl Math. *Res:* Design and analysis of algorithms; concrete complexity theory; deterministic scheduling theory; applications of combinatorial mathematics. *Mailing Add:* AT&T Res Labs 180 Park Ave Rm C239 Florham Park NJ 07932-0971. *Fax:* 973-360-8178; *E-Mail:* dsj@research.att.com

JOHNSON, DAVID W, JR, CERAMIC PROCESSING, ELECTRONIC CERAMICS. *Current Pos:* supvr, 84-88, DEPT HEAD, BELL LABS, 88- *Personal Data:* b Windber, Pa, Sept 23, 42; m 64; c Analee J & Bradley D. *Educ:* Pa State Univ, BS, 64, PhD(ceramic sci), 68. *Honors & Awards:* Ross Coffin Purdy Award, Am Ceramic Soc, 81 & Fulroth Award, 84; Taylor lectr, Pa State Univ, 87, Nat Acad Eng, 93. *Prof Exp:* Mem tech staff, Bell Tel Labs, 68-83. *Concurrent Pos:* Adj prof mat sci, Stevens Inst Technol, 82- *Mem:* Nat Acad Eng; Am Ceramic Soc (vpres, 90-92, treas, 92-93, pres elect, 93-94); AAAS; Am Soc Metals; Mat Res Soc; Metall Soc. *Res:* Dielectric relaxation in doped strontium titanate; characterization of fine oxide particles; magnetic ceramics; ionic conductors; sol gel glasses; oxide superconductors. *Mailing Add:* Bell Labs Rm 1F-206 Box 636 Murray Hill NJ 07974. *E-Mail:* dwj@bell-labs.com

JOHNSON, DAVID WILLIS, FOOD PRODUCTS. *Current Pos:* PRES, CHIEF EXEC OFFICER & DIR, CAMPBELL SOUP CO, 90- *Personal Data:* b Tumut, Australia, Aug 7, 32; m 66, Sylvia Raymonde Wells; c David Ashley Lawrence, Justin Christopher Kendall & Harley Alista Kent. *Educ:* Univ Sydney, B econs, 54, dipl educ, 55; Univ Chicago, MBA, 58. *Prof Exp:* Exec trainee, Ford Motor Co, Australia; mgt trainee, Colgate-Palmolive, Sydney, 59-60, prod mgr, 61, asst to managing dir, 62, brands mgr, 63, gen prod mgr, 64-65, asst gen mgr & mktg dir, 66, chmn & managing dir, 67-72; pres, Warner-Lambert/Parke Davis Asia, 73-76; pres, Personal Prod Div, Warner Lambert Co, Morris Plains, NJ, 77, pres, Am Chicle Div, 78, pres specialty foods group, 80-81, vpres, 80-82; exec vpres & gen mgr, Entenmann's Div, Warner-Lambert Co, Bayshore, NY, 79, pres & chief exec officer, 82; pres & chief exec officer, Entenmann's Inc & Gen Foods Corp, 82-87; chmn, pres & chief exec officer, Gerber Prod Co, 87-89, chmn & chief exec officer, 89-90. *Concurrent Pos:* Mem bd dirs, Colgate-Palmolive Co; adv coun, Univ Notre Dame Col Bus Admin; chmn bd, Campbell Soup Co, 93. *Mem:* Am Bakers Asn; Grocery Mfrs Am. *Mailing Add:* Campbell Soup Co World Hq Campbell Pl Camden NJ 08103-1799

JOHNSON, DELWIN PHELPS, analytical chemistry; deceased, see previous edition for last biography

JOHNSON, DENNIS DUANE, NEUROSCIENCES. *Current Pos:* From asst prof to assoc prof, 66-75, head, Dept Pharmacol, 86-92, PROF PHARMACOL, UNIV SASK, 75-, ASST DEAN, COL MED, 81-, ASSOC VPRES RES, 92- *Personal Data:* b Can, Mar 11, 38; c 4. *Educ:* Univ Sask, BSP, 60, MSc, 62; Univ Wash, PhD(pharmacol), 65. *Concurrent Pos:* Lectr pharmacol, Univ Sask, 65 66; counr, Med Res Coun Can, 87-; mem adv comt, Pharmaceut Mfrs Asn Can, 88-; bd dirs, Med Res Coun Can, 87-92, Sask Res Coun, 92, VIDO, 92, Nat Res Coun Plant Biotechnology Inst, 92, Royal Soc Eval Unit, 92, Ag-West Biotechnology, 92, Univ Sask Technol, Inc, 92. *Mem:* Nat Cancer Inst Can; Am Soc Neurosci; Am Soc Pharmacol & Exp Therapeut; Pharmacol Soc Can. *Res:* Pharamcology and biochemistry of epilepsy; neurochemistry of neuropharmacology. *Mailing Add:* Univ Sask Kirk Hall Rm 217 117 Science Pl Saskatoon SK S7N 5C8 Can

JOHNSON, DEWAYNE CARL, PHYSICS. *Current Pos:* asst prof, 65-69, ASSOC PROF PHYSICS, UNIV WIS-MILWAUKEE, 70- *Personal Data:* b Minneapolis, Minn, Sept 15, 35. *Educ:* Univ Minn, Minneapolis, BS, 57, MS, 60, PhD(elec eng), 63. *Prof Exp:* Mem tech staff physics, Bell Tel Labs, 64-65. *Mem:* Am Phys Soc. *Res:* Low energy electron diffraction. *Mailing Add:* Dept Physics Univ Wis Milwaukee WI 53201

JOHNSON, DEWEY, JR, BIOCHEMISTRY, NUTRITION. *Current Pos:* RETIRED. *Personal Data:* b Sapulpa, Okla, Sept 23, 26; m 53, Patricia R; c Joseph, Paul, Mary Anne (Crane) & Richard E. *Educ:* Colo State Univ, BS, 50; Univ Conn, MS, 55; Rutgers Univ, PhD, 58; Nat Registry Clin Chemists. *Prof Exp:* Asst poultry nutrit, Rutgers Univ, 55-58; assoc animal nutrit, Lime Crest Res Lab, Limestone Prod Corp Am, NJ, 58-62; nutritionist, Food & Drug Res Lab, 62-63; biochemist, Equitable Live Assurance Soc US, New York, 63-68, dir clin lab, 68-79; supv anal chemist, Metrop Life Ins Co, NY, 81-89, underwriter, 89-92. *Concurrent Pos:* Chemist, Environ Protection Agency. *Mem:* Am Soc Animal Sci; Am Dairy Sci Asn; Poultry Sci Asn. *Res:* Metabolism of amino acids; metabolism of drugs; biochemical changes in alcoholism; automated clinical chemistry techniques; folic acid and vitamin B12 metabolism; extraction and detection of pesticides. *Mailing Add:* 12 Barbara Pl Edison NJ 08817

JOHNSON, DIANNA AMMONS, NEUROBIOLOGY. *Current Pos:* PROF & DIR RES, DEPT OPHTHAL & DEPT ANAT & NEUROBIOL, UNIV TENN, MEMPHIS, 96- *Personal Data:* b Many, La, Oct 21, 43; m 65; c 1. *Educ:* Centenary Col, BS, 64; Univ Kans, PhD(neurobiol), 72. *Hon Degrees:* DSc, Centenary Col, 96. *Honors & Awards:* Distinguished Prof Women's Award, Univ Tex, Houston, 96. *Prof Exp:* Fel psychobiol, Univ Calif, Irvine, 72-74; from asst prof to prof neurobiol, Med Sch, Univ Tex, Houston, 74-96, asst dean res training, 88-96. *Mem:* Asn Res Vision Opthal; Soc Neurosci; Neurochem Soc; Soc Cell Biol; Am Soc Biol Chem; Asn Women in Sci; fel AAAS; Int Soc Develop Neurosci. *Res:* The nature of chemical transmission in neuronal tissue; mechanisms of neurotransmitter release, identification of functional neurotransmitters, modulation of chemical transmission by intrinsic and extrinsic factors; development of in vitro techniques for biochemical analysis of neurotransmitter systems; neurochemistry of the retina. *Mailing Add:* Univ Tenn Link Bldg Rm 530 855 Monroe Ave Memphis TN 38163

JOHNSON, DONAL DABELL, SOILS, MICROBIOLOGY. *Current Pos:* RETIRED. *Personal Data:* b Rigby, Idaho, July 20, 22; m 45; c 3. *Educ:* Brigham Young Univ, BS, 48; Cornell Univ, MS, 50, PhD(soils), 52. *Prof Exp:* Asst agron, Cornell Univ, 48-51; from asst prof to assoc prof agron, Colo State Univ, 52-62, coordr, Nigeria Proj, 64-69, dean, Col Agr Sci, 68-87, assoc & dep dir, Exp Sta, 69-87. *Concurrent Pos:* Trustee & chmn, Consortium Int Develop, 74-; chmn, Great Plains Agr Coun, 77. *Mem:* Sigma Xi; Fel AAAS; Am Soc Agron; Soil Sci Soc Am. *Res:* Nitrogen transformations in soil. *Mailing Add:* 1812 Orchard Pl Ft Collins CO 80521

JOHNSON, DONALD CHARLES, ENDOCRINOLOGY. *Current Pos:* from asst prof to prof, 63-96, res prof human reproduction, 78-96, EMER PROF OBSTET, GYNEC & PHYSIOL, SCH MED, UNIV KANS, 96- *Personal Data:* b Black River Falls, Wis, Jan 30, 27; m 52, Eleanore J Latuvnik; c 1. *Educ:* Univ Wis, BS, 49; Univ Iowa, MS, 50, PhD(zool), 56. *Prof Exp:* Asst zool, Univ Iowa, 53-56, res assoc, 56-58, res asst prof, 59-63.
Mem: AAAS; Endocrine Soc; Am Physiol Soc; Soc Gynec Invest; Soc Study Reprod; Sigma Xi. *Res:* Reproductive physiology and endocrinology; comparative physiology of gonadotrophins; control gonadal steroidogenic enzymes; reproductive toxicology. *Mailing Add:* Dept Obstet & Gynec Univ Kans Med Ctr Kansas City KS 66160. *Fax:* 913-588-5677; *E-Mail:* djohnsol@kumc.edu

JOHNSON, DONALD CURTIS, ORGANIC CHEMISTRY. *Current Pos:* scientific specialist fiber chem, 77-82, sci adv, 82-90, SR SCI ADV, WEYERHAEUSER CO, 90- *Personal Data:* b Minneapolis, Minn, Mar 21, 35; m 56; c 3. *Educ:* Hamline Univ, BS, 57; Univ Minn, PhD(org chem), 62. *Prof Exp:* Res aide org chem, Inst Paper Chem, 61-67, res assoc & chmn dept chem, 67-77, prof org chem, 70-77. *Concurrent Pos:* Chmn, Gordon Res Conf Chem & Physics of Paper, 72-74; co-ed, J Wood Chem & Technol, 81. *Mem:* Am Chem Soc; Tech Asn Pulp & Paper Indust. *Res:* Cellulose chemistry, including reactions in solution and mechanisms of chain degradation; lignin chemistry, particularly delignification processes with selective oxidants; bacterial cellulose production and applications. *Mailing Add:* 33936 134th Ave SE Auburn WA 98092

JOHNSON, DONALD ELWOOD, COMPUTER SCIENCE, SOFTWARE SYSTEMS. *Current Pos:* from instr to assoc prof, NCent Col, 61-78, chairperson math, 69-73 & 75-78, prof math, 78-82, chairperson, Div Natural Sci & Math, 78-83, prof & chairperson comput sci, 82-88, prof comput sci, 82-94, PROF MATH & COMPUT SCI, NCENT COL, 94- *Personal Data:* b Joliet, Ill, July 23, 35; m 56; c 2. *Educ:* NCent Col, BA, 57; Univ Wis-Madison, MS, 59; Ill Inst Technol, PhD(math), 73. *Prof Exp:* Asst mathematician, Argonne Nat Lab, 59-61. *Mem:* Math Asn Am; Inst Elec & Electronics Engrs Comput Soc; Am Asn Univ Prof. *Mailing Add:* 405 Forrest Ave Naperville IL 60540. *E-Mail:* dej@nccseq.noctrl.edu

JOHNSON, DONALD EUGENE, ANIMAL NUTRITION. *Current Pos:* assoc prof, 72-80, PROF ANIMAL SCI & NUTRIT & DIR METAB LAB, COLO STATE UNIV, FOOTHILLS CAMPUS, 80- *Personal Data:* b Sykeston, NDak, Nov 17, 38; m 61; c 3. *Educ:* NDak State Univ, BS, 60, MS, 63; Colo State Univ, PhD(animal nutrit), 66. *Honors & Awards:* Brody Mem Lectr; Blankenbaker Lectr. *Prof Exp:* Res asst animal nutrit, NDak State Univ, 61-63 & Colo State Univ, 63-66; res assoc, Cornell Univ, 66-68; asst prof ruminant nutrit, Univ Ill, Urbana, 68-72. *Mem:* AAAS; Am Soc Animal Sci. *Res:* Animal energy metabolism; metabolic rat variation; rumen function; body composition; methane emissions. *Mailing Add:* 209 Animal Sci Colo State Univ Ft Collins CO 80523. *Fax:* 770-491-5326; *E-Mail:* djohnson@ceres.agsci.colostate.edu

JOHNSON, DONALD GLEN, MATHEMATICS. *Current Pos:* from assoc prof to prof, 65-88, EMER PROF MATH, NMEX STATE UNIV, 88- *Personal Data:* b Detroit, Mich, Jan 29, 31; m 75, Patricia Traynor; c Randall, Edyth & Claudia. *Educ:* Albion Col, AB, 53; Mich State Univ, MS, 57; Purdue Univ, PhD(math), 59. *Prof Exp:* From asst prof to assoc prof math, Pa State Univ, 59-65. *Mem:* Am Math Soc; Math Asn Am; Nat Coun Teachers Math. *Res:* Lattice ordered rings; rings of continuous functions. *Mailing Add:* PO Box 1134 Glen Rock NJ 07452. *E-Mail:* john597@ibm.net

JOHNSON, DONALD L(EE), METALLURGICAL ENGINEERING. *Current Pos:* assoc prof metall, 63-75, PROF MECH ENG, METALL PROG, UNIV NEBR, LINCOLN, 75- *Personal Data:* b Denver, Colo, Feb 19, 27; m 47; c 4. *Educ:* Colo Sch Mines, MetE, 50, MS, 56; Univ Nebr, Lincoln, PhD(chem eng), 69. *Prof Exp:* Trainee, Allis Chalmers Mfg Co, 50-51; metall engr, Mine & Smelter Supply Co, 53-56; asst prof metall eng, Wash State Univ, 56-59; sr metallurgist, NAm Rockwell Corp, 60-63. *Concurrent Pos:* Consult, Brunswick Corp, 69-; Univ Nebr Res Coun-NASA-Ames Res Ctr fel, Univ Nebr, Lincoln, 71-72. *Mem:* Am Soc Metals; Nat Asn Corrosion Engrs. *Res:* Gas-metal equilibria; hydrogen transport in metallic alloys; polarization analysis of corrosion in aqueous systems; leaching kinetics. *Mailing Add:* 13 Samuel Clemens Rd Muscatine IA 52761-8769

JOHNSON, DONALD LEE, CHEMICAL ENGINEERING, POLYMER & CARBOHYDRATE CHEMISTRY. *Current Pos:* vpres res & develop, 89-96, VPRES DISCOVERY RES, GRAIN PROCESSING CORP, 96- *Personal Data:* b Aurora, Ill, Mar 9, 35; m 60, Virginia A Wesoloski; c 4. *Educ:* Univ Ill, Urbana, BS, 62; Wash Univ, DSc(chem eng), 66. *Prof Exp:* Res engr, Eng Res Dept, A E Staley Mfg Co, 65-67, group leader, Spec Prod Develop Dept, 67-70, Indust Prod Dept, 70-75, dir, Indust Prod Res & Develop Dept, 75-80, dir chem renewable resources, 80-87. *Mem:* Nat Acad Eng; Am Inst Chem Engrs; Tech Asn Pulp & Paper Industs; Am Asn Cereal Chemists; Sigma Xi; Am Chem Soc; Inst Food Technologists. *Res:* Physical chemistry of surfaces; polymer engineering as applied to paper, film and foil converting; biochemical engineering; biomass utilization; business assessment of biomass utilization plan, organize and direct product development; commercialize products, and develop strategies for biomass utilization in agriculture, chemical, and industrial commerce. *Mailing Add:* Dept Res & Develop Grain Processing Corp 1600 Oregon St Muscatine IA 52761. *Fax:* 319-264-4130

JOHNSON, DONALD R, METEOROLOGY. *Current Pos:* From proj asst to proj assoc, Univ Wis-Madison, 59-64, from asst prof to assoc prof, 64-66, prof, 70-, chmn dept, 73-76, assoc dir, Space Sci & Eng Ctr, 77-, EMER PROF METEOROL, UNIV WIS-MADISON. *Personal Data:* b McPherson, Kans, Apr 1, 30; m 53; c 3. *Educ:* Bethany Col, BS, 52; Univ Wash, BS, 53; Univ Wis, MS, 60, PhD(meteorol), 65. *Concurrent Pos:* Vis assoc prof, Pa State Univ, 68-69; chief ed, Monthly Weather Review, 77-80. *Mem:* Nat

Weather Asn; Am Meteorol Soc; Am Geophys Union. *Res:* Dynamic climatology and meteorology; secondary and general circulation studies. *Mailing Add:* Dept Atmospheric Ocean & Space Sci Bldg Univ Wis 1225 W Dayton St Madison WI 53706-1612

JOHNSON, DONALD RALPH, VERTEBRATE ECOLOGY. *Current Pos:* assoc prof, 68-75, PROF BIOL, UNIV IDAHO, 75- *Personal Data:* b Newport, Wash, Aug 18, 31; m 55; c 3. *Educ:* Univ Idaho, BS, 53, MS, 58; Colo State Univ, PhD(wildlife ecol), 62. *Prof Exp:* From asst prof to assoc prof biol, Ft Lewis Col, 61-65; assoc prof, Minot State Col, 65-68. *Mem:* Am Soc Mammal; Sigma Xi. *Res:* Small mammal ecology; effects of 2, 4-D on rodent food habits; energy relations of pikas; diets of sympatric lizards; osprey ecology. *Mailing Add:* Dept Biol Sci Univ Idaho 375 S Line St Moscow ID 83843-4140

JOHNSON, DONALD REX, MOLECULAR SPECTROSCOPY, RADIO ASTRONOMY. *Current Pos:* DIR, NAT MEASUREMENT LAB & TECHNOL SERV, NAT INST STAND & TECHNOL, 90-; DIR, NAT TECH INFO SERV. *Personal Data:* b Tacoma, Wash, July 19, 38; m 59; c 2. *Educ:* Univ Puget Sound, BS, 60, Univ Idaho, MS, 62; Univ Okla, PhD(physics), 67. *Prof Exp:* Physicist, Nat Bur Stand, 67-76, prog analyst, 76-78, dep dir progs, 78-80, dep dir resources & opers, 80-82, actg dir, Nat Measurements Lab, 82-90. *Concurrent Pos:* Technol mgt, technol transfer, state and local economic develop. *Mem:* Am Phys Soc; Am Astron Soc; AAAS; Am Soc Testing & Mat; Int Astron Union. *Res:* Molecular radio astronomy; microwave spectroscopy of free radicals and transient chemical species in the gas phase. *Mailing Add:* Nat Tech Info Serv Forbes Bldg No 200 Springfield VA 22161

JOHNSON, DONALD RICHARD, CLINICAL CHEMISTRY, POLYMER SCIENCE. *Current Pos:* res chemist, Polychem Dept, Res & Develop Div, Du Pont, 53-59, res suprv, 59-62, prod mgr, Instrument Prod Div, 62-65, res mgr, 65-71, mgr res & eng, Photo Prod Dept, 71-74, mgr, New Prod Scouting Res Div, 75-80, dir new prod res & develop clin systs, 80-83, dir new technol res, Diag & Biores Prod Div, Du Pont Biomed Prod Dept, 83-86, CONSULT, NEW PROD RES & DEVELOP, DU PONT, 86-; PRES, TECHNOL CONVERSION, 86- *Personal Data:* b Duluth, Minn, Jan 15, 29; m 56; c 2. *Educ:* Univ Minn, BA, 49; Univ Wis, PhD(anal chem), 54. *Honors & Awards:* IR-100 Award, Automatic Clin Anal, 79, Automated Sample Processor, Du Pont, 79; DuPont Lavoisier Medal, 93. *Prof Exp:* Chemist, Mat Packaging Sect, Forest Prod Lab, USDA, 52-53. *Concurrent Pos:* Chmn, Gordon Res Conf Anal Chem, 77; Du Pont Corp Planning Group Life Sci Res, 80-81; chmn, Indust Adv Bd, Ctr Biopolymers at Interfaces, Dept Bioeng, Univ Utah; bd dirs, Antivirals, Inc. *Mem:* AAAS; Am Chem Soc; Sigma Xi; Am Asn Clin Chemists. *Res:* Chemical instrumentation; thermal analysis; clinical, analytical, physical and polymer chemistry; infrared spectroscopy; immunodiagnostics and biomaterials; antisense therapeutics; DNA probes. *Mailing Add:* 1005 S Hilton Rd Wilmington DE 19803

JOHNSON, DONALD ROSS, urban entomology, mosquito control, for more information see previous edition

JOHNSON, DONALD W, veterinary medicine, for more information see previous edition

JOHNSON, DONALD W, AERONAUTICS. *Honors & Awards:* Aerodyn Decelerator Syst Award, Am Inst Aeronaut & Astronaut, 91. *Mailing Add:* 29561 S 585 Rd Grove OK 74344-7832

JOHNSON, DONOVAN EARL, MICROBIOLOGY, BIOCHEMISTRY. *Current Pos:* From res asst to res assoc microbiol, 66-74, proj leader microbiol, Northern Regional Res Lab, 74-81, RES MICROBIOLOGIST, US GRAIN MKT RES LAB, AGR RES SERV, USDA, 81- *Personal Data:* b Holdrege, Nebr, June 26, 42; m 65; c 2. *Educ:* Univ Nebr, BS, 64, MS, 66; Univ Wis-Madison, PhD(microbiol), 72. *Concurrent Pos:* Adj prof chem, Bradley Univ, 74. *Mem:* Sigma Xi; Am Soc Microbiol; Soc Invert Path. *Res:* Biological insecticides; microbiology of insect pathogens; physiology of bacterial sporulation. *Mailing Add:* 1515 College Ave Manhattan KS 66502. *Fax:* 785-537-5584; *E-Mail:* johnson@usgmrl.ksu.edu

JOHNSON, DOUGLAS ALLAN, PLANT PHYSIOLOGY, RANGE ECOLOGY. *Current Pos:* PLANT PHYSIOLOGIST RANGE PLANT IMPROV, FORAGE & RANGE RES LAB, AGR RES SERV, USDA, 76- *Personal Data:* b Montevideo, Minn, Dec 6, 49; m 72; c 3. *Educ:* Augustana Col, SDak, BA, 71; Utah State Univ, MS, 73, PhD(range ecol), 75. *Honors & Awards:* Outstanding Achievement Award, Soc Range Mgr, 96. *Prof Exp:* Res asst tundra plant water rel, Dept Range Sci, Utah State Univ, 71-75; res assoc, Dept Biol, Augustana Col, 75- *Concurrent Pos:* NSF grant, 75-76, USDA grant, 79-81, US-Spain grant, 84-88; Nat Defense Educ Act fel, 71-73; Commonwealth Sci & Indust Res Orgn Australia vis scientist award, 81-82; USDA-Coop State Res Serv grant, 85-88, 87-89 & 92-95; grant, Western Regional IPM, 85-88, USDA-OICD, 91 & 93. *Mem:* Crop Sci Soc Am; fel Am Soc Agron; Soc Range Mgt. *Res:* Development of superior forage plants for the Intermountain West of US; defining physiological basis of range legumes resistance to drought stress; nitrogen fixation in range legumes. *Mailing Add:* USDA-ARS Forage & Range Res Lab Utah State Univ Logan UT 84322-6300. *Fax:* 435-797-3075; *E-Mail:* daj@cc.usu.edu

JOHNSON, DOUGLAS L, chemical engineering, for more information see previous edition

JOHNSON, DOUGLAS WILLIAM, REMOTE SENSING, ATMOSPHERIC SPECTROSCOPY. *Current Pos:* SR STAFF SCIENTIST, SUN MICROSYSTS, 96- *Personal Data:* b Marion, Ind, Sept 15, 53; m 75; c 2. *Educ:* Rensselaer Polytech Inst, BS, 75; Univ Fla, PhD(astron), 80. *Prof Exp:* Teaching asst physics, Univ Fla, 75-80; teaching res assoc, Battelle Northwest, 80-82, res scientist, Battelle Mem Inst, 83-84, sr res scientist, 84-87, prin res scientist, 87-89; sr staff scientist, AER Inc, 89-96. *Mem:* Am Astron Soc; AAAS; Am Geog Union; Sigma Xi; NY Acad Sci; Am Soc Photogammetry & Remote Sensing. *Res:* Integration of remotely sensod imaging data of diverse types using imaging sattuore to aid in interpretation and understanding. *Mailing Add:* Sun Microsyst 2 Elizabeth Dr Chelmsford MA 01824

JOHNSON, DUDLEY PAUL, MATHEMATICS, MATHEMATICAL STATISTICS. *Current Pos:* from asst prof to assoc prof, 71-90, PROF MATH, UNIV CALGARY, 90- *Personal Data:* b Burbank, Calif, Sept 22, 40; m 64, Ann Benedict; c Eric A & Amanda G. *Educ:* Yale Univ, BA, 62; Mass Inst Technol, PhD(math), 66. *Prof Exp:* asst prof math, Univ Calif, 66-71. *Res:* Stochastic processes. *Mailing Add:* 16 Varsplain Pl NW Calgary AB T3A 0C7 Can. *E-Mail:* dpjohnso@acs.ucalgary.ca

JOHNSON, E(WELL) CALVIN, ELECTRICAL ENGINEERING. *Current Pos:* CORP STAFF, UBC, INC, 89- *Personal Data:* b Tampa, Fla, Apr 18, 26; div; c Cynthia. *Educ:* Ga Inst Technol, BEE, 47; Mass Inst Technol, SM, 49, EE, 50, ScD(elec eng), 51. *Prof Exp:* Res asst, Mass Inst Technol, 47-51; sr engr, Res Labs Div, Bendix Corp, 51-54, proj engr, 54-56, suprvy engr, 56-58, head comput dept, 58-62, mgr info & control systs lab, 62-65, asst gen mgr, 65-67, vpres res & dir labs div, 67-69, vpres eng & res, 69-73; vpres res & develop, Gould, Inc, 73-75; consult, 75-80; pres, Vincent Corp, 80-85, consult, 85-87; dir res & develop, Aerosonic Corp, 88-89. *Mem:* Fel Inst Elec & Electronics Engrs. *Res:* Feedback control systems; analog and digital computers; machine-tool control; photogrammetric instruments; aerospace information and control systems; automotive electronics; industrial automation systems. *Mailing Add:* UBC Inc PO Box 18751 Tampa FL 33679

JOHNSON, EARNEST J, OPTICS. *Current Pos:* AT MOTOROLA INC. *Personal Data:* b Philipsburg, Pa, Feb 23, 31; m 56; c 8. *Educ:* Pa State Univ, BS, 53; Purdue Univ, MS, 54, PhD(physics), 64. *Prof Exp:* Staff mem, NAm Aviation, Inc, 55-56 & Hughes Aircraft Co, 56-58; mem res staff, Lincoln Lab, Mass Inst Technol, 64-74; mem staff, GTE Lab, Waltham, Mass, 74- *Mem:* Optical Soc Am; Am Phys Soc. *Res:* Study of band structure of solids by observation of optical absorption and luminescence and effects of doping, magnetic fields and strains; laser materials; quantum electronics; fiber optic subsystems. *Mailing Add:* EL508 2100 E Elliot Rd Motorola Inc Tempe AZ 85284

JOHNSON, EDGAR MCCARTHY, RESEARCH PSYCHOLOGY. *Current Pos:* Res psychologist, US Army Res Inst, 70-78, chief, Human Factors Sect, 78-80, dir, Systs Res Lab, 80-82, tech dir, 82-93, CHIEF PSYCHOLOGIST, US ARMY RES INST, 82-, DIR, 93- *Personal Data:* b Jacksonville, Fla, Oct 29, 41; m 67, Fatima Nunes; c Victoria C & David M. *Educ:* Ga Inst Technol, BS, 64; Tufts Univ, MS, 67, PhD(exp psychol), 69. *Honors & Awards:* Franklin V Taylor Award, Inst Elec & Electronics Engrs, 84. *Mem:* Fel Am Psychol Asn; fel Am Psychol Soc; fel Human Factors & Ergonomics Soc; Inst Elec & Electronics Engrs; Ergonomics Soc; Sigma Xi. *Mailing Add:* US Army Res Inst 5001 Eisenhower Ave Alexandria VA 22304-4811

JOHNSON, EDWARD A, PHYSIOLOGY. *Current Pos:* JAMES B DUKE PROF & CHMN, DEPT PHYSIOL, DUKE UNIV SCH MED. *Educ:* Univ Sheffield, MD, 53. *Mailing Add:* Dept Physiol Duke Univ Sch Med PO Box 3005 Durham NC 27710

JOHNSON, EDWARD ARNOLD, VEGETATION SCIENCES. *Current Pos:* from asst prof to assoc prof, 79-93, PROF BIOL SCI, UNIV CALGARY, 93- *Personal Data:* b Long Branch, NJ, Aug 24, 43; m 94, Kiyoko Miyanishi; c Joanne Sonia. *Educ:* Univ Wis, BSc, 68; Univ NH, MSc, 72; Univ Sask, PhD, 77. *Honors & Awards:* William S Cooper Award, Ecol Soc Am, 86. *Concurrent Pos:* Assoc ed, Vegetation Sci, 90-97 & Can J Forest Res, 92-; dir, Kananaskis Field Stas, 92- *Mem:* Int Asn Veg Sci; Ecol Soc Am; Sigma Xi; Am Soc Naturalists. *Res:* Plant population dynamics; forest fire behavior and ecological effects; ecological mechanics, aerodynamics and small particle dispersal models; ecological effects of natural disturbances; contributed many articles to professional journals. *Mailing Add:* Dept Biol Sci Univ Calgary Calgary AB T2N 1N4 Can

JOHNSON, EDWARD MICHAEL, INITIATION OF DNA REPLICATION, CHROMOSOME STRUCTURE. *Current Pos:* PROF MOLECULAR BIOL & PATH, MT SINAI SCH MED, 85- *Personal Data:* b Kenosha, Wis, Apr 9, 45. *Educ:* Pomona Col, BA, 67; Yale Univ, PhD(pharmacol), 71. *Honors & Awards:* Fac Res Award, Am Cancer Soc, 82-87. *Prof Exp:* Fel, Rockefeller Univ, 71-73, from asst prof to assoc prof cell biol, 75-85; res assoc, Sloan-Kettering Cancer Ctr, 73-75. *Concurrent Pos:* Spec fel, Leukemia Soc Am, 73-75; adj prof genetics, Cornell Grad Sch Med Sci, 79, Rockefeller Univ, 85- *Mem:* Am Soc Cell Biol; Am Soc Pharmacol & Exp Therapeut; NY Acad Sci; Am Soc Biochem & Molecular Biol. *Res:* Control of DNA replication in mammalian cells; structure and chromosomal organization of individual genes, including ways in which hormones and other developmental signals regulate gene activity during development; regulation of gene expression in higher organisms. *Mailing Add:* Brookdale Ctr for Molecular Biol & Dept Path Mt Sinai Sch Med PO Box 1194 One Gustave L Levy Pl New York NY 10029. *Fax:* 212-534-7491; *E-Mail:* johnson@msvax.mssm.edu

JOHNSON, EDWIN C, NEUROPHYSIOLOGY, SINGLE ION CHANNEL RECORDING. *Current Pos:* HEAD, ELECTROPHYSIOL DEPT, SALK INST, 92- *Personal Data:* b Morristown, NJ, Nov 4, 58. *Educ:* Purdue Univ, BS, 79, PhD(electrophysiol), 84. *Prof Exp:* Res fel phototransduction, Brandeis Univ, 84-87; assoc prof med physiol, Marshall Univ Sch Med, 87-92. *Mem:* Soc Neurosci; Biophys Soc; Soc Gen Physiologists. *Res:* Neurophysiology; single ion channel recording. *Mailing Add:* Neuro Sci Inc 505 Coast Blvd S La Jolla CA 92037-4641. Fax: 619-452-9279

JOHNSON, EDWIN WALLACE, physical chemistry, for more information see previous edition

JOHNSON, EINER WESLEY, JR, ORTHOPEDIC SURGERY. *Current Pos:* From instr to assoc prof , 52-71, PROF ORTHOP SURG, MAYO GRAD, UNIV MINN, SCH MED, 71- *Personal Data:* b Bemidji, Minn, July 5, 19; m 51; c 4. *Educ:* Univ Minn, BA, 41, BS, 42, BM, 44, MD, 45, MA, 50. *Concurrent Pos:* Consult, Mayo Clin, Rochester Methodist Hosp & Rochester-St Mary's Hosp. *Mem:* Am Acad Orthop Surgeons; Clin Orthop Soc; Am Orthop Asn; Mid-Am Orthop Asn. *Mailing Add:* 201 First Ave SW No 411 Rochester MN 55902-3155

JOHNSON, ELIJAH, PHYSICAL CHEMISTRY. *Current Pos:* CHEMIST, OAK RIDGE NAT LAB, 76- *Personal Data:* b Eutawville, SC, Jan 1, 48. *Educ:* Penn State Univ, BS, 69; Univ Ill, PhD(chem), 76. *Concurrent Pos:* E P Wigner fel, Oak Ridge Nat Lab, 77- *Mem:* Am Chem Soc; Am Phys Soc. *Res:* Theoretical and experimental studies of liquids and amorphous and polymeric materials using statistical mechanics and x-ray and neutron scattering. *Mailing Add:* PO Box 5406 Oak Ridge TN 37831

JOHNSON, ELIZABETH BRIGGS, research reactors, nuclear criticality safety; deceased, see previous edition for last biography

JOHNSON, ELLIS LANE, OPERATIONS RESEARCH. *Current Pos:* COCA-COLA PROF INDUST & SYSTS ENG, GA INST TECHNOL, 90- *Personal Data:* b Athens, Ga, July 26, 38; m 62; c 1. *Educ:* Ga Inst Technol, BS, 60; Univ Calif, Berkeley, MA, 62, PhD(eng sci), 65. *Honors & Awards:* Lanchester Prize ORSA/IMT, 83; Dantzig Prize, Soc Indust & Appl Math, 85. *Prof Exp:* Asst prof admin sci, Yale Univ, 64-68; mem res staff math sci, Thomas J Watson Res Ctr, IBM Corp, 68-93. *Concurrent Pos:* Vis assoc prof, Univ Waterloo, 60-61, adj prof, 72-78; vis engr sci develop, IBM, France, 73-74. *Mem:* Nat Acad Eng; Math Prog Soc. *Res:* Theory and algorithms for integer programming; study of combinatorial polyhedra and mathematical programming; character recognition. *Mailing Add:* Indust & Syst Eng Dept Ga Inst Technol 225 North Ave NW Atlanta GA 30332-0205

JOHNSON, ELMER MARSHALL, EMBRYOLOGY & TOXICOLOGY, ENVIRONMENAL HEALTH. *Current Pos:* PROF ANAT & CHMN DEPT, JEFFERSON MED COL, THOMAS JEFFERSON UNIV, 72-, DIR, DANIEL BAUGH INST ANAT, 72- *Personal Data:* b Midlothian, Ill, June 16, 30; m 51, 76, Sharon Coyler; c Mark, Kim, Erik & Lora. *Educ:* Agr & Mech Col Tex, BS, 54, MS, 55; Univ Calif, Berkeley, PhD(anat), 59. *Prof Exp:* Asst zool, microtech & bot, Agr & Mech Col Tex, 53-55; asst gross anat & histol, Univ Calif, 55-58; instr anat & physiol, Contra Costa Col, 58-59; assoc prof anat, Univ Fla, 60-68, prof anat sci, 68-71; prof human morphol & chmn dept, Col Med, Univ Calif, Irvine, 71-72. *Concurrent Pos:* Asst researcher histochem, Surg Gen, US Army, 54; dir, March of Dimes & NIH grant's & NIEHS pre & postdoctoral training prog. *Mem:* AAAS; Teratology Soc (pres, 74-75); Am Asn Anatomists; Soc Toxicol; Am Chem Soc; Europ Teratology Soc; Am Col Toxicol. *Res:* Experimental teratology and nutrition; reproductive physiology; molecular biology; electron microscopy; histochemistry; developmental toxicity risk estimation; safety evaluation; in vitro toxicology. *Mailing Add:* Dept Anat & Develop Biol Jefferson Med Col Baugh Inst Anat 1020 Locust St Philadelphia PA 19107. Fax: 215-923-3808

JOHNSON, ELMER ROGER, CHEMISTRY. *Current Pos:* assoc prof, 46-55, prof, 55-78, EMER PROF CHEM, SDAK STATE UNIV, 78- *Personal Data:* b Erwin, SDak, Oct 4, 11; m 40; c 4. *Educ:* SDak State Col, BS, 33; Univ Wis, PhD(chem), 40. *Prof Exp:* Asst gen chem, Univ Wis, 37-40; res chemist, Tex Co, NY, 40-46. *Mem:* AAAS; Am Chem Soc; Sigma Xi. *Res:* Fuel composition and antiknock quality; synthesis of fuel components and additives; synthesis of additives for lubricating oils; the Lange gold sol test; factors influencing the preparation of the gold sol and its use in the Lange test. *Mailing Add:* Chem Dept Col Sta SDak State Univ Brookings SD 57007

JOHNSON, ELSIE ERNEST, anesthesiology; deceased, see previous edition for last biography

JOHNSON, EMMETT JOHN, MICROBIOLOGY. *Current Pos:* assoc prof, 67-70, PROF MICROBIOL & IMMUNOL, MED SCH, TULANE UNIV, 70- *Personal Data:* b New Orleans, La, Apr 17, 29; m 55; c 2. *Educ:* Loyola Univ of the South, BS, 52; La State Univ, MS, 54, PhD(bact), 57. *Prof Exp:* Nat Res Coun fel, Sch Med, Stanford Univ, 57-58; from asst prof to assoc prof microbiol, Med Sch, Univ Miss, 58-65; res scientist, Exobiol Div, Ames Res Ctr, NASA, 65-66; res assoc, Bruce Lyon Mem Res Inst, Oakland, Calif, 66-67. *Concurrent Pos:* Res assoc microbiol, Stanford Med Sch, 57-58; teaching assoc, 65-66, lectr, 66-67; Lederle Med Fac award, 62-65; res consult, Oak Ridge Nat Lab, 63-64 & 67-; res assoc molecular biol, Pasteur Inst, Paris, France, 74-75. *Mem:* AAAS; fel Am Acad Microbiol; Am Soc Microbiol; Am Soc Biol Chemists; Am Chem Soc. *Res:* Molecular mechanisms of genetic and biochemical regulation; biochemical basis of chemolithotrophic autotrophy; genetic and biochemical characterization of common enterobacterial antigens. *Mailing Add:* Dept Microbiol & Immunol Tulane Univ Med Sch 1430 Tulane Ave New Orleans LA 70112

JOHNSON, ERIC F, BIOCHEMISTRY. *Current Pos:* Asst mem, 77-82, assoc mem, 83-90, FEL, SCRIPPS RES INT, 90- *Personal Data:* b Cedar Rapids, Iowa, May 3, 46. *Educ:* Univ Tex, Austin, BS, 64; Univ Ill, PhD(chem), 72. *Mem:* Am Soc Pharmacol & Exp Therapeut; AAAS; Am Chem Soc; Am Soc Biochem & Molecular Biol. *Mailing Add:* Scripps Res Inst 10550 N Torrey Pines Rd La Jolla CA 92037. Fax: 765-285-2351

JOHNSON, ERIC G, JR, LASERS. *Current Pos:* GEN PHYSICIST, BOULDER LABS, NAT BUR STAND, 62- *Personal Data:* b Klamath Falls, Ore, June 17, 36; div; c 2. *Educ:* Mass Inst Technol, BS, 57; Harvard Univ, MA, 60, PhD(physics), 63. *Mem:* Sigma Xi; Laser Inst Am. *Res:* Measurement theory; unitary matrix field theory; laser properties measurements. *Mailing Add:* 6730 Lakeview Dr Boulder CO 80303-3133

JOHNSON, ERIC RICHARD, PROTEIN CHEMISTRY, ENZYMOLOGY. *Current Pos:* from asst prof to assoc prof, 76-88, PROF CHEM, BALL STATE UNIV, 88- *Personal Data:* b Elkhart, Ind, Mar 11, 47; m 90; c 3. *Educ:* Rose-Hulman Inst Technol, BS, 69; Univ Minn, PhD(biochem), 74. *Prof Exp:* Asst chemist, Uniroyal, Inc, 68; USPHS fel biochem, Univ Minn, 69-74; res assoc biochem, Duke Univ Med Ctr, 74-76. *Concurrent Pos:* Fel, Nat Inst Environ Health Sci, Duke Univ Med Ctr, 75-76; vis assoc prof biol chem, Univ Calif, Los Angeles, 84-85; res fel, USAF, 88. *Mem:* Am Soc Biochem & Molecular Biol; Sigma Xi. *Res:* Protein and peptide chemistry; high pressure liquid chromatography of protein and peptides; protease enzymology. *Mailing Add:* Dept Chem Ball State Univ Muncie IN 47306-0445. E-Mail: 00erjohnson@bsuvax1.bitnet

JOHNSON, ERIC ROBERT, ANALYTICAL CHEMISTRY, CHEMICAL INSTRUMENTATION. *Current Pos:* MGR LAB COMPUT NETWORK, WAYNE STATE UNIV, 77- *Personal Data:* b Windom, Minn, Nov 17, 47; m 69. *Educ:* Hamline Univ, BS, 69; Fla State Univ, PhD(anal chem), 75. *Prof Exp:* Res assoc anal chem, Mich State Univ, 74-76; mem staff, Mass Spectrometry Div, Varian Assocs, 76-77. *Mem:* Am Chem Soc; Soc Appl Spectros; Sigma Xi. *Res:* Application of minicomputers to laboratory instrumentation; design of special purpose digital, analog and hybrid instrumentation systems; study of atomic absorption, emission and fluorescence spectroscopic methods of trace metal analysis. *Mailing Add:* 213 Bobby Dr Franklin TN 37069

JOHNSON, ERIC VAN, ORNITHOLOGY. *Current Pos:* From asst prof to assoc prof, 69-79, PROF BIOL, CALIF POLYTECH STATE UNIV, SAN LUIS OBISPO, 79- *Personal Data:* b Medford, Mass, Mar 11, 43; div; c Kristina M & Eric L. *Educ:* Brown Univ, AB, 64; Cornell Univ, PhD(wildlife sci), 69. *Mem:* Cooper Ornith Soc; Am Ornith Union; Wilson Ornith Soc. *Res:* Avian taxonomy, behavior and population ecology; endangered species biology. *Mailing Add:* Dept Biol Sci Calif Polytechnic State Univ San Luis Obispo CA 93407

JOHNSON, ERNEST F(REDERICK), (JR), CHEMICAL ENGINEERING. *Current Pos:* from asst prof to prof, Princeton Univ, 48-86, assoc dean fac, 62-66, dir grad studies, Dept Chem Eng, 69-74, chmn dept, 77-78, assoc, Plasma Physics Lab, 55-88, clerk fac, 83-86, sr adv pres, 88-91, EMER PROF CHEM ENG, PRINCETON UNIV, 86- *Personal Data:* b Jamestown, NY, Apr 4, 18; m 44, M Ruth McMullin; c David (deceased), Carolyn (Walton), Arthur & Melissa. *Educ:* Lehigh Univ, BS, 40; Univ Pa, PhD(chem eng), 49. *Honors & Awards:* Jubilee Medal, Am Inst Chem Engrs, 83. *Prof Exp:* From res & develop engr to tech suprv synthetic org chem mfg, Barrett Div, Allied Chem & Dye Corp, 40-46. *Concurrent Pos:* Consult chem engr, 50-; trustee, Assoc Univs, Inc, 62-68, chmn, 65-67; dir, Autodynamics, Inc, 67-85. *Mem:* Fel AAAS; Am Chem Soc; fel Am Inst Chem Engrs; fel Am Inst Chemists. *Res:* Thermodynamic and transport properties of fluids; automatic process control; industrial wastes management; technological aspects of controlled thermonuclear fusion. *Mailing Add:* Dept Chem Eng Princeton Univ Eng Quadrangle Princeton NJ 08544

JOHNSON, ERNEST WALTER, DIABETES, ENDOCRINOLOGY. *Current Pos:* DIR, CTR GRANTS & CONTACTS, PA STATE UNIV, 91- *Personal Data:* b Paterson, NJ, Dec 15, 43; m 77; c 4. *Educ:* Muhlenberg Col, BS, 65; Univ Vt, PhD(physiol, biophys), 70. *Prof Exp:* Res assoc physiol, Med Ctr, Univ Colo, 70-72; asst prof, 72-75; AAAS fel & legis asst health sci, US Senate, 75-76; grants assoc, NIH, 76-77, sect chief diabetes, 77-79, br chief diabetes, Nat Inst Arthritis, Metab & Digestive Dis, 79-84, dir, Div Diabetes, Endocrinol & Metab Dis, Nat Inst Diabetes, Digestive & Kidney Dis, 84-91. *Concurrent Pos:* NIH fel, Med Ctr, Univ Colo, 70-72; prin investr, Nat Inst Neurol & Commun Disorders & Stroke, 73-75. *Mem:* AAAS; Am Diabetes Asn. *Res:* Etiology and pathophysiology of diabetes; hormone synthesis, secretion, action and metabolism; metabolic regulation; insulin delivery systems; islet cell transplantation; neurosecretary processes; receptor activation and inhibition; neurotrophic interactions; synaptic transmission. *Mailing Add:* Milton S Hershey Med Ctr Pa State Univ PO Box 850 Hershey PA 17033

JOHNSON, EUGENE A, BIOSTATISTICS. *Current Pos:* assoc prof & dir biomed data processing unit, 64-69, PROF BIOMET, COL MED SCI, UNIV MINN, MINNEAPOLIS, 69-, DIR GRAD STUDY, 80- *Personal Data:* b Crosby, Minn, Feb 24, 25; m 47; c 4. *Educ:* Univ Minn, BA, 49, MA, 50, PhD(biostatist), 56. *Prof Exp:* From asst prof to assoc prof biostatist, Univ Minn, Minneapolis, 56-60, assoc prof indust eng, 60-62; prof math & head dept, Gustavus Adolphus Col, 62-64. *Mem:* Am Statist Asn; Biomet Soc; Inst Math Statist; Sigma Xi. *Res:* Biomedical computing; computing in biology; mathematics; operations research. *Mailing Add:* 1580 Fulham St Falcon Heights MN 55108-1312

JOHNSON, EUGENE MALCOLM, JR, PHARMACOLOGY. *Current Pos:* asst prof, 76-78, ASSOC PROF PHARMACOL, SCH MED, WASH UNIV, 78- *Personal Data:* b Baltimore, Md, Oct 20, 43; m 65; c 2. *Educ:* Univ Md, BS, 66, PhD(med chem), 70. *Prof Exp:* Fel pharmacol, Sch Med, Wash Univ, 70-73; asst prof, Med Col Pa, 73-76. *Res:* Autonomic pharmacology; role of sympathetic nervous system in hypertension; effect of drugs on development of the sympathetic nervous system. *Mailing Add:* Dept Pharmacol Wash Univ Sch Med 660 S Euclid Ave St Louis MO 63110-1093. *Fax:* 314-362-7058

JOHNSON, EUGENE W, ALGEBRA. *Current Pos:* from asst prof to assoc prof, 66-75, PROF MATH, UNIV IOWA, 75- *Personal Data:* b El Paso, Tex, May 25, 39; m 59; c 1. *Educ:* Univ Calif, Riverside, BA, 63, MA, 64, PhD(algebra), 66. *Prof Exp:* Asst prof math, Eastern NMex Univ, 66. *Mem:* Am Math Soc; Math Asn Am. *Res:* Noetherian rings and abstract ideal theory. *Mailing Add:* Dept Math Univ Iowa Iowa City IA 52240

JOHNSON, EVERT WILLIAM, FORESTRY, PHOTOGRAMMETRY. *Current Pos:* from instr to assoc prof forestry, 50-67, asst, 50-53, asst forester, 53-57, prof, 80-86, EMER PROF FORESTRY, AUBURN UNIV, 86- *Personal Data:* b Astoria, NY, Apr 6, 21; m 50; c 3. *Educ:* Univ NH, BS, 43; Yale Univ, MF, 47; Syracuse Univ, PhD, 57. *Prof Exp:* Forester chg aerial surv, Sable Mt Corp, Vt, 47-50. *Concurrent Pos:* Fel, Soc Am Foresters. *Mem:* Soc Am Foresters; Am Soc Photogram; Sigma Xi. *Res:* Applications of photogrammetry, statistics and computer science to forest measurements. *Mailing Add:* 743 Heard Ave Auburn AL 36830-6023

JOHNSON, F BRENT, VIROLOGY. *Current Pos:* from asst prof to assoc prof, 72-80, PROF MICROBIOL, BRIGHAM YOUNG UNIV, 80-; LAB DIR, RICHARDS LABS, 86- & MICROVIR LABS, 89- *Personal Data:* b Monroe, Utah, Mar 31, 42; m 65, Paula Forbush; c Brian, Matthew, Christopher, Wesley & Stephanie. *Educ:* Brigham Young Univ, BS, 66, MS, 67, PhD(microbiol), 70. *Prof Exp:* Fel virol, NIH, 70-72. *Concurrent Pos:* NIH res grants, 73 & 76; res grants, Air Force Off Sci Res, 77-78 & 79-82, Thrasher Fund, 87-90. *Mem:* Am Soc Microbiol; AAAS; Sigma Xi; Am Soc Virol. *Res:* Viral replication; structure of viruses and biology of virus infections; diagnostic virology. *Mailing Add:* 887 Widtsoe Bldg Brigham Young Univ Provo UT 84602

JOHNSON, F CLIFFORD, GENETICS, ECOLOGY. *Current Pos:* PROF ZOOL, UNIV FLA, 70- *Personal Data:* b Ft Worth, Tex, Nov 4, 32; m 58; c 3. *Educ:* Univ Tex, BA, 55, MA, 60, PhD(zool), 61. *Prof Exp:* Instr zool, Duke Univ, 60-61; asst prof genetics, Va Polytech Inst, 61-62; asst prof biol & chmn dept, NMex Inst Mining & Technol, 62-66, assoc prof, 67-70. *Res:* Genetics of polymorphic variation. *Mailing Add:* Dept Zool Univ Fla 223 Bartram Hall Gainesville FL 32611-2009

JOHNSON, FATIMA NUNES, DEVELOPMENT OF SPECIFICATIONS FOR FOOD CHEMICALS & DRUGS. *Current Pos:* sr staff officer, 90-91, STUDY DIR, INST MED, NAT ACAD SCI, WASH, DC, 92- *Personal Data:* b Rizal, Philippines, Jan 1, 39; m 67, Edgar M; c Victoria C & David M. *Educ:* Adamson Univ, Manila, BS, 59; Boston Col, MS, 61, PhD(org chem), 64. *Prof Exp:* Proj leader org med chem, Arthur D Little, Inc, Mass, 64-69; res chemist, Org Chem Labs, Edgewood Arsenal, Md, 69-70; scientist drug stand, US Pharmacopeia, Rockville, Md, 71-90; chemist, Drug Enforcement Admin, Washington, DC, 91-92. *Mem:* Am Chem Soc; Asn Off Anal Chemists Int. *Res:* Organo-fluorine compounds; organometallics; molecular rearrangements; nitrogen heterocyclics. *Mailing Add:* 5315 Renaissance Ct Burke VA 22015. *Fax:* 202-334-2316

JOHNSON, FLOYD HOWARD, INTERNET TECHNOLOGIES, ISSUES RAISED BY THE COMPUTING SCIENCES. *Current Pos:* ASST PROF, DEPT COMPUT SCI, NORTHWESTERN COL, 92- *Personal Data:* b San Fernando, Calif, Nov 24, 50; m 74, Sandra L Courson; c 3. *Educ:* Univ Evansville, MS, 86; Univ Nebr, MSEd, 93. *Prof Exp:* Prof comput info systs, Bartlesville Wesleyan Col, 83-87; asst prof comput sci & info technol, Univ Nebr, 87-92. *Mem:* Asn Comp Mach; Asn Christians Math Sci; Inst Elec & Electronics Engrs Comput Soc. *Res:* Internet, both as a technology and as its impact on society. *Mailing Add:* 303 Fourth St NE Orange City IA 51041. *Fax:* 712-737-7247; *E-Mail:* floydj@netins.net

JOHNSON, FRANCIS, PHARMACOLOGY. *Current Pos:* PROF PHARMACOL & CHEM, STATE UNIV NY STONY BROOK, 74- *Personal Data:* b Bristol, Eng, Mar 12, 30; m 55; c 3. *Educ:* Glasgow Univ, BSc, 51, PhD(org chem), 54. *Prof Exp:* Fel org chem, Boston Univ, 54-57; from res chemist to assoc scientist, Eastern Res Lab, Dow Chem Co, 57-63, res scientist, 69-74. *Concurrent Pos:* Eve lectr, Boston Univ, 56-70; consult, Qm Res Corps, US Army, 58-; & Dow Chem Co, 74-; vis scientist, Oxford Univ, 66-67; consult res dir, Ganes Chemicals Inc, NJ, 90- *Mem:* Am Chem Soc; Royal Soc Chem; assoc Royal Inst Chem; fel Royal Soc Arts; NY Acad Sci. *Res:* Synthetic organic chemistry, especially natural product and aliphatic areas; medicinal chemistry. *Mailing Add:* SUNY Stony Brook Grand Chem Bldg Rm 607 Stony Brook NY 11794-3400

JOHNSON, FRANCIS SEVERIN, SPACE PHYSICS, METEOROLOGY. *Current Pos:* actg pres, Univ Tex, Dallas, 69-71, prof & dir, Ctr Advan Studies, 71-74, Cecil H & Ida M Green hons prof natural sci, 74-89, EMER PROF, UNIV TEX, DALLAS, 90- *Personal Data:* b Omak, Wash, July 20, 18; m 43, Maurine Green; c Sharan (Fry). *Educ:* Univ Alta, BSc, 40; Univ Calif, Los Angeles, MA, 42, PhD(meteorol), 58. *Honors & Awards:* Space Sci Award, Am Inst Aeronaut & Astronaut, 66; Henryk Arctowski Medal, Nat Acad Sci, 72; Except Sci Achievement Medal, NASA, 73; John A Fleming Award, Am Geophys Union, 77. *Prof Exp:* Physicist, US Naval Res Lab, 46-55; space physicist, Lockheed Missiles & Space Co, 55-62; prof & dir, Earth & Planetary Sci Lab, Southwest Ctr Advan Studies, 62-69; asst dir Astron, Atmospheric, Earth & Ocean Sci, NSF, Washington, DC, 79-83. *Concurrent Pos:* Consult, NASA, 60-79; mem, Panel Adv Cent Radio Propagation Lab, Nat Bur Stand, 62-65, mem panel on weather & climate modification, 64-70, mem adv comt to Air Force Systs Command panel on re-entry physics, 65-68, mem comt solar-terrestrial res, 66-79, chmn, 71-74, mem comt adv to Environ Sci Serv Admin, 66-71, mem space sci bd, 67-80, mem geophys res bd, 71-75, mem comt adv to Nat Oceanic & Atmospheric Admin, 71-72, mem, Climate Res Bd, Nat Acad Sci, 77-79; mem adv panel atmospheric sci, NSF, 62-66; chmn, US Comn IV, Int Union Radio Sci, 64-67, secy, US Nat Comt, 67-70, vchmn, 70-73, chmn, 73-76; mem, Air Force Sci Adv Bd, 68-79; mem, Nat Adv Comt Oceans & Atmosphere, 71-73; mem, climatic impact comt, Nat Acad Sci, 72-76, mem bd Atmospheric Sci & Climate, 84-87, mem comt solar physics, Nat Acad Sci, 86-88; mem Aerocibo Adv bd, Nat Astron & Ionospher Ctr, 85-88; vpres, Comt Space Res, Int Coun Sci Unions, 75-80. *Mem:* Am Meteorol Soc; Am Geophys Union; Am Inst Aeronaut & Astronaut; Inst Elec & Electronics Engrs; Sigma Xi. *Res:* Upper atmospheric and magnetospheric physics; space science; planetary atmospheres; upper atmosphere and space physics; planetary science; solar radiation; synoptic and physical meteorology. *Mailing Add:* 13619 Sprucewood Dr Dallas TX 75240

JOHNSON, FRANK BACCHUS, PATHOLOGY. *Current Pos:* pathologist, Armed Forces Inst Path, 52-60, chief basic sci div, 60-72, chief, Histochem Br, 72-74, CHMN, DEPT CHEM PATH, ARMED FORCES INST PATH, 74- *Personal Data:* b Washington, DC, Feb 1, 19; m 47; c 2. *Educ:* Univ Mich, BS, 40; Howard Univ, MD, 44. *Honors & Awards:* Citation Admin & Tech Proficiency, Vet Admin, 58, Commendation Outstanding Contributions Histochem, 64. *Prof Exp:* From intern to resident path, Med Ctr, Jersey City, 44-46; dir clin labs, Howard Univ, 46-48; res assoc, Univ Chicago, 50-52. *Concurrent Pos:* AEC fel med sci, Univ Chicago, 48-50. *Mem:* Am Crystallog Soc; Am Chem Soc. *Res:* Histochemistry in pathology. *Mailing Add:* USG Dept Defense Armed Forces Inst Path Washington DC 20306

JOHNSON, FRANK JUNIOR, ANALYTICAL CHEMISTRY. *Current Pos:* anal chemist, 62-69, head serv, 69-86, CHIEF, PE SERV BR, TENN AUTHORITY, 86. *Personal Data:* b Rosendale, Mo, Aug 24, 30; m 51; c 3. *Educ:* Northwest Mo State Col, BS, 52; Univ Mo, MSc, 61. *Prof Exp:* Instr agr chem, Univ Mo, 55-62. *Mem:* Asn Off Anal Chemists (pres-elect 85-86 & pres 86-87); Am Chem Soc; Fertilizer Soc. *Res:* Fertilizer chemistry; investigation of new or improved analytical methods pertaining to fertilizer and related materials. *Mailing Add:* 205 Westmeade Ct Florence AL 35630

JOHNSON, FRANKLIN M, GENETICS. *Current Pos:* RES GENETICIST, NAT INST ENVIRON HEALTH SCI, 77- *Personal Data:* b Cloquet, Minn, Nov 1, 40; m 81, Dorothy Moore; c Erik, David & Olen. *Educ:* Univ Minn, Duluth, BA, 62; Univ Hawaii, MS, 64; Univ Tex, Austin, PhD(zool), 66. *Prof Exp:* NIH fel, 66-67; res scientist, Univ Tex, Austin, 67-68; asst prof genetics, NC State Univ, 68-74, sr geneticist, Res Triangle Inst, 74-77. *Mem:* AAAS; Genetics Soc Am; Soc Environ Toxicol Chem; Am Soc Human Genetics. *Res:* Genetic variability in natural populations; genotype-environment relationships; developmental variation in the skeleton; mutagenesis; genetic risk; carcinogenesis. *Mailing Add:* Environ Toxicol Prog Nat Inst Environ Health Sci Research Triangle Park NC 27709. *Fax:* 919-541-1460

JOHNSON, FRED LOWERY, JR, INDUSTRIAL ORGANIC CHEMISTRY. *Current Pos:* RETIRED. *Personal Data:* b San Angelo, Tex, Oct 24, 27; m 49, Dorothy; c Ellen, Mary & Fred. *Educ:* Univ Tex, BS, 51, PhD(chem), 59. *Prof Exp:* Sr process chemist, Am Cyanamid Co, La, 59-62; res chemist, Jefferson Chem Co, Inc, 62-64, sr res chemist, 64-68, proj chemist, 68-76, sr proj chemist, Texaco Chem Co, 76-87. *Mem:* Am Chem Soc; Sigma Xi. *Res:* Catalytic research and process development for petrochemicals. *Mailing Add:* 3002 Yellowpine Terr Austin TX 78757-1629

JOHNSON, FRED M, LASER PHYSICS. *Current Pos:* PROF, DEPT PHYSICS & ASTRON, CALIF STATE UNIV, 71- *Educ:* City Col New York, BS, 49; Columbia Univ, MA, PhD(physics), 58. *Mem:* Am Phys Soc; Int Astron Union. *Mailing Add:* Dept Physics & Astron Calif State Univ Fullerton CA 92634

JOHNSON, FREDERIC ALLAN, INORGANIC CHEMISTRY, PHYSICAL CHEMISTRY. *Current Pos:* RETIRED. *Personal Data:* b Concord, NH, Mar 6, 32; m 56; c 3. *Educ:* Univ NH, BS, 54, MS, 55; Univ Wis, PhD(chem), 58. *Prof Exp:* Lab instr, Univ NH, 54; chemist, Redstone Arsenal Res Div, Rohm & Haas Co, 58-62, group leader anal chem, 62-70; assoc prof chem, Auburn Univ, 70-92. *Mem:* Am Chem Soc. *Res:* Fluorine and metal coordination chemistry; nuclear magnetic resonance; kinetics. *Mailing Add:* 821 Heard Ct Auburn AL 36830-6243

JOHNSON, FREDERIC DUANE, FOREST ECOLOGY, DENDROOGY. *Current Pos:* Radioisotopes technologist, 52-56, from instr to asst prof forest mgt, 56-67, assoc prof forest ecol, 67-72, PROF FOREST ECOL, UNIV IDAHO, 72- *Personal Data:* b Chicago, Ill, Oct 24, 25; m 48, Virginia Stinchcomb; c 5. *Educ:* Ore State Col, BS, 50; Univ Idaho, MS, 52. *Concurrent Pos:* Adj prof, Inst Agron Vet, Morocco. *Mem:* Ecol Soc Am; fel Soc Am Foresters. *Res:* Forest ecology-temperate and tropical, ecologic accessment; temperate and tropical dendrology. *Mailing Add:* Col Forestry Univ Idaho Moscow ID 83843-4199

JOHNSON, FREDERICK ALLAN, NUCLEAR PHYSICS. *Current Pos:* Defence Sci Serv officer nuclear physics, Suffield Exp Sta, 55-59, Defence Sci Serv Officer Chem, Biol & Radiation Labs, 59-71, DEFENCE SCI SERV OFFICER NUCLEAR PHYSICS, DEFENCE RES BD, DEFENCE RES ESTAB, 71- *Personal Data:* b Winnipeg, Man, Nov 7, 23. *Educ:* Univ Man, BSc, 45; McGill Univ, PhD(nuclear physics), 52. *Prof Exp:* Res assoc nuclear physics, Radiation Lab, McGill Univ, 52-53; sr engr, Can Aviation Electronics Co, 53-55. *Mem:* Am Phys Soc; Can Asn Physicists. *Res:* Spectroscopy of nuclear radiations from cyclotron-produced cadmium and silver isotopes; auger transitions in silver; industrial design of radiation detectors; nanosecond pulse electronics; neutron time-of-flight spectroscopy; beam pulsing and deflection; pulse-shape discrimination circuits for neutron identification; neutron activation; radiological protection and health physics. *Mailing Add:* Six Esquimalt Ave Nepean ON K2H 6Z3 Can

JOHNSON, FREDERICK ARTHUR, JR, GEOLOGY. *Current Pos:* GEOL ADV, EXXON CO, 76- *Personal Data:* b Pittsburgh, Pa, Sept 8, 23; m 46; c 1. *Educ:* Harvard Univ, BS, 44; Univ Chicago, MS, 49, PhD(geol), 51. *Prof Exp:* From assoc geologist to sr geologist stratig sect, Explor Dept, Humble Oil & Ref Co, 51-60, supvry geologist, 60-66; sect supvr struct geol & basin interpretation, Esso Prod Res Co, 66-67; sr explor geologist, Humble Oil & Refining Co, 67-76. *Mem:* Sigma Xi; AAAS; Geol Soc Am; Soc Econ Paleont & Mineral; Am Asn Petrol Geol. *Res:* Carbonate rock; stratigraphic and structural geology of Permian Basin, west Texas; structural geology of Rocky Mountains; regional geology of Alaska, eastern USSR and western Canada. *Mailing Add:* 2753 W Long Dr Apt F Littleton CO 80120

JOHNSON, FREDERICK CARROLL, APPLIED MATHEMATICS, RESOURCE MANAGEMENT. *Current Pos:* chief, Math Anal Div, 84-87, ASSOC DIR COMPUT, NAT INST STAND & TECHNOL, 87- *Personal Data:* b Sheridan, Wyo, Oct 23, 40; m 64; c 1. *Educ:* Univ NDak, BS, 62; Univ Wash, MS & PhD(appl math), 66. *Honors & Awards:* Silver Medal, Dept Commerce, 78. *Prof Exp:* Res analyst real-time data processing, DBA Systs, Inc, 66-68; res scientist appl math, Boeing Sci Res Labs, 68-73; mathematician, Nat Bur Stand, 73-77, chief, Math Anal Div, 77-82; partner, Nat Res Consult, 82-84. *Mem:* Soc Indust & Appl Math; Inst Elec & Electronics Engrs; Asn Comput Mach; Am Fisheries Soc; Sigma Xi. *Res:* Applications of mathematical modeling to physical systems; high performance computing; scientific visualization for mathematical modeling. *Mailing Add:* Nat Inst Stand & Technol Bldg 820 Rm 672 Gaithersburg MD 20899

JOHNSON, G ALLAN, MEDICAL IMAGING. *Current Pos:* Assoc physics, 78, from asst prof to assoc prof, 78-83, PROF PHYSICS, DEPT RADIOL, DUKE UNIV MED CTR, 88- *Personal Data:* b Champaigne, Ill, Jan 17, 47; m 69; c 2. *Educ:* St Olaf Col, BA, 69; Duke Univ, PhD(physics), 74. *Concurrent Pos:* Dir diag physics, Dept Radiol, Duke Univ Med Ctr, 78. *Mem:* Sigma Xi; Am Phys Soc; Am Asn Physicists Med. *Res:* Implementation and enhancement of new imaging technologies in medicine; magnetic resonance microscopy and its extension to basic sciences. *Mailing Add:* Duke Univ Med Ctr Box 3302 Durham NC 27710

JOHNSON, GARLAND A, BIOCHEMISTRY, PHARMACOLOGY. *Current Pos:* RES ASSOC, UPJOHN CO, 64- *Personal Data:* b Laona, Wis, July 16, 36; m 58; c 4. *Educ:* Carroll Col, Wis, BS, 58; Ohio State Univ, MSc, 60, PhD(physiol chem), 63. *Prof Exp:* Res assoc biochem, Res Found, Ohio State Univ, 63; staff fel, Nat Inst Neurol Dis & Blindness, 63-64. *Mem:* AAAS; Am Soc Pharmacol & Exp Therapeut. *Res:* Metabolism of catecholamines and serotonin; effect of drugs on biogenic amines. *Mailing Add:* 2566 Villa Lane Cincinnati OH 45208-1121

JOHNSON, GARY DEAN, GEOLOGY. *Current Pos:* from asst prof to assoc prof, 71-86, chmn dept, 80-83, PROF GEOL, DARTMOUTH COL, 87- *Personal Data:* b Sioux City, Iowa, Dec 2, 42; m 65; c 1. *Educ:* Iowa State Univ, BS, 64, MS, 67, PhD(geol), 71. *Prof Exp:* Instr geol, Iowa State Univ, 69-71. *Concurrent Pos:* Res assoc, Iowa State Univ, 71-72. *Mem:* Geol Soc Am; Soc Econ Paleont & Mineral; Int Asn Sedimentologists. *Res:* Stratigraphy and sedimentology; Cenozoic terrestrial deposits of Asia and Africa; geology of the Himalayas; paleopedology; geochronology. *Mailing Add:* Dept Earth Sci Dartmouth Col Hanover NH 03755

JOHNSON, GARY L, MOLECULAR BIOLOGY, CELL GROWTH & DIFFERENTIATION. *Current Pos:* PROF & SR RES SCIENTIST, NAT JEWISH CTR, 88- *Personal Data:* b Oxford, Nebr, Sept 18, 49. *Educ:* Calif State Univ, Northridge, BS, 71; Univ Colo, PhD(pharmacol), 76. *Prof Exp:* Fel, Univ Calif, San Francisco, 76-79; asst prof, Univ Mass, 79-87, prof, Med Ctr, Dept Biochem, 87-88. *Mem:* Am Soc Microbiol; Am Soc Biochem & Molecular Biol. *Mailing Add:* Nat Jewish Ctr Immunol & Respiratory Med 1400 Jackson St Denver CO 80206-2761. *Fax:* 303-398-1225

JOHNSON, GARY LEE, ELECTRICAL ENGINEERING. *Current Pos:* From asst prof to prof, 66-94, EMER PROF ELEC ENG, KANS STATE UNIV, 94- *Personal Data:* b Osage City, Kans, Nov 20, 38; m 60, Jolene Hazen; c Kirk & Janel. *Educ:* Kans State Univ, BS, 61, MS, 63; Okla State Univ, PhD, 66. *Concurrent Pos:* Consult, Kansas City Power & Light Co, 71-72. *Mem:* Inst Elec & Electronics Engrs; Am Wind Energy Asn; Int Tesla Soc. *Res:* Power systems; wind electric systems. *Mailing Add:* 1630 Osage St Manhattan KS 66502-4048

JOHNSON, GEAROLD ROBERT, ENGINEERING DESIGN, ENGINEERING COMPUTER GRAPHICS. *Current Pos:* from asst prof to prof, 73-84, G T ABELL CHAIR, COLO STATE UNIV, 84- *Personal Data:* b Des Moines, Iowa, Jan 11, 40; m 62; c 2. *Educ:* Purdue Univ, BS, 62, MS, 68, PhD(mech eng), 72. *Prof Exp:* Engr, aerospace, Boeing Co, 62-66; NATO fel fluid mech, von Karman Inst, 70-71. *Concurrent Pos:* Vis prof, Univ Kent, Canterbury, UK, 78-79, Calif Inst Technol, 84; vis scientist, Shape Data Ltd, Cambridge, UK, 85-86; dir, NTU-Eurosud Found, Paris, 92-93. *Mem:* Inst Elec & Electronics Engrs; Inst Elec & Electronics Engrs Comput Soc; Math Asn Am; Am Soc Eng Educ. *Res:* Application of computers to engineering problems such as solar energy, fluid mechanics, solid modeling, etc; uses of computer technology to support engineering education in design. *Mailing Add:* Nat Tech Univ 700 Centre Ave Ft Collins CO 80526-1842. *E-Mail:* gerry@longs.lance.colostate.edu

JOHNSON, GEORGE, JR, MEDICINE, SURGERY. *Current Pos:* from asst prof to prof, 61-73, CHIEF, DIV GEN SURG, SCH MED, UNIV NC, CHAPEL HILL, 69-, ROSCOE B G COWPER PROF SURG, 73-, VCHMN, DEPT SURG, 77- *Personal Data:* b Wilmington, NC, Apr 6, 26; m 50; c 4. *Educ:* Univ NC, BS, 49; Cornell Univ, MD, 52; Am Bd Surg, dipl, 60; Am Bd Thoracic Surg, dipl, 63. *Prof Exp:* Instr surg, Cornell Univ, 58-59. *Concurrent Pos:* Ed, NC Med J. *Mem:* Am Col Surgeons; Soc Univ Surgeons; Soc Vascular Surgeons; Am Asn Surg of Trauma; Asn Acad Surgeons. *Res:* Vascular and thoracic surgery; hemodynamics associated with cirrhosis of the liver; local and systematic hemodynamics of an arteriovenous fistula; gall bladder surgery. *Mailing Add:* Dept Surg Univ NC Sch Med CB No 7210 Chapel Hill NC 27599-7210

JOHNSON, GEORGE ANDREW, VETERINARY MEDICINE FOOD SCIENCE. *Current Pos:* PROF FOOD & ANIMAL SCI & CHAIRPERSON, NC AGR & TECH STATE UNIV, 78- *Personal Data:* b Brooklyn, NY, June, 39; m 65; c George & Stacey. *Educ:* Tuskegee Inst, Ala, DVM, 61; Cornell Univ, Ithaca, MS, 72. *Prof Exp:* Exec staff officer, USDA, Wash, DC, 70-72; assoc dean, Sch Agr & Natural Resources, Wash Tech Inst, 72-74; assoc dir, Univ DC, 74-77; mem adv coun, Pub Sch Syst, DC, 77-79. *Concurrent Pos:* Consult, Am Coun Comn Accreditation Serv Experience, 72; dean, Wash Tech Inst, 72-73, prof vet sci & chmn, 73-74; chairperson, Animal Sci, 79-, NC Agr & Tech State Univ. *Mem:* Am Vet Med Asn; Am Meat Sci Asn; Am Pub Health Asn; Nat Inst Food Technologists; Am Lab Animal Soc. *Res:* Detectability of sex flavor in a mildly seasoned comminuted product served cold as affected by concentration of boar meat. *Mailing Add:* Dept Animal Sci NC Agr & Tech State Univ Greensboro NC 27411. *Fax:* 910-334-7288

JOHNSON, GEORGE FREDERICK, ORGANIC CHEMISTRY. *Current Pos:* RETIRED. *Personal Data:* b Harmony, Minn, July 15, 16; m 41. *Educ:* Iowa State Univ, BS, 38; Ohio State Univ, PhD(chem), 43. *Prof Exp:* Proj leader, Process Develop Lab, Carbide & Carbon Chem Co, Union Carbide Corp, 53-55, group leader, Chem Div, 55-71, develop scientist chem & plastics, Res & Develop Dept, 71-76, site adminr, agr prod div, Res & Develop Dept, 76-82. *Mem:* Am Chem Soc. *Mailing Add:* 1336 Morningside Dr Charleston WV 25314-1958

JOHNSON, GEORGE LEONARD, GEOLOGICAL OCEANOGRAPHY. *Current Pos:* SR SCIENTIST, UNIV ALASKA, FAIRBANKS, 94- *Personal Data:* b Englewood, NJ, May 18, 31; m 89; c 3. *Educ:* Williams Col, BA, 53; NY Univ, MS, 65; Univ Copenhagen, PhD(marine geol), 75. *Prof Exp:* Res asst marine geol, Lamont-Doherty Geol Observ, 57-65; oceanogr, US Naval Oceanog Off, Md, 65-75; sci adminr arctic prog, Off Naval Res, 75-80, dir arctic progs, Phys Sci Admin, 80-85, dir geophys sci, 85-94. *Concurrent Pos:* Consult, Polar Res Bd, Natural Acad Sci, 75-, Panel Polar Eng, Nat Res Coun, 77- & Comn Tectonic Chart World, 77-; sci consult, Intergovt Oceanog Comn, Int Hydrographic Off, 75-; chmn, Arctic Geol-Geophys Comt, Arctic Geol Comt, Lithosphere Comn, secy, US-USSR Ocean Bilateral, Int Arctic Sci Comt, W G Arctic Marine Geol, Nansen Arctic Drilling Prog. *Mem:* Am Geophys Union; Arctic Inst NAm; Polar Soc. *Res:* Geophysics with specialization in marine geomorphology and physiography of the world's oceans; arctic and antarctic marine geology; naval arctic research; polar regions. *Mailing Add:* 7708 Lake Glen Dr Glendale MD 20769

JOHNSON, GEORGE PATRICK, TECHNOLOGY ASSESSMENT, CIVIL ENGINEERING. *Current Pos:* prog mgr tech assessment, NSF, 74-84, sr policy analyst, 84-88, head, Off Europe, 88-90, sr policy analyst, 90-95, PROG MGR SBIC, NSF, 95- *Personal Data:* b Pine Bluff, Ark, June 16, 32; m 67, Jean M Lennon; c Heather, Patrick & Margaret. *Educ:* Univ Miss, BSCE, 54; Stanford Univ, MS, 67, Engr, 69, PhD(civil eng), 71. *Prof Exp:* Res civil engr int develop, C S McCandless & Co, 65-67; oper analyst housing res, Stanford Res Inst, 67-69; res engr water resources, INTASA, Inc, 69-71; water resource engr, US Army Eng Inst Water Resources, 71-74. *Concurrent Pos:* Consult, Rand Corp, 70-71. *Mem:* AAAS; Sigma Xi. *Res:* Technology assessment methods and utilization; policy research and analysis; water resources planning; technological forecasting; futures research; structural modeling; decision analysis for public policy. *Mailing Add:* SBIR Prog NSF 4201 Wilson Blvd Arlington VA 22230. *Fax:* 703-306-0337; *E-Mail:* gpjohnson@nsf.gov

JOHNSON, GEORGE PHILIP, MATHEMATICAL ANALYSIS. *Current Pos:* RETIRED. *Personal Data:* b Minneapolis, Minn, Nov 13, 26; m 51; c 4. *Educ:* Univ Minn, BS, 48, MA, 49, PhD(math), 56. *Prof Exp:* Asst math & statist, Univ Minn, 48-51, instr math, 55-56; mathematician, Nat Security Agency, 51-54; sr mathematician, Stand Oil Co Calif, 56-60; assoc prof, Wesleyan Univ, 60-64 & Univ South, 64-65; chmn dept, Oakland Univ, 65-70, prof, 65-94, dean, Grad Sch, 69-81. *Concurrent Pos:* Off Naval Res assoc, 63-64; consult-evaluator, NCent Asn Cols & Schs, 72-91. *Mem:* Am Math Soc; Math Asn Am; Sigma Xi. *Res:* Abstract harmonic analysis; numerical analysis and computing. *Mailing Add:* 654 W Buell Rd Rochester MI 48309

JOHNSON, GEORGE ROBERT, ANIMAL HUSBANDRY. *Current Pos:* RETIRED. *Personal Data:* b Caledonia, NY, Aug 2, 17; m 42; c 4. *Educ:* Cornell Univ, BS, 39; Mich State Univ, MS, 47, PhD, 54. *Prof Exp:* Pub sch teacher, NY, 39-42; asst county agt agr, Canton, NY, 42-43; from instr to assoc prof animal husb, Cornell Univ, 43-55; from assoc prof animal sci to prof animal sci & chmn dept, Ohio State Univ, 55-83. *Mem:* Am Soc Animal Sci. *Res:* Administration in animal science, especially teaching, research and extension; sheep production and management. *Mailing Add:* 251 Fairlawn Dr Columbus OH 43214

JOHNSON, GEORGE S, CELL BIOLOGY, MOLECULAR BIOLOGY. *Current Pos:* RES CHEMIST, NAT CANCER INST, NIH, 74- *Personal Data:* b Cokato, Minn, Aug 25, 43. *Educ:* Mich State Univ, PhD(biochem), 69. *Mem:* Am Soc Biol Chem; Am Soc Microbiologists. *Res:* Oncology. *Mailing Add:* Nat Cancer Inst Executive Plaza N Rm 832 Bethesda MD 20892-7450. *Fax:* 301-496-8333

JOHNSON, GERALD, III, CARDIOVASCULAR PHYSIOLOGY, NUCLEAR CARDIOLOGY. *Current Pos:* ASSOC PROF, DEPT MED, UNIV OKLA HEALTH SCI CTR, 90- *Personal Data:* b Liberty, Tex, Aug 16, 45; m 85, Delynda J Wall. *Educ:* Park Col, BS, 68; Univ Okla, MA, 71, PhD(autonomic physiol), 80. *Prof Exp:* Clin & res electrophysiologist, Children's Med Ctr, 80-82; res assoc, Dept Physiol, Oral Roberts Univ Sch Med, 82-84, asst prof, 84-88; sr res fel, Ischemia-Shock Res Inst, Jefferson Med Col, 88-90. *Concurrent Pos:* Consult, Oral Roberts Univ Sch Med, 81-82, City of Faith Hosp, 82, McGee Rehab Inst, 90; lab dir, W K Warren Med Res Inst, 90-; fel, Circ Coun, Am Heart Asn; sci consult, Bristol-Myers Squibb Pharmaceut Res Inst, 90, Bracco Diags Adv Panel, 95, Cis Bio Int Adv Panel, 95. *Mem:* Am Heart Asn; Am Soc Nuclear Cardiol; Int Soc Heart Res; Sigma Xi; NY Acad Sci; Soc Nuclear Med; Am Physiol Soc. *Res:* Improvement of diagnostic imaging in normal and cardiovascular disease states; clearance kinetics of novel radiopharmaceuticals are studied with regard to their efficacy in providing diagnostic information about myocardial perfusion, function and viability. *Mailing Add:* 6465 S Yale Ave Suite 1010 Tulsa OK 74136. *Fax:* 918-481-7957

JOHNSON, GERALD GLENN, JR, MATERIALS SCIENCE. *Current Pos:* asst prof solid state sci, 65-71, ASSOC PROF COMPUT SCI, PA STATE UNIV, 71- *Personal Data:* b Renovo, Pa, Nov 10, 39; m 63; c 2. *Educ:* John Carroll Univ, BS, 62; Pa State Univ, PhD(mat sci, physics), 65. *Prof Exp:* Jr physicist, Erie Registor Corp, 60-62. *Concurrent Pos:* Mem, Nat Res Coun. *Mem:* AAAS; Am Phys Soc; Am Crystallog Asn; Am Soc Testing & Mat; Sigma Xi. *Res:* Information retrieval as applied to x-ray powder diffraction identification systems; high resolution powder diffraction techniques using Guinier Cameras and automatic microdensitometers. *Mailing Add:* Dept Comput Sci Col Sci Eng Pa State Univ 220 Pond Lab University Park PA 16802

JOHNSON, GERALD WINFORD, CIVIL ENGINEERING. *Current Pos:* ASST PROF CIVIL ENG, UNIV MINN, MINNEAPOLIS, 69-, ASSOC PROF, 80- *Personal Data:* b Minneapolis, Minn, Oct 31, 32; m 58; c 3. *Educ:* Purdue Univ, BS, 55; Ohio State Univ, MS, 60; Univ Wis-Madison, PhD(civil eng), 69. *Prof Exp:* Field serv engr, Boeing Co, Wash, 60-61; programmer analyst, Syst Develop Corp, Calif, 61-65. *Mem:* Am Soc Civil Engrs; Am Cong Surv & Mapping; Am Soc Photogram; Arctic Inst N Am; Am Inst Navig. *Res:* Reliability of atmospheric refraction in polar astronavigation; cartography and map rectification in north Greenland; application of computers to survey net adjustments. *Mailing Add:* Dept Civil Eng Univ Minn 500 Pillsbury Dr SE Minneapolis MN 55455

JOHNSON, GLEN ERIC, OPTIMAL MECHANICAL DESIGN. *Current Pos:* PROF & CHAIR, DEPT MECH & AEROSPACE ENG, UNIV DAYTON, 93- *Personal Data:* b Rochester, NY, May 29, 51; m 75, Kathryne De Loach; c Edward & Eric. *Educ:* Worcester Polytech Inst, BS, 73; Ga Inst Technol, MSME, 74; Vanderbilt Univ, PhD(mech eng), 78. *Honors & Awards:* Ralph Teetor Award, Soc Automotive Engrs, 84. *Prof Exp:* Mech eng, Machine Design, Tenn Eastman Co, 74-76; asst prof, mech eng, Vanderbilt Univ, 78-79 & Univ Va, 79-81; assoc prof, Vanderbilt Univ, 81-89; assoc prof, Univ Mich, 89-93, dir, Design Lab, 91-93. *Concurrent Pos:* Co-prin investr, US Dept Transp, 80-81; prin investr, NSF, 80-; assoc ed, J Mech Design, Am Soc Mech Engrs, 81-82, J Mech Trans Automation Design, 82-83; chair, Design Div, Am Soc Mech Engrs, 93-94, mem, Bd Commun, 94-98. *Mem:* Am Soc Mech Engrs; Am Soc Eng Educ. *Res:* Development of algorithmic and ad hoc optimization strategies; application of optimization theory to the design of mechanical systems and machines; machine design; system modeling and analysis; noise and vibration control. *Mailing Add:* 300 College Park Dayton OH 45469-0210. *E-Mail:* gjohnson@engr.udayton.edu

JOHNSON, GLENN M, ENGINEERING. *Current Pos:* proj engr, 65-68, GROUP MGR, ROY WESTON INC, 72-, VPRES, Roy Weston Inc. *Personal Data:* b US citizen. *Educ:* Pa State Univ, BS, 64; Northwestern Univ, MS, 65; Am Acad Environ Engrs, dipl. *Prof Exp:* Surveyor, US Forest Serv, 60; designer & draftsman, Chicago Bridge & Iron Co, 61-62; asst proj engr, Nat Forge Co, 62-63. *Mem:* Am Soc Civil Engrs; Am Water Resources Asn. *Res:* Water resources engineering; resource economics; wastewater management systems design. *Mailing Add:* Roy Weston Inc One Weston Way West Chester PA 19380

JOHNSON, GLENN RICHARD, PLANT BREEDING. *Current Pos:* plant breeder maize & area res dir, 65-89, PRIN RES DIR, DEKALB GENETICS CORP, 89- *Personal Data:* b Geneseo, Ill, Feb 19, 38. *Educ:* Iowa State Univ, BS, 60, PhD(plant breeding), 65. *Mem:* AAAS; Sigma Xi; Am Soc Agron; Am Genetic Asn; NY Acad Sci. *Res:* Plant breeding, including applied statistical techniques in relation to plant breeding problems. *Mailing Add:* DeKalb Genetics Corp 101 Tomaras Ave Savoy IL 81674

JOHNSON, GORDON CARLTON, PHYSICAL CHEMISTRY, SURFACTANTS. *Current Pos:* CONSULT, SURFACTANTS, 84- *Personal Data:* b Newport, RI, Feb 9, 29; m 56; c 3. *Educ:* City Col New York, BChE, 52; Pace Univ, MBA, 83. *Prof Exp:* Develop engr, Silicones Div, Union Carbide Corp, 52-62, proj leader silicone prod develop & tech serv, 62-66, group leader, 66-77, technol mgr, 77-84. *Concurrent Pos:* Consult, Paper Recycling. *Mem:* Am Chem Soc; Am Oil Chemists' Soc. *Res:* Silicone chemistry; polymer synthesis and characterization; emulsification; resin catalysis and cure; rheology; textile applications; paper release coating; fiber lubricant; surfactants; fiber intermediates; ethylene oxide derivates; paper deinking. *Mailing Add:* 50 Cedar Hollow Rd Wakefield RI 02879-1435

JOHNSON, GORDON E, PHARMACOLOGY. *Current Pos:* prof & head dept, 73-86, PROF PHARMACOL, UNIV SASK, 86- *Personal Data:* b Welland, Ont, Sept 21, 34; m 58; c 6. *Educ:* Univ Toronto, BScPhm, 57, MA, 59, PhD(pharmacol), 61. *Prof Exp:* Med Res Coun Can fel physiol, Karolinska Inst, Sweden, 62-63; from asst prof to prof pharmacol, Univ Toronto, 63-73. *Mem:* Am Soc Pharmacol & Exp Therapeut; Pharmacol Soc Can; Am Soc Clin Pharmacol; Can Soc Clin Pharmacol; Can Hypertension Soc. *Res:* Catecholamines; thermoregulation and influence of environmental temperature on drug action; drug metabolism. *Mailing Add:* Dept Pharmacol Univ Sask Saskatoon SK S7N 0W0 Can

JOHNSON, GORDON GUSTAV, MATHEMATICS. *Current Pos:* assoc prof, 71-74, PROF MATH, UNIV HOUSTON, 74- *Personal Data:* b Chicago, Ill, June 23, 36; m 57, Nancy M; c Cathy L (Hendricks), Kim M (Bates), Carl G & David H. *Educ:* Ill Inst Technol, BS, 58; Univ Tenn, PhD(math), 64. *Prof Exp:* Asst prof math, Univ Ga, 64-69; assoc prof, Va Polytech Inst, 69-71. *Concurrent Pos:* Managing ed, Houston J Math, 74-79, 84-89; fel, Oak Ridge Inst Nuclear Studies, 63-64; sr resident res, Nat Res Coun, 78-79; assoc, Johnson Space Ctr, NASA, 78-80 & NASA Hq, 80-81; ed, Houston J Math, 74-; vis prof, Emory Univ, 83-84, IDA, 90-92. *Mem:* Swedish Math Soc; Sigma Xi; Am Math Soc; Math Asn Am. *Res:* Analysis; granted one patent. *Mailing Add:* 2010 Fairwind Rd Houston TX 77062

JOHNSON, GORDON LEE, GENERAL CHEMISTRY. *Current Pos:* PROF CHEM, KENYON COL, 62-, CHMN DEPT, 86- *Personal Data:* b Newark, Ohio, Dec 21, 32; m 58, 66; c 2. *Educ:* Ohio Univ, BA, 54; Univ Ill, PhD(inorg chem), 58. *Concurrent Pos:* Chmn, Chem Dept, Kenyon Col, 68-69 & 70-75; NSF fac fel, Iowa State Univ Sci & Technol, 69-70; vis prof, Iowa State Univ, 69-70, Ohio State Univ, 83-84; vis scientist, Oak Ridge Nat Lab, 75-76; NSF proj dir, 85-87. *Mem:* Sigma Xi; Am Chem Soc. *Res:* Metal-ion hydrolysis of esters-bioinorganic chemistry; titanium in molten salt systems; synthetic heme type compounds bioinorganic chemistry; author of 13 articles and books. *Mailing Add:* Box 3 Gambier OH 43022-0003

JOHNSON, GORDON OLIVER, SOLID STATE PHYSICS. *Current Pos:* asst prof, 74-77, assoc prof, 77-80, PROF PHYSICS, WALLA WALLA COL, 80- *Personal Data:* b Portland, Ore, June 2, 44; m 71; c 3. *Educ:* Walla Walla Col, BS, 66; Calif Inst Technol, MS, 67, PhD(elec eng), 72. *Prof Exp:* Res assoc elec eng, Purdue Univ, 72-74. *Mem:* Inst Elec & Electronics Engrs; Am Asn Physics Teachers. *Res:* Magnetic materials; processes of magnetization; magneto resistance phenomena. *Mailing Add:* Dept Physics Walla Walla Col 204 S College Ave College Place WA 99324. *E-Mail:* johngo@wwc.edu

JOHNSON, GORDON V, SOIL FERTILITY. *Current Pos:* assoc prof, 77-83,PROF AGRON, OKLA STATE UNIV, 83-; DIR AGRON SERV & STATE SOIL SPECIALIST, EXTEN, 78- *Personal Data:* b Harvey, NDak, Jan 9, 40; m 62; c 2. *Educ:* NDak State Univ, BS, 63; Univ Nev, MS, 66; Univ Nebr, PhD(agron), 69. *Prof Exp:* From asst prof to assoc prof agr chem & soils, Univ Ariz, 69-77. *Mem:* Int Turfgrass Soc; Crop Sci Soc Am; Am Soc Agron; Soil Sci Soc Am. *Res:* Evaluation of micro-nutrient supplying status of soils; evaluation of interferences in the spectrophotometric determination of iron with ethylenediamine Di (o-hydroxyphenylacetic acid); turfgrass management and nutrition; subirrigation of turfgrass; soil-turfgrass systems for tertiary sewage effluent treatment; effects of temperature and nitrogen on turfgrass root decline; soil fertility and soil salinity. *Mailing Add:* Dept Agron Okla State Univ Stillwater OK 74078-0001

JOHNSON, GORDON VERLE, PLANT PHYSIOLOGY. *Current Pos:* asst prof, 65-70, ASSOC PROF BIOL, UNIV NMEX, 70- *Personal Data:* b Long Beach, Calif, Sept 5, 33; m 60; c 4. *Educ:* Univ Calif, Berkeley, BS, 55, MS, 59; Univ Ariz, PhD(agr chem, soils), 65. *Prof Exp:* Res assoc bot, Ore State Univ, 63-64, asst prof, 64-65. *Mem:* AAAS; Am Soc Plant Physiol; Sigma Xi. *Res:* Absorption and metabolism of iron by plants; physiological effects of stress on plants; algal nutrition; biological nitrogen fixation; plant tissue and cell culture. *Mailing Add:* Dept Biol Univ NMex Main Campus 1 University Campus Albuquerque NM 87131-0001

JOHNSON, GROVER LEON, PHYSICAL CHEMISTRY. *Current Pos:* CONSULT, 90- *Personal Data:* b Bunn, Ark, Jan 9, 31; m 62; c 3. *Educ:* Rice Inst, BA, 53; Univ Tex, PhD(phys chem), 60. *Prof Exp:* Sr res chemist corrosion, Socony Mobil Oil Co, 60-64; asst prof chem, Univ Tex, Arlington, 64-90. *Concurrent Pos:* Consult, Socony Mobil Oil Co, 64- *Mem:* Am Chem Soc. *Res:* Electrochemistry; corrosion. *Mailing Add:* 1716 Cheryl Lane Arlington TX 76013

JOHNSON, GUY, JR, MATHEMATICAL ANALYSIS. *Current Pos:* assoc prof, 66-69, PROF MATH, SYRACUSE UNIV, 69- *Personal Data:* b Dallas, Tex, Mar 11, 22; m 42, Jean Steward; c Guy III, Kenneth & Bonnie. *Educ:* Agr & Mech Col Tex, BS, 43, MS, 52; Harvard Univ, MBA, 47; Rice Inst, PhD, 55. *Prof Exp:* Asst eng, Tex Eng Exp Sta, 48-50; from instr to assoc prof math, Rice Univ, 54-66. *Concurrent Pos:* Vis prof, Syracuse Univ, 64-66. *Mem:* Am Math Soc; Math Asn Am. *Res:* Potential theory. *Mailing Add:* 10 Pumpkin Hook W Henrietta NY 14586

JOHNSON, GUY HENRY, NUTRITION, FOOD SCIENCES. *Current Pos:* DIR, NUTRIT, GRAND METROP FOOD SECTOR, 89- *Personal Data:* b Chicago, Ill, Oct 24, 49; m 77, Jean G Graham; c Adel M & Tess H. *Educ:* Univ Ill, Urbana-Champaign, BS, 71, PhD(nutrit sci), 76. *Prof Exp:* Res assoc, Ky State Univ, 76-79; nutrit specialist, Gerber Prods Co, 79-85, dir, Infant Nutrit, 85-89. *Mem:* Am Oil Chemists Soc; Inst Food Technologists; fel Am Col Nutrit; Am Inst Nutrit; Am Soc Clin Nutrit; Sigma Xi. *Res:* Use current information in nutrition to develop and market nutritionally improved food products and provide effective nutrition educational materials. *Mailing Add:* Dir Nutrit Pilsbury Co 330 University Ave SE Minneapolis MN 55414-2130. *Fax:* 612-330-1851

JOHNSON, HAL G(USTAV), ORGANIC CHEMISTRY, MARKETING. *Current Pos:* from assoc prof to prof, 71-84, EMER PROF MKT, NORTHERN ILL UNIV, 84- *Personal Data:* b Saginaw, Mich, Apr 30, 15; m 40, Elizabeth Schreiner; c Judith L, David & John B. *Educ:* Beloit Col, BS, 36, MS, 38; Univ Wis, PhD(org chem), 41. *Prof Exp:* Instr chem, Beloit Col, 35-38; asst, Univ Wis, 38-41; org chemist, Com Solvents Corp, Ind, 41-45; asst gen mgr, Dykem Co, St Louis, Mo, 45-46; mgr org intermediate & pharmaceuts, Org Develop Dept, Monsanto Chem Co, 46-49, asst dir, Gen Develop Dept, 49-52, dir res & develop, Western Div, Calif, 52-54, dir develop dept, Res & Eng Div, 54-57; dir chem & rubber div, Bus & Defense Serv Admin, US Dept Com, Washington, DC, 57-58; vpres, Vick Chem Co, 57-59; chem & mgt consult, 59-62; vpres mkt & sales, SW Potash Div, Am Metal Climax, Inc, 62-66; mgt consult, Hal Johnson Assocs & Barnes Res Assocs, 66-69; dir chem develop, Chem Plastics Group, Develop Div, Borg Warner Corp, 69-71. *Concurrent Pos:* Educ & mgt consult; guest prof int & indust mkt, Linkoping Univ, Sweden, 77-78; mem, bd dir, Marsh Prod, Batavia, Ill, 84-; chmn, bd dir, Ill Bus Hall of Fame, Macomb. *Mem:* AAAS; Am Chem Soc; Com Develop Asn. *Mailing Add:* 1060 S Adams St Lancaster WI 53813

JOHNSON, HARLAN BRUCE, PHYSICAL CHEMISTRY. *Current Pos:* RETIRED. *Personal Data:* b Indianapolis, Ind, July 3, 22; m 44; c 4. *Educ:* Purdue Univ, BS, 43; Iowa State Col, MS, 48; Kans State Col, PhD(chem), 52. *Prof Exp:* Org res chemist, Eastman Kodak Co, 43-44; prod supvr, Tenn Eastman Corp, 44-46; asst, Atomic Res Inst, 46-48; from instr to asst prof chem, Ft Hays Kans State Col, 48-52; prof & head dept, Washburn Univ, 52-57, chmn sci div, 56-57; res supvr, Petro-Tex Chem Corp, 57-67, asst dir res, 66-67; dir res, Columbia Nitrogen Corp, 67-70; mem staff, PPG Industs, Inc, 70-93. *Mem:* Am Chem Soc; Am Inst Chem Engrs; Sigma Xi. *Res:* Electrolytic solutions; thermodynamics; petrochemicals; electrochemistry. *Mailing Add:* 1038 N Jefferson No 9 Medina OH 44256-1203

JOHNSON, HARLAN PAUL, MARINE GEOLOGY, GEOPHYSICS. *Current Pos:* Res assoc prof, 80-90, PROF, UNIV WASH, 90-, AFFIL PROF, DEPT GEOL SCI, 94- *Personal Data:* b Chicago, Ill, Dec 18, 39; m 72; c 2. *Educ:* Univ Ill, BS, 63; Southern Ill Univ, MS, 66; Univ Wash, PhD(geophysics), 72. *Concurrent Pos:* Vis prof, Inst Geol, Univ Rennes, France, 81. *Mem:* Am geophys Union; fel Geol Soc Am. *Res:* Origin and evolution of oceanic crust; rock magnetism; source of marine magnetic anomalies. *Mailing Add:* Sch Oceanog Univ Wash Seattle WA 98195. *E-Mail:* johnson@ocean.washington.edu

JOHNSON, HAROLD DAVID, PHYSIOLOGY. *Current Pos:* asst zool, 51-52, from asst to prof dairy husb, 52-77, PROF ENVIRON PHYSIOL, UNIV MO-COLUMBIA, 77- *Personal Data:* b Verona, Mo, Feb 28, 24; m 49; c 4. *Educ:* Drury Col, BS, 49; Univ Mo, MA, 52, PhD(dairy husb), 56. *Honors & Awards:* Animal Biometeorol Award, Am Meteorol Soc, 72; Peterson Award, Int Soc Biometeorol, 72; Gamma Sigma Delta Fac Res Award, 75. *Prof Exp:* Asst biol, Drury Col, 48-49; drug rep, Kendall Co, Ind, 49-50. *Concurrent Pos:* Mem comt bioclimatol & meteorol, Agr Bd, Nat Acad Sci. *Mem:* AAAS; Am Soc Animal Sci; Am Physiol Soc; Am Dairy Sci Asn; Int Soc Biometeorol. *Res:* Environmental physiology; investigations on effects of climate and environment on growth and production; related biochemical and physiological reactions of cattle and smaller laboratory mammals. *Mailing Add:* Dept Animal Sci Col Agr Univ Mo 114 Animal Sci Res Ctr Columbia MO 65211

JOHNSON, HAROLD HUNT, MATHEMATICS. *Current Pos:* RETIRED. *Personal Data:* b Gary, Ind, Sept 20, 29; m 58, Betsy Ancker; c Ruth, David, Paul & Marty. *Educ:* San Jose State Col, BA, 51; Univ Calif, MA, 56, PhD(math), 57. *Prof Exp:* Instr math, Stanford Univ, 57-58 & Princeton Univ, 58-61; assoc prof, Univ Washington, 61-74; vis assoc prof math, George Washington Univ, 74-76; prof math, Trinity Col, 77-92. *Mem:* Am Math Soc; Math Asn Am. *Res:* Differential geometry; systems of exterior differential forms; infinite pseudo-groups. *Mailing Add:* 222 Harbour Dr No 311 Naples FL 33940. *E-Mail:* harold29@naplesnet.com

JOHNSON, HARRY MCCLURE, meteorology, oceanography, for more information see previous edition

JOHNSON, HARRY WILLIAM, JR, ORGANIC CHEMISTRY. *Current Pos:* From instr to assoc prof & chmn dept, Univ Calif, 54-67, prof, 67-88, dean, Grad Div, 74-80, assoc dean, Grad Div, 82-90, EMER PROF CHEM, UNIV CALIF, RIVERSIDE, 88- *Personal Data:* b Waverly, Fla, Jan 2, 27; m 57, Margaret Ann Dahlgren; c Anne E (Johnston), Jill A & Gail L. *Educ:* Mass Inst Technol, SB, 51; Univ Ill, PhD(chem), 54. *Mem:* AAAS; Am Chem Soc; Royal Soc Chem. *Res:* Organic reaction mechanisms; reactions of heterocycles; isocyanate and isocyanide chemistry. *Mailing Add:* 2555 Flanders Rd Riverside CA 92507. *E-Mail:* johnson.ucr@ucr.campus.mci.net

JOHNSON, HERBERT GARDNER, ASTHMA, CHRONIC AIRWAYS DISEASES. *Current Pos:* RETIRED. *Personal Data:* b Wessington, SDak, Mar 22, 33; m 53; c 3. *Educ:* Univ Ill, Urbana, BS, 58, MS, 59; Univ Mich, Ann Arbor, PhD(immunol), 69. *Prof Exp:* Res asst biochem, Upjohn Co, Kalamazoo, Mich, 59-66, res assoc immunol, 69-75, res scientist, 75-78, sr res scientist, 78-84, sr scientist, 84-95. *Concurrent Pos:* Vis scholar pharmacol, Univ Calif, San Francisco, 80-81. *Mem:* Am Asn Immunologists; Am Asn Physiologists; Am Soc Microbiol. *Res:* Role of lipoxygenase metabolites of arachidonic acid in chronic airways diseases; immunopharmacology of lipid mediators and their pharmacologic control as related to airways, smooth muscle and glands. *Mailing Add:* 829 Berkshire Dr Kalamazoo MI 49001

JOHNSON, HERBERT GORDON, PLANT PATHOLOGY. *Current Pos:* RETIRED. *Personal Data:* b Granite Falls, Minn, Apr 11, 16; m 41, Jean Hegel; c Newton H & Barbara J (Pozner). *Educ:* Univ Minn, BS, 39, PhD, 53. *Prof Exp:* Agt barberry eradication, USDA, 39-40; plant pathologist & horticulturist, Yoder Bros, Inc, 40-42 & 45-48; asst plant path, Univ Minn, 48-53; plant pathologist, Green Giant Co, 53-56; assoc prof plant path, Univ Minn, St Paul, 56-64, prof, 64-80, exten plant pathologist, 56-80. *Mem:* Am Phytopath Soc. *Res:* Applied plant pathology. *Mailing Add:* 2175 Rosewood Lane S St Paul MN 55113

JOHNSON, HERBERT WINDAL, GENETICS, PLANT BREEDING. *Current Pos:* PROF AGRON & HEAD DEPT AGRON & PLANT GENETICS, INST AGR, UNIV MINN, ST PAUL, 64- *Personal Data:* b Tenn, July 3, 20; m 48; c 3. *Educ:* Univ Tenn, BSc, 43; Univ Nebr, MSc, 48, PhD(agron), 50. *Prof Exp:* Instr genetics, Univ Nebr, 47-48; agronomist plant breeding, USDA, NC, 48-53, res agronomist, Crops Res Div, Agr Res Serv, 53-64. *Mem:* Fel Am Soc Agron. *Res:* Quantitative genetics; plant breeding procedures. *Mailing Add:* 11081 Pleasant Valley Rd Sun City AZ 85351

JOHNSON, HERMAN LEONALL, HUMAN NUTRITIONAL STATUS. *Current Pos:* RES PHYSIOLOGIST HUMAN RES, WESTERN HUMAN NUTRIT RES CTR, USDA, PRESIDIO OF SAN FRANCISCO, 80- *Personal Data:* b Whitehall, Wis, Apr 1, 35; m 76, Barbara A Badger. *Educ:* N Cent Col, Ill, BA, 59; Va Polytech Inst & State Univ, Blacksburg, MS, 61, PhD(biochem-nutrit), 63. *Prof Exp:* Res biochemist, S R Noble Res Fedn, Ardmore, Okla, 63-65; nutrit chemist human res, US Army Med Res & Nutrit Lab, Denver, 65-74 & US Army Western Inst of Res Ctr, Presidio, San Francisco, 74-80. *Mem:* Am Inst Nutrit; Am Col Nutrit; Am Col Sports Med; Am Soc Clin Nutrit; AAAS; NY Acad Sci. *Res:* New and improved methods for determining human body composition and energy metabolism-expenditure; effects of nutritional status on body composition and energy metabolism in humans especially during weight loss. *Mailing Add:* 256 Alden Ave Rohnert Park CA 94928-3704. *Fax:* 415-556-1432

JOHNSON, HILDING REYNOLD, ANALYTICAL CHEMISTRY. *Current Pos:* RETIRED. *Personal Data:* b Sweden, Feb 14, 20; US citizen; m 47. *Educ:* Clarkson Col Technol, BS, 42. *Prof Exp:* Chemist, Heyden Chem Corp, 42-48; group leader anal chem, Heyden Newport Chem Corp, 48-70; supvr, Tenneco Chem, Inc, 70-75, mgr anal serv, 75-81. *Mem:* Am Chem Soc. *Mailing Add:* 19 Lois Ct Wayne NJ 07470-4206

JOHNSON, HOLLIS RALPH, ASTRONOMY, SPECTROSCOPY & SPECTROMETRY. *Current Pos:* assoc prof, Ind Univ, Bloomington, 63-69, chmn dept, 78-82 & 90-93, prof, 69-94, EMER PROF ASTRON, IND UNIV, BLOOMINGTON, 94- *Personal Data:* b Tremonton, Utah, Dec 2, 28; m 54, Grete M Leed; c Carol A (Harrison), Wayne L, Lyle D, Charlotte (Willian), Lise M (Tyner) & Richard L. *Educ:* Brigham Young Univ, BA, 55, MA, 57; Univ Colo, PhD(astrogeophys), 60. *Prof Exp:* NSF fel, Paris, France, 60-61; res assoc astron, Yale Univ, 61-63. *Concurrent Pos:* Vis scientist, High

Altitude Observ, Nat Ctr Atmospheric Res, 71-72; sr fel, Nat Res Coun, NASA Ames Res Ctr, Moffett Field, Calif, 82-83; F C Donders vis prof, Univ Utrecht, Netherland, 89; vis prof, Niels Bohr Inst, Univ Copenhagen, 90 & 94-97. *Mem:* Int Astron Union; Sigma Xi; Am Astron Soc; AAAS; Am Asn Univ Professor. *Res:* Theory of spectral line formation; stellar chromospheres; cool giant stars; chemical composition of stars; molecular opacities; radiative transfer. *Mailing Add:* Dept Astron Ind Univ Swain Hall W 319 Bloomington IN 47405

JOHNSON, HOLLISTER, JR, CHEMISTRY. *Current Pos:* RETIRED. *Personal Data:* b Watertown, NY, Jan 14, 29; wid; c William & Katherine J (Kristansen). *Educ:* Univ Rochester, BS, 59. *Prof Exp:* Res assoc, Eastman Kodak Res Labs, 53-86, consult, 86-89. *Mem:* Am Chem Soc. *Res:* Solution formulation and coating technology. *Mailing Add:* 302 Killarney Dr Rochester NY 14616

JOHNSON, HORACE RICHARD, PHYSICS, ELECTRICAL ENGINEERING. *Current Pos:* exec vpres, 58-68, pres, 68-87, VCHMN BD, WATKINS-JOHNSON CO, 88- *Personal Data:* b Jersey City, NJ, Apr 26, 26; m 50; c 5. *Educ:* Cornell Univ, BEE, 46; Mass Inst Technol, PhD(physics), 52. *Prof Exp:* Asst physics, Cornell Univ, 46-47; asst, Mass Inst Technol; head, Microwave Tube Dept, Res Lab, Hughes Aircraft Co, 52-57. *Concurrent Pos:* Lectr, Univ Calif, Los Angeles, 56-57; lectr, Stanford Univ, 58-68, assoc, Dept Elec Eng, 68-; mem bd dirs, Nat Asn Mfrs. *Mem:* Nat Acad Eng; Am Phys Soc; Sigma Xi; fel Inst Elec & Electronics Engrs; Res Soc Am. *Res:* Microwave spectroscopy; electron devices; microwave systems; author of 21 technical publications; granted 3 patents. *Mailing Add:* Watkins-Johnson Co 3333 Hillview Ave Palo Alto CA 94304-1223

JOHNSON, HORTON ANTON, MEDICINE, PATHOLOGY. *Current Pos:* RETIRED. *Personal Data:* b Cheyenne, Wyo, Nov 12, 26. *Educ:* Colo Col, AB, 49; Columbia Univ, MD, 53; Am Bd Path; dipl, 58. *Honors & Awards:* Lederle Med Fac Award. *Prof Exp:* Intern, Univ Mich, 53-54; resident path, 54-57; resident, Pondville Hosp, Walpole, Mass, 57-58; res assoc, Brookhaven Nat Lab, 58-60; asst prof, Univ Utah, 60-63; scientist & attend pathologist, Brookhaven Nat Lab, 63-70; prof path, State Univ NY, Stony Brook, 70-72; prof, Sch Med, Ind Univ, Indianapolis, 72-75; prof path & chmn dept, Sch Med, Tulane Univ, 75-84; dir path, St Lukes-Roosevelt Hosp Ctr, 84-91; prof path, Columbia Univ, 84-91. *Mem:* Radiation Res Soc; Am Asn Path; Biophys Soc; Col Am Path; Int Acad Path. *Res:* Radiation pathology; kinetics of cell proliferation; thermal injury; information theory. *Mailing Add:* 3 Lincoln Ctr Plaza 28G New York NY 10023

JOHNSON, HOWARD (LAURENCE), MEDICINAL CHEMISTRY, PHARMACOLOGY. *Current Pos:* chemist pharmaceut chem, 65-71, sr pharmacol chemist, 72-78, MGR BIOPHYS CHEMOMETRICS, LIFE SCI RES, STANFORD RES INST, 78- *Personal Data:* b San Leandro, Calif, Jan 4, 33; m 56; c 4. *Educ:* Univ Calif, BS, 56, PhD, 63. *Prof Exp:* Pharmaceut educ fel, 59-61; fel chem pharmacol, Nat Heart Inst, 63-65. *Concurrent Pos:* Clin lab officer, US Air Force, 57-59; res assoc, Univ Calif, Med Ctr, 72-; Fed Aviation Admin licensed private pilot, 81- *Mem:* AAAS; Am Chem Soc; Am Pharmaceut Asn; Acad Pharmaceut Sci; Am Soc Pharmacol & Exp Therapeut. *Res:* Chemistry, pharmacology of autonomic agents; extrapyramidal central nervous system pharmacology; drug distribution, metabolism and mechanisms of action; structure activity relationships; biochemical pharmacology of biogenic amines; histamine; drug-receptor interaction. *Mailing Add:* 612 Princeton Dr Sunnyvale CA 94087

JOHNSON, HOWARD ARTHUR, SR, MATHEMATICS, OPERATIONS RESEARCH. *Current Pos:* CHIEF EXEC OFFICER, ASSOC CONSULTS, FT WALTON BEACH, FLA, 74- *Personal Data:* b Ind, Dec 16, 23; m 47; c 2. *Educ:* Franklin Col Ind, AB, 49; Wesleyan Univ, MA, 50. *Prof Exp:* Physicist, Naval Ord Plant, Ind, 50-54; opers analyst, Air Proving Ground Command, 54-58; chief opers anal, Hq, 3rd Air Force, Eng, 58, dept chief opers anal, Hq, US Air Forces Europe, 58-61, dir, Opers Model Eval Group Air Force (OMEGA), 61-63; sr staff scientist & mgr comp effectiveness res div, Spindletop Res, Inc, 63-67; res dir, Vitro Servs Div, Vitro Corp Am, 67-68; sci asst to dir testing, Hq, Armament Develop & Test Ctr, 68-70, sci asst electronics test, 70-73, sr opers res scientist, Hq, USAF Tactical Air Warfare Ctr, Elgin AFB, Fla, 73-84. *Concurrent Pos:* Consult, Supreme Hq, Allied Powers Europ, 59-61, Ministry Defense, WGer, 61, USAF, 64-65, Univ Ky Med Ctr, 66-67 & Gulf South Res Inst, 68-84; mem, Int Exec Serv Corps, 84- *Mem:* Opers Res Soc Am; Mil Opers Res Soc; Am Statist Asn; Sigma Xi; Int Test & Eval Asn; Armed Forces Commun & Electronics Asn. *Res:* Solution of non-recurring operational problems for command or management decision utilizing the scientific method and a quantitative multi-disciplinary approach. *Mailing Add:* 10409 Huntington Dr Eden Prairie MN 55347

JOHNSON, HOWARD B(EATTIE), CERAMICS ENGINEERING, PHYSICAL CHEMISTRY. *Current Pos:* tech dir, 82-88, VPRES & TECH DIR, CONSOL CERAM PRODS, INC, 88- *Personal Data:* b Willits, Calif, Apr 27, 36; m 62; c 4. *Educ:* Univ of the Pac, BS, 58; Univ Minn, MS, 66; Univ Utah, PhD(ceramic eng), 66. *Prof Exp:* Res chemist, PPG Indust, Inc, 60-63; sr ceramist, Pittsburgh Corning Corp, 66-69; dir process develop, 69-77; dir res, Vesuviys Crucible Co, 77-82. *Mem:* Am Ceramic Soc; Am Chem Soc; Sigma Xi. *Res:* Manufacturing inorganic thermal insulation materials and alumina graphite refractories, vacuum formed disposable refractories for steel and aluminum; kinetics and thermodynamics of gas-solid reactions; electrical properties of ceramic materials. *Mailing Add:* 838 Cherry St Cincinnati OH 45107-1316

JOHNSON, HOWARD ERNEST, FRESH WATER ECOLOGY, TOXICOLOGY. *Current Pos:* RETIRED. *Personal Data:* b Livingston, Mont, Sept 21, 35; m 59; c 3. *Educ:* Mont State Univ, BS, 59, MS, 61; Univ Wash, PhD(fisheries), 67. *Prof Exp:* From asst prof to assoc prof, Mich State Univ, 67-75, prof fisheries 75-81, coordr environ contamination, Pesiticide Res Ctr, 78-81, dir, Inst Water Res, 78-81; res assoc, Mont Environ Qual Coun, 81-84; coordr, Clark Fork River Proj, Off Gov, Mont, 84-89; chief, Bur Fish Mgt, Mont Fish Wildlife & Parks, 89-95. *Concurrent Pos:* Panel mem, Comt Water Qual Criteria, Nat Acad Sci, 71-72; coordr toxic substances, Mich Serv & Educ Admin Grant Prog, 78- *Mem:* Am Fisheries Soc; Am Inst Fisheries Res Biologists. *Res:* Toxicity tests with aquatic organisms; production and culture of fish. *Mailing Add:* 1041 University Helena MT 59601

JOHNSON, HOWARD MARCELLUS, LYMPHOCYTE FUNCTION, SOLUBLE MEDIATORS. *Current Pos:* PROF COMP EXP PATH, UNIV FLA, 83- *Educ:* Ohio State Univ, PhD(immunol), 62. *Mailing Add:* Dept Microbiol & Cell Sci Bldg 981 1052 McCarty Hall Univ Fla No Name & Museum Roads Box 110700 Gainesville FL 32611. *Fax:* 352-392-5922

JOHNSON, HOWARD P, HYDROLOGY & WATER RESOURCES. *Current Pos:* From asst prof to prof, 59-80, head agr eng, 80-88, ANSON MARSTON DISTINGUISHED PROF, IOWA STATE UNIV, 88- *Personal Data:* b Odebolt, Iowa, Jan 27, 23; m 52; c 3. *Educ:* Iowa State Univ, BS, 49, MS, 50, PhD(agr & civil eng), 59; Univ Iowa, MS, 54. *Honors & Awards:* Hancor Soil & Water Eng Award, Am Soc Agr Engrs, 78. *Concurrent Pos:* Vis prof, Univ Mo, Columbia, 66-67; dir, Am Soc Agr Engrs, 76. *Mem:* Fel AAAS; fel Am Soc Agr Engrs; Soil Conserv Soc Am; Am Soc Eng Educ. *Res:* Hydrology, water quality and soil mechanics problems related to irrigation, drainage, erosion control and small watersheds. *Mailing Add:* 1801 20th St Apt N8 Ames IA 50010-5178

JOHNSON, HUGH MITCHELL, X-RAY, ASTRONOMY. *Current Pos:* RETIRED. *Personal Data:* b Des Moines, Iowa, Mar 4, 23; m 51, Jeanette Ringstad. *Educ:* Univ Chicago, AB, 48, SB, 49, PhD(astron), 53. *Prof Exp:* Asst astron, Yerkes Observ, Univ Chicago, 50-53; asst prof, Univ Iowa, 54-59; assoc prof & assoc astronr, Univ Ariz, 60-62; assoc scientist, Nat Radio Astron Observ, 62-63; staff scientist & mem res lab, Lockheed Missiles & Space Co, 63-86. *Concurrent Pos:* Res assoc, Yerkes Observ, Univ Chicago, 53-60; vis fel, Australian Nat Univ, 58-59; lectr, Stanford Univ, 71-75 & 80-82. *Mem:* Am Astron Soc; Int Astron Union. *Res:* Nebulae; galaxies; x-ray astronomy; x-ray, uv, photographic, ir and microwave. *Mailing Add:* 1017 Newell Rd Palo Alto CA 94303

JOHNSON, I BIRGER, ENGINEERING. *Current Pos:* RETIRED. *Personal Data:* b Brooklyn, NY, Sept 29, 13; m 42, Johanna Mortensen; c Bruce E & Richar B. *Educ:* Polytech Univ, BEE, 37, MEE, 39. *Honors & Awards:* William Martin Habirshaw Award, Inst Elec & Electronics Engrs, 66, Centennial Award, 84 & Lamme Medal, 86. *Prof Exp:* Grad & res asst elec eng, Polytech Univ, 37-39; mgr & instr elec eng, Gen Elec, 39-78, consult, 78-88. *Mem:* Nat Acad Eng; Inst Elec & Electronics Engrs; Int Conf Large High Voltage Elec Syst. *Res:* Contributions to the reliability and economy of extra high voltage electric power systems in the analysis of lightning and switching surge phenomena and in the protection and coordination of insulation systems. *Mailing Add:* The Commons 1786 Union St No 210 Niskayuna NY 12309-4120

JOHNSON, IRVING, PHYSICAL CHEMISTRY. *Current Pos:* chemist, 57-79, SR CHEMIST, ARGONNE NAT LAB, 79- *Personal Data:* b Chicago, Ill, Oct 23, 18; m 42, Alice Huffman; c Thomas C & Karl B. *Educ:* Cornell Univ, BA, 41; Columbia Univ, MA, 43, PhD(phys chem), 47. *Prof Exp:* Asst chem, Columbia Univ, 41-42, lect demonstr, 42-43; lectr chem, 43-44, asst, Div War Res, 44-45; from asst prof to assoc prof chem, Okla Agr & Mech Col, 46-53; prin res engr, Ford Motor Co, 53-57. *Mem:* Am Chem Soc; Am Inst Chemists. *Res:* Kinetics; light scattering; aerosols; thermodynamics of high temperature systems; electrochemistry; chemistry of nuclear fuels; fuel reprocessing. *Mailing Add:* 276 Woodstock Ave Clarendon Hills IL 60514. *E-Mail:* johnsoni@juno.com

JOHNSON, IRVING STANLEY, ONCOLOGY, ENDOTHELIAL CELL BIOLOGY. *Current Pos:* BIOMED RES CONSULT, 88- *Personal Data:* b Grand Junction, Colo, June 30, 25; m 49, Alwyn N Ginther; c Rebecca L, Bryan G, Kirsten S & Kevin B. *Educ:* Washburn Univ, MS, 48; Univ Kans, PhD(develop biol), 53. *Honors & Awards:* Cain Award Preclin Res, Am Asn Cancer Res; First Annual Corp Award Leadership Biomed Res, US Cong. *Prof Exp:* Asst instr anat, Washburn Univ, 47-48; asst instr parasitol, embryol & zool, Univ Kans, 48-50, asst zool, 50-53; asst dir, Biol-Pharmacol Res Div, Eli Lilly Res Labs, 53-68, dir, Biol Res Div, 68-72, exec dir, 72-73, vpres res, 73-88. *Concurrent Pos:* Ed bd, Chemico-Biol Interactions, 68-73; mem consult panel, Nat Cancer Prog, 71; ed adv bd, Cancer Res, 71-73, assoc ed, 74-; mem develop therapeut comt, Nat Cancer Inst, 78- *Mem:* Fel AAAS; Am Asn Cancer Res; Am Soc Cell Biologists; Immunol Soc; NY Acad Sci. *Res:* Anti-tumor chemotherapy; antiviral chemotherapy; tissue culture techniques; experimental embryology; oncogenic viruses; maintenance of biological function in tissue culture; recombinant DNA and public policy. *Mailing Add:* RR 1 Box 35 Stonington ME 04681-9702. *Fax:* 941-472-4782

JOHNSON, IVAN M, ZOOLOGY, PHYSIOLOGY. *Current Pos:* asst prof, 71-78, ASSOC PROF BIOL, CONCORDIA COL, 78- *Personal Data:* b Mansfield, Wash, May 30, 40; m 62; c 2. *Educ:* Whitworth Col, Wash, BS, 62; Univ Mont, PhD(zool), 69. *Prof Exp:* Asst zool, Univ Mont, 63-69; Nat Inst Gen Med Sci fel biol, Yale Univ, 69-71. *Mem:* Sigma Xi; Raptor Res Found. *Res:* Osmoregulation of vertebrates. *Mailing Add:* Dept Biol Concordia Col 901 Eighth St S Moorhead MN 56562-0001

JOHNSON, J(OSEPH) ALAN, ENDOCRINOLOGY. *Current Pos:* USPHS fel, 69-71, from asst prof to assoc prof, 71-85, PROF PHYSIOL, UNIV MO-COLUMBIA, 85-, RES PHYSIOLOGIST, VET ADMIN HOSP, 74- *Personal Data:* b W Palm Beach, Fla, Feb 1, 33; m 56, Janice Van de Water; c Robert A & Gary F. *Educ:* Butler Univ, BA, 63; Ind Univ Med Ctr, PhD(physiol), 68. *Mem:* Am Physiol Soc; Endocrine Soc; Am Soc Nephrol; Soc Exp Biol & Med; Am Heart Asn. *Res:* Cardiovascular and endocrine physiology; mechanisms in the production of hypertension in animal models. *Mailing Add:* Res Serv 151 Truman Mem Vet Admin Hosp Columbia MO 65201-5297. *Fax:* 573-884-4276

JOHNSON, J DAVID, MUSCLE BIOCHEMISTRY, CALCIUM BINDING PROTEINS. *Current Pos:* PROF MED BIOCHEM, MED CTR, OHIO STATE UNIV, 83- *Educ:* Mich State Univ, PhD(biophysics), 77. *Mem:* Am Soc Biochem & Molecular Biol; Biophys Soc. *Res:* Role of calcium binding proteins in health and disease; cardiovascular drugs. *Mailing Add:* Dept Med Biochem Med Ctr 333 Hamilton Hall Ohio State Univ 1645 Neil Ave Columbus OH 43210-1218. *Fax:* 614-292-4118; *E-Mail:* jdjohnso@magnus.acs.ohio-state.edu

JOHNSON, J(AMES) DONALD, ENVIRONMENTAL CHEMISTRY, ANALYTICAL CHEMISTRY. *Current Pos:* From asst prof to prof water chem, 61-90, EMER PROF ENVIRON CHEM, SCH PUB HEALTH, UNIV NC, CHAPEL HILL, 90- *Personal Data:* b Inglewood, Calif, Aug 1, 35; m 55, Joanne Wolf; c 2. *Educ:* Univ Calif, Los Angeles, BS, 57; Univ NC, PhD(anal chem), 62. *Honors & Awards:* Tanner Award Water Res, US Environ Protection Agency Sci Adv Bd. *Concurrent Pos:* Vis lectr, NC Wesleyan Col, 63-64; environ fel, Gothenburg Univ, Sweden, 70-71 & Nobel symp, 71; chmn, Environ Chem Div, Am Chem Soc, 87-88. *Mem:* Am Chem Soc. *Res:* Chemistry of natural aqueous solutions; analysis and kinetics of chlorine and bromine; drinking, cooling, and waste-water disinfection chemistry. *Mailing Add:* 100 Highland Trail Chapel Hill NC 27516

JOHNSON, J(AMES) R(OBERT), CERAMICS ENGINEERING. *Current Pos:* CONSULT, 79- *Personal Data:* b Cincinnati, Ohio, Jan 2, 23; m 45; c Cathy (Speer), Barbara (Kallusky), Randy, John, Jamie (Myers) & Brian. *Educ:* Ohio State Univ, BCerE, 47, MSc, 48, PhD(ceramic eng), 50. *Hon Degrees:* DSc, Univ Wis, Stout, 93. *Honors & Awards:* Pace Award, 59; Engrs Achievement Award, Am Soc Mech Engrs, 80; Greaves-Walker Award, 85; JRJ Award, 85; Prakken Award, 89. *Prof Exp:* Asst instr ceramic eng, Ohio State Univ, 49-50; asst prof, Univ Tex, 50-51; tech adv, Ceramic Lab, Oak Ridge Nat Lab, 51-56; mgr, nuclear lab, Cent Res Labs, 3M Co, 56-62, dir phys sci res, 62-72, exec scientist & dir adv res progs lab, 72-79. *Concurrent Pos:* Adj prof, Univ Minn & Univ Wis-Stout; 3m William L McKnight distinguished prof, Univ Minn, Duluth, 89-90; Nelva Runnalls res award, Univ Wis, 90. *Mem:* Nat Acad Eng; hon mem Am Ceramic Soc (pres, 73); Sigma Xi; Nat Inst Ceramic Engrs; AAAS. *Res:* Ceramics; metallurgy; solid state physics; inorganic chemistry; diffusion; glass; nuclear fuels; pioneer auto catalytic converters. *Mailing Add:* 1189 Tamarind Way Boca Raton FL 33486. *Fax:* 561-394-2340

JOHNSON, J(OSEPH) STUART, electrical engineering; deceased, see previous edition for last biography

JOHNSON, JACK (LAMAR), ANALYTICAL CHEMISTRY. *Current Pos:* SR RES CHEMIST, RES LABS, GEN MOTORS CORP, 59- *Personal Data:* b Elkhart, Ind, Mar 30, 30; m 56; c 2. *Educ:* Western Mich Univ, BS, 52; Wayne State Univ, MS, 54, PhD(anal chem), 59. *Prof Exp:* Anal chemist, Ethyl Corp, Mich, 54. *Mem:* AAAS; Am Chem Soc. *Res:* Chemical microscopy; microchemical techniques of analysis; development of instrumental methods for microanalysis and characterization of micro samples; x-ray diffraction analysis of materials. *Mailing Add:* 26026 Newport Ave Warren MI 48089-1327

JOHNSON, JACK DONALD, RESEARCH ADMINISTRATION, ENVIRONMENTAL SCIENCE. *Current Pos:* assoc dean, Col Agr, 81-84, DIR, OFF ARID LANDS STUDIES, UNIV ARIZ, 71-, DIR, AID NATURAL RESOURCES PROG, 74-, DIR, SLANDRAU SCI CTR. *Personal Data:* b Huntington, Ore, Aug 23, 31; m 58; c 4. *Educ:* San Diego State Col, BA, 59; Univ Minn, MS, 67, PhD(environ health), 71. *Prof Exp:* Proj engr, Humphrey, Inc, 56-60; sect chief aerospace, Martin-Marietta Corp, 60-63; syst engr, Jet Propulsion Labs, Calif Inst Technol, 63-66; res fel, Univ Minn, 67-70. *Concurrent Pos:* Desertification consult, AID, 74; asst coordr, Interdisciplinary Progs, Univ Ariz, 71-, dir off technol trans, 85-; vpres, Ariz Technol Develop Corp, 87- *Mem:* AAAS; Am Water Resources Asn; Am Geophys Union; Inst Environ Sci; Inst Int Develop; Sigma Xi. *Res:* Desertification; less developed country development; utilization of arid land resources; hydrology; natural resources mangement; biomass and bioenergy development. *Mailing Add:* 7380 E Snyder Rd Tucson AZ 85715-6208

JOHNSON, JACK WAYNE, SOLID STATE CHEMISTRY, CATALYSIS. *Current Pos:* res chemist, Exxon Res & Eng, 77-79, sr chemist, 79-81, staff chemist, 81-83, SR STAFF CHEMIST, INORG CHEM, CORP RES LABS, EXXON RES & ENG, 83- *Personal Data:* b Cannon Falls, Minn, July 8, 50; m 73; c 3. *Educ:* Carleton Col, BA, 72; Univ Wis-Madison, MS, 74, PhD(inorg chem), 76. *Prof Exp:* NSF fel inorg chem, Cornell Univ, 76-77. *Mem:* Am Chem Soc; Sigma Xi; Clay Minerals Soc. *Res:* Intercalation chemistry and layered solids; solid state chemistry; pillared clays; catalysis in petroleum refining. *Mailing Add:* 9 Sunrise Circle Clinton NJ 08809. *E-Mail:* jwjohns@erenj.com

JOHNSON, JAMES ALLEN, JR, HEALTH POLICY & APPLIED SOCIAL SCIENCES. *Current Pos:* PROF & CHMN, HEALTH ADMIN & POLICY & ASSOC PROF FAMILY MED, MED UNIV SC, 89- *Personal Data:* b Selma, Ala, Nov 13, 54; m 80, Peggy D Fore; c Allen, Adam & Elizabeth. *Educ:* Univ SAla, BA, 78, MS, 80; Auburn Univ, MPA, 82; Fla State Univ, PhD, 87. *Honors & Awards:* Res & Mgt Award, Asn Mgt, 88. *Prof Exp:* Resident, Vet Admin Hosp, 82-83; sr assoc pub admin, Fla Ctr Productivity, 83-86; asst prof health admin, Memphis State Univ, 86-89. *Concurrent Pos:* Instr, Fla State Univ, 83-86 & Tusculum Col, 87-89; bd mem, Alliance for Blind, 87-89; consult, Upjohn Healthcare Serv, 87-90; ed, J Mgt Pract, 88-90; health ed, J Health & Human Resources, 88- *Mem:* Acad Mgt; Am Pub Health Asn; Am Col Healthcare Execs; Nat Social Sci Asn; Am Soc Pub Admin. *Res:* Health policy and delivery systems; applied behavioral science research in health delivery; risk behavior, and acquired immunodeficiency syndrome policy and prevention. *Mailing Add:* Dept Health Admin & Policy Med Univ SC Charleston SC 29425. *Fax:* 803-792-3327

JOHNSON, JAMES BLAKESLEE, BIOLOGICAL CONTROL, SYSTEMATICS. *Current Pos:* PROF ENTOM, DEPT PLANT, SOIL & ENTOM SCI, UNIV IDAHO, 81- *Personal Data:* b Jan 25, 51; m 93, Linda Margaret Wilson; c Shannon & Heather. *Educ:* Univ Mich, BS, 73; Univ Calif, Berkeley, PhD(entom), 82. *Mem:* Entom Soc Am; Coleopterist's Soc; Hymenopterist's Soc; Am Inst Biol Sci; Int Orgn Biol Control; AAAS. *Res:* Biological control of arthropod pests using predators and parasites; Russian wheat aphid; biosystematics of green lacewings. *Mailing Add:* Div Entom Univ Idaho Moscow ID 83844

JOHNSON, JAMES DANIEL, THEORETICAL PHYSICS, STATISTICAL MECHANICS. *Current Pos:* fel, Los Alamos Nat Lab, 74-76, staff mem physics, 76-89, proj leader, 85-89, dep group leader, 89-90, actg group leader, 90-91, PRIN INVESTR, LOS ALAMOS NAT LAB, 81-, DEPT GROUP LEADER, PHYSICS, 91- *Personal Data:* b Toledo, Ohio, Mar 21, 44; m 66, Suzanne Darling; c Ian Johnson. *Educ:* Case Inst Technol, BS, 66; State Univ NY, Stony Brook, MA, 68, PhD(physics), 72. *Prof Exp:* Res assoc physics, Rockefeller Univ, 72-74. *Concurrent Pos:* mem US Deleg, Nuclear Testing Talks, 88. *Mem:* Am Phys Soc; AAAS. *Res:* Exact models and rigorous results in statistical mechanics; equation of state studies for materials of interest to energy development programs and to detonation physics. *Mailing Add:* T-1 MS-B221 Los Alamos Nat Lab Los Alamos NM 87545. *Fax:* 505-665-5757; *E-Mail:* jdt1@lanl.gov

JOHNSON, JAMES EDWARD, RADIATION BIOPHYSICS. *Current Pos:* from asst prof to assoc prof, 68-74, PROF ANIMAL SCI & RADIATION BIOL, COLO STATE UNIV, 74- *Personal Data:* b Warren, Pa, Jan 3, 36; m 59; c 3. *Educ:* Houghton Col, BS, 57; Univ Rochester, MS, 59; Colo State Univ, PhD(radiation biol), 65. *Prof Exp:* Chemist, E I du Pont de Nemours & Co, 57; res asst biophys, Univ Rochester, 59-62; instr radiation physics & radiation safety officer, Colo State Univ, 62-66, asst prof animal sci & radiation biol, 66-67; res assoc biophys, Harvard Med Sch, 67-68. *Concurrent Pos:* Lectr, Oak Ridge Mobile Lab, 65-73. *Mem:* Health Physics Soc. *Res:* Alkali metal metabolism; whole-body counting; environmental radioactivity. *Mailing Add:* Dept Radiol Sci 135 Gen Serv Bldg Ft Collins CO 80523

JOHNSON, JAMES EDWIN, PHYSICAL CHEMISTRY. *Current Pos:* RETIRED. *Personal Data:* b Berwind, WVa, June 5, 17; m 55; c 2. *Educ:* Emory & Henry Col, BS, 42; Va Polytech Inst, MS, 49, PhD, 52. *Prof Exp:* Instr chem, Emory & Henry Col, 46-48; res chemist, Chemstrand Corp, 52-62; from assoc prof to prof chem, Appalachian State Univ, 61-83. *Mem:* Am Chem Soc. *Res:* Solid State physics; physical chemistry of high polymers. *Mailing Add:* 160 Blanwood Dr Boone NC 28607

JOHNSON, JAMES ELVER, PHYSICAL-ORGANIC CHEMISTRY, PHOTOCHEMISTRY. *Current Pos:* from asst prof to assoc prof, 70-77, PROF CHEM, TEX WOMAN'S UNIV, 77- *Personal Data:* b Montevideo, Minn, Dec 27, 37; m 78, Kimberly A Neal; c Evan, Elaine, Kirk & Kristin. *Educ:* Univ Minn, BChem, 61, MS, 62; Univ Mo, PhD(chem), 66. *Prof Exp:* Asst prof chem, Sam Houston State Univ, 66-70. *Concurrent Pos:* Dir, Tex Womens Univ Sci Learning Res Ctr. *Mem:* Am Chem Soc; Royal Soc Chem; Sigma Xi; Int Am Photochem Soc; Nat Asn Adv Health Professions. *Res:* Photochemistry of hydroxamic acid derivatives; kinetics and mechanisms of nucleophilic substitution at the carbon-nitrogen double bond; mechanisms of Z-E isomerization at the carbon-nitrogen double bond. *Mailing Add:* Dept Chem & Physics PO Box 425859 Tex Woman's Univ Denton TX 76204-5859. *Fax:* 817-898-2382

JOHNSON, JAMES HARMON, CLINICAL CHILD PSYCHOLOGY, CHILDHOOD PSYOPATHOLOGY. *Current Pos:* assoc prof clin psychol, 79-87, PROF PSYCHOL, UNIV FLA, 87- *Personal Data:* b Martin, Tenn, March 30, 43; m 67; c 2. *Educ:* Murray State Univ, BS, 66, MS, 68; Northern Ill Univ, PhD(psychol), 76. *Prof Exp:* Instr child psychol, Univ Tex Med Br, 72-75; asst prof psychol, Univ Wash, Seattle, 75-79. *Concurrent Pos:* Assoc ed, J Clin Child Psychol, 82-86; mem, Sect Clin Child Psychol, Am Psychol Asn, 82-87, pres, 87; mem, planning comt, Nat Conf Training Clin Child Psychologists, 83-85; conf coordr, Fla Conf Child Health Psychol, 88- *Mem:* Am Psychol Asn; Soc Pediat Psychol. *Res:* Linking stress to problems of both physical health and psychological adjustment; assessment of stress; variables that mediate the impact of stress on individuals; the relationship between stress and fluctuations in health status of those with chronic illness; child psychopathology; effects of stress on children. *Mailing Add:* Dept Clin & Health Psychol Univ Fla PO Box 100165 Gainesville FL 32610-0165

JOHNSON, JAMES LESLIE, CHEMISTRY. *Current Pos:* RETIRED. *Personal Data:* b Kipling, NC, Feb 13, 21; m 45; c 2. *Educ:* Univ NC, BS, 43; Univ Ill, PhD(chem), 49. *Prof Exp:* Chemist, Stamford Res Labs, Am Cyanamid Co, 43-46; chemist, 49-62, from div dir to vpres, Upjohn Co, 62-83. *Mem:* AAAS; Am Chem Soc; Sigma Xi. *Res:* Natural products; spectroscopy; quality control; clinical chemistry. *Mailing Add:* 5400 Glen Harbor Dr Kalamazoo MI 49009-9535

JOHNSON, JAMES M(ELTON), chemical engineering, for more information see previous edition

JOHNSON, JAMES NORMAN, SOLID MECHANICS. *Current Pos:* MEM TECH STAFF, LOS ALAMOS NAT LAB, 76- *Personal Data:* b Tacoma, Wash, Sept 6, 39; m 59, Carol A Berry; c Kevin R, Kerry J & Timothy J. *Educ:* Univ Puget Sound, BS, 61; Wash State Univ, PhD(physics), 66. *Prof Exp:* Res fel physics, Wash State Univ, 66-67; mem tech staff, Sandia Labs, 67-73; staff consult, Terra Tek, Inc, 73-76. *Concurrent Pos:* NATO sr scientist, Cavendish Lab, Cambridge, UK, 85-86. *Mem:* Am Geophys Union; Sigma Xi; Am Phys Soc. *Res:* Theory of wave propagation and dynamic failure in solids including geophysical materials; constitutive relations for solids; initiation of solid explosives. *Mailing Add:* Los Alamos Nat Lab MS-B221 Los Alamos NM 87545. *Fax:* 505-665-5757; *E-Mail:* jnj@lanl.gov

JOHNSON, JAMES W(INSTON), CORROSION, ELECTROCHEMISTRY. *Current Pos:* From instr to assoc prof, 58-67, chmn, Dept Chem Eng, 79-90, PROF CHEM EMG, UNIV MO, ROLLA, 67- *Personal Data:* b Quinton, Okla, May 25, 30; m 53, Vera Hamman; c Christopher & Victor. *Educ:* Univ Mo, Rolla, BS, 57, MS, 58; Univ Mo-Columbia, PhD(chem eng), 61. *Concurrent Pos:* Fel electrochem lab, Univ Pa, 62-63. *Mem:* Am Inst Chem Engrs; Sigma Xi. *Res:* Electrochemical oxidation and reduction of hydrocarbons; kinetics of metal dissolution and deposition; corrosion; adsorption of hydrocarbon mixtures on molecular sieves. *Mailing Add:* Dept Chem Eng Univ Mo Rolla MO 65409-1230. *E-Mail:* jwj@umr.edu

JOHNSON, JANICE KAY, physical science, science education, for more information see previous edition

JOHNSON, JAY ALLAN, WOOD SCIENCE, ENGINEERING MECHANICS. *Current Pos:* SCI SPECIALIST WOOD COMPOSITE MAT, WEYERHAEUSER CO, 77- *Personal Data:* b Two Harbors, Minn, July 15, 41; m 71. *Educ:* Univ Minn, BS, 64; Col Environ Sci & Forestry, Syracuse Univ, MS, 71; Univ Wash, PhD(wood sci), 73. *Prof Exp:* Asst prof wood physics, Va Polytech Inst & State Univ, 73-77. *Mem:* AAAS; Soc Wood Sci & Technol; Forest Prods Res Soc; Am Soc Testing & Mat. *Res:* Development of wood particulate materials; modeling stress development in wood during drying; evaluation of fracture mechanics for testing procedures for wood and wood based materials. *Mailing Add:* Col Forest Resources AR-10 Univ Wash Seattle WA 98195

JOHNSON, JEAN ELAINE, PSYCHOLOGY, STRESS & COPING. *Current Pos:* RETIRED. *Personal Data:* b Wilsey, Kans, Mar 11, 25. *Educ:* Kans State Univ, BS, 48; Yale Univ, MS, 65; Univ Wis-Madison, MS, 69, PhD(social psychol), 71. *Honors & Awards:* Distinguished Contrib Nursing Sci, Am Nurses Found & Am Nurses Asn, 83; First Distinguished Researcher Award, Oncol Nursing Soc, 92; Outstanding Contrib Nursing & Health Psychol, Am Psychol Asn, 93. *Prof Exp:* Instr nursing, var nursing schs, 48-60; in-serv coordr nursing, Gen Rose Hosp, Denver, Colo, 60-63; res asst nursing res, Sch Nursing, Yale Univ, 65-67; from assoc prof to prof res & nursing & dir, Ctr Health Res, Col Nursing, Wayne State Univ, 71-79; prof nursing, Univ Rochester, 79-95; vis prof, Col Nursing, Univ Utah, 96-97. *Concurrent Pos:* Assoc dir nursing oncol & clin nursing chief oncol, Strong Mem Hosp, 79-93; mem, Behav Med Study Sect, NIH, 82-86; site dir, Robert Wood Johnson Clin Nurse Scholars Prog, 84-91; mem, Breast Cancer Prog Integration Panel, US Army Med Res & Develop Command, 93-96. *Mem:* Inst Med-Nat Acad Sci; AAAS; Sigma Xi; Am Nurses' Asn; Oncol Nursing Soc; Acad Behav Med Res; Am Psychol Asn. *Res:* Development of psychological theories about reactions to threatening events, and clinical tests of the effects on patient welfare of care activities deduced from such theories. *Mailing Add:* Sch Nursing Univ Rochester Med Ctr Rochester NY 14642. *Fax:* 716-473-1059

JOHNSON, JEAN LOUISE, MOLYBDENUM ENZYMES. *Current Pos:* res assoc, 74-86, RES ASST PROF BIOCHEM, MED CTR, DUKE UNIV, 86- *Personal Data:* b Memphis, Tenn, June 17, 47; m 69; c 2. *Educ:* Cornell Col, BA, 69; Duke Univ, PhD(biochem), 74. *Mem:* Am Soc Biol Chemists. *Res:* Structure and role of molybdenum cofactor in molybdoenzymes; molybdenum cofactor biosynthesis; molybdenum cofactor deficiency disease. *Mailing Add:* Dept Biochem Duke Univ Med Ctr Durham NC 27710-0001. *Fax:* 919-684-8919

JOHNSON, JEFFERY LEE, NEUROPHYSIOLOGY. *Current Pos:* Asst prof, 70-76, ASSOC PROF PHYSIOL & PHARMACOL, SCH MED, UNIV SDAK, 76- *Personal Data:* b Milwaukee, Wis, Mar 6, 41; m 68; c 1. *Educ:* Lakeland Col, BS, 64; Ind Univ, Indianapolis, PhD(physiol), 68. *Concurrent Pos:* NIH grants, Inst Psychiat Res, Med Ctr, Ind Univ, Indianapolis, 68-70. *Mem:* AAAS; Soc Neurosci. *Res:* Axoplasmic flow; regeneration; transmitter systems; topographic distribution of amino acids and enzymes in nervous system; electrophysiological analysis of nervous system activity. *Mailing Add:* Dept Physiol & Pharmacol Univ SDak Sch Med 414 E Clark St Vermillion SD 57069-2390

JOHNSON, JEROME H, ELECTRICAL ENGINEERING. *Current Pos:* prof & coordr eng sci, Univ Redlands, 58-77, EMER PROF ENG, 77- *Personal Data:* b Moscow, Idaho, Nov 22, 18; m 43; c 3. *Educ:* Univ Idaho, BS, 42; Ore State Univ, MS, 47, PhD(elec eng), 53. *Prof Exp:* Asst prof elec eng, Univ Wyo, 46-47 & Wash State Univ, 47-53; staff mem res, Sandia Corp, 53-58. *Mem:* Inst Elec & Electronics Engrs; Sigma Xi. *Res:* High energy shock excited pulse generators; solid state lasers; digital-analog computer elements. *Mailing Add:* 1718 Rossmont Dr Redlands CA 92373

JOHNSON, JERRY WAYNE, AGRONOMY. *Current Pos:* from asst prof to assoc prof, 77-86, PROF CROP & SOIL SCI, UNIV GA, 86- *Personal Data:* b Perry, Ga, July 22, 48; m 68. *Educ:* Univ Ga, BSA, 70; Purdue Univ, MS, 72, PhD(agron), 74. *Prof Exp:* Res asst hybrid wheat, Purdue Univ, 70-74; asst prof plant breeding & genetics, Univ Md, 74-77. *Mem:* Am Soc Agron; Crop Sci Soc Agron. *Res:* Development of barley and wheat varieties that are early and have disease resistance and milling and baking quality; a better feed barley being developed with a higher protein content. *Mailing Add:* Dept Crop & Soil Sci Univ Ga Griffin 1109 Experiment St Griffin GA 30223-1797

JOHNSON, JOE W, HYDRAULIC ENGINEERING. *Current Pos:* RETIRED. *Personal Data:* b July 19, 08; US citizen. *Educ:* Univ Calif, Berkeley, BSCE, 31, MSCE, 34. *Honors & Awards:* Int Coastal Eng Award, 87; Outstanding Civil Eng Medal, Japanese Dept Army, 91. *Prof Exp:* Res sediment transport by flowing water, Waterways Exp Sta, Vicksburg, Miss, 34-35 & Soil Conserv Serv, Washington, DC, 42-75; from instr to prof, Univ Calif, Berkeley, 42-75, emer prof hydraul eng, 77-88. *Concurrent Pos:* Ed, Proc Int Conf Coastal Eng, 50-76 & Shore & Beach, 74-88; hon mem, Soc Engrs, Taiwan, Repub China. *Mem:* Nat Acad Eng; hon mem Am Soc Civil Engrs; Am Shore & Beach Preserv Asn; hon mem Chinese Soc Civil Engrs. *Res:* Coastal engineering sediment problems. *Mailing Add:* 2605 Windsor Rd Apt 101 Victoria BC V8S 5H9 Can

JOHNSON, JOHN ALAN, PROCESS CONTROL. *Current Pos:* PRIN SCIENTIST, IDAHO NAT ENG LAB, 79-; CONSULT SCI, 96- *Personal Data:* b Gary, Ind, Jan 30, 43; m 65; c 2. *Educ:* Grinnell Col, BA, 65; Carnegie-Mellon Univ, MS, 67, PhD(physics), 70. *Prof Exp:* Asst prof physics, Kenyon Col, 69-76, Wittenberg Univ, 76-79. *Concurrent Pos:* Adj prof, Idaho State Univ, Univ Idaho. *Mem:* Acoust Soc Am; Am Welding Soc; Int Neural Network Soc; Am Soc Metall Int. *Res:* Nondestructive evaluation; ultrasonics; microcomputers; process sensing and control. *Mailing Add:* Box 1625 Idaho Nat Eng Lab Idaho Falls ID 83415-2209

JOHNSON, JOHN ARNOLD, SKIN METABOLISM, PHOTOSENSITIVITY. *Current Pos:* ASSOC PROF DERMAT, SCH MED, CREIGHTON UNIV, 75- *Personal Data:* b Cusson, Minn, Dec 6, 24; m 51; c 6. *Educ:* Univ Minn, BA, 51, MS, 64, PhD(med biochem), 71. *Prof Exp:* Chemist, Bemis Bros Bag Co, 55-60; scientist biomed res, Univ Minn, 60-71; asst prof dermat, 71-73, ASSOC PROF DERMAT & BIOCHEM, MED CTR, UNIV NEBR, OMAHA, 73- *Mem:* AAAS; Am Chem Soc; Soc Invest Dermat. *Res:* In vivo skin glucose metabolism in humans; enzymic determination of glucose, oligoglucosides and glycogen in animal tissues; mechanisms of photoprotection. *Mailing Add:* Dermat Dept Nebr Univ 600 S 42nd St Med Ctr Omaha NE 68198-4360

JOHNSON, JOHN CHRISTOPHER, JR, ECOLOGY, ORNITHOLOGY. *Current Pos:* RETIRED. *Personal Data:* b Gunnison, Colo, Nov 28, 24; m 48; c 3. *Educ:* Ohio State Univ, BS, 47; Univ Okla, MS, 52, PhD(zool), 57. *Prof Exp:* Pub sch teacher, Ohio, 48; teacher, Sch Dependents, Ramey AFB, PR, 48-49; instr, Univ Okla, 50-56; from asst prof to assoc prof zool, Pittsburgh State Univ, 56-62, actg chmn dept biol, 60-62, from prof to emer prof, 62-87. *Concurrent Pos:* Actg dir, Rocky Mountain Biol Lab, Colo, 54, trustee, 64-, dir, 67-70, registr, 75- *Mem:* Am Ornithologists' Union; Soc Syst Zool; Am Inst Biol Sci. *Res:* Vertebrate zoology; bioecology; ornithology. *Mailing Add:* Dept Biol Pittsburg State Univ Pittsburg KS 66762

JOHNSON, JOHN E(DWIN), CIVIL & STRUCTURAL ENGINEERING. *Current Pos:* from asst prof to assoc prof civil eng, 65-72, PRES ENG FORENSICS & TESTING, PROF CIVIL & ENVIRON ENG, UNIV WIS-MADISON, 72- *Personal Data:* b Detroit, Mich, Jan 18, 31; m 53, 83; c 6. *Educ:* Gonzaga Univ, BSCE, 56; Stanford Univ, MSCE, 57; Purdue Univ, PhD, 63. *Honors & Awards:* Z W Craine Award; NSF Award. *Prof Exp:* Design engr, Detroit Edison Co, 58-60; instr, Purdue Univ, 60-62; res engr, Dow Chem Co, 62-65. *Concurrent Pos:* Consult to over 100 companies, 65-; various fels. *Mem:* Am Soc Civil Engrs; Am Soc Eng Educ; Am Concrete Inst; Nat Soc Prof Engrs; Am Soc Testing & Mat; Sigma Xi; Am Inst St Construct. *Res:* Composite behavior; use of plastics as structural materials; analysis and testing of the physical behavior of engineering materials; large number of papers, articles, design manuals and one textbook. *Mailing Add:* 9236 W US Hwy Apt 18 Cambridge WI 53523

JOHNSON, JOHN E, JR, ELECTRON MICROSCOPY. *Current Pos:* ASST PROF NEUROSCI, TULANE UNIV, 79- *Personal Data:* b Ft Worth, Tex, Aug 21, 45. *Educ:* Tulane Univ, PhD(neurosci), 73. *Mailing Add:* 2340 Mistletoe Ave Ft Worth TX 76110-1147

JOHNSON, JOHN HAL, ORGANIC & FOOD CHEMISTRY. *Current Pos:* PROF FOOD SCI & NUTRIT, BRIGHAM YOUNG UNIV, 69- *Personal Data:* b Benjamin, Utah, July 1, 30; m 58; c 4. *Educ:* Brigham Young Univ, BS, 55, MS, 57; Ohio State Univ, PhD(food sci), 63. *Honors & Awards:*

Virginia F Cutler Lectr, 78. *Prof Exp:* Lab instr chem, Brigham Young Univ, 59-60; res asst food chem, Agr Exp Sta, Ohio State Univ, 60-63; asst biochemist food sci, Agr Exp Sta, Univ Fla, 63-68. *Mem:* Inst Food Technologists; Sigma Xi. *Res:* Chemical reactions occurring in foods during processing and storage; effects on functional qualities of cooker extruded soy enriched cereal flours; development of cereal-based complemented foods. *Mailing Add:* Brigham Young Univ 2218 E SFLC Provo UT 84602

JOHNSON, JOHN HAROLD, LIQUID CHROMATOGRAPHY, SPECTROSCOPY. *Current Pos:* SR RES INVESTR, ANALYTIC DEVELOP, KRAFT GEN FOODS, 88- *Personal Data:* b Chicago, Ill. *Educ:* Monmouth Col, Ill, BA, 68; Univ Ark, PhD(organ chem), 74. *Prof Exp:* Sr scientist, US Environ Protection Agency, 73-77; res investr, Nalco Environ & Chem Sci Corp, 77-78; supvr chem anal, G D Searle Co, 78-80; group leader, Anal Develop, Dupont Critical Care, 80-88. *Concurrent Pos:* Lectr, Fac Inst, Argonne Nat Lab, 76-79 & Am Chem Soc Speakers Tour, 77. *Mem:* Acad Pharmaceut Sci; Am Chem Soc; Am Inst Chemists; Asn Off Anal Chemists. *Res:* Separation techniques as applied to food componets water soluble polymers; basic studies into new chromatographic separation, spectroscopic and laboratory automation techniques as applied to food analyis and structure identification. *Mailing Add:* 320 Juniper Parkway Libertyville IL 60048-3527

JOHNSON, JOHN HARRIS, ENGINES & DIESEL ENGINES, AIR POLLUTION. *Current Pos:* from asst prof to prof, 70-80, chmn dept, 86-93, DISTINGUISHED PRESIDENTIAL PROF, MICH TECHNOL UNIV, 81-, DIR, ENG, EXTEN COL ENG, 93- *Personal Data:* b Fond du Lac, Wis, Feb 10, 37; m 90, Eleanor Housding; c Jill A & Karin M. *Educ:* Univ Wis-Madison, BS, 59, MS, 60, PhD(mech eng), 64. *Honors & Awards:* Arch T Colwell Merit Award, Soc Automotive Engrs, 83 & 96, Horning Mem Award, 92. *Prof Exp:* Res asst mech eng, Univ Wis-Madison, 59-64; proj engr, US Army Tank-Automotive Ctr, 64-66; chief engr appl eng res, Int Harvester Co, Ill, 66-70. *Concurrent Pos:* Coordr, Res Coun Air Pollution Res Comt, 68-87; mem, Mine Health Res Adv Comt, Dept Health, Educ & Welfare, 79-81; consult, US Environ Protection Agency, 71-77, US Bur Mines, 77-79, NASA, 78-81, Nat Acad Sci, 79-81, Off Tech Assess, US Cong, 79, A D Little, 80-81, Stanford Res Inst, 81-82 & Fleetguard, Inc, 88-; mem bd dir, Soc Automotive Engrs, 82-85; mem, Nat Res Coun, 86-89, Dept Labor, 88 & Fuel Econ Comt, 91-92. *Mem:* Fel Soc Automotive Engrs; Combustion Inst; Am Soc Mech Engrs; Air Pollution Control Asn; Am Soc Eng Educ; Am Conf Govt Indust Hygienists. *Res:* Experimental combustion studies; computer calculations of single fuel drop motion and vaporization; computer cycle analysis; hybrid engine research; emissions and air pollution; instantaneous temperature measurements in internal combustion engines; tribology; diesel particulate emissions measurement and control; wear particle measurement; pollutants in underground mining; cooling system modeling. *Mailing Add:* Dept Mech Eng & Eng Mech Mich Technol Univ 1400 Townsend Dr Houghton MI 49931. *Fax:* 906-487-2822

JOHNSON, JOHN IRWIN, JR, ZOOLOGY. *Current Pos:* from assoc prof to prof biophys, psychol & zool, 65-81, PROF ANAT, MICH STATE UNIV, 81- *Personal Data:* b Salt Lake City, Utah, Aug 18, 31. *Educ:* Univ Notre Dame, AB, 52; Purdue Univ, MS, 55, PhD(psychol), 57. *Prof Exp:* Instr psychol, Purdue Univ, 56-57; from instr to asst prof, Marquette Univ, 57-60; USPHS spec res fel lab neurophysiol, Univ Wis, 60-63; Fulbright res scholar physiol, Univ Sydney, 64-65. *Concurrent Pos:* NIH career develop award, 65-72. *Mem:* AAAS; Am Soc Zool; Soc Neurosci; Am Asn Anat; Am Soc Mammalogists; hon mem Anat Asn Australia & New Zealand. *Res:* Brain function; neuroanatomy; animal behavior. *Mailing Add:* Dept Anat Mich State Univ East Lansing MI 48824-1316. *Fax:* 517-336-2443

JOHNSON, JOHN LEROY, microbiology; deceased, see previous edition for last biography

JOHNSON, JOHN LOWELL, PLASMA PHYSICS. *Current Pos:* RETIRED. *Personal Data:* b Butte, Mont, Mar 18, 26; m 51, Barbara M Hynds; c Lowell J, Lesley J (Gelb) & Jennifer R (Goodall). *Educ:* Mont State Univ, BS, 49; Yale Univ, MS, 50, PhD(physics), 54. *Prof Exp:* Vis mem res staff, Plasma Physics Lab, Princeton Univ, 55-68, vis res physicist, 68-71, vis sr res physicist, 71-85, prin res scientist, 85-96. *Concurrent Pos:* Sr scientist, Atomic Power Dept, Westinghouse Elec Corp, 54-64, fel physicist, Res Labs, 64-68, adv scientist, 68-79, consult scientist, Res & Develop Ctr, 79-85. *Mem:* Am Phys Soc. *Res:* Theoretical plasma physics associated with the controlled thermonuclear research program with principal emphasis directed towards investigation of the magnetohydrodynamic properties of toroidal confinement configurations. *Mailing Add:* 540 Ewing St Princeton NJ 08540

JOHNSON, JOHN MARSHALL, PHYSIOLOGY. *Current Pos:* from asst prof to assoc prof, 75-89, PROF PHYSIOL, UNIV TEX HEALTH SCI CTR, SAN ANTONIO, 89- *Personal Data:* b McCamey, Tex, Aug 10, 44; m 70; c 2. *Educ:* Rice Univ, BA, 66; Univ Tex Southwestern Med Sch, PhD(physiol), 72. *Prof Exp:* Sr fel, Sch Med, Univ Wash, 72-74, res assoc physiol, 74-75. *Mem:* Am Heart Asn; fel Am Physiol Soc; NY Acad Sci; AAAS; Am Col Sports Med. *Res:* Reflex control of the circulatory system; cardiovascular physiology regulation of cutaneous blood flow. *Mailing Add:* Dept Physiol Univ Tex Health Sci Ctr 7703 Floyd Curl Dr San Antonio TX 78284-7756. *Fax:* 210-567-4410

JOHNSON, JOHN MORRIS, BOTANY & CYTOLOGY, PLANT TAXONOMY. *Current Pos:* assoc prof, 69-74, chmn, Natural Sci & Math Div, 85-93, PROF BIOL, WESTERN ORE STATE COL, 74- *Personal Data:* b Boise, Idaho, Mar 16, 37; m 59; c 2. *Educ:* Col Idaho, BS, 59; Ore State Univ, MS, 61, PhD(bot, tissue cult), 64. *Prof Exp:* From asst prof to assoc prof biol, Cent Col Iowa, 64-69. *Concurrent Pos:* USPHS fel, Univ Chicago, 65-66. *Mem:* AAAS; Bot Soc Am; Am Soc Cell Biologists. *Res:* Plant tissue culture; behavior and function of nucleus and nucleolar vacuoles; plant taxonomy of Oregon plants; ecology of wet-land species especially Juncus. *Mailing Add:* Biol Dept Western Ore State Col Monmouth OR 97361

JOHNSON, JOHN RICHARD, BIOPHYSICS, HEALTH PHYSICS. *Current Pos:* mgr, Health Physics Dept, Life Sci Ctr, 88-93, chief scientist, Health Protection Dept, 93-96, EMER SCIENTIST, LIFE SCI CTR, PAC NW LAB, 96-; PRES, INT DOSEMETRY INSTRUMENTS & SERVS, INC, 96- *Personal Data:* b Edmonton, Alta, July 6, 42; m 67, Carell Brown; c Richard A & Lisa S. *Educ:* Univ BC, BS, 67, MS, 70, PhD(physics), 73. *Honors & Awards:* Distinguished Achievement Award, Can Radiation Protection Asn, 87; Outstanding Serv Award, Int Radiation Protection Asn, 92. *Prof Exp:* Res officer, Chalk River Nuclear Lab, 73-81, head, Biomed Res Br, 81-84, head, Dosimetric Res Br, Health Sci Div, 84-88. *Concurrent Pos:* Dir, Can Radiation Protection Asn, 82-83; adj prof, McMaster Univ, 84-90 & Wash State Univ, 91-; mem, Nat Coun Radiation Protection & Measurements. *Mem:* Radiation Res Soc; Health Physics Soc; Can Radiation Protection Asn (pres, 84-85); Soc Radiation Protection; Soc Risk Anal. *Res:* Dosimetric and metabolic models for internal dosimetry including radon daughters; improvement of techniques for measuring internal contamination in humans; instrumentation for internal dosimetry and exposure monitoring; internal contamination control and risk assessment for toxic materials. *Mailing Add:* Batelle Pac NW Lab PO Box 999 K3-53 Richland WA 99352. *Fax:* 509-375-2019; *E-Mail:* jr_johnson@pnl.gov

JOHNSON, JOHNNY ALBERT, LATTICES, RINGS. *Current Pos:* from asst prof to assoc prof, 68-78, PROF MATH, UNIV HOUSTON-UNIVERSITY PARK, 78- *Personal Data:* b El Paso, Tex, Mar 6, 38; m 55, Betty J Smith; c Johnny A & Brenda L. *Educ:* Univ Calif, Riverside, BA, 65, MA, 66, PhD(math), 68. *Prof Exp:* NSF fel, Univ Calif, Riverside, 65-68. *Concurrent Pos:* Univ Houston res initiation grant, 69; sr engr, Jet Propulsion Lab, Calif Inst Technol, 69-71; assoc managing ed, Houston J Math, 74-84, ed, 84-; Univ Houston res grant, 78, leave grant, 80. *Mem:* Math Asn Am; Am Math Soc. *Res:* Commutative algebra. *Mailing Add:* Dept Math Univ Houston-University Park Houston TX 77204-3476. *E-Mail:* JJohnson@uh.edu

JOHNSON, JOHNNY R(AY), APPLIED MATHEMATICS, ELECTRICAL ENGINEERING. *Current Pos:* RETIRED. *Personal Data:* b Chatham, La, Dec 19, 29; m 60, 90, Barbara Freeman; c Todd Michael, John Fitzgerald & Shauna Renee. *Educ:* La Polytech Inst, EE, 51; Auburn Univ, MS, 53, PhD(math), 59. *Honors & Awards:* Centennial Medal, Inst Elec & Electronics Engrs. *Prof Exp:* Electronic engr, Pitman-Dunn Lab, Frankford Arsenal, 53-54; asst prof math, La Polytech Inst, 58-62; assoc prof, Appalachian State Teachers Col, 62-63; from assoc prof to prof elec eng, La State Univ, Baton Rouge, 70-83; eng specialist, Gen Dynamics, 83-84; prof math, Univ NAla, 84-95. *Mem:* Sigma Xi. *Res:* Special functions; boundary value problems; analog and digital filters. *Mailing Add:* 222 Meadowcrest Dr Florence AL 35630

JOHNSON, JOSEPH ANDREW, III, TURBULENCE, NONEQUILIBRIUM FLOW. *Current Pos:* DISTINGUISHED PROF SCI & ENG, PROF PHYSICS & PROF MECH ENG, FLA A&M UNIV, 91-, DIR, CTR NONLINEAR & NONEQUILIBRIUM AEROSCI, 92- *Personal Data:* b Nashville, Tenn, May 26, 40; m 61, Lynette M Edmonds; c Christopher E, Bradley R, Kyla G & Tayari J. *Educ:* Fisk Univ, BA, 60; Yale Univ, MS, 61, PhD(physics), 65. *Hon Degrees:* DSc, Fisk Univ, 91. *Honors & Awards:* Bouchet Award, Am Phys Soc, 95. *Prof Exp:* Mem tech staff, Bell Labs, Whippany, NJ, 65-68; vis asst prof eng & appl sci, Yale Univ, 68-69; chmn & prof physics, Southern Univ, Baton Rouge, La, 69-72; assoc prof physics, Rutgers Univ, 73-81; prof physics, City Col NY, 81-93, Kayser prof sci & eng, 91-93. *Concurrent Pos:* Consult, Sikorsky Aircraft Corp, 62-65; Gen Appl Sci Lab, 68-69, Von Karman Gas Dynamic Facil, 69-77, Fermi Nat Lab, 73, Yale Univ, 73-75, Bell Labs, 75-76, Res & Develop Ctr, Gen Elec Corp, 78-80 & Grambling State Univ, 80-83. *Mem:* Assoc fel Am Inst Aeronaut & Astronaut; fel Am Phys Soc; Third World Acad Sci. *Res:* Experimental and theoretical studies of turbulence in fluids and plasmas, nonequilibrium processes, and fundamental interactions. *Mailing Add:* Fla A&M Univ Ctr Nonlinear & Nonequilibrium Aerosci 1800-3 E Dirac Dr Tallahassee FL 32310

JOHNSON, JOSEPH EGGLESTON, III, INTERNAL MEDICINE, INFECTIOUS DISEASE. *Current Pos:* interim exec vpres, 94-95, SR VPRES, AM COL PHYSICIANS, 93-; ADJ PROF MED, UNIV PA, 94- *Personal Data:* b Elberton, Ga, Sept 17, 30; m 56; c Joseph IV, Judith A & Julie M. *Educ:* Vanderbilt Univ, BA, 51, MD, 54. *Prof Exp:* Intern, Osler Med Serv, Johns Hopkins Hosp, 54-55, fel med, 58-59, asst resident, 57-58 & 59-60, res physician, 60-61; from instr to asst prof, Sch Med, Johns Hopkins Univ, 61-66, asst dean student affairs, 63-66; from assoc prof to prof, Col Med, Univ Fla, 66-72, chief, Infectious Dis Div, 68-72, assoc dean, 70-72; prof med & chmn dept, Bowman Gray Sch Med, 72-85; dean & prof internal med, Med Sch, Univ Mich, 85-93. *Concurrent Pos:* Am Col Physicians Mead Johnson scholar, 60-61; John & Mary R Markle scholar acad med, 62-67; prog dir, USPHS Med Student Res Training Grant, 63-66; prin investr, Off Surgeon Gen, US Dept Army res grant, 66-71; consult, US Army Biol Lab, Ft Detrick, Md, 66-71; dir, Nat Insts Allergy & Infectious Dis training grant & contract

Food & Drug Admin, 67-72, sabbatical, London Clin Res Ctr, 70-71, Royal Soc Med traveling fel, 70-71; chmn bd gov, Am Bd Int Med, 77-83; mem, Federated Coun Internal Med, 78-, chmn, 82-83; adj prof med, Univ Pa, 94- *Mem:* Am Asn Immunologists; Am Soc Microbiol; Soc Exp Biol & Med; fel Royal Soc Med; Am Clin & Climat Asn; Asn Am Physicians; Int Dis Soc Am; Am Col Physicians (pres, 82-83); Asn Prof Med (pres 82-83). *Res:* Pathogenesis of staphylococcal infection; role of bacterial hypersensitivity and immunity in infection; epidemiology of hospital and laboratory acquired infection; pulmonary host defense mechanisms; adverse drug reactions; epidemiology and mechanisms. *Mailing Add:* Am Col Physicians Independence Mall W Sixth St at Race Philadelphia PA 19106. *Fax:* 215-351-2829; *E-Mail:* jjohnson@mail.acponline.org

JOHNSON, JOYCE M, PSYCHIATRY. *Current Pos:* dep chief med officer, 94, asst surgeon gen, 94-95, DIR, OFF PHARMACOL & ALTERNATIVE THER, USPHS, 96- *Personal Data:* b Baton Rouge, La, Jan 30, 52. *Educ:* Luther Col, BA, 72; Univ Iowa, MA, 76; Mich State Univ, DO, 80. *Mailing Add:* 5700 Fishers Lane Rockwall 2 Bldg Suite 740 Rockville MD 20857. *Fax:* 301-480-3045; *E-Mail:* jjohnson@samhsa.gov

JOHNSON, JULIAN FRANK, POLYMER CHEMISTRY. *Current Pos:* RETIRED. *Personal Data:* b Baxter, Kans, Aug 20, 23; m 43. *Educ:* Col Wooster, BA, 43; Brown Univ, PhD(chem), 51. *Honors & Awards:* Am Chem Soc Award in Chromatog, 70. *Prof Exp:* Supvry res chemist, Chevron Res Corp, 50-68; from assoc prof to prof chem, Univ Conn, 68-89, assoc dir, Inst Mat Sci, 71-89. *Concurrent Pos:* Lectr, Exten Div, Univ Calif, Berkeley, 60-68. *Mem:* Am Chem Soc; Am Phys Soc; Am Soc Rheol; Brit Soc Rheol. *Res:* Physics of polymers; rheology; chromatography. *Mailing Add:* Life Care Ctr 6151 Vegas Dr Las Vegas NV 89108

JOHNSON, KAREN ELISE, PHYSICS, HISTORY OF PHYSICS. *Current Pos:* asst prof, 88-92, ASSOC PROF PHYSICS, ST LAWRENCE UNIV, 92-, HENRY PRIEST CHAIR PHYSICS, 95- *Personal Data:* b Balston Spa, NY, Oct 3, 50. *Educ:* Grinnell Col, BA, 72; Univ Minn, MS, 76, PhD(hist sci), 86. *Prof Exp:* Asst prof physics, Bates Col, 86-88; vis asst prof, Cath Univ, 87. *Mem:* Am Asn Physics Teachers; Hist Sci Soc; Sigma Xi. *Res:* History of 20th century physics; nuclear and chemical physics; history of women in science. *Mailing Add:* Dept Physics St Lawrence Univ Canton NY 13617

JOHNSON, KAREN LOUISE, BOTANY, PLANT ECOLOGY. *Current Pos:* cur bot, 72-91, CHIEF CUR, NATURAL HIST, MAN MUS MAN & NATURE, 91- *Personal Data:* b Flint, Mich, Feb 4, 41. *Educ:* Swarthmore Col, BA, 63; Univ Ill, Urbana, MS, 65, PhD(bot), 70. *Prof Exp:* Instr biol, Colby Col, 66-68; fel bot, Univ Man, 69-72. *Mem:* Ecol Soc Am. *Res:* Alpine plant communities and soils; vegetation mapping and description; establishment of ecological reserves and natural areas; boreal forest plant geography. *Mailing Add:* 190 Rupert Winnipeg MB R3B 0N2 Can

JOHNSON, KEITH E, STATISTICAL PROCESS CONTROL. *Current Pos:* STATISTICIAN, BELL SOUTH TELECOMMUN, 84- *Personal Data:* m 65, 84, 90, Martha Watson; c Kristin & Kathryn. *Educ:* Univ Wis-Stevens Point, BS, 65; Univ Wis-Madison, MS, 67; Univ Ga, PhD(math & topology), 71. *Prof Exp:* Asst prof math, Univ Southern Ala, 71-73; math analyst, SCent Bell, 74-84. *Mailing Add:* 3535 Colonnade Pkwy Rm S9C1 Birmingham AL 35243. *E-Mail:* keith.e.johnson@bridge.bellsouth.com

JOHNSON, KEITH EDWARD, ANALYTICAL CHEMISTRY. *Current Pos:* from asst prof to assoc prof, 66-72, PROF INORG & ANAL CHEM, UNIV REGINA, 72- *Personal Data:* b Feltham, Eng, Jan 4, 35; m 60; c 2. *Educ:* Univ London, BSc & ARCS, 56; Univ London, DIC & PhD(phys chem), 59, DSc(chem), 74. *Prof Exp:* Res assoc anal chem, Univ Ill, 59-62; asst lectr phys chem, Sir John Cass Col, Eng, 62-63, lectr, 63-66. *Concurrent Pos:* Vis prof, Univ Calif, Riverside, 72-73, Sask Power Corp, 79-80 & Oak Ridge Nat Lab, Oak Ridge, Tenn, 87-88. *Mem:* Electrochem Soc; fel Chem Inst Can; Am Chem Soc. *Res:* Molten salt electrochemistry; coordination of transition metal ions in melts; structural studies of inorganic complexes; water and soil trace analysis; pyrazolone chemistry; azolium ion chemistry; superacidic melts. *Mailing Add:* Dept Chem Univ Regina Regina SK S4S 0A2 Can. *Fax:* 306-585-4894; *E-Mail:* kejohnso@max.cc.uregina.ca

JOHNSON, KENNETH, research management, organic chemistry, for more information see previous edition

JOHNSON, KENNETH ALAN, ELEMENTARY PARTICLE PHYSICS. *Current Pos:* from asst prof to assoc prof, 58-65, PROF PHYSICS, MASS INST TECHNOL, 65- *Personal Data:* b Duluth, Minn, Mar 26, 31; m 54; c 1. *Educ:* Ill Inst Technol, BS, 52; Harvard Univ, AM, 54, PhD(physics), 55. *Prof Exp:* Res fel & lectr physics, Harvard Univ, 55-57; NSF fel, Univ Copenhagen, 57-58. *Concurrent Pos:* Guggenheim fel, 71-72. *Mem:* Fel Am Phys Soc; fel Am Acad Arts & Sci; Sigma Xi; fel AAAS. *Res:* Quantum electrodynamics; quantum field theory; elementary particle physics. *Mailing Add:* Dept Physics Mass Inst Technol Cambridge MA 02139

JOHNSON, KENNETH ALLEN, CELL MOTILITY, ENZYME MECHANISMS. *Current Pos:* ASST PROF BIOCHEM, PA STATE UNIV, 79- *Personal Data:* b Davenport, Iowa, Mar 10, 49; m 70; c 2. *Educ:* Univ Iowa, BS, 71; Univ Wis, PhD(molecular biol), 75. *Prof Exp:* Fel biophysics, Univ Chicago, 75-79. *Concurrent Pos:* Guest scientist, Brookhaven Nat Lab, 81- *Mem:* Biophys Soc; Am Soc Cell Biol. *Res:* Cell motility, especially structure, mechanism and regulation of the dynein adenosine tryphosphatase in cilia and flagella; microtubule assembly pathway; rapid transient kinetic analysis of enzyme reaction pathways; DNA polymerization mechanism. *Mailing Add:* Mole Cell Biol 106 Althouse Lab Pa State Univ University Park PA 16802

JOHNSON, KENNETH DUANE, PLANT PHYSIOLOGY. *Current Pos:* From asst prof to assoc prof, 72-80, PROF BIOL, SAN DIEGO STATE UNIV, 80- *Personal Data:* b Los Angeles, Calif, Jan 18, 44; m 66; c 2. *Educ:* Univ Calif, Santa Barbara, BA, 66, PhD(biol), 69. *Mem:* Am Soc Plant Physiol; Sigma Xi. *Res:* Plant cell biology; biochemistry of growth and development; glycoprotein processing. *Mailing Add:* Dept Biol San Diego State Univ San Diego CA 92182-0001

JOHNSON, KENNETH EARL, chemistry; deceased, see previous edition for last biography

JOHNSON, KENNETH GEORGE, GEOMORPHOLOGY, SEDIMENTATION. *Current Pos:* from asst prof to assoc prof, 66-78, chmn dept, 66-93, PROF GEOL, SKIDMORE COL, 78-, DIR, ENVIRON STUDIES PROG, 92- *Personal Data:* b Oneonta, NY, Feb 22, 30; m 53, D Nancy Feather; c Lisa F, Craig A & Ilse D. *Educ:* Union Col, NY, BS, 52; Mich State Univ, MS, 57; Rensselaer Polytech Inst, PhD(geol), 68. *Honors & Awards:* Skidmore Fac Res lectr, 81. *Prof Exp:* Geologist, Western Hemisphere Explor Div, Gulf Oil Corp, 58-61 & Bolivian Gulf Oil Co, 61-64. *Concurrent Pos:* Treas, Eastern Sect, Am Asn Petrol Geologists, 93-94. *Mem:* Soc Econ Paleontologists & Mineralogists; Nat Asn Geol Teachers; Geol Soc Am; Am Quaternary Asn. *Res:* Applications of geomorphology to military geology and petroleum exploration; photogeology in petroleum exploration; coastal depositional systems and nearshore marine processes. *Mailing Add:* Dept Geol Skidmore Col Saratoga Springs NY 12866. *Fax:* 518-584-3023

JOHNSON, KENNETH GERALD, INTERNAL MEDICINE. *Current Pos:* PROF COMMUNITY MED, MT SINAI SCH MED, 74- *Personal Data:* b New York, NY, Feb 12, 25; m 50. *Educ:* Manhattan Col, BS, 44; State Univ NY, MD, 50; Dartmouth Col, MA, 74. *Hon Degrees:* ;. *Prof Exp:* From intern to chief resident internal med, Yale-New Haven Med Ctr, 50-54; from instr to assoc prof, Yale Univ, Sch Med, 54-64; chief of med, Atomic Bomb Casualty Comn, Japan, 64-67; prof community med & dir, Div Epidemiol Res, Cornell Univ, Med Col, 67-71; prof community med, chmn dept & assoc dean, Dartmouth Med Sch, 71-74. *Concurrent Pos:* James Hudson Brown fel med physics, 51-52; Nat Heart trainee, 53-54; consult cardiologist, Yale-New Haven Med Ctr & Hosp of St Raphael, New Haven, Conn, 55-65; vis lectr, Hiroshima Univ, Col Med, 64-67; assoc attend physician, New York Hosp, 67-; sr prog consult, Robert Wood Johnson Found, 75-; chmn, NY State Comn Formulate Plan for Pub Med Schs, 75-76; sr prog consult, Robert Wood Johnson Found, 75-; consult, Am Col Obstet & Gynecol, 76-, Surgeon Army, 77-, Dean, State Univ NY, Binghamton clin campus, 77-, NY State Dept Health, 77-, Greenwall Found, 83- & Commonwealth Fund, 85- *Mem:* Fel Am Col Cariol; Am Soc Aging; fel Am Col Prev Med; Am Pub Health Asn. *Res:* Research and development of health services. *Mailing Add:* Health Serv Res Ctr PO Box 2230 Kingston NY 12401-0227

JOHNSON, KENNETH HARVEY, VETERINARY PATHOLOGY. *Current Pos:* NIH training fel, Univ Minn, 60-65, from asst prof to assoc prof, 65-73, head sect path, 74-76, act chmn dept vet pathobiol, 76-77, chmn dept vet pathobiol, 77-83, PROF VET PATH, COL VET MED, UNIV MINN, ST PAUL, 73- *Personal Data:* b Hallock, Minn, Feb 17, 36; m 60; c Jeffrey, Gregory & Sandra. *Educ:* Univ Minn, BS, 58, DVM, 60, PhD(vet path), 65. *Honors & Awards:* Norden Award, 70; Beecham Award for Res Excellence, 89; Ralston Purina Small Animal Res Award, 90. *Concurrent Pos:* Path consult, Minn Mining & Mfg Co, 66-71 & Medtronic, Inc, 72-80; USPHS biomed sci support grant, 68-93; consult, Natural-Y Surg Specialties, Inc, Los Angeles. *Mem:* Am Asn Investigative Path; Int Soc Amyloidosis; Fedn Am Soc Exp Biol; hon mem Am Col Vet Path. *Res:* Amyloidosis; feline diseases; ultrastructural studies; polymer tumorigenesis in mice; diabetes mellitus in cats. *Mailing Add:* Dept Vet Pathobiol Univ Minn Col Vet Med St Paul MN 55108. *Fax:* 612-624-8707; *E-Mail:* johns049@maroon.tc.umn.edu

JOHNSON, KENNETH LANGSTRETH, MECHANICAL ENGINEERING. *Current Pos:* RETIRED. *Personal Data:* b Barrow in Furness, UK, Mar 19, 25; m 54, Dorothy Rosemary; c Marian R, Hilary C & Andrew R. *Educ:* Manchester Univ, UK, BS, 44, MS, 49, PhD, 55. *Honors & Awards:* Mayo D Hersey Award, Am Soc Mech Engrs, 91. *Prof Exp:* Tech asst, Rotol Ltd, 44-49; asst lectr, Manchester Univ, 49-54; from lectr to prof, Cambridge Univ, 54-92. *Mem:* Fel Inst Mech Engrs; fel Royal Acad Eng; hon fel Am Soc Tribology & Lubrication Engrs. *Res:* Contributed articles to journals. *Mailing Add:* 1 New Sq Cambridge CB1 1EY England. *E-Mail:* kln1000@eng.com.ac.uk

JOHNSON, KENNETH MAURICE, JR, NEUROPHARMACOLOGY. *Current Pos:* from asst prof to assoc prof, 77-87, PROF PHARMACOL, UNIV TEX MED BR, 87- *Personal Data:* b Houston, Tex, Dec 7, 44; m 68; c 2. *Educ:* Stephen F Austin State Univ, BS, 67; Univ Houston, PhD(biophys sci), 74. *Prof Exp:* Instr physics, Houston Independent Sch Dist, 67-69; fel pharmacol, Med Col Va, 75-77. *Concurrent Pos:* Fel, Nat Inst Drug Abuse, 76-77; prin investr, Nat Inst Drug Abuse, 79-; NIDA pharmacol review subcomt, 88-92. *Mem:* AAAS; Am Soc Pharmacol & Exp Therapeut; Soc Neurosci; Sigma Xi. *Res:* Neurochemical and behavioral pharmacology of cannabinoids, opiates, hallucinogens, dissociative anesthetics and psychomotor stimulants; biochemistry of excitatory amino acid receptors, regulation of neurotransmitter synthesis, release and receptor; neuroendocrine effects of psychoactive drugs. *Mailing Add:* Dept Pharmacol & Toxicol Univ Tex Med Br 10th & Market St Galveston TX 77550-1031. *Fax:* 409-772-9642

JOHNSON, KENNETH OLAFUR, NEUROPHYSIOLOGY, BIOMEDICAL ENGINEERING. *Current Pos:* asst prof physiol & biomed eng, 71-72, assoc prof neurosci, 81-87, PROF NEUROSCI & BIOMED ENG, JOHNS HOPKINS UNIV, 87- *Personal Data:* US citizen. *Educ:* Univ Wash, BS, 61; Syracuse Univ, MS, 65; Johns Hopkins Univ, PhD(biomed eng), 70. *Prof Exp:* staff mem, Univ Melbourne, 72-80. *Mem:* AAAS; Soc Neurosci. *Res:* Neural mechanisms in sensation and perception. *Mailing Add:* Mind-Brain Inst Johns Hopkins Univ Med Sch 720 Rutland Ave Baltimore MD 21205-2109

JOHNSON, KENNETH OSCAR, PETROLEUM. *Current Pos:* SR VPRES, COASTAL CORP, 88- *Personal Data:* b Center City, Minn, Apr 11, 20; m 45, Margery Wheeler; c Eric W. *Educ:* Univ Minn, BS, 42. *Prof Exp:* Engr, Exxon Corp, 42-74, heavy fuels mgr, Supply Dept, 68-72, wholesale fuels sales mgr, Mkt Dept, 72-74; chmn & chief exec officer, Belcher Oil Co, 74-88. *Concurrent Pos:* Bd dirs, Coastal Corp & Petrol Indust Found. *Res:* Granted patents in petroleum engineering. *Mailing Add:* 845 Admiralty Parade Naples FL 34102

JOHNSON, KENNETH PETER, NEUROLOGY. *Current Pos:* PROF & CHMN, UNIV MD, 81- *Personal Data:* b Jamestown, NY, Mar 12, 32; m 56, Jacquelyn; c Peter, Thomas, Diane & Douglas. *Educ:* Upsala Col, BA, 55; Jefferson Med Col, MD, 59; Am Bd Psychiat & Neurol, dipl. *Honors & Awards:* Weil Award, Am Asn Neuropath, 67; Zimmerman Lectr, Stanford Univ, 81. *Prof Exp:* Intern, Buffalo Gen Hosp, 59-60; resident, Hosp Cleveland, 63-65; asst prof neurol, Case Western Res Univ, 68-71, assoc prof, 71-74; prof, Univ Calif, San Francisco, 74-81. *Concurrent Pos:* Res career develop award, NIH, 68-73; chief neurol, Vet Admin Hosp, Baltimore, 81-83. *Mem:* Fel Am Neurol Asn; Am Acad Neurol; Am Soc Virol; Am Clin & Climat Asn; Am Cong Rehab Med; Am Soc Neurorehab; Teratology Soc; Soc Exp Neuropath; Int Soc Neuroimmunol. *Res:* Neurology. *Mailing Add:* 22 S Greene St Baltimore MD 21201-1544

JOHNSON, KENNETH SUTHERLAND, HYDROGEOLOGY, ECONOMIC & ENVIRONMENTAL GEOLOGY. *Current Pos:* GEOLOGIST, OKLA GEOL SURV, 62-, ASSOC DIR, 78- *Personal Data:* b Brooklyn, NY, Sept 16, 34; m 59, Dorothea Joyal; c Lisa, David & Mark. *Educ:* Univ Okla, BS, 59 & 61, MS, 62; Univ Ill, Urbana, PhD(geol), 67. *Prof Exp:* Teaching asst, Univ Okla, 58-61. *Concurrent Pos:* Teaching asst, Univ Ill, Urbana, 65-67; consult geologist, 68-; vis prof geol & geol eng, Univ Okla, 73-; dir, Okla Mining & Mineral Resources Res Inst, 78-80; chmn, Okla Hazardous Waste Mgt Coun, 81-93; mem, Environ Adv Bd US Army CEng, 92-96. *Mem:* AAAS; Geol Soc Am; Am Asn Petrol Geologists; Am Inst Prof Geologists; Am Inst Mining, Metall & Petrol Engrs; Asn Eng Geologists; Int Asn Hydrogeologists. *Res:* Economic geology; stratigraphy; field mapping of geologic structures and mineral resources; photogeology; environmental geology; earth-science education; geology of evaporites and redbeds; disposal of radioactive and industrial wastes; hydrogeology; Karst. *Mailing Add:* Okla Geol Surv 100 E Boyd Rm N-131 Norman OK 73019. *Fax:* 405-325-7069; *E-Mail:* ksjohnson@ou.edu

JOHNSON, KENT J, IMMUNOPATHOLOGY. *Current Pos:* ASSOC PROF PATH, SCH MED, UNIV MICH, 83- *Personal Data:* b Minot, NDak, Nov 4, 46. *Educ:* Univ Conn, MD, 76. *Mem:* Am Asn Immunologists; Am Asn Pathologists. *Mailing Add:* Dept Path Univ Mich Sch Med 1335 E Catherine St Box 0602 Ann Arbor MI 48109-0602. *Fax:* 313-764-4308

JOHNSON, KURT EDWARD, DEVELOPMENTAL BIOLOGY. *Current Pos:* assoc prof, 77-82, PROF ANAT, MED CTR, GEORGE WASHINGTON UNIV, 82- *Personal Data:* b Needham, Mass, July 6, 43; m 82, Julie M Okkema; c Melissa, Abraham, Justine & Alexander. *Educ:* Johns Hopkins Univ, BS, 65; Yale Univ, MPhil, 69, PhD(develop biol), 70. *Prof Exp:* Fel develop biol, Yale Univ, 70-71; asst prof anat, Med Ctr, Duke Univ, 71-77. *Mem:* AAAS; Sigma Xi; Am Soc Cell Biologists; Soc Develop Biologists. *Res:* Experimental morphogenesis; experimental analysis of amphibian gastrulation. *Mailing Add:* Dept Anat George Washington Univ Med Sch 2300 I St NW Washington DC 20037-2337

JOHNSON, KURT P, MECHANICAL ENGINEERING. *Current Pos:* VPRES ENG, B F GOODRICH AERO MOTION DIV, 92- *Personal Data:* b Chicago, Ill, Oct 6, 38; m 61; c 1. *Educ:* Northwestern Univ, BS, 60, PhD(mech eng), 63. *Prof Exp:* Sr staff engr, McDonnell Douglas Astronaut Co, 63-75, dir corp diversification technol, McDonnell Douglas Corp, 76-84, dir eng & opers, 84-89, dir laser commun systs, 89-90; group vpres eng, Farrel Corp, 90-92. *Concurrent Pos:* NSF fel. *Mem:* Soc Mfg Engrs. *Res:* Energy systems; transportation systems technology. *Mailing Add:* 197 Ridgedale Ave Cedar Knolls NJ 07927

JOHNSON, L(AWRENCE) D(AVID), civil engineering, material science; deceased, see previous edition for last biography

JOHNSON, L(EE) ENSIGN, ELECTRICAL ENGINEERING, BIOENGINEERING. *Current Pos:* from instr to assoc prof, 59-72, assoc provost, 70-75, PROF ELEC ENG, VANDERBILT UNIV, 72- *Personal Data:* b New River, Tenn, May 26, 31; m 55; c 4. *Educ:* Vanderbilt Univ, BE, 53, BD, 59; Case Western Reserve Univ, MS, 63, PhD, 64. *Prof Exp:* Prod line mgr, Aladdin Electronics, Div Aladdin Indust, 55-59. *Mem:* Inst Elec & Electronics Engrs. *Res:* Physiological control systems; iron kinetics in humans; reliability modeling and engineering. *Mailing Add:* Vanderbilt Univ Sta B Nashville TN 37235

JOHNSON, LADON JEROME, ANIMAL HUSBANDRY. *Personal Data:* b Gardner, NDak, Sept 11, 34. *Educ:* NDak State Univ, BS, 56, MS, 57; Ohio State Univ, PhD(animal sci), 65. *Prof Exp:* Res asst animal sci, Ohio State Univ, 56-57; asst county agent com agr, NDak Coop Exten Serv, 59-61; res asst animal sci, Ohio Agr Res & Develop Ctr, 61-64, tech aide, 64-65; from asst exten animal husbandman to exten animal husbandman, Coop Exten Ser, NDak State Univ, 66-74, prof animal husb, 74-93. *Mem:* AAAS; Am Soc Animal Sci. *Res:* Physiological differences associated with different gaining ability of beef cattle; effect of stage of maturity on yield and nutritive value of corn silage; improvement of corn silage by chemical additives. *Mailing Add:* 2437 Lilac Lane Fargo ND 58102

JOHNSON, LARRY CLAUD, PHYSICS. *Current Pos:* MEM JOINT CENT TEAM, INTER JOINT WORKS SITE, 95- *Personal Data:* b Roby, Tex, Aug 24, 36; m 56; c 2. *Educ:* Tex Christian Univ, BA, 58; Mass Inst Technol, SM, 60; Princeton Univ, PhD(astrophys), 66. *Prof Exp:* Res assoc, Plasma Physics Lab, Princeton Univ, 66-69, mem res staff, 69-95. *Mem:* AAAS; Am Phys Soc. *Res:* Plasma physics; plasma spectroscopy and laser scattering; atomic collision cross sections. *Mailing Add:* ITER Joint Works Site 11025 N Torey Pines Rd La Jolla CA 92037. *Fax:* 619-546-8602

JOHNSON, LARRY DON, physics, for more information see previous edition

JOHNSON, LARRY K, MATHEMATICS EDUCATION. *Current Pos:* asst prof, 63-67, ASSOC PROF MATH, CENT MO STATE COL, 67- *Personal Data:* b Howard, Kans, Aug 6, 36; m 57, Deloris Eisele; c Larry K, Gregory, Clayton, Deborah & Veronica. *Educ:* Kans State Teachers Col, Emporia, BSEd & AB, 58, MS, 60; Univ Ga, EdD(math educ), 63. *Prof Exp:* Instr math educ, Univ Ga, 61-63. *Mem:* Math Asn Am; Nat Coun Teachers Math. *Res:* Mathematics education. *Mailing Add:* Dept Math WCM 121 Cent Mo State Univ Warrensburg MO 64093

JOHNSON, LARRY RAY, INDUSTRIAL ENGINEERING. *Current Pos:* from asst prof to assoc prof indust eng, 63-76, PROF INDUST ENG, MISS STATE UNIV, 76- *Personal Data:* b Atlanta, Ga, Dec 18, 35; m 58; c 3. *Educ:* Ga Inst Technol, BCerE, 58, BIE, 60, MSIE, 62; Okla State Univ, PhD(indust eng), 69. *Prof Exp:* Assoc mfg res engr, Lockheed-Ga Co, 61-63. *Mem:* Am Inst Indust Engrs. *Res:* Hospital systems; occupational safety and health; energy conservation; work methods. *Mailing Add:* Dept Indust Eng Miss State Univ Mississippi State MS 39762

JOHNSON, LARRY REIDAR, PULMONARY EPIDEMIOLOGY. *Current Pos:* asst prof physiol, 76-82, SR RES ASSOC, ORE HEALTH SCI UNIV, 82- *Personal Data:* b Seattle, Wash, Jan 5, 45; m 68, Elaine C Varekamp; c Carolyn & Daniel. *Educ:* Univ Wash, Seattle, BS, 66; State Univ NY, Buffalo, PhD(physiol), 73. *Prof Exp:* Res assoc, Harvard Sch Pub Health, Boston, Mass, 72-76. *Concurrent Pos:* Proj coordr, Ore Health Sci Univ Lung Health Study, 86- *Mem:* Am Physiol Soc; Am Thoracic Soc. *Res:* Epidemiology of pulmonary function, quality control of spirometry; pulmonary software maintenance and development. *Mailing Add:* Dept Physiol L334A Ore Health Sci Univ 3181 SW Sam Jackson Park Rd Portland OR 97201-3098. *Fax:* 503-494-5407; *E-Mail:* johnsnla@ohsu.edu

JOHNSON, LAVELL R, BIOCHEMISTRY, ORGANIC CHEMISTRY. *Current Pos:* PRES, JOHNSON RES, 71- *Personal Data:* b Salt Lake City, Utah, Jan 16, 35; m 58; c 6. *Educ:* Univ Utah, BS, 59; Brigham Young Univ, PhD(biochem), 65. *Prof Exp:* Sr scientist biochem, Ames Co Div, Miles Labs, 64-68; assoc res dir dept med, Latter-Day Saints Hosp, 68-71. *Mem:* AAAS; Am Chem Soc. *Res:* Mechanism of action of adrenocorticotropic hormone; pregnenolone synthesis by adrenal preparations; analysis of growth hormone, testosterone, metanephrine, insulin and adrenocorticotropic hormone. *Mailing Add:* Johnson Res 3201 Teton Dr Salt Lake City UT 84109

JOHNSON, LAWRENCE ALAN, PROCESSING OF CROPS. *Current Pos:* assoc prof, 85-88, PROF FOOD TECHNOL, CTR CROPS UTILIZATION RES, IOWA STATE UNIV, 88- *Personal Data:* b Columbus, Ohio, Apr 30, 47; m 69, Bernice; c Bradley & David. *Educ:* Ohio State Univ, BSc, 69; NC State Univ, MSc, 71; Kans State Univ, PhD(food sci), 78. *Honors & Awards:* ADM Award, Am Oil Chemists Soc, 87; Utilization Res Award, United Soybean Bd, 93. *Prof Exp:* Res asst food sci, NC State Univ, 69-71; food adv, US Army QM Corp, 71-73; res chemist food prod develop, Dwight P Joyce Res Ctr, Durkee Foods, 73-75; res asst grain sci, Food Sci, Kans State Univ, 75-78; asst res chemist, Food Protein Res & Develop Ctr, Tex A&M Univ, 78-83, assoc res chemist, 83-85. *Mem:* Am Asn Cereal Chemists; Inst Food Technologists; Am Oil Chemists Soc; Am Soc Agr Engrs. *Res:* Developing new product or processing technologies to utilize agricultural products; product applications include both food and non-food industrial products; processes include new techniques in crop separations, ingredient conversions, and food refabrication; oil extraction. *Mailing Add:* Dept Food Sci & Human Nutrit Food Sci Bldg Iowa State Univ Ames IA 50011. *Fax:* 515-294-6261; *E-Mail:* ljohnson@iastate.edu

JOHNSON, LAWRENCE ARTHUR, REPRODUCTIVE PHYSIOLOGY. *Current Pos:* Chemist, Agr Res Serv, USDA, 64-66, res chemist, 66-72, res physiologist animal sci, 72-90, RES LEADER, GERMPLASMA & GAMETE PHYSIOL LAB, AGR RES SERV, USDA, 90- *Personal Data:* b Luck, Wis, July 9, 36; m 59; c 3. *Educ:* Univ Wis, River Falls, BS, 61; Univ Minn, St Paul, MS, 63; Univ Md, PhD(animal physiol & biochem), 68. *Honors & Awards:* Outstanding Res Award in Physiol & Endocrinol, Am Soc Animal Sci, 91. *Mem:* Soc Study Reproduction; Am Soc Animal Sci; Soc Anal Cytol; Int Embryo Transfer Soc. *Res:* Reproductive physiology and biochemistry of mammalian semen and fertilization processes; artificial insemination; frozen semen; sex pre-selection. *Mailing Add:* Germplasm & Gamete Physiol Lab USDA Agr Serv BARC-EAST Bldg 200 Beltsville MD 20705

JOHNSON, LAWRENCE LLOYD, IMMUNOGENETICS. *Current Pos:* asst mem, 84-89, ASSOC MEM, SARANAC LAKE, NY, 90- *Personal Data:* b Bangor, Maine, Dec 30, 41; m 76; c 1. *Educ:* Univ Maine, BA, 64, MA, 73, PhD(zool), 80. *Prof Exp:* Fel, McArdle Lab, Univ Wis-Madison, 80-83, lectr, Lab of Genetics, 83-84. *Res:* Genetics of mammalian histocompatibility antigens; developmental immunogenetics; theoretical genetics. *Mailing Add:* RR 1 Saranac Lake NY 12983

JOHNSON, LAWRENCE ROBERT, ANALYTICAL CHEMISTRY, PHYSICAL CHEMISTRY. *Current Pos:* CONSULT, 94- *Personal Data:* b Gyor, Hungary, Feb 14, 31; US citizen. *Educ:* Eotvos Lorand Univ, Budapest, dipl, 53; Columbia Univ, PhD(chem), 61. *Prof Exp:* Res chemist, Lever Bros Res Ctr, NJ, 56-57; AEC res asst, Columbia Univ, 57-59; group leader polymer res radioisotopes, Rohm & Haas Co, Pa, 60-62; asst prof instrumental, anal & phys chem, Lafayette Col, 62-65; assoc prof anal & phys chem, Union Col, Ky, 65-78, actg head dept, 69-73; consult, 78-81; chemist water treat, City Utilities Co, Corbin, Ky, 81-93. *Res:* Kinetics of polymer adsorption, flocculation and deflocculation; radioisotopes; instrumental analysis; electrochemistry and electroanalysis; atomic absorption spectrophotometry. *Mailing Add:* 701 Rose Lane Corbin KY 40701

JOHNSON, LAYNE MARK, INFORMATION SCIENCE & SYSTEMS. *Current Pos:* microbial ecologist, 84-87, sr info scientist, 87-91, MGR TECH INFO, AM CYANAMID CO, PEARL RIVER, NY, 91- *Personal Data:* b Northfield, Minn, June 4, 53; m 78. *Educ:* Dana Col, BA, 75; Iowa State Univ, MS, 78, PhD(microbiol), 80. *Prof Exp:* Postdoctoral fel, Univ Okla, Norman, 80-82; sr res microbiologist, Cytox Corp, Allentown, Pa, 82-84. *Mem:* Soc Indust Microbiol; Pharmaceut Mfg Asn. *Res:* Management of published information, including scientific literature and patents pertaining to drug development processes within the pharmaceutical industry; manage state-of-the-art end user search program. *Mailing Add:* Wyatt-Ayerst 401 N Middletown Rd Bldg 160 Rm 101-C Pearl River NY 10965

JOHNSON, LEANDER FLOYD, SOIL-BORNE PLANT DISEASES. *Current Pos:* RETIRED. *Personal Data:* b Lecompte, La, Aug 3, 26; m 48; c 2. *Educ:* Southwestern La Inst, BS, 48; La State Univ, MS, 51, PhD(plant path), 53. *Prof Exp:* Instr bot, Univ Tenn, Knoxville, 53-54, from asst prof to prof plant path, 54-90. *Mem:* Am Phytopath Soc; Sigma Xi. *Res:* Biological control of plant diseases; methods of approach and basic concepts of soil microbiology. *Mailing Add:* 2004 Plumb Ridge Rd Knoxville TN 37932

JOHNSON, LEE FREDERICK, MOLECULAR BIOLOGY. *Current Pos:* from asst prof to assoc prof, 75-85, PROF BIOCHEM, OHIO STATE UNIV, 85-, PROF MOLECULAR GENETICS, 87-, CHMN MOLECULAR GENETICS, 90- *Personal Data:* b Philadelphia, Pa, Jan 10, 46; m 67, Ann Lester; c Adam & Karl. *Educ:* Muhlenberg Col, BS, 67; Yale Univ, MPhil, 69, PhD(molecular biophysics), 72. *Prof Exp:* Fel cell biol, Mass Inst Technol, 71-75. *Concurrent Pos:* Fel, Am Cancer Soc, 72-74, fac res award, 80-85; mem, Molecular, Cellular & Develop Biol Progs, Ohio State Univ, 76-; molecular biol panel, NSF, 80-84. *Mem:* Am Soc Cell Biol; Am Soc Biochem & Molecular Biol; Am Soc Microbiol. *Res:* Regulation of growth, RNA metabolism and gene expression in cultured mammalian cells; genetic engineering. *Mailing Add:* Dept Molecular Genetics Ohio State Univ Columbus OH 43210. *Fax:* 614-292-4466; *E-Mail:* johnson.6@osu.edu

JOHNSON, LEE H(ARNIE), CIVIL ENGINEERING. *Current Pos:* prof civil eng & dean, Sch Eng, 50-72, EMER DEAN & W R IRBY PROF ENG, TULANE UNIV, LA, 72- *Personal Data:* b Houston, Tex, Jan 4, 09; m 40; c 2. *Educ:* Rice Inst, BA, 30, MA, 31; Harvard Univ, MS, 32, ScD(civil eng), 35. *Prof Exp:* Asst civil eng, Harvard Univ, 32-35; asst eng aide, US Waterways Exp Sta, Miss, 35-36; jr engr & asst to engr in charge design & specifications, US Eng Off, Ala, 36-37; prof civil eng & dean, Sch Eng, Univ Miss, 37-50. *Concurrent Pos:* Teacher calculus, Newman Sch, La, 79-87. *Mem:* Am Soc Civil Engrs; Am Soc Eng Educ. *Res:* Mathematical simplification of design of statically indeterminate structures; new technique of slide rule operation for duplex-type slide rules; simplified nomography; creative approach to engineering education. *Mailing Add:* 211 Fairway Dr New Orleans LA 70124

JOHNSON, LEE MURPHY, MATHEMATICS. *Current Pos:* From asst prof assoc prof, 67-83, PROF MATH, NORTHERN ARIZ UNIV, 83- *Personal Data:* b Lufkin, Tex, Sept 11, 34; m 57; c 1. *Educ:* Univ Tex, Austin, BSChE, 57, MA, 65, PhD(math), 68. *Prof Exp:* Res chem engr, Humble Oil & Refining Co, 57-62. *Mem:* Am Math Soc; Math Asn Am. *Res:* General measure theory. *Mailing Add:* 5717 N Aztec St Flagstaff AZ 86011-0001

JOHNSON, LEE W, MATHEMATICS. *Current Pos:* Asst prof, 67-74, ASSOC PROF MATH, VA POLYTECH INST & STATE UNIV, 74- *Personal Data:* b Appleton, Minn, Oct 25, 38; m 63. *Educ:* La State Univ, BS, 63, MS, 65; Mich State Univ, PhD(math), 67. *Mem:* Am Math Soc; Soc Indust & Appl Math. *Res:* Numerical analysis and approximation theory. *Mailing Add:* Dept Math Va Polytech Inst & State Univ Blacksburg VA 24061

JOHNSON, LELAND GILBERT, DEVELOPMENTAL PHYSIOLOGY, LARVAL ECOLOGY. *Current Pos:* From asst prof to assoc prof, 64-73, PROF BIOL, AUGUSTANA COL, SDAK, 73- *Personal Data:* b Roseau, Minn, Oct 16, 37; m 78; c 3. *Educ:* Augustana Col, SDak, BA, 59; Northwestern Univ, MS, 61, PhD(biol sci), 65. *Concurrent Pos:* NSF sci fac fel, Queen Mary Col, 70-71; George C Marshall fel, Biol Inst, Odense Univ, Denmark, 77, Fulbright scholar, 83, Australian Inst Marine Sci, 89, 90, 91, 92 & 95; Leigh Marine Lab, Univ Auckland, NZ, 96; Lohthus distinguished prof. *Mem:* AAAS; Western Soc Naturalists; Soc Develop Biol; Asn Biol Lab Educ; Sigma Xi. *Res:* Developmental physiology; effects of temperature on developmental processes; author of two general biology texts and a developmental biology laboratory manual; thyroxine affects on invertebrate development. *Mailing Add:* Dept Biol Augustana Col Sioux Falls SD 57197. *E-Mail:* johnson@inst.augie.edu

JOHNSON, LENNART INGEMAR, MATERIALS & PROCESS ENGINEERING, SPECIFICATIONS & STANDARDS. *Current Pos:* chmn composites comt, 86-88, CONSULT, SOC AUTOMOTIVE ENGRS, 89- *Personal Data:* b Minneapolis, Minn, Dec 23, 24; m 61, Grant; c 1. *Educ:* Univ Minn, BS, 48. *Honors & Awards:* Leadership & Serv Award, Soc Automotive Engrs, Dedication & Distinction Award. *Prof Exp:* Sr engr, Ordinance Div, Honeywell, 49-67, prin engr, 67-69, supvr, Eng Plastics Lab, 69-87, staff eng, Defense Systs Div, 87-88. *Mem:* Soc Automotive Engrs; Am Inst Chem Engrs; fel Am Inst Chemists. *Res:* Development of casting resins involving urethane and epoxy polymers; development of stain-free injection molding of thermoplastic polymers; development of material specifications. *Mailing Add:* 14109 M Terr Minnetonka MN 55345

JOHNSON, LEO FRANCIS, LASERS. *Current Pos:* RETIRED. *Personal Data:* b White Plains, NY, Nov 6, 28; m 62, Barbara Harman; c David, Kathleen, Mark & Christopher. *Educ:* Univ Vt, BA, 51; Syracuse Univ, MS, 55, PhD(physics), 59. *Prof Exp:* Tech engr, Gen Elec Co, 51-53; res asst physics, Syracuse Univ, 54-59; mem tech staff physics, Bell Tel Labs, 59-86; consult, Amoco Laser Co, 87-89 & Amoco Res Ctr, 89-94; res assoc, Ctr Res Electro-Optics & Lasers, Univ Cent Fla, 90-91. *Mem:* Fel Am Phys Soc; Sigma Xi. *Res:* Photoconductivity of semiconductors; optical spectroscopy of rare earth and transition metal ions in crystals; investigations of laser phenomena in crystals; interference diffraction gratings; sub-micron surface structures; distributed feedback lasers. *Mailing Add:* 150 Riverwood Ave Bedminster NJ 07921

JOHNSON, LEON JOSEPH, SOIL MINERALOGY. *Current Pos:* asst prof soil technol, 59-67, assoc prof, 67-80, PROF SOIL MINERAL, PA STATE UNIV, 80- *Personal Data:* b Detroit, Mich, Jan 17, 29; m 52; c 3. *Educ:* Pa State Univ, BS, 54, MS, 55 PhD(agron), 57. *Prof Exp:* Res geologist, Cities Serv Res & Develop Co, 57-59. *Mem:* Am Soc Agron; Clay Minerals Soc. *Res:* Weathering of soil minerals; formation of soil profiles; clay mineralogy. *Mailing Add:* 116 Agr Sci Bldg Pa State Univ University Park PA 16802

JOHNSON, LEONARD EVANS, GEOPHYSICS. *Current Pos:* PROG DIR, CONTINENTAL DYNAMICS, NSF, 74- *Personal Data:* b Ogden, Utah, Nov 13, 40; m 87; c 1. *Educ:* Mass Inst Technol, BS, 62; Univ Calif, San Diego, MS, 67, PhD(geophys), 71. *Prof Exp:* Res assoc geophys, Boeing Sci Res Labs, 62-65; vis fel, Coop Inst Res Environ Sci, Univ Colo, 71-73; vis prof, Univ Calif, Berkeley, 73-74; assoc prog dir, Continental Lithosphere, NSF, 74-79, prog dir geophys, 79-82, prog dir seismol, 82-84, prog dir, 84-89. *Concurrent Pos:* Prof lectr, George Washington Univ, 77-86; mem comt math geophys, Int Union Geod & Geophys; assoc dir, Off Sci & Technol Centers Develop, NSF, 88. *Mem:* Am Geophys Union; Seismol Soc Am; AAAS. *Res:* Theoretical and observational seismology, inverse problems in geophysics. *Mailing Add:* 806 S Overlook Dr Alexandria VA 22305

JOHNSON, LEONARD ROY, PHYSIOLOGY. *Current Pos:* THOMAS A GERWIN PROF & CHMN, DEPT PHYSIOL, UNIV TENN COL MED, MEMPHIS, 90- *Personal Data:* b Chicago, Ill, Jan 31, 42; c 3. *Educ:* Wabash Col, BA, 63; Univ Mich, Ann Arbor, PhD(physiol), 67. *Hon Degrees:* MD, Copernicus Med Sch, Cracow, 90. *Honors & Awards:* Hoffmann-LaRoche Prize, Am Physiol Soc, Horace W Davenport Distinguished Lectr; NIH Merit Award; RD McKenna Mem lectr, Can Asn Gastroenterol. *Prof Exp:* NIH fel & instr physiol, Sch Med, Univ Calif, Los Angeles, 67-69; from asst prof to assoc prof, Sch Med, Univ Okla, 69-72; prof physiol, Univ Tex Med Sch, Houston, 72-89. *Concurrent Pos:* Res grant, Univ Okla, 70-73; G A Manahan Trust grant, 70-72; NIH res career develop award, 72-77, grant, 73-; ed, Am J Physiol, 79-85; mem, Vet Admin Merit Rev Bd, 87-91; NIH study sect gastroenterol clin nutrit, 80-82; nat bd med examiners, Physiol Test Comt, 83-91, chmn, 88-91. *Mem:* Am Gastroenterol Asn; Am Physiol Soc; Endocrine Soc; Soc Exp Biol & Med; hon mem Polish Physiol Soc; Am Soc Cell Biol. *Res:* Role of polyamines in mucosal growth and cell migration; regulation of growth of gastrointestinal mucosa and gastrin receptor binding. *Mailing Add:* Dept Physiol Univ Tenn Med Col 894 Union Ave Memphis TN 38163. *Fax:* 901-448-7126

JOHNSON, LEROY DENNIS, organic chemistry; deceased, see previous edition for last biography

JOHNSON, LEROY FRANKLIN, NUCLEAR MAGNETIC RESONANCE. *Current Pos:* NUCLEAR MAGNETIC RESONANCE INSTRUMENTS CONSULT, 94- *Personal Data:* b Seattle, Wash, Feb 4, 33; m 56, Margaret Lindsley; c Noel L & Brett N. *Educ:* Ore State Univ, BS, 54, MS, 56. *Honors & Awards:* Excep Achievement Award, Am Chem Soc, 92. *Prof Exp:* Dept mgr, Varian Assocs, 57-72; vpres, Nicolet Magnetics Corp, 72-83; mgr, Appln Labs, sr scientist & mgr, Analytical Nuclear Magnetic Resonance, Gen Elec Nuclear Magnetic Resonance Instruments, 83-92; analytical nuclear magnetic resonance mgr, Broker Instruments Western Region, 92-94. *Concurrent Pos:* Teacher of NMR short courses, Am Chem Soc, 66-; chmn, Exp Nuclear Magnetic Resonance Conf, 78. *Mem:* Am Chem Soc; Soc Appl Spectros; Int Soc Magnetic Resonance. *Res:* Applications of nuclear magnetic resonance spectroscopy; development of nuclear magnetic resonance instrumentation; utilization of minicomputers with nuclear magnetic resonance instruments. *Mailing Add:* 10155 Western Dr Cupertino CA 95014. *E-Mail:* ffdr20a@prodigy.com

JOHNSON, LESLIE KILHAM, ZOOLOGY. *Current Pos:* res biologist, 88-89, LECTR, PRINCETON UNIV, 89- *Personal Data:* b New York, NY, June 9, 45; m 76; c 1. *Educ:* Harvard Univ, BA, 67; Univ Calif, Berkeley, PhD(zool), 74. *Prof Exp:* Grad fel zool, NSF, 71-74; res fel, Alexander von Humboldt, Zool Inst, Wurzburg, Ger, 74-75; asst prof zool, Univ Iowa, 75-80, assoc prof biol, 80-88; biologist, Smithsonian Tropical Res Inst, 87-88. *Concurrent Pos:* Mem, bd dir, Orgn Trop Studies, 79-88; res assoc, Smithsonian Trop Res Inst, 83-88. *Mem:* Sigma Xi; Asn Trop Biol; Soc Study Evolution. *Res:* Behavioral ecology; aggressive behavior; learning; foraging patterns of social insects; sexual selection in insects. *Mailing Add:* Dept Ecol & Evolution Biol Princeton Univ Princeton NJ 08544-0001

JOHNSON, LESLYE, ALLERGY RESEARCH. *Current Pos:* BR CHIEF, ENTERIC DIS BR, NAT INST ALLERGY & INFECTIOUS DIS, NIH, 89- *Mailing Add:* Solar Bldg Rm 3A22 6003 Executive Blvd Rockville MD 20852

JOHNSON, LITTLETON WALES, FOOD SCIENCE. *Current Pos:* CONSULT, 88- *Personal Data:* b Concord Wharf, Va, Oct 17, 29; m 51, Nancy Taylor; c Susan (Allen), Karen (Beottgea) & Robert T. *Educ:* Va Polytech Inst, BS, 56, MS, 58. *Prof Exp:* Asst processing engr, Hercules Powder Co, 55-58; assoc prof food technol, Va Polytech Inst, 58-61; plant mgr, Dulany Foods, Inc, 61-67; opers mgr, Glidden-Durkee Div, SCM Corp, 67-69, dir mfg, Food Serv Group, 69-71, Regional mgr, 71-76; vpres, Mrs Smith's Frozen Food Co, Kellogg Co, 76-80, sr vpres mfg, 80-88. *Concurrent Pos:* Dir, Bowman Apple Prod Co, Inc. *Mem:* Am Frozen Food Inst; Sigma Xi; Am Mgt Asn; Nat Food Processors Asn. *Res:* Food processing techniques; statistical quality control; submerged acetic fermentations. *Mailing Add:* 292 Continental Dr Pottstown PA 19464

JOHNSON, LLOYD N(EWHALL), PETROLEUM & CHEMICAL ENGINEERING. *Current Pos:* coordr Oil & Gas Technol, Bee County Col, 79-81. *Personal Data:* b Eureka, Kans, Nov 16, 21; m 45, Marilla Ruebhausen; c Louise. *Educ:* Univ Kans, BS, 44; Univ Tex, Austin, PhD(petrol eng), 70. *Prof Exp:* Indust chemist, Hercules Powder Co, 44-45; res engr, Core Labs, Inc, 46-52, supvr reservoir fluids lab, Venezuela, 52-55; res engr, petrol res comt, Univ Tex, 55-63, instr math, 63-64; asst prof petrol & natural gas eng, Tex A&I Univ, 65-77. *Concurrent Pos:* Consult engr, 64- *Mem:* Simulation Coun; Soc Petrol Engrs. *Res:* Drilling problems; reserves; completion methods; production methods and controls; mathematical models; scientific data processing; economic development and improved recovery in petroleum reservoirs; engineering methods. *Mailing Add:* PO Box 2254 Station One Kingsville TX 78363

JOHNSON, LOERING M, CONTROL SYSTEMS DESIGN & ANALYSIS, ENGINEERING QUALITY SYSTEMS DOCUMENTATION. *Current Pos:* PRIN ENGR, LMJ ENTERPRISES, 93- *Personal Data:* b Dickinson, NDak, Sept 22, 26; m 52, Maral Austin; c Mairi V, Marueen K, Marc D & Mara E. *Educ:* Univ NDak, BS, 52; Rennselaer Polytech Inst, MS, 61. *Prof Exp:* Engr elec syst design, EI DuPont de Nemours Inc, 52-53; eng, elec syst design, Combustion Eng Inc, 55-58, supvr comput appl, 58-60, mgr, inst control & elect syst, 60-70, mgr stand, 70-80, mgr records control, 80-82, mgr off automation, 82-85; assoc prof teaching, Univ Hartford, 86-93. *Concurrent Pos:* Secy, Nuclear Power Eng Comt, 66-78; mem, Stand Bd, Inst Elec & Electronics Engrs, 78-81; Dir, Nat Soc Prof Engrs, 81-84. *Mem:* Nat Soc Prof Engrs; fel Inst Elec & Electronics Engrs; Sigma Xi. *Res:* Published numerous papers and book section on instrumentation and control, standards, and technical writing. *Mailing Add:* PO Box 372 Tariffville CT 06081-0372. *Fax:* 860-658-7962

JOHNSON, LOUISE H, MATHEMATICS EDUCATION. *Current Pos:* RETIRED. *Personal Data:* b Minneota, Minn, Oct 22, 27. *Educ:* Augsburg Col, BA, 49; Univ Northern Colo, MA, 61, DEduc, 71; Univ Ill, MA, 63. *Prof Exp:* Teacher high schs, Minn, 49-62; assoc dean lib arts & sci, St Cloud State Univ, 74-76, prof math, 63-90, dean lib arts & sci, 76-90, dean sci & technol, 84-90. *Mem:* Nat Coun Teachers Math. *Mailing Add:* 2030 Stockinger Dr St Cloud MN 56303

JOHNSON, LOWELL BOYDEN, PLANT MOLECULAR BIOLOGY, PLANT TISSUE CULTURE. *Current Pos:* from asst prof to assoc prof, 68-82, PROF PLANT PATH, KANS STATE UNIV, 82- *Personal Data:* b Dwight, Ill, Oct 12, 35; m 56, Wanda M Thorndyke; c Linda R (Butler) & David E. *Educ:* Univ Ill, BS, 57; Purdue Univ, West Lafayette, MS, 62, PhD(plant path), 64. *Prof Exp:* Asst res plant pathologist, Univ Calif, Davis, 64-68. *Concurrent Pos:* Vis scholar, Div Biol Sci, Univ Mich, Ann Arbor, 85 & Dept Biol, Ind Univ, Bloomington, 92. *Mem:* AAAS; Am Phytopath Soc; Am Soc Plant Physiol; Int Soc Plant Molecular Biol. *Res:* Plant transformation; plant cell culture and regeneration; alfalfa molecular genetics. *Mailing Add:* Dept Plant Path Kans State Univ Throckmorton Hall Manhattan KS 66506-5502. *Fax:* 785-532-5692; *E-Mail:* ljohnson@plantpath.pp.ksu.edu

JOHNSON, LOYD, SOIL & WATER MANAGEMENT, AGRICULTURAL EXPERIMENT STATION MANAGEMENT. *Current Pos:* CONSULT, 93- *Personal Data:* b Somerville, Ala, Mar 18, 27; m 52, Ester Banegas; c Theresa A, Thomas P & Loyd C. *Educ:* Ala Polytech Inst, BS, 50, MS, 55. *Honors & Awards:* Kishida Int Award, Am Soc Agr Engrs, 95. *Prof Exp:* Asst dist supt farm develop, Tela RR Co, 51-52 & 56; asst agr eng, Ala Agr Exp Sta, Auburn, 53-54; asst engr, Gen Off, United Fruit Co, 56-57, sr proj engr, Cia Agricola Guatemala, 56-60; agr engr, Rockefeller Found, 60-82, Winrock Int, 82-90; remote sensing bananas, Honduras, 92-93; develop & mgt, Ethiopian Exp Stas, 93, Pakistan, 94. *Concurrent Pos:* Agr engr, Int Rice Res Inst, 60-68, NC State Univ, 67-68, Int Ctr Trop Agr, Colombia, 68-77; vis scientist, La State Univ, 74-75, Int Fertilizer Develop Ctr, 81-82; rice specialist, Ecuador Nat Inst for Land & Cattle Investigations, 77- & Int Agr Develop Serv, 78-81; irrig specialist, Bangladesh, 82-83; agr exp sta develop & mgt specialist, Indonesia, 84, small farm mach, 85; res sta develop specialist, Burma, 86-89, Pakistan, 90. *Mem:* Am Soc Agr Engrs; Indian Soc Agr Eng; Nat Soc Prof Engrs; Soc Am Mil Engrs. *Res:* Rice specialist and development of irrigation, fertilizer, drainage, roads, bridges, sanitation, machine and processing systems for agricultural experiment stations and food production in the lowland tropics; machinery management. *Mailing Add:* 287 Herman Bailey Rd Somerville AL 35670

JOHNSON, LYNWOOD ALBERT, INDUSTRIAL ENGINEERING, OPERATIONS RESEARCH. *Current Pos:* assoc prof, 66-68, prof, 68-93, EMER PROF INDUST ENG, GA INST TECHNOL, 94- *Personal Data:* b Macon, Ga, Oct 4, 33. *Educ:* Ga Inst Technol, BIE, 55, MS, 59, PhD(indust eng), 65. *Prof Exp:* Indust engr, E I du Pont de Nemours & Co, Inc, 55-57; from instr to asst prof indust eng, Ga Inst Technol, 58-64; supvr opers res, Kurt Salmon Assocs, Inc, 64-66. *Concurrent Pos:* Vis prof, Thayer Sch Eng, Dartmouth Col, 67, Dept Systs & Indust Eng, Univ Ariz, 81-82; Dept Mech Eng, Univ Wash, 85. *Mem:* Inst Indust Engrs; Ist Opers Res & Mgt Sci; Am Prod & Inventory Control Soc. *Res:* Production systems analysis; inventory systems; optimization methods; decision theory. *Mailing Add:* 6881 Glenlake Pkwy NE No G Atlanta GA 30328. *E-Mail:* ljohnson@isye.gatech.edu

JOHNSON, MALCOLM PRATT, INORGANIC CHEMISTRY. *Current Pos:* MGR MKT, DIXIE CHEM CO, 80-, VPRES INT MKT. *Personal Data:* b New Haven, Conn, Aug 9, 41; m 64, Patricia; c David & Christopher. *Educ:* Amherst Col, BA, 63; Northwestern Univ, PhD(inorg chem), 67. *Prof Exp:* Res chemist, Chem Div, Union Carbide Corp, 66-69, res chemist, Linde Div, Tarrytown, NY, 69-71; gen mgr, Gulf Coast Div, Humphrey Chem Co, 71-77; mgr com develop, Southwest Specialty Chem Inc, 77-80. *Mem:* Am Chem Soc; NY Acad Sci. *Res:* Oxygen and nitrogen complexes of transition metals; organometallic chemistry; homogeneous catalysis; Lewis basicity; polyethylenimine chemistry; infrared spectroscopy. *Mailing Add:* Dixie Chem Co PO Box 130410 Houston TX 77219

JOHNSON, MARIE-LOUISE T, DERMATOLOGY, MEDICAL EDUCATION. *Current Pos:* CLIN PROF DERMAT, SCH MED, YALE UNIV, 80-; PVT PRACT, 93- *Personal Data:* b New York, NY, July 26, 27. *Educ:* Manhattanville Col, BA, 48; Yale Univ, PhD(microbiol), 54, MD, 56. *Prof Exp:* From instr to asst prof med, Sch Med, Yale Univ, 58-64, actg head, Div Dermat, 61-62; chief dermat, Atomic Bomb Casualty Comn, Hiroshima & Nagasaki, 64-67; assoc prof, Sch Med, NY Univ, 67-69, assoc prof clin dermat, 69-70, from assoc prof to prof dermat, 74-80; assoc prof internal med, Dartmouth Med Sch, 71-74; chief, Dermat Serv, Bellevue Hosp, 74-80; vpres med affairs, Benedictine Hosp, Kingston, NY, 80-82; dir med educ, 80-93. *Concurrent Pos:* Pres, Maternity & Early Childhood Found; chief, Dermat Serv, Vet Admin Hosp, White River Jet, Vt, 71-74, chief, Ambulatory Serv, 73-74; head, Div Educ & Commun, Nat Prog Dermat, 73-75; chmn, Med & Sci Comt, Dermat Found, 74-75 & Coun Educ Affairs, Am Acad Dermat, 80-82; mem, Eval Comt, Am Acad Dermat, 76-82, bd dirs, 77-80, Task Force Manpower, 86-89; vis lectr, 79th All-Japan Dermat Meeting, Hiroshima & Postgrad Course Venereal Dis, Yugoslavia, 80, XVI Int Cong Dermat, Tokyo, 82; deleg, Cong Int Physicians Against Nuclear War, Cambridge, 82, Third Cong, Neth, 83, Seventh Cong, Moscow, 87, Eighth Cong, 88 & Ninth Cong, Japan, 89; mem bd dirs, Am Dermat Asn, 86- *Mem:* Inst Med-Nat Acad Sci; Am Dermat Asn (vpres, 91-); Am Acad Dermat; Soc Invest Dermat; Int Physicians Prev Nuclear War; NY Acad Med; AMA; Soc Trop Dermat. *Res:* Epidemiology studies of late radiation effects in Hiroshima and Nagasaki; population studies as with the Health and Nutrition Examination Survey; prevalence of Hansen's Disease in Pohnpei, Micronesia; author of 6 scientific publications. *Mailing Add:* 368 Broadway Suite 202 Kingston NY 12401. *Fax:* 914-331-4191

JOHNSON, MARK ALAN, DYNAMICS & CONTROL, SOLID MECHANICS. *Current Pos:* MECH ENGR, GEN ELEC CORP RES & DEVELOP, 96- *Educ:* Univ Nebr, BS, 89; MS, 92; Cornell Univ, PhD(eng mech), 96. *Mem:* Am Soc Mech Engrs. *Mailing Add:* 1 Research Circle Niskayuna NY 12309

JOHNSON, MARK EDWARD, STATISTICS, OPERATIONS RESEARCH. *Current Pos:* CHMN & PROF, DEPT STATIST, UNIV CENT FLA, 90- *Personal Data:* b Chicago, Ill, June 27, 52; m 76. *Educ:* Univ Iowa, BA, 73, MS, 74, PhD(indust & mgt eng), 76. *Prof Exp:* staff mem statist,

Los Alamos Nat Lab, 76-88; prof indust eng, Ga Tech, 88-90. *Mem:* Am Statist Asn; Math Asn Am; Inst Math Statist. *Res:* Applied statistics; random variate generation; Monte Carlo methods; probability distributions. *Mailing Add:* Dept Statist Univ Cent Fla PO Box 25000 Orlando FL 32816-2370

JOHNSON, MARK SCOTT, PROGRAMMING LANGUAGES, COMPILER TECHNOLOGY. *Current Pos:* DIR ENG, SOFTWARE CORP, 97- *Personal Data:* b Oakland, Calif, Apr 16, 51. *Educ:* Univ Calif, BS, 73, MS, 74; Univ BC, PhD(comput sci), 78. *Prof Exp:* Asst prof, San Francisco State Univ, 78-80; mem tech staff, Hewlett-Packard Labs, 80-86; mgr lang prods, Sun Microsysts, 86-90; mgr prof serv, Microtec Res Inc, 90-93; sr engr mgr, Sun Microsysts, 93-95; chief tech officer, Vivid Studios, 95-97. *Concurrent Pos:* Vchair, Sigplan, Asn Comput Mach, 83-87, chair, 87-89, chair Sig bd, 90-92, mem coun, 90-92; mem, Spec Interest Group Planning Languages & Spec Interest Group Software Eng. *Mem:* Asn Comput Mach. *Res:* Develop and teach course in software engineering, software development methods, and programming tools and environments, particulary software debugging. *Mailing Add:* Softwine Corp 900 Larkspur Landing Circle No 270 Larkspur CA 94939. *E-Mail:* msj@mri.com

JOHNSON, MARTIN R, CHEMISTRY. *Current Pos:* ASST PROF ORG CHEM, GEORGE WASHINGTON UNIV, 92- *Personal Data:* b Chicago, Ill, Nov 24, 58. *Educ:* Reed Col, BA, 81; Univ Tex, PhD, 89. *Prof Exp:* Amgen, Inc, 82; Reed Energy Assoc, 83; fel, Robert A Welch Found, 85-88; fel, Chem Dept, Northwestern Univ, 89-92. *Mem:* Am Chem Soc; Sigma Xi; assoc mem Am Soc Mech Engrs. *Mailing Add:* Dept Chem George Washington Univ 2035 H St NW Washington DC 20052-0001

JOHNSON, MARVIN ELROY, PARTICLE PHYSICS. *Current Pos:* STAFF SCIENTIST, FERMI NAT ACCELERATOR LAB, 73- *Personal Data:* b Red Wing, Minn, Nov 3, 45; m 70, Anna Jean Slaughter; c David. *Educ:* Univ Minn, BS, 67; Yale Univ, MPhil, 69, PhD(physics), 73. *Mem:* Sigma Xi. *Res:* Heavy quark physics with emphasis on CP violation. *Mailing Add:* Nat Accelerator Lab MS 357 Batavia IL 60510. *E-Mail:* mjohnson@fnal.fnal.gov

JOHNSON, MARVIN FRANCIS LINTON, PHYSICAL CHEMISTRY. *Current Pos:* CONSULT, 85- *Personal Data:* b Chicago, Ill, June 6, 20; m 43, Jane Brown; c David L, Gail J (Davies) & Mark A. *Educ:* Loyola Univ, Ill, BS, 40, MS, 42. *Prof Exp:* Res chemist, Res & Develop Dept, Sinclair Refining Co, 41-50, res chemist, Sinclair Res Labs, 50-69, sr res chemist, Harvey Tech Ctr, Atlantic Richfield Co, 69-73, res assoc, 73-79, sr res assoc, 79-84, sr res adv, 84-85. *Concurrent Pos:* Chmn, subcomt Phys Chem Catalysts, Am Soc Testing & Mat, 80-85. *Mem:* Catalysis Soc; Am Chem Soc. *Res:* Heterogeneous catalysis; adsorption of gases by catalysts; pore structures of catalysts; physical-chemical characterizations of catalysts. *Mailing Add:* 1124 Elder Rd Homewood IL 60430

JOHNSON, MARVIN M, KINETICS, CATALYSIS. *Current Pos:* Sr res engr, Phillips Res Ctr, 56-65, mgr hydrocarbon process, 65-68, res assoc, 68-74, sr res assoc, 74-78, sr scientist catalysis, 78-86, consult, 86-89, RES & DEVELOP FEL, PHILLIPS RES CTR, 89-, CORP RES FEL 90-; PROF CHEM ENG, OKLA STATE UNIV, 89- *Personal Data:* b Salt Lake City, Utah, Mar 21, 28; m 51; c 4. *Educ:* Univ Utah, BS, 50, PhD(chem eng), 56. *Honors & Awards:* Nat Medal Technol, 86; Achievement Award, Indust Res Inst, 93. *Concurrent Pos:* Adj prof chem eng, Univ Kans, 81-82; vis prof, Colo Sch Mines, 82. *Mem:* Nat Acad Eng; Am Inst Chem Engrs; Sigma Xi; Nat Soc Prof Engrs; Am Chem Soc. *Res:* New catalysts and processes related to production and refining of petroleum and petrochemicals. *Mailing Add:* 354 PL Phillips Res Ctr Bartlesville OK 74004

JOHNSON, MARVIN MELROSE, INDUSTRIAL ENGINEERING, ENGINEERING STATISTICS. *Current Pos:* VIS PROF & PROG COORDR INDUST ENG, SDAK SCH MINES & TECHNOL, 89- *Personal Data:* b Neligh, Nebr, Apr 21, 25; m 51; c 5. *Educ:* Purdue Univ, BS, 49; Univ Iowa, MS, 66, PhD(indust eng), 68. *Prof Exp:* Supvr qual control, Chicago Bumper Div, Houdaille Hershey, 49-52; sr indust engr, Bell & Howell Co, 52-54; chief indust engr, Pioneer Cent Div, Bendix Corp, 54-57, supvr systs & procedures, 57-59, staff asst to asst gen mgr, 59-64; lectr indust & mgt eng, Univ Iowa, 64, instr, 65-66; assoc prof mech eng, Univ Nebr, Lincoln, 68-70, assoc prof, 70-77, prof indust & mgt systs eng, 77-88. *Concurrent Pos:* Indust eng consult, Lincoln, Nebr & Davenport, Iowa, 64-; consult, Pioneer Cent Div, Bendix Corp, 64-68 & Brunswick Corp, 69-; prof & advisor, USAID-Univ Nebr-Omaha Contract-Kabul Univ, Afghanistan, 75-76; vis prof Indust eng, Univ PR, Mayaguez, 82-83. *Mem:* Fel Am Inst Indust Engrs; Am Soc Mech Engrs; Am Statist Asn; Am Soc Eng Educ; Inst Mgt Sci; Opers Res Soc Am; Sigma Xi. *Res:* Systems; vegetable protein isolate; replaceable energy sources; operations research; applied statistics; simulation; quality control and reliability; production planning and control. *Mailing Add:* 329 Fox Run Dr Rapid City SD 57701

JOHNSON, MARY FRANCES, INORGANIC CHEMISTRY. *Current Pos:* PROF & CHAIRPERSON CHEM DEPT, FONTBONNE COL, 72- *Personal Data:* b Green Bay, Wis, Nov 17, 40. *Educ:* Marquette Univ, BS, 63, MS, 65; St Louis Univ, PhD(inorg chem), 72. *Mem:* Am Chem Soc; Sigma Xi. *Res:* Spectroscopy and synthesis of lanthanide chelates involving nitrogen donor ligands. *Mailing Add:* 4334 Virginia Ave St Louis MO 63111-1150

JOHNSON, MARY FRANCES, CLINICAL TRIALS, SURVIVAL ANALYSIS. *Current Pos:* VPRES, G H BESSELAAR ASSOC, 86- *Personal Data:* b Milford, Conn, Nov 21, 51; m 78. *Educ:* Tufts Univ, BS, 73; Yale Univ, MPH, 75, PhD(biostatist), 78. *Prof Exp:* Data analyst, Dept Epidemiol & Public Health, Yale Univ, 73-74, res asst, Conn Cancer Epidemiol Unit, 75-76; student ed, Yale J Biol & Med, Yale Univ, 75-78, teaching asst, Div Biostatist, 75-77; math statistician, Div Biomet, Bur Drugs, Food & Drug Admin, 78-86. *Concurrent Pos:* Consult, Waterford Conserv Comn, Conn, 74-75. *Mem:* Am Statist Asn; Biomet Soc. *Res:* Design and statistical analysis of therapeutic drug trials and epidemiological studies; applications of parametric and non-parametric models for failure time data. *Mailing Add:* 171 Sayre Dr Princeton NJ 08540

JOHNSON, MARY IDA, NEUROBIOLOGY, PEDIATRIC NEUROLOGY. *Personal Data:* b Harlingen, Tex, Oct 30, 42; m 75; c 3. *Educ:* Wash State Univ, BS, 64; Johns Hopkins Univ, MD, 68. *Prof Exp:* Intern & resident, Johns Hopkins Hosp, 68-71; fel neurol, Wash Univ Sch Med, 71-74, res asst prof neurol, 74-84, assoc prof pediat, anat & neurol, 84-89. *Mem:* Soc Neurosci; Child Neurol Soc; Am Acad Neurol; Soc Pediat Res; Am Neurol Asn. *Res:* Differentiation of neuronal form, growth cone function, dendritic development; development of neurotransmitter function in the autonomic nervous system. *Mailing Add:* Univ Ariz Health Sci Ctr 1501 N Campbell Ave Tucson AZ 85724. *Fax:* 520-626-2883; *E-Mail:* mjohnson@peds.arizona.edu

JOHNSON, MARY KNETTLES, BACTERIOLOGY. *Current Pos:* assoc prof, 67-80, PROF MICROBIOL, SCH MED, TULANE UNIV, LA, 80- *Personal Data:* b Detroit, Mich, Sept 2, 29; m 55; c 2. *Educ:* La State Univ, BS, 54, MS, 55, PhD(bact), 57. *Prof Exp:* Res assoc pharmacol, Stanford Univ, 57-58; asst prof microbiol, Sch Med, Univ Miss, 58-65. *Concurrent Pos:* Instr, Millsaps Col, 58-61. *Mem:* Fel Am Acad Microbiol; Am Soc Microbiol. *Res:* Bacterial physiology; mechanisms of pathogenicity. *Mailing Add:* Dept Microbiol Tulane Univ Sch Med 1430 Tulane Ave New Orleans LA 70112-2699

JOHNSON, MARY LYNN MILLER, FUEL SCIENCE, AIR POLLUTION. *Current Pos:* CONSULT CHEM, 94- *Personal Data:* b Pampa, Tex, Mar 12, 38; m 57, James J Jr; c Melinda A & James J III. *Educ:* Univ Tex, El Paso, BS, 58; NMex State Univ, MS, 61; Pa State Univ, PhD(fuel sci), 70. *Prof Exp:* Chemist, El Paso City-County Health Unit, Tex, 59-60 & 61-63 & Tex State Health Dept, 63-64; independent consult air pollution, 64-68; asst prof chem, Univ Tex, Arlington, 68-75; instr chem, Hockaday Sch, Dallas, 75-86; instr chem, Brookhaven Col, Dallas, 80-87 & 91-94; instr chem, Highland Park High Sch, Dallas, 86-94. *Concurrent Pos:* Fel, Am Inst Chemists. *Mem:* Combustion Inst; Am Chem Soc; Am Inst Chemists. *Res:* Investigation of odor counteractants; combustion reactions, especially in the afterburning region, oxides of carbon and sulfur; analytical methods for measurement of air pollutants; air pollution chemistry; flame chemistry; combustion, new energy sources and air pollution. *Mailing Add:* 3004 Croydon Denton TX 76201

JOHNSON, MARYL RAE, CARDIOLOGY. *Current Pos:* ASSOC MED DIR, RUSH HEART FAILURE & CARDIAC TRANSPLANT PROG, 94-; ASSOC PROF, RUSH UNIV, 94- *Personal Data:* b Ft Dodge, Iowa, Apr 15, 51. *Educ:* Iowa State Univ, BS, 73; Univ Iowa, MD, 77; Am Bd Internal Med, dipl. *Honors & Awards:* Clin Investr Award, NIH, 81, New Investr Res Award, 86. *Prof Exp:* From intern to resident, Univ Iowa Hosps, 77-81, assoc cardiol, Univ Iowa Hosps & Clin, 82-86, asst prof med, Cardiovasc Div, 86-88, med dir cardiac transplantation, Univ Iowa Hosp, 86-88; prof med, Loyola Univ, 88-92, assoc med dir cardiac transplantation, 88-94. *Concurrent Pos:* Mem, Nat Heart Lung Blood Adv Coun, 79-83; biomed res tech rev comt, NIH, 90-93, chairperson, 92-93; assoc ed, J Heart & Lung Transplantation, 95- *Mem:* AMA; AAAS; Am Col Physicians; Int Soc Heart & Lung Transplantation; Am Heart Asn; Am Fedn Clin Res; Am Col Cardiol; Am Soc Transplant Physicians. *Mailing Add:* Dept Med Loyola Univ Med Ctr 2160 S First Ave Maywood IL 60153-3304

JOHNSON, MELVIN ANDREW, MEDICAL PHYSIOLOGY. *Current Pos:* prof, 74-85, ADJ PROF PHYSIOL, SCH MED, WRIGHT STATE UNIV, 85- *Personal Data:* b Springfield, Ohio, Sept 4, 29; m 53; c 2. *Educ:* Cent State Univ, BS, 50; Miami Univ, MS, 55; Jefferson Med Col, PhD(med physiol), 69. *Prof Exp:* Asst anat, Western Reserve Univ, 51-53; grad asst zool, Miami Univ, 54-55; instr biol, Grambling Col, 55-59; from instr to assoc prof, 61-72, chmn dept, 69-85, PROF BIOL, CENT STATE UNIV, 72-, DEAN, COL ARTS & SCI, 85- *Concurrent Pos:* Am Heart Asn res grant, 70-72; prog dir minority biomed support grant, NIH, 72-88, prin investr, 72-77 & 80-88, ad hoc consult, Div Res Resources, 73-80; item writer, Educ Testing Serv, 75-77; prog dir, NASA grant, 77-79; res reviewer, Ohio Affiliate, Am Heart Asn, 85-87; prog dir, NIMH grant, NIH, 90- *Mem:* Nat Inst Sci (pres, 79-81, treas, 84-); AAAS; Am Physiol Soc; Sigma Xi; Am Heart Asn; Fedn Am Socs Exp Biol & Med. *Res:* Hemodynamic and metabolic responses to hemorrhagic stress following surgical alterations in liver and splenic tissue; effect of certain atmospheric pollutants on small mammals; effect of calcium channel blockers on peripheral circulation. *Mailing Add:* Col Arts & Sci 589 Wilson Dr Xenia OH 45385-1835

JOHNSON, MELVIN CLARK, TOXICOLOGY, PHARMACOLOGY. *Current Pos:* RETIRED. *Personal Data:* b Newark, NJ, Aug 29, 38; m 75, Yvonne Harrison; c Marion, Denise & Eric. *Educ:* Rutgers Univ, BS, 62; McGill Univ, MS, 68; Howard Univ, PhD(pharmacol), 72; Am Bd Toxicol, dipl. *Prof Exp:* From assoc scientist to scientist pharmacol, Warner-Lambert Res Inst, 62-70; toxicologist med dept, Hercules, Inc, 72-76; dir toxicol, Am

Cyanamid Co, 77-87, mgr health & safety affairs, Agr Div, 87-94. *Mem:* Am Inst Biol Sci; Am Acad Clin Toxicol; NY Acad Sci; Soc Toxicol. *Res:* Toxicology and pharmacology; safety of food additives, pesticides, animal drugs, food packaging materials and other consumer products; evaluation of potential exposures. *Mailing Add:* 101 Highland Ridge Rd Manalapan NJ 07726. *Fax:* 609-275-3523

JOHNSON, MELVIN WALTER, JR, AGRONOMY, GENETICS. *Current Pos:* ASSOC PROF AGRON, PA STATE UNIV, UNIVERSITY PARK, 65- *Personal Data:* b Chicago, Ill, May 27, 28; m 54; c 2. *Educ:* Univ Ill, BS, 50; Univ Wis, MS, 51, PhD(plant breeding), 54. *Prof Exp:* Asst agron, Univ Wis, 50-54; asst prof & asst agronomist, WVa Univ, 56-60, assoc prof & assoc agronomist, 60-65. *Mem:* Am Soc Agron; AAAS. *Res:* Plant breeding; plant genetics; corn breeding; basic and applied corn breeding and genetics research. *Mailing Add:* 607 Outer Dr State College PA 16801

JOHNSON, MICHAEL D, HUMAN PHYSIOLOGY. *Current Pos:* Researcher renal hypertension, 76-79, from asst prof to assoc prof, 79-88, PROF HUMAN PHYSIOL, WVA UNIV SCH MED, 88- *Personal Data:* b Chicago, Ill, Dec 29, 48. *Educ:* Wash State Univ, BS, 70; Univ Mich, PhD(physiol), 76. *Mem:* Am Physiol Soc. *Mailing Add:* Dept Physiol WVa Univ Sch Med Morgantown WV 26506-0001. *Fax:* 304-293-3850

JOHNSON, MICHAEL EVART, BIOPHYSICS. *Current Pos:* from asst prof to assoc prof, Med Ctr, 76-84, PROF MED CHEM, UNIV ILL, CHICAGO, 84-, ASSOC DEAN, 86- *Personal Data:* b Cody, Wyo, Sept 4, 45; m; c 1. *Educ:* Univ Wyo, BS, 68; Northwestern Univ, MS, 70, PhD(biophys), 73. *Prof Exp:* Res assoc & NIH fel biophys, Univ Pittsburgh, 73-75. *Concurrent Pos:* Guest scientist, Argonne Nat Lab, 75-; estab investr, Am Heart Asn, 79-84. *Mem:* Biophys Soc; AAAS; Am Chem Soc; Sigma Xi. *Res:* Sickling mechanism in sickle cell anemia; applications of magnetic resonance and computer aided molecular modeling in molecular structure analysis and design. *Mailing Add:* 2809 Girard Ave Evanston IL 60201-1708

JOHNSON, MICHAEL L, PROTEIN CHEMISTRY. *Current Pos:* From res asst prof to assoc prof, 80-85, ASSOC PROF PHARMACOL, UNIV VA, 85-, DIR, BIOPHYSCS PROG & DIABETES RES & TRAINING CTR, 85- *Personal Data:* b Myrtle Point, Ore, Nov 12, 47. *Educ:* Univ Conn, PhD(biophysics), 74. *Mem:* Biophys Soc; Calorimetry Soc; Am Soc Biol Chemists. *Res:* Computer applications. *Mailing Add:* Dept Pharmacol Univ Va Jordan Hall Rm 448 Charlottesville VA 22908-0001. *Fax:* 804-982-3878

JOHNSON, MICHAEL PAUL, PLANT ECOLOGY. *Current Pos:* MEM STAFF, SCI EDUC ADMIN, USDA, 80- *Personal Data:* b Oakland, Calif, Sept 13, 37; m 71; c 3. *Educ:* Univ Calif, Davis, BS, 59; Univ Ore, PhD(biol), 66. *Prof Exp:* Instr bot, San Francisco State Col, 60-61; asst prof ecol, Kent State Univ, 65-68; asst prof biol sci, Fla State Univ, 68-72; assoc prof biol, Kans State Univ & assoc dir, Konza Prairie Res Natural Area, 72-80. *Mem:* Soc Study Evolution; Ecol Soc Am; Brit Ecol Soc; Am Soc Naturalists; Sigma Xi. *Res:* Population biology; ecological genetics; botany; ecology. *Mailing Add:* Dept Computer Sci Ore State Univ Corvallis OR 97331

JOHNSON, MICHAEL ROSS, ORGANIC & STRUCTURAL CHEMISTRY, SYNTHETIC & NATURAL PRODUCTS CHEMISTRY. *Current Pos:* PRES & CHIEF EXEC OFFICER, PARNASSUS PHARMACEUT, INC, 94- *Personal Data:* b Detroit, Mich, Oct 27, 44; m 64; c 2. *Educ:* Univ Calif, Berkeley, BS, 67; Univ Calif, Santa Barbara, PhD(org chem), 70. *Prof Exp:* Res chemist, Pfizer Inc, 71-73, sr res scientist, 73-76, sr res investr & proj leader, 76-80, mgr, Cent Nerv Syst & Metab Dis Res, 81-85, asst dir med chem & dir chem, 87-89; vpres, Div Chem, Glaxo, Inc, 89-94. *Concurrent Pos:* NSF undergrad res fel, Calif State Col, Los Angeles, 64; NDEA Title IV fel, Univ Calif, Santa Barbara, 68-70, NIH fel, Berkeley, 70-71, distinguished res fel, 89- *Mem:* Am Chem Soc; Sigma Xi; NY Acad Sci; AAAS; Am Soc Pharmacol & Exp Therapeut; Pharmaceut Mfrs Asn. *Res:* Mechanism and stereochemistry of carbonium ion, carbanion, organometallic and hydride reduction reactions; synthesis of pharmacologically active heterocycles and natural products; synthesis of cannabinoid derived therapeutants; rational rug design. *Mailing Add:* 102 Hazlenut Ct Chapel Hill NC 27516

JOHNSON, MIKKEL BORLAUG, THEORETICAL NUCLEAR, PARTICLE PHYSICS. *Current Pos:* STAFF MEM PHYSICS & LAB FEL, LOS ALAMOS NAT LAB, UNIV CALIF, 72- *Personal Data:* b Waynesboro, Va, Jan 2, 43; m 65; c 2. *Educ:* Va Polytech Inst, BS, 66; Carnegie-Mellon Univ, MS, 68, PhD(physics), 71. *Honors & Awards:* Humboldt Award Sr US Scientists, 86. *Prof Exp:* Consult physics, Rand Corp, 67 & 68; res assoc, Cornell Univ, 70-72. *Concurrent Pos:* Assoc ed nuclear physics, North-Holland Publ Co, 75-; vis prof, Dept Physics, State Univ NY, Stony Brook, 81-82; consult, Oak Ridge Nat Lab, 86. *Mem:* Fel Am Phys Soc. *Res:* Effective interactions in nuclear physics; intermediate energy nuclear theory. *Mailing Add:* 118 Piedra Loop Los Alamos NM 87544. *Fax:* 505-665-7920; *E-Mail:* mjohnson@lanl.gov

JOHNSON, MILES F, SYSTEMATIC BOTANY. *Current Pos:* from asst prof to assoc prof, 68-80, PROF BIOL, VA COMMONWEALTH UNIV, 80- *Personal Data:* b Frederic, Wis, Mar 9, 36; m 63, 81. *Educ:* Wis State Univ, River Falls, BS, 58; Univ Wis-Madison, MS, 62; Univ Minn, Minneapolis, PhD(bot), 68. *Prof Exp:* High sch teacher, Wis, 58-60; teaching asst bot, Univ Wis-Madison, 60-62, instr bot & zool, 62-64; teaching asst bot, Univ Minn, Minneapolis, 64-67, instr, 68. *Mem:* Bot Soc Am; Am Soc Plant Taxon; Int Soc Plant Taxon. *Res:* Taxonomy and systematics of Compositae; genus Ageratum; flora of Virginia. *Mailing Add:* Dept Biol Va Commonwealth Univ Box 2012 Richmond VA 23284-9004

JOHNSON, MILLARD WALLACE, JR, PAPER PHYSICS, RHEOLOGY. *Current Pos:* from asst prof to prof eng mech, 58-94, EMER PROF ENG MECH & MATH, UNIV WIS-MADISON, 94- *Personal Data:* b Racine, Wis, Feb 1, 28; m 53, Ruth Gifford; c Millard W, Jeannette (Brooks), Charles G & Peter A. *Educ:* Univ Wis, BS, 52, MS, 53; Mass Inst Technol, PhD(math), 57. *Prof Exp:* Instr math, Mass Inst Technol, 53-58. *Concurrent Pos:* Mem staff, Math Res Ctr, Univ Wis, 58-; mem exec comt, Rheol Res Ctr, Univ Wis, 69-; mem adv bd, Int Math & Statist Libr, 71-93. *Mem:* Soc Rheol; Soc Indust & Appl Math; fel Am Soc Mech Engrs; Brit Soc Rheol. *Res:* Research papers in applied mathematics, rheology, elasticity and paper mechanics. *Mailing Add:* Univ Wis 1415 Engineering Dr Madison WI 53706. *Fax:* 608-238-0019; *E-Mail:* mwjohnsl@facstaff.wisc.edu

JOHNSON, MILTON R(AYMOND), JR, ELECTRONICS ENGINEERING. *Current Pos:* RETIRED. *Personal Data:* b Shreveport, La, Nov 5, 19; m 42; c 3. *Educ:* La Polytech Inst, BS, 40; Okla State Univ, MS, 51; Tex A&M Univ, PhD, 63. *Prof Exp:* Design engr, Gen Elec Co, 41-47; from asst prof to assoc prof, La Tech Univ, 47-54, prof elec eng, 54-86, head dept, 80-85. *Concurrent Pos:* Consult, Delta Res & Develop Corp, 52-60; NSF sci fac fel, 60-61. *Mem:* Am Soc Eng Educ; Inst Elec & Electronics Engrs. *Res:* Electromechanical energy converters; automatic control systems. *Mailing Add:* 6130 Kilbourn Chicago IL 60646-5020

JOHNSON, MORRIS ALFRED, PLANT BIOCHEMISTRY. *Current Pos:* PROF, FOX VALLEY TECH COL, 89- *Personal Data:* b International Falls, Minn, Aug 3, 37; m 61, Catherine Kiefer; c Raymond, Sigmond, Armond & Normond. *Educ:* NDak State Univ, BS, 60, MS, 62; Ore State Univ, PhD(biochem), 66. *Prof Exp:* Asst prof & res fel biochem, Inst Paper Chem, 66-73, chmn dept, 70-79, assoc prof, 73-89, res assoc, 74-89. *Mem:* Am Chem Soc; Am Soc Plant Physiol; fel Am Inst Chemists; Sigma Xi; Int Plant Growth Substances Asn; Plant Growth Regulator Soc of Am. *Res:* Intermediary metabolism and oxidative phosphorylation in plants; natural plant growth and development regulators; biochemistry of tree callus and suspension cultures. *Mailing Add:* W 7805 School Rd Greenville WI 54942. *Fax:* 920-735-2582; *E-Mail:* johnson.@foxvalley.tec.wi.us

JOHNSON, MURRAY LEATHERS, medicine, mammalogy; deceased, see previous edition for last biography

JOHNSON, MYRLE F, PHYSICAL CHEMISTRY. *Current Pos:* RETIRED. *Personal Data:* b Jerico Springs, Mo, Dec 12, 18; m 57; c 2. *Educ:* Southwest Mo State Col, AB, 41; Univ Wis, PhD(phys chem), 50. *Prof Exp:* Assoc prof chem, Southwest Mo State Col, 50-53; from res chemist to sr res chemist, Eastman Kodak Co, 53-71, res assoc, 71-83. *Mem:* Am Chem Soc. *Res:* Rheology and colloid chemistry. *Mailing Add:* 29 Margate Dr Rochester NY 14616-5503

JOHNSON, NANCY EBERSOLE, HUMAN & MINERAL NUTRITION. *Current Pos:* CHMN, DEPT FOOD SCI & HUMAN NUTRIT, UNIV HAWAII, 86- *Personal Data:* b Sioux Falls, NDak, Dec 12, 25. *Educ:* Iowa State Univ, BS, 47, MS, 49; Univ Wis, Madison, PhD(nutrit sci), 69. *Prof Exp:* From asst prof to prof nutrit, Col Agr & Life Sci, Univ Wis, 69-86. *Mem:* Inst Food Technologists; Am Inst Nutrit; AAAS. *Res:* Human and mineral nutrition. *Mailing Add:* 6750 Hawaii Kai Dr Apt 1102 Honolulu HI 96825-1452. *Fax:* 808-956-4024

JOHNSON, NED KEITH, ORNITHOLOGY. *Current Pos:* From asst prof to assoc prof, Univ Clif, Berkeley, 62-74, asst cur birds, Mus Vert Zool, 62-63, actg dir, 81, PROF ZOOL, UNIV CALIF, BERKELEY, 74-, VCHMN DEPT, 68-, CUR BIRDS, MUS VERT ZOOL, 63- *Personal Data:* b Reno, Nev, Nov 3, 32; m 52; c 4. *Educ:* Univ Nev, BS, 54; Univ Calif, PhD(zool), 61. *Concurrent Pos:* NSF res grants, 65- *Mem:* Am Soc Zool; Am Ornith Union; Cooper Ornith Soc; Soc Study Evolution; Soc Syst Zool; Am Soc Naturalists. *Res:* Biosystematics; distribution and ecology of New World birds. *Mailing Add:* 3101 Valley Life Sci Bldg Univ Calif Berkeley CA 94720-3140

JOHNSON, NEIL FRANCIS, PATHOLOGY, CYTOLOGY. *Current Pos:* GROUP SUPVR EXP PATH, MOLECULAR & CELLULAR TOXICOL, INHALATION TOXICOL RES INST, 86- *Personal Data:* b Heighington, Co Durham, UK, Mar 15, 48; m 70; c 3. *Educ:* London Univ, BSc, 69; City Univ, London, MSc, 71; Glasgow Univ, PhD(exp path), 76. *Prof Exp:* Res asst ocular path, Tennent Inst Ophthal, Glasgow Univ, 71-77; scientist exp path, Pneumoconiosis Unit, Penarth, Med Res Coun, UK, 77-84; lectr gen path, Inst Sci & Technol, Univ Wales, 80-84; vis scientist exp path, Los Alamos Nat Lab, 84-86; scientist Toxicol Univ, Med Res Coun, UK, 86. *Concurrent Pos:* Chmn, Task Group: Molecular Biol Carcinogenesis, Med Res Coun, 89-91; clin assoc prof, Col Pharm, Univ NMex, 91- *Mem:* Am Soc Testing & Mat; Soc Toxicol; Royal Col Pathologists. *Res:* Determining the cells at risk from carcinogenesis from inhaled materials with particular emphasis on radon progeny and natural and manmade mineral fibers. *Mailing Add:* Inhalation Toxicol Res Inst PO Box 5890 Albuquerque NM 87185. *Fax:* 505-845-1189; *E-Mail:* njohnson@tll-1.tli.org

JOHNSON, NOAH R, PROPERTIES OF HIGHLY EXCITED NUCLEI. *Current Pos:* RES PROF, UNIV TENN, 95- *Personal Data:* b Kingsport, Tenn, Oct 15, 28; m 50, Rosemary McElroy; c Kurt, Gregory & Gwendolyn. *Educ:* ETenn State Univ, BS, 50; Fla State Univ, PhD, 56. *Prof Exp:* Pub sch teacher, Tenn, 50-52; nuclear chemist, Oak Ridge Nat Lab, 56-80, group leader nuclear physics, 80-90, sr scientist, 91-94. *Concurrent Pos:* Fulbright scholar & Guggenheim fel, Niels Bohr Inst, Copenhagen, 62-63. *Mem:* Fel Am Phys Soc; Sigma Xi; Am Chem Soc. *Res:* Nuclear spectroscopy and reactions; coulomb excitation; Doppler-shift lifetime measurements; studies of high-angular momentum behavior in nuclei; development of complex gamma-ray detector systems. *Mailing Add:* Oak Ridge Nat Lab PO Box 2008 Oak Ridge TN 37831-6371. *Fax:* 423-574-1268; *E-Mail:* johnson@orph01.phy.ornl.gov

JOHNSON, NOBLE MARSHALL, ELECTRONIC DEFECTS IN SEMICONDUCTORS, HYDROGEN IN SEMICONDUCTORS. *Current Pos:* Mem res staff, 76-85, sr mem res staff, 85-87, PRIN SCIENTIST, ELECTRONIC MAT LAB, XEROX PALO ALTO CTR, XEROX CORP, 87- *Personal Data:* b San Francisco, Calif, Feb 23, 45. *Educ:* Univ Calif, Davis, BS, 67, MS, 70; Princeton Univ, PhD(eng & appl sci), 74. *Honors & Awards:* Distinguished Sr US Scientist Award, Alexander Von Humboldt Found, Ger, 87. *Concurrent Pos:* Vis lectr, Dept Elec Eng & Comput Sci, Sch Eng & Appl Sci, Princeton Univ, 86; mem coun, Mat Res Soc, 86-88; distinguished sr US scientist, Inst Appl Physics, Univ Erlangen-Nurnberg, Ger, 88. *Mem:* Fel Am Phys Soc; sr mem Inst Elec & Electronics Engrs; Mat Res Soc. *Res:* Electronic materials and devices particularly on electronic defects in semi-conductors, metal-insulator-semiconductor structures, deep-level transient spectroscopy, hydrogen in semi-conductors and synthesis and processing of electronic materials; co-edited 4 books, contributed over 250 articles to professional journals and patentee in field. *Mailing Add:* Xerox Palo Alto Res Ctr 3333 Coyote Hill Rd Palo Alto CA 94304. *E-Mail:* njohnson@parc.xerox.com

JOHNSON, NORMAN ELDEN, FOREST MANAGEMENT, SILVICULTURE. *Current Pos:* forest entomologist, Forestry Res Ctr,56-66, forest bioprotection leader, 66-69, WEYERHAUSER CO, TACOMA, 84- *Personal Data:* b Mesa, Ariz, Apr 26, 33; m 54; c 2. *Educ:* Ore State Univ, BSF, 55, MS, 57; Univ Calif, PhD, 61. *Prof Exp:* Forestry aid, US Forest Serv, 51-52; forest engr, Southwest Lumber Mills, 54-55, forest entom asst, 55; forestry res mgr, Southern Forestry Res Ctr, Weyerhaeuser Co, Ark, 69-75, mgr, regional forestry & res, 75-78, vpres, Far E region, Indonesia, 78-80, NC region, New Bern, NC, 80-84. *Concurrent Pos:* Assoc prof dept entom, Cornell Univ, 67-69; adj prof, Sch Forestry Resources, NC State Univ, 72; assoc ed, J Appl Forestry; mem bd dir, Pacific Sci Ctr, Sci Adv Coun, NC State Univ & Ore State Univ; chmn, Coop Forestry Adv Comt, US Dept Agr, McIntire-Stennis Res Prog; mem, Pres Reagan's Agr 7 Forestry Mission, Honduras, 82-83 & Zaire, 85; mem bd dir & Long Range Res Planning Comt, Wash Technol Ctr, US Nat Comt, Man & Biosphere Prog. *Mem:* Soc Am Foresters. *Res:* Forest plantation management. *Mailing Add:* 27229 Eighth Ave S Des Moines WA 98198

JOHNSON, NORMAN L, GEOMETRY. *Current Pos:* asst prof, 69-78, PROF MATH, UNIV IOWA, 78- *Personal Data:* b Tillamook, Ore, July 27, 39; m 64; c 3. *Educ:* Portland State Univ, BA, 64; Wash State Univ, MA, 66, PhD(math), 68. *Prof Exp:* Asst prof math, Eastern Wash State Col, 68-69. *Concurrent Pos:* Researcher, NSF fel, 71-72; res fel, Univ Bergen, 73-74; Sci Res Coun researcher, Great Britain, 78- *Res:* Finite projective planes; classification of semitranslation planes and their construction; translation planes; collineation groups. *Mailing Add:* Dept Math Univ Iowa Iowa City IA 52242-0001

JOHNSON, NORMAN LLOYD, STATISTICS. *Current Pos:* RETIRED. *Personal Data:* b Ilford, Eng, Jan 9, 17; m 64, Regina C Elandt. *Educ:* Univ Col London, BSc, 36 & 37, MSc, 38, PhD(statist), 48, DSc, 63. *Honors & Awards:* Shewhart Medal, Am Soc Qual Control, 84; Willes Mem Medal, Am Statist Asn, 92. *Prof Exp:* Asst lectr statist, Univ Col London, 38-39, 45-46, lectr, 46-56, reader, 56-62; prof, Univ NC, Chapel Hill, 62-82, chmn dept, 71-76, emer prof statist, 82- *Concurrent Pos:* Vis assoc prof, Univ NC, Chapel Hill, 52-53; vacation consult, Road Res Lab, Eng, 56-59; vis prof, Case Inst Technol, 60-61, Univ NSW, Australia, 69; co-ed in chief, Encycl Statist Sci (10 vols), 82-88. *Mem:* Fel Inst Math Statist; fel Am Statist Asn; Am Soc Qual Control; fel Royal Statist Soc; Biomed Soc; Int Statist Inst. *Res:* Systems of frequency distributions; checks on completeness of samples; reliability. *Mailing Add:* Dept Statist Univ NC Chapel Hill NC 27599-3260. *Fax:* 919-962-1279

JOHNSON, OLIVER, ELECTRON DENSITY IN METALS, PHOTOELECTRON SPECTROSCOPY. *Current Pos:* RETIRED. *Personal Data:* b Edgetts, Mich, Mar 6, 19; m 46, Phyllis Hewitt; c Peter, Mark, Douglas & Michael. *Educ:* NMich Univ, BSc, 39; Univ Mich, PhD, 42. *Prof Exp:* Manhattan Proj, Iowa State Univ, Ames, 43-46; res chemist, Emeryville Res Ctr, Shell Develop Co, 46-70; vis prof, Res Inst Catalysis, Honkaido Univ, Sapporo, Japan, 71-72 & 83, Inst Physics, Uppsala Univ, Sweden, 72-73, Dept Phys Chem, Univ Cambridge, Mass, 75-76, Dept Chem, Univ Ga, Athens, 75-76, Chem Ctr, Lund Inst Technol, Sweden, 80-81, Cavendish Lab, 80-81, Inst Catalysis Res, France, 81-82, Inst Molecular Sci, Okazaki, Japan, 82-83 & Dalian Inst Chem Physics, China, 84; vis prof, Inst des Recherches sur la Catalyse, Villeursbanne, France, 81-82, Inst Molecular Sci, Japan, 82-83 & Dalian Inst Chem Physics, China, 84. *Concurrent Pos:* Res prof, Univ Pittsburgh. *Mem:* Sigma Xi; Am Chem Soc. *Res:* Development of interstitial electron model for electronic structure of metals and metal alloys; interpretation of heterogeneous catalysis with above model; concept of variable ionic radii for anions. *Mailing Add:* 1626 Hillcrest San Luis Obispo CA 93401

JOHNSON, OLIVER WILLIAM, VERTEBRATE ZOOLOGY, PHYSIOLOGY. *Current Pos:* RETIRED. *Personal Data:* b Maud, Okla, Mar 30, 30; m 58; c 1. *Educ:* Fresno State Col, AB, 55; Ore State Univ, MS, 59, PhD(zool), 65. *Prof Exp:* Instr ecol, Ore State Univ, 59-61; asst prof zool, Ariz State Col, 61-63; res assoc entom, Ore State Univ, 63-64; from assoc prof to prof zool, Northern Ariz Univ, 64-89. *Mem:* AAAS; Am Soc Mammalogists; Am Soc Ichthyologists & Herpetologists; Sigma Xi. *Res:* Amphibian and reptilian temperature adaptation; biochemical taxonomy. *Mailing Add:* 63 Pine Ridge Dr Flagstaff AZ 86001

JOHNSON, ORLAND EUGENE, NUCLEAR PHYSICS. *Current Pos:* Res assoc, 56, from asst prof to prof, 56-96, EMER PROF PHYSICS, PURDUE UNIV, 96- *Personal Data:* b Gary, Ind, July 25, 23; m 46. *Educ:* Ind Univ, AB, 49, MS, 51, PhD(physics), 56. *Mem:* Am Phys Soc. *Res:* Beta and gamma spectroscopy; nuclear scattering and reactions. *Mailing Add:* Dept Physics Purdue Univ West Lafayette IN 47901

JOHNSON, OSCAR WALTER, ORNITHOLOGY, ECOLOGY. *Current Pos:* ADJ PROF BIOL, MONT STATE UNIV, 90- *Personal Data:* b Chicago, Ill, Mar 28, 35; m 55; c 2. *Educ:* Mich State Univ, BS, 57; Wash State Univ, MS, 59, PhD(zool), 64. *Prof Exp:* Asst prof biol, Western State Col Colo, 63-65; from asst prof to prof biol, Moorhead State Univ, 65-90. *Concurrent Pos:* Grantee, NSF, 65-66 & 67-69, Ariz State Univ, 71-72, Med Sch, Univ Ariz, 75, Res Corp, 73, AEC & Dept Energy, Univ Hawaii, 70, 73, 78, 79, & 80, Nat Geog Soc, 82, 84, 87, 88, 90, 92 & 96; mem, Int Comn Avian Anatomical Nomenclature, 73- *Mem:* Am Ornith Union; Cooper Ornith Soc; Wilson Ornith Soc; Asn Field Ornith. *Res:* Ecology and behavior in shorebirds, particularly long-distance migrant species of the insular Pacific. *Mailing Add:* Dept Biol Mont State Univ Bozeman MT 59717. *Fax:* 406-994-3190

JOHNSON, OWEN W, SOLID STATE PHYSICS. *Current Pos:* RETIRED. *Personal Data:* b Provo, Utah, Mar 31, 31; m 57; c 3. *Educ:* Univ Utah, BA, 57, PhD(physics), 62. *Prof Exp:* Asst res prof physics, Univ Utah, 62-64, asst prof ceramic eng, 64-65, from asst prof to prof physics, 65-96, adj assoc prof mat sci, 68-96. *Mem:* Am Phys Soc. *Res:* Electronic and optical properties of oxides and semiconductors; infrared spectroscopy; electronic properties of thin films. *Mailing Add:* Dept Physics Univ Utah 201b Fletcher Bldg Salt Lake City UT 84112

JOHNSON, PATRICIA ANN J, CLINICAL NEUROPSYCHOLOGY, PSYCHOLOGY. *Current Pos:* PVT PRACT, 77- *Personal Data:* b New York, NY, Oct 10, 43; m 64, Malcolm T; c David M & Christopher P. *Educ:* Univ Houston, BS, MA, PhD(psychol), 77. *Prof Exp:* Exec dir & clin neuropsychologist, 77-80; Found Land & Learning Opportunities, 77-80. *Concurrent Pos:* NIH fel, 74-77; clin asst prof psychol, Univ Houston, 78-; clin instr, Univ Tex, Houston, 93- *Mem:* Nat Acad Neuropsychol; Int Neuropsychol Soc; Soc Personality Assessment; Am Psychol Asn; Biofeedback Soc Am. *Res:* Etiology and neuropsychology of learning and language disorders in children. *Mailing Add:* 3722 N Main Baytown TX 77521-3304. *Fax:* 713-427-6252

JOHNSON, PATRICIA R, cell culture, genetic obesity, for more information see previous edition

JOHNSON, PAUL CHRISTIAN, PHYSIOLOGY. *Current Pos:* head dept, 67-87, PROF PHYSIOL, COL MED, UNIV ARIZ, 67- *Personal Data:* b Ironwood, Mich, Feb 3, 28; m 55, Genevieve Shanklin; c Ciri, Philip & Christopher. *Educ:* Univ Mich, BS, 51, MA, 53, PhD(physiol), 55. *Hon Degrees:* DrMed(hon), Univ Limburg, Maastricht, Neth. *Honors & Awards:* Eugene M Landis Res Award, Microcirc Soc, 78; Carl J Wiggers Award, Am Physiol Soc, 81. *Prof Exp:* Instr physiol, Univ Mich, 55-56; instr, Western Res Univ, 56-58; from asst prof to assoc prof, Sch Med, Ind Univ, 58-67. *Concurrent Pos:* NIH fel, 65-66; mem physiol study sect, NIH, 68-72; mem steering comt, circulation sect, Am Physiol Soc, 71-74, chmn, 74, mem coun, 78-82, chmn publs comt, 85-89. *Mem:* AAAS; Am Physiol Soc; Microcirc Soc (pres, 67-68). *Res:* Local regulation of blood flow, microcirculation; capillary filtration and exchange. *Mailing Add:* Dept Bioeng Univ Calif-San Diego 9500 Gilman Dr La Jolla CA 92093-0412

JOHNSON, PAUL H(ILTON), CHEMICAL ENGINEERING. *Current Pos:* RETIRED. *Personal Data:* b Nevis, Minn, May 2, 16; div; c Robert P & Patricia J. *Educ:* Univ Minn, BChE, 38. *Prof Exp:* Process engr, Minn Gas Co, 38-41; res engr, Phillips Petrol Co, 41-54, asst chief, Res & Develop Dept, 54-60, mgr, Petrol Process Br, 60-69, mgr, Carbon Black Br, Res Ctr, 69-81; consult carbon black environ health, process & feed stock, 81-91. *Mem:* Am Chem Soc. *Res:* Process development; petroleum refining; petrochemicals; carbon black environmental health; carbon black feed stock; characterization, evolution. *Mailing Add:* 1951 Southview Bartlesville OK 74003. *Fax:* 918-337-0769; *E-Mail:* hil38phs@aol.com

JOHNSON, PAUL HICKOK, BIOPHYSICS, GENETICS. *Current Pos:* sr molecular biologist, 81-84, DIR, DEPT MOLECULAR BIOL, SRI INT, 84- *Personal Data:* b Syracuse, NY, Mar 3, 43; m 81; c 4. *Educ:* State Univ NY Buffalo, BA, 65, PhD(biochem), 70. *Prof Exp:* Am Cancer Soc fel, Calif Inst Technol, 70-74; asst prof biochem & molecular biol, Wayne State Univ, 74-78, assoc prof biochem, 78-81. *Concurrent Pos:* USPHS grant molecular biol, Wayne State Univ, 74-77; NIH Genetics Study Sect, 78-82. *Mem:* AAAS; Am Chem Soc; Am Asn Microbiol; Sigma Xi; Am Soc Biochem & Molecular Biol. *Res:* Protein and nucleic acid biochemistry; genetic engineering; protein drug development; enzymology. *Mailing Add:* Dept Cell & Molecular Biol SRI Int Bldg 20501 Berlix Biosci PO Box 4099 15049 San Pablo Ave Richmond CA 94804-0099. *Fax:* 510-669-4246

JOHNSON, PAUL LORENTZ, COMPUTER SOFTWARE. *Current Pos:* res assoc, 75-77, comput scientist, 77-91, CHEMIST, ARGONNE NAT LAB, 91- *Personal Data:* b Hawarden, Iowa, Sept 19, 41; m 71; c 3. *Educ:* St Olaf Col, BA, 63; Wash State Univ, PhD(phys chem), 68. *Prof Exp:* Fel, Univ Ill, Urbana-Champaign, 68-69; res assoc, Univ Ariz, 69-71, Mich State Univ, 71-72; Royal Norwegian Coun Sci & Indust res fel, Univ Bergen, Norway, 72-73; res assoc, Univ Ariz, 73-75. *Concurrent Pos:* Instr, Lansing Community Col, 72. *Mem:* Asn Comput Mach; Am Crystallog Asn; Sigma Xi. *Res:* Neutron and x-ray crystallographic experiments applied to structures of organic, biological and inorganic interest; one-dimensional conducting compounds; portability of computer software; scientific applications of computers; analytical chemistry. *Mailing Add:* Anal Chem Lab Argonne Nat Lab 9700 S Cass Ave Argonne IL 60439-4831. *E-Mail:* pj@ anl.gov

JOHNSON, PAUL W, FORESTRY. *Current Pos:* CHIEF, NATURAL RESOURCES CONSERV SERV, USDA, 94- *Educ:* Univ Mich, BS & MS. *Mailing Add:* Natural Resources Conserv Serv USDA PO Box 2890 Washington DC 20013-2890

JOHNSON, PETER DAVID, SURFACE STATES, THIN FILMS. *Current Pos:* assoc physicist, 83-86, PHYSICIST, PHYSICS DEPT, BROOKHAVEN NAT LAB, 86- *Personal Data:* b Wellingborough, Eng, Jan 30, 52; m 81, Lynn Smith; c Robert & Catherine. *Educ:* Imp Col London, BS, 72; Warwick Univ, PhD(physics), 77. *Prof Exp:* Fel, Warwick Univ, 76-81, AT&T Bell Labs, 81-82. *Concurrent Pos:* adj prof, Mat Sci Dept, Stony Brook, 91- *Mem:* Fel Am Phys Soc; Am Vacuum Soc; Mat Res Soc. *Res:* Spin resolved electronic structure of surfaces, thin films and related multilayers. *Mailing Add:* Physics Dept Brookhaven Nat Lab Upton NY 11973. *Fax:* 516-282-2739; *E-Mail:* pdj@solids.phy.bnl.gov

JOHNSON, PETER DEXTER, applied physics, for more information see previous edition

JOHNSON, PETER GRAHAM, GEOMORPHOLOGY. *Current Pos:* From asst prof to assoc prof, 69-85, PROF GEOMORPHOL, UNIV OTTAWA, 85- *Personal Data:* b St Helens, Eng, Aug 28, 45; m 67; c 2. *Educ:* Univ Leeds, BSc, 66, PhD(geog), 69. *Mem:* Geol Asn Can; Asn Am Geog; Arctic Inst NAm; Can Asn Geog. *Res:* Alpine hydrology; rock glacier mechanics and drainage systems; ice cored landform formation and degradation, southwest Yukon Territory; glacier hydrology. *Mailing Add:* Dept Geog Univ Ottawa Ottawa ON K1N 6N5 Can

JOHNSON, PHILIP L, ECOLOGY. *Current Pos:* EXEC DIR, ARTIC RES COMM, WASHINGTON DC, 88- *Personal Data:* b Oneonta, NY, May 26, 31; m 73, Judy Rodgers. *Educ:* Purdue Univ, BS, 53, MS, 55; Duke Univ, PhD(bot), 61. *Prof Exp:* Instr bot, Univ Wyo, 59-61; res botanist, Range Res, US Forest Serv, Wyo, 61-62; res ecologist, Cold Regions Res & Eng Lab, NH, 62-67; assoc prof forest resources, Univ Ga, 67-70; div dir environ systs & resources, NSF, 70-74; exec dir, Oak Ridge Assoc Univs, 74-81; exec dir, John E Gray Inst, Lamar Univ, 81-86. *Concurrent Pos:* Vis asst prof biol, Dartmouth Col, 63 & 65-; res collabr, Brookhaven Nat Lab, 63-65; mem NH Pesticide Control Bd, 65-67; mem primary productivity comt, Int Biol Prog, 67-68, adv comt tundra biome, 68-70, deciduous forest biome coord comt, 68-70; assoc prog dir, environ biol prog, NSF, 68-69; mem environ biol panel foreign currency prog, Smithsonian Inst, 69-70; vchmn interagency comt ecol res, Fed Coun Sci & Technol-Coun Environ Qual, 72; mem US Comt Man & Biosphere Prog, 73-74; mem fel adv panel environ affairs, Rockefeller Found, 74-76; mem exec comt, East Tenn Cancer Res Ctr, Knoxville, 75-78; mem regional comt Southeastern Plant Environ Lab, 75-77; mem, US Comn, UNESCO, 78-80; Gov's Task Force Advan Labor & Mgt Relations, 84-86 & Houston Dist Export Coun, 85-86; mem polar res bd, Nat Acad Sci, 81-85. *Res:* Production and processes in arctic and alpine tundra; aerial sensing of ecological patterns; mineral cycling in ecosystems applications of environmental sciences; interdisciplinary research and training; regional economic development. *Mailing Add:* 118 Maid Marion Pl Williamsburg VA 23185

JOHNSON, PHILIP M, PHYSICAL CHEMISTRY, MOLECULAR SPECTROSCOPY. *Current Pos:* from asst prof to assoc prof, 68-78, PROF CHEM, STATE UNIV NY STONY BROOK, 78- *Personal Data:* b Vancouver, Wash, Oct 22, 40; m 64; c 2. *Educ:* Univ Wash, BS, 62; Cornell Univ, PhD(phys chem), 67. *Prof Exp:* NIH fel, Univ Chicago, 66-68. *Concurrent Pos:* Vis fel, Joint Inst Lab Astrophys, Colo, 75-76; Guggenheim fel, 82-83. *Mem:* Am Phys Soc. *Res:* Ultraviolet and vacuum ultraviolet spectroscopy; evolution of electronic energy in molecules; multiphoton ionization spectroscopy. *Mailing Add:* Dept Chem State Univ NY Stony Brook NY 11794

JOHNSON, PHILLIP EUGENE, MATHEMATICS. *Current Pos:* asst prof, 71-76, ASSOC PROF MATH, UNIV NC, CHARLOTTE, 76- *Personal Data:* b Bostic, NC, Feb 25, 37; m 59, Carolyn Long; c Marc. *Educ:* Appalachian State Teachers Col, BS, 59; George Peabody Col, MA, 63, PhD(math), 68; Am Univ, MA, 66. *Prof Exp:* High sch teacher, Va, 60-63; instr math, Univ Richmond, 63-65; from instr to asst prof, Vanderbilt Univ, 66-71. *Concurrent Pos:* Vis asst prof, NC State Univ, 71. *Mem:* Math Asn Am; Nat Coun Teachers Math; Am Math Soc. *Res:* Mathematics history and education. *Mailing Add:* Dept Math Univ NC Charlotte NC 28223

JOHNSON, PHYLLIS ELAINE, MASS SPECTROMETRY, TRACE METAL NUTRITION. *Current Pos:* res leader, Nutrit Biochem & Metab Unit, Human Nutrit Res Ctr, 87-91, assoc dir, Pac West Area, 91-96, CHEMIST, USDA AGR RES SERV, 79-, ASSOC DIR, BELTSVILLE AREA, 96- *Personal Data:* b Grafton, NDak, Feb 19, 49; m 69, Robert S T; c Erik & Sara. *Educ:* Univ NDak, BS, 71, PhD(phys chem), 76. *Honors & Awards:* Arthur S Flemming Award, 89; Wise Award, 93. *Prof Exp:* Lab instr chem & biochem, Mary Col, NDak, 71-72; fel, Univ NDak, 75-77, chemist, 77-79, clin instr, Sch Med, 81-91. *Mem:* Am Chem Soc; Am Inst Nutrit; Soc Exp Biol & Med; Sigma Xi; Am Soc Clin Nutrit; Int Soc Trace Element Res Humans (Secy, 92-98). *Res:* Trace metal absorption; biological metal-ligand complexes; lactation and infant nutrition; absorption, metabolism and bioavailability of trace metals, especially iron, zinc, copper and manganese, are investigated in humans using stable and radioactive metal isotopes as tracers. *Mailing Add:* USDA-ARS Beltsville Area Off Bldg 003 Rm 223 10300 Baltimore Ave Beltsville MD 20705. *Fax:* 301-504-5863; *E-Mail:* johnsonp@ars.usda.gov

JOHNSON, PHYLLIS TRUTH, INVERTEBRATE PATHOLOGY. *Current Pos:* RETIRED. *Personal Data:* b Salem, Ore, Aug 8, 26. *Educ:* Univ Calif, PhD(parasitol), 54. *Honors & Awards:* Bronze Medal, US Dept Com, 81. *Prof Exp:* Parasitologist med entom, Bur Vector Control, State Dept Health, Calif, 48-50; entomologist, Dept Entom, Walter Reed Army Inst Res, Washington, DC, 50-55; entomologist, Entom Res Br, USDA, 55-58; med entomologist, Gorgas Mem Lab, 59-63; from asst res pathobiologist to assoc res pathobiologist, Univ Calif, Irvine, 64-70; res fel, Calif Inst Technol, 70-71; consult, Off Environ Sci, Smithsonian Inst, 71-72; biologist, Nat Marine Fisheries Serv, 72-90. *Concurrent Pos:* Consult, US Naval Med Res Unit 3, Cairo, Egypt, 57-; res assoc, USDA, 58-63; mem comt animal models & genetic stocks, Nat Res Coun, 71-75. *Mem:* Sigma Xi; fel AAAS; Soc Invert Path (vpres, 78-80 & pres, 81-82); Am Soc Trop Med & Hyg; Am Soc Parasitol. *Res:* Leishmaniasis; taxonomy of Siphonaptera and Anoplura; pathological processes in invertebrates; viruses in crustaceans; histopathology of crustaceans. *Mailing Add:* 4721 E Harbor Dr Friday Harbor WA 98250-9349

JOHNSON, PORTER W, HIGH ENERGY PHYSICS, MATHEMATICAL PHYSICS. *Current Pos:* from asst prof to assoc prof, 69-83, chmn, Physics Dept, 84-95, PROF PHYSICS, ILL INST TECHNOL, 83- *Personal Data:* b Chattanooga, Tenn, Sept 4, 42; m 63, Frances Mabry; c Erik & Deborah. *Educ:* Case Inst Technol, BS, 63; Princeton Univ, MA, 65, PhD(physics), 67. *Prof Exp:* Fel, Case Western Reserve Univ, 67-69. *Mem:* Am Phys Soc; Am Asn Physics Teachers. *Res:* Study of structure of nonlinear equations involved in applications in elementary particle physics; dynamical symmetry breaking in quantum field theory. *Mailing Add:* Dept Physics Ill Inst Technol Chicago IL 60616-3573. *E-Mail:* physjohnson@iitvax

JOHNSON, PRESTON BENTON, electrical engineering, for more information see previous edition

JOHNSON, QUINTIN C, CRYSTALLOGRAPHY. *Current Pos:* PRES, MAT DATA, INC, 84- *Personal Data:* b Excelsior, Minn; c 2. *Educ:* St Olaf Col, BA, 57; Univ Calif, Berkeley, PhD(chem), 61. *Prof Exp:* Chemist, Lawrence Livermore Nat Lab, 60-75, actg dep dept head chem, 75-76, assoc dept head chem, 76-80, div leader, 80-84, sect leader, 84-86. *Mem:* AAAS; Am Crystallog Asn (vpres, 80, pres, 81); Am Phys Soc. *Res:* Automation of powder diffraction; PC software for materials characterization. *Mailing Add:* Mat Data Inc PO 791 Livermore CA 94550

JOHNSON, R(ICHARD) A(LLAN), ELECTRICAL ENGINEERING. *Current Pos:* RETIRED. *Personal Data:* b Winnipeg, Man, Mar 21, 32; m 57; c 3. *Educ:* Univ Man, BSc, 54, MSc, 56. *Prof Exp:* From asst prof to assoc prof, Univ Man, 55-66, actg dir planning, 69-70, head, Elec Eng Dept, 73-76, provost, 77-82, assoc vpres planning & anal, 82-87, assoc vpres, 87-92, prof elec eng, 66-97, vprovost progs, 92-97. *Concurrent Pos:* Pres, APEM, 79; chmn, Comt Accepting Eng Curric, Can Coun Prof Eng, 60-62, dir, 80-82; mem, Can Accreditation Bd, 64-67. *Mem:* Inst Elec & Electronics Engrs. *Res:* Circuits and systems theory; nonlinear oscillations; chaos and catastrophe theory and applications. *Mailing Add:* 208 Admin Bldg Univ Man Winnipeg MB R3T 2N2 Can

JOHNSON, R R, NUCLEAR PHYSICS. *Current Pos:* FAC MEM, DEPT PHYSICS, UNIV BC, 68- *Personal Data:* b Cloquet, Minn, Aug 7, 38. *Educ:* Univ Minn, BS, 60, MS, 62, PhD, 65. *Mem:* Am Phys Soc. *Mailing Add:* Dept Physics Univ BC Vancouver BC V6T 2A6 Can

JOHNSON, RALEIGH FRANCIS, JR, NUCLEAR MEDICINE, RADIOLOGICAL PHYSICS. *Current Pos:* asst prof radiol & nuclear med & physicist, 72-84, asst prof radiol & magnetic resonance imaging & tech dir, 84-91, ASSOC PROF RADIOL & MAGNETICS RESONANCE IMAGING PHYSICS DIR, UNIV TEX MED BR, GALVESTON, 91- *Personal Data:* b Hazard, Ky, Jan 24, 41; m 63; c 2. *Educ:* Berea Col, AB, 64; Univ Miami, MS, 65; Purdue Univ, PhD(radiol physics), 69. *Prof Exp:* Assoc radiol & nuclear med & physicist, Duke Univ & Vet Admin Hosp, 69-72. *Concurrent Pos:* Consult, Scientists & Engrs for Appalachia, 71- *Mem:* Health Physics Soc; Nuclear Med Soc; Sigma Xi; Creation Res Soc; Am Asn Physicists in Med; Soc Magnetic Resonance Med; Soc Magnetic Resonance Imaging. *Res:* Oblique imaging techniques in magnetic resonance imaging; quality control of magnetic resonance imaging systems; magnetic resonance imaging using contrast enhancement labeled agents; evaluation of high energy collimators for scintillation gamma cameras; evaluation of microprocession controlled automatic well-type scintillation counting system; evaluation of multipeak scintillation imaging; caordiac magnetic resonance imaging; 3D MRI imaging and 3D video display techniques. *Mailing Add:* Magnetic Resonance Imaging Div Med Br Univ Tex Rte D65 Galveston TX 77550

JOHNSON, RALPH ALTON, GENERAL ATMOSPHERIC SCIENCES. *Current Pos:* ENVIRON ODOR CONSULT, 83- *Personal Data:* b Alton, Ill, Sept 14, 19; m 54; c 1. *Educ:* Hastings Col, BA, 40; Univ Colo, MS, 42; Univ Minn, PhD(chem), 49. *Prof Exp:* Jr chemist, Manhattan Proj, Hanford Eng Works, E I du Pont de Nemours & Co, 44-45; from instr to asst prof anal chem, Univ Ill, 48-55; sr res chemist, Shell Develop Co, 55-83. *Mem:* Am Chem Soc; Air Pollution Control Asn; Am Soc Testing & Mat; Sigma Xi. *Res:* Psychophysics, odor measurement; wastewater processing and analysis; precipitation studies; spectrophotometric and electron microscopic investigations; neutron activation analysis. *Mailing Add:* 13135 Bohme Houston TX 77079

JOHNSON, RALPH M, JR, NUTRITION. *Current Pos:* RETIRED. *Personal Data:* b Ririe, Idaho, Apr 19, 18; m 40, Gwen Wilson; c Karen (Babcock), Christian & Wilford. *Educ:* Utah State Agr Col, BS, 40; Univ Wis, MS, 44, PhD(biochem), 48. *Prof Exp:* Asst prof biochem, Col Med, Wayne State Univ, 48-59; from assoc prof to prof physiol chem, Ohio State Univ, 59-68, dir & res prof, Inst Nutrit & Food Technol, 60-68, dir, 63-68, dean, Col Biol Sci, 66-68; dean, Col Sci & prof chem, Utah State Univ, 68-84. *Concurrent Pos:* Res assoc prof, Ohio State Univ, 59-60, dir labs, 59-63. *Mem:* Am Soc Biochem & Molecular Biol; Am Inst Nutrit. *Res:* Role of the essential unsaturated fatty acids; lipid metabolism; metabolism of phosphorous compounds; hormonal and hereditary factors in carcinogenesis; biochemical role of vitamin E. *Mailing Add:* 2044 N 13th E Logan UT 84321

JOHNSON, RALPH STERLING, JR, MATERIALS SCIENCE, METALLURGICAL ENGINEERING & CORROSION ENGINEERING. *Current Pos:* MANAGING PARTNER, R S J ASSOCS CONSULT ENGRS, 93- *Personal Data:* b Shickshinny, Pa, Apr 2, 26; m 51, Margaret Master; c Ralph III (deceased). *Educ:* Univ Akron, BS, 57, MS, 60; Univ Mich, Ann Arbor, PhD(mat sci & metall eng), 70. *Honors & Awards:* Apollo Achievement Award, NASA, 69. *Prof Exp:* Sr res engr mat & mfg res, Res & Develop Dept, Goodyear Aerospace Corp, 49-61; sr staff engr, Seismic Equip Dept, Bendix Aerospace Systems Div, Ann Arbor, 62-72; consult mat corrosion & mfg processes, Res & Eng Dept, Bechtel Nat, Inc, San Francisco, 73-79 & Aramco, Dhahran, Saudi Arabia, 79-81; consult mat corrosion & mfg processes & mem, Corrosion Task Force, Sohio Alaska Petrol Co, Anchorage, 81-84; sr consult, Brit Petrol, Dallas, Tex, 84-86; mgr, Mat Eng, Mead Paper Co, 86-92. *Concurrent Pos:* Mem water qual task force, Bechtel Power Corp, 75-79; mem, Sci Adv Comn, Alaska Found, Univ Alaska, 83-85; consult, Arctic Res Comn. *Mem:* Nat Asn Corrosion Engrs; Sigma Xi; Am Soc Metals; Tech Assoc Pulp & Paper Indust. *Res:* Materials performance and corrosion of materials in flue gas desulfurization systems; feedwater and steam generating systems in steam electric plants; oil field production facilities materials of construction and corrosion control; corrosion control pulp & paper. *Mailing Add:* 26 Timberlane Dr Chillicothe OH 45601-1941. *Fax:* 740-775-0475

JOHNSON, RALPH T, JR, SOLID STATE PHYSICS, RESEARCH SUPERVISION. *Current Pos:* RETIRED. *Personal Data:* b Salina, Kans, Apr 29, 35; m 58; c 4. *Educ:* Kans State Univ, BS, 57, MS, 59, PhD(physics), 64. *Prof Exp:* Physicist, Aircraft Nuclear Propulsion Dept, Gen Elec Co, 57-58; asst physics, Kans State Univ, 58-63; proj officer, Air Force Weapons Lab, 63-65; staff mem solid state physics, Sandia Nat Labs, 65-70, res supvr elec transport & electronic properties mat, 70-85, mgr measurement stand, 85-97. *Concurrent Pos:* Mem energy conversion panel, NMex Gov Energy Task Force, 74; mem nat res coun bd, Assessment Nat Bur Stand, Panel Basic Stand, 87-90. *Mem:* Am Phys Soc; Sigma Xi. *Res:* X-ray diffraction topography; dislocations and martensitic transformations; rocketborne magnetometers and optical spectrometers; semiconductor radiation defects, ionization effects and neutron detectors; electrical properties of amorphous semiconductors; thermoelectrics; solid electrolytes; electronic properties of dielectric materials. *Mailing Add:* 6601 Arroyo del Oso NE Albuquerque NM 87109

JOHNSON, RANDOLPH MELLUS, BIOCHEMICAL PHARMACOLOGY, NEUROPHARMACOLOGY. *Current Pos:* DEPT HEAD, NEUROBIOL, ROCHE BIOSCI, 95- *Personal Data:* b Los Angeles, Calif, Sept 6, 50; m 80, Charlyn L Hawelu; c Maile, Lani & Peter. *Educ:* Calif State Univ, Long Beach, BS, 74, MA, 78; Univ SC, PhD(pharmacol), 84. *Prof Exp:* Res assoc endocrine pharmacol, Sch Med, Univ Va, 84-87, res asst prof endocrine pharmacol, 87-88; scientist biomolecular pharmacol, Genentech, Inc, 88-91; staff researcher II, Syntex Discovery, 91-92, res sect & proj team leader, 92-95. *Concurrent Pos:* Nat Res Serv award, 86-88; consult, Quantex Corp, 89-91. *Mem:* Am Soc Pharmacol & Exp Therapeut; Am Soc Biochem & Molecular Biol; Endocrine Soc; AAAS; Soc Neurosci; Western Pharmacol Soc (secy, 96-). *Res:* Biomolecular mechanisms of growth factors, neurotransmitters and novel experimental therapeutics as it relates to second messenger formation and protein phosphorylation events in cell activation. *Mailing Add:* Dept Neurobiol Ctr Biol Res/Roche Biosci Neurobiol Unit 3401 Hillview Ave Palo Alto CA 94304. *Fax:* 650-852-3111; *E-Mail:* randy.johnson@roche.com

JOHNSON, RANDY ALLAN, HIGH ENERGY PHYSICS. *Current Pos:* ASSOC PHYSICIST, BROOKHAVEN NAT LAB, 76- *Personal Data:* b Minneapolis, Minn, Aug 9, 47; m 78. *Educ:* Princeton Univ, AB, 69; Univ Calif, Berkeley, PhD(physics), 75. *Prof Exp:* Fel physics, Lawrence Berkeley Lab, 75-76. *Mem:* Sigma Xi. *Res:* Particle scattering at high energies. *Mailing Add:* 745 Avon Fields Lane Cincinnati OH 45229-1538

JOHNSON, RAY EDWIN, SOIL FERTILITY. *Current Pos:* from asst prof to assoc prof agron, soil fertil & soil chem, 67-73, PROF AGRON, SOIL FERTIL & SOIL CHEM, WESTERN KY UNIV, 73- *Personal Data:* b East View, Ky, Aug 9, 36; m 85; c 1. *Educ:* Univ Ky, BS, 57, MS, 59; NC State Univ, PhD(mineral nutrit), 62. *Prof Exp:* Res assoc, Mineral Nutrit Pioneering Res Lab, USDA, 62-63, res plant physiologist, US Regional Soybean Lab, Crops Res Div, Agr Res Serv, Ill, 63-67. *Mem:* Am Soc Agron; Sigma Xi. *Res:* Mineral nutrition and interaction in plants; relationship of fertilizer response to soil test results. *Mailing Add:* Dept Agr Western Ky Univ 1 Big Red Way St Bowling Green KY 42101-3576

JOHNSON, RAY LELAND, PHYSICAL CHEMISTRY, ENVIRONMENTAL & ANALYTICAL CHEMISTRY. *Current Pos:* asst prof, 69-77, assoc prof & actg chmn, 77-79, PROF CHEM, DIV NATURAL SCI, HILLSDALE COL, 80-, CHAIR CHEM, 92- *Personal Data:* b LaGrange, Ohio, Nov 7, 39; m 62, Penelope Rees; c 3. *Educ:* Kent State Univ, BS, 61; Ohio Univ, PhD(phys chem), 66. *Prof Exp:* Sr res chemist, PPG Industs Inc, 66-69. *Concurrent Pos:* Consult, Hillsdale Waste Water Treatment Plant, 70-; W K Kellogg Found res grant water qual studies, 71-73. *Mem:* AAAS; Am Chem Soc. *Res:* Thermodynamics and kinetics; surface and colloid chemistry; solution chemistry; chemical investigations of water quality in lakes and streams; chemical methods of waste water treatment and analysis; development of multimedia and hypermedia materials for use in chemical education. *Mailing Add:* Dept Chem Hillsdale Col Hillsdale MI 49242. *Fax:* 517-437-3923; *E-Mail:* ray.johnson@ac.hillsdale.edu

JOHNSON, RAY O, electro-optics, optical signal processing, for more information see previous edition

JOHNSON, RAYMOND C, JR, ELECTRONICS. *Current Pos:* RETIRED. *Personal Data:* b Galveston, Tex, Sept 29, 22; c 9. *Educ:* Tex A&M Univ, BS, 45; Univ Fla, MS, 49. *Prof Exp:* From asst prof to prof elec eng, Univ Fla, 46-90, sect head, Electronic Res Sect, 59-90. *Concurrent Pos:* Dir, Electronic Commun Lab, 76- *Res:* Electronics systems. *Mailing Add:* 204 NW 32nd St Gainesville FL 32607

JOHNSON, RAYMOND EARL, ZOOLOGY. *Current Pos:* CONSULT, NAT WILDLIFE FEDN, 74- *Personal Data:* b Peru, Nebr, Oct 26, 14; m 41. *Educ:* Doane Col, BA, 36; Univ Nebr, MA, 38; Univ Mich, PhD(zool), 42. *Prof Exp:* Aquatic biologist, US Fish & Wildlife Serv, Univ Minn, 45-46, fisheries res supvr, 47-51, asst fed aid supvr, Bur Sport Fisheries & Wildlife, 51-56, chief fish div, 56-58, chief br fed aid, 58-59, asst dir, Bur Sport Fisheries & Wildlife, 59-71, chief off environ qual, 71-72; dep div dir, NSF, 72-74. *Mem:* Am Soc Ichtyologists & Herpetologists; Am Fisheries Soc; Am Soc Limnol & Oceanog; Wildlife Soc; Sigma Xi. *Res:* Taxonomy and distribution of freshwater fishes in North America; fisheries management; life history of freshwater fishes. *Mailing Add:* Jefferson No 1725 900 N Taylor St Arlington VA 22203

JOHNSON, RAYMOND LEWIS, MATHEMATICS. *Current Pos:* From asst prof to assoc prof, Univ Md, 68-78, assoc chmn grad studies, 87-90, chmn, 91-96, PROF MATH, UNIV MD, 80- *Personal Data:* b Alice, Tex, June 25, 43; m 65, Claudette Smith; c Malcolm. *Educ:* Univ Tex, Austin, BA, 63; Rice Univ, PhD(math), 69. *Concurrent Pos:* Gen Res Bd grant, 68 & 71; sabbatical leave, Inst Mittag-Leffler, DJursholm, 74-75, Howard Univ, 76-78 & McMaster Univ, Hamilton, Can, 83-84. *Mem:* Am Math Soc; Math Asn Am; Nat Asn Math. *Res:* Parabolic partial differential equations; representation theorems; spaces of functions defined by difference conditions; harmonic analysis. *Mailing Add:* Dept Math Univ Md College Park MD 20742. *Fax:* 301-314-0827; *E-Mail:* rlj@math.umd.edu

JOHNSON, RAYMOND NILS, ANALYTICAL CHEMISTRY. *Current Pos:* from res assoc anal chem to group leader, Wyeth-Ayerst Res, Inc, 69-75, sect head anal chem, 75-78, asst dir anal res & develop, 78-83, assoc dir, 83-84, dir anal res & serv, 85, asst vpres, 85-87, sr dir, 88-95, ASST VPRES ANALYTICAL RES & DEVELOP, WYETH-AYERST RES INC, 95- *Personal Data:* b New York, NY, July 26, 41; m 65, Lola McLuckey; c Jennifer & Sarah. *Educ:* Franklin & Marshall Col, AB, 63; Middlebury Col, MS, 65; Clarkson Univ, PhD(chem), 69. *Mem:* Am Chem Soc; Acad Pharmaceut Sci; Sigma Xi. *Res:* Pharmaceutical analysis using liquid chromatography and mass spectrometry; emphasis placed on analysis of novel chemical derivatives and development of analytical methods that are precise, accurate and specific; automation; raw material characterization; stability of raw materials and dosage forms. *Mailing Add:* Anal Res & Div Wyeth-Ayerst Res Inc 401 N Middletown Rd Pearl River NY 12979. *Fax:* 914-732-5189

JOHNSON, RAYMOND ROY, SYSTEMATIC BOTANY, VERTEBRATE ZOOLOGY. *Personal Data:* b Phoenix, Ariz, June 19, 32; m 76, Lois T Haight; c Elaine, Donna, Wayne, Korin & Catherine. *Educ:* Ariz State Univ, BS, 55; Univ Ariz, MS, 60; Univ Kans, PhD(bot), 64. *Prof Exp:* Asst prof biol, Western NMex Univ, 64-65; assoc prof biol, Univ Tex, El Paso, 65-68; from assoc prof to prof biol, Prescott Col, 68-74; res scientist, Grand Canyon, Nat Park Serv, Univ Ariz, 74-75, sr res scientist, 76-79, sr res scientist, Coop Nat Park Resources Study Unit, 80-92. *Concurrent Pos:* Prof, Renewable Nat Res, Univ Ariz, 80-95. *Mem:* Am Ornith Union; Am Soc Mammal. *Res:* Plant taxonomy, conservation biology; animal distribution; riparian ecology; desertification and arid land ecology; avian ecology; biogeography of North American Southwest. *Mailing Add:* 3755 S Hunters Run Tucson AZ 85730. *Fax:* 520-298-8418; *E-Mail:* rjohnson@worldnet.att.net

JOHNSON, REYNOLD B, COMPUTER PERIPHERALS. *Current Pos:* PRES, EDUC ASSOCS, 71- *Personal Data:* b Kingston, Minn, July 16, 06; c 3. *Educ:* Univ Minn, BS, 29. *Honors & Awards:* Nat Medal Technol, 86; Comput Pioneer Award, Inst Elec & Electronics Engrs, 87, Magnetic Soc Award, 88. *Prof Exp:* Res scientist, IBM, 34-71, res fel, 71. *Mem:* Nat Acad Eng. *Mailing Add:* Educ Eng Assocs 548 E Crescent Dr Palo Alto CA 94301

JOHNSON, RICHARD ALLEN, PHYSICAL CHEMISTRY. *Current Pos:* Scientist, Control Anal Res & Develop Unit, 71-73, res scientist, 73-74, sr res scientist, 74-76, MGR PROD CONTROL, UPJOHN CO, 76- *Personal Data:* b Panama City, Fla, Aug 13, 45; m 68; c 2. *Educ:* Ill Inst Technol, BS, 67; Mich State Univ, PhD(chem physics), 71. *Mem:* Am Chem Soc; Am Phys Soc. *Res:* Molecular spectroscopy of solids; solid state chemistry; physical characterization of pharmaceutical solids; application of computers to online data acquisition from analytical laboratory instrumentation. *Mailing Add:* 7689 Fieldwood Point Mattawan MI 49071

JOHNSON, RICHARD CLAYTON, APPLIED PHYSICS. *Current Pos:* CONSULT, MICRO J INC. *Personal Data:* b Eveleth, Minn, May 9, 30; div; c 2. *Educ:* Ga Inst Technol, BS, 53, MS, 58, PhD(physics), 61. *Prof Exp:* From asst res physicist to sr res physicist, Ga Inst Technol, 56-79, head, Radar Br, 63-68, prin res physicist, 67-79, chief, Electronics Div, 68-72, mgr, Systs & Tech Dept, 72-75, assoc dir, Eng Exp Sta, 75-79, prin res engr, 79-87. *Concurrent Pos:* Distinguished lectr, Inst Elec & Electronics Engrs, Antennas & Propagation Soc, 78-79, pres, 80. *Mem:* Am Phys Soc; fel Inst Elec & Electronics Engrs; Sigma Xi. *Res:* Radar and radiometry systems; antenna research and development; microwave theory and techniques; microwave spectroscopy; electromagnetic compatibility. *Mailing Add:* Micro J Inc 7069 Regalview Circle Dallas TX 75248

JOHNSON, RICHARD D, CHEMISTRY. *Personal Data:* b Zanesville, Ohio, Oct 28, 34; m 69, Catherina Collins; c 4. *Educ:* Oberlin Col, BA, 56; Carnegie Inst Technol, MS, 61, PhD(chem), 62; Mass Inst Tech, SM, 82. *Honors & Awards:* Except Serv Medal, NASA, 77. *Prof Exp:* Fel phys org chem, Univ Calif, Los Angeles, 61-62; sr scientist, Jet Propulsion Lab, Calif Inst Technol, 62-63; chief, Flight Exp Off, Life Sci, NASA, 75-76, chief, Biosystems Div, 76-85, res scientist, Ames Res Ctr, 63-85; sr technol consult, SRI Int, 85-90, prin, 90-93. *Concurrent Pos:* Lectr, Stanford Univ, 74-86; Sloan fel, 81-82. *Mem:* AAAS; Am Inst Aeronaut & Astronaut; Am Chem Soc; Inst Elec & Electronics Engrs. *Res:* Exobiology and the detection of extraterrestrial life; Apollo lunar sample analysis; 1976 Viking Mars life detection experiment; space colonies; 1976 Stanford-Ames study on space settlements; space shuttle experiments; space biomedical experiments; space commercialization; aerospace technology; human factors; technology management. *Mailing Add:* 11564 Arroyo Oaks Dr Los Altos CA 94024

JOHNSON, RICHARD DEAN, PHARMACEUTICAL LICENSING, TECHNOLOGY TRANSFER & BUSINESS DEVELOPMENT. *Current Pos:* ADJ GRAD PROF, SCH PHARM, UNIV MO, KANSAS CITY, 94-, PRES, PHARM FOUND, 96- *Personal Data:* b DeKalb, Ill, July 8, 36; m 69, Paula Jennings; c Janet, Julie, Richard Jr & Brodie. *Educ:* Univ Calif, Berkeley, BS, 60, PharmD, 61, MS, 62; Univ Calif, San Francisco, PhD(pharm chem), 65; Rockhurst Col, Kansas City, MBA, 84. *Honors & Awards:* Marion Labs President's Award, 80 & 81. *Prof Exp:* Pharmacist, Alta Vista Drug Co, 60-61; teaching asst, Univ Calif, San Francisco, 62-64; res chemist & sect head, Allergan Pharmaceut Co, 65-67; assoc med serv, Syntex Labs, Inc, 67-68, dir regulatory affairs, 68-73; dir corp licensing, Marion Labs, Inc, 73-79, vpres licensing, 80-83, corp pres, Marion Labs, Inc, 84-89, Marion Merrell Dow, Inc, 89-90; adj prof, Sch Pharm Univ Mo, Kansas City, 90-94. *Concurrent Pos:* Borden Co grad award, Univ Calif, San Francisco, 61-62; fels, Am Found Pharmaceut Educ & Henry S Wellcome Mem, 63-65; mem, Pres Comn Exec Interchange, White House, 70-71; lectr, Bus Sch, Univ SC, 75-77 & Bus Sch, Rockhurst Col, Kansas City, 83; mem bd dir, Tanabe-Marion Labs, 84-90, Dey Labs, 85-89, US Biosci Inc, 89-90, US Pharmaceut Rev Comt, 90-, Immuno Pharmaceut Inc, 91-94 & Microbiologix Biotech Inc, 95-; trustee, Univ MO, Kansas City Sch Pharm Found, 92-96 & Univ Kansas City, 96- *Mem:* AAAS; Am Pharmaceut Asn; Am Chem Soc; Acad Pharmaceut Sci; Licensing Exec Soc; Am Asn Pharmaceut Sci. *Res:* Thermal titration; thermal electric methods for studying physical and chemical properties of solutions of pharmaceutical interest. *Mailing Add:* 222 W Gregory Apt 235 Kansas City MO 64114-1127. *Fax:* 816-444-4894; *E-Mail:* yjohnson@cctr.umkc.edu

JOHNSON, RICHARD EVAN, ORNITHOLOGY, ZOOGEOGRAPHY. *Current Pos:* Asst prof, 72-78, dir, Charles R Conner Mus, 72-92, ASSOC PROF ZOOL, WASH STATE UNIV, 78-, RES DIR, CONNER MUS, 93- *Personal Data:* b Pomona, Calif, Nov 9, 36. *Educ:* Univ Calif, Berkeley, BS, 58; Univ Mont, MS, 68; Univ Calif, Berkeley, PhD(zool), 72. *Concurrent Pos:* Ed, The Murrelet, 76-80. *Mem:* Am Ornithologists Union; Cooper Ornith Soc; Wilson Ornith Soc; Soc Study Evolution; Soc Syst Zool; Am Soc Mammalogists. *Res:* Zoogeography, ecology and speciation of birds; evolution of arctic and alpine ecosystems; mammals of the Northwest; biogeography of alpine plants. *Mailing Add:* Dept Zool Wash State Univ Pullman WA 99164-0001

JOHNSON, RICHARD HARLAN, METEOROLOGY. *Current Pos:* from asst prof to assoc prof, 80-86, PROF ATMOSPHERIC SCI, COLO STATE UNIV, 86- *Personal Data:* b Portland, Ore, Nov 4, 45; m 65, LaVonne Bolstad; c Chris & Brian. *Educ:* Ore State Univ, BS, 67; Univ Chicago, MS, 69; Univ Wash, PhD(atmospheric sci), 75. *Prof Exp:* Res meteorologist, Nat Hurricane Res Lab, 76-77; asst prof atmospheric sci, Univ Wis-Milwaukee, 77-79. *Concurrent Pos:* Bd trustees, Univ Corp Atmospheric Res. *Mem:* Am Meteorol Soc; AAAS; Japan Meteorol Soc; Am Geophys Union. *Res:* Atmospheric convection and the planetary boundary layer; mesoscale meteorology; synoptic meteorology; study of precipitating clouds and their interaction with the atmospheric circulation on various scales. *Mailing Add:* 4216 Breakwater Ct Ft Collins CO 80525

JOHNSON, RICHARD JOSEPH, PROTEIN CHEMISTRY, COMPLEMENT ACTIVATION & INFLAMMATION. *Current Pos:* sr res assoc, Baxter Healthcare, 86-87, res scientist, 87-90, sr res scientist, 90-93, BAXTER RES SCIENTIST, BAXTER HEALTHCARE, 93- *Personal Data:* b Pittsburgh, Pa, 1954; m 82, Beverly A Banks; c Matthew, Timothy & Sara-Ann. *Educ:* Pa State Univ, BA, 76; Duquesne Univ, MS, 78, PhD(biochem), 82. *Prof Exp:* Fel, Univ Calif, San Diego/Vet Admin Med Ctr, 82-86. *Mem:* AAAS; Am Asn Immunologists. *Res:* Role of complement and particularly C5A in mediating an inflammatory response, particularly in a biomaterials setting such as during hemodialysis and C5A-receptor interaction; areas of cell capture technology in the transplantation area, flow cytometry analysis of PBL and molecular biology. *Mailing Add:* 442 W Quigley Mundelein IL 60060

JOHNSON, RICHARD LAWRENCE, organic chemistry, for more information see previous edition

JOHNSON, RICHARD LEON, SIGNAL PROCESSING, RADIO DIRECTION FINDING. *Current Pos:* INST SCIENTIST ELECTROMAGNETICS, SOUTHWEST RES INST, 70- *Personal Data:* b Enid, Okla, June 12, 38; m 62, Ethel Osborne; c Andrew & Blake. *Educ:* Univ Tex, Arlington, BSEE, 63; Southern Methodist Univ, MSEE, 66; Okla State Univ, PhD(elec eng), 70. *Prof Exp:* Aerosyst engr electronics, Gen Dynamics Corp, Ft Worth, Tex, 64-66; res asst, Okla State Univ, 66-70. *Concurrent Pos:* mem, Wave Propagation Stands Comt Antennas & Propagation Soc, Inst Elec & Electronics Engrs, 91- *Mem:* Int Union Radio Sci; fel Inst Elec & Electronics Engrs; Nat Soc Prof Engrs. *Res:* Superresolution spectrum estimation; digital signal processing; antennas and radio wave propagation analysis. *Mailing Add:* Inst Scientist Res Inst Electromagnetics Div 6220 Culebra DWR 28510 San Antonio TX 78228

JOHNSON, RICHARD NED, MANUFACTURING & PROCESSING, INFORMATION ANALYSIS. *Current Pos:* DIR MFG TECHNOL, ILL INST TECHNOL RES INST, 96- *Personal Data:* m 86; c 2. Karen L Friedman; c Jana, David & Rachel. *Educ:* Univ Wis-Madison, BS, 64, PhD(eng mech), 72; Case Inst Technol, MS, 68; Roosevelt Univ, MBA, 78. *Prof Exp:* Researcher, Lewis Res Ctr, NASA, 64-70; res assoc, Univ Wis-Madison, 70-71; mgr mat eng, GATX/GARD, 71-82; mgr mat & mfg res, Borg Warner Res, 82-88; mgr indust eng, Packer Eng, 89; assoc dir, Northwestern Univ, 90-96. *Concurrent Pos:* Consult, Psych Systs, 82-84; vpres, Axionixx, 89-92. *Mem:* Soc Mfg Engrs; Technol Transfer Soc. *Res:* Gear and bearing manufacturing; manufacturing technology information analysis; advanced aerospace alloys materials characterization and testing. *Mailing Add:* 15W755 Shepard Lane Burr Ridge IL 60521. *Fax:* 312-567-4329; *E-Mail:* rjohnson@iitri.com

JOHNSON, RICHARD NORING, BIOMEDICAL ENGINEERING. *Personal Data:* b Wethersfield, Conn, Apr 12, 34; m 60; c 2. *Educ:* Tri-State Col, BSc, 61; Worcester Polytech Inst, MSc, 65; Univ Va, DSc(biomed eng), 69. *Prof Exp:* Instr elec technol, Hartford State Tech Col, 61-65; res assoc neurol, Schs Eng & Med, Univ Va, 69-70, instr, 70-71, asst prof biomed eng & neurol, 72-77, assoc prof, 77-79; prof biomed eng & neurol, Sch Med, Univ NC, Chapel Hill, 79-81. *Concurrent Pos:* Fel biomed eng, Johns Hopkins Univ, 71-72. *Mem:* AAAS; Am Soc Eng Educ; Soc Neurosci; Biomed Eng Soc; Am Epilepsy Soc. *Res:* Neurophysiological control systems; neural models. *Mailing Add:* Adaptive Health Care Tech Inc PO Box 614 Marstons Mills MA 02648

JOHNSON, RICHARD RAY, AGRONOMY, SOIL SCIENCE. *Current Pos:* staff agronomist, 80-84, SR PRIN SCIENTIST, DEERE & CO, 84- *Personal Data:* b Carrol, Iowa, Nov 18, 47; m 68; c 2. *Educ:* Iowa State Univ, BS, 69, MS, 70; Univ Minn, PhD(plant physiol), 74. *Prof Exp:* Asst prof crop prod, Univ Ill, Urbana, 74-77, assoc prof, 77-80. *Mem:* Fel Crop Sci Soc Am; fel Am Soc Agron; Soil Sci Soc Am; Weed Sci Soc; Am Soc Agron Eng. *Res:* Applying new technology in crop production to the design and marketing of agricultural equipment. *Mailing Add:* 2030 E 45th St Davenport IA 52807

JOHNSON, RICHARD T, NEUROLOGY, VIROLOGY. *Current Pos:* assoc prof microbiol, 69-74, Dwight D Eisenhower-United Cerebal Palsy prof neurol, 69-89, PROF MICROBIOL, SCH MED, JOHNS HOPKINS UNIV, 74-, PROF & DIR NEUROL, 89-; NEUROLOGIST IN CHIEF, JOHNS HOPKINS HOSP, 89- *Personal Data:* b Grosse Pointe Farms, Mich, July 16, 31; m 54; c 4. *Educ:* Univ Colo, AB, 53, MD, 56. *Honors & Awards:* Weil Award, Am Asn Neuropath, 67; Sydney Farber Res Award, 74 & 76; Humboldt Prize, 75; Weinstein-Goldson Award, 79; Gordon Wilson Medal, 80; Charcot Award, Int Fed MS Soc, 85; Smadel Medal, 86; MS Medal, Asn British Neurol, 86; Outstanding Serv Award, Nat Mult Sclerosis Soc, 89; Soriano Award, World Fed Neurol, 93. *Prof Exp:* Teaching fel neurol & neuropath, Harvard Med Sch, 59-61; fel microbiol, John Curtin Sch Med, Canberra, Australia, 62-64; from asst prof to assoc prof neurol, Sch Med, Case Western Reserve Univ, 64-69. *Concurrent Pos:* First neurol asst, Univ Newcastle, Eng, 61-62; assoc neurologist, Cleveland Metrop Gen Hosp, Ohio, 64-69; asst neurologist, Highland View Hosp, Cleveland, 64-69; mem comn, Asn Res Nervous & Ment Dis, 64, 69-77; hon prof, Univ Peruana Cayetano Heredia, 80; jt appointment, Dept Molecular Microbiol &

Immunol, Johns Hopkins Sch Hyg & Pub Health, 84-; prof, neurosci, Johns Hopkins Hosp, 89. *Mem:* Inst Med-Nat Acad Sci; Am Soc Clin Invest; Am Asn Neuropath; Am Neurol Asn; Asn Am Physicians. *Res:* Clinical neurology; pathogenesis of viral infections of the nervous system; neurologic complications of HIV infection. *Mailing Add:* Dept Neurol Johns Hopkins Univ Med Sch Baltimore MD 21287

JOHNSON, RICHARD T(ERRELL), MECHANICAL ENGINEERING. *Current Pos:* PROF & CHMN MECH ENG, WICHITA STATE UNIV, 89- *Personal Data:* b Shreveport, La, July 28, 39; m 88, Mary Quermann; c Deborah, Patricia, Jenifer & Rebecca. *Educ:* Mo Sch Mines, BSME, 62, MS, 64; Univ Iowa, PhD(mech eng), 67. *Honors & Awards:* Delos Lab Develop Award, Am Soc Eng Educ. *Prof Exp:* Instr eng mech, Univ Mo-Rolla, 62-64; instr mech eng, Univ Iowa, 64-66; from asst prof to prof mech eng, Univ Mo-Rolla, 67-89, dir, Inst Flexible Mfg & Indust Automation, 84-88. *Mem:* Am Soc Mech Engrs; Soc Automotive Engrs; Sigma Xi; Soc Mfg Engrs; Am Soc Eng Educ; Combustion Inst. *Res:* Mechanical engineering design; control systems and instrumentation; alternate fuels for transportation engines; improved efficiency of combustion engines; manufacturing automation and systems integration; applications of artificial intelligence and expert systems to design and manufacturing. *Mailing Add:* Mech Eng Dept Wichita State Univ Box 133 Wichita KS 67260-0133. *Fax:* 316-978-3236; *E-Mail:* johnson@me.twsu.edu

JOHNSON, RICHARD WILLIAM, BIO-ORGANIC CHEMISTRY, ELECTRO-ORGANIC CHEMISTRY. *Current Pos:* SECT MGR, ROHM & HAAS CO, 83- *Personal Data:* b Denver, Colo, July 11, 50; m 75, Katharine Kappaut; c Matthew, Kevin, David & Donald. *Educ:* Northwestern Univ, BA & MS, 72; Columbia Univ, MPhil, 74, PhD(chem), 76. *Prof Exp:* Asst prof org chem, Harvard Univ, 77-83. *Mem:* Am Chem Soc. *Res:* New synthetic procedures based on organic electrochemical reactions; haptea-antibody interactions as model systems for enzymes; polymeric additives for PVC. *Mailing Add:* 119 Sandywood Dr Doylestown PA 18901-2951

JOHNSON, ROBERT A, CIRCUIT THEORY, ACOUSTICS. *Current Pos:* var positions, 57-84, prin engr & sales mgr, 84-96, CONSULT, ROCKWELL INT, 96- *Personal Data:* b Chicago, Ill, Sept 27, 32; US citizen; M, Lois O'Loughlin. *Educ:* Univ Calif, Los Angeles, BS, 55, MS, 63. *Mem:* Fel Inst Elec Electronics Engrs. *Res:* Electromechanical filters; awarded 14 US patents; author, co-author and series editor of numerous books. *Mailing Add:* Rockwell Int Filter Prod 2990 Airway Ave Costa Mesa CA 92626

JOHNSON, ROBERT ALAN, SOLID STATE PHYSICS, MATERIALS SCIENCE. *Current Pos:* PROF MAT SCI, UNIV VA, 69- *Personal Data:* b New York, NY, Jan 2, 33; m 54, Joyce W; c 3. *Educ:* Harvard Univ, AB, 54; Rensselaer Polytech Inst, PhD(physics), 62. *Prof Exp:* Scientist physics, Brookhaven Nat Lab, 62-69. *Mem:* Fel Am Phys Soc; AAAS; Am Inst Mining, Metall & Petrol Engrs; Mat Res Soc; Sigma Xi. *Res:* Theoretical study of interatomic forces, defects, surfaces and radiation damage in metals; use is made of computer simulation techniques and computer solutions of kinetic equations. *Mailing Add:* Dept Mat Sci Thornton Hall Univ Va Charlottesville VA 22903. *Fax:* 804-982-5660; *E-Mail:* raj@virginia.edu

JOHNSON, ROBERT ANDREW, ANT ECOLOGY & BEHAVIOR, ENVIRONMENTAL ASSESSMENTS & THREATENED & ENDANGERED SPECIES. *Current Pos:* ADJ FAC BOT, ARIZ STATE UNIV, 91- *Educ:* Univ Ill, Champaign-Urbana, BS, 78, MS, 80; Ariz State Univ, Tempe, PhD(zool), 89. *Prof Exp:* Contractecologists, Mus Northern Ariz, 80-83. *Concurrent Pos:* Prin investr, SW Parks & Monument Asn, 90-91, Nat Geog Soc, 93-94; contract ecologist, Johnson & Assocs, 87-; vol, US Fish & Wildlife Serv, 92- *Mem:* Ecol Soc Am; Am Soc Naturalists; Soc Study Evolution; Asn Study Animal Behav. *Res:* Community structure and distribution patterns of ants, especially as they relate to soil texture and interactions with other ants; ecology of rare cactus species. *Mailing Add:* Dept Plant Biol Az State Univ Box 871601 Tempe AZ 85287-1601. *Fax:* 602-965-6899; *E-Mail:* Bitnet: atm2d@asuacad

JOHNSON, ROBERT BRITTEN, GEOLOGY. *Current Pos:* chmn dept geol, Colo State Univ, 69-73, prof geol prog, 73-77, head earth resources actg dept, 79-80, prof geol, 67-88, EMER PROF GEOL, COLO STATE UNIV, 88- *Personal Data:* b Cortland, NY, Sept 24, 24; m 47, Garnet Brown; c Robert Jr, Richard & Elizabeth. *Educ:* Syracuse Univ, AB, 49, MS, 50; Univ Ill, PhD(geol), 54. *Honors & Awards:* E B Burwell Jr Mem Award, Geol Soc Am, 89; C B Holdredge Award, Asn Eng Geologists, 90. *Prof Exp:* Asst, Syracuse Univ, 47-50; asst, State Geol Surv, Ill, 51-53, asst geologist, 53-54; asst prof geol & staff geologist, Syracuse Univ, 54-55; sr geologist & geophysicist, C A Bays & Assocs, 55-56; from asst prof to prof geol, Purdue Univ, 56-66; prof geol & head dept geol & geog, DePauw Univ, 66-67. *Concurrent Pos:* Lectr, Univ Ill, 55-56; indust consult, 62-; mem comt A2L01, Transp Res Bd; mem comt A2L05, Transp Res Bd, 75-86, chmn comt A2L01, 76-82; geologist, US Geol Surv, 76-88, Elderhostel fac, 91- *Mem:* Sr fel Geol Soc Am; Asn Eng Geologists; Int Asn Eng Geol. *Res:* Engineering geology, especially landslides and geophysical and remote sensing applications. *Mailing Add:* Dept Earth Resources Colo State Univ Ft Collins CO 80523. *Fax:* 970-491-6307; *E-Mail:* arby@picea.cnr.colostate.edu

JOHNSON, ROBERT CHANDLER, ANALYTICAL SCIENCE, GENERAL PHYSICS. *Current Pos:* Res physicist, E I du Pont de Nemours & Co, Inc, 62-73, res physicist, res & develop planning, 73-75, res physicist, thermal analysis, 75-78, res supvr analytical sci, 78-93, RES & DEVELOP MGR, CENT RES & DEVELOP DEPT, E I DU PONT DE NEMOURS & CO INC, 93- *Personal Data:* b Detroit, Mich, Oct 19, 30; m 55, Mary J Wood; c Andrew, Douglas, Sarah & Michael. *Educ:* Univ Mich, BS, 52; State Univ Iowa, MA, 57; Stanford Univ, PhD(physics), 62. *Concurrent Pos:* Vis scientist, Am Inst Physics, 72-75. *Mem:* Fel NAm Thermal Anal Soc (secy, 79-81 & pres, 85-86); Am Phys Soc; Am Chem Soc; Mat Res Soc. *Res:* Magnetic field effects on triplet excitons; exciton physics of organic crystals; Kapitza resistance in liquid helium; low temperature physics; thermal analysis; x-ray synchrotron applications at Advanced Photon Source. *Mailing Add:* 2526 Blackwood Rd Wilmington DE 19810-3638

JOHNSON, ROBERT E, PHYSICAL CHEMISTRY. *Current Pos:* RES SCIENTIST, G D SEARLE, 88- *Personal Data:* b Los Angeles, Calif, Mar 23, 45. *Educ:* Johns Hopkins Univ, BS, 67, MS, 69, PhD(biochem), 75. *Prof Exp:* Fel, Chem Dept, Univ Ariz, 75-77, asst prof biochem, 80-88; res chemist, Vet Hosp Kans City, 77-80. *Mem:* Am Chem Soc. *Mailing Add:* G D Searle & Co Rm P-320 4901 Searle Pkwy Skokie IL 60077-1099

JOHNSON, ROBERT ED, MEDICINAL CHEMISTRY. *Current Pos:* RES CHEMIST, GROUP LEADER, SECT HEAD & ASSOC RES DIR MED CHEM, STERLING RES GROUP, 68- *Personal Data:* b Highland Park, Ill, Nov 14, 42; m 64; c 2. *Educ:* Univ Wis, BS, 64; Univ Minn, PhD(org chem), 68. *Mem:* Am Chem Soc; NY Acad Sci; AAAS. *Res:* Synthesis of novel heterocyclic and aromatic compounds that may have useful medicinal properties. *Mailing Add:* Sterling Res Group 270 Richard Way Collegeville PA 19426-0900

JOHNSON, ROBERT EDWARD, PLANETARY SCIENCE. *Current Pos:* PROF ENG PHYSICS, UNIV VA, 71-, JOHN LLOYD NEWCOMB PROF. *Personal Data:* b Chicago, Ill, July 3, 39; m 70; c 2. *Educ:* Colo Col, BA, 61; Wesleyan Univ, MA, 63; Univ Wis, Madison, PhD(physics), 68. *Prof Exp:* Res fel, Queen's Univ, Belfast, Ireland, 68-69; asst prof physics, Southern Ill Univ, 69-71. *Concurrent Pos:* Consult, Dept Physics, Denver Univ, 70, Bell Tel Lab, 79-89 & Uppsala Univ, 85-95; NATO fel, Univ Copenhagen, 76; vis scientist, Ctr Earth & Planetary Physics, Harvard Univ, 77-78; NSF & NASA grants prin investr, 78-; fac fel, Argonne Nat Lab, 82. *Mem:* Am Phys Soc; Am Geol Phys Union; Am Astron Soc. *Res:* Atomic and molecular physics; problems of interest in the Jovian magnetosphere, and interaction of ionizing radiations with solids and surfaces. *Mailing Add:* Thornton Hall B103 Eng Physics Univ Va Charlottesville VA 22901. *Fax:* 804-924-1353; *E-Mail:* rej@rinqlala.ede

JOHNSON, ROBERT EUGENE, PHYSIOLOGY, NUTRITION. *Current Pos:* VIS PROF PHYSIOL, UNIV VT, 84- *Personal Data:* b Conrad, Mont, Apr 8, 11; m 35, Margaret; c Thomas & Charles. *Educ:* Univ Wash, BS, 31; Oxford Univ, BA, 34, DPhil(biochem), 35; Harvard Univ, MD, 41. *Prof Exp:* Asst & assoc, Fatigue Lab, Harvard Univ, 35-42, asst prof indust physiol, 42-46; dir, Med Nutrit Lab, US Army, 46-49; prof physiol, Univ Ill, Urbana, 49-73; prof biol, Knox Col, 73-79, coordr, Knox-Rush Med Prog, 73-79; pres, Horn of the Moon Enterprises, Montpelier, VT, 79- *Concurrent Pos:* Head, dept physiol, Univ Ill, 49-60, dir hons prog, 58-67; NSF sr res fel, 57-58; Guggenheim fel, 64-65; consult physician, Presby-St Lukes Hosp, Chicago, 73-84. *Mem:* Am Physiol Soc; Am Soc Clin Invest; Hist Sci Soc; Sigma Xi. *Res:* Physiological responses in man to stresses of work, environment and diet; metabolism of poikilotherms; history of environmental physiology. *Mailing Add:* Five E Terrace South Burlington VT 05403

JOHNSON, ROBERT F, TEXTILE ENGINEERING. *Current Pos:* RETIRED. *Personal Data:* b Crestwood, Ky, Mar 20, 29; div; c 4. *Educ:* Univ Ky, BS, 51; Ga Inst Technol, MS, 58; Swiss Fed Inst Technol, DSc(indust & eng chem), 63. *Prof Exp:* Res chemist, Dow Chem Co, 58-65; assoc prof textile eng, Ga Inst Technol, 65-66; res sect mgr, Phillips Petrol Co, 66-68, consult, 69-70; prof textile eng & dir, Chem Processes Lab, Textile Res Ctr, Tex Tech Univ, 68-72; prof textiles & clothing, Univ Minn, 72-92, dir Grad Studies, 81-85. *Mem:* Am Asn Textile Chem & Colorists; Am Chem Soc; Brit Soc Dyers & Colourists; Am Coun Consumer Interests. *Res:* Physical and chemical properties of textile materials; chemistry of dyes; characterization of fire hazards of clothing. *Mailing Add:* 1500 Sixth St S Minneapolis MN 55454

JOHNSON, ROBERT GLENN, ELECTROPHYSICS. *Current Pos:* RETIRED. *Personal Data:* b Green Mountain, Iowa, Dec 12, 22; m 49, Elizabeth G; c 5. *Educ:* Case Inst Technol, BS, 47; Iowa State Col, PhD(physics), 52. *Honors & Awards:* H W Sweatt Award, Honeywell Inc, 68 & 85. *Prof Exp:* Asst physics, Iowa State Col, 49-52; proj engr, Bendix Aviation Corp, 52-55; sr res physicist, Honeywell Sensors & Systs Develop Ctr, Bloomington, Minn, 55-67, staff scientist, 67-90. *Concurrent Pos:* Adj prof, Dept Geol & Geophys, Univ Minn. *Mem:* Inst Elec & Electronics Engrs; AAAS; Sigma Xi; Geol Soc Am. *Res:* Corona degradation of materials; paleoclimatology; gas discharge phenomena; ultraviolet light sensor technology; silicon microstructures. *Mailing Add:* 12814 March Circle Minnetonka MN 55305-2742

JOHNSON, ROBERT GUDWIN, ORGANIC CHEMISTRY. *Current Pos:* from inst to assoc prof 54-65, chmn dept chem, 66-75 & 84-86, PROF CHEM, XAVIER UNIV, OHIO, 65- *Personal Data:* b Milwaukee, Wis, Nov 23, 27; m 58; c 4. *Educ:* Marquette Univ, BS, 49; Iowa State Col, PhD(chem), 54. *Prof Exp:* Asst chem, Iowa State Col, 49-53. *Concurrent Pos:* Vis prof, Purdue Univ, 60 & 63. *Mem:* Am Chem Soc. *Res:* Hunsdiecker-Borodine reaction; oxygen-containing heterocycles; hypolipidemic agents; anti-cancer compounds; aromatic substitution. *Mailing Add:* 2106 Townhill Dr Cincinnati OH 45238-3219

JOHNSON, ROBERT H, DENTISTRY. *Current Pos:* PROF PERIODONT, UNIV WASH SCH DENT, SEATTLE, 81- *Personal Data:* b Montreal, Que, June 23, 36; m 70, Barbara J Young. *Educ:* McGill Univ, BSc, 58, DDS, 62; Ind Univ, MSD, 64; Univ Wash, cert periodontics, 71; Am Bd Oral Med, dipl; FRCD(C). *Prof Exp:* Asst prof dent, McGill Univ, 64-66; asst prof dent & dir hosp dent serv, Med Ctr, Univ Ky, 66-69; from assoc prof to prof dent, Univ Western Ont, 71-80, chmn div periodont, 78-881. *Concurrent Pos:* Chief oral diag clin, Montreal Gen Hosp, 64-66; vis prof, Oral Med, Univ Glasgow, 91-92. *Mem:* Am Acad Periodont; fel Am Acad Oral Path. *Res:* Chemotherapeutic plaque and inflammation control; maintenance dental implants; mechanical toothbrushes. *Mailing Add:* Dept Periodont Box 35744 Univ Wash Sch Dent Seattle WA 98195-7444

JOHNSON, ROBERT JOSEPH, anatomy, for more information see previous edition

JOHNSON, ROBERT KARL, ICHTHYOLOGY. *Current Pos:* PROF, DEPT BIOL, UNIV CHARLESTON, 93- *Personal Data:* b Worthington, Minn, May 7, 44; m 75, Patricia H Peyton. *Educ:* Occidental Col, AB, 66; Univ Calif, San Diego, PhD(marine biol), 72. *Prof Exp:* Res assoc ecol, Chesapeake Biol Lab, Univ Md, 71-72; asst cur fishes, Field Mus Natural Hist, 72-75, assoc cur, 75-81, chmn dept zool, 81-84, cur fishes, 81-86; dir, Grad Prog Marine Biol, Grice Marine Biol Lab, 86-93. *Concurrent Pos:* Asst prof earth sci, Univ Notre Dame, 74; adj asst prof biol sci, Northern Ill Univ, 74-79, adj assoc prof, 79-; mem Comt Evolutionary Biol, Univ Chicago, 76-86. *Mem:* Am Soc Ichthyologists & Herpetologists; Soc Syst Zool; AAAS. *Res:* Systematics, ecology and zoogeography of marine fishes. *Mailing Add:* Grice Marine Biol Lab 205 Fort Johnson Charleston SC 29412

JOHNSON, ROBERT L(AWRENCE), MECHANICAL ENGINEERING, TRIBOLOGY. *Current Pos:* RETIRED. *Personal Data:* b Glasgow, Mont, June 18, 19; m 45, Josephine M Saetre; c Robert L Jr, Elizabeth M (Kaluza) & Richard P. *Educ:* Mont State Univ, BS, 42. *Honors & Awards:* IR 100 Award, 66 & 73; Alfred E Hunt Award, Am Soc Lubrication Engrs, 61 & 65, Nat Award, 71; Medal for Except Sci Achievement, NASA, 73; Tribology Gold Medal, Brit Inst Mech Engrs, 76; Mayo D Hersey Award, Am Soc Mech Engrs, 77. *Prof Exp:* Mech engr, Langley Mem Aeronaut Lab, Nat Adv Comt Aeronaut, NASA, 42-43, from mech engr to supvr mat res eng, 43-71, chief lubrication br, Lewis Res Ctr, 63-75. *Concurrent Pos:* Lubrication consult, 62-; chmn, Gordon Res Conf Friction, Lubrication & Wear, 74; US deleg & chmn group experts wear eng mat, Orgn Econ Coop & Develop, 64-73; adj prof mech eng, Rensselaer Polytech Inst, 75-87. *Mem:* Am Soc Testing & Mat; Soc Automotive Engrs; fel & hon mem Soc Tribologists & Lubrication Engrs (pres, 68-69); fel Brit Inst Mech Engrs. *Res:* Lubrication, friction and wear tribology in seals, bearings and other mechanical components and lubricants for extreme environments. *Mailing Add:* 5304 W 62nd St Edina MN 55436

JOHNSON, ROBERT L, ENGINEERING. *Current Pos:* RETIRED. *Personal Data:* b Winslow, Ariz, May 16, 20. *Educ:* Univ Calif, Berkeley, BS, 41, MS, 42. *Honors & Awards:* James H Wyld Mem Award, Am Rocket Soc. *Prof Exp:* From mem staff to vpres, Manned Orbiting Lab, Douglas Aircraft Co, 46-69; asst secy army for res & develop, Dept Army, 69-73; corp vpres eng & res, McDonnell Douglas Corp, 73-75, pres, McDonnell Douglas Astronaut Co, 75-80, corp vpres aerospace group exec, 80-87. *Concurrent Pos:* Mem, Eng Adv Coun, Univ Calif. *Mem:* Nat Acad Eng; fel Am Inst Aeronaut & Astronaut. *Mailing Add:* 30881 Greens East Dr Laguna Niguel CA 92677

JOHNSON, ROBERT LEE, PHYSIOLOGY. *Current Pos:* from instr to assoc prof, 57-69, PROF INTERNAL MED, SOUTHWESTERN MED CTR, UNIV TEX, DALLAS, 69- *Personal Data:* b Dallas, Tex, Apr 28, 26; m 52; c 2. *Educ:* Southern Methodist Univ, BS, 47; Northwestern Univ, MD, 51. *Honors & Awards:* Sci Accomplishment Award, Thoracic Soc, 96. *Prof Exp:* Intern, Cook Co Hosp, Chicago, 51-55; res fel internal med, Southwestern Med Sch, Univ Tex, 55-56; res fel physiol, Grad Sch Med, Univ Pa, 56-57. *Concurrent Pos:* Assoc ed, J Clin Invest, 72-77; prog chmn, Cardiopulmonary Coun, Am Heart Asn, 79-81 & chmn, 85-87, mem, Cardiovasc Develop Res Study Comt, 81-83; mem Heart Lung & Blood Inst Rev Comt, 85- *Mem:* Am Asn Physicians; Am Fedn Clin Res; Am Thoracic Soc; Am Physiol Soc; Am Soc Clin Invest; Am Heart Asn. *Res:* Exercise physiology; adaptation to high altitude; control of capillary circulation and diffusing surface in the lung. *Mailing Add:* Univ Tex Southwestern Med Ctr 5323 Harry Hines Blvd Dallas TX 75235-9034. *Fax:* 214-648-8027; *E-Mail:* rjohn2@mednet.swmed.edu

JOHNSON, ROBERT LEROY, MATHEMATICS. *Current Pos:* asst prof, 68-72, assoc prof, 72-80, PROF MATH, AUGUSTANA COL, ILL, 80- *Personal Data:* b Chicago, Ill, Sept 22, 40; m 63; c 2. *Educ:* Augustana Col, Ill, AB, 62; Univ Kans, MA, 65, PhD(math), 67. *Prof Exp:* Asst prof math, Iowa State Univ, 67-68. *Mem:* Math Asn Am; Am Math Soc; Sigma Xi. *Res:* Topological rings. *Mailing Add:* Dept Math Augustana Col Rock Island IL 61201

JOHNSON, ROBERT M, METALLURGICAL ENGINEERING. *Current Pos:* Asst prof eng mech & mat sci, Univ Tex, Arlington, 67-71, assoc prof mat sci, 71-79, assoc dean, Grad Sch, 80-93, actg provost res & dean grad sch, 93-94, assoc dean eng res, 95-96, PROF MECH ENG & MAT SCI, UNIV TEX, ARLINGTON, 79- *Personal Data:* b Oklahoma City, Okla, Mar 28, 39; m 63; c Dana L. *Educ:* Univ Okla, BS, 62, MMetEng, 65, PhD(eng sci), 67. *Concurrent Pos:* Sr scientist, Vought Corp Advanced Technol Ctr, 77-78. *Mem:* Am Soc Metals; Am Soc Eng Educ; Sigma Xi. *Res:* Basic deformation processes in mechanical metallurgy; dislocation mechanisms; fracture mechanics; corrosion; superplasticity; granted one patent. *Mailing Add:* Mech Eng Dept Univ Tex Arlington TX 76019

JOHNSON, ROBERT MICHAEL, BIOCHEMISTRY. *Current Pos:* instr, Med Sch, Wayne State Univ, 72-73, asst prof, 73-79, assoc prof, 79-92, PROF BIOCHEM, MED SCH, WAYNE STATE UNIV, 92- *Personal Data:* b Brooklyn, NY; c 1. *Educ:* Fordham Col, AB, 61; Columbia Univ, PhD(biochem), 70. *Prof Exp:* NIH fel, Cornell Univ, 71-72. *Concurrent Pos:* Vis prof, Int Cell Path, Bicetre, France, 82. *Mem:* Sigma Xi; Am Heart Assoc; Am Soc Biol Chemists; Soc Rheology; AAAS; Am Soc Hemat. *Res:* Biochemistry of biological membranes; protein structure, erythrocyte function. *Mailing Add:* Dept Biochem Wayne State Univ Med Sch 540 E Canfield Rd Detroit MI 48201-1908

JOHNSON, ROBERT OSCAR, APPLIED MATHEMATICS. *Current Pos:* PROF COMPUT SCI, FROSTBURG STATE UNIV, 90- *Personal Data:* b Detroit, Mich, May 7, 26; m 61; c 3. *Educ:* Univ Mich, Ann Arbor, BS(eng) & BS(math), 46, MS, 49; Univ Ill, Urbana, MS, 52; Ohio State Univ, PhD(math), 75. *Prof Exp:* Sr engr, ITT Labs, 50-52; procurement rep aircraft systs, Repub Aviation, Inc, 52-53; admin engr, Teterboro Div, Bendix Corp, 54-58; proposal mgr altitude control systs, Aerospace Div, Walter Kidde & Co, Inc, 58-62; mgr advan design, Arde, Inc, 62-63; res specialist, Columbus Div, NAm Rockwell, Inc, 64-68; prof math, Franklin Univ, 68-86, div chmn, Eng Technol, 81-85; prof comput sci, Marshall Univ, 86-90. *Concurrent Pos:* Teaching assoc, dept math, Ohio State Univ, 64-69; prof engr, Data Control Ctr, Ohio State Hwy Dept, 69-75. *Mem:* Asn Comput Mach; Inst Elec & Electronics Engrs; Math Asn Am. *Res:* Mathematical modeling. *Mailing Add:* PO Box 30011 Gahanna OH 43230-0011. *E-Mail:* rjohnson@freenet.columbus.oh.us

JOHNSON, ROBERT REINER, ORGANIC CHEMISTRY. *Current Pos:* RETIRED. *Personal Data:* b Chicago, Ill, June 8, 32; m 67; c 1. *Educ:* Brown Univ, ScB, 54; Rice Univ, PhD(chem), 58. *Prof Exp:* Res assoc chem, Johns Hopkins Univ, 58-59; group leader, Brown & Williamson Tobacco Corp, 59-67, scientist, 67-91. *Mem:* Am Chem Soc. *Res:* Physical organic chemistry and chemistry of natural products. *Mailing Add:* 503 Penwood Dr Louisville KY 40206-3031

JOHNSON, ROBERT S, MATHEMATICS. *Current Pos:* From instr to assoc prof, 65-75, PROF MATH & HEAD DEPT, WASHINGTON & LEE UNIV, 75- *Personal Data:* b Pikeville, Ky, Nov 23, 37. *Educ:* Georgetown Col, BS, 59; Univ NC, MA, 62, PhD(ring theory), 66. *Mem:* Am Math Soc; Sigma Xi. *Res:* Group theory and ring theory; conditions implying commutativity. *Mailing Add:* Dept Math Washington & Lee Univ Lexington VA 24450

JOHNSON, ROBERT SHEPARD, NUMERICAL ANALYSIS. *Current Pos:* ENGR, RCA CORP, 59- *Personal Data:* b Wilkinsburg, Pa, Nov 24, 28; m 59; c 3. *Educ:* Northwestern Univ, BS, 50, MS, 51; Univ Pa, PhD(math), 59. *Prof Exp:* Res assoc, Inst Coop Res, Univ Pa, 53-59. *Mem:* Am Math Soc; Soc Indust & Appl Math. *Res:* Approximation theory; moments. *Mailing Add:* 2102 Brandeis Ave Riverton NJ 08077-3513

JOHNSON, ROBERT WALTER, ECOLOGY. *Current Pos:* ASSOC PROF BIOL, HOFSTRA UNIV, 59-61 & 65- *Personal Data:* b New York, NY, Mar 11, 30; m 61; c 2. *Educ:* Hofstra Univ, BA, 58, MA, 59; Cornell Univ, PhD(wildlife mgt), 73. *Prof Exp:* Res asst nematol, USDA, 56-57. *Concurrent Pos:* Marine conserv biologist, Town Oyster Bay, NY, 67-; terrestrial ecologist, Grumman Ecosyst Corp, 74-; pres, R W Johnson & Assoc, Environ Anal Inc, 74- *Mem:* Wildlife Soc; Ecol Soc Am. *Res:* Estuarine ecology; ecology of marsh birds; environmental impact analysis. *Mailing Add:* Dept Biol Hofstra Univ 1000 Fulton Ave Hempstead NY 11550-1091

JOHNSON, ROBERT WARD, marine sciences, operations research, for more information see previous edition

JOHNSON, ROBERT WELLS, ALGEBRAIC NUMBER THEORY, DIOPHANTINE EQUATIONS. *Current Pos:* From instr to assoc prof, 64-75, prof, 75-90, ISAAC HENRY WING PROF MATH, BOWDOIN COL, 90- *Personal Data:* b Hartford, Conn, Apr 21, 38; m 64, Alison Krotter; c Clare, Gail & Lynn. *Educ:* Amherst Col, AB, 59; Mass Inst Technol, MS, 61, PhD(math), 64. *Mem:* Math Asn Am; Am Math Soc. *Res:* Algebra and number theory; diophantine equations of exponential type; binary linear recurrences. *Mailing Add:* Bowdoin Col Math 8600 College Sta Brunswick ME 04011-8486. *Fax:* 207-725-3750; *E-Mail:* johnson@polar.bowdoin.edu

JOHNSON, ROBERT WILLIAM, JR, ORGANIC CHEMISTRY. *Current Pos:* CONSULT, 93- *Personal Data:* b Jacksonville, Fla, Oct 9, 27; m 57; c 4. *Educ:* Univ Fla, BS, 53, PhD(org chem), 59; Purdue Univ, MS, 56. *Prof Exp:* Res chemist, Ethyl Corp, 59-62; supt, Compound Develop Dept, Chem Div, Union Bag-Camp Paper Corp, 62-65, supt, Prod Develop Dept, 65-67; mgr, Chem Div, Prod Develop Dept, Union Camp Corp, 67-73, sr chemist, Process Chem Dept, 73-86, tech assoc, 86-92. *Mem:* Am Chem Soc; Am Oil Chemists Soc; NY Acad Sci; fel Am Inst Chemists; Am Inst Chem Engrs. *Res:* Tall oil; fatty acids; organic synthesis; organometallics; separation technology; instrumental methods of analysis; rosin and derivatives; hydrogenation. *Mailing Add:* 227 Groveland Circle Savannah GA 31405

JOHNSON, RODNEY L, PEPTIDES, AMINO ACIDS. *Current Pos:* ASSOC PROF MED CHEM, UNIV MINN, 82- *Educ:* Univ Kans, PhD(med chem), 75. *Mailing Add:* HSUF 8-172 Univ Minn 308 Harvard St SE Minneapolis MN 55455-0343. *Fax:* 612-624-2974

JOHNSON, ROGER A, MECHANISMS OF HORMONE ACTION. *Current Pos:* PROF PHYSIOL & BIOPHYS & VCHMN DEPT PHYSIOL & BIOCHEM, STATE UNIV NY, STONY BROOK, 86- *Personal Data:* b Geneva, Ill, Feb 4, 43. *Educ:* Iowa State Univ, BS, 64; Univ Southern Calif, PhD(pharmacol), 68. *Prof Exp:* Fel, Vanderbilt Univ Med Sch, 68-70, from instr to assoc prof physiol, 70-86. *Mem:* Am Soc Biochem & Molecular Biol. *Mailing Add:* Dept Physiol & Biophys State Univ NY Health Sci Ctr Stony Brook NY 11794-8661. *Fax:* 516-444-3432

JOHNSON, ROGER D, JR, MATHEMATICS. *Current Pos:* asst prof, 56-61, ASSOC PROF MATH, GA INST TECHNOL, 61- *Personal Data:* b Richmond, Va, May 27, 30; m 55; c 3. *Educ:* Dartmouth Col, AB, 51; Univ Va, MA, 53, PhD(math), 56. *Prof Exp:* Instr math, Univ Va, 55-56. *Mem:* Am Math Soc; Math Asn Am. *Res:* Homology theory and its relationship to certain topics of general topology such as connectedness and dimension. *Mailing Add:* Ga Inst Technol Atlanta GA 30332-0001

JOHNSON, ROGER W, VIROLOGY, CELL CULTURE. *Current Pos:* DIR OPERS, WHITTAKER BIOPROD, 81- *Personal Data:* b Kalamazoo, Mich, May 4, 29; m 58; c Andrew & Paul. *Educ:* Valparaiso Univ, BS, 52; Univ Ky, MS, 58, PhD(microbiol), 63. *Prof Exp:* Microbiologist, Biol Labs, US Army, 63-69, prin investr, Biol Defense Res Ctr, 69-72; head dept virus prod, Frederick Cancer Res Ctr, Nat Cancer Inst, 72-81. *Mem:* AAAS; Am Soc Microbiol; Sigma Xi. *Res:* Parameters of seed stock development; scale up and production of oncogenic or suspected oncogenic viruses from tissue culture; large scale culture of mammalian cells. *Mailing Add:* 7003 Summerfield Dr Rte 7 Frederick MD 21701

JOHNSON, ROLLAND PAUL, ACCELERATORS. *Current Pos:* PRIVATE CONSULT, 97- *Personal Data:* b Stewartville, Minn, Jan 1, 41; m 90, Linda Even; c Jenifer & Russell. *Educ:* Univ Calif, Berkeley, AB, 64, PhD(physics), 70. *Prof Exp:* Res asst physics, Lawrence Berkeley Lab, Univ Calif, Berkeley, 67-70, res assoc, 70-74; physicist, Fermi Nat Accelerator Lab, 74-90; sr accelerator physicist, Maxwell Labs, Brobeck Div, 91-92; sr staff scientist, Cebaf, 93-96. *Concurrent Pos:* Vis scientist, Inst High Energy Physics, Serpukhov, USSR, 72-73 & Europ Orgn Nuclear Res, Geneva, Switz, 80-81; mem, Univ Chicago Rev Comt, High Energy Physics Div, Argonne Nat Lab, 84-86; adj prof, Univ Houston, 90-91, Ill Univ, 90-92, William & Mary, 93-; adv US Dept Energy, 94-96. *Mem:* Am Phys Soc. *Res:* Accelerators; experimental particle physics; experimental high energy physics. *Mailing Add:* 45 Jonquil Lane Newport News VA 23606. *E-Mail:* roljohn@aol.com

JOHNSON, RONALD CARL, INORGANIC CHEMISTRY. *Current Pos:* From asst prof to assoc prof, 61-73, assoc dean, 90-92, PROF CHEM, EMORY UNIV, 73- *Personal Data:* b Milwaukee, Wis, Sept 5, 35; m 60, Susan Anderson; c Erica & Laura. *Educ:* Lawrence Col, BS, 57; Northwestern Univ, PhD(chem), 61. *Mem:* AAAS; Am Chem Soc. *Res:* Reactions of compounds of transition metals; mechanisms of reactions. *Mailing Add:* Dept Chem Emory Univ Atlanta GA 30322

JOHNSON, RONALD ERNEST, PHYSICAL OCEANOGRAPHY. *Current Pos:* asst prof, 68-78, ASSOC PROF OCEANOG, OLD DOMINION UNIV, 78-, ASSOC DIR GRAD STUDIES, 85- *Personal Data:* b Portland, Ore, Oct 14, 39; m 68, Roberta K Kallgren; c Robert R & Ronald R. *Educ:* Ore State Univ, BS, 62, MS, 63, PhD(phys oceanog), 72. *Prof Exp:* Assoc sr engr, Lockheed-Calif Co, 63-64. *Mem:* Sigma Xi; Am Geophys Union. *Res:* Circulation and distribution of intermediate waters of the worlds oceans; waves and tides. *Mailing Add:* Dept Oceanog Old Dominion Univ Norfolk VA 23529-0276. *Fax:* 757-683-5303; *E-Mail:* rej@ocean.odu.edu

JOHNSON, RONALD GENE, RADIATION BIOPHYSICS, RADIOLOGICAL HEALTH. *Current Pos:* asst prof, 70-74, assoc prof, 74-78, PROF PHYSICS, MALONE COL, 78-, EXEC VPRES, 81- *Personal Data:* b Detroit, Mich, Nov 14, 41; m 64; c 2. *Educ:* Eastern Mich Univ, AB, 63; Univ Kans, MS, 68, PhD(radiation biophys), 70. *Prof Exp:* High sch teacher, Mich, 64 & Ohio, 64-65. *Concurrent Pos:* Radiation biologist, Aultman Hosp, 73-; consult, Med Physics Serv, Inc, 73-; vis assoc prof radiation biophys, Univ Kans, 76-77; assoc prof clin radiation biophys radiol, Northeastern Ohio Univs Col Med, 78- *Mem:* Am Asn Physics Teachers; Sigma Xi. *Res:* Effect of glucose on the sensitivity of Escherichia coli to Mitomycin C; radiation repair mechanisms; radiation-induced atrophy of bone; quality control in diagnostic radiology; effects of diagnostic x-rays during first trimester of pregnancy. *Mailing Add:* Pres of Col Malone Col 515 NW 25th St Canton OH 44709

JOHNSON, RONALD ROY, BIOCHEMISTRY, ANIMAL NUTRITION. *Current Pos:* RETIRED. *Personal Data:* b De Smet, SDak, Dec 8, 28; m 55, Sally Shamel; c Denetia, Jennifer, Mellisa & Scott. *Educ:* SDak State Col, BS, 50, MS, 52; Ohio State Univ, PhD(biochem), 54. *Prof Exp:* Asst, Exp Sta, SDak State Col, 50-52; from asst prof to prof animal sci, Ohio Agr Res & Develop Ctr, 55-69; prof animal sci & indust, Okla State Univ, 69-74; prof animal sci & head dept, Univ Tenn, Knoxville, 74-81; assoc dir, Okla Agr Exp Sta, Okla State Univ, 81-89, prof animal sci, 89-93. *Concurrent Pos:* Consult, Nutrit Surv Team, Comt Nutrit Nat Defense, Spain, 58 & Chile, 60; USPHS sr fel, Univ Calif, Berkeley, 65-66. *Mem:* Am Soc Animal Sci; Am Dairy Sci Asn; Am Inst Nutrit. *Res:* Nutrition, physiology and biochemistry of Rumen microorganisms and ruminant animals; nutrition of farm livestock. *Mailing Add:* 8 Narrows Dr Holiday Island AR 72632

JOHNSON, RONALD SANDERS, PHYSICAL BIOCHEMISTRY, INORGANIC BIOCHEMISTRY. *Current Pos:* asst prof biochem & phys biochem, 81-87, ASSOC PROF BIOCHEM, SCH MED, EAST CAROLINA UNIV, 87- *Personal Data:* b Chicago, Ill, March 9, 52. *Educ:* Northwestern Univ, BA, 73, PhD(biochem & molecularbiol), 78. *Prof Exp:* Instr biochem & res tech, Northwestern Univ, 78; fel, NIH & Miller Inst Basic Res Sci, Univ Calif, Berkeley, 78-81. *Mem:* Am Chem Soc; Sigma Xi; Am Soc Biol Chemists. *Res:* Application of biophysical techniques to explore the mechanism of gene regulation in the bacterium E coli, encompassing protein-nucleic acid as well as protein-protein interactions. *Mailing Add:* Dept Biochem Sch Med East Carolina Univ Rm 5W-37 Greenville NC 27858

JOHNSON, ROSS BYRON, ENVIRONMENTAL GEOLOGY, FUELS GEOLOGY. *Current Pos:* CONSULT GEOLOGIST, 74- *Personal Data:* b Ladd, Ill, June 4, 19; m 42. *Educ:* Univ NMex, BS, 46, MS, 48. *Prof Exp:* Geologist, US Geol Surv, 48-62, res geologist, 62-74. *Mem:* Fel Geol Soc Am; Sigma Xi. *Res:* Formation of sand dunes, rock glaciers, joints, and faults and their effects on the environment and engineering structures; stratigraphic, structural, and igneous geology; geologic mapping and photo-geology; petroleum and coal resources of the Southern Rocky Mountains and adjacent high plains of Colorado and New Mexico. *Mailing Add:* 240 Quay St Lakewood CO 80226

JOHNSON, ROSS GLENN, CELL BIOLOGY. *Current Pos:* Asst prof cytol & zool, 68-73, assoc prof zool, Univ Minn-Minneapolis, 73-76, assoc prof, 76-80, PROF GENETICS & CELL BIOL, UNIV MINN-ST PAUL, 80- *Personal Data:* b McKeesport, Pa, Oct 5, 42; m 64; c 2. *Educ:* Augustana Col, Ill, BA, 64; Iowa State Univ, MS, 66, PhD(cell biol), 68. *Concurrent Pos:* NIH Predoctoral Fel, Bush sabbatical fel. *Mem:* AAAS; Am Soc Cell Biol. *Res:* Involvement of cell junctions in cell communication; structure and function of cell organelles. *Mailing Add:* Dept Genetics & Cell Biol Univ Minn 1445 Gortner Ave St Paul MN 55108-1095. *Fax:* 612-625-5754

JOHNSON, ROY ALLEN, ORGANIC CHEMISTRY. *Current Pos:* SR SCIENTIST, UPJOHN CO, 65- *Personal Data:* b Bemidji, Minn, July 26, 37; m 63; c 2. *Educ:* Univ Minn, BCh, 59, PhD(org chem), 65; Univ BC, MSc, 61. *Concurrent Pos:* Vis scientist, Mass Inst Technol, 82-83; chem forum lectr, 90. *Mem:* Am Chem Soc; AAAS; NY Acad Sci. *Res:* Synthetic organic chemistry; prostaglandin chemistry; microbial oxidations; stereochemistry, phospholipid chemistry and superoxide chemistry. *Mailing Add:* 2122 Frederick Ave Kalamazoo MI 49008-1621

JOHNSON, ROY ANDREW, MEASURE THEORY, REAL FUNCTIONS. *Current Pos:* from asst prof to assoc prof, 66-84, PROF MATH, WASH STATE UNIV, 84- *Personal Data:* b Oak Park, Ill, Mar 20, 39; m 67, Carole Schulte; c Jennifer & Mark. *Educ:* St Olaf Col, BA, 60; Univ Iowa, PhD(math), 64. *Prof Exp:* Asst lectr math, Univ Lagos, 64-65; asst prof, Univ Col, Addis Ababa, 65-66. *Concurrent Pos:* Vis prof, Univ Lodz, Poland, 85-86. *Mem:* Am Math Soc; Math Asn Am; Nat Coun Teachers Math. *Res:* Products of Borel measures; extensions of the usual real topology. *Mailing Add:* Dept Math Wash State Univ Pullman WA 99164-3113. *E-Mail:* johnson@delta.math.wsu.edu

JOHNSON, ROY RAGNAR, PLASMA PHYSICS, SOLID STATE PHYSICS. *Current Pos:* inertial confinement fusion prog ADC, 92-94, INERTIAL CONFINEMENT FUSION PROG, CLASSIFICATION/RECORDS MGR, LAWRENCE LIVERMORE NAT LAB, 94- *Personal Data:* b Chicago, Ill, Jan 23, 32; m 63, Martha A Mattson; c Linnea M & Kaisa A. *Educ:* Univ Minn, BSEE, 56, MSEE, 56, PhD(elec eng), 59. *Prof Exp:* Asst solid state physics, Univ Minn, 54-56; sr basic res scientist, Boeing Sci Res Lab, 59-72; tech dir, KMS Fusion Inc, 72-91 & Innovation Assocs, 91-92. *Concurrent Pos:* Lectr, Univ Wash, 59-60; vis scientist, Royal Inst Technol, Sweden, 63-64; mem bd indust adv, Rose Hulman Inst Technol, 82- *Mem:* AAAS; fel Am Phys Soc; Inst Elec & Electronics Engrs; NY Acad Sci; Am Inst Aeronaut & Astronaut. *Res:* Fluids physics; solids fluctuations; inertial confinement fusion. *Mailing Add:* 1141 Concannon Blvd Livermore CA 94550. *Fax:* 510-423-6212; *E-Mail:* johnson3@llnl.gov

JOHNSON, RUSSELL CLARENCE, MEDICAL MICROBIOLOGY. *Current Pos:* from instr to assoc prof, 62-74, PROF MICROBIOL, MED SCH, UNIV MINN, MINNEAPOLIS, 74- *Personal Data:* b Wausau, Wis, Aug 3, 30; m 55, Patricia A Struck; c 3. *Educ:* Univ Wis, BS, 57, MS, 58, PhD(microbiol), 60. *Honors & Awards:* Gold Medal Award, Slovak Med Soc, 93. *Prof Exp:* Res assoc microbiol, Univ Wis, 60; Nat Acad Sci-Nat Res Coun res assoc, 60-61; res microbiologist, Ft Detrick, Md, 61-62. *Concurrent Pos:* USPHS spec fel, 63-65, res grant, 66-; mem, Subcomt Taxon Leptospira & Subcomt Taxon Spirochaetales, Int Comt Syst Bact, 69-95; mem comn viral infections, Armed Forces Epidemiol Bd, 70-73. *Mem:* AAAS; Am Soc Microbiol; Soc Exp Biol & Med; Am Leptospirosis Res Conf; fel Am Acad Microbiol; fel Infectious Dis Soc Am. *Res:* Biology of pathogenic spirochetes and ehrlichia. *Mailing Add:* Dept Microbiol Univ Minn Med Sch Minneapolis MN 55455. *Fax:* 612-626-0623; *E-Mail:* johnson@lenti.med.umn.edu

JOHNSON, RUSSELL DEE, JR, OPERATIONS RESEARCH. *Current Pos:* physicist, 56-62, SR SCIENTIST, OPERS RES, INC, 62- *Personal Data:* b Granite City, Ill, Dec 10, 28; m 53; c 4. *Educ:* Univ Rochester, BS, 50; Univ Calif, PhD(phys chem), 54. *Prof Exp:* Chemist, Dow Chem Co, Mich, 53-56. *Mem:* Am Chem Soc; Sigma Xi. *Res:* Weapons systems analysis; applied game theory. *Mailing Add:* 1902 Ventura Ave Wheaton MD 20902-2930

JOHNSON, SAMUEL BRITTON, OPHTHALMOLOGY. *Current Pos:* PROF & CHMN, OPHTHAL DEPT, UNIV MISS MED CTR, 56- *Personal Data:* b Canyon, Tex, Apr 25, 26; m 82, Barbara Herfurth; c Margaret N (Sudduth), Lee S & Alice B. *Educ:* WTex A&M Col, BS, 46; Tulane Univ, MD, 48; dipl ophthal, 50; Am Bd Ophthal, dipl, 53. *Concurrent Pos:* Trustee, Miss Sch for Deaf, Miss Sch for Blind & Miss Voc Rehab for Blind; lectr, Law Sci Acad, 59-81; asst prof eye path, Univ Miss; mem bd, Royal Maid Industs/ Signature Works (for blind). *Mem:* Am Col Surgeons; Asn Res Vision & Ophthal; Sigma Xi. *Res:* Eye pathology. *Mailing Add:* Dept Ophthal McBryde Eye Rehab Bldg Univ Miss 2500 N State St Jackson MS 39216. *Fax:* 601-984-5031

JOHNSON, SAMUEL EDGAR, II, MARINE ECOLOGY. *Personal Data:* b San Jose, Calif, Sept 27, 44; m 70. *Educ:* Stanford Univ, BS, 66, PhD(biol), 73. *Honors & Awards:* Arthur C Giese Award, Stanford Univ, 73. *Prof Exp:* Scholar biophys ecol, Dept Bot, Univ Mich, 72-73; asst prof zool, Clark Univ, 73-81; exec dir, Nat Conservancy, 81-87; dir spec projs, Ore Hist Soc, 87-89; dir planned giving, Ore Health Sci Univ Found, 91-93. *Concurrent Pos:* Res assoc, New Eng Res Inc, 73- *Mem:* Am Soc Zoologists; Ecol Soc Am; Am Meteorol Soc; Sigma Xi; Int Biometeorol Soc. *Res:* Biophysical ecology, microclimatology and biometeorology of the marine rocky intertidal region with emphasis on heat and mass transfer processes as they affect intertidal organisms, particularly amphipods and molluscs; estuarine ecology and coastal zone resource management. *Mailing Add:* 1449 SW Davenport St Portland OR 97201

JOHNSON, SAMUEL Y, NEOTECHTRONICS. *Current Pos:* GEOLOGIST, CENT REGION, GEOL HAZARDS TEAM, US GEOL SURV, COLO, 97- *Personal Data:* b San Diego, Calif, Aug 12, 51. *Educ:* Univ Calif, BS, 76; Univ Wash, MS, 78, PhD(geol sci), 82. *Prof Exp:* Asst prof, Wash State Univ, 82-84. *Mem:* Geol Soc Am; Am Geophys Union; Soc Sedimentary Geol; Seismol Soc Am; Int Asn Sedimetologists; Am Asn Petrol Geologists. *Mailing Add:* US Geol Surv MS 966 Box 25046 DF Denver CO 80025

JOHNSON, SARAH DURSTON, B MESON PHYSICS, PROTON-ANTIPROTON COLLIDER PHYSICS. *Current Pos:* ASST PROF PHYSICS, UNIV LA VERNE, 97- *Personal Data:* b Weymouth, Eng, Oct 21, 64; m 93, Mark W. *Educ:* State Univ NY, Albany, BS, 86; Univ Rochester, MA, 88, PhD(physics), 93. *Prof Exp:* Postdoctoral res, Niels Bohr Inst, 93-94; vis asst prof physics, Hobart & William Smith Col, 94-95; asst prof physics, State Univ NY, Geneseo, 95-97. *Concurrent Pos:* Vis res assoc, Univ Rochester, 94-97. *Mem:* Am Phys Soc; Am Asn Physics Teachers; Sigma Xi. *Res:* Experimental particle physics. *Mailing Add:* Dept Math & Physics Univ La Verne La Verne CA 91750. *Fax:* 909-392-2709; *E-Mail:* johnsosa@ulv.edu

JOHNSON, SHIRLEY MAE, REPRODUCTIVE PHYSIOLOGY. *Current Pos:* lab technician, Endocrine Res Unit, 65-70, asst to vpres, Off Res Develop, 71, UNIV PROF FAMILY MED, COL OSTEOP MED, MICH STATE UNIV, 72- *Personal Data:* b Ironwood, Mich, May 26, 40; m 75. *Educ:* Northern Mich Col, BS, 62; Mich State Univ, MS, 65, PhD(physiol), 70; Univ Mich, MPH, 72. *Prof Exp:* Teacher pub sch, Grand Rapids, Mich, 62-63. *Concurrent Pos:* Res consult, Mich Cancer Found, 70; educ consult, Tri-County Family Planning Ctr, Lansing, Mich, 75- *Mem:* Am Pub Health Asn; Am Asn Sex Educr, Counr & Therapists; Sigma Xi. *Res:* Influence on health care of knowledge, attitudes, concerns and beliefs patients have toward reproductive physiology and family planning; contraceptive use and advertising. *Mailing Add:* Dept Family & Community Med B2 Mich State Univ East Lansing MI 48824

JOHNSON, STANLEY HARRIS, AUTOMATIC CONTROL SYSTEMS. *Current Pos:* from asst prof to assoc prof, 73-79, PROF, DEPT MECH ENG & MECH, LEHIGH UNIV, 79- *Personal Data:* b Fresno, Calif, Dec 3, 38; m 65; c 1. *Educ:* Univ Calif, Berkeley, BS, 62, MS, 67, PhD(mech eng), 73. *Prof Exp:* Design engr physics res, Lawrence Radiation Lab, 61-65; syst engr comput sales, Int Bus Mach Co, 65-67; sr engr comput control, Mobil Res & Develop Corp, 67-70. *Concurrent Pos:* Fac fel, Dryden Flight Res Ctr, 74 & 75; DuPont assoc prof, DuPont Univ Sci & Eng grant, 78-80. *Mem:* Am Soc Mech Engrs; Am Asn Univ Prof. *Res:* Numerical simulation of dynamical systems; development of the methodology of simulation; simulation validity and verification; numerical solution of partial differential equations; application of optimal control theory. *Mailing Add:* Dept Mech Eng & Mech Lab 19 Lehigh Univ Bethlehem PA 18015

JOHNSON, STANLEY O(WEN), NUCLEAR ENGINEERING. *Current Pos:* VPRES & DIR, ASPEN SECURITY ADV INC, 85- *Personal Data:* b Bismarck, NDak, Dec 28, 30; div; c 2. *Educ:* Univ Colo, BS, 53. *Prof Exp:* Student engr, Westinghouse Elec Corp, 53-54, scientist, Bettis Atomic Power Lab, 54-60, supvr nuclear reactor kinetics, 60-61; group leader reactor safety & dynamics anal, Atomic Energy Div, Phillips Petrol Co, 61-63, sect chief anal & data processing, 63-68, mgr, Spert Proj, 68-69; mgr, Idaho Nuclear Corp, 69-71, Aerojet Nuclear Co, 71-73; pres, Intermountain Technol, Inc, 73-86; dir, ITI-Japan, Inc, 81-86; vpres, Rockwood Growth Fund Inc, 85-91. *Concurrent Pos:* Dir, Ene-Con, Inc, 78-81. *Mem:* Fel Am Nuclear Soc; Nat Soc Prof Engrs. *Res:* Nuclear reactor safety research; nuclear reactor dynamics; computer simulation of nuclear reactors. *Mailing Add:* 1312 Azalea Dr Idaho Falls ID 83404

JOHNSON, STANLEY R, AGRICULTURAL ECONOMICS, ECONOMETRICS. *Current Pos:* PROF ECON & DIR, CTR AGR & RURAL DEVELOP, IOWA STATE UNIV, AMES, 85-, VPROVOST EXTEN, 96- *Personal Data:* b Burlington, Iowa, Aug 26, 38; m 93, Maureen Kilkenny; c Peter & Ben. *Educ:* Western Ill Univ, BA, 61; Tex Tech Univ, MS, 62, Tex A&M Univ, PhD, 66. *Hon Degrees:* LHD, Western Ill Univ, 88. *Honors & Awards:* Chancellor's Award for Outstanding Res, 80; Int Hon Award, Off Int Coop & Develop, USDA, 87; Wilton Park Int Serv Award, 93. *Prof Exp:* Asst prof econ, 64-66, from assoc prof to prof econ & agr econ, 67-85, chmn, Dept Econ, 72-74; assoc prof agr econ, Univ Conn, Storrs, 66-67. *Concurrent Pos:* Vis assoc prof agr econ, Univ Calif-Davis, 70, Purdue Univ, 71-72; economist, Agr Can, Ottawa, 75; vis prof econ, Univ Ga, 75-76, Univ Calif-Berkeley, 81; exec dir, Food & Agr Policy Res Inst, 84-; prof, Univ Mo, Columbia, 85-; chmn bd, Midwest Agribus Trade Res & Info Ctr, 87-; adminr, Iowa State Univ USSR All-Union Acad Agr Sci Exchange Agreement, 88-93; chmn bd dirs, Inst Policy Reform, 90-; assoc ed, Am J Agr Econ; academician VI Lenin All-Union Acad Agr Sci, Moscow, Russ, 91, Ukraine, 93. *Mem:* Fel Am Agr Econ Asn. *Res:* Policy issues in agriculture and rural development; published extensively in economic theory, econometrics, consumer demand, and agricultural price, trade, and policy analysis. *Mailing Add:* VProvost Exten 315 Beardshear Ames IA 50011-2020. *Fax:* 515-294-9781; *E-Mail:* vpforext@exnet.iastate.edu

JOHNSON, STEPHEN ALLEN, COMBUSTION RESEARCH & DEVELOPMENT. *Current Pos:* area mgr, 83-90, VPRES, APPL COMBUSTION TECHNOLS, PHYS SCI INC, 90- *Personal Data:* b Worcester, Mass, April 26, 48; m 70; c 2. *Educ:* Worcester Polytech Inst, BS, 70. *Prof Exp:* Res & develop, E F Laurence Mfg Co, 70-71; sr res engr, Riley Stoker Corp, 71-76; group supvr, Babcock & Wilcox Co, 76-81; prog mgr, Sci Applns, Inc, 81-83. *Mem:* Am Inst Chem Engrs; Combustion Inst. *Res:* Developed advanced combustion processes to achieve 80 percent reduction; exploring mineral matter transformations in flames to predict and control ash deposition problems in large furnaces; developing processes to control emissions in coal-fueled diesel and gas turbine engines and waste incinerators; effects of fuels on equipment operation; development of technologies to control emission of nitrogen oxides; sulfur dioxide & airbone toxic. *Mailing Add:* 20 New EngBus Ctr Andover MA 01810

JOHNSON, STEPHEN THOMAS, TOOLING ENGINEERING. *Current Pos:* TOOL DESIGNER, BOEING, 92- *Personal Data:* b Washington, DC, May 31, 54; m 83. *Educ:* Northeastern Univ, BMET, 78. *Prof Exp:* Draftsman, Hollingsworth & Vose, 73-74; tech aide, US Army Natick Res & Develop, 75-78; tool designer, Boeing Aircraft Co. 78-81, propulsion engr, 81; sr tool designer, Sikorsky Aircraft Co, United Technologies, 81-92. *Mem:* Am Soc Metals; Am Soc Mech Eng. *Res:* Advanced tooling and fabrication concepts for composite aircraft parts. *Mailing Add:* 13713 SE 237th Pl Kent WA 98042

JOHNSON, STURE ARCHIE MANSFIELD, medicine, for more information see previous edition

JOHNSON, SUSAN BISSEN, FATTY ACIDS. *Current Pos:* RES TECHNOLOGIST, MAYO CLIN, ROCHESTER, MINN, 91- *Personal Data:* b Austin, Minn, July 20, 51; m 77. *Educ:* Mankato State Univ, BS, 73. *Prof Exp:* Jr scientist, Hormel Inst, Univ Minn, 73-77, from asst to assoc, 77-85, scientist, 85-91. *Concurrent Pos:* Consult, Travenol Lab, 84-85. *Mem:* Am Soc Clin Pathologists. *Res:* Study and measurement of electrophysiologic properties of the heart; metabolism of fatty acids in normal and disease conditions. *Mailing Add:* Mayo Clin St Mary's Hosp 1216 Second St SW Mary Brigh-2 Surgical Servs Rochester MN 55902

JOHNSON, SUSAN E, CELL BIOLOGY, BONE BIOLOGY. *Current Pos:* sr res scientist, 92-95, ASSOC RES FEL, RHONE-POULENC RORER, 95- *Personal Data:* b White Plains, NY, July 16, 53. *Educ:* State Univ NY, Albany, BS, 78, MS, 84, PhD(molecular biol), 89. *Prof Exp:* NIH fel, State Univ NY, Albany, 89; Am Heart & Lung fel, Wistar Inst, 89-92. *Mem:* AAAS; Am Soc Cell Biol; Sigma Xi; Am Soc Bone & Min Res; Fed Am Soc Exper Biol. *Res:* Osteoblast differentiation. *Mailing Add:* Rhone-Poulenc Rorer N-W 15 500 Arcola Rd Collegeville PA 19426-0107. *Fax:* 610-454-3340; *E-Mail:* johnsse@rpr.rpna.com

JOHNSON, SYLVIA MARIAN, SYNTHESIS & PROCESSING. *Current Pos:* Mat scientist, 82-86, sr mat scientist, 86-88, PROG MGR CERAMICS, SRI INT, 88- *Personal Data:* b Sydney, Australia, Aug 29, 54; m 85; c 2. *Educ:* Univ New South Wales, BSc Hons, 77; Univ Calif, Berkeley, MS, 79, PhD(eng & mat sci), 83. *Mem:* Am Ceramic Soc; AAAS; Metall Soc. *Res:* Synthesis of oxide and non-oxide ceramic powders; processing of ceramics, especially silicon nitride; characterization and evaluation of structural ceramics; joining of ceramics. *Mailing Add:* SRI Int 333 Ravenswood Ave Menlo Park CA 94025-3493

JOHNSON, TERRELL KENT, GENETICS, INSECT CELL CULTURE. *Current Pos:* chemist, 89-92, SR CHEMIST, SIGMA CHEM CO, 92- *Personal Data:* b Inglewood, Calif, Nov 23, 47; m 80, Barbara Schmidt; c Alexandra. *Educ:* Univ Calif, San Diego, BA, 70; Calif State Univ, Northridge, MS, 72; Univ Tex, Austin, PhD(zool), 76. *Prof Exp:* Res fel genetics, Calif State Technol, 76-77; USPHS trainee, Kans State Univ, 77-79, res assoc, 79-89. *Mem:* Genetics Soc Am; Soc Develop Biol; Sigma Xi; Tissue Cult Asn. *Res:* Media development for insect cell; development of toxicology assays. *Mailing Add:* Tissue Cult Sigma Chem Co PO Box 14508 St Louis MO 63178

JOHNSON, TERRY CHARLES, MOLECULAR BIOLOGY, TUMOR BIOLOGY. *Current Pos:* prof & dir, Div Biol, 77-92, UNIV DISTINGUISHED PROF & DIR, CANCER CTR, KANS STATE UNIV, 92- *Personal Data:* b St Paul, Minn, Aug 8, 36; m 58, Mary A Wilhelmy; c James, Gary & Jean. *Educ:* Hamline Univ, BS, 58; Univ Minn, Minneapolis, MS, 61, PhD(microbiol), 64. *Prof Exp:* USPHS res asst, Univ Minn, Minneapolis, 58-64; USPHS fel molecular biol, Univ Calif, Irvine, 64-66; from asst prof to assoc prof, Med Sch, Northwestern Univ, Chicago, 66-73, prof virol, 73-77. *Concurrent Pos:* Co-dir, Bioserve Space Technol; consult, Digene, College Park, Md; dir, Howard Hughes Med Inst Undergrad Sci Initiative, Kans State Univ. *Mem:* AAAS; Am Soc Cell Biol; Am Soc Neurochem; Am Soc Microbiol; Sigma Xi; NY Acad Sci. *Res:* Regulation of cell cycling, tumor suppressors, signal transduction, oncogene expression, membrane biology, cloning. *Mailing Add:* Div Biol Kans State Univ Ackert Hall Manhattan KS 66506-0001. *Fax:* 785-532-6653; *E-Mail:* terryj@ksavw.ksu.edu

JOHNSON, TERRY R(OBERT), NUCLEAR FUEL CYCLE. *Current Pos:* CHEM ENGR, ARGONNE NAT LAB, 75- *Personal Data:* b Chicago, Ill, Nov 16, 32; m 56; c 4. *Educ:* Rice Univ, BA, 54, BS, 55; Univ Mich, MS, 56, PhD(chem eng), 59. *Prof Exp:* Assoc chem engr, Argonne Nat Lab, 58-74; sr process engr, Aglomet, Inc, 74-75. *Concurrent Pos:* Vis prof, Iowa State Univ, 70. *Mem:* Am Inst Chem Engrs; Am Nuclear Soc; Sigma Xi. *Res:* Radiation chemistry of aqueous systems; nuclear fuel recovery; chemistry of liquid metals and salts; open-cycle MHD. *Mailing Add:* 1424 S Main Wheaton IL 60187-6482

JOHNSON, TERRY WALTER, JR, MYCOLOGY. *Personal Data:* b Waukegan, Ill, Jan 13, 23; m 48; c 3. *Educ:* Univ Ill, BS, 48; Univ Mich, MS, 49, PhD(bot), 51. *Prof Exp:* Instr bot, Univ Mich, 50-51; mycologist, Chem Corps Biol Labs, Camp Detrick, 51-53; asst prof biol, Univ Miss, 53-54; from asst prof to prof bot, Duke Univ, 54-85, chmn dept, 63-71. *Concurrent Pos:* Guggenheim fel, 60-61; mem systs panel, NSF, 63-66; ed-in-chief, Mycologia, 81- *Mem:* Bot Soc Am; Mycol Soc Am; Brit Mycol Soc. *Res:* Aquatic phycomycetes; Mycetozoa; marine fungi. *Mailing Add:* 3505 Manford Dr Durham NC 27707

JOHNSON, THEODORE REYNOLD, AGING, CANCER BIOLOGY. *Current Pos:* PROF BIOL, ST OLAF COL, 77- *Personal Data:* b Willmar, Minn, Mar 20, 46; m 70, Michelle Flaherty; c Carrie, Eric & Daniel. *Educ:* Augsburg Col, BA, 68; Univ Ill Med Ctr, MS, 70, PhD(microbiol), 73. *Prof Exp:* Res asst microbiol, Rush-Presby St Lukes Hosp, 68-72; asst prof biol, Mankato State Univ, 72-77. *Concurrent Pos:* Consult, St Joseph's Hosp, 74-77 & Donaldson Corp, 80-; vis scientist, Trudeau Inst, 83-84 & Oak Ridge Nat Lab, 91. *Mem:* Am Soc Microbiol; AAAS; Sigma Xi. *Res:* Biodegradation of toxic wastes and in soil; cancer and immune systems of hibernating animals; aging and cancer immunity; soil microbiology. *Mailing Add:* Dept Biol St Olaf Col Northfield MN 55057. *Fax:* 507-646-3104; *E-Mail:* johnson@stolaf.edu

JOHNSON, THOMAS, QUALITY CONTROL, ECONOMETRICS. *Current Pos:* assoc prof, 74-78, PROF ECON & STATIST, NC STATE UNIV, 78- *Personal Data:* b Halletsville, Tex, Feb 12, 36; m 56, Cleta Anderson; c David, Michael & Mark. *Educ:* Univ Tex, Austin, BA, 57; Tex Christian Univ, MA, 62; NC State Univ, MES, 67, PhD(economet & statist), 69. *Prof Exp:* Nuclear engr, Convair, Fortworth, Tex, 57-61; eng specialist, LTV-Vought Aeronaut Div, Dallas, Tex, 61-64; oper analyst, Res Triangle Inst, 64-69. *Concurrent Pos:* Asst prof econ & statist, Southern Methodist Univ, Dallas, Tex, 69-74, assoc prof, 74. *Mem:* Am Statist Asn; Am Soc Qual Control; Am Econ Asn; Am Agr Econ Asn. *Res:* Statistics and mathematics applications to management and economic issues; analysis of dynamics of social and biological systems; resource economics; data analysis. *Mailing Add:* Dept Agr & Resource Econ NC State Univ Box 8109 Raleigh NC 27695. *Fax:* 919-515-1824; *E-Mail:* tom__johnson@ncsu.edu

JOHNSON, THOMAS CHARLES, LIMNOLOGY, GEOLOGICAL PROCESSES IN LARGE LAKES. *Current Pos:* PROF & DIR, LARGE LAKES OBSERV, UNIV MINN, 94- *Personal Data:* b Virginia, Minn, Aug 15, 44; m 90, Katherine Taylor Whittaker; c Heidi Lena & Ryan Kent. *Educ:* Univ Wash, BS, 67; Scripps Inst Oceanog, PhD(oceanog), 75. *Prof Exp:* From asst prof to assoc prof, Univ Minn, 75-83; from assoc prof to prof, Duke Univ, 83-94, dir, NC Oceanog Consortium, 83-94. *Concurrent Pos:* Fulbright scholar, France, 93-94. *Mem:* Fel Geol Soc Am; AAAS; Am Soc Limnol & Oceanog; Am Geophys Union; Soc Int Limnol. *Res:* Paleoclimate and sedimentological research on large lakes of the world, including North America, East Africa, Central America, and Central Asia. *Mailing Add:* Large Lakes Observ Univ Minn Duluth MN 55812. *Fax:* 218-726-6979; *E-Mail:* tcj@umn.edu

JOHNSON, THOMAS EUGENE, GENETICS OF AGING, GENETICS OF ALCOHOL ABUSE. *Current Pos:* fel molecular, cellular & develop biol, 77-82, assoc prof, Inst Behav Genetics, 88-96, PROF, UNIV COLO, BOULDER, 96- *Personal Data:* b Denver, Colo, June 19, 48; m 82, Victoria Simpson; c P Andrew & Ariel R. *Educ:* Mass Inst Technol, BS, 70; Univ Wash, PhD(genetics), 75. *Honors & Awards:* Ewald Busse Award for Biomed Geront, 93; Nathan Shock Award, 95. *Prof Exp:* Fel genetics, Cornell Univ, 75-77; asst prof, Dept Molecular Biol & Biochem, Univ Calif, 82-88. *Mem:* Genetics Soc Am; AAAS; fel Geront Soc Am; Am Aging Asn; Am Fedn Aging Res; Res Soc Alcoholism. *Res:* Genetics of aging in the nematode; genetics of alcohol sensitivity in the mouse. *Mailing Add:* Lab Molecular Genetic Inst Behav Genetics Univ Colo Boulder CO 80309-0447. *Fax:* 303-492-8063; *E-Mail:* johnsont@ibg.colorado.edu

JOHNSON, THOMAS F, SPORTS MEDICINE. *Current Pos:* RETIRED. *Personal Data:* b Philadelphia, Pa, Mar 10, 17. *Educ:* Springfield Col, BS, 40; NY Univ, MA, 46; Univ Md, PhD(phys educ), 67. *Prof Exp:* Assoc Dean, Grad Sch, Howard Univ, 74-78. *Mem:* Am Physiol Soc. *Mailing Add:* 130 Ingraham St NW Washington DC 20011-6618

JOHNSON, THOMAS RAYMOND, CELL BIOLOGY. *Current Pos:* SR RES ASSOC, CASE WESTERN RESERVE UNIV, 73- *Personal Data:* b Washington, DC, July 8, 44; m 73, Candice E Brown; c 2. *Educ:* Harvard Univ, BA, 66; Case Western Reserve Univ, PhD(biol), 71. *Prof Exp:* Instr, Univ Ill, Chicago Med Ctr, 71-73. *Mem:* AAAS. *Res:* Expression of insulin gene family; relationship of insulin-like growth factors to cancer. *Mailing Add:* 3062 Huntington Shaker Heights OH 44120. *Fax:* 216-368-1357

JOHNSON, THYS B(RENTWOOD), MINING ENGINEERING, OPERATIONS RESEARCH. *Current Pos:* DIR APPL RES, NAT RESOURCES RES INST & PROF INDUST ENG, UNIV MINN, DULUTH, 85- *Personal Data:* b Duluth, Minn, Mar 20, 34; m 58; c 3. *Educ:* Univ Minn-Minneapolis, BS, 54, MS, 58; Univ Calif, Berkeley, PhD(opers res), 68. *Prof Exp:* Mining engr, Minn Ore Opers, US Steel Corp, 58-61, mathematician, 61-64; mining methods res engr, US Bur Mines, 64-68, mining engr, 68, supvry mining engr, 68-69, supvry opers res analyst, 69-72; prof mining eng, Colo Sch Mines, 72-, head dept, 74-85. *Mem:* Opers Res Soc Am; Am Inst Mining, Metall & Petrol Engrs. *Res:* Research and development of operations research techniques as applied to problems of the mineral industry; developed mathematical and dynamic programming techniques for open pit mine planning and production scheduling. *Mailing Add:* University MN Duluth MN 55811

JOHNSON, TIMOTHY JAY, FOURIER TRANSFORM INFRARED SPECTROSCOPY. *Current Pos:* applns scientist, 92-93, SR RES & DEVELOP SCIENTIST, BRUKER OPTICS, 96- *Personal Data:* b Minneapolis, Minn, Mar 25, 59; m 97. *Educ:* Carleton Col, BA, 81; Wash State Univ, PhD(chem physics), 87. *Prof Exp:* Fel, Max-Planck Inst, Ger, 88-90, staff scientist, 90-92; sr res assoc, York Univ, Toronto, 93-96. *Concurrent Pos:* Lectr instrumental chem, York Univ, 94-96. *Mem:* Am Phys Soc; Am Geophys Union; Am Radio Relay League; Optical Soc Am; Am Inst Chemists. *Res:* Fundamental physical properties of gas phase species, particularly those of atmospheric importance; more accurate and sensitive ways to measure such species. *Mailing Add:* Bruker Optics 19 Fortune Dr Billerica MA 01821-3923

JOHNSON, TIMOTHY JOHN ALBERT, MEMBRANE BIOCHEMISTRY. *Current Pos:* OWNER, SCIENCE FOR KIDS, 92- *Educ:* Univ Wis, PhD(biochem), 74. *Prof Exp:* Asst prof, Colo State Univ, 79-92. *Res:* Gluteraldehyde fixations; collidal gold labbing of membrane proteins. *Mailing Add:* 1337 Stonehenge Dr Ft Collins CO 80525

JOHNSON, TIMOTHY WALTER, PHYSICAL CHEMISTRY & POLYMER CHEMISTRY. *Current Pos:* res chemist, 73-81, RES ASSOC, PHILLIPS PETROLEUM CO, 81- *Personal Data:* b Newington, Conn, Sept 17, 41; m 66, Linda Anderson; c Anne & Loretta. *Educ:* Trinity Col, BS, 63, MS, 65; Purdue Univ, PhD, 70. *Prof Exp:* Res assoc, Northwestern Univ, 69-73. *Mem:* Sigma Xi; Am Chem Soc; Soc Plastics Engrs; Adhesion Soc. *Res:* Physical chemistry of polymer solutions; polymer rheology; electrical properties of polymers; electrically conductive polymers; polymer morphology; polymer properties; polymer composites; surface science; adhesion; size exclusion chromatography. *Mailing Add:* Res & Develop Dept Chem & Polymers Lab Phillips Petroleum Co Bartlesville OK 74004. *E-Mail:* twjohns@bvemx.ppco.com

JOHNSON, TOM MILROY, INTERNAL MEDICINE. *Current Pos:* CHIEF EXEC OFFICER, KALAMAZOO CTR MED STUDIES, MICH, 94- *Personal Data:* b Northville, Mich, Jan 16, 35; m 59; c 2. *Educ:* Col Wooster, BA, 56; Northwestern Univ, Ill, MD, 61. *Prof Exp:* Am Thoracic Soc fel pulmonary dis, Med Ctr, Univ Mich, 67-68; asst prof med, 68-71, assoc prof med, Col Human Med, Mich State Univ, 71-77; prof internal med & dean, Sch Med, Univ NDak, 77-88. *Concurrent Pos:* Asst dean, Grand Rapids Campus, Univ Mich, 71-77. *Mem:* Am Thoracic Soc; fel Am Col Physicians; Am Col Chest Physicians. *Res:* Relationship of community and university medical education; pulmonary disease. *Mailing Add:* 1804 Highland Nist Lane San Antonio TX 78251-3105

JOHNSON, TORRENCE VAINO, PLANETARY SCIENCES, ASTRONOMY. *Current Pos:* Nat Res Coun resident res assoc planetology, Calif Inst Technol, 71-73, sr scientist, 73-74, group supvr, Optical Astron Group, 74-85, res scientist, 80-81, SR RES SCIENTIST, JET PROPULSION LAB, CALIF INST TECHNOL, 81- *Personal Data:* b Rockville Centre, NY, Dec 1, 44; m 67; c 2. *Educ:* Washington Univ, BS, 66; Calif Inst Technol, PhD(planetary sci), 70. *Hon Degrees:* Dr, Univ Padua, Italy, 97. *Honors & Awards:* Sci Achievement Medal, NASA, 80 & 81; Fel, Am Geophys Union. *Prof Exp:* Mem res staff planetary astron, Planetary Astron Lab, Mass Inst Technol, 69-71. *Concurrent Pos:* Mem, Uranus Sci Adv Comt, NASA, 73-75, Outer Planets Probe Working Group, 74-76; scientist, Proj Galileo, NASA, 77- & mem, Voyager Imaging Sci Team, 78-; vis assoc prof planetary sci, Calif Inst Technol, 81-83; pres, Planetology Sect, Am Geophys Union, 90-92. *Mem:* Sigma Xi; AAAS; Am Astron Soc (secy-treas, 77-); Int Astron Union; Am Geophys Union. *Res:* Telescopic observations of planetary surfaces and atmospheres; laboratory studies of silicates and ices; interpretation of planetary spacecraft data. *Mailing Add:* Jet Propulsion Lab 183-501 4800 Oak Grove Dr Pasadena CA 91109

JOHNSON, VARD HAYES, geology; deceased, see previous edition for last biography

JOHNSON, VERN RAY, EDUCATIONAL ADMINISTRATION, SOCIAL TECHNOLOGY. *Current Pos:* assoc prof elec eng, 67-79, ASSOC DEAN, COL ENG & MINES, UNIV ARIZ, 79- *Personal Data:* b Salt Lake City, Utah, Feb 25, 37; m 59; c 4. *Educ:* Univ Utah, BS, 60, PhD(elec eng, physics), 65. *Prof Exp:* Res asst, Microwave Devices Lab, Utah, 60-64; res engr, Microwave Electronics Div, Teledyne, Inc, 64-67. *Mem:* Inst Elec & Electronics Engrs; Am Soc Eng Educ; Am Soc Qual Control. *Res:* Microwave acoustic amplification; photoelastic interactions in solid materials; surface wave acoustics; engineering manpower system simulation and demand projections; communication; application of engineering techniques to social problems; total quality management. *Mailing Add:* Col Eng & Mines Univ Ariz Tucson AZ 85721

JOHNSON, VERNER CARL, ENVIRONMENTAL GEOLOGY, EXPLORATION GEOPHYSICS. *Current Pos:* asst prof, 77-84, ASSOC PROF, MESA STATE COL, GRAND JUNCTION, COLO, 84- *Personal Data:* b Chicago, Ill, Sept 14, 43; c Richard & Seyha. *Educ:* Southern Ill Univ, BA, 67, MS, 70; Univ Tenn, PhD(geol), 75. *Prof Exp:* Instr, Calif State Univ, 72-74; proj geophysicist, Gulf Res & Develop Corp, 74-76; asst prof, Mesa Col, 76-77. *Concurrent Pos:* Geologist, Bendix Field Eng Corp, 77-83. *Mem:* Am Asn Petrol Geologists; Am Geophys Union; Geol Soc Am; Soc Explor Geophysicists; Nat Ground Water Asn; Comput Oriented Geol Soc. *Res:* Application of geophysical methods in ground water. *Mailing Add:* Mesa State Col PO Box 2647 Grand Junction CO 81502. *Fax:* 970-248-1324; *E-Mail:* verner@mesa5.mesa.colorado.edu

JOHNSON, VINCENT ARNOLD, ZOOLOGY, PHYSIOLOGY. *Current Pos:* from asst prof to assoc prof, 67-72, PROF BIOL, ST CLOUD STATE UNIV, 72- *Personal Data:* b York, Nebr, Jan 5, 28; m 53, Lucille M Strohm; c Krista E, Cydna R & Curtis J. *Educ:* Univ Nebr, BSc, 52, MSc, 55, PhD(zool, physiol), 64. *Prof Exp:* Spec instr biol, Univ Tex, 57-61; asst prof, Augustana Col, Ill, 64-67. *Mem:* Am Soc Zool; Soc Protozoologists; AAAS; Sigma Xi. *Res:* Cellular growth and metabolism. *Mailing Add:* Dept Biol Sci St Cloud State Univ St Cloud MN 56301

JOHNSON, VIRGIL ALLEN, agronomy, for more information see previous edition

JOHNSON, W REED, NUCLEAR ENGINEERING. *Current Pos:* proj engr reactor facil, Univ Va, 58-62, proj dir, Philippine Atomic Energy Comn Proj, 62-64, res dir, 64-66, assoc prof, 66-68, asst dir reactor facil, 66-74, PROF NUCLEAR ENG, UNIV VA, 68- *Personal Data:* b Chattanooga, Tenn, Sept 3, 31; m 56; c 3. *Educ:* Va Mil Inst, BS, 53; Univ Va, DSc(eng physics), 62. *Prof Exp:* Shielding engr, Elec Boat Div, Gen Dynamics Corp, 54-55; nuclear engr, Alco Prod, Inc, 55-57. *Concurrent Pos:* Proj engr, Div Reactor Licensing, US Atomic Energy Comn, 68-69; mem, Atomic Safety & Licensing Appeal Bd, 74- *Mem:* Fel Am Nuclear Soc; Am Soc Eng Educ. *Res:* Radiation shielding; reactor safety; experimental engineering. *Mailing Add:* 115 Falcon Dr Charlottesville VA 22901-2035

JOHNSON, W THOMAS, NUTRITIONAL BIOCHEMISTRY. *Current Pos:* Res prof biochem, 85-87, RES CHEMIST, HUMAN NUTRIT RES CTR, USDA, 87- *Personal Data:* b Butte, Montana, 45; m 87. *Educ:* Univ NDak, PhD(biochem), 76; Mont State Univ, BS(physics), 68. *Mem:* Am Inst Nutrit; Am Soc Biochem & Molecular Biol; AAAS. *Res:* Effects of nutrients on biological membranes; roles of nutrients in transmembrane signalling. *Mailing Add:* USDA Human Nutrit Res Ctr PO Box 7166 University Sta Grand Forks ND 58202

JOHNSON, WALLACE DELMAR, ORGANIC CHEMISTRY. *Current Pos:* Res chemist, 61-64 & 68-72, patent liaison, 72-84, LICENSING COORD, PHILLIPS PETROL CO, 84- *Personal Data:* b Idaho Falls, Idaho, June 5, 39; m 58; c 6. *Educ:* Brigham Young Univ, BS, 61; Univ Utah, PhD(org chem), 69. *Mem:* Am Chem Soc; Sigma Xi; AAAS. *Res:* Organophosphorus chemistry; synthesis of rubbers and plastics. *Mailing Add:* 3700 Redbud Lane Bartlesville OK 74006-4916

JOHNSON, WALLACE W, PHARMACOLOGY, DENTISTRY. *Current Pos:* Asst dent, 57-58, from instr to assoc prof oper dent, 58-65, PROF OPER DENT, COL DENT, UNIV IOWA, 65- *Personal Data:* b LaMoure, NDak, Nov 23, 26; m 51; c 4. *Educ:* NDak State Col, BS, 50; Univ Iowa, DDS, 57, MS, 58. *Mem:* Am Dent Asn; Am Col Dentists; Am Asn Dent Res; Am Asn Dent Schs. *Res:* Drugs and their use in dentistry; educational research; dental materials research. *Mailing Add:* 720 Greenwood Dr Iowa City IA 52246

JOHNSON, WALTER C(URTIS), ELECTRONIC MATERIALS & DEVICES. *Current Pos:* from instr to prof, Princeton Univ, 37-81, chmn dept, 51-65, Arthur LeGrand Prof Eng, 63-81, EMER PROF ELEC ENG, PRINCETON UNIV, 81- *Personal Data:* b Weikert, Pa, Jan 6, 13; m 34, Caroline Shirk; c Walter C Jr, William S & David E. *Educ:* Pa State Col, BSE, 34, EE, 42. *Honors & Awards:* Western Elec Award for Excellence in Eng Educ, Am Soc Eng Educ, 67. *Prof Exp:* Stud elec engr, Gen Elec Co, NY, 34-37. *Concurrent Pos:* Resident vis, Bell Labs, 68, consult. *Mem:* Am Soc Eng Educ; Am Phys Soc; fel Inst Elec & Electronics Engrs. *Res:* Semiconductor materials and devices; charge transport and trapping in insulators; insulator reliability; electronic properties of interfaces between semiconductors and insulators. *Mailing Add:* 20 McCosh Circle Princeton NJ 08540

JOHNSON, WALTER CURTIS, JR, BIOPHYSICAL CHEMISTRY. *Current Pos:* asst prof, 68-72, assoc prof, 72-78, PROF BIOPHYS, ORE STATE UNIV, 78- *Personal Data:* b Princeton, NJ, Feb 11, 39; m 60, Susan M Scheller; c Walter C III & Heather L. *Educ:* Yale Univ, BA, 61; Univ Wash, PhD(phys chem), 66. *Honors & Awards:* Milton Harris Award. *Prof Exp:* NSF fel, Univ Calif, Berkeley, 66-68. *Concurrent Pos:* NSF grant circular dichroism & conformation of biopolymers, 68-; USPHS grant, protein conformation & function, 74-; mem panel equip, NIH, 79, 83, 84; mem panel biol instrumentation, NSF, 80-82; mem BBCA panel, NIH, 88-91; advisory bd Biopolymers. *Mem:* Biophys Soc. *Res:* Spectroscopic properties of biopolymers, principally their circular dichroism, their conformation and resulting biological function. *Mailing Add:* Dept Biochem & Biophys Ore State Univ Agr & Life Sci 2011 Corvallis OR 97331-7503

JOHNSON, WALTER HEINRICK, JR, PHYSICS, MASS SPECTROMETRY. *Current Pos:* from asst prof to assoc prof, Univ Minn, 58-68, prof physics, 68-93, actg chmn, Dept Physics, 69-70 & 83, assoc dean, 71-77, actg dean, 77-79, assoc dean, 91-93, EMER PROF PHYSICS, UNIV MINN, MINNEAPOLIS, 93- *Personal Data:* b Minneapolis, Minn, Sept 20, 28; m 58, Harriet Willingham; c Bradford & Lee. *Educ:* Univ Minn, BA, 50, MA, 52, PhD(physics), 56. *Prof Exp:* Res assoc, Univ Minn, 56-57; exp physicist, Knolls Atomic Power Lab, Gen Elec Co, 57-58. *Concurrent Pos:* Mem, Comn on Atomic Masses & Fundamental Constants, Int Union Pure & Appl Physics, 66-72, Comn on Atomic Weights, 71-85 & secy, 72-75. *Mem:* AAAS; fel Am Phys Soc; Am Vacuum Soc; Am Asn Physics Teachers. *Res:* Mass spectroscopy; measurement of atomic masses; nuclear binding energy; neutron cross-section measurements. *Mailing Add:* Sch Physics & Astron 116 Church St SE Minneapolis MN 55455. *E-Mail:* cork@maroon.tc.umn.edu

JOHNSON, WALTER HUDSON, NEURAL NETWORKS, ROBOTICS. *Current Pos:* PROF PHYSICS & CHMN, DEPT PHYSICS, SUFFOLK UNIV, 73- *Personal Data:* b Fayetteville, NC, Dec 21, 42; m 77, Lea A Nemanich; c Erin & Adam. *Educ:* Rice Univ, BA, 65; Harvard Univ, MS, 67, PhD(physics), 73. *Concurrent Pos:* Researcher high energy physics, Harvard Univ, 73-79. *Mem:* Int Neural Network Soc; Inst Elec & Electronics Engrs; Am Phys Soc. *Res:* Neural networks, image processing, autoware media, robot control; ellipsometry, detection of environmental gases; high energy particle physics; high pressure liquids, propagation of ultrasonic waves. *Mailing Add:* 59 Jerusalem Rd Dr Cohasset MA 02025. *Fax:* 617-573-8513; *E-Mail:* w.john@acad.suffolk.edu

JOHNSON, WALTER K, ENVIRONMENTAL & CIVIL ENGINEERING. *Current Pos:* RETIRED. *Personal Data:* b Minneapolis, Minn, Aug 28, 23; m 50, Geneva L Olson; c Kristine, Karen & Konstance. *Educ:* Univ Minn, BCE, 48, MSCE, 51, PhD(sanit eng), 63; Am Acad Environ Eng, dipl, 65. *Honors & Awards:* Radebaugh Award, Cent States Water Pollution Control Asn, 65. *Prof Exp:* Civil engr, Greeley & Hansen, Consult Engrs, 48-49; asst, Univ Minn, 49-51; sanit engr, Infilco, Inc, Ariz, 51-52 & Toltz, King, Duvall & Anderson, Consult Engrs, Minn, 52-55; lectr civil eng, Univ Minn, Minneapolis, 55-63, from asst prof to prof, 63-75; dir planning, Metro Waste Control Comn, St Paul, 75-89. *Concurrent Pos:* Environ Protection Agency res fel, Brit Water Pollution Res Lab, Stevenage, Eng, 70. *Mem:* Am Soc Civil Engrs; Am Acad Environ Eng; Am Water Works Asn; Water Environ Asn. *Res:* Biological treatment of waste waters and the removal of nitrogen and phosphorus from waste waters by biological and chemical means. *Mailing Add:* 5321 29th Ave S Minneapolis MN 55417

JOHNSON, WALTER LEE, agronomy; deceased, see previous edition for last biography

JOHNSON, WALTER RICHARD, PHYSICS. *Current Pos:* from asst prof to assoc prof, 58-67, PROF PHYSICS, UNIV NOTRE DAME, 67- *Personal Data:* b Richmond, Va, Feb 25, 29; m 52. *Educ:* Univ Mich, BSE, 52, MS, 53, PhD(physics), 58. *Prof Exp:* Instr physics, Univ Mich, 57-58. *Mem:* Am Physics Soc. *Res:* Hydrodynamics; atomic physics; quantum electrodynamics. *Mailing Add:* Dept Physics Univ Notre Dame Notre Dame IN 46556

JOHNSON, WALTER ROLAND, JET ENGINE TECHNOLOGIES, ELECTRONICS. *Current Pos:* METALLURGIST & CONSULT, 69- *Personal Data:* b Boston, Mass, Feb 10, 27; m 62, Janet L Campbell; c Meryl A, Leah K & Christa H. *Educ:* Mass Inst Technol, BS, 58. *Prof Exp:* Metallurgist, Missile Systs Div, Raytheon Co, 58-69. *Concurrent Pos:* Chmn, QUBE Resources. *Mem:* Am Soc Metals. *Res:* Aerospace; electronics; metallurgy. *Mailing Add:* 35 Norseman Ave Gloucester MA 01930. *E-Mail:* wjohnson@user1.channel1.com; *Website:* http://wwv.channel1.com/metallurgist/

JOHNSON, WARREN THURSTON, entomology, plant pathology; deceased, see previous edition for last biography

JOHNSON, WARREN VICTOR, BIOCHEMISTRY. *Current Pos:* asst prof chem, molecular biol & biochem, 87-92, ASSOC PROF BIOCHEM & MOLECULAR BIOL, UNIV WIS-GREENBAY, 92- *Personal Data:* b Duluth, Minn, Sept 26, 51; m 73; c 3. *Educ:* Univ Minn, Duluth, BA, 73; Univ Wis-Milwaukee, MS, 78; Univ Iowa, PhD(biochem), 84. *Prof Exp:* Teacher sci & math, St Michael's Sch, Duluth, Minn, 74-75 & Strandquist High Sch, Minn, 75-76; teaching asst chem, Univ Wis-Milwaukee, 76-78; res asst biochem, Univ Iowa, 78-84; postdoctoral fel, Revlon Biotech Res Ctr, Rockville, Md, 84-86; postdoctoral assoc biochem, Univ Minn, Duluth, 86-87. *Mem:* Am Soc Biochem & Molecular Biol; Am Chem Soc. *Res:*

Structure, function and gene of the developmentally regulated glycoprotein fetuin; role of the carbohydrated moieties of glycoproteins; proteolytic processing; molecular diagnosis of phylogenetic relationships. *Mailing Add:* Univ Wis 2420 Nicolet Dr Green Bay WI 54311-7001. *E-Mail:* johnsonw@uwgb.edu

JOHNSON, WARREN W, pathology, for more information see previous edition

JOHNSON, WAYNE DOUGLAS, ELECTRON TRANSPORT. *Current Pos:* PROJ LEADER, DOW CHEM CO, 79- *Personal Data:* m 72; c 3. *Educ:* Lebanon Valley Col, BS, 73; Univ Del, PhD(physics), 78. *Prof Exp:* Res fel, Univ Pa, 78-79. *Mem:* Am Phys Soc. *Res:* Electron transport. *Mailing Add:* New Ventures Dow N Am 100 Larkin Ctr Midland MI 48674

JOHNSON, WAYNE JON, AUTOMOTIVE ENGINEERING. *Current Pos:* sr res engr, Ford Motor Co, 69-73, prin res eng assoc, Dept Physics, 73-82, prin staff engr, Electronic Syst Dept, 82-87, MGR, CONTROL SYST DEPT, FORD MOTOR CO, 87- *Personal Data:* b Elroy, Wis, May 14, 39; m 64; c 3. *Educ:* Univ Wis, BS, 61, MS, 62, PhD(elec eng), 68. *Prof Exp:* Engr, Res Dept, Collins Radio Co, Cedar Rapids, 60 & 61, res engr, 62-64; sr res engr, Lab di Cibernetica, Naples, Italy, 68-69. *Mem:* Inst Elec & Electronics Engrs; Soc Automotive Engrs; Eng Soc Detroit. *Res:* Nonlinear wave propagation; superconducting devices; semiconductor device physics; combustion research on internal combustion engines; plasma probing techniques; electromagnetic interference phenomena; networking and distributed computing techniques applied to the automobile; dynamic control systems. *Mailing Add:* Mgr Ford Motor Co Mail Drop 1170 Sci Res Lab PO Box 2053 Dearborn MI 48121

JOHNSON, WAYNE ORRIN, AGRICULTURAL CHEMISTRY. *Current Pos:* Group leader, 69-76, mgr res farms & liaison activ, 76-79, mgr hybrid crops, 79-83, pres, Rohm & Haas Seeds, 83-85, RES MGT BIOCIDES & SPEC POLYMERS, AGR PROD RES, AGR CHEM, ROHM & HAAS CO, 85- *Personal Data:* b Valley City, NDak, May 26, 42; m 65; c 1. *Educ:* Concordia Col, BA, 64; Mich State Univ, MS, 66; Univ Ore, PhD(org chem), 69. *Mem:* Am Chem Soc; Plant Growth Regulator Working Group; Am Seed Trade Asn. *Res:* Synthetic structure-activity chemistry related to biological sciences, especially pesticidal research; microbiology; polymer chemistry. *Mailing Add:* 4 Beth Dr Lower Gwynedd PA 19002-1928

JOHNSON, WENDEL J, ANIMAL ECOLOGY, ZOOGEOGRAPHY. *Current Pos:* From asst prof to assoc prof, 69-86, PROF BIOL, UNIV WIS CTR-MARINETTE, 86- *Personal Data:* b Oak Park, Ill, July 13, 41; m 82; c 3. *Educ:* Mich State Univ, BS, 63, MS, 65; Purdue Univ, PhD(mammalian ecol), 69. *Concurrent Pos:* Sigma Xi grant-in-aid, 64, 70; Wis Alumni Res Found fel, 70. *Mem:* AAAS; Ecol Soc Am; Am Soc Mammal. *Res:* Zoogeographical analysis of reptiles and amphibians in the Northern Peninsula of Michigan; population dynamics of small mammals in Isle Royale National Park; population regulation in small mammals; environmental problems from human numbers; Green Bay lampreys. *Mailing Add:* Dept Biol Sci Univ Wis Ctr Syst 750 Bayshore Marinette WI 54143

JOHNSON, WHITNEY LARSEN, STATISTICS, COMPUTER SCIENCE. *Current Pos:* dir mgt info serv, 72-86, dir, 86-92, EMER PROF DATA & TEL SYSTS, NORTHERN MICH UNIV, 92- *Personal Data:* b Brigham City, Utah, July 11, 27; m 54; c 11. *Educ:* Utah State Univ, BS, 54; Univ Minn, Minneapolis, MS, 57. *Prof Exp:* Assoc prof statist, Va Polytech Inst & State Univ, 62-68; adminr automated data processing systs, State Coun Higher Educ, Va, 69-72. *Concurrent Pos:* Coordr comput ctr, Va Polytech Inst & State Univ, 62-64 & dir, 64-68. *Mem:* Am Statist Asn; Asn Comput Mach; Int Asn Comput Educ. *Res:* Moments of serial correlation coefficients and computing networks on regional and statewide basis; management information for education. *Mailing Add:* 313 Lakewood Lane Marquette IN 49855

JOHNSON, WILEY CARROLL, JR, PLANT BREEDING. *Current Pos:* assoc prof, 57-69, PROF PLANT BREEDING, AUBURN UNIV, 69- *Personal Data:* b Asheville, NC, Jan 1, 30; m 51; c 2. *Educ:* Wake Forest Col, BS, 49; NC State Col, BS, 51, MS, 53; Cornell Univ, PhD(plant breeding), 56. *Prof Exp:* Res agronomist, Cornell Univ, 56-57. *Mem:* Am Soc Agron; Crop Sci Soc Am; Am Genetics Asn. *Res:* Genetics and breeding of clovers. *Mailing Add:* Coastal Plain Exp Sta PO Box 748 Tifton GA 31793-0748

JOHNSON, WILLIAM, MICROBIOLOGY. *Current Pos:* asst prof microbiol, 70-74, assoc prof, 74-80, PROF MICROBIOL, COL MED, UNIV IOWA, 80- *Personal Data:* b Boston, Mass, Oct 6, 41; m 65; c 3. *Educ:* Marietta Col, BS, 63; Miami Univ, MS, 65; Rutgers Univ, PhD(microbiol), 68. *Prof Exp:* Nat Acad Sci-Nat Res Coun fel, Army Biol Res Ctr, Ft Detrick, Md, 68-70. *Mem:* AAAS; Am Soc Microbiol; NY Acad Sci; Am Acad Microbiol. *Res:* Pathogenic microbiology; microbial toxins. *Mailing Add:* Dept Microbiol Univ Iowa Col Med 3403 Bowen Sci Iowa City IA 52242-1109

JOHNSON, WILLIAM ALEXANDER, POULTRY SCIENCE. *Current Pos:* from asst prof to assoc prof poultry breeding, 52-65, PROF POULTRY BREEDING, LA STATE UNIV, BATON ROUGE, 65-, HEAD DEPT, 81- *Personal Data:* b Ennis, Tex, June 22, 22; m 46; c 2. *Educ:* La State Univ, BS, 43, MS, 47; Univ Minn, PhD(poultry breeding), 52. *Prof Exp:* Instr poultry husb, La State Univ, 47-49, asst, Univ Minn, 49-52. *Mem:* Poultry Sci Asn; World Poultry Sci Asn; Am Genetics Asn; Sigma Xi; Nat Asn Cols & Teachers Agr. *Res:* Poultry breeding and genetics; environmental physiology; catfish breeding and genetics. *Mailing Add:* 8455 Sage Hill Rd St Francisville LA 70775-4725

JOHNSON, WILLIAM BOWIE, HALL EFFECT, ELECTRONIC BAND STRUCTURE. *Current Pos:* SR PHYSICIST PHYSICS, LAB PHYS SCI, 82- *Personal Data:* b Washington, DC, Sept 25, 54; m 87; c 1. *Educ:* George Mason Univ, BS, 76; Univ Md, MS, 78, PhD(physics), 82. *Mem:* Am Phys Soc; Inst Elec & Electronics Engrs. *Res:* Characterization of the electrical properties of materials at low temperatures and high magnetic fields; materials under development include semimagnetic semiconductors, quasicrystals, silicon carbide, gallium arsenide and rare earth semiconductors. *Mailing Add:* 1730 Tarrytown Ave Crofton MD 21114

JOHNSON, WILLIAM BUHMANN, MATHEMATICAL ANALYSIS. *Current Pos:* prof, 84-89, DISTINGUISHED PROF MATH, TEX A&M UNIV, 89-, A G & M E OWN CHAIR, 84- *Personal Data:* b Palo Alto, Calif, Dec 5, 44; m 68, Janet Lund; c Darren & Tamar. *Educ:* Southern Methodist Univ, BA, 66; Iowa State Univ, PhD(math), 69. *Prof Exp:* Asst prof math, Univ Houston, 69-71; from asst prof to prof, Ohio State Univ, 71-84. *Concurrent Pos:* Vis prof math, Univ Tex, Austin, 75 & Tex A&M Univ, College Station, 81; fel, Inst Advan Studies, Hebrew Univ, Jerusalem, 77-78; ed, Trans Am Math Soc, 82-86, Ill J Math, 87-93, Geometric & Functional Anal, 91-, positivity, 96- *Mem:* Am Math Soc; Math Asn Am. *Res:* Functional analysis; isomorphic theory of Banach spaces; probability theory. *Mailing Add:* Dept Math Tex A&M Univ College Station TX 77843. *E-Mail:* johnson@math.tamu.edu

JOHNSON, WILLIAM CONE, INTERNAL MEDICINE. *Current Pos:* MED DIR RESPIRATORY THER SERV & PULMONARY FUNCTION LABS, WTEX MED CTR HOSP, ABILENE, 70- *Personal Data:* b Eastland, Tex, Nov 20, 26; m 56; c 3. *Educ:* NTex State Univ, BS, 49; Univ Tex, MD, 54; Am Bd Internal Med, dipl, 63; Am Bd Pulmonary Dis, dipl, 68. *Prof Exp:* From intern to chief resident, John Sealy Hosp, Univ Tex Hosps, 54-58; chief med serv, 1604th USAF Hosp, 58-60, pulmonologist, Wilford Hall Hosp, Aerospace Med Div, Lackland AFB, Tex, 60-61, chief pulmonary & infectious dis serv, 61-63; med dir inhalation ther serv, Scott & White Mem Hosp, Temple, Tex, 63-65, dir pulmonary physiol labs, 63-68; dir respiratory ther serv & pulmonary physiol labs, Hendrick Mem Hosp, Abilene, 68-69; clin asst prof med, Univ Tex Health Sci Ctr, Dallas, 69- *Concurrent Pos:* Consult, Sect Clin Physiol, Scott & White Clin, Temple, 63-68, inhalation ther serv, Scott & White Mem Hosp, 65-68; med examr, Fed Aviation Agency, 66-; consult, Vet Admin Hosps, 65-, WTex Med Ctr Hosp, 68-, Hendrick Mem Hosp, Abilene, 68-69 & 70- & Shannon WTex Mem Hosp, San Angelo, 69; mem bd dirs, WTex Med Ctr Res Found, 69; med dir, Work Eval & Rehab Unit, Methodist Hosp Dallas, 69-70; med dir, respiratory ther serv, Cox Mem Hosp, Abilene, 70-75, Rolling Plains Mem Hosp, Sweetwater, 70-, Root Mem Hosp, Colorado City, Tex, 70, Med Ctr Hosp, Big Spring, 73-74, Shepperd Mem Hosp, Burnet, Tex, 76-80, Morris Mem Hosp, Coleman, Tex, 80-; clin asst prof med, Univ Tex, Southwestern Med Sch Dallas, 69-; clin assoc prof med, Tex Tech Univ, Sch Med, 74- *Mem:* AAAS; Am Asn Inhalation Therapists; fel Am Col Chest Physicians; fel Am Col Physicians; Am Fedn Clin Res. *Res:* Pulmonary physiology. *Mailing Add:* 6250 Reg Plaza Suite 1030 Abilene TX 79606-5223

JOHNSON, WILLIAM CRAIG, PHASE TRANSFORMATIONS. *Current Pos:* PROF MAT SCI, UNIV VA, 93- *Personal Data:* b Evergreen Park, Ill, Nov 4, 54; m, Lisa Ann Dole; c Hannah, Ian & Norah. *Educ:* Mich Technol Univ, BS, 76, MS, 78, PhD(metall eng), 80. *Honors & Awards:* Robert Lansing Hardy Gold Medal, Metall Soc, Am Inst Mining Metall & Petrol Engrs, 83; Bradley Stoughten Outstanding Young Teacher, Am Soc Metals, 88, Henry Marion Howe Award, 88. *Prof Exp:* Prof mat sci, Carnegie Mellon Univ, 82-93. *Concurrent Pos:* Guest prof metall physics, Tech Univ Berlin, 90-91. *Mem:* Am Soc Metals Int; Metall Soc; AAAS. *Res:* Influence of stress on phase transformations, diffusion and thermodynamics, especially in crystalline systems. *Mailing Add:* Dept Med Sci Thornton Hall Univ Va Charlottesville VA 22903-2442. *Fax:* 804-982-5799; *E-Mail:* wcjzc@virginia.edu

JOHNSON, WILLIAM E, JR, MEDICAL ENTOMOLOGY. *Current Pos:* RETIRED. *Personal Data:* b Plano, Tex, July 20, 30; m 53; c 3. *Educ:* Huston-Tillotson Col, BS, 51; Univ Okla, MS, 53, PhD(zool), 61. *Prof Exp:* Instr biol, Tuskegee Inst, 55-57; mus asst, Univ Okla, 57-60; chmn div sci & math, Albany State Col, 60-69; asst vpres acad affairs, Ala State Univ, 69-74, dean grad studies, 74-80, prof biol, 69-80; at Dept Vet Sci, Tuskegee Inst, 80-93. *Mem:* Am Mosquito Control Asn. *Res:* Mosquito ecology. *Mailing Add:* 3348 W Tuskegee Circle Montgomery AL 36108

JOHNSON, WILLIAM EVERETT, PHARMACOLOGY. *Current Pos:* assoc prof, 65-72, PROF PHARMACOL, COL PHARM, WASH STATE UNIV, 72- *Personal Data:* b Wallowa, Ore, Oct 22, 21; m 46; c 4. *Educ:* Wash State Univ, BS, 51, MS, 53, PhD(pharmacol), 58. *Prof Exp:* From instr to asst prof pharm, Col Pharm, Univ Wyo, 53-58, from assoc prof to prof pharmacol, 58-65. *Res:* Pharmacology of the cardiovascular system and mechanism of action of teratogens. *Mailing Add:* 1661 S Seacrest Lane Coupeville WA 98239-9634

JOHNSON, WILLIAM HILTON, QUATERNARY GEOLOGY. *Current Pos:* From instr to assoc prof, 68-87, PROF GEOL, UNIV ILL, URBANA, 87- *Personal Data:* b Indianapolis, Ind, Feb 14, 35; m 56; c 3. *Educ:* Earlham Col, AB, 56; Univ Ill, MS, 61, PhD(geol), 62. *Concurrent Pos:* Partic, Ill State Geol Surv. *Mem:* Geol Soc Am; Sigma Xi; Nat Asn Geol Teachers; Am Quaternary Asn. *Res:* Sedimentology and stratigraphy of Pleistocene deposits and glacial geology; relict Pleistocene periglacial forms; geomorphology. *Mailing Add:* Dept Geol Univ Ill 1301 W Green St Urbana IL 61801-2919

JOHNSON, WILLIAM HOWARD, AGRICULTURAL ENGINEERING. *Current Pos:* RETIRED. *Personal Data:* b Sidney, Ohio, Sept 3, 22; m 43, Wyoma J Swift; c Lawrence A, Cheri E (Graham) & Dana S (Heston). *Educ:* Ohio State Univ, BS, 48, MS, 53; Mich State Univ, PhD(agr eng), 60. *Prof Exp:* From instr to prof agr eng, Ohio Agr Res & Develop Ctr, assoc chmn dept, 53-68, actg chmn dept, 68-69; vis scientist & lectr, Tex A&M Univ, 69-70; prof agr eng & head dept, Kans State Univ, 70-81, dir, Eng Exp Sta, 81-87. *Concurrent Pos:* Agr eng consult, 57- *Mem:* Fel Am Soc Agr Engrs (pres, 86-87). *Res:* Power and machinery area of agricultural engineering; determination of functional requirements and design; efficiency of harvesting and tillage machine components. *Mailing Add:* 1532 Williamburg Dr Manhattan KS 66503

JOHNSON, WILLIAM HUGH, CROP PROCESS ENGINEERING, SYSTEM DESIGN AND ANALYSIS. *Current Pos:* Res instr, 56-61, from asst prof to prof agr eng, 61-83, ASST DIR, NC AGR RES SERV, NC STATE UNIV, 83- *Personal Data:* b Fayetteville, NC, Sept 14, 32; m 58, Glenda Noble; c William C & Richard C. *Educ:* NC State Univ, BS, 54, MS, 56, PhD(agr eng), 61. *Honors & Awards:* Philip Morris Distinguished Achievement in Tobacco Sci, 73. *Concurrent Pos:* Partic & spec reporter, Fourth Int Tobacco Sci Cong, Athens, 66, Fifth Int Tobacco Sci Cong, Hamburg, 70; consult, Indian Inst Technol, Ford Found Proj, Kharagpur, India, 66. *Mem:* Am Soc Agr Engrs; Sigma Xi. *Res:* Bioengineering of plant materials; energy and mass transfer relations during processing; physical, chemical and enzymatic changes in response to dynamic process variables; health-related modifications of tobacco; systems engineering; biological engineering; solar and heat energy recovery systems engineering. *Mailing Add:* PO Box 7625 Raleigh NC 27695-7625. *Fax:* 919-515-2717; *E-Mail:* wjohnson@cals1.cals.ncsu.edu

JOHNSON, WILLIAM JACOB, inorganic chemistry, for more information see previous edition

JOHNSON, WILLIAM JOSEPH, IMMUNOLOGY. *Current Pos:* dir res develop, 88-91, dir proj acquisition planning & mgt, 91-93, SR DIR PROJ MGT, G D SEARLE, 93- *Personal Data:* b Junction City, Kans, Feb 20, 54. *Educ:* Mankato State Univ, BA, 76; Univ Wis, MS, 79, PhD(microbiol), 80. *Honors & Awards:* Fel, Leukemia Soc, 82. *Prof Exp:* Fel macroface cell biol, Duke Univ, 80-82, asst med res prof, 82-84; assoc sr investr immunol, Smith Kline, 84-87, sr investr immunol, 87-88. *Mem:* Am Soc Immunologists. *Mailing Add:* G D Searle & Co 4901 Searle Pkwy A2E Skokie IL 60077-2980. *Fax:* 847-982-4690

JOHNSON, WILLIAM K, ORGANIC CHEMISTRY. *Current Pos:* CONSULT, 87- *Personal Data:* b Kalamazoo, Mich, Jan 4, 27; m 52; c 1. *Educ:* Univ Mich, BS, 50, MS, 51, PhD(pharm chem), 54. *Prof Exp:* Chemist res & eng div, Monsanto Co, 53-60, proj mgr, Org Develop Dept, 60-65, mgr mkt res, Org Div, 65-67, mgr commercial develop plasticizers & gen chem, 67-69, mgr technol gen chem, 69-71, dir res & commercial develop, Process Chem Group, Monsanto Indust Chem Co, 71-76, mgr markets & prod, 76-79, mgr mkt res & planning, Monsanto Intermediates Co, 79-82; mgr mkt res & planning, SRI Int, 83-85; dir petrochemicals, Catalytica Assocs, 85-87. *Mem:* Am Chem Soc; Commercial Develop Asn; Ger Chem Soc; Chem Mkt Res Asn. *Res:* Organometallics and organic synthesis; intermediates and fine chemicals. *Mailing Add:* 7356 Via Laguna San Jose CA 95135-1341

JOHNSON, WILLIAM LAWRENCE, RUMINANT NUTRITION, FORAGE UTILIZATION. *Current Pos:* From asst prof to assoc prof, 66-82, PROF ANIMAL SCI, NC STATE UNIV, 82- *Personal Data:* b Keene, NH, Aug 28, 36; m 58, 84, Thais A Bellomo; c Maya (Bellomo), Laisa (Bellomo), Warren, Susan & Steven. *Educ:* Univ NH, BS, 58; Cornell Univ, MS, 64, PhD(dairy cattle nutrit), 66. *Concurrent Pos:* Dairy husb res specialist, Nat Agrarian Univ, La Molina, Peru, 66-69, co-leader forage & animal nutrit prog, Agr Mission to Peru, 70-73; prin investr small ruminants collab res, Indonesia, Morocco & Brazil, 78-88; res & inst develop adv, Nat Inst for Agr Res, Lima, Peru, 88-; vis scientist, Empresa Brasileira de Pesquisa Agropecuaria, Brazil, 92; campus coordr, Ctr World Environ & Syst Develop, Duke, NC State Univ & Univ NC, 93- *Mem:* Am Soc Animal Sci; Int Goat Asn. *Res:* Factors influencing utilization of forages, and roughage by products, including tropical feedstuffs, by cattle, sheep and goats; sustainability of livestock-based agriculture in tropical ecosystems. *Mailing Add:* Dept Animal Sci NC State Univ Raleigh NC 27695-7621. *Fax:* 919-515-7780

JOHNSON, WILLIAM LEWIS, SOLID STATE PHYSICS. *Current Pos:* PROF PHYSICS & CHMN DEPT, WESTMINSTER COL, PA, 71- *Personal Data:* b Bryan, Tex, July 6, 40; m 63; c 1. *Educ:* Univ Southern Miss, BA, 62; Naval Postgrad Sch, MS, 66, PhD(physics), 69. *Prof Exp:* Instr physics, Naval Postgrad Sch, 63-69; res assoc, Univ Ill, 69-71. *Mem:* Am Phys Soc; Am Asn Physics Teachers; Sigma Xi. *Res:* Critical point phenomena; laboratory automation. *Mailing Add:* Dept Physics Westminster Col New Wilmington PA 16172

JOHNSON, WILLIAM LEWIS, SOLID STATE PHYSICS, MATERIALS SCIENCE. *Current Pos:* from asst prof to prof mat sci, 77-88, RUBEN & DONNA METTLER PROF ENG & APPL SCI, CALIF INST TECHNOL, 89- *Personal Data:* b Bowling Green, Ohio, July 26, 48; m 84; c Jessica. *Educ:* Hamilton Col, BA, 70; Calif Inst Technol, PhD(appl physics), 74. *Honors & Awards:* Hume Rothery Award, Am Metals Soc & Am Inst Mech Engrs, 95; Gold Medal, Int Symp Mech Alloyed Nancrystalline & Amorphous Metals, 95. *Prof Exp:* Fel appl physics, Calif Inst Technol, 74-75; fel, T J Watson Res Ctr, IBM Corp, 75-77. *Concurrent Pos:* Consult, Jet Propulsion Lab, Calif Inst Technol, Pasadena, 80-, Gen Motors, 83-, Hughes Res Labs, 84-, Lawrence Livermore Lab, 84-92; Alexander von Humbolt sr scientist award, 88. *Mem:* Am Phys Soc; AAAS; Am Soc Metals; Mat Res Soc. *Res:* Low temperature physics; superconductivity; amorphous materials; bulk metallic glasses; properties of metastable metallic materials. *Mailing Add:* Keck Lab Eng Calif Inst Technol Pasadena CA 91125. *Fax:* 626-795-6132; *E-Mail:* wlj@yperfine.caltech.edu

JOHNSON, WILLIAM RANDOLPH, JR, POLYMER CHEMISTRY, THEORETICAL CHEMISTRY. *Current Pos:* ADJ PROF CHEM, HAMPDEN-SYDNEY COL, 94- *Personal Data:* b Oxford, NC, July 25, 30; m 54; c 3. *Educ:* NC Col Durham, BS, 50; Univ Notre Dame, MS, 52; Univ Pa, PhD(chem), 58. *Prof Exp:* Instr, Prairie View A&M Col, 52-53; prof, Fla A&M Univ, 58-61; chemist, W R Grace & Co, 61-63; chemist, Philip Morris Ops Ctr, 63-75, mgr, Chem Res Div, 75-79, mgr spec affairs, 81-90, sr scientist, 90-94. *Concurrent Pos:* Adj prof chem, 63-73, exec in residence, Va Union Univ, 79-81. *Res:* Polymer synthesis; smoke chemistry; smoke formation mechanisms; pyrolysis mechanisms. *Mailing Add:* 1001 Spottswood Rd Richmond VA 23220

JOHNSON, WILLIAM ROBERT, MATERIALS SCIENCE. *Current Pos:* SR STAFF SCIENTIST, GEN ATOMICS, 90- *Personal Data:* b Buffalo, Okla, Sept 24, 39; m 61; c 2. *Educ:* San Jose State Col, BS, 64; Stanford Univ, MS, 67, PhD(mat sci), 69. *Prof Exp:* Scientist & prod mgr vacuum metallization, St Clair-Field Inc, Mt View, Calif, 69-70; assoc scientist, General Atomics, 70-71, staff assoc, 71-72, sr engr, 72-73, staff engr, 73-81, mgr mats eval, 81-90. *Mem:* Am Soc Metals. *Res:* Structure of materials; mechanical behavior of materials (fracture, creep and stress rupture); environmental effects on materials. *Mailing Add:* 12243 Riesling Ct San Diego CA 92131

JOHNSON, WILLIAM S(TANLEY), MECHANICAL & ENVIRONMENTAL ENGINEERING. *Current Pos:* from asst prof to assoc prof, 67-77, PROF MECH ENG, UNIV TENN, 77- *Personal Data:* b Camden, Tenn, Dec 9, 39; m 67, Jacquelyn Smith; c Steve & Kathryn. *Educ:* Univ Tenn, Knoxville, BS, 61; Clemson Univ, MS, 65, PhD(eng), 67. *Prof Exp:* Asst design engr, Pratt & Whitney Aircraft Div, United Aircraft Corp, 61-62. *Mem:* Am Soc Mech Engrs; Am Soc Heating Vent & Air Conditioning Engrs; Am Soc Eng Educ. *Res:* Application of pulse-jet flow in low area ratio ejectors; determination of velocity characteristics of two-dimensional fluid jets; boundary layer control on submarine surfaces; energy conservation analysis in buildings; heat pump evaluations. *Mailing Add:* Dept Mech & Aerospace Eng Univ Tenn Knoxville TN 37996-2210. *Fax:* 423-974-5274; *E-Mail:* wsjohnson@utk.edu

JOHNSON, WILLIAM SUMMER, organic chemistry; deceased, see previous edition for last biography

JOHNSON, WILLIAM W, GEOPHYSICS. *Current Pos:* CONSULT, 85- *Personal Data:* b Provo, Utah, July 11, 34; m 69; c 2. *Educ:* Brigham Young Univ, BS, 56; Univ Utah, MS, 58; Univ Pittsburgh, PhD(geophys), 65. *Prof Exp:* Sr res scientist, Sinclair Oil Corp, 65-69; prin res geophysicist, Atlantic Richfield Co, 69-85. *Concurrent Pos:* Res assoc, Lamont-Doherty Geol Observ, Columbia Univ, 66-67. *Mem:* AAAS; Soc Explor Geophysicists. *Res:* Propagation of elastic waves in anisotropic media; geological interpretation of gravity and magnetic data; seismic wave propagation. *Mailing Add:* 707 Parkview Circle Richardson TX 75080

JOHNSON, WILLIAM WAYNE, GENETICS. *Current Pos:* asst prof, 63-68, ASSOC PROF BIOL, UNIV NMEX, 68- *Personal Data:* b Minneapolis, Minn, Oct 12, 34. *Educ:* Univ Minn, BS, 57, MS, 59, PhD(zool), 63. *Prof Exp:* Interim asst prof biol, Univ Fla, 62-63. *Mem:* AAAS; Genetics Soc Am; Am Inst Biol Sci; Sigma Xi. *Res:* Experimental population genetics of Drosophila. *Mailing Add:* Dept Biol Univ NMex Main Campus 1 University Campus Albuquerque NM 87131-0001

JOHNSON, WILLIS HUGH, zoology; deceased, see previous edition for last biography

JOHNSON, WOODROW E, COMPUTER SCIENCE. *Current Pos:* CONSULT, COMPUT CODE CONSULTS, 73- *Personal Data:* b Chisolm, Minn, Feb 28, 25; m 46; c 5. *Educ:* Univ Minn, BS, 50. *Prof Exp:* Res engr, High Speed Flight Sta, Nat Adv Comt Aeronaut, 51-53; staff mem, Los Alamos Sci Lab, 53-58; staff mem, Gen Atomic Div, Gen Dynamics Corp, 58-59; staff mem, Los Alamos Sci Lab, 59-60; staff mem, Gen Atomic Div, Gen Dynamics Corp, 60-65; prin res scientist, Honeywell Inc, 65-67; Systs, Sci & Software, 67-71 & Sci Applns Inc, 71-73. *Mem:* Am Phys Soc; Am Sci Affiliation; *Res:* Use of high speed computers for the numerical treatment of radiation flow, neutronics and hydrodynamics; one, two and three dimensional hydrodynamic, strength of materials and radiation codes to solve problems in high energy fluid dynamics. *Mailing Add:* 114 Brompton Rd Garden City NY 11530

JOHNSON, WOODROW ELDRED, PHYSICS. *Current Pos:* RETIRED. *Personal Data:* b Forest Lake, Minn, Oct 22, 17; m 42; c 4. *Educ:* Hamline Univ, BS, 37; Brown Univ, MS, 39, PhD(physics), 42. *Hon Degrees:* DS, Hamline Univ, 61. *Prof Exp:* Asst, Brown Univ, 37-40; from instr to asst prof physics, Syracuse Univ, 41-44, asst prof, 46-47; sr physicist, Tenn Eastman Corp, 44-46 & Manhattan Proj, Oak Ridge Nat Lab, 47-49; sect mgr, Bettis Atomic Power Lab, Westinghouse Corp, 49-51, mgr tech opers, Prototype Reactor Facil, Idaho, 51-53, asst to dir develop, 53-54, corp tech consult, Matahorn Proj, Princeton Univ, 54, corp mem, Indust Atomic Power Study Group, 54-55, proj mgr, Pa Adv Reactor Proj, Atomic Power Dept, 55-59, dir projs, 59-61, gen mgr, 61-64, gen mgr, Astronuclear Lab, 64-68, corp vpres, 67-85, vpres & gen mgr, Astronuclear-Underseas Div, 68-71, vpres & gen mgr, Transp Div, 71-85. *Mem:* Nat Acad Eng; Inst Elec & Electronics Engrs; Am Nuclear Soc; Nat Asn Mfg; Am Phys Soc. *Res:* Photoelectricity; electron diffraction; physics of thin metallic films; effect of radiation on solids. *Mailing Add:* 114 Brompton Rd Garden City NY 11530

JOHNSON-LUSSENBURG, CHRISTINE MARGARET, VIROLOGY, MOLECULAR BIOLOGY. *Current Pos:* RETIRED. *Personal Data:* b Hawkesbury, Ont, Jan 29, 31; m 53, 72; c 6. *Educ:* McGill Univ, BSc, 52, MSc, 53; Univ Ottawa, PhD, 67. *Prof Exp:* Asst prof microbiol, Univ Ottawa, 67-78, assoc prof, 78-93. *Mem:* Can Soc Microbiologists; Am Soc Microbiol. *Res:* Structural and antigenic studies of components involved in virus replication, including myxoviruses, herpesvirus and coronavirus. *Mailing Add:* 1928 Oakdean Crescent Gloucester ON K1J 6H3 Can

JOHNSON-WINEGAR, ANNA, MICROBIAL TOXINS. *Current Pos:* microbiologist, 85-90, SCI ADMINR, US ARMY MED MAT DEVELOP ACTIV, 90- *Personal Data:* b Frederick, Md, May 27, 45; m 80. *Educ:* Hood Col, BA, 76; Catholic Univ Am, MS, 79, PhD(microbiol), 81. *Prof Exp:* Med technician res, US Army Med Res Inst Infectious Dis, 66-76, microbiologist, 76-85. *Concurrent Pos:* Reviewer, Appl Environ Microbiol, 83-; mem, Comt on Status of Women Microbiologists & Fed Orgn Prof Women, 83-; guest lectr var insts. *Mem:* Fel Am Soc Microbiologists; AAAS; Int Soc Toxinol; NY Acad Sci; Sigma Xi. *Res:* Purification and biochemical analysis of bacterial toxins; immunology of toxin-derived components; pathogenesis of toxins; fermentation techniques; animal models; genetic control of toxin production. *Mailing Add:* 7184 Stillwater Ct Frederick MD 21702-9491

JOHNSON-WINT, BARBARA PAULE, MORPHOGENESIS, CELL INTERACTIONS. *Current Pos:* ASST PROF, SCH MED, HARVARD UNIV, 85- *Educ:* Mich State Univ, PhD(zool), 76. *Mailing Add:* 4307 Carol Ave Cortland IL 60112

JOHNSTON, A SIDNEY, NUCLEAR PHYSICS. *Current Pos:* SR PATENT ATTY, DIGITAL EQUIP CORP, 78- *Personal Data:* b Hinton, WVa, Apr 4, 37. *Educ:* Va Polytech Inst, BS, 59; Carnegie-Mellon Univ, MS, 61, PhD(physics), 65; Chicago Kent Col Law, JD, 78. *Prof Exp:* Sr scientist physics, Westinghouse Astronuclear, 65-68; asst prof, Pratt Inst, 68-74; mem staff, Dept Nuclear Med, Michael Reese Hosp, 74-78. *Concurrent Pos:* Private law pract, 78- *Mem:* AAAS; Am Phys Soc. *Res:* Nuclear engineering; solid state physics; science and society. *Mailing Add:* 51 Quaboag Rd Acton MA 01720

JOHNSTON, ALAN ROBERT, OPTICAL PHYSICS. *Current Pos:* Res scientist, 56-62, res group supvr optical physics, 62-71, MEM TECH STAFF, JET PROPULSION LAB, 71- *Personal Data:* b Long Beach, Calif, June 26, 31; m 56; c 3. *Educ:* Calif Inst Technol, BS, 52, PhD(physics), 56. *Mem:* Optical Soc Am; Sigma Xi. *Res:* Fiber optic systems; optoelectronic sensors. *Mailing Add:* 1226 Olive Lane La Canada Flintridge CA 91011

JOHNSTON, ANDREA, MATHEMATICS. *Current Pos:* RETIRED. *Personal Data:* b Minneapolis, Minn, Mar 13, 21. *Educ:* St Mary Col, Kans, BA, 48; Cath Univ, MS, 52, PhD(math), 54. *Prof Exp:* Chmn, Dept Math, St Mary Col, Kans, 54-90. *Res:* Mathematics. *Mailing Add:* Mother House St Mary Col Leavenworth KS 66048-5082

JOHNSTON, ARCHIBALD CURRIE, GEOPHYSICS. *Current Pos:* from asst prof to assoc prof, 79-88, PROF GEOL SCI, MEMPHIS STATE UNIV, 88-, DIR RES, CTR EARTHQUAKE RES & INFO, 92- *Personal Data:* b Charlotte, NC, May 19, 45; m 92, Jill Diana Stevens. *Educ:* Rhodes Col, BS, 67; Dartmouth Col, 67-68; Univ Col PhD(geol sci & geophysics), 79. *Prof Exp:* Capt, USAF, 68-73; Dir, Ctr Earthquake Res & Info, Memphis State Univ, 79-92. *Concurrent Pos:* Grants, NSF, US Nuclear Regulatory Comn, TVA, US Geol Survey, Electric Power Res Inst, Memphis Light, Gas & Water Utility; chmn panel regional seismic networks comt seismol, Nat Acad Sci, 88-90; mem, Nat Earthquake Prediction Evaluation Coun, 90-; mem adv panel, Br Global Seismol & Geomagnetism, Nat Earthquake Info Ctr, 88-90; dir, Ctr Excellence State Tenn, 84-92; consult, Lawrence Livermore Nat Lab, Berkeley, Electric Power Res Inst, Palo Alto, US Army Corps Engrs, Vicksburg, Miss, Tenn Tech Found, Knoxville, Geomatrix Consult Inc, San Francisco, Law Environ, Atlanta, Battelle Inst, Seattle, SKB-Swedish Nuclear Fuel & Waste Mgt Co, Stockholm, Geol Survey Can, Ottawa,, Ctr Earthquake Res Australia, Univ Queensland. *Mem:* AAAS; Am Geophys Union; Seismol Soc Am (vpres, 91-92, pres, 92-93). *Mailing Add:* Ctr Earthquake Res & Info Univ Memphis Memphis TN 38152

JOHNSTON, BYRON E, SPECIALTY CHEMICAL INTERMEDIATES & REAGENTS. *Current Pos:* mgr res & develop, 85-89, SR SCIENTIST, ALBRIGHT & WILSON AM, 89- *Personal Data:* b Terry, Mont, Dec 3, 40; m 63, Shirley A Hauck; c Blaine & Heather. *Educ:* Mass Inst Technol, BS, 63; Univ Calif, Berkeley, PhD(org chem), 67. *Prof Exp:* Sr res chemist, Mobil Chem Co, 67-75, res assoc, 75-80, supv chemist, 80-85. *Mem:* Am Chem Soc. *Res:* Preparation and utilization of organophosphorus intermediates and reagents; process development and optimization for these materials. *Mailing Add:* Albright & Wilson Am PO Box 4439 Glen Allen VA 23058-4439. *Fax:* 804-550-4385

JOHNSTON, C EDWARD, AQUACULTURE. *Current Pos:* RETIRED. *Personal Data:* b Ont; m 64, Marcia; c Heather, Andrew & Melanie. *Educ:* Univ NB, BA, 64, PhD(biol), 68. *Prof Exp:* Asst prof, Prince Wales Col, 68-69; from asst prof to prof biol, Univ Pei, 69-84. *Concurrent Pos:* Vis prof, Biol Sta, NB, 79-80, Mem Univ, Nfld, 86-87 & Univ Man, 93-94. *Mem:* Am Fisheries Soc; Can Aqua Soc; Fish & Wildlife Soc. *Res:* Effect of low pH on parr-smolt transformation of Atlantic salmon; effect of temperature regimes on salmonid physiology; rapid and slow acclimation procedures on ionoregulatory mechanisms of rainbow trout; Atlantic salmon reproductive physiology and ichthyoplankton; Alosa aestivalis reproductive biology; thyroid physiology; blood chemistries; alkaline phosphatase. *Mailing Add:* Biol Dept Univ PEI Charlottetown PQ C1A 4P3 Can

JOHNSTON, CLIFF T, SOIL SCIENCE. *Current Pos:* ASSOC PROF AGRON, PURDUE UNIV, 93- *Personal Data:* b Colorado Springs, Colo, Oct 3, 55; m 77, Gail A Huxley; c Nathaniel C, Jessica H & Julie M. *Educ:* Univ Calif, Riverside, BSc, 79, PhD(soil & environ chem), 83. *Prof Exp:* Fel, Los Alamos Nat Lab, 83-85; from asst prof to assoc prof, Dept Soil Sci, Univ Fla, 85-93. *Concurrent Pos:* Vis prof, Cath Univ, Leuven, Belg, 92; assoc ed, Clay Mineral Soc, 93- *Mem:* Am Chem Soc; Clay Minerals Soc; Coblentz Soc; Soil Sci Soc Am. *Res:* Agronomy. *Mailing Add:* Crop Soil & Environ Sci Purdue Univ West Lafayette IN 47907-1968. *Fax:* 765-496-1368; *E-Mail:* cjohnston@dept.agry.purdue.edu

JOHNSTON, COLIN DEANE, CIVIL ENGINEERING, MATERIALS SCIENCE. *Current Pos:* assoc prof, 67-78, PROF CIVIL ENG, UNIV CALGARY, 78- *Personal Data:* b Northern Ireland, Apr 28, 40; m 67; c 2. *Educ:* Queen's Univ, Belfast, BSc, 62, PhD(civil eng), 67, DSc, 96. *Honors & Awards:* Wason Medal, Am Concrete Inst, 77. *Prof Exp:* Site engr, Govt Northern Ireland, 66-67; tech mgr concrete prod, Pre-Mix Concrete, Ltd, 67. *Mem:* Fel Am Concrete Inst; Am Soc Testing & Mat; Brit Concrete Soc; Transp Res Bd; Int Union Testing & Res Labs Mats & Structs. *Res:* Concrete, fiber reinforced concrete, durability, deicing salts, fly ash, silica fume, and chemical admixtures in concrete, asphalt concrete; structural and paving applications. *Mailing Add:* Dept Civil Eng Univ Calgary Calgary AB T2N 1N4 Can

JOHNSTON, CYRUS CONRAD, JR, INTERNAL MEDICINE, ENDOCRINOLOGY. *Current Pos:* fel endocrinol & metab, Ind Univ, Indianapolis, 59-61, from instr to assoc prof med, 61-69, assoc dir, Gen Clin Res Ctr, 62-67, dir, 67-88, dir, Div Endocrinol & Metab, 68-94, prof med, Med Ctr, 69-97, DISTINGUISHED PROF MED, IND UNIV, INDIANAPOLIS, 97- *Personal Data:* b Statesville, NC, July 16, 29; m 60; c 2. *Educ:* Duke Univ, AB, 51, MD, 55; Am Bd Internal Med, dipl. *Honors & Awards:* Sandoz Award for Geront Res, 93; Frederic C Bartter Award, Am Soc Bone & Mineral Res, 96. *Prof Exp:* Intern med, Duke Hosp, 55-56; resident, Barnes Hosp, St Louis, 56-57. *Concurrent Pos:* Vpres bd trustees, Nat Osteoporosis Found, 92-; assoc ed, BONE, 95- *Mem:* AAAS; Am Fedn Clin Res; Endocrine Soc; fel Am Col Physicians; Am Soc Bone & Mineral Res; Sigma Xi; Asn Osteobiol; Am Asn Cancer Educ; Am Col Clin Adminr; AMA; Cent Soc Clin Res. *Res:* Metabolism of bone both in human subjects and in the experimental animal; osteoporosis. *Mailing Add:* Emerson Hall Rm 421 Ind Univ Sch Med 545 Barnhill Dr Indianapolis IN 46202-5124. *Fax:* 317-274-4311; *E-Mail:* cjohnsto@mdep.iupui.edu

JOHNSTON, DANIEL, CELLULAR MECHANISMS OF LEARNING & MEMORY. *Current Pos:* from asst prof to assoc prof, 77-86, PROF NEUROSCI, BAYLOR COL MED, 86- *Personal Data:* b Passaic, NJ, Dec 9, 47. *Educ:* Univ Va, BS, 70; Duke Univ, PhD(biomed eng), 74. *Prof Exp:* Res asst, Univ Minn, Minneapolis, 74-77. *Mem:* Soc Neurosci; Am Physiol Soc. *Res:* Mechanisms of epilepsy. *Mailing Add:* Dept Neurosci Baylor Col Med One Baylor Plaza Houston TX 77030-3498. *Fax:* 713-799-8544

JOHNSTON, DAVID CARL, HIGH TEMPERATURE SUPERCONDUCTIVITY, SOLID STATE PHYSICS. *Current Pos:* PROF & SR PHYSICIST, AMES LAB, IOWA STATE UNIV, 87- *Personal Data:* b Flint, Mich, May 19, 47. *Educ:* Univ Calif, Santa Barbara, BA, 69; Univ Calif, San Diego, PhD(physics), 75. *Prof Exp:* Asst res physicist, Univ Calif, San Diego, 75-78; res staff, Exxon Res & Eng Co, 78-87. *Concurrent Pos:* Vis scientist, Nat Res Inst Metals, Tokyo, 91. *Mem:* Fel Am Phys Soc; AAAS; Am Asn Univ Prof. *Res:* Solid state physics and chemistry; synthesis and characterization of new materials; high temperature superconductivity in copper oxides and mechanism; magnetic, electronic transport, x-ray diffraction and thermal measurements. *Mailing Add:* Dept Physics & Astron Iowa State Univ Ames IA 50011. *Fax:* 515-294-0689; *E-Mail:* johnston@ameslab.gov

JOHNSTON, DAVID HERVEY, SEISMOLOGY, ROCK PHYSICS. *Current Pos:* SR RES SPECIALIST GEOPHYSICS, EXXON PROD RES CO, 79- *Personal Data:* b Syracuse, NY, Aug 25, 51; m 72, Linda Kaznova; c Elizabeth. *Educ:* Mass Inst Technol, SB, 73, PhD(geophysics), 79. *Concurrent Pos:* Distinguished lectr, Soc Petrol Engrs, 92-93. *Mem:* Am Geophys Union; Soc Explor Geophysicists (secy-treas, 89-90); Soc Petrol Engrs. *Res:* Reflection seismology; seismic processing; velocity analysis and interpretation; applications of geophysics to oil reservoir development and production; rock physics; relationship of rock microstructure to acoustic, electrical and flow properties; extraction of rock properties from seismic data; structure and evolution of planetary interiors; reservoir geophysics. *Mailing Add:* Exxon Prod Res Co PO Box 2189 Houston TX 77252-2189

JOHNSTON, DAVID OWEN, PHYSICAL CHEMISTRY. *Current Pos:* RETIRED. *Personal Data:* b Franklin, Tenn, July 27, 30; wid; c Kathy, Susie, David E & Beth. *Educ:* George Peabody Col, BS, 51; Mid Tenn State Col, MA, 58; Univ Miss, PhD(chem), 63. *Prof Exp:* Teacher pub schs, Tenn, 51-53 & 54-58; instr phys sci, Mid Tenn State Col, 58-60; from asst prof to prof chem, David Lipcomb Col, 63-86, Justin Potter distinguished prof, 86-91. *Concurrent Pos:* Fel res, Vanderbilt Univ, 65, 66, 69. *Mem:* Am Chem Soc. *Res:* Transport properties of rare earth salts in nonaqueous solvents; kinetics of inorganic oxidation-reduction reactions. *Mailing Add:* 1492 Clairmont Pl Nashville TN 37215

JOHNSTON, DAVID WARE, AVIAN PHYSIOLOGY, AVIAN ECOLOGY. *Current Pos:* RETIRED. *Personal Data:* b Miami, Fla, Nov 23, 26; m 48; c 3. *Educ:* Univ Ga, BS, 49, MS, 50; Univ Calif, PhD, 54. *Prof Exp:* Assoc prof, Mercer Univ, 54-59 & Wake Forest Col, 59-63; assoc prof biol sci & zool, Univ Fla, 63-74, prof zool, 74-79; at biol dept, George Mason Univ, 79-88. *Mem:* Ecol Soc Am; Cooper Ornith Soc; Am Ornith Union; Nat Audubon Soc. *Res:* Fat deposition in birds; pesticide levels in birds; ecology of insular avifaunas. *Mailing Add:* 5219 Concordia St Fairfax VA 22032

JOHNSTON, DEAN, TUMOR IMMUNOLOGY. *Current Pos:* ASST PROF DERMATOL, NY UNIV MED CTR, 82- *Personal Data:* b South Bend, Ind, Apr 12, 47. *Educ:* Wayne State Univ, PhD(biochem), 74. *Mem:* Am Soc Biol Chemists; AAAS. *Mailing Add:* Dept Health Sci Hunter Col City Univ NY 425 E 25th St New York NY 10010

JOHNSTON, DENNIS ADDINGTON, BIOSTATISTICS. *Current Pos:* Asst biomathematician & asst prof biomath, 72-78, ASSOC BIOMATHEMATICIAN & ASSOC PROF BIOMATH, UNIV TEX M D ANDERSON CANCER CTR, 78- *Personal Data:* b Oak Ridge, Tenn, Sept 17, 44; m 66; c 2. *Educ:* Arlington State Col, BS, 65; Univ Tex, Austin, MS, 66; Tex Tech Univ, PhD(math), 71. *Concurrent Pos:* adj assoc prof, Dept Statist, Rice Univ, 73-; mem fac, Grad Sch Biomed Sci, Univ Tex, Houston, 73- *Mem:* Am Statist Asn; Inst Elec & Electronics Engrs. *Res:* Biomedical image processing; consultant in mathematical and statistical models; biostatistics; automated chromosome analysis. *Mailing Add:* 2010 Ramada Dr Houston TX 77062

JOHNSTON, DON RICHARD, chemical physics, for more information see previous edition

JOHNSTON, E(LWOOD) RUSSELL, JR, CIVIL ENGINEERING. *Current Pos:* head dept, 72-77, PROF CIVIL ENG, UNIV CONN, 63- *Personal Data:* b Philadelphia, Pa, Dec 26, 25; m 51; c 2. *Educ:* Univ Del, BCE, 46; Mass Inst Technol, MS, 47, ScD(civil eng), 49. *Prof Exp:* Asst civil eng, Mass Inst Technol, 46-47; struct designer, Fay, Spofford & Thorndike, 47-49; from asst prof to prof, Lehigh Univ, 49-57; prof, Worcester Polytech Inst, 57-63. *Concurrent Pos:* Guest prof, Swiss Fed Inst Technol, Zurich, 70 & 77. *Mem:* Am Soc Civil Engrs; Am Soc Eng Educ; Int Asn Bridge & Struct Engrs; Am Acad Mech. *Res:* Structural engineering; applied mechanics; vibrations. *Mailing Add:* PO Box 525 Storrs CT 06268-0525

JOHNSTON, ERNEST RAYMOND, MATHEMATICS. *Current Pos:* from assoc prof to prof math, 55-76, head dept math sci, 63-72, EMER PROF MATH, IND UNIV-PURDUE UNIV, INDIANAPOLIS, 76- *Personal Data:* b Dahinda, Ill, Feb 9, 07; m 39. *Educ:* Ill State Norm Univ, BEd, 38; Univ Ill, MS, 39; Univ Minn, PhD(math), 54. *Prof Exp:* Teacher & prin, Pub Schs, Ill, 26-37; teacher, High Sch, Ill, 39-40; instr math, Austin Jr Col, Minn, 40-42 & Univ Minn, 42-44; mech engr, Naval Ord Lab, Md, 44-47; asst prof math & mech, Univ Minn, 47-51, lectr math, 51-53; prof, Wis State Col, Whitewater, 53-55. *Mem:* Am Math Soc; Math Asn Am. *Mailing Add:* 215 Valley View Dr Kerrville TX 78028-6246

JOHNSTON, FRANCIS E, CHILD GROWTH DEVELOPMENT. *Current Pos:* PROF ANTHROP, UNIV PA, 73- *Personal Data:* b Paris, Ky, Oct 9, 31; m 55, Patricia Honshul; c 3. *Educ:* Univ Ky, BA, 59, MA, 60; Univ Pa, PhD(anthrop), 62. *Prof Exp:* From instr phys anthrop to asst prof anthrop, Univ Pa, 60-66, asst cur phys anthrop, Univ Mus, 63-66; fel, Univ London Inst Child Health, 66-67; assoc prof anthrop, Univ Tex, Austin, 68-71; prof anthrop, Temple Univ, 71-73. *Concurrent Pos:* Consult growth & develop, Nat Ctr Health Statist, 63-; fel, Inst Cancer Res, 67-68 & 75-; managing ed, Am J Phys Anthrop, 77- *Mem:* Am Asn Phys Anthrop; Am Anthrop Asn; Brit Soc Study Human Biol; Human Biol Coun; fel Royal Soc Med; Am Inst Nutrit. *Res:* Child growth and development; population biology; human genetics; ecology of nutrition in human populations. *Mailing Add:* Dept Anthrop Univ Pa 325 Museum Philadelphia PA 19104-6398. *Fax:* 215-898-7462

JOHNSTON, FRANCIS J, CHEMICAL KINETICS, RADIATION CHEMISTRY. *Current Pos:* ASSOC PROF CHEM, UNIV GA, 60- *Personal Data:* b Ferryville, Wis, Sept 20, 24; m 48, Joyce Domke; c Michael F. *Educ:* Univ Wis, BS, 47, PhD(chem), 52. *Prof Exp:* Chemist, E I du Pont de Nemours & Co, 52-54; from asst prof to assoc prof chem, Univ Louisville, 54-60. *Mem:* Am Chem Soc; Sigma Xi. *Res:* Experimental studies of the effects of ionizing radiation in heterogeneous systems. *Mailing Add:* 140 Oakdale Rd Athens GA 30606-4818

JOHNSTON, G(ORDON) W(ILLIAM), ENGINEERING PHYSICS. *Current Pos:* PROF, FLUIDS & COMPUTATIONAL FLUIDS, INST AEROSPACE STUDIES, UNIV TORONTO, 70- *Personal Data:* b Toronto, Ont, Dec 10, 26; m 55; c 2. *Educ:* Univ Toronto, BSc, 48, MASc, 50, PhD(aerophys), 53. *Prof Exp:* Design engr, A V Roe, Co, Ltd, Can, 49-51; asst, Defense Res Bd Can, 52-53; res supvr sci lab, Res Div, Ford Motor Co, Mich, 53-54, head gas dynamics sect, 54-55; proj engr, De Haviland Aircraft Can, Ltd, 55-63, dir short take off & landing res proj, 60-63, head adv proj group, 63-70. *Concurrent Pos:* Mem assoc comt aerodyn noise, Nat Res Coun Can; lectr, Inst Aerophys, Univ Toronto, 57-59; aerodyn consult, Plasma Dynamics Dept, United Aircraft Res Labs, Conn, 67-70. *Mem:* Can Aeronaut Inst. *Res:* Transonic and low-speed aerodynamics; boundary layer control; stability and control of fixed and rotating wing aircraft configurations; slipstream wing aerodynamics. *Mailing Add:* 79 Valecrest Dr Toronto ON M9A 4P5 Can

JOHNSTON, GEORGE I, ELECTRICAL ENGINEERING. *Current Pos:* dir res, Instrument Serv, Med Sch, 58-76, ASSOC PROF & DIR, INSTRUMENT & SAFETY SERV, UNIV ORE, 76- *Personal Data:* b Bryn Mawr, Pa, May 29, 29; m 61; c 1. *Educ:* Johns Hopkins Univ, BS, 55. *Prof Exp:* Electronics technician, Sch Med, Johns Hopkins Univ, 48-55; med electronics engr, NIH, 55-58. *Concurrent Pos:* Asst sanit engr, USPHS. *Mem:* Inst Elec & Electronics Engrs; Sigma Xi. *Res:* Biomedical engineering. *Mailing Add:* 5462 SW Dover Lane Portland OR 97225

JOHNSTON, GEORGE LAWRENCE, PLASMA PHYSICS, THEORETICAL PHYSICS. *Current Pos:* RES SCIENTIST, PLASMA FUSION CTR, MASS INST TECHNOL, 80- *Personal Data:* b Los Angeles, Calif, Nov 11, 32; m 59. *Educ:* Calif Inst Technol, BS, 54; Univ Calif, Los Angeles, MS, 62, PhD(physics), 67. *Hon Degrees:* JD, Harvard Univ, 57. *Prof Exp:* Mem tech staff, Space Technol Labs, Inc, 57-60 & Aerospace Corp, 60-64; asst res physicist, Univ Calif, Los Angeles, 67-69; asst prof physics, Sonoma State Univ, 69-74, assoc prof, 74-80. *Concurrent Pos:* Res assoc, Mass Inst Technol, 75-77; adv comnr, Calif Energy Comn, 77-78. *Mem:* Am Phys Soc; AAAS; Sigma Xi. *Res:* Plasma kinetic theory; nonlinear plasma theory; mathematical physics; free electron lasers; relativistic electron beams. *Mailing Add:* 12 Billings St Acton MA 01720-2702

JOHNSTON, GEORGE ROBERT, CYTOGENETICS. *Current Pos:* from asst prof to assoc prof, 67-77, PROF BIOL, CALIF STATE UNIV, HAYWARD, 77- *Personal Data:* b Salt Lake City, Utah, July 4, 34; m 59; c 3. *Educ:* Univ Utah, BS, 59, MS, 61, PhD(genetics), 64. *Prof Exp:* Fel genetics, Univ Calif, Berkeley, 64-65; asst prof zool, Univ Wyo, 65-67. *Concurrent Pos:* Consult pediat, Kaiser Hosp, Oakland, Calif, 73-; consult, Biomed Div, Lawrence Livermore Lab, 75- *Mem:* Fel AAAS; Asn Cytogenetics Technologists. *Res:* Human chromosome identification linked to clinical defects and the structure of mammalian chromosomes. *Mailing Add:* Dept Biol Calif State Univ 25800 Carlos Bee Blvd Hayward CA 94542-3000

JOHNSTON, GEORGE TAYLOR, OPTICAL PHYSICS. *Current Pos:* PROG MGR, OPTICAL COATING LAB, INC, 82- *Personal Data:* b Princeton, WVa, Apr 18, 42; m 66; c 2. *Educ:* Mich State Univ, BS, 62, MS, 65, PhD(physics), 67; Univ Dayton, MS, 74. *Prof Exp:* Res assoc physics, Brown Univ, 67-69; asst prof, Univ Dayton, 69-72, res physicist, Univ Dayton, Res Inst, 72-81; sr scientist, Rocketdyne, Div Rockwell Int, 81-82. *Mem:* Optical Soc Am; Soc Photo-optical Instrumentation Engrs. *Res:* Optical properties of materials; optical instrumentation and metrology; analysis, test and evalutation of high energy laser optical components and component materials, including optical thin films and laser damage mechanisms in coatings, mirrors and transparent materials. *Mailing Add:* 1829 Sherwood Ct Santa Rosa CA 95405

JOHNSTON, GERALD ANDREW, AERONAUTICS, ASTRONAUTICS. *Current Pos:* RETIRED. *Personal Data:* b Chicago, Ill, July 17, 31; m 54, Jacquelyn Egan; c Jan, Colleen, Jeffrey, Gregory & Steven. *Educ:* Univ Calif, Los Angeles, BS, 56, MS, 72. *Prof Exp:* Jr engr, Shell Oil Co, 52-54; test engr, Robinson Aviation, 55-56; assoc engr & tech dir, Douglas Aircraft Co, 56-68; dir & vpres gen mgr, McDonnell Douglas Astronaut, 68-87; pres & chief exec officer, McDonnell Douglas Corp, 88-95. *Concurrent Pos:* Stress analyst, NAm Aviation, 55; trustee, St Louis Univ, 88. *Mailing Add:* 4141 Stonebridge Lane Rancho Santa Fe CA 92091-4556

JOHNSTON, GERALD SAMUEL, NUCLEAR MEDICINE. *Current Pos:* CHMN, DEPT NUCLEAR MED, WASH HOSP CTR, WASHINGTON, DC, 93- *Personal Data:* b Johnstown, Pa, Aug 4, 30; m 56, Dorothy Jones; c Joy (Biciocchi), Jill (Verna), Jana (Moritzkat), Gerald Jr, Amy (Tapparo) & Douglas. *Educ:* Univ Pittsburgh, BS, 52, MD, 56. *Prof Exp:* Intern rotating, Walter Reed Gen Hosp, US Army, 56-57, resident internal med, Brooke Gen Hosp, San Antonio, 57-60, comdr, Mobile Army Surg Hosp, Korea, 61-62, chief nuclear medicine, Walter Reed Gen Hosp, 63-69, nuclear med, Letterman Gen Hosp, San Francisco, 69-71; dir nuclear med, NIH, 71-82;

prof med, radiol, oncol & chief nuclear med, Univ Md, Baltimore, 82-93, actg chmn diag radiol, 89-92. *Concurrent Pos:* Clin assoc prof med, Georgetown Univ, 74-; prof radiol & nuclear med, Uniformed Serv, Univ Health Sci, Bethesda, Md, 79- *Mem:* Soc Nuclear Med; Am Col Physicians; Am Med Asn; Am Col Radiol; Am Col Nuclear Med. *Res:* Renal function; renal transplantation; nuclear medicine applications to renal function and cardiac function; nuclear medicine applications in oncology. *Mailing Add:* 22 S Greene St Baltimore MD 21201-1544

JOHNSTON, GORDON ROBERT, ORGANIC CHEMISTRY. *Current Pos:* CONSULT REGULATORY COMPLIANCE & OCCUP SAFETY HEALTH ASN, 91- *Personal Data:* b Portland, Ore, July 13, 28; m 60, Elizabeth Mary Ann Lane; c Catherine, Therese, William & Dennis. *Educ:* Univ Portland, BS, 50, MS, 52; Univ Ill, PhD(org chem), 56. *Prof Exp:* Res org chemist, Dow Chem Co, 56-58; res assoc org chem, Med Sch, Univ Ore, 58-60; res chemist, Crown Zellerbach Corp, 60-62; res chemist, Aerojet-Gen Corp, 62-63; res fel, Calif Inst Technol, 63-64; asst prof org chem, Col Women, San Diego, 64-66; asst prof chem, Pa State Univ, 66-91. *Concurrent Pos:* Trainee, Mass Inst Technol, 76-77. *Mem:* Am Chem Soc; Asn Consult Chemists & Chem Engrs. *Mailing Add:* PO Box 281 Beaver PA 15009-0281. *Fax:* 412-774-5394

JOHNSTON, HARLIN DEE, PETROLEUM CHEMISTRY, PILOT PLANT. *Current Pos:* res chemist, Phillips Petrol Co, 68-73, sr res chemist, 74-82, sect supvr, 83-90, TECH BR MGR, PHILLIPS RES CTR, PHILLIPS PETROL CO, 91- *Personal Data:* b Ogden, Utah, Mar 16, 42; m 63, Ann Thurston; c Matthew, Jennifer, Kelly & Jason. *Educ:* Brigham Young Univ, BA, 65, PhD(inorg chem), 68. *Mem:* Am Chem Soc; Sigma Xi. *Res:* Pilot plant design, operation, and supervision; heterogenous catalysis of solid-gas and solid-liquid-gas systems; laboratory and pilot plant automation. *Mailing Add:* Phillips Res Ctr Phillips Petrol Co Bartlesville OK 74004. *Fax:* 918-661-8761; *E-Mail:* hdjohns@ppco.com

JOHNSTON, HAROLD SLEDGE, PHYSICAL CHEMISTRY. *Current Pos:* RETIRED. *Personal Data:* b Woodstock, Ga, Oct 11, 20; m 48, Mary Ella Stay; c Shirley, Linda, David & Barbara (Dial). *Educ:* Emory Univ, AB, 41; Calif Inst Technol, PhD(chem), 48. *Hon Degrees:* DSc, Emory Univ, 65. *Honors & Awards:* Gold Medal Award, Calif Sect, Am Chem Soc, 56, Pollution Control Award, 74, Award Chem Contemporay Technol Probs, 85; Bourke Lectr, Faraday Soc, 61; George B Kistiakowsky Lectr, Harvard Univ, 73; G N Lewis Lectr, Univ Calif, 75; Cassett Found Lectr, Temple Univ, 78; Tyler Prize, 83; Award Chem Serv to Soc, Nat Acad Sci, 93; Nat Medal of Sci, 97. *Prof Exp:* Asst, Nat Defense Res Comt, Calif Inst Technol, 42-45, assoc prof chem, 56-57; from instr to assoc prof, Stanford Univ, 47-56; dean, Col Chem, Univ Calif, Berkeley, 66-70, prof chem, 57-91. *Concurrent Pos:* Res grants, Off Naval Res, 50-56, M W Kellogg Co, 51-53, Stand Oil Calif, 55-57, NSF, 59-68 & 75-78, USPHS, 63-70, Mat & Molecular Res Div, Lawrence Berkeley Lab, 66- & others; Guggenheim fel, Belg, 60-61; NATO vis prof, Univ Rome, Italy, 64; nat lectr, Sigma Xi, 73; assoc ed, J Geophys Res, 77-81; Acad Senate Fac res lectr, Univ Calif, Berkeley, 88-89. *Mem:* Nat Acad Sci; fel AAAS; Am Chem Soc; fel Am Phys Soc; Am Acad Arts & Sci; fel Am Geophys Union; Sigma Xi. *Res:* Fast gas phase reactions; kinetic isotope effects; photochemistry; unimolecular reactions; atmospheric chemistry; author of 2 books and numerous publications. *Mailing Add:* Dept Chem Univ Calif Berkeley CA 94720. *Fax:* 510-643-2156

JOHNSTON, HERBERT NORRIS, CHEMISTRY. *Current Pos:* assoc chief, Battelle Mem Inst, 52-68, chief polymer & paper technol div, Columbus Lab, 68-72, mgr polymer & paper chem, 72-78, MGR INDUST MKT OFF, COLUMBUS LABS, BATTELLE MEM INST, 78- *Personal Data:* b Cleveland, Ohio, Aug 9, 28; m 50; c 2. *Educ:* Ohio Univ, BS, 49. *Prof Exp:* Res chemist coatings res, Glidden Co, 49-52. *Mem:* Am Chem Soc; Sigma Xi; Tech Asn Pulp & Paper Indust; Am Mkt Asn; Am Mgt Asn. *Res:* Coatings, polymers, adhesives and inks for paper, wood and metals; powdered polymers, service life of polymeric materials, processing of plastics. *Mailing Add:* 1883 Andover Rd Columbus OH 43212-1001

JOHNSTON, JAMES BAKER, MARINE SCIENCES, SCIENCE EDUCATION. *Current Pos:* ecologist, 76-85, SUPV ECOLOGIST, US FISH & WILDLIFE SERV, US DEPT INTERIOR, 85- *Personal Data:* b Baton Rouge, La, Sept 10, 46; m 70; c 3. *Educ:* La State Univ, Baton Rouge, BS, 70, MEd, 71; Univ Southern Miss, PhD(sci educ, biol), 73. *Honors & Awards:* Edward H Hillard Award, Nat Wildlife Fedn, 72. *Prof Exp:* Oceanographer marine biol, Bur Land Mgt, New Orleans, 74-76. *Concurrent Pos:* Math instr & NSF consult, Prentiss Inst & Jr Col, 72-73; marine res asst, Univ Southern Miss, Gulf Univs Res Consortium, 72-73; marine fisheries mgt consult, Miss Marine Res Coun, 73-74; consult, Environ Can, 84-86. *Mem:* Ecol Soc Am; Explorers Club; Estuarine Res Fedn; Coastal Soc. *Res:* Characterization and geophysical mapping of offshore reefs and banks; marine fisheries management; ecosystem characterization and system analysis of coastal regions; development of marine science education programs; studies on wetlands and coastal barriers. *Mailing Add:* 100 Moray Dr Slidell LA 70461

JOHNSTON, JAMES BENNETT, APPLIED BIOCHEMISTRY, BIOCHEMICAL TECHNOLOGY. *Current Pos:* FOUNDER & EXEC VPRES, JWT, INC, 95- *Personal Data:* b San Diego, Calif, Dec 31, 43; m 69, Margaret J Rosenberry; c Mary E & Amy R. *Educ:* Univ Md, College Park, BS, 66; Univ Wis-Madison, PhD(biochem), 70. *Prof Exp:* Fel, Inst Pasteur, Paris, 70-71; res fel, Univ Kent, Canterbury, UK, 71-74; vis asst prof, Univ Ill, Urbana, 74-76, asst prof, 76-83; sr investr, Smith Kline & Fr, 83-87; res fel, Enzymatics, Inc, 87-89, dir res, 89-94. *Concurrent Pos:* Consult, Cetus Corp, 76-80, Ill Environ Protection Agency, 76-81, Pan Am Health Orgn, 80- & AgroBiotics Corp, 81-; prin investr, var grants, 77- *Mem:* Am Chem Soc; Am Soc Microbiol; Am Asn Clin Chem. *Res:* Recovery, detection and identification of environmental mutagens, especially in potable waters, and the genetics of hydrocarbon degradation by bacteria; manipulation of bacterial DNA to improve biodegradations for waste treatment or for the production of specialty chemicals; invention and development of instrument-dependent, quantitative diagnostic devices. *Mailing Add:* 1309 Cedar Rd Ambler PA 19002. *Fax:* 600-861-8247; *E-Mail:* jbj2@lehigh.edu

JOHNSTON, JAMES P(AUL), MECHANICAL ENGINEERING, FLUID DYNAMICS. *Current Pos:* from asst prof to assoc prof, 61-73, prof, 73-, EMER PROF MECH ENG, STANFORD UNIV. *Personal Data:* b Pittsburgh, Pa, May 11, 31; m 57; c 5. *Educ:* Mass Inst Technol, BS & MS, 54, ScD(mech eng), 57. *Honors & Awards:* Robert T Knapp Award, Am Soc Mech Engrs, 75. *Prof Exp:* Res engr, Ingersoll-Rand Co. NJ, 58-61. *Concurrent Pos:* Instr, Night Grad Sch Prog, Lehigh Univ, 59-60; Am Soc Mech Engrs-Freeman fel, 67; vis res scientist, Nat Phys Lab, Teddington, Eng, 67-68. *Mem:* AAAS; Am Soc Mech Engrs; Am Inst Aeronaut & Astronaut. *Res:* Fluid dynamics of real fluids, particularly two and three-dimensional turbulent boundary layers; effects of coordinate system rotation on the turbulent boundary layer; fluid flow in ducts, diffusers and tubomachinery. *Mailing Add:* Stanford Univ Mech Eng Dept Stanford CA 94305

JOHNSTON, JEAN VANCE, ORGANIC CHEMISTRY. *Current Pos:* from instr to assoc prof chem, 42-74, EMER ASSOC PROF CHEM, CONN COL, 74- *Personal Data:* b Shippensburg, Pa, Feb 17, 12. *Educ:* Smith Col, AB, 34; Yale Univ, PhD(org chem), 38. *Prof Exp:* Asst chem, Smith Col, 39; instr pvt sch, Conn, 40; asst prof chem, Furman Univ, 40-42. *Concurrent Pos:* Fel, Pa State Univ, 69-70; assoc prof, Shippensburg Univ, 76 & 77. *Mem:* Am Chem Soc; Sigma Xi. *Res:* Synthesis of organic compounds of medicinal interest; amidines. *Mailing Add:* 505 W King St Shippensburg PA 17257

JOHNSTON, JOHN, RUBBER CHEMISTRY. *Current Pos:* DIR APPLNS ENG, TESA TAPE INC, 89- *Personal Data:* b Newcastle-on-Tyne, Eng, Nov 8, 35; US citizen; m 47, 77, Naruse Nozawa; c Ian, Trevor & Alan. *Educ:* Hull Col Technol, BSc, 58. *Prof Exp:* Teacher, Co Educ Authorities, Hull, Eng, 48-49; chemist, Stand Oil Co, Saltend, 49-50 & T J Smith & Nephew Ltd, Hull, 50-58; res chemist, Arno Adhesive Tape Inc, 59-67, asst dir res pressure sensitive adhesives, 67, dir res, 68-71, dir res & develop, 71-73, vpres res, Develop & Tech Opers, 73-75; dir, Tech Serv, Johnson & Johnson, 75-77; dir res, Tuck Industs, 77-89. *Concurrent Pos:* Lectr, Purdue Univ, NRegional Campus, 65-71; chmn tech comt, Pressure Sensitive Tape Coun, 74-76 & planning comt; vchmn, Adhesive Tape Tech Comt, Nat Elec Mfr Asn. *Mem:* Am Chem Soc; Am Soc Testing & Mat; Inst Elec & Electronics Engrs. *Res:* Theory and practice of pressure sensitive adhesives. *Mailing Add:* 7600 Compton Ct Charlotte NC 28270. *Fax:* 704-553-5677

JOHNSTON, JOHN B(EVERLEY), CONTOUR MODEL OF OPERATIONAL SEMANTICS, SYNTAX-DIRECTED COMPILING EDITORS. *Current Pos:* PROF COMPUT SCI, NMEX STATE UNIV, 71- *Personal Data:* b Los Angeles, Calif, Aug 11, 29; m 66, Leatrice H Shaw; c Sharilee M. *Educ:* Calif Inst Technol, BS, 51, PhD(math), 55. *Prof Exp:* Instr math, Cornell Univ, 55-57; asst prof, Univ Kansas City, 57-58; from asst prof to assoc prof, Univ Kans, 58-64; mathematician, Gen Elec Res & Develop Ctr, NY, 64-68; assoc prof comput sci, Ind Univ, Bloomington, 68-69; info scientist, Gen Elec Res & Develop Ctr, NY, 69-71. *Mem:* Asn Comput Mach; Sigma Xi. *Res:* Structure of computation; computer languages; structure of computer systems. *Mailing Add:* Dept Comput Sci NMex State Univ Las Cruces NM 88001. *E-Mail:* jbj@nmsu.edu

JOHNSTON, JOHN ERIC, POLYMER & ANALYTICAL CHEMISTRY, LUBRICANTS & FUELS. *Current Pos:* head, Viscosity Index Modifier Res Group, Exxon Chem Co, 81-88, head, Polyalkene Tech, 88-89, component mgr viscosity modifiers, 90-91, LEADER, DISCHARGE ELIMINATION TASK FORCE, EXXON CHEM CO, 89-, SECT HEAD, ADVAN FUELS & LUBRICANTS, EXXON RES & ENG CO, CORP RES, 91- *Personal Data:* b Detroit, Mich, Feb 5, 48; m 85, Cathleen A Higgins. *Educ:* Univ Notre Dame, BS, 70; Univ Akron, PhD(polymer sci), 75. *Prof Exp:* Fel polymer sci, Ctr Macromolecular Res, 75; sr chemist polymer synthesis & characterization, Union Carbide Corp, 76-80. *Concurrent Pos:* Vis comt mem, NSF Advan Technol Educ Prog. *Mem:* Am Chem Soc; Soc Automotive Engrs; AAAS. *Res:* Basic research related to fuel and lubricant additives, combustion characteristics, lube tribology & rheology, genetic algoritm application to molecular design. *Mailing Add:* Exxon Chem Co PO Box 536 Linden NJ 07036

JOHNSTON, JOHN MARSHALL, BIOCHEMISTRY. *Current Pos:* from instr to assoc prof, 55-66, PROF BIOCHEM, UNIV TEX HEALTH SCI CTR, DALLAS, 66-, PROF OBSTET & GYNEC, 74- *Personal Data:* b North Platte, Nebr, Nov 14, 28; m 53; c 3. *Educ:* Hastings Col, BA, 49; Univ Colo, PhD, 53. *Prof Exp:* Res assoc, Walter Reed Inst Res, 53-55. *Concurrent Pos:* NSF sr res fel, Univ Lund, 62-63. *Mem:* AAAS; Am Chem Soc; Am Soc Biol Chemists; Sigma Xi. *Res:* Lipid metabolism in absorption; fetal lung maturation, partuition and membranes. *Mailing Add:* Dept Biochem Southwest Med Sch 5323 Harry Hines Dallas TX 75235-9051. *Fax:* 214-648-8683

JOHNSTON, JOHN O'NEAL, BIOCHEMICAL ENDOCRINOLOGY, NEUROENDOCRINE PHARMACOLOGY. *Current Pos:* res endocrinologist, 71-73, sect head endocrinol, 73-81, SR RES ENDOCRINOLOGIST, ENDOCRINOL, MARION MERRELL DOW RES INST, MARION MERRELL DOW INC, 81-, RES SCI & GROUP LEADER ENDOCRINOL, 93-, CHIEF SCIENTIST. *Personal Data:* b Baltimore, Md, July 21, 39; m 77; c 2. *Educ:* Univ Md, College Park, BS, 61, MS, 65, PhD(reproductive physiol), 70. *Prof Exp:* Res asst reproductive physiol, Agr Res Serv, USDA, 61-65; res asst, Dept Animal Sci, Univ Md, 65-69; res scientist fertil res, Upjohn Co, 69-71. *Concurrent Pos:* Consult vet pharmaceut, Jensen-Salsbery Labs, Kansas, Mo, 72-79; biol consult, Life Sci Div, Res Triangle Park, NC, 75-78; sci adv bd, Cincinnati Zoo, 85- *Mem:* Soc Study Reproduction; Am Soc Andrology; NY Acad Sci; AAAS; Endocrine Soc. *Res:* Development of therapeutic agents for control of male and female fertility; regulation of hormonal action via receptor mechanism in target tissues; animal growth stimulants; neuroendocrine pharmacology of animal behavior; development of enzyme inhibitors for regulation of endocrine dependent cancer, endocrine hypertension and reproductive processes. *Mailing Add:* Endocrine Assoc 9 Crooked Creek Milford OH 45150

JOHNSTON, JOHN SPENCER, ENTOMOLOGY. *Current Pos:* ASSOC PROF GENETICS, TEX A&M UNIV, 79- *Personal Data:* b Phoenix, Ariz, May 27, 44; m 66; c 1. *Educ:* Univ Wash, BS, 66; Univ Ariz, PhD(genetics), 72. *Prof Exp:* NIH fel, Univ Tex, Austin, 72-75; asst prof biol, Baylor Univ, Waco, 75-79. *Concurrent Pos:* Res grant, Energy Res Develop Asn & Univ Tex, Austin, 73- *Mem:* AAAS; Genetics Soc Am; Evolution Soc Am; Soc Am Naturalists. *Res:* Ecological genetics of Drosophila species. *Mailing Add:* Entom Dept Tex A&M Univ College Station TX 77843-0100

JOHNSTON, KATHARINE GENTRY, INDUSTRIAL ORGANIC CHEMISTRY. *Current Pos:* RETIRED. *Personal Data:* b Minneapolis, Kans, Jan 19, 21; m 50; c 2. *Educ:* Kans State Univ, BS, 42, MS, 50. *Prof Exp:* Res chemist, Org Div, Monsanto Chem Co, 51-71; staff scientist clin diag, Ames Co, Div Miles Labs, 71-86. *Mem:* Sigma Xi; AAAS; Am Chem Soc. *Res:* Organic and enzymatic reactions in clinical diagnostic systems; complex formation and stabilization; ion temperature polymerization. *Mailing Add:* 1633 Woodfield Court Elkhart IN 46514-4708

JOHNSTON, KENNETH JOHN, ASTRONOMY. *Current Pos:* Nat Acad Sci-Nat Res Coun res assoc astron, 69-71, astronomer, Naval Res Lab, 71-93, ASTRONOMER, US NAVAL OBSERV, 93- *Personal Data:* b New York, NY, Oct 9, 41; m 66. *Educ:* Manhattan Col, BEE, 64; Georgetown Univ, PhD(astron), 69. *Mem:* Am Astron Soc; Int Astron Union. *Res:* Radio astronomy; variable stars. *Mailing Add:* US Naval Observ 3450 Massachusetts Ave NW Washington DC 20392-5420

JOHNSTON, LA VERNE ALBERT, BOTANY. *Current Pos:* RETIRED. *Personal Data:* b Hallettsville, Tex, Mar 7, 30; m 61; c 2. *Educ:* Baylor Univ, AB, 51, MA, 57; Southwestern Baptist Theol Sem, MRE, 54. *Prof Exp:* Teacher, Gonzales Ind Sch Dist, 51-52; instr & asst prof biol, Baylor Univ, 54-60; res asst bot, Univ Tex, Austin, 76-80 & 83-90. *Concurrent Pos:* Tech writer, 80-83; pres, Johnston Enterprises. *Mem:* Am Inst Biol Sci; Bot Soc Am. *Res:* Phycology; angiosperm taxonomy. *Mailing Add:* 10412 Double Spur Loop Austin TX 78759

JOHNSTON, LAURANCE S, SPINAL CORD RESEARCH. *Current Pos:* DIR, PARALYZED VET AM SPINAL CORD RES & EDUC FOUND, 92- *Personal Data:* b St Paul, Minn, Aug 4, 50; m 75, Pauline Gogola. *Educ:* Hamline Univ, BS, 72; Northwestern Univ, Evanston, MS, 73, PhD(biochem & molecular biol), 77; George Mason Univ, MBA, 85. *Prof Exp:* Fel, Dept Biochem & Molecular Biol, Northwestern Univ, 76-77; fel, Chicago Med Sch, 77-78; consumer safety officer, Off Compliance, Bur Foods, Food & Drug Admin, Washington, DC, 78-81; health scientist adminr & exec secy, Nat Inst Child Health & Human Develop, NIH, 81-86, dir, Div Sci Rev, 86-92. *Mem:* Soc Res Adminr; Nat Coun Univ Res Adminr; Soc Neurosci; Am Paraplegia Soc. *Res:* Foundation funding source for spinal cord research and education grants. *Mailing Add:* Paralyzed Vet Am 801 18th St NW Washington DC 20006. *Fax:* 202-416-7641

JOHNSTON, LAWRENCE HARDING, OPTICAL PHYSICS. *Current Pos:* prof, 67-88, EMER PROF PHYSICS, UNIV IDAHO, 88- *Personal Data:* b Tse-Nan-Fu, China, Feb 11, 18; US citizen; m 42, Mildred Hillis; c Mary, Margaret, Daniel, Lois & Karen. *Educ:* Univ Calif, AB, 40, PhD(physics), 50. *Prof Exp:* Res assoc, Radiation Lab, Mass Inst Technol, 40-43; from instr to assoc prof physics, Univ Minn, Minneapolis, 50-61; sr scientist, Aerospace Corp, 61-63; sr staff mem, Stanford Linear Accelerator Ctr, 63-67. *Mem:* Fel Am Phys Soc; fel Am Sci Affil. *Res:* Far infrared physics; molecular spectroscopy; microwave radar; atom bomb development; proton linear accelerator development; nuclear and high energy particle physics; proton-proton scattering; submillimeter wave laser stark spectroscopy. *Mailing Add:* 917 E Eighth St Moscow ID 83843. *E-Mail:* johnston@uidaho.edu

JOHNSTON, MALCOLM CAMPBELL, TERATOLOGY, DEVELOPMENTAL BIOLOGY. *Current Pos:* PROF ORTHODONT & ANAT, SCH DENT & MED, UNIV NC, 76- *Personal Data:* b Montague, PEI, Feb 13, 31; m 55. *Educ:* Univ Toronto, DDS, 54, MScD, 56; Univ Rochester, PhD(anat), 65. *Prof Exp:* Res assoc clin res, Cleft Palate Res & Treat Ctr, Hosp Sick Children, Toronto, 56-60; asst & assoc prof hist, Sch Dent & Med, Univ Toronto, 64-69; vis scientist, NIH, Bethesda, Md, 69-76. *Concurrent Pos:* Sect ed, Cleft Palate J, 81- *Mem:* Sigma Xi; Am Cleft Palate Asn; Teratology Soc; Am Asn Anatomists. *Res:* Normal and abnormal embryonic craniofacial development in mice, with limited studies on man. *Mailing Add:* Anat Dept Univ NC Sch Med Chapel Hill NC 27599-7090

JOHNSTON, MANLEY RODERICK, ORGANIC POLYMER CHEMISTRY. *Current Pos:* Sr chemist, 3M Co, 68-72, res specialist, 72-73, supvr, 73-78, tech mgr, Bldg Serv & Cleaning Prod Div, 78-82, lab mgr, Nonwovens Technol Ctr, 82-83, dir Life Sci Res Lab, 83-86, dir, Disposible Prod Div, 86-89, TECH DIR, 3M CO, EUROPE, 89- *Personal Data:* b Edmonton, Alta, Oct 2, 42; m 67; c Cindy & Christine. *Educ:* Univ Alta, BSc, 64; Univ Ill, Urbana, MS, 66 & PhD (org chem), 69. *Mem:* Am Chem Soc; Royal Soc Chem. *Res:* Small ring compounds; organic coatings; metal finishing; adhesion; high temperature polymers; fibers; polymerization catalysts; fluorine chemistry. *Mailing Add:* 352 Quail Rd St Paul MN 55110

JOHNSTON, MARGARET IRENE, IMMUNOLOGY. *Current Pos:* prog officer, Develop Therapeut Br, NIH, 87-88, chief, Targeted Drug Discovery Sect, 88-89, chief, Develop Therapeut Br, 90-91, assoc dir, Basic Res & Develop Prog, 91-93, ACTG DIR, DIV AIDS, NAT INST ALLERGY & INFECTIOUS DIS, NIH, 93- *Educ:* Carnegie Mellon Univ, BS, 72; Tufts Univ, PhD(biochem), 77. *Prof Exp:* Assoc, Rega Inst Med Res, Cath Univ Leuven, Belg, 77-78; staff fel, Lab Chem, Nat Inst Diabetes, Digestive & Kidney Dis, NIH, 78-80, sr staff fel, 80-82; asst prof, Dept Biochem, Uniformed Serv Univ Health Sci, 82-87, adj assoc prof, 87-93. *Concurrent Pos:* Prin investr, Uniformed Serv Univ Health Sci, 83-86, NSF, 83-86 & NIH, 84-87. *Mem:* AAAS; Am Soc Biochem & Molecular Biol; Am Soc Microbiol; Asn Women Sci; Int Soc AIDS Res; Int Soc Antiviral Res. *Res:* Human immunovirus/acquired immunodeficiency syndrome therapeutics and vaccine design, evaluation, development; human immunovirus/acquired immunodeficiency syndrome basic research and pathogenesis. *Mailing Add:* Int AIDS Vaccine Initiative 1401 First St NW Suite 1220 Washington DC 20005. *Fax:* 202-408-1818

JOHNSTON, MARILYN FRANCES MEYERS, BIOCHEMISTRY, IMMUNOLOGY. *Current Pos:* fel path & med, 79-80, from asst prof to assoc prof, 80-91, PROF PATH, MED SCH, ST LOUIS UNIV, 91- *Personal Data:* b Buffalo, NY, Mar 30, 37. *Educ:* Dameon Col (Rosary Hill Col), BS, 66; St Louis Univ, PhD(biochem), 70, MD, 75. *Prof Exp:* NIH fel, Wash Univ, 70-72; instr biochem, Sch Med, St Louis Univ, 72-75; resident path, Sch Med, Washington Univ, 72-75 & St John's Mercy Med Ctr, 77-79; med dir, Mo-Ill Regional Red Cross, 83-88. *Concurrent Pos:* AMA J Goldberger fel, St Louis Univ, 74; prin investr; vchmn inspection & accreditation, Am Asn Blood Banks, 83-, mem comt transfusion pract, 84-89; med dir blood bank, Transfusion Serv, Apheris, St Louis Univ Hosp. *Mem:* Am Asn Blood Banks; Col Am Pathologists; Am Asn Immunologists; Int Soc Blood Transfusion; Sigma Xi; Am Soc Clin Path. *Res:* Transfusion medicine; red cell surface antigens; erythoporetin. *Mailing Add:* Sch Med St Louis Univ Hosps 3635 Vista at Grand Blvd PO Box 15250 St Louis MO 63110-0250

JOHNSTON, MARSHALL CONRING, SYSTEMATIC BOTANY. *Current Pos:* res scientist bot, 59-61, assoc prof, 61-72, PROF BOT, UNIV TEX, AUSTIN, 72- *Personal Data:* b San Antonio, Tex, May 10, 30; m 61; c 2. *Educ:* Univ Tex, BS, 51, MA, 52, PhD(bot), 55. *Prof Exp:* Fel, Rice Inst, 55; asst prof biol, Sul Ross State Col, 58-59. *Concurrent Pos:* Sci asst, Univ Munich, 68-69; dir, Rare Plant Study Ctr, 72- *Mem:* AAAS; Bot Soc Am; Am Soc Plant Taxon; Int Soc Plant Taxon; Am Inst Biol Sci; Sigma Xi. *Res:* Distribution of vegetation types; systematics and historical biogeography of vascular plants of southwestern United States and northern Mexico; flora of Texas. *Mailing Add:* 10412 Double Spur Loop Austin TX 78759

JOHNSTON, MELVIN ROSCOE, FOOD TECHNOLOGY. *Current Pos:* RETIRED. *Personal Data:* b McAlester, Okla, June 23, 21; m 46; c 2. *Educ:* Agr & Mech Col Tex, BS, 48; Ore State Col, MS, 50; Univ Mo, PhD, 56. *Prof Exp:* Instr food technol, Ore State Col, 48-50; food technologist, Libby, McNeil & Libby, 50-52; from instr to asst prof hort, Univ Mo, 52-59; prof food technol & adv dept, Univ Tenn, Knoxville, 59-73; chief, Fruit & Veg Br, Div Food Technol, Bur Foods, Food & Drug Admin, Health Educ & Welfare, 73-80, chief, Plant & Protein Prods Br, 80-86. *Mem:* Fel Inst Food Technologists; Sigma Xi. *Res:* Implementation and support of regulatory action; food color technology; freezing; freeze-drying and thermal processing of foods; ammonia damage to frozen foods. *Mailing Add:* 23 Country Club Circle New Braunfels TX 78130-5376

JOHNSTON, MILES GREGORY, SHOCK, INFLAMMATION. *Current Pos:* ASSOC PROF PATH, UNIV TORONTO, 81- *Educ:* Univ Toronto, PhD(exp path), 78. *Mailing Add:* Sunnybrook Health Sci Ctr Rm S-111 2075 Bayview Ave North York ON M4N 3M5 Can. *Fax:* 416-480-5737

JOHNSTON, MILTON DWYNELL, JR, PHYSICAL CHEMISTRY, MOLECULAR SPECTROSCOPY. *Current Pos:* asst prof, 73-80, ASSOC PROF CHEM, UNIV SFLA, 80- *Personal Data:* b Hillsboro, Ore, Nov 4, 43. *Educ:* Portland State Univ, BA, 65; Princeton Univ, AM, 68, PhD(chem), 69. *Prof Exp:* Res assoc nuclear magnetic resonance, Univ Ariz, 70-71; res assoc, Tex A&M Univ, 71-73. *Mem:* Am Chem Soc; Royal Soc Chem; Sigma Xi; NY Acad Sci; Am Phys Soc. *Res:* Nuclear magnetic resonance solvent effects; theory of nuclear magnetic resonance spectral parameters; theory of liquids and liquid solutions and of intermolecular forces. *Mailing Add:* 12204 N 53rd St Tampa FL 33617-1448

JOHNSTON, NORMAN JOSEPH, ORGANIC POLYMER CHEMISTRY, POLYMER MATRIX COMPOSITES TECHNOLOGY. *Current Pos:* Nat Acad Sci-Nat Res Coun resident res fel, NASA, 66-67, aerospace technologist & chemist, 67-70, head polymer sect, 70-80, sr scientist, 81-88, chief scientist-mats, 88-90, MGR, COMPOSITES TECHNOL, LANGLEY RES CTR, NASA, 91- *Personal Data:* b Charles Town, WVa, Dec 15, 34; m

57, Joy McCeney; c Jennifer, Robin, Susan & Carol. *Educ:* Shepherd Col, BS, 56; Univ Va, PhD(org chem), 63. *Honors & Awards:* NASA Except Serv Medal. *Prof Exp:* Chemist insulating mat dept, Gen Elec Co, 61-63; asst prof chem, Va Polytech Inst & State Univ, 63-66. *Mem:* Am Chem Soc; Soc Aerospace Mat & Process Engrs; Am Soc Composites. *Res:* Synthesis and characterization of high performance polymers and their evaluation as composite matrices; toughened high performance composites; resin property-composite property relationships; composite fabrication technology. *Mailing Add:* NASA Langley Res Ctr Mail Stop 226 Hampton VA 23681-0001. *Fax:* 757-864-8312; *E-Mail:* norm_johnston@qmgate.larc.nasa.gov

JOHNSTON, NORMAN PAUL, ANIMAL NUTRITION, REPRODUCTION BIOLOGY. *Current Pos:* PROF ANIMAL SCI, BRIGHAM YOUNG UNIV, 71- *Personal Data:* b Salt Lake City, Utah, Apr 5, 41; m 66; c 5. *Educ:* Brigham Young Univ, BA, 66; Ore State Univ, MS, 67, PhD(avian nutrit), 71; Univ Utah, MBA, 69. *Prof Exp:* Animal nutritionist, Brookfield Prod Inc, 69-70. *Mem:* Sigma Xi; Poultry Sci; Am Soc Animal Sci; World Poultry Sci. *Res:* Poultry reproduction, in particular artificial insemination; animal nutrition - rabbits, goats, poultry; international agriculture. *Mailing Add:* Agron Dept Brigham Young Univ 275 Widb Provo UT 84602-1049

JOHNSTON, NORMAN WILSON, POLYMER CHEMISTRY. *Current Pos:* VPRES TECHNOL & ENG, LIBBEY-OWENS-FORD CO. *Personal Data:* b Pittsburgh, Pa, June 18, 42; m 65; c 3. *Educ:* Clarion State Col, BS, 64; Univ Akron, PhD(polymer sci), 68. *Prof Exp:* Chemist polymer chem, Ethyl Corp, 65; sr chemist, Union Carbide Corp, 68-71, proj scientist, 71-72, group leader adhesives, coatings & moldings, 72-76; assoc dir res & develop, Owens-Corning Fiberglass Corp, 76-77, lab dir, 77-79, res dir, 78-81, mgr bus & tech planning, 81- *Mem:* Am Chem Soc. *Res:* Polymer structure: property relationships, polymer synthesis, coatings, adhesives, fire retardance, molding and extrusion, composites, polymer blends, degradable plastics, cement, foams, insulation. *Mailing Add:* Solvay Automotive 2565 W Maple Rd Troy MI 48084-7114

JOHNSTON, PATRICIA V, PROSTAGLANDINS & IMMUNITY. *Current Pos:* asst prof, 57-62 & 68-79, PROF FOOD SCI, UNIV ILL, 79- *Personal Data:* b Liverpool, Eng, Mar 15, 52. *Educ:* John Morrees Univ, Eng, MRSC, 54; Univ Ill, PhD(food sci), 57. *Prof Exp:* Res asst prof biochem, Univ Col, London, 62-68. *Mem:* Am Oil Chemists Soc; Soc Neurochem; AAAS; Am Inst Nutrit. *Res:* Prostaglandins and immunity. *Mailing Add:* 382C Agr Eng Sci Bldg Dept Food Sci 1304 W Pennsylvania Urbana IL 61801. *Fax:* 217-333-9329

JOHNSTON, PAUL BRUNS, MEDICAL MICROBIOLOGY. *Current Pos:* ASSOC PROF MICROBIOL, SCH MED, UNIV LOUISVILLE, 64- *Personal Data:* b Chicago, Ill, Apr 2, 27; wid; c 3. *Educ:* Northwestern Univ, BS, 49; Loyola Univ, Ill, MS, 51; Univ Chicago, PhD(microbiol), 57. *Prof Exp:* Virologist, US Naval Med Res Unit 2, Taiwan, 57-60; asst prof microbiol, Jefferson Med Col, 60-64. *Concurrent Pos:* Instr, Univ Chicago, 57-60. *Mem:* Am Soc Microbiol; Soc Exp Biol & Med; Tissue Cult Asn; Am Asn Immunol. *Res:* Nature of latent virus infections; simian foamy virus immunology; adenoviruses. *Mailing Add:* Dept Microbiol Sch Med Univ Louisville 2301 S Third St Louisville KY 40292-0001. *Fax:* 502-852-7531; *E-Mail:* john01@ulkyvm.louisville.edu

JOHNSTON, PAULINE KAY, SCIENCE POLICY, INFORMATION DISSEMINATION. *Current Pos:* SR CHEMIST, US ENVIRON PROTECTION AGENCY, 87- *Personal Data:* b Elgin, Ill, Mar 17, 51; m 75, Laurance S. *Educ:* Univ Ill Champaign, BS, 73; Northwestern Univ, MS, 74, PhD(biol sci), 79. *Prof Exp:* Environ scientist, Sci Appln Int Corp, 79-85; sr chemist, US Consumer Prod Safety Comn, 85-87. *Mem:* Am Chem Soc. *Res:* Reviews scientific information related to indoor air quality issues and provides input to scientific policy decisions in this area. *Mailing Add:* US Environ Protection Agency 6604J 401 M St SW Washington DC 20460

JOHNSTON, PERRY MAX, VERTEBRATE EMBRYOLOGY. *Current Pos:* From asst prof to assoc prof zool, 49-54, PROF ZOOL, UNIV ARK, FAYETTEVILLE, 54-, CHMN DEPT, 66- *Personal Data:* b Edgewood, Tex, Feb 6, 21; m 43; c 4. *Educ:* NTex State Col, BS, 40, MS, 42; Univ Mich, PhD(zool), 49. *Concurrent Pos:* Res partic, Oak Ridge Inst Nuclear Studies, 53-54. *Mem:* Am Soc Zool; Am Micros Soc; Sigma Xi. *Res:* Vertebrate embryology; embryology of centrarchid fishes; utilization of radioisotopes by vertebrate embryos. *Mailing Add:* 1923 E Joyce St No 153 Fayetteville AR 72703

JOHNSTON, PETER RAMSEY, FLUID FILTRATION. *Current Pos:* RETIRED. *Personal Data:* b Tampa, Fla, Aug 19, 26; m 49, Helen Clark; c Frederick, Rebecca, Terrance & Christopher. *Educ:* Miami Univ, Ohio, BA, 48. *Prof Exp:* Sr proj eng, Ametek, Inc, 80-92. *Concurrent Pos:* Prod develop filter media, Com Filters, Gelman Scis & Ametek, 72-92. *Mem:* Am Chem Soc; Am Inst Chem Engrs; fel Am Soc Testing & Mat; Am Filtration Soc. *Res:* Liquid filtration; electrochemistry; polymer chemistry; author of books, encyclopedia articles, and many papers on filtration. *Mailing Add:* 302 Morningside Dr Carrboro NC 27510-1249

JOHNSTON, RAYMOND F, PHYSIOLOGY, PHARMACOLOGY. *Current Pos:* asst path, 45-47, asst physiol, 47-49, PROF PHYSIOL, MICH STATE UNIV, 49- *Personal Data:* b Fenton, Mo, June 29, 13; m 35; c 1. *Educ:* Univ Mo, BS, 35; Mich State Univ, MS, 48, DVM, 49; Univ Minn, PhD, 59. *Prof Exp:* Instr voc agr, Univ Mo, 35-45. *Concurrent Pos:* Sr mem team vet to Indonesia, 60-62. *Mem:* Fel Am Vet Med Asn. *Res:* Toxicology; cardiovascular physiology; neurophysiology; biomedical communications. *Mailing Add:* 4583 Sequoia Terr Okemos MI 48864

JOHNSTON, RICHARD BOLES, JR, PEDIATRICS, IMMUNOLOGY. *Personal Data:* b Atlanta, Ga, Aug 23, 35; m 60; c 3. *Educ:* Vanderbilt Univ, BA, 57, MD, 61. *Hon Degrees:* MS, Univ Pa, 86. *Prof Exp:* NIH fel, Harvard Med Sch, 67-68, USPHS training grant, 68-69, NIH spec fel, 69-70; from asst prof to assoc prof pediat & microbiol, Univ Ala, Birmingham, 70-77; dir dept pediat, Nat Jewish Hosp & Res Ctr, Denver, 77-86; prof pediat, Sch Med, Univ Colo, 77-86, vchmn dept, 80-86; chmn, Dept Pediat, Univ Pa Sch Med, 86-90, William Bennett prof, 86-92. *Concurrent Pos:* Macy Found scholar, Rockefeller Univ, NY, 76-77; vis prof, Rockefeller Univ, NY, 83-84; chmn bd trustees, Int Pediat Res Found, 83-87 & 95. *Mem:* Inst Med-Nat Acad Sci; Am Asn Immunologists; Asn Am Physicians; Am Soc Clin Invest; Am Pediat Soc (pre, 96-97); Soc Pediat Res (pres, 80-81); fel AAAS. *Res:* Mechanisms of resistance to infection; phagocyte function; complement. *Mailing Add:* Dept Pediat Yale Univ Sch Med 333 Cedar St New Haven CT 06520

JOHNSTON, RICHARD FOURNESS, SYSTEMATICS, ECOLOGY. *Current Pos:* from asst prof to prof zool, Univ Kans, 58-92, from assoc cur to cur birds, Mus Natural Hist, 63-92, chmn, Dept Zool, 79-82, EMER PROF ZOOL, UNIV KANS, 92- *Personal Data:* b Oakland, Calif, July 27, 25; m 48, Lora Bliler; c Regan E, Janet V & Cassandra I. *Educ:* Univ Calif, BA, 50, MA, 53, PhD, 55. *Honors & Awards:* Coues Award, Am Ornith Union, 75. *Prof Exp:* Instr biol, NMex State Univ, 56-57. *Concurrent Pos:* Ed, Syst Zool, Soc Syst Zool, 67-70; cur birds, Mus Natural Hist, 67-92; prog dir syst biol, NSF, 68-69; ed, Annual Rev Ecol & Systematics, 68-92, Current Ornith, 81-86. *Mem:* Fel AAAS; Ecol Soc Am; fel Am Ornith Union; Soc Study Evolution; Soc Syst Zool (pres, 77-79); Cooper Ornith Soc. *Res:* Systematics; evolutionary biology; behavior and ecology of pigeons. *Mailing Add:* Univ Kans 602 Dyche Hall Lawrence KS 66045-2454. *Fax:* 785-864-5335; *E-Mail:* rfj@ukanvm

JOHNSTON, RICHARD H, HYDROGEOLOGY, IMPACT OF DEVELOPMENT ON LARGE AQUIFER SYSTEMS. *Current Pos:* RETIRED. *Personal Data:* b Philadelphia, Pa, Apr 7, 29; m 66, Mary L Flaherty; c Richard. *Educ:* Pa State Univ, BS, 57; Univ Wyoming, MA, 59. *Prof Exp:* Geologist, US Geol Surg, 59-69, groundwater hydrologist, 69-84, consult, 84-95. *Mem:* Fel Geol Soc Am; Int Asn Hydro-geologists. *Res:* Regional aquifer systems; Karst hydrogeology; ground-water budgets. *Mailing Add:* 108 Tolomato Trace St Simons Island GA 31522-1812

JOHNSTON, ROBERT BENJAMIN, BIOCHEMISTRY. *Current Pos:* RETIRED. *Personal Data:* b North Platte, Nebr, Mar 21, 22; m 44, Rogene M Mohnike; c Marie (Snyder) & Jeffrey. *Educ:* Hastings Col, AB, 44; Univ Chicago, PhD(biochem), 49. *Prof Exp:* Instr physiol chem, Yale Univ, 53; from asst prof to prof chem, Univ Nebr, Lincoln, 53-87. *Concurrent Pos:* USPHS spec fel, Max Planck Inst Cell Chem, Munich, 61-62 & Inst Microbiol Biochem, Erlansen, 78-79. *Mem:* AAAS; Am Chem Soc; Brit Biochem Soc; Am Soc Biol Chemists; Sigma Xi. *Res:* Enzyme mechanisms and biological synthesis of peptide bonds; amino acid racemases; releasing factors; enkephalins; peptide antibiotics. *Mailing Add:* 3900 J St Lincoln NE 68510

JOHNSTON, ROBERT E, BEHAVIOR, ETHOLOGY & PHEROMONES. *Current Pos:* From asst prof to assoc prof, 70-87, PROF PSYCHOL & BIOL, CORNELL UNIV, 87- *Personal Data:* b Philadelphia, Pa, Apr 16, 42; m 70, Joan E Colsey; c Alexander E & Robert A. *Educ:* Dartmouth Col, AB, 64; Rockefeller Univ, PhD(behav & life sci), 70. *Concurrent Pos:* Vis prof, Dept Zool, Univ Tex, 80, USSR Acad Sci, A N Severtson Inst Evolutionary Animal Morphol & Ecol, 91; prin investr, numerous grants. *Mem:* Animal Behav Soc; Sigma Xi; Am Soc Mammalogists; Soc Study Reproduction. *Res:* Mechanisms and evolution of behavior, especially reproductive and aggressive behavior; communication, including olfactory (pheromones), auditory and visual signals; relationships between hormones and behavior; neural mechanisms of olfaction; human ethology; human evolution; animal cognition. *Mailing Add:* Dept Psychol 211 Uris Hall Cornell Univ Ithaca NY 14853-7601

JOHNSTON, ROBERT EDWARD, MICROBIOLOGY, VIROLOGY. *Current Pos:* PROF MICROBIOL & IMMUNOL, UNIV NC, 89- *Personal Data:* b Houston, Tex, Sept 19, 47; m 76. *Educ:* Rice Univ, BA, 68; Univ Tex, Austin, PhD(microbiol), 73. *Prof Exp:* Med Res Coun fel microbiol, Queens Univ, 73-76; asst prof microbiol, NC State Univ, 76-80, assoc prof, 80-89. *Concurrent Pos:* NIH Young investr grant, NC State Univ, 78-81. *Mem:* Am Soc Microbiol; Am Soc Virol; AAAS. *Res:* Host cell influence on virus replication; viral pathogenesis; design of viral vaccines and vaccine vectors. *Mailing Add:* Dept Microbiol & Immunol Campus Box 7290 Univ NC Chapel Hill NC 27599

JOHNSTON, ROBERT HOWARD, mathematics; deceased, see previous edition for last biography

JOHNSTON, ROBERT WARD, PHYSICS, ACADEMIC ADMINISTRATION. *Current Pos:* RETIRED. *Personal Data:* b Buffalo, NY, May 27, 25; m 59, Catherine Pratt; c David R & Brian H. *Educ:* Cornell Univ, BEE, 46, PhD(physics), 52. *Prof Exp:* Asst physics, Cornell Univ, 46-51, physicist, Aeronaut Lab, 47-48; physicist, Electronics Lab, Gen Elec Co, NY, 51-57; mgr sci & tech rels, Adv Res & Develop Div, Avco Corp, Mass, 57-59; asst prog dir physics, NSF, 59-60, assoc prog dir, 60-61, spec asst to asst dir math, phys & eng sci div, 61, spec asst to assoc dir res, 61-65, exec asst to dir, Washington, DC, 65-69; vchancellor res, Wash Univ, 69-73; assoc exec officer, Nat Acad Sci-Nat Res Coun, 73-82, dir personnel & appts, 82-85, dep dir admin, 85-87. *Mem:* AAAS; Am Phys Soc. *Res:* Soft x-ray spectroscopy; magnetic materials; solid state physics; research administration. *Mailing Add:* 12705 Huntsman Way Potomac MD 20854

JOHNSTON, ROGER GLENN, LIGHT SCATTERING, INTERFEROMETRY. *Current Pos:* fel flow cytometry, 83-85, staff mem biophys, 85-90, STAFF MEM, CHEM SCI & TECHNOL DIV, LOS ALAMOS NAT LAB, 90- *Personal Data:* b Lincoln, Nebr, Feb 15, 54. *Educ:* Carleton Col, BA, 77; Univ Colo, Boulder, MS, 83, PhD(physics), 83. *Honors & Awards:* Res & Develop 100 Award, 95. *Prof Exp:* Grad student chem physics, Univ Colo, 77-83. *Concurrent Pos:* Prin investr, Los Alamos Nat Lab, 86-, proj leader, 88-, sect & team leader, 94-; consult, 90- *Mem:* Am Phys Soc; Am Indust Security. *Res:* Process development; development of new techniques and instrumentation for electro-optics, interferometry, light scattering, biometrics, and flow cytometry; vulnerability assessment of security devices. *Mailing Add:* Los Alamos Nat Lab MS J565 Los Alamos NM 87545. *Fax:* 505-665-4631; *E-Mail:* roger_johnston@cls-mac.lanl.gov

JOHNSTON, RONALD HARVEY, ELECTRONICS ENGINEERING. *Current Pos:* asst prof, 70-77, ASSOC PROF ELECTRONICS, UNIV CALGARY, 77- *Personal Data:* b Drumheller, Alta, May 11, 39; m 69. *Educ:* Univ Alta, BSc, 61; Univ London, DIC & PhD(elec eng), 67. *Prof Exp:* Eng trainee, Can Gen Elec, 61-62; res asst electronics, Queen's Univ, Belfast, 64-67; mem scientific staff res & develop, Northern Elec Co Ltd, 67-69. *Mem:* Inst Elec & Electronics Engrs. *Res:* Frequency multipliers; transistor amplifiers and multipliers; microwave measurements; semiconductor circuits. *Mailing Add:* Elec Eng Dept Univ Calgary Calgary AB T2N 1N4 Can

JOHNSTON, ROY G, STRUCTURAL ENGINEERING, EARTHQUAKE ENGINEERING. *Current Pos:* FOUNDER, EXEC VPRES & SECY, BRANDOW & JOHNSTON ASSOCS, 45- *Personal Data:* b Chicago, Ill, Jan 7, 14. *Educ:* Univ Southern Calif, BS, 35. *Prof Exp:* Staff mem, Los Angeles Co Building Dept, 35; consult eng, Clyde Deuel, 35-41; staff mem, Los Angeles Off, Lummus Co, 41-45. *Concurrent Pos:* Consult earthquake studies; mem earthquake Study, Vet Admin, Jet Propulsion Lab, Univ Southern Calif & Kaiser Hosps; dir, Earthquake Eng Res Inst, 79-81; mem, State Bldg Stand Comn, 86-94. *Mem:* Nat Acad Eng; fel Am Soc Civil Engrs; fel Am Concrete Inst; fel Earthquake Eng Res Inst (vpres, 81). *Res:* Structual design of over 10,000 projects; earthquake engineering. *Mailing Add:* Brandow & Johnston Assocs 1660 W Third St Los Angeles CA 90017

JOHNSTON, RUSSELL SHAYNE, PLASMA PHYSICS, APPLIED MATHEMATICS. *Current Pos:* ASSOC PROF PHYSICS, JACKSON STATE UNIV, 83- *Personal Data:* b Ft William, Ont, Nov 4, 48; m 76; c 3. *Educ:* McGill Univ, BSc, 70; Princeton Univ, PhD(plasma physics), 75. *Prof Exp:* Res asst plasma physics, Plasma Physics Lab, Princeton Univ, 70-74; res fel plasma physics, Lawrence Berkeley Lab, Univ Calif, 74-76; asst prof appl physics, Columbia Univ, 76-83. *Mem:* Am Phys Soc. *Res:* Theoretical plasma physics, particularly nonlinear interactions among waves and particles. *Mailing Add:* Dept Physics & Atmospheric Sci Jackson State Univ Jackson MS 39217

JOHNSTON, STEPHEN CHARLES, HUMAN PERFORMANCE, EXERCISE IN HEALTH. *Current Pos:* Vis asst prof 84-87, asst prof, 87-91, ASSOC PROF EXERCISE & SPORT SCI, UNIV UTAH, 91. *Personal Data:* b Vancouver, Wash, Sept 15, 50. *Educ:* Univ Utah, BS, 74, PhD(physiol exercise), 85. *Concurrent Pos:* Exercise consult, Holy Cross Hosp, Salt Lake City, Utah, 83- & Neuropsychol Dept, Vet Admin Hosp, Salt Lake City, Utah, 85-; dir physiol, Sports Med Coun, US Ski Team, 87-91, dir, Sport Sci, 91-; adj asst prof, Div Foods & Nutrit, Univ Utah, 87-, dir, Human Performance Res Lab, 87-; chair, Sports Med Comt, SW Alliance for Health, Phys Educ, Recreation & Dance, 89-91; adj assoc prof, Dept Bioeng & Div Foods & Nutrit, Univ Utah. *Mem:* AAAS; Am Asn Univ Professors; Am Alliance Health, Phys Educ, Recreation & Dance; Am Col Sports Med. *Res:* Effects of exercise and environment on the muscular, cardiovascular, respiratory, nervous and thermoregulatory systems of the human body; work with training response and optimization of training in elite athletes. *Mailing Add:* Dept Exercise & Sport Sci Univ Utah Salt Lake City UT 84112

JOHNSTON, TAYLOR JIMMIE, AGRONOMY, PLANT PHYSIOLOGY. *Current Pos:* From asst prof to assoc prof, Mich State Univ, 68-76, from asst dean to assoc dean, 81-91, PROF CROP SCI, MICH STATE UNIV, 76-, PROF CROP & SOIL SCI, 91- *Personal Data:* b Newbern, Tenn, May 11, 40; m 66, Paulette Meyer; c Bryan & Blair. *Educ:* Univ Tenn, Martin, BS, 63; Univ Ill, MS, 65, PhD(agron), 68. *Mem:* Am Soc Agron; Crop Sci Soc Am; Sigma Xi; Nat Asn Col & Teachers Agr; AAAS. *Res:* Photosynthesis of soybeans and general crop physiology and ecology. *Mailing Add:* Col Agr & Natural Resources Mich State Univ 286 PSS Bldg East Lansing MI 48824-1325

JOHNSTON, TUDOR WYATT, PLASMA PHYSICS. *Current Pos:* PROF, INST NAT RES SCI ENERGIE, UNIV QUE, 73- *Personal Data:* b Montreal, Que, Jan 17, 32; m 58; c 3. *Educ:* McGill Univ, BEng, 53; Cambridge Univ, PhD(eng physics), 58. *Prof Exp:* Sr res scientist, Microwave & Plasma Physics Lab, RCA Victor Co, Ltd, 58-67, Plasma & Space Physics Lab, 67-69; assoc prof physics, Univ Houston, 69-73. *Concurrent Pos:* Vis prof, Tex A&M Univ, 67; consult, RCA, 70, Can Dept Commun, 71, KMS Fusion, 80-81, Laser Lab, Univ Rochester, 81-; vis prof, Univ Rochester, 85. *Mem:* Fel Am Phys Soc; Can Asn Physicists. *Res:* Plasma theory; computer simulation; nonlinear wave-plasma; laser-plasma interaction. *Mailing Add:* INRS-Energie CP 1020 Varennes PQ J3X 1S2 Can

JOHNSTON, WALTER EDWARD, STATISTICS. *Current Pos:* ASSOC PROF, SOUTHWEST TEX STATE UNIV, SAN MARCOS, 80- *Personal Data:* b Clarksville, Ark, Apr 8, 39; m 60; c 3. *Educ:* Tex A&M Univ, BS, 60, MS, 65, PhD(statist), 70. *Prof Exp:* Teacher, Tex High Sch, 60-61; from asst prof to prof exp statist, Clemson Univ, 67-78. *Mem:* Am Statist Asn. *Res:* Application of statistical methods in agricultural and biological research. *Mailing Add:* 111 Pin Oak Dr Buda TX 78610

JOHNSTON, WARREN E, LAND ECONOMICS, COMMERCIAL AGRICULTURE. *Current Pos:* PROF AGR ECON, UNIV CALIF, DAVIS, 63- *Personal Data:* b Woodland, Calif, May 27, 33; m 59; c 2. *Educ:* Univ Calif, Davis, BS, 59; NC State Col, MS, 63; NC State Univ, PhD(agr econ & statist), 64. *Concurrent Pos:* Alexander von Humboldt res fel, WGer, 69-70; Fulbright res scholar, NZ, 76-77; dir, Am Agr Econ Asn, 85-88 & Int Agribus Mgt Asn, 91-94. *Mem:* Am Agr Econ Asn (pres, 90-91); Int Asn Agr Econ; Am Soc Farm Managers & Rural Appraisers; Int Agribus Mgr Asn. *Res:* Agricultural, natural resources and environmental economics and public policy; commercial and sustainable agriculture; land economics; land markets; adjustments to policy and economic changes. *Mailing Add:* Dept Agr Econ Univ Calif Davis CA 95616. *Fax:* 916-756-5614; *E-Mail:* wejohnston@ucdavis.edu

JOHNSTON, WILBUR DEXTER, JR, PHYSICS, ELECTRICAL ENGINEERING. *Current Pos:* mem tech staff, AT&T Bell Labs, 66-79, supvr, Solid State Mat, 80-96, TECH MGR, LIGHTWAVE DEVICE RES, LUCENT TECHNOL BELL LABS, 96- *Personal Data:* b New Haven, Conn, July 6, 40; m 63; c 2. *Educ:* Yale Univ, BS, 61; Mass Inst Technol, PhD(physics), 66. *Prof Exp:* Res asst electronics, Mass Inst Technol, 61-66. *Mem:* AAAS; Inst Elec & Electronics Engrs; Electrochem Soc. *Res:* Optical communications; laser physics; non-linear optics; semiconductor lasers; solar cells; heterojunction and compound semiconductor device physics; vapor phase epitaxial growth of semiconductor materials; materials science. *Mailing Add:* Oak Knoll Rd Mendham NJ 07945

JOHNSTON, WILLIAM CARGILL, SOLID STATE PHYSICS. *Current Pos:* chmn dept, 68-74, PROF PHYSICS, GEORGE MASON UNIV, 74-, DEAN SUMMER SESSION, 70- *Personal Data:* b Clarinda, Iowa, Aug 31, 17; m 47; c 4. *Educ:* Davidson Col, BA, 39; Univ Va, MS, 42, PhD(physics), 43. *Prof Exp:* Res engr, Westinghouse Elec Corp, 43-68. *Concurrent Pos:* Instr physics, Carnegie Inst Technol, 45- *Mem:* Sigma Xi. *Res:* Flame velocity measurements; fundamental combustion; solidification of metals. *Mailing Add:* 10927 Stuart Mill Rd Oakton VA 22124-1009

JOHNSTON, WILLIAM DWIGHT, INORGANIC CHEMISTRY. *Current Pos:* RETIRED. *Personal Data:* b Bellevue, Pa, Jan 17, 28; m 50; c 3. *Educ:* Univ Pittsburgh, BS, 49, MS, 51, PhD(chem), 53. *Prof Exp:* Res engr, Res Labs, Westinghouse Elec Corp, 53-57, adv chemist, 57-62; res chemist, Pittsburgh Corning Corp, 62-65, asst dir res, 65-69, dir res & develop, 69-74, tech dir int opers, 74-89. *Mem:* Am Chem Soc; Am Ceramic Soc. *Res:* Glass research; solid state chemistry; crystallography; semiconductors; magnetic materials; inorganic preparations; phase diagrams; thermodynamics; metal chelates. *Mailing Add:* 2416 Collins Rd Pittsburgh PA 15235

JOHNSTON, WILLIAM V, PHYSICAL CHEMISTRY & METALLURGY. *Current Pos:* RETIRED. *Personal Data:* b Berkeley, Calif, May 6, 27; m 51, Marian Stewart; c David, Donald, Carol & Cynthia. *Educ:* Col Wooster, BA, 50; Univ Pittsburgh, PhD(phys chem), 55. *Prof Exp:* Asst, Univ Pittsburgh, 50-55; sr cryogenic operator, Ohio State Univ, 52; res assoc, Knolls Atomic Power Lab, Gen Elec Co, 55-61; res specialist, Atomics Int Div, NAm Aviation Corp, 61-62, group leader phys metall, Sci Ctr, 62-69, prin scientist, NAm Rockwell Corp, 69, mem tech staff, Rocketdyne Div, 69-72; nuclear engr, US AEC, 72-74; br, chief, Fuel Behav Res Br, US Nuclear Regulatory Comn, 74-80, asst dir div eng, 80-85, chief, Eng Br, 85-86, dep dir div reactor safety, 86-90. *Concurrent Pos:* Chmn working group on nuclear safety, Orgn Econ Coop & Develop/Int Energy Agency, 75-80; chmn, Halden Reactor Proj, Orgn Econ Coop & Develop, 81. *Mem:* Am Chem Soc; Am Inst Mining, Metall & Petrol Engrs; fel AAAS; Am Nuclear Soc. *Res:* Metal physics; calorimetry; nuclear fuels; solid electrolytes; solution thermodynamics; nuclear safety; nuclear materials. *Mailing Add:* 2 Ruth Lane Downingtown PA 19335

JOHNSTON, WILLIAM WEBB, PATHOLOGY, CYTOLOGY. *Current Pos:* Res training prog grant, Duke Univ, 60-61, res fel path, 61-63, assoc, 63-65, from asst prof to assoc prof, 65- 72, PROF PATH, MED CTR, DUKE UNIV, 72-, DIR CYTOPATH, 66-, FAC CLIN CANCER TRAINING PROG, 66- *Personal Data:* b Statesville, NC, Aug 26, 33. *Educ:* Davidson Col, BS, 54; Duke Univ, MD, 59; Am Bd Path, dipl. *Honors & Awards:* Ortho Award, Can Soc Cytol, 72. *Concurrent Pos:* Consult path, Durham Vet Admin Hosp, 66-; mem bd dirs, Am Cancer Soc, Durham County. *Mem:* Am Asn Path; Am Soc Cytol (pres, 81-82); fel Am Soc Clin Path; fel Int Acad Cytol. *Res:* Basic diagnostic methods in cytopathology. *Mailing Add:* Dept Path Duke Univ Med Ctr Box 3322 Durham NC 27710

JOHNSTONE, C(HARLES) WILKIN, NUCLEAR PHYSICS, INSTRUMENTATION. *Current Pos:* RETIRED. *Personal Data:* b Alamosa, Colo, Aug 22, 16; m 47; c 2. *Educ:* Colo Col, AB, 38; Dartmouth Col, AM, 40. *Prof Exp:* Asst physics, Colo Col, 37-38, Dartmouth Col, 38-40 & Pa State Col, 40-41; proj engr, Navy Dept Proj, Sperry Gyroscope Co, NY, 41-44, Naval Res Lab, Washington, DC, 44-45, in charge marine radar design & develop, NY, 45-47; mem staff electronics res, Los Alamos Sci Lab, Calif, 47-56; develop proj engr, Schlumberger Well Serv, 56-60, sect head nuclear physics, 60-68, sr develop proj engr, Eng Physics Dept, 66-82. *Mem:* Inst Elec & Electronics Engrs. *Res:* Specialized electronic circuits for IFF, radar and nuclear research, and instrumentation; radioactivity techniques and apparatus for well logging. *Mailing Add:* 2055 Brentwood Dr Houston TX 77019

JOHNSTONE, DONALD BOYES, MICROBIOLOGY. *Current Pos:* RETIRED. *Personal Data:* b Newport, RI, July 25, 19; m 49; c 3. *Educ:* RI State Col, BS, 42; Rutgers Univ, MS, 43, PhD(microbiol), 48. *Prof Exp:* Bacteriologist, Woods Hole Oceanog Inst, 42-43 & 46; from asst prof to prof microbiol, Univ Vt, 48-85, microbiologist, Agr Exp Sta, 48-85, chmn dept agr biochem, 59-85, dean grad col, 69-85. *Mem:* AAAS; Am Soc Microbiol; fel Am Acad Microbiol. *Res:* Marine bacteriology; antibiotics from higher plants; isolation of streptomycin producing actinomycetes; vitamin B-12 sources; whey utilization; azotobacter metabolism; classification; fluorescent pigments; extra-cellular polysaccharides; pesticide degradation. *Mailing Add:* Eight Rudgate Rd Colchester VT 05446

JOHNSTONE, DONALD LEE, BACTERIOLOGY, MICROBIOLOGY. *Current Pos:* Asst prof civil eng & asst sanit scientist, Res Div, Col Eng, 69-76, ASSOC PROF CIVIL & ENVIRON ENG, WASH STATE UNIV, 76- *Personal Data:* b Bluefield, WVa, Feb 4, 39; m 62; c 1. *Educ:* Eastern Wash State Univ, BA, 64; Wash State Univ, MS, 66, PhD(aquatic bact), 70. *Concurrent Pos:* Mem, Int Conf Dis Nature Communicable to Man, 64; vis fac, Battelle, PNL. *Mem:* Am Soc Microbiol; Air & Waste Mgt; Am Water Works Soc; Sigma Xi. *Res:* Interaction of bacteria and soil; microbial degradation of contaminants in groundwater systems; survival of intestinal bacteria in the aquatic environment; effects of hydrocarbons on indicator bacteria in groundwater; ecology of fresh water bacteria. *Mailing Add:* Civil & Environ Eng Wash State Univ 1 SE Stadium Way Pullman WA 99164-0001

JOHNSTONE, JAMES G(EORGE), GEOLOGY, CIVIL ENGINEERING & GEOTECHNOLOGY. *Current Pos:* from asst prof to prof, 57-83, EMER PROF CIVIL ENG, COLO SCH MINES, 83- *Personal Data:* b LaPorte, Ind, July 29, 20; wid; c Nancy L (Ratay). *Educ:* Colo Sch Mines, Geol Eng, 48; Purdue Univ, MSE, 52. *Honors & Awards:* Alfred J Ryan Award, 90. *Prof Exp:* Asst prof geol & civil eng & res engr, Purdue Univ, 48-55; eng geologist, Geophoto Servs, Colo, 55-57. *Concurrent Pos:* Asst to plant engr, Ford Motor Co, Detroit, 42-45. *Mem:* Am Soc Civil Engrs; Sigma Xi; Nat Soc Prof Engrs (vpres, 75-76). *Res:* Soil mechanics; engineering geology; applications of geology to engineering projects; computer science. *Mailing Add:* 1805 S Balsam St 177 Lakewood CO 80232-6774

JOHNSTONE, JOHN WILLIAM, JR, CHEMISTRY. *Current Pos:* RETIRED. *Personal Data:* b Brooklyn, NY, Nov 19, 32; m 56, Claire Lundberg; c Thomas E, James R & Robert A. *Educ:* Hartwick Col, BA, 54. *Hon Degrees:* DSc, Hartwick Col, 91. *Prof Exp:* Staff mem, Hooker Chem Corp, 54-75, group vpres, 73-75; pres, Airco Alloys, Div Airco, Inc, 76-79; vpres & gen mgr indust prods, sr vpres chem group, Olin Corp, 79-80, corp vpres & pres chem group, Stamford, Conn, 80-85, pres, 85-87, chief operating officer, 86-87, pres & chief exec officer & chmn, 88-96. *Concurrent Pos:* Bd dirs, Am Brands, Phoenix Home Life Ins Co. *Mem:* Am Mgt Asn; Soc Chem Indust; Soap & Detergent Asn; Chem Mfrs Asn. *Res:* Chemical products development. *Mailing Add:* 467 Carter St New Canaan CT 06840

JOHNSTONE, ROSE M, BIOCHEMISTRY. *Current Pos:* from asst prof to assoc prof, 65-76, chmn dept biochem, 80-90, PROF BIOCHEM, McGILL UNIV, 77-, GILMAN-CHNEY PROF BIOCHEM, 85- *Personal Data:* b Lodz, Poland, May 14, 28; Can citizen; m 53; c 2. *Educ:* McGill Univ, BSc, 50, PhD(biochem), 53. *Honors & Awards:* Queen's Jubilee Medal, 77. *Prof Exp:* Res assoc biochem, McGill Univ & Montreal Gen Hosp Res Inst, 53-65, asst prof, 61-65. *Concurrent Pos:* Nat Cancer Inst Can fel, 54-57, res grant, 65-; Med Res Coun grant, 65-, NIH, 88- *Mem:* Can Fedn Biol Soc; Can Biochem Soc; Am Soc Biol Chemists; AAAS; fel Royal Soc Can (treas); Can Soc Cell Biol. *Res:* Transport of organic substances into mammalian cells; development and cloning of transport systems; reconstitution of transport systems; membrane remodeling during development of red cells; targeting of proteins for externalization during red cell maturation; exosomes and their protein content. *Mailing Add:* Dept Biochem Rm 810 McGill Univ 3655 Drummond Montreal PQ H3G 1Y6 Can. *Fax:* 514-398-7384

JOHNSTON-FELLER, RUTH M, COLOR SCIENCE. *Current Pos:* RES ASSOC, MELLON INST, 75- *Personal Data:* b Polo, Ill, Mar 31, 23; m 75, Robert L. *Educ:* Univ Ill, AB, 47. *Honors & Awards:* Bruning Award, Fedn Soc Paint Technol, 70; Macbeth Award, Int-Soc Color Coun, 84, Dorothy Nickerson Award, 88; Mattiello Lect, Fedn Soc Coatings Technol, 85; George Baugh Heckel Award, Fedn Soc Coatings Technol, 89. *Prof Exp:* Anal chemist, USDA, 44-46, Univ Ill, 46-47 & A E Staley Co, 47; res chemist, Pittsburgh Plate Glass Indust, 47-51, proj leader, 56-67; res chemist, Rohm & Haas Co, Pa, 53-54; asst dir, color ctr, Davidson & Hemmendinger, 67-69; dir, applns serv, Kollmorgen Corp, 69-73; mgr, coatings & colorimetry, Ciba-Geigy Corp, 73-85. *Concurrent Pos:* Lectr color sci, Univ Utah, Lehigh Univ, Clemson Univ & Ciba-Geigy Corp, 73-75; consult, pvt & inst, 75-; mem, bd dir, Paint Res Inst, 79-81. *Mem:* Am Chem Soc; Optical Soc Am; Am Inst Conserv Hist & Artistic Works; Am Soc Testing & Mat; Fedn Soc Coatings Technol; Int-Soc Color Coun. *Res:* Characterization of pigments and dyes in organic coatings; photochemically-induced fading of such systems; optical behavior of colorants in colored paint, plastic, textile and artists' materials. *Mailing Add:* Carnegie-Mellon Res Inst 220 N Dithridge St No 706 Pittsburgh PA 15213

JOINER, R(EGINALD) GRACEN, MIDDLE ATMOSPHERE RESEARCH, SPACE RADIATION EFFECTS. *Current Pos:* Physicist, US Naval Ordnance Lab, 59-64, physicist, Off Naval Res, 64-80, supvry phys sci adminr, 80-82, PROG MGR SPACE PHYSICS, OFF NAVAL RES, 82- *Personal Data:* b Hawkinsville, Ga, Feb 10, 33; m 52; c 2. *Educ:* Univ Ga, BS, 58, MS, 59. *Mem:* Am Geophys Union. *Res:* Extremely low frequency-very low frequency radio propagation; ionosphere; space. *Mailing Add:* 2988 Poplar Trail Annapolis MD 21401

JOINER, WILLIAM CORNELIUS HENRY, SOLID STATE PHYSICS. *Current Pos:* from asst prof to assoc prof, 65-73, PROF PHYSICS, UNIV CINCINNATI, 73-, HEAD DEPT, 74- *Personal Data:* b Camden, NJ, June 8, 36; m 64. *Educ:* Rutgers Univ, BA, 57, PhD(physics), 62. *Prof Exp:* Sr physicist, Aerospace Div, Westinghouse Elec Co, 61-65, fel physicist, 65. *Mem:* Am Phys Soc; Sigma Xi. *Res:* Superconductivity; low temperature physics. *Mailing Add:* 7290 Green Farms Dr Cincinnati OH 45224

JOIST, HEINRICH J, HEMATOLOGY, COAGULATION DISORDERS. *Current Pos:* PROF MED & PATH, DIV BMT, ONCOL HEMAT, ST LOUIS MED CTR, 83-, DIR HEMOSTASIS & THROMBOSIS LABS, 83-; CO-DIR, REGIONAL HEMOPHILIA COMP DIAG & TREATMENT CTR, MO, ILL, 77- *Personal Data:* b Bergisch, Gladbach, Ger, Jan 9, 35. *Educ:* McMaster Univ, PhD(exp path), 77; Univ Cologn, Ger, MD, 82. *Res:* Hematology; coagulation disorders. *Mailing Add:* St Louis Health Sci Ctr Path Dept 3635 Vista Ave PO Box 15250 St Louis MO 63110. *Fax:* 314-268-5110

JOKELA, JALMER JOHN, FOREST GENETICS. *Current Pos:* RETIRED. *Personal Data:* b Ely, Minn, Sept 20, 21; m 53; c 3. *Educ:* Univ Minn, BSF, 47, MS, 51; Univ Ill, PhD(agron), 63. *Prof Exp:* Agr aide, Lake States Forest Exp Sta, 46; asst, Univ Minn, 49-51; asst, Univ Ill, Urbana, 47-49 & 51-59, res assoc, 59-69, from instr to assoc prof forest res, 59-86. *Mem:* Soc Am Foresters; Sigma Xi. *Res:* Genetics and breeding of cottonwoods; silviculture; mensuration. *Mailing Add:* 1661 Saari Rd Ely MN 55731-8238

JOKERST, NAN MARIE, OPTICS, SOLID STATE PHYSICS. *Current Pos:* ASST PROF ELEC ENG, GA INST TECHNOL, 89- *Personal Data:* b St Louis, Mo, May 11, 61; m 88. *Educ:* Creighton Univ, BS, 82; Univ Southern Calif, MS, 84, PhD(elec eng), 89. *Concurrent Pos:* Consult, Foster-Miller, Inc, 90-; NSF presidential young investr, 90. *Mem:* Optical Soc Am; Inst Elec & Electronics Engrs; Am Phys Soc; Sigma Xi. *Res:* Monolithic deposition of GaAs and InP onto host substrates such as silicon, glass, lithium niobate, polymers for optoelectronic integrated circuits; solar cells; semiconductor lasers; nonlinear optics in semiconductors. *Mailing Add:* Sch Elec Eng Ga Inst Technol Atlanta GA 30332

JOKINEN, EILEEN HOPE, INVERTEBRATE ZOOLOGY, PARASITOLOGY. *Current Pos:* vis asst prof gen ecol & invert zool, 80-86, asst dir, 87-93, INTERIM DIR, CONN INST WATER RESOURCES, UNIV CONN, STORRS, 93- *Personal Data:* b Detroit, Mich, July 22, 43. *Educ:* Wayne State Univ, BS, 65, PhD(zool), 71. *Prof Exp:* Instr introd biol, Wayne Co Community Col, Detroit, Mich, 71-72; instr comp anat, Univ Mich, Dearborn, Mich, 72; asst & assoc prof invert zool, ecol, parasitol, comp anat, embryol & introd zool, Suffolk Univ, Boston, Mass, 72-80. *Mem:* Am Malacol Soc; Am Soc Zoologists; Am Inst Biol Sci. *Res:* Freshwater malacology; community ecology of freshwater littoral zone benthos; biogeography of freshwater snails. *Mailing Add:* Inst water Resources Univ Conn U-18 Storrs CT 06269-4018. *Fax:* 860-486-5408

JOKIPII, JACK RANDOLPH, THEORETICAL PHYSICS, ASTROPHYSICS. *Current Pos:* PROF ASTRON & PLANETARY SCI, UNIV ARIZ, 74- *Personal Data:* b Ironwood, Mich, Sept 10, 39; m 64; c 3. *Educ:* Univ Mich, BS, 61; Calif Inst Technol, PhD(physics), 65. *Prof Exp:* Res assoc physics, Enrico Fermi Inst Nuclear Studies, Univ Chicago, 65-67, asst prof, Inst & Univ, 67-69; assoc prof theoret physics, Downs Lab Physics, Calif Inst Technol, 69-73. *Concurrent Pos:* Alfred P Sloan Found fel, 69. *Mem:* Fel Am Phys Soc; Am Geophys Union; Int Astron Union. *Res:* Theoretical space physics; cosmic ray acceleration and propagation; interpretation of space vehicle observations; solar physics; interstellar physics. *Mailing Add:* Dept Planetary Sci Univ Ariz Tucson AZ 85721

JOKL, ERNST, PHYSIOLOGY. *Current Pos:* DISTINGUISHED PROF REHAB, PHYSIOL & PHYS EDUC, UNIV KY, 54- *Personal Data:* b Breslau, Ger, Aug 3, 07; nat US; m 33; c 2. *Educ:* Breslau Univ, MD, 31; Univ Witwatersrand, MB & BCh, 36. *Honors & Awards:* Buckston Browne Brit Empire Prize, 42; Medal, Brit Harveian Soc, 42; Res Awards, Ger Soc Sports Med & Int Coun Mil Sport. *Prof Exp:* Asst exp med, Breslau Univ, 30-31; sr res fel, Int Inst High Altitude Physics, Switz, 31; dir, Res Inst Med & Sport, Breslau Univ, 31-33; sr med officer, Dept Educ & mem, Nat Adv Coun Phys Educ, Union SAfrica, 38-44, med consult, Dir Gen Med Serv & Aviation Med, Union Defense Force, 40-44. *Concurrent Pos:* Pres res comt, Int Coun Sport & Phys Educ, UNESCO; hon prof physiol & med, Univs WBerlin, Frankfurt & Cologne; Nat Libr Med res grant fel, Bethesda. *Mem:* Fel Am Col Cardiol; Brit Med Asn; Sigma Xi. *Res:* Clinical physiology of exercise and rehabilitation. *Mailing Add:* 1121 Tanbark Rd Lexington KY 40515

JOKLIK, G FRANK, RESEARCH ADMINISTRATION. *Current Pos:* PRES & CHIEF OPERATING OFFICER, MK GOLD, INC, 95- *Personal Data:* b Vienna, Austria, May 30, 28. *Educ:* Univ Sydney, BSc, 49, PhD(geol), 53. *Prof Exp:* Fulbright scholar, Columbia Univ, 53-54; mgr, Amax, Inc, 63-72, corp vpres, 72-74; sr vpres, Metals Mining Standard Oil Co, Ohio, 82-87; pres & chief exec officer, B P Minerals Am, 87-89; explor geologist, Kennecott Corp, NY, 54-63, vpres, 74-79, pres, Salt Lake City, 80-87, pres & chief exec officer, 89-93. *Concurrent Pos:* Dir, First Security Corp; mem bd, Am Mining Cong, Am Inst Mining, Metall & Petrol Engrs & Australian Inst Mining & Metall. *Mem:* Nat Acad Eng. *Mailing Add:* 60 E S Temple Suite 2100 Salt Lake City UT 84111. *Fax:* 801-297-6940

JOKLIK, WOLFGANG KARL, MOLECULAR BIOLOGY, VIROLOGY. *Current Pos:* James B Duke prof microbiol & immunol & chmn dept, 68-92, JAMES B DUKE PROF MICROBIOL, DUKE UNIV, 92- *Personal Data:* b Vienna, Austria, Nov 16, 26; m 55, 77, Patricia Hunter; c Richard G & Vivien H. *Educ:* Univ Sydney, BSc, 48, MSc, 49; Oxford Univ, DPhil(biochem), 52. *Prof Exp:* Fel microbiol, Australian Nat Univ, 52-62; USPHS traveling fel, 59-60; from assoc prof to prof cell biol, Albert Einstein Col Med, 62-68. *Concurrent Pos:* Pres, Virol Div, Am Soc Microbiol, 68-89 & group counr, Group IV, 81-83; chmn, Virol Study Sect, NIH, 73-75, mem, Rec DNA Adv Comt, 82-87; ed-in-chief, Virol 76-93; mem exec comt, Int Comn Taxon Viruses, 78-84; assoc ed, J Biol Chem, 78-89; mem, Coun Res & Clin Awards, Am Cancer Soc, 80-83 & 88-91; ed-in-chief, Microbiol Rev, 90-94. *Mem:* Nat Acad Sci; Inst Med of Nat Acad Sci; Am Soc Microbiol; Am Med Sch Microbiol Chmns Asn (pres, 79); Am Soc Virol (pres, 82-83); Am Soc Biochem & Molecular Biol. *Res:* Biochemistry of virus multiplication, including the mechanisms of nucleic acid replication, transcription and translation of genetic information, regulation of gene expression and the mechanisms of protein synthesis; molecular virology; molecular genetics. *Mailing Add:* Dept Microbiol Duke Univ Med Ctr Durham NC 27710. *Fax:* 919-684-8735; *E-Mail:* joklik@abacus.mc.duke.edu

JOLESZ, FERENC ANDRAS, RADIOLOGY, NEUROLOGY. *Current Pos:* Milton res fel physiol, Harvard Med Sch, 80, res fel, 80-82, res assoc, 81-82, clin fel radiol, 82-85, from asst prof to assoc prof, 85-96, PROF RADIOL, HARVARD MED SCH, 96-; DIR, IMAGE GUIDED THER PROG, BRIGHAM & WOMEN'S HOSP, BOSTON, 93- *Personal Data:* b Budapest, Hungary, May 21, 46; m, Anna Szolnoki; c Marta & Klara. *Educ:* Semmelweis Med Sch, MD, 71; Am Bd Radiol, cert, 87; Am Bd Neuroradiol, cert, 88. *Hon Degrees:* Dr, Pannon Agr Univ, 96. *Honors & Awards:* Visions in Med Award, Gen Elec Med Systs, 91. *Prof Exp:* Intern, Semmelweis Med Sch, Hungary, 70-71; instr, Dept Physiol, Col Phys Educ, Hungary, 71-73, asst prof, 73-74, adj prof, 74-75; resident neurosurg, Inst Neurosurg, Hungary, 75-79; res fel neurol, Mass Gen Hosp, 79-80. *Concurrent Pos:* Lectr, Semmelweis Med Sch, 69-71, Col Phys Educ, Hungary, 71-75, Harvard Med Sch, 84-, Brigham & Women's Hosp, 85-, Children's Med Hosp, Boston, 85- & Wellesley Col, 85-86; resident radiol, Brigham & Women's Hosp, 82-85, radiologist, 85-, dir, Neuro Imaging Sect, 87-88, dir, Div Magnetic Resonance Imaging, 88-, mem res comt, Dept Radiol, 90-; consult, Dana Farber Cancer Inst, 85-, Children's Hosp Boston, 86- & W Roxbury Vet Admin Hosp, 87-; grantee, Milton Fund, 87-88, NIH, 90-94, Nat Multiple Sclerosis Soc, 91-94, Off Naval Res, 92-94, Whitaker Found, 92-95 & Nat Cancer Inst, 95-; mem res comt, Harvard Laser Ctr, 90-; assoc ed, J Acad Radio, 94-; ed, J Magnetic Resonance Imaging & Magnetic Resonance Med. *Mem:* Inst Med-Nat Acad Sci; Soc Magnetic Resonance Med; sr mem Am Soc Neuroradiol; Asn Univ Radiologists; Soc Magnetic Resonance Imaging; Radiol Soc NAm. *Res:* Brain morphology; white matter function and pathology; magnetic resonance imaging methods; interventional/surgical applications of magnetic resonance imaging. *Mailing Add:* 20 Rawson Rd Brookline MA 02146. *E-Mail:* jolesz@bwh.harvard.edu

JOLICOEUR, PIERRE, BIOMATHEMATICS, BIOMETRICS. *Current Pos:* from asst prof to assoc prof biol, 61-72, chmn, Dept Biol Sci, 73-77, PROF BIOL, UNIV MONTREAL, 72- *Personal Data:* b Montreal, Que, Apr 5, 34; m 69; c Lucie, Francine & Andre'. *Educ:* Univ Montreal, BA, 53, BSc, 56; Univ BC, MA, 58; Univ Chicago, PhD(paleozool), 63. *Concurrent Pos:* Vis assoc prof, Univ Kans, 66; vis assoc scientist, NIH, 67. *Mem:* Fel AAAS; Biomet Soc. *Res:* Biological applications of mathematics and statistics, multivariate analysis; allometry and nonlinear growth curves; vertebrate zoology; ecology of animal populations. *Mailing Add:* Dept Biol Sci Univ Montreal PO Box 6128 Montreal PQ H3C 3J7 Can. *Fax:* 514-343-2293

JOLIVETTE, PETER LAUSON, NUCLEAR STRUCTURES. *Current Pos:* asst prof, 76-83, ASSOC PROF PHYSICS, HOPE COL, 83- *Personal Data:* b Madison, Wis, May 27, 41; m 67; c 2. *Educ:* Univ Wis-Madison, BS, 63, PhD(physics), 71; Purdue Univ, MS, 65. *Prof Exp:* Res assoc, Univ Notre Dame, 70-76, vis asst prof physics, 75. *Mem:* Am Inst Physics; Am Asn Physics Teachers. *Res:* Low and intermediate energy nuclear physics; isospin and charge symmetry effects. *Mailing Add:* Dept Physics Hope Col Holland MI 49423

JOLLES, MITCHELL IRA, SOLID MECHANICS, FRACTURE MECHANICS. *Current Pos:* chmn dept, 88-91, PROF MECH ENG, WIDENER UNIV, 88- *Personal Data:* b Bronx, NY, Feb 10, 53. *Educ:* Polytech Inst, Brooklyn, BS & MS, 73; Va Polytech Inst & State Univ, PhD(eng mech), 76. *Honors & Awards:* Ralph R Teetor Award, Soc Automotive Engrs, 79; Jimmie Hamilton Award, Am Soc Naval Engrs, 89. *Prof Exp:* Lectr eng sci & mech, 73-74, Va Polytech Inst & State Univ, instr, 74-76; asst prof aerospace & mech eng, Univ Notre Dame, 77-79; assoc prof mech & aero eng/nuclear eng, Univ Mo, 79-82; head, Fracture Mech Sect, Naval Res Lab, 82-88. *Concurrent Pos:* Res assoc, Nat Aeronaut & Space Admin, 73-74, Dept Defense, 73-74, NSF, 73-76, Energy Res & Develop Admin, 75-76, Air Force Flight Dynamics Lab, 75 & Cabot Corp, 77; prin investr, NSF, 78-82, Exxon Educ Found, 78-79, Student Competition Relevant Eng, 78-79 & Argonne Nat Lab, 80-82; lectr, George Washington Univ, Eng Ed, 83-88; consult, Mat Eng Assoc, 83-88; adj fac, Va Polytech Inst & State Univ, 84-88. *Mem:* Am Asn Univ Prof; Am Soc Eng Educ; Sigma Xi. *Res:* Fracture mechanics; experimental mechanics; constitutive theory and material damage models; structural integrity methodology; nonlinear systems. *Mailing Add:* 1145 Putnam Blvd Wallingford PA 19086

JOLLEY, DAVID KENT, SIGNAL PROCESSING ALGORITHMS, GEOLOCATION TECHNIQUES. *Current Pos:* VPRES ENG, ASTECH, INC, 88- *Personal Data:* b Park City, Utah, Jan 25, 44; m 70; c 4. *Educ:* Univ Utah, BA, 66, PhD(physics), 73. *Prof Exp:* Sr engr, ESL Inc, 72-82, dept mgr, 84-88; sr engr, Advent Inc, 82-84. *Res:* Development of signal processing algorithms and signal processing systems for government agencies primarily in the areas of reconnaissance and surveillance. *Mailing Add:* Nichols Res Corp 5272 S College Dr Suite 300 Murray UT 84123

JOLLEY, HOMER RICHARD, public health administration, research administration, for more information see previous edition

JOLLEY, JOHN ERIC, MATERIALS SCIENCE. *Current Pos:* CONSULT, 85- *Personal Data:* b Blackpool, Eng, June 26, 29; nat US; m 55, Faith Bishop; c Susan, Linda & Melissa. *Educ:* Univ Liverpool, BS, 50, PhD(phys chem), 53. *Prof Exp:* Fel, Univ Rochester. 53-55 & Univ Calif, Berkeley, 55-57; res chemist film dept, Res Lab, E I du Pont de Nemours & Co, Inc, 58-60, res chemist cent res dept, 60, res supvr, 60-64, tech mgr develop dept, Exp Sta, 64-67, res fel, photog & electronic prod dept, 67-85. *Mem:* Sigma Xi; Am Ceramic Soc; Int Soc Hybrid Microelectronics; Soc Info Display. *Res:* Kinetics; radical reactions; solubility; polymer chemistry; electronic materials; magnetism; photographic science; glasses; ceramics; rheology. *Mailing Add:* 20 Boulder Brook Dr Wilmington DE 19803. *E-Mail:* ejolley@tower_hill.pvt.k12.de.us

JOLLEY, ROBERT LOUIS, ENVIRONMENTAL CHEMISTRY. *Current Pos:* chemist, 56-73, CHEM ECOLOGIST, OAK RIDGE NAT LAB, 73- *Personal Data:* b Little Rock, Ark, July 11, 29; m 50; c 2. *Educ:* Friends Univ, BA, 50; Univ Tenn, Knoxville, PhD(ecol), 73. *Prof Exp:* Asst chem, Friends Univ, 49-50 & Univ Chicago, 50-51; chemist, Southwest Grease & Oil Co, 51-55. *Concurrent Pos:* County comnr, Anderson County, Tenn, 59- *Mem:* Am Chem Soc; AAAS; Sigma Xi. *Res:* Measurement and identification of organic constituents in natural and polluted waters; determination of chlorination effects and analysis of chloro-organics in process effluents and condenser cooling waters for electric power plants; evaluation of treatment technologies for low-level radioactive waste and hazardous waste. *Mailing Add:* 120 N Seneca Rd Oak Ridge TN 37830-4898

JOLLEY, WELDON BOSEN, PHYSIOLOGY. *Current Pos:* ADV, NUCLEIC ACID RES INST, 95- *Personal Data:* b Gunnison, Utah, Sept 8, 26; m 54, 83; c 5. *Educ:* Brigham Young Univ, AB, 52; Univ Southern Calif, PhD(cell physiol), 59. *Prof Exp:* Res assoc, Univ Southern Calif, 53-59, instr, 58-59, asst prof physiol & co-dir, Surg Res Lab, 59-71; prof physiol, biophys & surg & assoc dir, Surg Res Lab, Loma Linda Univ, 71-80; prof physiol, Jerry L Pettis Vet Admin Hosp, 80-95. *Concurrent Pos:* Instr, Compton Col, 56; dir, Bio Nuclear Corp; mem bd, Life Resources, Inc & ICN Pharmaceut Inc; pres, Nucleic Acid Res Inst, 85-; mem bd dirs, SPI Pharm, Inc, sr vpres bd dirs, ICN Pharm, Inc. *Mem:* AAAS; AMA; Am Fedn Clin Res; Am Physiol Soc; Transplantation Soc. *Res:* Antiviral agents; immunologic modulators; cancer immunology; transplantation of skin, pancreas, heart, kidneys; endotoxic and hemorrhagic shock; biological effects of pulsed electromagnetic fields. *Mailing Add:* 3825 Woodbine Orange CA 92867

JOLLICK, JOSEPH DARRYL, MICROBIAL GENETICS, MEDICAL MICROBIOLOGY. *Current Pos:* asst prof, Sch Med, 78-80, ASSOC PROF MICROBIOL, COL OSTEOP MED, OHIO UNIV, 80- *Personal Data:* b Denbo, Pa, May 15, 41; m 63; c 2. *Educ:* Calif State Col, BS, 63, Am Univ, MS, 66; WVa Univ, PhD(microbiol), 69. *Prof Exp:* Biologist, Nat Cancer Inst, 63-64; Nat Res Coun grant, Biol Sci Lab, Ft Detrick, 69-70; instr, Sch Med, Wayne State Univ, 70-72, asst prof microbiol, 72-77. *Concurrent Pos:* NIH grant, Wayne State Univ, 74- *Mem:* AAAS; Am Soc Microbiol; Am Asn Univ Prof. *Res:* Genetics of Caulobacter; mechanism and transfer of antibiotic resistance in Serratia and Pseudomonas. *Mailing Add:* Biomed Sci Col Osteop Med Ohio Univ Athens OH 45701

JOLLIE, MALCOLM THOMAS, COMPARATIVE ANATOMY, ZOOLOGY. *Current Pos:* RETIRED. *Personal Data:* b Lakewood, Ohio, July 11, 19; m 50; c 2. *Educ:* Western Reserve Univ, BS, 41; Univ Colo, MS, 43; Stanford Univ, PhD(comp anat), 54. *Prof Exp:* Asst biol, Univ Colo, 41-43; mus technician birds & asst zool, Univ Calif, 43-45; instr sci, Western NMex Teachers Col, 45-47; asst & assoc prof zool, Univ Idaho, 47-56 & Univ Pittsburg, 56-65; prof biol, Northern Ill Univ, 65-88. *Res:* Comparative anatomy relating to origin and phylogeny of chordates and vertebrates; systematic ornithology and ichthyology. *Mailing Add:* 19074 N 91st St Scottsdale AZ 85255

JOLLIE, WILLIAM PUCETTE, ANATOMY, CELL & DEVELOPMENTAL BIOLOGY. *Current Pos:* PROF ANAT & CHMN DEPT, MED COL VA, VA COMMONWEALTH UNIV, 69- *Personal Data:* b Passaic, NJ, June 27, 28; m 50; c 2. *Educ:* Lehigh Univ, BA, 50, MS, 52; Harvard Univ, PhD(biol), 59. *Prof Exp:* Lectr histol & embryol, Queen's

Univ, Ont, 59-61; From asst prof to prof anat, Sch Med, Tulane Univ, 61-69. *Mem:* Am Asn Anatomists; Am Soc Cell Biologists; Teratology Soc. *Res:* Controlling mechanisms for placental transport; visualization of placental transport mechanisms; maternal accommodations to implantation and placental formation; effects of alcohol on acquisition of neonatal immunity. *Mailing Add:* Dept Anat Va Commonwealth Univ PO Box 980709 MCV Sta 11th & Marshall St Richmond VA 23298-0709. *Fax:* 804-828-9477; *E-Mail:* jollie@gems.vcu.edu

JOLLOW, DAVID J, TOXICOLOGY. *Current Pos:* PROF PHARMACOL & DIR ENVIRON HAZARDS ASSESSMENT RES, UNIV SC, 92- *Personal Data:* b Sidney, Australia, May 5, 36. *Educ:* Monarch Univ, Australia, PhD(biochem), 67. *Res:* Toxicology. *Mailing Add:* Dept Pharmacol Med Univ SC 171 Ashley Ave Charleston SC 29401-5801

JOLLS, CLAUDIA LEE, PLANT ECOLOGY, PLANT POPULATION BIOLOGY. *Current Pos:* asst prof, 84-89, ASSOC PROF, BIOL DEPT, ECAROLINA UNIV, 90- *Personal Data:* b Detroit, Mich, May 20, 53. *Educ:* Univ Mich, Ann Arbor, BS, 75; Univ Colo, Boulder, PhD(biol), 80. *Prof Exp:* Teaching asst ecol, bot & human physiol, Dept Environ Pop & Organismic, Univ Colo, 75-80; fel plant pop biol, Mich State Univ, 80-81; resident terrestrial ecologist, Biol Sta, Univ Mich, 81-84. *Concurrent Pos:* Res asst plant ecol, Dept Environ, Pop & Organismic, Univ Colo at Audubon-Whittel Res Ranch, Ariz, 76; adv, Traineeship Prog, Mt Res Sta, Inst Arctic & Alpine Res, Univ Colo, NSF, 77 & 78; fel, Kellogg Biostation, Mich State Univ, 81; prog coordr, Naturalist-Ecologist Training Prog, Biol Sta, Univ Mich, 81-84, res assoc & vis fac, 85, 87, 89, 91, 93; res assoc, Univ Colo, 88; Helms res award, Chap Sigma Xi, ECarolina Univ, 90. *Mem:* Am Inst Biol Sci; Bot Soc Am; Ecol Soc Am; Sigma Xi. *Res:* Plant ecology and population biology: conservation biology, population dynamics, breeding biology, forest succession; field-based studies in wetlands; northern hardwoods, alpine tundra, dunes. *Mailing Add:* Dept Biol ECarolina Univ Greenville NC 27858-4353

JOLLS, KENNETH ROBERT, PHASE BEHAVIOR, COMPUTER GRAPHICS. *Current Pos:* assoc prof chem eng, Iowa State Univ, 70-90, PROF CHEM ENG, 90- *Personal Data:* b Baltimore, Md, Oct 19, 33; c 1. *Educ:* Duke Univ, AB, 58; NC State Univ, BSChE, 61; Univ Ill, MS, 63, PhD(chem eng), 66. *Prof Exp:* Asst chem eng, Univ Ill, 61-65; from asst prof to assoc prof, Polytech Inst Brooklyn, 65-70. *Concurrent Pos:* Vis prof chem eng, Univ Calif, Berkeley, 81-83 & Cornell Univ, 84. *Mem:* Am Inst Chem Engrs; Sigma Xi; Am Chem Soc; Asn Comput Mach. *Res:* Fluid mechanics; thermodynamics; application of electronic instrumentation in chemical engineering; computer graphics; scientific visualization. *Mailing Add:* Dept Chem Eng Sweeney Hall Iowa State Univ Ames IA 50011-2230

JOLLY, ALISON BISHOP, PRIMATE BEHAVIOR. *Current Pos:* VIS LECTR, PRINCETON UNIV, 87- *Personal Data:* b Ithaca, NY, May 9, 37; m 63; c 4. *Educ:* Cornell Univ, BA, 58; Yale Univ, PhD(zool), 62. *Prof Exp:* Res assoc zool, NY Zool Soc, 62-64; res assoc, Sch Biol, Univ Sussex, 68-81; guest investr, Rockefeller Univ, 82-87. *Concurrent Pos:* NSF res grant, 62-64. *Mem:* Int Primatol Soc (pres); Wildlife Preserv Trust Int; Animal Behav Asn; Sigma Xi; Am Primatology Asn; fel AAAS; fel Am Acad Arts & Sci. *Res:* Conservation of natural ecosystems in Madagascar; primate behavior, particularly that of prosimians; evolution of human behavior. *Mailing Add:* Dept EE Biol Princeton Univ Princeton NJ 08544-1003. *Fax:* 609-258-1334

JOLLY, CLIFFORD J, PHYSICAL ANTHROPOLOGY, PRIMATOLOGY. *Current Pos:* from asst prof to assoc prof, 67-75, PROF PHYS ANTHROPOLOGY, NY UNIV, 75- *Personal Data:* b Southend, Eng, Jan 21, 39; m 61; c 2. *Educ:* Univ London, BA, 60, PhD(phys anthrop), 65. *Prof Exp:* Res asst phys anthropology, Univ Col, London, 63-65, asst lectr, 65-67. *Concurrent Pos:* Vis res fel, Makerere Univ Col, Uganda, 65-66. *Mem:* Soc Study Human Biol; Zool Soc London; Royal Anthrop Inst; Sigma Xi. *Res:* Primate functional anatomy; serology and biology. *Mailing Add:* 60 Eighth St Hoboken NJ 07030-5057

JOLLY, JANICE LAURENE WILLARD, economic geology, petrology, for more information see previous edition

JOLLY, STUART MARTIN, systems design, for more information see previous edition

JOLLY, WAYNE TRAVIS, PETROLOGY, VOLCANOLOGY. *Current Pos:* asst prof, 71-75, ASSOC PROF GEOL, BROCK UNIV, 75- *Personal Data:* b Jacksonville, Tex, Aug 15, 40. *Educ:* Univ Tex, Austin, BFA, 63, MA, 67; State Univ NY Binghamton, PhD(geol), 70. *Prof Exp:* Fel geol, Univ Sask, 70-71. *Mem:* Geol Soc Am; Geol Asn Can; Mineral Asn Can. *Res:* Geochemical petrology and metamorphic petrology of volcanic rocks with emphasis on prehnite-pumpellyite facies and origin of Archean volcanics. *Mailing Add:* Dept Geol Sci Brock Univ St Catharines ON L2S 3A1 Can

JOLLY, WILLIAM LEE, INORGANIC CHEMISTRY. *Current Pos:* instr, Univ Calif, 52-53, chemist, Radiation Lab, 53-55, from asst prof to assoc prof, 55-62, prof, 62-91, EMER PROF CHEM, UNIV CALIF, BERKELEY, 91- *Personal Data:* b Chicago, Ill, Dec 27, 27; m 95, Jane Weidringer; c 3. *Educ:* Univ Ill, BS, 48, MS, 49; Univ Calif, PhD(chem), 52. *Mem:* AAAS; Am Chem Soc; Royal Soc Chem. *Res:* Liquid ammonia chemistry; chemistry of the volatile hydrides; studies of the bonding in transition metal complexes; x-ray photoelectron spectroscopy; chemistry of the photographic process. *Mailing Add:* Dept Chem Univ Calif Berkeley CA 94720-1460

JOLLY-WOODRUFF, SUSAN, THEORETICAL CHEMISTRY. *Current Pos:* CONSULT. *Personal Data:* b Wakefield, RI, Aug 18, 40; m 63; c 2. *Educ:* Oberlin Col, AB, 62; Johns Hopkins Univ, MAT, 63; Univ Calif, Irvine, PhD(chem), 77. *Prof Exp:* Mem staff chem & fel, Los Alamos Sci Lab, 77-93. *Mem:* Am Chem Soc. *Res:* Chemical dynamics; chemical kinetics; classical trajectory methodology; quantum chemistry; potential energy surfaces; surface chemistry; computer capabilities. *Mailing Add:* 120 Dos Brazos Los Alamos NM 87544-2431

JOLY, LOUIS PHILIPPE, PHARMACEUTICAL CHEMISTRY. *Current Pos:* RETIRED. *Personal Data:* b Montreal, Que, July 23, 28; m 54; c 3. *Educ:* Laval Univ, BA, 49, BSc, 53; Univ Bordeaux, France, PhD, 65. *Prof Exp:* Lectr, Col Pharm, Univ Laval, 57-58, assoc prof, 58-71, prof med chem, 71-94. *Concurrent Pos:* Chief pharmacist, Robert Giffard Hosp Ctr, 57-69; consult, Neuropsychopharmacol Res Univ, 69- *Mem:* AAAS; NY Acad Sci; Am Pharmaceut Asn; Can Pharmaceut Asn. *Res:* Synthesis and essay by cell culture methods of new alkylating agents as antineoplastics; biotransforms of long acting psychotropic drugs. *Mailing Add:* 1324 Rue Marechal Foch Quebec PQ G1S 2C4 Can

JONA, FRANCO PAUL, SURFACE PHYSICS, SURFACE CHEMISTRY. *Current Pos:* PROF ENG, STATE UNIV NY STONY BROOK, 69- *Personal Data:* b Pistoia, Italy, Oct 10, 22; nat US; m 52; c Fred & Franco. *Educ:* Swiss Fed Inst Technol, dipl, 45, PhD(physics), 49. *Prof Exp:* Instr physics, Univ Bern, 45-46 & Swiss Fed Inst Technol, 46-52; res assoc, Pa State Univ, 52-54, asst prof, 54-57; res physicist res labs, Westinghouse Elec Corp, 57-59; staff physicist res lab, Int Bus Mach Corp, NY, 59-69. *Mem:* Fel Am Phys Soc; Swiss Phys Soc. *Res:* Ferroelectricity; crystallography; elasticity; piezoelectricity; crystal growth; surface studies; epitaxy; ultrathin films. *Mailing Add:* Col Eng State Univ NY Stony Brook NY 11790. *Fax:* 516-632-8052; *E-Mail:* franco@ccvm.sunysb.edu

JONAH, CHARLES D, RADIATION CHEMISTRY. *Current Pos:* fel, 71-74, asst scientist, 74-77, CHEMIST RADIATION CHEM, ARGONNE NAT LAB, 77- *Personal Data:* b Lafayette, Ind, Mar 19, 43; m 69, Margaret Martin. *Educ:* Oberlin Col, BA, 65; Columbia Univ, PhD(chem), 70. *Prof Exp:* Fel phys chem, Columbia Univ, 69-71. *Mem:* Am Phys Soc; Am Chem Soc. *Res:* Mechanism of reactions; fast kinetic measurements; instrumentation; radiation chemistry of aqueous systems solvation of electrons. *Mailing Add:* Chem Div Argonne Nat Lab 9700 S Cass Ave Argonne IL 60439. *Fax:* 630-252-4993; *E-Mail:* jonah@anlchm.chm.anl.gov

JONAH, MARGARET MARTIN, CELL SURFACE BIOLOGY. *Current Pos:* asst prof, 76-84, ASSOC PROF BIOL, ROSARY COL, 84-; RESIDENT ASSOC, ARGONNE NAT LAB, 76- *Personal Data:* b Berkeley, Calif, Oct 25, 42; m 69, Charles D. *Educ:* Pomona Col, Calif, BA, 64; Columbia Univ, PhD(chem biol), 71. *Prof Exp:* Res fel biochem, Northwestern Univ, Ill, 71-73; appointee biol, Argonne Nat Lab, 73-75, res assoc, 75-76. *Concurrent Pos:* prin investr, NSF, Inst Land Info grantee, 88-91, NIH area grantee, 89-93. *Mem:* AAAS; Am Inst Biol Sci; Am Chem Soc; Am Soc Microbiol; Int Radiation Res Soc; Sigma Xi; Am Asn Dent Res. *Res:* Functions of lipids in membrane formation and surface specificity; metabolism of streptococcus mutans; interactions of biologically active molecules with lipids; cell surface receptors; role of heavy metals in cell metabolism; cadmium metabolism in mammals. *Mailing Add:* Dept Natural Sci Dominican Univ River Forest IL 60305-1066

JONAK, ZDENKA L, CELLULAR & MOLECULAR BIOLOGY. *Current Pos:* Sr investr immunol, Smith Kline Beecham Pharmaceut, 84-85, sr investr cell biol, 85-88, asst dir cellular biochem & immunol, 88-93, ASSOC DIR CELLULAR BIOCHEM, SMITH KLINE BEECHAM PHARMACEUT, 93- *Personal Data:* b Iomouc, Czechoslavakia, Mar 9, 46; US citizen; m 69, Gerald J; c Peter, Elizabeth & Thomas. *Educ:* Charles Univ, Prague, Czechoslavakia, BS, 68; Yale Univ, MS, 71, PhD(biol-biochem), 75. *Prof Exp:* Res fel immunol, Joseph Stokes Jr Res Inst, Children's Hosp, 75-78; res investr immuno-biochem group, Wistar Inst Anat & Biol, 78-80; res assoc human genetics, Univ Pa, 80-84. *Concurrent Pos:* Fel, NSF, 73-74. *Mem:* AAAS; Am Asn Immunol; Fed Am Soc Exp Biol; Sigma Xi. *Res:* Humane immune system particularly cellular and molecular biology of B-cells and the consequences of alterations resulting in disease status; generation of fully human monoclonal antibodies to specific targets. *Mailing Add:* Smith Kline Beecham Dept Molecular Immunol 709 Swedeland Rd King of Prussia PA 19406-2799. *Fax:* 610-270-4899

JONAS, ALBERT MOSHE, PATHOLOGY, COMPARATIVE MEDICINE. *Current Pos:* sr staff scientist & dir, Lab Animal Med & Comp Path, Jackson Lab, 82-86, chief, Sci Resources, 83-86, PRES, RES ANIMAL CONSULTS, INC, 87-; CHMN, BD DIRS, VETCOR, 97- *Personal Data:* b New Haven, Conn, Oct 3, 31; m 54; c 3. *Educ:* Univ Toronto, DVM, 55; Am Col Vet Path, dipl, 63. *Hon Degrees:* MA, Yale Univ, 74. *Prof Exp:* Pvt pract, 55-61; res asst path, Sch Med, Yale Univ, 61-63, dir animal care, 61-78, from instr to asst prof, 63-68, assoc prof animal sci & chief lab, 68-73, assoc prof path, 71-73, prof animal sci & path, 73-74, prof comp med, Div Health Sci Res & Path & chief sect comp med, 74-77, prof comp med & path & chmn sect comp med, 77-78; first dean, Vet Sch Tufts Univ, 78-81, prof exp path, Med Sch, 78-82, chmn comp med & lab animal sci, Vet Sch, 81-82. *Concurrent Pos:* Mem coun, Inst Lab Animal Resources, Nat Acad Sci, 65-69; mem, Am Asn Accreditation Lab Animal Care, 68-75; mem animal res adv comt, Div Res Resources, NIH, 72-76; mem adv comt comp path, Armed Forces Inst Path, 73-76; chmn comt, Longterm Holding of Lab Rodents, Inst Lab Animal Res, Nat Acad Sci, 73-76 & mem, Orgn Comt Symp on Lab Animal Housing, 74-75; mem tech rev comt, Bioassay Prog, Nat Cancer Inst,

77-78, eval panel, Primate Res Ctrs Prog, NIH, 77-78, cause & prev sci rev comt, Nat Cancer Inst, 78-81, adv bd, Northeast Regional Primate Ctr, 79-82, comt vet med sci, Nat Acad Sci, 79-80; fel, Japanese Soc Prom Sci, 83; vis prof, Univ Tokyo, 83; vis prof, Dept Path, Pritzker Sch Med, Univ Chicago, 90-95, actg chair comput med, 91-95, actg dir, Animal Resources Ctr, 91-95. *Mem:* Am Asn Lab Animal Sci; Am Vet Med Asn; Int Acad Path; Am Col Vet Path; Soc Pharmacol & Environ Path. *Res:* Naturally occurring diseases in laboratory animals with specific interests in animal model systems; pulmonary pathology including pulmonary hemodynamics and infectious diseases with emphasis in pathogenesis. *Mailing Add:* 17 Cumberland St Boston MA 02115

JONAS, ANA, BIOCHEMISTRY. *Current Pos:* NIH trainee, 70-72, from asst prof to assoc prof, 72-84, PROF BIOCHEM, UNIV ILL, URBANA, 84- *Personal Data:* b Rokiskis, Lithuania, Nov 24, 43; US citizen; m 68, Jiri. *Educ:* Univ Ill, Chicago, BS, 66, Urbana, PhD(biochem), 70. *Honors & Awards:* Lyman Duff Lectr, Am Heart Asn, 96. *Concurrent Pos:* NATO fel, Max Planck Med Res Inst, Heidelberg, WGer, 73; res grants, Nat Heart Lung & Blood Inst, 73-, consult, 78-91; estab investorship, Am Heart Asn, 74-79; res grants, Am Heart Asn, 80-83, consult, 85-; Max Baer res award, 78-88; Coun Arteriosclerosis fel, Am Heart Asn; Fogarty fel, Ctr Molecular Biophys, Nat Ctr Res in Sci, Orleans, France, 81; adv bd, J Lipid Res, 84-; consult, Nat Res Coun, 89-92. *Mem:* Am Heart Asn; Am Soc Biochem & Molecular Biol; Am Chem Soc. *Res:* Structure and function of high density serum lipoproteins; protein-lipid interactions; interfacial-lipolytic enzymes; protein folding and dynamics. *Mailing Add:* 190 Med Sci Bldg Univ Ill 506 S Mathews Urbana IL 61801. *E-Mail:* a-jonas@uiuc.edu

JONAS, EDWARD CHARLES, CLAY MINERALOGY. *Current Pos:* from asst prof to prof, 54-, EMER PROF GEOL, UNIV TEX, AUSTIN. *Personal Data:* b San Antonio, Tex, July 24, 24; m 49; c 3. *Educ:* Rice Inst, BS, 44; Univ Ill, MS, 52, PhD(geol), 54. *Prof Exp:* Asst geologist, Ill State Geol Surv, 52-54. *Concurrent Pos:* Fulbright sr res award, NZ, 60-61. *Mem:* Fel AAAS; fel Geol Soc Am; fel Mineral Soc Am; Geochem Soc; Mineral Soc Gt Brit & Ireland. *Res:* Mineralogy of clays and uranium deposits in the Texas Gulf Tertiary. *Mailing Add:* Rte 1 Box 117 Marchaca TX 78652

JONAS, HERBERT, PLANT PHYSIOLOGY. *Current Pos:* assoc prof pharmacog, Col Pharm, 58-69, chmn dept, 58-68, prof plant physiol, Col Biol Sci, 69-85, EMER PROF BIOL, COL BIOL SCI, UNIV MINN, ST PAUL, 85- *Personal Data:* b Duesseldorf, Ger, May 23, 15; nat US; m 42, Charlotte Hoffmann. *Educ:* Univ Calif, BS, 41, PhD(plant physiol), 50. *Prof Exp:* Nat Res Coun & AEC fel plant physiol, Biol Div, Oak Ridge Nat Lab, 51-52; res assoc pharmacol, Sch Med, Univ Va, 52-54, res assoc, Cancer Res Lab, 54-58. *Concurrent Pos:* Electronics instr, US Naval Installations, Calif, 42-46. *Mem:* AAAS. *Res:* Physiology, biophysics; medicinal plants; secondary plant metabolites; sensitive plants; teaching; plant-man interrelations; economic botany; fresh water algae. *Mailing Add:* 3090 Hamline Ave N St Paul MN 55113

JONAS, JIRI, PHYSICAL CHEMISTRY, MOLECULAR SPECTROSCOPY. *Current Pos:* vis scientist, Univ Ill, Urbana, 63-65, from asst prof to assoc prof, 66-72, sr staff mem mat res, 70-92, dir, Sch Chem Sci, 83-93, PROF CHEM, UNIV ILL, URBANA, 72-, DIR, BECKMAN INST ADVAN SCI & TECHNOL, 93-, PROF, CTR ADVAN STUDY, 96- *Personal Data:* b Prague, Czech, Apr 1, 32; US citizen; m 68, Ana Masiulis. *Educ:* Tech Univ Prague, BS, 56; Czech Acad Sci, PhD(chem), 60. *Honors & Awards:* Joel Henry Hildebrand Award, Theoret & Exp Chem of Liquids, Am Chem Soc, 83; US Scientist Award, Alexander von Humboldt Found, WGer. *Prof Exp:* Res assoc chem, Czech Acad Sci, 60-63. *Concurrent Pos:* Fels, Alfred P Sloan Found, 67-69 & J S Guggenheim Found, 72-73; assoc mem, Ctr Advan Study, Univ Ill, 76-77. *Mem:* Nat Acad Sci; Am Chem Soc; fel Am Phys Soc; fel AAAS; fel Am Inst Chemists; fel Am Acad Arts & Sci. *Res:* Nuclear magnetic resonance; raman spectroscopy; dynamic structure of liquids; glasses, molecular solids and biopolymers; high pressure research; behavior of materials under extreme conditions of pressure and temperature. *Mailing Add:* 166 Roger Adam Lab 1209 W California Urbana IL 61801. *Fax:* 217-244-8371; *E-Mail:* j__jonas@uiuc.edu

JONAS, JOHN JOSEPH, ORGANIC CHEMISTRY. *Current Pos:* assoc mgr indust prod, Res & Develop Div, Kraft Inc, 51-77, SCI MGT CONSULT, RES & DEVELOP DIV, KRAFT, INC, 77- *Personal Data:* b Budapest, Hungary, Dec 9, 14; nat US; m 41; c 3. *Educ:* Pazmany Peter Univ, PhD(chem, physics, math), 37. *Prof Exp:* Asst & instr org & pharmaceut chem, Pazmany Peter Univ, 36-39; chemist, Darmol Pharmaceut Co, Budapest, 39-43; chemist, Hungary Viscose Corp, 43-45; asst div leader pharmaceut & nutrit res, Inst Heiligenberg, Ger, 46-51. *Concurrent Pos:* Consult, Protein Resources Study, NSF, 75-76. *Mem:* Am Chem Soc; Inst Food Technol; Am Inst Chemists. *Res:* Metabolic diseases of dairy cattle; seaweed hydrocolloids; food emulsifying systems; high protein foods; dairy analogues, vegetable proteins, synthetic nutrients. *Mailing Add:* Rte 2 Box 246 Meadows of Dan VA 24120

JONAS, JOHN JOSEPH, PHYSICAL METALLURGY, MECHANICAL METALLURGY. *Current Pos:* From asst prof to prof phys metall, McGill Univ, 60-85, assoc dean, Fac Grad Studies & Res, 71-75, CSIRA prof steel processing, 85-96, BIRKS PROF METALL, MCGILL UNIV, 92- *Personal Data:* b Montreal, Que, Dec 12, 32; m 60, Holly Higgins; c Jennifer, Jeremy, Jonathan & Jodie. *Educ:* McGill Univ, BEng, 54; Cambridge Univ, PhD(mech sci), 60. *Honors & Awards:* Frank Garofalo Mem Lectr, Northwestern Univ, 80; Reaumur Silver Medal, Fr Metall Soc, 80; Hatchett Medal & Award, Metals Soc UK, 82; Dofasco Mat Eng Award, Can Inst Mining & Metal, 82, Alcan Award, 90; Gold Medal, Can Metal Physics Asn, 83; Michael Tenenbaum Award, Iron & Steel Soc, Am Inst Mining Metall & Petrol Engrs, 89 & 96, Robert W Hunt Silver Medal, 97; Gold Medal, French Soc Metall & Mat, 91; Sawamura Award, Iron & Steel Inst Japan, 92 & 95; Officer Order of Can, 93. *Concurrent Pos:* Chmn res & develop, adv panel, Atomic Energy Can, 92 & 93; co-dir, McGill Metals Processing Ctr. *Mem:* Fel Am Soc Metals; Am Inst Mining, Metall & Petrol Engrs; Iron & Steel Inst Japan; fel Can Inst Mining & Metall; fel Royal Soc Can; fel Can Acad Eng. *Res:* Mechanical metallurgy; elevated temperature deformation of metals and crystalline materials; microstructural changes and stress-strain rate-temperature relationships during hot working; plastic instability; thermal activation analysis, textures, yield surfaces and formabilty. *Mailing Add:* Dept Metall Eng McGill Univ 3450 University St Montreal PQ H3A 2A7 Can. *Fax:* 514-398-4492; *E-Mail:* johnj@minmet.lan.mcgill.ca

JONAS, LEONARD ABRAHAM, PHYSICAL CHEMISTRY. *Current Pos:* SR RES SCIENTIST, HUGHES ASSOC, 87- *Personal Data:* b New York, NY, Feb 6, 20; m 42; c 2. *Educ:* Brooklyn Col, AB, 40; Univ Md, MS, 69, PhD(phys chem), 70. *Prof Exp:* Phys chemist, US Army Res & Develop Ctr, 42-80; sr res scientist, Nat Cancer Inst, Frederick Cancer Res Facil, Litton Bionetics, Inc, 80-87. *Concurrent Pos:* Consult air purification, Sch Hyg & Pub Health, Johns Hopkins Univ, 83- *Mem:* Am Carbon Soc; Am Soc Testing & Mat; AAAS; Am Chem Soc; Sigma Xi. *Res:* Equilibrium gas adsorption; adsorption kinetics; aerosol physics and filtration; heterogeneous catalysis; physical protection against carcinogens. *Mailing Add:* 12607 Timber Grove Rd Reisterstown MD 21136-1823

JONAS, ROBERT JAMES, ANIMAL ECOLOGY, WILDLIFE MANAGEMENT. *Current Pos:* coordr wildlife biol, 77-81, chmn, Dept Biol, 81-82, PROF ZOOL, WASH STATE UNIV, 66- *Personal Data:* b Marinette, Wis, June 8, 26; m 50; c 3. *Educ:* Univ Idaho, BS, 50, MS, 55; Mont State Univ, PhD(wildlife mgt), 64. *Prof Exp:* Instr biol, Lewis-Clark Norm Col, 55-57; asst prof, Whitman Col, 64-65 & Univ Idaho, 65-66. *Concurrent Pos:* Danforth Assoc, 68-; environ specialist, Nat Park Serv, 75-76. *Mem:* AAAS; Sigma Xi (vpres, 74-75); Wildlife Soc. *Res:* Populations of wild animals; human impact on natural ecosystems; wild turkeys. *Mailing Add:* 823 E Fifth St Moscow ID 83843

JONASSEN, HANS BOEGH, INORGANIC CHEMISTRY. *Current Pos:* From instr gen & anal chem to asst prof chem, Tulane Univ, 43-48, assoc prof inorg chem, 48-52, prof inorg chem, 52-80, chmn dept chem, 62-68. *Personal Data:* b Seelze, Ger, Aug 18, 12; nat US; m 39; c 3. *Educ:* Tulane Univ, BS, 42, MS, 44; Univ Ill, PhD(chem), 46. *Concurrent Pos:* Sci liaison officer, London Br, Off Naval Res, 58-59; mem adv coun col chem, NSF-Am Chem Soc, 62-67; Reilly centennial lectr, Univ Notre Dame, 65; Francis P Dwyer Mem lectr, Univ New South Wales, 67; Australian-Am Educ Found sr scholar, Univ Sydney, 71. *Mem:* AAAS; Am Chem Soc. *Res:* Inorganic and metalorganic chemistry; complex ions; homogenous and heterogeneous catalysis. *Mailing Add:* Tulane Univ 7729 Belfast St New Orleans LA 70125

JONCAS, JEAN HARRY, VIROLOGY, INFECTIOUS DISEASES. *Current Pos:* res asst, Univ Montreal, 60-70, res assoc virol, Inst Microbiol & Hyg, 71-76, head, Infectious Dis Sect, Ste Justine Hosp, Montreal, 70-76, head, Dept Microbiol, 77-85, PROF MICROBIOL & IMMUNOL, SCH MED, UNIV MONTREAL, 70-, HEAD VIROL RES LAB, STE JUSTINE HOSP, MONTREAL, 85- *Personal Data:* b Montreal, Que, June 27, 30; m 55, Anita Houde; c Maryse, Genevieve, Francois, Nathalie & Simon. *Educ:* Jean de Brebeuf Col, BA, 48; Univ Montreal, MD, 55, PhD(microbiol, immunol), 67; Royal Col Physicians & Surgeons, Can, cert pediat, 59, cert microbiol, 76. *Prof Exp:* Fel, Sch Med, Wayne State Univ, 56. *Concurrent Pos:* Clin asst, Montreal Children's Hosp, 59-70, consult, 70-; lectr, Sch Med, Univ Montreal, 64-67, asst prof, 67-70; demonstr, Dept Pediat, McGill Univ, 70-; mem adv comt infection, Immunity & Ther, Defence Res Bd Can, 70-74; Med Res Coun Can grant, 70-86; Nat Defence Res grant, 70-76; Fed Prov pub health res grant, 71-75; Nat Cancer Inst Can grant, 75-81; health & welfare contract, Epstein Barr Virus Nat Ctr, 85- *Mem:* Am Soc Microbiol; Int Soc Antiviral Res; fel Infectious Dis Soc Am; Can Infectious Dis Soc. *Res:* Etiology and epidemiology of infectious mononucleosis; the Epstein-Barr herpes virus; cell-virus relationship; Epstein-Barr virus and oncogenesis; diagnosis of viral infections by rapid immunological methods and molecular biology; pediatric infectious diseases, epidemiology, diagnosis and treatment. *Mailing Add:* Dept Microbiol & Immunol St Justine Hosp 3175 Ste-Catherine Rd Montreal PQ H3T 1C5 Can. *Fax:* 514-345-4801

JONEJA, MADAN GOPAL, TERATOLOGY, ULTRASTRUCTURAL CELL BIOLOGY. *Current Pos:* From lectr to assoc prof, Queens Univ, 65-76, chmn grad studies anat, 70-80, head, Dept Anat, 81-96, PROF ANAT, QUEENS UNIV, ONT, 76- *Personal Data:* b Lyallpur, India, Dec 25, 36; Can citizen; m 65, Asha Rajpal; c Mala & Navin. *Educ:* Panjab Univ, India, MSc, 58; Queen's Univ, Ont, PhD(biol), 65. *Mem:* Teratology Soc; Am Asn Anatomists; Can Asn Anatomists (pres, 93-95). *Res:* Cytological mechanisms of teratogenesis; scan electron microscope and transmission electron microscope of in vitro differentiation of the neural tube and cytoskeleton. *Mailing Add:* Dept Anat & Cell Biol Queen's Univ Kingston ON K7L 3N6 Can. *E-Mail:* jonejam@post.queensu.ca

JONES, ALAN A, POLYMER CHEMISTRY. *Current Pos:* from asst prof to assoc prof, 74-88, chmn dept, 81-87, actg provost, 87-88, PROF CHEM, CLARK UNIV, 81- *Personal Data:* b Jamestown, NY, Nov 15, 44; m 72. *Educ:* Colgate Univ, AB, 66; Univ Wis, PhD(phys chem), 72. *Prof Exp:* Res instr polymer chem, Dartmouth Col, 72-74. *Concurrent Pos:* Vis prof, Univ Wis, 85. *Mem:* Am Chem Soc; Am Phys Soc. *Res:* The dynamic properties of macromolecules in solution and in the bulk are probed by nuclear magnetic resonance spectroscopy or dielectric response and discussed in terms of models relating specific motions to the experimental observations. *Mailing Add:* Dept Chem Clark Univ Worcester MA 01610-1473

JONES, ALAN LEE, PLANT PATHOLOGY. *Current Pos:* From asst prof to assoc prof, 68-77, PROF PLANT PATH, MICH STATE UNIV, 77-. *Personal Data:* b Albion, NY, June 23, 39; m 67; c 2. *Educ:* Cornell Univ, BS, 61, MS, 63; NC State Univ, PhD(plant path), 68. *Honors & Awards:* Nat Award in Agr, Am Phytopath Soc, 78. *Concurrent Pos:* Sabbatical leaves, Plant Protection Inst, Agr Res Ctr, USDA, Beltsville, Md, 74-75, Bayer Agr, Leverkusen, Fed Repub Ger, 82 & Dept Plant Path, NY State Agr Exp Sta, Cornell Univ, Geneva, NY, 89. *Mem:* AAAS; Can Phytopath Soc; fel Am Phytopath Soc. *Res:* Epidemiology and control of tree fruit diseases; phytobacteriology; fungicide and antibiotic resistance in tree fruit pathogens. *Mailing Add:* Dept Bot & Plant Path Mich State Univ East Lansing MI 48824-1312. *Fax:* 517-353-5598

JONES, ALAN RICHARD, PHYSICAL CHEMISTRY, CHEMICAL ENGINEERING. *Current Pos:* Res scientist, Union Camp Corp, 67-69, leader paper prod group, 69-74, leader chem processes group, 74-78, asst tech dir, 78-83, tech dir, 83-85, div tech dir, 85-93, ASST DIR APPLN ENG, UNION CAMP CORP, 93-. *Personal Data:* b Denver, Colo, Dec 25, 39; m 64, Susan M Lowell; c Deborah A & Andrew T. *Educ:* Univ Colo, BSChE, 62; Lawrence Univ, MS, 64, PhD, 67. *Honors & Awards:* Hugh D Camp Award, Union Camp Corp, 73. *Mem:* Am Inst Chem Engr; Tech Asn Pulp & Paper Indust; AAAS; Am Soc Testing & Mat. *Res:* Mechanical and optical properties of paper, characterization of papermaking pulps, development and optimization of pulping, by-product chemical, and papermaking processes; environmental regulation; pollution prevention. *Mailing Add:* Union Camp Corp PO Box 570 Savannah GA 31402

JONES, ALBERT CLEVELAND, FISHERY SCIENCE. *Current Pos:* asst dir, Trop Atlantic Biol Lab, Nat Marine Fisheries Serv, 65-71, prog mgr, Off-in-Chg, 72-76, asst dir fishery mgt, 76-84, dir Miami Lab, 84-85, dir econ & statist, 85-90, DIR RES MGT DIV, SOUTHEAST FISHERIES SCI CTR, NAT MARINE FISHERIES SERV, 90-. *Personal Data:* b Coalinga, Calif, Aug 18, 29; m 55, Patricia Curry; c Thomas A, Michael R & Mark D. *Educ:* Univ Wash, BS, 51; Univ Calif, MA, 54, PhD(zool), 59. *Prof Exp:* Asst, Ore Fish Comn, 49-50, biologist, 51; biologist, Fisheries Res Inst, Wash, 52; asst, Sagehen Creek Wildlife Fisheries Sta, Univ Calif, 53-54, asst zool, Univ, 54-58; asst ichthyol, Calif Acad Sci, 58-59; res asst prof fisheries, Univ Miami, 59-65. *Concurrent Pos:* Ministry of Agr, Fisheries & Food fel, Eng, 64-65; adj assoc prof, Univ Miami, 68-76, adj prof, 76-. *Mem:* Am Fisheries Soc; Am Soc Ichthyol & Herpet; Am Inst Fishery Res Biologists. *Res:* Population dynamics; biometrics; ecology; fishery science research; stock assessment; fishery biology and statistics; living mariine resource management. *Mailing Add:* 8950 SW 62 Ct Miami FL 33156. *Fax:* 305-361-4219; *E-Mail:* albert.jones@noaa.gov

JONES, ALFRED, PLANT GENETICS. *Current Pos:* RETIRED. *Personal Data:* b Richmond, Va, Mar 25, 32; m 62; c 2. *Educ:* Va Polytech Inst, BS, 53; NC State Col, MS, 57, PhD(plant breeding & path), 61. *Prof Exp:* Res asst cotton breeding, Field Crops Dept, NC State Col, 61-62; res geneticist, Veg & Ornamentals Res Br, Plant Sci Res Div, US Veg Breeding Lab, USDA, 62-89. *Concurrent Pos:* L M Ware Res Award, Am Soc Hort Sci, 79. *Mem:* Am Soc Hort Sci; Am Genetic Asn; Crop Sci Soc Am; Am Soc Agron; Sigma Xi. *Res:* Cytogenetics of sweetpotato, especially nature of ploidy in Ipomoea and its relation to speciation, recombination and breeding systems; quantitative genetic techniques of breeding for disease and insect resistant types. *Mailing Add:* 2421 Pristine View Rd Charleston SC 29414

JONES, ALICE J, SOIL & WATER CONSERVATION. *Current Pos:* from asst prof to assoc prof, 85-95, PROF SOIL & WATER CONSERVE UNIV NEBR, LINCOLN, 95-. *Personal Data:* b Michigan City, Ind, Apr 9, 53; m 88, Lloyd N Mielke; c Janet & Steve. *Educ:* Mich Tech Univ, BS, 78; Mont State Univ, MS, 78; Utah State Univ, PhD(soil physics), 82. *Prof Exp:* Instr, Mont State Univ, 80-81, asst prof, 83-85; asst prof, Mont Col Sci & Tech, 81-83. *Concurrent Pos:* Vis scientisit, Univ Alaska, 84; dir sustainable agr res & educ, USDA, 93-95. *Mem:* Fel Soil & Water Soc (vpres, 91-92); Soil Sci Soc Am; Am Soc Am; Sigma Xi; Int Soil Tillage Res Orgn. *Res:* Soil and water conservation in combination with an emphasis on sustainable agriculture, topics include soil erosion, soil-plant-water relations and compaction. *Mailing Add:* Dept Agronomy Univ Nebr 254 Keim Hall E Campus Lincoln NE 68583-0915. *Fax:* 402-472-7904; *E-Mail:* ajones@unlinfo.unl.edu

JONES, ALISON M, FERMENTATION. *Current Pos:* SR RES SCIENTIST, CARGILL, INC, 95-. *Personal Data:* b Saskatoon, Sask, Mar 29, 64; m, John G Peters. *Educ:* Univ Sask, BSc, 86; McGill Univ, PhD(microbiol), 91. *Prof Exp:* Res assoc, Dept Biochem, Brandeis Univ, 91-92, Biotechnol Res Inst, Nat Res Coun Can, 93-95; postdoctoral fel, Dept Appl Microbiol & Food Sci, Univ Sask, 92-93. *Mem:* Am Soc Microbiol; Soc Indust Microbiol. *Res:* Fermentation. *Mailing Add:* Cargill Cent Res PO Box 5699 Minneapolis MN 55440

JONES, ALISTER VALLANCE, AERONOMY, AURORA. *Current Pos:* CONTRACTOR, CAN SPACE SCI PROG, 97-. *Personal Data:* b Christchurch, NZ, Feb 4, 24; m 51, Catherine Fergusson; c Elizabeth (Villeneuve), Catriana V (Gallant) & Alasdair F. *Educ:* Univ NZ, BSc, 45, MSc, 46; Cambridge Univ, PhD(physics), 50. *Prof Exp:* Nat Res Coun Can fel, 49-51; from asst prof to prof physics, Univ Sask, 53-68; sr res officer, Upper Atmosphere Res Sect, Astrophys Br, Nat Res Coun Can, 68-76, prin res officer, Planetary Sci Sect, 76-89, guest worker, solar terrestrial physics, Herzberg Inst Astrophys, 89-97. *Concurrent Pos:* Ed, Physics Can, Can Asn Physicists, 63-66, assoc ed, Aeronomy & Space Physics, Can J Physics, 79-; prin investr, Canopus Proj, 80-89; chmn, Div 2, Int Asn Geomag & Aeronomy, 87-91. *Mem:* Can Asn Physicists; Royal Soc Can. *Res:* Infrared, auroral and airglow spectroscopy. *Mailing Add:* Can Space Agency 100 Sussex Dr PO Box 7275 Ottawa ON K1L 8E3 Can. *Fax:* 613-952-0974; *E-Mail:* jones@canott.dan.sp-agency.ca

JONES, ALLAN W, BIOLOGY, PHYSIOLOGY. *Current Pos:* assoc prof, 72-78, PROF PHYSIOL, SCH MED, UNIV MO-COLUMBIA, 78-, CHAIR, DEPT PHYSIOL, 83-, ASSOC DIR, DALTON CARDIOVASC RES CTR, 86-. *Personal Data:* b Scranton, Pa, June, 3, 37; m 91, Elaine F Smith; c Christian, Heather, Nicol, Jay M, Rachel & Jill. *Educ:* Princeton Univ, BSE, 59; Univ Pa, PhD(physiol), 65. *Honors & Awards:* Merit Award, NIH, 86. *Prof Exp:* Trainee & instr physiol, Sch Med, Univ Pa, 65-66; fel, Oxford Univ, 66-68; assoc, Sch Med, Univ Pa, 68-69, asst prof, 69-72, assoc dir, Bockus Res Inst, Grad Hosp, 70-72. *Concurrent Pos:* Estab investr, Am Heart Asn, 74-79; chair, ECS Study Sect, NIH, 89-90. *Mem:* Am Pharmacol Soc; Am Physiol Soc; Coun High Blood Pressure Res; Int Soc Hypertension; Am Soc Hypertension. *Res:* Hypertension; electrolyte metabolism of arteries; cardiovascular research; pharmaco-mechanical coupling in arteries; effects of ischamia and exercise on arteries. *Mailing Add:* Dept Physiol Univ Mo MA415 Med Sci Bldg Columbia MO 65212-0001. *Fax:* 573-884-4276

JONES, ALMUT GITTER, PLANT TAXONOMY. *Current Pos:* Asst prof bot, 74-75 & 79-88, CUR HERBARIUM, UNIV ILL, URBANA, 73-, ASSOC PROF PLANT BIOL, 89-. *Personal Data:* b Oldenburg, WGer, Sept 8, 23; US citizen; wid. *Educ:* Univ Ill, Urbana, BS, 58, MS, 60, PhD(bot), 73. *Mem:* Am Soc Plant Taxonomists; Am Bot Soc; Int Asn Plant Taxon. *Res:* Taxonomy, phytogeography and biosystematics of Aster, Compositae; flora of Illinois. *Mailing Add:* Dept Plant Biol Univ Ill 505 S Goodwine Ave Urbana IL 61801-3707. *Fax:* 217-333-9758

JONES, ALUN RICHARD, PHYSICS, RADIATION DOSIMETRY. *Current Pos:* RETIRED. *Personal Data:* b Ipoh, Malaya, May 6, 28; Can citizen; m 55, Betty J Seays; c 2. *Educ:* Univ Bristol, BSc, 52; McGill Univ, MSc, 54. *Prof Exp:* Mem, Physics Div, Electronics Br, Atomic Energy Can Ltd, 54-56; mem, Biol & Health Div, Dosimetric Res Br, Atomic Energy Can Ltd, 56-90, sr res officer, 65-90. *Concurrent Pos:* Exchange worker, Inst Cancer Res, UK, 62-63; consult to pres comn, Three Mile-Island, 79. *Mem:* Health Physics Soc. *Res:* External dosimetry of gamma and beta rays; thermoluminescence dosimetry; monitoring of alpha, beta and gamma contamination; detectors of ionising radiation (Geiger Mueller counters and silicon junction detectors); radiation protection. *Mailing Add:* Box 711 Deep River ON K0J 1P0 Can

JONES, ANITA KATHERINE, COMPUTER SCIENCE. *Current Pos:* DIR, DEFENSE RES & ENG, DEPT DEFENSE, 94-. *Personal Data:* b Ft Worth, Tex; m, William A Wulf; c Karin & Ellen. *Educ:* Rice Univ, AB, 64; Univ Tex, MA, 66; Carnegie-Mellon Univ, PhD(comput sci), 73. *Prof Exp:* Programmer, IBM Corp, 66-68; asst prof, 73-78, assoc prof comput sci, Carnegie-Mellon Univ, 78-81; vpres & founder, Tartan Labs, Pittsburgh, Pa, 81-87; prof & dept chair, Comput Sci, Univ Va, 88-94. *Concurrent Pos:* Consult, NSF, Defense Advan Res Proj Agency, Nat Res Coun & Indust; trustee, Mitre Corp; dir Sci Appln Int Corp. *Mem:* Nat Acad Eng; fel Inst Elec & Electronic Engrs; Sigma Xi; Asn Comput Mach. *Res:* Design and implementation of programmed systems on computers, including enforcement of security policies on computers, operating systems and scientific data bases. *Mailing Add:* Defense Res & Eng Pentagon 3E1014 Washington DC 20301

JONES, BARBARA, INFRARED ASTRONOMICAL INSTRUMENTATION. *Current Pos:* res physicist, 80-83, PROF PHYSICS, UNIV CALIF, SAN DIEGO, 83-. *Personal Data:* b Ipswich, Eng, Feb 19, 48. *Educ:* Univ Col, London, PhD(physics), 77. *Prof Exp:* Postdoctoral, Univ Minn, 77-80. *Mem:* Fel Am Phys Soc; Am Astron Union; Am Asn Univ Women; Am Asn Physics Teachers; Int Astron Union. *Res:* Study of luminous infrared galaxies and active galactic nuclei through observations with novel infrared instrumentation. *Mailing Add:* Univ Calif San Diego CASS 0424 La Jolla CA 92093-0424

JONES, BARBARA ELLEN, NEUROSCIENCE, NEUROANATOMY. *Current Pos:* from asst prof to assoc prof, 77-89, PROF NEUROL, MCGILL UNIV, 89-. *Personal Data:* b Philadelphia, Pa, Dec 19, 44; m 72, John Galaty; c James. *Educ:* Univ Del, BA, 66, PhD(psychol), 71. *Prof Exp:* Fel neurochem, Col France, Paris, 70-72; res assoc psychiat, Univ Chicago, 72-74; vis lectr med physiol, Univ Nairobi, 74-75; res assoc & asst prof psychiat, Univ Chicago, 75-77. *Concurrent Pos:* Scholar, Med Res Coun Can, 78-83; scholar, Ctr Med Res, Que, 83-86; vis scientist human anat, Oxford Univ, UK, 84-85 & physiol, Ctr Med Univ, Geneva, Switz, 91-92. *Mem:* Soc Neurosci; Asn Psychophysiol Study Sleep. *Res:* Neuroanatomical and neurochemical substrates of mechanisms of the sleep-waking cycle; neurophsiology. *Mailing Add:* Dept Neurol & Neurosurg McGill Univ Montreal/Neurol Inst Montreal PQ H3A 2B4 Can. *Fax:* 514-398-8106

JONES, BARCLAY G(EORGE), NUCLEAR ENGINEERING, MECHANICAL ENGINEERING. *Current Pos:* res asst, Univ Ill, 58-60, instr nuclear eng, 63-66, from asst prof to assoc prof, 66-72, PROF NUCLEAR & MECH ENG, UNIV ILL, URBANA-CHAMPAIGN, 72-,

HEAD, 87- *Personal Data:* b Lafleche, Sask, May 6, 31; US citizen; m 59; c 4. *Educ:* Univ Sask, BE, 54; Univ Ill, MS, 60, PhD(nuclear eng), 66. *Prof Exp:* Athlone fel, Eng Elec Co, Rugby, Eng, 54-55; Atomic Energy Res Estab, Harwell, 55-57; engr, Nuclear Div, Canadair Ltd, Montreal, Que, 57-58. *Concurrent Pos:* Consult, WVa Pulp & Paper Co, Va, 68, Arnold Res Orgn, Inc, Tullahoma, Tenn, 74-80, Argonne Nat Lab, 76- & Fauske & Assocs, Burr Ridge, Ill, 81-85; assoc chairperson nuclear eng, Univ Ill, Urbana, 81-86, actg head, 86-87; Helliburton educ award, 83. *Mem:* Am Nuclear Soc; Can Soc Mech Engrs; Am Soc Mech Engrs; Eng Inst Can; Am Inst Aeronaut & Astronaut; Sigma Xi; Am Soc Eng Educ. *Res:* Experimental fluid mechanics and heat transfer, reactor safety, two-phase flow, turbulence, simulation & training. *Mailing Add:* 310 E Holmes St Urbana IL 61801-6732

JONES, BARRY N, molecular biology, for more information see previous edition

JONES, BENJAMIN A(NGUS), JR, AGRICULTURAL ENGINEERING. *Current Pos:* RETIRED. *Personal Data:* b Mahomet, Ill, Apr 16, 26; m 49, Georgeann Hall; c Nancy K (Richardson) & Ruth A (Sommers). *Educ:* Univ Ill, BS, 49, MS, 50, PhD(civil eng), 58. *Honors & Awards:* Hancor Award, Am Soc Agr Engrs, 77. *Prof Exp:* Asst agr eng, Univ Ill, 49-50; actg chmn, Dept Agr Eng, Univ Vt, 50-51, asst prof & asst agr engr, Agr Exten Serv, 50-52; from instr to assoc prof, Ill Agr Exp Sta, Univ Ill, Urbana-Champign, 52-64, prof agr eng & head soil & water div, 64-73, assoc dir, 73-92, emer prof agr eng, 92, emer assoc dir, 92. *Concurrent Pos:* Consult engr, Ill Drainage Dists. *Mem:* fel, Am Soc Agr Engrs; Soil Conserv Soc Am; Sigma Xi; Coun Agr Sci & Technol. *Res:* Agricultural land drainage and irrigation; agricultural hydrology and the hydraulics of erosion control structures. *Mailing Add:* 2012 B Eagle Ridge Ct Urbana IL 61802-8617

JONES, BENJAMIN FRANKLIN, JR, MATHEMATICS. *Current Pos:* from asst prof to prof, 62-74, NOAH HARDING PROF MATH, RICE UNIV, 74- *Personal Data:* b Apr 15, 36; US citizen; m 57; c 3. *Educ:* Rice Univ, BA, 58, PhD(math), 61. *Prof Exp:* Temp mem, Courant Inst Math Sci, NY Univ, 61-62. *Concurrent Pos:* Mem, Inst Advan Study, 65-66; vis prof, Univ Minn, 69-70; vis mem, Math Inst, Oxford Univ, 85-86. *Mem:* Am Math Soc; Math Asn Am. *Res:* Partial differential equations; singular integral operators. *Mailing Add:* Dept Math Rice Univ 6100 Main St Houston TX 99005-1892. *Fax:* 713-285-5231

JONES, BENJAMIN LEWIS, BIOCHEMISTRY. *Current Pos:* sr res chemist, Campbell Inst Res Technol, 84-85, res scientist, 85-90, sr res scientist, 90-93, RES PROG LEADER, CAMPBELL INST RES TECHNOL, 93- *Personal Data:* b Muncy Valley Twp, Pa, Aug 19, 52; m 80, Betty R Mann; c 1. *Educ:* Pa State Univ, BS, 74; Univ Tenn, MS, 78, PhD(biochem), 80. *Prof Exp:* Res assoc, Kettering Res Lab, 80-82; res chemist, Lipid Metab Lab, Vet Admin Hosp, 82-84. *Mem:* Am Soc Biochem & Molecular Biol; Am Chem Soc; Inst Food Technologists. *Res:* Developing beef and chicken type reaction flavors using yeast extracts, meats, enzymes and natural chemicals; processing methods and conditions for production of reaction flavors; scale up of reaction flavors. *Mailing Add:* Campbell Res & Develop Box 57X Campbell Pl Camden NJ 08103-1702. *Fax:* 609-342-4858

JONES, BERNE LEE, BIOCHEMISTRY, PROTEIN CHEMISTRY. *Current Pos:* res chemist, biochem, 77-89, SUPVRY RES CHEMIST BIOCHEM, USDA, 89- *Personal Data:* b Rochester, Ind, May 30, 41; m 63, Holly McBride; c Anne, Jennifer & Andrew. *Educ:* Wabash Col, BA, 63; Wash State Univ, PhD(chem), 67. *Prof Exp:* Fel biochem, Univ Colo, 67-69 & Univ Alta, 69-72; asst prof plant sci, Univ Man, 72-77. *Concurrent Pos:* Prof agron, Univ Wis, Madison, 89- *Mem:* Am Asn Brewing Chemists. *Res:* Biochemistry of cereal proteins; enzymology of malting; endoproteinase biochemistry; plant endoproteinase inhibitors. *Mailing Add:* Cereal Crops Res Unit 501 N Walnut St Madison WI 53705. *Fax:* 608-264-5528; *E-Mail:* bljones@macc.wisc.edu

JONES, BERWYN E, ANALYTICAL CHEMISTRY. *Current Pos:* quality control off, 85-90, NAT QUAL MGT COORDR, NAT WATER QUAL LAB, US GEOL SURV, DENVER, 90- *Personal Data:* b Scottsbluff, Nebr, Mar 11, 37; m 58, Janet Sue Hall; c Roderick H & Bruce G. *Educ:* Nebr Wesleyan Univ, BA, 58; Kans State Univ, PhD(anal chem), 65. *Prof Exp:* From instr to assoc prof chem, Monmouth Col, Ill, 63-75; prof, Upper Iowa Univ, Fayette, 75-77; assoc prof, Longwood Col, 77-78; res chemist, 78-80, asst lab dir, Nat Water Qual Lab, US Geol Surv, Atlanta, 80-85. *Concurrent Pos:* Vis asst prof, Univ Ill, 69-70; res assoc, Argonne Nat Lab, 70-71. *Mem:* AAAS; Am Chem Soc; Soc Appl Spectros; Sigma Xi; Am Soc Qual Control. *Res:* Absorption and fluorescence spectroscopy; chromatography; atomic emission spectroscopy; molecular fluorescence spectroscopy; quality assurance of chemical analysis; total quality management. *Mailing Add:* 30926 Shawnee Lane Evergreen CO 80439. *Fax:* 303-236-4937; *E-Mail:* bercoyn@usgs.gov

JONES, BLAIR FRANCIS, GEOLOGY. *Current Pos:* geologist, US Geol Surv, 55, Deposits Br, 56-57, res geologist, Water Resources Div, 58-74, res adv geochem, Washington, DC, 74-77, Reston, 81-84; SR SCIENTIST, WATER RESOURCES DIV, US GEOL SURV, NAT CTR, 83- *Personal Data:* b Apr 14, 34; m 55; c 2. *Educ:* Beloit Col, BA, 55; Johns Hopkins Univ, PhD, 63. *Honors & Awards:* Meritorious Serv Award, Dept Interior, 81 & Distinguished Serv Award, 86. *Prof Exp:* Lab instr geol, Beloit Col, 54-55. *Concurrent Pos:* Instr, Rockford Col, 54; vis prof, State Univ NY Binghamton, 70; guest investr, Rothamsted Exp Sta, Herpenden, Herts, UK, 72. *Mem:* Fel Geol Soc Am; Geochem Soc; fel Mineral Soc Am; Am Geophys Union; Clay Minerals Soc; Sigma Xi; Mineral Soc UK. *Res:* Hydrogeochemistry; sedimentary petrology; geochemistry of weathering; brines, lacustrine sediments and evaporites; solutes in natural water. *Mailing Add:* 7905 Glenbrook Rd Bethesda MD 20814-2403

JONES, BRIAN HERBERT, materials science, mechanical engineering, for more information see previous edition

JONES, BURTON FREDRICK, ASTROMETRY. *Current Pos:* asst res astronomer, 75-79, asst astronomer & prof, 79-87, ASTRONOMER & PROF, LICK OBSERV, UNIV CALIF, SANTA CRUZ, 87- *Personal Data:* b Manistique, Mich, Oct 28, 42; m 82, Mary Berger; c Kristine & Michelle. *Educ:* Univ Chicago, BS, 65, MS, 68, PhD(astron), 70. *Prof Exp:* Fel astron, Lick Observ, Univ Calif, 70-71; sr res fel, Royal Greenwich Observ, 72-74; res fel, Univ Tex, 74-75. *Mem:* Int Astron Union; Am Astron Soc; Astron Soc Pac. *Res:* Stellar proper motions; cluster membership. *Mailing Add:* Lick Observ Univ Calif Santa Cruz CA 95064. *Fax:* 408-426-3115; *E-Mail:* jones@helius.ucsc.edu

JONES, C ROBERT, CELL PHYSIOLOGY. *Current Pos:* from instr to asst prof physiol, 63-68, assoc prof cell biol, 68-74, chmn dept biol sci, 74-84, PROF CELL BIOL, LEHMAN COL, 68- *Personal Data:* b Scranton, Pa, May 8, 33; m 57; c 4. *Educ:* Univ Scranton, BS, 54; Fordham Univ, MS, 56, PhD(physiol), 62. *Prof Exp:* Res asst chemother, Sloan-Kettering Inst Cancer Res, 58-59; fel, Fordham Univ, 62-63. *Concurrent Pos:* Lectr, Bronx Community Col, 62-63; NSF res grant, Div Metab Biol, 64-66. *Mem:* AAAS; Entom Soc Am. *Res:* Activity of respiratory enzymes during the metamorphosis of holometabolous insects; identification of Lysosomes in insect tissues; mammalian physiology. *Mailing Add:* 138 Woodbrook Rd White Plains NY 10605

JONES, CARL E, physiology, biophysics, for more information see previous edition

JONES, CARL JOSEPH, BIOCONTROL, IMMUNOPARASITOLOGY. *Current Pos:* asst prof vet med entom, 89-93, Assoc Prof, 93-97, PROF MED, UNIV ILL, 97- *Personal Data:* b Ithaca, NY, Jan 1, 49; m 82, Frances Woollard; c Heather M, Wendy A & Christopher M. *Educ:* Cornell Univ, BS, 70; Univ Wyo, MS, 79, PhD(entom), 82. *Prof Exp:* Experimentalist, Dept Entom, Cornell Univ, 70-74, res specialist, 75-77; postdoctoral res assoc, Dept Entom, Univ Fla, 82; biol adminr, Off Entom, State Fla, 82-89. *Concurrent Pos:* Adj fac mem, Gulf Coast Community Col, 89; affil, Ill Natural Hist Surv Ctr Econ Entom, 91- *Mem:* Entom Soc Am; Sigma Xi. *Res:* Biological control of arthropods, physiological interactions of vertebrates and their hematophagous arthropod parasites; behavior and ecosystem dynamics of ticks; population dynamics and physiology of anautogenous muscoid flies; genetics of dispersal in arthropods. *Mailing Add:* Dept Vet Pathobiol Col Vet Med Univ Ill Urbana IL 61801

JONES, CAROL A, BIOPHYSICS. *Current Pos:* Fel biophys, USPHS, 69-71, res assoc biophys & genetics, 71-74, asst prof, 74-80, ASSOC PROF BIOPHYS & GENETICS, UNIV COLO HEALTH SCI CTR, 80-; SR FEL, ELEANOR ROOSEVELT INST CANCER RES, 80- *Personal Data:* b Kremmling, Colo, Sept 10, 36; m 55; c 7. *Educ:* Univ Colo, BA, 63, PhD(biophys), 69. *Mem:* AAAS; Am Soc Human Genetics; Am Asn Immunol. *Res:* Cell biology; somatic cell genetics; cell surface molecules. *Mailing Add:* E Roosevelt Inst Cancer Res 1899 Gaylord St Denver CO 80206. *Fax:* 303-333-8423

JONES, CHARLES, ROTARY ENGINES, TECHNICAL MANAGEMENT. *Current Pos:* CONSULT ENGR, 91- *Personal Data:* b New York, NY, Feb 27, 26; m 50, Gisele A Guerin; c Corinne & Leslie. *Educ:* Columbia Univ, BS, 50, MS, 53. *Honors & Awards:* Edward N Cole Award, Soc Automotive Engrs, 87, Forest McFarland Award, 91. *Prof Exp:* Sect head, Appl Mech, Curtiss-Wright Corp, 55-62, chief design engr, 62-68, chief engr, 68-69, dir res eng, 69-84, chief technologist, John Deere Technologies Int, 84-91. *Concurrent Pos:* Adj lectr, Stevens Inst Technol, 86-87. *Mem:* Fel Soc Automotive Engrs. *Res:* Rotary engines design and development; author of over 30 technical publications; awarded 76 patents. *Mailing Add:* 37 Harbor Circle Centerport NY 11721. *Fax:* 516-261-1002; *E-Mail:* cenptjones@aol.com

JONES, CHARLES E, MOLECULAR PHYSICS, ATOMIC PHYSICS. *Current Pos:* RETIRED. *Personal Data:* b Oklahoma City, Okla, June 10, 28; m 49; c 5. *Educ:* Univ Ark, Fayetteville, BS, 51, MS, 55; Tex A&M Univ, PhD(physics), 65. *Prof Exp:* Jr thermo engr, Convair Aircraft Co, 51-52; aerodyn engr, McDonnell Aircraft Co, 52-53; instr physics, Mo Sch Mines, 55-57 & Tex A&M Univ, 57-61; asst & assoc prof, Univ Ark, 61-70; prof physics & head dept, Etex State Univ, 70-91. *Concurrent Pos:* Consult, NSF-Agency Int Develop Summer Inst, 69. *Mem:* Am Asn Physics Teachers; Am Phys Soc. *Res:* Atoms and molecules in inert matrices at low temperatures by means of absorption and emission spectroscopy. *Mailing Add:* 18959 Shoreline Way Fayetteville AR 72703

JONES, CHARLES MILLER, JR, PHYSICS. *Current Pos:* CONSULT, 95- *Personal Data:* b Atlanta, Ga, Feb 25, 35; m 57; c 2. *Educ:* Ga Inst Technol, BS, 57; Rice Univ, MA, 59, PhD(physics), 61. *Prof Exp:* Res assoc, Rice Univ, 61-62; physicist, Oak Ridge Nat Lab, 62-94, tech dir, Holifield Heavy Ion Res Facil, 83-92, oper mgr, Physics Div, 92-94. *Mem:* AAAS. *Res:* Nuclear structure, especially reactions and scattering in the light nuclei; tests of fundamental symmetries using nuclear reactions; application of superconductivity to particle accelerators; physics and technology of electrostatic particle accelerators. *Mailing Add:* 1345 Oak Ridge Turnpike No 358 Oak Ridge TN 37830. *Fax:* 423-483-8944

JONES, CHARLES WELDON, GENE REGULATION, STEROID HORMONE ACTION. *Current Pos:* PROF & CHAIR BIOL, BETHEL COL, 82- *Personal Data:* b Providence, RI, May 25, 53. *Educ:* Harvard Univ, AB, 75, AM, 77, PhD(biol), 80. *Prof Exp:* Fel biochem, Stanford Univ Sch Med, 80-82. *Concurrent Pos:* Prin investr, Bethel Col, 82-; scholar biol, Harvard Univ, 88-89; vis scientist, Mayo Clin, 95-96. *Mem:* Genetics Soc Am; Col Res Asn Biol (secy, 92-93); AAAS; Asn Biol Lab Educr; Am Sci Affil; Coun Undergrad Res. *Res:* Understanding the regulation and expression of genes in higher organisms, specifically steroid hormone-induced gene in the fruit fly, Drosophila Melanogaster. *Mailing Add:* Bethel Col 3900 Bethel Dr St Paul MN 55112-6999. *Fax:* 612-638-6001; *E-Mail:* wjones@bethel.edu

JONES, CLARENCE S, PHYSICS, ENGINEERING. *Current Pos:* RETIRED. *Personal Data:* b Rigby, Idaho, Aug 21, 26; m 48; c 3. *Educ:* Univ Utah, BA, 50, MA, 52. *Prof Exp:* Mem staff, Los Alamos Sci Lab, 52-55; mem tech staff, Ramo-Wooldridge Corp, Calif, 55-57; chief engr, Res & Develop Labs, Link Div, Gen Precision, Inc, 57-62; mgr equip eng, Sylvania Elec Prod Inc, 62-64; vpres eng, ESL Inc, 64-70; pres, Anal Develop Assocs Corp, 70-76; chmn bd, Anal Develop Assocs Corp Labs, 76-86. *Mem:* AAAS; Sigma Xi. *Res:* Design and execution of physical experiments in nuclear physics and electronics; design of electronic systems and circuits; administration of scientific and engineering activities. *Mailing Add:* 991 S Springer Rd Los Altos CA 94024

JONES, CLARIS EUGENE, JR, POLLINATION BIOLOGY, BIOSYSTEMATICS. *Current Pos:* From asst prof to assoc prof, 69-77, PROF BOT, CALIF STATE UNIV, FULLERTON, 77-, CHAIR, DEPT BOT, 89- *Personal Data:* b Dec 15, 49; m 66, Teresa D Wagner; c Douglas E, Philip C & Elizabeth L. *Educ:* Ohio Univ, BS, 64; Ind Univ, PhD(bot), 69. *Concurrent Pos:* Dir, Faye A MacFadden Herbarium, Calif State Univ, 69-; Fullerton Arboretum, 70-80. *Mem:* Am Soc Plant Taxonomists; Int Asn Plant Taxon; Ecol Soc Am; Soc Study Evolution; Bot Soc Am; AAAS. *Res:* Pollination ecology of rare or endangered plant species, especially with reference to their coevolution with specific pollinators, insular biogeography in the Hawaiian Islands, biosystematics studies in the family Cucurbitaceae, and the honeybee dance language. *Mailing Add:* Dept Biol Sci Calif State Univ Fullerton CA 92834. *Fax:* 714-773-3426; *E-Mail:* cejones@fullerton.edu

JONES, CLIFFORD KENNETH, STRATEGIC PLANNING, PROJECT MANAGEMENT. *Current Pos:* DIR, NORTHROP GRUMMON, 97- *Personal Data:* b London, Eng, Dec 29, 32; US citizen; m 57; c 2. *Educ:* Univ London, BSc, 57, PhD(physics), 60. *Prof Exp:* Mem staff superconductor develop prog, Westinghouse Res & Develop Ctr, 62-67, mgr cryogenics, 67-75, mgr spec projs, 75-80, dir strategic planning, 80-88, mgr spec projs, 88-97. *Concurrent Pos:* Asst prof physics, Univ Calif, Los Angeles. *Mem:* Fel Am Phys Soc; Inst Elec & Electronics Engrs. *Res:* Cryogenics and fusion power technology; co-authored more than 80 publications in physical acoustics, metal physics and superconducting technology. *Mailing Add:* Northrop Grummon 1310 Beulah Rd Pittsburgh PA 15235

JONES, CLIVE GARETH, PLANT-INSECT-MICROBIAL INTERACTIONS, CHEMICAL ECOLOGY. *Current Pos:* CHEM ECOLOGIST, INST ECOSYSTEM STUDIES, MILLBROOK, 80- *Personal Data:* b Cirencester, Eng, March 3, 51; m 92, Donna J Rutlin; c Gordon & Heather. *Educ:* Univ Salford, Eng, BSc, 74; Univ York, Eng, DPhil(biol), 78. *Prof Exp:* Fel res, Dept Entom, Univ Ga, 78-80. *Concurrent Pos:* Travelling fel, Brit Ecol Soc, 87; Winston Churchill fel, 90; Guggenheim fel, 94. *Mem:* Fel AAAS; Entomol Soc Am; Ecol Soc Am; Int Soc Chem Ecol; Brit Ecol Soc. *Res:* Chemical ecology and plant-insect-microbial interactions; ecosystem effects of organisms; ecological theory; effects of stress damage to plants; ecosystem engineering gy species. *Mailing Add:* Inst Ecosystem Studies Box AB Millbrook NY 12545

JONES, CLYDE J, MAMMALIAN ECOLOGY, TAXONOMY. *Current Pos:* PROF SCI, TEX TECH UNIV, 82- *Personal Data:* b Scottsbluff, Nebr, Mar 3, 35. *Educ:* Hastings Col, BA, 57; Univ NMex, MS, 60, PhD(biol). 64. *Prof Exp:* Asst cur biol, Univ NMex, 62-65; asst prof, Tulane Univ, 65-70; zoologist, Bur Sport Fisheries & Wildlife, Nat Mus Natural Hist, 70-73, dir, Nat Fish & Wildlife Lab, 73-79; dir, Denver Wildlife Res Ctr, 79-82. *Concurrent Pos:* Res investr field studies, Rio Muni, WAfrica, Nat Geog Soc, 66-68; res assoc, Delta Regional Primate Res Ctr, 67-70; biologist, Antarctic Inspection, Oper Deepfreeze, 71-; res assoc, Smithsonian Inst, 71- *Mem:* Am Soc Mammal; Soc Syst Zool; Ecol Soc Am. *Res:* Systematics, taxonomy, biogeography, biodiversity and conservation mammals; conservation and management of specimens in museums. *Mailing Add:* Biol Sci Tex Tech Univ Lubbock TX 79409-0001

JONES, DALE ROBERT, PHYSICS. *Current Pos:* From asst prof to assoc prof, 53-62, PROF PHYSICS, UNIV CINCINNATI, 62- *Personal Data:* b Galesburg, Ill, June 17, 24. *Educ:* Univ Cincinnati, BSc, 48; Wash Univ, PhD, 53. *Mem:* Am Phys Soc; Sigma Xi. *Res:* Cosmic rays; atomic physics. *Mailing Add:* Dept Physics ML11 Univ Cincinnati Cincinnati OH 45221-0001

JONES, DALLAS WAYNE, PHYSICS. *Current Pos:* PRES, AMER TECH INST, 85- *Personal Data:* b Tiplersville, Miss, Sept 13, 38. *Educ:* Memphis State Univ, BS, 60; Univ Va, MS, 62, PhD(physics), 66. *Prof Exp:* Teaching asst physics, Univ Va, 60-63, res asst, 63-65; res physicist, US Naval Res Lab, 65-69; assoc prof physics, Memphis State Univ, 69-85, dir, Ctr Nuclear Studies, 73-85. *Mem:* Am Phys Soc. *Res:* Quantum physics; nuclear spectroscopy; reactor technology. *Mailing Add:* 2773 Johnson Rd Memphis TN 38139

JONES, DANE ROBERT, PHYSICAL CHEMISTRY. *Current Pos:* from asst prof to assoc prof, 76-85, PROF CHEM, CALIF POLYTECH STATE UNIV, SAN LUIS OBISPO, 85- *Personal Data:* b Park City, Utah, Nov 27, 47; m 74. *Educ:* Univ Utah, BA, 69; Stanford Univ, PhD(phys chem), 74. *Prof Exp:* Res assoc phys chem, Phys Chem Inst, Univ Uppsala, 74-75; res assoc & instr phys chem, Univ Utah, 75-76. *Mem:* Am Chem Soc. *Res:* Light scattering; surfaces and molecular complexes. *Mailing Add:* 1501 Fourth St Los Osos CA 93402

JONES, DANIEL DAVID, PLANT PHYSIOLOGY, PHYCOLOGY. *Current Pos:* From asst prof to assoc prof, 70-88, PROF BIOL, UNIV ALA, BIRMINGHAM, 88- *Personal Data:* b Olney, Ill, Feb 23, 43; m 65; c Christine A & Keith A. *Educ:* Purdue Univ, BS, 65, MS, 67; Mich State Univ, PhD(plant physiol), 70. *Concurrent Pos:* Interim chair, Dept Biol, Univ Ala, Birmingham, 74, grad prog dir biol, 81- *Mem:* Am Soc Plant Physiol; Am Inst Biol Scientists; Am Soc Microbiol. *Res:* Microbiology of Wastewater treatment and composting; gene-probe based detection of specific microbes. *Mailing Add:* Dept Biol Univ Ala 109 CH Birmingham AL 35294. *Fax:* 205-975-6097; *E-Mail:* biof002@uabdpo.dpo

JONES, DANIEL DAVID, RESEARCH & REGULATORY POLICY ON FOOD & AGRICULTURAL BIOTECHNOLOGY, AGRICULTURAL-HEALTH SCIENCES ADMINISTRATION. *Current Pos:* biotechnologist & dep dir, Off Agr Biotechnol, 87-96, NAT PROG LEADER, BIOTECHNOL USDA COOP STATE RES, EDUC & EXTEN SERV, 96- *Personal Data:* b Cedar Rapids, Iowa, Jan 9, 43; m 75, Mary J Edwards. *Educ:* Univ Iowa, BS, 65; Univ Mich, PhD(biochem), 70. *Prof Exp:* Res assoc, Chem Dept, Georgetown Univ, 71-72, Brookhaven Nat Lab, 73; biomed specialist, Info Syst Prog, Gen Elec Co, 73-75; staff assoc, Asn Am Med Col Div Biomed Res, 75-76; consumer safety officer, US Food & Drug Admin, Div Food & Color Additives, 76-80; br chief & food technologist, USDA Food Safety & Inspection Serv Stand & Labeling Div Stand Br, 80-86. *Concurrent Pos:* Consult protein sequence & struct, Carnegie Mellon Univ, 75-76; team leader, construct site review, Ind Univ Inst Molecular Cell Biol, 90; chmn biotech workshop, US Off Tech Assessment & Nat Agr Biotech Coun, 90. *Mem:* Am Chem Soc; Sigma Xi; NY Acad Sci. *Res:* Development of government policy, guidelines, regulations, and research thrusts for the application of modern biotechnology to agricultural research and production, research biosafety, food processing and safety, health and the environment. *Mailing Add:* 4138 Orchard Dr Fairfax VA 22032. *Fax:* 202-401-1602; *E-Mail:* ddjones@reeusda.gov

JONES, DANIEL ELVEN, PHYSICAL CHEMISTRY, COMPUTER SCIENCE. *Current Pos:* LAB SUPRV, STOCKHAUSEN LA, LTD, 96- *Personal Data:* b New Orleans, La, Sept 9, 43; m 65, Diana Mitchen; c Dana L & David M. *Educ:* La State Univ, Baton Rouge, BS, 65; Univ Calif, Berkeley, PhD(phys chem), 70; Tulane Univ, New Orleans, MSE, 96. *Prof Exp:* Res chemist, Am Cyanamid Co, 70-71, res comput specialist, 71-76; res chemist, Freeport-McMoRan, 76-78, sr res chemist, 79-93; res assoc, Tulane Univ, 93-94; sr prod chemist, Nalco Chem Co, 94-96. *Concurrent Pos:* Prof engr chem eng, 96. *Mem:* Am Chem Soc; Math Asn Am; Sigma Xi; Nat Soc Prof Engrs. *Res:* Carbon-13 Fourier transform nuclear magnetic resonance; application of digital computers and computing techniques for improvement of analytical instrumentation; uranium recovery from phosphoric acid; anaerobic biodegradation kinetics. *Mailing Add:* 37 Park Timbers Dr New Orleans LA 70131. *Fax:* 504-535-6711; *E-Mail:* 71233.506@compuserve.com

JONES, DANIEL PATRICK, HISTORY OF SCIENCE, HISTORY OF TECHNOLOGY. *Current Pos:* PROF OFFICER, DIV RES & EDUC, NAT ENDOWMENT HUMANITIES, WASHINGTON, DC, 84- *Personal Data:* b Lima, Ohio, Aug 21, 41; m 64, Carol Jackson; c Colin A. *Educ:* Univ Louisville, BS, 63; Harvard Univ, AM, 65; Univ Wis-Madison, PhD(hist sci), 69. *Prof Exp:* Macy fel hist med & biol sci, Johns Hopkins Univ, 69-70; asst prof hist sci, Ore State Univ, 70-78; vis prof, Ctr Humanistic Studies, Med Ctr, Univ Ill, 78-80, asst prof hist sci, 80-84. *Mem:* AAAS; Hist Sci Soc; Am Chem Soc; Am Asn Hist Med; Soc Hist Technol. *Res:* History of biochemistry and organic chemistry, 19th and early 20th century; relationships between science and society; history of public health. *Mailing Add:* Div Res & Educ Nat Endowment Humanities 1100 Pennsylvania Ave NW Washington DC 20506. *Fax:* 202-606-8394; *E-Mail:* djones@neh.fed.us

JONES, DANIEL SILAS, JR, PHYSICAL CHEMISTRY, X-RAY CRYSTALLOGRAPHY. *Current Pos:* asst prof, 73-78, ASSOC PROF CHEM, UNIV NC, CHARLOTTE, 78- *Personal Data:* b Charlotte, NC, Nov 16, 43; m 67, Linda Hood; c Amanda. *Educ:* Wake Forest Col, BS, 65; Harvard Univ, AM, 66, PhD, 70. *Prof Exp:* Teaching-res assoc, State Univ NY, Buffalo, 70-71; Nat Acad Sci-Nat Res Coun resident res assoc, Lab Struct Matter, Naval Res Lab, Washington, DC, 71-73. *Mem:* Am Chem Soc; Am Crystallog Asn. *Res:* Crystal and molecular structures by single crystal x-ray diffraction techniques. *Mailing Add:* Dept Chem Univ NC Charlotte NC 28223-0001. *E-Mail:* fch00dsj@unccvm.uncc.edu

JONES, DAVID A, JR, ORGANIC CHEMISTRY, PEPTIDE SYNTHESIS. *Current Pos:* PRES & CHIEF EXEC OFFICER, D J BIOTECH INC, 95- *Personal Data:* b McCook, Nebr, Feb 9, 37; m 76, E Ann Hallinan; c Katherine, Sean, David & Christopher. *Educ:* Tex A&M Univ, BS, 58; NMex State Univ, MS, 64; Purdue Univ, PhD(org chem), 68. *Prof Exp:* Mem staff, Dept Med Chem, G D Searle & Co, 68-81, res scientist II, 77-86; sr serv eng, Appl Biosysts Div, Perkin-Elmer Corp, 86-95. *Mem:* AAAS; Am Chem Soc. *Res:* Organometallic chemistry of silicon, magnesium, lithium; organic chemistry of phosphorus; amino acid and peptide chemistry; protein sequencing and instrumentation. *Mailing Add:* 135 Barton Ave Evanston IL 60202. *Fax:* 847-328-1565; *E-Mail:* biotech@mcs.net

JONES, DAVID ALWYN, ECOLOGICAL GENETICS OF CYANOGENESIS IN PLANTS, CHEMICAL ECOLOGY. *Current Pos:* PROF & CHMN, DEPT BOT, UNIV FLA, 89- *Personal Data:* b Colliers Wood, Eng, June 23, 34; m 59, Hazel C Lewis; c Catherine S (Thompson), Edmund M & Hugh F. *Educ:* Univ Cambridge, UK, BA, 57, MA, 60; Univ Oxford, UK, DPhil(genetics), 63. *Prof Exp:* Lectr genetics, Univ Birmingham, UK, 61-73; prof, Univ Hull, UK, 73-89, head, Dept Plant Biol & Genetics, 83-89. *Concurrent Pos:* Res grants, Sci & Eng Coun, Natural Environ Res Coun, Royal Soc, Ministry Agr Fisheries & Food, USDA Forest Serv; co-ed, J of Chem Ecol, 94- *Mem:* Brit Asn Advan Sci; fel Inst Biol; Int Soc Chem Ecol (pres, 87-88); Am Soc Naturalists; Soc Study Evolution; Genetical Soc UK; AAAS; Bot Soc Am. *Res:* First clear demonstration of chemical defense (cyanogenesis) by plants against herbivores using genetic variation; established criteria by which chemical defense can be proved; ecological genetics, chemical ecology and plant breeding. *Mailing Add:* Dept Bot Univ Fla 220 Bartram Hall PO Box 118526 Gainesville FL 32611-8526. *Fax:* 352-392-1175; *E-Mail:* djones@botany.ufl.edu

JONES, DAVID B, PATHOLOGY. *Current Pos:* From asst prof to assoc prof, 50-62, PROF PATH, STATE UNIV NY UPSTATE MED CTR, 62- *Personal Data:* b Canton, China, Dec 1, 21; US citizen; m 44; c 3. *Educ:* Syracuse Univ, AB, 43, MD, 45; Am Bd Path, dipl. *Mem:* Am Asn Pathologists & Bacteriologists; Am Soc Cytol; Sigma Xi. *Res:* Electron microscopy. *Mailing Add:* 226 Lockwood Rd Syracuse NY 13214-2035

JONES, DAVID HARTLEY, BIOCHEMISTRY. *Personal Data:* b Kansas City, Mo, Feb 10, 39; m 65; c 3. *Educ:* Bethany Nazarene Col, BS, 61; Univ Okla, MS, 64; Cornell Univ, PhD(biochem), 68. *Prof Exp:* USPHS fel biochem, Univ Calif, Los Angeles, 67-69; asst prof, Albany Med Col, Union Univ, 69-75, assoc prof, 75-78; assoc prof biochem, Oral Roberts Univ, 78-80. *Mem:* AAAS. *Res:* Oxidative phosphorylation in mitochondria; functional state transitions in the mammary gland; mitochondrial biogenesis during functional state transitions in the mammary gland. *Mailing Add:* 424 Shady Dr Grove City PA 16127

JONES, DAVID LAWRENCE, GEOLOGY, PALEONTOLOGY. *Current Pos:* PROF GEOL, DEPT GEOL, UNIV CALIF-BERKELEY. *Personal Data:* b Chicago, Ill, Nov 12, 30; m 53; c 4. *Educ:* Yale Univ, BS, 52; Stanford Univ, MS, 53, PhD, 56. *Prof Exp:* GEOLOGIST, WESTERN REGION, US GEOL SURV, 55- *Mem:* Geol Soc Am; Paleont Soc. *Res:* Molluscan paleontology; Cretaceous of the Pacific coast region of North America; stratigraphy, structural, biostratigraphy and molluscan paleontology of upper Mesozoic rocks of the Pacific Coast of North America. *Mailing Add:* Dept Geol Univ Calif-Berkeley Berkeley CA 94720

JONES, DAVID LLOYD, energy planning, meteorology & climatology, for more information see previous edition

JONES, DAVID ROBERT, PHYSIOLOGY OF DIVING ANIMALS, CARDIOVASCULAR DYNAMICS. *Current Pos:* PROF ZOOL, UNIV BC, 69- *Personal Data:* b Bristol, Eng, Jan 28, 41; Can citizen; m 62, Valerie Gibson; c Melanie & Vivienne. *Educ:* Southampton Univ, UK, BSc, 62; Univ E Anglia, UK, PhD(biol), 65. *Honors & Awards:* Fry Medal, Can Soc Zool, 91; Killiam Res Prize, 93. *Prof Exp:* Res fel biol, Univ E Anglia, UK, 65-66; lectr zool, Univ Bristol, UK, 66-69. *Concurrent Pos:* Sr fel, Killiam Found, Can, 73 & 90; comt mem, Can Soc Zoologists, 85-88; vis prof, Univ Melbourne, Australia, 88; mem, Grant Selection Comt, Nat Sci & Eng Res Coun Can, 90-94. *Mem:* Am Soc Zoologists; Am Physiol Soc; Soc Exp Biol; Can Soc Zoologists; Can Physiol Soc; Royal Soc Can. *Res:* Control of cardiovascular and respiratory responses to diving, altitude and exercise in birds and mammals; cardiovascular dynamics of invertebrates and vertebrates. *Mailing Add:* Zool Dept Univ BC 6270 University Blvd Vancouver BC V6T 1Z4 Can. *Fax:* 604-822-2416; *E-Mail:* jones@zoology.ubc.ca

JONES, DEAN PAUL, HYPOXIA, TOXICOLOGY. *Current Pos:* from asst prof to assoc prof, 79-91, PROF BIOCHEM, EMORY UNIV, 91- *Personal Data:* b Hazard, Ky, Sept 13, 49; m; c 2. *Educ:* Ore Health Sci Univ, PhD(biochem), 76. *Honors & Awards:* Levy Res Award. *Mem:* Am Soc Biochem & Molecular Biol; Am Soc Cell Biol; Am Physiol Soc; Am Chem Soc; AAAS; Soc Toxicol. *Res:* Oxygen metabolism in health and disease; diet and cancer; functions of glutathione in detoxification of carcinogens and other toxic compounds. *Mailing Add:* Biochem Sch Med Rollins Res Ctr Rm 4131 Emory Univ 1510 Clifton Rd Atlanta GA 30322-1100. *Fax:* 404-727-3231

JONES, DENNY ALAN, METALLURGY, ELECTROCHEMISTRY. *Current Pos:* PROF METALL ENG, UNIV NEV, 79- *Personal Data:* b Port Angeles, Wash, Jan 20, 38; m 62, Wanda Wallaace; c Regina, Gillian, Michael & Bryce. *Educ:* Univ Nev, BS, 60; Univ Ariz, MS, 62; Rensselaer Polytech Inst, PhD(mat sci), 67. *Prof Exp:* Res engr, Gen Elec Co, Wash, 62-63; res chemist, Kaiser Aluminum & Chem Corp, 66-68; res scientist, Battelle-NW Labs, 68-72; asst prof metall eng, Univ Hawaii, 72-74; res engr, US Steel Res Lab, 74-79. *Concurrent Pos:* Consult, Elec Power Res Inst, 79-86 & 93-, US Dept Energy, 85-89, Fed Trade Comn, 85-86; vis res prof, Desert Res Inst, 88-89; vis scientist, Idaho Nat Eng Lab, 88; Participating Guest, Lawrence Livermore Nat Lab, 94-97. *Mem:* Am Soc Metals; Nat Asn Corrosion Engrs; Electrochem Soc. *Res:* Stress corrosion cracking and corrosion fatigue of steel in aqueous and ammonia solutions; electrochemical studies of aqueous corrosion of stainless steels and aluminum. *Mailing Add:* Univ Nev 170 Reno NV 89557. *Fax:* 702-784-1766

JONES, DEREK WILLIAM, DENTAL MATERIALS. *Current Pos:* assoc prof dent biomat, 75-77, prof-in-chg dent biomat, 77-79, PROF & ACTG CHMN, DEPT APPL ORAL SCI & HEAD DIV DENT BIOMAT SCI, FAC DENT, DALHOUSIE UNIV, 79-, ASST DEAN RES & PROF, COL PHARM. *Personal Data:* b Birmingham, Eng, Dec 9, 33; Can citizen; m 57; c 4. *Educ:* Univ Birmingham, BSc, 65, PhD(dent mat sci), 70; Inst Ceramics, AICeram, 70, FICeram, 78; Brit Royal Soc Chem, CChem, FRSC, 85. *Honors & Awards:* Wilmer Souder Distinguished Scientist Award, Int Asn Dental Res, 88. *Prof Exp:* Instr dent technol & mat, Univ Birmingham, 65-75. *Concurrent Pos:* Vis lectr, Mathew Boulton Tech Col, 61-68; examr, City & Guilds London Inst, 66-73; mem comt & consult, Brit Stand Comt Dent Mat, 70-75; Brit expert rep, Int Stand Orgn, 73-75, Can rep, 75-, comt mem coun dent mat & devices, 77-, chmn Can adv comt, tech comt 106; chmn comt dent, Can Stand Asn, 78-; mem, Can Stand Steering Comt Health Care Technol, Can Stand Comt Implant Mat, 79 & Med Res Coun, Can Grants Comt, 81; dent schs rep, Dent Mat Group, Int Asn Dent Res; chmn, Can Stand Asn Tech Comt Dentistry, Can Adv Comt, Int Standards Orgn; mem secretariat, Int Stand Comt, 79-; vis prof at six dental schs, lectr in eleven countries; pres, Dental Mat Group Chap, CADR/IADR, 88-92, vpres-pres, Can Asn Dent Res, 90-95, pres, Int Dent Mat Group, IADR, 90-91, chmn, Dent Mat Group Prog, 88; meem, Nat Adv Panel Adv Indust Mat, Fed Govt Can, 90- *Mem:* Can Asn Dent Res; Int Asn Dent Res; Soc Biomat; Inst Ceramics; Royal Soc Chem. *Res:* Development of test methodology; evaluating mechanical-physical properties of materials to optimize clinical and laboratory use; biological factors relative to clinical performance; studies of hard and soft polymers, ceramics and metals; author of over 193 scientific publications. *Mailing Add:* Dalhousie Univ 5981 University Ave Halifax NS B3H 3J5 Can

JONES, DONALD AKERS, ACTUARIAL SCIENCE. *Current Pos:* Asst prof, 59-65, assoc prof, 65-91, EMER PROF MATH, UNIV MICH, ANN ARBOR, 91- *Personal Data:* b Topeka, Kans, Dec 27, 30; m 56; c 4. *Educ:* Iowa State Univ, BS, 52; Univ Iowa, MS, 56, PhD(math), 59. *Mem:* Am Statist Asn; Soc Actuaries; Am Acad Actuaries. *Res:* Actuarial science. *Mailing Add:* Dept Math Ore St Univ Corvallis OR 97331-4605

JONES, DONALD EUGENE, ANALYTICAL CHEMISTRY. *Current Pos:* from asst prof to assoc prof, 63-76, head dept, 76-82, PROF CHEM, WESTERN MD COL, 76- *Personal Data:* b South Bend, Ind, Aug 1, 34; m 55; c 3. *Educ:* Manchester Col, AB, 57; Purdue Univ, PhD(anal chem), 63. *Prof Exp:* Chemist, Bendix Corp, Ind, 57; res chemist, E I du Pont de Nemours & Co, 60; instr chem, Wabash Col, 61-63. *Concurrent Pos:* Vis assoc prof, Purdue Univ, 71-72; chem consult, Carroll County Gen Hosp, 74-79, USN, 84- *Mem:* Am Chem Soc. *Res:* Fluorescence of materials as applied to analytical procedures; trace analysis of materials; computer applications to chemical analysis; analytical chemistry as applied to clinical situations. *Mailing Add:* NSF Esie Arlington VA 22230

JONES, DONLAN F(RANCIS), ELECTRICAL ENGINEERING, COMPUTER SCIENCES. *Current Pos:* MATH TEACHER, OUR LADY LAKE GRAMMAR SCH, 91- *Personal Data:* b San Francisco, Calif, Feb 5, 30; m 57, Angela M Guerra; c Kathleen A, Robert F, Michael P & Terese M (Kemble). *Educ:* Univ Santa Clara, BEE, 52; Univ Calif, Los Angeles, MS, 54; Stanford Univ, Engr, 72. *Prof Exp:* Res engr, Hughes Aircraft Co, 52-56; asst prof elec eng, Univ Santa Clara, 56-63; adv develop engr, Sylvania Electronics Systs Div, Gen Tel & Electronics Corp, 63-65, eng specialist, 65-69; eng mgr, Comput Terminal Prods, Tektronix, Inc, 69-74, eng mgr, 4081 & MEG systs, 74-78, eng mgr, mass storage syst, 78-81, eng mgr, data commun, info display div, 81-84, appln mkt mgr, Graphics Work Sta Div, 85-91; math instr, Clackamas Community Col. *Concurrent Pos:* Adv develop engr, Sylvania Electronics Systs Div, Gen Tel & Electronics Corp, 57-63; NSF sci fac fel, 61-62; consult, Sonoma State Hosp, Calif, 62-63. *Mem:* Sigma Xi. *Res:* Application of computers to engineering and non-scientific problems; threshold logical design; graphic computer systems. *Mailing Add:* 427 Laurel St Lake Oswego OR 97034

JONES, DOUGLAS EMRON, PHYSICS. *Current Pos:* from asst prof to assoc prof, 64-74, prof, 74-, EMER PROF PHYSICS, BRIGHAM YOUNG UNIV. *Personal Data:* b Long Beach, Calif, Aug 19, 30; m 55; c 5. *Educ:* Brigham Young Univ, BS, 57, MS, 59, PhD(physics), 64. *Honors & Awards:* Karl G Maeser Res Award. *Prof Exp:* Technician radio repair, Southern Calif Edison Co, 54-55; apprentice engr, Collins Radio Co, 56, group supvr, 57; space scientist, Jet Propulsion Lab, Calif Inst Technol, 59-62. *Mem:* Am Geophys Union; Am Phys Soc. *Res:* Solar physics; interplanetary magnetic fields; planetary atmospheres; experimental space physics; measurement of microwave emission of planets; magnetic fields of comets and planets and in interplanetary space; space plasma simulations; soft x-ray studies of the sun. *Mailing Add:* Dept Physics & Astron Brigham Young Univ Provo UT 84602

JONES, DOUGLAS EPPS, GEOLOGY, PALEONTOLOGY. *Current Pos:* DIR, ALA MUS NATURAL HIST, 84- *Personal Data:* b Tuscaloosa, Ala, May 28, 30; m 55; c 3. *Educ:* Univ Ala, BS, 52; La State Univ, PhD(geol), 59. *Prof Exp:* Res geologist, La Geol Surv, 55-58; from asst prof to prof geol, 58-66, head, Dept Geol & Geog, 66-69, dean, Col Arts & Sci, 69-84, actg acad vpres, 88-90, PROF GEOL, UNIV ALA, 66- *Mem:* Geol Soc Am; Paleont Soc; Am Asn Petrol Geologists. *Res:* Stratigraphy and paleontology of Gulf Coastal plain region of the United States. *Mailing Add:* 823 N Overlook Rd Tuscaloosa AL 35406

JONES, DOUGLAS L, CARDIOVASCULAR PHYSIOLOGY, REGULATORY & INTEGRATIVE PHYSIOLOGY. *Current Pos:* From asst prof to assoc prof physiol, 81-91, PROF PHYSIOL & MED, UNIV WESTERN ONT, 91- *Personal Data:* b Calgary, Alta, Nov 3, 48; m 71; c Cara M, Sean A & Brian M. *Educ:* Univ Alta, BSc, 72; Univ Alta, MSc, 74; Univ Calgary, PhD(med physiol), 77. *Concurrent Pos:* Lady Davis scholar, 75; Med Res Coun fel, 78, 79 & 86-; L L scholar, 80; career scientist, Ont Ministry Health, 86 & 89; assoc scientist, J P Robarts Res Inst, London, 86-91, scientist, 91-; vis res fel, Univ Melbourne, Australia, 93-94. *Mem:* Fel Am Col Cardiol; Am Heart Asn; Am Phys Soc; Can Physiol Soc; AAAS; Soc Neurosci; Can Asn Neurosci. *Res:* Cardiovascular physiology; regulatory and integrative physiology; electrophysiology; neuroscience; electrocardiology. *Mailing Add:* Dept Physiol & Med Univ Western Ont London ON N6A 5C1 Can. *Fax:* 519-661-3827; *E-Mail:* dljones@physiology.uwo.ca

JONES, DOUGLAS LINWOOD, ENGINEERING, SOLID MECHANICS. *Current Pos:* Univ fel eng, George Washington Univ, 66-67, from instr to asst prof eng & appl sci, 67-71, from asst res prof to assoc res prof, 71-77, assoc prof, 77-82, chmn mech engr curric, 81-85, PROF ENG, GEORGE WASHINGTON UNIV, 82- *Personal Data:* b Limeton, Va, Dec 26, 37; m 75, Mary O'Brien. *Educ:* George Washington Univ, BME, 63, MSE, 65, DSc, 70. *Honors & Awards:* George Washington Award, George Washington Univ, 85. *Concurrent Pos:* Consult, Seal & Co, 70-71, Comsat Labs, 74-76, Eng Servs Co, 76-81, Ensco, Inc, 77-78, Systs Technol Labs, Inc, 80-82, Du Pont Corp, 82-85, Alcoa, 83, Intelsat Corp, 86-88, NKF Eng, 90 & US Dept Transp, 90-; prin or co-prin investr res grants, NASA, Dept Defense, NSF. *Mem:* Am Acad Mech; Am Soc Testing & Mat; Am Soc Mech Engrs; Am Soc Eng Educ; Soc Exp Mech; Sigma Xi. *Res:* Fatigue, fracture and fracture mechanics of metals and composite materials; computer aided engineering, computer aided design and optimization; fractography and failure analysis; experimental stress analysis; evaluation and development of constitutive relations in continuum mechanics; analysis and testing of composite materials. *Mailing Add:* Acad Ctr T723 George Wash Univ Washington DC 20052. *Fax:* 202-994-0238; *E-Mail:* jones@seas.gwu.edu

JONES, DUVALL ALBERT, VERTEBRATE ZOOLOGY, HERPETOLOGY. *Current Pos:* PROF BIOL, ST JOSEPH'S COL, 73- *Personal Data:* b Hurlock, Md, Oct 17, 33; m 66, Dorothy A Paul; c Genevieve I & Nathalie R. *Educ:* Western Md Col, AB, 55; Univ Md, MS, 61; Univ Fla, PhD(zool), 67. *Prof Exp:* Asst prof biol, James Madison Univ, 60-62; asst prof biol, head dept & chmn div natural sci & math, Ferrum Col, 62-65; asst prof biol & actg head dept, West Liberty State Col, 66-67; asst prof, Carnegie-Mellon Univ, 67-73. *Concurrent Pos:* Scaife grant. *Mem:* AAAS; Am Soc Zool; Am Soc Ichthyol & Herpet; Genetics Soc Am; Nat Sci Teachers Asn; Am Ornithologists Union. *Res:* Physiological ecology of amphibians; environmental genetics; bile pigments and their effects; ornithology. *Mailing Add:* Dept Biol St Joseph's Col Rensselaer IN 47978. *Fax:* 219-866-6300

JONES, E(DWARD) M(CCLUNG) T(HOMPSON), microwave electronics, for more information see previous edition

JONES, EARLE DOUGLAS, ELECTRONICS. *Current Pos:* REG MTG DIR, KOREA, 88- *Personal Data:* b Birmingham, Ala, Apr 10, 31; m 61. *Educ:* Ga Inst Technol, BS, 56; Stanford Univ, MS, 58. *Prof Exp:* Asst math, Ga Inst Technol, 55-56; exec dir, SRI-ASIA, 86-88. *Mem:* Inst Elec & Electronics Engrs; Sigma Xi. *Res:* Space electronics; communication systems research in satellite meteorology; display devices and digital control research; bioengineering. *Mailing Add:* 380 Conil Way Menlo Park CA 94028

JONES, EDWARD DAVID, PLANT ENTOMOLOGY. *Current Pos:* from asst prof to prof, 58-87, Henry & Mildred Uihlein prof plant path, 87-88, EMER PROF, DEPT PLANT PATH, CORNELL UNIV, 88- *Personal Data:* b Rockland, Wis, May 8, 20; m 47; c 4. *Educ:* Univ Wis, BS, 46, MS, 47, PhD(plant path), 53. *Prof Exp:* Instr plant path, Univ Wis, 48-53; plant pathologist, Red Dot Foods, Inc, 53-58. *Concurrent Pos:* In-chg found & cert seed potato prog NY state, 60-, Uihlein Farm, Cornell Univ, 61-, Henry Uihlein II tissue cult facil at Uihlein Farm, Lake Placid, NY, 77- *Mem:* Am Phytopath Soc; hon Potato Asn Am (vpres, 81-82, pres, 84-85); Sigma Xi. *Res:* Production of disease-free nuclear seed stocks by tissue culture; disease problems relating to the production of seed potatoes. *Mailing Add:* PO Box 260 Big Hills Lake Wild Rose WI 54984

JONES, EDWARD GEORGE, NEUROBIOLOGY. *Current Pos:* PROF & CHMN, UNIV CALIF IRVINE, 84- *Personal Data:* b Upper Hutt, NZ, Mar 26, 39; m 63, Elizabeth S Oldham; c Christopher & Philippa. *Educ:* Univ Otago, NZ, MB, ChB, 62, MD, 70; Oxford Univ, DPhil(anat), 68. *Hon Degrees:* Dr, Univ Salamanca, Spain, 97. *Honors & Awards:* Symington Mem Prize, Anat Soc Gt Brit & Ireland, 68; Rolleston Mem Prize, Oxford Univ, 70; Cajal Prize, Am Asn Anatomists, 89. *Prof Exp:* Demonstr anat, Univ Otago, NZ, 64-65, from asst lectr to lectr, 65-70, assoc prof, 71-72; assoc prof anat, Wash Univ, 72-75, prof anat & neurobiol, Sch Med, 75-84, prof neurosci, 81-84. *Concurrent Pos:* Nuffield Dom demonstr, Oxford Univ, 65-68, lectr, Balliol Col, 66-68; NZ Med Res Coun grant, Sch Med, Otago Univ, 69-71; assoc ed, J Comp Neurol, 75-80; Green vis prof, Med Br, Univ Tex, Galveston, 78; Macy Found sr fac scholar, Monash Univ, Australia, 78-79; dir, James O'Leary Div Exp Neurol & Neurol Surg, Wash Univ, George H & Ethel Ronzon scholar in neurosci & sr scientist, McDonnell Ctr Study Higher Brain Function, 81-84, assoc, Neurosci Res Prog, 84-93; assoc ed, J Neurosci, 81-88; dir, Neurol Systs Lab, Frontier Res Prog, Riken, Japan, 88-96. *Mem:* Anat Soc Gt Brit & Ireland; Am Asn Anatomists; Soc Neurosci; AAAS. *Res:* Structure, function and development of sensory systems particularly in primates and with emphasis on cerebral cortex and thalamus. *Mailing Add:* Dept Anat & Neurobiol Irvine Hall 114 Col Med Univ Calif Irvine Irvine CA 92697

JONES, EDWARD GRANT, CHEMICAL PHYSICS. *Current Pos:* res asst prof chem, 75-77, RES ASSOC PROF CHEM, WRIGHT STATE UNIV, 77- *Personal Data:* b Toronto, Ont, Feb 16, 42; m 72; c 3. *Educ:* Univ Toronto, BSc, 65, MSc, 67, PhD(phys chem), 69. *Prof Exp:* Vis res scientist, Ohio State Univ Res Found, 69-71; res assoc, Purdue Univ, 71-72; consult, Systs Res Labs, 71-72, sr res chemist & proj mgr, 72-75. *Concurrent Pos:* Consult, Systs Res Labs, 75- *Mem:* Sr mem Am Chem Soc; sr mem Am Soc Mass Spectrometry. *Res:* Gas phase kinetics; ion-neutral collision phenomena; unimolecular decomposition; chemiluminescence; thermal degradation of polymers; kinetics of polymerization. *Mailing Add:* 4850 N Piqua Troy Rd Troy OH 45373-9702

JONES, EDWARD O(SCAR), JR, MECHANICAL ENGINEERING. *Current Pos:* RETIRED. *Personal Data:* b Dothan, Ala, June 18, 22; m 47; c 2. *Educ:* Auburn Univ, BS, 43 & 46; Univ Ill, MS, 49. *Prof Exp:* Tooling engr, Consol Vultee Aircraft Corp, 43-45; from instr to prof mech eng, Auburn Univ, 46-92, asst dean eng, 74-78, asst dept head, 65-92. *Mem:* Soc Automotive Engrs; Soc Exp Stress Anal. *Res:* Experimental stress analysis, especially thin-shell pressure vessels. *Mailing Add:* 744 Sherbrook Dr Auburn AL 36830

JONES, EDWARD RAYMOND, AGRICULTURAL BUSINESS & MANAGEMENT, GENERAL AGRICULTURE. *Current Pos:* from asst prof to assoc prof, 69-77, PROF AGRON, DEL STATE COL, 77- *Personal Data:* b Steubenville, Ohio, Jan 27, 43; m 64, Brenda; c Kelly. *Educ:* Ohio State Univ, BS, 65; Pa State Univ, MS, 67, PhD(agron), 69. *Honors & Awards:* Merit Award, Forage & Grassland Coun, 88. *Concurrent Pos:* Adj prof plant sci, Univ Del, Newark. *Mem:* Am Soc Agron; Am Forage & Grassland Coun. *Res:* Forage crop management and utilization. *Mailing Add:* Del State Univ Dover DE 19901-2277

JONES, EDWARD STEPHEN, ORGANIC CHEMISTRY, ORGANOFLUORINE CHEMISTRY. *Current Pos:* RETIRED. *Personal Data:* b Boston, Mass, Apr 17, 31; m 56, Mary B Diuito; c Geraldine A, Stephen M & Lori E. *Educ:* Northeastern Univ, BS, 53; Purdue Univ, MS, 56; Wayne State Univ, PhD(org chem), 61. *Prof Exp:* Res chemist, Gen Chem Div, Allied Chem Corp, NJ, 60-69, sr res chemist, Specialty Chem Div, Buffalo, 69-80; sr res chemist, Halocarbon Prod Corp, 80-96. *Mem:* Am Chem Soc. *Res:* Organic fluorine chemistry; applications, process research and development; basic research; product research and development. *Mailing Add:* 224 Oakhurst Dr North Augusta SC 29841

JONES, EDWIN C, JR, ELECTRICAL ENGINEERING, EDUCATION. *Current Pos:* from asst prof to assoc prof, Iowa State Univ, 66-72, prof, 72-95, UNIV PROF ELEC ENG, IOWA STATE UNIV, 95- *Personal Data:* b Parkersburg, WVa, June 27, 34; m 60, Ruth Miller; c Charles, Cathleen & Helene. *Educ:* WVa Univ, BS, 55; Imp Col, Univ London, Dipl, 56; Univ Ill, Urbana, PhD(elec eng), 62. *Honors & Awards:* Centennial Medal, Inst Elec & Electronics Engrs, 84, Accreditation Activ Award, 86. *Prof Exp:* Teaching asst elec eng, Univ Ill, 58-59; from instr to asst prof elec eng, Univ Ill, 60-66. *Concurrent Pos:* Engr, Gen Elec Co, 55, 62 & Westinghouse Elec Co, 59; proc chmn, Nat Electronics Conf, 65, prog chmn, 68, secy, 69, awards chmn, 69-70, vpres continuing educ, 71; secy, Inst Elec & Electronics Engrs Educ Soc, 70-78, vpres, 73-74, pres, 75-76; mem, Eng Accreditation Comn, 80-84, bd dirs, Accreditation Bd Eng & Technol, 84-87; ed, Inst Elec & Electronics Engrs Trans Educ, 81-84. *Mem:* Fel Inst Elec & Electronics Engrs; fel Am Soc Eng Educ; fel AAAS; Soc Hist Technol; fel Accreditation Bd Eng & Technol. *Res:* Circuit theory; experimental engineering techniques; educational methods; technology and social change. *Mailing Add:* Dept Elec & Comput Eng Iowa State Univ Ames IA 50011. *E-Mail:* n2ecj@iastate.edu

JONES, EDWIN C, electrical engineering; deceased, see previous edition for last biography

JONES, EDWIN RUDOLPH, JR, SOLID STATE PHYSICS, SCIENCE EDUCATION. *Current Pos:* From asst prof to assoc prof, 65-77, PROF PHYSICS, UNIV SC, 77- *Personal Data:* b Lumberton, NC, Aug 3, 38; m 60; c 4. *Educ:* Clemson Univ, BS, 60; Univ Wis, MS, 62, PhD(physics), 65. *Concurrent Pos:* Vis prof, Univ de El Salvador, 78; mem, Comt Undergrad Educ, Am Asn Physics Teachers, 91-94, chair, 93-94; Comt Physics, High Sci, 97- *Mem:* Am Phys Soc; Am Asn Physics Teachers; Soc Photo-Optical Instrumentation Engrs. *Res:* Low temperature magnetic properties of solids; three dimensional imaging for video and computer displays; author of two textbooks. *Mailing Add:* Dept Physics Univ SC Columbia SC 29208. *E-Mail:* rjones@psc.psc.sc.edu

JONES, ELDON MELTON, medicinal chemistry; deceased, see previous edition for last biography

JONES, ELEANOR GREEN DAWLEY, MATHEMATICS. *Current Pos:* PROF MATH, NORFOLK STATE COL, 67-, READER, COL BD ADVAN PLACEMENT EXAM MATH, 89- *Personal Data:* b Norfolk, Va, Aug 10, 29; m 51, 67; c Edward A III & Everette B Jr. *Educ:* Howard Univ, BS, 49, MS, 50; Syracuse Univ, PhD(math), 66. *Prof Exp:* Instr, Hampton Inst, 55-62, assoc prof, 66-67; teaching asst, Syracuse Univ, 64-66. *Concurrent Pos:* Bd gov, Math Asn Am, 83-86; exec bd, Nat Asn Mathematicians, 88-; bd dir, Asn Women Math, 90- *Mem:* Am Math Soc; Math Asn Am; Nat Asn Math (vpres, 75-80); Asn Women Math; Sigma Xi. *Res:* Abelian groups and their endomorphism rings; direct decompositions and quasi-endomorphisms of torsion free abelian groups. *Mailing Add:* 6301 Bucknell Circle Virginia Beach VA 23464. *Fax:* 757-683-8427; *E-Mail:* eÖjones@vger.nsu.edu

JONES, ELIZABETH W, MOLECULAR GENETICS, CELL BIOLOGY. *Current Pos:* ADJ PROF PSYCHIAT, UNIV PITTSBURGH, 85- *Personal Data:* b Seattle, Wash, Mar 8, 39. *Educ:* Univ Wash, BS, 60, PhD(genetics), 64. *Prof Exp:* USPHS trainee, Univ Wash, 60-64; res assoc, Mass Inst Technol, 64-67, instr, 67-69; asst prof biol & microbiol, Case Western Reserve Univ, 69-74; assoc prof, 74-82, PROF BIOL SCI, CARNEGIE-MELLON UNIV, 82- *Concurrent Pos:* USPHS res grant, 70-, res career develop award, 71-74, 75-77; NIH Genetics Training Comt, 72-73, Genetics Study Sect, 76-80 & 84-86, chair, 90; assoc ed, Genetics, 80-, Yeast, 85-, Ann Rev Genetics, 90- *Mem:* Fel AAAS; Genetics Soc Am (vpres, 86, pres, 87); Am Soc Microbiol; Am Soc Cell Biol. *Res:* Organization and expression of genetic material in yeast; protein targeting and organellar assembly. *Mailing Add:* Dept Biol Sci Carnegie-Mellon Univ 4400 Fifth Ave Box 65 Pittsburgh PA 15213-2683. *Fax:* 412-268-7129

JONES, ELMER EVERETT, ORGANIC CHEMISTRY. *Current Pos:* RETIRED. *Personal Data:* b Hinsdale, Ill, Sept 2, 26; m 56, F Alice Williamson; c Laura A. *Educ:* Univ Chicago, PhB, 48, BS, 50; Washington Univ, PhD, 57. *Prof Exp:* Asst, Washington Univ, 50-55; res assoc, Tannhauser Lab, Boston Dispensary, 56-58; asst prof chem, Northeastern Univ, 58-62, assoc prof chem, 62-90. *Mem:* Am Chem Soc; Sigma Xi. *Mailing Add:* 67 Brook Rd Weston MA 02193-1766

JONES, ERIC DANIEL, SOLID STATE PHYSICS. *Current Pos:* mem staff solid state physics res, Sandia Corp, Sandia Nat Labs, 65-68, supvr laser effects res, 68-82, mem staff laser res, 82-85, mem tech staff Sandia Semiconductor Physics, 85-90, DISTINGUISHED MEM TECH STAFF, SANDIA NAT LABS, 90- *Personal Data:* b Oakland, Calif, Jan 6, 36; m 57, Mary A Hackworth; c Jennifer, Eric Jr, Kelly, Kim & Suzanne. *Educ:* Ore State Univ, BS, 57; Univ Wash, MS, 59, PhD(physics), 62. *Prof Exp:* Mem tech staff, Bell Tel Labs, NJ, 62-65. *Concurrent Pos:* Mem, Adv Comt-Optics Prog, Idaho State Univ, 70-76, Adv Comt Grad Studies, Elec & Comput Eng, Univ NMex, 76-88, bd ed, Rev Sci Instruments, 86-89, Users' Comt for the Francis Bitter Nat Magnet Lab, Mass Inst Technol, 90-93, External Adv Comt, Nat High Magnetic Field Lab, Fla State Univ, 91-94; pres, Albuquerque Chap Laser Inst Am, 72-76; adj prof, Physics Dept, Univ NMex, Albuquerque, NMex, 85-; secy-treas, Instruments & Measurement Sci Top Group, Am Phys Soc, 88-90; Woodrow Wilson fel, 60; chmn, User's Comt, Nat High Magnetic Field Lab, 93-95. *Mem:* Fel Am Phys Soc; sr mem Inst Elec & Electronics Engrs. *Res:* Study of ferromagnetism, antiferromagnetism, paramagnetism in insulators and metals by the use of nuclear magnetic resonance techniques; high power laser energy deposition in solids; ultrashort laser pulse generation and applications; magneto-optics of semiconductors, and pressure effects in semiconductors; semiconductor physics. *Mailing Add:* Sandia Nat Labs Semiconductor Physics Res 1113 MS0601 PO Box 5800 Albuquerque NM 87185-0350. *Fax:* 505-844-3211; *E-Mail:* edjones@sandia.gov

JONES, ERIC MANNING, HYDRODYNAMICS, ASTROPHYSICS. *Current Pos:* Staff mem hydrodyn, 69-75, group leader, 76-81, LAB FEL, LOS ALAMOS NAT LAB, 82- *Personal Data:* b Goldsboro, NC, Mar 25, 44. *Educ:* Calif Inst Technol, BS, 66; Univ Wis-Madison, PhD(astron), 69. *Concurrent Pos:* Nat Res Coun Comt on Nuclear Winter; co-ed with Ben R Finney, Interstellar Migration and the Human Experience, Univ of Calif Press, 85. *Mem:* Am Astron Soc. *Res:* Supernova remnants; interstellar medium; nuclear explosion phenomenology; numerical hydrodynamics; space development. *Mailing Add:* Los Alamos Nat Lab F 659 PO Box 1663 Los Alamos NM 87545

JONES, ERIC WYNN, VETERINARY SURGERY. *Current Pos:* vdean, Col Vet Med, Miss State Univ, 78-83, interim dean, 83-84, from asst to vpres, 84-86, prof, 86-87, PROF VET MED, MISS STATE UNIV, 87- *Personal Data:* b St Martins, Eng, Sept 24, 24; US citizen; m 48; c 1. *Educ:* MRCVS, 46; Cornell Univ, PhD(vet surg), 50; Am Col Vet Surg, dipl, 71; Am Col Vet Anesthesiol, dipl, 78. *Hon Degrees:* FRCVS, London, 87. *Prof Exp:* Consult, Col Vet Med, Miss State Univ, 74-78. *Concurrent Pos:* Dir clin res, 56-77. *Mem:* Am Vet Med Asn; Brit Vet Asn; Am Soc Anesthesiol; Am Vet Med Anesthesiol; Am Acad Vet Pharmacol & Toxicol; Am Asn Equine Practrs. *Res:* Drug and biologic and model development; program and facilities consulting national and international; spleen function in infectious anemia; enteritis; mechanical ventilators; malignant hyperthermia; drug testing. *Mailing Add:* Col Vet Med PO Drawer 9825 Miss State Univ Mississippi State MS 39762

JONES, ERNEST ADDISON, PHYSICS. *Current Pos:* from asst prof to prof physics, 50-85, EMER PROF PHYSICS, VANDERBILT UNIV, 85- *Personal Data:* b Columbia, Ky, June 5, 18; m 43. *Educ:* Western Ky State Teachers Col, BS, 42; Vanderbilt Univ, MS, 43; Ohio State Univ, PhD(phys chem), 48. *Prof Exp:* Res physicist, Manhattan Dist, Columbia Univ, 43-45; res chemist, Carbide & Carbon Chem Co, 48-50. *Mem:* Am Phys Soc; Optical Soc Am. *Res:* Infrared and Raman spectroscopy. *Mailing Add:* 2811 Wimbledon Rd Nashville TN 37215

JONES, ERNEST AUSTIN, JR, PETROLEUM GEOLOGY. *Current Pos:* RES GEOLOGIST, MOBIL CORP, 89- *Personal Data:* b Orange, NJ, Mar 24, 60. *Educ:* Princeton Univ, AB, 83; Harvard Univ, AM, 89, PhD(geol), 89. *Prof Exp:* Geologist, US Geol Surv, 84-87. *Mem:* Am Asn Petrol Geologists. *Res:* Development of diagenetic models to predict sandstone reservoir quality; clastic petrology and hydrogeology, Anadarko basin, Denver basin, Llamos basin & NW Shelf, Australia. *Mailing Add:* 4242 N Capistrano Dr Dallas TX 75287

JONES, ERNEST OLIN, RADIOLOGICAL PHYSICS. *Current Pos:* assoc prof radiol, Col Med, Univ Nebr, Omaha, 68-72, prof radiol, Col Med, 72-, assoc prof radiol, Col Dent, 69-, EMER PROF RADIOL, COL MED & DENT, UNIV NEBR, OMAHA. *Personal Data:* b Atlanta, Ga, Feb 1, 23; m 46; c 2. *Educ:* Emory Univ, AB, 48, MS, 49; US Naval Postgrad Sch, MS, 59; NC State Univ, PhD(nuclear eng), 64; Am Bd Radiol, dipl radiol physics, 75. *Prof Exp:* Dep dir nuclear med, Walter Reed Army Inst Res, 64-67, dir, Div Biometrics, 67-68. *Mem:* Soc Nuclear Med; Am Asn Physicists Med; Asn Mil Surgeons US; Am Col Nuclear Physicians; Am Col Med Physics; fel Am Col Radiol. *Res:* Radiation therapy dosimetry; diagnostic x-ray dosage reduction, medical computer applications. *Mailing Add:* Box 4334 Pagosa Springs CO 81157

JONES, EUGENE LAVERNE, GEOPHYSICS, GEOCHEMISTRY. *Current Pos:* RETIRED. *Personal Data:* b Adona, Ark, Sept 20, 28; m 50; c 4. *Educ:* Univ Ark, BS, 51, MS, 52; Univ Okla, PhD, 61. *Prof Exp:* Petrol geologist, Gulf Oil Corp, 52-54; asst prof geol & head dept, Ark Polytech Col, 54-60; sr res geologist, Field Res Lab, Socony Mobil Oil Co, Inc, 60-64, mgr geol-geochem res & tech serv, Mobil Res & Develop Corp, 64-71, vpres & explor mgr, Mobil North Sea Inc, London, 71-73 & Mobil Explor Norway, Inc, 73-75, adv, 78-79, mgr explor res, Mobil Res & Develop Corp, 75-88, mgr explor, Prod Res Div, 79-88. *Concurrent Pos:* Instr, Oklahoma City Univ, 58; fel, Nat Sci Found, 58-59. *Mem:* AAAS; Am Asn Petrol Geologists; Sigma Xi; Geol Soc London. *Res:* Palynology; sedimentation; petroleum exploration, geology, geochemistry and geophysics; stratigraphy. *Mailing Add:* 915 Green Hills Rd Duncanville TX 75137

JONES, EVAN EARL, BIOCHEMISTRY. *Current Pos:* asst prof nutrit biochem, 66-69, asst prof animal sci & biochem, 69-71, ASSOC PROF BIOCHEM, 71- & PROF ANIMAL SCI, NC STATE UNIV, 77- *Personal Data:* b Wray, Colo, June 8, 35; m 55. *Educ:* Colo State Univ, BS, 60; Univ Ill, MS, 62, PhD(biochem), 64. *Prof Exp:* Fel biochem, Inst Microbiol, Rutgers Univ, 64-66. *Concurrent Pos:* Vis scholar, Stanford Univ, 75-76. *Mem:* AAAS; Am Chem Soc; Am Soc Biol Chemists; Am Soc Microbiol. *Res:* Amino acid biosynthesis, arginine; metabolic control mechanisms. *Mailing Add:* Dept Animal Sci & Biochem NC State Univ Box 7621 Raleigh NC 27695-7621. *Fax:* 919-515-7780

JONES, EVERET CLYDE, MARINE BIOLOGY. *Current Pos:* RETIRED. *Personal Data:* b West Plains, Mo, Jan 26, 23; m 70, Marlene Knotts; c Michael. *Educ:* Hastings Col, AB, 49; Univ Miami, Fla, MS, 52. *Prof Exp:* Fishery biologist, Nat Marine Fisheries Serv, 55-73; asst prof biol, Northeast Mo State Univ, 74-77, asst prof sci, 79-87. *Mem:* Am Inst Fishery Res Biologists. *Res:* Systematics, ecology and zoogeography of marine copepods; mechanisms controlling distribution of marine plankton and tunas; behavior and systematics of sharks; chemistry of marine algae. *Mailing Add:* 3343 S Southlyn Pl Springfield MO 65804-6435

JONES, EVERETT, FLUID MECHANICS, HEAT TRANSFER. *Current Pos:* prof, 69-95, EMER PROF AEROSPACE ENG, UNIV MD, COLLEGE PARK, 95- *Personal Data:* b Albany, NY, Jan 25, 30; m 57; c 3. *Educ:* Rensselaer Polytech Inst, BAE, 56, MAE, 60; Stanford Univ, PhD(aeronaut & astronaut), 68. *Prof Exp:* Advan study scientist, Lockheed Missiles & Space Co, 56-57; res asst aeronaut eng, Rensselaer Polytech Inst, 57-59; sr thermodynamicist, Lockheed Missiles & Space Co, 59-61, sr engr, 61-64, res specialist, 64-69; engr, US Naval Surface Weapons Ctr, 77-83. *Concurrent Pos:* Res asst, Dept Aeronaut & Astronaut Sci, Stanford Univ, 66-68, res assoc, 68-69; lectr heat transfer, San Jose State Col, 67-68; fac res fel, NASA-ASER fac res prog, 70, US Army fac res eng prof, 83 & David W Taylor res prog, Naval Ship Res Ctr, 85. *Mem:* Am Inst Aeronaut & Astronaut; NY Acad Sci. *Res:* Fluid mechanics, heat transfer and aerodynamics; emphasis on applications for aerospace vehicles, computational fluid mechanics and blood flow. *Mailing Add:* 10969 Hilltop Lane Columbia MD 21044

JONES, EVERETT BRUCE, HYDROLOGY, WATER RESOURCES ENGINEERING. *Current Pos:* PROJ MGR ENG GROUP, JACOBS ENG GROUP, 91- *Personal Data:* b Ft Collins, Colo, Sept 23, 33; m 56, Margie Raben; c Elizabeth G & Janet L. *Educ:* Univ Wyo, BS, 55; Pa State Univ, MS, 59; Colo State Univ, PhD(watershed mgt), 64. *Prof Exp:* Chief water develop, Wyo Natural Resources Bd, 59-61; engr-hydrologist, Douglas W Barr, Consult Hydraul Engrs, Minn, 64-65; asst dir inst for res on land & water resources, in-chg of water resources ctr & asst prof meteorol, Pa State Univ, 65-68; coordr water resources, Environ Serv Oper, EG&G, Inc, 69; vpres, M W Bittinger & Assocs, Inc, 70-77, pres, 77; pres, Resource Consults, Inc, 77-87; mgr, Water Resources Dept, Environ Sci & Eng Inc, 87-88; assoc, Bishop-Brogden Assocs, Lakewood, Colo, 88-90; dist mgr, Groundwater

Tech, Inc, Englewood, Colo, 90-91. *Concurrent Pos:* Asst interstate streams comnr, State Wyo, 61; vpres, Wyo Well. *Mem:* Am Soc Civil Engrs; Am Meteorol Soc; Am Geophys Union. *Res:* Groundwater hydrology; surface-water hydrology and hydrometeorology, especially water resources management aspects. *Mailing Add:* 495 Spring Creek Dr Divide CO 80814

JONES, FABER BENJAMIN, POLYMER CHEMISTRY. *Current Pos:* mgr, Chem Appln Br, Phillips Petrol Co, 64-79, mgr, Polymer Appln Br, 79, dir polymer mat res, 80-81, div mgr polymer mat res, 82-86, vpres, planning & budgeting, 86-90, VPRES RES & DEVELOP, PHILLIPS PETROL CO, 90- *Personal Data:* b Dec 4, 32; US citizen; m 54; c 4. *Educ:* Ohio State Univ, BSc, 54. *Prof Exp:* Asst div chief polymer res, Battelle Mem Inst, 53-63; tech dir adhesives res, Evans Adhesives Corp, 63-64. *Mem:* Am Chem Soc; Adhesion Soc; Soc Plastic Engrs. *Res:* Polymer research and technology, especially on adhesives, coatings and reinforced plastic systems. *Mailing Add:* 2412 Kyles Court Bartlesville OK 74006-6339

JONES, FLOYD BURTON, TOPOLOGY. *Current Pos:* prof math, 62-78, EMER PROF MATH, UNIV CALIF, RIVERSIDE, 78- *Personal Data:* b Cisco, Tex, Nov 22, 10; m 36, Madeleine Maire; c Phyllis, Marion, Clay & Lesley. *Educ:* Univ Tex, BA, 32, PhD(math), 35. *Prof Exp:* Instr pure math, Univ Tex, 32-40, asst prof to assoc prof, 40-50; prof math, Univ NC, 50-62. *Concurrent Pos:* Res assoc, Underwater Sound Lab, Harvard Univ, 42-44; sr fel, NSF, 57-58; mem, Inst Advan Study, Australian Nat Univ, 57-58, vis fel, 68; Fulbright-Hays fel, NZ, 75; vis fel, Univ Houston, 77; Mary Moody northern chair, VMI, 79; distinguished vis scientist, Auburn Univ, 82. *Mem:* Am Math Soc; Math Asn Am. *Res:* Pointset theoretic topology. *Mailing Add:* 3775 Modoc Dr No 74 Univ Calif Santa Barbara CA 93105-4474

JONES, FRANCIS THOMAS, PHYSICAL CHEMISTRY. *Current Pos:* from asst prof to assoc prof chem, 64-71, head, Dept Chem & Chem Eng, 79-90, PROF CHEM, STEVENS INST TECHNOL, 71- *Personal Data:* b Pottsville, Pa, Oct 19, 33; m 81, Nuran Kumbaraci; c Anne & Marian. *Educ:* Pa State Univ, BS, 55; Polytech Inst Brooklyn, PhD(phys chem), 60. *Hon Degrees:* MEng, Stevens Inst Technol, 75. *Prof Exp:* Gen Elec Co Ltd fel radiation chem, Univ Leeds, 60-62; chemist, Union Carbide Corp, 62-64. *Concurrent Pos:* Adj assoc prof anesthesiol, NY Med Col, 77-89. *Mem:* Am Chem Soc. *Res:* Radiation chemistry; photochemistry; catalysis; mass spectrometry; kinetics; instrumentation design. *Mailing Add:* 692 Stewart St Ridgefield NJ 07657. *Fax:* 201-216-8240; *E-Mail:* fjones@stevens_tech.edu

JONES, FRANCIS TUCKER, CHEMISTRY. *Current Pos:* RETIRED. *Personal Data:* b Rocklin, Calif, Jan 17, 05; m 42; c 3. *Educ:* Pac Univ, Ore, AB, 28; Univ Ore, AM, 31; Cornell Univ, PhD(chem micros), 34. *Prof Exp:* Asst chem, Pac Univ, Ore, 26-28; teacher pub sch, Ore, 28-29; asst chem, Univ Ore, 29-31 & Cornell Univ, 32-34; prof, Pac Univ, Ore, 34-42; chemist, Mkt & Nutrit Div, Agr Res Serv, USDA, 42-74. *Mem:* Am Chem Soc; Sigma Xi. *Res:* Physical and analytical chemistry; chemical microscopy applied to determination of optical and crystallographic properties and phase relations; scanning electron microscopy. *Mailing Add:* 912 Regal Rd Berkeley CA 94708-1428

JONES, FRANK CULVER, COSMIC RAY PHYSICS, THEORETICAL ASTROPHYSICS. *Current Pos:* Nat Acad Sci-Nat Res Coun resident res assoc, Theoret Studies Group, 63-65, physicist, 65-77, astrophysicist, Lab High Energy Astrophys, 77-93, head, Theoret High Energy Astrophys Off, 95, SCIENTIST, LAB HIGH ENERGY ASTROPHYS, GODDARD SPACE FLIGHT CTR, NASA, 95- *Personal Data:* b Ft Worth, Tex, July 30, 32; m 55, Andythe Grube; c Chery (Mattis) & Timothy. *Educ:* Rice Inst, BA, 54; Univ Chicago, MS, 55, PhD(physics), 61. *Prof Exp:* Res assoc physics, Univ Chicago, 60; res assoc, Princeton Univ, 60-61, instr, 61-63. *Concurrent Pos:* Vis scientist, Max Planck Inst Nuclear Physics, 77; secy, Astrophys Div, Am Phys Soc, 88-92; coun mem, Am Phys Soc, 94-97. *Mem:* Fel AAAS; fel Am Phys Soc; Am Astron Soc; Am Geophys Union. *Res:* Physics of the origin of cosmic rays and related astrophysical problems; statistical physics of cosmic ray origin and propagation in the galaxy. *Mailing Add:* Code 665 Lab for High Energy Astrophys NASA Goddard Space Flight Ctr Greenbelt MD 20771. *Fax:* 301-286-1682; *E-Mail:* frank.c.jones@gsfc.nasa.gov

JONES, FRANK NORTON, POLYMER SYNTHESIS, ORGANIC COATINGS. *Current Pos:* PROF & DIR, COATINGS RES CTR, NSF, 90- *Personal Data:* b Columbia, Mo, Dec 27, 36; div; c David. *Educ:* Oberlin Col, AB, 58; Duke Univ, PhD(org chem), 62. *Honors & Awards:* Roon Found Prizes, 86, 87 & 91; Matiello lectr, 95. *Prof Exp:* Instr org chem, Duke Univ, 61-62; fel, Mass Inst Technol, 62-63; res chemist, Cent Res Dept, E I Du Pont Co, 63-68, staff chemist, 68-70, res supvr, 70-73; tech mgr, Celanese Polymer Specialties Co, 73-79; res & develop mgr, Cargill, Inc, 79-83; prof & chair, Dept Polymers & Coatings, NDak State Univ, 83-90. *Mem:* Am Chem Soc; Fedn Soc Coatings Technol. *Res:* Synthetic polymer chemistry; polymer structure/property relationships; polymeric materials; coatings. *Mailing Add:* Coatings Res Inst Eastern Mich Univ Ypsilanti MI 48197. *Fax:* 313-483-0085; *E-Mail:* frank.jones@emich.edu

JONES, FRANKLIN DEL, COMBAT STRESS, PSYCHOPHARMACOLOGY. *Current Pos:* CLIN PROF, UNIFORMED SERVS, UNIV HEALTH SCI, 75- *Personal Data:* b Hereford, Tex, Sept 22, 35; m 57, June Kim; c Gregory, Geoffrey, Gresham & Giselle. *Educ:* Baylor Univ, BS, 57; Univ Tex, Dallas, MD, 61. *Prof Exp:* Resident psychiat, Walter Reed Army Med Ctr, 61-65, dir res ward, 68-73; clin prof, Georgetwon Univ Med Sch, 73-94; psychiat & Neurol consult, Army Surgeon Gen, 77-81. *Concurrent Pos:* Intern med & surg, Ireland Army Hosp, Ft Knox, Ky, 61-62; chief psychiat sev, Walter Reed Army Med Ctr, 71-73 & forensic psychiat, 73-77, dir pyschiat educ, 73-77 & 85-88; clin consult psychiat, 73-, psychiat & neurol consult, Surgeon Gen Army, 77-81; secy-treas, Neuropsychiat & Human Serv Found, 95- *Mem:* World Psychiat Asn (pres, 77-83, secy, 83-89); fel Am Psychiat Asn. *Res:* Studies of combat stress in Vietnam, Egypt and Israel; post-traumatic stress disorder in combat veterans and rape victims; psychopharmacology of eating disorders and performance; use of BEAM (brain electrical activity mapping) in ADHD; author of six books. *Mailing Add:* 6508 Tall Tree Terr Rockville MD 20852-3733. *Fax:* 301-881-3732

JONES, FRANKLIN M, SCIENCE EDUCATION. *Current Pos:* RETIRED. *Personal Data:* b Reidsville, NC, Mar 10, 33; m 63; c 2. *Educ:* Appalachian State Teachers Col, BS, 55, MA, 60; Univ NC, MEd, 60; Univ Ga, EdD(sci educ), 66. *Prof Exp:* Teacher, High Sch, Va, 55-56 & NC, 56-58; prof chem, Ferrum Jr Col, 60-64; assoc prof, Radford Univ, 66-68, prof phys sci, 68-96. *Mailing Add:* Dept 28 Pine View Dr Radford VA 24141

JONES, FREDERICK GOODWIN, PERMANENT MAGNETS, POWDER METALLURGY. *Current Pos:* PRES, F G JONES ASSOC, LTD, 84- *Personal Data:* b Utica, NY, Nov 6, 35; m 59; c 3. *Educ:* Cornell Univ, BMetE, 59; Univ Mich, Ann Arbor, MSE & PhD(metall), 69. *Prof Exp:* Staff engr, Crucible Steel Co Am, 59-65; sr develop engr, magnetism, Gen Elec Co, 69-73; sr develop engr, Hitachi Magnetics Corp, 73-84. *Concurrent Pos:* Tech consult, NAm, Western Europ, Far East, 84- *Mem:* Am Inst Mining, Metall & Petrol Engrs; Am Foundrymen's Soc; Am Inst Elec & Electronics Engrs; Sigma Xi. *Res:* Permanent magnet materials; rare earth-transitional metal alloys; hydrogen-metal reactions; low alloy steels; high temperature alloys. *Mailing Add:* 820 Wright Ave Alma MI 48801-1129

JONES, GALEN EVERTS, MARINE MICROBIOLOGY, MICROBIAL BIOGEOCHEMISTRY. *Current Pos:* prof microbiol, 66-91, dir, Jackson Estuarine Lab, 66-72 & 83-87, EMER PROF, UNIV NH, 91-; CONSULT, 91- *Personal Data:* b Milwaukee, Wis, Sept 9, 28; m 54, 86, Eleonore A Angell; c Galen R, Swenith & Christopher. *Educ:* Dartmouth Col, AB, 50; Williams Col, MA, 52; Rutgers Univ, PhD(microbiol), 56. *Prof Exp:* Asst, Williams Col, 50-52; res asst, Tex Gulf Sulfur, Rutgers Univ, 52-55; from jr res microbiologist to asst res microbiologist, Div Marine Biol, Scripps Inst Oceanog, Univ Calif, 55-63, Rockefeller fel, 55-57; assoc prof biol, Boston Univ, 63-66. *Concurrent Pos:* Res grants, Nat Inst Allergy & Infectious Dis, 57-59, Div Water Supply & Pollution Control, USPHS, 59-62, 63-66 & NSF 72-74, 75-76 & 77-78, 81-85 & Sea Grant, 83-85, NOAA, 87-91; consult, Eli Lilly & Co, Ind, 58-59, Bendix-Pac, Calif, 60, Arthur D Little Co, Mass, 69-70 & 73-74 & Normandeau Assocs, Inc, NH, 70-71; Off Naval Res contract, 63-64 & 66-68; nonresident assoc microbiol, Woods Hole Oceanog Inst, 64-72, lectr, Marine Biol Lab, Woods Hole, 71-72, 74-75 & 76-77; mem, Nat Sea-Grant Univ Comt, 65-67; dir, Jackson Estuarine Lab, Univ NH, 66-72, chmn dept, 75-80 & Marine Sci Labs, 85-87, Interim Sea Grant, 86-87; mem, Santa Barbara Oil Spill Panel, Exec Off of the Pres, 69-70; mem adv panel biol oceanog, NSF, 71-72 & mem oceanog adv panel, 74-75; vis prof oceanog, Univ Liverpool, 72-73; mem, Inst Ecol Adv Panel to Nat Comn Water Qual, Washington, DC, 74-76; mem exec panel, Oceanog Div, NSF, 80; vis prof, Scripps Inst Oceanog, Univ Calif, 81. *Mem:* Fel AAAS; fel Am Acad Microbiol; Sigma Xi; Am Soc Microbiol; Oceanog Soc. *Res:* Biochemicals and trace elements in sea water; chemosynthesis; fractionation of stable isotopes in microorganisms; biogeochemistry; elemental composition of bacteria. *Mailing Add:* 6684 Michaeljohn Dr La Jolla CA 92037

JONES, GARTH, NUCLEAR PHYSICS. *Current Pos:* from asst prof to assoc prof, 61-69, PROF PHYSICS, UNIV BC, 69- *Personal Data:* b Victoria, BC, Mar 27, 32. *Educ:* Univ BC, BA, 53, MSc, 55, PhD(physics), 59. *Prof Exp:* Jr sci officer electronics, Atomic Energy Can, Ltd, 55-56; Rutherford Mem fel, Clarendon Lab, Oxford Univ, 60, Nat Res Coun Can overseas fel nuclear physics, 60-61. *Concurrent Pos:* Guggenheim fel, 67-68. *Mem:* Can Asn Physicists; Am Phys Soc. *Res:* Nuclear reactions; positron annihilation; intermediate energy physics. *Mailing Add:* Dept Physics Univ BC Vancouver BC V6T 1Z1 Can

JONES, GARTH WICKS, MICROBIOLOGY. *Current Pos:* scholar, 74-75, ASST PROF MICROBIOL, UNIV MICH, ANN ARBOR, 75- *Personal Data:* b Aberdare, Wales, Sept 23, 40; m 64; c 3. *Educ:* Univ Reading, BSc, 69, PhD(microbiol), 72. *Prof Exp:* Sr sci officer microbiol, Inst Res Animal Dis, Brit Agr Res Coun, 72-75. *Mem:* Soc Gen Microbiol; Brit Soc Appl Bact; Am Soc Microbiol. *Res:* Nature and function of the adhesive properties of bacteria, particularly enteric pathogens, and the composition of the eukaryotic cell components with which bacterial adhesive substances interact. *Mailing Add:* Dept Microbiol 6643 Med Sci Bldg 2 Univ Mich Med Sch 1301 Catherine Rd Ann Arbor MI 48109-0608

JONES, GARY EDWARD, genetics, cell biology, for more information see previous edition

JONES, GEOFFREY MELVILL, NEUROSCIENCES, AEROSPACE MEDICINE. *Current Pos:* assoc prof, McGill Univ, 61-68, prof physiol & dir, 68-88, Hosmer res prof, 78-91, EMER PROF PHYSIOL, MCGILL UNIV, CAN, 91- *Personal Data:* b Shelford, Eng, Jan 14, 23; m 53, Jenny Marigold Burnaby; c Kathanne, Francis, Andrew & Dorothy. *Educ:* Cambridge Univ, BA, 44, MA, 47, MB, BCh, 49. *Honors & Awards:* Harry G Armstrong Award Res Aerospace Med, Aerospace Med Asn, 68; Arnold D Tuttle Award, 71; Skylab Achievement Award, NASA, 74; Dohlman Medal, Dohlman Soc, 87; Quinquennial Gold Medal, Barany Soc, 88; Wilbur Franks Award, 88; Ashton Graybiel Lectr Award, US Naval Aerospace Med Res Lab, 89; Stewart Mem

Lectr Award, Royal Aeronaut Soc London, 89; Buchanan-Barbour Award, 90; McLaughlin Medal, Royal Soc Can, 91. *Prof Exp:* House surgeon, Middlesex Hosp, London, 49-50; surgeon, Ear, Nose & Throat, Addenbrookes Hosp, Cambridge, 50-51; sci med officer, RAF Inst Aviation Med, Eng, 51-55; sci officer, Med Res Coun, Gt Brit, 55-61; dir aviation med, Aerospace Med Res Unit, 61-88. *Concurrent Pos:* Adj prof, Col France, 79 & 95, clin neurosci, Univ Calgary, 91-; vis prof, Stanford Univ, 71-72, Col de France, Paris, 79, Univ Tex, Galveston, 82 & Univ Calgary, 83; sr res assoc, Nat Acad Sci, 71-72; assoc mem, Ctr Studies Age & Aging, McGill Univ & Dept Neurol & Neurosurg. *Mem:* Can Physiol Soc; UK Physiol Soc; Am Soc Neurosci; fel Can Aeronaut & Space Inst; fel Royal Soc Can; fel Royal Soc London; fel Royal Aeronaut Soc London; fel Am Aerospace Med Asn; Can Soc Aerospace Med Soc. *Res:* Neurophysiology of postural control, vestibular and oculomotor systems; respiration at high altitude; long duration flying fatigue; high altitude bail out; pilot disorientation; adaptive plasticity in brainstem reflexes; cognitive management of subcortical reflexes; author of numerous publications. *Mailing Add:* 1419 Eighth St NW Calgary AB T2M 3K4 Can

JONES, GEORGE HENRY, BIOCHEMISTRY, MOLECULAR BIOLOGY. *Current Pos:* ASSOC VPRES RES & GRAD STUDIES & DEAN GRAD SCH ARTS & SCI, EMORY UNIV, 90- *Personal Data:* b Muskogee, Okla, Feb 21, 42; m 65. *Educ:* Harvard Univ, BA, 63; Univ Calif, Berkeley, PhD(biochem), 68. *Prof Exp:* Helen Hay Whitney Found fels, NIH, 68-70 & Univ Geneva, 70-71; asst prof zool, Univ Mich, Ann Arbor, 71-74, assoc prof biol sci & cell & molecular biol, 74-90. *Mem:* AAAS. *Res:* Mammalian protein biosynthesis, specifically initiation mechanisms; immunoglobulin biosynthesis; cellular regulatory mechanisms. *Mailing Add:* Grad Sch Arts & Sci 202 Admin Bldg Emory Univ Atlanta GA 30322-2690. *Fax:* 404-727-4990

JONES, GEORGE R, SOLID STATE PHYSICS. *Current Pos:* RES PHYSICIST, INFO & SIGNAL PROCESSING SENSOR, CTR NIGHT VISION & ELECTRO OPTICS, 66- *Personal Data:* b Los Angeles, Calif, Aug 16, 30; m 52; c 6. *Educ:* Western Md Col, BS, 51; Cath Univ, MS, 53, PhD(physics), 63. *Prof Exp:* Jr electronics engr, Davies Labs, Inc, 52-54; physicist, Diamond Ord Fuze Labs, 54-63, res physicist, Harry Diamond Labs, 63-66. *Concurrent Pos:* Consult, Am Mach & Foundry, 61-62; lectr, Am Univ, 69-71. *Mem:* Am Phys Soc; Inst Elec & Electronics Engrs; AAAS. *Res:* Optical spectra of rare earth doped solids; magnetic properties of solids; electromagnetic theory; electromagnetic instrumentation for solid state measurements; artificial intelligence (visual) and mathematical modeling of human vision processes; applied parallel distributed processors and neural networks. *Mailing Add:* 113 Northway Greenbelt MD 20770-1711

JONES, GERALD MURRAY, DAIRY SCIENCE. *Current Pos:* assoc prof, 74-79, PROF DAIRY SCI, VA POLYTECH INST & STATE UNIV, 79-, EXTEN DAIRY SCIENTIST, 74- *Personal Data:* b Gouverneur, NY, Apr 17, 41; m 63; c 3. *Educ:* Cornell Univ. BS, 62; Univ Maine, MS, 64; Pa State Univ, PhD(dairy sci), 68. *Honors & Awards:* West Agron Award Mastitis Res, Am Dairy Sci Asn. *Prof Exp:* Asst prof animal sci, Macdonald Col, McGill Univ, 68-74. *Mem:* Nat Mastitis Coun; Am Dairy Sci Asn. *Res:* Milking management, practices and systems; mastitis; calf nutrition and management; dairy cattle nutrition; dairy herd management. *Mailing Add:* 1010 Madison Lane Blacksburg VA 24060

JONES, GERALD WALTER, PHOTOGRAPHIC CHEMISTRY, POLYMER APPLICATIONS. *Current Pos:* SR ENGR, IBM CORP, 81- *Personal Data:* b Utica, NY, June 25, 42; m 77, Terry Jones. *Educ:* Hartwick Col, BA, 64; Syracuse Univ, PhD(org chem), 70. *Prof Exp:* Lab asst chem, Hartwick Col, 64-65; fel, Ohio State Univ, 70-74; res chemist, GAF Corp, 74-81. *Mem:* Am Chem Soc. *Res:* Photolysis of alpha, beta-unsaturated ketones and carbene chemistry; photographic science, resilient sheet vinyl flooring and photoresists; photoresists. *Mailing Add:* 1070 Forest Hill Rd Apalachin NY 13732

JONES, GIFFIN DENISON, ORGANIC CHEMISTRY. *Current Pos:* res chemist, Phys Res Lab, 47-56, dir. 56-68, dir, E C Britton Lab, 68-70, RES SCIENTIST, PHYS RES LAB, DOW CHEM CO, 70- *Personal Data:* b Fond du Lac, Wis, Dec 16, 18; m 39; c 4. *Educ:* Univ Wis, BS, 39; Univ Ill, PhD(org chem), 42. *Prof Exp:* Instr org chem, Univ Iowa, 42-44; res chemist, Cent Res Labs, Gen Aniline & Film Corp, Pa, 44-47. *Concurrent Pos:* Civilian with Off Sci Res & Develop, 44. *Mem:* Am Chem Soc. *Res:* Polymers; organic reaction mechanism. *Mailing Add:* 4002 Cambridge St Midland MI 48642-3694

JONES, GILBERT FRED, MARINE ECOLOGY, HISTOLOGY. *Current Pos:* Biologist, Mainland Shelf Surv, Allan Hancock Found, 57-64, from instr to asst prof, 64-70, ASSOC PROF BIOL, UNIV SOUTHERN CALIF, 70- *Personal Data:* b Oakland, Calif, Apr 3, 30; m 51; c 6. *Educ:* Col of the Pac, AB, 52; Univ Wis, MS, 54; Univ Southern Calif, PhD(biol), 67. *Mem:* Am Soc Limnol & Oceanog; Marine Biol Asn UK. *Res:* Benthic marine ecology, particularly population ecology; marine nematodes. *Mailing Add:* 1717 Campus Rd Los Angeles CA 90041

JONES, GLENN CLARK, ORGANIC & POLYMER CHEMISTRY, TECHNICAL MANAGEMENT. *Current Pos:* from res chemist to sr res chemist, 62-84, RES ASSOC, TENN EASTMAN CO, 84- *Personal Data:* b Raleigh, NC, Aug 22, 35; m 65; c 2. *Educ:* Wake Forest Col, BS, 57; Duke Univ, PhD(chem), 62. *Prof Exp:* Res assoc org chem, Duke Univ, 61-62. *Mem:* Am Chem Soc; Sigma Xi. *Res:* Base catalyzed rearrangements; polymer feasibility studies; free radical chemistry; organic electrochemistry; hydroquinone, solvent and powder coatings. *Mailing Add:* 3620 Hemlock Park Dr Kingsport TN 37663-2057

JONES, GORDON ERVIN, PHYSICS. *Current Pos:* chancellor, 92-93, PROF PHYSICS & DEAN SCI & MATH, COL CHARLESTON, 91- *Personal Data:* b Greenwood, Miss, July 23, 36; m 61, Linda Dry; c Gordon S & Chad M. *Educ:* Miss State Univ, BS, 58; Duke Univ, PhD(physics), 64. *Prof Exp:* From asst prof to assoc prof physics, Miss State Univ, 64-72, prof, 72-91. *Mem:* Am Phys Soc; Am Asn Physics Teachers; Am Asn Higher Educ. *Res:* Microwave spectroscopy. *Mailing Add:* Sch Sci & Math Col Charleston 66 George St Charleston SC 29424

JONES, GORDON HENRY, organic chemistry, for more information see previous edition

JONES, GRAHAM ALFRED, AGRICULTURAL MICROBIOLOGY. *Current Pos:* asst prof dairy sci, Univ Sask, 63-68, from assoc prof to prof dairy & food sci, 67-82, lectr microbiol, 75-79, assoc, Dept Microbiol, Sch Med, 79-92, head dept, 81-92, PROF APPL MICROBIOL & FOOD SCI, UNIV SASK, 82-, ASSOC DEAN AGR, 94- *Personal Data:* b London, Eng, May 8, 35; m 63, Judy Guignion; c Alison M, Kevin G, Susan E & Jennifer D. *Educ:* Univ Leeds, BSc, 57; McGill Univ, MSc, 58, PhD(agr bact), 63. *Honors & Awards:* Queen's Jubilee Medal, 77. *Prof Exp:* Lectr agr bact, McGill Univ, 58-60. *Concurrent Pos:* Vis prof, Nat Res Coun Can, 74; vis scientist, Agr Res Coun Inst Animal Physiol, Babraham, Eng, 78-79, Agr Can, 92-93. *Mem:* Am Soc Microbiol; Can Soc Microbiol (secy-treas, 70-73, pres, 82-83); Agr Inst Can; Can Soc Animal Sci. *Res:* Rumen microbiology; agricultural fermentations. *Mailing Add:* Dept Appl Microbiol & Food Sci Univ Sask Saskatoon SK S7N 5A8 Can. *Fax:* 306-966-8894; *E-Mail:* jonesg@sask.usask.ca

JONES, GUILFORD, II, PHYSICAL ORGANIC CHEMISTRY, PHOTOCHEMISTRY. *Current Pos:* from asst prof to assoc prof, 71-82, dept chmn, 89-93, PROF CHEM, BOSTON UNIV, 82- *Personal Data:* b Jackson, Tenn, Nov 24, 43; m 66; c Jason G & David D. *Educ:* Rhodes Col, BS, 65; Univ Wis-Madison, PhD(chem), 70. *Prof Exp:* NIH fel, Yale Univ, 69-71. *Mem:* Am Chem Soc; Sigma Xi. *Res:* Photochemical conversion of energy; mechanisms and applications of photochemical reactions; dye photochemistry; photoeffects for polymer-bound chromophores; photoactive peptides. *Mailing Add:* Dept Chem Boston Univ Boston MA 02215

JONES, GUY LANGSTON, PLANT BREEDING. *Current Pos:* asst prof dept agron, NC State Univ, 52-58, assoc prof field crops, 58-61, prof crop sci, 61-65, head agron exten, 65-75, head crop sci exten, 75-85, prof crop sci, 61-85, EMER PROF, NC STATE UNIV, 85-, TOBACCO PROD & AGRON EXTEN PROGS, 71- *Personal Data:* b Kinston, NC, June 7, 23; m 48; c 2. *Educ:* NC State Col, BS, 47, MS, 50; Univ Minn, PhD, 52. *Honors & Awards:* Agron Exten Educ Award, Am Soc Agron. *Prof Exp:* Supt br sta, NC Agr Exp Sta, 47-49; asst dept agron & plant genetics, Univ Minn, 50-52. *Concurrent Pos:* Ministry Agr, Venezuela, 59, Inst Tobacco, Dominican Repub, 63, Agency Int Develop, Guatemala, 64-65 & Philippines, 64-65 & Food & Agr Orgn, Arg, 74, Inst Soil Sci, Nanjing, China, 83-85 & 91, Guatemala, 87 & 88, Dominican Repub, 87 & 88, Mex, 87-91; assoc ed, Agron J. *Mem:* Fel Am Soc Agron; Sigma Xi; Crop Sci Soc Am. *Res:* Tobacco genetics; tobacco variety evaluation; agronomy extension. *Mailing Add:* 3435 Blue Ridge Rd NC State Univ Raleigh NC 27612-8014

JONES, GWILYM STRONG, MAMMALOGY, VERTEBRATE ECOLOGY. *Current Pos:* PROF BIOL, NORTHEASTERN UNIV, 76- *Personal Data:* b Cincinnati, Ohio, May 4, 42; m 67; c 3. *Educ:* Hanover Col, BA, 64; Purdue Univ, MS, 67; Ind State Univ, PhD(mammal syst), 81. *Prof Exp:* Res investr, Naval Med Res Unit 2, Taiwan, 67-69; mus specialist, Smithsonian Inst, 70-71. *Concurrent Pos:* Collabr mammal div, Smithsonian Inst, 70; adv, Chinese Asn Conserv Nature & Natural Resources, 69-70; grants, Am Inst Biol Sci, 70, Theodore Roosevelt Mem Fund & Am Mus Natural Hist, 74, US Dept Health & Human Serv, 78 & 81, NH Fish Game Dept, 80-86, Pub Archeol Lab, Brown Univ, 80, Nature Conservancy, 84 & US Fish Wildlife Serv, 83. *Mem:* Am Soc Mammalogists; Soc Syst Zool; Sigma Xi; Soc Marine Mammalogy; Wildlife Soc. *Res:* Mammalian systematics; vertebrate food habits; ectoparasites and demographics. *Mailing Add:* Dept Biol Northeastern Univ 360 Huntington Ave Boston MA 02115-5096

JONES, HAROLD LESTER, ORGANIC CHEMISTRY. *Current Pos:* asst prof, 69-76, assoc prof, 76-86, PROF CHEM, COLO COL, 86-, CHMN, 81-82, 85- *Personal Data:* b Nampa, Idaho, June 19, 43; m 65, Pamela A Potter; c Rhiannon & Dorothy. *Educ:* Ore State Univ, BS, 65; Univ Colo, PhD(chem), 69. *Prof Exp:* Res asst, Univ Colo, 68. *Concurrent Pos:* Res assoc, Univ Colo, 72. *Mem:* Am Chem Soc. *Res:* Nuclear magnetic resonance; small ring chemistry, bicyclic systems and cyclopropanols; free radical reactions in cyclopropanols; photochemistry of bicyclic-spiro-compounds. *Mailing Add:* 818 E Boulder Colorado Springs CO 80903-1989

JONES, HAROLD TRAINER, mathematical analysis; deceased, see previous edition for last biography

JONES, HELENA L, ANATOMY, MEDICAL SCIENCES. *Current Pos:* ASST PROF BIOL, UNIV WIS-EAU CLAIRE, 75- *Personal Data:* b Columbus, Ohio, June 26, 40; m 65; c 2. *Educ:* Ohio State Univ, BSc, 62, PhD(anat) 68. *Prof Exp:* Instr anat, Med Ctr, Ind Univ, Indianapolis, 68-69; NIH staff fel, Nat Inst Environ Health Sci 72-75. *Concurrent Pos:* Consult, Adv Comt Estab Med Histol Technicians Assoc Degree, 76-; fels biomed sci, Washington, DC, 77 & 78; mem review panels, NSF; Eau Claire Community cancer grant, 80, 81 & 82. *Mem:* Am Asn Anatomists; Sigma Xi; NY Acad Sci. *Res:* Skin cancer; endocrinology; bone. *Mailing Add:* 5729 Elm Rd Rte 3 Eau Claire WI 54701

JONES, HOBART WAYNE, ANIMAL BREEDING. *Current Pos:* RETIRED. *Personal Data:* b Logansport, Ind, Apr 15, 21; m 43; c 4. *Educ:* Purdue Univ, BSA, 43; Ohio State Univ, MSA, 46, PhD(animal prod), 60. *Prof Exp:* from assoc prof to prof animal sci, Purdue Univ, 50-89. *Mem:* Am Soc Animal Sci. *Res:* Animal production; swine nutrition and environmental studies. *Mailing Add:* 104 N Sharon Chapel Rd West Lafayette IN 47906

JONES, HOWARD ST CLAIRE, JR, ELECTRONICS ENGINEERING, MICROWAVE PHYSICS. *Current Pos:* PVT CONSULT, 91- *Personal Data:* b Richmond, Va, Aug 18, 21; m 46. *Educ:* Va Union Univ, BS, 43; Howard Univ, cert eng, 44; Bucknell Univ, MSEE, 73. *Hon Degrees:* DSc, Va Union Univ, 71. *Prof Exp:* Electronic scientist microwave electronics, Diamond Ord Fuze Lab, Washington, DC, 53-59, supvry electronic engr, 59-68, chief microwave res & develop, 68-80, tech consult, Harry Diamond Labs, MD, 80-81; at Dept Elec Eng, Howard Univ, 82-83; Dept Defense, 83-91. *Concurrent Pos:* Instr physics & math, Hilltop Radio-Electronics Inst, Washington, DC, 46-53; asst prof electronic eng, Sch Eng, Howard Univ, 58-63; tech consult, Phelps Dodge Electronics, Conn, 68-69; Secy of Army fel, 72. *Mem:* Fel Inst Elec & Electronics Engrs; fel AAAS; Antenna & Propagation Soc; Microwave Theory & Techniques Soc. *Res:* Microwave research and development; directing, planning and coordinating research and development programs which involve theoretical and applied microwave research; management of programs and projects relating to major electronic systems. *Mailing Add:* 3001 Veazey Terr NW Apt 1310 Washington DC 20008

JONES, IRA, ZOOLOGY, PARASITOLOGY. *Current Pos:* from asst prof to assoc prof, 69-77, PROF BIOL, CALIF STATE UNIV, LONG BEACH, 77- *Personal Data:* b Bartow, Fla, Jan 22, 34; m 57; c 2. *Educ:* Benedict Col, BS, 55; Atlanta Univ, MS, 57; Wayne State Univ, PhD(biol), 66. *Prof Exp:* Instr biol, Savannah State Col, 57-59; assoc prof, Fla Agr & Mech Univ, 64-66 & Inter-Am Univ PR, 66-69. *Concurrent Pos:* USPHS fel, 61; grant, Caribbean Inst & Study Ctr for Latin Am, 68-69; Sigma Xi res grant, 68-69; PR Nuclear Ctr grant, 69; consult, Nat Commun Dis Ctr, 69; Calif State Univ Long Beach Found grant, 69-71; dir & consult parasitol, Jones Biomed & Lab, Long Beach, Ca, 77- *Mem:* Fel Inst Biol Sci; Soc Protozool. *Res:* Research on the endosymbionts of Sipunculids, including, zoogeography of parasitism, host specificity, life cycles of parasites and the cytochemistry and ultra-structure of Sipunculids sporozoa. *Mailing Add:* Dept Biol Calif State Univ 3702 Csulb Long Beach CA 90840-0004

JONES, IRVING WENDELL, STRUCTURAL ENGINEERING & MECHANICS. *Current Pos:* assoc prof, 69-72, PROF CIVIL ENG, HOWARD UNIV, 72- *Personal Data:* b Washington, DC. *Educ:* Howard Univ, BS, 53; Columbia Univ, MS, 57; Polytech Inst Brooklyn, PhD(appl mech), 67. *Prof Exp:* Asst civil eng, Columbia Univ, 56-57; struct engr, Grumman Aerospace Corp, 57-62; asst aerospace & mech, Polytech Inst Brooklyn, 62-63; asst dir & partner, Appl Technol Assocs, Inc, 63-69. *Concurrent Pos:* Consult, Space Div, Fairchild-Hiller Corp, 62-64 & Dist Eng Serv, Inc, 77-; mem, Pressure Vessel Res Coun, Welding Res Found, 64-69; lectr, Grad Sch, Stevens Inst Technol, 68-69. *Mem:* Am Soc Civil Engrs (pres, 69); Am Soc Mech Engrs (pres, 64); Am Soc Eng Educ (pres, 69). *Res:* Developed methods for computer-aided structural analysis including high temperature effects; helped develop shock-absorbing mounts and foundations for sensitive shipboard equipment; developed analysis methods for effects of high temperature on aerospace structures. *Mailing Add:* 383 N St SW Washington DC 20024

JONES, IVAN DUNLAVY, FOOD SCIENCE. *Current Pos:* assoc horticulturist, Exp Sta, 31-45, prof hort, 45-61 & food sci, 61-70, EMER PROF FOOD SCI, NC STATE UNIV, 70- *Personal Data:* b Holdrege, Nebr, Dec 10, 03; m 96, Ruby Buck; c Lucia & Ivan Jr. *Educ:* Nebr Wesleyan Univ, AB, 26; Univ Minn, PhD(agr biochem), 31. *Prof Exp:* Instr agr biochem, Univ Minn, 29-30. *Concurrent Pos:* Consult dir, Spec Fund, UN, Brazil & Dominican Repub, 62; consult food sci & technol, 70-; vis prof, Middle East Tech Univ, Ankara, Turkey 79-80. *Mem:* Am Chem Soc; fel Inst Food Technol; fel Am Pub Health Asn; fel Am Inst Chem; Sigma Xi. *Res:* Chemical composition of fruits and vegetables and their processing by freezing, canning, dehydration and brining; estimation of chlorophylls and their metal derivatives; influence preservation technique on chlorophyll. *Mailing Add:* 22 Springmoor Dr Raleigh NC 27615

JONES, J(AMES) B(EVERLY), MECHANICAL ENGINEERING. *Current Pos:* prof mech eng & head dept, 64-88, EMER PROF, VA POLYTECH INST & STATE UNIV, CONSULT. *Personal Data:* b Kansas City, Mo, Aug 21, 23; m 45; c 2. *Educ:* Va Polytech Inst, BS, 44; Purdue Univ, MS, 47; PhD(mech eng), 51. *Prof Exp:* Asst mech engr, Eng Bd, US War Dept, Va, 44-45; asst instr mech eng, Purdue Univ, 45-47, instr, 47-51; serv engr, Babcock & Wilcox Co, 48; develop engr, Gen Elec Co, 51-52; asst prof mech eng, Purdue Univ, 51-54; sr proj engr, Allison Div, Gen Motors Corp, 53; assoc prof mech eng, Purdue Univ, 54-57, prof, 57-64. *Concurrent Pos:* NSF faculty fel, Swiss Fed Inst Technol, 61-62. *Mem:* Am Soc Mech Engrs; Am Soc Eng Educ; Am Inst Aeronaut & Astronaut; Sigma Xi. *Res:* Fluid mechanics; thermodynamics. *Mailing Add:* 1503 Palmer Dr Blacksburg VA 24060. *Fax:* 540-231-9100

JONES, J BENTON, JR, SOIL FERTILITY, PLANT NUTRITION. *Current Pos:* VPRES, MICRO-MACRO INT, INC, ATHENS, GA, 90- *Personal Data:* b Tyrone, Pa, Apr 4, 30; m 55; c 3. *Educ:* Univ Ill, BS, 52; Pa State Univ, MS, 56, PhD(agron), 59. *Hon Degrees:* Dr, Univ Hort, Budapest, Hungary, 87. *Prof Exp:* From assoc prof to prof agron, Ohio Agr Res & Develop Ctr, 59-68; div chmn, Dept Hort, Univ Ga, 74-79, prof agron, agr exten-agron, 68-79, mem, Inst Ecol, 75-89, prof, Dept Hort, 79-89; PRES, BENTON LABS, INC, ATHENS, GA, 69- *Concurrent Pos:* Chmn, Micronutrient Comt, 67-69, Soil Testing & Plant Anal Comt, Soil Sci Soc Am, 67-69, Coun Soil Testing & Plant Anal, 69-72, secy-treas, 72-; consult, St Louis Testing Labs, 67-75; assoc referee, Plant Anal Emission Spectros, Asn Off Anal Chemists, 69-83, Plant Preparation, 69-89; exec ed, Commun Soil Sci & Plant Anal, 69-, J Plant Nutrit, 79-; bd mem, Coun Agr Sci & Technol, 73-78, subcomt Environ Qual, 74-77, Agron Comt, Nat Fertilizer Solutions Asn, 76-80. *Mem:* Fel AAAS; fel Am Soc Agron; fel Soil Sci Soc Am; Int Soc Soil Sci; Am Soc Hort Sci; Asn Off Anal Chemists; Hydroponic Soc Am; Sigma Xi. *Res:* Soil and plant chemistry, especially the micronutrients; soil fertility and plant nutrition related to crop production; soil testing and plant analysis; techniques of analysis by emission spectroscopy; techniques of giving plants in soilless media and hydroponically; author of numerous articles, books and book chapters and videos. *Mailing Add:* 183 Paradise Blvd Suite 108 Athens GA 30607. *Fax:* 706-548-4891

JONES, J KNOX, JR, vertebrate zoology; deceased, see previous edition for last biography

JONES, J(OHN) L(LOYD), JR, ELECTRICAL ENGINEERING. *Current Pos:* RETIRED. *Personal Data:* b Henry, Ill, June 5, 18; m 43, Margaret Ruth Hunt; c Patricia (Crampton), Gary H & Elizabeth (Eller). *Educ:* Univ Ill, BS, 40, MS, 41; Univ Md, MS, 49, PhD, 63. *Prof Exp:* Physicist, US Naval Ord Lab, 42-63; assoc prof elec eng, Bradley Univ, 63-77. *Mem:* Acoust Soc Am; Am Soc Eng Educ. *Res:* Acoustics; circuit theory; electromagnetic theory; shock and vibration. *Mailing Add:* 1110 Warren St Henry IL 61537

JONES, J P, MATHEMATICS. *Current Pos:* From asst prof to prof, 68-96, EMER PROF MATH, UNIV CALGARY, 96- *Personal Data:* b Los Angeles, Calif, Sept 9, 41. *Educ:* Univ Wash, BS, 63, MS, 66, PhD(math), 68. *Honors & Awards:* Lester R Ford Award, Math Asn Am, 77. *Mem:* Am Math Soc; Math Asn Am; Asn Symbolic Logic; Can Math Soc; Fibonacci Asn. *Res:* Mathematical logic; number theory; recursive function theory; diophantine equations. *Mailing Add:* Dept Math & Statist Univ Calgary Calgary AB T2N 1N4 Can. *E-Mail:* jpjones@acs.ucalgary.ca

JONES, JACK EARL, AGRONOMY, PHYTOPATHOLOGY. *Current Pos:* From asst prof to prof, 50-90, EMER PROF COTTON BREEDING & GENETICS, LA STATE UNIV, BATON ROUGE, 90- *Personal Data:* b Elbert Co, Ga, July 30, 25; m 46, Henrietta Weathers; c Lynda J (Burdette). *Educ:* Univ Ga, BS, 48, MS, 50; La State Univ, PhD, 61. *Honors & Awards:* Cotton Genetics Res Award, 85; Doyle Chambers Res Award, 88. *Concurrent Pos:* Consult. *Mem:* Am Soc Agron; Crop Sci Soc Am; Sigma Xi. *Res:* Cotton breeding for superior fiber properties; resistance to diseases and insects; genetics of quantitative characters of cotton; cotton production practices. *Mailing Add:* 246 Maxine Dr Baton Rouge LA 70808-6831

JONES, JACK EDENFIELD, POULTRY SCIENCE. *Current Pos:* RETIRED. *Personal Data:* b Jacksonville, Fla, Oct 24, 29; m 59; c 3. *Educ:* Univ Fla, BS, 51, MS, 64, PhD(physiol), 66. *Prof Exp:* Supvr farm mgt, Farmers Home Admin, 56-58; sanitarian, St Johns County Health Dept, 58-61; asst dir res, Coop Mills, 66-68; from asst prof to assoc prof poultry, Clemson Univ, 68-76, prof, 76-89. *Mem:* Poultry Sci Asn. *Res:* Nutrition; physiological-environmental relationships with turkeys and game birds. *Mailing Add:* 357 Mountain View Dr Central SC 29630

JONES, JACK RAYMOND, reservoir engineering, pressure transient analysis, for more information see previous edition

JONES, JAMES DARREN, ACOUSTICS, VIBRATIONS. *Current Pos:* ASSOC PROF MEC ENG, PURDUE UNIV, 87- *Personal Data:* b Oak Ridge, Tenn, June 7, 59; m 82; c 2. *Educ:* Tenn Technol Univ, BS, 81; Va Polytech Inst & State Univ, MS, 82, PhD(mech eng), 87. *Prof Exp:* Res asst mech eng, Va Polytech Inst & State Univ, 81-82, instr, 83-87; res assoc, Acoust & Noise Reduction Div, NASA Langley Res Ctr, 82-83. *Concurrent Pos:* NSF res grant active vibration control, 88-91, presidential young investr award, 89-90, 90-91; res grants, various agencies, 88-91; consult, Douglas Aircraft Co, McDonnell Douglas Corp, 88, Artesian Indust, 88, 90-, Elgin Sweeper Co, 89. *Mem:* Acoust Soc Am; Am Inst Aeronaut & Astronaut; Am Soc Eng Educ; Am Soc Heating Vent Air-conditioning & Refrig Engrs; Am Soc Mech Engrs; Inst Noise Control Eng. *Res:* Acoustics, noise control, vibrations; active noise and vibration control; intelligent structures, distributed sensors and actuators; machinery noise, shell dynamics, structural/acoustics interactions; biomechanics, bionics, prosthetics; author of numerous publications on acoustics, noise control and vibrations. *Mailing Add:* 1077 Ray W Herrick Labs Purdue Univ West Lafayette IN 47907-1077. *Fax:* 765-494-0787

JONES, JAMES DONALD, BIOCHEMISTRY. *Current Pos:* asst to staff sect biochem, 60-61, CONSULT, SECT CLIN CHEM, MAYO CLIN, 61- *Personal Data:* b Fond du Lac, Wis, Oct 5, 30; m 56; c 3. *Educ:* Ripon Col, AB, 52; Univ Wis, MS, 56, PhD(biochem), 58. *Prof Exp:* Asst prof animal nutrit, Iowa State Univ, 58-60. *Concurrent Pos:* Mem, Am Bd Clin Chem, 73; prof lab med & assoc prof biochem, Mayo Med Sch. *Mem:* Am Chem Soc; Am Inst Nutrit; Am Asn Clin Chem; fel Am Inst Chemists; fel Nat Acad Clin Biochem. *Res:* Nitrogen and electrolyte metabolism in animals; biochemistry of the young; metabolism of guanidines; inborn errors of metabolism. *Mailing Add:* Sect Clin Chem Mayo Clin 200 First St SW Rochester MN 55905-0001

JONES, JAMES EDWARD, VETERINARY MEDICINE. *Current Pos:* CLINICIAN, OHIO AGR RES & DEVELOP CTR, 68- *Personal Data:* b Columbus, Ohio, June 5, 24; m 44; c 5. *Educ:* Ohio State Univ, DVM, 50, MS, 75. *Prof Exp:* Gen pract vet med, 50-68. *Mem:* Am Vet Med Asn; Sigma Xi. *Res:* Atrophic rhinitis in swine; epizootiology. *Mailing Add:* 17 Storms Rd Kettering OH 45429

JONES, JAMES HENRY, COMPARATIVE PHYSIOLOGY, RESPIRATORY-EXERCISE PHYSIOLOGY. *Current Pos:* from asst prof to assoc prof, 86-96, PROF PHYSIOL, UNIV CALIF, DAVIS, 96- *Personal Data:* b Phoenix, Ariz, Oct 23, 52. *Educ:* Univ Ariz, BS & BA, 74, MS, 76; Duke Univ, PhD(zool), 79; Colo State Univ, DVM, 83. *Honors & Awards:* Scholander Award, Am Physiol Soc, 86. *Prof Exp:* Lectr biol, Harvard Univ, 83-86. *Concurrent Pos:* Vis prof, Anat Inst, Univ Berne, Switz, 86 & Biosci Inst, Univ Sao Paulo, Brazil, 90. *Mem:* Am Physiol Soc; Am Soc Zoologists. *Res:* Elucidate mechanisms limiting aerobic and anaerobic exercise performance in animals, especially birds and mammals; understand allometric (body-size) relationships between structure and function. *Mailing Add:* VM Surg & Radiol Sci Univ Calif Davis CA 95616. *Fax:* 530-752-6042; *E-Mail:* jrjones@ucdavis.edu

JONES, JAMES HOLDEN, organic chemistry, for more information see previous edition

JONES, JAMES OGDEN, PALEONTOLOGY. *Current Pos:* vis asst prof, 77-78, asst prof & prog coordr, 78-82, ASSOC PROF GEOL, UNIV TEX, SAN ANTONIO, 84- *Personal Data:* b Punkin Ctr, Electra, Tex; m, Marilyn Felty; c James II & Alan R. *Educ:* Midwestern State Univ, BS, 62; Baylor Univ, MS, 66; Univ Iowa, PhD(geol), 71. *Prof Exp:* Geologist, Shell Oil Co, 59-60; lab asst geol, Midwestern State Univ, 60-62; teaching asst, Baylor Univ, 62-64 & Univ Iowa, 64-68; explor geologist, Texaco Inc, 66; asst prof, Univ Southern Miss, 71; from asst prof to assoc prof geol, Southern Ark Univ, 71-74, head dept, 71-77. *Concurrent Pos:* US Army Air Defense Artillery; consult resource evaluations oil, gas, water & environ, 71- *Mem:* Am Asn Petrol Geologists; Soc Sedimentary Geol; Nat Asn Geosci Teachers; fel Geol Soc Am; Sigma Xi; Am Geophys Union; Int Asn Sedimentologists; Am Inst Prof Geologists; Soc Ind Prof Earth Scientists. *Res:* Sedimentology and stratigraphy of Lower Permian shelf deposits of North Texas; cretaceous stratigraphy and sedimentology of Texas and Mexico; paleontology; cambrian-precambrian sedimentology. *Mailing Add:* Geol Dept Univ Tex San Antonio TX 78249-0663. *Fax:* 210-458-4469; *E-Mail:* jjones@lonestar.utsa.edu

JONES, JAMES ROBERT, ANIMAL HUSBANDRY, NUTRITION. *Current Pos:* EXTEN SPECIALIST, NC STATE UNIV, 64-, HEAD, SWINE EXTEN, 80- *Personal Data:* b Quicksand, Ky, Dec 8, 31; m 58; c 3. *Educ:* Univ Ky, BS, 53, MS, 57; Cornell Univ, PhD(animal husb), 61. *Prof Exp:* Experimentalist animal husb, Cornell Univ, 61-64. *Mem:* Am Soc Animal Sci; Am Registry Prof Animal Scientists. *Res:* Swine nutrition. *Mailing Add:* Dept Animal Sci NC State Univ Box 7621 Raleigh NC 27695-0001. *Fax:* 919-515-7780

JONES, JANICE LORRAINE, BIOPHYSICS, CELL PHYSIOLOGY. *Current Pos:* ASSOC PROF PHYSIOL, GEORGETOWN UNIV, 87- *Personal Data:* b Takoma Park, Md, Mar 10, 43; m 67, Ronald; c Michael & Catherine. *Educ:* St Bonaventure Univ, BS, 65; Johns Hopkins Univ, PhD(biophys), 70. *Prof Exp:* Asst prof med technol, Univ Vt, 70-74, res assoc, Dept Med, 78; from asst prof to assoc prof physiol, Sch Med, Case Western Res Univ, 78-87. *Concurrent Pos:* Prin investr, NIH, defibrillator waveshape optimization, 79- & defibrillator induced dysfunction, 81-87; consult, Physiocontrol Corp & Cardiac Pacemakers-NIH Study Sect; assoc ed, Biomed Electronics. *Mem:* Biophys Soc; Int Soc Heart Res; Am Physiol Soc; NAm Soc Pacing & Electrophysiol; fel Am Inst Med & Biol Eng. *Res:* Cardiac physiology; physiology of cardiac cells in tissue culture; electrically induced myocardial damage. *Mailing Add:* Dept Physiol Georgetown Univ DVA Med Ctr 50 Irving St Washington DC 20422

JONES, JEANETTE, MEDICAL MYCOLOGY, HISTOTECHNIQUES. *Current Pos:* from asst prof to assoc prof, 76-85, MEM GRAD FAC, ALA A&M UNIV, 76-, PROF BIOL, 86- *Personal Data:* b Ft Valley, Ga, Sept 19, 50. *Educ:* Ft Valley State Col, BSc, 72; Ohio State Univ, MSc, 73, PhD(bot, med mycol), 76. *Honors & Awards:* Honors Award, NASA, 85. *Prof Exp:* Instr biol, Ft Valley State Col, 72; univ fel, Ohio State Univ, 72-73, grad teaching assoc, 73-75. *Concurrent Pos:* Res apprenticeship org chem, Forestry Exp Lab, Macon, Ga, 72; consult, Ft Valley State Col, Ft Valley Ga, 76, Northeast Ala State Jr Col, Riville, Ala, 77, NIH, 78-81 & 83, NSF, 79-80, Nat Adv Coun, Sixteen Insts Health Sci Consortium, NC, 79-81 & Southern Asn Cols & Schs Reaffirmation Comt, 82; prin investr, Grad Traineeships, NSF, 79 & Biomed Res Training Prog, NIH, 80; adj prof, Sch Pharm, Fla A&M Univ, 85. *Mem:* Med Mycol Soc Am; Sigma Xi; Int Soc Human & Animal Mycosis; Am Soc Microbiol; Am Soc Allied Health Professionals; Mycol Soc Am; AAAS; Med Mycologists Am. *Res:* Isolation and control of growth of pathogenic fungi; nutrition, growth and morphogenesis of pathogenic fungi. *Mailing Add:* VP Res & Develop Admin Ala A&M Univ PO Box 285 Normal AL 35762-0285. *Fax:* 205-851-5030

JONES, JENNINGS HINCH, organic chemistry; deceased, see previous edition for last biography

JONES, JEROLD W, THERMAL SYSTEMS, FLUID SYSTEMS. *Current Pos:* asst prof arch eng, 73-76, assoc prof mech eng, 76-83, PROF MECH ENG, UNIV TEX, AUSTIN, 83- *Personal Data:* b Salt Lake City, Utah, July 6, 37; m 61; c 5. *Educ:* Univ Utah, BSME, 62, PhD(mech eng), 70; Stanford Univ, MS, 65. *Prof Exp:* Res scientist heat transfer, Ames Res Ctr, NASA, 62-66; fel, Ohio State Univ, 69-70, asst prof mech eng, 70-73. *Concurrent Pos:* Asst dir & prin investr, Ctr Energy Studies, Univ Tex, Austin, 75-84; mem, Steering Comt Energy Conserv Bldg, Nat Res Coun, 79-80. *Mem:* Am Soc Heating, Refrig & Air-Conditioning Engrs; Am Soc Mech Engrs. *Res:* Heat transfer and thermodynamics with particular applications in systems modeling; design and analysis for improving energy use efficiency of buildings and heating and air conditioning equipment. *Mailing Add:* 4707 Graystone Dr Austin TX 78731

JONES, JERRY LATHAM, CHEMICAL PROCESS, PRODUCT DEVELOPMENT. *Current Pos:* environ engr, SRI Int, 73-75, sr chem engr, 75-76, mgr environ control group, 76-78, dir environ & biochem eng, 78-82, dir chem eng lab, 82-89, DIR CHEM ENG, DEVELOP CTR, SRI INT, 90- *Personal Data:* b St Louis, Mo, Oct 20, 46; m 73; c 2. *Educ:* Cornell Univ, BS, 68, ME, 69; Stanford Univ, MS, 76. *Prof Exp:* Pilot plants supvr, Monsanto Biodize Systs, 69-71; eng. *Mem:* Am Inst Chem Engrs; Am Chem Soc; Water Pollution Control Fedn; Soc Indust Microbiol; Parenteral Drug Asn. *Res:* Manufacturing process development and evaluation; pharmaceuticals and specialty chemical product development; bioprocesses; pollution control technologies and thermal processes; separations technology. *Mailing Add:* Raychem Corp 106/8210 300 Constitution Dr Menlo Park CA 94025-1164

JONES, JERRY LYNN, analytical chemistry, educational administration; deceased, see previous edition for last biography

JONES, JESS HAROLD, VIBRATION, STATISTICAL ANALYSIS OF DYNAMIC DATA. *Current Pos:* RETIRED. *Personal Data:* b Melville, La, Mar 30, 35; m 58, Lessie Kenney; c Yvonne, Greg, Doug & Matt. *Educ:* La State Univ, BS, 58. *Prof Exp:* Engr, Brown Eng Co, 61-64, sr engr, 64; aerospace engr, George C Marshall Space Flight Ctr, NASA, 64-66, chief, Acoust Sect, 66-72, team leader, Unsteady Flow Team, 72-75, 87-92, team leader, Environ Mental Anal Br, 75-87, br chief, Induced Environ Br, 92-95. *Mem:* Acoust Soc Am; Am Soc Mech Engrs. *Res:* Theoretical and experimental investigations of the basic noise generation mechanisms of rocket exhaust flows and fluctuating pressure fields associated with space vehicles; analysis of random processes; fluid mechanics; wave propagation; sonic boom analysis; structural dynamics; rotating machinery; turbomachinery analysis; diagnostic analysis of dynamic data; fast fourier transforms analysis; ignition overpressure analysis and testing; acoustics. *Mailing Add:* 707 Fagan Springs Dr SE Huntsville AL 35801. *Fax:* 205-544-1215

JONES, JESSE W, CHEMISTRY. *Current Pos:* PROF CHEM, BISHOP COL, 67- *Personal Data:* b Troup, Tex, Jan 16, 31; m 55; c 5. *Educ:* Tex Col, BS, 54; NMex Highlands Univ, MS, 56; Ariz State Univ, PhD(org chem), 63. *Prof Exp:* Asst chem, NMex Highlands Univ, 54-55; asst biochem, Univ Utah, 55-56; asst prof chem, Tex Col, 56-58; res assoc, Ariz State Univ, 58-63; prof, Tex Col, 63-67, head dept, 63-64, head div natural sci, 64-67. *Concurrent Pos:* Nat Inst Gen Med Sci & Welch Found grants, 63-65. *Mem:* AAAS; Am Chem Soc. *Res:* Synthesis, mechanism of action and biochemical studies of certain nitrogen heterocycles. *Mailing Add:* Dept Chem Baylor Univ Box 7348 Waco TX 76706-9989

JONES, JOE MAXEY, IMMUNOPATHOLOGY. *Current Pos:* ASSOC PROF IMMUNOL, UNIV ARK MED SCI, 83- *Personal Data:* b Herpel, Ark, Mar 20, 42; m, Olcay Yeralan; c Kristina, Regan, Shannon & John. *Educ:* Wichita State Univ, BS, 64, MS, 66; Univ NC, Chapel Hill, PhD(immunol), 70. *Prof Exp:* Fel immunopath, Scripps Clin Res Found, 70-73, assoc, 73-77; head immunol & immunochem, Nat Ctr Toxicol Res, 77-80. *Concurrent Pos:* Res career develop award, Nat Cancer Inst, 79-84. *Mem:* Am Asn Immunologists; AAAS; Res Soc Alcoholism. *Res:* Tumor immunology; genetic control of immune responses. *Mailing Add:* Univ Ark Med Sci 4301 W Markham Slot 517 Little Rock AR 72205. *Fax:* 501-686-5874

JONES, JOHN, JR, mathematics; deceased, see previous edition for last biography

JONES, JOHN A(RTHUR), environmental sciences, aquatic ecology, for more information see previous edition

JONES, JOHN ACKLAND, ENTOMOLOGY. *Current Pos:* asst prof, 78-84, ASSOC PROF ENTOM, UNIV NEBR, LINCOLN, 84- *Personal Data:* b Alexandria, Va, Nov 6, 34; m 60, Shirley Goodell; c Ackland. *Educ:* Univ of the South, BS, 56; Univ Va, MS, 63; Iowa State Univ, PhD(entom), 73. *Prof Exp:* Instr zool, bot & limnol, Univ of the South, 57-58; med lab technician histol, US Army Med Serv Corps, 58-60; assoc prof zool & bot, Parsons Col, 63-66; state entomologist regulatory, Nebr Dept Agr, 73-78. *Mem:* Entom Soc Am; Sigma Xi. *Res:* Insect morphology and development; insect pests of shelter belts; horticultural pests. *Mailing Add:* Dept Entom Univ Nebr 202 Plant Indust Bldg Lincoln NE 68583-0816. *Fax:* 402-472-4687

JONES, JOHN BRYAN, ORGANIC CHEMISTRY, ORGANIC BIOCHEMISTRY. *Current Pos:* from asst prof to assoc prof, 63-74, PROF ORG CHEM, UNIV TORONTO, 74- *Personal Data:* b Colwyn Bay, NWales, Dec 11, 34; m 62; c 2. *Educ:* Univ Wales, BSc, 55, PhD(chem), 58; Oxford Univ, DPhil(chem), 60. *Prof Exp:* Fel org chem, Mass Inst Technol, 60-61; NIH res fel, Calif Inst Technol, 61-62; Imp Chem Indust fel, Oxford Univ, 62-63. *Mem:* Fel Am Chem Soc; Chem Inst Can. *Res:* Organic chemical applications of enzymes; immobilized enzymes. *Mailing Add:* Dept Chem Univ Toronto 80 St George St Toronto ON M5S 1A1 Can. *Fax:* 416-978-1553

JONES, JOHN EVAN, INTERNAL MEDICINE, ENDOCRINOLOGY. *Current Pos:* dir USPHS trainee, WVa Univ, 60-61, from instr to asst prof med, 61-63, from asst prof to assoc prof endocrinol, 63-70, chmn, Div Metab-Endocrinol, 67-74, PROF MED & ENDOCRINOL, SCH MED, WVA UNIV, 70-, DEAN SCH MED, 74- *Personal Data:* b Mt Pleasant, Utah, Oct 29, 30; m 54; c 3. *Educ:* Univ Utah, BS, 52, MD, 55; Am Bd Internal Med, dipl, cert endocrinol & metab, 73. *Prof Exp:* Dir USPHS trainee endocrinol, Univ Minn Hosps, 59. *Mem:* Fel Am Col Physicians; Endocrine Soc; Am Fedn Clin Res; Am Soc Clin Nutrit. *Res:* Mineral metabolism; thyroid metabolism; adrenal hormone metabolism. *Mailing Add:* Health Sci Med Col Va VCU Box MCV Stat 0549 Richmond VA 23298-0549. *Fax:* 804-371-7737

JONES, JOHN F(REDERICK), CHEMICAL ENGINEERING. *Current Pos:* CONSULT 87- *Personal Data:* b Scranton, Pa, Aug 19, 32; m 62; c 3. *Educ:* Pa State Univ, BS, 54; Univ Del, MS, 56; Univ Colo, PhD(chem eng), 60. *Prof Exp:* Chem engr, Esso Res & Eng Co, 56-58; instr chem eng, Univ Colo, 58-60; res chem eng, FMC Corp, 60-63, sr res chem engr, 63-68, asst mgr, Proj COED, 68-72, mgr, 72-74, dir, coal & coke technol, 74-75, bus venture & tech mgr, Philadelphia, 75-77, dir res & develop, Indust Chem Group, 77-87. *Mem:* Am Chem Soc; Am Inst Chem Engrs; Indust Res Inst; AAAS; Sigma Xi. *Res:* Petroleum refining; carbonization; gasification and liquefaction of coal; sewage and water treatment; industrial chemicals. *Mailing Add:* Maple St PO Box 116 Stowe VT 05672-0116

JONES, JOHN PAUL, PLANT PATHOLOGY. *Current Pos:* Plant pathologist, Delta Exp Sta, Agr Res Serv, USDA, 55-60, PROF PLANT PATH, UNIV ARK, FAYETTEVILLE, 60- *Personal Data:* b Warren, Ohio, Dec 10, 24; m 50; c 3. *Educ:* Ohio Univ, BS, 50; Univ Nebr, MA, 53, PhD, 56. *Concurrent Pos:* Plant pathologist, Arab Repub Egypt, 81- *Mem:* Am Phytopath Soc. *Res:* Phytopathology; diseases of field crops; etiology and control of cereal crops diseases. *Mailing Add:* 2147 Loren Circle Fayetteville AR 72701

JONES, JOHN PAUL, VEGETABLE PLANT PATHOLOGY. *Current Pos:* from asst prof to assoc prof, 58-69, PROF PLANT PATH, GULF COAST RES & EDUC CTR, UNIV FLA, 72- *Personal Data:* b Stockdale, Ohio, Feb 24, 32; m 61, Peggy J Baker; c 3. *Educ:* Ohio State Univ, BS, 53, MS, 55, PhD(plant path), 58. *Honors & Awards:* Presidential Gold Medal, Fla State Hort Soc, Council Award; Res Award, Fla Fruit & Veg Asn. *Prof Exp:* Plant path asst, Ohio Agr Exp Sta, 54-58. *Concurrent Pos:* Vis prof, Int Rice Res Inst, Philippines, 80-81. *Mem:* Am Phytopath Soc; Sigma Xi. *Res:* Nature and control of vegetable diseases; biology of plant pathogens. *Mailing Add:* Gulf Coast Res & Educ Ctr Univ Fla 5007 60th St E Bradenton FL 34203

JONES, JOHN PAUL, MATHEMATICS. *Current Pos:* asst prof, 71-74, ASSOC PROF MATH & HEAD DEPT, FROSTBURG STATE UNIV, 74- *Personal Data:* b Takoma Park, Md, Nov 17, 40; m 66; c 1. *Educ:* Alderson-Broaddus Col, BS, 62; WVa Univ, MA, 64; Pa State Univ, DEd(math), 71. *Prof Exp:* Instr math, Allegheny Col, 64-67. *Mem:* Am Math Soc; Math Asn Am. *Res:* Algebra-groups and rings. *Mailing Add:* Dept Math Frostburg State Univ Frostburg MD 21532

JONES, JOHN RICHARD, LIMNOLOGY. *Current Pos:* asst prof, 75-80, ASSOC PROF LIMNOL, UNIV MO-COLUMBIA, 80- *Personal Data:* b Bremerton, Wash, Aug 23, 47; m 69; c 1. *Educ:* Western Wash State Col, BA, 69; Iowa State Univ, MS, 72, PhD(limnol), 74. *Prof Exp:* Fel, Iowa State Univ, 74-75. *Mem:* Am Soc Limnol & Oceanog; Ecol Soc Am; Am Fisheries Soc; Sigma Xi. *Res:* Eutrophication process in lakes and reservoirs; attention to phosphorous and algal biomass. *Mailing Add:* Univ Mo Forest 1-30 Agr Bldg Columbia MO 65211-0001. *Fax:* 573-884-5070

JONES, JOHN TAYLOR, ceramics engineering, metallurgy, for more information see previous edition

JONES, JOHN VERRIER, rheumatology, immunology, for more information see previous edition

JONES, JOHNNYE M, ELECTRON MICROSCOPY, MYCOLOGY & PLANT PHYSIOLOGY. *Current Pos:* ASSOC PROF BIOL, HAMPTON UNIV, 79- *Personal Data:* b Henderson, Tex, Apr 3, 43. *Educ:* Prarie View A&M Univ, BS, 65; Atlanta Univ, MA, 70, PhD(bot & mycol), 79. *Prof Exp:* Instr biol & math, Carthage Public Schs, 65-67, Chicago Public Schs, 67-69, Morgan State Univ, Baltimore, Md, 70-74 & Mercer Univ, Atlanta, Ga, 75-79. *Concurrent Pos:* Fac fel, Nat Inst Gen Med Sci, NIH, 74; res assoc, Brookhaven Nat Lab, 79-81; dir, Minority Access Res Careers Hons Prog. *Mem:* Bot Soc Am; Mycol Soc Am; Nat Minority Health Affairs Asn; Electron Micros Soc Am; Nat Assoc Minority Med Educr. *Res:* Ultrastructural studies on certain species of fungi Ascomycetes and Oomycetes, especially developmental and physiological aspects. *Mailing Add:* Dept Biol Sci Hampton Inst Hampton VA 23668-0001

JONES, JOIE PIERCE, MEDICAL ULTRASONICS, ACOUSTICAL MICROSCOPY. *Current Pos:* PROF RADIOL SCI, UNIV CALIF, IRVINE, 77- *Personal Data:* b Brownwood, Tex, Mar 4, 41; m 65, Kay Becknell. *Educ:* Univ Tex, Austin, BA, 63, MS, 65; Brown Univ, PhD(physics), 70. *Prof Exp:* Sr scientist, Bolt Beranek & Newman, 70-75; assoc prof med physics, Case Western Reserve Univ, 75-77. *Concurrent Pos:* Consult, var pvt co & govt agencies, 71-; reviewer, NSF & NIH, 75-; mem, President's Sci & Technol adv comt, 76-79; vis prof, Kings Col, London, 82, 89 & 92, Univ Paris, 96. *Mem:* Acoust Soc Am; fel Am Inst Ultrasound Med; Am Asn Physicists Med; Inst Elec & Electronics Engrs. *Res:* Medical ultrasonics; ultrasonic tissue characterization; medical imaging; acoustical microscopy. *Mailing Add:* Dept Radiol Sci Univ Calif Irvine CA 92697-5000. *Fax:* 714-824-6532; *E-Mail:* jpjones@uli.edu

JONES, JOYCE HOWELL, EMBRYOLOGY, ANIMAL SCIENCE & NUTRITION. *Current Pos:* RETIRED. *Personal Data:* b Roanoke, Va, May 4, 44; m 68. *Educ:* Va Polytech Inst & State Univ, BS, 66, MS, 71, PhD(genetics), 74. *Prof Exp:* Jr high sch phys sci teacher, 69-70; asst prof biol, Ferrum Col, 74-77; exten specialist & asst prof poultry, Va Polytech Inst & State Univ, 77-96. *Mem:* Poultry Sci Asn; Am Genetic Asn; AAAS; Sigma Xi. *Res:* Genetical, physiological and behavioral relationships in avian and mammalian pre and postnatal development. *Mailing Add:* 15474 Windbreak Loop Happy Valley E Abingdon VA 24210

JONES, KAY H, ENVIRONMENTAL HEALTH, TOXICOLOGY. *Current Pos:* PRES ZEPHRY CONSULT, 90. *Personal Data:* b Spokane, Wash, Jan 13, 35; US citizen; c 6. *Educ:* Univ Washington, BS, 56; Univ Calif, Berkeley, MS, 61, PhD(sanit eng), 68. *Honors & Awards:* State-of-the-Art Civil Eng Award, Am Soc Civil Engrs, 75. *Prof Exp:* Mem staff, Nat Air Pollution Control Admin, Dept Health, Educ & Welfare, 67-70; mem, Off Air Prog, Environ Protection Agency, 70-74; consult, WHO, 74-75; mem, Coun Environ Qual, Exec Off Pres, 75-79; prof environ eng, Drexel Univ, Pa, 79-81; vpres, Roy Weston Inc, 81-90. *Mem:* Am Soc Civil Engrs; Air Pollution Central Asn. *Res:* Ambient air quality data analysis; air pollution impact analysis; population exposure modeling; environmental epidemiology; environmental toxicology; industrial hygiene; air pollution central engineering; risk assessment. *Mailing Add:* Zephyr Consult Suite 18 2600 Fairview Ave Seattle WA 98102

JONES, KEITH WARLOW, EXPERIMENTAL ATOMIC PHYSICS, APPLIED PHYSICS. *Current Pos:* from assoc physicist to physicist, 63-75, SR PHYSICIST, BROOKHAVEN NAT LAB, 75-, DIV HEAD, DEPT APPL SCI, 84- *Personal Data:* b Lincoln, Nebr, Aug 30, 28; m 54; c 3. *Educ:* Princeton Univ, AB, 50; Univ Wis, MS, 51, PhD(physics), 55. *Prof Exp:* Asst prof physics, Univ NC, 54-55; res assoc, Columbia Univ, 55-58; from asst prof to assoc prof, Ohio State Univ, 58-63. *Concurrent Pos:* Group leader, Dept Physics, Brookhaven Nat Lab, 76-84. *Mem:* Fel Am Phys Soc. *Res:* Beam foil spectroscopy; heavy ion-atom collisions; trace element and isotope identification techniques; micro-beam methods and applications; synchrotron radiation experiments. *Mailing Add:* Dept Appl Sci Bldg 815 Brookhaven Nat Lab Upton NY 11973

JONES, KENNETH CHARLES, ALGOLOGY, MOLECULAR GENETICS. *Current Pos:* From asst prof to assoc prof, 64-71, actg dean grad studies & res, 77-78, dept chmn, 79-80, PROF BIOL, CALIF STATE UNIV, NORTHRIDGE, 71- *Personal Data:* b San Pedro, Calif, July 20, 34; m 56; c 2. *Educ:* Univ Calif, Los Angeles, BA, 57, MA, 62, PhD(plant sci), 65. *Mem:* AAAS; Sigma Xi. *Res:* Chemical regulation of plant growth; genetic control mechanisms; physiology of germination of Chara. *Mailing Add:* Dept Biol Calif State Univ 11000 University Pkwy Northridge CA 91330

JONES, KENNETH LESTER, soil microbiology, history, for more information see previous edition

JONES, KENNETH WAYNE, CLINICAL MICROBIOLOGY. *Current Pos:* AT HEALTH LABS. *Personal Data:* b Decatur, Ill, Dec 22, 46; m 68; c 2. *Educ:* Southern Conn State Col, BS, 70; Univ NC, MPH, 74, PhD(public health microbiol), 76. *Prof Exp:* Microbiologist, Conn Health Dept, Greenwich, 71-73; res asst, Centers Dis Control, 75-76; chief microbiologist, RI Dept Health, 76- *Mem:* Sigma Xi; Am Soc Microbiol; Am Public Health Asn. *Res:* Diagnostic procedures in clinical and public health microbiology; microbiological methods for monitoring environmental quality. *Mailing Add:* Dept Health Labs 50 Orms St Providence RI 02904. *Fax:* 401-277-6984

JONES, KEVIN F, BACTERIAL PATHOGENESIS & VACCINE RESEARCH. *Current Pos:* DIR BACT RES, SIGA, NY, 96- *Personal Data:* b East Stroudsburg, Pa, Sept 20, 52. *Educ:* Moravian Col, BS, 74; Cornell Univ, MS, 77, PhD(immunol), 81. *Prof Exp:* Res fel streptoccoial pathogenesis, Rockefeller Univ, 81-85, asst prof immunol, 85-90; sr scientist, Lederle-Praxis Biol, 90-92; dir bact res, M-G Pharmaceut, 92-96. *Mem:* Am Soc Microbiol; Am Asn Immunologists; Int Soc Vaccines. *Mailing Add:* 610 W 110th St New York NY 10025

JONES, KEVIN MCDILL, UNDERGRADUATE TEACHING EXPERIMENTS IN OPTICS, RETARDATION IN MOLECULES. *Current Pos:* Postdoctoral fel, Hydrogen Maser Lab, 83-84, asst prof, 84-91, ASSOC PROF, DEPT PHYSICS, WILLIAMS COL, 91- *Personal Data:* b Washington, DC, Dec 31, 55; m 83, Moira O'Hara; c Sophie & Schuyler. *Educ:* Williams Col, BA, 77; Stanford Univ, PhD(physics), 84. *Concurrent Pos:* Consult, Lawrence Livermore Nat Lab, 87-88; dept chair, 92-; Vis, Nat

Inst Stand & Technol, Gaithersburg. *Mem:* Am Phys Soc; Sigma Xi; Optical Soc Am; Coun Undergrad Res; Am Asn Physics Teachers. *Res:* Laser spectroscopy of atoms and molecules. *Mailing Add:* Physics Dept Williams Col Williamstown MA 01267. *E-Mail:* kevin.jones@williams.edu

JONES, KEVIN SCOTT, SEMICONDUCTOR RESEARCH, TRANSMISSION ELECTRON MICROSCOPY STUDIES. *Current Pos:* asst prof, 87-89, ASSOC PROF SEMICONDUCTOR PROCESSING & STRUCT & CHARACTERIZATION MAT, DEPT MAT SCI & ENG, UNIV FLA, 89- *Personal Data:* b Gainesville, Fla, Feb 20, 58; m 83, Dauphin; c Britta, Ryan & Sean. *Educ:* Univ Fla, BS, 80; Univ Calif, Berkeley, MS, 85, PhD(mat sci eng), 87. *Prof Exp:* Tech proc engr, E I DuPont & Co, Wash Works Plant, 80-82; consult, TRW, Inc, 85-86; teaching & res asst, Univ Calif, Berkeley, 82-87; researcher, 87. *Concurrent Pos:* Co-organizer, Compound Semiconductor Growth, Processing & Devices 1990's, Japan/US Topical Conf, 87; organizer, meeting session electronic mat, 89, IX Int Conf Ion Implantation Technol, 92; NSF presidential young investr award, 90-95. *Mem:* Am Soc Metals; Electron Micros Soc Am; Mat Res Soc; Metall Soc; Electrochem Soc. *Res:* Processing and characterization of elemental and compound semiconductors; ion implantation; ion beam induced phase transformations; transmission electron microscopy. *Mailing Add:* Dept Mat Sci & Eng Univ Fla 214A Rhines Hall Gainesville FL 32611-6400

JONES, L(LEWELLYN) E(DWARD), HYDRAULIC ENGINEERING, NUMERO-GRAPHICAL METHODS. *Current Pos:* instr & lectr appl physics, 36-44, from asst prof to prof mech eng, 44-75, ENG ARCHIVIST & CUR, UNIV TORONTO, 70-, ASSOC, INST ENVIRON STUDIES, 71-, EMER PROF MECH ENG, 75- *Personal Data:* b Montreal, Can, Mar 25, 10; m 38, Dorothy I Mudge; c James L & William R. *Educ:* Univ Man, BScCE, 31, Univ Toronto, MASc, 33, PhD(hydraul), 41. *Honors & Awards:* Sons of Martha Medal, 65; Queen's Silver Jubilee Medal, 77. *Prof Exp:* Jr engr, Can Pac Rwy Co, 29-30 & Man Prov Govt, 31-33. *Concurrent Pos:* Hydraul engr, Hydro-Elec Power Comn Ont, 41-57; Ford Found res grant, 63; gen consult, 57- *Mem:* Can Soc Civil Eng; Am Soc Mech Engrs; Royal Can Inst; fel Brit Inst Mech Engrs; fel Eng Inst Can. *Res:* Applied physics; optics; photography; metrology; fluid mechanics; water resources; applied mathematics; data processing and interpretation; computers and numerical methods; technical publication; engineering history; optimal interpretation of experimental data; memorial authorship and calligraphy. *Mailing Add:* 29 Prince George Dr Islington ON M9A 1X9 Can. *Fax:* 416-971-2291

JONES, LARRY HUDSON, GENETICS, MOLECULAR BIOLOGY. *Current Pos:* from asst prof to assoc prof, 77-90, dept chair, 88-93, PROF BIOL, UNIV SOUTH, 90-, ASSOC DEAN COL, 93- *Personal Data:* b Dillon, SC, July 3, 48; m 88, Leslie Doster; c Houston H & Jonathan A. *Educ:* Wofford Col, BS, 70; Univ NC, Chapel Hill, PhD(bot), 76. *Prof Exp:* Res assoc biochem & microbiol, Cook Col, Rutgers Univ, 75-76; vis asst prof biol, Swarthmore Col, 76-77. *Concurrent Pos:* Vis res assoc, USDA Res Ctr, Florence, SC, 84; vis assoc prof biol, Reed Col, Portland, Ore, 89-90. *Mem:* Am Soc Plant Physiologists; Sigma Xi; Genetics Soc Am; Am Genetic Asn. *Res:* Tissue culture; effects of methylation of RNA on biological systems; coordination of protein synthesis in chloroplasts and mitochondria; plant hormones; genetics. *Mailing Add:* Dept Biol Univ South Sewanee TN 37383. *Fax:* 931-598-1318

JONES, LARRY PHILIP, VETERINARY PATHOLOGY. *Current Pos:* AT BIOL DEPT, UNIV TEX, EL PASO. *Personal Data:* b Hamilton, Mont, Dec 11, 34; m 59; c 2. *Educ:* Wash State Univ, BA, 57, DVM, 58; Am Col Vet Path, dipl, 68. *Prof Exp:* Res assoc path, Agr Res Lab, Univ Tenn, 58-60; asst prof vet path, Inst Trop Vet Med, 65-69; pathologist & head dept path, Tex Vet Med Diag Lab, 69- *Mem:* Am Vet Med Asn; Wildlife Dis Asn; Wildlife Soc; Sigma Xi. *Res:* Infectious diseases of domestic and wild ruminants. *Mailing Add:* Biol Sci Dept Univ Tex El Paso TX 79968-0001

JONES, LARRY WARNER, PLANT PHYSIOLOGY, ENVIRONMENTAL ENGINEERING. *Current Pos:* from asst prof to assoc prof bot, 65-73, dir Appl Sci Div, Hazardous Waste Res & Educ Inst, 85-96, PROF BOT & PLANT PHYSIOL & GENETICS, UNIV TENN, KNOXVILLE, 73-, ASSOC DIR, APPL SCI DIV, HAZARDOUS WASTE RES & EDUC INST, 96- *Personal Data:* b Huntington Co, Ind, Feb 14, 34; m 57, Martha A Crawford; c 3. *Educ:* Univ Ariz, BS, 55, MS, 59; Univ Tex, PhD(bot), 64. *Prof Exp:* Res scientist, Res Inst Adv Studies, Div Martin Co, 64-65. *Concurrent Pos:* Vis prof, Ore State Univ, 74-75; vpres, VeriTec Corp; consult, Waterways Exp Sta, US Army Corps Engrs, 76- *Mem:* Am Soc Plant Physiol; Am Pollution Control Asn; Water Pollution Control Fedn. *Res:* Immobilization and stabilization of hazardous wastes; environmental effects and monitoring; algal physiology; photosynthesis and hydrogen production. *Mailing Add:* Waste Mgt Inst Univ Tenn Knoxville TN 37996-0710. *Fax:* 423-974-3892

JONES, LAWRENCE RYMAN, ANALYTICAL CHEMISTRY. *Current Pos:* RETIRED. *Personal Data:* b Terre Haute, Ind, Jan 8, 21; m 43; c 2. *Educ:* Ind State Univ, BS, 46. *Prof Exp:* Res chemist, Com Solvents Corp, 43-75; res scientist, Int Mineral & Chem Corp, 75-86. *Concurrent Pos:* Chemist, St Anthony Hosp, 46-50. *Res:* Analytical method research. *Mailing Add:* 1219 E Alamito St Rockport TX 78382

JONES, LAWRENCE WILLIAM, HIGH ENERGY PHYSICS, COSMIC RAY PHYSICS. *Current Pos:* from instr to assoc prof, 52-63, chmn, Dept Physics, 82-87, PROF PHYSICS, UNIV MICH, ANN ARBOR, 63- *Personal Data:* b Evanston, Ill, Nov 16, 25; m 50, Ruth Drummond; c Douglas W, Carol (Dwyer) & Ellen (Dillman). *Educ:* Northwestern Univ, BS, 48, MS, 49; Univ Calif, PhD(physics), 52. *Prof Exp:* Asst, Univ Calif, 50-52. *Concurrent Pos:* Physicist, Lawrence Radiation Lab, Univ Calif, 50-52 & Midwestern Univs Res Asn, 56-57; consult, Space Tech Labs Inc, & Thompson-Ramo-Wooldridge Inc; vis scientist, Europ Orgn Nuclear Res, Geneva, Switz, 61-62, 65 & 85-, assoc, 88-; vis physicist, Brookhaven Nat Lab, Upton, NY, 63- & Fermi Nat Accelerator Lab, Batavia, Ill, 71-; Guggenheim Found fel, 65; vis prof, Westfield Col, London, 77, Tata Inst, Bombay, 79, Univ Sidney, 91, Univ Auckland, 91; chmn, Dept Physics, Univ Mich, 82-87; trustee, Univ Res Asn, 82-87; physicist, SSC Cent Design Group, Lawrence Berkeley Lab, 87; distinguished vis scholar, Univ Adelaide, 91; vis prof, Univ Sidney, 91, Univ Auckland, 91. *Mem:* Fel Am Phys Soc; AAAS; Int Asn Hydrogen Energy. *Res:* Strong interactions of elementary particles at high energies; cosmic ray physics at very high energies; hadron production of dileptons and prompt neutrinos; hydrogen energy systems; medical physics instrumentation; hadron production of charm mesons; electron positron interactions at high energies; high-energy hadron interactions at small (forward) angles. *Mailing Add:* Dept Physics Univ Mich Ann Arbor MI 48109-1120. *Fax:* 313-936-1817; *E-Mail:* lwjones@umich.edu

JONES, LEE BENNETT, ORGANIC CHEMISTRY. *Current Pos:* PROF CHEM, UNIV NEBR, 85- *Personal Data:* b Memphis, Tenn, Mar 14, 38; m 64, Vera Kramar; c David & Michael. *Educ:* Wabash Col, BA, 60; Mass Inst Technol, PhD(org chem), 64. *Hon Degrees:* DSc, Wabash Col, 92. *Prof Exp:* NSF fel chem, Calif Inst Technol, 64; from asst prof to assoc prof, Univ Ariz, 64-72, asst head dept, 71-73, head dept, 73-77, dean grad col, 77-80, prof chem, 72-85, provost, Grad Col & Health Sci, 80-82. *Mem:* AAAS; Am Chem Soc; Royal Soc Chem. *Res:* Photochemistry; carbonium ion reactions; nucleophilic substitutions; isotope effects. *Mailing Add:* Dept Chem Univ Nebr 3835 Holdrege 106 Varner Hall Lincoln NE 68583

JONES, LEEROY G(EORGE), environmental medicine, internal medicine; deceased, see previous edition for last biography

JONES, LEONIDAS JOHN, software systems, for more information see previous edition

JONES, LESTER TYLER, PHYSICAL CHEMISTRY, RESEARCH ADMINISTRATION. *Current Pos:* Sr chemist, Cent Res Labs, 3M Co, 65-72, res specialist, 72-73, supvr, 73-74, mgr, 74-82, mgr, Technol Assessment & Univ Rels, Corp Res Labs, 82-94, SR PATENT LIAISON SPECIALIST, 3M CO, 94- *Personal Data:* b Des Moines, Iowa, Dec 5, 39; m 62, Ardith Brocka; c Trent, Lance & Kevin. *Educ:* Univ Iowa, BS, 61; Wash State Univ, PhD(phys chem), 66. *Mem:* Am Chem Soc. *Res:* Corrosion of metals; nuclear quadruple resonance; charge transfer complexes; dye adsorption; controlled release; biomaterials; technology transfer; intellectual property. *Mailing Add:* 2215 S Shore Blvd St Paul MN 55110

JONES, LEWIS HAMMOND, IV, SEMICONDUCTOR PHYSICS, FREQUENCY TIMING GENERATORS. *Current Pos:* SR PROD ENGR, INTEGRATED CIRCUIT SYST, 94- *Personal Data:* b Cleveland, Ohio, Feb 26, 41. *Educ:* Ohio Wesleyan Univ, BA, 63; Univ Ill, MS, 65, PhD(physics), 71. *Prof Exp:* Vis scientist physics, Ctr Nuclear Energy, Saclay, France, 71-72 & Nat Lab, Frascati, Italy, 72-74; res assoc physics, Univ Md, College Park, 74-77; asst res physicist, Univ Calif, Irvine, 78-79; mem res staff, Fairchild Camera & Instrument Corp, Palo Alto, test eng staff, 85-87; sect head, Nat Semiconductor Corp, Santa Clara, Calif, 88-89; sr yield enhancement engr, Advan Micro Devices, Santa Clara, Calif, 89-92; test engr, EG&G Reticon, Sunnyvale, Calif, 92-94. *Mem:* Am Phys Soc; Inst Elec & Electronics Engrs. *Res:* Frequency timing generators; semiconductor characterization; semiconductor product engineering. *Mailing Add:* 693 Madrone Ave Sunnyvale CA 94086. *Fax:* 408-925-9460; *E-Mail:* jones@icst

JONES, LEWIS WILLIAM, BACTERIOLOGY. *Current Pos:* from instr to prof, 37-73, actg head dept, 60-63, EMER PROF BACT, UTAH STATE UNIV, 73- *Personal Data:* b Malad, Idaho, July 6, 06; m 28, Anna Evans; c Sidney L. *Educ:* Utah State Univ, BS, 36, MS, 37; Stanford Univ, PhD(bact, physiol), 52. *Prof Exp:* Pub sch prin, Idaho, 26-34. *Concurrent Pos:* NSF fac fel, 59-60. *Mem:* AAAS; Am Soc Microbiol; Am Pub Health Asn. *Res:* Effects of temperature, alkali salts, insecticides and herbicides upon soil microorganisms; gas production in pasteurized dairy products; anaerobic metabolism; denitrification. *Mailing Add:* 320 North 100 W Malad ID 83252

JONES, LILY ANN, MICROBIAL GENETICS, MOLECULAR BIOLOGY. *Current Pos:* Instr, 64-70, asst prof microbial genetics, 70-76, ASST PROF IMMUNOL & MICROBIOL, WAYNE STATE UNIV, 76- *Personal Data:* b Montevideo, Minn, July 6, 38; div; c 2. *Educ:* Univ Minn, BA, 60, MS, 63, PhD(microbiol), 64. *Mem:* AAAS; Am Soc Microbiol. *Res:* Genetics of Streptomyces; phylogeny of actinomycetes; bacterial resistance to antibiotics; life-cycle and structure of actinophage; bacteriophage classification & taxonomy. *Mailing Add:* Dept Immunol & Microbiol 7374 Scott Wayne State Univ Med Sch 540 E Canfield Detroit MI 48201-1928

JONES, LINCOLN D, ELECTRICAL ENGINEERING. *Current Pos:* RETIRED. *Personal Data:* b Los Angeles, Calif, Dec 4, 23; m 44; c 3. *Educ:* Univ Ariz, BS, 51, MS, 56; Stanford Univ, Engr, 64. *Prof Exp:* Instr elec eng, Univ Ariz, 51-54; asst prof, Calif State Polytech Col, 54-56; from asst prof to prof elec eng, San Jose State Univ, 56-94, emer prof, 94. *Mem:* Inst Elec & Electronics Engrs; Am Soc Eng Educ; Soc Comput Simulation. *Res:* Finding system models for second order nonlinear systems that exhibit jump resonance. *Mailing Add:* 1962 Schrader Dr San Jose CA 95124

JONES, LLEWELLYN CLAIBORNE, JR, ANALYTICAL CHEMISTRY. *Current Pos:* RETIRED. *Personal Data:* b Chester, Pa, Nov 4, 19; m 45, Doris Earon; c Richard C, Sallie (Wendt) & Susan C. *Educ:* Harvard Univ, BS, 43. *Prof Exp:* Res chemist, Houston Res Lab, Shell Oil Co, 43-44 & Wood River Res Lab, 44-46, group leader, 46-56, res chemist, Thorton Res Ctr, Shell Res, Ltd, Eng, 56-57, asst chief res physicist, Wood River Res Lab, 57-65, head analytic dept, Emeryville Res Ctr, Shell Develop Co, 65-69, head process develop dept, Res Ctr, Shell Berre, France, 69-70, head, Analytic Dept, Royal Dutch Shell Lab, Netherlands, 70-72, analytic mgr, 72-76, mgr loss Control-Logistics, 76-80. *Res:* Absorption spectroscopy; infrared and vacuum ultraviolet; ion exchange chromatography; instrumental methods of analysis. *Mailing Add:* 8203 E Del Caverna Scottsdale AZ 85258

JONES, LLOYD GEORGE, HORTICULTURE. *Current Pos:* RETIRED. *Personal Data:* b Hobart, La, Aug 6, 19. *Educ:* La State Univ, BS, 49, MS, 50; Purdue Univ, PhD(hort), 53. *Prof Exp:* Asst, La State Univ, 46-49; asst, Purdue Univ, 50-53; asst horticulturist, La State Univ, Baton Rouge, 53-55, assoc prof, 56-61, prof hort, Agr Exp Sta, 62. *Mem:* AAAS; Am Soc Plant Physiol; Am Soc Hort Sci. *Res:* Plant nutrition; soil fertility. *Mailing Add:* 34845 La Hwy 1019 Denham Springs LA 70726

JONES, LOIS MARILYN, GEOCHEMISTRY, GEOLOGY. *Current Pos:* RETIRED. *Personal Data:* b Berea, Ohio, Sept 6, 34. *Educ:* Ohio State Univ, BS, 55, MS, 59, PhD(geochem), 69. *Prof Exp:* Asst, Ohio State Univ, 53-55; res anal chem, Exp Sta, E I du Pont de Nemours & Co, Inc, 59-61; asst, Ohio State Univ, 61; lectr, Mem Univ Nfld, 61-63; res anal chemist, US Geol Surv, 63-66; res asst geochem, Ohio State Univ, 66-67, res assoc isotope geol, 69; asst prof geol, Univ Ga, 69-77; sr res scientist, Conoco, Inc, 77-82, res assoc, Petrol Res & Develop Dept, 82-90. *Concurrent Pos:* Prin investr, Tenn Copper Co grant, 69; proj leader, NSF grant, Inst Polar Studies, Ohio State Univ, & Univ Ga, 69-70. *Mem:* Am Asn Petrol Geologists; Am Geophys Union; Geochem Soc; Geol Soc Am; Int Asn Geochem & Cosmochem. *Res:* Isotope geochemistry in hydrocarbon exploration; rubidium-strontium geochronology; strontium isotopes as natural tracers; geochronology, geochemistry, and glacial history of the ice-free valleys and paleolimnology of the saline lakes, Antarctica. *Mailing Add:* 5520 Blackhawk Forrest Dr Westerville OH 43082

JONES, LORELLA MARGARET, elementary particle physics; deceased, see previous edition for last biography

JONES, LOUISE HINRICHSEN, APPLIED MATHEMATICS, COMPUTER SCIENCE. *Current Pos:* RETIRED. *Personal Data:* b Ames, Iowa, Dec 24, 30; m 52. *Educ:* Radcliffe Col, AB, 52, MA, 53; Univ Del, MA, 68, PhD(appl math), 70. *Prof Exp:* Physicist, Textile Fibers Dept, E I du Pont de Nemours & Co, Inc, 53-59, res physicist, 59-66; asst prof appl math & comput sci, Univ Del, 69-74; mem staff, E I du Pont de Nemours & co, Inc, 74-76, supvr, 76-85. *Mem:* Am Math Soc; Soc Indust & Appl Math; Asn Comput Mach. *Res:* Nonlinear eigenvalue problems; numerical solution of integral equations; automata theory; microprogramming; optimization. *Mailing Add:* 233 Cheltenham Rd Newark DE 19711

JONES, LYLE VINCENT, PSYCHOMETRICS. *Current Pos:* from assoc prof to prof, Univ NC, Chapel Hill, 57-87, alumni distinguished prof psychol, 69-92, dir, Thurstone Psychometric Lab, 57-74 & 79-92, RES PROF, UNIV NC, CHAPEL HILL, 92- *Personal Data:* b Grandview, Wash, Mar 11, 24; m 49; c 3. *Educ:* Univ Wash, BS, 47, MS, 48; Stanford Univ, PhD(psych), 50. *Prof Exp:* Fel, Univ Chicago, 50-51, asst prof psychol, 51-57. *Concurrent Pos:* Fel, Nat Res Coun, 50-51; vis assoc prof psychol, Univ Tex, 56-57; fel, Ctr Advan Study Behav Sci, 64-65 & 81-82; vchancellor & dean, The Grad Sch, Univ NC, Chapel Hill, 69-79. *Mem:* Inst Med Nat Acad Sci; fel Am Acad Arts & Sci; fel Psychomet Soc (pres, 63-64); Psychometric Soc (pres, 62-63); fel Am Statist Asn; Am Educ Res Asn; fel AAAS. *Res:* Psychological measurement; monitoring student achievement trends, especially in mathematics and science for minority students. *Mailing Add:* CB No 3270 Davie Hall Univ NC Chapel Hill NC 27599-3270

JONES, MAITLAND, JR, ORGANIC CHEMISTRY. *Current Pos:* from instr to assoc prof, 64-73, PROF CHEM, PRINCETON UNIV, 73- *Personal Data:* b New York, NY, Nov 23, 37; m 60; c 3. *Educ:* Yale Univ, BS, 59, MS, 60, PhD(chem), 63. *Prof Exp:* Fel chem, Univ Wis, 63-64. *Concurrent Pos:* Vis prof, Free Univ, Amsterdam, 73-74 & 78. *Mem:* Am Chem Soc. *Res:* Chemistry of reactive intermediates; carborange chemistry. *Mailing Add:* Dept Chem Princeton Univ Princeton NJ 08544

JONES, MALCOLM DAVID, RADIOLOGY. *Current Pos:* EMER PROF RADIOL, UNIV CALIF, 93- *Personal Data:* b Orange, Calif, Feb 16, 23; m 45; c 5. *Educ:* Univ Calif, AB, 43, MD, 46. *Prof Exp:* Intern, San Diego Naval Hosp, 46-47; from asst resident to resident radiol, Med Ctr, Univ Calif, San Francisco, 50-53, from asst prof to assoc prof, 54-65, from asst radiologist to assoc radiologist, 54-65, prof radiol & radiologist, 65-74; prof radiol & chmn dept, Univ Tex Health Sci Ctr San Antonio, 74-, prof, Dept Diag & Roentgenol, 77- *Mem:* AMA; Am Col Radiol. *Res:* Radiographic assessment of age changes in the primate spine. *Mailing Add:* 1015 Castlegate Lane Santa Ana CA 92705. *Fax:* 714-456-8386

JONES, MARGARET ZEE, NEUROPATHOLOGY, PATHOLOGY. *Current Pos:* from asst prof to assoc prof path, 70-78, PROF PATH, MICH STATE UNIV, 78- *Personal Data:* b Swedesboro, NJ, June 24, 36; m 59; c 3. *Educ:* Univ Pa, BA, 57; Med Col Va, MD, 61. *Prof Exp:* Clin asst, Sch Med, Univ Wash, 62-65; resident neuropath, Med Col Va, 66-67, from instr to asst prof, 67-69, actg dir, Div Neuropath, 68-69. *Concurrent Pos:* From intern to resident path & neuropath, Univ Wash, 62-65; lectr, Sch Med, Yale Univ, 69-; fel biochem, Nat Inst Neurol Dis & Stroke, Mich State Univ, 70-71, grant, 80-83, NIH grant, 80-87; grant, Nat Multiple Sclerosis Soc, 71-72; vis prof, Muscular Dystrophy Res Labs, Newcastle Gen Hosp, England, 76-77; hon consult, Western Gen Hosp & sr lectr, Univ Edinburgh, Edinburgh, Scotland, 83-84; mem Neurol Prog Comt, Nat Inst Neurol & Commun Disorders & Stroke, NIH, 85-88; mem, Inst Lab Animal Resources, Nat Res Coun, Nat Acad Sci, 85-88, Coun, 89-. *Mem:* Am Fedn Clin Res; Am Asn Neuropath; Soc Neurosci; Am Asn Pathologists. *Res:* Inherited metabolic diseases; developmental neurobiology; medical education; neuropathology, particularly developmental and neuromuscular disorders. *Mailing Add:* Dept Path Mich State Univ East Lansing MI 48824-0001. *Fax:* 517-336-1053

JONES, MARJORIE ANN, FETAL-MATERNAL INTERACTIONS, PROSTAGLANDINS. *Current Pos:* asst prof, 85-89, ASSOC PROF BIOCHEM, ILL STATE UNIV, 89- *Personal Data:* b Flint, Mich, Dec 11, 44; m 66; c 1. *Educ:* Cent Mich Univ, BS, 70, MS, 72; Univ Ill, MS, 73; Univ Tex, PhD(biochem), 82. *Prof Exp:* Res assoc biochem, Health Sci Ctr, Univ Tex, 82-84, sr res assoc, 84-85. *Mem:* Soc Study Reproduction; Int Embryo Transfer Soc; Am Fertility Soc; Soc Study Fertility; Am Chem Soc; NY Acad Sci. *Res:* Role of lipids in biological processes, especially the regulation and initiation of events involved in reproduction; interaction between developing embryo and the maternal system, with emphasis on signals exchanged between the two separate systems. *Mailing Add:* 305 Felmley Hall Normal IL 61761

JONES, MARK MARTIN, INORGANIC CHEMISTRY. *Current Pos:* from asst prof to assoc prof, 57-64, PROF INORG CHEM, VANDERBILT UNIV, 64- *Personal Data:* b Scranton, Pa, Jan 7, 28; m 51, Shirley Gleason; c Mark & Theodore. *Educ:* Lehigh Univ, BS, 48, MS, 49; Univ Kans, PhD(chem), 52. *Prof Exp:* Fel hydrazine chem, Univ Ill, 52-53, instr chem, 53-55; chemist, Picatinny Arsenal, 55-57, chief develop unit, Explosives Res Sect, 57. *Mem:* AAAS; Am Chem Soc; Soc Toxicol. *Res:* Therapeutic chelating agents for toxic heavy metals. *Mailing Add:* Dept Chem Vanderbilt Univ PO Box 1583 Nashville TN 37235. *Fax:* 615-322-4936; *E-Mail:* jonesmm0@ctrvax.vanderbilt.edu

JONES, MARTHA OWNBEY, BIOLOGICAL CHEMISTRY, ORGANIC CHEMISTRY. *Current Pos:* ASST PROF CHEM, UNION COL, 82- *Personal Data:* b Colfax, Wash, Dec 10, 40; m 68; c 1. *Educ:* Grinnell Col, BA, 62; Purdue Univ, PhD(chem), 75. *Prof Exp:* Instr, Purdue Univ, 66-67; from instr to asst prof chem, Drew Univ, 68-78; lectr org chem, Princeton Univ, 78-82. *Mem:* Am Chem Soc; AAAS; Sigma Xi; Am Asn Univ Profs. *Res:* Protein chemistry and enzymology; protein folding and the relationship between structure and biological activity of proteolytic enzymes. *Mailing Add:* 123 Mountainside Dr Randolph NJ 07869-3316

JONES, MARTIN L, PROBABILITY, MATHEMATICS. *Current Pos:* asst prof, 89-96, ASSOC PROF MATH, COL CHARLESTON, 96- *Personal Data:* b Hazelton, Ga. *Educ:* Warren Wilson Col, NC, BA, 79; Univ SC, MS, 83; Ga Inst Technol, PhD(math), 89. *Concurrent Pos:* Grad prog dir, Master Sci Prog Math, 92-94; vis prof, Univ de los Andes, Venezuela, 94-95, Univ de Oriente, Venezuela, 94 & Univ Costa Rica, 97-98; Fulbright lectr, Venezuela, 94-95. *Res:* Mathematical probability theory including optimal stopping theory, sequential decision theory and stochastic processes. *Mailing Add:* Dept Math Col Charleston 66 George St Charleston SC 29424-0001

JONES, MARVIN RICHARD, DEVELOPING PROCEDURES & EQUIPMENT FOR MAKING & TESTING PRODUCTS. *Current Pos:* CONSULT ENGR, 85- *Personal Data:* b Bristow, Okla, Nov 3, 14; m 35; c 3. *Honors & Awards:* Oil Drop Award, Am Soc Mech Engrs, 88, Silver Patent Award, 89. *Prof Exp:* Prod draftsman, Am Iron & Mach Works, 36-37; prod designer, Hughes Tool Co, 37-39; prod develop engr, Cameron Iron Works, Inc, 39-43, dir res & mgr eng serv, 56-79; chief engr, Oil Ctr Tool Co, 46-49; pres, Petrol Mech Develop Co, 49-55; vpres res & develop, Koomey Inc, 81-85. *Mem:* Fel Am Soc Mech Engrs; Soc Petrol Engrs. *Res:* Developing high pressure equipment for drilling and producing oil wells; author of numerous publications; granted 66 US patents and 81 foreign patents. *Mailing Add:* 414 Flintdale Rd Houston TX 77024-6300. *Fax:* 713-467-1860

JONES, MARVIN THOMAS, PHYSICAL CHEMISTRY. *Current Pos:* FAC MEM, DEPT CHEM, UNIV HOUSTON, VPROVOST & DEAN RES & GRAD STUDIES, 95- *Personal Data:* b St Louis, Mo, Apr 20, 36; m 58; c 2. *Educ:* Washington Univ, St Louis, AB, 58, PhD(phys chem), 61. *Prof Exp:* Res chemist, Exp Sta, Cent Res Dept, E I du Pont de Nemours & Co, Inc, 61-66; assoc prof chem, St Louis Univ, 66-69; assoc prof, Univ Mo, St Louis, 69-71, assoc dean, Col Arts & Sci, 76-86, actg dean, 78-79, interim assoc vchancellor Acad Affairs, 86-87, spec asst, Chancellor Budget Planning & Instnl Res, 87-88, prof chem, 71-, dep to chancellor, 88- *Concurrent Pos:* Res assoc, Univ Groningen, Neth, 75-76 & Sheffield Univ, Eng, 76. *Mem:* AAAS; Am Chem Soc; Am Phys Soc; Sigma Xi. *Res:* Spectroscopic techniques, especially magnetic resonance to study problems of chemical and physical interest; low dimensional synthetic metals. *Mailing Add:* Res & Grad Studies 1335 Perrace Hall Kent State Univ Kent OH 44242

JONES, MARY ELLEN, biochemistry; deceased, see previous edition for last biography

JONES, MAURICE HARRY, PHYSICAL CHEMISTRY, ORGANIC CHEMISTRY. *Current Pos:* EXEC DIR, CAN RES MGT ASN, 88- *Personal Data:* b London, Eng, Jan 7, 27; m 52, Eleanor C Holmes; c Derek R & Heather A. *Educ:* Univ London, BSc, 47, PhD(chem), 50. *Prof Exp:* Fel photochem, Nat Res Coun, Can, 50-52; Bakelite res fel polymerization, Univ Birmingham, 52-53; asst dir dept chem, Ont Res Found, Can, 54-63, dir dept phys chem, 63-72, dir, Dept Res Coord & Planning, 72-77, vpres interdept prog, 77-83, vpres opers, 83-84; consult, 84-88. *Mem:* Am Chem Soc; fel Chem Inst Can; Can Res Mgt Asn. *Res:* Polymerization; membranes; electroplating; pollution; research management. *Mailing Add:* 4642 Badminton Dr Mississauga ON L5M 2Y1 Can

JONES, MELTON RODNEY, GENETICS, BIOLOGY. *Current Pos:* DEAN ACAD SERV, JOHN TYLER COMMUNITY COL, 86- *Personal Data:* b Richmond, Va, Jan 13, 45; m 68; c 2. *Educ:* Am Univ, BS, 66; Howard Univ, MS, 68, PhD(zool), 72. *Prof Exp:* Div chmn, Natural Sci & Math, Shaw Univ, 72-75; asst prof biol, Univ Colo, Boulder, 75-77; asst to assoc dean basic sci, Ohio Univ, 77-78; dean, Community Col, Baltimore, 78-86; prof biol & chmn, Dept Sci, 78-86. *Concurrent Pos:* Asst to dean, Col Osteop med, Ohio Univ, 78-86. *Mem:* AAAS; Am Inst Biol Sci; Sigma Xi. *Res:* Biochemical genetics with respect to enzyme activity and gene dosage. *Mailing Add:* Acad Serv John Tyler Community Col Chester VA 23831-5399

JONES, MELVIN D, PROSTHODONTICS. *Current Pos:* MEM STAFF, UNIV CALGARY, 75- *Personal Data:* b Hardisty, Alta, Nov 16, 43; m 83; c 5. *Educ:* Univ Alta, DDS, 66; Ind Univ, Indianapolis, MSD, 69. *Prof Exp:* Asst prof dent, Univ Alta, 66-67; instr, Ind Univ, Indianapolis, 68-69; assoc prof dent, Univ Alta, 69-75. *Concurrent Pos:* Can Fund Dent Educ fel, 67-69; mem, Am Asn Dent Schs, 69-70; supvr audiovisual sect, Fac Dent, Univ Alta, 70-71; mentor, Calgary & Dist Grathological Soc. *Mem:* AAAS; Calgary & Dist Dent Soc; Can Dent Asn; Can Acad Restorative Dent; Am Acad Crown & Bridge Prosthodontics; Asn Prosthodontists Can. *Res:* Phosphate-bonded investments for regular gold castings; three dimensional recordings of mandibular movement; interactive video uses in teaching; audiovisual education; failures of cast restorations long term clinical study; myofacial pain syndrome clinical study; differential diagnosis of temporomandibular joint pain. *Mailing Add:* 1321 Hillside Dr Vestal NY 13850-1211

JONES, MERRELL ROBERT, COMPUTER SCIENCE, PHYSICS INSTRUCTION. *Current Pos:* From asst prof to prof physics, Southern Utah State Col, 66-83, chmn dept eng & phys sci, 73-76, dir, Comput Ctr, 74-82, PROF COMPUT SCI, SOUTHERN UTAH STATE COL, 83- *Personal Data:* b Salt Lake City, Utah, June 27, 38; m 59, Carol Ann Parry; c Ruth, Mark R, Daniel M, Stephen E, Rebecca & David P. *Educ:* Univ Utah, BS, 60, PhD(physics), 70. *Mem:* Asn Comput Mach; Digital Equip Corp Users Soc. *Res:* Computer science; computers in undergraduate instruction; methods and curricula in astronomy physics and computer science in elementary and secondary schools; piezoelectricity; point defects in crystals. *Mailing Add:* Dept Math & Comput Sci Southern Utah State Col Cedar City UT 84720. *Fax:* 435-865-8051; *E-Mail:* jones@suu.edu

JONES, MERRILL C(ALVIN), REAL TIME SOFTWARE, NERWORK-SYSTEM MANAGEMENT. *Current Pos:* electronics technician, Sandia Nat Labs, 48-52, measurement engr, 52-53, sect supvr metrol, 53-55, sect supvr & mem tech staff, 55-65, mem tech staff, 65-77, div supvr, 77-85, mem tech staff, 85-90, SR MEM TECH STAFF, SANDIA NAT LABS, 90- *Personal Data:* b Salona, Pa, Jan 4, 25; m 50; c 4. *Educ:* Univ NMex, BS, 52, MA, 70. *Prof Exp:* Eng technician, Indust Apparatus Div, Sylvania Elec Prod, Inc, 44-48. *Mem:* Comput Soc; Inst Elec & Electronics Engrs; Asn Comput Mach. *Res:* Measurement of electrical and physical quantities; application of computers to scientific and administrative disciplines; software design and maintenance; real time data collection and reduction; user-computer interface; computer languages/applications; network and system administration/management. *Mailing Add:* Sandia Nat Lab Div PO Box 5800 Albuquerque NM 87185-0965

JONES, MICHAEL E, NUCLEAR PHYSICS. *Current Pos:* DEP GROUP LEADER, LOS ALAMOS NAT LAB, 78- *Personal Data:* b Mobile, Ala, Sept 3, 52. *Educ:* Auburn Univ, BS, 73, PhD(physics), 78; Univ NC, MS, 74. *Mem:* Am Phys Soc. *Mailing Add:* B259 Los Alamos Nat Lab PO Box 1663 Los Alamos NM 87545. *Fax:* 505-665-3389

JONES, MICHAEL R, HUMAN NUTRITION. *Current Pos:* SR RES MGR NUTRIT, BAXTER HEALTH CARE CORP, 93- *Personal Data:* b Jacksonville, Tex, Mar 9, 46. *Educ:* Univ Calif, Los Angeles, PhD(org chem), 83. *Res:* Human nutrition. *Mailing Add:* Baxter Health Care Corp Renal Div 1620 Waukegan Rd McGaw Park IL 60085. *Fax:* 847-473-6923

JONES, MILLARD LAWRENCE, JR, CHEMICAL ENGINEERING. *Current Pos:* from asst prof to assoc prof chem eng, 66-90, EMER PROF CHEM ENG, UNIV TOLEDO, 90- *Personal Data:* b Aug 14, 33; m 59; c 2. *Educ:* Univ Utah, BS, 55; Univ Mich, Ann Arbor, MS, 58, PhD(chem eng), 61. *Prof Exp:* Res engr, Dow Chem Corp, 61-66. *Concurrent Pos:* Consult, Owens-Ill Corp, 67-87. *Mem:* Am Inst Chem Engrs. *Res:* Process dynamics and controls. *Mailing Add:* 2318 Densmore Dr Toledo OH 43606

JONES, MILTON BENNION, SOIL FERTILITY, RANGE SCIENCE & IMPROVEMENT. *Current Pos:* Assoc agronomist, Sta, 55-69, AGRONOMIST, HOPLAND FIELD STA & LECTR, UNIV CALIF, 69- *Personal Data:* b Cedar City, Utah, Jan 15, 26; m 51; c 4. *Educ:* Utah State Univ, BS, 52; Ohio State Univ, PhD(soil fertil), 55. *Concurrent Pos:* Res mineral nutrit of trop legumes, IRI Res Inst, Brazil, 63-65; teacher forage crops & range mgt, Univ Calif, Davis, 67-; res sulfur nutrit forage crops, CSIRO, Canberra, Australia, 74; lectr, Univ Evora, Portugal, 84, Dept Agr & Res, Basque Govt, 87. *Mem:* Fel Am Soc Agron, 87; Am Soc Range Mgt; fel Soil Sci Soc Am. *Res:* Range plant nutrition; range soils; range fertilization. *Mailing Add:* 3501 Leland Lane Ukiah CA 95482

JONES, MORRIS THOMPSON, BACTERIOLOGY. *Current Pos:* asst to chief extramural progs, Nat Inst Allergy & Infectious Dis, 56-57, asst chief, Nat Inst Arthritis & Metab Dis, 57-60, dep chief training br, 60-64, asst head spec foreign currency prog, Off Int Res, NIH, 64-68, CHIEF SPEC FOREIGN CURRENCY PROG, FOGARTY INT CTR, NIH, 68- *Personal Data:* b St Louis, Mo, Dec 17, 16; m 48; c 2. *Educ:* Univ Ill, AB, 40, MS, 41, PhD(bact), 44. *Prof Exp:* Appl res bacteriologist, Swift & Co, 44; res bacteriologist & food technologist, Automatic Canteen Co Am, 46-50; phys sci res adminr, Off Naval Res, 50-56. *Mem:* AAAS; Am Soc Microbiol; Am Chem Soc; Am Pub Health Asn; Sigma Xi. *Res:* High frequency cooking of foods; bacteriology of meat food products; solubility of dehydrated cream; incidence and distribution of Clostridum botulinium in soils of Illinois; sanitation and corrosion of stainless steels. *Mailing Add:* 6622 Fernwood Ct Bethesda MD 20817-3010

JONES, MORTON EDWARD, PHYSICAL CHEMISTRY. *Current Pos:* RETIRED. *Personal Data:* b Alhambra, Calif, Apr 12, 28; m 51; c 4. *Educ:* Univ Calif, BS, 49; Calif Inst Technol, PhD(chem), 53. *Prof Exp:* Mem tech staff, Tex Instruments, Inc, 53-61, sr scientist, Semiconductor Device Tech Sect, Device Res Dept, 61-65, dir, Mat Sci Res Lab, 65-71, dir, Phys Sci Res Lab, 71-79, dir, Resource Develop, 79-85. *Mem:* Sigma Xi. *Mailing Add:* 619 Northhill Dr Richardson TX 75080

JONES, NOEL DUANE, CRYSTALLOGRAPHY, DRUG DESIGN. *Current Pos:* res adv, 67-93, VPRES DRUG DESIGN, ELI LILLY & CO, 94- *Personal Data:* b Omaha, Nebr, Aug 4, 37; m 63, Katharine Holtom; c Evan & Leonard. *Educ:* Rensselaer Polytech Inst, BS, 59; Calif Inst Technol, PhD(chem), 64. *Prof Exp:* NIH fel, Univ Berne, 64-66. *Concurrent Pos:* Vis res scientist, Yale Univ, 84-85. *Mem:* Am Chem Soc; Am Crystallog Asn. *Res:* Structure-based design of biologically active compounds. *Mailing Add:* Molecular Structure Corp 3200 Res Forest Dr Woodlands TX 77381

JONES, NOLAN T(HOMAS), electrical engineering, for more information see previous edition

JONES, OLIVER WILLIAM, MEDICINE, BIOCHEMISTRY. *Current Pos:* assoc prof, 68-73, PROF MED & PEDIAT, SCH MED, UNIV CALIF, SAN DIEGO, 73-, DIR DIV MED GENETICS, 68- *Personal Data:* b Ft Smith, Ark, Feb 7, 32; m 55; c 4. *Educ:* Northeastern State Col, Okla, BS, 54; Univ Okla, MD, 57. *Prof Exp:* From intern to jr resident med, Med Ctr, Duke Univ, 57-59, sr resident, 60-61; res assoc biochem genetics, Nat Heart Inst, 61-63; asst prof med, Duke Univ, 65-66, asst prof biochem, 66-67, co-dir, Res Training Prog, Med Ctr, 66-68, assoc prof med & biochem, 67-68. *Concurrent Pos:* Arthritis & Rheumatism Asn fel, Duke Univ, 59-60; fel biochem, Stanford Univ, 63-65; NIH career develop award, 63-68; Nat Inst Arthritis & Metab Dis res grant, 65-68; Damon Runyon Found res grant, 68-71; Am Cancer Soc res grant, 69-73; NIH grants, 69-75. *Mem:* AAAS; Am Soc Human Genetics; Am Soc Cell Biol; Am Soc Biol Chemists; Soc Pediat Res. *Res:* Genetic counseling; regulation of pyrimidine biosynthesis; cytogenetics. *Mailing Add:* Dept Med Genetics 0639 Univ Calif San Diego 9500 Gilman Dr La Jolla CA 92093-0639. *Fax:* 619-534-7929

JONES, ORDIE REGINAL, CONSERVATION TILLAGE, WIND & WATER EROSION CONTROL. *Current Pos:* SOIL SCIENTIST, AGR RES SERV, BUSHLAND, TEX, US DEPT AGR, 71- *Personal Data:* b Memphis, Tex, Aug 7, 37; m 57; c 3. *Educ:* Tex Tech Univ, Lubbock, BS, 60; WTex State Univ, Canyon, MS, 71. *Concurrent Pos:* Field agronomist. *Mem:* Soil Sci Soc Am; Am Soc Agron; fel Soil & Water Conserv Soc; Int Soc Soil Sci. *Res:* Developing soil and water conservation practices for use in dryland cropping in semi-arid areas; cropping and tillage practices that conserv water, reduce erosion and increase water use efficiency of crops. *Mailing Add:* 2319 Larry St Amarillo TX 79016

JONES, ORVAL ELMER, WEAPON SAFETY, APPLIED MECHANICS. *Current Pos:* staff mem, Sandia Corp, 61-64, div supvr dynamic stress res, 64-68, mgr phys res dept, 68-71, dir solid state sci res, 71-74, dir nuclear security systs, 74-77, dir nuclear waste and environ progs, 77-78, dir eng sci, 78-82, vpres tech support, 82-83, vpres defense progs, 83-86, exec vpres tech progrs, 86-93, CONSULT, SANDIA NAT LABS, 93- *Personal Data:* b Ft Morgan, Colo, Apr 9, 34; m 54, Pauline A Lunka; c Carol, Sharon & Lawrence. *Educ:* Colo State Univ, BS, 56; Calif Inst Technol, MS, 57, PhD(mech eng), 61. *Prof Exp:* Tech staff mem, Res & Develop Labs, Hughes Aircraft Co, Calif, 56-57; res engr, Hydromech Lab, Calif Inst Technol, 60-61. *Concurrent Pos:* NSF fel, 59-60; vis lectr, Univ NMex, 64 & 68, hon consult mech eng, 91-92; distinguished assoc award, US Dept Energy, 93. *Mem:* Fel Soc Mech Eng; Am Phys Soc; Sigma Xi. *Res:* Response of piezoelectrics, ferroelectrics and semiconductor to shock loading; nuclear security safeguards and safety systems for transportation and storage of nuclear materials and weapons; underground repository and technology development for nuclear waste isolation; engineering applications of structural dynamics, transport phenomena, and rock mechanics. *Mailing Add:* 12321 Eastridge Dr NE Albuquerque NM 87112-4604. *E-Mail:* oejones@aol.com

JONES, OTHA CLYDE, CHEMICAL ENGINEERING, PHYSICAL CHEMISTRY. *Current Pos:* CONSULT ENG CONTRACTOR, 79- *Personal Data:* b Emporia, Kans, May 16, 08; m 31. *Educ:* Univ Utah, BS, 30, MS, 31. *Prof Exp:* Res engr, Monsanto Co, 31-37, group leader, 38-50, asst dir res, 50-64, mgr process tech monomers, 64-70, sr planning analyst, 70-73; mech engr, Arthur G McKee, Inc, 75-77; process engr, Fishstone, Inc, 78-79. *Mem:* Am Chem Soc Am; Inst Chem Engrs. *Res:* Production of phosphorus, inorganic phosphates, fluosilicates, phosphorus sulfides, vinyl chloride, polyethylene, and other polymers. *Mailing Add:* 736 Cedar Field Ct Chesterfield MO 63017-5727

JONES, OWEN LLOYD, PHYSICAL CHEMISTRY, RADIOCHEMISTRY. *Current Pos:* asst prof, 65-73, ASSOC PROF CHEM, US NAVAL ACAD, 73- *Personal Data:* b Hackensack, NJ, July 31, 35; c 6. *Educ:* Drew Univ, AB, 57; WVa Univ, MS, 60, PhD(phys chem), 67. *Prof Exp:* Instr chem, WVa Univ, 60-65. *Mem:* Am Chem Soc; Sigma Xi. *Res:* Solution kinetics; exchange rate studies using isotopic tracer techniques. *Mailing Add:* Dept Chem US Naval Acad Annapolis MD 21402-5088

JONES, OWEN THOMAS, molecular neurobiology, ion channels, for more information see previous edition

JONES, P(HILIP) H(ARRHY), sanitary engineering; deceased, see previous edition for last biography

JONES, PATRICIA PEARCE, IMMUNOLOGY. *Current Pos:* From asst prof to assoc prof, 78-90, PROF BIOL SCI, STANFORD UNIV, 90- *Personal Data:* b 1947; m, Robert T Schimke. *Educ:* Oberlin Col, BA, 69; Johns Hopkins Univ, PhD(biol), 74. *Honors & Awards:* Founder's Prize, Tex Instruments Found, 84. *Mem:* Am Asn Immunologists. *Res:* Immunogenetics; genetics, structure, function and expression of histocompatibility proteins. *Mailing Add:* Dept Biol Sci Stanford Univ Stanford CA 94305-5020

JONES, PATRICK RAY, PHYSICAL CHEMISTRY. *Current Pos:* MEM FAC CHEM, UNIV PAC, 74- *Personal Data:* b Austin, Tex, Oct 22, 43; m 68; c 2. *Educ:* Univ Tex, Austin, BA & BS, 66; Stanford Univ, PhD(chem), 71. *Prof Exp:* Res fel chem, Nat Acad Sci, 71-73; res fel chem, Calif Inst Technol, 73-74. *Concurrent Pos:* Vis scholar chem, Stanford Univ, 79-80. *Mem:* Am Chem Soc; Sigma XI. *Res:* Matrix isolation studies of oxygen, fluorine and chlorine atom reactions; electron-impact excitation of gases; combined liquid chromatography and mass-spectrometry; physical chemistry of organometallics. *Mailing Add:* Chem Dept Univ Pac Stockton CA 95211-0197

JONES, PAUL HASTINGS, GEOLOGY. *Current Pos:* CONSULT, 77- *Personal Data:* b Fostoria, Mich, Aug 31, 18; m 41, Romaine Frances Grohman; c Susan F, Roger P, Jeffrey T & Alan G. *Educ:* Mich State Col, BS, 41; La State Univ, MS, 51, PhD, 68. *Honors & Awards:* Meritorious Serv Award, US Dept Interior, 75. *Prof Exp:* Geophysicist, Halliburton Oil Well Cementing Co, Tex, 41-42; from geologist to geologist in charge groundwater invests, US Geol Surv, La, 42-52, dist geologist in charge, Pa, 52-55, tech adv, Groundwater Geol Surv, Int Co-op Admin, India, 55-57, dist geologist, Tenn, 58-59, res proj chief, Ground Water Br, Nat Reactor Testing Sta, Idaho, 59-62, chief radiohydrol sect, Water Resources Div, DC, 62-64, res hydrologist, Gulf Coastal Plain, 65-74; mem fac, dept geol, La State Univ, 74-77. *Concurrent Pos:* Consult, World Bank, 66 & 83-87, India, Nepal & Bangladesh, UN, 70; mem Nat Acad Sci adv team, India, 71. *Mem:* Soc Econ Geol; fel Geol Soc Am; Am Asn Petrol Geol; Soc Petrol Eng; Am Soc Test & Mat. *Res:* Quantitative interpretation of borehole geophysical logs; hydrogeology of deep sedimentary basins; role of geopressure in the fluid hydrocarbon regime; hydrology of waste disposal; enhanced production of petroleum and natural gas; geothermal resources of Northern Gulf of Mexico Basin. *Mailing Add:* 3256 McConnell Dr Baton Rouge LA 70809

JONES, PAUL KENNETH, BIOMETRICS, BIOSTATISTICS. *Current Pos:* sr instr, 72-73, asst prof, 73-80, ASSOC PROF EPIDEMIOL & BIOSTATIST, CASE WESTERN RES UNIV, 80- *Personal Data:* b Des Moines, Iowa, Jan 5, 43; m 71, Susan L Organ. *Educ:* Grinnell Col, BA, 64; Univ Iowa, MS, 69, PhD(statist), 72. *Prof Exp:* Res asst statist, Am Col Testing, 68-72. *Mem:* Am Statist Asn; Biomet Soc; Soc Epidemiol Res. *Res:* Quantitative methods in health care/health services research; statistical methods; regression, logistic regression. *Mailing Add:* Dept Epidemiol & Biostatist Case Western Res Univ Cleveland OH 44106-4945. *Fax:* 216-368-3970; *E-Mail:* pkj@hal.epbi.cwru.edu

JONES, PAUL RAYMOND, ORGANIC CHEMISTRY, HISTORY OF CHEMISTRY. *Current Pos:* From asst prof to assoc prof, 56-65, PROF CHEM, UNIV NH, 65- *Personal Data:* b Chicago, Ill, July 19, 30; m 58, Meredyth Manns; c Paul G, Amy E & Sarah R. *Educ:* Albion Col, BA, 52; Univ Ill, PhD, 56. *Concurrent Pos:* NSF sci fac fel, Max-Planck Inst, Gottingen, 64-65; Fulbright res fel, Chem Inst, Univ Freiburg, Ger, 73; vis prof, Deutsches Mus, Munich, Ger, 82-83; Fulbright Sr Res Fel, 91-92. *Mem:* Am Chem Soc; Hist Sci Soc. *Res:* Macrocycles; ring-chain tautomerism; anhydro dimers; history of chemistry. *Mailing Add:* Dept Chem Univ NH Parsons Hall Durham NH 03824-4724

JONES, PAUL RONALD, ORGANOMETALLIC CHEMISTRY. *Current Pos:* asst prof, 68-73, assoc prof, 73-79, PROF CHEM, UNIV NTEX, 79- *Personal Data:* b York, Pa, Dec 19, 40; m 67; Priscilla A Carney; c Kevin & Anne. *Educ:* Pa State Univ, BS, 62; Purdue Univ, PhD(chem), 66. *Honors & Awards:* W T Doherty Award, Dallas-Ft Worth Sect, Am Chem Soc, 85. *Prof Exp:* Res assoc chem, Univ Wis-Madison, 66-67. *Concurrent Pos:* Vis scientist, Korea Advan Inst Sci & Technol, 84. *Mem:* Am Chem Soc; Sigma Xi. *Res:* Organometallic chemistry, especially involving synthesis structure and reactions of group IV compounds; bonding in organometallic compounds; stereochemistry and mechanism of the reactions of subvalent organosilicon intermediates; polysilyl polyacetylenes. *Mailing Add:* Univ NTex PO Box 5068 Denton TX 76203. *Fax:* 817-565-4318; *E-Mail:* pjones@cas.unt.edu

JONES, PETER D, LIPID METABOLISM, FATS IN NUTRITION. *Current Pos:* from asst prof to assoc prof biochem, 72-83, asst dean, Acad Affairs, Col Med, 79-85, PROF BIOCHEM, UNIV TENN CTR HEALTH SCI, 83- *Personal Data:* b Palmerston North, NZ, Apr 27, 40; m 67; c 3. *Educ:* Victoria Univ Wellington, BS, 61, MS, 63; Duke Univ, PhD(biochem), 68. *Prof Exp:* Res assoc, Univ Ariz, 68-69; lectr, Victoria Univ Wellington, 69-72. *Mem:* AAAS; Sigma Xi; Nutrit Today Soc; Am Soc Biol Chemists. *Res:* Oxidative desaturation of long chain fatty acids; structure and function of the electron transport chains of the endoplasmic reticulum; nutritional role of fatty acids and lipids. *Mailing Add:* Dept Biochem Univ Tenn Col Med 800 Madison Ave Memphis TN 38163-0001

JONES, PETER FRANK, PHYSICAL CHEMISTRY, AEROSPACE ENGINEERING & SPACE TECHNOLOGY. *Current Pos:* SR RES ENGR, UNIV NMEX, 96- *Personal Data:* b Brooklyn, NY, Mar 15, 37; m 78, Susan Schon; c Lisa, Robin, Jennifer, Julieanne, William & Daniel. *Educ:* Univ Kans, BA, 60; Univ Chicago, MS, 61; Univ Calif, Los Angeles, PhD(high pressure spectros), 67. *Prof Exp:* Mem tech staff, Aerospace Corp, 66-73, head, Forensic Sci Sect, 73-74, Anal Sci Dept, 74-87, sr engr technol develop, 87-96. *Concurrent Pos:* Consult forensic sci & gunshot residue, 77. *Res:* Guide the planning and development of space technology for the Air Force Phillips Lab Space Technology Directorate. *Mailing Add:* Phillips Lab VT-O 3550 Aberdeen Ave SE Kirtland AFB NM 87117-5776. *E-Mail:* jonespf@plk.af.mil

JONES, PETER HADLEY, MEDICINAL CHEMISTRY, CARDIOVASCULAR DISEASES. *Current Pos:* PRES, MCD6 CONSULTS, 92- *Personal Data:* b Cleveland, Ohio, Aug 14, 34; m 57, Joan Miller; c Laura F (Nelson), Peter H Jr & David P. *Educ:* Harvard Univ, AB, 56; Univ Calif, Los Angeles, PhD(org chem), 60. *Prof Exp:* Sr res chemist, Abbott Labs, 60-70, assoc res fel, 70-71, mgr med chem, 71-75, head cardiovasc res, 75-79; vpres & dir res, Interx Corp, 79-80; sect had gastrointestinal dis, Searle Labs, G D Searle & Co, 80-85, dir med chem, 85-86, sr dir, Gastrointestinal Dis Res, 86-92. *Concurrent Pos:* Instr, Dept Biochem, Med Sch, Northwestern Univ, 69-73; adj prof med chem, Univ Ill, Chicago, 87- *Mem:* Am Chem Soc; AAAS; Sigma Xi; fel Am Inst Chemists; NY Acad Sci. *Res:* Reactions of diphenylcarbenes; chemistry of macrolide antibiotics; chemistry of hypertensive agents; development of new drugs for hypertension angina; chemical drug delivery systems; gastrointestinal drugs and diseases; polymer delivery systems. *Mailing Add:* MCD6 Consults 11125 Fleming Rd Woodstock IL 60098

JONES, PHILIP ARTHUR, ENTOMOLOGY. *Current Pos:* RETIRED. *Personal Data:* b Prince George, BC, Mar 1, 24. *Educ:* Univ BC, BSA, 49; Univ Wis-Madison, MS, 56, PhD(entom), 63. *Prof Exp:* Asst forest biologist sci serv, Can Dept Agr, 49-52; res asst forest entom, Univ Wis, 52-58; res officer, Forest Biol Div, Can Dept Agr, 58-60; from proj asst to proj assoc biol control, Univ Wis, 60-64; from asst prof to assoc prof entom, SDak State Univ, 65-74; tech dir, Agr Chem Div, FMC of Can Ltd, 74-77; environ scientist, Environ Can, 77-93. *Concurrent Pos:* Mem tech comt, Can Agr Chem Asn, 74-77. *Res:* Environmental assessment of toxic chemicals. *Mailing Add:* PO Box 1943 Vernon BC V1T 8Z7 Can

JONES, PHILLIP SANFORD, MATHEMATICS. *Current Pos:* from instr to prof, 47-82, EMER PROF MATH, UNIV MICH, ANN ARBOR, 82- *Personal Data:* b Elyria, Ohio, Feb 26, 12; m 35; c 4. *Educ:* Univ Mich, AB, 33, AM, 35, PhD(math), 48. *Hon Degrees:* LHD, Northern Mich Univ, 72. *Prof Exp:* Teacher pub sch, Mich, 34-37; teacher math, Edison Inst Technol, 37-43, Univ Mich, 43-44 & Ohio State Univ, 44-45. *Concurrent Pos:* Vis prof, Ain Shams Univ, Cairo, Egypt, 78. *Mem:* Nat Coun Teachers Math (pres, 60-62); Am Math Soc; Hist Sci Soc; Math Asn Am. *Res:* History and teaching of mathematics; development of the mathematical theory of linear perspective; development of number systems. *Mailing Add:* 1701 Shadford Rd Ann Arbor MI 48104-4523

JONES, PHILLIPS RUSSELL, PHYSICS. *Current Pos:* from asst prof to prof, 58-93, EMER PROF PHYSICS, UNIV MASS, AMHERST, 93- *Personal Data:* b Troy, NY, Aug 25, 30; m 52, Ereda L; c Linda, Kevin & Sharon. *Educ:* Univ Mass, BS, 51; Univ Conn, MA, 56, PhD(physics), 59. *Prof Exp:* Teacher, Mass Pub Sch, 52; asst physics, Univ Conn, 54-58. *Mem:* Am Phys Soc. *Res:* Experimental atomic physics. *Mailing Add:* Dept Physics Hasbrouck Lab Univ Mass Amherst MA 01003

JONES, PHYLLIS EDITH, NURSING. *Current Pos:* From asst prof to prof, 63-89, dean nursing, 79-88, EMER PROF NURSING, UNIV TORONTO, 89- *Personal Data:* b Barrie, Ont, Sept 16, 24. *Educ:* Univ Toronto, BScN, 50, MSc, 69. *Concurrent Pos:* mem bd, Von Metro Toronto; res referee, On Ministry Health, Nat Health Res & Develop Prog; consult, WHO; external examr, Univ Ibadan; hon mem, Finnish Soc Prof Nursing, 87. *Mem:* Can Pub Health Asn; fel Am Pub Health Asn; NAm Nursing Diag Asn. *Res:* Innovations in community health nursing, in collaboration with physician services; nursing diagnoses. *Mailing Add:* RR 2 Owensound ON N4K 5N4 Can

JONES, R E DOUGLAS, mathematics, for more information see previous edition

JONES, R NORMAN, SPECTROCHEMISTRY. *Current Pos:* PVT CONSULT CHEM SPECTROS, 77- *Personal Data:* b Manchester, Eng, Mar 20, 13; nat Can; m 39, Magda Kemeny; c R Kemeny & David L. *Educ:* Univ Manchester, BSc, 33, MSc, 34, PhD(chem), 36, DSc, 54. *Hon Degrees:* DSc, Univ Poznan, 72 & Tokyo Inst Technol, 82. *Honors & Awards:* Herzberg Award, Spec Soc Can; Fisher Award, Chem Soc Can. *Prof Exp:* Tutor biochem, Harvard Univ, 39-41; lectr chem, Queen's Univ, Can, 42-43, asst prof, 43-46; from assoc res officer to prin res officer, Nat Res Coun Can, 46-77. *Concurrent Pos:* Chmn, Molecular Spectros comn, Int Union Pure & Appl Chem, 67-71; secy task group comput use, Comt Data Sci & Technol, Int Coun Sci Unions, 67-75, mem bur, 70-74, mem adv comt, UNISIST-UNESCO, 74-77; guest prof, Tokyo Inst Technol, Japan, 79-82, guest researcher, 85-86; guest worker, Nat Res Coun Can, 79-; distinguished visitor, Univ Alta, 82-83, guest scientist, 92-; adj prof, Queen's Univ, Kingston, Ont, 84. *Mem:* Am Chem Soc; Royal Soc Can; Chem Inst Can; Royal Soc Chem; Int Union Pure & Appl Chem (vpres to pres, Phys Chem Div, 71-77, emer pres, 77-). *Res:* Molecular spectroscopy; use of ultraviolet, infrared and Raman spectroscopy for the elucidation of molecular structure, with special reference to steroids and other natural products; use of computers for data logging and as aids in evaluation, storage and retrieval of spectral data; molecular structure determination and analysis by vibrational spectroscopy. *Mailing Add:* 11027-87 Ave NW Suite 1003 Edmonton AB T6G 2P9 Can

JONES, RALPH WILLIAM, PHARMACEUTICAL CHEMISTRY. *Current Pos:* RETIRED. *Personal Data:* b Coin, Iowa, Aug 29, 21; m 45; c 3. *Educ:* St Louis Col Pharm, BS, 48; Purdue Univ, MS, 51. *Prof Exp:* Res pharmacist, Abbott Labs, 51-57, group leader sterile prod res, 57-61, sect head liquid-ointment prod res, 61-64, secy new prod comt, 63-64, dept mgr allied prod res, 64-66 & radiopharmaceut prod res & develop, 66-67, dept mgr liquid prods res & develop, 67-83. *Mem:* Am Pharmaceut Asn; Sigma Xi. *Res:* Basic and applied research on new pharmaceutical dosage forms and products; pharmacy, chemistry and allied medical sciences. *Mailing Add:* 716 Fairview Ave Libertyville IL 60048

JONES, REESE TASKER, PSYCHOPHARMACOLOGY, DRUG DEPENDENCE. *Current Pos:* asst prof to assoc prof res, Med Ctr, 67-76, PROF PSYCHIAT, UNIV CALIF, SCH MED, SAN FRANCISCO, 76- *Personal Data:* b Philadelphia, Pa, June 7, 32; m 56; c 3. *Educ:* Univ Mich, BS, 54, MD, 58. *Prof Exp:* Res psychiat, Langley Porter Neuropsychiat Inst, 62-67. *Concurrent Pos:* Staff psychiatrist, Langley Porter Neuropsychiat Inst, 67-; NIMH res career develop award, 67- *Mem:* Am Psychiat Asn; Psychiat Res Soc; Am Col Neuropsychopharmacol; Soc Biol Psychiat. *Res:* Objective indices of psychopathology; human neurophysiology; psychopharmacology; drug dependence. *Mailing Add:* Univ Calif Sch Med 401 Parnassus Ave San Francisco CA 94143-0984

JONES, RENA TALLEY, MICROBIOLOGY. *Current Pos:* INSTR BIOL, CHMN DEPT & PROJ DIR HEALTH CAREERS PROG, SPELMAN COL, 73- *Personal Data:* b Chipley, Ga, Aug 3, 37. *Educ:* Morris Brown Col, BA, 60; Atlanta Univ, MS, 67; Wayne State Univ, PhD(microbiol), 74. *Prof Exp:* Instr biol, Pub Schs, Ga, 60-66; NSF grant, Atlanta Univ, 66. *Mem:* Am Soc Microbiol; AAAS; Sigma Xi. *Res:* Staphylococcal and slime molds; enzymes; immunochemistry. *Mailing Add:* Dept Biol Spelman Col 350 Spelman Lane Atlanta GA 30314-4346

JONES, RICHARD BRADLEY, NUCLEAR SCIENCE, APPLIED MATHEMATICS. *Current Pos:* VPRES, HARTFORD STEAM BOILER INSPECTION, 92- *Personal Data:* b Norristown, Pa, June 21, 47. *Educ:* Va Polytech Inst & State Univ, BS, 70, MS, 71, PhD(nuclear eng), 74. *Prof Exp:* Lectr nuclear eng, Univ Calif, Santa Barbara, 74-75; fel appl math, Univ Ill, 75-77; mem tech staff, nuclear risk anal, Sandia Lab, 77-78; asst prof comput sci, State Univ NY, Plattsburgh, 78-81; consult, 81-92. *Concurrent Pos:* Consult, W Alton Jones Cell Sci Ctr, 78, Chem-Nuclear Syst Inc, 78; vis prof appl math, Univ Florence, Italy, 81. *Mem:* Am Nuclear Soc; Am Soc Eng Educ; Soc Indust & Appl Math; AAAS. *Res:* Applied mathematics; mathematical modeling of cell regeneration; computer animation effects in education; systems design. *Mailing Add:* 111 Fairwood Rd Bethany CT 06524

JONES, RICHARD CONRAD, BOTANY. *Current Pos:* RETIRED. *Personal Data:* b Lebanon, NH, Feb 25, 16; m 41, Dorothy Jordan; c Richard E. *Educ:* Dartmouth Col, AB, 38; Univ NH, MS, 42; State Col Wash, PhD(bot), 44. *Prof Exp:* Asst, Agr Exp Sta, Univ NH, 44-45, instr bot, 45-46, asst, 46-48; prof biol, State Univ NY Col New Paltz, 48-66, actg dean, 66-67, dean col, 67-68, vpres acad affairs, 68; assoc univ dean, State Univ NY Albany, 68; pres, State Univ NY Col Cortland, 68-78; exec dir, Montshire Mus Sci, 79-80. *Concurrent Pos:* With NSF Inst Bot, Cornell Univ, 57 & NSF Genetics, Cold Springs Harbor, 59; res fel, State Univ NY Col New Paltz, 58 & 60. *Mem:* AAAS; Bot Soc Am; Mycol Soc Am. *Res:* Genetics; alteration of generations in biological systems. *Mailing Add:* PO Box 223 Etna NH 03750

JONES, RICHARD DELL, CARDIOVASCULAR PHYSIOLOGY, BIOMATERIALS. *Current Pos:* DIR PHYSIOL, DIV SURG RES, ST LUKE'S HOSP, 75- *Educ:* Case Western Reserve Univ, PhD(physiol), 62. *Mailing Add:* Div Surg Res St Luke's Hosp 3108 Lincoln Blvd Cleveland Heights OH 44118-2036. *Fax:* 216-368-8194

JONES, RICHARD ELMORE, PHYSICAL PHARMACY. *Current Pos:* VPRES DEVELOP, PHARMETRIX CORP, 89- *Personal Data:* b Rochester, NY, July 16, 44; m 69; c 1. *Educ:* Dartmouth Col, AB, 65; Stanford Univ, PhD(phys chem), 70. *Prof Exp:* Sr progammer & analyst, Syntex Corp, 69-71; staff researcher, 71-77, sr staff researcher, 77-78, dept head, Inst Pharmaceut Sci, Syntex Res, 78-84; dir pharmaceut res & develop, Genentech Inc, 84-88; vpres develop, Liposome Technol Inc, 88-89. *Concurrent Pos:* Adj prof, Univ Pac Sch Pharm, 74-75, 80-84. *Mem:* Am Chem Soc; AAAS; NY Acad Sci; Am Asn Pharmaceut Scientists. *Res:* Percutaneous absorption; experimental design in formulation problems; pharmaceutical aerosols; protein drug delivery. *Mailing Add:* 4250 El Camino Real No C323 Palo Alto CA 94306

JONES, RICHARD EVAN, COMPARATIVE ENDOCRINOLOGY, REPRODUCTIVE BIOLOGY. *Current Pos:* from asst prof to assoc prof, 69-80, PROF BIOL, UNIV COLO, BOULDER, 80- *Personal Data:* b Sacramento, Calif, May 13, 40; m 80; c 4. *Educ:* Univ Calif, Berkeley, BA, 61, MA, 64, PhD(zool), 68. *Prof Exp:* Asst prof behav sci, Hershey Med Ctr, Pa State Univ, 68-69. *Concurrent Pos:* Res career develop award, NIH, 74-79. *Res:* Control of ovarian follicular growth; reptilian reproduction; control of uterine contraction. *Mailing Add:* Dept EPO Biol Univ Colo Campus Box 334 Boulder CO 80309

JONES, RICHARD EVAN, JR, PHYSICAL CHEMISTRY, INORGANIC CHEMISTRY. *Current Pos:* assoc prof, 70-80, PROF CHEM, LEWIS & CLARK COMMUNITY COL, 80- *Personal Data:* b Oak Park, Ill, Aug 3, 40; m 64; c 1. *Educ:* Monmouth Col, BA, 62; Univ Hawaii, PhD(chem), 70. *Prof Exp:* Lab asst qual control, Ralph Wells & Co, 61-62; res scientist, Continental Can Co, 62-64; lab mgr plastics, Gat Ke Corp, 64-66; NDEA Title IV fel, 67. *Mem:* Am Chem Soc. *Res:* Aqueous-nonaqueous solvent extraction of metals; better methods for presentation of chemistry in lower division courses. *Mailing Add:* Lewis & Clark Community Col 5800 Godfrey Rd Godfrey IL 62035. *E-Mail:* richardj81@adl.com

JONES, RICHARD HUNN, BIOSTATISTICS, COMPUTER SCIENCE. *Current Pos:* dir, Sci & Comput Ctr, 75-82, PROF BIOMET, UNIV COLO SCH MED, DENVER, 75- *Personal Data:* b Ridley Township, Pa, Oct 31, 34; m 81, Julie Ann Marshall; c 4. *Educ:* Pa State Univ, BS, 56, MS, 57; Brown Univ, PhD(appl math), 61. *Prof Exp:* NSF fel, Univ Stockholm, 61-62; from asst prof to assoc prof statist, Johns Hopkins Univ, 62-68; prof info & comput sci, Univ Hawaii, 68-75, chmn dept, 70-73. *Concurrent Pos:* Consult, Swed Meteorol & Hydrol Inst, 62, RCA Serv Co, Fla, 62-66, Tripler Army Hosp, Hawaii, 69-73, Nat Bur Stand, Boulder, Colo, 79-85 & Nat Ctr Atmospheric Res, Boulder, Colo, 84-86. *Mem:* Biomet Soc; fel Am Statist Asn; Am Meteorol Soc. *Res:* Time series analysis; stochastic processes; statistical data analysis. *Mailing Add:* Dept Biomet & Prev Med Sch Univ Colo PO Box B-119 Denver CO 80262. *Fax:* 303-270-3183

JONES, RICHARD LAMAR, INSECT PHYSIOLOGY, INSECT BEHAVIOR. *Current Pos:* assoc prof insect physiol, 77-84, PROF & HEAD, DEPT ENTOM, UNIV MINN, 84- *Personal Data:* b Charleston, Miss, May 31, 39; m 64; c 2. *Educ:* Miss State Univ, BS, 63, MS, 65; Univ Calif, Riverside, PhD(insect toxicol), 68. *Prof Exp:* Insect physiologist, Southern Grain Insect Res Lab, Agr Res Serv, USDA, 68-77; res assoc, Univ Ga, 69-77. *Concurrent Pos:* Fulbright Scholar, Univ Leiden, Netherlands, 80. *Mem:* AAAS; Entom Soc Am; Am Chem Soc. *Res:* Investigation of chemicals associated with insect behavior. *Mailing Add:* Dept Med Univ Alberta 2E434 WMC Alberta BC T6G 2B7 Can. *Fax:* 403-492-6384

JONES, RICHARD LEE, materials science engineering, metallurgical engineering; deceased, see previous edition for last biography

JONES, RICHARD LEE, LUNG PHYSIOLOGY. *Current Pos:* Lectr, Univ Alta, 71-73, asst prof, 73-77, assoc prof physiol, 77-86, PROF, UNIV ALTA, 86- *Personal Data:* b Mendota, Ill, June 27, 44; m 80; c 1. *Educ:* St Thomas Col, BS, 66; Marquette Univ, MS, 69, PhD(physiol), 70. *Concurrent Pos:* Dir, Pulmonary Lab, Univ Hosp, 73-; sci assoc, Royal Alexandria Hosp, 77- *Mem:* Sigma Xi; Am Physiol Soc; Am Col Chest Physicians; NY Acad Sci; Can Soc Clin Invest. *Res:* High frequency ventilation; regional lung function; exercise training in patients with lung disease. *Mailing Add:* Univ Alta Edmonton AB T6G 2B7 Can

JONES, RICHARD THEODORE, MEDICINE, BIOCHEMISTRY. *Current Pos:* from asst prof to assoc prof exp med & biochem, 61-66, PROF BIOCHEM & CHMN DEPT, MED SCH, UNIV ORE, 66- *Personal Data:* b Portland, Ore, Nov 9, 29; m 53; c 3. *Educ:* Univ Ore, BS, 53, MS & MD, 56; Calif Inst Technol, PhD(chem), 61. *Prof Exp:* Intern med, Hosp Univ Pa, 56-57. *Concurrent Pos:* Former mem biochem comt, Nat Bd Med Examrs; med scientist, Training Comt, Nat Inst Gen Med Serv; mem, Biochem Training Comt, NIH, Med Scientist Training Comt, Sickle Cell Ctr Rev Comt & Blood Res Rev Group; actg pres, Univ Ore Health Sci Ctr, 77-78, spec consult to pres, 78-79. *Mem:* Am Soc Hemat; Int Soc Hemat; Am Fedn Clin Res; Am Soc Biol Chemists. *Res:* Medical and biochemical genetics, structure and function of normal and abnormal hemoglobins and other human proteins. *Mailing Add:* Dept Biochem Ore Health Sci Univ L224 3181 SW San Jackson Park Rd Portland OR 97201. *Fax:* 503-494-8393

JONES, RICHARD VICTOR, SOLID STATE PHYSICS. *Current Pos:* from asst prof to assoc prof appl physics, Harvard Univ, 57-71, assoc dean div eng & appl physics, 69-71, dean grad sch arts & sci, 71-72, PROF APPL PHYSICS, HARVARD UNIV, 71- *Personal Data:* b Oakland, Calif, June 8, 29; c 3. *Educ:* Univ Calif, AB, 51, PhD(physics), 56. *Hon Degrees:* MA, Harvard, 61. *Prof Exp:* Sr engr, Shockley Semiconductor Lab, Beckman Instruments, Inc, 55-57. *Concurrent Pos:* Guggenheim fel, 60-61; vis MacKay Prof, Univ Calif, Berkeley, 67-68. *Mem:* Inst Elec & Electronics Engrs. *Res:* Optical physics and electromagnetic phenomena; electronic and optical materials; ceramics; theory and application of magnetism and ferroelectricity. *Mailing Add:* 21 Kensington Rd Arlington MA 02174. *E-Mail:* jones@deas.harvard.edu

JONES, ROBERT ALLAN, OPTICAL FABRICATION, COMPUTER CONTROLLED MANUFACTURING. *Current Pos:* CONSULT, 95- *Personal Data:* b Guilford, Conn, Feb 25, 38; m 60; c 2. *Educ:* Union Col, BS, 59; Syracuse Univ, MS, 64. *Honors & Awards:* Dennis Gabor Award, Soc Photo-Optical Instrumentation Engrs, 85; Eng Excellence Award, Optical Soc Am, 89; Advan Technol Award, Litton Corp, 90. *Prof Exp:* Physicist, Rome Air Develop Ctr, 60-64; sr staff engr, Perkin-Elmer Corp, 64-84; prin engr, Itek Optical Systs, 84-95. *Mem:* Fel Optical Soc Am; Sigma Xi. *Res:* Directing the fabrication of large aspheric optics using advanced equipment and techniques; developing new fabrication processes by conducting analyses, computer simulations and experiments; author of numerous technical publications; awarded three patents. *Mailing Add:* One Melissa Dr Westford MA 01886

JONES, ROBERT CHARLES, DESIGN OF DISPLAYS, DESIGN OF ASPHERICAL ASYMMETRIC LENSES FOR COLOR TELEVISIONS. *Current Pos:* PROG MGR, FIDELITY TECHNOL CORP, 92-, ENGR, 96- *Personal Data:* b Pottsville, Pa, Dec 11, 38; div; c Eric C & Jared R. *Educ:* Lehigh Univ, BSEE, 61; Drexel Univ, MSEE, 65. *Prof Exp:* Sr engr, Philco-Ford Corp, Philadelphia, 61-70; Syst design engr, Univac-Sperry Rand Corp, 70-72; mgr optical design eng, Gen Elec Co, Syracuse, NY, 72-87, syst engr, Valley Forge, Pa, 87-89, consult, China, 89-91. *Mem:* Optical Soc Am. *Res:* Front end design and process development of new state of the art color cathode ray tubes; directed technical personnel and initiated product research and development on a variety of consumer electronic products; fabrication of electron guns for CRTs. *Mailing Add:* 2501 Kutztown Rd Reading PA 19605-2961. *Fax:* 610-921-9446

JONES, ROBERT CLARK, OPTICS. *Current Pos:* RETIRED. *Personal Data:* b Toledo, Ohio, June 30, 16; m 38, 77. *Educ:* Harvard Univ, AB, 38, AM, 39, PhD(physics), 41. *Honors & Awards:* Lomb Medal, Optical Soc Am, 44, Frederic Ives Medal, 72; Thomas Young Medal & Prize, Brit Inst Physics, 77. *Prof Exp:* Mem tech staff, Bell Tel Labs, 41-44; sr physicist, Polaroid Corp, 44-67, res fel physics, 67-82. *Mem:* Fel Optical Soc Am; fel Acoust Soc Am; fel Soc Photog Sci & Eng (vpres, 59-63); fel Am Acad Arts & Sci. *Res:* Theoretical physics; theoretical optics; detectivity and detective quantum efficiency of radiation detectors; theoretical models of photographic films; theory of absorption of light by developed photographic films. *Mailing Add:* 1716 Cambridge St Apt 27 Cambridge MA 02138

JONES, ROBERT EDWARD, PHYSICS. *Current Pos:* RETIRED. *Personal Data:* b Yonkers, NY, Jan 14, 23; m 48; c 2. *Educ:* Oberlin Col, BA, 48; Univ Mich, MA, 49; Pa State Univ, PhD(physics), 53. *Prof Exp:* Res asst eng res, Ionosphere Res Lab, Pa State Univ, 52-53, instr physics, 53-54, assoc prof & actg dir, 54-55; assoc prof, Linfield Col, 55-63, from actg head to head dept, 56-74, chmn, Div Natural Sci & Math, 74-79, prof, 63-87, emer prof physics, Linfield Col, 87. *Concurrent Pos:* Physicist, Linfield Res Inst, 56-, actg dir, 65-68; physicist, Field Emission Corp, 61-63. *Mem:* AAAS; Am Asn Physics Teachers; Optical Soc Am. *Res:* Physics of the upper atmosphere. *Mailing Add:* 915 NW Sunnywood Ct McMinnville OR 97128

JONES, ROBERT F, GENERAL SURGERY, SURGICAL ONCOLOGY. *Current Pos:* RETIRED. *Personal Data:* b Dallas, Tex, Dec 30, 26; m 53, Jerri Monnier; c 4. *Educ:* Univ Tex, Dallas, MD, 52; Am Bd Surg, cert, 64. *Prof Exp:* Res fel surg, Univ Tex Southwestern Med Sch, Dallas, 55, USPHS fel, 62-63; from instr to assoc prof, Univ Tex Health Sci Ctr, Dallas, 63-74; from assoc prof to prof surg, Med Sch, Univ Wash, 74-92. *Concurrent Pos:* Fel surg oncol, MD Anderson Hosp, Houston, 61-62; Am Cancer Soc advan clin fel, 63-66; NIH res fel, Rosnell Park Mem Inst, Buffalo, 67-68. *Mem:* Am Col Surgeons; Am Soc Clin Oncol; Am Asn Cancer Educ; Am Cancer Soc; Soc Surg Oncol. *Res:* Viral and surgical oncology; tumor immunology; clinical cancer. *Mailing Add:* 20105 SE 32nd St Issaquah WA 98029. *Fax:* 425-391-1827

JONES, ROBERT JAMES, CROP PHYSIOLOGY, AGRONOMY. *Current Pos:* asst prof corn physiol, 78-80, ASSOC PROF ENTOM, FISHERIES & WILDLIFE, UNIV MINN, 80- *Personal Data:* b Dawson, Ga, June 10, 51; m 70; c 1. *Educ:* Ft Valley State Col, BS, 73; Univ Ga, MS, 75; Univ Mo, PhD(crop physiol), 78. *Prof Exp:* Soil conservationist, Soil Conserv Serv, 70-73. *Mem:* Crop Sci Soc Am; Am Soc Agron; Am Soc Plant Physiologists. *Res:* Corn physiology; major interest in the relationship between photosynthesis and dark respiration during plant ontogeny and as affected by nutritional and environmental stress factors. *Mailing Add:* Dept Agron Univ Minn Rm 411 Borlaug Hall 1991 Upper Bufford Cir St Paul MN 55108-6024. *Fax:* 612-625-1268

JONES, ROBERT L, SOIL MINERALOGY. *Current Pos:* Res assoc, 62-64, from asst prof to assoc prof, 64-73, PROF SOIL MINERAL & ECOL, UNIV ILL, URBANA, 73- *Personal Data:* b Wellston, Ohio, Jan 26, 36; m 58; c 3. *Educ:* Ohio State Univ, BSc, 58, MSc, 59; Univ Ill, PhD(soil mineral), 62. *Mem:* Am Soc Agron; Mineral Soc Am; Soc Environ Geochem Health. *Res:* Soil mineral analysis techniques; applied mineralogy in soil genesis studies; biogeochemistry. *Mailing Add:* Dept Agron Univ Ill Urbana IL 61801. *E-Mail:* r-jones9@uiuc.edu

JONES, ROBERT LEROY, human biology, physiology & health psychophysiology, for more information see previous edition

JONES, ROBERT MILLARD, SOLID MECHANICS. *Current Pos:* dir, Composite Mat & Struct Ctr, 85-87, PROF ENG SCI & MECH, VA POLYTECH INST & STATE UNIV, 81- *Personal Data:* b Mattoon, Ill, Aug 8, 39; m 63, Donna Thomas; c Mark, Karen & Christopher. *Educ:* Univ Ill, Urbana, BS, 60, MS, 61, PhD(theoret & appl mech), 64. *Prof Exp:* Instr theoret & appl mech, Univ Ill, Urbana, 63-64; mem tech staff, Aerospace Corp, 64-70; assoc prof solid mech, Inst Technol, Southern Methodist Univ, 70-74, prof, 75-81. *Concurrent Pos:* Consult, Lockheed Missile & Space Co, 76 & 79, USAF Mat Lab, 71-79, Boeing, 80, Bell Helicopter, 85, Atlantic Res, 86-87, Health Techn, 87 & TRW, 93. *Mem:* Assoc fel Am Inst Aeronaut & Astronaut; Am Acad Mech; fel Am Soc Mech Engrs; Am Soc Composites. *Res:* Shell buckling; shell stress analysis; mechanics of composite materials; finite element; stress analysis of axisymmetric solids. *Mailing Add:* Eng Sci & Mech Dept Va Polytech Inst & State Univ Blacksburg VA 24061-0219. *E-Mail:* rmjones@vt.edu

JONES, ROBERT SIDNEY, marine biology, ichthyology, for more information see previous edition

JONES, ROBERT THOMAS, AERONAUTICAL ENGINEERING. *Current Pos:* RETIRED. *Personal Data:* b Macon, Mo, May 28, 1910; m 64; c 6. *Hon Degrees:* ScD, Univ Colo, 71. *Honors & Awards:* Reed Award, Inst Aeronaut Sci, 46; Inventions & Contrib Award, NASA, 75; Langley Medal, Smithsonian Inst, 81; Prandtl Ring Award, Ger Soc Aviation & Astronaut; President's Award Distinguished Fed Civil Serv; Excalibur Award, US Cong; Fluid Dynamics Prize, Am Phys Soc, 86. *Prof Exp:* Aeronaut res scientist, NACA, Langley Field, Va, 34-46, res scientist, Ames Res Ctr, NACA-NASA, Moffett Field, Calif, 46-62; sr staff scientist, Avco-Everett Res Lab, Everett, Mass, 62-70; sr staff scientist, NASA, Ames Res Ctr, Calif, 70-81, res assoc, 81-96; staff mem, Stanford Univ, 86-96. *Concurrent Pos:* Consult prof, Stanford Univ, 81. *Mem:* Nat Acad Sci; Nat Acad Eng; hon fel Am Inst Aeronaut & Astronaut; fel Am Acad Arts & Sci. *Res:* High speed wing theory. *Mailing Add:* 25005 La Loma Dr Los Altos Hills CA 94022

JONES, ROBERT WILLIAM, GEOLOGY. *Current Pos:* from instr to asst prof, 58-66, ASSOC PROF GEOL, UNIV IDAHO, 66- *Personal Data:* b Seattle, Wash, Jan 20, 27; m 53; c 3. *Educ:* Univ Wash, Seattle, BS, 50, MS, 57, PhD(geol), 59. *Prof Exp:* Ground water geologist, US Geol Surv, 51-55. *Mem:* Geol Soc Am; Am Asn Petrol Geol; Nat Asn Geol Teachers; Int Asn Volcanology; Sigma Xi. *Res:* Petrology and structure of igneous and metamorphic rocks. *Mailing Add:* 1414 E First St Moscow ID 83843

JONES, ROBERT WILLIAM, HIGH ENERGY LASERS, FREE ELECTRON LASERS. *Current Pos:* res physicist, US Army Missile Command, 71-83, proj engr, 83-86, chief, Free Electron Laser Div, Ground Based Laser Proj, Off, 86-88, CHIEF, LASER SENSOR DIV, AOA PROJ OFF, US ARMY STRATEGIC DEFENSE COMMAND, 88- *Personal Data:* b Dyersburg, Tenn, Sept 7, 44; m 69; c 1. *Educ:* Univ Ala, BA, 67, MS, 72, PhD(physics), 83. *Prof Exp:* Physicist, Teledyne-Brown Eng, 68-70; teaching asst physics, Univ Ala, Huntsville, 70-71. *Concurrent Pos:* Consult, Eng Math Co, 79-88; instr, Univ Ala, Huntsville, 85-86; chmn, Systems Eng & Tech Assistance Task Force, US Army Strategic Defense Command, 90- *Mem:* Optical Soc Am; Sigma Xi. *Res:* High energy repetitively pulsed and continuous wave lasers; resonator design and transverse mode formation; free electron laser. *Mailing Add:* 807 Argonne Terr SE Huntsville AL 35802-3650

JONES, ROBIN L(ESLIE), PHYSICAL METALLURGY, MATERIALS ENGINEERING. *Current Pos:* proj mgr, Elec Power Res Inst, 78-80, prog mgr nuclear systs & mat, 80-85, sr prog mgr, Corrosion Control, 85-93, dir, Mat & Chem Dept, 93-95, VPRES NUCLEAR POWER, ELEC POWER RES INST, 95- *Personal Data:* b Stanley, Eng, May 19, 40; m 65; c 1. *Educ:* Cambridge Univ, BA, 62, MA, 66, PhD(metall), 66. *Prof Exp:* Sr res metallurgist, Res Labs, Franklin Inst, 66-71, group leader, Metall Lab, 71-72; mgr metall prog, SRI Int, 72-78. *Mem:* Am Soc Mech Engrs; Nat Asn Corrosion Engrs; Am Inst Mining, Metall & Petrol Engrs; Am Soc Testing & Mat. *Res:* Physical and mechanical metallurgy, particularly the relations between mechanical properties and fine microstructure; fracture mechanics; ductile fracture of metallic materials; corrosion; environmentally assisted fracture of metals and ceramics; corrosion cracking damage in nuclear power plant materials. *Mailing Add:* Elec Power Res Inst 3412 Hillview Ave Palo Alto CA 94303

JONES, ROBIN RICHARD, PATHOLOGY, BIOCHEMISTRY. *Current Pos:* Spec instr, Univ Ark, 65-69, from asst prof to assoc prof path, 67-88, asst prof med technol, 74-76, PROF PATH, MED SCH, UNIV ARK, 88- *Personal Data:* b Little Rock, Ark, Oct 18, 37. *Educ:* Univ Ark, BS, 61, MD, 62, MS, 66, PhD(biochem), 67. *Mem:* Sigma Xi. *Res:* Vitamin E deficiency; muscular dystrophy; interactive videodisc in pathology education. *Mailing Add:* UAMS 4301 W Markham St Slot 517 Little Rock AR 72205-7101

JONES, ROGER, BOTANY. *Current Pos:* From asst prof to assoc prof, 67-85, PROF BIOL, TRENT UNIV, 85- *Personal Data:* b Kimbolton, Herefordshire, Eng, Mar 19, 40; m 65; c 2. *Educ:* Univ Wales, BSc, 62, PhD(ecol), 67; Kans State Univ, MSc, 64. *Mem:* Brit Ecol Soc; Soc Int Limnol. *Res:* Plant ecology; paleolimnology. *Mailing Add:* Dept Biol Trent Univ PO Box 4800 Peterborough ON K9J 7B8 Can

JONES, ROGER ALAN, NUCLEIC ACID CHEMISTRY. *Current Pos:* from asst prof to assoc prof, 77-88, PROF CHEM, RUTGERS UNIV, 88- *Personal Data:* b York, Pa, Mar 25, 47; div; c 1. *Educ:* Univ Del, BS, 69; Univ Alta, PhD(chem), 74. *Honors & Awards:* Fac Res Award, Am Cancer Soc, 86-91. *Prof Exp:* NIH fel, Dept Chem, Mass Inst Technol, 75-76. *Mem:* AAAS; Am Chem Soc. *Res:* Synthesis and characterization of modified and/or isotopically labelled oligonucleotides to study DNA polymorphism. *Mailing Add:* Dept Chem Rutgers Univ Piscataway NJ 08854

JONES, ROGER C(LYDE), ELECTRICAL ENGINEERING, PLASMA PHYSICS. *Current Pos:* actg dir, Appl Res Lab, Univ Ariz, 64-65, adj prof radiol, 78-87, prof elec eng, 64-89, prof radiation-oncol, 87-89, EMER PROF, UNIV ARIZ, 89- *Personal Data:* b Lake Andes, SDak, Aug 17, 19; m 52; c 2. *Educ:* Univ Nebr, BS, 49; Univ Md, MS, 53, PhD, 63. *Prof Exp:* Electronic engr, Naval Res Lab, 49-50, electronic scientist, 50-57; sr staff engr, Melpar Inc, Westinghouse Air Brake Co, 57-58, consult proj engr, Antenna & Radiation Systs Lab, 58-59, head physics sect, Phys Sci Lab, 59-64, chief scientist physics, Electronics-Physics Res Ctr, 64. *Concurrent Pos:* Guest prof, Kraeftforskningsinstituttet, Aarhus, Denmark, 82-83. *Mem:* Fel AAAS; Am Phys Soc; sr mem Inst Elec & Electronics Engrs; Optical Soc Am; Bioelectromagnetics Soc. *Res:* General physical electronics; infrared engineering; gas and solid state lasers; hyperthermia; bioelectromagnetics. *Mailing Add:* 5809 E Third St Tucson AZ 85711-1519

JONES, ROGER FRANKLIN, REINFORCED THERMOPLASTICS, THERMOPLASTICS ALLOYS. *Current Pos:* PRES, FRANKLIN POLYMERS, INC, 89- *Personal Data:* b Philadelphia, Pa, Oct 31, 30; m 53, Caryl J Reisgen; c Ellen (Starliper), Evan R & Mitchell R. *Educ:* Haverford Col, BS, 52. *Honors & Awards:* Honor Scroll, Am Inst Chemist, 72. *Prof Exp:* Process eng, E I DuPont De Nemours Co, Inc, 52-54; lieutenant, US Navy, 55-58; develop engr, Atlantic Refining Co, 58-60; sr staff supvr polymer res, Avisun Corp, 60-67; pres & gen mgr, LNP Corp, 67-81; chmn & pres, Inolex Chem Co, 81-83; prin, Concord Assocs Mgt Consults, 83-84; managing dir eng plastics, BASF Corp, 84-89. *Concurrent Pos:* Group mgr chem, Beatrice Foods Co, 76-81. *Mem:* Am Inst Chemists (vchmn 80-81, secy, 81-84); Am Chem Soc; Soc Chem Indust; fel Soc Plastics Engrs; Sigma Xi. *Res:* The development of novel reinforced and modified thermoplastic composites; surfactants and polymer intermediates. *Mailing Add:* Franklin Polymers Inc Four Kenny Circle Broomall PA 19008

JONES, ROGER L, ERGODIC THEORY, MARTINGALES. *Current Pos:* From asst prof to assoc prof, 74-84, PROF MATH, DEPAUL UNIV, 84- *Personal Data:* b Holland Patent, NY, June 2, 49; m 74. *Educ:* State Univ NY, Albany, BS, 71; Rutgers Univ, PhD(math), 74. *Mem:* Am Math Soc; Math Asn Am. *Res:* Classical harmonic analysis and its application to problems in ergodic theory and probability; maximal inequalities. *Mailing Add:* DePaul Univ 2219 Kenmore Chicago IL 60614-3504

JONES, ROGER STANLEY, HIGH ENERGY PHYSICS. *Current Pos:* ASSOC PROF PHYSICS, UNIV MINN, MINNEAPOLIS, 67- *Personal Data:* b New York, NY, June 17, 34; m 56; c 2. *Educ:* City Col New York, BS, 55; Univ Ill, MS, 57, PhD(physics), 61. *Prof Exp:* Res assoc physics, Univ Ill, 61-62; USAF Off Sci Res fel, Nat Comt Nuclear Energy Labs, Frascati, 62-63; from asst physicist to assoc physicist, Brookhaven Nat Lab, 64-67. *Mem:* Am Phys Soc; Sigma Xi. *Res:* High energy experimental physics and elementary particle physics; epistemology and symbolism of physics. *Mailing Add:* Dept Physics Univ Minn Minneapolis MN 55455

JONES, RONALD DALE, computer science, for more information see previous edition

JONES, RONALD GOLDIN, ORGANIC CHEMISTRY. *Current Pos:* from asst prof to assoc prof, 61-67, PROF ORG CHEM, GA STATE UNIV, 67- *Personal Data:* b Yorkville, Ga, Nov 29, 33; m 57, Sara E Sanford; c Laurilyn D. *Educ:* Emory Univ, BA, 55, MS, 57; Ga Inst Technol, PhD(org chem), 61. *Prof Exp:* Chem prod develop & qual control, Southern Latex Corp, Ga, 51-55. *Mem:* Am Chem Soc; Sigma Xi. *Res:* Applications of nuclear magnetic resonance spectroscopy in organic chemistry and polysaccharides of microbial origin; organic reaction mechanisms. *Mailing Add:* Ga State Univ University Plaza Atlanta GA 30303. *Fax:* 404-651-1416

JONES, RONALD MCCLUNG, PHYSIOLOGICAL ECOLOGY, RESPIRATORY PHYSIOLOGY. *Current Pos:* FEL PHYSIOL, DARTMOUTH MED SCH, HANOVER, 78- *Personal Data:* b Palo Alto, Calif, May 6, 51; m 74; c 1. *Educ:* Swarthmore Col, BA, 72; Univ Calif, Riverside, PhD(biol), 78. *Mem:* AAAS; Am Inst Biol Sci; Am Soc Zool; Sigma Xi. *Res:* Physiological ecology of vertebrates. *Mailing Add:* 13175 Franklin Ave Mountain View CA 94040

JONES, ROSEMARY C, PULMONARY DISEASE. *Current Pos:* ASST PROF PATH, SCH MED, HARVARD UNIV, 80- *Personal Data:* b Caerleon, Wales, UK, Dec 26, 41. *Educ:* Univ London, PhD(exp path), 80. *Mailing Add:* Mass Gen Hosp 149 13th St Charlestown MA 02129-2060. *Fax:* 617-726-4176

JONES, ROY CARL, JR, MATHEMATICS. *Current Pos:* ASST PROF MATH, FLA TECHNOL UNIV, 69- *Personal Data:* b New York, NY, Aug 3, 39; m 64; c 4. *Educ:* Case Inst Technol, BS, 62; Western Res Univ, MS, 64, PhD(math), 66. *Prof Exp:* Asst prof, Univ Fla, 66-69. *Mem:* Am Math Soc; Math Asn Am. *Res:* Approximation theory, characterizing and finding best uniform or Tchebycheff approximations; numerical methods including developing algorithms or iterative procedures that converge to the best approximations. *Mailing Add:* Dept Math Univ Cen Fla Box 25000 Orlando FL 32816-0001

JONES, RUFUS SIDNEY, MEMBRANE SCIENCE & TECHNOLOGY, ELECTRO-OPTICALLY ACTIVE POLYMERS. *Current Pos:* RETIRED. *Personal Data:* b Warrenton, NC, May 9, 40; m 68, Martha E Ownbey; c Laura R. *Educ:* Duke Univ, BS, 62; Purdue Univ, PhD(org chem), 68. *Prof Exp:* Res chemist, Celanese Corp, 68-72, sr res chemist, 72-80, res assoc, 81-82, qual adminr, 82-83, proj leader/res supvr, 83-87; prog mgr, Hoechst Celenese Corp, 88-89, dir, Technol & Bus Develop, 90-97. *Mem:* Am Chem Soc; NAm Membrane Soc. *Res:* Synthesis, characterization, and application of novel polymers for use in devices and systems which rely upon a unique functional polymer property rather than a structural property; materials for optical data storage; gas and liquid separations. *Mailing Add:* 123 Mountainside Dr Randolph NJ 07869. *Fax:* 704-588-7393

JONES, RUSSEL C(AMERON), CIVIL ENGINEERING. *Current Pos:* UNIV RES PROF, UNIV DEL, 87- *Personal Data:* b Tarentum, Pa, Oct 18, 35; m 58. *Educ:* Carnegie Inst Technol, BS, 57, MS, 60, PhD(sci of mat), 64. *Prof Exp:* Struct designer, Hunting, Larsen & Dunnels Engrs, Pa, 57-59, assoc engr, Missiles & Space Systs Div, Douglas Aircraft Co, 60; asst prof civil eng, Mass Inst Technol, 63-66, assoc prof, 66-71; prof & chmn dept, Ohio State Univ, 71-77; dean, Sch Eng, Univ Mass, 77-81; vpres acad affairs, Boston Univ, 81-87. *Mem:* AAAS; Am Soc Eng Educ; Nat Soc Prof Engrs; Metall Soc; Am Soc Testing & Mat. *Res:* Science of materials; composite materials; building systems; housing; construction management; engineering education. *Mailing Add:* Univ Res Prof Univ Del 360 A Dupont Hall Newark DE 19716. *Fax:* 302-831-6504

JONES, RUSSELL HOWARD, MATERIALS SCIENCE, METALLURGY. *Current Pos:* sr res scientist, 73-80, staff scientist metall, 80-90, MGR STRUCT RES SEC SCIENTIST, PAC NORTHWEST LAB, BATTELLE MEM INST, 90- *Personal Data:* b Oakland, Calif, July 7, 44; m 68; c 3. *Educ:* Calif State Polytech Col, BS, 67; Univ Calif, Berkeley, MS, 68, PhD(metall), 71. *Prof Exp:* Engr metall, Westinghouse Elec Corp, 71-73. *Mem:* Am Soc Metals; Am Inst Mining, Metall & Petrol Engrs; Mat Res Soc; Electrochem Soc. *Res:* High temperature alloys; radiation damage and stress corrosion; ceramic and metal matrix composites. *Mailing Add:* Pattelle Northwest Lab PO Box 999 MSIN P8-15 Richland WA 99352. *Fax:* 509-376-0418

JONES, RUSSELL K, VETERINARY PUBLIC HEALTH. *Current Pos:* RETIRED. *Personal Data:* b Port Chester, NY, Aug 17, 22; m 49; c 4. *Educ:* Cornell Univ, DVM, 45; Purdue Univ, PhD(path), 54. *Prof Exp:* From instr to assoc prof, Agr Exp Sta, Sch Vet Sci & Med, Purdue Univ, 48-60, assoc prof path, 60-65, prof vet path, 65-88. *Mem:* Am Vet Med Asn; Conf Res Workers Animal Dis. *Res:* Diagnostics, including microbiology and pathology; zoonoses. *Mailing Add:* 1707 Fernleaf Dr West Lafayette IN 47906

JONES, RUSSELL LEWIS, PLANT PHYSIOLOGY. *Current Pos:* from asst prof to assoc prof, 66-74, PROF PLANT BIOL, UNIV CALIF, BERKELEY, 74- *Personal Data:* b Dyserth, Wales, May 10, 41; c 3. *Educ:* Univ Col Wales, BSc, 62, PhD(bot), 65. *Prof Exp:* AEC fel, Mich State Univ-AEC Plant Res Lab, 65-66. *Concurrent Pos:* Peer panel mem, adv, Panel Develop Biol, NSF, 70-73; assoc ed, Annual Rev Plant Physiol, 72-; Guggenheim Mem Found fel, 72-73; Miller res prof, Univ Calif, Berkeley, 75-76, chmn, Col Letters & Sci Comt on Courses, 76-79, actg chmn, Dept Instruction Biol, 77-78, mem exec comt, Miller Inst Basic Res, 77-81, chmn dept bot, 81-86, mem comt res, 81-, chmn, Col Letters & Sci Comt Res, 83-84; actg dir, Univ Calif Herbarium, 82-83; mem, Plant Growth & Develop Panel, USDA CRGO, 84-86, prog mgr, 87-88; Alexander von Humbolt sr scientist, Univ Göttingen, Fed Repub Ger, 86-87; mem, Life sci Peer Rev Panel, NASA, 87-; Life Sci Div Working Group, 88- *Mem:* Am Soc Plant Physiol; Int Plant Growth Substances Asn. *Res:* Biochemistry and physiology of the action of gibberellic acid and calcium. *Mailing Add:* Dept Plant Biol Univ Calif 345 Mulford Hall Berkeley CA 94720-0001

JONES, RUSSELL STINE, PATHOLOGY. *Current Pos:* DIR LABS, DEPT PATH, IMPERIAL POINT MED CTR, FT LAUDERDALE, 72- *Personal Data:* b Corvallis, Ore, June 5, 14; m 40; c 8. *Educ:* Univ Ore, MD, 40; Am Bd Path, dipl, 48. *Prof Exp:* Intern, Ancker Hosp, Minn, 40-41; resident path, Hosp & Clins, Univ Ore, 41-44; from instr to asst prof, Col Med, Univ Tenn, 47-52; assoc prof, Med Sch, Univ Ore, 52-54; prof, Col Med, Univ Utah, 54-66, dir clin labs, 60-66; prof path, Univ Mo-Kansas City, 66-70; dir labs, Dept Path, Providence Hosp, Ore, 70-72. *Concurrent Pos:* Dir labs, WTenn Tuberc Hosp, Memphis, 48-52; consult, Vet Admin Hosp, Memphis, 48-52. *Mem:* Am Asn Cancer Res; Am Rheumatism Asn; Am Soc Clin Pathologists; Am Asn Blood Banks; Int Acad Path. *Res:* Arthritis and rheumatic diseases; experimental tumors; adrenal steroids; scurvy; mycoplasmal infections; activation analysis; radiobiology. *Mailing Add:* 6401 N Federal Hwy Ft Lauderdale FL 33308-1405

JONES, SAMUEL B, JR, BOTANY, HORTICULTURE. *Current Pos:* CO-OWNER, PICCADILLY FARM PERENNIAL NURSERY, 91- *Personal Data:* b Roswell, Ga, Dec 18, 33; m 55; c 3. *Educ:* Auburn Univ, BS, 55, MS, 61; Univ Ga, PhD(bot), 64. *Honors & Awards:* Silver Shield Award, Nat Coun State Garden Clubs. *Prof Exp:* Teacher, SCobb High Sch, 58-59; instr bot, Auburn Univ, 59-61; asst prof, Univ Southern Miss, 64-67; from asst prof to prof bot, Univ Ga, 67-91, dir, Bot Garden, 81-84. *Concurrent Pos:* NSF res grants; Calloway Found res grant. *Mem:* Garden Writers Asn Am; Am Soc Plant Taxonomists; Am Asn Nurserymen. *Res:* Systematics of higher plants; landscaping with native plants; flora of southeastern United States; the genus Hosta (Liliacene); shade gardening; perennials. *Mailing Add:* 1971 Whippoorwill Rd Bishop GA 30621

JONES, SAMUEL O'BRIEN, chemistry, chemical engineering; deceased, see previous edition for last biography

JONES, SAMUEL STIMPSON, PHYSICAL CHEMISTRY. *Current Pos:* RETIRED. *Personal Data:* b Buckingham Co, Va, Apr 9, 23. *Educ:* Hampden-Sydney Col, BS, 43; Cornell Univ, PhD(phys chem), 50. *Prof Exp:* Chemist, Manhattan Proj, Monsanto Chem Co, 44-46; res assoc phys chem, Knolls Atomic Power Lab, Gen Elec Co, 50-57, radiation chemist, Vallecitos Atomic Lab, 57-61, radiation effects specialist, Defense Syst Dept & Electronics Lab, 61-63 & tech specialist, Hanford Labs, 63-65; res assoc Pac Northwest Lab, Battelle Mem Inst, Wash, 65-70; sr staff res scientist, Ctr Technol, Kaiser Aluminum & Chem Corp, 70-81; mgr carbon & mat res, 81-83, indust carbon consult, Anaconda Aluminum Co & Arco Metals Co, 83, Allied Signal, 84-96, R&D Carbon, Switz, 84-96. *Mem:* AAAS; Am Chem Soc; NY Acad Sci; Am Carbon Soc. *Res:* Radiochemistry; complex ions; radiation chemistry; radiation effects on electronic materials; graphite physics and chemistry; chemistry and physics of carbon. *Mailing Add:* PO Box 43698 Tucson AZ 85733

JONES, SANFORD L, REPRODUCTIVE ENDOCRINOLOGY. *Current Pos:* RETIRED. *Personal Data:* b Bulan, Ky, Sept 22, 25; m 56; c 3. *Educ:* Eastern Ky State Col, BS, 50; Univ Ky, MS, 56; Univ Tenn, PhD(physiol, biochem), 60. *Prof Exp:* Secondary teacher, Perry Co Schs, Ky, 50-55; res assoc physiol, Univ Tenn, 60-61; from asst prof to prof biol, Eastern Ky Univ, 61-92, chmn dept, 79-92. *Mem:* Am Soc Zool; Sigma Xi. *Res:* Effects of antithyroid compounds on metabolism of thyroxine; absorption of iodinated compounds in amphibians and reptiles; radioimmunoassay of luteinizing hormone. *Mailing Add:* 204 Bristol Dr Richmond KY 40475

JONES, SHARON LYNN, NEUROPHARMACOLOGY, NEUROANATOMY. *Current Pos:* ASST PROF PHARMACOL, UNIV OKLA, 90- *Personal Data:* b Pasadena, Calif, Dec 19, 60. *Educ:* Univ NMex, BS, 83; Univ Iowa, PhD(pharmacol), 87. *Mem:* Soc Neurosci; Int Asn Study Pain; Am Pain Soc; Sigma Xi. *Res:* Organization and function of endogenous pain suppression systems that modulate spinal nociceptive transmission by using anatomical, pharmacological and physiological techniques. *Mailing Add:* Dept Pharmacol Univ Okla PO Box 26901 Oklahoma City OK 73126-0901

JONES, STANLEY B, MEDICAL ADMINISTRATION. *Current Pos:* CONSULT HEALTH POLICY, 89- *Personal Data:* b July 27, 38. *Educ:* Dartmouth Col, BA, 60. *Prof Exp:* From staff mem to assoc dir, Div Computer Res & Technol, HEW, NIH, 64-69, chief, Planning Systs Br & dir, Off Mgt Policy, Health Serv & Ment Health Admin, 69-71; prog develop officer, Inst Med-Nat Acad Sci, 77-78; founding partner, Fullerton, Jones & Wolkstein, Health Policy Alternatives, 78-80 & 83-86; vpres, Wash Representation, Blue Cross & Blue Shield Asn, 80-83; pres, Consol Consult Group & vpres, Consol Healthcare, Inc, 86-89. *Concurrent Pos:* Fel, Inst Soc, Ethics & Life Sci, Hastings Ctr, 78-89; mem, Robert Wood Johnson Fel Bd & Bd Ment Health & Behav Med, Inst Med-Nat Acad Sci, 80-86, DC Gen Hosp Comn, 85-87 & Robert Wood Johnson Rev Comt Prog Promote Long-Term Care Ins Elderly, 88; chmn, Ad Hoc Comt Educ Health Professionals & Invitational Workshop Utilization Mgt, Inst Med-Nat Acad Sci, 87 & Panel Long Range Planning Dis Res, 89; dir, Health Ins Reform Proj, George Wash Univ, 94- *Mem:* Inst Med-Nat Acad Sci. *Res:* Author of various publications on health care administration. *Mailing Add:* PO Box 1847 Shepherdstown WV 25443-1848

JONES, STANLEY BENNETT, GEOPHYSICS. *Current Pos:* RETIRED. *Personal Data:* b San Francisco, Calif, Jan 14, 22; m 46; c 2. *Educ:* Univ Calif, PhD(physics), 50. *Prof Exp:* Physicist, Radiation Lab, Univ Calif, 48-50; res physicist oil field res, Chevron Oil Field Res Co, 50-58, sect supvr, Well Logging & Basic Prod Sect, 58-63, sect supvr, Geophys Sect, 63-68, mgr, Geophys Div, Chevron Oil Field Res Co, 68-76, mgr, Develop & Implementation Div, Chevron Geosci Co, 77-78, geophys res consult, Chevron Oil Field Res Co, 79-80, mgr, Systs & Eng Serv Div, Chevron Oil Field Res Co, 81-85; assoc dir tech servs, Soc Explor Geophysicists, 85-89. *Mem:* Am Phys Soc; Am Geophys Union; Soc Explor Geophys; Europ Asn Explor Geophys; Soc Explor Geophysicists (vpres, 84-85). *Res:* Cosmic rays; meson physics; oil well logging, oil producing and geophysics research. *Mailing Add:* 7823 California Ave Whittier CA 90602-2708

JONES, STANLEY C(ULVER), CHEMICAL ENGINEERING, PERMEABILITY MEASUREMENT. *Current Pos:* CONSULT, WESTERN ATLAS LOGGING SERV, 94- *Personal Data:* b Spokane, Wash, Aug 31, 33; m 57, Barbara Larson; c 3. *Educ:* Wash State Univ, BSE, 56; Univ Mich, MSE, 59, PhD(chem eng), 62. *Honors & Awards:* Advan Technol Achievement Award, Litton Ind, 92; Henry Mattson Tech Serv Award, Soc Petrol Engrs, 89. *Prof Exp:* Engr, Kaiser Aluminum & Chem Corp, 56-58; adv res engr, Denver Res Ctr, Marathon Oil Co, 62-71, sr res scientist, 71-75, res assoc, 75-86; res & develop dept, Core Labs, 86-94. *Mem:* Soc Petrol Engrs; Sigma Xi; Am Inst Chem Engrs; Soc Core Analysts. *Res:* Anodizing processes for aluminum alloys; behavior of a pulsed extraction column; movement of water through aquifers in contact with natural gas; secondary and tertiary oil recovery processes; reservoir rock properties; petroleum production. *Mailing Add:* 875 Front Range Rd Littleton CO 80120

JONES, STANLEY E, APPLIED MATHEMATICS, ENGINEERING MECHANICS. *Current Pos:* RES PROF, UNIV ALA, 91- *Personal Data:* b Mt Vernon, NY, July 20, 39; m 94, Barbara A Evans; c Lara E & Robert T. *Educ:* Univ Del, BA, 63, MS, 66, PhD(appl sci), 67. *Honors & Awards:* Siam lectr, 83. *Prof Exp:* Prof eng mech, Univ Ky, 67-87; dept head Eng Mech, Univ Ala, 87-89; distinguished vis prof, USAF Acad, 89-91. *Concurrent Pos:* Vis prof, Univ Iowa, 69 & Ga Inst Tech, 79-80; consult, Marshall Space Flight Ctr, NASA, 70, USAF, Eglin AFB, Fla, 81-, NSF, 83 & Nat Water Resources Inst, 84; lectr, Naval Surface Weapons Ctr, 94. *Mem:* Am Soc Mech Engrs; Am Soc Mech. *Res:* Fluid transients, plasticity analysis and nonlinear mechanics; co-author one book and author of approximately 100 research papers. *Mailing Add:* Dept Aerospace & Eng Mech Univ Ala Tuscaloosa AL 35487-0278. *Fax:* 205-348-8573

JONES, STANLEY LESLIE, ANALYTICAL CHEMISTRY. *Current Pos:* RETIRED. *Personal Data:* b Waltham, Mass, Mar 22, 19; m 48, Anna B Ames; c Cheryl, Ronald, Marion, Arthur & Peter. *Educ:* Tufts Col, BS, 41, MS, 47; Harvard Univ, AM, 49, PhD(anal chem), 51. *Prof Exp:* Res chemist drying oils, Bird & Son, Inc, 41-42; jr chemist chem anal, US Navy Yard, Mass, 42-44; res chemist, Merck & Co, Inc, 50-55; appl res chemist, Knolls Atomic Power Lab, Gen Elec Co, 55-60, consult chemist, 60-81. *Mem:* Am Chem Soc; AAAS; Sigma Xi. *Res:* Analytical research; colloid science. *Mailing Add:* 1413 Fox Hollow Rd Schenectady NY 12309-2509

JONES, STANLEY TANNER, PHYSICS. *Current Pos:* From asst prof to assoc prof, 70-83, PROF PHYSICS, UNIV ALA, 83-, ASST DEAN, COL ARTS & SCI, 99- *Personal Data:* b Palo Alto, Calif, Mar 10, 45; m 77, Charlotte Horton; c Patrick, Tanner & Laurie (Norwierski). *Educ:* Stanford Univ, BS, 66; Univ Ill, Urbana, MS, 68, PhD(physics), 70. *Mem:* Am Phys Soc. *Res:* Elementary particle physics. *Mailing Add:* Dept Physics Univ Ala PO Box 870324 Tuscaloosa AL 35487-0324. *Fax:* 205-348-9642; *E-Mail:* sjones@as.ua.edu

JONES, STEPHEN BENDER, CIRCULATORY, MEDICAL EDUCATION. *Current Pos:* res assoc physiol, 75-76, asst prof, 76-82, ASSOC PROF, STRITCH SCH MED, LOYOLA UNIV, CHICAGO, 82- *Personal Data:* b Lansing, Mich, Oct 19, 45; m 70; c 3. *Educ:* Cent Mich Univ, BS, 67, MS, 69; Univ Mo-Columbia, PhD(physiol), 75. *Prof Exp:* Teaching asst biol, Cent Mich Univ, 67-68, asst instr, 68-69, instr, 69-71. *Concurrent Pos:* Vis prof, NRC, Ottawa, Can, 71, Dept Pharmacol, Univ Melbourne, Australia, 87. *Mem:* Sigma Xi; Am Physiol Soc; Shock Soc. *Res:* Neural control of circulation in developing control; control of peripheral neurotransmitter; plasma catacholamines. *Mailing Add:* Dept Physiol Burn Shock Trauma Inst Loyola Univ Med Ctr 2160 S First Ave Maywood IL 60153. *Fax:* 708-327-2813

JONES, STEPHEN THOMAS, ORGANIC CHEMISTRY. *Current Pos:* Res chemist, Lorillard, Inc, 68-70, supvr prod develop, 70-72, mgr prod develop, 72-77 & opers & planning, 77-83, dir mkt res, 83-92, DIR PROD DEVELOP, LORILLARD, INC, 92- *Personal Data:* b Washington, DC, Feb 12, 42; m 63, Wanda Aldridge; c Scott R. *Educ:* E Carolina Univ, AB, 64; Emory Univ, PhD(org chem), 68. *Mem:* Am Chem Soc. *Res:* Steroid synthesis; syntheses of hydroazulenes; syntheses of heterocyclic compounds; tobacco chemistry. *Mailing Add:* Lorillard Res Ctr PO Box 21688 Greensboro NC 27420

JONES, STEPHEN WALLACE, NEUROSCIENCES. *Current Pos:* ASST PROF PHYSIOL, DEPT PHYSIOL, CASE WESTERN RES UNIV, CLEVELAND, OHIO, 86- *Personal Data:* b Steubenville, Ohio, Nov 7, 53. *Educ:* Mich State Univ, BS, 74; Cornell Univ, PhD(neurobiol), 80. *Prof Exp:* Assoc teaching fel muscular dystrophy, Dept Neurobiol & Behav, Cornell Univ, 79-82; teaching fel NIH, Dept Neurobiol & Behav, State Univ NY, Stony Brook, 82-84, res asst prof, 84-86. *Concurrent Pos:* Lectr neurobiol, Cornell Univ, 81. *Mem:* Biophys Soc; Soc Neurosci; AAAS. *Res:* Electrophysiology and pharmacology of vertebrate neurons, primarily in autonomic ganglia; voltage-clamp analysis of voltage-dependent currents and of the actions of neurotransmitters. *Mailing Add:* Dept Physiol & Biophys Case Western Reserve Univ Cleveland OH 44106. *Fax:* 219-368-5586

JONES, STEVEN WAYNE, MEMBRANE RECEPTOR BIOCHEMISTRY, SIGNAL TRANSDUCTION MECHANISMS. *Current Pos:* DIR MOLECULAR BIOL, CORTECH, INC, 88- *Personal Data:* b Glenwood Springs, Colo, Nov 12, 53; m 79, Paula J Hoisington; c Harrison W & Benjamin J. *Educ:* Western Ill Univ, BS, 77; Univ Nebr, PhD(biochem), 83. *Prof Exp:* Fel, Leopold Schepp Found, 83-84, Harvard Univ, 83-88 & NIH, 84-87. *Mem:* AAAS; fel Am Soc Microbiol; Protein Soc; fel Am Asn Biochem & Molecular Biol; fel Fedn Am Soc Exp Biol. *Res:* G protein-linked membrane receptors that are implicated in human diseases; signal transduction events associated with these receptors; discovery of novel, human therapeutics. *Mailing Add:* 4317 W 110th Pl Westminster CO 80030. *Fax:* 303-650-1217; *E-Mail:* sjones@.cortech.com

JONES, SUSAN MURIEL, EPITHELIAL TRANSPORT, RENAL HORMONES. *Current Pos:* CONSULT, PROBLEM-SOLVING INSTRNL MAT PROJ, NSF, 91-; PROF PHARM, HIST, ANAT & PHYSIOL, TOURO COL, DIX HILLS, NY, 91- *Educ:* State Univ NY, PhD(pharmacol), 78. *Prof Exp:* Asst prof, Med Col, Cornell Univ, 87-91. *Mem:* Am Physiol Soc; NY Acad Sci. *Mailing Add:* 57 Windmill Ct Huntington Station NY 11746

JONES, T(HOMAS) BENJAMIN, ELECTRICAL ENGINEERING. *Current Pos:* RETIRED. *Personal Data:* b Madison, Md, Aug 26, 12; m 47; c 2. *Educ:* Johns Hopkins Univ, BE, 33, Dr Eng, 37. *Prof Exp:* Asst instr elec eng, Johns Hopkins Univ, 36-37; mem tech staff, Bell Tel Lab, NY, 37-41; foreign wire rels engr, C & P Tel Co, Md, 41-44, personnel supvr, 44-45, commercial mgr, 45-46; from asst prof to assoc prof elec eng, Johns Hopkins Univ, 46-56; mem tech staff, Bell Tel Labs, 56-58, tech supvr, 58-67, dielectrics specialist, 67-73; sr assoc, Trident Eng Assocs, 73-88. *Concurrent Pos:* Proj engr bur ships, US Navy, 46-50, res contract dir, Off Naval Res, 48-54; res contract dir, Army Ord Corps, 54-56; consult, E I du Pont de Nemours & Co, Inc, 54-56. *Mem:* Inst Elec & Electronics Engrs. *Res:* Dielectrics and insulation; electrical capacitors; electrical discharges, arcs and welding; electrical measurements; oxidation of impregnated paper insulation. *Mailing Add:* 5309 River Crescent Dr Annapolis MD 21401

JONES, TAPPEY HUGHES, CHEMICAL ECOLOGY, MICRO ANALYTICAL ORGANIC CHEMISTRY. *Current Pos:* STAFF FEL RES, LAB BIOPHYS CHEM, NAT HEART, LUNG & BLOOD INST, BETHESDA, MD, 87- *Personal Data:* b Norfolk, Va, June 6, 48. *Educ:* Va Mil Inst, BS, 70; Univ NC, PhD(org chem), 74. *Prof Exp:* Postdoctoral fel res, Chem Dept, Cornell Univ, 75-77; asst prof teaching & res, Chem Dept, Furman Univ, 77-79; postdoctoral fel res, Entom Dept, Univ Ga, Athens, 79-81; asst prof teaching & res, Chem Dept, US Naval Acad, 81-85; asst prof teaching & res, Chem Dept, Col William & Mary, 85-87. *Mem:* Am Chem Soc. *Res:* Over 64 publications, with more than 50 of them in the area of insect natural products; venom chemistry of myrmicine ants; developed a number of structure proof methods and syntheses for micro-scale organic analysis. *Mailing Add:* Dept Chem Va Mil Inst Lexington VA 24450-0304

JONES, THEODORE CHARLES, GENETICS, BIOCHEMISTRY. *Current Pos:* CONSULT, 79-; BIOLOGIST, ENVIRON PROTECTION AGENCY, 79- *Personal Data:* b Pittsburgh, Pa, Nov 9, 39; m 62; c 2. *Educ:* Amherst Col, AB, 61; Univ Wash, PhD(genetics), 67. *Prof Exp:* Fel, Univ Wis, 67-69; asst prof biol, Amherst Col, 69-72, Mt Holyoke Col, 72-79. *Mem:* Genetics Soc Am; Am Soc Microbiol; Sigma Xi. *Res:* Regulation of enzyme synthesis and enzyme localization in microorganisms. *Mailing Add:* 201 First St SW V234 Washington DC 20024-4267

JONES, THEODORE HAROLD DOUGLAS, BIOCHEMISTRY, MICROBIOLOGY. *Current Pos:* from asst prof to assoc prof, 70-82, PROF CHEM, UNIV SAN FRANCISCO, 82- *Personal Data:* b Belfast, North Ireland, Oct 30, 38; m 76, Jeanie Schmit. *Educ:* Univ Edinburgh, BSc, 59; Mass Inst Technol, PhD(biochem), 66. *Prof Exp:* Res asst biochem, Detroit Inst Cancer Res, 59-61; Damon Runyon Fund Cancer Res fel, Harvard Med Sch, 66-68; NIH traineeship aging res, Retina Found, 68-70. *Concurrent Pos:* Damon Runyon fel. *Mem:* NY Acad Sci; AAAS. *Res:* Biochemistry of differentiation, particularly events occurring during germination of spores of the cellular slime molds; biochemistry of membrane proteins and their changes during differentiation; clinical enzymology; peptide hormones in microorganisms; processing of peptide hormones. *Mailing Add:* Dept Chem Univ San Francisco San Francisco CA 94117-1080

JONES, THEODORE SIDNEY, petroleum geology; deceased, see previous edition for last biography

JONES, THOMAS CARLYLE, VETERINARY PATHOLOGY, COMPARATIVE PATHOLOGY. *Current Pos:* clin assoc, Med Sch, Harvard Univ, 57-63, assoc clin prof path, 63-71, prof comp path, New Eng Regional Primate Res Ctr, Harvard Med Sch, 71-82, EMER PROF COMP PATH, HARVARD UNIV, 82- *Personal Data:* b Boise, Idaho, Sept 29, 12; wid; c 3. *Educ:* Wash State Univ, BS & DVM, 35. *Hon Degrees:* DSc, Ohio State Univ, 70. *Prof Exp:* Officer in chg, US Army Vet Res Lab, Front Royal Qm Depot, Va, 39-46, chief vet path sect, Armed Forces Inst Path, Washington, DC, 46-50, chief vet dept, Army Med Field Lab, Heidelberg, Ger, 50-53, chief vet path sect, Armed Forces Inst Path, 53-57; dir dept path, Angell Mem Animal Hosp, Boston, 57-67. *Concurrent Pos:* Master res, Grad Coun, George Washington Univ, 47-51; res assoc path, Cancer Res Inst, New Eng Deaconess Hosp, 57-67; consult, Armed Forces Inst Path, 58- & Nat Cancer Inst, 61-62; mem comt path training, Nat Inst Gen Med Sci, 60-63; mem comt animal health, Nat Acad Sci-Nat Res Coun, 62-65; mem consult staff, Peter Bent Brigham Hosp, Boston, 62-78; mem adv comt animal resources, NIH, 65-68; mem vis comt sch vet med, Tufts Univ, 83-87. *Mem:* Am Vet Med Asn; Am Col Vet Pathologists (secy-treas, 48-50 & 53-60, pres, 62-63); Am Asn Path; Int Acad Path (pres, 70-71); Conf Res Workers Animal Dis. *Res:* Genetics and cytogenetics applied to disease in animals. *Mailing Add:* 1301 Arenal Ct Santa Fe NM 87501

JONES, THOMAS EVAN, analytical chemistry, inorganic chemistry, for more information see previous edition

JONES, THOMAS HUBBARD, PHYSICAL CHEMISTRY, LIGHT-SENSITIVE MATERIALS. *Current Pos:* PROJ LEADER, ILL TOOL WORKS, ITW TECHNOL CTR, GLENVIEW, 90- *Personal Data:* b Batavia, Ill, June 8, 36; m 58; c 2. *Educ:* Augustana Col, Ill, BA, 58; Univ Minn, Minneapolis, PhD(phys chem), 63. *Prof Exp:* Res chemist, Photo Prod Res Lab, E I Du Pont de Nemours & Co, Inc, 63-69; proj chemist, Richardson Co, Melrose Park, 69-78, res supvr, 78-80, res assoc, 80-82; sr chemist, Turtle Wax Inc, Chicago, 84-86; sr chemist, London Chem Co, Bensenville, Ill, 86-90. *Mem:* Am Chem Soc. *Res:* Photopolymerization; applications of polymers and photopolymers in printed circuit resists. *Mailing Add:* 1032 Douglas Ave Naperville IL 60540-4320

JONES, THOMAS S, GENERAL EARTH SCIENCES. *Current Pos:* PHYS SCIENTIST, US GEOL SURV, 96- *Personal Data:* b Oakland, Md, Nov 11, 29; m 55, Diane Stavridis; c 3. *Educ:* Univ Ill, BS, 50, MS, 51; Pa State Univ, PhD(metall), 61. *Prof Exp:* Res asst metall, Gen Elec Res Lab, 51-56; res assoc, Pa State Univ, 61-62; sr res metallurgist, Allegheny Ludlum Res Ctr, 62-70; staff metallurgist, US Bur Mines, 71-74, phys scientist, 74-96. *Mem:* Am Inst Mining Metall & Petrol Engrs. *Res:* Phase equilibria in metal and oxide systems at high temperatures; kinetics of reduction in metallurgical systems; steelmaking. *Mailing Add:* 4212 Braeburn Dr Fairfax VA 22032. *Fax:* 703-648-7757

JONES, THOMAS SCOTT, NONDESTRUCTIVE TESTING, NDT OF COMPOSITE MATERIALS & STRUCTURES. *Current Pos:* sr nondestruct testing eng, 87-89, mgr res & eng, 89-92, VPRES, INDUST QUAL INC, 92- *Personal Data:* b Newport News, VA, May 30, 53; m 75, D Diane Glass; c Kristine M & Heather S. *Educ:* Va Polytechnic Inst & State Univ, BS, 75, MS, 77. *Honors & Awards:* Charles W. Briggs Award, Am Soc Testing Mat, 97. *Prof Exp:* From engr to lead engr, McDonnell Aircraft Co, 77-87. *Concurrent Pos:* Chmn, Aerospace Comn, Am Soc Nondestruct Testing, 89-91, E07.02 Ref Radiol Images, Am Soc Testing Mats, 90-93, E07.06 Ultrasonic Method, 92-; secy, E-7 Nondestructive Testing, Am Soc Testing & Mat Comt. *Mem:* Fel Am Soc Nondestructive Testing; Soc Advan Mat & Process Eng; Int Soc Optical Eng; Am Soc Testing & Mats. *Res:* Nondestructive testing technology; research and development of ultrasonic characterization of materials; simulation of radiographic imaging and infrared thermography applications. *Mailing Add:* 640 E Diamond Ave Suite C Gaithersburg MD 20877-5323. *Fax:* 301-948-9037; *E-Mail:* tsjones@indqual.com

JONES, THOMAS V, RESEARCH ADMINISTRATION. *Current Pos:* RETIRED. *Personal Data:* b Pomona, Calif, July 21, 20. *Educ:* Stanford Univ, BS, 42. *Hon Degrees:* LLD, George Washington, 67. *Honors & Awards:* Reed Aeronaut Award, Am Inst Aeronaut & Astronaut, 85; Wright Bros Mem Trophy, Nat Aeronaut Asn, 89. *Prof Exp:* Tech adv, Brazilian Air Ministry, Rio de Janeiro, 47-51; mem staff, Rand Corp, 51-53; asst to chief engr, Northrop Corp, 53-58, sr vpres develop planning, 58-59, pres, 59-60, chief exec officer, 60-89, chmn bd, 63-90, mem, Bd Dirs, 90-91. *Concurrent Pos:* Prof & dept head, Aeronaut Inst Technol, Brazil, 51-53; mem bd dirs, MCA, Inc; chmn bd govs, Aerospace Indust Asn, 85. *Mem:* Nat Acad Eng; Aerospace Indust Asn; hon fel Am Inst Aeronaut & Astronaut. *Mailing Add:* 650 N Sepulveda Blvd Los Angeles CA 90049

JONES, THOMAS WALTER, THEORETICAL ASTROPHYSICS. *Current Pos:* from asst prof to assoc prof, 78-84, CHMN, DEPT ASTRON, 81-, PROF ASTRON, UNIV MINN, 84- *Personal Data:* b Odessa, Tex, June 22, 45; m 68, Karen G Cronquist; c Walter B. *Educ:* Univ Tex, Austin, BS, 67; Univ Minn, MS, 69, PhD(physics), 72. *Prof Exp:* Asst res physicist, Univ Calif, San Diego, 72-75; asst scientist, Nat Radio Astron Observ, 75-77, assoc scientist, 77. *Mem:* Am Astron Soc; Int Astron Union; Sigma Xi; Royal Astron Soc. *Res:* Studies of physical processes in cosmic radio and infrared sources; active galaxies and quasars; numerical hydrodynamics; supernova remnants; cosmic rays. *Mailing Add:* Dept Astron Univ Minn Minneapolis MN 55455. *Fax:* 612-626-2029; *E-Mail:* twj@ast1.spa.umn.edu

JONES, TIMOTHY ARTHUR, NEUROPHYSIOLOGY. *Current Pos:* ASSOC PROF, SCH MED, UNIV MO, COLUMBIA, 94- *Educ:* Univ Calif, PhD(physiol), 80. *Prof Exp:* From asst prof to assoc prof physiol, Univ Nebr, Lincoln, 82-94, assoc prof, Dept Spec Educ & Commun Dis, 88-94. *Concurrent Pos:* NASA res assoc award, Stanford Univ, 80 & 81; fac fel, Army Equip Feng Estab, NASA, 88 & 90; mem, Comn Gravitational Physics, Int Union Psychol Sci. *Res:* Ontogeny of sensory systems; gravitational physiology. *Mailing Add:* 207 Allton Bldg De375 Dept Surg & Physiol Univ Mo Med Sch Columbia MO 65212

JONES, TODD KEVIN, MEDICAL CHEMISTRY, SYNTHETIC METHODS IN ORGANIC CHEMISTRY. *Current Pos:* ASST DIR MED CHEM, LIGAND PHARACEUT, 92- *Personal Data:* b Denver, Colo; m 80. *Educ:* Colo Sch Mines, Golden, BS, 80; Univ Ill, Urbana, PhD(org chem), 85. *Prof Exp:* NIH fel, Harvard Univ, 85-87; sr res chemist, Merck Res Labs, 87-91, res fel, 91-92. *Mem:* Am Chem Soc; AAAS. *Res:* Synthesizing small organic molecules that interact with intracellular receptors. *Mailing Add:* Ligand Pharaceut 9393 Towne Centre Dr Suite 100 San Diego CA 92121

JONES, TREVOR O, ENGINEERING. *Current Pos:* chmn bd, 87-94, pres & chief exec officer, 93-94, MEM BD DIRS, LIBBEY-OWENS-FORD, 94-; CHMN & CHIEF EXEC OFFICER, INT DEVELOP CORP, 94- *Personal Data:* b Maidstone, Eng; m, Jennie. *Honors & Awards:* Hooper Mem Prize, Brit Inst Elec Engrs, 50; Arch T Colwell Award, Soc Automotive Engrs, 74 & 75, Vincent Bendix Automotive Electronics Eng Award, 76, Buckendale Lectr, 86 & Edward N Cole Automotive Eng Award, 88; Safety Award Eng

Excellence, US Dept Transp, 78; H H Bliss Award, 91. *Prof Exp:* Dir, Delco Electronics Div, Gen Motors, 59-70, Automotive Electronic Control Systs, 70-72, Advan Prod Eng, 72-74, Gen Motors Proving Ground, 74-78; vpres eng, Automotive Worldwide Sector, TRW Inc, 78-79, group vpres & gen mgr, Transp Electronics Group, 79-85, group vpres strategic progs, Automotive Worldwide Sector, 85, group vpres sales & mkt, 85-87. *Concurrent Pos:* Mem, Safety Res for a Changing Hwy Environ Comt, Nat Acad Eng, Nat Interests in an Age of Global Technol Comt; pres, Int Develop Corp; mem, Nat Motor Vehicle Safety Adv Coun, 71-, vchmn, 72; mem, Nat Hwy Safety Adv Comt, 75-78, chmn, 78; mem, Transp Res Bd Comt, Nat Res Coun. *Mem:* Nat Acad Eng; fel Brit Soc Elec Engrs; fel Am Inst Elec & Electronics Engrs; fel Soc Automotive Engrs; Brit Inst Elec Engrs. *Res:* Automotive safety and electronics; granted several patents. *Mailing Add:* Int Develop Corp Orangewood Pl Suite 450 3690 Orange Pl Beachwood OH 44122

JONES, ULYSSES SIMPSON, JR, SOIL FERTILITY, ATMOSPHERIC CHEMISTRY & PHYSICS. *Current Pos:* head, Dept Agron & Soils, 60-71, prof, 71-83, EMER PROF AGRON & SOILS, CLEMSON UNIV, 83- *Personal Data:* b Portsmouth, Va, Feb 14, 18; m 41, Ann G Plummer; c Josephine (Allen). *Educ:* Va Polytech Inst, BS, 39; Purdue Univ, MS, 42; Univ Wis, PhD(soils), 47. *Prof Exp:* Asst, Purdue Univ, 39-42; chemist, F S Royster, 42; asst, Univ Wis, 46-47; assoc prof, Miss State Univ, State Col Miss, 47-53; agronomist, Olin Corp, 53-60. *Concurrent Pos:* Head, Dept Phys Sci, Univ Florence, Italy, 45; guest prof, Oak Ridge Inst Nuclear Studies, 50 & Univ Ark, 52; consult, A G Edwards, 62, J P Stevens, 75, Blount Int, 83, UN Develop Prog, 83 & Gilbert, 88-93; Fulbright lectr, Aegean Univ, 76-77, Univ Zimbabwe, 86-87 & Estonian Agr Univ, 93; vis prof, Univ Philippines, 79-80; vis scientist, Int Rice Res Inst, 80; dir, Rural Develop Inst, Cuttington Univ, Liberia, W Africa, 83-85; prof chem, Little Rock Univ. *Mem:* Fel Soil Sci Soc Am; fel Am Soc Agron; Am Chem Soc; Entom Soc Am. *Res:* Availability of phosphates in soils; soil acidity and organic matter; limestone availability to crops and reaction in soil; use of radioactive elements for soil and fertilizer studies; insecticide and fertilizer mixtures for leaf feeding and pest control; trends in sulfur supply in air, rainwater and soil; environmental impact and monitoring of acid precipitation. *Mailing Add:* 111 Strawberry Lane Clemson SC 29631. *Fax:* 864-656-3443

JONES, VERNON DOUGLAS, PHARMACOLOGY. *Current Pos:* ATTORNEY AT LAW, 75- *Personal Data:* b Florence, Ala, July 15, 37; m 61; c 1. *Educ:* Florence State Univ, BA, 58; Vanderbilt Univ, PhD(pharmacol), 64; Univ NMex, JD, 74. *Prof Exp:* NIH fel pharmacol, Sch Med, Vanderbilt Univ, 64-65; NIH fel, Med Col, Cornell Univ, 65-67; asst prof pharmacol, Sch Med, Univ NMex, 67-71, asst prof psychiat, 71-73, clin assoc, Dept Psychiat, 73-, pharmacologist, Ment Health Ctr, 73- *Res:* Drugs in criminal and civil law. *Mailing Add:* 1400 Central SE Suite 3100 Albuquerque NM 87106

JONES, VICTOR ALAN, FOOD ENGINEERING, FOOD SCIENCE. *Current Pos:* From asst prof to prof, 62-93, EMER PROF FOOD ENG, NC STATE UNIV, 93- *Personal Data:* b Fremont, Mich, Feb 24, 30; m 54; c 4. *Educ:* Mich State Univ, BS, 52, MS, 59, PhD(agr eng), 62. *Concurrent Pos:* Vis prof, Ore State Univ, 71. *Mem:* Am Soc Agr Engrs; Inst Food Technologists; Am Dairy Sci Asn; Sigma Xi. *Res:* Unit operations and control for ultrahigh temperature pasteurization or sterilization of foods; packaging materials and equipment. *Mailing Add:* 618 Richard Dr Cary NC 27513

JONES, WALTER H(ARRISON), CHEMISTRY. *Current Pos:* from assoc prof to prof aeronaut syst, 69-75, dir, Corpus Christi Ctr, 69-75, PROF CHEM, UNIV WFLA, 75- *Personal Data:* b Griffin, Sask, Sept 21, 22; US citizen; wid. *Educ:* Univ Calif, Los Angeles, BS, 44, PhD(phys org chem), 48. *Prof Exp:* Res assoc, Univ Calif, Los Angeles, 48; chemist, Western Regional Res Lab, USDA, 48-51 & Los Alamos Sci Lab, 51-54; sr res engr, NAm Aviation, Inc, 54-56; mgr, Chem Dept, Aeronutronic Div, Ford Motor Co, 56-60; panel chmn, Inst Defense Anal, 60-63; head, Propulsion Dept, Aerospace Corp, 63-64; sr scientist & head adv tech, Hughes Aircraft Co, 64-68. *Concurrent Pos:* Chmn, Thermochem Panel, Joint Army-Navy-Air Force-Adv Res Proj Agency, NASA, 60-62; consult, Fla Energy Comt & Solar Energy Ctr, 74-79, Eng Soc Comn Energy, 82-83 & Naval Surface Weapons Ctr, 82-; vis prof, Univ Toronto, 78-79 & 94; consult, Eng Soc Comn Energy, 82-83 & Naval Surface Weapons Ctr, 82-; vis res chemist, Univ Calif, Los Angeles, 94- *Mem:* Am Chem Soc; fel Am Inst Chemists; NY Acad Sci; AAAS; Int Solar Energy Soc; World Asn Theoret Org Chemists. *Res:* Chemical kinetics; polymer chemistry; thermodynamics; combustion; propulsion; missile and space systems analysis and engineering; energy systems analyses; quantum chemistry; chemistry at high pressures. *Mailing Add:* 355 Calle Loma Norte Santa Fe NM 87501. *Fax:* 850-474-3130

JONES, WAYNE E, PHOTOCHEMISTRY, PHOTOINDUCED ELECTRON TRANSFER. *Current Pos:* ASST PROF, STATE UNIV NY, BINGHAMTON, 93- *Personal Data:* b Springfield, Mass, June 25, 65; m 88, Michele L Brault; c Meghan & Erin. *Educ:* St Michael's Col, BS, 87; Univ NC, Chapel Hill, PhD, 91. *Prof Exp:* Teaching asst, Univ NC, Chapel Hill, 87-88, res asst, 88-91; fel, Univ Tex, Austin, 92-93. *Mem:* Am Chem Soc; AAAS; Sigma Xi. *Mailing Add:* Dept Chem State Univ NY Binghamton NY 13902

JONES, WESLEY MORRIS, PHYSICAL CHEMISTRY. *Current Pos:* GUEST SCIENTIST & LAB AFFIL, 86- *Personal Data:* b Raymond, Wash, Apr 29, 19; m 54, Dorothy Frenz; c 3. *Educ:* Univ Calif, AB, 40, PhD(chem), 46. *Prof Exp:* Asst chem, Univ Calif, 40-42; staff mem, Los Alamos Nat Lab, 43-86. *Concurrent Pos:* Res fel, Calif Inst Technol, 57-58. *Mem:* Sigma Xi. *Res:* Low temperature specific heats; thermodynamics; gas kinetics; physical chemistry of tritium and hydrogen isotope effects; diffusion; thermochemical cycles for hydrogen production; plutonium environmental chemistry. *Mailing Add:* 4753 Sandia Dr Los Alamos NM 87544

JONES, WILBER CLARK, INORGANIC CHEMISTRY. *Current Pos:* From asst prof to assoc prof, 66-77, chmn, Physics Sci Dept, 74-94, PROF CHEM, CONCORD COL, 77- *Personal Data:* b Grove City, Pa, Jan 21, 41; m 62, Carolee Paul; c Wendy & Tracy. *Educ:* Westminster Col, Pa, BS, 62; Univ Tenn, PhD(chem), 66. *Mem:* Am Chem Soc. *Res:* Synthesis and structural studies on coordination compounds. *Mailing Add:* Dept Phys Sci Concord Col Athens WV 24712. *Fax:* 304-384-9044; *E-Mail:* jones@math.concord.wvnet.edu

JONES, WILBUR DOUGLAS, JR, BIOLOGY, CLASSIFICATION, IDENTIFICATION & GENETICS OF MYCOBACTERIA. *Current Pos:* RETIRED. *Personal Data:* b Augusta, Ga, July 3, 27; m 52, Buell Keith; c Wilbur K & Robert W. *Educ:* Emory Univ, AB, 49; WVa Univ, MS, 51; Med Col Ga, PhD(microbiol), 68. *Prof Exp:* Asst, WVa Univ, 51; instr sci, Truett-McConnell Jr Col, 51-53; bacteriologist, Ga State Health Dept, 53-60, chief bacteriologist, Training Lab, 60-62; res microbiologist, Ctr Dis Control, USPHS, 62-90. *Mem:* Am Soc Microbiol; fel Am Acad Microbiol. *Res:* Genetics and phage typing of the mycobacteria; genetics and molecular biology of the mycobacteriophages. *Mailing Add:* 4182 Smithfield Dr Tucker GA 30084

JONES, WILLIAM B, APPROXIMATION THEORY & NUMERICAL ANALYSIS. *Current Pos:* actg asst prof math, Univ Colo, 63-64, asst prof appl math, 64-68, assoc prof math, 68-73, assoc chmn dept, 72-74, chmn dept, 87-90, PROF MATH, UNIV COLO, BOULDER, 73- *Personal Data:* b Spring Hill, Tenn, Sept 24, 31; m 56, Martha Hadley; c 5. *Educ:* Jacksonville State Col, BA, 53; Vanderbilt Univ, MA, 55, PhD(math), 63. *Honors & Awards:* Gold Medal Award, US Dept Com, 65. *Prof Exp:* Mathematician, Nat Bur Stand, 58-63. *Concurrent Pos:* Consult, Nat Bur Stand, 64-65 & Environ Sci Servs Admin, 65-70; consult, Off Telecommun-Inst Telecommun Sci, 70-73, mathematician, 70-71; vis prof, Univ Kent, Canterbury, UK, 77; vis Fulbright prof, Univ Trondeim, Norway, 84-85, Fulbright res scholar, 91-92; Fulbright res-scholar award, 84-85; award grant, Norwegian Marshall Fund, 84-85. *Mem:* Am Math Soc; Math Asn Am; Soc Indust & Appl Math. *Res:* Numerical analysis; approximation theory; continued fractions; Pade Approximants; moment theory. *Mailing Add:* Univ Colo Boulder CO 80309-0395. *Fax:* 303-492-7707; *E-Mail:* wjones@euclid.colo.edu

JONES, WILLIAM B(ENJAMIN), JR, ELECTRICAL ENGINEERING. *Current Pos:* RETIRED. *Personal Data:* b Fairburn, Ga, Sept 17, 24; m 48, Mary Hammond; c William B III, Katherine P Boerstler & Joseph L. *Educ:* Ga Inst Technol, BS, 45, MS, 48, PhD(elec eng), 53. *Prof Exp:* Engr, radar develop, R I Sarbacher & Assoc, 47-48; from instr to assoc prof elec eng & res assoc, Ga Inst Technol, 48-54; res engr, Hughes Aircraft Co, 54-58; prof elec eng, Ga Inst Technol, 58-67; head dept, Tex A&M Univ, 67-84, prof elec eng, 67-90. *Concurrent Pos:* Vis prof, Univ Fla, 84-85. *Mem:* Sr mem Inst Elec & Electronics Engrs; Optical Soc Am; Am Soc Eng Educ. *Res:* Communications theory and systems; optical communication systems. *Mailing Add:* 43 Hyalite Rd Dahlonega GA 30533-8831

JONES, WILLIAM B, ASSISTIVE DEVICES FOR HANDICAPPED, POLYMER FRACTURE. *Current Pos:* CHIEF ENGR, B J ENTERPRISES, 89- *Personal Data:* b Littlefield, Tex, June 10, 37; m 56; c 6. *Educ:* Tex Tech Univ, BS, 59, MS, 60; Univ Utah, PhD(mech eng), 70. *Prof Exp:* Teaching asst mech eng, Tex Tech Univ, 59-60, assoc prof, 82-89; mem tech staff, Rocketdyne Div, Rockwell Int, 60-75; mat res engr, Wright AFB Aero Labs, 75-82. *Concurrent Pos:* Res asst mech eng, Univ Utah, 66-69; consult, Lockheed Propulsion Co, 67-69, Textron, Bell Helicopter, 74-75 & Fredrick R Harris, 78-79; lectr, Kent State Univ, 78-82 & Univ Calif, Los Angeles, 79-85. *Mem:* Adhesion Soc; Soc Aerospace Mat & Process Engrs; Am Chem Soc; Am Solar Energy Soc. *Res:* Fracture mechanics of polymers and adhesive joints; materials and processes for adhesives and advanced composite materials. *Mailing Add:* 1200 W 14th St Littlefield TX 79339

JONES, WILLIAM BARCLAY, physics, for more information see previous edition

JONES, WILLIAM DAVIDSON, INORGANIC CHEMISTRY, ORGANIC CHEMISTRY. *Current Pos:* PROF CHEM, UNIV ROCHESTER, 80- *Personal Data:* b Folsom, Pa, Oct. 26, 53; m 77; c 3. *Educ:* Mass Inst Technol, BS, 75; Calif Tech, PhD, 79. *Prof Exp:* Nat Sci Found Postdoctoral, chem, Univ Wis, Madison, 79-80. *Concurrent Pos:* Ap Sloan fel, Sloan Found, 84; Camille & Henry Dreyful fel, 85-88; Guggenheim fel, John S Guggenheim, 88; Fulbright fel, 88-89; Royal Soc fel, 88-89. *Mem:* Am Chem Soc. *Res:* Inorganic and organometallic chemistry; mechanism and thermodynamics of carbon-hydrogen bond activity by homogeneous transition metal complexes. *Mailing Add:* Dept Chem Univ Rochester Rochester NY 14627-0216

JONES, WILLIAM DENVER, RELATIVISTIC ELECTRON BEAMS. *Current Pos:* assoc prof, 70-72, PROF PHYSICS, UNIV SFLA, 72- *Personal Data:* b Jenkinjones, WVa, Apr 14, 35; div; c Mark A & Lisa G. *Educ:* Berea Col, BA, 58; Vanderbilt Univ, MA, 61, PhD(physics), 63. *Prof Exp:* Res assoc plasma physics, Thermonuclear Div, Oak Ridge Nat Lab, 63-70. *Concurrent Pos:* AEC & Energy Res Develop Admin res contracts, 71-76; Air Force Cambridge Res Labs contract, 72-74; consult, Solarkit Fla, Tampa, 75-80, Naval Res Lab, 84-86. *Mem:* Fel Am Phys Soc; Am Asn Physics Teachers; Sigma Xi. *Res:* Basic and applied research in plasmas; particularly pulsed power, applied research in alternative energy sources, with emphasis on solar energy. *Mailing Add:* Dept Physics Univ SFla Tampa FL 33620. *Fax:* 813-974-5813

JONES, WILLIAM ERNEST, PHYSICAL CHEMISTRY & SPECTROSCOPY, ATOMIC & MOLECULAR PHYSICS. *Current Pos:* ACAD VPRES & PROF CHEM, UNIV WINDSOR, 91- *Personal Data:* b Sackville, NB, Can; m 58, Norma Florence Reid; c Mary E, Jennifer A, Sarah A & K Martha. *Educ:* Mt Allison Univ, BSc, 58, MSc, 59; McGill Univ, PhD(phys chem), 63. *Prof Exp:* Res assoc, Mt Allison Univ, 59-60; from asst prof to prof phys chem, Dalhousie Univ, 62-89, chmn chem dept, 74-83, chmn Dalhousie Senate, 83-89; prof chem & dean sci, St Mary's Univ, 89-91. *Mem:* Chem Inst Can; Sigma Xi; Can Asn Physicists; Spectros Soc Can. *Res:* Kinetics; spectroscopy; surface chemistry; catalysis; gas phase kinetics of atoms and free radicals; atomic and molecular spectroscopy. *Mailing Add:* Acad VP Univ Windsor 401 Sunset Ave Windsor ON N9B 3P4 Can. *Fax:* 519-973-7070; *E-Mail:* wjones@uwindsor.ca

JONES, WILLIAM HOWRY, ORGANIC CHEMISTRY. *Current Pos:* RETIRED. *Personal Data:* b Lancaster, Pa, Nov 6, 20; m 59; c 4. *Educ:* Juniata Col, BS, 42; Columbia Univ, MA, 44; Mass Inst Technol, PhD(org chem), 47. *Prof Exp:* Lab asst chem, Juniata Col, 39-42; lab asst, Columbia Univ, 42-44, lectr, 43, asst, Manhattan Proj, SAM Labs, 44-45; asst, Anti-Malarial Proj, Mass Inst Technol, 45-46; Du Pont fel nuclear alkylation, Univ Ill, 47-48, instr chem, 48-49; res chemist, Merck Inc, 49-59, res assoc, Merck Sharp & Dohme Res Labs, 59-85. *Mem:* Am Chem Soc; fel NY Acad Sci. *Res:* Synthesis of physiologically active compounds; reaction mechanisms; synthesis of substituted diamines and quinoline derivatives; catalytic hydrogenation; high pressure research. *Mailing Add:* 115 Hazelwood Ave Metuchen NJ 08840-2112

JONES, WILLIAM J, ENGINEERING PHYSICS. *Current Pos:* SR STAFF RES ASSOC, ENERGY LAB, MASS INST TECHNOL, 72- *Personal Data:* b New York, NY, Mar 23, 15; m 42; c 3. *Educ:* Tufts Univ, BS, 41; Newark Col Eng, MS, 50. *Prof Exp:* Lectr physics, Harvard Univ, 63-72. *Res:* High energy physics; energy technologies issues and policies. *Mailing Add:* 92 Bullough Park Newton MA 02160

JONES, WILLIAM JONAS, JR, ORGANIC CHEMISTRY, TEXTILE FIBERS. *Current Pos:* Res chemist, E I du Pont de Nemours & Co Inc, 66-74, sr res chemist, 74-85, res assoc, 85-92, SR RES ASSOC, DACRON RES LAB, E I DU PONT DE NEMOURS & CO INC, 92- *Personal Data:* b Whaleyville, Va, Nov 18, 41; m 80, Annette Hudson. *Educ:* Col William & Mary, BS, 63; Duke Univ, PhD(org chem), 66. *Mem:* Am Chem Soc. *Res:* Heterocyclic organic compounds; polymers; chemistry of textile fibers; fiber engineering; polyester filling products. *Mailing Add:* 417 Falcon Circle Greenville NC 27834

JONES, WILLIAM MAURICE, SYNTHETIC INORGANIC & ORGANOMETALLIC CHEMISTRY. *Current Pos:* from asst prof to assoc prof, 56-65, chmn dept, 68-73, prof chem, 65-90, DISTINGUISHED SERV PROF, UNIV FLA, 90- *Personal Data:* b Campbellsville, Ky, Jan 12, 30; m 56; c 3. *Educ:* Union Univ, Tenn, BS, 51; Univ Ga, MS, 53; Univ Southern Calif, PhD(org chem), 55. *Prof Exp:* Instr chem, Univ Southern Calif, 55-56. *Concurrent Pos:* Sloan fel, 63-67; NATO sr sci fel, 71; mem ed bd, Chem Rev, 71-74, J Organic Chem, 74-79 & Petrol Res Fund Adv Bd, 86-93, chmn, 90-93. *Mem:* Am Chem Soc. *Res:* Mechanisms of organic reactions; strained allenes and their transition metal complexes; transition metal complexes of conjugated carbocyclic carbenes; transition metal organometallic rearrangements. *Mailing Add:* Dept Chem Univ Fla Gainesville FL 32611

JONES, WILLIAM PHILIP, EXPERIMENTAL NUCLEAR PHYSICS. *Current Pos:* Res assoc, 69-71, STAFF SCIENTIST PHYSICS, IND UNIV, BLOOMINGTON, 71- *Personal Data:* b Chicago, Ill, Oct 2, 42; m 64, Mary Ann Verbeeck; c Catherine M (Gottlieb) & Robert W. *Educ:* Univ Notre Dame, BS, 64; Univ Mich, MS, 65; PhD(physics), 69. *Mem:* Am Phys Soc; Sigma Xi; AAAS. *Res:* Medium energy nuclear physics; charged-particle reactions; properties of nuclear energy levels; cyclotron orbit dynamics; charged particle beam optics. *Mailing Add:* 308 S High St Bloomington IN 47401. *Fax:* 812-855-6645; *E-Mail:* jones@iucf.indiana.edu

JONES, WILLIAM VERNON, COSMIC PHYSICS, ASTROPHYSICS. *Current Pos:* Res assoc physics, La State Univ, Baton Rouge, 67, res instr, 69-70, from asst prof to prof physics & astron, 70-88, EMER PROF PHYSICS & ASTRON, LA STATE UNIV, BATON ROUGE, 88-; CHIEF SCIENTIST COSMIC & HELIOTROPHIC PHYSICS, NASA HQ, WASHINGTON, DC, 88- *Personal Data:* b Yellville, Ark, Jan 25, 35; m 55, Freda Daniel; c Rebecca L (Melancon), Donna K (Jones-Lorio) & Sharon L (Rivet). *Educ:* Univ Tulsa, BS, 63; La State Univ, Baton Rouge, PhD(physics), 67. *Prof Exp:* Guest res assoc, Max Planck Inst Extraterrestrial Physics, 67-68. *Concurrent Pos:* Alexander von Humboldt res stipend, 67-68; res physicist, Goddard Space Flight Ctr, NASA, 75-76; vis res scientist, Univ Tokyo Inst Cosmic Res, 81; vis sr scientist, Jet Propulsion Lab, 86-87, NASA Hq, 85-88. *Mem:* Am Inst Physics; Am Phys Soc; Am Geophys Union. *Res:* Electromagnetic cascade measurements; properties of high-energy nuclear interactions; Monte Carlo simulations of study nuclear cascade processes; cosmic ray composition and energy spectra; heliospheric physics. *Mailing Add:* Code SS Space Physics Div NASA Hq Washington DC 20546

JONES, WINTON D, JR, MEDICINAL CHEMISTRY, ORGANIC CHEMISTRY. *Current Pos:* SCIENTIST, HOECHST MARION ROUSSEL, 91- *Personal Data:* b Terre Haute, Ind, June 23, 41; m 64, Sandra Myrdock; c 2. *Educ:* Butler Univ, BS, 63, MS, 66; Univ Kans, PhD(med chem), 70. *Prof Exp:* Org chemist, Merrell-Dow Pharmaceut, Inc, Dow Chem Co, 80-91. *Concurrent Pos:* Cong sci consult, 79-80. *Mem:* Am Chem Soc. *Res:* Medicinal chemistry, antiallergic agents; synthesis of central nervous system, cardiotonic agents, antihypertensives, antiviral and anti-cancer agents. *Mailing Add:* Hoechst Marion Roussel 2110 Galbraith Rd Cincinnati OH 45215

JONES-LEE, REBECCA ANNE, AQUATIC TOXICOLOGY, WATER QUALITY. *Current Pos:* VPRES, G FRED LEE & ASSOCS, 89- *Personal Data:* b Menominee, Mich, Jan 23, 51. *Educ:* Southern Methodist Univ, BS, 73; Univ Tex, Dallas, MS, 75, PhD(environ sci), 78. *Honors & Awards:* Charles B Dudley Award, Am Soc Testing & Mat, 84. *Prof Exp:* Res asst prof civil eng, Colo State Univ, 78-81; coordr aquatic biol, Fluor Engrs, Irvine, Calif, 82; res assoc & lectr environ eng, Tex Tech Univ, Lubbock, 82-84; assoc prof environ eng, water qual & aquatic toxicol, NJ Inst Technol, 84-89. *Concurrent Pos:* Proj assoc, G Fred Leed & Assoc, 78- *Res:* Chemical and biological aspects of surface and groundwater supplies and quality; sources, significance and fate of chemical contaminants in the environment; chemical and biological aspects of water pollution control in surface and groundwaters, rivers, lakes, estuaries and the oceans. *Mailing Add:* G Fred Lee & Assocs 27298 E El Macero Dr El Macero CA 95618

JONG, ING-CHANG, SOLID MECHANICS. *Current Pos:* AT MECH ENG DEPT, UNIV ARK. *Personal Data:* b Yunlin, Taiwan, Feb 5, 38; US citizen; m 66; c David & Vida. *Educ:* Nat Taiwan Univ, BS, 61; SDak Sch Mines & Technol, MS, 63; Northwestern Univ, Evanston, PhD(theoret & appl mech), 65. *Prof Exp:* From asst prof to assoc prof eng sci, Univ Ark, Fayetteville, 65-74, prof, 74- *Concurrent Pos:* Prin investr, eng res initiation grant, NSF, 67-69, eng mech res grant, 69-71. *Mem:* Am Soc Mech Engrs; Am Soc Eng Educ; Am Acad Mech; Sigma Xi. *Res:* Nonconservative stability of damped structures; vibrations and dynamic stability of structural systems exhibiting yielding and hysteresis; senior author of three books. *Mailing Add:* 2684 Stanton Ave Fayetteville AR 72703. *Fax:* 501-575-6982; *E-Mail:* icj@engr.uark.edu

JONG, SHUNG-CHANG, MYCOLOGY. *Current Pos:* sr mycologist, Am Type Cult Collection, 69-71, cur fungi, 71-73, cur & head mycol & bot dept, 74-94, dir, Mycol & Protistol Prog, 94-96, DIR, MICROBIOL DIV, AM TYPE CULT COLLECTION, 97- *Personal Data:* b Taiwan, Nov 12, 36; US citizen; m 65, Chiu-Hwa; c Maria, Cynthia & Victoria. *Educ:* Nat Taiwan Univ, BS, 60; Western Ill Univ, MS, 66; Wash State Univ, PhD(mycol), 69. *Honors & Awards:* Agr Award Int Sci & Technol Cooperation, Ministry; J Roger Porter Award, 97 Agr, PR China, 88. *Prof Exp:* Asst plant pathologist, Taiwan Agr Res Inst, 61-63; asst instr mycol, Nat Taiwan Univ, 63-65. *Concurrent Pos:* Sci Found grants, 75- *Mem:* Brit Mycological Soc; Chinese Med & Health Asn; Int Soc Human & Animal Mycol; Med Mycol Soc Am; Mycol Soc Am; Int Asn Plant Tissue Culture; Int Mushroom Soc for Tropics; Int Soc Plant Molecular Biol; Japan Antibiotics Res Asn; Sigma Xi; Soc Fermentation Technol; US Fedn Culture Collections. *Res:* Preservation and industrial applications of living fungi; biology of fungi in culture. *Mailing Add:* Microbiol Div Am Type Cult Collection 12301 Parklawn Dr Rockville MD 20852

JONNARD, AIMISON, CHEMICAL ENGINEERING. *Current Pos:* CHIEF, ENERGY & CHEM DIV, US INT TRADE COMN, 71- *Personal Data:* b Sewanee, Tenn, Aug 3, 16; m 61; c 4. *Educ:* Kans State Univ, BS, 38; Columbia Univ, MS, 39; Univ Pittsburgh, PhD(chem eng), 49. *Prof Exp:* Engr, Exp Sta, E I du Pont de Nemours & Co, 39-41; instr chem eng, Kans State Univ, 41-45; sr technologist, Shell Chem Co, 49-54, mgr mkt anal, 54-59; mgr mkt res & develop, US Indust Chem Co Div, Nat Distillers & Chem Co, 59-61; vpres, Celanese Chem Co, 61-63; sr corp planner, Exxon Chem Co, 63-71. *Mem:* Am Chem Soc; Am Inst Chem Engrs. *Res:* Chemical economics. *Mailing Add:* 1202 Old Stable Rd McLean VA 22102-2419

JONSEN, ALBERT R, MEDICAL ETHICS, MEDICAL EDUCATION. *Current Pos:* PROF, DEPT MED HIST & ETHICS, UNIV WASH, SCH MED, 88-, CHMN DEPT, 89- *Personal Data:* b San Francisco, Calif, Apr 4, 31; m 76, Mary Elizabeth Carolan. *Educ:* Gonzaga Univ, BA, 55, MA, 56; Univ Santa Clara, STM, 63; Yale Univ, PhD, 67. *Honors & Awards:* McGovern Award, Am Osler Soc; Annual Award, Soc Health & Human Value; Davies Award, Am Col Physicians; Convocation Medal, Am Col Cardiol. *Prof Exp:* Assoc prof theol & philos, Univ San Francisco, 67-72, pres, 69-72; prof med ethics, Sch Med, Univ Calif, San Francisco, 72-88. *Concurrent Pos:* Mem, Nat Comt Protection Human Subj Biomed Behavioral Res, 74-78, pres Comt Study Ethical Problems in Med, 79-82; consult, Am Bd Internal Med, 78-; mem, Nat Bd Med Examnrs, 85-87; bd dir, Sierra Found, 86- *Mem:* Inst Med-Nat Acad Sci; fel Inst Soc Ethics & Life Sci; Soc Health Human Values (pres, 86); Am Soc Law & Med. *Res:* Ethics of care for dying; genetics; history of bioethics. *Mailing Add:* Dept Med Hist & Ethics A-205 Health Ctr Univ Wash Sch Med Seattle WA 98195. *Fax:* 206-685-7515; *E-Mail:* arjonsen@u.washington.edu

JONSSON, BJARNI, UNIVERSAL ALGEBRA, LATTICE THEORY. *Current Pos:* distinguished prof math, 66-93, EMER DISTINGUISHED PROF MATH, VANDERBILT UNIV, 93- *Personal Data:* b Draghals, Iceland, Feb 15, 20; m 50, 70, Harriet Parker; c Eric M, Meryl S & M Kristin. *Educ:* Univ Calif, Berkeley, AB, 43, PhD(math), 46. *Hon Degrees:* DSc, Univ Iceland, 86. *Prof Exp:* From instr to asst prof, Brown Univ, 46-56; from assoc prof to prof, Univ Minn, 56-66. *Concurrent Pos:* Vis prof, Univ Iceland, 54-55; vis assoc prof, Univ Calif, Berkeley, 55-56, vis prof & res mathematician, 62-63. *Mem:* Am Math Soc; Asn Symbolic Logic; Am Asn Univ Prof. *Res:* Universal algebra; lattice theory. *Mailing Add:* Dept Math Vanderbilt Univ Nashville TN 37240. *E-Mail:* jonsson@math.vanderbilt.edu

JONSSON, HALDOR TURNER, JR, BIOCHEMISTRY. *Current Pos:* asst prof chem, 66-70, ASSOC PROF BIOCHEM, MED UNIV SC, 70- *Personal Data:* b State College, Pa, Jan 5, 29; m 64; c 2. *Educ:* Tex A&M Univ, BS, 52, MS, 61; Baylor Univ, PhD(biochem), 65. *Prof Exp:* Res asst plastics & resins, Shell Chem Corp, 56-59; res asst biochem, Tex A&M Univ, 59-61 & Col Med, Baylor Univ, 61-65; res assoc, Sch Med, Boston Univ, 65-66. *Concurrent Pos:* Clin chem consult, Vet Admin Hosp, Charleston, 66- *Mem:* Am Chem Soc; Am Soc Biol Chem; Am Oil Chemists' Soc; NY Acad Sci. *Res:* Gonadotropins and their influence on ovarian function; role of prostoglandins and essential fatty acids in wounds; gas-liquid chromatography; long term effects of pesticides on mammals. *Mailing Add:* Dept Biochem Med Univ SC 171 Ashley Ave Charleston SC 29425-0001

JONSSON, JOHN ERIK, engineering; deceased, see previous edition for last biography

JONSSON, WILBUR JACOB, mathematics, for more information see previous edition

JONTE, JOHN HAWORTH, GEOCHEMISTRY, INORGANIC CHEMISTRY. *Current Pos:* RETIRED. *Personal Data:* b Moscow, Idaho, Oct 21, 18; m 42; c 4. *Educ:* Univ of the Pac, AB, 40; Wash State Univ, MS, 42; Univ Ark, PhD(chem), 56. *Prof Exp:* Jr chemist, US Bur Mines, Nev, 42-44 & Shell Develop Co, Calif, 44-46; instr chem, Iowa State Univ, 46-51; instr geol, Univ Ark, 54-55; res chemist, Texaco Inc, Tex, 55-61, group leader geochem, 61-66; assoc prof geochem & anal, SDak Sch Mines & Technol, 66-69, prof chem & head dept, 69-85, emer prof chem, 85-95. *Concurrent Pos:* Consult, 85- *Mem:* AAAS; Am Chem Soc; Geochem Soc; Am Ins; Sigma Xi. *Res:* Method development of drugs in biological fluids incorporating analytical instrumentation such as gas and liquid chromatography, fluorescence, techniques specializing in electroanalytical chemistry and computerized data reduction; laboratory information management, system management, system analysis and robotics based on implementation of information and method development. *Mailing Add:* 35 Wild Turkey Rd Sedona AZ 86351

JONZON, ANDERS, NEONATOLOGY, PEDIATRIC CARDIOLOGY. *Current Pos:* CONSULT & LECTR NEONATOLOGY, DEPT PEDIAT, UNIVERSITY HOSP, UNIV UPPSALA, 84-, CONSULT & LECTR PEDIAT CARDIOL & PEDIAT INTENSIVE CARE, 90- *Personal Data:* b Stockholm, Sweden, May 6, 48; m 72; c 3. *Educ:* Uppsala Univ, MedKand, 70, MedDr(physiol), 72, Lakarexamen, 77. *Concurrent Pos:* Julius Comroe Jr fel, Cardiovasc Res Inst, Univ Calif, San Francisco, 84-86. *Mem:* Europ Soc Pediat Res; Scand Physiol Soc; Am Physiol Soc. *Res:* Positive pressure breathing; control of respiration; lung development. *Mailing Add:* Dept Pediat Univ Hosp Uppsala S-751 85 Sweden. *Fax:* 46-18-665583

JOOS, BARBARA, animal physiology, for more information see previous edition

JOOS, BELA, THEORETICAL SOLID STATE PHYSICS. *Current Pos:* from asst prof to assoc prof, 84-96, PROF PHYSICS, UNIV OTTAWA, 96- *Personal Data:* b Montreal, Que, Aug 7, 53. *Educ:* Loyola Montreal, BSc, 74; McGill Univ, PhD(physics), 79. *Prof Exp:* Res fel, Univ Calif, Berkeley, 79-81; res assoc, Simon Fraser Univ, 81-82, asst prof, 82-84. *Concurrent Pos:* Assoc ed, Can J Physics, 84-93; hon assoc ed, Physics Can, 96- *Mem:* Can Asn Physicists; Am Phys Soc; Mats Res Soc. *Res:* Theoretical solid state physics; structural properties of surfaces, interfaces and monolayers; properties of strained materials including soft materials rubber, membranes, etc; dislocation kinetics. *Mailing Add:* Dept Physics Univ Ottawa Ottawa ON K1N 6N5 Can. *Fax:* 613-562-5190; *E-Mail:* joos@physics.uottawa.ca

JOOS, HOWARD ARTHUR, pediatrics, pediatric cardiology, for more information see previous edition

JOOS, RICHARD W, BIOCHEMISTRY. *Current Pos:* RES SPECIALIST, 3M CTR, MINN MINING & MFG CO, 67- *Personal Data:* b Cologne, Minn, Sept 22, 34; m 60; c 4. *Educ:* Col St Thomas, BS, 58; Univ Minn, PhD(biochem), 64. *Prof Exp:* Teaching asst biochem, Univ Minn, 58-62, res assoc med, 62-66; biochemist, Vet Admin Hosp, Minneapolis, 66-67. *Concurrent Pos:* Instr, Univ Minn Dent Sch, 71- *Mem:* Int Asn Dent Res. *Res:* Ion binding to macromolecules; humoral factors against bacteria; preventive agents for dental disease; dental materials. *Mailing Add:* 3934 Denmark Ave St Paul MN 55123

JOP, KRZYSZTOF M, TOXICOLOGY IDENTIFICATION EVALUATION, HAZARDOUS WASTE SITE ECOLOGICAL RISK ASSESSMENT. *Current Pos:* PROG MGR, SPRINGBORN LABS, 86 - *Personal Data:* b Krakow, Poland, Aug 15,50; m, Susan Bellevue. *Educ:* Jagiellonian Univ, Doctorat(hydrobiol), 80. *Prof Exp:* Res scientist, NTex State, 82-86; lab mgr, Battelle, 86-88. *Mem:* Soc Environ Toxicol & Chem; NAm Benthol Soc. *Res:* Provide technical expertise and management of industrial and municipal wastewater programs and hazardous site programs. *Mailing Add:* 16 Rocky Knook Lane Marion MA 02738

JOPLIN, KARL HENRY, MOLECULAR ASPECTS OF INSECT DEVELOPMENT, INVOLVEMENT OF HEAT SHOCK PROTEINS IN ENVIRONMENTAL STRESS. *Current Pos:* ASST PROF, E TENN STATE UNIV, 94- *Personal Data:* b Charleston, WVa, July 23, 48; m 69, Claire F Brown; c Amber R & Mikal L. *Educ:* Univ Wash, BSc, 73; Ohio State Univ, MSc, 82, PhD(molecular cellular & develop biol), 89. *Prof Exp:* Res assoc, Dept Entom, Ohio State Univ, 89-94. *Mem:* AAAS; Soc Develop Biol; Entom Soc Biol. *Res:* Differential expression of diapause-specific genes in the brains of diapausing pupae. *Mailing Add:* Biol Dept E Tenn State Univ PO Box 10001 Johnson City TN 37614-0002. *E-Mail:* kjoplin@magnus.acs.ohio-state.edu

JOPPA, LEONARD ROBERT, GENETICS, CYTOGENETICS. *Current Pos:* RES GENETICIST PLANTS, AGR RES SERV, USDA, 67- *Personal Data:* b Billings, Mont, Sept 29, 30; m 59, Catherine A Osborn; c Teresa, William R, Barbara L & Margaret A. *Educ:* Mont State Univ, BS, 57, PhD(genetics), 67; Ore State Univ, MS, 62. *Honors & Awards:* Res Award, Sigma Xi, 85. *Prof Exp:* Asst agron, Mont Agr Exp Sta, 57-62, asst agronomist, 62-64, res asst agron, 64-67. *Mem:* Fel AAAS; fel Am Soc Agron; Crops Sci Soc Am; Genetics Soc Am; Genetics Soc Can; Sigma Xi. *Res:* Genetics and cytogenetics of wheat and its relatives. *Mailing Add:* 90 24th Ave N Fargo ND 58102

JOPPA, RICHARD M, ELECTRICAL ENGINEERING ELECTRONICS, CONSTRUCTION PROJECT MANAGEMENT. *Current Pos:* RETIRED. *Personal Data:* b Littleton, Colo, Sept 29, 29; m 52; c 1. *Educ:* Colo State Univ, BS, 51; Univ Ill, MS, 57, PhD(elec eng), 63. *Prof Exp:* USAF, 51-71, instr elec eng, USAF Inst Technol, 57-59, chief space phycyics br, res directorate, Air Force Spec Weapons Ctr, NMex, 60-61, asst chief space vehicle div, test directorate, 62-64, from asst prof to assoc prof elec eng, USAF Acad, 64-68, chief anal br, survivability div & dir, vulnerability assessment directorate, Air Force Spec Weapons Ctr, Kirtland AFB, 68-71; elec-electronics engr, Los Alamos Nat Labs, Univ Calif, 71-90. *Concurrent Pos:* NSF fel, Univ Santa Clara, 67. *Mem:* Sr mem Inst Elec & Electronics Engrs; Nat Soc Prof Engrs. *Res:* Telemetry; instrumentation; information theory; circuit theory; experiment design, test and integration; control systems; electromagnetic environment energy conversion; research and development financial management; construction project management. *Mailing Add:* 10 Timber Ridge St Los Alamos NM 87544

JOPSON, HARRY GORGAS MICHENER, ZOOLOGY. *Current Pos:* from asst prof to assoc prof, 36-46, prof biol, 46-81, EMER PROF, BRIDGEWATER COL, 81- *Personal Data:* b Philadelphia, Pa, June 23, 11; m 33; c 2. *Educ:* Haverford Col, BS, 32; Cornell Univ, MA, 33, PhD(vert zool), 36. *Hon Degrees:* ScD, Bridgewater Col, 77. *Prof Exp:* Instr biol, Iowa State Teachers Col, 36. *Concurrent Pos:* Asst dir, Overseas Oper, United Seamen's Serv, 43-46; trustee, Rockingham Co Bd Educ, 57-76, chmn, 74-76; trustee, Nat Parks & Conserv Asn, 65-80. *Mem:* Am Soc Ichthyol & Herpet; Am Soc Mammal; Am Ornith Union. *Res:* Salamanders of southeastern United States; vertebrate natural history. *Mailing Add:* PO Box 26 Bridgewater VA 22812

JORCH, HARALD HEINRICH, physics, semiconductor surface, for more information see previous edition

JORDAN, ALBERT RAYMOND, PHYSICS. *Current Pos:* dean, 57-72, EMER DEAN, GRAD SCH, COLO SCH MINES, 72- *Personal Data:* b Alma, Kans, Oct 4, 06; m 32; c 3. *Educ:* Univ Colo, BA, 29, MA, 33, PhD(physics), 40. *Honors & Awards:* Mines Medal. *Prof Exp:* Instr physics, Univ Colo, 30-36 & Colo Agr & Mech Col, 36-37; from asst prof to assoc prof, Mont State Col, 37-41; physicist, Naval Ord Lab, Washington, DC, 41-42; from assoc prof to prof physics, Mont State Col, 42-52; sr res physicist, Denver Res Inst, Colo, 52-57. *Concurrent Pos:* Physicist, Curtiss-Wright Res Lab, 44-45. *Mem:* Am Geophys Union; Am Meteorol Soc. *Res:* Barometry and anemometry, atmospheric acoustics; geophysics. *Mailing Add:* 1603 S Uinta Way Denver CO 80231

JORDAN, ALEXANDER WALKER, III, ENDOCRINOLOGY, REPRODUCTIVE PHYSIOLOGY. *Current Pos:* STAFF FEL ENDOCRINOL, FOOD & DRUG ADMIN, HEW, 78- *Personal Data:* b Richmond, Va, Apr 12, 45; m 72. *Educ:* Roanoke Col, BS, 67; Univ Richmond, MA, 69; Rutgers Univ, PhD(zool), 75. *Prof Exp:* Fel endocrinol, Dept Physiol & Biophysics, Colo State Univ, 75-78. *Concurrent Pos:* Fel, Rockefeller Found, 75-77. *Mem:* Sigma Xi; Soc Study Reproduction. *Res:* Reproductive endocrinology; investigation into the mechanism of action of peptide hormones and prostaglandins on steroidogenesis. *Mailing Add:* Div Reproduction & Urol Drug PDTS FDA 5600 Fishers Lane HFD-580 Rm 17B20 Rockville MD 20857. *Fax:* 301-443-9282

JORDAN, ANDREW G, AGRICULTURAL RESEARCH. *Current Pos:* mgr mkt & processing technol, 76-81, asst dir tech serv, 82-83, DIR TECH SERV, NAT COTTON COUN, 83- *Personal Data:* b Wrens, Ga, May 18, 39; m; c 3. *Educ:* Univ Ga, BS, 62; Clemson Univ, MS, 72, PhD(eng), 77. *Prof Exp:* Systs engr, Western Elec Co, 62-65; supvr, Advan Technol Training, Lockheed-Ga Aircraft Corp, 65-70; res scientist & instr, Agr Eng, Clemson Univ, 71-76. *Concurrent Pos:* Cong task force rural transp; joint cotton breeding policy comt. *Mem:* Agr Res Inst; Am Soc Agr Engrs. *Res:* Agricultural engineering. *Mailing Add:* Nat Cotton Coun PO Box 12285 Memphis TN 38182

JORDAN, ANDREW STEPHEN, MATERIALS SCIENCE OF COMPOUND SEMICONDUCTORS, PHYSICAL CHEMISTRY. *Current Pos:* mem tech staff, 65-84, supvr, Heterostructure Mat Group, 84-90, DISTINGUISHED MEM TECH STAFF, AT&T BELL LABS, 91- *Personal Data:* b Mezokovesd, Hungary, May 1, 36; US citizen; m 68, Priscilla Theisz; c Daniel R & William B. *Educ:* Pa State Univ, BS, 59; Univ Pa, PhD(metall), 65. *Prof Exp:* Engr, Philco Corp, Pa, 59-62; res engr, Westinghouse Res Labs, Pa, 62-63. *Concurrent Pos:* Vis prof, Univ Tokyo, 92. *Mem:* Am Asn Crystal Growth. *Res:* Crystal growth of compound semiconductors; chemical thermodynamics of optoelectronic materials with special emphasis on phase diagrams; impurity incorporation and defect chemistry; reliability of devices; crystal growth modeling; physical characterization; epitaxial growth; diffusion. *Mailing Add:* 428 White Oak Ridge Rd Short Hills NJ 07078. *Fax:* 732-396-4037

JORDAN, ANGEL G, ELECTRICAL ENGINEERING, COMPUTER ENGINEERING. *Current Pos:* Instr, Dept Elec Eng, Carnegie Mellon Univ, 56-58, res fel, Mellon Inst Indust Res, 58-59, from asst prof to assoc prof, Dept Elec Eng, 59-66, prof, 66-76, actg chmn, Biomed Eng Prog, 76-78, head, Dept Elec & Comput Eng, 69-79, dean, Carnegie Inst Technol, 79-83, actg pres, Mellon Inst, 83-85, actg dir, Software Eng Inst, 86, actg dean, Mellon Col Sci, 87-88, prof elec & comput eng, 90-97, JOSEPH F KEITHLEY & NANCY P KEITHLEY PROF ELEC & COMPUT ENG, CARNEGIE MELLON UNIV, 97- *Personal Data:* b Pamplona, Spain, Sept 19, 30; nat US; m 56; c 3. *Educ:* Univ Zaragoza, Spain, MS, 52; Univ Madrid, Spain, PhD(physics), 56; Carnegie Mellon Univ, MS, 59, PhD(elec eng), 59. *Hon Degrees:* Dr, Polytech Univ Madrid. *Honors & Awards:* Sr Scientist Award, NATO. *Concurrent Pos:* Adj asst prof electronics, Naval Ord Sch, Madrid, Spain, 53-56; vis prof, Indian Inst Technol, Kampur, India, 71; vis sr scientist, Health & Safety Exec, Sheffield, Eng, 76; provost, Carnegie Mellon Univ, 83-90. *Mem:* Nat Acad Eng; Inst Elec & Electronics Engrs; fel AAAS; Am Soc Eng Educ; Am Phys Soc; Sigma Xi. *Res:* Solid state devices; integrated circuits; thin films; high definition television; flat panel displays; intelligent sensors; robotics; automation; knowledge engineering and software engineering focusing on technological change and technology transfer. *Mailing Add:* Wean Hall 4618 Carnegie Mellon Univ 5000 Forbes Ave Pittsburgh PA 15213

JORDAN, ARTHUR KENT, ELECTROMAGNETIC INVERSE SCATTERING, OPTICAL INTEGRATED CIRCUITS. *Current Pos:* ELECTRONICS ENGR REMOTE SENSING DIV, OFF NAVAL RES, 73-, PROG MGR, 86- *Personal Data:* b Philadelphia, Pa, Dec 28, 32; m 65, Mary F Baily; c Thomas B, Edward M & Elizabeth A. *Educ:* Pa State Univ, BSc, 57; Univ Pa, MSc, 71, PhD(elec eng), 72. *Prof Exp:* Res engr, Res Div, Philco Corp, 58-61; engr, Astro-Electronics Div, Radio Corp Am, 62-64; physicist, Aerospace Physics Lab, Gen Elec Co, 64-69; res asst, Moore Sch Elec Eng, Univ Pa, 69-73. *Concurrent Pos:* Res fel, Dept Elec Eng, Univ Pa, 71-73; mem, Advan Res Workshop Electromagnetic Imaging, NATO, WGer, 83; vis scientist, Mass Inst Technol, 89- *Mem:* Fel Inst Elec & Electronics Engrs; Electromagnetics Acad; Sigma Xi; Am Phys Soc; fel Optical Soc Am; Soc Indust & Appl Math; Inst Elec & Electronics Engrs Antennas & Propagation Soc; Inst Elec & Electronics Engrs Lasers & Electro-Optics Soc; Int Union Radio Sci; AAAS. *Res:* Electromagnetic inverse scattering theory; electromagnetic field theory; quantum electronics; optical waveguides and devices; remote sensing theory; author of numerous publications; holder of two US patent. *Mailing Add:* Naval Res Lab Remote Sensing Div Code 7227 Washington DC 20375-5351. *Fax:* 202-767-9130; *E-Mail:* jordan@ccf.nrl.navy.mil

JORDAN, BRIGITTE, MEDICAL ANTHROPOLOGY, CROSSCULTURAL OBSTETRICS. *Current Pos:* SR RES SCIENTIST, PALO ALTO RES CTR, XEROX CORP, 89- *Personal Data:* b Ger. *Educ:* Calif State Univ, Sacramento, BA, 69, MA, 71; Univ Calif, Irvine, PhD(soc sci), 75. *Honors & Awards:* Margaret Mead Award, Soc Appl Anthrop, 80. *Prof Exp:* Asst prof, Dept Anthrop & Community Med, Mich State Univ, 75-80, assoc prof, Dept Anthrop & Pediat, 80-88. *Concurrent Pos:* Res assoc, Feminist Women's Health Ctr, Santa Ana, Calif, 72-75; prin investr res grant, Crosscult Invest Childbirth Pract, Nat Inst Child Health & Human Develop, NIH, 77-79 & Cult Influences Response Physicians Diag, NSF, 84-86; mem exec bd, Soc Med Anthrop, 85-; consult, WHO, Geneva, Switz. *Mem:* Fel Am Anthrop Asn; Soc Appl Anthrop; Soc Med Anthrop; Soc Visual Anthrop. *Res:* Design of culturally appropriate maternal and child health care delivery systems; integration of traditional and western medicine in developing countries; methodology, including videographic methods for documentation and analysis; patient-practitioner relationship; alternate systems of health care delivery; symbolic language of advertising; status of women; Maya Indians of Yucatan, Mexico. *Mailing Add:* PO Box 198 LaHonda CA 94020

JORDAN, BYRON DALE, COMPUTER VISION, COLORIMETRY. *Current Pos:* HEAD, OPTICS SECT, PULP & PAPER RES INST CAN, 77- *Personal Data:* b Akron, Ohio, Jan 24, 47; Can citizen; m 69, Kate Ronsheim; c Crispin & Alayne. *Educ:* Hiram Col, BA, 69; McMaster Univ, PhD(physics), 75. *Honors & Awards:* Richard S Hunter Prize & Process & Prod Qual Div Tech Award, Tech Asn Pulp & Paper Indust, 93. *Prof Exp:* Physicist, Welwyn Res Ltd, 75-77. *Concurrent Pos:* Auxiliary prof chem eng, McGill Univ, 85- *Mem:* Am Phys Soc; Optical Soc Am; Tech Asn Pulp & Paper Indust; Inst Elec & Electronics Engrs; Soc Photo-Optical Instrumentation Engrs; Am Math Soc. *Res:* Paper physics; optical properties of paper; application of image processing to study random textures and fiber morphology; colorimetry and optical methods of quality control. *Mailing Add:* Pulp & Paper Res Inst Can 570 St John's Blvd Pointe Claire PQ H9R 3J9 Can. *Fax:* 514-630-4134; *E-Mail:* jordan@paprican.ca

JORDAN, CARL FREDERICK, ECOLOGY. *Current Pos:* adj assoc prof, 84-89, RES ASSOC, INST ECOL, UNIV GA, 74-, SR RES ECOLOGIST, 79-, ADJ PROF, 89- *Personal Data:* b New Brunswick, NJ, Dec 10, 35; m 67; c 2. *Educ:* Univ Mich, BS, 58; Rutgers Univ, MS, 64, PhD(ecol), 66. *Honors & Awards:* Mercer Award, Ecol Soc Am, 73. *Prof Exp:* Assoc scientist, P R Nuclear Ctr, AEC, 66-69; from asst ecologist to assoc ecologist, Radiol & Environ Res Div, Argonne Nat Lab, 69-74. *Concurrent Pos:* Vis scientist, Ecol Ctr, Venezuelan Inst Sci Invest, 74- *Mem:* AAAS; Ecol Soc Am; Soil Sci Soc Am; Sigma Xi. *Res:* Movement of chemical elements in soil; radiation recovery and mineral cycling in the tropical rain forest; application of systems analysis techniques to ecology; shifting agriculture in the Amazon Basin; laungya agriculture in Thailand. *Mailing Add:* Inst Ecol Univ Ga 126 Ecology Bldg Athens GA 30602-2202. *Fax:* 706-542-6040

JORDAN, CHARLES LEMUEL, METEOROLOGY. *Current Pos:* RETIRED. *Personal Data:* b Ash Grove, Mo, May 28, 22; m 51; c 6. *Educ:* Univ Chicago, PhB, 48, BS, 49, SM, 51, PhD(meteorol), 56. *Prof Exp:* Meteorol aide, US Weather Bur, Philippines & Japan, 46-47, res meteorologist, Nat Hurricane Res Proj, 56-57; asst meteorol, Chicago, 51-54; tech consult, Air Weather Serv, USAF, Washington, DC, 54-55; assoc prof meterol, 57-63, chmn dept, 63-70, prof meterol, emer prof, Fla State Univ, 63-90. *Mem:* AAAS; fel Am Meteorol Soc; Am Geophys Union. *Res:* Tropical meteorology and climatology; synoptic meteorology; hurricanes. *Mailing Add:* Dept Meteorol Fla State Univ Tallahassee FL 32306-3034

JORDAN, CHRIS SULLIVAN, BIOLOGY. *Current Pos:* RETIRED. *Personal Data:* b Yangchow, China, Aug 6, 24; US citizen; m 47; c 3. *Educ:* Drake Univ, BA, 48; Univ Iowa, MS, 51, PhD(zool), 55. *Prof Exp:* Clin lab technologist, Vet Admin Hosp, Iowa City, Iowa, 52-55; supvr bact & parasitol, Terrell's Labs, Tex, 55-56; prof biol, Howard Payne Col, 56-63; prof, Houston Baptist Col, 63-67; chmn, Div Sci & Math, Dallas Baptist Col, 67-93. *Concurrent Pos:* Res grant, NIH, 59-62. *Mem:* Am Inst Biol Sci; AAAS; Am Soc Parasitol; Am Soc Microbiol; Sigma Xi. *Res:* Parasitology and medical bacteriology. *Mailing Add:* 1214 Hilltop Lindale TX 75771

JORDAN, CONSTANCE (LOUISE) BRINE, NUTRITION. *Current Pos:* prof home econ & head dept, Framingham State Col, 56-73, dean grad studies, 73-78, prof 78-84, EMER PROF, FOOD & NUTRIT, FRAMINGHAM STATE COL, 84- *Personal Data:* b Newton, Mass, Dec 26, 19; m 57; c John Jr (deceased), Kirk, Kathleen, Elizabeth & Mary. *Educ:* Harvard Univ, MPH, 48; Cornell Univ, PhD(food, nutrit), 54. *Hon Degrees:* DSc, Framingham State Col, 87. *Prof Exp:* Chief dietitian, Newton-Wellesley Hosp, 43-45; asst dir sch lunch, Pub Schs, Newton, 45-46; asst nutrit, Harvard Univ, 46-48; assoc prof food & nutrit, Univ RI, 48-56. *Concurrent Pos:* Anna Cora Smith fel, Cornell Univ, 53; consult, Arthur D Little, Inc & Mkt Res Corp Am, 54-58. *Mem:* AAAS; Am Dietetic Asn; Am Home Econ Asn. *Res:* Absorption of calcium; institutional dietary studies; nutritional status; nontraditional education at graduate level. *Mailing Add:* 8 Beacon Natick MA 01760

JORDAN, CRAIG ALAN, GRANT ADMINISTRATION, COMMUNICATIONS SCIENCES. *Current Pos:* HEALTH SCIENTIST ADMINR, NAT INST DEAFNESS & OTHER COMMUN DISORDERS, 90- *Personal Data:* b Elyria, Ohio, June 27, 55; m, Cheryl Berry; c Cameron & Casey. *Educ:* Ohio State Univ, BS, 77; Univ Tex, Galveston, PhD(med microbiol), 84. *Prof Exp:* Sr staff fel, Nat Inst Neurol Dis & Stroke, 84-90. *Concurrent Pos:* Actg dir, Div Extramural Activ, Nat Inst Deafness & Other Commun Disorders, 96-, actg chief, Sci Review Br, 96- *Mem:* AAAS; Asn Res Otolaryngol. *Res:* Scientific evaluation of applications dealing with communication sciences and disorders; voice, speech, language, taste, smell, balance and hearing; viral replication in the central nervous system and gene expression by oligodendrocytes and glial cells. *Mailing Add:* EPS Rm 400C Nat Inst Deafness & Other Commun Disorders Bethesda MD 20892. *Fax:* 301-402-6250; *E-Mail:* cj34b@nih.gov

JORDAN, DAVID CARLYLE, BACTERIOLOGY. *Current Pos:* RETIRED. *Personal Data:* b Brampton, Ont, July 11, 26; m 54, Marian Bayne; c Mark, Scott & Peter. *Educ:* Univ Toronto, BSA, 50, MSA, 51; Mich State Univ, PhD, 55, Can Col Microbiol, RM, 79. *Prof Exp:* Asst res, Ont Agr Col, Univ Guelph, 50-52; lectr bact, 52-56; from asst prof to prof microbiol, 56-87, chmn dept, 71-81. *Concurrent Pos:* Nuffield traveling fel, 59. *Mem:* Can Soc Microbiol. *Res:* Bacterial physiology as related to Rhizobium species; Rhizobium taxonomy; antibiotic mode of action. *Mailing Add:* Eight Young St Guelph ON N1G 1M2 Can. *E-Mail:* djordan@uoguelph.ca

JORDAN, DAVID M, ORGANIC CHEMISTRY. *Current Pos:* From assoc prof to prof, 65-96, EMER PROF CHEM, STATE UNIV NY COL POTSDAM, 96- *Personal Data:* b Ashtabula, Ohio, Aug 19, 37; m 61; c 2. *Educ:* Col Wooster, BA, 59; Ohio State Univ, PhD(chem), 65. *Mem:* Am Chem Soc; Sigma Xi. *Res:* Diazoacetophenone decompositions; reaction of ketenes; techniques for thin-layer chromatography on cylindrical surfaces; styryl azide decompositions. *Mailing Add:* 372 Outer Main St Potsdam NY 13676

JORDAN, DIANE KATHLEEN, MEDICAL CYTOGENETICS. *Current Pos:* res asst, 87-91, ASST RES SCIENTIST, UNIV IOWA, 91-, ASST DIR, CYTOGENETICS LAB, 91- *Personal Data:* b Peoria, Ill, Jan 3, 54; m 76, John M. *Educ:* Bradley Univ, BS, 76; Univ Iowa, PhD(genetics), 87. *Prof Exp:* supvr, Cytogenetics Lab, Wash Univ, St Louis, 76-79. *Concurrent Pos:* Co-dir, Med Cytogenetics Prog, Univ Iowa, 91-94, adj lectr, Dept Path, 92- *Mem:* Am Col Med Genetics; Am Soc Human Genetics; Asn Cytogenetic

Technologists; Orgn Clin Lab Geneticists. *Res:* Cancer cytogenetics; chromosomal abnormalities and fragile site formation in tumors; numerical chromosome changes in leukemia and prostate cancer patients. *Mailing Add:* Cytogenetics Lab W-101GH Dept Pediat Univ Iowa 200 Hawkins Dr Iowa City IA 52242-1083

JORDAN, DONALD J, ENGINEERING. *Current Pos:* RETIRED. *Personal Data:* b New York, NY, 16. *Educ:* NY Univ, BS, 38. *Prof Exp:* Power plant staff engr, Chance Vought Aircraft, 44-48; mem staff, Pratt & Whitney, 48-71, eng mgr, 71-75; eng mgr, Power Systs Div, United Technologies, 75-78. *Mem:* Nat Acad Sci; Nat Acad Eng. *Mailing Add:* 113 Evergreen Lane Glastonbury CT 06033

JORDAN, DUANE PAUL, MECHANICAL ENGINEERING. *Current Pos:* asst prof mech eng, 64-67, ASSOC PROF MECH ENG, TEX TECH UNIV, 67- *Personal Data:* b Glendale, Calif, July 17, 35; m; c 2. *Educ:* Stanford Univ, BS, 57, MS, 58, PhD(mech eng), 61. *Honors & Awards:* Dedicated Serv Award, Am Soc Mech Engrs, 88. *Prof Exp:* Mech engr, Lawrence Radiation Lab, Univ Calif, 60-63; sr engr, integrated controls dept, Electronics Assocs, Inc, 63-64. *Concurrent Pos:* Consult, Lawrence Radiation Lab, 63-65; Profit Index Systs, Inc, 66-84, Fanning, Fanning, Agnes Consult Engrs, 76-78 & Tex Indust Comn, 78-79. *Mem:* Am Soc Mech Engrs; Am Soc Eng Educ. *Res:* Thermal, physical and social economic systems analysis and simulation using digital and analog computer techniques. *Mailing Add:* Dept Mech Eng Tex Tech Univ PO Box 41021 Lubbock TX 79409

JORDAN, EDWARD DANIEL, RELIABILITY ENGINEERING. *Current Pos:* from assoc prof to prof nuclear eng, Catholic Univ Am, 59-68, dir info syst & planning off, 68-83, prof, 83-92, EMER PROF MECH ENG, CATHOLIC UNIV AM, 92- *Personal Data:* b Bridgeport, Conn, Mar 14, 31; m 57, Margaret A Moran; c Christopher E, Kathleen M, Daniel E, David E & Margaret J. *Educ:* Fairfield Univ, BS, 53; NY Univ, MS, 55; Univ Md, PhD(nuclear eng), 65. *Prof Exp:* Reactor physicist nuclear eng, Foster Wheeler Corp, 55-57; US Atomic Energy Comn, 57-59. *Mem:* Sigma Xi. *Res:* Computer modeling of complex engineering system reliability. *Mailing Add:* 4010 Shinnecock Dr New Bern NC 28562

JORDAN, ELKE, MOLECULAR BIOLOGY, GENETICS. *Current Pos:* grants assoc, Nat Cancer Inst, NIH, 72-73, coordr collab res, 73-76, prog admin, Nat Inst Gen Med Sci, 76-78, dep dir, genetics prog, 78-81, assoc dir prog activ, 81-88, dir, Off Human Genome Res, 88-89, DEP DIR, NAT CTR HUMAN GENOME RES, NIH, 89- *Personal Data:* b Ger, Apr 8, 37. *Educ:* Goucher Col, BA, 57; Johns Hopkins Univ, PhD(biochem), 62. *Hon Degrees:* DSc, Goucher Col, 92. *Prof Exp:* Fel, Harvard Univ, 62-64; fel, Univ Cologne, 64-68; res assoc, univ Wis-Madison, 68-69 & Univ Calif, Berkeley, 69-72. *Concurrent Pos:* NIH fel, 62-65; fel, Helen Hay Whitney Found, 65-68. *Mem:* Genetics Soc Am; fel AAAS; Am Soc Microbiol; Am Soc Human Genetics. *Res:* Gene regulation in prokaryotes, genetic recombination. *Mailing Add:* Nat Ctr Human Genome Res NIH Bethesda MD 20892

JORDAN, FRANK, BIO-ORGANIC CHEMISTRY, BIOPHYSICAL CHEMISTRY. *Current Pos:* asst prof, 70-75, assoc prof, 75-79, PROF CHEM, RUTGERS UNIV, NEWARK, 79- *Personal Data:* b Budapest, Hungary, Jan 28, 41; US citizen; m 65, Rosy R Schechter; c Michael J & Lisa J. *Educ:* Drexel Univ, BS, 64; Univ Pa, PhD(chem), 67. *Prof Exp:* NATO fel quantum chem, Univ Paris, France, 67-68; NIH fel bio-org chem, Chem Dept, Harvard Univ, 68-70. *Concurrent Pos:* NIH grants, USPHS, 74-82 & 84-; NSF grants, 82-92. *Mem:* Am Chem Soc; AAAS; Sigma Xi; Biophys Soc; Am Soc Biol Chem. *Res:* Enzyme mechanism studies on enzymes sythesizing and utilizing thiamine diphosphate, purine nucleoside phosphorylase, glyoxalase I and serine proteases. *Mailing Add:* Dept Chem Rm 1010 Rutgers Univ Newark Col Arts 73 Warren St Newark NJ 07102. *Fax:* 973-648-1264; *E-Mail:* frjordan@andromeda.rutgers.edu

JORDAN, FREDDIE L, BIOCHEMISTRY, NEUROSCIENCES. *Current Pos:* res assoc, 88-89, vis asst prof, Oral Biol Dept, 89-95, DIR, STUDENT AFFAIRS & ADJ PROF, ORAL BIOL DEPT, OHIO STATE UNIV, 95- *Personal Data:* b Yazoo City, Miss, Aug 14, 54; m; c 3. *Educ:* Jackson State Univ, BS, 78; Meharry Med Col, PhD(biochem), 86. *Prof Exp:* Postdoctoral fel neurobiol, Meharry Med Col, 86-88. *Concurrent Pos:* Vis asst prof, Oral Biol Dept, Ohio State Univ, 89-; vis scientist, Fedn Am Socs Exp Biol, Soc Cell Biol, 90- *Mem:* Soc Neurosci; Int Asn Dent Res; Soc Cell Biol; AAAS. *Res:* Transmembrane signalling in the cerebral cortex. *Mailing Add:* Student Affairs Col Dent Ohio State Univ 305 W 12th Ave Box 199 Columbus OH 43210-1241

JORDAN, GARY BLAKE, ELECTRONICS PROGRAM MANAGEMENT, MARKETING. *Current Pos:* DIR, JORDAN & ASSOCS, 89-; ELECTRONIC ENGR, ANALYSIS & TECHNOL, INC, 94- *Personal Data:* b Urbana, Ill, Feb 3, 39; m 68, Gloria J Heppler; c Gareth K & Glynis J. *Educ:* Ohio Univ, BS, 61; Pac Southern Univ, DEE, 77; Sussex Col Technol, Eng, PhD(elec eng), 77. *Prof Exp:* Sr prog mgt engr, Ford Aerospace, 75-79; prog mgr, ESL Subsid TRW Inc, 79-87, Cubic Corp, 87-89, Sci Atlanta, 88-89. *Concurrent Pos:* Exec vpres, EW Orgn, 69-75; dir, Nat Intel Agency, 76-79. *Mem:* Fel Am Biog Inst; sr mem Soc Tech Commun; corp mem Radio Soc Gt Brit; Armed Forces Commun & Electronics Asn; AAAS; assoc mem US Naval Inst; Am Radio Relay League; Inst Elec & Electronics Engrs. *Res:* Electronic warfare as applied to electronics in the battlefield and on battlefield training ranges; spread spectrum, digital and advanced communications systems. *Mailing Add:* 13392 Fallen Leaf Rd Poway CA 92064

JORDAN, GEORGE LYMAN, JR, surgery; deceased, see previous edition for last biography

JORDAN, GEORGE SAMUEL, MATHEMATICS. *Current Pos:* From asst prof to assoc prof, 71-84, PROF MATH, UNIV TENN, KNOXVILLE, 84-, ASSOC HEAD DEPT, 80- *Personal Data:* b Dallas, Tex, Apr 11, 44; m 66. *Educ:* Southern Methodist Univ, BA, 66; Univ Wis-Madison, MS, 69, PhD(math), 71. *Mem:* Am Math Soc; Math Asn Am; Sigma Xi; Soc Ind & Appl Math. *Res:* Integral and differential equations; Tauberian theory; functions of a complex variable. *Mailing Add:* Dept Math Ayres Hall Univ Tenn Knoxville TN 37916

JORDAN, HAROLD VERNON, MICROBIOLOGY. *Current Pos:* RETIRED. *Personal Data:* b Boston, Mass, Aug 18, 24; m 50; c 3. *Educ:* Univ NH, BS, 49; Univ Md, MS, 52, PhD(microbiol), 56. *Prof Exp:* Res scientist oral microbiol, Nat Inst Dent Res, 49-69; res scientist oral microbiol, Forsyth Dent Ctr, 69-87. *Concurrent Pos:* Vis scientist, Royal Dent Sch, Malmo, Sweden, 65-66. *Mem:* AAAS; fel Am Col Dent; Am Soc Microbiol; Int Asn Dent Res. *Res:* Lactic acid bacteria, metabolism and taxonomy; microbiology of dental caries and periodontal disease; gnotobiotic techniques in dental research; oral microbiology. *Mailing Add:* 16 Sheppards Quay Brewster MA 02631-2557

JORDAN, HARRY FREDERICK, COMPUTER SCIENCE, ELECTRICAL ENGINEERING. *Current Pos:* From asst prof to assoc prof, 66-80, PROF ELEC ENG & COMPUT SCI, UNIV COLO, BOULDER, 80- *Personal Data:* b Tacoma Park, Md, Mar 6, 40; m 62; c 2. *Educ:* Rice Univ, BA, 61; Univ Ill, MS, 63, PhD(physics), 68. *Mem:* Asn Comput Mach; Am Phys Soc; Inst Elec & Electronics Engrs. *Res:* Computer systems architecture; parallel algorithm design; optical computing; parallel processor design. *Mailing Add:* 6623 Lefthand Canyon Dr Jamestown CO 80455-9709

JORDAN, HELEN ELAINE, VETERINARY PARASITOLOGY. *Current Pos:* prof vet parasitol, 69-93, EMER PROF, COL VET MED, OKLA STATE UNIV, 93- *Personal Data:* b Bridgewater, Va, July 19, 26. *Educ:* Bridgewater Col, BA, 49; Va Polytech Inst, MS, 55; Univ Ga, DVM, 55, PhD(parasitol), 62. *Prof Exp:* From asst prof to assoc prof vet parasitol, Univ Ga, 55-69. *Mem:* Am Soc Parasitol; Am Vet Med Asn; Am Asn Vet Parasitol; World Asn Vet Parasitol. *Res:* Life cycle study of flukes; surveillance and epidemiology parasites in wild and domestic animals; parasite-host interactions and parasite ecology. *Mailing Add:* Dept Vet Parasitol & Pub Health Okla State Univ Col Vet Med Stillwater OK 74078. *E-Mail:* hjordan@ums.ucc.okstate.edu

JORDAN, HOWARD EMERSON, electrical engineering, for more information see previous edition

JORDAN, JAMES A, JR, APPLIED MATHEMATICS. *Current Pos:* CHIEF EXEC OFFICER, AS TECH CUPPERTINO, 93- *Personal Data:* b Berkeley, Calif, Dec 28, 36; m 61; c 2. *Educ:* Ohio State Univ, BSc, 58; Univ Mich, MSc, 59, PhD(physics), 64. *Prof Exp:* Physicist, USAF Aeronaut Res Lab, 60; asst res physicist, Univ Mich, 60-64; asst prof atomic physics, Rice Univ, 64-70; sci staff mem, IBM Houston Sci Ctr, 69-71, mgr appl math, 71-74, mgr power syst analysis, IBM Palo Alto Sci Ctr, 74-93. *Mem:* Inst Elec & Electronics Engrs. *Res:* Optical data processing, computer holography; network analysis; atomic collisions; atomic spectroscopy; scientific computations; simulation and control of power systems; data management. *Mailing Add:* 21914 Granada Ave Cupertino CA 95014

JORDAN, JAMES HENRY, MATHEMATICS. *Current Pos:* from asst prof to assoc prof, 62-70, PROF MATH, WASH STATE UNIV, 70-, CHMN, PROG SCI & MATH TEACHING, 77- *Personal Data:* b Sacramento, Calif, Oct 16, 31; m 58; c 3. *Educ:* Southern Ore Col, BS, 53; Univ Ore, MA, 58; Univ Colo, PhD(math), 62. *Prof Exp:* Teacher elem sch, Ore, 53-56. *Mem:* Math Asn Am; Am Math Soc. *Res:* Number theory in general, specifically Kth power reciprocity, consecutive residues, Gaussian integers and simple continued fractions. *Mailing Add:* Dept Pure & Appl Math Wash Univ Pullman WA 99164-2930

JORDAN, JAMES N, earth science, for more information see previous edition

JORDAN, JOHN PATRICK, BIOCHEMISTRY. *Current Pos:* ADMINR COOP, STATE RES SERV, USDA, WASHINGTON, DC, 83-, CTR DIR, SOUTHERN REGIONAL RESOURCE CTR, AGR RES SERV, USDA, NEW ORLEANS, LA. *Personal Data:* b Salt Lake City, Utah, Apr 23, 34; m 54; c 8. *Educ:* Univ Calif, Davis, BS, 55, PhD(comp biochem), 63. *Honors & Awards:* Bond Award, Am Oil Chem Soc, 67. *Prof Exp:* From asst prof to assoc prof chem, Okla City Univ, 62-68; assoc prof biochem, Colo State Univ, 68-71, assoc dean, Col Natural Sci & dir biol core curric, 68-72, dir, Proj Biocotie, 70-83, prof biochem, 71-83, dir, Univ Exp Sta, 72-83. *Concurrent Pos:* Grant dir, NASA res grant, 63-; prin investr, Frontiers Sci Found Okla, Inc res grant, 64-65; Okla Heart Asn res grant, 65-66; NIH res grant, 65-68; consult space med, NASA, 65-70; NIH biomed sci support grant, 69-; NSF curric res grant, 71-; Boettcher Found res grant, 70-71; gen chmn ann meeting, Am Inst Biol Sci, 71. *Mem:* Fel AAAS; fel Am Inst Chem; Brit Biochem Soc; Am Physiol Soc; Soc Exp Biol & Med. *Res:* Intermediary metabolism, particularly the effects of artificial atmospheres on metabolism; curricular development, especially in biology and chemistry; research administration. *Mailing Add:* Ctr Dir Southern Regional Resource Ctr USDA Agr Res Serv PO Box 19687 New Orleans LA 70179. *Fax:* 202-720-8987

JORDAN, JOHN WILLIAM, INDUSTRIAL CHEMISTRY. *Current Pos:* mgr res labs, NL Indust, Inc, 51-56, tech dir, 57-76, consult, Baroid Div, 76-82, CONSULT CLAY-ORGANIC COMPLEXES, NL INDUSTS, INC, 82- *Personal Data:* b Pittsburgh, Pa, Apr 25, 12; m 36, 79, Norine E Holt; c Emily (Oaks), Frank W, John C, Edward H & Andrew S. *Educ:* Marietta Col, AB, 34; Columbia Univ, PhD(chem), 38. *Hon Degrees:* ScD, Marietta Col, 59. *Honors & Awards:* Pioneer Clay Sci, Develop Clay-Organic Complexes, Clay Minerals Soc, 90. *Prof Exp:* Asst food anal & colloid chem, Columbia Univ, 35-38; fel asst tech glassware, Mellon Inst, 38-39, sr fel lead, 41-51; chemist, Pittsburgh Corning Corp, Pa, 39-41. *Concurrent Pos:* Dir, Enenco, Inc, 62-76. *Mem:* AAAS; Am Chem Soc; Clay Minerals Soc (pres, 73-74). *Res:* Chemistry of hydrous ferric oxides; structural glass products; synthetic resins and coatings; oil well drilling fluids; organic complexes of clay minerals for gellants and rheological control agents; developed abherent coatings. *Mailing Add:* 1505 Butlercrest Houston TX 77080-7613

JORDAN, KENNETH A(LLAN), AGRICULTURAL ENGINEERING, BIOSYSTEMS ENGINEERING. *Current Pos:* PROF, UNIV ARIZ, TUCSON, 86- *Personal Data:* b Plainfield, NJ, June 30, 30; m 52, Phyllis Deck; c Jeanette A, Genevieve J, Kenneth A Jr & David M. *Educ:* Purdue Univ, BS, 52, MS, 54, PhD(agr eng), 59. *Prof Exp:* Res instr, Purdue Univ, 57-58; from asst prof to assoc prof farm struct, NC State Univ, 58-67; prof farm struct, Univ Minn, St Paul, 67-84. *Concurrent Pos:* Vis prof, Univ Tokyo, 71; dir, Microprocessor Instrumentation Lab Sensor Technol Develop. *Mem:* Sigma Xi; Am Soc Agr Engrs; Inst Elec & Electronics Engrs; Japan Soc Biol Control; Am Soc Heating, Refrig & Air-Conditioning Eng. *Res:* Animal shelter and greenhouse simulation; weather pattern frequency; plant and animal modeling; machine vision; sensor technology development; transpiration; C3,C4,CAM plants; micropropagation. *Mailing Add:* Univ Ariz 403 Shantz Bldg 38 Tucson AZ 85721. *Fax:* 520-621-3963; *E-Mail:* kenjord@ccit.arizona.edu

JORDAN, KENNETH DAVID, PHYSICAL CHEMISTRY, THEORETICAL CHEMISTRY. *Current Pos:* from asst prof to assoc prof, 78-85, PROF CHEM, UNIV PITTSBURGH, 85- *Personal Data:* b Norwood, Mass, Feb 25, 48; m 81, Sandra Horwitz; c Erin & Kate. *Educ:* Northeastern Univ, BA, 70; Mass Inst Technol, PhD(chem), 74. *Prof Exp:* J W Gibbs instr eng & appl sci, Yale Univ, 74-76, asst prof, 76-78. *Concurrent Pos:* Vis asst prof, Univ Utah, 76 & 77; Alfred P Sloan Found fel, 77-79; Camille & Henry Dreyfus Found teacher scholar, 77-82; John Simon Guggenheim fel, 81-82; prog dir theoretical chem physics, NSF, 84-85; adj prof, Carnegie-Mellon Univ, 88-; chmn, Theoret Chem Subdiv, Phys Chem Div, Am Chem Soc, 90-91; vis prof, Australian Nat Univ, 91 & Univ Utah, 94 & 95; fel, Joint Inst Lab Astrophics, 97. *Mem:* Am Chem Soc; fel Am Phys Soc; Sigma Xi. *Res:* Theoretical studies of the electronic structure of molecules; electron transmission spectroscopic studies of temporary anions; energy transfer in reactions of excited atoms with molecules; properties of atomic and molecular clusters. *Mailing Add:* Dept Chem Univ Pittsburgh Pittsburgh PA 15260. *E-Mail:* jordan@a.psc.edu

JORDAN, KENNETH GARY, PHYSICAL CHEMISTRY, TECHNICAL FIBERS. *Current Pos:* Chemist, E I du Pont de Nemours & Co, Inc, 57, res chemist, Dacron Technol Div, NC, 63-68, sr res chemist, 69-70, Dacron Textile Res Lab, Wilmington, 70-75, textile fibers end use mkt specialist, 75-77, develop assoc, 77-78, mkt rep, 78-81, sr mkt rep, 81, from account mgr to sr account mgr, Indust Fibers Div, 82-91, EXEC ACCT MGR, E I DU PONT DE NEMOURS & CO, INC, 92- *Personal Data:* b Anderson, SC, Nov 18, 35; m 57, Joyce Hackaby; c Kenneth G Jr & Christopher A (deceased). *Educ:* Clemson Univ, BS, 57, MS, 61, PhD(phys chem), 63. *Mem:* Am Chem Soc. *Res:* Semiconductor properties of polymers; polyester catalysis and kinetics; new polymer technology; synthetic fiber and fabric characterization and evaluation; industrial fiber sales and development. *Mailing Add:* 4502 Lanier Ave Anderson SC 29624

JORDAN, KENNETH L(OUIS), JR, ELECTRICAL ENGINEERING, COMMUNICATIONS. *Current Pos:* CHIEF SCIENTIST, SCI APPLN, INC, 79-, COOP VPRES, 92- *Personal Data:* b Portland, Maine, May 10, 33; m 62; c 3. *Educ:* Rensselaer Polytech Inst, BEE; Mass Inst Technol, SM, 56, ScD(elec eng), 61. *Prof Exp:* Staff mem commun, Lincoln Lab, Mass Inst Technol, 60-67, asst group leader, 67-68, group leader, 68-76; prin dep asst secy res & develop, Off Secy Air Force, The Pentagon, 76-79. *Mem:* Fel Inst Elec & Electronics Engrs. *Res:* Random processes; modulation and coding; satellite communications. *Mailing Add:* Sci Appln Inc 1710 Goodridge Dr McLean VA 22102. *Fax:* 703-356-0959

JORDAN, LARRY, MOTOR CONTROL PHYSIOLOGY. *Current Pos:* Researcher neuropharmacol, 70-72, from asst prof to assoc prof, 72-85, PROF & DEPT HEAD NEUROSCI, UNIV MAN, 85- *Personal Data:* b Paris, Tex, Mar 18, 44. *Educ:* Univ Tex, BA, 66; SW Med Sch, Dallas, PhD(physiol), 71. *Concurrent Pos:* Distinguished lectr, Hollfelder Found, 89. *Mem:* Can Asn Neurosci (treas, 83-85); AAAS; Am Physiol Soc; Can Physiol Soc; Soc Neurosci. *Mailing Add:* Fac Med Dept Physiol Univ Man 730 William Ave BMSB34 Winnipeg MB R3E 3J7 Can. *Fax:* 204-774-9417

JORDAN, LAWRENCE M, COMPUTER SCIENCE. *Current Pos:* assoc prof comput sci, 88-89, ASSOC PROF BIOMED ENG, UNIV TENN, MEMPHIS, 90- *Personal Data:* b Greensboro, NC, Apr 6, 36. *Educ:* Fisk Univ, BA, 57; Princeton Univ, PhD(physics), 64. *Honors & Awards:* Bronze Medal, US Dept Transp, 79, Group Achievement Award, Emergency Transp Proj, 85. *Prof Exp:* Instr physics, Colgate Univ, Hamilton, NY, 62-64, asst prof, 64-66; staff scientist & sr scientist, Avco Space Syst Div, Lowell, Mass, 66-70; physicist, Electronics Res Ctr & Transp Syst, NASA, 70-76; oper res analyst, Transp Syst Ctr, Cambridge, Mass, 76-88. *Concurrent Pos:* Mgr neurosci, 3-D Micros Lab, 89; prin investr, Nat Inst Arthritis & Musculoskeletal & Skin Dis, 92-94; mem subcomt grad prog, Univ Tenn, 93. *Mem:* Am Phys Soc. *Res:* Novel densitometric techniques for osteoporosis; computer assisted ultrasound diagnosis of liver and kidney disease; a vector mode doppler ultrasound technique; author of 30 publications. *Mailing Add:* Biomed Eng Dept Univ Tenn 899 Madison Ave Rm 801 Memphis TN 38163

JORDAN, LOWELL STEPHEN, PLANT PHYSIOLOGY. *Current Pos:* RETIRED. *Personal Data:* b Vale, Ore, Apr 23, 30; m 50, 80, Catalina N Memita; c Gary S, Diane L (Hankla), Lauraly N (Ramos), James L & Sharon T (Luster). *Educ:* Ore State Univ, BS, 54; Univ Minn, PhD(agron, bot), 57. *Prof Exp:* Asst agron, Univ Minn, 54-57; asst prof plant indusrts, Southern Ill Univ, 57-59; from asst to assoc prof plant physiologist, Univ Calif, Riverside, 59-70, physiologist & prof, 70-93, emer physiologist & prof hort sci, 93. *Mem:* Fel Weed Sci Soc Am; Am Soc Plant Physiol; Am Soc Hort Sci; Am Coun Sci & Health; Coun Agr Sci & Technol. *Res:* Weed science; herbicide physiology, mechanism of action and metabolism in plants. *Mailing Add:* Dept Bot & Plant Sci Univ Calif Riverside CA 92521

JORDAN, MARK H(ENRY), CIVIL ENGINEERING. *Current Pos:* CONSULT ENGR, 76- *Personal Data:* b Lawrence, Mass, Apr 10, 15; m 39; c 2. *Educ:* US Naval Acad, BS, 37; Rensselaer Polytech Inst, BCE, 41, MCE, 42, MS, 65, PhD(mgt), 68. *Prof Exp:* Line admin, US Navy, 42-60; officer in charge, Naval Civil Engrs Corps Officers Sch, Pt Hueneme, Calif, 60-63; assoc prof civil eng, construct & mgt, Univ Mo, 66-67; dean continuing studies, Rensselaer Polytech Inst, 67-72, prof civil eng, 68-77. *Concurrent Pos:* Mem, Rensselaer County Charter Comn, 69-71; arbitrator, Am Arbit Asn, 70- *Mem:* Fel Am Soc Civil Engrs; Am Soc Eng Educ; Nat Soc Prof Engrs; Soc Am Mil Engrs; Am Cons Engrs Coun; Am Arbit Asn. *Res:* Industrial management, application of contemporary management concepts to engineering construction. *Mailing Add:* 46 East Rd Troy NY 12180

JORDAN, MARY ANN, MICROTUBULES, VINCA ALKALOIDS. *Current Pos:* postdoctoral fel, Univ Calif, Santa Barbara, 78-82, asst res biologist, 82-90, assoc res biologist, 91-75, RES BIOLOGIST, UNIV CALIF, SANTA BARBARA, 95-, ADJ PROF, 96- *Personal Data:* b Minneapolis, Minn, July 31, 40; m 84, David S Johnson; c Andrea (Lommen) & Kate (Lommen). *Educ:* Univ Minn, BA, 62; Univ Rochester, MS, 64, PhD(biol), 69. *Prof Exp:* Temp asst prof, Univ Wyo, 68-69; researcher biol, Univ Mich, 71-72 & Utah State Univ, 74-77. *Mem:* AAAS; Am Soc Cell Biol; Am Asn Cancer Res. *Res:* Microtubule structure and function; regulation by drug and physiological compounds; cell death and mechanism of action of anti-mitotic drugs, vinblastine and taxol. *Mailing Add:* Dept Molecular Cellular & Develop Biol Univ Calif Santa Barbara CA 93106. *Fax:* 805-893-4724; *E-Mail:* jordan@lifesci.lscf.ucsb.edu

JORDAN, MARY LUCILLE, SCIENCE LAW. *Current Pos:* CHMN, FED MINE SAFETY & HEALTH REV COMN, 94- *Educ:* St Bonaventure Univ, BA, 71; Anitoch Sch Law, JD, 76. *Prof Exp:* Atty, Off Fed Regist, Nat Archives & Records Admin; sr staff atty, United Mine Workers Am, 77-94. *Mailing Add:* Fed Mine Safety & Health Rev Comn 1730 K St NW Sixth Floor Washington DC 20006

JORDAN, NEAL F(RANCIS), ENGINEERING PHYSICS. *Current Pos:* sr res engr, 65-68, res assoc, 68-84, MGR SUBSURFACE IMAGING EXXON PROD RES, TEX, 84- *Personal Data:* b Franklinville, NY, July 8, 32; m 55, 94, Vaida Mikits; c Kirk G & Sarah E (Towler). *Educ:* Cornell Univ, BEngPhys, 55; Purdue Univ, MS, 59, PhD(eng sci), 63. *Prof Exp:* Instr continuum mech, Purdue Univ, 60-63; res engr, Jersey Prod Res Co, Okla, 63-65. *Concurrent Pos:* Consult, Gen Tech Corp, Ind, 59-63. *Mem:* Soc Eng Sci; Soc Explor Geophys. *Res:* Geophysics; nonlinear theories of continuous media; elastic wave propagation; exploration applications of potential fields. *Mailing Add:* 330 Knipp Houston TX 77024

JORDAN, PAUL H, JR, GASTROENTEROLOGY, SURGERY. *Current Pos:* PROF SURG, BAYLOR COL MED, 64- *Personal Data:* b Bigelow, Ark, Nov 22, 19; m 44; c 3. *Educ:* Univ Chicago, BS, 41, MD, 44; Univ Ill, MS, 50. *Prof Exp:* Asst prof surg, Sch Med, Univ Calif, Los Angeles, 55-58; assoc prof, Sch Med, Univ Fla, 59-64; chief staff, 69-70, chief surg, Vet Admin Hosp, Houston, 64-83. *Concurrent Pos:* Fel, NIH, 58-59. *Mem:* Am Surg Asn; Soc Exp Biol & Med; Soc Univ Surg; Am Col Surg; Am Gastroenterol Asn. *Res:* Gastrointestinal physiology. *Mailing Add:* Baylor Col Med One Baylor Plaza SM 1639 Houston TX 77030-2717

JORDAN, PETER ALBION, ECOLOGY, WILDLIFE MANAGEMENT. *Current Pos:* ASSOC PROF, DEPT FISHERIES & WILDLIFE, UNIV MINN, ST PAUL, 74- *Personal Data:* b Oakland, Calif, Jan 2, 30; div; c 3. *Educ:* Univ Calif, Berkeley, AB, 55, PhD(zool), 67. *Prof Exp:* Asst specialist studies migratory deer, Univ Calif, Berkeley, 55-61, teaching asst zool, 61-62, instr, 62-63; res assoc ecol moose & wolves, Purdue Univ, 63-66; asst prof wildlife ecol, Sch Forestry, Yale Univ, 67-74. *Concurrent Pos:* Bd dirs, Minn Zoo. *Mem:* Wildlife Soc; Am Soc Naturalists; Am Soc Mammal. *Res:* Behavior, population dynamics and food habits of wild ungulates and carnivores; impact of herbivorous mammals upon forest vegetation; sodium acquisition and aquatic feeding by forest herbivores; management of big game; ecosystem processes; integration of wildlife habitat with timber management. *Mailing Add:* Fisheries 200 Hodson Hall Univ Min 1980 Folwell Ave St Paul MN 55108-1037

JORDAN, PETER C H, THEORETICAL CHEMISTRY. *Current Pos:* asst prof chem, 64-70, assoc prof, 70-81, PROF CHEM, BRANDEIS UNIV, 81- *Personal Data:* b London, Eng, May 3, 36; US citizen; m 79, Barbara Palmer. *Educ:* Calif Inst Technol, BS, 57; Yale Univ, PhD(quantum mech), 60. *Prof Exp:* NSF fel, 60-62; asst res chemist, Univ Calif, San Diego, 62-64. *Concurrent Pos:* Guggenheim fel, 71-72; Marion & Jaspar Whiting fel, 78-79; vis prof, Dept Biol, Konstanz Univ, 78-79; vis scientist, Univ Houston, 86-87, Univ Groningen, 93-94. *Mem:* AAAS; Am Phys Soc; Biophys Soc; Am Chem Soc. *Res:* Statistical mechanics; quantum chemistry; irreversible thermodynamics; membrane transport. *Mailing Add:* Dept Chem Brandeis Univ Waltham MA 02154. *E-Mail:* jordan@binah.cc.brandeis.edu

JORDAN, RICHARD CHARLES, MECHANICAL ENGINEERING. *Current Pos:* Eng Exp Sta, Univ Minn, Minneapolis, 37-41, asst dir, 41-44, from asst prof to prof mech eng, 41-76, dir, Indust Labs, 44-45, head, Dept Mech Eng, 50-76 & Sch Mech & Aerospace Eng, 66-76, assoc dean, Inst Technol, 77-80, EMER PROF MECH ENG, UNIV MINN, MINNEAPOLIS, 76- *Personal Data:* b Minneapolis, Minn, Apr 16, 09; m 35, Freda Laudon; c Mary Ann, Carol & Linda. *Educ:* Univ Minn, BAeroE, 31, MS, 33, PhD(mech eng), 40. *Honors & Awards:* Wolverine Award, Am Soc Heat, Refrig & Air-Conditioning Engrs, 49, F Paul Anderson Medal & E K Campbell Award, 66. *Prof Exp:* Head, Air Conditioning Div, Minneapolis Br, Am Radiator & Stand Sanit Corp, 33-36; instr petrol eng, Univ Tulsa, 36-37. *Concurrent Pos:* Consult, Corps Engrs, US Army, 51-52; adv, Panel Eng Sci, NSF, 54-57, chmn, 56-57; mem, Div Eng & Indust Res, Nat Acad Sci-Nat Res Coun, 54-74, chmn div, 61-65, mem-at-large, 65-74, chmn, ad hoc comt eng develop countries, 59-61 & ad hoc comt eng & soc sci, 61-65; deleg, Int Cong Refrig, Paris, 55, Copenhagen, 59, Munich, 63, Madrid, 67, Wash, 71 & Moscow, 75; US deleg, Int Inst Paris, 57-63, US Nat Comt, Moscow & Prague, 58 & 59-63, tech bd, 63-67; Am Stand Asn deleg, Int Stand Orgn, London, 58; deleg, World Power Conf, Melbourne, 62; mem, CENTO Surv Mission, Iran, Pakistan & Turkey, 63; vchmn eng & accreditation comt, Region VII, Eng Coun Prof Develop, 64-66, chmn eng accreditation comt, Region VIII, 66-69; consult, AID, 64-, Int Power Technol, 79-, Onan Corp, 83- & var indust orgn; mem adv comt int orgns & progs, Off Int Rels, Nat Acad Sci, 65-; mem, Fulbright Prog Long-Range Planning Team, US-Brazil Prog, 67; chmn study group indust res, US-Brazil Sci Coop Prog, Nat Acad Sci, Rio de Janeiro & Washington, DC, 67 & Belo Horizonte, Brazil & Houston, 68; mem, Conf Strategy for Technol Develop Latin-Am, 69; mem bd dirs, Onan Corp Div, McGraw-Edison Corp, 72-83; energy consult, Control Data Corp, 77-84; World Bank consult alt energy resources, Brazil, 76; chmn, comt rev prog, Div Conserv & Community Syst, Nat Res Coun, 80- *Mem:* Nat Acad Eng; fel AAAS; fel Am Soc Mech Engrs; Nat Soc Prof Engrs; fel Am Soc Heat, Refrig & Air-Conditioning Engrs (treas, 50, vpres, 51-52, pres, 53). *Res:* Air filtration; dust analyses; conditions of comfort; heat transmission; refrigeration; quantitative and qualitative analysis of atmospheric dust; solar energy; engineering. *Mailing Add:* 18418 Horseshoe Circle Rio Verde AZ 85263-7036. *E-Mail:* jordan409@aol.com

JORDAN, ROBERT KENNETH, ULTRA-FINE INORGANIC PARTICLES. *Current Pos:* DIR ENG RES & DEVELOP, ENG RES INST, GANNON UNIV, 80-, DIR METALLIDING INST, SCIENTIST IN RESIDENCE, 83- *Personal Data:* b Clearfield, Pa, Dec 12, 25; m 48; c 3. *Educ:* Tufts Col, BS, 54. *Prof Exp:* Chemist, energy res & develop, Olin-Mathieson Chem Co, 54-56; mgr, nuclear div & asst mgr chem, plastics & metals, res div, Curtiss-Wright Corp, 56-60; mgr new prod, Gen Tire Chem-Plastics, 60-65; proj mgr new prod, US Steel Corp, 65-73; consult, energy-indust, Brookhaven Nat Lab, 74-80. *Concurrent Pos:* Expert deleg, NATO, Comm Challenges of Modern Soc Conf, Steel Indust, 75-78; indust consult, 75-82. *Res:* Metallurgical (Metalliding), ceramics, minerals extraction, metals processes, organic and inorganic fluorides, organic nitrogenous and inorganic phosphorous fertilizers research and development; crude oil conversion to petrochemicals, organic intermediates, polymers and plastics-elastomers; metals surface and subsurface alloying. *Mailing Add:* Gannon Univ Erie PA 16541. *Fax:* 814-455-2631

JORDAN, ROBERT LAWRENCE, ANATOMY, TERATOLOGY. *Current Pos:* Asst prof, 70-74, ASSOC PROF ANAT, MED COL VA, 74- *Personal Data:* b Miami, Fla, May 7, 41; div; c 2. *Educ:* Fla Southern Col, BS, 65; Univ Fla, 65-66; Univ Cincinnati, PhD(anat), 69. *Concurrent Pos:* USPHS fel teratology & toxicol, Kettering Lab, Univ Cincinnati, 69-70; vis prof anat, St Georges Med Sch, Greneda, West Indies, 79- *Mem:* Teratology Soc; Am Asn Anat; Sigma Xi. *Mailing Add:* Dept Anat Sci St Georges Univ PO Box 7 St Georges Grenada. *Fax:* 473-444-2887

JORDAN, ROBERT MANSEAU, ANIMAL SCIENCE. *Current Pos:* RETIRED. *Personal Data:* b Minneapolis, Minn, Feb 13, 20; m 42; c 3. *Educ:* Univ Minn, BS, 42; SDak State Col, MS, 49; Kans State Col, PhD(animal nutrit), 53. *Honors & Awards:* Animal Mgt Award, Am Soc Animal Sci, 83,. *Prof Exp:* Instr animal husb, Univ Minn, 42; sales rep, Lyon Chem, Minn, 45; instr, SDak State Col, 48-49, from asst prof to assoc prof, 49-54; from asst prof to assoc prof, Univ Minn, St Paul, 54-64, prof animal husb, 64- *Concurrent Pos:* Mem, Comt Nutrient Req Horses, Nat Res Coun, 78, chmn, Comt Nutrient Req Sheep, 80-85. *Mem:* Fel Am Soc Animal Sci; Brit Soc Animal Prod; Equine Nutrit & Physiol Soc; Acad Natural Sci. *Res:* Use of hormones in animal production; digestibility studies; sheep nutrition; protein, calcium and phosphorus energy requirements for growth, reproduction, lactation and work of horses; copper toxicity studies with horses; pasture research involving development of low alkaloid varieties of canary grass and energy intakes by lamb grazing legume or grass pastures; silage studies and non-protein sources of nitrogen for horses; milk replacer studies for the committee for lamb nutrition and management; nutrition requirements for Angora goats. *Mailing Add:* Dept Animal Sci Univ Minn 122 Peters Hall St Paul MN 55108. *Fax:* 612-625-5789

JORDAN, ROBERT R, GEOLOGY. *Current Pos:* STATE GEOLOGIST & DIR, DEL GEOL SURV, 69-; PROF GEOL, UNIV DEL, 88- *Personal Data:* b New York, NY, June 5, 37; m 58; c 2. *Educ:* Hunter Col, AB, 58; Bryn Mawr Col, MA, 62, PhD(geol), 64. *Honors & Awards:* Autometric Award, Am Soc Photogrammetry, 76; Cert of Merit, Am Asn Petrol Geologists, 87, Distinguished Serv Award, 88; Presidential Cert of Merit, Am Inst Prof Geologists, 90. *Prof Exp:* From geologist to asst state geologist, Del Geol Surv, 58-69; from instr to assoc prof geol, Univ Del, 62-88. *Concurrent Pos:* Chmn, Del State Boundary Comn, 71-; gov rep, Outer Continental Shelf, Dept Interior, 74-77 & Policy Comt, 85-, chmn, 93-94; mem, Comt Offshore Energy Technol & Alaska OCS Comt, 92-94, Nat Acad Sci-Nat Res Coun, 78-80, US Nat Comt Geol, 90-; regional coordr, Asn Am Petrol Geologists, 78-84; mem, NAm Comn Stratig Nomenclature, 78, vchmn-secy, 78-82 & 89-90, chmn, 82-83 & 90-91; house of delegates, Am Asn Petrol Geologists, 90-; pres-elect, Del Acad Sci, 90, pres, 91. *Mem:* Asn Am State Geol (secy-treas, 77-81, vpres, 81-82, pres-elect, 82-83, pres, 83-84); Am Inst Prof Geol; fel Geol Soc Am; Soc Econ Paleont & Mineral; hon mem Am Asn Petrol Geologists; Nat Asn Geol Teachers; Sigma Xi; Am Geol Inst (treas, 92-93). *Res:* Sedimentary petrology; stratigraphy; geology of the Atlantic Coastal Plain; ground water supplies. *Mailing Add:* Del Geol Surv Univ Del Newark DE 19717-0001

JORDAN, RUSSELL THOMAS, VIROLOGY, IMMUNOCHEMISTRY. *Current Pos:* PRES, MED-X-CONSULT, FT COLLINS, 77- *Personal Data:* b Geneseo, NY; m 46; c 6. *Educ:* Univ Ark, BS, 49, MS, 51; Univ Mich, PhD(virol), 53. *Prof Exp:* Rackham res fel, Sch Med, Univ Mich, 53, asst prof bact, 53-54; clin asst prof infectious dis, Sch Med, Univ Calif, Los Angeles, 54-59; chief, Dept Exp Immunol, Nat Jewish Hosp, Denver, 60-63; dir res & labs, Biomed Res Labs Div, Bio-Organic Chem Inc, 63-71; vpres sci & technol, C F Kettering Found, dir, C F Kettering Lab & vpres, Kettering Sci Res, Inc, 71-73; pres & chmn bd, Vipont Chem & Res Ctr, 73-75; res dir, Chemex Corp, 75-77. *Concurrent Pos:* Chmn dept microbiol, City of Hope Med Ctr, Calif, 54-60; lectr, Univ Calif, Los Angeles, 56-59; res fel immunochem, Calif Inst Technol, 58-59; asst prof, Sch Med, Univ Colo, Denver, 61-71; chief space biomed res, Aerospace Group, Martin-Marietta Corp, Colo, 66-71. *Mem:* Am Asn Immunol; Soc Exp Biol & Med; Am Asn Cancer Res; Sigma Xi; NY Acad Sci. *Res:* Microbiology; interference phenomenon; infection and resistance; virus induced neoplasms; immunochemistry of cancer; immunochemical properties of tumor specific antigens and antibodies. *Mailing Add:* 1809 Indian Meadows Lane Ft Collins CO 80525

JORDAN, SCOTT WILSON, PATHOLOGY. *Current Pos:* from asst prof to assoc prof, 65-82, PROF PATH, SCH MED, UNIV NMEX, 82- *Personal Data:* b Iola, Kans, Aug 22, 34; m 55; c 3. *Educ:* Univ Kans, AB, 56, MD, 59. *Prof Exp:* From intern to resident path, Med Ctr, Univ Kans, 59-63; pathologist, Nat Acad Sci-Nat Res Coun Atomic Bomb Casualty Comn, 63-65. *Concurrent Pos:* USPHS fel, Med Ctr, Univ Kans, 60-63; consult, Midwest Res Inst, Mo, 62-63 & Nat Cancer Inst, 74-77. *Mem:* Am Soc Cytol (past pres); Am Asn Path; Int Acad Path; fel Am Bd Path. *Res:* Pathology of radiation injury; diagnostic cytology; digital image analysis. *Mailing Add:* Dept Path Univ NMex Sch Med Albuquerque NM 87131-0001. *Fax:* 505-277-7224

JORDAN, STANLEY CLARK, PEDIATRICS, PEDIATRIC NEPHROLOGY. *Current Pos:* ASST PROF PEDIAT, UNIV CALIF, LOS ANGELES, 80- *Personal Data:* b Elkin, NC, Apr 13, 47; m 76; c 1. *Educ:* Univ NC, Chapel Hill, AB, 69, MD, 73. *Prof Exp:* Asst clin prof pediat, Univ Southern Calif, 79-80. *Concurrent Pos:* Prin investr, NIH clin investr award, 80-83. *Mem:* Am Soc Pediat Nephrol. *Res:* Renal immmunopathology and transplantation immunology. *Mailing Add:* Cedars-Sinai Med Ctr 8700 Beverly Blvd Los Angeles CA 90048-1804

JORDAN, STEVEN LEE, COMPUTER GRAPHICS, MATHEMATICS EDUCATION. *Current Pos:* From asst prof to assoc prof math, 70-96, ASSOC PROF ORAL & MAXILLOFACIAL SURG, UNIV ILL, CHICAGO, 87-, PROF MATH, 95- *Personal Data:* b Jersey City, NJ, Feb 17, 43; m 66; c 2. *Educ:* Princeton Univ, AB, 65; Univ Calif, Berkeley, MA, 67, PhD(math), 70. *Concurrent Pos:* NSF res grant, 70-72; Carnegie Found res grant, 75-76; HEW res grant, 85-86, Dept Educ grants, 86-; co-dir, UIC/CCC Partnership Prog, 87-; consult to bds educ & biochem labs. *Mem:* Am Math Soc; Math Asn Am; Sigma Xi; Nat Coun Teachers Math. *Res:* Differential geometry and complex manifolds; all levels of mathematics teacher education; history of mathematics; applications of computer graphics, statistics, and modelling to radiology and oral surgery. *Mailing Add:* Math Dept Univ Ill M/C 249 851 S Morgan Chicago IL 60607

JORDAN, STUART DAVIS, SOLAR PHYSICS. *Current Pos:* res scientist, Lab Astron & Solar Physics, 68-84, head, Solar Physics Br, 84-89, SR STAFF SCIENTIST, GODDARD SPACE FLIGHT CTR, NASA, 89- *Personal Data:* b St Louis, Mo, July 25, 36; m 61, Elizabeth Roemar; c John S & James W. *Educ:* Washington Univ, BS, 58; Univ Colo, Boulder, PhD(physics, astrophys), 68. *Prof Exp:* Res adminr plasma dynamics, Air Force Off Sci Res, 59-63; res asst, Joint Inst Lab Astrophys, 63-68. *Concurrent Pos:* Actg chief solar physics, NASA Hq, 74; proj scientist, Solar Optical Telescope, 76-85; coordr, Nonthermal Stellar Atmospheres, NASA, 78-93. *Mem:* Am Astron Soc; Int Astron Union; Sigma Xi. *Res:* Spectral line formation in solar atmosphere; shock wave heating of solar atmosphere; energy balance and temperature structure of stellar atmospheres. *Mailing Add:* Code 680 Lab Astron & Solar Physics Goddard Space Flight Ctr Greenbelt MD 20771

JORDAN, THOMAS FREDRICK, THEORETICAL PHYSICS. *Current Pos:* PROF PHYSICS, UNIV MINN, DULUTH, 70- *Personal Data:* b Duluth, Minn, June 4, 36; div. *Educ:* Univ Minn, Duluth, BA, 58; Univ Rochester, PhD(physics), 62. *Prof Exp:* Res assoc physics, Univ Rochester, 61-62, instr, 62-63; NSF fel, Berne, 63-64; from asst prof to assoc prof, Univ Pittsburgh, 64-70. *Concurrent Pos:* Sloan Found fel, 65-67. *Res:* Mathematical physics; quantum mechanics; field theory; relativistic particle dynamics; scattering theory; elementary particle interactions; quantum theory of optical coherence; hydrodynamics of Great Lakes circulation; general relativity. *Mailing Add:* Dept Physics Univ Minn Duluth MN 55812

JORDAN, THOMAS HILLMAN, GEOPHYSICS. *Current Pos:* HEAD DEPT, EARTH ATMOSPHERIC & PLANETARY SCIS, MASS INST TECHNOL, 88- *Personal Data:* b Coco Solo, CZ, Oct 8, 48; m 73; c 1. *Educ:* Calif Inst Technol, BS, 69, MS, 70, PhD(geophys), 72. *Honors & Awards:* James B Macelwane Award, Am Geophys Union, 83. *Prof Exp:* Asst prof geophys, Princeton Univ, 72-75; assoc prof geophys, Scripps Inst Oceanog, Univ Calif, San Diego, 75-88. *Concurrent Pos:* Alfred P Sloan fel, physics, 80-82. *Mem:* Fel Am Geophys Union; Geol Soc Am. *Res:* Structure of the earth's interior; earthquake processes; mantle dynamics; wave propagation; inverse theory. *Mailing Add:* Dept Earth Sci Mass Inst Technol 77 Massachusetts Ave Cambridge MA 02139-4307. *Fax:* 617-253-7651

JORDAN, THOMAS L, BACTERIOLOGY. *Current Pos:* FAC BIOL, NC AGR & TECH STATE UNIV, 81- *Personal Data:* b Yazoo City, Miss, Apr 27, 43; m 79; c 1. *Educ:* Rockhurst Col, Kansas City, Mo, BA, 64; Univ Wis-Madison, MS, 68, PhD(bact), 72. *Prof Exp:* NIH fel bact, Univ Wash, Seattle, 72-75; fac biol, Alcorn State Univ, Miss, 76-78, Dillard Univ, New Orleans, 78-81. *Concurrent Pos:* Fel, Marine Biol Lab, 79, Sch Med, Tulane Univ, 80-81; asst res prof, Univ SC, Columbia, 83-84. *Mem:* Am Soc Microbiol. *Res:* Relationship between energy metabolism and starvation induced arrest of the cell cycle in Caulobacter crescentus. *Mailing Add:* Dept Biol NC Agr & Tech State Univ 1601 E Market St Greensboro NC 27401-3209. *Fax:* 910-334-7105

JORDAN, TRUMAN H, PHYSICAL CHEMISTRY. *Current Pos:* from asst prof to assoc prof, 66-77, PROF CHEM, CORNELL COL, 77- *Personal Data:* b Wayne, Mich, Nov 18, 37; m 61, Linda Wilcox; c Jennifer, Jackie & Joy. *Educ:* Albion Col, BA, 59; Harvard Univ, MA, 62, PhD(chem), 64. *Prof Exp:* NASA fel & res assoc crystallog, Univ Pittsburgh, 64-66. *Concurrent Pos:* NIH fel, Nat Bur Stand, 72-73; vis prof, Univ Iowa, 78-79 & 86-87. *Mem:* AAAS; Am Chem Soc; Am Crystallog Asn; Int Asn Dent Res. *Res:* Molecular structure by means of x-ray crystallography; dental chemistry. *Mailing Add:* 600 First St W Mt Vernon IA 52314. *E-Mail:* truman@cornell_iowa.edu

JORDAN, V CRAIG, ENDOCRINE PHARMACOLOGY. *Current Pos:* PROF CANCER PHARMACOL, ROBERT B LURIE CANCER CTR, NORTHWESTERN UNIV MED SCH, 93-, DIR BREAST CANCER RES PROG, 93- *Personal Data:* b New Braunfels, Tex, July 25, 47; m 93, Monica Morrow; c Helen & Alexandra. *Educ:* Univ Leeds, Eng, BS(Hons), 69, PhD(pharmacol), 72, DSc, 85. *Honors & Awards:* Bruce Cain Mem Award, Am Asn Cancer Res, 89; Inaugural Brinker Int Breast Cancer Award, Susan G Komen Breast Cancer Found, 92; Cameron Prize, Univ Edinburgh, Scotland, 93; Sir John Gaddum Mem Award, Brit Pharmacol Soc, 93; Am Soc Pharmacol & Exp Therapeut Award, 93; William L McGuire Mem Award, San Antonio, 94; Ital-Am Award for Sci Excellence in Med, 95; Sixth Cino Del Duca Award Oncol, Paris, 97. *Prof Exp:* Vis scientist, Worcester Found Exp Biol, 72-74; fac lectr pharmacol, Univ Leeds, 74-78; head endocrinol unit, Ludwig Inst Cancer Res, Switz, 79-80; from asst prof to prof human oncol, Clin Cancer Ctr, Univ Wis, 80-85, prof human oncol & pharmacol, 85-93. *Concurrent Pos:* Dir breast cancer res prog, Northwestern Univ. *Mem:* Endocrine Soc; Soc Surg Oncol; fel Royal Soc Chem; Brit Pharm Soc; Am Asn Cancer Res; Am Soc Pharmacol & Exp Therapeut. *Res:* Development of taroxifer and understanding of the molecular mechanisms of estrogen and antiestrogen acid. *Mailing Add:* Robert B Lurie Cancer Ctr Northwestern Univ Med Sch 303 E Chicago Chicago IL 60611. *Fax:* 312-908-1372

JORDAN, WADE H(AMPTON), JR, electrochemical kinetics, batteries, for more information see previous edition

JORDAN, WAYNE ROBERT, PLANT PHYSIOLOGY, BIOCHEMISTRY. *Current Pos:* DIR, TEX WATER RESOURCES INST, TEX A&M UNIV. *Personal Data:* b Kankakee, Ill, Jan 7, 40; m 60, Dorothy M Cailteux; c 6. *Educ:* Univ Ill, Urbana, BS, 61, MS, 62; Univ Calif, Davis, PhD(plant physiol), 68. *Honors & Awards:* Dep Chancellor's Award Res, Tex A&M Univ, 83. *Prof Exp:* From asst prof to prof, 68-75, prof crop physiol, Tex Agr Exp Sta, 75-, resident dir, Black Land Res Ctr, 80-83. *Concurrent Pos:* Assoc ed, Agron J, 78-81. *Mem:* Am Soc Plant Physiol; fel Crop Sci Soc Am; fel Am Soc Agron; Am Water Resources Asn; Am Water Works Asn. *Res:* Plant water relations; drought resistance; root physiology; hormonal regulation of abscission; perception and transduction of environmental stimuli. *Mailing Add:* Tex Water Resources Inst Tex A&M Univ 301 Scoates Hall MS 2118 College Sta TX 77843-2118. *Fax:* 409-845-8554

JORDAN, WILLARD CLAYTON, NUCLEAR PHYSICS. *Current Pos:* SCIENTIST, LOCKHEED MISSILES & SPACE RES LABS, PALO ALTO, 64- *Personal Data:* b Richmond, Ind, May 13, 22; m 46; c 2. *Educ:* Miami Univ, BA, 45; Univ Mich, MS, 48, PhD, 54. *Prof Exp:* Res assoc, Argonne Nat Lab, 51-53, asst physicist, Exp Nuclear Physics, 53-54; physicist, Res Labs, Bendix Corp, 54-64. *Concurrent Pos:* Asst, Univ Mich, 48-53; vis physicist, Lawrence Radiation Lab, Univ Calif, 58-64. *Mem:* Am Phys Soc; Am Nuclear Soc; Am Asn Physics Teachers; Sigma Xi. *Res:* Radioactive decay; nuclear reactors; thermonuclear research; space physics. *Mailing Add:* 24 Oak St Los Altos CA 94022-2266

JORDAN, WILLIAM D(ITMER), MECHANICAL ENGINEERING. *Current Pos:* RETIRED. *Personal Data:* b Selma, Ala, Feb 5, 22; m 47, Carolyn Carter; c William Jr, Lucy & Rebecca. *Educ:* Univ Ala, BS, 42, MS, 49; Univ Ill, PhD(theoret & appl mech), 52. *Prof Exp:* Asst prof eng mech, Univ Ala, 46-50, asst theoret & appl mech, Univ Ill, 50-52, from assoc prof eng mech to prof, Univ Ala, 52-86, head Dept Eng Mech, 61-86; from assoc prof eng mech to prof, Univ Ala, 52-86, head Dept Eng Mech, 61-86. *Concurrent Pos:* Distinguished eng fel, Univ Ala, 88. *Mem:* Am Soc Eng Educ; fel Am Soc Mech Engrs; Am Soc Mech Engrs; Am Acad Mech; Nat Soc Prof Engrs. *Res:* Strength of materials; structures; stress analysis; thermal stresses; buckling. *Mailing Add:* Dept Eng Mech PO Box 870278 Tuscaloosa AL 35487

JORDAN, WILLIAM MALCOLM, HISTORY OF GEOLOGY. *Current Pos:* assoc prof, 66-69, chmn, 67-72, PROF GEOL, MILLERSVILLE UNIV, 69- *Personal Data:* b Brooklyn, NY, June 19, 36; m 63; c 2. *Educ:* Columbia Univ, BA, 57, MA, 61; Univ Wis, PhD(geol), 65. *Prof Exp:* Res geologist, Jersey Prod Res Co, Okla, 64-65, Esso Prod Res Co, Tex, 65-66. *Concurrent Pos:* Secy/treas, Hist Geol Div, Geol Soc Am. *Mem:* Am Asn Petrol Geologists; Geol Soc Am; Hist Sci Soc; Nat Asn Geol Teachers; Soc Econ Paleont & Mineral; Hist Earth Sci Soc. *Res:* Mature clastic sediments; paleocurrents and paleoclimatology; sedimentary facies and petroleum accumulation; history of geology. *Mailing Add:* Dept Earth Sci Millersville Univ PO Box 1002 Millersville PA 17551-0302

JORDAN, WILLIAM R, III, ECOLOGICAL RESTORATION, HISTORY OF IDEAS ABOUT RELATIONSHIP BETWEEN HUMANS & ENVIRONMENT. *Current Pos:* OUT REACH PROG MGR, ARBORETUM UNIV WIS-MADISON, 77- *Personal Data:* b Denver, Colo, Apr 30, 44; m 66, Barbara K Post; c 1. *Educ:* Marquette Univ, BS, 66; Univ Wis-Madison, PhD(bot), 71, MA, 74. *Prof Exp:* Newswriter, Publ & Outreach Prog, Am Chem Soc, 75-76. *Concurrent Pos:* Consult, Environ Adv Prog, Quest Found, 91-; vis scholar, NSF, Univ NTex, 93-94. *Mem:* Soc Ecol Restoration. *Res:* Ecological restoration as a technique for research, a teaching technique and a performing art; history of ideas about the relationship between human being and the rest of nature, through intellectual history, anthropology, literature and the arts. *Mailing Add:* Univ Wis Arboretum 1207 Seminole Hwy Madison WI 53711. *Fax:* 608-262-5209

JORDAN, WILLIAM STONE, JR, PUBLIC HEALTH & EPIDEMIOLOGY. *Current Pos:* dir, 76-87, EMER DIR & VOL, MICROBIOL & INFECTIOUS DIS PROG, NAT INST ALLERGY & INFECTIOUS DIS, 87- *Personal Data:* b Fayetteville, NC, Sept 28, 17; m 47, Marion Anderson; c William S III & Marion A. *Educ:* Univ NC, AB, 38; Harvard Univ, MD, 42. *Prof Exp:* From intern to asst resident, 2nd Med Serv, Boston City Hosp, 42-43, resident, 46-47; from instr to assoc prof prev med, Sch Med, Western Res Univ, 48-58, from instr to asst prof med, 48-58; prof prev & internal med & chmn dept prev med, Sch Med, Univ Va, 58-67; prof med & community med, Univ Ky, 67-74, dean, Col Med, 67-74. *Concurrent Pos:* Teaching fel prev med & med, Sch Med, Western Res Univ, 47-48; dir comn acute respiratory dis, Epidemiol Bd, US Armed Forces; consult, Surgeon Gen; mem, comn epidemiol & vet follow-up studies, Nat Acad Sci, 65-72; mem infectious dis adv comt, Nat Inst Allergy & Infectious Dis, 67-71; mem, Panel Rev Viral & Rickettsial Vaccines, Food & Drug Admin, 75-91; consult, Nat Vaccine Prog Off, Pub Health Servs, 91- *Mem:* Am Epidemiol Soc; Am Soc Clin Invest; Am Asn Immunol; Asn Am Physicians; Am Soc Microbiol; Infectious Dis Soc Am. *Res:* Etiology and epidemiology of acute respiratory disease; accelerated development of new vaccines. *Mailing Add:* NIH Solar Bldg Rm 2C37 Bethesda MD 20892

JORDAN-MOLERO, JAIME E, PLANT PHYSIOLOGY, WEED CONTROL. *Current Pos:* Res asst agr, Univ PR, 63-69, asst agronomist agr res, 69-79, asst dir, Agr Exp Sta, 77-79, asst dean & dir, 79-84, ASSOC PROF AGR RES, AGR EXP STA, UTUADO REGIONAL COL, UNIV PR, 79- *Personal Data:* b Utauado, PR, Jan 5, 41; m 72; c 3. *Educ:* Univ PR, BS, 63, MS, 70; Univ Ill, Urbana-Champaign, PhD(agron), 77; Harvard Univ, IEM, 84. *Concurrent Pos:* Prof crop physiol, Mayaguez Campus, Univ PR, 77-; prof tropical crops, Los Angeles Montana Regional Col-Utuado PR. *Mem:* Am Soc Agr Sci; Weed Sci Soc Am. *Res:* Crop nutrition; coffee genetics and selection; plant physiology; weed control physiology and ecology; citrus breeding. *Mailing Add:* Agr Exp Sta Call Box 2500 Utuado PR 00641. *Fax:* 787-894-2891

JORDEN, JAMES ROY, FORMATION EVALUATION, WELL LOGGING. *Personal Data:* b Oklahoma City, Okla, Apr 16, 34; m 56, Shirley A Swan; c Philip T & David E. *Educ:* Univ Tulsa, BS, 57. *Honors & Awards:* Distinguished Serv Award, Soc Petrol Engrs, 88, DeGolyer Distinguished Serv Medal, 91. *Prof Exp:* Mem eng staff, Shell Oil Co, 60-81, sr tech specialist petrophys eng, Head Off Prod, 81-85, mgr, Petrol Eng Res, Shell Develop Co, 85-88, mgr tech training, 88-93, mgr CPI training, Head Off Explor & Prod, 93-95. *Concurrent Pos:* Dir, Soc Petrol Engrs, 79-82; bd chmn, Soc Petrol Engrs Serv Corp, 85, pres, 86 & 89-90; treas, Soc Petrol Engrs Found, 91-92, sr vpres, 93-95, pres, 95- *Mem:* Hon mem Soc Petrol Engrs (pres, 84). *Res:* Co-author of a three-volume series on formation evaluation and well logging. *Mailing Add:* 10926 Piping Rock Lane Houston TX 77042-2728

JORDEN, ROGER M, ENVIRONMENTAL ENGINEERING, WATER CHEMISTRY. *Current Pos:* PRES, CLEAR CORP, 87- *Personal Data:* b Carthage, Mo, Nov 15, 35; m 75, Joan E; c Cherlynne. *Educ:* Univ Tex, Austin, BS, 59; Univ Ariz, MS, 62; Univ Ill, Urbana, PhD(civil eng), 68. *Honors & Awards:* Eddy Award, Water Pollution Control Fedn, 76. *Prof Exp:* Res asst hydrol, Inst Water Utilization, Univ Ariz, 59-62; res assoc, Travelers Res Inst, 62-64; res assoc sanit eng, Univ Ill, Urbana, 64-67, res fel, 67-68; asst prof environ eng, Univ Colo, Boulder, 68-75, assoc prof, 75-76; proj mgr, Elec Power Res Inst, Calif, 76-79; proj mgr water mgt, Colo Ute Elec Asn, Inc, 79-81; consult water mgt, 82-87. *Mem:* AAAS; Am Water Works Asn; Water Pollution Control Fedn; Am Chem Soc. *Res:* Coagulation-flocculation of dilute colloidal suspensions; physical-chemical removal of trace elements; environmental transport of trace elements; water pollution control in oil shale; side-stream lime softening; water management of zero discharge water systems in power plants. *Mailing Add:* Clear Corp 1750 30th St Boulder CO 80301

JORDIN, MARCUS WAYNE, PHARMACOLOGY. *Current Pos:* RETIRED. *Personal Data:* b Idaho Falls, Idaho, May 23, 27; m 56; c 2. *Educ:* Idaho State Col, BS, 49; Purdue Univ, MS, 52, PhD(pharmacol), 54. *Prof Exp:* Assoc prof, Sch Pharm, Univ Ark, Little Rock, 54-62, prof pharmacol & head dept, 62-90. *Mem:* Am Pharmaceut Asn. *Res:* Central nervous system drugs; tranquilizers and psychic energizers. *Mailing Add:* 309 Brookside Dr Little Rock AR 72205

JORDON, ROBERT EARL, DERMATOLOGY, IMMUNOLOGY. *Current Pos:* AT DERMAT DEPT, UNIV TEX HEALTH SCI CTR. *Personal Data:* b Buffalo, NY, May 7, 38; m 69; c 1. *Educ:* Hamilton Col, BA, 60; State Univ NY Buffalo, MD, 65; Univ Minn, Minneapolis, MS, 70. *Prof Exp:* Asst prof dermat & immunol, Mayo Med Sch Med, Univ Minn, Rochester, 71-77; prof & chmn sect dermat, Med Col Wis, 77- *Concurrent Pos:* Training grant dermat, Mayo Clin, 68-69; Nat Inst Arthritis, Metab & Digestive Dis res fel, Univ Minn, 72-73; vis asst prof & assoc mem grad fac, Univ Minn, Minneapolis, 71- *Mem:* AAAS; Am Asn Immunol; Am Fedn Clin Res; Soc Invest Dermat; Sigma Xi. *Res:* Immunopathology of bullous skin diseases using immunofluorescence, and complement research technics. *Mailing Add:* Dermat Dept Univ Tex Health Sci Ctr 6431 Fannin Suite 1204 Houston TX 77030-1501. *Fax:* 713-794-1836

JORDY, GEORGE Y, ENERGY. *Current Pos:* MEM STAFF, ENERGY RES DEPT, OFF PROG ANALYSIS, DEPT ENERGY, 80- *Personal Data:* b Pittsburgh, Pa, May 2, 32. *Educ:* Carnegie Mellon Univ, BS, 54; Univ Pennsylvania, MBA, 55; Univ Maryland, PhD,(math education), 76. *Mailing Add:* 20207 Grazing Way Gaithersburg MD 20879

JORGENSEN, CLIVE D, ENTOMOLOGY. *Current Pos:* Field dir ecol res, 60-63, from instr to assoc prof zool & entom, 63-73, PROF ZOOL, BRIGHAM YOUNG UNIV, 73-, CHMN DEPT, 74- *Personal Data:* b Orem, Utah, July 14, 31; m 55; c 3. *Educ:* Brigham Young Univ, BS, 54, MS, 57; Ore State Univ, PhD(entom), 64. *Concurrent Pos:* US Atomic Energy Comn res grant, 63-66; USDA res grant, 65-67; NSF grant, asst prof zool, Iowa State Univ, 71-72; coordr biol instr, Brigham Young Univ, 72-74. *Mem:* AAAS; Entom Soc Am; Am Soc Mammal. *Res:* Ecological research. *Mailing Add:* 1155 E 140 N Orem UT 84057

JORGENSEN, ERIK, ENVIRONMENTAL MANAGEMENT, FORESTRY. *Current Pos:* CONSULT PROF FORESTER, 87- *Personal Data:* b Denmark, Oct 28, 21; nat Can; m 46; c 2. *Educ:* Royal Vet & Agr Col, Denmark, MF, 46. *Prof Exp:* Asst forest path, Royal Vet & Agr Col, Denmark, 49-53, amanuensis, col & proj leader, Forest Exp Sta, 53-55; res officer in chg plantation dis, Can Dept Agr, 55-59; agr prof forest path, Univ Toronto, 59-63, assoc prof, Shade Tree Res Lab, 63-67, prof forestry, 67-73, in chg lab, 63-72; chief urban forestry prog, Forest Mgt Inst, Can Forestry Serv, Dept Environ, 73-78; dir & prof environ biol, Univ Guelph Arboretum, 78-86. *Mem:* Can Phytopath Soc; Arboricult Res & Educ Acad (pres, 76-78). *Res:* Urban forestry management and planning; environmental impact on/and by trees; tree diseases, physiology and breeding; arboriculture. *Mailing Add:* 507-172 Metcalfe St Guelph ON N1E 6J5 Can

JORGENSEN, GEORGE NORMAN, BIOCHEMISTRY, VIROLOGY. *Current Pos:* RETIRED. *Personal Data:* b Omaha, Nebr, Feb 22, 36; m 70; c 2. *Educ:* Univ Nebr, BS, 57; Univ Ill, MS, 68, PhD(biochem), 72. *Prof Exp:* Lab technician, Shell Chem Co, 57-58; res asst radiation biol, M D Anderson Hosp & Tumor Inst, 59-66; res assoc biochem virol, Baylor Col Med, 72-76; res assoc biol, Rice Univ, 77-78; res assoc, Univ Tex Med Sch Houston, Obstet Gynec, 79-80. *Mem:* Am Chem Soc; AAAS; Sigma Xi. *Res:* Studies of enzymes of snail metabolism such as urease, super oxide desmutase and mannitol oxidase concerned with comparative aspects of nitrogen metabolism and energy sources of snails; isolation and studies of hormone relaxin. *Mailing Add:* 8302 Greenbush St Houston TX 77025

JORGENSEN, HELMUTH ERIK MILO, PHYSICAL CHEMISTRY. *Current Pos:* from assoc prof to prof, 69-84, adj prof, 86-90, EMER PROF, HUDSON VALLEY COMM UNITY COL, 90- *Personal Data:* b Odense, Denmark, June 19, 27; nat US; m 53; c 3. *Educ:* Polytech Inst Brooklyn, BS, 50; Rutgers Univ, PhD(phys chem), 59. *Prof Exp:* Develop chemist, Sterling-Winthrop Res Inst, 50-51; res chemist, Schering Corp, 52-53; develop chemist, Am Cyanamid Co, 53-54; asst, Rutgers Univ, 54-58; res chemist, Distillation Prod Industs, Eastman Kodak Co, 58-60; assoc res chemist, Sterling-Winthrop Res Inst, NY, 60-69. *Mem:* Am Chem Soc. *Res:* Physical chemistry of polymers and colloids; new methods of teaching chemistry. *Mailing Add:* 66 Van Levven Br S Rensselaer NY 12144

JORGENSEN, JAMES D, SOLID STATE PHYSICS. *Current Pos:* Fel, Argonne Nat Lab, 75-77, asst physicist to physicist, 77-90, SR PHYSICIST, ARGONNE NAT LAB, 90- *Personal Data:* b Salina, Utah, Mar 23, 48; m 70, Ramona; c 6. *Educ:* Brigham Young Univ, BS, 70, PhD(physics), 75. *Honors & Awards:* Warren Diffraction Physics Award, 91; Barrett Award in Powder Diffraction, 97. *Concurrent Pos:* Mem, US Nat Comt Crystallog, Neutron Scattering Comn. *Mem:* Fel Am Phys Soc; Am Crystallog Asn; Int Union Crystallog. *Res:* Powder neutron diffraction at pulsed neutron sources; ternary superconductors; neutron diffraction at high pressure; oxide superconductors; colossal magnetoresistive materials; battery and fuel cell materials. *Mailing Add:* Mat Sci Div Argonne Nat Lab Bldg 223 Argonne IL 60439

JORGENSEN, JAMES H, PATHOLOGY, MICROBIOLOGY. *Current Pos:* from instr to assoc prof path & microbiol, Health Sci Ctr, 73-84, DIR CLIN MICROBIOL LABS, UNIV HOSP, UNIV TEX, 75-, PROF PATH, MED, MICROBIOL & CLIN LAB SCI, HEALTH SCI CTR, 84- *Personal Data:* b Dallas, Tex, July 11, 46; m 78, Jane Drummond. *Educ:* NTex State Univ, BA, 69, MS, 70; Univ Tex, PhD, 73. *Honors & Awards:* Becton-Dickinson & Co Award Clin Microbiol, 92. *Prof Exp:* Res assoc, Shriners Hosp for Crippled Children, 70-73; assoc dir, Bexar Co Hosp, 73-75. *Concurrent Pos:* James W McLaughlin Pre-Doctoral fel, Infection & Immunity, Med Branch Univ Tex, 71-73; consult microbiologist, Audie Murphy Vet Admin Hosp, San Antonio, 73-; chair, Nat Comt Clin Lab Stand Subcomt Antimicrobial Susceptibility Testing, 91- *Mem:* Fel Infectious Diseases Soc Am; fel Am Acad Microbiol; Am Soc Microbiol. *Res:* Rapid microbiology testing methods; anti-microbial susceptibility testing; Streptococcus pneumoniae and Haemophilus influenzae. *Mailing Add:* Dept Path Tex Med Sch Univ Tex 7703 Floyd Curl Dr San Antonio TX 78284-6200

JORGENSEN, JENS ERIK, MECHANICAL ENGINEERING, SYSTEMS ANALYSIS. *Current Pos:* asst prof, 68-73, assoc prof, 73-79, PROF MECH ENG, UNIV WASH, 79-, BOEING PROF MFG, 87- *Personal Data:* b Oslo, Norway, July 2, 36; US citizen; m 62; c 2. *Educ:* Mass Inst Technol, SB, 59, MS, 63, ScD(mech eng), 69. *Honors & Awards:* Ralph Teetor Award, Soc Automotive Engrs, 71. *Prof Exp:* Res engr, Cadilac Gage Co, Calif, 59-61; res engr, MHD Inc, Calif, 62; res asst mech eng, Mass Inst Technol, 63-65, instr, 65-68. *Concurrent Pos:* Nat Insts Health fel bioeng, 69; consult, Wash Iron Works, 69-70, Pac Northwest Forest & Range Exp Sta, US Forest Serv, 71-77, Weyerhaeuser Co, 79-81, Metro, 81-83 & Boeing Com Airlines, 83-85. *Mem:* Am Soc Mech Engrs; Soc Mfg Engrs; Sigma Xi. *Res:* Fluid power systems analysis; design and analysis of fluidic devices; control systems analysis; instrumentation design and performance analysis; design and control of large scale off road equipment for logging in national forests; manufacturing systems analysis and automation of manufacturing processes. *Mailing Add:* Dept Mech Eng Univ Wash Box 35260 Seattle WA 98195-2600

JORGENSEN, NEAL A, AGRICULTURAL ADMINISTRATION, DAIRY SCIENCE. *Current Pos:* From asst prof to prof diary sci, Col Agr & Life Sci, Univ Wis-Madison, 68-84, assoc dean, 84-91, asst dir, 84, assoc dir, 84-89, exec dir, 90-91, EXEC ASSOC DEAN & DIR, COL AGR & LIFE SCI, UNIV WIS-MADISON, 91- *Personal Data:* b Luck, Wis, Feb 3, 35; m 55; c 1. *Educ:* Univ Wis-River Falls, BS, 60; Univ Wis-Madison, MS, 62, PhD(dairy sci), 64. *Concurrent Pos:* Mem, Comt Animal Nutrit, Nat Res Coun, 81-88, Bd Agr, 90-; chair, Animal Systs Subcomt, Exp Sta Comt Orgn & Policy, 89- *Mem:* Am Dairy Sci Asn (pres, 90-91); Am Soc Animal Sci. *Res:* Agricultural administration; dairy cattle nutrition and management; preservation and utilization of forage crops; fiber requirements, amount, source, physical form; vitamin D and calcium metabolism. *Mailing Add:* Col Agr & Life Sci Univ Wis Rm 140 Agr Hall Madison WI 53706. *Fax:* 608-262-4556

JORGENSEN, PALLE E T, OPERATOR ALGEBRAS, MATHEMATICAL PHYSICS. *Current Pos:* PROF MATH, UNIV IOWA, 83- *Personal Data:* b Copenhagen, Denmark, Oct 8, 47; US citizen; m 75, Soon M Park; c Anton, Greta & Tina. *Educ:* Univ Aarhus, Denmark, AB, 68, MS, 70, PhD(math), 73. *Prof Exp:* Fel math, Univ Wash, 73-74 & Univ Pa, 74-77; asst prof, Stanford Univ, 77-80; assoc prof, Aarhus, 79-82; vis assoc prof, Univ Pa, 82-84. *Concurrent Pos:* Res fel, Danish Res Coun, 76-77 & NSF, 77-; ed, D Reidel Publ Co, 82-; ed, Am Math Soc, 88-; speaker, US-Japan Operator Algebra Conf, Philadelphia, 88. *Mem:* Danish Acad Sci; Am Math Soc; Danish Math Soc; Soc Indust & Appl Math; fel Royal Swed Acad Sci; NY Acad Sci. *Res:* Modern analysis; operator algebras, spectral theory, harmonic analysis, differential geometry, and mathematical physics; various monographs published. *Mailing Add:* Dept Math MacLean Hall Univ Iowa Iowa City IA 52242. *Fax:* 319-335-0627; *E-Mail:* jorgen@math.uiowa.edu

JORGENSEN, PAUL J, MATERIALS SCIENCE, CHEMISTRY. *Current Pos:* chmn, Ceramics Dept, Stanford Res Inst, 68-74, dir, Mat Res Ctr, 74-76, exec dir phys sci, 76-77, vpres phys & life sci, 77-80, sr vpres sci group, 80-88, exec vpres & chief operating officer, 88-94, EXEC VPRES, SRI INT, 94- *Personal Data:* b Midway, Utah, Sept 1, 30; m 59, Ardelle M Bloom; c Paula, Mark, Janet, LaDell, Brett & Scott. *Educ:* Brigham Young Univ, BS, 54; Univ Utah, PhD(mat sci), 60. *Honors & Awards:* I R 100 Award, 67. *Prof Exp:* Ceramist, Gen Elec Res Lab, 60-68. *Concurrent Pos:* Lectr, Univ Calif, Berkeley, 69-70; consult, GTE Sylvania, Inc, 71-; mem, Comt High Temp Chem, Nat Res Coun-Nat Acad Sci, 71-74 & Nat Mat Adv Bd, 81-84; chmn, Adv Coun, Col Eng, Univ Utah, 83-84; mem, bd dirs, Mirage Systs, 84-, SRI Int, 86-, Plant Cell Res Inst, 87-91, Devco, 87-93, David Sarnoff Res Ctr, 88-94; mem, adv coun, Kansai Res Inst, 87-93; mem, Int Panel Adv Technol, Singapore Inst Stand & Indust Res, 90-94. *Mem:* Fel Am Ceramic Soc; AAAS; Sigma Xi; Am Electronics Asn; Am Mgt Asn. *Res:* Kinetics of transport processes in ceramics, including sintering, solute segregation, grain growth, diffusion, electrical conductivity, oxidation, corrosion and permeation. *Mailing Add:* 333 Ravenswood Ave Menlo Park CA 94025

JORGENSEN, T, JR, MOLECULAR PHYSICS. *Current Pos:* RETIRED. *Personal Data:* b Long Ridge, Conn, Nov 13, 05. *Educ:* Univ Nebr, BS, 29, MS, 31; Harvard Univ, PhD(physics), 35. *Prof Exp:* Fac mem, Dept Physics, Univ Nebr, 34-75. *Mem:* Am Phys Soc. *Mailing Add:* 4932 High St Lincoln NE 68506

JORGENSEN, WILLIAM L, ORGANIC CHEMISTRY, THEORETICAL CHEMISTRY. *Current Pos:* C P WHITEHEAD PROF CHEM, YALE UNIV, 90- *Personal Data:* b New York, NY, Oct 5, 49. *Educ:* Princeton Univ, AB, 70; Harvard Univ, PhD(chem physics), 75. *Honors & Awards:* Ann Medal, Int Acad Quantum Molecular Sci, 86. *Prof Exp:* From asst prof to prof org chem, Purdue Univ, 75-90, H C Brown prof chem, 85-90. *Concurrent Pos:* Dreyfus teacher-scholar, Camille & Henry Dreyfus Found fel, 78-83; A P Sloan Found fel, 79-81; A C Cope scholar, 90. *Mem:* Am Chem Soc; AAAS. *Res:* Theoretical organic chemistry; computer simulations of molecular liquids and solutions; computer assisted synthetic analysis. *Mailing Add:* Dept Chem Yale Univ New Haven CT 06511-8118

JORGENSON, EDSEL CARPENTER, ZOOLOGY, NEMATOLOGY. *Current Pos:* RETIRED. *Personal Data:* b Kamas, Utah, Mar 11, 26; m 47; c 6. *Educ:* Univ Utah, BS, 53, MS, 56. *Prof Exp:* Nematologist, USDA, 54-62, res nematologist, Utah State Univ, 62-67, zoologist, Utah Exp Sta, 67-70, zoologist, Calif Exp Sta, 70-87. *Mem:* Soc Nematol; Orgn Trop Am Nematol; Am Phytopath Soc. *Res:* Nematode ecology, control, biology and interactions. *Mailing Add:* 7604 Branding Iron Ct Bakersfield CA 93309

JORGENSON, GORDON VICTOR, THIN FILMS. *Current Pos:* prin res scientist, Honeywell Inc, 78-79, sr prin res scientist, 80-84, res staff scientist, 84-90, SECT CHIEF, HONEYWELL INC, 91- *Personal Data:* b Sunburg, Minn, Jan 3, 33; m 57; c 2. *Educ:* St Olaf Col, BA, 54. *Prof Exp:* Physicist, Wright Air Develop Ctr, Wright-Patterson AFB, 54-55; prin lab attendant, Univ Minn, 56-57; assoc scientist, Gen Mills, Inc, 57-61, sr scientist, 61-63; sr scientist, Appl Sci Div, Litton Indust, Inc, 63-66; sr physicist, NStar Res & Develop Inst, 66-75; sr physicist, Midwest Res Inst, 75-78. *Mem:* Soc Photo-Optical Instrumentation Engrs; Am Vacuum Soc. *Res:* Surface physics research utilizing sputtering; effects of solar-wind bombardment of bodies in space; electrohydrodynamics; research in vacuum deposited thin films; optical coating technology. *Mailing Add:* 14609 Summit Oaks Dr Burnsville MN 55337

JORGENSON, JAMES WALLACE, CHROMATOGRAPHY, ELECTROPHORESIS. *Current Pos:* From asst prof to assoc prof, 79-87, PROF CHEM, UNIV NC, CHAPEL HILL, 87- *Personal Data:* b Kenosha, Wis, Sept 9, 52; m 78. *Educ:* Northern Ill Univ, BS, 74; Ind Univ, PhD(chem), 79. *Mem:* Am Chem Soc; AAAS. *Res:* Chemical separations: fundamental studies of gas chromatography; liquid chromatography and electrophoresis. *Mailing Add:* Chem Dept Venable Hall Univ NC Chapel Hill NC 27599-3290

JORIZZO, JOSEPH L, IMMUNODERMATOLOGY, NEUTROPHILS & IMMUNE COMPLEX REACTIONS IN THE SKIN. *Current Pos:* PROF & CHMN DEPT DERMAT, BOWMAN GRAY SCH MED, WAKE FOREST UNIV, WINSTON-SALEM, NC, 86-, DIR DERMAT RESIDENCY PROG, 87- *Personal Data:* b Rochester, NY, Oct 6, 51; c 1. *Educ:* Boston Univ, AB, 72, MD, 75; Am Bd Dermat, 79. *Honors & Awards:* Royal Soc Med Trust Lectureship, UK, 94. *Prof Exp:* Intern internal med, NC Mem Hosp, 75-76, resident dermat, 76-78, chief resident, 78-79; clin asst prof, Dept Dermat, Univ Tex Med Br, Galveston, 79-80, from asst prof to assoc prof, 80-86. *Concurrent Pos:* Consult, Vet Admin Clin, Winston-Salem, NC, 86- *Mem:* Soc Invest Dermat; Am Acad Dermat; Am Dermat Asn; fel Am Col Physicians; AMA; Int Soc Trop Dermat; Asn Profs Dermat. *Res:* Histamine induced localized vasculitis in patients with reactive vascular dermatoses; circulating immune complex-mediated aspects of secondary syphilis; dermatologic aspects of circulating immune complexes; dermatologic aspects of rheumatoid arthritis; histamine related mediators of inflammation; immunologic investigations in Behcet's disease and bowel disease; immune enhancers, prostaglandin synthesis blockers; collagen vascular diseases-experimental therapies for cutaneous aspects. *Mailing Add:* Dept Dermat Bowman Gray Sch Med Med Ctr Blvd Winston-Salem NC 27157-0001

JORNE, JACOB, ELECTROCHEMISTRY, MICROELECTRONICS PROCESSING. *Current Pos:* PROF CHEM ENG, UNIV ROCHESTER, 82- *Personal Data:* b Tel-Aviv, Israel, July 24, 41; US citizen; m 85, Judith A Love; c Ariel, Eli & Alexander. *Educ:* Technion Israel Inst Technol, BSc, 63, MSc, 67; Univ Calif, Berkeley, PhD(chem eng), 72. *Honors & Awards:* Battery Res Award, Electrochem Soc, 89, Carl Wagner Mem Award, 93. *Prof Exp:* Res asst chem eng, Lawrence Berkeley Lab, 67-72; prof, Wayne State Univ, 72-82. *Concurrent Pos:* Adj prof, Wayne State Univ, 84-; consult, Eastman Kodak Co. *Mem:* Electrochem Soc; Am Inst Chem Engrs. *Mailing Add:* Dept Chem Eng Univ Rochester Rochester NY 14627. *Fax:* 716-442-6686; *E-Mail:* jorne@che.rochester.edu

JORNS, MARILYN SCHUMAN, ENZYMOLOGY. *Current Pos:* assoc prof biochem, 82-87, dir, Molecular Biol & Biotechnol Grad Prog, 91-95, PROF BIOCHEM, HAHNEMANN UNIV SCH MED, 87- *Personal Data:* b New York, NY, Aug 24, 43; m 71. *Educ:* State Univ NY Binghamton, BA, 65; Univ Mich, MS, 67, PhD(biochem), 70. *Honors & Awards:* Linus Pauling Award, 87. *Prof Exp:* Am Cancer Soc fel chem, Univ Konstanz, 70-72; res assoc biochem, Univ Tex Health Sci Ctr Dallas, 72-75; asst prof chem, Ohio State Univ, 75-82. *Mem:* Am Soc Photobiol; Am Chem Soc; Am Soc Biol Chemists; AAAS. *Res:* Mechanism of catalysis by flavoproteins. *Mailing Add:* Dept Biochem Allegheny Univ Philadelphia PA 19102-1192. *Fax:* 215-246-5836

JORSTAD, JOHN LEONARD, METALLURGY. *Current Pos:* Technician, Metall Lab, Reynolds Metals Co, 57-65, res scientist, 65-68, develop engr, Prod Develop Lab, 68-81, dept mgr, 81-85, MGR INGOT & FOUNDRY TECHNOL, REYNOLDS METALS CO, 85- *Personal Data:* b Richmond, Va, Sept 17, 35; c 3. *Honors & Awards:* Achievement Award, NAm Die Casters Asn, 87; Award of Sci Merit, Am Foundrymen's Soc, 90. *Concurrent Pos:* Chmn, Cast Metals Coun, Soc Mfg Engrs, 78-81 & Tech Coun, Am Foundrymen's Soc, 90-92; mem, Tech Coun, NAm Die Casters Asn, 91- *Mem:* Fel Am Soc Metals Int; Am Foundrymen's Soc; NAm Die Casters Asn; Soc Mfg Engrs; Soc Automotive Engrs; Am Soc Testing & Mat. *Res:* Aluminum casting alloys; casting processes and processing parameters; casting applications for automotive use, especially engines. *Mailing Add:* 9112 Donora Dr Richmond VA 23229

JORTNER, JOSHUA, PHYSICAL CHEMISTRY. *Current Pos:* assoc prof, 65-66, PROF, TEL AVIV UNIV, 66-, HEINEMANN PROF CHEM, 73- *Personal Data:* b Poland, Mar 14, 33; m 60, Ruth Sanger; c 2. *Educ:* Hebrew Univ Jerusalem, PhD. *Honors & Awards:* Weizmann Prize, 73; Rothschild Prize, 76; Kolthof Prize, 76; Israel Prize in Chem, 82; Wolf Prize, 88. *Prof Exp:* Instr, Dept Phys Chem, Hebrew Univ Jerusalem, 61-62, sr lectr, 63-65. *Concurrent Pos:* Res assoc, Univ Chicago, 62-64; head, Inst Chem, Tel Aviv Univ, 66-72, dep rector, 66-69, vpres, 70-72; vis prof, H C Orsted Inst, Univ Copenhagen, 74, Univ Calif, Los Angeles & Berkeley, 75; vis prof chem, Univ Copenhagen, 78. *Mem:* Foreign assoc Nat Acad Sci; Israel Acad Sci & Humanities (vpres, 80-86, pres, 86-); Int Acad Quantum Sci; Am Philos Soc; Polish Acad Sci; Romanian Acad Sci; foreign mem Royal Danish Acad Sci & Lett; Europ Acad Sci & Arts; foreign fel Am Acad Arts & Sci. *Res:* Intramolecular radiationless transitions. *Mailing Add:* Sch Chem Tel Aviv Univ Ramat-Aviv Tel Aviv 69978 Israel

JORY, FARNHAM STEWART, PHYSICS. *Current Pos:* RETIRED. *Personal Data:* b Berkeley, Calif, Dec 6, 26; div; c 2. *Educ:* Univ Calif, AB, 48; Swiss Fed Polytech, dipl, 51; Univ Chicago, MS, 54, PhD(physics), 55. *Prof Exp:* Asst, Enrico Fermi Inst Nuclear Studies, Ill, 52-55; researcher physics, Univ Md, 56-57; res geophysicist, Inst Geophys, Univ Calif, Los Angeles, 57-58; mem tech staff, Space Tech Labs, Thompson-Ramo-Wooldridge Corp, 58-59; asst prof physics, Long Beach State Col, 59-60; consult physics, 60-85. *Concurrent Pos:* Vis asst prof, Univ Calif, Los Angeles, 57-58; physicist, Lawrence Berkeley Lab, 60. *Mem:* AAAS; NY Acad Sci. *Res:* Cosmic-ray and upper-atmosphere physics; geomagnetism and solarterrestrial relationships. *Mailing Add:* 3550 Pacific Ave Apt 1406 Livermore CA 94550

JORY, HOWARD ROBERTS, MICROWAVE ELECTRON TUBES, ELECTRON ACCELERATOR SYSTEMS FOR CANCER THERAPY. *Current Pos:* res & develop engr, 62-72, eng mgr, 72-76, DEVELOP MGR, VARIAN ASSOCS, 76- *Personal Data:* b Berkeley, Calif, Dec 8, 31; m 57, Carol Proudfoot; c Kevin, Craig & Thomas. *Educ:* Univ Calif, Berkeley, BS, 54, MS, 55, PhD(elec eng), 60. *Prof Exp:* Officer, US Army Electronics Res & Develop Lab, 60-62. *Concurrent Pos:* Consult, High Power Microwave Study Panel, Naval Res Lab, 76; chmn, Subcomt Electron Tubes, Inst Elec & Electronics Engrs, 83. *Mem:* Fel Inst Elec & Electronics Engrs; Sigma Xi. *Res:* Commercial gyrotrons; high power millimeter wave generators used in magnetic fusion laboratories. *Mailing Add:* Communication & Power Ind 811 Hansen Way Palo Alto CA 94303

JOSE, JORGE V, PHYSICS. *Current Pos:* asst prof to assoc prof, 80-88, PROF PHYSICS, NORTHEASTERN UNIV, 88-, DIR, CTR INTERDISCIPLINARY RES COMPLEX SYSTS, 95- *Personal Data:* b Mexico City, Mex, Sept 13, 49; m; c 3. *Educ:* Nat Univ Mex, BS, 72, MS, 73, PhD(physics), 76. *Prof Exp:* Res assoc physics, Brown Univ, 74-76, asst prof res, 76-77; James Franck fel physics, Univ Chicago, 77-79; asst prof res, Rutgers Univ, 79-80. *Concurrent Pos:* Guest scholar, Kyoto Univ, Japan, 79; consult, Exxon Res Eng, 82; vis scientist, Schlumberger, Dallas, 84 & Inst Physics, Mex, vis prof, 81 & 85. *Mem:* Am Phys Soc; AAAS; Mex Physics Soc. *Res:* Theoretical condensed matter physics. *Mailing Add:* Physics Dept Northeastern Univ Boston MA 02115

JOSE, PEDRO A, PEDIATRIC NEPHROLOGY. *Current Pos:* PROF PEDIAT, GEORGETOWN UNIV, 83- *Personal Data:* b Dingras, Ilocos Norte, Phillippines, Dec 4, 42; m, Nora Doctor; c Kristina M & Maria E. *Educ:* Univ Santo Tomas, MD, 65; Georgetown Univ, PhD(physiol), 76. *Honors & Awards:* William Peck Mem Award, Resin Kidney Dis, Interstate Postgrad Med Soc, 72; Apolinario Mabinin Award, Asn Philippine Physicians Am, 90. *Mem:* Soc Pediat Res; Am Fedn Clin Res; Am Soc Nephrology; Am Soc Pediat Nephrology. *Res:* Role of dopamine and adrenergic receptors on sodium transport in specific nephron segments during development in normotensive and spontaneously hypertensive rat. *Mailing Add:* Dept Pediat Georgetown Univ Hosp 3800 Reservoir Rd NW Washington DC 20057

JOSEFSON, CLARENCE MARTIN, CHEMICAL EDUCATION, COMPUTATIONAL CHEMISTRY. *Current Pos:* PROF CHEM, MILLIKIN UNIV, 73-, CHMN, 91- *Personal Data:* b Chicago, Ill, Apr 11, 43; m 66, Carol Fellows; c Rebecca, James & Jennifer. *Educ:* Univ Ill, Urbana, BS, 65; Southern Ill Univ, Carbondale, PhD(phys chem), 73. *Concurrent Pos:* Vis asst prof, Inst Environ Studies, Univ Ill, 80-81; vis res scientist pharmacol, Univ Gothenburg, Sweden, 88. *Mem:* Am Chem Soc; AAAS. *Res:* Developing project-based laboratories for undergraduate chemistry; computational chemistry of psycoactive drugs; adsorption of trace organic compounds onto polymers. *Mailing Add:* Dept Chem Millikin Univ Decatur IL 62522. *Fax:* 217-424-3993; *E-Mail:* cjosefson@mail.millikin.edu

JOSELYN, JO ANN CRAM, SOLAR PHYSICS, SPACE PHYSICS. *Current Pos:* Physicist res ionospheric physics, 68-75, physicist res magnetospheric physics, 75-76, physicist res solar wind, 76-78, PHYSICIST SOLAR & GEOMAGNETIC FORECASTING, SPACE ENVIRON SERVS CTR, SPACE ENVIRON LAB, NAT OCEANIC & ATMOSPHERIC ADMIN, 78- *Personal Data:* b St Francis, Kans, Oct 5, 43. *Educ:* Univ Colo, BS, 65, MS, 67, PhD(astrogeophys), 78. *Concurrent Pos:* US deleg, Study Group Six, Consult Comt Ionospheric Radio, 81 & 83; topic reporter, Div 5, Int Asn Geomagnetism & Aeronomy. *Mem:* Am Geophys Union; Union Radio Scientists Int; AAAS; Sigma Xi; Am Inst Aeronaut & Astronaut. *Res:* Astro geophysics, especially solar physics and solar wind physics; also solar-terrestrial relationships, especially geomagnetism. *Mailing Add:* 390 Hollyberry Ln Boulder CO 80303

JOSENHANS, JAMES GROSS, SOLID STATE ELECTRONICS. *Current Pos:* MEM TECH STAFF, BELL TEL LAB, 63- *Personal Data:* b Toledo, Ohio, Dec 19, 32; m 61; c 2. *Educ:* Univ Toledo, BSc, 56; Ohio State Univ, MSc, 58, PhD(elec eng), 62. *Prof Exp:* Engr, Storer Broadcasting Co, Ohio, 51-53; teaching asst physics, Univ Toledo, 53-56; from res asst to res assoc, Electron Device Lab, Ohio State Univ, 57-62, asst prof elec eng, 62-63. *Mem:* Am Phys Soc; Inst Elec & Electronics Engrs; Sigma Xi; Am Acoust Soc; Audio Engr Soc. *Res:* Silicon integrated circuit development strategies to satisfy projected telephone systems needs. *Mailing Add:* 397 Diamond Hill Rd Berkeley Heights NJ 07922

JOSEPH, ALFRED S, PHYSICS. *Current Pos:* RETIRED. *Personal Data:* b Cortland, NY, June 27, 32; m 56; c 2. *Educ:* Union Col, NY, BS, 56; Case Inst Technol, MS, 60, PhD(physics), 62. *Prof Exp:* Instr, Case Inst Technol, 58-62; sr physicist, Atomics Int Div, Corp Eng, Rockwell Int, 62, mem tech staff, 62-68, group leader, sci ctr, 68-72, dir solid state electronics, 72-76, sr tech adv, Autonetics, 76-77, sr eng exec technol appln, 77-80. *Concurrent Pos:* Consult, Gen Elec Co, Ohio, 59-61. *Mem:* Am Phys Soc. *Res:* Studies of the electronic properties of metals through the de Haas-van Alphen effect; superconducting phenomena; semiconductors and semiconductor devices. *Mailing Add:* 688 Laguna Dr Simi Valley CA 93065

JOSEPH, BERNARD WILLIAM, VEHICLE EMISSION. *Current Pos:* RETIRED. *Personal Data:* b Detroit, Mich, June 7, 29; m 51; c 3. *Educ:* Wayne State Univ, BA, 68. *Honors & Awards:* Arch T Colwell Award, Soc Automotive Engrs, 74. *Prof Exp:* Assoc sr res physicist, Res Labs, Gen Motors Corp, 51-80, sr develop engr, eng staff, 80-86. *Mem:* Optical Soc Am; Soc Photog Scientists & Engrs. *Res:* Optical properties of materials, optical design, radiometry, photometry and photochemistry; exhaust emission measurement; optical engineering. *Mailing Add:* 37239 Glenbrook Dr Clinton Township MI 48036. *E-Mail:* bjoseph@industry-dm.com

JOSEPH, DANIEL D, MECHANICAL ENGINEERING, FLUID MECHANICS RHEOLOGY. *Current Pos:* asst prof, 62-63, from asst prof to assoc prof fluid mech, 63-68, PROF AEROSPACE ENG & MECH, UNIV MINN, 68-, REGENTS' PROF, 94- *Personal Data:* b Chicago, Ill, Mar 26, 29; m 90, Kay Jaglo; c 3. *Educ:* Univ Chicago, MA, 50; Ill Inst Technol, BS, 59, MS, 60, PhD(mech eng), 63. *Honors & Awards:* GI Taylor Medal, Soc Eng Sci, 90; Bingham Medal, Soc Rheology, 90; Timashenko Medal, Am Soc Mech Engrs, 95; Thomas Baron Fluid Particle Syst Award, Am Inst Chem Engrs, 96. *Prof Exp:* Asst mech eng, Ill Inst Technol, 59-62,. *Concurrent Pos:* Guggenheim fel, 69 & 70; assoc ed seven journals. *Mem:* Nat Acad Sci; Nat Acad Eng; Soc Natural Philol; Am Soc Mech Engrs; Am Phys Soc; Am Acad Arts & Sci. *Res:* Fluid mechanics, flow through porous media and hydrodynamic stability; applied mathematics; theory of hydrodynamic stability and bifurcation theory; rheology of viscoelastic fluids; multi-phase flow. *Mailing Add:* Dept Mech & Aerospace Eng Univ Minn Minneapolis MN 55455. *Fax:* 612-626-1558; *E-Mail:* joseph@aem.umn.edu

JOSEPH, DAVID WINRAM, ELEMENTARY PARTICLE PHYSICS. *Current Pos:* from asst prof to assoc prof, 63-68, PROF PHYSICS, UNIV NEBR-LINCOLN, 68- *Personal Data:* b Evanston, Ill, June 28, 30; m 60; c 3. *Educ:* Roosevelt Col, BS, 52; Univ Chicago, MS, 57, PhD(elem particle physics), 59. *Prof Exp:* Physicist, Ballistic Res Labs, Aberdeen Proving Ground, Md, 53-55; res assoc physics, Purdue Univ, 59-61; res assoc, US Naval Res Lab, Washington, DC, 61-63. *Mem:* Fel Am Phys Soc. *Res:* Group and algebraic methods. *Mailing Add:* Dept Physics & Astron Univ Nebr Lincoln NE 68588

JOSEPH, DONALD J, OTOLARYNGOLOGY. *Current Pos:* Assoc prof, 67-71, PROF SURG, UNIV MO, SCH MED, COLUMBIA, 71-, CHIEF OTOLARYNGOL, 67- *Personal Data:* b Summerfield, Ill, Sept 24, 22; m 45; c 2. *Educ:* St Louis Univ, MD, 46; Baylor Univ, MS, 53. *Honors & Awards:* Bronze Star Medal, 57. *Concurrent Pos:* Consult, US Army Surgeon Gen, 61-64; mem comt hearing & bioacoust, Nat Res Coun, 61-67; communicative sci study sect, NIH, 62-64. *Mem:* Fel Am Acad Ophthal & Otolaryngol; fel Am Col Surg; fel Am Laryngol, Rhinol & Otol Soc. *Res:* Communicative sciences; audiology; speech pathology. *Mailing Add:* 1026 Merrill Dr Box 159 Lebanon IL 62254-0159

JOSEPH, EARL CLARK, II, STRATEGIC MANAGEMENT. *Current Pos:* DIR COMPETITIVE ANAL & SNZ PROD MGR, CRAY RES, 95- *Personal Data:* b St Paul, Minn, Mar 2, 56; m 74, Holly J Smith. *Educ:* Univ Minn, BS, 78, PhD(strategic mgt), 83. *Prof Exp:* Systs planner, Sperry-Univac, 83-84, financial planner, 84-85; prog mgt, Unisys, 86-88; mkt req & res, Cray Res, Inc, 88-92; dir strategic planning, Concurrent Comput Corp, 92-95. *Concurrent Pos:* Vis lectr, Metro Univ, Minn, 83 & AT&T Mgt Training Ctr, Mankato Univ & St Thomas Col, 85. *Res:* The development and application of strategic management tools for use in exploring the potential future of products proposed for research and currently being developed; future product planning for computer systems of all types. *Mailing Add:* 365 Summit Ave St Paul MN 55102

JOSEPH, J MEHSEN, MEDICAL MICROBIOLOGY, IMMUNOLOGY. *Current Pos:* DIR, COMMUNITY HEALTH SURRVEILLANCE & LABS ADMIN, 87-; ASSOC PROF MICROBIOL, UNIV MD, 72- *Personal Data:* b Whitesville, WVa, Sept 30, 28; m 51, LaRue E Voshell; c Dorothy, Richard, Katherine, Susan, Barbara & Donna. *Educ:* WVa Univ, BA, 48, MSc, 49; Univ Md, PhD(bact, chem), 54; Univ Toledo, BSc, 55. *Honors & Awards:* Barnett Cohen Award, Microbiol. *Prof Exp:* Asst zool & anat, WVa Univ, 48-49; asst prof microbiol, Univ Toledo, 51-54; dir res, Biol Res Inst, 54-57; asst dir bur labs, 63-76, dir labs, Md State Dept Health & Ment Hyg, 77-87. *Concurrent Pos:* Div head bur labs, Md State Dept Health & Ment Hyg, 57-63; assoc epidemiol, Johns Hopkins Univ, 79- *Mem:* Hon mem Am Soc Microbiol (secy, 74); Brit Soc Microbiol; Tissue Cult Asn; Am Pub Health Asn; Am Acad Microbiol. *Res:* Disinfectants; antiseptics; microbiology of acid mine waters; lysozyme activity in relation to oral infections; public health microbiology; isolation methods for genus Clostridium; acute and chronic toxicity of chlorinated phenols; disease transmission by anesthetizing apparatus; evaluation of fungicidal compounds; diagnostic virology and tissue culture. *Mailing Add:* Md State Labs Admin 201 W Preston St Baltimore MD 21201. *Fax:* 410-333-5403

JOSEPH, J WALTER, JR, MECHANICAL ENGINEERING. *Current Pos:* mech engr, Savannah River Lab, E I Du Pont De Nemours & Co Inc, 54-65, mech engr, Reactor Tech Dept, 65-71, asst chief supvr, 71-76, chief supvr, 76-78, supt, Traffic & Transp Dept, 78-80, supt, LStartup Proj Team, 80-83, supt, Equip Engr Dept, supt, Site Quality Dept, 83-85, SAVANNAH RIVER PLANT, E I DU PONT DE NEMOURS & CO, INC, 85- *Personal Data:* b Oak Park, Ill, Oct 8, 28; m 53; c 2. *Educ:* NC State Col, BS, 50; Pa State Univ, MS, 54. *Prof Exp:* Asst eng res, Pa State Univ, 50-51, thermal res lab, 53-54. *Res:* Participatve leadership nuclear reactor project management; mechanical and welding development supporting nuclear operations; remote equipment, nuclear waste management; isotopic heat sources; shipping containers; resistance welding; high pressure gas technology. *Mailing Add:* 340 Cherbourg Pl Aiken SC 29801

JOSEPH, JAMES, MARINE BIOLOGY. *Current Pos:* Scientist, Inter-Am Trop Tuna Comn, 58-63, prin scientist, 64-69, dir, 69, RES ASSOC, INST MARINE RES, SCRIPPS INST OCEANOG, 69-; AFFIL PROF, UNIV WASH, 69-; RES ASSOC, INST MARINE INS, SCRIPPS INST OCEANOG, 69- *Personal Data:* b Los Angeles, Calif, Oct 28, 30; m 58, Patricia Duffy; c Michael & Jerry. *Educ:* Humboldt State Col, BS, 56, MS, 58; Univ Wash, PhD, 66. *Hon Degrees:* Dr, Honoris Causa, Universite de Bretagne Occidental, France. *Honors & Awards:* Nautilus Award, Marine Technol Soc; Dave Wallace Award, Nautilus Press; Roger Revelle Perpetual Award Marine Sci. *Concurrent Pos:* Served on various panels, comts, etc concerning marine sci and fisheries & as adv to all levels of govt; US Nat Acad Scis, Ocean Studies Bd Comt Fisheries; affil prof, Univ Wash, 69- *Mem:* Am Inst Fishery Res Biol; Sigma Xi. *Res:* Dynamics of the stocks of marine fishes and mammals and effects of man's exploitation of them; development of international arrangements for the conservation of living marine resources. *Mailing Add:* IATTC Scripps Inst Oceanog La Jolla CA 92037. *Fax:* 619-546-7133

JOSEPH, JEYMOHAN, NEUROIMMUNOLOGY, ENDOTHELIAL CELL BIOLOGY. *Current Pos:* res assoc neuroimmunol, 85-87, instr, 87-89, ASST PROF NEUROIMMUNOL, THOMAS JEFFERSON UNIV, 89- *Personal Data:* b Jodhpur, India, Jan 20, 53; m 87; c 1. *Educ:* Univ Wis-Madison, PhD(immunol), 83. *Prof Exp:* Res assoc oncol, Wis Clin Cancer Ctr, 83-85. *Mem:* Int Soc Neuroimmunol; Am Asn Immunologists; AAAS; NY Acad Sci. *Res:* Role of endothelial cells in immune and inflammatory events following virus infection. *Mailing Add:* Dept Neurol Rm 511 Col Bldg Thomas Jefferson Univ 1025 Walnut St Philadelphia PA 19107-5083. *Fax:* 215-955-5515

JOSEPH, JOHN MUNDANCHERIL, CHROMATOGRAPHY, SPECTROSCOPY. *Current Pos:* GROUP LEADER ANALYTICAL CHEM & DOSAGE FORM ANALYSIS, BRISTOL-MYERS SQUIBB PHARMACEUT RES INST, 81- *Personal Data:* b Kerala, India, Feb 21, 47; US citizen; m 81; c 3. *Educ:* Kerala Univ, India, BS, 68; Univ Jabalpur, India, MS, 71; Drexel Univ, Philadelphia, MS & PhD(biochem), 80. *Prof Exp:* Lectr chem, Kerala Univ, India, 68-69; chemist, McDowell Distillery, Kerala, 71-73, Midvale Heppenstal, Philadelphia, 73-75; teaching & res asst biochem, Drexel Univ, Philadelphia, 75-80. *Concurrent Pos:* Fel biochem, Drexel Univ, Philadelphia, 75-81. *Mem:* Sigma Xi; Am Asn Pharmaceut Scientists; Am Chem Soc. *Res:* Examination of the stereochemical requirements for the biological activity of cholesterol in terms of its metabolism to other functional sterols and its proper fit into biological membranes, investigated in both enzymatic and functional membranous systems; chemical synthesis of cholesterol analogues; conformational and configurational analysis of sterols by hydrogen and carbon 13-nuclear magnetic resonance; in-vitro dissolution testing; pharmaceutical testing and regulatory affairs. *Mailing Add:* Dept Anal Lab Bristol-Myers 1 Squibb Dr PO Box 191 New Brunswick NJ 08903

JOSEPH, PETER D(ANIEL), ELECTRICAL ENGINEERING. *Current Pos:* mem tech staff, TRW Systs & Energy Group, 61-64, head, Guidance Sect, 64-66, mgr, Syst Anal & Software Dept, 66-70, mgr, Sensor Design & Anal Dept, 70-76, LAB MGR, TRW SYSTS & ENERGY GROUP, 76-

Personal Data: b Brooklyn, NY, Jan 21, 36; m 57; c 1. *Educ:* Mass Inst Technol, SB & SM, 58; Purdue Univ, PhD(elec eng), 61. *Prof Exp:* Instr elec eng, Purdue Univ, 58-61. *Mem:* Inst Elec & Electronics Engrs; Am Inst Aeronaut & Astronaut. *Res:* Guidance of missiles and space vehicles; optimal control theory; optimal filter theory; electro-optical sensors. *Mailing Add:* 2740 W 233 St Torrance CA 90505-3112

JOSEPH, PETER MARON, MEDICAL PHYSICS. *Current Pos:* assoc prof, 83-91, PROF RADIOL PHYSICS, UNIV PA, PHILADELPHIA, 91- *Personal Data:* b Ridley Park, Pa, Mar 26, 39. *Educ:* Lafayette Col, BS, 59; Harvard Univ, MA, 61, PhD(physics), 67. *Hon Degrees:* MPh, Univ Pa, 87. *Honors & Awards:* Sylvia Greenfield Prize, Am Asn Physicists Med. *Prof Exp:* Instr physics, Cornell Univ, 67-70; asst prof, Carnegie-Mellon Univ, 70-72; NIH fel, Memorial-Sloan Kettering Cancer Ctr, 72-73; instr radiol, Columbia-Presby Med Ctr, 73-75, asst prof, 75-80; assoc prof diag images physics, Univ Md, Baltimore, 80-82. *Mem:* AAAS; Am Phys Soc; Am Asn Physicists in Med; fel Inst Elec & Electronics Engrs; Soc Magnetic Resonance Med; Radiol Soc NAm. *Res:* High energy electromagnetic phenomena; experimental tests of quantum electrodynamics; photo production of vector mesons; energy range relations; x-ray spectra and attenuation curves; radiographic image quality; computerized axial tomography; magnetic resonance image; air pollution and asthma. *Mailing Add:* Radiol Dept Hosp Univ Pa 3400 Spruce St Philadelphia PA 19104. *E-Mail:* joseph@rad.hup.upenn.edu

JOSEPH, RAMON R, GASTROENTEROLOGY, ENDOSCOPY. *Current Pos:* MED DIR, HENRY FORD MED CTR, 87- *Personal Data:* b New York, NY, May 17, 30; m 56, Mary A Kowalchik; c Ricardo G, Maria A (Thompson) & Lisa M (Benson). *Educ:* Manhattan Col, BS, 52; Cornell Univ, MD, 56. *Prof Exp:* Intern med, Meadowbrook Hosp, Hempstead, 56-57; resident, 59-62, staff physician, 62-64, asst dir, Dept Med, Wayne Co Gen Hosp, 64-73; dir, Gastroenterol Sect, Wayne Co Gen Hosp, Westland, 61-63, dir, Dept Med, 73-85; assoc prof internal med, Univ Mich, Ann Arbor, 68-75, asst dean, Med Sch, 73-84, prof internal med, 75-84. *Concurrent Pos:* Fel, Wayne Co Gen Hosp, 61-62; consult, Annapolis Hosp, Wayne, 62-88, St Mary Hosp, Livonia, 62-, Mich Dept Educ, 69-73; from instr to prof internal med, Univ Mich, Ann Arbor, 62-75; chmn res dept, Wayne Co Gen Hosp, 64-85, pres med staff, 71-72; chair, gastroenterol, St Mary Hosp, 85-90. *Mem:* AAAS; fel Am Col Physicians; NY Acad Sci; Asn Am Med Col; AMA; Am Gastroenterol Asn; Am Soc Internal Med; Am Soc Gastrointestinal Endoscopy. *Res:* Origin and nature of human serum lactic dehydrogenase; multiple molecular forms of enzyme amylase; biochemical diagnosis in gastroenterology; endoscopic aspects of gastroenterology. *Mailing Add:* 13755 W Montoya Viadu Ct Apt W 35605 Warren Rd Sun City West AZ 85375. *Fax:* 313-728-1920

JOSEPH, RICHARD ISAAC, SOLID STATE PHYSICS. *Current Pos:* from asst prof to assoc prof, 66-70, PROF ELEC ENG, JOHNS HOPKINS UNIV, 70- *Personal Data:* b Brooklyn, NY, May 25, 36; m 61; c 3. *Educ:* City Col New York, BS, 57; Harvard Univ, PhD(physics), 62. *Prof Exp:* Sr res scientist solid state physics, Raytheon Co, 61-66. *Mem:* AAAS; Am Phys Soc. *Res:* Statistical mechanics; theory of magnetism and properties of magnetic materials; microwave physics; theory of solid state; exchange interactions in solids; critical phenomena; solitons; non-linear wave equations. *Mailing Add:* 2106 Uffington Rd Baltimore MD 21209

JOSEPH, ROSALINE RESNICK, MEDICINE, HEMATOLOGY. *Current Pos:* prof med & chief Hematol & Oncol Dept, 77-96, PROF MED, MED COL PA, 96- *Personal Data:* b New York City, NY, Aug 21, 29; m 54; c 2. *Educ:* Cornell Univ, AB, 49; Women's Med Col Pa, MD, 53; Temple Univ, MS, 58. *Prof Exp:* Instr hematol, Med Ctr, Temple Univ, 57-60, assoc med, 60-63, assoc prof med, 63-77, course coordr reticulo-endothelial, Syst Interdisciplinary Course Comt, 68-73. *Concurrent Pos:* Prof clin oncol, Am Cancer Soc, 89-94. *Mem:* Am Fedn Clin Res; Am Soc Hematol; Fel Am Col Physicians; Am Asn Cancer Educ; Am Soc Clin Oncol. *Res:* New modalities in the treatment of cancer and hematologic disorders. *Mailing Add:* Med Col Pa 3300 Henry Ave Philadelphia PA 19129

JOSEPH, ROY D, APPLIED MATHEMATICS. *Current Pos:* asst prof, 73-80, ASSOC PROF ELEC ENG, SPACE INST, UNIV TENN, 80- *Personal Data:* b Fremont, Ohio, July 26, 37; m 69. *Educ:* Fenn Col, BEE, 60; Case Inst Technol, MSEE, 62, PhD(eng), 65. *Prof Exp:* Res assoc, Case Inst Technol, 65-66; asst prof eng, State Univ NY, Stony Brook, 66-72. *Mem:* Inst Elec & Electronics Engrs; Soc Indust & Appl Math; Am Asn Univ Professors. *Res:* Active network synthesis; optimal control signal processing; digital signal processing. *Mailing Add:* Dept Elec Eng Space Inst Univ Tenn MS 21 Tullahoma TN 37388-8897

JOSEPH, SAMMY WILLIAM, MICROBIOLOGY, MEDICAL BACTERIOLOGY. *Current Pos:* chmn dept, 81-89, PROF, DEPT MICROBIOL, UNIV MD, 81- *Personal Data:* b Jacksonville, Fla, Oct 10, 34; m 67, Marianne Gertrude Cotte; c Jeffrey Keith & Jennifer Michelle. *Educ:* Univ Fla, BSA, 56; St John's Univ, NY, MS, 64, PhD(microbiol), 70. *Prof Exp:* Asst head, Serol Br, US Naval Med Sch, Nat Naval Med Ctr, 57-58, head, Bact Serol & Mycol Br, US Naval Hosp, St Albans, NY, 58-63, head, Bact & Mycol Br, 63-67; Navy contract fel bact, St John's Univ, NY, 67-70; microbiologist & asst OIC, Naval Med Res Unit 2, Jakarta Detachment, Indonesia, 70-73; exec officer comndg officer, Naval Unit, Ft Detrick, 74-75, dep chmn, Microbiol Dept, Naval Med Res Inst, 75-78, prog mgr infectious dis, Naval Med Res & Develop Command, Nat Naval Med Ctr, 78-81. *Concurrent Pos:* Vis scientist, Off Naval Res, London, 77 & Naval Med Res Inst, Bethesda, Md, 95. *Mem:* Am Soc Microbiol; fel Am Acad Microbiol; AAAS; NY Acad Sci; Am Soc Clin Path; Sigma Xi. *Res:* Studies on bacteria of clinical significance, particularly those causing gastroenteritis; purification and characterization of bacterial toxins; role of antibiotics in treatment; bacterial adherence to surfaces; genetic basis of pathogenic mechanisms; bacterial taxonomy and systematic classification; studies of food-bourne disease caused by bacteris. *Mailing Add:* 5914 Granby Rd Rockville MD 20855. *Fax:* 301-345-8519; *E-Mail:* sj13@umail.umd.edu

JOSEPH, SOLOMON, INDUSTRIAL CHEMISTRY. *Current Pos:* RETIRED. *Personal Data:* b Brooklyn, NY, Nov 3, 10; m 35; c 2. *Educ:* Columbia Univ, BS, 35, MA, 37; Polytech Inst Brooklyn, PhD(chem), 44. *Prof Exp:* Lab instr chem, Yeshiva Col, 35-38; chemist, NY Bd Transp, 39-45; dir res, Bri-Test, Inc, 45-50; chief chemist, Camp Chem Co, 51-52; chemist, Res Div, Penetone Co, NJ, 52-60; chief chemist, Chem Div, John Sexton & Co, Mich, 60-63; teacher chem, NY Bd Educ, 63-80. *Concurrent Pos:* Instr, Yeshiva Col, 45-50; lectr & adj prof chem, City Univ New York, 67-70. *Mem:* Sigma Xi; Am Chem Soc. *Res:* Emulsion of waxes, resins and polishes; cryoscopic studies of acids and bases in selenium oxychloride; protective coatings; synthetic detergents; corrosion prevention; sanitation chemicals; chemical specialties. *Mailing Add:* 1044 E Fifth St Brooklyn NY 11230-3325

JOSEPH, STANLEY ROBERT, MEDICAL ENTOMOLOGY, INSECT PEST MANAGEMENT. *Current Pos:* RETIRED. *Personal Data:* b Jacobus, Pa, May 21, 30; m 56, Minna Louise Messick; c Minna L (Leydorf), Jane C & John H. *Educ:* Gettysburg Col, BA, 52; Pa State Univ, MS, 54; Univ Md, PhD(entom), 68. *Prof Exp:* From asst entomologist to assoc entomologist, Md State Bd Agr, 56-73; entomologist, pest mgt sect, Md Dept Agr, 73-79, chief, Mosquito Control Sect, 80-92. *Mem:* Sigma Xi; Am Mosquito Control Asn. *Res:* Methods and insecticides for use in mosquito control in Maryland; ultra low volume insecticide applications with air and ground equipment; biology of Culiseta melanura in Maryland; insect physiology; toxicology of malathion to vertebrates. *Mailing Add:* 1631 Generals Hwy Annapolis MD 21401

JOSEPH, STEPHEN C, HEALTH SCIENCES. *Current Pos:* RETIRED. *Personal Data:* b New York, NY, Nov 25, 37. *Educ:* Harvard Col, BA, 59; Yale Univ, MD, 63; Johns Hopkins Univ, MPH, 68; Am Bd Pediat, dipl, 68. *Honors & Awards:* Pub Serv for Med Award, Am Col Physicians, 89. *Prof Exp:* Intern pediat, Boston Children's Hosp, 63-64, asst resident, 66-67; fel, Comp Child Care Proj, Dept Pediat, Sch Med, Johns Hopkins Univ, 67-68; prof pediat & community health, Univ Ctr Health Sci, Yaounde, Cameroon, 71-73; dir med educ & planning & consult to pres, Univ Wyo, 73-74; asst med, Children's Hosp Med Ctr, 74-78, dep asst adminr, Human Resources Develop, Bur Develop Support, Agency Int Develop, 78-81; consult & lectr, Int Develop Res Ctr, Can, 81-82; chief pediat, Grenfell Regional Health Serv, St Anthony, Can, 82-83; spec coordr child health & survival, UN Children's Fund, 83-86; comnr health, NY, 86-90; dean, Sch Pub Health, Univ Minn, 91-93; asst secy defense health affairs, US dept defense, 93-97. *Concurrent Pos:* Dir, Off Int Health Progs, Harvard Sch Pub Health, 74-78, lectr, Dept Maternal & Child Health, 74-78; asst med, Children's Hosp Med Ctr, 74-78; mem, Nat Coun Int Health, 75-78; actg asst adminr, Bur Develop Support, Agency Int Develop, 81; mem bd trustees, US Conf Local Health Officers, 87-89; mem, Nat Adv Comt HIV, Ctrs Dis Control, 88-91; Sol Fleischman vis prof med, Harvard Community Health Plan, 90. *Mem:* Inst Med-Nat Acad Sci; fel Am Pub Health Asn; fel Am Acad Pediat. *Res:* Author of over 350 publications. *Mailing Add:* Dept Defense Rm 3E-346 Washington DC 70301. *Fax:* 703-614-3537

JOSEPHS, JESS J, MUSICAL ACOUSTICS. *Current Pos:* prof, 56-87, EMER PROF PHYSICS, SMITH COL, 87- *Personal Data:* b New York, NY, Jan 4, 17; m 62; c 2. *Educ:* NY Univ, AB, 38, MSc, 40, PhD(phys chem), 43. *Prof Exp:* Res assoc, Northwestern Univ, 45-46, instr phys chem, 46-47; asst prof phys sci, Univ Chicago, 47-50; asst prof physics, Boston Univ, 50-56. *Mem:* Am Phys Soc; Am Asn Physics Teachers; Audio Eng Soc; Sigma Xi. *Res:* Solid state physics, psychoacoustics; acoustical study of the violin; distortion in electronically reproduced music. *Mailing Add:* 3300 Darby Rd C1004 Haverford PA 19041-1066

JOSEPHS, MELVIN JAY, PLANT PHYSIOLOGY, INFORMATION SCIENCE. *Current Pos:* RETIRED. *Personal Data:* b New York, NY, Apr 26, 26; m 48, Myra J Albert; c 2. *Educ:* Rutgers Univ, BSc, 50, MSc, 52, PhD(plant physiol, bot), 54. *Prof Exp:* Plant physiologist, Dow Chem Co, Mich, 54-60; assoc ed, Chem & Eng News, Am Chem Soc, 60-66, managing ed, Environ Sci & Technol, 66-69, managing ed, Chem & Eng News, 69-73; asst dir, Prod & Prog Mgt, Nat Tech Info Serv, US Dept Com, 73-76 & 78-86; chief, Toxicol Data Bank, Nat Libr Med, HEW, 76-78; exec dir, Am Soc Plant Physiologist, 86-93. *Mem:* Sigma Xi; AAAS. *Res:* Boron nutrition and organic acid content; growth regulators; herbicides; algae; aquatic plants. *Mailing Add:* 9109 Friars Rd Bethesda MD 20817

JOSEPHS, ROBERT, BIOPHYSICS, STRUCTURAL BIOLOGY. *Current Pos:* SR SCIENTIST & ASSOC, POLYMER DEPT, WEIZMAN INST, 77-, PROF MOLECULAR GENETICS & CELL BIOL, UNIV CHICAGO, 90- *Personal Data:* b Philadelphia, Pa, June 29, 37; m 74, 90. *Educ:* Univ Ill, BS, 59; Hebrew Univ, MSc, 62; Johns Hopkins Univ, PhD(biol), 66. *Honors & Awards:* Res Career Develop Award, NIH. *Prof Exp:* Res assoc muscle biol, Johns Hopkins Univ, 66-67; fel, MRC Lab Molecular Biol, 68-69; fel struct biol, Weizman Inst, 70-73, assoc prof biophys & theoret biol, Univ Chicago. *Concurrent Pos:* NIH grant, 78- *Mem:* Electron Micros Soc Am; Biophys Soc. *Res:* Structural biology; sickle cell anemia; electron crystallography; cryoelectron microscopy. *Mailing Add:* Dept Molecular Genetics & Cell Biol Univ Chicago 920 E 58th St Chicago IL 60637. *E-Mail:* bob@befvax.uchicago.ede

JOSEPHSON, ALAN S, MEDICINE, IMMUNOLOGY. *Current Pos:* From asst prof to assoc prof, 63-73, PROF MED, STATE UNIV NY DOWNSTATE MED CTR, 73- *Personal Data:* b Bronx, NY, Nov 30, 30; m 55, Adeline Goldberg; c 3. *Educ:* NY Univ, AB, 52, MD, 56; Am Bd Internal Med, dipl, 66; Am Bd Allergy & Immunol, dipl, 75, re-cert, 87, dipl diag lab immunol, 91. *Concurrent Pos:* Nat Inst Allergy & Infectious Dis trainee fel, NY Univ, 58-60. *Mem:* Am Fedn Clin Res; Am Asn Immunologists; fel Am Col Physicians; fel Am Acad Allergy & Immunol; Clin Immunol Soc; Harvey Soc; AAAS. *Res:* Immunologic properties of penicillin; proteins of secretions; immunologic properties of air pollutants. *Mailing Add:* Dept Med State Univ NY Downstate Med Ctr Brooklyn NY 11203. *Fax:* 718-270-1831; *E-Mail:* ajosephson@aol.com

JOSEPHSON, BRIAN DAVID, PHYSICS. *Current Pos:* Dir res, 67-72, reader, 72-74, PROF PHYSICS, CAMBRIDGE UNIV, 74- *Personal Data:* b Cardiff, Eng, Jan 4, 40. *Educ:* Cambridge Univ, BA, 60, MA, 64, PhD(physics). *Hon Degrees:* DSc, Univ Wales, 74, Exeter Univ, 83. *Honors & Awards:* Nobel Prize in Physics, 73; Fitz London Award, 72; Guthrie Medal, 72; van der Pol Medal, 72; Elliot Cresson Medal, 72; Hughes Medal, 72; Holweck Medal, 73; Faradax Medal, 82; Sir George Thompson Medal, 84. *Concurrent Pos:* Fel, Trinity Col, Cambridge, 62-; vis fac, Maharishi Europ Res Univ, 75; co-ed, Consciousness & the Phys World, 80; vis prof, Dept Comput Sci, Wayne State Univ, 83, Indian Inst Sci, Bangalore, 84, Univ Mo, Rolla, 87. *Mem:* Hon foreign mem Am Acad Arts & Sci; hon mem Inst Elec & Electronics Engrs; fel Royal Soc. *Mailing Add:* Cavendish Lab Univ Cambridge Madingley Rd Cambridge CB3 0HE England

JOSEPHSON, EDWARD SAMUEL, FOOD SCIENCE & FOOD IRRADIATION, RESEARCH ADMINISTRATION. *Current Pos:* ADJ PROF, DEPT FOOD SCI & NUTRIT, UNIV RI, 86- *Personal Data:* b Boston, Mass, Sept 30, 15; m 38, Blanche Andelman; c Nancy E (Wall), Betty L (King) & William J. *Educ:* Harvard Univ, AB, 36; Mass Inst Technol, PhD(biochem), 40; Indust Col Armed Forces, dipl, 62. *Honors & Awards:* Merton Singer Award, Res & Develop Assocs Mil Food & Packaging Systs, 92; Outstanding Achievement Cert, Int Atomic Energy Agency, 93. *Prof Exp:* Williams-Waterman fel, Mass Inst Technol, 40-43; biochemist, NIH, 44-52 & US Army Chem Corp, 52-54; chief, Biol & Chem Br, Qm Res & Eng Command, 54, asst chief, Chem & Plastics Div, 54-56, assoc sci dir develop, 56-61, spec asst food & food irradiation, 61-62; assoc dir food radiation, Food Div & dir, Radiation Lab, 62-72, dep tech dir, Food Serv Systs Prog, US Army Natick Res & Develop Labs, 72-75; sr lectr, Dept Appl Biol Sci, Mass Inst Technol, 76-89. *Concurrent Pos:* Asst prof, Oglethorpe Univ, 43-44 & Med Sch, Emory Univ, 45; lectr, Am Univ, 50-54; adv on preserving food by ionizing radiation, Int Atomic Energy Agency, UN, 64-, Food & Agr Orgn, UN, 64-, Israel AEC, 65-85, Inter-Am Nuclear Energy Comn, Orgn Am States, 68-69, Ministry Econ, Iran, 69-75, Dept Atomic Energy, India, 67-71, Nuclear Energy Comn, Chile, 82-84 & Ministry Light Indust, China, 84; vchmn, Inter-Dept Comt Radiation Preserv Food, 70-71; consult, Universal Sci & Eng, 76-; lectr, Ctr Lifelong Learning, Harvard Univ, 77-82; sci adv, NH House Reps, 77-78. *Mem:* AAAS; Am Chem Soc; Inst Food Technol; Sigma Xi; Coun Agr Sci & Technol; Am Coun Sci & Health; Res & Develop Assocs Mil Food & Packaging Systs. *Res:* Chemotherapy of malaria and other tropical diseases; enzymes; vitamins; nutrition; microbiology; food preservation by ionizing radiations. *Mailing Add:* Dept Food Sci & Nutrit Univ RI 530 Liberty Lane West Kingston RI 02892. *Fax:* 401-874-2994

JOSEPHSON, LEONARD MELVIN, PLANT BREEDING, AGRONOMY. *Current Pos:* prof agron, 54-71, prof plant & soil sci, 71-79, EMER PROF PLANT & SOIL SCI, UNIV TENN, KNOXVILLE, 79- *Personal Data:* b Ashland, Wis, Dec 4, 13; m 40, 83, Cledous H Hansard; c Louise & Jon Baard. *Educ:* Univ Wis, BS, 36, PhD(plant path, agron), 41. *Prof Exp:* Agt, USDA, Wis, 33-36, purchasing seed grain agt, Minn, 36-37; asst, Univ Wis, 37-39; secy & field rep, Malt Res Inst, 39-43; from asst agronomist to agronomist, Exp Sta, Univ Ky, 43-51; maize breeder, Union SAfrica, 51-54. *Concurrent Pos:* Consult, Univ Tenn-AID, India, SAfrica, 56, 82 & 88, Arg, 82 & 84; res agronomist, USDA, 54-71. *Mem:* AAAS; fel Am Soc Agron; Am Phytopath Soc; Am Genetics Asn; Genetics Soc Am; fel Crop Sci Soc Am. *Res:* Corn breeding, breeding methods and genetics; corn pathology; corn insects. *Mailing Add:* Dept Plant & Soil Sci Univ Tenn Knoxville TN 37916

JOSEPHSON, ROBERT KARL, COMPARATIVE PHYSIOLOGY. *Current Pos:* PROF BIOL, UNIV CALIF, IRVINE, 71- *Personal Data:* b Somerville, Mass, July 12, 34; m 56; c 3. *Educ:* Tufts Univ, BS, 56; Univ Calif, Los Angeles, PhD(zool), 60. *Prof Exp:* NATO fel, Univ Tubingen, 61; from asst prof to assoc prof zool, Univ Minn, 62-65; from assoc prof to prof biol, Case Western Reserve Univ, 65-71. *Concurrent Pos:* Guggenheim fel, 77-78; mem, Marine Biol Lab Corp. *Mem:* AAAS; Am Soc Zool; Brit Soc Exp Biol; Soc Gen Physiol; Soc Neurosci; Sigma Xi; Soc Biophys; Am Physiol Soc. *Res:* Mechanical power and efficiency of muscle. *Mailing Add:* Dept Psychobiol Sch Biol Sci Univ Calif Irvine CA 92717-4550. *Fax:* 714-824-2447

JOSEPHSON, RONALD VICTOR, FOOD SCIENCE, NUTRITION. *Current Pos:* coordr, 92-93, ASSOC PROF & PROF FOODS & NUTRITION, SAN DIEGO STATE UNIV, 75- *Personal Data:* b Bellefonte, Pa, May 19, 42; m 69, Judith Pinkerton; c Kirsten E & Erika L. *Educ:* Pa State Univ, BS, 64; Univ Minn, St Paul, MS, 66, PhD(food sci), 70. *Prof Exp:* Asst prof dairy technol, Ohio State Univ, 70-71, asst prof food sci & nutrit, 71-75. *Concurrent Pos:* Prin investr grants, Nat Oceanic & Atmospheric Admin, US Army, Nat Fisheries Inst, 77-; chmn, Basic Symp Comt, Inst Food Technol, 85-87; pres, San Diego Chap, Sigma Xi, 86-87. *Mem:* Am Dairy Sci Asn; Inst Food Technol; Sigma Xi. *Res:* Chemistry, analysis and storage stability of foods; milk and dairy foods, fish and seafoods, medical foods, and human and cow's milk proteins. *Mailing Add:* Dept Exercise & Nutrit Sci San Diego State Univ San Diego CA 92182. *Fax:* 619-594-6553

JOSHI, ARAVIND KRISHNA, COMPUTER & INFORMATION SCIENCE. *Current Pos:* assoc ling anal, 58-61, from asst prof to assoc prof elec eng & ling, 61-72, PROF COMPUT & INFO SCI & CHMN DEPT, UNIV PA, 72- *Personal Data:* b Poona, India, Aug 5, 29; m 63; c 2. *Educ:* Univ Poona, BE, 51; Indian Inst Sci, Bangalore, dipl, 52; Univ Pa, MS, 58, PhD(elec eng), 60. *Prof Exp:* Res asst electronics, Indian Inst Sci, Bangalore, 52-53 & Tata Inst Fundamental Res, Bombay, 53; prof engr, Radio Corp Am, NJ, 54-58. *Concurrent Pos:* Assoc, transformations & discourse anal proj, NSF, 58-; consult info theory & ling, Philco Res Lab, Pa, 62-63; ling consult, Western Reserve, 64-; Guggenheim fel, 71-72; mem, Inst Advan Study, 71-72. *Mem:* Asn Comput Mach; fel Inst Elec & Electronics Engrs; Am Math Soc; Sigma Xi. *Res:* Information theory; structural analysis of natural languages and formal linguistics; natural language processing; artificial intelligence; mathematical linguistics. *Mailing Add:* Moore Sch Univ Pa Philadelphia PA 19104

JOSHI, BHAIRAV DATT, PHYSICAL CHEMISTRY, QUANTUM CHEMISTRY. *Current Pos:* from asst prof to assoc prof, 70-84, PROF CHEM, STATE UNIV NY COL GENESEO, 85- *Personal Data:* b Dungrakot, Almora, India, Mar 5, 39; US citizen; m 67, Barbara Ravenell. *Educ:* Univ Delhi, BS, 59, MS, 61; Univ Chicago, MS, 63, PhD(chem), 64. *Prof Exp:* Fel chem, Dept Phys, Univ Chicago, 65-66, lectr, Indian Inst Technol, Kanpur, 66-67; reader, Univ Delhi, 67-69; res assoc, State Univ NY Stony Brook, 69-70. *Mem:* Am Chem Soc; Sigma Xi. *Res:* Quantum mechanical studies of the electronic structure of small atoms and molecules; use of computers in undergraduate education. *Mailing Add:* 3 Mohawk Ave Geneseo NY 14454-9511. *Fax:* 716-245-5288; *E-Mail:* joshi@uno.cc.geneseo.edu

JOSHI, CHANDRASHEKHAR JANARDAN, PHYSICS OF BEAMS. *Current Pos:* PROF, DEPT PHYSICS, UNIV CALIF, LOS ANGELES, 80- *Personal Data:* b India, July 22, 53. *Educ:* London Univ, BS, 74; Hall Univ, Eng, PhD(appl physics), 81. *Prof Exp:* Res physicist, Nat Res Coun, Ottawa, Can, 78-80. *Mem:* Am Phys Soc; Inst Elec & Electronics Engrs. *Res:* Physics of beams. *Mailing Add:* Electrical Eng Dept, Eng IV Bldg, UCLA Los Angeles CA 90024

JOSHI, JAY B, MOLECULAR NEUROBIOLOGY, NEUROPEPTIDE GENE EXPRESSION. *Current Pos:* CHIEF MOLECULAR BIOL, VET ADMIN MED CTR, 92-, ASSOC PROF MOLECULAR BIOL, MICROBIOL DEPT, GEORGE WASHINGTON UNIV SCH MED & PUB HEALTH, 93- *Personal Data:* b Bombay, India, Dec 22, 49; m 75, Bharati. *Educ:* Univ India, Bombay, BS, 72, MS, 76, PhD(molecular biol), 80. *Prof Exp:* Res fel, Virol Lab, Univ Nebr, 80-82, res assoc fel, 82-84; sr staff fel, Lab Biochem Genetics, Nat Heart Lung & Blood Inst, 85-90, chief, Molecular Biol Unit, 90-92. *Mem:* Am Soc Biochem & Molecular Biol; AAAS; Soc Neurosci; Soc Exp Biol & Med. *Res:* Molecular neurobiology; neuropeptide geneexpression; molecular neurovirology. *Mailing Add:* Molecular Biol Lab Vet Admin Med Ctr Res Bldg Rm 1F145 50 Irving St NW Washington DC 20422. *Fax:* 202-462-2006; *E-Mail:* jayjoshi@gwis2.circ.gwu.edu

JOSHI, JAYANT GOPAL, BIOCHEMISTRY. *Current Pos:* assoc prof, 70-79, PROF BIOCHEM, UNIV TENN, KNOXVILLE, 79- *Personal Data:* b Poona, India, July 22, 32; m 58; c 2. *Educ:* Univ Poona, BSc, 52, MSc, 54, PhD(biochem), 57. *Prof Exp:* Indian Coun Med Res-Rockefeller Found fel biochem, Nutrit Res Labs, Coonoor, India, 56-58; jr sci officer, Cent Food Tech Res Inst, Mysore, 58-59; res fel, Duke Univ, 59-64; sci pool officer, Nat Chem Labs, Poona, India, 64-66; assoc, Duke Univ, 66-68, asst prof, 68-70. *Concurrent Pos:* Vis scientist, Inst Clin Chem, Uppsala, Sweden, 72 & 73; consult, Biol Div, Oak Ridge Nat Labs; rev panel, Environ Protection Agency, 89- *Mem:* Am Soc Biol Chemists; Am Soc Microbiol. *Res:* Comparative biochemistry; mechanism of enzyme action; pyridine nucleotide, metabolism, biosynthesis and regulation, biochemical change induced by ultraviolet light; metal toxicity. *Mailing Add:* Dept Biochem Univ Tenn Knoxville TN 37916-0001

JOSHI, MADHUSUDAN SHANKARRAO, REPRODUCTIVE PHYSIOLOGY, ENDOCRINOLOGY. *Current Pos:* mem fac, 77-80, assoc prof, 80-85, PROF, DEPT ANAT, UNIV NDAK, 85- *Personal Data:* b Jamkandi, India, Oct 21, 28; m 53; c 2. *Educ:* Karnatak Univ, India, BSc, 49; Univ Bombay, MSc, 53; Weizmann Inst Sci, PhD(biol), 70. *Honors & Awards:* Golden Apple Award, Am Med Students Asn, 82 & 89. *Prof Exp:* Asst res officer physiol reprod, Cancer Res Ctr, Parel, Bombay, 56-66; asst prof anat, State Univ NY Downstate Med Ctr, 70-77. *Mem:* Soc Study Fertil UK; Soc Study Reproduction; Am Asn Anat; Am Physiol Soc. *Res:* Mechanisms involved in fertilization and implantation; study of hormone dependent enzymes in uterus and in oviduct; proteins in cerebrospinal fluid; sperm maturation. *Mailing Add:* Dept Anat Univ NDak Sch Med 501 N Columbia Rd Grand Forks ND 58203-2817

JOSHI, MUKUND SHANKAR, PHARMACEUTICAL CHEMISTRY, ORGANIC CHEMISTRY. *Current Pos:* res scientist, 76-87, ASSOC DIR, BIOPROCESS RES & DEVELOP, UPJOHN CO, 87- *Personal Data:* b India, June 11, 47; m 73; c 2. *Educ:* VJ Tech Inst, Bombay, India, 69; Univ Md, MS, 73, PhD(chem engr), 76. *Prof Exp:* Vis scientist, Danish Atomic Energy Comn, 75-76. *Mem:* Am Inst Chem Engrs; Am Chem Soc. *Res:* Chemical process research and development work to commercially manufacture pharmaceutical products; synthesis of steroids and prostaglandins; feasibility studies risk analysis, economic evaluation and supervision of laboratory; bioengineering and biomedical eng. *Mailing Add:* Pharmacia & Upjohn Co 1200-38-001 7000 Portage Rd Kalamazoo MI 49001-0102

JOSHI, NAYAN H, SYNTHETIC INORGANIC & ORGANOMETALLIC CHEMISTRY, SYNTHETIC ORGANIC & NATURAL PRODUCTS CHEMISTRY. *Current Pos:* SR RES CHEMIST, ATOTECH USA INC, 88- *Personal Data:* b Gondal, India, July 31, 52; US citizen; m 83, Pragna K Patel; c Devang & Jayraj. *Educ:* Saurashta Univ, India, BS, 73, MS, 75; Gujarat Univ, India, PhD(elec chem), 80. *Honors & Awards:* MASCOT Award, Electrochem Soc India, 80. *Prof Exp:* Anal chemist, Brooke Bond India Ltd, 73-75; jr lectr chem, UP Arts & Sci Col, Pilvai, India, 75-80; chief chemist, Samrat Chem, Keshad, India, 80-81; sr chemist, Gujarat Steel Tubes, Ahmedabad, India, 81-84; production supvr, Fema Electronics, NJ, 84-88. *Mem:* Am Electroplaters & Surface Finishers Soc. *Res:* Improvement of metallization process for electronic applications as well as metallization of non-conductors for electromagnetic shielding and decorative applications; surface modification of polymers. *Mailing Add:* 2168 Summers Glen Rock Hill SC 29732. *Fax:* 803-817-3502

JOSHI, RAMESH CHANDRA, MATERIAL SCIENCE, GEOTECHNICAL ENGINEERING. *Current Pos:* PROF GEOTECH ENG, UNIV CALGARY, 77- *Personal Data:* b May 6, 32; Can citizen; m 55; c 3. *Educ:* Rajputana Univ, India, BE, 56; Punjab Univ, India, MSc, 66; Iowa State Univ, MSc, 68, PhD(civil eng), 70. *Prof Exp:* Exec engr, Rajasthan Pub Works Dept, India, 56-66; res assoc, Eng Res Inst, Iowa State Univ, 66-70; sr proj engr, Woodward Clyde Consults, 70-77. *Concurrent Pos:* Adj lectr, Univ Mo, 76-77; vis fel, Japan Soc Promotion Sci, 90-91. *Mem:* Fel Am Soc Civil Eng; Can Geotech Soc; Int Soc Soil mech & Found Eng; Eng Inst Can. *Res:* Coal ash, particularly fly ash, utilization; model testing of piles; leachgate migration control; properties of frozen soil; soft soil fabric and consolidation. *Mailing Add:* Univ of Calgary, 2500 University Dr NW Dept Civil Eng Calgary AB T2N 1N4 Can

JOSHI, RAVINDRA PRABHAKAR, MICRO & NANO ELECTRONICS, HIGH SPEED HIGH POWER SEMI-CONDUCTOR SWITCHES. *Current Pos:* asst prof, 89-95, ASSOC PROF, OLD DOM UNIV, 95- *Personal Data:* b Allahabad, India, Sept 23, 60; m 93, Bela Dange. *Educ:* Indian Inst Technol, BTech, 83, MTech, 85; Ariz State Univ, PhD(elec eng), 88. *Prof Exp:* Res assoc, Ariz State Univ, 85-88, fel, 88-89. *Concurrent Pos:* Prin investr, Dept Energy, 92-93, Off Naval Res, 94-; res consult, Tetra Corp, NMex, 94, Mission Res Corp, Calif, 95; vis fac, Phillips Lab, 95; vis scientist, Oak Ridge Nat Lab, 96; prin investr, NASA & Dept Energy, 96. *Mem:* Sr mem Inst Elec & Electronics Engrs; Am Phys Soc; Int Soc Opt Engrs. *Res:* Semiconductor device simulation; physics and modeling of sub-micron semiconductor devices; optical interactions in semiconductors; ultrafast processes in photo excited semiconductor plasmas; high field non-linear electron transport; gas discharge phenomena. *Mailing Add:* Dept Elec & Comput Eng Old Dom Univ Norfolk VA 23529. *Fax:* 757-683-3220; *E-Mail:* rpj@ecesun.ee.odu.edu

JOSHI, SADANAND D, HORIZONTAL DRILLING, RESERVOIR ENGINEERING. *Current Pos:* PRES, JOSHI TECHNOLOGIES, INC, 88- *Personal Data:* b Panwel, India, Mar 15, 50; US citizen; m 79; c 2. *Educ:* WCE Col, India, BE, 72; Indian Inst Technol, MTech, 74; Iowa State Univ, Ames, PhD(mech eng), 78. *Prof Exp:* Res engr, Phillips Petrol Co, 80-88. *Concurrent Pos:* Indust teacher, Univ Tulsa, 88-, Am Asn Petrol Geologists & Soc Petrol Engrs, 89- *Mem:* Am Soc Mech Engrs; Soc Petrol Engrs. *Res:* Drilling mechanism and petroleum production research using horizontal drilling; author of one book. *Mailing Add:* 10631 S Erie Ave Tulsa OK 74137-7234

JOSHI, SEWA RAM, veterinary medicine, for more information see previous edition

JOSHI, SHARAD GOPAL, REPRODUCTIVE ENDOCRINOLOGY & PHYSIOLOGY. *Current Pos:* DIR, FERTIL STUDIES LAB, ALBANY MEM HOSP, 88- *Personal Data:* b Nagpur, India. *Educ:* Univ Nagpur, India, BS, 52, MS, 54; Univ Bombay, PhD(biochem), 59. *Honors & Awards:* Edward Tyler Award, Int Soc Reproductive Med, 81. *Prof Exp:* Fel endocrinol, Worcester Fedn & Harvard Med Sch, 59-63; assoc prof reproductive physiol, Inst Med Sci, India, 63-65; staff scientist endocrinol, Syntex Inst Hormone Biol, 65-66 & Southwest Fedn Res & Educ, 66-73; assoc prof obstet, gynec & biochem, Albany Med Col, 73-82, prof obstet & gynec, 82-88. *Mem:* Endocrine Soc; Soc Study Reproduction; Int Soc Reproductive Med; NY Acad Sci. *Res:* Hormonal control and role of endometrium in human pregnancy; fertility control in human subjects; effects of toxic agents on human pregnancy; role of human endometrium and placenta in pregnancy; development of in vivo and in vitro models to study human placenta and endocrine-related functions; monitoring human reproductive functions and tumor growth using biochemical markers. *Mailing Add:* Fertil Studies Lab Albany Mem Hosp 600 Northern Blvd Albany NY 12204

JOSHI, SURESH MEGHASHYAM, CONTROL SYSTEMS RESEARCH, SPACECRAFT DYNAMICS RESEARCH. *Current Pos:* SR RES SCIENTIST, LANGLEY RES CTR, NASA, 83- *Personal Data:* b Poona, India; US citizen. *Educ:* Banaras Univ, India, BS, 67; Indian Inst Technol, MS, 69; Rensselaer Polytech Inst, PhD(elec eng), 73. *Honors & Awards:* DuMont Prize, RPI, 73; Control System Technol Award, Inst Elec & Electronics Engrs, 95. *Prof Exp:* Eng, Stone & Webster Corp, 72-73; post doc res fel, Nat Res Coun, Langley Res Ctr, NASA, 73-75; assoc prof elec & mech eng, Old Dominion Univ Res Found, 75-83. *Concurrent Pos:* Adj prof, George Wash Univ, 86-, & Pa State Univ, 86-91; chmn, aerospace syst & tech panel, Am Soc Mech Engrs, 87-91; mem, tech comt astrodyn, Am Inst Aeronautics & Astronauts, 88-90; mem, bd govs, Inst Elec & Electronics Engrs, 89-94; vis prof, Univ Va, 92-93. *Mem:* Fel Inst Elec & Electronics Engrs; Am Soc Mech Engrs; fel Am Inst Aeronautics & Astronauts. *Res:* Multivariable control theory and its application to NASA's advanced aerospace systems concepts which include very large satellites such as large space antennas and space station and advanced aircraft; author of approximately 140 technical articles and two books. *Mailing Add:* NASA Langley Res Ctr Mail Stop 132 Hampton VA 23681

JOSHI, UMESHWAR PRASAD, HIGH SPEED DATA COMMUNICATIONS, COMPUTER ARCHITECTURES. *Current Pos:* vis scientist, 88-89, assoc scientist, 89-94, APPL SCIENTIST, FERMI NAT ACCELERATOR LAB, 94- *Personal Data:* b Kathmandu, Nepal, Dec 28, 53. *Educ:* Indian Inst Technol, Kanpur, MSc, 76; Univ Calif, Santa Barbara, PhD(elem particle physics), 84. *Prof Exp:* Res assoc, Rutgers Univ, 84-88. *Res:* High-speed data communications with primary emphasis on data acquisition systems for high energy physics experiments. *Mailing Add:* MS 318 Fermilab PO Box 500 Batavia IL 60510

JOSHI, VASUDEV CHHOTALAL, BIOCHEMISTRY. *Current Pos:* asst prof, 72-78, ASSOC PROF BIOCHEM, BAYLOR COL MED, 78- *Personal Data:* b Borsad, Gujarat, June 26, 38; m 65; c 3. *Educ:* Madras Univ, BPharm, 59; Andhra Univ, MPharm, 61; Indian Inst Sci, PhD(biochem), 65. *Prof Exp:* Res assoc biochem, Med Ctr, Duke Univ, 66-70, assoc in pediat, 70-72. *Concurrent Pos:* Ford Found fel, Indian Inst Sci, Bangalore, 65-66; Fulbright fel, US Educ Found in India, 66; NIH grant, Med Ctr, Duke Univ, 66-70; vis assoc prof, Mass Inst Technol, 80-81; res career develop award, USPHS, 78-83. *Mem:* Brit Biochem Soc; Am Soc Biol Chemists; Soc Biol Chemists, India. *Res:* Enzymatic mechanism of fatty acid synthesis in bacteria and animal tissues; hormonal regulation of fatty acid synthetase and stearoyl coenzyme A desaturase in liver; lipid metabolism in cultured cells; mechanism of insulin action. *Mailing Add:* 9315 Meaux Dr Houston TX 77031

JOSHI, VIJAY S, MATHEMATICS. *Current Pos:* ASSOC PROF MATH, VA INTERMONT COL, 92- *Personal Data:* b Pune, India, May 25, 39; US citizen; m 62, Rohini Kumari V; c Swati & Madhavi. *Educ:* Gujarat Univ, India, BS, 59, MS, 62, PhD(physics), 69. *Prof Exp:* Teacher math, JK High Sch, NC, 71-73; instr physics, Fayetteville Tech Community Col, 73-81; instr math, Durham Tech Community Col, 81-92. *Mem:* Am Asn Physics Teachers; Math Asn Am; Nat Coun Teachers Math. *Mailing Add:* Va Intermont Col 1013 Moore St Bristol VA 24201-4298. *Fax:* 540-669-5763; *E-Mail:* vijayj1729@naxs.com

JOSHUA, HENRY, ORGANIC CHEMISTRY, SEPARATION SCIENCE. *Current Pos:* RES & DEVELOP MGR, AURA INDUST INC, 93- *Personal Data:* b Hamburg, Ger, Dec 8, 34; US citizen; m 68; c 3. *Educ:* Bar-Ilan Univ, Israel, BS, 59; NY Univ, MS, 62, PhD(chem), 64. *Prof Exp:* Res chemist, Res Div, Col Eng, NY Univ, 60-61; res fel chem, Princeton Univ, 64-65; sr res chemist, Merck Res Labs, 65-78, res fel, 78-91, sr res fel, 91-93. *Mem:* Am Chem Soc; Asn Off Anal Chemists. *Res:* Chromatographic methods development; development of instrumentation for liquid chromatography, laboratory automation and environmental analysis. *Mailing Add:* Aura Indust Inc PO Box 898 Staten Island NY 10314. *Fax:* 718-983-9107

JOSIAS, CONRAD S(EYMOUR), ELECTRICAL ENGINEERING. *Current Pos:* PRES, JOSIAS ASSOCS, INC, 79- *Personal Data:* b New York, NY, June 12, 30; m 63; c 3. *Educ:* NY Univ, BEE, 51; Polytech Inst Brooklyn, MEE, 55. *Honors & Awards:* Award, NASA Inventions & Contrib Bd, 64. *Prof Exp:* Engr electronic develop, Airborne Instruments Lab, Inc, NY, 51-56; from res engr, missile guid systs to eng group supvr, space electronics group, space sci div, Jet Propulsion Lab, Calif Inst Technol, 56-65; pres, Analog Technol Corp, Pasadena, 65-79. *Concurrent Pos:* Instr, Pasadena City Col, 59-61. *Mem:* Sr mem Inst Elec & Electronics Engrs. *Res:* Electronic devices and systems; scientific instruments for laboratory and space applications; analytical instruments for industrial laboratories. *Mailing Add:* 4733 Hillard Ave La Canada Flintridge CA 91011

JOSIASSEN, RICHARD CARLTON, PSYCHOPATHOLOGY, NEUROPHYSIOLOGY. *Current Pos:* ASSOC PROF PSYCHIAT, MED COL PA, 87- *Personal Data:* b Oroville, Calif, Apr 29, 47. *Educ:* Westmont Col, BA, 69; Fuller Theol Sem, MA, 75; Fuller Grad Sch Psychol, PhD(psychol), 79. *Prof Exp:* Consult, Dept Defense, 69-73; from asst prof to assoc prof psychiat, Temple Univ Med Sch, 80-87. *Concurrent Pos:* Fel neurosci, NIMH, 80-82; vis asst prof, Dept Neurol, Hahnemann Univ, 81-; assoc secy gen, IV World Congress & Biol Psychiat, Philadelphia, 85. *Mem:* Soc Biol Psychiat; Am Psychopathol Asn; Soc Res Psychopathol; NY Acad Sci. *Res:* Neurophysiological mechanisms which underlie major mental illness. *Mailing Add:* Allegheny Univ Eastern Pa Psychiat Inst 3200 Henry Ave Philadelphia PA 19129. *Fax:* 215-843-1910

JOSLIN, ROBERT SCOTT, PHARMACEUTICAL CHEMISTRY. *Current Pos:* AT JOSLIN & ASSOC LTD. *Personal Data:* b Indianapolis, Ind, May 28, 29; m 84; c 3. *Educ:* Purdue Univ, BS, 51, MS, 55, PhD(phys pharm), 59. *Honors & Awards:* Lunsford Richardson Award, 57. *Prof Exp:* Assoc pharmaceut chemist, Eli Lilly & Co, 53-54; sr pharmaceut chemist, 58-65; dir prod improv, William H. Rorer, Inc, 65-68; dir depts pharmaceut sci, Res Div & asst dir res, 68-74; assoc dir pharmaceut & chem develop, G D Searle & Co, 74-78; dir pharmaceut & anal res & develop, Baxter Labs, 78. *Concurrent Pos:* Consult, 78- *Mem:* Fel Am Inst Chemists; Am Chem Soc; fel Acad Pharmaceut Sci; Int Pharmaceut Fedn; NY Acad Sci; fel Am Asn Pharmaceut Scientists. *Res:* Pharmaceutical formulation; biopharmaceutics; process and product development. *Mailing Add:* Joslin & Assoc Ltd 291 Deer Trail Ct Ste C Barrington IL 60010-1773

JOSLYN, DENNIS JOSEPH, INSECT CYTOGENETICS, EVOLUTIONARY GENETICS OF INSECTS. *Current Pos:* from asst prof to assoc prof, 79-93, PROF ZOOL (GENETICS), RUTGERS UNIV, 93-, ASSOC DEAN FAC, 93- *Personal Data:* b Chicago, Ill, Apr 29, 47; m 76; c 2. *Educ:* St Procopius Col, BS, 69; Univ Ill, Urbana, MS, 73, PhD(zool), 78. *Prof Exp:* Asst res scientist insect genetics, Univ Fla, 76-79; res assoc, Insects Affecting Man & Animals Res Lab, USDA, 76-79. *Mem:* Genetics Soc Am; Am Genetic Asn; Am Mosquito Control Asn. *Res:* Evolutionary genetics and insect cytogenetics; genetics of insects of medical, veterinary and agricultural importance; biology of eukaryotic chromosomes; molecular carcinogenesis. *Mailing Add:* Dept Biol Camden Col Arts & Sci Rutgers Univ Camden NJ 08102

JOSS, PAUL CHRISTOPHER, THEORETICAL ASTROPHYSICS, ATMOSPHERIC PHYSICS. *Current Pos:* from asst prof to assoc prof, 73-83, assoc head, Astrophys Div, Dept Physics, 83-88, PROF, DEPT PHYSICS, MASS INST TECHNOL, 83-, MEM, CTR THEORET PHYSICS, 73- *Personal Data:* b Brooklyn, NY, May 7, 45; m 92, Karen E Murray; c Susan E & Matthew A. *Educ:* Cornell Univ, BA, 66, PhD(astron, space sci), 71. *Honors & Awards:* Helen B Warner Prize, Am Astron Soc, 80. *Prof Exp:* Mem, Inst Advan Study, 71-73. *Concurrent Pos:* Vis scientist, Dept Nuclear Physics, Weizmann Inst Sci, 74-75 & 78, Inst Astron, Univ Cambridge, 77 & 93 & inst, theoret physics, Univ Calif, Santa Barbara, 92; Alfred P Sloan res fel, 76-80; vis staff mem, Los Alamos Nat Lab, 79; consult, Visidyne, Inc, 79-82 & 92-93, spec asst to pres, 93- & Los Alamos Nat Lab, 80-92; mem, Adv Comt, Inst Geophys & Planetary Physics, Los Alamos Nat Lab, 87-92; mem, High Energy Astrophys Mgt Opers Working Group, Nat Aeronaut & Space Admin, 88-90; mem, Sci Coun Astron & Space Physics, Univ Space Res Asn, 88-92; pres, Joss Consult Assoc, 92-; ed-in-chief, The Astrophys J, 97- *Mem:* Am Astron Soc; Am Phys Soc; Int Astron Union. *Res:* Theoretical and observational studies of compact x-ray sources; theoretical research on the structure and evolution of stars and binary stellar systems, supernovae, extragalactic astrophysics, the spectra of quasars, and the origin and orbital evolution of comets; theoretical and observational studies of atmospheric physics and global climatic change. *Mailing Add:* Mass Inst Technol Rm 6-203 Cambridge MA 02139. *Fax:* 978-794-5633

JOSSEM, EDMUND LEONARD, PHYSICS. *Current Pos:* from asst prof to assoc prof, 56-64, chmn dept, 67-80, PROF PHYSICS, OHIO STATE UNIV, 64- *Personal Data:* b Camden, NJ, May 19, 19. *Educ:* City Col New York, BS, 38; Cornell Univ, MS, 39, PhD(physics), 50. *Prof Exp:* Asst physics, Cornell Univ, 40-42, instr, 42-45; mem staff, Los Alamos Sci Lab, 45-46; asst physics, Cornell Univ, 46-50, res assoc, 50-55, actg asst prof, 55-56. *Concurrent Pos:* Staff physicist, Comn Col Physics, 63-64, exec secy, 64-65, chmn, 66-71; mem, Nat Adv Coun Educ Professions Develop, 67-70; mem bd dirs, Mich-Ohio Educ Lab, 67-69; mem physics survey comt, panel on educ, Nat Acad Sci-Nat Res Coun, 70-72; mem comn physic educ, Int Union Pure & Applied Physics, 81-; mem hon bd, Int Conf X-ray & Atomic Inner Shell Physics, 81-82. *Mem:* Fel AAAS; Am Phys Soc; Am Asn Physics Teachers (vpres, 71-72, pres, 73-74); Sigma Xi. *Res:* Solid state physics; x-ray physics. *Mailing Add:* 174 W 18th Ave Columbus OH 43210-1106

JOSSI, JACK WILLIAM, OCEANOGRAPHY, ECOLOGY. *Current Pos:* Phys oceanogr trop oceanog, Washington Biol Lab, US Dept Interior, 62-65, oceanogr, Trop Atlantic Biol Lab, 65-70, mgr, Fishery Climat Prog, Southeast Fisheries Ctr, 71-72, chief, Continuous Plankton Recorder Surv, Marine Resources Monitoring, Assessment & Prediction Field Group, US Dept Com, 72-74, asst chief, 74-78, res oceanogr ocean climat, Atlantic Environ Group, 78-91, SUPVRY OCEANOGR, NAT OCEANIC & ATMOSPHERIC ADMIN, US DEPT COM, 91- *Personal Data:* b Portland, Ore, Apr 4, 37; c 3. *Educ:* Pac Univ, BS, 59; Univ Wash, Seattle, BS, 62; Univ Miami, MS, 72. *Concurrent Pos:* Fel, Univ Miami, 67-68; consult, Smithsonian Inst, 70; mem, Standing Comt Oceanog, Nat Marine Fisheries Serv, US Dept Com, 71- *Mem:* Marine Biol Asn UK. *Res:* Ocean climatology; modeling and forecasting of distribution and abundance of living marine resources. *Mailing Add:* 670 Boston Neck Rd Narragansett RI 02882

JOST, DANA NELSON, PHYCOLOGY, ENVIRONMENTAL BIOLOGY. *Current Pos:* RETIRED. *Personal Data:* b Arlington, Mass, May 11, 25; m 47; c 3. *Educ:* Univ Mass, BS, 49; Harvard Univ, PhD(biol), 53. *Prof Exp:* Instr, Framingham State Col, 53-55, from asst prof to assoc prof, 55-59, chmn dept, 64-76, prof biol, 59-90. *Mem:* AAAS; Phycol Soc Am; Bot Soc Am; Int Phycol Soc; Mycol Soc Am; Am Inst Biol Sci. *Res:* Growth and reproduction of chlorophycean algae; evolution of microorganisms; environmental influences on algal growth; distribution and identification of freshwater periphyton. *Mailing Add:* 4 William J Heights Framingham MA 01701-6134

JOST, ERNEST, PHYSICAL CHEMISTRY. *Current Pos:* PRES, CHEMET CORP, 80- *Personal Data:* b El Ferrol, Spain, Sept 6, 28; US citizen; m 55; c 4. *Educ:* Univ Berne, license, 55, PhD(phys chem), 58. *Prof Exp:* Mem tech staff, Metals & Controls Div, Tex Instruments Inc, 58-61; mgr develop, Ciba A G, Switz, 61-62; dir res & develop, Mat & Elec Prod Group, Tex Instruments Inc, Attleboro, 62-74, dir prod res dept, 74-80. *Concurrent Pos:* Consult, Nat Acad Sci, 71. *Mem:* Electrochem Soc; Royal Chem Soc. *Res:* Metallurgy; electrochemistry; diffusion; solid state physics; semiconducting ceramics. *Mailing Add:* Nine Mirimichi St Plainville MA 02762. *Fax:* 508-695-4180

JOST, HANS PETER, TRIBOLOGY, CENTRALIZED LUBRICATION SYSTEMS. *Current Pos:* managing dir, 55-89, CHMN, K S PAUL GROUP, 74-, ASSOC TECHNOL GROUP LTD & ENG & GEN EQUIP LTD, 77- *Personal Data:* b Berlin, Ger, Jan 25, 21; Brit citizen; m 48, Margaret Kadesh; c Jennifer Margot & Gillish Frances. *Educ:* Univ Manchester Inst Sci & Technol, HNC, 43. *Hon Degrees:* DSc, Univ Salford, 70, Univ Bath, 90; DTech, Coun Nat Acad Awards, 87; DrSc, Slovak Univ, Bratislava, 87; DEng, Univ Leeds, 89. *Honors & Awards:* Comdr of the Order of the Brit Empire, HM the Queen, 69; Georg Vogelpohl Insignia, Ger Tribology Soc, 79; First Nuffield Medal, Inst Prod Engrs, 81; Merit Medal, Hungarian Sci Soc Mech Engrs, 83; Gold Insignia of the Order of Merit, Supreme Coun of State of the Polish Repub, 86. *Prof Exp:* Methods engr, K & L Steelfounders & Engr Ltd, 43; chief planning engr, Datim Mach Tool Co Ltd, 46-49; gen mgr & dir, Trier Bros Ltd, 49-55. *Concurrent Pos:* Managing dir, Centralube Ltd, 55-77, chmn, 74-77; chmn, Lubrication Educ & Res Working Group, Dept Educ & Sci, 64-65, Comt Tribology, Ministry, Technol, Dept Trade & Indust, 66-74, Peppermill Brass Foundry Ltd, 70-76 & Indust Technol Mgt Bd, Dept Trade & Indust, 72-74; lubrication consult, Richard Thomas & Baldwins Ltd, 69-76; dir, Williams Hudson Ltd, 67-75 & Stothert & Pitt Plc, 71-85; mem, Comt Terotechnol, Dept Trade & Indust, 71-72, Found Sci & Technol, 85 & Parliamentary Group Eng Develop, 86; hon indust prof, Liverpool Polytechnic, 83, hon prof mech eng, Univ Wales, 86. *Mem:* Fel Am Soc Mech Engrs; fel Soc Mfg Engrs; fel Inst Metals; hon mem Inst Plant Engrs; hon mem Chinese Mech Eng Soc; hon fel Inst Elec Engrs. *Res:* Surface finish measurement; oil-free steam cylinder lubrication; solid lubricants and surface treatments; tribology. *Mailing Add:* K S Paul Prods Ltd Angel Lodge Labs & Works Eley Estate London N18 3DB England. *Fax:* 44-181-807-2023

JOST, JEAN-PIERRE, BIOCHEMISTRY CELL & MOLECULAR BIOLOGY. *Current Pos:* GROUP LEADER, FRIEDRICH MIESCHER INST, SWITZ, 71- *Personal Data:* b Avenches, Switz, Oct 10, 37; US citizen; m 68, Tse Y Chim; c Isabelle King Yi & Alain King Ho. *Educ:* Swiss Fed Inst Technol, MS, 61, PhD(biol, biochem), 64. *Prof Exp:* Proj assoc, McArdle Mem Lab Cancer Res, Univ Wis-Madison, 64-66, fel, Lab Molecular Biol, 67-68; molecular biologist, Nat Jewish Hosp & Res Ctr, Denver, 68-71. *Concurrent Pos:* Asst prof, Dept Biophys & Genetics, Med Sch, Univ Colo, Denver, 68-71; res grants, Am Cancer Soc, 69, NIH, Health, Educ & Welfare & NSF, 70. *Res:* Hormonal regulation of the expression of specific genes in eukaryotes, DNA methylation and genes expression and cell differentiation; transgenes inactivation in plants and animals linked to DNA methylation. *Mailing Add:* Friedrich Miescher Inst Postfach 2543 CH-4002 Basel Switzerland. *Fax:* 41-61-721-4091; *E-Mail:* jost@imi.ch

JOST, PATRICIA COWAN, BIOPHYSICAL CHEMISTRY, MOLECULAR BIOLOGY. *Current Pos:* Res assoc molecular genetics, 66-68, SR RES ASSOC MOLECULAR BIOL, INST MOLECULAR BIOL, UNIV ORE, 68- *Personal Data:* b St Louis, Mo. *Educ:* Memphis State Univ, BS, 52; Univ Ore, PhD(biol), 66. *Concurrent Pos:* NIH fel, Univ Ore, 66-68; co-dir, Biophys Prog, NSF, 84-86. *Mem:* Biophys Soc. *Res:* Membrane structure; reporter groups and magnetic resonance; membrane biology, lipid-lipid and lipid-protein interactions. *Mailing Add:* 750 E 27th St Eugene OR 97405

JOSTLEIN, HANS, VACUUM ENGINEERING, EXPERIMENTAL PHYSICS. *Current Pos:* PHYSICIST RES & ACCELERATION SUPPORT, FERMI NAT ACCELERATOR LAB, 79- *Personal Data:* b Munich, WGer, Dec 27, 40; m 67; c 3. *Educ:* Technische Hochschule München, Dipl Eng, 65, Ludwigs Maximilian Univ, W Germany, PhD(physics), 69. *Prof Exp:* Fel high energy res, Univ Munich, 69-70; res asst, Univ Rochester, 70-73; asst prof, State Univ NY, Stony Brook, 73-79. *Res:* High energy particle physics, specifically muon; muon inelastic scattering; higgs mass pair production for leptons and hadrons to test quark theory; drell-yan processes and resonance production; very high lumosity pair production. *Mailing Add:* 122 Fermlab PO Box 500 MS 208 Batavia IL 60510

JOTHY, SERGE, MOLECULAR AND CELL BIOLOGY. *Current Pos:* from asst prof to assoc prof, 78-90, ASSOC MEM, CTR CLIN IMMUNOBIOL & TRANSPLANTATION, FAC MED, MCGILL UNIV, 89-, ASSOC MEM, DEPT ONCOL, 92-, PROF DEPT PATH, 91-; SR PATHOLOGIST, ROYAL VICTORIA HOSP, MONTREAL, 84- *Personal Data:* b Bordeaux, France, May 18, 44; Can & French citizen; m, Marie Francoisen; c Vanessa & Antoine. *Educ:* Univ Bordeaux, France, MD, 68, MS, 72; McGill Univ, PhD(exp med), 76. *Prof Exp:* Asst prof biophys, Dept Med Biophys, Univ Bordeaux, France, 68-70; res asst, Dept Physiol, Univ Montreal, 70-71. *Concurrent Pos:* Asst pathologist, Royal Victoria Hosp, Montreal, 78-82; vis scientist, Pasteur Inst, Paris, France, 86-87. *Mem:* AAAS; Am Soc Cancer Rese; Am Soc Investigative Path; Int Acad Path; Int Soc Oncodevelopmental Biol & Med; World Asn Soc Path. *Res:* Cellular and molecular biology of cell adhesion proteins; molecular biology of alterations of met oncogene; colon and breast cancer. *Mailing Add:* McGill Univ Dept Path 3775 University St Montreal PQ H3A 2B4 Can

JOUBERT, WAYNE DAVID, NUMERICAL ANALYSIS, NUMERICAL LINEAR ALGEBRA. *Current Pos:* postdoctoral fel, 92-95, TECH STAFF MEM, LOS ALAMOS NAT LAB, 95-, PRIN INVESTR, 96- *Personal Data:* b Opelousas, La, Jan 28, 59; m 96, Shirley Bleasdale. *Educ:* Univ Southwestern La, BSc, 81; Univ Tex, PhD(math), 90. *Honors & Awards:* R & D 100 Award, 97. *Prof Exp:* Postdoctoral fel, Univ Tex, 90-92. *Concurrent Pos:* Collabr, Advan Comput Lab, Los Alamos Nat Lab, 90-91; Schlumberger Found fel, 91. *Mem:* Soc Indust & Appl Math; Am Math Soc; Math Asn Am; Sigma Xi. *Res:* Numerical analysis; numerical linear algebra; iterative linear system solvers; software development and parallel computing; oil reservoir simulation; ground water modeling; radiation diffusion modeling. *Mailing Add:* Group CIC-19 MS B256 Los Alamos Nat Lab Los Alamos NM 87545. *Fax:* 505-667-1126; *E-Mail:* wdj@lanl.gov

JOUBIN, FRANC RENAULT, chemistry, for more information see previous edition

JOULLIE, MADELEINE M, ORGANIC CHEMISTRY. *Current Pos:* From instr to assoc prof, 53-77, PROF CHEM, UNIV PA, 77- *Personal Data:* b Paris, France, Mar 29, 27; nat US; m 59, Richard Prange. *Educ:* Simmons Col, BS, 49; Univ Pa, MS, 50, PhD, 53. *Honors & Awards:* Lindback Award; Garvan Medal; Am Inst Chem Award. *Mem:* AAAS; Am Chem Soc; Sigma Xi. *Res:* Mechanisms of organic reactions; heterocyclic chemistry; synthesis of potential antimetabolites; peptide synthesis; peptide mimetics. *Mailing Add:* Chem Dept Univ Pa Philadelphia PA 19104

JOUNG, JOHN JONGIN, CHEMICAL PROCESS ENGINEERING, BIOENGINEERING. *Current Pos:* SR RES ENGR, AMOCO CORP, 81- *Personal Data:* b Korea, June 29, 41; m 68; c 2. *Educ:* Seoul Nat Univ, BS, 63, MS, 67; Univ NMex, PhD(chem eng), 70. *Prof Exp:* Res fel, Ames Lab, 70-71; res supvr, Univ Chicago, 71-76; sr scientist, Colgate-Palmolive Co, 76-78; sci adv, Am Hosp Supply Corp, 78-81. *Concurrent Pos:* Vcmndg officer, Chem Smoke Generator Co, Korea, 63-65; assst investr, Korea Inst Sci & Technol, 67-68. *Mem:* Am Inst Chem Engrs; Am Chem Soc; Soc Plastics Engrs; Am Mgt Asn. *Res:* Process and product research in the areas of chemical, polymer, energy and health care business; cancer and clinical pathology; process development for chemical and biological products, including recombinant DNA products; polymer applications for biomedical and personal care products; reaction engineering. *Mailing Add:* 6095 Millbridge Lane Lisle IL 60532

JOURDIAN, GEORGE WILLIAM, BIOCHEMISTRY, MICROBIOLOGY. *Current Pos:* From instr to assoc prof biol chem & biochem, 61-74, res assoc internal med, 65-74, PROF BIOL CHEM, MED SCH, UNIV MICH, ANN ARBOR, 65- *Personal Data:* b Northampton, Mass, Apr 21, 29; m 54; c 2. *Educ:* Amherst Col, BA, 49; Univ Mass, MS, 53; Purdue Univ, PhD(bact), 58. *Concurrent Pos:* Arthritis Found fel, 58-61; Fogarty Sr Int fel, 78-79. *Mem:* Am Soc Biol Chem; Am Chem Soc; Soc Complex Carbohydrates. *Res:* Biochemistry of glycosaminoglycans and glycoproteins. *Mailing Add:* Univ Mich Med Ctr 4633 Kresge Bldg I 200 Zina Pitcher Pl Ann Arbor MI 48109-0001

JOURNEAY, GLEN EUGENE, MEDICINE. *Current Pos:* RETIRED. *Personal Data:* b Orange, Tex, June 14, 25; m 48, Betty Cooper; c Carol A (Kaler), David G, Stephen D, Nancy C (Jackson) & Janet E (Slack). *Educ:* Rice Univ, Houston, BA, 45, BS, 47; Univ Tex, Austin, PhD(org chem), 52, Galveston, MD, 60. *Honors & Awards:* M D Anderson Excellency in Oncol Award, 85. *Prof Exp:* Res chemist, Monsanto Chem, 51-56; physician, Beeler Manske Clin, Toxicity, 61-93; physician pvt pract, 63-93. *Concurrent Pos:* Vis prof biomed eng, Univ Tex, Austin, 64-66, lectr, 66- *Mem:* AMA; Am Acad Family Physicians; Am Chem Soc; fel Am Inst Chemists. *Res:* Cyanoethylation; hydrocyanic acid reactions; toxicity of acrylonitrile and acrylamide; neurotoxicity; environmental toxicology. *Mailing Add:* 3908 Sierra Dr Austin TX 78731-3912. *Fax:* 512-345-0047; *E-Mail:* journeay@mail.utexas.edu

JOVANCICEVIC, VLADIMIR, ELECTROCHEMISTRY, CORROSION & PASSIVITY. *Current Pos:* res chemist mat sci, 87-89, SR RES CHEMIST, W R GRACE & CO, COLUMBIA, MD, 89- *Personal Data:* b Belgrad, Yugoslavia, Dec 14, 47; m 69; c 1. *Educ:* Univ Belgrad, BSc 72, MSc 76; Univ Paris VI, France, PhD(phys chem), 80. *Honors & Awards:* W R Grace Res Award. *Prof Exp:* Res asst electrochem, Inst Tech Sci, Belgrad, 75-78; res assoc, Elec France, 80-81, Nat Ctr Sci Res, Paris, 81-82; sr scientist mat sci, Sasilor-Sollac, Thionville, France, 82-84; sr res assoc electrochem, Tex A&M Univ, 84-87. *Mem:* Electrochem Soc; Am Chem Soc; Nat Asn Chem Engrs. *Res:* Investigation of the physico-chemical properties of metal-solution interfaces; spectroscopic characterization of the structure, composition and reactivity of the adsorbed and thin surface layers as related to the corrosion, passivation and electrodeposition; corrosion in cooling toxiers and boiler systems. *Mailing Add:* W R Grace & Co Res Div 7500 Grace Dr Columbia MD 21044-4041

JOVANOVIC, DRASKO D, HIGH ENERGY PHYSICS. *Current Pos:* RES SCIENTIST, FERMI NAT ACCELERATOR LAB, 68- *Personal Data:* b Belgrade, Yugoslavia, May 24, 30. *Educ:* Belgrade Univ, BS, 53; Univ Chicago, MS, 56, PhD(physics), 59. *Mem:* Fel Am Phys Soc. *Mailing Add:* Fermi Nat Accelerator Lab PO Box 500 Batavia IL 60510

JOVANOVIC, M(ILAN) K(OSTA), MECHANICAL ENGINEERING. *Current Pos:* prof, 68-84, EMER PROF MECH ENG, WICHITA STATE UNIV, 84- *Personal Data:* b Belgrade, Yugoslavia, Oct 29, 13; nat US; m 54, Muriel Hedblom; c 1. *Educ:* Univ Belgrade, Dipl Ing, 38, Dipl Phys, 45; Northwestern Univ, MS, 54, PhD(mech eng), 57. *Prof Exp:* Asst thermodyn & physics, Univ Belgrade, 39-46, instr physics, 46-47, asst prof thermodyn, 47-51, assoc prof thermodyn & refig mach & asst dean, Sch Mech Eng, 51-52; instr physics, Univ Ill, 55; assoc prof mech eng, SDak Sch Mines & Technol, 56-58; from assoc prof to prof, Okla State Univ, 58-63; prof, Univ Alaska, 63-65; prof, US Naval Acad, 65-68. *Res:* Thermodynamics. *Mailing Add:* 1026 N Pinecrest Wichita KS 67208

JOVANOVICH, JOVAN VOJISLAV, HIGH ENERGY & NUCLEAR PHYSICS, NUCLEAR POWER. *Current Pos:* from asst prof to assoc prof, 65-79, PROF PHYSICS, UNIV MAN, 79- *Personal Data:* b Belgrade, Yugoslavia, July 30, 28; m 55, Anica Vladisavljevich; c Goran & Vera. *Educ:* Univ Belgrade, BSc, 50, Univ Man, MSc, 56; Washington Univ, St Louis, PhD(physics), 61. *Prof Exp:* Asst physics, Inst Brois Kidric, Belgrade, Yugoslavia, 50-54, Univ Belgrade, 53-55 & Univ Man, 55-57; asst, Wash Univ, 57-61; res assoc, Brookhaven Nat Lab, 61-64; develop officer, Oxford Univ, Nuclear Physics Lab, 64-65. *Concurrent Pos:* Vis scientist, Orgn Europ Nuclear Res, 71-72 & 78-79. *Mem:* Am Phys Soc; Can Asn Physicists; Can Radiation Protect Asn; Can Nuclear Soc. *Res:* Investigation of properties of neutral K mesons; elementary inelastic proton-proton interaction; search for quarks, pion properties; Chernobyl accident; sustainable development and nuclear power; raditation protection. *Mailing Add:* Dept Physics Univ Man Winnipeg MB R3T 2N2 Can. *Fax:* 204-269-8489; *E-Mail:* jovan@physics.umanitoba.ca

JOVANOVICH, KIM DAYNE, FIBER OPTIC SENSOR RESEARCH & DEVELOPMENT, OPTICAL TELECOMMUNICATION SYSTEM DEVELOPMENT. *Current Pos:* PRES, OMNI TECHNOL INC, 94- *Personal Data:* b New Orleans, La, Jan 16, 51; m 74, Janet Meynier; c Brett, Eric & Mark. *Educ:* Tulane Univ, BS, 72; Univ Southern Miss, MS, 78. *Prof Exp:* Capt, Sch Appl Aerospace Sci, USAF, 72-77; sr commun engr, Comput Sci Corp, 77-80; dir fiber optics res, Litton Data Systs Div, 80-91; staff electrooptics engr, Naval Res Lab, Stennis Space Ctr, NASA, 90-91; tech dir, Omnicron Telecommun, 91-94. *Concurrent Pos:* Adj prof elec eng, Univ New Orleans, 80-; tech dir, Omnicron Telecommu, 91-; adj prof, Univ Col, Tulane, 93- *Mem:* Inst Elec & Electronics Engrs. *Res:* Use of fiber optics to measure various physical phenomenon and environmental conditions; high speed laser and fiber optic telecommunication and network design. *Mailing Add:* 450 31st St Suite A Kenner LA 70065

JOWETT, DAVID, STATISTICS, BOTANY. *Current Pos:* assoc prof, 70-72, PROF MATH, UNIV WIS-GREEN BAY, 72- *Personal Data:* b Liverpool, Eng, Oct 14, 34; m 57; c 2. *Educ:* Univ Wales, BSc, 56, PhD(bot), 59. *Prof Exp:* Demonstr agr bot, Univ Col NWales, 56-59; sr sci officer, Plant Breeding, EAfrican Agr & Forestry Res Orgn, Uganda, 59-65; from asst prof to assoc prof statist, Iowa State Univ, 65-70. *Concurrent Pos:* Rockefeller Found fel, Iowa State Univ, 62-63; Intern, Acad Admin, Am Coun Educ, 76-77. *Mem:* AAAS; Brit Ecol Soc; Am Statist Asn; Inst Math Statist; Am Soc Nat; fel Royal Statist Soc; Sigma Xi. *Res:* Heavy metal resistance and tolerance of low nutrient levels in plants; improved varieties hybrids of sorghum for Africa; sorghum agronomy crown rust epiphytology; biostatistics; biomathematics; statistical computing. *Mailing Add:* Dept Math Univ Wis 2420 Nicolet Dr Green Bay WI 54311-7003

JOY, DAVID CHARLES, ELECTRON MICROSCOPY, MATERIALS SCIENCE. *Current Pos:* DISTINGUISHED SCIENTIST & PROF, OAK RIDGE NAT LAB & UNIV TENN, 87- *Personal Data:* b Colchester, Eng, Nov 15, 43; US citizen; m 79, Carolyn McCrory. *Educ:* Cambridge Univ, BA, 66; Oxford Univ, DPhil(metall), 69. *Honors & Awards:* Burton Medal, Electron Micros Soc Am, 78; Birks Award, Microbeam Anal Soc, 85, Castaing Award, 93. *Prof Exp:* Fac metall, Oxford Univ, 69-74; mem tech staff electron micros, Bell Tel Labs, 74-87. *Concurrent Pos:* Res fel, Imperial Chem Industs, 69-71 & Oxford Univ, 69-72; Warren res fel, Royal Soc London, 72-74; gen ed, J Micros, 81-91. *Mem:* Electron Micros Soc Am; Royal Micros Soc London. *Res:* Electron microscopy and electron spectroscopy applied to microstructural and microchemical analysis; computer modeling of electron-solid interactions; electron holography. *Mailing Add:* EM Facil F241 Walters Life Sci Bldg Univ Tenn Stadium Dr M-407 Knoxville TN 37966-0840. *Fax:* 423-974-3642; *E-Mail:* joy@utkvs.utk.edu

JOY, EDWARD BENNETT, ANTENNA MEASUREMENTS, RADOME ELECTROMAGNETIC DESIGN. *Current Pos:* From asst prof to assoc prof, 70-80, PROF ELEC ENG, GA INST TECHNOL, SCH ELEC ENG, 80-; PRES; JOY ENG CO, 81- *Personal Data:* b Troy, NY, Nov 15, 41; m 66, Patricia Huddles; c Frederick & Rebecca. *Educ:* Ga Inst Technol, BEE, 63, MS, 67, PhD(elec eng), 70. *Honors & Awards:* Young Scientist Year, URSI Comm A, 72. *Concurrent Pos:* Prin investr, US Army, USAF, Elec Power Res Inst, NSF & Joint Ser Electronics Prog, 70-; lectr, US, Can, Europe, Mid East & Far East; consult, Martin Marietta Aerospace, Sci Atlanta, Ford Aerospace, Harris Corp, Fed Aviation Admin, Westinghouse Elec, Sperry Corp, Gen Elec Corp & Alcoa, 70-; distinguished scientist lectr, Govt India, 82; tech coordr, Antenna Measurement Techniques Asn, 84-85, co-host ann meeting, 88; fel, Inst Elec & Electronics Engrs, Antennas & Propagation Soc, 89. *Mem:* Fel Inst Elec & Electronics Engrs; Antenna Measurement Techniques Asn (vpres, 83-84); Sigma Xi. *Res:* Development of the theory, technique and application of far- field, anechoic chamber, compact and near-field antenna measurements; radome analysis, design and measurement; earth grounding of power delivery systems; holds three patents; over 120 publications. *Mailing Add:* Ga Inst Technol Sch Elec & Comput Eng Atlanta GA 30332-0250. *Fax:* 404-894-5935

JOY, GEORGE CECIL, III, INORGANIC CHEMISTRY. *Current Pos:* Res chemist, Allied-Signal Inc, 74-76, group leader, 76-81, mgr appl catalysis res, 81-86, dir, Tech Dept, Automotive Catalyst Div, 87-90, RES SCIENTIST, RES & TECH DIV, ALLIED-SIGNAL INC, 90-, DIR RES & TECHNOL, EUROPE. *Personal Data:* b Lincoln, Nebr, Apr 22, 48; m 70; c 1. *Educ:* Grinnell Col, BA, 70; Northwestern Univ, MS, 71, PhD(inorg chem), 75. *Mem:* Am Chem Soc; Nat Catalysis Soc; Soc Automotive Engrs; Inst Chem Engrs (UK). *Res:* Studies in heterogeneous catalysis; inorganic aspects of preparation and characterization of catalysts. *Mailing Add:* 151 Mendham Rd Bernardsville NJ 07924

JOY, JOSEPH WAYNE, PHYSICAL OCEANOGRAPHY. *Current Pos:* RETIRED. *Personal Data:* b Iowa City, Apr 12, 30; m 58; c 3. *Educ:* State Col Wash, BA, 55; Univ Calif, San Diego, MS, 58. *Prof Exp:* Res oceanogr, Marine Phys Lab, Univ Calif, San Diego, 56-61; oceanogr, Marine Adv, Bendix Corp, 61-66; res oceanogr, Meteorol Res, Inc, 66-67; sr scientist,

Westinghouse Ocean Res Lab, Calif, 67-70; specialist oceanog, Scripps Inst Oceanog, Univ Calif, San Diego, 70-74; staff oceanogr, Intersea Res Corp, 74-84; comput spec, Nat Marine Fisheries Serv, Nat Oceanic & Atmospheric Admin, US Dept Com, 84-88; comput spec, US Navy Personnel Res & Develop Ctr, San Diego, Calif, 88-92, opers res analyst, 92-94. *Mem:* AAAS; Am Geophys Union; Am Meteorol Soc. *Res:* Surface waves and currents; radar oceanography; radar as oceanographic tool. *Mailing Add:* 1210 Agate St San Diego CA 92109

JOY, KENNETH WILFRED, plant physiology, for more information see previous edition

JOY, MICHAEL LAWRENCE GRAHAME, BIOMEDICAL ENGINEERING. *Current Pos:* Asst prof elec eng, 70-76, ASSOC PROF BIOMED & ELEC ENG, UNIV TORONTO, 76-, ASSOC CHMN, ELEC & COMPUT ENG, 93- *Personal Data:* b Toronto, Ont, July 31, 40; m 67, Jane Andras; c Robert, Gwendolyn & Eleanor. *Educ:* Univ Toronto, BSc, 63, MASc, 68, PhD(elec eng), 70. *Mem:* Can Med & Biol Eng Soc; Inst Elec & Electronics Engrs; Soc Magnetic Resonance. *Res:* Electric current density imaging by magnetic resonance. *Mailing Add:* Inst Biomed Eng Univ Toronto Toronto ON M5S 1A4 Can

JOY, ROBERT JOHN THOMAS, INTERNAL MEDICINE, PHYSIOLOGY. *Current Pos:* prof mil med & hist & chmn dept, 76-81, prof, 81-96, EMER PROF MED HIST, UNIFORMED SERV UNIV HEALTH SCI, 96- *Personal Data:* b South Kingstown, RI, Apr 5, 29; m 52, 85, Janet Brady; c Robert L F & Lisa. *Educ:* Univ RI, BS, 50; Yale Univ, MD, 54; Harvard Univ, MA, 65. *Honors & Awards:* Osler Medal, Am Asn Hist Med, 54; Hoff Mem Medal Mil Med, 59; J S Billings Award, 66; Clements Award, 80. *Prof Exp:* Med Corps, US Army, 54-81, intern, Walter Reed Gen Hosp, 54-55, resident, 56-58, chief, Bioastronaut Br, Army Med Res Lab, Ft Knox, Ky, 59-61, comdr & mem res staff, Army Res Inst Environ Med, 61-63, chief med res team, Walter Reed Army Inst Res, Vietnam, 65-66, dep dir, US Army Res Inst Environ Med, Mass, 66-68, chief Med Res Div, US Army Med Res & Develop Command, Washington, DC, 68-69, dep biol & med res, Directorate of Defense Res & Eng, 69-71, dep dir, 71-75, dir & comdr, Walter Reed Army Inst Res, 75-76. *Concurrent Pos:* Ed, J Hist Med & Allied Sci, 82-87. *Mem:* Am Asn Hist Med; fel AAAS; Am Physiol Soc; fel Am Col Physicians; Osler Soc. *Res:* Environmental physiology and medicine; history of medicine; military medical history; research administration and management. *Mailing Add:* 5821 Highland Dr Chevy Chase MD 20815

JOY, ROBERT MCKERNON, neuropharmacology, neurotoxicology; deceased, see previous edition for last biography

JOY, VINCENT ANTHONY, INTERNAL MEDICINE. *Current Pos:* clin asst prof med, 69-81, EMER PROF, CORNELL UNIV, MED COL, 81- *Personal Data:* b New York, NY, Feb 22, 20; m 52; c 7. *Educ:* Fordham Univ, BS, 46; Duke Univ, MD, 50. *Prof Exp:* Staff internist, Vet Admin Hosp, East Orange, NJ, 53-54; staff internist & admitting officer, Vet Admin Hosp, New York, 54-59; med dir clin res, Int Div, E R Squibb & Sons, 59-67; sr med dir basic clin res, Int Div, Merck, Sharp & Dohme, Rahway, NJ, 67- *Concurrent Pos:* Asst physician, Bellevue Hosp, 60-69; clin asst physician, New York Hosp, 69-; dir, Med Clin, Nasau County Hosp, 84-87. *Res:* Gastroenterology; influence of the vagus nerve on gastric secretion; various classes of drugs on the parietal cell; action of decarboxylase inhibitor in the treatment of patients with Parkinson's disease, including administration of L-dopa to determine action of inhibitor as a means of reducing requirements; lipid-lowering and uricosuric effects of clofibrate-type drugs; beta-blockers. *Mailing Add:* 12640 N 89th St Scottsdale AZ 85260

JOYCE, BLAINE R, PHYSICAL CHEMISTRY. *Current Pos:* CONSULT & PRES, ACTIVATED TECH SERV CO, 86- *Personal Data:* b Jeannette, Pa, Nov 13, 25; m 55; c 3. *Educ:* Univ Pittsburgh, BS, 49; Univ Toledo, MS, 65. *Prof Exp:* Res assoc activated carbon, Mellon Inst, 49-51; develop engr, Union Carbide Corp, 53-60, group leader activated carbon, 60-65, mgr activated carbon prod eng, 65-68, sr develop engr, Carbon Prod Div, 68-80, tech dir activated carbon, 80-86. *Mem:* Am Chem Soc. *Res:* Production and applications of arc carbons for lighting and metal processing applications; development of activated carbon products and cost studies for business product planning. *Mailing Add:* 453 Cranston Dr Berea OH 44017

JOYCE, EDWIN A, JR, MARINE SCIENCE. *Current Pos:* RETIRED. *Personal Data:* b Hampton, Va, Feb 23, 37; m 78, Mary D Woodbery; c Chris, Kelly, Beth, Trip, Kathy, Carson & Kim. *Educ:* Butler Univ, BA, 59; Univ Fla, Gainesville, MS, 61. *Prof Exp:* Marine biologist, Fla Bd Conserv, 61-67; sr fisheries biologist, Fla Dept Natural Resources, 67-68, supvr, Marine Res Lab, 68-72, chief, Bur Marine Sci & Technol, 72-75, dir, Div Marine Resources, 75-88. *Mem:* Am Fisheries Soc; fel Am Inst Fishery Res Biologists; Sigma Xi; Nat Shellfisheries Asn. *Res:* Research and publications on shellfish issues and administrative activities in fishery management and research supervision. *Mailing Add:* 14130 N Meridian Rd Tallahassee FL 32312

JOYCE, GERALD F, MOLECULAR EVOLUTION. *Current Pos:* asst prof, 89-92, assoc prof, 92-96, PROF, DEPT CHEM & MOLECULAR BIOL, SCRIPPS RES INST, 96- *Personal Data:* b Manhattan, Kans, Nov 28, 56. *Educ:* Univ Chicago, BS, 78; Univ Calif, San Diego, MD & PhD(nucleic acids), 84. *Honors & Awards:* Molecular Biol Award, Nat Acad Sci, 94. *Prof Exp:* Fel, Salk Inst, 85-89. *Mem:* Am Chem Soc; Int Soc Study Origins Life. *Res:* Molecular biology; biochemistry. *Mailing Add:* Dept Molecular Biol Scripps Res Inst 10550 N Torrey Pines Rd La Jolla CA 92037

JOYCE, GLENN RUSSELL, PLASMA PHYSICS. *Current Pos:* SR RES SCIENTIST, NAVAL RES LAB, 81- *Personal Data:* b St Louis, Mo, June 24, 39; m 62; c 1. *Educ:* Cent Methodist Col, BA, 61; Univ Mo, MS, 63, PhD(physics), 66. *Prof Exp:* Res assoc, Univ Iowa, 66-68, from assoc prof to prof physics, 68-81. *Concurrent Pos:* Vis assoc prof, Hunter Col, 74; res scientist physics, Max Planck Inst Plasma Physics, 69; vis res scientist, Goddard Space Flight Ctr, NASA, 75-79. *Mem:* Am Phys Soc. *Res:* Plasma theory; interaction of test particles with plasmas; particle simulation of plasmas; numerical simulation and kinetic theory of plasmas. *Mailing Add:* Naval Res Lab Code 4790 4555 Overlook Ave SW Washington DC 20375

JOYCE, JAMES MARTIN, ATOMIC COLLISIONS, COMPUTER APPLICATIONS. *Current Pos:* dir accelerator lab, 70-76, from asst prof to assoc prof, 70-79, PROF PHYSICS, ECAROLINA UNIV, 79-, DIR DIGITAL SYST, 76- *Personal Data:* b Bayonne, NJ, Jan 27, 42; m 65; c 2. *Educ:* LaSalle Col, BA, 63; Univ Pa, MS, 64, PhD(physics), 67. *Prof Exp:* Res assoc nuclear physics, Univ NC, Chapel Hill, 67-70. *Mem:* Am Phys Soc; Sigma Xi. *Res:* Experimental atomic physics and applied physics; computer systems and interface design; physics applied to medicine. *Mailing Add:* 106 Valley Lane Greenville NC 27858-4944

JOYCE, JOHN RANDAL, INSTRUMENT DESIGN & AUTOMATION. *Current Pos:* LIMS MGR, DIV CONSOL LAB SERV, COMMONWEALTH VA, 93- *Educ:* Univ Tulsa, BS, 77; Tex A&M Univ, PhD(anal chem), 83. *Prof Exp:* Proj leader, Instrument Develop & Automation Group, Dow Chem Co, 83-93. *Concurrent Pos:* Contrib ed, sci comput & automation, Gordon Publ, 94- *Res:* Internet and laboratory automation; coordinate LIMS development and instrument automation activities for state laboratory. *Mailing Add:* DGS Div Consol Lab Serv 1 N 14th St Richmond VA 23219. *Fax:* 804-371-0666; *E-Mail:* jjoyce@dgs.state.va.us

JOYCE, NANCY C, CELL BIOLOGY, PHARMACOLOGY OF THE CORNEAL ENDOTHELIUM. *Current Pos:* asst scientist, 87-92, ASSOC SCIENTIST, SCHEPENS EYE RES INST, 92-, ASST PROF RES, HARVARD, UNIV, 92- *Personal Data:* b New Haven, Conn, Aug 28, 45. *Educ:* Alburtos Magnis Col, BA, 67; Yale Univ, PhD(cellular biol), 85. *Prof Exp:* Res fel, Yale Univ, 85-87. *Mem:* Asn Res Vision & Ophthal; Am Soc Cell Biol; AAAS. *Res:* Cell biology; pharmacology of the corneal endothelium. *Mailing Add:* Schepens Eye Res Inst Pharmacol Unit 20 Staniford St Boston MA 02114-2500. *Fax:* 617-720-1069

JOYCE, RICHARD ROSS, ASTRONOMY. *Current Pos:* SUPPORT SCIENTIST ASTRON, KITT PEAK NAT OBSERV, 73- *Personal Data:* b Wilmington, Del, June 28, 44; m 79, Sandra Owen. *Educ:* Williams Col, BA, 65; Univ Calif, Berkeley, PhD(physics), 70. *Prof Exp:* Res asst physics, Lawrence Radiation Lab, Univ Calif, Berkeley, 66-70; fel astron, State Univ NY, Stony Brook, 70-72, lectr, 72-73. *Mem:* Am Phys Soc; Astron Soc Pac; Am Astron Soc. *Res:* Infrared detector development; telescope optimization for infrared use; study of heavily obscured and/or cool sources in infrared; study of infrared emission line sources. *Mailing Add:* Kitt Peak Nat Observ PO Box 26732 Tucson AZ 85726-6732

JOYCE, WILLIAM, CHEMISTRY. *Current Pos:* engr, Union Carbide, 57-68, prod mgr, Chem & Plastics Group, 71-74, opers mgr, 74-76, dir, Polyolefins Opers, 76-78, vpres, Marketing, 78-79, vpres, licensing/technol, 79, pres, Silicones & Urethane Intermediates Div, 82-85, pres, Polyolefins Div, 85-92, exec vpres opers, 92-93, BD DIR, UNION CARBIDE CORP, 92-, PRES & CHIEF OPER OFFICER, 93-, CHMN, 96- *Personal Data:* b Greensburg, Pa, Dec 15, 35; m, Kathleen; c William, Susan & Diana. *Educ:* Pa State Univ, BS, 57; NY Univ, MBA, 71, PhD, 74. *Honors & Awards:* Nat Medal Technol, Pres Clinton, NSF, '93; Indust Achievement Award, Plastics Acad, 94. *Concurrent Pos:* Dir-at-large, chmn & immediate past chmn, bd dirs, Soc Plastics Indust, 88-91; bd dirs, Chem Mfr Asn, Am Plastics Coun, Melville Corp & Reynolds Metals Co; bd trustees, Univ Res Asn, Inc. *Mem:* Nat Acad Eng; Inst Elec & Electronics Engrs. *Mailing Add:* Union Carbide Corp 39 Old Ridgebury Rd L4 Danbury CT 06817

JOYCE, WILLIAM B(AXTER), THEORETICAL PHYSICS. *Current Pos:* mem tech staff, AT&T Bell Labs, 66-81, distinguished mem tech staff, 82-88, FEL, LUCENT BELL LABS, 88- *Personal Data:* b Columbus, Ohio, Oct 17, 32; m 58; c 4. *Educ:* Cornell Univ, BEP, 55; Ohio State Univ, PhD(physics), 66. *Prof Exp:* Mgr advan technol, Accuray Corp, Ohio, 63-66. *Mem:* Am Phys Soc. *Res:* Applied theoretical physics. *Mailing Add:* Lucent Bell Labs 2D-350 Murray Hill NJ 07974

JOYNER, CLAUDE REUBEN, MEDICINE. *Current Pos:* DIR DEPT MED, ALLEGHENY GEN HOSP, PITTSBURGH, 72-; PROF MED, MED COL PA, 88- *Personal Data:* b Winston-Salem, NC, Dec 4, 25; m 50; c 2. *Educ:* Univ NC, BS, 47; Univ Md, MD, 49; Am Bd Internal Med, dipl, 57; Am Bd Cardiovasc Dis, dipl, 63. *Prof Exp:* Resdient med, Bowman Gray Sch Med, 50; Nat Heart Inst trainee & asst instr, Sch Med, Univ Pa, 52-53, from instr to assoc prof, 53-71; prof med, Hahnemann Med Col, 71-72; clin prof med, Univ Pittsburgh, 72-88. *Concurrent Pos:* Attend cardiologist, Vet Admin Hosp, Philadelphia, 65-; mem coun arteriosclerosis, Am Heart Asn. *Mem:* Fel AAAS; Am Heart Asn; fel Am Col Physicians; Am Fedn Clin Res; fel Am Col Cardiol. *Res:* Academic medicine; cardiology; phonocardiography; ultrasound. *Mailing Add:* Allegheny Gen Hosp 320 E North Ave Pittsburgh PA 15212-4772

JOYNER, H(OWARD) SAJON, ENGINEERING. *Current Pos:* PRES, KINETIC CORP, 77- *Personal Data:* b Ft Worth, Tex, June 6, 39; m 69, Mary E Yankoff; c 3. *Educ:* Univ Tex, Austin, BS, 62, MA, 64; Univ Mo, Rolla, MS, 67, PhD, 70. *Prof Exp:* Nuclear engr, Gen Dynamics-Ft Worth, 64; asst prof mech eng, Wichita State Univ, 69-75; dir planning, res & develop, Univ Kans Sch Med, Wichita, 75-77. *Concurrent Pos:* Adj prof, Wichita State Univ. *Res:* Thermal systems, especially anti-ice systems on aircraft wings and tails. *Mailing Add:* Kinetic Corp PO Box 8161 Wichita KS 67208

JOYNER, JOHN T, III, internal medicine, for more information see previous edition

JOYNER, POWELL AUSTIN, RESEARCH MANAGEMENT. *Current Pos:* RETIRED. *Personal Data:* b Dallas, Tex, July 20, 25; m 52, Walli Schaper. *Educ:* Centenary Col, BS, 46; Univ Iowa, PhD(phys chem), 51. *Prof Exp:* Asst, Univ Iowa, 46-50; res chemist, Minneapolis-Honeywell Regulator Co, 50-52; head, Anal Sect, Callery Chem Co, 52-53; head, Measurements Div, 53-54; sr res scientist, Res Ctr, Minneapolis-Honeywell Regulator Co, 54-56, res supvr, 56-58, head, Chem Sect, 58-60, proj mgr fuel cell controls, 60-62, staff scientist, Honeywell Res Ctr, 62-63; asst dir, Res Div, Allis Chalmers Mfg Co, 63-64, gen mgr space & defense sci, 64-67, dir planning & eval, 67-68; dir res, Trane Co, 68-79, vpres res, 79-85; mgr advan projs, Elec Power Res Inst, 85-95. *Mem:* Am Chem Soc; AAAS; Int Ground Source Heat Pump Asn; Am Soc Heating, Refrig & Air Conditioning Engrs. *Res:* Raman effect; humidity instrumentation; hydrophyllic films; phase studies; thermochemistry; molten salts; fuel cells; air pollution; air conditioning; combustion; refrigeration; ground source heat pumps. *Mailing Add:* 1224 Fairbrook Dr Mountain View CA 94040

JOYNER, RALPH DELMER, INORGANIC CHEMISTRY. *Current Pos:* RETIRED. *Personal Data:* b Derby, Va, Aug 31, 28; m 50; c 3. *Educ:* Miami Univ, BS, 50, MS, 51; Case Inst Technol, PhD(inorg chem), 61. *Prof Exp:* Chemist, Monsanto Co, Ohio, 51-52, res chemist, Mound Lab, 52-58, chemist, Solvay Process Div, Allied Chem Corp, NY, 61; sr res chemist, Chem Div, Pittsburgh Plate Glass Co, Ohio, 61-62, res assoc, 62, res supvr, 62-65; from asst prof to prof inorg chem, Ball State Univ, 65-88, dept chmn, 86-88. *Concurrent Pos:* Instr night sch, Univ Dayton, 52-54; res assoc & grad student adv, Case Inst Technol, 62-63. *Mem:* Am Chem Soc; Sigma Xi. *Res:* Silicon and germanium coordination compounds. *Mailing Add:* 4501 N Wheeling Ave Muncie IN 47304

JOYNER, RONALD WAYNE, CARDIAC ELECTROPHYSIOLOGY, NEUROPHYSIOLOGY. *Current Pos:* PROF PEDIAT & PHYSIOL, EMORY UNIV, 87- *Personal Data:* b Wake Forest, NC, Mar 21, 47; m 69; c 1. *Educ:* Univ NC, BS, 69; Duke Univ, MD, 74, PhD(physiol), 73. *Prof Exp:* Asst prof physiol, Duke Univ, 76-77; asst prof physiol, Univ Iowa, 77-87. *Mem:* Biophys Soc. *Res:* Mechanisms of propagation of cardiac action potentials related to cardiac arrythmias, by electrophysiological and numerical simulation techniques; synaptic transmission and motor control in squid. *Mailing Add:* Dept Pediat & Physiol Emory Univ 2040 Ridgewood Dr Atlanta GA 30322. *Fax:* 404-727-6024

JOYNER, WEYLAND THOMAS, JR, NUCLEAR PHYSICS, ELECTRONICS. *Current Pos:* PROF PHYSICS, HAMPDEN-SYDNEY COL, 67- CHMN DEPT, 69- *Personal Data:* b Suffolk, Va, Aug 8, 29; m 55; c 3. *Educ:* Hampden-Sydney Col, BS, 51; Duke Univ, MA, 52, PhD(physics), 55. *Prof Exp:* Asst physics, Duke Univ, 51-53, fel, 53-54; physicist, Dept of Defense, 54-57; asst prof, Hampden-Sydney, Col, 57-59, assoc prof, 59-63, prof, 63-66; staff physicist, Univ Mich, Ann Arbor, 66-67. *Concurrent Pos:* Consult, Oak Ridge Inst Nuclear Studies, 60-66; res partic, Ames Lab, AEC, 64, 65; vis prof, Pomona Col, 65 & Dartmouth Col, 81; dir col physics prog, Am Inst Physics, 67-68; chmn physics comt, Col Entrance Exam Bd, 71-72; NASA sr fel, 84 & 85. *Mem:* Am Phys Soc; Am Asn Physics Teachers; Inst Elec & Electronics Engrs; fel AAAS. *Res:* Positron lifetimes; picosecond circuitry; x-ray fluorescence; silicon deep impurity devices; radon. *Mailing Add:* Box 608 Hampden-Sydney VA 23943

JOYNER, WILLIAM B, GEOPHYSICS. *Current Pos:* GEOPHYSICIST, US GEOL SURV, 64- *Personal Data:* b Casper, Wyo, Dec 27, 29; m 52, Mary L MacElhose. *Educ:* Harvard Univ, AB, 51, AM, 52, PhD(geophys), 58. *Prof Exp:* Geophysicist, Humble Oil & Refining Co, 58-63; sr scientist, Vela Uniform Prog, Dunlap & Assocs, Inc, 64. *Mem:* Am Geophys Union; Soc Explor Geophys; Geol Soc Am; Seismol Soc Am; Earthquake Eng Res Inst. *Res:* Solid earth geophysics; gravity and terrestrial magnetism; terrestrial heat flow and temperatures within the earth; engineering seismology. *Mailing Add:* 472 Virginia Ave San Mateo CA 94402-2236. *Fax:* 650-329-5163; *E-Mail:* joyner@esg.wr.usgs.gov

JOYNER, WILLIAM HENRY, JR, COMPUTER SCIENCE. *Current Pos:* RES STAFF MEM COMPUT SCI, IBM THOMAS J WATSON RES CTR, 73- *Personal Data:* b Washington, DC, Sept 21, 46; m 68; c 2. *Educ:* Univ Va, BS, 68; Harvard Univ, SM, 69, PhD(appl math), 73. *Mem:* Asn Comput Mach. *Res:* Computer program verification; automated theorem proving; machine description languages; VLSI design. *Mailing Add:* IBM Res Box 218 Yorktown Heights NY 10598

JOYNER, WILLIAM LYMAN, PHYSIOLOGY. *Current Pos:* PROF PHYSIOL & CHMN DEPT, COL MED, E TENN STATE UNIV, 89- *Personal Data:* b Farmville, NC, June 10, 39; m 82, Chris Eccleston; c William J, Candace D, Andrew W & Evan C. *Educ:* Davidson Col, BS, 65; Univ NC, MSPH, 67, PhD(physiol), 71. *Prof Exp:* Res technician animal med, Univ NC, 65-67, res assoc physiol, 67-69; trainee, Med Ctr, Duke Univ, 71-73; from asst prof to assoc prof physiol, Col Med, Univ Nebr Med Ctr, 73-83, prof, 83-89,. *Concurrent Pos:* Pharm travel grantee, Microcirculatory Soc, 75; pres, Microcircular Soc Inc, 87. *Mem:* Am Physiol Soc; Microcurculatory Soc; AAAS; Soc Exp Biol & Med; Royal Soc Med; Europ Soc Microcirculation. *Res:* Cardiovascular physiology particularly the microcirculation, molecular transport, vascular reactivity and controlling mechanisms; hypertension, diabetes and alterations in blood coagulation and hemostasis related to hemodynamic responses of the microcirculation in various tissues. *Mailing Add:* Dept Physiol ETenn Univ Col Med PO Box 70576 Johnson City TN 37614. *Fax:* 423-439-7189

JOYNSON, REUBEN EDWIN, JR, PHYSICS. *Current Pos:* RETIRED. *Personal Data:* b Winfield, Kans, Dec 27, 26; m. *Educ:* Kans State Univ, BS, 49, MS, 50; Mass Inst Technol, PhD(physics), 54. *Prof Exp:* Res physicist, Continental Oil Co, 54-60; consult physicist, Comput Lab, Gen Elec Co, 60-63, physicist, Res & Develop Ctr, 63-87. *Mem:* AAAS; Am Phys Soc; Sigma Xi. *Res:* X-ray diffraction; digital computer design and programming; cryogenics; thin film devices; artificial intelligence; visual image processing. *Mailing Add:* 251 Alplaus Ave PO Box 118 Alplaus NY 12008

JOYNT, ROBERT JAMES, NEUROLOGY. *Current Pos:* RETIRED. *Personal Data:* b LeMars, Iowa, Dec 22, 25; m 53; c 6. *Educ:* Westmar Col, BA, 49; Univ Iowa, MD, 52, MS, PhD(anat), 63; Am Bd Psychiat & Neurol, dipl, 59. *Hon Degrees:* DSc, Westmar Col, 64. *Honors & Awards:* Netter Award, Am Acad Neurol, 88; George W Jacoby Award, Am Neurol Asn, 92. *Prof Exp:* Assoc neurol, Univ Iowa, 57-58, from asst prof to assoc prof, 58-66; prof neurol & anat & chmn dept neurol, Med Ctr, Univ Rochester, 66-84, dean, Sch Med & Dent, 85-90, vprovost, 85-89, vpres, health affairs, 89-94. *Concurrent Pos:* Mem res training grant comt, Nat Inst Neurol Dis & Blindness, 63-67 & neurol study sect, div res grants, NIH, 67-72; bd adv, off biometry & epidemiol, NINCDS, 76-84; ed, Arch Neurol, 82-; mem, Bd Regents, Nat Library Med, 92- *Mem:* Am Neurol Asn; Am Acad Neurol; Am Electroencephalog Soc; Am Med Asn; Inst Med; fel AAAS. *Res:* Investigation of fluid control by central nervous system; correlation of performance tests with lesions in brain damaged patients; Alzheimer's disease. *Mailing Add:* Sch Med & Dent Univ Rochester Rochester NY 14642

JOYS, TERENCE MICHAEL, RECOMBINANT DNA, VACCINES. *Current Pos:* ASSOC PROF IMMUNOL, TEX TECH HEALTH SCI CTR, 76- *Personal Data:* b Hull, Eng, Jan 19, 35; m 60; c 3. *Educ:* Leeds Univ, Eng, BSc, 57; London Univ, Eng, PhD(microbiol gen), 61. *Prof Exp:* Instr bact, Univ Minn, 64-65; asst prof bact genetics, Univ Ore Med Sch, 65-76; assoc prof med microbiol, Penn State Univ, 76. *Concurrent Pos:* Career develop award, US Pub Health Dept, 69-74; vis scientist, Max Planck Inst, Munich, Ger, 90. *Mem:* Am Soc Microbiol; Am Acad Microbiol; Southern Asn Agr Scientists. *Res:* Structure of bacterial flagellan filament protein and its use in vaccine development. *Mailing Add:* Dept Microbiol Tex Tech Univ Sch Med 3601 Fourth St Lubbock TX 79430-0002

JU, FREDERICK D, THEORETICAL & APPLIED MECHANICS. *Current Pos:* RETIRED. *Personal Data:* b Shanghai, China, Sept 21, 29; US citizen; m 56, Ruby Nee Chen; c Wilfred, Manfred & Winifred. *Educ:* Univ Houston, BS, 53; Univ Ill, MS, 56, PhD(theoret & appl mech), 58. *Honors & Awards:* Prof Soc Theoret & Appl Mech Award, 86; Chinese Soc Nat Sci Award, 86. *Prof Exp:* From asst prof to prof, Univ NMex, 58-94, chmn dept, 73-76 & 89-92 pres prof, 85-92, Halliburton prof mech eng, 92- *Concurrent Pos:* Consult, Los Alamos Nat Lab, 62-, vis staff mem, 72-; nat vis prof, Nat Sci Coun, Repub of China, 71-72; prin investr, Air Force Off Sci Res, 61-72 & 81-, Off Naval Res, 81- *Mem:* Fel Am Soc Mech Engrs; Soc Eng Sci; Sigma Xi. *Res:* Fracture diagnosis in structures; thermo-mechanical cracking from friction loading; structural safety of reactor; reliability of tribo-coatings. *Mailing Add:* Dept Mech Eng Univ NMex Albuquerque NM 87131-1361

JU, JIN SOON, PROTEIN NUTRITION, AGING & NUTRITION. *Current Pos:* DIR & PROF NUTRIT, KOREA NUTRIT INST, HALLYM UNIV, CHUN-CHON, KOREA, 87- *Personal Data:* b Ham-hung, Ham-nam Prov, Oct 20, 21; m 48; c 2. *Educ:* Seoul Nat Univ, MD, 47, PhD(nutrit), 59. *Honors & Awards:* Korea Nat Acad Sci Award, 85. *Prof Exp:* Researcher nutrit, Nat Chem Lab, Korea, 47-50; prof nutrit, Nat Fisheries Col, Pusan, Korea, 50-53; prof, 53-87, emer prof biochem & nutrit, Korea Univ Med Col, Seoul, Korea, 87- *Concurrent Pos:* Dir, Korea Geront Ctr, Hallym Univ, Seoul, 90- *Mem:* Am Inst Nutrit; Int Union Nutrit Sci; Pac Sci Asn; Korea Nat Acad Sci. *Res:* Protein metabolism in human and animals, especially protein requirement of Korean. *Mailing Add:* 691-8 Jayang-dong Hallym U Hanyang Villa No 203 Sueng-dong-ku Seoul 133-192 South Korea. *Fax:* 822 633 0018

JUANG, JER-NAN, TEST METHODS FOR SPACE STRUCTURES, LINEAR ALGEBRA. *Current Pos:* SR RES SCIENTIST, LANGLEY RES CTR, NASA, 82- *Personal Data:* b Tou-Liu, Taiwan, July 21, 45; US citizen; m 77, Lily; c Philo & Derek. *Educ:* Nat Cheng Kung Univ, Taiwan, BS, 69; Tenn Technol Univ, MS, 71; Va Polytech Inst, PhD(eng mech), 74. *Honors & Awards:* Merit Awards, Am Soc Mech Engrs; Spec Achievment, NASA; Dirk Brouwer Award, Am Astronaut Soc, 91; Mech & Control Award, Am Inst Aeronaut & Astronaut, 93. *Prof Exp:* Res assoc, Va Polytech Inst, 74-75; tech staff engr, Comput Sci Corp, 75-77; staff engr, Martin Marietta Corp, 77-79, sr staff engr, 81-82; tech staff res, Jet Propulsion Lab, 79-81. *Concurrent Pos:* Assoc ed, J Astronaut Sci, 86-89, J Guidance, Control & Dynamics, 88-91, J Vibration & Acoust, 91-; mem, Tech Comt Composite Mats, Am Astronaut soc, 82-, Tech Comt Composite Large Space Struct, 87-; adj prof, Univ Colo, Boulder, 88-91. *Mem:* Fel Am Astronaut Soc; fel Am Inst

Aeronaut & Astronaut; Soc Indust & Appl Math. *Res:* Active and passive control, tracking, modal parameter identification, system realization, and other dynamic problems for large space structures; nonlinear control problems and parameter estimation in distributed-parameter systems. *Mailing Add:* NASA Langley Res Ctr MS 230 Hampton VA 23681

JUANG, LING LING, NUMERICAL ANALYSIS. *Current Pos:* COMPUT PROCESS CONTROL SPECIALIST, GEN ELEC CO, 80- *Personal Data:* b Taipei, Taiwan, Oct 10, 49; m 73; c 1. *Educ:* Nat Taiwan Univ, BS, 72; State Univ NY Stony Brook, MS, 73, PhD(appl math), 76. *Prof Exp:* Syst analyst heat transfer prob, KLD Assoc, Inc, 75-76; asst mathematician energy models, Brookhaven Nat Lab, 76-80. *Mem:* Am Commun Mach; Soc Mfg Eng. *Res:* Economic-energy modeling of depletable resources; computer aided manufacturing system design. *Mailing Add:* 4293 Berryhill Lane Cincinnati OH 45242

JUBB, GERALD LOMBARD, JR, PEST MANAGEMENT. *Current Pos:* PROF ENTOM, AGR EXP STA, VA POLYTECH INST, 89-, ASSOC DIR, VA AGR EXP STA, 89- *Personal Data:* b Ayer, Mass, Jan 3, 43; m 67, Carole Frost; c Thomas & Carrie. *Educ:* NMex Highlands Univ, BA, 65; Univ Ariz, MS, 67, PhD(entom), 70. *Prof Exp:* NSF trainee entom, Univ Ariz, 67-70; from asst prof to prof entom, Erie Co Field Res Lab, Pa State Univ, 70-84; prof entom & ctr head, Western Md Res & Educ Ctr, Univ Md, 84-89. *Concurrent Pos:* Pres, Entom Soc Pa, 72, pres, secy & treas, Eastern Br, 78-81, 89 & gov bd, 85-88. *Mem:* Entom Soc Am; NY Entom Soc; Acarological Soc Am; Sigma Xi. *Res:* Insects and mites attacking grapes; economic injury levels; monitoring techniques; pesticide impact in vineyards; small fruit pest management. *Mailing Add:* Agr Exp Sta Va Polytech Inst Blacksburg VA 24061-0402. *Fax:* 540-231-4163; *E-Mail:* jubbg@vtm1.cc.vt.edu

JUBERG, RICHARD KENT, MATHEMATICS. *Current Pos:* from instr to prof, 58-91, EMER PROF MATH, UNIV CALIF, IRVINE, 91- *Personal Data:* b Cooperstown, NDak, May 14, 29; m 56, 89, Sandra Vakerics; c Alison, Kevin, Hilary & Ian. *Educ:* Univ Minn, BS, 52, PhD(math), 58. *Prof Exp:* Temp mem, Courant Inst Math Sci, NY Univ, 57-58. *Concurrent Pos:* NSF sci fac fel, Pisa, 65-66; vis prof, Univ Sussex, 72-73, Math Inst Technol, Gothenburg, Sweden, 81. *Mem:* Am Math Soc. *Res:* Problems in analysis and partial differential equations. *Mailing Add:* 9356 Mesa Verde Dr No D Montclair CA 91763-1918. *E-Mail:* rkjuberg@uci.edu

JUBERTS, MARIS, ELECTRO-MAGNETICS, ROBOTICS IN MILITARY & SPACE STATION APPLICATIONS. *Current Pos:* GROUP LEADER, INTELLIGENT SYSTS DIV, NAT INST STAND & TECHNOL, 90- *Personal Data:* b Feb 5, 41. *Educ:* George Washington Univ, MS, 69. *Prof Exp:* Group leader electromech, Goddard Space Flight Ctr, 88-90. *Mem:* Am Welding Soc. *Mailing Add:* Nat Inst Stand & Technol Bldg 220 Rm B214 Gaithersburg MD 20899. *E-Mail:* juberts@cme.nist.gov

JUBY, PETER FREDERICK, MEDICINAL CHEMISTRY. *Current Pos:* RETIRED. *Personal Data:* b Great Yarmouth, Eng, Oct 27, 35; US citizen; m 70; c 2. *Educ:* Univ Nottingham, BSc, 57, PhD(org chem), 61. *Prof Exp:* Nat Res Coun Can fel, 60-62; sr res scientist, Bristol Labs, Inc, 62-76, prin investr, 76-82, dir gastrointestinal chem, Bristol-Myers Co, 82-87, dir CNS Therapeut Area Opers, 87-94. *Mem:* Am Chem Soc. *Res:* Natural product chemistry; biosynthesis of alkaloids; synthesis of medicinal agents; arthritis; allergies; gastrointestinal diseases. *Mailing Add:* 130 Cedar Heights Dr Jamesville NY 13078

JUCHAU, MONT RAWLINGS, PHARMACOLOGY, TOXICOLOTY & TERATOLOGY. *Current Pos:* assoc prof, 73-80, PROF PHARMACOL, SCH MED, UNIV WASH, 80- *Personal Data:* b Virginia, Idaho, Nov 11, 34; m 60, Elizabeth Herrick; c Curtis M, Lauri, Christopher T, Michelle & Nanette. *Educ:* Idaho State Univ, BS, 60; Wash State Univ, MS, 63; Univ Iowa, PhD(pharmacol), 66. *Honors & Awards:* Delbert-Putnam Award, 59; Rexall Award, 60. *Prof Exp:* Pharmacist, Trolinger Pharm, Tick Klock Drug, 60-63; from instr to asst prof biochem pharmacol, State Univ NY, Buffalo, 66-69; asst prof, 69-73. *Mem:* AAAS; Am Soc Pharmacol & Exp Therapeut; Int Soc Biochem Pharmacol; Soc Toxicol; Teratology Soc. *Res:* Investigation of the biotransformation of drugs in the human foetoplacental unit. *Mailing Add:* Sch Med Univ Wash Box 357280 Seattle WA 98195. *E-Mail:* jachau@u.washington.edu

JUD, HENRY G, ELECTRICAL ENGINEERING. *Current Pos:* RETIRED. *Personal Data:* b Rochester, NY, Sept 19, 34; wid; c 4. *Educ:* Valparaiso Univ, BS, 56; Univ Pittsburgh, MS, 59, PhD(elec eng), 62. *Prof Exp:* Electronics technician, Western Elec Co, 56-57; specialist missile systs, Autonetics Div, NAm Aviation Inc, 62-64; from asst prof to assoc prof elec eng, Valparaiso Univ, 64-68; staff engr, IBM Fed Systs Div, NY, 68-70, advan engr, 70-71, develop engr, 71-76, develop engr, IBM Corp, Md, 76-85; sr staff systs eng, Unisys Corp, 85-89, dir systs technol, 89-94. *Mem:* Inst Elec & Electronics Engrs. *Res:* Missile system error analysis; automatic control; random input control systems; computer systems design. *Mailing Add:* 15327 Waterloo Rd Amissville VA 20106

JUDAY, GLENN PATRICK, FOREST ECOLOGY, CONSERVATION. *Current Pos:* vis assoc prof, Agr & Forestry Exp Sta, 81-87, ASST PROF FOREST ECOL, UNIV ALASKA, FAIRBANKS, 87- *Personal Data:* b Elwood, Ind, May 4, 50; m 71; c 4. *Educ:* Purdue Univ, BS, 72; Ore State Univ, Phd(plant ecol), 77. *Prof Exp:* Fel ecol & conserv, Ore State Univ, 76-77; coordr ecol reserves, Joint Fed-State Land Use Planning Comn, Alaska, 77-78, Arctic Environ Info & Data Ctr, Univ Alaska, 78 & Inst Northern Forestry, Forest Serv, USDA, 78-81. *Concurrent Pos:* Pres, Natural Areas Asn, 85-87, 87-88. *Mem:* AAAS; Ecol Soc Am; Soc Am Foresters; Natural Areas Asn. *Res:* Systematic plan for conserving ecological reserves using vegetation, wildlife, and geologic classifications; old-growth forest structure, including stocking, basal area, age height and spacing; post-glacial primary succession; fire effects research. *Mailing Add:* 4837 Palo Verde Ave Fairbanks AK 99709

JUDAY, RICHARD EVANS, ORGANIC CHEMISTRY. *Current Pos:* from asst prof to prof chem, 47-77, EMER PROF CHEM, UNIV MONT, 77- *Personal Data:* b Madison, Wis, May 28, 18. *Educ:* Harvard Univ, BA, 39; Univ Wis, PhD(org chem), 43. *Prof Exp:* Asst res chemist, Gen Chem Co, NY, 43-44 & Ortho Pharmaceut Corp, 44-47. *Mem:* Fel AAAS; Am Chem Soc; Am Soc Limnol & Oceanog. *Res:* Water quality; chemical limnology. *Mailing Add:* Dept Chem Univ Mont Missoula MT 59812-1006

JUDD, BRIAN RAYMOND, THEORETICAL PHYSICS, ATOMIC PHYSICS. *Current Pos:* chmn, Physics Dept, 79-84, prof, 66-96, EMER PROF PHYSICS, JOHNS HOPKINS UNIV, 97- *Personal Data:* b Chelmsford, Eng, Feb 13, 31. *Educ:* Oxford Univ, BA, 52, MA & DPhil, 55. *Honors & Awards:* Frank H Spedding Award, Rare Earth Res, 88. *Prof Exp:* Fel, Magdalen Col, Oxford Univ, 55-62; instr physics, Univ Chicago, 57-58; chemist, Lawrence Radiation Lab, Univ Calif, Berkeley, 59-62; assoc prof spectros, Univ Paris, 62-64; staff mem nuclear chem, Lawrence Radiation Lab, Univ Calif, Berkeley, 64-66. *Concurrent Pos:* Consult, Argonne Nat Lab, 77-88; hon fel, Brasenose Col, Oxford, 83- *Mem:* Fel Am Phys Soc. *Res:* Theoretical studies of atoms, molecules and solid state physics, particularly application of group theory. *Mailing Add:* Dept Physics & Astron Johns Hopkins Univ Baltimore MD 21218-2686. *Fax:* 410-516-7239

JUDD, BURKE HAYCOCK, GENETICS. *Current Pos:* RETIRED. *Personal Data:* b Kanab, Utah, Sept 5, 27; m 53, Barbara A Gaddy; c Sean M, Evan P & Timothy B. *Educ:* Univ Utah, BS, 50, MS, 51; Calif Inst Technol, PhD(genetics), 54. *Prof Exp:* Am Can Soc Fel, Univ Tex, Austin, 54-56, from instr to assoc prof zool, 56-69, prof, 69-79; chief, Lab Genetics, Nat Inst Environ Health Sci, Res Triangle Park, NC, 79-95. *Concurrent Pos:* Geneticist, AEC, Washington, DC, 68-69; mem panel genetic biol, NSF, 69-72; assoc ed, Genetics, 73-78; Gosney vis prof, Div Biol, Calif Inst Technol, 75-76; dir, Genetics Inst, Univ Tex, Austin, 77-79; adj prof biol, Univ NC, Chapel Hill, 79- & Prog Genetics, Duke Univ, Durham, NC, 80-; corresp ed, Molecular & Gen Genetics, 86-95. *Mem:* Fel AAAS; Genetics Soc Am (vpres, 79 & pres, 80); Am Soc Nat (secy, 68-70). *Res:* Chromosome organization; gene function and regulation; recombination mechanism; genetics of Drosophila. *Mailing Add:* 411 Clayton Rd Chapel Hill NC 27514. *Fax:* 919-942-7463; *E-Mail:* bjudd@aol.com

JUDD, DAVID LOCKHART, THEORETICAL PHYSICS. *Current Pos:* group leader, 51-66, lectr, Dept Physics, 53-61, from dept head to head, Physics Div, 63-70, assoc dir, 67-70, SR LECTR, DEPT PHYSICS, UNIV CALIF, BERKELEY, 62-, SR RES PHYSICIST, LAWRENCE BERKELEY LAB, 70- *Personal Data:* b Chehalis, Wash, Jan 8, 23; m 45; c 2. *Educ:* Whitman Col, AB, 43; Calif Inst Technol, MS, 47, PhD(physics), 50. *Hon Degrees:* DSc, Whitman Col, 74. *Prof Exp:* Staff mem, Physics Div, Los Alamos Sci Lab, 45-46; staff mem theoret physics, Nuclear Energy Div, Rand Corp, 49-51. *Concurrent Pos:* Consult, Northrop Aircraft Co, 47-49, Radiation Lab, Univ Calif, 50-51, Rand Corp, 51-55 & W M Brobeck & Assocs, 60; mem adv comt, Electronuclear & Physics Div, Oak Ridge Nat Lab, 63-65. *Mem:* Fel Am Phys Soc; Sigma Xi. *Res:* Theoretical and mathematical physics; accelerator theory; ion optics; plasma and particle physics; nonlinear mechanics. *Mailing Add:* Lawrence Berkeley Lab Univ Calif Berkeley CA 94720

JUDD, FLOYD L, HIGH ENERGY PHYSICS, OPTICS. *Current Pos:* RETIRED. *Personal Data:* b Janesville, Wis, Jan 25, 34; m 62; c 3. *Educ:* Carroll Col, BS, 56; Iowa State Univ, MS, 60, PhD, 66. *Prof Exp:* Asst prof, Northwestern State Col, La, 59-62, 64-67; asst prof, Fresno State Col, 67-70, assoc prof physics, 70-71; prof physics & chmn, Calif State Univ, Fresno, 71-77. *Mailing Add:* Dept Physics Calif State Univ 2345 E San Ramon Fresno CA 93740

JUDD, FRANK WAYNE, POPULATION ECOLOGY, PHYSIOLOGICAL ECOLOGY. *Current Pos:* prof biol & dir, Coastal Studies Lab, 84-96, CHAIR, DEPT BIOL, UNIV TEX, PAN AM, 96- *Personal Data:* b Wichita Falls, Tex, Aug 23, 39; m 69; c 2. *Educ:* Midwestern State Univ, BS, 65; Tex Tech Univ, MS, 68, PhD(zool), 73. *Prof Exp:* Teaching asst biol, Dept Biol, Tex Tech Univ, 65-68, res asst & instr, 69-71; instr, Biol Dept, Pan Am Univ, 68-69, from asst prof to prof, 72-82, dir, Coastal Studies Lab, 84-91. *Concurrent Pos:* Adj prof, Dept Biol Sci, Tex Tech Univ, 83-; vis prof, Dept Wildlife & Fisheries Sci, Tex A&M Univ, 89- *Mem:* Am Soc Ichthyologists & Herpetologists; Am Soc Mammalogists; Ecol Soc Am; Herpetologists' League. *Res:* Ecology of the coastal zone of southern Texas and northern Mexico; barrier island ecology; black mangrove distribution; oyster reef distribution; tortoise demography. *Mailing Add:* Dept Biol Univ Tex-Pan Am 1201 W University Dr Edinburg TX 78539-2999

JUDD, GARY, PHYSICAL METALLURGY, ELECTRON MICROSCOPY. *Current Pos:* Res asst, Rensselaer Polytech Inst, 66-67, from asst prof to prof, 67-, actg chmn, Dept Mat Eng, 74-75, vprovost, Plans & Resources, 75-78, actg provost & vpres, Acad Affairs, 82-83, 85-86, vprovost, Acad Affairs, 79-93, DEAN, GRAD SCH, RENSSELAER POLYTECH INST, 79-,

DEAN FAC, 93- Personal Data: b Humene, Czech, Sept 24, 42; US citizen; m 64, Rosalind S Dixter; c Robin, Jennifer & Jason. Educ: Rensselaer Polytech Inst, BMetE, 63, PhD(phys metall), 67. Concurrent Pos: Consult, Oak Ridge Nat Lab, 68-70 & Watervliet Arsenal, 69-78; metall eng consult ed, McGraw-Hill Sci & Technol Encycl, 75- Mem: Fel Am Soc Metals Int; Minerals Metals & Mat Soc; Sigma Xi; Microbeam Anal Soc; AAAS. Res: Structure sensitive properties of materials, particularly strengthening mechanisms, precipitation kinetics, defect structures, biomaterials and corrosion; electron probe microanalysis; scanning electron microscopy; forensic science. Mailing Add: Pittsburgh Bldg Rensselaer Polytech Inst Troy NY 12181. Fax: 518-276-4061; E-Mail: gary_judd@rpi.edu

JUDD, JOSEPH T, HUMAN NUTRITIONAL RESEARCH, LIPIDS. Current Pos: RES LEADER, DIET & HUMAN PERFORMANCE LAB, HUMAN NUTRIT RES CTR, USDA, BELTSVILLE, 77- Personal Data: b Nashville, Tenn, Apr 22, 35. Educ: NC State Univ, PhD(nutrit), 63. Res: Human nutrition; lipids. Mailing Add: Lipid Nutrit Lab Bldg 308-E Rm 126A USDA Human Nutrit Res Ctr Beltsville MD 20705. Fax: 301-504-9192

JUDD, LEWIS LUND, PSYCHIATRY, CHILD PSYCHIATRY. Current Pos: assoc prof, Univ Calif, 70-73, actg chmn dept, 74-75, co-chmn dept, 75-77, PROF PSYCHIAT, UNIV CALIF, SAN DIEGO, 73-, MARY GILMAN MARSTON PROF PSYCHIAT, 92- Personal Data: b Los Angeles, Calif, Feb 10, 30; m 74; c 3. Educ: Univ Utah, BS, 54; George Washington Univ, 54-56; Univ Calif, Los Angeles, MD, 58. Hon Degrees: DSc, Med Col Ohio, Toledo. Honors & Awards: William C Menninger Award, Am Col Physicians, 95. Prof Exp: Intern internal med, Ctr Health Sci, Univ Calif, Los Angeles, 58-59, resident psychiat, 59-60, 62-64, asst prof psychol & psychiat, 65-70, assoc prof, 70. Concurrent Pos: Fel child psychiat, Ctr Health Sci, Univ Calif, Los Angeles, 64-65, State Calif fel, 66, NIMH fels, 67-69, Scottish Rites Comt on Res in Schizophrenics, 69; supvr psychiat, Adolescent Outpatient Unit, Marion Davies Pediat Clin, Ctr Health Sci, Univ Calif, Los Angeles, 65-70, supvr psychiat consult serv, Dept Pediat, 65-70, asst attend physician, Hosp, 65-70, psychiat consult, Dept Phys Med & Rehab, 67-70, dir educ, child & adolescent psychiat, Dept Psychiat, 68-70; psychiat consult, Calif State Bd Rehab, Sacramento, 65-70; mem, Adv Comt Eval Drug Abuse Progs, Co San Diego, 70; dir, Univ Calif Drug Abuse Progs, 70-73; vchmn & dir clin progs, Dept Psychiat, 75, chmn, Dept Radiol, 78, Univ Calif, San Diego, 70-73, chmn, Social & Behav Sci Course, Sch Med, 70-; psychiat consult, San Diego Co Dept Pub Health, 72-; chief psychiat serv, Vet Admin Med Ctr, San Diego, 72-78; pres med staff, Med Ctr, Univ Calif, San Diego, 82-84; dir, NIMH, Dept Health & Human Serv, 88-90; counr, Am Asn Chmn Depts Psychiat, 92-94; Int Acad Biomed & Drugs Res, 93- Mem: Inst Med-Nat Acad Sci; Am Orthopsychiat Asn; Soc Res Child Develop; Am Soc Adolescent Psychiat; Psychiat Res Soc; fel Am Psychiat Asn (vpres, 92-94); fel Am Col Neuropsychopharmacol; fel Am Col Psychiatrists; Am Acad Child Psychiat; Asn Acad Psychiat; Soc Neurosci. Res: Substance abuse in adolescents; developmental psychopathology; epidemiology of deviant populations; clinical psychopharmacology; author of numerous publications. Mailing Add: Dept Psychiat Univ Calif San Diego 9500 Gilman Dr La Jolla CA 92093-0603. Fax: 619-534-7653; E-Mail: ljudd@acsd.edu

JUDD, O'DEAN P, LASERS & OPTICS, ATOMIC & MOLECULAR PHYSICS. Current Pos: PRIVATE TECH ADV & CONSULT, 94- Personal Data: b Austin, Minn, May 26, 37. Educ: St Johns Univ, BS, 59; Univ Calif, Los Angeles, MS, 61, PhD(physics), 68. Prof Exp: Staff physicist, Hughes Res Lab, 59-67 & 69-72; fel plasma physics, Univ Calif, Los Angeles, 68-69; assoc group leader, Theoret Div, Los Alamos Nat Lab, Univ Calif, 72-75, group leader advan laser res, 75-77, mem staff, Appl Photochem Div, 77-82, chief scientist, Defense Res, 82-87; chief scientist, strategic defense initiative, Pentagon, Washington, DC, 87-90; chief scientist energy & environ, Los Alamos Nat Lab, 90-93; Nat Intel Officer Sci & Technol, Nat Intel Covn, Wash DC, 93-94. Concurrent Pos: Hughes masters fel, 59, Hughes fel, 64; consult, 72-744; consult, 80-; adj prof physics, Univ NMex, 81-; fel, Los Alamos Nat Lab, 90- Mem: Am Phys Soc; fel Inst Elec & Electronics Engrs; fel AAAS; fel Inst Advan Eng. Res: Non-linear optics; laser physics, atomic and molecular physics; plasma physics; quantum electronics and laser chemistry, theoretical and experimental; 3 US patents and numerous publications; national defense policy and intelligence. Mailing Add: 101 Zuni Los Alamos NM 87544

JUDD, ROBERT LEE, BIOCHEMICAL PHARMACOLOGY. Current Pos: ASST PROF PHARMACOL, NORTHEAST LA UNIV SCH PHARM, 93- Personal Data: b Kingsport, Tenn, Aug 23, 64. Educ: Hendrix Col, BA, 86; Northeast La Univ, PhD(pharmacol & toxicol), 90. Prof Exp: Researcher, Endocrine Res Unit, Mayo Clin, 90-93. Mem: AAAS; Am Soc Pharmacol & Exp Therapeut; Am Diabetic Asn. Res: Diabetes research; fatty acid transport. Mailing Add: Northeast La Sch Pharm 700 University Ave Monroe LA 71203

JUDD, ROSS LEONARD, HEAT TRANSFER, FLOW INDUCED VIBRATIONS. Current Pos: lectr, 63-67, from asst prof assoc prof, 67-74, assoc prof, 67-80, PROF MECH ENG, McMASTER UNIV, 80- Personal Data: b London, Ont, June 3, 36; m 62 Joyce E Swerdfeger; c Mary Ellen & David. Educ: Univ Western Ont, BESc, 58; McMaster Univ, MEng, 63; Univ Mich, PhD(heat transfer), 68. Honors & Awards: R R Teetor Award, Soc Automotive Engrs; L Stuart Laughland Medal, Univ Western Ont. Prof Exp: Develop engr, Civilian Atomic Power Dept, Can Gen Elec, 58-61. Mem: Am Soc Mech Engrs; Soc Automotive Engrs. Res: Boiling heat transfer; two phase flow; flow induced vibrations; heat pipes. Mailing Add: Dept Mech Eng McMaster Univ Hamilton ON L8S 4L8 Can. Fax: 905-572-7544

JUDD, STANLEY H, ENVIRONMENTAL HEALTH, COMPUTERIZED HEALTH & SAFETY INFORMATION MANAGEMENT SYSTEMS. Current Pos: INDUST HYG CONSULT, 90-; RESOURCE CONSULT, HFP ACOUST CONSULTS, 91- Personal Data: b Denver, Colo, Feb 12, 28; m 50, 77, Dorothy Newington; c Richard A & Nancy E. Educ: Univ Calif, Los Angeles, BS, 49; Univ Calif, Berkeley, MPH, 56; Am Bd Indust Hyg, cert, 66. Prof Exp: Chemist, State Calif Dept Pub Health, 49-50, 53-56 & US Army Environ Health Lab, 50-52; res chemist, Chevron Res Corp, Calif, 56-58, indust hygienist, 58-65, sr indust hygienist, 65-69, environ health & pollution engr, 69-78, staff indust hygienist, 78-80, mgr, Health Surveillance Serv, 80-88, sr consult toxicol & health info res, Chevron Environ Health Ctr, Richmond, Calif, 89-90. Concurrent Pos: Mem fac, Inst Noise Control Eng & Inst Safety & Syst Mgt, Univ Southern Calif Extension; mem fac, Ctr Occup & Environ Health, Univ Calif, Berkeley; lectr & nat secy, Am Indust Hyg Asn, 90-93. Mem: Am Indust Hyg Asn; Am Acad Indust Hyg; Am Chem Soc. Res: Engineering noise control at the source to prevent hearing loss, interference with communications and annoyance; safe handling of pesticide and petrochemical products including facilities designs; occupational health information systems design; biomedical surveillance. Mailing Add: 220 Lombard St No 823 San Francisco CA 94111-1113. E-Mail: 71520.3435@compuserve.com

JUDD, WALTER STEPHEN, PLANT SYSTEMATICS. Current Pos: ASSOC PROF BOT, DEPT BOT, UNIV FLA, 78- Personal Data: b Fairbanks, Alaska, Apr 14, 51; m 72. Educ: Mich State Univ, BS, 73, MS, 74; Harvard Univ, PhD(biol), 79. Mem: Am Soc Plant Taxonomists; Int Asn Plant Taxon; Am Bryological & Lichenological Soc; Bot Soc Am. Res: Systematics and evolution of flowering plants with specific interest in the Ericaceae and Melastomataceae; floras of the West Indies and Florida. Mailing Add: Dept Bot Univ Fla 220 Bartram Hall Gainesville FL 32611-2009

JUDD, WILLIAM ROBERT, ROCK MECHANICS, GEOTECHNICAL ENGINEERING. Current Pos: prof rock mech, Sch Civil Eng, 66-87, head geotech eng, 76-87, EMER PROF CIVIL ENG, PURDUE UNIV, 88-; CONSULT ENG GEOLOGIST, 50- Personal Data: b Denver, Colo, Aug 16, 17; m 42, Rachel Douglas; c Judith (Soden), Jeanne (Wadley), Dayna (Grandmason), Pamels & Connie. Educ: Univ Colo, AB, 41. Honors & Awards: Spec Award Outstanding Contrib Rock Mech Res, US Nat Comt Rock Mech, 82; Alex du Toit Mem Lectr, SAfrica & Rhodesia, 67; Distinguished Pract Award, Geol Soc Am, 89; Hans Cloos Medal, Int Asn Eng Geologists, 94. Prof Exp: Eng geologist, US Bur Reclamation, head geol sect I, Off Chief Engr, 44-60; head basing technol group, Rand Corp, Calif, 60-65. Concurrent Pos: Eng geologist, Water Conserv Bd, Colo, 41-42 & Denver & Rio Grande West Rwy, 42-44; instr, Lowry AFB, 46-51; consult geologist & engr, 50-; mem adv bd, mountain & arctic warfare, US Army, 56-62; consult to various US & foreign govt agencies & comts & pvt industs, 58-; founder & chmn, US Nat Comt Rock Mech, 63-69, chmn panel awards, 74-78, sr adv panel res, 77-81; mem panel geophys, USAF Sci Adv Bd, 64-68; geo-sci ed, Am Elsevier Publ Co Inc, 66-71; reviewer, Appl Mech Reviews, 68-73; chmn, Panel Ocean Sci Comt Int Coop, 71-85; ed-in-chief, Int J Eng Geol, 72-92, honorary ed, 96-; tech dir, Underground Explor & Rock Properties Info Ctr, 72-80; mem, Exec Coun, US Comt Large Dams, 77-83, comt Earthquakes, 76-90, Nat Res Coun Comt Dam Safety, 77-78 & Comt Safety Existing Dams, 82-83; mem Adv Bd Applied Phys Math and Biol Sci, NSF, 79-81. Mem: Fel SAfrican Inst Mining & Metall; fel Am Soc Civil Engrs; fel Geol Soc Am; Int Soc Eng Geologists; Am Arbit Asn; hon mem India Soc Eng Geol; hon mem Asn Eng Geologists; Sigma Xi. Res: Seismic effects on underground openings, dam safety; rock tunnels. Mailing Add: 10 Elder Ct Lafayette IN 47905

JUDD, WILLIAM WALLACE, ENTOMOLOGY. Current Pos: asst prof, Univ Western Ont, 50-51, assoc prof, 52-64, prof, 65-81, EMER PROF ZOOL, UNIV WESTERN ONT, 81- Personal Data: b Windsor, NS, Oct 22, 15; m 46; c 4. Educ: McMaster Univ, BA, 38; Univ Western Ont, MA, 40; Univ Toronto, PhD(zool), 46. Prof Exp: Agr asst, Can Dept Agr, 37-42; asst meteorol, Dept Transport, Ottawa, 42-45; lectr zool, McMaster Univ, 46-48, asst prof, 48-50. Res: Aquatic insects; insect morphology. Mailing Add: Dept Zool Univ Western Ont London ON N6A 5B7 Can

JUDGE, DARRELL L, PHYSICS. Current Pos: lectr math, Univ Southern Calif, 61-63, vis asst prof, 65-66, from asst prof to assoc prof, 66-75, PROF PHYSICS, UNIV SOUTHERN CALIF, 75- Personal Data: b Albion, Ill, Nov 2, 34; m 59; c 3. Educ: Eastern Ill State Col, BS, 56; Univ Southern Calif, MS, 63, PhD(physics), 65. Honors & Awards: NASA Except Scientific Achievement Medal & NASA Pub Serv Group Achievement Award to Pioneer 10 Scientific Instrument Team, 74. Prof Exp: Mem tech staff, Thompson-Ramo-Wooldridge Corp, 58-59. Concurrent Pos: Consult, Space Physics Dept, Thompson-Ramo-Wooldridge Corp, 60-71, Douglas Aircraft Co, 61 & Planetary Atmospheres Adv Subcomt, Space Sci & Applns Steering Comt, NASA, 69-70. Mem: Am Geophys Union; Am Phys Soc. Res: Space physics and spectroscopy. Mailing Add: Dept Physics Space Sci Ctr SHS 270 Univ Southern Calif Univ Park Los Angeles CA 90089

JUDGE, JOSEPH MALACHI, POLYMER CHEMISTRY, INFORMATION RETRIEVAL. Current Pos: TECHNOL TRANSFER AGENT, NAT TECHNOL TRANSFER CTR, 93- Personal Data: b Carbondale, Pa, June 10, 30; m 57; c 5. Educ: Kings Col, Pa, BS, 52; Univ Notre Dame, PhD(chem), 58. Prof Exp: Res chemist, Polychems Dept, E I du Pont de Nemours & Co, 55-58; res chemist, Armstrong World Indust, 58-80, mgr, Tech Info Ser, 80-86 & Techol Transfer, 86-89; technol info consult, Lanxide Corp, 89-91; mgr database construct, Comput Appl Serv, Inc, 92. Mem: AAAS; Am Soc Info Sci; Am Chem Soc. Res: Vinyl polymerization; polymeric blends; polyvinyl chloride modifications; structure to dynamic properties relationships; elastomer synthesis; high energy radiation; information retrieval. *Mailing Add:* 436 Manor View Dr Millersville PA 17551

JUDGE, LEO FRANCIS, JR, MICROBIOLOGY. *Current Pos:* RETIRED. *Personal Data:* b Washington, DC, Jan 6, 27; m 49; c 4. *Educ:* Univ Md, BS, 53, MS, 55, PhD(bact), 58. *Prof Exp:* Asst bact, Univ Md, 53-57; mgr microbiol serv, Procter & Gamble Co, 57-88. *Mem:* Am Soc Microbiol; Soc Indust Microbiol; Am Soc Testing & Mat; Cosmetic Toiletry & Fragrance Asn. *Res:* Bacterial metabolism and physiology; microbial associations; medical microbiology; antiseptics and disinfectants. *Mailing Add:* 8982 Mockingbird Lane Cincinnati OH 45231

JUDGE, MAX DAVID, ANIMAL SCIENCE, FOOD SCIENCE. *Current Pos:* RETIRED. *Personal Data:* b Shirley, Ind, Oct 14, 32; m 53; c 3. *Educ:* Purdue Univ, BS, 54, PhD(animal physiol), 62; Ohio State Univ, MSc, 58. *Prof Exp:* From inst to prof animal sci, Purdue Univ, 58-97. *Concurrent Pos:* Res fel, Univ Wis, 64-65. *Mem:* Am Meat Sci Asn; Am Soc Animal Sci; Inst Food Technol. *Res:* Physiological and endocrine control of muscle properties and subsequent utilization of muscle as a food. *Mailing Add:* 7 Cougar Run Hilton Head Island SC 29926

JUDGE, ROGER JOHN RICHARD, AERONAUTICAL ENGINEERING, ASTRONAUTICAL ENGINEERING. *Current Pos:* STAFF SCIENTIST, IRT CORP, 79- *Personal Data:* b London, Eng, Nov 22, 38; US citizen; m 74; c 2. *Educ:* Univ Nottingham, BSc, 60, PhD(physics), 64. *Prof Exp:* Staff scientist, Bell Can Labs, 63-67; fel, Nat Res Coun Can, 67-69; res physicist, Univ Calif, San Diego, 69-75; prin engr, Orincon Corp, 78-79. *Concurrent Pos:* Vis prof, Univ Ottawa, 67-69 & Univ Calif, San Diego, 75- *Mem:* Am Geophys Union. *Res:* Upper atmosphere and space physics; spacecraft technology; nuclear survivability. *Mailing Add:* 1301 Virginia Way La Jolla CA 92037

JUDIS, JOSEPH, biochemical pharmacology, for more information see previous edition

JUDISH, JOHN PAUL, CHEMICAL PHYSICS. *Current Pos:* Engr Van de Graaff Accelerator, 51-74, RES STAFF MEM PHYSICS, OAK RIDGE NAT LAB, 75- *Personal Data:* b Canonsburg, Pa, May 23, 26; m 58; c 3. *Educ:* Univ Pittsburgh, BS, 50; Univ Tenn, PhD(physics), 74. *Mem:* Am Phys Soc; Inst Elec & Electronics Engrs. *Res:* Atomic and molecular physics; visible and vuv spectroscopy; interaction of optical radiation with gases; lasers; excitation and ionization of gases by high energy ions; superconducting resistance at high frequencies. *Mailing Add:* 107 Wendover Circle Oak Ridge TN 37830

JUDISH, ROBERT M, ELECTRICAL ENGINEERING. *Current Pos:* Tech staff, Microwave Metrol Group, 80-93, GROUP LEADER, NAT INST STAND & TECHNOL, 93- *Personal Data:* b Dec 8, 52. *Educ:* Colo State Univ, MA, 78. *Mem:* Am Soc Qual Control; Inst Elec Engrs. *Mailing Add:* Nat Inst Stand & Technol 325 Broadway Boulder CO 30303. *E-Mail:* judish@boulder.nist.gov

JUDKINS, JOSEPH FAULCON, JR, SANITARY ENGINEERING. *Current Pos:* DIR WATER RESOURCES RES INST, AUBURN UNIV, 89- *Personal Data:* b Richmond, Va, May 12, 38; m 61; c 3. *Educ:* Va Polytech Inst, BS, 61, MS, 65, PhD(civil eng), 67. *Prof Exp:* Asst prof civil eng, Auburn Univ, 67-71, Gottlieb assoc prof, 71-77, Gottlieb prof civil eng, 77-81; pvt eng pract, 81-89. *Mem:* Am Soc Civil Engrs; Water Pollution Control Fedn; Am Water Works Asn. *Res:* Industrial and domestic waste treatment; water supply engineering. *Mailing Add:* 211 Cary Dr Auburn AL 36830

JUDKINS, RODDIE REAGAN, COAL CONVERSION SYSTEMS. *Current Pos:* mgr, Fossil Energy Mat Prog Mgr, 86-88, MGR, FOSSIL ENERGY PROG, OAK RIDGE NAT LAB, 88- *Personal Data:* b Sunbright, Tenn, Dec 31, 41; div; c 3. *Educ:* Tenn Polytech Inst, BS, 63, MS, 65; Ga Inst Technol, PhD(phys chem), 70. *Prof Exp:* Eng assoc, Union Carbide Corp, 64, 65 & 66; instr chem, Ga Inst Technol, 65-70; plant mgr, Nuclear Chem & Metals Corp, 70-73; tech assoc, E R Johnson Assocs, Inc, 73-77; develop engr, Union Carbide Corp, 77-81; task leader, 81-84; task leader, Martin Marietta Energy Systs, 84-86. *Mem:* Am Soc Metals Int; Sigma Xi; Am Soc Mech Engrs. *Res:* Materials of construction for coal conversion and utilization systems; thorium metal process development and improvement; corrosion mechanisms in coal liquefaction processes; nuclear fuel fabrication technology and economics. *Mailing Add:* 9917 Rainbow Dr Knoxville TN 37922-5108

JUDSON, CHARLES LEROY, INSECT PHYSIOLOGY. *Current Pos:* asst prof, 62-70, assoc prof entom, 70-77, ASSOC, EXP STA, UNIV CALIF, DAVIS, 55-, PROF ENTOM, 77-; VECTOR CONTROL SPECIALIST, CALIF DEPT PUB HEALTH, 55- *Personal Data:* b Lodi, Calif, Oct 21, 26; m 50; c 3. *Educ:* Univ Calif, BA, 51, PhD(entom), 56. *Mem:* Entom Soc Am. *Res:* Insect biochemistry; physiology of hatching; mosquito eggs. *Mailing Add:* 742 Plum Pl Davis CA 95616

JUDSON, CHARLES MORRILL, ANALYTICAL CHEMISTRY. *Current Pos:* RETIRED. *Personal Data:* b Washington, DC, July 2, 19; m 44; c Molly & Ellen. *Educ:* Swarthmore Col, BA, 40; Univ Pa, MS, 42, PhD(phys chem), 47. *Prof Exp:* Asst instr chem, Univ Pa, 40-42; res chemist, Columbia Univ, 42-44; res chemist, Stand Oil Co, Ind, 44-45; res chemist, Am Cyanamid Co, 47-54, group leader, 54-57, mgr chem physics sect, 57-62; chief anal develop sect, Anal & Control Div, Consol Electrodyn Corp, 62-63, dir eng, 63-70; res scientist, Granville Phillips Co, 70-71; consult mass spectrometry, 71-73; scientist, Analog Technol Corp, 73-76, chief scientist, 76-79; mgr, Microtrace Anal Serv, 75-77; res assoc, Univ Southern Calif, 79-80; dir, Mass Spectrometry Lab, Univ Kans, 80-89. *Mem:* Am Chem Soc; Am Phys Soc; Am Soc Mass Spectrometry; Soc Appl Spectros. *Res:* Mass spectrometry; instruments; radio-tracers; electrolytes; surface agents. *Mailing Add:* 608 Seabrook Pl Lawrence KS 66046

JUDSON, HORACE AUGUSTUS, organic chemistry, for more information see previous edition

JUDSON, SHELDON, ARCHAEOLOGICAL GEOLOGY. *Current Pos:* assoc prof, Princeton Univ, 55-64, Knox Taylor prof, 64-87, chmn, Dept Geol & Geophys Sci, 70-82, chmn, Univ Res Bd, 72-77, EMER PROF GEOL, PRINCETON UNIV, 87- *Personal Data:* b Utica, NY, Oct 18, 18; m 43, 90, Pamela Rhodes; c Stephanie, Lucy & Anne. *Educ:* Princeton Univ, AB, 40; Harvard Univ, AM, 46, PhD(geol), 48. *Prof Exp:* From instr to assoc prof geol, Univ Wis, 48-55. *Concurrent Pos:* Fund Advan Educ fel, 54-55; Guggenheim & Fulbright fels, Italy, 60-61; Guggenheim fel, 66-67. *Mem:* Geol Soc Am; Sigma Xi. *Res:* Glacial geology; geomorphology; use of geologic studies in archaelogy. *Mailing Add:* Dept Geosci Princeton Univ Princeton NJ 08544

JUDSON, WALTER EMERY, MEDICINE. *Current Pos:* assoc prof, 56-65, PROF MED, SCH MED, UNIV IND, INDIANAPOLIS, 65- *Personal Data:* b Roxbury, Mass, June 5, 16; m 43; c 3. *Educ:* Tufts Univ, BS, 38; Johns Hopkins Univ, MD, 42; Am Bd Internal Med, dipl, 50; Am Bd Cardiovasc Dis, cert, 50. *Prof Exp:* Asst med, Sch Med, Boston Univ, 48-49, from instr to asst prof, 50-55. *Mem:* Fel Am Col Physicians; AMA; Am Heart Asn; Am Fedn Clin Res; Sigma Xi. *Res:* Cardiovascular research. *Mailing Add:* Indiana Univ Hosp 550 N Univ Blvd Rm 5640 Indianapolis IN 46202-5203

JUDZIEWICZ, EMMET JOSEPH, TAXONOMY & CONSERVATION OF VASCULAR PLANTS. *Current Pos:* SR CONSERV BIOLOGIST, WIS DEPT NATURAL RESOURCES, 95- *Personal Data:* b Milwaukee, Wis, Dec 8, 53. *Educ:* Univ Wis-Parkside, BA, 79; Univ Wis-Madison, MS, 85, PhD(bot), 87. *Prof Exp:* Postdoctoral fel, Dept Bot, Smithsonian Inst, 87-91; asst scientist, Dept Bot, Univ Wis-Madison, 91-95. *Concurrent Pos:* Res assoc Dept Bot, Milwaukee Pub Mus, 97- *Mem:* Am Soc Plant Taxonomists; Int Union Conserv Nature. *Res:* Taxonomy, ecology and conservation of New World bamboos; inventory and conservation of vascular plants of the western Great Lakes region. *Mailing Add:* PO Box 144 Mountain WI 54149

JUENGE, ERIC CARL, PHARMACEUTICAL & ORGANOMETALLIC CHEMISTRY. *Current Pos:* RETIRED. *Personal Data:* b Weehawken, NJ, Jan 12, 27; m 54, 71; c 3. *Educ:* NY Univ, BA, 51, PhD(chem), 57. *Prof Exp:* Jr chemist pharmaceut, Hoffmann-La Roche, Inc, 51-52; asst, NY Univ, 55-56; res chemist organometallic field, Ethyl Corp, La, 56-59; sr chemist agr chem, Spencer Chem Co, 59-61; from assoc prof to prof chem, Kans State Col, Pittsburg, 61-74; res assoc, Coop State Res Serv, Ft Valley State Col, 74-75; asst res prof chem, 75-78; chemist, Div Drug Anal, Food & Drug Admin, 78-89. *Mem:* Am Chem Soc. *Res:* Organic chemistry; agricultural chemistry; chemical nitrogen fixation; methods research in pharmaceutical chemistry. *Mailing Add:* 1351 N Second St No 10 Belleville IL 62226

JUERGENS, JOHN LOUIS, INTERNAL MEDICINE. *Current Pos:* CONSULT CARDIOVASC DIS & INTERNAL MED, MAYO CLIN, 56- *Personal Data:* b Mankato, Minn, Mar 29, 25; m 48; c 4. *Educ:* Univ Minn, Minneapolis, BS, 46, MS, 56; Harvard Univ, MD, 49. *Prof Exp:* Asst prof med, 62-67, assoc prof clin med, 67-78, PROF MED, MAYO SCH MED, UNIV MINN, 78- *Concurrent Pos:* Fel internal med, Mayo Grad Sch Med, Univ Minn, 53-56. *Mem:* Fel Am Col Physicians. *Res:* Peripheral vascular diseases. *Mailing Add:* Mayo Clin Rochester MN 55905-0002

JUERGENSMEYER, ELIZABETH B, CELL BIOLOGY, PROTOZOOLOGY. *Current Pos:* assoc prof, 69-80, PROF BIOL & FAC MODERATOR, JUDSON COL, ILL, 80- *Personal Data:* b Columbia, Mo, May 28, 40; m 63; c 2. *Educ:* Ore State Univ, BS, 62; Univ Ill, Urbana, MS, 64, PhD(biol), 67. *Prof Exp:* Asst, Univ Ill, Chicago Circle, 65-68; asst prof, Harper Col, 68-69. *Mem:* AAAS; Am Inst Biol Sci; Soc Protozool; Genetics Soc Am; Am Soc Microbiol. *Res:* Comparative genetics of tetrahymena. *Mailing Add:* Math & Sci Judson Col 1151 N State St Elgin IL 60123-1404

JUHASZ, STEPHEN, MECHANICS. *Current Pos:* CONSULT, 84- *Personal Data:* b Budapest, Hungary, Dec 26, 13; nat US. *Educ:* Royal Inst Technol, Budapest, dipl Ing, 36; Royal Inst Technol, Sweden, MSc, 49, Tekn Lic, 51. *Prof Exp:* Mgr & engr, Oeconomia Ltd, Combustion & Salgotarjan Coal Mines, Hungary, 36-46; mem staff, Royal Inst Technol, Stockholm, 49-51 & Univ Toronto, 51-52; res assoc, Fuels Res Lab, Mass Inst Technol, 52-53; exec ed, Appl Mech Rev, 53-60, ed, 60-; dir, Southwest Res Inst, 60-84. *Mem:* Fel Am Soc Mech Engrs; Sigma Xi; Am Inst Aeronaut & Astronaut; fel Am Asn Advan Sci. *Res:* Heat transfer; boiler availability; information retrieval. *Mailing Add:* 6100 NW Loop 410 No 402 San Antonio TX 78238

JUHASZ, STEPHEN EUGENE, PSYCHIATRY. *Current Pos:* RETIRED. *Personal Data:* b Kecskemet, Hungary, Sept 20, 23; Can citizen; m 65. *Educ:* Med Univ Budapest, MD, 51; McGill Univ, PhD, 62. *Prof Exp:* Instr bact, Med Univ Budapest, 51-54, lectr, 54-56, asst prof, 56; res assoc, Royal Edward Laurentian Hosp, 57; res asst, McGill Univ, 58-62; guest researcher, Univ Lausanne, 62-63; staff researcher, Res Inst Exp Biol & Med, Borstel, WGer, 63-64; asst prof microbiol, Univ BC, 64-66; assoc prof microbiol, Stritch Sch Med, Loyola Univ, 67-70, prof, 70-72; res microbiologist, Vet Admin Hosp, Hines, 67-72, resident psychiat, 72-75; instr psychiat, Stritch Sch Med, Loyola Univ, 75-78; attend psychiatrist, Alexian Bros Med Ctr, 75-93. *Mem:* Sigma Xi. *Res:* Bacterial cytology; spheroplasts and L forms of Salmonella; morphogenetics of mycobacteria; phage typing and lysogeny in mycobacteria; transduction and transformation in mycobacteria. *Mailing Add:* 5415 N Sheridan Rd No 1001 Chicago IL 60640

JUHL, WILLIAM G, CHEMICAL ENGINEERING. *Current Pos:* group leader res, 55-64, process tech mgr, 65-74, PROCESS TECHNOL DIR, MONSANTO CO, 74- *Personal Data:* b Luverne, Minn, June 30, 24; m 56; c 2. *Educ:* Univ Minn, BChE, 45; Iowa State Col, PhD(chem eng), 53. *Prof Exp:* Res engr, Lion Oil Co, 53-55. *Mem:* Am Inst Chem Engrs; Am Chem Soc. *Res:* Process development studies of hydrocarbons, conversion and petrochemical production. *Mailing Add:* 203 Millcreek Dr El Dorado AR 71730

JUHOLA, CARL, ELECTRICAL ENGINEERING. *Current Pos:* RETIRED. *Personal Data:* b Bismarck, NDak, Jan 28, 20; m 44, Margaret M Adams; c Roger, David & Margaret J. *Educ:* Univ Wash, Seattle, BSEE, 43. *Prof Exp:* Surveyor, US Bur Reclamation, 40-41; plant engr, Boeing Aircraft Co, Seattle, 41-43; eng exec, electronic develop, United Shoe Mach Corp, 46-61, dept mgr, indust & mach develop, 61-70; dir, Comput Control Lab, USM Corp, 70-73, mgr, Electronics Lab, 73-81, & Ctr Technol Innovation, 81-84. *Concurrent Pos:* Mgt consult. *Mem:* Sr mem Inst Elec & Electronics Engrs; Sigma Xi. *Res:* Management; electronic controls; dielectric heating; fasteners; packaging adhesive systems; development of minicomputer and micro-computer control systems; robotics and computer-aided design; computer-aided manufacturing systems. *Mailing Add:* RR 2 Box 399 East Lebanon ME 04027

JUKES, THOMAS HUGHES, BIOCHEMISTRY, NUTRITION. *Current Pos:* PROF IN RESIDENCE MED PHYSICS, NUTRIT SCI & RES BIOCHEMIST, SPACE SCI LAB, UNIV CALIF, BERKELEY, 63-, PROF BIOPHYSICS, 81- *Personal Data:* b Hastings, Eng, Aug 25, 06; nat US; m 42, Marguerite Esposito; c Kenneth, Caroline & Mavis. *Educ:* Univ Toronto, BSA, 30, PhD(biochem), 33. *Hon Degrees:* DSc, Univ Guelph, 72. *Honors & Awards:* Borden Award, Poultry Sci Asn, 47; Kenneth A Spencer Award, Am Chem Soc, 76, Agr & Food Chem Award, 79; Bruce F Cain Mem Award, Am Assoc for Cancer Res, 87; Klaus Schwarz Medal, Int Asn Bioinorg Sci, 88; Distinguished scientist Achievement Award, Am Counc Sci & Health, 93. *Prof Exp:* Nat Res Coun fel biochem, Univ Calif, 33-34, instr poultry husb, 34-39, asst prof, 39-42; dir sect nutrit & physiol res, Lederle Labs Div, Am Cyanamid Co, 42-59, dir chem res, Agr Div, 59-63. *Concurrent Pos:* Consult, Chem Warfare Serv, 43-45 & NASA, 69-70; vis sr res fel biochem, Princeton Univ, 62-63; chmn, Interdisciplinary Sci Comn F on Life Sci, Comt Space Res, Int Coun Sci Unions, 78-84; assoc ed, J Molecular Evolution, 86-, biog ed, J Nutrit, 83-. *Mem:* Am Soc Biol Chem; Soc Exp Biol & Med; fel Am Soc Animal Sci; fel Poultry Sci Asn; fel Am Inst Nutrit; Sigma Xi. *Res:* Vitamin B complex; choline; pantothenic and folic acid; vitamin B12 and antibiotics in nutrition; folic acid antagonists; proteins; genetic code; biochemical evolution; molecular evolution; trace elements; neutral theory of molecular evolution. *Mailing Add:* Dept Integrative Biol Univ Calif Berkeley CA 94720. *Fax:* 510-643-9761

JULES, LEONARD HERBERT, ORGANIC CHEMISTRY. *Current Pos:* RETIRED. *Personal Data:* b Cleveland, Ohio, Oct 5, 22; m 53; c 2. *Educ:* Univ Southern Calif, AB, 48, MS, 49. *Prof Exp:* Res chemist, Sahyun Labs, 50-55; res chemist, Purex Corp, 55-58; res chemist, Nat Res & Chem Co, 58-62; res chemist, Philip A Hunt Chem Corp, 62-69, plant mgr, 69-85. *Concurrent Pos:* Consult, 85- *Mem:* Am Chem Soc; Soc Photog Sci & Eng. *Res:* Pharmaceuticals; organic intermediates; organic chlorine bleaches; surfactants; asphalt additives; corrosion inhibitors; photographic chemicals. *Mailing Add:* 6035 Wooster Ave Los Angeles CA 90056-1433

JULESZ, BELA, VISION, PHYSIOLOGICAL OPTICS. *Current Pos:* STATE NJ PROF PSYCHOL & DIR, LAB VISION RES, RUTGERS UNIV, BUSCH CAMPUS, 89- *Personal Data:* b Budapest, Hungary, Feb 19, 28; US citizen; m 53. *Educ:* Budapest Tech Univ, dipl, 50; Hungarian Acad Sci, Dr Ing, 56. *Honors & Awards:* Dr H P Heinken Prize, Royal Neth Acad Arts & Sci, 85; Karl Spencer Lashley Award, Am Philos Soc, 89. *Prof Exp:* Asst prof, Dept Tel Commun, Budapest Tech Univ, 50-51; res engr microwave syst, Inst Telecommun Res Inst, Budapest, 51-56; mem tech staff, AT&T Bell Labs, 56-64, head, Sensory & Perceptual Processes Dept, 64-83 & Visual Perception Res Dept, 83-89. *Concurrent Pos:* Vis prof exp psychol, Mass Inst Technol, 69, Fed Tech Univ, Zurich, 75-76, vis prof, Biol Dept, Calif Tech Inst, Pasadena, 85-; Fairchild distinguished scholar, Calif Inst Technol, 77-78 & 87; neurosci assoc, Neurosci Inst, 82; MacArthur Found fel, 83-88. *Mem:* Nat Acad Sci; Inst Elec & Electronics Engrs; fel Optical Soc Am; Psychonomic Soc; fel Am Acad Arts & Sci; fel AAAS; fel Soc Exp Psychologists; hon mem Hungarian Acad Sci. *Res:* Visual perception; binocular depth perception; pattern recognition; optical data processing; psychophysics and neurophysiology of vision; mathematical models; clinical problems of strabismus. *Mailing Add:* Lab Vision Res Rutgers Univ Psychol Bldg-Busch Campus Piscataway NJ 08854. *Fax:* 732-445-6715; *E-Mail:* julesz@gandalf.rutgers.edu

JULIAN, DONALD BENJAMIN, PHOTOGRAPHIC CHEMISTRY, CHEMICAL MICROSCOPY. *Current Pos:* RETIRED. *Personal Data:* b Pelham, Mass, June 6, 22; m 45, Anna Keedy; c Helen J (Heffer), Margaret J (Leonard) & Donna L. *Educ:* Univ Mass, BS, 45. *Prof Exp:* Jr chemist, Eastman Kodak Res Labs, 45-48, from res chemist to sr res chemist, 48-62, res assoc chem, 62-74, sr res assoc, 74-80. *Mem:* Am Chem Soc; Soc Photog Scientists & Engrs. *Res:* Determination of image structure of color photographic films and papers by optical microscope methods; dispersions of oil soluble couplers and other components in aqueous gelatin; chemistry and physics of color photography. *Mailing Add:* 1079 Shoemaker Rd Webster NY 14580-8764

JULIAN, GLENN MARCENIA, SOLID STATE PHYSICS. *Current Pos:* from asst prof to assoc prof, 68-79, PROF PHYSICS, MIAMI UNIV, 80- *Personal Data:* b Knoxville, Tenn, Oct 1, 39; m 68, Elizabeth Jane Kaltenbach; c Daniel, Cynthia & Gerald. *Educ:* Carnegie-Mellon Univ, BS, 61, MS, 63, PhD(physics), 67. *Mem:* Am Phys Soc; Am Geophys Union; Sigma Xi; Am Asn Physics Teachers. *Res:* Studies of magnetic ordering by moessbauer spectroscopy. *Mailing Add:* Dept Physics Miami Univ Oxford OH 45056. *Fax:* 513-529-5629; *E-Mail:* juliangm@muohio.edu

JULIAN, GORDON RAY, CHEMISTRY. *Current Pos:* RETIRED. *Personal Data:* b Wenatchee, Wash, May 29, 28; m 52; c 2. *Educ:* Univ Utah, BS, 50; Univ Ore, MA, 55, PhD(chem), 60. *Prof Exp:* Res fel pharmacol, Harvard Med Sch, 60-62, res assoc, 62-64; from asst prof to prof chem, Mont State Univ, 64-86. *Concurrent Pos:* NIH res grant, 65-68; foreign vis scientist, Szeged, Hungary, 74-75; vis prof, Friedrich Miescher Inst, Basel, Switz, 75-76. *Mem:* AAAS; Am Chem Soc. *Res:* Biochemical processes at elevated temperature; in vitro protein synthesis; early biochemical events in plant development. *Mailing Add:* 3369 Bear Canyon Rd Bozeman MT 59715-6669

JULIAN, MAUREEN M, physical chemistry, crystallography, for more information see previous edition

JULIAN, WILLIAM H, MATHEMATICS. *Current Pos:* PROF MATH, NMEX STATE UNIV, 69- *Personal Data:* b Chicago, Ill, Sept 27, 39. *Educ:* Mass Inst Technol, BS, 61, PhD(math), 65. *Mem:* AAAS; Am Math Soc; Sigma Xi. *Res:* Research in mathematics as applied to astrophysics; rotation of Halley's Comet. *Mailing Add:* Math Dept NMex State Univ Las Cruces NM 88003

JULIANO, PETER C, POLYMER CHEMISTRY. *Current Pos:* Chemist, 68-71, tech coordr, 71-72, MGR RES & DEVELOP, POLYMER PHYSICS & ENG BR, GEN ELEC CO, 76- *Personal Data:* b New Kensington, Pa, Oct 10, 41; m 65; c 3. *Educ:* St Vincent Col, BS, 63; WVa Univ, MS, 65; Univ Akron, PhD(polymer sci), 68. *Concurrent Pos:* Chmn, Gordon Conf Elastomers, 81. *Mem:* Acct Control Syst; Soc Plastic Engrs. *Res:* Synthesis and properties of block polymers; use of organometallic and organosiloxane intermediates for polymer forming reactions. *Mailing Add:* Res & Develop Ctr Gen Elec Co One Research Circle KWD 275 Niskayuna NY 12301

JULIANO, RUDOLPH LAWRENCE, CELL BIOLOGY & ADHESION MOLECULES, BIOPHYSICS. *Current Pos:* PROF & CHAIR PHARMACOL, UNIV CHAPEL HILL, 86- *Personal Data:* b New York, NY, July 18, 41; m 63; c 2. *Educ:* Cornell Univ, BS, 63; Univ Rochester, PhD(biophys), 70. *Prof Exp:* Engr, Radio Corp Am, 63-64; sci teacher, US Peace Corps, Philippines, 64-66; cancer res scientist cell biol, Roswell Park Mem Inst, 70-72; investr cell biol, Res Inst, Hosp Sick Children, Toronto, 72-80; asst prof, Dept Med Biophys, Univ Toronto, 73-; assoc prof pharmacol, Univ Tex Med Sch, Houston, 78-82, prof pharmacol, 86. *Concurrent Pos:* Mem, Oversight Panel, NSF, 85, Prog Comt, Am Asn Cancer Res, 91, NC Biotechnol Ctr, 93-94. Prog Comt, Am Soc Pharmacol & Exp Therapeut, 94-97; chmn, Gordon Res Conf, 87, NY Acad Sci Symp, 87; assoc ed, Cancer Res, 81-89, Molecular Pharmacol, 90-95; ed, Advan Drug Delivery Revs, 87-92. *Mem:* AAAS; Biophys Soc; Can Biochem Soc; Am Asn Cancer Res; Am Soc Cell Biol; Am Soc Pharmacol & Exp Therapeut. *Res:* Signal transduction processes mediated by cell adhesion receptors; drug delivery systems. *Mailing Add:* Dept Pharmacol Univ NC Med Sch Chapel Hill NC 27514

JULIEN, HIRAM PAUL, PHYSICAL CHEMISTRY. *Current Pos:* RETIRED. *Personal Data:* b Syracuse, NY, Oct 21, 29; m 51, 83; c 4. *Educ:* DePauw Univ, AB, 51; Mass Inst Technol, PhD(phys chem), 55. *Prof Exp:* Asst phys chem, Mass Inst Technol, 51-55; res chemist, Prod Res, Esso Res & Eng Co, 55-58, group head, 58-59; mgr, Adv Studies Dept, Bonded Abrasives Div, Carborundum Co, 59-61, Mgr, Develop Dept, 62-64, mgr, Ceramics & Metall Dept, Res & Develop Div, 64-67; mgr, Advn Technol & Testing Dept, Jim Walter Res Corp, 67-81. *Mem:* Am Chem Soc. *Res:* Thermodynamics; automotive and jet fuels; bonded abrasives; high temperature materials and composites; building materials; cellular plastics; mineral fibers; inorganic fillers. *Mailing Add:* 700 Starkey Rd No 822 Largo FL 34641-2302

JULIEN, HOWARD L, HEAT TRANSFER, FLUID MECHANICS. *Current Pos:* CONSULT. *Personal Data:* b Oak Park, Ill, Dec 13, 42; m 65; c 2. *Educ:* Ill Inst Technol, BS, 64, MS, 67; Stanford Univ, PhD(heat & mass transfer), 69. *Prof Exp:* From assoc sr res engr to sr res engr, Gen Motors Res Labs, 69-77; prin engr, Kaiser Engrs, Inc, 77-88; assoc prof mech eng, Univ NMex, 89- *Mem:* Am Soc Mech Engrs; Sigma Xi; Soc Automotive Engrs; Am Nuclear Soc. *Res:* Basic experimental/analytical convective heat transfer research; gas turbine heat transfer; experimental fluid mechanics; thermodynamic cycle analysis of alternative automotive power plants; heat transfer in nuclear waste processing and storage facilities; cooling of solid state lasers. *Mailing Add:* Met 1300-G El Paseo No 278 Las Cruces NM 88001

JULIEN, JEAN-PAUL, food chemistry; deceased, see previous edition for last biography

JULIEN, JEAN-PIERRE, MOLECULAR NEUROBIOLOGY. *Current Pos:* RES ASSOC & ASSOC PROF NEUROL, MCGILL UNIV, 89- *Personal Data:* b Montreal, Que, Nov 20, 52. *Educ:* Univ Que, BSc, 76; McGill Univ, PhD(biochem), 82. *Honors & Awards:* Phil Gold Award, 96-97. *Prof Exp:* Med Res Coun Can fel, Nat Inst Med Res, London, 82-85; res assoc & asst prof biochem, Univ Montreal, 85-89. *Concurrent Pos:* Dir, Transgenic Core Facil, Can Neurosci Net. *Mem:* Am Soc Cell Biol; AAAS. *Res:* Transgenic mouse-models of neurofilament-induced pathology; neurofilament expression and function. *Mailing Add:* Dept Neurol McGill Univ Montreal Gen Hosp Res Inst 1650 Cedar Ave Montreal PQ H3G 1A4 Can. *Fax:* 514-934-8265

JULIEN, LARRY MARLIN, PHYSICAL CHEMISTRY. *Current Pos:* Asst prof, 66-73, ASSOC PROF CHEM, MICH TECHNOL UNIV, 73- *Personal Data:* b Nora Springs, Iowa, Aug 16, 37; m 59; c 2. *Educ:* Wis State Univ, River Falls, BS, 62; Univ Iowa, MS, 65, PhD(chem), 66. *Mem:* Am Chem Soc. *Res:* Thermodynamics; molecular spectroscopy and wood-bark surface properties. *Mailing Add:* Dept Chem Mich Technol Univ Houghton MI 49931

JULIEN, ROBERT M, PHARMACOLOGY, ANESTHESIOLOGY. *Current Pos:* STAFF ANESTHESIOLOGIST, ST VINCENT HOSP & MED CTR, 83- *Personal Data:* b Port Townsend, Wash, Mar 24, 42. *Educ:* Univ Wash, Seattle, PhD(pharmacol), 70; Univ Calif, MD, 77. *Prof Exp:* Anesthesiologist, Ore Health Sci Univ, 80-83. *Mailing Add:* 1212 SW Hessler Dr Portland OR 97201-2807. *Fax:* 503-297-2085

JULIENNE, PAUL SEBASTIAN, THEORETICAL SPECTROSCOPY, SCATTERING THEORY. *Current Pos:* res chemist, Phys Chem Div, 74-77, RES CHEMIST, MOLECULAR PHYSICS DIV, NAT BUR STANDARDS, 77- *Personal Data:* b Spartanburg, SC, May 8, 44; m 68, Marietta Lenear; c Marianne & Alicia. *Educ:* Wofford Col, BS, 65; Univ NC, Chapel Hill, PhD(chem), 69. *Prof Exp:* Nat Acad Sci-Nat Res Coun res assoc, Nat Bur Standards, 69-71, res chemist quantum chem, 71-73; res physicist, Plasma Physics Div, Naval Res Lab, Washington, DC, 73-74. *Mem:* Fel Am Phys Soc; Am Geophys Union. *Res:* Molecular spectroscopy, photodissociation, line broadening theory; atomic collision theory; collisions of laser cooled atoms. *Mailing Add:* B268 Physics Bldg Nat Inst Standards & Technol Gaithersburg MD 20899. *Fax:* 301-975-3038; *E-Mail:* pjulienne@nist.gov

JULIUS, STEVO, MEDICINE. *Current Pos:* from instr to assoc prof, 65-74, PROF INTERNAL MED & DIR, HYPERTENSION UNIT, MED CTR, UNIV MICH, ANN ARBOR, 74-, PROF PHYSIOL, 80- *Personal Data:* b Kovin, Yugoslavia, Apr 15, 29; m; c 2. *Educ:* Univ Zagreb, MD, 53, DMSc, 64. *Hon Degrees:* MD, Univ Goteborg, Sweden, 79. *Honors & Awards:* Astra Award, Int Soc Hypertension; Arthur C Corcoran Mem Lectr, Coun High Blood Pressure, Am Heart Asn. *Prof Exp:* Intern, Univ Zagreb Hosp, 53-54, resident internal med, 55-60; res asst med, Med Ctr, Univ Mich, Ann Arbor, 61-62; sr instr, Univ Zagreb Hosp, 62-64. *Concurrent Pos:* Mem, Coun Epidemiol & Med Adv Bd-Coun High Blood Pressure Res, Am Heart Asn. *Mem:* Am Col Cardiol; Am Heart Asn; Am Fedn Clin Res; Int Soc Cardiol; Am Physiol Soc; Int Soc Hypertension; Am Asn Physicians. *Res:* Hemodynamics of borderline hypertensions; patho-physiology of hypertension; insulin resistance; pathophysiology of coronary risk in hypertension. *Mailing Add:* Dept Internal Med Univ Mich Hosp 3918 Taubman Ctr Ann Arbor MI 48109-0356

JULIUSSEN, J EGIL, COMPUTER SCIENCE, INFORMATION SCIENCE. *Current Pos:* PRES, COMPUT INDUST ALMANAC INC, 86- *Personal Data:* b Stavanger, Norway, May 4, 43; US citizen; c 4. *Educ:* Purdue Univ, BS, 69, MS, 70, PhD(elec eng), 72. *Prof Exp:* Engr, Norden, Div United Technols, 72-73; sr mem tech staff elec eng, Tex Instruments, Inc, 73-81. *Concurrent Pos:* Chmn, Future Comput Inc, 81-86 & Store Bd Inc, 86-90. *Mem:* Inst Elec & Electronics Engrs; Asn Comput Mach. *Res:* Computer technology trends; technology forecasting; computer market analysis, trends and projections. *Mailing Add:* 225 Allen Way Incline Village NV 89451

JULL, ANTHONY JOHN TIMOTHY, RADIOISOTOPE DATING, ACCELERATOR MASS SPECTROMETRY. *Current Pos:* res assoc, 81-84, RES SCIENTIST GEOCHEM, DEPT GEOSCI, UNIV ARIZ, 81- *Personal Data:* b Leeds, Eng, Dec 18, 51; Can citizen. *Educ:* Univ BC, BSc, 72; Univ Bristol, PhD(chem), 76. *Prof Exp:* Teaching res asst geochem, Org Geochem Unit, Univ Bristol, 75-76; res fel geochem, dept mineral & petrol, Univ Cambridge, 76-79, NATO fel, 77-79; vis scientist geochem, Max Planck Inst Chem, Mainz, 79-81. *Mem:* Am Geophys Union; Meteoritical Soc; Royal Soc Chem; Geol Soc Am. *Res:* Radiocarbon dating by accelerator mass spectrometry; studies of cosmogenic redionuclides in meteorites and terrestrial samples; development of Carbon 14 sample preparation methods for accelerator dating; isotope and light element geochemistry. *Mailing Add:* 1170 N Catalina Ave Tucson AZ 85712. *Fax:* 520-621-9619

JULL, EDWARD VINCENT, ELECTROMAGNETIC WAVE THEORY. *Current Pos:* assoc prof, 72-80, PROF ELEC ENG, UNIV BC, 80- *Personal Data:* b Calgary, Alta, Aug 8, 34; m 65, Anne Kjellberg; c Victoria, Charlotta, Walter & Philip. *Educ:* Queen's Univ Ont, BSc, 56; Univ London, PhD(elec eng), 60. *Hon Degrees:* DSc, Univ London, 79. *Honors & Awards:* J T Bolljahn Award, Inst Elec & Electronics Engrs, 65. *Prof Exp:* Jr res officer, Radio & Elec Eng Div, Nat Res Coun Can, 56-57; asst prof elec eng, Univ Alta, 60-61; asst res officer, Radio & Elec Eng Div, Nat Res Coun Can, 61-72, assoc ed, 67-72. *Concurrent Pos:* Guest researcher, Lab Electromagnetic Theory, Tech Univ Denmark, 63-65 & Microwave Dept, Royal Inst Technol, Sweden, 65, guest prof, Electromagnetic Theory Div, 91-92; chmn, Can comn VI, Int Union Radio Sci, 73-76, assoc ed, Radio Sci, 80-83, chmn Can Mem Comt, 80-86; vis res officer, Nat Res Coun Can, 79-80; int dir, Electromagnetics Soc, 81-86. *Mem:* Fel Inst Elec & Electronics Engrs; Int Union Radio Sci (vpres, 87-90, pres, 90-93); Electromagnetics Acad. *Res:* Antennas; antenna far-field/near-field prediction; electromagnetic diffraction theory; geometrical theory of diffraction; electromagnetic diffraction gratings; seismic pulse diffraction; beam diffraction. *Mailing Add:* Dept Elec Eng Univ BC Vancouver BC V6T 1Z4 Can. *Fax:* 604-822-5949; *E-Mail:* jull@ee.ubc.ca

JULL, GEORGE W(ALTER), ELECTRONICS ENGINEERING. *Current Pos:* SR CONSULT, COMMUN RES DIRECTORATE, 75- *Personal Data:* b Calgary, Alta, Can, June 22, 29; m 56; c 1. *Educ:* Univ Alta, BS, 51; Univ London, DIC & PhD(elec eng), 55. *Prof Exp:* Defense scientist, High Frequency Systs, Defense Res Telecommun Estab, 55-71; prog mgr, Info Directorate, 71-75. *Mem:* Optical Soc Am; Inst Elec & Electronics Engrs. *Res:* Advanced communications systems techniques; coherent optical systems; new voice, video and data systems analysis; telecommunications policy research. *Mailing Add:* 72 Stinson Ave Nepean ON K2H 6N4 Can

JULLIEN, GRAHAM ARNOLD, SIGNAL PROCESSING, ELECTRONIC SYSTEMS. *Current Pos:* from asst prof to assoc prof, 69-78, PROF ELEC ENG, UNIV WINDSOR, 78- *Personal Data:* b Wolverhampton, Eng, June 16, 43; m 70; c 2. *Educ:* Loughborough Univ Technol, BTech, 65; Univ Birmingham, MS, 67; Univ Aston, PhD(elec eng), 69. *Prof Exp:* Engr, English Elec Co, 65-66; res asst elec eng, Univ Aston, 67-69. *Concurrent Pos:* Univ grant, Windsor Univ, 69-70, Nat Res Coun Can grant, 69-72, operating grants, 69-, travel fel, 75; sr res engr, Cent Res Labs, EMI Ltd, UK, 75-76; Nat Sci & Eng Res Coun grant, Can, 80-86; pres, Micrel Ltd, 74- *Mem:* Inst Elec & Electronics Engrs; Am Soc Eng Educ. *Res:* Digital signal processing; image processing; high speed digital hardware; microprocessor systems. *Mailing Add:* Dept Elec Eng Univ Windsor Windsor ON N9B 3P4 Can

JULYAN, FREDERICK JOHN, ANATOMY, HISTOLOGY. *Current Pos:* RETIRED. *Personal Data:* b Cleveland, Ohio, May 21, 27; m 60; c 4. *Educ:* Western Reserve Univ, AB, 50; Ohio State Univ, PhD(zool), 62. *Prof Exp:* Instr zool, Capital Univ, 60-61; from instr to asst prof anat, Ohio State Univ, 62-66; from asst prof to assoc prof, 67-73, prof anat, Chicago Col Osteop Med, 74-75, chmn dept, 73-75; prof & chmn dept anat, Kirksville Col Osteop Med, Kirksville, MO, 75-92. *Mem:* AAAS. *Res:* Teaching techniques. *Mailing Add:* RR 1 PO Box 320 Kirksville MO 63501

JUMARIE, GUY MICHAEL, INFORMATION THEORY & APPLICATIONS, INFORMATION SCIENCE & CONTROL SYSTEMS. *Current Pos:* assoc prof appl math, 70-76, PROF APPL MATH & STATIST, UNIV QUE, MONTREAL, 76- *Personal Data:* b Dakar City, Senegal, Mar 18, 39; Fr & Can citizen; m 62, Nadia Arbatchevski; c Catherine. *Educ:* Univ Paris, BSc, 60 & 61, Dr Math, 62; Univ Lille, D Univ, 72, DSc (physics), 81. *Honors & Awards:* Silver Medal, Soc Encouragement Invention Res, 75. *Prof Exp:* Engr missile guidance, SNIA, Paris, 62-66, res engr aeronauts, 66-68; group leader, syst eng comput, MATRA, Paris, 68-70. *Concurrent Pos:* Lectr, Univ Paris, 63-66, invited prof, Nat Inst Statist, Morocco, 74-79, Fed Univ, Rio de Janeiro, 84, Nat Automic Univ Mex, 83, Int Theoret Physics, Univ Stuttgart, Ger, 87, invited lectr, Int Ctr Theoret Physics, 78, 87 & 96. *Mem:* Int Asn Cybernetics; Austrian Soc Cybernetic Study. *Res:* Application of theory of relative information and theory of information of deterministic functions to such questions as systems science, automatic control, approximate reasoning, robotics, computer vision and nonlinear physics. *Mailing Add:* 365 Rue de Chateauguay Apt 252 Longueuil PQ J4H 3X5 Can. *Fax:* 514-987-8935; *E-Mail:* jumanie.guy@ugam.ca

JUMARS, PETER ALFRED, BIOLOGICAL OCEANOGRAPHY. *Current Pos:* from asst prof to assoc prof, 75-83, PROF OCEANOG, UNIV WASH, 83- *Personal Data:* b Dinkelsbuhl, Ger, June 3, 48; US citizen; m; c 1. *Educ:* Univ Del, BA, 69; Univ Calif, San Diego, PhD(oceanog), 74. *Prof Exp:* Res assoc oceanog, Allan Hancock Found, Univ Southern Calif, 74-75. *Concurrent Pos:* Sci officer, Environ Sci div, Off Naval Res, 80-82; ed, Limnol & Oceanog, 86. *Mem:* AAAS; Am Soc Limnol & Oceanog; Am Statist Asn; Am Geophys Union. *Res:* Biological-physical interactions, deposit feeding, succession, spatial scales of community processes; biology of polychaetes. *Mailing Add:* Sch Oceanog WB-10 Univ Wash 3900 Seventh Ave NE Seattle WA 98195-0001

JUMP, J ROBERT, COMPUTER ARCHITECTURE. *Current Pos:* from asst prof to assoc prof, 68-79, PROF ELEC ENG, RICE UNIV, 80- *Personal Data:* b Kansas City, Mo, Feb 15, 37; m 62, Gerry L Becker; c Stephen & Kathryn. *Educ:* Univ Cincinnati, BS, 60, MS, 62; Univ Mich, MS, 65, PhD(comput sci), 68. *Prof Exp:* Elec engr, Avco Corp, 60-61 & IBM Corp, 62-64. *Concurrent Pos:* assoc ed, Inst Elec & Electronics Engrs Trans Computs, 79-81, ed, Inst Elec & Electronics Engrs Trans Parallel & Distributed Systs, 91-93; master, Lovett Col, 84-89; prog dir, NSF, 93- *Mem:*

Inst Elec & Electronics Engrs; Asn Comput Mach. *Res:* Digital systems design; parallel computing; simulation of computer systems. *Mailing Add:* Elec Eng Dept Rice Univ PO Box 1892 Houston TX 77251. *E-Mail:* jrj@rice.edu

JUMP, JOHN AUSTIN, MYCOLOGY, PLANT PATHOLOGY. *Current Pos:* chmn dept, 58-78, prof biol, 58-78, EMER PROF, ELMHURST COL, 78- *Personal Data:* b Easton, Md, Dec 28, 13; m 43; c 2. *Educ:* Swarthmore Col, AB, 34; Univ Pa, PhD(bot), 38. *Prof Exp:* Instr biol, Md State Teachers Col, Frostburg, 38-43; mem res dept, Jos E Seagram & Sons, 43-44; res assoc, Univ Pa, 44-46; from asst prof to assoc prof biol, Univ Notre Dame, 46-58. *Res:* Plant mimicry; Mesembryanthemacea. *Mailing Add:* 230 Larch Ave Elmhurst IL 60126

JUMP, LORIN KEITH, genetics, plant breeding, for more information see previous edition

JUMPER, CHARLES FREDERICK, PHYSICAL CHEMISTRY. *Current Pos:* from asst prof to assoc prof, 62-69, PROF CHEM, THE CITADEL, 69-, HEAD DEPT, 82- *Personal Data:* b Prosperity, SC, Mar 24, 35; m 67; c 1. *Educ:* Univ SC, BS, 56, MS, 57; Fla State Univ, PhD(phys chem), 61. *Prof Exp:* Instr chem, Univ SC, 60-61; res assoc, Bell Tel Labs NJ, 61-62. *Mem:* Am Chem Soc; Sigma Xi. *Res:* Hydrogen bonding; nuclear magnetic resonance; ion exchange; kinetics of very fast reactions; structure of liquids; vibrational spectroscopy. *Mailing Add:* 26 Meander Row Charleston SC 29412

JUMPER, ERIC J, GAS DYNAMICS, LASER PHYSICS. *Current Pos:* PROF, DEPT AEROSPACE & MECH ENG, UNIV NOTRE DAME, 89- *Personal Data:* b Washington, DC, Aug 18, 46; m 67, Marjorie L Stanko; c Eric J Jr & Christine A. *Educ:* Univ NMex, BS, 68; Univ Wyo, MS, 69; Air Force Inst Technol, PhD(mech eng, laser physics), 75. *Prof Exp:* Lab mech engr, Human Eng Div, 65-70 Aerospace Med Res Lab, Wright-Patterson AFB, Ohio, 69-72, aerodynamicist fluid dynamics & laser physics, Technol Div, Air Force Weapons Lab, 74-76, assoc prof, Dept Aeronaut, USAF Acad, 76-81, prof, Dept Aeronaut & Astronaut, Air Force Inst Technol, Wright-Patterson AFB, 81-87, chief, Laser Devices Div, Air Force Weapons Lab, Kirtland AFB, NMex, 87-89. *Concurrent Pos:* Co-coodr, Shroud of Turin Proj, 74-84, bd dir, 78-86; consult laser probs, Air Force Weapons Lab, 76-85; ed, Aeronaut Dig, USAF Acad, 78-81, assoc ed, 81-83; consult heat transfer, Broadcast Prod Div, Harris Corp, 79-82. *Mem:* Assoc fel Am Inst Aeronaut & Astronaut; Am Soc Eng Educ. *Res:* Supersonic drag predictions; physical chemistry of heterogeneous reactions; gas dynamics of lasers; laser-target interaction physics; unsteady aerodynamics; aero-optics; unsteady aerodynamics; laser-fluid interactions. *Mailing Add:* Dept Aerospace & Mech Eng Notre Dame IN 46556. *E-Mail:* eric.j.jumper.1@nd.edu

JUMPER, SIDNEY ROBERTS, RESOURCES, AGRICULTURAL MARKETING. *Current Pos:* assoc prof, 67-72, head, Dept Geog, 77-95, PROF GEOG, UNIV TENN, 72- *Personal Data:* b Gaston, SC, Dec 10, 30; m 54, Mary J Scarcela; c 1. *Educ:* Univ SC, AB, 51, MS, 53; Univ Tenn, PhD(geog), 60. *Honors & Awards:* Distinguished Geog Educ, Nat Geog Soc, 89. *Prof Exp:* Instr geog, Univ SC, 52-53; instr Univ Tenn, 56-57; from asst prof to prof, Tenn Technol Univ, 57-67, head dept geog, philos & sociol, 62-67. *Concurrent Pos:* Ed, Southeastern Geogr, Asn Am Geographers, 75-79; Chmn Bd, Tenn Geog Alliance, Inc, 86-; Tenn State geogr. *Mem:* Asn Am Geographers; Nat Geog Soc; Sigma Xi. *Res:* Marketing of agricultural products, particularly fresh fruits and vegetables; economic geography; geography education. *Mailing Add:* Dept Geog Univ Tenn Knoxville TN 37996-1420

JUNCOSA, MARIO LEON, APPLIED MATHEMATICS, NUMERICAL ANALYSIS. *Current Pos:* mathematician, 53-70, SR MATHEMATICIAN, RAND CORP, 70- *Personal Data:* b Lima, Peru, Sept 18, 21; US citizen; m 46, Vera Pabo; c Raymond, William, Adrian, Alexander & Sylvia. *Educ:* Hofstra Col, BA, 43; Cornell Univ, MS, 45, PhD(appl math), 48. *Prof Exp:* Asst physics, Cornell Univ, 43-47, asst mech, 45-47, instr, 47-48; math, Johns Hopkins Univ, 48-50; mathematician, Exterior Ballistics Lab & Comput Lab, Ballistics Res Labs, Aberdeen Proving Ground, Md, 49-53. *Concurrent Pos:* Instr, Univ Southern Calif Exten, 54; instr & lectr Univ Calif Exten, Los Angeles, 56-58; ed in chief, Asn Comput Mach J, 59-63; consult math & comput sci adv group, AEC, 63-72; chmn satellite tracking accuracy panel, Nat Acad Sci Adv Comt to Air Force Systs Command, 67-69; mem comput adv panel, Nat Ctr Atmospheric Res, 68-75; mem adv coun, Southwest Regional Lab Educ Res & Develop, 68-72; consult, Div Comput Res, NSF, 71-75; lectr, Grad Sch Bus, Calif State, Long Beach, 79-81, fel, 96; vis lectr & vis assoc prof, Econ Dept, Univ Calif, Los Angeles, 81-89, lectr Col Eng, 83-85. *Mem:* Soc Indust & Appl Math. *Res:* Applied math, probability, statistics, ordinary and partial differential equations and applications, general numerical and problem analysis, digital computation, mathematical programing and applications, privacy in computerized data banks, and mathematical applications in medicine; models; analyses of terrorism; chaos and aggregation in combat models. *Mailing Add:* 1122 El Medio Ave Pacific Palisade CA 90272-2421. *E-Mail:* marie_uncosa@rand.org

JUNEJA, VIJAY KUMAR, EFFECT OF MULTIPLE FOOD FORMULATIONS ON FATE OF BACTERIA IN FOODS, THERMAL INACTIVATION OF SPORE FORMING BACTERIA IN FOODS. *Current Pos:* LEAD SCIENTIST & FOOD MICROBIOLOGIST, USDA, 91- *Personal Data:* b Jammu, India, July 1, 56; US citizen; m 85, Poonam; c Komal & Nikhil. *Educ:* G B Pant Univ, BVSc & AH, 78; Univ Tenn, Knoxville, MS, 88, PhD(food technol & sci), 91. *Hon Degrees:* BVSC & AH, GB Pant Univ, 88. *Prof Exp:* Vet surgeon animal husbandry, Punjab, India, 78-85. *Mem:* Inst Food Technologists; Int Asn Milk Food & Environ Sanitarians. *Res:* Effect of multiple food formulations on the growth of spoilage and pathogenic bacteria in foods; food fermentations; diagnostic microbiology techniques including immunological and molecular biology methods. *Mailing Add:* USDA Eastern Regional Res Ctr 600 E Mermaid Lane Wyndmoor PA 19038. *Fax:* 215-233-6581; *E-Mail:* vjuneja@arserrc.gov

JUNG, CHAN YONG, TRANSMEMBRANE TRANSPORT, INSULIN ACTIONS. *Current Pos:* CHIEF BIOPHYS RES, VET ADMIN MED CTR, BUFFALO, 75- *Personal Data:* b Chungju, Korea, Aug 12, 28; US citizen. *Educ:* Univ Rochester, NY, PhD(biophys), 64. *Prof Exp:* Res assoc radiation biol, Univ Rochester, 64-65; res assox pharmacol, Univ Louisville, 65-67; res asst prof biophys, State Univ NY, Buffalo, 67-74, res assoc prof, 74-77, assoc prof, 77-81, PROF BIOPHYS, STATE UNIV NY, BUFFALO, 81-, RES PROF MED, 83- *Mem:* Am Biophys Soc; Am Soc Biol Chem; Am Diabetes Asn; NY Acad Sci; AAAS; Red Cell Club. *Res:* Molecular elucidation of membrane-related functions; transmembrane solute translocation; information transduction; receptor-ligand interactions; insulin-mediated stimulation of glucose transport function in peripheral tissues. *Mailing Add:* Vet Admin Med Ctr Bldg 20 Rm 215 3495 Bailey Ave Buffalo NY 14215

JUNG, DENNIS WILLIAM, ION TRANSPORT, MITOCHONDRIA. *Current Pos:* RES SCIENTIST PHYSIOL, DEPT PHYSIOL CHEM, OHIO STATE UNIV, 76- *Educ:* Univ Ill, PhD(biol), 74. *Res:* Heart biochemistry. *Mailing Add:* Dept Med Biochem Ohio State Univ 1645 Neil Ave Columbus OH 43210-1218

JUNG, DONALD T, PHARMACOKINETICS, BIOPHARMACEUTICS. *Current Pos:* ASSOC DIR CLIN PHARAMACOL, ROCHE BIOSCI, 87- *Personal Data:* b Los Angeles, Calif, Apr 10, 53; m 84, Young M Lee; c Stacy & Brian. *Educ:* Univ Calif, Davis, BS, 74; Univ Calif, San Francisco, MS, 78; Univ Ariz, PhD(pharmaceut sci), 80. *Prof Exp:* Asst prof pharmacokinetics, Univ Ill, Chicago, 81-87. *Concurrent Pos:* Adj asst prof pharmacokinetics, Univ Ill, Chicago, 87- *Mem:* Am Asn Pharmaceut Sci; Acad Pharmaceut Sci; Am Pharmaceut Asn; Drug Info Asn. *Res:* Effect of disease states on pharmacokinetics, pharmacokinetic/pharmacodynamic modeling, drug metabolism drug interaction, bio equivalence, clinical trials. *Mailing Add:* 3401 Hillview Ave A2-230 Palo Alto CA 94304. *Fax:* 650-855-5560; *E-Mail:* donald.jung@roche.com

JUNG, FREDERIC THEODORE, PHYSIOLOGY. *Current Pos:* RETIRED. *Educ:* Univ Chicago, PhD(physiol), 25; Northwestern Univ, MD, 32. *Prof Exp:* At dept ed, J AMA. *Mailing Add:* 1555 Oak Ave Evanston IL 60201-4233

JUNG, GERALD ALVIN, AGRONOMY, PLANT ECOLOGY. *Current Pos:* RETIRED. *Personal Data:* b Milwaukee, Wis, July 16, 30; m 57. *Educ:* Univ Wis, BS, 52, MS, 54, PhD, 58. *Honors & Awards:* Res Award, Northeast Br, Am Soc Agron, 84; Goddard Mem lectr, Univ Tenn, 88; John Peters Mem lectr, WVa Univ, 90. *Prof Exp:* Biologist, Chem Warfare Lab, Ft Detrick, Md, 54-56; asst prof agron, WVa Univ, 58-62, assoc prof, 62-67, prof agron & genetics, 67-70; tech adv for soil fertility & physiol & biochem technol, USDA, 71-81, res agronomist & res leader, US Regional Pasture Res Lab, Agr Res Serv, 70-94. *Concurrent Pos:* Adj prof agron, Pa State Univ; mem, Presidium, 12th Int Grassland Cong, Moscow, USSR, 74; Pa Forage & Grassland Coun res award, 87. *Mem:* Fel Am Soc Agron; Am Forage & Grassland Coun; Soc Cryobiol; fel Crop Sci Soc Am. *Res:* Forage crop adaptation and production on marginal lands; nutritional value of forage crops as influenced by soils and fertilizers; physiology of cold tolerance of alfalfa. *Mailing Add:* 22 Oyster Bay Pl Hilton Head SC 29926

JUNG, GLENN HAROLD, OCEANOGRAPHY, METEOROLOGY. *Current Pos:* assoc prof oceanog, 58-65, prof oceanog, 65-83, EMER PROF, NAVAL POSTGRAD SCH, 83- *Personal Data:* b Lyons, Kans, Oct 11, 24; m 48, Jean Clements; c Lynn (Parsons), Lawrence E, Leslie M, Richard B & K Dale. *Educ:* Mass Inst Technol, SB, 49, SM, 52; Tex A&M Univ, PhD(phys oceanog), 55. *Prof Exp:* Asst meteorol, Mass Inst Technol, 50-51; mem staff, Div Indust Co-op, 52; asst oceanog, Tex A&M Univ, 53-54; assoc oceanog & asst prof phys oceanog & phys meteorol, 55-57. *Concurrent Pos:* Consult, Texas Co, La, 58 & UN Naval Oceanog Off, 65 & 66; vis fac mem, Inst Phys Oceanog, Univ Copenhagen, 71-72; Naval Postgrad Sch, 87-88 & 90-91. *Mem:* Sigma Xi. *Res:* Energy transfer by sea and air, especially across air-sea boundary; oceanographic analysis and forecasting. *Mailing Add:* 25750 Rio Vista Dr Carmel CA 93923

JUNG, HILDA ZIIFLE, PHYSICAL CHEMISTRY, PLASMA PHYSICS. *Current Pos:* RETIRED. *Personal Data:* b Gretna, La, Sept 7, 22; m 68, Julius R Jung Jr. *Educ:* Tulane Univ, BS, 43. *Prof Exp:* Release clerk, Higgins Aircraft Co, 43-44; res physicist, Southern Regional Res Ctr, USDA, 44-79. *Mem:* Sigma Xi; Am Chem Soc; AAAS. *Res:* Physical and physical chemical reactions and properties of natural polymers; kinetics of reactions; crystalline orientation; elasticity; low temperature plasma reactions; application of statistical techniques. *Mailing Add:* 109 Kennedy Dr Gretna LA 70053

JUNG, JAMES MOSER, ORGANIC CHEMISTRY. *Current Pos:* PROF CHEM & CHMN DEPT, CAMPBELL UNIV, 62- *Personal Data:* b Kannapolis, NC, May 25, 28; m 58; c 5. *Educ:* Davidson Col, BS, 49; Univ NC, PhD(org chem), 62. *Mem:* AAAS. *Res:* Preparation, properties and cyclization of azomethines. *Mailing Add:* Dept Chem Campbell Univ Buies Creek NC 27506-9999

JUNG, JOHN ANDREW, JR, ORGANIC CHEMISTRY, CATALYSIS. *Current Pos:* STAFF CHEMIST, INTERMEDIATES DIV, EXXON CHEM, 81- *Personal Data:* b Jersey City, NJ, May 3, 38. *Educ:* St Peter's Col, BS, 61; Univ Iowa, PhD(org chem), 66. *Prof Exp:* Res chemist, US Army Ballistic Res Labs, Md, 66-67, M W Kellogg Co, 67-71; sr res chemist, Chem Systs Inc, 72-81. *Mem:* Am Chem Soc; Catalysis Soc; Sigma Xi. *Res:* Oxo process catalysis. *Mailing Add:* 6628 Milstone Dr Baton Rouge LA 70808

JUNG, LAWRENCE KWOK LEUNG, IMMUNOLOGY, MEDICAL SCIENCE. *Current Pos:* sr clin scientist, 82-86, ASST MEM, OKLA MED RES FOUND IMMUNOL PROG, 86-; ASST PROF & CHIEF, CLIN IMMUNOL SERV, OKLA CHILDREN'S MEM HOSP, 86- *Personal Data:* b Canton, China, Aug 6, 50; Can citizen; m 77; c 2. *Educ:* Univ Sask, BSc, 71, MD, 75; FRCP(C), 80; Am Acad Pediat, dipl, 80. *Prof Exp:* Sr resident pediatrician, Hosp Sick Children, Toronto, 75-77; sr resident pediatrician, McMaster Univ Med Ctr, Toronto, 77-78, pediat immunol fel, 78-80; res fel, Sloan-Kettering Inst Cancer Res, 80-82; res fel, dept pediat, Okla Children's Mem Hosp, 82-84. *Concurrent Pos:* Prin investr, NIH grants, 84- *Mem:* Am Asn Immunologists; Clin Immunol Soc; NY Acad Sci; AAAS; AMA. *Res:* The role of human T cell differentiation antigens on T cell ontogeny, activation and differentiation in normal and immunodeficiency states. *Mailing Add:* Dept Pediat Immunol 55 Lake Ave Worcester MA 01605-2377. *Fax:* 508-856-5500

JUNG, MICHAEL ERNEST, SYNTHETIC ORGANIC CHEMISTRY, NATURAL PRODUCTS CHEMISTRY. *Current Pos:* from asst prof to assoc prof, 74-83, PROF CHEM, UNIV CALIF, LOS ANGELES, 83- *Personal Data:* b New Orleans, La, May 14, 47; m 69. *Educ:* Rice Univ, BA, 69; Columbia Univ, PhD(chem), 73. *Prof Exp:* NATO fel, Swiss Fed Inst Technol, 73-74. *Concurrent Pos:* Camille & Henry Dreyfus Teacher-Scholar grant, 78-83; Alfred P Sloan Found Res fel, 79-81; Fulbright-Hays grant, US Res Scholar Award, 80-81; mem, Cancer Ctr, Univ Calif, Los Angeles. *Mem:* Am Chem Soc; Royal Chem Soc; Sigma Xi. *Res:* Organic synthesis, particularly of biologically interesting natural products; development of new synthetic methods; chemistry of organic compounds of group IVb metals, such as silicon and tin, and their use in organic synthesis. *Mailing Add:* Dept Chem Univ Calif 405 Hilgard Ave Los Angeles CA 90024-1569

JUNG, RODNEY CLIFTON, TROPICAL MEDICINE, CLINICAL PARASITOLOGY. *Current Pos:* Asst zool, Tulane Univ, 39-42, asst parasitol, 48-50, from instr to prof trop med, 50-74, clin prof med, 74-91, EMER PROF TROP MED, TULANE UNIV, 92- *Personal Data:* b New Orleans, La, Oct 9, 20; m 86. *Educ:* Tulane Univ, BS, 41, MD, 45, MS, 50, PhD(parasitol), 53. *Honors & Awards:* Geiger Medal Pub Health. *Concurrent Pos:* Markle scholar, 53-58; dir health, City of New Orleans, 63-70 & 79-; sr vis physician, Charity Hosp, La; consult, US Quarantine Serv. *Mem:* Am Soc Trop Med & Hyg; Am Soc Parasitologists; fel Am Col Physicians; Royal Soc Trop Med & Hyg; hon mem Brazilian Soc Trop Med. *Res:* Clinical aspects of parasitic infections. *Mailing Add:* Crescent City Phys Inc Touro Infirmary Buckam Clin 3434 Prytania St Suite 460 New Orleans LA 70115-3615

JUNGA, FRANK ARTHUR, SOLID STATE PHYSICS. *Current Pos:* Grad prog student, 56-63, RES SCIENTIST SOLID STATE PHYSICS, LOCKHEED RES LAB, 63- *Personal Data:* b Patchogue, NY, May 15, 34; m 56. *Educ:* Yale Univ, BS, 56; Univ Calif, Berkeley, MA, 59, PhD(physics), 63. *Mem:* Am Phys Soc. *Res:* Basic mechanisms involved in optical and/or electrical phenomena in semiconductors; photoconductivity; photovoltaic effects; laser phenomena; radiation effects in semiconductors; research on surface phenomena in compound semiconductors. *Mailing Add:* Lockheed Res Lab Bldg 202 Dept H154 3251 Hanover St Palo Alto CA 94304-1187

JUNGALWALA, FIROZE BAMANSHAW, BIOCHEMISTRY, NEUROCHEMISTRY. *Current Pos:* prin res assoc neurol, Harvard Univ, 75-90, ASSOC PROF NEUROSCI, HARVARD MED SCH, 90- *Personal Data:* b India, Aug 28, 36; US citizen. *Educ:* Gujarat Univ, India, BSc, 56, MSc, 58; Indian Inst Sci, Bangalore, PhD(biochem), 63. *Honors & Awards:* Career Develop Award, NIH. *Prof Exp:* BIOCHEMIST, EUNICE KENNEDY SHRIVER CTR MENT RETARDATION, INC, 71- *Concurrent Pos:* Res fel physiol chem, Univ Wis-Madison, 64-66; res fel psychiat, Washington Univ, St Louis, 66-68; Nat Multiple Sclerosis Soc res fel, Inst Animal Physiol, Cambridge, Eng, 68-70; assoc ed, J Lipid Res; mem, Neurol Dis Prog Proj Rev, NIH, 85- *Mem:* Int Soc Neurochem; Am Soc Neurochem; Fedn Am Socs Exp Biol. *Res:* Lipids; role of lipids in membrane formation and organization; cerebral membranes, systhesis function and breakdown of lipids in health and diseases. *Mailing Add:* Dept Biomed Sci E K Shriver Ctr Ment Retardation 200 Trapelo Rd Waltham MA 02254. *Fax:* 781-893-4824

JUNGAS, ROBERT LEANDO, ENERGY METABOLISM. *Current Pos:* assoc dean preclin educ, 85-90, PROF PHYSIOL, UNIV CONN HEALTH CTR, 74- *Personal Data:* b Mt Lake, Minn, Sept 25, 34; m 57, Lois Gering. *Educ:* St Olaf Col, BA, 56; Harvard Univ, PhD(biochem), 61. *Prof Exp:* Instr biochem, Harvard Med Sch, 63-65, assoc 65-68, asst prof, biol chem, 68-71, assoc prof, 71-74. *Concurrent Pos:* USPHS training grant biochem, Harvard Med Sch, 60-63. *Mem:* Am Soc Biol Chemists; Biochem Soc. *Res:* Action of hormones on adipose tissue metabolism. *Mailing Add:* Dept Physiol MC 3505 Univ Conn Health Ctr 263 Farmington Ave Farmington CT 06030. *Fax:* 860-679-1269; *E-Mail:* yukonrlj@aol.com

JUNGBAUER, MARY ANN, INORGANIC CHEMISTRY. *Current Pos:* adj assoc prof, 69-72, assoc prof, 72-92, CHMN, DEPT PHYS SCI, BARRY UNIV, 80-, PROF CHEM, 92- *Personal Data:* b Phoenix, Ariz, Aug 10, 34; c 1. *Educ:* Immaculate Heart Col, BA, 57; Univ Notre Dame, MS, 61, PhD(inorg chem), 64. *Prof Exp:* Teacher, Pub Schs, 56-59; instr chem, Immaculate Heart Col, 63-67; asst prof chem, Drew Univ, 67-69. *Mem:* Am Chem Soc; Sigma Xi. *Mailing Add:* 704 Jeronimo Dr Coral Gables FL 33146. *Fax:* 305-899-3439; *E-Mail:* jungbaver@buaxp1.barry.edu

JUNGCK, GERALD FREDERICK, TOPOLOGY. *Current Pos:* Instr, 59-61, from asst prof to assoc prof, 61-82, PROF MATH, BRADLEY UNIV, 82-, DEPT CHAIR, 89- *Personal Data:* b Dubuque, Iowa, Mar 1, 29; m 59; c 2. *Educ:* Wartburg Col, BA, 56; Univ Wis, MA, 59; State Univ NY, Binghamton, PhD(math), 78. *Concurrent Pos:* NSF fac fel, Rutgers Univ, 68. *Mem:* Math Asn Am. *Res:* Fixed point theorems for commuting mappings on metric spaces; local homeomorphisms. *Mailing Add:* 1505 W Lincolnwood Peoria IL 61614-2616

JUNGCK, JOHN RICHARD, MOLECULAR EVOLUTION. *Current Pos:* FROM ASSOC PROF TO PROF & CHMN DEPT BIOL, BELOIT COL, 79- *Personal Data:* b Moorhead, Minn, Aug 17, 44; m 65; c 1. *Educ:* Univ Minn, BS, 66, MS, 68; Univ Miami, PhD(biol & chem), 73. *Prof Exp:* Asst prof biol, Merrimack Col, 71-75; from asst prof to assoc prof, Clarkson Col, 75-79. *Concurrent Pos:* Assoc ed, Bulletin of Math Biol, 82-86; ed, Am Biol Teacher, 84-85; Fulbright Scholar, Chiang Mai Univ, Thailand, 85-86; ed midwest bioscene, Asn Midwestern Col Biol Teachers, 88- *Mem:* Soc Study Evolution; Int Soc Study Origins Life; Soc Math Biol; Nat Asn Biol Teachers; Soc Systematic Zool. *Res:* Origins of and mathematical properties of the genetic code; computer analysis of nucleic acid and protein sequences; genetic language; algorithms for analyzing sequence data; philosophy of biology; computer assisted learning-strategic simulations; combinatorics and finite mathematics. *Mailing Add:* Biol Dept Beloit Col 700 College St Beloit WI 53511-5595

JUNGCLAUS, GREGORY ALAN, ANALYTICAL CHEMISTRY, ENVIRONMENTAL CHEMISTRY. *Current Pos:* SR CHEMIST, MIDWEST RES INST, 81- *Personal Data:* b Yankton, SDak, Dec 16, 47; m 66; c 2. *Educ:* Univ SDak, BA, 70, MA, 72; Ariz State Univ, PhD(chem), 75. *Prof Exp:* Res assoc chem, Mass Inst Technol, 75-77; sr res scientist, Ford Motor Co, 77-78; res chemist, Battelle Columbus Labs, 78-81. *Mem:* Am Chem Soc; Am Soc Mass Spectrom; Meteoritical Soc; Sigma Xi. *Res:* Technical direction of projects concerning analytical method development and application; agent demilitarization and installation restoration; gas chromatographic mass spectrometry. *Mailing Add:* 8904 W 132nd St Shawnee Mission KS 66213

JUNGE, DOUGLAS, BIOPHYSICS, APPLIED MATHEMATICS. *Current Pos:* from asst prof to assoc prof, 67-79, PROF ORAL BIOL, SCH DENT, UNIV CALIF, LOS ANGELES, 79- *Personal Data:* b Milwaukee, Wis, Jan 16, 38; m 60; c 2. *Educ:* Calif Inst Technol, BS, 59; Univ Calif, Los Angeles, PhD(physiol), 65. *Prof Exp:* Asst res zoologist, Scripps Inst Oceanog, 65-67. *Concurrent Pos:* NIH grant, 68-71 & contract, 69-71; NSF grant, 72-74; ed, J Theoret Neurobiol, 81- *Mem:* Am Physiol Soc; Biophys Soc; Soc Neurosci. *Res:* Electrophysiology of excitable membranes; ionic properties of nerve; computer analysis of BMG signals in painful or tender muscles; neurosciences. *Mailing Add:* 10756 Massachusetts Ave Los Angeles CA 90024

JUNGER, MIGUEL C, ACOUSTICS, APPLIED MECHANICS. *Current Pos:* partner, 55-59, pres, 59-90, CHMN BD & PRIN SCIENTIST, CAMBRIDGE ACOUST ASSOC, 90- *Personal Data:* b Dresden, Ger, Jan 29, 23; nat US; m 60, Ellen Sinclair; c M Sebastian & A Carlotta (Luke). *Educ:* Mass Inst Technol, BS, 44, MS, 46; Harvard Univ, ScD(appl mech), 51. *Honors & Awards:* Trent-Crede Medal, Acoust Soc Am; Raleigh lectr, Am Soc Mech Engr, 87; Per Bruel Gold Medal, 92. *Prof Exp:* Res fel, Harvard Univ, 51-55. *Concurrent Pos:* Sr vis lectr, Mass Inst Technol, 68-78; vis prof, Compiegne Technol Univ, France 75 & 77-81; consult, Off Naval Res, London, 75. *Mem:* Fel Acoust Soc Am; fel Am Soc Mech Engr. *Res:* Physical acoustics, particularly underwater sound; dynamics of elastic systems in an acoustic medium; noise control; mechanical vibrations and shock. *Mailing Add:* 90 Fletcher Rd Belmont MA 02178

JUNGERMAN, JOHN (ALBERT), PHYSICS. *Current Pos:* res physicist, 51-69, dir, Crocker Nuclear Lab, 69-80, chmn, Physics Dept, 83-87, PROF PHYSICS, UNIV CALIF, DAVIS, 60- *Personal Data:* b Modesto, Calif, Dec 28, 21; m 48; c 4. *Educ:* Univ Calif, AB, 43, PhD(physics), 49. *Prof Exp:* Asst physics, Univ Calif, 43-44, res physicist, Radiation Lab, 44-45, Los Alamos Sci Lab, 45-46 & Lawrence Berkeley Lab, 46-49; AEC fel, Cornell Univ, 49-50; res physicist, Lawrence Berkeley Lab, staff, Univ Calif, 50-51. *Concurrent Pos:* Assoc prof, Univ Grenoble, France, 72; consult, Int Atomic Energy Agency, Univ Chile, 82. *Mem:* Fel Am Phys Soc; Sigma Xi. *Res:* Charged particle induced fission; beta ray spectroscopy; sector-focused cyclotrons; particle scattering; medical physics; physics and society. *Mailing Add:* Dept Physics Univ Calif Davis CA 95616

JUNGERMANN, ERIC, SURFACE ACTIVE AGENTS, ANTIMICROBIAL AGENTS. *Current Pos:* PRES, JUNGERMANN ASSOCS, INC, 78- *Personal Data:* b Mainz, Ger, Sept 8, 23; US citizen; m 51, Eva Schlein; c 1. *Educ:* City Col New York, BS, 49; Polytech Inst Brooklyn, MS, 53, PhD(org chem), 57. *Honors & Awards:* Award of Merit, Am Oil Chemists Soc, 71; Soc Cosmetic Chemists Award, 75. *Prof Exp:* Res chemist, Colgate-Palmolive Co, 46-57; sect head chem synthesis, Armour Indust Chem Co, 57-59, mgr res, Soap Div, 59-65, dir household res & develop, Armour & Co, 65-71, vpres res & develop, Armour Dial Inc, 71-75; dir corp develop, Helene Curtis Indust, 75-78; sr vpres technol, Neutrogena Corp, 83-92. *Concurrent Pos:* Assoc ed, J Am Oil Chemists Soc; mem sci adv bd, Lowes Corp, 79-85; mem bd dirs, Lee Pharmaceut Corp, 79-89. *Mem:* Am Oil Chemists' Soc; Soc Cosmetic Chemists; Am Chem Soc. *Res:* Soap, detergent and cosmetic technology, both from the fundamental and practical viewpoint; fat based surfactants; fatty acid derivatives; soaps; hair and skin care products; antimicrobials; organophosphorus compounds. *Mailing Add:* 2323 N Central Ave Suite 1001 Phoenix AZ 85004

JUNGHANS, RICHARD PAUL, HEMATOLOGY, ONCOLOGY. *Current Pos:* ASSOC PROF MED, NEW ENG DEACONESS HOSP, 91- *Personal Data:* bn Ft Atkinson, Wis, Feb 28, 51. *Educ:* Univ Calif, Berkeley, PhD(molecular biol & virol), 75. *Res:* Hematology; oncology; molecular biology; virology. *Mailing Add:* Biotherapy Develop Prog Harvard Med Sch Dept Med Div Hemat & Oncol New England Deaconess Hosp 99 Brookline Ave Rm 301 Boston MA 02215

JUNGKIND, DONALD LEE, MEDICAL MICROBIOLOGY, CLINICAL LABORATORY ADMINISTRATION. *Current Pos:* from asst prof to assoc prof, 73-88, PROF PATH & MICROBIOL, SCH MED, THOMAS JEFFERSON UNIV, 88-, DIR, CLIN MICROBIOL LAB, 73- *Personal Data:* b Washington, DC, Apr 16, 43; m 65; c 4. *Educ:* Lamar State Univ, BS, 65; Univ Houston, MS, 68; Univ Tex Med Br Galveston, PhD(microbiol), 72. *Prof Exp:* Fel clin microbiol, Sch Med, Temple Univ, 72-73. *Concurrent Pos:* Pres, Microbiol Consult, Inc, 78- *Mem:* Am Soc Microbiol; Am Soc Clin Path; Asn Clin Scientists. *Res:* Diagnostic microbiology and immunology with emphasis on automation of procedures; microbial physiology and effects of antimicrobial agents on cells; sexually transmitted diseases. *Mailing Add:* Clin Microbiol Lab Thomas Jefferson Med Col 1025 Walnut St Philadelphia PA 19107-5001

JUNGMANN, RICHARD A, MOLECULAR BIOLOGY. *Current Pos:* res assoc, 63-68, from asst prof to assoc prof biochem, 68-74, PROF BIOCHEM, MED SCH, NORTHWESTERN UNIV, 74-, PROF MOLECULAR BIOL, 80- *Personal Data:* b Volklingen, Switz, Oct 29, 28; nat US; m 61, Suzanne Houriet. *Educ:* Univ Saarland, 48-50; Univ Basel, PhD, 58. *Prof Exp:* Res staff mem biochem, Worcester Found Exp Biol, Mass, 58-59; dir org res, McGean Chem Co, Ohio, 59-63. *Concurrent Pos:* Lectr, Cleveland State Univ, 60-63; sr res investr biochem, Dept Res, Chicago Wesley Mem Hosp, 63-68; consult, McGean Chem Co, 63-64, dept med, Med Sch, Northwestern Univ, 65- *Mem:* AAAS; Am Chem Soc; fel Am Inst Chem; Swiss Chem Soc; Endocrine Soc. *Res:* Role of signal transduction in gene expression. *Mailing Add:* Northwestern Univ Med Sch 303 E Chicago Ave Chicago IL 60611. *Fax:* 312-503-7107; *E-Mail:* rjungman@nwu.edu

JUNI, ELLIOT, BACTERIAL PHYSIOLOGY. *Current Pos:* PROF MICROBIOL, MED SCH, UNIV MICH, ANN ARBOR, 66- *Personal Data:* b NY, Aug 6, 21; m 44; c 2. *Educ:* City Col New York, BEE, 44; Western Reserve Univ, PhD(microbiol), 51. *Prof Exp:* Asst prof bact, Univ Ill, 51-56; from assoc prof to prof, Sch Med, Emory Univ, 56-66. *Mem:* AAAS; Am Soc Microbiol; Am Soc Biol Chem. *Res:* Bacterial metabolism; taxonomy. *Mailing Add:* Dept Microbiol Univ Mich Med Sch Sci Bldg II Ann Arbor MI 48109-0001

JUNK, WILLIAM A(RTHUR), JR, CHEMICAL ENGINEERING. *Current Pos:* CHEM ENGR, STANDARD OIL CO, 52- *Personal Data:* b Uniontown, Pa, Mar 12, 24; m 56; c 2. *Educ:* Pa State Col, BS, 48; Univ Ill, MS, 50, PhD(chem eng), 52. *Mem:* Am Chem Soc. *Res:* Physical properties of hydrocarbons; separation processes. *Mailing Add:* 18344 Aberdeen Ave Homewood IL 60430

JUNKER, BOBBY RAY, ATOMIC PHYSICS. *Current Pos:* physicist, 77-83, dir, Physic Div, 83-86, DIR MATH, PHYS SCI DIRECTORATE, OFF NAVAL RES, 86- *Personal Data:* b San Antonio, Tex, Aug 29, 43; c 3. *Educ:* Univ Southwestern La, BS, 65; Univ Tex, Austin, MA, 67, PhD(chem), 69. *Prof Exp:* Instr chem, Univ Tex, Austin, 69-70; res assoc physics, Univ Pittsburgh, 70-72; asst prof physics, Univ Ga, 72-76. *Mem:* Am Phys Soc; Sigma Xi; AAAS. *Res:* Theoretical atomic physics, including electron-atom and ion- atom collisions. *Mailing Add:* Off Naval Res Code 111 800 N Quincy St Arlington VA 22217

JUNKER, MICHAEL LEE, MODELING & SIMULATION, ON & IN-LINE PROCESS ANALYZERS. *Current Pos:* res chemist, DSM Copolymer, Inc, 83-86, group leader, 86-93, tech mgr, 93-96, SR SCIENTIST, DSM COPOLYMER INC, 96- *Personal Data:* b St Louis, Mo, Jan 1, 43; m 64, Linda Ann Blakely; c Penelope A (Piercy) & Mark Louis. *Educ:* Ind Univ, AB, 64; Purdue Univ, MS, 67; Univ SC, PhD(phys chem), 73; La State Univ, MSChE, 77. *Prof Exp:* Asst prof anal chem, Newberry Col, 66-72; instr, Univ SC, 72-73; vis prof, Univ NC, 73-74, vis prof phys chem, Univ Nebr, 74-75; develop engr OnLine Analyzers, Celanese Corp, 77-83; sr staff engr high-density polyethylene, Cities Serv Corp, 80-83. *Concurrent Pos:* Instr comput prog, McNeese State Univ, 82. *Mem:* Am Chem Soc; Instrument Soc Am. *Res:* Investigating new technologies and working to integrate them into the plants. *Mailing Add:* 1040 S Eugene St Baton Rouge LA 70806

JUNKHAN, GEORGE H, MECHANICAL ENGINEERING. *Current Pos:* From instr to asst prof, 57-66, ASSOC PROF MECH ENG, IOWA STATE UNIV, 66- *Personal Data:* b Peoria, Ill, Jan 30, 29; m 56; c 2. *Educ:* Iowa State Univ, BS, 55, MS, 59, PhD(mech eng, appl mech), 64. *Mem:* Am Soc Mech Engrs; Am Soc Eng Educ; Sigma Xi. *Res:* Heat transfer and fluid mechanics, particularly testing of turbomachinery and experimental heat transfer. *Mailing Add:* 320 Riverside Dr Ames IA 50010-5973

JUNKINS, JERRY R, administration; deceased, see previous edition for last biography

JUNKINS, JOHN LEE, AEROSPACE ENGINEERING, APPLIED MATHEMATICS. *Current Pos:* distinguished chair holder, 85-89, GEORGE J EPPRIGHT ENDOWED CHAIR PROF, TEX A&M UNIV, 89-, DIR, CTR MECH & CONTROL. *Personal Data:* b Carters, Ga, May 23, 43; m 65; c 2. *Educ:* Auburn Univ, BSAE, 65; Univ Calif, Los Angeles, MS, 67, PhD(eng), 69. *Honors & Awards:* Mech & Control of Flight Award, Am Inst Aeronaut & Astronaut, 88, John Leland Atwood Award, 88, Von Karman Lect, 97. *Prof Exp:* Aerospace engr, NASA, 62-65; engr & scientist aerospace eng, McDonnell Douglas Astronaut Co, 65-70; assoc prof, Univ Va, 70-78; prof eng mech, Va Polytech Inst, 78-85. *Concurrent Pos:* Consult, US Naval Surface Weapons Labs, 70-73, US Army Topog Maps Command, 71-74, Univ Space Res Asn, 75-76, US Engr Topog Lab, 77-, US Defense Mapping Agency, 77-, Univ Va, 78-; prin investr, Apollo 15-17 Lunar Sci Team, 74-77; assoc ed, J Astronaut Sci, 77- *Mem:* Nat Acad Eng; Am Inst Aeronaut & Astronaut; Am Geophys Union; Am Astronaut Soc; Am Soc Photogram; Int Acad Astronaut. *Res:* Satellite dynamics and control; mathematical modeling of dynamical systems; geophysics; remote sensing; author of over 330 publications and 3 textbooks; granted patent. *Mailing Add:* Dept Aerospace Eng Tex A&M Univ College Station TX 77843

JUO, PEI-SHOW, BIOCHEMISTRY, MOLECULAR BIOLOGY. *Current Pos:* assoc prof, 68-74, PROF BIOL, STATE UNIV NY COL, POTSDAM, 74- *Personal Data:* b Shantung, China, Feb 6, 30; m 65. *Educ:* Taiwan Prov Chung Hsing Univ, BS, 57; Univ Toronto, MS, 63; Univ NH, PhD(virol), 66. *Prof Exp:* Res biochemist, Kitchawan Res Lab, 66-67 & Gulf South Res Inst, 67-68. *Mem:* AAAS; Am Soc Microbiol. *Res:* Purification and characterization of proteins and other macromolecules; immunological and electrophoretic analysis of protein antigens. *Mailing Add:* Dept Biol State Univ NY 44 Pierrepont Ave Potsdam NY 13676-2200

JUODKA, BENEDIKTAS, BIOCHEMISTRY. *Current Pos:* Lectr, 68-69, sr lectr, 69-71, HEAD BIOCHEM DEPT, VILNIUS UNIV, LITHUANIA, 71-, PROF 82-, VICE-RECTOR, 91-; PRES, LITHUANIAN ACAD SCI, 92- *Personal Data:* b Utena, Lithuania, Jan 13, 43; m 68, Tiina Pusse; c Robert. *Educ:* Moscow State Univ, MS, 65, PhD, 68. *Honors & Awards:* Lithuania State Award in Sci. *Concurrent Pos:* Mem Sci Coun, Vilnius, 91-93; adv res & educ, Lithuanian Govt, Vilnius, 93-94. *Mem:* Lithuanian Acad Sci; NY Acad Sci; Latvian Acad Sci. *Res:* Chemistry and biochemistry of nucleic acids. *Mailing Add:* Lithuanian Acad Sci Gedimino pr 3 Vilnius 2600 Lithuania. *Fax:* 370-2-61-11-79; *E-Mail:* benediktas.juodka@cz.vu.lt

JUOLA, ROBERT C, STATISTICS, MATHEMATICS. *Current Pos:* assoc chmn dept, 70-77, PROF MATH, BOISE STATE UNIV, 70- *Personal Data:* b Astoria, Ore, Aug 8, 40; m 63; c 2. *Educ:* Univ Ore, BS, 62; Mich State Univ, MS, 64, PhD(statist), 68. *Prof Exp:* Res engr, Boeing Co, 64-66; asst prof math, Univ Tex, Austin, 68-70. *Mem:* AAAS; Inst Math Statist; Am Statist Asn; Sigma Xi. *Res:* Design of experiments; sequential experimentation. *Mailing Add:* Dept Math Boise State Univ 1910 University Boise ID 83725

JUORIO, AUGUSTO VICTOR, NEUROPHARMACOLOGY. *Current Pos:* res pharmacologist, 73-77, head basic studies, 77-83, SR SCIENTIST, NEUROPSYCHIAT RES UNIT, UNIV SASK, SASKATOON, 83-, PROF, DEPT PSYCHIAT, 95- *Personal Data:* b Buenos Aires, Arg, July 13, 34; m 61; c 2. *Educ:* Univ Buenos Aires, BSP, 58, BSc, 61, PhD(pharmacol), 67. *Prof Exp:* Demonstr pharmacol, Fac Pharm Biochem, Univ Buenos Aires, 59-63; res fel, Inst Animal Physiol, Babraham, Cambridge, Eng, 63-66; asst prof, Fac Pharm Biochem, Univ Buenos Aires, 66-68; res fel, Univ Col, Univ London, 68-73. *Mem:* Am Soc Pharmacol & Exp Therapeut; Brit Pharmacol Soc; Int Soc Neurochem; Can Col Neuropsychopharmacol; Pharmacol Soc Can; Soc Neurosci; Int Brain Res Orgn; Am Soc Neurochem. *Res:* Molecular mechanisms of neurotransmitter action in the central nervous system and of drugs used to alleviate abnormal mental conditions; neuroprotective mechanisms in neural cultures and in animal models. *Mailing Add:* Neuropsychiat Res Unit CMR Bldg Univ Sask Saskatoon SK S7N 0W0 Can. *E-Mail:* juorio@sask.usask.ca

JUPNIK, HELEN, OPTICS. *Current Pos:* res physicist, Am Optical Co, 43-48, sr res physicist, 48-58, supvr thin films, 58-59, chief physicist, 59-65, mgr thin film develop, 65-67, MGR THIN FILM TECH, SCI INSTRUMENT DIV, AM OPTICAL CORP, 67- *Personal Data:* b Kenosha, Wis, Sept 30, 15. *Educ:* Univ Wis, BA & MA, 37; Univ Rochester, PhD(physics), 40. *Prof Exp:* Asst physics, Univ Wis, 37; asst instr, Univ Rochester, 37-40; Huff fel, Bryn Mawr Col, 40-41; Berliner res docentship fel, 41-42; asst, Princeton Univ, 42; physicist, Nat Res Corp, 42-43. *Mem:* Am Phys Soc; fel Optical Soc Am; Am Vacuum Soc; NY Acad Sci. *Res:* Physical optics; evaporation and properties of thin films; microscopy. *Mailing Add:* 40 Meadowview Lane Buffalo NY 14221

JURA, MICHAEL ALAN, ASTROPHYSICS. *Current Pos:* asst prof, 74-77, assoc prof, 77-81, PROF ASTRON, UNIV CALIF, LOS ANGELES, 81- *Personal Data:* b Oakland, Calif, Sept 11, 47; m 74; c 1. *Educ:* Univ Calif, Berkeley, BA, 67; Harvard Univ, MA, 69, PhD(astron), 71. *Prof Exp:* Res assoc astron, Goddard Space Flight Ctr, NASA, 71 & Princeton Univ Observ, 73-74. *Concurrent Pos:* Alfred P Sloan Found fel, 77-79. *Mem:* Int Astron Union; Am Astron Soc. *Res:* Physics of the interstellar medium and problems in star formation. *Mailing Add:* Dept Astron Univ Calif 405 Hilgard Ave Los Angeles CA 90024

JURAN, JOSEPH M, QUALITY MANAGEMENT. *Current Pos:* chmn, 79-87, EMER CHMN, JURAN INST INC, 87- *Personal Data:* b Braila, Rumania, Dec 24, 04; US citizen; m 26; c 4. *Educ:* Univ Minn, BS, 24; Loyola Univ, JD, 35. *Hon Degrees:* DSc, Roch Inst Tech & Univ Minn, 92; LLD, Univ New Haven, 92. *Honors & Awards:* Order of the Sacred Treasure, Emperor of Japan, 81; Nat Medal Technol, President of the US, 92. *Prof Exp:* engr, Western Elec Co, 24-41; asst adminr, Foreign Econ Admin, US Govt, 41-45; prof & chmn indust eng, NY Univ, 45-51; consult, 51-79. *Concurrent Pos:* Mem var int & US comts, Am Soc Qual Control. *Mem:* Nat Acad Eng; Am Soc Mech Engrs; Am Soc Qual Control; Am Inst Indust Engrs; Sigma Xi. *Res:* Pioneer in creating consulting in quality, world-wide, concept of quality improvement; author of 15 books, 40 videocassettes, numerous training manuals, and over 200 published papers. *Mailing Add:* 11 River Rd PO Box 811 Wilton CT 06897-0811. Fax: 203-834-9891

JURAND, JERRY GEORGE, PERIODONTOLOGY, IMMUNOLOGY. *Current Pos:* assoc prof, 65-70, PROF PERIODONT, COL DENT, UNIV TENN, MEMPHIS, 70- *Personal Data:* b Gostyn, Poland, Apr 23, 23; US citizen; m 50, Ruth Kujus; c Lydia, Robert & Darlene. *Educ:* Univ Erlangen, DMD, 56; Univ Tenn, Memphis, DDS, 65. *Prof Exp:* Cancer res scientist, Roswell Park Mem Inst, 58-62; res assoc immunol, St Jude Childrens Res Hosp, Memphis, 62-65. *Concurrent Pos:* Consult, St Jude Children's Res Hosp, 65- *Mem:* AAAS; NY Acad Sci; Int Asn Dent Res; Am Dent Asn. *Res:* Immunohistochemical identification and localization of antibodies in humans and animals; tumor immunology; immunological reactions in etiology of periodontal disease; growth factors in oro-facial development; collagen in normal and diseased gingiva. *Mailing Add:* Col Dent Univ Tenn Memphis TN 38163

JURASEK, LUBOMIR, PROTEIN CHEMISTRY, MICROBIOLOGY. *Current Pos:* CONSULT, 97- *Personal Data:* b Uzhorod, Czech, June 2, 31; m 57; c 3. *Educ:* Purkyne Univ Brno, MSc, 54, PhD(biol), 63. *Prof Exp:* Res officer mycol, State Forest Prod Res Inst, Bratislava, Czech, 54-64; fel enzymol, Nat Res Coun Can, 64-66; res scientist microbiol, State Forest Prod Res Inst, 66-68; res assoc protein chem, Univ Alta, Edmonton, 68-75; prin scientist & head, Biol Chem Sect, Pulp & Paper Res Inst Can, 75-97. *Concurrent Pos:* Lectr, Dept Biochem, Univ Alta, 73-75. *Res:* Molecular mechanism of biological degradation of cellulose, hemicelluloses and lignin; lignin degrading enzymes; molecular modelling of eignin. *Mailing Add:* 29 Nobel Kirkland PQ H9H 4J5 Can

JURASKA, JANICE MARIE, BIOPSYCHOLOGY. *Current Pos:* NIMH fel, 78-79, assoc prof, 86-94, PROF, DEPT PSYCHOL, UNIV ILL, 94- *Personal Data:* b Berwyn, Ill, Feb 9, 49; m 86, William T Greenough. *Educ:* Lawrence Univ, BA, 71; Univ Ill, Champaign, MA, 75; Univ Colo, PhD(biopsychol), 77. *Prof Exp:* Asst prof biopsychol, Dept Psychol, Ind Univ, 80-85, assoc prof, 85. *Mem:* Fel Am Psychol Soc; Int Soc Develop Psychobiol; Soc Neurosci; Int Acad Sex Res. *Res:* Plasticity and development of the nervous system (anatomy) and of behavior; sex differences in the brain; effects of the estrous cycle. *Mailing Add:* Dept Psychol Univ Ill 603 E Daniel Champaign IL 61820

JURCH, GEORGE RICHARD, JR, PHYSICAL ORGANIC CHEMISTRY. *Current Pos:* from asst prof to assoc prof, 66-80, PROF CHEM, UNIV SFLA, 80- *Personal Data:* b New Britain, Conn, Feb 1, 34; m 61, Molly I Brown; c George III, Steven & Carol. *Educ:* Univ Fla, BS, 57; Univ Ky, MS, 61; Univ Calif, San Diego, PhD(chem), 65. *Prof Exp:* Res chemist, IBM Corp, Ky, 61; NIH fel chem, Yale Univ, 65-66, res assoc, 66. *Mem:* Am Chem Soc; Sigma Xi. *Res:* Radical-cation intermediates; free radicals; sulfur chemistry, nonaqueous solvent interactions with biological systems; nuclear magnetic resonance conformation studies. *Mailing Add:* Dept Chem Univ SFla Tampa FL 33620. Fax: 813-974-3203

JURD, LEONARD, CHEMISTRY. *Current Pos:* Res chemist, 59-70, RES LEADER NAT PROD CHEM, AGR RES SERV, USDA, 70- *Personal Data:* b Sydney, Australia, Dec 3, 25; US citizen; m 61; c 2. *Educ:* Univ Sydney, BSc, 47; Univ Nottingham, England, PhD(org chem), 53. *Hon Degrees:* DSc, Univ Sydney, 71. *Honors & Awards:* Agr Chem Award, Am Chem Soc, 77. *Mem:* Phytochem Soc NAm (pres, 62); Am Chem Soc. *Res:* Isolation and structure of biologically active plant products. *Mailing Add:* 1054 Park Hills Rd Berkeley CA 94708-1745

JURETSCHKE, HELLMUT JOSEPH, SOLID STATE PHYSICS. *Current Pos:* From instr to assoc prof, 50-59, actg head dept, 65-66, head dept, 66-77, PROF PHYSICS, POLYTECH UNIV, 59- *Personal Data:* b Berlin, Ger, Aug 9, 24; nat US; m 50, Ruth M Tarno; c Susan & Annette. *Educ:* Harvard Univ, BS, 44, MA, 47, PhD(physics), 50. *Concurrent Pos:* NSF Fac Fel, Grenoble 64-65; vis fel, Royal Melbourne Inst Technol & Univ Melbourne, 85. *Mem:* Fel Am Phys Soc; Am Asn Physics Teachers; Sigma Xi; Am Crystallog Asn. *Res:* Surface properties of metals; electronic structure of metals; dynamical theory of x-rays. *Mailing Add:* 41 Eastern Pkwy Brooklyn NY 11238. *E-Mail:* hjuretsc@photon.poly.edu

JURF, AMIN N, PHYSIOLOGY. *Current Pos:* Res scientist, 61-66, from instr to asst prof, 66-74, assoc prof renal physiol, 74-76, ASST PROF PHYSIOL, UNIV MD, BALTIMORE CITY, 76- *Personal Data:* b Syria, Dec 3, 32; US citizen; m 58; c 3. *Educ:* Western Md Col, BA, 59; Univ Md, PhD(physiol), 66. *Res:* Neuro-renal physiology; salt and water metabolism. *Mailing Add:* Dept Physiol Univ Md Sch Med Baltimore MD 21201

JURGELSKI, WILLIAM, JR, EXPERIMENTAL CARCINOGENESIS, TOXICOLOGY. *Current Pos:* EMERGENCY RM PHYSICIAN, CRAVEN COUNTY HOSP, NEWBERN, NC, 90- *Personal Data:* b Englishtown, NJ, May 25, 31; m 54; c 2. *Educ:* Rutgers Univ, BS, 53, MS, 55, PhD(genetics), 58; Duke Univ, MD, 67. *Prof Exp:* Geneticist, Fed Exp Sta in PR, Agr Res Serv, USDA, 57-60; pharmacologist, Food & Drug Admin, 60-63; res assoc path, Med Ctr, Duke Univ, 63-67, intern, 67-68; med officer, Nat Inst Environ Health Sci, 68- *Concurrent Pos:* Fel neuropath, Duke Univ, 67-68. *Mem:* AAAS; Am Asn Pathologists; Am Asn Cancer Res. *Res:* Carcinogenesis and and pediatric cancer; the marsupial as an experimental animal. *Mailing Add:* 3211 Oak Knob Ct Hillsborough NC 27278

JURGENS, MARSHALL HERMAN, ANIMAL SCIENCE & NUTRITION, ANIMAL HUSBANDRY. *Current Pos:* from asst prof to assoc prof, 68-78, PROF, ANIMAL SCI DEPT, IOWA STATE UNIV, 78- *Personal Data:* b Minden, Nebr, Dec 26, 41; m 64; c 2. *Educ:* Univ Nebr, BS, 64, MS, 66, PhD(animal sci), 69. *Prof Exp:* Res asst, animal sci dept, Univ Nebr, 64-67, asst instr, 66. *Mem:* Am Soc Animal Sci; Am Asn Feed Microscopists. *Res:* Nutrient-energy relationships in diet of the growing-finishing pig. *Mailing Add:* Animal Sci Iowa State Univ Ames IA 50011-2010

JURGENSEN, DELBERT F(REDERICK), JR, CHEMICAL ENGINEERING. *Current Pos:* RETIRED. *Personal Data:* b St Paul, Minn, Mar 31, 09; m 28; c 3. *Educ:* Univ Minn, BChE, 31, MS, 32, PhD(chem eng), 34. *Prof Exp:* Chemist, Pure Oil Co, 34-35; res supvr, US Gypsum Co, 35-42; chief engr, Chem Warfare Serv Develop Lab, Mass Inst Technol, 42-45; dir chem res & develop & chief engr, Spec Projs Dept, Am Mach & Foundry Co, NY, 46-52, spec asst to vpres res & develop, 60-64; dir eng & develop, Congoleum Nairn Inc, 52-56; vpres develop & res, Blaw-Knox Co, Pittsburgh, 56-60; consult mgt engr, 64- *Mem:* Am Chem Soc; Asn Res Dirs; Am Inst Chemists; Am Inst Chem Engrs. *Res:* Technical administration; heat transfer; development of equipment and processes for industrial promotion; commercial development and research and development administration; chemical process industries. *Mailing Add:* 10777 W Sample Rd Coral Springs FL 33065-3771

JURIC, DAMIR, FLUID DYNAMICS & HEAT TRANSFER, NUMERICAL METHODS. *Current Pos:* POSTDOCTORAL ASSOC, LOS ALAMOS NAT LAB, 96- *Personal Data:* b Dusseldorf, Ger, June 10, 65. *Educ:* Worcester Polytech Inst, BS, 87, MS, 90; Univ Mich, PhD(mech eng), 96. *Prof Exp:* Aerodyn engr, Pratt & Whitney Aircraft, 87-91. *Mem:* Am Soc Mech Engrs; Am Inst Aeronaut & Astronaut; Am Soc Eng Educ. *Res:* Fluid dynamics and heat transfer in multiphase, multicomponent processes with interdisciplinary applications in materials; chemical processing, manufacturing, combustion; thermal management, multiphase flows in microgravity. *Mailing Add:* Los Alamos Nat Lab MSB216 Los Alamos NM 87545. Fax: 505-665-5926; *E-Mail:* djuric@lanl.gov

JURICA, GERALD MICHAEL, ATMOSPHERIC PHYSICS. *Current Pos:* ASSOC PROF ATMOSPHERIC SCI, TEX TECH UNIV, 75- *Personal Data:* b Detroit, Mich, Sept 24, 41; m 78; c 3. *Educ:* Univ Detroit, BEE, 63; Univ Ariz, MS, 66, PhD(atmospheric sci), 70. *Prof Exp:* Res assoc, Univ Ariz, 67-70; asst prof, Purdue Univ, 70-75. *Mem:* Am Meteorol Soc; Sigma Xi. *Res:* Satellite meteorology; cloud physical processes. *Mailing Add:* Dept Geosci Tex Tech Univ Lubbock TX 79409-0001

JURICIC, DAVOR, MECHANICAL SYSTEMS DESIGN, COMPUTER AIDED DESIGN. *Current Pos:* PROF MECH ENG, UNIV TEX, AUSTIN, 78- *Personal Data:* b Split, Yugoslavia, Aug 2, 28; m 53; c 1. *Educ:* Univ Belgrade, BSc, 52, DSc, 64. *Prof Exp:* Analyst aircraft struct, Icarus-Belgrade, Yugoslavia, 53-58; res fel aeroelasticity, Inst Aeronaut, Zarkovo-Belgrade, 58-63; from asst prof to assoc prof aeronaut eng, Univ Belgrade, 63-68; from assoc prof to prof mech eng, SDak State Univ, 68-75; vis prof appl mech, Stanford Univ, 75-78. *Concurrent Pos:* Consult, Elec Power Res Inst, Palo Alto, Flow Res, Inc, Kent, Wash, 76-, Southern Res Inst, Birmingham, Joy Mfg Co, Los Angeles & Dresser Industs, Houston, 78- *Mem:* Am Soc Eng Educ; Ger Soc Appl Math & Mech; Am Soc Mech Engrs; Sigma Xi. *Res:* Aircraft vibration and flutter; dynamics of railway vehicles; dynamics and stability of bipedal locomotion; modeling and simulation of dynamic systems; mechanical systems design; electrostatic precipitators. *Mailing Add:* 2011 Mistywood Dr Austin TX 78746

JURINAK, JEROME JOSEPH, SOIL PHYSICAL CHEMISTRY, ENVIRONMENTAL ASSESSMENT. *Current Pos:* dept head, 78-83, prof, 67-93, EMER PROF SOIL CHEM, COL AGR, UTAH STATE UNIV, 93- *Personal Data:* b Cleveland, Ohio, June 3, 27; m 54, Mary A Zychowski; c Jeff, Jane, David & Victoria. *Educ:* Colo State Univ, BS, 51; Utah State Univ, MS, 54, PhD(soil chem), 56. *Prof Exp:* Jr soil chemist, Univ Calif, Davis, 56-58, from asst to assoc soil chemist, 58-67. *Concurrent Pos:* Danforth teaching fel; consult, USAID, UNESCO, Orgn Am States & pvt indust; vis prof, Rural Univ Rio de Janeiro, Brazil, 75, 77 & Haryana Univ, India; div chmn, Soil Sci Soc Am, 75; vis prof, Univ Calif, Davis, 91. *Mem:* Fel Am Soc Agron; fel Soil Sci Soc Am; Int Soc Soil Sci; fel Am Inst Chem; Coun Agr Sci

Technol; fel AAAS. *Res:* Reclamation of disturbed soils and geologic material; trace element chemistry and transport in soils; salt-affected soils; environmental soil chemistry; surface chemistry. *Mailing Add:* Dept Plants Soils & Biometeorol Utah State Univ Logan UT 84322-4820. *Fax:* 435-750-3376

JURINSKI, NEIL B(ERNARD), INDUSTRIAL HYGIENE, ENVIRONMENTAL CHEMISTRY. *Current Pos:* PRES, NUCHEM CO, INC, 75- *Personal Data:* b Peekskill, NY, Oct 28, 38; m 62; c 3. *Educ:* State Univ NY, Albany, BS, 60; Univ Miss, PhD(phys chem), 63; Am Bd Indust Hyg, cert, 74. *Prof Exp:* Res assoc chem, Mich State Univ, 63-64; asst prof, Boston Col, 64-69; res scientist, Chem Div, J M Huber Corp, 69-72; environ chemist, US Army Environ Hyg Agency, 72-76; sr indust hygienist, SRI Int, 76-77; indust hygienist, Tracor Jitco, Inc, 77-80. *Concurrent Pos:* Consult, 70- *Mem:* Am Indust Hyg Asn; Am Acad Indust Hyg; Am Chem Soc; Royal Soc Chem; Int Hazard Control Mgt Asn; NY Acad Sci. *Res:* Industrial hygiene surveys and consultation; hazardous and toxic chemical problems; waste disposal and processing; carcinogen/mutagen safety; environmental sampling and analysis; material handling and processing. *Mailing Add:* 9321 Raintree Rd Burke VA 22015

JURIST, JOHN MICHAEL, BIOPHYSICS. *Current Pos:* PRES, CRM INC, 82- *Personal Data:* b Williamsport, Pa, Oct 13, 43; m 64; c 2. *Educ:* Univ Calif, Los Angeles, AB, 64, MS, 66, PhD(biophys), 68. *Prof Exp:* Proj assoc med physics, 68-69, asst prof orthop surg & space sci & eng, 69-71, asst prof orthop surg, Univ Wis-Madison, 71-76; res assoc, Mont State Univ, 76-77, sr res engr, 77-78, assoc res biophysicist, 78-80, adj pro med sci, 80-82. *Concurrent Pos:* NASA fel, Univ Wis-Madison, 68-69; prin investr, NIH grants, 70-78; biophysicist, St Vincent Hosp, Billings, 76-82; consult, Deaconess Hosp, Billings, 84-85, Mont State Bd Health, 87- *Mem:* AAAS; Geront Soc; NY Acad Sci; Orthop Res Soc; Aerospace Med Asn. *Res:* Osteoporosis; nondestructive evaluation of skeletal status; application of computers to medical practice; medical thermography. *Mailing Add:* 2520 17th St W Billings MT 59102. *Fax:* 406-245-6775

JURKA, JERZY W, BIOINFORMATICS, COMPUTATIONAL MOLECULAR BIOLOGY. *Current Pos:* PRES, GENETIC INFO RES INST, 94- *Personal Data:* b Ponikiew, Poland, June 4, 50; US citizen; m 81, Elzbieta Nowak; c Michael, Matthew & Timothy. *Educ:* Jagiellonski Univ, Poland, MSc,73; Univ Warsaw, DSc, 79. *Prof Exp:* Vis scientist, Dept Med Physics, Karolinska Inst, Univ Stockholm, 82-83; postdoctoral fel, Dept Microbiol & Immunol, Univ Mich, 83-84, Dept Biochem & Biophysics, Univ Houston, 84-86; res fel, Dept Biostat, Dana Farber Cancer Inst, Harvard Sch Pub Health, 86-87; scientist, Bionet, 87-89; res scientist, Linus Pauling Inst Sci & Med, 89-90, dir comput resources, 90-92, asst dir res, 92-94, dir bioinformatics, 94-95. *Concurrent Pos:* Prin investr, Dept Energy, 91-97, NIH, 92-95 & 96- *Mem:* Int Soc Molecular Evolution; AAAS. *Res:* Identification and systematic studies of mobile elements and their impact on eukaryotic genomes, using computer assisted analyses of DNA sequence data. *Mailing Add:* 1190 Eureka Ave Los Altos CA 94024. *E-Mail:* jurka@gnomic.stanford.edu

JURKAT, MARTIN PETER, MANAGEMENT SCIENCE, MATHEMATICS. *Current Pos:* staff scientist, Davidson Lab, 64-76, dir, Ctr Munic Studies & Servs, 76-78, prof, 78-80, ALEXANDER CROMBIC HUMPHREYS PROF MGT SCI, STEVENS INST TECHNOL, 80- *Personal Data:* b Berlin, Germany, July 23, 35; m 58; c 3. *Educ:* Swarthmore Col, BA, 57; Univ NC, MA, 60; Stevens Inst Technol, PhD(math), 72, MEng, 83. *Prof Exp:* Statistician, Marketer's Res Serv, Inc, 59-60; asst engr, Res Lab, Burroughs Corp, 60-61; sr systs analyst, ITT Info Systs Div, 61-64. *Concurrent Pos:* Consult, Tank Automotive Command, US Army. *Mem:* Opers Res Soc Am; Comput Soc Inst Elec & Electronics Engrs; Asn Comput Mach. *Res:* Mathematical modelling; simulation; off-road vehicle design and modelling; computer graphics; transportation systems; operations research; expert systems. *Mailing Add:* 706 Hudson St Hoboken NJ 07030

JURKAT, WOLFGANG BERNHARD, mathematical analysis, for more information see previous edition

JURKIEWICZ, MAURICE J, SURGERY. *Current Pos:* PROF SURG, SCH MED, EMORY UNIV, 73- *Personal Data:* b Claremont, NH, Sept 24, 23; m 51; c 2. *Educ:* Univ Md, DDS, 46; Harvard Univ, MD, 52. *Prof Exp:* Instr surg, Sch Med, Washington Univ, 57-59; from asst prof to prof surg, Col Med, Univ Fla, 59-73, chief plastic surg, 64-73. *Concurrent Pos:* Clin fel plastic surg, Barnes Hosp, St Louis, Mo, 58-59; mem bd sci counr, Nat Inst Dent Res, 66-71; chief surg serv, Vet Admin Hosp, Gainesville, 68-73; lectr & consult, Naval Hosp, 69-70; consult plastic surg, Walter Reed Hosp, Washington, DC, 70- *Mem:* AAAS; Am Col Surg; AMA; Am Soc Plastic & Reconstruct Surg; Plastic Surg Res Coun. *Res:* Wound healing; congenital malformations; general and reconstructive surgery; head and neck surgery. *Mailing Add:* 25 Prescott St Atlanta GA 30308. *Fax:* 404-686-5974

JURKUS, ALGIRDAS PETRAS, ELECTRONICS. *Current Pos:* RES SCIENTIST ELECTRONICS, NAT RES COUN CAN, 60- *Personal Data:* b Klaipeda, Lithuania, June 11, 35; Can citizen. *Educ:* Univ Montreal, BASc, 57; Univ Sheffield, PhD(elec eng), 60. *Mem:* Inst Elec & Electronics Engrs. *Res:* Establishment and maintenance of primary national standards and development of precise methods of measurement, at high and microwave frequencies, of various electromagnetic quantities. *Mailing Add:* Inst Nat Measurement Standards Nat Res Coun Ottawa ON K1A 0R6 Can

JURMAIN, ROBERT DOUGLAS, PHYSICAL ANTHROPOLOGY. *Current Pos:* Asst prof, 75-79, ASSOC PROF ANTHROP, SAN JOSE STATE UNIV, 79- *Personal Data:* b Worcester, Mass, July 20, 48; m 74. *Educ:* Univ Calif, Los Angeles, AB, 70; Harvard Univ, PhD(anthrop), 75. *Mem:* Am Asn Phys Anthropologists. *Res:* Paleopathology of prehistoric human osteological remains; comparative biomechanical studies of primate limb skeletons; paeloanthropological research of early hominids in East Africa. *Mailing Add:* Biol Sci San Jose State Univ 1 Washington Sq San Jose CA 95192-0001

JURRIS, ERIC R, TECHNOLOGY TRANSFER. *Current Pos:* DIR, OFFICE TECHNOL TRANSFER, CITY OF HOPE NAT MED CTR, 86- *Personal Data:* b Ohio. *Res:* Technology transfer. *Mailing Add:* City of Hope Nat Med Ctr 1500 E Duarte Rd Duarte CA 91010

JURS, PETER CHRISTIAN, ANALYTICAL CHEMISTRY. *Current Pos:* from asst prof to assoc prof, 69-78, PROF CHEM, PA STATE UNIV, 78- *Personal Data:* b Oakland, Calif, Apr 13, 43; m 67; c 3. *Educ:* Stanford Univ, BS, 65; Univ Wash, PhD(chem), 69. *Honors & Awards:* Computers in Chem Award, Am Chem Soc, 90. *Concurrent Pos:* Prog dir chem anal, Chem Div, NSF, 83-84. *Mem:* Am Chem Soc; AAAS; Asn Comput Machinery. *Res:* Computer methods in analytical chemistry; structure-activity studies; computer applications in chemistry; studies of relations between molecular structure and biological activity (pharmacological effects, carcinogenic potential, odor); chemical applications of pattern recognition; computer-assisted structure elucidation. *Mailing Add:* Dept Chem Pa State Univ University Park PA 16802. *E-Mail:* pcj@psu.edu

JURSINIC, PAUL ANDREW, biophysics, for more information see previous edition

JURTSHUK, PETER, JR, MICROBIAL PHYSIOLOGY, BIOCHEMISTRY. *Current Pos:* assoc prof, 70-76, undergrad chmn biol, 77-81, PROF BIOL, UNIV HOUSTON, 76 - *Personal Data:* b New York, NY, July 28, 29; m 71, Rebecca J Jones; c Peter III & Larissa. *Educ:* NY Univ, AB, 51; Creighton Univ, MS, 53; Univ Md, PhD(microbiol), 57. *Honors & Awards:* Distinguished Serv Award, Am Soc Microbiol, 82. *Prof Exp:* Asst microbiol, Univ Md, 53-56; asst prof pharmacol, Brooklyn Col Pharm, 57-59; fel enzyme chem, Inst Enzyme Res, Univ Wis, 59-63; from asst prof to assoc prof, Univ Tex, Austin, 63-70. *Mem:* AAAS; fel Am Acad Microbiol; Am Soc Microbiol; Am Chem Soc; Am Soc Biochem & Molecular Biol. *Res:* Isolation and characterization of oxidases and oxygenating enzyme complexes from microorganisms; aspects of the microbiological oxidase reaction relating to cellular bioenergetics; microbial taxonomy specifically, on Bacillus and Azotobacter species. *Mailing Add:* Dept Biol Univ Houston Houston TX 77204-5513. *Fax:* 713-743-2636

JURY, ELIAHU I(BRAHAM), ELECTRICAL ENGINEERING. *Current Pos:* From instr to prof elec eng, 53-81, EMER PROF, UNIV CALIF, BERKELEY, 81-; EMER RES PROF, DEPT ELEC & COMPUT ENG, UNIV MIAMI, 880. *Personal Data:* b Bagdad, Iraq, May 23, 23; nat US; m 49; c 2. *Educ:* Israel Inst Technol, EE, 47; Harvard Univ, MS, 49; Columbia Univ, EngScD, 53. *Hon Degrees:* DrSc Tech, Swiss Fed Inst Tech, Zörich, Switz, 82. *Honors & Awards:* Rufus Oldenburger Medal, Amer Soc Mech Engrs, 86; Technol Founder Award, Am Technol Soc, 90; Phoebe H Hearst Medal, Univ Calif, Berkeley, 91; Heritage Medal, Am Contrib Coun, 93. *Concurrent Pos:* Res engr, Columbia Univ, 53-54; consult, Bell Tel Labs, 56 & Convair Div, Gen Dynamics Corp, 57; vis lectr, Northwestern Univ, 57, Univ Mich, 58, Univ Paris, 58-59, Imperial Col Sci, London, 64-65; distinguished scholar, Univ Miami, 88. *Mem:* Fel mem Inst Elec & Electronics Engrs. *Res:* Sampled-data and discrete systems; automatic control; circuit theory; transform methods; information theory; digital and sampled-data control systems. *Mailing Add:* Dept Elec Eng Univ Miami PO Box 248294 Coral Gables FL 33124

JURY, WILLIAM AUSTIN, SOIL PHYSICS, ENVIRONMENTAL PHYSICS. *Current Pos:* from asst prof to assoc prof, 74-82, PROF SOIL PHYSICS, DEPT SOIL & ENVIRON SCI, UNIV CALIF, RIVERSIDE, 82- *Personal Data:* b Highland Park, Mich, Aug 8, 46; m 72. *Educ:* Univ Mich, BS, 68; Univ Wis, MS, 70, PhD(physics), 73. *Prof Exp:* Proj assoc soil physics, Dept Soil Sci, Univ Wis, 73-74. *Concurrent Pos:* Mem, Nat Comn, Nat Res Coun/Inst Ecol, 74-75; consult, Rockwell Hanford Oper, 76-79 & County of San Diego, 78-79. *Mem:* Am Soc Agron; Soil Sci Soc Am; Int Soil Sci Soc; Am Geophys Union; AAAS. *Res:* Measurement and modeling of water, heat and chemical transport through and reactions in soil. *Mailing Add:* Dept Soil Univ Calif 900 University Ave Riverside CA 92521-0101

JUSINSKI, LEONARD EDWARD, SOLID STATE PHYSICS, PHYSICAL CHEMISTRY. *Current Pos:* PHYSICIST, SRI INT, 83- *Personal Data:* b Oakland, Calif, Aug 12, 55; m 77; c 4. *Educ:* Univ San Francisco, BS, 77. *Prof Exp:* Physicist, USAF Weapons Lab, 77-81; engr, Varian Assocs, 82. *Res:* Laser-induced fluorescence; multi-photon ionization; author/co-author of 45 publications. *Mailing Add:* 3432 Little Ct Fremont CA 94538

JUSKO, WILLIAM JOSEPH, PHARMACY. *Current Pos:* assoc prof, 72-77, vchmn dept, 84-87, PROF PHARMACEUT, SCH PHARM, STATE UNIV NY, BUFFALO, 77- *Personal Data:* b Salamanca, NY, Oct 26, 42; m 64, 96, Malgorzata Sidor; c 3. *Educ:* State Univ NY, Buffalo, BS, 65, PhD(pharmaceut), 70. *Hon Degrees:* Dr, Med Acad Crakow, 87. *Honors & Awards:* Rawls Palmer Award, Am Soc Clin Pharmacol & Therapeut, 87;

Russell Miller Award, Am Col Clin Pharm 88, Distinguished Serv Award, 89. *Prof Exp:* Pharmacologist, Vet Admin Hosp, Boston, 70-72. *Concurrent Pos:* Dir, Clin Pharmacokinetics Lab, Millard Fillmore Hosp, Buffalo, 72-81; Fulbright fel, 78; consult, Wyeth Labs, Biogen, Bristol Myers Squibb. *Mem:* Fel Am Pharmaceut Asn; fel AAAS; Am Soc Clin Pharmacol & Therapeut; Am Soc Microbiol; fel Am Asn Pharmaceut Sci; Am Soc Pharmacol & Exp Therapeut; fel Am Col Clin Pharmacol. *Res:* Basic and clinical pharmacokinetics and pharmacodynamics; biopharmaceutics; drug analysis and pharmacodynamics; chemotherapy. *Mailing Add:* Sch Pharm Dept Pharmaceut State Univ NY Buffalo Buffalo NY 14260. *Fax:* 716-645-3693; *E-Mail:* wjjusko@acsu.buffalo.edu

JUST, GEORGE, ORGANIC CHEMISTRY. *Current Pos:* from asst prof to assoc prof, 58-70, PROF ORG CHEM, McGILL UNIV, 70- *Personal Data:* b Kobe, Japan, May 17, 29; nat Can; m 55; c 3. *Educ:* Swiss Fed Inst Technol, Ing Chim, 51; Univ Western Ont, PhD(chem), 56. *Prof Exp:* Res chemist, Univ Calif, Los Angeles, 56-57 & Monsanto Can, Ltd, 57-58. *Mem:* Am Chem Soc; fel Chem Inst Can. *Res:* Natural products synthesis. *Mailing Add:* 801 Sherbrooke W McGill Univ Dept Chem Montreal PQ H3A 2K6 Can

JUST, JOHN JOSEF, DEVELOPMENTAL BIOLOGY, ENDOCRINOLOGY. *Current Pos:* asst prof biol, 70-74, ASSOC PROF BIOL, UNIV KY, 74- *Personal Data:* b Botschar, Jugoslavia, Nov 17, 38; US citizen; m 65, Jeannette Kraus; c Sharon, Diane & Steven. *Educ:* DePaul Univ, Chicago, BS, 62, MS, 64; Univ Iowa, PhD(zool), 68. *Prof Exp:* Teaching asst, DePaul Univ, 62-64; NIH fel, Iowa Univ, 65-68; fel biochem, Fla State Univ, 68-70. *Concurrent Pos:* Schmitt fel, Dept Zool, Univ Iowa, 63-64; NIH fel, Dept Chem, Fla State Univ 68-70; vis prof, Univ Bern, 76-77. *Mem:* AAAS; Am Zoologist; Sigma Xi. *Res:* Biochemical and morphological methods are used to study hormonal influence on development with particular emphasis on amphibian metamorphosis; physiological triggers for hatching of embryos. *Mailing Add:* Sch Biol Morgan Bldg Univ Ky Lexington KY 40506. *Fax:* 606-257-1717

JUST, KURT W, THEORETICAL PHYSICS. *Current Pos:* assoc prof, 61-66, PROF PHYSICS, UNIV ARIZ, 66- *Personal Data:* b Oels, Ger, May 19, 27; m 53, Sigrid Walther; c Stefan, Klemens & Felix. *Educ:* Free Univ Berlin, Dr rer nat, 54, Dr habil, 58. *Honors & Awards:* First Prize, Gravity Res Found, 65. *Prof Exp:* Asst physics, Free Univ Berlin, 50-60. *Concurrent Pos:* Sci counsr, Free Univ Berlin, 60-63; consult, Edgerton, Germeshausen & Grier, Nev, 63-64. *Mem:* Int Soc Gen Relativity & Gravitation. *Res:* Quantum field theory; quantized theory of gravity. *Mailing Add:* 1213 N Nema Ave Tucson AZ 85712. *E-Mail:* just@albert.physics.arizona.edu

JUST, RICHARD, RESOURCE ECONOMICS. *Current Pos:* chmn dept, 92-95, PROF AGR ECONS, UNIV MD, COL PARK, 85-, DISTINGUISHED UNIV PROF, 95- *Personal Data:* b Tulsa, Okla, Feb 18, 48; m 67, 89, Janet L Humphries; c Angela, David & Ronald. *Educ:* Okla State Univ, BS, 69; Univ Calif, Berkeley, MA, 71, PhD(agr econs), 72. *Honors & Awards:* Res Award, Am Agr Econ, 74, 77, 80, 81, 83, 89, 92 & 94. *Prof Exp:* Comput programmer, Okla State Univ, 66-69, assoc prof agr econs, 72-75; prof agr econs, Univ Calif, Berkeley, 75-85. *Concurrent Pos:* Consult, World Bank, 76-93, US Gen Acct Off, 79-95, Safeway Stores, Inc, 83-86, Pillsbury, 88, Price Waterhouse, 87-91 & Agtrol, 90, Drexel, 87-95, Oak Ridge Nat Lab, 76-81, Sostram, 94-95. *Mem:* Am Econ Asn; Economet Soc; fel Am Agr Econ Asn; Western Agr Econ Asn. *Res:* Welfare economics, distributional effects of agricultural policy; interaction and macroeconomic policy, land price determination, biotechnology, multi output production modeling, effects of exchange rates on agriculture, futures markets; trans-boundary resource issues. *Mailing Add:* Dept Agr & Resource Econ Univ Md College Park MD 20742-5535. *Fax:* 301-314-9879

JUSTEN, LEWIS LEO, physical chemistry, analytical chemistry, for more information see previous edition

JUSTER, NORMAN JOEL, ORGANIC CHEMISTRY, SOLID-STATE ORGANIC CHEMISTRY. *Current Pos:* INDEPENDENT CONSULT, 93- *Personal Data:* b New York, NY, Feb 19, 24; m 60, Marian R Friedman; c Jeanette, Debbi, Cindy, Robyn & Becky. *Educ:* Univ Calif, Los Angeles, BA, 43; MS, 47, PhD(org chem), 50. *Honors & Awards:* Sprenger Medal, Am Asn Consult Chemists, 71; Mfg Chemists Asn Award, 74; J Ray Risser Award, 78; Res Medal, Nat Oceanic & Atmoshperic Admin, 88. *Prof Exp:* Mem chem fac, John Muir Col, 47-55; dept phys sci, Pasadena City Col, org chem, 56-60; sr chemist & head org sect, Motorola, Inc, 60-61, mgr org-polymer labs, Semiconductors Div, 61; prof org chem, Pasadena City Col, 61-84, chmn, Dept Chem & dean, Div Phys Sci, 78-84,; vis prof, Univ Calif, Los Angeles, 84-92. *Concurrent Pos:* Res dir & consult, Photo Prod Res Lab, E I du Pont de Nemours & Co, 49-52; consult, Witco Chem Co, 53, Silverton & SIlverton, 68-78, McInherry Enterprises, 69-72 & Oncol Div, Med Res Inst Calif, 74-84; vis prof chem, Univ Calif, Los Angeles, 59-65, 67-68, 75-77 & Univ Hawaii, 73-74 & 80; res dir & consult, Motorola Semiconductor Prod, Inc, 61-65; Nat Defense Educ Act lectr, 63; res dir & consult, Energy Conversion Devices, 64; vis prof, Univ Ky, 65-66; vis lectr, Weizmann Inst Sci, Israel, 66; ed, Southern Calif Sect, Am Chem Soc, 78-84, chair, 89-91, nat coun, Am Chem Soc, 90-93. *Mem:* AAAS; Am Chem Soc; Asn Consult Chemists & Chem Eng; Soc Plastics Eng; Sigma Xi; fel NY Acad Sci. *Res:* Electronic behavior of organic solids; reactions between organic solids; studies of electret phenomena; molecular modeling for electronic properties of organic solids; syntheses of small, strained molecules; polymerization of acetylenic moieties studies. *Mailing Add:* Dept Chem & Biochem 513 N Rexford Dr Beverly Hills CA 90210-3309

JUSTESEN, DON ROBERT, NEUROPSYCHOLOGY. *Current Pos:* RETIRED. *Personal Data:* b Salt Lake City, Utah, Mar 8, 30; m 58, Patricia A Larson; c Richard, Jouille, Tracy & Anthony. *Educ:* Univ Utah, BA, 55, MA, 57, PhD, 60. *Prof Exp:* Asst prof psychol & head dept, Westminster Col, 59-62; career res scientist & dir, Neuropsychol Res Labs, Vet Admin Hosp, 62; prof psychiat & neuropsychol, Med Sch, Univ Kans, 71- *Concurrent Pos:* From asst prof to prof psychiat, Med Sch, Univ Kans, 63-71; from lectr to prof, Univ Mo, Kansas City, 63-75; vis prof, Univ Colo, 65; consult, NASA, 70-72; mem, Subcomt C-95-1 Safety Stand Non-ionizing Radiation, Am Nat Stand Inst, 75-88; assoc ed, J Microwave Power & Electromagnetic Energy, 75-88; mem, Comn A, Nat Acad Sci Int Union Radio Sci & chmn, Comt Man & Radiation, Inst Elec Electronics Engrs, 78-79; sci adv, Elec Power Res Inst, 84-87; mem, USA/USSR Sci Exchange, Non-Ionizing Radiation, 84-89; ed-in-chief, Bioelectromagnetics, 88- *Mem:* Fel Am Psychol Asn; fel AAAS; Soc Neurosci; Bioelectromagnetics Soc (pres, 84-85). *Res:* Neurophysiological correlates of behavior; biothermal correlates of emotion and arousal; biological and psychological response to non-ionizing electromagnetic radiation; philosophy of science. *Mailing Add:* 12416 Ewing Ci Grandview MO 64030

JUSTHAM, STEPHEN ALTON, CLIMATOLOGY, METEOROLOGY. *Current Pos:* chmn, Dept Geog, Kutztown Univ, 85-89, asst provost, 89-91, actg assoc vchancellor acad & student affairs, 91-92, PROF GEOG, KUTZTOWN UNIV, 83-91 & 92- *Personal Data:* b New Kensington, Pa, May 22, 37; m 68, Claudia M Fulton; c Kristin M & Cheryl L. *Educ:* Indiana Univ Pa, BS, 64, MA, 70; Univ Ill, PhD(geog), 74. *Honors & Awards:* Merit Award, Am Soc Landscape Architects, 83. *Prof Exp:* Teacher geog polit sci, Washington Twp Sch Dist, Apollo, Pa, 64-66; teacher civics, New Kensington-Arnold Sch Dist, 66-68; assoc prof geog, Ball State Univ, 71-83. *Mem:* Am Meteorol Soc; Am Geophys Union; Asn Am Geogr; Royal Meteorol Soc. *Res:* Climatology and meteorology of severe weather phenomena, specifically tornado preparedness programs; wind resource inventory and modeling. *Mailing Add:* Dept Geog Kutztown Univ Kutztown PA 19530. *Fax:* 610-683-1352; *E-Mail:* justham@kutztown.edu

JUSTICE, JAMES HORACE, exploration geophysics, for more information see previous edition

JUSTICE, KEITH EVANS, ECOLOGY. *Current Pos:* asst prof biol sci, Univ Calif, Irvine, 65-67, assoc dean grad div, 68-69, actg dean, 69-71, dean spec progs, 74-77, dean prof studies, 77-81, assoc prof ecol & evolutionary biol, 67-87, EMER PROF, UNIV CALIF, IRVINE, 87- *Personal Data:* b Arkansas City, Kans, Feb 6, 30; m 57; c 3. *Educ:* Univ Ariz, BS, 55, MS, 56, PhD(zool), 60. *Prof Exp:* Res assoc pop genetics, Columbia Univ, 59-60 & Ariz-Sonora Desert Mus, 60-62; proj engr, Melpar Inc, 62-65. *Concurrent Pos:* Res assoc, Univ Ariz, 60-62; vpres, Rocky Mt Biol Lab, Crested Butte, Colo, 66-71. *Mem:* Am Soc Mammal; Sigma Xi. *Res:* Population dynamics and behavior of desert rodents; computer assisted instruction. *Mailing Add:* 2652 E Kael St Mesa AZ 85203

JUSTIN, JAMES ROBERT, AGRONOMY, FIELD CROPS. *Current Pos:* assoc specialist, 67-75, SPECIALIST, CROPS & SOILS EXTEN, RUTGERS UNIV, NEW BRUNSWICK, 75- *Personal Data:* b Scranton, Pa, Oct 14, 33; m 57; c 2. *Educ:* Pa State Univ, BS, 55, MS, 57; Tex A&M Univ, PhD(plant breeding), 63. *Prof Exp:* Instr agron, Tex A&M Univ, 60-63; exten agronomist, Univ Minn, 63-67, from instr to asst prof agron, 64-67. *Mem:* Am Forage & Grassland Coun; Am Soc Agron; Crop Sci Soc Am; Am Soybean Asn; Asn Off Seed Certifying Agencies. *Res:* Improvement of field crop and seed production; variety testing and production research with soybeans and variety testing with forages. *Mailing Add:* 35 Rath Lane New Brunswick NJ 08816

JUSTUS, DAVID ELDON, IMMUNOLOGY, PARASITOLOGY. *Current Pos:* Fel microbiol, Sch Med, 69-70, ASST PROF MICROBIOL & IMMUNOL, UNIV LOUISVILLE, 70- *Personal Data:* b Van Buren, Mo, May 22, 36; m 60; c 5. *Educ:* Southeast Mo State Col, BS, 63; Univ Mo-Columbia, MS, 65; Univ Okla, PhD(med parasitol), 68. *Mem:* Am Soc Microbiol; Am Soc Trop Med & Hyg; Reticuloendothelial Soc. *Res:* Anaphylactic antibody and mast cell responses in mice infected with Trichinella spiralis. *Mailing Add:* Dept Microbiol Univ Louisville Sch Med 2301 S Third St Louisville KY 40292-0001

JUSTUS, JERRY T, DEVELOPMENTAL BIOLOGY. *Current Pos:* PROF BIOL, GRAND CANYON UNIV, 91- *Personal Data:* b Chicago, Ill, Oct 13, 32. *Educ:* Franklin Col, AB, 57; Ind Univ, MA, 62, PhD(endocrinol, develop biol), 65. *Prof Exp:* Teacher zool, Ind Univ, 60-61, res asst endocrinol, 61-63, res fel develop biol, 64-65; sr cancer res scientist, Springville Labs, Roswell Park Mem Inst, 66-68; from asst prof to assoc prof zool, Ariz State Univ, 68-91. *Concurrent Pos:* Am Cancer Soc Inst grant, 67-68; United Health Found grant, 67-68; Am Heart Asn grant, 67-69 & 76-78; estab investr, Am Heart Asn, 71-76. *Mem:* AAAS; NY Acad Sci; Am Soc Zool; Soc Develop Biol. *Mailing Add:* Nat Sci Grand Canyon Univ 3300 W Camelback Rd Phoenix AZ 85017-3030

JUSTUS, PHILIP STANLEY, GEOLOGY, REGULATORY GEOLOGY. *Current Pos:* geologist, US Nuclear Regulatory Comn, 80-81, sect leader, High-Level Radioactive Waste Mgt, 81-92, sr on-site licensing rep, 92-94, SR GEOLOGIST, US NUCLEAR REGULATORY COMN, 94- *Personal Data:* b New York, NY, Jan 17, 41; m 62; c 2. *Educ:* City Col New York, BS, 62; Univ NC, Chapel Hill, MS, 66, PhD, 71. *Prof Exp:* Teaching asst geol, Univ NC, 62-67, student dir seismog sta, 64-66; instr astron & phys geog, US Mil

Acad, 67-68, asst prof astron & geol, 68-70; fel, Rice Univ, 70-71; from asst prof to assoc prof geol, Fairleigh Dickinson Univ, 71-80. *Concurrent Pos:* Assoc ed, Geol Sect, NJ Acad Sci Bull & contrib ed, NJ Sci Teachers Asn Bull, 73-80; res fel, Univ London, 77. *Mem:* AAAS; Geol Soc Am; Am Geophys Union; Sigma Xi; Int Asn Eng Geol. *Res:* Textural development and crystallization of diabase dikes; determining structural metamorphic evolution of the Brevard fault zone, Blue Ridge Mountains, North Carolina; radioactive waste disposal safety evaluations; regulatory geology case studies; geological hazards risk assessment for facilities design and performance assessments. *Mailing Add:* US Nuclear Regulatory Comm Mailstop T7-C6 Washington DC 20555. *E-Mail:* psj@nre.gov

JUTAMULIA, SUGANDA, electro-optics, photonics, for more information see previous edition

JUTILA, JOHN W, IMMUNOLOGY, MEDICAL MICROBIOLOGY. *Current Pos:* from asst prof to prof microbiol & microbiologist, Mont State Univ, 61-89, dean, Col Letters & Sci, 74-78, vpres res, 78- 89, coordr develop, 90-93, EMER PROF, MONT STATE UNIV, 93- *Personal Data:* b Mullan, Idaho, May 21, 31; m 53; c 4. *Educ:* Mont State Univ, BA, 53, MA, 54; Univ Wash, PhD(microbiol), 60. *Prof Exp:* Bacteriologist, Rocky Mountain Lab, Mont, 56-57. *Concurrent Pos:* Fel, Univ Wash, 60-61; NIH grants, 62-69 & 70-76. *Mem:* Fel AAAS; fel Am Acad Microbiol; Am Soc Microbiol; Soc Ext Biol & Med; Am Asn Immunol. *Res:* Pathogenesis of wasting syndromes in mice; immunobiology of the congenitally athymic mouse and immune cell interactions with tumor cells in vivo and tissue culture systems. *Mailing Add:* 516 S Grand Ave Bozeman MT 59715

JUTILA, MARK ARTHUR, INFLAMMATORY DISEASE, DEVELOPMENTAL IMMUNOLOGY. *Current Pos:* ASST PROF IMMUNOL, MONT STATE UNIV, 89- *Personal Data:* b Seattle, Wash, Jan 31, 59; m 81, Kathryn Campbell; c Jamie, Kelly & Aaron. *Educ:* Mont State Univ, BS, 82; Wash State Univ, MS, 84, PhD(immunol & vet sci), 86. *Prof Exp:* Teaching asst, Wash State Univ, 82-86, res asst, Vet Sch, 86; fel path, Stanford Univ Sch Med, 86-89. *Concurrent Pos:* Fel, NIH Training Grant, Dept Path, Stanford Univ Sch Med, 86-88; sr fel, Am Cancer Soc, Calif Div, 88-89. *Res:* Inflammatory disease and cancer, the molecular basis for the recruitment of host defense cells from the blood into various tissues of the body. *Mailing Add:* Vet Molecular Biol Lab Mont State Univ S 19th & Lincoln Bozeman MT 59717-0001. *Fax:* 406-994-4303

JUVET, RICHARD SPALDING, JR, PLASMA DESORPTION MASS SPECTROMETRY, CHROMATOGRAPHIC METHODS & COMPUTER INTERFACING. *Current Pos:* Prof, 70-95, EMER PROF ANALYTICAL CHEM, ARIZ STATE, 95- *Personal Data:* b Los Angeles, Calif, Aug 8, 30; m 55, 84, Evelyn R Elthon; c Victoria, David, Stephen & Richard P. *Educ:* Univ Calif, Los Angeles, BS, 52, PhD(chem), 55. *Honors & Awards:* Sci Exchange Agreement Award, Czech, Hungary, Romainia & Yugoslavia, 77. *Prof Exp:* From instr to assoc prof anal chem, Univ Ill, Urbana, 55-70; res chemist, E I Du Pont de Nemours, 55. *Concurrent Pos:* Vis prof, Univ Calif, Los Angeles, 60, Cambridge Univ, Eng, 64-65, Nat Taiwan Univ, 68, Ecole Polytechnique, France, 76-77, Univ Vienna, Austria, 89-90; NSF sr fel, Cambridge Univ, Eng, 64-65; mem, Air Pollution Chem & Physics Adv Comt, US HEW, 69-72; chmn, Div Anal Chem, Am Chem Soc, 72-73, nat counr, 78-89, Coun, Comt Reagent Chem, 85-95; Sci Exchange Agreement Award lect & travel Eastern Europe, 77. *Mem:* Am Chem Soc (secy-treas, 69-71); fel Am Inst Chemists; Sigma Xi; Am Radio Relay League; Int Platform Asn. *Res:* New applications of gas chromatography; liquid chromatography detectors; photochemistry; organic structural determinations and functional group analysis; chelate chemistry of polyhydroxy compounds; optical rotation measurements in study of metal chelates; inorganic gas chromatography; computer interfacing; plasma desorption mass spectrometry. *Mailing Add:* Dept Chem & Biochem Ariz State Univ Tempe AZ 85287-1604. *Fax:* 602-965-2747; *E-Mail:* rsjuvet@imap3.asu.edu

JWO, CHIN-HUNG, MECHANICAL SYSTEM ANALYSIS, PRODUCT RESEARCH & DEVELOPMENT. *Current Pos:* SR MECH ENGR, SYMBOL TECHNOL, BOHEMIA, NY, 93- *Personal Data:* b Taiwan, Nov 12, 56; m 84, Emily Chang; c Kevin & Doris. *Educ:* Feng Chia Univ, Taiwan, BS, 79; Univ Fla, ME, 85, PhD(mech eng), 89. *Prof Exp:* Advan develop engr, NCR, Ithaca, 89-91, prin engr, NCR E&M- Atlanta, 91-93. *Mem:* Assoc mem Am Soc Mech Engrs. *Res:* Opto-mechanical systems design and analysis for bar code scanners; mechanical packaging for hand-held terminals; electronic packaging; product development for retail and industrial usages. *Mailing Add:* 10 Vineyard Way Mt Sinai NY 11766. *Fax:* 516-244-4618

JYUNG, WOON HENG, PLANT PHYSIOLOGY. *Current Pos:* from asst prof to assoc prof biol, 64-74, chmn dept, 76-91, PROF BIOL, UNIV TOLEDO, 74- *Personal Data:* b Korea, Mar 12, 34; m 61; c 2. *Educ:* Seoul Nat Univ, BS, 57; Mich State Univ, MS, 59, PhD(hort physiol), 63. *Prof Exp:* Res assoc hort physiol, Mich State Univ, 63-64. *Mem:* AAAS; Am Soc Plant Physiol; Japanese Soc Plant Physiol. *Res:* Mechanisms of ion uptake by plant cells; zinc metabolism in higher plants; biology of aging. *Mailing Add:* Dept Biol Univ Toledo Toledo OH 43606

K

KAAE, JAMES LEWIS, MATERIALS SCIENCE. *Current Pos:* SR TECH ADV, GA TECHNOL, 82- *Personal Data:* b Bell, Calif, Oct 28, 36; m 65; c 1. *Educ:* Univ Calif, Los Angeles, BS, 59, MS, 61, PhD(eng), 65. *Prof Exp:* Int res fel, Welding Inst, Eng, 65-67; staff mem, metall, Gulf Energy & Environ Systs, Inc, 67-73; tech adv, Gen Atomic Co, 73-82. *Concurrent Pos:* Mem, Boiler & Pressure Vessel Code Comt, Am Soc Mech Engrs, 85-87; lectr, Univ Calif, San Diego, 87-89. *Mem:* Am Carbon Soc; AAAS; Sigma Xi; Am Soc Metals; Am Ceramic Soc. *Res:* Structure, properties and irradiation behavior of pyrolytic carbon; welding metallurgy of steels; behavior of materials under high-temperature cyclic loading; behavior of coated particle nuclear fuels; chemical vapor deposition of carbides and nitrides; mechanical properties of materials. *Mailing Add:* 613 Solana Glen Ct Solana Beach CA 92075

KAAS, JON HOWARD, PSYCHOPHYSIOLOGY NEUROANATOY BEHAVIOR & NEUROPHYSIOLOGY. *Current Pos:* assoc prof, 73-79, PROF PSYCHOL, VANDERBILT UNIV, 79- *Personal Data:* b Fargo, NDak, Sept 13, 37; m 63, Borbra Martin; c Jon & Lisa. *Educ:* Northland Col, BA, 59; Duke Univ, PhD(psychol), 65. *Honors & Awards:* Iavitsneurosci Investr Award, 87; Distinguished Sci Contrib Award Am Psychol Asn, 94; Krieg Corticol Discoverer Award, 88. *Prof Exp:* Trainee neurophysiol, Univ Wis-Madison, 65-68, asst prof, 68-73. *Mem:* Soc Neurosci; In Brain Res Orgn. *Res:* Visual and sensory systems; brain functions and evolution. *Mailing Add:* Dept Psychol Vanderbilt Univ 132 Wesley Hall Nashville TN 37240-0009

KAATTARI, STEPHEN L, COMPARATIVE IMMUNOLOGY. *Current Pos:* PROF IMMUNOL, COL WILLIAM & MARY, SCH MARINE SCI, 93- *Personal Data:* b Palo Alto, Calif, Sept 22, 51. *Educ:* Univ Calif, Davis, BS, 73, PhD(microbiol), 79. *Prof Exp:* Res fel cellular immunol, Ore Health Sci Univ, 79-82; from asst prof to prof immunol, Dept Microbiol, Ore State Univ, 82-92. *Mem:* Int Soc Develop & Comp Immunol; Am Asn Immunol; Am Soc Microbiol. *Mailing Add:* Dept Environ Sci Sch Marine Sci Col William & Mary Glouchester Point VA 23062-1346. *Fax:* 804-642-7186

KAATZ, MARTIN RICHARD, PHYSICAL GEOGRAPHY, GEOMORPHOLOGY. *Current Pos:* From asst prof to assoc prof, 52-64, chmn dept, 62-76, prof, 65-82, EMER PROF GEOG, CENT WASH UNIV, 83- *Personal Data:* b Cleveland, Ohio, Apr 16, 24; m 47, Carla Hemsing; c Allen, Larry & David. *Educ:* Univ Mich, BA, 48, MA, 49, PhD(geog), 52. *Concurrent Pos:* Fulbright prof, Trinity Col, Univ Dublin, 65-66. *Mem:* Asn Am Geogr; Am Quaternary Asn; AAAS. *Res:* Significance of mass wasting and periglacial landforms to the modern environment; irrigation and drought in Central Washington. *Mailing Add:* Cent Wash Univ 400 E Eighth Ellensburg WA 98926

KABACK, DAVID BRIAN, RECOMBINANT DNA, DEVELOPMENTAL BIOLOGY. *Current Pos:* asst prof, 78-85, ASSOC PROF MICROBIOL, NJ MED SCH, UNIV MED & DENT NJ, 85- *Personal Data:* b New York, NY, May 4, 50; m 91, Stephanie Apt; c Alexis R & Julia I. *Educ:* State Univ NY Stony Brook, BS, 71; Brandeis Univ, PhD(biol), 76. *Honors & Awards:* Nat Res Serv Award, Pub Health Serv. *Prof Exp:* Res fel chem, Calif Inst Technol, 76-78. *Concurrent Pos:* Damon Runyon-Walter Winchell Cancer Res Fel. *Mem:* Am Soc Microbiol; Harvey Soc; Genetics Soc Am. *Res:* Molecular genetics of yeast meiosis and sporulation; organization of eucaryotic genes and chromosomes; meiosis. *Mailing Add:* Dept Microbiol & Molecular Genetics NJ Med Sch Univ Med & Dent NJ 185 S Orange Ave Newark NJ 07103. *E-Mail:* kaback@umdnj.edu

KABACK, HOWARD RONALD, BIOCHEMISTRY. *Current Pos:* PROF, DEPTS PHYSIOL, MICROBIOL & MOLECULAR GENETICS, UNIV CALIF, LOS ANGELES, 89-, INVESTR, HOWARD HUGHES MED INST, 89- *Personal Data:* b Philadelphia, Pa, June 5, 36; m 57; c 3. *Educ:* Haverford Col, BA, 58; Albert Einstein Col Med, MD, 62. *Honors & Awards:* Selman A Waksman Award, 73; Lewis Rosenstiel Award, 74; Harvey Lectr, 88; Nathan Kaplan Mem Lectr, Univ Calif, 88; Kenneth Cole Award, Am Biophys Soc, 88; Philips Lectr, Haverford Col, 89; George A Feigen Mem Lectr, Stanford Univ, 89; Harold Lambert Lectr, Columbia Univ, 93; Jacques & Giselle Weismen Lectr, Israel, 93 & 94; 3M Life Sci Award, 93. *Prof Exp:* Intern pediat, Bronx Munic Hosp Ctr, 62-63; staff assoc, Lab Biochem, Nat Heart Inst, NIH, 64-66, sr res investr, 66-69; assoc mem, Dept Biochem, Roche Inst Molecular Biol, 70-72, mem, 72-89, head, Lab Membrane Biochem, 77-89, head, Dept Biochem, 83-89. *Concurrent Pos:* Edward John Noble Found fel, 62-64; Edward John Noble Found fel physiol, Albert Einstein Col Med, 64-66; res fel biochem, Nat Heart Inst, 64-66; adj assoc prof, Columbia Univ, NY, 73-85, adj prof, 85-89, adj prof, Grad Sch & Univ Ctr, City Univ New York, 76-89; Lady Davis vis prof, Hebrew Univ, Israel, 80, Albert Alberman vis prof, Technion-Israel Inst Technol, 81, Wellcome vis prof, Univ Idaho, 87-88; nat lectr, Am Soc Microbiol, 81; adj prof microbiol, NJ Med Sch, 86-89; mem, Bd Sci Coun, Nat Inst Diabetes, Digestive & Kidney Dis, 87-91, chmn bd, 91-92; mem ad hoc, NIH Study Sect, 90; vis prof prog lectr, Univ Fla, 94; distinguished lectr, Robert Wood Johnson Med Sch, 96; guest speaker, Mt Sinai Deans Lect Series, 96. *Mem:* Nat Acad Sci; Fedn Am Socs Exp Biol; NY Acad Sci; Am Soc Microbiol; Biophys Soc; fel Am Acad Arts & Sci; AAAS; Am Soc Biol Chemists; Am Chem Soc; Soc Gen Physiologists. *Res:* Transport; membranes; genetics. *Mailing Add:* Howard Hughes Med Inst Univ Calif McDonald Res Libr PO Box 951662 675 Circle Dr Los Angeles CA 90095-1662

KABACK, MICHAEL M, PEDIATRICS, MEDICAL GENETICS. *Current Pos:* CHIEF, DIV MED GENETICS, DEPT PEDIAT, SCH MED, UNIV CALIF, SAN DIEGO, 86- *Personal Data:* b Sept 1, 38. *Educ:* Haverford Col, BA, 59; Univ Pa, MD, 63; Am Bd Pediat, dipl; Am Bd Med Genetics, dipl. *Honors & Awards:* William Allen Mem Award, Am Soc Human Genetics, 93. *Prof Exp:* Res assoc, Nat Inst Neurol Dis & Blindness, 64-66; instr, Johns Hopkins Univ, 68-69, asst prof pediat, 69-72; assoc chief, Div Med Genetics, Harbor Med Ctr, Univ Calif, Los Angeles, Med Ctr, 72-86, from assoc prof to prof pediat med, 72-86; chair, Dept Pediat, Univ Calif, San Diego, 86-91. *Concurrent Pos:* Dir, Calif Tay-Sachs Dis Prev Prog, 72, Int Tay-Sachs Ctr, 79. *Mem:* Inst Med-Nat Acad Sci; fel Am Col Med Genetics; fel Am Acad Pediat; fel AAAS; Am Soc Human Genetics (pres, 91); Am Pediat Soc (pres-elect, 97). *Res:* Public health considerations in human (medical) genetics; technical, psychosocial and ethics-legal aspects of genetic screening. *Mailing Add:* Children's Hosp & Health Ctr 8110 Birmingham Way San Diego CA 92123

KABACK, STUART MARK, ORGANIC CHEMISTRY. *Current Pos:* Chemist, Tech Info Div, Esso Res & Eng Co, 60-63, Chem Res Div, 63 & Tech Info Div, 63-68, sr res chemist, Chem Corp Serv, 68-70, sr res chemist, Res Corp Serv, 70-76, res assoc, 76-85, mem staff, Anal & Info Div, 78-83, sr res assoc, 85-90, MEM STAFF, RES SER DIV, EXXON RES & ENG CO, 84-, SCI ADV, 90- *Personal Data:* b Elizabeth, NJ, June 12, 34; m 55, Marilyn Feldman; c Robin N (McGowan) & Gilbert P. *Educ:* Columbia Univ, AB, 55, AM, 56, PhD(org chem), 60. *Concurrent Pos:* mem, Patent Info User's Group; mem, Chem Abstracts Serv Comt, Am Chem Soc, 96- *Mem:* Am Chem Soc; Chem Struct Asn. *Res:* Information retrieval and analysis; patent information on petrochemicals, polymer chemistry; petroleum technology. *Mailing Add:* 222 Denman Rd Cranford NJ 07016. *Fax:* 908-474-3230; *E-Mail:* smkabac@erenj.com

KABADI, BALACHANDRA N, PHYSICAL PHARMACY, PHARMACEUTICAL CHEMISTRY. *Current Pos:* SR RES SCIENTIST ANALYSIS CONTROL, E R SQUIBB & SONS, 68- *Personal Data:* b Gadag, Mysore, India, July 15, 33; m 50; c 4. *Educ:* Karnatak Univ, India, BSc, 58; Univ Bombay, BSc, 60; Univ Wash, MS, 62, PhD(pharm), 65. *Prof Exp:* Fel chem, Univ SC, 65-66 & Sch Pharm, Univ Mich, 66-67; asst prof pharm, Col Pharm, Fla A&M Univ, 67-68. *Mem:* Am Pharmaceut Asn; Am Chem Soc. *Res:* Isolation, identification of compounds from natural plant products; pharmaceutical complexation reactions of phenols and water soluble hydrophilic polymers of nonionic nature; analytical chemistry-analysis of pharmaceutical products involving spectrophotometric methods; reference standards. *Mailing Add:* 34 Colin Dr South River NJ 08882-2406

KABAK, IRWIN WILLIAM, OPERATIONS RESEARCH, INDUSTRIAL ENGINEERING. *Current Pos:* prof statist & oper res, 96, EMER PROF STATIST, NY UNIV, 96- *Personal Data:* b New York, NY, May 21, 36; m 57; c 2. *Educ:* NY Univ, BIndE, 56, MIndE, 58, PhD(opers res), 64. *Prof Exp:* Mfg trainee & cost control analyst, Mergenthaler Linotype Co, 56-57; opers res engr, Esso Res & Eng Co, 56-58; mem tech staff & specialist traffic studies, Bell Tel Labs, 58-64; from asst prof to prof opers res, NY Univ, 65-89; pres, Modelmetrics, Inc, 67-89; mem bd dirs, NJ Automobile Full Ins Underwriting Asn, 89-96. *Concurrent Pos:* Consult various indust & govt; instr & adj asst prof, NY Univ, 63-65; lectr, City Univ New York, 64-65, Am Mgt Asn, 66-69, Purchasing Agents Asn NY, 67 & Diebold Group, 67; corp dir, Taxtronics Inc, 69-; consult & corp dir, Hardboard Fabricators Inc, 70; vis prof, Polytech Inst NY & CW Post Col, 71-72, Rutgers Univ, 78; exec mgt consult, Stat-A-Matrix, 85- *Mem:* Am Inst Indust Engrs; Inst Mgt Sci; Opers Res Soc Am; Nat Soc Prof Engrs. *Res:* Applications of applied probability in queueing, inventory, reliability and simulation; operations management and finance; model building, testing and evaluating quality and production. *Mailing Add:* 109 Stephenville Pkwy Edison NY 08820

KABALKA, GEORGE WALTER, ORGANIC CHEMISTRY, ORGANOMETALLIC CHEMISTRY. *Current Pos:* PROF CHEM, UNIV TENN, KNOXVILLE, 70-, PROF RADIOL, 84- *Personal Data:* b Wyandotte, Mich, Feb 1, 43; m 68; c 2. *Educ:* Univ Mich, BS, 65; Purdue Univ, PhD(chem), 70. *Prof Exp:* Res assoc, Purdue Univ, 69-70. *Concurrent Pos:* Consult, Oak Ridge Nat Lab, 76-, Oak Ridge Assoc Univ, 77-, Brookhaven Nat Lab, 81-, CTI Corp, Knoxville, Tenn, 85-; dir basic sci res, Inst Biomed Imaging, Univ Tenn Hosp, 88-; consult, Squibb Inst, 87-89; bd dir, Int Isotope Soc, 86-, Radiopharmaceut Coun Soc Nuclear Med, 87-89; chancellor's res award, Univ Tenn, 84 & sci alliance res award, 86-93. *Mem:* Am Chem Soc; Soc Nuclear Med; Int Isotope Soc; Soc Magnetic Resonance. *Res:* Organic synthesis; synthesis of radiopharmaceuticals containing short-lived radionuclides; organometallic reaction mechanisms; magnetic pharmaceuticals; pharmaceutical chemistry. *Mailing Add:* Dept Chem Univ Tenn Knoxville TN 37916-1600. *Fax:* 423-974-2997; *E-Mail:* inskabalka@utkvx.utk.edu

KABARA, JON JOSEPH, PHARMACOLOGY, CLINICAL BIOCHEMISTRY. *Current Pos:* prof pharmacol & assoc dean, 69-70, prof med, Col Osteop, 70-87, EMER PROF MED, MICH STATE UNIV, 87- *Personal Data:* b Chicago, Ill, Nov 26, 26; m 92, Betty Zane Tubor; c 6. *Educ:* St Mary's Col, Minn, BS, 48; Univ Miami, MS, 50; Univ Chicago, PhD(pharmacol), 59. *Prof Exp:* Asst biochem, Univ Ill, 48; asst chem, Univ Miami, 48-49, microbiol, 50-53; asst med, Univ Chicago, 53-57; from asst prof to prof chem, Univ Detroit, 57-68. *Concurrent Pos:* Consult, Med-Chem Labs Technol Exchange. *Mem:* AAAS; Am Chem Soc; NY Acad Sci; Am Soc Clin Path; Am Asn Clin Chem. *Res:* Cancer and virus chemotherapy; sterol biogenesis and metabolism; biochemistry of the central nervous system; radiobiology and clinical chemistry; biochemistry; venom research; pharmacology in dental research of food preservation and cosmetic; granted 19 US patents and 20 foreign patents. *Mailing Add:* 405 W Wachter Rd Galena IL 61036. *E-Mail:* jonkab@aol.com

KABAT, DAVID, BIOCHEMISTRY, GENETICS. *Current Pos:* asst prof, 69-72, ASSOC PROF BIOCHEM, MED SCH, UNIV ORE, 72- *Personal Data:* b Minneapolis, Minn, Oct 15, 40; m 62; c 2. *Educ:* Brown Univ, ScB, 62; Calif Inst Technol, PhD(biochem), 67. *Prof Exp:* NIH res assoc biophys, Mass Inst Technol, 67-69. *Mem:* Am Soc Biol Chemists. *Res:* Biochemical genetics of growth and differentiation. *Mailing Add:* Dept Biochem Ore Health Sci Univ Sch Med 3181 SW Sam Jackson Park Rd Portland OR 97201-3098. *Fax:* 503-494-8393

KABAT, ELVIN ABRAHAM, BIOCHEMISTRY. *Current Pos:* res assoc biochem, 41-46, from asst prof to assoc prof bact, 46-52, microbiologist, Columbia Presbyterian Hosp, 56-85, prof, 52-85, Higgins prof, 83-85, EMER PROF & HIGGINS EMER PROF MICROBIOL, COL PHYSICIANS & SURGEONS, COLUMBIA UNIV, 85- *Personal Data:* b New York, NY, Sept 1, 14; m 42; c Jon, Geoffrey & David. *Educ:* City Col New York, BS, 32; Columbia Univ, AM, 34, PhD(biochem), 37. *Hon Degrees:* DL, Univ Glasgow, 76; PhD, Univ Orleans, France, 82; PhD, Weizman Inst Sci, Rehovot, Israel, 82. *Honors & Awards:* Nat Medal of Sci, 91; Lilly Award, Am Soc Microbiologists, 49; Award, Nat Multiple Sclerosis Soc, 62; Karl Landsteiner Mem Award, 66; L G Horwitz Prize, Harvey Soc, 77; R E Dyer Lectr Award, NIH, 79; Philip Levine Award, Soc Clin Path, 82; Nat Medal Sci, 91. *Prof Exp:* Lab asst immunochem, Presby Hosp, 33-37; instr path, Med Col, Cornell Univ, 38-41. *Concurrent Pos:* Rockefeller Found fel, Inst Phys Chem, Univ Uppsala, 37-38; Fogarty scholar, NIH, 74-75; mem subcomt shock, Nat Res Coun, 51-53, panel on plasma, 53-59, comt plasma & plasma substitutes, 59-71; biochem adv panel, Am Inst Biol Sci, Off Naval Res, 57-62; Philips lectr, Haverford Col, 60, 74; prof, Col France, 64; mem expert adv panel on immunol, WHO, 65-82; expert, Nat Cancer Inst, NIH, 75-81; res award, City of Hope, 74. *Mem:* Nat Acad Sci; AAAS; Am Chem Soc; Am Soc Microbiol; Harvey Soc (vpres, 75-76, pres, 76-77). *Res:* Immunochemistry; organic reactions in qualitative analysis; mechanisms of immune reactions; antibody purification; physical chemistry of antibodies; serum and spinal fluid proteins; blood group substances; allergy; multiple sclerosis; dextrans; structure and immunological specificity; secondary structure of proteins; lectin; nature of antibody combining sites; cloning and sequencing of antibody variable regions. *Mailing Add:* Col Physicians & Surgeons Columbia Univ New York NY 10032

KABAT, HUGH F, PHARMACY ADMINISTRATION. *Current Pos:* prof, 84-96, EMER PROF COL PHARM, UNIV NMEX, ALBUQUERQUE, 96- *Personal Data:* b Manitowoc, Wis, Oct 3, 32; m 56, 80, Sally P Gutteridge; c Edward, Patrick, James, Charles Steaderman, John Steaderman & Mark Steaderman. *Educ:* Univ Mich, BS, 54, MS, 56; Univ Colo, PhD(pharm admin), 61. *Honors & Awards:* Mead-Johnson Award, Am Soc Hosp Pharmacists, 69; Hallie Bruce Mem lectr, 69; Dorothy Dillon Mem lectr, 90. *Prof Exp:* Chief pharm serv, Alaska Native Hosp, USPHS, 56-58; from asst prof to assoc prof pharm technol, Univ Minn, Minneapolis, 61-69, head dept clin pharm, 69-74, prof clin pharm, 69-80, asst dean admin, 74-80, assoc dean, Acad Affairs, 80-84, prof, Col Pharm, 80-86. *Concurrent Pos:* Consult, Vet Admin Hosp, Minneapolis, Hennepin Co Med Ctr, St Paul Ramsey Med Ctr, Data Dynamics & Mkt Measurements, Vet Affairs Med Ctr, Univ NMex Hosp, Alpha Data Servs, NIH; contrib ed, Geriatric Nursing, 65-68, Drug Intel, 67-74, Int Pharmaceut Abstr, 64-81, Topics in Hosp Pharm Mgt, 86-, Ediciones Mayo, 87-90 & Hosp Pharm, 90- *Mem:* Am Pharmaceut Asn; Am Soc Hosp Pharmacists; Am Asn Cols Pharm (pres elect); Am Pub Health Asn. *Res:* Drug utilization review; patient compliance; clinical pharmacy; drugs and the aging; problem based-student centered learning. *Mailing Add:* Col Pharm Univ NMex Albuquerque NM 87131. *Fax:* 505-272-6749; *E-Mail:* hkabat@unm.edu

KABAYAMA, MICHIOMI ABRAHAM, POLYMER CHEMISTRY. *Current Pos:* RETIRED. *Personal Data:* b Kanazawa, Japan, Apr 18, 26; m 51; c 5. *Educ:* Sir George Williams Col, BSc, 52; Univ Montreal, MSc, 56, DSc, 58. *Prof Exp:* Control chemist, Monsanto Can, 51-53; demonstr, Univ Montreal, 53-56; res chemist, Dupont Can, 58 & E I Dupont de Nemours & Co, 58-65; res chemist, Ethicon, Inc, 65-67; res chemist, Res & Develop Labs, Northern Elec Co Ltd, 67-69, mgr transducer & polymer mat develop, 69-71, Bell-Northern Res Labs, 71-74, mgr plastics eng, Mfg Res Centre, 74-76; tech dir, Soc Plastics Indust Can, 76-85, Vinyl Coun Can, 85-88; mgr recycling, Twinpak Inc, 88-89; mgr environ affairs, Tetra Pak Inc, 90-95. *Mem:* Soc Plastics Engrs; fel Chem Inst Can. *Res:* Physical properties and structure of polymers; thermodynamics of solutions of polymers; calorimetry of polymer solutions; plastic material and processing technology; new methods and applications; combustibility and toxicity of combustion products; occupational health and safety; recycling. *Mailing Add:* 434 Winona Dr Toronto ON M6C 3T7 Can

KABE, DATTATRAYA G, MATHEMATICAL STATISTICS, OPERATIONS RESEARCH. *Current Pos:* RETIRED. *Personal Data:* b Belgaum, India, Dec 30, 26; m 54, Ansuya; c Uday, Aruna & Prakash. *Educ:* Univ Bombay, BSc, 48, MSc, 52; Univ Karnatak, India, MSc, 55; Wayne State Univ, PhD(statist), 64. *Prof Exp:* Lectr statist, Vijay Col, India, 52-53 & Karnatak Univ, India, 53-61; assoc math, Wayne State Univ, 61-64; assoc prof math & statist, Northern Mich Univ, 65-66 & Dalhousie Univ, 66-68; assoc prof, St Mary's Univ, NS, 68-75, prof math & statist, 75-92. *Concurrent Pos:* Nat Res Coun Can grants & Can Math Cong res scholar; prof statist, NMex State Univ, 80-81, Bowling Green State Univ, 87-88. *Mem:* Can Statist Asn. *Res:* Distribution theory; design of experiments; multivariate analysis; Pascal computer programming language; sampling techniques; math programming. *Mailing Add:* Dept Comput Scis & Math St Mary's Univ Halifax NS B3H 3C3 Can

KABEL, RICHARD HARVEY, TRIBOLOGY, MECHANICAL ENGINEERING. *Current Pos:* PRES, RICH-LO-CONSULT CORP, 87- *Personal Data:* b Detroit, Mich, Dec 18, 32; m 60; c 2. *Educ:* Gen Motors Inst, BSME, 61. *Honors & Awards:* Coop Eng Colwell Medal, Soc Automotive Engrs. *Prof Exp:* Res engr eng oils, Gen Motors Res Labs, 61-67, sr res engr, 67-87, group leader, 74-78, staff res engr eng oils, 78-81, sr staff res engr, eng oils, Gen Motors Res Labs, 81-87. *Concurrent Pos:* Gen Motors rep, Lub Rev Comt, US Army & Soc Automotive Engrs; Soc Automotive Engrs fel, bd dr. *Mem:* Soc Automotive Engrs; Am Soc Testing & Mat. *Res:* Engine oils, formulation of engine oils, field performance, and methods to evaluate them. *Mailing Add:* 11051 Jonathan Lane Romeo MI 48065

KABEL, ROBERT L(YNN), CHEMICAL REACTION ENGINEERING, SCALE-UP. *Current Pos:* from asst prof to assoc prof, 63-74, PROF CHEM ENG, PA STATE UNIV, 74- *Personal Data:* b Champaign, Ill, Apr 3, 32; m 58, Barbara J Robb; c Joseph R & Douglas A. *Educ:* Univ Ill, BS, 55; Univ Wash, PhD(chem eng), 61. *Honors & Awards:* Western Elec Fund Award Excellence Instr, Am Soc Eng Educ, 83, Corcoran Award, Chem Eng Div, 89; Nat Catalyst Award, Chem Mfrs Asn, 84. *Prof Exp:* Staff mem, Space Systs Div, USAF, 61-63. *Concurrent Pos:* Royal Norweg Coun Sci & Indust Res fel, Tech Univ, Norway, 71-72; consult, Exxon Res & Eng, 76-80; vis lectr, Pahlavi Univ, Iran, 78; invitational prof, Ariz State Univ, 84-85; vis prof, Univ NSW, Australia, 88 & 89; Chalalongkorn Univ, Thailand, 89; Erskine fel, Univ Canterbury, NZ, 89. *Mem:* Am Chem Soc; fel Am Inst Chem Engrs; Am Asn Univ Profs; Am Soc Eng Educ. *Res:* Reaction kinetics; adsorption; thermodynamic equilibria; heterogeneous catalysis; chemical reactor dynamics; aerospace life support systems; thermal conductivity; mathematical modeling of natural processes; mass transfer at the earth's surface; air pollution meteorology; scaleup of chemical processes. *Mailing Add:* 132A Fenske Lab Pa State Univ University Park PA 16802

KABIR, PRABAHAN KEMAL, SYMMETRY, HIGH ENERGY PHYSICS. *Current Pos:* PROF PHYSICS, UNIV VA, 71- *Personal Data:* b Calcutta, India, June 30, 33. *Educ:* Univ Delhi, BSc, 51, MSc, 53; Cornell Univ, PhD(theoret physics), 57. *Prof Exp:* Mem Inst Advan Study, Princeton Univ, 56-57; res fel physics, Univ Birmingham, 57-58; sr reader nuclear physics, Univ Calcutta, 58-60; asst prof physics, Carnegie Inst Technol, 60-63; vis scientist, Europ Org Nuclear Res, Geneva, 63-65; prin sci officer, Sci Res Coun, UK, 65-71. *Concurrent Pos:* Mem, Ctr Advan Study, Univ VA, 70-73; sr res fel, Univ Sussex, 74; ed, Physics Letters B, 78-81; vis prof, Harvard Univ, 83. *Mem:* Fel Am Phys Soc. *Res:* Application of concepts of symmetry to the classification of elementary particles and investigation of the broken mirror-symmetries of physical laws. *Mailing Add:* Physics Bldg 319 Univ Va McCormick Rd Charlottesville VA 22901. *Fax:* 804-924-4576; *E-Mail:* pkk@virginia.edu

KABISCH, WILLIAM THOMAS, ANATOMY. *Current Pos:* RETIRED. *Personal Data:* b Bureau, Ill, Nov 10, 19; m, Linda Thompson; c Mary E, Nancy L & Sally A. *Educ:* Augustana Col, AB, 48; Univ Chicago, SM, 51, PhD(anat), 54. *Prof Exp:* Asst, Univ Chicago, 49-53, from instr to asst prof anat, 54-62; asst to exec officer, AAAS, 62-67, asst exec officer, 67-70; assoc prof anat, Sch Med, Southern Ill Univ, 70-71; from asst dean to assoc dean, 70-72, prof, 73-92, emer prof & assoc dean res, 92-94. *Concurrent Pos:* Lederle med fac award, 56-59; dir, Eastern Tech Off & sr staff mem, Enviro-Med Calif, Inc, 72-73. *Mem:* AAAS. *Res:* Gross anatomy; phagocytosis; bone regeneration; research administration. *Mailing Add:* PO Box 5143 Springfield IL 62705

KABLAOUI, MAHMOUD SHAFIQ, CHEMISTRY. *Current Pos:* From chemist to sr res chemist, 67-80, group leader, 80-87, MGR CHARGE BIOTECHNOL, COAL GASIFICATION & MEMBRANE SEPARATION, BEACON RES LAB, TEXACO INC, 87- *Personal Data:* b Tarshiha, Palestine, Apr 15, 38; US citizen; m 65; c 3. *Educ:* Am Univ Beirut, BSc, 60; Univ SC, PhD(org chem), 67. *Mem:* Am Chem Soc; Sigma Xi; Am Soc Microbiol. *Res:* Organic synthesis, petrochemicals; aromatization reactions, organic nitrogen compounds and fuels and lubricants technology; biotechnology area involving fermentation, enzyme catalysis and photobioconversion. *Mailing Add:* 6 Amherst Lane Wappingers Falls NY 12590

KABLER, J D, internal medicine; deceased, see previous edition for last biography

KABLER, MILTON NORRIS, SURFACE SCIENCE, OPTICAL PROPERTIES. *Current Pos:* physicist, Naval Res Lab, 62-69, assoc supt, Mat Sci Div, 75-77, head, Optical Mat Br, 69-79, head, Optical Probes Br, 79-85, HEAD SYNCHROTRON RAD SECT, NAVAL RES LAB, 86- *Personal Data:* b Roanoke, Va, Apr 30, 32; m 57, Angelita Suiter; c Stephen L & Cynthia L. *Educ:* Va Polytech Inst, BS, 55; Univ NC, Chapel Hill, PhD(physics), 59. *Honors & Awards:* Pure Sci Award, Sigma Xi-Naval Res Lab, 73. *Prof Exp:* Res asst prof physics, Univ Ill, Urbana, 59-62. *Concurrent Pos:* Vis scientist, Clarendon Lab, Oxford Univ, 73-74. *Mem:* Fel Am Phys Soc; Sigma Xi; AAAS; Optical Soc Am; Am Vacuum Soc. *Res:* Electronic and optical properties of materials; dynamics of photochemical processes; defects, excitons, semiconductors, radiation effects, surfaces, insulators; optical technologies; synchrotron radiation; research management. *Mailing Add:* Code 6686 Naval Res Lab Washington DC 20375-5345

KABOS, PAVEL, HIGH FREQUENCY MAGNETISM. *Current Pos:* postdoctoral fel, 82-84, sr res scientist, 92-95, PROF PHYSICS, COLO STATE UNIV, 95- *Personal Data:* b Kosice, Czech, July 24, 47; m 72, Dagmar Kabosova-Hamakova; c Peter. *Educ:* Slovack Tech Univ, MS, 70, PhD(solid state physics), 79, DSc, 94. *Prof Exp:* Asst prof elec eng, Electro Tech Fac, Slovak Tech Univ, 71-83. *Concurrent Pos:* Assoc prof elec eng, Slovak Tech Univ, 83- *Mem:* Sr mem Inst Elec & Electronics Engrs. *Res:* Ferromagnetic resonance; spin wave instabilities; magnetic excitations in finite-size magnetic samples; multilayers and superlattices; Brillouin light scattering; microwave ferrites; nonlinear magnetics; microwave magnetism; solitons. *Mailing Add:* Dept Physics Colo State Univ Ft Collins CO 80523. *Fax:* 970-491-7947; *E-Mail:* kabos@lamar.colostate.edu

KACEW, SAM, DRUG-INDUCED CHANGES IN NEWBORNS. *Current Pos:* PROF PHARMACOL, DEPT PHARMACOL, UNIV OTTAWA, 75- *Personal Data:* b Poland, 46. *Educ:* McGill Univ, Montreal, BS, 67; Univ Ottawa, MS, 70, PhD(pharmacol), 73. *Res:* Toxicology of newborns. *Mailing Add:* Dept Pharmacol Univ Ottawa Fac Med 451 Smyth Rd Ottawa ON K1H 8M5 Can

KACHANOV, MARK L, FRACTURE & DAMAGE MECHANICS, MICROMECHANICS OF MATERIALS. *Current Pos:* assoc prof, 82-88, PROF MECH ENG, TUFTS UNIV, 88- *Personal Data:* b Moscow, USSR, Aug 6, 46; US citizen. *Educ:* Leningrad Univ, BS & MS, 64; Leningrad Polytech Inst, Cand Sci, 74; Brown Univ, PhD, 81. *Prof Exp:* Asst prof mech & mat sci, Rutgers Univ, 80-82. *Concurrent Pos:* Vis scientist, Stanford Res Inst, Nat Inst Standards & Technol, Shell Res Lab, Holland & Gen Elec Labs; consult, SRI Int, Gen Tel Labs & Shell Labs; prin investr, Dept Energy, Dept Transp, US Army & Alcoa Found. *Mem:* Am Acad Mech. *Res:* Mechanics of solids with multiple cracks and other defects; micromechanics of brittle materials; fractures accompanied by damage and microcracking; mechanics of damage. *Mailing Add:* 47 Iroquois Rd Arlington MA 02174

KACHHAL, SWATANTRA KUMAR, INDUSTRIAL ENGINEERING, OPERATIONS RESEARCH. *Current Pos:* From instr to assoc prof, 74-85, CHMN DEPT, UNIV MICH, DEARBORN, 85-, PROF INDUST & MFG SYST ENG, 87- *Personal Data:* b India, July 7, 47; m 77; c 3. *Educ:* Univ Roorkee, India, BS, 68; Univ Minn, MS, 71, PhD(indust eng & opers res), 74. *Concurrent Pos:* Consult, Corning Glass Works, 78-80 & Henry Ford Hosp, 80- *Mem:* Am Inst Indust Eng. *Res:* Facilities planning; warehousing; automated and mechanized storage systems; applications of operations research in healthcare. *Mailing Add:* Dept Indust & Mfg Syst Eng Univ Mich Dearborn MI 48128-1491

KACHIKIAN, ROUBEN, microbiology, analytical chemistry; deceased, see previous edition for last biography

KACHINSKY, ROBERT JOSEPH, WATER SUPPLY & WASTEWATER DISPOSAL ENGINEERING. *Current Pos:* Staff engr, 65-75, proj dir, 75-77, VPRES, CAMP DRESSER & MCKEE INC, 77- *Personal Data:* b Boston, Mass, May 3, 37; m 63; c 4. *Educ:* Northeastern Univ, BS, 63, MS, 75. *Mem:* Fel Am Soc Civil Engrs; Am Acad Environ Engrs; Water Pollution Control Fedn; Am Waterworks Asn. *Res:* Wastewater treatment & disposal engineering. *Mailing Add:* Camp Dresser & McKee Inc 10 Cambridge Ctr Cambridge MA 02142

KACKER, RAGHU N, STATISTICAL QUALITY ENGINEERING, INDUSTRIAL EXPERIMENTATION. *Current Pos:* MATH STATISTICIAN, NAT INST STANDARDS & TECHNOL, GAITHERSBURG, MD, 88- *Personal Data:* b India, June 24, 51; US citizen; m 79; c 2. *Educ:* Univ Delhi, India, BS, 71; Agra Univ, India, MStatist, 73; Univ Guelph, Can, MS, 75; Iowa State Univ, PhD(statist), 79. *Prof Exp:* Instr statist, Iowa State Univ, Ames, Iowa, 75-79; asst prof statist, Va Polytech Inst, Blacksburg, 79-80; tech staff qual assurance, AT&T Bell Labs, Holmdel, NJ, 80-85, distinguished tech staff qual assurance, 85-88. *Mem:* Am Statist Asn; Am Soc Qual Control; Am Soc Testing & Mat; Am Ceramic Soc. *Res:* Accelerate advanced materials formulation and processing through statistical quality engineering; engineering designs of instruments for measurement and for processing respond linearly to changes in input signals and make such designs robust to unavoidable noise factors. *Mailing Add:* 10704 Tuckahoe Way Gaithersburg MD 20878

KACSER, CLAUDE, THEORETICAL PHYSICS. *Current Pos:* asst prof, 64-67, ASSOC PROF PHYSICS, UNIV MD, COLLEGE PARK, 67- *Personal Data:* b 1934. *Educ:* Oxford Univ, BA, 55, MA & PhD(physics), 59. *Prof Exp:* Res fel physics, Magdalen Col, Oxford Univ, 58-59; instr, Princeton Univ, 59-61; res fel, Magdalen Col, Oxford Univ, 61-62; asst prof, Columbia Univ, 62-64. *Mem:* Am Asn Physics Teachers. *Res:* Pedagogy; special relativity, thermodynamics. *Mailing Add:* Dept Physics Univ Md College Park MD 20742

KACZMARCZYK, WALTER J, BIOCHEMICAL GENETICS. *Current Pos:* asst prof to assoc prof genetics, 69-76, PROF GENETICS & BIOCHEM, WVA UNIV, 76-, BIOCHEM GENETICIST, 69- *Personal Data:* b New Britain, Conn, Jan 3, 39; m 77, Linda Snider; c Christopher, Jeanne & Anne. *Educ:* Fairfield Univ, BS, 61; St John's Univ, NY, MS, 63; Hahnemann Med Col, PhD(biochem genetics), 67. *Prof Exp:* Nat Acad Sci fel biochem, Plum Island Animal Dis Lab, USDA, 66-69. *Mem:* AAAS; Genetics Soc Am; Am Chem Soc. *Res:* Molecular biology of endothia parasitica; biochemistry of Heterosis; fungal viruses; TGF-B; soluable phosphate. *Mailing Add:* Dept Genetics Develop Biol WVa Univ Box 6168 Morgantown WV 26506-6057

KACZOROWSKI, GREGORY JOHN, MEMBRANE BIOCHEMISTRY, MEMBRANE BIOPHYSICS. *Current Pos:* sr res biochemist, 80-84, res fel, 84-86, assoc dir, 86-87, DIR, DEPT MEMBRANE BIOCHEM & BIOPHYS, MERCK INST THERAPEUTIC RES, 88- *Personal Data:* b South Bend, Ind, Nov 20, 49; m 82, Maria L Garcia. *Educ:* Univ Notre Dame, BS, 72; Mass Inst Technol, PhD(biochem), 77. *Prof Exp:* Helen Hay Whitney fel, Roche Inst Molecular biol, 77-80. *Mem:* Am Soc Biol Chemists; Am Chem Soc; Biophys Soc; AAAS; NY Acad Sci. *Res:* Membrane biochemistry study of ion channels, especially calcium and potassium channels, as well as ion transporting systems in electrically excitable membranes by a combination of biochemical and biophysical techniques; therapeutic drug development with ion channels as targets. *Mailing Add:* Dept Membrane Biochem & Biophys Merck Res Labs Rm 80N-31C Merck Inst PO Box 2000 Rahway NJ 07065-0900. *Fax:* 732-594-3925; *E-Mail:* gjk@mfrck.com

KACZYNSKI, DON, METALLURGICAL ENGINEERING. *Current Pos:* Supvr res & develop, 84-90, DIR TECH, BERYLLIUM MINING, BRUSH WELLMAN ENG MATS, 90- *Personal Data:* b Fremont, Mich, Apr 16, 48; m 85, Sandra L Braunworth. *Educ:* Mich Technol Univ, BS, 71, MS, 73; Colo Sch Mines, PhD(metall eng), 78. *Prof Exp:* Metallurgist, Hanna Mining Co, 77-80, res metallurgist, 80-81, sr res metallurgist, 81-84. *Mem:* Am Soc Metals Int; Am Inst Mining; Electrochem Soc. *Res:* Controlling the morphology of beryllium oxide powders, removing chlorine from copper ores, froth flotation of borate minerals and concentration of iron ores. *Mailing Add:* Brush Wellman Inc 14710 W Portage River S Rd Elmore OH 43416

KADABA, PANKAJA KOOVELI, NEUROCHEMISTRY, MEDICINAL CHEMISTRY. *Current Pos:* assoc res, 68-90, RES PROF MED CHEM & PHARAMACEUT, COL PHARM, UNIV KY, 90- *Personal Data:* b Perumbavoor, India, May 15, 28; m 54, Prasad; c Lini (Raja Gopalan). *Educ:* Travancore Univ, India, BSc, 47, MSc, 49; Univ Delhi, PhD(org chem), 54. *Prof Exp:* Lectr chem, Am Mission Med Col, Vellore, India, 49-50 & Univ Delhi, 50-53; guest scholar, Univ Ky, 54-55, instr biochem, 64-65; res assoc, Brown Univ, 57-60; assoc prof chem, Morehead State Univ, 65-66; asst prof, Christian Bros Col, 66-68. *Concurrent Pos:* Fulbright-Smith-Mundt fel, 53-54; vis assoc prof chem, Univ Ljubljana, Yugoslavia, 73-74; vis scientist, Mat Res Lab, Wright Patterson AFB, Dayton, Ohio, 82; prin investr, Res Proj Grant, Nat Inst Neurol Commun Dis & Stroke, NIH, 82-91; chmn, 9th Int Cong Heterocyclic Chem, Tokyo, Japan, 83; mem, Res Bd Adv, Am Biog Inst, 86-; assoc, Sanders-Brown Ctr Aging, Univ Ky, 90-93; pres, Kand K Bio Sci, Inc. *Mem:* Am Chem Soc; Int Soc Heterocyclic Chem; India Chemists & Chem Engrs Club; Am Asn Pharmaceut Scientists. *Res:* Chemistry of heterocyclic compounds, their synthesis, reaction mechanisms and biological activity; 1,2,3-triazoles, tetrazoles, aziridinesand 1,2,3-triazolines; role of protic and dipolar aprotic solvents in heterocyclic synthesis via 1,3-cycloaddition reactions; borohydride reductions of heterocyclic compounds; direct esterification of acids with alcohols using borontrifluoride-etherate catalyst; rational design of anticonvulsants, their structure-activity relationships, metabolism and pharmacology, mechanism of action and anti-epileptic drug development; nmda antagonists; author of over 80 published papers and abstracts; holder of six patents; antiischemic drugs; antiparkinsonian drugs. *Mailing Add:* Div Med Chem Univ Ky Col Pharm Lexington KY 40536-0082. *Fax:* 606-257-7585

KADABA, PRASAD KRISHNA, PHYSICS, ELECTRONICS. *Current Pos:* assoc prof, 59-62, PROF ELEC ENG & DIR RES, UNIV KY, 62- *Personal Data:* b Bangalore, India, Feb 14, 24; m 54; c 1. *Educ:* Univ Mysore, BS, 43, MS, 44; Calif Inst Technol, MS, 46; Univ Calif, Los Angeles, PhD(physics), 49. *Honors & Awards:* sr Fulbright-Hays Award, Yugoslav-Am Bi-Nat Comn, 74. *Prof Exp:* Sci officer electronics, Nat Phys Lab, India, 50-52, asst supt, Tech Develop Estab, 52-53; asst prof elec eng, Univ Ky, 54-57 & Newark Col Eng, 57-59. *Concurrent Pos:* Alumni fel physics, Mich State Univ, 53-54; consult, Fed Pac Elec Co, NJ, 58; scholar, Univ Calif, Los Angeles, 58-59; AEC traveling fel, India, 63-64; Ky Res Found spec fel, 63-64; mem conf elec insulation & dielec phenomena, Nat Res Coun; consult, IBM, Ky; resident assoc, Argonne Nat Lab; prin investr microwave proj, Ky Tobacco Res Inst, 71-72; res fel to Yugoslavia, Int Res & Exchange Bd, 73; vis scientist, Johnson Space Ctr, Houston, 75; prin investr proj, Off Water Resources Res Inst, 76-; Oak Ridge Assoc Univs fel, 76; prin investr microwave spectros proj, Ky Tobacco Res Inst, 77-78; vis prof, intergovernment personnel act prog, Air Force Off Sci Res, Wright Patterson AFB Mat Lab, 80-81, Avionics Lab, 81-82. *Mem:* Am Soc Eng Educ; Brit Inst Elec Eng; sr mem Inst Elec & Electronics Engrs. *Res:* Microwave absorption of organic liquids; non resonant absorption of compressed gases and molecular nature of materials; nuclear quadrupole resonance and nuclear magnetic resonance studies; biological effects of microwaves; pollution studies. *Mailing Add:* 3411 Brookhaven Dr Lexington KY 40502

KADABA, PRASANNA V, MECHANICAL ENGINEERING, DESIGN OF THERMAL SYSTEMS. *Current Pos:* ASSOC PROF MECH ENG, GA INST TECHNOL, 69- *Personal Data:* b Gundlupet, India, July 4, 31; US citizen; m 66, Usha Rani Rajgobal; c Vaibhav. *Educ:* Univ Mysore, BE, 52 & 54, Univ Ky, MS, 56, Ill Inst Technol, PhD(mech eng), 64. *Honors & Awards:* Appreciation Award, Am Soc Heating, Refrig & Air-Conditioning Engrs, 84 & 85. *Prof Exp:* Asst mech eng, Univ Ky, 54-56; asst mech eng, Ill Inst Technol, 56-60, instr, 60-63; sr res engr, Roy C Ingersol Res Ctr, Borg-Warner Corp, 63-67; sr res scientist, Res & Develop Ctr, Westinghouse Elec Corp, Pa, 67-69. *Concurrent Pos:* Vis prof, Univ Carabobo, Valencia, Venezuela, 73 & 75; adv, Vol Int Tech Assistance, 77-; guest worker, Nat Bur Stand, Gaithersburg, MD, 78; consult, Lawrence Berkeley Lab, Berkeley, CA, 79-80, Copeland Corp, Emerson Elec, Sidney, Ohio, 84, IPA fel, Lewis Res Ctr, NASA, Cleveland Ohio, 86; fac fel, Marshall Space Flight Ctr, NASA, Huntsville, 82, Lewis Res Ctr, Cleveland, Ohio, 87; vis prof, Univ Cincinnati, 87-90; mem, tech comt, TC6-3 & TC 9.6, Am Soc Heating Refrig & Air Conditioning Engrs; mem, Metric Comt, Am Soc Testing Mats. *Mem:* Fel Am Soc Mech Engrs; fel Am Soc Heating, Refrig & Air-Conditioning Engrs; Sigma Xi; Am Inst Chem Engrs; Am Soc Testing Mats. *Res:* Solar energy; refrigeration; air conditioning; heat transfer; thermodynamics; mechanical systems for buildings; thermal systems design; energy conservation; productivity and efficiency; photovoltaic total energy system; heat exchangers; optimization; space power coupled photovoltaic heat engine design; thermal sciences laboratory development; second law applications to thermal systems and thermoeconomics. *Mailing Add:* George W Woodruff Sch Mech Eng Ga Inst Technol Atlanta GA 30332-0405. *Fax:* 404-894-3733; *E-Mail:* prasanna.kadaba@me.yatech.edu

KADAN, RANJIT SINGH, FOOD BIOCHEMISTRY, MICROBIOLOGY. *Current Pos:* SR FOOD SCIENTIST, SOUTHERN REGIONAL RES CTR, AGR RES SERV, USDA, NEW ORLEANS, 75- *Personal Data:* b Karnal, Haryana State, India, Jan 1, 35; m 66, Savitri; c Nina S. *Educ:* Punjab Univ, DVM, 58; Kans State Univ, MS, 62; Rutgers Univ, New Brunswick, PhD(food sci), 67. *Prof Exp:* Vet surgeon, Punjab State, India, 58-60; res asst food, Food Sci Dept, Rutgers Univ, 62-67, sr group leader, 67-73; group leader food res, Quaker Oats Co, Barrington, Ill, 66-69, sr group leader, 70-73; mgr, Food Products Res, Lubin Maselli Lab, Chicago, 73-75. *Concurrent Pos:* Consult, Volunteers Tech Assistance, 66- *Mem:* Inst Food Technologists; Am Oil Chemists Soc; Am Asn Cereal Chemists; Am Dairy Sci Asn; NY Acad Sci. *Res:* Diversified food research activities in the areas of dairy, cereals, oil seeds, snacks, long shelf life food products, beverages, toxic constituents of foods including microbiol toxins, nutritional attributes of foods and value added novel foods from agricultural crops. *Mailing Add:* USDA Southern Regional Res Ctr PO Box 19687 New Orleans LA 70179. *Fax:* 504-286-4419; *E-Mail:* rkadan@nola.srrc.usda.gov

KADAN, SAVITRI SINGH, EMERGENCY MEDICINE, OBSTETRICS & GYNECOLOGY. *Current Pos:* EMERGENCY RM PHYSICIAN, ALEXIAN BROTHERS HOSP, ELKGROVE, 74- *Personal Data:* b Sonepat, Haryana, India, Aug 12, 34; m 66; c 1. *Educ:* Bihar Univ, India, MD, 58; Dipl, 64; Patna Med Col, Patna Univ, India, MS, 71. *Prof Exp:* Asst prof obstet & gynec, Patna Med Col, 64-67; intern, St Fransic Hosp, Evanston, Ill, 68-69; resident, Lutheran Gen Hosp, Park Ridge, Ill, 69-70; emergency rm physician, Northwest Community Hosp, 73; dir, Cook County Venereal Dis Clin, Maywood, Ill, 74-75; resident, Clarity Hosp, La State Univ, New Orleans, 75-77. *Concurrent Pos:* Fel Family pract, Am Acad Family Pract, 78. *Mem:* Am Acad Family Pract. *Res:* Obstetrics; gynecology. *Mailing Add:* 8554 Fordham Ct New Orleans LA 70127

KADANE, JOSEPH BORN, APPLIED STATISTICS, MATHEMATICAL STATISTICS. *Current Pos:* assoc prof, 71-72, PROF STATIST & SOCIAL SCI, DEPT STATIST, CARNEGIE-MELLON UNIV, 72-, LEONARD J SAVAGE PROF, 85- *Personal Data:* b Washington, DC, Jan 10, 41; m 92, Caroline Mitchell. *Educ:* Harvard Univ, BA, 62; Stanford Univ, PhD(statist), 66. *Prof Exp:* Asst prof statist, Yale Univ, 66-68; staff analyst, Ctr Naval Anal, 68-71. *Concurrent Pos:* Res staff mem, Cowles Found Res Econ, Yale Univ, 66-68. *Mem:* Fel Am Statist Asn; fel Inst Math Statist; fel Royal Statist Soc; fel AAAS; Biometric Soc; Econometric Soc. *Res:* Theory and use of statistics in economics, political science, sociology, demography, law, medicine, archeology, oceanography, environment. *Mailing Add:* Dept Statist Carnegie-Mellon Univ Pittsburgh PA 15213. *E-Mail:* radane@stat.cmu.edu

KADANKA, ZDENEK KAREL, CYTOGENETICS, BIOCHEMISTRY. *Current Pos:* PVT PRACT, 85- *Personal Data:* b Rajhrad, Czech, May 24, 33; m 60; c 2. *Educ:* Purkyne Univ, Brno, dipl chem & RNDr, 57, dipl med & MUDr, 63; Inst Postgrad Studies for Physicians & Pharmacists, Prague, dipl, 66. *Prof Exp:* Lectr histol & embryol, Med Fac, Purkyne Univ, Brno, 59-63; physician allergy & diabetes, Sanatorium, Luhacovice, Czech, 63-66, intern, 66-69; sr res asst, Connaught Med Res Labs, Univ Toronto, 69-71, res assoc Karyology, 71-85. *Concurrent Pos:* Gertrude I'Anson fel, Connaught Med Res Labs, Univ Toronto, 69-70; NIH grants, 71-72. *Res:* Karyologic data; cell membrane changes; transformation of human and animal cells cultured in vitro. *Mailing Add:* 64 Gwendolen Crescent Willowdale ON M2N 2L7 Can

KADANOFF, LEO P, THEORETICAL PHYSICS, APPLIED MATHEMATICS. *Current Pos:* PROF PHYSICS, UNIV CHICAGO, 78- *Personal Data:* b New York, NY, Jan 14, 37; m 58; c 3. *Educ:* Harvard Univ, AB, 57, AM, 58, PhD(physics), 60. *Honors & Awards:* Buckley Prize, Am Phys Soc, 77; Wolf Found Award, 80; Boltzmann Medal, Int Union Pure & Appl Physics, 89. *Prof Exp:* Res fel, Bohr Inst Theoret Studies, Copenhagen, 60-62; from asst prof to prof physics, Univ Ill, Urbana, 62-69; univ prof physics, Brown Univ, 69-78, prof eng, 71-78. *Concurrent Pos:* A P Sloan Found fel, 62-67; vis prof, Cambridge Univ, Eng, 65; mem adv comt, Inst Theoret Physics, Santa Barbara, 78-81, Schlumberger Doll Res Lab, 81-86, Univ Minn, 86-; dir, Mat Res Lab, Univ Chicago, 81-84; mem, Bd Physics & Astron, Nat Res Coun, 83-; vchmn, Sci & Tech Adv Comt, Argonne Nat Lab, 83-84. *Mem:* Nat Acad Sci; fel Am Phys Soc; fel Am Acad Arts & Sci; fel AAAS. *Res:* Solid state and many particle theory; development of urban growth models; phenomena near phase transitions; behavior of dynamical systems; turbulence chaos; author of over 160 articles and books. *Mailing Add:* Dept Physics James Franck Inst Univ Chicago 5640 S Ellis Ave Chicago IL 60637

KADAR, DEZSO, PHARMACOLOGY. *Current Pos:* Res asst pharmacol & toxicol, Connaught Med Res Lab, 60-65, demonstr, 65-68, lectr, 68-70, asst prof, 70-76, ASSOC PROF PHARMACOL, UNIV TORONTO, 76- *Personal Data:* b Zazar, Transylvania, July 21, 33; Can citizen; m 57; c 2. *Educ:* Univ Toronto, BS, 59, MS, 66, PhD(pharmacol), 68. *Concurrent Pos:*

Mem, Drug Adv Comt, Ont Col Pharmacists, 72-, Comt Drugs & Therapeut, St Joseph's Hosp, 74- & Coun Fac Pharm, Univ Toronto, 73- *Mem:* Pharmacol Soc Can. *Res:* Drug metabolism and disposition in man and animals; microsomal drug oxidation in vitro. *Mailing Add:* Dept Pharmacol Univ Toronto Fac Med Toronto ON M5S 1A8 Can

KADE, CHARLES FREDERICK, JR, MEDICAL & HEALTH SCIENCES. *Current Pos:* RETIRED. *Personal Data:* b Sheboygan, Wis, Apr 4, 14; m 46; c 6. *Educ:* Carleton Col, BA, 36; NDak State Univ, MS, 38; Univ Ill, PhD(biochem), 41. *Prof Exp:* Asst chem, Carleton Col, 35-36 & NDak State Univ, 36-38; asst, Univ Ill, 38, 39-41, fel, 41-43; dir biochem res, Frederick Stearns & Co, 43-47; res chemist, Sterling-Winthrop Res Inst, 47-49; dir div med sci, McNeil Labs, Inc, 49-60, vpres & dir res, 60-66; vpres, Johnson & Johnson Int, 66-79; vpres, Janssen Res & Develop, Inc, 72-79; consult, 79-89. *Mem:* AAAS; Am Chem Soc; Asn Res Dirs; Am Pharmaceut Asn; Soc Indust Chem; Am Inst Chemists. *Res:* Intermediary metabolism of amino acids; protein and amino acid requirements of the dog; preparation of hydrolysates for intravenous use. *Mailing Add:* 983 Butler Pike Blue Bell PA 19422

KADEKARO, MASSAKO, BODY FLUID BALANCE & VASOPRESSIN, OXYTOCIN & ANGIOTENSIN II. *Current Pos:* PROF & DIR NEUROSURG RES LAB, DIV NEUROSURG, MED BR, UNIV TEX, GALVESTON, 84- *Personal Data:* b Brazil, Jan 18, 39; m 79, Francis A Kutyna. *Educ:* Univ Sao Paulo, Brazil, PhD(neural regulation of gastric secretion), 70. *Prof Exp:* Vis scientist, Lab Cerebral Metabol, Nat Inst Mental Health, Bethesda, Md, 77-84. *Concurrent Pos:* Mem, Neurol Study Sect, NIH. *Mem:* Soc Neurosci; Am Physiol Soc; NY Acad Sci; Sigma Xi; AAAS. *Res:* Neural regulation of water balance; modulatory influence of nitric oxide on neural ciruciltry regulating water drinking behavior; vasopressin and oxytocin secretion and arterial blood pressure. *Mailing Add:* Div Neurosurg Univ Tex Med Br Galveston TX 77555-0517

KADER, ADEL ABDEL, PLANT PHYSIOLOGY, HORTICULTURE. *Current Pos:* asst res plant physiol, 72-77, from asst prof to assoc prof, 78-82, PROF POMOL, UNIV CALIF, DAVIS, 82- *Personal Data:* b Cairo, Egypt, Mar 1, 41; US citizen; m 63; c 2. *Educ:* Univ Ain Shams, Cairo, BSc, 59; Univ Calif, Davis, MSc, 62, PhD(plant physiol), 66. *Honors & Awards:* Asgrow Award, Am Soc Hort Sci, 78; Nat Food Processors Award, Am Soc Hort Sci, 80. *Prof Exp:* Lectr hort, Univ Ain Shams, Cairo, 66-71; consult, Agr Inst, Kuwait, 71-72. *Mem:* Fel Am Soc Hort Sci(pres, 96); Am Soc Plant Physiologists; Inst Food Technologists; Int Soc Hort Sci; Coun Agr Sci & Technol. *Res:* Postharvest biology and technology of horticultural crops; quality evaluation and maintenance of harvested fruits; controlled atmospheres. *Mailing Add:* Dept Pomol Univ Calif Davis CA 95616-8683. *E-Mail:* aakader@ucdavis.edu

KADESCH, ROBERT R, PHYSICS. *Current Pos:* From asst prof to assoc prof physics, 56-65, assoc dean col lett & sci, 66-68, PROF PHYSICS, UNIV UTAH, 65- *Personal Data:* b Cedar Falls, Iowa, May 14, 22; m 43, 83; c 3. *Educ:* Iowa State Teachers Col, BS, 43; Univ Rochester, MS, 49; Univ Wis, PhD(physics), 55. *Concurrent Pos:* Staff assoc, NSF, Washington, DC, 68-69; vis res physicist, Lawrence Hall Sci, Univ Calif, Berkeley, 73-74. *Res:* Personalized computer-assisted video disc instruction; learning theory; formal thinking. *Mailing Add:* 48 W Broadway Salt Lake City UT 84101

KADEY, FREDERIC L, JR, ECONOMIC GEOLOGY, INDUSTRIAL MINERALS EXPLORATION & EVALUATION. *Current Pos:* CONSULT INDUST MINERALS, 83- *Personal Data:* b Toronto, Ont, June 21, 18; US citizen; m 50, Brenda Boocock; c Brenda (King) & Frederic L III. *Educ:* Rutgers Univ, BSc, 41; Harvard Univ, MA, 47. *Honors & Awards:* Hardinge Award, Am Inst Mining, Metall & Petrol Engrs, 86. *Prof Exp:* Res petrogr, Res Lab, US Steel Corp, 47-51; mineralogist & petrogr, Johns-Manville Res & Eng Ctr, NJ, 51-66, chief fillers sect, 66-71, res assoc geol, Res Ctr, 71-72; explor mgr, Manville Corp, Colo, 72-83. *Concurrent Pos:* Geol field asst, Sinclair Oil Co, 46; teaching fel mineralogy, Harvard Univ, 46-47; Nat Defense exec reservist, Emergency Minerals Admin, US Dept Interior, 73-90. *Mem:* Fel AAAS; distinguished mem Soc Mining, Metall & Explor; Mineral Soc Am; Sigma Xi; Am Inst Prof Geologists. *Res:* Microscopy, particle size analysis; technology of mineral fillers and hydro-thermal silicate reactions; economic evaluation of industrial minerals; exploration of diatomite, perlite, talc & kaolin deposits. *Mailing Add:* 14127 Aster Ave Wellington FL 33414-8506

KADIN, ALAN MITCHELL, SUPERCONDUCTING THIN FILMS & DEVICES, THIN FILM DEPOSITION & PROPERTIES. *Current Pos:* ASSOC PROF ELEC ENG, UNIV ROCHESTER, 87- *Personal Data:* b Brooklyn, NY, Dec 7, 52. *Educ:* Princeton Univ, BA, 74; Harvard Univ, MA, 75, PhD(physics), 79. *Prof Exp:* Res assoc, State Univ NY, Stony Brook, 79-80, Univ Minn, 81-83; res physicist, Energy Conversion Devices, Inc, 83-87. *Concurrent Pos:* Prin investr, NSF, 89-96; mem, Tech Adv Bd, CVC Prods, Inc, 91-95. *Mem:* Am Phys Soc. *Res:* Superconducting thin films and devices; nonequilibrium phenomena; thin film deposition and properties; magnetic materials. *Mailing Add:* Dept Elec Eng Univ Rochester Rochester NY 14627. *E-Mail:* kadin@ee.rochester.edu

KADIRVEL, VELMURUGAN, CIRCUIT DESIGN, LOGIC DESIGN. *Current Pos:* DESIGN ENGR, MOTOROLA SEMICONDUCTOR PROD SECT, 92- *Personal Data:* b Madras, India, Aug 15, 67. *Educ:* Anna Univ, India, BE, 89; Tex A&M Univ, MS, 92. *Mem:* Inst Elec & Electronics Engrs; Inst Elec & Electronics Engrs Comput Soc. *Mailing Add:* 3324 N Lakeharbor Lane G306 Boise ID 81703-6255. *E-Mail:* vzgr20@email.sps.mot.com

KADIS, BARNEY MORRIS, BIOCHEMISTRY. *Current Pos:* RETIRED. *Personal Data:* b Omaha, Nebr, Dec 26, 27. *Educ:* Univ Nebr, BA, 52; Iowa State Univ, PhD(chem), 57. *Prof Exp:* Asst chem, Iowa State Univ, 52-57; asst prof, Dubuque Univ, 57-58; res chemist, Col Med, Univ Nebr, 58-60; assoc prof chem, State Univ NY, Albany, 60-61; res asst prof obstet & gynec, Col Med, Univ Nebr, Omaha, 61-66, asst prof biochem, 62-66; assoc prof biol sci, Southern Ill Univ, 69-70, assoc prof, 70-74, chmn, Dept Dent Med, 70-73, prof biochem, 74-82; prof bio-chem, Sch Med, Mercer Univ, 82-94. *Concurrent Pos:* Fel, Inst Hormone Biol, Syntex Res, 66-67; fel anat, Sch Med, Stanford Univ, 67-69; vis prof, Univ Calif Med Ctr, 75-76. *Mem:* AAAS; Am Chem Soc; Endocrine Soc; Am Soc Biochem & Molecular Biol; Sigma Xi; Am Col Sports Med; Am Soc Bone & Mineral Res; Am Soc Cell Biol. *Res:* Metabolism of bone cells in culture. *Mailing Add:* 13023 Frances St Omaha NE 68144

KADIS, SOLOMON, MICROBIOLOGY. *Current Pos:* RETIRED. *Personal Data:* b Baltimore, Md, May 17, 23; m 58; c 2. *Educ:* St John's Col, Md, BA, 50; Univ Va, MA, 51; Vanderbilt Univ, PhD(cellular physiol), 57. *Prof Exp:* Asst, Vanderbilt Univ, 55-57; res assoc cellular physiol & microbiol, US Vitamin & Pharmaceut Corp, NY, 57-60 & Geront Res Inst, 60-61; assoc prof microbiol & immunol, Sch Med, Temple Univ, 71-72; prof med microbiol, Col Vet Med, Univ Ga, 72-90. *Concurrent Pos:* Asst mem, Res Labs, Albert Einstein Med Ctr, 61-63, assoc mem, 63-73. *Mem:* AAAS; Am Soc Microbiol; Am Acad Microbiol; Sigma Xi; Conf Res Workers in Animal Dis. *Res:* Bacterial physiology and toxin production and action; role of bacterial tox is in pathogenesis of respiratory disease; role of dietary iron in susceptibility of animals to bacterial infectious diseases. *Mailing Add:* 7 Deauville Ct No 2A Baltimore MD 21208

KADIS, VINCENT WILLIAM, MICROBIOLOGY, BIOCHEMISTRY. *Current Pos:* RETIRED. *Personal Data:* b Seinai, Lithuania, Sept 25, 22; Can citizen; m 58, Eileen M Crookes. *Educ:* Univ Sask, BA, 55; Purdue Univ, MSc, 57, PhD(microbiol, biochem), 60. *Prof Exp:* Microbiologist, Alta Dept Agr, Can, 57-61, dir, Food Lab Serv, 61-90; pvt consult, 90-91. *Concurrent Pos:* Consult, anal fields of foods & other agr commodities, food qual-safety anal & planning anal labs. *Mem:* Fel Am Pub Health Asn; Am Inst Food Technologists; Sigma Xi; Can Inst Food Sci & Technol (pres, 77-78); Am Soc Microbiol. *Res:* Bacteriophage of lactic cultures; Q-fever infection in humans and animals; detection and persistence of chlorinated insecticides in human and animal blood; insecticide residues in food; food sanitation, quality and safety; laboratory planning and design. *Mailing Add:* Unit 903-109 St Edmonton AB T6J 6R1 Can

KADISH, KARL MITCHELL, ANALYTICAL CHEMISTRY. *Current Pos:* from asst prof to assoc prof, 76-81, assoc chmn, 79-84, PROF CHEM, UNIV HOUSTON, 81- *Personal Data:* b Detroit, Mich, Feb 4, 45; c 2. *Educ:* Univ Mich, BS, 67; Pa State Univ, PhD(chem), 70. *Honors & Awards:* Sigma Xi Res Award, 88. *Prof Exp:* Vis asst prof chem, Univ New Orleans, 70-71; res asst, Nat Ctr Sci Res, France, 71-72; asst prof chem, Calif State Univ, Fullerton, 72-76. *Concurrent Pos:* Pres, Intersci Consults, USA, 75-; vis prof, Univ Louis Pasteur, Strasbourg, France, 80-81, Univ Rome La Torgavata, Italy, 90 & 91, Ecole Superieure Chem, Lyon, France, 84 & Univ Dijon, France, 85, 87, 88, 91 & 93; secy, Comn V.5 Electroanal Chem, Int Union Pure & Appl Chem, 88-92, mem, Anal Div Comt, 94- *Mem:* Am Chem Soc; Electrochem Soc; Sigma Xi; fel Royal Soc Chem. *Res:* Over 275 publications; analytical chemistry; electro-and bioanalytical chemistry; rates and mechanisms of electron transferin; biologically important compounds; reactions of porphyrin metal complexes; redox reactions of transition metal complexes and dinuclears metal-metal bonded complexes; spectroelectrochemistry; fullerene chemistry. *Mailing Add:* Dept Chem Univ Houston Houston TX 77204-5641

KADISON, RICHARD VINCENT, MATHEMATICS. *Current Pos:* KUEMMERLE PROF MATH, UNIV PA, 64- *Personal Data:* b New York, NY, July 25, 25; m 56, Karen M Holm; c Lars David. *Educ:* Univ Chicago, MS, 47, PhD, 50. *Hon Degrees:* Dr, Univ d'Aix-Marseille, 85, Univ Copenhagen, 87. *Prof Exp:* Nat Res Coun fel math, Inst Advan Study, 50-51, mem, Off Naval Res Contract, 51-52; from asst prof to prof, Columbia Univ, 52-64. *Concurrent Pos:* Fulbright res grant, Denmark, 54-55; Sloan fel, 58-62; Guggenheim fel, 69-70. *Mem:* Nat Acad Sci; foreign mem Royal Danish Acad Sci & Lett; Sigma Xi; foreign mem Norweg Acad Sci & Lett; Am Math Soc. *Res:* Spectral theory; group representations; topological algebra; non-commutative analysis; von Neumann algebras; c-algebras; math physics. *Mailing Add:* Dept Math Univ Pa 209 S 33rd St Philadelphia PA 19104-6395. *Fax:* 215-573-4063; *E-Mail:* liming@math.upenn.edu

KADKADE, PRAKASH GOPAL, PLANT PHYSIOLOGY, PLANT BIOCHEMISTRY. *Current Pos:* MEM TECH STAFF PLANT PHYSIOL, GEN TEL & ELECTRONICS LAB, 74- *Personal Data:* b Goa, India, Sept 10, 41; US citizen; m 70; c 1. *Educ:* Bombay Univ, BSc, 62, MSc, 64; St Louis Univ, PhD(biol), 70. *Prof Exp:* Fel plant biochem, St Louis Univ, 70-71; vis scientist natural prod, Cent Am Res Inst, 71-73; sr res chemist cereal chem, Anheuser Busch, Inc, 73-74. *Concurrent Pos:* Vis scientist plant biochem, Cent Am Res Inst, 74; vis prof molecular biol, Cath Univ, PR, 74. *Mem:* AAAS; Am Inst Biol Sci; Am Inst Plant Physiologists; Int Soc Plant Cell & Tissue Cult; Sigma Xi. *Res:* Understanding of mechanisms of light actions on certain plant biological and chemical processes. *Mailing Add:* GTE Labs 45 Lambert Circle Marlborough MA 01752-1518

KADKO, DAVID C, MARINE SCIENCES. *Current Pos:* assoc prof, 90-96, PROF, ROSENSTIEL SCH MARINE & ATMOSPHERIC CHEM, UNIV MIAMI, 96- *Educ:* Brooklyn Col, BS, 73; Columbia Univ, MA, 74, MPhil, 75, PhD(oceanog), 81. *Prof Exp:* Nat Res Coun fel, US Geol Surv, Menlo Park, Calif, 81-83; res assoc, Ore State Univ, 83-88, asst prof, 89-90. *Concurrent Pos:* Doctoral fel, NSF, 75-78; Fulbright fel, 96. *Mem:* Am Soc Limnol & Oceanog; Am Geophys Union; Sigma Xi. *Res:* Author of numerous publications. *Mailing Add:* Div Marine & Atmospheric Chem Univ Miami 4600 Rickenbacker Causeway Miami FL 33149-1098

KADLEC, JOHN A, WILDLIFE MANAGEMENT, ECOLOGY. *Current Pos:* head dept, 74-80, PROF WILDLIFE SCI, COL NATURAL RESOURCES, UTAH STATE UNIV, 74- *Personal Data:* b Racine, Wis, Sept 22, 31; m 54; c 4. *Educ:* Univ Mich, BSF, 52, MS, 56, PhD(wildlife mgt), 60. *Prof Exp:* Res biologist, Mich Dept Conserv, 58-63 & US Bur Sport Fisheries & Wildlife, 63-67; res assoc & asst prof wildlife mgt, Univ Mich, Ann Arbor & prog coordr anal ecosyst, Int Biol Prog, 68-71, from assoc prof to prof resource ecol, 71-74. *Mem:* AAAS; Wildlife Soc; Ecol Soc Am. *Res:* Applications of population ecology and systems ecology to resource management, especially wildlife; animal habitat studies; wetland ecology. *Mailing Add:* Wildlife Mgt Utah State Univ Logan UT 84322-0001

KADLEC, ROBERT HENRY, CHEMICAL ENGINEERING. *Current Pos:* From asst prof to assoc prof, 61-70, prof 70-, EMER PROF CHEM ENG, UNIV MICH, ANN ARBOR. *Personal Data:* b Racine, Wis, June 11, 38; m 79, D Kay; c 5. *Educ:* Univ Wis, BS, 58; Univ Mich, MS, 59, PhD(chem eng), 62. *Concurrent Pos:* Ed, Am Inst Chem Engrs J, 76-85. *Mem:* Am Inst Chem Engrs; Water Pollution Control Fedn; Soc Wetland Sci; Nat Soc Prof Engrs; Int Asn Water Qual. *Res:* Chemical reactors, water quality; mathematical modelling; simulation; wetlands; wastewater. *Mailing Add:* Dept Chem Eng 2300 Hayward Dow Bldg Univ Mich Campus Ann Arbor MI 48109-2136

KADLUBAR, FRED F, TOXICOLOGY, ONCOLOGY. *Current Pos:* chemist, Div Molecular Biol, 76-79, dir, Div Biochem Toxicol, 79-89, ASSOC DIR RES, NAT CTR TOXICOL RES, 89- *Personal Data:* b Dallas, Tex, Mar 1, 46; m 68; c 2. *Educ:* Univ Dallas, BA, 68; Univ Tex, Austin, PhD(chem), 73. *Prof Exp:* Fel, McArdle Lab Cancer Res, Univ Wis, Madison, 73-76. *Concurrent Pos:* Adj prof, Dept Biochem, Dept Pharmacol & Toxicol, Univ Ark, Little Rock, 77-; mem, Working Cadre Nat Bladder Cancer Proj, 80-84. *Mem:* Am Asn Cancer Res; Sigma Xi; AAAS; Am Chem Soc; Am Soc Biol Chemists. *Res:* Biochemical mechanisms of chemical carcinogenesis with emphasis on aromatic amines and nitroaromatics and liver, bladder, and colon carcinogenisis; detoxification by glutathione and structure properties of carcinogen DNA adducts. *Mailing Add:* Off Res Div Molecular Epidemiol Nat Ctr Toxicol Res Jefferson AR 72079. *Fax:* 870-543-7136

KADNER, CARL GEORGE, INSECT PHYSIOLOGY. *Current Pos:* Instr biol, 36-41, prof & chmn dept, 41-78, EMER PROF BIOL, LOYOLA MARYMOUNT UNIV, 78- *Personal Data:* b Oakland, Calif, May 23, 11; m 39, Beth Moran; c Robert J, Grace K (Wickersham) & Carl L. *Educ:* Univ San Francisco, BS, 33; Univ Calif, Berkeley, MS, 36, PhD(med entom), 41. *Concurrent Pos:* Parasitologist, US Army, 43-46. *Mem:* Entom Soc Am; Sigma Xi. *Res:* Nutritional requirements of Dipteran larvae. *Mailing Add:* 8100 Loyola Blvd Los Angeles CA 90045-2639

KADNER, ROBERT JOSEPH, BIOCHEMICAL GENETICS. *Current Pos:* from asst prof to assoc prof, 69-80, PROF MICROBIOL, SCH MED, UNIV VA, 80- *Personal Data:* b Los Angeles, Calif, Mar 19, 42; m 67, Carole F Mashburn; c Kristen E & Robert J. *Educ:* Loyola Univ, Los Angeles, BS, 63; Univ Calif, Los Angeles, PhD(biol chem), 67. *Prof Exp:* Nat Cancer Inst fel microbiol, Med Sch, NY Univ, 67-69. *Concurrent Pos:* Res career develop award, NIH, 75-80; lectr microbiol, Am Soc Microbiol Found, 88-89; mem, Personal C Rev Panel, Am Cancer Soc, 89-93. *Mem:* Am Soc Microbiol; Genetics Soc Am; Am Soc Biol Chemists. *Res:* Genetics and biochemistry of transport in Escherichia coli; bacterial genetics and regulation. *Mailing Add:* Dept Microbiol Sch Med Univ Va Charlottesville VA 22908-0001. *Fax:* 804-982-1071

KADO, CLARENCE ISAO, MOLECULAR BIOLOGY, PLANT PATHOLOGY. *Current Pos:* from asst prof to assoc prof, 66-76, PROF PLANT PATH, UNIV CALIF, DAVIS, 76-, DIR, FALLEN LEAF LAKE CONF, 85- *Personal Data:* b Santa Rosa, Calif, June 10, 36; m 63; c 2. *Educ:* Univ Calif, Berkeley, BS, 59, PhD, 64. *Honors & Awards:* Rolex Award, 89. *Prof Exp:* Res fel virus lab, Univ Calif, Berkeley, 64-67; asst res biochemist, 67-68. *Concurrent Pos:* Vis prof, Univ Colo, Boulder, 73, Ctr Etude Radiobiol Molecular, Belg, Univ Hawaii, Honolulu, 82 & Friedrich Miescher Inst, Basel, Switz, 92; NATO sr fel, Ctr Study Nuclear Energy, Mol, Belg, 74-75; sabbatical leave, Dept Molecular, Cellular & Develop Biol, Univ Colo, Boulder, 75. *Mem:* AAAS; Am Soc Microbiol; fel Am Phytopath Soc; NY Acad Sci; Sigma Xi; fel Am Acad Microbiol; Am Soc Molecular Biol & Biochem; Am Chem Soc; Int Soc Molecular Plant-Microbe Interaction. *Res:* Molecular biology of host-pathogen interactions; molecular mechanism of tumorigenesis and abnormal growth in higher cells; plant bacteriology. *Mailing Add:* Dept Plant Path Univ Calif Davis CA 95616

KADOR, PETER FRITZ, MEDICINAL CHEMISTRY. *Current Pos:* Staff fel cataract res, Nat Eye Inst, NIH, 76-79, res chemist, 79-85, Chief Molecular Pharmacol, 85-91, CHIEF LAB OCULAR THERAPEUT, NAT EYE INST, NIH, 91- *Personal Data:* b Regensburg, Ger, Oct 3, 49; US citizen; m 76; c 2. *Educ:* Capital Univ, BA, 72; Ohio State Univ, PhD(med chem), 76. *Honors & Awards:* Rhoto Cataract Res Award, 81; Alcon Res Found award, 86; Fed Cross Merit Ger Gov, 94; Kinoshita Lect, Nat Found Eye Res, 95. *Concurrent Pos:* Trustee, Asn Ocular Pharmacol & Therapeut, 95-, Nat Found Eye Res, 96- *Mem:* Am Chem Soc; Asn Res Vision & Ophthal; Am Diabetes Asn; Asn Ocular Pharmacol & Therapeut; Int Soc Eye Res. *Res:* Cataract development; drug effects on the lens; aldose reductase inhibitors; diabetic complications; ocular pharmacology. *Mailing Add:* 9419 Jongroner Ct Potomac MD 20854. *Fax:* 301-402-2399; *E-Mail:* kador@helix.nih.gov

KADOTA, T THEODORE, MATHEMATICS, COMMUNICATIONS. *Current Pos:* RETIRED. *Personal Data:* b Ehime-ken, Japan, Nov 14, 30; US citizen; m 56; c 3. *Educ:* Yokohama Nat Univ, BS, 53; Univ Calif, Berkeley, MS, 56, PhD(elec eng), 60. *Prof Exp:* Teaching asst, Univ Calif, Berkeley, 55-56, res asst, 56-60; mem staff math, AT&T Bell Labs, Inc, 60-93. *Mem:* Fel Inst Elec & Electronics Engrs. *Res:* Mathematical research in communication and information theory, specifically, application of probability theory and stochastic processes to detection, estimation, information theory; model making; theorem proving. *Mailing Add:* 6750 Hawaii Kai Dr Honolulu HI 96825

KADOUM, AHMED MOHAMED, ENTOMOLOGY, TOXICOLOGY. *Current Pos:* ASST PROF ENTOM, KANS STATE UNIV, 66- *Personal Data:* b Oct 28, 37; m 65; c 2. *Educ:* Univ Alexandria, BSc, 58; Univ Nebr, MSc, 63, PhD(entom), 66. *Prof Exp:* Instr chem, Univ Alexandria, 58-60; res asst entom, Univ Nebr, 62-65; instr toxicol, 65-66. *Res:* Pesticidal chemistry and toxicology. *Mailing Add:* 1511 University Dr Manhattan KS 66502

KADOWITZ, PHILLIP J, PHARMACOLOGY. *Current Pos:* from asst prof to assoc prof, 71-78, PROF PHARMACOL, TULANE UNIV MED SCH, 78- *Personal Data:* b Newark, NJ, Mar 20, 41. *Educ:* Rutgers Univ, BS, 63; Sch Med, Marquette Univ, PhD(pharmacol), 68. *Prof Exp:* Fel pharmacol, Univ Iowa, 68-71. *Concurrent Pos:* Chmn, Cardiopulmonary Coun, Am Heart Asn, 90-92. *Mem:* Am Heart Asn; Am Soc Pharmacol & Exp Therapeut. *Mailing Add:* Dept Pharmacol Tulane Univ Sch Med 1430 Tulane Ave New Orleans LA 70112-2699

KADYK, JOHN AMOS, PHYSICS. *Current Pos:* EXP PHYSICIST, LAWRENCE BERKELEY LAB, UNIV CALIF, 59- *Personal Data:* b Springfield, Ill, Nov 10, 29; m 57, Ann Ford; c Lisa & John. *Educ:* Williams Col, AB, 52; Mass Inst Technol, BS, 52; Calif Inst Technol, PhD(physics), 57. *Prof Exp:* Instr physics, Univ Mich, 57-59. *Mem:* Am Phys Soc. *Res:* High energy physics; colliding beams. *Mailing Add:* MS 50A-2160 Lawrence Berkeley Lab Univ Calif One Cyclotron Rd Berkeley CA 94720. *Fax:* 510-486-5105; *E-Mail:* kadyk@csa.lbl.gov

KAEDING, WARREN WILLIAM, organic chemistry; deceased, see previous edition for last biography

KAELBER, CHARLES THEODORE, PSYCHOPATHOLOGY. *Current Pos:* CHIEF PSYCHOPATH RES, NIMH, NIH, 87- *Personal Data:* b Cardington, Ohio, Feb 25, 38. *Educ:* Harvard Univ, MPH, 67, DrPH, 69; Case Western Reserve Univ, MD, 75. *Mem:* Am Psychiat Asn. *Mailing Add:* NIMH NIH 10C09 Parklon Bldg 5600 Fisher's Ln Rockville MD 20857. *Fax:* 301-443-4045; *E-Mail:* ckaelber@nih.gov

KAELBER, WILLIAM WALBRIDGE, neurology; deceased, see previous edition for last biography

KAELBLE, DAVID HARDIE, INTELLIGENT SYSTEMS, TECHNICAL MANAGEMENT. *Current Pos:* DIR, ARROYO COMPUT CTR, 80- *Personal Data:* b Pine City, Minn, June 2, 28; m 51; c 5. *Educ:* Univ Minn, Minneapolis, BSc, 51. *Honors & Awards:* Adhesion Award, Am Soc Test & Mat, 63. *Prof Exp:* Res chemist, Cent Res Labs, 3M Co, 51-56, sr res chemist, 56-61, res specialist, 61-69; mem tech staff, Sci Ctr, Rockwell Int Corp, 69-75, group leader polymer & Composites Group, 75-80. *Concurrent Pos:* Mem comt damping nomenclature, Am Standards Asn, 63-65 & comt adhesion, Nat Res Coun, 71; chmn, Gordon Conf Adhesion, 71; chmn, Gordon Conf Thermosetts, 81. *Mem:* Am Chem Soc; Soc Rheol. *Res:* Adhesion phenomena including surface chemistry, rheology, and fracture mechanics; polymer physical chemistry and mechanical properties; biophysics and composite material properties; cognitive science; computer modeling; intelligent systems; technical management. *Mailing Add:* Arroyo Comput Ctr 730 Blue Oak Ave Thousand Oaks CA 91320

KAELBLE, EMMETT FRANK, ANALYTICAL CHEMISTRY, SPECTROSCOPY. *Current Pos:* ASSOC, CHELAN ASSOCS, 87- *Personal Data:* b St Louis, Mo, July 31, 31; m 55; c 3. *Educ:* DePauw Univ, BA, 53; Univ Ill, MS, 55, PhD(anal chem), 57. *Prof Exp:* From res chemist to sr res chemist, Monsanto Indust Chem Co, 57-64, res group leader, Res Dept, Inorg Chem Div, Monsanto Co, 64-78, sr res group leader, appl tech, 78-86. *Mem:* Am Chem Soc; Soc Appl Spectros. *Res:* X-ray spectroscopy; chromatography; other instrumental and chemical analytical techniques. *Mailing Add:* 641 Windrush Dr Kirkwood MO 63122-3054

KAELLIS, JOSEPH, HEAT TRANSFER. *Current Pos:* CONSULT, PVT PRACT, 81- *Personal Data:* b Philadelphia, Pa, July 6, 25. *Educ:* City Col New York, BS, 49; Univ Mo, MS, 50; Ill Inst Technol, PhD(chem eng), 70. *Prof Exp:* Asst engr, Griscom Russel Co, 50-55; assoc engr, Argonne Nat Lab,

55-77, Advan Reactors Div, Westinghouse Elec Corp, 72-74, C F Braun & Co, 74-76 & TRW Inc, 77-80; chief engr, Basic Technol Inc, 80-81. *Concurrent Pos:* Pres, Kaellis Eng. *Mem:* Am Inst Chem Engrs; Am Nuclear Soc; Sigma Xi. *Res:* Computer technique used to determine the simultaneous transient developing mass momentum boundary layer resulting from the flow of a fluid through a channel having walls which dissolve. *Mailing Add:* 5700 Etiwanda Ave No 287 Tarzana CA 91356-2550

KAEMPFFER, FREDERICK AUGUSTUS, THEORETICAL PHYSICS. *Current Pos:* Lectr, 48, from asst prof to prof, 49-85, EMER PROF PHYSICS, UNIV BC, 86- *Personal Data:* b Gorlitz, Germany, Nov 29, 20; nat Can; m 44; c 2. *Educ:* Univ Gottingen, dipl physics, 43, Dr rer nat(physics), 48. *Mem:* Am Phys Soc. *Res:* Theory of fields. *Mailing Add:* 2054 Western Pkwy Vancouver BC V6T 1V5 Can

KAESBERG, PAUL JOSEPH, VIROLOGY. *Current Pos:* From instr to asst prof biomet & physics, Univ Wis-Madison, 49-54, from asst prof to prof biochem, 55-62, prof biophys & biochem, 63-82, chmn, Biophys Lab, 69-87, William W Beeman prof, 82-86, chmn, Inst Molecular Virol, 87-88, prof molecular virol & biochem, 87-90, EMER PROF MOLECULAR VIROL & BIOCHEM, UNIV WIS-MADISON, 90- *Personal Data:* b Engers, Ger, Sept 26, 23; nat US; m 53; c 3. *Educ:* Univ Wis, BS, 45, PhD(physics & math), 49. *Hon Degrees:* DSc, Univ Leiden, Neth, 75. *Concurrent Pos:* Res career investr, USPHS, NIH Res, 63-; assoc ed, Virol; consult, NIH, NSF & US Dept Agr. *Mem:* Nat Acad Sci; Biophys Soc; Sigma Xi; Am Soc Microbiol; Am Soc Virol (pres, 87-88); Am Soc Biol Chem & Molecular Biol; Gt Brit Soc Gen Microbiol. *Res:* Structure and synthesis of viruses and macromolecules; author of numerous publications. *Mailing Add:* Molecular Virol Inst Univ Wis Madison WI 53706

KAESER, R S, INSTRUMENT & MEASUREMENT SCIENCE. *Current Pos:* RETIRED. *Personal Data:* b Pittsfield, Ill, Jan 14, 28. *Educ:* Ill Col, BS, 50. *Prof Exp:* Staff scientist, Nat Inst Stand & Technol, 62-92. *Mem:* Am Phys Soc. *Mailing Add:* 5800 Dimes Rd Rockville MD 20855-1729

KAESLER, ROGER LEROY, MICROPALEONTOLOGY. *Current Pos:* From asst prof to assoc prof, 65-73, PROF GEOL & DIR MUS INVERT PALEONT, UNIV KANS, 73- *Personal Data:* b Ponca City, Okla, June 22, 37; div; c 3. *Educ:* Colo Sch Mines, GeolE, 59; Univ Kans, MS, 62, PhD(micropaleont), 65. *Mem:* Paleont Soc; Soc Syst Zool; Geol Soc Am; Am Soc Naturalists. *Res:* Paleoecology of Ostracoda; quantitative methods in paleontology and applied aquatic biology. *Mailing Add:* 120 Lindley Hall Lawrence KS 66045-2124

KAESZ, HERBERT DAVID, ORGANOMETALLIC CHEMISTRY. *Current Pos:* from asst prof to assoc prof, 60-68, PROF INORG CHEM, UNIV CALIF, LOS ANGELES, 68- *Personal Data:* b Alexandria, Egypt, Jan 4, 33; nat US; m 58; c 3. *Educ:* NY Univ, BA, 54; Harvard Univ, MA, 56, PhD, 59. *Honors & Awards:* US Scientist Award, Alexander von Humboldt Sr, Fed Repub Ger, 88. *Prof Exp:* Fel inorg chem & adv prog high sch teachers, Harvard Univ, 58-60. *Concurrent Pos:* Assoc ed, Inorg Chem, Am Chem Soc, 68- *Mem:* Am Chem Soc; Royal Soc Chem; fel AAAS; fel Japan Soc Prom Sci. *Res:* Chemistry of transition metals, especially organometallic complexes, polynuclear metal carbonyl cluster complexes and hydrides; pathways of homogeneous catalysis; organometallic chemical deposition; coal liquefaction. *Mailing Add:* Dept Chem & Biochem Univ Calif Los Angeles CA 90095-1569

KAETZEL, MARCIA ALDYTH, CALMODULIN, CALMODULIN BINDINGS PROTEINS. *Current Pos:* FEL CELL BIOL, SCH MED, UNIV TEX, 85- *Educ:* Baylor Col Med, PhD(cell biol), 85. *Mailing Add:* Dept Molecular & Cel Physiol Univ Cincinnati 231 Bethesda Ave PO Box 670576 Cincinnati OH 45267-0576. *Fax:* 513-558-5738

KAFADAR, KAREN, DATA ANALYSIS, ROBUST METHODS. *Current Pos:* assoc prof, 94-97, PROF MATH, UNIV COLO, DENVER, 97- *Personal Data:* b Evergreen Park, Ill, July 6, 53. *Educ:* Stanford Univ, BS & MS, 75; Princeton Univ, PhD(statist), 79. *Prof Exp:* Asst prof statist, Ore State Univ, 79-80; math statistician, Statist Eng Div, Nat Bur Stand, 80-83; mem tech staff, Hewlett-Packard, 83-90. *Concurrent Pos:* Consult, OEA, Inc, 77- *Mem:* Am Statist Asn; Inst Math Statist. *Res:* New methodology in data analysis particularly robust methods and treatment of outliers; experimental design; spectrum analysis; statistical engineering design. *Mailing Add:* Math Dept Univ Colo Denver Campus Box 170 PO Box 173364 Denver CO 80217-3364

KAFAFI, ZAKYA HUSSEIN, LIGHT-EMITTING MATERIALS & DEVICES, NONLINEAR & LINEAR SPECTROSCOPIES. *Current Pos:* SR RES SCIENTIST, US NAVAL RES LAB, 86- *Educ:* Univ Houston, BSc, 69; Rice Univ, MA, 72, PhD(chem), 72. *Honors & Awards:* IR-100 Award, 86. *Prof Exp:* Asst prof, Al-Azhar Univ, 79-81; vis prof, Rice Univ, 81-86. *Concurrent Pos:* Pres, Spectros Assoc, 85-89. *Mem:* Am Chem Soc; Optical Soc Am; Soc Photo-Optical Instrumentation Engrs; Soc Info Display; Mat Res Soc. *Res:* Nonlinear optical organic materials; light-emitting material and devices; matrix isolation spectroscopy; metal aluminum cluster chemistry; inert bond activation. *Mailing Add:* Naval Res Lab Code 5611 Washington DC 20375

KAFALAS, PETER, LASER TECHNOLOGY. *Current Pos:* RETIRED. *Personal Data:* b Newburyport, Mass, Dec 6, 25; m 57, Eleanor Juco; c 2. *Educ:* Harvard Univ, AB, 50; Mass Inst Technol, PhD(inorg chem), 54. *Prof Exp:* Assoc chemist, Argonne Nat Lab, 54-59; staff mem, Mitre Corp, Mass, 59-61; sr scientist, Tech Opers, Inc, 61-65; staff mem, Lincoln Lab, Mass Inst Technol, 65-86. *Concurrent Pos:* Consult, Laser Technol. *Mem:* Am Chem Soc; Optical Soc Am. *Res:* Nuclear chemistry, deuteron reactions and neutron reactions; spectroscopy, high-speed spectrography of plasmas; laser technology, laser Q-switching with saturable dyes; laser propagation studies; laser vaporization of fog droplets; laser beam diagnostics. *Mailing Add:* 24 Hickory Rd Sudbury MA 01776

KAFATOS, FOTIS C, DEVELOPMENTAL BIOLOGY. *Current Pos:* DIR-GEN, EUROP MOLECULAR BIOL LAB, 93- *Personal Data:* b Crete, Greece, Apr 16, 40; nat US; m 67; c 2. *Educ:* Cornell Univ, AB, 61; Harvard Univ, MA, 62, PhD(biol), 65. *Hon Degrees:* DSc, Univ Athens, 92, Univ Thessaloniki, 94. *Honors & Awards:* Walter Bauer Mem Lectr, Helen May Whitney Found, 78; Rosenberger Distinguished Lectr, Univ Rochester, 81; G J Mendel Hon Gold Medal Merit Biol Sci, Acad Sci Czech Repub, 95. *Prof Exp:* Tutor, Harvard Univ, 62-63, from instr to prof biol, 65-94, chmn cellular & develop biol, 78-81; prof biol & dir, Inst Molecular Biol & Biotechnol, Res Ctr Crete, 82-93. *Concurrent Pos:* Mem, Develop Biol Panel, NSF, 70-72; adj prof biol, Univ Athens, 72-82, Univ Crete, 82-; distinguished lectr, Univ Tex, 77; mem, Cell Biol & Nucleic Acids & Protein Synthesis Adv Comt, Am Cancer Soc, 83-86; mem, Nat Sci Adv Bd, Greece, 88- *Mem:* Nat Acad Sci; fel AAAS; Am Soc Cell Biol; Soc Develop Biol (pres, 81-82); fel Am Acad Arts & Sci; Europ Molecular Biol Orgn; Genetics Soc Am; Am Soc Zoologists; Int Soc Develop Biologists; Hellenic Biochem & Biophys Soc; Hellenic Soc Biol Sci; Human Genome Orgn. *Res:* Molecular and cellular aspects of development, cell differentiation during insect metamorphosis; molecular evolution; over 240 papers in refereed journals. *Mailing Add:* Europ Molecular Biol Lab Meyerhofstrass Nol 69117 Heidelberg Germany

KAFATOS, MINAS, ASTROPHYSICS. *Current Pos:* from asst prof to assoc prof, 75-84, PROF PHYSICS, GEORGE MASON UNIV, 84- *Personal Data:* b Crete, Greece, Mar 25, 45; m 71; c 3. *Educ:* Cornell Univ, BA, 67; Mass Inst Technol, PhD(physics), 72. *Prof Exp:* Res assoc astrophysics, Joint Inst for Lab Astrophys, Univ Colo, 72-73 & Nat Res Coun, Nat Acad Sci, 73-75. *Concurrent Pos:* Res scientist astrophys, Goddard Space Flight Ctr, NASA, 75- *Mem:* Am Astron Soc; Am Phys Soc; Int Astron Union; Royal Astron Soc. *Res:* Black holes; quasars; active galaxies; interstellar medium; mass loss and long period variables; forbidden line calculations; symbiotic stars; cosmic rays; supernovae; quantum physics. *Mailing Add:* CSI Inst George Mason Univ 4400 University Dr Fairfax VA 22030

KAFER, ENID ROSEMARY, ANESTHESIOLOGY. *Current Pos:* assoc prof physiol & anesthesiol, 73-82, PROF ANESTHESIOL, SCH MED, UNIV NC, CHAPEL HILL, 82-, DIR NEUROANESTHESIOL, 82- *Personal Data:* b Sydney, Australia, May 27, 37. *Educ:* Univ Sydney, BS, 59, MB & BS, 62, MD, 70, FRACP, FRCA, ABA. *Honors & Awards:* Peter Bancroft Award, 70. *Prof Exp:* Med resident, Royal Prince Alfred Hosp, Sydney, 62-63, anesthetic registr, 64; res fel, Dept Med, Univ Sydney, 65-66, lectr, 67, Life Ins Med Res fel, 68-69; sr registr, Dept Anesthetics, Royal Postgrad Med Sch, London, 69-71; fel physiol, Univ Calif, San Francisco, 71-72, asst prof, Dept Anesthesia, 72-73; consult respiratory & anesthesia diseases panel, Food & Drug Admin. *Concurrent Pos:* Mem, Res Rev Comt, NC Heart Asn, 76-79. *Mem:* Fel Royal Australian Col Physicians; Am Physiol Soc; Am Soc Anesthesiologists; Sigma Xi; fel Royal Col Anesthetists; Am Asn Med Instrumentation. *Res:* Load adjustment mechanisms of the respiratory system, including examination of neural and muscle factors, and effects of changing chemical stimuli, chemoreceptor denervation and the effects of general anesthesia on respiratory control. *Mailing Add:* Dept Anesthesiol Sch Med Univ NC CB-7010 Chapel Hill NC 27599-7010. *Fax:* 919-966-4873

KAFER, ETTA (MRS E R BOOTHROYD), MITOTIC RECOMBINATION, ANEUPLOIDY. *Current Pos:* RETIRED. *Personal Data:* b Zurich, Switz, July 31, 25; m 57, E Roger Boothroyd; c Arnold Ian, Karin Jean & Derek Brian. *Educ:* Univ Zurich, dipl, 48, PhD(genetics), 52. *Honors & Awards:* Award of Excellence, Genetics Soc Can, 87. *Prof Exp:* Res asst microbial genetics, Glasgow Univ, 53-55, res fel, 55-56, res fel, Carnegie Inst, 56; res assoc, McGill Univ, 58-63, from lectr to prof molecular genetics, 59-92. *Concurrent Pos:* Adj prof, Biosci Dept, Simon Fraser Univ; assoc mem, Inst Molecular Biol & Biochem, 91- *Mem:* Genetics Soc Am; Genetics Soc Can; Swiss Genetics Soc; Environ Mutogen Soc. *Res:* Microbial genetics; mitotic and meiotic recombination; molecular genetics of nucleases; DNA repair mutants and gene cloning in fungi; assays for environmentally induced nondisjunction; genetics of fungi used for biotechnology. *Mailing Add:* 23233 52nd Ave RR 13 Langley BC V2Z 2R6 Can. *Fax:* 604-291-5583

KAFESJIAN, R(ALPH), CHEMICAL ENGINEERING, PHYSICAL CHEMISTRY. *Current Pos:* SR ENGR, BAXTER HEALTHCARE, 86- *Personal Data:* b Chicago, Ill, Mar 28, 34; m 55; c 3. *Educ:* Purdue Univ, BS, 55; Univ Louisville, MChE, 57, PhD(chem eng), 61. *Prof Exp:* Instr chem physics & chem eng, Univ Louisville, 57-60; res chem engr, Monsanto Res Corp, 61-63, sr res chem engr, 63-67, res group leader, 67-69; biomed res lab, Am Hosp Supply Corp, 69-71; task leader corp technol, 71-77, sr scientist, 78-80, prin scientist, 81-86. *Mem:* AAAS; Am Chem Soc; assoc Am Inst Chem Engrs; Nat Asn Corrosion Engrs; Biomat Soc; Sigma Xi. *Res:* High temperature materials, reactions, processes and technology; electrochemical energy conversion methods; corrosion; electrochemistry; biomedical materials and devices. *Mailing Add:* Baxter Healthcare 17221 Red Hill MS 22 Irvine CA 92714

KAFKA, MARIAN STERN, NEUROSCIENCE, PHYSIOLOGY. *Current Pos:* USPHS fel, Endocrinol Br, Nat Heart & Lung Inst, 65-68, physiologist, Hypertension-Endocrine Br, 68-74, sect biochem & pharmacol, Biol Psychiat Br, 74-82, physiologist, Clin Neurosci Br, 82-85, exec secy, Cellular Neurobiol & Psychopharmacol, 85-90, CHIEF CLIN, EPIDEMIOL & SERV REV BR, DIV EXTRAMURAL ACTIV, NIMH, USPHS, 90- *Personal Data:* b Richmond, Va, Mar 30, 27; m 52; c 3. *Educ:* Conn Col, BA, 48; Univ Chicago, PhD(physiol), 52. *Prof Exp:* Asst physiol, Sch Med, Univ Chicago, 48-52; res asst, Sch Med, Emory Univ, 52-53, Ill Neuropsychiat Inst, Univ Ill, Chicago, 53-54 & Sch Med, Yale Univ, 54-57. *Concurrent Pos:* Marie J Mergler fel physiol, Univ Chicago, Ill, 50; mem, pub info comt, Fedn Am Socs Exp Biol, 77-82; mem, coun NIMH-Nat Inst Neurol & Commun Dis Assembly Scientists, 81-82, pres, 82-83 & mem, clin res rev comt, NIMH, 82-84; mem, Comt Intramural Prog Dir's Conf, NIH, 82-85; reviewer, Med Res Coun Can & NSF & numerous sci publns. *Mem:* Am Physiol Soc; Endocrine Soc; Biophys Soc; AAAS; Sigma Xi; Soc Neurosci; Int Soc Chronobiol. *Res:* Interaction between neurotransmitters, hormones and receptors on neurons and blood cells; central nervous system control of circadian rhythms. *Mailing Add:* NIMH NIH 9C-26 7834 Aberdeen Rd Bethesda MD 20814-1102

KAFKA, ROBERT W(ILLIAM), DEFENSE ELECTRONICS SYSTEMS, COMMAND & CONTROL SYSTEMS. *Current Pos:* RETIRED. *Personal Data:* b Chicago, Ill, Oct 30, 37; m 66; c 2. *Educ:* Univ Ill, BSEE, 58, MSEE, 59, PhD(elec eng), 63. *Prof Exp:* Instr elec eng, Univ Ill, 60-63; mem tech staff, Guidance & Control Dept, Aerospace Corp, 63-66; mgr, Advan Systs Prog Off, Systs Div, Hughes Aircraft Co, 66-94. *Mem:* Inst Elec & Electronics Engrs; Sigma Xi. *Mailing Add:* 2749 Puente St Fullerton CA 92835

KAFKA, TOMAS, EXPERIMENTAL, ELEMENTARY PARTICLE PHYSICS. *Current Pos:* from res asst prof to res assoc prof, 82-91, RES PROF, TUFTS UNIV, 91- *Personal Data:* b Praha, Czech, Oct 15, 36; US citizen; m 96, Suzanne H Costanza. *Educ:* Univ Karlova, Praha, Promovany Fyzik, 60; State Univ NY, Stony Brook, PhD(physics), 74. *Prof Exp:* Res assoc, State Univ NY, Stony Brook, 74-82. *Mem:* Am Phys Soc. *Res:* Hadron-hadron, lepton-hadron, and photon-hadron interactions at high energies; proton decay; cosmic rays; particle astronomy. *Mailing Add:* Dept Physics & Astron Tufts Univ Medford MA 02155. *E-Mail:* kafka@tuhep3.phy.tufts.edu

KAFRAWY, ADEL, POLYMER & ORGANIC CHEMISTRY, CELLULOSE TECHNOLOGY. *Current Pos:* sr scientist, 81-91, GROUP LEADER, JOHNSON & JOHNSON, 91- *Personal Data:* b Cairo, Egypt, Oct 15, 43; US citizen; m 75; c 2. *Educ:* Cairo Univ, BSc, 64; Univ Rochester, MS, 71; Univ Mo-Columbia, PhD(org chem), 74; Syracuse Univ, MBA, 83. *Prof Exp:* Demonstr chem, Cairo Univ, 64-68; assoc phys org chem, Syracuse Univ, 74-75; assoc org chem, State Univ NY Col Environ Sci & Forestry, Syracuse, 75-77; res chemist, Cellulose Res, ITT Rayonier, Inc, 77-81. *Res:* Biomedical application of polymers; controlled drug release systems; absorbable biomedical polymers. *Mailing Add:* 16 Cooke Ave Kingston MA 02364

KAFRI, ODED, MOIRE EFFECT, AUTHENTICATION. *Current Pos:* PRES SYNCRONYS, ISRAEL, 94- *Personal Data:* b Tel-Aviv, Israel, Dec 13, 44; m 66; c 2. *Educ:* Technion, BSc, 69, DSc, 73. *Prof Exp:* Asst, Dept Chem, Technion, 69-71, instr, 71-73; instr appl physics, Hebrew Univ, Jerusalem, 73-74; res scientist assoc, Dept Chem, Univ Wis-Madison, 74-76; res scientist, Nuclear Res Ctr-Negev, Beer Sheva, 76-82, group leader, Optical-Non-Destructive Testing, 78-86; pres, Rotlex Optics Ltd, Arava, Israel, 86-89; pres, Fontech Ltd, 90-94. *Concurrent Pos:* Adv energy, Nat Res Coun, Israel, 78-82; sr res scientist, Nuclear Res Ctr-Negev, Beer Sheva, 82-89; sr physicist, Corp Technol, Allied Corp, Mt Bethel, NJ, 83-84. *Mem:* Optical Soc Am; Int Soc Optical Eng. *Res:* Optical metrology: invention of moire deflectometry, a method used in several industries like ophthalmological industry, wind tunnels, lasers industries and research labs; theoretical aspects of metrology and information theory; author or co-author of one book, over 100 scientific publications and holder of over 20 patents; developed a method to print data on paper and to send data from personal computer to paper fax; telecommunication. *Mailing Add:* Ehud 3 Beer Sheva 84234 Israel. *Fax:* 972-627-4695

KAGAN, BENJAMIN, REGULATORY AFFAIRS. *Current Pos:* CONSULT, REGULATORY AFFAIRS, 77- *Personal Data:* b New York, NY, Mar 9, 21; m 43, Helen L Hallem; c Tobias & Debra. *Educ:* DePaul Univ, BS, 47; Pa State Univ, MS, 50. *Prof Exp:* Org res chemist, Army Chem Ctr, Md, 50-62; res anal chemist, Div Food Chem, Bur Drugs, Food & Drug Admin, 62-66, chemist, Div Oncol & Radiopharmaceut Drug Prod, 66-73, supvry chemist, 73-77. *Concurrent Pos:* Lectr regulatory affairs, 79-85; Fla Sect, (counr, 82-92, pres, Am Inst Chemists, 92-94). *Mem:* Emer mem AAAS; emer mem Am Chem Soc; fel Am Inst Chemists; NY Acad Sci; Royal Soc Chem. *Res:* Organo-phosphorous and sulfur compounds; nitrogen heterocycles; radiopharmaceuticals. *Mailing Add:* PO Box 352948 Palm Coast FL 32135-2948

KAGAN, BENJAMIN M, PEDIATRICS, INFECTIOUS DISEASE. *Current Pos:* prof-in-residence, 55-90, vchmn dept, 74-90, EMER PROF PEDIAT, SCH MED, UNIV CALIF, LOS ANGELES, 90- *Personal Data:* b Washington, Pa, July 18, 13; m 40, Katherine Hamburger; c Christopher & Robert. *Educ:* Washington & Jefferson Col, AB, 33; Johns Hopkins Univ, MD, 37; Am Bd Nutrit & Am Bd Pediat, cert & recert. *Honors & Awards:* Distinguished Serv Award, US Army, 45; Citation, Am Acad of Pediat, 78. *Prof Exp:* Instr, St Phillip Sch Pub Health Nursing, 40-42, Marine Biol Lab, Woods Hole, 34; intern, Sinai Hosp, Baltimore, 37-38; res contagion, Willard Parker Hosp, 38; resident pediat, Babies Hosp, New York, 38-40; instr pediat, Med Col Va, 40-42; asst, Columbia Univ, 46; from clin asst prof to clin prof, Univ Ill, 47-54; prof, Northwestern Univ, 54-55. *Concurrent Pos:* Mem staff, Michael Reese Hosp, 46-55, attend pediatrician, & dir, Pediat Res Dept, Inst Med Res, 46-55, chmn dept pediat, 51-55; dir & chmn pediat, Cedars Sinai Med Ctr, 55-; official examr, mem exec comt & chmn written exam comt, Am Bd Pediat; dir, Cystic Fibrosis Ctr, 60- *Mem:* AAAS; Am Pediat Soc; Soc Pediat Res; Soc Exp Biol & Med; AMA; fel Am Acad Pediat; fel Am Col Physicians; fel Am Col Chest Physicians; fel Infectious Dis Soc Am; fel Pediat Infectious Dis. *Res:* Nutrition and infectious disease; cystic fibrosis; 142 publications in refereed journals. *Mailing Add:* Dept Pediat Cedars Sinai Med Ctr Univ Calif 8700 Beverly Blvd Los Angeles CA 90027-1809

KAGAN, BRUCE L, PSYCHOPHARMACOLOGY, ELECTRO PHYSIOLOGY. *Current Pos:* Asst prof, 86-92, ASSOC PROF PSYCHIAT, UNIV CALIF, LOS ANGELES, 92- *Personal Data:* b New York, NY, Aug 1, 53; m 89. *Educ:* Yale Univ, BA, 75; Yeshiva Univ, MD, 82, PhD(physiol, biophys), 82. *Mem:* Fel Am Psychiat Asn; Biophys Soc; Int Soc Traumatic Stress Studies; Am Soc Clin Psychopharmacol. *Res:* Channel forming toxins including colicins, diphtheria toxin, yeast killer, defeunsins, amylin, prions. *Mailing Add:* 760 Westwood Pl Los Angeles CA 90024. *E-Mail:* bkagan@np.h.mednet.ucla.edu

KAGAN, FRED, MEDICINAL CHEMISTRY, ORGANIC CHEMISTRY. *Current Pos:* RETIRED. *Personal Data:* b Chicago, Ill, Dec 24, 20; m 45; c 6. *Educ:* Univ Ill, BS, 42; Mass Inst Technol, PhD(org chem), 49. *Prof Exp:* Res org chemist, Stand Oil Co Ind, 49-52; res org chemist, Upjohn Co, 52-68, mgr cent nerv syst res, 68-78, group mgr, 78-81, dir exp sci & therapeut, 81-82, vpres therapeut, clin res & biotechnol, 82-86. *Mem:* Am Chem Soc; Royal Soc Chem; NY Acad Sci. *Res:* Synthesis; psychopharmacology, drug development from test tube thru obtaining an NDA and obtaining international registrations. *Mailing Add:* 2225 Chevy Chase Kalamazoo MI 49008-2225

KAGAN, HARVEY ALEXANDER, CONSTRUCTION MANAGEMENT, FORENSIC ENGINEERING. *Current Pos:* ASSOC, S T HUDSON INT, INC, 87- *Personal Data:* b New York, NY, Sept 25, 37; m 68; c 2. *Educ:* Columbia Univ, BS, 58; Univ Ill, MS, 59; NY Univ, EngScD(civil eng), 65; Purdue Univ, MS, 80. *Prof Exp:* Struct engr, Repub Aviation Corp, 59-61; asst civil engr, New York City Bd Educ, 61; struct test engr, Martin Co Div, Martin-Marietta Corp, 61-62, eng specialist, 65-66; test engr, Vertol Div, Boeing Co, 62; struct mech engr, Grumman Aircraft Corp, 66; from asst prof to assoc prof civil eng, Rutgers Univ, 66-74; sr civil engr, C F Braun & Co, 74-75; assoc prof & prog chmn, Univ Evansville, 75-77; sr consult, Wagner-Hohns-Inglis, 78-81; sr consult, Hill Int, Inc, 81-82; pres, Construct Adv Group, Inc, 82-84; prof civil eng, Rutgers Univ, 84-87. *Concurrent Pos:* NSF res grant, 67-68. *Mem:* Am Soc Civil Engrs; Am Concrete Inst; Sigma Xi. *Mailing Add:* 18 Tanager Way Medford NJ 08055

KAGAN, HERBERT MARCUS, BIOCHEMISTRY. *Current Pos:* asst prof, 69-72, assoc prof, 72-80, PROF BIOCHEM, SCH MED, BOSTON UNIV, 80- *Personal Data:* b Boston, Mass, Aug 18, 32; m 62; c 2. *Educ:* Univ Mass, Amherst, BS, 54, MS, 56; Tufts Univ, PhD(biochem), 66. *Prof Exp:* Instr microbiol, Purdue Univ, 56-58; res assoc pharmacol, Sch Med, Boston Univ, 59-60; biologist, Arthur D Little, Inc, 60-61; Am Cancer Soc res fel biochem, Harvard Med Sch, 66-69. *Concurrent Pos:* Am Cancer Soc res fel biochem, Harvard Med Sch, 66-69; Fel, Arteriosclerosis Coun, Am Heart Asn; merit award, NIH, 88- *Mem:* AAAS; Am Soc Biol Chemists; Am Heart Asn; Sigma Xi. *Res:* Enzymology; protein chemistry; structure-function relationships of enzymes; connective tissue proteins; stereospecifity in catalysis. *Mailing Add:* Dept Biochem Boston Univ Sch Med 80 E Concord St Boston MA 02118-2394. *Fax:* 617-638-4459; *E-Mail:* kagan@med-biochm.bu.edu

KAGAN, IRVING GEORGE, PARASITOLOGY, IMMUNOLOGY. *Current Pos:* chief Helminth Unit, 57-62, chief Parasitol Unit, 62-66, DIR PARASITOL DIV, CTRS DIS CONTROL, 67- *Personal Data:* b New York, NY, June 1, 19; m 40; c 2. *Educ:* Brooklyn Col, AB, 40; Univ Mich, MA, 47, PhD(zool), 50. *Honors & Awards:* Henry Baldwin Ward Medal, Am Soc Parasitol, 65; Behring-Bilharz Medal, 81. *Prof Exp:* Asst prof zool, Univ Pa, 52-57. *Concurrent Pos:* Nat Res Coun fel, Univ Chicago, 50-52; mem, Scientific Working Group, Epidemiology, WHO, 78. *Mem:* Am Soc Trop Med & Hyg; Am Soc Parasitol; Am Asn Immunol; Am Micros Soc; Sci Res Soc Am. *Res:* Immunodiagnosis of parasitic infections and the immunology of the host parasite interaction. *Mailing Add:* 1074 Oakdale Rd NE Atlanta GA 30307

KAGAN, JACQUES, ORGANIC CHEMISTRY, BIOLOGICAL CHEMISTRY. *Current Pos:* from asst prof to assoc prof, 65-73, PROF CHEM & BIOL, UNIV ILL, CHICAGO, 73- *Personal Data:* b Paris, France, Nov 11, 33; US citizen; m 65, Peggy A Ziegler; c 2. *Educ:* Sorbonne, BS, 56; Rice Univ, PhD(chem), 60. *Honors & Awards:* Cooley Award, Am Soc Plant Taxon, 64. *Prof Exp:* Res assoc, Mass Inst Technol, 60-61; res chemist, Amoco Chem Co, Ind, 61-62; res scientist & Welch Found fel, Univ Tex, 62-65. *Concurrent Pos:* Vis prof, Univ Geneva, 71-72 & Univ Haute-Alsace, 80; Fulbright grant, 80 & 87; Museum Nat d'Histoire Naturelle, Paris, 87. *Mem:* Am Chem Soc; Am Soc Photobiol. *Res:* Organic synthesis and reaction mechanisms; photochemistry and photobiology; environmental chemistry. *Mailing Add:* 1620 Washington Ave Wilmette IL 60091-2419. *E-Mail:* jkagan@uic.edu

KAGAN, JEROME, DEVELOPMENTAL PSYCHOLOGY. *Current Pos:* PROF, DEPT PSYCHOL, HARVARD UNIV, 64- *Personal Data:* b Newark, NJ, Feb 25, 29; m 51; c 1. *Educ:* Rutgers Univ, BS, 50; Yale Univ, PhD(psychol), 54; Harvard Univ, MA, 64. *Honors & Awards:* Distinguished Sci Award, Am Psychol Asn, 87. *Prof Exp:* Chmn, Dept Psychol, fels res inst, 57-64. *Mem:* Nat Acad Sci; Am Psychol Asn; Soc Res Child Develop; Am Asn Advan Sci. *Res:* Cognitive and emotional development of children; role of temperament in personality development. *Mailing Add:* Dept Psychol Harvard Univ 33 Kirkland St Cambridge MA 02138

KAGAN, JOEL (DAVID), MATHEMATICS. *Current Pos:* asst prof, 70-84, ASSOC PROF MATH, UNIV HARTFORD, 84- *Personal Data:* b New York, NY, Aug 18, 43; div; c 2. *Educ:* Rutgers Col, BA, 66; Stevens Inst Technol, MS, 67 & 84, PhD(math), 70. *Prof Exp:* Instr math, Stevens Inst Technol, 68-70. *Mem:* Soc Symbolic Logic; Math Asn Am. *Res:* Algebraic logic; algebraic structures arising from theories in the sentential and predicate calculus with identity connective. *Mailing Add:* Math Phys & Comput Sci Univ Hartford 200 Bloomfield Ave West Hartford CT 06117-1599

KAGAN, MICHAEL Z, HIGH-PERFORMANCE LIQUID CHROMATOGRAPHY, SEPARATION SCIENCES. *Current Pos:* RES SCIENTIST, WYETH-AYERST RES, 90- *Personal Data:* b Moscow, USSR, Feb 26, 50; US citizen; m, Natasha; c Michael & Nicole. *Educ:* Moscow Inst Chem Technol, USSR, MS, 73; Inst BioOrg Chem, USSR Acad Sci, PhD(bioorg chem), 77. *Prof Exp:* Res scientist, Inst Animal Morphol & Ecol, USSR, 77-88; fel, Harvard Univ, 88-90. *Mem:* Am Chem Soc. *Res:* Synthesized synthetic analogs and isolated physiologically active compounds by high-performance liquid chromatography and other separation techniques. *Mailing Add:* 4 Mackenzie Lane Plainsboro NJ 08536

KAGANSKY, LARISA, spectroscopy & spectrometry, material properties & physical chemistry, for more information see previous edition

KAGARISE, RONALD EUGENE, PHYSICS. *Current Pos:* RETIRED. *Personal Data:* b East Freedom, Pa, July 17, 26; m 47; c 3. *Educ:* Duke Univ, BA, 48; Pa State Col, MS, 49, PhD(physics), 51. *Prof Exp:* Res assoc physics, Pa State Col, 51-52; head chem spectros sect, Naval Res Lab, 52-66; prog dir phys chem, NSF, 66-68; supt chem div, Naval Res Lab, 68-76; dir div mat res, NSF, Washington, DC, 76-77; asst dir math & phys sci, 77-79; div dir mat res, 79-83. *Mem:* Am Phys Soc; Sigma Xi; Am Chem Soc; Coblentz Soc. *Res:* Rotational isomerism; molecular constants; structure. *Mailing Add:* 602 Pine Rd Ft Washington MD 20744

KAGAWA, YUKIO, COMPUTATIONAL ACOUSTICS, NUMERICAL ANALYSIS. *Current Pos:* prof, 70-90, EMER PROF ELEC ENG, TOYAMA UNIV, JAPAN, 90-; PROF ELEC & ELECTRONICS ENG, OKAYAMA UNIV, 90- *Personal Data:* b Yamagata, Japan, May 8, 35; m 90, Karube Sachiko. *Educ:* Tohoku Univ, Sendai, Japan, BEng, 58, MEng, 60, DrEng, 63. *Honors & Awards:* Ishikawa Prize, Union Japanese Scientists & Engrs, 89. *Prof Exp:* Postdoctoral fel mech eng, Polytech Inst, Brooklyn, NY, 64-65; postdoctoral fel acoust eng, Tech Univ Norway, 66-68; res fel acoust eng, Inst Sound & Vibration Res, Southampton Univ, UK, 68-70. *Concurrent Pos:* Leverhulme fel, Univ NSW, Australia, 78; vis prof, Indian Inst Technol, Delhi, India, 82 & Inst Acoust, Academia Sineca, China, 84; mem bd dirs, Japan Soc Simulation Technol, 86-, vpres, 96- *Mem:* Fel Inst Elec & Electronics Engrs; fel Inst Acoust UK; Inst Electronic Info & Commun Engrs Japan. *Res:* Numerical modelling and simulation of electrical acoustical and vibration systems by means of finite element and boundary element method; electrical impedance and ultrasonic computed tomography as an inverse or optimization problem. *Mailing Add:* Dept Elec & Electronics Eng Okayama Univ Okayama 700 Japan. *Fax:* 81-86-252-5734; *E-Mail:* kagawa@calc.elec.okayamau.ac.jp

KAGEL, RONALD OLIVER, ANALYTICAL CHEMISTRY. *Current Pos:* ENVIRON CONSULT, 93- *Personal Data:* b Milwaukee, Wis, Jan 16, 36; m 59, Lois Jeanne Kaercher; c Jennifer, Kathryn & Sharon. *Educ:* Univ Wis, BS, 58; Univ Minn, PhD(phys chem), 64. *Honors & Awards:* Anachem Award, Am Inst Chem, 88. *Prof Exp:* Res chemist, Dow Chem Co, 64-67, proj leader, Chem Res Lab, 67-69, group leader, 69-71, sr res chemist, 71-72, sr anal specialist, 72-74, supvr spec anal group, 74-76, supt environ control, 76-77, environ syst group leader surface anal, 77-78, res mgr surface anal, 78-79, mgr, Regulatory Affairs-Water, 79-81, mgr, States Environ Activ, 81, dir environ qual, 81-85, environ dir, Eng Res & Comput Serv, 85-88, environ counsult, 88-93. *Concurrent Pos:* Mem fac, Saginaw Valley Col, 64-67; mem adv bd, Raman Newslett, 68-75; secy, Ad-hoc Subpanel Laser Excited Raman Spectra, Nat Res Coun, 68, mem, Numerical Data Adv Bd, Joint Comt Atomic & Molecular Structure-Subcomt Laser Raman Spectros, 70-80; mem, Ad-hoc Panel Micro-Raman Spectros, Nat Bur Stand, 74; assoc ed, Appl Spectros, 75-80; secy, Int Fourier Trans Conf, 77, CMA leader, Task Group Environ Monitoring, 76-81; mem adv comt, Critical Mat Register, State Mich Dept Nat Res, 76-79, CMA work group leader, Environ Audits, 82-84; liaison coordr, Am Soc Testing & Mat, 79-81; chmn, Natural Resources Comt, State Govt Affairs Coun, 81, Groundwater Subcomt, 84-85 & Bd dirs, Coalition Responsible Waste Incineration, 87 & 90-; mem, Environ Qual Comn, Synthetic Org Chem Mfg Asn, 82-85. *Mem:* Fel Am Inst Chemists; Sigma Xi; Am Chem Soc; AAAS; NY Acad Sci; Coblentz Soc. *Res:* Molecular structure elucidation, structure catalysis and bulk mechanistic studies; remote detection of ambient air emissions by infrared Fourier transform and Raman spectroscopy; infrared chemiluminescence applications; environmental measurements of trace compounds; combustion chemistry and incineration; dioxin. *Mailing Add:* 4 Hannah Ct Midland MI 48642. *Fax:* 517-631-4477

KAGEN, HERBERT PAUL, ORGANIC CHEMISTRY. *Current Pos:* RETIRED. *Personal Data:* b Worcester, Mass, May 6, 29; c Bradley, Beth, Michael & Ruth. *Educ:* Mass Inst Technol, SB, 52; Univ RI, MS, 54; Wayne State Univ, PhD, 60. *Prof Exp:* From asst prof to assoc prof chem, Detroit Inst Technol, 57-67; prof org chem, WVa State Col, 67-90, chmn, Dept Chem, 68-71 & 87, dir chem technol, 75-90; field serv prof environ health & assoc dir & supvr Environ Analysis Chem Lab, Inst Environ Health, Univ Cincinnati Med Ctr, 87-95. *Concurrent Pos:* Consult, Chem Serv Corp, 57-, Union Carbide Corp, WVa State Bd Educ & Kanawha County Bd Educ; Mich Heart Asn fel, 60; adj prof, WVa Univ, 70-71; dir, NSF-Coop Col Sch Sci Prog for high sch chem teachers, 70-71; dir, WVa RESA III Prog Gifted High Sch Sr, 75; fac adv, NSF-SOS Prog, Kanawha Valley, 73; adj prof, Grad Studies, WVa Col, 75-77; vis prof, Inst Environ Health Med Ctr, Univ Cincinnati, 87-88; assoc dir & supvr, Anal Chem Lab, 88-89. *Mem:* Am Chem Soc; Nat Sci Teachers Asn; Am Asn Univ Prof; Sigma Xi. *Res:* Reaction of lactides; organic nitrogen chemistry; preparation of lactides; chemical education; environmental. *Mailing Add:* 7017 Mayfield Ave Cincinnati OH 45243

KAGEN, LAWRENCE J, RHEUMATOLOGY, MUSCLE DISORDERS. *Current Pos:* ATTEND PHYSICIAN, HOSP SPEC SURG, 79-; PROF MED, MED COL, CORNELL UNIV, 79- *Personal Data:* b New York, NY, Feb 2, 36. *Educ:* NY Univ, MD, 60. *Res:* Inflammatory muscle disease. *Mailing Add:* 535 E 70th St New York NY 10021

KAGETSU, T(ADASHI) J(ACK), CHEMICAL ENGINEERING. *Current Pos:* CONSULT, 87- *Personal Data:* b Vancouver, BC, Apr 22, 31; m 57, Kanaye K Tsuchida; c Nolan & Naomi. *Educ:* Univ Toronto, BASc, 54, MASc, 55, PhD(appl chem), 57. *Prof Exp:* Asst res chem engr, metals div, Union Carbide Corp, 57-60, res chem engr, 60-61, assoc engr, nuclear div, 61-64, proj engr, mining & metals div, 64-67, staff engr, 67-75, mgr, process eng, 75-77, mgr design eng, 77-78, asst dir tech, Metals Div, 78-86. *Res:* Kinetics of metal dissolution in aqueous media; fused salt electrolysis; gas-solid mass transfer and heat transfer; hydrometallurgy and pyrometallurgy; process simulation by computers. *Mailing Add:* Consult 435 Dutton Dr Lewiston NY 14092

KAGEY-SOBOTKA, ANNE, ALLERGIES. *Current Pos:* From instr to asst prof, 77-85, ASSOC PROF MED, SCH MED, JOHNS HOPKINS UNIV, 85- *Personal Data:* b Atlanta, Ga, June 11, 40. *Educ:* Vanderbilt Univ, BA, 62; Johns Hopkins Univ, PhD(microbiol), 77. *Mem:* Am Asn Immunol; fel Am Acad Allergy; Int Col Allergists. *Mailing Add:* J H Asthma & Allergy Ctr Dept Med 5501 Hopkins Bayview Blvd Baltimore MD 21224

KAGHAN, WALTER S(EIDEL), CHEMICAL ENGINEERING. *Current Pos:* RETIRED. *Personal Data:* b New York, NY, Apr 16, 19; m 47; c 3. *Educ:* City Col New York, BChE, 40; NY Univ, MChE, 48; Purdue Univ, PhD(chem eng), 52. *Prof Exp:* Res chem engr, St Regis Paper Co, 40-41; assoc chem engr, E I du Pont de Nemours & Co, 42-43; process engr, Kellex Corp, 44-45; dir, Resinous Res Assoc, 45-48; asst prof chem eng, Rose Polytech Inst, group leader & asst sect chief, Develop Sect, Olin Corp, 51-59, dir develop sect, Film Res & Develop Dept, 59-63, dir res & develop, Film Div, 63-75; consult chem engr, 75-86. *Mem:* Am Soc Plastics Engrs; Am Inst Chem Engrs; NY Acad Sci; Am Chem Soc. *Res:* Cellophane; polymers; plastics extrusion; rheology; polyolefins; packaging. *Mailing Add:* 4315 Brandywine Dr Sarasota FL 34241-6108

KAGIWADA, HARRIET HATSUNE NATSUYAMA, applied mathematics, systems science, for more information see previous edition

KAGIWADA, REYNOLD SHIGERU, ELECTRONICS ENGINEERING, SOLID STATE PHYSICS. *Current Pos:* mem prof staff, TRW Systs Group, 72-75, scientist, 75-76, sect head, 76-77, sr scientist, 77-80, mgr, Microwave Prod Dept, 80-83, mgr, Advan Microelectronics Lab, 83-87, asst proj mgr/ dep proj mgr, 87-88, prog mgr, 88-89, mimic chief scientist, 89-94, ADVAN TECHNOL MGR, MICROWAVE TECHNOL DEPT OPER, TRW ELECTRONIC SYSTS GROUP, 94-, ADVAN TECHNOL MGR & ADVAN TECHNOL DIRECTORATE, TRW SPACE & ELECTRONIC GROUP. *Personal Data:* b Los Angeles, Calif, July 8, 38; m 61, Harriet H Natsuyama; c 2. *Educ:* Univ Calif, Los Angeles, BS, 60, MS, 63, PhD(physics), 66. *Honors & Awards:* Gold Medal Recipient, Ramo Technol Transfer Award, 85. *Prof Exp:* Asst prof physics, Univ Calif, Los Angeles, 67-69 & Univ Southern Calif, 69-72. *Mem:* Inst Elec & Electronics Engrs; Asn Old Crows. *Res:* Gallium-arsenic devices; integrated circuits; millimeter-wave devices; microwave acoustic devices; low temperature physics; superconductivity; liquid helium; ultrasonics; acoustics; microwave physics. *Mailing Add:* TRW Space & Electronics Group & Electronic Systs & Technol Div One Space Park Redondo Beach CA 90278. *Fax:* 310-812-7011; *E-Mail:* reynold__kagiwadg@gmail4.nloa.trw.ccm

KAHAN, ARCHIE M, METEOROLOGY. *Current Pos:* CONSULT METEOROLOGIST, 79-; SR SCIENTIST, OPHIR CORP, 87- *Personal Data:* b Denver, Colo, Jan 18, 17; m 44; c 2. *Educ:* Univ Denver, BA, 36, MA, 40; Calif Inst Technol, MS, 42; Agr & Mech Col Tex, PhD(meteorol oceanog), 59. *Honors & Awards:* Award, Am Meteorol Soc, 62. *Prof Exp:* Jr engr, Denison Dist, Corps Engrs, 38-41; hydrologist, US Weather Bur, 45-46; supvr hydrologist in-chg, Mo River Forecast Ctr, 46-51; assoc dir, Am Inst Aerological Res, 51-53; asst prof meteorol, Agr & Mech Col Tex, 53-54; exec dir, Tex A&M Res Found, 54-63, dir, Tex Eng Exp Sta, 62-63; dir, Univ Okla Res Inst, 63-65; gen phys scientist, US Bur Reclamation, 65-70, chief off atmospheric resources mgt, 70-79, assoc chief, div res, 78-79. *Concurrent Pos:* Consult, President's Adv Comt Weather Control, 54 & NSF Panel Weather

Modification, 65; mem, Adv Comt Weather Modification, State of Colo, 72-83; sr scientist, Ophir Corp, 87- *Mem:* Am Soc Civil Engrs; AAAS; Am Meteorol Soc; Am Geophys Union. *Res:* Hydrology; hydrometeorology; oceanography; research administration; development of cloud seeding technology for water resource enhancement. *Mailing Add:* 610 S Eldridge Lakewood CO 80228

KAHAN, BARRY D, IMMUNOLOGY, SURGERY. *Current Pos:* PROF, DEPT SURG, UNIV TEX MED SCH, 77- *Personal Data:* b Cleveland, Ohio, July 25, 39; m 62. *Educ:* Univ Chicago, BS, 60, PhD(physiol), 64, MD, 65. *Prof Exp:* Intern, Mass Gen Hosp, 65-66; staff assoc, NIH, 66-68; surg residency, 68-72; asst prof, 72-74, assoc prof surg, Northwestern Univ, 74-77. *Mem:* AAAS; Am Asn Immunol; Soc Univ Surg; fel Am Col Surg; Transplantation Soc; Am Surg Asn. *Res:* Electron microscopy; protein biochemistry; transplantation antigens; delayed-typed hypersensitivity; transplantation and tumor-specific antigens. *Mailing Add:* Dept Surg Univ Tex Med Sch PO Box 20036 Houston TX 77225

KAHAN, I HOWARD, avian pathology, bacteriology, for more information see previous edition

KAHAN, LAWRENCE, BIOCHEMISTRY, IMMUNOLOGY. *Current Pos:* Fel biochem, 70-73, from asst prof to assoc prof, 73-83, PROF PHYSIOL CHEM, UNIV WIS-MADISON, 83-, DIR HYBRIDOMA FAC & VCHMN, DEPT PHYSIOL CHEM, 85- *Personal Data:* b Los Angeles, Calif, May 16, 44; m 69; c 2. *Educ:* Univ Calif, Berkeley, BA, 65; Brandeis Univ, PhD(biochem), 71. *Concurrent Pos:* Fel, Am Cancer Soc, 70-72; res grant, NIH, 75-; consult, NSF, 77-80, 82-85 & 87-; NSF res grant, 80-83. *Mem:* Am Soc Biochem & Molecular Biol; Am Chem Soc. *Res:* Structure and function of bacterial and eukaryote ribosomes; cancer associated enzymes; molecular biology. *Mailing Add:* 4106 Hiawatha Dr Madison WI 53711-3040. *Fax:* 608-262-5253

KAHAN, LINDA BERYL, NEUROPHYSIOLOGY. *Current Pos:* MEM FAC, DEPT BIOL, EVERGREEN STATE COL, 71- *Personal Data:* b San Francisco, Calif, Sept 28, 41. *Educ:* Univ Calif, Berkeley, BA, 63; Stanford Univ, MA, 65, PhD(biol), 67. *Prof Exp:* Fel neurophysiol, Univ Miami, 67-68; asst prof, Antioch Col, 68-71. *Mem:* AAAS; Sigma Xi. *Res:* Physiology and anatomy of invertebrate nervous systems; neural control of behavior. *Mailing Add:* Natural Sci Evergreen State Col Olympia WA 98505-0001. *E-Mail:* kahanl@elwha.evergreen.edu

KAHAN, SIDNEY, DEVELOPMENT NEW FOOD PRODUCT. *Current Pos:* RETIRED. *Personal Data:* b New York, NY, Oct 14, 15; m 44, Ruth Shaw; c Barbara (Hoffman), Judith (Kampmann) & Martha. *Educ:* Columbia Univ, BS, 35; Polytech Inst Brooklyn, MS, 49. *Prof Exp:* Jr chemist ores & metals, Am Smelting & Refinng Co, 36-38; jr chemist food chemist, US Food Drug Admn, 38-55; chief food technologist, Food Chem Prod Develop, B Manischewitz Co, 55-60; chief chemist food chem, Fitelson Lab Inc, 60-82, consult, 82-95. *Concurrent Pos:* Consult food chem, Kahansultants Inc, 82-95. *Mem:* Fel asn anal chemists; Am Chem Soc; Inst Food Technologists. *Res:* Adulteration of various food products. *Mailing Add:* 66 Peachtree Lane Roslyn Heights NY 11577-2416

KAHAN, WILLIAM M, MATHEMATICS, COMPUTER SCIENCE. *Current Pos:* prof comput sci, 69-72, PROF MATH, ELEC ENG & COMPUT SCI, UNIV CALIF, BERKELEY, 72- *Personal Data:* b Toronto, Ont, June 5, 33; m 54; c 2. *Educ:* Univ Toronto, BA, 54, MA, 56, PhD(numerical anal), 58. *Honors & Awards:* A M Turing Award, Asn Comput Mach, 89. *Prof Exp:* Nat Res Coun Can fel, Cambridge Univ, 58-60; from asst prof to prof math & comput sci, Univ Toronto, 60-68. *Concurrent Pos:* Nat Res Coun Can res grant, 64-69; vis assoc prof, Stanford Univ, 66; consult, IBM, NY, 67, 72-73, 84-; Hewlett-Packard, Corvallis, Or, 74-86 & Intel, Santa Clara, Calif, 77-, Apple, 87- *Mem:* Am Math Soc; Asn Comput Mach; Soc Indust & Appl Math. *Res:* Large matrix calculations; trajectory problems; error analysis; design computer arithmetic units; execution-time diagnostic systems for scientific computer systems; general purpose programs to solve standard problems in numerical analysis with highest reliability on electronic computer; IEEE standards 754 and 854 for floating-point arithmetic. *Mailing Add:* Dept Elec Eng & Comput Sci 733 Soda Hall Univ Calif Berkeley CA 94720-1776

KAHANA, SIDNEY H, THEORETICAL PHYSICS. *Current Pos:* vis scientist, 65-66, SCIENTIST PHYSICS, BROOKHAVEN NAT LAB, 67- *Personal Data:* b Winnipeg, Man, July 23, 33; m 57; c 2. *Educ:* Univ Man, BSc, 54, MSc, 55; Univ Edinburgh, PhD(physics), 57. *Honors & Awards:* Sr Award, Alexander Von Humboldt Stiftone. *Prof Exp:* From asst prof to assoc prof physics, McGill Univ, 57-67; vis scientist, Niels Bohr Inst, 59-61. *Concurrent Pos:* Vis scientist, Atomic Energy Can, 57-62, 63 & 64; Guggenheim fel, John Simon Mem Found, 74-75. *Mem:* Fel Am Phys Soc. *Res:* Nuclear theory; structure and reactions; intermediate energy; baryon-anti-baryon systems; many body problems. *Mailing Add:* Dept Physics Brookhaven Nat Lab Upton NY 11973

KAHANER, DAVID KENNETH, APPLIED MATHEMATICS, COMPUTER METHODS. *Current Pos:* mem staff, 79-80, GROUP LEADER, NAT BUR STAND, 81- *Personal Data:* b New York, NY, Sept 12, 41; m 64; c 2. *Educ:* City Col New York, BS, 62; Stevens Inst Technol, MS, 64, PhD(math), 68. *Prof Exp:* Mem staff numerical anal, Los Alamos Nat Lab, 68-80. *Concurrent Pos:* Vis prof, Univ Mich, 72-73, Univ Torino, Italy, 77, Swiss Fed Inst Technol, 77-78 & Vienna Tech Univ, 78. *Mem:* Am Math Soc; Asn Comput Mach. *Res:* Numerical analysis; computing methods; mathematical software. *Mailing Add:* Dir Asian Tech Info Prog Unit 45002 Box 319 APO AP 96337-0007

KAHL, JONATHAN D W, AIR POLLUTION METEOROLOGY, POLAR METEOROLOGY & CLIMATOLOGY. *Current Pos:* asst prof, 90-94, ASSOC PROF ATMOSPHERIC SCI, UNIV WIS-MILWAUKEE, 94- *Personal Data:* b Shirley, Mass, May 7, 59; m 87, Carol J Waldvogel; c Joseph J & Samantha R. *Educ:* Univ Mich, BA, 81, MS, 83, PhD(atmospheric sci), 87. *Prof Exp:* Nat Res Coun res assoc, Nat Oceanic & Atmospheric Admin-Geophys Monitoring Climatic Chg, 87-89. *Concurrent Pos:* Prin investr, Elec Power Res Inst, Nat Oceanic & Atomspheric Admin, NSF & Defense Nuclear Agency; resident res assoc, Nat Res Coun, 87; res assoc, Coop Inst Res Environ Sci, Univ Colo. *Mem:* Am Meteorol Svc; AAAS; Am Geophys Union. *Res:* Meteorological aspects of air pollution, particularly long-range transport, polar meteorology; arctic boundary layer. *Mailing Add:* Dept Geosci Univ Wis PO Box 413 Milwaukee WI 53201. *Fax:* 414-229-5452; *E-Mail:* kahl@csd.uwm.edu

KAHLE, ANNE B, GEOPHYSICS, REMOTE SENSING. *Current Pos:* mem tech staff, Jet Propulsion Lab, 74-75, supvr, Geol Group, 75-91, MGR, GEOL & VOLCANOLOGY PROG, 88-, SR RES SCIENTIST, 89-, US ASTER, SCI TEAM LEADER, JET PROPULSION LAB, 91- *Personal Data:* b Auburn, Wash, Mar 30, 34; m 57, James Kahle; c Sheree (Luttrel), Richard, Vicki & Jeffrey. *Educ:* Univ Alaska, BS, 55, MS, 61; Univ Calif, Los Angeles, PhD(meteorol), 75. *Honors & Awards:* Gen James Gordon Steese Prize. *Prof Exp:* Res asst, Rand Corp, Calif, 61-63, from asst phys scientist to phys scientist, 63-67, sr phys scientist, 67-74. *Mem:* Sigma Xi; Am Geophys Union; AAAS; Geol Soc Am. *Res:* Remote sensing of geology; volcanology geomagnetic field; solar-terrestrial relationships; atmospheric physics; gravity; atmospheric radiation. *Mailing Add:* 19767 Grandview Dr Topanga CA 90290. *E-Mail:* anne@aster.jpl.nasa.gov

KAHLE, CHARLES F, GEOLOGY. *Current Pos:* from asst prof to assoc prof, 65-74, PROF GEOL, BOWLING GREEN STATE UNIV, 74- *Personal Data:* b Toledo, Ohio, June 2, 30; m 57; c 6. *Educ:* St Joseph's Col, Ind, BS, 53; Miami Univ, Ohio, MS, 57; Univ Kans, PhD(geol), 62. *Prof Exp:* Geologist, Mobil Petrol Co, Okla, 57-58; asst prof geol, Okla State Univ 62-63 & Univ Toledo, 63-65. *Mem:* Geol Soc Am; Soc Econ Paleont & Mineral. *Res:* Carbonate geology; stratigraphy; scanning electron microscopy; sedimentation. *Mailing Add:* Dept Geol Bowling Green State Univ 1001 E Wooster St Bowling Green OH 43403-0001

KAHLER, ALBERT COMSTOCK, III, NUCLEAR PHYSICS. *Current Pos:* sr scientist exp physics, 81-91, FEL SCIENTIST EXP PHYSICS, BETTIS ATOMIC POWER LAB, WESTINGHOUSE ELEC CORP, 91- *Personal Data:* b Bay Shore, NY, June 10, 51; m 72; c 1. *Educ:* Gettysburg Col, BA, 73; Univ Tenn, PhD(physics), 78. *Prof Exp:* Res assoc physics, Cyclotron Inst, Tex A&M Univ, 78-81. *Mem:* Am Phys Soc. *Res:* Nuclear structure studies using gamma-ray spectroscopy techniques. *Mailing Add:* Bettis Atomic Power Lab Westinghouse Elec Corp PO Box 79 West Mifflin PA 15122

KAHLER, ALEX L, GENETICS, PLANT BREEDING. *Current Pos:* PRES & FOUNDER, BIOGENETIC SERV, INC, 88- *Personal Data:* b Scottsbluff, Nebr, July 4, 39; m 63, Judith Ann; c Alexander L & Jonathan L. *Educ:* Univ Calif, Davis, BS, 65, MS, 67, PhD, 73. *Prof Exp:* Staff res assoc genetics, Univ Calif, Davis, 65-80; prof plant sci, SDak State Univ, Brookings, 80-; plant geneticist, Northern Grain Insects Res Lab, Agr Res Serv, USDA, 80-86 & 86-88. *Concurrent Pos:* Mgr biotechnol & sr res geneticist, Garst, Slater, Iowa, 86-88. *Mem:* AAAS; Am Genetics Asn; Soc Study Evolution; Genetics Soc Am; Crop Sci Soc Am; Sigma Xi. *Res:* Determining the extent and distribution of genetic variability within and between populations and with measuring the forces which are responsible for the observed variability; improving corn populations for resistance to insects and diseases. *Mailing Add:* Biogenetic Serv Inc 2308 Sixth St E PO Box 710 Brookings SD 57006

KAHLER, RICHARD LEE, CARDIOVASCULAR PHYSIOLOGY. *Current Pos:* HEAD CARDIOVASCULAR DIV, SCRIPPS CLIN & RES FOUND, 68- *Personal Data:* b Milltown, NJ, Jan 2, 33; m 58; c 3. *Educ:* Yale Univ, MD, 57. *Prof Exp:* From asst prof to assoc prof med, Yale Univ, 65-68; assoc prof med, Sch Med, Univ Calif, San Diego, 68- *Concurrent Pos:* NIH res career develop award, 65-68. *Mem:* AAAS; Am Physiol Soc; Am Heart Asn; Am Col Physicians; Am Col Cardiol; Sigma Xi. *Res:* Cardiovascular pharmacology. *Mailing Add:* PO Box 104 Rancho Santa Fe CA 92067-0104. *Fax:* 619-756-1485

KAHLON, PREM SINGH, BIOLOGY, PLANT GENETICS. *Current Pos:* PROF BIOL, TENN STATE UNIV, 66-, DIR MONITORING & ASSESSMENT RES CTR PROG. *Personal Data:* b Lyallpur, India, June 16, 36; m 67, Darshi; c Paul & Jay. *Educ:* Punjab Univ, India, BS, 56; La State Univ, MS, 62, PhD(plant breeding), 64. *Prof Exp:* Asst prof biol, Talladega Col, 64-65; prof, Alcorn Agr & Mech Col, 65-66. *Mem:* Genetics Soc Am; Indian Soc Genetics & Plant Breeding; Tissue Cult Asn Am. *Res:* Inheritance studies in rice, especially cooking quality; mutation genetics; chemical mutagenesis; in vitro culture of soybean and cell genetics. *Mailing Add:* Dept Biol Tenn State Univ 3500 John Merritt Blvd Nashville TN 37209-1561

KAHLON, TALWINDER SINGH, NUTRITION, BIOCHEMISTRY. *Current Pos:* Nutritionist, 84-87, RES CHEMIST, WESTERN REGIONAL RES CTR, USDA, 84- *Personal Data:* b Ludhiana, Punjab, India, Feb 25, 45; US citizen; m; c Ashwinder & Pushpinder. *Educ:* Univ Minn, PhD(nutrit), 74. *Concurrent Pos:* Guest staff scientist, Lawrence Berkeley Lab, 83-; assoc ed, Cereal Chem J, 91- *Mem:* Am Inst Nutrit; fel Am heart Asn; Am Asn Cereal Chemist. *Res:* Cholesterol-lowering by cereal fibers and fractions. *Mailing Add:* Western Reg Res Ctr 800 Buchanan St Albany CA 94710-1198. *Fax:* 510-559-5777

KAHN, A CLARK, BIOCHEMISTRY. *Current Pos:* dir lab, 85-86, PRES & LAB DIR, ENVIRON EVALUATIONS & LAB SERV, ANA-QUAL LABS. *Personal Data:* b Pittsburgh, Pa, Dec 16, 37; m 90; c 2. *Educ:* Univ NH, BA, 61, MS, 63; Pa State Univ, PhD(biochem), 66. *Prof Exp:* Lab officer clin chem & biochemist, USPHS Hosp, 66-68; supvr clin path, ICI Am, 68-76; dir res & develop, Precision Systs, 76-77; dir labs, New Eng Med Labs, 77-78; dir clin path, Int Res & Develop Corp, 78-81; sr chemist, Palasades Nuclear Power Plant, 81-84. *Mem:* AAAS; Am Chem Soc; Am Asn Clin Chem; Am Soc Vet Clin Pathologists; Nat Registry Clin Chemists. *Res:* Clinical laboratory medicine, particularly electrolyte chemistry and intestinal absorption, malabsorption syndrome; laboratory animal clinical pathology; toxicology of hazardous materials. *Mailing Add:* 506 River Rd Paw Paw MI 49079

KAHN, ALAN RICHARD, bioengineering, physiology, for more information see previous edition

KAHN, ALBERT, DEVELOPMENTAL BIOLOGY. *Current Pos:* assoc prof, 70-92, EMER PROF BIOL & LECTR, GENETICS INST, COPENHAGEN UNIV, 92 - *Personal Data:* b Wuerburg, Ger, May 21, 31; nat US; m 66, Anne-Marie J Hercuard; c Sophie E & Rachel A. *Educ:* Cornell Univ, BS, 53; Univ Calif, Los Angeles, PhD(bot), 58. *Prof Exp:* Jr res botanist, Univ Calif, Los Angeles, 58-59; fels, NSF, Stockholm, 59-61 & USPHS, 61-62; res fel biol, Calif Inst Technol, 62-64; assoc prof, Purdue Univ, 64-70. *Res:* Chloroplast pigments; genetic control of chloroplast development. *Mailing Add:* Genetics Dept Copenhagen Univ Inst Molecular Biol Oster Farimagsgade 2A DK 1353 Copenhagen K Denmark

KAHN, ARNOLD HERBERT, physics, for more information see previous edition

KAHN, ARTHUR B, MANAGEMENT INFO SYSTEMS. *Current Pos:* ASSOC PROF, INFO QUANT STUDIES, UNIV BALTIMORE, 78- *Personal Data:* b New York, NY, Feb 11, 31; m 56, Gilda Tilow; c 3. *Educ:* City Col New York, BS, 51; Johns Hopkins Univ, MSE, 54, PhD(dynamic meteorol), 59. *Prof Exp:* Res asst dynamic meteorol, Johns Hopkins Univ, 51-54, staff asst, 54-58; sr engr, Air Arm Div, Westinghouse Elec Corp, 58-63, fel engr, Systs Div 63-68, fel engr, Info Processing Dept, 68-70, adv engr, 71-78. *Concurrent Pos:* Founder & chmn prog eval & rev tech proj, SHARE, 62-64; vis assoc prof, Univ Wis-Madison, 68-71. *Mem:* Asn Comput Mach; Sigma Xi; Opers Res Soc Am. *Res:* Determination of what the nonspecialist should know about computers and development of ways and means to educate him; application of structured system development methods to creative activities. *Mailing Add:* 4120 Balmoral Circle Baltimore MD 21208-2116. *Fax:* 410-837-4899; *E-Mail:* abkahn@ube.umd.edu

KAHN, BERND, RADIOCHEMISTRY. *Current Pos:* DIR, ENVIRON RESOURCES CTR & PROF NUCLEAR ENG & HEALTH PHYSICS, GA INST TECHNOL, 74- *Personal Data:* b Pforzheim, Germany, Aug 16, 28; nat US; m 61, Gail Pressman; c Jennifer & Elizabeth. *Educ:* Newark Col Eng, BS, 50; Vanderbilt Univ, MS, 52; Mass Inst Technol, PhD(chem), 60. *Prof Exp:* Assoc chemist radiochem, Oak Ridge Nat Lab, 51-54; radiochemist, USPHS, 54-69; radiochemist, Radiochem & Nuclear Eng Br, Environ Protection Agency, Nat Environ Res Ctr, 69-74. *Concurrent Pos:* Mem, Nat Coun Radiation Protection & Measurements. *Mem:* Health Physics Soc; Am Chem Soc; Am Phys Soc. *Res:* Analytical radiochemical methods; behavior of radionuclides in the environment; radioactive effluents from nuclear power stations. *Mailing Add:* Environ Resources Ctr Ga Inst Technol Atlanta GA 30332

KAHN, CARL RONALD, ENDOCRINOLOGY. *Current Pos:* PROF MED, HARVARD MED SCH, 84- *Personal Data:* b Louisville, Ky, Jan 14, 44; m 66; c 2. *Educ:* Univ Louisville, BA, 64, MD, 68. *Honors & Awards:* Davis Rumbough Mem Award, Juv Diabetes Found, 77; Pfizer Biomed Res Award, 86; Edwin B Astwood Lectr, Endocrine Soc, 87. *Prof Exp:* Sr investr, 73-78, chief cellular & molecular physiol, Diabetes Br, Nat Inst Arthritis & Metab Dis, NIH, 78-81; dir res, Joslin Diabetes Ctr, 81- *Concurrent Pos:* Mem, Med Sci Adv Bd, Juv Diabetes Found, 78-; chief, Div Diabetes & Metabolism, Brigham & Women's Hosp, 81. *Mem:* Am Soc Clin Invest; Am Fedn Clin; Asn Am Physicians; Nat Coun Am Soc Clin Invest (pres-elect, 87). *Res:* Endocrine Soc; Am Diabetes Asn. *Res:* Insulin action and alterations in insulin action in disease states; hypoglycemia and insulin-like peptides in blood. *Mailing Add:* Joslin Diabetes Ctr One Joslin Pl Boston MA 02115-5394. *Fax:* 617-732-2593

KAHN, DANIEL STEPHEN, MATHEMATICS. *Current Pos:* asst prof to assoc prof, 64-78, PROF MATH, NORTHWESTERN UNIV, ILL, 78- *Personal Data:* b Brooklyn, NY, Nov 20, 35. *Educ:* Princeton Univ, AB, 57; Mass Inst Technol, PhD(math), 64. *Prof Exp:* Res instr math, Univ Chicago, 62-64. *Mem:* Am Math Soc. *Res:* Algebraic topology, especially field of stable homotopy theory. *Mailing Add:* Dept Math Northwestern Univ 2033 Sheridan Rd Evanston IL 60208-2730

KAHN, DAVID, SOLID STATE PHYSICS, ELECTROCHEMISTRY. *Current Pos:* res assoc, 70-87, sr mem tech staff, 87-93, DIR MEASUREMENT TECHNOL, AMP, INC, 93- *Personal Data:* b Peoria, Ill, Feb 4, 26; m 57, Dorothy Gwon; c Alan, Edward & Harold. *Educ:* Univ Ill, BS, 45; Univ Chicago, MS, 50, PhD(physics), 53. *Prof Exp:* Solid state physicist, Lewis Lab, Nat Adv Comt Aeronaut, 53-56; staff scientist, Res Inst Advan Study, 56-59, sr scientist, 59-70. *Concurrent Pos:* Am Cancer Soc res fel, Norsk Hydro's Inst Cancer Res, Norway, 54-55. *Mem:* Am Phys Soc; Mat Res Soc; Am Soc Metals; NY Acad Sci. *Res:* X-ray diffraction; magnetic susceptibility; electrometallurgy; conductive polymers; stress relaxation in metals; electro deposition modeling. *Mailing Add:* Res Div AMP Inc Mail Stop 21-01 PO Box 3608 Harrisburg PA 17105-3608. *Fax:* 717-541-3036

KAHN, DAVID, PHYSICS. *Current Pos:* CONSULT, 86- *Personal Data:* b New York, NY, Apr 27, 33; m 52; c 3. *Educ:* Brooklyn Col, BS, 57; Yale Univ, MS, 59, PhD(physics), 62. *Prof Exp:* Sr scientist, Raytheon Co, 62-66 & electronics res ctr, NASA, 66-71; group head, Modelling & Anal Group, US Dept Transp, 71-74, sect chief technol, Transp Systs Ctr, 74-86. *Mem:* Am Phys Soc; sr mem Inst Elec & Electronics Engrs; Sigma Xi. *Res:* Kinetic theory and plasma physics; wave propagation in highly rarefied gases; plasma density discontinuity wave coupling; traffic flow theory. *Mailing Add:* 238 Biddle Dr Exton PA 19341-1707

KAHN, DONALD JAY, ORGANIC CHEMISTRY. *Current Pos:* RETIRED. *Personal Data:* b Baltimore, Md, Aug 10, 30; m 60, Ruth Revzen; c 3. *Educ:* Princeton Univ, BA, 52; Univ Chicago, PhD(org chem), 57. *Prof Exp:* Asst org chem, Univ Chicago, 52-55; chemist, Esso Res & Eng Co, 57-60, proj leader & sr chemist, 60-63, sect head, 63-67, mgr aviation tech serv, Exxon Int Inc, 68-71, environ conserv sr adv, Exxon Corp, 71-77, solar energy gen mgr, Exxon Enterprises Inc, 78-81, sr technol adv, 81-84, strategic planning, 84-86. *Concurrent Pos:* Consult, Technol Mgt. *Mem:* Am Chem Soc; Sigma Xi. *Res:* Reaction mechanisms; free radical organic chemistry and polymerization; chemical additives for lubricants; industrial lubricants, greases, wax products and asphalt products; solar photovoltics. *Mailing Add:* 62 Spring St Metuchen NJ 08840

KAHN, DONALD R, CARDIOVASCULAR SURGERY, THORACIC SURGERY. *Current Pos:* RETIRED. *Personal Data:* b Birmingham, Ala, May 21, 29; c 4. *Educ:* Birmingham-Southern Col, BA, 50; Univ Ala, BA, 57, MD, 54. *Prof Exp:* Intern, St Louis City Hosp, 54-55; resident, Med Ctr, Univ Mich, Ann Arbor, 55-59, instr thoracic surg, Med Sch, 63-64, from asst prof to assoc prof surg, 64-71; head, Div Thoracic & Cardiovasc Surg, Med Ctr, Univ Wis-Madison, 71-80, prof surg & chmn cardiovasc med, Univ WKis Hosp, 71-80. *Concurrent Pos:* Am Thoracic Soc fel, 61-64; asst, Sch Med, Washington Univ, 54-55; dir clin invest lab, directorate med res, Chem Warfare Lab, 56-58. *Mem:* Fel Am Col Surg; Am Heart Asn; Am Thoracic Soc; Am Asn Thoracic Surg; Soc Thoracic Surg. *Mailing Add:* 2012 Magnolia Ave Birmingham AL 35205

KAHN, DONALD W, MATHEMATICS. *Current Pos:* from asst prof to assoc prof, 64-84, PROF MATH, UNIV MINN, MINNEAPOLIS, 84- *Personal Data:* b New York, NY, Nov 21, 35; m 56, Phyllis Lorberblatt; c 2. *Educ:* Cornell Univ, BA, 57; Yale Univ, PhD(math), 61. *Prof Exp:* Ritt instr math, Columbia Univ, 61-64. *Concurrent Pos:* Vis Fulbright prof, Univ Heidelberg, 65, Univ Toulouse, 88-89. *Mem:* Am Math Soc. *Res:* Algebraic topology. *Mailing Add:* Univ Minn Sch Math Minneapolis MN 55455

KAHN, ELLIOTT H, ECONOMIC STUDIES, APPLIED MECHANICS. *Current Pos:* mgr, 76-92, CONSULT, COOPERS & LYBRAND, 92- *Personal Data:* b Brooklyn, NY, Feb 27, 26; m 52; c 3. *Educ:* City Col New York, BCE, 45; Polytech Inst Brooklyn, MCE, 48. *Honors & Awards:* Robert Ridgeway Award, Am Soc Civil Engrs, 45. *Prof Exp:* Res engr, Repub Aviation Corp, NY, 45-47; staff engr, D B Steinman, 47-51; sr engr, W L Maxson Corp, 51-57, mgr reliability anal sect, 57-61; sr tech staff scientist, Kollsman Instrument Corp, Syosset, 61-76. *Concurrent Pos:* Lectr & consult engr, var times. *Mem:* AAAS; NY Acad Sci; Nat Soc Prof Engrs; Am Soc Civil Engrs; Inst Elec & Electronics Engrs; Am Inst Aeronaut & Astronaut. *Res:* Applied mechanics and systems engineering in the fields of structures, reliability, traffic, instruments, laser safety and electro-optical systems. *Mailing Add:* 280 Henry St Brooklyn NY 11201. *Fax:* 718-624-2434

KAHN, FREDERIC JAY, ELECTRO-OPTICAL DEVICES & SYSTEMS, LIQUID CRYSTALS. *Current Pos:* PRES, KAHN INT, 92- *Personal Data:* b Brooklyn, NY, Sept 1, 41; m 67; c 2. *Educ:* Rensselaer Polytech Inst, BEE, 62; Harvard Univ, AM, 63, PhD(solid state physics), 68. *Prof Exp:* Res asst magneto-optics garnets & orthoferrites, Gordon McKay Lab, Harvard Univ, 65-68; spec researcher liquid crystal displays, Quantum Device Res Lab, Cent Res Lab, Nippon Elec Co, Kawasaki, Japan, 68-69; mem tech staff liquid crystal mat, displays & related technol, Optical Control Devices Dept, Solid State Lab, Bell Labs, 70-73; lab proj mgr, Hewlett Packard Lab, 74-82, dept mgr, optical mat & polymers, Mat Res Lab, 82-83, dept mgr Storage Physics Dept, Mass Memory Lab, 83-84; vpres, Technol, Greyhawk Systs Inc, 84-92. *Concurrent Pos:* Prin investr, Joint Serv VHSIC, 81-83. *Mem:* Am Phys Soc; Inst Elec & Electronics Engrs; fel Soc Info Display; Int Soc Optical Eng. *Res:* Liquid crystal display materials, devices and systems; electron-beam and x-ray resists for high resolution lithography; optical memory materials and systems; optical fiber properties and devices; optical disc memories and erasable media; research and development on very high information content (resolution) imaging systems for display, hard copy generation and optical processing based on laser and optical beam addressed liquid crystal projection light valves. *Mailing Add:* 782 Southampton Dr Palo Alto CA 94303

KAHN, HAROLD A, CHRONIC DISEASE, EPIDEMIOLOGY. *Current Pos:* CONSULT EPIDEMIOL, 78- *Personal Data:* b New York, NY, Jan 4, 20; m 40, Lenora Polsky; c 3. *Educ:* City Col New York, BS, 39; Am Univ, MA, 49. *Prof Exp:* Statistician heart dis res, Nat Heart & Lung Inst, 50-51, med care needs, USPHS, 51-57, res adminr, NIH, 57-60, heart dis res, 60-71, chief off biomet & epidemiol, Nat Eye Inst, 71-75; prof epidemiol, Sch Hyg & Pub Health, Johns Hopkins Univ, 75-78. *Concurrent Pos:* Fel Coun Epidemiol, Am Heart Asn, 64-; USPHS award, 57; Lady Davis vis prof epidemiol, Hebrew Univ, Jerusalem, 80; vis prof epidemiol, Loma Linda Univ, 82, Johns Hopkins Univ, 85- *Mem:* Fel Am Statist Asn; Soc Epidemiol Res. *Res:* Nutrition and other risk factors in relation to chronic disease; problems of validating dietary data collected in field surveys. *Mailing Add:* 3405 Pendleton Dr Silver Spring MD 20902

KAHN, HENRY SLATER, CARDIOVASCULAR EPIDEMIOLOGY, OBESITY. *Current Pos:* asst prof community & prev med, 74-78, ASSOC PROF FAMILY & PREV MED, EMORY UNIV SCH MED, 78-, ASSOC PROF, SCH PUB HEALTH, 91- *Personal Data:* b Poughkeepsie, NY, May 6, 43; m 70, Mary Gillmor; c Jeremy G & Daniel K (Gillmor). *Educ:* Harvard Univ, AB, 64, MD, 68. *Prof Exp:* Med epidemiologist, US Ctrs Dis Control, 72-74. *Concurrent Pos:* Attend physician, Grady Mem Hosp, 73-; vis scientist, Nat Ctr Chronic Dis Prev & Health Prom, Ctrs Dis Control, 86-89; prin investr, Health & Body Size Study, Nat Heart Lung & Blood Inst, NIH, 90-94; clin prof community health & prev med, Morehouse Sch Med, Atlanta, Ga, 91-; sr res fel Epidemiol, Am Cancer Soc, 95- *Mem:* Fel Am Col Physicians; Am Pub Health Asn; Am Heart Asn; Soc Epidemiol Res; Soc Gen Internal Med. *Res:* Prevention of chronic diseases especially those related to obesity; epidemiology of body-fat distribution; efficient, humane models of primary medical care. *Mailing Add:* Dept Family & Prev Med Emory Univ Sch Med 69 Butler St Atlanta GA 30303-3219. *Fax:* 404-616-6847; *E-Mail:* hkahn@emory.edu

KAHN, JACK HENRY, ENGINEERING PHYSICS. *Current Pos:* RETIRED. *Personal Data:* b Bolivar, Tenn, Nov 1, 23; m 52, Sue Upchurch; c Elizabeth, George & Andrew. *Educ:* Univ Tenn, BS, 47, MS, 49, PhD(physics), 51. *Prof Exp:* Classification analyst, Declassification Br, US AEC, 51-55, asst chief, 55-68, chief, 68-73, staff asst, 73-75, asst chief, Weapons Prog Br Div Classification, 75-79, physicist, US Dept Energy, 79-88; consult, Hist Assocs, Inc, 88-92; consult, SAIC, 93-95. *Mem:* Am Phys Soc; Sigma Xi. *Res:* Nuclear physics. *Mailing Add:* 3212 Red Deer Ct Plano TX 75093

KAHN, JEFFREY, APPLIED MATHEMATICS. *Current Pos:* PROF, MATH DEPT, RUTGERS UNIV. *Honors & Awards:* George Polya Prize, Soc Indust & Appl Math, 96. *Mailing Add:* Math Dept-Hill Ctr-Busch Campus Rutgers Univ New Brunswick NJ 08903

KAHN, JOSEPH STEPHAN, PLANT BIOCHEMISTRY. *Current Pos:* from asst prof to prof, 61-89, EMER PROF BOT & BIOCHEM, NC STATE UNIV, 89- *Personal Data:* b Ger, Aug 12, 29; m 70; c 2. *Educ:* Univ Calif, BS, 55; Univ Ill, PhD, 58. *Prof Exp:* Res assoc physiol, Univ Ill, 58-59; res assoc biol, Johns Hopkins Univ, 59-61. *Concurrent Pos:* Fulbright fel, India, 78. *Mem:* Am Soc Plant Physiol; AAAS; Biophys Soc; Am Soc Biol Chem. *Res:* Electron transport and pathway of adenosine triphosphate formation in chloroplasts; localization of enzyme systems in chloroplasts; modification of protozoal membranes by drugs. *Mailing Add:* 102 Planters Wood Lane Carey NC 27511

KAHN, LAWRENCE F, STRUCTURAL ENGINEERING, CIVIL ENGINEERING. *Current Pos:* asst prof, 76-80, ASSOC PROF STRUCT ENG, GA INST TECHNOL, 80- *Personal Data:* b Oakland, Calif, Jan 26, 45; m 71; c 2. *Educ:* Stanford Univ, BS, 66; Univ Ill, Champaign-Urbana, MS, 67; Univ Mich, Ann Arbor, PhD(civil eng), 76. *Honors & Awards:* Raymond Reese Res Prize, Am Soc Civil Eng, 80. *Prof Exp:* Struct engr undersea struct, US Naval Civil Eng Lab, 67-71; struct engr power plant, Bechtel Power Corp, 76. *Concurrent Pos:* Prin investr, NSF grant, 77-85; consult, Wiss-Janney-Elstner Assocs. *Mem:* Fel Am Soc Civil Engrs; fel Am Concrete Inst; Earthquake Eng Res Inst; Masonry Soc. *Res:* Earthquake engineering; computer aided engineering/computer aided design/computer aided mechanics; reinforced concrete structures; masonry structures; experimental analysis. *Mailing Add:* 105 Woodfall Way SW Lilborn GA 30247

KAHN, LEO DAVID, BIOPHYSICAL CHEMISTRY. *Current Pos:* RETIRED. *Personal Data:* b Everett, Mass. *Educ:* Mass Inst Technol, SB, 54; Yale Univ, PhD(chem), 59. *Prof Exp:* Res chemist, Eastern Regional Res & Develop Lab, USDA, 58-84. *Mem:* AAAS; Am Chem Soc; Biophys Soc; NY Acad Sci; Sigma Xi. *Res:* Physical chemistry of proteins; electronic instrumentation for use in chemical investigations. *Mailing Add:* 15-38 Chandler Dr Fairlawn NJ 07410-2714

KAHN, LEONARD B, SURGICAL PATHOLOGY. *Current Pos:* CHMN DEPT LABS, LONG ISLAND JEWISH MED CTR, 80-; PROF PATH, STATE UNIV NY, STONY BROOK, 80-; PROF PATH, ALBERT EINSTEIN COL. *Personal Data:* b Johannesburg, SAfrica, July 20, 37; m 63; c 3. *Educ:* Witwatersrand Univ, Johannesburg, MB, BCh, 60; Univ Cape Town, M Med Path, 65; MRCPath, 77, FRCPath, 86. *Prof Exp:* Intern med & surg, Johannesburg Gen Hosp, 61-62; resident path, Univ Cape Town, 62-66; resident & fel clin asst, Sch Med, Washington Univ, St Louis, 67-69; assoc prof, Dept Path, Sch Med, Univ Cape Town, 74-77; prof & dir surg & path, Sch Med, Univ NC, Chapel Hill, 77-80. *Concurrent Pos:* Cecil John Adams Mem travelling fel, Univ Cape Town, 67. *Mem:* Int Acad Path; Gastrointestinal Path Club; Int Skeletal Soc; Arthur Purdy Stout Soc Surg Pathologists; Col Am Pathologists. *Res:* Clinical pathologic, including immunologic and ultrastructural studies of a variety of human neoplasma, especially those involving lymphoreticular tissues, bone, soft tissue and gastrointestinal tract including salivary glands. *Mailing Add:* Path Dept Albert E Einstein Col 1300 Morris Park Ave Bronx NY 10461-1926

KAHN, MANFRED, CERAMIC SCIENCE, ELECTRICAL ENGINEERING. *Current Pos:* RETIRED. *Personal Data:* b Frankfurt am Main, Ger, Feb 21, 26; nat US; m 60, Eileen M; c William, Douglas & Stephen. *Educ:* Univ Wis, BSEE, 54; Rensselaer Polytech Inst, MSEE, 59; Pa State Univ, PhD(ceramic sci), 69. *Prof Exp:* Mem tech staff, Ceramic Dept, Sprague Elec Co, 54-74; sr scientist, AVX Ceramics Inc, 74-82; dept head, Hurry County Tech Col, 82-83; sect head, Naval Res Lab, Washington, DC, 83-96. *Mem:* Inst Elec & Electronics Engrs; fel Am Ceramic Soc. *Res:* Surface layer capacitors; ohmic contacts and hybrid microcircuits; multilayer capacitors; pilot plant production; base metal electrodes; process development; pilot plant and production; circuits and applications engineering; piezo electric sensors, programed transmission control devices. *Mailing Add:* 3412 Austin Ct Alexandria VA 22310. *Fax:* 202-767-1344; *E-Mail:* kahn@anvil.navy.mil

KAHN, MARVIN WILLIAM, OTHER MEDICAL & HEALTH SCIENCES. *Current Pos:* PROF PSYCHOL, UNIV ARIZ, 69- *Personal Data:* b Cleveland, Ohio, Feb 1, 26; m 82. *Educ:* Pa State Univ, BS, 48, MS, 49, PhD (psychol), 52. *Prof Exp:* From instr to asst prof psychol, Yale Univ, 52-54; from asst prof psychol to assoc prof psychiat, Univ Colo Sch Med, 54-64; prof psychol, Ohio Univ, 64-69. *Mem:* Am Psychol Asn. *Mailing Add:* Psychol Dept Univ Ariz PO Box 210068 Tucson AZ 85721-0068

KAHN, MILTON, CHEMISTRY. *Current Pos:* RETIRED. *Personal Data:* b Philadelphia, Pa, Nov 21, 18; m 40; c 1. *Educ:* Univ Calif, BS, 41; Wash Univ, PhD(chem), 50. *Prof Exp:* Anal chemist, Paraffine Co, Inc, 42-43; res chemist, Los Alamos Sci Lab, 43-46; from asst prof to assoc prof chem, Univ N Mex, 48-57, prof, 57-81. *Mem:* AAAS; Am Chem Soc. *Res:* Isotopic exchange reactions; hot atom chemistry; chemical behavior of substances at low concentrations; radiochemistry. *Mailing Add:* 4201 Hannett Ave NE Albuquerque NM 87110-4941

KAHN, NORMAN, NEUROPHARMACOLOGY, DENTAL & MEDICAL EDUCATION. *Current Pos:* from instr to asst prof, Columbia Univ, 62-72, assoc prof pharmacol, 72-80, assoc prof dent, 74-81, prof dent, Sch Dent & Oral Surg, 81-92, assoc dean acad affairs, 89-95, acting dean, 95-96, PROF PHARMACOL, COL PHYSICIANS & SURGEONS, COLUMBIA UNIV, 81-, EDWIN ROBINSON PROF DENT & ORAL SURG, 92- *Personal Data:* b New York, NY, Dec 28, 32; m 58, Dale Krasnow. *Educ:* Columbia Univ, AB, 54, DDS, 58, PhD(pharmacol), 64. *Prof Exp:* Dent intern, Montefiore Hosp, Bronx, NY, 58-59. *Concurrent Pos:* NIH trainee neuropharmacol, Columbia Univ, 59-62; Nat Inst Neurol Dis & Blindness spec fels, Columbia Univ, 62-64 & Pisa, 65-66; NIH career develop award, 67-71; vis assoc prof anesthesiol, Univ Calif, Los Angeles, 78; chmn, Inst Rev Bd, Columbia Presby Med Ctr, NY; hon res fel, Univ Col London, 86. *Mem:* Am Dent Asn; Am Physiol Soc; Int Asn Dent Res. *Res:* Physiology and pharmacology of autonomic nervous system; medical and dental education. *Mailing Add:* Col Physicians & Surgeons Columbia Univ New York NY 10032. *E-Mail:* mks@columbia.edu

KAHN, PETER B, THEORETICAL PHYSICS. *Current Pos:* from asst prof to assoc prof, 61-71, chmn dept, 74-86, PROF PHYSICS, STATE UNIV NY STONY BROOK, 71- *Personal Data:* b New York, NY, Mar 18, 35; m 56, 89, Victoria McLane; c Miriam, David & Jeffrey. *Educ:* Union Col, NY, BS, 56; Northwestern Univ, PhD(physics), 60. *Prof Exp:* Res assoc physics, Univ Iowa, 60-61. *Concurrent Pos:* Sr Weizmann fel, 67-68. *Mem:* Fel Am Phys Soc. *Res:* Mathematical biology; statistical theory of energy level distributions; innovation in physics curricula; dynamical systems. *Mailing Add:* Dept Physics State Univ NY Stony Brook NY 11794

KAHN, PETER JACK, MATHEMATICS. *Current Pos:* asst prof to assoc prof, 65-75, PROF MATH, CORNELL UNIV, 75- *Personal Data:* b Santiago, Chile, Dec 1, 39; US citizen; m 63. *Educ:* Oberlin Col, BA, 60; Princeton Univ, PhD(math), 64. *Prof Exp:* Actg instr math, Univ Calif, Berkeley, 63, instr, 64-65. *Concurrent Pos:* Mem, Inst Advan Study, 69-7; Humboldt sr scientist, Univ Heidelberg, 74-75. *Mem:* Am Math Soc. *Res:* Algebraic and differential topology. *Mailing Add:* White Hall Cornell Univ White Hall Ithaca NY 14853-0001

KAHN, RAYMOND HENRY, endocrinology, histology; deceased, see previous edition for last biography

KAHN, ROBERT ELLIOT, COMPUTER SCIENCES, ELECTRICAL ENGINEERING. *Current Pos:* PRES, CORP NAT RES INITIATIVES, 86- *Personal Data:* b Brooklyn, NY, Dec 23, 38; m 80. *Educ:* City Col New York, BEE, 60; Princeton Univ, MA, 62, PhD(elec eng), 64. *Honors & Awards:* Harry Goode Mem Award, Am Fedn Info Processing Soc, 86; Koji Kobayashi Comput & Commun Award, Inst Elec & Electronic Engrs, Alexander Graham Bell Medal, 97; Marconi Award; Pres Award, Am Chem Soc; Nat Medal of Technol, 97. *Prof Exp:* Mem tech staff, Bell Tel Labs, 60-62; asst prof elec eng, Mass Inst Technol, 64-66; sr scientist, Bolt Beranek & Newman, 66-72; dir dept, div & prog mgr, Defense Advan Res Proj Agency, Info Processing Tech Off, 72-85. *Concurrent Pos:* Mem, Air Force Sci Adv Bd,

87- & Comput Sci & Technol Bd, Nat Acad Sci. *Mem:* Nat Acad Eng; fel Inst Elec & Electronics Engrs; fel Am Asn Artificial Intel. *Res:* National information infrastructure including networking. *Mailing Add:* Corp Nat Res Initiatives 1895 Preston White Dr Suite 100 Reston VA 20191-5434

KAHN, ROBERT PHILLIP, PLANT PATHOLOGY, PLANT QUARANTING. *Current Pos:* CONSULT, PLANT PROTECTION & QUARANTINE, 85- *Personal Data:* b Chicago, Ill, Apr 20, 24; m 49, Judith Aronson; c 4. *Educ:* Univ Ill, BA, 48, PhD(plant path), 51. *Prof Exp:* Asst bot, Univ Ill, 48-52; from plant pathologist to supvry plant pathologist, Chem Warfare Labs, Ft Detrick, 52-57; plant pathologist & sr staff, Animal & Plant Health Inspection Serv, USDA, 57-85. *Concurrent Pos:* Officer-in-chg, EAfrican Plant Quarantine Sta, Kenya, 70-72. *Mem:* Am Phytopath Soc; Int Soc Plant Pathol; Am Inst Biol Sci; AAAS; Brit Soc Plant Path. *Res:* Virology; plant quarantine pathology; plant tissue culture; agriculture; tropical plant pathology; international exchange of plant germplasm; plant protection and quarantine. *Mailing Add:* 14104 Flint Rock Terr Rockville MD 20853. *Fax:* 301-871-3965; *E-Mail:* r.kahn@cgnet.com

KAHN, SAMUEL GEORGE, NUTRITION SCIENCE ADMINISTRATION, NUTRITION POLICY. *Current Pos:* nutrit adv, Res Off & Univ Rels, Tech Assistance Bur, 71-74, sr nutrit adv, Off Nutrit, Sci & Tech Bur, 74-95, SR HEALTH-NUTRIT ADV, OFF HEALTH NUTRIT, GLOBAL BUR, AID, 95- *Personal Data:* b Belleville, NJ, May 20, 29; m 60, Irma Berger; c Kenneth & Edith. *Educ:* Ill Wesleyan Univ, BS, 51; Univ Ill, MS, 53 & 54, PhD(animal nutrit), 55. *Prof Exp:* Asst animal nutrit, Univ Ill, 52-55; res assoc, Radio Carbon Lab, 55-56; asst biochem, Squibb Inst Med Res, 56-58, sect head nutrit res, Div Agr Sci, 58-59, sr res scientist, 59-67, res supvr & head nutrit res, 67-69; assoc prof nutrit, food & chmn, Drexel Inst Technol, 69-71. *Concurrent Pos:* Hon prof nutrit, Rutgers Univ, 67-70; adj prof, Va Polytech Inst & State Univ, 74; secy, Int Vitamin A Consult Group, 74-77, Int Nutrit Anemia Consult Group, 76-; ed, Am Inst Nutrit-Nutrit Notes, 79-; mem, Joint Res Comt, Pres Bd Int Food & Agr Develop, 80-83; mem, Joint Subcomt Human Nutrit Res, Exec Off Pres US, 79-83, mem, Nat Comt Human Nutrit Res, 83-; mem, Subcomt Nutrit Group Control Iron Deficiency, UN, 89-95, Food Safety Workgroup, Off Sci & Technol Policy/Fed Coord Coun Sci Eng & Technol, 91-93. *Mem:* Am Soc Nutrit Sci; fel NY Acad Sci; Am Physiol Soc; Soc Exp Biol & Med; Am Soc Clin Nutrit; Am Chem Soc. *Res:* Vitamin and lipid metabolism; atherosclerosis; animal nutrition; nutrition, health and population; international nutrition. *Mailing Add:* 11827 Goya Dr Potomac MD 20854

KAHN, TRACY LYNN, CITRUS DIVERSITY & GERMPLASM, PRODUCTIVE BOTANY. *Current Pos:* NIH fel, Univ Calif, Berkeley, 87-88, vis researcher, Riverside, 89-93, staff res assoc, 94-95, SR MUS SCIENTIST & LECTR BIOL, UNIV CALIF, RIVERSIDE, 95- *Personal Data:* b Ann Arbor, Mich, May 13, 55; m 83, Norman C Ellstrand; c Nathan. *Educ:* Univ Mich, BS, 77, PhD(bot), 87. *Concurrent Pos:* Adj fac biol, Univ Redlands, 90-92, Riverside Community Col, 92 & Chaffey Col, 93-95; vis researcher, Swedish Agr Univ, 93. *Mem:* Bot Soc Am. *Res:* Reproductive questions associated with pollination and fruit set in citrus and another subtropical fruit, the cherimoya. *Mailing Add:* Bot & Plant Sci Univ Calif Riverside CA 92521-0124

KAHN, WALTER K(URT), ELECTRICAL ENGINEERING, ELECTROPHYSICS. *Current Pos:* PROF ENG & APPL SCI, GEORGE WASHINGTON UNIV, 69- *Personal Data:* b Mannheim, Ger, Mar 24, 29; US citizen; m 62; c 2. *Educ:* Cooper Union, BEE, 51; Polytech Inst Brooklyn, MEE, 54, DEE, 60. *Prof Exp:* Engr radar, Wheeler Labs, NY, 51-54; res assoc, microwave res inst, Polytech Inst Brooklyn, 54-60, asst prof elec eng, 60-62, from assoc prof to prof electrophysics, 62-69. *Concurrent Pos:* Liaison scientist, Off Naval Res, London, 67-68; mem comn 6, Int Union Radio Sci; ed, Trans, Antennas & Propagation, Inst Elec & Electronics Engrs, 77-80; dir, Anro Eng,Inc, 82- & Inst Info Sci & Technol, 83-92. *Mem:* AAAS; fel Inst Elec & Electronics Engrs; Optical Soc Am; Soc Photo Optical Instruments Engrs. *Res:* Optical resonators and fiberoptics; lasers; microwave antennas and antenna arrays; waveguide junctions and directional couplers; microwave measurements; monopulse, radar systems; fiber optics. *Mailing Add:* Dept Elec Eng & Comput Sci George Wash Univ Washington DC 20052. *Fax:* 202-994-0227; *E-Mail:* wkkahn@seas.gwu.edu

KAHNE, STEPHEN JAMES, control theory, systems engineering, for more information see previous edition

KAHNG, SEUN KWON, ELECTRICAL ENGINEERING, SOLID STATE ELECTRONICS. *Current Pos:* ASST DIV CHIEF, EXP TESTING TECHNOL DIV, NASA, LANGLEY, 89- *Personal Data:* b Seoul, Korea, Jan 16, 36; US citizen; m 70; c 2. *Educ:* Seoul Nat Univ, BSEE, 58; Univ Va, MEE, 63, PhD(elec eng), 67. *Prof Exp:* Res fel transducers, Langley Res Ctr, NASA, 67-68; from asst prof to assoc prof, Univ Okla, 68-78, prof elec eng, 78-89, dir elec eng, 80-89. *Concurrent Pos:* Res fel, Langley Res Ctr, NASA, 75-76. *Mem:* Inst Elec & Electronics Engrs; Optical Soc Am. *Res:* Solid state electronic devices; piezoresistive silicon sensors; silicon-on-sapphire sensors; piezoelectric sensors. *Mailing Add:* 36 Valmoore Dr Poquoson VA 23662

KAHRIZI, MOJTABA, COMPUTER PROGRAMMING, VERY LARGE SCALE INTEGRATION TECHNOLOGY. *Current Pos:* RES ASSOC PHYSICS, CONCORDIA UNIV, 90-, TECH OFFICER ELEC & COMPUT ENG, 94- *Personal Data:* b Arak, Iran, Jan 26, 49; Can citizen; m 73; c 2. *Educ:* BSc, Tehran Univ, 73, MSc, 75; MSc, Concordia Univ, 80, PhD(physics), 85. *Prof Exp:* Lectr, Arak Col Sci, Iran, 75-78; Lab instr physics, Concordia Univ, 78-83, fac mem, 83-85; postdoctoral fel physics, St Francis Xavier Univ, 85-87, asst prof, 87-90. *Mem:* Can Asn Physicists; Can Inst Neutron Scattering. *Res:* Investigating magnetic resonance properties of electron nuclear spin coupled systems in condensed matters physics; magnetic and structural phase transitions in solid state materials, particularly high-Tc superconductors and rare-earth metals, using magnetic and dilatometric measurements. *Mailing Add:* Elec & Comput Eng Dept Concordia Univ 1455 de Maisonneuve W Montreal PQ H3G 2P7 Can

KAHRS, MARK WILLIAM, DIGITAL AUDIO SIGNAL PROCESSING & COMPUTER MUSIC, COMPUTER-AIDED DESIGN. *Current Pos:* ASST PROF ELEC & COMPUT ENG, RUTGERS UNIV, 88- *Personal Data:* b Rome, Italy, Oct 25, 52; US citizen; m 87, Diane Litman; c Noah. *Educ:* Univ Calif, San Diego, AB, 74; Univ Rochester, MS, 79, PhD(comput sci), 84. *Prof Exp:* Res programmer, Ctr Comput Res Music & Acoust, 75-77; researcher, Inst Res Coord Acoust Music, 77-78; mem tech staff, AT&T Bell Lab, 83-87. *Mem:* Inst Elec & Electronics Engrs; Asn Comput Mach; Audio Eng Soc; Acoust Soc Am. *Res:* Interaction between computer architecture and hardware design of digital signal processing (especially computer music and digital audio) and programming language design and implementation particularly for use in computer aided design. *Mailing Add:* PO Box 1390 Piscataway NJ 08855-1390. *E-Mail:* kahrs@caip.rutgers.edu

KAHRS, ROBERT F, VETERINARY MEDICINE, VETERINARY EPIDEMIOLOGY. *Current Pos:* DIR NAT CTR IMPORTS & EXPORTS, USDA. *Personal Data:* b Lynbrook, NY, June 28, 30; m 53; c 4. *Educ:* Cornell Univ, DVM, 54, MS, 63, PhD(virol biomet), 65. *Honors & Awards:* Nat Academias Pract. *Prof Exp:* Asst vet, pvt pract, Interlaken, NY, 54-55; vet, Attica, NY, 55-61; res asst vet virol & biomet, NY State Vet Col, Cornell Univ, 61-65, res assoc vet epidemiol & microbiol, 65-66, asst prof vet epidemiol, 66-70, assoc prof vet epidemiol, 70-78; prof vet epidemiol & chmn, Dept Vet Prev Med, Univ Fla, 78-; dean, Univ Mo, Col Vet Med, 92. *Mem:* Am Vet Med Asn; US Animal Health Asn; Am Vet Epidemiol Soc. *Res:* Epidemiology of virus diseases of livestock. *Mailing Add:* USDA Import Export Products 4700 River Rd Unit 40 Riverdale MD 20737

KAIGHN, MORRIS EDWARD, EMBRYOLOGY, VIROLOGY. *Current Pos:* SR RES INVESTR, PASADENA FOUND MED RES, 75-; AT FREDERICK CANCER RES FACIL, NAT CANCER INST; CONSULT, BIOL RES FACIL, IJAMSVILLE MD, 95- *Personal Data:* b Camden, NJ, Aug 6, 22; m 79. *Educ:* Brooklyn Col, BS, 56; Mass Inst Technol, PhD(biol), 62. *Prof Exp:* Asst investr embryol, Carnegie Inst, 64-67; res assoc, NY Blood Ctr, 67-70, assoc investr embryol, 70-72; sr scientist cell ctr, 72-75. *Concurrent Pos:* Fel virol, Univ Toronto, 62-64. *Mem:* Am Asn Cancer Res; Am Soc Cell Biol; Tissue Cult Asn. *Res:* Isolation and characterization of epithelial cells; immortalization of epithelial cells by oncogenes; clonal culture of differentiated human liver prostate and cancer cells; growth control by steroids and peptide growth factors; cell biology. *Mailing Add:* Biol Res Facil 10075-20 Gyler Pl Ijamsville MD 21754

KAILATH, THOMAS, ELECTRICAL ENGINEERING, APPLIED MATHEMATICS. *Current Pos:* assoc prof elec eng, Stanford Univ, 63-68, dir, Info Systs Lab, 71-81, assoc chmn, Dept Elec Eng, 81-87, PROF ELEC ENG, STANFORD UNIV, 68-, HITACHI AM PROF ENG, 88- *Personal Data:* b Poona, India, June 7, 35; m 62, Sarah; c Ann, Paul, Priya & Ryan. *Educ:* Univ Poona, BE, 56; Mass Inst Technol, SM, 59, ScD(elec eng), 61. *Hon Degrees:* DEng, Linkoping Univ, Sweden, 90, Strathclyde Univ, Scotland, 92. *Honors & Awards:* Eng Achievement Award, Nat Fedn Asian Indian Orgns, 86; Tech Achievement & Soc Award, Signal Processing Soc, Inst Elec & Electronics Engrs, 89 & 91, Educ Medal, 95, DG Fink Prize, 96. *Prof Exp:* Res specialist, Jet Propulsion Lab, Calif Inst Technol, 61-62. *Concurrent Pos:* Ed, Prentice-Hall Series on Info & Systs Sci, 63-; vis prof, India Inst Sci, Bangalore, 69-70, Katholieke Univ Leuven, 77 & Tech Univ, Delft, 81; Guggenheim fel, Indian Inst Sci, 69-70; consult, Govt India, 70-71; Churchill fel, Statist Lab, Churchill, Eng, 77; chmn bd dirs, Integrated Systs, Inc, 80-89, vchmn, 89-; Erna & Jacob Michael vis chair theoret math, Weizmann Inst, 84; Royal Soc guest res prof, Imp Col, London, 89. *Mem:* Nat Acad Eng; fel Inst Math Statist; fel Inst Elec & Electronics Engrs; hon fel Inst Electronics & Telecommun Engrs India; Am Math Soc; Soc Indust & Appl Math; Am Acad Arts & Sci; Indian Nat Acad Eng. *Res:* Information theory; communications; computation; control; linear systems; statistical signal processing; very large scale integration systems; stochastic processes; linear algebra; operator theory; author or co-author of over 300 research papers. *Mailing Add:* Durand 117 Stanford CA 94305. *Fax:* 650-723-8473; *E-Mail:* kailath@stanford.edu

KAIMAL, JAGADISH CHANDRAN, METEOROLOGY. *Current Pos:* RETIRED. *Personal Data:* b Kuala Lumpur, Malaysia, Nov 18, 30; US citizen; m 57; c 3. *Educ:* Benares Hindu Univ, BSc, 53; Univ Wash, MS, 59, PhD(meteorol), 61. *Prof Exp:* Res physicist, Air Force Cambridge Res Labs, 61-76; chief, Atmospheric Studies Prog, Wave Propagation Lab, Energy Res Lab, Nat Oceanic & Atmospheric Admin, 76-92. *Mem:* Am Meteorol Soc. *Res:* Experimental investigations of turbulent fluctuations in the atmospheric boundary layer and the study of the fluxes of momentum and heat within this layer. *Mailing Add:* 13 John St Hamilton NY 13346-1317

KAIN, RICHARD YERKES, ELECTRICAL ENGINEERING. *Current Pos:* assoc prof, 66-77, PROF ELEC ENG, UNIV MINN, MINNEAPOLIS, 77- *Personal Data:* b Chicago, Ill, Jan 20, 36; m 61, 81; c 3. *Educ:* Mass Inst Technol, SB, 57, SM, 59, ScD(elec eng), 62. *Prof Exp:* Asst elec eng, Mass Inst Technol, 57-60, from instr to asst prof, 60-66. *Concurrent Pos:* Ford fel eng, 62-64; consult, Honeywell Corp, 75-89, Secure Computing Technol

Corp, 89- *Mem:* AAAS; Asn Comput Mach; Inst Elec & Electronics Engrs; Sigma Xi; Computer Prof Social Responsibility. *Res:* Computer systems; computer architecture; secure computer systems. *Mailing Add:* Dept Elec Eng Univ Minn 200 Union St SE Minneapolis MN 55455

KAINE, BRIAN PAUL, EVOLUTION OF THERMOPHILIC ORGANISMS. *Current Pos:* RES ASSOC, UNIV ILL, 81- *Educ:* Northwestern Univ, PhD(biol sci), 81. *Res:* T RNA gene structure in archaebacteria. *Mailing Add:* B 103 Chem & Life Scis Lab Univ Ill 601 S Goodwin Ave Urbana IL 61821

KAINSKI, MERCEDES H, FOOD SCIENCE, NUTRITION. *Current Pos:* RETIRED. *Personal Data:* b Kewaunee Co, Wis, Jan 26, 23; m 64. *Educ:* Univ Wis, BS, 44, MS, 55, PhD(foods), 57. *Prof Exp:* Control chemist, Wilson Res Lab, Ill, 44; with res lab, Carnation Co, Wis, 45-47; teacher pub schs, Wis, 48-53; assoc prof foods & nutrit, Kans State Univ, 57-65; assoc prof home econ, Bowling Green State Univ, 65-67; prof food & nutrit, Univ Wis, Stout, 67-85. *Mem:* Am Home Econ Asn; Inst Food Technol; Am Dietetic Asn. *Res:* Minerals, iron and copper in pork; magnesium and fat metabolism; iron, phenols and organic acid in potatoes. *Mailing Add:* 1712 Fifth St W No 108 Menomonie WI 54751

KAISEL, S(TANLEY) F(RANCIS), electronics; deceased, see previous edition for last biography

KAISER, ARMIN DALE, BIOCHEMISTRY, GENETICS. *Current Pos:* from asst prof to assoc prof, 59-66, PROF BIOCHEM, SCH MED, STANFORD UNIV, 66-, PROF DEVELOP BIOL, 89- *Personal Data:* b Piqua, Ohio, Nov 10, 27; m 53; c 2. *Educ:* Purdue Univ, BSc, 50; Calif Inst Technol, PhD(biol), 54. *Honors & Awards:* Award in Molecular Biol, US Steel Found, 70; Lasker Award, 80; Waterford Biomed Sci Award, 81. *Prof Exp:* From instr to asst prof microbiol, Wash Univ, 56-59. *Concurrent Pos:* Am Cancer Soc fel, 54-56; mem, Genetics Study Sect, NIH, 63-68; NSF sr fel, 64-65; mem, Genetic Biol Panel, NSF, 69-72. *Mem:* Nat Acad Sci; Genetics Soc Am; Am Soc Biol Chemists; Am Acad Arts & Sci. *Res:* Bacteriophage genetics; nucleic acid biochemistry; biochemistry of morphogenesis; author and co-author of over 100 publications. *Mailing Add:* Dept Biochem Stanford Univ Sch Med Stanford CA 94305-5427

KAISER, C WILLIAM, SURGERY. *Current Pos:* CHIEF SURG, VET ADMIN MED CTR, MANCHESTER, NH, 81-; ASST PROF SURG, HARVARD MED SCH, 81- *Personal Data:* b Troy, NY, Dec 7, 39; m 66; c 3. *Educ:* Colgate Univ, AB, 61; Tufts Univ, MD, 65. *Prof Exp:* Surg resident, Boston City Hosp, 68-72; assoc dir surg, Tufts Surg Serv, 72-76; assoc chief surg, Vet Admin Med Ctr, Northport, NY, 76-78; chief surg, Pondville Hosp, 78-81. *Mem:* Soc Surg Alimentary Tract; Asn Acad Surg; Asn Vet Admin Surgeons. *Res:* Surgical oncology. *Mailing Add:* Vet Admin Med Ctr 718 Smyth Rd Manchester NH 03104-7004

KAISER, CARL, MEDICINAL CHEMISTRY. *Current Pos:* RETIRED. *Personal Data:* b Baltimore, Md, Feb 8, 29; m 53; c 3. *Educ:* Univ Md, BS, 51, MS, 53, PhD(pharmaceut chem), 55. *Prof Exp:* Lab asst pharmaceut chem, Univ Md, 51-53; Smith Kline & French fel, Univ Va, 55-57; sr med chemist, Smith Kline & French Labs, 57-65, med chem group leader, 65-68, sr investr, 68-72, asst dir chem, 72-79, assoc sci dir, 79-81, sr fel, 81-86; dir med chem, Nova Pharm Corp, 86-94. *Mem:* Am Chem Soc; Am Pharmaceut Asn. *Res:* Design and synthesis of potential drug products, especially substances affecting the central and autonomic nervous systems, enzyme inhibitors, antimetabolites, drug metabolism and small ring compounds. *Mailing Add:* 8470 Woodland Rd Millersville MD 21108-1756

KAISER, CHARLES FREDERICK, DEVELOPMENTAL & HEALTH PSYCHOLOGY, STRESS MANAGEMENT. *Current Pos:* asst prof, 72-77, assoc prof, 77-91, PROF PSYCHOL, COL CHARLESTON, 91- *Personal Data:* b Dec 30, 42; m 66, Judith Hammelburger; c Edward & Michael. *Educ:* City Col, City Univ New York, BS, 64, MA, 67; Univ Houston, PhD(psychol), 73. *Prof Exp:* Fel, Univ Houston, 66-72. *Concurrent Pos:* Fel, Dept Psychiat, Baylor Col Med, 66-70; adj asst prof, Dept Phys Med & Rehab, Med Univ SC, 81-89; mem comt, Asn Appl Psychophysiol & Biofeedback, 83-93, bd mem, 86-89; grant, Nat Hazards Res & Appln Info Ctr, 93. *Mem:* Int Stress Mgt Asn; Am Psychol Soc; SEastern Psychol Asn. *Res:* Research in personality and cognitive abilities of gifted adolescents; stress and depression in college students, gifted adolescents and children; published articles in various journals; personality and behaviors associated with substance abuse and natural disasters. *Mailing Add:* Col Charleston Dept Psychol 66 George St Charleston SC 29424. *Fax:* 803-953-5590; *E-Mail:* kaiserc@cofc.edu

KAISER, CHRISTOPHER B, HISTORY & PHILOSOPHY OF SCIENCE, PHYSICS. *Current Pos:* from asst prof to assoc prof, 77-88, PROF, WESTERN THEOL SEM, HOLLAND, 88- *Personal Data:* b Greenwich, Conn, Oct 16, 41; m 70, Martha W Mercaldi; c Justin, Matthew & Patrick. *Educ:* Harvard Univ, BA, 63; Univ Colo, PhD(astrogeophys), 68; Edinburgh Univ, PhD(theology), 74. *Honors & Awards:* John Templeton Found Prize Outstanding Bks Sci & Relig, 95. *Prof Exp:* Lectr physics, Gordon Col, 68-71 & Edinburgh Univ, 73-74; with Systs Develop, QEI Inc, Bedford, Mass, 75-76. *Concurrent Pos:* Mem, Gravity Res Found, 68-; resident mem, Ctr Theol Inquiry, Princeton, NJ, 84, 87. *Mem:* Soc Hist Technol. *Res:* History of science as influenced by religious belief and practice; history of interaction between theological beliefs and scientific progress. *Mailing Add:* Western Theol Seminary 101 E 13th St Holland MI 49423. *Fax:* 616-392-7717

KAISER, DAVID GILBERT, PHARMACEUTICAL CHEMISTRY, DRUG METABOLISM. *Current Pos:* chemist, Upjohn Co, 59-69, res head drug metab, 69-79, res mgr drug metab, 79-85, dir drug metab res, 85-86, SR RES CONSULT, UPJOHN CO, 86- *Personal Data:* b Detroit, Mich, Aug 25, 28; m 61; c 2. *Educ:* Detroit Inst Technol, BS, 52; Purdue Univ, MS, 54, PhD(pharmaceut chem), 59. *Prof Exp:* Fel radiochem, Univ Mich, 59. *Mem:* AAAS; Am Chem Soc; Am Pharmaceut Asn; Sigma Xi; Am Soc Mass Spectrometry; NY Acad Sci. *Res:* Drug metabolism and analytical chemistry. *Mailing Add:* 6605 Robinswood Dr Portage MI 49024-3138

KAISER, DEBRA LEE, HIGH TEMPERATURE SUPERCONDUCT CRS, FERROELECTRIC OXIDE THIN FILMS. *Current Pos:* MAT RES ENGR, NAT INST STAND & TECHNOL, 88- *Personal Data:* b Hinsdale, Ill, Oct 9, 57; m 87, Frank W Gayle; c Carly L & Andrew J. *Educ:* Lehigh Univ, BS, 79; Colo Sch Mines, MS, 80; Mass Inst Technol, ScD, 85. *Prof Exp:* Fel, IBM, 85-87. *Mem:* Mat Res Soc; Fedn Mat Socs; Am Asn Crystal Growth. *Res:* Metal-organic chemical vapor deposition of ferroelectric oxide thin films for photonic applications; crystal growth, detwinning and magneto-optical characterization of high temperature superconductors. *Mailing Add:* Nat Inst Stand & Technol Bldg 223 Rm A329 Gaithersburg MD 20899. *Fax:* 301-990-8729; *E-Mail:* debra.kaiser@nist.gov

KAISER, EDWARD WILLIAM, JR, PHYSICAL CHEMISTRY. *Current Pos:* sr res scientist, Ford Motor Co, 74-80, prin res assoc, 80-86, staff scientist, 86-95, SR STAFF TECH SPECIALIST, FORD MOTOR CO, 95- *Personal Data:* b Minneapolis, Minn, May 10, 42; m 68, Jacqueline Sersen; c Elizabeth. *Educ:* Northwestern Univ, BA, 64; Harvard Univ, MA, 66, PhD(chem), 70. *Honors & Awards:* Donald Julius Groen Prize, Inst Mech Engrs, 86. *Prof Exp:* NATO fel, Southampton Univ, 69-70; temp mem tech staff, Bell Labs, 70-72; assoc scientist, Xerox Corp, 72-74. *Mem:* Am Phys Soc; Am Chem Soc; Combustion Inst. *Res:* Chemical kinetics; combustion research; emissions from spark-ignition engines. *Mailing Add:* 7 Windham Lane Dearborn MI 48120. *E-Mail:* ekaiser@ford.com

KAISER, EDWIN MICHAEL, ORGANIC CHEMISTRY. *Current Pos:* from asst prof to prof chem, 70-95, CURSTORS DISTINGUISHED TEACHING PROF, UNIV MO, COLUMBIA, 95- *Personal Data:* b Youngstown, Ohio, Oct 15, 38; m 60, Judith A Boyer; c Kim, Kay, Karla, Kevin & Kurt. *Educ:* Youngstown Univ, BS, 60; Purdue Univ, PhD(org chem), 64. *Prof Exp:* Res assoc org chem, Duke Univ, 64-66. *Concurrent Pos:* Dir, Hon Col, 84-91. *Mem:* Am Chem Soc; Sigma Xi. *Res:* Organometallic derivatives of methylated heterocycles; condensations and cyclizations in nonaqueous media. *Mailing Add:* 123 Chem Bldg Univ Mo Columbia MO 65211. *Fax:* 573-882-2754; *E-Mail:* chemed@showme.missouri.edu

KAISER, GEORGE C, THORACIC SURGERY. *Current Pos:* from asst prof to assoc prof, 63-70, PROF SURG, SCH MED, ST LOUIS UNIV, 70- *Personal Data:* b Bronx, NY, July 30, 28; m 53; c 3. *Educ:* Lehigh Univ, AB, 49; Johns Hopkins Univ, MD, 53. *Prof Exp:* Intern surg, Johns Hopkins Hosp, Baltimore, Md, 53-54; resident, Vet Admin Hosp, Ft Howard, Md, 54; clin assoc, clin of surg, Nat Heart Inst, 54-56; resident surg, Med Ctr, Ind Univ, 56-61, from instr to asst prof, 61-63. *Concurrent Pos:* Staff surgeon, Vet Admin Hosp, Indianapolis, Ind, 61; dir St Louis Univ surg serv, Vet Admin Hosp, 63-65. *Mem:* Soc Thoracic Surg; AMA; Am Col Surg; Int Cardiovasc Soc; Am Asn Thoracic Surg; Sigma Xi. *Res:* General and thoracic surgical problems, including research in cardiac physiology. *Mailing Add:* St Louis Univ Hosp PO Box 15250 St Louis MO 63110-0250

KAISER, GERARD ALAN, THORACIC SURGERY, CARDIOVASCULAR SURGERY. *Current Pos:* PROF SURG & CHIEF, DIV THORACIC & CARDIOVASCULAR SURG, SCH MED, UNIV MIAMI, 71- *Personal Data:* b Brooklyn, NY, Dec 9, 32; m 55; c 3. *Educ:* Princeton Univ, AB, 54; Columbia Univ, MD, 58. *Prof Exp:* Intern, Presby Hosp, NY, 58-59, asst resident gen surg, 59-62, resident, 64-65; resident thoracic surg, Vet Admin Hosp & Bellevue Hosp Ctr, NY, 66 & Presby Hosp, 67; instr surg, Columbia Univ, 67-68; asst prof, Mt Sinai Sch Med, 68-69; assoc prof, Columbia Univ, 69-71. *Concurrent Pos:* Fel, NY Tuberc & Health Asn, 66-67; Glorney-Raisbeck fel, NY Acad Med, 68-69; asst surg, Columbia Univ, 65-67; asst vis prof, Delafield Hosp, 68; asst attend surg, Columbia-Presby Med Ctr, 68, assoc attend surg, 69-71; vis asst surg, Elmhurst Hosp, 68-69 & Harlem Hosp Ctr, 69-71; asst attend surg, Mt Sinai Hosp, 68-69; consult, Vet Admin Hosp, 68-71; active attend & chief div thoracic & cardiovasc surg, Jackson Mem Hosp; Otto G Storm estab investr, Am Heart Asn, 70. *Mem:* Soc Univ Surgeons; Soc Thoracic Surgeons; Asn Acad Surg; Am Fedn Clin Res; Int Cardiovasc Soc; Sigma Xi. *Res:* Cardiovascular physiology and pharmacology, especially electrophysiology. *Mailing Add:* Univ Miami Exec Res PO Box 016960 R114 Miami FL 33101

KAISER, HINRICH, systematics, for more information see previous edition

KAISER, IVAN IRVIN, BIOCHEMISTRY. *Current Pos:* From asst prof to assoc prof biochem, 67-75, prof biochem & chem, 75-78, chmn biochem, 79-84, PROF MOLECULAR BIOL & CHEM, UNIV WYO, 85- *Personal Data:* b Stuart, Nebr, Nov 21, 38; m 66, 94, Annette Greenberg; c Sally & Julie. *Educ:* Wayne State Col, BA, 62; Iowa State Univ, PhD(biochem), 67. *Honors & Awards:* Burlington Northern Award, Univ Wyo, 92. *Mem:* Am Chem Soc; Am Soc Biol Chemists; Sigma Xi; AAAS; Int Soc Toxinology; Protein Soc. *Res:* Structure and function of ribonucleic acids; selenium biochemistry; natural toxins. *Mailing Add:* Dept Molecular Biol Univ Wyo PO Box 3944 University Sta Laramie WY 82071-3944. *Fax:* 307-766-5098

KAISER, JACK ALLEN CHARLES, REMOTE SENSING, INSTRUMENTATION. *Current Pos:* res physisist, 72-93, SUPVRY RES PHYSICIST, NAVAL RES LAB, 93- *Personal Data:* b Chicago, Ill, Nov 15, 35; m 63, 91, Dorothy C Darnes; c Cynthia (Ferguson) & Scott. *Educ:* Ill Inst Technol, BS, 57; Univ Chicago, PhD(geophys), 69. *Prof Exp:* Weather forecaster, USAF, 58-60; res asst, Univ Chicago, 62-69, res assoc, 69-72. *Concurrent Pos:* Prin investr, Naval Res Lab, 74-81. *Mem:* Am Meterol Soc; Am Geophys Union; Sigma Xi. *Res:* Experiments on air-sea interaction and upper ocean dynamics, ocean remote sensing, ocean waves, ocean measurement techniques. *Mailing Add:* 12002 Kingfield Ct Upper Marlboro MD 20772

KAISER, JAMES F(REDERICK), ELECTRICAL ENGINEERING. *Current Pos:* RETIRED. *Personal Data:* b Piqua, Ohio, Dec 10, 29; m 54, Margo; c 4. *Educ:* Univ Cincinnati, EE, 52; Mass Inst Technol, SM, 54, ScD, 59. *Honors & Awards:* Centennial Medal, Inst Elec & Electronics Engrs, 84, Tech Achievement Award, Acoustics, Speech & Signal Processing, 78, Soc Award, 81. *Prof Exp:* Asst, Servomech Lab, Mass Inst Technol, 52-55, from instr to asst prof elec eng, 55-60; mem tech staff, Bell Tel Labs Inc, Digital Systs Res Dept, Bell Core, 59-84, distinguished mem tech staff, 84-90. *Mem:* Fel Inst Elec & Electronics Engrs; Asn Comput Mach; AAAS; Soc Indust & Appl Math; Acoust Soc Am; Europ Asn Signal Processing. *Res:* Theory of control and signal processing systems; system optimization; application of digital computations to continuous systems; digital signal processing; continuous system modeling; vocal tract modeling; speech technology research. *Mailing Add:* Dept Elec & Comput Eng Rutgers Univ Piscataway NJ 08855

KAISER, JOSEPH ANTHONY, PHARMACOLOGY. *Current Pos:* RETIRED. *Personal Data:* b Baltimore, Md, Mar 22, 26; m 51, Louise Bentley; c Joseph A Jr, Thomas M & Kathleen K (Evans). *Educ:* Univ Md, BS, 50, MS, 52, PhD(pharmacol), 55. *Prof Exp:* Sr res pharmacologist, Pfizer Therapeut Inst, NJ, 55-58; exp therapeut res sect, Lederle Labs, Am Cyanamid Co, 58-63; pharmacologist, Drug Rev Br, Div Toxicol Eval, Bur Sci Stand & Eval, Food & Drug Admin, 63-64, res pharmacologist, Div Pharmacol, Bur Sci Res, 64-66; exec secy pharmacol & endocrinol fels rev sect, NIH, 66-69, from asst chief to dep chief, Career Develop Rev Br, 69-73, exec secy spec progs, 73-74, exec secy, Pharmacol Study Sect, Div Res Grants, 74-95. *Mem:* Am Soc Pharmacol & Exp Therapeut. *Res:* Pharmacology-toxicology; antibiotics; anticholinergics, antihistamines, antiparasiticides and anti-tubercular agents; health science administration; toxicological evaluation. *Mailing Add:* 1017 Tracy Dr Colesville MD 20904-2183. *Fax:* 301-594-7601; *E-Mail:* jkq@nihorg.bitnet

KAISER, KLAUS L(EO) E(DUARD), ORGANIC CHEMISTRY, STRUCTURE-ACTIVITY RELATIONSHIPS. *Current Pos:* head, Org Prop Sect, 80-84, RES SCIENTIST, CAN CTR INLAND WATERS, ENVIRON CAN, 72-, CHIEF, NEARSHORE-OFFSHORE INTERACTIONS PROJ, 84-; ADJ PROF, DEPT CHEM, BROCK UNIV, 90- *Personal Data:* b Kempten, Ger, June 17, 41; Can citizen; m, Dianne E; c Anita C, Edward L & Andrew W. *Educ:* Tech Univ, Munich, cand chem, 64, dipl chem, 66, Dr rer nat(chem), 68. *Prof Exp:* Fel organometallic chem, Fonds Ger Chem Indust, 68-69 & Nat Res Coun, McMaster Univ, Ont, 69-71. *Concurrent Pos:* From alt mem to mem, Water Qual Objectives Subcomt, Int Jt Comn, 74-78; mem, Task Force Polychlorinated Biphenyls, Environ Can & NHW Can, 75-76 & Task Force Mirex, 76-77; liaison mem, Task Force Ecol Effects Non-Phosphate Detergent Builders, Int Jt Comn, 78-80; assoc ed, J Great Lakes Res, 80-93; ed, Quant Struct Activity Relationship in Environ Toxicol, 84; co-ed, Acta Hydrochimica et Hydrobiologica, 85-; quant struct activ relationships, Environ Toxicol-II, 87; pres, Int Assoc Great Lakes Res, 87-88; Chief, Nearshore-Offshore Interactions Proj, 87-; co-chair, Fate of Toxics Comt, Lake Ont-Niagara River Mgt Plan, 89-92; editor-in-chief, Water Qual Res J Can, 94-; chief, Environ Stand & Statist Proj, 94-96; assoc ed, Environ Toxicol Chem, 97-; dir, Environ & Rubber Chem Div, CIC, 97- *Mem:* Int Asn Great Lakes Res; Ger Chem Soc; Soc Environ Toxicol Chemists; fel Chem Inst Can. *Res:* Chemistry of contaminants in the biosphere, including their analysis, bioaccumulation, metabolic and photochemical transformation and their toxicity; quantitative structure-activity correlation (QSAR) of contaminants; organometallic and environmental chemistry. *Mailing Add:* Nat Water Res Inst PO Box 5050 Burlington ON L7R 4A6 Can. *Fax:* 905-336-6430; *E-Mail:* klaus.kaiser@cciw.ca

KAISER, MARY AGNES, ANALYTICAL CHEMISTRY. *Current Pos:* res chemist, E I du Pont de Nemours & Co, 77-80, res supvr, 80-84, sr supvr, 84-89, test mgr, 89-94, SR RES ASSOC, E I DU PONT DE NEMOURS & CO, 94- *Personal Data:* b Pittston, Pa, June 11, 48; m 79, Cecil Dybowski; c Marta M. *Educ:* Wilkes Univ, BS, 70; St Joseph's Univ, Pa, MS, 72; Villanova Univ, PhD(chem), 76. *Prof Exp:* Assoc chem, Univ Ga, 76-77. *Concurrent Pos:* Prog chair, Eastern Anal Symp, 96. *Mem:* Am Chem Soc; Sigma Xi. *Res:* Analytical chemistry of separations; spectroscopy; environmental chemistry. *Mailing Add:* Corp Ctr Anal Sci E I du Pont de Nemours & Co Inc PO Box 80256 Wilmington DE 19880-0256

KAISER, MICHAEL LEROY, RADIO ASTRONOMY. *Current Pos:* RADIO ASTRONR, GODDARD SPACE FLIGHT CTR, NASA, 69- *Personal Data:* b Keokuk, Iowa, Dec 28, 41; m 68; c 2. *Educ:* Univ Iowa, BA, 64; Univ Md, College Park, MS, 73. *Prof Exp:* Comput programmer astron, Nat Radio Astron Observ, 64-65; sci analyst astron celestial mech, Wolf Res & Develop Corp, 65-69. *Mem:* Am Astron Soc; Am Geophys Union; Int Union Radio Scientists; Inst Elec & Electronics Engrs. *Res:* Planetary radio physics; magnetospheric physics. *Mailing Add:* NASA/GSFC Code 695 Greenbelt MD 20771

KAISER, NICHOLAS, ASTRONOMY. *Current Pos:* assoc prof, 88-90, PROF ASTRON, CAN INST THEORET ASTROPHYS, UNIV TORONTO, 90- *Personal Data:* b Sept 15, 54. *Educ:* Leeds Univ, BSc, 78; Univ Calif, PhD(astron), 82. *Honors & Awards:* Helen Warner Prize, Am Astron Soc, 89; Gerhard Herzberg Medal, Can Asn Physicists, 93. *Prof Exp:* Lindemann fel, Univ Calif, Berkeley, 83; fel, Univ Calif, Santa Barbara & Berkeley, 84, Univ Cambridge, 85-86, Sci & Eng Res Coun advan fel, 86-88. *Concurrent Pos:* Sr vis, Univ Sussex, 85; prin investr, Natural Sci & Eng Res Coun Can, 88, 91 & 93; fel cosmol prog, Can Inst Advan Res, 88-; Steacie fel, 91-92. *Res:* Observational cosmology; galaxy formation; large scale structure; bulk flows; gravitational lensing. *Mailing Add:* Inst Astron 2680 Woodlawn Dr Honolulu HI 96822

KAISER, PETER, ELECTRICAL ENGINEERING. *Current Pos:* mem staff, Guided Waves Res Lab, 66-79, SUPVR, LIGHTWAVE TECH GROUP, BELL LABS, 79- *Personal Data:* b Aschaffenburg, W Ger, 1938; m 66; c 2. *Educ:* Munich Tech Univ, Diplom Ing, 63; Univ Calif, Berkeley, MS, 65, PhD(elec eng), 66. *Prof Exp:* NATO fel, 63-64. *Mem:* Inst Elec & Electronics Engrs; Optical Soc Am. *Res:* Frequency independent antennas; optical communication; guided wave transmission. *Mailing Add:* Bellcore Rm 3Z379 331 Newman Springs Rd Red Bank NJ 07701

KAISER, PETER KONRAD, GEOMECHANICS & GEOTECHNICAL ENGINEERING, ROCK MECHANICS & GROUND CONTROL. *Current Pos:* PROF MINING ENG, CHAIR ROCK MECH & GROUND CONTROL, LAURENTIAN UNIV, 87-, DIR, GEOMECH RES CTR, 90- *Personal Data:* b Schaffhausen, Switz, Mar 31, 47; Can citizen; m 72, Katharina Lutz; c Mirjam Lynn & Michael Stefan. *Educ:* Eidgenoessische Tech Hochschule, Zurich, dipl, 72, Univ Alta, PhD(civil eng), 79. *Honors & Awards:* Distinguished Serv Award, Can Inst Mining, 91; J F Franklin Award, Can Geotech Soc, 94; Schlumberger Award, Int Soc Rock Mech. *Prof Exp:* From asst prof to prof civil eng, Univ Alta, 77-87. *Concurrent Pos:* Geotech consult civil & mining applns, 80-; vis prof, Ger, Japan, France, 83, 89, 93; hon prof mining, Northeastern Univ, Shenyang, China. *Mem:* Tunnelling Asn Can (vpres, 84-88); Int Soc Rock Mech (vpres, 91-95); Am Soc Civil Eng; Can Geotech Soc; Am Inst Mining Engrs; Swiss Geol Soc. *Res:* Geomechanics of underground excavations; rock support under static and dynamic loading; rock mass response monitoring including microseismics for civil and mining engineering; nuclear waste disposal; ground tunnelling; dam stability; groundwater flow. *Mailing Add:* Laurentian Univ Ramsey Lake Rd F217 Sudbury ON P3E 2C6 Can. *Fax:* 705-675-4838; *E-Mail:* pkaiser@nickel.laurentian.ca

KAISER, QUENTIN C, SOLID STATE PHYSICS. *Current Pos:* RETIRED. *Personal Data:* b Ridgewood, NY, Sept 12, 21; m 45, Evelyn B Burkland; c Susan J, Donald A & Richard C. *Educ:* Hofstra Col, BA, 49; Okla Agr & Mech Col, MS, 50. *Prof Exp:* Physicist, Res Lab, Harry Diamond Labs, 50-53, supvry electronics scientist, Develop Lab, 53-59, physicist, Microminiaturization Br, 59-61, supvr res & develop, 61-63, br chief & supvry physicist, 63-80. *Mem:* Am Phys Soc; Inst Elec & Electronics Engrs. *Res:* Dielectric measurements; proximity fuze design; solid state devices. *Mailing Add:* 4114 Byrd Ct Kensington MD 20895

KAISER, REINHOLD, MAGNETIC RESONANCE. *Current Pos:* RETIRED. *Personal Data:* b Duisburg, Ger, Nov 19, 27. *Educ:* Univ Gottingen, dipl physics, 53, Dr rer nat, 54. *Prof Exp:* Ger Res Coun fel, Imp Col, Univ London, 55; Can Res Coun fel, Dalhousie Univ, 56; from asst prof to prof, Univ NB, 57-91, 66-91, emer prof physics, 92. *Concurrent Pos:* Res fel, Harvard Univ, 64 & Shell Develop Co, Calif, 65; guest prof, Swiss Fed Inst Technol, 71-72. *Res:* Acoustics; magnetic resonance. *Mailing Add:* 30 Jason Ct Fredericton NB E3B 6Y3 Can. *E-Mail:* reka@unb.ca

KAISER, ROBERT, CHEMICAL ENGINEERING, APPLIED CHEMISTRY. *Current Pos:* PRES, ARGOS ASSOC INC, 77-; PRES & FOUNDER, ENTROPIC SYSTS, INC, WINCHESTER, MASS, 86- *Personal Data:* b Strasbourg, France, June 22, 34; US citizen; m 70, Madeleine Butty; c Pierre J & Martine L. *Educ:* Mass Inst Technol, SB, 56, MS, 57, ScD(chem eng), 62. *Prof Exp:* Res engr, M W Kellogg Co, 61, res chemist, Res & Develop Ctr, Pullman, Inc, NJ, 62-65, res engr, 65-66; sr staff scientist, Res & Tech Labs, Space Systs Div, Avco Corp, Lowell, 66-71, group leader, Advan Processes Dept, Systs Div, 71-74; consult engr, 74-77. *Concurrent Pos:* Vis scientist, Mass Inst Technol, 82-86. *Mem:* Am Chem Soc; Am Inst Chem Engrs; Inst Environ Sci; Soc Automotive Engrs. *Res:* Oil/water separation; magnetic liquids; applied surface chemistry; fine powder technology; process development; technology assessment and forecasting; industrial market research; precision cleaning. *Mailing Add:* PO Box 397 Winchester MA 01890-0597

KAISER, ROBERT L, tropical medicine, epidemiology; deceased, see previous edition for last biography

KAISER, THOMAS BURTON, PLASMA PHYSICS. *Current Pos:* PHYSICIST PLASMA PHYSICS, LAWRENCE LIVERMORE LAB, 76- *Personal Data:* b St Louis, Mo, May 11, 40; m 67, Phyllis Holmstrom; c Jonathan. *Educ:* St Edward's Univ, BS, 62; Univ Md, College Park, MS, 71, PhD(physics), 73. *Prof Exp:* Sr analyst programming, LTV Aerospace Corp, Mass, 66-68; res assoc space physics, Goddard Space Flight Ctr, Md, 73-75. *Concurrent Pos:* Resident res assoc, Nat Acad Sci-Nat Res Coun, 73-75. *Mem:* AAAS; Am Phys Soc; Sigma Xi. *Res:* Theoretical plasma physics; computational physics; magnetic and inertial confinement fusion. *Mailing Add:* Lawrence Livermore Lab L-630 PO Box 808 Livermore CA 94550. *E-Mail:* tkaiser@llul.gov

KAISER, WILLIAM RICHARD, COAL HYDROGEOLOGY, AQUEOUS GEOCHEMISTRY. *Current Pos:* RES SCIENTIST, BUR ECON GEOL, UNIV TEX, 72- *Personal Data:* b Racine, Wis, Aug 15, 37; m 70, Mary Collinson; c Jennifer & Rebecca. *Educ:* Univ Wis-Madison, BA, 59, MS, 62; Johns Hopkins Univ, PhD(geol), 72. *Prof Exp:* Geologist micropaleont, Exxon Co, USA, 62-63, geologist petrol geol, 65-68; geologist igneous & metamorphic petrog, Ghana Geol Surv, Accra, Ghana, 63-65. *Concurrent Pos:* Lectr, Dept Geol Sci, Univ Tex, Austin, 78-80; mem, Lignite Subcomt & Fossil Energy Adv Comt, Dept Energy, 78; chmn exec comt, Tex Univ Coal Res Consortium, 83-85; mem, Steering Comt Coal Res Assesment, Dept Energy, 89- *Mem:* Geol Soc Am; Am Assoc Petrol Geologists; Am Geophys Union. *Res:* Depositional systems; geology of Gulf Coast (Texas) lignite; hydrogeology; underground coal gasification; low-temperature aqueous geochemistry; brine equilibria in the predication of reservoir quality; retardation of radionuclides; coalbed methane. *Mailing Add:* 4921 Strass Dr Austin TX 78731. *Fax:* 512-471-0140

KAISER, WOLFGANG A, TELECOMMUNICATIONS. *Current Pos:* PROF TELECOMMUN, UNIV STUTTGART, 67- *Personal Data:* b Schoental, Ger, Feb 22, 23; m 51; c 2. *Educ:* Univ Stuttgart, dipl ing, 51, Dr ing, 55. *Hon Degrees:* Dr ing Eh, Univ Munich, 85. *Prof Exp:* Res engr telecommun, Stand Elektrik Lorenz, 54-57, lab head, 57-63, res & develop dir, 63-67. *Concurrent Pos:* Chmn, Res Coun, Muenchner Kreis, Munich, 77-; mem, Acad Sci, Heidelberg, 82. *Mem:* Fel Inst Elec & Electronics Engrs. *Res:* Evolution of telecommunications; optical transmission systems; wideband networks for speech, text, data, pictures; television; digital audio; data communication in local and metropolitan area networks. *Mailing Add:* Inst Fnachrichtenuebertag Breitscheid St 2 70563 Stuttgart Germany

KAISER-KUPFER, MURIEL I, OPHTHALMIC GENETICS RESEARCH. *Current Pos:* sr staff fel, Nat Inst Child Health & Human Develop, NIH, 72-74, med officer ophthal & pediat, Clin Br, Nat Eye Inst, 74-81, chief, Sect Ophthalmic Genetics & Pediat Ophthal, Clin Br, 81-89, BR CHIEF, OPHTHALMIC GENETICS & CLIN SERV BR, NAT EYE INST, NIH, BETHESDA, 89-, DEP CLIN DIR, 91- *Personal Data:* b New York, NY, May 25, 36. *Educ:* Wellesley Col, BA, 57; Hopkins Med Sch, MD, 61; Am Bd Pediat, cert, 67; Am Bd Ophthal, cert, 74. *Prof Exp:* Residency pediat, Johns Hopkins Hosp, Baltimore, 61-65, fel child psychiat, 65-66, asst dir & instr, Comprehensive Care Clin, Dept Pediat, 66-68; residency, Ophthal & Consult Congenital Defects Clin, Sch Med, Univ Wash, 68-70; consult eye care delivery facill, Comprehensive Health Care Ctr, 70-71; asst prof, Dept Obstet & Gynec, Sch Med, George Washington Univ, 71-72. *Concurrent Pos:* Vis prof, Pan Am Ophthal Asn, 76; comt mem, Pharm & Therapeut Comt Clin Ctr, NIH, 77-89. *Mem:* Am Acad Ophthal; Nat Soc Prev Blindness; Asn Res Vision & Ophthal; Am Ophthal Soc. *Res:* Child psychiatry; ophthalmic genetics research. *Mailing Add:* NIH Nat Eye Inst Ophthal Genetics & Clin Serv Br Bldg 10 Rm 10N226 Bethesda MD 20892

KAISERMAN, HOWARD BRUCE, ENZYME STABILIZATION, SURFACTANT & PROTEIN INTERACTIONS. *Current Pos:* RES SCIENTIST BIOCHEM, UNILEVER RES, 88- *Personal Data:* b Philadelphia, Pa, Oct 10, 57; m 91, Robyn Greenberg. *Educ:* Skidmore Col, BA, 80; Emory Univ, PhD(chem), 84. *Prof Exp:* Postdoctoral fel biochem, Dept Biol, Johns Hopkins Univ & NIH, 84-88. *Mem:* Am Chem Soc; Am Soc Biochem & Molecular Biol. *Res:* Influence of chemical agents on protein denaturation with the ultimate goal of protecting proteins from denaturants; storage stability of proteins in aggressive environments. *Mailing Add:* 135 Owatonna St Haworth NJ 07641

KAISERMAN-ABRAMOF, ITA REBECA, NEUROBIOLOGY, NEUROCYTOLOGY. *Current Pos:* ASSOC PROF ANAT, SCH MED, CASE WESTERN RESERVE UNIV, 71- *Personal Data:* b Belo Horizonte, Brazil, Sept 11, 33; div; c 1. *Educ:* Univ Minas Gerais, BS, 55, MS, 56, PhD(biol sci), 62. *Prof Exp:* Actg dept chmn biol, Univ Minas Gerais, 62-63, assoc prof cytol, histol & embryol, 65-66; teaching asst histol, Sch Med, Harvard Univ, 66-67; asst prof anat, Sch Med, Boston Univ, 67-71. *Mem:* Am Inst Biol Sci; Am Soc Cell Biol; Am Asn Anatomists. *Res:* Cytological investigations of the mammalian brain, including visual and motor cerebral cortex and cerebellum; use of electron microscopy with experimental and quantitative analysis of connectivity; anophthalmic mutant mice and mechanisms involved in epilepsy. *Mailing Add:* Dept Anat Case Western Res Univ Sch Med 2109 Adelbert Rd Cleveland OH 44106

KAISTHA, KRISHAN K, toxicology, clinical chemistry, for more information see previous edition

KAITA, ROBERT, PLASMA PHYSICS. *Current Pos:* Res assoc, Plasma Physics Lab, Princeton Univ, 78-80, res staff, 80-84, res physicist, 84-90, PRIN RES PHYSICIST, PLASMA PHYSICS LAB, PRINCETON UNIV, 90- *Personal Data:* b Tokyo, Japan, Sept 2, 52; US citizen; m 80, Chiu-Tze Lin; c Courtney L & Constance L. *Educ:* State Univ NY, Stony Brook, BSc, 73; Rutgers Univ, PhD(physics), 78. *Concurrent Pos:* Chancellor's vis prof, Univ Mo, Rolla, 94. *Mem:* Am Phys Soc; Sigma Xi; AAAS. *Res:* Tokamak heating with neutral particle beams and radiofrequency waves; probe beams and particle detectors as plasma diagnostics; computer simulations of thermonuclear plasmas. *Mailing Add:* Princeton Univ Plasma Physics Lab Box 451 Princeton NJ 08543. *Fax:* 609-243-2418; *E-Mail:* kaita@pppl.gov

KAIZER, HERBERT, ONCOLOGY, BONE MARROW TRANSPLANTATION. *Current Pos:* COLEMAN-FANNIE MAY CANDIES FOUND PROF PEDIAT, MED & IMMUNOL, RUSH UNIV & DIR, BONE MARROW TRANSPLANT CTR, RUSH PRESBY, ST LUKE'S, 88- *Personal Data:* b Boston, Mass, Sept 30, 30; m 54; c 3. *Educ:* Boston Univ, AB, 51, PhD(exp psychol), 56; Stanford Univ, MD, 65. *Prof Exp:* Assoc psychologist, Int Bus Mach, Inc, 56-58; mem tech staff, Thompson, Ramo, Woolridge, Inc, 58-59; intern & asst resident, Johns Hopkins Hosp, 65-67; fel microbiol, Johns Hopkins Univ, 67-69; sr fel pediat, Univ Tex M D Anderson Hosp & Tumor Inst, 69-70; asst prof pediat & oncol, Sch Med, Johns Hopkins Univ, 70-88. *Mem:* AAAS; Am Soc Microbiol. *Res:* Autologous bone marrow transplantation in cancer. *Mailing Add:* Rush Presby St Luke's 1653 W Cong Pkwy Chicago IL 60612

KAJANDER, RICHARD EMIL, SYNTHETIC & EXOTIC FIBER STRUCTURES. *Current Pos:* SR RES ENGR, SCHULLER INT, 91- *Personal Data:* b Detroit, Mich, Dec 10, 51. *Educ:* Mich Technol Univ, BS, 74, BS, 75 & MS, 76. *Prof Exp:* Process engr, Proctor & Gamble Co, 76-78; res engr, Am Can Co, 78-81; sr develop engr, Dexter Corp, 81-83; proj mgr, Tambrands Inc, 83-90. *Concurrent Pos:* Consult coating process develop, 84-86. *Mem:* Am Chem Soc; Tech Asn Pulp & Paper Indust. *Res:* Papermaking process and specialty paper product development; granted 6 US patents. *Mailing Add:* Schuller Int 331 N Dulton Dr Toledo OH 43615

KAJFEZ, DARKO, ELECTRICAL ENGINEERING. *Current Pos:* Assoc prof elec eng, 67-70, PROF ELEC ENG & RES ENGR, UNIV MISS, 70- *Personal Data:* b Delnice, Yugoslavia, July 8, 28; m 54; c 2. *Educ:* Univ Ljubljana, EE, 53; Univ Calif, Berkeley, PhD(eng), 67. *Concurrent Pos:* Vis prof elec eng, Univ Ljubljana, 76-77; consult, Harris-Farinan, San Carlos, Calif, 80-83. *Mem:* Inst Elec & Electronics Engrs; Int Union Radio Sci; Inst Elec Engrs Brit. *Res:* Microwave circuits and antennas. *Mailing Add:* Dept Elec Eng Univ Miss University MS 38677

KAJI, AKIRA, BIOCHEMISTRY. *Current Pos:* assoc, 63, from asst prof to assoc prof, 64-72, PROF MICROBIOL, SCH MED, UNIV PA, 72- *Personal Data:* b Tokyo, Japan, Jan 13, 30; m 58, Katayana Hideko; c Kenneth, Eugene, Naomi & Amy. *Educ:* Univ Tokyo, BS, 53; Johns Hopkins Univ, PhD(biochem), 58. *Prof Exp:* Res assoc microbiol, Sch Med, Vanderbilt Univ, 60-61. *Concurrent Pos:* Res fel ophthal, Sch Med, Johns Hopkins Univ, 58-59, res fel, McCollum Pratt Inst, 59-60; Helen Hay Whitney Found fel, 61-63; vis investr, Rockefeller Inst, 59; vis scientist, Oak Ridge Nat Lab, 62; Helen Hay Whitney estab investrship, 64-69; John Simmon Guggenheim Scholar, Imperial Cancer Res Fund Lab, London & prof, Tokyo Univ, 69-; vis prof, Kyoto Univ, 86-87; Fogarty int fel, 86-87; sci counr, Nat Eye Inst, 87-92. *Mem:* Am Soc Biol Chemists; Am Soc Microbiol; Japanese Cancer Soc; Japanese Biochem Soc. *Res:* Sulfur metabolism; neurochemistry; mechanism of enzyme action; tumorgenesis; protein biosynthesis; nucleic acids; antivirus agents; anti-cancer agents. *Mailing Add:* 334 Fillmore St Jenkintown PA 19046. *Fax:* 215-573-2221

KAJI, HIDEKO (KATAYAMA), BIOCHEMISTRY, PHARMACOLOGY. *Current Pos:* assoc prof, 76-83, PROF, JEFFERSON MED COL, THOMAS JEFFERSON UNIV, 83- *Personal Data:* b Tokyo, Japan, Jan 1, 30; m 58, Akira; c Kenneth, Eugene, Naomi & Amy. *Educ:* Tokyo Col Pharmaceut Sci, BS, 54; Univ Nebr, MS, 56; Purdue Univ, PhD(pharmacol), 58. *Prof Exp:* Eli Lilly fel, Sch Med, Johns Hopkins Univ, 58-59; from instr to asst prof, Sch Med, Vanderbilt Univ, 60-62; vis scientist, Oak Ridge Nat Lab, 62-63; assoc, Sch Med, Univ Pa, 63-64, res assoc, 65-66, asst mem biochem, Inst Cancer Res, 66-76. *Concurrent Pos:* Vis prof, Wistar Inst, 84-85; bd mem, sci counr, NIH, 87-91; consult, Nippon Paint Co Ltd, 89- *Mem:* Am Soc Biol Chemists; Am Soc Pharmacol & Exp Therapeut. *Res:* Mechanism of macromolecular synthesis; transport mechanism; genetic regulatory mechanisms of oncogenesis and AIDS. *Mailing Add:* Dept Pharmacol Jefferson Med Col 1020 Locust St Philadelphia PA 19107. *Fax:* 215-923-7343; *E-Mail:* kajil@jeflin.tju.edu

KAK, AVINASH CARL, COMPUTER ENGINEERING. *Current Pos:* From asst prof to assoc prof, 70-77, PROF ELEC ENG, ROBOT VISION LAB, PURDUE UNIV, 77- *Personal Data:* b Srinagar, Kashmir, Oct 22, 44; m 76; c 2. *Educ:* Indian Inst Technol, PhD(elec eng), 70. *Concurrent Pos:* Ed-in-chief, Comput Vision & Image Understanding J, 94- *Mem:* Am Asn Artificial Intel; Inst Elec & Electronics Engrs. *Res:* Sensory aspects of robotic intelligence; computer vision; spatial reasoning; robot cognition; image processing; various forms of imaging. *Mailing Add:* Sch Elec Eng Purdue Univ West Lafayette IN 47907. *E-Mail:* kaka@purdue.edu

KAK, SUBHASH CHANDRA, NEURAL NETWORKS, ARTIFICIAL INTELLIGENCE. *Current Pos:* assoc prof elec eng, 79-83, PROF ELEC & COMPUT ENG, LA STATE UNIV, 83- *Personal Data:* b Srinagar, India, Mar 26, 47; m 79, Navnidhi Saklani; c Abhinav & Arushi. *Educ:* Kashmir Univ, BS, 67; Indian Inst Technol, Delhi, PhD(elec eng), 70. *Honors & Awards:* Sci Acad Medal, Indian Nat Sci Acad, 77; Kothari Award, Kothari Sci & Res Inst, 77. *Prof Exp:* Lectr elec eng, Indian Inst Technol, Delhi, 71-74, asst prof, 74-79. *Concurrent Pos:* Acad visitor, Imp Col, Univ London, 75-76; guest researcher, Bell Labs, Murray Hill, 76 & Tata Inst Fundamental Res, Bombay, 77-78; guest ed, Inst Elec & Electronics Engrs Comput, 83; vis prof, Indian Inst Technol, Delhi, 85-86, Harvard Univ, 95; consult, UN Develop Prog, 86 & 89-90; guest ed, Info Sci, 93 & Circuits, Systs & Signal Processing, 93. *Mem:* AAAS. *Res:* Information theory; quantum physics; cognitive science; artificial intelligence; neural computing; cryptology and study of ancient scripts; history and philosophy of science. *Mailing Add:* Dept Elec & Comput Eng La State Univ Baton Rouge LA 70803-5901. *Fax:* 504-388-5200; *E-Mail:* kak@ee.lsu.edu

KAKAR, ANAND SWAROOP, CONDUCTIVE COATINGS, SURFACE CHEMISTRY. *Current Pos:* DIR RES, GRAFO COLLOIDS, 81- *Personal Data:* b India, Oct 14, 37; US citizen; m 69; c 1. *Educ:* Banaras Hindu Univ, BSc, 60; Indian Inst Technol, MTech, 64; Wayne State Univ, MS, 71, PhD(phys chem), 78. *Prof Exp:* Lectr chem eng, Indian Inst Technol, Delhi, 65-68; technician, Can Gen Elec, 68-69 & Mercury Paint Co, 71-72; mfg develop engr, Ford Motor Co, Mt Clemons, Mich, 72-74; res asst, Wayne State Univ, 74-78; staff chemist, Acheson Colloids, Mich, 78-81. *Mem:* Electrochem Soc; Am Inst Chem Engrs. *Res:* Heat transfer and hold-up fluidized beds; zone refining and single crystal growth; optical and electrical properties of semiconductor; photovoltaic cells; electroless deposition; size reduction; colloidal dispersion; conductive coatings; solid film lubricants; surface preparation and analysis. *Mailing Add:* 412 Boena Vista St Emlenton PA 16373. *Fax:* 412-867-5974

KAKAR, RAJESH KUMAR, STATISTICS, DATA PROCESSING. *Current Pos:* ASST PROF BUS STATIST, ARIZ STATE UNIV, 78- *Personal Data:* b New Delhi, India, Oct 2, 50; m 77. *Educ:* Univ Delhi, BSc, 70, MS, 72; Tex Tech Univ, DBA(bus statist), 78. *Prof Exp:* Instr bus statist, Tex Tech Univ, 72-78. *Mem:* Am Statist Asn; Inst Mgt Sci; Am Inst Decision Sci. *Res:* Empirical bayesian estimation; assessment of subjective probabilities; forecasting; manpower models; auditing software. *Mailing Add:* 4891 E Butler Dr Paradise Valley AZ 85253

KAKEFUDA, TSUSYOSHI, INTERNATIONAL COOPERATION ON CANCER RESEARCH & TREATMENT. *Current Pos:* MED OFFICER, NAT CANCER INST, 67- *Personal Data:* b Jan 20, 29; c 2. *Educ:* Tokyo Univ, MD, 52, PhD(path), 58. *Concurrent Pos:* City of Hope Med Ctr, 60-67. *Mem:* Am Asn Cancer Res. *Res:* Cancer etiology. *Mailing Add:* 14901 River Rd Potomac MD 20854

KAKIS, FREDERIC JACOB, PHYSICAL ORGANIC CHEMISTRY, FOOD SCIENCE. *Current Pos:* PRES & CHIEF EXEC OFFICER, FORENSIC CONSULT SERVS, 96- *Personal Data:* b Drama, Greece, Nov 1, 30; US citizen; m 52; c 4. *Educ:* City Col New York, 60; Stanford Univ, PhD(org chem), 64. *Honors & Awards:* Prof Develop Award, NSF, 77. *Prof Exp:* Chmn dept, Chapman Col, 63-68, assoc prof, 66-71, prof chem, 71-89, chmn, Div Natural Sci, 78-80, assoc vpres, 83-89, exec vpres, Impact General Inc, 89-96. *Concurrent Pos:* Grants, NSF, 65, Petrol Res Found, 65, 66, 76 & 77, Res Corp, 66, 67, 70 & Union Oil Found, 74, 75, 76 & 77; res fel, Oak Ridge Nat Lab, 66; assoc prof, Calif State Col, Long Beach, 66-67 & Calif State Univ, Fullerton, 66-70; res fel, NASA-Ames Res Ctr & Stanford Univ, 69; environmentalist, Defense Contract Admin Serv, 70; vis prof, Lab Org Synthesis, Polytech Sch, Paris, 70-71; NSF res fel, Univ Calif, Riverside; vis prof, Univ Calif, Los Angeles & Univ Calif, Riverside; Fulbright award, 80; dir, Nat Inst Forensic Studies, 89-96. *Mem:* AAAS; Am Chem Soc; fel Am Inst Chemists; Royal Soc Chem; NY Acad Sci; Inst Food Technologists; Soc Cosmetic Chemists. *Res:* Study of reaction mechanisms by isotopic labelling; air pollution research; synthetic and mechanistic organic chemistry; heterogeneous catalysis and adsorption; food dehydration. *Mailing Add:* 1534 Harding St Orange CA 92867

KAKO, KYOHEI JOE, PHYSIOLOGY. *Current Pos:* RETIRED. *Personal Data:* b Tokyo, Japan, May 29, 28; Can citizen; m 62, Johanna M Kako; c Chris & Anthony. *Educ:* Tokyo Jikei Univ, MD, 53; FRCP. *Prof Exp:* Resident internal med, Tokyo Jikei-Kai Tokyo Hosp, 54-56; res asst med, Sch Med, Wash Univ, 56-57; res assoc, Wayne State Univ, 59-61; from asst prof to prof physiol, Fac Med, Univ Ottawa, 64-93. *Concurrent Pos:* Mo Heart Asn fel, 57-59; fel, Kanton Hosp, Univ Zurich, 61-63; Alexander von Humboldt fel, I Med Clin, Univ Munich, 63-64; med res assoc, 68-88, residency, Mt Sinai Hosp, 81-82. *Mem:* Am Physiol Soc; Can Cardiovasc Soc; fel Am Col Cardiol; fel Am Col Physicians; fel Am Col Chest Physicians; Royal Col Physicians Can. *Res:* Heart muscle biochemistry; lipid and carbohydrate metabolism; cardiomyopathies; cellular & subcellular function, membrane, calcium fluxes. *Mailing Add:* 580 Mariposa Ave Univ Ottawa Fac Med Rockcliffe Park ON K1M 0S2 Can

KAKU, MICHIO, THEORETICAL HIGH ENERGY PHYSICS, NUCLEAR PHYSICS. *Current Pos:* from asst prof to assoc prof, 73-82, PROF PHYSICS, CITY COL NEW YORK, 82- *Personal Data:* b San Jose, Calif, Jan 24, 47. *Educ:* Harvard Univ, BA, 68; Univ Calif, Berkeley, PhD(physics), 72. *Prof Exp:* Lectr physics, Princeton Univ, 72-73. *Concurrent Pos:* Vis prof, NY Univ, 88, Inst Advan Study, Princeton, 90. *Mem:* Fel Am Phys Soc. *Res:* High energy and nuclear physics; unified field theories; quantum gravity and supergravity; kinetics and neutron transport theory; reactor physics; gauge field theory of superstrings, which will include general covariance and $SU(3) \times SU(2) \times U(1)$ as subsets, making it a candidate for a unified field theory of all known interactions. *Mailing Add:* Dept Physics City Col New York New York NY 10031. *E-Mail:* kaku@scisun.sci.ccny.cuny.edu

KAKUTANI, SHIZUO, MATHEMATICS. *Current Pos:* RETIRED. *Personal Data:* b Osaka, Japan, Aug 28, 11; m 52; c 1. *Educ:* Tohoku Univ, Japan, MA, 34; Osaka Univ, PhD(math), 41. *Hon Degrees:* MA, Yale Univ, 53. *Prof Exp:* Res mem, Inst Adv Study, 40-42; asst prof, Osaka Univ, 42-48; res mem, Inst Advan Study, 48-49; from asst prof to assoc prof, Yale Univ, 49-53, prof math, 53- *Mem:* Am Math Soc; Math Soc Japan. *Res:* Functional analysis; probability and stochastic processes. *Mailing Add:* 32 Round Hill Rd North Haven CT 06473

KALAB, MILOSLAV, BIOCHEMISTRY. *Current Pos:* RETIRED. *Personal Data:* b Urcice, Czech, June 12, 29; m 56; c 2. *Educ:* Brno Tech Univ, BSc, 50; Slovak Tech Univ, Bratislava, MSc, 52; Slovak Acad Sci, PhD(chem), 57. *Honors & Awards:* Pfizer Inc Award, Am Dairy Sci Asn, 82. *Prof Exp:* Res scientist, Chem Inst, Slovak Acad Sci, 57-58; from asst prof to assoc prof, Sch Med, Palacky Univ, Czech, 58-65, assoc prof, Dept Natural Sci, 65-66; Nat Res Coun Can fel, 66-68; res scientist, Food Res Inst, Agr Can, 68-95. *Concurrent Pos:* Ed-in-chief, Food Struct. *Mem:* Am Dairy Sci Asn; Can Inst Food Sci & Technol; Micros Soc Can; Electron Micros Soc Am; Inst Food Technologists. *Res:* Food proteins; milk protein gelation, composition, texture; microstructure of dairy products using electron microscopy. *Mailing Add:* Agr Food Can Ottawa ON K1A 0C6 Can

KALABOKIDIS, KOSTAS D, FOREST FIRES, GEOGRAPHIC INFORMATION SYSTEMS. *Current Pos:* res asst & instr, 89-91, RES ASSOC, COLO STATE UNIV, 92-, ASST PROF FOREST FIRE SCI, 93- *Personal Data:* b Thessaloniki, Greece, Nov 2, 58; c 1. *Educ:* Aristotelian Univ, Greece, BS, 81; Univ Mont, MS, 85; Colo State Univ, PhD(forest fire sci/geog info systs), 92. *Prof Exp:* Res asst, Univ Mont, 83-85. *Mem:* Am Soc Photogram & Remote Sensing; Int Asn Wildland Fire; Soc Am Foresters. *Res:* Wildland fire management, fire behavior modeling, fuel management, prescribed burning, fire suppression, fire ecology, geographic information systems, remote sensing and statistics. *Mailing Add:* Dept Forest Sci Colo State Univ Ft Collins CO 80523. *Fax:* 970-491-6754

KALAFUS, RUDOLPH M, SATELLITE NAVIGATION ENGINEERING. *Current Pos:* AT TRIMBLE NAVIG. *Personal Data:* b Jackson, Mich, Dec 17, 37; m 65, Lois Aptekar; c 2. *Educ:* Univ Mich, BS(elec eng) & BS(eng math), 60, MS, 63, PhD(elec eng), 66. *Honors & Awards:* Johannes Kepler Award, Inst Navig, 92. *Prof Exp:* Electronics engr, Transp Systs Ctr, US Dept Transp, 70-81, head satellite navig group, 82-87; dir differential GPS dept, Trimble Navig, 88-91, mktg mgr landing & tracking systs, 92-93. *Concurrent Pos:* Chmn, Radio Tech Comn Maritime Serv. *Mem:* Inst Elec & Electronics Engrs; Inst Navig. *Res:* Satellite navigation development; differential GPS techniques development; integrity monitoring techniques development; GPS-based landing system development; aviation applications development. *Mailing Add:* Trimble Navigation 645 N Mary Ave Sunnyvale CA 94088. *Fax:* 408-481-2097

KALAI, EHUD, GAME THEORY, MATHEMATICAL ECONOMICS. *Current Pos:* from asst prof to prof, 76-82, MORRISON CHAIR PROF DECISION SCI, KELLOGG SCH MGT, NORTHWESTERN UNIV, 82-, PROF MATH, 90-, DIR, KELLOG CTR STRATEGIC DECISION MAKING, 96- *Personal Data:* b Tel-Aviv, Israel, Dec 7, 42; US citizen; m 67, Marilyn Lott; c Kerren L & Adam K. *Educ:* Univ Calif Berkeley, AB, 67; Cornell Univ, MS, 71 & PhD(math), 72. *Prof Exp:* Asst prof decision theory & oper res, Dept Statist, Tel-Aviv Univ, 72-76; Oscar Morgonstern res prof math econ & game theory, NY Univ, 91. *Concurrent Pos:* Consult, Div Common, Israeli Army, 74-75; prin investr, NSF grants, 79-; mem bd dirs, First Savings Am & Fed Savings & Loan Asn, 86-89; ed, Games & Econ Behav, 88-; vis prof econ, Calif Inst Technol, 93, Sherman Fairchild distinguished scholar, 94. *Mem:* Am Math Soc; fel Econometrics Soc. *Res:* Author of over 50 journal and book articles on game-theory, decision theory, and mathematical economics; non-cooperative and cooperative games and their application to economics and other social sciences, including: bargaining and strategic interaction, social choice theory and learning in dynamic interaction. *Mailing Add:* Kellog Sch Mgt Northwestern Univ Evanston IL 60208. *Fax:* 847-467-1220; *E-Mail:* kalai@nwu.edu

KALANT, HAROLD, PHARMACOLOGY, CELL PHYSIOLOGY. *Current Pos:* from assoc prof to prof, 64-89, EMER PROF PHARMACOL, UNIV TORONTO, 89- *Personal Data:* b Toronto, Ont, Nov 15, 23; m 48, Oriana Josseau. *Educ:* Univ Toronto, MD, 45, BSc, 48, PhD(path chem), 55. *Honors & Awards:* Jellinek Mem Award Res on Alcoholism, 72; Int Gold Medal Res Award, Raleigh Hills Found, 81; Ann Res Award, Res Soc Alcoholism (USA), 83; Upjohn Award, Pharmacol Soc Can, 85; Nathan B Eddy Mem Medal Award, 86. *Prof Exp:* Sect head, Defense Res Med Labs, Can, 56-59. *Concurrent Pos:* Nat Res Coun Can fel biochem, Cambridge Univ, 55-56; asst res dir, Ont Alcoholism Res Found, 59-62, assoc res dir, 62-89, emer res dir biol sci, 89-; mem res comt NAm Asn of Alcoholism Progs, 62-67; mem alcoholism study sect, NIMH, Washington, DC, 70-74; res comt non-med use drugs, Dept Nat Health & Welfare, Can, 70-72; mem sci adv bd, Int Coun Alcoholism & Addictions, Lausanne, 72-; mem expert adv panel on drugs of dependence, WHO, 74-84; mem, Comn Prob Drug Dependence, US, 78-, Bd Can Ctr Substance Abuse, 89-93; chmn, Bd Sci Counr, Nat Inst Alcohol Abuse & Alcoholism, 83-88; assoc ed, Can J Physiol Pharmacol, 75-81, pharmacol field ed, J Stud Alcohol, 85- *Mem:* Pharmacol Soc Can; Int Soc Biomed Res Alcoholism (pres, 90-94); fel Royal Soc Can; AAAS. *Res:* Pharmacology of ethanol and other addictive drugs; cell membrane chemistry and physiology; drug-behavior interactions in drug tolerance and dependence. *Mailing Add:* Dept Pharmacol Univ Toronto Toronto ON M5S 1A8 Can. *Fax:* 416-978-6395

KALANTAR, ALFRED HUSAYN, DATA ANALYSIS. *Current Pos:* asst prof, 64-69, ASSOC PROF CHEM, UNIV ALTA, 69- *Personal Data:* b Chicago, Ill, Dec 13, 34; m 61, Louise Fluhr; c Thomas, Daniel, Michael & Louise (Larochelle). *Educ:* Rutgers Univ, BSc, 56; Cornell Univ, PhD(chem), 63. *Prof Exp:* NSF res fel chem, Calif Inst Technol, 63-64. *Concurrent Pos:* Adj assoc prof, State Univ NY Binghamton, 70-71; vis scientist, Nat Res Coun, Ottawa, 85. *Res:* Analysis of errors in parameters extracted from data; effects of weighting on efficiency of data analysis. *Mailing Add:* Dept Chem Univ Alta Edmonton AB T6G 2G2 Can. *Fax:* 403-492-8231; *E-Mail:* kalantar@gpu.srv.ualberta.ca

KALASINSKY, VICTOR FRANK, PHYSICAL CHEMISTRY, SPECTROSCOPY. *Current Pos:* from asst prof to assoc prof, 77-85, PROF CHEM, MISS STATE UNIV, 85- *Personal Data:* b Columbus, Ohio, Dec 30, 49; m 74; c 2. *Educ:* Mass Inst Technol, SB, 72; Univ SC, PhD(phys chem), 75. *Honors & Awards:* Res Award,. *Prof Exp:* Asst prof chem, Furman Univ, 76-77. *Concurrent Pos:* Vis scientist, NIH, 87-88. *Mem:* Am Chem Soc; Am Phys Soc; Soc Appl Spectros; Coblentz Soc; Sigma Xi. *Res:* Raman, infrared and microwave spectroscopy; chemical structure and conformation; intramolecular and intermolecular interactions; applications of the laboratory computer; GC/FTIR and HPLC/FTIR. *Mailing Add:* 4709 Mercury Dr Rockville MD 20853-3128

KALATHIL, JAMES SAKARIA, ATMOSPHERIC PHYSICS, PHYSICS. *Current Pos:* PROF PHYSICS, CALIF POLYTECH STATE UNIV, SAN LUIS OBISPO, 65- *Personal Data:* b Shertallai, India, Dec 4, 35; US citizen; c 2. *Educ:* Univ Madras, BS, 56; Southern Ill Univ, MS, 63; Univ Nev, PhD(atmospheric physics), 77. *Prof Exp:* Instr physics, Frostburg State Col, Md, 63-65. *Mem:* Am Meteorol Soc; Am Asn Physics Teachers; Am Geophys Union. *Res:* Cumulus cloud models; history of meteorology; effects of solar activity on weather and climate; climatology. *Mailing Add:* Dept Physics Calif Polytech State Univ San Luis Obispo CA 93407-0001

KALB, G WILLIAM, MINERALOGY, ANALYTICAL CHEMISTRY. *Current Pos:* PRES, TRADET INC, 70- *Personal Data:* b Akron, Ohio, Dec 10, 43; m 65; c 2. *Educ:* Col Wooster, BA, 65; Ohio State Univ, MS, 67, PhD(mineral), 69. *Honors & Awards:* Bituminous Coal Res Award, Am Chem Soc, 72. *Prof Exp:* Lab mgr mineral, Geol Surv, 69-70. *Mem:* Am Chem Soc; Am Soc Testing & Mat; Geol Soc Am. *Res:* Determination of volatile trace metals in coal; development of analytical methods for the collection and measurement of volatilized mercury in high 502 concentration gas streams. *Mailing Add:* RR4 Box 77 Wheeling WV 26003

KALB, JOHN W, HIGH VOLTAGE POWER EQUIPMENT. *Current Pos:* PRES, LOW COUNTRY CANDLES, 81- *Personal Data:* b Columbus, Ohio, June 6, 18. *Educ:* Swarthmore Col, BS, 40. *Prof Exp:* Sr develop engr, Ohio Brass Co, 40-63, dir res, 63-81. *Mem:* Nat Acad Eng; fel Inst Elec & Electronics Engrs. *Mailing Add:* 101 Pier Pont Condos 100 Floyd St St Simons Island GA 31522

KALBACH, CONSTANCE, REACTION PHENOMENOLOGY, RADIOACTIVE WASTE DISPOSAL. *Current Pos:* vis scholar, 81-85, SR RES SCIENTIST, DEPT PHYSICS, DUKE UNIV, 85- *Personal Data:* b Chicago, Ill, Jan 12, 44; m 75, William D Walker. *Educ:* Univ Rochester, BS, 65, PhD(nuclear physics), 70. *Prof Exp:* Vis res assoc, Nuclear Structure Res Lab, Univ Rochester, & lectr chem, Nazareth Col Rochester, 70-71, fel chem, Univ Rochester, 71-73; guest researcher, Dept Physics, Tech Univ Munich, 72; sr res collabr physics, French AEC, 73-74; asst prof physics, Univ Tenn & res consult physics div, Oak Ridge Nat Lab, Union Carbide, 74-75; guest researcher, Triangle Univs Nuclear Lab, 75-81. *Concurrent Pos:* Vis asst prof, Dept Chem, NC State Univ, 77; consult, 78-; mem, NC Low Level Radioactive Waste Mgt Authority, 87-, vchmn, 89- *Mem:* Am Chem Soc; Sigma Xi. *Res:* Statistical models of nuclear reactions especially preequilibrium particle emission; nuclear level densities. *Mailing Add:* Physics Dept Duke Univ Durham NC 27708-0305

KALBERER, JOHN THEODORE, JR, PHYSIOLOGY, BIOLOGY. *Current Pos:* grants assoc, Div Res Grants, NIH, 66-67, spec asst to assoc dir extramural activities, 67-73, assoc dir prog planning, Nat Cancer Inst, 74-78, dep dir, Off Med Appln Res, 79-83, coordr dis prev & health prom, off dir, 83-86, DEP DIR, DIV OF DIS PREV, OFF DIR, NIH, 87- *Personal Data:* b New York, NY, Mar 15, 36. *Educ:* Adelphi Univ, AB, 56; Creighton Univ, MS, 57; NY Univ, PhD(biol, physiol), 66; Dartmouth Col, Inst Grad, 81. *Prof Exp:* Res assoc path, Beth Israel Med Ctr, NY, 57-66. *Mem:* Am Soc Zool; Am Asn Anat; Aerospace Med Asn; Am Acad Polit & Soc Sci; NY Acad Sci; Soc Epidemiol Res; Sigma Xi. *Res:* Decompression sickness, especially as it relates to fat embolization to the lung; role of vasoactive substances as they relate to stress conditions; science and society; disease prevention and health promotion. *Mailing Add:* NIH Rm 258 Bldg 1 Bethesda MD 20892. *Fax:* 301-480-9654; *E-Mail:* jk137n@nih.gov

KALBFLEISCH, GEORGE RANDOLPH, PARTICLE PHYSICS, HIGH ENERGY PHYSICS. *Current Pos:* PROF PHYSICS, UNIV OKLA, NORMAN, 79- *Personal Data:* b Long Beach, Calif, Mar 14, 31; m 54, Ruth Ann Adams; c 4. *Educ:* Loyola Univ, Calif, BS, 52; Univ Calif, Berkeley, PhD(physics), 61. *Prof Exp:* Qual control supvr, United Can & Glass, Hunt Foods, Inc, Calif, 52-56; anal chemist, Hales Testing Labs, 57; technician, Lawrence Radiation Lab, Univ Calif, 57-59, asst, 59-61, physicist, 61-64; assoc physicist, Brookhaven Nat Lab, 64-67, physicist, 67-76; physicist, Fermi Nat Accelerator Lab, 76-79. *Concurrent Pos:* Consult, Anamet Testing Labs, 62-64; mem bd overseers, URA Fermilab, 89-95. *Mem:* Fel Am Phys Soc. *Res:* Neutrino interactions; muon and pion physics; photon physics; superconducting magnets; beauty and charm physics; magnetic monopole search. *Mailing Add:* Dept Physics & Astron Univ Okla Norman OK 73019. *Fax:* 405-325-7557; *E-Mail:* grk@phyast.nhn.ou.edu

KALBFLEISCH, JAMES G, MATHEMATICAL STATISTICS. *Current Pos:* Lectr math, 64-66, from asst prof to assoc prof statist, 66-71, chmn dept, 75-79, PROF STATIST, UNIV WATERLOO, 71- *Personal Data:* b Galt, Ont, Sept 12, 40; m 63; c 3. *Educ:* Univ Toronto, BSc, 63; Univ Waterloo, MA, 64, PhD(math), 66. *Concurrent Pos:* Adj prof, York Univ, 67; Dept Univ Affairs res grant, 67-70; Nat Res Coun Can res grant, 67-; vis prof, Univ Essex, 68-69; C D Howe fel, 68-69; prof statist, Univ Man, 70-71. *Mem:* Biomet Soc; fel Int Statist Inst; Royal Statist Soc; fel Am Statist Asn. *Res:* Statistical inference; combinatorial mathematics. *Mailing Add:* Dept Statist Univ Waterloo Waterloo ON N2L 3G1 Can

KALBFLEISCH, JOHN DAVID, STATISTICAL INFERENCE & METHODOLOGY, APPLICATIONS IN MEDICINE & EPIDEMIOLOGY. *Current Pos:* assoc prof, 73-79, chair, 84-90, PROF STATIST & ACTUARIAL SCI, UNIV WATERLOO, 79-, DEAN, FAC MATH, 90- *Personal Data:* b Grand Valley, Ont, July 16, 43; m, Sharon Allen; c Michael Allen, Kirby Ann & Heidi Kathryn. *Educ:* Univ Waterloo, BSc, 66, MMath, 67, PhD(statist), 69. *Honors & Awards:* Gold Medal, Statist Soc Can, 94. *Prof Exp:* Res assoc, Univ Col, London, 69-70; asst prof, State Univ NY, Buffalo, 70-73. *Concurrent Pos:* Vis prof, Univ Wash, 79-80, Univ Mich, 87 & Univ Calif, San Francisco, 88; assoc ed, Annuals Statist, 80-82; sr assoc ed, Can J Statist, 81-84, assoc ed, 84-89. *Mem:* Int Statist Inst; fel Am Statist Asn; fel Inst Math Statist; fel Royal Soc Can. *Res:* Mathematical statistics and statistical methodology with particular attention to applications in medicine and epidemiology. *Mailing Add:* Fac Math Univ Waterloo Waterloo ON N2L 3G1 Can. *Fax:* 519-746-0274; *E-Mail:* jdkalbfl@math.uwaterloo.ca

KALDJIAN, MOVSES J(EREMY), STRUCTURAL MECHANICS, CIVIL ENGINEERING. *Current Pos:* from instr to assoc prof solid mech, 57-76, ASSOC PROF CIVIL ENG, UNIV MICH, 76- *Personal Data:* b Beirut, Lebanon, Dec 26, 25; US citizen; m 58; c 3. *Educ:* Am Univ, Beirut, BA, 48, BSc, 49; Univ Man, MSc, 52; Univ Mich, PhD(civil eng), 60. *Prof Exp:* Off engr, Trans-Arabian Pipeline Co, Lebanon, 49-50; civil engr, Dom Bridge Co Ltd, Can, 52-53; lectr struct, Queen's Univ, Ont, 53-54. *Concurrent Pos:* Partic, Ford Found comput proj, 61 & Ford Fac Develop adv comt grant, 62; vis prof, Univ Mich-US AID Prog & Indian Inst Technol, Kanpur, 62-64; consult, G C Optronics & Palmer-Shile. *Mem:* Am Soc Civil Engrs. *Res:* Numerical techniques in structural mechanics including finite element methods; response of buildings and dams to earthquake forces; ship structures in ice fields and some experimentation with holography. *Mailing Add:* 2927 Sheffield Ct Ann Arbor MI 48105

KALDOR, ANDREW, CLUSTER SCIENCE, CATALYSIS LASER PHYSICS. *Current Pos:* sr res chemist appl physics, 74-77, head chem physics group, 77-81, DIR RESOURCE CHEM LAB, CORP RES LAB, EXXON RES & ENG CO, 81- *Personal Data:* b Budapest, Hungary, Oct 11, 44; US citizen; m 67; c 2. *Educ:* Univ Calif, Berkeley, BS, 66; Cornell Univ, PhD(chem), 70. *Honors & Awards:* Silver Medal, Dept Com, 73; Frontiers Chem Lectr, Case Western Reserve, 79; Edwin G Baetjer Lectr, Princeton, 83. *Prof Exp:* Mem staff laser chem, Nat Bur Standards, 70-74. *Concurrent Pos:* Nat Acad Sci-Nat Res Coun fel, Nat Bur Standards, 70-72; chmn bd trustee, Gordon Res Conf, 89-90. *Mem:* AAAS; Am Chem Soc; Am Vacuum Soc; Am Phys Soc. *Res:* Laser chemistry; laser isotope separation; chemical physics; reaction dynamics; molecular spectroscopy; surface chemistry; chister science; materials science. *Mailing Add:* Exxon Res & Develop Lab Div 8400 4045 Scenic Hwy Baton Rouge LA 70821-2226

KALDOR, GEORGE, PHYSIOLOGY. *Current Pos:* assoc prof physiol, 65-69, prof physiol & biophys, Med Col Pa, 69-75, clin path, 70-75, CHIEF, CLIN LAB SERV, VETERANS ADMIN HOSP, ALLEN PARK, MICH, 75-; PROF PATH, WAYNE STATE UNIV, DETROIT, 75- *Personal Data:* b Budapest, Hungary, Feb 10, 26; nat US; m 63; c 3. *Educ:* Med Univ Budapest, MD, 50; Am Bd Clin Chem, dipl, 64; Am Bd Path, dipl clin path, 65, dipl chem path, 78. *Prof Exp:* Asst prof clin biochem, Med Univ Budapest, 54-56; res assoc biochem & head phys chem, Isaac Albert Res Inst, Jewish Chronic Dis Hosp, 59-65. *Concurrent Pos:* Res fel biochem, Mass Gen Hosp, 57-58 & McArdle Mem Lab, Wis, 58-59. *Mem:* Am Soc Biol Chem; Am Physiol Soc; Am Soc Exp Path; fel Am Soc Clin Pathologists; fel Royal Soc Health. *Res:* Biochemistry of muscular contraction and relaxation; computer assisted medical decision making. *Mailing Add:* Dept Path Vet Admin Med Ctr 4646 John R St Detroit MI 48201-1916

KALE, HERBERT WILLIAM, II, ornithology, conservation; deceased, see previous edition for last biography

KALELKAR, MOHAN SATISH, PHYSICS. *Current Pos:* from asst prof to assoc prof, 78-95, assoc chmn dept, 85-89, PROF PHYSICS, RUTGERS UNIV, PISCATAWAY, 95- *Personal Data:* b Bombay, India, Apr 24, 48. *Educ:* Harvard Col, BA, 68; Columbia Univ, MA, 70, PhD(physics), 75. *Prof Exp:* Res assoc physics, Columbia Univ, 75-77, asst prof, 77-78. *Mem:* Am Phys Soc; Am Asn Physics Teachers. *Res:* Experimental work in elementary particle physics; neutrino interactions and electron-positron collisions. *Mailing Add:* Physics Dept Rutgers Univ PO Box 849 Piscataway NJ 08855-0849. *Fax:* 732-445-4343; *E-Mail:* kalelkar@ruthep.rutgers.edu

KALENDA, NORMAN WAYNE, ORGANIC CHEMISTRY. *Current Pos:* RETIRED. *Personal Data:* b Grand Rapids, Mich, Nov 27, 28; m 57. *Educ:* Univ Mich, BS, 51; Univ Ill, PhD(chem), 55. *Prof Exp:* Res chemist, Mellon Inst, 54-55; res chemist, Eastman Kodak Co, 57-90. *Mem:* Am Chem Soc. *Res:* Organic chemistry; photographic chemistry. *Mailing Add:* 66 Parkmere Rd Rochester NY 14617

KALENSHER, BERNARD EARL, POTENTIAL THEORY, FLUID MECHANICS. *Current Pos:* SR ANALYTICAL PHYSICIST, PHRASOR SCI, INC, 77- *Personal Data:* b Beaumont, Tex, May 4, 27. *Educ:* Univ Tex, PhD(physics), 54. *Prof Exp:* Sr res engr, Jet Propulsion Lab, Calif Inst Technol, 54-60; sr physicist, Electro-Optical Systs, Xerox Corp, 61-76. *Mem:* Am Phys Soc. *Res:* Theory modification of blackbody radiation law as applied to the thermal radiation from micron size, spherical, liquid metal droplets; mathematical analysis of pressure-time history of gas flow between chambers of a dual-chamber thruster and the vacuum of outer space; statistical analyses of charged droplet distributions; determined minimum and maximum allowed twist of a rifle barrel; authored two published articles. *Mailing Add:* 551 B Linwood Ave Monrovia CA 91016-2659. *Fax:* 626-357-3203

KALER, ERIC WILLIAM, COLLOIDS, SURFACTANTS. *Current Pos:* from assoc prof to prof, 89-96, DEPT CHAIR, UNIV DEL, 96- *Personal Data:* b Burlington, Vt, Sept 23, 56; m 79; c 2. *Educ:* Calif Inst Technol, BS, 78; Univ Minn, PhD(chem eng), 82. *Honors & Awards:* McGraw Award, Am Soc Eng Educ, 95. *Prof Exp:* Res assoc, Chevron Oil Field Res Co, 78; intern, Oak Ridge Nat Lab, 79; res & teaching asst chem eng, Univ Minn, 78-82; from asst prof to assoc prof chem eng, Univ Wash, 82-89. *Concurrent Pos:* Presidential young investr, 84-89. *Mem:* Am Inst Chem Engrs; Am Chem Soc; Am Crystallog Asn; AAAS. *Res:* Colloid and surfactant science; complex fluid thermodynamics; materials synthesis; small-angle scattering. *Mailing Add:* Dept Chem Eng Univ Del Newark DE 19716. *E-Mail:* kaler@che.udel.edu

KALER, JAMES BAILEY, ASTRONOMY. *Current Pos:* From asst prof to assoc prof, 64-76, PROF ASTRON, UNIV ILL, URBANA, 76- *Personal Data:* b Albany, NY, Dec 29, 38; m 60, Maxine; c 4. *Educ:* Univ Mich, Ann Arbor, AB, 60; Univ Calif, Los Angeles, PhD(astron), 64. *Concurrent Pos:* Guggenheim fel, 72-73. *Mem:* Am Astron Soc; Int Astron Union; Astron Soc Pac. *Res:* Planetary nebulae; nebular spectrophotometry; interstellar medium; chemical abundances. *Mailing Add:* 103 Astron Bldg Univ Ill 1002 W Green Urbana IL 61801. *Fax:* 217-244-7638; *E-Mail:* kaler@astro.uiuc.edu

KALEY, GABOR, PHYSIOLOGY, EXPERIMENTAL PATHOLOGY. *Current Pos:* assoc prof, 64-70, PROF PHYSIOL, NY MED COL, 70-, CHMN DEPT, 72- *Personal Data:* b Budapest, Hungary, Nov 16, 26; m 53; c 2. *Educ:* Columbia Univ, BS, 50; NY Univ, MS, 57, PhD(exp path), 60. *Honors & Awards:* Landis Award; Semmelweis Award. *Prof Exp:* Resident asst surg, Bellevue Hosp, New York, 55-56; res asst path, NY Univ Med Ctr, 56-60, from instr to asst prof, 61-62. *Concurrent Pos:* USPHS fel, NY Univ Med Ctr, 60-62; prin investr, NIH Grants, 74- *Mem:* Am Physiol Soc. *Res:* Cardiovascular physiology; hypertension; juxtaglomerular cells; renal-adrenal relationships; renen-angiotens in system; erythropoietin; inflammation; microcirculation and prostaglandins; endotoxins; endothelial cells; nature and mechanisms of action of a variety of biochemical and hormonal factors that regulate the function of small blood vessels and local blood flow. *Mailing Add:* Dept Physiol NY Med Col Valhalla NY 10595

KALEY, ROBERT GEORGE, II, GAS CHROMATOGRAPHY, MASS SPECTROMETRY. *Current Pos:* Sr res chemist, Indust Chem Co, 73-78, res group leader, 78-81, sr res specialist, Corp Res & Develop Staff, 81-85, prod & environ safety mgr, 85-86, MGR, ENVIRON TECH SUPPORT, CORP ENVIRON POLICY STAFF, MONSANTO CO, 86- *Personal Data:* b Litchfield, Ill, Nov 8, 45; m 81; c 3. *Educ:* Purdue Univ, BS, 68; Univ Ill, MS, 71, PhD(anal chem), 74. *Mem:* Am Chem Soc; Am Soc Mass Spectrometry; AAAS. *Res:* Spectrochemical analysis; gas chromatography-mass spectrometry; environmental analysis. *Mailing Add:* Monsanto A2NE 800 N Lindbergh Blvd St Louis MO 63167

KALF, GEORGE FREDERICK, BIOCHEMISTRY. *Current Pos:* prof biochem, 66-86, prof path, 79-86, PROF BIOCHEM & MOLECULAR BIOL, JEFFERSON MED COL, THOMAS JEFFERSON UNIV, 86- *Personal Data:* b New Britain, Conn, Dec 22, 30; m 53; c 2. *Educ:* Upsala Col, BS, 52; Pa State Univ, MS, 54; Yale Univ, PhD(biochem), 57. *Prof Exp:* Enzymologist, Chem & Physics Sect, Animal Dis & Parasite Res Div, USDA, 59; from asst prof to assoc prof biochem, NJ Col Med & Dent, 60-66. *Concurrent Pos:* Nat Found fel, Yale Univ, 57-59; investr, Am Heart Asn, 63-68; adj prof pharm & toxicol, Rutgers Univ, 82. *Mem:* Am Soc Biol Chem; Am Asn Cancer Res; Brit Biochem Soc; Soc Toxicol; Int Soc Study Xenobiotics. *Res:* Carcinogenesis; biochemical oncology; benzene toxicity. *Mailing Add:* Dept Biochem & Molec Biol Jefferson Med Col Thomas Jefferson Univ 233 S Tenth St Philadelphia PA 19107-5566. *Fax:* 215-955-5393

KALFAYAN, BERNARD, ANATOMICAL PATHOLOGY. *Current Pos:* RETIRED. *Educ:* Am Univ, Beirut, MD, 39. *Prof Exp:* Pathologist, Gunderson Clinic, Ltd. *Mailing Add:* 174 S Collier Blvd Apt 902 Marco FL 33937-4330

KALFF, JACOB, HYDROBIOLOGY. *Current Pos:* From asst prof to assoc prof, 65-76, PROF BIOL, MCGILL UNIV, MONTREAL, 77-, DIR, LIMNOL RES CTR, DEPT BIOL, 82- *Personal Data:* b Velsen, Neth, Dec 20, 35; Can citizen; m 59; c Derek, Sarah & Anna. *Educ:* Univ Toronto, BSA, 59, MSA, 61; Ind Univ, PhD(limnol), 65. *Concurrent Pos:* Vis scientist hydrobiol, Inst Nat Rech Agron, France, 72-73, CSIC, Blanes, Spain; consult, Ecol Adv Comt, Baie James Energy Corp, 77-84; vis prof, Dept Bot, Univ Nairobi, Kenya, 79-80; vis scientist, CNRS, Toulouse, France, 86-87; regional ed, Hydrobiol. *Mem:* AAAS; Am Soc Limnol & Oceanog; Int Asn Theoret & Appl Limnol. *Res:* Ecology of algae, bacteria and aquatic higher plants with an emphasis on their productivity and their role in the nutrient and contaminant cycling in lakes. *Mailing Add:* Dept Biol McGill Univ 1205 Dr Penfield Montreal PQ H3A 1B1 Can. *Fax:* 514-398-5069

KALFOGLOU, GEORGE, SURFACE POLYMER CHEMISTRY, APPLICATION OF POLYMER SOLUTIONS & POLYMER GELS IN ENHANCED OIL RECOVERY. *Current Pos:* RES CHEMIST, RES ASSOC & SR RES ASSOC, TEXACO INC, 68- *Personal Data:* b Istanbul, Turkey, June 12, 39; m 68, Margo Yoanidis; c Daisy & Mary. *Educ:* Robert Col, Istanbul, BS, 63; NC State Univ, PhD(chem), 68. *Mem:* AAAS; Am Chem Soc; Soc Petrol Engrs; Sigma Xi. *Res:* Solution thermodynamics; colloidal chemistry; chemical treatment of water-sensitive minerals; physical and interfacial properties of surfactants; design enhanced petroleum recovery processes in hard brines and elevated temperatures by utilizing proper surfactant systems; tertiary oil recovery by micellar/polymer systems, caustic/polymer floods, thermally stable polymers, design of polymer gels for profile modification and water shut-off treatments; granted 35 patents. *Mailing Add:* 523 Greenpark Dr Houston TX 77079-6415. *Fax:* 713-954-6911

KALIA, MADHU P, NEUROBIOLOGY. *Current Pos:* Assoc prof, 74-78, PROF PHARMACOL & NEUROSURG, THOMAS JEFFERSON UNIV, 78- *Personal Data:* b Kashmir, India, Sept 11, 40. *Educ:* Univ Delhi, MD, 64, PhD(neurophysiol), 68. *Mem:* Soc Neurosci; Am Physiol Soc; Am Asn Anatomists; German Physiol Soc. *Res:* Respiratory control; cardiovascular control. *Mailing Add:* Jefferson Med Col 1015 Chestnut St Suite 1400 Philadelphia PA 19107-4302. *Fax:* 215-955-6492

KALIAGUINE, SERGE, ENGINEERING EDUCATION. *Current Pos:* PROF CHEM ENG, UNIV LAVAL, ST FOY, QUE. *Honors & Awards:* Urgel Archambault Phys Sci & Math Prize, Can-Fr Asn Advan Sci, 94. *Res:* Physical science and math. *Mailing Add:* Dept Chem Eng Univ Laval St Foy Quebec PQ G1K 7P4 Can

KALIAKIN, VICTOR NICHOLAS, GEOMECHANICS, STRUCTURAL MECHANICS. *Current Pos:* ASST PROF CIVIL ENG, UNIV DEL, 90- *Personal Data:* b Los Angeles, Calif, Nov 1, 56; m 90. *Educ:* Univ Calif, Davis, BS, 78, PhD(eng mech), 85; Univ Calif, Berkeley, MS, 79. *Prof Exp:* Postdoctoral civil eng, Univ Calif, Davis, 85-86; vis asst prof civil eng, Univ Ariz, 86-87; mem tech staff, Sandia Nat Labs, 87-90. *Concurrent Pos:* Mem, Comt Inelastic Behav, Am Soc Civil Engrs, 91- & Comt Aerospace Struct & Mat; mem, Comt Modeling Tech Geomech, Transp Res Bd. *Mem:* Assoc mem Am Soc Civil Eng; Am Acad Mech; Am Soc Eng Educ; Int Asn Comput Mech. *Res:* Computational mechanics applied to problems in: geotechnical engineering, composite material and structural engineering. *Mailing Add:* Dept Civil & Environ Eng Univ Del Newark DE 19716. *Fax:* 302-831-3640; *E-Mail:* kaliakin@ce.udel.edu

KALICA, ANTHONY R, VIROLOGY, LUNG DISEASES. *Current Pos:* Biologist, Epidemiol Sect, Lab Infectious Dis, Nat Inst Allergy & Infectious Dis, NIH, 64-67, chemist & electron microscopist, Respiratory viruses Sect, 67-74, microbiologist, Epidemiol Sect, 74-83, microbiologist, Interstitial Lung Dis Br, Nat Heart Lung & Blood Inst, 83-85, prog adminr, Occup & Immunol Lung Dis Prog, 85-87, CHIEF, INTERSTITIAL LUNG DIS BR, NAT HEART LUNG & BLOOD INST, NIH, 87- *Personal Data:* b Albany, NY, June 14, 39; m 64, Sandra J Smith; c Paul R & Joseph R. *Educ:* Siena Col, BS, 62; Cath Univ Am, MS, 64; Univ Md, PhD(microbiol), 74. *Mem:* Am Soc Microbiol; Am Soc Virol; Int Aquired Immune Deficiency Syndrome Soc. *Res:* Molecular and cellular aspects of gastrointestinal and respiratory virus infections; managed about 70 million dollars worth of biomedical research on interstitial lung disease, occupational lung disease, and lung disease associated with infection of the human immunodeficiency syndrome. *Mailing Add:* 11548 Paramus Dr Gaithersburg MD 20878. *Fax:* 301-594-7487

KALIL, FORD, ENGINEERING PHYSICS. *Current Pos:* aerospace technologist, Goddard Space Flight Ctr, 63-68, sr tech asst to br head, Manned Flight Planning & Anal Div, 68-74, sr tech consult, Network Procedures & Eval Div, networks directorate, 74-78, systs mgr cosmic background explorer proj, eng directorate, 78-80, TECH ENGR & OPERS MGR & PRES, GODDARD SPACE FLIGHT CTR, NASA, 80- *Personal Data:* b Akron, Ohio, Jan 5, 25; m 50; c 3. *Educ:* Univ Akron, BEE, 50; Vanderbilt Univ, MS, 51, PhD(physics), 58. *Prof Exp:* Physicist, USPHS, 51-53; staff mem, Los Alamos Sci Lab, 53-55; supvr lab, Martin Co, 58-59, gen supvr test eval, 59, mgr, 59-60, design engr, 60-63. *Concurrent Pos:* Adj prof, Drexel Inst, 58-; mem, Apollo Exten Syst, Commun & Navig Traffic Control Panel, 65 & Apollo Exten Syst Working Group, NASA, 65- *Mem:* Am Inst Aeronaut & Astronaut; Am Phys Soc; Sigma Xi. *Res:* Aerospace technology; mission and systems analysis; orbital mechanics; electron and radiation physics; management. *Mailing Add:* 9108 Bridgewater St College Park MD 20741-4008

KALIMI, MOHAMMED YAHYA, ENDOCRINOLOGY. *Current Pos:* from asst prof to assoc prof, 79-89, PROF, DEPT PHYSIOL, MED COL VA, RICHMOND, 89- *Personal Data:* b Surat, India; US citizen; m 85, Robina; c Omar. *Educ:* Bombay Univ, BS, 61, MS, 64, PhD(biochem), 70. *Honors & Awards:* Res & Career Develop Award, NIH, 80. *Prof Exp:* Res fel, Inst Cancer Res, Columbia Univ, 72-74; res assoc, dept cell biol, Baylor Col Med, Houston, 74-75; res asst prof, dept biochem, Albert Einstein Col Med, Bronx, NY, 75-79. *Concurrent Pos:* Vis prof, City of Hope Med Ctr, Los Angeles, 83-84. *Mem:* Am Physiol Soc; Endocrine Soc; AAAS. *Res:* Mechanism of steroid hormone action; isolation, characterization and purification of glucocorticoid receptors; interaction of the steroid-receptor complex with genomic components; developmental and aging related changes in the steroid receptors. *Mailing Add:* Box 551 MCV Sta Richmond VA 23298-0551. *Fax:* 804-828-7382

KALIN, ROBERT, MATHEMATICS EDUCATION. *Current Pos:* from instr to prof math educ, 56-89, chmn math educ prog, 74-78, EMER PROF MATH EDUC, FLA STATE UNIV, 89- *Personal Data:* b Everett, Mass, Dec 11, 21; wid, Madelyn Pildish; c Susan L, John B, Richard D & Sandra K. *Educ:* Univ Chicago, BS, 47; Harvard Univ, MAT, 48; Fla State Univ, PhD(math educ), 61. *Honors & Awards:* Serv Award, Math Asn Am, 91. *Prof Exp:* Teacher high sch, Mass, 48-49 & pub sch, Mo, 49-52; statistician, Naval Air Tech Training Ctr, Okla, 52-53; test specialist math, Educ Testing Serv, NJ, 53-55, res assoc math educ, 55; exec asst, Comn Math Col Bd, 55-56. *Concurrent Pos:* Dir, NSF Acad Year Insts, 69-71; governor, Nat High Sch & Jr Col Math Clubs, 72-75, pres, 78-80; pres, Fla Asn Math Educr, 84-86; secy & treas, Fla Sect, Math Asn Am, 85-91. *Mem:* Nat Coun Teachers Math; Math Asn Am. *Res:* Comparison of mathematical performance of elementary school children in Federal Republic of Germany, United Kingdom and USA since 1978; television-text instructional system for elementary school teachers; analytic geometry; elementary mathematics texts for grades 1-8; secondary geometry text. *Mailing Add:* 7 Stoneleigh Pl Brownsville TN 38012-2458. *Fax:* 901-772-3954

KALINA, ROBERT E, OPHTHALMOLOGY. *Current Pos:* RETIRED. *Personal Data:* b New Prague, Minn, Nov 13, 36; m 59; c 2. *Educ:* Univ Minn, BA, 57, BS, 60, MD, 60. *Honors & Awards:* Sr Hon Award, Am Acad Ophth. *Prof Exp:* Intern med, Univ Ore, 60-61; resident ophthal, 61-66; fel retina, Children's Hosp, San Francisco, 66-67 & Harvard Med Sch, 67; chief, Harborview Med Ctr, 68-69; actg chmn, Univ Wash, Seattle, 70-71, prof & chmn Ophthal, 70-96. *Concurrent Pos:* Consult, Vet Admin Hosp, 69-; Pub Health Hosp, 69- & Madigan Gen Hosp, US Army, 69-; med dir, Lions Eye Bank, 69-93; assoc head, Ophthal Div, Children's Orthopedic Hosp, 75-84; dir, Am Bd Ophthal, 82-89. *Mem:* Am Acad Ophthal; Am Col Surgeons; Nat Soc Prev Blindness; Asn Res Vision & Ophth; AMA. *Res:* Diseases and surgery of the retina. *Mailing Add:* Univ Wash Dept Ophthal Box 356485 Seattle WA 98195-6435

KALINOWSKI, MATHEW LAWRENCE, petroleum chemistry; deceased, see previous edition for last biography

KALINSKY, ROBERT GEORGE, PHYCOLOGY, ENVIRONMENTAL BIOLOGY. *Current Pos:* ASST PROF BIOL, LA STATE UNIV, SHREVEPORT, 74- *Personal Data:* b Cleveland, Ohio, Sept 18, 45; m 71. *Educ:* Univ Dayton, BS, 67; Ohio State Univ, MSc, 69, PhD(bot), 73. *Prof Exp:* Lectr bot, Ohio State Univ, 73-74. *Concurrent Pos:* Biol consult, Dames & Moore Engrs, Cincinnati, 73-74. *Mem:* Sigma Xi; Phycol Soc Am; Brit Phycol Soc; Bot Soc Am. *Res:* Systematic revision of the diatom genus Nitzschia; ecological studies of the major waterways of Northwestern Louisiana. *Mailing Add:* Dept Biol Sci La State Univ One Univ Pl Shreveport LA 71115-2301

KALISCH, GERHARD KARL, ANALYSIS, PARTIAL DIFFERENTIAL EQUATIONS. *Current Pos:* RETIRED. *Personal Data:* b Breslau, Ger, Dec 21, 14; nat US; m 42, Leonora Liph; c John M & Margaret J. *Educ:* Univ Iowa, BA, 38, MS, 39; Univ Chicago, PhD(math), 42. *Prof Exp:* Asst, Inst Adv Study, 41-42; instr math, Univ Kans, 42-44 & Cornell Univ, 44-46; from asst prof to prof, Univ Minn, 46-65; prof math, Univ Calif, Irvine, 65-91. *Mem:* AAAS; Am Math Soc; Math Asn Am; Math Soc France. *Res:* Analysis; partial differential equations. *Mailing Add:* 4530 Roxbury Rd Corona del Mar CA 92625

KALISH, DAVID, OPTICAL FIBERS, SYSTEMS ENGINEERING. *Current Pos:* mem tech staff mat eng & chem, Bell Tel Labs, Inc, 71-73, supvr metall eng, 73-79, supvr lightguide glass technol, 80-85, supvr lightguide syst eng, 86-88, head mat eng & chem dept, 89, OPTICAL FIBER DEVELOP & ENG DIR, BELL LABS, 90- *Personal Data:* b New York, NY, Aug 15, 39; c 1. *Educ:* Mass Inst Technol, SB, 60, SM, 64, ScD, 66. *Prof Exp:* Engr, ManLabs, Inc, 60-63; instr metall, Mass Inst Technol, 63-65; staff scientist, ManLabs, Inc, 65-68; scientist & team leader phys metall, Lockheed-Ga Co, 68-71. *Concurrent Pos:* Vis assoc prof, Ga Inst Technol, 70, lectr mech eng, 73-81. *Mem:* Am Soc Metals. *Res:* Optical fibers for communications and systems engineering, optical fibers measurements and fabrication. *Mailing Add:* Lucent Technol Bell Labs 2000 NE Expressway Norcross GA 30071. *Fax:* 770-798-4655; *E-Mail:* dkalish@lucent.com

KALISH, HERBERT S(AUL), METALLURGICAL ENGINEERING. *Current Pos:* CONSULT, 91- *Personal Data:* b New York, NY, Aug 11, 22; m 50, Lili Grossman; c Martin S & John M. *Educ:* Univ Mo, BS, 43, MetE, 53; Univ Pa, MS, 48. *Hon Degrees:* MetE, Univ Mo, Rolla, 53. *Honors & Awards:* Award of Merit, Am Soc Testing & Mat; Distinguished Serv to Powder Metall Award, Metal Powder Indust Fedn. *Prof Exp:* Metall observer open hearth steel, Carnegie-Ill Steel Corp, 43; res engr, Alloy Develop, Battelle Mem Inst, 43-44 & 46; asst, Thermodyn Res Lab, Univ Pa, 46-48; res metallurgist lead alloys, Elec Storage Battery Co, 48; sr engr spec prod, Sylvania Elec Prod, Inc, 48-50, engr-in-charge, Zirconium Sect, 50-52, sect head appl metall, 52-55, eng mgr metal fabrication & assembly, 55-57; eng mgr, Sylvania-Corning Nuclear Corp, 57; sect chief mat, Nuclear Fuel Res Labs, Olin Mathieson Chem Corp, 57-60, chief nuclear metall, Nuclear Fuel Res, 60-62; mgr, Com Fuel Dept, United Nuclear Corp, Conn, 62-65; asst to pres, Hertel Cutting Technologies Inc, 65-71, vpres, 71-91. *Concurrent Pos:* Trustee, Am Soc Metals, 85-88; vpres & treas, Photogrs Eye Inc. *Mem:* Fel Am Soc Metals; Sigma Xi; Am Soc Test & Mat; Am Inst Mining, Metall & Petrol Engrs; Soc Mining Metall & Explor; Am Powder Metall Inst. *Res:* Nuclear materials; high temperature materials; powder metallurgy, particularly alloy development; physical metallurgy; fabrication research; cemented carbide. *Mailing Add:* 65 Falmouth St Short Hills NJ 07078

KALISKI, MARTIN EDWARD, MICROPROCESSOR-BASED CONTROL, SYSTEMS THEORY. *Current Pos:* PROF ELEC & ELECTRONIC ENG, CALIF POLYTECH UNIV. *Personal Data:* b New York, NY, Oct 22, 45; m 69. *Educ:* Mass Inst Technol, BS, 66 & 68, SM, 68, PhD(elec eng), 71. *Prof Exp:* Asst prof comput sci, City Col New York, 71-73; from asst prof to assoc prof elec eng, Northwestern Univ, 76-90. *Concurrent Pos:* Fulbright scholar, France, 80-81. *Mem:* Inst Elec & Electronics Engrs; Sigma Xi. *Res:* Systems theory; industrial automation & robotics; microprocessor-based control; software engineering. *Mailing Add:* Elec & Electronic Eng Dept Calif Polytech State Univ San Luis Obispo CA 93407

KALISS, NATHAN, IMMUNOLOGY. *Current Pos:* Am Cancer Soc sr fel, Jackson Lab, 47-50, staff scientist cancer res, 50-59, asst dir res, 58-62 & 75-76, sr staff scientist, 59-76, EMER SR STAFF SCIENTIST, JACKSON LAB, 76-, GUEST INVESTR. *Personal Data:* b New York, NY, Aug 1, 07; m 28, Rebecca Weiss; c Anthony M, Jeffrey D & William E. *Educ:* City Col New York, BS, 29; Columbia Univ, MA, 31, PhD(zool), 38. *Honors & Awards:* Silver Medal, Am Med Assoc, Sci Res Exhibit, 55. *Prof Exp:* Asst zool, Columbia Univ, 31-38 & Univ Pa, 39-40; asst path, Med Col, Cornell Univ, 41-43; instr zool, George Washington Univ, 46-47. *Concurrent Pos:* Med statistician, US Vet Admin, 46-47; vis fel, Sloan-Kettering Inst, 48; instr biol, Brooklyn Col, 48; ed, Transplantation, 50-70; Guggenheim fel, 56-57; res assoc surg, Harvard Med Sch, 66-73. *Mem:* Soc Exp Biol & Med; Am Asn Cancer Res; Transplantation Soc; Reticuloendothelial Soc; fel AAAS; fel NY Acad Sci. *Res:* Homograft immunity; etiology of carcinogenesis; biology of cancer; immunology of tissue grafting. *Mailing Add:* Seely Rd Bar Harbor ME 04609-1506

KALIVODA, FRANK E, JR, MECHANICAL ENGINEERING. *Current Pos:* mgr prod eval, 73-81, MGR ENG, COPELAND CORP, 81- *Personal Data:* b Cicero, Ill, Mar 17, 30; m 57; c 3. *Educ:* Ill Inst Technol, BSME, 54, MSME, 58. *Prof Exp:* Coop trainee prod, Link-Belt Corp, 49-52; asst res engr, Heat-Power Res Dept, Armour Res Found, 54-58; sr res engr, Roy C Ingersoll Res Ctr, Borg-Warner Corp, 58-65; mgr component develop, Res Div, Cummins Engine Co, 65, mgr adv fuel systs, Eng Div, 65-66, mgr thermosci, Res Div, 66-68; mgr res & develop, South Wind Div, Stewart Warner Corp, 68-70, chief engr, 70-73. *Concurrent Pos:* Instr quality control & mfg processes, Edison State Univ, 75-78. *Mem:* Am Soc Mech Engrs; Am Soc Heating, Refrig & Air-Conditioning Engrs; Sigma Xi; Am Soc Qual Control. *Res:* Development of air conditioners, heat exchangers, compressors, combustion heaters, hydraulic equipment, engine fuel injectors and pumps; research on engine heat transfer, hydrodynamic bearings; manufacturing processes; reliability engineering. *Mailing Add:* 406 E Robinwood St Sidney OH 45365

KALKA, MORRIS, MATHEMATICAL ANALYSIS. *Current Pos:* MEM FAC MATH, TULANE UNIV, 80- *Personal Data:* b Landsberg, Ger, May 4, 49; US citizen; m 71. *Educ:* Yeshiva Univ, BA, 71; NY Univ, MS, 73, PhD(math), 75. *Prof Exp:* Instr math, Univ Utah, 75-77; asst prof math, Johns Hopkins Univ, 77-80. *Mem:* Am Math Soc. *Res:* Study of holomorphic functions of several complex variables using methods of differential geometry and partial differential equations. *Mailing Add:* 3610 Nashville Ave New Orleans LA 70125

KALKOFEN, WOLFGANG, ASTROPHYSICS. *Current Pos:* PHYSICIST, SMITHSONIAN ASTROPHYS OBSERV, SMITHSONIAN INST, 63-, PHYSICIST, CTR FOR ASTROPHYS, HARVARD COL OBSERV, 74- *Personal Data:* b Mainz, Ger, Nov 15, 31; US citizen; m 60; c 2. *Educ:* Univ Frankfurt, BS, 56; Harvard Univ, MA, 61, PhD(physics), 63. *Honors & Awards:* sr US scientist award, Alexander vom Humboldt Found, 79. *Prof Exp:* Engr, Raytheon Mfg Co, 57-59. *Concurrent Pos:* Res fel, Harvard Col Observ, 64-66; vis lectr astron, Yale Univ, 65; lectr, Harvard Univ, 65-; vis fel, Univ Heidelberg, 79-80. *Mem:* Am Astron Soc; AAAS; Int Astron Union. *Res:* Theoretical astrophysics; radiative transfer; gas dynamics. *Mailing Add:* Smithsonian Astrophys Observ Harvard Univ Cambridge MA 02138

KALKSTEIN, LAURENCE SAUL, APPLIED CLIMATOLOGY, BIOCLIMATOLOGY. *Current Pos:* assoc prof geog & climat, 75-88, PROF GEOG & CLIMAT, UNIV DEL, 88- *Personal Data:* b Brooklyn, NY, Jan 29, 48; m 71, Rhona Finkel; c Adam J. *Educ:* Rutgers State Univ, BA, 69; La State Univ, MA, 72, PhD(geog, climat), 74. *Prof Exp:* Instr geog, La State Univ, 73; asst prof geog & ecosystems anal, Univ Calif, Los Angeles, 73-75. *Concurrent Pos:* Prin investr, climate & socio-econ assessment, Nat Oceanic & Atmospheric Admin, 80-86; vis scientist, Nat Oceanic & Atmospheric Admin, 82-83; Environ Protection Agency Climate Change Div, 89-90; coordr, global warming/human health prog, Environ Protection Agency, synoptic climatology-pollution relationships, climate- visibility relationships, Salt River Proj & Southern pine beetle- climate anal, US Forest Serv, 85-; mem, Comt Appl Climatol, Am Meteorol Soc, Comn Climatol, World Metrol Orgn; ed, Climate Res. *Mem:* Asn Am Geographers; Am Meteorol Soc. *Res:* Climate's impact on human health and well-being; impact of climate on organism population fluctuations; development of applied climatological indices; socio-economic impacts of a global warming. *Mailing Add:* Dept Geog Univ Del Newark DE 19716-2541. *Fax:* 302-831-6654; *E-Mail:* larryk@udel.edu

KALKWARF, DONALD RILEY, BIOPHYSICAL CHEMISTRY. *Current Pos:* res assoc Chem Dept, Pac NW Nat Labs, 65-66, mgr Radiation Chem Unit, Environ & Radio Sci Dept, 66-68, res assoc Radiol Sci Dept, 68-78, staff scientist Biol & Chem Dept, 78-90, STAFF SCIENTIST, NAT SECURITY & DEFENSE DIRECTORATE, PAC NW NAT LAB, 90- *Personal Data:* b Portland, Ore, Aug 17, 24; m 49, Betsy Rider; c 4. *Educ:* Reed Col, BA, 47;

Northwestern Univ, PhD(chem), 51. *Prof Exp:* Chemist, Gen Elec Co, 51-53, sr scientist, 54-62, res specialist, 62-65. *Mem:* Am Chem Soc; Sigma Xi. *Res:* Radiation biochemistry; synthetic biomembranes; electron spin resonance spectroscopy; controlled release of pharmaceuticals; kinetics of pollutant transformation. *Mailing Add:* 1201 Birch Richland WA 99352

KALKWARF, KENNETH LEE, PERIODONTOLOGY. *Current Pos:* assoc dean adv educ, 87-88, DEAN DENT SCH, UNIV TEX HEALTH SCI CTR, SAN ANTONIO, 88- *Personal Data:* b Lincoln, Nebr, Apr 12, 46; m 74; c 2. *Educ:* Univ Nebr, DDS, 70, MS, 73. *Prof Exp:* Asst prof periodont, Col Dent, Univ Nebr, 73-78; assoc prof, Col Dent, Univ Okla, 78-81; prof periodont & dir grad periodont, Col Dent, Univ Nebr, 81-87, dir grad & postgrad studies, 83-87. *Concurrent Pos:* Consult, Nebr Vet Admin Hosp, Lincoln, 73-, Grand Island, 81-87, Omaha, 86-; Cent Regional Dent Testing Serv, 80-87; Periodont Case Reports, 82- Cent Community Col, Hastings, Nebr, 83-87, J Periodontol, 84-; vis prof, Independent Univ Guadalajara, Mex, 80-82; adv bd, Southeast Nebt Community Col, 81-87; mem, Nebr Bd Dent Examr, 85-87. *Mem:* Int Asn Dent Res; Am Acad Periodont; Am Asn Dent Schs; Am Dent Asn; fel, Am Col Dentists. *Res:* Longitudinal evaluation of periodontal therapy; histologic evaluation of oral wound healing. *Mailing Add:* Dent Sch Univ Tex Health Sci Ctr 7703 Floyd Carl Dr San Antonio TX 78284-7906

KALLAHER, MICHAEL JOSEPH, MATHEMATICS. *Current Pos:* assoc dean sci, Wash State Univ, 79-84, from asst prof to assoc prof, 69-76, chmn dept, 84-92, PROF MATH, WASH STATE UNIV, 76- *Personal Data:* b Cincinnati, Ohio, Sept 4, 40; m 63, Donalyn M Lavaway; c Joy, Michael, Christopher, Daniel & Raymond. *Educ:* Xavier Univ Ohio, BS, 61; Syracuse Univ, MS, 63, PhD(math), 67. *Prof Exp:* Instr math, Syracuse Univ, 66-67; fel, Univ Man, 67-68, asst prof, 68-69. *Concurrent Pos:* Fulbright-Hays fel, Fulbright Comn, 75-76. *Mem:* AAAS; Am Math Soc; Math Asn Am; Sigma Xi; NY Acad Sci; Soc Indust & Appl Math. *Res:* Non-associative algebras; finite geometries, particularly finite projective planes and finite affine planes. *Mailing Add:* Dept Math Wash State Univ Pullman WA 99164-2930. *E-Mail:* kallaher@alpha.math.wsu.edu

KALLAI-SANFACON, MARY-ANN, BIOCHEMISTRY, ENDOCRINOLOGY. *Current Pos:* HEAD BIOCHEM, JEAN-TALON HOSP, MONTREAL, 91- *Personal Data:* b Montreal, Que, Apr 16, 49; m 77; c 2. *Educ:* McGill Univ, Montreal, BSc, 70; Laval Univ, Que, MSc, 73; Univ Toronto, PhD(physiol), 77. *Prof Exp:* Res fel biochem, Erindale Col, Univ Toronto, 77-78; res fel, Ayerst Res Lab Montreal, 78-80, sr scientist, 80-82; dir, Lab Med Anal, BioEndo Labs, 82-83; dir, Clin Chem Lab, Louis-H Lafontaine Hosp, 83-85; sect head pharmacol & toxicol, Clin Chem Lab, Sacre-Coeur Hosp, Montreal, 85-91. *Concurrent Pos:* Indust fel, Nat Res Coun Can, 78-80; grant, Med Res Coun, 85; mem, Prof Affairs Comt, Asn Biochem Que, 85-91, Ad Hoc Comt Drugs Workplace, Order of Chemists of Que, 91; lectr, Continuous Educ Prog Med Technologists, Pharmacol & Toxicol, 89; tutor in pharmacol & toxicol for postdoctoral trainees in clin chem, 89-90; councr, Can Soc Clin Chemists, 91-93. *Mem:* Can Soc Clin Chem (secy, 95-98); Am Asn Clin Chem; Can Acad Clin Biochem. *Res:* Lipid metabolism; the development of hypolipidemic agents and the elucidation of their mode of action; carbohydrate metabolism; development of oral hypoglycaemic agents; hypertension; development of antihypertensive agents particularly those associated with angiotensin converting enzyme inhibition; pharmacology and toxicology. *Mailing Add:* Jean-Talon Hosp Biochem 1385 Rue Jean-Talon Est Montreal PQ H2E 1S6 Can. *Fax:* 514-495-6772

KALLAL, R(OBERT) J(OHN), CHEMICAL ENGINEERING. *Current Pos:* chem engr plastics develop, 49-55, asst tech supt, 55-58, sr supvr res & develop, 58-70, asst plants tech mgr, 70-74, res mgr, 74-75, PLANNING MGR, E I DU PONT DE NEMOURS & CO, INC, 75- *Personal Data:* b Chesterfield, Ill, Feb 1, 21; m 46; c 5. *Educ:* Univ Ill, BS, 43, MS, 46; Mass Inst Technol, ScD(chem eng), 49. *Prof Exp:* Asst munitions develop, Univ Ill, 43-45; asst chem eng, Mass Inst Technol, 46-47, instr, 47. *Mem:* AAAS; Am Chem Soc; Am Inst Chem Engrs. *Res:* Organic and inorganic chemical process development. *Mailing Add:* 518 Kerfoot Farm Rd Wilmington DE 19803-2444

KALLAND, GENE ARNOLD, REPRODUCTIVE ENDOCRINOLOGY. *Current Pos:* from asst prof to assoc prof, 66-76, chairperson dept, 72-75, PROF BIOL, CALIF STATE UNIV, DOMINGUEZ HILLS, 71- *Personal Data:* b Ashland, Wis, Dec 15, 36; c 2. *Educ:* Calif State Univ, Northridge, BA, 62; Ind Univ, PhD(zool), 66. *Prof Exp:* Assoc engr, Rocketdyne Div, NAm Aviation, Inc, 57-62. *Concurrent Pos:* Vis asst prof, Univ Southern Calif, 71; res assoc endocrinol, Harbor-Univ Calif, Los Angeles Med Ctr, 75-80. *Mem:* AAAS; Sigma Xi. *Res:* computer use in science instruction; biology of childhood and adolescence; amphibian hatching mechanisms. *Mailing Add:* 3603 S Walker Ave San Pedro CA 90731-6053

KALLANDER, JOHN WILLIAM, COMPUTER SCIENCE. *Current Pos:* RETIRED. *Personal Data:* b Bessemer, Mich, June 20, 27; m 69, Norma Thornton. *Educ:* Mich Technol Univ, BS, 48; Univ Cincinnati, MS, 50, PhD(appl sci), 52. *Prof Exp:* Develop engr analog computs, Gen Elec Co, 52; res physicist magnetic amplifiers, 53-56, US Naval Res Lab, high-energy radiation effects, 56-61, proj leader, proj sect, 61-63, consult prog lang & physics to head res comput ctr, 63-64, head prog systs sect, 64-68, supvry mathematician, 68-82. *Concurrent Pos:* Consult. *Mem:* Sigma Xi; Inst Elec & Electronics Engrs; Asn Comput Mach. *Res:* Digital computer systems analysis and programming; data base management analysis and programming. *Mailing Add:* 2436 Nolen Dr Flint MI 48504-4679

KALLELIS, THEODORE S, PHARMACOGNOSY. *Current Pos:* assoc prof, 65-71, chmn dept pharmacog & toxicol, 65-69, prof, 71-80, EMER PROF PHARMACOG, TEMPLE UNIV, 80- *Personal Data:* b Peabody, Mass, Oct 12, 12; m 47. *Educ:* Tufts Univ, BS, 35; Mass Col Pharm, BS, 52; Temple Univ, MS, 52; Univ Md, PhD, 56. *Prof Exp:* Assoc prof pharm & chmn dept, Fordham Univ, 56-65. *Mem:* Am Chem Soc; Sigma Xi; Am Pharmaceut Asn; Am Soc Pharmacog; NY Acad Sci. *Res:* Isolation of plant constituents. *Mailing Add:* 921 Beverly Rd Jenkintown PA 19046

KALLEN, FRANK CLEMENTS, VERTEBRATE ANATOMY. *Current Pos:* from asst prof to assoc prof, 64-75, PROF ANAT, STATE UNIV NY BUFFALO, 75- *Personal Data:* b Colonie, NY, May 27, 28; m 58; c 2. *Educ:* Cornell Univ, BA, 49, PhD(zool), 61. *Prof Exp:* Instr anat, Sch Med & Dent, Univ Rochester, 60-64. *Mem:* Am Asn Anat; Am Soc Mammal. *Res:* Blood volume, fluid balance, hibernation, hypothermia and functional morphology in bats and other vertebrates. *Mailing Add:* Dept Anat Sci State Univ NY 303 Sherman Hall Buffalo NY 14214

KALLEN, ROLAND GILBERT, MEDICINE, BIOCHEMISTRY. *Current Pos:* from asst prof to assoc prof biochem, 65-77, PROF BIOCHEM & BIOPHYS, SCH MED, UNIV PA, 79- *Personal Data:* b Glasgow, Scotland, July 3, 35; US citizen; m 63, Stephanie Ebin; c Jared & Caleb. *Educ:* Amherst Col, AB, 56; Columbia Univ, MD, 60; Brandeis Univ, PhD(biochem), 65. *Hon Degrees:* MS, Univ Pa. *Prof Exp:* Intern, NY Univ-Bellevue Med Ctr, 60-61. *Concurrent Pos:* Fogerty Int fel, 81. *Mem:* Am Chem Soc; Am Soc Biochem & Molecular Biol; Biophys Soc. *Res:* Mechanisms and regulation of voltage-sensitive sodium channels; mechanisms of hormone action; mechanisms and regulation of gene expression. *Mailing Add:* Dept Biochem and Biophys Sch Med Univ Pa Philadelphia PA 19104-6059. *Fax:* 215-573-7058; *E-Mail:* rgk@mbio.med.upenn.edu

KALLEN, THOMAS WILLIAM, INORGANIC CHEMISTRY. *Current Pos:* from asst prof to assoc prof, 70-80, PROF CHEM, STATE UNIV NY COL BROCKPORT, 80- *Personal Data:* b Hammond, Ind, Oct 26, 38; m 89, Mary Hussang; c Michael & Amber. *Educ:* Beloit Col, BS, 65; Wash State Univ, PhD(chem), 68. *Prof Exp:* Res assoc chem, Georgetown Univ, 68-70. *Mem:* Sigma Xi; Am Chem Soc. *Res:* Kinetics and mechanisms of substitution reactions and oxidation-reduction reactions of transition-metal complex ions; catalysis by transition-metal ions; ion-exchange chromatography. *Mailing Add:* 8 Old Elm Dr Brockport NY 14420

KALLENBACH, ERNST ADOLF THEODOR, HISTOLOGY, ELECTRON MICROSCOPY. *Current Pos:* instr anat, 63-64, asst prof, 64-67, assoc prof path, 67-77, assoc prof anat, 77-81, PROF ANAT, COL MED, UNIV FLA, 81- *Personal Data:* b Minden, Ger, Feb 21, 26; m 57; c 3. *Educ:* George Williams Col, BSc, 58; McGill Univ, MSc, 60, PhD(anat), 63. *Prof Exp:* Res assoc histol, McGill Univ, 60-63. *Concurrent Pos:* Assoc ed, Anat Rec. *Mem:* Am Asn Anatomists; Electron Micros Soc Am. *Res:* Lymphocyte production in thymus gland; presence and arrangement of cytoplasmic fibrils within epithelial cells; formation of enamel; fine structure of enamel organ. *Mailing Add:* 7903 SE County Rd 234 Gainesville FL 32641

KALLENBACH, NEVILLE R, BIOPHYSICAL CHEMISTRY. *Current Pos:* from assoc prof to assoc prof, 64-71, PROF BIOL, UNIV PA, 71- *Personal Data:* b Johannesburg, SAfrica, Jan 30, 38; US citizen; m 59; c 1. *Educ:* Rutgers Univ, BS, 58; Yale Univ, PhD(chem), 61. *Prof Exp:* NSF fel biophys chem, Univ Calif, San Diego, 61-62, NIH fel, 62-64. *Concurrent Pos:* Guggenheim Mem Found fel, 72-73. *Mem:* Biophys Soc; Am Soc Biol Chemists. *Res:* Structure and function of nucleic acids. *Mailing Add:* Dept Chem NY Univ 4 Washington Pl New York NY 10003

KALLENBERGER, WALDO ELBERT, LEATHER CHEMISTRY, HALOPHILIC BACTERIOLOGY. *Current Pos:* Jr res assoc, 76-78, res assoc, 78-81, SR RES ASSOC, TANNERS LAB, UNIV CINCINNATI, 81-, ASST DIR, LEATHER INDUSTS AM LAB, 85- *Personal Data:* b Mercer Co, Ohio, Feb 25, 50; m 72, Janet E Hemmingson; c Carolyn & John. *Educ:* Valparaiso Univ, BA, 72; Univ Cincinnati, MS, 81, PhD(tan chem), 85. *Honors & Awards:* Alsop Award, Am Leather Chem Asn, 85. *Concurrent Pos:* Consult, 89-; coun rep, Am Leather Chemists Asn, 91-, comt chair, Alsop Comt, 94. *Mem:* Am Leather Chemist Asn; Am Chem Soc. *Res:* Leather processing, testing and product function; chromium conservation, environmental issues, analytical methods and halophilic bacteria in cured hide quality. *Mailing Add:* PO Box 210014 Cincinnati OH 45221-0014. *Fax:* 513-556-2377 (Office), 513-522-9838 (Home); *E-Mail:* kallenwe@ucbeh.san.uc.edu

KALLEND, JOHN SCOTT, CRYSTALLOGRAPHY. *Current Pos:* dept chair, 91-95, PROF MAT ENG, ILL INST TECHNOL, 78-, DEAN, UNDERGRAD COL, 95- *Personal Data:* b Bromley, Eng, Sept 30, 45; m 69, Gail Walker; c Alex, James, Peter & Matthew. *Educ:* Univ Cambridge, BA, 67, MA, 70, PhD(metall), 71. *Prof Exp:* Univ demonstr mat sci, Univ Cambridge, 72-77. *Concurrent Pos:* Consult, Naval Res Lab, 82-84, Argonne Nat Lab, 90; affil, Ctr Mat Sci, Los Alamos Nat Lab, 87-93. *Mem:* Inst Mat; Am Soc Metals; Mineral Metals & Mat Soc; Am Soc Eng Educ. *Res:* Relations between crystallographic texture and anisotropy in polycrystalline materials; software development for analysis of x-ray and neutron texture data. *Mailing Add:* Undergraduate Col Ill Inst Technol 3300 S Federal St Chicago IL 60616-3732. *Fax:* 312-567-3135; *E-Mail:* kallend@charlie.iit.edu

KALLER, BRIAN FRANCIS, total synthesis of natural products, for more information see previous edition

KALLER, CECIL LOUIS, MATHEMATICS, EDUCATION. *Current Pos:* RETIRED. *Personal Data:* b Humboldt, Sask, Mar 26, 30; m 62, Theresa A Fricke; c Kevin P, Damon M, Brian F & Alan M. *Educ:* Univ Sask, BA & BEd, 54, MA, 56; Purdue Univ, PhD(math statist), 60. *Prof Exp:* Teacher elem & high schs, Sask, 48-52; from asst prof to assoc prof math, Univ Sask, 60-65, from assoc prof to prof, Univ Regina, 65-70, chmn dept, 65-70; prof math & pres, Notre Dame Univ of Nelson, BC, 70-76; mathematician, Okanagan Col, BC, 76-92. *Concurrent Pos:* Asst res statistician, Educ Div, Dom Bur Statist, Ottawa, 55; res statistician, UpJohn Co, Kalamazoo, 58, 59 & 60. *Mem:* Am Math Soc; Math Asn Am; Am Statist Asn; Biomet Soc; Sigma Xi; Can Math Soc. *Res:* Mathematical statistics and probability theory; statistical models in biological sciences. *Mailing Add:* 536 Southerland Ave Kelowna BC V1Y 5X3 Can

KALLEY, GORDON S, applied ai, office automation; deceased, see previous edition for last biography

KALLFELZ, FRANCIS A, NUTRITION. *Current Pos:* From asst prof to assoc prof, dept large animal med obstet & surg, 66-80, PROF CLIN NUTRIT, DEPT CLIN SCI, NY STATE COL VET MED, CORNELL UNIV, 80- *Personal Data:* b Syracuse, NY, July 17, 38; m 65, Leonie Heidi Gantner; c 3. *Educ:* Cornell Univ, DVM, 62, PhD(phys biol), 66. *Mem:* Am Vet Med Asn; Am Inst Nutrit; Soc Nuclear Med; Am Acad Vet Nutritionists; Am Col Vet Nutrit. *Res:* Alkaline earth metabolism, the role of vitamin D in calcium metabolism; applications of radioisotopes in clinical veterinary medicine; mineral metabolism in domestic animals; metabolic diseases. *Mailing Add:* Dept Clin Sci Col Vet Med Cornell Univ C2-289 VMTH Ithaca NY 14853. *Fax:* 607-253-3056; *E-Mail:* fak1@cornell.edu

KALLFELZ, JOHN MICHAEL, nuclear engineering, for more information see previous edition

KALLIANPUR, GOPINATH, MATHEMATICS. *Current Pos:* AT DEPT STATIST, UNIV NC, CHAPEL HILL. *Personal Data:* b Mangalore, India, Apr 16, 25; m 53; c 1. *Educ:* Univ Madras, BA, 45, MA, 46; Univ NC, PhD(math statist), 51. *Prof Exp:* Lectr statist, Univ Calif, 51-52; mem, Inst Advan Study, 52-53; reader statist, Indian Statist Inst, Calcutta, 53-56; vis assoc prof, Mich State Univ, 56-59; assoc prof math, Ind Univ, 59-61; prof statist, Mich State Univ, 61-63; prof math & statist, Univ Minn, Minneapolis, 63- *Mem:* AAAS; fel Inst Math Statist. *Res:* Probability theory; stochastic processes; statistics. *Mailing Add:* 1301 Wildwood Dr Chapel Hill NC 27514

KALLIN, CATHERINE, STRONGLY CORRELATED ELECTRON SYSTEMS. *Current Pos:* asst prof, McMaster Univ, 86-90, assoc chair, 88-90, assoc prof, 90-96, PROF PHYSICS, MCMASTER UNIV, 96- *Personal Data:* b BC, Sept 4, 54; m 83, John Berlinsky; c Ann. *Educ:* Univ BC, BSc, 79; Harvard Univ, AM, 81, PhD(physics), 84. *Prof Exp:* Postdoctoral fel, Inst Theoret Physics, Univ Calif, Santa Barbara, 84-86. *Concurrent Pos:* Alfred P Sloan res fel, Sloan Found, 87; vis scientist, AT&T Bell Labs, NJ, 88, Univ BC, 91 & Cornell Univ, 92-93; trustee, Aspen Ctr Physics, 94-97; assoc, Can Inst Advan Res, 95-; EWR Steacie fel, Natural Sci & Eng Res Coun Can, 96; John Simon Guggenheim fel, 96; vis prof, Stanford Univ, 96-97; dir acad affairs, Can Asn Physicists, 97- *Mem:* Fel Am Phys Soc; Can Asn Physicists. *Res:* Theory of highly correlated electronic systems, including high temperature super conductivity, frustrated antiferromagnets, anions and the two-dimensional electron gas in the limit of large magnetic fields and low temperatures. *Mailing Add:* Dept Physics McMaster Univ 1280 Main St W Hamilton ON L8S 4M1 Can. *E-Mail:* kallin@mcmaster.ca

KALLIO, REINO EMIL, microbial physiology; deceased, see previous edition for last biography

KALLIOKOSKI, JORMA OSMO KALERVO, ECONOMIC GEOLOGY. *Current Pos:* head, Geol Eng Dept, 68-81, PROF GEOL, MICH TECHNOL UNIV, 68- *Personal Data:* b Harma, Finland, Nov 23, 23; nat US; m 49; c 3. *Educ:* Univ Western Ont, BSc, 47; Princeton Univ, PhD(geol), 51. *Prof Exp:* Geologist, Geol Surv Can, 49-53 & Newmont Explor, Ltd, 53-56; from asst prof to assoc prof geol, Princeton Univ, 56-68. *Concurrent Pos:* Bus ed, Econ Geol Publ Co, 71-77. *Mem:* Geol Soc Am; Soc Econ Geol (secy, 65-67, pres elect, 79, pres, 80); Can Inst Mining & Metall; Geol Soc Finland; Am Inst Min Metall. *Res:* Relationship between structure and mineral deposits; Precambrian geology in Canada, the United States and Venezuela; uranium geology. *Mailing Add:* 1010 Seventh Ave Houghton MI 49931

KALLMAN, BURTON JAY, BIOCHEMISTRY, NUTRITION. *Current Pos:* RETIRED. *Personal Data:* b New York, NY, Nov 1, 27; m 58; c 2. *Educ:* Bethany Col, WVa, BS, 47; Univ Southern Calif, MS, 51, PhD(biochem), 58. *Prof Exp:* Instr chem, Sch Dent, Univ Southern Calif, 52-53, res assoc, Sch Med, 53-58; fel, Attend Staff Asn, Los Angeles County Gen Hosp, 58-59; biochemist, Fish-pesticide Res Lab, US Fish & Wildlife Serv, 59-63 & Vet Admin Ctr, 63-67; biochemist, TRW Inc, 67-76; sr scientist, Sci Appln Inc, 76-80; prin, Interdisciplinary Sci Assoc, Inc, 80-82; dir, Appl Biol Sci Labs, 82-85; dir, sci & technol, nat nutrit foods assoc, 85-96. *Concurrent Pos:* Consult, Childrens Asthma Res Inst, 62-63, Behav Health Serv, 74-76, US State Dept, 78, IWG Corp, 80-, Sci Appln Inc, 80- *Mem:* AAAS; Am Chem Soc. *Res:* Adrenocorticotropic hormone release; thyroid hormone metabolism and physiology; pesticide biochemistry and pharmacology; immunochemistry; bioconversion of energy; fate and effects of petroleum on marine ecosystems; potential health effects of shale oil industry. *Mailing Add:* 23214 Robert Rd Torrance CA 90505

KALLMAN, KLAUS D, GENETICS, ICHTHYOLOGY. *Current Pos:* RETIRED. *Personal Data:* b Berlin, Ger, July 20, 28; US citizen; m 65. *Educ:* Queens Col, NY, BS, 52; NY Univ, MS, 55, PhD(genetics), 59. *Prof Exp:* Res assoc, NY Aquarium, 60-62, geneticist, Osborn Labs Marine Sci, 63-92, head, Genetics Labs, 86-92; res assoc ichthyol, Am Mus Nat Hist, NY, 65-92. *Concurrent Pos:* USPHS fel, 59-61; lectr, City Col New York, 60-66. *Mem:* Genetics Soc Am; Am Soc Zool; Am Soc Ichthyol & Herpet. *Res:* Tissue transplantation; sex determination; evolution; pigment cell biology. *Mailing Add:* 282 Putnam Ave Freeport NY 11520

KALLMAN, MARY JEANNE, PSYCHOBIOLOGY, PSYCHOPHARMACOLOGY. *Current Pos:* assoc prof psychol & pharmacol, 83-91, ADJ ASSOC PROF PSYCHOL, PHARMACOL, UNIV MISS, 91-, RES SCIENTIST, ELI LILLY & CO, GREENFIELD, IN, 91- *Personal Data:* b Alexandria, Va, May 27, 48; m 69. *Educ:* Lynchburg Col, BS, 70; Univ Ga, MS, 74, PhD(biopsychol), 76. *Prof Exp:* Res asst psychiat, Med Ctr, Univ Miss, 73-74; fel, Med Col Va, 76-79, res assoc, 79-80, asst prof pharmacol, 80-83. *Concurrent Pos:* Mem adj fac, Dept Psychol, Va Commonwealth Univ, 75-76. *Mem:* AAAS; Soc Neurosci; Soc Stimulus Properties Drugs; Am Psychol Asn; Am Asn Pharmacol & Exp Therapeut; Behav Pharmacol Soc. *Res:* State dependency of drugs and stimulus control; central nervous system function and sites of drug action; comparative and developmental central nervous system differences; central sensory processing; psychophysiology; behavioral toxicology and teratology. *Mailing Add:* 1569 E 300 W Greenfield IN 46140

KALLMAN, RALPH ARTHUR, MATHEMATICS. *Current Pos:* asst prof, 67-73, ASSOC PROF MATH, BALL STATE UNIV, 73- *Personal Data:* b Holdrege, Nebr, Sept 17, 34. *Educ:* Univ Minn, BA, 56, MA, 61, PhD(math), 65. *Prof Exp:* Asst prof math, Univ Minn, Duluth, 65-67. *Mem:* Am Math Soc; Math Asn Am; Asn Comput Mach. *Res:* Real and functional analysis; probability and statistics; computational combinatorics; computational probability and statistics. *Mailing Add:* 4045 Hutchinson Muncie IN 47303

KALLMAN, ROBERT FRIEND, RADIOBIOLOGY. *Current Pos:* res assoc, Stanford Univ, 56-60, dir radiobiol res div, 59-77, from asst prof to assoc prof, 60-72, prof, 72-92, EMER PROF RADIOL, STANFORD UNIV, 92- *Personal Data:* b New York, NY, May 21, 22; m 48, 69, Ingrid Moelhede; c Timothy R, Robin L & Lars P. *Educ:* Hofstra Col, AB, 43; NY Univ, MS, 49, PhD, 52. *Prof Exp:* Instr biol, Brooklyn Col, 47-48; asst res physiologist, Univ Calif, 52-56. *Mem:* AAAS; Radiation Res Soc (pres, 76-77); Am Asn Cancer Res; Am Asn Lab Animal Sci; fel NY Acad Sci; Sigma Xi; Am Soc Therapeut Radiol & Oncol; Soc Anal Cytol. *Res:* Radiation effects in mammals; mechanisms of biological action of radiation; experimental cancer therapy; carcinogenesis. *Mailing Add:* 735 San Rafael Pl Stanford CA 94305. *E-Mail:* rkallman@leland.stanford.edu

KALLO, ROBERT MAX, PHYSICAL CHEMISTRY. *Current Pos:* RETIRED. *Personal Data:* b San Francisco, Calif, Oct 6, 23; m 47; c 2. *Educ:* Univ Calif, Berkeley, BS, 45, PhD, 50. *Prof Exp:* From instr to assoc prof, Calif State Univ, Fresno, 50-60, prof chem, 60- *Res:* Thermodynamics. *Mailing Add:* 5236 N Poplar Ave Fresno CA 93704

KALLOK, MICHAEL JOHN, CARDIOVASCULAR PHYSIOLOGY, PULMONARY MECHANICS. *Current Pos:* sr engr, Medtronic Inc, 79-81, sr scientist, 81-85, tachycordia res scientist, 85-87, sr res scientist, 87-88, dir, Physiol Res Lab, 88-92, DIR RES CLIN RES, REGULATORY AFFAIRS, MEDTRONIC HEART VALVE DIV, MEDTRONIC INC, 92- *Personal Data:* b Gary, Ind, Apr 9, 48; m 71, Mary Parker; c Michael, Maureen & Meghan. *Educ:* Univ Colo, BS, 70; Purdue Univ, MS, 74; Univ Minn, PhD(biomed eng), 78. *Honors & Awards:* Beckton Dickenson Career Achievement Award, Asn Advan Med Instrumentation, 85. *Prof Exp:* Design engr, Pratt & Whitney Aircraft, 70-71; instr math, Andrean High Sch, 71-72; staff eng, Chicago Metallic Corp, 72-74; res asst, Univ Minn, 74-77; res fel, Mayo Clin, 77-79. *Concurrent Pos:* Eng consult, Ind Health Eng Assocs, Inc, 76; instr physiol, Mayo Med Sch, 79; assoc fel, Medtronic Inc, 83-88, fel, 88-89. *Mem:* Am Physiol Soc; Am Soc Mech Engrs; Biomed Eng Soc; fel Am Heart Asn; fel Am Col Cardiol; fel Am Inst Med & Biol Eng. *Res:* Pulmonary mechanics; cardiac tachyarrhythmia mechanisms; detection and therapy of ventricular tachycardia and ventricular fibrillation; applications of engineering for medicine and physiology. *Mailing Add:* Medtronic Inc 7000 Central Ave NE Minneapolis MN 55432-3568. *Fax:* 612-574-2890

KALLOS, GEORGE J, ANALYTICAL CHEMISTRY. *Current Pos:* RETIRED. *Personal Data:* b Greece, May 21, 36; US citizen; m 63; c 2. *Educ:* Cent Mich Univ, BS, 60; Univ Detroit, MS, 62. *Prof Exp:* Res chemist, Dow Chem Co, 63-71, sr res chemist, 71-75, sr res specialist, 75-78, assoc scientist chem, 78-95. *Concurrent Pos:* Chmn, Carcinogen Safety Monograph Rev Panel, Nat Cancer Inst, 78. *Mem:* Am Chem Soc; Sigma Xi. *Res:* Development of new analytical technology for trace analysis; application of mass spectrometry to the elucidation of organic structure; monitoring of environmental pollutants. *Mailing Add:* 20 Winfred Pl Saginaw MI 48602

KALLSEN, HENRY ALVIN, ENGINEERING ECONOMY, SAFETY. *Current Pos:* prof civil eng & asst dean eng, Univ Ala, 65-72, actg head dept, 85-86, prof, 72-91, EMER PROF INDUST ENG, UNIV ALA, 91- *Personal Data:* b Jasper, Minn, Mar 25, 26; m 50, Harriet Burger; c Margaret (Lucas), Laura (Weathers), Thomas & Alice (Weekley). *Educ:* Iowa State Univ, BS, 48; Univ Wis, MS, 52, PhD, 56. *Prof Exp:* Asst engr, Wabash RR Co, 48-49; from instr to asst prof civil eng, Univ Wis, 49-59; from assoc prof to prof, La Polytech Inst, 59-64, actg head dept, 62-63; asst exec secy, Am Soc Eng Educ,

64-65. *Concurrent Pos:* Mem adv res coun, La Hwy Dept, 62-64; consult bd eng educ, Comn Higher Educ, State of Tenn, 69; co-dir sch transp proj, Ala Dept Econ & Community Affairs, 87-90. *Mem:* Sigma Xi; Am Soc Civil Engrs. *Res:* Engineering economy; geometronics; safety; computer science. *Mailing Add:* 3727 13th St E Tuscaloosa AL 35404

KALLUNKI, JACQUELYN ANN, BOTANY. *Current Pos:* Herbarium aide, NY Bot Garden, 75-76, curatorial asst, 79-80, herbarium mgr, 81-86, admin cur, 86-90, ASST DIR HERBARIUM, NY BOTANICAL GARDEN, 91- *Personal Data:* b Laurium, Mich, July 3, 48. *Educ:* Univ Mich, BS, 71; Univ Wis-Madison, MS, 74, PhD, 79. *Concurrent Pos:* Assoc ed, Brittonia, 80-90, ed-in-chief, 91-94; mem, Systematics Collections Comt, Am Soc Plant Taxonomists, 89-91; lectr, Yale Univ Sch Forestry, 90 & 91; grantee, NSF, 91-93 & 93-95, Nat Geog Soc, 93-94, Collection Serv Activ, NY Botanical Garden, 95-98; Fulbright scholar award, 95. *Mem:* Am Soc Plant Taxonomists. *Mailing Add:* NY Botanical Garden Bronx NY 10458-5126

KALLWASS, HELMUT KARL WALTER, ENZYMOLOGY, MOLECULAR BIOLOGY. *Current Pos:* STAFF SCIENTIST II, GENZYME CORP, 92- *Personal Data:* b Wolfenbuettel, Ger, Sept 21, 59. *Educ:* Univ Braunschweig, Ger, dipl, 86, Dr rer nat(biochem), 88. *Prof Exp:* Postdoctoral Fel, Ger Sci Found, 88-90, Dept Chem, Univ Toronto, 90-92. *Mem:* Am Chem Soc; Am Soc Biochem & Molecular Biol. *Res:* Enzyme and protein research that meets the multiple needs of an innovative biomedical company, particularly in drug discovery, diagnostic product development and chiral synthesis; multidisciplinary approach combines enzymology, protein chemistry, molecular biology and cell biology. *Mailing Add:* Genzyme Corp 1 Kendall Sq Cambridge MA 02139-1562. *Fax:* 617-252-7550; *E-Mail:* hkallwass@genzyme.com

KALM, MAX JOHN, ORGANIC CHEMISTRY, PHARMACEUTICAL CHEMISTRY. *Current Pos:* RETIRED. *Personal Data:* b Munich, Ger, Nov 27, 28; US citizen; m 69, Lila J Dayhoff; c Denise P & Deborah A. *Educ:* Univ Calif, Berkeley, BS, 52, PhD(chem), 54. *Prof Exp:* Res assoc chem, Univ Mich, 54-55; sr investr, G D Searle & Co, 55-65; dir sci liaison, Cutter Labs, Inc, 65-71, dir qual control, 71-74, dir qual assurance, 74-77, vpres qual assurance, 77-82, vpres qual assurance, Schering Corp, 82-92. *Concurrent Pos:* Mem adv comt, Dept Health, Calif, 76-78. *Mem:* AAAS; Am Chem Soc; Acad Pharmaceut Sci; fel Am Inst Chem; Pharmaceut Mfrs Asn; Parenteral Drug Asn; Am Pharm Asn; NY Acad Sci. *Res:* Photochemistry of benzene; psycho-stimulants and anorexics; synthesis of steroids with hormonal activity. *Mailing Add:* 9 Bennett Pl Westfield NJ 07090-2311. *E-Mail:* mkalm2@juno.com

KALMA, ARNE HAERTER, NUCLEAR RADIATION EFFECTS, OPTICAL SENSORS. *Current Pos:* VPRES, MAXWELL TECHNOL, 90- *Personal Data:* b Long Branch, NJ, May 26, 41; m 65; c 1. *Educ:* Rensselaer Polytech Inst, BS, 63, MS, 65, PhD(nuclear sci eng), 68. *Prof Exp:* Res scientist physics, Univ Paris, 68-69; res scientist group leader physics, IRT Corp, 69-79; mem staff, Northrop Res & Technol Ctr, 79-84; group leader electro optics, Mission Res Corp, 84-90. *Mem:* Am Phys Soc; Optical Soc Am; Inst Elec & Electronics Engrs; Sigma Xi. *Res:* Radiation effects in materials, particularly infrared detectors, optical materials and semiconductors; design and use of radiation hard fiber optics systems; radiation testing; nuclear radiation effects; optical sensors. *Mailing Add:* Maxwell Technol 8888 Balboa Ave San Diego CA 92123. *E-Mail:* arne@maxwell.com

KALMAN, CALVIN SHEA, HIGH ENERGY PHYSICS. *Current Pos:* chmn dept, 83-89, PROF PHYSICS, SIR GEORGE CAMPUS, CONCORDIA UNIV, 75- *Personal Data:* b Montreal, Que, Oct 29, 44; m 66, Rica-Judith M Miller; c Samuel A & Benjamin M. *Educ:* McGill Univ, BSc, 65; Univ Rochester, MA, 67, PhD(physics), 71. *Prof Exp:* Asst prof, Loyola Col Montreal, 68-75. *Concurrent Pos:* Vis assoc prof, Ind Univ, 76-77. *Mem:* Am Asn Physics Teachers; Inst Particle Physics. *Res:* Supersymmetric Gauge Field Theory, subquark structure. *Mailing Add:* Dept Physics Concordia Univ Montreal PQ H3G 1M8 Can. *Fax:* 514-848-2828; *E-Mail:* kalman@vax2.concordia.ca

KALMAN, GABOR J, PLASMA & MANY BODY PHYSICS. *Current Pos:* RES PROF PHYSICS, BOSTON COL, 70- *Personal Data:* b Budapest, Hungary, Dec 12, 29; US citizen; c 2. *Educ:* Polytech Univ, Budapest, dipl, 52; Israel Inst Technol, DSc, 61. *Prof Exp:* From jr res scientist to res scientist, Cent Res Inst Physics, Budapest, Hungary, 52-56; res assoc, Israel Inst Technol, 57-58, lectr physics, 58-61; prof, Univ Paris, 61-66, dir res, Nat Ctr Sci Res, 66-68; vis prof, Brandeis Univ, 66-70. *Concurrent Pos:* Dir, Orsay Summer Inst Plasma Physics, France, 62; vis fel, Joint Lab Astrophys, 65-66; expert, Air Force Cambridge Res Lab, 67-68; vis scientist, Paris Observ, Meudon, France, 73-74 & Ionosphere Res Group, Nat Ctr Sci Res, Orleans, France, 74; sr vis fel, Univ Oxford, 75; exchange prof, Univ Paris, 76; assoc, Ctr Astrophys, Harvard Univ, 73-77; dir, NATO Advan Study Inst Strongly Coupled Plasmas, Orleans, France, 77; res leader, Int Ctr Theoret Physics, 81 & 84; co-dir, NSF-CNRS Workshop Spectral Diag Turbulence Solar Flares, Boston, 82; prin investr grants & contracts, NSF, Dept Energy, Air Force Off Sci Res, Air Force Geophys Lab & Israel-US Binat Found NATO. *Mem:* AAAS; European Phys Soc; fel Am Phys Soc; Fr Phys Soc; fel NY Acad Sci. *Res:* Strongly coupled plasmas; plasma physics; many body response functions; plasma astrophysics; models for high density; astrophysical many body systems; solid state plasmas; many body physics. *Mailing Add:* Dept Physics Boston Col Chestnut Hill MA 02167. *Fax:* 617-552-8478; *E-Mail:* kalman@bcvms.bc.edu

KALMAN, RUDOLF EMIL, MATHEMATICS, ENGINEERING. *Current Pos:* grad res prof & dir Ctr Math Syst Theory, 71-92, EMER GRAD RES PROF & DIR, CTR MATH SYST THEORY, UNIV FLA, 92- *Personal Data:* b Budapest, Hungary, May 19, 30; nat US; m 59; c 2. *Educ:* Mass Inst Technol, SB, 53, SM, 54; Columbia Univ, DSci, 57. *Honors & Awards:* Rufus Oldenburger Medal, Am Soc Mech Eng, 76; Medal of Honor, Inst Elec & Electronics Engrs; Kyoto Prize; Steele Prize. *Prof Exp:* Asst, Servomechanisms Lab, Mass Inst Technol, 53-54; res engr process control res, E I du Pont de Nemours & Co, Del, 54-55; instr, Columbia Univ, 55-57; staff engr, IBM Corp, NY, 57-58; staff mathematician, Res Inst Adv Studies, 58-62, head, Ctr Control Theory, 62-64; prof eng mech & elec eng, Stanford Univ, 64-67, prof math syst theory & opers res, 67-71. *Concurrent Pos:* Prof math system theory, Swiss Fed Inst Technol, Zurich, 73- *Mem:* Nat Acad Sci; Nat Acad Eng; Hungarian Acad Sci; Am Math Soc; Inst Elec & Electronics Engrs; Acad Sci Inst France. *Res:* Automatic control; network and information theory; mathematical statistics; automata; nonlinear dynamic systems; calculus of variations; stochastic processes; engineering science; algebraic system theory; innovative statistics. *Mailing Add:* Ctr Math Theory Univ Fla Gainesville FL 32611

KALMAN, THOMAS IVAN, BIO-ORGANIC CHEMISTRY, ENZYMOLOGY & ANTIVIRAL & CANCER CHEMOTHERAPY. *Current Pos:* adj asst prof & sr res assoc health sci, 66-70, from asst prof to assoc prof biochem pharmacol, 70-93, PROF MED CHEM, STATE UNIV NY, BUFFALO, 93- *Personal Data:* b Budapest, Hungary, Jan 20, 36; nat US; m 63, Marietta S Szeben; c Rob P & Nicolette C. *Educ:* Tech Univ Budapest, Dipl ChE, 59; State Univ NY, Buffalo, PhD(biochem, pharmacol), 68. *Honors & Awards:* Scholar Award, Am Cancer Soc, 96. *Prof Exp:* Res chemist, Hungary, 59-62; res asst, Res Found, State Univ NY, 63-66; fel, NIH, 67-68. *Concurrent Pos:* NIH res career develop award, 71-76; vis assoc prof, Dept Pharmacol, Sch Med, Yale Univ, 75-76; vis prof, Dept Pharmacol & Dept Med Chem, Med Col Va, 96-97. *Mem:* AAAS; Am Chem Soc; NY Acad Sci; fel Am Inst Chem; Am Asn Cancer Res; Sigma Xi. *Res:* Mechanisms of enzyme and drug action; design and synthesis of selective enzyme inhibitors; biosynthesis of purine and pyrimidine nucleotides; folic acid metabolism; drug design; experimental chemotherapy; cancer research; antiviral agents. *Mailing Add:* 955 Pinetree Ct East Amherst NY 14051. *Fax:* 716-645-2393

KALMANSON, KENNETH, MATHEMATICS. *Current Pos:* ASST PROF MATH, MONTCLAIR STATE COL, 70- *Personal Data:* b Brooklyn, NY, Mar 26, 43; m 66; c 1. *Educ:* Brooklyn Col, BS, 64; City Col New York, PhD(math), 70. *Prof Exp:* Teacher high schs, NY, 65-66. *Mem:* Am Math Soc; Math Asn Am. *Res:* Combinatorial geometry, especially extreme Hamiltonian lines with respect to metric spaces. *Mailing Add:* Montclair Univ Upper Montclair NJ 07043

KALMBACH, SYDNEY HOBART, PHYSICS. *Current Pos:* from assoc prof to prof, 52-84, EMER PROF PHYSICS, NAVAL POSTGRAD SCH, 84- *Personal Data:* b Fond du Lac, Wis, June 8, 13; m 40; c 1. *Educ:* Marquette Univ, BS, 34, MS, 39. *Prof Exp:* Asst prof physics, Elmhurst Col, 40-43 & US Naval Acad, 47-52. *Mem:* Am Phys Soc; Am Asn Physics Teachers. *Res:* Infrared spectroscopy; atmospheric optics. *Mailing Add:* Portola Rd Pebble Beach CA 93953

KALME, JOHN S, MATHEMATICS. *Current Pos:* CONSULT, 82- *Personal Data:* b Riga, Latvia, June 20, 38; US citizen. *Educ:* Univ Pa, BA, 61, MA, 64, PhD(math), 66. *Prof Exp:* Teaching fel math, Univ Pa, 61-64; instr, Drexel Inst, US Naval Acad, Annapolis, 65-66, from asst prof to assoc prof math, 69-79; consult & comput prog, David Taylor, US Naval Ship Res & Develop Ctr, Annapolis, 79-82. *Res:* Mathematical analysis, chiefly probability theory and integral operators; stochastic processes, time series analysis; use of time series analysis in source and path identification of structure-borne noise on ships; vibration analysis. *Mailing Add:* Dept Math US Naval Acad Annapolis MD 21402

KALMUS, GERHARD WOLFGANG, DEVELOPMENTAL BIOLOGY. *Current Pos:* asst prof develop, 77-83, assoc prof, 83-93, PROF BIOL, ECAROLINA UNIV, 93- *Personal Data:* b Berlin, Germany, Dec 19, 42; m 67, Karen Biehl. *Educ:* Univ Calif, Berkeley, BA, 67; Rutgers Univ, Camden, MS, 74; Rutgers Univ, New Brunswick, PhD(zool), 77. *Prof Exp:* Res asst physiol, Univ Pa, 67-68; asst proj mgr transl, Info Intersci Inc, 69-70; teacher biol, Quakertown Community High Sch, 72; res asst embryol, Temple Univ, 73; teaching asst zool, Rutgers Univ, 73-77. *Mem:* AAAS; Soc Integrative Comp Biol; Am Inst Biol Sci; Soc In Vitro Biol; Soc Develop Biol; Sigma Xi. *Res:* Transplantation immunology; chick primordial germ cells; fetal alcohol syndrome; differentiation in cell culture. *Mailing Add:* Dept Biol ECarolina Univ Greenville NC 27858-4353. *Fax:* 919-328-4178; *E-Mail:* bikalmus@bcuvm.cis.ecu.edu

KALNAY, EUGENIA, NUMERICAL WEATHER PREDICTION, GENERAL CIRCULATION MODELING. *Current Pos:* DEVELOP DIV CHIEF, NAT METEROL CTR, NAT OCEANIC & ATMOSPHERIC ADMIN, 87-, DIR, ENVIRON MODELING CTR, 87- *Personal Data:* b Buenos Aires, Arg, Oct 10, 42; US citizen; m 81, Mal C Dick; c 1. *Educ:* Univ Buenos Aires, Lic, 65; Mass Inst Technol, PhD(meteorol), 71. *Honors & Awards:* Except Sci Achievement Medal, NASA, 81; Silver Medal, Dept Com, 90, Gold Medal, Develop Div, 93; Jules G Charney Award, Am Meteorol Soc, 95; Sr Exp Serv Presidential Rank Award, 96. *Prof Exp:* Asst prof meteorol, Univ Montevideo, Uruguay, 71-73; res assoc, Mass Inst Technol, 73-74, from asst prof to assoc prof, 75-78; sr res meteorologist, Goddard Lab Atmosphere, NASA, 79-83, head, Global Modeling & Simulation Br, 83-86. *Concurrent Pos:* Prin investr, NASA res projs, 73-; adj prof meteorol, Univ Md, 80-83; mem, First Global Atmospheric Res Prog Global Exp Panel, Nat Acad Sci, 83-93; assoc ed, J Atmospheric Sci, 84-90; assoc ed, Monthly Weather Rev, 90 & Quart J Royal Meteorol Soc, 92; mem, Bd Atmospheric Sci & Climate, Nat Acad Sci, 93. *Mem:* Nat Acad Eng; fel Am Meteorol Soc. *Res:* Heads development division of national meteorological center where all improvements to atmospheric models and data assimilation are developed and implemented giving guidance to the National Weather Service forecasts; use of satellite data; data assimilation; atmospheric predictability; ensemble forecasting. *Mailing Add:* Nat Ctr Environ Prediction Nat Oceanic & Atmospheric Admin Washington DC 20233. *Fax:* 301-763-8545; *E-Mail:* eugenia@noaa.gov

KALNIN, ILMAR L, MATERIALS SCIENCE. *Current Pos:* RETIRED. *Personal Data:* b Riga, Latvia, Jan 23, 26; US citizen; m 54; c 3. *Educ:* Westminster Col, Pa, BA, 52; Ill Inst Technol, PhD(chem), 57. *Prof Exp:* Mem tech staff, Bell Tel Labs, 57-62; res scientist, Am-Stand Co, 62-66; sr res scientist, Celanese Res Co, 66-67, res assoc, 67-86, res assoc, Hoechst-Celanese Co, 86-91. *Concurrent Pos:* Tech consult. *Mem:* Am Chem Soc; Am Ceramic Soc; Am Soc Testing & Mat; Mat Res Soc. *Res:* Functional polymers; structural composites; fiber reinforced plastics; electronic ceramics. *Mailing Add:* 135 Haas Rd Basking Ridge NJ 07920-1098

KALNINS, ARTURS, MECHANICS. *Current Pos:* assoc prof mech, 65-67, PROF MECH, LEHIGH UNIV, 67- *Personal Data:* b Riga, Latvia, Feb 13, 31; US citizen; m 56. *Educ:* Univ Mich, BS, 55, MS, 56, PhD(eng mech), 60. *Prof Exp:* Res asst eng mech, Univ Mich, 56-58; res engr appl mech, Univ Calif, Berkeley, 58-60; asst prof eng & appl sci, Yale Univ, 60-65. *Concurrent Pos:* Assoc ed, J Acoust Soc Am, 70-; Fulbright-Hayes fel, Univ Innsbruck, 77. *Mem:* Am Soc Mech Engrs; Acoust Soc Am. *Res:* Stress analysis, pressure vessel design. *Mailing Add:* 1984 Sunrise Lane Bethlehem PA 18015

KALNITSKY, GEORGE, BIOCHEMISTRY. *Current Pos:* from instr to assoc prof, 46-57, PROF BIOCHEM, UNIV IOWA, 57- *Personal Data:* b Brooklyn, NY, Oct 22, 17; m 40; c 3. *Educ:* Brooklyn Col, BA, 39; Iowa State Col, PhD(physiol bact), 43. *Prof Exp:* Asst, Iowa State Col, 42-43, res assoc, 43; res assoc & instr biochem, Univ Chicago, 43-45. *Concurrent Pos:* Univ col med travelling fel, Oxford Univ, 56-57; Guggenheim fel, Weizmann Inst Sci, Israel, 65-66; Welcome res travel award, 80. *Mem:* Fel AAAS; Am Chem Soc; Soc Exp Biol & Med; Am Soc Biol Chemists; Sigma Xi. *Res:* Bacterial metabolism; intermediary carbohydrate metabolism; mechanism of action of enzymes; proteolytic enzymes; intracellular proteases, lung, and protease inhibitors. *Mailing Add:* Dept Biochem Univ Iowa Basic Sci Bldg Iowa City IA 52242-1000. *Fax:* 319-335-9570

KALOGERIS, THEODORE J, GASTROINTESTINAL PHYSIOLOGY, ABSORBTION & TRANSPORT OF LIPIDS. *Current Pos:* NIH fel, 92-95, RES ASST PROF, DEPT SURGERY & PHYSIOL, LA STATE UNIV MED CTR, 95- *Personal Data:* b Salina, Kans, Oct 1, 55. *Educ:* Univ Calif, San Diego, BA, 76; Univ Calif, Davis, MS, 83, PhD(nutrit), 88. *Prof Exp:* Nat Heart Asn fel, Dept Foods & Nutrit, Purdue Univ, 88-91. *Concurrent Pos:* NIH first award, 97- *Mem:* Sigma Xi; Am Physiol Soc; Am Soc Nutrit Scis; Am Gastroenterol Asn. *Res:* Regulation of intestinal lipoproteins; role of oxidized lipoproteins in mediating endothelial dysfunction, regulation of expression of endothelial cell adhesion molecules. *Mailing Add:* Dept Physiol & Biophys La State Univ Med Ctr 1501 Kings Hwy Shreveport LA 71130

KALOGEROPOULOS, THEODORE E, HIGH ENERGY PHYSICS. *Current Pos:* from asst prof to assoc prof, 62-69, PROF PHYSICS, SYRACUSE UNIV, 69- *Personal Data:* b Megalopolis, Greece, Jan 20, 31; m 54. *Educ:* Dipl physics, Nat Univ Athens, 54; dipl electronics, Radio-Eng Sch, Athens, 51; Univ Calif, Berkeley, PhD(physics), 59. *Prof Exp:* Res assoc physics, Lawrence Radiation Lab, Univ Calif, 59; instr, Columbia Univ, 59-62. *Concurrent Pos:* Vis physicist, Argonne Nat Lab, 65, Brookhaven Nat Lab, 60-85; vis prof, Nuclear Res Ctr Democritos, 69-70. *Mem:* Am Phys Soc; AAAS. *Res:* Elementary particle physics; investigations on antinucleon-nucleon interactions, using emulsions, bubble chambers, spark chambers, counters and drift chambers; medical applications of antiprotons; optimization algorithms and applications. *Mailing Add:* Dept Physics Syracuse Univ Syracuse NY 13244

KALONJI, GRETCHEN, ATOMISTIC COMPUTER SIMULATIONS. *Current Pos:* from asst prof to assoc prof, mat sci, Mass Inst Technol, 82-90, KYOCERA PROF, UNIV WASH, 90- *Personal Data:* US citizen. *Educ:* Mass Inst Technol, BS, 80, PhD(mat sci), 82. *Honors & Awards:* Presidential Young Investr Award, NSF, 84. *Prof Exp:* Mat engr, Nat Bur Standards, 79-81. *Mem:* Am Ceramics Soc; Mat Res Soc; Am Phys Soc; AAAS. *Res:* Theory of defects in crystalline solids; computer simulation techniques in materials science; rapid solidification of ceramics. *Mailing Add:* 2310 E Valley St Seattle WA 98112

KALOOSTIAN, GEORGE H, ENTOMOLOGY. *Current Pos:* RETIRED. *Personal Data:* b Kaisarea, Turkey, Jan 12, 12; nat US; m 35; c 2. *Educ:* Fresno State Col, BA, 35; Ore State Col, MS, 39. *Prof Exp:* Res leader, Calif, Fruit & Veg Insect Res, Agr Res Serv, USDA, 38-40, Wash, 40-48, Utah, 48-57, Ga, 57-61, res leader, Calif, 61-79. *Mem:* Entom Soc Am; Am Phytopath Soc; Sigma Xi. *Res:* Life history and control of dried fruit insects; plant and insect survey methods; insects in relation to fruit tree diseases caused by virus and mycoplasmalike organisms. *Mailing Add:* 4066 Mt Vernon Ave Riverside CA 92507-4804

KALOS, MALVIN HOWARD, THEORETICAL PHYSICS, COMPUTER SCIENCE. *Current Pos:* DIR, CORNELL THEORY CTR & PROF DEPT PHYSICS, CORNELL UNIV, 89- *Personal Data:* b New York, NY, Aug 5, 28; m 49; c 2. *Educ:* Queens Col, NY, BS, 48; Univ Ill, MS, 49, PhD(physics), 52. *Honors & Awards:* Eugene Feenberg Award, 89. *Prof Exp:* Res assoc physics, Univ Ill, 52-53 & Cornell Univ, 53-55; adv scientist, Nuclear Develop Corp, 55-64; res prof, Courant Inst Math, 64-89. *Concurrent Pos:* Lectr, Univ Paris, 70-77. *Mem:* Am Phys Soc; fel NY Acad Sci; AAAS; fel Am Nuclear Soc. *Res:* Nuclear physics; statistical physics; neutron interactions; parallel computers; application of computers to physics, especially Monte Carlo methods. *Mailing Add:* 521 ETC Bldg Cornell Univ Hoy Rd Ithaca NY 14853

KALOTA, DENNIS JEROME, ORGANIC CHEMISTRY, FLUORINE CHEMISTRY. *Current Pos:* Sr res chemist, Monsanto Co, 74-80, res specialist, 80-84, sr res specialist, 84-88, SCI FEL, MONSANTO CO, 88- *Personal Data:* b North Tonawanda, NY, Nov 15, 45; m 67, Kathleen A Gill; c Kevin, Michele & Lisa. *Educ:* Niagara Univ, BS, 68; Univ Detroit, MS, 71, PhD(chem), 74. *Mem:* Am Chem Soc; Sigma Xi. *Res:* New products research and process development for amino acids and polyamino acids; direct fluorination of polyethers; chlorination, nitration, hydrolysis, and amination of aromatics; synthesis of polycarboxylates; electrochemistry; enzymatic and heterogeneous catalysis. *Mailing Add:* Monsanto Co 800 N Lindbergh Blvd St Louis MO 63167. *Fax:* 314-694-4575

KALOW, WERNER, PHARMACOLOGY, PHARMACO GENETICS. *Current Pos:* from lectr to assoc prof, 52-62, chmn dept, 66-77, PROF PHARMACOL, UNIV TORONTO, 62- *Personal Data:* b Cottbus, Ger, Feb 15, 17; nat Can; m 46, 91, Patricia M Arnold; c Peter & Barbara. *Educ:* Univ Koenigsberg, MD, 41. *Honors & Awards:* Upjohn Award, Pharmacol Soc Can, 81; Oscar B Hunter Award, 93; Res Recognition Award, Can Anaesthetists Soc, 93. *Prof Exp:* Sci asst, Univ Berlin, 47-48, Free Univ Berlin, 49; res fel pharmacol, Univ Pa, 50, instr, 51. *Concurrent Pos:* Dir biol res, C H Boehringer Sohn, Ingelheim, WGer, 65-66. *Mem:* Am Soc Pharmacol & Exp Therapeut; NY Acad Sci; Can Physiol Soc; Pharmacol Soc Can (secy-treas, 56-58, pres, 63-64); Ger Pharmacol Soc; Can Anaesthetists Soc; Pac Rim Asn Clin Pharmacogenetics (pres, 89-94); fel Royal Soc Can. *Res:* Bile secretion; serum cholinesterase; curare; local anesthetics; caffeine metabolism; malignant hyperthermia; genetics and drug response; ethnicity and drug metabolism. *Mailing Add:* Dept Pharmacol Univ Toronto Toronto ON M5S 1A8 Can. *Fax:* 416-867-6395; *E-Mail:* w.kalow@utoronto.ca

KALPAKJIAN, SEROPE, MANUFACTURING ENGINEERING. *Current Pos:* PROF MECH & MAT ENG, ILL INST TECHNOL, 63- *Personal Data:* b Istanbul, Turkey, May 6, 28; US citizen; m 62; c Claire & Kent. *Educ:* Robert Col, Istanbul, BSc, 49; Harvard Univ, SM, 51; Mass Inst Technol, SM, 53. *Honors & Awards:* Centennial Medallion, Am Soc Mech Engrs. *Prof Exp:* Res engr, Mass Inst Technol, 53-54; res supvr metal forming, Cincinnati Milacron, Inc, 57-63. *Concurrent Pos:* Consult, Ill Inst Technol Res Inst, 63-80, Continental Can Co, 69-76, Xerox Corp, 79 & A Finkl & Sons, 84-86; cor ed, J Mfg, 90- *Mem:* Fel Am Soc Mech Engrs; fel Am Soc Metals; fel Soc Mfg Engrs; Int Inst Prod Eng Res. *Res:* Grinding and lubrication; machining and forming; manufacturing processes. *Mailing Add:* Dept Mech Mat & Aerospace Eng Ill Inst Technol 3300 S Federal Chicago IL 60616-3732. *Fax:* 312-567-7230; *E-Mail:* skalpakjian@charlie.cns.iit.edu

KALRA, JAWAHAR, CLINICAL PATHOLOGY, MEDICAL BIOCHEMISTRY. *Current Pos:* From asst prof to assoc prof, 85-91, actg head, 90-91, PROF & HEAD, DEPT PATH, COL MED, UNIV SASK, 91-; DIR PATH LABS, ROYAL UNIV HOSP, 91-; CHIEF, DEPT LAB MED, SASKATOON DIST HEALTH BD, 93- *Personal Data:* b Aligarh, India, Apr 2, 49; Can citizen; m 86, Kamla Katyal; c Neil & Natasha. *Educ:* Aligarh Univ, India, BSc, 67, MSc, 69; Mem Univ Nfld, 72, PhD(biochem), 76, MD, 81; Can Soc Clin Chemists, cert, 86; Royal Col Physicians & Surgeons Can, cert, 86; FACB, 87; FRCPC, 87; FICA, 88; FACA, 89; FCACB, 89. *Honors & Awards:* Med Chem Award, Can Soc Clin Chem, 91, 92; Man of Yr, Am Biog Inst Res Asn, 94. *Prof Exp:* Lab instr 3rd & 4th yr biochem lab courses, Mem Univ, Nfld, 72-74, res asst, Mem Univ Res Unit, Fac Med, 74-76, res assoc, 76-77; Burrough-Wellcome scholar, 79; jr resident, Dept Lab Med, Ottawa Civic Hosp, 82-83 & 84, Dept Med, 83, actg chief resident internal med, endocrinol & metab, Hosp, 84, sr resident, Dept Med, 84-85 & Dept Lab Med, 85. *Concurrent Pos:* active med staff, Royal Univ Hosp, 85-, mem Med Adv Comt, 90-; Schering travelling award, Can Soc Clin Invest, 88; dir residency training progs gen & anat path, Univ Sask, 90-91, postgrad training prog, Dept Path, 90- & mem, Adv Comt Acad Enrichment Progs, Col Med, 90-; mem bd dirs, Parkinson's; dep gov, mem bd gov, Am Biog Inst Res Asn, 95. *Mem:* Int Soc Free Radical Res-Oxygen Soc; Am Soc Clin Pathologists; Int Soc Heart Res; NY Acad Sci; Nat Acad Clin Biochem; Am Asn Clin Chem; Can Med Asn; Can Asn Med Biochem (pres, 93-). *Res:* Role of oxygen free radicals in various clinical diseases especially heart failure, atheroscleccrsis and Parkinson's disease; earlier work on cardiac glycoside (digoxin) biotransformation and thyroid function testing along with lab utilization studies. *Mailing Add:* Dept Path Royal Univ Hosp Saskatoon SK S7N 0X0 Can. *Fax:* 306-655-2200

KALRA, S(URINDRA) N(ATH), COMMUNICATIONS. *Current Pos:* assoc prof, 67-69, PROF ELEC ENG, UNIV WATERLOO, 69- *Personal Data:* b Lahore, India, May 12, 27; nat Can; m 59; c 2. *Educ:* Panjab Univ, India, BS, 46; Univ Ill, MS, 47, PhD, 50. *Prof Exp:* Reader in electronics, Phys Res Lab, India, 50-52; fel, Nat Res Coun Can, 52-53, head high frequency physics lab, Div Appl Physics, 53-62; assoc prof elec eng, Univ Windsor, 62-67; dir interdisciplinary studies in commun, 65-67. *Mem:* Sr mem Inst Elec & Electronics Engrs; Brit Inst Elec Engrs. *Res:* Communication sciences; electronics; computers. *Mailing Add:* 103-30 Blue Springs Dr Univ Waterloo Waterloo ON N2J 4T2 Can

KALRA, SATYA PAUL, NEUROENDOCRINOLOGY & ENDOCRINOLOGY, BEHAVIOR. *Current Pos:* from asst prof to to assoc prof, 71-82, PROF REPRODUCTIVE BIOL, COL MED, UNIV FLA, 82- *Personal Data:* b Mari Indus, WPakistan, Jan 1, 39; m 69; c 1. *Educ:* Univ Delhi, BSc, 60, MSc, 62, PhD(physiol), 66. *Prof Exp:* Res asst physiol reproduction, Univ Delhi, 66-68. *Concurrent Pos:* Ford Found fel anat, Col Med, Univ Calif, Los Angeles, 68-69 & fel physiol, Southwestern Med Sch, Univ Tex Health Sci Ctr, Dallas, 69-71; NIH grant obstet & gynec, Univ Fla, 71- *Mem:* Endocrine Soc; Am Physiol Soc; Soc Gynec Invest; Int Soc Neuroendocrinol; Int Soc Neurosci; Am Andrology Soc; Soc Neurosci. *Res:* Neuroendocrinology of reproduction; regulation of pituitary gonadotropin functions by gonadal steroids; monoamines and hypothalamic releasing hormones; neuroendocrine and feeding and sexual behavior. *Mailing Add:* Dept Neurosci Univ Fla Col Med JHM HC 1600 SW Archer Rd PO Box 100924 Gainesville FL 32610-0294. *Fax:* 904-392-8347

KALRA, VIJAY KUMAR, BIOCHEMISTRY. *Current Pos:* From asst prof to assoc prof, 71-84, PROF BIOCHEM & SEN, FAC SENATE, SCH MED, UNIV SOUTHERN CALIF, 84- *Personal Data:* b Multan, WPakistan, Aug 26, 42; m 71; c 2. *Educ:* Univ Delhi, BSc, 61, MSc, 63, PhD(chem), 67. *Concurrent Pos:* USDA res fel, Ctr Advan Studies Chem of Natural Prod, Univ Delhi, 67; USPHS res fel, Sch Med, Univ Southern Calif, 67-70. *Mem:* Am Chem Soc; Am Soc Biol Chem. *Res:* Structure and function of membranes; oxidative phosphorylation, mechanism of transport of amino acids in bacterial and mammalian cells; sterol metabolism in animal and human cells and relationship to atherosclerosis; structure and function of membranes of red blood cells and sickle cells; structure and function of endothelial cells. *Mailing Add:* Dept Biochem Univ Southern Calif Sch Med 2011 Zonal Ave Los Angeles CA 90033-1034. *Fax:* 213-342-2764

KALRA, YASH PAL, SOIL CHEMIST. *Current Pos:* HEAD ANALYTICAL SERVS, FORESTRY CAN, EDMONTON, 67- *Personal Data:* b Gunjial, Punjab, India, Oct 28, 40; c Moneesh & Navita. *Educ:* Agra Univ, Kanpur, India, BSc, 61, MSc, 63; Univ Manitoba, Winnipeg, MSc, 67. *Concurrent Pos:* Res fel, Indian Coun Agr Res, 61-63, Univ Man, 63-64; grantee, Prime Minister India, 63, Nat Res Coun Can, 64-66; mem safety comt, Northern Forestry Ctr, 70-72; mem chem exec, Professional Inst Pub Serv Can, 84-, exec, Edmonton Br, 91-; chmn, registration comt, Environ Soil Sci Conf, Can Land Reclamation Asn/Can Soc Soil Sci, 92; mem biol serv/environ sci adv comt, Northern Alta Inst Technol, Edmonton, 93- *Mem:* Can Soc Soil Sci (secy, 93-); Int Soc Soil Sci; Soil Sci Soc Am; Am Soc Agronomy; Indian Soc Soil Sci; Soc Ind Foresters; Asn Off Analytical Chemists; Int Soc Soil Sci; Western Inviron Agr Lab Asn (secy & treas, 81-82, 85-86); Prof Inst Pub Serv Can; Coun Soil Testing Plant Anal. *Mailing Add:* Forestry Can 5320 122nd St Edmonton AB T6H 3S5 Can

KALSBECK, JOHN EDWARD, PEDIATRIC NEUROSURGERY. *Current Pos:* From instr to assoc prof, 62-80, PROF SURG NEUROSURG, IND UNIV, INDIANAPOLIS, 80- *Personal Data:* b Grand Rapids, Mich, May 20, 27; m 59; c 3. *Educ:* Calvin Col, AB, 49; Univ Mich, MD, 53; Am Bd Neurol Surg, dipl, 68. *Concurrent Pos:* NIH fel, Nat Hosp, Queen Sq, London, 60-61; consult, New Castle State Hosp, 63- *Mem:* Am Asn Neurol Surg; Cong Neurol Surg. *Mailing Add:* Ind Univ Med Ctr 702 Barnhill Dr RM 2517 Indianapolis IN 46202-5210

KALSER, MARTIN, GASTROENTEROLOGY. *Current Pos:* assoc prof, 59-63, CHIEF, DIV GASTROENTEROL, UNIV MIAMI, 61-, PROF GASTROENTEROL & PHYSIOL, SCH MED, 63- *Personal Data:* b Pittsburgh, Pa, Jan 7, 23; m 53; c 3. *Educ:* Univ Pittsburgh, BS, 42, MD, 46; Univ Ill, MS, 51, PhD(physiol), 53; Am Bd Internal Med, dipl, 55; Am Bd Gastroenterol, dipl, 57. *Prof Exp:* From instr to assoc prof gastroenterol, Grad Sch Med, Univ Pa, 54-56. *Concurrent Pos:* Res fel clin sci, Univ Ill, 50-53; res fel gastroenterol, Grad Sch Med, Univ Pa, 54-55; consult, Montefiore Hosp, Pittsburgh, 47-50, Vet Admin Clin, Dayton, Ohio & dean's comt, Col Med, Univ Cincinnati, 50-52, Cook County Hosp, Chicago, 52-53, Grad Hosp, Philadelphia, 54-55; mem comn enteric infections, Armed Forces Epidemiol Bd, 63-67. *Mem:* AMA; Am Gastroenterol Asn; Am Col Physicians. *Res:* Internal medicine; physiology. *Mailing Add:* 12145 SW 69th Pl Miami FL 33156-5431

KALSER, SARAH CHINN, PHARMACOLOGY. *Current Pos:* LIVER DIS PROG DIR, NAT INST ARTHRITIS, DIABETES & DIGESTIVE & KIDNEY DIS, NIH, 68- *Personal Data:* b Connellsville, Pa, June 11, 29; m 52. *Educ:* Pa State Univ, BS, 51; Northwestern Univ, MS, 53; Univ Pittsburgh, PhD(pharmacol), 61. *Prof Exp:* Biochemist, Med Labs, US Army Chem Ctr, 53-58; res asst pharmacol, Sch Med, Univ Pittsburgh, 58-60, from instr to asst prof, 61-68. *Mem:* AAAS; Am Gastroenterol Asn; Am Asn Study Liver Dis; Am Soc Exp Pharmacol & Therapeut. *Res:* Glutathione synthesis in trauma; atropine metabolism; drug metabolism in hypothermia and in cold acclimatization. *Mailing Add:* 6012 Rossmore Dr Bethesda MD 20814-2266. *Fax:* 301-402-1278

KALSNER, STANLEY, PHARMACOLOGY. *Current Pos:* PROF & CHMN DEPT PHYSIOL, CITY UNIV NEW YORK MED SCH, 85- *Personal Data:* b New York, NY, Aug 21, 36; m 63; c 3. *Educ:* NY Univ, AB, 58; Univ Man, PhD(pharmacol), 66. *Prof Exp:* Asst pharmacologist, Schering Corp, 62; from asst prof to prof pharmacol, Univ Ottawa, 67-85. *Concurrent Pos:* Fel pharmacol, Cambridge Univ, 66-67; Med Res Coun Can grant, 67-; Ont Heart Found grant, 70- *Mem:* Pharmacol Soc Can; Am Soc Pharmacol & Exp Therapeut. *Res:* Autonomic and cardiovascular pharmacology and physiology; biogenic amines; supersensitivity of autonomic effectors to drugs and denervation; receptor mechanisms; coronary artery disease; vascular smooth muscle; hypertension. *Mailing Add:* City Univ New York Med Sch 138th St & Convent Ave New York NY 10031-9100. *Fax:* 212-650-7726

KALSOW, CAROLYN MARIE, OCULAR MICROBIOLOGY & IMMUNOLOGY. *Current Pos:* RES ASSOC PROF, UNIV ROCHESTER, 86- *Personal Data:* b Elgin, Ill, July 9, 43; m 81, Richard W Krause; c Jeff, Paul, Michael, John & Carolyn. *Educ:* Iowa State Univ, BS, 65; Univ Tex Med Br, MA, 67; Univ Louisville, PhD(microbiol), 70. *Prof Exp:* Instr microbiol, Univ Louisville, 70-71, lectr biol, 70-72, res assoc ophthal, 71-72, instr, 72-73, asst prof, 73-79, assoc prof, 79-81; adj assoc prof, Hope Col, 81-85. *Concurrent Pos:* Vis asst prof med microbiol, SFla Med Sch, 72; vis scientist, A Study Sect, 82-86, C Study Sect, 92- *Mem:* Am Uveitis Soc; Asn Res Vision & Ophthal; Sigma Xi; AAAS; Am Asn Immunol; Int Soc Eye Res; Am Uveitis Soc; Europ Pineal Soc; Asn Vet Immunol; Int Ocular Soc. *Res:* Ocular immunology and microbiology. *Mailing Add:* Ophthal Dept Univ Rochester Box 314 Rochester NY 14642. *Fax:* 716-273-1043

KALT, MARVIN ROBERT, RESEARCH GRANTS & CONTRACTS POLICY. *Current Pos:* exec secy grants & contracts rev, Nat Inst Aging, NIH, 80-82, chief, sci rev, 82-90, dept dir, 90-94, DIR, DIV EXTRAMURAL ACTIV, NAT CANCER INST, NIH, 94-; MEM, SR EXEC SERV, US AM, 90- *Personal Data:* b Elizabeth, NJ, Aug 25, 45; m 67; c 1. *Educ:* Lafayette Col, AB, 67; Case Western Res Univ, PhD(anat), 71. *Prof Exp:* USPHS fel cell & molecular biol, Dept Biol, Yale Univ, 71-73; asst prof anat, Univ Conn Health Ctr, 73-80. *Concurrent Pos:* Prin investr grant awards, USPHS, Nat Inst Child Health Human Develop, 73-77, NSF, 77-80; mem rev policy comt, Off of the Dir, NIH, 82-90, referral & training officer, Nat Inst Aging, 80-83. *Mem:* Am Soc Cell Biol; Sigma Xi. *Res:* Vertebrate germ cell development; vertebrate morphogenesis; cell biology; gerontology; federal grants and contract review and administration; human subjects and animal welfare policy; national scientific research policy. *Mailing Add:* Nat Cancer Inst NIH Suite 600 EPN Bethesda MD 20892-7405. *Fax:* 301-402-0956; *E-Mail:* kaltm@dea.nci.nih.gov

KALTENBACH, CARL COLIN, REPRODUCTIVE PHYSIOLOGY. *Current Pos:* VDEAN & DIR, AGR EXP STA, UNIV ARIZ, 89- *Personal Data:* b Buffalo, Wyo, Mar 22, 39; m 64, Ruth Johnson; c 2. *Educ:* Univ Wyo, BSc, 61; Univ Nebr, MSc, 63; Univ Ill, PhD(animal physiol), 67. *Prof Exp:* Australian Wool Bd fel, Univ Melbourne, 67-69; prof animal physiol, Univ Wyo, 69-89, actg head, Div Animal Sci, 78, assoc dir res, Col Agr, 80, assoc dean & dir, Wyo Agr Exp Sta, 84. *Mem:* AAAS; Am Soc Animal Sci; Soc Study Fertil; Soc Study Reprod; Sigma Xi. *Res:* Luteotrophic and steroidogenotrophic properties of pituitary hormones; corpus luteum function; radioimmunoassay for protein and steroid hormones; experimental surgery; fetal growth and development. *Mailing Add:* 727 E Via Entrada Tucson AZ 85718-4733

KALTENBACH, JOHN PAUL, BIOCHEMISTRY. *Current Pos:* asst prof, 56-60, Northwestern Univ, assoc prof path & biochem, 60-80, dir, Dent Sch Interview Prog, 77-79, actg dir admin, 78-79, prof path, 80-82, EMER PROF PATH, MED SCH, NORTHWESTERN UNIV, 82- *Personal Data:* b Rockford, Ill, Feb 28, 20; m 94, Dawn L Deck; c John C. *Educ:* Beloit Col, BS, 44; Univ Iowa, MS, 48, PhD, 50. *Prof Exp:* Brittingham fel cancer res, McArdle Mem Lab, Wis, 50-52; USPHS fel, Karolinska Inst, Stockholm, Sweden, 53-54; chief, Cell Metab Lab, Vet Admin Res Hosp, Chicago, Ill, 54-56. *Mem:* AAAS. *Res:* Metabolism of whole cells, normal and neoplastic; metabolism of ischemic myocardium; effect of D-serine on rat renal proximal tubules. *Mailing Add:* W7746 Tubbs Lane Spooner WI 54801

KALTENBACH-TOWNSEND, JANE, HISTOLOGY, ENDOCRINOLOGY. *Current Pos:* from asst prof to prof, Mt Holyoke Col, 58-70, chmn dept, 80-86, prof biol, 70-93, EMER PROF BIOL, MT HOLYOKE COL, 93- *Personal Data:* b Chicago, Ill, Dec 21, 22; m 66, Robert L. *Educ:* Beloit Col, BS, 44; Univ Wis, MA, 46; Univ Iowa, PhD(zool), 50. *Prof Exp:* Teaching asst zool, Univ Wis, 44-47; teaching asst & instr, Univ Iowa, 47-50; res asst & proj assoc path, Univ Wis, 50-53; Am Cancer Soc res fel, Wenner-Grens Inst, Univ Stockholm, 53-56; asst prof zool, Northwestern Univ, 56-58. *Concurrent Pos:* Mem, Corp Marine Biol Lab; guest investr, Kristinebergs Zool Sta, Swed, 54-55; Naples Staziona Zool, Italy, 55, Fla State Univ, 60, Oakland Univ, Mich, 64, Brown Univ, 66. *Mem:* Fel AAAS; Am Asn Anatomists; Am Inst Biol Sci; Am Soc Zoologists; Sigma Xi; Soc Exp Biol & Med. *Res:* Thyroxine and other hormonal controls of amphibian metamorphosis; localization of peptides in amphibian brain, gut and skin (immunohistochemistry); localization of specific sugars in skin of aquatic and terrestrial frogs (lectin histochemistry). *Mailing Add:* Dept Biol Sci Mt Holyoke Col South Hadley MA 01075. *Fax:* 413-538-2327; *E-Mail:* jtownsen@mhc.mtholyoke.edu

KALTENBORN, HOWARD SCHOLL, MATHEMATICS. *Current Pos:* prof & chmn dept, 46-72, EMER PROF MATH, MEMPHIS STATE UNIV, 72- *Personal Data:* b Pittsburgh, Pa, Jan 21, 07; m 37, Helen Houghtaling; c Alice & Sara. *Educ:* Carnegie Inst Technol, BS, 28; Univ Mich, MS, 31, PhD(math), 34. *Prof Exp:* Instr math, Carnegie Inst Technol, 29-32 & Univ Mich, 34-37; instr appl math, Univ Tex, 38-39; assoc prof math, La Polytech Inst, 39-43 & Univ Idaho, 45-46. *Res:* Mathematical analysis; mathematics education. *Mailing Add:* 169 S Mendenhall Rd Memphis TN 38117

KALTENBRONN, JAMES S, ORGANIC CHEMISTRY. *Current Pos:* RES CHEMIST, PARKE, DAVIS & CO, 60- *Personal Data:* b New Baden, Ill, Nov 21, 34. *Educ:* Univ Ill, BS, 56; Mass Inst Technol, PhD(org chem), 60. *Mem:* Am Chem Soc. *Res:* Medicinal chemistry; natural products; stereochemistry. *Mailing Add:* 3555 Green Brier Dr Ann Arbor MI 48105

KALTER, HAROLD, GENETICS, TERATOLOGY. *Current Pos:* From asst prof to prof, 58-94, EMER PROF RES PEDIAT, COL MED, UNIV CINCINNATI, 94- *Personal Data:* b New York, NY, Feb 26, 24; m 45; c 3. *Educ:* Sir George Williams Col, BA, 49; McGill Univ, MSc, 51, PhD(genetics), 53. *Concurrent Pos:* Nat Cancer Inst fel, McGill Univ, 53-55; res assoc, Children's Hosp Res Found, 55-94; mem, Human Embryol & Develop Study Sect, NIH, 66-70; ed, Teratol, 67-76; mem Secy's Comn Pesticides, 69; adv comt, 2, 4, 5-T, Environ Protection Agency, 71; consult, Comt Biol Effects Atmospheric Pollutants, Nat Res Coun Panel Vapor Phase Organic Air Pollutants from Hydrocarbon, 71; mem adv comt, Dept Safety Assessment, Merck Inst Therapeut Res, 75-80; mem, Panel Qual Criteria Water Reuse, Nat Acad Sci, 79-81; ed, Issues & Rev in Teratology, 82-94. *Mem:* Teratology Soc. *Res:* Experimental mammalian teratology. *Mailing Add:* Children's Hosp Res Found Elland Ave & Bethesda Cincinnati OH 45229. *Fax:* 513-559-9669; *E-Mail:* kalterh@email.uc.edu

KALTER, SEYMOUR SANFORD, VIROLOGY. *Current Pos:* chmn, Dept Microbiol, 63-66, dir, Div Microbiol & Infectious Dis, 66-88, DIR VIR REF LAB, 88- *Personal Data:* b New York, NY, Mar 19, 18; m 82, Yvette L; c Susan P (Gershman), Steven P, Debra I & Chartore (deceased). *Educ:* St Joseph's Col, Pa, BS, 40; Univ Kans, MA, 43; Syracuse Univ, PhD(med bact), 47; Am Bd Microbiol, dipl. *Prof Exp:* Asst instr bact, Univ Kans, 41-43; asst med bact, Sch Med, Univ Pa, 43-45; from instr to assoc prof microbiol, State Univ NY Upstate Med Ctr, 45-56; chief, Virus Diag Methodology Unit, Commun Dis Ctr, USPHS, Ga, 56-61; chief, Virol Sect, US Air Force Sch Aerospace Med, Brooks AFB, Tex, 61-63; dir, Dept Virol & Infectious Dis, Southwest Found Biomed Res, 64-88. *Concurrent Pos:* Bacteriologist, Syracuse Dept Health, NY, 45-56; asst prof prev med, Sch Med, Emory Univ, 56-60; lectr, Med Sch, Baylor Univ, 61-63; adj prof, Trinity Univ & Univ Tex Health Sci Ctr, San Antonio, adj prof pediat & microbiol; adj prof, Dent Sci Inst, Univ Tex Health Sci Ctr, Houston; consult, Pan Am Sanit Bur; consult, Neurol Inst, Univ Cologne & Off Pesticide Progs, Environ Protection Agency; consult simian & pox viruses, WHO, chmn, comt simian viruses; consult virol, Univ Tex Syst Cancer Ctr, Houston; mem bd dir, Cancer Ther & Res Found, San Antonio; mem, Fedn US Culture Collections. *Mem:* Fel AAAS; Am Acad Microbiol; Soc Exp Biol & Med; Am Asn Immunol; fel Am Pub Health Asn. *Res:* Enteroviruses; respiratory viruses; oncogenic viruses; virus diagnosis; simian virology; comparative primate virology; oncogenic viruses; latent viruses. *Mailing Add:* Virus Ref Lab Inc 7540 Louis Pasteur San Antonio TX 78229-4018. *Fax:* 210-614-7355

KALTHOFF, KLAUS OTTO, DEVELOPMENTAL BIOLOGY. *Current Pos:* assoc prof, 78-80, PROF ZOOL, UNIV TEX, AUSTIN, 80- *Personal Data:* b WGer, Feb 5, 41; m 65, Karin Losskarn; c Christian, Ulrich & Philipp. *Educ:* Univ Hamburg, BA, 64; Univ Freiburg, MA, 67, PhD(zool), 71. *Prof Exp:* Asst prof zool, Univ Freiburg, 71-76, assoc prof, 76-77. *Mem:* Europ Develop Biologist Orgn; Soc Develop Biol; AAAS. *Res:* Role of localized cytoplasmic determinants in embryogenesis using insect embryos and ultraviolet irradiation, microinjection and molecular techniques. *Mailing Add:* Dept Zool Univ Tex Austin TX 78712. *Fax:* 512-471-9651; *E-Mail:* kkaethoff@mail.utexas.edu

KALTOFEN, ERICH L, COMPUTER ALGEBRA, ALGORITHM DESIGN & ANALYSIS. *Current Pos:* PROF MATH, NC STATE UNIV, 96- *Personal Data:* b Linz, Austria, Dec 21, 55; m 81, Hoang T Nguyen. *Educ:* Rensselaer Polytech Inst, MS, 79, PhD(comput sci), 82. *Prof Exp:* Lectr comput sci, Univ Del, 81-82; from asst prof to assoc prof, Rensselaer Polytech Inst, 84-92, prof, 92-95. *Concurrent Pos:* Res assoc, Kent State Univ, 82; vis scientist, Tektronix Inc, 85; res fel, Math Sci Res Inst, 85; secy, Spec Interest Group Symbolic & Algebraic Monipolation, Asn Comput Mach, 86-87, vchmn, 87-88, chmn, 93- *Mem:* Asn Comput Mach; Soc Indust & Appl Math. *Res:* Computational algebra and number theory; design and analysis of sequential and parallel algorithms; symbolic manipulation systems and languages. *Mailing Add:* Dept Math NC State Univ Raleigh NC 27695-8205. *Fax:* 919-515-3798; *E-Mail:* kaltofen@eos.ncsu.edu

KALTON, ROBERT RANKIN, crop breeding; deceased, see previous edition for last biography

KALU, DIKE NDUKWE, PHYSIOLOGY. *Current Pos:* asst prof, 75-80, ASSOC PROF PHYSIOL, UNIV TEX HEALTH SCI CTR, SAN ANTONIO, 80- *Personal Data:* b Nigeria, Jan 3, 38; m 67; c 3. *Educ:* Univ London, BS, 67, PhD(biochem), 71. *Prof Exp:* Sci officer, Royal Postgrad Med Sch, Univ London, 67-71; fel Sch Med, Johns Hopkins Univ, 72-75. *Concurrent Pos:* Fel, Inst Med Lab Sci, UK. *Mem:* Inst Med Lab Sci UK; AAAS; The Endocrine Soc; Fed Am Soc Exp Biol; NY Acad Sci. *Res:* Hormonal control of calcium and skeletal metabolism and the effects of aging. *Mailing Add:* Dept Physiol Univ Tex Health Sci Ctr 7703 Floyd Curl Dr San Antonio TX 78284-7756. *Fax:* 210-567-4410

KALUZIENSKI, LOUIS JOSEPH, X-RAY ASTRONOMY. *Current Pos:* STAFF SCIENTIST HIGH ENERGY ASTROPHYS, NASA HQ, 78- *Personal Data:* b Union Beach, NJ, July 28, 48. *Educ:* Rutgers Univ, BA, 70; Univ Md, MS, 74, PhD(physics), 77. *Prof Exp:* Grad res asst x-ray astron, Goddard Space Flight Ctr, Univ Md, 74-77, res assoc, 77-78. *Mem:* Am Astron Soc. *Res:* Transient x-ray sources; x-ray binaries. *Mailing Add:* 914 Melvin Rd Annapolis MD 21403

KALVINSKAS, JOHN J(OSEPH), CHEMICAL PROCESS DESIGN & DEVELOPMENT, ENVIRONMENTAL ENGINEERING. *Current Pos:* TASK MGR, GROUP SUPVR & MEM TECH STAFF, JET PROPULSION LAB, CALIF INST TECHNOL, 74- *Personal Data:* b Philadelphia, Pa, Jan 14, 27; m 55, Louanne M Adams; c Adrian J. *Educ:* Mass Inst Technol, BS, 51, MS, 52; Calif Inst Technol, PhD(chem eng), 59. *Prof Exp:* Res engr, Eastern Lab, E I du Pont de Nemours & Co, NJ, 52-55, 59-60; asst chem eng, Calif Inst Technol, 55-59; res specialist, Rocketdyne Div, Rockwell Int Corp, 60-61, supvr basic studies, 61-64, group scientist propellant eng, 64-67, dir environ health systs, Life Sci Opers, 67-70; pres, Resource Dynamics Corp, 70-74; proj mgr, Holmes & Narver Inc, 74. *Concurrent Pos:* Corp res dir, Monogram Indust, Inc, 72; consult, Rockwell Int, 72-74, Kinetics Technol Int, Pasadena, Calif, 82-84. *Mem:* NY Acad Sci; Am Chem Soc; Am Inst Chem Engrs; Sigma Xi. *Res:* Chemical reaction kinetics; machine computation; chemical engineering process design; heat transfer; rocket propulsion; environmental engineering; coal beneficiation; bioconversion and bioenergy; hazardous material disposal; environmental monitoring. *Mailing Add:* 316 Pasadena Ave Apt 3 South Pasadena CA 91030-2939

KALYAN-RAMAN, KRISHNA, NEUROLOGY. *Current Pos:* CLIN PROF NEUROL, UNIV CHICAGO, PRITZKER SCH MED, 95- *Personal Data:* b Madras, India, June 2, 35; m 63; c 2. *Educ:* Univ Madras, MBBS, 58, DM, 71; Univ Delhi, MD, 62. *Prof Exp:* Asst prof med, Thanjavur Med Col, Madras Univ, 62-65; asst prof neurol & hon asst, Inst Neurol, Govt Gen Hosp, Madras, 69-71; clin asst prof, Sch Med, State Univ NY, Buffalo, 71-72, from asst prof to assoc prof neurol, 72-76; from assoc prof to prof neurol, Col Med, Univ Ill, Peoria, 76-95. *Concurrent Pos:* Neurologist, E J Meyer Mem Hosp, Buffalo, 71-; neurologist, Outpatient Serv, Vet Admin Hosp, Buffalo, 72-; consult neurologist, West Seneca Develop Ctr, 73-; vis lectr, Inst Neurol, Govt Gen Hosp, 75-, mem staff, St Francis Hosp Med Ctr, Methodist Med Ctr Ill & Proctor Community Hosp, Peoria, 76-; dir, Muscular Dystrophy Asn Neuromuscular Clin, Col Med, Univ Ill, Peoria, 79-; Attend Neurol, Univ Ill Hosps, 95-96. *Mem:* Neurol Soc India; Am Acad Neurol; fel Am Col Physicians; assoc Am Asn Electromyog & Electrodiag. *Res:* Nerve and muscle involvement in systemic disorders and effects of upper motor neurone lesions on histochemical pattern of muscle. *Mailing Add:* 110 St Francis Circle Oak Brook IL 60521

KAM, GAR LAI, DIGITAL SIGNAL, SPEECH ANALYSIS. *Current Pos:* AT AT&T BELL LABS, WHIPPANY, NJ. *Personal Data:* b Canton, China, Aug, 36; US citizen; m 69; c 1. *Educ:* Nat Taiwan Univ, BSEE, 61; Univ Tenn, MSEE, 66. *Prof Exp:* Sr electronics engr, Lockheed Co, Ga, 66-69; mem tech staff, Hughes Aircraft Co, 69-71; engr III, Jet Propulsion Lab, Calif Inst Technol, 71; sr engr, Martin-Marietta Aerospace Corp, 71-74; eng specialist, Singer-Kearfott Co, 74-80; prin engr, Xybion Corp, 80- *Mem:* Inst Elec & Electronics Engrs; sr mem Am Inst Aeronaut & Astronaut. *Res:* Developing models and algorithms of complex aerospace engineering applications and implementing these models and algorithms in comprehensive computer simulations for system performance analyses. *Mailing Add:* 16 Cold Hill Rd Morris Plains NJ 07950

KAM, JAMES TING-KONG, COMPUTER MODELING, OPERATIONS RESEARCH. *Current Pos:* PRIN HYDROLOGIST, MORRISON KNUDSEN, 85- *Personal Data:* b Hong Kong, July 29, 45; US citizen; m 74, Winna Wong; c Kelvin K & Theresa P. *Educ:* Univ Man, Can, BSc, 68; Univ Calif, Berkeley, PhD(soil physics & hydrol), 74. *Prof Exp:* Res fel, Water Eng, Univ Calif, Davis, 74-75; hydrologist, Geol Eng, Morrison Knudsen, 75-79; sr engr hydrol, Sci Applns Inc, 79-81; staff specialist, consult, hydrol & geol, Davy McKee-Davy Inc, 81-85. *Concurrent Pos:* Hydro/environ consult, 84-85. *Mem:* Am Soc Civil Engrs; Nat Water Well Asn; Environ Assessment Asn. *Res:* Computer modeling and analyses of hydrologic and geological engineering problems; general civil (hydrologic) engineering design, contaminant transport and fate analysis, risk assessment, environmental assessment and remedial design. *Mailing Add:* 2430 35th Ave San Francisco CA 94116

KAM, MOSHE, DECISION THEORY, NEURAL NETWORKS. *Current Pos:* asst prof, 87-90, ASSOC PROF, ELEC & COMPUT ENG DEPT, DREXEL UNIV, 90-, ASST DEPT HEAD DEVELOP, ELEC & COMPUT ENG, 90- *Personal Data:* b Tel Aviv, Israel, Oct 3, 55. *Educ:* Tel Aviv Univ, BSc, 77; Drexel Univ, MS, 85, PhD(elec eng), 87. *Prof Exp:* Res & develop engr, Israeli Defense Forces, 76-83. *Concurrent Pos:* Vpres, Reshet Inc, 87-; NSF presidential young investr, 90; assoc ed, Transactions on Systs, Man & Cybernet, Inst Elec & Electronics Engrs, 92-; assoc ed, Pattern Recognition, 92- *Mem:* Inst Elec & Electronics Engrs; Int Neural Network Soc; Sigma Xi. *Res:* Synthesis of optimal sensor fusion architectures; design and construction of mobile robots; design of efficient algorithms for multiaccess communications; automatic writer identification for questioned documents. *Mailing Add:* Dept Elec & Comput Eng 7-412 Drexel Univ Philadelphia PA 19104. *Fax:* 215-895-1695

KAMACK, H(ARRY) J(OSEPH), CHEMICAL ENGINEERING. *Current Pos:* RETIRED. *Personal Data:* b Conn, Dec 5, 18. *Educ:* Ga Inst Technol, BS, 41; Univ Del, MS, 56. *Prof Exp:* Chem engr, Gen Chem Co, 41 & Ord Dept, US Army, 42; chem engr, E I DuPont de Nemours & Co, Inc, 42-46, res engr, 46-54, process design engr, 54-69, sr design consult, 69-73, prin design consult, 73-78. *Mem:* Am Inst Chem Engrs. *Res:* Chemical plant design; atomic energy design; particle size reduction and measurement. *Mailing Add:* 490 Stamford Dr Apt 304 Newark DE 19711-2774

KAMAL, ABDUL NAIM, PARTICLE PHYSICS. *Current Pos:* from asst prof to assoc prof physics, 64-73, dir, Theoret Physics Inst, 79-80, chmn physics, 80-84, actg chmn, 88-89, McCalla prof, 90-91, PROF PHYSICS, UNIV ALTA, 73- *Personal Data:* b Dhaka, Bangladesh, Oct 28, 35; div; c 3. *Educ:* Univ Dhaka, BSc, 55, MSc, 56; Univ Liverpool, PhD(theoret physics), 62. *Prof Exp:* Lectr physics, Univ Dhaka, 62-63; fel theoret physics, Univ Liverpool, 63 & Theoret Physics Inst, Edmonton, Alta, 63-64. *Concurrent Pos:* Sr sci officer, Rutherford Lab, UK, 68-69, vis scientist, 71 & 78; vis scientist, Int Ctr Theoret Physics, Trieste, Italy, 72; vis prof, Stanford Linear Accelerator Ctr, 79, vis scientist, 84-85. *Mem:* Am Phys Soc; Can Asn Physicists. *Res:* Theoretical particle physics; weak and strong interactions. *Mailing Add:* Dept Physics Univ Alta Edmonton AB T6G 2J1 Can. *Fax:* 403-492-0714; *E-Mail:* kamal@phys.ualberta.ca

KAMAL, MOUNIR MARK, ENGINEERING MECHANICS. *Current Pos:* Assoc sr res engr, Gen Motors Res Labs, 65-67, sr res engr, 67-68, supv res engr, 68-71, asst head dept, 71-77, head, Dept Eng Mech, 77-82, tech dir mech & elec eng, 82-87, EXEC DIR ENG SCI, GEN MOTORS RES LABS, 88- *Personal Data:* b Beirut, Lebanon, Feb 13, 36; US citizen; m 62, Mary E Merrow; c 3. *Educ:* Robert Col, Istanbul, BS, 56; Univ Mich, Ann Arbor, MS, 58, MS, 62, PhD(eng), 65. *Honors & Awards:* Distinguished Serv Awards, Am Soc Mech Engrs, Soc Automotive Engrs. *Concurrent Pos:* Mem, Univ Mich Indust Comt, 70-78. *Mem:* Sigma Xi; Soc Automotive Engrs; Am Soc Mech Engrs; Am Acad Mech; fel Soc Mfg Engrs; fel AAAS. *Res:* Mechanical engineering; internal combustion engines; fluid mechanics and vehicle structural mechanics; vehicle crash dynamics. *Mailing Add:* 30230 Jefferson St Clair Shores MI 48082

KAMAL, MUSA RASIM, POLYMER ENGINEERING, MATERIALS SCIENCE ENGINEERING. *Current Pos:* assoc prof, 67-73, chmn chem eng, 83-93, PROF CHEM ENG, MCGILL UNIV, 73-; DIR, BRACE RES INST, 87- *Personal Data:* b Tulkarm, Jordan, Dec 8, 34; m 61, Nancy J Edgar; c Rammie & Basim. *Educ:* Univ Ill, BS, 58; Carnegie Inst Technol, MS, 59, PhD(chem eng), 62. *Honors & Awards:* Int Educ Award, Soc Plastics Engr, 84; Kuwait Prize, Appl Sci & Technol, 83; CANPLAST Award, Soc Plastics Indust, Can, 85, Indust Leader Yr, 95. *Prof Exp:* Teacher elem sch, Kuwait, 52-54; res chem engr, Stamford Res Labs, Am Cyanamid Co, Conn, 61-65, group leader, Wallingford Develop Lab, 65-67. *Concurrent Pos:* Vis prof, Am Univ of Beirut, 74-75; dir, Microecon & Sectoral Sect, Morocco Indust Develop Plan, Dar Al-Handasah Consults, 79; pres, Talkarm Enterprises Ltd, 78- *Mem:* Am Inst Chem Engrs; Am Chem Soc; fel Soc Plastics Engrs; Soc Rheol; NY Acad Sci; Sigma Xi; fel Chem Inst Can; Am Acad Mech; AAAS; fel Royal Soc Can; Can Acad Sci. *Res:* Polymer engineering; plastics processing; injection molding; rheology; heat transfer; non-Newtonian flow; thermoset and thermoplastic processing; weatherability of plastics systems; properties of polymers; microstructure development and control in plastics processing; polymer crystallization and morphology; composites; computer simulation; project evaluation and planning. *Mailing Add:* Dept Chem Eng McGill Univ 3480 University St Montreal PQ H3A 2A7 Can. *Fax:* 514-398-6678

KAMAL, MUSA RASIM, PLASTICS. *Current Pos:* assoc prof chem eng, McGill Univ, Que, 67-73, chmn, Chem Eng Dept, 83-93, PROF CHEM ENG, MCGILL UNIV, 73-, DIR, BRACE RES INST, 86- *Personal Data:* b Tulkarm, Jordan, Dec 8, 34; m 61, Nancy J Edgar; c Rammie & Basim. *Educ:* Univ Ill, BSc, 58; Carnegie-Mellon Univ, ME, 59, PhD(eng), 61. *Honors & Awards:* Kuwait Prize, Kuwait Foun Advan Sci, 83; Int Educ Award, Soc Plastics Engrs, 84; Can Plast, Award, 85. *Prof Exp:* Res chem engr, Cent Res Labs, Am-Cyanimd Co, 61-65, res group leader plastics, 65-67. *Concurrent Pos:* Dir, Microeconomics Develop Plan, Rabat, Morocco, 77; pres, Tulkarm Enterprises, Montreal, 77-; mem bd govs, Can Plastics Inst, Toronto, 86- *Mem:* Fel Royal Soc Can; fel Chem Inst Can; fel Soc Plastics Engrs; Am Inst Chem Engrs; Am Chem Soc; Am Inst Physics; Soc Rheology; Soc Plastics Indust Can; Polymer Processing Soc Int; Can Soc Chem Eng. *Res:* Laminar polymer blends; processing of plastics, blends and composites; injecton and blow molding; polymer characterizaton; author of over 300 articles; awarded six patents. *Mailing Add:* Dept Chem Eng McGill Univ 3610 University St Montreal PQ H3A 2B2 Can. *Fax:* 514-398-6678; *E-Mail:* kamal@chemeng.lan.mcgill.ca

KAMAN, CHARLES HENRY, COMPUTER SCIENCE. *Current Pos:* CONSULT, 81- *Personal Data:* b Brookline, Mass, 1943. *Educ:* Harvard Col, AB, 65; Polytech Inst Brooklyn, MS, 67, PhD(syst sci), 74. *Prof Exp:* Consult engr comput archit, Digital Equip Corp, Tewksbury, 69-81. *Mem:* Asn Comput Mach; Inst Elec & Electronics Engrs; Soc Indust & Appl Math; Am Math Soc; Math Asn Am. *Res:* Computer architecture; computer implementation; programming languages and semantics; computer algorithms; application of theoretical computer science to practical computer design and implementation. *Mailing Add:* 274 Dedham St Newton Highlands MA 02161-2045

KAMAN, CHARLES HURON, AERONAUTICAL ENGINEERING. *Current Pos:* pres, 45-90, CHMN & CHIEF EXEC OFFICER, KAMAN CORP, 90- *Personal Data:* b Washington, DC, June 15, 19; m 45; c 3. *Educ:* Cath Univ, BAeroE, 40. *Hon Degrees:* DSc, Univ Colo, 84 & Univ Hartford, 85; LLD, Univ Conn, 85. *Honors & Awards:* Asn Award, Navy Helicopter Asn, 75; Dr Alexander Klemin Award, Am Helicopter Soc, 81; Fleet Adm Chester W Nimitz Award, Navy League US, 86; Nat President's Award, Naval Res Asn, 87; Pioneer Award, Asn Unmanned Vehicle Systs, 93; Nat Medal of Technol, 96. *Prof Exp:* Aerodyn, Hamilton Stand Div, United Aircraft Corp, 40-45. *Concurrent Pos:* Chmn, Helicopter Coun, Aerospace Indust Asn, 54 & Vertical Lift Aircraft Coun, 64; bd regents, Cath Univ Am, bd gov; bd dirs, Conn Bus & Indust Asn; dir, Emhart Corp, Hartford Nat Corp, Conn Nat Bank, Inst Living & Security Conn Ins Co; adv bd, World Affairs Ctr Honors; founder, Univ Hartford; indust comt mem, Greater Hartford YMCA; pres & dir, Fidelco Guide Dog Found Coun, 64; corporator, Inst Living, Hartford Hosp. *Mem:* Nat Acad Eng; hon mem Navy Helicopter Asn; hon fel Am Helicopter Soc; fel Am Inst Aeronauts & Astronauts. *Mailing Add:* Kaman Corp Blue Hills Ave PO Box 1 Bloomfield CT 06002

KAMAN, ROBERT LAWRENCE, BIOCHEMISTRY. *Current Pos:* asst prof biochem, 73-77, ASST PROF BASIC HEALTH SCI, TEX COL OSTEOP MED, NTEX STATE UNIV, 77- *Personal Data:* b New York, NY, June 26, 41; m 67; c 2. *Educ:* Univ Pa, AB, 63; Va Polytech Inst, MS, 67, PhD(biochem), 69. *Prof Exp:* NIH fel biochem, Sch Med, Univ Mich, 69-72, res assoc, Sch Pub Health, 72-73. *Mem:* Am Osteop Acad Sports Med; Am Col Sports Med; Am Asn Fitness Dirs. *Res:* Chemotherapy for atherosclerosis; effect of exercise on health and fitness; diet and exercise; exercise programs for firemen; exercise and alcohol rehabilitation. *Mailing Add:* Dept Physiol Tex Col Osteop Med 3500 Camp Bowie Blvd Ft Worth TX 76107-2644

KAMAT, PRASHANT V, COLLOID & SURFACE SCIENCE, SEMICONDUCTOR NANOCLUSTERS. *Current Pos:* from asst prof specialist to assoc prof specialist, 83-92, PRIN INVEST, NOTRE DAME RADIATION LAB, 83-, PROF SPECIALIST PHYS CHEM, 92- *Personal Data:* b Binaga, Karnataka, India, Jul 6, 53; m 83, Shobha; c Neha & Neeta. *Educ:* Bombay Univ, MS & PHD, 79. *Honors & Awards:* Award, Japan Soc Promotion Sci, 96. *Prof Exp:* Res asst, catalysis, Hindustan Lever Res Ctr, Bombay, 77-79; res assoc phys chem, chem dept, Boston Univ, 79-81, Univ Tex, Austin, 81-83. *Concurrent Pos:* Reviewer, Am Chem Soc Pubs, 83- *Mem:* Sigma Xi; Am Chem Soc; Soc Electroanal Chem; Electrochem Soc; Interam Photochem Soc. *Res:* Investigating dynamics of interfacial processes in semiconductor particulate systems; surface photochemistry and heterogeneous photocatalysis; conducting polymers; polymer modified electrodes; excited state behavior of polymers and dyes; electrochemistry and interfacial processes; solar energy conversion; semiconductor, nanoclusters and thin films. *Mailing Add:* Radiation Lab Univ Notre Dame Notre Dame IN 46556. *Fax:* 219-631-8068; *E-Mail:* kamat@marconi.rad.nd.edu

KAMATH, KRISHNA, PETROLEUM ENGINEERING, PHYSICAL CHEMISTRY. *Current Pos:* PETROL ENGR, MORGANTOWN ENERGY TECHNOL CTR, US DEPT ENERGY, 76- *Personal Data:* b Shertallai, India, Aug 24, 20; m 69. *Educ:* Univ Travancore, India, BSc, 41; Banaras Univ, MSc, 44; Pa State Univ, MS, 57, PhD(petrol eng), 60. *Prof Exp:* Anal chemist, Govt India, 44-46; res chemist, Alembic Chem Works, India, 47-49; prof chem, Petlad Col, India, 49-52; sr sci asst phys chem, Nat Chem Lab India, Poona, 52-54; res engr, Gulf Res & Develop Co, 59-61; asst prof petrol technol & chmn dept, Indian Sch Mines & Appl Geol, Dhanbad, 61-63; vis assoc prof petrol eng, Stanford Univ, 63-66; res engr, Continental Oil Co, Okla, 66-68 & IIT Res Inst, 69-72; environ protection engr, Ill Environ Protection Agency, 74-76. *Concurrent Pos:* Adj assoc prof petrol eng, WVa Univ, Morgantown, 77- *Mem:* AAAS; Am Chem Soc; Soc Petrol Engrs; Am Water Works Asn. *Res:* Preparative electrochemistry; education; surface and colloid chemistry relating to petroleum recovery and multiphase fluid flow through porous media; enhanced petroleum recovery; surface and colloid chemistry. *Mailing Add:* 1519 W Polk St Chicago IL 60607-3120

KAMATH, SAVITRI KRISHNA, BIOCHEMISTRY, CLINICAL NUTRITION. *Current Pos:* from asst prof to assoc prof, 72-81, PROF NUTRIT, UNIV ILL MED CTR, 81-, DEPT HEAD, 79- *Personal Data:* b Kanhangad, India, Sept 22, 30; US citizen; m 69. *Educ:* Bombay Univ, BSc, 50; Univ Baroda, MSc, 63; Iowa State Univ, PhD(nutrit), 67. *Prof Exp:* Lectr chem, St Agnes Col, India, 51-58; reader nutrit, Univ Baroda, 67-69; res biochemist, Hektoen Med Res Inst, Chicago, 71-72. *Mem:* Am Dietetic Asn; Soc Nutrit Educ; NY Acad Sci; fel Am Col Nutrit; Am Inst Nutrit. *Res:* Ascorbic acid, lipid metabolism; nutrition and cancer; nutritional assessment of population groups; dietetic education and practice. *Mailing Add:* Dept Nutrit & Med Diet M/C 518 Univ Ill 808 S Wood St Rm 167 Chicago IL 60612-3742. *Fax:* 312-413-0319

KAMATH, VENKATESH, GAS CHROMATOGRAPHY-MASS SPECTROSCOPY ANALYSIS OF FRAGRANCES & FLAVORS, GAS CHROMATOGRAPHY ANALYSIS OF FRAGRANCES & FLAVORS. *Current Pos:* ANALYTICAL RES DIR, ROBERTET FRAGRANCES, 91- *Personal Data:* b Nerlkatte, India, Mar 28, 36; m, Ajita Nayak; c Arun, Vanita (Brauer) & Sangeeta (Tyerech). *Educ:* Madras Univ, India, BS, 57. *Prof Exp:* Prod chemist, Calico Chems, India, 57-60; prod supvr, Union Carbide, India, 61-67; technician, Shawinigan Chems, Can, 67-69; asst chemist, Ciba-Geigy Ltd, NY, 69-73; sr chemist, Int Flavors & Fragrances, NJ, 73-85; tech dir, J Manheimer Inc, NY, 85-87 & Takasago Inc, 87-91. *Mem:* Am Chem Soc. *Res:* Analysis of essential oils; granted patents on sandalwood chemicals. *Mailing Add:* 125 Bauer Dr Oakland NJ 07436

KAMATH, YASHAVANTH KATAPADY, PHYSICAL CHEMISTRY, POLYMER CHEMISTRY. *Current Pos:* fel, 72-74, staff scientist, 74-76, sr scientist, 76-87, PRIN SCIENTIST, TEXTILE FINISHING, TEXTILE RES INST, 87- *Personal Data:* b Katapady, India, Apr 15, 38; m 72; c 1. *Educ:* Univ Bombay, BSc, 59 & 61, MSc, 64; Univ Conn, PhD(phys chem), 73. *Honors & Awards:* Lit Award, Soc Cosmetic Chemists. *Prof Exp:* Assoc lectr plastic technol, Dept Chem Technol, Univ Bombay, 63-66. *Mem:* Am Chem Soc; Fiber Soc. *Res:* Surface chemical properties of human hair; effect of polymers and surfactants on the surface wettability of human hair; fractography of human hair; compressibility of fiber bundles; environmental fading of dyes in nylon; microspectrophotocetry of dyes in monofilaments; mechanisms of formaldehyde release in durable press fabric; finish distribution in fibers and textiles. *Mailing Add:* Textile Res Inst 601 Prospect Ave PO Box 625 Princeton NJ 08540-0625

KAMB, WALTER BARCLAY, MINERALOGY, GLACIOLOGY. *Current Pos:* From asst prof to assoc prof geol, Calif Inst Technol, 56-62, chmn, Div Geol & Planetary Sci, 72-83, vpres & provost, 87-89, PROF GEOL & GEOPHYS, CALIF INST TECHNOL, 62- *Personal Data:* b San Jose, Calif, Dec 17, 31; m 57; c 4. *Educ:* Calif Inst Technol, BS, 52, PhD(geol), 56. *Honors & Awards:* MSA Award, Mineral Soc Am, 68; Seligman Award, Int Glaciol Soc, 77. *Concurrent Pos:* Guggenheim Mem Found fel, 60; Sloan fel, 63. *Mem:* Nat Acad Sci; Geol Soc Am; Am Geophys Union; Mineral Soc Am; Am Asn Petrol Geologists; AAAS; fel Am Acad Arts & Sci. *Res:* Crystallography; tectonophysics; structural geology and petrology; glaciology; mineralogy and x-ray crystallography; crystal optics. *Mailing Add:* Div Geol & Planetary Sci Calif Inst Technol 1201 E California Blvd Pasadena CA 91109

KAMBARA, GEORGE KIYOSHI, ophthalmology, for more information see previous edition

KAMBAYASHI, TATSUJI, ALGEBRAIC GEOMETRY. *Current Pos:* PROF MATH, TOKYO DENKI UNIV, 87- *Personal Data:* b Kyoto, Japan, Nov 8, 33; m 63, Mami Yasuda. *Educ:* Univ Tokyo, ScB, 57; Northwestern Univ, PhD(math), 62. *Prof Exp:* Instr math, Brown Univ, 61-63; lectr, Ind Univ, 63-64, asst prof, 64-67; from assoc prof to prof math, Northern Ill Univ, 67-87. *Concurrent Pos:* Mem res staff, Res Ctr Physics & Math, Pisa, Italy, 65-67; res mem, Res Inst Math Sci, Kyoto Univ, Japan, 72-73; res grant, NSF, 73-80. *Mem:* Am Math Soc; Math Soc Japan. *Res:* Algebraic groups. *Mailing Add:* Math Sci Dept Tokyo Denki Univ Hiki-gun Saitama 350-03 Japan. *Fax:* 813-3322-0801; *E-Mail:* tac@r.dendai.ac.jp

KAMBOH, MOHAMMAD ILYAS, GENETICS OF CARDIOVASCULAR DISEASE. *Current Pos:* Res assoc, Univ Pittsburgh, 85-86, asst prof, 87-91, assoc prof, 91-96, PROF, HUMAN GENETICS, UNIV PITTSBURGH, 97- *Personal Data:* b Punjab, Pakistan, Nov 1, 56; US citizen; m 84, Shaheen Anwar; c Hafsa I, Sundas I & Ali M. *Educ:* Univ Punjab, BS, 76, MS, 79; Australian Nat Univ, PhD(human genetics), 84. *Concurrent Pos:* Prin investr, NIH, 88-92 & 91-96, Nat Dairy Prom Res Bd, 90-, Lupus Found Am, 93-95; mem, Pittsburgh Cancer Inst, Nutrit Res Sci & Nat Dairy Prom & Res Bd, 93-96. *Mem:* AAAS; Am Soc Human Genetics; Human Genetics Soc Australasia; Am Soc Phys Anthrop; Am Heart Asn; Int Electrophoresis Soc; NY Acad Sci. *Res:* Evaluate the role of genes in determining risk for cardiovascular disease and Alzheimer's disease in the general population; author of 125 publications. *Mailing Add:* 1265 Cardinal Dr Pittsburgh PA 15243. *Fax:* 412-383-9844; *E-Mail:* ikamboh@helix.pitt.edu

KAMBOUR, ROGER PEABODY, PHYSICAL CHEMISTRY, POLYMER PHYSICS. *Current Pos:* CUMIRP RES PROF, POLYMER SCI & ENG DEPT, UNIV MASS, AMHERST, 94- *Personal Data:* b Wilmington, Mass, Apr 1, 32; m 58, 84, Barbara J Vivier; c Annaliese S, Christian R & Joshua V. *Educ:* Amherst Col, BA, 54; Univ NH, PhD(chem), 60. *Honors & Awards:* Union Carbide Chem Award, Am Chem Soc, 68; Ford High Polymer Physics Prize, Am Phys Soc, 85. *Prof Exp:* Res assoc, Gen Elec Res & Develop Ctr, 60-70 & 75-94, mgr polymer studies unit, 70-74. *Mem:* Nat Acad Eng; fel Am Phys Soc; Am Chem Soc. *Res:* Diffusion of gases and vapors in polymers; polymer crazing and fracture; properties of block polymers; crystallization; polymer flame retardance; polymer blend thermodynamics; mobility and toughness in plasticized resins; properties of reactive cyclic oligomers and resultant polymers. *Mailing Add:* Corp Res & Develop Gen Elec Co PO Box 8 Schenectady NY 12301. *E-Mail:* kambour@crd.ge.com

KAMBYSELLIS, MICHAEL PANAGIOTIS, DEVELOPMENTAL GENETICS. *Current Pos:* asst prof, NY Univ, 71-73, assoc prof develop biol, 73-80, PROF BIOL, NY UNIV, 80- *Personal Data:* b Antissa, Greece, Mar 1, 35. *Educ:* Nat Univ Athens, BSc, 60; Yale Univ, MS, 65; Univ Tex, PhD(zool), 67. *Prof Exp:* Res asst genetics, Univ Tex, 65-67, res assoc, 67-68; res fel insect physiol, Harvard Univ, 68-70, lectr biol, 71. *Concurrent Pos:* Vis prof, Athens Univ, Greece, 74-75. *Mem:* AAAS; Genetics Soc Am; Am Inst Biol Sci; NY Acad Sci; Soc Develop Biol. *Res:* Physiological genetics; Drosophila genetics and evolution; insect tissue transplantations; Drosophila ovarian development; insect tissue cultures; hormonal control of insect reproduction. *Mailing Add:* Dept Biol NY Univ 100 Washington Sq E New York NY 10003-6688

KAMEGAI, MINAO, COMPUTATIONAL PHYSICS. *Current Pos:* sr physicist, 66-93, CONSULT, LAWRENCE LIVERMORE LAB, 93- *Personal Data:* b Koshu, Korea, July 7, 32; US citizen; m 85, Meera McCuaig; c Stephani M & Sharon A. *Educ:* Univ Hawaii, BA, 57; Univ Chicago, MS, 60, PhD(physics), 63. *Prof Exp:* Res assoc nuclear physics, Enrico Fermi Inst, Univ Chicago, 63; physicist, Knolls Atomic Power Lab, Gen Elec Co, 63-66. *Concurrent Pos:* Vis scientist, Nat Chem Lab, Tsukuba Res Ctr, Tsukuba City, Ibaraki, Japan; consult, Kamegai & Assocs. *Mem:* Am Phys Soc; Sigma Xi. *Res:* Theoretical and computational physics; materials science, hydrodynamics and laser optics; computer modeling in shock hydrodynamics. *Mailing Add:* 908 Florence Rd Livermore CA 94550. *Fax:* 510-455-5247

KAMEGO, ALBERT AMIL, PHYSICAL ORGANIC CHEMISTRY. *Current Pos:* sr eng specialist, 77-94, LORAL VOUGHT SYSTS, CORE LABS, INC, 85- *Personal Data:* b Detroit, Mich, June 11, 41; m 73. *Educ:* Wayne State Univ, BS, 64; Calif State Univ, Long Beach, MS, 68; Univ Calif, Santa Barbara, PhD(chem), 74. *Prof Exp:* Chemist paints, Ford Motor Co, 65-67; from teaching asst chem to staff res assoc, Univ Calif, Santa Barbara, 68-73; fel chem, State Univ NY Buffalo, 73-75; lectr chem, Univ Mont, 75-76; instr chem, Univ Tex, Arlington, 76-77. *Mem:* Am Chem Soc. *Mailing Add:* 832 Spring Brook Dr Bedford TX 76021-4304

KAMEL, HYMAN, MATHEMATICS. *Current Pos:* PROF MATH, WIDENER COL, 67- *Personal Data:* b Philadelphia, Pa, Dec 2, 19; m 41, 68; c 2. *Educ:* Univ Pa, AB, 41, NY Univ, MS, 44; Univ Pa, PhD(math), 52. *Prof Exp:* Instr math, Univ Pa, 50-52 & Cornell Univ, 52-54; asst prof, Rensselaer Polytech Inst, 54-61; assoc prof, Howard Univ, 61-67. *Mem:* Am Math Soc; Math Asn Am; Sigma Xi. *Res:* Functional analysis. *Mailing Add:* 2316 Waverly St Philadelphia PA 19146

KAMEMOTO, FRED ISAMU, ZOOLOGY, COMPARATIVE ENDOCRINOLOGY. *Current Pos:* from asst prof to prof, 62-94, EMER PROF ZOOL, UNIV HAWAII, 95- *Personal Data:* b Honolulu, Hawaii, Mar 8, 28; m 63, Alice T Asayama; c Kenneth, Garett & Janice. *Educ:* George Washington Univ, AB, 50, MS, 51; Purdue Univ, PhD(zool), 54. *Prof Exp:* Res assoc zoophysiol, Wash State Col, 57-59; asst prof zool, Univ Mo, 59-62. *Concurrent Pos:* Vis res scholar, Ocean Res Inst, Univ Tokyo, 68-69; vis scholar, Dept Biol, Wesleyan Univ, Middletown, Conn, 75-76; vis sr scientist, Dept Fisheries, Nihon Univ, Tokyo, 86; vis foreign researcher, Trop Biosphere Res Ctr, Univ Ryukyus, Japan, 94. *Mem:* AAAS; Am Soc Zoologists; Sigma Xi; Zool Soc Japan. *Res:* Neurosecretion and osmoregulation; crustacean biology. *Mailing Add:* Dept Zool Univ Hawaii 2538 The Mall Honolulu HI 96822. *Fax:* 808-956-9812

KAMEMOTO, HARUYUKI, HORTICULTURE. *Current Pos:* From asst horticulturist to horticulturist, 50-86, prof hort & chmn dept, 69-75, EMER PROF HORT, UNIV HAWAII, 86- *Personal Data:* b Honolulu, Hawaii, Jan 18, 22; m 52; c 3. *Educ:* Univ Hawaii, BS, 44, MS, 47; Cornell Univ, PhD, 50. *Honors & Awards:* Gold Medal, Malayan Orchid Soc, 63; Norman Jay Colman Award, 77; Orchid Soc Thailand Medal of Honor, 78; Alex Laurie Award, 82; Childers Award, 84; Gold Medal, Am Orchid Soc, 89. *Concurrent Pos:* Fulbright award, 56-57; consult, Food & Agr Orgn, UN, 71, 80. *Mem:* Fel AAAS; fel Am Soc Hort Sci; fel Am Orchid Soc; Int Aroid Soc; Am Genetic Asn; Bot Soc Am. *Res:* Cytogenetics and breeding of tropical ornamentals. *Mailing Add:* 3246 Lower Rd Honolulu HI 96822

KAMEN, DEAN, ELECTROMECHANICAL ENGINEERING. *Current Pos:* PRES & OWNER, DEKA RES & DEVELOP CORP. *Personal Data:* b Apr, 1951. *Hon Degrees:* DSc, Worcester Polytech Inst, 92, NH Col, 97. *Honors & Awards:* Hoover Medal, Am Soc Mech Engrs, 95; John W Hyatt Award, Soc Plastics Engrs, 96. *Prof Exp:* Founder, Auto Syringe Inc, 76; owner & chmn, Enstrom Helicopter Corp, 85-90. *Concurrent Pos:* Chmn, Teletrol Energy Syst, Inc; founder, Sci Enrichment Encounters, 85, Inspiration & Recognition Sci & Technol, 89, US First, 89. *Mem:* Nat Acad Eng; fel Am Inst Med & Biol Engrs. *Res:* Inventing and commercializing biomedical devices and fluid measurement and control systems; popularizing engineering among young people; holds more than 30 patents. *Mailing Add:* Deka Res & Develop 340 Commercial St Manchester NH 03101

KAMEN, EDWARD WALTER, ENGINEERING, MATHEMATICS. *Current Pos:* asst prof, 71-76, ASSOC PROF ELEC ENG, GA INST TECHNOL, 76-; AT DEPT ELEC ENG, UNIV FLA, GAINESVILLE. *Personal Data:* b Mansfield, Ohio, Oct 2, 45. *Educ:* Ga Inst Technol, BEE, 67; Stanford Univ, MS, 69, PhD(elec eng), 71. *Prof Exp:* Engr, Argo Systs Inc, Calif, 70-71. *Concurrent Pos:* NSF res initiation grant, Ga Inst Technol, 72-74; res specialist, Inst Res Info & Automatic Control, France, 72- *Mem:* AAAS; Inst Elec & Electronics Engrs. *Res:* Mathematical system theory; network theory; receiver systems. *Mailing Add:* Elec Eng Dept Ga Inst Technol Atlanta GA 30332

KAMEN, GARY P, MOTOR CONTROL, NEUROMUSCULAR PHYSIOLOGY. *Current Pos:* ASSOC PROF, BOSTON UNIV, 88- *Educ:* Univ Mass, PhD(exercise sci), 79. *Prof Exp:* Assoc prof, Ind Univ. *Mem:* AAAS; fel Am Col Sports Med; Int Soc Biomech; Soc Neurosci; Sigma Xi; Am Physiol Soc. *Res:* Neuromuscular physiology and motor control with applications in gerontology, sports medicine and rehabilitation medicine; consulting in sports medicine; exercise science. *Mailing Add:* Dept Exercise Sci Massachusetts Univ Amherst MA 01003. *Fax:* 413-545-2906

KAMEN, MARTIN DAVID, PHYSICAL BIOCHEMISTRY. *Current Pos:* prof, 74-78, EMER PROF BIOL SCI, UNIV SOUTHERN CALIF, 78-; EMER PROF CHEM, UNIV CALIF, SAN DIEGO, 78- *Personal Data:* b Toronto, Ont, Aug 27, 13; nat US; wid; c 1. *Educ:* Univ Chicago, BS, 33, PhD(phys chem), 36. *Hon Degrees:* Dr, Univ Paris, 69; ScD, Univ Chicago, 69, Wash Univ, 77, Univ Ill, Chicago Circle, 78, Univ Freiburg, Ger, 79 & Brandeis Univ, 88. *Honors & Awards:* Am Chem Soc Award, 63; C F Kettering Award, Am Soc Plant Physiol, 69; Merck Award, Am Soc Biol Chemists, 82; Einstein Award, 96; Fermi Award, 96. *Prof Exp:* Fel nuclear chem, Radiation Lab, Univ Calif, 37-39, res assoc, 39-41; marine test engr, Kaiser Cargo, Calif, 44-45; assoc prof biochem, Wash Univ, 45-46, assoc prof chem & chemist, Mallinckrodt Inst, 45-57; prof biochem, Brandeis Univ, 57-61; prof chem, Univ Calif, San Diego, 61-74, chmn dept, 71-73. *Concurrent Pos:* NSF sr fel, 56; Guggenheim fel, 56 & 72; Fogarty scholar, 88-89. *Mem:* Nat Acad Sci; Am Chem Soc; Am Soc Biol Chemists; Am Acad Arts & Sci; fel Am Inst Chem; Am Philos Soc. *Res:* Application of biophysical chemical methods, including isotopic tracer methodology, to study bacterial metabolism; energy storage, especially in photosynthesis; comparative biochemical iron proteins. *Mailing Add:* 300 Hot Springs Rd Apt B-58 Montecito CA 93108

KAMENETZ, HERMAN LEO, physical medicine & rehabilitation, for more information see previous edition

KAMENEVA, MARINA VITALY, ENGINEERING. *Current Pos:* vis prof, 91-96, ASST PROF SURG, UNIV PITTSBURGH, 96- *Personal Data:* m 66, Boris A Kushner; c Yulia & Alexander. *Educ:* Moscow State Univ, MS, 68, PhD(fluid mech), 72. *Prof Exp:* Jr res fel, Res Inst Mech, Moscow State Univ, USSR, 68-75, sr investr, 75-89. *Mem:* Biomed Eng Soc; Am Soc Artificial Internal Organs. *Res:* Hemodynamic and hemorheological investigations concentrating on the study of mechanical properties of blood in cardiovascular patient and artificial heart recipients blood trauma in heart-assist devices and methods of its reduction; author of over 80 publications. *Mailing Add:* Univ Pittsburgh Med Ctr 300 Technol Dr Pittsburgh PA 15219. *Fax:* 412-647-6059; *E-Mail:* marina@vms.cis.pitt.edu

KAMEN-KAYE, MAURICE, GLOBAL PALEOGEOGRAPHY. *Current Pos:* CONSULT GEOLOGIST, 68- *Personal Data:* b London, Eng, Aug, 17, 05; m 38, Dorothy Allers. *Educ:* Royal Col Sci, London, BSc, ARES, 26; Royal Sch Mines, London, ARSM(petrol geol), 29. *Prof Exp:* Explor geologist, Caracas Petrol Corp, Venezuela, 30-40, chief geologist, 40-50; consult geologist, US & Canada, 50-53; chief geologist, Sedimentary Sect, Province Sask, Can, 54; explor res geologist, Conorada Petrol Corp, NY, 65-67; explor res geologist, Amerada Petrol Corp, Tulsa, 65-67. *Mem:* Fel Geol Soc Am; Am Asn Petrol Geologists; Soc Explor Geophys. *Res:* Architecture & petroleum productivity of sedimentary basins; global paleogeography; petroleum geology of African borderlands of the Indian Ocean. *Mailing Add:* One Waterhouse St Apt 5 Cambridge MA 02138

KAMENTSKY, LOUIS A, BIOPHYSICS, PATHOLOGY. *Current Pos:* pres, 88-92, CHMN & CHIEF SCIENTIST, COMPUCYTE CORP, 92- *Personal Data:* b Newark, NJ, July 28, 30; m 55; c Lee, Howard & Ellen. *Educ:* Newark Col Eng, BS, 52; Cornell Univ, PhD(eng physics), 56. *Hon Degrees:* Dr, NJ Inst Tech, 92. *Prof Exp:* Res asst physics, Brookhaven Nat Lab, 51; res asst eng physics, Cornell Univ, 52-54; mem staff, Electronics Res Lab, Columbia Univ, 54-55; mem staff, Bell Tel Labs, Inc, 56-60 & Watson Lab, IBM Corp, 60-68; pres, Bio/Physics Systs, Inc, 68-76; vpres res & develop, Ortho Instruments, 76-80, vpres res, Ortho Diagnostics Systs, 80-88; dir, Cambridge Res Lab, 83-88. *Concurrent Pos:* Physicist, Res Lab, US Steel Corp, 53; vis scientist, Karolinska Inst, 66; adj assoc prof, Dept Path, Med Ctr, NY Univ, 69-73; consult, Dept Path, Mem Hosp for Cancer, NY, 73-93; sr res scientist, Res Lab Electronics, Mass Inst Technol, 80-88. *Mem:* AAAS; Inst Elec & Electronics Engrs; NY Acad Sci; Int Soc Alternative & Augmentative Commun. *Res:* Information and computer theories; solid state physics; optics; pattern recognition; medical instrumentation; research administration; analytic cytometry. *Mailing Add:* 180 Beacon St Boston MA 02116. *E-Mail:* lakam@shore.net

KAMIEN, C ZELMAN, mechanical engineering, for more information see previous edition

KAMIEN, ETHEL N, PLANT PHYSIOLOGY, HUMAN SEXUALITY. *Current Pos:* from instr to assoc prof biol, 60-66, chmn dept biol & phys sci, 65-75, PROF BIOL, UNIV LOWELL-NORTH CAMPUS, 66- *Personal Data:* b New York, NY, July 1, 30; m 55; c 2. *Educ:* Brooklyn Col, BA, 50; Univ Wis, MS, 52, PhD(bot), 54. *Prof Exp:* Asst bot, Univ Wis, 50-54; instr hort, Purdue Univ, 54-58. *Concurrent Pos:* Coop teacher, Ed Serv, Inc, 65-; mem, US Sex Info & Educ Coun. *Mem:* Am Soc Plant Physiol; Am Inst Biol Sci; Am Asn Sex Educrs, Counrs & Therapists; Sigma Xi; AAAS. *Res:* Chemical control of plant growth; plant tissue culture. *Mailing Add:* 29 Arbutus Ave Chelmsford MA 01824

KAMIL, ALAN CURTIS, ANIMAL BEHAVIOR, BEHAVIORAL ECOLOGY. *Current Pos:* PROF BIOL & PSYCHOL, SCH BIOL SCI, UNIV NEBR, 92- *Personal Data:* b Bronx, NY, Nov 20, 41; m 63; c 2. *Educ:* Hofstra Univ, BA, 63; Univ Wis-Madison, MS, 66, PhD(psychol), 67. *Prof Exp:* From asst prof to assoc prof, Univ Mass, Amherst, 67-79, prof psychol & zool, 79-92. *Concurrent Pos:* Vis assoc prof psychol, Univ Calif, Berkeley, 76-77; prin investr grants, NSF, 71- & NIH, 78-79 & 88- *Mem:* Animal Behav Soc; Ecol Soc Am; Am Ornithologists Union; fel Am Psychol Asn. *Res:* Mechanisms of foraging behavior. *Mailing Add:* 3210 S 27th St Lincoln NE 68502

KAMILLI, DIANA CHAPMAN, ARCHAEOMETRY, PETROLOGY. *Current Pos:* INDEPENDENT CONSULT GEOL, ARCHEOL GEOL & MAT ANAL, 83- *Personal Data:* b New York, NY, Sept 5, 41; m 69; c 2. *Educ:* Vassar Col, BA, 63; Rutgers Univ, MS, 66, PhD(igneous petrol, metamorphic petrol), 68. *Prof Exp:* Instr geol, Vassar Col, 68; asst prof mineral, City Col New York, 68-69; asst prof geol, Wellesley Col, 69-75, chmn dept geol, 69-74; res assoc archeol mat anal, Mass Inst Technol & res fel archeol mat anal, Harvard Univ Peabody Mus, 75-77; res assoc archeol mat anal, Univ Colo Mus, 77-83. *Concurrent Pos:* NSF grant, Colo Plateau, 71; Fisher fel fund & fac grants, Wellesley Col, 71-72; consult, Sardis Expedition, Harvard Univ, 74-76, Amax Molybdenum Co, 76-77 & 79-80; NSF res grant, 75. *Mem:* Geol Soc Am; Mineral Soc Am; Soc Am Archaeol. *Res:* Petrology and geochemistry of granitic and metagranitic rocks, New Jersey, Ontario and Colorado; mineralogic and chemical analysis of ancient mesopotamian, North and Central American ceramics; geochemistry and correlation of Ubaid, Samarran and Halaf ceramics, Mesopotamia. *Mailing Add:* 5050 N Siesta Dr Tucson AZ 85750

KAMILLI, ROBERT JOSEPH, ECONOMIC GEOLOGY, GEOCHEMISTRY. *Current Pos:* geologist, US Geol Surv Mission, Jeddah, Saudi Arabia, 83-87, mission chief geologist, 87-89, res geologist, 89-96, SCIENTIST-IN-CHARGE, SW FIELD OFF, US GEOL SURV, TUCSON, ARIZ, 96- *Personal Data:* b Philadelphia, Pa, June 14, 47; m 69, Diana F Chapman; c Ann Chapman & Robert Chapman. *Educ:* Rutgers Univ, BA, 69; Harvard Univ, AM, 71, PhD(geol), 76. *Prof Exp:* geologist, AMAX Inc, 76-79, asst resident geologist, 79-80, proj geologist, 80-83; adj prof, Univ Colo, Boulder, 81-83. *Concurrent Pos:* Consult geologist, Huampar Mines, 73-76 & Buenaventura Mines, 75-76; secy, Soc Econ Geologists, Int Exchange Lectr Comt, 94-; counr, Ariz Geol Soc, 94- *Mem:* Fel Geol Soc Am; AAAS; fel Soc Econ Geologists; Soc Mining Engrs. *Res:* Investigation of the origin of vein and intrusion-related metal deposits, especially molybdenum, tin, tungsten, gold and silver; emphasis on the geochemistry of such ore deposits. *Mailing Add:* 5050 N Siesta Dr Tucson AZ 85750-9652. *Fax:* 520-670-5571; *E-Mail:* bkamilli@strider.swfo.arizona.edu

KAMINER, BENJAMIN, PHYSIOLOGY. *Current Pos:* PROF PHYSIOL & CHMN DEPT, SCH MED, BOSTON UNIV, 70- *Personal Data:* b Slonim, Poland, May 1, 24; m 48; c 2. *Educ:* Univ Witwatersrand, MB, BCh, 46; Royal Col Physicians & Surgeons, dipl child health, 50. *Prof Exp:* Intern med, surg & pediat, Johannesburg Hosp, SAfrica, 47-48; house physician & registr pediat, Edgeware Hosp, London, Eng, 49-50; res asst endocrinol, Postgrad Med Sch, Univ London, 50-51; from lectr to sr lectr physiol, Med Sch, Univ Witwatersrand, 51-59; investr muscle, Inst Muscle Res, 59-69; lectr anat, Harvard Med Sch, 69-70. *Concurrent Pos:* Rockefeller Found fel, 59-60. *Mem:* Soc Gen Physiol; Biophys Soc; Am Soc Cell Biol; Am Physiol Soc; Corp Marine Biol Lab. *Res:* Physiology and biochemistry of muscle; endoplasmic reticulum and intracellular calcium regulation. *Mailing Add:* Dept Physiol Boston Univ Sch Med 80 E Concord St Boston MA 02118-2394. *Fax:* 617-638-4253

KAMINETZKY, HAROLD ALEXANDER, OBSTETRICS & GYNECOLOGY. *Current Pos:* RETIRED. *Personal Data:* b Chicago, Ill, Sept 6, 23; m 57; c 2. *Educ:* Univ Ill, BS, 48, MD, 50; Am Bd Obstet & Gynec, dipl. *Prof Exp:* From instr to prof, Col Med, Univ Ill, 54-68; prof obstet & Gynec, chmn Dept Col Med & Dent NJ, Newark, 68-85, from actg dean to dean, 72-74; dir, Pract Activ, Am Col Obstet & Gynec, 85-94. *Concurrent Pos:* Mem cancer adv comt, Chicago Bd Health; ed, Int J Gynaecology & Obstet, 78; prog dir, Greater Newark Family Planning Prog, 70-81; pres, Am Col Obstet & Gynecologists, 78; pres, 10th World Cong of Obstet & Gynecol, 82. *Mem:* AMA; Am Col Obstet & Gynec; Am Col Surg; Sigma Xi; Am Gynecologists & Obstetricians Soc. *Res:* Experimental dysplasia and carcinogenesis of the uterine cervix; maternal nutrition; vitamin profiles of mothers and newborns at parituition; nutrition during pregnancy. *Mailing Add:* ACOG 409 12th St SW Washington DC 20024

KAMINKER, JEROME ALVIN, TOPOLOGY, MATHEMATICAL ANALYSIS. *Current Pos:* from asst prof to assoc prof, 73-79, PROF MATH, IND UNIV-PURDUE UNIV, 79- *Personal Data:* b Chicago, Ill, May 10, 41; m 67; c 2. *Educ:* Univ Calif, Berkeley, BA, 63; Univ Calif, Los Angeles, MA, 65, PhD(math), 68. *Prof Exp:* Asst prof math, Ind Univ, Bloomington, 68-73. *Concurrent Pos:* Vis prof, Univ Calif, Los Angeles, 83; mem, Math Sci Res Inst, 84-85. *Mem:* Am Math Soc; Sigma Xi. *Res:* Development of relations between algebraic topology and functional analysis; application of K-theory to the theory of linear operators on Hilbert space. *Mailing Add:* Ind Univ-Purdue Univ Indianapolis IN 46202-3216

KAMINOW, IVAN PAUL, FIBER OPTICS, SEMICONDUCTOR LASERS. *Current Pos:* mem tech staff, Bell Labs, Inc, 54-84, DEPT HEAD, AT&T BELL LABS, INC, 84- *Personal Data:* b Union City, NJ, Mar 3, 30; m 52; c 3. *Educ:* Union Univ NY, BS, 52; Univ Calif, Los Angeles, MS, 54; Harvard Univ, AM, 57, PhD(appl physics). 60. *Honors & Awards:* Quantum Electronics Award, Inst Elec & Electronics Engrs, 83; Charles Hard Townes Award, Am Optical Soc, 95, Tyndall Award, 97. *Prof Exp:* Mem tech staff, Hughes Aircraft Co, 52-54. *Concurrent Pos:* Vis lectr, Princeton Univ, 68, & Univ Calif, Berkeley, 77; mem, Eval Panel, Optical Physics Div, Nat Acad Sci-Nat Bur Stand, 72-75, Ctr for Electronics & Elec Eng, 84-87; assoc ed, J Quantum Electronics, 77-83; adj prof, Columbia Univ, 86; vis prof, Univ Tokyo, 90. *Mem:* Nat Acad Eng; fel Am Phys Soc; fel Optical Soc Am; fel Inst Elec & Electronics Engrs; Am Bd Laser Surg. *Res:* Microwave antennas; ferrites; high pressure physics; ferroelectrics; optical lasers and communication techniques; light modulation; Raman scattering; photopolymers; integrated optics; optical fibers; semiconductor lasers; photonic networks. *Mailing Add:* Lucent Technol/Bell Labs 791 Holmdel Rd Holmdel NJ 07733. *Fax:* 732-888-7007; *E-Mail:* ipk@hoh.1.att.com

KAMINS, THEODORE I, SOLID-STATE ELECTRONICS, SILICON INTEGRATED CIRCUITS. *Current Pos:* mem tech staff, 74-81, proj leader elec eng, 81-95, DEPT SCIENTIST, HEWLETT-PACKARD LAB, 95- *Personal Data:* b San Francisco, Calif, Nov 11, 41. *Educ:* Univ Calif, Berkeley, BS, 63, MS, 64, PhD(elec eng), 68. *Honors & Awards:* Electronics Div Award, Electrochem Soc, 89. *Prof Exp:* Act asst prof elec eng, Univ Calif, Berkeley, 68-69; mem res staff, Fairchild Semiconductor, 69-74. *Concurrent Pos:* Vis lectr, Dept Elec Eng, Stanford Univ, 74; consult, Stanford Electronic Lab, Stanford Univ, 75-82; vis scholar, Ctr Integrated Systs, Stanford Univ, 86-87, consult prof, Dept Elec Eng, 90- *Mem:* Fel Inst Elec & Electronics Engrs; fel Electrochem Soc. *Res:* Research and development of materials and devices for silicon integrated circuits; especially, polycrystalline silicon, silicon-on-insulator, photodiode arrays, epitaxial techniques, silicon-germanium devices; author of books on device electronics and polycrystalline silicon. *Mailing Add:* Hewlett-Packard Co PO Box 10350 Palo Alto CA 94303-0867

KAMINSKAS, EDVARDAS, PHARMOCOLOGY, MOLECULAR BIOLOGY. *Current Pos:* PHYSICIAN-IN-CHIEF, HEBREW REHAB CTR AGED, 81- *Personal Data:* b Kaunas, Lithuania, Sept 12, 35; US citizen; m 65. *Educ:* Seton Hall Univ, NJ, AB, 55; Sch Med, Yale Univ, MD, 59. *Prof Exp:* Intern & fel hemat, Michael Reese Hosp, Chicago, Ill, 61-63; resident med, Vet Admin Res Hosp, Chicago, Ill, 61-63; chief med, US Air Force Hosp, 63-65; res fel, Mass Inst Technol, 65-68; from instr to asst prof med, Harvard Med Sch, Beth Israel Hosp, 68-74; from assoc prof to prof, Univ Wis, Mt Sinai Med Ctr, 74-81; assoc prof med, Harvard Med Sch, Beth Israel Hosp, 81- *Mem:* Am Soc Biol Chemists; Am Asn Cancer Res; Am Fedn Clin Res; Geront Soc Am; Am Geriat Soc; AAAS. *Res:* Regulation of tumor cell growth; effects of anti-neoplastic agents on tumor cells; molecular biology of Alzheimer's disease cells. *Mailing Add:* Hebrew Rehabil Ctr Aged Harvard Univ 1200 Centre St Boston MA 02131-1011. *Fax:* 617-325-8069

KAMINSKI, DONALD LEON, SURGERY. *Current Pos:* Asst prof, 71-75, assoc prof, 75-80, PROF SURG, ST LOUIS UNIV, 80- *Personal Data:* b Elba, Nebr, Nov 9, 40; m 65; c 4. *Educ:* Creighton Univ, BS, 62, MD, 66. *Mem:* Am Physiol Soc; Am Gastroenterol Soc; Soc Univ Surgeons; Asn Acad Surg; Am Col Surgeons. *Res:* Gastrointestinal physiology, studying the hormonal control of hepatic bile flow. *Mailing Add:* Dept Surg St Louis Univ Med Ctr 3635 Vista Grand Blvd PO Box 15250 St Louis MO 63110-0250. *Fax:* 573-771-1945

KAMINSKI, EDWARD JOZEF, CHEMISTRY. *Current Pos:* res technologist, Dent Sch, Northwestern Univ, 56-60, res assoc path, 64-67, asst prof, 67-71, assoc prof, 71-79, PROF PATH, DENT & MED SCH, NORTHWESTERN UNIV, 79- *Personal Data:* b Torun, Poland, Mar 24, 26; US citizen; m 51, Krystyna; c Norbert E & Yvonne K. *Educ:* Northwestern Univ, PhB, 60, PhD(chem), 64, Am Bd Toxicol, dipl. *Prof Exp:* Res technologist, Royal Cancer Hosp, London, Eng, 51-53; res asst path, Mt Sinai Hosp, Toronto, Can, 53-56. *Concurrent Pos:* Consult toxicology, 64- *Mem:* Soc Toxicol; Am Chem Soc; Inst Biomed Sci; AAAS. *Res:* Toxicology of materials used in the human body and the nature of the foreign body reaction; study on the mechanism of absorption of substances from the environment. *Mailing Add:* Dept Path Northwestern Univ Dent & Med Sch Chicago IL 60611-3010. *Fax:* 773-508-8240

KAMINSKI, JAMES JOSEPH, MEDICINAL & THEORETICAL CHEMISTRY. *Current Pos:* res chemist, Schering Corp, 78-80, sect leader, 80-91, SR PRIN SCIENTIST, SCHERING PLOUGH CORP, 92- *Personal Data:* b Buffalo, NY, June 5, 47; m 68, Yvonne Buchina. *Educ:* State Univ NY Col Fredonia, BS, 69; Univ NH, PhD(org chem), 72. *Prof Exp:* Sr res chemist, Interx Res Corp, 72-78. *Concurrent Pos:* Adj assoc prof, Ctr Drug Discovery, Univ Fla, Gainesville, Fla; chair-elect, Med & Natural Prod Chem, Am Asn Pharmaceut Scientists, 91. *Mem:* Am Chem Soc; fel Am Asn Pharmaceut Scientists. *Res:* Physical-chemical approach to pharmaceutical problems; chemical modification of drug to improve drug delivery and development of soft medicinal agents; computer-assisted drug design. *Mailing Add:* Schering-Plough Res Inst 2015 Galloping Hill Rd Kenilworth NJ 07033. *E-Mail:* james.kaminski@spcorp.com

KAMINSKI, JOAN M, ORGANIC CHEMISTRY. *Current Pos:* res chemist, Mobil Res & Develop Corp, 77-80, sr res chemist, 81-84, assoc, 84-87, res assoc, 88-91, planning assoc, 91-93, SR RES ASSOC, MOBIL RES & DEVELOP CORP, 93- *Personal Data:* b Darby, Pa, May 3, 47. *Educ:* West Chester State Col, BA, 69; Drexel Univ, PhD(org chem), 75. *Prof Exp:* Asst res chemist, Univ Ill, Urbana, 67 & 69; teaching asst chem, Drexel Univ, 70-74; Nat Res Coun-Agr Res Serv res assoc org chem, 74-75, res scientist org chem, Fats & Proteins Res Found, Eastern Regional Res Ctr, Agr Res Serv, USDA, 75-77. *Mem:* Am Chem Soc. *Res:* Lubricants-new product development, petroleum chemistry. *Mailing Add:* 148 Weatherby Rd Mullica Hill NJ 08062

KAMINSKI, PAUL G, LOW OBSERVABLES TECHNOLOGY & APPLICATION, KALMAN FILTERING. *Personal Data:* b Cleveland, Ohio, Sept 16, 42; m, Julie Crafts; c Laura D & Garrett K. *Educ:* USAF Acad, BS, 64; Mass Inst Technol, MS, 66; Stanford Univ, PhD(aeronaut/astronaut eng), 71. *Prof Exp:* Spec asst under secy defense, USAF, 77-81, dir low observable technol, Off Dept Chief of Staff Res & Develop, 81-85; pres & chief operating officer, Technol Strategies & Alliances, 85-93, chmn & chief exec officer, 93-94, under secy defense acquisition & technol, 94-97. *Concurrent Pos:* Dir, Dyncorp, 88-, Geodynamics Inc, 88-, Delfin Systs, 91-, ISY Corp, 92-, Mich Develop Corp, 93-, Atlantic Aerospace & Electronics Corp, 93- & Charles Stark Draper Lab, 93-; chmn, Defense Sci Bd, 93- *Mem:* Nat Acad Eng; Am Inst Aeronaut; AAAS; Sigma Xi; Inst Elec & Electronics Engrs. *Res:* Kalman filtering, with application to navigation systems; internal guidance systems and terminal guidance systems for precision guided munitions; stealth technology to include design, analysis and testing; synthetic aperture radar and applications to reconnaissance and surveillance; square root filtering and smoothing; numerical methods. *Mailing Add:* 6691 Rutledge St Fairfax Station VA 22039

KAMINSKI, ZIGMUND CHARLES, MEDICAL MICROBIOLOGY, INFECTIOUS DISEASES. *Current Pos:* DIR CLIN MICROBIOL, UNIV HOSP, 68- *Personal Data:* b Hartford, Conn, Jan 15, 29. *Educ:* Univ Conn, BA, 52; Hahnemann Med Col, MS, 54, PhD(microbiol), 57; Am Bd Med Microbiol, dipl pub health & med microbiol, 72. *Prof Exp:* From instr to asst prof microbiol, Col Med, Seton Hall Univ, 57-65; asst prof, Med Sch, Univ Med & Dent, NJ, 68-71, assoc prof microbiol & path, 71- *Mem:* Am Soc Microbiol; Acad Clin Lab Physicians & Scientists; NY Acad Sci; Infectious Dis Soc Am. *Res:* Mycobacterial infections. *Mailing Add:* Pathol & Lab Med Univ Med & Dent NJ 150 Bergen St Newark NJ 07103

KAMINSKY, LAURENCE SAMUEL, BIOLOGICAL SCIENCES, TOXICOLOGY. *Current Pos:* PROF, STATE UNIV NY, 85- *Personal Data:* b Cape Town, SAfrica, Dec 25, 40; m 66, Sylvia Singer; c Philip & Rena. *Educ:* Univ Cape Town, BS, 62, Hons, 63, PhD(chem), 66. *Honors & Awards:* Frank Blood Award, Soc Toxicol. *Prof Exp:* Res assoc biochem, Sch Med, Yale Univ, 67-68; assoc prof med biochem, Med Sch, Univ Cape Town, 68-75; prin res scientist biochem, 75-77, dir biochem toxicol, 78-83, chief biochem genetic toxicol, NY State Dept Health, 83- *Concurrent Pos:* Vis res prof biochem, State Univ NY Albany, 74; adj assoc prof, Albany Med Col, 76- *Mem:* Brit Biochem Soc; Am Soc Biochem & Molecular Biol; Soc Toxicol; Int Soc Study Xenobiotics. *Res:* Investigations into the role of of the heme proteins hepatic microsomal cytochrome P-450 in the metabolism of drugs; toxifying and detoxifying properties of cytochromes P-450. *Mailing Add:* Wadsworth Ctr NY State Dept Health Albany NY 12201-0509. *Fax:* 518-486-1505; *E-Mail:* laurence.kaminsky@wadsworth.org

KAMINSKY, MANFRED STEPHAN, EXPERIMENTAL PHYSICS, SURFACE PHYSICS. *Current Pos:* PROP, SURFACE TREATMENT SCI INT, 86- *Personal Data:* b Koenigsberg, Ger, June 4, 29; m 57, Elisabeth M Moellering; c Cornelia K & Mark P. *Educ:* Univ Rostock, Dipl, 51, Univ Marburg, Ger, PhD(physics), 57. *Honors & Awards:* E W Mueller Lectr, Univ Wis-Milwaukee, 78. *Prof Exp:* Asst physics, Univ Rostock, 50-52, lectr, Med Tech Sch, 52; res asst, Phys Inst, Univ Marburg, 53-57, sr asst, 57-58; res assoc, Argonne Nat Lab, 58-59, asst physicist, 59-62, assoc physicist, 62-70, dir, Surface Sci Ctr, 74-80, sr physicist, 70-86. *Concurrent Pos:* Invited prof, Inst Energy, Univ Quebec, Montreal-Varennes, 76-83; Coop US scientist, Div Int Prog, NSF, 78-83; mem, Task Group Plasma-Wall Interactions, Off Fusion Energy, Dept Energy, 79-80; chmn, Steering Comt Fusion Technol, Int Union Vacuum Sci, Technol & Appln, 81-83; res fel, Japanese Soc Prom Sci, 82; proj mgr, US Dept Energy E Cut Tribology Proj & mgr tribology proface, Argonne Nat Lab, 84-86; consult, Off Tech Assessment, US Cong, 86, Nat Res Coun, Coun Tribol, 86-88. *Mem:* AAAS; fel Am Phys Soc; Am Chem Soc; Sigma Xi; hon mem Am Vacuum Soc; Res Soc Am; Europ Phys Soc; Ger Phys Soc. *Res:* Atomic and ionic impact phenomena on solids; channeling phenomena; nuclear polarization; surface science in thermonuclear research; mass spectrometry; tribology; ultrahigh vacuum technology; ionic processes in electrolytic solutions; radiation effects on solid surfaces; surface effects in controlled fusion devices; author of numerous books on surface physics. *Mailing Add:* 906 South Park Hinsdale IL 60521

KAMINSKYJ, SUSAN GAIL WILLETS, FUNGAL BIOLOGY. *Current Pos:* RES BIOLOGIST, PURDUE UNIV, 94- *Educ:* Univ Toronto, BSc, 78, MSc, 82; York Univ, PhD(biol), 94. *Honors & Awards:* Alice Wilson Award, Royal Soc Can, 95. *Prof Exp:* Res assoc, Univ Western Ont, 82-84; res assoc, York Univ, 84, res tech, 84-89. *Res:* Author of numerous articles. *Mailing Add:* Dept Biol Purdue Univ West Lafayette IN 47907-1392

KAMIYAMA, MIKIO, IMMUNOCHEMISTRY, IMMUNOHEMATOLOGY. *Current Pos:* PROF, SCH GRAD MED EDUC, SETON HALL, 88- *Personal Data:* b Kyoto, Japan, Mar 25, 36; m 71; c 3. *Educ:* Kyoto Prefectural Univ, BS, 62; Univ Tokyo, PhD(biochem) & DMSc, 67. *Prof Exp:* Fel biochem, Princeton Univ, 67-68; res assoc microbiol, Albert Einstein Med Ctr, 68; res assoc biochem, State Univ NY, Buffalo, 69-70; sr researcher molecular biol, Inst Molecular Path, Univ Paris, 71-74; res assoc hemat, St Luke's Roosevelt Hosp Ctr & Columbia Univ, 74-77, attend staff immunol, 77-88; dir res, Blood Res Inst, St Michael's Med Ctr, 88- *Concurrent Pos:* Vis lectr biochem, Inst Physiol Chem, Univ Marburg, 72-73. *Mem:* Am Asn Immunologists; sr mem Am Fedn Clin Res; Asn Med Lab Immunologists; NY Acad Sci; Harvey Soc; Am Heart Asn Coun Thrombosis; Int Soc Thrombosis & Haemostasis. *Res:* Immunological and biochemical characterization of platelet glycoproteins; cell membrane studies; monoclonal antibody preparations directed to human platelet glycoproteins; non-radioactive immune assays. *Mailing Add:* Blood Disorder Ctr Overlook Hosp 99 Beauvoir Ave Summit NJ 07902-0220. *Fax:* 908-522-2977

KAMM, DONALD E, NEPHROLOGY, PHYSIOLOGY. *Current Pos:* from instr to asst prof, 66-71, ASSOC PROF MED, SCH MED & DENT, UNIV ROCHESTER, 71- *Personal Data:* b Rochester, NY, July 10, 29; m 56; c 4. *Educ:* Cortland State Col, BS, 51; Albany Med Col, MD, 60. *Prof Exp:* Intern & resident med, Beth Israel Hosp, Boston, 60-62. *Concurrent Pos:* NIH res fel renal physiol, Sch Med, Boston Univ, 62-64; NIH fel metab, Harvard Med Sch, 64-66. *Mem:* Am Fedn Clin Res; Am Physiol Soc Nephrology; Int Soc Nephrology. *Res:* Effects of potassium balance on the regulation of urea production and renal ammonia production. *Mailing Add:* Dept Med Nephrol Unit Sch Med Univ Rochester Rochester NY 14642-0001

KAMM, GILBERT G(EORGE), CHEMICAL ENGINEERING. *Current Pos:* CONSULT, 88- *Personal Data:* b Emington, Ill, Aug 6, 25; m 54; c 1. *Educ:* Univ Ill, BS, 49. *Prof Exp:* Group leader metals, Res Div, Am Nat Can Co, Ill, 58-66, mgr metals sect, Res & Develop Ctr, 66-68, asst to assoc dir, Mat Sci Sect, 68-71, assoc dir, Princeton Res Ctr, 71-78, assoc dir metall, 79-81, dir, metal mat technol, 82-84, dir mat technol, Barrington Tech Ctr, 84-88. *Mem:* Am Chem Soc; Electrochem Soc; Am Soc Metals. *Res:* Metal cleaning and plating; corrosion, especially electrolytic tin plate and other metals used in containers; metallurgical properties of container materials; plastic-metal composites; energy related research in pulp and paper processes; organic coatings and sealing compounds. *Mailing Add:* 21032 N Crestview Dr Barrington IL 60010-2924

KAMM, JAMES A, economic entomology, for more information see previous edition

KAMM, JEROME J, BIOCHEMICAL PHARMACOLOGY. *Current Pos:* SECT HEAD, HOFFMANN-LA ROCHE, INC, 67- *Personal Data:* b New York, NY, June 4, 33; m 56. *Educ:* Brooklyn Col, BS, 54; Georgetown Univ, MS, 59, PhD(biochem), 64. *Prof Exp:* Chemist, Nat Heart Inst, 55-64; sr biochemist, Smith, Kline & French Labs, 64-67. *Mem:* AAAS; Am Chem Soc; Acad Pharmaceut Sci; NY Acad Sci; Am Soc Pharmacol & Exp Therapeut; Sigma Xi. *Res:* Drug metabolism and mechanisms of drug metabolism; toxicology. *Mailing Add:* Dept Toxicol Hoffmann-La Roche Inc Nutley NJ 07110-1150. *Fax:* 973-235-4795

KAMM, ROGER DALE, BIOMEDICAL ENGINEERING, FLUID MECHANICS. *Current Pos:* Instr, 77, lectr & res assoc, 77-78, asst prof to assoc prof, 78-88, PROF MECH ENG, MASS INST TECHNOL, 88- *Personal Data:* b Ashland, Wis, Oct 10, 50; m 74, Judith Brown; c Peter M. *Educ:* Northwestern Univ, BS, 72; Mass Inst Technol, SM, 73, PhD(mech eng), 77. *Mem:* Am Soc Mech Engrs; Am Inst Med & Biol Eng; Am Physiol Soc; Biomed Eng Soc. *Res:* Biomedical fluid mechanics, specifically physiology and pathophysiology of venous circulation, respiratory tract and eye. *Mailing Add:* Dept Mech Eng Mass Inst Technol 77 Massachusetts Ave Cambridge MA 02139-4307. *Fax:* 617-258-8559

KAMMANN, KARL PHILIP, JR, CHEMISTRY. *Current Pos:* PROD DEVELOP MGR, KEIL CHEM DIV, FERRO CORP, 75- *Personal Data:* b St Louis, Mo, Mar 30, 36; m 60; c 4. *Educ:* Washington Univ, AB, 57; La State Univ, MS, 60, PhD(chem), 62. *Prof Exp:* Sr res chemist, Cities Serv Co, 62-64; group leader, Emery Indust, Inc, 64-74. *Mem:* Am Chem Soc; Am Oil Chemists Soc; Am Soc Lubrication Engrs. *Res:* Sulfurization and chlorosulfurization; fats and oils, and derivatives. *Mailing Add:* 3430 W Atherton Lane White Pine TN 37890-4910

KAMMASH, TERRY, NUCLEAR ENGINEERING & ENGINEERING MECHANICS, APPLIED PHYSICS. *Current Pos:* asst aircraft propulsion lab, Eng Res Inst, 54-55, from instr to assoc prof nuclear eng & eng mech, 55-67, prof nuclear eng, 67-77, STEPHEN S ATWOOD PROF NUCLEAR ENG & ACTG CHMN DEPT, UNIV MICH, ANN ARBOR, 77- *Personal Data:* b Salt, Jordan, Jan 27, 27; nat US; m 56. *Educ:* Pa State Univ, BS, 52, MS, 54; Univ Mich, PhD(nuclear eng), 58. *Honors & Awards:* Arthur Holly Compton Award & Am Nuclear Soc, 77. *Prof Exp:* Asst aerodyn, Pa State Univ, 52-53, instr eng mech, 53-54. *Concurrent Pos:* Vis scientist, Lawrence Radiation Lab, 62-63, 63-67. *Mem:* Fel Am Phys Soc; fel Am Nuclear Soc; Am Soc Eng Educ; Soc Eng Sci. *Res:* Magnetohydrodynamics; plasma physics; plasticity and physics of ionized gases; controlled fusion; space application of fusion energy. *Mailing Add:* Dept Nuclear Eng Univ Mich Ann Arbor MI 48109

KAMMEN, HAROLD OSCAR, BIOCHEMISTRY. *Current Pos:* asst res biochemist, 64-69, assoc res biochemist, 69-89, HEALTH & SAFETY COORDR, UNIV CALIF, BERKELEY, 90- *Personal Data:* b New York, NY, July 28, 27; m 59, Miriam Wexler; c Shira L & Seth J. *Educ:* Bethany Col, WVa, BS, 46; Stanford Univ, PhD(chem), 60. *Prof Exp:* Res asst biochem, M D Anderson Hosp, Tex, 56-59; fel pharmacol, Sch Med, Yale Univ, 59, res asst, 59. *Concurrent Pos:* Lectr, Univ Calif, Berkeley, 71, 75-81. *Mem:* AAAS; Am Soc Microbiol; Am Soc Biol Chem; fel Am Acad Sci. *Res:* Enzymes and regulation of nucleic acid metabolism. *Mailing Add:* Bldg 158 Richmond Field Sta Univ Calif 1301 S 46th St Richmond CA 94804-4603. *Fax:* 510-231-9520; *E-Mail:* kammen@uclink.berkeley.edu

KAMMER, ANN EMMA, neurobiology; deceased, see previous edition for last biography

KAMMERAAD, ADRIAN, EXPERIMENTAL BIOLOGY, RESEARCH ADMINISTRATION. *Current Pos:* RETIRED. *Personal Data:* b Holland, Mich, Feb 25, 12; wid; c 3. *Educ:* Hope Col, AB, 33; Yale Univ, PhD(exp embryol), 40. *Prof Exp:* Asst zool, Yale Univ, 33-36; instr, Dartmouth Col, 36-38; asst anat, Sch Med, La State Univ, 38-40, instr, 40-42; sci dir, Van Patten Pharmaceut Co, 46-50; dir res & prod control, Kremers-Urban Co, 50-56; in chg pharmaceut prod develop, Dow Chem Co, 56-60, dir pharm lab, 59-60, in chg res admin, 60-62, mgr drug regulatory sect, Res Ctr, 62-77. *Concurrent Pos:* Instr, Sch Med, Northwestern Univ, 47-50. *Res:* Administration and supervision of drug regulatory activities. *Mailing Add:* 9115 Washington Blvd Indianapolis IN 46240

KAMMERDIENER, JOHN LUTHER, NON-PROLIFERATION, WEAPONS PHYSICS. *Current Pos:* tech staff mem, 72-95, LAB FEL, LOS ALAMOS NAT LAB, 95- *Personal Data:* b Perrin, Tex, July 6, 37; m 75, Ellen Leonard; c Kristin, Susan & Michael. *Educ:* US Mil Acad, West Point, BS, 61; Univ Calif, MS, 66, PhD(appl sci), 72. *Honors & Awards:* Award of Excellence, Dept Energy, 85 & 92. *Res:* Classified weapons research and development and providing technical advice and analysis to US government policy makers. *Mailing Add:* 102 Monte Rey N Los Alamos NM 87544. *Fax:* 202-665-2227; *E-Mail:* jlk@lanl.gov

KAMMERER, CANDACE MARIE, GENETIC EPIDEMIOLOGY. *Current Pos:* from fel scientist to asst scientist, 81-89, ASSOC SCIENTIST, SW FOUND BIOMED RES, 90-; ASSOC PROF, UNIV TEX HEALTH SCI CTR, SAN ANTONIO, 90- *Personal Data:* b Iowa City, Iowa, Nov 20, 53. *Educ:* Colo State Univ, BS, 75; Ohio State Univ, PhD(genetics), 79. *Prof Exp:* Asst prof biol, Franklin & Marshall Col, 79-80; fel scientist, Univ Cincinnati Med Sch, 80-81. *Concurrent Pos:* mem, Int & Coop Proj Study Sect, NIH, 93-97. *Mem:* Am Soc Human Genetics; Am Heart Asn; Genetics Soc Am; Int Genetics Epidemiol Soc; AAAS; Tex Genetics Soc. *Res:* Genetic epidemiology of atherosclerosis, hypertension and osteoporosis using data on human families and animal models. *Mailing Add:* SW Found Biomed Res PO Box 28141 San Antonio TX 78228-0147. *Fax:* 210-670-3337; *E-Mail:* candy@darwin.sfbr.org

KAMMERER, WILLIAM JOHN, MATHEMATICS. *Current Pos:* CONSULT, 90- *Personal Data:* b Rochester, NY, Oct 8, 31; m 57; c 2. *Educ:* Univ Rochester, BA, 54; Univ Wis, Madison, MS, 55, PhD(math), 59. *Prof Exp:* Asst prof oper res, Case Western Reserve Univ, 59-60; from asst prof to prof math, Ga Inst Technol, 60-90. *Concurrent Pos:* Soc Indust & Appl Math lectr, 71-72. *Mem:* Am Math Soc; Soc Indust & Appl Math; Asn Comput Mach. *Res:* Numerical analysis; approximation theory and optimization. *Mailing Add:* 3430 Pin Oak Circle Atlanta GA 30340

KAMMERMEIER, MARTIN A, SPEECH PATHOLOGY. *Current Pos:* from instr to asst prof, 62-73, PROF SPEECH PATH, ST CLOUD STATE UNIV, 73-, CHMN DEPT SPEECH SCI, PATH & AUDIOL, 70- *Personal Data:* b Cold Spring, Minn, Oct 23, 31; m 59; c 3. *Educ:* St Cloud State Col, BS, 58, MS, 63; Univ Minn, Minneapolis, PhD(speech path), 69. *Prof Exp:* Speech therapist, Pub Sch, 58-62. *Mem:* Am Speech & Hearing Asn. *Res:* Acoustic analysis of the voices of speakers with a variety of central nervous system disorders. *Mailing Add:* Dept Commun Disorders St Cloud State Univ St Cloud MN 56301-4498

KAMMERMEYER, KARL, CHEMICAL ENGINEERING. *Current Pos:* prof chem eng & head dept, 49-73, EMER PROF CHEM ENG, UNIV IOWA, 73- *Personal Data:* b Nurnberg, Ger, June 15, 04; nat US; m 30; c 1. *Educ:* Univ Mich, BSChE & BS(math), 29, MSE, 31, DSc(chem eng), 32. *Prof Exp:* Res assoc eng, Univ Mich, 30-32; develop engr, Standard Oil Co, Inc, 33-36; refinery chief chemist & chem engr, Pure Oil Co, Ohio, 36-39; asst prof chem eng, Drexel Inst, 39-42; dir res, Publicker Industs Inc, 42-47; mgr res & develop, Chem Div, Glenn L Martin Co, 47-49. *Concurrent Pos:* Sci consult, US Dept Com, Ger, 46; consult, Vet Admin Hosp, Iowa City; chmn, Gordon Res Conf Separation & Purification, 57. *Mem:* AAAS; Am Chem Soc; fel Am Inst Chem Engrs; Am Soc Eng Educ; Sigma Xi. *Res:* Separation processes; membrane separations and distillation; air purification in submarines and space capsules; genetic engineering for technologists. *Mailing Add:* Dept Chem Eng Univ Iowa Iowa City IA 52240

KAMMERUD, RONALD CLAIRE, SOLAR ENERGY. *Current Pos:* SOLAR ENERGY RES PHYSICIST, LAWRENCE BERKELEY LAB, 76- *Personal Data:* b Monroe, Wis, July 10, 42; m 63; c 2. *Educ:* Drexel Univ, BS, 66; Ind Univ, Bloomington, MS, 69, PhD(physics), 70. *Prof Exp:* Res assoc exp high energy physics, Ohio State Univ, 70; res assoc exp high energy physics, Fermi Nat Accelerator Lab, 73-76. *Mem:* Am Phys Soc; Int Solar Energy Soc. *Res:* Heat transfer analysis as applied to passive solar building energy analysis. *Mailing Add:* 4032 Waterhouse Rd Oakland CA 94602

KAMMLER, DAVID W, NUMERICAL ANALYSIS, APPROXIMATION THEORY. *Current Pos:* from asst prof to assoc prof, 71-78, PROF MATH, SOUTHERN ILL UNIV, CARBONDALE, 78- *Personal Data:* b Belleville, Ill, Oct 29, 40; m 65, Ruth Kuhnert; c Timothy & Daniel. *Educ:* Southern Ill Univ, Carbondale, BA, 62; Southern Methodist Univ, MS, 69; Univ Mich, Ann Arbor, PhD(math), 71. *Prof Exp:* Mem tech staff, Tex Instruments Inc, 65-68. *Concurrent Pos:* Fel, Rome Air Develop Ctr, 80-81. *Mem:* Am Math Soc; Soc Indust & Appl Math; Math Asn Am; Sigma Xi. *Res:* Approximation with sums of exponentials; transient analysis; numerical analysis; discrete fourier analysis. *Mailing Add:* Dept Math Southern Ill Univ Carbondale IL 62901-4408. *Fax:* 618-453-5300

KAMMULA, RAJU G, TOXICOLOGY, PHYSIOLOGY. *Current Pos:* VET MED OFFICER/TOXICOLOGIST, DRAERD/FOOD & DRUG ADMIN, 79- *Personal Data:* b May 1, 35; m 66; c 3. *Educ:* Madras Univ, DVM, 57; Univ Minn, PhD(physiol), 64. *Prof Exp:* Res asst, Univ Minn, 59-64; prof physiol, Col Vet Med, Tuskegee Univ, 64-76; vet practr, Calif, 76-78. *Mem:* Am Physiol Soc; Am Vet Med Asn; Am Col Toxicol; DC Vet Med Asn. *Res:* Pharmacology. *Mailing Add:* DRAERD Food & Drug Admin 9200 Corporate Blvd Rm 310-T M/S HFZ-470 Rockville MD 20850. *Fax:* 301-427-1977

KAMON, ELIEZER, ERGONOMICS, OCCUPATIONAL HEALTH. *Current Pos:* PROF PHYSIOL, PA STATE UNIV, 74- *Personal Data:* b Jerusalem; US citizen; m 67; c 3. *Educ:* Israel State Col, T dipl, 52; Hebrew Univ, Jerusalem, MSc, 59, PhD(zool), 64. *Prof Exp:* Res asst occup health, Univ Pittsburgh, 66-67, res assoc, 68-73. *Concurrent Pos:* Fel ergonomics, Loughboro Univ Technolog, 65. *Mem:* Am Physiol Soc; Am Indust Hyg Asn; fel Am Col Sports Med; Ergonomics Soc; Human Factors Soc. *Res:* Human thermal physiology and man's adaptability to his working conditions as they relate to muscular strength, cardiovascular capacity and respiratory functions. *Mailing Add:* 453 Park Lane State College PA 16803-3208

KAMOUN, MALEK, LABORATORY MEDICINE. *Current Pos:* ASST PROF PATH & LAB MED, DEPT IMMUNOL & HEMAT, UNIV PA, 83- *Educ:* Pierre & Marie Curie Univ, Paris, France, MD, 75. *Res:* Lymphocyte growth and differentiation. *Mailing Add:* Dept Path Univ Pa Hosp 3400 Spruce St Philadelphia PA 19104-4274. *Fax:* 215-349-5090

KAMOWITZ, HERBERT M, MATHEMATICS. *Current Pos:* assoc prof, 66-70, PROF MATH, UNIV MASS, BOSTON, 70- *Personal Data:* b Brooklyn, NY, Dec 31, 31; m 55, Elaine Heyman; c David L, Sylvia J & Anne L. *Educ:* City Col New York, BS, 52; Brown Univ, ScM, 54, PhD(math), 60. *Prof Exp:* Assoc scientist math, Res & Advan Develop Div, Avco Corp, 57-60, sr scientist, 60-61, from staff scientist to sr staff scientist, 61-66. *Concurrent Pos:* Vis scientist, Pure Math Dept, Weizmann Inst Sci, Rehovot, Israel, 73 & 80. *Mem:* Am Math Soc. *Res:* Functional analysis. *Mailing Add:* Dept Math Univ Mass Dorchester MA 02125. *E-Mail:* hkamo@cs.umb.edu

KAMP, DAVID ALLEN, ORGANIC CHEMISTRY, POLYMER CHEMISTRY. *Current Pos:* CONSULT, ORG & POLYMER CHEM, RAYCHEM CORP, 80-; SCIENTIST & GROUP LEADER, LANDEC CORP, 90- *Personal Data:* b St Louis, Mo, Sept 26, 47; m 73, Phaik-Foon. *Educ:* Univ Calif, Los Angeles, BSc, 70; Univ Ore, PhD(chem), 76; Univ Calif, Santa Cruz, cert hazardous mat mgt, 91. *Prof Exp:* Assoc chem, Cornell Univ, 76-77; staff scientist, Res & Develop Ctr, Gen Elec Co, 77-80 & Raychem Corp, 80-87. *Mem:* Am Chem Soc; Asn Consult Chemists & Chem Engrs; Prof & Tech Consults Asn; Int Soc Optical Eng. *Res:* Organic synthesis; organic and polymer chemistry; materials science. *Mailing Add:* 886 Ticonderoga Dr Sunnyvale CA 94087-2252

KAMPAS, FRANK JAMES, PHYSICAL CHEMISTRY, SOLID STATE PHYSICS. *Current Pos:* DIR ENCAPSULATION, AM PHYS SOC, 90- *Personal Data:* b Buffalo, NY, Apr 24, 46. *Educ:* Univ Pa, BA & MS, 68; Stanford Univ, PhD(physics), 74. *Prof Exp:* Res assoc chem, Univ Wash, 74-77; res assoc, Molecular Sci Div, Brookhaven Nat Lab, 77-78, from asst scientist to scientist, Dept Energy & Environ, Mat Sci Div, 78-85; sr scientist, Chronar Co, 85-86, mgr, Process Develop Group, 86-87, mgr, process develop & eng, 88-89. *Mem:* Am Phys Soc; Mat Res Soc; Inst Elec & Electronic Engrs. *Res:* Physics of organic molecules in the solid state and in solution; plasma chemistry as applied to thin film deposition; optical spectroscopy; solar cell device physics. *Mailing Add:* 1614 E Butler Pike Ambler PA 19002

KAMPE, DENNIS JAMES, ELECTRON MICROSCOPY. *Current Pos:* Staff scientist, Carbon Prod Div, Union Carbide Corp, 72-73, dept head micros & phys testing, 73-75, res scientist, 75-82, sr staff scientist, 83-90, res scientist, 91-94, SR RES SCIENTIST, CARBON PROD DIV, UNION CARBIDE CORP, 95- *Personal Data:* b Brooklyn, NY, July 16, 45; div; c Keri & Matthew. *Educ:* State Univ NY Stony Brook, BESc, 67; Univ Va, MMSc, 69, PhD(mat sci), 72. *Mem:* Electron Micros Soc Am; Am Soc Testing & Mat; Mining Eng; Asn Iron & Steel Engrs; Am Inst Mech Engrs; Iron & Steel Soc. *Res:* Carbon an graphite materials in steel making processes and si and p production. *Mailing Add:* UCAR Carbon PO Box 6116 Cleveland OH 44101. *Fax:* 216-676-2623

KAMPEN, EMERSON, chemistry; deceased, see previous edition for last biography

KAMPER, ROBERT ANDREW, PHYSICS. *Current Pos:* RETIRED. *Personal Data:* b Surbiton, Eng, Mar 14, 33; nat US; m 55; c 3. *Educ:* Oxford Univ, BA, 54, MA & DPhil(physics), 57. *Honors & Awards:* Arnold O Beckman Award, Instrument Soc Am, 74; Gold Medal, US Dept Com, 75. *Prof Exp:* Imp Chem Industs res fel, Oxford Univ, 57-61; physicist, Cent Elec Generating Bd, Eng, 61-63; physicist, Cryogenics Div, Nat Bur Stand, 63-74, assoc chief, Electromagnetics Div, 74-78, chief electromagnetic technol div, 78-94, dir, Boulder Labs, 82-94. *Concurrent Pos:* Fulbright travel grant, Univ Calif, Berkeley, 58-59. *Mem:* Fel Inst Elec & Electronics Engrs. *Res:* Cryoelectronics; superconductivity; electrical measurement technique; electron spin resonance. *Mailing Add:* 439 17th St Boulder CO 80302

KAMPHOEFNER, FRED J(OHN), ELECTRONICS. *Current Pos:* RETIRED. *Personal Data:* b San Francisco, Calif, Mar 23, 21; m 60. *Educ:* Univ Calif, BS, 43; Stanford Univ, MA, 47, PhD, 49. *Prof Exp:* Res assoc, Radio Res Lab, Harvard Univ, 43-45 & Stanford Univ, 46-49; mgr, Control Systs Lab, SRI Int, 49-71, dir, Eng Sci Lab, 71-86, dep dir, Advan Technol Div, 86-90. *Concurrent Pos:* Res analyst, Opers Res Off, Johns Hopkins Univ, 52. *Mem:* Sigma Xi; sr mem Inst Elec & Electronics Engrs. *Res:* Instrumentation; data systems; bioengineering; mechanized data entry and non-impact printing. *Mailing Add:* 175 Ravenswood Ave Atherton CA 94027-3416

KAMPHUIS, J(OHN) WILLIAM, COASTAL & OCEANOGRAPHIC ENGINEERING. *Current Pos:* from asst prof to assoc prof, 68-72, PROF CIVIL ENG, QUEEN'S UNIV, ONT, 74- *Personal Data:* b Vollenhove, Neth, Sept 9, 38; Can citizen; m 60; c 2. *Educ:* Queen's Univ, Ont, BSc, 61, MSc, 63, PhD(civil eng), 66; Delft Technol Univ, dipl hydraul eng, 64. *Prof Exp:* Asst res officer, Nat Res Coun Can, 65-68. *Concurrent Pos:* Lectr, Carleton Univ, 65-68; specialist consult coastal eng, 69- *Mem:* Am Soc Civil Engrs; Int Asn Hydraul Res; Can Soc Civil Engrs. *Res:* Wave mechanics; interaction of waves and coasts; coastal sediment transport by waves and tides; model analysis; tidal propagation and numerical analysis; marina design. *Mailing Add:* Dept Civil Eng Ellis Hall Queen's Univ Kingston ON K7L 3N6 Can. *Fax:* 613-545-2128

KAMPINE, JOHN P, ANESTHESIOLOGY, PHYSIOLOGY. *Current Pos:* PROF & CHAIR, DEPT ANESTHESIOL, FROEDTRET MEM LUTHERAN HOSP, 79- *Educ:* Med Col Wis, MD & PhD. *Mem:* Inst Med-Nat Acad Sci. *Mailing Add:* Dept Anesthesiol Froedtret Mem Lutheran Hosp 9200 W Wisconsin Ave Milwaukee WI 53226. *Fax:* 414-257-8047

KAMPMEIER, JACK A, ORGANIC CHEMISTRY, EDUCATION. *Current Pos:* From instr to assoc prof, Univ Rochester, 60-71, chmn dept, 75-79, assoc dean grad studies, Col Arts & Sci, 82-86, dean, Col Arts & Sci, 88-91, PROF CHEM, UNIV ROCHESTER, 71-, ASSOC DIR, NSF SCI & TECHNOL, CTR PHOTO INDUCED CHARGE TRANSFER, 91- *Personal Data:* b Cedar Rapids, Iowa, June 11, 35; m 58, Anne Derk; c Scott, Margaret & Stephen. *Educ:* Amherst Col, BA, 57; Univ Ill, PhD(org chem), 60. *Concurrent Pos:* NSF sci fac fel, Univ Calif, Berkeley, 71-72; NSF fel, 58-60; Fulbright-Hays, sr res fel, Univ Freiburg, 79-80; sr scientist, NATO, 79-80. *Mem:* Am Chem Soc; Sigma Xi. *Res:* Mechanistic organic chemistry; free radical reactions; organometallic reactions; photochemistry; electron transfer reactions. *Mailing Add:* Dept Chem Univ Rochester Rochester NY 14627-1001. *Fax:* 716-473-6889; *E-Mail:* kamp@chem.chem.rochester.edu

KAMPRATH, EUGENE JOHN, SOIL FERTILITY. *Current Pos:* From asst prof to prof, NC State Univ, 55-81, William Neal Reynolds prof soil sci, 81-96, head dept, 90-96, WILLIAM NEAL REYNOLDS EMER PROF, NC STATE UNIV, 96- *Personal Data:* b Seward, Nebr, Jan 9, 26; m 56, Katherine Arnold; c John & Sara. *Educ:* Univ Nebr, BS, 50, MS, 52; NC State Col, PhD(soils), 55. *Hon Degrees:* DSc, Univ Nebr, 87. *Honors & Awards:* Soil Sci Appl Res Award, Soil Sci Soc of Am, 86. *Concurrent Pos:* Dir, Soil Testing Div, State Dept Agr, NC, 57-62; ed-in-chief, Soil Sci Soc Am, 69-74. *Mem:* Fel Am Soc Agron; fel Soil Sci Am; Sigma Xi. *Res:* Soil fertility; soil chemistry relationships in soils as they affect availability of nutrients to plants. *Mailing Add:* Dept Soil Sci Box 7619 NC State Univ Raleigh NC 27695-7619

KAMPSCHMIDT, RALPH FRED, BIOCHEMISTRY, IMMUNOLOGY. *Current Pos:* RETIRED. *Personal Data:* b Gerald, Mo, May 6, 23; m 54, Frances Jackson; c Kimberly, Kit, Coby & Kerry. *Educ:* Univ Mo, BS, 47, MS, 49, PhD(agr chem), 51. *Prof Exp:* Instr animal husb, Univ Mo, 47-51; res chemist biochem, Armour & Co, 51-55; sect head, Samuel Roberts Noble Found Inc, 55-85. *Mem:* Fel AAAS; Am Asn Cancer Res; Soc Exp Biol & Med; hon mem Reticuloendothelial Soc; NY Acad Sci. *Res:* Cancer research; iron metabolism; reticuloendothelial system; endotoxin; monokines. *Mailing Add:* 2614 Ridgeway St Ardmore OK 73401

KAMRA, OM PERKASH, RADIATION GENETICS, CYTOGENETICS. *Current Pos:* assoc prof, 63-72, PROF RADIATION BIOL, DALHOUSIE UNIV, 72- *Personal Data:* b Lahore, India, Mar 18, 35; m 59; c 2. *Educ:* Univ Delhi, BSc, 54; NC State Univ, MS, 56; Wash State Univ, PhD(genetics), 59; Univ Lund, dipl, 59. *Honors & Awards:* Travel Award, Can Genetics Soc, 63. *Prof Exp:* Fel Swedish Agr Res Coun, 59; secy, Food & Agr Orgn-Swedish Int Training Ctr Genetics, Univ Lund, 59-60; res officer radiation genetics, Atomic Energy Estab, Trombay, India, 60-61; res assoc plant genetics, Univ Man, 61-63. *Concurrent Pos:* Fel, Swedish Agr Res Coun, 59-60; chmn biol subcomt, Atlantic Prov Inter-Univ Comt Sci, 67-68; consult, Int Atomic Energy Agency, Vienna, 69-70 & UN Develop Prog, Indonesia, 72; mem comt int exchange, Nat Res Coun, 73-76; vis prof, Belgium Nuclear Res Estab, 77, 78 & 81. *Mem:* Sigma Xi. *Res:* Cytology; genetics; mutations; food additives; effect of laser beams on biological systems. *Mailing Add:* 1588 Cambridge St Halifax NS B3H 4A6 Can

KAMRAN, MERVYN ARTHUR, ENTOMOLOGY, ECOLOGY. *Current Pos:* asst prof biol to assoc prof, 68-79, PROF BIOL, DOWLING COL, 79- *Personal Data:* b Sialkot, Pakistan, Nov 8, 38. *Educ:* Punjab Univ, Pakistan, BS, 57, MS, 59; Univ Hawaii, PhD(entom), 65. *Prof Exp:* Lectr biol, Pakistan Ed Serv, Lahore, 59-61; Pakistan AEC scholar, Cent Treaty Orgn Inst Nuclear Sci, Tehran, Iran, 61; res fel entom, Int Rice Res Inst, Philippines, 65-67; asst prof entom, Pa State Univ, 68. *Mem:* AAAS; Am Entom Soc; Entom Soc Am. *Res:* Ecology and biological control of insect pests; taxonomy of tachinid flies. *Mailing Add:* Dept Math & Sci Dowling Col 150 Idle Hour Blvd Oakdale NY 11769-1906

KAMRIN, MICHAEL ARNOLD, PUBLIC EDUCATION IN SCIENCE, SCIENCE POLICY. *Current Pos:* from asst prof to prof natural sci, 67-89, PROF, INST ENVIRON TOXICOL, MICH STATE UNIV, 82-, PROF, RES DEVELOP, 90- *Personal Data:* b Brooklyn, NY, Aug 5, 40; m 64, Ritva Nieminen; c Kari & Edward. *Educ:* Cornell Univ, BA, 60; Yale Univ, MS, 62, PhD(chem), 65. *Honors & Awards:* Mem Medal, Univ Turku, Finland; Pub Commun Award, Soc Toxicol. *Prof Exp:* Res assoc biol, Biol Div, Oak Ridge Nat Lab, 63-64, consult, 65-66; NIH trainee, Hopkins Marine Sta, Stanford Univ, 66-67. *Concurrent Pos:* Vis scientist, Mich Legis Off Sci Adv, 80-81; docent, Univ Turku, Finland, 96- *Mem:* Fel AAAS; Am Chem Soc; Sigma Xi; Soc Environ Toxicol & Chem; Soc Toxicol; Soc Risk Anal. *Res:* Risk assessment, risk management, risk communication; science education for non-scientists; science policy. *Mailing Add:* Inst Environ Toxicol C-231 Holden Hall Mich State Univ East Lansing MI 48824-1206. *E-Mail:* kamrin@msu.edu

KAMYKOWSKI, DANIEL, BIOLOGICAL OCEANOGRAPHY. *Current Pos:* assoc prof 79-86, PROF MARINE EARTH & ATMOSPHERIC SCI, NC STATE UNIV, 86- *Personal Data:* b Chicago, Ill, Nov 23, 45; m 72, Sara-Joan Zentara; c Zachary & Terra-Lynn. *Educ:* Loyola Univ, Chicago, BS, 67; Univ Calif, San Diego, PhD(oceanog), 73. *Prof Exp:* Killam res assoc oceanog, Dalhousie Univ, 73-75; asst prof bot & marine sci, Univ Tex, Austin, 75-79. *Mem:* Am Soc Limnol & Oceanog; Am Geophys Union; Phycol Soc Am; Oceanog Soc. *Res:* Physiology and behavior of marine dinoflagellates in response to physical processes; global patterns in hydrographic factors, plant nutrients and phytoplankton species composition; phytoplankton physiology in the upper mixed layer of the ocean. *Mailing Add:* Dept Marine Earth & Atmospheric Sci NC State Univ Box 8208 Raleigh NC 27695-8208. *Fax:* 919-515-7802; *E-Mail:* dan_kamykowski@ncsu.edu

KAN, JOSEPH RUCE, SPACE PLASMA PHYSICS. *Current Pos:* asst prof, 72-76, assoc prof, 76-81, head, Space Physics & Atmospheric Sci Prog, 77-80, PROF GEOPHYS, GEOPHYS INST, UNIV ALASKA, 81- *Personal Data:* b Shanghai, China, Feb 10, 38; US citizen; c 3. *Educ:* Nat Cheng-Kung Univ, Taiwan, BS, 61; Wash State Univ, MS, 66; Univ Calif, San Diego, PhD(appl physics), 69. *Prof Exp:* Fel space physics, Dartmouth Col, 69-72. *Concurrent Pos:* Consult, Aerospace Corp, 80-81; vis prof, Inst Geophys & Planetary Physics, Univ Calif, Los Angeles, 80-81; assoc ed, J Geophys Res, 84- *Mem:* AAAS; Sigma Xi; Am Phys Soc; Am Geophys Union. *Res:* Space physics; plasma physics. *Mailing Add:* 2568 Talkeetra Ave Fairbanks AK 99709

KAN, LOU SING, PHYSICAL CHEMISTRY, BIOPHYSICS. *Current Pos:* fel chem, 71-74, res assoc, 74-77, asst prof, 77-81, ASSOC PROF, DIV BIOPHYS, SCH HYG & PUB HEALTH, JOHNS HOPKINS UNIV, 81- *Personal Data:* b Honan, China, Feb 28, 43; m 70. *Educ:* Nat Taiwan Univ, BS, 64; Duquesne Univ, PhD(phys chem), 70. *Prof Exp:* Asst chem, Nat Taiwan Univ, 65; asst phys chem, Duquesne Univ, 66-70, fel, 70-71. *Concurrent Pos:* Vis fel, Mellon Inst, Carnegie-Mellon Univ, 70-71. *Mem:* Am Chem Soc; Biophys Soc; Sigma Xi. *Res:* Studies of structure and backbone conformations of oligoribonucleotides and deoxyribonucleotides; conformation of nucleic acids; modified nucleic acids. *Mailing Add:* Inst Chem Acad Sinica Nankang Taipei Taiwan

KAN, PETER TAI YUEN, ORGANIC CHEMISTRY. *Current Pos:* from res chemist to sr res chemist, Wyandotte Chem Corp, 57-68, res assoc, 68-76, res supvr, 76-85, RES MGR, BASF WYANDOTTE CORP, 86- *Personal Data:* b Canton, China, Apr 12, 27; US citizen; m 51; c 2. *Educ:* Gannon Col, BS, 49; Univ Mich, MS, 51; Wayne State Univ, PhD(org chem), 58. *Prof Exp:* Sr anal chemist, R P Scherer Corp, Mich, 51-55. *Mem:* AAAS; Am Chem Soc; fel Am Inst Chem. *Res:* Isocyanates; isocyanurates; polyurethanes; organo-metallics; general organic synthesis. *Mailing Add:* 47200 Ann Arbor Rd W Plymouth MI 48170

KAN, YUET WAI, GENETICS, HEMATOLOGY. *Current Pos:* assoc prof, Dept Med & Lab Med, 72-77, PROF, DEPT MED & LAB MED, UNIV CALIF, SAN FRANCISCO, 77-, LOUIS K DIAMOND PROF HEMAT, 83- *Personal Data:* b Hong Kong, China, June 11, 36; US Citizen; m 64; c 2. *Educ:* Univ Hong Kong, MB & BS, 58, DSc, 80; FRS, 81; FRCP, 83. *Hon Degrees:* MD, Univ Cagliari, Italy, 81; DSc, Chinese Univ, Hong Kong, 81 & Univ Hong Kong, 87. *Honors & Awards:* Damashek Award, Am Soc Hemat, 79; Stratton Lectr, Int Soc Hemat, 80; George Thorn Award, Howard Hughes Med Inst, 80; Chinese Am Physicians Soc Award, 82; Allan Award, Am Soc Human Genetics, 84; Gairdner Found Int Award, 84; Lita Annenberg Hazen Award, 84; Waterford Award, 87; Am Col Physicians Award, 88; Warren Alpert Award, 89; San Remos Int Award, 89; Cotlove Award, Acad Clin Lab Physicians & Scientists, 93. *Prof Exp:* Intern, Univ Dept Med, Queen Mary Hosp, Hong Kong, 58-59, resident, 59-60; resident med, Presby Univ Hosp, Pittsburgh, Pa, 62-63; res assoc, Dept Biol, Mass Inst Technol, 63-64; res fel hemat, Dept Med, Royal Victoria Hosp, McGill Univ, 64-66; assoc med, Presby-Univ, Pa Hosp, Philadelphia, 66-67; res assoc, Children's Hosp Med Ctr, Dept Pediat, Harvard Med Sch, 67-70, asst prof pediat, 70-72. *Concurrent Pos:* Chief, Hemat Serv, San Francisco Gen Hosp, 72-79; investr, Howard Hughes Med Inst Lab Study Human Genetic Dis, San Francisco, 76-; res assoc, Cancer Res Inst, Univ Calif, San Francisco, 80-94, head, Div Genetics & Molecular Hemat, Dept Med, 83-89, chief, Div Molecular Med & Diag, Dept Lab Med, 89-, sr staff, Cardiovasc Res Inst, 93-; dir, Inst Molecular Biol, Univ Hong Kong, 90-, hon prof, 90- *Mem:* Nat Acad Sci; Am Fedn Clin Res; Am Soc Clin Invest; Asn Am Physicians; fel Royal Soc London; Third World Acad Sci; Am Soc Hemat (pres, 89-90); Am Soc Human Genetics; Asn Chinese Geneticists Am (pres, 88-89); foreign mem Chinese Acad Sci; fel Royal Col Physicians; Soc Chinese Bioscientists Am (secy-treas, 91-92, pres-elect, 97-98); fel Am Acad Arts & Sci; fel AAAS; Molecular Med Soc. *Res:* Control of globin synthesis and genetic defects in homoglobinopathies and thalassemia. *Mailing Add:* 20 Yerba Buena Ave San Francisco CA 94127

KANA, DANIEL D(AVID), ENGINEERING MECHANICS, MECHANICAL ENGINEERING. *Current Pos:* RETIRED. *Personal Data:* b Cuero, Tex, Sept 22, 34; m 58, Gladys A Psencik; c 3. *Educ:* Univ Tex, BS, 58, PhD(eng mech), 67; Univ NMex, MS, 61. *Prof Exp:* From res engr to sr res engr, SW Res Inst, 61-70, group leader, 70-71, mgr struct dynamics & acoust, 71-83, inst engr, 83-96. *Mem:* Fel Am Soc Mech Engrs; fel Am Inst Aeronaut & Astronaut. *Res:* Liquid and structure dynamic interaction; linear and non-linear vibrations; dynamic response and stability of structures; general structural dynamics and acoustics; environmental testing; earthquake engineering. *Mailing Add:* 10410 Mt Hope St San Antonio TX 78230

KANABROCKI, EUGENE LADISLAUS, BIOCHEMISTRY. *Current Pos:* Asst chief chemist, Clin Lab, Hines Vet Admin Hosp, 46-48, asst chief biochemist, 48-56, biochemist nuclear med, 56-73, chief clin chemist, Four Hosp Complex, 73-83, RES CHEMIST, NUCLEAR MED SERV, HINES VET ADMIN HOSP, 83- *Personal Data:* b Chicago, Ill, Apr 18, 22; m 50; c 2. *Educ:* DePaul Univ, BS, 47; Loyola Univ Chicago, MS, 69; Jagiellonian Univ, Poland, DSc, 83; Nat Registry Clin Chem, cert. *Concurrent Pos:* Consult, 56-; res assoc, Loyola Univ Chicago; chemist, US Customs Lab, Chicago; WHO investr, Int Atomic Energy Agency. *Mem:* Am Chem Soc; Int Soc Chronobiol; Sigma Xi; Health Physics Soc. *Res:* Etiology of arteriosclerosis; chronobiology; trace elements. *Mailing Add:* 151 Braddock Dr Melrose Park IL 60160-2406

KANADE, TAKEO, ARTIFICIAL INTELLIGENCE. *Current Pos:* sr res scientist, Dept Comput Sci & Robotics Inst, Carnegie Mellon Univ, 80-82, assoc prof tenure, 82-85, prof, 85-94, DIR, ROBOTICS INST, CARNEGIE MELLON UNIV, 92-; U A & HELEN WHITAKER CHAIRED PROF COMPUT SCI & ROBOTICS, 93- *Personal Data:* b Hyogo, Japan, Oct 24, 45; c 2. *Educ:* Kyoto Univ, BE, 68, ME, 70, PhD(elec eng), 73. *Honors & Awards:* AVIRG Award, Audio Visual Info Res Group in Japan, 80; AT&T Spec Group Award, 88; Hosa Bunka Kikin Found Award, 94; Joseph F Engelberger Award, 95. *Prof Exp:* Asst prof, Dept Info Sci, Kyoto Univ, Japan, 73-76, assoc prof, 76-80. *Concurrent Pos:* Chmn, Comt Robotics, Inst Elec & Electronics Engrs Comput Soc, 82-83; found chief ed, Int J Comput Vision, 85-; mem, Aeronaut & Space Eng Bd, Nat Res Coun, 92-95 & 92-96, Int Found Robotics Res, 93- *Mem:* Nat Acad Eng; Int Soc Intelligent Automation; Asn Comput Mach; fel Inst Elec & Electronics Engrs; fel Am Asn Artificial Intel; Robotics Soc Japan; Inst Electronics & Commun Engrs Japan; Sigma Xi; Intelligent Automation Soc; Robotics & Automation Soc. *Res:* Computer science; artificial intelligence; image understanding; robotics; vision; manipulator; navigation; sensors; medical imaging and graphics; granted 7 patents. *Mailing Add:* Robotics Inst 1 Carnegie Mellon Univ 5000 Forbes Ave Pittsburgh PA 15213

KANAKKANATT, ANTONY, POLYMER CHEMISTRY. *Current Pos:* res asst, 65-67, SR ASSOC INDEXER, CHEM ABSTRACTS SERV, 67- *Personal Data:* b Cochin, India, Mar 6, 35; m 65; c 3. *Educ:* Univ Kerala, India, BSc, 56; Marquette Univ, MS, 60; Univ Akron, PhD, 63. *Prof Exp:* Sr res chemist, Monsanto Co, 63-65. *Mem:* Am Chem Soc. *Res:* Catalytic isomerization; sequence distribution in polypeptides; reinforcement in elastomers. *Mailing Add:* 1216 Shady Hill Dr Columbus OH 43221

KANAKKANATT, SEBASTIAN VARGHESE, POLYMER PHYSICS. *Current Pos:* PRES, UNIQUE TECHNOL, INC, 83- *Personal Data:* b Kerala, India, Jan 20, 29; US citizen; m 58; c 1. *Educ:* Univ Madras, BSc, 50; Univ Akron, MS, 65, PhD(polymer physics), 69. *Prof Exp:* Instr chem, Univ Madras, 50-52 & Univ Addis Ababa, 52-64; from asst prof to assoc prof, 69-80, asst dir environ mgt lab, 76-80, prof gen technol, Univ Akron, 80- *Concurrent Pos:* Bd chmn, Unique Technol, Inc, 82-83. *Mem:* Am Chem Soc; Rheol Soc; Sigma Xi. *Res:* Diffusion in polymeric matrices used in the controlled release of pesticides, herbicides, fertilizers and photochromic dyes; cancer therapeutic agents. *Mailing Add:* 2459 Audubon Rd Akron OH 44320

KANAL, LAVEEN NANIK, INTELLIGENT SYSTEMS. *Current Pos:* pres, 69-70, MANAGING DIR L N K CORP, RIVERDALE, 70-; EMER PROF, UNIV MD, 96- *Personal Data:* b Dhond, India, Sept 29, 31; m 60, Agnes Raclare Cordis; c Shobhi, Jaya & Gyan. *Educ:* Univ Wash, BS, 51, MS, 53; Univ Pa, PhD(elec eng), 60. *Honors & Awards:* King-Sun Fu Award, Int Asn Pattern Recognition, 92. *Prof Exp:* Develop engr, Can Gen Elec Co, Ont, 53-55; instr elec eng, Moore Sch Elec Eng, Univ Pa, 55-60; mgr mach intel lab, Gen Dynamics/Electronics, NY, 60-62; res mgr info sci, Philco Appl Res Lab, Philco-Ford Corp, 62-65; mgr advan eng & res activ, Commun & Electronics Div, Philco-Ford Corp, 65-69; porf comput sci, Univ Md, College Park, 70-96. *Concurrent Pos:* Lectr, Wharton Grad Sch, Univ Pa, 63-64, vis assoc prof, 64-66, vis prof, 66-74; adj prof, Lehigh Univ, 65-70; admin comt, Systs & Cybernet, Inst Elec & Electronics Engrs, 72-74, 77-81 bd govs, info theory group, 73-79. *Mem:* Fel AAAS; Asn Comput Mach; fel Int Asn Pattern Recognition Soc; Soc Mfg Engrs; fel Inst Elec & Electronics Engrs; fel Am Asn Artificial Intel; Soc Photooptical Engrs; Sigma Xi. *Res:* Information science; machine recognition of patterns; stochastic learning models; statistical classification theory and applications of artificial intelligence; pattern recognition and image processing in remote sensing and automated digital cartography. *Mailing Add:* 302 Notley Ct Silver Spring MD 20905

KANAMORI, HIROO, SEISMOLOGY, GEOPHYSICS. *Current Pos:* PROF GEOPHYS, CALIF INST TECHNOL, 72- *Personal Data:* b Tokyo, Japan, Oct 17, 36; m 64; c 2. *Educ:* Univ Tokyo, BS, 59, MS, 61, PhD(geophys), 64. *Prof Exp:* Res fel geophys, Calif Inst Technol, 65-66; from assoc prof to prof, Univ Tokyo, 66-72. *Concurrent Pos:* Vis assoc prof geophys, Mass Inst Technol, 69-70. *Mem:* Fel Am Geophys Union; Seismol Soc Am; Seismol Soc Japan. *Res:* Mechanism of earthquakes; earthquake prediction; application of seismology to earthquake engineering. *Mailing Add:* Geophys & Plantary Sci 252-21 Calif Inst Technol Pasadena CA 91125

KANAMUELLER, JOSEPH M, INORGANIC CHEMISTRY. *Current Pos:* asst prof chem, 66-72, assoc prof, 72-80, PROF CHEM, WESTERN MICH UNIV, 80- *Personal Data:* b Chicago, Ill, July 4, 38. *Educ:* St Joseph's Col Ind, BS, 60; Univ Minn, PhD(inorg chem), 65. *Prof Exp:* Res assoc inorg chloramine chem, Univ Fla, 65-66. *Concurrent Pos:* Vis prof inorg chem, Vienna Tech Univ, Austria, 74. *Mem:* AAAS; Am Chem Soc. *Res:* Synthetic inorganic chemistry, especially sulfur-nitrogen and phosphorus-nitrogen compounds. *Mailing Add:* Dept Chem Western Mich Univ Kalamazoo MI 49008

KANAREK, ROBIN BETH, REGULATION OF FOOD INTAKE, NUTRITION & BEHAVIOR. *Current Pos:* Assoc prof, 83-89, PROF PSYCHOL & ADJ PROF NUTRIT, TUFTS UNIV, 89- *Personal Data:* b Apr 8, 46; m 86; c 2. *Educ:* Antioch Col, BA, Rutgers Univ, MS, PhD(psychol), 74. *Concurrent Pos:* Prin investr, NIH Res Grants, 78-; ed-in-chief, Nutrit & Behav, 80-87. *Mem:* Am Inst Nutrit; Behav Pharmacol Soc; Am Col Nutrit; NY Acad Sci; N Am Soc Study Obesity; Soc Study Ingestive Behav. *Res:* Physiological psychology; author. *Mailing Add:* Dept Psychol Tufts Univ 490 Boston Ave Medford MA 02155-5532. *Fax:* 617-627-3178

KANARIK, ROSELLA, MATHEMATICS. *Current Pos:* instr, Los Angeles City Col, 53-56, counr, 56-62, from assoc prof to prof, 62-74, EMER PROF MATH, LOS ANGELES CITY COL, 74- *Personal Data:* b Hungary, Feb 7, 09; US citizen; m 36; c 2. *Educ:* Univ Pittsburgh, BA, 30, MA, 31, PhD(math), 34. *Prof Exp:* Asst math, Univ Pittsburgh, 31-33; teacher 46-53. *Mem:* Am Math Soc; Math Asn Am. *Res:* Differential equations; group theory. *Mailing Add:* 238 S Mansfield Ave Los Angeles CA 90036-3017

KANAROWSKI, S(TANLEY) M(ARTIN), CHEMISTRY-GENERAL, ANALYTICAL CHEMISTRY. *Current Pos:* RETIRED. *Personal Data:* b Beausejour, Man, Dec 12, 12; nat US; wid; c Stanley M Jr, Nancy (Ciaffari) and Janice E. *Educ:* Univ Toledo, BS, 34. *Prof Exp:* From chemist to chief chemist, Dept Liquor Control, Ohio, 36-42; consult & sr chemist, Ord Plant, Firestone Tire & Rubber Co, Nebr, 42-43, asst dir, Corp Gen Lab, Ohio, 43, chief factory prod chem engr, 43-46, res & develop compounding chem engr, 46-49; lab dir & asst res & develop mgr, Fremont Rubber Co, 49-52; res & develop chem engr, Glass Fibers Inc, 52-53; chief res & develop chemist-engr & qual control mgr, Dairypak Butler Inc, 53-60; chief chemist, Northern Region, Enforcement Div, Ohio, 60-62; res & develop chem engr, Consol Paper Co, 62-63; sewage & indust wastes chemist, City of Toledo, 63-64; proj engr & head chemist, Invests Sect, Ohio River Div Labs, Chem & Thermal Effects Br, US Army Eng Div Corps Eng, 64-69, proj leader & prin investr, Eng Mat Div, US Army Construct Eng Res Lab, Corps Engrs, 69-86. *Concurrent Pos:* Mat appln res chemist-engr. *Mem:* Am Chem Soc; Am Inst Chem Engrs; Am Defense Preparedness Asn. *Res:* Construction materials application research and development including design of testing equipment; sealants application; waterproofing materials and films; reflective solar control films for windows; maple gymnasium floor finishes; paint-test kit for paint quality evaluation; prevention of windblown rain penetration; collective protection centers against chemical-biological warfare; reflection cracking in pavements; chemical hazardous materials and disposal; rubber and synthetic rubber products, elastomers, polymers, coatings, plastics, glass fibers, resins and paperboard; compoinding; quality control; laboratory and factory operations; materials problems consultant; 30 research publications nationally and internationally. *Mailing Add:* 1329 Excaliber Lane Sandy Spring MD 20860-1117

KANASEWICH, ERNEST RAYMOND, GEOPHYSICS. *Current Pos:* from asst prof to assoc prof, 63-71, from asst chmn to actg chmn dept, 69-74, PROF PHYSICS, UNIV ALTA, 71- *Personal Data:* b Eatonia, Sask, Mar 4, 31; m 69; c 2. *Educ:* Univ Alta, BSc, 52, MSc, 60; Univ BC, PhD(geophys), 62. *Prof Exp:* Seismologist, Tex Instruments-Geophys Serv, Inc, 53-58; fel, Univ BC, 62-63. *Concurrent Pos:* Mem cubcomt glaciol, Nat Res Coun, 63-, subcomt seismol, 67-; mem adv comt explor tech, Northern Alta Inst Technol, 64- & subcomt phys methods appl to geol probs, Nat Adv Comt Res Geol Sci, 65-; vis assoc prof, Dept Earth & Planetary Sci, Calif Inst Technol, 70-71. *Mem:* Am Geophys Union; Soc Explor Geophys; Seismol Soc Am; Can Asn Physicists. *Res:* Gravity; seismology; isotope dating techniques; glaciology. *Mailing Add:* Dept Physics Univ Alta Edmonton AB T6G 2M7 Can

KANATZAR, CHARLES LEPLIE, ZOOLOGY. *Current Pos:* asst prof biol, MacMurray Col, 46-48, prof & head dept, 48-61, dean fac, 61-67, dean col, 67-74, EMER DEAN, MACMURRAY COL, 74- *Personal Data:* b St Elmo, Ill, Apr 12, 14; wid; c Constance J (Buhrmann) & Phyllis R (Rock). *Educ:* Eastern Ill State Teachers Col, BEduc, 35; Univ Ill, MS, 36, PhD(protozool), 40. *Hon Degrees:* DH, Mac Murray Col, 86. *Prof Exp:* Asst zool, Univ Ill, 35-38. *Concurrent Pos:* Pres, Ill State Acad Sci, 59-60; mem bd adv, Ill State Mus, 62-74, chmn, 70-74; mem bd dirs, Ill State Mus Soc, 85-91. *Res:* Free-living protozoa; general zoology; general education in science. *Mailing Add:* 1841 Mound Rd Jacksonville IL 62650

KANATZIDIS, MERCOURI G, SOLID STATE CHEMISTRY. *Current Pos:* ASST PROF CHEM, MICH STATE UNIV, 87- *Personal Data:* b Thessaloniki, Greece, Aug 6, 57; m 87. *Educ:* Univ Thessaloniki, BS, 79; Univ Iowa, PhD(chem), 84. *Prof Exp:* Res assoc chem, Univ Mich, 84-85 & Northwestern Univ, 85-87. *Concurrent Pos:* NSF presidential young investr, 89; Alfred P Sloan Found fel, 91. *Mem:* Am Chem Soc; Am Crystallog Soc; Mat Res Soc. *Res:* Inorganic chemistry systhesis of novel molecular and solid state compounds of sulfur, selenium and tellurium; intercalation chemistry; conductive polymers; solid state chemistry; crystallography. *Mailing Add:* Dept Chem Mich State Univ East Lansing MI 48824

KANCIRUK, PAUL, SCIENTIFIC DATABASE MANAGEMENT. *Current Pos:* res assoc aquatic ecol, 78-84, sr res assoc, 84-90, PROG MGR, OAK RIDGE NAT LAB, 91- *Personal Data:* b New York, NY, Oct 10, 47. *Educ:* City Col New York, BS, 69; Fla State Univ, PhD, 76. *Honors & Awards:* Bronze Medal, Environ Protection Agency, 85. *Prof Exp:* Marine biol, Nova Ocean Sci Ctr, 76-77. *Concurrent Pos:* Liason, Cudaza Comt, Nat Res Lab, 93- *Mem:* Ecol Soc Am. *Res:* Management and analysis of large environmental data bases in support of global change research, including research into biogeochemical cycles, general circulation model and atmospheric chemistry. *Mailing Add:* Environ Sci Div MS 6407 Oak Ridge Nat Lab Oak Ridge TN 37831

KANCZAK, NORBERT M, ANATOMY. *Current Pos:* ASSOC PROF ANAT, SCH DENT MED, UNIV PITTSBURGH, 70- *Personal Data:* b Buffalo, NY, Feb 12, 31; m 58; c 4. *Educ:* State Univ NY Buffalo, BA, 58, PhD(anat), 64. *Prof Exp:* Sr instr anat, Sch Med, Tufts Univ, 65-66, asst prof, 66-70. *Concurrent Pos:* Nat Inst Arthritis & Metab Dis fel, Ohio State Univ, 63-64, Nat Cancer Inst fel, 64-65. *Res:* Morphology and physiology of transitional epithelium; oncology of transitional cell carcinoma; electron microscopic histochemistry. *Mailing Add:* Univ Pittsburgh Sch Med Dent Pittsburgh PA 15261

KANDA, MOTOHISA, ELECTROMAGNETICS, ANTENNA THEORY. *Current Pos:* SECT CHIEF, ELECTROMAGNETIC FIELDS DIV, NAT INST STAND & TECHNOL, BOULDER, COLO, 71- *Personal Data:* b Kanagawa, Japan, Sept 10, 43; US citizen; m 71, Yoko Umeda; c Michael Y, Carol T, Mark H, Matthew N. *Educ:* Keio Univ, BS, 66; Univ Colo, MS, 68, PhD(elec & comput eng), 71. *Honors & Awards:* Bronze Medal, Dept Com, 81 & 92, Silver Medal, 88. *Prof Exp:* Res technician, Keio Univ, Tokyo, 65-66; tech asst, Electrotech Lab, Tokyo, 66; res asst, Univ Colo, Boulder, 67-71. *Concurrent Pos:* Assoc adj prof, Univ Colo, 74-78, adj prof, 78-; vchmn, Comt A, Int Union Radio Sci, 87-, chmn, 90-92, vchmn, Int Comn A, 93- *Mem:* Fel Inst Elec & Electronics Engrs; Int Union Radio Sci; Sigma Xi. *Res:* Electromagnetic field strength calibrations procedures and their associated accuracy statements; directs calibration services for near field parameters: field strength, antenna factor, pattern, gain; technical design and analysis of international intercomparisons of electromagnetic field standard parameters. *Mailing Add:* Electromagnetic Fields Div Nat Inst Stand & Technol 325 Broadway Boulder CO 80303-3328. *Fax:* 303-497-6665; *E-Mail:* mkanda@boulder.nist.gov

KANDASAMY, SATHASIVA B, NEUROSCIENCE, MARINE PHARMACOLOGY. *Current Pos:* vis scientist, 86-92, PROJ MGR & SUPVR RES PHARMACOLOGIST, ARMED FORCES RADIOBIOL INST, 92- *Personal Data:* b Madras, India, Jan 16, 45. *Educ:* Univ Madras, India, BSc, 65, MSc, 68; Pasteur Inst, Paris, PhD(pharmacol), 75. *Honors & Awards:* Int Union Pharmacologists Award, 74. *Prof Exp:* Res fel, Ciba-Geigy, Basel, Switz, 74-75; asst prof pharmacol, Univ Benin, Nigeria, 76-78; asst prof res, Alfaten Med Sch, Lybia, 78-79; vis scientist marine pharmacol, Univ Okla, 79-80, vis scientist thermoregulation, NASA, 81-84; assoc prof pharmacol, Baneras Hindu Univ, India, 84-85. *Concurrent Pos:* Nat Res Coun assoc, 83-85. *Mem:* Soc Neurosci; Am Soc Pharmacol & Exp Therapeut. *Res:* Neuroscience; marine pharmacology. *Mailing Add:* Behav Sci Dept Armed Forces Radiobiol Inst Bethesda MD 20889-5145. *Fax:* 301-295-0313

KANDEL, ABRAHAM, COMPUTER SCIENCES. *Current Pos:* assoc prof, 78-80, dir comput sci, dept math & comput sci, 78-84, DIR & PROF COMPUT SCI, FLA STATE UNIV, 80-, CHMN DEPT, 84- *Personal Data:* b Tel-Aviv, Israel, Oct 6, 41; US citizen; m 66; c 3. *Educ:* Technion-Israel Inst Technol, BSc, 66; Univ Calif, Santa Barbara, MSc, 68; Univ NMex, PhD(elec eng, comput sci), 77. *Honors & Awards:* Gold Medal Lifetime Achv, Moisil Int Found, 96- *Prof Exp:* From instr to assoc prof comput sci, NMex Inst Mining & Technol, 70-78. *Concurrent Pos:* Vis sr lectr, Ben Gurion Univ Negev & Tel-Aviv Univ, Israel, 76-77; consult, Sandia Labs, Albuquerque, NMex, 76, TASC Corp, Mass & EL-AL, Tadiran; distinguished vis, Inst Elec & Electronics Engrs-Comput Soc, 81-85. *Mem:* Sr mem & fel, Inst Elec & Electronics Engrs; Asn Comput Mach; Pattern Recognition Soc; Am Soc Eng Educ; fel AAAS; fel NY Acad Sci; Sigma Xi. *Res:* Fuzzy sets and systems; computer architecture; performance evaluation; pattern recognition; fault-tolerant systems; switching, microprocessors and logic design; expert systems; applied artificial intelligence. *Mailing Add:* CSE Dept Univ SFla 4204 E Fowler Ave Tampa FL 33620

KANDEL, ERIC RICHARD, NEUROBIOLOGY, PSYCHIATRY. *Current Pos:* prof, Col Physicians & Surgeons, 74-83, UNIV PROF, COLUMBIA UNIV, 83-; SR INVESTR, HOWARD HUGHES MED INST, 84- *Personal Data:* b Vienna, Austria, Nov 7, 29; nat US; m 56; c 2. *Educ:* Harvard Univ, AB, 52; NY Univ, MD, 56. *Hon Degrees:* DSc, Hahnemann Univ & State Univ NY, 86; DHL, Johns Hopkins Univ, 86. *Honors & Awards:* Moses Award, 59; Lester N Hofheimer Prize, Am Psychiat Asn, 77, Spec Presidential Commendation, 86, Distinguished Serv Award, 89; Karl Spencer Lashley Prize in Neurobiol, Am Philos Soc, 81; NY Acad Sci Award in Biol & Med Sci, 82; Albert Lasker Basic Med Res Award, 83; Howard Crosby Warren Medal, Soc Exp Psychologists, 84; J Murray Luck Award for Sci Reviewing, Nat Acad Sci, 88; Nat Medal Sci, 88. *Prof Exp:* Intern, Montefiore Hosp, NY, 56-57; res assoc, Lab Neurophysiol, NIH, 57-60; dir, Mass Ment Health Ctr, 60-65, res psychiat, 60-62, 63-64; from assoc prof to prof physiol & psychiat, Sch Med, NY Univ, 65-74. *Concurrent Pos:* Numerous lectrs, US & foreign, 59-90; teaching fel psychiat, Harvard Med Sch, 60-61, Milton res fel, 61-62; USPHS spec fel, Lab Gen Neurophysiol, Col France, 62-63; res assoc, Med Sch, Harvard Univ, 63-64, instr, 64-65; mem, Comt Life Sci, Nat Acad Sci-Nat Res Coun, 68-69; chief, Dept Neurobiol & Behav, Pub Health Res Inst, NY, 68-74; mem, Neuropsychol Res Rev Comt, NIMH, 69-72; assoc ed, J Neurophysiol, 77-80, J Neurosci, 81-83. *Mem:* Nat Acad Sci; Inst Med; Am Acad Arts & Sci; fel AAAS; Am Philos Soc; hon mem Am Neurol Asn; Int Brain Res Orgn; Am Psychiat Asn; Soc Neurosci (pres, 80-81). *Res:* Electrophysiology of central neurons; neurosecretion; cellular mechanisms of behavior; neuronal plasticity; author or co-author of 7 books and over 220 publications. *Mailing Add:* Ctr Neurobiol & Behav-Col Physicians & Surgeons Columbia Univ 722 W 168th St Res Annex New York NY 10032. *Fax:* 212-960-2474; *E-Mail:* erk5@columbia.edu

KANDEL, RICHARD JOSHUA, PHYSICAL CHEMISTRY. *Current Pos:* RETIRED. *Personal Data:* b New York, NY, Apr 30, 24; m 48, Jeanne Zieph; c 4. *Educ:* NY Univ, BS, 46, PhD(chem), 50. *Prof Exp:* Instr gen chem, NY Univ, 49-50; mem staff phys chem, Los Alamos Sci Lab, 50-67; mem staff chem prog br, Div Res, 67-69, chief radiation, Isotope & Phys Chem Br, 69-75, chief chem & atomic physics br, div phys res, US Energy Res & Develop Admin, 75-77; chief, Fundamental Interactions Br, Div Chem Sci, US Dept Energy, 77-86. *Mem:* Am Chem Soc. *Res:* Mass spectrometry; kinetics; radiation chemistry. *Mailing Add:* 818 Fordham St Rockville MD 20850

KANDHAL, PRITHVI SINGH, PAVEMENT MATERIALS, ASPHALT TECHNOLOGY. *Current Pos:* ASSOC DIR, NAT CTR ASPHALT TECHNOL, AUBURN UNIV, 88- *Personal Data:* b Bikaner, India, May 6, 35; US citizen; m 58, Ummed Kumari; c Ravindra K & Mitra S. *Educ:* Univ Rajasthan, India, Bachelor Engineering, 57; Iowa State Univ, MS, 69. *Honors & Awards:* W J Emmons Award, Asn Asphalt Paving Technologists, 89. *Prof Exp:* Asst dist engr, Rajasthan Pub Works Dept, India, 57-65, dist engr, 65-68; hwy engr, Berger Assocs, Camp Hill, Pa, 69-70; chief asphalt engr, Pa Dept Transp, Harrisburg, 70-88. *Concurrent Pos:* Chmn, Transp Res Bd Comt A2D02 Asphalt Mixtures, 82-88, Subcomt Joint & Crack Sealers, Am Soc Testing & Mat, 88-94, Subcomt Bituminous Mat, Am Soc Civil Engrs, 89-93; dir-at-large, Asn Asphalt Paving Techonolgists. *Mem:* Asn Asphalt Paving Technologists; Am Soc Testing & Mat; Transp Res Bd; Am Soc Civil Engrs. *Res:* Author of over 100 publications; highway pavement materials; mix design; construction; maintenance; hot mix asphalt materials. *Mailing Add:* 635 Woody Dr Auburn AL 36832

KANDINER, HAROLD J(ACK), chemical engineering; deceased, see previous edition for last biography

KANDOIAN, A(RMIG) G(HEVONT), ENGINEERING. *Current Pos:* INDEPENDENT CONSULT, TELECOMMUN ENG, 73- *Personal Data:* b Van, Armenia, Nov 28, 11; nat US; m 45; c 3. *Educ:* Harvard Univ, BS, 34, MS, 35. *Hon Degrees:* DEng, Newark Col Eng, 67. *Honors & Awards:* Award, Inst Elec & Electronics Engrs, 65. *Prof Exp:* From jr engr to head dept radio commun equip, Int Tel & Tel Corp, 35-46, head radio commun lab, Fed Telecommun Labs, Inc, 46-58, vpres commun systs, Int Tel & Tel Labs, 58-59, vpres & gen mgr, 60-64, vpres eng, 64-65; vpres & gen mgr, Commun Systs Inc, Comput Sci Corp, 65-66, pres, 66-67, exec staff vpres, 67-68; vpres & dir, Scanwell Labs, Inc, 68-70; consult telecommun, US Dept Commerce, 70, dir off telecommun, 70-73. *Concurrent Pos:* Exec secy, Cable Television Tech Adv Comt, Fed Commun Comn; mem, Panel on Telecommun Res in US, Nat Acad Eng. *Mem:* Fel Inst Elec & Electronics Engrs. *Res:* Radio aids to air navigation; instrument landing systems; radio antenna systems, particularly in the range; design of radio transmitters and receivers for the very high frequency regions; radio ranges for point to point flight of aircraft; radar components; radio communication systems; satellite communication. *Mailing Add:* 195 Orchard Pl Ridgewood NJ 07450

KANDUTSCH, ANDREW AUGUST, BIOCHEMISTRY. *Current Pos:* Res fel biochem, Roscoe B Jackson Mem Lab, 54-55, res assoc, 55-57, staff scientist, 57-64, asst dir res, 65-66, dep dir, 81-85, SR STAFF SCIENTIST, JACKSON LAB, 64- *Personal Data:* b Kennan, Wis, Oct 10, 26; m 52; c 2. *Educ:* Ripon Col, BA, 50; Univ Wis, MS, 52, PhD(biochem), 54. *Mem:* Am Soc Biol Chemists. *Res:* Animal sterols and their metabolism; sterol biosynthesis and its regulation; membrane structure and function; relationships between sterols, cancer and atherosclerosis; regulation of dolichol biosynthesis; regulation of the cell replication cycle. *Mailing Add:* Jackson Lab Bar Harbor ME 04609-0800

KANE, AGNES BREZAK, CELL INJURY, EXPERIMENTAL CARCINOGENESIS. *Current Pos:* from asst prof to assoc prof path, 82-95, PROF PATH, BROWN UNIV, 95-, CHAIR PATH, 96- *Personal Data:* b Danbury, Conn, Nov 3, 46. *Educ:* Swarthmore Co, BA, 68; Temple Univ, MD, 74, PhD(exp path), 76. *Prof Exp:* Fel, Karolinska Inst, Stockholm, Swed, 76-77; staff pathologist, Temple Univ Hosp, 79-82. *Concurrent Pos:* Res career develop award, NIH, 81-86; sci consult, RI Comn Safety & Occup Health, 86-; consult, Identify Occup Dis which pose a major health threat to workers in RI, 87-90; mem, Environ Health Sci Rev Comt, Nat Inst Environ Health Sci, NIH, 88-92; mem, Mine Health Safety Res Adv Comt, Ctr Dis Control/Nat Inst Occup Safety & Health, 93- *Mem:* Sigma Xi; Am Asn Pathologists; Int Acad Path; AAAS; Am Med Womens Asn; Am Thoracic Soc. *Res:* Experimental pathology. *Mailing Add:* Dept Path & Lab Med Brown Univ Providence RI 02912

KANE, BERNARD JAMES, ORGANIC CHEMISTRY. *Current Pos:* Chemist, 57-62, mgr develop terpene chem, 62-71, DIR RES, GLIDDEN-DURKEE, DIV SCM CORP, 71- *Personal Data:* b New York, NY, Sept 22, 32; m 55; c 6. *Educ:* Iona Col, BS, 54; Adelphi Col, MS, 56. *Honors & Awards:* D P Joyce Award, Glidden-Durkee, Div SCM Corp, 70. *Mem:* Am Chem Soc. *Res:* Terpene chemical and organic research and development. *Mailing Add:* 333 Ocean Blvd Atlantic Beach FL 32233-5279

KANE, DANIEL E(DWIN), CHEMICAL ENGINEERING, STERILIZATION ENGINEERING. *Current Pos:* RETIRED. *Personal Data:* b Iowa Park, Tex, Aug 12, 23; m 53, Inga Brolin; c Jeffrey & Daniel. *Educ:* Iowa State Univ, BS, 47; Lawrence Col, MS, 50, PhD(chem eng), 53. *Prof Exp:* Chem engr, Phillips Petrol Co, 47-48; sr chem engr, Fibreboard Paper Prod Corp, 53-59; res assoc res & develop, Nat Vulcanized Fibre Co, 59-66, tech mgr, NVF Co, 66-70; supvr paper/coatings, Bus Equip Div, SCM Corp, 70-73, mgr pilot prod, 73-76; group leader mfg technol, Miles Inc, 76-80, mgr process develop, 80-82, mgr sterilization eng, 82-89. *Concurrent Pos:* pharmaceutical process validation, GMPs. *Mem:* Tech Asn Pulp & Paper Indust; Am Chem Soc. *Res:* Kraft chemical recovery; vulcanized fibre; saturating and specialty papers; water and air pollution abatement; reprographics; coatings; hospital supplies; intravenous solutions; steam sterilization of intravenous solutions and process equipment; ETO sterilization; sterilize in place; clean in place. *Mailing Add:* 18680 Quailridge Rd Cottonwood CA 96022

KANE, DANIEL JAMES, ULTRAFAST LASER DIAGNOSTICS, DIODE LASER SPECTROSCOPY. *Current Pos:* SR RES SCIENTIST, SW SCI INC, 92- *Educ:* Mont State Univ, BS, 83; Univ Ill, MS, 86, PhD(physics), 89. *Prof Exp:* Fel, Los Alamos Nat Labs, 89-92. *Mem:* Am Phys Soc; Optical Soc Am. *Res:* Development of devices to measure ultrashort laser pulses and trace gas detection using diode lasers. *Mailing Add:* 1570 Pacheco St Suite E-11 Santa Fe NM 87505-3937

KANE, E(NEAS) D(ILLON), ENGINEERING. *Current Pos:* RETIRED. *Personal Data:* b San Francisco, Calif, Jan 8, 17; m 44; c 8. *Educ:* Univ Calif, BS, 38, PhD(mech eng), 49; Kans State Col, MS, 39. *Prof Exp:* Student & design engr, Westinghouse Mfg Co, Philadelphia, 39-40; mech engr, Radiation Lab, Univ Calif, 42-43; group engr, Clinton Eng Works, Tenn Eastman Corp, Oak Ridge, 43-45; asst prof eng design, Univ Calif, 45-47, lectr, 47-48, assoc prof, 50-51, assoc prof, Radiation Lab, 51-52; supvr process eval, Calif Res & Develop Co, 52-53; res, Calif Res Corp, 54-63; mgr prod res, Chevron Res Co, 63-64, vpres prod res, 65-67, pres, 67-70, vpres res, 70-76; asst secy exec comt, Stand Oil Co, Calif, 64-65, vpres technol, 75-82. *Mem:* Nat Acad Eng; Am Soc Mech Engrs. *Res:* Flow of gases at low pressures; process design and evaluation in nuclear energy and petroleum refining; oil field research. *Mailing Add:* 781 Balra Dr El Cerrito CA 94530

KANE, EDWARD R, TECHNICAL MANAGEMENT. *Current Pos:* RETIRED. *Personal Data:* b Schenectady, NY, Sept 13, 18; m 48, Doris Peterson; c Christine K (Plant) & Susan K (Booth). *Educ:* Union Col, BS, 40; Mass Inst Technol, PhD(phys chem), 43. *Honors & Awards:* Int Paladium Medal, Soc Indust Chem, 79. *Prof Exp:* Pres, E I du Pont de Nemours & Co, 73-79, dir, 69-89. *Concurrent Pos:* Trustee, Union Col, 72-77; mem gov bd, JP Morgan, 79-88; dir, Inco Ltd, 81-89, Tex Instruments, 80-89, Mead Corp, 80-88; mem corp, Mass Inst Technol, 79-89; coun mem, Nat Acad Eng, 86-; mem gov bd, Nat Res Coun, 90- *Mem:* Nat Acad Eng (treas, 86-); Soc Chem Indust (pres, 79-80). *Mailing Add:* Old Kennett Rd Wilmington DE 19807

KANE, GORDON LEON, HIGH ENERGY PHYSICS, ASTROPHYSICS. *Current Pos:* asst prof, 65-75, PROF PHYSICS, UNIV MICH, ANN ARBOR, 75- *Personal Data:* b St Paul, Minn, Jan 19, 37; m 58, Lois E Kliffer; c Hal & Mollie. *Educ:* Univ Minn, BA, 58; Univ Ill, MS, 61, PhD(physics), 63. *Prof Exp:* Res assoc physics, Johns Hopkins Univ, 63-65. *Concurrent Pos:* Guggenheim Mem Found fel, 71-72; consult, Brookhaven Nat Lab & Standord Linear Accelerator Ctr; ed, Phys Rev; Delphysius lectr, Univ Calif, Santa Cruz; mem, US Deleg Japan Joint Working Group Space Sci Comt. *Mem:* Fel Am Phys Soc; Hist Sci Soc. *Res:* Theoretical high energy physics; supersymmetry; Higgs physics; dark matter. *Mailing Add:* Dept Physics Univ Mich Ann Arbor MI 48109. *Fax:* 313-763-2213; *E-Mail:* gkane@umich.edu

KANE, GORDON PHILO, PESTICIDE FORMULATION. *Current Pos:* CONSULT, 87- *Personal Data:* b New York, NY, Dec 8, 25; m 52, Saxon B; c Kathleen, Gordon & John. *Educ:* Adelphi Univ, BA, 49; Polytech Inst Brooklyn, MS, 53. *Prof Exp:* Chemist, Warner-Lambert Pharmaceut Corp, NY, 51-54; indust chemist, Barrett Div, Allied Chem Corp, 56; res dir, Valchem Div, United Merchants & Mfrs, SC, 56-62, res scientist, Res Ctr, 62-64; sr org chemist, Columbia Nitrogen Corp, 64-68; sr chemist, Ciba-Geigy Corp, 68-73, group leader, 73-78, sr staff chemist, 78-87. *Mem:* Am Chem Soc; fel Am Inst Chemists. *Res:* Pesticide formulation and process development. *Mailing Add:* 38127 Monticello Dr Prairieville LA 70769

KANE, HARRISON, geotechnical engineering, for more information see previous edition

KANE, HENRY EDWARD, GEOLOGY. *Current Pos:* from asst prof to prof, 61-83, EMER PROF GEOL, BALL STATE UNIV, 83- *Personal Data:* b New Orleans, La, Dec 18, 17; m 53, Gertrude Mattson; c Denarie A & Karen O. *Educ:* La State Univ, BS, 45, MS, 48; Univ Calif, Los Angeles, PhD, 65. *Prof Exp:* Geol scout, Tex Co, 44; field geologist, Miss River Comn, 45; asst, La State Univ, 46-48; subsurface geologist, Stanolind Oil & Gas Co, Standard Oil Co Ind, 48; asst, Univ Calif, Los Angeles, 49-51; geologist, Lloyd Corp Ltd, 52-56; asst prof geol, Lamar State Col Technol, 56-60 & Ft Hays Kans State Col, 60-61. *Concurrent Pos:* Res grants, Shell Res & Develop Co, Shell Oil Co, 56-59, Univ Calif, Los Angeles, 64-65, Ball State Univ, 65-67, 68-69 & 70-71, Ind Acad Sci, 66 & Non-Western Studies, 67; Univ Sci Improv Prog grant, 70-71; Partic, NSF teachers cong, Univ Ore, 59, Am Univ, 61, field geol inst, Ind Univ, 60, res adv undergrad res prog, 59 & NSF geol of Gulf Coast, Rice Univ, 67. *Mem:* Fel Geol Soc Am. *Res:* Recent sedimentation, microfaunas, quaternary geomorphology and geology of the Gulf Coast and the Southern Rockies; fluviatile geomorphology; Kentucky River Basin; geology, Eastern Indiana. *Mailing Add:* 4109 N Redding Rd Muncie IN 47304

KANE, HOWARD L, organic chemistry; deceased, see previous edition for last biography

KANE, JAMES FRANCIS, MICROBIAL PHYSIOLOGY, MICROBIAL GENETICS. *Current Pos:* SCI FEL, SMITH KLINE BEECHAM, 92- *Personal Data:* b Philadelphia, Pa, Nov 22, 42; m 66, Roselyn M Passmore; c Maryellen, James R & Catherine. *Educ:* St Joseph's Col, BS, 64; State Univ NY, Buffalo, PhD(biol), 69. *Prof Exp:* Fel, Baylor Col Med, 68-70; from asst prof to assoc prof, Ctr Health Sci, Univ Tenn, 70-81; sr scientist, Bethesda Res Labs, 81-82; sr res specialist, Monsanto, 82-84, sr res group leader, 84-88, sci fel, 88-92. *Concurrent Pos:* USPHS fel, Baylor Col Med, 68-70; NSF grant, 73-78; adv & consult, Commun Media, Am Soc Microbiol, 79-81; vchmn,

Dept Microbiol & Immunol, Ctr Health Scis, Univ Tenn, 80-81; adj prof molecular biol, Wash Univ, 88-92. *Mem:* Am Soc Microbiol; Soc Indust Microbiol; Am Soc Biochem & Molecular Biol. *Res:* Study the effects of metabolic stress on the quantity and quality of heterlogous proteins produced by E coli in high density fermentations. *Mailing Add:* 709 Swedeland Rd UE3839 King of Prussia PA 19406. *Fax:* 610-270-7449; *E-Mail:* james_f_kane@sbhrd.com

KANE, JAMES JOSEPH, ORGANIC CHEMISTRY. *Current Pos:* asst prof, Wright State Univ, 64-65, coordr, 65-66, asst prof, 66-70, assoc prof chem, 70-92, EMER PROF, WRIGHT STATE UNIV, 92- *Personal Data:* b New York, NY, Mar 4, 29; m 67, Margaret Miller. *Educ:* Upsala Col, BS, 54; Ohio State Univ, PhD(org chem), 60. *Prof Exp:* Res chemist, E I du Pont de Nemours & Co, 60-64. *Mem:* Am Chem Soc; Sigma Xi. *Res:* Chemistry of small and medium carbocyclic and heterocyclic systems; polymers with high thermal stability. *Mailing Add:* 925 Talus Dr Yellow Springs OH 45387-1199

KANE, JOHN JOSEPH, RADIOLOGY. *Current Pos:* From instr to assoc prof, 57-66, prof radiol, 66-77, EMER PROF RADIOL, MED UNIV SC, 77- *Personal Data:* b Key West, Fla, Jan 13, 15; m 39, Myrtle Paplin; c Jean. *Educ:* Col Charleston, BS, 35; Med Col SC, MD, 38; Am Bd Radiol, dipl, 57. *Concurrent Pos:* Radiologist, Med Univ Hosp, 57-77; consult, Mat Air Transp Serv, US AFB, Charleston, 62-85. *Mem:* Emer fel Am Col Radiol; Radiol Soc NAm. *Res:* Cardiac radiology. *Mailing Add:* 1875 Capri Dr Charleston SC 29407-7603

KANE, JOHN POWER, MEDICINE, BIOCHEMISTRY. *Current Pos:* asst resident, Hosps, 59-60, asst prof, 71-76, ASSOC PROF MED, CARDIOVASC RES INST, UNIV CALIF, SAN FRANCISCO, 76-, PROF MED & BIOCHEM & BIOPHYSICS, 82- *Personal Data:* b West Point, NY, July 15, 32; m 66; c 3. *Educ:* Ore State Univ, BS, 55; Univ Ore, MS & MD, 57; Univ Calif, San Francisco, PhD(biochem), 71. *Prof Exp:* Intern med, Santa Clara County Hosp, San Jose, 57-58; asst resident internal med, Hosps, Stanford Univ, 58-59. *Concurrent Pos:* Am Heart Asn estab investr, Cardiovasc Res Inst, Univ Calif, San Francisco, 71-76; mem coun arteriosclerosis, Am Heart Asn, estab investr. *Mem:* AAAS; Am Chem Soc; Biophys Soc; Am Soc Clin Invest; Am Fedn Clin Res; Am Asn Physicians. *Res:* Structure and function of serum lipoproteins; lipid and carbohydrate metabolism; arteriosclerosis; genetics. *Mailing Add:* Dept Med & Biochem 1327M Univ Calif San Francisco CA 94143-0130

KANE, JOHN ROBERT, NUCLEAR PHYSICS. *Current Pos:* Res assoc, 64-68, asst prof, 68-71, assoc prof nuclear physics, 71-78, PROF, COL WILLIAM & MARY, 79- *Personal Data:* b Washington, DC, May 16, 36; m, Kay. *Educ:* Loyola Col, Md, BS, 59; Carnegie-Mellon Univ, MS, 62, PhD, 64. *Mem:* Am Phys Soc. *Res:* Muonic and hadronic atom x-ray studies; muonium in vacuum measurements; rare kaon decays. *Mailing Add:* Dept Physics Col William & Mary Williamsburg VA 23187. *E-Mail:* kane@wmheg.physics.wm.edu

KANE, JOHN VINCENT, JR, three particle reactions, nuclear electronics, for more information see previous edition

KANE, MARTIN FRANCIS, GEOPHYSICS. *Current Pos:* RETIRED. *Personal Data:* b Portland, Maine, Sept 9, 28; m 57, Jacqueline S Morin; c 5. *Educ:* St Francis Xavier Univ, BSc, 51; St Louis Univ, PhD, 70. *Prof Exp:* Geophysicist, Regional Geophys Br, US Geol Surv, 52-63 & Astrogeol Br, 64-67, supvry geophysicist, Regional Geophys Br, 68-70, geologist-in-charge, Marine Geol Br, 70-71, chief, Regional Geophys Br, 72-78, res scientist, 78-83, chief geophysicist, US Geol Surv Mission Jeddah Saudi Arabia, 84-86, consult, 86-90. *Mem:* Geol Soc Am; Am Geophys Union. *Res:* Regional geophysics; marine geophysics; planetary geophysics. *Mailing Add:* 9998 W Florida Ave Lakewood CO 80232

KANE, ROBERT B, MATHEMATICS. *Current Pos:* from asst prof to assoc prof, 60-69, dean sch educ, 89-92, PROF MATH & EDUC, PURDUE UNIV, 69-, DIR TEACHER EDUC, 75- *Personal Data:* b Oak Park, Ill, July 27, 28; m 60; c 5. *Educ:* Univ Ill, BS, 50, MS, 58, PhD(math educ), 60. *Prof Exp:* Teacher pub schs, Ill, 50-51; mgr trainee, Stand Oil Co, 53-55, indust engr, 55-57; res asst, Bur Educ Res, Univ Ill, 59-60. *Concurrent Pos:* Consult sch dists, 61-; vis res prof, Univ Canterbury, 69. *Mem:* Nat Coun Teachers Math; Am Educ Res Asn. *Res:* Linguistic factors in learning and teaching mathematics; cognitive development and mathematics learning. *Mailing Add:* Dept Curric Purdue Univ West Lafayette IN 47907-1442

KANE, RONALD S(TEVEN), THERMAL FLUID ANALYSIS, ENERGY SYSTEMS. *Current Pos:* ASST VPRES ACAD AFFAIRS, NJ INST TECHNOL, 90- *Personal Data:* b New York, NY, Feb 11, 44; m 68; c 2. *Educ:* City Col New York, BME, 65, MME, 69; City Univ New York, PhD(eng), 73. *Prof Exp:* Mech engr heat transfer, Pratt & Whitney Aircraft, 65-66; proj engr mech, Esso Res & Eng, 66-70; grad asst fluid mech, City Col New York, 70-73; consult thermal sci, Polytech Design Co, 73-74; from asst prof to prof mech eng, Manhattan Col, 74-85, chmn dept & grad dir reactor admin, 81-85; grad dean grad studies, res & continuing prof educ, prof mech eng, Stevens Inst Technol, 85-90. *Concurrent Pos:* Res asst, City Col New York Res Found, 70-73; consult, Polytech Design Co, Foster Wheeler Energy Corp, 74-; reviewer, McGraw-Hill Publ Co, 76-; consult, Burns & Roe, 80-; consult, Transnuclear Corp, Gen Elec, 85- *Mem:* Am Soc Mech Engrs; Am Inst Chem Engrs; Sigma Xi; Am Soc Eng Educ. *Res:* Drag reduction in particulate suspensions; coal gasification; liquid metal heat transfer and fluid mechanics; ocean thermal energy conversion; heat pipe development; new energy resource development; advanced reactor safety. *Mailing Add:* 98 Algonquin Trail Oakland NJ 07436-3733

KANE, STEPHEN SHIMMON, CHEMISTRY. *Current Pos:* RETIRED. *Personal Data:* b Chicago, Ill, Nov 5, 17; m 46; c 2. *Educ:* Univ Chicago, BS, 37, PhD(org chem), 41. *Prof Exp:* Res chemist, Phillips Petrol Co, Okla, 40-42 & Apex Smelting Co, Chicago, 42-44; instr chem, Jersey City Jr Col, 46-48, San Bernardino Valley Col, 48-50 & East Los Angeles Col, 50-59; res chemist, Zolatone Process, Inc, 59-63; instr chem, East Los Angeles Col, 63-68; asst dean instr, West Los Angeles Col, 68-75, dean student serv, 75-80. *Mem:* AAAS; Am Chem Soc; Soc Coating Technol. *Res:* Organic coatings; petroleum; aluminum magnesium metallurgy; organic synthesis. *Mailing Add:* 4333 Redwood Ave No 5 Marina Del Rey CA 90292-7642

KANE, SUSAN ELIZABETH, MULTIDRUG RESISTANCE, EXPRESSION VECTORS. *Current Pos:* Asst res scientist, 90-96, ASSOC RES SCIENTIST, CITY OF NEW HOPE NAT MED CTR, 96- *Personal Data:* b Tucson, Ariz, Aug 8, 57. *Educ:* Stanford Univ, BS, 79; Johns Hopkins Univ, PhD(biol), 86. *Concurrent Pos:* Fel Am Cancer Soc, Nat Cancer Inst, NIH, 87-90, staff fel, 90. *Mem:* Am Asn Cancer Res; Am Asn Advan Sci; Am Soc Cell Biol; Asn Women Sci. *Res:* Multidrug resistance (MDR) which develops in cancer patients during chemotherapy, the mechanisms by which MDR works; gene therapy to protect normal cells against toxic side-effects of chemotherapy. *Mailing Add:* Dept Cell & Tumor Biol City Hope Nat Med Ctr 1500 E Duarte Rd Duarte CA 91010. *Fax:* 813-301-8972; *E-Mail:* skane@smtplink.coh.org

KANE, THOMAS R(EIF), MECHANICS, AEROSPACE ENGINEERING. *Current Pos:* prof, 61-97, EMER PROF ENG MECH, STANFORD UNIV, 97- *Personal Data:* b Vienna, Austria, Mar 23, 24; nat US; m 51; c 2. *Educ:* Columbia Univ, BS, 49 & 50, MS, 52, PhD(appl mech), 53. *Hon Degrees:* Dr Tech Sci, Tech Univ Vienna, Austria, 90. *Honors & Awards:* Dirk Brouwer Award, Am Astron Soc; Alexander von Humboldt Prize. *Prof Exp:* Res assoc, Columbia Univ, 52-53; from asst prof to assoc prof mech eng, Univ Pa, 53-60. *Concurrent Pos:* Fulbright lectr, Victoria Univ Manchester, 58-59; vis prof, Fed Univ Rio de Janeiro, 71-72. *Mem:* Am Soc Mech Engrs; Am Astronaut Soc. *Res:* Dynamics; human motion; mechanics of continua. *Mailing Add:* Dept Mech Eng Durand Bldg Rm 275 Stanford Univ Stanford CA 94305-3030

KANE, WALTER REILLY, NUCLEAR PHYSICS. *Current Pos:* res assoc, 58-60, from asst physicist to assoc physicist, 60-66, PHYSICIST, BROOKHAVEN NAT LAB, 66- *Personal Data:* b Ithaca, NY, Nov 3, 26; m 53, Margaret Gunn; c Katherine S. *Educ:* Stanford Univ, BS, 49; Univ Wash, MS, 51; Harvard Univ, PhD(physics), 59. *Prof Exp:* Physicist, Nat Bur Stand, 51-52, Avco Mfg Corp, 56-57; mem staff, Los Alamos Sci Lab, 52-54. *Mem:* Fel Am Phys Soc; sr mem Inst Nuclear Mat Mgt. *Res:* Nuclear spectroscopy; neutron physics. *Mailing Add:* Dept Advan Technol Brookhaven Nat Lab Upton NY 11973-5000. *Fax:* 516-344-7533; *E-Mail:* wkane@bnl.gov

KANE, WILLIAM J, ORTHOPEDIC SURGERY, PHYSIOLOGY. *Current Pos:* Ryerson prof orthop surg & chmn dept, 71-78, PROF ORTHOP SURG, MED SCH, NORTHWESTERN UNIV, 78- *Personal Data:* b Brooklyn, NY, Feb 22, 33; m 60, Elizabeth Knoll; c Kathleen, William, Stephen, Patricia & Anne. *Educ:* Col of the Holy Cross, AB, 54; Columbia Univ, MD, 58; Univ Minn, Minneapolis, PhD(orthop surg), 65. *Honors & Awards:* Kappa Delta Award, Am Acad Orthop Surg, 66. *Prof Exp:* From instr to assoc prof orthop surg, Univ Minn, Minneapolis, 64-71. *Mem:* Am Orthop Asn; Am Acad Orthop Surg; Scoliosis Res Soc (pres, 79-80); Int Soc Study Lumbar Spine; Am Col Surgeons; NAm Spine Soc. *Res:* Bone blood flow; degenerative diseases of the spine; pelvic fractures; scoliosis. *Mailing Add:* 825 S Eighth St Minneapolis MN 55404. *Fax:* 612-333-6922

KANE, WILLIAM THEODORE, x-ray diffraction, spectroscopy, for more information see previous edition

KANE-BERMAN, JOCELYNE DENISE LAMB, HEALTHCARE ADMINISTRATION. *Current Pos:* CHIEF DIR, HEALTH DEPT, WEST CAPE, SAFRICA, 96- *Personal Data:* b Johannesburg, SAfrica, Mar 26, 33. *Educ:* Univ Cape Town, MB ChB, 56, MPA, 78. *Prof Exp:* Intern, Groote Schuur Hosp, SAfrica, 57, from med supt to chief dir, 70-95; med officer, Cape Prov Admin, 60-70. *Concurrent Pos:* Sr lectr, Dept Community Health, Univ Cape Town, 78-; trustee, Health Systs Trust, SAfrica, 92-; found mem, Coun Health Servs Accreditation, 94- *Mem:* Foreign assoc Inst Med-Nat Acad Sci; Med Asn SAfrica (pres, 96-97). *Mailing Add:* Health Dept Prov Admin Dorp St Cape Town West Cape South Africa

KANEDA, TOSHI, BIOCHEMISTRY, MICROBIOLOGY. *Current Pos:* res fel, 84-92, RES MICROBIOLOGIST, ALTA RES COUN, 60-, HEAD BIOL, 81-, EMER RES FEL, 92- *Personal Data:* b Utsunomiya-shi, Japan, May 21, 25; m 59; c 2. *Educ:* Tokyo Inst Technol, BEng, 50; Univ Tokyo, DSc(biochem), 62. *Prof Exp:* Fel microbiol, Prairie Regional Lab, Nat Res Coun Can, 56-58; fel biochem, Sch Med, Western Res Univ, 58-60. *Concurrent Pos:* Med Res Coun Can grant, 64-; hon prof med bact, Univ Alta, 75-, Heilongjiang Acad Sci, China, 88- *Mem:* Am Chem Soc; Can Biochem Soc. *Res:* Microbiology of fossil fuels; low temperature microbiology; biosynthesis and functions of iso and anteiso series of fatty acids in bacteria. *Mailing Add:* 312-5465 201st St Langley BC N3A 1P8 Can

KANEHIRO, YOSHINORI, SOIL SCIENCE. *Current Pos:* Asst soils & agr chem, Univ Hawaii, 42-48, jr soil scientist, 48-57, from asst soil scientist & asst prof to assoc soil scientist & assoc prof, 57-70, soil scientist & prof soil sci, 70-83, EMER SOIL SCIENTIST & EMER PROF SOIL SCI, UNIV HAWAII, 84- *Personal Data:* b Puuloa, Hawaii, Oct 6, 19; m 47; c 2. *Educ:* Univ Hawaii, BS, 42, MS, 48, PhD(soil sci), 64. *Concurrent Pos:* Tech consult, Olin Mathieson Chem Corp, 57; res soil scientist, Agr Res Serv, USDA, Ft Collins, Colo, 68-69. *Mem:* Am Soc Agron; Soil Sci Soc Am; Sigma Xi. *Res:* Nitrogen transformation in soils; minor elements, especially zinc in soils; clay mineralogy of soils. *Mailing Add:* Dept Agron & Soil Sci Univ Hawaii 1910 East-West Rd Honolulu HI 96822

KANEKO, HISASHI, ELECTRICAL ENGINEERING. *Current Pos:* res staff, NEC Corp, 56-60, res mgr, 62-68, gen mgr, Transmission Div, 70-85, vpres, 85-89, sr vpres, 89-93, pres & chief exec officer, NEC Am, NY, 91-93, exec vpres, 93-94, PRES, NEC CORP, TOKYO, 94- *Personal Data:* b Tokyo, Japan, Nov 19, 33; m, Motoko Washino; c Satoshi, Makoto & Hajime. *Educ:* Univ Tokyo, BSEE, 56, PhD(eng), 67; Univ Calif, MSEE, 62. *Honors & Awards:* Kajii Mem Prize, Elec Comn Asn, Japan, 79; Achievement Award, Inst Electronics Info & Commun Engrs, 85; E H Armstrong Award, Inst Elec & Electronics Engrs, 92. *Prof Exp:* Res asst, Univ Calif, Berkeley, 60-62; mem tech staff, Bell Tel Labs, 68-70. *Concurrent Pos:* Bd dirs, Nat Eng Consort Corp, 89- *Mem:* Foreign assoc Nat Acad Eng; fel Inst Elec & Electronics Engrs; Inst Electronics Info & Commun Engrs; Eng Acad Japan. *Res:* Author of 4 publications; granted 70 Japanese patents and 4 US patents; electrical engineering. *Mailing Add:* NEC Corp 571 Shiba Minatoku Tokyo 108-01 Japan

KANEKO, JIRO JERRY, PHYSIOLOGY, CLINICAL BIOCHEMISTRY. *Current Pos:* Asst specialist, Exp Sta, 56-59, from asst prof to assoc prof, 59-69, PROF CLIN PATH & CHMN DEPT, SCH VET MED, UNIV CALIF, DAVIS, 69- *Personal Data:* b Stockton, Calif, Nov 20, 24; m 50; c 3. *Educ:* Univ Calif, AB, 52, DVM, 56, PhD(comp path), 59. *Hon Degrees:* DVSc, Belg, 80. *Concurrent Pos:* Lectr, 57-59. *Mem:* Soc Exp Biol & Med; Am Physiol Soc; Am Asn Clin Chem; Am Col Vet Pathologists; Sigma Xi; Am Chem Soc. *Res:* Biochemistry of erythrocyte and hemoglobin of animals; blood dyscrasias of animals; metabolic diseases; kinetics of erythropoiesis and granulopoiesis; organ functions. *Mailing Add:* Dept Vet Med & Clin Path Dept PMI Univ Calif Davis CA 95616. *Fax:* 530-752-3349

KANEKO, THOMAS MOTOMI, ORGANIC CHEMISTRY, POLYMER CHEMISTRY. *Current Pos:* RETIRED. *Personal Data:* b Tokyo, Japan, Aug 15, 14; US citizen; m 57. *Educ:* Univ Utah, BSChE, 36, PhD(metall), 56. *Prof Exp:* Assayer, Nev Mines Div, Kennecott Copper Corp, 36-39; res chemist, Cent Res Labs, Mitsubishi Chem Industs Ltd, Japan, 39-41; res engr, Res & Planning Dept, Mitsubishi Rayon Co, Ltd, 50-52; res metallurgist, Union Carbide Nuclear Div, 56-57; res chemist, Nat Distillers & Chem Corp, 57-59; res metallurgist, Basf Wyandotte Corp, 59-65, sr res chemist, 65-78, res assoc, 78-84. *Concurrent Pos:* Task force chmn, Am Soc Test & Mat, 77- *Mem:* Fel AAAS; Am Chem Soc; fel Am Inst Chem; NY Acad Sci; Weed Sci Soc Am. *Res:* Extractive metallurgy; reaction kinetics; colloid and surfactant chemistry; surfactant applications research in the formulating and evaluating of detergents, pesticides and metal processing compounds. *Mailing Add:* 1224 Bracebridge Ct Campbell CA 95008

KANE-MAGUIRE, NOEL ANDREW PATRICK, INORGANIC CHEMISTRY. *Current Pos:* from asst prof to assoc prof, 73-85, PROF CHEM, FURMAN UNIV, 85- *Personal Data:* b Brisbane, Queensland, Australia, May 4, 42; m 69; c 1. *Educ:* Univ Queensland, BSc, 63, Hons, 64, PhD(chem), 69. *Prof Exp:* Assoc inorg chem, Boston Univ, 68-69 & Wayne State Univ, 69-70; assoc, Carleton Univ, 70-73. *Mem:* Am Chem Soc. *Res:* Reaction mechanisms of inorganic compounds; transition metal photochemistry. *Mailing Add:* 111 Bexhill Ct Greenville SC 29609-1403

KANEMASU, EDWARD TSUKASA, AGRICULTURE. *Current Pos:* PROF & HEAD, AGRON DEPT, UNIV GA, 89- *Personal Data:* b Hood River, Ore, Nov 16, 40; c 3. *Educ:* Mont State Univ, BS, 62, MS, 64; Univ Wis-Madison, PhD(soil physics), 69. *Honors & Awards:* Agron Res Award, Am Soc Agron; Fel, AAAS. *Prof Exp:* From asst prof to assoc prof, Kans State Univ, 69-78, prof agron, Evapo-transportation Lab, 78-89. *Mem:* AAAS; fel Am Soc Agron; Am Meteorol Soc. *Res:* Stomatal diffusion resistance as influenced by leaf water potential and light; evapo-transpiration and water use efficiency of agronomic crops. *Mailing Add:* Col Agr & Environ Sci Off Int Agr 303 Lumpkin House Athens GA 30602

KANES, WILLIAM H, TECTONICS. *Current Pos:* assoc prof, 71-75, dir, Earth Sci & Resource Inst, 75, PROF GEOL, UNIV SC, 75-, DISTINGUISHED PROF EARTH RESOURCES, 85- *Personal Data:* b New York, NY, Oct 15, 34; m 59, 84; c 6. *Educ:* City Col New York, BS, 56; Univ WVa, MS, 58, PhD(geol), 65. *Prof Exp:* Sr res geologist, Exxon Prod Res Co, 60-66, area geologist, Exxon Stan Libya, 67-69; asst prof geol, WVa Univ, 69-70. *Concurrent Pos:* NSF resident res prof, Acad Sci Res & Technol, Cairo, Egypt, 76-77; vis prof fel, Univ Col Swansea, Univ Wales, 77-80, hon prof fel, Univ Col Aberystwyth, 79-83 & Univ Col Swansea, 80-86, co-dir, Earth Resources Inst, Univ Col Swansea, 80-86; co-dir, ESRI-UK, Univ Bristol, 86-88, hon prof fel, 86-89; vis prof & adv, Postgrad Res Inst Sedimentology & exec dir, ESRI-UK, Univ Reading, 89- *Mem:* Assoc Am Asn Petrol Geol; Soc Econ Paleontologists & Mineralogists; fel Geol Soc Am; fel AAAS; Am Geophys Union. *Res:* Stratigraphy, sedimentation and structural geology in the Appalachian Region; African and circum Mediterranean regional geology and tectonics; South American tectonics and petroleum geology; tectonics and petroleum geology of Eastern Europe and the USSR. *Mailing Add:* Dept Geol Univ SC 901 Sumpter St Columbia SC 29208-0001

KANESHIGE, HARRY MASATO, CIVIL ENGINEERING. *Current Pos:* from asst prof to assoc prof, 58-74, PROF CIVIL ENG, OHIO UNIV, 74- *Personal Data:* b Aiea, Oahu, Hawaii, July 11, 29; m 63, 81, Susan Fleming; c Loren & Michael. *Educ:* Univ Wis, BS, 51, MS, 52, PhD(civil eng), 59. *Prof Exp:* Instr civil eng, Univ Wis, 54-56, 57-58, proj assoc, 56-57. *Mem:* AAAS; Am Soc Civil Engrs; Am Water Works Asn; Water Pollution Control Fedn. *Res:* Environmental health and sanitation; surveying and mapping; water and wastewater treatment. *Mailing Add:* Dept Civil Eng Ohio Univ Stocker Ctr Athens OH 45701

KANESHIRO, EDNA SAYOMI, CELL BIOLOGY, BIOCHEMISTRY. *Current Pos:* from asst prof to assoc prof, 72-82, PROF BIOL, UNIV CINCINNATI, 82- *Personal Data:* b Hilo, Hawaii, Dec 20, 37. *Educ:* Syracuse Univ, BS, 57, MS, 62, PhD(zool), 68. *Prof Exp:* USPHS fel cell biol, Univ Chicago, 68-70; NSF fel biochem, Bryn Mawr Col, 70-72. *Concurrent Pos:* Mem corp, Marine Biol Lab, Woods Hole, 73-; sr res microbiologist, Nat Inst Allergy & Infectious Dis, 80-81. *Mem:* Am Soc Cell Biol; Soc Protozoologists; AAAS; Am Soc Trop Med & Hyg; Sigma Xi; Am Asn Univ Profs. *Res:* Structure and function of protozoans; membrane structure and function; lipid biochemistry; opportunistic infections (pneumocystis). *Mailing Add:* Dept Biol Sci Univ Cincinnati 231 Bethesda Ave Cincinnati OH 45221-0006. *Fax:* 513-556-5280; *E-Mail:* kaneshir@ucbeh

KANESHIRO, KENNETH YOSHIMITSU, EVOLUTIONARY BIOLOGY. *Current Pos:* COORDR, HAWAIIAN DROSOPHILA PROJ, DEPT ENTOM, UNIV HAWAII, 70-, DIR, HAWAIIAN EVOLUTIONARY BIOL PROG, 85- *Personal Data:* b Honolulu, Hawaii, Dec 15, 43; m 67; c 2. *Educ:* Univ Hawaii, BA, 65, MS, 68, PhD(entom), 74. *Mem:* Entom Soc Am; Soc Study Evolution; Am Soc Naturalists. *Res:* Basic mechanisms of speciation processes in Hawaiian Drosophila; tools and techniques for the formulation of a biosystematic classification of the endemic Hawaiian Drosophilidae; sexual behavior and inferences of directions of evolution. *Mailing Add:* 3050 Maile Way Honolulu HI 96822

KANEY, ANTHONY ROLLAND, GENETICS. *Current Pos:* from asst prof to assoc prof, 69-80, PROF BIOL, BRYN MAWR COL, 80- *Personal Data:* b Centralia, Ill, Mar 8, 40. *Educ:* Wabash Col, AB, 61; Univ Ill, Urbana, PhD(microbiol), 66. *Prof Exp:* Res assoc microbiol, Univ Ill, Urbana, 66-67; asst prof biol, Univ PR, San Juan, 67-69. *Concurrent Pos:* NATO Fel, Biol Inst Carlsberg Found, Copenhagen, 76-77. *Mem:* Genetics Soc Am; Soc Protozool. *Res:* Developmental genetics of Tetrahymena thermophila. *Mailing Add:* Dept Biol Bryn Mawr Col Bryn Mawr PA 19010

KANFER, JULIAN NORMAN, BIOCHEMISTRY. *Current Pos:* dept head, 75-86, PROF BIOCHEM, FAC MED UNIV MAN, 75- *Personal Data:* b Brooklyn, NY, May 23, 30; m 87, Beverly McNamara; c Rachel & Brian. *Educ:* Brooklyn Col, BS, 54; George Washington Univ, MS, 58, PhD(biochem), 61. *Honors & Awards:* Vis Scientist Award, Med Res Coun Can, 83, 84 & 86. *Prof Exp:* Lab asst biol, Brooklyn Col, 54-55; chemist, Nat Inst Neurol Dis & Blindness, 55-61, biochemist, 62-69; assoc biochemist, Mass Gen Hosp, Boston, 69-71, biochemist, 71-75; dir biochem, Eunice Kennedy Shriver Ctr, 71-75. *Concurrent Pos:* NIH res fel, Harvard Med Sch, 61-62, NSF res fel, 62-63; assoc prof, Med Sch, Duke Univ, 68-69 & Harvard Med Sch; adj assoc prof Brandeis Univ; mem med adv bd, Nat Tay-Sachs Found; vis prof, Univ Pittsburg Med Ctr, 93-94. *Mem:* AAAS; Am Chem Soc; Am Soc Biol Chem; Am Soc Neurochem; Int Soc Neurochem. *Res:* Sphingolipid metabolism in relationship to the sphingolipidosis; membrane phospholipids of brain; alzheimers disease, multiple sclerosis; signal transduction; second messengers. *Mailing Add:* Dept Biochem Univ Man Winnipeg MB R3T 2N2 Can. *Fax:* 204-783-0864

KANG, C YONG, VIROLOGY, MOLECULAR BIOLOGY. *Current Pos:* DEAN SCI, FAC SCI PROF, DEPT ZOOL & PROF, DEPT MICROBIOL & IMMUNOL, UNIV WESTERN ONT, 92- *Personal Data:* b Hadong, Korea, Nov 28, 40; Can citizen; m 66; c 3. *Educ:* Malling Agr Col, Denmark, DiplVSci, 63; Kon-Kuk Univ, Seoul, Korea, BSA, 65; McMaster Univ, Hamilton, Can, PhD(virol), 71. *Hon Degrees:* Dsc, Carleton Univ, 91. *Prof Exp:* Asst viral oncol, McArdle Lab, Univ Wis, 71-74; from asst prof to assoc prof virol, Southwestern Med Sch, Univ Tex, 74-82; prof & chmn, Dept Microbiol & Immunol, Fac Med, Univ Ottawa, 82-92. *Concurrent Pos:* Sci consult, Virus Res Inst, Cambridge, Mass & Korea, Green Cross Corp, Seoul, Korea. *Mem:* Am Soc Virol; Am Soc Microbiol; AAAS; Can Soc Microbiologists; Genetic Soc Can; NY Acad Sci; fel Royal Soc Can. *Res:* Studies of molecular mechanisms of viral interference mediated by defective interfering virus particles; investigation of molecular genetics of Hantaviruses; studies on cellular transformation by reticuloendotheliosis virus transforming gene rel; development of acquired immunodeficiency syndrome vaccine. *Mailing Add:* Deans Off Western Sci Ctr Univ Western Ont London ON N6A 5B7 Can

KANG, CHANG-YUIL, idiotype, viral immunology, for more information see previous edition

KANG, CHIA-CHEN CHU, fuel science, petroleum science, for more information see previous edition

KANG, DAVID SOOSANG, PEDIATRICS, GENETICS. *Current Pos:* from asst prof to assoc prof, 77-88, PROF PEDIAT & GENETICS, COL MED, RUSH UNIV, 88- *Personal Data:* b Yiryong, Korea, Nov 7, 31; US citizen; m 58; c 4. *Educ:* Seoul Nat Univ, MD, 53, PhD(pharmacol), 63. *Prof Exp:*

Asst prof genetics, Ill Inst Technol, 71-75. *Mem:* Am Soc Human Genetics. *Res:* Genetic and biochemical studies of genetic disease and common diseases: interrelations of basic amino acids and their metabolites in urea cycle disorder, and role of protein-bound homocystine in common diseases. *Mailing Add:* Rush-Presby St Luke's Med Ctr 1753 W Congress Pkwy Chicago IL 60612-3809

KANG, HONGLING, ACOUSTICS & NOISE VIBRATIONS. *Current Pos:* ENG SPECIALIST, UNITED TECHNOLS, 92- *Personal Data:* m 84, Aiming Sun; c John. *Educ:* Tianjin Univ, BS, 82, MS, 84; Wayne State Univ, PhD(mech eng), 90. *Prof Exp:* Asst prof, Tianjin Univ, 84-85; struct engr, Acme Eng & Mfg Co, 90-92. *Mem:* Am Soc Mech Engrs; Soc Automotive Engrs; Inst Noise Control Eng. *Res:* Noise and vibration of automobile components and their systems; noise and vibration control of automobile subsystems; finite element analysis and mechanical system analysis of the mechanical system with linear and non-linear characteristics. *Mailing Add:* 9129 Stonehouse Livonia MI 48150. *Fax:* 313-593-9703; *E-Mail:* hongling@uta.com

KANG, IK-JU, ATOMIC PHYSICS. *Current Pos:* assoc prof, Carbondale, 67-69, assoc prof, Edwardsville, 69-70, PROF PHYSICS, SOUTHERN ILL UNIV, EDWARDSVILLE, 70-, CHMN, 80- *Personal Data:* b Korea, Nov 13, 28; m 55; c 3. *Educ:* Yonsei Univ, Korea, BS, 55, MS, 57; Northwestern Univ, PhD(physics), 62. *Prof Exp:* Instr physics, Yonsei Univ, 55-59; res assoc, Brandeis Univ, 62-63; asst prof, Univ Mass, Amherst, 63-67. *Mem:* Am Phys Soc; Am Asn Physics Teachers. *Res:* Theoretical atomic physics and scattering theory. *Mailing Add:* Dept Physics Southern Ill Univ Edwardsville IL 62026

KANG, JOOHEE, superconductivity, thin film technology, for more information see previous edition

KANG, JUNG WONG, POLYMER ORGANIC CHEMISTRY. *Current Pos:* RETIRED. *Personal Data:* b Tokyo, Japan, July 25, 33; nat US; m 55; c 3. *Educ:* Kinki Univ, Japan, BSc, 56; Osaka Univ, MSc, 59, PhD(org chem), 62. *Prof Exp:* Instr chem, Nara Med Col, Japan, 62-63; fel org chem, Harvard Univ, 63-64; fel organometallic chem, Univ NC, 64-66; res assoc, McMaster Univ, 66-70; res scientist chem to assoc scientist, Firestone Tire & Rubber Co, 70-82, res assoc, 83-96. *Mem:* Am Chem Soc; Japanese Chem Soc; Korean Chem & Chem Eng NAm. *Res:* Polymer chemistry; organometallic chemistry. *Mailing Add:* Heritage House No 206 6710 Hawaii Kai Dr Honolulu HI 96825

KANG, KENNETH S, microbial physiology, for more information see previous edition

KANG, KEWON, genetics, for more information see previous edition

KANG, KYUNGSIK, ELEMENTARY PARTICLE PHYSICS, THEORETICAL PHYSICS. *Current Pos:* Res assoc, 64-66, from asst prof to assoc prof, 66-73, PROF PHYSICS, BROWN UNIV, 73- *Personal Data:* b Jochiwon, Korea, July 12, 36; m 63, Hai-Lanne Hahm; c Peter, Michael & David. *Educ:* Seoul Nat Univ, BS, 59; Ind Univ, PhD(theoret physics), 64. *Honors & Awards:* Camellia Medal, Legion of Honor, Korea, 85. *Concurrent Pos:* Vis prof, Univ Paris, 72-73, 86-87 & 94; vis scientist, Europ Orgn Nuclear Res, 73 & 87; vis physicist, Fermi Nat Accelerator Lab, 74, 77 & 81, Argonne Nat Lab, 68 & 84, Brookhaven Nat Lab, 68 & 79 Neils Bohr Inst, 71 & 87, Los Alamos Nat Lab, 77 & 86; hon prof, Yanbian Univ, Yanji, China, 90; invited chair prof, Korea Advan Inst Sci & Technol, 93. *Mem:* Korean Phys Soc; Korean Scientists & Engrs Am (pres, 82-83); fel Am Phys Soc. *Res:* Phenomenological descriptions of high energy elementary particle physics; grand unification theories; flavor dynamics; composite models; electroweak gauge theories; lepton-induced reactions; supersymmetric string theories; cosmology. *Mailing Add:* Dept Physics Brown Univ Providence RI 02912. *E-Mail:* kang@brownvm.bitnet

KANG, MOHINDER, EVALUATION OF GLYCOPROTEIN PROCESSING INHIBITORS AS ANTI HUMAN IMMUNODEFICIENCY VIRUS & ANTI METASTATIC AGENTS, DRUG METABOLISM STUDIES IN MICE & INVESTIGATION OF TARGETING OF DRUGS TO DIFFERENT TISSUES. *Current Pos:* SR RES BIOCHEMIST, DEPT ONCOL, HOECHT MARION ROUSSEL INC, 88- *Personal Data:* m; c 2. *Educ:* Punjab Agr Univ, BS, 66; Panjab Univ, BS Hons, 67, MS Hons, 69; Tex Tech Univ, PhD(biochem), 76. *Prof Exp:* Res scholar-Cum-Demonstr, Dept Biochem, Panjab Univ, 70-71; res asst, Dept Chem, Tex Tech Univ, 72-75, instr & res asst, 75-76; fel, Dept Biochem, Univ Tex Health Sci Ctr, 76-79; vis fel, Lab Viral Carcinogenesis DCCP, Nat Cancer Inst, NIH, 79-82, staff fel, Lab Biochem & Metab, Nat Inst Arthritis, Diabetes & Digestive & Kidney Dis, 82-86, biotechnol fel, Lab Molecular Biol, Div Cancer Biol & Diag, Nat Cancer Inst, 86-88. *Concurrent Pos:* Vpres, Biochem Soc, Panjab Univ, Chandigarh, India, 70-71; prin investr, Nat Cancer Inst, NIH, 80-81. *Mem:* Am Soc Biol Chemists; Soc Biol Chemists India; Am Chem Soc; AAAS; Am Asn Cancer Res; Soc Complex Carbohydrates. *Res:* Glycolipid and glycoprotein biosynthesis in vitro as well as in mammalian cell and viruses; lipid metabolism in brain and primary cultures from rat brain; isolation, purification and characterization of intermediates in glycoprotein biosynthesis and the effects of glycosylation of proteins in virus replication and infectivity; granted 3 US patents. *Mailing Add:* Hoechst Marion Roussel Inc Oncol Dept 2110 E Gal;braith Cincinnati OH 45215

KANG, MOHINDER SINGH, MEDICAL & HEALTH SCIENCES. *Current Pos:* SR RES BIOCHEM DEPT CELL BIOL, MARION MERRELL DOW RES INST, 88- *Personal Data:* c 2. *Educ:* Punjab Agr Univ Ludhiana India, BS, 66; Punjab Univ Chandigarh India, BS(Hon), 67, MS(Hon), 69; Tex Tech Univ, Lubback, PhD(biochem), 76. *Prof Exp:* Res scholar, Dept Biochem, Panjab Univ India, 70-71; grad res asst, Dept Chem, Tex Tech Univ, 72-76; fel, Dept Biochem, Univ Tex Health Sci Ctr, 76-79; vis fel, Lab Viral Carcinogenesis, Nat Chem Inst, NIH, 79-82; staff fel, Lab Biochem & Metab, Nat Inst Arthritis, Diabetes, & Digestive & Kidney Dis, NIH, 82-86; biotechnol fel, Lab Molecular Biol Div Cancer Biol & Diag, Nat Cancer Inst, NIH, 86-88. *Concurrent Pos:* Vpres biochem soc, Panjab Univ Chandigarh, India, 70-71. *Mem:* Am Soc Biol Chemists; Am Chem Soc; AAAS; Am Asn Cancer Res; Soc Complex Carbohydrates. *Res:* Evaluation of glycoprotein processing inhibitors as anti human immunodeficiency virus (HIV) and anti metastatic agents; drug metabolism studies in mice and investigation of targeting of drugs to different tissues. *Mailing Add:* Dept Cell Biol Merrell Dow Res Inst Cincinnati OH 45215

KANG, SUNG-MO STEVE, COMPUTER-AIDED DESIGN, MODELING & SIMULATION OF VERY LARGE SCALE INTEGRATION. *Current Pos:* PROF ELEC & COMPUT ENG, UNIV ILL, URBANA-CHAMPAIGN, 85-, ASSOC DIR MICROELECTRONICS, 88-, PROF COMPUTER SCI, 90-, HEAD, DEPT ELEC & COMPUT ENG, 95- *Personal Data:* b Seoul, Korea, Feb 25, 45; US citizen; m 72; c 2. *Educ:* Fairleigh Dickinson Univ, BS, 70; State Univ NY, Buffalo, MS, 72; Univ Calif, Berkeley, PhD(elec eng), 75. *Honors & Awards:* Meritorious Serv Award, Inst Elec & Electronics Engrs Computer Soc, 90; Humboldt Res Award for Sr US Scientists, 96. *Prof Exp:* Asst prof elec eng, Rutgers Univ, 75-77; mem tech staff, AT&T Bell Labs, Murray Hill, 77-81, supvr, 82-85. *Concurrent Pos:* Vis prof, Swiss Fed Inst Technol, Lausanne, 89; consult, Teltech, Inc, 89-, MCC, Austin, 89, Motorola Inc, AT&T Bell Labs, 90, Avant!, 96-; mem bd dirs, Anagram Inc, 92-96. *Mem:* Fel Inst Elec & Electronics Engrs; Inst Elec & Electronics Engrs Circuits & Systs Soc (pres, 91); Inst Elec & Electronics Engrs Computer Soc; Inst Elec & Electronics Engrs Lasers & Electrooptical Soc; AAAS; Am Soc Eng Educ; Asn Comput Mach. *Res:* Computer-aided design of very-large scale integrated circuits and systems; modeling and simulation of optoelectronic and novel devices and circuits; analog and digital microelectronics; optical communications. *Mailing Add:* Dept Elec & Comput Eng Univ Ill 1406 W Green St Urbana IL 61801. *Fax:* 217-244-7075; *E-Mail:* kang@ece.uiuc.edu

KANG, SUNGZONG, BIOPHYSICS, BIOCHEMISTRY. *Current Pos:* from instr to asst prof, 68-72, ASSOC PROF, MT SINAI SCH MED, CITY UNIV NEW YORK, 72- & BRONX VET ADMIN MED CTR, 80- *Personal Data:* b Puyo, Korea, Mar 1, 37; m 65. *Educ:* Univ Tubingen, PhD(chem), 64. *Prof Exp:* Res assoc chem, Univ Tubingen, 64-66, Univ Notre Dame, 66-67 & NY Univ, 67-68. *Concurrent Pos:* Vis prof, Max Plank Inst Biophys Chem, Gottingen, 76-77, Max Plank Inst Physiol, Dortmund, 77-78, Seoul Nat Univ, 78-79 & AID, 78-79; Fogarty sr int scholar, 76-77; Alexander von Humboldt US sr scientist fel, 77-78. *Mem:* AAAS; Am Chem Soc; NY Acad Sci; Am Soc Pharmacol & Exp Therapeut. *Res:* Stability, structure and function of biological macromolecules, membranes, proteins and nucleic acids; brain research; molecular pharmacology; quantum biochemistry. *Mailing Add:* Hanhyo Inst CPO Box 1751 Seoul South Korea. *Fax:* 82-2-791-1705

KANG, TAE WHA, INDUSTRIAL TOXICOLOGY, MEDICAL TECHNOLOGY. *Current Pos:* DIR LAB, BIO-SCI RES INST, 78- *Personal Data:* b Chejoodo, Korea; m 73; c 2. *Educ:* Yonsei Univ, BS, 70; Ill Inst Technol, PhD(biol), 76. *Prof Exp:* Fel molecular biol, Univ Edinburgh, 76-77; chmn biochem, Bio-Technics Labs, Inc, 77-78. *Concurrent Pos:* Adj prof, Am Int Univ, 79-80 & Pac Western Univ, 82- *Mem:* Sigma Xi; Am Soc Microbiol; AAAS. *Res:* Testing of food, drug and cosmetics: product label validation and shelf-life stability studies (Rx drugs and OTC products); pre-clinical studies of new drugs and toxicological assessment of environment chemicals (acute, subchronic & chronic animal studies); mutagenicity and carcinogenicity studies of food additives and color additives; safety tests and potency assay of human leukocyte interferon; water and wastewater tests. *Mailing Add:* Bio-Sci Res Inst Inc 4813 Cheyenne Way Chino CA 91710-5510. *Fax:* 909-590-8948; *E-Mail:* bio-science@bio-scienceresearch

KANG, YUAN-HSU, CELL BIOLOGY. *Current Pos:* CHIEF ELECTRON MICROS SECT, NAVAL MED RES INST, 84- *Educ:* Brigham Young Univ, PhD(zoology), 72. *Res:* Natural killer cells; reticuendothelial cells in septic shock. *Mailing Add:* Pathobiol Div Naval Med Res Inst 8905 Wisconsin Ave Bethesda MD 20889-5607. *Fax:* 301-295-0535

KANGAS, DONALD ARNE, CHEMISTRY OF EMULSION POLYMERIZATION. *Current Pos:* CONSULT, 96- *Personal Data:* b Detroit, Mich, Feb 12, 29; m 54, Sirkka Halinen; c 5. *Educ:* Mich Technol Univ, BS, 50; Mich State Univ, MS, 58. *Prof Exp:* Anal chemist, R P Scherer Corp, 50-51; develop chemist, US Army-Chem Corp, 51-53; sr res specialist, Dow Chem USA, 53-80, res assoc polymer, 80-92, consult, 93-96. *Res:* Hydrophobic colloids formed from vinyl monomers; kinetics of polymerization; characterization of dispersion; morphology of particles; properties of films and composites; hydrophillic polyelectrolytes from ionizable vinyl monomers; kinetics characterization and properties. *Mailing Add:* 5112 Nurmi Dr Midland MI 48640. *Fax:* 517-832-2959

KANGOVI, SACH, COMPUTATIONAL & EXPERIMENTAL FLUID MECHANICS, FLUID FILTRATION & ABSORBENCY. *Current Pos:* PRIN SCIENTIST, JOHNSON & JOHNSON, 91- *Personal Data:* b Bangalore, India, Aug 25, 48; m 78, Sita; c Shreya. *Educ:* Jabalpur Univ, BE, 69; Indian Inst Sci, ME, 71; Rutgers Univ, PhD (mech & aeronaut eng), 77. *Honors & Awards:* Minta Martin Award, Am Inst Aeronaut & Astronaut, 75. *Prof Exp:* Sr scientist, Nat Aeronaut Lab, 71-82; res scientist, Paramatic Filter Corp, 82-89; sr tech specialist, Boeing, 89-90. *Mem:* AAAS; Am Soc Mech Engrs. *Res:* Application of computational & experimental fluid mechanics, fluid absorbency and fluid filtration to problems of practical interest especially in health care industry. *Mailing Add:* 63 Saratoga Dr N Cranbury NJ 08512

KANICK, VIRGINIA, radiology, for more information see previous edition

KANIECKI, THADDEUS JOHN, ORGANIC CHEMISTRY. *Current Pos:* TECH DIR, DIAMOND CHEM CO INC, 88- *Personal Data:* b Brooklyn, NY, Mar 24, 31; m 55, Florenc Florek; c Marianne, Walter & John. *Educ:* NY Univ, BA, 53, MS, 55, PhD(org chem), 60. *Prof Exp:* Res assoc, Res & Develop Div, Lever Bros Co, NJ, 60-67; res supvr, Armour-Dial Inc, Chicago, 67-69, res mgr, 69-72; sect mgr, Am Cyanamid Co, 72-75; sr chemist res & develop, Stauffer Chem Co, 75-81; sr tech serv rep, Brent Chem Corp, 81-82, dir res & develop, 82-84; dir res & develop, Clenesco Div, Chemed Corp, 84-87, dir opers, Clenesco Prod Corp, 87-88. *Mem:* Am Chem Soc; Soc Cosmetic Chem; Am Soc Testing & Mat. *Res:* Synthesis and applications of surface active molecules; detergents, toiletries and consumer products, both basic and applied research; preparation and uses of disinfectants, sanitizers and biocides. *Mailing Add:* Two Van Alen Pl Pompton Plains NJ 07444

KANIG, JOSEPH LOUIS, PHARMACEUTICS. *Current Pos:* Assoc pharm, Columbia Univ, 49-51, from asst prof to assoc prof, 51-62, dir, Aerosol Res Labs, 58-67, DIR, INDUST PHARM LAB, COLUMBIA UNIV, 59-, PROF PHARM, 62-, DEAN COL, 65- *Personal Data:* b New York, NY, July 11, 21; m 47; c 3. *Educ:* LI Univ, BS, 42, Columbia Univ, MS, 49; NY Univ, PhD, 60; Am Bd Pharm, dipl. *Concurrent Pos:* Consult, UNESCO, 62-65 & pharmaceut, chem & cosmetic industs; mem, NY State Coun Hosp Pharmacists. *Mem:* Fel AAAS; fel Am Col Apothecaries; fel Am Inst Chem; Am Pharmaceut Asn; Soc Cosmetic Chem. *Res:* Pharmaceutical sciences; industrial pharmaceutical processing; product development and research in dosage design and evaluation; process machinery and evaluative instruments; biopharmaceutics. *Mailing Add:* 3810 Mission Hills Rd Apt 205 Northbrook IL 60062-5751

KANIK, ISIK, ATOMIC & MOLECULAR PHYSICS, ULTRA VIOLET EMISSIONS & ABSORPTIONS IN ATMOSPHERES OF STARS & PLANETS. *Current Pos:* RES SCIENTIST, JET PROPULSION LAB, 92- *Personal Data:* b Istanbul, Turkey, May 24, 58; US citizen; m 82, Isinsu Acikgoz; c Michael T. *Educ:* Mid E Tech Univ, BSc, 80; Univ Calif, MS, 84, PhD(physics), 88. *Prof Exp:* Postdoctoral researcher, Univ Calif, 88-89; asst prof physics, Erciyes Univ, Turkey, 89-90; resident res assoc, Nat Res Coun, NASA, 90-92. *Concurrent Pos:* Res adv, Nat Res Coun, 93-; prin investr, Jet Propulsion Lab, NASA, 93-; task mgr, USAF, 95-; adj prof physics, Calif State Univ, 97- *Mem:* Am Phys Soc. *Res:* Electron-impact excitation; electron-impact-induced emission and photon absorption processes to understand ultra violet emission; photoabsorption occuring in upper atmospheres of stars and solar system bodies. *Mailing Add:* Calif Inst Technol Jet Propulsion Lab 4800 Oak Grove Dr MS 183-601 Pasadena CA 91109. *Fax:* 818-393-4605; *E-Mail:* ikanik@jpluvs.jpl.nasa.gov

KANITZ, MARY HELEN HITSELBERGER, MEDICAL RESEARCH. *Current Pos:* RES BIOLOGIST, DEPT HEALTH & HUMAN SERV, NAT INST OCCUP SAFETY & HEALTH, 92- *Personal Data:* b Washington, DC, Feb 19, 57; m 91, David E; c Julia R. *Educ:* Georgetown Univ, BS, 79; Univ Ill, Col Med, PhD(pharmacol), 86. *Prof Exp:* Chemist, Agr Res Ctr, US Dept Agr, Beltsville, MD, 79-80; res fel, Dept Path & Pharmacol, Northwestern Univ Med Sch, 87-90; scientist, Cancer Res Div, Lilly Res Labs, Eli Lilly & Co, 90-92. *Concurrent Pos:* Prin investr, NIH, 87-90. *Mem:* Am Asn Cancer Research; Asn Women Cancer; Am Soc Cell Biol; NY Acad Sci; Asn Women Sci; AAAS. *Res:* Biochemical; molecular; immunological; in vitro primary cell culture establishment. *Mailing Add:* Nat Inst Occup Safety & Health Div Biomed & Behav Sci Mail Stop C23 44676 Columbia Pkwy Cincinnati OH 45226-1998. *Fax:* 513-533-0510; *E-Mail:* mhkz@niobbs1.cm.cdc.gov

KANIZAY, STEPHEN PETER, GEOLOGY. *Current Pos:* RETIRED. *Personal Data:* b Cleveland, Ohio, Feb 3, 24; m 48, Freda L Barthol; c Jeff, Kelly & Theodore. *Educ:* Miami Univ Ohio, AB, 49, MS, 50; Colo Sch Mines, DSc, 56. *Prof Exp:* From instr to asst prof geol, Colo Sch Mines, 52-58; geologist, Eng Geol Br, US Geol Surv, 58-83. *Concurrent Pos:* Consult, 54-58. *Mem:* Am Geophys Union. *Res:* Engineering and structural geology; rock and soil mechanics. *Mailing Add:* 625 S Parfet St Lakewood CO 80215

KANJOLIA, RAVI K, COMPOUND SEMICONDUCTORS, PRECURSOR CHARACTERIZATION. *Current Pos:* TECH MGR, EPICHEM INC, 96- *Personal Data:* b Raj, India, Nov 16, 54; US citizen; m 84, Sarita Gupta; c Kunal. *Educ:* Univ Rajasthan, India, BSc, 73, MSc, 75; B H Univ, India, PhD(chem), 81. *Prof Exp:* Postdoctoral fel, Univ Ala, Birmingham, 82-84, asst prof chem, 84-87; tech mgr, Morton Int, 87-96. *Mem:* Am Chem Soc; Mat Res Soc; Am Ceramic Soc. *Res:* Synthesis, purification and characterization of organometallic compounds; therochemistry of volatile sources of aluminum, gallium, indium, phosphorous, arsenic and antimony; application of organometallic compounds in electronic devices. *Mailing Add:* 26 Ward Hill Ave PO Box 8230 Haverhill MA 01835. *Fax:* 978-374-6474; *E-Mail:* kanjolir@epichem.com

KANKEL, DOUGLAS RAY, DEVELOPMENTAL BIOLOGY, NEUROBIOLOGY. *Current Pos:* MEM FAC BIOL DEPT, YALE UNIV, 74- *Personal Data:* b Waterbury, Conn, Jan 22, 44. *Educ:* Brown Univ, PhD(biol), 70. *Prof Exp:* Res fel neurobiol, Calif Inst Technol, 70-74. *Mailing Add:* Dept Biol Yale Univ UPO Box 208103 New Haven CT 06520-8103

KAN-MITCHELL, JUNE, CELLULAR IMMUNITY, SKIN & OCULAR MELANOMA. *Current Pos:* ASST PROF MICROBIOL, UNIV SOUTHERN CALIF SCH MED, 85-, ASSOC PROF PATH, 90- *Personal Data:* b Hong Kong, June 3, 49; US citizen; m 67, Malcolm S; c Ian D. *Educ:* Smith Col, BA, 71; Yale Univ, PhD(pharmacol), 77. *Concurrent Pos:* Assoc ed, J Lab Clin Invests, Human Antibodies & Hybridomas & Vaccine Res; prin investr, Nat Eye Inst. *Mem:* Am Asn Cancer Res; Asn Res Vision & Ophthal; Fedn Am Soc Exp Biol; Am Asn Immunol. *Res:* Melanocyte transformation; immune response to melanoma in man; Identification of antigens of skin and ocular melanomas that are immunogenic to human and their usefulness in diagnosis and treatment. *Mailing Add:* Dept Pathol Univ Calif San Diego Sch Med 9500 Gilman Dr 0063 LaJolla CA 92093-0063. *Fax:* 619-534-5792

KANNAN, RAUI, EDUCATION. *Current Pos:* PROF MATH, CARNEGIE MELLON UNIV. *Honors & Awards:* Leroy P Steele Prize, Am Math Soc, 92. *Mailing Add:* Dept Math Carnegie-Mellon Univ Pittsburgh PA 15213-3816

KANNAPPAN, PALANIAPPAN, MATHEMATICS & FUNCTIONAL EQUATIONS, QUASIGRAPHS & LOOPS. *Current Pos:* assoc prof, 67-77, PROF MATH, UNIV WATERLOO, 77- *Personal Data:* b Nattarasan Kottai, India, June 28, 34; m 52, Ronganayaki; c 5. *Educ:* Annamalai Univ, Madras, BSc(Hons), 55, MA, 57; Univ Wash, Seattle, MS & PhD(math), 64. *Prof Exp:* Lectr math, Annamalai Univ, Madras, 55-61; reader, 64-67; asst, Univ Wash, 61-64. *Concurrent Pos:* Fulbright scholar, 61; consult, Dept Univ Affairs, Can, 68-69 & Nat Res Coun Can, 69- *Mem:* Am Math Soc; Indian Math Soc; Indian Acad Sci; Japan Math Soc. *Res:* Functional analysis and functional equations; linear algebra and quasigroups; information theory. *Mailing Add:* Dept Pure Math Univ Waterloo Waterloo ON N2L 3G1 Can. *E-Mail:* plkannappan@watdragon.uwaterloo.ca

KANNEL, WILLIAM B, CARDIOVASCULAR DISEASES, INTERNAL MEDICINE. *Current Pos:* chief sect epidemiol & prev med, 79-90, PROF MED & PUB HEALTH, SCH MED, BOSTON UNIV, 79- *Personal Data:* b Brooklyn, NY, Dec 13, 23; m 42; c 4. *Educ:* Ga Med Col, MD, 49; Harvard Univ, MPH, 59. *Hon Degrees:* MD, Gothenberg Univ, 85. *Honors & Awards:* Dana Award, 72 & 86; Einthoven Award, 73; Gaidner Int Award, 76; Paul Dudley White Award, 77; Copernicus Award, 77; Ciba Award, 81; J D Bruce Award, Am Col Physicians, 82; Distinguished Serv Award, Am Col Cardiol, 88. *Prof Exp:* Intern & resident, USPHS Hosp, Staten Island, NY, 49-50, 53-56; clin investr heart dis epidemiol study, NIH, Framingham, Mass, 50-51; med officer, Newton Heart Prog, Mass, 51-52; assoc dir, Framingham Unit, NIH, 56-65, dir, 65-79. *Concurrent Pos:* Fel, Harvard Med Sch, 56-59; asst med, Peter Bent Brigham Hosp, 56-62; instr, Harvard Med Sch, 59-60, assoc prev med, 60-70, lectr, 70-; consult, Cushing State Hosp, 56-73 & Framingham Union Hosp, 64- *Mem:* Fel Am Col Prev Med; fel Am Heart Asn; fel Am Col Physicians; fel Am Col Cardiol; fel Am Col Epidemiol. *Res:* Cardiovascular epidemiology; investigation of factors of risk and natural history of coronary heart disease, hypertension, stroke and peripheral vascular disease; preventive medicine. *Mailing Add:* Boston Univ Framingham Study Five Thurber St Framingham MA 01701

KANNENBERG, LLOYD C, PHYSICS, OPTICS. *Current Pos:* from instr to assoc prof, Lowell Technol Inst, 68-77, PROF PHYSICS, UNIV LOWELL, 77- *Personal Data:* b Sarasota, Fla, Mar 23, 39; m 63, Susan Lippman; c Susanna. *Educ:* Mass Inst Technol, SB, 61; Univ Fla, MS, 63; Northeastern Univ, PhD(physics), 67. *Prof Exp:* Instr physics, Lowell Technol Inst, 66-67 & Northeastern Univ, 67-68. *Concurrent Pos:* Vis res assoc, Northeastern Univ, 72-80. *Mem:* Am Phys Soc; Int Soc Gen Relativity & Gravitation; Sigma Xi; Math Asn Am. *Res:* General relativity, field theory. *Mailing Add:* 115 Meadowbrook Rd Weston MA 02193

KANNENBERG, LYNDON WILLIAM, MAIZE BREEDING, POPULATION IMPROVEMENT. *Current Pos:* from asst prof to prof, 65-96, EMER PROF CORN BREEDING, UNIV GUELPH, 97- *Personal Data:* b Chicago, Ill, Oct 15, 31; m 54, Barbara M Wallace; c William W, Debra A, Susan E, Jeanne M & Catherine M. *Educ:* Mich State Univ, BSc, 57, MS, 59; Univ Calif, Davis, PhD(genetics), 64. *Prof Exp:* NIH fel, Univ Calif, Davis, 64-65. *Concurrent Pos:* mem, Grants Comt, Nat Res Coun Can, 71-73; mem, Expert Comt Plant Gene Resources, 83-96; maize consult, Can Int Develop Agency, Bangladesh, 85; vis lectr, China, 88. *Mem:* Am Soc Agron; Genetics Soc Can; Sigma Xi; Can Soc Agron. *Res:* Development and improvement of short season corn breeding populations as sources for inbred lines with different genetic backgrounds than current commercial germplasm. *Mailing Add:* Dept Crop Sci Univ Guelph Guelph ON N1G 2W1 Can. *Fax:* 519-763-8933; *E-Mail:* lkannenb@crop.uoguelph.ca

KANNEWURF, CARL RAESIDE, SOLID STATE ELECTRONICS. *Current Pos:* Res assoc physics, 60-62, from asst prof to assoc prof elec eng, 63-71, PROF ELEC ENG & COMP SCI, NORTHWESTERN UNIV, EVANSTON, 71- *Personal Data:* b Waukegan, Ill, Mar 24, 31; m 83, Patricia L Sharpe. *Educ:* Lake Forest Col, BA, 53; Univ Ill, MS, 54; Northwestern Univ, PhD(physics), 60. *Mem:* Am Phys Soc; Sigma Xi; sr mem Inst Elec & Electronics Engrs; Mat Res Soc. *Res:* Study of various electrical and optical phenomena in semiconductors, metals, molecular metals and conducting polymers; transport phenomena and superconductivity; development of optical materials and devices. *Mailing Add:* Northwestern Univ EE-CS Evanston IL 60208-3118

KANNINEN, MELVIN FRED, ENGINEERING MECHANICS, MATERIAL SCIENCE ENGINEERING. *Current Pos:* OWNER & PROPRIETOR, MFK CONSULT, 95- *Personal Data:* b Ely, Minn, Jan 31, 35; m 57; c 2. *Educ:* Univ Minn, BS, 57, MS, 59, Stanford Univ PhD(Eng Mech), 66. *Prof Exp:* Researcher, Battelle's Columbus Lab, 66-75, sr researcher, 75-79, res leader, 79-83; inst scientist, SW Res Inst, 83-91, prog dir eng mech, 91-95. *Concurrent Pos:* Mem, Nat Mat Adv Bd, Nat Res Coun & numerous prof soc & govt adv comts; lectr, numerous US & foreign univs. *Mem:* Nat Acad Eng; Am Soc Testing & Mat; Int Asn Struct Mech; Am Welding Soc; fel Am Soc Mech Engrs; Soc Eng Sci. *Res:* Fracture mechanics for fast fracture arrest; elastic-plastic fracture mechanics; lifetime predictions for fiber reinforced composites; residual stress and cracking of welds; applications to nuclear pressure vessels, cryogenic storage tanks, railroad equipment, gas transmission pipelines, plastic pipe and joints; author of more than 150 technical publications. *Mailing Add:* 7322 Ashton Pl San Antonio TX 78229

KANNOWSKI, PAUL BRUNO, ZOOLOGY. *Current Pos:* from asst prof to prof biol, Univ NDak, 57-90, chmn dept, 63-70 & 82-88, dir, Inst Ecol Studies, 65-81, EMER PROF BIOL, UNIV NDAK, 91- *Personal Data:* b Grand Forks, NDak, Aug 11, 27; m 53, Phyllis Mosher; c Katherine & Mark. *Educ:* Univ NDak, BS, 49, MS, 52; Univ Mich, PhD(zool), 57. *Honors & Awards:* Prof Award, Wildlife Soc, 89. *Prof Exp:* Asst biol, Univ NDak, 50-52; instr, Bowling Green State Univ, 56-57. *Concurrent Pos:* Res assoc, Harvard Univ, 66-67; NSF sr fel, 66-67; vis scientist, Smithsonian Trop Res Inst, 67, 68; entom consult, Lystads Pest Control, Inc, 68-75; ed, Prairie Naturalist, 68-; natural resources consult, US Congressman Mark Andrews, NDak, 69-70. *Mem:* Am Inst Biol Sci; Am Soc Zoologists; AAAS; Entom Soc Am; Ecol Soc Am. *Res:* Ecology; biogeography; animal behavior; myrmecology; chemical communication. *Mailing Add:* Dept Biol Univ NDak Grand Forks ND 58202-9019. *Fax:* 701-777-2623

KANO, ADELINE KYOKO, CHEMISTRY, ACADEMIC ADMINISTRATION. *Current Pos:* Instr chem & jr chemist, Colo State Univ, 55-60, asst chemist, 60-66, asst prof, 60-73, ADMIN ASST & FAC AFFIL, COLO STATE UNIV, 73- *Personal Data:* b Mitchell, Nebr, Nov 22, 27. *Educ:* Univ Nebr, BA, 48. *Mem:* Am Chem Soc; Sigma Xi. *Res:* Factors imposed on chicks and rats, their alleviation and relation to blood and tissue content of amino acids. *Mailing Add:* 1013 Cragmore Dr Ft Collins CO 80521-4331

KANOFSKY, ALVIN SHELDON, ELEMENTARY PARTICLE PHYSICS. *Current Pos:* From asst prof to assoc prof, 67-76, PROF PHYSICS, LEHIGH UNIV, 76- *Personal Data:* b Philadelphia, Pa, July 5, 39; m 64, Donna Mikolik; c Robert & Nathan. *Educ:* Univ Pa, BA, 61, MS, 62, PhD(physics), 66. *Concurrent Pos:* Res collabr, Brookhaven Nat Lab, Fermilab; pres, Res & Develop Co. *Mem:* Fel Am Phys Soc; Sigma Xi; AAAS; Rotary Int Chambers Com. *Res:* Research in eta decay; proton-proton scattering; mu magnetic moment, Glauber calculations in particles, high energy particle channeling in crystals, particle-nuclei interactions, hypernuclei, jet production, cosmic rays and instrumentation; accelerator research; intermediate energy physics; radiation effects. *Mailing Add:* Dept Physics Lehigh Univ 16 Memorial Dr E Bethlehem PA 18015

KANOFSKY, JEFFREY RONALD, CHEMISTRY & BIOCHEMISTRY OF SINGLET OXYGEN. *Current Pos:* STAFF PHYSICIAN, EDWARD HINES JR VET ADMIN HOSP, 80- *Personal Data:* b Chicago, Ill, Apr 30, 46; m 72, Donna A Cohen. *Educ:* Ill Inst Technol, BS, 68, MS, 70, PhD(chem), 72; Rush Med Col, MD, 75. *Prof Exp:* Residency internal med, Univ Ill Hosp, 75-78; fel hemat & oncol, Univ Chicago, 78-80; asst prof med, Stritch Sch Med, Loyola Univ, 80-86, assoc prof, 86-88, assoc prof med & biochem, 88-91, prof med, molecular & cellular biochem, Stritch Sch Med, Loyola Univ, 91- *Mem:* Fel Am Col Physicians; Am Soc Hemat; Am Soc Clin Oncol; Am Asn Cancer Res; Am Soc Photobiol; Oxygen Soc. *Res:* Study of biochemical and photochemical mechanisms of singlet-oxygen generation in biological systems. *Mailing Add:* Hines Vet Admin Hosp PO Box 278 Hines IL 60141. *Fax:* 708-216-2319

KANOJIA, RAMESH MAGANLAL, MEDICINAL CHEMISTRY. *Current Pos:* assoc scientist, Ortho Pharmaceut Corp, 66-70, scientist, 70-76, sr scientist, 77-79, RES FEL, ORTHO PHARMACEUT CORP, 80- *Personal Data:* b Mangrol, India, Feb 15, 33; m 67; c Preeti & Amee. *Educ:* Bombay Univ, BSc, 54, BScTech, 56, MScTech, 61; Univ Wis, PhD(pharmaceut chem), 66. *Honors & Awards:* Philip B Hoffman Award, Johnson & Johnson Co, 77. *Prof Exp:* Instr pharmaceut chem, Bombay Univ, 58-59, hon lectr tech pharmaceut & fine chem, 59-60; res asst pharmaceut chem, Sch Pharm, Univ Wis, 61-66. *Mem:* Am Chem Soc. *Res:* Isolation, characterization and synthesis of natural and synthetic organic medicinal compounds; antifertility compounds of natural and synthetic origin; synthesis of cardiovascular-active drugs; antiinfective agents. *Mailing Add:* R W Johnson Pharmaceut Res Inst Raritan NJ 08869. *Fax:* 908-526-6469

KANOPOULOS, NICK, VLSI DESIGN, INTERGRATED CIRCUIT TESTING. *Current Pos:* from engr to sr engr, 82-85, coordr, 85-87, MGR, RES TRIANGLE INST, 87- *Personal Data:* b Drama, Greece, Aug 11, 56; US citizen; m 90, Athiya Giannopoulos; c Nichole & Tasos. *Educ:* Univ Patras, Greece, BS, 79; Duke Univ, MS, 80, PhD(elect eng), 84. *Prof Exp:* Res asst, Duke Univ, 79-81; engr, Bendix Corp, 81-82. *Concurrent Pos:* Adj assoc prof, Duke Univ, 85- *Mem:* AAAS; sr mem, Inst Elec & Electronics Engrs. *Res:* Design of very large scale, application specific integrated circuits; design of parallel signal processor architectures for high-performance, real-time applications; developed design for testability and built in self-test techniques and structures; design of fault secure circuits for high reliability applications. *Mailing Add:* Design Res Triangle Inst 3040 Corwallis Rd Herbert Bldg Durham NC 27709. *Fax:* 919-541-6515; *E-Mail:* nick@rti.rti.org

KANOST, MICHAEL ROBERT, INSECT IMMUNE RESPONSE, INSECT HEMOLYMPH PROTEINS. *Current Pos:* asst prof, 91-95, ASSOC PROF BIOCHEM, KANS STATE UNIV, 95- *Personal Data:* b Cheyenne, Wyo, Nov 17, 56; m 77; c 4. *Educ:* Colo State Univ, BS, 79; Purdue Univ, PhD(entom), 83. *Prof Exp:* Postdoctoral fel, Queen's Univ, 83-86; res assoc, Univ Ariz, 86-89, res asst prof, 89-91. *Mem:* Am Soc Biochem & Molecular Biol; AAAS. *Res:* Structure and function of insect hemolymph proteins involved in immune responses. *Mailing Add:* Kans State Univ Willard Hall 103 Manhattan KS 65506. *Fax:* 785-532-7278; *E-Mail:* kanost@ksu.edu

KANO-SUEOKA, TAMIKO, MOLECULAR BIOLOGY. *Current Pos:* from asst prof to assoc prof, 73-85, PROF MOLECULAR CELLULAR & DEVELOP BIOL, UNIV COLO, 85-, SR RES ASSOC, 85- *Personal Data:* b Kyoto, Japan, June 26, 32; m 56, Noboru; c 1. *Educ:* Kyoto Univ, Japan, BA, 56; Radcliffe Col, MA, 60; Univ Ill, Urbana, PhD(molecular biol), 63. *Prof Exp:* Res asst biol, Calif Inst Technol, 56-58; res assoc biochem, Princeton Univ, 63-67, res staff, 68-72. *Mem:* Am Soc Biochem & Molecular Biol; Am Asn Cancer Res; Am Tissue Cult Asn. *Res:* Regulation of growth of normal and neoplastic mammary cells, in particular the involvement of membrane phospholipids in the control of cell proliferation. *Mailing Add:* Dept Molecular Cellular & Develop Biol Univ Colo Boulder CO 80309-0347. *E-Mail:* tamiko@stripe.colorado.edu

KANT, FRED H(UGO), CHEMICAL ENGINEERING. *Current Pos:* RETIRED. *Personal Data:* b Vienna, Austria, Jan 11, 30; nat US; m 52; c 2. *Educ:* Columbia Univ, BS, 51, MS, 53, DEngSc, 57. *Prof Exp:* Sr staff adv, New Areas Staff, Esso Res & Eng Co, 54-66, dir new invests res lab, Linden, 66-69, proj mgr, Corp Res Staff, 69-72, sr staff adv, 72-75, planning mgr, Govt Res, 75-78, sr staff adv, Corp Res, Exxon Res & Eng Co, 78-80, sr tech adv, Exxon Corp, 80-84. *Concurrent Pos:* Consult, 84- *Mem:* Am Chem Soc; AAAS; NY Acad Sci. *Res:* Fuels process; staff research coordination, planning and project evaluation in new areas; research administration. *Mailing Add:* 400 W 119th St Apt 15S New York NY 10027-7108

KANT, GLORIA JEAN, BIOMEDICAL RESEARCH. *Current Pos:* chemist, Dept Psychiat, Walter Reed Army Inst Res, 70-71, neurochemist, Dept Microwave Res, 71-77, asst chief, Neuroendocrinol & Neurochem Br, 77-87, CHIEF, DEPT MED NEUROSCI, WALTER REED ARMY INST RES, 87- *Personal Data:* b Chicago, Ill, June 6, 44. *Educ:* Mich State Univ, BS, 65; Univ Wis, PhD(physiol chem), 69. *Prof Exp:* Res fel, Dept Food Sci, Univ Wis, 69-70. *Mem:* Sigma Xi; Soc Neurosci; AAAS; Women Neurosci; Am Soc Pharmacol & Exp Therapeut; Int Soc Psychoneuroendocrinol; Int Behav Neurosci Soc. *Res:* Basic biomedical research; effects of stress on physiology and behavior. *Mailing Add:* 1124 Dennis Ave Silver Spring MD 20901-2171

KANT, JEFFREY A, MOLECULAR DIAGNOSIS, HEMATOPATHOLOGY. *Current Pos:* dir, Hemat Sect, 83-93, DIR, MOLECULAR DIAG SECT, UNIV PA MED CTR, 86- *Personal Data:* b Boston, Mass, Oct 4, 46; m 69, Julia Gibson; c Benjamin & Peter. *Educ:* Princeton Univ, AB, 68; Univ Chicago, PhD(biochem), 74, MD, 75. *Prof Exp:* Expert consult, Path Lab, Nat Cancer Inst, NIH, 79-83. *Mem:* Am Soc Hemat; Am Soc Human Genetics; Acad Clin Lab & Physicians & Scientists; Am Acad Path; Can Acad Path; AAAS. *Res:* Diagnostic applications of molecular biology inherited genetic disorder and hematopoietic neoplasia. *Mailing Add:* Dept Path Univ Pittsburgh Med Ctr 3550 Terrace St Pittsburgh PA 15261. *Fax:* 215-662-7529; *E-Mail:* jeff_kant.labmed@pathla.med.upenn.edu

KANT, KENNETH JAMES, PHYSIOLOGY, VETERINARY MEDICINE. *Current Pos:* PVT PRACT, VET MED, MOUNTAIN HWY VET HOSP, 87- *Personal Data:* b Elyria, Ohio, July 14, 35; m 58, Elaine Marquard; c Kenneth C, Kyle J, Karyl F & Kristin M A. *Educ:* Ohio State Univ, BS, 58; Univ Ill, Urbana, MS, 64, PhD(physiol), 67; Univ Tenn, Dir, 83. *Prof Exp:* From instr to asst prof physiol, State Univ NY Buffalo, 67-74; assoc prof physiol, Univ Tenn, Knoxville, 74-84. *Mem:* Am Vet Med Asn. *Res:* Neurophysiology and behavior, especially limbic structures. *Mailing Add:* 2216 E Lamar Alexander Pkwy Maryville TN 37804

KANTACK, BENJAMIN H, ENTOMOLOGY, AGRONOMY. *Current Pos:* from asst prof to prof entom, 62-91, exten entomologist, 63-91, EMER PROF ENTOM, SDAK STATE UNIV, 91- *Personal Data:* b Greenleaf, Kans, Sept 26, 27; m 53; c 7. *Educ:* Kans State Univ, BS, 51; Okla State Univ, MS, 54; Univ Nebr, PhD(entom), 63. *Honors & Awards:* F O Butler Award. *Prof Exp:* Trainee agron, Libby, McNeill & Libby, Hawaii, 51-52; asst entom, Okla State Univ, 52-54; instr & entomologist, Univ RI, 54-55; entomologist, USDA, Ga, 55-58; instr entom, Univ Nebr, 58-62. *Mem:* Entom Soc Am. *Res:* Stored grain, vegetable and field crop insects; livestock ecto parasites. *Mailing Add:* 1907 Derdall Dr Brookings SD 57006

KANTAK, KATHLEEN MARY, PSYCHOBIOLOGY. *Current Pos:* AT DEPT PSYCHOL, BOSTON UNIV. *Personal Data:* b Syracuse, NY, Nov 11, 51; m 75; c 2. *Educ:* State Univ NY Potsdam, BA, 73; Syracuse Univ, PhD (biopsychol), 77. *Prof Exp:* Res asst prof biopsychol, Syracuse Univ, 78; res assoc behav neurochem, Univ Wis-Madison, 78-81; res assoc psychol, Tufts Univ, 81- *Concurrent Pos:* Pvt invest, Nat Inst Drug Abuse grant. *Mem:* Soc Neurosci; Sigma Xi; Int Soc Res Aggression; Behav Pharmacol Soc. *Res:* Neurochemical correlates of aggression in terms of how these measures are affected by nutritional factors; nutritional aspects of drug abuse; animal models of tardiue dyskinesia. *Mailing Add:* Dept Psychol Boston Univ 64 Cummington St Boston MA 02215

KANTER, GERALD SIDNEY, PHYSIOLOGY. *Current Pos:* from instr to assoc prof physiol, 52-63, lectr biochem, 53-55, asst to dean, 66-67, asst dean, 67-69, PROF PHYSIOL, ALBANY MED COL, 63-, ASSOC DEAN, 69-*Personal Data:* b New York, NY, Dec 7, 25; m 56; c 2. *Educ:* Long Island Univ, BS, 47; Univ Rochester, PhD(physiol), 52. *Prof Exp:* Jr instr physiol, Sch Med, Univ Rochester, 52. *Concurrent Pos:* Chief physiol br, US Army Inst Environ Med, 63-64. *Mem:* AAAS; Am Physiol Soc; Sigma Xi. *Res:* Body fluid and electrolyte regulation; kidney function; thirst; temperature regulation and environmental physiology. *Mailing Add:* Physiol Albany Med Col 47 New Scotland Ave Albany NY 12208

KANTER, HELMUT, ELECTRON PHYSICS. *Current Pos:* mem tech staff, Lab Div, 64-74, MEM STAFF, ELECTRONIC RES LAB, AEROSPACE CORP, 74- *Personal Data:* b Hamburg, Ger, Jan 19, 28; US citizen. *Educ:* Univ Marburg, MS, 53, PhD(physics), 56. *Prof Exp:* Res physicist, Res Labs, Westinghouse Elec Corp, 57-64. *Mem:* Am Phys Soc; Ger Phys Soc. *Res:* Electron scattering; photo and secondary electron emission; electron transport; photoconductivity; imaging tubes. *Mailing Add:* Aerospace Corp MS M2246 PO Box 92957 Los Angeles CA 90009

KANTER, IRA E, ENGINEERING PHYSICS. *Current Pos:* sr engr NERVA nuclear reactors, Astronuclear Labs, Westinghouse, 63-69, sr engr chem eng, 69-77, sr engr chem physics, Res & Develop Labs, 77-87, SR ENGR ENVIRON CONTROL OFFICER, SOLID OXIDE FUEL CELLS, SCI & TECH CTR, WESTINGHOUSE, 87- *Personal Data:* b Chicago, Ill, Oct, 31, 31; m 68; c 2. *Educ:* Ill Inst Technol, BS, 53, MS, 54. *Prof Exp:* Asst chem engr, US Army Chem Corps, 54-56; engr high temperature, Vanguard X405 Rocket, Flight Propulsion Lab, Gen Elec, 57-59; res staff high temperature chem, Univ Wis, 60-61. *Concurrent Pos:* Environ sci. *Mem:* Am Nuclear Soc; Inst Elec & Electronics Engrs; Air & Waste Mgt Asn; Int Technol Inst. *Res:* Radio-chemical reactions for synthesis; chemical thermodynamics; inertially and magnetically confined fusion reactor blanket systems; radio-gas waste treatment and storage; glow discharge chemistry; physical chemistry; pollution control systems. *Mailing Add:* 1172 Colgate Dr Monroeville PA 15146

KANTER, IRVING, RADAR, ELECTRONIC COUNTER MEASURES & COUNTER COUNTER MEASURES. *Current Pos:* RETIRED. *Personal Data:* b New York, NY, Oct 30, 24; m 51; c 5. *Educ:* Brooklyn Col, AB, 44; Brown Univ, PhD(appl math), 53. *Prof Exp:* Physicist, Kellex Corp, 44-45, Union Carbide & US Army, 45-47; systs specialist, Lockheed Aircraft Corp, 51-54; systs engr, RCA, 54-66; consult engr, Raytheon Co, 66-92. *Concurrent Pos:* Adj lectr, Univ Calif, Los Angeles, Temple Univ, Univ Pa & Northeastern Univ. *Mem:* Fel Inst Elec & Electronics Engrs; Inst Elec & Electronics Engrs Aerospace & Electronic Systs; Inst Elec & Electronics Engrs Info Theory Soc. *Res:* Detection and estimation; monopulse radar. *Mailing Add:* 9 Bushnell Dr Lexington MA 02173

KANTER, MANUEL ALLEN, INTERNATIONAL TRAINING. *Current Pos:* CONSULT, EDUC, TRAINING, SCI & TECHNOL. *Personal Data:* b Boston, Mass, Jan 18, 24; m 90; c 4. *Educ:* Northeastern Univ, BS, 44; Ill Inst Technol, MS, 49, PhD, 55. *Prof Exp:* Assoc chemist, Argonne Nat Lab, 46-68, training coordr, Argonne Ctr Educ Affairs, 69-75, dir, Int Atomic Energy Agency Nuclear Power Training, 75-86, consult educ, training, sci, technol & energy econs, 86-95. *Mem:* Am Nuclear Soc. *Res:* High temperature chemistry; galvanomagnetic effects; actinide compounds; diffusion; nuclear material safeguards. *Mailing Add:* 5733 Sheridan Rd No 17C Chicago IL 60660. *E-Mail:* mankan@juno.com

KANTHA, LAKSHMI, OCEANIC CIRCULATION. *Current Pos:* RES SCIENTIST, DYNALYSIS PRINCETON, 80- *Personal Data:* US citizen; m 74; c 1. *Educ:* Bangalore Univ, BE, 67; Indian Inst Sci, ME, 69; Mass Inst Technol, PhD(aerospace & astron), 73. *Prof Exp:* Fel, Johns Hopkins Univ, 74-75, assoc res scientist, 75-79, res scientist, 79-80. *Mem:* Am Meteorol Soc; Am Geophys Union. *Res:* Turbulence and wave motions in the atmosphere and the oceans; ocean circulation in the coastal regions; oceanic mixing and influence of the ice cover on polar oceans; numerical and experimental modeling of oceanic and atmospheric processes. *Mailing Add:* 837 Trail Ridge Dr Louisville CO 80027

KANTOR, FRED STUART, IMMUNOLOGY. *Current Pos:* from instr to prof, 62-83, PAUL B BEESON PROF MED, SCH MED, YALE UNIV, 83-*Personal Data:* b New York, NY, July 2, 31; m 58, Linda; c 3. *Educ:* Union Col NY, BS, 52; NY Univ, MD, 56; Am Bd Internal Med, dipl, 64; Am Bd Allergy, dipl, 66, Yale Univ, MA, 73. *Prof Exp:* Intern, Ward Med Serv, Barnes Hosp, St Louis, Mo, 56-57; res assoc, Nat Inst Allergy & Infectious Dis, 57-59; asst res med, Grace New Haven Hosp, Sch Med, Yale Univ, 59-60. *Concurrent Pos:* Whitney fel, Sch Med, Yale Univ, 60-61 & NY Univ, 61-62; USPHS career develop awardee, 62-; vis scientist with Dr Gustave Nossal, Walter & Eliza Hall Inst, Melbourne, Australia, 68-69; mem coun, Am Heart Asn. *Mem:* Asn Am Physicians; Am Soc Clin Invest; Am Acad Allergy; Am Asn Immunol. *Res:* Immune response in man, including both delayed and immediate types of immunity; immunity to Lyme disease and other tick-borne infections. *Mailing Add:* Sch Med Dept Int Med Yale Univ 333 Cedar St New Haven CT 06510-3219

KANTOR, GEORGE JOSEPH, BIOPHYSICS, MOLECULAR BIOLOGY. *Current Pos:* from asst prof to assoc prof, 70-80, PROF BIOL SCI, WRIGHT STATE UNIV, 80- *Personal Data:* b Titusville, Pa, Jan 24, 37; m 66; c 3. *Educ:* Slippery Rock State Col, BS, 58; NMex Highlands Univ, MS, 62; Pa State Univ, PhD(biophys), 67. *Prof Exp:* NIH fel biophys, Pa State Univ, 67-68; fel, Biomed Res Group, Los Alamos Sci Lab, 68-70. *Mem:* Biophys Soc; AAAS; Sigma Xi; Tissue Culture Asn; Am Soc Photobiol. *Res:* Effects of radiation on biological systems with emphasis on human cells cultured in vitro; DNA repair in human cells. *Mailing Add:* Dept Biol Sci Wright State Univ 3640 Colonel Glenn Dayton OH 45435-0001. *Fax:* 513-873-3301; *E-Mail:* gkantor@wsu.bitnet

KANTOR, GIDEON, NEUROMUSCULAR ELECTRICAL STIMULATION. *Current Pos:* LECTR, ELECTROENVIRON ENG, CATH UNIV, WASHINGTON DC, 95- *Personal Data:* b Vienna, Austria, Mar 30, 25; US citizen; m 67; c 2. *Educ:* NY Univ, BEE, 48; Polytech Univ NY, MEE, 50; Cornell Univ, PhD(elec eng), 63. *Honors & Awards:* Bicentennial Medal, Inst Elec & Electronics Engrs, 84. *Prof Exp:* Res assoc, Microwave Res Inst, Brooklyn, 50-55; res asst, Cornell Univ, 55-59; physicist, Air Force Cambridge Lab, 59-65; staff mem, Avco, Lowell, 65-68 & Mitre, Bedford, 68-72; physicist, Ctr Devices & Radiol Health, Food & Drug Admin, Rockville, 72-95. *Concurrent Pos:* Engr, Gen Elec, Ithaca, 55-56. *Mem:* Fel Inst Elec & Electronics Engrs; Sigma Xi. *Res:* Neuromuscular electrical stimulation with emphasis on the role of electrical parameters such as current and phase charge on safety and effectiveness. *Mailing Add:* PO Box 553 Garrett Park MD 20896

KANTOR, HARVEY SHERWIN, INFECTIOUS DISEASES, MICROBIOLOGY. *Current Pos:* assoc prof med & dir div infectious dis, 75-85, ASSOC PROF PATH, CHICAGO MED SCH, 78-, DIR, DIV MED MICROBIOL, 85-; CHIEF, MED MICROBIOL LAB, VET ADMIN MED CTR, NORTH CHICAGO, 85- *Personal Data:* b New York, NY, Apr 30, 38; div. *Educ:* Wash Univ, MD, 62; Am Bd Internal Med, dipl, 68. *Prof Exp:* Asst med, Sch Med, Wash Univ, 62-63; res fel, New Eng Med Ctr Hosp, Tufts Univ, 66-69, asst, Sch Med, 66-69; res educ assoc, Vet Admin, 70-71; asst prof med & microbiol, Univ Ill Med Ctr, 71-75. *Concurrent Pos:* Actg dir div infectious dis, Cook County Hosp, 72-74; consult, Highland Park Hosp, Highland Park & US Naval Hosp, Great Lakes, Ill, 75-; chief infectious dis sect, Vet Admin Med Ctr, North Chicago, 75-85; dir, Internal Med & Infectious Dis & Travel Health Serv, Dept Internal Med, Tex Tech Univ, 93-*Mem:* Fel Am Col Physicians, assoc prof med & pathol, 75-93, chief, Med Microbiol Lab, 85-93; Sigma Xi; Am Fedn Clin Res; Am Soc Microbiol; NY Acad Sci; fel Infectious Dis Soc Am; Assoc Hosp Epidemiologists Am. *Res:* Bacterial toxins and their mechanism of action; their influence on cyclic nucleotides and prostaglandin interactions; hospital infection control. *Mailing Add:* Dept Int Med Tex Tech Univ Health Sci Ctr 800 W Fourth St Odessa TX 79763

KANTOR, PAUL B, VALUE INFORMATION, NETWORKED INFORMATION ENVIRONMENT. *Current Pos:* PRES, TANTALUS INC, 77-; PROF, RUTGERS STATE UNIV NJ, 91- *Personal Data:* b Washington, DC, Nov 27, 38; m 62, Carole Kaplowitz; c Michael & David. *Educ:* Columbia Univ, AB, 59; Princeton Univ, PhD(physics), 63. *Prof Exp:* Res assoc physics, Brookhaven Nat Lab, 63-65; vis asst prof, State Univ NY, Stony Brook, 65-67; asst prof, Case Western Res Univ, 67-69, assoc prof physics, 69-74, assoc prof oper res, Libr & Info Sci, 74-77, prog dir, Complex Systs Inst, 73-74, sr res assoc systs eng, 77-81. *Concurrent Pos:* Guest physicist, Brookhaven Nat Lab, 65-; adj assoc prof libr & info sci, Kent State Univ, 78-81; sr lectr, Weatherhead Sch Mgt, Case Western Res Univ, 81-; distinguished vis scholar, Online Comput Libr Ctr, Ohio, 87; vis prof, Info Systs, Rutgers Univ, 90; mem, Ctr Opers Res, Rutgers Univ. *Mem:* Am Phys Soc; Am Statist Asn; Am Soc Info Sci; NY Acad Sci; Am Libr Asn. *Res:* Value of information; information retrieval, large databases; distributed detection and decision systems; industrial learning phenomena; networked information environment. *Mailing Add:* Rutgers Univ 4 Huntington St New Brunswick NJ 08903. *Fax:* 732-545-6930; *E-Mail:* kantor@scils.rutgers.edu

KANTOR, SIDNEY, PARASITOLOGY, PROTOZOOLOGY. *Current Pos:* RETIRED. *Personal Data:* b New York, NY, Feb 1, 24; m 49, 73; c 5. *Educ:* George Washington Univ, BA, 47, MA, 49; Univ Ill, PhD(zool), 56. *Prof Exp:* Invert zoologist, Acad Natural Sci, Pa, 51-53; asst parasitol, Col Vet Med, Univ Ill, 53-55; coop agent, USDA, Ill, 55-56; from parasitologist to group leader, Am Cynamid Co, 56-73; sr res biologist protozool chemother, Agr Res Div, 70-73, prin res biologist, 77-89. *Mem:* Am Soc Parasitol; Soc Protozool; Sigma Xi. *Res:* Parasitic chemotherapy; veterinary entomology. *Mailing Add:* 4A Van Buren Dr Cranbury NJ 08512

KANTOR, SIMON WILLIAM, POLYMER CHEMISTRY, ORGANIC CHEMISTRY. *Current Pos:* RES PROF, UNIV MASS, AMHERST, 82-*Personal Data:* b Brussels, Belg, Mar 23, 25; nat US; m 89, Karen C Duncan; c Michael & Sharon. *Educ:* City Col NY, BS, 45; Duke Univ, PhD(org chem), 49. *Honors & Awards:* Gold Patent Medallion, Gen Elec Co, 66. *Prof Exp:* Fel, Duke Univ, 49-51; res assoc, Gen Elec Co, Schenectady, NY, 51-60, sect mgr, 60-65, br mgr, 65-72; vpres res & develop, GAF Corp, Wayne, 72-82. *Mem:* AAAS; Am Chem Soc. *Res:* Organic reactions of carbanions; organosilicon polymers; synthesis of aromatic condensation polymers; liquid crystal polymers. *Mailing Add:* Polymer Sci & Eng Dept Univ Mass Amherst MA 01003. *Fax:* 413-545-0082; *E-Mail:* swkantor@polysci.umass.edu

KANTOROVICH, LEONID VITALJEVICH, MATHEMATICS, ECONOMICS. *Current Pos:* HEAD DEPT SCI, INST SYST STUDIES, MOSCOW, 76- *Personal Data:* b Leningrad, Russia, Jan 19, 12; m 38, Natalia V Iljina; c Ien & Vsevolod. *Educ:* Leningrad Univ, ScD, 35. *Hon Degrees:* Numerous from foreign univs, 35- *Honors & Awards:* Nobel Prize in Econs, 75. *Prof Exp:* From instr to prof, Inst Indust Construct Eng, 30-39, Leningrad Univ, 32-60; head, Math Inst, USSR Acad Sci, 48-60, head, Math-Econs Dept, Inst Siberian Br, 61-71; head res lab, Inst Nat Econ Control, Moscow,

71-76. *Concurrent Pos:* Prof & head chair Comput Math, Novosibizu Univ, 61-71; mem, State Comt Sci & Technol, 75- *Mem:* USSR Acad Sci; fel Econometric Soc; Hungarian Acad Sci; Nat Acad de Ingen, Mexico; Yugoslavian Acad Arts & Scis; Am Acad Arts & Scis. *Res:* Author of numerous published articles. *Mailing Add:* Russian Acad Scis Int Nat Econ Mgt 14 Leninsky Prospect Moscow Russia

KANTOROVITZ, SHMUEL, OPERATOR THEORY. *Current Pos:* PROF MATH, BAR ILAN UNIV, ISRAEL, 72- *Personal Data:* b Casablanca, Morocco, Sept 17, 35; m 60; c 4. *Educ:* Hebrew Univ Israel, MSc, 56; Univ Minn, Minneapolis, PhD(math), 62. *Prof Exp:* Instr math, Princeton Univ, 62-63; mem, Inst Advan Study, 63-64; asst prof, Yale Univ, 64-67; from assoc prof to prof math, Univ Ill, Chicago Circle, 70-78. *Concurrent Pos:* Dept chmn, Bar Ilan Univ, 77-79 & 85-87. *Mem:* Am Math Soc. *Res:* Functional analysis. *Mailing Add:* Bar Ilan Univ 52900 Ramat Gan Israel

KANTOWITZ, BARRY H, ERGONOMICS, HUMAN INFORMATION PROCESSING. *Current Pos:* CHIEF SCIENTIST, HUMAN FACTORS TRANSP CTR, BATTELLE, 87-; AFFIL PROF, PSYCHOL DEPT, UNIV WASH, 88- *Personal Data:* b New York, NY, Aug 25, 43. *Educ:* City Univ NY City Col, BA, 65; City Univ NY Queens Col, MA, 67; Univ Wis, PhD(exp psychol), 69. *Prof Exp:* Asst prof, Purdue Univ, 69-72, assoc prof, 72-79, dir, human Factors Grad Training Prog, Psychol Dept, 77-87, prof, Psychol Sci Dept, 79-87, prof Indust Eng Dept, 81-87. *Concurrent Pos:* Sr lectr ergonomics, Inst Indust Org, Univ Trodheim, Norway, 76-77; Am Soc Elec Engrs fel, Ames Res Ctr, NASA, 82, human factors sci adv, Aviation Safety Reporting Syst, 91-; courtesy appointment, Dept Aeronaut & Astronaut, Stanford Univ, 84; vis prof psychol, Univ Lulea, Sweden Tech, 86; ed, Transp Human Factors J, 97. *Mem:* Fel Am Psychol Soc; fel Am Psychol Asn; Psychonomic Soc; Human Factors Soc; Soc Automotive Engrs. *Res:* Human attention; mental workload; human-machine interaction; human factors; intelligent vehicle highway systems. *Mailing Add:* Battelle-Human Factors Transp Ctr 4000 NE 41st St Seattle WA 98105. *Fax:* 206-528-3555; *E-Mail:* kantowbh@battelle.org

KANTOWSKI, RONALD, PHYSICS. *Current Pos:* from asst prof to assoc prof, 68-81, PROF PHYSICS, UNIV OKLA, 81- *Personal Data:* b Shreveport, La, Dec 18, 39; m 61, Anita E Clarke; c Andrew, Leila & Matthew. *Educ:* Univ Tex, Austin, BS, 62, PhD(physics), 66. *Prof Exp:* Res scientist med, Univ Tex Med Br, Galveston, 62-63; teaching asst physics, Univ Tex, Austin, 63-66, asst prof, 66-67; res assoc, Southwest Ctr Advan Studies, 67-68. *Mem:* Am Phys Soc. *Res:* Gravity theories; quantum field theory. *Mailing Add:* Dept Physics & Astron 440 W Brooks Norman OK 73019. *Fax:* 405-325-7557; *E-Mail:* kantowski@ou.edu

KANTROWITZ, ADRIAN, SURGERY. *Current Pos:* PROF SURG, COL MED, WAYNE STATE UNIV, 70- *Personal Data:* b New York, NY, Oct 4, 18; m 48; c 3. *Educ:* NY Univ, AB, 40; Long Island Col Med, MD, 43; Am Bd Surg, dipl. *Honors & Awards:* H L Moses Prize, Montefiore Alumnus, 49; Exhibit Prize, NY State Med Soc, 52; Theodore & Susan B Cummings Award, Am Col Cardiol, 67; Gold Plate Award, Am Acad Achievement, 66; Max Berg Award, 69. *Prof Exp:* Intern, Jewish Hosp, Brooklyn, 44; surg resident, Mt Sinai Hosp, 47; resident, Montefiore Hosp, 48-50; from asst prof to prof surg, State Univ NY Col Med, 55-70. *Concurrent Pos:* USPHS fel cardiovasc res & teaching fel physiol, Dept Physiol, Western Reserve Univ, 51-52; dir cardiovasc surg, Maimonides Med Ctr, Brooklyn, 55-64, dir surg, 64-70; chmn dept surg, Sinai Hosp, Detroit, 70- *Mem:* Fel NY Acad Sci; Am Chem Soc; Int Soc Angiol; Am Soc Artificial Internal Organs (pres, 68-69); Harvey Soc. *Res:* Cardiac pacemakers; heart transplants; human balloon pump; partial human mechanical heart. *Mailing Add:* 70 Gallogly Rd Auburn Hills MI 48326-1222

KANTROWITZ, ARTHUR (ROBERT), GAS DYNAMICS, LASER PROPULSION. *Current Pos:* PROF ENG, THAYER SCH ENG, DARTMOUTH COL, 78- *Personal Data:* b Bronx, NY, Oct 20, 13; m 43, 80, Lee Stuart; c 3. *Educ:* Columbia Univ, BS, 34, MA, 36, PhD(physics), 47. *Hon Degrees:* DE, Mont Col Mineral Sci & Technol, 75; DSc, NJ Inst Technol, 81. *Honors & Awards:* Theodore Roosevelt Asn Medal of Honor, Distinguished Serv Sci, 67; Carl F Kayan Medal, Columbia Univ, 73; Messenger lectr, Cornell Univ, 78; Fluid & Plasma Dynamics Award & Medal, Am Inst Aeronaut & Astronaut, 81, Aerospace Contrib to Soc Award & Medal, 90; MHD Faraday Mem Medal, UNESCO, 83. *Prof Exp:* Physicist, Nat Adv Comt Aeronaut, 36-46; from assoc prof to prof aeronaut eng & eng physics, Cornell Univ, 46-56; founder, dir, chief exec officer & chmn, Avco Everett Res Lab, 55-78, sr vpres bd dir, Avco Corp, 56-79. *Concurrent Pos:* Vis lectr, Harvard Univ, 52; Fulbright scholar & Guggenheim fel, Cambridge Univ & Univ Manchester, 54; vis inst prof & fel, Sch Advan Study, Mass Inst Technol, 57; mem adv coun, Dept Aeronaut Eng, Princeton Univ, 59-77; eng adv bd mem, Stanford Univ, 66-82 & Rensselaer Polytech Inst, 81-86; hon trustee, Univ Rochester, 71; mem bd overseers, Thayer Sch Eng, Dartmouth Col, 75-82; presidential advisory group, Anticipated Advances in Sci & Technol, Sci Court Task Force chmn, 75-76; hon life mem, Bd Gov, Technion, 78; hon prof, Huazhang Inst Technol, Wuhan, China, 80. *Mem:* Nat Acad Sci; Nat Acad Eng; Am Phys Soc; fel Am Inst Aeronaut & Astronaut; fel Am Acad Arts & Sci; Int Acad Astronaut. *Res:* Physical gas dynamics; magneto-hydrodynamics power; high power lasers; cardiac assist devices; strategic technology; social control of technology. *Mailing Add:* 4 Downing Rd Hanover NH 03755-1902. *Fax:* 603-643-3377; *E-Mail:* ark@dartmouth.edu

KANTROWITZ, EVAN R, BIOCHEMISTRY. *Current Pos:* From asst prof to assoc prof chem & biochem, 72-84, PROF BIOCHEM, BOSTON COL, 84-, CHMN DEPT BIOCHEM, 92- *Personal Data:* b Fall River, Mass, Aug 18, 49. *Educ:* Boston Univ, BA, 71, MS, 73; Harvard Univ, PhD(chem), 76. *Mem:* Am Chem Soc; AAAS; Protein Soc; Am Soc Biochem & Molecular Biol. *Mailing Add:* Dept Chem Boston Col Merkert 239 Chestnut Hill MA 02167. *Fax:* 617-552-4558

KANTROWITZ, IRWIN H, GEOLOGY, HYDROLOGY. *Current Pos:* From geologist to chief hydrologist, 59-80, DISTRICT CHIEF, US GEOL SURV, FLA, 80- *Personal Data:* b Brooklyn, NY, Oct 12, 37. *Educ:* Brooklyn Col, BS, 58; Ohio State Univ, MS, 59. *Concurrent Pos:* Mem, US Geol Surv Water Resources Adv Bd. *Mem:* Fel Geol Soc Am; Am Geophys Union; Asn Groundwater Scientists & Engrs. *Mailing Add:* 4142 Chelmsford Rd Tallahassee FL 32308

KANTZ, PAUL THOMAS, JR, PHYCOLOGY. *Current Pos:* From asst prof to assoc prof, 67-81, dept chair, 88-90, PROF BIOL, CALIF STATE UNIV, SACRAMENTO, 81- *Personal Data:* b Jacksonville, Tex, Jan 21, 41; m 62; c 3. *Educ:* Univ Tex, BA, 63, MA, 65, PhD(phycol), 67. *Mem:* Phycol Soc Am; Bot Soc Am; NY Acad Sci; Sigma Xi. *Res:* Taxonomy and morphology of blue green algae. *Mailing Add:* 525 42nd St Sacramento CA 95819-2818

KANTZES, JAMES (GEORGE), PLANT PATHOLOGY. *Current Pos:* From instr to assoc prof, 52-69, PROF PLANT PATH, COL AGR, UNIV MD, 69- *Personal Data:* b Bertha, Pa, Mar 29, 24; m 54; c 3. *Educ:* Univ Md, BS, 51, MS, 54, PhD(plant path), 57. *Mem:* Am Phytopath Soc; Sigma Xi. *Res:* Agriculture; control of vegetable diseases. *Mailing Add:* 751 Richwill Dr Salisbury MD 21801-5627

KANWAL, RAM PRAKASH, GENERALIZED FUNCTIONS. *Current Pos:* assoc prof, 59-62, PROF MATH, PA STATE UNIV, 62- *Personal Data:* b India, July 4, 24; m 54, Vilma; c Neeru & Neeraj. *Educ:* Punjab Univ, India, BA, 45, MA, 48; Ind Univ, PhD, 57. *Prof Exp:* Asst, Ministry of Agr, Govt India, 48-50; lectr math, Daynand Anglo Vernacular Col, India, 50-51; asst prof, Birla Col, Pilani, 51-52; asst lectr, Indian Inst Technol, Kharagpur, 52-54; res assoc appl math, Ind Univ, 54-57; asst prof, Math Res Ctr, Univ Wis, 57-59; sr scientist, Oak Ridge Nat Lab, 59. *Concurrent Pos:* Vis prof, Tech Univ Denmark, 65-66 & Royal Inst Technol, Stockholm, 66. *Mem:* Soc Indust & Appl Math; Allahabad Math Soc. *Res:* Hydrodynamics; aerodynamics; magnetohydrodynamics; elasticity; diffraction; integral and differential equations. *Mailing Add:* Dept Math Pa State Univ 204 McAllister Bldg University Park PA 16802-6401. *Fax:* 814-865-3735; *E-Mail:* kanwal@math.psu.edu

KANWAR, YASHPAL SINGH, RENAL PATHOLOGY & IMMUNOPATHOLOGY. *Current Pos:* from asst prof to assoc prof, 81-83, PROF PATH & RENAL MED, NORTHWESTERN UNIV MED SCH, 84- *Personal Data:* b Punjab, India, June 1, 47. *Educ:* Univ Punjab, India, MD, 70; Univ Ill, Chicago, PhD(biochem & path), 76. *Prof Exp:* Residency, Univ Ill, Chicago, 71-75; fel renal cell biol & path, Yale Univ, 76-80. *Concurrent Pos:* Res career develop award, NIH, 82-89. *Mem:* AAAS; Am Soc Cell Biol; Am Soc Nephrology; Am Asn Path. *Res:* Renal pathology and immunopathology. *Mailing Add:* Dept Path Ward 6085 Northwestern Univ Med Sch 303 E Chicago Ave Chicago IL 60611-3072. *Fax:* 312-503-8240

KANZELMEYER, JAMES HERBERT, ANALYTICAL CHEMISTRY. *Current Pos:* CONSULT, 87- *Personal Data:* b Manila, Philippines, Aug 9, 26; m 49; c 9. *Educ:* Univ Calif, AB, 47; Ore State Col, PhD(anal chem), 55. *Prof Exp:* Chemist, Beacon res labs, Tex Co, 47-49; instr chem, Ore State Col, 53-54; asst prof, NMex Highlands Univ, 54-57; anal res chemist, St Joe Zinc Co, 57-63, chief chemist smelting div, 63-80, chief chemist, Corp Anal Serv, St Joe Minerals Corp, 80-87. *Concurrent Pos:* Mem, Nat Res Coun Eval Panel, Anal Chem Div, Nat Bur Standards, 75-78. *Mem:* Am Soc Testing & Mat; Sigma Xi. *Res:* Analytical chemistry of zinc-containing materials, including chemical, optical-emission and x-ray spectrographic methods. *Mailing Add:* 5219 Webb St Aliquippa PA 15001-4943

KANZLER, WALTER WILHELM, ANIMAL BEHAVIOR, BIOETHICS. *Current Pos:* from instr to asst prof, 66-76, assoc prof biol, 76-84, PROF BIOL & CHMN, WAGNER COL, 84- *Personal Data:* b Jersey City, NJ, Sept 17, 38. *Educ:* Montclair State Univ, BA, 60, MA, 63; Marshall Univ, MA, 64; Univ Cincinnati, PhD(ecol, behav), 72. *Prof Exp:* Instr biol, Union City High Schs, NJ, 60-65; asst prof, Trenton State Col, 65-66. *Concurrent Pos:* NASA fel, 69-70; NSF grant, Nat Primate Ctr, Univ Calif, Davis, 71 & Am Mus Natural Hist, 94; sr res assoc, Nat Ctr Bioethics, Drew Univ, 76; consult, Scientists Ctr Animal Welfare, 80-; adj prof biol, St John's Univ, Staten Island, NY, 89- & St Peter's Col, Jersey City, NJ, 90- *Mem:* Animal Behav Soc; Sigma Xi; AAAS; Nat Wildlife Fed. *Res:* Insect, gerbil and primate behavior, zoo animal behavior; history of biology and medicine; social issues in biology and medicine. *Mailing Add:* Dept Biol Wagner Col Staten Island NY 10301-4495

KAO, CHARLES K, FIBER OPTICS. *Current Pos:* vchancellor & pres, 87-96, HON PROF ENG, CHINESE UNIV, HONG KONG, 96- *Personal Data:* b Shanghai, China, Nov 4, 33; US citizen; m 59, Mary-wan Wong; c Simon M & Amanda M. *Educ:* Univ London, BSc, 57, PhD(elec eng), 65. *Hon Degrees:* DSc, Chinese Univ Hong Kong, 85, Univ Sussex, 90 & Univ Durham, 94; Dr, Soka Univ, 91 & Univ Padova, Italy, 94; DEng, Univ Glasgow, 92. *Honors & Awards:* Morey Award, Am Ceramic Soc, 76; Stewart Ballantine Medal, Franklin Inst, 77; Morris H Liebmann Mem Award, Inst

Elec & Electronics Engrs, 78, Alexander Graham Bell Medal, 85; L M Ericsson Int Prize, Sweden, 79; Gold Medal, Armed Forces Commun & Electronics Asn, 80; Int Prize New Mat, Am Phys Soc, 89; Faraday Medal, Inst Elec Engrs, 89; Gold Medal, Int Soc Optical Eng, 92; Japan Prize, Sci & Tech Found, Japan, 96. *Prof Exp:* Develop engr, Stand Tel & Cables Ltd, London, 57-60; prin res engr, Stand Telecommun Lab Ltd; prof, Electronics Dept, Chinese Univ Hong Kong, 70-74; chief scientist, Electro-Optical Prod Div, ITT, Roanoke, Va, 74-81, vpres, & dir eng, 81-83; exec scientist & dir res, Advan Tech Ctr, Shelton, Conn, 83-87. *Concurrent Pos:* Adj prof & fel, Trumbull Col, Yale Univ, 85; Marconi int fel, 85. *Mem:* Nat Acad Eng; fel Inst Elec & Electronics Engrs; Royal Swed Acad Eng Sci; fel Inst Elec Engrs UK; fel Royal Acad Engrs UK; fel Acad Sinica Taiwan. *Mailing Add:* Chinese Univ Hong Kong Shatin New Territories Hong Kong People's Republic of China. *Fax:* 852-2603-7663; *E-Mail:* ckao@ie.cuhk.edu.hk

KAO, CHIEN YUAN, NEUROTOXINS, SMOOTH MUSCLES. *Current Pos:* asst to assoc prof pharmacol, 57-69, PROF PHARMACOL, STATE UNIV NY DOWNSTATE MED CTR, 69-, PROF NEUROSCI, 74- *Personal Data:* b Shanghai, China, Dec 20, 27; nat US; m 57; c 2. *Educ:* Univ Southern Calif, BA, 48; State Univ NY, MD, 52. *Prof Exp:* Intern & asst path, NY Hosp-Cornell Med Ctr, 52-53, res assoc neurol, Col Physicians & Surgeons, Columbia Univ, 53-54; instr, State Univ NY Downstate Med Ctr, 55-56; asst, Rockefeller Inst, 56-57. *Concurrent Pos:* Fel physiol, State Univ NY Downstate Med Ctr, 54-55. *Mem:* Am Physiol Soc; Am Soc Pharmacol & Exp Therapeut; Soc Gen Physiol; Biophys Soc. *Res:* Tetrodotoxin, saxitoxin and related toxins on sodium channel; ionic-channel functions of mammalian smooth muscles, and actions of drugs thereon. *Mailing Add:* Dept Pharmacol State Univ NY Health Sci Ctr 450 Clarkson Ave Box 29 Brooklyn NY 11203-9967. *Fax:* 718-270-3309

KAO, FA-TEN, SOMATIC CELL & HUMAN MOLECULAR GENETICS. *Current Pos:* Asst prof, Univ Col Med Ctr, 67-70, assoc prof, 70-81, PROF BIOCHEM BIOPHYS & GENETICS, UNIV COLO HEALTH SCI CTR, DENVER, 81-; SR FEL, ELEANOR ROOSEVELT INST CANCER RES, 65. *Personal Data:* b Hankow, China, Apr 20, 34; nat US; m 60, Betty C Tang; c Alan S. *Educ:* Nat Taiwan Univ, BS, 55; Univ Minn, St Paul, PhD(genetics), 64. *Concurrent Pos:* Nat Cancer Inst fel, Univ Colo Med Ctr, Denver, 65-67; Int Union Against Cancer-Eleanor Roosevelt Int Cancer fel, Univ Oxford, 73-74; res scientist, Europ Molecular Biol Lab, Heidelberg, 85; hon consult prof med molecular genetics, Harbin Med Univ, People's Rep China, 87; vis prof human molecular genetics, Tonji Med Univ, People's Repub China, 88. *Mem:* Genetics Soc Am; Am Soc Cell Biol; Am Soc Human Genetics; Am Asn Cancer Res; Tissue Cult Asn; AAAS. *Res:* In vitro genetic studies of somatic mammalian cells; somatic cell and molecular genetic analysis of the human genome; mapping of human genes; use of recombinant DNA technology in human genetic studies; molecular analysis of genetic diseases. *Mailing Add:* Eleanor Roosevelt Inst Cancer Res 1899 Gaylord St Denver CO 80206-1210. *Fax:* 303-333-8423

KAO, JOHN Y, ANIMAL & EXPLORATORY DRUG METABOLISM. *Current Pos:* SR RES FEL, DEPT ANIMAL & EXPLOR DRUG METAB, MERCK SHARP & DOHME RES LABS, 91- *Personal Data:* b Hong Kong, Dec 12, 48; m; c 2. *Educ:* Univ Surrey, Eng, BSc, 73, PhD(biochem), 77. *Honors & Awards:* Frank Blood Award, Soc Toxicol, 87. *Prof Exp:* NIH fel, Lab Reprod & Develop Toxicol, Nat Inst Environ Health Sci, 77-80; staff scientist, Biol Div, Oak Ridge Nat Lab, 80-86; sr investr, Dept Drug Metab, SmithKline Beecham Pharmaceut, 86-91. *Concurrent Pos:* Fac mem, Traveling Lect Prog, Oak Ridge Assoc Univs, 84-86; mem, Arthropod Repellent Subcomt & Bd Environ Studies & Toxicol, Nat Res Coun, 86-87. *Mem:* Soc Toxicol; Int Soc Study Xenobiotics; Am Asn Pharmaceut Scientists; Am Soc Pharmacol & Exp Therapeut. *Res:* Absorption, metabolism and toxicokinetics of xenobiotics; mechanisms of chemical toxicity and safety evaluation; dermatotoxicology, percutaneous absorption and transdermal delivery of drugs; drug development, drug metabolism and pharmacokinetics; author of numerous technical publications. *Mailing Add:* Drug Safety & Metab Div Wyeth-Ayerst Res CN 8000 Princeton NJ 08543-8000. *Fax:* 732-594-1416

KAO, KUNG-YING TANG, biochemistry; deceased, see previous edition for last biography

KAO, KWAN CHI, SEMICONDUCTORS & DIELECTRICS. *Current Pos:* assoc prof, 66-68, PROF ELEC ENG, UNIV MAN, 69- *Personal Data:* b Chungshan, China, Oct 11, 26; Can citizen; m 93, Leatrice; c 7. *Educ:* Univ Nanking, BSc, 48; Univ Mich, MSc, 50; Univ Birmingham, Eng, PhD (elec eng), 57,. *Hon Degrees:* DSc, Univ Birmingham, Eng, 84. *Prof Exp:* Res fel mat sci, Univ Col Swansea, UK, 57-58; res engr non-linear control syst, Nelson Res Lab, Eng Elec Co Ltd, Eng, 58-60; group leader & sr res engr dielec mats, Brush Elec Eng Co, Ltd, Eng, 60-61; sr lectr elec eng, Univ Salford, Eng, 62-65. *Concurrent Pos:* Vis prof, Nat Defense Acad Japan, 80-81, Nat Univ Singapore & Xian Jiaotong Univ, China, 81; external referee, Res Grants Comts Can Coun & Natural Sci & Eng Res Coun Can, Ottawa, 76- *Mem:* Fel Inst Elec Engrs UK; fel Inst Physics UK; sr mem Inst Elec & Electronics Engrs; Can Asn Physicists; Sigma Xi; Asn Prof Engrs Can. *Res:* Electronic and optical properties of semiconductors and insulators (crystalline, poly-crystalline, micro-crystalline, and non-crystalline, organic and inorganic) in bulk and film forms with and without doping, and their applications for devices; high-field conduction and breakdown phenomena in dielectrics; photo-electric properties of polymers and ceramics incorporated with various impurities. *Mailing Add:* Dept Elec & Comput Eng Univ Man Winnipeg MB R3T 2N2 Can. *Fax:* 204-261-4639

KAO, MING-HSIUNG, ANIMAL PHYSIOLOGY. *Current Pos:* Asst prof, 81-88, ASSOC PROF BIOL, MEM UNIV NFLD, 88- *Personal Data:* b Taipei, Taiwan, Jan 10, 44; Can citizen; c 2. *Educ:* Nat Taiwan Univ, BSc, 64; Mem Univ Nfld, MSc, 70, PhD(biol), 79. *Res:* Protein & glycoprotein antifreeze activities in marine teleosts. *Mailing Add:* Dept Biol Sci Mem Univ Nfld Elizabeth Ave St John's NF A1C 5S7 Can

KAO, RACE LI-CHAN, MYOCARDIAL METABOLISM, CARDIOVASCULAR DISEASE. *Current Pos:* DIR SURG RES, ALLEGHENY-SINGER RES INST, 83-, CAROL H LONG CHAIR EXEC SURG RES, 92- *Personal Data:* b Chungking, China, Dec 1, 43; m 69; c 2. *Educ:* Nat Taiwan Univ, BS, 65; Univ Ill, MS, 71, PhD(biochem & physiol), 72. *Prof Exp:* Res assoc animal sci, Univ Ill, 72; res assoc physiol, M S Hershey Med Ctr, 72-75, asst prof, 75-77; asst prof surg & physiol, Univ Tex Med Br, 77-82; assoc prof surg, Wash Univ, 82-83; prof, Med Col Pa, 88-92. *Concurrent Pos:* Mem, Coun Circulation, Am Heart Asn. *Mem:* Am Heart Asn; Am Physiol Soc; AAAS; Am Soc Artificial Internal Organs; Int Soc Heart Res; NY Acad Sci. *Res:* Utilizing isolated heart muscle cells, isolated perfused organs, and several animal models to study regulation of myocardial metabolism, gene expression, hypertrophy, function, and the recovery of the failing heart. *Mailing Add:* E Tenn Univ Col Med Box 70575 Johnson City TN 37614-0575. *Fax:* 423-439-7450

KAO, SAMUEL CHUNG-SIUNG, MATHEMATICAL STATISTICS, MATHEMATICS. *Current Pos:* STATISTICIAN, BROOKHAVEN NAT LAB, 74- *Personal Data:* b Kaohsiung, Taiwan, June 12, 41; c 2. *Educ:* Nat Taiwan Univ, BS, 64; Nat Tsing Hua Univ, MS, 66; Columbia Univ, PhD(statist), 72. *Prof Exp:* Lectr math, Nat Tsing Hua Univ, 66-67; statist assoc, Biomet Res, NY State Psychiat Inst, 71-73; asst prof statist, Univ Mass, Amherst, 73-74. *Mem:* Am Statist Asn; Inst Math Statist; Biomet Soc; Sigma Xi; NY Acad Sci. *Res:* Sequential experimentation; robust statistical procedures; applied probability. *Mailing Add:* 26 Cornwallis Rd East Setauket NY 11733

KAO, TAI-WU, COMMUNICATION. *Current Pos:* From asst prof to assoc prof, 65-77, PROF ELEC ENG, LOYOLA MARYMOUNT UNIV, 77- *Personal Data:* b China, Jan 5, 35; m 59; c 5. *Educ:* Nat Taiwan Univ, BS, 58; Chiao Tung Univ, MS, 61; Univ Utah, PhD(elec eng), 65. *Concurrent Pos:* Consult, Teledyne Systs Control Syst, 65-68, DWP, Los Angeles, 71-72, Dept Navy, 73-74 & TRW, 75- *Mem:* Inst Elec & Electronics Engrs. *Res:* Electromagnetics and semiconductors; communication systems. *Mailing Add:* 7101 W 80th St Los Angeles CA 90045

KAO, TIMOTHY WU, FLUID MECHANICS, CIVIL ENGINEERING. *Current Pos:* Asst prof space sci, 64-66, assoc prof atmospheric sci, 66-70, PROF CIVIL ENG, CATH UNIV AM, 70-, CHMN, DEPT CIVIL ENG, 81- *Personal Data:* b Shanghai, China, July 20, 37; US citizen; m 65; c 2. *Educ:* Univ Hong Kong, BSc, 59; Univ Mich, MSE, 60, PhD(eng mech), 63. *Concurrent Pos:* Prin investr, NSF grants, 65-95 & Off Naval Res Contracts, 74-92. *Mem:* Am Meteorol Soc; fel Am Soc Civil Engrs. *Res:* Physical oceanography; air-sea interaction; mountain waves; environmental fluid mechanics. *Mailing Add:* Dept Civil Eng Cath Univ Am 620 Michigan Ave Washington DC 20064-0001

KAO, WEN-HONG, ELECTROCHEMISTRY, ENERGY STORAGE & TRANSFER SYSTEMS. *Current Pos:* SR CHEMIST, ADVAN BATTERY RES, JOHNSON CONTROLS INC, 88- *Personal Data:* b Taipei, Taiwan, Mar 15, 54; m 79, Shu-jen Fang; c Yvonne, Peter & Jonathan. *Educ:* Nat Tsing Hua Univ, Hsinchu, Taiwan, BS, 76; Ohio State Univ, Columbus, PhD(anal chem), 84. *Prof Exp:* Lead scientist res & develop, Rayovac Corp, 84-88. *Concurrent Pos:* Res fel, Ohio State Univ, 84. *Mem:* Am Chem Soc; Electrochem Soc. *Res:* Chemical and electrochemical analysis of battery electrode materials and systems; models of chemical and electrochemical reactions; production-related battery problems. *Mailing Add:* 5356 W Silverleaf Lane Brown Deer WI 53223-1651

KAO, WINSTON WHEI-YANG, COLLAGEN & EXTRACELLULAR MATRIX COMPONENTS, CORNEAL WOUND-HEALING. *Current Pos:* assoc prof, Dept Ophthal, 82-90, PROF OCULAR MOLECULAR BIOL, UNIV CINCINNATI COL MED, 90- *Personal Data:* m 72, Candace W C Wang; c Edward & Charles. *Educ:* Univ Pa, PhD(biochem), 74. *Honors & Awards:* Edward McCormick Award, Res Prevent Blindness, 86. *Prof Exp:* Asst prof, Dept Ophthal, Univ Pittsburgh, 77-82. *Mem:* Asn Res Vision & Ophthal; Am Soc Biochem & Molecular Biol; AAAS; Int Soc Eye Res; Int Soc Differentiation. *Res:* Metabolism of extra-cellular matrix during corneal wound healing; the role of cornea-specific K12 keratin in the maintenance of the integrity of corneal epithelium. *Mailing Add:* Dept Ophthal Eden & Bethesda Ave Cincinnati OH 45267-0527. *Fax:* 513-558-3108

KAO, YI-HAN, PHYSICS. *Current Pos:* from asst prof to assoc prof, 63-71, PROF PHYSICS, STATE UNIV NY, STONY BROOK, 71- *Personal Data:* b Foochow, China, Jan 27, 31; m 57; c 2. *Educ:* Nat Taiwan Univ, BS, 55; Okla State Univ, MS, 58; Columbia Univ, PhD(physics), 62. *Prof Exp:* Res assoc physics, Thomas J Watson Lab, Int Bus Mach Corp, 62-63. *Mem:* Am Phys Soc. *Res:* Low temperature solid state physics; superconductivity; physics of thin films; transport phenomena. *Mailing Add:* Dept Physics State Univ NY 239 Fronczak Hall Amherst NY 14260

KAO, YUEN-KOH, CHEMICAL ENGINEERING, CONTROL ENGINEERING. *Current Pos:* asst prof, 75-81, ASSOC PROF CHEM ENG, UNIV CINCINNATI, 81- *Personal Data:* b Liaoning, China, Apr 3, 41; US citizen; m 66; c 2. *Educ:* Nat Taiwan Univ, BS, 64; Northwestern Univ, MS, 68, PhD(chem eng), 73. *Prof Exp:* Assoc chem eng, Rensselaer Polytech Inst, 73-75. *Concurrent Pos:* Consult, Mound Lab, Monsanto Res Corp, 77, Columbia Gas, 76 & R Katzen Asn, 80. *Mem:* Am Inst Chem Engrs; Sigma Xi; Electrochem Soc. *Res:* Process simulation and control; electrochemical engineering; boiling heat transfer; reaction engineering. *Mailing Add:* 6622 E Farmacres Dr Cincinnati OH 45237

KAPADIA, ABHAYSINGH J, PHARMACY. *Current Pos:* res assoc, 65-74, MGR STABILITY TESTING & PROD EVAL, A H ROBINS CO INC, 74- *Personal Data:* b Bombay, India, Mar 14, 29; m 55; c 2. *Educ:* L M Col Pharm, Ahmedabad, India, 52; Univ Mich, Ann Arbor, MS, 58; Univ Tex, Austin, PhD(pharm), 63. *Prof Exp:* Res chemist, Univ Mich, 57-58; sect head anal res, Alcon Labs, 63-65. *Mem:* Am Pharmaceut Asn. *Res:* Analytical methods development; stability testing of pharmaceuticals; preformulation studies of pharmaceuticals; drug plastic interactions. *Mailing Add:* 2221 Walhala Dr Richmond VA 23236

KAPANIA, RAKESH KUMAR, STRUCTURAL MECHANICS, PLATES & SHELLS. *Current Pos:* asst prof, 85-90, ASSOC PROF AEROSPACE STRUCT, VA POLYTECH INST & STATE UNIV, 90- *Personal Data:* b Nakodar, Punjab, Aug 3, 56; m 85; c 1. *Educ:* Punjab Univ, India, BS, 77; Indian Inst Sci, MS, 79; Purdue Univ, PhD(aerospace), 85. *Prof Exp:* Grad asst aerospace struct, Purdue Univ, 79-85. *Concurrent Pos:* NASA-ASEE fel, NASA-Langley Res Ctr, 85. *Mem:* Am Inst Aeronaut & Astronaut; Am Soc Civil Engrs; Soc Indust & Appl Math. *Res:* Application and development of state-of-the-art computational methods to solve problems in aeroelasticity, wave propagation in composites, impact response of laminated structures and plates and shells with emphasis on finite element method. *Mailing Add:* 404 Seminole Dr Blacksburg VA 24060-7813. *Fax:* 540-231-9632; *E-Mail:* rak@vtvm1.cs.vt.edu

KAPANY, NARINDER SINGH, PHYSICS, OPTICS. *Current Pos:* CHMN BD & PRES, KAPTRON INC, 73- *Personal Data:* b Moga, India, Oct 31, 27; nat US; m 54; c 2. *Educ:* DAV Col, Dehra Dun, BS, 48; Imp Col, London, dipl, 52; Univ London, PhD(optics), 54. *Prof Exp:* Supvr, Ord Factory, India, 49-51; lens designer, Barr & Stroud Optical Co, Scotland, 52; res assoc physics, Imp Col, London, 54-55; res assoc, Inst Optics, Rochester, 55-57; mgr optics sect, Ill Inst Technol Res Inst, 57-61; pres & dir res, Optics Technol, Inc, 61-73. *Concurrent Pos:* Consult, Bausch & Lomb Optical Co, 55-57, Argus Camera Co, 55-57 & Johns Hopkins Hosp, 56-57; res assoc, Palo Alto Med Res Found, Calif, 62-; vis scholar, Stanford Univ, 73-74; regents prof, Univ Calif, Santa Cruz, 76-77, dir, Ctr Innovation & Entrepreneurial Develop, 78. *Mem:* AAAS; fel Am Phys Soc; fel Optical Soc Am; sr mem Inst Elec & Electronics Engrs; fel Brit Inst Phys; Sigma Xi. *Res:* Geometrical and physical optics; fiber optics with applications in medicine, photoelectronics, photography, high-speed photography; infrared fiber optics communications, local area networks; laser and its applications; image evaluation and optical information processing; photoelectronics; aspherics; interference microscopy; refractometry; solar energy. *Mailing Add:* Tech & Advan Develop AMP 2525 E Bayshore Rd Palo Alto CA 94303

KAPECKI, JON ALFRED, PHYSICAL ORGANIC CHEMISTRY, PHOTOGRAPHIC SCIENCE. *Current Pos:* sr chemist, Eastman Kodak Co, 72-80, res assoc, 80-85, lab head, 85-89, SR LAB HEAD, EASTMAN KODAK CO, 89- *Personal Data:* b Chicago, Ill, June 8, 42; m 82, Jeanne Kaeding. *Educ:* Col St Thomas, BS, 64; Univ Vienna, Dipl, 64; Univ Ill, Urbana, PhD(org chem), 69. *Prof Exp:* NIH fel chem, Cornell Univ, 68-71, fel, 71-72. *Concurrent Pos:* Mem staff, X-ray Clinic, State Univ NY, Albany, 75-76; lectr, Univ Rochester, 72-80, sr lectr, 80-84, vis assoc prof, 84-86. *Mem:* Am Chem Soc; Soc Imaging Sci & Technol. *Res:* Organic cycloaddition mechanisms; solid state reactions; molecular orbital theory; computer applications to organic chemistry; models for reactive intermediates; reaction mechanisms; image and image modifying chemistry; qsar; information theory. *Mailing Add:* 161 Crosman Terr Rochester NY 14620. *Fax:* 716-588-7611; *E-Mail:* kapecki@kodak.com

KAPER, HANS G, APPLIED MATHEMATICS, MATHEMATICAL ANALYSIS. *Current Pos:* div dir, 87-91, SR MATHEMATICIAN, ARGONNE NAT LAB, 69- *Personal Data:* b Alkmaar, Neth, June 10, 36; US citizen; m 62; c 2. *Educ:* State Univ Groningen, Neth, MSc, 60, PhD(math), 65. *Prof Exp:* Asst prof appl math, State Univ Groningen, Neth, 65-66, assoc prof, 67-69; res assoc, Stanford Univ, 66-67. *Concurrent Pos:* Vis prof, Univ van Amsterdam, Neth, 76-77, Univ Vienna, Austria, 77, Northwestern Univ, 78-80 & 84-85, Univ Claude Bernard-Lyon I, France, 93 & Univ Toulouse 3, Toulouse, France, 96; adj prof, Northern Ill Univ, 83- *Mem:* Am Math Soc; Soc Indust & Appl Math; Math Soc Neth; corresp mem Royal Neth Acad Sci. *Res:* Applied analysis; scientific computing. *Mailing Add:* Math & Comput Sci Div Argonne Nat Lab 9700 S Case Ave Argonne IL 60439. *Fax:* 630-252-5986; *E-Mail:* kaper@mcs.anl.gov

KAPER, JACOBUS M, BIOCHEMISTRY, MOLECULAR BIOLOGY. *Current Pos:* biochemist, Plant Sci Res Div, 62-69, RES CHEMIST, PLANT PROTECTION INST, AGR RES SERV, USDA, 69- *Personal Data:* b Madjalenka, Indonesia, Dec 9, 31; US citizen; m 55; c 1. *Educ:* Univ Leiden, BS, 51, Drs, 54, PhD(biochem), 57. *Prof Exp:* Asst biochem, Univ Leiden, 54-57, sr res biochemist, 59-62; res fel, Virus Lab, Univ Calif, 57-59. *Concurrent Pos:* Fel, Neth Orgn Pure Res, 57-58; USPHS trainee, 58; assoc res prof, George Washington Univ, 62-69; prin investr, NIH res grants, 62-69 & USDA res grant, 78-81, 82-85 & 85-87. *Mem:* Am Soc Virol; Am Chem Soc; Am Soc Biol Chemists; Am Soc Microbiol; corresp mem Royal Neth Acad Sci; Int Soc Plant Molecular Biol. *Res:* Molecular organization and stabilizing interactions of viruses; structural biochemistry of proteins nucleic acids; divided genome viruses; mechanisms of viral disease regulation. *Mailing Add:* 115 Hedgewood Dr Greenbelt MD 20770-1610

KAPER, JAMES BENNETT, VACCINE DEVELOPMENT, INFECTIOUS DISEASES. *Current Pos:* asst prof med & microbiol, Univ Md, 81-84, asst prof biol chem, 83-85, assoc prof med, microbiol & biol chem, 84-90, CHIEF, BACT GENETICS SECT, CTR VACCINE DEVELOP, UNIV MD, 83-, PROF MED, MICROBIOL & BIOCHEM, 90- *Personal Data:* b Havre de Grace, Md, Aug 25, 52. *Educ:* Univ Md College Park, BS, 73, PhD(microbiol), 79. *Prof Exp:* Lab technician, England Labs, Beltsville, Md, 74-75; res asst, micros dept, Univ Md, College Park, 75-79; res fel, Dept Microbiol & Immunol, Univ Wash, 79-81. *Concurrent Pos:* Adj prof micros, Univ RI, 82-83; consult, NIH, 82-83, 88- & WHO, 84. *Mem:* Am Soc Microbiol; AAAS. *Res:* Development of vaccines and improved diagnostic tests for infectious diseases using recombinant DNA techniques. *Mailing Add:* Dept Microbiol Sch Med Univ Md 655 W Baltimore St Baltimore MD 21201-1559

KAPETANAKOS, CHRISTOS ANASTASIOS, PLASMA PHYSICS. *Current Pos:* PROF PHYSICS, INST PLASMA PHYSICS, UNIV CRETE, 93-, ACTING DIR, 93- *Personal Data:* b Sparta, Greece, Jan 2, 36; US citizen; div; c Tassos & Yula. *Educ:* Nat Univ Greece, Bachelor, 60; Mass Inst Technol, MS, 64; Univ Md, PhD(physics), 70. *Honors & Awards:* Outstanding Performance Award, Naval Res Lab, 72, Res Publ Awards, 73, 76, 79, 86 & 90. *Prof Exp:* Res physicist plasma physics, Univ Tex, 70-71; supvry res physicist plasma physics, Naval Res Lab, 71-80, head, Beam Dynamics Prog, 80-85, head, Adv Beam Technol Br, 85-89, sect head 89-92. *Concurrent Pos:* Energy Res & Develop Admin grant, 75-77, Dept Energy, 77-80, Off Naval Res, 80-84, SDID, 84, Defense Adv Res Proj Agency, 84 & Spawar, 85- *Mem:* Fel Am Phys Soc; fel Wash Acad Sci. *Res:* Supervise and contact research on intense, relativistic electron and ion beams and fusion reactors based on reversed magnetic field configurations; free electron lasers and ultra-high current accelerators. *Mailing Add:* LET Corp 4431 MacArthur Bvd Washington DC 20007 Greece. *Fax:* 202-767-3950

KAPETANOVIC, IZET MICHAEL, DRUG METABOLISM, EPILEPSY. *Current Pos:* PHARMACIST, PRECLIN EPILEPSY BR, NIH, 78- *Educ:* Northwestern Univ, Chicago, PhD(pharmacol), 78. *Mailing Add:* Park Bldg Rm 445 Bethesda MD 20892. *Fax:* 301-402-4924

KAPICA, SHARON KELLY, ENVIRONMENTAL HEALTH, BIOCHEMISTRY. *Current Pos:* PROF CHEM, CO COL MORRIS, 79-, CHMN BIOL & CHEM, 86- *Personal Data:* b Chicago, Ill, June 17, 43; div; c Kelly, Meghan & Tracey. *Educ:* Col St Elizabeth, BS, 65; Univ Chicago, MS, 68. *Honors & Awards:* Catalyst Award, Chem Mfr Asn, 91. *Prof Exp:* Res assoc, Med Sch, Univ Ill, 67-70; instr biol, Col St Elizabeth, 74-75. *Concurrent Pos:* Consult, 86- *Mem:* Am Chem Soc. *Mailing Add:* 12 Fletcher Pl Madison NJ 07940. *Fax:* 973-328-5361; *E-Mail:* skapica@ccm.edu

KAPIKIAN, ALBERT ZAVEN, EPIDEMIOLOGY, VIROLOGY. *Current Pos:* actg head epidemiol, 64-67, EPIDEMIOLOGIST, LAB INFECTIOUS DIS, NAT INST ALLERGY & INFECTIOUS DIS, 57-, HEAD, EPIDEMIOL SECT & ASST CHIEF, 67- *Personal Data:* b New York, NY, May 9, 30; m 60, Catherine Forth Andrews; c Albert Kaloust, Thomas Firth & Gregory Baird. *Educ:* Queens Col, NY, BS, 52; Cornell Univ, MD, 56. *Honors & Awards:* Kabakjian Award, Armenian Students' Asn Am, 74; Stitt Award, Asn Mil Surgeons US, 74; Behring Diag Award, Am Soc Microbiol, 87; Diag Virol Award (Murex), Pan Am Soc Clin Virol, 93. *Prof Exp:* Intern, Meadowbrook Hosp, Hempstead, NY, 56-57. *Concurrent Pos:* Guest worker virol, Royal Postgrad Med Sch, Univ London, 70; res prof, Child Health & Develop, Sch Med & Health Serv, George Washington Univ, 77- *Mem:* Am Pub Health Asn; Am Soc Microbiol; Am Epidemiol Soc Pres, 96-97; fel Infectious Dis Soc Am; fel AAAS. *Res:* Epidemiologic investigations of infectious diseases; viral gastroenteritis. *Mailing Add:* 11201 Marcliff Rd Rockville MD 20852. *Fax:* 301-496-8312

KAPILA, ASHWANI KUMAR, ASYMPTOTICS. *Current Pos:* from asst prof to assoc prof, 76-88, PROF MATH, RENSSELAER POLYTECH INST, 88- *Personal Data:* b Ludhiana, India, Aug 26, 46; US citizen; m 71; c 2. *Educ:* Punjabi Univ, India, BS, 68; Univ Sask, Can, MS, 70; Cornell Univ, PhD(theoret & appl mech), 75. *Prof Exp:* Instr & res assoc mech, Cornell Univ, 74-76. *Concurrent Pos:* Vis asst prof, Northwestern Univ, 78; Math Res Ctr, Univ Wis-Madison, 79-80; vis assoc prop, Inst Math Appln, Univ Minn, 86-87. *Mem:* Combustion Inst; Soc Indust & Appl Math. *Res:* Applied mathematics, especially asymptotics, perturbation theory and numerics; application to problems in mechanics, chemically reactive flows and combustion theory. *Mailing Add:* Dept Math Sci Rensselaer Polytech Inst Troy NY 12180-3590

KAPLAN, ABNER, AERONAUTICS. *Current Pos:* RETIRED. *Personal Data:* b New York, NY, June 21, 23; m 50; c 3. *Educ:* Calif Inst Technol, BS, 48, MS, 49, PhD(aeronaut), 54. *Prof Exp:* Res engr, Struct Res Group, Northrop Aircraft Corp, 52-55; mem tech staff & mgr, Struct Dept, TRW Systs Group, 55-70, staff engr, 70-92. *Mem:* Am Soc Mech Engrs; Am Inst Aeronaut & Astronaut. *Res:* Nonlinear buckling; thin shells; pressure vessels. *Mailing Add:* 4012 Stalwart Dr Rancho Palos Verdes CA 90274

KAPLAN, ALAN MARC, IMMUNOLOGY. *Current Pos:* PROF & CHMN, DEPT MICROBIOL & IMMUNOL, SCH MED, UNIV KY, 82- *Personal Data:* b Brooklyn, NY, Dec 10, 40; m 72; c 1. *Educ:* Tufts Univ, BS, 63; Purdue Univ, PhD(immunol), 69. *Prof Exp:* Res asst tumor immunol, Sloan-Kettering Inst, 63-65; asst prof, Med Col Va, 72-75, assoc prof surg & microbiol, 75-79, coordr, Tumor Immunol Sect, 74-82, prof surg & microbiol, 79-82, chmn, Dept Microbiol, 81-82, assoc dir res, Va Commonwealth Univ Cancer Ctr, 80-82. *Concurrent Pos:* Can Med Res Coun fel immunol, Univ Toronto, 69-72. *Mem:* Am Soc Microbiol; NY Acad Sci; Can Soc Immunol; Am Asn Immunol; Am Asn Cancer Res; Reticuloendothelial Soc. *Res:* Tumor and cellular immunology; autoimmunity; immunoadjuvants; immunogenetics; macrophage differentiation. *Mailing Add:* Dept Microbiol & Immunol Univ Ky Col Med MS411 Lexington KY 40536-0084

KAPLAN, ALEX, PHYSIOLOGY, CHEMISTRY. *Current Pos:* assoc prof biochem, Univ Wash, 60-69, prof biochem & lab med & dir, Chem Div, 69-80, dir, Hosp Chem Labs, 60-80, EMER PROF LAB MED, SCH MED, UNIV WASH, 80-d. *Personal Data:* b New York, NY, May 22, 10; m 40; c 3. *Educ:* Univ Calif, Los Angeles, AB, 32; Univ Calif, PhD(physiol), 36. *Prof Exp:* Res assoc, Mt Zion Hosp, San Francisco, 37-39; asst physiol, Univ Calif, 39-40; asst dir, Harold Brunn Inst Cardiovasc Res, San Francisco, 40-42; chief lab, Vio-Bin Corp, 46-50; asst dir dept biochem, Michael Reese Hosp, Ill, 50-57; chief chemist, Children's Hosp, San Francisco, 57-60. *Mem:* AAAS; Soc Exp Biol & Med; Am Physiol Soc; Am Asn Clin Chem (pres, 71). *Res:* Lipid metabolism; clinical chemistry. *Mailing Add:* 6207 Brooklyn Ave NE Seattle WA 98115

KAPLAN, ALEXANDER E, OPTICS, THEORETICAL PHYSICS. *Current Pos:* PROF DEPT ELEC & COMPUT ENG, JOHNS HOPKINS UNIV, 87- *Personal Data:* b Kiev, USSR, June 9, 38; US citizen. *Educ:* Moscow Phys-Tech Inst, MS, 61; USSR Acad Sci, Moscow & Gorky State Univ, PhD(physics & math), 67. *Prof Exp:* Mem res staff, USSR Acad Sci, Moscow, 63-79; mem res staff, Francis Bitter Nat Magnet Lab, Mass Inst Technol, 79-82; prof elec eng, Purdue Univ, 82-87. *Concurrent Pos:* Vis scientist, Max Planck Inst, Garching, WGer; consult, Bell Labs, 80-81, Los Alamos Nat Lab, 81 & Honeywell, 82; prin investr res proj, Off Sci Res, USAF, 80-, Mat Res Lab, NSF, 82-87 & CST Ind, 86-87. *Mem:* Am Phys Soc; fel Optical Soc Am; Lasers & Electroptical Soc. *Res:* Quantum electronics and nonlinear optics, nonlinear and quantum optics of a single electron; theory of two-level systems in a strong field; self-focusing and self-bending effects; theory of solitons; interaction of light with nonlinear interfaces and theory of cavityless optical bistability; light induced nonreciprocity, sagnac effect in nonlinear ring resonators and optical gyroscopes; nonlinear optical effects in superlattices; x-ray radiation by fast electron beams in periodical structrees (in particular in superlattices); four-wave mixing instabilities and multistability; the switching and steering of laser beams; x-ray nonlinear optics. *Mailing Add:* Dept Elec Eng Barton Hall Johns Hopkins Univ 34th & Charles St Baltimore MD 21218. *E-Mail:* sasha@super.ece.jhu.edu

KAPLAN, ALLEN P, MEDICINE. *Current Pos:* CHMN, DEPT MED, STATE UNIV NY, STONY BROOK HEALTH SCI CTR, 87- *Personal Data:* b Jersey City, NJ, Oct 27, 40; c 2. *Educ:* Columbia Univ, BA, 61; Downstate Med Sch, MD, 65; Am Bd Internal Med, cert, 72, Rheumat, cert, 72, Allergy & Clin Immunol, cert, 74, Diag Lab Immunol, cert, 86. *Prof Exp:* Intern med, Strong Mem Hosp, Rochester, NY, 65-66, asst resident med, 66-67; clin assoc, Nat Inst Arthritis & Metab Dis, NIH, Bethesda, Md, 67-69, head, Allergic Dis Sect, Lab Clin Invest, 72-78; res fel med, Peter Bent & Robert B Brigham Hosps, Harvard Med Sch, 69-72; prof med & head, Div Allergy, Rheumat & Clin Immunol, State Univ NY, Stony Brook, 78-87. *Concurrent Pos:* Spec fel, NIH, 70-72; prof lectr, Dept Biochem, Georgetown Univ, Washington, DC, 76-78; prof med & head, Div Allergy, Rheumat & Clin Immunol, Northport Vet Admin Hosp, NY, 78-87; grants, NIH, 78-; mem study sect, Nat Heart, Lung & Blood Inst, NIH, 81-85, Am Rheumatism Asn, 81-84, Am Heart Asn, 83-87; chmn, Res Coun, Am Acad Allergy & Immunol, 81-84; dir, Am Bd Allergy & Clin Immunol, 85-88; mem, Allergy, Immunol & Transplantation Res Comt, Nat Inst Allergy & Infectious Dis, 88-, chmn, 90- *Mem:* AAAS; Am Col Rheumat; Am Asn Immunologists; Am Thoracic Soc; Am Soc Exp Path; Am Soc Pharmacol & Exp Therapeut; Am Soc Hemat; Am Soc Clin Res; fel Am Acad Allergy; fel Am Col Physicians. *Res:* Coagulation, fibrinolysis and inflammation; immunochemistry and immunopathology; biochemical mechanisms of allergic reactions; cytokines, mast cells and rheumatic disease; author or co-author of over 180 publications. *Mailing Add:* Dept Med State Univ NY Health Sci Ctr Stony Brook NY 11794-8160

KAPLAN, ANN ESTHER, BIOCHEMISTRY, BIOPHYSICS. *Current Pos:* biochemist, 72-77, RES BIOCHEMIST, NAT CANCER INST, 77- *Personal Data:* b New York, NY, Dec 28, 26. *Educ:* Hunter Col, BA, 47; Mt Holyoke Col, MA, 49; Univ Pa, PhD(biochem), 59. *Prof Exp:* Instr neurol, Albert Einstein Col Med, 62-63; res assoc, Rockefeller Inst, 63-65; asst prof doctoral fac biochem, City Univ New York, 65-67; sr res assoc, Salk Inst Biol Studies, 67-72. *Concurrent Pos:* Dazian Found fel microbiol, Sch Med, NY Univ, 59-60; NIH sr fel physiol, Albert Einstein Col Med, 60-62; chmn & comr rep, sci manpower comn, Am Soc Exp Biol, 78-81. *Mem:* AAAS; Am Chem Soc; NY Acad Sci; Am Soc Biol Chem; Biophys Soc; Am Soc Physiol; Soc Gen Physiologists. *Res:* Biosynthesis of lipids in biological membranes; serum lipid factors in cell growth; oxygenase pathway in heart mitochondria; lactate dehydrogenase in central nervous system and serum in experimental allergic encephalomyelitis; modification of lactate dehydrogenase in hepatocyte lines with neoplastic transformation; aerobic glycolysis in neoplastic cell lines. *Mailing Add:* 4242 East-West Hwy Apt 514 Chevy Chase MD 20815-5950

KAPLAN, ARNOLD, LYSOSOMOLOGY, ORGANELLE BIOGENESIS. *Current Pos:* CHMN, DEPT BIOL SCI, UNIV ARK, FAYETTEVILLE. *Personal Data:* b New York, NY, Dec 20, 39; m 63; c 2. *Educ:* City Col New York, BS, 61; George Washington Univ, MS, 63, PhD(biochem), 66; Univ Calif, PhD(biochem), 68. *Prof Exp:* From asst prof to assoc prof, Med Sch, St Louis Univ, 68-84, prof microbiol, 84- *Concurrent Pos:* NIH fel, 66-68 & spec res fel, 70-72; fel, Nat Cancer Soc, 66-68; vis scientist biophys, Weissman Inst, 72; vis assoc prof pediat, Wash Univ Med Sch, 76; consult, Weissman Inst, Calbiochem, Monsanto & Childrens Inst; prog dir, Cell Biol Prog, NSF, 86. *Mem:* Am Soc Biol Chemists; Am Soc Cell Biol. *Mailing Add:* Dept Biol Sci 632 Sci Eng Univ Ark Fayetteville AR 72701-1202

KAPLAN, ARTHUR LEWIS, HEALTH PHYSICS, NUCLEAR ENGINEERING. *Current Pos:* CONSULT, ENVIRON ENG ASSOC, 93- *Personal Data:* b Boston, Mass, Mar 13, 33; m 57; c 2. *Educ:* Mass Inst Technol, BS, 54, MS, 55. *Prof Exp:* Proj engr, Aircraft Nuclear Propulsion Prog, Wright Air Develop Ctr, Ohio, 55-57; physicist, Tech Opers, Inc, 57-60; physicist & unit mgr, Gen Elec Co, 60-64; physicist & proj leader, Tech Opers Res, 64-69; tech dir, Systs Sci & Eng, Inc, 69-72; consult engr, Gen Elec Co Nuclear Fuel Dept, Gen Elec Co, Cleveland, 72-78, mgr licensing & compliance, Mfg Dept, 78-81, mgr environ control, Lighting Bus Group, 81-90, sr environ eng, Gen Elec Lighting, 91-93. *Mem:* Health Physics Soc. *Res:* Theoretical and experimental radiation shielding; biological effects of ionizing radiation; long range environmental effects of radioactive fallout; radiation effects in electronics and materials; health physics and radiation safety; health physics, licensing and compliance in uranium fabrication plants; environmental safety engineering. *Mailing Add:* 25422 Bryden Rd Cleveland OH 44122

KAPLAN, BARRY B, MOLECULAR NEUROBIOLOGY. *Current Pos:* assoc prof, 84-88, DIR, MOLECULAR NEUROBIOL, UNIV PITTSBURGH SCH MED, 88-, PROF, 94- *Personal Data:* b Bronx, NY, Sept 28, 46. *Educ:* Hofstra Univ, BS, 68, MS, 69; Cornell Univ, PhD(cell & molecular biol), 74. *Prof Exp:* Res fel molecular neurobiol, Andrews Geront Ctr, Univ Southern Calif, 74-76; asst prof microscopic anat, Cornell Med Col, 76-84. *Mem:* Soc Neurosci; Int Brain Res Orgn; Am Soc Neurochem; Int Soc Neurochem. *Res:* Molecular neurobiology. *Mailing Add:* Univ Pittsburgh Sch Med Western Psychiatric Hosp Room E1240 Pittsburgh PA 15261. *Fax:* 412-624-8997

KAPLAN, BARRY HUBERT, oncology, biochemistry, for more information see previous edition

KAPLAN, BERNARD, mathematical physics; deceased, see previous edition for last biography

KAPLAN, BERTON HARRIS, EPIDEMIOLOGY. *Current Pos:* PROF SOCIAL EPIDEMIOL, UNIV NC, CHAPEL HILL, 60- *Personal Data:* b Winchester, Va, June, 30; c 2. *Educ:* Va Polytech Inst, BS, 51; Univ NC, Chapel Hill, MS, 52, PhD(sociol), 62. *Concurrent Pos:* Fel, Social Res Coun, 65-66. *Mem:* AAAS; Soc Behav Med; Am Anthrop Asn; Am Sociol Asn; Soc Epidemiol Res. *Res:* Behavioral factors in coronary disease. *Mailing Add:* 1904 Rolling Rd Chapel Hill NC 27514

KAPLAN, DANIEL ELIOT, SOLID STATE PHYSICS, PLASMA PHYSICS. *Current Pos:* Res scientist, 58-67, SR STAFF SCIENTIST, LOCKHEED PALO ALTO RES LAB, 67- *Personal Data:* b San Mateo, Calif, Aug 17, 32; m 59; c 4. *Educ:* Univ Calif, AB, 53, MA, 55, PhD(physics), 58. *Mem:* Am Phys Soc; Sigma Xi. *Res:* Paramagnetic and ferrimagnetic resonance; plasma resonance phenomena. *Mailing Add:* 27000 Appaloosa Way Los Altos Hills CA 94022

KAPLAN, DANIEL MOSHE, ELEMENTARY PARTICLE PHYSICS. *Current Pos:* asst prof, 87-90, ASSOC PROF PHYSICS, NORTHERN ILL UNIV, 90- *Personal Data:* b Philadelphia, Pa, May 21, 53; m 86; c 1. *Educ:* Haverford Col, BA, 74; State Univ NY, Stony Brook, PhD(physics), 79. *Prof Exp:* Res asst, State Univ NY, Stony Brook, 74-78; res assoc, Columbia Univ, 79-82; assoc scientist, Fermilab, 82-84; comput res specialist, Fla State Univ, 84-86. *Mem:* Am Phys Soc; Sigma Xi. *Res:* Elementary particle physics carrying out a series of fixed-target experiments studying the interactions of quarks at large momentum transfer. *Mailing Add:* Physics Dept Ill Inst Tech Chicago IL 60616

KAPLAN, DAVID GILBERT, PHYSICAL CHEMISTRY. *Current Pos:* TAX LAW SPECIALIST, INTERNAL REVENUE SERV, LOS ANGELES, CALIF, 87- *Personal Data:* b Chicago, Ill, Nov 13, 44; m 71; c 2. *Educ:* Univ Ill, Urbana, BS, 65; Univ Southern Calif, PhD(phys chem), 72; JD, Loyola Sch Law, 80. *Prof Exp:* Fel biochem, Sch Med, Univ Calif, Los Angeles, 72-74; res coordr radiopharm, Sch Pharm, Univ Southern Calif, 75-76; unit head gelatin res, Banner Gelatin Prod Corp, 76-81; patent chemist, Union Oil Calif, 81-83; sr scientist, Cilgo Inc, Pomona, Calif, 83-87. *Mem:* Am Chem Soc. *Res:* Studies on the viscoelastic behavior of connective tissue and lipid metabolism of biological systems. *Mailing Add:* 4215 Los Springs Dr Agoura Hills CA 91301-5328

KAPLAN, DAVID JEREMY, OPERATIONS RESEARCH, SYSTEMS ANALYSIS. *Current Pos:* OPERS RES ANALYST, NAVAL RES LAB, 69- *Personal Data:* b Honolulu, Hawaii, Oct 8, 34; c 3. *Educ:* State Univ Iowa, BA, 56; Univ Calif, Berkeley, MA, 58. *Prof Exp:* Mathematician, Ames Res

Ctr, NASA, 58-60; mathematician syst anal, Stanford Res Inst, 60-69. *Mem:* Fel AAAS; Sigma Xi; Opers Res Soc Am; Math Asn Am. *Res:* Developing the symbolic framework that underlies command and control systems; data-driven language representations that form the interface between signal coordinating systems and their environment. *Mailing Add:* Naval Res Lab 5583 Washington DC 20375-0001

KAPLAN, DAVID L, statistics, demography; deceased, see previous edition for last biography

KAPLAN, DAVID LEE, BIODEGRADATION-BIOTRANSFORMATIONS, BIOPOLYMERS. *Current Pos:* RES MICROBIOLOGIST & CHEMIST, NATICK RES & DEVELOP CTR, US ARMY, 79- *Personal Data:* b Glen Cove, NY, Mar 18, 53. *Educ:* Univ Albany, BS, 75; State Univ NY, PhD(biochem), 78. *Prof Exp:* Teaching asst biol, Col Environ Sci & Forestry, State Univ NY, 76, res asst, 76-78, res assoc fel, Res Found, 78-79. *Concurrent Pos:* Reviewer, NSF grants, 80-, Environ Sci & Technol J, US Army Res Off grants & US Army Toxic & Hazardous Mat Agency proposals, 83- & US Environ Protection Agency grants, 84- *Mem:* Am Soc Microbiol; Am Soc Indust Microbiol; AAAS; Water Pollution Control Fedn; Sigma Xi. *Res:* Applied and environmental microbiology and biochemistry; prevention of deterioration and contamination of materials; biotransformations and biochemical reactions of natural and synthetic organic compounds in soils and waters; analytical chemistry techniques for separations and indentification of organic compounds; sewage sludge stabilization; enzymatic reactions with aromatic compounds; pollution abatement; installation restoration approaches for hazardous wastes. *Mailing Add:* 25 Hallock Point Rd Stow MA 01775-1570

KAPLAN, DONALD ROBERT, PLANT MORPHOLOGY. *Current Pos:* from asst prof to assoc prof, 68-77, PROF BOT, UNIV CALIF, BERKELEY, 77- *Personal Data:* b Chicago, Ill, Jan 17, 38; m 64, Dorothy Thunouer; c Andrew Martin & Timothy Douglas. *Educ:* Northwestern Univ, BA, 60; Univ Calif, Berkeley, PhD(bot), 65. *Prof Exp:* Asst prof biol sci, Univ Calif, Irvine, 65-68. *Concurrent Pos:* NSF fel, Royal Bot Garden, Eng, 65; Guggenheim fel, 87-88; Alexander von Humboldt sr US scientist award, Heidelburg, Ger, 88-89; Sigma Xi nat lectr, 96-97. *Mem:* AAAS; Bot Soc Am; Int Soc Plant Morphol; Am Soc Cell Biol; fel Linnean Soc London; Sigma Xi. *Res:* Comparative and developmental morphology of plants. *Mailing Add:* Dept Plant Biol 111 Genetics Plant Biol Bldg Univ Calif Berkeley CA 94720. *E-Mail:* koplandr@nature.berkeley.edu

KAPLAN, EDWARD LYNN, MATHEMATICAL PROGRAMMING. *Current Pos:* from assoc prof to prof, 61-81, EMER PROF MATH, ORE STATE UNIV, 81- *Personal Data:* b Philadelphia, Pa, May 11, 20; div. *Educ:* Carnegie Inst Technol, BS, 41; Princeton Univ, PhD(math), 51. *Prof Exp:* Mathematician, US Naval Ord Lab, 41-48; asst, Princeton Univ, 48-50; mem tech staff, Bell Tel Labs, 50-57; mathematician, Lawrence Radiation Lab, Univ Calif, 57-61. *Mem:* Am Math Soc. *Res:* Random sequences; elliptic-integral tables; probability; statistics; Monte Carlo methods; computation; mathematical programming; optimization; musical symbology. *Mailing Add:* 727 NW 11th St Corvallis OR 97330

KAPLAN, EHUD, NEUROPHYSIOLOGY, SENSORY PROCESS. *Current Pos:* PROF, JULIET DORIS STEIN RES PREVENT BLINDNESS, MT SINAI MED SCH, 96- *Personal Data:* b Jerusalem, Israel, Dec 29, 42; m 66; c 2. *Educ:* Hebrew Univ, Jeruselem, Israel, BA, 67; Syracuse Univ, PhD(neurophysiol), 73. *Prof Exp:* Res asst vision, Hadassah Hosp, Jerusalem Israel, 63-65 & Syracuse Univ, 68-73; fel, Rockefeller Univ, 73-76, asst prof to assoc prof, 77-96. *Concurrent Pos:* Instr, Marine Biol Lab, Woods Hole, Mass, 77- *Mem:* NY Acad Sci; Asn Res Vision & Opthal; Sigma Xi. *Res:* Information processing by the brain especially in the visual system; the way photoreceptors transduce light into electrical energy. *Mailing Add:* Mt Sinai Med Sch 1 Gustave Levy Pl New York NY 10029

KAPLAN, EMANUEL, BIOCHEMISTRY. *Current Pos:* RETIRED. *Personal Data:* b Clearfield, Pa, Mar 12, 10; m 34; c 2. *Educ:* Johns Hopkins Univ, AB, 31, ScD(biochem), 34. *Prof Exp:* Spec asst biochem, Sch Hyg & Pub Health, Johns Hopkins Univ, 30-32, asst, 31-34; chief div chem, Bur Labs, Baltimore City Health Dept, 34-57, asst dir, 57-65; chief, Div Biochem, Bur Labs, Md State Dept Health, 65-76. *Concurrent Pos:* Instr, Sch Nursing, Sinai Hosp, 39-44. *Mem:* Am Chem Soc; fel Am Pub Health Asn; Am Asn Clin Chem. *Res:* Environmental chemistry; clinical chemistry; completely edible dentifrice. *Mailing Add:* 3 Stonehenge Circle Apt 1 Baltimore MD 21208

KAPLAN, EPHRAIM HENRY, ANALYTICAL CHEMISTRY. *Current Pos:* RETIRED. *Personal Data:* b New York, NY, Nov 16, 18; m 52; c 3. *Educ:* City Col New York, BS, 38; Univ Iowa, MS, 40; Univ Pittsburgh, PhD(org chem, biochem), 45; Northwestern Univ, MM, 74. *Prof Exp:* Asst sci aide, Eastern Regional Res Lab, Bur Agr & Indust Chem, USDA, 41-42; org chemist, Bur Mines, Pittsburgh, 42-45; res assoc, Polytech Inst Brooklyn, 47-49; Res Corp fel enzyme chem, Inst Enzyme Res, Univ Wis, 49-50; res assoc, Med Sch, Northwestern Univ, 50-53; res chemist, Vico Prod Co, 53-56; res assoc, Inst Tuberc Res, Univ Ill, 56-57; tech dir, Hodag Chem Corp, 57-60; res chemist, Velsicol Chem Corp, Chicago, 60-69; toxicologist & supvr Biochem Sect, Chicago Bd Health, 70-89. *Mem:* Am Chem Soc. *Res:* Surface active chemicals; enzymes; proteins; intermediary metabolism; sorption of vapors by and permeation through polymers; organic synthesis; analysis of hydrocarbon mixtures; pesticides; instrumental, drug and clinical analysis. *Mailing Add:* 9526 Kostner Ave Skokie IL 60076-1330

KAPLAN, ERVIN, INTERNAL MEDICINE, NUCLEAR MEDICINE. *Current Pos:* RETIRED. *Personal Data:* b Independence, Iowa, June 19, 18; m 45; c 2. *Educ:* Univ Ill, BS, 47, MS & MD, 49; Am Bd Internal Med, dipl; Am Bd Nuclear Med, dipl. *Honors & Awards:* First Prize Award, Gema Czerniak; Award Nuclear Med & Radiopharmacol, Ahavat Zion Found, Israel, 74. *Prof Exp:* Intern, Mt Sinai Hosp, Chicago, 49-50; clin asst, Univ Ill Col Med, 52-53, clin instr, 53-57, from clin asst prof to prof med & physiol, 59-88; resident internal med, Vet Admin Hosp, 50-52, actg assoc dir radioisotope serv, 52-59, chief, 59-70, sr physician, 71-75, chief nuclear med serv, 59-88, dept dir nuclear med, Great Lakes Dist, 86-88. *Concurrent Pos:* Physician-in-charge, Radioisotope Clin & assoc attend physician, Mt Sinai Hosp, Chicago, 53-59, consult, 67-84; physician-in-charge, Radioisotope Lab, Michael Reese Hosp, Chicago, 56-59; assoc attend physician, Cook County Hosp, 59-64, attend physician, 64-; bd trustees & chmn standing comt, Technol Nuclear Med, Soc Nuclear Med, 60-67; consult nuclear med, Louis Weiss Mem Hosp, 70-78; lectr, Chicago Med Sch, 71-78 & Stritch Sch Med, Loyola Univ; mem, Post World Cong Nuclear Med, Vet Gen Hosp, Taiwan, 74-78; dist dir, Nat Asn Vet Admin Physicians, 76-80; mem, Liaison Comt between Soc Nuclear Med & World Fedn Nuclear Med & Biol, 78; vis prof, Albert Einstein Col Med, 82; sci corresp, Rev Biol & Nuclear Med, Uruguay; dep dir nuclear med, US Vet Admin Hosp Region 4; adj prof elec eng & comput sci, Col Eng, Univ Ill, Chicago. *Mem:* AAAS; Soc Exp Biol & Med; Soc Nuclear Med; Am Col Nuclear Physicians. *Res:* Application of radioisotopes in medicine and biological research. *Mailing Add:* 2600 Wilmette Ave Wilmette IL 60091. *E-Mail:* ohgng@aol.com

KAPLAN, EUGENE HERBERT, PARASITOLOGY, SCIENCE EDUCATION. *Current Pos:* from lectr to assoc prof, 58-74, PROF BIOL, HOFSTRA UNIV, 75-, DIR, MARINE LAB, 80- *Personal Data:* b Brooklyn, NY, June 26, 32; m 58, Breena Lubou; c Julie & Susan. *Educ:* Brooklyn Col, BS, 54; Hofstra Col, MS, 56; Ny Univ, PhD(sci educ), 63. *Honors & Awards:* Marine Educ Award, Nat Marine Educr Asn, 89. *Prof Exp:* Teacher high sch, NY, 56-58. *Concurrent Pos:* NSF sci fac fel, 63-64; UNESCO expert elem sci, Israel, 71-72. *Mem:* Am Soc Parasitol; Nat Asn Res Sci Teaching; Asn Marine Labs Caribbean; Caribbean Aquacult Asn. *Res:* Marine ecology, especially coral reef invertebrates; effects of dredging on benthos; introductory science courses for non-science majors; measuring aspects of scientific thinking; comparisons of hybridfishes suitable for aquaculture. *Mailing Add:* Dept Biol Hofstra Univ 1000 Fulton Ave Hempstead NY 11550-1091

KAPLAN, FRED, ORGANIC CHEMISTRY. *Current Pos:* from instr to assoc prof, 61-68, PROF CHEM, UNIV CINCINNATI, 68- *Personal Data:* b Brooklyn, NY, Sept 2, 34; m 73; c 4. *Educ:* NY Univ, BA, 55; Yale Univ, PhD(chem), 60. *Prof Exp:* USPHS res fel chem, Swiss Fed Inst Technol, 59-60; univ fel, Calif Inst Technol, 60-61. *Mem:* AAAS; Am Chem Soc; Am Asn Univ Professors. *Res:* Applications of ion cyclotron resonance spectroscopy; gas phase ion-molecule reactions; gas phase properties of organic species; electron deficient species. *Mailing Add:* Dept Chem Univ Cincinnati 2600 Clifton Ave Cincinnati OH 45221-2872

KAPLAN, GEORGE HARRY, ASTROMETRY, RADIO & OPTICAL INTERFEROMETRY. *Current Pos:* ASTRONR, US NAVAL OBSERV, 71- *Personal Data:* b Hagerstown, Md, Apr 24, 48; m 72, Carol Zyskowski. *Educ:* Univ Md, BS, 69, MS, 76, PhD, 85. *Mem:* AAAS; Am Astron Soc; Sigma Xi; Int Astron Union. *Res:* Radio and optical astrometry; radio and optical interferometry; earth rotation; solar system dynamics and ephemerides; astronomical reference frames; celestial navigation. *Mailing Add:* US Naval Observ 3450 Massachusetts Ave NW Washington DC 20392-5420. *E-Mail:* ghk@newcomb.usno.navy.mil

KAPLAN, GERALD, ANALYTICAL CHEMISTRY. *Current Pos:* Res scientist, Johnson & Johnson Res Ctr, 67-71, sr res scientist anal chem, 71-72, group leader methods develop, 72-75, asst mgr, 75-79, mgr anal labs, 79-88, dir, 89, mgr, 90-95, MGR, PROD DEVELOP ORAL CARE, JOHNSON & JOHNSON CONSUMER PRODS, 95- *Personal Data:* b Brooklyn, NY, Dec 21, 39; m 67, Marilyn Hollender; c Andrew, Michael, Jason & Laura. *Educ:* Columbia Univ, BS, 61, MS, 63; Rutgers Univ, PhD(pharmaceut chem), 68. *Mem:* Am Chem Soc; Sigma Xi. *Res:* Separations sciences; oral care product development, floss & toothbrushes. *Mailing Add:* Johnson & Johnson Consumer Prod 199 Grandview Rd Skillman NJ 08558-9418

KAPLAN, HAROLD IRWIN, PSYCHIATRY, PSYCHOANALYSIS. *Current Pos:* PROF PSYCHIAT, SCH MED, NY UNIV, 80- *Personal Data:* b Brooklyn, NY, Oct 1, 27; m 81, Nancy Barrett; c Phillip, Peter & Jennifer. *Educ:* NY Med Col, MD, 49; Am Bd Psychiat & Neurol, dipl, 57; NY Univ, BA, 88. *Honors & Awards:* Distinguished Serv Award, Asn Psychiat Outpatient Centers Am, 82. *Prof Exp:* Intern med, Brooklyn Jewish Hosp, 49-50; resident psychiat, Bronx Vet Admin Hosp, 50-53, Mt Sinai Hosp, New York, 52-53; from instr to prof psychiat, New York Med Col, 54-80. *Concurrent Pos:* Attend psychiatrist, Metrop Hosp, 54-80, Flower & Fifth Hosp, 54-80 & Bird S Coler Hosp, 54-80; attend psychiatrist, Univ Hosp & Bellevue Hosp, New York Univ Med Ctr, NY; consult psychiatrist, Lenox Hill Hosp, New York, NY, 95- *Mem:* Am Psychiat Asn; Am Acad Psychoanal; Am Col Physicians; NY Acad Med; Am Med Writers Asn. *Res:* Education of women physicians; psychiatric education research; psychosomatic medicine; author or editor of 52 textbooks on psychiatry or psychiatric subjects. *Mailing Add:* 50 E 78th St New York NY 10021

KAPLAN, HAROLD M, PHYSIOLOGY. *Current Pos:* RETIRED. *Personal Data:* b Boston, Mass, Sept 4, 08; m 34; c 3. *Educ:* Dartmouth Col, AB, 30; Harvard Univ, AM, 31, PhD(physiol), 33. *Prof Exp:* Asst instr zool, Harvard Univ, 33-34; instr physiol, Middlesex Univ, 34-37, prof, Med Sch, 37-45 &

Vet Sch, 45-47; prof physiol, Brandeis Univ, 45-47; assoc prof, Univ Mass, 47-49; chmn dept, Southern Ill Univ, Carbondale, 49-71, prof physiol, 49-77. *Concurrent Pos:* Pvt res with Dr E V Enzmann, Biol Labs, Harvard Univ, 35-37; writer, Wash Inst Med, 46-49; vis prof, Sch Med, Southern Ill Univ, 77- *Mem:* Fel AAAS; Am Physiol Soc; Am Soc Zool; Am Asn Lab Animal Sci (pres, 96-97); Electron Micros Soc Am. *Res:* Laboratory animal medicine. *Mailing Add:* Sch Med Southern Ill Univ Carbondale IL 62901. *Fax:* 618-453-1919; *E-Mail:* hkaplan@dom.siu.edu

KAPLAN, HARRY ARTHUR, neurosurgery; deceased, see previous edition for last biography

KAPLAN, HARVEY, THEORETICAL PHYSICS. *Current Pos:* from asst prof to assoc prof, 59-65, PROF PHYSICS, SYRACUSE UNIV, 65- *Personal Data:* b New York, NY, Nov 29, 24; m 47; c 3. *Educ:* City Col New York, BS, 48; Univ Calif, PhD(physics), 52. *Prof Exp:* Res assoc, Mass Inst Technol, 52-54; asst prof physics, Univ Buffalo, 54-59. *Mem:* Am Phys Soc. *Res:* Theory of solid state; dynamical systems. *Mailing Add:* Dept Physics Syracuse Univ Syracuse NY 13244

KAPLAN, HARVEY, BIOCHEMISTRY. *Current Pos:* asst prof biochem, 71-76, assoc prof, 76-79, prof, 79-88, PROF CHEM, UNIV OTTAWA, 88- *Personal Data:* b New York, NY, May 24, 40; Can citizen; m 66; c 2. *Educ:* Queen's Univ, Ont, BSc, 62; Univ Ottawa, PhD(kinetics), 66. *Prof Exp:* Nat Res Coun Can fel, 66-67; fel, Lab Molecular Biol, Cambridge Univ, 67-68; asst res officer biochem, Nat Res Coun Can, 68-71. *Mem:* Can Biochem Soc. *Res:* Kinetics and mechanism of enzyme action; structure and function of serine proteases; ionization constants and reactivity of functional groups in proteins. *Mailing Add:* Dept Chem Univ Ottawa 10 Marie Curie Ottawa ON K1N 6N5 Can. *Fax:* 613-562-5180

KAPLAN, HARVEY ROBERT, PHARMACOLOGY. *Current Pos:* Assoc dir, Dept Pharmacol, 67-80, DIR CARDIOVASC SECT, WARNER-LAMBERT RES INST, 80- *Personal Data:* b New Brunswick, NJ, Aug 21, 41; m 64; c 2. *Educ:* Philadelphia Col Pharm, BSc, 63; Univ Conn, MSc, 65, PhD(pharmacol), 66. *Concurrent Pos:* NIH fel, Univ Pittsburgh, 66-67. *Mem:* AAAS; NY Acad Sci; Am Soc Pharmacol & Exp Therapeut. *Res:* Cardiovascular and autonomic pharmacology; cardiac arrhythmias and antiarrhythmic drugs; central cardiovascular mechanisms; evaluation and assay of synthetics as well as natural products isolated form both plant and animals. *Mailing Add:* Dept Sci Affairs Parke-Davis Pharmaceut Res Div Warner Lambert Co 2800 Plymouth Rd Ann Arbor MI 48105-2430

KAPLAN, HELEN SINGER, PSYCHIATRY, SEXUAL DISORDERS. *Current Pos:* coordr undergrad teaching psychiat, 70-76, CLIN PROF PSYCHIAT, CORNELL UNIV MED COL, 70-; ATTEND PSYCHIATRIST, PAYNE WHITNEY CLIN, NY HOSP, 70- *Personal Data:* b Vienna, Austria, Feb 6, 29; US citizen; div; c 3. *Educ:* Syracuse Univ, BFA, 49; Columbia Univ, MA, 51, PhD(psychol), 55; NY Med Col, MD, 59; Am Bd Psychiat & Neurol, dipl. *Honors & Awards:* Outstanding Prof Contrib Field Sexuality, Am Asn Sex Educrs & Counrs, 83. *Prof Exp:* Instr, Dept Pharmacol & Physiol, NY Med Col, 59-61; fel psychiat, Bellevue Hosp, 61-62; NY Med Col, Metropolitan Hosp Ctr, 62-64; Nat Inst Mental Health career teacher psychiat, NY Med Col, Metrop Hosp Ctr, 64-66; from asst prof to assoc prof psychiat, NY Med Col, 66-70; chmn behav sci topic teaching block, 69-70. *Concurrent Pos:* Assoc attend psychiatrist, Metrop, Flower Fifth & B S Coler Hosp, 66-70; dir, Human Sexuality Prog, Payne Whitney Clin, 70-, Helen S Kaplan Assocs, 70- *Mem:* Am Psychol Asn; fel Am Psychiat Asn; Psychosom Soc; Acad Psychoanal; Sigma Xi; AMA; Am Group Psychother Asn; Asn Advan Behav Ther; NY Acad Sci; Am Asn Sex Educrs & Counrs; NY Acad Med. *Res:* Psychopharmacology; psychosomatic medicine; treatment of sexual disorders; psychiatric education. *Mailing Add:* 960 Fifth Ave New York NY 10021-1708

KAPLAN, HENRY J, OPHTHALMOLOGY. *Current Pos:* PROF & CHMN, DEPT OPHTHAL & VISUAL SCI, SCH MED, WASH UNIV, ST LOUIS, MO, 88- *Personal Data:* b New York, NY, Dec 29, 42; m 66; c 3. *Educ:* Columbia Univ, AB, 64; Cornell Univ, MD, 68; Am Bd Ophthal, cert, 79. *Honors & Awards:* Honor Award, Am Acad Ophthal, 84; Sci Award, Alcon Res Inst, 87; Sr Honor Award, Am Acad Ophthal, 94. *Prof Exp:* Intern med, Lakeside Hosp, Univ Hosps, Cleveland, Case Western Res Univ, 68-69; surg resident, Bellevue Hosp, NY Univ Med Ctr, New York, NY, 69-70; res fel immunol, NIH, Dept Cell Biol, Univ Tex Med Sch, Dallas, 72-74, asst prof, Dept Cell Biol, 74-75; assoc prof, Dept Ophthal, Sch Med, Emory Univ, Atlanta, Ga, 79-84, prof, 84-88. *Concurrent Pos:* Affil scientist path & immunol, Yerkes Regional Primate Res Ctr, Atlanta, Ga, 81-; Olga Keith Weiss Scholar, Res Prevent Blindness Inc, 84; dir res, Dept Ophthal, Sch Med, Emory Univ, Atlanta, Ga, 84-88, assoc prof, Dept Microbiol, 85-88; adj prof, Dept Small Animal Med, Univ Ga, Athens, 85-; mem, Visual Dis Study Sect A-1, Nat Eye Inst, NIH, 85-89, chmn, 87-89; ophthalmologist-in-chief, Barnes Hosp, 88-96 & 96-; active staff ophthalmologist, St Louis Children's Hosp, 88-; assoc attend ophthalmologist, Jewish Hosp, St Louis, 88-96; mem bd dirs, Wash Univ Physician Network, 89-, Partners Health Plan, 89-; assoc examr, Am Bd Ophthal, 90- *Mem:* Asn Res Vision & Ophthal; fel Am Acad Ophthal; AAAS; AMA; NY Acad Sci; Am Asn Immunologists; Am Uveitis Soc; fel Am Col Surgeons; Am Soc Contemp Ophthal. *Res:* Retina-vitreous; immunology-uveitis; author or co-author of over 80 publications. *Mailing Add:* Dept Ophthal Sch Med Wash Univ 660 S Euclid Ave Box 8096 St Louis MO 63110-1093. *Fax:* 314-362-2575; *E-Mail:* kaplan@am.seer.wwotl.edu

KAPLAN, IRVING, theoretical physics; deceased, see previous edition for last biography

KAPLAN, ISSAC R, GEOCHEMISTRY. *Current Pos:* assoc prof geol & geophys, 65-69, PROF GEOL & GEOCHEM, UNIV CALIF, LOS ANGELES, 69-; PRES, GLOBAL GEOCHEM CORP, 77- *Personal Data:* b Baranowicze, Poland, July 10, 29; m 55; c 2. *Educ:* Univ Canterbury, BSc, 52, MSc, 53; Univ Southern Calif, PhD(biogeochem), 61. *Prof Exp:* Res officer oceanog, Commonwealth Sci & Indust Res Orgn, Australia, 53-57; res fel geochem, Calif Inst Technol, 61-62; guest lectr & Ziskind scholar microbiol & geochem, Hebrew Univ, Israel, 63-65. *Concurrent Pos:* Assoc ed, Geochem Soc, 66-70 & Chem Geol, 66-67; mem planetary biol subcomt, Space Sci & Appln Steering Comt, NASA, 67-; Guggenheim Mem Found res fel, Mineral Res Labs, Commonwealth Sci & Indust Res Orgn, Japan, New Caledonia, NZ & Australia, 70-71; assoc ed, Marine Chem, 72- & Geochem J, 76-; mem exobiol panel, Space Sci Bd, Nat Acad Sci. prin investr lunar return mat, Apollo 11, 12, 14 & 15; chmn, Org Geochem Div, Geochem Soc, 76-77. *Mem:* Geochem Soc; fel Am Inst Chemists; Am Asn Petrol Geologists; fel AAAS; Am Chem Soc; fel Geol Soc Am. *Res:* Biogeochemistry of recent sediments; factors controlling the distribution of elements in the ocean; isotope geochemistry and organic geochemistry of terrestrial rocks and meteorites; biological fractionation of stable isotopes; atmospheric chemistry and atmospheric pollution. *Mailing Add:* Global Geochem Corp 6919 Eton Ave Canoga Park CA 91303

KAPLAN, JEROME I, SOLID STATE PHYSICS. *Current Pos:* PROF PHYSICS, IND UNIV-PURDUE UNIV INDIANAPOLIS, 74- *Personal Data:* b New York, NY, July 28, 26; m 65; c 1. *Educ:* Univ Mich, BS, 50; Univ Calif, Berkeley, PhD(physics), 54. *Honors & Awards:* Fulbright lectr, Univ Col, Rhodesia & Nyasaland, 63-64. *Prof Exp:* Res scientist, Naval Res Lab, DC, 54-59; res assoc physics, Brandeis Univ, 59-62, asst prof, 62-63; assoc res prof, Brown Univ, 64-67; res fel, Battelle-Columbus, 67-74; res assoc, Krannert Inst Cardiol, 74-80. *Concurrent Pos:* Louis Lipsky fel physics, Weizmann Inst, 56-57; consult, Lincoln Lab, Mass Inst Technol, Hercules Chem Co, 61; sr fel, Indianapolis Ctr Advan Res, 80-87; vis scientist, Naval Res Lab, 81. *Mem:* Am Phys Soc. *Res:* Magnetic properties of solids; nuclear and ferromagnetic wave resonance; electron, nuclear and ferromagnetic spin resonance phenomena; magnetic resonance in liquids and liquid crystals; nuclear magnetic resonance in heart muscle; solar heating design; nuclear magnetic resonance theory. *Mailing Add:* 4417 N Pennsylvania Indianapolis IN 46205

KAPLAN, JERRY, CELL BIOLOGY. *Current Pos:* PROF PATH, MED CTR, UNIV UTAH, 80- *Educ:* Purdue Univ, PhD(biol sci), 71. *Res:* Membrane dynamics; biochemistry. *Mailing Add:* Med Ctr Rm 5C124 Univ Utah Col Med Salt Lake City UT 84132-0001. *Fax:* 801-581-4517

KAPLAN, JOEL HOWARD, IMMUNOTOXICOLOGY, HEALTH RISK ASSESSMENT. *Current Pos:* RES SCIENTIST, BUR TOXIC SUBSTANCE ASSESSMENT, NY STATE DEPT HEALTH, 87- *Personal Data:* b New York, NY, Apr 6, 41. *Educ:* City Col New York, BS, 62; Johns Hopkins Univ, PhD(biochem), 67. *Prof Exp:* Nat Cancer Inst fel cancer biochem, McArdle Lab Cancer Res, 67-69; staff scientist med sci, Gen Elec Res & Develop Ctr, 69-85. *Concurrent Pos:* Vis scientist, Johns Hopkins Sch Hyg & Pub Health, 85-87. *Mem:* Am Asn Immunol; AAAS. *Res:* Health risk assessment of toxic substances, immunotoxicology; in vitro methods in cell-mediated immunity; electrokinetic properties of lymphocyte subpopulations; cancer-immunodiagnosis. *Mailing Add:* NY State Dept Health 2 University Pl Albany NY 12203

KAPLAN, JOEL HOWARD, CHEMICAL ENGINEERING. *Current Pos:* RETIRED. *Personal Data:* b Paterson, NJ, Sept 8, 38; c 2. *Educ:* Newark Col Eng, BS, 61, MS, 62, DSc(chem eng), 66. *Prof Exp:* Res chem engr, Am Cynamid Co, Bound Brook, 66-69, group leader, Process Anal Sect, 69-71, mgr, Systs Anal Dept, 71-80, proj leader process develop, Org Chem Div, 80-83; mgr mat & res planning, Lonza Inc, Fairlawn, 83-90, dir corp plant opers, 90-94. *Concurrent Pos:* Adj prof chem eng, NJ Inst Technol, 78- *Mem:* Am Inst Chem Engrs; Am Chem Soc; NY Acad Sci. *Res:* Kinetics and reactor design of industrial processes; process development; application of computer control to industrial processes; research management concerned with plant and laboratory automation and development of research strategy models; inventory and production planning systems, MRP II. *Mailing Add:* 26 Bianculli Dr South Plainfield NJ 07080

KAPLAN, JOHN ERVIN, PHAGOCYTOSIS, THROMBOSIS. *Current Pos:* Fel, Albany Med Col, State Univ NY, 75-77, instr, 76-77, from asst prof to assoc prof physiol, 77-87, assoc prof, Grad Sch Pub Health, 84-90, vchmn, 90-91; PROF PHYSIOL & CELL BIOL, ALBANY MED COL, 86-, PROF, STATE UNIV NY, ALBANY, GRAD SCH PUB HEALTH, 90-, ASSOC DEAN GRAD STUDIES, 91- *Personal Data:* b Chicago, Ill, Dec 4, 50; m 73; c 2. *Educ:* Univ Ill, BS, 72; Albany Med Col, PhD(physiol), 76. *Concurrent Pos:* Prin investr res grants, New York Heart Asn, 77-78 & 90-, NIH, 78- & Shared Instrumentation Prog, 79-82; Sinsheimer Fund Scholar, 80-83; res career develop award, 80-85; dir, NIH Prog Proj, 91- *Mem:* Sigma Xi; Reticuloendothelial Soc; Am Heart Asn; Am Physiol Soc; Am Soc Cell Biol. *Res:* Mechanisms by which macrophages and adhesive proterms act as physiological anti-thrombotic mechanisms, and the role of these mechanisms in sepsis, trauma, intravascular coagulation and vascular injury; interaction of platelets and endothelial cells; fibronectin receptors. *Mailing Add:* Dept Physiol & Cell Biol A-134 Albany Med Col 47 New Scotland Rd Albany NY 12208. *Fax:* 518-262-5669

KAPLAN, JOSEPH, PEDIATRICS, HEMOTOLOGY & ONCOLOGY. *Current Pos:* From asst prof to assoc prof pediat, 72-87, PROF PEDIAT, IMMUNOL & MICROBIOL, WAYNE STATE UNIV, 87-, PROF MED, 88- *Personal Data:* b Boston, Mass, March 7, 41; m 86; c 2. *Educ:* NY Univ, BA, 62; Johns Hopkins Univ, MD. 66. *Mem:* Am Asn Immunologists; Am Pediat Soc; Am Soc Hematol. *Res:* Clinical immunology; role of natural killer cells in health and disease such as in prevention of graft-version hour disease and bone marrow graft rejection. *Mailing Add:* Dept Pediat Children's Hosp Wayne State Univ 3901 Beaubien Blvd Detroit MI 48201. *Fax:* 313-993-7158

KAPLAN, LAWRENCE, BOTANY. *Current Pos:* assoc prof, 65-68, PROF BIOL, UNIV MASS, BOSTON, 68- *Personal Data:* b Chicago, Ill, Apr 14, 26; m 46; c 1. *Educ:* Univ Iowa, BA, 49, MS, 51; Univ Chicago, PhD(bot), 56. *Prof Exp:* Assoc cur, Mus Useful Plants, Mo Bot Gardens, 55; instr biol, Wright Jr Col, 56; asst prof, Roosevelt Univ, 57-65. *Concurrent Pos:* Ed, Econ Bot, 91- *Mem:* Fel AAAS; Bot Soc Am; Sigma Xi; Soc Econ Bot (pres, 87); Soc Am Archeol. *Res:* Ethnobotany; systematics. *Mailing Add:* Dept Biol Univ Mass 100 Morrissey Blvd Boston MA 02125

KAPLAN, LAWRENCE JAY, BIOCHEMISTRY, FORENSIC SCIENCE. *Current Pos:* from asst prof to assoc prof, 71-84, PROF CHEM, WILLIAMS COL, 84-, CHMN, CHEM DEPT & CO-CHMN, PROG BIOCHEM & MOLECULAR BIOL, 88- *Personal Data:* b Newark, NJ, Mar 20, 43; m 65; c 2. *Educ:* Univ Pittsburgh, BS, 64; Purdue Univ, PhD(chem), 70. *Prof Exp:* Fel, Univ Mass, Amherst, 70-71. *Concurrent Pos:* Res scientist, Weizmann Inst, Israel, 76-77; vis assoc prof, Biochem Dept, Brandeis Univ, 80-81. *Mem:* AAAS; Am Chem Soc; Am Soc Biochem & Molecular Biol. *Res:* Physical biochemistry of proteins; conformational transitions of macromolecules; structure of chromatin. *Mailing Add:* Dept Chem Williams Col Williamstown MA 01267

KAPLAN, LEONARD, ORGANIC CHEMISTRY, CATALYSIS. *Current Pos:* proj scientist, 74-75, res scientist, 75-79, SR RES SCIENTIST, UNION CARBIDE CORP, 79- *Personal Data:* b Brooklyn, NY, July 18, 39. *Educ:* Cooper Union, BChE, 60; Univ Ill, PhD(org chem), 64. *Prof Exp:* Res assoc org chem, Columbia Univ, 64-65; instr, Univ Chicago, 65-67, asst prof, 67-74. *Concurrent Pos:* NSF fel, 64-65; Alfred P Sloan Found fel. *Mem:* Am Chem Soc; The Chem Soc. *Res:* Homogeneous catalysis; organometallic chemistry; mechanistic and physical organic chemistry; exploratory synthesis; free radical chemistry. *Mailing Add:* 227 Walker Dr Apt 679 Dunbar WV 25064

KAPLAN, LEONARD LOUIS, PHARMACEUTICAL QUALITY ASSURANCE, CONSULTING. *Current Pos:* PRES, PHARMA QUAL ASSOC, 95- *Personal Data:* b New York, NY, Oct 10, 28; m 68; Susan Orent; c Robert & Marc. *Educ:* NY Univ, BA, 48, PhD(statist, mgt sci), 68; Ohio State Univ, BScPharm, 52; City Col New York, MBA, 63. *Prof Exp:* Res assoc pharm, Sterling-Winthrop Res Inst, 55-59; dir develop, Walker Labs Div, Richardson-Merrell, 59-63, group mgr, Vick Div Res, 63-69; dir res & develop, Health Care Div, Ortho Pharm Corp, Johnson & Johnson-Domestic Oper Co, 69-78, dir res & develop, Advan Care Prods, 78-83, vpres, 84-89; vpres res & develop, Over The Counter Drugs, Sterling Drug, 89-90; sr vpres bus & tech develop, D M Graham Labs, 91-95. *Concurrent Pos:* Adj assoc prof, Brooklyn Col Pharm, 66-69 & Col Pharm, Rutgers Univ, 79- *Mem:* Acad Pharmaceut Sci; Soc Cosmetic Chemists; Am Asn Clin Chemists; Am Asn Prof Pharmacists; Am Pharm Asn. *Res:* Pharmaceutical research specializing in areas of analgesics, oral hygiene, sports medicine, dermatology and deodorancy; contraceptives; diagnostics. *Mailing Add:* 1 Minuteman Ct East Brunswick NJ 08816. *Fax:* 609-951-9196

KAPLAN, LEWIS DAVID, atmospheric sensing for numerical weather prediction, for more information see previous edition

KAPLAN, MANUEL E, INTERNAL MEDICINE, HEMATOLOGY. *Current Pos:* chief hemat & oncol, 69-93, STAFF PHYSICIAN, VET ADMIN MED CTR, MINN, 93-; PROF MED, MED SCH UNIV MINN, MINNEAPOLIS, 73- *Personal Data:* b New York, NY, Nov 6, 28; m 55, Rita Goldman; c 3. *Educ:* Univ Ariz, BS, 50; Harvard Med Sch, MD, 54. *Prof Exp:* Intern med, Boston City Hosp, 54-55, from asst resident to sr resident, 55-59; res assoc, Mt Sinai Hosp, NY, 62-63, asst dir hemat, 63-65; asst prof med, Sch Med, Wash Univ, 65-69; assoc prof, Univ Minn, Minneapolis, 69-73. *Concurrent Pos:* Fel microbiol, Thorndike Mem Lab, Boston City Hosp, 59-62; USPHS res grants, 63-64 & 66-, career develop award, 67-69; res fel microbiol, Col Physicians & Surgeons, Columbia Univ, 63-65; chief hemat, Jewish Hosp St Louis, 65-69. *Mem:* AAAS; Am Fedn Clin Res; Am Soc Clin Invest; Am Soc Hemat; Am Asn Immunol. *Res:* Immunohematology; lymphocyte structure and function; hematopoiesis. *Mailing Add:* Dept Hematol/Oncol Vet Admin Med Ctr 1 Vet Dr Minneapolis MN 55417-2300. *Fax:* 612-725-2149; *E-Mail:* kapla008@maroon.tc.umn.edu

KAPLAN, MARK STEVEN, PHOTOGRAPHIC CHEMISTRY, DRY MEDIA. *Current Pos:* Sr res scientist, 71-87, res assoc spec mat, 87-93, SUPV SCIENTIST, IMAGE & HARDCOPY TECHNOL, EASTMAN KODAK CO, 94- *Personal Data:* b New York, NY, Feb 25, 47; m 88, Drane; c 2. *Educ:* Bucknell Univ, BS & MS, 67; Univ Ore, PhD(org chem), 71. *Mem:* Am Chem Soc; Am Defense Preparedness Asn. *Res:* Novel lithographic systems; use of lasers in graphic arts; photoresists; chemical defense research; dry or processless media; patentee in field. *Mailing Add:* Eastman Kodak Co HE PLANT Rochester NY 14653-7207. *E-Mail:* markap@kodak.com

KAPLAN, MARSHALL HARVEY, AERONAUTICS, ASTRONAUTICS. *Current Pos:* CONSULT, SPACETECH INC. *Personal Data:* b Detroit, Mich, Nov 5, 39; m 61; c 2. *Educ:* Wayne State Univ, BS, 61; Mass Inst Technol, SM, 62; Stanford Univ, PhD(aeronaut, astronaut), 68. *Honors & Awards:* Outstanding Res Award, Pa State Univ, 78. *Prof Exp:* Mem tech staff, Hughes Res Lab, Calif, 62-64; mem tech staff, Space Systs Div, Hughes Aircraft Co, 64-65; sr engr, Western Develop Labs, Philco Corp, 65-66; from asst prof to prof aerospace eng, Pa State Univ, 68-82. *Mem:* Am Inst Aeronaut & Astronaut; Am Astronaut Soc; Am Soc Eng Educ. *Res:* Space systems synthesis and engineering; astrodynamics; propulsion; satellite dynamics and control. *Mailing Add:* 8029 Rising Ridge Rd Bethesda MD 20517

KAPLAN, MARTIN CHARLES, DIGITAL IMAGE SCANNERS, COMPUTER IMAGE PROCESSING. *Current Pos:* RES SCIENTIST PHYSICS & IMAGE PROCESSING, KODAK RES LABS, 82- *Personal Data:* b 1953. *Educ:* Mass Inst Tech, BSc(physics) & BSc(math), 75, PhD(physics), 80. *Prof Exp:* NSF grad fel physics, Mass Inst Technol, 75-78, IBM grad fel, 78-79; asst physicist, Brookhaven Nat Lab, 80-82. *Mem:* Am Phys Soc; AAAS; Sigma Xi. *Res:* Digital image scanning of film and paper; computer image processing and photographic science related to amateur and professional photography; color science. *Mailing Add:* Kodak Res 1/65/RL/ 01801 Rochester NY 14650-1801. *Fax:* 716-477-6811; *E-Mail:* mckaplan@kodak.com

KAPLAN, MARTIN L, COMPARATIVE PHYSIOLOGY, INSECT PATHOLOGY. *Current Pos:* from asst prof to assoc prof, 62-71, asst dean Sch Gen Studies, 70-75, PROF BIOL, QUEENS COL, NY, 71- *Personal Data:* b New York, NY, Apr 7, 23; m 48; c 2. *Educ:* Brooklyn Col, AB, 49; NY Univ, MS, 54, PhD(exp zool), 58. *Prof Exp:* Lectr biol, Brooklyn Col, 53-56, tutor, 56-57; instr biol, Fairleigh Dickinson Univ, 57-58, asst prof anat, Sch Dent, 58-59; assoc path, St Vincent's Hosp, New York, 59-62. *Concurrent Pos:* Lectr, Sch Gen Studies, Brooklyn Col, 59-62. *Mem:* AAAS; Am Soc Zool; Sigma Xi. *Res:* Histogenesis and biochemistry of melanotic tumors in Drosophila. *Mailing Add:* Dept Biol Queens Col Flushing NY 11367

KAPLAN, MARTIN L, PHYSICAL ORGANIC CHEMISTRY. *Current Pos:* RETIRED. *Personal Data:* b New York, NY, Dec 27, 35; m 64; c 1. *Educ:* City Col NY, BS, 56; Fla State Univ, MS, 60; Seton Hall Univ, JD, 70. *Prof Exp:* Res technician microbiol, Columbia Univ, 56-57 & Sloan-Kettering Inst Cancer Res, 57-58; res assoc phys chem, Fla State Univ, 60; chemist, Richfield Oil Corp, 60-62; vol sci teaching, US Peace Corps, 62-64; assoc mem staff, Bell Labs, 64-77, mem staff, 77-94. *Concurrent Pos:* Atty at law, NJ, 70- *Mem:* Am Chem Soc. *Res:* Mechanisms of organic reactions; rates of conformational isomerization of organic molecules by nuclear magnetic resonance; epoxy resin reactions; reactions by singlet oxygen with polymers; electrical conductivity of organic molecules and polymers. *Mailing Add:* 19436 Wilderness Dr West Linn OR 97068-2024

KAPLAN, MAURICE, psychiatry, for more information see previous edition

KAPLAN, MELVIN, ORGANIC CHEMISTRY. *Current Pos:* CONSULT, URETHANES & DIISOCYANATES, M KAPLAN ASSOCS, BUFFALO, 89- *Personal Data:* b Brooklyn, NY, Nov 11, 27; m 53; c 4. *Educ:* Brooklyn Col, BS, 50; Ohio State Univ, PhD(org chem), 54. *Prof Exp:* From proj leader to res supvr urethane applns, Indust Chem Div, Allied Chem Corp, Buffalo, 54-70, mgr tech serv & develop urethanes, Specialty Chem Div, 70-81, mgr res serv, 81-89. *Mem:* Am Chem Soc; Am Soc Testing & Mat; Int Isocyanate Inst; Soc Plastics Indust. *Res:* Isocyanate and urethane polymer chemistry; plastics; organic synthesis; kinetics of chemical reactions; blowing agents; plastic foams. *Mailing Add:* 292 Culpepper Rd Buffalo NY 14221

KAPLAN, MELVIN HYMAN, RHEUMATOLOGY, IMMUNOLOGY. *Current Pos:* dir, Div Rheumatology & Immunol, 74-81, PROF MED, MED SCH, UNIV MASS, 74- *Personal Data:* b Malden, Mass, Dec 23, 20. *Educ:* Harvard Univ, AB, 42, MD, 52. *Prof Exp:* Intern med, Boston City Hosp, 52-53; asst bact & immunol, Harvard Med Sch, 53-54; from asst prof to prof, Sch Med, Case Western Reserve Univ, 58-74. *Concurrent Pos:* Resident, Med Boston City Hosp, Harvard, 52-53, res fel, House Good Samaritan, Boston, 53-54; USPHS res career award, 64-74; res assoc, House Good Samaritan, Boston, 54-57; instr, Harvard Med Sch, 54-56, assoc, 57-58; estab investr, Am Heart Asn, 54-64; assoc mem, Comn Streptococcal Dis, Armed Forces Epidemiol Bd, US Dept Defense, 56-72; temp adv, WHO, 65-66; assoc ed, J Lab & Clin Med, 63-69, J Clin & Exp Immunol, Exp Path. *Mem:* Am Soc Clin Invest; Am Asn Immunol; Am Col Rheumatol; Infectious Dis Soc Am. *Res:* Microbiology; pathogenesis of rheumatic diseases, rheumatic fever, lupus, rheumatoid arthritis, particularly in the role of immunologic mechanisms; clinical immunology and rheumatology. *Mailing Add:* 1550 Worcester Rd Apt 519 Framingham MA 01701

KAPLAN, MICHAEL, RADIATION CHEMISTRY. *Current Pos:* EDUC TESTING SERV, 87- *Personal Data:* b New York, NY, Nov 7, 37; m 68; c 2. *Educ:* Rensselaer Polytech Inst, BS, 59; Columbia Univ, MA, 61, PhD(electron spin resonance), 65. *Prof Exp:* Mem tech staff, RCA Labs, 65-87. *Mem:* Am Chem Soc; Am Phys Soc; NY Acad Sci; fel Am Inst Chemists. *Res:* Electron spin resonance of organic materials; interaction of charged particles with thin films; electron-beam lithography; x-ray lithography. *Mailing Add:* 45 Copper Mine Rd Princeton NJ 08540

KAPLAN, MORTON, NUCLEAR REACTIONS, HYPERFINE INTERACTIONS. *Current Pos:* assoc prof, 70, PROF CHEM, CARNEGIE MELLON UNIV, 71- *Personal Data:* b Chicago, Ill, Nov 21, 33; m 57, Sandra Solon; c David & Susan. *Educ:* Univ Chicago, AB, 54, SM, 56; Mass Inst Technol, PhD(phys chem), 60. *Prof Exp:* Res assoc chem, Mass Inst Technol, 60; res staff, Lawrence Radiation Lab, 60-62; from asst prof to assoc prof, Yale Univ, 62-70. *Concurrent Pos:* Alfred P Sloan res fel, 65-69; vis scientist, Univ Oxford, 71-72. *Mem:* Am Phys Soc; Am Chem Soc; AAAS. *Res:* Nuclear reactions induced by heavy ions; Mossbauer effect; perturbed angular correlations of gamma rays; magnetic properties and chemical bonding at low temperatures; nuclear spectroscopy; low temperature nuclear orientation. *Mailing Add:* Carnegie Mellon Univ 4400 Fifth Ave Pittsburgh PA 15213-2683

KAPLAN, MURRAY LEE, NUTRITION, METABOLISM. *Current Pos:* from assoc prof to prof food & nutrit, 81-90, PROF FOOD SCI & HUMAN NUTRIT, IOWA STATE UNIV, 90- *Personal Data:* b Jan 9, 41; m 65; c 2. *Educ:* Alfred Univ, NY, BA, 62; City Univ NY, PhD(biol), 72. *Prof Exp:* Lectr biol, Brooklyn Col, 66-71; res assoc nutrit, Dept Food Sci & Human Nutrit, Mich State Univ, 71-74; asst prof nutrit, Rutgers Univ, 74-80. *Concurrent Pos:* NIH res fel, Dept Food Sci & Human Nutrit, Mich State Univ, 72-74; interim dir, Ctr Designing Foods Improve Nutrit, Iowa State Univ, 88-92; vis prof pediat, Baylor Col Med, Houston, 95. *Mem:* AAAS; Am Inst Nutrit; NY Acad Sci; NAm Asn Obesity. *Res:* Role of early nutritional experiences on the development of regulation of carbohydrate, lipid metabolism and obesity; Adipocyte metabolism; redesign of fatty acids in pork. *Mailing Add:* Dept Food Sci & Human Nutrit Iowa State Univ Ames IA 50011. *Fax:* 515-294-6193

KAPLAN, NORMAN M, INTERNAL MEDICINE. *Current Pos:* from instr to assoc prof, 61-70, PROF MED, HEALTH SCI CTR, UNIV TEX, DALLAS, 70-, HEAD HYPERTENSION SECT, 78- *Personal Data:* b Dallas, Tex, Jan 2, 31; m 50; c 6. *Educ:* Univ Tex, BS, 50, MD, 54; Am Bd Internal Med, dipl & cert endocrinol & metab. *Prof Exp:* Res physician, Parkland Mem Hosp, Dallas, 55-58. *Concurrent Pos:* USPHS res fel, Clin Endocrinol Br, Nat Heart Inst, 60-61; USPHS grants, 62-70; dep vpres res progs, Am Heart Asn, 75-76; NIH acad award, 79-84. *Mem:* Am Fedn Clin Res; Endocrine Soc; Am Col Physicians; Am Soc Clin Invest; Coun High Blood Pressure Res. *Res:* Mechanisms controlling biosyntheses of adrenal cortical hormones particularly aldosterone; relationship of renin-angiotension system to hypertension; sodium restriction and other non-drug modalities in treatment of hypertension. *Mailing Add:* Univ Tex Health Sci Ctr 5323 Harry Hines Blvd Dallas TX 75235-8899. *Fax:* 214-631-5340

KAPLAN, PHYLLIS DEEN, CHEMISTRY, BIOCHEMISTRY. *Current Pos:* MGT CONSULT, 90- *Personal Data:* b Everett, Wash, Feb 9, 31; c Harold D & Madeleine M. *Educ:* Univ Wash, BA, 53; Brandeis Univ, MA, 56; Univ Cincinnati, PhD(chem), 66. *Prof Exp:* Spectroscopist chem, Syntex Corp, 67-68; res assoc, Med Ctr, Univ Cincinnati, 68-71, asst prof environ health, 71-77; sr res toxicologist, Am Cyanamid Co, 77-82; consult engr, Am Stand Testing Prog, 82-83; adminr preclin int res & develop, Allergan, 83-87, dir int res & develop Europe & Middle East, 87-90. *Concurrent Pos:* Am Chem Soc Petrol Res Fund grant, Univ Cincinnati, 65-66; Nat Inst Occup Safety & Health res grant, 71-76; lectr, Col Arts & Sci, Univ Cincinnati, 72-73 & Col Nursing, 73-74; adj prof, NY Univ, 82-83; consult, Baker Chem Co; dir tech affairs, Invitro Int, Inc, 90 & 92; dir tech affairs, Lahaye Labs, Inc, 92-96. *Mem:* Int Soc Ocular Toxicol; Am Chem Soc; Sigma Xi; Asn Res Vision Ophthal. *Res:* Metabolism, binding and structural identity of transition metal compounds in the body, with a special interest in elucidating the mechanisms determining toxicity and essentiality of metals within living systems; pharmaceutical product development; eye and skin care; inhalation toxicology. *Mailing Add:* 526 First Ave Suite 525 Seattle WA 98104. *Fax:* 206-233-9072; *E-Mail:* pdkapl@eskimo.com

KAPLAN, RAPHAEL, SOLID STATE PHYSICS. *Current Pos:* RETIRED. *Personal Data:* b New York, NY, Mar 26, 36. *Educ:* Syracuse Univ, AB, 57; Brown Univ, PhD(physics), 63. *Prof Exp:* Physicist, Semiconductors Br, Solid State Div, US Naval Res Lab, 63- *Mem:* Am Phys Soc. *Res:* Spin resonance of color centers in irradiated crystals; far infrared and millimeter wave spectroscopy in semiconductors and other materials. *Mailing Add:* US Naval Res Lab Code 6863 Washington DC 20375

KAPLAN, RAYMOND, SOLID STATE PHYSICS. *Current Pos:* ASST PROF PHYSICS, FORDHAM UNIV, 81- *Personal Data:* b New York, NY, Jan 26, 29; m 65; c 2. *Educ:* City Col New York, BS, 50; Columbia Univ, MA, 52, PhD(physics), 59. *Prof Exp:* Jr res physicist, Univ Calif, 58-59; res physicist, Airborne Instruments Lab, 60-62; asst prof physics, Adelphi Univ, 62-64; res physicist, US Rubber Co, NJ, 64-68; asst prof, Cooper Union, 68-71, assoc prof physics, 71-77; adj assoc prof physics, York Col, 77-79; asst prof physics, Maritime Col, State Univ NY, 79-80. *Concurrent Pos:* Consult, Info Div, Am Inst Physics & Electronic Semiconductor Co. *Mem:* Am Phys Soc; Am Asn Physics Teachers; NY Acad Sci. *Res:* Superconductivity; cryogenics. *Mailing Add:* 1610 Croton Lake Yorktown Heights NY 10598

KAPLAN, RICHARD E, AEROSPACE ENGINEERING, FLUID MECHANICS. *Current Pos:* From asst prof to assoc prof, Univ Southern Calif, 64-73, dir, Systs Simulation Lab, 69-71, dir, Eng Comput Lab, 82-83, dept chmn, 83-86, assoc dean, 84-86, VPROVOST RES & ACAD COMPUT, 87-, PROF AEROSPACE ENG, UNIV SOUTHERN CALIF, 73- *Personal Data:* b Philadelphia, Pa, July 4, 38; m 60; c 2. *Educ:* Mass Inst Technol, BS & MS, 61, ScD(aerospace eng), 64. *Concurrent Pos:* Fulbright lectr & Guggenheim fel, 71-72; Fulbright lectr, 75-76. *Mem:* Am Inst Aeronaut & Astronaut; Am Phys Soc; Am Soc Eng. *Res:* Fluid dynamic stability theory and turbulence experimentation; numerical methods in fluid mechanics; digital techniques in turbulence experimentation; aerosonics and jet noise. *Mailing Add:* Aerospace Eng Univ Southern Calif 854 W 36th Pl Los Angeles CA 90089

KAPLAN, RICHARD STEPHEN, MEDICAL ONCOLOGY. *Current Pos:* ASSOC PROF ONCOL & MED, UNIV MD, 79- *Personal Data:* b Pittsburgh, Pa, Aug 24, 45; m 70. *Educ:* Univ Pittsburgh, BA, 66; Univ Miami, MD, 70; Am Bd Internal Med, dipl, 74; Am Bd Med Oncol, dipl, 75. *Prof Exp:* Clin assoc oncol, Nat Cancer Inst, 71-73; fel, Univ Miami, 74-75, asst prof oncol, 75-79. *Concurrent Pos:* Surgeon, USPHS, 71-73; consult oncologist, Miami Vet Admin Hosp & sr staff mem, Comprehensive Cancer Ctr, Fla, 75-79; sr investr, Nat Cancer Inst, 79-81. *Mem:* Fel Am Col Physicians; Am Asn Cancer Res; Am Soc Clin Oncol; NY Acad Sci; AAAS; Am Soc Hemat; Am Fed Clin Res. *Res:* Clinical and laboratory research in clinical oncology: neuro-oncology, malignant lymphomas and gastrointestinal malignancy. *Mailing Add:* Cancer Ther Eval Prog Nat Cancer Inst EPN 741 Bethesda MD 20892-7436

KAPLAN, ROBERT A, ENGINEERING PHYSICS. *Current Pos:* OWNER, QUANTRONIX, 65- *Personal Data:* b Brooklyn, NY, June 20, 35. *Educ:* Cornell Univ, BS, 57; Polytech Univ, PhD(physics), 61. *Prof Exp:* Res scientist, Wheeler Labs, 57-65. *Mem:* Am Phys Soc. *Mailing Add:* One Gracie Terr No 6F New York NY 10028

KAPLAN, ROBERT JOEL, DERMATOLOGY. *Current Pos:* PVT PRACT, MEMPHIS, TENN, 79- *Personal Data:* b New York, NY, Sept 13, 47. *Educ:* Franklin & Marshall Col, BA, 69; Univ Tenn, Memphis, MD, 73. *Prof Exp:* Tech asst, Englewood Hosp, 68-69; internship, Geisinger Med Ctr, Danville, Pa, 73-74; residency, Univ Tenn, 74-77, asst prof dermat, 77-79. *Mem:* Am Acad Dermat; AMA. *Res:* Clinical studies involving cutaneous levels of cyclic adenosine monophate in atopic dermatitis. *Mailing Add:* 910 Madison Suite 922 Memphis TN 38103-3460. *Fax:* 901-523-0779

KAPLAN, ROBERT LEWIS, OPERATIONS ANALYSIS, MARKET RESEARCH. *Current Pos:* PRES, RUMSON CORP, 81- *Personal Data:* b Long Branch, NJ, Oct 5, 28; m 60, Jean Gaithir; c 1. *Educ:* US Mil Acad, BS, 53; Mass Inst Technol, MS, 60. *Prof Exp:* Vpres opers res, Actuarial Res Corp, 76-80. *Concurrent Pos:* Dep dir mat plans & prog & dep chief staff res, develop & aquisition, Hq, Dept Army, 63-88. *Mem:* Am Inst Aeronaut & Astronaut; Am Helicopter Soc; Sigma Xi. *Res:* Low speed aeronautical research c/w v-stol, helicopters, and aircushion vehicles; command and control operations research; quantitative measurement of subjective judgements. *Mailing Add:* PO Box 1943 Middleburg VA 20118-1943

KAPLAN, ROBERT S, EXTRACTIVE METALLURGY, CHEMICAL METALLURGY. *Current Pos:* res supvr metall, Resource Recovery, 76-78, staff minimum policy rev, 78-79, mgr extractive nonfuel minerals processes, 80-82, MGR RECYCLING TECHNOL, BUR MINES, US DEPT INTERIOR, 82- *Personal Data:* b New York, NY, July 13, 40; m 67; c 2. *Educ:* Univ Mich, BSE, 62, MSE, 64; Carnegie-Mellon Univ, PhD(metall, mat sci), 68. *Prof Exp:* Res metallurgist, Battelle Columbus Labs, 68-71; staff metallurgist, Bur Mines, US Dept Interior, 71-76; proj mgr res recovery, Off Tech Assess, US Cong, 76. *Mem:* Am Inst Mining, Metall & Petrol Engrs. *Res:* Iron-making slags; decarburization of steels; steel refining; inclusions in steels; recovery of metals from nonferrous metal scrap and wastes. *Mailing Add:* Horizon Eng Serv Ltd 5436 Doral Dr Wilmington DE 19808

KAPLAN, RONALD M, COMPUTER SCIENCE, COMPUTATIONAL LINGUISTICS. *Current Pos:* consult, 73-74, res scientist psycholing, Palo Alto Res Ctr, 74-86, RES FEL, XEROX CORP, 86- *Personal Data:* b Los Angeles, Calif, July 15, 46; m 70; c 2. *Educ:* Univ Calif, Berkeley, BA, 68; Harvard Univ, MA, 70, PhD(social psychol), 75. *Honors & Awards:* Software Syst Award, Am Comput Mach, 92. *Prof Exp:* Consult, Rand Corp, 68-72 & Info Sci Inst, Univ Southern Calif, 72-73. *Concurrent Pos:* Res assoc, Harvard Univ, 73-74; vis scholar cognitive sci, Mass Inst Technol, 78; consult prof ling, Stanford Univ, 88-; mem adv comt sci & technol ctrs, NSF, 88-91; fel in residence, Neth Inst, Advan Study, Humanities & Social Sci, 95-96. *Mem:* Fel Asn Comput Mach; Asn Comput Ling (vpres, 78, pres, 79); Linguistics Soc Am; Am Asn Artificial Intel; Cognitive Sci Soc. *Res:* Computational models of human language comprehension; linguistics; psycholinguistics. *Mailing Add:* Xerox Palo Alto Res Ctr 3333 Coyote Hill Rd Palo Alto CA 94304. *E-Mail:* kaplan.parc@xerox.com

KAPLAN, RONALD S, BIOENERGETICS. *Current Pos:* from asst prof to assoc prof, 86-96, PROF PHARMACOL, COL MED, UNIV SOUTH ALA, 96- *Personal Data:* b New York, NY, July 12, 51; m 87; c 3. *Educ:* NY Univ, BA, 73, MS, 75, PhD(biol), 81. *Prof Exp:* Fel, Johns Hopkins Sch Med, 80-86. *Mem:* AAAS; Am Chem Soc; Biophys Soc; Am Soc Biochem & Molecular Biol; Am Diabetes Asn. *Res:* Elucidate the structure, function and mechanisms of regulation of mitochondrial transport proteins in normal and diseased States. *Mailing Add:* Dept Pharmacol Col Med Univ SAla MSB Rm 3130 Mobile AL 36688. *Fax:* 334-460-6798; *E-Mail:* kaplanr@sungcg.usouthal.edu

KAPLAN, SAMUEL, MATHEMATICS. *Current Pos:* PROF MATH, PURDUE UNIV, 61- *Personal Data:* b Detroit, Mich, Sept 13, 16; m 53; c 2. *Educ:* Univ Mich, BS, 37, MS, 38, PhD(math), 42. *Prof Exp:* Instr math, Univ Mich, 46; Rackham fel, Princeton Univ, 46-47; researcher, Inst Adv

Study, 47-48, 56-57; from asst prof to prof, Wayne State Univ, 48-61. *Mem:* Am Math Soc. *Res:* Homology theory; topological groups; topological spaces; duality; functional analysis. *Mailing Add:* 8516 Johnson Mill Rd Purdue Univ Bahama NC 27503

KAPLAN, SAMUEL, CARDIOLOGY. *Current Pos:* dir, Pediat Cardiol Training Prog, 87-95, PROF PEDIAT, UNIV CALIF, LOS ANGELES, 87- *Personal Data:* b Johannesburg, SAfrica, Mar 28, 22; nat US; m 52, Molly E McKenzie. *Educ:* Univ Witwatersrand, MD, 49, MB, BCh, 44. *Honors & Awards:* Theodore & Susan Cummings Humanitarian Award, 72, 75, 76, 78 & 84; Samuel Kaplan Visionary Award, Am Heart Asn. *Prof Exp:* Lectr physiol, Univ Witwatersrand, 46-47, lectr internal med, 47-49; registr cardiol, Postgrad Med Sch, Univ London, 49-50; sr res assoc pediat, Univ Cincinnati, 51-54, from asst prof to assoc prof internal med, 54-82, assoc prof pediat, 61-66, prof pediat, 66-87, prof internal med, 82-87. *Concurrent Pos:* Consult, NIH; dir div cardiol, Children's Hosp, Cincinnati, Ohio, 53-87. *Mem:* Soc Pediat Res; Am Pediat Soc; Am Fedn Clin Res. *Res:* Hemodynamics and extracorporeal circulation; cardiac complications of human immune virus infection. *Mailing Add:* Dept Pediat Cardiol Univ Calif Sch Med Los Angeles CA 90095

KAPLAN, SAMUEL, MOLECULAR BIOLOGY, GENETICS. *Current Pos:* PROF & CHMN, DEPT MICROBIOL & MOLECULAR GENETICS, UNIV TEX MED SCH, 89- *Personal Data:* b Yonkers, NY, Feb 13, 34. *Educ:* Cornell Univ, BS, 59; Univ Calif, San Diego, PhD(chem), 63. *Honors & Awards:* A O Stark Award, Miami Univ, Ohio, 85; Karski Award, Am Soc Microbiol, 86; Oliver H Smith Award, Markell Univ, 88. *Prof Exp:* From asst prof to assoc prof microbiol, Univ Ill, 68-73, prof & dir, Sch of Life Sci, 73-89. *Mem:* Am Soc Microbiol; Genetics Soc Am; AAAS. *Res:* Molecular biology; genetics. *Mailing Add:* Dept Microbiol Univ Tex Med Sch PO Box 20708 FB 765 Houston TX 77225

KAPLAN, SANDRA SOLON, CLINICAL PATHOLOGY, HEMATOLOGY. *Current Pos:* asst res prof path & med, 70-78, from asst prof to assoc prof, 78-90, PROF PATH, SCH MED, UNIV PITTSBURGH, 91- *Personal Data:* b Pittsburgh, Pa, Sept 9, 34; m 57; c David B & Susan E. *Educ:* Roosevelt Univ, BS, 55; Boston Univ, MD, 59. *Prof Exp:* Res assoc, Yale Univ, 65-69. *Concurrent Pos:* USPHS res fel hemat, Children's Hosp, San Francisco, 62-63; USPHS res training grant, Med Sch, Yale Univ, 63-64; res worker, Sir William Dunn Sch Path, Oxford Univ, 71-72; dir hemat, Magee Womens Hosp, Pittsburgh, 78-; med dir, Hemat Lab, Med Ctr, Univ Pittsburgh. *Mem:* Am Soc Hemat; Am Soc Clin Path; Am Soc Investigative Path; Soc Leukocyte Biol. *Res:* Mechanisms of leukocyte activation associated with phagocytosis; mechanisms of chemotaxis and bacterial killing by leukocytes. *Mailing Add:* 326 Orchard Dr Mt Lebanon PA 15228

KAPLAN, SANFORD SANDY, STRATIGRAPHY, SEDIMENTATION. *Current Pos:* PRES, EARTHSOURCE CONSULT, INC, 87; RES ASSOC PROF, UNIV NEBR, LINCOLN, 89- *Personal Data:* b New York, NY, Oct 2, 50; m, Connie; c Elicia, Todd, Wendi, Shira & Bryan. *Educ:* Lafayette Col, AB, 71; Lehigh Univ, MS, 76; Univ Pittsburgh, PhD(geol), 81; Salve Regina Col, MA, 87. *Prof Exp:* Teaching asst, Lehigh Univ, 75-76; lectr gen geol, Univ Nebr, Lincoln, 77-78; vis lectr coal geol, Univ Pittsburgh, 80; geologist, Coal Prep Div, Pittsburgh Mining Technol Ctr, US Dept Energy, 79-80; geologist, Penzoil Explor & Prod Co, 80-86. *Concurrent Pos:* Surface Warfare Officer, USN, 69-; vis lectr geol, Northampton Co Area Community Col, 74-75. *Mem:* Am Asn Petrol Geologists; Geol Soc Am; Soc Econ Paleontologists & Mineralogists; Sigma Xi; AAAS; Am Econ Asn; Int Asn Sedimentologists. *Res:* Interpreting ancient environments of deposition of sedimentary sequences especially those containing coal, oil and gas and deducing their tetonic setting from such evidence; environmental geology; site assessments; hydrology. *Mailing Add:* 5701 Judith Dr Lincoln NE 68517-9792. *Fax:* 402-472-4917; *E-Mail:* skaplan@unlinfo.unl.edu

KAPLAN, SELIG N(EIL), NUCLEAR PHYSICS & ENGINEERING. *Current Pos:* Physicist, Lab, Univ Calif, Berkeley, 57-68, lectr, 62-65, from asst prof to prof, 65-92, SR PHYSICIST, LAWRENCE BERKELEY LAB, UNIV CALIF, BERKELEY, 68-, EMER PROF NUCLEAR ENG, 92- *Personal Data:* b Chicago, Ill, June 30, 32; m 54; c 2. *Educ:* Univ Ariz, BS, 52; Univ Calif, MA, 54, PhD(physics), 57. *Mem:* Am Phys Soc; Am Nuclear Soc. *Res:* Nuclear instrumentation; neutronics; interaction of muons with nuclei. *Mailing Add:* Dept Nuclear Eng Univ Calif Berkeley CA 94720

KAPLAN, SELNA L, PEDIATRICS, ENDOCRINOLOGY. *Current Pos:* from asst prof to assoc prof, 66-74, PROF PEDIAT, SCH MED, UNIV CALIF, SAN FRANCISCO, 74- *Personal Data:* b Brooklyn, NY, Apr 8, 27. *Educ:* Brooklyn Col, BA, 48; Wash Univ, MA, 50, PhD(anat), 53, MD, 55. *Honors & Awards:* Ayerst Award, Endocrinol Soc, 87 & Koch Award, 95. *Prof Exp:* Asst anat, Sch Med, Wash Univ, 51-52; instr pediat, Col Physicians & Surgeons, Columbia Univ, 61-63, assoc, 63-65, asst prof, 65-66. *Concurrent Pos:* NIH fel, 58-61, career develop award, 62-71. *Mem:* Endocrine Soc; Soc Pediat Res; NY Acad Sci; Am Pediat Soc. *Res:* Growth disorders in children; immunochemistry of pituitary human growth hormone; ontogenesis of human fetal hormones; pubertal development. *Mailing Add:* 60 Allston Way San Francisco CA 94127

KAPLAN, SOLOMON ALEXANDER, MEDICINE. *Current Pos:* PROF PEDIAT, MED CTR, UNIV CALIF, LOS ANGELES, 68- *Personal Data:* b SAfrica, Feb 5, 24; nat US; m 57. *Educ:* Univ Witwatersrand, MB & BCh, 46. *Prof Exp:* Instr pediat, Univ Cincinnati, 51-53; from asst prof to assoc prof, State Univ NY, 53-59; from assoc prof, Sch Med, Univ Southern Calif, 59-68. *Concurrent Pos:* Res fel pediat, Univ Cincinnati, 49-51. *Mem:* AAAS; Am Physiol Soc; Soc Pediat Res; Am Pediat Soc; Brit Soc Endocrinol. *Res:* Pediatrics; endocrinology; biochemistry. *Mailing Add:* Dept Pediat Univ Calif Med Ctr Health Sci Los Angeles CA 90024-1752

KAPLAN, STANLEY, TERATOLOGY, HUMAN DEVELOPMENT. *Current Pos:* from asst prof to assoc prof, Med Col Wis, 69-82, vchmn, 72-82, actg chmn, 82-84, PROF CELLULAR BIOL & ANAT, MED COL WIS, 82-, ASSOC CHMN, 84- *Personal Data:* b Canton, Ohio, Apr 28, 36; div; c Wayne, Lisa & Dean. *Educ:* Univ Miami, BS & BEd, 62, PhD(teratology), 67. *Prof Exp:* Instr & fel, Col Med, Univ Fla, 66-67, asst prof anat sci, 67-69. *Concurrent Pos:* Vis prof, Univ Man, Can, 74 & Hebrew Univ, Israel, 89; prin investr, NIH, 85-86. *Mem:* Am Asn Anat; Am Soc Zool; Am Inst Biol Sci; Europ Teratology Soc; Teratology Soc; Toxicol Soc. *Res:* Mechanisms by which chemical and physical environmental agents produce congenital malformations. *Mailing Add:* Dept Cellular Biol & Anat Med Col Wis 8701 Watertown Plank Rd Milwaukee WI 53226. *Fax:* 414-266-8496; *E-Mail:* skaplan@post.its.mcw.edu

KAPLAN, STANLEY A, PHARMACEUTICAL RESEARCH & DEVELOPMENT, ADMINISTRATION. *Current Pos:* SR VPRES, ALPHARMA INC, BALTIMORE, MD, 92- *Personal Data:* b New York, NY, Sept 28, 38; m 60, Lois Haber; c Lisa, Michelle & Martin. *Educ:* Columbia Univ, BS, 59, MS, 61; Univ Calif, San Francisco, PhD(pharmaceut chem), 65. *Prof Exp:* Postdoctoral fel, NIH, 65; several positions, dept dir & assoc div dir exp therapeut, Hoffmann-La Roche Inc, Nutley, NJ, 66-84; exec dir develop, Med Res Div, Lederle Labs, Am Cyanamid, 84-87; sr vpres res & develop, Liposome Technol, Inc, 87-89; pres & chief oper officer, Pharmetrix Corp, 89-92. *Mem:* Am Asn Pharmaceut Scientists; Am Soc Clin Pharmacol & Therapeut; Am Col Clin Pharmacol; Am Soc Pharmacol & Exp Therapeut; AAAS; NY Acad Sci; Controlled Release Soc. *Res:* Pharmacokinetics; biopharmaceutics; drug metabolism; drug development; novel drug delivery systems; analytical methodology; design and implement programs to develop new drugs and drug products; over 90 publications, presentations or chapters in books. *Mailing Add:* Alpharma Inc 333 Cassell Dr Suite 3500 Baltimore MD 21224. *Fax:* 410-558-7262

KAPLAN, STANLEY BARUCH, MEDICINE, RHEUMATOLOGY. *Current Pos:* from asst resident to chief resident, 58-62, from instr to assoc prof, 61-73, PROF MED & RHEUMATOL, SCH MED, UNIV TENN, MEMPHIS, 73- *Personal Data:* b Memphis, Tenn, Jan 6, 31. *Educ:* Univ Tenn, MD, 54. *Prof Exp:* Intern med, Jefferson Med Col, 55. *Concurrent Pos:* Fel rheumatol, Sch Med, Univ Tenn, 60-62; attend physician, Vet Admin Hosp, 67- *Mem:* AMA; Am Col Rheumatol. *Res:* Clinical investigation in rheumatic diseases. *Mailing Add:* Univ Tenn 920 Madison Ave Suite 434 Memphis TN 38103

KAPLAN, STANLEY MEISEL, PSYCHIATRY. *Current Pos:* from instr to prof, 52-90, actg dir, 75-77, EMER PROF PSYCHIAT, COL MED, UNIV CINCINNATI, 90- *Personal Data:* b Cincinnati, Ohio, May 10, 22; m 50, Mickey Jarson; c Steven, Barbara & Richard. *Educ:* Univ Cincinnati, BS, 43, MD, 46. *Prof Exp:* Intern med, Cincinnati Jewish Hosp, 46-47, resident, 47-48, resident psychiat, Cincinnati Gen Hosp, 49-51. *Concurrent Pos:* Res fel, May Inst, 48-49; fel psychosom, Cincinnati Gen Hosp, 51-52; NIMH spec res fel, 54-56 & Inst Psychoanal, 61-67. *Mem:* AAAS; Am Psychosom Soc; Am Med Asn; fel Am Psychiat Asn; Am Psychoanal Asn. *Res:* Psychosomatic medicine; psychiatry; psychoanalysis. *Mailing Add:* Dept Psychiat Univ Cincinnati Col Med Cincinnati OH 45267. *Fax:* 513-558-4805

KAPLAN, THOMAS ABRAHAM, SOLID STATE THEORY. *Current Pos:* prof, 70-95, EMER PROF PHYSICS, MICH STATE; UNIV, 96- *Personal Data:* b Philadelphia, Pa, Feb 24, 26; m 56, Patricia Roe; c Melissa, Andrea & Laurie. *Educ:* Univ Pa, BS, 48, PhD(physics), 54. *Honors & Awards:* Alexander von Humboldt Sr Scientist Award, 81. *Prof Exp:* Res asst physics, Willow Run Res Ctr, Univ Mich, 54-55, res assoc, Eng Res Inst, 55-56; res assoc, Pa State Univ at Brookhaven Nat Lab, 56-59; staff mem, Lincoln Lab, Mass Inst Technol, 59-70. *Concurrent Pos:* Consult, Naval Res Lab, Washington, DC, 79 & 80; vis scientist, Max-Planck-Institut fur Festkorperforschung, Stuttgart, Ger, 81-82, 83-84, 88-89; Institut fur Festkorperforschung der KFA Julich, Ger, 82; distinguished vis prof, Univ Tsukuba, Japan, 89. *Mem:* Fel Am Phys Soc; Sigma Xi; Union Concerned Scientists. *Res:* Quantum theory of solids; numerical solution of models of highly-correlated-electron systems, e.g. Heisenberg spin models, Hubbard models; cluster models for spin and charge density in quantum antiferromagnets; theory of novel Mott insulators called electrides. *Mailing Add:* Dept Physics & Astron Mich State Univ East Lansing MI 48824. *Fax:* 517-353-0690; *E-Mail:* kaplan@msupa.msu.edu

KAPLAN, WILFRED, MATHEMATICS. *Current Pos:* from instr to prof, 40-86, EMER PROF MATH, UNIV MICH, ANN ARBOR, 88- *Personal Data:* b Boston, Mass, Nov 28, 15; m 38, Ida Roettinger; c Roland & Muriel. *Educ:* Harvard Univ, AB, 36, AM, 36, PhD(math), 39. *Prof Exp:* Instr math, Col William & Mary, 39-40. *Concurrent Pos:* Res assoc, Brown Univ, 44-45; Guggenheim Found fel, 49-50. *Mem:* AAAS; Am Phys Soc; Am Math Soc; Math Asn Am; Math Soc France. *Res:* Non-linear differential equations; dynamics; Riemann surfaces; statistical mechanics. *Mailing Add:* 2072 East Hall Univ Mich Ann Arbor MI 48109-1109

KAPLAN, WILLIAM, medical mycology, for more information see previous edition

KAPLAN, WILLIAM DAVID, GENETICS. *Current Pos:* RETIRED. *Personal Data:* b New York, NY, Aug 24, 14; m 52; c 2. *Educ:* Brooklyn Col, BA, 36; Harvard Univ, MA, 37; Univ Calif, PhD(zool), 51. *Prof Exp:* Chief genetics sect, City Hope Res Inst, 53-58, chmn dept genetics, 58-62, asst chmn & sr res geneticist, dept biol, 62-83. *Concurrent Pos:* Agr Res Coun sr res fel, Inst Animal Genetics, Univ Edinburgh, 51-53; Fulbright res scholar, Norsk Hydro's Inst Cancer Res, Oslo, Norway, 63-64; lectr, Univ Calif, 51; vis prof, Univ Calif, Los Angeles, 62-63; vis prof, Max-Planck Inst Biol Cybernet, Tubingen, Ger, 74-75; Consult, 83- *Mem:* Genetics Soc Am; AAAS; Behav Genetics Asn; Soc Neurosci; Sigma Xi; Am Soc Human Genetics. *Res:* Mutation and biochemical genetics; Drosophila melanogaster; mammalian cytology; behavioral genetics. *Mailing Add:* 186 E Camino Real Arcadia CA 91006

KAPLANSKY, IRVING, MATHEMATICS. *Current Pos:* dir, 84-92, EMER DIR MATH, MATH SCI RES INST, BERKELEY, 92- *Personal Data:* b Toronto, Ont, Mar 22, 17; m 51; c 3. *Educ:* Univ Toronto, BA, 38, MA, 39; Harvard Univ, PhD(math), 41. *Hon Degrees:* DMath, Univ Waterloo, 68; DSc, Queens Univ, Ont, 69. *Honors & Awards:* Steele Prize, Am Math Soc. *Prof Exp:* Instr math, Harvard Univ, 41-44; res mathematician, Appl Math Group, Nat Defense Res Comt, Columbia Univ, 44-45; from instr to prof math, Univ Chicago, 45-69, chmn dept, 62-67, George Herbert Mead distinguished serv prof, 69-84. *Concurrent Pos:* Guggenheim Found fel, 48-49. *Mem:* Nat Acad Sci; Am Math Soc; Math Asn Am. *Res:* Algebra. *Mailing Add:* Math Sci Res Inst 1000 Centennial Dr Berkeley CA 94720

KAPLER, JOSEPH EDWARD, BIOLOGY. *Current Pos:* from asst prof to prof biol, 57-89, EMER PROF BIOL, LORAS COL, 89- *Personal Data:* b Cresco, Iowa, Mar 13, 24; m 59; c 4. *Educ:* Loras Col, BS, 48; Marquette Univ, MS, 53; Univ Wis, PhD(entom), 58. *Prof Exp:* Instr biol, Loras Col, 48-51; asst zool, Marquette Univ, 51-53, instr, 53-54; instr biol, Loras Col, 54-55; asst entom, Univ Wis, 55-57. *Mem:* Entom Soc Am. *Res:* Biology and ecology of forest insects. *Mailing Add:* Dept Biol Loras Col 1450 Alta Vista Dubuque IA 52001

KAPLITA, PAUL V, PHARMACOLOGY. *Current Pos:* sr res investr, 90-92, PRIN RES INVESTR, STERLING-WINTHROP, 92- *Personal Data:* b Bridgeport, Conn. *Educ:* Univ Conn, BS, 76; State Univ NY, Buffalo, PhD(pharmacol), 81. *Prof Exp:* Res fel pharmacol, Dartmouth Med Sch, 82-85; sr res assoc, Nova Pharmaceut Corp, 85-87, staff scientist, 87-90. *Mem:* Am Soc Pharmacol & Exp Therapeut; Soc Neurosci. *Mailing Add:* Boehringer Ingelheim Pharmaceut Inc 900 Ridgebury Rd PO Box 368 Ridgefield CT 06877-0368

KAPLON, MORTON FISCHEL, PHYSICS. *Current Pos:* RETIRED. *Personal Data:* b Philadelphia, Pa, Feb 11, 21; m 46; c 3. *Educ:* Lehigh Univ, BS, 41, MS, 47; Univ Rochester, PhD(physics), 51. *Prof Exp:* Res assoc physics, Univ Rochester, 51-52, from asst prof to prof, 52-71, assoc dean, Col Arts & Sci, 63-65, chmn, Dept Physics & Astron, 64-69; assoc provost, City Col New York, 71-75, vpres admin affairs, 75-86. *Concurrent Pos:* NSF sr fel, 59-60. *Mem:* AAAS; Am Phys Soc; Am Geophys Union; Ital Phys Soc; Am Astron Soc. *Res:* Cosmic ray physics; fundamental particle physics; high energy nuclear physics. *Mailing Add:* 1047 Johnston Dr Bethlehem PA 18017

KAPLOW, LEONARD SAMUEL, FLOW CYTOMETRY. *Current Pos:* assoc prof path & lab med, 70-75, PROF PATH & LAB MED, SCH MED, YALE UNIV, 75-; DIR, MED TECH PROG, HOUSATONIC COMMUNITY COL, 77- *Personal Data:* b New York, NY, Feb 11, 20; m 55; c 2. *Educ:* Rutgers Univ, BS, 41; Univ Vt, MS, 55, MD, 59. *Hon Degrees:* MS, Yale Univ, 75. *Prof Exp:* Asst prof path, Med Col Va, 63-64; assoc clin fac, Quinnipiac Col, 68-78. *Concurrent Pos:* Pathologist, Vet Admin Med Ctr, 64-66, chief clin path, 66-74, actg assoc chief staff, 74-77, chief lab serv, 74-; chmn hemat, Nat Comt Clin Lab Standards, 73-76; pres, Asn Vet Admin Chiefs Lab Servm 78-80. *Mem:* Fel Am Soc Clin Pathologists; fel Col Am Pathologists; Histochem Soc (pres, 84); Int Acad Path; NY Acad Sci; Royal Micros Soc. *Res:* Development and clinical application of cytochemical assays for leukocyte enzymes; discoverer of dialysis induced leukopenia. *Mailing Add:* VA Hosp W Spring St West Haven CT 06516

KAPNER, ROBERT S(IDNEY), chemical engineering, physical chemistry; deceased, see previous edition for last biography

KAPOOR, AMRIT LAL, MEDICINAL CHEMISTRY, PHARMACEUTICAL CHEMISTRY. *Current Pos:* res fel chem, 63-66, PROF PHARMACEUT CHEM, COL PHARM & ALLIED HEALTH PROFESSIONS, ST JOHN'S UNIV, NY, 66- *Personal Data:* b Amritsar, India, Oct 15, 31; m 59; c 2. *Educ:* Punjab Univ, India, BS, 52, MS, 54; Swiss Fed Inst Technol, ScD(pharmaceut chem), 56. *Prof Exp:* Teaching fel, Sorbonne, 56-57; fel, Wayne State Univ, 57-58; sci officer, Nat Chem Labs, India, 58-59; chief chemist, Merck, Sharpe & Dohme Int, NY, 59-63. *Mem:* AAAS; Am Chem Soc; Am Pharmaceut Asn. *Res:* Natural products; synthesis of biologically active peptides and polypeptides. *Mailing Add:* Dept Pharm St John's Univ 8150 Utopia Pkwy Jamaica NY 11439-0001

KAPOOR, BRIJ M, PLANT CYTOLOGY. *Current Pos:* from asst prof to assoc prof, 68-80, chmn dept, 72-77 & 89-93, PROF BIOL, ST MARY'S UNIV, NS, 80- *Personal Data:* b Chawli, India, Mar 3, 36; m 63, Suder Shan; c Anil, Sunil & Vimal. *Educ:* Univ Delhi, BSc, 57, MSc, 59, PhD(cytol), 63. *Prof Exp:* Nat Res Coun Can res assoc plant biosyst, Univ Montreal, 63-65; NSF res assoc cytogenetics, Univ Colo, 65-66, vis prof biol, 66-67, asst prof, 67-68. *Mem:* Bot Soc Am; Genetics Soc Can; Am Inst Biol Sci; Soc Econ Bot. *Res:* Cytomorphological development of the endosperm of angiosperms; cytomorphological studies of the genus Solidago; cytogenetics of Eastern North American plants with special emphasis on compositae. *Mailing Add:* Dept Biol St Mary's Univ Halifax NS B3H 3C3 Can

KAPOOR, INDER PRAKASH, METABOLISM, INSECT TOXICOLOGY. *Current Pos:* res chemist, 73-75, group leader, 76-80, mgr, 80-85, DIR, PLANT INDUST DISCOVERY, AM CYANAMID CO, 85- *Personal Data:* b Multan, India, Sept 9, 37; m 70; c 2. *Educ:* Univ Delhi, BSc, 57; Univ Ill, Urbana, PhD(entom), 70. *Prof Exp:* Tech asst entom, Ministry Food & Agr, India, 57-66; res asst, Univ Calif, Riverside, 66-68; from res asst to res assoc entom metab, Univ Ill, Urbana, 68-72. *Mem:* Am Chem Soc. *Res:* Metabolism of pesticides in the environment and its elements; biological screening and development of new pesticides, plant growth regulants and biotechnology research. *Mailing Add:* 335 Penn-Titusville Rd Pennington NJ 08534

KAPOOR, NARINDER N, ZOOLOGY, PHYSIOLOGY. *Current Pos:* asst prof, 73-76, ASSOC PROF BIOL, CONCORDIA UNIV, 76- *Personal Data:* b Calcutta, India, Sept 4, 37; Can citizen; m 69, Nitish Mehta; c 3. *Educ:* Panjab Univ, India, BSc, 60, MSc, 61; McMaster Univ, PhD(animal behav & physiol), 68. *Honors & Awards:* 2nd Prize Outstanding Electronmicros, Polaroid Int Competition, 84; Grand Prize, Photomicro Graphy Contest, Bethesda Res Lab, Md, 89; Excellence in Plecoptera Res Award, NAm Plecoptera Soc, 90. *Prof Exp:* Lectr zool, Govt Col, Panjab, India, 61-62; demonstr physiol, McMaster Univ, 63-68; lectr, Univ Waterloo, 68-69, asst prof, 69-73. *Concurrent Pos:* Grad prog dir biol, Concordia Univ, 88-91 & 94- *Mem:* Int Soc of Plecoptera. *Res:* Respiratory physiology and behavior of stream animals; morphology, osmoregulation, scanning and transmission electron microscopy; Plecoptera; sense organs and feeding behavior. *Mailing Add:* Dept Biol Concordia Univ 1455 de Maisonneuve Blvd Montreal PQ H3G 1M8 Can. *Fax:* 514-848-2881; *E-Mail:* kapoorn@vax2.concordia.ca

KAPOOR, S F, MATHEMATICS. *Current Pos:* from asst prof to assoc prof, 67-81, PROF MATH, WESTERN MICH UNIV, 81- *Personal Data:* b Bombay, India, Sept 7, 34. *Educ:* Univ Bombay, BSc, 55, MSc, 57, LLB, 63; Mich State Univ, PhD(math), 67. *Prof Exp:* Staff asst, State Bank India, 58-61; lectr math, Kirti Col, Univ Bombay, 61-63; asst, Mich State Univ, 63-67. *Mem:* Math Asn Am. *Res:* Topology; graph theory. *Mailing Add:* 3475 Kenbrooke Ct Kalamazoo MI 49006

KAPOOR, VIKRAM J, PHYSICS. *Current Pos:* dir grad studies, 83-86, PROF ELEC & COMPUT ENG, UNIV CINCINNATI, 83-, DEPT HEAD, 86- *Personal Data:* b India, July 23, 45; US citizen. *Educ:* Univ Delhi, BS, 66, MS, 68; Lehigh Univ, MS, 72, PhD(physics), 76. *Honors & Awards:* Thomas D Callinan Award, Electrochem Soc, 91. *Prof Exp:* Sr design engr & mem res staff, Fairchild Semiconductor Corp, 76-78; asst prof elec eng, Case Western Res Univ, 78-81, dir, Solid State Integrated Circuit Lab, 78-83, assoc prof, 81-83. *Concurrent Pos:* Mem, Subcomt State-of-the-Art Compound Semiconductor Technol, Electrochem Soc, 83-87; mem, Nat Comn Semiconductor Mfg & Industr Competitiveness, Dept Com, 88-90. *Mem:* Am Phys Soc; sr mem Inst Elec & Electronics Engrs; Nat Soc Prof Engrs; Am Soc Eng Educ; fel Electrochem Soc; Am Vacuum Soc. *Res:* Solid state electronics; microwave/millimeterwave engineering; high Tc superconductors for microwave electronics. *Mailing Add:* Dept Elec & Comput Eng Univ Toledo Toledo OH 43606

KAPOR, MITCHELL DAVID, MANAGEMENT. *Current Pos:* CHMN, ELECTRONIC FRONTIER FOUND INC, 90- *Personal Data:* b Brooklyn, NY, Nov 1, 50; m 72, 83, Ellen M Poss. *Educ:* Yale Univ, BA, 71; Beacon Col, MA, 78. *Hon Degrees:* DHL, Boston Univ, 85, Mass Sch Prof Psychol, 90; DCS, Suffolk Univ, 88. *Honors & Awards:* Distinguished Info Sci Award, Data Processing Mgt Asn, 90. *Prof Exp:* Consult, 78-80; prod mgr, Personal Software, 80; pres, Lotus Develop Corp, 82-84, chmn, 84-86; chmn, ON Tech Inc, 87-90. *Concurrent Pos:* Adj res fel, Kennedy Sch Govt, Harvard Univ, 92- *Res:* Computer science. *Mailing Add:* 238 Main St Cambridge MA 02142

KAPOS, ERVIN, OPERATIONS RESEARCH & SYSTEMS ANALYSIS, WARGAMING & SIMULATION MILITARY COMMAND & CONTROL. *Current Pos:* PRES, KAPOS ASSOCS INC, 84- *Personal Data:* b Brashov, Rumania, June 21, 31; US citizen; m 52, June Ellenwood; c Valerie. *Educ:* Ind Univ, AB, 54. *Honors & Awards:* Meritorious Pub Serv Award, Secy Navy. *Prof Exp:* Assoc math, Ind Univ, 53-58; analyst, Opers Eval Group, Mass Inst Technol, 58-59, rep to oper test & eval force, US Pac Fleet, 59-60, rep to comdr 1st Fleet, 60-61, head command & control sect, Ctr Naval Anal, 62-66, rep to comdr-in-chief, US Pac Fleet, 66-67, dir, Southeast Asia Combat Anal Div, Opers Eval Group, 67-68 & Marine Corps Anal Group, 68-69, dir Opers Eval Group, 69-72; exec vpres & dir, Washington Opers, Ketron, Inc, 72-80, pres, 80-83. *Concurrent Pos:* Assoc mem, Defense Sci Bd, 74-76, 82-87; panel mem marine bd, Nat Acad Sci, 78-80; mem, adv bd, Nat Security Agency, 79-82; mem, panels sci & tech policy & crisis mgt, Ctr Strategic & Int Studies. *Mem:* Am Math Soc; Opers Res Soc Am; fel Mil Opers Res Soc. *Res:* Military operations research, particularly in command, control and communications; surveillance, intelligence and electronic warfare; human information processing and problem-solving; gaming simulation; military command and control. *Mailing Add:* 908 Turkey Run Rd McLean VA 22101

KAPP, JUDITH A, PATHOLOGY. *Current Pos:* STAFF, WINSHIP CANCER CTR, 93- *Prof Exp:* Assoc path-immunol, Harvard Med Sch, 73-76; from asst prof to assoc prof, 76-84, Depts Path, Microbiol & Immunol, Sch Med, Washington Univ, prof, 84-91; assoc staff, Jewish Hosp, St Louis, MO, 76-91. *Concurrent Pos:* Assoc ed, J Immunol, 79-83; res career develop award, NIH, 79-84; mem, Transplantation Biol & Immunol Comt, Nat Inst Allergy & Infectious Dis, NIH, 80-84, Cancer Preclin Prog Proj Rev Comt, Nat Cancer Inst, 86-88; mem, immunobiol study sect, Nat Inst Allergy & Infectious Dis, NIH, 88-; mem comt fundamental res, Nat Multiple Sclerosis Soc, 88- *Mem:* Sigma Xi; Am Asn Immunologists; Am Asn Pathologists. *Res:* Immunology; microbiology; author or co-author of over 140 publications. *Mailing Add:* Dept Path Winship Cancer Ctr Emory Univ Sch Med S Clin Bldg 1327 Clifton Rd NE Atlanta GA 30322. *Fax:* 404-778-5016

KAPP, ROBERT WESLEY, JR, TOXICOLOGY, GENETICS. *Current Pos:* PRES, ROBERT KAPP ASSOCS, 89- *Personal Data:* b Point Pleasant, NJ; m 67; c 3. *Educ:* Syracuse Univ, AB, 67; George Washington Univ, MS, 74, PhD(genetic toxicol), 79. *Prof Exp:* Head cytogenetics, Nat Naval Med Ctr, Md, 69-72; med technician med, Group Health Asn, Washington, DC, 69-73; staff scientist toxicol, Hazleton Lab Am, Va, 73-78, sr toxicologist, 78-79; assoc dir, Toxicol Lab, Exxon Corp, 79-82, dir, 82-89. *Concurrent Pos:* Vis fac, Cancer Ctr, Med Br, Univ Tex, 78-, adj prof genetic toxicol, 85-; consult, Genetic Toxicol Ctr, 79-; mem, Dominant Lethal Comt & Sperm Anal Comt, Genetic Toxicol Prog, Environ Protection Agency, 79-; chmn, Med Toxicol Comt, Am Soc Testing & Mat, 79-; reviewer, Nat March of Dimes, 80-; consult, Dept Health & Human Servs, 80-82, bd sci counrs, Nat Toxicol Prog, Nat Inst Occup Safety & Health, 82-; rev panel, Energy Health Sci, Environ Protection Agency, 81-; adj prof genetic toxicol, Med Br, Univ Tex, 85- *Mem:* NY Acad Sci; Soc Toxicol; Am Soc Testing & Mat; Am Col Toxicol; Sigma Xi; Environ Mutagen Soc. *Res:* Development of clinical and nonclinical methodology to determine occupational carcinogenesis and mutagenesis; evaluation of general and genetic toxicological procedures for safety assessment; laboratory and research management. *Mailing Add:* 11700 Aberdeen Midlothian VA 23113

KAPPAGODA, C TISSA, CARDIOLOGY, PHYSIOLOGY. *Current Pos:* PROF MED, UNIV CALIF, DAVIS, 90- *Educ:* Univ Leeds, Eng, PhD(cardiovasc physiol), 72. *Hon Degrees:* FRCP(Lond), 88, FRCP(C), 80. *Prof Exp:* Prof med cardiol, Univ Alta, 78-90. *Mem:* Physiol Soc Am; Physiol Soc Gt Brit; fel Am Col Cardiol. *Res:* reflex regulation of the circulatiai and exercin physiology. *Mailing Add:* Univ Calif TB172 Davis CA 95616

KAPPAS, ATTALLAH, METABOLISM, PHARMACOLOGY. *Current Pos:* assoc prof & physician, 67-71, sr physician, 71-74, PROF ROCKELLER UNIV, 71-, PHYSICIAN-IN-CHIEF, 74-, SHERMAN FAIRCHILD PROF, 81-, VPRES, 83- *Personal Data:* b Union City, NJ, Nov 4, 26; m 63; c 3. *Educ:* Columbia Univ, AB, 47; Univ Chicago, MD, 50; Am Bd Internal Med, dipl, 58. *Hon Degrees:* DSc, NY Med Col, 78. *Honors & Awards:* Spec Award Clin Pharmacol, Burroughs Wellcome Fund, 73; Sir Henry Hallet Dale Mem Lectr, Med Sch, Johns Hopkins Univ, 75; Pfizer Lectr, Peter Bent Brigham Hosp, Harvard Med Sch, 77; Res Award, Am Soc Pharmacol & Exp Therapeut, 78; Pfizer Lectr, Hershey Med Ctr, Pa State Univ, 80; Glaxo Lectr, Cornell Univ Med Col, 84. *Prof Exp:* Intern med, Univ Serv, Kings County Hosp, New York, 50-51; med resident, Peter Bent Brigham Hosp, 54-56; assoc, Sloan-Kettering Inst, 56-57; from asst prof to assoc prof, Sch Med, Univ Chicago, 57-67. *Concurrent Pos:* Res fel, Sloan-Kettering Inst, 51-54; Commonwealth Fund fel, Courtauld Inst, Middlesex Hosp Med Sch, London, Eng, 61-62; John Simon Guggenheim Found fel & guest investr, Rockefeller Univ, 66-67; vis prof clin pharmacol, Med Sch, Johns Hopkins Univ, 75; Vincent Astor prof clin sci, Mem Sloan-Kettering Cancer Ctr, Cornell Univ Med Col, 79-81; Nicholson exchange fel, Karolinska Inst, 85. *Mem:* Am Soc Clin Invest; Endocrine Soc; Harvey Soc; Asn Am Physicians; Am Clin & Climat Asn; Am Soc Pharmacol & Exp Therapeut; fel Am Col Physicians; Endocrine Soc. *Res:* Metabolic-genetic diseases; hormone biology; drug metabolism toxicology and disorders of porphyrin-heme metabolism. *Mailing Add:* Rockefeller Univ Hosp 1230 York Ave New York NY 10021-6259

KAPPE, DAVID SYME, PHYSICAL CHEMISTRY, RADIOCHEMISTRY. *Current Pos:* res dir, 67-85, CHMN & CEO, KAPPE ASSOCS, INC, 86- *Personal Data:* b Philadelphia, Pa, Sept 28, 35; c 3. *Educ:* Univ Md, College Park, BS, 59; Pa State Univ, PhD(phys chem), 65. *Prof Exp:* Phys sci aid, Metall Div, Nat Bur Standards, 58-59; chief radiation appln sect, Hittman Assocs, Inc, 66-67. *Concurrent Pos:* Consult, Am Acad Environ Eng-Environ Protection Agency Manpower Training Prog, 71; tech rev res proposals, USEPA, 75, monitoring progs hazardous waste incinerators. *Mem:* Am Chem Soc; Am Inst Physics; Am Water Works Asn; Water Pollution Control Fedn. *Res:* Reclamation of spent nuclear reactor fuels; measurement of thermal neutron cross sections; development and application of radionuclide-phosphor self-luminescent light sources; treatment of domestic, industrial and agricultural waste-waters; sludge composting. *Mailing Add:* Kappe Assoc Inc 100 Wormans Mill Ct Frederick MD 21701-8721

KAPPEL, ELLEN SUE, MARINE GEOLOGY, GEOPHYSICS. *Current Pos:* ASSOC DIR, OCEAN DRILLING PROG, JOINT OCEANOG INSTS INC, 86-, PROG DIR, US SCII SUPPORT PROG, 88- *Personal Data:* b Brooklyn, NY, Oct 22, 59; m 89, Stuart A Berman; c Daniel C & Emily J. *Educ:* Cornell Univ, AB, 80; Columbia Univ, MA, 82, MPhil & PhD(geol), 85. *Prof Exp:* Postdoctoral assoc res scientist, Lamont-Doharty Earth Observ, Columbia Univ, 85-86. *Concurrent Pos:* Chair, Tellers Comt, Am Geophys Union. *Mem:* Am Geophys Union; Geol Soc Am. *Res:* Relationship between midocean ridge tectonics and hydrothermal mineralization. *Mailing Add:* 5610 Gloster Rd Bethesda MD 20816. *E-Mail:* ekappel@brook.edu

KAPPENMAN, RUSSELL FRANCIS, STATISTICS. *Current Pos:* MATH STATISTICIAN, NORTHWEST & ALASKA FISHERIES CTR, SEATTLE, 76- *Personal Data:* b Lennox, SDak, Sept 2, 38; m 64; c 4. *Educ:* Univ SDak, BA, 60; Univ Iowa, MS, 62; State Univ NY Buffalo, PhD(statist), 69. *Prof Exp:* Asst prof statist, Pa State Univ, 69-76. *Mem:* Am Statist Asn. *Res:* Statistical inference. *Mailing Add:* 17014 NE 100th St Redmond WA 98052

KAPPERS, LAWRENCE ALLEN, SOLID STATE PHYSICS. *Current Pos:* from asst prof to assoc prof, 73-93, PROF PHYSICS, UNIV CONN, 93- *Personal Data:* b Hingham, Wis, May 27, 41; m 63, Jean Buteyn. *Educ:* Cent Col, Iowa, BA, 63; Univ Mo, Columbia, MS, 66, PhD(physics), 70. *Prof Exp:* Air Force Off Sci res fel physics, Univ Minn, Minneapolis, 70-72; NSF res assoc, Okla State Univ, 72-73. *Mem:* Am Phys Soc. *Res:* Electronic structure of defects in ionic crystals; optical absorption; luminescence and electron paramagnetic resonance; production and decay mechanisms of color centers, additive coloration and radiation damage; lasers; high pressure diamond anvil studies. *Mailing Add:* Dept Physics Univ Conn Storrs CT 06269-3046. *Fax:* 860-486-3346; *E-Mail:* kappers@uconnnm.uconn.edu

KAPPLER, JOHN W, MEDICINE. *Current Pos:* INVESTR, HOWARD HUGHES MED INST, 85-; PROF, HEALTH SCI CTR, UNIV COLO, 85- *Mem:* Nat Acad Sci. *Mailing Add:* Nat Jewish Ctr Dept Med & Basic Immunol 1400 Jackson St Denver CO 80206. *Fax:* 303-398-1396; *E-Mail:* j.kappler@ispop.njc.org

KAPPLER, JOHN W, IMMUNOLOGY, MICROBIOLOGY. *Current Pos:* PROF MICROBIOL & IMMUNOL, UNIV COLO, DENVER. *Honors & Awards:* Louisa Gross Horwitz Prize, Columbia Univ, 94. *Mailing Add:* Univ Colo Howard Hughes Med Inst Denver CO 80262

KAPPMEYER, KEITH K, ADMINISTRATION. *Current Pos:* VPRES TECHNOL, USX CORP, PITTSBURGH. *Honors & Awards:* Albert Victor Bleininger Award, Am Ceramic Soc, 92. *Mailing Add:* USX Corp 600 Grant St Pittsburgh PA 15219-2702

KAPPUS, KARL DANIEL, MEDICAL ENTOMOLOGY, EPIDEMIOLOGY. *Current Pos:* res entomologist, Nat Commun Dis Ctr, 67-69, biologist, 69-76, EPIDEMIOLOGIST, CTR DIS CONTROL, 76- *Personal Data:* b Cleveland, Ohio, July 2, 38. *Educ:* Ohio State Univ, BSc, 60, MSc, 62, PhD(entom), 64. *Prof Exp:* Res asst mosquito biol, Res Found, Ohio State Univ, 61-64; Nat Res Coun fel arbovirus infection, US Army Biol Labs, 65-66; res assoc mosquito biol, Res Found, Ohio State Univ, 66-67. *Mem:* Am Soc Trop Med & Hyg; Entom Soc Am; Sigma Xi. *Res:* Animal photoperiodism; viral infection in arthropods; mosquito behavior; viral zoonoses; epidemiology of viral infections; human intestinal protozoa; disease eradication. *Mailing Add:* 216 Glendale Decatur GA 30030-1918

KAPRAL, FRANK ALBERT, BACTERIAL HOST-PARASITE INTERACTIONS. *Current Pos:* assoc prof, 56-69, actg chmn dept, 73-78, PROF MED MICROBIOL, OHIO STATE UNIV, 69- *Personal Data:* b Philadelphia, Pa, Mar 12, 28; m 51, Marina Garay; c Frederick, Gloria & Robert. *Educ:* Philadelphia Col Pharm & Sci, BS, 52; Univ Pa, PhD(med microbiol), 56. *Prof Exp:* From asst instr to assoc microbiol, Univ Pa, 52-56. *Concurrent Pos:* NIH grants, Ohio State Univ, 67-, NIH training grant, 68-71; assoc microbiol, Philadelphia Gen Hosp, 62-64; chief microbiol res, 64-66; chief microbiol, 65-66; asst chief microbiol res, Vet Admin Hosp, Philadelphia, 62-66. *Mem:* AAAS; Am Soc Microbiol; Am Asn Immunol; Infectious Dis Soc; Soc Exp Biol & Med; Am Acad Microbiol. *Res:* Pathogenesis of staphylococcal infections; bacterial host-parasite interactions; bacterial toxins; lipids as immune mechanisms. *Mailing Add:* Dept Med Microbiol & Immunol 2166A Graves Hall Ohio State Univ Columbus OH 43210-1239. *Fax:* 614-292-9805

KAPRAL, RAYMOND EDWARD, THEORETICAL CHEMISTRY. *Current Pos:* asst prof to assoc prof, 69-80, PROF CHEM, UNIV TORONTO, 80- *Personal Data:* b Swoyersville, Pa, Mar 21, 42; m 64; c 1. *Educ:* King's Col, Pa, BS, 64; Princeton Univ PhD(chem), 67. *Honors & Awards:* Noranda Award, Chem Inst Can, 81, Joh Potanyi Award, 96. *Prof Exp:* Res assoc chem, Princeton Univ, 67 & Mass Inst Technol, 68-69. *Concurrent Pos:* Killian res fell Can Coun, 94-96. *Mem:* Fel Am Phys Soc; Chem Inst Can; fel Royal Soc Can. *Res:* Statistical mechanics; quantum mechanics; chemical kinetics. *Mailing Add:* Dept Chem Univ Toronto 80 St George St Toronto ON M5S 3H6 Can. *Fax:* 416-978-5325; *E-Mail:* rkapral@gatto.chem.utoronto.ca

KAPRAUN, DONALD FREDERICK, PHYCOLOGY. *Current Pos:* assoc prof bot & phycol, 71-77, PROF BIOL, UNIV NC, WILMINGTON, 77- *Personal Data:* b Spring Valley, Ill, Sept 13, 45; m 75. *Educ:* Eastern Ill Univ, BS, 66; Univ Tex, PhD(bot), 69. *Prof Exp:* Asst prof bot, Univ Southwestern La, 69-71. *Mem:* Phycol Soc Am; Int Phycol Soc; Brit Phycol Soc. *Res:* Ecology and reproductive periodicity of benthic marine algae in North Carolina. *Mailing Add:* Dept Biol Univ NC 601 S College Rd Wilmington NC 28403-3201

KAPRELIAN, EDWARD KARNIG, PHOTOGRAPHY, PATENTS. *Current Pos:* PRES, KAPRELIAN RES & DEVELOP CO, 73- *Personal Data:* b Union Hill, NJ, June 20, 13; m 36, Lucy Ainilian; c Charles, Harold & Helen (Ward). *Educ:* Stevens Inst Technol, ME, 34. *Prof Exp:* Patent exam, US

Patent Off, 36-42; physicist, Bd Econ Warfare, 42-45; patent adv, Off Chief Signal Officer, 45-46; chief photog res br, US Army Signal Eng Lab, 46-52; dir res & eng, Kalart Co, 52-55; dir res, Kaprelian Res & Develop Co, 55-57; dept dir res, US Army Signal Res & Develop Lab, 57-62, tech dir, US Army Limited War Lab, 62-67; vpres & tech dir, Keuffel & Esser Co, Morristown, 68-73. *Concurrent Pos:* Mem, Nat Acad Sci-Nat Res Coun, 52-58. *Mem:* Fel Soc Photog Sci & Eng (pres, 48-52); Optical Soc Am; Am Soc Mech Eng; Soc Motion Picture & TV Eng; sr mem Inst Elec & Electronics Engrs. *Res:* Applied physics; photographic processes and apparatus; electronics; patent law; optical instruments. *Mailing Add:* 15 Lowery Lane Mendham NJ 07945-3403

KAPRON, FELIX PAUL, FIBER OPTICS. *Current Pos:* DIR, OPTICAL SYST TECH & FIBER OPTICS DEPT, BELLCOR, 88- *Personal Data:* b St Catharines, Ont, Nov 29, 40; US citizen; m 71. *Educ:* Univ Toronto, BASc, 62; Univ Waterloo, MSc, 63, PhD(physics), 67. *Prof Exp:* Physicist, Corning Glass Works, 67-72; sr scientist & mgr, Bell-Northern Res, 73-82; staff scientist, Electro-Optical Prod Div, Int Tel & Tel, 82-87. *Concurrent Pos:* Lectr, Carleton Univ, 76-82. *Mem:* Optical Soc Am; Soc Photo-Optical Instrumentation Engrs; Can Asn Physicists; sr mem Inst Elec & Electronics Engrs. *Res:* Optical communications and sensors; fiber-optical waveguides; optical devices properties of solids, particularly emitters, modulators, detectors and couplers. *Mailing Add:* 5 Hillcrest Dr Denville NJ 07834

KAPSALIS, ANDREAS A, IMMUNODIAGNOSTIC ASSAYS. *Current Pos:* SR RES SCIENTIST DIAGNOSTICS, ABBOTT LABS, 76- *Personal Data:* b Vitina, Arkadia, Greece, Nov 6, 36; m, Glenda Hawley; c Terri & Effie. *Educ:* Univ Athens, Bacheloris, 60; Univ Chicago, MS, 64; Univ Ill, PhD(immunochem), 74. *Prof Exp:* Res asst, Chicago Col Osteop, 64-65; res assoc allergy res, Michael Reece Hosp, Chicago, 65-68; res assoc, Baxter Labs, 68-72; immunologist cancer res, West Side Vet Admin Hosp, Univ Ill, 74-76. *Mem:* AAAS; Am Chem Soc; Am Asn Clin Chem; NY Acad Sci. *Res:* Development of immunodiagnostic assays for viral diseases and for therapeutic drug monitoring. *Mailing Add:* 1005 Hinman Ave Evanston IL 60202

KAPSALIS, JOHN GEORGE, FOOD SCIENCE, BIOCHEMISTRY. *Current Pos:* CONSULT, 87- *Personal Data:* b Mytilene, Greece, Jan 27, 27; US citizen; m 56, Athena; c Ellen & Gina. *Educ:* Athens Col Agr, BS, MS, 54; Univ Fla, MAgr, 55; Tex A&M Univ, PhD(food sci), 59. *Honors & Awards:* Sci Dir Silver Key Award Res, US Army Natick Lab, 69. *Prof Exp:* Asst prof & fel dairy tech, Ohio State Univ, 59-60; food technologist, Armed Forces Food & Container Inst, US Army Natick Res & Develop Labs, 60-62, res chemist, 62-63, chief, food biochem lab, 63-74, chief, Biochem Br, Sci & Advan Technol Lab, 74-87. *Concurrent Pos:* Secy Army res & study fel, 65-66. *Mem:* Am Chem Soc; Sigma Xi; fel Am Inst Chemists; NY Acad Sci. *Res:* Quality parameters of dehydrated foods; effect of water vapor equilibrium on chemical and rheological properties of foods; nondestructive methods of measurement in foods; chemical and rheological properties of lipids. *Mailing Add:* 5776 Deauville Lake Circle C-308 Naples FL 34112

KAPUR, BHUSHAN M, TOXICOLOGY, CLINICAL BIOCHEMISTRY. *Current Pos:* CONSULT, TOXICOL DIV CLIN PHARMACOL & TOXICOL, HOSP SICK CHILDREN, TORONTO, 95- *Personal Data:* b Amritsar, India, Feb 23, 38; m 68; c 2. *Educ:* Bombay Univ, BSc, 59; Univ Basel, PhD(org chem), 67; ARIC, 72, MRIC, 76, FRSC, 79, FACB, 83, FCACB, 89. *Prof Exp:* Res assoc, Univ Basel, 67; fac pharm, Univ Toronto, 68-71; sr chemist, Addiction Res Found, 71-72, dir labs, clin inst, 72-95. *Concurrent Pos:* Lectr, Dept Clin Biochem, Fac Med, Univ Toronto, 74 & 76-78, asst prof, 78; instr, Toronto Inst Med Technol, 74-79. *Mem:* Soc Toxicol; The Chem Soc; Can Soc Clin Chem; Am Asn Clin Chem; Can Soc Sci; Soc Forensic Toxicol. *Res:* Natural product chemistry; clinical biochemistry; toxicology; biochemical changes due to alcohol use. *Mailing Add:* 2374 Canso Rd Oakville ON L6J 5W6 Can. *Fax:* 905-849-4389

KAPUR, KAILASH C, QUALITY & PRODUCTIVITY IMPROVEMENT, DESIGN OF EXPERIMENTS. *Current Pos:* DIR & PROF INDUST ENG, UNIV WASH, SEATTLE, 92- *Personal Data:* b India, Aug 17, 41; US citizen; m 69, Geraldine Palmer; c Anjali J & Jay P. *Educ:* Delhi Univ, India, BS, 63; India Inst Technol, MTech, 65; Univ Calif, Berkeley, MS, 67, PhD(oper res & indust eng), 69. *Honors & Awards:* Allan Chop Tech Advan Award, Am Soc Qual Control, 87; Craig Award, Am Soc Qual Control, 89. *Prof Exp:* Sr res engr res, Gen Motors Res Labs, 69-70; from asst prof to assoc prof teaching & res, Wayne State Univ, 70-80, assoc chmn, 75-76, prof, 80-89; sr reliability engr res, Tank Automotive Command, 78; dir & prof teaching & res, Univ Okla, 89-92. *Concurrent Pos:* Vis scholar, Ford Motor Co, 73; vis assoc prof, Univ Waterloo, 77-78. *Mem:* Fel Inst Indust Engrs; Opers Res Soc Am; Inst Mgt Sci; fel Am Soc Qual Control. *Res:* Quality engineering; product and process design optimization; reliability engineering; design of experiments; author of various publications. *Mailing Add:* Indust Eng Univ Wash Box 352650 Seattle WA 98195-2650. *Fax:* 206-685-3072; *E-Mail:* kkapur@u.washington.edu

KAPUR, SHAKTI PRAKASH, HUMAN ANATOMY, HISTOLOGY. *Current Pos:* res assoc, 71-72, asst prof, 72-78, ASSOC PROF ANAT, GEORGETOWN UNIV, 78- *Personal Data:* b Ludhiana, Panjab, India, Aug 20, 32; m 66; c 2. *Educ:* Panjab Univ, India, BSc, 53, MSc, 54; McGill Univ, PhD(zool), 64. *Prof Exp:* Lectr biol, Govt Col, Panjab, 55-61; sr teaching asst zool, McGill Univ, 61-64; exp biologist, Ayerst Drug Res Labs, Can, 64-66; asst prof zool, Panjab Univ, India, 66-71. *Mem:* Sigma Xi; Am Asn Anatomists; Soc Exp Biol & Med; AAAS. *Res:* Electron microscopy; histochemistry of thyroid-parathyroid; endocrine mechanisms controlling calcium homeostasis; calcification in biological systems; zinc homeostasis; immunocytochemistry; radioimmunoassay. *Mailing Add:* Dept Anat Georgetown Univ Sch Med 3900 Reservoir Rd NW Washington DC 20007-2187

KAPUSCINSKI, JAN, fluorescence spectroscopy, for more information see previous edition

KAPUSTA, GEORGE, AGRONOMY, WEED CONTROL. *Current Pos:* assoc prof, 64-80, PROF AGRON, SOUTHERN ILL UNIV, 80- *Personal Data:* b Max, NDak, Nov 20, 32; m 58; c 4. *Educ:* NDak State Univ, BS, 54; Univ Minn, MS, 57; Southern Ill Univ, PhD(bot), 75. *Honors & Awards:* Outstanding Res & Exten Award, Land of Lincoln Soybean Asn, 78. *Prof Exp:* Agronomist, NDak State Univ, 58-64. *Mem:* Agron Soc Am; Soil Sci Soc Am; fel Weed Sci Soc Am; Sigma Xi. *Res:* Weed control in field and forage crops; minimum and zero-tillage; culture, especially plant density and geometry, cultivars and growth regulators; nitrification inhibition; symbiotic nitrogen fixation. *Mailing Add:* 1274 W No Name Rd Carbondale IL 62901

KAPUSTA, JOSEPH IRVING, HIGH ENERGY NUCLEAR PHYSICS. *Current Pos:* from asst prof to assoc prof, 82-86, PROF PHYSICS, UNIV MINN, 86- *Personal Data:* b Antigo, Wis, June 21, 52. *Educ:* Univ Wis, Madison, BA, 74; Univ Calif, Berkeley, MA, 76, PhD(physics), 78. *Prof Exp:* Postdoctoral res assoc, Lawrence Berkeley Lab, 78-79, Los Alamos Nat Lab, 79-81; NATO-NSF fel & sci assoc, Europ Ctr Nuclear Res, 81-82. *Concurrent Pos:* Prog dir, Univ Calif, Santa Barbara, 93. *Mem:* AAAS; fel Am Phys Soc. *Res:* Theoretical studies of the properties of high temperature and density of nuclear and subnuclear matter and its realization in high energy nuclear collisions, stars and the early universe. *Mailing Add:* Sch Phys & Aston Univ Minn 116 Church St SE Minneapolis MN 55455. *Fax:* 612-624-4578; *E-Mail:* kapusta@physics.spa.umn.edu

KARAALI, ORHAN, NEURAL NETWORKS, SPEECH PROCESSING SYSTEMS. *Current Pos:* staff engr, 89-94, sr staff engr, 94-96, PRIN STAFF ENGR, MOTOROLA INC, 96- *Personal Data:* b Istanbul, Turkey, Oct 3, 60; US citizen. *Educ:* Univ Wis, BS, 82, MS, 84; Fla Atlantic Univ, PhD(comput eng), 89. *Prof Exp:* Lectr micro processors, Univ Wis-Milwaukee, 83-84; sr hardware engr, ATT-Paradyne Corp, 84-87; res engr, Modcomp/AEG, 88-89. *Mem:* Sigma Xi. *Res:* Neural network architectures and algorithms, neural network implementations and applications, microprocessor and digital signal processor architectures and applications; developing neural network technologies for speech synthesis. *Mailing Add:* 1301 E Algonquin Rd Schaumburg IL 60196. *Fax:* 847-576-0541

KARABATSOS, GERASIMOS J, ORGANIC CHEMISTRY. *Current Pos:* From asst prof to assoc prof, 59-66, chmn dept, 75-86, PROF CHEM, MICH STATE UNIV, 66- *Personal Data:* b Chomatada, Greece, May 17, 32; US citizen; m 56; c 4. *Educ:* Adelphi Col, BA, 54; Harvard Univ, PhD(org chem), 59. *Honors & Awards:* Petrol Chem Award, Am Chem Soc, 71. *Concurrent Pos:* Sloan Found res fel, 63-66; NSF sr fel, 65-66; sci dir, Greek Atomic Energy Comn, 74-75. *Mem:* Am Chem Soc; corresp mem Acad Athens; The Chem Soc. *Res:* Carbonium ions; nuclear magnetic resonance spectroscopy; isotope effects; stereochemistry of enzymatic reactions. *Mailing Add:* Dept Chem Mich State Univ East Lansing MI 48823

KARACAN, ISMET, SLEEP DISORDERS. *Current Pos:* ASSOC CHIEF STAFF, RES & DEVELOP & DIR, SLEEP RES LAB, VET ADMIN MED CTR, HOUSTON, 73-; PROF PSYCHIAT & DIR, SLEEP DISORDER & RES CTR, BAYLOR COL MED, TEX MED CTR, HOUSTON, 73- *Personal Data:* b Istanbul, Turkey, July 23, 27; m 62; c 5. *Educ:* Univ Istanbul, BS, 48, MD, 53; State Univ NY Downstate Med Ctr, DSc(med), 65; Turkish Bd Neuropsychiat, 60; Am Bd Psychiat & Neurol cert psychiat, 63. *Honors & Awards:* Nathaniel Kleitman Prize, Asn Sleep Dis Ctrs, 81. *Prof Exp:* From assoc prof to prof psychiat & dir, Sleep Labs, Univ Fla, Gainville, 66-73. *Mem:* Fel Am Psychiat Asn; AMA; AAAS; fel Am Col Physicians; Sleep Res Soc (pres, 76-79); NY Acad Sci; Am Col Neuropsychopharmacol; Brit Asn Psychopharmacol. *Res:* Psychological and physiological mechanisms of male impotence; neurophysiological and biochemical mechanisms responsible for male erectile failure; pharmacology of human sleep. *Mailing Add:* Baylor Col Med Psych Houston TX 77030

KARADBIL, LEON NATHAN, RESOURCE MANAGEMENT. *Current Pos:* RETIRED. *Personal Data:* b New York, NY, Apr 2, 20; m 41; c 3. *Educ:* City Col New York, BS, 40. *Prof Exp:* Asst sect chief, Census Bur, US Dept Com, 40-42, economist & statistician, War Prod Bd, 42-45, economist, Civilian Prod Admin, 45-46, statistician, War Assets Admin, 46-48, economist, Econ Coop Admin, 48-51, indust specialist, Nat Prod Auth, Defense Prod Admin, 51-53 & Off Defense Mobilization, 53-57; consult & analyst, Opers Res Off, Johns Hopkins Univ, 57-61; opers analyst & study chmn opers res, Res Anal Corp, Va, 61-72; study chmn, Gen Res Corp, Va, 72-76; dir, Emergency Preparedness Div, Int Trade Admin, US Dept Com, 76-85. *Concurrent Pos:* Consult, Opers Res Off, Johns Hopkins Univ, 57-58; sr fel, Nat Defense, Univ Ft McNair, Wash. *Mem:* Opers Res Soc Am. *Res:* Military operations research in logistics and costing; analysis of industrial resources. *Mailing Add:* 6909 Winterberry Lane Bethesda MD 20817

KARADI, GABOR, CIVIL ENGINEERING. *Current Pos:* assoc prof, 67-69, prof eng mech, 69-77, PROF CIVIL ENG & CHMN DEPT, UNIV WIS-MILWAUKEE, 77- *Personal Data:* b Budapest, Hungary, Sept 12, 24; m 51; c 2. *Educ:* Tech Univ Budapest, BSc, 50, MSc, 54, PhD(civil eng), 60;

Hungarian Acad Sci, DSc(hydraul), 64. *Prof Exp:* Asst hydraul engr, Hungarian Dept Hydraul Eng, 50-51; sr engr, Inst Water Resources Eng, Budapest, 54-58; sr engr, Inst Hwy Eng, 58-59; sr engr, Water Resources Co, 59-60, chief develop engr, 60-63; lectr civil eng, Univ Khartoum, 63-64, sr lectr, 65-66; vis assoc prof, Northwestern Univ, Evanston, 66-67. *Concurrent Pos:* Consult, Agr Res Inst, 60-63, Inst Chem Eng, Budapest, Hungary, 61-63 & Northwestern Univ, Evanston, 67-68; mem US comn, Int Comn Irrig & Drainage, 68. *Mem:* Am Soc Civil Engrs; Am Water Resources Asn. *Res:* Hydrodynamics of groundwater flow; watershed hydrology; urban hydrology. *Mailing Add:* Dept Civil Eng Univ Wis PO Box 784 Milwaukee WI 53201

KARADY, GEORGE GYORGY, POWER ELECTRONICS, TRANSMISSION & DISTRIBUTION. *Current Pos:* dir energy conversion & sr consult engr, Ariz State Univ, 77-78, chief elec consult engr, 79-82, chief engr comput technol, 82-84, mgr elec systs, Ebasco Serv Inc, 84-86, SRP CHAIR PROF, ARIZ STATE UNIV, 86- *Personal Data:* b Budapest, Hungary, Aug 17, 30; US citizen. *Educ:* Tech Univ Budapest, Dipl Eng, 52, Dr Eng, 60. *Hon Degrees:* Dr, Tech Univ Budapest, Hungary, 96. *Honors & Awards:* T&D Comt Outstanding Working Group Chmn Award, 88; Working Group Recognition Award, Inst Elec & Electronics Engrs Power Eng Soc, 93. *Prof Exp:* Assoc prof elec eng, Tech Univ Budapest, 52-68; lectr, Univ Salford, 68-69; prog mgr res, Hydro Que Inst Res, Montreal, Can, 69-77. *Concurrent Pos:* Consult high voltage res, Inst Elec Energy Res, Budapest, 58-63; dep secy, Hungarian Elec Asn, 61-62, vchmn, 63-65, exec bd, 65-66; consult power syst anal, Elec Bd, Budapest, 63-69, vis prof, Univ Iraq, Baghdad, 66-68; adj prof, Univ Montreal, 71-77 & McGill Univ, 72-77; adj prof, Polytech Inst Brooklyn, 78-86; vpres, US Nat Comt, CIGRE, 81-85, secy/treas, 85-93, tech comt, 94- *Mem:* Fel Inst Elec & Electronics Engrs; Conf Int Grandes Reseaux Electriques; Soc Aerospace Engrs; Natural Sci & Eng Res Coun Can. *Res:* Power electronics, high voltage technic, insulation pollution and special insulators; high voltage thyristor valves and high voltage direct current technology; rectifier and inverter systems; pulsed power supplies. *Mailing Add:* Elec Eng Dept Ariz State Univ Tempe AZ 85287-5706. *Fax:* 602-965-0745; *E-Mail:* karady@asuvax.eas.asu.edu

KARADY, SANDOR, ORGANIC CHEMISTRY. *Current Pos:* chemist, Merck & Co, 57-59, res chemist, 66-75, sr chemist, 75-78, res fel, 78-83, SR INVESTR, RES LABS, MERCK & CO, 66-, SR RES FEL, 83- *Personal Data:* b Budapest, Hungary, Aug 18, 33; US citizen; m 63; c 2. *Educ:* Eotvos Lorand Univ, Lorand, Budapest, BSc, 56; Mass Inst Technol, PhD(org chem), 63. *Honors & Awards:* Thomas Alva Edison Patent Award, 85. *Prof Exp:* Chemist, Pharmaceut Res Labs, Budapest, Hungary, 55-56. *Concurrent Pos:* NIH fel, Mass Inst Technol, 63-64, Inst Org Chem, Gif sur Yvette, France, 64-65. *Mem:* Am Chem Soc. *Res:* Synthetic organic chemistry; natural products; pharmaceuticals; cephalosporin chemistry; heterocycles; synthetic electrochemistry; thienamycins. *Mailing Add:* 348 Longview Dr Mountainside NJ 07092-2005

KARAFIN, LESTER, UROLOGY. *Current Pos:* PROF UROL, MED COL PA, 64- *Personal Data:* b Philadelphia, Pa, Sept 26, 26; m 50; c 3. *Educ:* Temple Univ, MD, 49, MSc, 56. *Concurrent Pos:* Consult, Vet Admin Hosp, Philadelphia, 64-; prof, Med Ctr, Temple Univ. *Mem:* AMA; Am Urol Asn. *Res:* General urology. *Mailing Add:* Med Col Pa 3300 Henry Ave Philadelphia PA 19129-1121

KARAGIANES, MANUEL TOM, TOXICOLOGY EXPERIMENTAL SURGERY, BIOMATERIAL. *Current Pos:* res scientist, 67-70, res assoc, 70-78, mgr, Inhalation Technol & Toxicol, 78-85, MGR SPECIAL OPERATIONS FACILITY, PAC NW LABS, BATTELE MEM INST, 85- *Personal Data:* b Boise, Idaho, Sept 22, 32; m 57; c 3. *Educ:* Wash State Univ, BS, 61, DVM, 63. *Honors & Awards:* I-R 100 Award, 71. *Prof Exp:* Pvt pract, Sunset Animal Clin, Idaho, 63-67. *Res:* Development of intravascular implant operations for bioengineering-biomaterials research; use of porous metals as bone substitutes for orthopedic and dental prostheses. *Mailing Add:* 519 Holly St Richland WA 99352

KARAGOZIAN, ANN RENEE, GASEOUS JETS. *Current Pos:* From asst prof to assoc prof, 82-93, PROF ENG & APPL SCI, DEPT MECH & AEROSPACE ENG, UNIV CALIF, LOS ANGELES, 93- *Educ:* Univ Calif, BS, 78; Calif Inst Technol, MS, 79, PhD(mech eng), 82. *Concurrent Pos:* Mem tech staff, Aerospace Corp & Hughes Aircraft Co; consult, Rand Corp & Pac-Sierra Res Corp; mem, Panel on Molten Salt Oxidation, Dept Energy, 91; mem, Defense Sci Study Group, 94-96; assoc ed, J Propulsion & Power, 96- *Mem:* Assoc fel Am Inst Aeronaut & Astronaut. *Res:* Effects of heat release on diffusion flame-vortex pair interactions; gaseous jet in supersonic crossflow. *Mailing Add:* Dept Mech & Aerospace Eng Univ Calif Los Angeles CA 90095-1597

KARAKASH, JOHN J, ELECTRICAL ENGINEERING. *Current Pos:* from asst prof to prof elec eng, Lehigh Univ, 46-62, head dept, 55-68, distinguished prof elec eng, 62-81, dean eng, 66-76, EMER DISTINGUISHED PROF ELEC & COMPUT ENG, LEHIGH UNIV, 81-, EMER DEAN 81- *Personal Data:* b Istanbul, Turkey, June 14, 14; nat US; m 45; c 1. *Educ:* Duke Univ, BS, 37; Univ Pa, MS, 38. *Hon Degrees:* DEng, Lehigh Univ, 71. *Honors & Awards:* Noble Robinson Award, Lehigh Univ, 48, Hillman Award, 63 & 80; Distinguished Engr Award, Nat Soc Prof Engrs, 65; Centennial Award, Inst Elec & Electronics Engrs, 84. *Prof Exp:* Instr, Univ Pa, 38-40; with Am TV Inc, Ill, 40-42; ed dir, 6th Serv Comn, Signal Corps Radar Sch, 42-44; instr & proj engr, Moore Sch Elec Eng, Univ Pa, 44-46. *Concurrent Pos:* Consult, Bell Tel Labs, NY, 50-55; proj engr, Signal Corps, 50-54, proj dir, 54-61; mem hon adv bd, Pergamon Inst; mem, Nat Accreditation Coun Eng Cols; consult, Dept Educ, Commonwealth of PR, 72-76 & Gen State Authority, Commonwealth of Pa, 74-77; resident consult, Int Bus Mach, 80- *Mem:* Fel Inst Elec & Electronics Engrs. *Res:* Electrical networks; microwaves; transmission line theory; filter networks. *Mailing Add:* Packard Lab Bldg 19 IBM Lehigh Univ Col Engr & Phys Sci Bethlehem PA 18015

KARAKASHIAN, ARAM SIMON, SOLID STATE PHYSICS, OPTICAL DEVICES. *Current Pos:* From asst prof to assoc prof, 70-82, chmn, 87-93, ASST CHMN, DEPT PHYSICS & APPL PHYSICS, UNIV MASS, LOWELL, 93-, PROF PHYSICS, 82- *Personal Data:* b Philadelphia, Pa, Nov 16, 39; m 75, Barbara Burke; c John & Elizabeth. *Educ:* Temple Univ, BA, 61, MA, 63; Univ Md, PhD(physics), 70. *Concurrent Pos:* Chmn, NEng Sect, Am Phys Soc, 93-94. *Mem:* Am Phys Soc; Sigma Xi; Mat Res Soc. *Res:* Optical properties of metals and semiconductors; surface plasma oscillations; photonic and optoelectronic devices. *Mailing Add:* Dept Physics & Appl Physics Univ Mass Lowell MA 01854. *Fax:* 978-934-3068; *E-Mail:* karakasha@woods.uml.edu

KARAKAWA, WALTER WATARU, capsular polysaccharides; deceased, see previous edition for last biography

KARAL, FRANK CHARLES, JR, APPLIED MATHEMATICS. *Current Pos:* post doctoral fel (math), 57-59, assoc res scientist, Courant Inst Math Sci, 59-61, from asst prof to assoc prof, 61-70, PROF MATH, NY UNIV, 71-, UNDERGRAD CHMN DEPT, 85- *Personal Data:* b Philadelphia, Pa, Aug 3, 26. *Educ:* Univ Colo, BS, 46; Univ Tex, Austin, PhD(physics), 50. *Prof Exp:* Res physicist, Defense Res Lab, 49-50; res engr, Hughes Aircraft Co, 50-51; res physicist, Defense Res Lab, 51-52; sr res technologist, Mobil Oil Corp, 52-57. *Concurrent Pos:* Geophysics consult. *Mem:* Am Math Soc; Am Phys Soc; Am Geophys Union. *Res:* Geophysics; electromagnetic theory; computer assisted instruction. *Mailing Add:* Buckner Village No 10-B 7111 Alabama St El Paso TX 79904-3905

KARALIS, JOHN PETER, COMPUTER SCIENCES. *Current Pos:* SR VPRES CORP DEVELOP, TEKTRONIX INC, 92- *Personal Data:* b Minneapolis, Minn, July 6, 38; m 63, Mary Curtis; c Amy Curtis & Theodore Curtis. *Educ:* Univ Minn, BA, 60, JD, 63. *Prof Exp:* Pvt pract, Minneapolis, 63-70 & 83-85; assoc gen coun, Honeywell Inc, 70-83, vpres, 82-83; sr vpres & gen coun, Sperry Corp, 85-87; vpres & gen coun, Apple Computer Inc, 87-89; off coun, Brown & Bain, 89-92. *Concurrent Pos:* Bd dirs, Sony, Tektronix Corp; mem bd adv, Ctr Study Law, Sci & Technol, Ariz State Univ Col Law, Tempe, 83-, adj prof, 90-91. *Mailing Add:* 7878-66E Gainey Ranch Rd Scottsdale AZ 85258-1754

KARAM, JIM DANIEL, MOLECULAR GENETICS, BIOCHEMISTRY. *Current Pos:* PROF & CHMN BIOCHEM, TULANE UNIV, 91- *Personal Data:* b Kumasi, Ghana. *Educ:* Am Univ Beirut, BS, 58; Univ NC, PhD(biochem), 65. *Prof Exp:* Res asst biochem, Am Univ Beirut, 59-60; res asst prof, Genetics & Cell Biol Sect, Univ Conn, 67-68; res assoc, Sloan-Kettering Inst Cancer Res, 68-71; from assoc prof to prof biochem, Med Univ SC, 71-91. *Concurrent Pos:* USPHS fel, Cold Spring Harbor Lab Quant Biol, 65-67; USPHS res career develop award, 74- *Mem:* Genetics Soc Am; Am Soc Biol Chemists; Am Soc Microbiol. *Res:* Genetic control of DNA replication of phage T4. *Mailing Add:* Dept Biochem Tulane Univ Med Ctr 1430 Tulane Ave New Orleans LA 70112-2699. *Fax:* 504-584-1611

KARAM, JOHN HARVEY, ENDOCRINOLOGY. *Current Pos:* res fel, 60-63, asst prof, 63-74, ASSOC PROF INTERNAL MED, UNIV CALIF, SAN FRANCISCO, 74- *Personal Data:* b Shreveport, La, July 20, 29; m 55; c 2. *Educ:* St Louis Univ, BS, 49; Tulane Univ, MD, 53. *Prof Exp:* Resident physician internal med, Bronx Vet Admin Hosp, Bronx, NY, 54-56; res fel endocrinol, Hammersmith Hosp, London, Eng, 59-60. *Concurrent Pos:* Fulbright vis prof, Univ Baghdad, 65-67. *Mem:* Endocrine Soc; Am Fedn Clin Res; Am Diabetes Asn; Am Col Physicians. *Res:* Diabetes mellitus, particularly relating to disorders of insulin secretion; obesity and factors relating to insulin insensitivity; hypoglycemia and its management. *Mailing Add:* 1141 HSW Box 0540 Univ Calif San Francisco CA 94143

KARAM, RATIB A(BRAHAM), NUCLEAR ENGINEERING, MATHEMATICS. *Current Pos:* PROF NUCLEAR ENG, GA INST TECHNOL, 72- *Personal Data:* b Miniara, Lebanon, Mar 8, 34; US citizen; m 60; c 1. *Educ:* Univ Fla, BChE, 58, MSE, 60, PhD(nuclear eng), 63. *Prof Exp:* Res asst nuclear field, Fla, 58-63; asst nuclear engr, Argonne Nat Lab, 63-67, assoc nuclear engr, 67-72. *Mem:* Am Nuclear Soc; Am Phys Soc. *Res:* Fast reactor physics; neutron transport; alternate fuel cycles; new breeder concepts and heterogeneity effects. *Mailing Add:* 2415 Ashbourne Dr Lawrenceville GA 30243

KARAS, JAMES GLYNN, HORTICULTURE, BIOLOGY. *Current Pos:* ASSOC PROF BIOL SCI, YOUNGSTOWN STATE UNIV, 69- *Personal Data:* b Chicago, Ill, Feb 24, 33. *Educ:* Univ Ill, BS, 56; Mich State Univ, MS, 58, PhD(hort, bot), 62. *Prof Exp:* Teaching asst hort, Mich State Univ, 56-61, res assoc biochem, hort & bot, 62-64, asst prof natural sci, 64-67; asst prof hort, NMex State Univ, 67-69. *Mem:* Am Soc Hort Sci; Am Inst Biol Sci. *Res:* Plant physiology; grauperceptions in plants; natural products; electron microscopy; plant nutrition; seed germination. *Mailing Add:* Dept Biol Sci Youngstown State Univ 410 Wick Ave Youngstown OH 44555-0001

KARAS, JOHN ATHAN, SCIENCE COMMUNICATIONS. *Current Pos:* PRES, JONATHAN KARAS & ASSOCS, 60-; PRES, SCI HOUSE, 65- *Personal Data:* b Lebanon, Pa, Apr 7, 22; m 58, Marion L Vanderyn; c Maria L & Anthony J. *Educ:* Lehigh Univ, BS, 43, MS, 47. *Hon Degrees:* DSc, Lowell Tech Inst, 60. *Honors & Awards:* Bausch & Lomb Sci Medal. *Prof Exp:* Instr physics, Lehigh Univ, 43-44, 45-50, Manhattan Proj, 44-45; asst prof, Univ NH, 51-57. *Concurrent Pos:* Sci dir, WBZ-TV, Boston, Mass; asst, USAF Cambridge Res Ctr, 43-44; res proj dir, Univ NH; consult commun of sci & technol; pres, Neutral Territory, 83- *Mem:* AAAS; Am Phys Soc; Am Asn Physics Teachers. *Res:* Accident reconstruction; science and information films and television programs; science museum design and concepts. *Mailing Add:* 216 Summer St Manchester MA 01944

KARASAKI, SHUICHI, DEVELOPMENTAL BIOLOGY, ARTHRITIS. *Current Pos:* MEM STAFF, KORIYAMA INST MED IMMUNOL, JAPAN, 84- *Personal Data:* b Kure, Japan, Nov 27, 31; m 61, Taeko Yamamoto; c Taro. *Educ:* Nagoya Univ, Japan, BSc, 54, MSc, 56, PhD(biol), 59. *Prof Exp:* Asst prof chem, Col Gen Educ, Nagoya Univ, 59-61; vis investr, Biol Div, Oak Ridge Nat Lab, Tenn, 61-65; staff mem, Putnam Mem Hosp Inst Med Res, Bennington, Vt, 65; mem staff, Montreal Cancer Inst, Notre Dame Hosp, 65-79 & Dept Pathol, Chiba Cancer Ctr, Res Inst, Japan, 79-84. *Concurrent Pos:* From assoc prof to prof anat, Univ Montreal, 68-79; res assoc, Nat Cancer Inst Can, 70-79. *Mem:* Soc Develop Biol; Am Soc Cell Biol; Am Asn Cancer Res; Int Soc Differentiation; NY Acad Sci; AAAS; Histochem Soc; Micros Soc Am. *Res:* Immunocytochemistry of human tissue cells in culture; cell biology of arthritis; cancer. *Mailing Add:* Koriyama Inst Med Immunol 2-11-1 Zukei Koriyama 963 Japan

KARASEK, FRANCIS WARREN, ANALYTICAL CHEMISTRY. *Current Pos:* PROF CHEM, UNIV WATERLOO, 68- *Personal Data:* b Council Bluffs, Iowa, Dec 11, 19; m 42; c 7. *Educ:* Elmhurst Col, BS, 42; Ore State Col, PhD(chem), 52. *Prof Exp:* Sr chemist, Res & Develop Labs, Pure Oil Co, 42-48; mgr instrument develop, Phillips Petrol Co, 51-68. *Mem:* Am Chem Soc; Am Soc Mass Spectrometry. *Res:* Mass spectroscopy; chromatography; analytical instrumentation; ion mobility spectrometry; environmental sciences. *Mailing Add:* 26209 S Nottingham Dr Sun Lakes AZ 85248-9287

KARASEK, MARVIN A, BIOCHEMISTRY. *Current Pos:* asst prof, 60-68, assoc prof biochem & res dermat, 68-85, PROF BIOCHEM IN DERMAT, SCH MED, STANFORD UNIV, 86- *Personal Data:* b Chicago, Ill, Mar 8, 31. *Educ:* Purdue Univ, BS, 53; Univ Calif, PhD(biochem), 56. *Prof Exp:* Asst prof biochem, Tufts Univ, 57-60. *Concurrent Pos:* Boston Med Found fel, 58-61. *Mem:* AAAS; Soc Invest Dermat; Soc Cell Biol. *Res:* Protein synthesis; nucleotide metabolism; biochemistry of virus infections; blood vessel metabolism; sebaceous gland metabolism. *Mailing Add:* Dept Dermat Stanford Univ Palo Alto CA 94305

KARASZ, FRANK ERWIN, POLYMER SCIENCE, BIOPHYSICAL CHEMISTRY. *Current Pos:* assoc prof, Univ Mass, 67-71, co-dir Mat Res Lab, 73-85, prof polymer sci & eng, 71-86, SILVIO O CONTE PROF, UNIV MASS, AMHERST, 92- *Personal Data:* b Vienna, Austria, July 23, 33; c 2. *Educ:* Univ London, BSc, 54, DSc(chem), 72; Univ Wash, PhD(phys chem), 58. *Honors & Awards:* Mettler Award, NAm Thermal Analysis Soc, 75; High Polymer Physics Prize, Am Phys Soc, 84. *Prof Exp:* Fel, Univ Ore, 58-59; sr res fel, Basic Physics Div, Nat Phys Lab, Eng, 59-61; res chemist, Gen Elec Co, 61-67. *Concurrent Pos:* Adj prof mat sci, Eng Dept, Univ Fla. *Mem:* Nat Acad Eng; Am Phys Soc; Am Chem Soc. *Res:* Physical chemistry of polymers; thermodynamics and statistical thermodynamics of liquids; biological macromolecules. *Mailing Add:* Dept Polymer Sci & Eng Univ Mass Amherst MA 01003. *Fax:* 413-253-5295

KARATZAS, IOANNIS, STOCHASTIC PROCESSES & CONTROL. *Current Pos:* asst prof, 80-83, ASSOC PROF MATH STATIST, COLUMBIA UNIV, 83- *Personal Data:* b Kallithea, Greece, May 29, 51; m 75. *Educ:* Nat Tech Univ Athens, dipl, 75; Columbia Univ, MSc, 76, PhD(math statist), 80. *Prof Exp:* Vis asst prof appl math, Brown Univ, 79-80. *Concurrent Pos:* Vis scientist, MIT, 84-85. *Mem:* Sigma Xi; Inst Math Statist; Inst Elec & Electronics Engrs. *Mailing Add:* 448 Riverside Dr New York NY 10027

KARAVOLAS, HARRY J, BIOCHEMISTRY NEUROSTEROIDS & HORMONE BIOCHEMISTRY. *Current Pos:* from asst prof to assoc prof, 68-75, PROF BIOMOLECULAR CHEM & CHMN DEPT, SCH MED, UNIV WIS-MADISON, 75- *Personal Data:* b Peabody, Mass, Feb 21, 36; m 62, Barbara Katsaras; c Chris. *Educ:* Mass Col Pharm, BS, 57, MS, 59; St Louis Univ, PhD(biochem), 63. *Prof Exp:* Res fel biol chem, Harvard Med Sch, 63-66, res assoc & tutor biochem sci, Harvard Univ, 66-68. *Concurrent Pos:* vis lectr biol chem, Harvard Univ Med Sch, 75; vis prof, London Univ, Ludwig, Cancer Inst, 84; Chair basic sci, Univ Wis Sch Med, 89- *Mem:* AAAS; Am Chem Soc; Am Soc Biol Chem; Soc Neurosci; Endocrine Soc. *Res:* Mechanism of action of steroid hormones; steroid metabolic patterns in neural and pituitary tissues; enzymology. *Mailing Add:* Dept Biomolecular Chem Sch Med Univ Wis 1300 University Ave Madison WI 53706. *Fax:* 608-262-5253

KARAYANNIS, NICHOLAS M, INORGANIC CHEMISTRY. *Current Pos:* res chemist to sr res chemist, 70-76, Amoco Chem Co, 70-72, res assoc, 76-88, SR RES ASSOC, AMOCO CHEM CO, 88- *Personal Data:* b Athens, Greece, May 30, 31; m 55; c 2. *Educ:* Nat Tech Univ Athens, BS, 55; Univ London, PhD(chem), 60. *Prof Exp:* Sci collabr, Hellenic Nat Defense Gen Staff, 61-62 & Greek Ministry of Coord, 62-65; NIH res fel anal chem, Johns Hopkins Univ, 65-67; US Army Edgewood Arsenal res fel inorg chem, Drexel Univ, 67-70. *Mem:* AAAS; Am Chem Soc; NY Acad Sci; Greek Tech Chamber. *Res:* Coordination chemistry; metal complexes of neutral and acidic phosphoryl ligands and aromatic amine oxides; catalysis; catalysts for olefin polymerization; analytical chemistry, high pressure gas chromatography; organic chemistry, redox systems; bioinorganic chemistry. *Mailing Add:* 15 Pebblewood Trail Naperville IL 60563-9060

KARCHER, GUIDO GEORGE, CODES & STANDARDS FOR PRESSURE EQUIPMENT, PRESSURE VESSEL TANKAGE & PIPING DESIGN. *Current Pos:* CONSULT ENGR, 94- *Personal Data:* b Brookly, NY, Oct 20, 34; m 61, Patricia A Ennis; c Carol A, Maureen P & Richard T. *Educ:* Pratt Inst, BME, 60; Rensselaer Polytech Inst, MSME, 64. *Honors & Awards:* J Hall Taylor Medal, Am Soc Mech Engrs, 95. *Prof Exp:* Sr engr, Exxon Res & Eng Co, 66-75, eng assoc, 75-80, sr eng assoc, 80-89, eng adv, 89-94. *Concurrent Pos:* Chmn, Comt Pressure Vessels & Tanks, Am Petrol Inst, 82-88; vchmn, Boiler & Pressure Vessel Main Comt, Am Soc Mech Engrs, 92-; chmn, Pressure Vessel Res Coun, 94- *Mem:* Am Petrol Inst; fel Am Soc Mech Engrs; Am Welding Soc. *Res:* Developed several unique designs for heavy wall pressure vessels, high temperature valves and storage tanks; developed design criteria for steels in the creep range and the design of thin wall expansion joints. *Mailing Add:* 38 N Boom Way Little Egg Harbor NJ 08087-2312. *Fax:* 609-294-2686; *E-Mail:* ggkaacher@aol.com

KARCHER, RAYMOND, ANALYTICAL INSTRUMENTATION FOR THE CLINICAL LABORATORY, PROCESS AUTOMATION. *Current Pos:* CLIN CHEMIST, WILLIAM BEAUMONT HOSP, 70- *Personal Data:* b Corpus Christi, Tex, Dec 31, 43. *Educ:* John Carroll Univ, BS, 65; Purdue Univ, PhD(anal chem), 71. *Concurrent Pos:* Adj asst prof electronics, Wayne State Univ, 71-86; inspector, Lab Improvement Prog, Col Am Pathol, 80-; adj assoc prof, Clin Lab Instrumentation, Oakland Univ, 90- *Mem:* Am Asn Clin Chem; Am Chem Soc; Am Soc Clin Pathologists; Clin Lab Mgt Asn. *Res:* Techniques for separation of isoenzymes using electrophoretic or chromatographic methods and in automating laboratory processes for high volume testing. *Mailing Add:* 35213 Glengary Circle Farmington Hills MI 48331. *Fax:* 248-551-3694; *E-Mail:* rkascher@smtpgw.beaumont.edu

KARCHMER, JEAN HERSCHEL, ANALYTICAL CHEMISTRY. *Current Pos:* RETIRED. *Personal Data:* b Dallas, Tex, Dec 28, 14; m 39; c 2. *Educ:* Southern Methodist Univ, BS, 36. *Prof Exp:* Jr engr, Dept Agr, Tex, 38; chief chemist, Nat Chemsearch Co, 39-42; asst chemist, Tenn Valley Authority, Ala, 42-44; sr analyst & res chemist, Humble Oil & Refining Co, 44-50, sr res chemist, 50-55, res specialist, 55-63, res assoc, 63-77, consult anal chem, Exxon Res & Eng Co, 78-84. *Concurrent Pos:* Consult chemist, 84- *Mem:* Am Chem Soc. *Res:* Analytical chemistry of sulfur compounds; analysis of petroleum, coal, polymers; elemental analysis; polarography. *Mailing Add:* 3018 Castlewood Houston TX 77025-3216

KARCZMAR, ALEXANDER GEORGE, PHARMACOLOGY, PHYSIOLOGY. *Current Pos:* prof pharmacol & exp therapeut & chmn dept, Stritch Sch Med, Loyola Univ, 56-85, sr co-dir, Inst Mind, Drugs & Behav, 65-85, assoc dean, grad sch traing, 81-86, assoc dean res, 82-86, EMER PROF, LOYOLA UNIV, 86- *Personal Data:* b Warsaw, Poland, May 9, 18; nat US; m 46; c 2. *Educ:* Warsaw & Free Polish Univ, Med Sci, 39; Columbia Univ, MA, 41, PhD(biophysics, embryol), 46. *Honors & Awards:* Sixth Ann Carl F Schmidt Hon Lectr, Philadelphia, 81; Otto Loewi Lectr, Ix Int Symp on Cholinergic Syst, Ger, 95. *Prof Exp:* Res fel, Amherst Col, 44-45; teaching fel, Columbia Univ, 45-46; from instr to assoc prof pharmacol, Sch Med, Georgetown Univ, 46-53; assoc mem, Sterling-Winthrop Res Inst, 53-56. *Concurrent Pos:* Am Philos Soc grant, NY Univ, 42-44; NIH grants, 47-85; consult, Emerson Drug Co, 52, Melpar Inc, 57-60, Hines Vet Admin Hosp, 57-, Ill State Psychiat Inst, 60-, US Army Res Develop Co, 80-, US Defense Off 80-85, Inst Biol Sci, Nat Acad Sci, 85- & Off Surgeon Gen, 87-; Guggenheim fel, 68-69; mem, Pharmacol Sect, NIH, 68-72, Multi Sclerosis Study Sect, 72-74 & Alzheimer Dis Study Sect, 83; vis prof, Sorbonne, Paris, 69 & 75 & Polish Acad Sci, 79; mem nat toxicol panel, Nat Res Coun, 80, toxicol comt, Nat Acad Sci, 81; hon prof, Kurume Univ, 80-; sr Fulbright scholar, 87-88; actg med dir, Found 41, Australia, 88-89; health specialist, Hines Vet Admin Hosp, Ill, 96-; co-dir res initiative, Am Vets Reactivation Ctr, Ill, 96- *Mem:* AAAS; Am Soc Pharmacol & Exp Therapeut; Soc Exp Biol & Med; fel Am Col Neuropsychopharmacol; Int Brain Res Orgn; Soc Neurosci. *Res:* Physiology and pharmacology of synaptic transmission; cholinesterases and anticholinesterase drugs; cholinergic system, its role in transmission, development, trophic phenomena, teratology, aging, and behavior; neuropsychopharmacology; author of over 400 publications. *Mailing Add:* Res Serv 2160 Edward Hines Jr Vet Admin Hosp Hines IL 60141. *Fax:* 708-216-2319

KARDAMI, ELISSAVET, MUSCLE CELL BIOLOGY, CARDIAC MUSCLE CELL BIOLOGY. *Current Pos:* asst prof, 87-92, ASSOC PROF CELL BIOL, UNIV MAN, 92- *Personal Data:* b Corinth, Greece, Jan 4, 52. *Educ:* Univ Athens, Greece, dipl, 75; King's Col, London, PhD(cell biophys), 79. *Prof Exp:* Res fel, Inst de Pasteur, 80-83 & Univ Calif, Berkeley, 83-86. *Mem:* Soc Cell Biol; Int Soc Heart Res. *Res:* Muscle cell biology; cardiac muscle cell biology. *Mailing Add:* Univ Man, St Boniface Gen Hosp Res Ctr 351 Tache Ave Winnipeg MB R2H 2A6 Can. *Fax:* 204-233-6723

KARDOS, GEZA, MECHANICAL ENGINEERING. *Current Pos:* prof, 71-96, EMER PROF ENG & CONSULT, CARLETON UNIV, 96- *Personal Data:* b Tolna, Hungary, Mar 2, 26; Can citizen; m 49; c 3. *Educ:* Univ Sask, BSc, 48; McGill Univ, ME, 57, PhD(mech eng), 65. *Honors & Awards:* Fred Merryfield Design Award, Am Soc Eng Educ, 83. *Prof Exp:* Jr res officer fire hazards, Nat Res Coun Can, 48-50; proj engr, Tamper Ltd, 50-54; proj engr, Aviation Elec Ltd, 54-56, eng supvr, 56-62, staff engr, 65-66; site mgr, HARP, McGill Univ, 62-63; assoc prof design, McMaster Univ, 66-71. *Concurrent Pos:* Assoc dir res, Ctr Appl Res & Eng Design, McMaster Univ, 67-69; vis prof, Royal Col Arts; consult, Vitro-Tech, Monterey, Mex, 80-82; vis scholar, Univ Stellenbosch, SA; consult, Nat Res Coun, Can Energy Group, 83-84, BBC Eng Res Ltd, 86 & Elma Eng Serv, 87-; vis assoc prof, Stanford Univ, 71; Wighton fel, 92. *Mem:* Fel Am Soc Mech Engrs; Am Soc Eng Educ. *Res:* Mechanical pressure elements; high strain rates; design and computer aided design; case method of engineering teaching; metal physics; fracture mechanics; creative problem solving; systematic design. *Mailing Add:* Eng Fac Carleton Univ Ottawa ON K1S 5B6 Can. *E-Mail:* geza_kardos@carleton.ca

KARDOS, JOHN LOUIS, COMPOSITE MATERIALS, POLYMER SCIENCE. *Current Pos:* from asst prof to assoc prof, Wash Univ, 65-74, dir, Mat Res Lab, 70-91, chmn, Mat Sci & Eng Prog, 71-91, prof, 74-93, actg chmn, 77-78, CHMN CHEM ENG, WASH UNIV, 91-, FRANCIS F AHMANN PROF CHEM ENG, 93- *Personal Data:* b Colfax, Wash, Apr 19, 39; m 66, Janice M Sega; c Joseph, Joanna & Gina. *Educ:* Pa State Univ, BS, 61; Univ Ill, MS, 62; Case Inst Technol, PhD(polymer physics), 65. *Honors & Awards:* Mat Eng & Sci Div Award, Am Inst Chem Engrs, 81. *Concurrent Pos:* Chmn, Gordon Conf on Composite Mat, 83. *Mem:* Am Chem Soc; Soc Rheology; Am Phys Soc; Am Inst Chem Engrs; Soc Plastics Engrs; Soc Advan Mat Process Eng. *Res:* Chemistry, physics and processing science of composite materials; structure-property relations in reinforced plastics; process modelling for composite materials; materials characterization techniques. *Mailing Add:* Campus Box 1198 St Louis MO 63130. *Fax:* 314-935-7211

KARDOS, OTTO, CHEMISTRY. *Current Pos:* res assoc, 64-69, sr res assoc, 69-72, CONSULT, M&T CHEM INC, 72- *Personal Data:* b Vienna, Austria, Feb 7, 07; nat US; m 30; c 1. *Educ:* Univ Vienna, PhD(chem), 32. *Honors & Awards:* Heussner Award, Am Electroplaters Soc, 56-57. *Prof Exp:* Electrochemist, Galvapol, Vienna, 35-38; electroplating consult, France, 38-42; res electrochemist, Conmar Prod, NJ, 43-44; res electrochemist, Hanson-Van Winkle-Munning Co, 44-52, chief res electrochemist, 53-58, sr scientist, 58-64. *Mem:* Am Chem Soc; Electrochem Soc; Am Electroplaters Soc. *Res:* Electrodeposition of metals. *Mailing Add:* 10004 Vernon Ave Huntington Woods MI 48070

KARECKI, DAVID RALPH, PHYSICS, INFRARED & NEAR INFRARED SPECTROSCOPIES. *Current Pos:* SCIENTIST, UNISEARCH ASSOCS INC, 84- *Personal Data:* b Chicago, Ill, May 29, 46; Can citizen; m 86, Kathryn Mahony. *Educ:* Mich State Univ, BS, 68; Simon Fraser Univ, MSc, 72, PhD(physics), 80. *Prof Exp:* Postdoctoral, Emory Univ, 80-83. *Res:* Trace gas monitoring with infrared and near infrared spectroscopy. *Mailing Add:* 1043 Royal York Rd Etobicoke ON M8X 2G5 Can. *Fax:* 905-669-8652; *E-Mail:* karecki@interlog.com

KAREEM, AHSAN, PROBABILISTIC DYNAMICS, STRUCTURAL ENGINEERING. *Current Pos:* PROF CIVIL ENG, UNIV NOTRE DAME, 90- *Personal Data:* b Lahore, Pakistan, Sept 29, 47; m; c 2. *Educ:* WPakistan Univ Eng & Technol, BSc, 68; Univ Hawaii, Honolulu, MSc, 75; Colo State Univ, PhD(civil eng), 78. *Prof Exp:* Design engr, Harza Eng Co Int, Pakistan, 68-71; res assoc, Colo State Univ, 77-78; from asst prof to prof civil eng, Univ Houston, 78-90. *Concurrent Pos:* Gen consult, Aerovironment Inc, 79-; pres young investr, White House Off Sci & Technol, NSF, 83. *Mem:* Am Soc Civil Engrs; Sigma Xi; Am Inst Aeronaut & Astronaut. *Res:* Analysis and design of civil engineering and ocean engineering structures subjected to stochastic excitation due to wind, waves and earthquakes; reliability based design and digital simulation of civil engineering systems; design of vibration mitigation devices; wind energy. *Mailing Add:* 51875 Quail Valley Dr Granger IN 46530

KAREIVA, PETER MICHAEL, INSECT POPULATION BIOLOGY, AGRICULTURAL ECOLOGY. *Current Pos:* PROF, DEPT ZOOL, UNIV WASH, SEATTLE; ASST PROF THEORET ECOL & MATH MODELLING, BROWN UNIV, 81- *Personal Data:* b Utica, NY, Sept 20, 51. *Educ:* Duke Univ, BS, 73; Univ Calif, Irvine, MS, 76; Cornell Univ, PhD(ecol & evolution), 81. *Prof Exp:* Lectr environ biol, Calif State Univ, Los Angeles, 76. *Mem:* Ecol Soc Am; Entom Soc Am. *Res:* Population biology of herbivorous insects; mathematical models of insect dispersal; the influence of vegetation texture on herbivore dynamics. *Mailing Add:* Zool Dept NJ-15 Univ Wash 3900 Seventh Ave NE Seattle WA 98195-0001

KAREL, KARIN JOHNSON, ORGANOMETALLIC CHEMISTRY. *Current Pos:* CHEMIST, CENT RES & DEVELOP, E I DU PONT DE NEMOURS & CO, 80- *Personal Data:* b Portland, Ore, Aug 9, 50; m 72; c 3. *Educ:* Univ Chicago, BS, 72; Princeton Univ, MA, 74, PhD(chem), 78. *Prof Exp:* NSF fel, Univ Ill, 78-79. *Mem:* Am Chem Soc. *Res:* Organometallic reagents for organic synthesis; preparation and characterization of novel organometallic species. *Mailing Add:* 104 Country Club Dr Wilmington DE 19803-2918

KAREL, MARCUS, FOOD SCIENCE, CHEMICAL ENGINEERING. *Current Pos:* res assoc food tech, Mass Inst Technol, 57-61, from asst prof to prof food eng, 61-88, head, Dept Nutrit Food Sci, 74-79, prof chem & food eng, 88-89, EMER PROF CHEM ENG, MASS INST TECHNOL, 89- *Personal Data:* b Lwow, Poland, May 17, 28; US citizen; m 58; c 4. *Educ:* Boston Univ, AB, 55; Mass Inst Technol, PhD, 60. *Hon Degrees:* ScD, Technion Israel Inst Technol, Haifa, Israel, 91. *Honors & Awards:* William V Cruess Award, Inst Food Technol, 70, Nicholas Appert Medal, 86-; Food Eng Award, Am Soc Agr Engrs & Dairy & Food Industs Supply Asn, 78. *Concurrent Pos:* Consult var food & chem co, 60-; distinguished vis prof, Rutgers Univ, 86-; prof food sci, State NJ, Rutgers Univ, 89-96. *Mem:* Nat Acad Sci Arg; fel Inst Food Technol; fel Brit Inst Food Sci & Technol; NY Acad Sci; Am Inst Chem Eng; hon fel Int Asn Eng & Food; Am Chem Soc. *Res:* Food engineering; autoxidation of lipids; diffusion of gases and vapors through polymeric membranes; physicochemical properties of foods; heat and mass transfer aspects of food processing; controlled drug release. *Mailing Add:* Mass Inst Technol Rm 66-468 Cambridge MA 02160. *E-Mail:* karel@highway1.com

KAREL, MARTIN LEWIS, NUMBER THEORY. *Current Pos:* asst prof, 80-83, ASSOC PROF, RUTGERS UNIV, CAMDEN COL ARTS & SCI, 83- *Personal Data:* b Baltimore, Md, Mar 15, 44; m 72; c 3. *Educ:* Johns Hopkins Univ, BA, 66; Univ Chicago, MA, 67, PhD(math), 72. *Prof Exp:* Asst math, Inst Advan Study, Princeton Univ, 72-73, mem, 73-74; asst prof math, Univ NC, Chapel Hill, 74-80. *Concurrent Pos:* NSF fel, 75-80 & 81-86; res assoc, Univ Ill, Urbana-Champaign, 79; mem, Inst Advan Study, Princeton, 83. *Mem:* Am Math Soc. *Res:* Arithmetical theory of automorphic forms. *Mailing Add:* Camden Col Arts & Sci Dept Math Rutgers Univ Camden NJ 08102. *E-Mail:* karel@camden.rutgers.edu

KARFAKIS, MARIO GEORGE, ROCK MASS CHARACTERIZATION, MINE SUBSIDENCE. *Current Pos:* asst prof, 88-93, ASSOC PROF MINING ENG, VA POLYTECH INST & STATE UNIV, 93- *Personal Data:* b Iskenderun, Turkey, Sept 12, 50; m 83, Diane Stearns; c 2. *Educ:* Univ Grenoble, France, BS, 75; Univ Wis-Madison, MS, 78, PhD(mining eng), 83. *Prof Exp:* Res asst rock mech, Univ Wis, 76 & 78-79, res assoc, 77 & teaching asst mining eng, 80-83; asst prof mining eng, Univ Wyo, 83-88. *Concurrent Pos:* Consult, Chrome-Alloy Eng Instrumentation Wastewater Treatment plant, 78, site eval, Wash, Rockwell Int, 80 & DEQ Subsidence Eval, Wyo, 85, 87, 88. *Mem:* Instrument Soc Am; Int Soc Rock Mech; Sigma Xi; assoc mem Am Inst Mining, Metall & Petrol Engrs. *Res:* Rock fracture mechanics; effects of aqueous environment on fracturing; rock fragmentation; coal mine ground control; insitu stress determination. *Mailing Add:* 2107 Broken Oak Dr Blacksburg VA 24060. *Fax:* 540-231-4070; *E-Mail:* mario@vtvm1

KARG, GERHART, PHYSICAL CHEMISTRY, COSMETIC CHEMISTRY. *Current Pos:* mgr cosmetic & treat prod, 92-93, mgr treatment prod, 94-96, MGR FRAGRANCE & TOILETRIES PROD, BENCKISER, 96- *Personal Data:* b New York, NY, Jan 21, 36; m 66, Barbara Coyle; c Kathryn, Janet, Lawrence, Michael & Sharon. *Educ:* Manhattan Col, BS, 57; Polytech Inst Brooklyn, PhD(phys chem), 63. *Prof Exp:* Res chemist, M W Kellogg Co, 62-64; res chemist, Ultra Chem Co Div, Witco Chem Co, 64-69; develop chemist, Avon Prod Inc, 69-70, sr phys chemist, 71-78, sr develop chemist, 78-88; sr prod develop chemist, Pfizer, Inc, 88-90, mgr cosmetic & treat prod, Coty Res & Develop, 90-92. *Mem:* Soc Cosmetic Chemists. *Res:* Photochemistry; surface chemistry; hair properties; skin care. *Mailing Add:* Benckiser Int Develop Ctr 410 American Rd Morris Plains NJ 07950-2451

KARGER, BARRY LLOYD, ANALYTICAL CHEMISTRY. *Current Pos:* From asst prof to assoc prof, 63-72, PROF CHEM, NORTHEASTERN UNIV, 72-, DIR, BARNETT INST CHEM ANALYSIS & MAT SCI, 73-, JAMES L WATER PROF ANALYTICAL CHEM, 85- *Personal Data:* b Boston, Mass, Apr 2, 39; m 61; c 2. *Educ:* Mass Inst Technol, BS, 60; Cornell Univ, PhD(anal chem), 63. *Honors & Awards:* Gulf Res Award, 71; Steven Dal Nogare Mem Award, Delaware Valley Chromatog Form, 75; Chromatography Award, Am Chem Soc, 82; Tswett Mem Medal, USSR, 80; Tswett Medal, USA, 87; Fisher Award, Am Chem Soc, 89; Martin Medal, 90. *Concurrent Pos:* NIH res grant, 69-; NSF res grant, 66-85; Fed Water Pollution Control Admin res grant, 67-70; Off Naval Res grants, 69-74; sci adv, Food & Drug Admin, 73-76; consult, Technicon Instruments Corp, 77-82, Cambridge Anal, 85-87, Beckman 88-, Genentech 87- *Mem:* Fel AAAS; Am Chem Soc; NY Acad Sci; Sigma Xi. *Res:* High performance liquid chromatography; biochemical applications of high performance liquid chromatography; fundamentals of biopolymer separations; capillary electrophoresis, sequencing, electrophoresis and mass spectrometry; separation science. *Mailing Add:* 341 Mugar Bldg Northeastern Univ 360 Huntington Ave Boston MA 02115-5005. *Fax:* 617-373-2855

KARGL, THOMAS E, BIOCHEMISTRY. *Current Pos:* From asst prof to assoc prof, 59-70, head dept, 64-68, PROF CHEM, BELLARMINE COL, 70- *Personal Data:* b Des Plaines, Ill, Feb 25, 32; m 57; c 8. *Educ:* St Ambrose Col, BA, 54; Purdue Univ, MS, 56, PhD(biochem), 59. *Mem:* Sigma Xi. *Res:* Carotenoid pigments of tomatoes; Lewis acid catalyzed reactions of methyl vinyl ketone; structure determination of complex polyenes; slow release fertilizers. *Mailing Add:* Chem Dept Bellarmine Col 2001 Newburg Rd Louisville KY 40205-1863

KARI, LILA, THEORY & DNA COMPUTING, FORMAL LANGUAGES. *Current Pos:* vis prof, 93-96, ASST PROF COMPUT SCI, UNIV WESTERN ONT, 96- *Personal Data:* b Tulcea, Romania, Oct 22, 64. *Educ:* Univ Bucharest, Romania, MSc, 87; Univ Turku, Finland, PhD(math & comput sci), 91. *Prof Exp:* Researcher, Inst Informatics, Romania, 87-90; Acad Finland, 90-93. *Mem:* Asn Comput Mach; Can Math Soc; Europ Asn Theoret Comput Sci. *Res:* DNA computing, solving computational problems by solely manipulating DNA strands in test tubes; finding a mathematical model of DNA computing and experimentally solving hard mathematical problems using molecular biology tools. *Mailing Add:* Dept Comput Sci Univ Western Ont London ON N6A 5B7 Can. *Fax:* 519-661-3515; *E-Mail:* lila@csd.uwo.ca

KARICKHOFF, SAMUEL WOODFORD, PHYSICAL CHEMISTRY. *Current Pos:* RES CHEMIST, ENVIRON RES LAB, ENVIRON PROTECTION AGENCY, 71- *Personal Data:* b Buckhannon, WVa, Oct 22, 43; m 64; c 2. *Educ:* WVa Wesleyan Col, BS, 65; Fla State Univ, PhD(phys chem), 71. *Mem:* Am Chem Soc; Soc Environ Toxicol & Chem. *Res:* Fate and transport of pollutants in the environment; computer modeling of chemical reactions. *Mailing Add:* 135 Holly Point Dr Watkinsville GA 30677

KARIEL, HERBERT G, SOCIAL GEOGRAPHY, ENVIRONMENTAL PERCEPTION. *Current Pos:* RETIRED. *Personal Data:* b Plaueu, Ger; US & Can citizen. *Educ:* Univ Ore, BS, 49, ME, 54; Univ Iowa, PhD(geog), 62. *Prof Exp:* Asst prof geog, Western Wash State Univ, 62-65; assoc prof, Calif State Univ, Haywood, 65-67; prof, Univ Calgary, 67- *Concurrent Pos:* Lectr quan methods, Inst Advan Study Geog, 66; vis prof geog, Hebrew Univ Jerusalem, 94. *Mem:* Soc Sigma Xi; Asn Am Geographers. *Res:* In the realm of social geography focus is on tourism and its social and cultural impact, environmental noise and its perception, news in newspapers and the circulation information. *Mailing Add:* 4500-39th St NW Apt 205 Calgary AB T3A 0M5 Can. *Fax:* 403-282-6561; *E-Mail:* hgkariel@acs.ucalgary.ca

KARIG, DANIEL EDMUND, GEOLOGY. *Current Pos:* asst prof, 74-75, assoc prof, 75-80, PROF GEOL SCI, CORNELL UNIV, 80- *Personal Data:* b Irvington, NJ, July 20, 37; m 71; c 1. *Educ:* Colo Sch Mines, GeolE, 59, MSc, 64; Scripps Inst Oceanog, PhD(earth sci), 70. *Prof Exp:* NSF grant & asst res geologist, Scripps Inst Oceanog, 70-71; asst prof geol sci, Univ Calif, Santa Barbara, 71-74. *Mem:* Geol Soc Am; Am Geophys Union; Sigma Xi; Geol Soc Malaysia. *Res:* Marine geology and geophysics of marginal basins and island arc systems; genesis of rift zones; environmental problems in streams and small lagoons; structure and evolution of island arcs and young mountain belts. *Mailing Add:* Dept Geol Sci 2122 Snee Hall Cornell Univ Ithaca NY 14853-1504

KARIM, AZIZ, PHARMACEUTICAL CHEMISTRY. *Current Pos:* sr res investr drug metab, Dept Biochem Res, G D Searle & Co, 69-72, group leader, 72-74, res fel, Dept Drug Metab, 74-79, DIR CLIN BIOAVAILABILTY & PHARMACOKINETICS, G D SEARLE & CO, 79- *Personal Data:* b Dar es Salaam, Tanzania, Aug 20, 39; m 64; c 2. *Educ:* Univ London, BPharm, 64, PhD(pharmaceut chem), 67. *Prof Exp:* NIH fel, Univ Wis, 67-69. *Mem:* Am Chem Soc; Pharmaceut Soc Gt Brit; Am Soc Clin Pharmacol & Therapeut; Am Soc Exp Pharmacol & Therapeut; Acad Am Pharm Sci. *Res:* Drug metabolism; study of biotransformation and pharmacokinetics of drugs; isolation and structural elucidation of natural products possessing biological activities. *Mailing Add:* Dept Drug Metab G D Searle & Co 4901 Searle Pkwy Chicago IL 60077-2980. *Fax:* 847-982-4734

KARIM, GHAZI A, ENGINEERING, COMBUSTION. *Current Pos:* assoc prof, 68-69, PROF MECH ENG, UNIV CALGARY, 69- *Personal Data:* b Baghdad, Iraq, 34. *Educ:* Univ Durham, BSc, 56; Univ London, DIC & PhD(mech eng), 60. *Hon Degrees:* DSc, Univ London, 72. *Honors & Awards:* Unwin Award in Mech Eng, Eng, 60. *Prof Exp:* Trainee prime movers, Eng Elec Co, 56-57; res asst mech eng, Imp Col, Univ London, 57-60; consult engr, Ministry of Indust Repub Iraq, 60-61; UN tech fels, 61-62; lectr mech eng, Imp Col, Univ London, 62-68, chmn, Combustion Res Group, 64-68. *Concurrent Pos:* Consult, C N G Ltd, 80-, Nova Corp, 83, Canterra Energy Ltd, 84, PetroCanada, 85 & Alternative Fuel Systs, 94- *Mem:* Soc Automotive Engrs; Combustion Inst; Am Soc Mech Engrs. *Res:* Utilization of natural gas and other gaseous fuels for power in internal combustion engines; chemical kinetics of common gaseous fuels; air pollution from combustion processes; fire and explosion research; engineering education; liquid natural gas utilization; thermodynamics; coal, oil sands and heavy oil. *Mailing Add:* Dept Mech Eng Univ Calgary Calgary AB T2N 1N4 Can. *Fax:* 403-282-8406; *E-Mail:* karim@enme.ucalgary.ca

KARIM, KHONDKAR REZAUL, ATOMIC & MOLECULAR PHYSICS, ASTROPHYSICS. *Current Pos:* RES ASSOC, KANS STATE UNIV, 85- *Personal Data:* b Bangladesh, Feb 8, 50; c 1. *Educ:* Dhaka Univ, BS, 72, MS, 74; Univ Ore, MS, 80, PhD(physics), 83. *Prof Exp:* Res assoc, Univ Ore, 83-85. *Mem:* Am Phys Soc. *Res:* Dielectronic recombination; plasma diagnostics; x-ray and Auger transition rates; resonant transfer and excitation; electron and position scattering in rare gases. *Mailing Add:* Physics Dept Ill State Univ Normal IL 61790

KARIM, MOHAMMAD A, OPTOELECTRONICS, COMPUTER & ELECTRICAL ENGINEERING. *Current Pos:* asst prof, Univ Dayton, 86-88, assoc prof, 89-91, DIR & PROF, ELECTRO-OPTICS PROG, UNIV DAYTON, 90-, CHAIR & PROF ELEC & COMPUT ENG, 94- *Personal Data:* b Sylhet, Bangladesh, June 1, 53; US citizen; m 77, Setara; c Lutfi, Lamya & Aliya. *Educ:* Univ Dacca, Bangladesh, BS, 76; Univ Ala, MS, 78, MS, 79, PhD(elec eng), 81. *Prof Exp:* Asst prof, Univ Ark, 81-82, Wichita State Univ, 83-86. *Concurrent Pos:* Guest ed, Optical Eng, 90, 91, 93, 95 & 98, Optical & Laser Technol, 94. *Mem:* Fel Optical Soc Am; fel Soc Photo-instrumentation Engrs; Am Soc Eng Educ; Inst Elec & Electronics Engrs. *Res:* Pattern recognition, optical computing, information processing and optical systems design. *Mailing Add:* 8710 Castlecreek Dr Centerville OH 45458. *E-Mail:* mkarim@engr.udayton.edu

KARIM, MUNAWAR, ELECTRO MAGNETISM. *Current Pos:* from asst prof to assoc prof, 83-93, PROF PHYSICS, ST JOHN FISHER COL, 93- *Personal Data:* b Calcutta, India, Oct 7, 45; nat US. *Educ:* Dacca Univ, Bangladesh, BSc, 65, MSc, 66; Lehigh Univ, MS, 69; Univ Ore, PhD, 75. *Prof Exp:* Lectr, Univ Ife, Nigeria, 76-79, Ahmadu Bello Univ, Nigeria, 79-80; res assoc, Univ Rochester, 80-83. *Concurrent Pos:* Vis scientist, Univ Rochester, 83-; vis prof, Inst Physics della Spazio Interplanetario, Italy, 86-89, Univ Rome, 90; co-prin investr, NSF, 88-94; Fullbright scholar, Quaid-i-Azam Univ, Pakistan, 97. *Mem:* Am Phys Soc; Am Asn Physics Teachers. *Res:* Effects of gravitational curvature on the quantum electrodynamic properties of electrons; electronic instrumentation; high vacuum techniques; applications of solar energy. *Mailing Add:* Dept Physics St John Fisher Col Rochester NY 14618. *E-Mail:* karim@sjfc.edu

KARIMAN, KHALIL, PULMONARY IMMUNOLOGY, OXYGEN TRANSPORT. *Current Pos:* ASST PROF MED, MED CTR, DUKE UNIV, 80- *Personal Data:* b Mashad, Iran, Feb 1, 44. *Educ:* Mashad Med Sch, Iran, MD, 68. *Mem:* Am Fedn Clin Res; Am Thoracic Soc; fel Am Col Chest Physicians; NY Acad Sci. *Mailing Add:* 1100 Palmer Grove Ch Rd Hillsborough NC 27278

KARIN, SIDNEY, COMPUTER SCIENCE. *Current Pos:* DIR, CTR ADV COMPUTATIONAL SCI & ENG, UNIV CALIF, SAN DIEGO, 96- *Personal Data:* b Baltimore, Md, July 8, 43. *Educ:* City Col NY, BE, 66; Univ Mich, MSE, 67, PhD(nuclear eng), 73. *Prof Exp:* Comput programmer/nuclear engr, ESZ Assocs, Inc, 68-72; sr engr & sect leader, Gen Atomics, 73-75, mgr, Fusion Div Comput Ctr, 75-82, dir, Info Systs Div, 82-85, dir, San Diego Supercomput Ctr, 85-96, vpres advan comput, 87-96. *Concurrent Pos:* Mem comput rev panel, Fusion Energy Div, Oak Ridge Nat Lab, 80 & Plasma Physics Lab, Princeton Univ, 83-85; mem, Tech Adv Group Supercomput Ctrs, NSF, 84-85, ann rev panel, Comput Ctr, Lawrence Livermore Nat Lab, 86 & Indust Liaison Coun, Dept Nuclear Eng & Eng Physics, Univ Wis, 87-89; mem, Sci Comput Systs Tech Adv Panel, 84-89; mem, Nat Res Coun Panel, Nat Bur Stand Comput, 86, Comput Sci Res Prog Rev Panel, Nat Res Coun-NASA, 87 & Comput Sci & Technol Bd, Nat Res Coun, 88-93; chmn, Nat Res Coun Rev Panel Comput, Nat Bur Stand Comput, 87-88. *Mem:* AAAS; Asn Comput Mach; Inst Elec & Electronics Engrs. *Res:* Scientific computing; computer systems; computer hardware and software; networking and communications; distributed computing; computational science and engineering. *Mailing Add:* Univ Calif San Diego 9500 Gilman Dr La Jolla CA 92093-0505. *Fax:* 619-534-5056

KARINATTU, JOSEPH J, CLINICAL BIOCHEMISTRY, PATHOLOGY. *Current Pos:* PHYSICIAN-RESEARCHER, EAST CENT ILL EDUC FOUND & UNIV ILL, CHAMPAIGN, 80- *Personal Data:* b Kerala, India, Aug 6, 38; US citizen; m 63; c 2. *Educ:* Univ Kerala, BSc, 61; Univ Delhi, MSc, 63; St Thomas Inst, MS, 65, PhD(biochem), 67; Univ Autonoma, MD, 80. *Prof Exp:* Biochemist, Jewish Hosp, Cincinnati, 67-69; biochemist, St Therese Hosp, 69-78. *Concurrent Pos:* Biochemist consult, Our Lady of Mercy Hosp, Cincinnati, Ohio, 66-69; vis prof clin chem, Col of Lake County, Grayslake, Ill, 73- *Mem:* AMA; Am Chem Soc; fel Am Asn Clin Scientists; Am Asn Clin Chemists; NY Acad Sci. *Res:* Diagnostic methods in laboratory medicine; trace metals. *Mailing Add:* 52 Maywood Dr Danville IL 61832-2921

KARINEN, ARTHUR ELI, PHYSICAL GEOGRAPHY, CARTOGRAPHY. *Current Pos:* from asst prof to prof, 59-86, chmn dept, 67-72, EMER PROF GEOG, CALIF STATE UNIV, CHICO, 86- *Personal Data:* b Comptche, Calif, Feb 25, 19; m 46, Florence Wickstrom; c Sandra, Nancy, Patricia & Judith. *Educ:* Univ Calif, Berkeley, AB, 44, MA, 48; Univ Md, College Park, PhD(geog), 58. *Prof Exp:* Cartogr, US Govt, 42-43; instr geog, Ohio State Univ, 46-47; asst prof, Univ Md, 48-59. *Concurrent Pos:* Fulbright lectr, Univ Finland, 70, lectr, 80; vis prof, Helsinki Sch Econ, 79-80. *Mem:* Corresp mem Finnish Geog Soc; Asn Am Geogrs; Am Cong Surv & Mapping; AAAS. *Res:* Geography of Europe and California; world food production; Finnish settlement in the US. *Mailing Add:* 834 Arbutus Ave Chico CA 95926

KARINS, JAMES PETER, OPTICAL PROCESSING FOR PATTERN RECOGNITION, IMAGE PROCESSING. *Current Pos:* prog mgr, 92-96, DIR RECOGNITION SYSTS, DATA SYSTS DIV, LITTON, 96- *Personal Data:* b Albany, NY, Feb 12, 57; m, Linda S Hoffman; c James III & Dylan. *Educ:* State Univ NY, BS, 78, MS, 79, PhD(physics), 81. *Prof Exp:* Mem tech staff, Philips Lab, 81-83; staff engr, GE Electronics Lab, 83-90; sr scientist, Mission Res Corp, 90-92. *Mem:* Int Soc Optical Eng; Am Phys Soc; Am Defense Preparedness Asn; Asn Old Crows. *Res:* Pattern recognition, optical processing, spatial light modulators and magneto-optics; infrared systems, infrared sensors and detectors; modeling and simulation. *Mailing Add:* 29851 Agoura Rd Agoura Hills CA 91301. *Fax:* 818-707-4356; *E-Mail:* jkarins@vines.littondsd.com

KARIPIDES, ANASTAS, INORGANIC CHEMISTRY, PHYSICAL CHEMISTRY. *Current Pos:* asst prof, 68-73, ASSOC PROF CHEM, MIAMI UNIV, 73- *Personal Data:* b Canton, Ohio, July 4, 37. *Educ:* Oberlin Col, BA, 59; Univ Ill, MS, 61, PhD(chem), 64. *Prof Exp:* Res chemist, David Sarnoff Res Ctr, RCA Corp, NJ, 64-66; fel, Cornell Univ, 66-68. *Res:* Co-ordination chemistry; spectroscopy; crystallography. *Mailing Add:* 3631 Kehr Rd Oxford OH 45056-1618

KARIV-MILLER, ESSIE, ORGANIC ELECTROCHEMISTRY. *Current Pos:* PROF CHEM, UNIV MINN, 81- *Personal Data:* b Sofia, Bulgaria. *Educ:* Hebrew Univ, Jerusalem, MSc, 63; Weizman Inst Sci, PhD(chem), 69. *Honors & Awards:* Int Exchange Award, Nat Acad Sci, 87; Career Adv Award, NSF, 87. *Prof Exp:* Sr lectr chem, Tel Aviv Univ, 69-77. *Res:* Studies of the electrochemical behavior of organic compounds; synthesis by means of electrochemistry; conducting organic solids; chemistry of organic radicals. *Mailing Add:* Dept Chem 139 Smith Hall Univ Minn 207 Pleasant St SE Minneapolis MN 55455-0431

KARIYA, TAKASHI, BIOCHEMISTRY. *Current Pos:* RETIRED. *Personal Data:* b Belmont, Calif, June 23, 25; m 51; c 2. *Educ:* Drake Univ, BS, 52, MA, 54. *Prof Exp:* Res asst atherosclerosis res, Merrell Dow Res Inst, Dow Chem Co, 55-61, biochemist, 61-65, sect head, Lipid Metab Sect, Biochem Dept, Merrell-Nat Labs, Div Richardson-Merrell, Inc, 65-80, sr pharmacologist, Pharmacol Dept, 80-86. *Mem:* NY Acad Sci. *Res:* Pharmacological control of metabolism of cholesterol and other lipids in relation to the treatment of atherosclerosis; biochemical approaches to the regulation of cardiovascular function by pharmaceutical agents. *Mailing Add:* 5809 Bluespruce Lane Cincinnati OH 45224

KARK, ROBERT ADRIAAN PIETER, NEUROLOGY, NEUROCHEMISTRY. *Current Pos:* pres, 91-93, CLIN DIR, PERFORMING ARTS MED ASN, CENT NY, 90- *Personal Data:* b Boston, Mass, Dec 3, 40; m 78, Dori Urch; c Aimee, Rebecca, Candace, Colin & Marci. *Educ:* Oxford Univ, BA, 62, MA, 67; Harvard Univ, MD, 65. *Prof Exp:* Asst prof neurol, Reed Neurol Res Ctr, Neuropsychiat Inst, Univ Calif, Sch Med, 72-80, chief of Neuro-Psychiat Inst Hosp, Los Angeles, & dir, Ataxia Ctr, 80-83; assoc prof neurol, La State Univ, Sch Med, Shreveport, 83-90; chief, Neurol Serv, Vet Admin Med Ctr, Shreveport, 83-90. *Concurrent Pos:* Clin assoc & guest scientist neurol & neurochem, Med Neurol Br, Nat Inst Neurol Dis & Stroke, NIH, 68-71; investr, Neurobiochem Group, Ment Retardation Prog, Neuropsychiat Inst, Univ Calif, Los Angeles, 72-83, assoc co-dir, Clin Neuromuscular Dis, 74-76, dir, Friedreichs Ataxia Clin, 75-83; consult, Wadsworth Vet Admin Hosp, 73- & Friedreichs Ataxia Group Am, 75-; mem, Med Adv Bd, Nat Ataxia Found, 75-; mem, Med Adv Bd, Nat Ataxia Found, Western Regional Chap, 77-82 & Joseph's Dis Found, 78-; mem, Comt Bioethical Concensus, Med Soc State NY, 91-; Epilepsy clin-fel, Bowman Gray Sch Med, 88 & 93; fel, Aspen Inst Seminar Med & Soc, 93. *Mem:* Am Acad Neurol; Am Fedn Clin Res; Am Soc Neurochem; Int Soc Neurochem; Am Soc Neurosci; fel Am Col Physicians. *Res:* Enzymatic defects, metabolic changes, pathophysiology and treatment of inherited forms of ataxia, mental retardation and neuromuscular disease; neurochemistry of mercurial poisoning; biochemical aspects of neuromuscular trophic effects; biomedical ethics; epilepsy clinical studies; dementias clinical studies; multiple sclerocis clinical studies. *Mailing Add:* 5112 West Taft Rd Suite F Liverpool NY 13088. *Fax:* 315-449-2667

KARKALITS, OLIN CARROLL, JR, CHEMICAL ENGINEERING. *Current Pos:* DEAN, COL ENG & TECHNOL, MCNEESE STATE UNIV, 72- *Personal Data:* b Pauls Valley, Okla, May 31, 16; m 61, Barbara Robinson; c Kay A & Karen S. *Educ:* Rice Inst, BS, 38; Univ Mich, MS, 41, PhD(chem eng), 50. *Prof Exp:* Jr res chemist, Shell Oil Co, 37-42; instr chem eng, Univ Mich, 45-47; group leader process develop, Am Cyanamid Co, 48-56; supvr res, Petro-Tex Chem Corp, 56-63, mgr, 63-66, asst dir technol, 66-72. *Mem:* AAAS; fel Am Inst Chem Engrs; Am Soc Eng Educ; Nat Soc Prof Engrs. *Res:* Catalysis; geothermal energy. *Mailing Add:* Dean Engr & Tech McNeese State Univ 4100 Ryan St Lake Charles LA 70609. *Fax:* 318-475-5286; *E-Mail:* ckarkal@huey.engr.mcneese.edu

KARKHECK, JOHN PETER, PHYSICS. *Current Pos:* PROF PHYSICS & DEPT CHAIR, MARQUETTE UNIV, 93- *Personal Data:* b New York, NY, Apr 26, 45; m 69, Kathleen Mary Shiel; c Lorraine, Michelle & Eric. *Educ:* Le Moyne Col, BS, 66; State Univ NY Buffalo, MS, 72; State Univ NY Stony Brook, PhD(physics), 78. *Prof Exp:* Physics assoc, Brookhaven Nat Lab, 75-79; from asst prof to prof, GMI Eng & Mgt Inst, 81-89, dir physics, 88-89, head, Dept Sci & Math, 89-93. *Concurrent Pos:* Fel, State Univ NY, Stony Brook, 78, res assoc, 79-81; consult, Brookhaven Nat Lab, 79-85, STS, 83, BID Ctr, 85, 87; guest scientist, RWTH Aachen, 83-85, Rijksuniversiteit Utrecht, 86; acad assoc, 88 & 90, Mich State Univ, vis scholar, 89. *Mem:* Am Phys Soc; AAAS; Am Asn Physics Teachers; Sigma Xi. *Res:* Transport theory; energy modeling; kinetic theory; optical properties of composites; optoelectronics; physics education. *Mailing Add:* Dept Physics Marquette Univ PO Box 1881 Milwaukee WI 53201-1881. *E-Mail:* karkheck@vms.csd.mu.edu

KARKLINS, OLGERTS LONGINS, GEOLOGY, PALEONTOLOGY. *Current Pos:* RETIRED. *Personal Data:* b Tukums, Latvia, Oct 3, 24; US citizen; m 56, Vija Lejnieks; c Leva. *Educ:* Columbia Univ, BS, 57, Univ Minn, MS, 61, PhD, 66. *Prof Exp:* Geologist biostratig paleont, US Geol Surv, 63-89. *Concurrent Pos:* Asst prof lectr, Col Gen Studies, George Washington Univ, 69-72. *Mem:* Int Bryozool Asn; Sigma Xi. *Res:* Invertebrate paleontology; biostratigraphy; use of paleobiology, stratigraphy and paleogeography of Paleozoic Ectoprocta in regional correlations. *Mailing Add:* 11301 Hawhill End Potomac MD 20854

KARL, DAVID M, OCEANOGRAPHY. *Current Pos:* From asst prof to assoc prof, Univ Hawaii, 78-87, chmn, Oceanic Biol Res Div, Hawaii Inst Geophysics, 86-90, chmn, Biol Oceanog Div, SOEST, 90-91, PROF OCEANOG, UNIV HAWAII, 87- *Educ:* State Univ Col, Buffalo, BA, 71; Fla State Univ, Tallahassee, MS, 74; Univ Calif, San Diego, PhD(oceanog), 78. *Concurrent Pos:* Fel, Am-Scand Found, 76; mem affil fac, Bermuda Biol Sta Res, 95- *Mem:* Am Geophys Union; Sigma Xi; Oceanog Soc; Am Soc Microbiol; Am Soc Limnol & Oceanog. *Mailing Add:* Sch Ocean & Earth Sci & Technol Univ Hawaii 1000 Pope Rd Honolulu HI 96822. *Fax:* 808-956-5059; *E-Mail:* dkarl@soest.hawaii.edu

KARL, GABRIEL, THEORETICAL PHYSICS. *Current Pos:* from asst prof to assoc prof physics, 69-75, PROF PHYSICS, UNIV GUELPH, 75- *Personal Data:* b Cluj, Romania, Apr 30, 37; Can citizen; m 65, Dorothy; c 1. *Educ:* Univ Cluj, BA, 58; Univ Toronto, PhD(chem), 64. *Honors & Awards:* Ger-Can Res Prize, 92. *Prof Exp:* Fel molecular physics, Univ Toronto, 64-66; fel high energy physics, Oxford Univ, 66-69. *Concurrent Pos:* Vis scientist, Europ Orgn Nuclear Res, Geneva, 74, 83 & 92; vis prof, Univ Munich, 93. *Mem:* Am Phys Soc; Can Asn Physicists; fel Royal Soc Can. *Res:* High energy physics; atomic physics. *Mailing Add:* Dept Physics Univ Guelph Guelph ON N1G 2W1 Can. *E-Mail:* kgabriel@uoguelph.ca

KARL, HERMAN ADOLF, MARINE GEOLOGY, SEDIMENTOLOGY. *Current Pos:* Nat Res Coun res assoc marine geol, 77, MARINE GEOLOGIST, PAC-ARCTIC BR MARINE GEOL, US GEOL SURV, 77- *Personal Data:* b New York, NY, Mar 24, 47; m 70. *Educ:* Colgate Univ, BS, 69; Univ Nebr, MS, 71; Univ Southern Calif, PhD(geol sci), 77. *Prof Exp:* Explor geologist petrol explor, Humble Oil & Refining Co, 71; res geologist, Esso Prod Res Co, 72. *Mem:* AAAS; Geol Soc Am; Soc Econ Paleontologists & Mineralogists; Int Asn Sedimentologists; Am Geophys Union; Sigma Xi. *Res:* Dynamics of depositional processes and sediment transport on continental margins. *Mailing Add:* 655 Woodland Ave Menlo Park CA 94025

KARL, MICHAEL M, CLINICAL MEDICINE. *Current Pos:* dir clin affairs, dept med, 87-93, PROF CLIN MED, SCH MED, WASHINGTON UNIV, 72- *Personal Data:* b Milwaukee, Wis, Jan 30, 15; m; c 2. *Educ:* Univ Wis, BS, 36; Univ Louisville, MD, 38; Am Bd Internal Med, cert, 46. *Honors & Awards:* Laureate Award, Am Col Physicians, 88; Ralph O Claypoole Sr Mem Award, Am Col Physicians, 90; Irene & Michael Karl Lectr. *Prof Exp:* Intern, St Louis City Hosp, Sch Med, Washington Univ, 38-42, resident internal med, 40-42; pract internal med, Md Med Group, St Louis, Mo, 42-87. *Concurrent Pos:* Dir, Third Yr Med Clerkship, St Louis City Hosp, 42-44 & Dept Med, Jewish Hosp St Louis, 63-64; med dir, Red Cross Mobile Blood Unit, 42-44; mem, Munic Nursing Bd, City St Louis, 60-62; consult internal med, USAF, 62-64; counr, Soc Internal Med, 67; co-organizer, Jeff-Vander-Lou Med Clin, 67-72; pres, Fac Ctr, Wash Univ, 69, mem exec fac, Sch Med, 75-76 & 85-86; chmn, Comt Serv to Elderly, Nat Coun Jewish Fedns, 76-81; mem, White House Conf Families, 78-80; Am Col Physicians rep, Coun Med Specialty Socs, 86-; mem, Accreditation Coun Continuing Med Educ, 87-, chmn, 91; mem prog comt, Inst Med-Nat Acad Sci, 88-90; Irene & Michael Karl prof endocrinol. *Mem:* Inst Med-Nat Acad Sci; fel & master Am Col Physicians; AMA; Cent Soc Clin Res; Am Asn Study Liver Dis; Am Soc Internal Med. *Mailing Add:* Dept Med Wash Univ Sch Med 660 S Euclid Ave Box 8121 St Louis MO 63110

KARL, PETER I, SIGNAL TRANSDUCTION, AMINO ACID TRANSPORT. *Current Pos:* instr physiol, 85-88, asst prof, 88-94, ASSOC PROF PHYSIOL, CORNELL UNIV MED COL, 94- *Personal Data:* b Seoul, Korea, June 13, 54; US citizen. *Educ:* Mid Tenn State Univ, BS, 76, MS, 78; Miss State Univ, PhD(animal physiol), 81. *Prof Exp:* Res assoc, Ctr Blood Res, 81-82; Harvard Med Sch, 81-84; res fel, Beth Israel Hosp, 82-84. *Concurrent Pos:* Res physiologist, N Shore Univ Hosp, 84-; co-prin investr, N Shore Univ Hosp, Cornell Univ Med Ctr, 90-, prin investr, 93- *Mem:* Am Physiol Soc; Am Chem Soc; Res Soc Alcoholism; Int Soc Biomed Res Alcoholism; NY Acad Sci. *Res:* Determine placental nutrient transport, metabolism and endocrine functions which contribute to normal development of the fetus. *Mailing Add:* 350 Community Dr Northshire Univ Hosp Cornell Univ Med Col Manhasset NY 11030. *Fax:* 516-562-2496

KARL, RICHARD C, SURGERY. *Current Pos:* RETIRED. *Personal Data:* b Albany, NY, Feb 16, 20; m 44; c 3. *Educ:* Columbia Univ, AB, 42; Cornell Univ, MD, 44; Am Bd Surg, dipl, 52. *Prof Exp:* Instr anat, Med Col, Cornell Univ, 46-47, asst surg, 48-51, from instr to assoc prof, 52-70; prof surg & chmn dept, Dartmouth Med Sch, 70-91. *Concurrent Pos:* From asst to assoc attend surgeon, NY Hosp, 54-70; dir, Second Surg Div, Bellevue Hosp, NY, 63-67; dir surg, North Shore Hosp, 67-70; consult, NY Vet Admin Hosp, 63-70, USPHS Hosp, Staten Island, 64-70 & Vet Admin Hosp, White River Junction, Vt, 70-; dir surg, Dartmouth-Hitchcock Affil Hosps, 70-91. *Mem:* Fel Am Col Surg. *Res:* Academic educational surgery. *Mailing Add:* Etna NH 03750

KARL, ROBERT RAYMOND, JR, ATMOSPHERIC CHEMISTRY, PHYSICS. *Current Pos:* STAFF SCIENTIST, LOS ALAMOS NAT LAB, 76- *Personal Data:* b Sewickley, Pa, June 15, 45; c 2. *Educ:* Pa State Univ, BS, 67; Cornell Univ, PhD(phys chem), 74. *Prof Exp:* Res assoc surface adsorption, Chem Dept, Pa State Univ, 66-67; res asst molecular struct, Chem Dept, Cornell Univ, 68-73, res asst chem laser, 73-74; postdoctoral, spectros, Isotope Sepn, State Univ NY, Binghamton, 74-76. *Mem:* Am Inst Physics; Am Chem Soc; Am Phys Soc. *Res:* Spectroscopy, photochemistry; remote atmospheric sensing; remote lidar sensing; fluorescence spectroscopy; remote beamdiagnostics; remote exoarmospheric diagnostics of weapons tests and ionospheric plasmas. *Mailing Add:* 146 Piedra Loop Los Alamos NM 87544

KARL, SUSAN MARGARET, REGIONAL GEOLOGY OF ALASKA, MARINE GEOLOGY & GEOCHEMISTRY. *Current Pos:* GEOLOGIST, US GEOL SURV, 77- *Personal Data:* b Pittsburg, Pa, Oct 7, 51; m 85, Steve Teller; c Tamara & Rusty. *Educ:* Middlebury Col, BA 73; Stanford Univ, PhD(geol), 82. *Honors & Awards:* Harold Stearns Award, Geol Soc Am, 78. *Concurrent Pos:* Mem, proj 187, Int Geol Correlation Prog, ODP Leg 129; secy, Alaska Geol Soc. *Mem:* Geol Asn Can; Am Geophys Union; Geol Soc Am. *Res:* Geochemistry, sedimentology and environmental interpretation of siliceous rocks; sedimentologic analysis of turbidite deposits; paleoenvironmental analysis of sedimentary basins; sedimentary and tectonic processes in accretionary complexes; Paleozoic-Mesozoic North Pacific rim paleoceanography in Japan-Russia-Alaska. *Mailing Add:* US Geol Surv 4200 University Dr Anchorage AK 99508

KARL, THOMAS RICHARD, CLIMATOLOGICAL TIME SERIES, SECULAR CLIMATE CHANGE. *Current Pos:* meteorologist, Climate Res & Appln, 80-92, SR SCIENTIST, NAT CLIMATE DATA CTR, 92- *Personal Data:* b Evergreen Park, Ill, Nov 22, 51; m 73; c 2. *Educ:* Northern Ill Univ, BS, 73; Univ Wis-Madison, MS, 74. *Honors & Awards:* Bronze Medal, Dept Com, 87, Gold Medal, 91. *Prof Exp:* Meteorologist air qual res, Environ Sci Res lab, 75-79; meteorologist weather forecasting & anal, Nat Weather Serv, 79-80. *Concurrent Pos:* Rapporteur, Climat Time Series, World Meteorol Orgn, 83- *Mem:* Am Metrol Soc; Am Geophys Union. *Res:* The analysis and reconstruction of the 20th century climate record for identifying climate change for basic climate research; design and management strategies of various environmentally sensitive systems. *Mailing Add:* Global Climate Lab Fed Bldg Nat Climatic Data Ctr 151 Patton Ave Asheville NC 28801-5001

KARLANDER, EDWARD P, BOTANY. *Current Pos:* RETIRED. *Personal Data:* b Manchester, Vt, Nov 30, 31; wid; c 6. *Educ:* Univ Vt, BS, 60; Univ Md, MS, 62, PhD, 64. *Prof Exp:* From res asst to res assoc, Univ Md, College Park, 60-65, asst prof, 66-69, assoc prof algal physiol, 69-90, asst chmn dept, 82-90. *Concurrent Pos:* Prog officer NSF, 79-80; actg dir, Md Water Resources Res Ctr, 80-81. *Mem:* Phycol Soc Am; Am Inst Biol Sci. *Res:* Ecological biophysics; algal physiology; responses of organisms to light; cell growth. *Mailing Add:* 107 Lakeside Dr Greenbelt MD 20770

KARLE, HARRY P, PLANT PATHOLOGY, VITICULTURE. *Current Pos:* from asst prof to assoc prof, 62-69, prof plant path & chmn dept plant sci, 69-86, ASSOC DEAN AGR OPERS, CALIF STATE UNIV, FRESNO, 86- *Personal Data:* b Sanger, Calif, Jan 4, 27; m 56; c 4. *Educ:* Fresno State Col, BS, 50; Univ Calif, Davis, MS, 59, PhD(plant path), 65. *Prof Exp:* Instr, High Sch, Calif, 50-51; foreman viticulture, Fresno State Col, 51-53; lab helper plant path, Univ Calif, Davis, 54-55, lab asst, 55-58, res asst, 58-59, lab technician, 59-62. *Concurrent Pos:* Consult res & study comt, Calif Raisin Adv Bd, 65-84. *Mem:* AAAS; Am Phytopath Soc; Am Soc Hort Sci; Am Inst Biol Sci; Am Soc Agron; Sigma Xi. *Res:* Grape diseases; non-cultivation studies. *Mailing Add:* 1275 E Portals Ave Fresno CA 93710

KARLE, ISABELLA LUGOSKI, MOLECULAR BIOLOGY, CONFORMATION PEPTIDES. *Current Pos:* physicist, 46-59, HEAD, X-RAY ANALYSIS SECT, US NAVAL RES LAB, 59- *Personal Data:* b Detroit, Mich, Dec 2, 21; m 42, Jerome; c Louise (Hanson), Jean M & Madeline (Towney). *Educ:* Univ Mich, BS, 41, MS, 42, PhD(phys chem), 44. *Hon Degrees:* DSc, Univ Mich, 76, Wayne State Univ, 79 & Univ Md, 86; LHD, Georgetown Univ, 84. *Honors & Awards:* Sci Res Soc Am Award, 67; Hillebrand Award, Am Chem Soc, 69, Garvan Award, 76; Fed Woman's Award, US Govt, 73; Dexter Conrad Award, Off Naval Res, 80; Pioneer Award, Am Inst Chemists, 84; Gregori Aminoff Prize, Royal Swedish Acad Sci, 88; Rear Admiral William S Parsons Award, Navy League of US, 88; Mich Women's Hall Of Fame, 89; Bijroet Medal, Univ Utrecht, Neth, 90; Vincent du Vigneaud Award, Gordon Conf, 92; Bower Award, Franklin Inst Philadelphia, 93; Nat Medal of Sci, 95; Chem Prize, Nat Acad Sci, 95. *Prof Exp:* Assoc chemist, Univ Chicago, 44; instr, Univ Mich, 44-46. *Concurrent Pos:* Mem, Nat Comt Crystallog, Nat Acad Sci-Nat Res Coun, 74-77; mem, Exec Comt, Am Peptide Symposium, 76-81; mem adv bd, Off Chem & Chem Tech, Nat Res Coun, 78-81, Corp Vis Comt, Mass Inst Technol, 82-90; mem bd, Int Orgn & Progs, Nat Acad Sci, 80-83. *Mem:* Nat Acad Sci; Am Philos Soc; Biophys Soc; Am Crystallog Asn (vpres, 75, pres, 76); Am Chem Soc; Am Acad Arts & Sci. *Res:* Application of electron and x-ray diffraction to structure problems; phase determination in crystallography; elucidation of molecular formulae; peptides; configurations and conformations of natural products and biologically active materials. *Mailing Add:* Lab Struct Matter Code 6030 US Naval Res Lab Washington DC 20375-5000. *Fax:* 202-767-6874

KARLE, JEAN MARIANNE, X-RAY CRYSTALLOGRAPHY. *Current Pos:* DEPT PHARMACOL, WALTER REED ARMY INST RES, WASHINGTON, 83- *Personal Data:* b Washington, DC, Nov 14, 50. *Educ:* Univ Mich, BS, 71; Duke Univ, PhD(chem), 76. *Prof Exp:* Pub health serv fel, Nat Inst Arthritis, Diabetes, Digestive & Kidney Dis, NIH, 76-78, staff fel, Nat Cancer Inst, 78-83. *Mem:* Am Chem Soc; Am Asn Cancer Res; Int Soc Study Xenobiotics; Am Crystallographic Asn; Am Soc Trop Med Hyg. *Res:* Three-dimensional structure of biologically active small molecules; chiral chromatographic methods development; drug development of antimalarials; computational chemistry. *Mailing Add:* Dept Pharmacol Walter Reed Army Inst Res Washington DC 20307

KARLE, JEROME, CRYSTALLOGRAPHY. *Current Pos:* head, Electron Diffraction Sect, 46-58, head, Diffraction Br, 58-67, CHIEF SCIENTIST, LAB FOR STRUCT OF MATTER, US NAVAL RES LAB, 67- *Personal Data:* b New York, NY, June 18, 18; m 42, Isabella Lugoski; c Louise (Hanson), Jean & Madeleine (Tawney). *Educ:* City Col New York, BS, 37; Harvard Univ, MS, 38; Univ Mich, MS, 42, PhD(phys chem), 44. *Hon Degrees:* LHD, Georgetown Univ, 84; DHC, Univ Md, City Univ NY, 86, Univ Mich, 89. *Honors & Awards:* Nobel Prize in Chem, 85; Sigma Xi Award, 59; Chair of Sci Award, 68; Hillebrand Award, Am Chem Soc, 69; Robert Dexter Conrad Award, 86; Patterson Award, Am Crystallog Asn, 86; Albert A Michelson Award, 86; Rear Admiral William S Persons Award, 86; Townsend Harris Award, 86; Nat Libr Med Medal, 86; Thomas Edison Mem lectr, 86; Karl Herzfeld Mem Lectr, Cath Univ Am, 86; Paul Harteck Series Lectr, Rensselear Polytech Inst, 86; numerous named lectureships at US & foreign univs, 87- *Prof Exp:* Lab asst, State Dept Health, NY, 39-40; res assoc, Manhattan Proj, Chicago, 43-44 & US Navy Proj, Mich, 44-46. *Concurrent Pos:* Lectr, Univ Col, Univ Md, 51-71, Nat Ctr Excellence Educ, 87-89; prof, Univ Md, 51-70; mem, Nat Res Coun, 54-56 & 67-87; chmn, USA Nat Comt Crystallog, Nat Acad Sci-Nat Res Coun, 73-75; mem exec comt, Int Union Crystallog, 78-87, pres, 81-84; chmn, Chem Sect, Nat Acad Sci, 88-91, mem, Comt Human Rights, 91- *Mem:* Nat Acad Sci; Am Chem Soc; fel Am Phys Soc; Am Crystallog Asn (treas, 50-52, vpres, 71, pres, 72); Am Math Soc; Am Philos Soc; Sigma Xi; hon mem Int Acad Sci; fel AAAS; Int Soc Quantum Biol & Pharmacol. *Res:* Structure of atoms, molecules, glasses, crystals and solid surfaces. *Mailing Add:* Lab Struct Matter Code 6030 US Naval Res Lab Washington DC 20375-5341. *Fax:* 202-767-6874

KARLEKAR, BHALCHANDRA VASUDEO, MECHANICAL ENGINEERING. *Current Pos:* PROF MECH ENG, ROCHESTER INST TECHNOL, 66- *Personal Data:* b Baroda, India, Jan 19, 39; m 64; c 2. *Educ:* Univ Baroda, BE, 58; Univ Ill, Urbana, MS, 59, PhD(mech eng), 62. *Prof Exp:* Lectr mech eng, Indian Inst Technol, 62-63; consult, Ibcon Pvt Ltd, Bombay, 63-66. *Concurrent Pos:* Consult, Eastman Kodak Co, 66-70, A Burgart Inc, 70-71, Xerox, 74-77 & Chapin Co, 78; actg chmn, Chapin Co, 76-77; chmn energy task force, Rochester Inst Technol, prof & head mech engr dept. *Mem:* Am Soc Mech Engrs; Am Soc Eng Educ; Sigma Xi. *Res:* Heat transfer; energy conservation. *Mailing Add:* 30 Kitty Hawk Dr Pittsford NY 14534

KARLEN, DOUGLAS LAWRENCE, SOIL & CROP MANAGEMENT, SOIL QUALITY. *Current Pos:* Res soil scientist, Coastal Plains Soil & Water Conserv Res Ctr, 78-87, RES SOIL SCIENTIST, NAT SOIL TILTH LAB, USDA AGR RES SERV, 87- *Personal Data:* b Monroe, Wis, Aug 28, 51; m 73, Linda S (Bender); c Sarah, Steve & Holly. *Educ:* Univ Wis-Madison, BS, 73; Mich State Univ, MS, 75; Kans State Univ, PhD(agron), 78. *Honors & Awards:* Scarseth Mem Award, Scarseth Mem Found, 77. *Concurrent Pos:* Adj prof, Agron Dept, Clemson Univ, 83-; collab & prof, Agron Dept, Iowa State Univ, 87-; assoc ed, Crop Sci Soc Am, 87-93, tech ed, 94- *Mem:* Fel Am Soc Agron; fel Soil Sci Soc Am; fel Crop Sci Soc Am; Coun Agr Sci & Technol; Soil & Water Conserv Soc Am; Coun Soil Testing & Plant Anal. *Res:* Evaluation of the interactions among soil, crop, water and nutrient management practices as they affect nutrient losses from the soil and assessing the effects of conservation tillage and other management practices on soil tilth and soil quality. *Mailing Add:* Nat Soil Tilth Lab USDA-ARS 2150 Pammel Dr Ames IA 50011. *Fax:* 515-294-8125; *E-Mail:* dkarlen@nstl.gov

KARLER, RALPH, PHARMACOLOGY. *Current Pos:* Res instr, 59-63, from asst prof to assoc prof, 63-76, PROF PHARMACOL, COL MED, UNIV UTAH, 76- *Personal Data:* b Mishawaka, Ind, Nov 11, 28; m 53. *Educ:* Univ Chicago, AB, 47; Ind Univ, BA, 50; Univ Calif, MS, 53, PhD(physiol), 59. *Concurrent Pos:* USPHS spec res fel, 61-62, USPHS res career develop award, 62-72. *Mem:* Am Soc Pharmacol & Exp Therapeut; assoc Am Physiol Soc; Int Soc Biochem Pharmacol. *Res:* Pharmacology of drugs affecting the nervous system and muscle; role of calcium in contraction; drug metabolism. *Mailing Add:* Dept Pharmacol Rm 2C 234 Univ Utah Sch Med Salt Lake City UT 84132-0001

KARLIN, ALVAN A, EVOLUTION, SYSTEMATICS. *Current Pos:* AT DEPT BIOL, UNIV ARK, LITTLE ROCK. *Personal Data:* b Newark, NJ, May 3, 50; m; c 2. *Educ:* Rutgers Univ, AB, 72; Ind State Univ, MA, 75; Miami Univ, PhD(zool), 78. *Prof Exp:* Staff Biologist Genetics, Tall Timbers Res Sta, 78- *Concurrent Pos:* Adj asst prof, Fla State Univ, 79- *Mem:* Soc Study Evolution; Soc Syst Zoologists; Am Soc Ichthyologists & Herpetologists; Soc Study Amphibians & Reptiles; Sigma Xi. *Res:* Evolutionary biology, population genetics and ecological genetics; vertebrate biology and sociobiology. *Mailing Add:* Dept Biol Univ Ark 2801 S University Ave Little Rock AR 72204-1000

KARLIN, ARTHUR, RECEPTORS, CHANNELS. *Current Pos:* From res asst to res assoc neurol, Columbia Univ, 62-64, from asst prof to assoc prof physiol, 65-74, assoc prof neurochem, 74-78, PROF BIOCHEM & NEUROL, COLUMBIA UNIV, 78-, DIR CTR MOLECULAR RECOGNITION & HIGGINS PROF BIOCHEM, MOLECULAR BIOPHYS, PHYSIOL & CELLULAR BIOPHYS & NEUROL, 89- *Personal Data:* b Philadelphia, Pa, Jan 14, 36; m 58, 77, Cynthia Rollings; c 6. *Educ:* Swarthmore Col, BA, 57; Rockefeller Univ, PhD(biol), 62. *Honors & Awards:* Louis & Bert Freedman Found Award Res Biochem, NY Acad Sci, 85. *Concurrent Pos:* New York City Health Res Coun career scientist award, Columbia Univ, 70-72; mem bd rev, Fedn Proc, 74, JBC, 79-84, 87-92, Proteins, 86-, J Neurosci, 90-95, Neuron, 96-; chmn, Gordon conf molecular pharmacol, 75; Grass traveling scientist, 79; Quastel vis prof, McGill Univ, 84; Krantz lectr pharmacol & exp therapeut, Univ Maryland, 85; dir, MBL neurobiol course, 85-89; mem adv comt, Max-Planck Inst Med Res, Heidelberg, 93- *Mem:* Am Soc Biol Chem; Am Soc Pharmacol & Exp Therapeut; Soc Neurosci; fel AAAS; Soc Gen Physiologists. *Res:* Structure and function of receptors for neurotransmitters; molecular mechanisms of binding, gating and ion-conduction. *Mailing Add:* Ctr Molecular Recognition Col Phys & Surg Columbia Univ 630 W 168th St New York NY 10032. *Fax:* 212-305-5594; *E-Mail:* ak12@columbia.edu

KARLIN, KENNETH DANIEL, INORGANIC CHEMISTRY. *Current Pos:* PROF INORG CHEM, JOHNS HOPKINS UNIV, BALTIMORE, 90- *Personal Data:* b Pasadena, Calif, Oct 30, 48; c 2. *Educ:* Stanford Univ, BS, 70; Columbia Univ, PhD(inorg chem), 75. *Honors & Awards:* Buck-Whitney Award, 91. *Prof Exp:* Res assoc & NATO fel organometallic chem, Cambridge Univ, Eng, 75-77; prof inorg chem, State Univ NY Albany, 77-90. *Concurrent Pos:* Hon US Ramsey fel, 76-77. *Mem:* Am Chem Soc; The Chem Soc; fel AAAS. *Res:* Bioinorganic chemistry; chemistry of copper I; binuclear and trinuclear copper complexes; activation of molecular oxygen; models for copper metalloproteins; multimetal centers in hydrolysis reactions; metal-peroxide complex reactions. *Mailing Add:* Dept Chem Johns Hopkins Univ Baltimore MD 21218-3261

KARLIN, SAMUEL, MATHEMATICAL STATISTICS, STATISTICS. *Current Pos:* prof math & statist, 56-74, prof math, 74-78, ROBERT GRIMMITT PROF MATH, STANFORD UNIV, 78- *Personal Data:* b Yonava, Poland, June 8, 24; nat US; m 47; c 3. *Educ:* Ill Inst Technol, BS, 44; Princeton Univ, PhD(math), 47. *Hon Degrees:* DSc, Technion-Israel Inst Technol, Haifa, Israel, 85. *Honors & Awards:* Wilkes Lectr, Princeton Univ, 77, Seymour Sherman Mem Lectr, 78; Gibbs Lectr, 83; Am Math Soc 1st Mahalanobis Mem Lectr, 83; Indian Statist Inst & 11th Fisher Mem Lectr, London, 83; Nat Medal Sci, 89; Britton Lectr, McMasters Univ, Ont, Can, 90. *Prof Exp:* Asst prof math, Calif Inst Technol, 49-50 & 51-54, assoc prof, 54-56; vis asst prof, Princeton Univ, 50-51; dean, Fac Math & chmn, Dept Math, Weizmann Inst Sci, Rehovot, Israel, 70-76. *Concurrent Pos:* Consult, Rand Corp, Calif, 48-; Andrew D White prof-at-large, Cornell Univ, 75-81. *Mem:* Nat Acad Sci; Am Math Soc; Inst Math Statist (pres-elect, 77, pres, 78-79); Am Statist Asn; Am Soc Human Genetics; Genetic Soc Am; Am Naturalist Soc; Human Genome Orgn; hon mem Am Philos Soc. *Res:* Problems in mathematics, statistics, genetics and biology. *Mailing Add:* Dept Math Stanford Univ Stanford CA 94305

KARLINER, JERROLD, STRUCTURE ELUCIDATION, APPLIED SPECTROSCOPY. *Current Pos:* group leader spectros, Ciba-Geigy Corp, 68-78, dept head, Anal Res Dept, 78-90, dept head, Spectros Dept, 90-93, EXEC DEPT, ANALYTICAL DEVELOP & SERV, CIBA-VISON CORP, 93- *Personal Data:* b Stanislawow, Poland, Mar 5, 40; US citizen; m 63; c 2. *Educ:* City Col New York, BS, 62; Stanford Univ, PhD(org mass spectrometry), 66. *Prof Exp:* Res assoc mass spectrometry, Lederle Labs Div, Am Cyanamid Co, 66-68. *Mem:* Am Chem Soc; Am Soc Mass Spectrometry. *Res:* Structure elucidation of organic compounds by physical methods; analysis and characterization of organic compounds and analytical and physical methods; analytical methods development. *Mailing Add:* 660 Boxwood Terr Alpharetta GA 30202

KARLL, ROBERT E, ORGANIC CHEMISTRY. *Current Pos:* Res chemist, Standard Oil Co (Ind), 49-54, group leader, 54-65, SECT LEADER, AMOCO CHEM CORP, 65- *Personal Data:* b Davenport, Iowa, Apr 29, 24; m 46; c 3. *Educ:* St Ambrose Col, BS, 45; Univ Iowa, MS, 47, PhD(org chem), 49. *Mem:* Am Chem Soc. *Res:* Surfactants; motor oil additives; tertiary oil chemicals. *Mailing Add:* 1171 Lexington Lane Batavia IL 60510-3358

KARLOF, JOHN KNOX, MATHEMATICS. *Current Pos:* PROF MATH SCI, UNIV NC, 87- *Personal Data:* b Rochester, NY, Nov 9, 46; m 69; c 2. *Educ:* State Univ NY Col Oswego, BA, 68; Univ Colo, MA, 70, PhD(math), 73. *Prof Exp:* Asst prof math, Univ Nebr, Omaha, 74-77, assoc prof, 77-80; assoc prof math & comput sci, State Univ NY, Stony Brook, 80-87. *Mem:* Am Math Soc; Math Asn Am. *Res:* Gaussian channel coding theory; algebraic coding theory; group theory. *Mailing Add:* Dept Math Sci Univ NC Wilmington NC 28403-3297

KARLOVITZ, BELA, MECHANICAL & ELECTRICAL ENGINEERING. *Current Pos:* PARTNER, COMBUSTION & EXPLOSIVES RES, INC, 53- *Personal Data:* b Papa, Hungary, Nov 9, 04; nat US; m 29; c 3. *Educ:* Budapest Tech Univ, ME, 26; Swiss Fed Inst Technol, EE, 28. *Honors & Awards:* Gold Medal, Combustion Inst, 70; Int MHD Faraday Mem Medal, 86. *Prof Exp:* Sect engr, Elec Power Co, Hungary, 29-38; res engr, Westinghouse Elec Corp, 38-47; sect chief, US Bur Mines, 47-53. *Mem:* Am Phys Soc; Combustion Inst. *Res:* Magnetohydrodynamic power generation; combustion; turbulent flames; propulsion systems; electrically augmented flames; high power dispersed electrical discharge; plasma phenomena. *Mailing Add:* 1290 Boyce Rd A-431 Upper St Clair PA 15241

KARLOW, EDWIN ANTHONY, PHYSICS. *Current Pos:* CONSULT, 90- *Personal Data:* b Glendale, Calif, May 13, 42; m 64; Cress; c Marvin A & Norman E. *Educ:* Walla Walla Col, BS, 66; Wash State Univ, MS, 68, PhD(physics), 71. *Prof Exp:* Chmn dept math & physics, Columbia Union Col, 72-78; chmn dept physics, Loma Linda Univ, 78-90. *Mem:* Am Asn Physics Teachers; Am Phys Soc; Am Sci Affil; Nat Sci Teachers Asn. *Res:* Analog and digital processing of signals; acoustic reflection spectroscopy. *Mailing Add:* Dept Physics La Sierra Univ Riverside CA 92515. *E-Mail:* ekarlow@lasierra.edu

KARLSON, ESKIL LEANNART, BIOPHYSICS, ZOOLOGY. *Current Pos:* PRES ION EXCHANGE, LIFE SUPPORT INC, 71- *Personal Data:* b Johnkeping, Sweden; Jan 5, 20; US citizen; m 42; c 3. *Educ:* Univ Pittsburgh, BS, 46, MS, 48; Occidental Univ, St Louis, DSc(physics, zool), 70. *Prof Exp:* Lab leader develop radiation instrumentation, Savana River Plant, AEC, 50-55; group leader, Reactor Inst, Greenwich Plant, AMF Inc, 55-57; chief appl physics atomic bomb tests, Las Vegas Labs, EG&G, 57-61; pres gas analyzers, Precision Res, 61-67; vpres res ozone systs, Pollution Control Industs, 67-71. *Concurrent Pos:* Consult to reactor control, 74-77; res & develop adv ozone, Iconex, Inc, Stamford, Conn, 75-78; consult ion exchange, Facet Enterprises, Tulsa, Okla, 77-78. *Mem:* Optical Soc Am; Inst Soc Am; Health Physics Soc; Am Nuclear Soc. *Res:* Developed first digital pressure transducer, first eight gas analyzer, first automatic inbedable heat pump; developed first continuous separation system for oil, blood or water employing the chromatographic phenomena; developed the first sterilizer employing ozone as the sterilizing agent. *Mailing Add:* 4634 State St Erie PA 16509

KARLSON, KARL EUGENE, surgery, for more information see previous edition

KARLSON, RONALD HENRY, MARINE ECOLOGY, BENTHIC ECOLOGY. *Current Pos:* asst prof, 78-84, ASSOC PROF INVERT ECOL, UNIV DEL, 84- *Personal Data:* b Coalinga, Calif, Oct 13, 47; m 77, Susan Ray; c James H & Tavenner A. *Educ:* Pomona Col, BA, 69; Duke Univ, MA, 72, PhD(zool), 75. *Prof Exp:* Fel, Johns Hopkins Univ, 76-78. *Concurrent Pos:* Prin investr, NSF grants, 76-78, 82-84, Mer Res Grant/Australian Res Coun, 93; vis fac, coral reef ecol, Discovery Bay Marine Lab, Univ WI-Jamaica, 84; vis scientist, Dept Zool, Univ Adelaide, 85, Victorian Inst Marine Sci, 86, Sch Biol Sci, Univ Sydney, 86, Australian Inst Marine Sci, 86, Mountain Lake Biol Sta, Univ Va, 90, Dept Marine Biol, James Cook Univ, NQueensland, 93-94; travel fel, Lizard Island, 93. *Mem:* Soc Int Comp Biol; AAAS; Am Soc Naturalists; Ecol Soc Am; Int Bryol Asn; Int Soc Reef Studies. *Res:* Clonal life history strategies and the effects of dispersal, recruitment and disturbance on benthic invertebrates. *Mailing Add:* Biol Dept Univ Del Newark DE 19716. *Fax:* 302-831-2281; *E-Mail:* rkarlson@udel.edu

KARLSSON, ERIC ALLAN, POWER SEMICONDUCTOR DEVICES, HIGH VOLTAGE SEMICONDUCTOR DEVICES. *Current Pos:* STAFF SCIENTIST, SONOMA RES CO, 91- *Personal Data:* b San Francisco, Calif, Dec 3, 50. *Educ:* Univ Calif, Davis, BS, 73; San Francisco State Univ, MS, 80. *Prof Exp:* Process/prod engr, Fairchild Semiconductor, 77-79; res scientist, Lawrence Berkeley Lab, 80-81; sr engr, Fairchild Semiconductor, 81-83, Allen-Bradley Co, 83-84; proj engr, Burroughs Corp, 84-85; eng mgr, Tag Semiconductors, 85-86, dir res & develop & eng, 86-88; sr res scientist, Raytheon Res, 88-89; eng mgr, Microsemi, 89-90; tech dir, Lite-on Semiconductor, 90-91. *Concurrent Pos:* Consult, Allen-Bradley Co, 84-85; Microsemi Corp, 90, UDT Sensors Inc, 90, BKC Semiconductors, 92- *Res:* Semiconductor device development, including process development and simulation, device design and simulation. *Mailing Add:* 1380 Thompson Ave Napa CA 94558. *Fax:* 707-252-8362; *E-Mail:* sonomarc@delphi.com

KARLSSON, STURE KARL FREDRIK, FLUID MECHANICS. *Current Pos:* from asst prof to assoc prof eng, 60-71, PROF ENG, BROWN UNIV, 71- *Personal Data:* b Sodra Vi, Sweden, Oct 11, 25; US citizen; m 49; c 2. *Educ:* Johns Hopkins Univ, PhD(aeronaut), 58. *Prof Exp:* Fel aeronaut, Johns Hopkins Univ, 58-59; NATO fel, Royal Inst Technol Sweden, 59-60. *Mem:* Am Phys Soc. *Res:* Turbulent flows; laminar stability. *Mailing Add:* Div Eng Brown Univ Providence RI 02912

KARLSSON, ULF LENNART, anatomy, neurobiology, for more information see previous edition

KARLSTROM, ERNEST LEONARD, HERPETOLOGY, ECOLOGY. *Current Pos:* assoc prof, 61-64, PROF BIOL, UNIV PUGET SOUND, 64- *Personal Data:* b Seattle, Wash, May 18, 28; m 50; c 3. *Educ:* Augustana Col, AB, 49; Univ Wash, Seattle, MS, 52; Univ Calif, Berkeley, PhD(zool), 56. *Prof Exp:* Assoc zool, Univ Calif, Berkeley, 55-56; from asst prof to assoc prof biol, Augustana Col, 56-61. *Concurrent Pos:* Arctic Inst NAm res grant, 59-61; NSF basic res grants, 62-64. *Mem:* Am Soc Ichthyol & Herpet; Sigma Xi; Western Soc Naturalists. *Res:* Comparative anatomy of reptiles; ecology and systematics of amphibians; basic marine ecology; radioactive tracer methods; ecological recovery Mount Saint Helens, Washington. *Mailing Add:* Dept Biol Univ Puget Sound Tacoma WA 98416-0001

KARMALI, RASHIDA A, NUTRITION, ENDOCRINE PATHOPHYSIOLOGY. *Current Pos:* PATENT ATTY, PENNIE & EDMONDS, 94- *Personal Data:* Univ Newcastle-upon-Tyne, Eng, PhD(biochem), 76, JD, 93. *Prof Exp:* Assoc res prof, Cook Col, Rutgers Univ, 84-89; vis assoc prof, Sloan-Kettering Cancer Ctr, 84-92. *Concurrent Pos:* Adj assoc prof, Sloan-Kettering Cancer Ctr, 80-90, consult, 90-93; student legal specialist, City Law, Dept Tort Div, NY, 90-91. *Mailing Add:* 13 W 13th St Apt 3A N New York NY 10011. *Fax:* 212-949-9795

KARMAS, GEORGE, ORGANIC CHEMISTRY. *Current Pos:* asst, 44-64, RES FEL, ORTHO PHARMACEUT CORP, RARITAN, 64- *Personal Data:* b Rochester, NY, Dec 18, 20; m 51, Virginia Savage. *Educ:* Univ Rochester, BS, 42; NY Univ, MS, 45; Polytech Inst Brooklyn, PhD(org chem), 55. *Prof Exp:* Res chemist, Manhattan Dist Proj, Iowa State Col, 42-44. *Mem:* Am Chem Soc; Sigma Xi. *Res:* Synthetic medicinal chemistry, especially antimicrobials; heterocyclic and steroid chemistry. *Mailing Add:* 757 Cedarcrest Dr Bound Brook NJ 08805-1103

KARMAZYN, MORRIS, HEART RESEARCH, EICOSANOIDS. *Current Pos:* assoc prof, 89-90, PROF PHARMACOL & TOXICOL & CAREER INVESTR, HEART & STROKE FOUND ONT, UNIV WESTERN ONT, 90- *Personal Data:* b Wloclawek, Poland, Apr 5, 50; Can citizen; m 88. *Educ:* Loyola Col, BSc, 74; McGill Univ, MSc, 76, PhD(physiol), 79. *Honors & Awards:* Merck Frosst Award, 90. *Prof Exp:* Fel physiol, Univ Man, 78-81; from asst prof to assoc prof pharmacol, Dalhousie Univ, 81-89. *Concurrent Pos:* Vis scientist, Weis Ctr Res, Geisinger Clin, Danville, Pa, 87-88. *Mem:* Int Soc Heart Res; Am Soc Pharmacol & Exp Ther; Can Pharmacol Soc; Am Heart Asn; AAAS. *Res:* Study of the role of eicosanoids and Na/H exchange in cardiac injury associated with ischemia and reperfusion. *Mailing Add:* Dept Pharmacol & Toxicol Univ Western Ont Med Sci Bldg London ON N6A 5C1 Can

KARMEN, ARTHUR, MEDICINE, CLINICAL PATHOLOGY. *Current Pos:* PROF & CHMN DEPT LAB MED, ALBERT EINSTEIN COL MED, 71- *Personal Data:* b New York, NY, Feb 25, 30; m 55; c 3. *Educ:* NY Univ, AB, 50, MD, 54. *Honors & Awards:* Sloan Award Cancer Res, 57; Van Slyke

Award, Am Asn Clin Chemists, 79; Tswett Medal Chromatography, 82. *Prof Exp:* Resident & intern med, Bellevue Hosp, NY, 54-56; res investr, Nat Heart Inst, 56-63; assoc prof radiol, radiol sci & med, Johns Hopkins Univ, 63-68; prof path & med, Sch Med & dir clin labs, Univ Hosp, NY Univ & Bellevue Hosp, 68-71. *Concurrent Pos:* Dir clin labs, Bronx Munic Hosp Ctr & Hosp Albert Einstein Col Med, 71- *Res:* Analytical biochemistry, clinical pathology and chemistry, lipid metabolism and clinical enzymology; nuclear medicine; biochemistry. *Mailing Add:* Lab Med Albert Einstein Col Med 1300 Morris Park Ave Bronx NY 10461-1926

KARMIOL, SOVERIN, DESIGN CELL CULTURE SYSTEMS. *Current Pos:* DIR RES & DEVELOP, CLONETICS CORP, BIOWHITTAKER INC, 93- *Personal Data:* b Lodz, Poland, May 1, 47; Can citizen. *Educ:* Univ Toronto, BSc, 69; Univ Windsor, MSc, 81; Univ Guelph, PhD(nutrit biochem), 89. *Prof Exp:* Post-doctoral fel, Dept Path, Univ Mich Med Sch, 89-93. *Mem:* Am Asn Cancer Res; Soc Invest Dermat; Am Soc Cell Biol; Cell Transplantation Soc; Soc In Vitro Biol. *Res:* Design in vitro cell systems. *Mailing Add:* 8830 Biggs Ford Rd Walkersville MO 21793. *E-Mail:* sov@biowhittaker.com

KARMIS, MICHAEL E, MINING ENGINEERING. *Current Pos:* asst prof, 78-81, ASSOC PROF MINING ENG, VA POLYTECH INST & STATE UNIV, 81- *Personal Data:* b Athens, Greece, June 9, 48; m 72; c 3. *Educ:* Univ Strathclyde, BSc, 71, PhD(rock mech), 74. *Prof Exp:* Royal Soc Brit fel rock mech, Dept Mining Eng, Univ Strathclyde, 74-75; asst prof mining eng, Nat Tech Univ Athens, Greece, 75-78. *Mem:* Am Inst Mining, Metall & Petrol Engrs; Inst Mining, Metall & Petrol Engrs; Int Soc Rock Mech. *Res:* Stress analysis around mining excavations using theoretical and experimental methods; design of instrumentation for monitoring underground stresses and strains; in-situ investigations; mining subsidence; geotechnical techniques; mine design. *Mailing Add:* 1227 Patton Ct Blacksburg VA 24060

KARN, JAMES FREDERICK, RANGE RUMINANT NUTRITION, FORAGE EVALUATION. *Current Pos:* RES ANIMAL SCIENTIST BEEF CATTLE NUTRIT, NORTHERN GREAT PLAINS RES LAB, AGR RES SERV, USDA, 76- *Personal Data:* b Columbus, Ohio, Jan 28, 39; m 60, Joy A Herren; c Anita S (Kaizer) & D Renee (Clarke). *Educ:* Ohio State Univ, BS, 62, MS, 64; Univ Nebr, PhD(ruminant nutrit), 76. *Prof Exp:* Res technician, North Platte Sta, Univ Nebr, 67-76. *Mem:* Am Soc Animal Sci; Soc Range Mgt; Am Soc Agron; Am Registry Prof Animal Scientists. *Res:* Improving the efficiency of producing beef cattle on rangelands; forage nutritive quality evaluation; clarifying the nutrient requirements of range cattle. *Mailing Add:* Northern Great Plains Res Lab PO Box 459 Mandan ND 58554

KARN, RICHARD WENDALL, CIVIL ENGINEERING. *Current Pos:* SR VPRES, GREINER, INC, 90- *Personal Data:* b Oakland, Calif, July 19, 27; m 49, Peggy J; c Pamela J & Robert A. *Educ:* Univ Calif, Berkeley, BS, 50. *Honors & Awards:* Kenneth Andrew Roe Award, Am Asn Eng Soc, 89. *Prof Exp:* Civil & hydraul engr, Flood Control & Water Conserv Dist, Alameda Co, 50-62, engr-mgr, 62-66; vpres, Bissell & Karn, Inc, 66-86, pres, 86-90. *Concurrent Pos:* Mem, Bd Dir, Civil Eng Res Found, Washington, DC. *Mem:* Fel Am Soc Civil Engrs (pres, 84-85); Am Asn Eng Soc; Civil Eng Res Found; Am Pub Works Asn; Nat Soc Prof Engrs. *Mailing Add:* 7 Twelve Oaks Dr Pleasanton CA 94588

KARN, ROBERT CAMERON, MAMMALIAN & BIOCHEMICAL GENETICS, MAMMALIAN SALIVARY PROTEINS. *Current Pos:* PROF & HEAD BIOL SCI, BUTLER UNIV, 86- *Personal Data:* b Berwyn, Ill, Mar 12, 45; m 66, Marianne Kane; c Colin E & Evan C. *Educ:* Ind Univ, BA, 67, MA, 70, PhD(zool), 72. *Prof Exp:* From instr to assoc prof med genetics, Sch Med, Ind Univ, 74-86, dir Genotyping Labs, Dept Med Genetics, 75-81, grad adv, 81-86. *Concurrent Pos:* NIH fel, Sch Med, Ind Univ, 74-75, career develop award, 77-82. *Mem:* Sigma Xi; Genetics Soc Am; Am Inst Biol Sci; Am Soc Biochem & Molecular Biol. *Res:* Molecular genetics of salivary and prostate proteins; evolution by gene duplication. *Mailing Add:* Biol Sci Dept Butler Univ 4600 Sunset Ave Indianapolis IN 46208-3485. *Fax:* 317-283-9519; *E-Mail:* karn@butleru.edu

KARNAKY, KARL JOHN, JR, EPITHELIAL TRANSPORT. *Current Pos:* ASSOC PROF ANAT & CELL BIOL, MED UNIV SC, 86- *Personal Data:* b Houston, Tex, Sept 2, 43. *Educ:* Rice Univ, PhD(biol), 72. *Prof Exp:* Asst prof anat & cell biol, Sch Med, Temple Univ, 76-80; asst prof physiol, Sch Med, Univ Tex, Houston, 80-86. *Mem:* Am Soc Biol Chemists. *Mailing Add:* Dept Anat & Cell Biol Med Univ SC 171 Ashley Ave Charleston SC 29425-2204

KARNAUGH, MAURICE, HEURISTIC SEARCH, KNOWLEDGE REPRESENTATION. *Current Pos:* RETIRED. *Personal Data:* b New York, NY, Oct 4, 24; m 70; c 2. *Educ:* City Col NY, BS, 48; Yale Univ, MS, 50, PhD(physics), 52. *Prof Exp:* Res staff, Bell Tel Labs, 52-66; res & develop mgr, Fed Systs Div, IBM, Yorktown Heights, NY, 66-70, res staff, 70-93. *Concurrent Pos:* Distinguished adj prof comput sci, Polytech Inst NY, 81- *Mem:* Fel Inst Elec & Electronics Engrs; Am Asn Artificial Intel; Sigma Xi. *Res:* Techniques for implementing knowledge based systems in computers; knowledge representations and search methods. *Mailing Add:* IBM Corp Res Div Watson Res Ctr PO Box 218 Yorktown Heights NY 10598

KARNER, FRANK RICHARD, GEOLOGY. *Current Pos:* From asst prof to assoc prof, 62-69, PROF GEOL, UNIV NDAK, 69- *Personal Data:* b Elmhurst, Ill, Aug 14, 34; m 58; c 5. *Educ:* Wheaton Col, BS, 57; Univ Ill, PhD(geol), 63. *Mem:* AAAS; Geol Soc Am; Sigma Xi. *Res:* Mineralogy and petrology of igneous, sedimentary and metamorphic rocks. *Mailing Add:* Geol Dept Univ NDak PO Box 8358 Grand Forks ND 58202-8358

KARNEY, CHARLES FIELDING FINCH, RADIO-FREQUENCY HEATING, DIVERTOR PHYSICS. *Current Pos:* res assoc, 77-79, res staff, 79-88, PRIN RES PHYSICIST, PLASMA PHYSICS LAB & LECTR/ PROF, DEPT ASTROPHYS, PRINCETON UNIV, 88- *Personal Data:* b Eng, Nov 7, 51; m. *Educ:* Cambridge Univ, Eng, BA, 72; Mass Inst Technol, SM, 74, PhD(elec eng & comp sci), 77. *Prof Exp:* Res assoc, Dept Elec Eng & Comp Sci, Mass Inst Technol, 77. *Mem:* Am Phys Soc. *Res:* Plasma physics, especially divertor physics and radio-frequency heating; intrinsic stochasticity with application to plasma physics. *Mailing Add:* Plasma Physics Lab Princeton Univ PO Box 451 Princeton NJ 08543-0451. *Fax:* 609-243-2662; *E-Mail:* karney@princeton.edu

KARNI, SHLOMO, ELECTRICAL ENGINEERING. *Current Pos:* from asst prof to prof, 61-69, dir grad studies, 71-87, PROF ELEC ENG, UNIV NMEX, 69-, DIR UNDERGRAD STUDIES, 87-, GRADNER-ZEMKE PROF, 93- *Personal Data:* b June 23, 32; US citizen; m 61, Michaela Jordan; c Gideon J & Sarah M. *Educ:* Israel Inst Technol, BS, 56; Yale Univ, MEng, 57; Univ Ill, PhD(elec eng), 60. *Prof Exp:* Testing engr, Palestine Power Co, 55-56; asst elec eng, Yale Univ, 56-57; from instr to asst prof, Univ Ill, 57-61. *Concurrent Pos:* Mem circuits group, Univ Ill, 60-61; consult, Los Alamos Nat Lab, Dept Energy, Westinghouse, Var Publ Houses & Kirtland AFB; vis prof, Univ Hawaii, 69-70, Tel Aviv Univ, 70-71 & Israel Inst Technol, 77-78. *Mem:* AAAS; fel Inst Elec & Electronics Engrs; Am Soc Eng Educ. *Res:* Theory; system theory; filters; engineering education. *Mailing Add:* Dept Elec Eng & Comput Eng Univ NMex Albuquerque NM 87131. *Fax:* 505-277-1439; *E-Mail:* karni@.unm.edu

KARNOPP, BRUCE HARVEY, ENGINEERING MECHANICS, APPLIED MATHEMATICS. *Current Pos:* asst prof eng mech, 68-77, ASSOC PROF ENG MECH & APPL MECH, UNIV MICH, ANN ARBOR, 77- *Personal Data:* b Milwaukee, Wis, June 13, 38; m 63; c 3. *Educ:* Mass Inst Technol, SB, 60; Brown Univ, ScM, 63; Univ Wis, PhD(eng mech), 65. *Prof Exp:* Engr, AC Spark Plug, Gen Motors Corp, Wis, 60-61; engr, Sanders Assocs, NH, 61; instr eng mech, Univ Wis, 62-65; asst prof, Univ Toronto, 65-68. *Mem:* Acoust Soc Am; Tensor Soc. *Res:* Variational methods in mechanics, vibrations and dynamics. *Mailing Add:* Dept Mech Eng & Appl Mech 2250 GG Brown Univ Mich Main Campus 2350 Haywood Ann Arbor MI 48109-2125

KARNOPP, DEAN CHARLES, MECHANICAL ENGINEERING. *Current Pos:* from asst prof to assoc prof syst dynamics & control, Mass Inst Technol, 64-69, prof syst dynamics & control, 69-80, PROF MECH ENG, UNIV CALIF, DAVIS, 80- *Personal Data:* b Milwaukee, Wis, June 12, 34; m 58; c 2. *Educ:* Mass Inst Technol, BS & MS, 57, PhD(mech eng), 61. *Honors & Awards:* Levy Medal, Franklin Inst, 69; Sr US Scientist Award, Humbolt Found, 75. *Prof Exp:* Asst appl mech, Mass Inst Technol, 57-59, instr, 59-61, asst prof & Ford fel, 61-63; develop engr, Siemens Schuckert Res Ctr, Ger, 63-64. *Concurrent Pos:* Vis prof, Univ Stuttgart, Ger, 75-76. *Mem:* Am Soc Mech Engrs. *Res:* Dynamic systems; random vibrations; search and optimization theory; control; computation; bond graph modeling of engineering systems. *Mailing Add:* 1217 Stanford Pl Davis CA 95616

KARNOSKY, DAVID FRANK, FOREST GENETICS. *Current Pos:* STAFF MEM, SCH FORESTRY, MICH TECH UNIV, HOUGHTON, 83- *Personal Data:* b Rhinelander, Wis, Oct 12, 49; m 70, Sheryl Bennett; c 2. *Educ:* Univ Wis-Madison, BS, 71, MS, 72, PhD(forest genetics), 75. *Prof Exp:* Forest geneticist, Cary Arboretum, NY Bot Garden, 75-83. *Mem:* Int Soc Arboriculture; Tissue Culture Asn; Soc Am Foresters; Int Tissue Cult Asn; Sigma Xi; Int Plant Propagators Asn. *Res:* Variation in air pollution tolerance of trees; cytogenetic and tissue culture studies of elms; developing urban hardy trees; interspecific hybridization of Ulmus and Larix species; forest biotechnology and gene transfer. *Mailing Add:* Sch Forestry Mich Tech Univ 1400 Townsend Dr Houghton MI 49931. *Fax:* 906-487-2897

KARNOVSKY, MANFRED L, BIOCHEMISTRY. *Current Pos:* from res assoc to assoc, 50-51, from asst prof to prof, 52-65, chmn dept, 69-73, Harold T White prof, 65-89, EMER HAROLD T WHITE PROF BIOL CHEM, HARVARD MED SCH, 89- *Personal Data:* b Johannesburg, SAfrica, Dec 14, 18; nat US; m 52; c 1. *Educ:* Univ Witwatersrand, BSc, 51, hons, 42, MSc, 43; Univ Capetown, PhD(org chem), 47. *Honors & Awards:* Glycerine Producers Asn Second Award, 53; Gold Medal, Reticuloendothelial Soc, 66. *Prof Exp:* Jr lectr chem, Univ Witwatersrand, 41-42; chief chemist & inspector, Brit Ministry Aircraft Prod, SAfrica, 42-43; asst, Univ Capetown, 44-47. *Concurrent Pos:* Res fel, Univ Wis, 47-48; Lederle med fac award, 55-58. *Mem:* Am Soc Biol Chemists; fel Am Acad Arts & Sci; Histochem Soc (secy, 82-85); Am Chem Soc; Am Soc Cell Biol. *Res:* Biochemistry of phagocytosis, pinocytosis and other transport phenomena; biochemistry of sleep. *Mailing Add:* Dept Biol Chem & Molecular Pharm Harvard Med Sch 25 Shattuck St Boston MA 02115-6092

KARNOVSKY, MORRIS JOHN, PATHOLOGY, CELL BIOLOGY. *Current Pos:* assoc, 61-63, from asst prof to assoc prof, 63-68, PROF PATH, HARVARD MED SCH, 68-, SHATTUCK PROF PATH ANAT, 72- *Personal Data:* b Johannesburg, SAfrica, June 28, 26; nat US; m 51, Shirley

Katz; c David & Nina. *Educ:* Univ Witwatersrand, BSc, 46, MB, BCh, 50, DSc, 84; Univ London, dipl clin path, 54. *Hon Degrees:* MA, Harvard Univ, 65. *Honors & Awards:* Rous-Whipple Award, Am Asn Pathologists, 81; Distinguished Scientist Award, Electron Micros Soc Am, 88; E B Wilson Award, Am Soc Cell Biol, 90; Maude Abbott Award, US & Can Acad Path, 94. *Prof Exp:* House officer med & surg, Johannesburg Gen Hosp, 51; asst resident path, Beth Israel Hosp, 55-56. *Concurrent Pos:* Res fel, Harvard Med Sch, 56-60; Lederle med fac award, 63-66; assoc, Peter Bent Brigham Hosp, 58-60; sci collabr, Sch Med, Univ Geneva, 61-63; mem study group path, USPHS, 65-69. *Mem:* Nat Acad Sci-Inst Med; fel Am Acad Arts & Sci; Am Soc Exp Path; Histochem Soc; Int Acad Path; Am Soc Cell Biol; fel AAAS; hon mem Ger Soc Cell Biol; Histochem Soc. *Res:* Histochemistry; electron microscopy; ultrastructural cytochemistry; cell surface topography and modulation; cell junctions; metabolism and structure of kidney; structure and function of capillaries; growth regulation in blood vessels; reactive oxygen species. *Mailing Add:* Dept Path Harvard Med Sch 25 Shattuck St Boston MA 02115

KARNS, CHARLES W(ESLEY), OPERATIONS ANALYSIS. *Current Pos:* RETIRED. *Personal Data:* b Waynesboro, Pa, July 15, 20; m 46; c 3. *Educ:* Dickinson Col, BA, 41; Northwestern Univ, MA, 48. *Prof Exp:* Asst math, Northwestern Univ, 46-51; mem staff, Opers Eval Group, Div Sponsored Res, Mass Inst Technol, 51-53, 54-62, Opers Res Group, 53-54; mem staff opers eval group, Ctr Naval Anal, Franklin Inst, 62-63, naval warfare anal group, 63-64, opers eval group, 64-67; mem staff, Opers Eval Group, Ctr Naval Anal, Univ Rochester, 67-71; staff asst off dep dir test & eval, Off Dir Defense Res & Eng, Off Secy Defense, 71-78; staff specialist prog & financial matters, Off Dir Test & Eval, Off Undersecy Defense Res & Eng, 78-85. *Mem:* Opers Res Soc Am; Math Asn Am. *Res:* Military operations research. *Mailing Add:* 8629 Redwood Dr Vienna VA 22180

KARO, DOUGLAS PAUL, APPLIED TECHNOLOGY, INFORMATION MANAGEMENT. *Current Pos:* TECH STAFF, DRAPER LAB, 89- *Personal Data:* b Seattle, Wash, Aug 24, 47; m 71, Rebecca Wall; c Alice J. *Educ:* Stanford Univ, BS, 69; Mass Inst Technol, PhD(physics), 73, MS, 80. *Prof Exp:* Physicist, Harry Diamond Lab, US Army, 71; sr staff scientist physics, Avco Everett Res Lab Inc, 73-78; staff mgt consult, Texton Defense Syst, 80-87; tech consult, Nat Sec, 87-89. *Mem:* Am Phys Soc; AAAS; Sigma Xi; Int Inst Strategic Studies; Am Inst Aeronaut & Astronaut. *Res:* Defense science and technology; systems analysis; management of research and development. *Mailing Add:* 7308 Churchill Rd McLean VA 22101. *E-Mail:* dkaro@draper.com

KARO, WOLF, INDUSTRIAL ORGANIC CHEMISTRY, POLYMER APPLICATIONS TO BIOTECHNOLOGY. *Current Pos:* RETIRED. *Personal Data:* b Altona-Hamburg, Ger, Apr 2, 24; nat US; m 55, Inge Heiman; c David N. *Educ:* Cornell Univ, AB, 45, PhD(org chem), 49. *Prof Exp:* Aeronaut res scientist jet fuel, Nat Adv Comt Aeronaut, 49-53; aeronaut res scientist fuel synthesis, Monomer-Polymer, Inc, 53-55; group leader contract res, synthesis & polymerization sects, Borden Chem Co, 55-68, develop mgr, Monomer-Polymer & Dajac Labs, 61-68; sr sci specialist, Scott Paper Co, 68-69; new prod mgr, Sartomer Resins, Inc, 70-71; supvr qual control, Lactona Corp Div, Warner-Lambert Pharmaceut Co, 72-75; sr chemist, Rohm & Haas Co, 75; res supvr, Haven Chem Co, 75-76; mgr res & develop, Polysci Inc, 76-93. *Mem:* AAAS; Am Chem Soc; Sigma Xi. *Res:* Reaction kinetics and mechanisms in organic chemistry; organic functional group synthesis; emulsion and anaerobic polymerization; adhesives; coatings; product and process development; materials for radiation-induced polymerization; anionic polymerization; organic polymer chemistry; monodispersed polymer latices for biotechnology; magnetizable latex and application; intraoccular materials. *Mailing Add:* 328 Rockledge Ave Huntingdon Valley PA 19006

KAROL, FREDERICK J, POLYMER CHEMISTRY. *Current Pos:* Chemist, Chem & Plastics Group, Union Carbide Corp, 56-59 & 62-65, proj scientist, 65-67, res scientist, 67-69, group leader chem & plastics, 69-78, res assoc & group supvr, 78-81, corp fel, 81-84, SR CORP FEL, UNION CARBIDE CORP, 84- *Personal Data:* b Norton, Mass, Feb 28, 33; m 58, Ruth Lindbom; c Mark, Donald & Cynthia. *Educ:* Boston Univ, BS, 54; Mass Inst Technol, PhD(org chem), 62. *Honors & Awards:* Chem Pioneer Award, Am Inst Chemists, 88; Perkin Medal, Soc Chem Indust, 89; Int Gold Medal, Soc Plastics Engrs, 90; Award for Creative Invention, Am Chem Soc, 91. *Mem:* Nat Acad Eng; Am Inst Chemists; Sigma Xi; Am Chem Soc. *Res:* Heterogeneous and polyolefin catalyses; mechanism of polymerization; production of high density polyethylene and low density polyethylene; polypropylene; new polymers. *Mailing Add:* 18 Hiland Dr Belle Mead NJ 08502

KAROL, MARK J, COMMUNICATIONS SYSTEMS RESEARCH, NETWORK SYSTEMS RESEARCH. *Current Pos:* mem tech staff, 85-92, DISTINGUISHED MEM TECH STAFF, AT&T BELL LABS, 93- *Personal Data:* b Jersey City, NJ, Feb 28, 59; m 87, Roxanne; c Robert & Kevin. *Educ:* Case Inst Technol, BS & BSEE, 81; Princeton Univ, MS, 82, MA, 83, PhD(elec eng), 86. *Concurrent Pos:* Assoc ed, Inst Elec & Electronics Engrs J Lightwave Technol, 91; secy, Tech Comt Comput Commun, Inst Elec & Electronics Engrs, 89-91, vchmn, 91-93, chmn, 93-95, gen chair, info comt, 94, Commun Soc Bd Gov, 96- *Mem:* Fel Inst Elec & Electronics Engrs; Math Asn Am. *Mailing Add:* Bell Labs Lucent Technologies, Rm 4F-529 101 Crawfords Corner Rd Holmdel NJ 07733-3030. *Fax:* 732-949-9118; *E-Mail:* mk@bell-labs.com

KAROL, MERYL HELENE, IMMUNOCHEMISTRY, TOXICOLOGY. *Current Pos:* res assoc epidemiol, 74-76, res asst prof toxicol, 76-78, assoc prof, 79-85, PROF IMMUNOTOXICOL, UNIV PITTSBURGH, 85- *Personal Data:* b New York, NY; m 63; c 3. *Educ:* Cornell Univ, BS, 61; Columbia Univ, PhD(microbiol), 67. *Honors & Awards:* Frank R Blood, 81; Rachel Carson Award, 93. *Prof Exp:* Fel biochem, State Univ NY, Stony Brook, 67-68, assoc mem, NIH Study Sect. *Mem:* Am Chem Soc; Am Thoracic Soc; AAAS; Soc Toxicol (pres, 94); NY Acad Sci; Am Asn Immunol. *Res:* Chemical and industrial allergens; environmental lung disease; occupational disease; diagnostic radioimmunoassays. *Mailing Add:* Dept Environ & Occup Health Univ Pittsburgh 260 Kappa Dr Pittsburgh PA 15238. *Fax:* 412-967-6611

KAROL, PAUL J(ASON), PHYSICAL CHEMISTRY, ANALYTICAL CHEMISTRY. *Current Pos:* from asst prof to assoc prof, 69-94, assoc dean sci, 81-86, PROF CHEM, CARNEGIE-MELLON UNIV, 94- *Personal Data:* b New York, NY, Mar 18, 41; m 63, Meryl; c Darcie, Deverin & Meredith. *Educ:* Johns Hopkins Univ, BA, 61; Columbia Univ, MS, 62, PhD(chem), 67. *Prof Exp:* Res assoc nuclear chem, Brookhaven Nat Lab, 67-69. *Concurrent Pos:* Res collabr, Brookhaven Nat Lab, 69-72; consult, Westinghouse Elec Corp, 72-85; mem Comt Nuclear Radiochem, Nat Res Coun, 81-87, assoc mem, Comn on Radiochem, Int Union Pure & Appl Chem, 85-93, titular mem, 93-97, chmn, 95-97; chmn, Div Nuclear Chem & Technol, Am Chem Soc, 96; vis prof, Lab Nat Di Disilia Nucleare, Padova. *Mem:* AAAS; Am Chem Soc; Am Phys Soc; Sigma Xi; fel Am Inst Chemists. *Res:* Mechanisms of high energy nuclear reactions; rapid radiochemical separations; column chromatography; positronium quenching; environmental chemistry. *Mailing Add:* Dept Chem 4400 Fifth Ave Pittsburgh PA 15213. *Fax:* 412-268-6945; *E-Mail:* pko3@andrew.cmu.edu

KAROL, ROBIN A, MONOCLONAL ANTIBODY PRODUCTION. *Current Pos:* Res immunologist, 82-85, SR RES IMMUNOLOGIST & GROUP LEADER, DEPT BIOMED PROD, E I DU PONT DE NEMOURS & CO INC, WILMINGTON, DEL, 85- *Personal Data:* b Bronx, NY, Sept 29, 51. *Mem:* AAAS; Am Asn Immunologists. *Mailing Add:* Chalfonte 2412 Granby Dr Wilmington DE 19810. *Fax:* 302-451-3487

KARON, JOHN MARSHALL, BIOSTATISTICS. *Current Pos:* STATISTICIAN, CTR DIS CONTROL, ATLANTA, 84- *Personal Data:* b Milwaukee, Wis, Nov 6, 41. *Educ:* Carleton Col, BA, 63; Stanford Univ, MS, 65, PhD(math), 68. *Prof Exp:* Asst prof math, Syracuse Univ, 68-70; res assoc, Stanford Univ, 70-71; asst prof math, Colo Col, 71-77; fel biostatist, Univ NC, 77-80, res assoc prof, 80-84. *Concurrent Pos:* Vis lectr, Tel Aviv Univ, 72-73. *Mem:* AAAS; Soc Indust & Appl Math; Am Statist Asn. *Res:* Evaluation of statistical methods; statistical epidemiology. *Mailing Add:* Univ NC 423 Blanton Rd Atlanta GA 30342

KAROW, ARMAND M(ONFORT), GENERAL PHARMACOLOGY, CRYOBIOLOGY. *Current Pos:* Res instr, Dept Surg, Med Col Ga, 68-71, res asst prof, 71-77, asst prof, Dept Pharmacol, 68-70, assoc prof, 70-75, dir grad studies, 73-80, RES ASSOC PROF, DEPT SURG, MED COL GA, 77-, PROF, DEPT PHARMACOL, 75- *Personal Data:* b New Orleans, La, Nov 11, 41; m 64, Ramona McClelland; c Christopher A & Jonathan C. *Educ:* Duke Univ, BA, 62; Univ Miss, PhD(pharmacol), 68. *Concurrent Pos:* Ed, Organ Preserv for Transplantation, 74, 81, Biophys of Organ Cryopreservation, 87; officer, Xytex Corp, Augusta, Ga, 75-; res grants, NIH & USPHS; fel, Nat Endowment Humanities, 80; Fogarty sr int fel award, NIH, 81. *Mem:* Fel AAAS; Am Soc Reproductive Med; Soc Cryobiol (secy, 77-80); Am Asn Tissue Banks; Europ Soc Human Reproduction & Embryol. *Res:* Cryopreservation of mammalian organs and tissues; mammalian reproductive biology. *Mailing Add:* Dept Pharmacol Med Col Ga Augusta GA 30912. *Fax:* 706-721-2347

KAROWE, DAVID NATHAN, PLANT-INSECT INTERACTIONS, ECOLOGICAL EFFECTS OF ELEVATED CARBON DIOXIDE. *Current Pos:* ASST PROF BIOL, VA COMMONWEALTH UNIV, 90- *Personal Data:* b Waltham, Mass, May 27, 57. *Educ:* Harvard Univ, BA, 79; Univ Mich, MS, 83, PhD(ecol), 88. *Prof Exp:* Fel, NATO-NSF, 88-89, Univ Mich, 89-90. *Concurrent Pos:* Vis asst prof, Univ Mich Biol Sta, 90- *Mem:* Soc Study Evolution; Chem Ecol Soc; Entom Soc Am. *Res:* Direct effects of elevated carbon dioxide on multiple trophic level systems and the potential for adaptive evolutionary response at each trophic level. *Mailing Add:* Dept Biol Va Commonwealth Univ Box 2012 Richmond VA 23284-9004. *Fax:* 804-367-0503; *E-Mail:* dkarowe@cabell.vcu.edu

KARP, ABRAHAM E, RESEARCH ADMINISTRATION, MATHEMATICS. *Current Pos:* RETIRED. *Personal Data:* b New York, NY, Mar 11, 15; m 40, Annette Greenfield; c Robert & Karen (Willson). *Educ:* City Col New York, BS, 36, MS, 37. *Prof Exp:* Mathematician, Aberdeen Proving Ground, Dept Army, 40-50, chief, Anal Sect Math Statist, 50-55, dir, AnalLab, 55-62, chief, Gaming Div, Strategy & Tactics Anal Group, 62-66; tech dir, opers res & systs anal progs, Nat Bur Stand, 66-69; dir, Ctr Criminal Justice Opers Res & Mgt, Law Enforcement Assistance Admin, 69-70; dir, Tech Anal Div, Nat Bur Stand, 70-71; pvt consult, Systs Anal & Opers Res, 71-80. *Concurrent Pos:* Mem, US Civil Serv Bd Exam, 63-71 & Army Math Steering Comt, 63-66; mem comt govt & bus exec policy & progs, Brookings Inst, 69-71; consult, prof bus orgn on prog develop & tech mgt, 72-85. *Mem:* Fel AAAS; Opers Res Soc Am. *Res:* Operations research and systems analysis in the areas of transportation, other public systems and military defense systems including the development of war gaming methodology. *Mailing Add:* 10308 Green Trail Dr N Boynton Beach FL 33436

KARP, ALAN H, ASTROPHYSICS, COMPUTER ARCHITECTURE. *Current Pos:* SR STAFF MEM, HEWLETT-PACKARD LABS, 92- *Personal Data:* b Syracuse, NY, Aug 6, 46; m 70, Nancy Hurtt; c Joseph S. *Educ:* Rensselaer Polytech Inst, BS, 68; Univ Md, College Park, PhD(astron), 74. *Prof Exp:* Fel astron, IBM Res, Yorktown Heights, NY, 74-76; asst prof physics, Dartmouth Col, 76-77; mem staff physics, IBM Sci Ctr, 77-92. *Concurrent Pos:* Consult, IBM Res, Yorktown Heights, NY, 76-77. *Mem:* Am Astron Soc; Asn Computer Mach; Inst Elec & Electronic Engrs Computer Soc; Soc Indust & Appl Math. *Res:* Algorithms for parallel processors; radiative transfer in moving stellar atmospheres; radiative transfer in planetary atmospheres containing dust. *Mailing Add:* 837 Ilima Ct Palo Alto CA 94304. *E-Mail:* alan_karp@hpl.hp.com

KARP, ARTHUR, HIGH FREQUENCY PHYSICS, MICROWAVE ELECTRONICS. *Current Pos:* SR ENGR, VARIAN ASSOCS INC, 77- *Personal Data:* b New York, NY, Apr 26, 28. *Educ:* City Col New York, BEE, 48; Mass Inst Technol, SM, 50; Cambridge Univ, PhD(elec eng), 62. *Honors & Awards:* B J Thompson Mem Prize, Inst Radio Engrs, 58. *Prof Exp:* Jr engr, A Alford Consult Engrs, Mass, 48; res asst electronics, Mass Inst Technol, 48-50; res asst cent lab, Int Tel & Tel, Paris, France, 50-51; mem tech staff, Bell Tel Labs, Inc, 51-56; engr lab, Cambridge Univ, 56-59; res engr, W W Hansen Labs, Stanford, 60-64; sr res engr, SRI Int, 64-77. *Concurrent Pos:* Consult, Sylvania Elec Prod Inc, Calif, 60-62, Varian Assocs, 62-63 & Goodyear Aerospace Corp, Ariz, 63-64. *Mem:* AAAS; Inst Elec & Electronics Engrs. *Res:* Electron devices; ultrahigh frequency, microwave and millimeter-wave techniques, components, circuits, electron tubes, bio-effects; color perception and display techniques including color encryption. *Mailing Add:* 1470 Sand Mill Rd Apt 301 Palo Alto CA 94304-2058

KARP, BENNETT C, NUCLEAR PHYSICS. *Current Pos:* DISTINGUISHED MEM TECH STAFF, AT&T BELL LABS, 84- *Personal Data:* b Brooklyn, NY, May 15, 54. *Educ:* State Univ NY, Binghampton, Ba, 76; Univ Pittsburgh, MS, 78, PhD(physics), 82. *Prof Exp:* Postdoc res assoc, Univ NC, 82-84. *Mem:* Am Phys Soc. *Mailing Add:* 812 Wellington Pl Aberdeen NJ 07747

KARP, HERBERT RUBIN, NEUROLOGY. *Current Pos:* asst prof med, 58-63, PROF NEUROL, SCH MED, EMORY UNIV, 63- *Personal Data:* b Atlanta, Ga, Apr 13, 21; m 48; c 3. *Educ:* Emory Univ, AB, 43; MD, 51; Am Bd Psychiat & Neurol, dipl, 60. *Prof Exp:* Intern & jr asst resident internal med, Grady Mem Hosp, 51-53; fel metab dis, Sch Med, Emory Univ, 53-54; resident neurol, Univ Hosp, Duke Univ, 54-56; clin & res fel, Harvard Med Sch, 56-57, res fel neuropath, 57-58. *Concurrent Pos:* Nat Inst Neurol Dis & Blindness spec trainee, 56-58; consult, Vet Admin Hosp, Atlanta, Ga. *Mem:* AAAS; Am Neurol Asn; fel Am Acad Neurol. *Res:* Cerebrovascular disease from the standpoint of further understanding of underlying pathophysiology as well as evaluation of current methods of therapy; age-dependent degenerative diseases of the nervous system. *Mailing Add:* 1821 Clifton Rd Atlanta GA 30329-4021

KARP, HOWARD, ANALYTICAL CHEMISTRY. *Current Pos:* RETIRED. *Personal Data:* b Pittsburgh, Pa, Sept 26, 26; m 52; c 4. *Educ:* Univ Pittsburgh, BS, 49. *Prof Exp:* assoc res consult chem, US Steel Corp, 49-85. *Concurrent Pos:* Mem, comt chem anal metals, Am Soc Testing & Mat. *Res:* Analytical chemistry as it pertains to steel chemistry. *Mailing Add:* 151 Kelvington Dr Monroeville PA 15146

KARP, LAURENCE EDWARD, OBSTETRICS & GYNECOLOGY, MEDICAL GENETICS. *Current Pos:* ASSOC PROF OBSTET & GYNEC, SCH MED, UNIV WASH, 77-; DIR EDUC OBSTET & GYNEC, SWED HOSP MED CTR, SEATTLE, 77- *Personal Data:* b Paterson, NJ, Apr 26, 39; m 62; c 2. *Educ:* NY Univ, MD, 63. *Prof Exp:* Instr obstet & gynec, Sch Med, Univ Tex, San Antonio, 69-70; sr fel reprod genetics, Sch Med, Univ Wash, 70-72, asst prof obstet & gynec, 72-76; assoc prof, Harbor Gen Hosp, Univ Calif, Los Angeles, 76-77. *Mem:* Fel Am Col Obstet & Gynec; AAAS; Am Soc Human Genetics. *Res:* Investigation of chromosomal anomalies in gametes and preimplantation embryos; also, advancement of procedures and techniques for prenatal diagnosis. *Mailing Add:* Div Perinatal Med Swed Hosp Med Ctr 747 Summit Seattle WA 98104-2132

KARP, RICHARD DALE, IMMUNOLOGY. *Current Pos:* from asst prof to assoc prof, 75-86, PROF BIOL SCI, UNIV CINCINNATI, 86- *Personal Data:* b Minneapolis, Minn, June 19, 43; m 68; c 3. *Educ:* Univ Minn, BA, 65, MS, 68, PhD(microbiol), 72. *Prof Exp:* Res assoc microbiol, Univ Minn, 66-72; NIH & C D Rogers fels, Univ Calif, Los Angeles, 73-75. *Mem:* Am Soc Microbiol; Am Soc Zoologists; Am Asn Immunologists; AAAS; NY Acad Sci; Int Soc Develop Comp Immunologists; Entom Soc Am. *Res:* Evolution of humoral and cell-mediated immunity. *Mailing Add:* Dept Biol Sci Univ Cincinnati Cincinnati OH 45221-0006. *Fax:* 513-556-5299

KARP, RICHARD M, COMPUTER THEORY, ALGORITHMS & COMPUTATIONAL COMPLEXITY. *Current Pos:* Prof comput sci & opers res, Univ Calif, Berkeley, 68-94, assoc chmn dept, 73-75, Miller res prof, 80-81, prof math, 80-94, fac res lectr, 81-82, EMER UNIV PROF, GRAD SCH, UNIV CALIF, BERKELEY, 94-; PROF COMPUT SCI & ENG & ADJ PROF MOLECULAR BIOTECHNOL, UNIV WASH, 95- *Personal Data:* b Boston, Mass, Jan 3, 35; m 79; c 1. *Educ:* Harvard Univ, AB, 55, SM, 56, PhD(appl math), 59. *Hon Degrees:* Dr, Univ Pa, 86, Technion, 89, Univ Mass, 90 & Georgetown Univ, 92. *Honors & Awards:* Lanchester Prize, Opers Res Soc Am & Inst Mgt Sci, 77; Fulkerson Prize, Am Math Soc, 79; Turing Award, Asn Comput Mach, 85; von Neumann lectr, Soc Indust & Appl Math, 87; von Neumann Theory Prize, Opers Res Soc Am, 90; Babbage Prize, 95; Nat Med Sci, 96; Centennial Medal, Harvard Univ, 97. *Prof Exp:* Mem res staff, Watson Res Ctr, Int Bus Mach Corp, 59-68; adj assoc prof indust & mgt eng, Columbia Univ, 67-68; res scientist, Int Comput Sci Inst, 88-94. *Concurrent Pos:* Vis assoc prof elec eng, Univ Mich, 64-65; vis assoc prof, Polytech Inst Brooklyn, 65-68, vis prof, 68; mem bd trustees, Int Comput Sci Inst, 88-; mem bd govs, Weizmann Inst Sci, 89-; mem nat adv bd, Comput Professionals Social Responsibility, 89- *Mem:* Nat Acad Sci; Nat Acad Eng; fel Am Acad Arts & Sci; Am Math Soc; fel Asn Comput Mach; Comput Prof Social Responsibility; Soc Indust & Appl Math; NY Acad Sci; fel AAAS. *Res:* Construction of computational algorithms and the determination of the inherent computational complexity of problems with particular emphasis on combinatorial problems. *Mailing Add:* Dept Comput Sci & Eng Univ Wash Box 352350 Seattle WA 98195

KARP, SAMUEL NOAH, applied mathematics, for more information see previous edition

KARP, STEWART, ANALYTICAL CHEMISTRY. *Current Pos:* asst prof, 68-71, assoc prof, 71-82, chmn, Dept Chem, 81-88, PROF CHEM, C W POST COL, LONG ISLAND UNIV, 82- *Personal Data:* b New York, NY, Mar 17, 32; m 57; c 2. *Educ:* Queens Col, NY, BS, 53; Polytech Inst Brooklyn, MS, 60, PhD(chem), 67. *Prof Exp:* Chemist, Sperry Gyroscope Co, 57-60; anal chemist, Colgate-Palmolive Co, 60-62; sr chemist, Am Cyanamid Co, 67-68. *Mem:* Am Chem Soc; Sigma Xi; AAAS. *Res:* Electroanalytical chemistry; analytical methods. *Mailing Add:* Dept Chem Long Island Univ C W Post Ctr Greenvale NY 11548

KARP, WARREN B, DENTISTRY. *Current Pos:* pediat res instr, Sch Med, Med Col Ga, 71-73, instr cell & molecular biol, 72-73, asst res prof pediat & asst prof cell & molecular biol, Sch Med & asst prof, Sch Grad Studies, 73-79, asst prof biochem, Sch Dent, 74-79, assoc res prof pediat, Sch Med, 79-88, assoc prof oral biol biochem & oral med, Sch Dent, 79-88, PROF PEDIAT, ORAL BIOL, ORAL DIAG/PATIENT SERV, BIOCHEM & MOLECULAR BIOL, SCH MED, DENT & GRAD STUDIES, MED COL GA, 88- *Personal Data:* b Brooklyn, NY, Feb 12, 44; m 76, Nancy Blanchard; c Heather & Michael. *Educ:* Pace Univ, BS, 65; Ohio State Univ, PhD(physiol chem), 70; Med Col Ga, DMD, 77. *Prof Exp:* Teaching asst physiol chem, Ohio State Univ, 66-68, res assoc, 68-70, res assoc pediat, 70-71. *Concurrent Pos:* Dir clin perinatal lab, 78-, licensed dietitian, cert nutrit spec. *Mem:* AAAS; Sigma Xi; Am Chem Soc; NY Acad Sci; Int Dent Res Soc; Am Inst Nutrit; Am Soc Clin Nutrit. *Res:* Environmental effects on human placental enzymology; human placental amino acid metabolism; the effect of bilirubin on brain metabolism; human placental lipid metabolism; human nutrition. *Mailing Add:* 402 Hastings Pl Augusta GA 30907. *Fax:* 706-721-7531

KARPATI, GEORGE, HISTOCHEMISTRY, MUSCLE BIOLOGY & NEUROSCIENCE. *Current Pos:* Assoc dir res, 85-91, DIR NEUROMUSCULAR RES, MONTREAL NEUROL INST, MCGILL UNIV, 84-, KILLAM CHAIR NEUROL, 85-, PROF PEDIAT, 90- *Personal Data:* Can citizen; c 2. *Educ:* Dalhousie Univ, MD, 60. *Honors & Awards:* Can Gov Gen Award, 93. *Concurrent Pos:* Coordr, Neuromuscular Res Group, Montreal Neurol Inst, 85-; chmn, Bd Examiners, Royal Col Physicians & Surgeons Can, 86-89; chmn sci adv bd, Muscular Dystrophy Asn Can, 91-94. *Mem:* Hon mem French Neurol Soc; Am Acad Neurol; Am Neurol Asn; Can Cong Neurol Sci; Histochem Soc; Royal Col Physicians & Surgeons Can; World Fedn Neurol. *Res:* Neuromuscular system using histochemical, cytochemical, immunological and physiological techniques; cell therapy of inherited muscle diseases; gene therapy of neurological diseases. *Mailing Add:* Montreal Neurol Inst Rm 633 Montreal PQ H3A 2B4 Can. *Fax:* 514-398-8310

KARPATKIN, SIMON, BIOCHEMISTRY, PHYSIOLOGY. *Current Pos:* from instr to assoc prof, 64-74, PROF MED, SCH MED, NY UNIV, 74- *Personal Data:* b Brooklyn, NY, Sept 6, 33; m 65. *Educ:* Brooklyn Col, BS, 54; NY Univ, MD, 58. *Prof Exp:* Intern med, Bellevue Hosp, NY Univ, 58-59, resident, 59-60; resident, Einstein Med Ctr, Bronx, 60-61. *Concurrent Pos:* Fel hemat, Sch Med, Wash Univ, 61-62; fel biochem, 62-64; USPHS trainee, 61-62; Am Cancer Soc fel, 62-64; res grants, Health Res Coun City of New York, 66, Muscular Dystrophy Asn Am, 66-68, NY Heart Asn, 67-70, NIH, 70-84 & NSF, 78-82; career scientist, Health Res Coun City of New York, 66-71. *Mem:* Am Soc Hemat; Am Fedn Clin Res; Am Soc Physiol; Am Soc Clin Invest; Am Soc Biol Chem. *Res:* Regulation and organization of glycolytic enzymes in platelets; platelet biochemical interactions during hemostasis; biochemical and physiological aspects of human platelet senescence; regulation of platelet production; autoimmune platelet disorders; role of platelets in cancer. *Mailing Add:* NY Univ Sch Med 550 First Ave New York NY 10016-6481

KARPEL, RICHARD LESLIE, MOLECULAR BIOLOGY, BIOPHYSICS. *Current Pos:* from asst prof to assoc prof, 76-95, PROF CHEM, UNIV MD, BALTIMORE CO, 95- *Personal Data:* b New York, NY, May 31, 44; m 68, Madeline A Blatt; c Emily. *Educ:* Queens Col, NY, BA, 65; Brandeis Univ, PhD(chem), 70. *Prof Exp:* Res assoc, Princeton Univ, 70-71, NIH res fel, 71-72, res assoc, 72-74, NIH res fel biochem sci, 74-76. *Concurrent Pos:* Sr fel, Nat Res Coun, Nat Cancer Inst, Frederick Cancer Res Facil, NIH, 82-83. *Mem:* AAAS; Am Chem Soc; Sigma Xi; Am Soc Biochem Molecular Biol. *Res:* Protein-nucleic acid interactions; nucleic acid-interactive enzymes; structure-function studies on nucleic acid helix-destabilizing proteins; retroviral nucleic acid binding proteins; metal-nucleic acid interactions. *Mailing Add:* Dept Chem & Biochem Univ Md 5401 Wilkens Ave Baltimore MD 21228-5398. *Fax:* 410-455-2608; *E-Mail:* karpel@umbc.edu

KARPETSKY, TIMOTHY PAUL, CHEMICAL WARFARE. *Current Pos:* vpres mkt, 89-91, PRES, ENVIRON TECHNOL GROUP INC, 91- *Educ:* Johns Hopkins Univ, PhD(org chem), 70. *Prof Exp:* Supvr phys scientist, Us Army Chem Res & Eng Ctr, 82-87; vpres eng, Bendix Corp, 87-89. *Res:* Convention compliance monitoring. *Mailing Add:* 8219 Ruxton Crossing Ct Baltimore MD 21204

KARPIAK, STEPHEN EDWARD, psychiatry, for more information see previous edition

KARPINSKI, MAREK M, COMPUTER SCIENCES. *Current Pos:* CHAIR PROF COMPUT SCI, UNIV BONN, GER, 89- *Educ:* Acad Scis, Warsaw, Poland, PhD, 73. *Honors & Awards:* Prize, Polish Math Soc, 74; Award, Polish Acad Sci, 76; Res Award, Humboldt Found, 82; Max Planck Res Prize, 94. *Concurrent Pos:* Mem, Int Comput Sci Inst, Berkeley, Calif. *Mem:* Am Math Soc; Soc Indust & Appl Math; Asn Comput Mach; Inst Elec & Electronics Engrs; AAAS. *Res:* Contributed over 100 articles to professional journals; author of 5 books. *Mailing Add:* Dept Comput Sci Univ Bonn Roemerstr 164 53117 Bonn Germany. *Fax:* 49-228-734440; *E-Mail:* marek@cs.bonn.edu

KARPLUS, MARTIN, PHYSICAL CHEMISTRY. *Current Pos:* prof, 66-79, THEODORE WILLIAM RICHARDS PROF CHEM, HARVARD UNIV, 79- *Personal Data:* b Vienna, Austria, Mar 15, 30; nat US; m 81; c 3. *Educ:* Harvard Univ, BA, 50; Calif Inst Technol, PhD(chem), 53. *Honors & Awards:* Fresenius Award, 65; Harrison Howe Award, Am Chem Soc, 67; Award Outstanding Contribution, Int Soc Quantum Biol, 79; Irving Langmuir Award, Am Phys Soc, 87; Theoret Chem Award, Am Chem Soc, 93. *Prof Exp:* NSF fel chem, Oxford Univ, 53-55; from instr to assoc prof phys chem, Univ Ill, 55-60; from assoc prof to prof, Columbia Univ, 60-66. *Concurrent Pos:* NSF sr fel, 65-66; vis prof, Univ Paris, 72-73 & 80-81, prof, 74-75; prof, Col France, Paris, 80-81, 87-88 & Univ Louis Pasteur, Strasbourg, 92 & 94-95; nat lectr, Biophys Soc, 91. *Mem:* Nat Acad Sci; Am Acad Arts & Sci; Int Acad Quantum Molecular Sci; foreign mem Neth Acad Arts & Sci. *Res:* Theory of molecular structure and spectra with emphasis on biologically important molecules; theoretical chemistry, including the electronic interpretation of nuclear magnetic resonance and spectra of molecules, the development of techniques for the evaluation of molecular properties; the formulation of detailed models for chemical reactions; author of numerous publications. *Mailing Add:* Dept Chem Harvard Univ 12 Oxford St Cambridge MA 02138. *Fax:* 617-496-3204

KARPLUS, WALTER J, COMPUTER SCIENCE, SYSTEM MODELING & SIMULATION. *Current Pos:* chmn, Comput Sci Dept, 71-79, PROF COMPUT, ELEC CIRCUITS & ELECTRONICS, UNIV CALIF, LOS ANGELES, 52- *Personal Data:* b Vienna, Austria, Apr 23, 27; nat US; m 69, Takako; c Maya & Anthony. *Educ:* Cornell Univ, BEE, 49; Univ Calif, MS, 51; Univ Calif, Los Angeles, PhD(elec eng), 55. *Honors & Awards:* Sr Sci Simulation Award, Soc Comput Simulation; Achievement Award, NASA; Silver Core Award, Int Fed Info Processing Soc. *Prof Exp:* Field party chief, Sun Oil Co, 49-50; res engr, Int Geophys Inst, 51-52. *Concurrent Pos:* Fulbright res fel, 61; Guggenheim fel, 68. *Mem:* Inst Elec & Electronics Engrs; Soc Comput Simulation; Asn Comput Mach; Am Inst Aeronaut & Astronaut. *Mailing Add:* Dept Comput Sci Univ Calif 3732 Boelter Hall Los Angeles CA 90024

KARR, ALAN FRANCIS, INFERENCE FOR STOCHASTVC PROCESSES. *Current Pos:* ASSOC DIR, NAT INST STATIST SCI, 92-; PROF STATIST & BIOSTATIST, UNIV NC, CHAPEL HILL, 93- *Personal Data:* b Bryn Mawr, Pa, July 12, 47. *Educ:* Northwestern Univ, BS, 69, MS, 70 & PhD(appl math), 73. *Prof Exp:* Prof math sci, Johns Hopkins Univ, 73-92. *Mem:* Fel Inst Math Statist; Am Statist Asn. *Res:* Statistical inference for stochastic processes; image analysis and processing; statistics and materials science. *Mailing Add:* PO Box 14162 Research Triangle Park NC 27709-4162. *Fax:* 919-541-7102; *E-Mail:* karr@rcc.rti.org

KARR, CLARENCE, JR, CHEMISTRY. *Current Pos:* RETIRED. *Personal Data:* b St Louis, Mo, May 12, 23; m 47; c 4. *Educ:* St Louis Univ, BS, 44; Johns Hopkins Univ, PhD(chem), 50. *Honors & Awards:* Award, US Dept Interior, 65 & 66. *Prof Exp:* Fel petrol chem, Mellon Inst, 50-55; supvry res chemist low temperature tar, US Bur Mines, 55-66, coal chemistry, 66-75; supvry res chemist coal liquefaction, Energy Res & Develop Admin, US Dept Energy, 75-77, res chemist synthetic fuels, 77-80, proj mgr advan gasification, Morgantown Energy Technol Ctr, 80-83. *Concurrent Pos:* Prin investr, Apollo 11, 12, 14 & 15 Lunar Sample Prog, 69-72. *Mem:* Fel Am Inst Chem; Am Chem Soc. *Res:* Composition of low temperature coal tar, petroleum; organic synthesis; chromatography; infrared ultraviolet spectroscopy; air pollution; coal minerals; synthetic fuels from coal; lunar mineral; liquid fuels from coal; coal gasification. *Mailing Add:* 624 Vista Pl Morgantown WV 26505

KARR, JAMES PRESBY, REPRODUCTIVE PHYSIOLOGY, STEROID BIOCHEMISTRY. *Current Pos:* cancer res scientist reproductive physiol, Roswell Park Mem Inst, 73-74 & 76-77, dep dir sci affairs cancer res, Nat Prostatic Cancer Proj, 78-84, assoc dir, Organ Systs Coord Ctr, 84-85, dir, Organ Systs Coord Ctr, 85-96, PROF PHYSIOL, NIAGRA UNIV, 82-; ASSOC DIR SCI AFFAIRS, ROSWELL PARK MEM INST, 89-; DIR, OFF INSTNL PROTOCOLS & SCI INTEGRITY, ROSWELL CANCER INST, 96- *Personal Data:* b Nashua, NH, July 24, 41; m 62; c 2. *Educ:* Univ Vt, BA, 64, MS, 66; Pa State Univ, PhD(reproductive physiol), 70. *Prof Exp:* Res assoc reproductive physiol, Pa State Univ, 70-71; asst prof animal breeding, Haille Selassie I Univ, 71-73; asst prof animal breeding & reproductive physiol, Am Univ, Beirut, 74-75. *Concurrent Pos:* Asst prof physiol, Univ Buffalo, 82- *Mem:* AAAS; Am Asn Cancer Res; NY Acad Sci; Soc Basic Urol Res (pres, 93-94). *Res:* Reproductive endocrinology, steroid biochemistry, plasma steroid binding proteins and hormone receptors in the normal physiology and disease states of the human prostate. *Mailing Add:* Roswell Park Cancer Inst Elm & Carlton St Buffalo NY 14263. *Fax:* 716-845-3545

KARR, JAMES RICHARD, WATER QUALITY, CONSERVATION BIOLOGY. *Current Pos:* dir, Inst Environ Studies, 91-95, PROF FISHERIES & ZOOL, UNIV WASH, 95-, ADJ PROF FISHERIES, ENVIRON HEALTH & PUB AFFAIRS. *Personal Data:* b Shelby, Ohio, Dec 26, 43; m 63, 84, Elena Serrano; c Elizabeth & Eric. *Educ:* Iowa State Univ, BSc, 65; Univ Ill, Urbana-Champaign, MSc, 67, PhD(zool), 70. *Prof Exp:* Fel, Princeton Univ, 70-71 & Smithsonian Trop Res Inst, 71-72; asst prof ecol, Purdue Univ, 72-75; from assoc prof to prof ecol, Univ Ill, Urbana-Champaign, 75-84; dep dir, Smithsonian Trop Res Inst, Balboa, Panama, 84-87, actg dir, 87-88; Harold H Bailey prof biol, Va Polytech Inst & State Univ, Blacksburg, Va, 88-91. *Concurrent Pos:* Mem, Eval Panel, Instrnl Sci Equip Prog, NSF, 75, Undergrad Res Participation, 76, conserv biol, 90; consult, Orgn Am States, 80; prin investr grants, NSF, Environ Protection Agency, Nat Geog Soc, Am Philos Soc, US Fish & Wildlife Serv, US Forest Serv & Off Water Resources Technol, Tenn Valley Authority, Dept Energy, 73-; affil, Ill Natural Hist Surv, 81-91; ed, Trop Ecol, 77-81, Ecol, 81-84 & Biosci, 85-94, Conserv Biol, 91, Ecosyst Health, 92-, Freshwater Biol, 93-, Ecol Appln, 95- *Mem:* Ecol Soc Am; fel Am Ornithologists Union; Wilson Ornith Soc; Int Soc Trop Ecol; fel AAAS; Am Inst Biol Sci. *Res:* Community ecology from both basic and applied perspectives with emphasis on studies of tropical forest birds and stream fishes, including a wide range of land use and water resource problems; improving knowledge of biological communities and to apply that knowledge to solution of selected environmental and natural resource problems. *Mailing Add:* Box 352200 Univ Wash Seattle WA 98195. *Fax:* 206-543-2025; *E-Mail:* jrkarr@u.washington.edu

KARR, REYNOLD MICHAEL, JR, ALLERGY, RHEUMATOLOGY. *Current Pos:* ASSOC PROF MED, UNIV WASH, 80- *Personal Data:* b New York, NY, June 24, 42; m 76; c 2. *Educ:* Johns Hopkins Univ, BA, 64; Univ Md, MD, 69. *Prof Exp:* Assoc prof med, Clin Immunol Sect, Sch Med, Tulane Univ, 76-80. *Concurrent Pos:* Vis consult, Vet Admin Hosp, New Orleans, 76-; vis physician, Charity Hosp, New Orleans, 76- *Mem:* Fel Am Col Physicians; Am Acad Allergy; Am Thoracic Soc; Am Rheumatism Asn. *Res:* Arthritis; occupational lung disease; bronchoprovocation. *Mailing Add:* Aland Arthritis Specialists 3128 Norton Ave Everett WA 98201-4216

KARR, TIMOTHY LAWRENCE, BIOCONTROL OF INSECT PESTS USING BACTERIAL-INDUCED MALE STERILITY. *Current Pos:* ASST PROF, UNIV ILL, 87-, FAC FEL, BECKMAN INST, 90- *Personal Data:* b Phoenix, Ariz, May 1, 53; m 84, Wendy Weintraub; c Michael. *Educ:* Univ Calif, Santa Barbara, BA, 76, PhD(chem), 81. *Prof Exp:* Res asst, Univ Calif, Santa Barbara, 77-81; fel, Jane Coffin Childs Mem Fund Med Res, 81-84; Weingart fel, Univ Calif, San Francisco, 85-86, Am Cancer Soc sr fel, 86-87. *Mem:* AAAS; Am Soc Cell Biol; Genetics Soc Am. *Res:* Molecular mechanisms of fertilization in insects; host-symbiosis in insects; cellular and molecular mechanisms of cytoplasmic incompatibility caused by an intracellular symbiont, welbachia pipentis. *Mailing Add:* Dept Organismal Biol & Anat Univ Chicago 1027 E 57th St Chicago IL 60637-1508. *Fax:* 217-244-8371; *E-Mail:* karr@ux1.cso.uiuc.edu

KARRAKER, ROBERT HARRELD, INORGANIC CHEMISTRY. *Current Pos:* assoc prof chem, 67-80, PROF CHEM, EASTERN ILL UNIV, 80- *Personal Data:* b Carbondale, Ill, May 6, 31; m 53; c 2. *Educ:* Southern Ill Univ, BA, 53; Iowa State Univ, PhD(inorg chem), 61. *Prof Exp:* Chemist, Olin-Mathieson Chem Corp, NY, 53-55; asst prof chem, Memphis State Univ, 61-67. *Mem:* Am Chem Soc; Sigma Xi. *Res:* Chemistry of rare earth elements. *Mailing Add:* 2740 Whipoorwill Dr Charleston IL 61920

KARRAS, THOMAS WILLIAM, LASERS, ELECTRO-OPTICS. *Current Pos:* physicist, Astro-Space Div, Gen Elec Co, King of Prussia, Pa, 64-72, mgr laser & plasma physics, 72-79, laser res, 79-84, mgr electro-optic anal, 85-87, mgr, Electro-Optics Anal & Develop, 88-92, tech leader, Martin Marietta Astro-Space, 93-95, DIV FEL, LOCKHEED-MARTIN MISSLILE & SPACE, KING OF PRUSSIA, PA, 96- *Personal Data:* b Chicago, Ill, Jan 4, 36; m 60, Demetra Bartus; c Larissa E & William A. *Educ:* Univ Chicago, BS, 57; Ill Inst Technol, MS, 61; Univ Calif, Los Angeles, PhD(physics), 64. *Prof Exp:* Physicist elec propulsion, Rocketdyne Div, NAm Aviation, 59-61. *Mem:* Am Phys Soc; Am Inst Aeronaut & Astronaut; Sigma Xi; Optical Soc Am; Int Soc Optical Eng. *Res:* Metal vapor lasers; nanosecond discharges; microwave photonics. *Mailing Add:* 231 Wooded Way Berwyn PA 19312. *Fax:* 610-354-2045; *E-Mail:* thomas.w.karras@lmco.com

KARREMAN, GEORGE, MATHEMATICAL BIOLOGY. *Current Pos:* from assoc prof to prof physiol, 62-83, EMER PROF MATH BIOL, SCH MED, UNIV PA, 83- *Personal Data:* b Rotterdam, Holland, Nov 4, 20; US citizen; m 53, Anna Halbertsma; c Grace, Frank & Hubert. *Educ:* Univ Leiden, BS, 39, Drs, 41; Univ Chicago, PhD(math biol), 51. *Prof Exp:* Instr math & physics, Col Tech Sci, Rotterdam, Holland, 46-48; res assoc math biol, Univ Chicago, 51-53, asst prof, 53-54; res assoc theoret biol, Int Muscle Res, Mass, 54-57; med res scientist, Eastern Pa Psychiat Inst, 57-62. *Mem:* Soc Math Biol (pres, 73-81). *Res:* Physiological irritability; biological energy transfer; quantum biology; system analysis of cardiovascular, central nervous renal and endocrine systems; cooperative phenomena; threshold mechanisms; bioelectric phenomena; adsorption mechanism. *Mailing Add:* 435 S Woodbine Ave Penn Valley PA 19072

KARREMAN, HERMAN FELIX, APPLIED MATHEMATICS. *Current Pos:* mem, Math Res Ctr, Univ Wis-Madison, 63-67, prof, Sch Bus, 65-83, prof, Col Eng, 68-83, EMER PROF, UNIV WIS-MADISON, 83- *Personal Data:* b Rotterdam, Neth, June 21, 13; US citizen; m 38, 74; c 2. *Educ:* Neth Sch Econ, Drs, 49. *Honors & Awards:* Lanchester Prize, Opers Res Soc Am, 60. *Prof Exp:* Staff employee, Royal Packet Navig Co, Dutch E Indies, 37-47; sr officer, Cent Planning Bur, Neth, 49-54; res assoc, Nat Bur Econ Res, NY, 54-56; res assoc, Economet Res Prog, Princeton Univ, 56-63. *Mem:* Opers Res Soc Am; Math Asn Am; Am Math Soc. *Mailing Add:* 3412 Blackhawk Dr Madison WI 53705-1404

KARREN, KENNETH W, STRUCTURAL DESIGN. *Current Pos:* CONSULT, 79- *Personal Data:* b Vernal, Utah, May 20, 32; m 53; c 7. *Educ:* Univ Utah, BS, 53, MS, 61; Cornell Univ, PhD(civil eng), 65. *Prof Exp:* Proj develop engr, Pipeline Div, Phillips Petrol, 56-57; chief engr, Otto Buehner Co, 57-61; asst prof civil eng, Brigham Young Univ, 61-62, prof, 65-70; grad student civil eng, Cornell Univ, 62-65; sr engr, Hercules Inc, 70-71; pres, Struct Engrs, Karren & Assocs, 78-79. *Concurrent Pos:* Consult, Hercules Inc, 66-75. *Mem:* Am Soc Civil Engrs. *Res:* Cold-forming of sheet steel led to provisions included in Am Iron and Steel Institute specifications. *Mailing Add:* 424 E 4750 N Provo UT 84604

KARRER, KATHLEEN MARIE, MOLECULAR BIOLOGY, DEVELOPMENTAL BIOLOGY. *Personal Data:* b Grosse Pointe Farms, Mich, June 16, 49. *Educ:* Marquette Univ, BS, 71; Yale Univ, PhD(biol), 76. *Honors & Awards:* John Spangler Nicholas Prize Exp Zool, Yale Univ, 77. *Prof Exp:* Fel biol, Ind Univ, 76-80; asst prof biol, Brandeis Univ, 80-89; Clare Booth Luce prof, Marquette Univ, 89-94. *Concurrent Pos:* Jane Coffin Childs Mem Fund Med Res fel, 76-78; NIH fel, 78-79. *Mem:* AAAS; Am Soc Cell Biol; Soc Protozoologists. *Res:* Eukaryotic chromosome structure and function; DNA rearrangement; molecular biology of ciliates; DNA methylation. *Mailing Add:* Dept Biol Marquette Univ PO Box 1881 Milwaukee WI 53201-1881. *Fax:* 414-288-7357; *E-Mail:* karrerk@vms.csd.mu.edu

KARRON, DANIEL B, MEDICAL IMAGING & GEOMETRIC MODELING. *Current Pos:* NETWORK CONSULT, DEPT SURG, NY UNIV MED CTR, 91-, RES ASSOC THREE-DIMENSIONAL ULTRASOUND FOR COMPUT-AIDED SURG, 93- *Personal Data:* b Brooklyn, NY, Oct 25, 56; m 87, Gail Schupak; c Sarah. *Educ:* NY Univ, BS, 84, MS, 88, PhD(bioeng), 93. *Prof Exp:* Sci graphics programmer & comput syst adminr, Inst Reconstruct Plastic Surg, 83-91. *Concurrent Pos:* Database adminr, Soc Rehab Facially Disfigured, 84-90; fel, Dept Appl Sci, NY Univ, 90-93, assoc, Ctr Neural Sci, 93- *Mem:* AAAS; Inst Elec & Electronics Engrs; Asn Comput Mach. *Res:* Development of a topologically correct method of modeling three-dimensional structures embedded in volumetric datasets. *Mailing Add:* Surg Dept Rm 1 RR 606 NY Univ Med Ctr 560 First Ave New York NY 10018. *Fax:* 212-263-7190; *E-Mail:* karron@nyu.edu

KARROW, PAUL FREDERICK, QUATERNARY GEOLOGY. *Current Pos:* prof civil eng, Univ Waterloo, 63-65, assoc prof earth sci, 65-69, chmn dept, 65-70, PROF EARTH SCI, UNIV WATERLOO, 69- *Personal Data:* b St Thomas, Ont, Sept 14, 30; m 62, Beth McCormick; c Douglas D, Niel A, Sheila E & Thomas P. *Educ:* Queen's Univ, Ont, BSc, 54; Univ Ill, PhD(geol), 57. *Honors & Awards:* W A Johnston Medal, Can Quaternary Asn, 95. *Prof Exp:* Geologist, Ont Dept Mines, 57-63. *Concurrent Pos:* Geologist, Geol Surv Can, 65-68, Ont Dept Mines, 64 & 73, Ont Geol Surv, 82 & 84-87; vis scientist, Scripps Inst Oceanog, La Jolla, Calif, 70 & 76, & BC Geol Surv, 92; vis prof, Univ SFla, Tampa, 84; dir, Quaternary Sci Inst, 87-89. *Mem:* Fel Geol Soc Am; Soc Econ Paleont & Mineral; fel Geol Asn Can; Int Asn Gt Lakes; Am Asn Quaternary Environ; Can Quaternary Asn. *Res:* Quaternary geology; glacial geology; geomorphology; urban geology; paleoecology; great lakes history; interglacial environments. *Mailing Add:* Dept Earth Sci Univ Waterloo Waterloo ON N2L 3G1 Can. *Fax:* 519-746-0183; *E-Mail:* pfkarrow@sciborg.u.waterloo.ca

KARSCH, FRED JOSEPH, REPRODUCTIVE ENDOCRINOLOGY, NEUROENDOCRINOLOGY. *Current Pos:* From asst prof to assoc prof, 72-82, PROF PHYSIOL, UNIV MICH, ANN ARBOR, 82- *Personal Data:* b New York, NY, Aug 8, 42; m 67; c 2. *Educ:* Juniata Col, BS, 64; Univ Maine, MS, 66; Univ Ill, PhD(animal sci, biochem & physiol), 70. *Concurrent Pos:* Ford Found fel, Med Sch, Univ Pittsburgh, 70-71, NIH fel, 71-72. *Mem:* Endocrine Soc; Soc Study Reprod; Soc Study Fertil. *Res:* Neuroendocrine control of gonadotropin secretion; seasonal reproduction; developmental endocrinology. *Mailing Add:* Physiol Med Sci 2 M7744 Univ Mich Med Sch 1301 Catherine Rd Ann Arbor MI 48109-0600

KARSON, JEFFREY ALAN, STRUCTURAL GEOLOGY. *Current Pos:* scholar, 79-80, ASST SCIENTIST, GEOL, WOODS HOLE OCEANOG INST, 80- *Personal Data:* b Akron, Ohio, Nov 3, 49; m 78; c 1. *Educ:* Case Inst Technol, BS, 72; State Univ NY, Albany, MS, 75, PhD(geol), 77. *Prof Exp:* Asst instr, State Univ NY, Albany, 72-75, res asst, 75-77; fel, Erindale Col & Univ Toronto, 77-79. *Concurrent Pos:* Vis lectr, Bridgewater State Col, Mass, 81- *Mem:* Geol Soc Am; Am Geophys Union. *Res:* Internal structure of the oceanic lithosphere via direct observation of the sea floor and structural analysis of ophiolites. *Mailing Add:* Dept Geol Duke Univ Durham NC 27706-8001

KARSTEN, KENNETH STEPHEN, PLANT PHYSIOLOGY, CHEMISTRY. *Current Pos:* CONSULT, INDUST MINERALS & CHEMICALS, 81- *Personal Data:* b Holland, Mich, July 24, 13; m 39; c 4. *Educ:* Hope Col, AB, 35; Univ Nev, MS, 37; Univ Wis, PhD(plant physiol), 39. *Prof Exp:* Chemist-analyst, Sullivan Mining Co, Idaho, 37; asst, Univ Wis, 37-39; tutor biol, Brooklyn Col, 39-41; dir org res, Niagara Sprayer & Chem Co, 41-45; insecticide chemist, Rohm and Haas Co, Pa, 45-47; dept mgr, R T Vanderbilt Co, Inc, 48-72, dir res & develop, 72-78, vpres res & develop, 78-81. *Mem:* Am Chem Soc. *Res:* Organic syntheses; insecticide and fungicide formulation and development; plant hormones; plant physiology; root activity and oxygen in relation to soil fertility; fungicides; bactericides; sap stain control chemicals; bacteriostats for soap. *Mailing Add:* 5397 Keysville Ave Spring Hill FL 34608-1839

KARSTENS, ANDRES INGVER, aerospace medicine, for more information see previous edition

KARTEN, HARVEY J, NEUROANATOMY. *Current Pos:* PROF NEUROSCI & PSYCHIAT, UNIV CALIF, SAN DIEGO, 86- *Personal Data:* b New York, NY, July 13, 35; m 64; c 3. *Educ:* Yeshiva Col, BA, 55, Albert Einstein Col Med, MD, 59. *Honors & Awards:* Herrick Award, Am Asn Anat, 68. *Prof Exp:* Intern med, Univ Utah, 59-60; resident psychiat, Univ Colo, 60-61; res assoc neurophysiol, Walter Reed Army Inst Res, 61-65; res assoc neuroanat, Mass Inst Technol, 65-73, sr res assoc, 73-74; prof psychiat & anat sci, State Univ NY, Stony Brook, 74-86, prof neurobiol, 79-86. *Concurrent Pos:* USPHS fel, Univ Colo, 60-61; NIMH career develop award, 61-65; Nat Inst Child Health & Human Develop career develop award, 65-74; res assoc, Lab Neuropsychol, Wash Sch Psychiat, 63-65; adj prof, Salk Inst & Univ Utah, 86. *Mem:* Am Soc Zool; Am Asn Anat; Soc Neurosci. *Res:* Neuroanatomy. *Mailing Add:* Dept Neurosci Univ Calif San Diego La Jolla CA 92093-0608

KARTEN, MARVIN J, MEDICINAL CHEMISTRY. *Current Pos:* HEALTH SCI ADMINR, NAT INST CHILD HEALTH & HUMAN DEVELOP, NIH, 71- *Personal Data:* b New York, NY, Apr 26, 31; m 56; c 2. *Educ:* Brooklyn Col, BS, 54; Univ Pittsburgh, PhD(chem), 58. *Prof Exp:* Res chemist, Monsanto Chem Co, Ohio, 58-59, Mass, 59-60; sr res chemist, USV Pharmaceut Corp, 60-67, group leader, 67-70. *Mem:* Am Chem Soc. *Res:* Medicinal chemistry; organic synthesis; synthesis and biological evaluation of new contraceptive agents. *Mailing Add:* 8600 Pelham Rd Bethesda MD 20817-3820. *Fax:* 301-496-0962

KARTHA, KUTTY KRISHNAN, PLANT BIOTECHNOLOGY, PLANT CELL & TISSUE CULTURE. *Current Pos:* vis scientist, Prairie Regional Lab, Nat Res Coun, Saskatoon, 73-74, asst res officer, Plant Biotechnol Inst, 74-76, assoc res officer, 76-81, head, Cell Technol Sect, 85-87, SR RES OFFICER, PLANT BIOTECHNOL INST, NAT RES COUN, 81-, GROUP LEADER, CEREAL BIOTECHNOL, 87-, ACTG RES DIR, 91- *Personal Data:* b Shertallai, India, Aug 9, 41; Can citizen; m 72; c 2. *Educ:* Saugar Univ, India, BSc, 62; Jawaharlal Nehru Agr Univ, India, MSc, 65; India Agr Res Inst, PhD(plant path), 69. *Honors & Awards:* George M Darrow Award, Am Soc Hort Sci, 81; Merit Award Excellence Res, Nat Res Coun, Can, 91; Award of Excellence Res, Treas Bd Can, 92; C J Bishop Award, Can Soc Hort Sci, 92. *Prof Exp:* Fel, Nat Inst Agr Res, France, 70-72. *Concurrent Pos:* Nat corresp, Int Asn Plant Tissue Cult, 82-86; ed, J Plant Physiol, 87; adj prof, Univ Sask, Saskatoon, 87-; mem, Can Agr Res Coun, 90-94. *Mem:* Int Asn Plant Tissue Cult; Can Soc Plant Physiologists. *Res:* Plant biotechnology especially the genetic engineering of crops such as cereals and strawberry; cryopreservation of plant cells and organs; plant tissue culture. *Mailing Add:* 214 Old Crescent Saskatoon SK S7H 4W9 Can

KARTHA, MUKUND K, RADIOLOGY, BIOPHYSICS. *Current Pos:* asst prof, 68-73, ASSOC PROF RADIOL, OHIO STATE UNIV, 73-, ASSOC PROF ALLIED MED PROF, 76- *Personal Data:* b Pattanakad, Kerala, India, July 31, 36; US citizen; m 63; c 2. *Educ:* Univ Kerala, BSc, 58; Univ Sagar, India, MSc, 61; Univ Western Ont, PhD(radiol physics), 69. *Prof Exp:* Sci officer radiol physics, India Atomic Energy Comn, 61-63; cancer res fel, Ont Cancer Found, 63-68. *Concurrent Pos:* Am Cancer Soc fel, Ohio State Univ, 70-71, Nat Cancer Inst fel, 74-77; co-dir, Radiation Ther Consult Prog, Cancer Res Ctr, Ohio State Univ, 73- *Mem:* Radiol Soc NAm; Radiation Res Soc; Am Asn Physicists in Med; Am Col Radiol; Am Soc Therapeut Radiol & Oncol; Am Oncol Assoc Inc (pres). *Res:* Experimental and clinical research in radiation therapy; investigation of cancer treatment using radiation; radiation therapy. *Mailing Add:* 5003 11th Ave Vienna WV 26105-3152

KARTHA, SREEDHARAN, DIFFERENTIATION, GROWTH REGULATION. *Current Pos:* ASST PROF GROWTH REGULATION, UNIV CHICAGO, 88- *Personal Data:* b Kerala, India, 1948; m 88, Sethulaksmi Pilla; c Neelima & Malini. *Educ:* Nehru Univ, India, PhD(cell biol), 78. *Prof Exp:* Res fel, Johns Hopkins Med Sch, Baltimore, 80-83. *Res:* Growth factors; oncogenes. *Mailing Add:* 5449 S Woodlawn Ave Chicago IL 60615. *Fax:* 773-702-5818

KARTZMARK, ELINOR MARY, physical chemistry, for more information see previous edition

KARUKSTIS, KERRY KATHLEEN, PHOTOSYNTHESIS, FLUORESCENCE SPECTROSCOPY. *Current Pos:* from asst prof to assoc prof, 84-93, PROF CHEM, HARVEY MUDD COL, 93- *Personal Data:* b Buffalo, NY, 55. *Educ:* Duke Univ, BS, 77, PhD(chem), 81. *Prof Exp:* Res fel chem, Lab Chem Biodynamics, Univ Calif, Berkeley, 81-84. *Mem:* Am Chem Soc; Biophys Soc; Am Soc Photobiol; Sigma Xi; Coun Undergrad Res. *Res:* Use of steady-state and time-resolved fluorescence and absorbance measurements to monitor the organization of chloroplast photosynthetic membranes and the processes of excitation transfer and electron transport in photosynthesis. *Mailing Add:* Dept Chem Harvey Mudd Col Claremont CA 91711-5990. *Fax:* 909-621-8465

KARULKAR, PRAMOD C, PHYSICS. *Current Pos:* FAB MGR, UNIV RES FOUND, MD, 93- *Personal Data:* b Maharashtra State, India, 50; US citizen. *Educ:* Univ Poona, BSc, 69; Indian Inst Technol, MSc, 71; Portland State Univ, MS, 75; Univ Wis, PhD(mat sci), 79. *Prof Exp:* Mem staff, Rockwell Int Corp, Anaheim, Calif, 80-84, Hughes Aircraft Co, Newport Beach, Calif, 84-85, Lincoln Lab, Mass Inst Technol, 85-93. *Concurrent Pos:* Res assoc, Saha Inst Nuclear Physics, India, 71-72; res scholar low temp physics, Indian Inst Technol, Bombay, 72-73; lectr elec eng, Calif State Polytech Univ, Pomona, 81-85. *Mem:* Sigma Xi; Am Phys Soc; Am Vacuum Soc; Inst Elec & Electronics Engrs; Electrochem Soc. *Res:* Fabrication and analysis of electronic materials; fabrication of solid state devices; fabrication of VLSI circuits; plasma processing; thin film technology; device physics; failure analysis. *Mailing Add:* 3816 Font Hills Dr Ellicott City MD 21042

KARUNAKARAN, THONTHI, MOLECULAR GENETIC ANALYSIS OF VIRULENCE FACTORS & GENES, MICROBIAL PHYSIOLOGY & BIOCHEMISTRY. *Current Pos:* RES SCIENTIST, UNIV TEX HEALTH SCI CTR, SAN ANTONIO, 90- *Personal Data:* b Chinnamanur, Tamilnadu, India, Apr 20, 62; m 91, Bheemappa G Devi. *Educ:* Vivekanda Col, Tiruvedagam West, BSc, 82; Madurai Kamaraj Univ, MSc, 84, PhD(microbiol), 90. *Prof Exp:* Jr res fel, Technotran Pvt Ltd, India, 85-86; sr res fel, Coun Sci & Indust Res, India, 87-90. *Concurrent Pos:* Vis fel, Nat Ctr Sci Res, France, 88. *Mem:* Am Soc Microbiol; Am Soc Dent Res. *Res:* Isolated and characterized a few genes from pathogenically and biotechnologically important microorganisms. *Mailing Add:* 51 Poplar Ct Buffalo NY 14226

KARUNASIRI, GAMANI, SOLID STATE ELECTRONICS, QUANTUM MECHANICS. *Current Pos:* RES ENG, UNIV CALIF, LOS ANGELES, 87- *Personal Data:* b Colombo, Sri Lanka, Apr 14, 56; m 84; c 2. *Educ:* Univ Colombo, Sri Lanka, BS, 79; Univ Pittsburgh, MS, 81, PhD(physics), 84. *Prof Exp:* Asst lectr physics, Univ Colombo, 79-80; res assoc, Microtonics Assocs, 85-87. *Mem:* Am Phys Soc; Inst Elec & Electronics Engrs. *Res:* Physics and device application of semiconductor; quantum wells and superlattices; characterization of the devices using photo current and fourier transform infrared spectroscopies. *Mailing Add:* 7506 Gaynor Ave Van Nuys CA 94106

KARUSH, FRED, MONOCLONAL ANTIBODIES, GENE EXPRESSION. *Current Pos:* from asst prof to assoc prof immunol, Dept Pediat, 50-57, prof immunochem, 57-85, prof microbiol, 60-85, EMER PROF, UNIV PA, 85- *Personal Data:* b Chicago, Ill, July 12, 14; m 36, Sally Scher; c Arnold, Gerald & Carl. *Educ:* Univ Chicago, BS, 35, PhD(chem), 38. *Prof Exp:* Res physicist, E I du Pont de Nemours & Co, Inc, NJ, 41-46. *Concurrent Pos:* Rockefeller fel enzyme kinetics, Mass Inst Technol, 39-40; Harrison fel biophysics, Univ Pa, 40-41; Am Cancer Soc sr fel, Col Med, NY Univ, 47-48, Sloan-Kettering Inst Cancer Res, 49 & Col Physicians & Surgeons, Columbia Univ, 50; res career award, NIH, 62-85. *Mem:* Am Chem Soc; Am Soc Biol Chem; Am Asn Immunol. *Res:* Photoelectric polarimetry; enzyme kinetics; physics of pigments; protein interactions; bacterial synthesis of proteins; molecular immunology; affinity analysis of monoclonal antibodies. *Mailing Add:* Dept Microbiol Univ Pa Sch Med Philadelphia PA 19104-6076. *Fax:* 215-898-9557; *E-Mail:* karush@a1.mscf.up.edu

KARUSH, WILLIAM, MATHEMATICS. *Current Pos:* prof math, 67-87, EMER PROF MATH, CALIF STATE UNIV, NORTHRIDGE, 87- *Personal Data:* b Chicago, Ill, Mar 1, 17; m 39; c 2. *Educ:* Univ Chicago, BS, 38, MS, 39, PhD(math), 42. *Prof Exp:* Mathematician, Geophys Lab, Carnegie Inst, 42-43; physicist, Metall Lab, Univ Chicago, 43-45, from instr to assoc prof math, 45-56; mem sr staff, Ramo-Wooldridge Corp, 56-57; sr opers res scientist, Syst Develop Corp, 58-62, prin scientist, 62-67. *Concurrent Pos:* Mathematician, Inst Numerical Anal, Nat Bur Standards, Univ Calif, Los Angeles, 49-52; mem tech staff, Res & Develop Labs, Hughes Aircraft Co, 53 & Ramo-Wooldridge Corp, 54-55; Ford fac fel, Univ Calif, Los Angeles, 55-56. *Mem:* Am Math Soc; Opers Res Soc Am. *Res:* Operations research; calculus of variations; applied mathematics. *Mailing Add:* 10439 Holman Ave Los Angeles CA 90024-6012

KARUZA, SARUNAS KAZYS, ATOMIC FREQUENCY STAND, NAVIGATION & COMMUNICATION SYSTEMS. *Current Pos:* MEM TECH STAFF, ELECTRONIC RES LABS, AEROSPACE CORP, 80- *Personal Data:* b Kaunas, Lithuania, Jan 19, 40; m 77; c 2. *Educ:* Univ Southern Calif, BSEE, 63, MSEE, 66, PhD(elec eng), 72. *Prof Exp:* Mem tech staff, Commun Div, Hughes Aircraft Co, 63-65, Ground Systs Div, 65-66, Aeronaut Systs Div, 66-67; dir & prof staff assoc, Environ Sci Lab, Rancho Los Amigos Hosp, 72-80. *Concurrent Pos:* Consult, Fullerton Internal Med Clin, 78; adj asst prof med & adj assoc prof biomed eng, Univ Southern Calif, 75- *Mem:* Sigma Xi; Inst Elec & Electronics Engrs. *Res:* Precision atomic frequency standards (cesium-rubidium) which are used in the Navstar Global Positioning System (GPS) satellites for world wide navigation; stability properties of these standards as they are influenced by their electronics and environmental factors; satellite communication systems. *Mailing Add:* Aerospace Corp PO Box 92957 Los Angeles CA 90009

KARVE, MOHAN DATTATREYA, INDUSTRIAL MICROBIOLOGY, MYCOLOGY. *Current Pos:* Asia-Pac area rep, 65-71, gen mgr, Northern Asia-Pac Area, 71-86, VPRES, JAPAN/KOREA, BUCKMAN LABS, INC, 86- *Personal Data:* b Kupwad, India, Aug 14, 39; m 67; c 2. *Educ:* Univ Poona, BSc, 59, Hons, 60, MSc, 61; Ohio State Univ, PhD(mycol), 65. *Mem:* Am Chem Soc; Tech Asn Pulp & Paper Indust. *Res:* Microbial physiology; fungal proteins and amino acids; microbial deterioration. *Mailing Add:* Buckman Labs Inc PO Box 80305 Memphis TN 38108-0305

KARWAN, MARK HENRY, MATHEMATICAL PROGRAMMING, MULTIPLE CRITERIA DECISION MAKING. *Current Pos:* From asst to assoc prof, 76-86, dept chmn, 87-92, assoc dean, Sch Eng & Appl Sci, 92-94, actg dean, 94-95, PROF OPERS RES, DEPT INDUST ENG, STATE UNIV NY, BUFFALO, 86-, DEAN, 96- *Personal Data:* b Cleveland, Ohio, Nov 16, 51; m 73, Sabina L Matarazzo; c Maria, Melinda, Monica & Mark W. *Educ:* Johns Hopkins Univ, BES, 74, MSE, 74; Ga Inst Technol, PhD(opers res), 76. *Concurrent Pos:* Prin investr, NSF, 78-82, 92-94 & Off Naval Res, 85-87; consult, Mgt Adv Servs Inc, 74, Health Care Plan Inc, 84-87, Praxair Inc, 87-; fac adv student chap, Inst Indust Engrs 849, 77-83; proj dir univ, Ctr Indust Effectiveness, Buffalo, 93- *Mem:* Opers Res Soc Am; Inst Mgt Sci; Inst Ind Eng. *Res:* Discrete optimization, routing and scheduling; multicriteria decision making; multilevel decentralized planning; redundancy in mathematical programming; industrial inspection; contributed papers to professional journals and patentee in field. *Mailing Add:* 412 Bonner Hall Sch Eng & Appl Sci State Univ NY Buffalo NY 14260-1900. *Fax:* 716-645-2495; *E-Mail:* indmark@ubvms.bitnet

KARWEIK, DALE HERBERT, ANALYTICAL CHEMISTRY. *Current Pos:* MEM FAC, DEPT CHEM, OHIO STATE UNIV, 80- *Personal Data:* b Milwaukee, Wis, May 27, 48; m 70; c 2. *Educ:* Univ Wis-Milwaukee, BS, 70; Purdue Univ, PhD(anal chem), 75. *Prof Exp:* Asst prof, Wayne State Univ, 75-80. *Mem:* Am Chem Soc. *Res:* Measurement of homogeneous electron transfer rates; electrochemistry of porphyrins and related compounds with mechanistic studies. *Mailing Add:* Dept Chem Ohio State Univ 120 W 18th Ave Columbus OH 43210-1106

KARZ, ROBERT STEPHEN, HEAT TRANSFER MODELLING, POLYMER RHEOLOGY & CONSTITUTIVE EQUATIONS. *Current Pos:* Assoc scientist, Xerox Corp, 72-77, scientist, 77-85, sr scientist, 85-87, PRIN SCIENTIST, XEROX CORP, 87- *Personal Data:* b Rochester, NY, June 6, 45; m 69, Myrna L Bentkover; c Sara & Lisa. *Educ:* Mass Inst Technol, SB, 67; Univ Ill, MS, 68, PhD(metall), 72; Univ Rochester, MBA, 85. *Mem:* Am Phys Soc. *Res:* Development of xerographic and thermal ink jet marking technologies; modelling of toner flows, heat transfer analysis, rheological measurements and developing print quality evaluation methods. *Mailing Add:* 1202 Fox Hollow Dr Webster NY 14580. *Fax:* 716-422-6509; *E-Mail:* karz@wbst311.xerox.com

KARZON, DAVID T, VIROLOGY, PEDIATRICS. *Current Pos:* PROF PEDIAT & CHMN DEPT, SCH MED, VANDERBILT UNIV, 68-, MED DIR, CHILDREN'S HOSP, UNIV, 71- *Personal Data:* b New York, NY, July 8, 20; m 50; c 2. *Educ:* Ohio State Univ, BS, 40, MS, 41; Johns Hopkins Univ, MD, 44; Am Bd Pediat, dipl; Am Bd Microbiol, dipl, 64. *Prof Exp:* Instr contagious dis, Johns Hopkins Univ Hosp, 45, 48, instr virol, Sch Med, 49-50; from asst prof to prof pediat, Sch Med, State Univ NY Buffalo, 52-68, from asst prof to prof virol, Dept Bact & Immunol, 54-68, dir, Virol Lab, 52-68. *Concurrent Pos:* Lowell Palmer fel, 52-54; res career develop award, NIH, 62-68; Markle scholar, 56-61; spec consult, Nat Commun Dis Ctr, USPHS, Atlanta, Ga, 59-62, mem surgeon-gen spec adv comt immunization pract, 64-70; consult res reagents comt, Nat Inst Allergy & Infectious Dis, 63-67, chmn, 66-67, mem virol & rickettsiol study sect, 67-69; prog consult growth & develop sect, Nat Inst Child Health & Human Develop, 64-68; assoc ed, Am J Epidemiol, 66-78; mem biol rev steering comt, Food & Drug Admin, 72- *Mem:* Soc Pediat Res; Soc Exp Biol & Med; Fedn Am Soc Exp Biol; Am Epidemiol Soc; Infectious Dis Soc; Am Asn Immunologists; Am Acad Microbiol; Am Soc Virol; Am Soc Microbiol. *Res:* Animal virology; tissue culture. *Mailing Add:* Dept Pediat Vanderbilt Univ Sch Med D7235 Med Ctr N Nashville TN 37232-2581. *Fax:* 615-343-9723

KAS, ARNOLD, MATHEMATICS. *Current Pos:* AT BOEING HELICOPTERS. *Personal Data:* b Washington, DC, July 18, 40. *Educ:* Johns Hopkins Univ, BA, 62; Stanford Univ, PhD(math), 66. *Prof Exp:* Instr math, Stanford Univ, 66-67; Air Force Off Sci Res fel, Math Inst, State Univ Leiden, 67-69; asst prof, Univ Calif, Berkeley, 69-73; assoc prof math, Ore State Univ, 73-80, prof, 80- *Res:* Complex manifolds; algebraic geometry. *Mailing Add:* 171 McGraw St Seattle WA 98109

KASABACH, HAIG F, SCIENCE ADMINISTRATION. *Current Pos:* sr geologist, 60-66, dep state geologist, 84-85, STATE GEOLOGIST, NJ GEOL SURV, 85- *Personal Data:* b New York, NY, Dec 5, 35; m 62, Carol Rodano; c Peter & Christopher. *Educ:* Univ Mich, BS, 57, MS, 59. *Prof Exp:* Supv geologist, NJ Div Water Res, 67-76; chief, NJ Bur Water Qual & Mgt, 77-79, NJ Bur Ground Water Mgt, 80-83. *Concurrent Pos:* Mem, Intergovt Task Force Water Monitoring, 92-; dir, Sterling Hill Mining Mus. *Mem:* Asn Am State Geologists; Am Inst Prof Geologists; Asn Eng Geologists; Am Inst Hydrol; Asn Ground Water Scientists & Engrs. *Res:* Hydrology and water resources. *Mailing Add:* NJ Geol Surv CN 427 Trenton NJ 08625. *Fax:* 609-633-1004

KASAHARA, AKIRA, METEOROLOGY, NUMERICAL WEATHER PREDICTIONS. *Current Pos:* prog scientist, 63-73, sr scientist, 73-96, SR RES ASSOC, NAT CTR ATMOSPHERIC RES, 96- *Personal Data:* b Tokyo, Japan, Oct 11, 26; US citizen; m 52, Yuko Matsukata; c 2. *Educ:* Univ Tokyo, BS, 48, MS, 50, DSc, 54. *Honors & Awards:* Award, Meteorol Soc Japan, 61; Fujiwara Award, Japan Meteorol Soc, 96. *Prof Exp:* Asst geophys inst, Univ Tokyo, 48-53, res assoc, 53-54; res assoc oceanog & meteorol, Agr & Mech Col Tex, 54-56; res assoc meteorol, Univ Chicago, 56-62; res scientist, Courant Inst Math Sci, NY Univ, 62-63. *Concurrent Pos:* Affil prof dept meteorol, Tex A&M Univ, 67-70; assoc ed, J Appl Meteorol, 67-72; vis lectr, Inst Meteorol, Univ Stockholm, Sweden, 71-72; external examr, Dept Meterol, Univ Nairobi, Kenya, 77-79; adj prof, Dept Meteorol, Univ Utah, 79- *Mem:* Am Geophys Union; Meteorol Soc Japan; fel Am Meteorol Soc; fel AAAS. *Res:* Dynamic meteorology; development of weather prediction methods with the numerical integration of thermo-hydro-dynamical equations. *Mailing Add:* Nat Ctr Atmospheric Res Box 3000 Boulder CO 80307-3000. *Fax:* 303-497-1700; *E-Mail:* rasahara@ncar.ucar.edu

KASAI, PAUL HARUO, PHYSICAL CHEMISTRY. *Current Pos:* Thomas J Watson res ctr, IBM Corp, Yorktown Heights, NY, 85-86, RES STAFF MEM, IBM ALMADEN RES CTR, 86- *Personal Data:* b Osaka, Japan, Jan 30, 32, nat US; m 59, Toko Hatori; c Yumi & Miki. *Educ:* Univ Denver, BS, 55; Univ Calif, Berkeley, PhD(chem), 59. *Prof Exp:* Mem res staff, Hitachi Cent Res Lab, Japan, 59-62; res inst, Union Carbide Corp, 62-66; assoc prof chem, Univ Calif, Santa Cruz, 66-67; mem res staff, Res Inst, Union Carbide Corp, 67-75, group leader, 75-77; sr scientist, Tarrytown Tech Ctr, 77-79; mgr tech support, IBM Instruments Inc, Danbury, 79-85. *Mem:* Am Chem Soc. *Res:* Magnetic resonance studies of polymer synthesis and degradation, organometallic complexes, reactions between atoms and small molecules in low temperature matrices, free radicals and surface states. *Mailing Add:* 18645 Castle Lake Dr Morgan Hill CA 95037. *Fax:* 408-927-3310; *E-Mail:* kasai@almaden.ibm.com

KASAMATSU, HARUMI, MOLECULAR BIOLOGY. *Current Pos:* PROF MOLECULAR BIOL, UNIV CALIF, LOS ANGELES, 84- *Educ:* Osaka Univ, Japan, PhD(molecular biol), 69. *Mailing Add:* Dept Biol Molecular Biol Inst Univ Calif 405 Hilgard Ave Los Angeles CA 90024-1301

KASAMEYER, PAUL WILLIAM, GEOPHYSICS. *Current Pos:* GEOPHYSICIST, LAWRENCE LIVERMORE NAT LAB, 74- *Personal Data:* b Detroit, Mich, Sept 9, 43; m 65; c 3. *Educ:* Mass Inst Technol, BS, 65, PhD(geophys), 71; Yale Univ, MS, 66. *Mem:* Soc Explor Geophysicists; Sigma Xi; Am Geophys Union. *Res:* Collection and interpretation of geophysical data; thermal modeling; magnetotellurics; experimental studies of gravity; earthquake hazards. *Mailing Add:* 692 Jefferson Ave Livermore CA 94550. *E-Mail:* kasameyer@llnl.gov

KASAP, SAFA O, MATERIALS SCIENCE ENGINEERING, ELECTRICAL ENGINEERING. *Current Pos:* PROF ENG, UNIV SASK, 86- *Educ:* Univ London, BS, 76, MS, 78, PhD(elec eng), 83. *Prof Exp:* Fac mem, Dept Elec Eng, Univ London, 83-86. *Mem:* Inst Elec & Electronics Engrs; Am Phys Soc. *Mailing Add:* Dept Elect Eng Univ Sask Saskatoon SK S7N 0W0 Can. *Fax:* 306-966-5407

KASARDA, DONALD DAVID, PROTEIN CHEMISTRY. *Current Pos:* res chemist, Food Qual Res Unit, 64-72, res leader, 72-85, RES CHEMIST, CROP IMPROV & UTILIZATION, WESTERN REGIONAL RES CTR, AGR RES SERV, USDA, 85- *Personal Data:* b Kingston, Pa, Oct 12, 33; m 64; c 1. *Educ:* King's Col, Pa, BS, 55; Boston Col, MS, 57; Princeton Univ, MA, 59, PhD (phys chem), 61. *Honors & Awards:* Thomas Burr Osborne Medal, Am Asn Cereal Chemists, 93. *Prof Exp:* Mem Tech Staff, Bell Tel Labs, NJ, 61-63; Cardiovasc Res Inst fel, Sch Med, Univ Calif, San Francisco, 63-64. *Concurrent Pos:* Assoc Exp Sta, Dept Agron & Range Sci, Univ Calif, Davis, 74- *Mem:* AAAS; Am Chem Soc; Am Asn Cereal Chem. *Res:* Protein chemistry; wheat genetics. *Mailing Add:* Western Regional Res Ctr USDA Albany CA 94710

KASARSKIS, EDWARD JOSEPH, NEUROLOGY. *Current Pos:* PROF CHIEF, NEUROL SERV, UAMC, 92- *Personal Data:* b Chicago, Ill, Oct 9, 46; m 69, Mary Lenroot; c Andrew, Peter, Larisa & Irina. *Educ:* Col St Thomas, BA, 68; Univ Wis-Madison, MD, 74, PhD(biochem), 75. *Prof Exp:* Resident internal med, Univ Wis-Madison Hosp, 74-76; resident neurol, Univ Va Hosp, 76-79; asst prof neurol, Sch Med, La State Univ, 79-80; from asst prof to assoc prof neurol, toxicol & nutrit, Univ Ky, 85-92. *Concurrent Pos:* Staff neurologist, Vet Admin Hosp, Lexington, Ky, 80-, chief neurol serv, 92- *Mem:* Sigma Xi; Am Acad Neurol; Soc Neurosci; Am Soc Neurochem; Int Soc Neurochem; Int Soc Bioinorg Sci; Am Neurol Asn. *Res:* Role of trace metals in the function of the brain; investigative factors that modify zinc metabolism; role of trace metals in Amyotrophic lateral sclerosis. *Mailing Add:* Dept Neurol Univ Ky Col Med 800 Rose St Lexington KY 40536-0084. *Fax:* 606-281-4817

KASBEKAR, DINKAR KASHINATH, PHYSIOLOGY, BIOCHEMISTRY. *Current Pos:* from asst prof to assoc prof physiol & biophys, 69-84, PROF PHYSIOL & BIOPHYS, SCH MED & DENT, GEORGETOWN UNIV, 84- *Personal Data:* b Bombay, India, Apr 3, 32; m 61; c 1. *Educ:* Univ Bombay, BSc, 52 & 54, MSc, 57; Univ Calif, PhD(biochem), 61. *Prof Exp:* Jr res biochemist, Univ Calif, San Francisco, 61-63, asst res biochemist, Cardiovasc Res Inst, 63-65; asst res physiologist, Univ Calif, Berkeley, 66-68. *Concurrent Pos:* San Francisco Heart Asn fel, 64-65; prin investr, Washington Heart Asn, 70-71, NSF, 70-; vis sr fel, Nat Inst Arthritis, Metab & Digestive Dis, NIH, 81. *Mem:* Biophys Soc; Am Physiol Soc; NY Acad Sci. *Res:* Ion transport, zymogen secretion, specifically in the area of gastric secretion. *Mailing Add:* 11330 Saddleview Ct Raleigh NC 27613-6807. *Fax:* 919-848-9824

KASCSAK, RICHARD JOHN, SLOW VIRUS & PERSISTENT INFECTIONS. *Current Pos:* RES SCIENTIST, NY STATE INST BASIC RES DEVELOP DISABILITIES, 75- *Personal Data:* b Whitestone, NY, Sept 20, 47; m 72; c Matthew & Melissa. *Educ:* St Francis Col, NY, BS, 69; Adelphi Univ, MS, 71; Cornell Univ Med Col, PhD(virol), 76. *Prof Exp:* Teaching asst, Adelphi Univ, NY, 69-71; training fel, Cornell Univ, 71-75. *Mem:* Am Soc Microbiol; Am Soc Virol. *Res:* Slow viral infections of the central nervous system with emphasis on the creation of model systems relevant to human disease; unconventional slow virus diseases; scrapie. *Mailing Add:* NY State Inst Basic Res Develop Disabilities 1050 Forest Hill Rd Staten Island NY 10314. *Fax:* 718-698-3803

KASE, KENNETH RAYMOND, RADIATION DOSIMETRY & SCHIELDING. *Current Pos:* head, Radiation Physics Dept, 92-95, ASSOC DIR, ENVIRON, SAFETY & HEALTH, STANFORD LINEAR ACCELERATOR CTR, 95- *Personal Data:* b Oak Park, Ill, July 13, 38; m 62; c 2. *Educ:* Ga Inst Technol, BS, 61; Univ Calif, Berkeley, MS, 63; Stanford Univ, PhD(biophys), 75; Am Bd Health Physics, cert, 69; Am Bd Radiol, cert, 81. *Honors & Awards:* Elda E Anderson Award, Health Physics Soc, 78. *Prof Exp:* Scientist reactors environ, Lockheed Missiles & Space Co, 61-62; health physicist radiation safety, Lawrence Livermore Lab, Univ Calif, 63-67, chief radiation safety, 67-69; health physicist, Stanford Linear Accelerator, Stanford Univ, 69-73; asst prof & chief dosimetry & radiation safety radiol physics, Harvard Med Sch, 75-84; prof & dir physics, Dept Radiation & Oncol, Med Ctr, Univ Mass, 85-91. *Concurrent Pos:* Ed, Health Physics J, Health Physics Soc, 77-82; adj prof, Lowell Univ, 78-91; mem, sci comt, Nat Coun Radiation, Protection & Measurement, 46 & 83-; mem, Nat Coun Radiation Protection & Measurement, 87-; sci vpres oper radiation safety, Nat Coun Radiation Protection & Measurement, 95- *Mem:* Fel Health Physics Soc; Am Asn Physicists Med (treas, 86-91); Radiation Res Soc; fel Am Col Radiol; fel Am Col Med Physics; Am Acad Health Physics (pres, 96). *Res:* Radiation measurement and dosimetry; biological effects of radiation; application of new treatment modalities to cancer therapy. *Mailing Add:* Stanford Linear Accelerator Co (SLAC) 2575 Sand Hill Rd Menlo Park CA 94025. *Fax:* 650-926-3030; *E-Mail:* krk@slac.stanford.edu

KASEL, JULIUS ALBERT, MICROBIOLOGY, VIROLOGY. *Current Pos:* PROF MICROBIOL & IMMUNOL, BAYLOR COL MED, 72- *Personal Data:* b Homestead, Pa, Dec 7, 23; m 50; c 3. *Educ:* Univ Pittsburgh, BS, 49; Georgetown Univ, MS, 58, PhD(microbiol, virol), 60. *Prof Exp:* Head med virol sect, Nat Inst Allergy & Infectious Dis, 50-72. *Concurrent Pos:* Assoc dir, Influenza Res Ctr. *Mem:* Infectious Dis Soc Am; Am Asn Immunologists; Am Soc Microbiol; Soc Exp Biol & Med; Soc Gen Microbiol; Sigma Xi; fel Am Acad Microbiol. *Res:* Virological research related to respiratory viral infections in man. *Mailing Add:* Baylor Cil Med 1926 Country Club Sugarland TX 77478-3910

KASER, J(OHN) D(ONALD), CHEMICAL ENGINEERING. *Current Pos:* RETIRED. *Personal Data:* b Oak Park, Ill, Nov 21, 29; div; c 2. *Educ:* Augustana Col, BA, 56; Univ Iowa, BS, 58, MS, 60, PhD(chem eng), 63. *Prof Exp:* Sr develop engr, Battelle-Northwest, 63-76; staff engr, Rockwell Hanford Oper, 76-80, prin engr, 80-89; fel eng, Westinghouse Hanford Col, 89. *Concurrent Pos:* Mem fac, Joint Ctr, Grad Study, 68-; mem steering comn on shallow land burial of radioactive waste, Dept Energy, 77-78. *Mem:* Am Inst Chem Engrs; Am Nuclear Soc. *Res:* Solidification and disposal of radioactive waste from nuclear fuel reprocessing; decontamination; solvent extraction; radioactive waste management; heat transfer. *Mailing Add:* 1140 Southeast Park Dr Colville WA 99114

KASETA, FRANCIS WILLIAM, SOLID STATE PHYSICS, AMATEUR RADIO. *Current Pos:* asst prof physics, 64-67, chmn dept, 77-83, ASSOC PROF PHYSICS, COL HOLY CROSS, 67- *Personal Data:* b Norwood, Mass, June 6, 33; m 60; c 4. *Educ:* Boston Col, BS, 55; Mass Inst Technol, PhD(solid state physics), 62. *Prof Exp:* Asst prof elec eng, Mass Inst Technol, 62-64. *Concurrent Pos:* Ford Found fel, 62-64; consult, Mass Inst Technol, 64-65. *Mem:* Am Phys Soc. *Res:* Dielectric breakdown; conduction processes in semiconductors and dielectrics; electrooptics. *Mailing Add:* 45 Concord Ave Norwood MA 02062

KASH, JEFFREY ALAN, OPTICAL EMISSION FROM SEMICONDUCTORS & DEVICES. *Current Pos:* RES SCIENTIST, T J WATSON RES CTR, IBM, 81- *Personal Data:* b Whittier, Calif, Oct 14, 53. *Educ:* Univ Calif, Berkeley, BA, 75, PhD, 81. *Mem:* Fel Am Phys Soc; Inst Elec & Electronics Engrs. *Mailing Add:* IBM T J Watson Res Ctr PO Box 218 Yorktown Heights NY 10598

KASH, KATHLEEN, SYSTEMS OF REDUCED DIMENSIONALITY, ULTRAFAST PHENOMENA. *Current Pos:* ASSOC PROF PHYSICS, CASE WESTERN RES UNIV, 93- *Personal Data:* b Corona, Calif, Nov 28, 53; m 78, David A Smith; c 2. *Educ:* Middlebury Col, BA, 75; Mass Inst Technol, PhD(physics), 82. *Prof Exp:* Fel, AT&T Bell Labs, 82-84; mem tech staff, Bellcore, 84-93. *Concurrent Pos:* Adj res prof physics, Dartmouth Col, 92-93. *Mem:* Am Phys Soc; Am Vacuum Soc. *Res:* Confinement of excitons to quantum wires and dots; carrier relaxation-diffusion in semiconductors; optical properties of quantum wells; strain confinement of excitons in semiconductors; solid state physics. *Mailing Add:* Dept Physics Case Western Res Univ 10900 Euclid Ave Cleveland OH 44106-7221. *Fax:* 216-368-4671; *E-Mail:* kxk43@po.cwru.edu

KASH, MICHAEL MASON, EFFECTS OF EXTERNAL FIELDS ON ATOMIC STRUCTURE. *Current Pos:* Asst prof, 88-94, ASSOC PROF PHYSICS, LAKE FOREST COL, 88-, CHAIRPERSON, DEPT PHYSICS, 95- *Personal Data:* b Cincinnati, Ohio, Aug 12, 55. *Educ:* Lake Forest Col, BA, 77; Mass Inst Technol, PhD(atomic physics), 88. *Mem:* Am Phys Soc; Sigma Xi. *Res:* Angular and specular distribution of fluorescence from lithium atoms that have been executed by photons and electrons; electromagnetic interactions of atomic electrons. *Mailing Add:* 555 Sheridan Rd Lake Forest IL 60045. *E-Mail:* kash@lfc.edu

KASHA, HENRY, HIGH ENERGY PHYSICS, COSMIC RAY PHYSICS. *Current Pos:* sr res assoc, 70-73, SR RES PHYSICIST, YALE UNIV, 73- *Personal Data:* b Warsaw, Poland. *Educ:* Hebrew Univ, Jerusalem, MSc, 54; Israel Inst Technol, DSc(physics), 60. *Prof Exp:* Lectr physics, Israel Inst Technol, 60-63; asst physicist, Brookhaven Nat Lab, 64-66, assoc physicist, 66-70. *Mem:* AAAS; Am Phys Soc. *Mailing Add:* Dept Physics Yale Univ PO Box 6666 New Haven CT 06520

KASHA, KENNETH JOHN, PLANT CYTOGENETICS, PLANT CELL CULTURE. *Current Pos:* asst prof crop sci & crop cytogeneticist, 66-69, assoc prof crop cytogenetics, 69-74, PROF CROP CYTOGENETICS, UNIV GUELPH, 74- *Personal Data:* b Lacombe, Alta, May 6, 33; m 58, Marion E Lenz; c Lorelei M & David J. *Educ:* Univ Alta, BSc, 57, MSc, 58; Univ Minn, PhD(plant genetics), 62. *Hon Degrees:* LLD, Univ Calgary, 86. *Honors & Awards:* Grindley Medal, Agr Inst Can, 77; E C Manning Award, 83; Nilsson-Ehle Lectr, Sweden, 87; Officer of Order of Can, 94; Award of Excellence, Genetics Soc Can, 94. *Prof Exp:* Teaching asst, Univ Minn, 60-61; res officer 2, Ottawa Res Sta, Can Dept Agr, 62-64, res officer 3, 64-66, res scientist 1, 66. *Concurrent Pos:* Orgn chmn, Int Symposium Haploids in Higher Plants, Guelph, 74; dir, Plant Biotech Ctr Guelph, Waterloo Biotech, 84-87; vis scientist, Plant Indust, Commonwealth Sci & Indust Orgn, Canberra, Australia, 85-86; prog chmn, XVI Int Cong Genetics, Toronto, 88; nat corresp, Int Asn Plant Cell & Tissue Cult, 90-94. *Mem:* Genetics Soc Am; Genetics Soc Can (secy, 66-69, dir, 70-72, vpres, 75, pres, 76); Am Soc Agron; fel Royal Soc Can; Int Asn Plant Cell & Tissue Cult; Can Soc Plant Molecular Biol. *Res:* Crop plant cytogenetics; haploidy in cereals; molecular cytology; interspecific hybridization and chromosome pairing in Hordeum, Triticum and Secale; linkage and RFLP mapping of barley; plant cell culture in cereals; male sterility and self-incompatibility; molecular biology. *Mailing Add:* Dept Crop Sci Univ Guelph Guelph ON N1G 2W1 Can. *Fax:* 519-763-8933

KASHA, MICHAEL, CHEMICAL PHYSICS, SPECTROSCOPY & MOLECULAR ELECTRONIC PHENOMENA. *Current Pos:* chmn, Dept Chem, 59-62, dir, Inst Molecular Biophys, 60-80, PROF PHYS CHEM, FLA STATE UNIV, 51-, ROBERT O LAWTON DISTINGUISHED PROF, 62- *Personal Data:* b Elizabeth, NJ, Dec 6, 20; m 47; c 1. *Educ:* Univ Mich, BS, 43; Univ Calif, PhD(phys chem), 45. *Hon Degrees:* DSc, Gonzaga Univ, 88, Univ Gdansk, 92. *Honors & Awards:* Phillips Lectr, Haverford Col, 59; Reilly Lectr, Univ Notre Dame, 59; S C Lind Lectr, Oak Ridge Nat Lab, 61; George Porter Medal, 90; Robert Mulliken Medal, Univ Chicago, 90. *Prof Exp:* Lab asst, Res Lab, Merck & Co, Inc, 38-41; res chemist, Plutonium Proj, Univ Calif, 44-46, univ fel & instr, 46, res assoc, 46-49; AEC fel, Univ Chicago, 49-50; Guggenheim fel & spec lectr, Univ Manchester, 50-51. *Concurrent Pos:* Vis prof chem, Harvard Univ, 59-60, vis prof biophys, 61; Charles F Kettering Res Award, Gen Motors Corp, 63-69; vis prof chem, Univ Mich, 69; Nat Sci Bd, Pres Carter, 79-84, France, 80-; exec comt, Inst La Vie, Paris, France, 80-; foreign coun, Inst Molecular Sci, Okazaki, Japan, 82-85; mem, Sci & Tech Adv Comt, Argonne Nat Lab, 83-88; sci adv to Gov Bob Graham, Fla, 83-87; Geoffrey Frew fel, Australian Acad Sci, 91. *Mem:* Nat Acad Sci; corresp mem Brazilian Acad Sci; foreign mem Ukrainian Acad Sci; fel Am Acad Arts & Sci; Int Acad Quantum Molecular Sci. *Res:* Molecular biophysics and electronic spectroscopy; triplet states of molecules; emission spectroscopy of molecules; classification of electronic transitions; spin-intercombinations; n-pi transitions; radiationless transitions; theoretical photochemistry; molecular excitons and energy transfer; biological molecular interactions. *Mailing Add:* Inst Molecular Biophys Fla State Univ Tallahassee FL 32306-3014

KASHAR, LAWRENCE JOSEPH, METALLURGY, MATERIALS SCIENCE. *Current Pos:* PRES, KASHAR TECH SERV, 91- *Personal Data:* b Brooklyn, NY, June 1, 33; m 81, Barbara C Fasiska; c Evan C, Summerlea J & Desa N. *Educ:* Rensselaer Polytech Inst, BMetE, 55; Stevens Inst Technol, MS, 59; Carnegie Inst Technol, MS, 61; Carnegie-Mellon Univ, PhD(metall, mat sci), 70. *Prof Exp:* Assoc metallurgist, AMAX Res & Develop Co, Inc, 55-59; res assoc, Carnegie Inst Technol, 60-64; sr res metallurgist, US Steel Appl Res Lab, 64-70; mem tech staff, B-1 Div, Rockwell Int, 71-72; staff engr, Orlando Div, Martin Marietta Corp, 73; dir, Metall Serv, Scanning Electron Anal Labs, Inc, 73-79, dir, Tech Serv, 79-83, vpres technol, 83-91. *Concurrent Pos:* Adj lectr, Univ Southern Calif, 75-81; vpres & secy, ATFA, Inc, 77-80; vpres, Litigation Consults Int, 78-81; chmn, Struct Anal Prog, Int Symp Testing & Failure Anal, 80-87; chmn, Westec Conf, Am Soc Metals, 83. *Mem:* Am Soc Metals; Am Soc Testing & Mat; Inst Elec & Electronics Engrs; Int Soc Testing & Failure Anal; Am Chem Soc; Electron Micros Soc Am; Am Welding Soc. *Res:* Causes and prevention of failures of metal structures; development of microanalytical and surface analysis techniques for practical materials problem solving such as particulates, pollution and asbestos. *Mailing Add:* 5117 Corning Ave Los Angeles CA 90056. *Fax:* 310-645-9859

KASHATUS, WILLIAM C, PATHOLOGY, HEMATOLOGY. *Current Pos:* from instr to assoc prof path, Hahnemann Med Col, 63-73, dir, Sch Med Technol, 64-71, vchmn dept, 73-79, PROF PATH, HAHNEMANN MED COL, 72- *Personal Data:* b Nanticoke, Pa, Apr 23, 29; m 54; c 2. *Educ:* Wilkes Col, BS, 51; Bucknell Univ, MS, 53; Hahnemann Med Col, MD, 59. *Prof Exp:* Instr chem, Bucknell Univ, 51-52. *Concurrent Pos:* Mary Bailey Heart Found fel, 56-58; Am Cancer Soc fel, 62-64; dir labs, Hahnemann Hosp, 64-70; mem tech adv bd, Southeast Pa Div, Am Red Cross, 68-72 & West Co, 69-71; med dir, SBCL, Philadelphia, 71- *Mem:* AMA; fel Col Am Path; Am Soc Clin Path; Acad Clin Lab Physicians & Scientists. *Res:* Hematology, especially cancer chemotherapy; blood banking, especially immunochematology; tissue typing. *Mailing Add:* Smith Kline Beecham Clin Lab 400 Egypt Rd Norristown PA 19403-3406

KASHDAN, DAVID STUART, PHARMACEUTICAL APPLICATIONS OF POLYMERS, DRUG DELIVERY METHODS. *Current Pos:* from res chemist to sr res chemist, 79-88, DIR, EASTMAN CHEM CO, 88- *Personal Data:* b New York, NY, Oct 21, 50; m 83, Letitia Jones; c 1. *Educ:* Stevens Inst Technol, BS, 72; Univ Vt, PhD(org chem), 77. *Prof Exp:* Vis instr org chem, Univ Vt, 76-77; res fel, Univ Calif, Berkeley, 77-79. *Mem:* Am Chem Soc. *Res:* Organic synthesis; synthetic methods; organolithium reagents and halogenation of aromatics; synthesis of morphinans and isoquinolines; development of new polymers for use in pharmaceutical applications; polymer chemistry, especially polycondensation polymers, celulosics, polyolefins. *Mailing Add:* 2064 Canterbury Rd Kingsport TN 37660-5027. *Fax:* 423-229-3896; *E-Mail:* dkashdan@eastman.com

KASHEF, A(BDEL-AZIZ) I(SMAIL), GEOTECHNICAL ENGINEERING, GROUNDWATER SCIENCES. *Current Pos:* vis prof soil mech & ground water, 62-67, prof, 67-80, EMER PROF CIVIL ENG, NC STATE UNIV, 80- *Personal Data:* b Cairo, Egypt, Feb 10, 19; m 48. *Educ:* Univ Cairo, BS, 40, MS, 48; Purdue Univ, PhD(soil mech), 51. *Prof Exp:* Irrig engr, Egyptian Govt, 40-45 & 48-51; instr struct, Univ Cairo, 45-48; sr lectr, Ein Shams Univ, 51-54 & Univ Cairo, 54-56; prof, Am Univ Beirut, 56-60. *Concurrent Pos:* Consult soil engr, 52-; mem water-well comt, Nat Prod Coun, Govt Egypt, 53, mem, Nat Hydraul Comt, 56, mem tech comt, River Harbors Comt, 60-62; soil consult, High Aswan Dam Auth, Egypt, 54-56; dir, Consult Eng Off, Saudi Arabia, 59-60; ed, Water Resources Bull, 70-73. *Mem:* Fel Am Water Resources Asn; fel Am Soc Civil Engrs; Am Geophys Union. *Res:* Water resources research, especially in ground-water field and geotechnical engineering. *Mailing Add:* 5504 N Hills Dr Raleigh NC 27612

KASHGARIAN, MICHAEL, PATHOLOGY, CELL BIOLOGY. *Current Pos:* asst resident path, 59-61, from instr to assoc prof, 62-74, vchmn dept, 76-89, PROF PATH & BIOL, YALE UNIV, 74- *Personal Data:* b New York, NY, Sept 20, 33; m 60, Jean Caldwel; c Michaele (Rose) & Thea (Obstler). *Educ:* NY Univ, BA, 54; Yale Univ, MD, 58. *Prof Exp:* Asst med, Sch Med, Wash Univ, 58-59. *Concurrent Pos:* Life Ins Med Res fel physiol, Univ Gottingen, 61-62; USPHS spec fel, 63-65 & res career award, 65-75; assoc pathologist, Yale New Haven Hosp, 63-66, asst attend pathologist, 66-69, attend pathologist, 69-, assoc chief pathologist, 76-86. *Mem:* Am Asn Path; Am Physiol Soc; Am Soc Clin Path; Am Soc Nephrol; Int Acad Path; fel AAAS. *Res:* Pathology and physiology of the kidney. *Mailing Add:* Dept Path Sch Med Yale Univ PO Box 208023 New Haven CT 06520-8023. *Fax:* 203-785-3348; *E-Mail:* michael.kashgarian@yale.edu

KASHIN, PHILIP, NEUROPHYSIOLOGY, CLINICAL RESEARCH. *Current Pos:* ASSOC DIR CLIN AFFAIRS, PFIZER HOSP PROD GROUP, 86- *Personal Data:* b New York, NY, Oct 27, 30; m 58; c Peter S, Thomas B & Sarah B. *Educ:* Brooklyn Col, BA, 53; Columbia Univ, MA, 58; NY Univ, MS, 61; Ill Inst Technol, PhD(physiol), 70. *Honors & Awards:* I R 100 Award, 67. *Prof Exp:* Res asst immunochem, Hosp for Spec Surg, New York, 61-62; res asst biochem, State Univ NY Downstate Med Ctr, 62-63; asst biochemist, IIT Res Inst, 63-64, assoc biochemist, 64-69, res biochemist, 69-70; Nat Inst Neurol Dis & Stroke spec res fel neurophysiol, Univ Ore, 70-71; asst prof biol, Queens Col, NY, 71-76; sr asst dir clin res, USV Pharmaceut Corp, 76-82; clin monitor, Abbott Lab, 83-84; asst dir, Pfizer Int Corp, 84-86. *Concurrent Pos:* Consult, 82-83. *Mem:* AAAS; NY Acad Sci; Am Physiol Soc. *Res:* Methods to assay mosquito repellents; cardiovascular and anti-infective clinical research; mechanism of action of carbon dioxide with neurotransmitters in the central nervous system; clinical research. *Mailing Add:* 47 Glen Cove Dr Glen Head NY 11545

KASHIWA, BRYAN ANDREW, NUMERICAL FLUID DYNAMICS. *Current Pos:* MEM STAFF, LOS ALAMOS NAT LAB, 79- *Personal Data:* b Oswego, NY, Feb 20, 52; m 69; c 3. *Educ:* Worcester Polytech Inst, BS, 73; Univ Wash, MS, 78, PhD, 87. *Prof Exp:* Engr, K2 Corp, 73-79. *Mem:* Am Soc Mech Engrs. *Res:* Application and development of methods in numerical fluid dynamics with emphasis on multifield flows. *Mailing Add:* PO Box 1663 MS B216 Los Alamos Nat Lab Los Alamos NM 87545

KASHIWA, HERBERT KORO, anatomy, histochemistry; deceased, see previous edition for last biography

KASHKARI, CHAMAN NATH, ELECTRICAL ENGINEERING. *Current Pos:* asst prof elec eng, 69-75, ASSOC PROF ELEC ENG, UNIV AKRON, 75- *Personal Data:* b Srinagar, India, Aug 27, 33; m 63; c 2. *Educ:* Univ Jammu & Kashmir, India, BA, 52; Univ Rajasthan, BS, 57; Univ Detroit, MS, 65; Univ Mich, Ann Arbor, PhD(elec eng), 69. *Prof Exp:* Asst engr, Gen Elec Co, India, 57-58, grad trainee, Eng, 58-60, plant engr, India, 61-64; teaching fel, Univ Detroit, 64-65 & Univ Mich, Ann Arbor, 66-69. *Concurrent Pos:* Energy consult, Govt Nepal, NSF, 75. *Mem:* Inst Elec & Electronics Engrs; Am Soc Eng Educ; Sigma Xi. *Res:* Energy planning in developing countries; solar energy; biogas plants; mini power plants; energy conservation; electric power systems engineering. *Mailing Add:* Dept Elec Eng Akron Univ Akron OH 44325

KASHKET, EVA RUTH, BACTERIOLOGY, BIOCHEMISTRY. *Current Pos:* assoc prof, 74-82, PROF MICROBIOL, SCH MED, BOSTON UNIV, 82- *Personal Data:* b Zagreb, Yugoslavia, Mar 1, 36; US citizen; m 57; c 2. *Educ:* McGill Univ, BSc, 56, MSc, 57; Harvard Univ, PhD(med sci), 63. *Prof Exp:* Res assoc, Dept Physiol, Harvard Med Sch, 57-74. *Concurrent Pos:* Fel biochem pharmacol, Sch Med Tufts Univ, 62-65. *Mem:* Am Soc Microbiol; Am Soc Biochem & Molecular Biol. *Res:* Bioenergetics, fermentations; clostridia, lactobacilli. *Mailing Add:* Dept Microbiol Boston Univ Sch Med 80 E Concord St Boston MA 02118-2307

KASHKET, SHELBY, BIOCHEMISTRY, NUTRITION. *Current Pos:* asst mem, 72-80, assoc mem, 81-96, SR INVESTR, FORSYTH DENT CTR, 96- *Personal Data:* b Montreal, Que, Feb 1, 31; m 57, Eva; c 2. *Educ:* McGill Univ, BSc, 52, MSc, 53, PhD(biochem), 56. *Prof Exp:* Res fel biochem, McGill Univ, 56-57; res fel bact, Harvard Med Sch, 57-59; asst biochemist, Mass Gen Hosp, 63-67; biochemist, USPHS, 67-70. *Concurrent Pos:* Res fel med, Harvard Med Sch, 59-60, res assoc, 60-77, lectr, 79- *Mem:* AAAS; Int Asn Dent Res; Am Chem Soc; Am Soc Biochem & Molecular Biol; Sigma Xi. *Res:* Metabolic effects of fluoride; oral biology; intermediary metabolism; biochemical and clinical methods; foods and dental disease; mechanisms of inflammation. *Mailing Add:* Forsyth Dent Ctr 140 The Fenway Boston MA 02115. *Fax:* 617-262-4021; *E-Mail:* skashket@forsyth.org

KASHKOUSH, ISMAIL I, UNDERWATER ACOUSTICS, MICROCONTAMINATION CONTROL. *Current Pos:* process engr, 93-94, mgr, 94-95, DIR, SUBMICRON SYSTS, 95- *Personal Data:* b Egypt, Nov 10, 58; m 90; c 3. *Educ:* Cairo Univ, Egypt, BS, 82, MS, 88; Clarkson Univ, PhD(eng sci), 93. *Prof Exp:* Teaching asst, Dept Mech Design, Cairo Univ, 82-86; instr solid mech, Acad Defense, Cairo, 87-88; res asst microcontamination control, Clarkson Univ, 88-93. *Concurrent Pos:* Assoc lectr, Dept Mech Design, Cairo Univ, 86-88; instr thermodyn & fluid mech, Clarkson Univ, 90 & 91. *Mem:* Electrochem Soc; Am Vacuum Soc; Mat Res Soc; Inst Environ Sci; Am Inst Chem Engrs. *Res:* Microcontamination control in the clean room environment using various removal techniques; detection of particulates on silicon wafers; research in different aspects of contamination; establishing numerical simulation of the surface cleaning using sonic methods; developing new models that accurately describe the cleaning mechanism; author of several publications. *Mailing Add:* 3117 S Fifth Ave Whitehall PA 18052

KASHNOW, RICHARD ALLEN, physics, for more information see previous edition

KASHY, EDWIN, EXPERIMENTAL NUCLEAR PHYSICS. *Current Pos:* assoc prof, 64-67, PROF PHYSICS, MICH STATE UNIV, 67- *Personal Data:* b Beirut, Lebanon, July 8, 34; US citizen; m 57; c 2. *Educ:* Rice Univ, BA, 56, MA, 57, PhD(physics), 59. *Prof Exp:* NSF fel physics, Mass Inst Technol, 59-60, instr, 60-62; asst prof, Princeton Univ, 62-64. *Concurrent Pos:* Guggenheim fel, Niels Bohr Inst, Copenhagen, 70-71. *Mem:* Am Phys Soc. *Res:* Experimental investigations of nuclear spectroscopy and nuclear reaction mechanisms by means of charged particle and gamma ray studies. *Mailing Add:* Cyclotron Lab Physics Mich State Univ East Lansing MI 48824

KASHYAP, MOTI LAL, INTERNAL MEDICINE, ENDOCRINOLOGY. *Current Pos:* PROF MED & PATH, CALIF COL MED, UNIV CALIF, IRVINE, 86- *Personal Data:* b Singapore, Feb 19, 39; m 70, Suman; c Keshni, Vikram & Ishaan. *Educ:* Univ Singapore, MB, BS, 64; McGill Univ, MS, 67; FRCP(C), 69, FACP, 78. *Honors & Awards:* Distinguished Physicians Award, Indian Med Asn, USA, 92; Distinguished Academician of the Year, Acad Med, Singapore, 96. *Prof Exp:* Intern med & surg, Teaching Hosps, Univ Singapore, 64-65; resident internal med & fel endocrinol & metab, Royal Victoria Hosp, McGill Univ, 65-69, lectr, Fac Med, 69-70; sr fel, Cardiovasc Res Inst, Moffit Hosp, Sch Med, Univ Calif, San Francisco, 70-71; sr lectr med physiol, Fac Med, Univ Singapore, 71-74; from asst prof to assoc prof, 74-81, prof med, Col Med, Univ Cincinnati, 81-86. *Concurrent Pos:* Sr res fel, Am Heart Asn, 70-71, fel, Arteriosclerosis Coun; assoc dir-Lipid Res Clin, Cincinnati, 74-; dir, Apolipoprotein Res Labs, Cincinnati, 74-86; dir, Coronary Primary Prevention Trial, NIH, 74-78; chief of geriatric res, Vet Admin Med Ctr, Long Beach, Calif, chief gerontol, Long Beach, Calif, 86-88, chief gerontol & dir cholesterol ctr, 88-; res awards, Nat Inst Health & Am Heart Asn; Irvine Page Young Investr Award, Am Heart Asn, 76. *Mem:* Am Fedn Clin Res; Int Soc Cardiol; Can Soc Endocrinol & Metab; Am Geriatrics Soc; fel Am Heart Asn; fel Acad Med, Singapore. *Res:* Lipoprotein metabolism and atherosclerotic cardiovascular disease; focus is on regulation of high density lipoproteins, their constituent apolipoproteins and their role in heart disease prevention. *Mailing Add:* Vet Admin Med Ctr 111GE 5901 E Seventh St Long Beach CA 90822. *Fax:* 562-494-5515

KASHYAP, RANGASAMI LAKSMINARAYANA, ELECTRICAL ENGINEERING. *Current Pos:* from asst prof to assoc prof, 66-74, PROF ELEC ENG, PURDUE UNIV, 74- *Personal Data:* b Mysore, India, Mar 28, 38. *Educ:* Univ Mysore, BSc, 58; Indian Inst Sci, Bangalore, Dipl, 61, MEng, 63; Harvard Univ, PhD(eng), 66. *Honors & Awards:* King Sun Fu Res Award, Int Asn Pattern Recognition, 90. *Prof Exp:* Res asst control systs, Harvard Univ, 63-65, teaching fel, 64, res fel eng, 65-66. *Concurrent Pos:* Gordon McKay fel, 62-63; consult, Gen Elec Co, Ind, 67-68. *Mem:* Fel Inst Elec & Electronics Engrs; Asn Comput Mach; Sigma Xi. *Res:* Systems science; pattern recognition; learning systems; statistical inference; image processing. *Mailing Add:* 642 Eden St West Lafayette IN 47906

KASHYAP, TAPESHWAR S, POPULATION GENETICS, POULTRY BREEDING. *Current Pos:* geneticist & head data processing dept, 59-73, DIR GENETICS DEVELOP, KIMBER FARMS INC, 73- *Personal Data:* b Kapurthala, India, Oct 15, 29; US citizen; m 59; c 2. *Educ:* Punjab Agr Col, India, BSc, 50; Univ Minn, St Paul, MSc, 56, PhD(animal husb), 58. *Prof Exp:* Asst animal husb, Univ Minn, St Paul, 55-58. *Concurrent Pos:* FAO consult, Poultry Proj POL/71/515, Poznan, Poland, 76-78; consult geneticist poultry res proj, Animal Sci Dept, Univ Nebr, 78-; systs consult, Bank Am, 81- *Mem:* Genetics Soc Am; Am Genetics Asn; AAAS. *Res:* Animal breeding; improving livestock performance with the aid of principles of genetics; statistical analysis of data, using modern computers, to evaluate and seek answers to various problems in poultry breeding. *Mailing Add:* 41532 Paseo Padre Pkwy Fremont CA 94539

KASI, LEELA PESHKAR, RADIOPHARMACEUTICAL CHEMISTRY, NUCLEAR MEDICINE. *Current Pos:* RETIRED. *Personal Data:* b Bombay, India, July 15, 39; US citizen; m 71. *Educ:* Univ Bombay, India, BS, 58; Univ Marburg, WGer, PhD(pharmaceut chem), 68. *Prof Exp:* Sr chemist pharmaceut quality control, Boehringer-Knoll Ltd, Bombay, India, 69-71; dir qual control, pharmaceut chem, Health Care Indust, Mich City, Ind, 72-77; from asst chemist radiopharmaceut chem to assoc chemist, M D Anderson Cancer Ctr, Univ Tex, 79-95, from asst prof to assoc prof nuclear med, 82-95. *Concurrent Pos:* Asst prof clin radiol, Univ Tex Med Sch, Houston, 82-93, mem grad fac, Grad Sch Biomed Sci, 84-89, assoc prof clin radiol, 93-; asst ed, J Nuclear Med, 84-89. *Mem:* Soc Nuclear Med; AAAS; Sigma Xi. *Res:* Development and evaluation (in vitro and in vivo) of new radiolabeled substances for use in diagnostic imaging, radioimmunotherapy or biokinetic studies in cancer patients; radioimmunoimaging, pharmacology and nuclear magnetic resonance; radiopharmaceutic chemistry. *Mailing Add:* 4710 McDermel Houston TX 77035

KASIANOWICZ, JOHN JAMES, BIOSENSORS, SOFTWARE DEVELOPMENT. *Current Pos:* fel, 87-91, PHYSICAL SCIENTIST BIOPHYS & PHYSICS, NAT INST SCI TECHNOL, NIH, 92- *Personal Data:* b Boston, Mass, Apr 22, 57. *Educ:* Boston Univ, BA, 79; State Univ NY, MA, 81, PhD(physiol & biophys), 87. *Prof Exp:* Lectr physics, Dept Physics, Eastern Nazarene Col, 82-83. *Mem:* Biophys Soc; Am Phys Soc; Mats Res Soc. *Res:* Experimental and theoretical investigations of ion transport in protein ion channels; developing novel methods to determine the structure-function relationship of membrane-bound proteins; emerging emphasis on potential applications of pore-forming proteins in biotechnology. *Mailing Add:* Nat Inst Sci Technol 222/A353 Gaithersburg MD 20899. *Fax:* 301-330-3447; *E-Mail:* john.kasianowicz@nist.gov

KASIK, JOHN EDWARD, MEDICINE, PHARMACOLOGY. *Current Pos:* assoc prof, 70-73, PROF MED, COL MED, UNIV IOWA, 73-, ASSOC DEAN, 80-; CHIEF OF STAFF, VET ADMIN MED CTR, IOWA CITY, 80- *Personal Data:* b Chicago, Ill, Aug 9, 27; m 45; c 6. *Educ:* Roosevelt Univ, BS, 49; Univ Chicago, MS, 53, MD, 54, PhD(pharmacol), 62; Am Bd Internal Med, dipl. *Honors & Awards:* Walter L Bierring Award, Am Thoracic Soc, Iowa, 76. *Prof Exp:* Intern, Clins Univ Chicago, 54-55, from jr asst to asst resident med, 55-56, from asst prof to assoc prof, Grad Sch Med, 59-70. *Concurrent Pos:* Miller fel, Univ Chicago, 57-59; Fulbright scholar, Oxford Univ, Dunn Sch, 66-67; med dir, Kirchwood Col-Vet Admin Hosp Iowa City Sch Respiratory Ther. *Mem:* Am Thoracic Soc; Am Fedn Clin Res; fel Am Col Physicians; fel Am Soc Clin Pharmacol & Therapeut; Am Acad Clin Toxicol. *Res:* Pharmacology of immunosuppressent drugs; pharmacology of antibiotics. *Mailing Add:* 2661 NE Newport Rd Solon IA 52333

KASINSKY, HAROLD EDWARD, BIOCHEMISTRY, ZOOLOGY. *Current Pos:* asst prof, 69-81, ASSOC PROF ZOOL, UNIV BC, 81- *Personal Data:* b New York, NY, Jan 20, 41; m 67, 84, Vicki Turay; c Yuri, Jeremy & Leah. *Educ:* Columbia Univ, BA, 61; Univ Calif, Berkeley, PhD(biochem), 67. *Prof Exp:* NIH fel, Dept Embryol, Carnegie Inst, 67-69. *Concurrent Pos:* Vis prof, Univ Calif, Berkeley, Univ Calgary, Univ Amsterdam & Polytech Univ Barcelona. *Mem:* AAAS; Int Soc Molecular Evolution; Soc Develop Biol; Can Soc Zool. *Res:* Comparative aspects of sperm protein diversity in vertebrates and invertebrates; characterization of sperm nuclear basic protein and their genes in reptiles, amphibians, fish, tunicates, mollusks, worms and plants. *Mailing Add:* Dept Zool Univ BC Vancouver BC V6T 1Z4 Can. *Fax:* 604-822-2416; *E-Mail:* kasinsky@zoology.ubc.ca

KASK, UNO, INORGANIC CHEMISTRY. *Current Pos:* from assoc prof to prof, 66-93, chmn dept, 70-72, EMER PROF CHEM, TOWSON STATE UNIV, 93- *Personal Data:* b Sadala, Estonia, Sept 16, 22; US citizen; m 70, Martha J Sage. *Educ:* Univ Ga, BS, 50; Univ Minn, MA, 56; Univ Tex, PhD(inorg chem), 63. *Prof Exp:* Instr chem, Armstrong Col, 52-55 & Eureka Col, 55-56; asst prof, Valdosta State Col, 56-57, Am Int Col, 57-60, Ind State Col, 61-62 & Univ Ga, 63-66. *Res:* Nonaqueous reactions and reaction mechanisms of transition metal compounds with liquid sulfur; chemical education and textbook writing. *Mailing Add:* 709 Fairway Dr Towson MD 21286. *Fax:* 410-821-1536; *E-Mail:* uakask@aol.com

KASKA, HAROLD VICTOR, GEOLOGY. *Current Pos:* RETIRED. *Personal Data:* b Brooklyn, NY, Jan 11, 26; m 50; c 3. *Educ:* NY Univ, BA, 50; Univ Ind, MA, 52. *Prof Exp:* Paleont asst, Univ Ind, 50-52; micropaleontologist, Dominion Oil Ltd, 52-53, chief paleontologist, 53-56; explor paleontologist, Calif Explor Co, 56-57; stratig paleontologist, Compania Guatemala Calif de Petroleo, 57-62; palynologist, Calif Explor Co, 62-65; paleontologist, Chevron Explor Co, 65-67; sr paleontologist, Standard Oil Co, Calif, 68-71; staff paleontologist, Chevron Overseas Petrol Inc, 71-85. *Mem:* Am Asn Petrol Geol; Am Inst Prof Geol; Paleont Soc; Am Asn Stratig Palynologist; Brit

Micropaleont Soc; Swiss Geol Soc. *Res:* palynology, paleozoic, mezoic and tertiary spores, pollen dinoflagellates and acritards; micropaleontology, Mesozoic and Tertiary foraminifera, planktonics, tintinnids, calcareous nannoplankton; application of micropaleontology and palynology to petroleum exploration, dating, correlation and facies studies. *Mailing Add:* 50 Nottingham Circle Clayton CA 94517

KASKA, WILLIAM CHARLES, CHEMISTRY. *Current Pos:* asst prof, 65-74, assoc prof, 74-79, PROF CHEM, UNIV CALIF, SANTA BARBARA, 79- *Personal Data:* b Ancon, CZ, May 13, 35; m 64; c 4. *Educ:* Loyola Univ, Calif, BS, 57; Univ Mich, PhD(chem), 63. *Prof Exp:* Res assoc chem, Pa State Univ, 63-64. *Mem:* Am Chem Soc; Sigma Xi. *Res:* Synthesis and chemistry of organomettalic compounds of the transition elements. *Mailing Add:* Dept Chem Univ Calif Santa Barbara CA 93106

KASKAS, JAMES, THEORETICAL PHYSICS. *Current Pos:* RETIRED. *Personal Data:* b Detroit, Mich, Jan 30, 39. *Educ:* Wayne State Univ, BS, 60, MS, 61, PhD(physics), 64. *Prof Exp:* From instr to assoc prof physics, Detroit Inst Technol, 63-89. *Mem:* Am Phys Soc; Am Asn Physics Teachers. *Res:* Elementary particle theory; quantum field theory. *Mailing Add:* 25533 Fairgrove St Trenton MI 48183-4447

KASLER, FRANZ JOHANN, ANALYTICAL CHEMISTRY. *Current Pos:* Asst prof, 59-65, ASSOC PROF CHEM, UNIV MD, COLLEGE PARK, 65- *Personal Data:* b Vienna, Austria, Jan 1, 30; m 64; c 2. *Educ:* Univ Vienna, PhD(org microanal), 59. *Mem:* AAAS; Am Chem Soc; Am Microchem Soc; Austrian Chem Soc; Sigma Xi. *Res:* Quantitative nuclear magnetic resonance; organic elemental analysis of classic and instrumental methods. *Mailing Add:* 4401 Briggs Chaney Beltsville MD 20705-1046

KASLICK, RALPH SIDNEY, PERIODONTICS, ORAL MEDICINE. *Current Pos:* DIR DENT, GOLDWATER MEM HOSP, MED CTR, NY UNIV, 88-; CLIN PROF PERIODONT, SCH DENT, 88-, PRES MED STAFF, 92- *Personal Data:* b Brooklyn, NY, Oct 17, 35; m 76, Jessica Hellinger; c Andrew. *Educ:* Columbia Univ, AB, 56, DDS, 59. *Honors & Awards:* Jour Award, Int Col Dent, 72; Medallion, Japan Stomatol Soc, 78. *Prof Exp:* From instr to prof periodont & oral med, Sch Dent, Fairleigh Dickinson Univ, 65-88, from asst dean to dean, 72-88. *Concurrent Pos:* Res grants from var indust firms & founds, 65-; res consult for var indust firms, 69- *Mem:* Fel Am Col Dent; Am Acad Periodont; Int Asn Dent Res; Sigma Xi; Am Asn Dent Schs. *Res:* Genetic studies of periodontal diseases in young adults; quantitative analysis of gingival fluid; clinical testing of therapeutic dentifrices, ointments and hygiene aids. *Mailing Add:* Goldwater Mem Hosp NY Univ Med Ctr Roosevelt Island New York NY 10044. *Fax:* 212-318-4370

KASLOW, CHRISTIAN EDWARD, organic chemistry; deceased, see previous edition for last biography

KASLOW, DAVID EDWARD, AEROSPACE SYSTEM ENGINEERING. *Current Pos:* ANALYST & MGR, VALLEY FORGE SPACE CTR, LOCKHEED MARTIN, 73-, SR STAFF ENGR & CHIEF ENGR. *Personal Data:* b Bloomington, Ind, Sept 27, 42. *Educ:* Ind Univ, Bloomington, AB, 64, MS, 66; Univ Mich, Ann Arbor, PhD(physics), 71. *Prof Exp:* Res assoc physics, Lehigh Univ, 71-73. *Mem:* Int Coun Syst Eng. *Mailing Add:* Valley Forge Space Ctr Lockheed Martin PO Box 8555 King of Prussia PA 19101

KASLOW, RICHARD ALAN, MEDICINE. *Current Pos:* CHIEF, EPIDEMIOL & BIOMET BR, NAT INST ALLERGY & INFECTIONS DIS, 80-; PROF EPIDEMIOL, MED & MICROBIOL, UNIV ALA, BIRMINGHAM, 95- *Personal Data:* b Omaha, Nebr, Mar 1, 43. *Educ:* Yale Col, BA, 65; Harvard Med Sch, MD, 69; Harvard Sch Pub Health, MPH, 76. *Honors & Awards:* A Conger Goodyear Prize, 65. *Prof Exp:* Epidemiologist, Sidney Farber Cancer Ctr, 75-76; chief, Arthritis & Immunol Dis Activ, Ctr Dis Control, 76-79; clin asst prof med, Emory Univ Sch Med, 76-79; sr surgeon, USPHS, 76-85, capt, 85-95. *Concurrent Pos:* Diabetes mellitus coord comt, 79-81, epidemiol comt, NIH, 79-; Reye Syndrome Task Force, 82-; Prev Activ, Hosp Infections Prog, Ctr Dis Control, 76-78; chmn adv comt, Study AIDS Natural Hist, NIH, 83-85; task force AIDS epidemiol, USPHS, 84-86, capt, 85-95; workshop on epidemiol & dis burden AIDS, Inst Med, Nat Acad Sci, 86, Human Immunodeficiency Virus Infection, Nat Inst Allergy & Infectious Dis, India, 86-; sr attend phys, Nat Inst Allergy & Infections Dis, 81-; adj prof, Uniformed Serv Univ Health Sci, 88-, George Washington Univ, 88-95, Johns Hopkins Sch Hygiene & Pub Health, 96- *Mem:* Am Col Physicians; Infectious Dis Soc; Am Epidemiol Soc; Am Col Epidemiol; Am Fed Clin Res; AAAS. *Res:* Epidemiologic research on infectious and immune disease including AIDS and other genital infections, Lyme disease, autoimmune diseases and asthma; immunogenetics of infectious and other diseases. *Mailing Add:* 212C Tidwell Hall Sch Pub Health 720 20th St S Birmingham AL 35294-0008

KASNER, FRED E, PHYSICAL CHEMISTRY. *Current Pos:* PROF CHEM, OLIVE-HARVEY COL, 71- *Personal Data:* b New York, NY, July 8, 26; m 53; c 1. *Educ:* City Col New York, BS, 48; Univ Chicago, MS, 49, PhD(phys chem), 61. *Prof Exp:* From instr to asst prof natural sci, Univ Chicago, 54-59; from instr to prof chem, Fenger Jr Col, 61-70. *Concurrent Pos:* Consult, USAF, 59; vis scholar, Northwestern Univ, 71; vis scientist, Argonne Nat Lab, 79. *Mem:* Am Chem Soc; Am Soc Testing & Mat. *Res:* Laser Raman spectroscopy of aqueous solutions; thermal conductivity and its temperature coefficient; heats of dilution of aqueous solutions of strong electrolytes. *Mailing Add:* 320 17th St Wilmette IL 60091-3224

KASNER, WILLIAM HENRY, PHYSICS. *Current Pos:* FEL SCIENTIST, GAS LASERS RES & DEVELOP, WESTINGHOUSE RES & DEVELOP CTR, 61- *Personal Data:* b Killbuck, Ohio, Jan 27, 29; m 51; c 1. *Educ:* Case Western Reserve Univ, BS, 51; Univ Pittsburgh, PhD(physics), 58. *Prof Exp:* Res assoc physics, Univ Md, 58-59, asst res prof, 59-61. *Mem:* Am Phys Soc. *Res:* Atomic physics, especially atomic and electronic collision phenomena; ultraviolet spectroscopy; gas discharges; optics; laser development and application. *Mailing Add:* 11686 Althea Dr Pittsburgh PA 15235

KASOWSKI, ROBERT V, SOLID STATE PHYSICS. *Current Pos:* CONSULT, 80- *Personal Data:* b Bremond, Tex, Feb 14, 44; m 69; c 1. *Educ:* Tex A&M Univ, BS, 66; Univ Chicago, PhD(physics), 69. *Prof Exp:* Physicist, E I du Pont de Nemours & Co, Inc, 69-80. *Mem:* Am Phys Soc. *Res:* Calculating the electronic properties of molecules adsorbed onto metal or semiconductor surfaces using linear combination of muffin tin orbitals method. *Mailing Add:* Brinton's Bridge Rd West Chester PA 19382

KASPAREK, STANLEY VACLAV, ORGANIC CHEMISTRY, MEDICINAL CHEMISTRY. *Current Pos:* PRES, CHEMINFO, 85- *Personal Data:* b Prague, Czech, June 11, 29. *Educ:* Charles Univ, Prague, Dr rer nat, 65. *Prof Exp:* Chemist, Res Inst Pharm & Biochem, Prague, 50-59 & Czech Acad Sci, 62-65; fel & chemist, Nat Res Coun Can, 65-67; abstractor, Chem Abstracts Serv, Ohio, 68; info scientist, Hoffmann-La Roche Inc, 68-81, tech fel, 82-85. *Mem:* Am Chem Soc. *Res:* Scientific information. *Mailing Add:* 3 Rockledge Pl Cedar Grove NJ 07009

KASPER, ANDREW E, JR, PALEOBOTANY. *Current Pos:* Asst prof, 70-75, ASSOC PROF BOT, RUTGERS UNIV, NEWARK, 75- *Personal Data:* b Bridgeport, Conn, Oct 29, 42; m 67, Nancy A Oste; c Christian & Emily. *Educ:* Duquesne Univ, BA, 65; Univ Conn, MS, 68, PhD(bot), 70. *Mem:* Bot Soc Am; Sigma Xi; Paleont Soc. *Res:* Description and classification of Devonian age plant fossils. *Mailing Add:* Dept Biol Sci Rutgers Univ 101 Warren St Newark NJ 07102

KASPER, CHARLES BOYER, CELL BIOLOGY. *Current Pos:* from asst prof to assoc prof, 65-82, PROF ONCOL, McARDLE LAB, UNIV WIS-MADISON, 82- *Personal Data:* b Joliet, Ill, Apr 27, 35; m 57, M Jeanne Charlton; c Lynda, David, Jenette & JoAnna. *Educ:* Univ Ill, BS, 58; Univ Wis, PhD(physiol chem), 62. *Prof Exp:* Asst prof biol chem, Univ Calif, Los Angeles, 64-65. *Concurrent Pos:* NIH fels, Univ Utah, 62-63 & Univ Calif, Los Angeles, 63-64. *Mem:* Am Soc Biol Chemists; Am Asn Cancer Res. *Res:* Regulation of enzymes responsible for the metabolic activation of chemical carcinogens; molecular basis of enzyme induction; molecular biology; toxicology. *Mailing Add:* Dept Oncol 421a McArdle Res Univ Wis Med Sch 1420 University N Madison WI 53706-1531. *Fax:* 608-262-2824

KASPER, DENNIS LEE, BACTERIAL DISEASES, IMMUNOCHEMISTRY. *Current Pos:* Edward H Kass prof med, 87-89, PROF MED HARVARD MED SCH 85-, WILLIAM ELLERY CHANNING PROF MED; ASSOC DIR CHANNING LAB, BRIGHAM & WOMEN'S HOSP, 82-, CO-DIR CHANNING LAB; CHEIF INFECTIOUS DIS, BETH ISRAEL HOSP, BOSTON, MASS, 81- *Personal Data:* b Feb 23, 43; m 67, Terri Wainess; c Adam, Jocelyn & Jacob. *Educ:* Univ Ill, Chicago, MD, 67. *Honors & Awards:* Squibb Award, Infectious Dis Soc Am; Res Career Develop Award, NIH, Merit Award. *Concurrent Pos:* Exec comt, Int Soc Infectious Dis; chmn, Bd Sci Counselors, Nat Inst Allergy & Infectious Dis. *Mem:* Am Soc Clin Invest; Asn Am Physicians; Am Fedn Clin Res; Am Asn Immunologists; Am Soc Microbiol; Infectious Dis Soc Am; Int Soc Anaerobic Bact (pres). *Res:* Infectious diseases; bacterial pathogenesis and vaccine development; primary efforts are in group B streptococcal infections and anaerobic bacterial infections; granted 15 US patents. *Mailing Add:* Dept Med Channing Lab Harvard Med Sch 180 Longwood Ave Boston MA 02115-5889. *Fax:* 208-262-2824

KASPER, GERHARD, AEROSOL SCIENCE & TECHNOLOGY, CONTAMINATION CONTROL. *Current Pos:* DIR, TECHNOL, ENG & QUAL, ELECTRONICS DIV, AIR LIQUIDE, WALNUT CREEK, CA, 93- *Personal Data:* b Salzburg, Austria, June 6, 49; m; c 2. *Educ:* Univ Vienna, Austria, PhD(physics), 77. *Prof Exp:* asst prof physics, Inst Exp Physics, Univ Vienna, Austria, 77-78; from res asst prof to asst prof elec engr, State Univ NY, Buffalo, 78-83; sr sci, Am Air Liquide Inc, Countryside, Ill, 83-85, dir res & develop, Chicago Res Ctr, 85-93. *Concurrent Pos:* Adj prof, Univ Vienna, Austria, 83-; chmn, particulate standards subcomt Semicond Equip & Mat Inst, 84-; ed-in-chief, J Aerosol Sci, 85- *Mem:* Europ Asn Aerosol Res; Am Asn Aerosol Res; Inst Environ Sci; Am Soc Testing & Mat. *Res:* Aerosol science and particle technology including instrumentation and measurement techniques; filtration; contamination control; surface-particle interactions; aerosol generation and sampling; dynamics of irregular particles. *Mailing Add:* Inst Mech Versahrenstechnik Univ Karlsruhe 76128 Karlsruhe Germany

KASPER, HORST MANFRED, PHYSICAL CHEMISTRY, SEMICONDUCTOR DEVICES. *Current Pos:* PATENT ATTY, KASPER & LAUGHLIN, 79- *Personal Data:* b Dusseldorf, Ger, June 3, 39; c Olaf & Kathy. *Educ:* Univ Bonn, Ger, dipl, 63, Dr, 65; Seton Hall Univ, JD, 78. *Prof Exp:* Staff mem, Lincoln Lab, Mass Inst Technol, 66-69; staff mem, Bell Telephone Labs, 70-76; patent atty, Allied Corp, 77-79. *Mem:* Fel Am Phys Soc; Electrochem Soc; Am Chem Soc; NY Acad Sci. *Res:* Physical chemistry of semiconductors. *Mailing Add:* 13 Forest Dr Warren NJ 07060. *Fax:* 908-668-5262

KASPER, JOHN SIMON, PHYSICAL CHEMISTRY. *Current Pos:* RETIRED. *Personal Data:* b Newark, NJ, May 27, 15. *Educ:* Johns Hopkins Univ, AB, 37, PhD(chem), 41. *Prof Exp:* Jr instr chem, Johns Hopkins Univ, 37-41; instr, St Louis Univ, 41-42; res chemist, Nat Defense Res Comt contract, Johns Hopkins Univ, 42-43 & Manhattan Dist Proj, SAM Labs, Columbia Univ, 43-45; res assoc, Res Lab, Gen Elec Co, 45-58, phys chemist, 58-80. *Mem:* AAAS; Am Chem Soc; Am Phys Soc; Am Crystallog Asn. *Res:* X-ray diffraction; structures of crystals; structural chemistry; fluorocarbon chemistry; gas adsorption; physical properties; aqueous solutions; neutron diffraction. *Mailing Add:* 18 Cumberland Pl Scotia NY 12302

KASPER, JOSEPH EMIL, SCIENCE EDUCATION. *Current Pos:* RETIRED. *Personal Data:* b Cedar Rapids, Iowa, May 2, 20; m 57; c 5. *Educ:* Coe Col, BA, 51; Univ Iowa, MS, 54, PhD(physics), 58. *Prof Exp:* Asst physics, Univ Iowa, 51-57, instr, 58; asst prof physics, Coe Col, 59-63, prof, 63-86. *Mem:* Am Phys Soc; Am Asn Physics Teachers. *Res:* Geomagnetic theory; cosmic radiation; soft radiations in upper atmosphere; rocketry. *Mailing Add:* 3344 Carlisle St NE Cedar Rapids IA 52402

KASPER, JOSEPH F, JR, NAVIGATION, APPLIED PHYSICS. *Personal Data:* b Baltimore, Md, Dec 9, 43; m 66; c 2. *Educ:* Mass Inst Technol, BS, 64, MS, 66, DSc(instrumentation), 68. *Prof Exp:* Mgr spec projs, Anal Sci Corp, 75-78, mgr, Navig Systs, 78-79, dir, Stratig Syst Div, 79-80, dir sea-launched ballistic missile, 80-90; pres & chief exec officer, Found Informed Med Decision Making, 90-94. *Mem:* Am Geophys Union; Inst Navig; Inst Elec & Electronics Engrs; Am Inst Aeronaut & Astronaut. *Res:* Mathematical modeling of very low frequency propagation anomalies; statistical description of geodetic phenomena; analysis of radio and inertial navigation error behavior; applied Kalman filtering. *Mailing Add:* 32 Elm St Norwich VT 05055

KASPERBAUER, MICHAEL J, PLANT PHYSIOLOGY, PHOTOBIOLOGY. *Current Pos:* res plant physiologist, Agr Res Serv, Pioneering Res Lab Plant Physiol, Beltsville, Md, 62-63, Crops Res Div, Lexington, Ky, 63-83, COASTAL PLAIN, WATER & PLANT RES, US DEPT AGR, FLORENCE, SC, 83- *Personal Data:* b Manning, Iowa, Oct 8, 29; m 62, Isabel M Giles; c Maria, John, Paul & Sandra. *Educ:* Iowa State Univ, BS, 54, MS, 57, PhD(plant physiol), 61. *Honors & Awards:* L M Ware Res Award, 90; Crop Sci Res Award, 90; Agronomic Res Award, 94. *Prof Exp:* NSF fel, Univ Md, 61-62. *Concurrent Pos:* Adj prof agron, Univ Ky, 65-83; assoc ed, Agron J, 75-83; prof plant physiol, Clemson Univ, 83- *Mem:* Am Soc Plant Physiol; fel Crop Sci Soc Am; fel Am Soc Agron; Am Soc Photobiol; Sigma Xi. *Res:* Interaction of light and temperature on plant growth, development and composition; phytochrome control of plant physiological processes; haploid and doubled haploid utilization in crop improvement. *Mailing Add:* 1717 Williamsburg Ct Lexington KY 40504

KASPEREK, GEORGE JAMES, BIOCHEMISTRY, EXERCISE. *Current Pos:* assoc prof, 78-88, PROF, BIOCHEM, SCH MED, ECAROLINA UNIV, 88- *Personal Data:* b Albert Lea, Minn, June 1, 44; m 66; c 2. *Educ:* Mankato State Col, BA, 66; Ore State Univ, PhD(org chem), 69. *Prof Exp:* Fel bioorg, Univ Calif, Santa Barbara, 69-72; asst prof biochem, Conn Col, 72-77, assoc prof, 77-78. *Concurrent Pos:* NIH fel, 76-77; vis prof, Sch Med, ECarolina Univ, 78-79. *Mem:* Am Col Sports Med. *Res:* Regulation of metabolism during exercise; amino acid metabolism; protein metabolism. *Mailing Add:* Dept Biochem Sch Med ECarolina Univ Greenville NC 27858-4354

KASPROW, BARBARA ANN, MICRO ANATOMY, REPRODUCTIVE BIOLOGY. *Current Pos:* ASST TO PRES, UNIV RES SYSTS, 79- *Personal Data:* b Hartford, Conn, Apr 23, 36. *Educ:* Albertus Magnus Col, BA, 58; Loyola Univ, Ill, PhD(anat), 69. *Prof Exp:* USPHS training scholar, Yale Univ, 59-60, res asst anat & reproductive biol, Sch Med, 61; res assoc, NY Med Col, 61-62; from res assoc to sr res & admin assoc, Inst Study Human Reproduction, Ohio, 62-67; sr res assoc, Stritch Sch Med, Loyola Univ, Chicago, 67-69, asst prof anat, 69-76; writer, Opers Specialist, 76-79. *Concurrent Pos:* Co-ed, Biol Reproduction, 73. *Mem:* AAAS; Am Asn Anatomists; Am Soc Zoologists; NY Acad Sci; Sigma Xi. *Res:* Reproductive phenomena in the mammalian female; growth mechanisms, pathologic variants in reproductive organs and endocrinologic interrelationships; cytophysiology; research administration; science education. *Mailing Add:* PO Box 385 Lombard IL 60148

KASRIEL, ROBERT H, MATHEMATICS. *Current Pos:* from asst prof to prof, 54-84, EMER PROF MATH, GA INST TECHNOL, 85- *Personal Data:* b Tampa, Fla, Oct 18, 18; m 46; c 2. *Educ:* Univ Tampa, BS, 40; Univ Va, MA, 49, PhD(math), 53. *Honors & Awards:* Ferst Res Award, Sigma Xi, 62. *Prof Exp:* Coordr war-training courses, Univ Tampa, 40-42; aeronaut res scientist, Nat Adv Comt Aeronaut, 52-54. *Mem:* Am Math Soc; Math Asn Am; Sigma Xi. *Res:* Analytic topology; fixed point theorems; mapping theorems. *Mailing Add:* Math Dept Ga Tech Atlanta GA 30332-0001

KASS, GUSS SIGMUND, COSMETIC CHEMISTRY, TOPICAL DRUGS. *Current Pos:* PRES, G S KASS & ASSOCS, LTD, 74- *Personal Data:* b Chicago, Ill, Oct 19, 15; m 38, Shirley Herron; c Barbara (Kipnis) & Marilyn (Ring). *Educ:* Univ Chicago, BS, 38. *Prof Exp:* Res chemist, Munic Tuberc Sanitarium, 38-39; chemist, Prod Corp Am, 39-40; res chemist, Acme Cosmetic Corp, 40-41; chief chemist, Duart Mfg Co, Ltd, Calif, 41-42 & 46-48; asst res dir, Helene Curtis Industs, Inc, 48-54; res dir & vpres, Lanolin Plus, Inc, 54-60; from tech dir to vpres & dir corp res & develop, Alberto-Culver Co, 60-74. *Concurrent Pos:* Lectr, Univ Chicago, 58; lectr, Sch Med, Univ Ill, 65-86. *Mem:* Am Acad Dermat; Am Chem Soc; fel Soc Cosmetic Chem; fel Am Inst Chem. *Res:* Cosmetics; toiletries; proprietary pharmaceuticals. *Mailing Add:* GS Kass & Assoc Ltd 8938 N Keeler Ave Skokie IL 60076

KASS, LEE B, BOTANY, HISTORY OF SCIENCE. *Current Pos:* lectr biol, 79-81, asst prof, 82-89, ASSOC PROF BOT, ELMIRA COL, 89- *Personal Data:* b New York, NY, May 23, 46; m 81, Robert S Hunt. *Educ:* City Col NY, BS, 69; Cambridge Univ, MA, 75; Cornell Univ, PhD(bot), 75. *Prof Exp:* Teaching asst, State Univ NY, 69-71; res fel, Girton Col, Cambridge Univ, 75-77, instr, 76, supvr, 77; NSF fel biol, Vanderbilt Univ, 77-78, res asst pharmacol, 78-79. *Concurrent Pos:* Lectr biol, Univ Tenn, 78-79; fac assoc & res technician, Sect Poultry & Avian Sci, Cornell Univ, 79-81; chair, Teaching Sect Slide Exchange, Bot Soc Am, 84, 87, mem comt, Careers Bot, 94; vis assoc prof, Cornell Univ, 90-91, 96-97 & 97-98, adj assoc prof, 94-; consult, Environ Mgmt Coun, Tomkins Co, 91-93; vis assoc prof biol & plant path, Mich State Univ, 94; Fulbright scholar natural sci, Col Bahamas, 96; prin investr, NSF, 96-97 & 97-98. *Mem:* Am Fern Soc; Am Inst Biol Sci; Asn Trop Biol; Bot Soc Am; Int Soc Hist Sci & Soc Studies Biol. *Res:* Rare plant species; ecology and reproductive biology of mangroves; history of botany and genetics; Bahama flora biochemistry. *Mailing Add:* Div Math & Natural Sci Elmira Col 1 Park Pl Elmira NY 14901. *Fax:* 607-564-9082; *E-Mail:* lbkbhwon@aol.com

KASS, LEON RICHARD, MEDICAL ETHICS. *Current Pos:* Henry R Luce prof lib arts of human biol, 76-84, prof, 84-90, ADDIE CLARK HARDING, PROF, COL & COMT SOCIAL THOUGHT, UNIV CHICAGO, 90- *Personal Data:* b Chicago, Ill, Feb 12, 39; m 61, Amy Apfel; c Sarah & Miriam. *Educ:* Univ Chicago, BS, 58, MD, 62; Harvard Univ, PhD(biochem, molecular biol), 67. *Prof Exp:* Intern med, Beth Israel Hosp, Boston, Mass, 62-63; staff assoc molecular biol, Nat Inst Arthritis & Metab Dis, 67-69, sr staff fel, 69-70; exec secy comt life sci & social policy, Nat Acad Sci, 70-72; tutor, St John's Col, Md, 72-76; Joseph P Kennedy, sr res prof bioethics, Kennedy Inst & assoc prof neurol & philos, Georgetown Univ, 74-76. *Concurrent Pos:* Guggenheim fel, 72-73; mem bd dir, Hastings Ctr, 70-96, fel, 70-; mem bd gov, US-Israel Binat Sci Found, 82-88; mem, Nat Humanities Coun, 84-91; fel, Nat Humanities Ctr, 84-85; William Brady Jr distinguished fel social thought, Am Enterprise Inst, 91-92. *Res:* Ethical and social implications of advances in biomedical science and technology; philosophy of biology and medicine; philosophical anthropology; ethics of everyday life. *Mailing Add:* Univ Chicago 1116 E 59th St Chicago IL 60637

KASS, ROBERT S, MEMBRANE BIOPHYSICS. *Current Pos:* from asst prof to assoc prof, 77-90, PROF PHYSIOL & PEDIAT, UNIV ROCHESTER, 90- *Personal Data:* b New York, NY, June 13, 46; m 82; c 2. *Educ:* Univ Ill, BSc, 68; Univ Mich, MSc, 69, PhD(physics), 72. *Prof Exp:* Fel physiol, Univ Mich, 72-74; fel membrane biophysics, Marine Biol Labs, Mass, 73; fel physiol, Yale Univ, 74-77. *Mem:* Biophys Soc; Am Heart Asn; Soc Gen Physiologists; NY Acad Sci. *Res:* Physiology and biophysics of excitable membranes with a particular interest in the membranes of heart muscle cells; regulation of ion channels by hormones and drug molecules. *Mailing Add:* Dept Physiol Univ Rochester Med Ctr 601 Elmwood Rd Box 642 Rochester NY 14642. *Fax:* 716-461-3529

KASS, SEYMOUR, ALGEBRA. *Current Pos:* dir eng prog, 84-85, PROF MATH, UNIV MASS, BOSTON, 82- *Personal Data:* b New York, NY, Apr 13, 26; m 55, Judith Marks; c Dan & Lia. *Educ:* Brooklyn Col, BA, 48; Stanford Univ, MS, 57; Univ Chicago, SM, 65; Ill Inst Technol, PhD(math), 66. *Prof Exp:* Mathematician, Curtiss Wright Corp, 52-55 & Stanford Res Inst, 55-57; from instr to asst prof math, Ill Inst Technol, 60-71; from assoc prof to prof, Boston State Col, 77-82, chmn dept, 72-75. *Concurrent Pos:* NSF res grant, 69 & 70. *Mem:* Am Math Soc; Math Asn Am; Sigma Xi. *Res:* Algebra; geometry; statistics. *Mailing Add:* 118 York Terr Brookline MA 02146-2322. *E-Mail:* kass@umbsky.cc.umb.edu

KASSAKHIAN, GARABET HAROUTIOUN, ENVIRONMENTAL CHEMISTRY-REMEDIATION, QUALITY ASSURANCE. *Current Pos:* mgr, qual assurance, 92-96, DIR, QUAL ASSURANCE, TETRA TECH INC, PASADENA, CALIF, 96- *Personal Data:* b Jerusalem, Palestine, Aug 15, 44; US citizen; m 69, Loussik Antonian; c Harutiun, Ardashes & Vazken. *Educ:* Yerevan State Univ, Armenia, MSc, 67; Harvard Univ, AM, 70, PhD(anal chem), 75. *Honors & Awards:* Willem Rudolfs Medal, Water Pollution Control Fedn, 82. *Prof Exp:* Sr teaching fel chem, Harvard Univ, 68-74; asst prof chem, Univ Mass, Boston, 75-78; environ chemist, Eldorado Nuclear Ltd, Ottawa, 78-80; mgr, Amerada Hess Corp, Woodbridge, NJ, 80-82; dir environ res & develop, Nayirit Syn Rubber Factory, Yerevan, Armenia, 82-85; assoc, Lockman & Assocs, Monterey Park, Calif, 85-87; sr environ scientist, Law Environ Inc, Burbank, Calif, 88-91. *Concurrent Pos:* Asst prof environ chem, Univ LaVerne, Calif, 85-87. *Mem:* Am Chem Soc; Water Environ Fedn; Am Soc Qual Control. *Res:* Uranium mine and mill tailings; methane gas mitigation; air and water pollution; radionuclides in environment; water purification; wastewater treatment; contaminated soil remediation; quality assurance; drinking water standards; data validation. *Mailing Add:* 1409 Valverde Pl Glendale CA 91208-1119

KASSAKIAN, JOHN GABRIEL, POWER ELECTRONICS, ELECTRICAL ENGINEERING. *Current Pos:* from asst prof to assoc prof elec eng, 73-84, assoc dir, Elec Power Syst Eng Lab, 79-83, PROF ELEC ENG, MASS INST TECHNOL, 84-, DIR, LAB ELECTROMAGNETIC & ELECTRONIC SYST, 91- *Personal Data:* b Mar 27, 43; US citizen; m 68, Wilma Riemenschneider; c 2. *Educ:* Mass Inst Technol, SB, 65, SM, 67, EE, 67, ScD(elec eng), 73. *Honors & Awards:* Centennial Medal, Inst Elec &

Electronics Engrs, 84, William E Newell Award, 87. *Prof Exp:* Tech rep to Univac naval data syst, USN, 69-71. *Concurrent Pos:* Sr staff scientist, Gould Labs, Gould Inc, 75, consult, 75-; consult, Lutron Electronics, 78-; mgr spec proj, Amerada Hess Corp, 80-85; dir, Ault Inc, 84-, Sheldahl Inc, 85- *Mem:* Fel Inst Elec & Electronics Engrs; Nat Acad Eng; Europ Power Electronics Asn; Sigma Xi. *Res:* Simulation, analysis, synthesis of electronic energy conversion systems; power semiconductor devices; manufacturing technolgies for electronic apparatus. *Mailing Add:* Mass Inst Technol Bldg 10-172 77 Massachusetts Ave Cambridge MA 02139-4309. *E-Mail:* jgk@mit.edu

KASSAL, ROBERT JAMES, PLASTICS FAILURE ANALYSIS, ORGANIC CHEMISTRY. *Current Pos:* res chemist, E I Du Pont de Nemours & Co, Inc, 63-68, sr res chemist, Plastics Dept, 68-69, res supvr, 69-75, mem staff, Elastomers Dept, 75-78, res assoc, Polymer Prod Dept, 75-85, sr res assoc & group leader, 85-90, RES FEL, POLYMER PROD DEPT, E I DU PONT DE NEMOURS & CO INC, 90- *Personal Data:* b Berwick, Pa, Oct 23, 36; m 58; c 4. *Educ:* Hofstra Univ, BA, 58; Univ Fla, PhD(org chem), 64. *Prof Exp:* Chemist, Am Cyanamid Co, 58-60; res asst fluorine chem, Univ Fla, 60-63. *Mem:* Soc Plastics Indust. *Res:* Fluorine chemistry; polymer preparation; fluorocarbon heterocyclic polymers; intermediates and monomer exploratory research; new product development; polymer synthesis; polymer modification; high performance composite development; novel elastomer systems; polymer toughening; solvent resistant polymers; engineering polymers; polymer compounding and processing; failure analysis of polymer systems; accelerated test method development; environmental effects on polymers. *Mailing Add:* Exp Sta Lab Bldg 323/205B E I Du Pont de Nemours & Co Inc PO Box 80323 Wilmington DE 19880-0323

KASSAM, SALEEM ABDULALI, SIGNAL PROCESSING, COMMUNICATION THEORY. *Current Pos:* From asst prof to prof, 75-93, SOLOMON & SYLVIA CHANP PROF, MOORE SCH ELEC ENG, UNIV PA, 93-, CHMN DEPT ELEC ENG, 92- *Personal Data:* b Dar es Salaam, Tanzania, June 16, 49; US citizen; m 78; c 3. *Educ:* Swarthmore Col, BS, 72; Princeton Univ, MSE & MA, 74, PhD(elec eng), 75. *Hon Degrees:* MA, Univ Pa, 80. *Concurrent Pos:* Prin investr, Air Force Off Sci Res res grants, Univ Pa, 76-, NSF grant, 77-79, Naval Res Lab grants, 78-80 & Off Naval Res grant, 80-; consult, RCA, 80-81, Interspec, 82-88, Naval Air Dev Cen, 87- & Bio Rad Inc, 89-90; vis assoc prof, Univ BC, 83; vis scholar, Princeton Univ, 92. *Mem:* Fel Inst Elec & Electronics Engrs; Sigma Xi. *Res:* Signal processing and communication theory; nonparametric detection; quantization, robust signal processing; image processing; microwave and ultrasonic imaging; spectrum estimation; author of numerous technical papers and two books. *Mailing Add:* Moore Sch Elec Eng Univ Pa Philadelphia PA 19104. *E-Mail:* kassam@ee.upenn.edu

KASSANDER, ARNO RICHARD, JR, RESEARCH ADMINISTRATION. *Current Pos:* assoc dir, Inst Atmospheric Physics, 54-57, dir, 57-73, head dept atmospheric sci, 58-73, VPRES RES, UNIV ARIZ, 72-, PROF ATMOSPHERIC SCI, 76- *Personal Data:* b Carbondale, Pa, Sept 10, 20; m 43, Sara Nollen; c Helen (Ruskin). *Educ:* Amherst Col, BA, 41; Univ Okla, MS, 43; Iowa State Col, PhD(physics), 50. *Hon Degrees:* DSc, Amherst Col, 71, Univ Ariz, 86. *Prof Exp:* Asst geologist, Tex Co, 41; asst geophys, Magnolia Petrol Co, 43; asst prof physics, Iowa State Col, 50-54. *Concurrent Pos:* Dir, Water Resources Res Ctr, Univ Ariz, 64-72; mem panel environ, President's Sci Adv Comt; trustee, Ariz Sonora Desert Mus; chmn, Univ Corp Atmospheric Res, 58-68; dir, First Interstate Bank Ariz, 72-92; dir, Burr Brown Res Corp, 74-91. *Mem:* Fel AAAS; Am Phys Soc; fel Am Meteorol Soc. *Res:* General geophysical instrumentation; recording and automatic analysis of statistical data. *Mailing Add:* 3341 E Fourth St Tucson AZ 85716

KASSCHAU, MARGARET RAMSEY, COMPARATIVE PHYSIOLOGY, CELL PHYSIOLOGY. *Current Pos:* CHAIR, BIOL SCI DEPT & PROF BIOL, PHILADELPHIA COL PHARM & SCI, 96- *Personal Data:* b Cambridge, Mass, Sept 9, 42; div; c Kristin & Michael. *Educ:* Univ Rochester, AB, 64; Univ SC, MS, 70, PhD(biol), 73. *Prof Exp:* Res asst biol, Oak Ridge Nat Lab, 64-67; guest worker parasitol, NIH, 73-74; fel res physics, M D Anderson Hosp & Tumor Inst, 74-75; from asst prof to prof biol, Univ Houston, Clearlake City, 75-96. *Concurrent Pos:* Prin investr, Sea Grant Col Prog, 78-80; vis res assoc, Med Sch, Stanford Univ, 80-81; prin investr, NSF Grant, RUI Prog, 87-91; NSF vis prof women, Harvard Med Sch, 90-91. *Mem:* Am Soc Zoologists; Am Soc Parasitologists; AAAS; Soc Environ Toxicol & Chem; Biophys Soc; Soc Toxinology. *Res:* Hemolysis by schistosoma parasites; cell to cell adhesion; aquatic toxicology of marine animals; cellular toxicology. *Mailing Add:* Philadelphia Col Pharm & Sci 600 S 43rd St Philadelphia PA 19104-4495. *Fax:* 713-283-3707

KASSIRER, JEROME PAUL, NEPHROLOGY, INTERNAL MEDICINE. *Current Pos:* ED-IN-CHIEF, NEW ENG J MED, 91- *Personal Data:* b Buffalo, NY, Dec 19, 32; c Amy, Richard, Wendy, Elizabeth, Winston & Samuel. *Educ:* Univ Buffalo, BA, 53, MD, 57. *Hon Degrees:* Var from US & foreign univs. *Prof Exp:* Asst physician, New Eng Med Ctr Hosp, Tufts Univ, 62-65, instr med & nephrol, Sch Med, 62-65, from asst prof to assoc prof med, 65-74, physician, 69-74, assoc physician-in-chief & assoc chmn, 71-76, actg chmn, 74-75 & 76-77, prof med, 74-, actg physician-in-chief, 76-77, assoc chmn & assoc physician-in-chief, 77-91. *Concurrent Pos:* Mem, Med Sci Panel, Am Inst Biol Sci, 77-80; co-ed, Kidney Int, Nephrology Forum, 78-91, Clin Prob Solving Hosp Pract, 85-91; bd sci counr, Nat Libr Med, 86-89. *Mem:* Inst Med-Nat Acad Sci; Am Col Informatics. *Res:* Renal, electrolytes and acid-base physiology; clinical nephrology; decision analysis and clinical cognition. *Mailing Add:* New Eng J Med 10 Shattuck St Boston MA 02115. *Fax:* 617-734-4457

KASSIS, SHOUKI, CELL BIOLOGY, CHEMISTRY. *Current Pos:* SR INVESTR CHEM, SMITH-KLINE BEECHAM LABS, 88- *Personal Data:* b Haiva, Pakistan, Feb 8, 47. *Educ:* Bingoway Univ, BA, 69; Tel Aviv Univ, MS, 73, PhD(microbiol), 79. *Prof Exp:* Researcher chem, NIH, 81-88. *Mem:* AAAS; Am Soc Cell Biol; Am Soc Biochem & Molecular Biol. *Res:* Cell biology; chemistry. *Mailing Add:* Immunol Dept Smith-Kline Beecham Labs 709 Swedeland Rd MCL-101 King of Prussia PA 19406-2799

KASSNER, JAMES LYLE, JR, CLOUD PHYSICS, INDUSTRIAL & MANUFACTURING ENGINEERING. *Current Pos:* PRES, KASSNER WOODCRAFT, INC, 81-; FACIL MGR, NAT WOODWORKS, INC, 91- *Personal Data:* b Tuscaloosa, Ala, May 1, 31; m 56, Wanda J Hulsart; c James D (deceased), Linda J, Christine C, Peter C & Kevin C. *Educ:* Univ Ala, BS, 52, MS, 53, PhD(physics), 57. *Prof Exp:* Asst physics, Univ Ala, 53-54, res assoc, 54-56; asst prof, Mo Sch Mines, 56-59; assoc prof, Univ Mo, Rolla, 59-66, dir, Grad Ctr Cloud Physics Res, 68-84, prof physics, 66-84; chief exec officer, Dexter D Hulsart, Inc, 84-89; mfg mgt, Fibreform Containers, 90-91. *Concurrent Pos:* Mem subcomt nucleation, Int Asn Meteorol & Atmospheric Physics; mem subcomn IV, Ions, Aerosols & Radioactivity, Int Comn Atmospheric Elec. *Mem:* Fel Am Phys Soc; Am Meteorol Soc; Am Geophys Union; Sigma Xi. *Res:* Atmospheric condensation; homogeneous and heterogeneous nucleation from the vapor; mobility of cluster ions; laboratory simulation of cloud formation; measurements on atmospheric particulates; nucleation of ice. *Mailing Add:* 11947 Graceland Acres Northport AL 35476

KASSNER, RICHARD J, BIOCHEMISTRY. *Current Pos:* asst prof, 69-74, ASSOC PROF CHEM, UNIV ILL, CHICAGO CIRCLE, 74- *Personal Data:* b Chicago, Ill, July 1, 39; m 62; c 3. *Educ:* Purdue Univ, BS, 61; Yale Univ, MS, 63, PhD(biophys chem), 66. *Prof Exp:* NIH fel chem, Univ Calif, San Diego, 66-68, instr, 68-69. *Res:* Structural basis for the properties of heme and iron-sulfur proteins; model systems for the active sites of hemeproteins; heme and chlorophyll biosynthesis. *Mailing Add:* Dept Chem Univ M/C Ill Univ Il 845 W Taylor Rm 4500 Chicago IL 60607-7061

KASSOY, DAVID R, FLUID MECHANICS, COMBUSTION. *Current Pos:* from asst prof to assoc prof, 69-78, asst vchancellor res, 88-92, PROF MECH ENG, UNIV COLO, BOULDER, 78-, ASSOC VCHANCELLOR ACAD AFFAIRS, 92- *Personal Data:* b Brooklyn, NY, Jan 29, 38; m 64, Carol Fuchs; c Andrew R & Erin A. *Educ:* Polytech Inst Brooklyn, BAE, 59; Univ Mich, MSAE, 61, PhD(aerospace eng), 65. *Prof Exp:* Asst res engr, Univ Calif, San Diego, 65-67, asst prof aerospace & mech eng sci, 68-69. *Concurrent Pos:* Guggenheim fel, 73, Fulbright Res fel, Tech Univ Delft, 83; vis fel, Sci & Eng Res Coun, Univ EAnglia, Eng, 82-83 & Japan Soc Prom Sci, Nagoya Univ, Japan, 85; vchmn exec comn, Div Fluid Dynamics, Am Phys Soc, 89-90, mem exec comn, 89-, chmn exec comt, 92-93. *Mem:* Fel Am Phys Soc; Soc Indust & Appl Math; Combustion Inst; Am Inst Aeronaut & Astronaut; Nat Asn State Univ & Land Grant Col. *Res:* Combustion theory; ignition and explosion; perturbation methods; theoretical fluid mechanics; solid rocket motor fluid dynamics; solidification of materials. *Mailing Add:* Acad Affairs B-40 Univ Colo Boulder CO 80309. *Fax:* 303-492-8861; *E-Mail:* kassoy@spot.colorado.edu

KASTELLA, KENNETH GEORGE, PHYSIOLOGY. *Current Pos:* RETIRED. *Personal Data:* b Kalispell, Mont, May 27, 33; div; c 1. *Educ:* Univ Wash, BS, 59, MS, 65, PhD(physiol), 69. *Prof Exp:* NIH training grant neurophysiol, Univ Wash, 69-70, res assoc, 70; asst prof physiol, Univ NMex, 70-76; assoc prof, Univ Alaska, 76-87; teaching assoc, Dept Biol Struct, Sch Med, Univ Wash, 87- *Mem:* AAAS; Inst Elec & Electronics Engrs; Biophys Soc. *Res:* Neurophysiology, especially central control of blood pressure; temperature regulation. *Mailing Add:* 643 1/2 Meadowood Ct Grand Junction CO 81504

KASTEN, FREDERICK H, CYTOLOGY. *Current Pos:* RETIRED. *Personal Data:* b New York, NY, Mar 7, 27; m 49; c 4. *Educ:* Univ Houston, BA, 50; Univ Tex, MS, 51, PhD(zool), 54. *Prof Exp:* Scientist cancer res, Roswell Park Mem Inst, NY, 54-56; asst prof zool, Agr & Mech Col, Tex, 56-61; res coordr & dir, Ultrastruct Cytochem Dept, Pasadena Found Med Res, 63-70; prof anat, Med Ctr, La State Univ, 70-94. *Concurrent Pos:* NSF sr fel, Giessen, Ger, 61-62; NSF sr fel, Inst Cancer Res, Villejuif, France, 62-63, NIH spec res fel, 62-63; from adj asst prof to adj assoc prof, Univ Southern Calif, 63-70; from asst clin prof to assoc clin prof, Loma Linda Univ, 65-70; partic, W Alton Jones Cell Sci Ctr, 71; consult, Nat Heart & Lung Inst, 71- & Nat Cancer Inst, 73-; assoc coordr, La Cancer Ctr, 73-78; rev ed, In Vitro, 75-78; vis prof anat, ETenn State Univ Med Sch, 79-80, Ain-Shams Univ Fac Med, Cairo Egypt, 87 & 90; pres, Biol Stain Comn, 86-, trustee, 73-; vis prof histol, Alex Univ Med Sch, Alexandria, Egypt, 86 & 87; adv bd, TCA Tech Manual, 74-80; res grants comt, Cancer Asn GNO, 75-; pres, Am Asn Dent Res, NO Sect, 83-84; vis prof zool, Jagiellonian Univ, Krakow, Poland, 89. *Mem:* Biol Stain Comn; Am Soc Cell Biol; AAAS; Ger Histochem Soc; Tissue Cult Asn; Sigma Xi. *Res:* Quantitative cytochemistry of nucleic acids; absorption curve analyses of stained cells; development of new staining techniques; electron microscopy; cytochemistry of viral infections; dye impurities; fluorescence microscopy; cancer; tissue culture; history of medicine. *Mailing Add:* 109 E Maple St PO Box 1157 Johnson City TN 37605-1157

KASTEN, PAUL R(UDOLPH), REACTOR EVALUATION, REACTOR TECHNOLOGY. *Current Pos:* RETIRED. *Personal Data:* b Jackson, Mo, Dec 10, 23; m 47, Eileen A Kiehne; c Susan E (Goebbert), Kim P & Jennifer L. *Educ:* Univ Mo Sch Mines, BS, 44, MS, 47; Univ Minn, PhD(chem eng), 50. *Honors & Awards:* Outstanding Serv Award, Oak Ridge Chap, Tenn Soc Prof Engrs, 88. *Prof Exp:* Staff mem, Oak Ridge Nat Lab, 50-55, sect chief, 55-61, assoc dept head, 61-63, assoc dir molten salt reactor prog, 65-70, dir, gas cooled reactor & thorium utilization progs & mgr, Alternate Fuel Cycle Eval, 77-79, dir gas cooled reactor progs, 79-85, tech dir, 85-88; guest dir, Inst Reactor Develop, Julich Res Ctr, WGer, 63-65; prof, Col Eng, Univ Tenn, Knoxville, 88-; consult, Oak Ridge Nat Lab, 88. *Concurrent Pos:* Lectr, Univ Tenn, Knoxville, 53-60, prof, 65- *Mem:* Fel Am Nuclear Soc; fel AAAS; Sigma Xi. *Res:* Nuclear engineering; very high temperature reactors; development of high temperature reactor models of fuel performance under normal and accident conditions. *Mailing Add:* 341 Louisiana Ave Oak Ridge TN 37830

KASTENBAUM, MARVIN AARON, BIOMETRICS, BIOSTATISTICS. *Current Pos:* CONSULT, 87- *Personal Data:* b New York, NY, Jan 16, 26; m 55, Helen Ganz; c Joan K (Jackson) & Robert H. *Educ:* City Col New York, BS, 48; NC State Col, MS, 50, PhD(statist), 56. *Prof Exp:* Asst statistician, US Bur Census, 48 & 50; chief statistician mkt res, Dun & Bradstreet, Inc, 52; biostatistician, Atomic Bomb Casualty Comm, 53-54; sr res statistician, Oak Ridge Nat Lab, Tenn, 56-70; dir statist, Tobacco Inst, 70-87. *Concurrent Pos:* Mem math res ctr, Univ Wis, 65-66; NSF vis lectr, 66-71; mem statist dept, Stanford Univ, 69; med statist, biomet & epidemiol consult. *Mem:* Fel AAAS; Biomet Soc (secy-treas, Eastern NAm region, 59-60, gen treas, 60-63); fel Am Statist Asn; Inst Math Statist; fel Royal Statist Soc; fel NY Acad Sci. *Res:* Medical statistics; biometry; epidemiology. *Mailing Add:* 16933 Timberlakes Dr SW Ft Myers FL 33908-4339

KASTENBERG, WILLIAM EDWARD, NUCLEAR ENGINEERING. *Current Pos:* PROF, NUCLEAR ENG DEPT, UNIV CALIF, BERKELY, 95-, DEPT CHMN, 95- *Personal Data:* b New York, NY, June 25, 39; m 92, Gloria Hauser; c Andrew, Joshua & Lillian. *Educ:* Univ Calif, Los Angeles, BS, 62, MS, 63; Univ Calif, Berkeley, PhD(eng), 66. *Prof Exp:* From asst prof eng to assoc prof eng & appl sci, Univ Calif, Los Angeles, 66-75, prof mech, aerospace & nuclear eng, 75-94, vchmn, Dept Chem, Nuclear & Thermal Eng, 77-78, asst dean grad studies, 81-85, chmn, 85-88. *Concurrent Pos:* Guest scientist, Karlsruhe Nuclear Res, Fed Repub Ger, 72-73; sr fel, Nat Res Coun, Washington, DC, 79-80; chmn nuclear reactor safety, Am Nuclear Soc, 84-85; mem, Nat Res Comn Reactor Safety, 85-86; dir, Risk & Syst Anal Control Toxics Prog, Univ Calif, Los Angeles, 89-95, chmn, Ctr Clean Technol, 92-94. *Mem:* Nat Acad Eng; fel AAAS; fel Am Nuclear Soc. *Res:* Nuclear reactor safety; fusion technology; risk assessment; toxic waste control; environmental risk assessment. *Mailing Add:* Nuclear Eng Dept Univ Calif 4155 Etcheverry Hall Berkeley CA 94720-1730

KASTENHOLZ, CLAUDE E(DWARD), ELECTRICAL ENGINEERING. *Current Pos:* RETIRED. *Personal Data:* b Milwaukee, Wis, Nov 27, 36; m 59; c 5. *Educ:* Marquette Univ, BEE, 58; Univ Southern Calif, MS, 60; Univ Wis, PhD(elec eng), 63; Pepperdine Univ, MBA, 70. *Prof Exp:* Mem tech staff, Hughes Aircraft Co, Calif, 58-60, sr staff engr, 67-75, sr scientist, 75-81, proj mgr, 82-96; res engr, Autonetics Div, NAm Aviation, Inc, 60-61; res asst circuit design, Univ Wis, 61-62; res specialist, Autonetics Div, NAm Rockwell Corp, 63-67. *Mem:* Inst Elec & Electronics Engrs. *Res:* Sonar systems engineering; fire control system design; system testing. *Mailing Add:* 16932 Nightingale Lane Yorba Linda CA 92886

KASTENS, KIM ANNE, MARINE GEOLOGY, MARINE GEOPHYSICS. *Current Pos:* RES ASSOC, LAMONT-DOHERTY EARTH OBSERV, COLUMBIA UNIV, 81-, SR RES SCIENTIST. *Personal Data:* b Menlo Park, Calif, May 19, 54. *Educ:* Yale Univ, BS, 75; Scripps Inst Oceanog, PhD(oceanog), 81. *Mem:* Am Geophys Union; Geol Soc Am; Sigma Xi. *Res:* Tectonic and sedimentological processes in the deep sea. *Mailing Add:* Lamont-Doherty Geol Observ Rt 9W 116 Oceonography Palisades NY 10964

KASTIN, ABBA J, ENDOCRINOLOGY, NEUROSCIENCES. *Current Pos:* assoc prof, 71-74, PROF MED, SCH MED, TULANE UNIV, 74-; CHIEF ENDOCRINOL, VET ADMIN HOSP, NEW ORLEANS, 68- *Personal Data:* b Cleveland, Ohio, Dec 24, 34. *Educ:* Harvard Col, AB, 56; Harvard Med Sch, MD, 60. *Hon Degrees:* Dr, Univ Nat Federico Villarreal, Lima, Peru, 84; DSc, Univ New Orleans, 84. *Honors & Awards:* Edward T Tyler Fertil Award, Int Fertil Soc, 75; Copernicus Medal, Poland, 79; William S Middleton Award, Vet Admin, 82; Talmage Lectr, Aspen Allergy Conf, 86. *Prof Exp:* Clin assoc endocrinol, NIH, 62-64; NIH spec fel, Sch Med, Tulane Univ, 64-65; clin investr med, Vet Admin Hosp, New Orleans, 65-68. *Concurrent Pos:* Mem med adv bd, Nat Pituitary Agency, 74-77; assoc mem grad fac, Univ New Orleans, 76-, consult prof, Dept Psychol, 86-; mem res adv comt, Nat Asn Retarded Citizens, 78-79; consult, Food & Drug Admin, 79-80; ed-in-chief, Peptides, 80-; Wellcome vis prof, Fedn Am Soc Exp Biol, ET State Univ, 89-90. *Mem:* Endocrine Soc; Am Physiol Soc; Soc Exp Biol & Med; Soc Neurosci; Int Soc Psychoneuroendocrinol; hon mem Endocrine Socs of Chile, Philippines, Peru, Poland & Hungary; Int Soc Neuroendocrinol; fel Int Behav Neurosci Soc; fel Am Col Endocrinol; Int Neuropeptide Soc (pres, 93-). *Res:* Blood-brain barrier; brain peptides; neuroendocrinology; hypothalamic hormones; author of more thatn 650 papers. *Mailing Add:* Vet Affairs Med Ctr 1601 Perdido St New Orleans LA 70146. *Fax:* 504-522-8559

KASTING, JAMES FRASER, ATMOSPHERIC EVOLUTION, RADIATIVE TRANSFER. *Current Pos:* PROF GEOSCI, PA STATE UNIV. *Personal Data:* b Schenectady, NY, Jan 2, 53; m 80; c 2. *Educ:* Harvard Univ, AB, 75; Univ Mich, MS(phys) & MS(atmospheric sci), 78, PhD(atmospheric sci), 79. *Prof Exp:* Res fel, Nat Ctr Atmospheric Res, 79-81; res fel, Ames Res Ctr, NASA, 81-83, res scientist, 83- *Mem:* Am Geophys Union; Int Soc Study Origin Life; fel AAAS. *Res:* Evolution of planetary atmospheres; history of the earth and why it is different from that of Mars and Venus. *Mailing Add:* Dept Geol Pa State Univ 403 Deike Bldg State College PA 16802-2713. *Fax:* 814-865-3191; *E-Mail:* kasting@essc.psh.edu

KASTL, PETER ROBERT, OPHTHALMOLOGY, BIOCHEMISTRY. *Current Pos:* Instr biochem, Tulane Univ, 75-81, instr ophthal, 77-81, asst prof, 81-85, assoc prof biochem & ophthal, 85-88, PROF BIOCHEM & OPHTHAL, TULANE UNIV, 89- *Personal Data:* b Alexandria, La, July 25, 49; m 74; c 2. *Educ:* Centenary Col La, BS, 71; Tulane Univ, MD, 74, PhD(biochem), 78. *Concurrent Pos:* Fel, Nat Inst Gen Med Sci, 75-76; NIH res grant, 81-83. *Mem:* Sigma Xi; AMA; Southern Med Asn; Am Acad Ophthal. *Res:* Microsomal treatment of ingested toxins; pharmacologic prevention of cataracts; design of new types of ophthalmologic prosthetic devices; tear analysis; contact lenses. *Mailing Add:* Dept Ophthal Tulane Med Ctr New Orleans LA 70112. *Fax:* 504-584-2684; *E-Mail:* pkastl@mailhost.tcs.tulane.edu

KASTNER, CURTIS LYNN, MEAT SCIENCE, MUSCLE BIOLOGY. *Current Pos:* PROF & RES COORDR, ANIMAL & FOOD SCI, KANS STATE UNIV, 75- *Personal Data:* b Altus, Okla, Sept 21, 44; m 66, Rebecca Diltz; c Jason & Justin. *Educ:* Okla State Univ, BS, 67, MS, 69, PhD(food sci), 72. *Honors & Awards:* US Key Res Scientist, AAAS, 84; Teacher Fel Award, Nat Asn Cols Teachers & Agr, 85; Signal Serv Award, Am Meat Sci Asn, 96. *Prof Exp:* Asst prof food sci, Wash State Univ, 72-75. *Concurrent Pos:* Sect chmn, Inst Food Technologists, 82, mem exec bd, Muscle & Food Div, 91; chmn, Am Meat Sci Asn Ann Conf, 88, chair, 89, exec bd, 88-89, pres, 93-94. *Mem:* Am Meat Sci Asn; Am Soc Animal Sci; Inst Food Technologists. *Res:* Technology, development, processing and preservation of meat and meat products, including hot processing, tenderization, microbial sampling, shelf life extension, packaging sanitation, microbiology, chemical residues, meat safety and low fat technology. *Mailing Add:* Dept Animal Sci & Indust Kans State Univ Weber Hall Manhattan KS 66506-0201. *Fax:* 785-532-7059

KASTNER, MARC AARON, SEMICONDUCTORS, HIGH-TEMPERATURE SUPERCONDUCTIVITY. *Current Pos:* from asst prof to prof, 73-89, DONNER PROF PHYSICS, MASS INST TECHNOL, 89- *Personal Data:* b Toronto, Ont, Nov 20, 45; m 67; c 2. *Educ:* Univ Chicago, BS, 67, MS, 69 & PhD(physics), 73. *Honors & Awards:* David Adler Lectr Award, Am Phys Soc, 95. *Prof Exp:* Res fel, Div Eng & Appl Physics, Harvard Univ, 72-73. *Concurrent Pos:* Head div atomic, condensed matter & plasma physics, Dept Physics, Mass Inst Technol, 83-87; counr, Am Phys Soc, 90-94; assoc dir, Consortium Superconducting Electronics 89-92; dir, Ctr Mat Sci & Eng, 93- *Mem:* Fel Am Phys Soc; AAAS. *Res:* Electronic and optical studies of amorphous semiconductors led to the Valence Alteration Model; measurements of conductivity of nanometer-size semiconductor devices; magnetic optical and transport studies of high-temperature superconductors. *Mailing Add:* Mass Inst Technol Rm 13-2142 Cambridge MA 02139

KASTNER, MIRIAM, GEOLOGY, OCEANOGRAPHY. *Current Pos:* from asst prof to assoc prof, 72-82, PROF GEOL, SCRIPPS INST OCEANOG, 82-, CHMN, GEOL RES DIV, 89- *Personal Data:* b Bratislava, Czech; US citizen; m, Bentor T. *Educ:* Hebrew Univ Jerusalem, Israel, BSc & MSc, 64; Harvard Univ, PhD(geol), 70. *Hon Degrees:* Dr, Univ Paris XI, 84. *Honors & Awards:* Newcomb Cleveland Prize, AAAS. *Prof Exp:* Fel geol, Harvard Univ, 70-71, Univ Chicago, 71-72. *Concurrent Pos:* Assoc ed, J Sedimentary Petrol, 80-88 & Appl Geochem, 86-89; distinguished lectr, Am Asn Petrol Geologists, 83 & 84; planning comt mem, Ocean Drilling Proj, 84-90; vis prof, Hebrew Univ, Jerusalem, Israel, 86; mem, NSF Adv Comt, Earth Sci, 86-88, steering comt, 2nd Conf Sci Ocean Drilling, 86-87; mem-at-large, Sect Geol & Geog, AAAS, 87-91; chmn, Gordon Res Conf Chem Oceanog, 89; counr, Geochem Soc, 90-93 & 93-94. *Mem:* Fel AAAS; Geochem Soc; fel Am Geophys Union; Int Asn Geochem & Cosmochem; Sigma Xi; Int Asn Sedimentologists. *Res:* Origin, mineralogy and geochemistry of silicates phosphates and carbonates in marine and non-marine environments; stable isotopes for diagenesis; processes that cause metal enrichment in oceanic sediments; surface chemistry in diagenesis; hydrothermal deposits in the submarine environment; the role of fluids in convergent plate margins; chemical paleoceanography. *Mailing Add:* Geol Res Div 0212 Scripps Inst Oceanog La Jolla CA 92093-0212. *Fax:* 619-534-0784; *E-Mail:* mkastner@ucsd.edu

KASTNER, SIDNEY OSCAR, PHYSICS. *Current Pos:* CONSULT SCIENTIST, 82- *Personal Data:* b Winnipeg, Man, Apr 20, 26; m 51; c 3. *Educ:* McGill Univ, BSc, 50; Syracuse Univ, MS, 55, PhD(physics), 60. *Prof Exp:* Jr res officer, Nat Res Coun Can, 50-52; physicist, Gen Elec Res Lab, 55-57; physicist, Goddard Space Flight Ctr, NASA, 59-82. *Mem:* AAAS; Am Phys Soc; NY Acad Sci; AAAS. *Res:* Atomic physics and spectroscopy; solar physics and astrophysics; theoretical calculations and applications of atomics physics to observe visible, ultraviolet and infrared spectra of astronomical sources; primarily fluorescent spectra of nebulae, cataclysmic, variables, symbiotic stars and novae. *Mailing Add:* 1-A Ridge Rd Greenbelt MD 20770

KASUBA, ROMUALDAS, MECHANICAL ENGINEERING, APPLIED MECHANICS. *Current Pos:* DEAN, COL ENG & ENG TECHNOL, NORTHERN ILL UNIV, 86- *Personal Data:* b Kaunas, Lithuania, Mar 23, 31; US citizen; m 61, Elena N Mekys; c Vida R & Dalia R (Metzger). *Educ:* Univ Ill, Urbana, BS, 54, MS, 57, PhD(mech eng), 62. *Prof Exp:* Res asst dynamics, Mech Eng Dept, Univ Ill, Urbana, 58-62; head, Stress & Dynamics Group Power Systs Div, TRW Inc, Ohio, 62-68; from assoc prof to prof mech eng, Cleveland State Univ, 68-86, chairperson, Dept Mech Eng, 78-85, dir, Eng Doctorate Prog, 85-86. *Concurrent Pos:* Corp consult, Warner & Swasey Corp, 69-76; lectr, US, Can & Venezuela; consult, Indust Fasteners Inst, 70-75 & Am Nat Stand Inst, 71-74; invited distinguished vis researcher, Tokyo Inst Technol, 94. *Mem:* Fel Am Soc Mech Engrs; Am Soc Eng Educ; Nat Soc Prof Engrs; Mfg Asn Am Gear; Sigma Xi. *Res:* Vibration and noise studies in industrial machines; dynamic loads in geared systems; development of optimum threaded fastener system; dynamic simulation of geared systems; dynamic simulation of machine tool structures and drives; application of finite element techniques; optimum fastener system; digital simulation of real rotating gear systems. *Mailing Add:* Col Eng & Eng Technol Northern Ill Univ Eng Bldg 321 De Kalb IL 60115. *Fax:* 815-753-1310; *E-Mail:* kasuba@ceet.niu.edu

KASUBE, HERBERT EMIL, MATHEMATICS EDUCATION. *Current Pos:* ASSOC PROF MATH, BRADLEY UNIV, PEORIA, ILL, 78- *Personal Data:* b Chicago, Ill, Mar 23, 49; m 71, DorAnn Stegeman; c Emilie D. *Educ:* MacMurray Col, BA, 71; Univ Ill, MA, 73; Univ Mont, PhD(math), 79. *Prof Exp:* Teaching asst math, Univ Ill, 71-75 & Univ Mont, 75-78. *Mem:* Sigma Xi; Math Asn Am; Am Math Soc; Nat Coun Teachers Math. *Res:* Discrete mathematics; number theory; college mathematics education. *Mailing Add:* Dept Math Bradley Univ 1501 W Bradley Ave Peoria IL 61625-0001. *E-Mail:* hkasube@bucc1.bradley.edu

KASUPSKI, GEORGE JOSEPH, diagnostic virology, molecular virology, for more information see previous edition

KASVINSKY, PETER JOHN, ENZYME REGULATION, CALCIUM CONTROL. *Current Pos:* asst prof, 79-82, dir res develop, 86-88, ASSOC PROF BIOCHEM, MARSHALL UNIV 82-, DIR RES DEVELOP & GRAD STUDIES, SCH MED, 88- *Personal Data:* b Bridgeport, Conn, Dec 7, 42; m 74; c 2. *Educ:* Bucknell Univ, BSc, 64; Univ Vt, PhD(biochem), 70. *Prof Exp:* Biochemist, US Army Aeromed Res Lab, 69-72; instr biochem, Sch Med, Wayne State Univ, 72-74; sr res assoc biochem, Univ Alta, 74-79, instr, Dept Biochem, 77-79. *Concurrent Pos:* Radiol control officer, US Army Aeromed Res Lab, 70-72; adj asst prof, 80-82, adj assoc prof biomed sci, WVa Univ, 82-; prin investr, NIH grants, 81. *Mem:* Am Chem Soc; AAAS; Can Biochem Soc; Am Soc Biol Chemists; Sigma Xi; Nat Coun Univ Res Admin. *Res:* Enzymology of covalent modification of proteins, enzyme regulation, structure function and allosteric control, especially as applied to the regulation of enzymes of glycogen metabolism. *Mailing Add:* Dept Sch Grad Studies Youngstown State Univ 410 Wick Ave Youngstown OH 44555-3091

KASZNIAK, ALFRED WAYNE, NEUROSCIENCE. *Current Pos:* from asst prof to assoc prof, Dept Psychiat, 79-82, assoc prof, Dept Psychol & Psychiat, 82-87, PROF, DEPTS PSYCHOL, NEUROL & PSYCHIAT, UNIV ARIZ COL MED, 87- *Personal Data:* b Chicago, Ill, June 2, 49; m 73, Mary E Beaurain; c Jesse & Elizabeth. *Educ:* Univ Ill, BS, 70, MA, 73, PhD, 76. *Prof Exp:* Instr, Dept Psychol, Rush Med Col, Chicago, 74-76, asst prof, Dept Psychol, 76-79; staff psychologist, Presby-St Lukes Hosp, 76-79, Univ Hosp, Tucson, 79- *Concurrent Pos:* Grantee, Nat Inst Aging, 78-83 & 89-94; trustee, Southern Ariz Chap, Nat Multiple Sclerosis Soc, 80-82; mem med adv bd, Fan Kane Fund for Brain-injured Children, Tucson, 80-82; dir & coordr, Clin Neuropsychol Prog; res fel, Gerontol Soc, 80; mem med & sci adv bd, Nat Alzheimers Dis & Related Disorders Asn, 81-84; mem, Human Develop & Aging Study Sect, Div Res Grants, NIH, 81-86; grantee, Nat Inst Ment Health, 84-94; mem, Vet Admin Geriat & Geront Adv Comt, 86-89; grantee, Robert Wood Johnson Found, 86-89; Ariz Gov Adv Comt on Alzheimers Dis, 88-92; chmn, Comn on Geront, Univ Ariz, 90-93, actg head, Dept Psychol, 92-93; mem bd gov, Int Neuropsychol Soc, 94. *Res:* Author of 3 books and various articles. *Mailing Add:* Dept Psychol Univ Ariz Tucson AZ 85721

KATARIA, YASH P, PULMONARY DISEASES, INTERNAL MEDICINE. *Current Pos:* assoc prof, 78-82, PROF INTERNAL MED, ECAROLINA UNIV SCH MED, 82-, VCHMN DEPT MED, 87- *Personal Data:* b 1936. *Educ:* Glancy Med Col, India, MD, 59; Liverpool Sch Med, Eng, DTM & H, 63; Welsh Nat Sch Med, Univ Wales, DTCD, 65; FRCP, 79. *Prof Exp:* Registr, Welsh Nat Sch Med, 67-69; assoc med, Chicago Med Sch, 70-71; from instr to asst prof med & pulmonary dis, Col Med, Ohio State Univ, 72-78. *Concurrent Pos:* Actg chmn dept med, E Carolina Univ Sch Med, 86-87, sect head pulmonary div, 78-; med dir, Spec Servs & Respiratory Ther, 88- *Mem:* Fel Am Col Chest Physicians; Am Lung Asn; NY Acad Sci; Am Fedn Clin Res; AMA; Sigma Xi. *Res:* Clinical and immunologic aspects of sarcoidosis exploring its pathogenesis and etiology; immunologic work involves studies of peripheral blood and bronchoalveolar lavage (BAL), T and B-cell quantitation; examination of sarcoidal granuloma for its cellular components and production of lymphokines, etc; production of Kreim antigen from auto logous BAL cells. *Mailing Add:* Dept Med Pulmonary Dis ECarolina Univ Sch Med Greenville NC 27858-4354

KATAYAMA, DANIEL HIDEO, MOLECULAR SPECTROSCOPY. *Current Pos:* PHYSICIST, AIR FORCE GEOPHYS LAB, 71- *Personal Data:* b Honolulu, Hawaii, Sept 26, 39; m 63. *Educ:* Univ Hawaii, BS, 62, MS, 64; Tufts Univ, PhD(physics), 70. *Prof Exp:* Physicist aeronomy, Air Force Cambridge Res Lab, 63-66; physicist solid state physics, Gillette Co, 70-71. *Concurrent Pos:* Vis scientist, Bell Lab, Murray Hill, NJ, 78-79 & Mass Inst Tech, Cambridge, 80-82. *Mem:* AAAS; Am Phys Soc; Optical Soc Am. *Res:* Laser induced fluorescence of molecules and ions; absorption-photoionization cross sections and spectroscopy of atmospheric gases in vacuum ultraviolet; phonon scattering in solids; elastic constants of materials. *Mailing Add:* 2 Fox-Run Rd Bedford MA 01730-1404

KATCHEN, BERNARD, BIOCHEMISTRY. *Current Pos:* RETIRED. *Personal Data:* b New York, NY, May 20, 28; m 51; c 2. *Educ:* City Col New York BS, 49; Ohio State Univ, MSc, 51; NY Univ, PhD(biochem), 56. *Prof Exp:* Chemist, Clairol Inc, 54-56; sr chemist, Nat Cash Register, 56-61; prin scientist, Schering Corp, 62-91. *Mem:* AAAS; Am Chem Soc; NY Acad Sci. *Res:* Pharmacokinetics; drug metabolism; biopharmaceutics. *Mailing Add:* 1271 Sand Castle Rd Sanibel FL 33957-3616

KATCHER, DAVID ABRAHAM, WRITING & EDITING. *Current Pos:* CONSULT, 80- *Personal Data:* b New York, NY, Apr 28, 15; m 47, 84, Gladys Uhl; c Philip R & Katherine L (Kravik). *Educ:* Univ Wis, BA, 36. *Prof Exp:* Tech ed, Naval Ord Lab, 41-43; founding ed, Physics Today, Am Inst Physics, 47-51; assoc ed, Opers Res Off, 51-56; assoc ed, Jour Opers Res Soc Am, 52; ed, Weapons Systs Eval Group, Inst Defense Anal, 56-60, exec secy, Jason Div, 60-66; mem sr staff, Opers Res Sect, Arthur D Little, Inc, Mass, 66-72; sr staff mem, Secretariat of Nat Adv Comt Oceans & Atmospheres, Nat Oceanic & Atmospheric Admin, 72-76; sr policy analyst, Off Sci & Technol Policy, Exec Off of the Pres, 76-77; spec asst to undersecy state for security assistance, Sci & Technol, Dept State, 77-80. *Mem:* AAAS. *Mailing Add:* 5608 Warwick Pl Chevy Chase MD 20815. *Fax:* 301-654-6946

KATCHMAN, ARTHUR, ORGANIC CHEMISTRY. *Current Pos:* RETIRED. *Personal Data:* b New York, NY, Oct 4, 24; m 60, Evelyn R Silver; c Ross N & Scott J. *Educ:* NY Univ, BA, 49; Polytech Inst Brooklyn, PhD(chem), 56. *Prof Exp:* Asst instr biochem, NY Med Col, 49-50, instr, 50-52, assoc, 52-54; res chemist, Hooker Chem Co, 55-56; res assoc, Polytech Inst Brooklyn, 57-58; res assoc, Gen Elec Res Lab, Gen Elec Co, 59-62, mgr mat physics & chem, Capacitor Dept, 63-66, mgr polymer chem, Chem Develop Oper, 66-68, mgr advan res, Plastics Dept, 68-70, mgr prod develop, Plastics Dept, 70-75, mgr chem develop, 76-79, mgr opers control & planning, 80-81, mgr, Div Qual Assurance, 81-84, mgr, Anal Chem, 84-86, mgr, Mat & Automation Develop, 87-90. *Concurrent Pos:* Hooker fel, 57-58. *Mem:* Am Chem Soc; Sigma Xi. *Res:* Mechanism and kinetics of polymerization; polymer structure and properties; stereospecific polymerization. *Mailing Add:* 6904 Country Lakes Circle Sarasota FL 34243-3803

KATCOFF, SEYMOUR, NUCLEAR CHEMISTRY, SCIENCE EDUCATION. *Current Pos:* SR CHEMIST, BROOKHAVEN NAT LAB, 48- *Personal Data:* b Chicago, Ill, Aug 19, 18; m 51, Edith Laporte; c Don & Joel. *Educ:* Univ Chicago, BS, 40, PhD(phys chem), 44. *Prof Exp:* Assoc chemist, Metall Lab, Univ Chicago, 43-45; staff mem, Los Alamos Sci Lab, 45-48. *Concurrent Pos:* Fel, Weizmann Inst Sci, 58-59 & Guggenheim fel, 67-68; vis scientist, City Col NY, 84-85. *Mem:* Am Chem Soc; Am Phys Soc; Sigma Xi. *Res:* High-energy nuclear reactions; nuclear track detectors; cross section measurements; neutron-rich isotope studies; nuclear spectroscopy; heavy ion reactions. *Mailing Add:* Brookhaven Nat Lab Upton NY 11973

KATEKARU, JAMES, ANALYTICAL CHEMISTRY, NUCLEAR CHEMISTRY. *Current Pos:* from asst prof to assoc prof, 69-80, PROF CHEM, CALIF POLYTECH STATE UNIV, 80- *Personal Data:* b Kauai, Hawaii, June 10, 35; m 64; c 2. *Educ:* Univ Ore, BS, 56; Univ Ariz, MS, 61; Univ Cincinnati, PhD(chem), 65. *Prof Exp:* Anal chemist, Food & Drug Admin, 62-63; res chemist, Rocketdyne Div, NAm Rockwell, 65-66; index ed, Chem Abstr Serv, 66-67; res mgr, Naval Radiol Defense Lab, 67-69. *Concurrent Pos:* Res consult, Trapelo West Div, Lab Electronics, 70-71. *Mem:* Am Chem Soc; Am Inst Physics. *Res:* Solvent extraction; polarography; rocket exhaust product analysis; catalysis of non-hypergollic propellant combinations; nuclear fallout phenomenology; detection and diagnosis of nuclear weapons. *Mailing Add:* 5 Chorro St #B San Luis Obispo CA 93405-1776

KATEN, PAUL C, MICROMETEOROLOGY, AIR POLLUTION. *Current Pos:* CONSULT, 85- *Personal Data:* b Lawrence, Mass, Feb 7, 43; m 68. *Educ:* Lowell Technol Inst, BS, 64; Trinity Col, MS, 68; Colo State Univ, PhD(atmospheric sci), 77. *Prof Exp:* Test engr, Pratt & Whitney Aircraft, 64-69; res assoc, Dept Atmospheric Sci, Ore State Univ, 77-84; exp scientist, Div Environ Mech, Commonwealth Sci & Indust Res Orgn, Canberra, Australia, 84-85. *Mem:* Am Meteorol Soc; Am Geophys Union; Air Pollution Control Asn. *Res:* Instrumentation development with recent applications to the dry-deposition of gases and particles; micrometeorology; turbulence; indoor air pollution; industrial hygiene; wind power resource assessment. *Mailing Add:* 12142 Caddy Row San Diego CA 92128-3268

KATER, STANLEY B, NEUROSCIENCES. *Current Pos:* PROF NEUROBIOL & ANAT, SCH MED, UNIV UTAH, 95- *Personal Data:* b Cleveland, Ohio, June 12, 43; div; c 1. *Educ:* Case Western Reserve Univ, BA, 65; Univ Va, PhD(biol), 68. *Prof Exp:* NIH fel biol, Univ Ore, 68-69; from asst prof to prof zool, Univ Iowa, 79-90; prof anat & neurobiol, Colo State Univ, 90-95. *Concurrent Pos:* Javits neurosci investr award, NIH sponsored res; Alexander Von Humboldt res scientist award. *Mem:* AAAS; Soc Neurosci. *Res:* Developmental neurobiology; control of neuronal growth cores. *Mailing Add:* Univ Utah Sch Med 50 N Medical Dr Rm 527 Wintrobe Bldg Salt Lake City UT 84132. *E-Mail:* sbkator@med.utah.edu

KATES, JOSEF, SCIENCE POLICY, SYSTEMS SCIENCE. *Current Pos:* PRES, JOSEF KATES ASSOCS, INC, 74-; BD DIR & DIR STRATEGY, IRD TELERIDE. *Personal Data:* b Vienna, Austria, May 5, 21; nat Can; m 44; c 4. *Educ:* Univ Toronto, BA, 48, MA, 49, PhD(physics), 51. *Hon Degrees:* LLD, Concordia Univ, Can, 81. *Prof Exp:* Supvr, Imp Optical Co, 42-44; proj engr, Rogers Electronic Tubes, 44-48; res engr, Univ Toronto, 48-54; pres, KCS Ltd & Traffic Res Corp, 54-66; dep managing partner, Kates, Peat, Marwick & Co, 67-68, assoc, 69-73. *Concurrent Pos:* Pres, Setak Comput Servs Co, 67-; mem, Sci Coun Can, 68-74, chmn, 75-78, chmn, Teleride Sage Corp, 78-; consult, US AEC; chancellor, Univ Waterloo, 79-85, emer chancellor, 93- *Mem:* Inst Mgt Sci; Can Oper Res Soc; fel Eng Inst Can; Sci, Eng & Technol Community Can; fel Inst Mgt Consult. *Res:* Application of scientific methods, especially computers and operations research to industrial, scientific and engineering problems particular to transportation and planning applications. *Mailing Add:* 3 Silverdale Crescent North York ON M3A 3G9 Can

KATES, MORRIS, LIPID CHEMISTRY, BIOMEMBRANES LIPIDMETABOLISM. *Current Pos:* prof chem, Univ Ottawa, 68-69, prof biochem, 69-89, vdean res, 78-82, chmn dept, 82-85, EMER PROF BIOCHEM, UNIV OTTAWA, 89- *Personal Data:* b Galati, Roumania, Sept 30, 23; Can citizen; m 57, Pirkko H Makinen; c Anna L, Marja & Ilona. *Educ:* Univ Toronto, BA, 45, MA, 46, PhD(biochem), 48. *Honors & Awards:* Supelco Award Lipid Res, Am Oil Chemists' Soc, 84; R A Morton Lectr, Biochem Soc London, 94. *Prof Exp:* Asst, Banting & Best Med Res, 48-49; Nat Res Labs fel, Nat Res Coun Can, 49-51, asst res officer, Div Appl Biol, 51-55, assoc res officer, 55-61, sr res officer, 61-68. *Concurrent Pos:* Vis scientist, Nat Inst Med Res, London, Eng, 59-60; co-ed, Can J Biochem, 74-84; vis prof, Univ Helsinki, 75, Obihiro Univ, Japan, 75 & 85, Kansai Med Sch & Kinki Univ, Osaka, Japan, 85; staff res lectr, Univ Ottawa, 81. *Mem:* Am Chem Soc; Am Soc Biol Chem; Can Biochem Soc; Brit Biochem Soc; Royal Soc Can; Am Oil Chemists' Soc. *Res:* Synthesis of lecithins and related compounds; structure of the alkaloid, gelsemine; plant lecithinases and plant phospholipids; glycerides; lipases; bacterial lipids; phospholipid desaturases; biosynthesis of phospholipids; diphytanyl glycerol ether lipids; glycolipids. *Mailing Add:* Dept Biochem Univ Ottawa 40 Marie Curie PVT Ottawa ON K1N 6N5 Can. *Fax:* 613-562-5191; *E-Mail:* mkates@oreo.uottawa.ca

KATES, ROBERT, LONG TERM POPULATION DYNAMICS, GLOBAL ENVIRONMENTAL CHANGE & SUSTAINABILITY OF BIOSPHERE. *Current Pos:* univ prof & dir, Alan Shawn Feinstein World Hunger Prog, 86-93, EMER UNIV PROF, BROWN UNIV, 93- *Personal Data:* b Brooklyn, NY, Jan 31, 29; m 48; c 3. *Educ:* Univ Chicago, MA, 58, PhD(geog), 62. *Hon Degrees:* DSc, Clark Univ, 93. *Honors & Awards:* Nat Medal Sci, 91; Honors Award, Asn Am Geographers. *Prof Exp:* From asst prof to prof, Grad Sch Geog, Clark Univ, 62-87. *Concurrent Pos:* Dir, Bur Resource Assessment & Land Use Planning, Univ Col, Dar Es Salaam, Tanzania; univ prof, Clark Univ, 74-80; chmn, Comn Human Rights, NAS, 76-79, mem, 79-85; fel, Woodrow Wilson Int Ctr Scholars, 79; Mac Arthur Prize fel, 81-85; fel distinguished scholar exchange, Comt Scholarly Common People's Rep China, 85; res prof, Ctr Technol, Environ & Develop, Clark Univ, 81-87; mem bd dirs, Comt Prob & Policy, Social Sci Res Coun & Comt Int Appl Syst Anal, Am Acad Arts & Sci, 82; mem, Nat Coun, Fedn Am Scientists & Bd Sci & Technol Int Develop, Nat Res Coun, 86-89, Comt Global Change, 89-92; vchmn, bd sustainable develop, Nat Res Coun, 95-; sr fel, econs & environ, H John Heinz III Ctr Sci; fac assoc, Col Atlantic; distinguished scientist, George Perkins Morse Inst, Clark Univ. *Mem:* Nat Acad Sci; Asn Am Geographers (pres, 93-94); fel AAAS; Fedn Am Sci; Am Acad Arts & Sci; Acad Europ. *Res:* The prevalance and persistence of hunger; long term population dynamics; sustainability of the biosphere, climate impact assessment; theory of the human environment; author of many books on hunger, environment and technology. *Mailing Add:* RR1 Box 169B Trenton ME 04605

KATH, WILLIAM LAWRENCE, WAVE PROPAGATION, ASYMPTOTIC METHODS. *Current Pos:* ASST PROF ENG SCI & APPL MATH, NORTHWESTERN UNIV, 84- *Personal Data:* b Pasadena, Calif, June 23, 57; m 84. *Educ:* Mass Inst Technol, SB, 78; Calif Inst Technol, PhD(appl math), 81. *Prof Exp:* NSF res fel appl math, Calif Inst Technol, 81-82, Von Karman instr, 82-84. *Concurrent Pos:* Prin investr, NSF Presidential young investr award, 85- *Mem:* Soc Indust & Appl Math; Sigma Xi. *Res:* Application of asymptotic and singular perturbation methods to linear and nonlinear wave propagation (and related phenomena) in fluids, fiber optics and quantum optical devices. *Mailing Add:* ES-AM McCormick Sch Eng Northwestern Univ Evanston IL 60208-0001

KATHAN, RALPH HERMAN, CLINICAL BIOCHEMISTRY. *Current Pos:* RETIRED. *Personal Data:* b Chicago, Ill, Feb 1, 29; m 93, Dorothy Ruth Susie Norfleet; c Arthur E & Kathryn (Elston). *Educ:* Univ Chicago, SB, 49; Univ Ill, MS, 59, PhD(biochem), 61. *Prof Exp:* Res asst biol chem, Univ Chicago, 48-49; biochemist res labs, Kraft Foods Div, Nat Dairy Prod Corp, 49-51; tech serv, Am Can Co, 56-57; res asst, Col Med, Univ Ill, 57-61, res assoc, 61-62, asst prof, 62-68, assoc prof biol chem, 68-91; chmn, Div Biochem, Cook Co Hosp, 71-91. *Concurrent Pos:* Consult comn influenza, Armed Forces Epidemiol Bd, 64-68. *Mem:* Nat Acad Clin Biochemists; Soc Complex Carbohydrates; Am Soc Biol Chem; Am Asn Clin Chem. *Res:* Protein structure; mechanisms of viral infection; bacterial metabolism; carbohydrate absorption; plasma expanders; diagnostic biochemistry. *Mailing Add:* 38 W 086 Glenoak Lane St Charles IL 60175. *E-Mail:* 75446.511@compuserve.com

KATHARIOU, SOPHIA, STUDY OF BACTERIAL PATHOGENESIS, SURFACE ANTIGENS OF BACTERIA. *Current Pos:* ASSOC PROF MICROBIOL, UNIV HAWAII, 90- *Personal Data:* b Assos Corinth, Greece, Jan 1, 54; m 89, Edward Lanwermeyer; c Atif & Stefan. *Educ:* Austin Col, BA, 75; Univ Calif, Berkeley, PhD(genetics), 81. *Prof Exp:* Res assoc, Cornell Univ, 81-83 & Univ Wuerzburg, 84-88; guest researcher, Ctr Dis Control, 88-90. *Concurrent Pos:* Mem grad fac, Cell, Molecular & Neurosci Prog, Univ Hawaii, 90-, Dept Food Sci & Human Nutrit, 93- *Mem:* Am Soc Microbiol; AAAS; Sigma Xi. *Res:* Expression of bacterial virulence factors and surface antigens; involvement of temperature in gene expression; bacterial growth and gene expression at low temperatures. *Mailing Add:* Univ Hawaii 2538 Mall Honolulu HI 96822. *Fax:* 808-956-5339; *E-Mail:* ksophia@hawaii.edu

KATHMAN, R DEEDEE, tardigradology, freshwater pollution assessment, for more information see previous edition

KATHOLI, CHARLES ROBINSON, BIOMATHEMATICS. *Current Pos:* asst prof biomath, 70-77, asst prof info sci, 73-76, ASSOC PROF BIOMATH, UNIV ALA, BIRMINGHAM, 77- *Personal Data:* b Charleston, WVa, Jan 2, 41; m 80; c 1. *Educ:* Lehigh Univ, BA, 63; Adelphi Univ, MS, 65, PhD(math, appl anal), 70. *Prof Exp:* Asst, Adelphi Univ, 64-66; instr math, Suffolk County Community Col, 66-67; instr, Adelphi Univ, 67-70. *Mem:* AAAS; Soc Indust & Appl Math; NY Acad Sci; Asn Comput Mach; Acoust Soc Am; Sigma Xi. *Res:* Mathematical modelling and computer simulations in the field of cardiovascular research; computational methods for special functions. *Mailing Add:* 315 Poinciana Dr Birmingham AL 35209-4127

KATHREN, RONALD LAURENCE, RADIOBIOLOGY, ENVIRONMENTAL ENGINEERING. *Current Pos:* PROF & DIR, US TRANSURANIUM & URANIUM REGISTRIES, WASH STATE UNIV, 92- *Personal Data:* b Windsor, Ont, June 6, 37; US citizen; m 64, Susan Krafft; c SallyBeth & Daniel. *Educ:* Univ Calif, Los Angeles, BS, 57; Univ Pittsburgh, MS, 62; Am Bd Health Physics, dipl, 66; Am Acad Environ Eng, dipl, 78; Soc Radiol Protection, cert appl health physics, 85; Am Bd Med Physics, dipl, 89. *Honors & Awards:* Elda E Anderson Award, Health Physics Soc, 77, Founders Award, 85; Arthur Humm Award, Nat Registry Radiation Protection Technologists, 88; Hartman Orator & Medallist, Radiol Centennial, 95. *Prof Exp:* Supvr health physicist, Mare Island Naval Shipyard, USN, 59-61; health physicist, Lawrence Radiation Lab, Univ Calif, 62-67; sect mgr & sr res scientist radiation dosimetry, Pac Northwest Div, Battelle Mem Inst, 67-72; corp health physicist, Portland Gen Elec Co, 72-78; staff scientist, PAC Northwest Div, Battelle Mem Inst, 78-87; dir, Health Physics, Hanford Environ Health Found, 87-89, dir, US Transuranium & Uranium Registries, 89-92, dir res, 90-92. *Concurrent Pos:* Abstractor, Chem Abstr, 62-78; lectr, Tri-Cities Univ Ctr, Univ Wash, 71-72; affil assoc prof, 78-95, coordr radiol sci, 80-82, 86-87 & affil prof, 95-; adj prof, Ore State Div Continuing Educ, 72-77; health physicist, Reed Col, 73-78; mem, Traineeship Adv Comt, US AEC, 73-74; mem, Nat Adv Comt Nuclear Technicians, Tech Educ Res Ctr, 75-81; ed, Health Physics J, Health Physics Soc, 76-80; mem, Radiation Adv Comt, 77-78; consult, Int Atomic Energy Agency tech expert, 77, US Nuclear Regulatory Comm, 77, US Adv Comt Reactor Safeguards, 78-, US Adv Comt Nuclear Wastes, 88- & US Transuranium & Uranium Registries, 84-87; mem panel examr, Am Bd Health Physics, 78-80; mem, Am Bd Health Physics, 82-84, secy-treas, 84; mem, Nat Coun Radiation Protection & Measurements Task Force on Alarm & Access Control Systs, 83-, chmn, SC 1-3 Comt Collective Dose, 90-; bd dir, Am Acad Health Physics, 85-86; lectr, Wash State Univ, 87-; mem, Comt Film Badge Dosimetry, Nat Res Coun, 88-89; int adv bd, J Radiation Protection, 88-; ed, Radiation Pro Dosimetry, 91-93; chmn, Nat Coun Radiation Protection & Measurements, Sci Comt SC-1 Collective Dose, 93-94; affil staff scientist, Pac NW Nat Lab, 96- *Mem:* Fel Health Physics Soc; Am Asn Physicists Med; AAAS; fel Soc Radiol Protection; Am Acad Health Physics (pres-elect, 97 & pres, 98); Sigma Xi; Health Physics Soc (pres-elect, 88-89 & pres, 89-90); Am Acad Environ Engrs. *Res:* Biokinetics and dosimetry of actinides; applied health physics; radiological dosimetry; environmental radioactivity; history of radiation protection and physics. *Mailing Add:* 100 Sprout Rd Richland WA 99352. *Fax:* 509-375-1817; *E-Mail:* rkathren@tricity.wsu.edu

KATO, IKUNOSHIN, PROTEIN CHEMISTRY. *Current Pos:* PROTEIN CHEMIST, CENTOCOR, INC, 83- *Educ:* Univ Osaka, Japan, PhD(biochem), 69. *Res:* Sequencing of protein; monoclonal antibody. *Mailing Add:* Takara Shuzo Co 3-4-1 SETA Otsu Shiga 520-21 Japan. *Fax:* 81-775-43-2312

KATO, SUSUMU, ATMOSPHERIC PHYSICS. *Current Pos:* VIS PROF, BANDUNG INST TECHNOL, INDONESIA, 92-; VCHMN, JAPAN-INDONESIA SCI & TECH FORUM, 92- *Personal Data:* b Saitama, Aug 27, 28; m, Kyoko-Kojo. *Educ:* Kyoto Univ, PhD. *Honors & Awards:* Tanakadate Prize, 59; Yamaji Sci Prize, 74; Appleton Prize, 87; Hasegawa Prize, 87; Fujiware Prize, 89; Japan Acad Award, 89. *Prof Exp:* Lectr, Fac Eng, Kyoto Univ, Osaka Univ, 55-61, asst prof, Ionosphere Res Lab, 61-62, assoc prof, 64-67, prof, 67-81, dir & prof, Radio Atmospheric Sci Ctr, 81-92, emer prof, 92-; res officer, Upper Atmosphere Sect, Commonwealth Sci & Indust Res Orgn, 62-64; vis prof, Dept Meteorol, Univ Calif, Los Angeles, 73-74. *Concurrent Pos:* Vis scientist, High Altitude Observ, Nat Ctr Atmospheric Res, 67-68 & 73-74. *Mem:* Nat Acad Eng. *Res:* Atmospheric tidal theory; observation of atmospheric waves. *Mailing Add:* 22-15 Fujimidai Otsu Shiga Prefecture 520 Japan

KATO, TOSIO, MATHEMATICS. *Current Pos:* PROF MATH, UNIV CALIF, BERKELEY, 62- *Personal Data:* b Kanuma, Japan, Aug 25, 17; m 44. *Educ:* Univ Tokyo, BS, 41, DSc(math physics), 51. *Honors & Awards:* Asahi Award, 60; Norbert Wiemer Prize, 80. *Prof Exp:* From asst to prof physics, Univ Tokyo, 43-62. *Mem:* Am Math Soc; Math Soc Japan. *Res:* Functional analysis and applications; mathematical physics. *Mailing Add:* Univ Calif Berkeley CA 94720-0001

KATO, WALTER YONEO, REACTOR SAFETY. *Current Pos:* assoc chmn & sr nuclear engr, Brookhaven Nat Lab, 75-80, dept chmn, 80-88, chmn, Dept Nuclear Energy, 88-91, sr scientist, 91-93, SR SCIENTIST, DEPT ADVAN TECHNOL, BROOKHAVEN NAT LAB, 93- *Personal Data:* b Chicago, Ill, Aug 19, 24; m 53, Anna Kurata; c Norman S, Cathryn J & Barbara J. *Educ:* Haverford Col, BS, 46; Univ Ill, MS, 49; Pa State Col, PhD(physics), 54. *Honors & Awards:* Order of Sacred Treasure, 3rd Class, Japanese Govt, 93. *Prof Exp:* Res assoc hydroqun, Ord Res Lab, Sch Eng, Pa State Col, 49-52; jr res assoc neutron physics, Brookhaven Nat Lab, 52-53; asst physicist nuclear & reactor physics, Argonne Nat Lab, 53; assoc physicist, Reactor Eng Div, 53-63, assoc physicist, Reactor Physics Div, 63-68, head, Fast Reactor Exps Sect, 63-70, sr physicist, 68-75, sr physicist, Appl Physics Div, 69-75,

Concurrent Pos: Fulbright res scholar, Japan Atomic Energy Res Inst & Univ Tokyo, 58-59; vis prof nuclear eng, Univ Mich, 74-75; consult, Off Nuclear Regulatory Res, Nuclear Regulatory Comn, 74-85. *Mem:* AAAS; Am Phys Soc; fel Am Nuclear Soc. *Res:* Hydrodynamics; cavitation studies; neutron resonance phenomenon; neutron total cross section measurements; neutron inelastic scattering studies; reactor physics; critical assembly experiments; fast reactor physics and safety; reactor safety research. *Mailing Add:* Brookhaven Nat Lab Upton NY 11973. *Fax:* 516-282-5266; *E-Mail:* kato1@bnl.gov

KATO, YASUSHI, BIOMATERIALS, BIOMEDICAL ENGINEERING. *Current Pos:* SR RES ENGR ARTIFICIAL INTERNAL ORGANS, CORVITA CORP, 91- *Personal Data:* b Tokyo, Japan, 1963. *Educ:* Cornell Univ, BS, 85; Rutgers Univ, PhD(biomed eng), 91. *Mem:* Soc Biomat; Am Soc Artificial Internal Organs. *Mailing Add:* Corvita Corp 8210 NW 27th St Miami FL 33122

KATOCS, ANDREW STEPHEN, JR, hypertension, ultrasound, for more information see previous edition

KATOH, ARTHUR, DEVELOPMENTAL BIOLOGY. *Current Pos:* dir oncol lab, Dept Radiother, 66-73, DIR, DIV NUCLEAR PATH & ONCOL, MERCY HOSP, 73- *Personal Data:* b Honolulu, Hawaii, Aug 24, 33; m 63, Dorothy Kurashige; c Ara, Austin & Ann. *Educ:* Syracuse Univ, AB, 54; Univ Ill, MS, 56, PhD(zool), 60; Univ Pittsburgh, MPH, 86. *Prof Exp:* NSF fel, 60-61; res assoc zool, Univ Ill, 61-62; asst prof biol, Univ Toledo, 62-63; res assoc, Argonne Nat Lab, 63-66. *Mem:* Soc Develop Biol; NY Acad Sci; Am Soc Cell Biol; Am Asn Cancer Res; Metastasis Res Soc. *Res:* Developmental biology; cellular differentiation in amphibian and chick embryos; cancer metastasis. *Mailing Add:* Div Nuclear Path & Oncol Mercy Hosp Pittsburgh PA 15219

KATON, JOHN EDWARD, PHYSICAL CHEMISTRY. *Current Pos:* assoc prof, 68-72, PROF CHEM, MIAMI UNIV, 72-, DIR MOLECULAR MICROS LAB, 84- *Personal Data:* b Toledo, Ohio, Jan 5, 29; m 55, Jeanette Scott; c Kent, Linden & Alison. *Educ:* Bowling Green State Univ, BA, 51; Kans State Univ, MS, 55; Univ Md, PhD(chem), 58. *Honors & Awards:* Chemist Award, Am Chem Soc, 79. *Prof Exp:* Sr res chemist, Monsanto Chem Co, 58-61, res group leader, Monsanto Res Corp, Ohio, 61-68. *Concurrent Pos:* Consult, US Air Force, 60-61 & 68-69 & NIH, 70; chmn, Fedn Anal Chem & Spectros Soc, 81. *Mem:* Am Chem Soc; Microbeam Analysis Soc; Soc Appl Spectros; Coblentz Soc; Soc Appl Spectros (pres, 76). *Res:* Molecular spectroscopy and structure; microspectroscopy; spectroscopic identification of materials. *Mailing Add:* 69 Hidden Creek Dr Oxford OH 45056. *Fax:* 513-529-2874

KATONA, PETER GEZA, BIOMEDICAL CONTROL SYSTEMS. *Current Pos:* VPRES, BIOMED ENG PROGS, WHITAKER FOUND, 91- *Personal Data:* b Budapest, Hungary, June 25, 37; US citizen; m 66, Jaroslava Blanar; c Andrew & Catherine. *Educ:* Univ Mich, BS, 60; Mass Inst Technol, SM, 62, ScD(elec eng), 65. *Honors & Awards:* Alexander von Humboldt Sr US Scientist Award, 87. *Prof Exp:* From instr to asst prof elec eng, Mass Inst Technol, 63-69; assoc prof biomed eng, Case Western Res Univ, 69-78, chmn dept, 80-87, prof, 78-91. *Concurrent Pos:* Ford res fel, 65-67; consult, Biosysts, Inc, Mass, 65-67 & Mass Gen Hosp, Boston, 66-69; Fogarty sr int fel, 78-79; vis scientist, Univ Heidelberg, WGer, 87-88; prog dir bioeng, NSF, 89-91; fel Cardiovasc Sect, Am Physiol Soc. *Mem:* Fel AAAS; Inst Elec & Electronics Engrs; Biomed Eng Soc (pres, 84-85); Am Physiol Soc; Am Soc Eng Educ; fel Am Inst Med & Biomed Eng. *Res:* Administration of research grant programs; neural control of the cardiovascular system; interaction of cardiovascular and respiratory control mechanisms; automated control of drug infusion. *Mailing Add:* Whitaker Fedn 1700 N Moore St Suite 2200 Rosslyn VA 22209. *E-Mail:* 00019@psilink.com

KATOVIC, VLADIMIR, ELECTROCHEMISTRY. *Current Pos:* assoc prof, 78-91, PROF INORG CHEM, WRIGHT STATE UNIV, 91- *Personal Data:* b Bihac, Croatia, Dec 19, 35; US citizen; m 71, Lois A Adcock; c Nina M. *Educ:* Univ Zagreb, BS, 61, PhD(chem), 65. *Prof Exp:* Res assoc inorg chem, Ohio State Univ, 68-71; assoc prof anal chem, Univ Zagreb, 71-76; res assoc inorg chem, Iowa State Univ, 76-78. *Mem:* Am Chem Soc; Croatian Chem Soc. *Res:* Synthetic and structural studies of coordination compounds of biological or catalytic interest; metal-metal bonding and metal-cluster compounds. *Mailing Add:* Chem Dept Wright State Univ Dayton OH 45435. *Fax:* 937-775-3301

KATOVICH, MICHAEL J, PHARMACODYNAMICS. *Current Pos:* assoc physiol, Col Med, Univ Fla, 76-77, Am Heart fel, 77-79, asst prof, Dept Pharmaceut Biol, 79-84, assoc prof, 84-88, PROF PHARMACODYNAMICS, COL PHARM, UNIV FLA, 89-, CHMN DEPT, 88- *Personal Data:* b San Jose, Calif, July 16, 48; m 90, Carol; c Megan & Sean. *Educ:* Univ Calif, Davis, BS, 70, MS, 73, PhD(physiol), 76. *Honors & Awards:* Irving I Hertzendorf Mem Award Physiol, 76. *Prof Exp:* Teaching asst, Dept Physiol, Univ Calif, 72-73, assoc, 73-74, res assoc, 74-75, res physiologist, 75-76. *Concurrent Pos:* Prin investr, Am Heart Asn, 79-81 & 84-94, Nat Inst Child Health & Human Develop, 83-95, NIH, 89-92; mem, Coun Complications, Am Diabetes Asn, 90. *Mem:* Sigma Xi; Aerospace Med Asn; Am Physiol Soc; Endocrine Soc; Am Diabetes Asn; Am Asn Cols Pharm. *Res:* Hypertension; metabolic phenomena; diabetes; environmental physiology with emphasis on temperature regulation; endocrinology; thirst control mechanisms; morphine dependency and withdrawal; acceleration biology; author of more than 150 technical publications. *Mailing Add:* Dept Pharmacodynamics Univ Fla Box 100487 JHMHC Gainesville FL 32610-0487. *Fax:* 904-392-9187

KATRITZKY, ALAN R, HETEROCYCLIC CHEMISTRY. *Current Pos:* KENAN PROF CHEM, UNIV FLA, 80-, DIR, CTR HETEROCYCLIC COMPOUNDS, 85- *Personal Data:* b London, Eng, Aug 18, 28; US citizen; m 52, Agnes J Kilian; c Margaret, Erika, Rupert & Freda. *Educ:* Univ Oxford, BSc, 52, MA, 54, DPhil, 54; Univ Cambridge, PhD, 58, ScD, 63. *Hon Degrees:* Dr, Nat Univ, Madrid, Spain, 86, Univ Poznan, Poland, 90, Univ Sdansk, Poland, 94, Univ E Anglia, UK, 95, Univ Toulouse, France, 96, Univ St Petersburg, Russia, 97. *Honors & Awards:* Tilden Medal, 75; Royal Soc Chem Award in Heterocyclic Chem, 82; Int Soc Heterocyclic Chem Award, 93; Fla Award, Am Chem Soc, 95. *Prof Exp:* Lectr, Pembroke Col, 56-58; univ demonstr, Univ Cambridge, 58-62, lectr, 62-63; prof chem, Univ E Anglia, 63-80, dean Sch Chem Sci, 63-70 & 76-80. *Concurrent Pos:* Fel, Churchill Col, 60-63; consult, 3M, 64-, Sandoz, 79-95, Exxon, 81-, Reilly, 81-, Pharmos, 83-, Nutrasweet, 87-, Monsanto, 89-, Bristol-Myers Squibb, 93-, Haughten Pharma, 95- *Mem:* Hon fel Italian Chem Soc; fel Royal Soc; foreign fel Royal Australian Inst Chem; hon fel Polish Chem Soc; foreign mem Polish Acad Sci; foreign mem Real Catalan Acad. *Res:* Heteroaromatic tautomerism & aromaticity; heteroaromatic rearrangements; electrophilic substitution; conformational analysis of heterocycles; intermolecular interactions; infrared intensites; cycloadditions to heterocyclic betaines; pyrylium & pyridinium chemistry; mechanism of nucleophlic substitution reactions. *Mailing Add:* Dept Chem Univ Fla Gainesville FL 32611. *Fax:* 904-392-9199; *E-Mail:* katritzk@pine.circa.ufl.edu

KATSAMPES, CHRIS PETER, pediatrics, for more information see previous edition

KATSANIS, D(AVID) J(OHN), PHYSICS, PRODUCTION OPERATIONS MANAGEMENT. *Current Pos:* SR PHYSICIST MECH, SHIELDING TECHNOLOGIES, INC, 91- *Personal Data:* b Philadelphia, Pa, Sept 28, 26; m 48; c 3. *Educ:* Temple Univ, BA, 52, MA, 54, PhD, 62, George Washington Univ, MEng, 80. *Prof Exp:* Physicist fluid dynamics, Naval Air Mat Ctr, 52-54; physicist ballistics, Frankford Arsenal, 54-57, chief, gas mech sect, 57-58, theoret ballistics sect, 58-59, systs ballistics sect, 59-63, LASH Proj, 63-65, advan concepts br, 65-66 & spec prods lab, 66-68, chief physicist, laser safety team, 68-69; chief physicist, US Army Small Arms Systs Agency, 69-73, chief, suppressive shielding, Edgewood Arsenal, 73-77, chief mech process, Chem Systs Lab, US Army Small Arms Systs Agency, Aberdeen Proving Ground, 77-81; physicist & chief producibility Eng Br, T&E Int, Inc, Bel-air, 81-86, sr physicist mech, 86-91. *Mem:* Am Phys Soc; Int Asn Bomb Technicians & Investigators; Asn US Army. *Res:* Weapon systems analysis; fluid dynamics; mechanics; thermodynamics; design of experiments; production technology; ventented suppressive shielding. *Mailing Add:* 4047 Heaps Sch Rd Pylesville MD 21132

KATSANIS, ELEFTHERIOS P, COLLOID CHEMISTRY, SURFACE CHEMISTRY. *Current Pos:* SR CHEMIST, PHILADELPHIA QUARTZ CO, 75- *Personal Data:* b Mytilene, Greece, Sept 28, 44; US citizen; div; c 1. *Educ:* Lehigh Univ, BS, 67, MS, 70; Clarkson Col Tech, PhD, 81. *Mem:* Am Chem Soc; Sigma Xi; Soc Petrol Engrs. *Res:* Preparation of hydrous metal oxide sols via precipitation techniques; zeolites; stabilization of colloidal dispersions and their application to practical systems; enhanced oil recovery; water chemistry. *Mailing Add:* 121 Green Hill Rd King of Prussia PA 19406-2045

KATSAROS, KRISTINA B, ATMOSPHERIC PHYSICS. *Current Pos:* res asst atmospheric sci, Univ Wash, 60 & 67-68, res assoc, 69-74, from res asst prof to res assoc prof, 74-83, assoc prof, 83-89, PROF ATMOSPHERIC SCI, UNIV WASH, 89- *Personal Data:* b Gothenburg, Sweden, July 24, 38; m 59, Michael A; c Anthony & Ester S. *Educ:* Univ Wash, BS, 60, PhD(atmospheric sci), 69. *Honors & Awards:* Sverdrup Gold Medal, Am Meteorol Soc, 97. *Prof Exp:* Dir, Dept Oceanog From Space, Fr Inst Explor Res Of The Sea, Ifremer, 92-97. *Concurrent Pos:* NDEA fel, 63-65; vis scientist, Riso Nat Lab, Denmark, 80, Royal Dutch Meteorol Soc, 84 & 85, Univ Paris, 87 & 90; vis prof women, NSF, 83-85. *Mem:* Am Geophys Union; fel Am Meteorol Soc; AAAS; Swed Geophys Soc; Europ Geophys Soc; Oceanog Soc. *Res:* Air-sea transfer processes, turbulent momentum transfer and its relation to sea slate, evaporation and the effects of sea spray radiative transfers; turbulent fluxes; free convection; remote sensing of atmosphere; scatterometry of passive microwave remote sensing of surface winds and storms over the sea. *Mailing Add:* Dept Atmospheric Sci 351640 Univ Wash Seattle WA 98195-1640. *Fax:* 206-543-0308; *E-Mail:* kutsaros@atmos.washington.edu

KATSEL, PAVEL LEON, REGULATION OF GENE EXPRESSION, CHEMICAL IDENTIFICATION OF PHEROMONES & GENE THERAPY. *Current Pos:* RES COORDR, VET ADMIN MED CTR, MT SINAI SCH MED, 92- *Personal Data:* b Irkutsk, USSR, Nov 19, 60; m, Bronislava Blyufer; c Nora & Leonard. *Educ:* Irkutsk State Univ, USSR, BS, 81, MS, 82, PhD(biochem & physiol), 90. *Prof Exp:* Jr researcher, Irkutsk State Univ, Inst Biol, 82-90, sr researcher, 90-92. *Concurrent Pos:* Asst prof, Irkutsk State Univ, 90-92. *Res:* Chemical communication during reproduction in fish; steroids and phorbol ester upregulation of rat cholecystokinin gene as a model for studying the mechanisms of eukaryotic transcriptional regulation; cationic lipid mediated gene transfer into the control nervous system and gastrointestinal tract. *Mailing Add:* Vet Admin Med Ctr 151 130 W Kingsbridge Rd Bronx NY 10468. *Fax:* 718-579-3348

KATSNELSON, LEV Z, KNOWN GOOD DIE, MULTI-CHIP MODULE. *Current Pos:* CHIEF SCIENTIST, MINCO TECH LABS INC, 93- *Personal Data:* m, Berta Ostrovskaya; c Zinoviy & Michael. *Educ:* Univ Latvia, BS, 63, MS, 65, PhD(appl math comput sci), 68. *Honors & Awards:* Latvian State Award In Sci & Technol, 80. *Prof Exp:* Res scientist, Dept Math, Latvia Univ,

68-73, sr res scientist, Ctr Comput Sci, 73-77, proj leader, 77-80, head lab, 80-87, head dept, Inst Math & Comput Sci, Latvia Univ, 87-92. *Concurrent Pos:* Assoc prof, Univ Latvia, 68-92; sr scientist, USSR Acad Scis, 72; Vis prof, Humboldt Univ, Berlin, 76, Dresden Tech Univ, Ger, 82 & 89, Kar Univ Prague, Czech, 88, Beer-Sheva Univ, Israel, 90. *Mem:* Int Soc Hybrid Microelectronics; Int Elec Packaging Soc; Inst Elec & Electronics Engrs. *Res:* Design and test known good die and multi chip modules; designed and developed numerical methods for analysis and optimization of linear and nonlinear integrated circuits; developed methods for optimal design of RC-filters; developed quasi-newton and adaptive algorithms for solving systems of ordinary differential equations and stiff systems. *Mailing Add:* Minco Tech Labs Inc 1805 Rutherford Lane Austin TX 78754. *Fax:* 512-837-6285

KATSOYANNIS, PANAYOTIS G, BIOCHEMISTRY. *Current Pos:* PROF BIOCHEM & CHMN DEPT, MT SINAI SCH MED, 68- *Personal Data:* b Greece, Jan 7, 24; nat US; m 55; c 2. *Educ:* Nat Univ Athens, MS, 48, PhD(chem), 52. *Honors & Awards:* 50th Anniversary Award, Am Diabetes Asn. *Prof Exp:* Res assoc, Med Col, Cornell Univ, 52-56, asst prof biochem, 56-58; assoc res prof, Sch Med, Univ Pittsburgh, 58-64; head, Div Biochem, Med Res Ctr, Brookhaven Nat Lab, 64-68. *Concurrent Pos:* Corresp mem, Nat Acad Greece. *Mem:* Am Chem Soc; Am Soc Biol Chem; NY Acad Sci; Royal Soc Chem; Brit Biochem Soc. *Res:* Biologically active polypeptides; isolation, characterization and synthesis; insulin synthesis. *Mailing Add:* Dept Biochem Box 1020 Mt Sinai Sch Med One Gustave L Levy Pl New York NY 10029-6574

KATSUMOTO, KIYOSHI, chemistry, for more information see previous edition

KATTA, JAYARAM REDDY, SOIL & ENVIRONMENTAL CHEMISTRY, WATER QUALITY. *Current Pos:* Res assoc, Univ Wyo, 86-87, res assoc III, Wyo Water Resources Ctr, 87-90, res assoc IV, 90-93, adj asst prof, 90-93, ADJ ASSOC PROF PLANT, SOIL & INSECT SCI, UNIV WYO, 92-, SR RES SCIENTIST, WYO WATER RESOURCES CTR, 93- *Personal Data:* b Hyderabad, India, July 10, 53; m 80, Jyothi Reni; c Sweatha & Swathi. *Educ:* Andhrapradesh Agr Univ, BS, 77, MS, 80; Colo State Univ, Ft Collins, PhD(soil & environ chem), 86. *Concurrent Pos:* Prin investr, US Dept Energy, 86-89, Wyo Water Resources Ctr, 88-91, US Geol Surv, 89-91, Elec Power Res Inst, 90-93, Abandoned Coal Mine Land Res Prog, 91-, US Geol Surv Merit Fund Prog, 92-, US Environ Protection Agency, 94- *Mem:* Am Soc Agron; Soil Sci Soc Am; Am Water Resources Asn; Sigma Xi. *Res:* Understanding geochemical processes of soils, groundwater systems, coal mine lands and hazardous wastes; application of chemical speciation, adsorption/disorption precipitation/dissolution processes to predict the fate of organic and inorganic contaminants in the vadose zone of contaminated soils and hazardous wastes and development of remediation methods for contaminated soils and groundwater; author of 2 books, several journal articles and publications. *Mailing Add:* 4413 Crow Dr Laramie WY 82070. *Fax:* 307-766-3785; *E-Mail:* katta@uwyo.edu

KATTAKUZHY, GEORGE CHACKO, RATES & PROPORTIONS, MODEL FITTING & PREDICTION. *Current Pos:* STATISTICIAN STATIST, HEALTH CARE FINANCING ADMIN, 78- *Personal Data:* b Kottayam, SIndia, Oct 1, 44; US citizen; m 74, Regini Titus; c Sandhya E, Anita M & Sarah M. *Educ:* Kerala Univ, Kerala, India, BSc, 66, MSc, 68; Temple Univ, MA, 73, PhD(math statist), 75. *Prof Exp:* Instr math, Temple Univ, Philadelphia, Pa, 72-75, lectr statist, 73-75; asst prof statist, Pahlavi Univ, Shiraz, Iran, 75-76; asst prof math, Philadelphia Col Pharm & Sci, 76-78. *Mem:* Am Statist Asn (treas, 89-90). *Res:* Variation in admission rates in selected disease catagories in medicare population 1986 to present. *Mailing Add:* 3611 Morningview Ct Ellicott City MD 21042. *Fax:* 410-966-1873

KATTAMIS, THEODOULOS ZENON, PHYSICS, METALLURGY. *Current Pos:* from asst prof to assoc prof, 69-75, PROF METALL, UNIV CONN, 75- *Personal Data:* b Kythrea, Cyprus, May 7, 35; US citizen; div; c Alexis & Nicholas. *Educ:* Univ Liege, Mining Engr, 60, Geol Engr, 61, Metall Engr, 62; Mass Inst Technol, MS, 63, ScD(metall), 65. *Honors & Awards:* Cert for Innovation in Metal Casting, NASA. *Prof Exp:* Res assoc metall, Mass Inst Technol, 65-69. *Concurrent Pos:* Grants, NASA, 72-74, NSF, 73-76 & Air Force Off Sci Res, 77-81; contract, Continental Can Co, 82-85. *Mem:* Am Soc Metals; Metall Soc; Am Foundrymen's Soc. *Res:* Solidification and properties of materials, composite materials, joining, powder metallurgy, thin coatings, single crystal growth and materials processing; microstructure-property relationships; materials science engineering. *Mailing Add:* Dept Metall & Mat Eng Univ Conn Storrs CT 06269-3136. *Fax:* 860-486-4745; *E-Mail:* tkattami@mail.ims.uconn.edu

KATTAN, AHMED A, HORTICULTURE, FOOD SCIENCE. *Current Pos:* From asst prof to prof hort, 55-62, HEAD, DEPT FOOD SCI, UNIV ARK, FAYETTEVILLE, 68-, EMER UNIV PROF, 88- *Personal Data:* b Cairo, Egypt, Mar 21, 25; nat US; m 51, Anna Phillips; c Jeanie, Mitchell & Michael. *Educ:* Cairo Univ, BSc, 45; Univ Md, MS, 50, PhD(hort), 52. *Honors & Awards:* Woodbury Award, Am Soc Hort Sci, 59; Gourley Award, 79. *Prof Exp:* Asst, Cairo Univ, 46-48, lectr, 53-54; asst veg crops, Univ Md, 51-52, res assoc, 52-53, asst prof, 54-55. *Concurrent Pos:* Exec vpres, Ozark Food Processors Assoc, 62-88. *Mem:* Fel Am Soc Hort Sci; Inst Food Technol. *Res:* Pre- and post-harvest physiology of horticultural crops; methods of quality evaluation of raw and processed fruits and vegetables; methods of handling and mechanical harvesting of fruits and vegetables. *Mailing Add:* 1625 Halsell Rd Fayetteville AR 72701

KATTAWAR, GEORGE W, OPTICAL PHYSICS. *Current Pos:* assoc prof, 68-73, PROF PHYSICS, TEX A&M UNIV, 73- *Personal Data:* b Beaumont, Tex, Aug 10, 37; m 61; c 3. *Educ:* Lamar State Col, BS, 59; Tex A&M Univ, MS, 61, PhD(physics), 64. *Prof Exp:* Theoretical physicist, Los Alamos Sci Lab, 63-64; sr res physicist, Esso Prod Res, 64-66; asst prof physics, NTex State Univ, 66-68. *Concurrent Pos:* Consult, Navy & Jet Propulsion Lab. *Mem:* Fel Optical Soc Am; Sigma Xi. *Res:* Electromagnetic scattering theory; hydrologic optics. *Mailing Add:* 4968 Smugglers Rd College Station TX 77845

KATTERMAN, FRANK REINALD HUGH, PLANT PHYSIOLOGY. *Current Pos:* assoc prof plant breeding, 67-70, PROF AGRON & PLANT GENETICS, UNIV ARIZ, 70-, PLANT BREEDER, AGR EXP STA, 74- *Personal Data:* b Paia, Hawaii, June 28, 29; m 56; c 5. *Educ:* Univ Hawaii, BA, 54; Tex A&M Univ, PhD(plant physiol), 60. *Prof Exp:* Plant physiologist, Agr Res Serv, USDA, 59-67. *Concurrent Pos:* Mem, Nat Cotton Coun Am. *Mem:* AAAS. *Res:* Composition and biochemistry of the nucleic acids in higher plants. *Mailing Add:* Dept Plant Sci Forbes 303 Univ Ariz Tucson AZ 85721-0001

KATTI, KATTESH V, MAIN GROUP-TRANSITION METAL CHEMISTRY FOR THE DESIGN OF NEW CATALYSIS NEW MONOMERS & POLYMERS FOR NUCLEAR WASTE REMEDIATION. *Current Pos:* res asst prof, 90-93; ASST PROF RADIOL, UNIV MO, 93- *Personal Data:* b Dharwad, Karnatak, India, Nov 11, 56; m, Kavita. *Educ:* Karnatak Univ, India, BS, 75; Mysore Univ India, MS, 79; Indian Inst Sci, PhD(chem), 85. *Prof Exp:* Merit fel, Nat Coun Educ Res & Training, New Delhi, India, 78-80; res fel, Dept Atomic Energy, India, 79-84; Alexander von Humboldt fel, Univ Gottingen, Ger, 85-87; res scientist, Univ Alta, 87-90. *Concurrent Pos:* Lectr several univs & industs, US, Ger, France & Neth, 85-; chief consult, Ligands Inc, 90-; dir, Agr Testing P-N Compounds, Monsanta, 92-; adj prof chem, Univ Mo, Columbia, 92-; co-prin investr, Dept Energy, 92-, Zynaxis Cell Sci Inc, 93- & DuPont Merck, 93- *Mem:* Am Chem Soc; Soc Nuclear Med; Sigma Xi; Int Asn Radiopharmacol. *Res:* Fundamental main group chemistry of phosphorus-nitrogen/sulfer-nitrogen and silicon-nitrogen compounds; application of the new main group frameworks as ligands in the coordination chemistry of transition metals which include paramagnetic metals and metallic radiosisotopes; design of new main group monomers and polymers for applications in materials science and radioactive waste treatment. *Mailing Add:* Ctr Radiol Res Rm 103 301 Business Loop 70 W Columbia MO 65203. *Fax:* 573-884-5679

KATTI, SHRINIWAS KESHAV, ANALYTICAL STATISTICS, APPLIED STATISTICS. *Current Pos:* RETIRED. *Personal Data:* b Bijapur, India, June 20, 36; US citizen; m 60; c 2. *Educ:* Univ Delhi, BA, 56; Iowa State Univ, MA, 58, PhD(statist), 60. *Prof Exp:* From asst prof to assoc prof statist, Fla State Univ, 60-69; prof, Univ Mo, Columbia, 69- *Concurrent Pos:* USAF fel, Fla State Univ, 60-62, USPHS fel, 64-66 & USDA fel, 67-69; consult, Underwriter's Nat Assurance Co, 62-64 & Scot Res Lab, Perkesie, 67-70; assoc ed, Biomet Soc, 67-72; vis prof, Univ New South Wales, 71. *Mem:* Biomet Soc; fel Am Statist Asn; Am Inst Biol Sci; Am Math Soc; Inst Math Statist; Sigma Xi. *Res:* Inference; methods of tested priors; adaptive estimators. *Mailing Add:* 8290 Lake Dr Suite 249 Miami FL 33166. *Fax:* 573-446-2209

KATTUS, J ROBERT, FAILURE ANALYSIS, METALLOGRAPHY. *Current Pos:* CONSULT METALLURGIST, AMC-VULCAN INC, 80- *Personal Data:* b Cincinnati, Ohio, Aug 25, 22; wid; c Josephine, Robert, Sandra, Laura & Patricia. *Educ:* Purdue Univ, BS, 44. *Honors & Awards:* Award of Merit, Am Soc Testing & Mat, 71; Allen Ray Putnam Award, Am Soc Metals Int, 90. *Prof Exp:* Metallurgist, US Naval Res Lab, 44-46 & Aluminum Industs Inc, 46-48; chief metallurgist, Anderson Elec Corp, 48-52; dir metall res, Southern Res Inst, 52-66; gen mgr, Bethea Castings Co, 66-68; consult metallurgist, 68-80. *Concurrent Pos:* Chmn, Test Methods Panel, Joint Comt Effects Temperature Properties Metals, Am Soc Testing & Mat, 63-68, chmn, Comt A-4 Iron Castings, 65-69; nat trustee, Am Soc Metals Int; mem, Eng Manpower Comn, 65-68. *Mem:* Fel Am Soc Testing & Mat; fel Am Soc Metals Int. *Res:* Elevated-temperature properties of metals under conditions of rapid heating and rapid loading simulating aerospace conditions; effects of composition and foundry practice on the quality of ferrous and non-ferrous castings. *Mailing Add:* AMC-Vulcan Inc 810 Fifth Ave N Birmingham AL 35203. *Fax:* 205-328-3015

KATUSIC, ZVONIMIR, PHARMACOLOGY. *Current Pos:* Res assoc consult, 87-89, SR ASSOC CONSULT, MAYO CLIN, ST MARYS HOSP, 90- *Personal Data:* b Belgrade, Yugoslavia, Aug 16, 52. *Educ:* Univ Belgrade, BS, 77, MS, 83, PhD(pharmacol & med), 87. *Mem:* Am Heart Asn; Am Physiol Soc; Am Soc Pharmacol & Exp Therapeut. *Res:* Pharmacology. *Mailing Add:* Dept Anesthesiol & Pharmacol Mayo Clin St Marys Hosp 200 SW First St Rochester MN 55905-0001

KATZ, ADRIAN I, INTERNAL MEDICINE, NEPHROLOGY & PHYSIOLOGY. *Current Pos:* asst prof & attend physician, 68-71, assoc prof, 71-74, PROF MED, SCH MED, UNIV CHICAGO, 75- *Personal Data:* b Bucharest, Romania, Aug 3, 32; m 65, Miriam Lesser; c Ron & Iris. *Educ:* Hebrew Univ Jerusalem, MD, 62. *Prof Exp:* House officer internal med, Belinson Med Ctr, Sch Med, Tel-Aviv Univ, 63-65; res fel med, Sch Med, Yale Univ, 65-67; res fel, Harvard Med Sch, 67-68. *Concurrent Pos:* Asst med, Peter Bent Brigham Hosp, Boston, 67-68; head sect nephrology, Univ Chicago, 73-82. *Mem:* Am Soc Clin Invest; Am Fedn Clin Res; Am Soc Nephrology; NY Acad Sci; fel Am Col Physicians; Asn Am Physicians. *Res:* Renal physiology, especially biochemical mechanisms of renal tubular sodium transport; renal handling of polypeptide hormones; kidney function in pregnancy; clinical nephrology; biochemistry. *Mailing Add:* Dept Med Box 453 Pritzker Sch Med Univ Chicago 5841 S Maryland Ave Chicago IL 60637. *Fax:* 773-702-5818; *E-Mail:* akatz@medicine.bsd.uchicago.edu

KATZ, ALAN CHARLES, REGULATORY AFFAIRS, RISK ASSESSMENT. *Current Pos:* MGR, TECH AFFAIRS, SANACHEM USA, INC, 97- *Personal Data:* b Kearny, NJ, Nov 10, 46; m 74, Marcia A Ellenwood; c Bryan J & Jeffrey A. *Educ:* Fairleigh Dickinson Univ, BS, 70, MS, 77; Am Bd Toxicol, dipl; Am Bd Forensic Examr, dipl. *Prof Exp:* Res asst, Rockefeller Univ, 71-72; toxicol res asst, Ortho Pharmaceut Corp, 72-74; pharmacologist, Cooper Lab Inc, 74-76; sr assoc scientist, Johnson & Johnson Res Found, 76-79; toxicologist & study dir, Stauffer Chem Co, 79-84; toxicologist, US Environ Protection Agency, 84-86; sr toxicologist, 86-87; exec dir toxicol & anal chem, Tech Assessment Syst Inc, 87-97. *Concurrent Pos:* Consult toxicol. *Mem:* Soc Comp Ophthal (pres, 92-96); NY Acad Sci; Int Soc Study Xenobiotics; Am Col Forensic Examrs; Soc Toxicol; Can Soc Toxicol. *Res:* Chemical and pharmaceutical fields; pharmacology and toxicology; program management. *Mailing Add:* 16090 Simon Kenton Rd Haymarket VA 20169

KATZ, ALAN JEFFREY, GENETIC TOXICOLOGY, BIOSTATISTICS. *Current Pos:* from asst prof to assoc prof, 75-85, PROF GENETICS, DEPT BIOL SCI, ILL STATE UNIV, 85- *Personal Data:* b Columbus, Ohio, Oct 2, 47; m 68; c 3. *Educ:* Ohio State Univ, BS, 69, MS, 70, PhD(genetics), 74. *Prof Exp:* NIH fel pop genetics, Dept Genetics & Cell Biol, Univ Minn, 74-75. *Concurrent Pos:* vis res fel, Swiss Fed Inst Toxicol, Schwerzenbach, 82, res grants, March Dimes, 82-86, NIH, 87-89. *Mem:* Genetics Soc Am; Biomet Soc; Environ Mutagens Soc; AAAS; Sigma Xi. *Res:* Identification and study of chemical mutagens and antimutagens in the somatic tissue of drosophila. *Mailing Add:* Dept Biol Sci Ill State Univ Campus Box 4120 Normal IL 61790-0001

KATZ, ALBERT BARRY, CLINICAL CHEMISTRY, DIRECTOR CLINICAL LABORATORY. *Current Pos:* EMER TEACHER CHEM, PALM BEACH SCH SYST FLA, 88- *Personal Data:* b New York, NY, Feb 25, 17; m 79, Anita; c Stephanie (Greenwald) & Jeffrey H. *Educ:* NY Univ, BS, 38, MS, 39, PhD(chem), 42. *Prof Exp:* Malarial control officer, Mediter Base Sect, Europ Theatre Opers, 42; chief clin lab, 43rd Gen Hosp, US Army, 43-46; mem adv coun, State NJ-Gov Brendan Byrne, 69-71; dir clin lab, Hackensack Clin Lab, 77-79; chief lab, S Palm Beach Utilities, Boca Raton, 81-85. *Concurrent Pos:* Fel, Dept Health Ky, 46. *Mem:* Fel Am Asn Clin Chem; Am Chem Soc; fel Am Inst Chemists; Nat Acad Clin Biochem; NY Acad Sci; Am Bd Clin Chem. *Res:* Hemosiderin pigment that was found in heart failure cells; methodology found to identify the heart failure cell that appeared in sputum. *Mailing Add:* 19285 Cedar Glen Dr Boca Raton FL 33434-5130

KATZ, ARNOLD MARTIN, MEDICINE, PHYSIOLOGY. *Current Pos:* PROF MED & EMER HEAD DIV CARDIOL, HEALTH CTR, UNIV CONN, 77- *Personal Data:* b Chicago, Ill, July 30, 32; m 59, Phyllis C Beck; c Paul, Sarah, Amy & Laura. *Educ:* Univ Chicago, BA, 52; Harvard Univ, MD, 56. *Hon Degrees:* Dr Med, Carol Davila Univ, 94. *Honors & Awards:* Res Achievement Award, Am Heart Asn, 89, Sci Coun Distinguished Achievement Award, 91, Louis N & Arnold M Katz Prize, Basic Sci Coun. *Prof Exp:* Intern med, Mass Gen Hosp, 56-57; res assoc, Nat Heart Inst, 57-59; asst resident, Mass Gen Hosp, 59-60; hon registr, Nat Heart Hosp, London, 60-61; res fel med, Med Sch, Univ Calif, Los Angeles, 61-64; asst prof physiol, Col Physicians & Surgeons, Columbia Univ, 63-67; assoc prof med & physiol, Univ Chicago, 67-69; Philip J & Harriet L Goodhart prof med-cardiol, Mt Sinai Sch Med, 69-77. *Concurrent Pos:* Mosely traveling fel Harvard Univ, 60-61; Am Heart Asn res fel, 61-63; estab investr, Am Heart Asn, 63-68, mem exec coun, Coun Basic Sci, 68-71; asst physician, Med Serv, Presby Hosp, 63-67; mem, Comt Myocardial Infarction, Nat Heart Inst, 66, Ad Hoc Comt Rev Proposals Myocardial Infarction Study Ctrs, 67, Heart Prog Proj B Comt, 67-69 & prog proj comt A, 80-; session chmn, Gordon Res Conf Cellular Control Cardiac Contraction, 68 & Gordon Res Conf Cardiac Muscle, 70; attend physician, Mt Sinai Hosp, 69-77, John Dempsey Hosp, Conn, 77-; consult, Vet Admin, 70-, St Francis Hosp & Med Ctr, 79-, Hartford Hosp, 79- & New Britain Gen Hosp, 81-; vchmn task group cardiac failure, Nat Heart, Blood, Lung & Blood Vessel Prog, NIH, 72; assoc ed, J Molecular & Cellular Cardiol, 79-86, ed in chief, 86-92; vis prof med, Dartmouth Med Sch, 90-91; bd sci counsellors, Nat Heart Lung Blood Inst, 89-92; chmn sci bd, Sarnoff Edow Med Sci, 92-93; chmn sci adv bd, Patrick & Catherin Weldon Donaghue Found, 94-; bd dir, Am Heart Asn, 93-94. *Mem:* Am Physiol Soc; Am Soc Pharmacol & Exp Therapeut; Cardiac Muscle Soc (pres, 69-71); Am Soc Biol Chemists; Sigma Xi; Asn Univ Cardiologists; fel Am Col Cardiol. *Res:* Cardiology; cardiovascular physiology; muscle biochemistry. *Mailing Add:* Cardiol Div Univ Conn Health Ctr 263 Farmington Ave Farmington CT 06030-1305. *Fax:* 860-679-3346; *E-Mail:* akatz@nso1.chc.edu

KATZ, BARRETT, NEURO-OPHTHALMOLOGY, NEURO-SURGERY. *Current Pos:* WAYNE & GLADYS VALLEY PROF & VCHMN, DEPT OPHTHAL, CALIF PAC MED CTR, 89- *Personal Data:* m 81, Deborah; c Matthew, Jacob, Nathaniel & Sarah. *Educ:* Colgate Univ, AB, 69; Case Western Res Univ, MD, 73. *Prof Exp:* Intern, Parkland Hosp, Dallas, 73-74; assoc, NIH, 74-75; resident neurol, Harvard Med Sch, Boston, 75-78, ophthal, Tufts Med Sch, Boston, 78-81; fel neuro-ophthal, Univ Calif, San Francisco, 81-82; asst prof ophthal neurol & neurosurg, Univ Ariz, Tucson, 82-84; assoc prof ophthal neurol & neurosurg, Univ Calif, San Diego, 84-89. *Concurrent Pos:* Sr scientist, Smith-Kettlewell Eye Res Inst, San Francisco, 84- *Mem:* Am Acad Neurol; Am Neurol Asn; Am Asn Ophthal; Asn Res Vision & Ophthal; Asn Univ Profs Ophthal. *Res:* Clinical neuro-ophthalmology; ocular motility. *Mailing Add:* Calif-Pac Med Ctr 2340 Clay St San Francisco CA 94115-1932. *Fax:* 415-885-8637

KATZ, BERNARD, BIOPHYSICAL RESEARCH. *Current Pos:* RETIRED. *Personal Data:* b Leipzig, Ger, Mar 26, 11. *Educ:* Univ Leipzig, MD, 34; Univ London, PhD, 38, DSc, 43. *Hon Degrees:* DSc, Univ Southampton, 71, Univ Melbourne, 71, Cambridge Univ, 80; PhD, Weizmann Inst Sci, 79. *Honors & Awards:* Nobel Prize in Med, 70; Baly Medal, Royal Col Physicians, 46-50; Herter Lectr, Johns Hopkins Univ, 58; Dumham Lectr, Harvard Univ, 61; Croonian Lectr, Royal Soc, 61; Feldberg Award, 65; Copley Medal, Royal Soc, 67; Baly Medal, Royal Col Physicians, 67; Cothenius Medal, Dutch Acad, 89. *Prof Exp:* Beit mem res fel, 38-39; Carnegie res fel, 39-42; dir res biophys & Henry Head res fel, Royal Soc, 46-50; reader physiol, Univ Col London, 50-51; prof biophys & head dept, 52-78. *Concurrent Pos:* Royal Australian Air Force, 42-45; Agr Res Coun, 67-77. *Mem:* Foreign assoc Nat Acad Sci; Royal Col Physicians; fel Royal Soc (vpres, 65, secy, 68-76); foreign mem Royal Danish Acad Sci & Lett; Am Acad Arts & Sci. *Mailing Add:* Dept Physiol Univ Col Gower St London WC1E 6BT England

KATZ, DAVID HARVEY, MEDICINE, IMMUNOLOGY. *Current Pos:* CHIEF EXEC OFF & PRES, QUIDEL, 81-; PRES & DIR, MED BIOL INST, LA JOLLA, 81- *Personal Data:* b Richmond, Va, Feb 17, 43; m 63; c 2. *Educ:* Univ Va, AB, 63, Duke Univ, MD, 68. *Prof Exp:* Med house officer, Johns Hopkins Hosp, 68-69; staff assoc immunol, NIH, 69-71; from instr to assoc prof immunol & path, Harvard Med Sch, 71-76; chmn & mem immunol staff, Scripps Clin & Res Found, 76-81. *Concurrent Pos:* Mem adv comt cancer ctrs, Nat Cancer Inst, 72-74; mem allergy & immunol study sect, NIH, 77; mem human cell biol adv panel, NSF, 77-78. *Mem:* Am Asn Immunologists; Am Soc Clin Invest; AAAS; Am Asn Pathologists; Am Fedn Clin Res. *Res:* Basic immunology; allergy; tumor immunology; developmental biology. *Mailing Add:* Dept Immunol Med Biol Inst Lidak Pharm 11077 N Torrey Pines Rd La Jolla CA 92037-1082

KATZ, EDWARD, microbiology, biochemistry; deceased, see previous edition for last biography

KATZ, ELI JOEL, PHYSICAL OCEANOGRAPHY. *Current Pos:* sr res assoc, 79-83, SR SCIENTIST, LAMONT-DOHERTY EARTH OBSERV, 84- *Personal Data:* b Brooklyn, NY, Jan 12, 37; m 57; c 3. *Educ:* Polytech Inst Brooklyn, BSME, 57; Pa State Univ, MS, 59; Johns Hopkins Univ, PhD(fluid mech), 62. *Prof Exp:* Res assoc mech, Johns Hopkins Univ, 62-63; vis lectr meteorol, Hebrew Univ, Jerusalem, 63-65; res specialist acoust, Gen Dynamics Corp, 65-66; asst scientist, Woods Hole Oceanog Inst, 66-69, assoc scientist phys oceanog, 70-78; sr lectr mech, Tel Aviv Univ, 69-70. *Concurrent Pos:* Co-ed, J Phys Oceanog, 86-91, chief ed, 92-96. *Mem:* Am Meteorol Soc. *Res:* Ocean dynamics and ocean role in world climate: specifically the Tropical Oceans. *Mailing Add:* Lamont-Doherty Earth Observ Columbia Univ Palisades NY 10964. *Fax:* 914-365-8157; *E-Mail:* ejk@lamont.ldeo.columbia.edu

KATZ, ERNST, SOLID STATE PHYSICS. *Current Pos:* from asst prof to prof, 47-80, EMER PROF PHYSICS, UNIV MICH, ANN ARBOR, 80- *Personal Data:* b Maehr-Ostrau, Austria, July 23, 13; Netherlands citizen; m 39, Katherine Musch; c Johan M. *Educ:* Univ Utrecht, BS, 33, MS, 37, PhD(physics), 41. *Prof Exp:* Asst physics, Rockefeller Biophys Res Group, 37-41, Univ Utrecht, 38-47; with Neth Instrument & Elec Apparatus Co, 41-45, dir res, 45-47. *Mem:* Fel Am Phys Soc. *Mailing Add:* 33 Ridgeway Ann Arbor MI 48104

KATZ, EUGENE RICHARD, GENETICS. *Current Pos:* From asst prof to assoc prof, Dept Biol, 70-80, assoc prof, 80-85, dean, Div Biol Sci, 88-96, PROF GENETICS MOLECULAR GENETICS & MICROBIOL, STATE UNIV NY, STONYBROOK, 85-, ASSOC DEAN, ARTS & SCI, 97- *Personal Data:* b Brooklyn, NY, Apr 10, 42; m 69, Anne Ballard; c Sarah H & David J. *Educ:* Univ Wis, Madison, BS, 62; Univ Cambridge, Eng, PhD(molecular genetics), 69. *Concurrent Pos:* Vis scientist, Mass Inst Technol, 70; dir, Grad Prog Cellular & Develop Biol, SUNY at Stony Brook, 75-80, Grad Prog Genetics, 80-88; vis prof, Univ Nijmegen, Netherlands, 77-78. *Mem:* AAAS. *Res:* Genetic control of development using the cellular slime mold; Dictyostelium discoideum as a model system; formal genetics and biochemical analysis of mutants affecting development. *Mailing Add:* Dept Molecular Genetics & Microbiol Sch Med State Univ NY Stony Brook NY 11794-5200. *Fax:* 516-632-6900; *E-Mail:* ekatz@ccmail.sunysb.edu

KATZ, FRANCES R, CARBOHYDRATE CHEMISTRY, PATENT AFFAIRS. *Current Pos:* DIR PUBL, INST FOOD TECHNOLOGISTS, 96- *Personal Data:* b LeRoy, Ill, Aug 16, 37; m 83, Allan; c Andrew. *Educ:* Ind Cent Univ, BS, 61; Univ Chicago, MBA-XP, 82. *Prof Exp:* Food technologist, Durkee Foods, SCM Corp, 61-65, Continental Coffee Co, 65-69, assoc ed, Putnam Publ Co, 69-74; ed dir, Gorman Publ Co, 74-78; vpres res, Am Maize Prod Co, 78-96. *Concurrent Pos:* External adv, Food Sci Dept, Univ Ill; bd govs, Food Update; Fiber Subcomt, Int Life Sci Inst. *Mem:* Am Chem Soc; Inst Food Technologists; Corn Refiner's Asn; Am Asn Cereal Chemists. *Res:* Carbohydrate research; applications of carbohydrates; formulation of research policy; corn genetics research. *Mailing Add:* Inst Food Technologists 221 N LaSalle Chicago IL 60601. *Fax:* 219-473-6607

KATZ, FRANK FRED, PARASITOLOGY. *Current Pos:* from asst prof to assoc prof, 62-70, actg chmn dept to chmn dept, 71-83, PROF BIOL, SETON HALL UNIV, 70-, ASSOC DEAN, COL ARTS & SCI, 85- *Personal Data:* b Philadelphia, Pa, July 19, 27; m 55; c 2. *Educ:* Philadelphia Col Pharm, BS, 51; Tulane Univ, MS, 53; Univ Pa, PhD(parasitol), 56. *Prof Exp:* Asst zool, Philadelphia Col Pharm, 51; asst instr parasitol, Univ Pa, 54-55; jr res assoc biol, Brookhaven Nat Lab, 55-56; sr parasitologist, Eaton Labs, Norwich

Pharmacal Co, 56-57; asst prof microbiol, Jefferson Med Col, 57-62. *Mem:* AAAS; Am Soc Parasitol; Am Soc Trop Med & Hyg; Micros Soc Am. *Res:* Helminthology; protozoology; experimental parasitology; biology of Strongyloides, Trichinella, Plasmodium and trypanosomes. *Mailing Add:* Dept Biol Seton Hall Univ 400 S Orange Ave South Orange NJ 07079

KATZ, FRED H, INTERNAL MEDICINE, ENDOCRINOLOGY. *Current Pos:* RETIRED. *Personal Data:* b Essen, Ger, Apr 7, 30; US citizen; m 60; c 3. *Educ:* Columbia Univ, AB, 52, MD, 56; Am Bd Internal Med, dipl, 64. *Prof Exp:* Asst prof med, Sch Med, Univ Chicago, 63-66; assoc prof med & chief endocrinol, Stritch Sch Med, Loyola Univ, 66-69; assoc prof med, Univ Colo, 69-75, head, Div Endocrinol, 72-76, prof med, 75-, clin prof med, 76- *Concurrent Pos:* Nat Found fel, Presby Hosp, New York, 59-60, Nat Inst Arthritis & Metab Dis trainee, 60-61; chief endocrinol, Vet Admin Hosp, Denver, 69-76; mem, Med Adv Bd, Coun High Blood Pressure, Cent Soc Clin Res. *Mem:* Endocrine Soc; Soc Exp Biol & Med; fel Am Col Physicians. *Res:* Steroid hormone metabolism, physiology and pharmacology. *Mailing Add:* 3535 Cherry Creek N Dr No 307 Denver CO 80209-3609

KATZ, GARY VICTOR, INHALATION TOXICOLOGY, INDUSTRIAL HYGIENE. *Current Pos:* toxicologist, 77-81, MGR, INHALATION TOXICOL, EASTMAN KODAK CO, 81-, UNIT DIR CHEM & REGULATORY INFO, 90- *Personal Data:* b New York, NY, July 12, 43; m 84; c 2. *Educ:* City Col New York, BS, 65; NY Univ, MS, 68, PhD(biol & environ health sci), 75. *Prof Exp:* From asst res to assoc res scientist inhalation toxicol & chem carcinogenesis, Dept Environ Med, NY Univ Med Ctr, 69-77. *Concurrent Pos:* Adj asst prof environ med, Dept Environ Med, NY Univ Med Ctr, 77-; tech assoc, Eastman Kodak Co, 81-, asst to the dir & div vpres, 88-; chmn, Chem Mfr Asn (CMA) Toxicol Task Group, 84-; mem, CMA Integrated Risk Info Syst Task Group, 88-; Am Indust Health Coun (ATHC) Air Toxics Work Group. *Mem:* Am Indust Hygiene Asn; Soc Risk Anal. *Res:* Chemical carcinogenesis; neurotoxicology; quantitative risk assessment. *Mailing Add:* Chem & Regulatory Info Eastman Kodak Co Rochester NY 14652-6267

KATZ, GEORGE MAXIM, ENGINEERING, NEUROPHYSIOLOGY. *Current Pos:* RETIRED. *Personal Data:* b Mar 26, 22; US citizen; m 49; c 2. *Educ:* City Col New York, BEE, 42; Polytech Inst Brooklyn, MEE, 57; Columbia Univ, EE, 61, PhD(physiol), 67. *Prof Exp:* Engr, Gen Elec Co, NY, 42-47; lectr elec eng, City Col New York, 47-50; sr engr, Advan Develop Lab, Allen B Dumont Co, NJ, 50-51; res assoc surg, Col Physicians & Surgeons, Columbia Univ, 52-61, sr res assoc & asst prof neurol, 62- *Concurrent Pos:* Consult, St Vincent's Hosp & Med Ctr, New York, 68- *Mem:* Biophys Soc. *Res:* Methodology and instrumentation for conducting research; mathematical analysis of data. *Mailing Add:* Merck Res Labs PO Box 2000 Rahway NJ 07605

KATZ, HERBERT M(ARVIN), CHEMICAL ENGINEERING. *Current Pos:* RETIRED. *Personal Data:* b Brooklyn, NY, Apr 4, 26; m 54; c 2. *Educ:* City Col New York, BChE, 49; Univ Cincinnati, MS, 50, PhD(chem eng), 54. *Prof Exp:* Asst chem engr, Argonne Nat Lab, 54-56; staff engr, Eng Ctr, Univ Columbia, 56-57; chem engr, Brookhaven Nat Lab, 57-67; chem engr, Res Div, W R Grace & Co, 67-68; chmn dept, Howard Univ, 68-73, prof chem eng, 73-86. *Concurrent Pos:* Consult, Nuclear Safety Asn & Brookhaven Nat Lab. *Mem:* Sigma Xi; Am Inst Chem Engrs. *Res:* Chemical reprocessing of nuclear reactor fuels; treatment of radioactive wastes; fluidized bed technology. *Mailing Add:* 101 Coast Blvd La Jolla CA 92037

KATZ, IRA, FOOD SCIENCE. *Current Pos:* proj leader, 67-71, groupleader, 71-73, dir, 73-80, VPRES & DIR, RES & DEVELOP, INT FLAVORS & FRAGRANCES, INC, 80- *Personal Data:* b New York, NY, Nov 10, 33; m 55; c 3. *Educ:* Univ Ga, BSA, 57; Univ Md, MS, 59, PhD, 62. *Prof Exp:* Res asst lipid chem, Univ Md, 61-62, res assoc, 62-65, asst prof, 65-67. *Mem:* AAAS; Am Dairy Sci Asn; Am Oil Chem Soc; Am Chem Soc; Inst Food Technologists; Sigma Xi. *Res:* Flavor of food and fragrance systems. *Mailing Add:* Int Flavors & Fragrances Inc 1515 Hwy 36 Union Beach NJ 07735

KATZ, IRVING, MATHEMATICS. *Current Pos:* from asst prof to assoc prof, 66-77, PROF MATH, GEORGE WASHINGTON UNIV, 77- *Personal Data:* b Brooklyn, NY, Oct 25, 33; m 57; c 3. *Educ:* Brooklyn Col, BS, 56; Ohio State Univ, MA, 58; Univ Md, PhD(math), 64. *Prof Exp:* Mathematician, Nat Security Agency, 58-59 & Opers Res Inc, 59-60; from instr to assoc prof, Am Univ, 61-66. *Mem:* Am Math Soc; Math Asn Am. *Res:* Matrix theory. *Mailing Add:* George Washington Univ Washington DC 20052-7528

KATZ, ISRAEL, MECHANICAL ENGINEERING, ENGINEERING MANAGEMENT. *Current Pos:* dean, Ctr Continuing Educ, 67-74, prof & dir advan eng progs, 74-88, PROF EMER ENG TECHNOL, NORTHEASTERN UNIV, 88- *Personal Data:* b New York, NY, Nov 30, 17; m 42; c 3. *Educ:* Northeastern Univ, BSME, 41; Mass Inst Technol, cert naval archit, 42; Cornell Univ, MME, 44. *Honors & Awards:* Pioneer Award, Am Soc Eng Educ, 78; New Eng Award, Eng Soc NEng, 93. *Prof Exp:* Test engr, Gen Elec Co, 38-42; engr-in-charge, submarine propulsion machinery, US Naval Diesel Eng Lab, Cornell Univ, 42-46, asst prof grad sch aeronaut eng, 46-48, assoc prof mech eng & prof-in-charge aircraft powerplants lab, 48-57; mgr-liason & consult engr, Gen Elec Advan Electronics Ctr, Cornell Univ, 57-63; dir, Benwill Pub Corp, 64-82. *Concurrent Pos:* Consult eng designer, Pratt & Whitney Aircraft Co, 47-52; consult, Ctr Advan Eng Study, Mass Inst Technol, 68-90; chmn subcomt res & educ comt Mat Sci Appln & Coord, Nat Res Count, 72-73; consult engr, Nat Acad Sci, 71-91; app, Bd Examiners, Dept Bldg Construct, Brookline, Mass, 94-, chmn, 96- *Mem:* Am Soc Eng Educ; Inst Elec & Electronics Engrs; AAAS; Sigma Xi. *Res:* Engineering thermodynamics; electromechanical systems; aerospace technology; continuing education for scientists and engineers; author of numerous publications; principle of aircraft propulsion machinery pitman. *Mailing Add:* 40 Auburn St Brookline MA 02146

KATZ, ISRAEL NORMAN, MATHEMATICS, STATISTICS. *Current Pos:* assoc prof appl math & comput sci, 67-74, PROF APPL MATH & SYSTS SCI, 74-, CHMN DEPT SYSTS SCI & MATH, WASHINGTON UNIV, 91- *Personal Data:* b New York, NY, Apr 14, 32; m 57, Judith Batt Katz; c Avi & Maidi. *Educ:* Yeshiva Univ, BA & MS, 52; Mass Inst Technol, PhD(math), 59. *Honors & Awards:* Burlington Northern Award, 89. *Prof Exp:* Asst math, Yeshiva Univ, 52-54; asst, Mass Inst Technol, 55-58, res asst, 58-59; sr staff scientist, Res & Adv Develop Div, Avco Corp, 59-63, chief math anal sect, 63-65, mgr math dept, 66-67. *Concurrent Pos:* Lectr, Math Asn Am; vis consult, Soc Indust & Appl Math. *Mem:* Opers Res Soc Am; Am Math Soc; Math Asn Am; Soc Indust & Appl Math; Asn Comput Mech. *Res:* Applied math; numerical analysis; facility location; finite elements; biomathematics; ordinary and partial differential equations; algorithms for parallel computation. *Mailing Add:* Dept Systs Sci & Math Washington Univ Box 1040 St Louis MO 63130. *Fax:* 314-935-6121; *E-Mail:* katz@zach.wustl.edu

KATZ, J LAWRENCE, BONE BIOMECHANICS, BONE BIOMATERIALS. *Current Pos:* DEAN ENG & PROF BIOMED ENG, CASE INST TECHNOL, CASE WESTERN RESERVE UNIV, 89- *Personal Data:* b Brooklyn, NY, Dec 18, 27; m 50; c 3. *Educ:* Polytech Inst Brooklyn, BS, 50, MS, 51, PhD(physics), 57. *Honors & Awards:* 3rd Annual Award for Outstanding Contributions to Tech Lit Biomat, Soc Biomat & Clemson Univ, 75; Outstanding Biomed Eng Educator Award, Am Soc Eng Educ, 88; George Winter Award for Outstanding Res, Europ Soc Biomat, 89. *Prof Exp:* Instr math, Polytech Inst Brooklyn, 52-56; from asst prof to prof physics, Rensselaer Polytech Inst, 61-73, prof biophys & biomed eng, 73-89, dir, Ctr Biomed Eng, 74-84, chmn, Dept Biomed Eng, 83-85. *Concurrent Pos:* Consult, Ernest F Fullam, Inc, NY, 58-83, Bio-Anal Labs, Inc, 61-83, Orthop Panel, Food & Drug Admin, 76-78 & Orthop Div, Johnson & Johnson Co, 79-80; NSF sci fac fel & hon res asst crystallog, Univ Col, London, 59-60; mem, eng in biol & med training comt, NIH, 68-71; vis prof, Univ Miami, 69-70, Sao Carlos Inst Physics & Chem, Univ Sao Paulo, Brasil, 78, Univ London, Eng, 85-86 & Fac Med Lariboisiere, Paris, 86; mem equip & mat for med radiation appln & chmn subcomt diag radiol, Am Nat Standards Inst, 69-74; consult & site vis, Nat Inst Dent Res & Nat Inst Gen Med Sci; partic vis sci prog physics, Am Asn Physics Teachers-Am Inst Physics, 70-71; prof surg, Albany Med Col, 75-89; Jerome Fischbach travel grant, Rensselaer Polytech Inst, 76; Guggenheim fel, Harvard Univ, 78, vis lectr orthop, Sch Med, 78; vis biophysicist, Orthopaedics Res Lab, Children's Hosp, Boston, 78; E Leon Watkins vis prof, Wichita State Univ, Kans, 78; mem, Coun Alliance Eng Med & Biol, 78-81; mem, Sci Rev & Eval Bd for Rehab Eng Res & Develop, Vet Admin, 81-83, 90-; assoc ed, Biomat, Biomech & Rehab Eng, Annals of Biomed Eng, 84-89; NIH sr int fel, 85-86; vis prof, Dept Mat, Queen Mary Col, Univ London, Eng, 85-86 & Lab Orthop Res, Fac Med Lariboisiere-Saint-Louis, Paris, France, 86. *Mem:* Am Crystallog Asn; Am Phys Soc; Int Asn Dent Res; Sigma Xi; Soc Biomat (pres, 78-79); Biomed Eng Soc (pres, 83-84). *Res:* Bone biomechanics and biomaterials, especially the correlation between structure and properties of the various calcified tissues and of synthetic materials used as implant biomaterials; biomechanics of calcified and connective tissues; electromechanical properties of bone and bone remodeling; rehabilitation engineering; scanning electron microscopy; X-ray diffraction and ultrasonic studies of bone and teeth; biomedical materials; rehabilitation engineering. *Mailing Add:* Dept Biomed Eng Case Western Reserve Univ Cleveland OH 44106-7220

KATZ, JACK, AUDIOLOGY, CENTRAL AUDITORY DISORDERS & PROCESSING. *Current Pos:* clin prof, 74-76, chmn commun dis & sci, 82-87, PROF COMMUN DIS & SCI, State Univ NY, BUFFALO, 76- *Personal Data:* b New York, NY, Mar 25, 34; m 56, Irma H Laufer; c Mark D & Miriam B. *Educ:* Brooklyn Col, BA, 56; Syracuse Univ, 57; Univ Pittsburgh, PhD(audiol), 61. *Honors & Awards:* Fulbright-Hays sr lectr, Ankara, Turkey, 72-73. *Prof Exp:* Therapist speech & hearing, Bd Educ, Cayuga Co, NY, 57-58; res audiologist, Univ Pittsburgh, 60-61; asst prof audiol, Northern Ill Univ, 61-62; asst prof speech path & audiol, Tulane Univ, 62-65; dir audiol lab, Menorah Med Ctr, Kansas City, 65-74. *Concurrent Pos:* Consult audiol, Univ Pittsburgh, 61-62, Menorah Med Ctr, 74-75, Roswell Park Mem Inst, 79-, Veteran Admin Med Ctr, Buffalo, NY, 84-; assoc clin prof, Univ Mo Kansas City, 70-74 & Univ Kans, 71-74, vis prof Univ Kans Med Ctr, 87-88; mem spec med staff, Chedoke-McMaster Hosps, Hamilton, Ont, 81-84; mem bd dir, Orton Soc Western NY, 87-90 & Buffalo Hearing Speech Ctr; vpres univ & labs, NY State Speech Lang-Hearing Asn, 81-85; adj prof, Dept Otolaryngol, State Univ NY, 92. *Mem:* Fel Am Speech-Lang-Hearing Asn; NY Acad Sci. *Res:* Evaluation of central auditory integrity, binaural hearing, low level adaptation, auditory perception, learning disabilities, listening problems in incarcerated populations and influence of conductive hearing loss. *Mailing Add:* Dept Commun Dis & Sci State Univ NY 105 Park Hall Buffalo NY 14260-0001. *Fax:* 716-645-2216

KATZ, JAY, PSYCHIATRY. *Current Pos:* Elizabeth Dollard prof law/med psychiat, Law Sch, 90-93, EMER PROF, YALE UNIV, 93-, HARVEY L KARP PROF LAW PSYCHOANALYSIS, 95-; TRAINING & SUPV PSYCHOANALYST, WESTERN NEW ENG INST PSYCHOANAL, 72- *Personal Data:* b Zwickau, Ger, Oct 20, 22; nat US; m 52; c 3. *Educ:* Univ Vt, BA, 44; Harvard Univ, MD, 49; Am Bd Psychiat & Neurol, dipl. *Honors & Awards:* Isaac Ray Award, Am Psychiat Asn, 75; William C Menninger Award, Am Col Physicians, 83; Am Soc Law & Med Award, 87. *Prof Exp:* Intern, Mt Sinai Hosp, NY, 49-50; asst resident psychiat, State Univ NY &

Northport Vet Admin Hosp, Long Island, 50-51; asst resident psychiat, Sch Med, Yale Univ, 53-54, chief resident outpatient clin, 54-55, from instr to asst prof psychiat, 55-58, asst prof psychiat & law, Law Sch, 58-60, assoc prof law & assoc clin prof psychiat, 60-67, adj prof law & psychiat, 67-84, John A Gorver prof law & psychoanalyst, 84-90. *Concurrent Pos:* Asst investr, USPHS res grant hypnotic dreams, 53-56; attend psychiatrist, Yale-New Haven Med Ctr, 57-; chmn, Adv Comt Ment Health, Woodbridge Bd Educ, Conn, 64-68; staff psychoanalyst, Psychoanal Clin, Western New Eng Inst Psychoanal, 66-69, trustee, 68-71; fel, Ctr Advan Psychoanal Studies, 67-; fel, Morse Col, Yale Univ, 68- *Mem:* Inst Med-Nat Acad Sci; fel Am Psychiat Asn; Am Orthopsychiat Asn; Am Col Psychiat; Am Psychoanal Asn. *Mailing Add:* Yale Law Sch New Haven CT 06520

KATZ, JONATHAN ISAAC, ASTROPHYSICS, APPLIED PHYSICS. *Current Pos:* assoc prof, 81-85, PROF PHYSICS, WASHINGTON UNIV, MO, 85- *Personal Data:* b New York, NY, Jan 5, 51; m 82, Lilly M Canel; c Sholomo, Alexander, Isaac, Rebecca & Joseph. *Educ:* Cornell Univ, AB, 70, MA, 71, PhD(astron), 73. *Prof Exp:* Mem staff astrophysics, Inst Advan Study, 73-76; assoc prof astron & geophysics, Univ Calif, Los Angeles, 76-81. *Concurrent Pos:* Consult, Lawrence Livermore Lab, 73-; SRI Int, 74-82 & adv coun, NASA, 83-86; Sloan Found fel, 77-79; MITRE, 82- *Mem:* Am Phys Soc. *Res:* Theoretical high energy astrophysics; capillarity, applied physics; gamma-ray astronomy including bursts, soft gamma repeaters and active galactic nuclei. *Mailing Add:* Dept Physics Washington Univ St Louis MO 63130. *Fax:* 314-935-6219; *E-Mail:* katz@wuphys.wustl.edu

KATZ, JOSE, INTERNAL MEDICINE, CARDIOLOGY. *Current Pos:* asst prof med & radiol, 88-94, DIR CARDIOVASC, MAGNETIC RESONANCE IMAGING & SPECTROS, COL PHYSICIANS & SURGEONS, COLUMBIA UNIV, 88-, ASSOC PROF MED & RADIOL, 94- *Personal Data:* m, Anke Ebsen; c David, Rachel, Hannah & Susan. *Educ:* Univ Ill, Urbana, BS, 63, MS, 64, PhD(theoret physics), 67; Free Univ Berlin, MD, 80. *Prof Exp:* Res assoc physics, Univ Hamburg, Ger, 67-69; asst prof, Inst Physics, Purdue Univ, 69-71; from asst prof to prof, Free Univ, Berlin, 71-82; resident internal med, Metrop Gen Hosp & Mt Sinai Med Ctr, Cleveland, Ohio, 82-85; cardio fel, Southwestern Med Sch, 85-88. *Concurrent Pos:* Prin investr nuclear magnetic resonance res, Col Physicians & Surgeons, Columbia Univ, 88-; staff attending, Columbia Presby Med Ctr, 88-; fel Coun Cardiovasc Radiol & Coun Clin Cardiol, Am Heart Asn. *Mem:* Fel Am Col Physicians; fel Am Col Cardiologists; fel Am Col Chest Physicians; fel Am Col Angiol; fel Am Heart Asn. *Res:* Nuclear magnetic resonance; technique development for the monitoring of intracellular sodium change, in biological systems without a shift reagent. *Mailing Add:* PO Box 637 Alpine NJ 07620. *Fax:* 212-305-4648; *E-Mail:* jk32@columbia.edu

KATZ, JOSEPH, BIOCHEMISTRY. *Current Pos:* from res assoc to sr res assoc, Inst Med Res, Cedars of Lebanon Hosp, 55-70, SR RES SCIENTIST, MED RES INST, CEDARS-SINAI MED CTR, 70- *Personal Data:* b Vilno, Lithuania, Jan 15; US citizen; c 5. *Educ:* Univ Calif, Berkeley, BS, 43, PhD, 49. *Prof Exp:* Asst res physiologist, Univ Calif, Berkeley, 53-55. *Concurrent Pos:* Res fel biochem, Univ Calif, Berkeley, 49-51, fel physiol, 51-53; advan res fel, Cedars-Sinai Med Ctr, 59-61; estab investr, Am Heart Asn, 61-66; adj prof, Univ Southern Calif, 69-88, Univ Calif, Los Angeles, 88- *Mem:* Am Chem Soc; Am Soc Biol Chemists; Am Nutrit Soc; Am Physiol Soc; Brit Biochem Soc. *Res:* Carbohydrate metabolism determination of pathways of glucose utilization; the interrelationship between lipogenesis and glucose utilization; plasma protein metabolism. *Mailing Add:* 2509 Bombadil Lane Davis CA 95916

KATZ, JOSEPH J, PHYSICAL CHEMISTRY. *Current Pos:* sr chemist, 46-82, EMER DISTINGUISHED SR SCIENTIST, ARGONNE NAT LAB, 82- *Personal Data:* b Detroit, Mich, Apr 19, 12; m 44, Celia S Weiner; c 4. *Educ:* Wayne State Univ, BS, 32; Univ Chicago, PhD(chem), 42. *Honors & Awards:* Nuclear Appln Award, Am Chem Soc, 61, Midwest Award, 69, Rumford Premium, Am Acad Arts & Sci, 92. *Prof Exp:* Chemist, Univ Chicago, 42-43, chemist metall lab, 43-46. *Concurrent Pos:* Guggenheim fel, 57-58; Am ed, J Inorg & Nuclear Chem; ed-in-chief, Inorg & Nuclear Chem Letters, 55-81. *Mem:* Nat Acad Sci; Am Chem Soc; Am Soc Photobiol; Sigma Xi. *Res:* Chemistry of uranium and transuranium elements; deterium isotope studies; chlorophyll chemistry; photosynthesis; solar energy. *Mailing Add:* Argonne Nat Lab 9700 S Cass Ave Argonne IL 60439. *Fax:* 630-252-9289; *E-Mail:* jjkatz@worldnet.att.net

KATZ, JOSEPH L, NUCLEATION, VAPOR PHASE FORMATION OF CERAMIC POWDER. *Current Pos:* dir, Energy Res Inst, 81-83, dept chmn, 81-84, PROF CHEM ENG, JOHNS HOPKINS UNIV, 79- *Personal Data:* b Colon, Panama, Aug 4, 38; US citizen; m 65, Liliane Capelluto; c Daniel P & Alan R. *Educ:* Univ Chicago, BS, 60, PhD(phys chem), 63. *Honors & Awards:* John W Graham Prize, 75; Maryland Chemist Award, 82. *Prof Exp:* Asst prof phys chem, Univ Copenhagen, 63-64; mem tech staff, NAm Rockwell Sci Ctr, 64-70; prof chem eng, Clarkson Col Technol, 70-79. *Concurrent Pos:* Guggenheim fel, 76-77; vis prof, Mass Inst Technol, 77. *Mem:* Fel AAAS; fel Am Phys Soc; Am Chem Soc; Am Inst Chem Engrs; Sigma Xi; Mat Res Soc; Combustion Inst. *Res:* Nucleation; equations of state; thermal conductivity; flame generation of ceramic powders; scale (calcite) inhibition. *Mailing Add:* Dept Chem Eng Johns Hopkins Univ Baltimore MD 21218. *Fax:* 410-516-5510; *E-Mail:* jlk@jhu.edu

KATZ, LARRY STEVEN, BEHAVIORAL ENDOCRINOLOGY, REPRODUCTIVE PHYSIOLOGY. *Current Pos:* asst prof, 89-95, ASSOC PROF ANIMAL SCI, RUTGERS STATE UNIV NJ, 95- *Personal Data:* b Albany, NY, Dec 3, 53; m 80, Barbara J Tarbell. *Educ:* Cornell Univ, BS, 76, MS, 79; Univ Calif, Davis, PhD(animal behav), 84. *Prof Exp:* NIH trainee, Colo State Univ, 84-85; researcher, Univ Calif, Davis, 85-86; res physiologist, Univ Calif, Berkeley, 86-89. *Concurrent Pos:* Co-founder, Coalition for Animals & Animal Res, 88; ed, Appl Animal Behav Sci, 93-; sect ed, Environ & Behav, J Animal Sci, 93-96. *Mem:* AAAS; Am Soc Animal Sci; Animal Behav Soc; Endocrine Soc; Soc Study Reproduction; Sigma Xi. *Res:* Describe the interactions between gonadal and pituitary hormones, reproductive function, sexual behavior and seasonal environmental changes, such as photoperiod in goats, sheep and deer. *Mailing Add:* Dept Animal Sci-Cook Col Rutgers Univ New Brunswick NJ 08903. *E-Mail:* katz@aesop.rutgers.edu

KATZ, LAURENCE BARRY, GASTROENTEROLOGY, CARDIOVASCULAR PHARMACOLOGY. *Current Pos:* prin scientist, 89-90, PROJ MGR, R W JOHNSON PHARMACEUT RES INST, 90- *Personal Data:* b Syracuse, NY, Oct 3, 54; m 81; c 2. *Educ:* Univ Pa, BA, 76; Philadelphia Col Pharm & Sci, MS, 79 & PhD(pharmacol), 82. *Prof Exp:* Res assoc toxicol, Univ Wis, 81-83; res scientist pharmacol, Ortho Pharmaceut Corp, 83-84, sr res scientist, 84-89. *Mem:* Am Soc Pharmacol & Exp Therapeut; Am Asn Advan Sci; Gastrointestinal Res Group; Sigma Xi. *Res:* Drugs useful in peptic ulcer disease and hypertension including prostaglandins, histamine H2-receptor antagonist and vasodilators. *Mailing Add:* Ohmeda Pharmaceut Prod Div 100 Mountain ve Murray Hill NJ 07947. *Fax:* 908-771-6161

KATZ, LEON, SCIENCE POLICY. *Current Pos:* RETIRED. *Personal Data:* b Poland, Aug 9, 09; Can citizen; m 41, Georgina Caverly; c Sylvan, Zender, David & M Faye. *Educ:* Queen's Univ, Ont, BSc, 34, MSc, 37; Calif Inst Technol, PhD(physics), 42. *Hon Degrees:* DSc, Univ Sask, 90. *Honors & Awards:* Officer Order of Can. *Prof Exp:* Res lead acid batteries, Monarch Battery Co, Ont, 31-33, plant foreman, 34-36; res engr, Westinghouse Elec Corp, 42-46; from assoc prof to prof physics, Univ Sask, 46-75, dir, Accelerator Lab, 61-75, head dept, 65-75; dir, Sci Policy Secretariat, Govt Sask, 75-80. *Concurrent Pos:* Mem, Sci Coun Can, 66-72; mem coun trustees, Inst Res Pub Policy, 74-89. *Mem:* Fel Am Phys Soc; Can Asn Physicist; fel Royal Soc Can. *Res:* Thermodynamics; radar; ratio of specific heats of gases; nuclear physics; chaos theory. *Mailing Add:* 203 Ball Crs Saskatoon SK S7K 6E1 Can

KATZ, LEON, ORGANIC CHEMISTRY, PACKAGING. *Current Pos:* CONSULT, 89- *Personal Data:* b Springfield, Mass, Aug 27, 21; m 47; c 3. *Educ:* Trinity Col, Conn, BS, 44; Univ Ill, PhD(org chem), 47. *Honors & Awards:* Packaging Hall of Fame, 92. *Prof Exp:* Chemist, Am Cyanamid Co, 47-49; mgr org chem, Schenley Labs, 49-53; res chemist, Gen Aniline & Film Corp, NY, 53-55, sect mgr dyes & pigments, 55-58, prod mgr pigments, 58-59, tech dir, 59-62, dir res, Dyestuff & Chem Div, 62-65, corp dir res, 65-66, vpres, 66-69; exec vpres, Rockwood Industs, Conn, 69-71; vpres corp develop, Polychrome Corp, Yonkers, NY, 71-73; vpres res & develop & packaging, Am Can Co, Greenwich, Conn, 73-82; sr vpres corp res & develop, James River Corp, 82-86, vpres corp technol, 87-88. *Mem:* AAAS; Indust Res Inst; Am Chem Soc; NY Acad Sci; Am Inst Chem; Sigma Xi. *Res:* Alkaloids; pharmaceuticals; dyestuffs; pigments; reprographics; photography; specialty chemicals packaging; pulp paper. *Mailing Add:* 195 Dogwood Ct Stamford CT 06903-4500

KATZ, LEWIS, X-RAY CRYSTALLOGRAPHY. *Current Pos:* from instr to prof phys chem, Univ Conn, 52-88, actg vpres grad educ & res, 81-83, assoc provost, 85-88, EMER PROF PHYS & CHEM, UNIV CONN, 88- *Personal Data:* b Fond du Lac, Wis, Mar 19, 23; m 48, Shirley Robbins; c Susan & Deborah. *Educ:* Univ Minn, BChem, 46, PhD(phys chem), 51. *Prof Exp:* Asst chem, Univ Minn, 46-50; res fel, Calif Inst Technol, 51-52. *Concurrent Pos:* NSF sci fac fel, Cambridge Univ, 61-62; guest scientist, Weizmann Inst, Univ Leyden & Univ Stockholm, 69. *Mem:* Am Chem Soc; Am Crystallog Asn. *Res:* X-ray diffraction by crystals. *Mailing Add:* Dept Chem Univ Conn Storrs CT 06269

KATZ, LEWIS E, physical metallurgy, materials science, for more information see previous edition

KATZ, LOUIS, molecular biology, computer science, for more information see previous edition

KATZ, MANFRED, POLYMER CHEMISTRY, TEXTILE CHEMISTRY. *Current Pos:* CONSULT, 95- *Personal Data:* b Ger, Feb 16, 29; nat US; m 53; c 4. *Educ:* Okla State Univ, BS, 50, MS, 51; Univ Del, PhD, 61. *Prof Exp:* Res supvr, E I Du Pont De Nemours & Co, Inc, 61-67, tech supvr, 67-71, from res assoc to sr res assoc, 71-86, res fel, 86-92; vis prof & dir, Polymer Sci Prog, Howard Univ, 92-95. *Mem:* AAAS; Am Chem Soc; Sci Res Soc Am; NY Acad Sci. *Res:* Condensation polymers; synthetic fibers; non-woven fabrics; composites; carbon fibers. *Mailing Add:* 310 Brockton Rd Sharpley Wilmington DE 19803

KATZ, MARVIN L(AVERNE), CHEMICAL ENGINEERING. *Current Pos:* RETIRED. *Personal Data:* b Tulsa, Okla, Dec 12, 35; m 55; c Laura, Donald & Stephen. *Educ:* Univ Mich, BS, 56, MS, 58, PhD(chem eng), 60. *Prof Exp:* Res engr, Sinclair Res Inc, 60-64, adminr sci comput, 64-69; mgr admin dept, NAm Producing Div, Atlantic Richfield Co, 69-72, mgr res & develop dept, 72-78, vpres res & develop dept, Arco Oil-Gas Co Div, 79-82, vpres planning & eval, 82-84, vpres eng, Arco Oil Gas Co Div, 84-86; vpres eng, Chief Petrol Co, 86-92. *Concurrent Pos:* Chmn, technol task group, Nat

Petrol Coun Comt on enhanced recovery techniques for oil & gas in the US, 76. *Mem:* Soc Petrol Engrs (pres, 80). *Res:* Fluid flow through porous media; heat transfer; computer science. *Mailing Add:* 6924 Leameadow Dallas TX 75248. *E-Mail:* marvdallas@aol.com

KATZ, MAX, FISHERIES. *Current Pos:* AFFIL PROF FISHERIES, UNIV WASH, 73-PRES, ENVIRON INFO SERV INC, 76- *Personal Data:* b Seattle, Wash, Mar 27, 19; m 46; c 4. *Educ:* Univ Wash, Seattle, BS, 39, MS, 42, PhD(fisheries biol), 49. *Prof Exp:* Fisheries biologist, State Dept Fisheries, Wash, 40-42; asst, Inst Paper Chem, Wis, 46-47; from fisheries res biologist to pollution biologist, USPHS, Cincinnati, 49-53, Corvallis, 53-60; actg assoc prof fisheries, Univ Wash, 60-66, res prof, 66-73, dir water resources info ctr, 71-73; res dir, Seattle Marine Labs, Inc, res dir, Parametrix, Inc, 74-76. *Concurrent Pos:* Hon assoc prof, Dept Fish & Game Mgt, Ore State Col, 54-60; consult, Calif Water Pollution Control Bd, 58, Rayonier, Inc, Wash, 59, Northwest Pulp & Paper Asn, 61, off resource develop, USPHS, 62-64, Simpson Timber Co, Wash, 63, Libby, McNeil & Libby, Ill, 63-65, Health Plating Co, Wash, 64-65 & various other companies. *Mem:* Am Fisheries Soc; Am Soc Ichthyol & Herpet; Am Inst Fishery Res Biol; Water Pollution Control Fedn; Marine Biol Asn UK; Sigma Xi. *Res:* Water quality requirements of fish; fish toxicology; biological effects of water pollution; blood parasites of fish; hematology of fish; fish diseases. *Mailing Add:* 730 A Heritage Village Southbury CT 06488-7311

KATZ, MICHAEL, PEDIATRICS, VIROLOGY. *Current Pos:* VPRES RES, MARCH OF DIMES BIRTH DEFECTS FOUND, 92- *Personal Data:* b Lwow, Poland, Feb 13, 28; nat US; m 86, Robin Roy; c Edward Alexander. *Educ:* Univ Pa, AB, 49; State Univ NY, MD, 56; Columbia Univ, MS, 63. *Honors & Awards:* Med Award, Jurzykowski Found, 84; Sr Scientist Award, Humboldt Found, 87. *Prof Exp:* Instr biol, Queen's Col, NY, 51-52; intern, Med Ctr, Univ Calif, Los Angeles, 56-57; resident pediat, Babies Hosp, New York, 60-62; instr, Col Physicians & Surgeons, Columbia Univ, 64-65, prof trop med, 70-92, prof pediat, 71-77, Reuben S Carpenter prof pediat & chmn dept, 77-92; assoc, Sch Med, Univ Pa, 65-66, asst prof, 66-70. *Concurrent Pos:* Hon lectr, Makerere Univ, Uganda & hon pediat specialist, Mulago Hosp, Kampala, Uganda, 63-64; consults, Peace Corps vols, Princeton Univ, 64, WHO, UNICEF & USAID; assoc vis pediatrician, Harlem Hosp Ctr, New York, & asst pediatrician, Babies Hosp, 64-65, assoc mem, Wistar Inst, Philadelphia, 65-70; assoc physician, Children's Hosp Philadelphia, 66-70; attend pediatrician, Presby Hosp, 70-77, dir pediat serv, 77-; mem, Subcomt Interactions Nutrit & Infections, Nat Acad Sci, 71-74, chmn, 74-75, consult, 75-80; vis prof, Inst Virol, Univ Wuerzbuerg, Ger, 88; mem, comt exam adverse effects of vaccines, 90-91; Emer Carpentier prof pediat & pub health, Columbia Univ. *Mem:* Inst Med-Nat Acad Sci; Am Soc Trop Med & Hyg; NY Acad Sci; Am Pediat Soc; Soc Pediat Res; Infectious Dis Soc Am; fel AAAS. *Res:* Relationship of malnutrition to infection; antibody production and other host defense responses in protein deficiency; etiology of diarrhea; rubella and vaccine production; nature of slow virus infections. *Mailing Add:* March of Dimes Birth Defects Found 1275 Mamaroneck Ave White Plains NY 10605. *Fax:* 914-997-4560; *E-Mail:* katzmi@pipeline.com

KATZ, MORRIS HOWARD, FOOD SCIENCE, BIOCHEMISTRY. *Current Pos:* PRES, M H KATZ CONSULT INC, 80- *Personal Data:* b Milwaukee, Wis, Jan 12, 20; m 54, Esther Nissenkoren; c Maynard S & Larry A. *Educ:* Univ Wis, BS, 43. *Prof Exp:* Chemist, Nat Syrup Prod Co, 46-47; chief chemist, Martin Food Prod, Inc, 47-49; asst res dir, Orange Crush Co, 49-52; mfg dir, B A Railton Co, 52-53; flavor res chemist, Fries & Fries, Inc, 53-58; sr chemist, Pillsbury Co, 58-59, head flavor sect, 59-61, sr scientist, 61-68, res assoc res labs, 68-80. *Concurrent Pos:* Guest lectr, Ill Inst Technol, 66 & 70; lectr flavor technol, Ctr Prof Advan, 74 & 76, Univ Minn, 76, Int Microwave Power Inst, 77 & Am Asn Cereal Chemists, 79. *Mem:* Am Chem Soc; Inst Food Technol; Soc Flavor Chemists. *Res:* Flavor chemistry; food texture, ingredient systems and processes; flavor and food products development. *Mailing Add:* 2700 S Yosemite Ave Minneapolis MN 55416-1856

KATZ, MORTON, ORGANIC CHEMISTRY, POLYMER CHEMISTRY. *Current Pos:* res chemist, Buffalo, 67-70, res chemist, Plastic Prod Dept, 70-85, SR RES CHEMIST, E I DU PONT DE NEMOURS & CO, INC, 85- *Personal Data:* b New York, NY, Apr 25, 34; m 61; c 3. *Educ:* State Univ NY Albany, BS, 56, MS, 61; Wayne State Univ, PhD(org chem), 68. *Prof Exp:* Teacher high sch, 56-58; technician, Gen Elec Res Lab, 59-61. *Mem:* Am Chem Soc. *Res:* Chemistry of bicyclic and tricyclic molecules; high temperature polymers; market research. *Mailing Add:* Electronics Dept E I du Pont de Nemours & Co Inc Circleville OH 43113

KATZ, MURRAY ALAN, NEPHROLOGY, MICROCIRCULATORY PATHOPHYSIOLOGY. *Current Pos:* from asst prof to assoc prof, 74-81, PROF NEPHROL, SCH MED, UNIV ARIZ, 81-, PROF PHYSIOL, 87-; ASST CHIEF STAFF RES, TUCSON VET AFFAIRS MED CTR, 82- *Personal Data:* b Albuquerque, NMex, June 15, 41; m 64; c 2. *Educ:* Johns Hopkins Univ, BA, 63, MD, 66. *Prof Exp:* Intern med, Osler Ward Serv, Johns Hopkins Univ Hosp, 66-67, resident, 67-68; fel nephrol, Univ Tex Southwestern Med Sch, 68-70; asst prof, Sch Med, Temple Univ, 71-74, actg chief nephrol, 73-74; Assoc Chief Staff Res, Tucson Vet Affairs Med Ctr, 82- *Concurrent Pos:* Res career develop award, Pub Health Serv, 71-76; clin investr award, Vet Admin, 76; staff physician med & nephrology, Vet Admin Hosp, Tucson, 74-; dir, B W Zweifach Microcirculation Labs, 86- *Mem:* Am Soc Nephrol; Am Fedn Clin Res; AAAS; Microcirculatory Soc; Am Physiol Soc; Int Soc Lymphology; W Soc Clin Invest (pres, 87); W Asn Physicians. *Res:* General microcirculatory physiology and pathophysiology; control of microcirculatory dynamics, hypertension, capillaropathies, vasculitis; diabetes. *Mailing Add:* Dept Internal Med & Physiol Univ Ariz Col Med Vet Admin Med Ctr Res Serv (151) Tucson AZ 85723

KATZ, NORMAN L, PHARMACOLOGY. *Current Pos:* asst prof, 72-81, ASSOC PROF PHARMACOL, UNIV ILL MED CTR, 81- *Personal Data:* b Boston, Mass. *Educ:* Mass Col Pharm, BS, 63; Albany Med Col, Union Univ, PhD(pharmacol), 69. *Prof Exp:* Fel neurophysiol, State Univ NY Albany, 69-72. *Mem:* Soc Neurosci; Am Soc Pharmacol Exp Therapeut. *Res:* Behavioral Pharmacology; regulation of feeding behavior. *Mailing Add:* Dept Pharmacodynamics M/C 865 Univ Ill 833 S Wood St Chicago IL 60612-4324

KATZ, OWEN M, FAILURE ANALYSIS, ELECTRON MICROSCOPY. *Current Pos:* MEM STAFF, BETTIS ATOMIC POWER LAB, ADV SCIENTIST. *Personal Data:* b Baltimore, Md, Dec 21, 32; m 54, Shirley; c 2. *Educ:* Carnegie-Mellon Inst, BS, 54, MS, 58; Univ Pittsburgh, PhD(metall eng), 63. *Concurrent Pos:* Adj prof metall eng, Univ Pittsburgh, 70-75. *Mem:* Fel Am Soc Metals Int; Electron Micros Soc Am; Int Metallog Soc. *Res:* Over 300 published failure analysis reports, over 20 journal articles and book contributions; metallurgy, lab management; microanalytical techniques. *Mailing Add:* Bettis Atomic Power Lab 5600 Munhall Rd No 703 Pittsburgh PA 15217

KATZ, PAUL K, INTERNAL MEDICINE, IMMUNOLOGY. *Current Pos:* ASST PROF MED, & CHIEF, ALLERGY DIV, GEORGETOWN UNIV HOSP, 84- *Educ:* Georgetown Univ, MD, 73. *Mailing Add:* Dept Med Georgetown Univ Hosp 3800 Reservoir Rd NW Washington DC 20007-2197

KATZ, RALPH VERNE, EPIDEMIOLOGY, GERONTOLOGY. *Current Pos:* assoc prof & head, Dept Restorative Dent, 82-89, PROF, DEPT BEHAV SCI & COMMUNITY HEALTH, UNIV CONN, 89- *Personal Data:* b Jersey City, NJ, Mar 20, 44; m 68, B J Frey; c Amos E. *Educ:* Trinity Col, Conn, BS, 65; Tufts Univ, DMD, 69; Univ Minn, MPH, 71, PhD(epidemiol), 76. *Prof Exp:* Chief, Div Prev Dent, Inst Dent Res, US Army, Washington, DC, 74-76; dir dent serv, Phys Med & Rehab Unit, Univ Minn, 72-74, assoc prof, Dept Health Ecol, Sch Dent, 76-82. *Concurrent Pos:* NIH & Nat Res Serv Awards fel, 70-74; assoc prof, Prog Dent Pub Health, Sch Pub Health, Univ Minn, 76-82, Dept Epidemiol, Grad Sch, 78-82, dir & prin investr, Cardiol Training Prog, 80-82, dir grad studies, Oral Health Serv Older Adults, 81-82; co-dir, Oral Epidemiol Training Grant, Nat Inst Dent Res, 85- & Minority Oral Health Res Ctr, 92-; lectr, Dept Epidemiol & Biostatist, Yale Univ. *Mem:* Am Public Health Asn; Int Asn Dent Res; Soc Epidemiol Res; Am Asn Dent Sch; Sigma Xi; fel Am Col Epidemiol. *Res:* Epidimiology of root caries and coronal caries; clinical trials of preventive agents for dental caries; oral health of older adults; cancer chemoprevention trials and risk factors for oral cancer/precancerous lesions. *Mailing Add:* Sch Dent Med Univ Conn Farmington CT 06032. *Fax:* 860-679-1342

KATZ, RANDY H, COMPUTER SCIENCE. *Current Pos:* teaching asst, Univ Calif, Berkeley, 76-77, res asst, 77-80, from asst prof to assoc prof, Comput Sci, 83-89, PROF, COMPUT SCI DIV, ELEC ENG & COMPUT SCI DEPT, UNIV CALIF, BERKELEY, 89-, CHMN, 96- *Personal Data:* b Aug 19, 55; US citizen. *Educ:* Cornell Univ, AB, 76; Univ Calif, Berkeley, MS, 78, PhD(comput sci), 80. *Honors & Awards:* Brice Colloquium Lectr, Rice Univ, 94; Distinguished Serv Award, Comput Res Asn, 95. *Prof Exp:* Consult time-sharing, Cornell Univ, 73-76; comput scientist, Bolt, Beranek and Newman Inc, 80, Comput Corp Am Inc, 80-81; asst prof, Comput Sci Dept, Univ Wis-Madison, 81-83. *Concurrent Pos:* Acad assoc, IBM Res Lab, 78; Consult, Xerox Palo Alto Res Ctr, 82-85, Res Triangle Inst, 83, Digital Equip Corp, 83-87, TMC Ltd, 84, Intermetrics Inc, 84, Tex Instruments Cent Res Lab, 85-86, USAF, 85-87, Microelectronics & Comput Technol Corp, 85, Electronic Design Automation Inc, 86-89, Software Alliance Inc, 88-92, Teknekron Corp, 88-92, Microtechnol Corp, 89-92; distinguished invited lectr, Univ Wis-Madison, 87, Univ Colo, Boulder, 88; prog mgr & dep dir, Comput Systs Technol Off, Advan Res Proj Agency, Dept Defense, 93-94; distinguished prof, Elec Eng & Comput Sci, Microelectronics Corp, 96- *Mem:* Fel Asn Comput Mach; fel Inst Elec & Electronics Engrs. *Res:* Design, implementation and integration of wireless computing systems; collaborative applications; video archive systems. *Mailing Add:* Comput Sci Div EECS Dept Univ Calif 637 Soda Hall Berkeley CA 94720-1776

KATZ, RICHARD WHITMORE, STATISTICS, ATMOSPHERIC SCIENCE. *Current Pos:* ASST PROF, DEPT ATMOSPHERIC SCI, ORE STATE UNIV, 79- *Personal Data:* b Williamsburg, Va, Sept 12, 48. *Educ:* Univ Va, BA, 70; Pa State Univ, PhD(statist), 74. *Honors & Awards:* Spec Achievement Award, Environ Data Serv, 75. *Prof Exp:* Statistician climatic & environ assessment, Environ Data Serv, Nat Oceanic & Atmospheric Admin, 74-75; scientist & statistician environ & societal impacts, Nat Ctr Atmospheric Res, 75-79. *Concurrent Pos:* Fel, Nat Ctr Atmospheric Res, 75-76; consult, NASA, 77; adj prof, Dept Econ, Univ Colo, 77-79; prin investr, NSF grant, 80-; consult, Lawrence Livermore Nat Lab, 81. *Mem:* Am Statist Asn; Inst Math Statist; AAAS; Am Meteorol Soc. *Res:* Meteorological statistics; probabilistic models for hydrological variables; applied probability theory; climatic impacts. *Mailing Add:* Dept Math & Comput Sci Calif State Univ Los Angeles CA 90032-8204

KATZ, ROBERT, PHYSICS. *Current Pos:* vchmn dept, 68-73, EMER PROF PHYSICS, UNIV NEBR, LINCOLN, 66- *Personal Data:* b New York, NY, July 17, 17; div; c Steven J & John H. *Educ:* Brooklyn Col, AB, 37; Columbia Univ, AM, 38; Univ Ill, PhD(physics), 49. *Prof Exp:* Radiologist, US Army Air Force, Wright Field, 39-43, physicist, 43-46; from asst prof to prof, Kans State Univ, 49-66. *Mem:* fel Am Phys Soc; Radiation Res Soc. *Res:* Radiography; precipitation static radio interference; cereal technology; nuclear physics; structure of particle tracks; theory of relative biological effectiveness. *Mailing Add:* 5850 Sunrise Rd Lincoln NE 68510-4049

KATZ, RONALD LEWIS, ANESTHESIOLOGY. *Current Pos:* chmn dept anesthesiol, 73-90, PROF ANESTHESIOL, MED SCH, UNIV CALIF, LOS ANGELES, 73- *Personal Data:* b New York, NY, Apr 22, 32; div; c Richard, Laura & Margaret. *Educ:* Univ Wis, BA, 48; Boston Univ, MD, 52; Am Bd Anesthesiol, dipl, 62; FRCPS, 81. *Prof Exp:* Intern, Staten Island Pub Health Serv, NY, 56-57; resident anesthesiol, Columbia-Presby Med Ctr Hosp, 57-59; instr, Col Physicians & Surgeons, Columbia Univ, 60-61, assoc, 61-62, from asst prof to prof, 62-73. *Concurrent Pos:* Fel pharmacol, Col Physicians & Surgeons, Columbia Univ, 59-60; Guggenheim fel, 68-69; consult, Coun Drugs, AMA, 62-; consult anesthesiol res grant comt, NIH, 65-, mem anesthesiol res training grant comt, 70-; vis prof, Royal Postgrad Med Sch, Univ London, 68-69. *Mem:* Am Soc Anesthesiol; fel Am Col Anesthesiol; Am Soc Pharmacol & Exp Therapeut; Am Physiol Soc; Sigma Xi. *Res:* Physiology; pharmacology; respiratory neurophysiology and neuropharmacology; cardiovascular physiology and pharmacology; neuromuscular transmission. *Mailing Add:* Dept Anesthesiol Univ Calif Sch Med 120 N State St Los Angeles CA 90033. *Fax:* 213-226-2794

KATZ, SAMUEL, GEOPHYSICS. *Current Pos:* from assoc prof to prof, 57-85, chmn dept, 63-68, EMER PROF GEOPHYS, RENSSELAER POLYTECH INST, 86- *Personal Data:* b Berlin, Ger, Feb 13, 23; nat US; m 53, Jean B Parker; c David R, Daniel M & Miriam E. *Educ:* Univ Mich, BS, 43; Columbia Univ, AM, 47, PhD, 55. *Honors & Awards:* Kunz Prize, NY Acad Sci, 53. *Prof Exp:* Mem staff, Radiation Lab, Mass Inst Technol, 43-46; asst, Lamont Geol Observ, Columbia Univ, 48-53; physicist, Stanford Res Inst, 53-56, sr physicist, 56-57. *Mem:* AAAS; Sigma Xi; Am Geophys Union. *Res:* Marine sciences; seismology; underwater sound propagation; high pressure; exploration geophysics. *Mailing Add:* 908 Karenwald Lane Schenectady NY 12309-6416

KATZ, SAMUEL LAWRENCE, VIROLOGY, PEDIATRICS. *Current Pos:* RETIRED. *Personal Data:* b Manchester, NH, May 29, 27; m, Catherine M Wilfert; c Samuel L Jr (deceased), John S, David L, Deborah S, Susan J, Penny J, Rachel A & Catherine C. *Educ:* Dartmouth Col AB, 48; Harvard Univ, MD, 52. *Hon Degrees:* DSc, Georgetown Univ, 96. *Honors & Awards:* Grulee Medal, Am Acad Pediat; Jacobi Award, Am Med Asn & Am Acad Pediat; Saint Geme Award, Am Pediat Soc & Soc Pediat Res; Bristol Award, Infectious Dis Soc Am; Distinguished Physician Award, Pediat Infectious Dis Soc. *Prof Exp:* Intern, Med Serv, Beth Israel Hosp, Boston, Mass, 52-53; jr asst resident, Children's Hosp Med Ctr, 53-54, resident, 55; asst resident, Children's Med Serv, Mass Gen Hosp, 54-55; exchange registr from Children's Hosp Med Ctr to pediat unit, St Mary's Hosp Med Sch, London, 56; instr pediat, Harvard Med Sch, 58-59, assoc, 59-63, tutor med sci, 61-63, asst prof pediat, 63-68; prof pediat & chmn dept, Sch Med, Duke Univ, 68-90, Wilburt C Davison prof, 72-97. *Concurrent Pos:* Nat Found Infantile Paralysis res fel pediat, Res Div Infectious Dis, Children's Hosp Med Ctr, Harvard Med Sch, 56-58; pediatrician-in-chief, Beth Israel Hosp, 58-61; assoc physician, Children's Med Ctr, 58-63, res assoc, Res Div Infectious Dis, 58-68, chief, Newborn Div, 61-68, sr assoc med, 65-68; consult coun drugs, AMA, 63-65; Nat Inst Allergy & Infectious Dis career develop award, 65-68; mem, Vaccine Develop Bd, Nat Inst Allergy & Infectious Dis, 67-71, Armed Forces Epidemiol Bd, Comn Immunization, 69-73, Gen Clin Res Ctr Comt, NIH, 71-74 & Nat Adv Coun Child Health & Human Develop, 74-77; chmn & pres, Asn Med Sch Pediat Dept, 77-79; chmn, adv comt Immunization Pract, USPHS,85-93; chmn bd dir, Burroughs Wellcome Fund, 95- *Mem:* Inst Med-Nat Acad Sci; Infectious Dis Soc Am; Am Asn Immunol; Am Pediat Soc (vpres, 85-86, pres, 86-87); Am Soc Clin Invest; Am Soc Virol; Am Acad Pediat. *Res:* Tissue culture studies of measles virus variants; development of live attenuated measles virus vaccine; central nervous system viral infections; AIDS & human immuno-deficiency virus infections. *Mailing Add:* Dept Pediat Duke Univ Sch Med Box 2925 Durham NC 27710. *Fax:* 919-681-8934; *E-Mail:* katz0004@mc.duke.edu

KATZ, SHELDON LANE, PHYSICS, RADAR SYSTEMS. *Current Pos:* sr mem eng staff, GE-Govt Electronic Systs Div, GE Aerospace, 84-92, PRIN MEM ENG STAFF, GE/MARTIN MARIETTA LOCKHEED MARTIN, GOVT ELECTRONIC SYSTS, MOORESTOWN, NJ, 92- *Personal Data:* b Philadelphia, Pa, Oct 6, 48; m 73, Ruth Rosenfeld; c Michelle, Gary & Jeffrey. *Educ:* Temple Univ, BA, 69, MA, 73, PhD(physics), 77. *Prof Exp:* Lab instr physics, Temple Univ, Philadelphia, 69-74, res asst, 74-77; vis lectr, Lafayette Col, 77-78, asst prof physics, 78-83; asst prof physics, Villanova Univ, 83-84. *Mem:* Am Phys Soc; Inst Elec & Electronics Engrs. *Res:* Dynamics of first and second order phase transitions; renormalization group; Monte Carlo simulations; radar performance analysis; phased array applications to radar meteorology; radar detection of aircraft wake vortices. *Mailing Add:* Lockheed Martin Govt Electronic Syst MS 108-210 Moorestown NJ 08057. *E-Mail:* skatz@motown.ge.com

KATZ, SIDNEY, PHYSICAL CHEMISTRY. *Current Pos:* res phys chemist, Ill Inst Technol Res Inst, 52-58, sci adv, 58-69, sr sci adv, 69-87, TECH CONSULT, IIT RES INST, 87- *Personal Data:* b Winnipeg, Man, Aug 17, 09; US citizen; m 37; c 2. *Educ:* Univ Man, BSc, 34, MSc, 35; McGill Univ, PhD(phys chem), 37. *Prof Exp:* Royal Soc Can traveling fel, London, 37-38; res chemist, British Thompson-Houston Co, Eng, 38-39, Pfanstiehl Chem Co, Ill, 40-41 & Goldsmith Bros, Chicago, 41-44; res assoc, Manhattan proj, 44-45; assoc prof chem, Inst Gas Technol, 45-52. *Concurrent Pos:* Lectr eng, Sci & Mgt War Training, Ill Inst Technol, 42-45. *Mem:* Am Chem Soc; Sigma Xi. *Res:* Light scattering; kinetics of gaseous reactions; kinetics and thermodynamics; spectroscopy; aerosol technology. *Mailing Add:* 5532 SS Shore Dr Apt 19F Chicago IL 60637-1922

KATZ, SIDNEY, PHYSIOLOGY, NEUROPHYSIOLOGY. *Current Pos:* from asst prof to assoc prof, 65-77, PROF PHYSIOL, MED UNIV SC, 77- *Personal Data:* b Brooklyn, NY, Dec 23, 30; m 57. *Educ:* NY Univ, BA, 57, MS, 59, PhD(physiol), 63. *Prof Exp:* Teaching asst neuroanat, Sch Med, NY Univ, 61-62, instr physiol, Col Dent, 62-63. *Concurrent Pos:* Nat Heart Inst fel, 63-65. *Mem:* Am Physiol Soc; Soc Neurosci. *Res:* Central control of respiration and circulation; modulation of medullary neuron discharge patterns; ionic permeabiltiy of muscle studies with electrophysiological methods; electrophysiology of spinal cord injury. *Mailing Add:* Dept Physiol Med Univ SC 171 Ashley Ave Charleston SC 29425-2658

KATZ, SIDNEY, MEDICINE. *Current Pos:* EMER PROF GERIAT, COLUMBIA UNIV, 89- *Personal Data:* b Cleveland, Ohio, Feb 4, 24; m 46; c 4. *Educ:* Case Western Res Univ, MD, 48; Brown Univ, MA, 84; Am Col Epidemiol, cert, 82. *Honors & Awards:* Sidney Katz lectr geriat/geront, Brown Univ; Robert Weiss Award. *Prof Exp:* Intern & resident internal med, Case Western Res Univ, Univ Hosp Cleveland, 48-50, Am Cancer Soc fel path, 50-51, from instr to prof, Dept Prev Med & Med, Sch Med, 52-71; prof med & dir, Off Health Serv Educ & Res, Col Human Med, Mich State Univ, 71-77, prof community health & chmn dept, 78-82; assoc dean med & prof community health & med, Brown Univ, 82-87; prof architectonic & med, Case Western Res Univ, 87-89. *Concurrent Pos:* Assoc dir, Dept Community Health, 69-71, dir, Univ Health Serv, Sch Med, Case Western Res Univ, 66-71; prof, Dept Med, 71-82, dir, Ctr Policy Anal in Aging & Long Term Care, Col Med, Mich State Univ, 80-82; spec adv, White House Conf Aging, 80-81, sr adv, US Prev Serv Task Force, 85-; dir, Long Term Care Geront Ctr, 82-87, assoc, Pop Studies & Training Ctr, Brown Univ, 84-87; consult, Health Care Financing Admin, Nat Ctr Health Statist, Nat Ctr Health Serv Res, Rand Corp, Dykewood Corp, Appl Mgt Sci, Inc, Morgan Mgt Systs, Inc, Geomet, Inc, Urban Inst, Herman Miller Res Corp. *Mem:* Inst Med-Nat Acad Sci; fel Geront Soc; Am Geriatrics Soc; Int Epidemiol Asn; Soc Epidemiol Res; AMA. *Res:* Clinical epidemiology; gerontology; author of 4 books and over 60 journal articles. *Mailing Add:* Stroud Ctr Columbia Univ New York NY 10032

KATZ, SIDNEY A, RADIOCHEMISTRY, ANALYTICAL CHEMISTRY. *Current Pos:* instr, 60-62, from asst prof to assoc prof, 62-71, PROF CHEM, RUTGERS UNIV, 71- *Personal Data:* b Camden, NJ, June 4, 35; m 57; c 2. *Educ:* Rutgers Univ, AB, 58; Univ Pa, PhD(chem), 62. *Prof Exp:* Chemist, R H Hollingshead Corp, 53-58; asst instr chem, Univ Pa, 58-60. *Concurrent Pos:* Res chemist, E I du Pont de Nemours & Co, Inc, 66; res assoc, Univ Pa Hosp, 60-70; prof, Temple Univ, 66-70; vis prof, The Univ, Reading, Berkshire, UK, 73; NATO sr fel sci, NSF, 73; consult, ACCU Test & Consult Lab, 74-75, John G Reutter & Assocs, 74-75, Rossnagel & Assocs, 77-78 & Jack McCormick & Assocs, 78; vis prof, Trace Anal Res Ctr, Dalhousie Univ, 77 & ATOMKI, Hungarian Acad Sci, 84. *Mem:* AAAS; Am Chem Soc; Am Nuclear Soc. *Res:* Environmental and biochemical effects of trace elements. *Mailing Add:* Dept Chem Rutgers Univ Camden NJ 08102

KATZ, SOL, PULMONARY DISEASES. *Current Pos:* Adj clin prof, Georgetown Univ, 45-58, assoc prof, 58-65, dir pulmonary dis, 70-78, PROF LECTR, GEORGETOWN UNIV, 58-, PROF MED & KOBER LECTR, 65-, PROF PULMONARY MED, 78- *Personal Data:* b New York, NY, Mar 29, 13; m 46, Beatrice Paul; c Paul, Rita & Judith. *Educ:* City Col New York, BS, 35; Georgetown Univ, MD, 39; Am Bd Internal Med, dipl, 48. *Hon Degrees:* DSc, Sch Med, Georgetown Univ, 79. *Honors & Awards:* John Maher Mem Laureate Award, Am Col Physicians, 83. *Concurrent Pos:* Chief med serv, Vet Admin Hosp, DC, 59-70; clin prof med, Sch Med, Howard Univ, 67-; consult, NIH, 58-, Children's Hosp, Walter Reed Army Hosp & Bethesda Naval Hosp; vis consult, Cardiothoracic Inst, Brompton Hosp, London, 74-75. *Mem:* Am Thoracic Soc; Am Col Physicians; Am Col Chest Physicians; Am Fedn Clin Res; Brit Thoracic Asn. *Res:* Pulmonary diseases. *Mailing Add:* Georgetown Univ Hosp 3800 Reservoir Rd NW Washington DC 20007-2196

KATZ, STEPHEN I, DERMATOLOGY. *Current Pos:* CHIEF, DERMAT BR, NAT CANCER INST, NIH, 74- *Mem:* Inst Med-Nat Acad Sci. *Mailing Add:* NIH Bldg 10 Rm 12N238 9000 Rockville Pike Bethesda MD 20892. *Fax:* 301-496-5370

KATZ, THOMAS JOSEPH, ORGANIC SYNTHESIS, MECHANISMS OF TRANSFORMATIONS. *Current Pos:* Instr, 59-61, from asst prof to assoc prof, 61-68, PROF CHEM, COLUMBIA UNIV, 68- *Personal Data:* b Prague, Czech, Mar 21, 36; US citizen; m 63, Meta Oehmsen; c Joshua. *Educ:* Univ Wis, BA, 56; Harvard Univ, MA, 57, PhD(chem), 59. *Honors & Awards:* Arthur C Cope Scholar Award, Am Chem Soc. *Concurrent Pos:* Sloan fel, 62-66; Guggenheim fel, 67-68. *Mem:* Am Chem Soc; Royal Soc Chem (UK). *Res:* Non-benzenoid aromatic compounds; organometallic compounds; organic synthesis; catalysis by metals; New materials. *Mailing Add:* Dept Chem Columbia Univ MC 3112 New York NY 10027. *Fax:* 212-932-1289

KATZ, VICTOR JOSEPH, HISTORY OF MATHEMATICS. *Current Pos:* assoc prof, 73-80, PROF MATH UNIV DC, 80- *Personal Data:* b Philadelphia, Pa, Dec 31, 42; m 69, Phyllis Friedman; c Sharon, Ari & Naomi. *Educ:* Princeton Univ, AB, 63; Brandeis Univ, MS, 65, PhD, 68. *Honors & Awards:* Watson Davis Prize, Hist Sci Soc, 95. *Prof Exp:* Asst prof, Fed City Col, 68-73. *Concurrent Pos:* Vis res assoc, Int Hist & Philos Sci, Univ Toronto, 78-79; vis prof, Math Dept, Boston Univ, 85-86; mem coun, Can Soc Hist & Philos Math, 87-89 & 90-92; vis mathematician, Math Asn Am, 94-95; co-prin investr, NSF Grant Inst His Math Use in Teaching, 95- *Mem:* Am Math Soc; Math Asn Am; Hist Sci Soc; Can Soc Hist & Philos Math. *Res:* History of mathematics; application of history to the teaching of mathematics. *Mailing Add:* 841 Bromley St Silver Spring MD 20902-3019. *Fax:* 202-274-5399; *E-Mail:* vkatz@udc.edu

KATZ, WILLIAM, SURFACE ANALYSIS, ION BEAM METHODS. *Current Pos:* OWNER, EVANS CENT, 90-; CO-OWNER, KATZ ANALYTICAL CTR, 91- *Personal Data:* b Dayton, Ohio, Dec 10, 53; m 79. *Educ:* Earlham Col, Richmond, Ind, BA, 75; Univ Ill, Urbana, MS, 77, PhD(anal chem), 79; State Univ NY, Albany, MBA, 86. *Prof Exp:* Res chemist, Exxon Res & Develop Lab, 78-80; mat scientist, Gen Elec, 80-84; mgr anal chem, 84-86; dir labs, Perkin Elmer Corp, 86-90. *Concurrent Pos:* Adj prof physics, State Univ NY, Albany, 81; chmn, Corp Affil Comt, Mat Res Soc. *Mem:* Am Inst Physics; Am Vacuum Soc; Am Chem Soc; Microbeam Anal Soc. *Res:* Application of ion beams for the characterization of electronic materials; ion-solid interactions; sputtering; secondary ionization mechanisms. *Mailing Add:* Katz Anal Ctr 11415 Valley View Rd Eden Prairie MN 55344

KATZ, WILLIAM J(ACOB), SANITARY & CHEMICAL ENGINEERING. *Current Pos:* CONSULT, 92- *Personal Data:* b Chicago, Ill, Jan 19, 25; m 48; c 3. *Educ:* Univ Ill, BS, 48; Univ Wis, MS, 49, PhD(chem eng), 53. *Honors & Awards:* Eddy Medal, Water Pollution Control Fedn, 55, Gascoigne Medal. *Prof Exp:* Proj assoc indust waste & treatment, Univ Wis, 49-52; dir sanit & indust wastes res & consult, Envirex Inc Div, Rexnord Inc, 53-63, tech dir & mgr water treatment & water pollution control res, 63-70, mgr, Ecol Div, Rex Chainbelt Inc Div, 70-75, vpres res & develop, Envirex Inc, 76-77; dir tech serv, Milwaukee Metrop Sewerage Dist, 77-81; pres, Environ Planning & Sci Div, Camp Dresser & McKee Inc, 81-92; pres, WJK Assocs, Ltd, 81-92. *Concurrent Pos:* Vis prof civil eng, Univ Wis, 65-67; adj prof civil eng, Marquette Univ. *Mem:* Water Pollution Control Fedn; Nat Soc Prof Engrs; Am Soc Civil Engrs; Am Inst Chem Engrs; Am Water Works Asn. *Res:* Water and industrial waste treatment; packing plant; mechanism of activated sludge; foundries; refineries. *Mailing Add:* 220 W Cherokee Circle Milwaukee WI 53217

KATZ, YALE H, METEOROLOGY. *Current Pos:* DIR, INST FOR TECHNOL COMMUNICATION, 82- *Personal Data:* b Milwaukee, Wis, Mar 15, 20; m 45, Rosella Joseph; c Donald S & Maxine R. *Educ:* Univ Wis, BS, 47, MS, 48; Pa State Col, MS, 51. *Prof Exp:* Asst, Univ Wis, 47-48; meteorologist, USAF Air Weather Serv, 51, specialist climatic res, 52-54, tech consult, 54-56; res assoc, Phys Res Labs, Univ Boston, 56-57; sr staff meteorologist, Itek Corp, 58-60; phys scientist, Rand Corp, Calif, 60-67; sr staff mem, TRW Systs Group, Redondo Beach, 67-73, sr systs engr, 73-76; dir, Appl Res Assocs, 76-77; tech dir, Soc Photo-Optical Instrumentation Engrs, 77-81; dir, Ctr Continuing Prof Educ & Training, Santa Barbara, Calif, 82-84. *Concurrent Pos:* Partner & assoc, Appl Res Assocs, 54-60, 76-77; lectr, Univ Chicago, 54; Air Force Sr Technol Specialist Sch, Mather AFB, 56, MIT, 56, Univ Calif, Los Angeles, 61, 63 & 65 & Univ Calif, San Diego, 70; ed, J Soc Photo-Optical Instrumentation Engrs, 70-72, assoc ed, Optical Eng, 72-78. *Mem:* Am Meteorol Soc; Am Geophys Union; fel Soc Photo-Optical Instrument Engrs (vpres, 71-75, gov, 70-71 & 75); Coun Eng Sci Soc Execs. *Res:* Development of educational programs for medical, legal and industrial professionals; applied optical and electro-optical engineering; environmental engineering; atmospheric pollution; statistical meteorology and climatology; solar energy utilization. *Mailing Add:* 2800 Woodridge Dr Bellingham WA 98226

KATZBERG, ALLAN ALFRED, ANATOMY. *Current Pos:* from assoc prof to prof, 69-83, EMER PROF ANAT, MED CTR, IND UNIV-PURDUE UNIV, INDIANAPOLIS, 83- *Personal Data:* b Can, July 6, 13; nat US; m 48, Betty J Bainbridge; c Allan, Susan, Mary L & Lynne. *Educ:* Univ Man, BSc, 43; Inst Divi Thomae, MS, 49; Univ Okla, PhD(med sci), 56. *Hon Degrees:* DSc, St Thomas Inst, 86. *Honors & Awards:* Eli Lilly Award, 72. *Prof Exp:* Instr histol & embryol, Sch Med, Univ Okla, 49-51, from instr to asst prof anat, 51-59; res assoc prof & head cellular biol sect, Aerospace Med Ctr, USAF, Brooks AFB, TX, 59-63, dep chief, Astrobiol Div, 60-63; assoc prof physiol, Med Sch, Univ Sask, 63-64; head anat div, Southwest Found for Res & Educ, 64-65, chmn dept, 65-68; assoc prof biol, Western Ill Univ, 68-69. *Concurrent Pos:* Consult, Arctic Aeromed Lab, USAF, 61, Fed Aviation Admin-USAF 6571st Aeromed Res Lab, Holloman AFB & Ford Motor Co, 67; actg chmn dept anat, Ind Univ-Purdue Univ, Indianapolis, 70-71. *Mem:* AAAS; Am Asn Anat; no mem Mex Soc Anat; fel Royal Micros Soc; Int Primatol Soc; Pan-Am Asn Anat. *Res:* Aging processes; tissue culture; regeneration; aerospace medicine; primate histology; cardiac muscle. *Mailing Add:* 944 E Main St Carmel IN 46032

KATZE, JON R, NEOPLASIA, Q NUCLEOSIDE. *Current Pos:* assoc prof microbiol & immunol, 76-83, PROF MICROBIOL & IMMUNOL, UNIV TENN, MEMPHIS, 83- *Personal Data:* b Portland, Ore, Nov 21, 39; m 82, Kathryn Altman; c Kendall, Prudence & Jack. *Educ:* Univ Calif, Berkeley, BS, 61, Univ Calif, Los Angeles, PhD(physiol chem), 66. *Prof Exp:* Postdoctoral biochem, Yale Univ, 66-69; asst prof microbiol, Univ Southern Calif, 69-76. *Mem:* AAAS; Am Soc Microbiol; Am Soc Biochem & Molecular Biol. *Res:* The association of defective Q nucleoside metabolism with neoplasia; the linkage of Q deficiency with tumor promotion; the wide distribution of Q base in the biosphere but absence of synthesis in eukaryotes. *Mailing Add:* Dept Microbiol & Immunol Univ Tenn 858 Madison Ave Memphis TN 38163-2129. *Fax:* 901-448-8462

KATZEN, RAPHAEL, CHEMICAL ENGINEERING. *Current Pos:* prin chem process, 53, pres consult & design, 53-96, CHMN, RAPHAEL KATZEN ASSOCS INT, INC, 96- *Personal Data:* b Baltimore, Md, July 28, 15; m 38; c 1. *Educ:* Polytech Inst Brooklyn, BChE, 36, MChE, 38, DChE(chem eng), 42. *Honors & Awards:* Chem Eng Prof Pract Award, Am Inst Chem Engrs, 86, Robert L Jacks Mem Award, 90; C D Scott Award, 97. *Prof Exp:* Dir res, Chem Prod, Northwood Chem Co, 37-40, tech supvr res & develop, Diamond Alkali Co, 42-44; proj mgr chem plant & mgr design & construct, Eng Div, Vulcan-Cincinnati, 44-53. *Concurrent Pos:* Mem adv bd, Expos Chem Indust, 55-; mem nat panel, Am Arbit Asn, 70-; instr chem eng, Polytech Inst Brooklyn. *Mem:* Nat Acad Eng; fel Am Inst Chem Engrs; fel Am Inst Chemists; Tech Asn Pulp & Paper Indust; Can Pulp & Paper Asn; fel Am Chem Soc. *Res:* Organosolv pulping process; new technology for enzymatic conversion of cellulosic materials to sugar and ethanol; advanced technology in scrubbing and recovery of sulfur dioxide emmissions; biomass conversion to fuels and chemicals technology. *Mailing Add:* Raphael Katzen Assocs Int Inc 2300 Wall St Suite K Cincinnati OH 45212-2783

KATZENELLENBOGEN, BENITA SCHULMAN, REPRODUCTIVE ENDOCRINOLOGY, CANCER BIOLOGY. *Current Pos:* NIH res fel endocrinol, Dept Physiol & Biophys, 70-71, from assoc prof to prof, 70-82, PROF PHYSIOL, CELL & STRUCT BIOL, COL MED, UNIV ILL, PHYSIOL & BIOPHYS, URBANA, 82- *Personal Data:* b New York, NY, Apr 11, 45; m 67, John A; c Deborah J & Rachel A. *Educ:* Brooklyn Col, BA, 65; Harvard Univ, MA, 66, PhD(biol), 70. *Honors & Awards:* Ernst Oppenheimer Mem Award, Endocrine Soc; Nat Young Scholar Award, Am Asn Univ Women, 81; Breast Cancer Res Award, Susan G Komen Found, 88 & 93; Merit Award, NIH, 91. *Concurrent Pos:* Vis prof, Dept Biochem & Biophys, Univ Calif, San Francisco, 77-78; endocrinol study sect, NIH, 79-83, NIH-Nat Inst Diabetes & Digestive & Kidney Dis Bd Sci Counselors, 85-89; publications comt, Endocrine Soc, 81-83, prog comt, 83-87; int org comt, Int Cong on Hormones & Cancer, 87-; Am Asn Cancer Res Task Force Endocrinol, 87-89; co-chmn Gordon Res Conf Hormone Action, 88; mem, Cent Comt, Int Soc Endocrinol, 88-96; mem adv comt, Biochem & Endocrinol, Am Cancer Soc, 89-93; mem coun, Endocrine Soc, 89-92; mem, Waterman Award Comt, NSF, 89-91. *Mem:* Am Physiol Soc; Endocrine Soc; Am Asn Cancer Res; Soc Study Reproduction; fel Am Acad Arts & Sci. *Res:* Regulation of the growth and function of reproductive tissues and tumors, especially breast cancer, by reproductive hormones and antihormones. *Mailing Add:* Dept Physiol & Biophys Univ Ill 524 Burrill Hall 407 S Goodwin Ave Urbana IL 61801-3704. *Fax:* 217-244-9906

KATZENELLENBOGEN, JOHN ALBERT, BIO-ORGANIC CHEMISTRY, SYNTHETIC ORGANIC CHEMISTRY. *Current Pos:* From asst prof to assoc prof, 69-79, PROF CHEM, UNIV ILL, URBANA, 79- *Personal Data:* b Poughkeepsie, NY, May 10, 44; m 67, Benita Schulman; c Deborah J & Rachel A. *Educ:* Harvard Univ, BA, 66, MA, 67, PhD(chem), 69. *Honors & Awards:* Teacher Scholar Award, Camille & Henry Dreyfus Found, 74-79; Paul C Abersold Award, Soc Nuclear Med, 95. *Concurrent Pos:* Sloan fel, 74-76; Guggenheim fel, 77-78; chmn, study sect, NIH. *Mem:* Fel AAAS; Am Chem Soc; NY Acad Sci; Am Soc Biol Chemists; fel Am Acad Arts & Sci; Soc Nuclear Med. *Res:* New synthetic methods; organometallic chemistry; natural product synthesis; mechanism of hormone action; affinity labeling; tumor localizing agents; radiopharmaceutical development; fluorescence; enzyme inhibitors; steroids; hormone receptors. *Mailing Add:* Sch Chem Sci Univ Ill 600 S Mathews Ave Urbana IL 61801. *Fax:* 217-333-7325; *E-Mail:* jkatzene@uiuc.edu

KATZIN, GERALD HOWARD, PHYSICS. *Current Pos:* from asst prof to assoc prof, 63-76 PROF PHYSICS, NC STATE UNIV, 76- *Personal Data:* b Winston-Salem, NC, Aug 2, 32; m 58; c 2. *Educ:* NC State Univ, BS, 54, MS, 56, PhD(relativity), 63. *Prof Exp:* Assoc nuclear reactor theory, Astra, Inc, Conn, 57-58. *Concurrent Pos:* NSF grant, 67. *Mem:* Am Phys Soc. *Res:* Study of the relations between symmetries and conservation laws; theoretical mechanics; Riemannian geometry and tensor analysis; differential geometry; general relativity; classical electrodynamics. *Mailing Add:* Dept Physics NC State Univ Raleigh NC 27695-8202

KATZIN, LEONARD ISAAC, PHYSICAL INORGANIC CHEMISTRY. *Current Pos:* RETIRED. *Personal Data:* b Eau Claire, Wis, Jan 18, 15; m 38, Alice Ginsburg; c Ruth N (Johnston), Martha R (Simon), Lisbeth E (Unger) & Judith H (Kaplan). *Educ:* Univ Calif, Los Angeles, AB, 35; Univ Calif, PhD(phys chem biol), 38. *Prof Exp:* Asst zool, Univ Calif, 35-37, fel, 38-40; jr biologist, USPHS, 40-41, asst biologist, 41-42; fel radiol, Sch Med & Dent, Univ Rochester, 42-43; res assoc, Metall Lab, Univ Chicago, 43-46; sr chemist, Argonne Nat Lab, 46-78. *Concurrent Pos:* Vis prof, Univ Chicago, 56-57; exchange fel, Atomic Energy Res Estab, Harwell, Eng, 58-59; exten lectr, Univ Ill, 61; vis prof inorg chem, Hebrew Univ Jerusalem, 69-70 & Inst Chem, Tel Aviv Univ, 69-70. *Mem:* AAAS; Am Phys Soc; Am Chem Soc; Sigma Xi. *Res:* Nuclear chemistry; heavy element chemistry; optical rotation; coordination chemistry; nuclear waste management. *Mailing Add:* 428 Hudson Lane Port Hueneme CA 93041-2140. *E-Mail:* 70053.1066@compuserve.com

KATZMAN, PHILIP AARON, BIOCHEMISTRY. *Current Pos:* Res instr, 32-36, sr instr, 36-41, from asst prof to prof, 41-74, EMER PROF BIOCHEM, MED SCH, ST LOUIS UNIV, 74- *Personal Data:* b Omaha, Nebr, May 18, 06; m 33; c 2. *Educ:* Kalamazoo Col, AB, 27; St Louis Univ, PhD(biochem), 32. *Concurrent Pos:* US Pharmacopoeia Comt, 40-50; lectr, Univ Kans, 52; Merck Sharpe & Dohme vis prof, Univ SDak, 63. *Mem:* AAAS; Am Soc Biol Chem; Am Chem Soc; Endocrine Soc; Soc Study Reproduction. *Res:* Chorionic gonadotropin; reproduction; antihormones; antibiotics; hydrolysis of conjugated steroids; biological properties of estrogens; molecular action of ovarian hormones. *Mailing Add:* One McKnight Pl No 144 St Louis Sch Med St Louis MO 63124

KATZMAN, ROBERT, NEUROLOGY. *Current Pos:* chair dept, 84-90, prof, 84-94, RES PROF NEUROSCI, UNIV CALIF, SAN DIEGO, 95- *Personal Data:* b Denver, Colo, Nov 29, 25; m 47; c 2. *Educ:* Univ Chicago, BS, 49, MS, 51; Harvard Med Sch, MD, 53; Am Bd Psychiat & Neurol, dipl & cert neurol, 59. *Honors & Awards:* S Weir Mitchell Award, Am Acad Neurol, 60; Potamkin Prize, co-recipient, 92; Ann Prize, Am Asn Neuropathologists, 62; Humanitarian Award & Allied Achievement Aging Award, Alzheimer's Dis & Related Dis Asn, 85; Henderson Mem Award, Geriat Soc, 86; George W Jacoby Award, Am Neurol Asn, 89; Distinguished Serv Award, Alzheimer's Asn, 89. *Prof Exp:* Intern, Harvard Med Serv, Boston City Hosp, 53-54; asst resident neurol, Neurol Inst, Columbia Presby Hosp, 54-56, chief resident neurologist, 56-57; instr neurol, Albert Einstein Col Med, 57-58, assoc, 58-60, from asst prof to prof, 60-84, chmn dept, 64-81, dir, Hosp, 74-84. *Concurrent Pos:* Nat Mult Sclerosis Soc fel, 57-59; USPHS sr fel neurophysiol, 61-62, USPHS career res develop award, 62-66; asst neurol, Columbia Univ, 56-57; guest scholar, Polytech Inst Brooklyn, 60-61; consult, Jewish Bd Guardians, 61-65; assoc attend neurologist, Bronx Munic Hosp Ctr, 62-64, attend neurologist, 64-84, dir neurol serv, 70-84; mem res rev panel, Nat Mult Sclerosis Soc, 64-70; asst examr, Am Bd Psychiat & Neurol, 63-70; chair, Neurochem Sect, Am Acad Neurol, 65-67; consult, Montefiore Hosp & Med Ctr, 66-82, attend neurologist, 82-84; mem, Neurol Prog Proj A Comn, Nat Inst Neurol & Commun Dis & Stroke, 69-72, chmn, Neurol Dis Prog Proj Rev Comt, 72-73, mem, Aging Rev Comt, 76-81, chmn, 80-81; mem, adv coun, Nat Inst Aging, 82-85, Adv Bd Alzheimer's Dis, US Cong, 87 & Adv Panel Alzheimer's Dis, Dept Health & Human Serv, 87-93; Florence Riford prof res, Alzheimer's Dis, Sch Med, Univ Calif, San Diego, 84-90, attend neurologist, San Diego Med Ctr & San Diego Vet Admin Med Ctr, 84-95. *Mem:* Inst Med-Nat Acad Sci; fel AAAS; fel Am Acad Neurol; Am Asn Neuropathologists; In Soc Neurochem; Soc Neurosci; Am Neurol Asn (pres, 84-85); Int Soc Alzheimer's Dis Res (pres 96-97). *Res:* Epidemiology, clinical-pathological correlation and risk factors for Alzheimer's Disease. *Mailing Add:* Dept Neurosci Univ Calif San Diego 9500 Gilman Dr La Jolla CA 92093-0949. *Fax:* 619-622-1016

KATZMANN, FRED L, ELECTRONICS. *Current Pos:* RETIRED. *Personal Data:* b Magdeburg, Ger, Apr 10, 29; US citizen; m 55; c 3. *Educ:* City Col New York, BEE, 52; Stevens Inst Technol, MSc, 62. *Prof Exp:* Res eng, Allen B DuMont Labs Div, Fairchild Camera & Instrument Corp, 52-59, eng mgr, Corp, 59-65; dir electronic instruments dept, Electronic Prod & Controls Div, Monsanto Co, 66-69, dir & gen mgr, 69-70; vpres mkt, Electronic Prods Div, Singer Co, 70-71; pres, Ballantine Labs, Inc, 71-89. *Mem:* Inst Elec & Electronics Engrs; Precision Measurement Asn; Int Standards Asn; Instrument Soc Am. *Res:* Electronic instrumentation, particularly oscilloscopes, voltmeters and digital frequency counters, ultra fast transient recording instrumentation systems and precise alternating current measurements. *Mailing Add:* Montclair Sci Instruments PO Box 182 Cedar Grove NJ 07009

KATZOFF, SAMUEL, AERODYNAMICS. *Current Pos:* RETIRED. *Personal Data:* b Baltimore, Md, Aug 3, 09. *Educ:* Johns Hopkins Univ, BS, 29, PhD(chem), 34. *Prof Exp:* Lab technician, Rockefeller Inst, 29-30; res chemist, Baltimore Paint & Color Works, 34-53; Jones fel biophys, Cold Spring Harbor, 35-36; physicist, Nat Adv Comt Aeronaut, NASA, 36-58, res scientist, 58-60, asst chief, Appl Mat & Physics Div, 60-64, from sr staff scientist to chief scientist, Langley Res Ctr, 64-72. *Concurrent Pos:* Ed, Proc Symposium Thermal Radiation Solids, 64 & Remote Measurement Pollution, 71; instr, Gifted Children, Hampton, Va, & John Hopkins Univ, 72- *Mem:* AAAS. *Res:* X-ray crystallography; x-ray studies of the molecular arrangements in liquids; colloids; general aerodynamics; stability; electrical analogies; wind-tunnel interference; cascades; helicopters; space sciences; thermal control of spacecraft. *Mailing Add:* 725 Mt Wilson Lane No 424 Baltimore MD 21208

KATZUNG, BERTRAM GEORGE, PHARMACOLOGY, MEDICINE. *Current Pos:* Lectr, Univ Calif, San Francisco, 60-62, from asst prof to assoc prof, 62-71, act chmn, 80-83, PROF PHARMACOL, MED CTR, UNIV CALIF, SAN FRANCISCO, 71-, VCHMN DEPT, 67- *Personal Data:* b Floral Park, NY, June 11, 32; m 57, Alice Camp; c Katharine & Brian. *Educ:* Syracuse Univ, BA, 53; State Univ NY, MD, 57; Univ Calif, PhD, 62. *Concurrent Pos:* Ed, Basic & Clin Pharmacol; Markle Scholar, 66-71; guest lectr, Sch Med, Stanford Univ, Univ Hawaii & Univ Calif, Berkeley. *Mem:* AAAS; Am Soc Pharmacol & Exp Therapeut; Biophys Soc; Soc Gen Physiologists; NY Acad Sci. *Res:* Cardiovascular pharmacology; electrophysiology; author and editor of 3 books. *Mailing Add:* 65 Knoll Rd San Rafael CA 94901-3626

KAUDER, OTTO SAMUEL, ORGANIC CHEMISTRY. *Current Pos:* chemist plastics additives, 52-59, res group leader, 59-68, patent liaison & toxicol supvr, 62-68, vpres res & develop, 68-79, TECH VPRES, ARGUS CHEM CORP, 79- *Personal Data:* b Vienna, Austria, Nov 26, 26; US citizen; m 56; c 2. *Educ:* City Col New York, BS, 46; Polytech Inst Brooklyn, MS, 49; Oxford Univ, DPhil(org chem), 52. *Prof Exp:* Chemist, Polychem Labs, NY, 46-48. *Mem:* Am Chem Soc. *Res:* Time-dependent properties of organic compounds and effect of additives and contaminants thereon; synthesis of organic compounds containing phosphorus, cadmium, tin and antimony. *Mailing Add:* 5382-C Venetia Ct Boynton Beach FL 33437-2113

KAUER, JAMES CHARLES, ORGANIC CHEMISTRY, NEUROCHEMISTRY. *Current Pos:* dir chem, 88-93, VPRES CHEM TECHNOL, CEPHALON INC, 94- *Personal Data:* b Cleveland, Ohio, Jan 17, 27; m 54; c Julie, Catherine, James, Frederic & Susanne. *Educ:* Case Western Res Univ, BS, 51; Univ Ill, PhD(chem), 55. *Prof Exp:* Res chemist, E I du Pont de Nemours & Co, Inc, 55-85, prin investr med chem, Dupont, 85-87. *Mem:* Am Chem Soc; Soc Neurosci; AAAS. *Res:* Organic synthesis; heterocycles; peptides; antiviral agents; neurotransmitter analogs; Neuropeptides; growth factors; enzyme inhibitors. *Mailing Add:* Savorys Mill Rd Kennett Square PA 19348. *E-Mail:* kauer@shrys.hslc.org

KAUER, JOHN STUART, SENSORY PHYSIOLOGY. *Current Pos:* prof neurosci, anat & cell biol & dir neurosurg res, 83-93, PROF NEUROSCI, NEW ENG MED CTR, TUFTS UNIV MED SCH, 93- *Personal Data:* b New York, NY, Dec 26, 43; m 85, Barbara R Talamo; c Jane & Joshua. *Educ:* Clark Univ, BA, 67, MA, 69; Univ Pa, PhD(anat), 73. *Honors & Awards:* Javits Award, NIH. *Prof Exp:* Fel neurophysiol, Sch Med, Yale Univ, 73-75, res assoc & dir lab studies, 76-78, asst prof, Sect Neurosurg, 78-80. *Mem:* Soc Neurosci; Am Asn Anatomists; Asn Chemoreception Sci; Europ Chemoreception Res Orgn. *Res:* Central synaptic organization of the olfactory and other sensory systems; mathematical models of neurophysiology; artificial olfactory systems. *Mailing Add:* Tufts Univ Med Sch Dept Neurosci 136 Harrison Ave Boston MA 02111. *E-Mail:* jkauer@pearl.tufts.edu

KAUFERT, JOSEPH MOSSMAN, MEDICAL ANTHROPOLOGY. *Current Pos:* PROF COMMUNITY MED, COMMUNITY HEALTH SCIS, FAC MED, UNIV MAN, 76- *Personal Data:* b Minneapolis, Minn, Feb 10, 43; m 70; c 1. *Educ:* Univ Minn, BA, 66; Northwestern Univ, MA, 68, PhD(polit sci, anthrop), 73. *Honors & Awards:* Keith L Were Award, Nat Media Develop Trust, 72. *Prof Exp:* Asst prof health admin, Baylor Univ, 71-72; asst prof med sociol & social psychiat, Med Sch, Univ Tex, San Antonio, 72-74; head soc sci sect, St Thomas Hosp Med Sch, Univ London, 74-76. *Concurrent Pos:* Leverhulme fel, Univ Birmingham, 73-74; consult, Welsh Off, Brit Health & Social Serv, UK, 74-76, Nat Haemophilia Soc UK, 74-76 & Ment Health Man, 77-78; adj prof, Dept Anthrop, Univ Man, 77-, prof, Dept Social & Prev Med, 85; vis health scientist, Univ Toronto, 85; vis prof Can Studies, Leeds Univ. *Mem:* Soc Social Med; fel Soc Appl Anthrop; Brit Sociol Asn; Soc Med Anthrop; Can Asn Med Anthrop (pres). *Res:* Social epidemiology; medical sociology; illness behavior; the sociology of disability; social gerontology. *Mailing Add:* Dept Community Health Sci Fac Med Univ Man Winnipeg MB R3T 2N2 Can. *Fax:* 204-772-8748

KAUFFELD, NORBERT M, entomology, apiculture, for more information see previous edition

KAUFFMAN, CAROL A, INFECTIOUS DISEASES, HOST-DEFENSE MECHANISMS. *Current Pos:* asst dean student affairs, 86-91, PROF MED, UNIV MICH, 81-; CHIEF, DIV INFECTIOUS DIS, VET ADMIN MED CTR, ANN ARBOR, MICH, 77- *Personal Data:* b Columbia, Pa, Oct 9, 43. *Educ:* Penn State Univ, BS, 65; Univ Mich, MD, 69. *Mem:* Am Asn Immunologists; Infectious Dis Soc Am; Am Soc Microbiol; Am Fedn Clin Res; Am Col Physicians; Cent Soc Clin Res. *Res:* Infections in the elderly; effects of aging and malnutrition in fabrile response to infection; antifungal therapy. *Mailing Add:* Vet Admin Med Ctr 2215 Fuller Rd Ann Arbor MI 48105. *Fax:* 313-769-7039

KAUFFMAN, ELLWOOD, DIGITAL COMPUTER PROGRAMMING, COMPUTER APPLICATIONS. *Current Pos:* PRES, MAINTENANCE DATABASE SYSTS, INC, 85-, DIR, PARHAM GROUP, 88- *Personal Data:* b Philadelphia, Pa, Mar 18, 28; m 50, Shirley Rosengarten; c Scott L, Geoffrey N, Jane R & Matthew W. *Educ:* Temple Univ, AB, 52. *Prof Exp:* Sr analyst, Remington Rand, Inc, NY, 52-55; comput applns officer, Chesapeake & Ohio Rwy Co, Va, 55-57; sr programmer digital comput, Elec Assocs, Inc, 57-58; comput consult, 58-59; pres, Appl Data Res, Inc, 59-63 & Comput Mgt Corp, 63-65; tech dir, Mgt Info Systs, Inc, 65-69; exec vpres, Mainstem, Inc, 65-78; exec vpres, K-Squared Systs, Inc, 78-84. *Mem:* Am Pub Work Asn. *Res:* Utility concept of computer problem solving; application of digital computing systems to the solutions of commercial and scientific problems; automatic programming procedures for digital computers; application of mainframe, mini- & personal computers to maintenance management applications. *Mailing Add:* 148 Library Pl Princeton NJ 08540

KAUFFMAN, ERLE GALEN, PALEOBIOLOGY, PALEOECOLOGY. *Current Pos:* AT GEOL SCI STOP, UNIV COLO, BOULDER. *Personal Data:* b Washington, DC, Feb 9, 33; m 56; c 3. *Educ:* Univ Mich, BS, 55, MS, 56, PhD(geol, paleont, stratig), 61. *Hon Degrees:* MS, Oxford Univ, 70. *Prof Exp:* Asst cur, US Nat Mus, Smithsonian Inst 60-61, assoc cur, 61-67, cur dept paleobiol, 67- *Concurrent Pos:* Lectr, George Washington Univ, 63-64, adj prof, 65-; NSF res grant, 63-71; Am Geol Inst vis lectr, 65-66; Smithsonian Res Found grants, 65-; Paleont Soc rep, Comt Earth Sci, Nat Res Coun-Nat Acad Sci, 65-71; vis prof, Oxford Univ, 70-71, Univ Tubingen, 74 & Univ Colo, 76-78; res assoc, Mus Paleontol, Univ Mich, 75-; adj prof, Univ Colo, 76- *Mem:* AAAS; Brit Palaeont Asn; Malacol Soc London; Int Palaeont Union; Paleont Soc. *Res:* Systematics, evolution and paleoecology of Mesozoic-Cenozoic Mollusca; ecology of Recent Mollusca; Mesozoic-Cenozoic stratigraphy, biostratigraphy and sedimentation. *Mailing Add:* Dept Geol Sci Ind Univ 1005 E Tenth St Bloomington IN 47405

KAUFFMAN, FREDERICK C, BIOCHEMISTRY, PHARMACOLOGY. *Current Pos:* DISTINGUISHED PROF PHARMACOL TOXICOL, RUTGERS UNIV, 88- *Personal Data:* b Chicago, Ill, July 9, 36; m 61; c 2. *Educ:* Knox Col, Ill, BA, 58; Univ Ill, Chicago, PhD(pharmacol), 65. *Prof Exp:* Asst prof & assoc pharmacol, SU NY, Buffalo, 67-74; assoc prof, 74-78, prof pharmacol, Sch Med, Univ MD, Baltimore, 78-88. *Concurrent Pos:* USPHS fel pharmacol, Wash Univ, 65-67. *Mem:* AAAS; Am Chem Soc; Am Toxicol Soc; Am Pharmacol Soc. *Res:* Biochemical pharmacology; neurochemistry. *Mailing Add:* Rutgers Univ 41 Gordon Rd Piscataway NJ 08854-5930. *Fax:* 732-445-6905

KAUFFMAN, GEORGE BERNARD, INORGANIC CHEMISTRY, HISTORY OF SCIENCE. *Current Pos:* from asst prof to assoc prof, 56-66, PROF CHEM, CALIF STATE UNIV, FRESNO, 66- *Personal Data:* b Philadelphia, Pa, Sept 4, 30; m 52, 69, Laurie Marks; c Ruth D (Bryskier), Judith M (Reposo), Robert Papazian, Teresa L (Baron) & Mary E (Yoder). *Educ:* Univ Pa, BA, 51; Univ Fla, PhD(chem), 56. *Honors & Awards:* Lev Aleksandrovich Chugaev Jubilee Dipl & Bronze Medal, USSR Acad Sci, 76; Nikolai Semenovich Kurnakov Jubilee Dipl & Bronze Medal, 90, Ilya Ilyich Chernyaev Jubilee Dipl & Bronze Medal, 91; Catalyst Award, Mfg Chemists Asn, 76; Dexter Award Hist of Chem, 78; Marc-Auguste Pictet Medal, Physics Soc Natural Hist Geneve, 92; George C Pimentel Award Chem Educ, Am Chem Soc, 93. *Prof Exp:* Asst chem, Univ Fla, 51-55; instr, Univ Tex, 55-56. *Concurrent Pos:* Res corp grant, 55, 57, 59 & 69; NSF res grants, 60 & 67-69, Zurich, 63 & Berkeley, 76-77; chmn, Div Hist Chem, Am Chem Soc, 69; Am Chem Soc Petrol Res Fund grant, 62 & 65; Am Philos Soc grant, 63 & 69; tour speaker, Am Chem Soc, 71; fel, John Simon Guggenheim Mem Found, 72-73, grant, 75; NSF undergrad res partic dir, 72; contributing ed, J Col Sci Teaching, 73-; co-ed, Topics Hist Chem, Lectures on Tape Series, Am Chem Soc, 75-78, ed, 78-81; vis scholar, Univ Calif, Berkeley, 76 & Univ Puget Sound, 78; contrib ed, The Hexagon, 80-, Polyhedron, 82-85, Indust Chemist, 85, J Chem Educ, 87- & Today's Chemist, 89-91, Today's Chemist at Work, 95-, Chem Heritage, 96-; Nat Endowment Humanities grant, 82-83; Strindberg fel, Svenska Inst, 82-83. *Mem:* AAAS; Am Chem Soc; Hist Sci Soc; Soc Study Alchemy & Chem; Sigma Xi. *Res:* Inorganic synthesis; stereochemistry; coordination compounds; chromatography separations; ion exchange; platinum metals; lanthanides; chemical education; unusual oxidation states; history of chemistry; biographies of chemists; translations of classics of chemistry. *Mailing Add:* Dept Chem Calif State Univ Fresno CA 93740-0070. *Fax:* 209-278-7139, 278-4402; *E-Mail:* george_k@csofresno.edu

KAUFFMAN, GLENN MONROE, PHYSICAL ORGANIC CHEMISTRY. *Current Pos:* PROF CHEM, EASTERN MENNONITE COL, 65-, CHMN DEPT, 66- *Personal Data:* b Goshen, Ind, Apr 8, 38. *Educ:* Goshen Col, BA, 61; Univ Pa, PhD(org chem), 66. *Concurrent Pos:* Acad exten grant, Univ Fla & Eastern Mennonite Col, 68-70; Res Corp res grant, Eastern Mennonite Col, 68-69; res fel, Univ Fla, 75-76. *Mem:* AAAS; Am Chem Soc. *Res:* Conformational analysis of cyclopentane compounds; mechanisms of epoxidation reactions and ring-opening reaction of epoxides; hydrogen-deuterium exchange of pyridine-N-oxides. *Mailing Add:* Dept Chem Eastern Mennonite Col Harrisonburg VA 22801

KAUFFMAN, GORDON LEE, JR, PHYSIOLOGY. *Current Pos:* PROF CELLULAR & MOLECULAR PHYSIOL & CHIEF, DIV GEN SURG, MILTON S HERSHEY MED CTR, PA STATE UNIV, 85- *Personal Data:* b Grand Rapids, Mich, Mar 30, 46; m, Christie L Van Sweden; c Gordon L III & Christian A. *Educ:* Wheaton Col, BS, 68; Univ Mich Med Sch, MD, 72. *Prof Exp:* Investr, Ctr Ulcer Res & Educ, Los Angeles, 79-81; staff surgeon, VA Wadsworth, Los Angeles, 77-85; asst prof surg, Sch Med, Univ Calif, Los Angeles, 79-83, assoc prof, 83-85. *Mem:* Am Physiol Soc; fel Am Col Surgeons; Am Surg Asn; Soc Surg Alimentary Tract. *Res:* Control of brain peptides on gastro-intestinal function. *Mailing Add:* Milton S Hershey Med Ctr Dept Surg PO Box 850 Hershey PA 17033-0850

KAUFFMAN, HAROLD, phytopathology, agronomy, for more information see previous edition

KAUFFMAN, JAMES FRANK, ELECTRICAL ENGINEERING. *Current Pos:* from asst prof to assoc prof, 70-89, PROF ELEC ENG, NC STATE UNIV, 89- *Personal Data:* b St Joseph, Mo, Jan 29, 37; m 64; c 2. *Educ:* Univ Mo-Rolla, BS, 60; Univ Ill, Urbana, MS, 64; NC State Univ, PhD(elec eng), 70. *Prof Exp:* Engr airborne radar, Westinghouse Elec Corp, 60-62; res asst lens antennas, Antenna lab, Univ Ill, Urbana, 64-65; sr engr, Electronics Res Lab, Corning Glass Works, 67-70. *Mem:* Inst Elec & Electronics Engrs; Sigma Xi. *Res:* Electromagnetics, especially antennas and microwave transmission. *Mailing Add:* 6932 Valley Lake Dr Raleigh NC 27612-1757

KAUFFMAN, JOEL MERVIN, LASER DYES & FLUORESCENT TAGS, SCINTILLATION FLUORS. *Current Pos:* from asst prof to assoc prof, 79-91, PROF CHEM, PHILADELPHIA COL PHARM & SCI, 91- *Personal Data:* b Philadelphia, Pa, Jan 3, 37; m 66, 81, Helen Ehrlich Plotkin; c Michael & Alec. *Educ:* Philadelphia Col Pharm, BS, 58; Mass Inst Technol, PhD(org chem), 63. *Prof Exp:* Chemist, Reaction Motors Div, Thiokol Chem Corp, 63-64; USPHS fel antiradiation drugs, Mass Col Pharm, 64-66; res chemist, ICI Am Inc, Mass, 66-69; res & develop dir, Pilot Chem Div, New Eng Nuclear Corp, Watertown, 69-76; res assoc, Mass Col Pharm, 77-79. *Concurrent Pos:* Consult liquid scintillation counting, 76- & laser dyes, 82-, automotive chem, Nat Motorist Asn. *Mem:* Am Chem Soc; Am Chem Univ Prof. *Res:* Synthesis of fluors, fluorescent dyes, laser dyes, scintillators, antiallergenic drugs, antimalarials, antimicrobials drugs and other medicinal chemicals; laser dyes; scintillators; blocked amino acids; heterocyclics; vinyl monomers; photochemical reactions; terpenes; peptides; boron cage compounds; antiradiation-anticancer drugs; radiation sensitizers; plasticizers; fatty acid derivatives; formulation of liquid scintillators, solubilizers, decontaminants. *Mailing Add:* 65 Meadowbrook Rd Wayne PA 19087. *E-Mail:* kauffman@hslc.org

KAUFFMAN, JOHN W, BIOPHYSICS. *Current Pos:* RETIRED. *Personal Data:* b Washington, DC, Mar 28, 25; m 59; c Steven W & Lee A (deceased). *Educ:* George Washington Univ, BS, 47; Univ Md, MS, 49; Univ Ill, PhD, 55. *Prof Exp:* Res physicist, US Naval Res Lab, 48-50; asst, Univ Ill, 50-55; prof biomed eng, Northwestern Univ, 55-90. *Res:* Biomaterials; consciousness studies. *Mailing Add:* 621 W Pl Nueva Green Valley AZ 85614

KAUFFMAN, LEON A, PULMONARY DISEASES, INTERNAL MEDICINE. *Current Pos:* ASSOC PROF MED, HAHNEMANN UNIV, 77- *Personal Data:* b Philadelphia, Pa, July 26, 34; m 69; c 2. *Educ:* Temple Univ, AB, 57, MD, 61; Am Bd Internal Med, dipl, 73, cert pulmonary med, 78. *Prof Exp:* Resident path, SDiv, Einstein Med Ctr, Philadelphia, 62-63; resident internal med, Hahnemann Med Col & Hosp, 63-65, fel pulmonary med & pulmonary physiol, 65-66, instr med, 66-68, sr instr & dir pulmonary function lab, 68-70, asst dir pulmonary dis div & dir respiratory intensive care unit, 69-73, asst prof med, 70-77; med dir sect respiratory ther, St Agnes Hosp, 73-78; chmn, Div Pulmonary Med, Metrop Hosp, Philadelphia, 73-83. *Concurrent Pos:* Pa Thoracic Soc fel pulmonary physiol & clin chest dis, 65-66; clin asst pulmonary med, Hahnemann Div, Philadelphia Gen Hosp, Pa, 66-78; mem ad hoc comt to evaluate med care in state tuberc hosp syst, Pa, 67; mem fel & res comt, Pa Thoracic Soc, 68-74; pulmonary consult, Shock & Trauma Unit, Hahnemann Med Col & Hosp, 70-82; attend pulmonary med, St Agnes Hosp, 73-. *Mem:* AMA; Am Thoracic Soc; fel Am Col Physicians; Am Soc Internal Med. *Res:* Respiratory intensive care and respiratory failure in man; design of systems for delivery of care and treatment of repiratory failure; respiratory therapy; clinical pulmonary physiology. *Mailing Add:* 1930 Pine St Philadelphia PA 19103-6626

KAUFFMAN, MARVIN EARL, GEOLOGY. *Current Pos:* RETIRED. *Personal Data:* b Lancaster, Pa, Aug 31, 33; m 53; c 7. *Educ:* Franklin & Marshall Col, BS, 55; Northwestern Univ, MS, 57; Princeton Univ, PhD, 60. *Prof Exp:* Asst geologist, Alaskan Br, US Geol Surv, 53; asst geologist, Bethlehem Steel Co, 53-55; prof geol, Franklin & Marshall Col, 59-88; exec dir, Am Geol Inst, 85-90; exec dir, Learning Ctr Appl Environ Technol, 90-91; prog dir, Nat Sci Found, 91-94. *Concurrent Pos:* NSF sci fel, State Univ Utrecht, 65-66; consult geologist various co; pres, Yellowstone-Bighorn Res Asn. *Mem:* Nat Asn Geol Teachers (past-pres); Int Asn Sedimentologists; Geol Soc Am; Am Inst Prof Geol; Am Asn Petrol Geol; AAAS. *Res:* Structure and stratigraphy of the Garnet Range and Marine Jurassic of western Montana; cambrian stratigraphy of southeastern Pennsylvania. *Mailing Add:* 540 Upper Continental Dr Red Lodge MT 59068

KAUFFMAN, RALPH EZRA, DRUG METABOLISM, PHARMACOKINETICS. *Current Pos:* PROF PEDIAT & PHARMACOL, SCH MED, WAYNE STATE UNIV, 82- *Educ:* Univ Kans, MD, 65. *Mailing Add:* Med Res Children's Mercy Hosp 2401 Gillham Rd Kansas City MO 64108

KAUFFMAN, RAYMOND F, CARDIOVASCULAR PHARMACOLOGY, ATHEROSCLEROSIS. *Current Pos:* sr pharmacologist cardiovasc res, 81-86, res scientist, 87-92, SR RES SCIENTIST CARDIOVASC RES, LILLY RES LABS, ELI LILLY & CO, 93- *Personal Data:* b Dayton, Ohio, Aug 20, 52; m 74, Jane M Clark; c Christopher & Carolyn. *Educ:* Univ Dayton, BS, 73; Univ Wis-Madison, PhD(biochem), 78. *Prof Exp:* Fel biochem, Enzyme Inst, Univ Wis, 79; fel, Hormel Inst, Univ Minn, 79-81. *Mem:* Am Chem Soc; Am Soc Pharmacol & Exp Therapeut; Sigma Xi; Am Heart Asn Arteriosclerosis Coun; NAm Vascular Biol Orgn. *Res:* Vascular occlusive disorders, including atherosclerosis and chronic restenosis following balloon angioplasty; discovery of new mechanisms/drugs for prevention of vascular proliferative disorders and for modulating serum lipoproteins. *Mailing Add:* Cardiovasc Res Lilly Corp Ctr Eli Lilly & Co Indianapolis IN 46285. *Fax:* 317-277-0892; *E-Mail:* kauffman_raymond_f@lilly.com

KAUFFMAN, ROBERT GILLER, MEAT SCIENCE. *Current Pos:* prof, 66-96, EMER PROF ANIMAL SCI, UNIV WIS-MADISON, 96-, UNIV WIS-MADISON, 81- *Personal Data:* b St Joseph, Mo, Dec 29, 32; m 55, Phyllis A Smith; c Rebecca Ruth (Henly) & Ellen (Campbell). *Educ:* Iowa State Univ, BS, 54; Univ Wis, MS, 58, PhD(animal sci), 61. *Honors & Awards:* Signal Serv Award, Am Meat Sci Asn. *Prof Exp:* Asst prof animal sci, Univ Ill, 61-66. *Mem:* Fel Am Soc Animal Sci; Am Meat Sci Asn; Inst Food Technol. *Res:* Lipid transport in striated muscle; composition of meat animals; re-and post rigor quality modification for meat animals. *Mailing Add:* Muscle Biol Lab, Univ Wis 1805 Linden Dr Madison WI 53706-1205. *Fax:* 608-265-3110; *E-Mail:* rgkauffm@facstaff.wisc.edu

KAUFFMAN, SHIRLEY LOUISE, PATHOLOGY. *Current Pos:* fel, 60, from asst prof to assoc prof, 61-70, PROF PATH, SU NY DOWNSTATE MED CTR, 70- *Personal Data:* b Grand Junction, Colo, Sept 10, 24. *Educ:* Univ Chicago, BS, 46, MS, 48; Univ Kans, MD, 55. *Prof Exp:* Asst path, Med Col, Cornell Univ, 55-57; Nat Cancer Inst trainee path, Francis Delafield Hosp, 57-59; instr, Albert Einstein Col Med, 59-60. *Concurrent Pos:* Provisional asst pathologist, NY Hosp, 55-57; vis prof, Dept Anat, Univ Berne, 69, Path Inst Rikshospitalet, Oslo, Norway, 76- & Inst Cancer Res Royal Marsden, Sutton Surrey, UK, 77. *Mem:* Am Soc Exp Path; NY Acad Sci; Int Soc Stereology; Am Asn Path & Bact. *Res:* Mammalian embryogenesis; lung morphometry; cell differentiation and proliferation; neoplasia. *Mailing Add:* 680 Hudson Terr Cliffside Park NJ 07010-3020

KAUFFMAN, STUART ALAN, MEDICINE, THEORETICAL BIOLOGY. *Current Pos:* assoc prof biochem-biol, 75-81, ASSOC PROF BIOCHEM & BIOPHYS, UNIV PA, 81- *Personal Data:* b Sacramento, Calif, Sept 28, 39; m 67; c 1. *Educ:* Dartmouth Col, BA, 61; Oxford Univ, BA, 63; Univ Calif, San Francisco, MD, 68. *Honors & Awards:* Norbert Wiener Gold Medal, Am Soc Cybernet, 70. *Prof Exp:* Vis scientist, Mass Inst Technol, 67-68; intern, Cincinnati Gen Hosp, 68-69; asst prof theoret biol, Univ Chicago, 69-73, assoc prof med, 70-73; res assoc, Lab Theoret Biol, Nat Cancer Inst, 73-75. *Concurrent Pos:* Fel genetics, Univ Cincinnati, 68-69. *Mem:* Philos Sci Asn. *Res:* Theory of organization of eukaryotic gene regulation networks; control of DNA synthesis. *Mailing Add:* Dept Biochem & Physiol Univ Pa Col Med Philadelphia PA 19104

KAUFMAN, ALBERT IRVING, MEDICAL PHYSIOLOGY, EPITHELIAL TRANSPORT. *Current Pos:* Instr, 66-69, asst prof, 69-80, ASSOC PROF PHYSIOL, STATE UNIV NY DOWNSTATE MED CTR, 80-, ASST DEAN, 90- *Personal Data:* b New York, NY, July 22, 38; m 62, Jeannetta Van Raalte; c Joshua & Rachel. *Educ:* Cooper Union, BEE, 61; Drexel Inst Technol, MS, 62; Temple Univ, PhD(physiol), 68. *Concurrent Pos:* Vis prof, Tokyo Metrop Inst Geront, 75-76. *Mem:* Sigma Xi; NY Acad Sci; AAAS; Am Physiolog Soc. *Res:* Transepithelial water and electrolyte movement. *Mailing Add:* SUNY Health Sci Ctr 450 Clarkson Ave Box 31 Brooklyn NY 11203

KAUFMAN, ALLAN N, PLASMA PHYSICS THEORY. *Current Pos:* assoc, 65-67, PROF PHYSICS, UNIV CALIF, BERKELEY, 67-, STAFF PHYSICIST, LAWRENCE BERKELEY LAB, 65- *Personal Data:* b Chicago, Ill, July 21, 27; m 57, Louise Lazarus; c Joel & Janet. *Educ:* Univ Chicago, PhB, 47, BS, 49, MS, 51, PhD(physics), 53. *Prof Exp:* Staff physicist, Lawrence Livermore Lab, 53-64; vis prof physics, Univ Calif, Los Angeles, 64-65. *Concurrent Pos:* Chmn, Div Plasma Physics, Am Phys Soc, 81-82; sr fel, Goddard Space Flight Ctr, 67. *Mem:* Fel Am Phys Soc. *Res:* Basic plasma physics theory. *Mailing Add:* Bldg 4/230 Lawrence Berkeley Lab 1 Cyclotron Rd Berkeley CA 94720

KAUFMAN, ALVIN B(ERYL), ELECTRICAL ENGINEERING, ELECTRONIC ENGINEERING. *Current Pos:* WRITING, CONSULT & LECTR, 81- *Personal Data:* b Jacksonville, Fla, Oct 9, 17; m 48, Irene Bleiberg; c Peter H & Debra Jo. *Educ:* Los Angeles City Col, AA, 38. *Prof Exp:* Res analyst, Douglas Aircraft Co, Calif, 39-52; group engr, Northrop Aircraft Corp, 52-55; chief develop engr, Arnoux Corp, 55-58; head, Mat & Devices Res Sect, Res & Analysis Dept, Litton Industs, 58-65, mem tech staff, Litton Systs Div, 65-70; sr mil systs engr, Lockheed Aircraft Corp, 70-74; proj engr, Inet Div, Teledyne Corp, 74-78; mem tech staff, Hughes Aircraft Co, 78-81. *Res:* Development of instrumentation equipment and systems; development and test of night vision systems, radar and uninterruptible power supply systems; technical writing; nuclear effects on guidance and control systems. *Mailing Add:* 22420 Philiprimm St Woodland Hills CA 91367

KAUFMAN, ARNOLD, research administration, biochemical engineering; deceased, see previous edition for last biography

KAUFMAN, BERNARD, BIOCHEMISTRY. *Current Pos:* ASSOC PROF BIOCHEM, MED CTR, DUKE UNIV, 68- *Personal Data:* b Chicago, Ill, Aug 17, 32; m 56; c 2. *Educ:* Univ Ill, BSc, 54, MSc, 56; Ind Univ, PhD(microbiol), 61. *Prof Exp:* Asst microbiol, Univ Ill, 54-56; asst, Ind Univ, 56-61; Arthritis & Rheumatism Found fel, Univ Mich, Ann Arbor, 61-64, lectr bot, 64-66; asst prof biochem, Johns Hopkins Univ, 66-68. *Mem:* AAAS; Am Soc Microbiol. *Res:* Elucidation of the reactions concerned in the synthesis of brain gangliosides; relationship of axonal gangliosides to myelination; chemistry and biosynthesis of cell surface glycolipids and glycoproteins. *Mailing Add:* Dept Biochem Box 3322 Duke Univ Sch Med Durham NC 27710-7599

KAUFMAN, BERNARD TOBIAS, biochemistry; deceased, see previous edition for last biography

KAUFMAN, BORIS, mechanical engineering, for more information see previous edition

KAUFMAN, C(HARLES) W(ESLEY), CHEMICAL ENGINEERING. *Current Pos:* CONSULT, CJC CONSULT, 70- *Personal Data:* b Thomas, WVa, Nov 26, 11; m 35, Colleen Over; c Janet B. *Educ:* Wash & Lee Univ, BS, 33; Univ Ariz, MS, 63, PhD, 67. *Prof Exp:* Chemist, Nat Fruit Prod Corp, 33-34; chem engr, Nat Canners Asn, 35-39; lab mgr food technol, Gen Foods Corp, 39-43, dir res, 44-48, vpres, 48-50, dir, 49-50; dir res, Kraft Foods Corp, 50-51, vpres res & develop, 51-57; dir, Nat Dairy Prod Corp, 58-61; vpres, Foremost Dairies, 61-62; assoc prof dairy sci, Univ Ariz, 64-67; vpres res & develop, Mars, Inc, 67-70. *Concurrent Pos:* Consult, Off Qm Gen, US Army, 40-44; lectr NY Univ, 47; vpres, Res & Develop Assoc Food & Container Inst, 50-52; mem bd trustees, Shimer Col, 58-63; vpres admin, Pima Community Col, Tucson, 70-71, assoc fac math & statist, 78- *Mem:* Inst Food Technol; hon mem Packaging Inst (pres, 59-60); fel Am Inst Chemists. *Res:* Food technology and engineering; colloid chemistry; research administration. *Mailing Add:* 2601 Camino Valle Verde Tucson AZ 85715

KAUFMAN, CHARLES, THEORETICAL PHYSICS. *Current Pos:* from asst prof to assoc prof, 64-81, PROF PHYSICS, UNIV RI, 81- *Personal Data:* b Brooklyn, NY, June 4, 37; c Eleanor D & Amelia D. *Educ:* Univ Wis, BS, 56; Pa State Univ, MS, 59, PhD(physics), 63. *Prof Exp:* Instr physics, Pa State Univ, 63-64. *Concurrent Pos:* Physicist, US Naval Underwater Systs Ctr, 69-71; guest lectr, Univ Vienna, 71-72; consult, Raytheon Corp, 78-81; fel, Off Naval Res-Am Soc Eng Educ, Naval Underwater Systs Ctr, New London, 83, 84, 91, 92 & 93; sr visitor, DAMTP, Univ Cambridge, 85-86. *Mem:* NY Acad Sci; Acoust Soc Am; Am Phys Soc; Am Asn Univ Professors. *Res:* Electrodynamics; quantum field theory; atomic and elementary particle physics; turbulence theory; quantum chaos; underwater acoustics. *Mailing Add:* Dept Physics Univ RI Kingston RI 02881-0817. *Fax:* 401-874-2380; *E-Mail:* chuck@uriacc.uri.edu

KAUFMAN, CLEMENS MARCUS, SILVICULTURE, FOREST ECOLOGY. *Current Pos:* dir sch forestry, 51-62, prof, 62-76, EMER PROF FORESTRY, UNIV FLA, 76- *Personal Data:* b Moundridge, Kans, Aug 27, 09; m 41; c 3. *Educ:* Bethel Col, Kans, AB, 36; Univ Minn, MS, 38, PhD(forestry), 43. *Prof Exp:* Asst, Div Forestry, Univ Minn, 39, asst forester, Agr Exten Serv, 40-42, asst, Cloquet Forest Exp Sta, 42-43; from asst res prof to assoc res prof forestry, NC State Col, 43-48, prof forest mgt, 48-51. *Concurrent Pos:* Res prog develop, Col Forestry, Univ NY, 79-81. *Mem:* Soc Am Foresters; Ecol Soc Am. *Res:* Physiological ecology; growth of slash pine. *Mailing Add:* 13026 NW 50th Ave Gainesville FL 32606

KAUFMAN, DANIEL, ORGANIC CHEMISTRY. *Current Pos:* RES DIR, KAUFMAN DEVELOP CO, 75- *Personal Data:* b Washington, DC, Mar 8, 20; m 43; c 5. *Educ:* Univ Md, MS, 41. *Prof Exp:* Asst, Univ Md, 41-42; chemist, US Bur Mines, Utah, 42-44, NC, 46-47; chemist, Manhattan Proj, Los Alamos, NMex, 44-46; res chemist, Nat Lead Co, 47-59; supvr inorg res, Res Div, Wyandotte Chem Corp, 59-68; res assoc, Kerr Mfg Co Div, Ritter Pfaudler Corp, 68-69, dir res & develop, Kerr Mfg Co Div, Sybron Corp, 69-71, vpres res & develop, 71-75. *Concurrent Pos:* Mem nat adv bd biomat res, Clemson Univ; US mem, Fedn Dentaire Int Comn, 75-77. *Mem:* Am Chem Soc; Int Asn Dent Res; AAAS. *Res:* Hydrogenation and hydrogenolysis of furfural; production of elemental boron; hydrometallurgy of manganese ores; titanium chemistry; cyclopentadienyl metal compounds; catalysis and olefin polymerization; metallurgical chemistry; dental materials. *Mailing Add:* 2242 Newquist Ct Camarillo CA 93010-1166

KAUFMAN, DAVID GORDON, PATHOLOGY, BIOCHEMISTRY. *Current Pos:* assoc prof, 75-80, PROF PATH, UNIV NC, 80- *Personal Data:* b Jersey City, NJ, May 28, 43; m 66; c 2. *Educ:* Reed Col, BA, 66; Wash Univ, MD, 68, PhD(exp path), 73. *Prof Exp:* Intern path, Barnes Hosp, Wash Univ, 68-69, resident, 69-70; res assoc carcinogenesis, Nat Cancer Inst, 70-73, res scientist, 73-75. *Concurrent Pos:* Mem, Path B Study Sect, NIH, 77-79, Chem Path Study Sect, 79-83; mem prototype explicit anal pesticides comt, Nat Acad Sci, 78-80; res career develop award, Nat Cancer Inst, 78-83, mem Cancer Ctr support rev comt, 84- *Mem:* Am Asn Cancer Res; Am Asn Pathologists; Am Soc Cell Biol; Am Col Toxicol; NY Acad Sci; Soc Toxicol. *Res:* Chemical carcinogenesis; eukaryotic DNA replication and repair; cell biology of respiratory tract and female genital tract tissues; toxicology. *Mailing Add:* Dept Path 228H Univ NC Med Sch 515 Brinkhaus-Bullitt Bldg Chapel Hill NC 27599-7525

KAUFMAN, DON ALLEN, ORGANIC CHEMISTRY. *Current Pos:* PROF ORG CHEM, KEARNEY STATE COL, 69- *Personal Data:* b Wahoo, Nebr, Aug 4, 40; m 63; c 1. *Educ:* Univ Nebr, BS, 61; Univ Colo, MBS, 65; Colo State Univ, PhD(chem), 69. *Prof Exp:* Instr gen sci, Omaha Pub Schs, Nebr, 61-63; instr chem, Chandler High Sch, Ariz, 63-64. *Concurrent Pos:* NSF fac prof develop grant, Univ Nebr-Lincoln, 77-78. *Mem:* Am Chem Soc. *Res:* Use of crown ethers in organic synthesis; stability of vinyl cations; pH of precipitation; synthesis and reactions of Bunte salts. *Mailing Add:* Dept Chem Kearney State Col Kearney NE 68849-0001

KAUFMAN, DONALD BARRY, IMMUNOLOGY, NEPHROLOGY. *Current Pos:* PROF MED, COL HUMAN MED, MICH STATE UNIV, 81- *Personal Data:* b Los Angeles, Calif, Aug 5, 37. *Educ:* Univ Calif, MD, 63. *Mailing Add:* Dept Pediat & Human Develop Mich State Univ B240 Life Sci East Lansing MI 48824-1317

KAUFMAN, DONALD DEVERE, SOIL MICROBIOLOGY, AGRICULTURAL CHEMISTRY. *Current Pos:* RETIRED. *Personal Data:* b Wooster, Ohio, Dec 2, 33; m 57. *Educ:* Kent State Univ, BA, 55, MA, 58; Ohio State Univ, PhD(plant path), 62. *Prof Exp:* Res technician plant path, Ohio Agr Exp Sta, 56-57, res asst, 58-62; soil microbiologist pesticides, Plant Indust Sta, USDA, 62-73, soil microbiologist, Agr Environ Qual Inst, Beltsville Agr Res Ctr W, Sci & Educ Admin-Agr Res, 73-84, res leader & soil microbiologist, Soil-Microbiol Systs Lab, Agr Environ Qual Inst, Agr Res Serv, 84-96. *Concurrent Pos:* Fulbright lectr soil microbiol, Khonkaen Univ, Thailand, 67-68. *Mem:* AAAS; Am Phytopath Soc; Am Soc Microbiol; Am Chem Soc; Weed Sci Soc Am. *Res:* Microbial decomposition of pesticides; effects of pesticides on soil microorganisms; soil microbiology of root diseases. *Mailing Add:* 1294 Grand Valley Rd Hanover PA 17331

KAUFMAN, DONALD WAYNE, MAMMALIAN ECOLOGY. *Current Pos:* from asst prof to assoc prof, 80-91, PROF BIOL, KANS STATE UNIV, 91- *Personal Data:* b Abilene, Tex, June 7, 43; m 67; c 1. *Educ:* Ft Hays Kans State Col, BS, 65, MS, 67; Univ Ga, PhD(zool), 72. *Honors & Awards:* Am Soc Mammalogists Award, 72. *Prof Exp:* Fel genetics, Univ Tex, 71-73; vis scientist, Savannah River Ecol Lab, Aiken, SC, 73-74; asst prof zool, Univ Ark, 74-75; asst prof biol, State Univ NY, Binghamton, 75-77; dir, Pop Biol & Physiol Ecol Prog, NSF, 77-80. *Concurrent Pos:* Mem rev panel, Environ Protection Agency, 81-85 & US Dept Agr, 95-96; assoc dir, Konza Prairie Res Natural Area, 81-85, actg dir, 85-86, dir, 90; res grant, NSF, 83-; mem, External Oversight Comt Pop Biol & Ecol Progs, NSF, 84; Kans Nongame Wildlife Adv Coun, 85-88; Kans Natural & Sci Areas Adv Bd, 85-88; proj dir, Konza Prairie Long-term Ecol Res Prog, 85-90; mem bd dirs, Am Soc Mammalogists, 89-92. *Mem:* Am Soc Mammalogists; Ecol Soc Am; AAAS; Soc Study Evolution; Am Inst Biol Scientists; Soc Conserv Biol. *Res:* Ecology of rodents, evolutionary ecology; grassland ecology; ecological effects of disturbances in grasslands; physical impacts of mammals on grassland ecosystems; mammalian herbivory; plant-mammal interactions. *Mailing Add:* Div Biol Ackert Hall Kans State Univ Manhattan KS 66506. *Fax:* 785-532-6653; *E-Mail:* kwkaufma@lter_konza.konza.ksu.edu

KAUFMAN, EDWARD GODFREY, DENTISTRY. *Current Pos:* From instr to assoc prof prosthodont, 46-66, from asst dean to assoc dean,69-84, PROF PROSTHODONT, COL DENT, NY UNIV, 67-, CHMN DEPT, 74-, DEAN, 84- *Personal Data:* b New York, NY, June 8, 19; m 38; c 3. *Educ:* UCLA 39, NY Univ, DDs, 43. *Concurrent Pos:* Pvt practice, 46-; res assoc, Mat Res Lab, Murry & Leone Guggenheim Inst Dent Res, 56-; Williams Ref Corp grant, 64-; pvt pract, 46-; Gordon Res Found grant, 57-60; consult dent asst training prog, NIH, 60-, co-prin investr, NIH Grant, 66-71; consult outpatient clin USPHS, 66- *Mem:* AAAS; Am Dent Asn; Am Soc Metals; Am Ceramic Soc; Sigma Xi. *Res:* Clinical and laboratory research in fields of dental materials, stress analysis and applied technology. *Mailing Add:* New York Col Dent 345 E 24th St New York NY 10010

KAUFMAN, ELAINE ELKINS, BIOSYNTHESIS. *Current Pos:* RES CHEMIST, NIMH, 70- *Personal Data:* b Cincinnati, Ohio, June 23, 23; m 48, Seymour; c Allan S, Emily (Watkins) & Leslie (Barrick). *Educ:* Wellesley Col, BA, 45; Duke Univ, PhD(biochem), 49. *Prof Exp:* Fel, USPHS, 47-48; res chemist, NIMH, 65-67 & NIH, 67-69. *Mem:* Sigma Xi; Am Soc Neurochem; Int Soc Neurochem; Am Soc Biochem & Molecular Biol. *Res:* Neuronal-astroglial interactions and interdependence; biosynthesis and degradation of the neuromodulator-hydroxybutyrate; biochemical basis for the physiological effects of -hydroxybutyrate. *Mailing Add:* NIH Bldg 36 Rm 1A21 9000 Rockville Pike Bethesda MD 20892-0001. *Fax:* 301-480-1668

KAUFMAN, ERNEST D, PHYSICAL CHEMISTRY. *Current Pos:* RETIRED. *Personal Data:* b Cologne, Germany, Sept 21, 31; US citizen; m 59; c 3. *Educ:* Ill Inst Technol, BS, 53; Loyola Univ, Ill, MS, 58, PhD(phys chem), 62. *Prof Exp:* Res chemist, Dearborn Chem Co, Ill, 53-57; sr engr, Cook Elec Co, 57-61; lectr phys sci, Roosevelt Univ, 61-62; from asst prof to assoc prof chem, St Mary's Col, Minn, 62-69; res chemist, Am Cyanamid Co, 69-74, prof leader, 74-77, proj mgr, 77-78, dir, Bradford Tech Ctr, Cyanamid Int, UK, 78-80, tech dir, Cyanamid BV, Neth, 80-82, dir, Chem Technol Assessment, 82-85, dir, New Prod Develop, 85-89, tech dir, Int Chem Div, 90-92. *Concurrent Pos:* Lectr phys chem, Mundelein Col, 61-62; Fulbright lectr, Univ Ceylon, 66-67. *Mem:* Am Chem Soc; Indust Mkt Res Asn; Indian Chem Soc; Soc Chem Indust; Royal Dutch Chem Soc; Licensing Executives Soc. *Res:* Polymerization kinetics; process development; sodium atom reactions; protein conformation; rotation of collagen model compounds; polymer-cellulose interactions. *Mailing Add:* 513 Vienna Ave Redford VA 24141-3833

KAUFMAN, FRANK B, PHYSICAL CHEMISTRY, ORGANIC CHEMISTRY. *Current Pos:* MEM RES STAFF PHYS CHEM, T J WATSON RES CTR, IBM CORP, 73- TECHNOL INTEGRATION. *Personal Data:* b June 23, 43; US citizen. *Educ:* Univ Rochester, BS, 65; Johns Hopkins Univ, PhD(chem), 71. *Prof Exp:* NIH fel phys chem, Royal Inst Great Brit, 70-72; vis prof, Univ Ill, 72-73. *Mem:* Am Chem Soc; NY Acad Sci. *Res:* Design, synthesis and properties of new monomeric and polymeric materials with novel electronic properties. *Mailing Add:* 721 Easton Ave Geneva IL 60134

KAUFMAN, GLENNIS ANN, SOCIAL ORGANIZATION, PLANT-ANIMAL INTERACTION. *Current Pos:* res asst biol, Kans State Univ, 81-84, grad asst, 84-90, instr gen biol, 91-92, asst scientist, 91-95, RES ASST PROF, KANS STATE UNIV, 96- *Personal Data:* b Deshler, Nebr, Nov 13, 47; m 67, Donald W; c Dawn M. *Educ:* Kans State Univ, BS, 84, PhD(biol), 90. *Honors & Awards:* A Brazier Howell Award, Am Soc Mammalogists, 89. *Prof Exp:* Res asst, Savannah River Ecol Lab, 68-71 & 73-74; res asst zool, Univ Tex, 71-73. *Concurrent Pos:* Mem, Conserv Land Mammals Comt, Am Soc Mammalogists, 88- & Educ & Grad Students Comt, 90- *Mem:* Am Soc Mammalogists; Am Behav Soc; Ecol Soc Am; Soc Study Evolution; Sigma Xi; Int Soc Behav Ecol. *Res:* Mammalian behavior and population biology; community organization of small mammals in grasslands; biostatistics; plant-small mammal interactions; fire ecology of small mammals. *Mailing Add:* Div Biol Kans State Univ Ackert Hall Manhattan KS 66506. *E-Mail:* gkaufman@lter-konza.konza.ksu.edu

KAUFMAN, HAROLD ALEXANDER, ORGANIC CHEMISTRY, AGRICULTURAL. *Current Pos:* RETIRED. *Personal Data:* b Brooklyn, NY, Jan 27, 33; m 56, Elaine Sommers; c Michele B & Roy S. *Educ:* Brooklyn Col, BS, 55; Univ Pittsburgh, PhD(chem), 61. *Prof Exp:* Instr chem, Brooklyn Col, 55; res chemist, AMP, Inc, 55-56; mgr pesticides synthesis, screening & develop, Mobil Chem Co, 61-76; vpres res & develop, J T Baker Chem Co, 76-95. *Mem:* Am Chem Soc; The Chem Soc; AAAS. *Mailing Add:* 142 Fountain Ave Piscataway NJ 08854

KAUFMAN, HAROLD RICHARD, PLASMA PHYSICS, MECHANICAL ENGINEERING. *Current Pos:* prof mech eng & physics, 74-84, chmn dept, 79-84, EMER PROF, COLO STATE UNIV, 84-; PRES, FRONT RANGE RES, 84- *Personal Data:* b Audubon, Iowa, Nov 24, 26; m 48, Elinor M; c Brian C, Karin T, Bruce R & Cynthia A. *Educ:* Northwestern Univ, BS, 51; Colo State Univ, PhD(mech eng), 71. *Honors & Awards:* James H Wyld Award, Am Inst Aeronaut & Astronaut, 69; Medal Except Sci Achievement, NASA, 71; Albert Nerken Award, Am Vacuum Soc, 91. *Prof Exp:* Res engr, Nat Adv Comt Aeronaut, NASA, Cleveland, Ohio, 51-58, mgr, Space Propulsion Res, 58-74. *Mem:* Assoc fel Am Inst Aeronaut & Astronaut; Am Phys Soc; Am Vacuum Soc. *Res:* Electric space propulsion; industrial broad-beam ion sources. *Mailing Add:* Front Range Res 1306 Blue Spruce Unit A Ft Collins CO 80524. *Fax:* 970-484-9350

KAUFMAN, HERBERT EDWARD, OPHTHALMOLOGY. *Current Pos:* BOYD PROF OPHTHAL & PHARMACOL & HEAD OPHTHAL, LA STATE UNIV MED CTR, NEW ORLEANS, 78- *Personal Data:* b New York, NY, Sept 28, 31; m 77; c 3. *Educ:* Princeton Univ, AB, 52; Harvard Med Sch, MD, 56; Am Bd Ophthal, dipl, 63. *Honors & Awards:* Knapp Award, AMA, 63; Albion O Bernstein Award, NY State Med Soc, 63; Lions Int Humanitarian Award, 68; Conrad Berens Award, 75; Proctor Award, 78; Jackson Mem Lectr, 79; Pocklington Lectr, 79; Proctor Lectr, 81; Twentieth Annual Edwin B Dunphy Lectr, 83; First Annual Wohl Lectr Ophthal, 83; R Townley Paton Award, 83; G Victor Simpson Lectr, 84; Peter Kronfeld Mem Lectr, 84. *Prof Exp:* Head & lectr ophthal, Uveitis Lab, Mass Eye & Ear Infirmary, 59-62; prof ophthal & pharmacol & chmn Ophthal, Col Med, Univ Fla, 62-77. *Concurrent Pos:* Dir outpatient clins, Univ Fla; bd dir, Eye Bank Asn Am; ed, Invest Ophthal; ed, Am J Ophthal & Chemotherapy, Metabolic Ophthal & Ann Ophthal; med dir, Eye & Ear Inst La, 79-84. *Mem:* AAAS; AMA; Asn Res Vision & Ophthal (secy-treas, 64-73, pres, 75); Am Asn Immunol; Am Fedn Clin Res; Am Acad Ophthal; Asn Univ Prof Ophthal; Am Soc Contemporary Ophthal; Int Soc Refractory Surg. *Mailing Add:* LSU Med Ctr 2020 Gravier St Suite B New Orleans LA 70112-2272

KAUFMAN, HERBERT S, MEDICINE, ALLERGY. *Current Pos:* NIH fel allergy & immunol, 64-66, CLIN INSTR DERMAT, MED CTR, UNIV CALIF, SAN FRANCISCO, 66- *Personal Data:* b Salina, Kans, Apr 30, 35; m, Vivian Janho; c 3. *Educ:* Univ Kans, BA, 57; Baylor Univ, MD, 61; Am Bd Pediat, dipl, 66, Am Acad Pediat Allergy, cert, 67; Am Bd Allergy & Immunol, dipl, 72, cert, 78. *Prof Exp:* Intern pediat, St Louis Childrens Hosp, Mo, 61-62, resident, 62-63; resident, Tex Childrens Hosp, 63-64. *Concurrent Pos:* Res grant, Univ Calif, San Francisco, 66-; comt mem & course chmn, Continuing Educ Dept, Pac Presby Med Ctr, 66-, dir pediat allergy clin, 66-68; consult, Dept Rehab, State of Calif & Letterman Gen Hosp, 66-; chief allergy & immunol clin, Dept Pediat, Children's Hosp, San Francisco, 68-71; mem prog clin immunol, Brit Allergy Soc, Oxford Univ, 77. *Mem:* AMA; Am Acad Allergy; Am Col Allergists; Brit Soc Allergy; Brit Soc Immunol; Am Thermography Asn. *Res:* Immunoglobin defects in allergic individuals; complement levels in allergic disease; organic components of mental illness; author of 60 peer reviewed published papers. *Mailing Add:* 2352 Post St San Francisco CA 94115-3424. *Fax:* 415-921-5990

KAUFMAN, HOWARD, CONTROL SYSTEMS. *Current Pos:* PROF CONTROLS, RENSSELAER POLYTECH INST, 69- *Personal Data:* b Saratoga Springs, NY, Apr 24, 40; m, Eve Bruskin; c David M, Jeffrey S & Deborah L. *Educ:* Rensselaer Polytech Inst, BEE, 62, MEE, 64, PhD(elec eng), 65. *Prof Exp:* Res engr, Cornell Aeronaut Lab, 65-68; systs engr, Gen Elec Corp Res & Develop, 68-69. *Concurrent Pos:* Consult, Gen Elec, 80-90, Intersci, 96-97; indust res partic, Gen Elec Corp Res & Develop, NSF, 82, fac intern, 93. *Mem:* Sr mem Inst Elec & Electronics Engrs; Sigma Xi. *Res:* Development and application of adaptive control algorithms that do not require explicit parameter identification; drug infusion systems; robotics; flight systems. *Mailing Add:* Elec Comput & Systs Eng Dept Rensselaer Poytech Inst Troy NY 12180-3590. *Fax:* 518-276-6261; *E-Mail:* kaufmh@rpi.edu

KAUFMAN, HOWARD NORMAN, MECHANICAL ENGINEERING, TRIBOLOGY. *Current Pos:* PVT CONSULT, 87- *Personal Data:* b Boston, Mass, Jan 2, 26; m 47; c 3. *Educ:* Northeastern Univ, BS, 45; Carnegie-Mellon Univ, MS, 52. *Honors & Awards:* Walter D Hodson Award, Am Soc Lubrication Engrs, 55. *Prof Exp:* Res fel engr mech eng & tribology, Westinghouse Sci & Technol Ctr, Westinghouse Elec Corp, 47-86. *Concurrent Pos:* Instr mech eng, Carnegie-Mellon Univ, 52-56 & Allegheny County Community Col, 66-69; lectr, Am Soc Lubrication Engrs, 82- *Mem:* Am Soc Lubrication Engrs. *Res:* Research and development in the field of friction, wear, and lubrication mechanics encompassing the theory, test, and application of journal and thrust bearings, rolling contact bearings and seals. *Mailing Add:* 1233 Northwestern Dr Monroeville PA 15146

KAUFMAN, HYMAN, MATHEMATICS. *Current Pos:* RETIRED. *Personal Data:* b Lachine, Que, Feb 2, 20; m 59. *Educ:* McGill Univ, BSc, 41, MSc, 45, PhD(physics), 48. *Prof Exp:* Lectr math, McGill Univ, 41-48; fel & asst instr elec eng, Yale Univ, 48-49; geophysicist, Continental Oil Co, 49-51; engr, Lab, Fox Electronics, Inc, 51-52; prof math, McGill Univ, 52-80. *Mem:* Soc Indust & Appl Math; Soc Explor Geophys; Asn Comput Mach; Math Asn Am; Inst Elec & Electronics Engrs. *Res:* Applied mathematics in engineering. *Mailing Add:* 400 Stewart Apt 2211 Ottawa ON K1N 6L2 Can

KAUFMAN, IRVING, ELECTRONICS ENGINEERING, MICROWAVES. *Current Pos:* RETIRED. *Personal Data:* b Geinsheim, Ger, Jan 11, 25; US citizen; m 50, Ruby Dordek; c Eve Deborah, Sharon Anne & Julie Ellen. *Educ:* Vanderbilt Univ, BE, 45; Univ Ill, MS, 49, PhD(elec eng), 57. *Honors & Awards:* Ann Achievement Award Outstanding Contrib Elec Eng, Inst Elec & Electronics Engrs, 68. *Prof Exp:* Engr, RCA Victor, 45-48; asst elec eng, Univ Ill, 48-49, instr, 49-53, res assoc, 53-56; mem tech staff, Ramo-Wooldridge & Space Tech Labs, TRW, Inc, 57-64, head microwave res, 61-64; prof eng, Ariz State Univ, 65-94, dir, Solid State Res Lab, 68-78. *Concurrent Pos:* Fulbright sr res fel, Italy, 64-65 & 73-74; collaborating scientist, Consiglio Nazionale delle Ricerche, Florence, Italy, 73-74; vis prof, Univ Auckland, NZ, 74; liaison scientist, Off Naval Res, London, 78-80; distinguished res award, Grad Col, Ariz State Univ, 86-87; collabr, Los Alamos Nat Lab, 89 & 91. *Mem:* Fel Inst Elec & Electronics Engrs; Sigma Xi. *Res:* Microwave electronics; electronic and optical device research; displays; non-destructive evaluation. *Mailing Add:* Dept Elec & Comput Eng Ariz State Univ Tempe AZ 85287-5706. *Fax:* 602-965-8325

KAUFMAN, JANICE NORTON, PSYCHIATRY. *Current Pos:* RETIRED. *Personal Data:* b Denver, Colo, June 22, 23; m 72, l Charles. *Educ:* Univ Utah, BA, 48, MD, 51; Am Bd Psychiat & Neurol, dipl, 58. *Prof Exp:* Intern med, Strong Mem Hosp, Rochester, NY, 51-52, resident psychiat, 52-55; from instr to assoc prof, Univ Colo Med Ctr, Denver, 55-72; dir, Denver Inst Psychoanal, 69-72, mem fac, 72-79; prof psychiat, Univ Colo Med Ctr, Denver, 72-79. *Concurrent Pos:* USPHS career teacher fel, 56-58; mem fac, Chicago Inst Psychoanal, 63-79. *Mem:* Fel Am Psychiat Asn; Am Psychoanal Asn. *Res:* Practice and teaching of psychoanalysis and psychiatry. *Mailing Add:* 1112 Santa Rufina Ct Solana Beach CA 92075

KAUFMAN, JOHN GILBERT, JR, COMPUTERIZED MATERIAL SCIENCE DATA, FRACTURE MECHANICS. *Current Pos:* vpres technol, 93-96, DIR, ALUMINUM ASN, 96- *Personal Data:* b Baltimore, Md, Oct 14, 31; m 53, Ruth; c John G III, Ruth A & Keith C. *Educ:* Carnegie Inst Technol, BSCE, 53, MS, 54; Carnegie Mellon Univ, MS, 75. *Honors & Awards:* Award of Merit, Am Soc Testing & Mat; Award of Merit, Am Soc Metals Int. *Prof Exp:* Mgr, eng properties, Aluminum Co Am, 54-83, technol develop, 84-89 & fabrication technol, 89-90; pres, Nat Mat Properties Data Network, 85-93. *Concurrent Pos:* Dir res & develop, Anaconda Aluminum Co, 80-83 & Arco Metals, Atlantic Richfield, 83-85; mem, Struct Comt, Nat Res Coun, 80-85 & Nat Mat Adv Bd Comt Appln Computers Mat Sci, 91-; chmn, Comt E24, Am Soc Testing & Mat, 80-84 & Comt E49, 86-88; pres, Mat Property Databases Mgt Comt, 87-93, chmn, 95; chmn, Codata Mat Property Database Comt, 95-; Mat Database Comt, Am Soc Metals, 96- *Mem:* Fel Am Soc Testing & Mat; fel Am Soc Metals; Sigma Xi; Am Soc Mech Engrs; Comt Data Sci & Technol; Asn Comput Mach; Aluminum Asn; hon mem Am Soc Testing & Mat. *Res:* Materials development, notably aluminum alloys; fracture mechanics and applications; networking of materials databases; metallurgy of aluminum alloys. *Mailing Add:* 3662 Pevensey Dr Columbus OH 43220. *Fax:* 614-459-3949; *E-Mail:* gkaufman@aluminum.org

KAUFMAN, JOSEPH J, UROLOGY, SURGERY. *Current Pos:* From asst prof to prof surg & urol, 66-76, CHIEF, DIV UROL, SCH MED, UNIV CALIF, LOS ANGELES, 70- *Personal Data:* b New Haven, Conn, Feb 10, 21; m 42; c 2. *Educ:* Univ Calif, Los Angeles, BA, 42; Univ Calif, San Francisco, MD, 45; Univ Guadalajara, Mex, MD Hons, 80. *Concurrent Pos:* Hon mem fac, Sch Med, Univ Chile, 66. *Mem:* Am Urol Asn; Int Soc Urol; Soc Clin Urol; Soc Univ Urol; Am Asn Genito-Urinary Surg. *Res:* Renovascular hypertension; kidney transplantation; urological oncology. *Mailing Add:* 3529 Cannon Rd N0 26-514 Oceanside CA 92056-4980

KAUFMAN, JOYCE J, QUANTUM CHEMISTRY, PSYCHOPHARMACOLOGY. *Current Pos:* ASSOC PROF ANESTHESIOL, SCH MED & PRIN RES SCIENTIST CHEM, JOHNS HOPKINS UNIV, 69- *Personal Data:* b New York, NY, June 21, 29; m 48, Stanley; c Jan C. *Educ:* Johns Hopkins Univ, BS, 49, MA, 59, PhD(chem, chem physics), 60; Sorbonne Univ, DES(theoret physics), 63. *Honors & Awards:* Gold Medal, Martin Co, 64, 65 & 66; Dame Chevalier, Nat Ctr Sci Res, France, 69; Garvan Medal, Am Chem Soc, 74; Lucy Pickett Award, 75; Md Chemist Award, 74. *Prof Exp:* Chemist, US Army Chem Ctr, Md, 49-52; res asst, Johns Hopkins Univ, 52-60; staff scientist, Res Inst Advan Studies, 60-62, head quantum chem group, 62-69. *Concurrent Pos:* Vis staff mem, Ctr Appl Quantum Mech, France, 62; Soroptimist fel int study, 62; mem heavy ion sources comt, Nat Acad Sci, 73-75; US deleg, Int Atomic Energy Symp, Vienna, Austria, 66; mem corresp, Acad Europ Sci, Arts & Letters. *Mem:* Am Chem Soc; fel Am Phys Soc; fel Am Inst Chem; Int Soc Quantum Biol. *Res:* Physicochemistry and theory of drugs which affect the central nervous system; computer systems; experimental chemical physics; chemical effects of nuclear transformation; isotopic exchange reactions of boron hydrides; quantum chemistry. *Mailing Add:* Dept Chem Johns Hopkins Univ Baltimore MD 21218. *Fax:* 410-516-8420; *E-Mail:* chm__zjjk@jhuvms.hcf.jhu.edu

KAUFMAN, KARL LINCOLN, pharmacy, medicinal chemistry; deceased, see previous edition for last biography

KAUFMAN, LARRY, THERMODYNAMICS, MATERIALS SCIENCE. *Current Pos:* LECTR, DEPT MAT SCI & ENG, MASS INST TECHNOL, 96-; CONSULT, 96- *Personal Data:* b Brooklyn, NY, June 6, 31; m 55; c 3. *Educ:* Polytech Inst Brooklyn, BMetE, 52; Mass Inst Technol, ScD(metall), 55. *Honors & Awards:* Rossiter Raymond Award, Am Inst Mining, Metall & Petrol Engrs, 64; Gibbs Triangle Award, Calphad, Inc, 89; Hume Rothery Prize, Inst Metals, London, 96. *Prof Exp:* Mem res staff, Lincoln Lab, Mass Inst Technol, 55-58; sr metallurgist, Mfg Labs, Inc, Alcan Aluminum Corp, 58-63, dir res, 63-76, vpres, 76-84, pres, 84-91, prin scientist, 91-96. *Concurrent Pos:* Ed-in-chief, Calphad, 77-95. *Mem:* Am Soc Metals; Am Inst Mining, Metall & Petrol Engrs; Sigma Xi. *Res:* Kinetics; phase equilibria; high pressure and temperature; transformations; computer calculation of phase diagrams. *Mailing Add:* 140 Clark Rd Brookline MA 02146

KAUFMAN, LEO, MEDICAL MYCOLOGY. *Current Pos:* microbiologist med res, USPHS, 59-62, in-chg, Fungus Serol Lab, Mycol Unit, 63-67, chief fungus immunol br, Mycol Div, Ctr Dis Control, 67-90, ASST CHIEF MYCOTIC DIS BR, DIV BACT & MYCOTIC DIS, USPHS, 90- *Personal Data:* b New York, NY, Jan 20, 30; m 52; c 3. *Educ:* Brooklyn Col, BS, 52; Univ Ky, MS, 55, PhD(bact), 59. *Honors & Awards:* Kimble Methodology Res Award, 74; Meridian Award, Med Mycol Soc Am, 84; Int Soc Human Animal Mycol Award, 85. *Prof Exp:* Instr bact, Univ Ky, 58-59. *Concurrent Pos:* Dir, Nat Ctr Fungal Serol; mem fac, Univ NC, Sch Pub Health, Ga State Univ & Emory Univ. *Mem:* Am Asn Immunol; Am Thoracic Soc; Am Soc Microbiol; Int Soc Human & Animal Mycol; Sigma Xi. *Res:* Immunological procedures for diagnosis of systemic fungus infections and for identification of fungal pathogens. *Mailing Add:* Ctr Dis Control G-11 Div Bact & Mycotic Dis Bldg 5 B-13 Atlanta GA 30333

KAUFMAN, LINDA, NUMERICAL ANALYSIS, COMPUTER SCIENCE. *Current Pos:* MEM TECH STAFF, BELL LABS, 76- *Personal Data:* b Fall River, Mass, Mar 20, 47; m 81. *Educ:* Brown Univ, ScB, 69; Stanford Univ, MS, 71, PhD(comput sci), 73. *Prof Exp:* Asst prof comput sci, Univ Colo, Boulder, 73-76. *Concurrent Pos:* Vis lectr comput sci, Univ Aarhus, 73-74; prin investr, NSF Grant, 76-; assoc ed, J Matrix Anal & Applns. *Mem:* Asn Comput Mach; Soc Indust & Appl Math. *Res:* Development of algorithms in numerical linear algebra and function minimization. *Mailing Add:* Bell Labs 700 Mountain Ave Rm 2C461 Murray Hill NJ 07974. *E-Mail:* lck@research.att.com

KAUFMAN, MARC P, PHYSIOLOGY & PSYCHOLOGY. *Current Pos:* assoc prof, 87-91, PROF INTERNAL MED & HUMAN PHYSIOL, UNIV CALIF, DAVIS, 91- *Personal Data:* b Dec 10, 47; m 74; c Scott & Michael. *Educ:* Univ Miami, PhD(physiol psychol), 77. *Prof Exp:* Asst prof physiol, Health Sci Ctr, Univ Tex, Dallas, 80-87. *Mem:* Am Physiol Soc. *Res:* Neural control of cardiovascular and respiratory system. *Mailing Add:* Div Cardiovasc Med Univ Calif TB-172 Davis CA 95616-8636. *Fax:* 530-752-3265, 754-8935

KAUFMAN, MARTIN, HISTORY OF AMERICAN MEDICINE & PUBLIC HEALTH. *Current Pos:* from asst prof to assoc prof hist, 69-76, chairperson dept, 82-90, PROF HIST, WESTFIELD STATE COL, 76- *Personal Data:* b Boston, Mass, Dec 6, 40; c Edward Brian & Linda Gail. *Educ:* Boston Univ, AB, 62; Univ Pittsburgh, MA, 64; Tulane Univ, PhD(hist), 69. *Prof Exp:* Instr hist, Worcester State Col, 68-69. *Concurrent Pos:* Vis prof, Univ Vt Col Med, 73-74; dir, Inst Mass Studies, 80- *Mem:* Am Asn Hist Med; Hist Sci Soc; Orgn Am Historians; Nat Educ Asn. *Res:* History of American medicine and public health; unorthodox medicine in the 19th century; history of medical education; biographies of physicians and nurses throughout history. *Mailing Add:* 666 Western Ave Westfield MA 01085

KAUFMAN, MAVIS ANDERSON, NEUROPATHOLOGY. *Current Pos:* from instr to asst prof, 53-69, assoc, 55-56, ASSOC PROF NEUROPATH, COL PHYSICIANS & SURGEONS, COLUMBIA UNIV, 69- *Personal Data:* b Yonkers, NY, July 14, 19. *Educ:* Radcliffe Col, AB, 41; NY Med Col, MD, 44. *Prof Exp:* Intern med & surg, Flower & Fifth Ave Hosp, 44-45; resident path, NY Postgrad Hosp, 45-46, resident med & surg, Northern Westchester Hosp, 46-47; resident internal med, Aultman Hosp, Canton, Ohio, 47-48; resident psychiat, Kings Co Hosp, NY, 48-50; resident path, Vet Admin Hosp, 50-53. *Concurrent Pos:* Assoc res scientist, NY State Psychiat Inst, 56-92. *Mem:* Am Asn Neuropath; Am Acad Neurol. *Res:* Surgical and autopsy specimens of central nervous system; demyelinating and degenerative diseases; effects of psychopharmacologic agents; effects of aging. *Mailing Add:* NY State Psychiat Inst 722 W 168th St New York NY 10032-2603

KAUFMAN, MIRON, POLYMER PHYSICS, SUPERCONDUCTORS. *Current Pos:* from asst prof to assoc prof, 85-95, PROF, CLEVELAND STATE UNIV, 95- *Personal Data:* b Oct 31, 50; US citizen; m 75; c 2. *Educ:* Tel Aviv Univ, Israel, BSc, 73, MSc, 77; Carnegie Mellon Univ, PhD(physics), 81. *Prof Exp:* Res physicist statist mech, Carnegie-Mellon Univ, 81-82; Bantrell fel surface physics, Mass Inst Technol, 83-85. *Concurrent Pos:* Vis asst prof, Boston Univ, 85. *Mem:* Am Phys Soc. *Res:* Research activity on condensed matter and statistical physics focused on following topics: random magnets, liquid mixtures, spin (ISING-POTTS) models, percolation, superconductivity, polymers and fractals; research methods: scaling theory of critical phenomena, renormalization-group technique. *Mailing Add:* Physics Dept Cleveland State Univ Cleveland OH 44115. *E-Mail:* m.kaufman@popmeil.csuohis.edu

KAUFMAN, MYRON JAY, PHYSICAL CHEMISTRY. *Current Pos:* assoc prof, 72-78, PROF CHEM, EMORY UNIV, 78- *Personal Data:* b New York, NY, Mar 24, 37; m 67. *Educ:* Rensselaer Polytech Inst, BS, 58; Harvard Univ, MS, 63, PhD(chem physics), 65. *Prof Exp:* Trainee, Gen Elec Co, 58-59; res fel chem, Harvard Univ, 64-66; asst prof, Princeton Univ, 66-72. *Mem:* Am Chem Soc. *Res:* Chemical kinetics; molecular beams; atmospheric chemistry; combustion; coal chemistry. *Mailing Add:* Dept Chem Emory Univ Atlanta GA 30322

KAUFMAN, NATHAN, PATHOLOGY. *Current Pos:* prof & head dept, 67-79, EMER PROF PATH, QUEEN'S UNIV, ONT, 81- *Personal Data:* b Lachine, Que, Aug 3, 15; m 46; c 5. *Educ:* McGill Univ, BSc, 37, MD & CM, 41; Am Bd Path, dipl, 50. *Prof Exp:* Intern, Royal Victoria Hosp, Montreal, 41-42; resident path, Jewish Gen Hosp, 46-47; asst resident, Cleveland City Hosp, 47-48; from instr to assoc prof, Med Sch, Western Res Univ, 48-60; prof, Sch Med, Duke Univ, 60-67. *Concurrent Pos:* Asst pathologist, Cleveland Metrop Gen Hosp, 48-52, pathologist in chg, 52-60; pathologist-in-chief, Kingston Gen Hosp, 67-79; mem grants comt path & morphol, Med Res Coun, 68-74, chmn, 71-74, mem coun, 71-77, exec, 71-74; consult, Lennox & Addington Co Gen Hosp, Napanee, Ont & Hotel Dieu Hosp, 69-79 & Ont Cancer Treatment & Res Found, Kingston Clin, 71-79; mem grants panel, Nat Cancer Inst Can, 70-74; ed, Lab Invest, 72-75; secy-treas, US-Can Div, Int Acad Path, 79. *Mem:* Int Acad Path (vpres, 72-74, pres-elect, 74-76, pres, 76-78); Can Asn Path; Am Asn Path; Soc Exp Biol & Med; US & Can Acad Path (pres, 73-74, secy-treas, 79-). *Mailing Add:* 185 Ontario St Unit 704 Kingston ON K7L 2Y7 Can

KAUFMAN, PAUL LEON, ophthalmology, glaucoma, for more information see previous edition

KAUFMAN, PETER BISHOP, PLANT PHYSIOLOGY. *Current Pos:* res assoc, 56-57, from instr to assoc prof bot, 56-73, cur, Bot Gardens, 57-73, PROF BOT, UNIV MICH, ANN ARBOR, 73-, PROF CELL & MOLECULAR BIOL & BIOENG PROG, 83- *Personal Data:* b San Francisco, Calif, Feb 25, 28; m 58; c 2. *Educ:* Cornell Univ, BS, 49; Univ Calif, PhD(bot), 54. *Honors & Awards:* Orr E Reynolds Award Distinguished Serv, Am Soc Gravitational & Space Biol. *Prof Exp:* Res technician hort, Cornell Univ, 45-49; res technician, Shell Develop Co, 49; res technician & asst bot, Univ Calif, 49-54; Muellhaupt scholar, Ohio State Univ, 54. *Concurrent Pos:* NSF grants, 59-61, 75 & 80-83; grants, Inst Plant Physiol, Univ Lund, 64-66, Am Cancer Soc, 68-71, Inst Environ Qual, Univ Mich, 71-72 & NASA, 79-88; vis prof cell, Molecular & Develop Biol, Univ Colo, Boulder, 74 & Nagoya Univ, Japan, 81; vis scientist, Int Rice Res Inst, Los Banos, Philippines, 81 & US Dept Agr, Beltsville, Md, 81, Univ Calgary, 85. *Mem:* Am Soc Plant Physiol; Soc Develop Biol; fel AAAS; Am Soc Gravitational & Space Biol; Int Plant Growth Substances Asn; Int Soc Plant & Molecular Biol. *Res:* Scanning electron microscopy, electron microprobe analysis and neutron activation analysis as related to silicification mechanisms in rice, oats, sugarcane and other grasses; studies on hormonal interactions and primary mode of action of gibberellin hormone regulation of stem elongation in grasses; mechanism of negative gravitropic response in grasses under NASA Space Biology programs; molecular biology of rice seed proteins, heat-shock proteins in rice; use of plant cell cultures for production of useful secondary compounds; development of life support systems for NASA space station and moon-mars bases; gravitropic response mechanism in snapdragon flowering shoots and in cereal grass shoots; natural products of medicinal value in plants. *Mailing Add:* Dept Biol Univ Mich Ann Arbor MI 48109-1048

KAUFMAN, RAYMOND, EXPERIMENTAL PHYSICS. *Current Pos:* DIR, DEL ELECTRONICS CORP, 86- *Personal Data:* b Aug 30, 17; US citizen; m 42; c 3. *Educ:* City Col New York, BS, 42, MS, 46; NY Univ, PhD(physics),50. *Prof Exp:* Sr asst physicist labs, US Signal Corps, 42-43; tutor physics, City Col New York, 43-44 & 47-49; asst physicist, Farrand Optical Co, Inc, 44-47, physicist, 49-58; dir res, Del Electronics Corp, Valhalla, NY, 58-76, pres & chief exec officer, 76-82, chmn bd, 82-85. *Concurrent Pos:* Assoc prof, City Col New York. *Mem:* Am Phys Soc; Am Asn Physics Teachers. *Res:* Ionization potentials of molecules; electron optics; mass spectroscopy; ultrahigh vacuum techniques; infrared; high voltage phenomena. *Mailing Add:* 3755 Henry Hudson Pkwy Riverdale NY 10463. *Fax:* 718-549-0529

KAUFMAN, RAYMOND H, OBSTETRICS & GYNECOLOGY, GYNECOLOGICAL PATHOLOGY & CYTOPATHOLOGY. *Current Pos:* from asst prof to assoc prof obstet, gynec & path, Baylor Med Col, 58-73, actg chmn, Dept Obstet & Gynec, 68-72, Ernst W Bertner chmn obstet & gynec, 73-93, PROF PATH, OBSTET & GYNEC, BAYLOR MED COL, 73- *Personal Data:* b Brooklyn, NY, Nov 24, 25; m 46, Patricia Judson; c Susan, Wendy, Murri & Elizabeth. *Educ:* Univ Md, MD, 48; Am Bd Obstet & Gynec, dipl. *Prof Exp:* Resident obstet & gynec, Beth Israel Hosp, NY, 48-53. *Concurrent Pos:* Fel path, Methodist Hosp, Houston, 55-58. *Mem:* Am Col Obstet & Gynec; fel Am Col Surg; Am Gynec & Obstet Soc; Am Cytol Soc; Ctr Asn Obstet & Gynec; Soc Gynec & Oncol. *Res:* Gynecologic pathology; cytopathology; relationship of virus to lower genital tract carcinoma. *Mailing Add:* Baylor Col Med 1 Baylor Plaza Houston TX 77030. *Fax:* 715-798-5015

KAUFMAN, SAMUEL, PHYSICAL & ANALYTICAL CHEMISTRY, CHEMICAL EDUCATION. *Current Pos:* RETIRED. *Personal Data:* b Toledo, Ohio, Jan 29, 13; m 41, Julia Rice. *Educ:* Univ Toledo, BEd, 37, BSc, 40, MSc, 47. *Prof Exp:* Control & prod supvr ceramics, Save Elec Corp, 37-38; control analyst, US Gypsum Co, 41; chemist, Engr Corps, US Army, 41-45; chemist, Nat Bur Stand, 45-48; res chemist, US Naval Res Lab, 48-75, consult, 76-82; consult, Univ Md, 82-95. *Concurrent Pos:* Instr, Montgomery Jr Col, 46-47. *Mem:* Am Chem Soc; Sigma Xi. *Res:* Isopycnic ultracentrifugation; lubricant additives; water pollution abatement; nonaqueous micelle formation and solubilization; reactions of amines in nonaqueous media; analysis of fluorine-bearing silicates; concrete curing agents; nonaqueous titrations; carbon fiber composites. *Mailing Add:* 919 Hyde Rd Silver Spring MD 20902

KAUFMAN, SEYMOUR, BIOCHEMISTRY, NEUROSCIENCES. *Current Pos:* chief sect cellular regulatory mechanisms, 54-68, CHIEF LAB NEUROCHEM, NIMH, 68- *Personal Data:* b NY, Mar 13, 24; m 48, Elaine Elkins; c Allan, Emily & Leslie. *Educ:* Univ Ill, BS, 45, MS, 46; Duke Univ, PhD(biochem), 49. *Honors & Awards:* Hillebrand Prize, 91. *Prof Exp:* Res fel, Sch Med, NY Univ, 49, from instr to asst prof, 50-53. *Concurrent Pos:* NSF travel award, Int Cong Biochem, Paris, 52. *Mem:* Nat Acad Sci; Am Chem Soc; Harvey Soc; Am Soc Neurochem; Int Soc Neurochem; Am Soc Biol Chemists; Am Acad Arts & Sci. *Res:* Mechanism of action of enzymes; intermediary metabolism of amino acids, phenylketonuria, neurotransmitter biosynthesis, tetrahydrobiopterin. *Mailing Add:* 10300 Rossmore Ct Bethesda MD 20814-2226

KAUFMAN, SHELDON BERNARD, NUCLEAR CHEMISTRY. *Current Pos:* from assoc chemist to chemist, 66-86, SR PHYSICIST, ARGONNE NAT LAB, 86- *Personal Data:* b Los Angeles, Calif, June 7, 29; wid; c 2. *Educ:* Univ Chicago, MS, 51, PhD, 53. *Prof Exp:* Res assoc chem, Columbia Univ, 55-57; from instr to asst prof, Princeton Univ, 57-66. *Mem:* Am Phys Soc; AAAS; Am Chem Soc. *Res:* Radiochemical studies of low and high energy nuclear reactions; hot-atom chemistry; tracer applications to inorganic chemistry; high-energy nuclear reactions; nuclear fission; pi-meson reactions; reactions of complex nuclei with energetic protons, pi-mesons, and heavy ions; nuclear fission. *Mailing Add:* 910 W Elm St Wheaton IL 60187-6216

KAUFMAN, SIDNEY, CRUSTAL STUDIES, GEOTHERMAL STUDIES. *Current Pos:* prof, 74-91, ADJ PROF GEOPHYS, CORNELL UNIV, 91- *Personal Data:* b Passaic, NJ, Aug 10, 08; wid; c Martha A (Selzman) & Susan J. *Educ:* Cornell Univ, AB, 30, PhD(physics, math), 34. *Honors & Awards:* Gold Medal Award, Soc Explor Geophys, 83; Hedberg Award, Southern Methodist Univ, 90. *Prof Exp:* Asst physics, Cornell Univ, 30-33, Coffin Found fel, 35; geophysicist, Shell Oil Co, 36-41, sr physicist, Shell Develop Co, 46-58, head geophys instrumentation dept, 58-61, sr res assoc, 61-65, asst to vpres, 65-74. *Concurrent Pos:* Prin physicist, Naval Res Labs, 46; consult, Adv Res Projs Agency, US Dept Defense, 61-73; mem geophys adv panel, Air Force Off Sci Res, 61-74, chmn, 64-66; mem comt seismol, Nat Acad Sci-Nat Res Coun, 66-71 & 74-77; consult, Energy Res & Develop Admin, 75-; dir, Geothermal Resources Coun, 73-77. *Mem:* Hon mem Soc Explor Geophys; Seismol Soc Am; Am Geophys Union; Sigma Xi; Europ Asn Explor Geophysicists. *Res:* Geophysical exploration; deep crustal seismic profiling; geothermal resource assessment. *Mailing Add:* 651 Bering Dr No 605 Houston TX 77057-2134. *E-Mail:* 71742.1310@compuserve.com

KAUFMAN, SOL, SIMULATION MODELING, EXPERT SYSTEMS. *Current Pos:* INDEPENDENT CONSULT, 90- *Personal Data:* b New York, NY, Mar 2, 28; m 54, Joyce Goldberg; c Bruce A, Wayne M, Jay S, Jessica L & Daniel K. *Educ:* Wash Univ, AB, 51; Cornell Univ, PhD(math), 65. *Prof Exp:* Physicist, Nat Bur Stand, 51-52; syst analyst & asst head opers, Res Dept, Cornell Aeronaut Lab/Calspan Corp, 53-62 & 65-73; coordr res & eval, Niagara Falls Community Ment Health Ctr, 73-74; cancer control network coordr, SUNY Buffalo, 74-79; mem staff, Falcon Res & Develop Co, 79-84; systs analyst, XMCO, Inc, 84-86 & Anal & Simulation, Inc, 86-93. *Concurrent Pos:* Lectr indust eng & social & prev med, State Univ NY, Buffalo, 70-82, res asst prof otolaryngol, 80- *Mem:* Math Asn Am; Asn Statist Asn. *Res:* Expert system application to simulation modeling; discrete event simulation, statistical analysis of complex survey data; cancer epidemiology and outcome analysis; public systems research; aerosol transport and diffusion models. *Mailing Add:* 1201 Stolle Rd Elma NY 14059

KAUFMAN, STANLEY, MATERIALS SCIENCE. *Current Pos:* mem tech staff, 70-77, SUPVR CHEM ENVIRON & SAFETY, CHEM GROUP, AT&T BELL LABS, 77-, ENVIRON & SAFETY OFFICER, 92- *Personal Data:* b New York, NY, Oct 30, 41; m 64; c 2. *Educ:* City Col NY, BS, 63; Brown Univ, PhD(chem), 70. *Honors & Awards:* Akzo Chemie Award, UK, 80. *Prof Exp:* Res scientist, Uniroyal Res Ctr, 68-70. *Mem:* Am Phys Soc; Nat Fire Protection Asn; Am Chem Soc. *Res:* Materials for communications use. *Mailing Add:* Bell Labs Lucent Technol 2000 Northeast Expressway Norcross GA 30071. *Fax:* 770-798-4655; *E-Mail:* stankaufman@lucent.com

KAUFMAN, STEPHEN J, CELL BIOLOGY, DEVELOPMENTAL BIOLOGY. *Current Pos:* asst prof microbiol, Univ Ill, 74-81, assoc prof cell biol, 77-81, assoc prof microbiol & cell biol, 81-93, PROF CELL BIOL, UNIV ILL, 93- *Personal Data:* b New York, NY, Jan 3, 43; div; c 2. *Educ:* State Univ NY, Binghamton, BA, 64, MA, 66; Univ Colo, PhD(microbiol), 71. *Prof Exp:* Fel molecular biol, Mass Inst Technol, 71-74. *Concurrent Pos:* Jane Coffin Childs Found fel, 71-73; Muscular Dystrophy Asn fel, 73-74, prin investr, 75-78; prin investr, Basil O'Connor Grant, 75-78; consult, Nat Birth Defect Found, 78-81; prin investr, NIH grant, 79-; sr fel, Fogarty Int Ctr, 84-85; vis scientist, Max Planck Inst for Biophys Chem, Goettingen, FRG, 84-85; ed, Exp Cell Res, 85-91; adj prof, Kwang-Ju Inst Technol, Korea, 94- *Mem:* AAAS; Soc Develop Biol; Am Soc Cell Biol; Am Soc Microbiol; Am Soc Biol Chem. *Res:* Muscle differentiation; development of specialized cells; role of integrins and extracellular matrix in muscle development. *Mailing Add:* Dept Cell & Struct Biol B107 CLSL Univ Ill Urbana IL 61801

KAUFMAN, STEPHEN P, ELECTRONICS. *Current Pos:* exec vpres, 82-84, chief oper officer, 84-86, PRES, ARROW ELECTRONICS INC, 84-, CHIEF EXEC OFFICER, 86-, CHMN, 94- *Personal Data:* b Cambridge, Mass, Nov 19, 41; m 69, Sharon K Malin; c Jeremy S. *Educ:* Mass Inst Technol, BS, 63; Harvard Univ, MBA, 65. *Prof Exp:* Asst to pres, Grand Steel & Mfg Co, 65-67; group controller, Chase Brass & Copper Co, 67-69; from assoc to partner, McKinsey & Co, 69-80; group vpres, Midland Ross Corp, 80-82. *Mailing Add:* Arrow Electronics 25 Hub Dr Melville NY 11747-3503

KAUFMAN, THOMAS CHARLES, GENETICS. *Current Pos:* INVESTR, HOWARD HUGHES MED INST, 90- *Personal Data:* b Chicago, Ill, July 28, 44; m 67; c 1. *Educ:* San Fernando Valley State Col, BA, 67; Univ Tex, Austin, MA, 69, PhD(genetics), 71. *Prof Exp:* Nat Res Coun Can res assoc zool, Univ BC, 71-73, lectr, 73-74; asst prof zool, 75-81, PROF GENETICS, IND UNIV, BLOOMINGTON, 81- *Concurrent Pos:* Adj prof med genetics, Med Sch, Ind Univ. *Mem:* AAAS; Genetics Soc Am. *Res:* Mutagenesis; genetic fine structure in eucaryotic organisms; cytology of dipteran polytene salivary gland chromosomes; position effect variegation and developmental genetics of drosophila; genetics and control of redundant genes. *Mailing Add:* 485 Serena Lane Bloomington IL 47401

KAUFMAN, VICTOR, ATOMIC PHYSICS. *Current Pos:* RETIRED. *Personal Data:* b New York, NY, Sept 27, 25; m 49, Vena Lovett; c Mark, Vail, Mona & Shawn. *Educ:* Kans State Univ, BS, 49, MS, 50; Purdue Univ, PhD(physics), 59. *Prof Exp:* Instr physics, Univ NDak, 50-55; res assoc, Purdue Univ, 59-60; physicist, Nat Bur Stand, 60-88. *Mem:* Fel Optical Soc Am. *Res:* Atomic emission spectroscopy; interferometry; wavelength standards by precision measurement and by calculation from atomic energy levels, analysis of the spectra of highly ionized atoms. *Mailing Add:* 11402 Cam Ct Kensington MD 20895

KAUFMAN, WILLIAM, FOOD ALLERGY, PSYCHOSOMATIC MEDICINE. *Current Pos:* RETIRED. *Personal Data:* b New York, NY, Dec 30, 10; m 40, Charlotte R Schnee. *Educ:* Univ Pa, BA, 31; Univ Mich, MA, 32, MD, 38, PhD(physiol), 37. *Honors & Awards:* Tom Spies Award Nutrit & Mem Lectr, Int Acad Prevent Med, 78; Merit Award, Am Col Allergy, Asthma & Immunol, 81. *Prof Exp:* Intern med, Barnes Hosp, St Louis, 38-39; asst resident & resident, Mt Sinai Hosp, NY, 39-40; Dazian Found fel physiol, Med Sch, Yale Univ, 40-42; pvt med pract, Bridgeport, Conn, 40-64; assoc med dir, L W Frohlich & Co-Intercon Int Inc, 64-65, med dir, 65-67, dir med affairs, 67-68; assoc med dir, Klemtner Casey, Inc, 69-70, dir med affairs, 70-71, vpres & dir med affairs, Klemtner Advert, Inc, 71, sr vpres & dir sci & med affairs, 71-81. *Concurrent Pos:* Am ed-in-chief, Int Arch Allergy Appl & Immunol, 55-67; film consult, Family Film Ctr Conn Inc, 67-74. *Mem:* Fel AAAS; fel Am Col Physicians; fel Am Col Allergy, Asthma & Immunol; fel Am Col Nutrit; fel Gerontol Soc Am; Nat Asn Sci Writers. *Res:* Reflex physiology; tissue conductivity; electrocardiography; psychosomatic medicine; food allergy; human nutrition including the treatment of osteoarthritis and rheumatoid arthritis with niacinamide (alone or in combination with other vitamins); gerontology. *Mailing Add:* 3180 Grady St Winston-Salem NC 27104-4008

KAUFMAN, WILLIAM CARL, JR, HUMAN PHYSIOLOGY, BIOPHYSICS. *Current Pos:* prof human adaptability & chmn dept, Univ Wis, 69-78, chmn res coun, 78-81, prof, 78-86, EMER PROF HUMAN BIOL, UNIV WIS, GREEN BAY, 86- *Personal Data:* b Appleton, Minn, Jan 21, 23; m 46, Patricia Hurley; c Jane & William C III. *Educ:* Univ Minn, BA, 48; Univ Ill, MS, 53; Univ Wash, PhD(physiol), 61. *Prof Exp:* Instr aviation physiol, Wright-Patterson AFB, 50-51, proj officer altitude suits, Aeromed Lab, 53-56, res biologist thermal environ, Aerospace Med Res Labs, 58-66, chief, Byodynamics Br, Aeromed Res Lab, Holloman AFB, 66-68; Nat Inst Med Res spec res fel, Hampstead Labs, London, Eng, 68-69. *Concurrent Pos:* Asst prof prev med, Ohio State Univ, 62-67; mem nuclear weapons effects res comt, Defense Atomic Support Agency, 65-68; consult to pvt indust; NIH special res fel, London, Eng, 68-69. *Mem:* AAAS; Aerospace Med Asn; Am Physiol Soc. *Res:* Temperature regulation and peripheral circulation; thermal and space environments; respiration; evaluation and development of cold weather protective equipment; evaluation and development of protective and recreational clothing. *Mailing Add:* 19228 NE 202nd St Woodinville WA 98072

KAUFMAN, WILLIAM MORRIS, ELECTRICAL ENGINEERING, AUTOMATED INSPECTION & TRANSPORTATION SAFETY. *Current Pos:* VPRES APPL RES, CARNEGIE MELLON UNIV, 85-, DIR, CARNEGIE MELLON RES INST, 85- *Personal Data:* b Pittsburgh, Pa, Dec 31, 31; m 53, Iris F Picovsky; c Nathan, Marjorie & Emily. *Educ:* Carnegie Inst Technol, BS & MS, 53, PhD(elec eng), 55. *Prof Exp:* Instr, Carnegie Inst Technol, 53-54, res engr, 54-55; engr, Westinghouse Elec Corp, 55-57, res mathematician, 57-59, supvry engr, 59-62; dir res, Gen Instrument Corp, 62-65; consult engr, Gen Elec Co, 65-66; mgr, Med Eng Dept, Hittman Assocs, Inc, 66-71; vpres eng, Ensco, Inc, 71-84; vpres new prod develop, Ocean Data Systs, Inc, 84-85. *Mem:* Inst Elec & Electronics Engrs. *Res:* The application of solid state materials to electronic and electromechanical systems; artificial organs; medical instrumentation; data acquisition and processing; transportation safety research; railroad track geometry automated inspection; robotic inspection of aircraft. *Mailing Add:* Carnegie Mellon Res Inst 4400 Fifth Ave Pittsburgh PA 15213. *Fax:* 412-268-3101; *E-Mail:* wk0e@andrew.cmu.edu

KAUFMAN-JACOBS, SUSAN E, BLOOD PRESSURE REGULATION, BODY FLUID HOMEOSTASIS. *Current Pos:* res assoc, 77-79, assoc prof med, 79-92, PROF MED, UNIV ALTA, 92- *Personal Data:* b Ottawa, Can, Aug 5, 43; m 68, 88, Harold Jacobs; c Naomi, Rachel & Oren. *Educ:* Univ Col, London, BS, 65; McGill Univ, Montreal, MS, 67; Univ BC, PhD(zool), 71. *Prof Exp:* Sci res coun fel, Univ Cambridge, 71-72; sr res worker, 73-74; premier asst, Univ Lausanne, 75-77. *Concurrent Pos:* Can Heart Found grant, 80-83; Alta Heritage Found med res grant, 83-95. *Mem:* Am Physiol Soc; AAAS; NY Acad Sci; Can Physiol Soc. *Res:* Integrative cardiovascular/renal physiology; mechanisms underlying control of blood pressure and intravascular volume with special reference to the homeostatic changes that occur during pregnancy. *Mailing Add:* Univ Alta 475 HMRC Edmonton AB T6G 2S2 Can. *Fax:* 403-492-7522; *E-Mail:* susan.jacobs@ualberta.ca

KAUFMANN, ALVERN WALTER, MATHEMATICS. *Current Pos:* RETIRED. *Personal Data:* b Cleveland, Ohio, Feb 21, 24; m 46; c 3. *Educ:* Greenville Col, BA, 47; Ohio State Univ, MA, 48, PhD, 60. *Prof Exp:* Instr math, Aurora Col, 48-50; instr math & physics, Cent Col, Kans, 50-52; teacher, Pub Sch, Ohio, 52-54; asst instr math, Ohio State Univ, 54-57; assoc prof math & physics, Roberts Wesleyan Col, 57-65, prof math, 65-81, acad dean, 74-81; prof math, Mt Vernon Nazarene Col, Ohio, 81-86. *Mem:* Math Asn Am; Am Sci Affil; Nat Coun Teachers Math. *Res:* Meaning and definition in mathematics. *Mailing Add:* 4401 SE Mohogany Run Winter Haven FL 33884

KAUFMANN, ANTHONY J, MICROBIOLOGY, BIOCHEMISTRY. *Current Pos:* assoc prof, 69-74, PROF BIOL, ST MARY'S UNIV, SAN ANTONIO, 74- *Personal Data:* b Millen, Ga, Aug 19, 36; m 66. *Educ:* Univ Ga, BS, 59, MS, 61; La State Univ, PhD(microbiol), 67. *Prof Exp:* Med microbiologist, Nat Communicable Dis Ctr, 62-63; fel microbiol, La State Univ, 63-67; assoc prof health sci, Etenn State Univ, 67-69. *Concurrent Pos:* Res assoc, La State Univ, 71; consult, Southwest Res Found & Inst, San Antonio, 71- *Mem:* AAAS; Am Soc Microbiol; Am Inst Biol Sci. *Res:* Microorganisms capable of degrading certain solid waste products such as cellulose, paper products and certain plastics. *Mailing Add:* St Mary's Univ One Camino Santa Maria San Antonio TX 78228-5433

KAUFMANN, ARNOLD FRANCIS, EPIDEMIOLOGY. *Current Pos:* vet epidemiologist, Ctr Dis Control, 63-67, vet pathologist, 68-70, chief bact zoonoses act, 71-90, CHIEF, MYCOTIC DIS BR, CTR DIS CONTROL, 90- *Personal Data:* b Dubuque, Iowa, Feb 24, 36; div; c 3. *Educ:* Iowa State Univ, DVM, 60; Univ Minn, MS, 68; Am Col Vet Path, dipl. *Prof Exp:* Vet, 62-63. *Mem:* Am Vet Med Asn; Am Asn Lab Animal Sci; Am Col Vet Pathologists. *Res:* Pathology and epidemiology of infectious diseases; molecular biology of leptospires. *Mailing Add:* 1381 Wood Pond Cove Stone Mountain GA 30083

KAUFMANN, ELTON NEIL, SCIENCE POLICY, MATERIALS SCIENCE. *Current Pos:* dir, Superconductivity Pilot Ctr, 89-91, ASSOC DIR, STRATEGIC PLANNING GROUP, OFF DIR, ARGONNE NAT LAB, 91- *Personal Data:* b Cleveland, Ohio, Mar 18, 43. *Educ:* Rensselaer Polytech Inst, BS, 64; Calif Inst Technol, PhD(physics), 69. *Prof Exp:* Mem tech staff, Bell Tel Labs, 68-81; Mats Div Leader, Lawrence Livermore Nat Lab, 81-89. *Concurrent Pos:* Ed, Hyperfine Interactions, 80-89, Ann Rev Mat Sci, 93- *Mem:* Fel Am Phys Soc; Metall Soc; Mat Res Soc (pres, 85); AAAS; Mat Res Soc Japan. *Res:* Hyperfine interactions using nuclear spectroscopic methods; particle-solid interactions including ion-beam channeling and ion-implantation; directed energy beam materials modification; superconductivity; research administration and policy. *Mailing Add:* Off Dir Argonne Nat Lab 9700 S Cass Ave Argonne IL 60439-4832. *Fax:* 630-252-3679; *E-Mail:* eltonk@anl.gov

KAUFMANN, GERALD WAYNE, ANIMAL BEHAVIOR, ECOLOGY. *Current Pos:* From instr to assoc prof, 64-79, PROF BIOL, LORAS COL, 79- *Personal Data:* b Dubuque, Iowa, Sept 18, 40; m 66; c 3. *Educ:* Loras Col, BS, 62; Iowa State Univ, MS, 64; Univ Minn, Minneapolis, PhD(biol), 71. *Mem:* Am Ornith Union; Wilson Ornith Soc. *Res:* Marsh ecology; behavior of soras and Virginia rails; behavior of Weddell seals; marsh and river ecology. *Mailing Add:* Dept Biol Loras Col 1450 Alta Vista Dubuque IA 52001-4399

KAUFMANN, JOHN HENRY, vertebrate zoology, behavioral ecology, for more information see previous edition

KAUFMANN, JOHN SIMPSON, CLINICAL PHARMACOLOGY, INTERNAL MEDICINE. *Current Pos:* CONSULT, 87- *Personal Data:* b Raleigh, NC, Apr 18, 31; m 59; c 3. *Educ:* Wake Forest Univ, BS, 53, MD, 56, PhD(pharmacol), 68; Am Bd Internal Med, dipl, 64. *Prof Exp:* Instr med, Wake Forest Univ, 62-64, instr pharmacol & assoc med, 64-70, from asst prof to assoc prof med & pharmacol, Bowman Gray Sch Med, 75-87. *Concurrent Pos:* USPHS spec fel & vis asst prof, Vanderbilt Univ, 68-70. *Mem:* AAAS. *Res:* Interaction of drugs in man; mechanisms of action of antihypertensive agents; platelet amine uptake and aggregation; actions of hematologic and oncolytic agents; neuronal amine uptake and psychoactive drugs. *Mailing Add:* 4210 Briarcliffe Rd Winston-Salem NC 27106

KAUFMANN, KENNETH JAMES, INSTRUMENTATION. *Current Pos:* MEM STAFF, WORTHINGTON GROUP, MCGRAW EDISON CO, 80- *Personal Data:* b New York, NY, May 2, 47. *Educ:* City Col NY, BS, 68; Mass Inst Technol, PhD(chem), 73. *Prof Exp:* Fel chem, Calif Inst Technol, 73-74, Bell Tel Labs, 74-75; asst prof chem, Univ Ill, Urbana, 76-80. *Mem:* Am Phys Soc; Am Chem Soc; Sigma Xi. *Res:* Picosecond kinetics of biological and chemical reaction. *Mailing Add:* 360 Foothill Rd No 6910 Bridgewater NJ 08807-0910

KAUFMANN, MAURICE JOHN, PLANT PATHOLOGY. *Current Pos:* mem fac biol, 63-70, from assoc prof to prof, 70-94, EMER PROF BIOL, BLUFFTON COL, 94- *Personal Data:* b Hopedale, Ill, Nov 11, 29. *Educ:* Bluffton Col, BS, 52; Univ Ill, MS, 55, PhD(plant path, bot), 57. *Prof Exp:* Plant pathologist, Agr Res Serv, USDA, Wis, 57-63. *Mem:* Am Phytopath Soc. *Res:* Diseases of soybeans and forage grasses. *Mailing Add:* 10465 Augsburger Rd Bluffton OH 45817-1198

KAUFMANN, MERRILL R, PHYSIOLOGICAL ECOLOGY, FOREST HYDROLOGY. *Current Pos:* PRIN PLANT PHYSIOLOGIST, ROCKY MOUNTAIN FOREST & RANGE EXP STA, US FOREST SERV, USDA, 77- *Personal Data:* b Paxton, Ill, June 17, 41; m 62, 93, Evelyn Clayson; c 2. *Educ:* Univ Ill, BS, 63; Duke Univ, MF, 65, PhD(forestry), 67. *Prof Exp:* Asst prof plant physiol & asst plant physiologist, Univ Calif, Riverside, 67-73, assoc prof plant physiol & assoc plant physiologist, 73-77. *Concurrent Pos:* Chair, Whole Plant Physiol Working Party, Int Union Forestry Res Orgn, 91- *Mem:* Int Union Forestry Res Orgn; Ecol Soc Am. *Res:* Physiological ecology of old-growth trees; plant-environment interaction; plant water relations; physiological effects on subalpine forest watersheds; ecosystem management strategies. *Mailing Add:* USDA Forest Serv Rocky Mountain Forest & Range 240 W Prospect Rd Ft Collins CO 80526. *Fax:* 970-498-1297

KAUFMANN, PETER G, STRESS PHYSIOLOGY PSYCHOSOMATIC MEDICINE & HEALTH PSYCHOLOGY. *Current Pos:* SPEC EXPERT TO CHIEF, BEHAV MED BR, NAT HEART LUNG & BLOOD INST, 83-, CHIEF, 92- *Personal Data:* b Europe, Feb 5, 42; US citizen; m, Aukse Liulevicius; c Vikoras, Arius & Vyga. *Educ:* Loyola Univ, BS, 64, MA, 66; Univ Chicago, PhD(psychol), 70. *Prof Exp:* Asst prof psychol, Emory & Henry Col, 70-72; scholar neurosci, Duke Univ Med Ctr, 72-75, assoc to asst med res prof, 75-83. *Concurrent Pos:* Lectr psychol, Loyola Univ, Chicago, 66-67, Montgomery Col, 91-92; adj assoc prof, George Mason Univ, 92. *Mem:* Soc Neurosci; Am Psychol Soc; Am Psychol Asn; fel Soc Behav Med; Am Psychosomatic Soc; Acad Behav Med Res. *Res:* Behavioral and neurol aspects of cardiovascular function; basic and clinical research related to biopsychosocial and sociocultural factors in somatic illness and stress-related disorders; treatment and prevention of cardiovascular diseases. *Mailing Add:* Nat Heart Lung & Blood Inst 6701 Rockledge Dr MSC 7936 Bethesda MD 20892-7936. *E-Mail:* pvk@cu.nih.gov

KAUFMANN, PETER JOHN, COSMETIC CHEMISTRY. *Current Pos:* VPRES PROD DEVELOP & RES & DEVELOP, ALMAY INC, 80- *Personal Data:* b Amsterdam, Holland, Oct 30, 35; US citizen; m 63, Arlene; c Mark & Cybele. *Educ:* Univ Ill, Urbana, BS, 59. *Prof Exp:* Chief chemist, Dr P Fahrney & Sons, Chicago, 63-65; res chemist cosmetics, Alberto-Culver Co, Ill, 65-67; lab dir, Marcelle Cosmetics Div, Borden, Inc, 67-70; dir prod develop, Max Factor & Co, 70-80. *Mem:* Am Chem Soc; Soc Cosmetic Chemists; Inst Food Technol. *Res:* Emulsion technology; formulation, development and manufacture of makeup and skin care products; efficacy and safety of cosmetics. *Mailing Add:* Estee Lauder 125 Pinelawn Rd Melville NY 11747-3145. *Fax:* 516-531-1565

KAUFMANN, RICHARD L, PHYSICS. *Current Pos:* From asst prof to assoc prof, 63-73, PROF PHYSICS, UNIV NH, 73- *Personal Data:* b Honolulu, Hawaii, June 11, 35; m 63; c 2. *Educ:* Calif Inst Technol, BS, 57; Yale Univ, MS, 58, PhD(chem), 60. *Mem:* Am Phys Soc. *Res:* Space physics. *Mailing Add:* Dept Physics Univ NH Durham NH 03824

KAUFMANN, WILLIAM B, ELEMENTARY PARTICLE PHYSICS. *Current Pos:* From asst prof to assoc prof, 69-87, PROF PHYSICS, ARIZ STATE UNIV, 87- *Personal Data:* b San Francisco, Calif, Nov 11, 36; m 68; c 2. *Educ:* Univ Calif, Berkeley, PhD(physics), 68. *Mem:* Am Phys Soc; AAAS. *Res:* Theoretical medium-energy nuclear physics. *Mailing Add:* Dept Physics Ariz State Univ Tempe AZ 85287-0001

KAUFMANN, WILLIAM KARL, MOLECULAR BIOLOGY. *Current Pos:* ASST PROF, DEPT PATH, UNIV NC, CHAPEL HILL, 88- *Personal Data:* b Richland, Wash, Aug 13, 51. *Educ:* Yale Univ, BS, 73; Univ NC, PhD(path), 79. *Prof Exp:* Fel biol, Lab Radiol & Environ Health, Univ Calif, San Francisco, 82-87. *Mem:* AAAS; Sigma Xi. *Res:* Mechanisms of DNA replication and repair and their importance in carcinogenesis. *Mailing Add:* Lineberger Cancer Ctr Univ NC-Chapel Hill CB 7295 Rm 351 Chapel Hill NC 27599-7295

KAUGERTS, JURIS E, LOW TEMPERATURE PHYSICS. *Current Pos:* SUPERCOLLIDER CENT DESIGN GROUP, 87- *Personal Data:* b Riga, Latvia, Sept 24, 40; US citizen; m 69; c 3. *Educ:* Stevens Inst Technol, BS, 62, MS, 64, PhD(physics), 72. *Prof Exp:* Presidential intern superconductivity, Lawrence Berkeley Lab, Univ Calif, 72-73; res assoc, Plasma Physics Lab, Princeton Univ, 73-75; asst physicist superconductivity, Brookhaven Nat Lab, 75-77, assoc physicist superconductivity, 77-79, physicist, 80-82; sr scientist, Oxford Superconducting Technol, 84-87. *Mem:* Am Phys Soc. *Res:* Superconducting accelerator magnet research, design and development. *Mailing Add:* 104 Hamburg Turnpike Pompton Lakes NJ 07442

KAUKER, MICHAEL LAJOS, PHARMACOLOGY, GENERAL & ANIMAL PHYSIOLOGY. *Current Pos:* PROF, DEPT PHYSIOL & PHARMACOL, UNIV SDAK, VERMILLION, 83- *Personal Data:* b Szerecseny, Hungary, Jan 24, 35; US citizen; m 94, Linda M Brahms; c 4. *Educ:* Univ Ala, Birmingham, PhD(pharmacol), 67. *Prof Exp:* NIH fel, Univ NC Chapel Hill, 67-79; from asst prof to assoc prof pharmacol, Ctr Health Sci, Univ Tenn, Memphis, 69-83. *Concurrent Pos:* Fulbright scholar, Semmelweis Univ Med, 95. *Mem:* Am Soc Pharmacol & Exp Therapeut; Soc Exp Biol & Med; Am Soc Nephrology; Int Soc Nephrology. *Res:* Electrolyte and water metabolism; renal micropuncture; mechanism of action of antidiuretic hormone; renal effects of diuretic drugs; regulation of body fluid compartments. *Mailing Add:* Dept Physiol & Pharmacol Sch Med Univ SDak Vermillion SD 57069. *Fax:* 605-677-5124

KAUL, MAHARAJ KRISHEN, engineering mechanics, applied mathematics, for more information see previous edition

KAUL, PUSHKAR NATH, PHARMACOLOGY, CLINICAL PHARMACOLOGY. *Current Pos:* DEPT CHEM, FITCHBURG STATE COL. *Personal Data:* b Srinagar, India, June 29, 33; m 61; c 4. *Educ:* Banaras Hindu Univ, BPharm, 54, MPharm, 55; Univ Calif, San Francisco, PhD(pharmacol, pharmaceut chem), 60. *Honors & Awards:* Aruna & Malaviya Prizes, 54; Lunsford Richardson Pharm Award, 60; Ebert Prize Cert, 62; Univ Okla Alumni Res Award, 69 & 70. *Prof Exp:* Asst prof pharmaceut, Birla Inst Technol, India, 55-57; asst pharmaceut chem, Med Ctr, Univ Calif, San Francisco, 57-58, asst pharmacol, 58-60; res assoc pharmacol & vis scientist, Med Sch, Univ Melbourne, 60-61; chief res pharmacol, Antibiotics Res Ctr, India, 61-65; group leader, Farbwerke Hoechst, Ger, 65-68; assoc prof pharmacol, res med & res pediat, Univ Okla, 68-75, prof pharmacol, 75-77, prof pharmacodyn & toxicol, 77-81; prof & chmn pharmacol & asst to pres, Res & Spec progs, Sch Med, Morehouse Univ, 81-84; off res admin, Atlanta Univ. *Concurrent Pos:* Lectr, Univ Poona, 62-63; dir marine pharmacol & adj prof pediat & res med, Univ Okla; dir drug metab, Cent State Hosp, Norman; chmn, Nat Task Force Marine Biomed. *Mem:* Assoc fel Royal Australian Chem Inst; Am Soc Pharmacol & Exp Therapeut; Int Soc Biochem Pharmacol; Acad Pharmaceut Sci. *Res:* Biotransformation of drugs; mechanism of drug action; screening of pharmacologically active substances from the sea; antibiotics; psychotropic drugs. *Mailing Add:* 1589 Whisperingwood Trail Stone Mountain GA 30088-1811. *Fax:* 770-498-2122

KAUL, RAJINDER K, MOLECULAR BASIS OF INHERITED DISORDERS, ENZYMOLOGY & PROTEIN CHEMISTRY. *Current Pos:* ACTG CHIEF SCI OFFICER, AEIVEOS SCI GROUP, 96- *Personal Data:* b Banihal, India, Mar 3, 51; US citizen; m 79, Chandrika Thussu; c Abhinau & Anand. *Educ:* Lucknow Univ, India, PhD(biochem), 78. *Prof Exp:* Lectr, Indian Inst Technol, Delhi, 78-79; res assoc, Univ Chicago, 79-84; from instr to asst prof genetics, Univ Ill, 84-89; sr res scientist, Miami Children's Hosp Res Inst, 89-96; assoc prof biol, Fla Int Univ, 90-96. *Concurrent Pos:* Sr res fel, Chicago Heart Asn, 85-87. *Mem:* Soc Inherited Metab Dis; Am Soc Human Genetics; NY Acad Sci; AAAS. *Res:* Molecular basis of canavan disease; identification of mutations that lead to canavan disease; creation of a mouse model for canavan disease; gene organization and regulation of aspartoacylase. *Mailing Add:* Aeiveos Sci Group 4010 Stone Way N Suite 220 Seattle WA 98103. *Fax:* 305-663-2461

KAUL, ROBERT BRUCE, BOTANY, TAXONOMY. *Current Pos:* from asst prof to assoc prof, 64-72, vdir, biol sci, 89-91, PROF BOT, UNIV NEBR, LINCOLN, 72- *Personal Data:* b Faribault, Minn, Jan 28, 35; m 76, Martha Naugler. *Educ:* Univ Minn, 57, PhD(bot), 64. *Prof Exp:* Asst bot, Univ Minn, 57-60, instr, 61-62. *Concurrent Pos:* Ed, Trans Nebr Acad Sci, 88- *Mem:* Bot Soc Am; Am Soc Plant Taxon; Am Inst Biol Sci. *Res:* Morphology and life history of angiosperms, especially trees and aquatic plants; floristics of the Great Plains. *Mailing Add:* Sch Biol Sci Univ Nebr Lincoln NE 68588-0118. *Fax:* 402-472-2083; *E-Mail:* rkaul@unlinfo.unl.edu

KAUL, S K, PURE MATHEMATICS. *Current Pos:* from asst prof to assoc prof, 63-71, PROF MATH, UNIV REGINA, 71- *Personal Data:* b Lucknow, India, Dec 25, 36, Can citizen; m 63, Radha; c 2. *Educ:* Univ Lucknow, BSc, 54, MSc, 55; Univ Delhi, PhD(math), 59. *Prof Exp:* Instr math, Hampton Inst, 58-59; instr math, Univ Rochester, 59-60, univ fel, 60-61; instr math, Univ Utah, 62. *Mem:* Am Math Soc; Can Math Cong; Math Asn Am. *Res:* Studying topological structures associated with differential equations, like flows, semi-flows and generalized dynamical systems and various stability notions using a flow associated with a semiflow and a semiflow associated with a generalized dynamical system; impulsive differential equations. *Mailing Add:* Dept Math Univ Regina Regina SK S4S 0A2 Can. *Fax:* 306-585-4020; *E-Mail:* kaul@math.uregina.ca

KAUL, SANJIV, CARDIOLOGY. *Current Pos:* asst prof, 84-88, ASSOC PROF MED, UNIV VA, 88- *Personal Data:* b Kashmir, India, Aug 18, 51; m 81; c 1. *Educ:* Univ Delhi, MBBS, 75. *Prof Exp:* Intern med, Chicago Med Sch, 77-78; resident med, Univ Vt, 78-80; fel cardiol, Univ Calif Sch Med, Los Angeles, 80-82 & Harvard Med Sch, 82-84. *Concurrent Pos:* Mem, Coun Clin Cardiol, Am Heart Asn, 85. *Mem:* Fel Am Col Physicians; fel Am Col Cardiol; fel Am Col Chest Physicians; Physicians for Social Responsibility; Am Fedn Clin Res; fel Am Heart Asn; Am Soc Echocardiography. *Res:* Assessment of regional myocardial flow-function relationships using non-invasive techniques. *Mailing Add:* Univ of VA Health Sci Ctr Cardiol Div Box 158 Charlottesville VA 22908

KAULA, WILLIAM MASON, GEOPHYSICS. *Current Pos:* RETIRED. *Personal Data:* b Sydney, Australia, May 19, 26; US citizen; m 49, 78, Gene Hurley; c Anne, Jacqueline, Charles & Marie. *Educ:* US Mil Acad, BS, 48; Ohio State Univ, MS, 53. *Hon Degrees:* DSc, Ohio State Univ, 75. *Honors & Awards:* Whitten Medal, Am Geophys Union; Brouwer Medal, Am Astron Soc. *Prof Exp:* Geodesist, Army Map Serv, Washington DC, 57-58, chief geod res & anal div, 58-60; geophysicist geod, Celestial Mech & Planetary Interiors, Goddard Space Flight Ctr, NASA, Md, 60-63; prof geophys, dept earth & space sci, Inst Geophys & Planetary physics, Univ Calif, Los Angeles, 63-92. *Concurrent Pos:* Chief, Nat Geodetic Survey, NOAA, Rockville, Md, 84-87. *Mem:* Nat Acad Sci; fel Am Geophys Union; Am Astron Soc; Geol Soc Am. *Res:* Gravitational fields of the earth and planets; origin and evolution of the earth, moon and planets; mantle convection; dynamics of the solar system. *Mailing Add:* Dept Earth & Space Sci Univ Calif Los Angeles CA 90095-1567. *Fax:* 310-825-2779; *E-Mail:* wkaula@ess.ucla.edu

KAUNE, WILLIAM TYLER, BIOENGINEERING. *Current Pos:* PRES, EM FACTORS, 93- *Personal Data:* b Everett, Wash, Aug 31, 40; m 72; c 2. *Educ:* Univ Wash, BS, 66; Stanford Univ, PhD(physics), 73. *Prof Exp:* Res asst high energy physics, Stanford Linear Accelerator Ctr, 68-72; res assoc, Univ Wash, 72-73; asst prof physics, Loyola Marymount Univ, 73-75; sr res engr, 75-80, staff engr bioeng, Pac Northwest Div, Battelle Mem Inst, 80-87; physicist, Nat Bur Standards, Boulder, Colo, 87-88; vpres, Enertech Consults, Campbell, Calif, 88-93. *Mem:* Bioelectromagnetics Soc; Inst Elec & Electronics Engrs. *Res:* Biological effects of electromagnetic radiation; exposure systems and dosimetry. *Mailing Add:* EM Factors 640 Jedwin Suite F Richland WA 99352

KAUNITZ, HANS, NUTRITION. *Current Pos:* RETIRED. *Personal Data:* b Vienna, Austria, Oct 20, 05; US citizen; m 43. *Educ:* Vienna Univ, MD, 30. *Honors & Awards:* Achievement award, Am Oil Chem Soc, 70; Presidential Merit Medal Philippines, 73; Big Sign Honor, Repub Austria, 73; Alton E Bailey Award, Am Oil Chem Soc, 81. *Prof Exp:* Attending physician & head clin lab, Dept Med, Sch Med, Univ Vienna, 35-38; assoc prof med & head clin lab, Univ Philippines, 38-40; clin prof path, Columbia Univ, 41-73. *Concurrent Pos:* NIH grants, 55-73; consult several food firms, 53-78; consult geront, Rutgers Univ, 78. *Mem:* Sigma Xi; Am Soc Exp Path; Harvey Soc; Am Oil Chem Soc; Am Inst Nutrit. *Res:* Biological effect of edible fats, especially medium chain triglycerides; function of cholesterol in arteriosclerosis; biological effects of sodium chloride; philosophy of science. *Mailing Add:* 630 W 168th St Dept Pathol Columbia Univ Col P&S New York NY 10032-3702

KAUP, DAVID JAMES, INTEGRABLE SYSTEMS, NONLINEAR STUDIES. *Current Pos:* From asst prof to prof physics, 67-87, from res asst prof to res assoc prof, 74-76, JOINT PROF MATH, COMPUT SCI & PHYSICS, CLARKSON UNIV, 87- *Personal Data:* b Marionville, Mo, Apr 8, 39; m 82; c 3. *Educ:* Univ Okla, BS, 60, MS, 62; Univ Md, PhD(physics), 67. *Concurrent Pos:* vis res geophysicist, Univ Calif Los Angeles, 81, vis prof math, Lab Phys Math, Univ Sci & Tech Langs, Montpellier, France, 87; consult, Varian Assocs, 83; res scientist, Dynamics Technol, 80-81. *Mem:* Am Phys Soc; Sigma Xi; Am Math Soc; Soc Indust Appl Math. *Res:* Soliton theory; inverse scattering; nonlinear optics; plasma physics; mathematical physics. *Mailing Add:* Dept Math Box 5815 Potsdam NY 13699-0001. *Fax:* 315-268-6670; *E-Mail:* kaup@sun.ncs.clarkson.edu

KAUP, EDGAR GEORGE, CHEMICAL ENGINEERING. *Current Pos:* sr chem engr, 65-69, resident eng mgr, 69-76, SR CHEM ENGR, BURNS & ROE, INC, BURNS & ROE CONSTRUCT CORP DIV, CONTRACTOR TO OFF SALINE WATER, US DEPT INTERIOR, 76- *Personal Data:* b Irvington, NJ, Oct 5, 27; m 53; c 2. *Educ:* Lehigh Univ, BS, 50; Neward Col Eng, BS, 58, MS, 63. *Prof Exp:* Phys chemist, Hoffmann-La Roche, NJ, 52-54; spectroscopist, Air Reduction Lab, 54-55, res chem engr, 55-62; develop engr, Celanese Plastic Co, 62-65. *Mem:* Am Chem Soc; Am Inst Chem Engrs; Am Soc Test & Mat. *Res:* Desalting and water pollution abatement; reverse osmosis evaluations and applications; water and waste treatment by ion exchange and evaporative methods. *Mailing Add:* Eight Essex Rd Essex Fells NJ 07021-1104

KAUPP, VERNE H, ELECTRICAL ENGINEERING. *Current Pos:* PROF ELEC ENG, UNIV ARK, 80- *Personal Data:* b Denver, Colo, Apr 15, 40; m 66; c 2. *Educ:* Univ Md, BS, 71; Univ Kans, DEng, 79. *Prof Exp:* Engr microwave sensor, Martin Marietta Corp, 71-75; eng consult microwave sensor, Earth Resources Technol, 75; sr res engr microwave remote sensing, Ctr for Res, Inc, 75-80. *Concurrent Pos:* Consult, Systs Technol/Appl Res Corp, 77-80, Ark Res Consults, Inc, 80- *Mem:* Inst Elec & Electronics Engrs; Sigma Xi; Am Soc Photogram & Remote Sensing; Am Soc Eng Educ. *Res:* Microwave remote sensing; electromagnetics; digital signal processing. *Mailing Add:* Univ Ark Dept Elec Eng Fayetteville AR 72701

KAUPPILA, RAYMOND WILLIAM, ENGINEERING MECHANICS. *Current Pos:* from asst prof to prof, 57-89, EMER PROF MECH ENG, MICH TECHNOL UNIV, 89- *Personal Data:* b Iron Mountain, Mich, Feb 17, 29; m 52; c 4. *Educ:* Univ Mich, BS(mech eng) & BS(eng math), 51; Mich Col Mining & Technol, MS, 61; Univ Mich, PhD, 68. *Prof Exp:* Maintenance, develop & inspection engr, Standard Oil Div, Am Oil Co, Ind, 51-55; plant engr, Cliffs Dow Chem Co, Mich, 55-57. *Concurrent Pos:* Design consult; expert witness, failure analysis. *Res:* Machine design; dynamics and vibrations of machinery; stress analysis; thermal stresses; plasticity in forming operations. *Mailing Add:* 424 W Ridge St Marquette MI 49855

KAUPPILA, WALTER ERIC, POSITRON & ELECTRON SCATTERING EXPERIMENTS. *Current Pos:* from asst prof to assoc prof, 72-83, PROF PHYSICS, WAYNE STATE UNIV, 83- *Personal Data:* b Hancock, Mich, Sept 11, 42; m 64, Margaret Thompson; c Eric & David. *Educ:* Mich Technol Univ, BS, 64; Univ Pittsburgh, PhD(physics), 69. *Prof Exp:* Res scientist, Joint Inst Lab Astrophys, Univ Colo, 69-71; asst prof physics, Univ Mo, Rolla, 71-72. *Concurrent Pos:* Co-prin investr, NSF supported res grants, 75- *Mem:* Fel Am Phys Soc; fel Sigma Xi. *Res:* Experimental studies of elastic, inelastic and total scattering for positrons and electrons colliding with atoms and molecules. *Mailing Add:* Dept Physics & Astron Wayne State Univ Detroit MI 48202. *Fax:* 313-577-3932; *E-Mail:* kauppila.hal.physics.wayne.edu

KAUS, PETER EDWARD, THEORETICAL PHYSICS. *Current Pos:* assoc prof, 62-67, PROF PHYSICS, UNIV CALIF, RIVERSIDE, 67- *Personal Data:* b Vienna, Austria, Oct 9, 24; nat US; m 50; c 3. *Educ:* Univ Calif, Los Angeles, BS, 47, MA, 52, PhD, 55. *Honors & Awards:* Sarnof Achievement Medal, 57. *Prof Exp:* Asst physics, Univ Calif, Los Angeles, 51-53; res physicist, Labs, Radio Corp Am, NJ, 54-58; asst prof physics, Univ Southern Calif, 58-62. *Concurrent Pos:* Consult, Hughes Aircraft Co, 58-59, Jet Propulsion Lab, Pasadena, 59-61 & Los Alamos Nat Lab, 80-; trustee, Aspen Ctr Physics, 64-, vpres, 70-82, pres, 81-83; Fulbright res scholar, Denmark, 65-66. *Mem:* Fel Am Phys Soc. *Res:* Field theory; elementary particle theory; biophysics; biologic rhythms. *Mailing Add:* 2825 Maude St Riverside CA 92506

KAUSHIK, AZAD, AUTOIMMUNITY-AUTOIMMUNE DISEASES, IMMUNOBIOLOGY. *Current Pos:* ASST PROF IMMUNOL, UNIV GUELPH, CAN, 91- *Personal Data:* b Dhauj, India, Sept 8, 55; m 82, Archana Sharma; c Manu. *Educ:* Pasteur Inst, DSc, 87; Haryana Agril Univ, MVSc, 78, BVSc, 76. *Prof Exp:* Asst prof immunol, Haryana Agril Univ, Hisar, India, 79-83; res assoc, Pasteur Inst, Paris, France, 83-87; res scientist, Mt Sinai Sch Med, NY, 87-90; asst prof, Med Sch, Univ Geneva, 90-91. *Mem:* Am Asn Immunologists; NY Acad Sci; Can Soc Immunol; Soc Fr Immunologists. *Res:* Natural autoimmunity and autoimmune disorders; immunoglobulin molecular genetics; idiotypy; protective immunity and clinical veterinary immunology. *Mailing Add:* Dept Pathobiol & Immunol Univ Guelph Guelph ON N1G 2W1 Can. *Fax:* 519-837-8542; *E-Mail:* akaushik@uoguelph.ca

KAUSHIK, NARINDER KUMAR, ECOLOGY, HYDROBIOLOGY. *Current Pos:* asst prof, 73-77, ASSOC PROF ENVIRON BIOL, UNIV GUELPH, 77- *Personal Data:* Can citizen; m; c 2. *Educ:* Univ Delhi, India, BS, 54, MS, 56; Univ Waterloo, MS, 66, PhD(biol), 69. *Prof Exp:* Res & sr res asst sanit biol, Cent Pub Health Eng Res Inst, 61-64; fel ecol, Univ Toronto, 69-71; asst prof biol, Univ Waterloo, 71-72. *Mem:* Can Water Resource Asn; NAm Benthol Soc; Can Soc Zoologists; Int Soc Theoret & Appl Limnol. *Res:* Role of autumn shed leaves in secondary production in streams; nitrogen transport and transformations in streams; use of limnocorrals for pesticide impact assessment; ecotoxicology. *Mailing Add:* Dept Environ Biol Univ Guelph Guelph ON N1G 2W1 Can

KAUSHIK, ROY, LOW POWER ELECTRONICS FOR PORTABLE COMPUTING & WIRELESS COMMUNICATION, VERY LARGE SCALE INTEGRATION TESTING & FAULT TOLERANCE. *Current Pos:* asst prof, 93-97, ASSOC PROF ELEC ENG, PURDUE UNIV, 97- *Personal Data:* b Calcutta, India, Aug 30, 61. *Educ:* Indian Inst Technol, BTech, 83; Univ Ill, Urbana-Champaign, PhD(elec & comput eng), 90. *Honors & Awards:* NSF Career Award, 95. *Prof Exp:* Mem tech staff, Tex Instruments, 90-93. *Concurrent Pos:* Adj fac, Univ Tex, Dallas, 92-93; prin investr, numerous govt & corp contracts & grants, 93-; assoc ed, Design & Test of Comput, Inst Elec & Electronics Engrs, 95-, Trans Circuits & Systs, 97-; vis prof, Intel Corp, 96. *Mem:* Sr mem Inst Elec & Electronics Engrs. *Res:* Low energy computing for portable applications where battery life is very important; reconfigurable/adaptive computing; very large scale integration testing, fault tolerance and nanoscale electronics. *Mailing Add:* Elec & Comput Eng Purdue Univ West Lafayette IN 47907-1285

KAUTZ, FREDERICK ALTON, II, LOW DENSITY GAS DYNAMICS, AEROTHERMODYNAMICS. *Current Pos:* res asst, 74-77, STAFF MEM, LINCOLN LAB, MASS INST TECHNOL, 86- *Personal Data:* b Knoxville, Tenn, Aug 27, 50; m 77, Carol A Messere; c Catherine & Elizabeth. *Educ:* Univ Tenn, BSc, 72; Mass Inst Technol, SM & NucE, 83. *Prof Exp:* Staff mem, Oak Ridge Nat Lab, 72-73; staff scientist, Off Sci & Weapons Res, Cent Intel Agency, 77-86. *Concurrent Pos:* Mem, Themophys Tech Comt, Am Inst Aeronaut & Astronaut, 87-90, secy, 87; mem, NASA-Langley ad hoc comt reentry plasmas, 88-; reviewer, J Spacecraft & Rockets, Am Inst Aeronaut & Astronaut, 89-92. *Mem:* NY Acad Sci; Am Inst Aeronaut & Astronaut; Am Phys Soc; Inst Elec & Electronics Engrs; Soc Indust & Appl Math; AAAS; Sigma Xi. *Res:* Low density gas dynamics; physics and chemistry of reentry and planetary entry plasmas; computational aerothermodynamics; spacecraft-environment interactions; missile aerodynamics. *Mailing Add:* Carnegie-Mellon Univ Grad Sch of Indust Admin Pittsburgh PA 15213-3890. *Fax:* 781-981-0783; *E-Mail:* kautz@andrew.cmu.edu

KAUZLARICH, JAMES J(OSEPH), MECHANICAL ENGINEERING, TRIBOLOGY. *Current Pos:* chmn dept, 63-75, PROF MECH ENG, UNIV VA, 63- *Personal Data:* b Des Moines, Iowa, Sept, 27, 27; m 52; c 4. *Educ:* Univ Iowa, BS, 50; Columbia Univ, MS, 52; Northwestern Univ, PhD(mech eng), 58. *Prof Exp:* Lab asst, Columbia Univ, 50-52; develop engr, Gen Elec Co, NY, 52-54; instr mech eng, Northwestern Univ, 54-57; from asst prof to assoc prof, Worcester Polytech Inst, 58-61; assoc prof, Univ Wash, Seattle, 61-63. *Concurrent Pos:* Engr, Boeing Corp, 62 & 63; vis res, Cambridge Univ, 70-71 & Swansea Univ, 84-85 & 88-89. *Mem:* Am Soc Eng Educ; fel Am Soc Mech Engrs; Am Soc Lubrication Engrs; Sigma Xi. *Res:* Fluid mechanics; heat transfer; rehabilitation engineering. *Mailing Add:* Dept Mech Eng Univ Va Charlottesville VA 22903-2442. *Fax:* 804-982-2037; *E-Mail:* jjk@uva.pcmail.virginia.edu

KAUZMANN, WALTER (JOSEPH), PHYSICAL CHEMISTRY, PROTEIN CHEMISTRY. *Current Pos:* RETIRED. *Personal Data:* b Mt Vernon, NY, Aug 18, 16; m 51, Elizabeth A Flagler; c Charles P, Eric F & Katherine E J. *Educ:* Cornell Univ, BA, 37; Princeton Univ, PhD(phys chem), 40. *Hon Degrees:* PhD, Univ Stockholm, 62. *Honors & Awards:* Linderstrom-Lang Medal, 66; Stein-Moore Award, Protein Soc, 93. *Prof Exp:* Fel, Westinghouse Elec & Mfg Co, 40-42; chemist, Nat Defense Res Comt, Bruceton, Pa, 42-43; engr, Manhattan Dist Proj, Los Alamos, 44-46; from asst to assoc prof chem, Princeton Univ, 46-63, chmn dept, 64-68, David B Jones prof chem, 63-82, chmn, Dept Biochem Sci, 80-82. *Concurrent Pos:* Guggenheim fel, 57 & 74-75; vis prof Univ Ibadan, 75; vis scientist, Nat Res Coun Can, Halifax, 83. *Mem:* Nat Acad Sci; Am Geophys Union; Am Acad Arts & Sci; Am Chem Soc; fel Am Phys Soc; Hist Sci Soc; fel AAAS; Am Math Soc; Protein Soc. *Res:* Physical chemistry of proteins; theory of water; properties of matter at high pressures; geochemistry; muscle physiology. *Mailing Add:* 302 N Harriston St Suite 152 Princeton NJ 08540

KAVALER, FREDERIC, PHYSIOLOGY. *Current Pos:* from instr to assoc prof, 58-65, PROF PHYSIOL, STATE UNIV NY DOWNSTATE MED CTR, 65- *Personal Data:* b New York, NY, Feb 2, 26; m 55; c 2. *Educ:* Columbia Univ, AB, 47; Johns Hopkins Univ, MD, 51. *Prof Exp:* Intern med, Maimonides Hosp, Brooklyn, 51-52; resident, Goldwater Mem Hosp, NY, 52-54; NY Heart Asn fel, 54-55; fel physiol, Col Med, Cornell Univ, 55-56, instr physiol, 56-57. *Mem:* Am Physiol Soc. *Res:* Electrophysiology of the heart; cardiac physiology. *Mailing Add:* State Univ NY Health Sci Ctr 450 Clarkson Ave Brooklyn NY 11203-2098

KAVALJIAN, LEE GREGORY, PLANT MORPHOLOGY. *Current Pos:* from instr to assoc prof biol sci, 54-64, PROF BIOL SCI, CALIF STATE UNIV, SACRAMENTO, 64- *Personal Data:* b Chicago, Ill, Feb 6, 26. *Educ:* Univ Chicago, PhB, 47, BS, 48, PhD(bot), 51. *Prof Exp:* Res assoc bot, Brooklyn Bot Garden, NY, 51-52; vis res assoc, Brookhaven Nat Lab, NY, 52; asst to chief chemist, Modern Agr Crop Serv, Calif, 53; Ford Found teaching intern natural sci, Univ Chicago, 53-54, instr, 54. *Res:* Plant tissue cultures; floral morphology; cytochemistry; ethnobotany. *Mailing Add:* Dept Biol 6077 Calif State Univ 6000 Jay St Sacramento CA 95819-6077. *E-Mail:* leek@csus.edu

KAVANAGH, KAREN L, MATERIAL SCIENCE ENGINEERING. *Current Pos:* ASSOC PROF ELEC ENG & MAT SCI, UNIV CALIF, SAN DIEGO, 93- *Personal Data:* b Halifax, NS, May 3, 56. *Educ:* Queens Univ, BSc, 78; Cornell Univ, MSc, 84, PhD(mat sci & eng), 87. *Honors & Awards:* Presidential Young Investr Award, NSF, 91. *Prof Exp:* Mem tech staff, Bell-Northern Res, 78-81; fel, Mass Inst Technol, 87-88, IBM Corp, 88. *Mem:* Mat Res Soc; Am Phys Soc; Am Vacuum Soc; Electron Micros Soc Am. *Res:* Electronic materials science defects and diffusion at semiconductor interfaces; structure-electronic property correlations. *Mailing Add:* Dept Elec & Comput Eng Univ Calif San Diego La Jolla CA 92093-0407. *Fax:* 619-534-0556

KAVANAGH, RALPH WILLIAM, NUCLEAR PHYSICS. *Current Pos:* From res fel to sr res fel, 56-60, from asst prof to assoc prof, 60-70, PROF PHYSICS, KELLOGG LAB, CALIF INST TECHNOL, 70- *Personal Data:* b Seattle, Wash, July 15, 24; m 48; c 5. *Educ:* Reed Col, BA, 50; Univ Ore, MA, 52; Calif Inst Technol, PhD, 56. *Mem:* Am Phys Soc. *Res:* Spectroscopy of light nuclei using electrostatic accelerators. *Mailing Add:* 106-38 Caltech Pasadena CA 91125. *Fax:* 626-564-8708; *E-Mail:* kav@krl.caltech.edu

KAVANAGH, ROBERT JOHN, RESEARCH MANPOWER. *Current Pos:* RETIRED. *Personal Data:* b Whitchurch, Hants, Eng, Oct 7, 31; m 56; c 2. *Educ:* Univ NB, BSc, 53; Univ Toronto, MASc, 54, PhD(elec eng), 57; Imp Col, London, DIC, 60. *Prof Exp:* Lectr elec eng, Univ Toronto, 57-59, asst prof, 60-62; from assoc prof to prof elec eng, Univ NB, 62-84, assoc dean, 69-71, actg vpres acad, 78-80, dean grad studies & res, 71-84; dir-gen, Scholarships & Int Prog, Natural Sci & Eng, Res Coun, 84-95. *Concurrent Pos:* NATO fel, Imp Col, Univ London, 59-60; guest worker, Control Eng Div, Warren Spring Lab, Eng, 68-69; vis scientist, Natural Sci & Eng Res Coun, 82-83. *Mem:* Sr mem Inst Elec & Electronics Engrs; fel NY Acad Sci. *Mailing Add:* 849 Mary's Island Ave Ottawa ON K2C 0H9 Can. *E-Mail:* rjk@nserc.ca

KAVANAU, JULIAN LEE, ETHOLOGY & NEUROSCIENCE, MEMORY & SLEEP. *Current Pos:* from asst prof to prof, 57-91, EMER PROF BIOL, UNIV CALIF, LOS ANGELES, 91- *Personal Data:* b Detroit, Mich, Jan 21, 22; c 3. *Educ:* Univ Mich, BS, 43; Univ Calif, MS & PhD(zool), 52. *Prof Exp:* Asst physics, Univ Mich, 41-43; physicist, Univ Calif, 43; mem res staff physics, Calif Inst Technol, 43-45; asst math, Univ Calif, Los Angeles, 46-47, asst zool, 49-51; USPHS fel, Wenner-Gren Inst, Stockholm, Sweden, 52-54; res assoc develop, Rockefeller Inst, 55-57. *Mem:* AAAS; Animal Behav Soc; Am Ornithol Union. *Res:* Instrumentation for behavior research; influences of environmental variables on mammalian activity; symmetry of curves and figures; behavior and evolution of psittaciforms; origin, evolution and functions of sleep; evolution of synaptic efficacy maintenance. *Mailing Add:* Dept Biol Univ Calif Los Angeles CA 90024-1606. *Fax:* 310-206-3987

KAVANAUGH, DAVID HENRY, SYSTEMATIC ENTOMOLOGY, BIOGEOGRAPHY. *Current Pos:* From asst cur to cur, Calif Acad Sci, 74-88, chmn dept, 79-83, dir res, 86-88, SR CUR ENTOM, CALIF ACAD SCI, 88- *Personal Data:* b San Francisco, Calif, Apr 7, 45; m 65, Beverly A Cooper; c Michael, Jeffrey, Thomas, Rebecca & Kathryn. *Educ:* San Jose State Univ, BA, 67; Univ Colo, Denver, MA, 70; Univ Alta, PhD(entom), 78. *Concurrent Pos:* Fel, Nat Res Con Can, 72-74; adj prof, Sonoma State Univ, Rohnert Park, Calif. *Mem:* Soc Syst Zool; Entom Soc Am; Coleopterists Soc; Am Entom Soc. *Res:* Classification, phylogeny, zoogeography and natural history of ground beetles; biogeography and evolution of high altitude biota, especially the coleoptera faunas of western North America; theory and practice of systematic zoology. *Mailing Add:* Dept Entom Calif Acad Sci San Francisco CA 94118. *Fax:* 415-750-7346; *E-Mail:* dkavanau@cas.calacademy.org

KAVARNOS, GEORGE JAMES, SOLID STATE MATERIALS. *Current Pos:* RES CHEMIST, NAVAL UNDERWATER SYSTS CHIEF NAVAL TRAINING, 89- *Personal Data:* b New London, Conn. *Educ:* Clark Univ, BA, 64; Univ RI, PhD(org chem), 68; Dipl, Am Bd Clin Chem. *Prof Exp:* NIH fel, Columbia Univ, 68-71; chief chemist, New London, Cyto-Roche, Div Hoffmann La-Roche, 71-74, assoc dir & clin chemist, Cyto Med Lab Inc, Norwich, 74-89. *Concurrent Pos:* Vpres, Bio-Anal Labs, 73-; adj prof chem, Univ RI, 78-; lectr, St Joseph Col, 85- *Mem:* Am Chem Soc; Am Asn Clin Chemists. *Res:* Photochemistry; clinical chemistry; photoinduced electron transfer material; science molecular modeling. *Mailing Add:* 121 Riverview Ave New London CT 06320

KAVASSALIS, TOM A, PHYSICAL CHEMISTRY. *Current Pos:* mgr planning & bus processes, 95-96, MEM RES, XEROX RES CTR, CAN, 87-, ASSOC CTR MGR, 96- *Personal Data:* b Toronto, Ont, Feb 3, 58; m 83; c 2. *Educ:* Univ Toronto, BSc, 80; Mass Inst Technol, PhD(phys chem), 85. *Prof Exp:* Chemist, Ont Hydro Res, 85-87. *Mem:* Am Chem Soc; Am Phys Soc. *Res:* Theoretical and computational methods for material science applications; simulation of surfactants; theories of polymer structure, morphology and dynamics; mechanical properties of polymers; theory of transport in fluids. *Mailing Add:* Xerox Res Ctr Can 2660 Speakman Dr Mississauga ON L5K 2L1 Can. *Fax:* 905-822-7021; *E-Mail:* kavassalis.xacc@xerox.com

KAVATHAS, PAULA, IMMUNOLOGY, GENETICS. *Current Pos:* ASST PROF, LAB MED, IMMUNOBIOL & GENETICS, SCH MED, YALE UNIV, 86- *Personal Data:* b Evanston, Ill, May 30, 50; m; c 2. *Educ:* Univ Wis-Madison, PhD(genetics), 80. *Res:* Immunobiology of T lymphocyte co-receptor molecule CD8. *Mailing Add:* Dept Lab Med Fitkin 617 Yale Univ Sch Med 333 Cedar st PO Box 208035 New Haven CT 06520-8035

KAVEH, MOSTAFA, STATISTICAL SIGNAL PROCESSING, IMAGE PROCESSING. *Current Pos:* various ranks, 75-85, PROF ELEC ENG, UNIV MINN, 85-, HEAD ELEC ENG, 90- *Personal Data:* b Karadj, Iran, Apr 18, 47. *Educ:* Purdue Univ, BS, 69, PhD(elec eng), 74; Univ Calif, Berkeley, MS, 70. *Honors & Awards:* Sr Award, Inst Elec & Electronics Engrs Signal Processing Soc, 86, Meritorious Serv Award, 88. *Prof Exp:* Postdoc res assoc, Purdue Univ, 75. *Concurrent Pos:* Consult. *Mem:* Fel Inst Elec & Electronics Engrs. *Res:* Sensor array signal processing. *Mailing Add:* 1625 E River Pkwy Minneapolis MN 55403

KAVENOFF, RUTH, BIOPHYSICAL CHEMISTRY, VIROLOGY. *Current Pos:* fel phys chem, 71-72 & 73-79, res assoc virol, 79-80, RES ASSOC BIOL, UNIV CALIF, SAN DIEGO, 80- *Personal Data:* b New York, NY, Aug 11, 44. *Educ:* Reed Col, BA, 67; Albert Einstein Col Med, PhD(cell biol), 71. *Prof Exp:* UN Int Agency Res Cancer-WHO fel virol, Univ Auckland, NZ, 72-73. *Concurrent Pos:* Anna Fuller Found fel, 74-75; NIH fel, 75-78. *Res:* Chromosome structure; nucleic acids. *Mailing Add:* Designer Genes Posters Ltd PO Box 100 Del Mar CA 92014. *Fax:* 619-755-7175; *E-Mail:* ttnx82a@prodigy.com

KAVESH, SHELDON, POLYMER PROCESSING, STRUCTURE & PROPERTIES. *Current Pos:* res assoc, 70-80, PRIN SCIENTIST, ALLIED CHEM CORP, MORRISTOWN, 80- *Personal Data:* b New York, NY, Jan 15, 33; m 57; c 2. *Educ:* Mass Inst Technol, BSChE, 57; Polytech Inst Brooklyn, MChE, 60; Univ Del, PhD(chem eng), 68. *Honors & Awards:* Gold Medal, Nat Assoc Sci Technol & Soc, 94. *Prof Exp:* Res engr, Celanese Corp Am, 57-60, Foster Grant Co, Inc, 60-62 & Avisun Corp, 62-65; proj leader polymers, Films Packaging Div, Union Carbide Corp, 68-70. *Mem:* Am Inst Chem Engrs; Am Phys Soc; Am Chem Soc. *Res:* Polymer physics; transport phenomena; materials science; fiber processing. *Mailing Add:* 16 N Pond Rd Whippany NJ 07981-1277. *Fax:* 973-455-5295

KAVVAS, LEVENT M, HYDROLOGY & WATER RESOURCES. *Current Pos:* assoc prof, 85-90, PROF HYDROL ENG, DEPT CIVIL & ENVIRON ENG, UNIV CALIF, DAVIS, 90- *Personal Data:* b Ankara, Turkey, May 24, 48; US citizen; m 76, Jale Calikoghn; c Eren & Erol. *Educ:* Mid E Tech Univ, Turkey, BS, 70; Colo State Univ, MS, 72; Purdue Univ, PhD(civil eng), 75. *Honors & Awards:* Res Award Foreign Specialists, Ministry Construct, Japan, 89. *Prof Exp:* Asst prof math, probability, stochastic processes, Indust Eng Dept, Mid E Tech Univ, 75-80, assoc prof math & probability, 80; vis assoc prof hydrol eng, Sch Civil Eng, Purdue Univ, 80-82; assoc prof, Dept Civil Eng, Univ Ky, 82-85. *Concurrent Pos:* Consult, PWRI, Ministry Construct, Japan, 90-, USAF, 91-92, Hydrol Eng Ctr, US Army Engrs, 94-95; assoc ed, J Hydrol, 91-, Hydrol Sci J, 94-; founding ed, J Hydrol Eng, Am Soc Civil Engrs, 94- *Mem:* Am Soc Civil Engrs; Am Geophys Union; Am Water Works Asn. *Res:* Mathematical modeling of hydrometeorological processes; regional scale modeling of coupled hydrologic-atmospheric processes; mathematical modeling of hydrologic processes such as overland flow, channel flow, unsaturated-saturated subsurface flow, snow melt runoff, contaminant transport, erosion; stochastic modeling of hydrologic processes. *Mailing Add:* 526 Isla Pl Davis CA 95616. *Fax:* 530-753-9584; *E-Mail:* mlkavvas@ucdavis.edu

KAWAHARA, FRED KATSUMI, ENVIRONMENTAL POLLUTION. *Current Pos:* org chemist, Anal Qual Control Lab, 68-71, spec consult, Method Develop & Qual Assurance Lab, 72-74, SPEC CONSULT OIL IDENTIFICATION, ANAL QUAL CONTROL LAB, ENVIRON PROTECTION AGENCY, 71-, EXPERT WITNESS, 80- *Personal Data:* b Penngrove, Calif, Feb 26, 21; m 52, 91, Anrea L Eary; c Robert K, Kiku S & Richard H. *Educ:* Univ Tex, BS, 44; Univ Wis, MS, 46, PhD(chem), 48. *Honors & Awards:* Group Super Serv Award, Bur Agr & Indust Chem, USDA, 52; Int Order Merit, IBC Cambridge, Eng, 88, First Five Hundred Gold Medal, 89. *Prof Exp:* Assoc chemist, USDA, 48-51; fel org chem, Univ Chicago, 51-53; sr res scientist, Stand Oil Co, Ind, 53-65, res chemist, 66-68. *Concurrent Pos:* Expert witness petroleum fuels; dep gov, Am Biographic Inst Res Asn. *Mem:* Fel Am Inst Chem; Am Chem Soc; Am Biographic Inst Res Asn; fel Int Biographic Asn. *Res:* Synthetic fuels, coal liquefaction; lubricants; phosphorus; fluorocarbons; gasoline additives; waxes; carcinogens; chromatography, infrared, ultraviolet, synthesis, identification; insecticides; greases; phenols; mercaptans; oil pollution; soy bean oil flavor reversion; aromatic amines; peroxides; methods development; auto-oxidation; laser-fiber optics; freon 113 substitute solvent; hydrodechlorinization of polychlorobiphenyls reaction mechanism. *Mailing Add:* Environ Protection Agency Environ Monitor & Systs Lab 26 W Martin Luther King Cincinnati OH 45268

KAWAI, MASATAKA, ELECTRICAL ENGINEERING, COMPUTER CONTROLLED EXPERIMENTS. *Current Pos:* ASSOC PROF ANAT, UNIV IOWA, 87- *Personal Data:* b Gifu, Japan, June 13, 43; m 69; c 2. *Educ:* Tokyo Univ, BSc, 66; Princeton Univ, PhD(biol), 71. *Prof Exp:* Res assoc, Columbia Univ, 71-78, asst prof muscle physiol, Dept Neurol, 78-83, asst prof anat & cell biol, 83-87. *Concurrent Pos:* Prin investr cross-bridge kinetics res, Dept Neurol, Columbia Univ, 76- *Mem:* Biophys Soc; Gen Physiol Soc. *Res:* Cross-bridge kinetics in chemically skinned muscle fibers by use of sinnsoidal analysis which changes the length and detects concomitant amplitude and phase shift in tension. *Mailing Add:* Dept Anat Univ Iowa Bowen Sci Bldg 1-670 Iowa City IA 52242

KAWAKAMIT, TOSHIAKI, IMMUNOLOGY, METABOLISM. *Current Pos:* Fel immunol & allergy res, 84-86, asst mem allergy res, 87-93, ASSOC MEM IMMUNOL, LA JOLLA INST, 93- *Personal Data:* b Matfu, Japan, Oct 25, 50. *Educ:* Univ Tokyo, BS, 76, MS, 78, PhD(immunol), 83. *Mem:* Am Asn Immunol; Am Chem Soc. *Res:* Immunology; metabolism. *Mailing Add:* La Jolla Inst Allergy & Immunol 10355 Science Center Dr San Diego CA 92121

KAWALEK, JOSEPH CASIMIR, JR, BIOCHEMISTRY, BIOCHEMICAL PHARMACOLOGY. *Current Pos:* RES CHEMIST, OFF RES, CTR VET MED, FOOD & DRUG ADMIN, 80- *Personal Data:* b Stockton, Calif, Dec 21, 45; m 72, Rosella M Seckel; c Kiera A & James A. *Educ:* St Francis Col, BS, 67; Univ Pittsburgh, PhD(biochem), 73. *Prof Exp:* Res asst biochem, Univ Pittsburgh, 70-73; res assoc, Hoffmann-La Roche, Inc, 74-76; staff scientist chem carcinogen, Frederick Cancer Res Ctr, Litton Bionetics, Inc, 76-80. *Mem:* Am Chem Soc; Am Inst Biol Sci; Sigma Xi; NY Acad Sci; Soc Toxicol; Am Col Toxicol; Am Acad Vet Comp Toxicol. *Res:* Factors affecting drug metabolism in food producing and companion animals. *Mailing Add:* 8401 Muirkirk Rd Laurel MD 20708. *E-Mail:* kawalek@bangate.fda.gov

KAWAMURA, HIROSHI, BRAIN MECHANISMS OF BEHAVIOR, CIRCADIAN RHYTHMS. *Current Pos:* PROF NEUROSCI, UNIV EASIA GRAD SCH, 92- *Personal Data:* b Antong, China, Jan 26, 27; Japanese citizen; m 71, Keiko Tsuruta; c 2. *Educ:* Univ Tokyo, MD, 54, DMed Sc(neurophysiol), 59. *Honors & Awards:* Mainischi Award, Mainischi Shinbunsha, Tokyo. *Prof Exp:* Instr neurophysiol, Brain Res Inst, Univ Tokyo, 59-61; assoc prof, Yokohama Univ Sch Med, 61-63; asst res anatomist, Dept Anat, Univ Calif, Los Angeles, 63-65; UNESCO fel neurophysiol, Inst Physiol, Univ Pisa, 65-66; res assoc, Dept Pharmacol, Univ Mich, 66-71; chief, Neurophysiol Lab, Mitsubishi Kasei Inst Life Sci, 72-81, dir, Dept Neurosci, 81-90, distingusihed scientist, 90-92. *Concurrent Pos:* Chief, Neurophysiol Sect, Lafayette Clin, 67-71; vis scientist, Dept Res Anesthesia, McGill Univ, 71-72; vis prof, Toho Univ Med Sch, 93-97. *Mem:* Am Physiol Soc; Soc Neurosci; AAAS; Soc Study Biol Rhythms. *Res:* Hypothalmic mechanisms of sleep-wakefulness and circadian rhythm generation of the suprachiasmatic nucleus; brain tissue transplantation, learning after brainstem transection. *Mailing Add:* 2-1-2 Ichigaya Sadoharacho Apt 208 Shinjuku-ku Tokyo 162 Japan

KAWAMURA, KAZUHIKO, INTELLIGENT ROBOTICS, INTELLIGENT TRAINING SYSTEMS. *Current Pos:* assoc prof elec eng & mgt technol, 80-88, ASSOC DIR, CTR INTEL SYSTS, VANDERBILT UNIV, 85-; PROF ELEC ENG & DIR GRAD STUDIES, 88-, PROF MGT TECHNOL, DEPT ELEC ENG, 88- *Personal Data:* b Nagoya, Japan, Feb 4, 39; m 71. *Educ:* Waseda Univ, Japan, BEng, 63; Univ Calif, Berkeley, MS, 66; Univ Mich, Ann Arbor, PhD(elec eng), 72. *Prof Exp:* Lectr elec eng, Univ Mich-Dearborn, 72-73; res specialist exp vehicles, Ford Motor Co, 73; prin researcher tech assessment, Columbus Div, Battelle Mem Inst, 73-81. *Concurrent Pos:* Sr res fel, Japan Soc Prom Sci, 80; vis prof, Kyoto Univ, Japan, 80-81; consult, Saudi Arabian Nat Ctr Sci & Technol, 81-83; orgn coordr, Int Asn Impact Assessment, 81-83; mem, AAAS Comt Sci, Eng, & Pub Policy, 83- *Mem:* Inst Elec & Electronics Engrs; AAAS; Sigma Xi; Am Asn Artificial Intel. *Res:* Expert systems; intelligent robotics; intelligent tutoring systems; risk analysis; computer vision. *Mailing Add:* 5908 Robert E Lee Dr Nashville TN 37215

KAWANISHI, HIDENORI, CELLULAR IMMUNOLOGY, IMMUNOCHEMISTRY. *Current Pos:* PROF MED, RUTGERS UNIV. *Educ:* Kyoto Med Sch, Japan, MD & PhD(exp path), 60. *Prof Exp:* Assoc prof med, Health Sci Ctr, State Univ NY, Stony Brook, 82- *Mailing Add:* 55 Grist Mill Dr Belle Mead NJ 08502

KAWASAKI, EDWIN POPE, CHEMICAL ENGINEERING, PHYSICAL CHEMISTRY. *Current Pos:* RETIRED. *Personal Data:* b Sikeston, Mo, Jan 25, 26; m 48; c 2. *Educ:* Case Inst Technol, BS, 54, MS, 58, PhD(chem eng), 60. *Prof Exp:* Res engr, res ctr, 54-58, supvr chem processing, 58-63, div head surface chem, 63-73, div head processing, 73-75, asst dir res, Repub Steel Res Ctr, 75-84. *Mem:* Nat Asn Corrosion Engrs. *Res:* Corrosion of ferrous metals; chemical processing; environmental control; iron and steel making. *Mailing Add:* 4250 Meadow Gateway Broadview Heights OH 44147

KAWATA, KAZUYOSHI, SANITARY ENGINEERING, ENVIRONMENTAL HEALTH. *Current Pos:* RETIRED. *Personal Data:* b Portland, Ore, Jan 2, 24; m 49, Marion J Sammis; c David, Ray & Jean. *Educ:* Ore State Col, BS, 49; Univ Minn, MS, 50; Univ Calif, Berkeley, MPH, 58; Johns Hopkins Univ, DrPH(sanit eng), 65. *Prof Exp:* Civil-sanit engr, Bd Missions, Methodist Church, 50-66; from asst prof to assoc prof, Johns Hopkins Univ, 66-80, prof environ health eng & prof int health, 80-89. *Concurrent Pos:* Consult, WHO, Bangladesh, 73 & Philippines, 75, consult & lectr, Egypt, 76; expert health sci, AID, 76-78, consult, 79-95; World Bank consult, 90-97. *Mem:* Am Soc Civil Engrs; Am Pub Health Asn; Am Water Works Asn; Water Environ Fedn; Am Acad Environ Engrs; Int Asn Water Qual. *Res:* Water and waste-water treatment processes; disinfection kinetics; tropical environmental health. *Mailing Add:* 415 Russell Ave No 717 Gaithersburg MD 20877

KAWATERS, WOODY H, air pollution impacts, waste management impacts, for more information see previous edition

KAWATRA, MAHENDRA P, PHYSICS. *Current Pos:* dir educ & comput technol, 80-83, PROF PHYSICS, MEDGAR EVERS COL, CITY UNIV NEW YORK, 71-, PROF MATH, 91- *Personal Data:* b Wazirabad, India, June 22, 35; US citizen; m 62, Ved; c Anjali, Anita & Sandhya. *Educ:* Univ Delhi, BSc, 55, MSc, 57, PhD(physics), 62. *Prof Exp:* Lectr physics, Univ Delhi, 57-63; Smith-Mundt scholar & Fulbright grant, Mass Inst Technol, 63-64; assoc res scientist, Courant Inst Math Sci, NY Univ, 64-66; asst prof, Fordham Univ, 66-71. *Concurrent Pos:* Res assoc, Univ Ill, 64; Smith-Mundt scholar, Mass Inst Technol. *Mem:* Am Phys Soc; NY Acad Sci. *Res:* Quantum-statistical mechanics; many-body problem; liquid helium; thin film and theory of superconductivity; low-temperature physics. *Mailing Add:* Hilldale Lane Sands Point NY 11050

KAWOOYA, JOHN KASAJJA, protein folding, reconstitution of proteins with lipids, for more information see previous edition

KAY, ALAN, PERSONAL COMPUTING. *Current Pos:* DISNEY FEL, WALT DISNEY IMAGINEERING RES & DEVELOP INC, 96- *Personal Data:* b May 17, 40; m 83, Bonnie Lynn. *Educ:* Univ Colo, BS, 66; Univ Utah, PhD, 69. *Honors & Awards:* J D Warnier Prize; Software Systs Award, Asn Comput Mach. *Prof Exp:* Apple fel, Apple Comput Inc, 84-96. *Concurrent Pos:* Chief scientist, Atari Inc, 84- *Mem:* Nat Acad Eng; fel Royal Soc Arts; fel AAAS. *Res:* Help children learn to think better. *Mailing Add:* Walt Disney Imagineering Res & Develop Inc 1401 Flower St PO Box 25020 Glendale CA 91221-5020

KAY, ALVIN JOHN, MATHEMATICAL ANALYSIS. *Current Pos:* from instr to assoc prof, 70-92, PROF MATH, TEX A&I UNIV, 92- *Personal Data:* b Luling, Tex, June 10, 38; m 67; c 4. *Educ:* Southwest Tex State Univ, BS, 61, MA, 65; Univ Houston, PhD(math), 75. *Prof Exp:* Teacher math, Woodsboro High Sch, 61-64; asst, Southwest Tex State Univ, 64-65; instr, San Jacinto Col, 65-69; asst, Univ Houston, 69-70. *Mem:* Am Math Soc. *Res:* Integral equations and product integral. *Mailing Add:* Dept Math Tex A&M Univ Kingsville TX 78363

KAY, CYRIL MAX, BIOCHEMISTRY. *Current Pos:* from asst prof to assoc prof, 58-67, PROF BIOCHEM, UNIV ALTA, 67- *Personal Data:* b Calgary, Alta, Oct 3, 31; m 53, Faye Bloomenthal; c Lewis E & Lisa (Sherman). *Educ:* McGill Univ, BSc, 52; Harvard Univ, PhD(biochem), 56. *Honors & Awards:* Ayerst Award Biochem, 70. *Prof Exp:* Fel, Life Ins Med Res Fund, Cambridge Univ, 56-57; res phys biochemist, Eli Lilly & Co, 57-58. *Concurrent Pos:* Med Res Coun Can vis prof, Weizmann Inst Sci, Rehovot, Israel, 69-70; co-dir, Med Res Coun Group Protein Struct & Function, Univ Alta, 74-95; mem, Protein Eng Network Ctr Excellence, 90. *Mem:* Fel NY Acad Sci; fel Royal Soc Can; Brit Biochem Soc; Am Soc Biol Chem; Can Biochem Soc; Biophys Soc; Order Can. *Res:* Protein physical chemistry; hydrodynamic and optical properties of macromolecules; correlation of physico-chemical properties with biological function for muscle proteins; de novo design of proteins. *Mailing Add:* 9408-143d St Edmonton AB T5R 0P7 Can. *Fax:* 403-492-0095; *E-Mail:* ckay@gpu.srv.ualberta.ca

KAY, DAVID CLIFFORD, COMBINATORICS, FINITE MATHEMATICS. *Current Pos:* AT DEPT MATH, UNIV NC. *Personal Data:* b Oklahoma City, Okla, July 26, 33; m 55, 78; c 3. *Educ:* Otterbein Col, BS, 55; Univ Pittsburgh, MS, 59; Mich State Univ, PhD(math), 63. *Prof Exp:* Asst prof math, Univ Wyo, 63-66. *Concurrent Pos:* Res Coun award, Univ Wyo, 65; dir, Reg NSF Conf, Convexity, Nat Sci Found, 71. *Mem:* Sigma Xi; Am Math Soc; Math Asn Am. *Res:* Problems regarding curve-curvature in metric spaces; axiomatic convexity, matroids and geometric problems in topological linear spaces. *Mailing Add:* Dept Math Univ NC Ashville NC 28804

KAY, DAVID CYRIL, PSYCHIATRY, PSYCHOPHARMACOLOGY. *Current Pos:* ASSOC PROF PSYCHIAT & PHARMACOL, BAYLOR COL MED, 80-; DIR DRUG ABUSE PROG, HOUSTON VET ADMIN HOSP, 80- *Personal Data:* b Sault Ste Marie, Mich, Sept 5, 32; m 61; c 4. *Educ:* Wheaton Col, Ill, BS, 54; Univ Ill, Chicago, MD, 58; Am Bd Psychiat & Neurol, dipl, 69. *Prof Exp:* Intern, Presby-St Luke's Hosp, Chicago, 58-59; staff physician, USPHS Hosp, Ft Worth, Tex, 59-61; res psychiatrist, Ill State Psychiat Inst, 61-64; chief exp psychiat unit, Addiction Res Ctr, Nat Inst Drug Abuse, 66-69, chief exp psychiat sect, 69-80. *Concurrent Pos:* USPHS Ment health career develop fel, 61-66; fel, Addiction Res Ctr, Nat Inst Ment Health, 64-66; vis lectr, Asbury Theol Sem, 64-66; clin assoc prof, Med Ctr, Univ Ky, 64-80. *Mem:* Am Soc Pharmacol & Exp Therapeut; Int Brain Res Orgn; Sigma Xi; Am Psychiat Asn; Am Soc Clin Pharmacol & Therapeut; Soc Neurosci. *Res:* Behavioral and physiological investigation of psychoactive drugs and individuals who abuse them; interaction of sleep with drugs and sexual function. *Mailing Add:* 1313 Campbell Rd Bldg C Houston TX 77055-6403. *Fax:* 713-973-0545

KAY, DENIS G, MOLECULAR BIOLOGY. *Current Pos:* Res fel, 87-90, SR RES SCIENTIST MOLECULAR BIOL, CLIN RES INST MONTREAL, 90- *Personal Data:* b Prince Edward Island, Can, Aug 14, 56. *Educ:* Dalhousie Univ, BS, 78, MS, 81; McGill Univ, PhD(biochem), 87. *Mem:* Am Soc Cell Biol; Am Soc Biochem & Molecular Biol. *Res:* Molecular biology. *Mailing Add:* Lab Molecular Biol Rm 502 Clin Res Inst Montreal 110 Pine Ave W Montreal PQ H2W 1R7 Can

KAY, EDWARD LEO, ORGANIC CHEMISTRY. *Current Pos:* RETIRED. *Personal Data:* b Cleveland, Ohio, Sept 23, 24; m 55; c 4. *Educ:* Case Western Reserve Univ, BS, 47, MS, 53, PhD(org chem), 55. *Prof Exp:* Res scientist org chem, Texaco Inc, 55-60; sr res assoc org chem, Firestone Tire & Rubber Co, 60-85. *Mem:* Am Chem Soc. *Res:* Organic chemicals synthesis; organic chemical process development; oxidation studies; vulcanization accelerators; adhesion studies; vapor phase oxidation of hydrocarbons; scrap rubber disposal processes; fire and smoke suppressants; guayule natural rubber processing; reinforcement of polyurethanes. *Mailing Add:* 79 S Tamarack Akron OH 44319-4546

KAY, ELIZABETH ALISON, BIOLOGY. *Current Pos:* From asst prof to assoc prof sci, Univ Hawaii, Manoa, 57-66, assoc dean, Grad Div, 75-79, actg vchancellor, 84-85, PROF ZOOL, UNIV HAWAII, MANOA, 70-; HON ASSOC MALACOL, B P BISHOP MUS, 58- *Personal Data:* b Kauai,

Hawaii, Sept 27, 28. *Educ:* Mills Col, BA, 50; Cambridge Univ, BA, 52, MA, 56; Univ Hawaii, PhD, 57. *Concurrent Pos:* Fulbright scholar, 50-52. *Mem:* Fel AAAS; Soc Syst Zool; Marine Biol Asn UK; Challenger Soc; Malacol Soc Australia; fel Linmean Soc. *Res:* Functional morphology of marine gastropods; molluscan ecology and systematics; biogeography. *Mailing Add:* Dept Zool Univ Hawaii Manoa 2538 The Mall Honolulu HI 96822-2270

KAY, ERIC, PHYSICAL CHEMISTRY, THIN FILM PLASTICS. *Current Pos:* PROF, DEPT MAT SCI & TECHNOL, STANFORD UNIV, 92- *Personal Data:* b Heidelberg, Ger, Nov 23, 26; nat US; m 53, Lorell Davs; c 3. *Educ:* Univ Calif, BS, 53; Univ Wash, Seattle, PhD(chem), 58. *Hon Degrees:* Dr, Univ Karlsruhe, Ger, 89. *Honors & Awards:* John Thornton Mem Award, Am Vacuum Soc, 89. *Prof Exp:* Res chemist, Best Co, Oakland, Calif, 48-52 & Lawrence Radiation Lab, Univ Calif, 52-54; asst phys chem, Univ Wash, Seattle, 54-55; staff res chemist, IBM Corp, 58-65, head, Mat Sci Dept, Res Lab, 65-92. *Concurrent Pos:* Vis prof, Univ Calif, Berkeley, 68-69; mem, Tech Rev Panel, Nat Bur Stand, 76-79 & rev comt, Argonne Univ Asn Math Sci & Technol Div, Argonne Nat Lab, 81-86 & Tech Rev bd, Nat Submicron Facil, Cornell Univ, 85-; US Sr Scientist Von Humboldt Award, 87-88. *Mem:* Fel Am Vacuum Soc; fel Am Phys Soc; Sigma Xi. *Res:* Ion impact phenomena on condensed phases; plasma chemistry; surface phenomena; chemistry and physics of thin films; surface magnetism; cluster science. *Mailing Add:* PO Box 28 Mendocino CA 95460. *Fax:* 707-937-3467; *E-Mail:* kayeric@almaden.ibm.com

KAY, FENTON RAY, T-E SPECIES MANAGEMENT, VERTEBRATE ZOOLOGY. *Current Pos:* ADJ ASSOC PROF, DEPT FISHERY & WILDLIFE SCI, NMEX STATE UNIV, 95-, RES SPECIALIST, GORNADA EXP RANGE, 96- *Personal Data:* b Pacoima, Calif, Oct 10, 42; div; c Aelene B & Jennifer M. *Educ:* Nev Southern Univ, BS, 67; Univ Nev, Las Vegas, MS, 69; NMex State Univ, PhD(biol), 75. *Prof Exp:* Res asst, Desert Res Inst, Univ Nev, Las Vegas, 70, US Int Biol Prog, Desert Biome, Dept Biol, NMex State Univ, 70-74; NIH trainee, Dept Physiol, Col Med, Univ Fla, 74-76; asst prof biol, Calif State Univ, Los Angeles, 76-78; habitat staff biol, Nev Dept Wildlife, 84-90; ind consult, Biol & Environ, 90-92; supvr, Natural Resource Data Bases, Ariz Game & Fish Dept, 92-93; sr environ scientist, Proteus Corp, 93-95; sr biologist/regional mgr, ECG Inc, 95-96. *Concurrent Pos:* Comput programmer & opers mgr, OAO Corp (White Sands Missile Range), 80-83; independent comput consult, 83-84; instr, Truckee Meadows Community Col, Reno, 84-89, Western Nev Community Col, Carson City, 88, Univ Nev, Reno, 88-89, West Coast Univ, Los Angeles, 92. *Mem:* Ecol Soc Am; Am Soc Mammalogists; Herpetologists League; Sigma Xi. *Res:* Thermal biology of desert animals; desert animal community composition; economic value of wildlife; application of geographic information systems to environmental problems, effects of rodents on desert grassland structure. *Mailing Add:* 4100 Cholla Rd Las Cruces NM 88011. *E-Mail:* kayrat@lascruces.com

KAY, H DAVID, CELLULAR IMMUNOLOGY, LEUKEMIA. *Current Pos:* RES COORDR & CO-DIR, DEPT INTERNAL MED, LAB GENE REGULATION RES, 91- *Personal Data:* b Glendale, Ohio, Sept 6, 43; m 68, Judy Willeke; c Carrie S & Emily J. *Educ:* Rensselaer Polytech Inst, BS, 66; Iowa State Univ, MS, 69, PhD(immunobiol), 72. *Prof Exp:* Asst tumor immunol, M D Anderson Hosp & Tumor Inst, Univ Tex, 72-73; assoc prof med & dir, Exp Immunol Lab, Med Ctr, Univ Nebr, 83-90, chmn, Immunol Coun, 84-90; legal consult, 90-91. *Concurrent Pos:* Lectr cellular immunol, Univ Nebr, Omaha, 88. *Mem:* Am Asn Immunologists; Am Rheumatism Asn; Am Asn Cancer Res; Am Fedn Clin Res; Int League Against Rheumatism. *Res:* Design and testing of novel antisense oligonucleotides for use in clinical research trials to treat and cure certain cancers such as leukemia, lymphoma and breast cancer. *Mailing Add:* 12829 O St Omaha NE 68137-1834. *Fax:* 402-559-8101; *E-Mail:* hdkay@unmcvm.unmc.edu

KAY, IRVIN (WILLIAM), APPLIED MATHEMATICS, ELECTROMAGNETISM. *Current Pos:* SR CONSULT, VERTECH INC, 96- *Personal Data:* b Savannah, Ga, Apr 19, 24; m 54, Marjorie Nimz; c Lily & Eli. *Educ:* NY Univ, BA, 48, MS, 49, PhD(math), 53. *Prof Exp:* Res assoc math, NY Univ, 52-58, from asst prof to assoc prof, 59-62; sr res mathematician, Conductron Corp, 62-64, dept head advan systs, 64-68, dir independent res & develop, 68-71; prof elec eng, Wayne State Univ, 71-73; staff mem, Inst Defense Anal, 73-96. *Mem:* Am Math Soc; Am Phys Soc. *Res:* Electromagnetic theory; systems analysis; optics. *Mailing Add:* 6111 Wooten Dr Falls Church VA 22044

KAY, JACK GARVIN, PHYSICAL & INORGANIC CHEMISTRY, NUCLEAR & ATMOSPHERIC CHEMISTRY. *Current Pos:* head dept, 69-85, PROF CHEM, DREXEL UNIV, 69- *Personal Data:* b Scott City, Kans, July 11, 30; m 52; c 2. *Educ:* Univ Kans, AB, 52, PhD(phys chem), 60. *Prof Exp:* From instr to asst prof inorg chem, Univ Ill, Urbana, 59-66; prof chem, Univ Toledo, 66-69, chmn dept, 66-68. *Concurrent Pos:* Consult, Chemotronics, Inc, Avco, Inc, Charlestown Twp, Chester County, Pa, Alex C Fergusson Co & Dwight & Wilson Co; prin investr, Atomic Energy Comn, 60-69 & NSF, 84-; rep Coun Chem Res, 80-; rep Pa Asn Cols & Univs on Task Force to Develop Pa Right-to-Know legis, 83-84. *Mem:* AAAS; Am Chem Soc; Am Phys Soc; Faraday Soc; fel Am Inst Chem; Am Geophys Union. *Res:* Electronic spectroscopy of gaseous diatomic molecules; matrix-isolation spectroscopy; flash heating and kinetic spectroscopy; flash photolysis; high temperature chemistry; solar furnaces; radiation chemistry; hot atom chemistry in inorganic crystals; nuclear and radiochemistry; radon and decay products in the atmosphere and oceans. *Mailing Add:* Drexel Univ 32nd & Chestnut Sts Philadelphia PA 19104

KAY, KENNETH GEORGE, INTRAMOLECULAR ENERGY TRANSFER, SEMICLASSICAL APPROXIMATIONS. *Current Pos:* PROF CHEM, BAR-ILAN UNIV, 87- *Personal Data:* b New York, NY, Oct 13, 43; m 68, Katherine Brody; c Victoria, Elizabeth & Jennifer. *Educ:* Polytech Inst, Brooklyn, BS, & MS, 65; Johns Hopkins Univ, PhD(chem), 70. *Prof Exp:* Res assoc chem, Univ Chicago, 70-71; from asst prof to prof, Kans State Univ, 71-81. *Concurrent Pos:* Vis assoc prof, Tel-Aviv Univ, 79-80; vis prof, Univ Toronto, 82-83. *Mem:* Am Phys Soc; Am Chem Soc. *Res:* Theory of molecular reaction dynamics; unimolecular dissociation; intramolecular vibrational energy transfer; quantum ergodic theory; theoretical models for photodecomposition reactions; Semiclassical approximations. *Mailing Add:* Chem Dept Bar Ilan Univ Ramat Gan Israel. *Fax:* 972-535-1250; *E-Mail:* kay@fen.cc.biu.ac.il

KAY, MARGUERITE M B, GERIATRICS & GERONTOLOGY, MEMBRANE BIOLOGY. *Current Pos:* REGENTS PROF, MICROBIOL & IMMUNOL & MED, COL MED, UNIV ARIZ, 90- *Personal Data:* b Washington, DC, May 13, 47. *Educ:* Univ Calif, Berkeley, BA, 70; Univ Calif, San Francisco, MD, 74; Nat Inst Aging, NIH, cert, 76. *Prof Exp:* Staff fel, Geront Res Ctr, Nat Inst Child Health & Human Develop, NIH Baltimore City Hosp, 74, USPHS Off & chief, High Resolution Membrane Lab, 75-77; chief, Lab Molecular & Clinical Immunol, Veterans Admin Wadsworth Med Ctr, Los Angeles Calif; prof med & prof med biochem & genetics & dir, Div Geriat Med,, Tex A&M Univ, Col Med, 81-90, prof micro biol & immunol, 81-91. *Concurrent Pos:* Consult, immuno-electron micros, Dept Basic & Clin Immunol & Microbiol, Med Univ SC, 74-81, biol consult, Electron Micros Lab, Enrico Fermi Inst, Univ Chicago, 74-75, reviewer, NSF & US-Israel Binational Sci Found, 77-, reviewer, NIH; NAm ed, Geront, 88- *Mem:* Am Soc Clin Invest; Am Soc Biol Chem; Am Asn Immunologists; Am Geriat Soc; Am Soc Cell Biol; Am Soc Hemat. *Res:* Molecular and cell biology of aging. *Mailing Add:* Dept Microbiol & Immunol Rm 644 LSN Univ Ariz Col Med 1501 N Campbell Ave Tucson AZ 85724-0001. *Fax:* 520-626-2100

KAY, MICHAEL AARON, ANALYTICAL CHEMISTRY, HEALTH-SAFETY & ENVIRONMENTAL CONSULTING. *Current Pos:* PRES, AMBRY, INC, 88- *Personal Data:* b San Francisco, Calif, May 7, 43; m 68, 76, Rachel A Foley; c Andrew & Daniel. *Educ:* Univ Calif, Berkeley, BS, 65; Mass Inst Technol, Cambridge, ScD, 70. *Prof Exp:* Radiochemist, US Naval Radiol Defense Lab, Calif, 65; sr chemist, Res Reactor Facility, Univ Mo, Columbia, 70-75, sr res scientist, 75-78; mem fac, Univ Mo, Columbia, 75-78; sr scientist, Rockwell Hanford Opers, Wash, 78-80; assoc prof chem & dir, Reed Reactor Facil, Reed Col, 80-86; mgr chem res & develop, Hannah Car Wash Int, 86-88. *Concurrent Pos:* Consult forensic sci & health physics, 81-; adj prof anal chem, Portland State Univ, Ore, 91- *Mem:* AAAS; Am Nuclear Soc; Am Chem Soc; Health Physics Soc; Inst Hazardous Mats Mgt; fel Am Instit Chemists. *Res:* Health, safety & environment compliance; environmental radiation monitoring; data quality assurance & quality control expert witness. *Mailing Add:* PO Box 22266 Milwaukie OR 97269-2266. *Fax:* 503-245-8529; *E-Mail:* mikekay@teleport.com

KAY, MORTIMER ISAIA, CRYSTALLOGRAPHY. *Current Pos:* head sea water-surfactant project, ocean thermal energy conversion, 79-80, PHYS SCIENTIST, US DEPT ENERGY, 81- *Personal Data:* b Bronx, NY, Aug 27, 30; m 64. *Educ:* Brooklyn Col, BA, 52; Purdue Univ, MS, 53; Univ Conn, PhD(phys chem), 58. *Prof Exp:* Asst chem, Purdue Univ, 52-53; asst, Univ Conn, 53-57; res assoc, Pa State Univ, 57-59; fel, Royal Norweg Coun Sci & Indust Res, 59-60; res scientist, NASA, 60-61; res assoc prof, Ga Inst Technol, 62-64; sr scientist & head neutron diffraction prog, PR Nuclear Ctr, 64-77, head, Mats Sci Div, PR Ctr Energy & Environ Res, 76-79. *Concurrent Pos:* Vis assoc physicist, Brookhaven Nat Lab, 57-59. *Mem:* AAAS; Am Chem Soc; Am Phys Soc; Am Crystallog Asn; Sigma Xi. *Res:* Molecular and crystal structure; diffraction studies of ferroelectric transitions; ocean thermal energy; pyroelectric energy conversion; surface chemistry; atomic energy. *Mailing Add:* 70 Oak Shade Rd Gaithersburg MD 20878-1048

KAY, PETER STEVEN, CLINICAL CHEMISTRY, INSTRUMENTATION. *Current Pos:* PRIN, STRATEGIC MGR ADV GROUP, 86- *Personal Data:* b Milwaukee, Wis, Sept 24, 37. *Educ:* Cornell Univ, AB, 59; Purdue Univ, PhD(org chem), 66. *Prof Exp:* Tech asst coal chem, US Steel Res Ctr, 59-60; teaching asst chem, Purdue Univ, 60-62; res chemist, Textile Fibers Dept, 66-69, col rels rep, Employee Rels Dept, 69-70; res chemist, Textile Fibers Dept, E I Du Pont de Nemours & Co, Inc, 70-72, mkt rep, 72-73, dist mgr, 73-76, nat sales mgr, Sci Instruments, Inst Prod, 76-77, mgr thermal anal, 77-79, mgr liquid chromatography, 79-80, nat sales mgr, Electronic Div, 80-82; dir mkt Harshaw Chem Co (Gulf Oil), 82-84; gen mgr x-ray prod, Picker Int, 85-86. *Mem:* AAAS; Am Chem Soc; Sigma Xi; fel Am Inst Chemists. *Res:* Kinetics and product distributions in solvolyses of allylic halides and esters; polyamide fibers; biocomponent fibers; polyamide textile fibers; robotics; digital x-ray techniques; clinical laboratory automated analyzers and medical imaging devices; general management consultation. *Mailing Add:* Six Mariners Cove Cincinnati OH 45249-1791

KAY, ROBERT EUGENE, EPITAXIAL CRYSTAL GROWTH, INFRARED DETECTORS. *Current Pos:* mgr, Biosci Dept, 61-80, TECH CONSULT, SEMICONDUCTOR TECHNOL DEPT AERONUTRONIC DIV, FORD AEROSPACE CORP, 61- *Personal Data:* b Missoula, Mont, Dec 23, 25; m 51, Beverly Buell; c Kimberly, Roberta & Gregory. *Educ:* Univ Calif, Los Angeles, BS, 48, PhD(bot sci), 52. *Prof Exp:* Asst bot, Univ Calif, Los Angeles, 51-52; supvry chemist, US Naval Radiol Defense Lab, 54-61. *Res:* Radiobiology; lipid metabolism; isolated perfused organs; adaptive enzyme systems; olfactory transduction in insects; model membrane systems; interactions of dyes with biological macromolecules; immobilized enzymes; organic semiconductors; infrared detectors; missile-vehicle integration; missile systs mgt; high temperature batteries; hetero epitaxial crystal growth. *Mailing Add:* 1515 Warwick Ln Newport Beach CA 92660

KAY, ROBERT LEO, PHYSICAL CHEMISTRY, SOLUTION CHEMISTRY. *Current Pos:* sr fel, Mellon Inst, 63-67, actg dir, Ctr Spec Studies, 73-74, head dept, 74-83, prof, 67-90, EMER PROF CHEM, CARNEGIE-MELLOW UNIV, 90- *Personal Data:* b Hamilton, Ont, Dec 13, 24; m 52, Ann D Morrow; c David (deceased), Theresa, Joanne & Robert Jr. *Educ:* Univ Toronto, MA, 50, PhD(phys chem), 52. *Prof Exp:* Merck fel, Rockefeller Inst, 52, res asst, 53-56; asst prof chem, Brown Univ, 56-63. *Concurrent Pos:* Ed, J Solution Chem, 71- *Mem:* Am Chem Soc; Biophys Soc. *Res:* Transport properties of electrolyte solutions; structure of liquids; electrophoresis; solutions at high pressure and temperature; dielectrics; thermodynamics; computer generation of scientific information. *Mailing Add:* Carnegie Mellon Univ 4400 Fifth Ave Pittsburgh PA 15213. *Fax:* 412-268-6945; *E-Mail:* rkga@andrew.cmu.edu

KAY, ROBERT WOODBURY, GEOCHEMISTRY. *Current Pos:* from asst prof to assoc prof, 76-86, PROF GEOL, CORNELL UNIV, 86- *Personal Data:* b New York, NY, Jan 21, 43; m 75, Suzanne Mahlburg; c Jennifer & Alexander. *Educ:* Brown Univ, AB, 64; Columbia Univ, PhD(geol), 70. *Prof Exp:* Asst prof geol, Columbia Univ, 70-75; asst res geophysicist, Univ Calif, Los Angeles, 75-76. *Concurrent Pos:* Consult geochem. *Mem:* Fel Geol Soc Am; Am Geophys Union; Geochem Soc. *Res:* Geochemistry of rare earth elements in volcanic rocks; regional geology of the Aleutian Islands, Alaska; chemistry of the lower crust. *Mailing Add:* Dept Geol Sci Snee Hall Cornell Univ Ithaca NY 14853

KAY, SAUL, surgical pathology, for more information see previous edition

KAY, SUZANNE MAHLBURG, PETROLOGY, MINERALOGY. *Current Pos:* res assoc geol, 76-82, sr res assoc, Inst Study Continents, 83-93, ASSOC PROF, CORNELL UNIV, 93- *Personal Data:* b Rockford, Ill, May 30, 47; m 75, Robert; c Jennifer & Alexander. *Educ:* Univ Ill, Urbana, BS, 69, MS, 72; Brown Univ, PhD(geol), 75. *Prof Exp:* Fel geol, Univ Calif, Los Angeles, 75-76. *Concurrent Pos:* Vis assoc petrol, Calif Inst Technol, 82; vis prof, Univ Buenos Aires, Arg, 89; Fulbright fel, 89-90. *Mem:* Fel Geol Soc Am; fel Mineral Soc Am; Am Geophys Union; Sigma Xi. *Res:* Study of natural and experimentally produced intergrowths in ternary and plagioclase feldspars, genesis of magmutic rocks in the Aleutian Islands, Alaska; study of lower crustal xenoliths; volcanism and tectonism in the Andes of Argentina and Chile. *Mailing Add:* Dept Geol Sci Cornell Univ Ithaca NY 14853

KAY, WEBSTER BICE, chemical engineering, physical chemistry; deceased, see previous edition for last biography

KAYA, AZMI, SYSTEMS ENGINEERING. *Current Pos:* asst prof to assoc prof, 70-97, EMER PROF MECH ENG, UNIV AKRON, 97- *Personal Data:* b Acik, Turkey, Feb 1, 33; m 64; c 1. *Educ:* Tech Col Men, Ankara, Dipl, 52; Univ Wis, Madison, MS, 62; Univ Minn, Minneapolis, MS & PhD, 70. *Prof Exp:* Control engr, Honeywell, Inc, 62-68; teaching assoc, Univ Minn, Minneapolis, 70. *Concurrent Pos:* NSF res grant, Univ Akron, 71-72; NATO vis expert, 74. *Mem:* Am Soc Mech Engrs; Sigma Xi; Inst Elec & Electronics Engrs; Am Soc Eng Educ; Tech Asn Pulp & Paper Indust. *Res:* Modeling, control and optimization of large scale systems; control theory applications; energy management systems. *Mailing Add:* Dept Mech Eng Univ Akron Akron OH 44325

KAYA, CALVIN MASAYUKI, ENVIRONMENTAL BIOLOGY OF FISHES. *Current Pos:* From asst prof to assoc prof zool, 71-82, PROF BIOL, MONT STATE UNIV, 82- *Personal Data:* b Maui, Hawaii, Sept 4, 42; m 67, Kathryn Nozaki; c Brandon & Rachel. *Educ:* Univ Hawaii, Manoa, BA, 64; Univ Wis-Madison, MA, 67, PhD(zool), 71. *Concurrent Pos:* Vis scientist fishery biol, Nat Marine Fisheries Serv, Honolulu Lab, 78-80 & 83. *Mem:* Am Fisheries Soc. *Res:* Ecology, reproduction and behavior of fishes, with recent focus on rare or threatened freshwater fishes. *Mailing Add:* Biol Dept Mont State Univ Bozeman MT 59717. *Fax:* 406-994-3190; *E-Mail:* ubick@gemini.oscs.montana.edu

KAYA, HARRY KAZUYOSHI, INSECT PATHOLOGY & NEMATOLOGY. *Current Pos:* from asst prof to assoc prof, 76-84, PROF, DEPT NEMATOL, UNIV CALIF, DAVIS, 84- *Personal Data:* b Honolulu, Hawaii, Nov 20, 40; m 64; c 2. *Educ:* Univ Hawaii, BS, 62, MS, 66; Univ Calif, Berkeley, PhD(insect path), 70. *Prof Exp:* Asst entomologist, Conn Agr Exp Sta, 71-76. *Mem:* Soc Invert Path; Entom Soc Am; Int Orgn Biol Control; Soc Nematol; fel Japan Soc Promotion Sci. *Res:* Biological control of insects; epizootiology in insect populations; use of microorganisms to control insects; insect nematology. *Mailing Add:* Entom Univ Calif Davis CA 95616-5200. *Fax:* 530-752-5809; *E-Mail:* hkkaya@ucdavis.edu

KAYANI, JOSEPH THOMAS, APPLIED MECHANICS, STRESS ANALYSIS. *Current Pos:* PRIN ENGR APPL MECH, EBASCO SERV, INC, 78- *Personal Data:* b Kuravilangad, India, Mar 8, 45; US citizen; m 69; c 2. *Educ:* Univ Kerala, India, BSc, 67; Polytech Inst Brooklyn, MS, 71; Polytech Inst NY, PhD(mech eng), 75. *Prof Exp:* Engr supvr construct, Telecommun Dept, Govt India, 67-69; mech engr, Acoust & Vibrations Lab, Souncoat Co, Inc, Brooklyn, 72-74, stress analysis, Nuclear Power Servs, Inc, New York, 74-75, Burns & Roe, Inc, 75-78. *Concurrent Pos:* Res asst, Polytech Inst Brooklyn, 73-75; fel fel, Polytech Inst New York, 75- *Mem:* Am Soc Mech Engrs; Am Acad Mech. *Res:* Stress and vibration analysis of pressure vessels and piping; nonlinear random vibrations; acoustics and noise control of machines and structural components. *Mailing Add:* 300 Ellen Pl Jericho NY 11753

KAYAR, SUSAN RENNIE, RESPIRATORY PHYSIOLOGY, MICROCIRCULATION & DIVING PHYSIOLOGY. *Current Pos:* RES PHYSIOLOGIST, NAVAL MED RES INST, NAT NAVAL MED CTR, BETHESDA, MD, 90- *Personal Data:* b Highland, Ill, May 17, 53. *Educ:* Univ Miami, BS, 74, PhD(biol), 78. *Honors & Awards:* Arne Zetterstrom Award Hydrogen Diving Res. *Prof Exp:* Res asst, Everglades Nat Park, 78-79; res assoc, Univ Colo, Boulder, 79-81; postdoctoral fel, Med Sch, Univ Colo, Denver, 81-84; res asst prof, Univ Bern, Switz, 84-89; instr, Univ Med Dent, NJ, 89-90. *Mem:* Am Physiol Soc; Microcirculatory Soc; AAAS. *Res:* Patented a process for facilitating diving decompression by biochemical elimnation of gases in divers. *Mailing Add:* Albert R Behnke Diving Med Res Ctr Naval Med Res Inst Nat Naval Med Ctr 8901 Wisconsin Ave Bethesda MD 20889-5607. *Fax:* 301-295-0782; *E-Mail:* kayar@mail2.nmri.nnmc.navy.mil

KAYDEN, HERBERT J, MEDICINE. *Current Pos:* Asst, NY Univ, 49-51, clin instr, 51-54, from asst prof to assoc prof, 54-70, PROF MED, SCH MED, NY UNIV, 70- *Personal Data:* b New York, NY, Jan 30, 20; m 51; c 2. *Educ:* Columbia Col, AB, 40; NY Univ, MD, 43. *Concurrent Pos:* From asst vis physician to assoc vis physician, Goldwater Mem Hosp, 50-56, vis physician, 56-, assoc dir, 58-62; from asst attend physician to assoc attend physician, NY Univ Hosp, 51-71, attend physician, 71-; from asst vis physician to assoc vis physician, Bellevue Hosp, 52-71, vis physician, 71-; attend physician, Manhattan Vet Admin Hosp, 56-; mem coun arteriosclerosis, Am Heart Asn. *Mem:* Am Soc Pharmacol & Exp Therapeut; Harvey Soc; Am Fedn Clin Res; fel Am Col Physicians; fel NY Acad Med. *Res:* Cardiovascular diseases, especially disorders of cardiac rhythm; pharmacology of antiarrhythmic drugs; lipid metabolism in humans, including studies of serum and tissue lipoproteins; vitamin E metabolism in humans. *Mailing Add:* Dept Med NY Univ Col Med 550 First Ave New York NY 10016-6402. *Fax:* 212-263-6571

KAYE, ALBERT L(OUIS), ELECTROCHEMICAL ENGINEERING. *Current Pos:* from assoc prof to prof, 67-74, spec asst to chancellor, 76-81, EMER PROF METALL ENG TECHNOL, PURDUE UNIV, 74- *Personal Data:* b New York, NY, Mar 16, 09; m 34; c 3. *Educ:* Mass Inst Technol, SB, 31, MS, 32, ScD(electrochem), 34. *Prof Exp:* Asst chem, Calif Inst Technol, 32-33; res assoc, Div Indust Coop, Mass Inst Technol, 34-37, secy comt corrosion metals, 35-37; metallurgist, Carnegie-Ill Steel Corp, Chicago, 37-41, mgr alloy bur, Metall Div, Chicago Dist, 41-44, metall engr, Pittsburgh, 44-45; vpres & gen mgr, Beckman Supply Co, 45-67. *Concurrent Pos:* Gerard Swope fel physics, Mass Inst Technol, 31-32; indust metall consult, 82-88; Paul Harris fel, Rotary Int, 86; mem, City of Hammond Redevelopment Comn, 66-70. *Mem:* AAAS; Am Soc Testing & Mat; Am Soc Metals; Am Inst Mining, Metall & Petrol Engrs; Royal Photog Soc of Gt Brit. *Res:* Development of alloy steels for automotive, aircraft and high temperature uses; electrochemistry of the alkaline-earth metals. *Mailing Add:* 6618 Forest Ave Hammond IN 46324-1003

KAYE, ALVIN MAURICE, REPRODUCTIVE ENDOCRINOLOGY, DEVELOPMENTAL BIOLOGY. *Current Pos:* mem res staff biochem cancer, Weizmann Inst Sci, 56-68, sr scientist biodynamics, 68-77, assoc prof & hormone res, 77-86, Joseph Moss prof molecular endocrinol & hormone res, 85-95, PROF MOLECULAR GENETICS, WEIZMANN INST SCI, 95- *Personal Data:* b New York, NY, Sept 18, 30; m 58, Myra Ockrent. *Educ:* Columbia Univ, AB, 51, AM, 55; Univ Pa, PhD, 56. *Honors & Awards:* Bernhard Zondek Mem Plenary Lectr, VI Int Cong Hormonal Steroids, 82. *Prof Exp:* Asst cytol, Columbia Univ, 51-52; asst cell physiol, Univ Pa, 53-55. *Concurrent Pos:* Corresp ed, J Steroid Biochem, Molecular Biol; chmn, Int Orgn Comt, Hormones & Cancer Congresses & mem, Prog Comt, Int Study Group Steroid Hormones. *Mem:* Israel Chem Soc; Biochem Soc Israel; Am Soc Cell Biol; Endocrine Soc; Sigma Xi; Biochem Soc UK. *Res:* Enzymic modification of nucleic acids and proteins; hormonal induction of protein synthesis; enzyme catabolism; mechanism of carcinogenesis by ethyl carbamate regulation of creatine kinase amd ornithine decarboxylase genes; hormones & osteoporosis; selective estrogen receptor modulators and cancer. *Mailing Add:* Dept Molecular Genetics Weizmann Inst Sci Rehovot 76100 Israel. *Fax:* 972-8-9344108; *E-Mail:* lhkaye@weizmann.weizmann.ae.il

KAYE, BRIAN H, PHYSICS. *Current Pos:* PROF PHYSICS & DIR INST FINE PARTICLES RES, LAURENTIAN UNIV, 68- *Personal Data:* b Hull, Eng, July 8, 32; m 57; c 4. *Educ:* Univ Hull, BSc, 53, MSc, 55; Univ London, PhD(physics), 62. *Prof Exp:* Sci officer, Brit Atomic Weapons Res Estab, 55-59; lectr physics, Univ Nottingham, 59-62; res officer, Welwyn Res Asn, 62-63; sr physicist, IIT Res Inst, 63-68. *Concurrent Pos:* Consult, Brit Atomic Energy Authority, 61-63; managing dir, Brian Kaye Assocs Ltd; educ & res consult. *Mem:* Am Soc Testing & Mat. *Res:* Particle size analysis of powders; physical and chemical properties of powder systems and aerosols; fractal geometry powder mixing; author of two books. *Mailing Add:* Dept Physics Laurentian Univ Sudbury ON P3E 2C6 Can

KAYE, DONALD, MEDICINE. *Current Pos:* PROF MED & CHMN DEPT, MED COL PA & CHIEF MED, HOSP, 69- *Personal Data:* b New York, NY, Aug 12, 31; m 55; c 4. *Educ:* Yale Univ, AB, 53; NY Univ, MD, 57; Am Bd Internal Med, dipl, 64, cert infectious dis, 74. *Honors & Awards:* Lindback Award. *Prof Exp:* From asst prof to assoc prof med, Cornell Univ, 63-69. *Concurrent Pos:* NIH fel, Cornell Univ Med Col, 60-62, spec fel, 62-63, NY Health Res Coun career scientist award, 66-69; from asst attend physician to assoc attend physician, NY Hosp, 63-69; hon prof, Fed Univ Bahia, Salvadore, Brazil. *Mem:* Asn Am Physicians; Asn Profs Med; Infectious Dis Soc Am; master Am Col Physicians; Am Soc Clin Invest. *Res:* Research in infectious diseases with special interest in pathogenesis of bacterial infections and host defense mechanisms against bacterial infection. *Mailing Add:* Med Col Penn 3300 Henry Ave Philadelphia PA 19035

KAYE, GEORGE THOMAS, SYSTEMS DESIGN. *Current Pos:* br head, 79-84, PROG MGR, NAVAL OCEAN SYSTS CTR, SAN DIEGO, 85- *Personal Data:* b Lorain, Ohio, Dec 11, 44; m 67; c 2. *Educ:* US Naval Acad, BS, 66; Univ Mich, MS, 72, PhD(oceanog), 74. *Prof Exp:* Asst res oceanogr, Sea Grant Prog, Univ Mich, 71-74; asst res oceanogr, Marine Phys Lab, Scripps Inst Oceanog, Univ Calif, San Diego, 74-78. *Mem:* Acoust Soc Am. *Res:* High-frequency sound scattering from biota and water density structures; theoretical acoustics; upper-ocean measurements with drifting arrays; acoustic noise generation by storms; model decomposition of internal waves; information processing and data fusion for systems application; optical propagation in the upper ocean. *Mailing Add:* Code D11 NCOSC RDTE Div 53560 Hull St San Diego CA 92152

KAYE, GORDON I, WASTE MANAGEMENT, CELL BIOLOGY. *Current Pos:* prof & chmn, Dept Anat, Albany Med Col, 76-87, prof path, 81-94, Alden March prof anat, cell biol & neurobiol, 87-94, ALDEN MARCH PROF PATH, ALBANY MED COL, 94- *Personal Data:* b New York, NY, Aug 13, 35; m 56, Nancy Weber; c Jacqueline & Vivienne. *Educ:* Columbia Col, AB, 55; Columbia Univ, AM, 57, PhD(anat), 61. *Honors & Awards:* Charles Huebschman Prize, Columbia Univ, 54; Tousimis Prize, 81; Raymond C Truex Distinguished lectr, Hahneman Med Col, 87. *Prof Exp:* Res assoc anat, Columbia Univ, 61-63, assoc surg path, 63-66, from asst prof to assoc prof , 66-76. *Concurrent Pos:* Career scientist, Health Res Coun New York, 63-72; dir, F H Cabot Lab Electron Micros, Columbia Univ, 63-76; consult, NY Vet Admin Hosp, 65-; metab & digestive dis res career award, Nat Inst Arthritis, 72-76; consult surg, 76-78; affil attend surg, Albany Med Ctr Hosp, 78-93; prof, Sch Pub Health, State Univ NY, Albany, 85-; pres & chief exec officer, Waste Reduction by Waste Reduction Inc, Troy, NY; chmn, NY State Low-Level Waste Group, 86-95. *Mem:* Am Soc Cell Biol; Am Asn Anat; Asn Anat Chmn (pres, 80-81); Harvey Soc; Sigma Xi. *Res:* Electron microscopy; fluid transport; epithelial-mesenchymal interactions in gastrointestinal tissue differentiation; collagen-glycoconjugate interaction in cornea; cell biology of soft tissue tumors; waste management technology. *Mailing Add:* Dept Path A-135 Albany Med Col Albany NY 12208. *Fax:* 518-262-5136, 271-2040; *E-Mail:* gordon_kaye@ccgateway.amc.edu

KAYE, HOWARD, POLYMER CHEMISTRY, INDUSTRIAL CHEMISTRY. *Current Pos:* DIR, POLYHEDRON LABS INC, 80- *Personal Data:* b New York, NY, Dec 9, 38; m 66; c 2. *Educ:* Polytech Inst Brooklyn, BS, 60, PhD(polymer chem), 65. *Prof Exp:* NIH fel, Cambridge Univ, 65-67; asst prof chem, Tex A&M Univ, 67-73; pres, Howard Kaye & Assoc, 73-80. *Concurrent Pos:* Consult chem indust. *Mem:* Fel Am Inst Chemists; Am Chem Soc; Soc Plastic Engrs; Royal Soc Chem; Am Soc Testing Mat; Royal Micros Soc. *Res:* Synthesis and properties of macromolecules; new syntheses for the manufacture of industrially important materials and chemicals; process and product improvement research; characterization of high polymers; automatic chemical analysis; chemical, physical and thermal testing of plastics. *Mailing Add:* Polyhedron Laba 10626 Kinghurst Houston TX 77099

KAYE, JACK ALAN, ATMOSPHERIC CHEMICAL MODELING, SATELLITE DATA ANALYSIS & SCIENCE PROGRAM MANAGEMENT. *Current Pos:* space scientist, Goddard Space Flight Ctr, 83-91, MGR, ATMOSPHERIC CHEM MODELING & ANALYSIS PROG, NASA HQ, 91- *Personal Data:* b Brooklyn, NY, Nov 3, 54; m 84, Dawn Bressler; c Rebecca, Hannah & Allison. *Educ:* Adelphi Univ, BA, 76; Calif Inst Technol, PhD(chem), 82. *Prof Exp:* Res assoc, Plasma Physics Div, Naval Res Lab, Washington, DC, 82-83. *Mem:* Am Chem Soc; Am Geophys Union. *Res:* Management of research program on computational modeling of atmospheric chemistry; analysis of in site and remotely-sensed data on atmospheric trace constituent composition. *Mailing Add:* NASA Hq Code YS Washington DC 20546. *Fax:* 202-358-2770; *E-Mail:* jackkaye@hq.nasa.gov

KAYE, JAMES HERBERT, RADIOCHEMISTRY. *Current Pos:* RES SCIENTIST RADIOCHEM, PAC NORTHWEST LABS, BATTELLE MEM INST, 63- *Personal Data:* b Seattle, Wash, Sept 3, 37; m 65; c 3. *Educ:* Univ Wash, BS, 58; Carnegie Inst Technol, MS, 61, PhD(nuclear chem), 63. *Mem:* Am Chem Soc; Am Nuclear Soc; AAAS. *Res:* Development of highly sensitive instrumentation and techniques for measurement of trace substances in the environment. *Mailing Add:* 2119 Newcomer Ave Richland WA 99352-1830

KAYE, JEROME SIDNEY, CELL BIOLOGY. *Current Pos:* from asst prof to prof biol, 59-92, EMER PROF BIOL, UNIV ROCHESTER, 92- *Personal Data:* b Hartford, Conn, June 15, 30; m 55. *Educ:* Columbia Univ, AB, 52, MA, 54, PhD, 57. *Prof Exp:* Instr zool, Univ Calif, Los Angeles, 57-59. *Concurrent Pos:* Lalor Found fel, 58. *Res:* Transacting factors controlling gene transcription. *Mailing Add:* 160 Commonwealth Rd Rochester NY 14618

KAYE, MICHAEL PETER, physiology, surgery, for more information see previous edition

KAYE, NANCY WEBER, EMBRYOLOGY, ANIMAL PHYSIOLOGY. *Current Pos:* res assoc, Albany Med Col, 76-82, asst prof, Dept Anat, 82-89, res asst prof, Dept Med, 82-89, CONSULT, DEPT MED, ALBANY MED COL, 89- *Personal Data:* b Englewood, NJ, Sept 14, 29; m 56, Gordon; c Jacqueline & Vivienne. *Educ:* Swarthmore Col, BA, 51; Hunter Col, MEd, 54; Columbia Univ, MA, 58, PhD(zool), 60. *Prof Exp:* Res worker, Col Physicians & Surgeons, Columbia Univ, 62-76. *Concurrent Pos:* Fel neuroanat, Columbia Univ, 60-61; vis lectr, Dept Biol, Rensselaer Polytech Inst, 84; consults, EM Consult Serv, 90-; asst secy, Waste Reduction by Waste by Waste Reduction, Inc, 93- *Mem:* Sigma Xi; AAAS; Am Soc Cell Biol; Asn Res Vision & Ophthal; Am Asn Anatomists; NY Acad Sci. *Res:* Spleen and liver pathobiology and fine structure; gene mapping connective tissue genes; fine structure of connective tissue; corneal fine structure and physiology. *Mailing Add:* 212 Pinewoods Ave Troy NY 12180. *Fax:* 518-271-2040

KAYE, NORMAN JOSEPH, APPLIED BUSINESS STATISTICS, MATH APPLIED TO BUSINESS. *Current Pos:* RETIRED. *Personal Data:* b Milwaukee, Wis, Apr 24, 23; m 47; c 8. *Educ:* Marquette Univ, BS, 48; Univ Mich, MBA, 51; Univ Wis, PhD(com), 56. *Prof Exp:* Asst instr math, Marquette Univ, 49-50, asst prof math & statist, 51-55, from assoc prof to prof grad statist, 56-87, emer prof grad statist, 88. *Concurrent Pos:* Commun & Statist consult, 51-88; dept chair, Mgt Dept, Marquette Univ, 56-57 & 69-71. *Mem:* Am Statist Soc. *Res:* Communications and applied statistics. *Mailing Add:* 3137 S 30th St Milwaukee WI 53215

KAYE, ROBERT, PEDIATRICS. *Current Pos:* PROF PEDIAT & CHMN DEPT, HAHNEMANN MED COL & HOSP, 73- *Personal Data:* b New York, NY, July 17, 17; m 42; c 3. *Educ:* Johns Hopkins Univ, AB, 39, MD, 43. *Prof Exp:* From intern to chief resident pediat, Johns Hopkins Hosp, 43-45; instr, Med Sch, Johns Hopkins Univ, 45; assoc physiol, Sch Pub Health, Harvard Univ, 46-47; instr pediat, Sch Med, Univ Pa, 48-50, assoc, 50-51, from asst prof to prof, 51-73. *Concurrent Pos:* Asst, Harvard Med Sch, 46-47; asst physician, Children's Hosp, 48-51, sr physician, 51-, dir clins & clin teaching, 52-57, dep physician-in-chief, 64; asst chmn dept, Sch Med, Univ Pa, 64-73; chmn, Nat Med Adv Bd, Juvenile Diabetes Found, 73-76. *Mem:* AAAS; Am Pediat Soc; Soc Pediat Res; AMA; Am Diabetes Asn. *Res:* Nutrition and metabolism. *Mailing Add:* 34th & Civic Center Blvd Philadelphia PA 19104

KAYE, SAMUEL, ORGANIC CHEMISTRY. *Current Pos:* RETIRED. *Personal Data:* b Canton, Ohio, Dec 18, 17; m 41, Aline B Emerman; c Donald, Michael, Robert & Ellen. *Educ:* Mt Union Col, BS, 40; Ohio State Univ, MS, 41, PhD(chem), 48. *Prof Exp:* Anal chemist, Repub Steel Corp, 41; inspector powder & explosives, Ind Ord Works, 42; aeronaut res scientist chem, Nat Adv Comt Aeronaut, 48-56; tech specialist, Aerojet Gen Corp, 56-57; staff scientist, Space Sci Dept, Gen Dynamics/Convair, 57-81, consult, 81-83. *Mem:* Am Chem Soc; Am Inst Aeronaut & Astronaut; fel Am Inst Chem; Combustion Inst. *Res:* Pollution detection; materials sciences; space manufacturing; high energy propellants. *Mailing Add:* 5626 Albalone Pl La Jolla CA 92037-7501

KAYE, SAUL, STERILIZATION, ASEPSIS. *Current Pos:* PRES, KAYE RES INC, 61- *Personal Data:* b Montreal, Que, May 23, 20; m 41; c 2. *Educ:* Brooklyn Col, BA, 41; Univ Chicago, MS, 69. *Honors & Awards:* Kilmer Award. *Prof Exp:* Chemist, Biol Labs, Chem Corps, US Army, 43-48; res assoc med, Univ Chicago, 48-50; chief decontamination br, Chem Corps, US Army, Ft Detrick, 50-56; res dir, Sterilants Ben Venue Labs, 56-58; res dir, US Movidyn Co, 58-61. *Mem:* AAAS; Am Chem Soc; Am Soc Microbiol; Sigma Xi; Soc Indust Microbiol; Parenteral Drug Asn. *Res:* Disinfection and sterilization, basic principles; methods of application; development of new methods and devices; aseptic processes. *Mailing Add:* 838 Mich Ave No 4A Evanston IL 60202

KAYE, SIDNEY, TOXICOLOGY. *Current Pos:* RETIRED. *Personal Data:* b Brooklyn, NY, Mar 10, 12; m 51, Carmen M; c Cynthia & Frederic. *Educ:* NY Univ, BS, 35, MSc, 39; Med Col Va, PhD(pharmacol), 56; Am Bd Clin Chem, dipl, 52; Nat Registry Clin Chem, cert, 68. *Honors & Awards:* Award of Merit, Am Acad Forensic Soc, 73, Gettler Outstanding Achievement Medal, 85; Milton Helpern Award, Nat Asn Med Examnrs, 89. *Prof Exp:* Teaching fel, NY Univ, 35-38; res asst toxicol lab, Off Chief Med Exam, New York, 38-41; instr path, Wash Univ, Sch Med, 46-47; toxicologist & dir toxicol labs, Off Chief Med Exam, Va, 47-62, dir, Richmond Poison Control Ctr, 58-62; prof toxicol, Pharmacol and Legal med & assoc dir, Inst Legal Med, Univ PR, San Juan, 62-82, emer prof pharmacol, Toxicol & Path, 82. *Concurrent Pos:* Toxicologist & assoc dir, Sci Crime Detection Lab, St Louis Police Dept, 46-47; from asst prof to assoc prof, Med Col Va, 47-62; mem subcomt alcohol & drugs, Nat Safety Coun, 52-; lectr, Armed Forces Inst Path, 58-62 & 71; coordr poison control ctrs, Community PR, 64-84; consult toxicologist, Vet Admin Hosp, Richmond, US Army Hosp, San Juan, 64-70, Vet Admin Hosp, San Juan, 69-, USAF Hosp, 71-75 & USN Hosp, 71-82; emer consult toxicol, Dept of US Army, 70-; exec res liaison officer, Defense Civil Prep Agency, Fed Emergency Mgt Admin, Dept Defense, 73- *Mem:* Assoc fel Am Soc Clin Path; Asn Mil Surg US; Soc Toxicol; Pan Am Med Asn; Sigma Xi; fel Am Acad Forensic Sci. *Res:* Analytical method for detection of lead poisoning; identification of seminal stains; diagnosis of poisoning; alcohol and its effects on man. *Mailing Add:* Med Sch Univ PR PO Box 865067 San Juan PR 00936-5067. *Fax:* 787-754-0710

KAYE, STEPHEN VINCENT, HEALTH PHYSICS, RADIOECOLOGY. *Current Pos:* GEN MGR, ANAL CORP, 93- *Personal Data:* b Rahway, NJ, Sept 17, 35; m 59; c 3. *Educ:* Rutgers Univ, BS, 57; NC State Univ, MS, 59; Univ Rochester, PhD(radiation biol), 66. *Prof Exp:* Res staff health physics & radioecol, Ecol Div & Health Physics Div, Oak Ridge Nat Labs, 60-72, proj supvr environ impacts, Environ Sci Div, 73-75, sect head radiol assessments, 75-77, div dir, Biol Div, 87-88, div dir, Health & Safety Res, 77-92. *Concurrent Pos:* Adv health physics fel, Univ Rochester, 63-66; mem nuclear fuel subgroup, Comt Nuclear & Alternative Energy Systs, Nat Res Coun, 76-78; chmn radiol data working group, US Dept Energy Reactor Safety Data Coord Group, 76-79; mem support group to develop proc guide for probabilistic risk assessment, Inst Elec & Electronics Engrs, Am Nuclear Soc, Nuclear Regulatory Comn, & nuclear indust, 81-82; mem, Environ Protection Agency High Level Radioactive Waste Comt, Sci Adv Bd, 82-84; mem, Tech Adv, Fla Phosphate Res Inst, 86-87; consult, US Vet Admin, 90- *Mem:* Health Physics Soc; Soc Risk Anal; Am Nuclear Soc; Sigma Xi; AAAS. *Res:* Transport of radionuclides in the environment and estimation of dose to man from ingestion or external exposure; assessments and comparisons of health and environmental issues related to all energy technologies. *Mailing Add:* DPRA 151 Lafayette Suite 310 Oak Ridge TN 37830

KAYE, WILBUR (IRVING), CHEMISTRY, INSTRUMENTATION. *Current Pos:* RETIRED. *Personal Data:* b Pelham Manor, NY, Jan 28, 22; m 44, Virginia Agett; c Roy A & Elsa K (Campbell). *Educ:* Stetson Univ, BS, 42; Univ Ill, PhD(chem), 45. *Prof Exp:* Asst chem, Univ Ill, 42-44; sr res chemist, Tenn Eastman Corp, 45-55; dir res, Sci Instruments Div, Beckman Instruments, Inc, Fullerton, 56-68; dir sci res, Corp Res Activ, 68-73, sr scientist, 73-80, prin staff scientist, Irvine, 80-87. *Concurrent Pos:* Beckman fel; consult. *Mem:* Am Chem Soc; Optical Soc Am; Soc Appl Spectros; fel AAAS. *Res:* Infrared and ultraviolet spectroscopy; chromatography; instrument development. *Mailing Add:* PO Box 3034 Princeville HI 96722

KAYES, STEPHEN GEOFFREY, IMMUNOPARASITOLOGY. *Current Pos:* asst prof neuroanat, Dept Anat & asst prof parasitol, 81-87, ASSOC PROF ANAT & CELL BIOL, 86-, ASSOC PROF PARASITOL, DEPT MICROBIOL, UNIV SOUTH ALA, 86-, PROF STRUCT & CELLULAR BIOL, 91- *Personal Data:* b Madison, Wis, May 1, 46. *Educ:* Univ Wis-Madison, BS, 71; Tulane Univ, MS, 73; Univ Iowa, PhD(anat), 77. *Prof Exp:* Fel immunol, Sch Med, Vanderbilt Univ, 77-81. *Concurrent Pos:* Res assoc, Vet Admin Med Ctr, 77-81. *Mem:* Am Soc Trop Med & Hyg; Am Soc Parasitologists; AAAS; Am Assoc Anat; Am Asn Immunol. *Res:* Immunologic basis of the host-parasite relationship by correlation of the host's immune status with the pathology elicited by the parasite. *Mailing Add:* Dept Struct & Cellular Biol Rm 2042 MSB Univ SAla Mobile AL 36688-0002. *Fax:* 334-460-6771; *E-Mail:* kayes@sungcg.usouthal.edu

KAYHART, MARION, GENETICS. *Current Pos:* from asst prof to assoc prof, 54-57, PROF BIOL & CHMN DEPT, CEDAR CREST COL, 57- *Personal Data:* b Butler, NJ, Sept 14, 26. *Educ:* Drew Univ, BA, 47; Univ Pa, MA, 49, PhD(zool), 54. *Prof Exp:* From instr to asst prof biol, Roanoke Col, 49-52. *Mem:* AAAS; Genetics Soc Am; Nat Asn Biol Teachers; Sigma Xi. *Res:* Radiation genetics. *Mailing Add:* 100 College Dr Cedar Crest Col Allentown PA 18104-6196

KAYLL, ALBERT JAMES, FORESTRY. *Current Pos:* prof & dir, Sch Forestry, 81-87, PROF, LAKEHEAD UNIV, 87- *Personal Data:* b Vancouver, BC, Jan 21, 35; m 62; c 2. *Educ:* Univ BC, BSF, 59; Duke Univ, MF, 60; Aberdeen Univ, PhD(fire ecol), 64. *Honors & Awards:* H R MacMillan Prize, 59. *Prof Exp:* Res scientist fire ecol, Can Dept Forestry, 60-68; asst prof fire ecol, Univ NB, 68-71, actg chmn, Dept Forest Resources, 75-76, assoc prof fire ecol, 71-77, co-dir, Fire Sci Ctr, 70-78, prof fire ecol & chmn, Dept Forest Resources, 77-80. *Concurrent Pos:* Mem fire mgt working group, NAm Forestry Comn, Food & Agr Orgn, UN, 73-75; Can Forestry Accreditation Bd, 89- *Mem:* Soc Am Foresters; Can Inst Forestry (pres, 87-88); Asn Univ Forestry Schs Can. *Res:* Ecological and physiological effects of fire on forest vegetation. *Mailing Add:* Sch Forestry Lakehead Univ 885 Oliver Rd Thunder Bay ON P7B 5E1 Can

KAYLOR, HOYT MCCOY, OPTICAL PHYSICS. *Current Pos:* Assoc prof, 52-58, prof physics, 58-81, PROF PHYSICS & MATH, BIRMINGHAM-SOUTHERN COL, 81- *Personal Data:* b Alexander City, Ala, Aug 17, 23; m 57; c 2. *Educ:* Birmingham-Southern Col, BS, 43; Univ Tenn, MS, 49, PhD(physics), 53. *Mem:* Fel AAAS; Am Phys Soc; Optical Soc Am; Am Asn Physics Teachers. *Res:* High dispersion infrared spectroscopy; physical properties of optical materials. *Mailing Add:* 1240 Greensboro Rd Birmingham AL 35208

KAYNE, FREDRICK JAY, BIOCHEMISTRY, CLINICAL CHEMISTRY. *Current Pos:* ASSOC PROF PATH & LAB MED, HAHNEMANN MED COL, 77- *Personal Data:* b Washington, DC, Jan 19, 41; m 65, Marlene; c Jonathan. *Educ:* Ill Inst Technol, BS, 62; Mich State Univ, PhD(biochem), 66. *Prof Exp:* NATO fel, Max Planck Inst Phys Chem, 67, res assoc phys chem, 67-69; asst prof phys biochem, Johnson Res Found, 69-74, assoc prof biochem & biophys, Univ Pa, 74-77. *Concurrent Pos:* Fulbright res fel, Max Planck Inst Biophys, 85-86. *Mem:* Am Asn Clin Chemists; Am Soc Biochem & Molecular Biol. *Res:* Enzyme mechanisms; chemical relaxation; clinical chemistry; laboratory medicine. *Mailing Add:* Dept Path Allegheny Univ Health Sci Broad & Vine Sts Philadelphia PA 19102-1178. *Fax:* 215-246-5433; *E-Mail:* kaynef@hal.hahnemann.edu

KAYNE, HERBERT LAWRENCE, PHYSIOLOGY. *Current Pos:* From instr to asst prof, 62-69, ASSOC PROF PHYSIOL, SCH MED, BOSTON UNIV, 69- *Personal Data:* b Chicago, Ill, Sept 22, 34; m 62; c 2. *Educ:* Univ Ill, BS, 55, MS, 58, PhD(physiol), 62. *Mem:* Am Physiol Soc; Biomet Soc. *Res:* Biostatistics. *Mailing Add:* Dept Physiol Boston Univ Sch Med 80 E Conard St Boston MA 02118-2307

KAYNE, MARLENE STEINMETZ, BIOCHEMISTRY, MOLECULAR BIOLOGY. *Current Pos:* ASST PROF MOLECULAR BIOL & CHMN DEPT BIOL, TRENTON STATE COL, 77- *Personal Data:* b Bronx, NY, July 6, 41; m 65. *Educ:* St John's Univ, BS, 62; Mich State Univ, PhD(biochem), 66. *Prof Exp:* Fel immunol, Max Planck Inst Exp Med, 67-69; res assoc enzym, Dept Biophysics, Univ Pa, 70-74 & Dept Biol, 74-77. *Concurrent Pos:* Ger Res Asn fel, 67-69; NSF res grants, 76-77 & 78- *Mem:* Sigma Xi. *Res:* Purification and characterization of procaryotic enzymes required in protein biosynthesis. *Mailing Add:* Dept Biol Trenton State Col Trenton NJ 08650

KAYS, M ALLAN, GEOLOGY, PETROLOGY. *Current Pos:* From asst prof to assoc prof, 61-80, PROF GEOL, UNIV ORE, 80- *Personal Data:* b Princeton, Ind, May 13, 34; m 55, Dorothy Tucker; c David, Timothy & Mary. *Educ:* Southern Ill Univ, BA, 56; Univ Washington, St Louis, MA, 58, PhD(geol), 61. *Concurrent Pos:* Vis geologist, Precambrian Geol Div, Dept Mineral Resources, Prov Sask, Can, 70-71; part-time geologist, US Geol Surv, 79, 80. *Mem:* Am Geophys Union; Geol Soc Am; Am Asn Univ Prof. *Res:* Petrology of xenoliths and their fused products in margins of basic intrusions; petrology and structural relations of Archaean supracrustal metamorphic and plutonic rocks, East Greenland; petrology of migmatized gneisses of Canada, Finland and East Greenland; metamorphism and structure of convergent plate marginal sequences in cordillera of western North America. *Mailing Add:* Dept Geol Sci Univ Ore Eugene OR 97403-1272. *Fax:* 541-346-4692; *E-Mail:* makays@oregon.uoregon.edu

KAYS, STANLEY J, HORTICULTURE, VEGETABLE CROP PHYSIOLOGY. *Current Pos:* ASSOC PROF VEG CROPS & POST-HARVEST, DEPT HORT, UNIV GA, 77- *Personal Data:* b Stillwater, Okla, Feb 3, 45. *Educ:* Okla State Univ, BS, 68; Mich State Univ, MS, 69, PhD(hort), 71. *Prof Exp:* Researcher plant biol, Dept Biol, Tex A&M Univ, 71; researcher, Sch Plant Biol, Univ Col Northern Wales, UK, 71-72; asst prof veg crops, Dept Hort, Univ Ga, Tifton, 73-75; assoc prof, Dept Hort Food Sci, Univ Ark, 76-77. *Concurrent Pos:* Grants, Nat Pecan Shellers, 76, Gilroy Foods Inc, 78, Woolfolk Chem Works Inc, 78, Sci Educ Adm, USDA, 81, AID 86; vis scientist, Dept Appl Biol, Cambridge Univ, Cambridge, Eng; vis scholar, Wolfson Col, Cambridge. *Mem:* Am Soc Hort Sci; Int Hort Soc; AAAS; Int Trop Root Crops Soc; Sigma Xi. *Res:* Developmental and post-harvest physiology of vegetable crops. *Mailing Add:* Dept Hort Univ Ga 1180 E Broad St Athens GA 30601-3040

KAYS, WILLIAM MORROW, MECHANICAL ENGINEERING. *Current Pos:* Res assoc, 47-51, Stanford Univ, from asst prof to assoc prof, 51-57, head dept, 61-72, dean eng, 72-84, PROF MECH ENG, STANFORD UNIV, 57- *Personal Data:* b Norfolk, Va, July 29, 20; m 47, 83, Judith Scholtz; c Nancy, Leslie, Margaret & Elizabeth. *Educ:* Stanford Univ, AB, 42, MS, 47, PhD(mech eng), 51. *Honors & Awards:* Am Soc Mech Engrs Mem Award, 65; Max Jacob Award, 92. *Concurrent Pos:* Fulbright lectr, Imp Col London, 59-60; NSF sr fel, 66-67. *Mem:* Nat Acad Eng; Fel Am Soc Mech Engrs; fel Am Soc Eng Educ. *Res:* Heat transfer to fluids, especially turbulent boundary layers. *Mailing Add:* Dept Mech Eng Stanford Univ Stanford CA 94305

KAYSER, BORIS JULES, THEORETICAL ELEMENTARY PARTICLE PHYSICS. *Current Pos:* assoc prog dir theoret physics, 72-75, PROG DIR THEORET PHYSICS, NSF, 75- *Personal Data:* b New York, NY, June 2, 38; m 60. *Educ:* Princeton Univ, AB, 60; Calif Inst Technol, PhD(physics), 64. *Prof Exp:* Res assoc physics, Univ Calif, Berkeley, 64-66; asst prof, State Univ NY Stony Brook, 66-69; asst prof, Northwestern Univ, Evanston, 69-74. *Mem:* Fel Am Phys Soc. *Res:* Weak interactions. *Mailing Add:* Div Physics NSF Rm 1015 4201 Wilson Blvd Arlington VA 22230

KAYSER, FRANCIS X, METALLURGICAL ENGINEERING. *Current Pos:* From asst prof to assoc prof, 63-75, PROF METALL, IOWA STATE UNIV, 75- *Personal Data:* b Toledo, Ohio, Feb 10, 27; m 52, Eileen M Mueller; c Joseph, Patricia, Christopher, Daniel & Gregory. *Educ:* Univ Notre Dame, BS, 48; Mass Inst Technol, MS, 50, DSc(metall), 63. *Honors & Awards:* Presidents Award, Am Soc Metals Int, 88. *Prof Exp:* Metallurgist, Unitcast Corp, Ohio, 48-49; res metallurgist, Res Labs Div, Gen Motors Corp, Mich, 50-55 & sci lab, Ford Motor Co, 55-58. *Concurrent Pos:* Assoc metallurgist, Inst Atomic Res, Ames Lab, 63-70, sr metallurgist, 70-81. *Mem:* Am Soc Metals; Sigma Xi. *Res:* Nature of solid solutions; diffraction; phase transformations in solids; elastic and plastic behavior of metallic and non-metallic materials. *Mailing Add:* 2818 Torrey Pines Rd Ames IA 50014-4547

KAYSER, RICHARD FRANCIS, TECHNICAL MANAGEMENT. *Current Pos:* ACTG DEP DIR CTR CHEM TECHNOL, NAT BUR STANDARDS TECHNOL, GAITHERSBURG. *Personal Data:* b Toledo, Ohio, Feb 24, 25; m 50; c 9. *Educ:* Univ Cincinnati, PhD(chem eng), 52. *Prof Exp:* Engr, Linde Div, Union Carbide Corp, 52-65, prod mgr, Silicones Div, 65-72, opers mgr, 72-74, dir, Res & Develop, Chem & Plastics Div, 74-80, vpres technol, Ethylene Oxide/Glycol Div, 80- *Mem:* Sigma Xi. *Res:* Silicones processes; low pressure oxo process and oxo alcohols; new ethylene oxide catalyst developments. *Mailing Add:* A111 Phys Bldg Nat Inst Standards Technol Gaithersburg MD 20899

KAYSER, ROBERT HELMUT, BIO-ORGANIC CHEMISTRY, BIO-ORGANIC CHEMISTRY. *Current Pos:* MEM STAFF US ENVIRON PROTECTION AGENCY, WASHINGTON, DC, 80- *Personal Data:* b Orange, NJ, Aug 21, 48; m 72; c 2. *Educ:* Stevens Inst Technol, BS, 70; Georgetown Univ, PhD(org chem), 75. *Prof Exp:* Res asst org chem, Georgetown Univ, 74; res assoc bio-org chem, Univ Md, Baltimore County, 74-80. *Mem:* Am Chem Soc. *Res:* Designing model systems in an attempt to mimic various enzymatic processes and elucidate enzymatic mechanisms. *Mailing Add:* 5355 Iron Pen Pl Columbia MD 21044-3310

KAYTON, MYRON, VEHICLE SYSTEM DESIGN, VEHICLE ELECTRONICS. *Current Pos:* PRES, KAYTON ENG CO, 81- *Personal Data:* b New York, NY, Apr 26, 34; m 54, Paula A Erde; c Elizabeth & Susan. *Educ:* Cooper Union, BS, 55; Harvard Univ, SM, 56; Mass Inst Technol, PhD(instrumentation), 60. *Honors & Awards:* Gano Dunn Medal, Cooper Union, 75; M B Carlton Award, Inst Elec & Electronics Engrs, 88. *Prof Exp:* Design engr, Res & Develop Div, Avco, 56-58; res asst navig systs, Draper Lab, Mass Inst Technol, 58-60; sect head, Guid & Control Div, Litton, 60-65; mgr, NASA Johnson Space Ctr, 65-69; sr staff mem, TRW Defense & Space Sector, 69-81. *Concurrent Pos:* Lectr, Univ Calif, Los Angeles, 69-88; distinguished lectr, Aeorspace & Electronic Systs Soc, Inst Elec & Electronics Engrs, 88-, pres, 93-94, corp bed dirs, 96-97. *Mem:* Fel Inst Elec & Electronics Engrs; Am Soc Mech Engrs; Inst Navig; Soc Automotive Engrs. *Res:* Electronic system design and testing for high-value vehicles and plants, emphasizing communications, navigation, control, fault-tolerance; author of three books, two encyclopedia articles and 60 technical papers. *Mailing Add:* Kayton Eng Co PO Box 802 Santa Monica CA 90406. *E-Mail:* m.kayton@ieee.org

KAZAHAYA, MASAHIRO MATT, managing experience of research & development engineers, computer-to-computer communication, for more information see previous edition

KAZAKIA, JACOB YAKOVOS, APPLIED MECHANICS. *Current Pos:* Res assoc, Lehigh Univ, 72-74, asst prof, 74-79, assoc prof, Ctr Appln Math, 79-87, PROF ENG MATH, LEHIGH UNIV, 87- *Personal Data:* b Istanbul, Turkey, Feb 27, 45; m 72; c 2. *Educ:* Istanbul Tech Univ, MS, 68; Lehigh Univ, PhD(appl mech), 72. *Mem:* Am Acad Mech; Am Soc Mech Engrs. *Res:* Nonlinear wave propagation in fluids; viscoelastic fluid flows; stability of liquid filled shells; run-up and spin-up problems. *Mailing Add:* Dept Mech Eng & Mech Lehigh Univ Bethlehem PA 18015

KAZAKS, PETER ALEXANDER, SCATTERING THEORY IN LOW & HIGH ENERGY PHYSICS. *Current Pos:* asst prof, 73-75, PROF PHYSICS, UNIV SFLA, 80- *Personal Data:* b Riga, Latvia, Feb 22, 40; US citizen; m 68; c 6. *Educ:* McGill Univ, BSc, 62; Yale Univ, MS, 63; Univ Calif, Davis, PhD(physics), 68. *Prof Exp:* Res assoc, Ohio Univ, 68-70; asst prof physics, St Lawrence Univ, 70-73. *Concurrent Pos:* NSF res partic, Univ Fla, 71; NSF grant, St Lawrence Univ, 71-72; Res Corp grant, 75; vis prof/scholar, Univ Penn, 85; chmn, Div Natural Sci, New Col, Univ SFla, 80-85; vis scholar, Harvard Univ, 91 & 96. *Mem:* Am Phys Soc. *Res:* Three-body models of nuclear reactions; electron-atom collision collisions; pion-nucleus scattering; proton-proton scattering; spin physics. *Mailing Add:* Div Nat Sci New Col Univ SFla Sarasota FL 34243

KAZAL, LOUIS ANTHONY, BIOCHEMISTRY, HEMATOLOGY. *Current Pos:* head sect blood plasma fractionation, Cardeza Found, Jefferson Med Col, 56-60, from asst prof to prof physiol, 57-78, assoc prof med & assoc dir Cardeza Found Hemat Res, 60-78, prof physiol, Col Grad Studies, 70-78, HON PROF PHYSIOL & HON ASSOC PROF MED, JEFFERSON MED COL, THOMAS JEFFERSON UNIV, 78- *Personal Data:* b Newark, NJ, July 2, 12; m 42, Marie Barry; c Marianne K (Livingston), Susan K (Bove), Alicia K (Ricci) & Louis A Jr. *Educ:* Seton Hall Col, BS, 35; Rutgers Univ, PhD(biochem, physiol), 40. *Honors & Awards:* Co-recipient Rorer Award, Am J Gastroenterol, 66. *Prof Exp:* Asst physiol & biochem, Rutgers Univ, 37-40; res biochemist, Merck Sharp & Dohme Inc, 40-50, dir biol develop, 50-54, mgr tech info, 54-55, tech asst to med dir, 55-56. *Concurrent Pos:* Chmn blood coagulation sessions, Fed Am Soc Exp Biol, 63-68. *Mem:* Am Chem Soc; Soc Exp Biol & Med; Am Soc Biol Chem; fel NY Acad Sci; Int Soc Thrombosis & Homeostasis; fel AAAS; Sigma Xi (pres, 67); Asn Clin Scientists. *Res:* Blood coagulation; proteins; blood group specific substances; ion-exchange resins; erythropoietin inhibitors; lipids; trypsin inhibitor; isolation and crystalization of pancreatic secretory trypsin inhibitor; gastric juice and saliva thromboplastin; fibrinogen-glycine; human typing serum; author of numerous publications and recipient of one US patent. *Mailing Add:* 18215 Organ Pipe Dr Sun City AZ 85373-1773

KAZAN, BENJAMIN, IMAGING & DISPLAY TECHNOLOGY. *Current Pos:* CONSULT, 84- *Personal Data:* b New York, NY, May 8, 17; div, Gerda Bloch Mosse; c David L. *Educ:* Calif Inst Technol, BS, 38; Columbia Univ, MA, 40; Munich Tech Univ, Dr rer nat, 61. *Honors & Awards:* Silver Medal, Am Roentgen Ray Soc, 57; Coolidge Award, Gen Elec Co, 58. *Prof Exp:* Radio engr, Signal Corps Eng Labs, 40-44, chief spec purpose tube sect, 44-50; physicist, RCA Labs, 50-58; head solid-state display sect, Res Labs, Hughes Aircraft Co, 58-61; chief scientist aerospace electronics div, Electro-Optical Systs, Inc, 61-68; mgr explor display dept, Thomas J Watson Res Ctr, IBM Corp, 68-74; head, Display Group, Xerox Corp, 74-84. *Concurrent Pos:* Ed, Advan in Image Pickup & Display, 72-84; assoc ed, Inst Elec & Electronics Engrs, Trans on Electron Devices, 78-84 & Advan Electronics & Electron Physics, 85-; consult adv group electron devices, Defense Dept, 73-82; adj prof, Univ RI, 70-74. *Mem:* Sigma Xi; Am Phys Soc; Inst Elec & Electronics Engrs; Soc Info Display. *Res:* Electronic image storage; image pickup and display devices; display technology; solid-state image devices. *Mailing Add:* 557 Tyndall St Los Altos CA 94022. *Fax:* 650-812-4471; *E-Mail:* kazan@parc.xerox.com

KAZANJIAN, ARMEN ROUPEN, PHYSICAL CHEMISTRY. *Current Pos:* RETIRED. *Personal Data:* b New Haven, Conn, Feb 13, 28; m 62; c 3. *Educ:* Northeastern Univ, BS, 51; Univ Calif, Los Angeles, PhD(phys chem), 65. *Prof Exp:* Chemist, Raw Mat Develop Lab, AEC, 51-56; res chemist, Rocketdyne Div, NAm Aviation, Inc, 56-60; res chemist, Rocket Power Inc, 66; res chemist, Rocky Flats Div, Dow Chem Co, 66-75; res chemist, Rocky Flats Div, Rockwell Int, 75-90. *Mem:* AAAS; Radiation Res Soc; Sigma Xi; Nuclear Soc Am. *Res:* Chemical effects of nuclear transformations; radiation chemistry; plutonium chemistry. *Mailing Add:* 1596 Snee-Oosh Rd La Conner WA 98257

KAZARIAN, LEON EDWARD, biomechanics, for more information see previous edition

KAZARINOFF, MICHAEL N, BIOCHEMISTRY. *Current Pos:* asst prof, 78-84, ASSOC PROF NUTRIT BIOCHEM, CORNELL UNIV, 85- *Personal Data:* b Ann Arbor, Mich, Mar 24, 49; m 70; c 3. *Educ:* Yale Univ, BS, 70; Cornell Univ, PhD(biochem), 75. *Prof Exp:* Fel biochem, Univ Calif, Berkeley, 75-76; fel microbiol, Univ Tex, Austin, 76-78. *Concurrent Pos:* Actg Dir, Div Nutrit Sci, Cornell Univ, 87-88; assoc dir, Pew Nat Nutrit Prog, 87-93. *Mem:* Am Chem Soc; AAAS; Am Inst Nutrit; Am Soc Biol Chem. *Res:* Enzymology; protein-coenzyme interactions; protein turnover; coenzyme mechanisms; purification and properties of enzymes of vitamin metabolism; nutrition and cancer. *Mailing Add:* Dept Biochem & Div Nutrit Sci Cornell Univ 230 Savage Hall Ithaca NY 14853-6301

KAZAZIAN, HAIG H, JR, PEDIATRIC GENETICS, HUMAN MOLECULAR GENETICS. *Current Pos:* SEYMOUR GREY PROF MOLECULAR MED GENETICS & CHMN, DEPT GENETICS, UNIV PA, PHILADELPHIA, 94- *Personal Data:* b Toledo, Ohio, July 30, 37. *Educ:* Dartmouth Col, AB, 59; Johns Hopkins Univ, MD, 62. *Honors & Awards:* Mead Johnson Award, Am Acad Pediat, 76. *Prof Exp:* Pediat intern, Univ Minn, 62-64; fel genetics, Johns Hopkins Univ, 64-68, pediat genetics residency, 68-69, from asst prof to prof pediat, 69-94, prof biol, 82-94, prof obstet & gynec, 85-94, prof med, 88-94, dir, Ctr Med Genetics, 89-93. *Concurrent Pos:* Staff assoc, NIH, 66-68. *Mem:* Inst Med-Nat Acad Sci; Am Pediat Soc; Am Soc Clin Invest; Am Soc Human Genetics; Asn Am Physicians. *Mailing Add:* Dept Genetics Clin Res Bldg Univ Pa 422 Curie Blvd Philadelphia PA 19104

KAZDA, LOUIS F(RANK), ELECTRICAL ENGINEERING. *Current Pos:* from instr to assoc prof, 47-60, prof elec eng, 60-81, PROF ELEC & COMPUT ENG, UNIV MICH, ANN ARBOR, 81- *Personal Data:* b Dayton, Ohio, Sept 21, 16; m 40; c 3. *Educ:* Univ Cincinnati, EE, 40, MSE, 43; Syracuse Univ, PhD(elec eng), 62. *Prof Exp:* Res & develop engr elec eng, Bendix Aviation Corp, 43-46. *Concurrent Pos:* Consult, Cook Res Labs, 51-53, Willow Run Labs, Mich, 54-, USAF, 57-59, Maxitrol Corp, 58-68, Clark Equipment Co, 60-62, Ford Motor Co, 62 & Conduction Corp, 63. *Mem:* AAAS; fel Inst Elec & Electronics Engrs. *Res:* Feedback control systems of linear, nonlinear or adaptive type; inertial navigation systems; application of system engineering techniques to societal problems. *Mailing Add:* 4569 Spanish Dagger Las Cruces NM 88001-9637

KAZDAN, JERRY LAWRENCE, GEOMETRY, PARTIAL DIFFERENTIAL EQUATIONS. *Current Pos:* from asst prof to assoc prof, 66-74, chair, 89-92, PROF MATH, UNIV PA, 74- *Personal Data:* b Detroit, Mich, Oct 31, 37. *Educ:* Rensselaer Polytech Inst, BS, 59; NY Univ, MS, 61, PhD(math), 63. *Prof Exp:* Instr math, NY Univ, 63; Benjamin Peirce instr, Harvard Univ, 63-66. *Concurrent Pos:* Vis assoc prof, Harvard Univ, 71-72; vis prof, Univ Calif, Berkeley, 74-76, Univ Paris, 81, Kyoto Univ, 85-86 & Max Planck Inst, 93. *Mem:* Am Math Soc. *Res:* Partial differential equations; differential geometry. *Mailing Add:* Dept Math Univ Pa 2095 33rd St Philadelphia PA 19104-6395. *E-Mail:* kazdan@math.upenn.edu

KAZEM, SAYYED M, MATERIALS TESTING, REFRIGERATION. *Current Pos:* asst prof, 80-87, ASSOC PROF HEAT POWER & MAT, MET DEPT, SCH TECHNOL, PURDUE UNIV, 87- *Personal Data:* b Kabul, Afghanistan, July 28, 38; US & Afghan citizen; m 72; c 4. *Educ:* Tulsa Univ, BS, 63, MS, 64; Purdue Univ, MS, 71. *Prof Exp:* Asst prof chem eng, Fac Eng, Kabul Univ, Afghanistan, 67-77. *Concurrent Pos:* Mem, Nat Res Coun, Kabul Univ, 71-73 & 75-77, head appl eng res & consult, Fac Eng, 75-77. *Mem:* Am Soc Mech Engrs; Am Soc Eng Educ; Am Soc Heating Refrig & Air-Conditioning Engrs. *Res:* Purification of vegetable oils; refrigeration, pressure drops and heat transfer; steam power plants; heat power; materials. *Mailing Add:* 1700 Ravina Rd West Lafayette IN 47906

KAZEMI, HOMAYOUN, PULMONARY MEDICINE. *Current Pos:* resident med, Mass Gen Hosp, 63, Am Heart Asn res fel, 64, chief pulmonary unit, 67-88, CHIEF, PULMONARY & CRITICAL CARE UNIT, MASS GEN HOSP, 88-; PROF MED, HARVARD MED SCH, HARVARD-MASS INST TECHNOL DIV HEALTH SCI & TECHNOL, 80- *Personal Data:* b Teheran, Iran, Sept 28, 34; US citizen; m 58, Katheryne McNulty; c Paul A & Laili N. *Educ:* Univ London , MB, 53; Lafayette Col, BA, 54; Columbia Univ, MD, 58. *Hon Degrees:* MSc, Harvard Univ, 90. *Honors & Awards:* P D Agarwal Orator, Calcutta, India, 87; R J Carabasi lectr, Texas A&M Sch Med, 91. *Prof Exp:* Intern, 58-59, asst res med, Bassett Hosp, 59-60, res fel, 60-61, Am Heart Asn res fel, 61-62. *Concurrent Pos:* Vis fel, Hammersmith Hosp, Royal Postgrad Med Sch, London, 65; consult, Brigham & Women's Hosp, Boston, 65-82, Nat Heart Lung & Blood Inst, 73-, Fed Aviation Agency, 87-88; vis prof, Peking Union Med Col, Beijing, China, 91; hon consult, Internal Med, Shang Hai First People's Hosp, China, 91- *Mem:* Am Thoracic Soc; Am Physiol Soc; Am Heart Asn; Am Soc Clin Invest. *Res:* Central chemical control of ventilation as it relates to biochemistry of the respiratory centers; role of brain metabolism & amino acid neurotransmitters in determining the central ventilatory drive; control of cardiorespiratory function during exercise; occupational lung disease. *Mailing Add:* Mass Gen Hosp Pulmonary Unit 32 Fruit St Boston MA 02114

KAZEMI, HOSSEIN, PETROLEUM ENGINEERING. *Current Pos:* adv res scientist, sr res scientist & res assoc, Marathon Oil Co, 69-80, mgr eng dept, 81-86, mgr, Reservoir Mgt Dept, Explor & Prod Technol Ctr, 86-88, ASSOC DIR, PROD TECHNOL, PROD TECHNOL CTR, MARATHON OIL CO, 88- *Personal Data:* b Iran, Mar 11, 38; m 64; c 3. *Educ:* Univ Tex, BS, 61, PhD(petrol eng), 63. *Honors & Awards:* Henry Matlson Technical Award, Soc Petrol Engrs, 80; John Franklin Carll Award, 87. *Prof Exp:* Sr res scientist, reservoir eng, Tulas Res Ctr, Sinclair Oil & Gas Co, 63-69, res scientist, Atlantic Richfield Co, 69. *Concurrent Pos:* Eng fel, Univ Tex, 61; lectr math, Univ Tulsa, 67-69; adj prof petrol eng, Colo Sch Mines, 81- *Mem:* Soc Petrol Engrs. *Res:* Solution mining; pressure transient testing of oil and gas wells; reservoir simulation; enhanced oil recovery, naturally fractured reservoirs. *Mailing Add:* 7446 S Jackson Ct Littleton CO 80122

KAZEROUNI, LEWA, MICROBIAL FERMENTATION & FREEZE DRYING, MEDIA DEVELOPMENT FOR MICROBIAL FERMENTATION. *Current Pos:* MICROBIOL CONSULT, ORE FREEZEDRY, 89- *Personal Data:* b Kuwait, Oct 18, 56; US citizen. *Educ:* Kuwait Univ, BS, 77; Ore State Univ, PhD(microbiol), 85. *Prof Exp:* Res microbiologist, Kuwait Inst Sci Res, 78-82; res asst, Ore State Univ, 82-86, res assoc, 87-88; res assoc, Southwestern Univ, Tex, 86-87. *Concurrent Pos:* Consult, K & K Inc, 89- *Mem:* Am Soc Microbiol; Inst Food Technologists. *Res:* Optimizing the fermentation conditions for growing microorganisms of industrial value; finding the best way to keep these cultures viable for long periods of time after being freeze dried and held at ambient temperature. *Mailing Add:* Ore Freeze Dry 525 25th Ave SW Albany OR 97321. *Fax:* 541-967-8768

KAZEROUNIAN, KAZEM, OPTIMIZATION, REDUNDANCY RESOLUTION. *Current Pos:* asst prof, 84-89, ASSOC PROF DESIGN & ROBOTICS, UNIV CONN, 89- *Personal Data:* b Shiraz, Iran, Nov 3, 56; US citizen; m 76; c 2. *Educ:* Univ Ill, BS, 80, MS, 81, PhD(mech design). *Prof Exp:* Res asst, Univ Ill, 80-84. *Concurrent Pos:* Consult, specialized mechanics, Gen Elec, Bran Rex & Rogers, Inc, 84-91; reviewer, Inst Elec & Electronics Engrs, Int J Robotics Res, Robotics & Automation, Am Soc Mech Engrs, 84-91. *Res:* Analysis and design optimization of robotic systems and mechanisms, theoretical and applied kinematics. *Mailing Add:* 165 Davis St Storrs Mansfield CT 06268

KAZES, EMIL, THEORETICAL PHYSICS. *Current Pos:* from asst prof to assoc prof, 59-66, PROF PHYSICS, PA STATE UNIV, 66- *Personal Data:* b Istanbul, Turkey, June 13, 26; nat US; m 54; c 3. *Educ:* Univ Wis, BS, 49, MS, 50; Univ Chicago, PhD(physics), 56. *Prof Exp:* Proj assoc physics, Univ Wis, 57-59. *Mem:* Fel Am Phys Soc. *Res:* Electrodynamics; general relativity; soluble field theories; elementary particle theory; pion nucleon interaction; current algebra. *Mailing Add:* 104 Davey Lab Dept Physics Pa State Univ University Park PA 16802-6300

KAZHDAN, DAVID, MATHEMATICS. *Current Pos:* PROF MATH, HARVARD UNIV, 77- *Personal Data:* b Moscow State Univ, MA, 67, PhD, 69. *Hon Degrees:* BA, Harvard Univ, 77. *Prof Exp:* Researcher, Moscow State Univ, 69-75, vis prof, 75-77. *Mem:* Nat Acad Sci. *Res:* Algebraic aspects of analysis. *Mailing Add:* Math Dept Sci Ctr 325 Harvard Univ Cambridge MA 02138

KAZI, ABDUL HALIM, RADIATION EFFECTS, NEUTRON SOURCES. *Current Pos:* prin investr, Army Pulse Radiation Facil, 66-87, dir, Nuclear Effects Directorate, US Army Combat Systs Test Activ, 87-95, DIR, RADIATION SIMULATION ANAL DIRECTORATE, ABERDEEN TEST CTR, 95- *Personal Data:* b Kreuzlingen, Switz, Jan 12, 35; US citizen; m 59, Patricia Stewart; c Aaron & Ethan. *Educ:* Am Univ, Cairo, Egypt, BSc, 54; Rensselaer Polytech Inst, MS, 56; Mass Inst Technol, SM, 59, PhD(nuclear eng), 61. *Prof Exp:* Staff mem, Gen Atomics, La Jolla, Calif, 61-63; sect chief, United Nuclear, White Plains, NY, 63-66. *Concurrent Pos:* Mem, NATO Panel VII & VIII Res Study Groups, 76-, Radiation Dosimetry Standards Comt, Am Soc Testing & Mat, 84- & Multi Serv Test & Res Investment Comt Nuclear Effects, 89- *Mem:* Am Nuclear Soc. *Res:* Design, operation and utilization of nuclear weapon radiation simulators; neutron sources; flash gamma accelerators; radiation dosimetry; radiation effects. *Mailing Add:* 2813 Rocks Rd Jarrettsville MD 21084

KAZIMI, MUJID S, THERMAL ENGINEERING, SAFETY ENGINEERING. *Current Pos:* from asst prof to assoc prof, 76-86, PROF NUCLEAR ENG, MASS INST TECHNOL, 86-, DEPT HEAD NUCLEAR ENG, 89- *Personal Data:* b Jerusalem, Palestine, Nov 20, 47; US citizen; m 73; c 3. *Educ:* Univ Alexandria, Egypt, BEng, 69; Mass Inst Technol, MS, 71, PhD(nuclear eng), 73. *Prof Exp:* Sr engr, Westinghouse Elec Corp, 73-74; assoc scientist, Brookhaven Nat Lab, 74-76. *Concurrent Pos:* Consult, Brookhaven Nat Lab, 76-, Elec Power Res Inst, 89-91 & Argonne Nat Lab, 89-91; pres, Asn Arab Am Univ Graduates, Inc, 80 & 87; chmn, High Level Waste Tech Adv Panel, Dept Energy, 90-95. *Mem:* Am Nuclear Soc; Am Soc Mech Engrs; Am Inst Chem Engrs; Am Soc Eng Educ. *Res:* Thermal design and safety of nuclear facilities, including nuclear power reactors, nuclear waste storage facilities and nuclear fusion research facilities. *Mailing Add:* Mass Inst Technol 77 Massachusetts Ave Cambridge MA 02139

KAZIMIERCZUK, MARIAN K, POWER ELECTRONICS, RADIO FREQUENCY TECHNOLOGY. *Current Pos:* from asst prof to assoc prof, 85-94, PROF ELEC ENG, WRIGHT STATE UNIV, 94- *Personal Data:* b Smolugi, Poland, Mar 3, 48; m 73, Alicja Nowowiejska; c Anna & Andrew. *Educ:* Tech Univ Warsaw, MSc, 71, PhD(electronics eng), 78, DSci, 84. *Honors & Awards:* Outstanding Engr & Scientists Award, Eng & Sci Found & Affil Socs Coun, 95. *Prof Exp:* Asst prof, Dept Electronics, Tech Univ Warsaw, 78-84; design engr, Design Automation, Inc, 84-85. *Concurrent Pos:* Vis prof, Va Polytech Inst & State Univ, 84-85; res award, Ministry Sci & Higher Educ, Poland, 84, Polish Acad Sci, 83. *Mem:* Sr mem Inst Elec & Electronics Engrs. *Res:* Energy conversion; published over 190 articles and granted 5 patents. *Mailing Add:* Dept Elec Eng Wright State Univ Dayton OH 45435. *Fax:* 937-775-5009

KAZMAIER, HAROLD EUGENE, ENVIRONMENTAL SCIENCES, ENVIRONMENTAL MANAGEMENT. *Current Pos:* CHIEF TECH ASSISTANCE, PESTICIDE BR, US ENVIRON PROTECTION AGENCY, 72- *Personal Data:* b Bowling Green, Ohio, Feb 17, 24; m 49; c 3. *Educ:* Ohio State Univ, BS, 49, MS, 51, PhD(bot), 60. *Prof Exp:* Asst plant path, Agr Exp Sta, Ohio State Univ, 50-52; sr res plant pathologist, Battelle-Columbus, 52-72. *Mem:* Am Phytopath Soc; Soc Nematol; Sigma Xi. *Res:* Pesticides; plant pest control; registration support data. *Mailing Add:* Four Evans Dr Wilmington MA 01887

KAZMAIER, PETER MICHAEL, ELECTRONIC MATERIALS, MOLECULAR MODELING. *Current Pos:* mem res staff chem, 79-92, SR MEM RES STAFF, XEROX RES CTR CAN, XEROX CORP, 92- *Personal Data:* b Neustadt, Ger, Apr 19, 51; Can citizen; m, Kathy; c 3. *Educ:* Univ Calgary, BSc Hons, 73; Queen's Univ, PhD(chem), 78. *Honors & Awards:* Chem Inst Can Prize, Chem Inst Can, 72; Arthur K Doolittle Award, Am Chem Soc, 93. *Prof Exp:* Killam fel chem, Univ BC, 78-79. *Concurrent Pos:* Mem comt, Can Soc Chem Publ, 91-; vis fel, Cornell Univ; adj assoc prof, Queen's Univ, Kingston. *Mem:* Chem Inst Can; Am Chem Soc. *Res:* Electronic materials; novel photogenerator materials; living free-radical polymerization; hole and electron; transport; use of molecular orbital calculations; author of more than 30 publication; granted 18 patents. *Mailing Add:* Xerox Res Ctr Can 2660 Speakman Dr Mississauga ON L5K 2L1 Can. *Fax:* 905-822-7022; *E-Mail:* pkaz.xrcc@xerox.com

KAZMANN, RAPHAEL GABRIEL, HYDROLOGY, HYDROLOGIC ENGINEERING. *Current Pos:* prof, 63-82, EMER PROF CIVIL ENG, LA STATE UNIV, 82- *Personal Data:* b Brooklyn, NY, Oct 16, 16; m 42, Mary C Beem; c Elisabeth P, Hollis B & William M. *Educ:* Carnegie-Mellon Univ, BS, 39. *Prof Exp:* Hydraul engr ground water, US Geol Surv, Washington, DC, 40-45; chief hydraul engr ground water explor, Ranney Method Water Supplies, Inc, Columbus, Ohio, 46-50; consult engr ground water, 50-63. *Concurrent Pos:* Consult, 82- *Mem:* Am Soc Civil Engrs; Soc Mining Engrs; Nat Groundwater Asn; Am Water Works Asn; Am Geophys Union. *Res:* Cyclic storage of fresh water in saline aquifers; storage and retrieval of heated and superheated water in saline aquifers; miscible displacement processes and their application to solution mining and deepwell disposal of wastes; monitoring of leachates from landfills; geomorphology and national water policy; book: Modern Hydrology 3rd ed pub 5/88. *Mailing Add:* 231 Duplantier Blvd Baton Rouge LA 70808. *E-Mail:* rkzam@aol.com

KAZMERSKI, LAWRENCE L, PHOTOVOLTAICS, SURFACE SCIENCE. *Current Pos:* sr scientist, 77-79, PRIN SCIENTIST, NAT RENEWABLE ENERGY LAB, SOLAR ENERGY RES INST, 79-, BR MGR, 80- *Personal Data:* b Chicago, Ill, June 9, 45; m 68, Kathleen E Scanlan; c Keira E & Timothy L. *Educ:* Univ Notre Dame, BSEE, 67, MSEE, 68, PhD(elec eng), 70. *Honors & Awards:* Peter Mark Mem Award, Am Vacuum Soc, 80; Res Develop IR-100 Award, 85; Res Develop R&D 100 Award, 89 & 92; William R Cherry Award, Inst Elec & Electronics Engrs, 93. *Prof Exp:* Res fel, Am Eng Coun, Notre Dame Radiation Lab, 71; asst prof teaching res, Univ Maine, Orono, 71-74, assoc prof, 74-77. *Concurrent Pos:* Adj prof, Univ Colo, 79-, Colo Sch Mines, 80-; ed, J Solar Cells, 79-91, Polycrystalline & Amorphous Thin Films & Devices, 80; chmn, Nat Am Vacuum Soc Symposium, 82, IEEE PVSC, 87. *Mem:* Am Vacuum Soc (pres, 91); fel Inst Elec & Electronics Engrs; fel Am Phys Soc; Sigma Xi. *Res:* Photovoltaic devices and solid-state physics, with emphasis on the correlation of compositional/chemical properties and electrical characteristics of interfaces in solar cells and other semiconductor devices; scanning tunneling microscopy and surface analysis. *Mailing Add:* Nat Renewable Energy Lab 1617 Cole Blvd Golden CO 80401. *Fax:* 303-231-1231; *E-Mail:* kaz@nrel.gov

KAZNOFF, ALEXIS I(VAN), METALLURGICAL ENGINEERING, CHEMICAL ENGINEERING. *Current Pos:* DIR MATS ENG, NAVAL SEA SYSTS COMMAND, 82- *Personal Data:* b Harbin, China, Oct 22, 33; US citizen; m 80. *Educ:* Univ Calif, Berkeley, BS, 55, PhD(phys metall), 61; Calif Inst Technol, MS, 56. *Prof Exp:* Scientist mat sci, Gen Elec Co, 60-64, mgr ceramics & electronic mat, 64-66, mat sci & develop, Nucleonics Lab, 66-69, metall & ceramics lab, Nuclear Technol & Appln Oper, 69-73, consult engr, prod & qual assurance oper, nuclear energy bus group, 73-75, mgr, 75-82. *Mem:* Am Soc Metals; Am Ceramic Soc; Am Chem Soc; Am Welding Soc; Am Mgt Asn. *Res:* Nuclear fuel technology; structural materials for nuclear plants and ships; nuclear materials; welding and materials processing; marine corrosion; corrosion control; fuels and lubricants. *Mailing Add:* 9809 Summerday Dr Burke VA 22015

KAZURA, JAMES, ONCOLOGY, TROPICAL HEALTH. *Current Pos:* ASSOC PROF MED, UNIV HOSP, CASE WESTERN RESERVE UNIV, 83- *Personal Data:* b Cleveland, Ohio, 1946. *Educ:* Ohio State Univ, MD, 72. *Mem:* Am Soc Trop Med & Hyg; Am Fedn Clin Res; Infectious Dis Soc Am. *Mailing Add:* Case Western Res Sch Med 2119 Abington Cleveland OH 44106-2333. *Fax:* 219-368-1825

KE, HUA ZHU, OSTEOPOROSIS, PHYSICAL FRAILTY. *Current Pos:* SR RES SCIENTIST, CENT RES DIV, PFIZER INC, 92-95, SR RES INVESTR, 96- *Personal Data:* b Maoming, China, Aug 25, 62; div; c Qiao Han & Hunter. *Educ:* Zhanjiang Med Col, BSc, 81; Guangdong Med Col, MD, 84. *Prof Exp:* Teaching asst anat, Guangdong Med Col, 84-88; postdoctoral fel bone biol, Univ Utah, 88-90, res assoc osteoporosis, 90-92. *Concurrent Pos:* Vis assoc prof bone biol & med, Guangdong Med Col, 95-96, vis prof, 96-; young investr travel award, Int Bone & Mineral Soc, 95. *Mem:* Am Soc Bone & Mineral Res; Int Bone & Mineral Soc; Int Soc Bone Morphometry; Endocrine Soc; Soc Chinese Bioscientists Am; Int Chinese Hard Tissue Soc. *Res:* Pathophysiology of osteoporosis and physical frailty; discovery and development of new therapies for osteoporosis, frailty and related diseases. *Mailing Add:* Div Metab Dis Pfizer Cent Res Eastern Pointe Rd Groton CT 06340. *Fax:* 860-441-4111; *E-Mail:* buazhu_ke@gioton.pfizer.com

KE, PAUL JENN, ANALYTICAL BIOCHEMISTRY, FOOD TECHNOLOGY. *Current Pos:* PROF BIOCHEM, MEM UNIV, 88- *Personal Data:* b Ahwei Prov, China, Jan 16, 34; Can citizen; m 61; c 2. *Educ:* Nat Cheng-Kung Univ, Taiwan, BEng, 59; Nat Taiwan Univ, MSc, 63; Mem Univ Nfld, MSc, 66; Univ Windsor, PhD(anal biochem), 72. *Prof Exp:* Res & develop chem engr, Taiwan Sugar Res Inst, Taiwan, 59-61; instr, Nat Taiwan Univ, 62-64; anal chemist, Fish Res Bd Can, 66-69; res scientist, Halifax Lab, Fisheries & Oceans Can, 72-83, sr scientist & head tech studies dept, 83-93. *Mem:* Chem Inst Can; Can Soc Chem Engrs; Inst Food Technologists; Can Inst Food Sci & Technol; Am Oil Chemists Soc; fel Can Sci Coun. *Res:* Biochemical study on kinetics of lipid oxidation and various rancidity reactions; methodological studies for determination of biochemical parameters and contaminates in various fishery products and waters; quality science studies for sea foods; preservation biochemistry investigation; fish engineering sciences. *Mailing Add:* Biochem Dept Mem Univ Nfld St John's NF A1C 3X9 Can. *Fax:* 709-737-4000

KEAGY, PAMELA M, FOLIC ACID & NUTRIENT BIOAVAILABILITY. *Current Pos:* PROJ LEADER FOOD QUAL RES, AGR RES SERV-USDA, 78- *Educ:* Univ Calif, Berkeley, PhD, 81. *Mem:* Am Inst Nutrit; Inst Food Technologists; Am Asn Cereal Chemists. *Mailing Add:* Western Region Res Ctr Agr Res Serv USDA Berkeley CA 94710-1100

KEAHEY, KENNETH KARL, VETERINARY PATHOLOGY. *Current Pos:* RETIRED. *Personal Data:* b Covington, Okla, Sept 17, 23; m 56; c 3. *Educ:* Okla State Univ, BS, 48, DVM, 54; Mich State Univ, PhD(vet path), 63. *Prof Exp:* Adv vet med, Imp Ethiopian Col Agr & Mech Arts, 54-56, head dept animal sci, 56-57, dean, 57-58, actg pres, 58-60; NIH fel, Mich State Univ, 60-63, from asst prof to prof vet path, 63-90, dir, Anal Health Diag Lab, 77-90. *Mem:* AAAS; Am Vet Med Asn. *Res:* Infectious diseases and nutritional deficiencies in swine. *Mailing Add:* 1817 Cahill Dr East Lansing MI 48823

KEAIRNS, DALE LEE, CHEMICAL ENGINEERING, RESEARCH ADMINISTRATION. *Current Pos:* sr engr, Res & Develop Ctr, 67-73, mgr, Fluidized Bed Eng, 73-78, mgr, fossil fuel & fluidized bed processing, 78-83, MGR, CHEM & PROCESS ENG, RES & DEVELOP CTR, WESTINGHOUSE ELEC CORP, 83- *Personal Data:* b Vincennes, Ind, Nov 20, 40; m 67; c 1. *Educ:* Okla State Univ, BS, 62; Carnegie Inst Technol, MS, 64, PhD(chem eng), 67. *Prof Exp:* Assoc develop engr, Oak Ridge Nat Lab, 62 & Gaseous Diffusion Plant, Tenn, 63. *Concurrent Pos:* Chmn, First Int Fluidization Conf, Eng Found, 75, co-chmn, 78; mem, fossil fuel adv comt, Oak Ridge Nat Lab, 79-83, chem & process eng adv comt, NSF, 82-83; mem, adv panel, chem eng dept, Univ Pittsburgh, 84-; mem, tech comt, Particulate Solids Res Inst; mem, adv comt, Carnegie Inst & Carnegie Libr, 84-85, coun, Carnegie Mus Nat Hist, 84- *Mem:* Am Inst Chem Engrs; Am Chem Soc; AAAS; Soc Hist Technol. *Res:* Hydrodynamic, heat transfer and reaction rate studies on fluidized bed systems; pilot plant engineering and design; gasification and fluidized bed combustion systems development; gas cleaning. *Mailing Add:* 5419 Northumberland Pittsburgh PA 15217-1128

KEAMMERER, WARREN ROY, PLANT ECOLOGY. *Current Pos:* ECOL CONSULT, KEAMMERER ECOL CONSULT, 73- *Personal Data:* b Gary, Ind, Nov 25, 46; m 70, Deborah Barton; c Holly. *Educ:* Capital Univ, BS, 68; NDak State Univ, PhD(bot), 72. *Prof Exp:* Lectr biol, Capital Univ, 71-72; fel ecol, Univ Colo, 72-73. *Concurrent Pos:* Consult with var projs. *Mem:* Ecol Soc Am; Brit Ecol Soc; Sigma Xi; Wilderness Soc; Soc Range Mgt. *Res:* Preparation of baseline plant ecological reports designed to provide necessary data for impact analysis and permit applications; study areas are located in eastern Wyoming, western Colorado, Utah, New Mexico, North Dakota and Montana; monitoring revegetation success on reclaimed lands using comprehensive microcomputer program. *Mailing Add:* 5858 Woodbourne Hollow Rd Boulder CO 80301

KEAN, CHESTER EUGENE, FOOD CHEMISTRY. *Current Pos:* RETIRED. *Personal Data:* b Chicago, Ill, Oct 16, 25; m 49, 72, Betty L Cochran; c John M, Carolyn E (Reichman), Jeffry J, Janice (Gilmour), Richard C Graden & Jeffery R Graden. *Educ:* Univ Ill, BS, 48; Ore State Col, MS, 50; Univ Calif, PhD(agr chem), 54. *Prof Exp:* Asst chem, Ore State Col, 48-50; food technologist, Univ Calif, 50-53; assoc technologist, Calif & Hawaiian Sugar Refining Corp, 53-58, technologist, 58-61, new prod technologist, 61-66, sr technologist, 66-78, chief chemist prod develop, C&H Sugar Co, Crockett, 78-86. *Mem:* Inst Food Technologists. *Res:* Copper clouding in wines; fungal amylases in butanol acetone fermentation; organic acids in wine; method for determining the sub-sieve particle size distribution of pulverized sugar; carbohydrate chemistry; product development based on sugar properties. *Mailing Add:* 667 Byrdee Way Lafayette CA 94549

KEAN, EDWARD LOUIS, GLYCOPROTEINS & GLYCOLIPIDS, RHODOPSIN GLYCOSYLATION. *Current Pos:* from sr instr to assoc prof, 65-79, PROF OPHTHAL & BIOCHEM, SCH MED, CASE WESTERN RES UNIV, 79-, DIR, CTR VISION RES, 91- *Personal Data:* b Philadelphia, Pa, Oct 19, 25; m 62; c 4. *Educ:* Univ Pa, BA, 49, PhD(biochem), 61; Drexel Univ, MS, 56. *Prof Exp:* Chemist, Sharp & Dohme Inc, 49-52 & Smith Kline & French Labs, 52-56; asst instr biochem, Univ Pa, 56-57; res assoc, Univ Mich, 61-64; sr cancer res scientist, Roswell Park Mem Inst, NY, 64-65. *Concurrent Pos:* Arthritis & Rheumatism Found fel, 61-64; Nat Inst Neurol Dis & Stroke & Nat Eye Inst res grants, 68-; exchange scientist, Japan, 81; exchange scientist fel, Japan Soc Prom Sci, 81; Fogarty sr int res fel, 86-87; Erna & Jakob Michael, Vis Professorship Award, Weizman Inst Sci, Israel, 86-87. *Mem:* Am Chem Soc; Asn Res Vision & Ophthal; Int Soc Eye Res; Soc Glycobiol; Am Soc Biochem Molecular Biol; AAAS. *Res:* Biosynsthesis, subcellular location and degradation of cytosine monophosphate-sialic acid; glycolipid sulfation and vitamin A deficiency; glycosylation, oligosaccharide structure and degradation of rhodopsin; activation, regulation, topography and kinetics of initial reactions of the dolichol pathway. *Mailing Add:* Dept Ophthal Rm 653 Wearn Bldg Case Western Res Univ Cleveland OH 44106. *Fax:* 216-844-7899; *E-Mail:* elka@po.cwru.edu

KEAN, VANORA MABEL, FORENSIC SEROLOGY, BLOODSTAIN PATTERN INTERPRETATION. *Current Pos:* FORENSIC BIOLOGIST, CTR FORENSIC SCI, MINISTRY OF SOLICITOR GEN, GOVT ONT, 90- *Personal Data:* b Manchester, Eng, June 3, 55; m 88, William J Cobban. *Educ:* Univ Manchester, Eng, Hons BSc, 76; Univ Aberdeen, Scotland, PhD(genetics), 81. *Prof Exp:* Teaching asst genetics, Dept Genetics, Univ Aberdeen, Scotland, 77-80; res fel, Fac Med, Univ Nfld, 81-83; res fel, Dept Genetics, Hosp Sick Children, Toronto, 83-84, res assoc, 84-85; res asst, Dept Optom & Vision Sci, Univ Manchester Inst Sci & Technol, Eng, 85-87. *Concurrent Pos:* Tutor molecular biol, Fac Med, Univ Nfld, 81-83, Univ Manchester Inst Sci & Technol, 85-87; teaching asst med genetics, Dept Genetics, Hosp Sick Children, Toronto, 84. *Mem:* Am Soc Human Genetics; Brit Soc Cell Biol; Geneticsl Soc UK; Can Soc Forensic Sci; Int Asn Bloodstain Pattern Analysts. *Res:* Plant and human cytogenetics; human genetic diseases, including Duchenne muscular dystrophy and retinitis pigmentosa; DNA recombinant technology. *Mailing Add:* Biol Sect Ctr Forensic Sci 25 Grosvenor St Toronto ON M7A 2G8 Can. *Fax:* 416-314-3225

KEANA, JOHN F W, ORGANIC CHEMISTRY. *Current Pos:* from asst prof to assoc prof, 65-77, PROF CHEM, UNIV ORE, 77- *Personal Data:* b St Joseph, Mich, Sept 14, 39; m 66; c 2. *Educ:* Kalamazoo Col, BA, 61; Stanford Univ, PhD(chem), 65. *Prof Exp:* NSF fel, Columbia Univ, 64-65. *Concurrent Pos:* Guggenheim fel; A P Sloan fel; res career award, NIH. *Mem:* Am Chem Soc; Soc Magnetic Res Med; Int Soc Heterocyclic Chem. *Res:* Biological membranes; new synthetic reactions; preparation and properties of unusual organic molecules; chemistry and biophysics of nitroxide free radical spin-labels; neurochemistry; magnetic research imaging; photoresists and electron beam lithography. *Mailing Add:* Dept Chem Univ Ore Eugene OR 97403

KEANE, J R, NEURO-OPHTHALMOLOGY, BRAIN STEM NEUROLOGY. *Current Pos:* from instr to assoc prof, 70-82, PROF NEUROL, UNIV SOUTHERN CALIF SCH MED, LOS ANGELES, 82- *Personal Data:* b Washington, DC, Mar 12, 37. *Educ:* Univ Utah, BS, 58; Harvard Med Sch, MD, 61. *Prof Exp:* Intern, Bellevue Hosp, Univ Calif Med Ctr, 61-62 & 64-65; resident neurol, NY Neurol Inst, Columbia-Presby, 65-67; fel res, Mt Sinai Hosp, NY, 67-68; fel neuro-ophthal, Univ Calif Med Ctr, San Francisco, 68-69. *Concurrent Pos:* Bd examr, Am Bd Neurol & Psychiat, 74- *Mem:* Am Acad Neurol; Am Neurol Asn. *Res:* Clinical-anatomic correlations, with emphasis on eye movement neuropathology. *Mailing Add:* Dept Neurol LAC-USC Med Ctr 1200 N State St Los Angeles CA 90033-4525

KEANE, JOHN FRANCIS, JR, BIOPHYSICS, PHYSIOLOGY. *Current Pos:* RETIRED. *Personal Data:* b Milford, Mass, Feb 3, 22; m 48; c 2. *Educ:* Boston Col, BS, 43; Fordham Univ, MS, 49; Univ St Louis, PhD(biol chem), 54. *Prof Exp:* Asst biol, Fordham Univ, 48-49 & Cytochem Sect, Sloan-Kettering Inst, 49-50; asst biol, Biophys Inst, Univ St Louis, 50-54, res assoc, 54-56; from instr to assoc prof physics, St Louis Col Pharm, 55-80. *Mem:* AAAS; NY Acad Sci. *Res:* Physical properties and chemical constitution of crystalline inclusions in giant Amoebae; ultraviolet microspectrography of normal and malignant, desquammated and cultured cells; protective and other action of chemical agents particularly aliphatic amides on biological and physical systems subjected to subfreezing temperatures. *Mailing Add:* 1105 Missouri Ave Kirkwood MO 63122-1013

KEANE, KENNETH WILLIAM, nutrition, biochemistry; deceased, see previous edition for last biography

KEANE, ROBERT W, NEUROIMMUNOLOGY, DEVELOPMENTAL NEUROBIOLOGY. *Current Pos:* ASSOC PROF PHYSIOL, SCH MED, UNIV MIAMI, 82- *Educ:* Univ Calif, Davis, PhD, 76. *Mem:* Soc Neurosci; Soc Develop Biol; Soc Cell Biol. *Mailing Add:* Dept Physiol & Biophys R430 Univ Miami Sch Med 1600 NW Tenth Ave Miami FL 33136-1015

KEANE, WILLIAM FRANCIS, NEPHROLOGY. *Current Pos:* from asst prof to assoc prof, 76-87, PROF MED, UNIV MINN, MINNEAPOLIS, 87- *Personal Data:* b New York, NY, Sept 21, 42; m 67, Stephanie M Gaherin; c Alicia A & Elizabeth G. *Educ:* Fordham Univ, BS, 64; Yale Univ, MD, 68.

Prof Exp: Intern, resident then chief med resident, Cornell NY Hosp Med Ctr, 68-73. *Concurrent Pos:* Pres, Minn Med Res Found, 89-; chmn, Dept Med, Hennepin Co Med Ctr, 92- *Res:* Nephrology. *Mailing Add:* Hennepin Co Med Ctr 701 Park Ave Minneapolis MN 55415

KEAR, BERNARD HENRY, MATERIALS & TECHNOLOGY. *Current Pos:* PROF MAT SCI & TECHNOL CHMN, DEPT MECH & MAT SCI & DIR ADVAN TECHNOL, CTR SURFACE ENG MAT, RUTGERS UNIV, 86-, DIR, CTR FOR NANOMAT RES, 95- *Personal Data:* b Port Talbot, SWales, July 5, 31; US citizen; m 59; c 4. *Educ:* Birmingham Univ, BSc, 54, PhD (mat sci), 57, DSc, 70. *Honors & Awards:* Howe Medal, Am Soc Metals, 70; Mathewson Gold Medal, Am Inst Mining, Metall & Petrol Engrs, 71; John Dorn Mem Lectr, 80; Henry Krumb Mem Lectr, 83. *Prof Exp:* Res metallurgist, Tube Investments Ltd, UK, 57-59; fel, Franklin Inst, Philadelphia, 59-63; mem staff, Com Prod Div, Pratt & Whitney Aircraft, 63-81; sci adv, Exxon Res & Eng Co, 81-86. *Concurrent Pos:* Chmn, Gordon Res Conf Phys Metall, 74; sr consult scientist, United Technologies Res Ctr, 77-81; chmn, Nat Mat Adv Bd, Nat Res Coun, 86-89; co-ed, J Nanostructured Mat. *Mem:* Nat Acad Eng; fel Am Soc Metals; Am Inst Mining, Metall & Petrol Engrs; Mat Res Soc; Am Ceramic Soc. *Res:* New phenomena associated with chemical vapor deposition and solidification of materials surfaces; laser processing of materials; structure and property relationships in nickel base superalloys; chemically synthesized nanophase materials; chemical vapor deposition, surface modification and structure-properties-processing relationships in crystalline solids; author of 230 technical publications; awarded 30 patents. *Mailing Add:* Dept Ceramics & Mat Eng Rutgers Univ PO Box 909 Piscataway NJ 08855-0909

KEAR, EDWARD B, JR, MECHANICAL ENGINEERING, SYSTEMS ANALYSIS. *Current Pos:* REGISTR & DEAN SPEC PROG SUMMER SCH, CLARKSON UNIV; PRES, CLARKSON DEVELOP CORP. *Personal Data:* b Yonkers, NY, Mar 23, 32; m 54; c 3. *Educ:* Clarkson Tech Univ, BME, 54; Cornell Univ, MS, 56, PhD, 69. *Prof Exp:* From asst prof to assoc prof control syst anal, Clarkson Col Technol, 58-76, assoc prof mech & indust eng, 76-, exec officer, mech eng dept, 71- *Mem:* Am Soc Eng Educ. *Res:* Control systems analysis; variation of hand-eye coordination with age. *Mailing Add:* 12 Bradley Dr Potsdam NY 13676

KEARL, WILLIS GORDON, FARM AND RANCH MANAGEMENT, MARKETING AND PRICES. *Current Pos:* RETIRED. *Personal Data:* b Laketown, Utah, May 11, 27. *Educ:* Utah State Univ, BS, 49, MS, 51; Univ Calif, Berkeley, PhD(agr econ), 68. *Prof Exp:* Agr economist, res water develop, Bur Agr Econ USDA, Utah State Univ, 50-51, res fluoride damage, 54-55, digest staff, Doan Agr Serv, 51, agr econ res, Econ Res Serv, USDA, Calif & Wyo, 58-62; first lieutenant radar maintenance, USAF, 51-53; prof ranch mgt, Range Econ & Livestock Mkt, Univ Wyo, 62-90. *Mem:* Am Agr Econ Asn; Am Soc Range Mgt; Am Soc Animal Sci; Am Agr Law Asn. *Res:* Ranch management and economics of range improvements. *Mailing Add:* Box 3983 Univ Sta Laramie WY 82071

KEARLEY, ERIC, BIOPHYSICS. *Current Pos:* Radiation physicist, Armed Forces Radiobiol Res Inst, USN, 75-78, sci dir, USN Dosimetry Ctr, 80-86, asst dir radiation health, Puget Sound Naval Shipyard, 86-89, head, Mil Req & Appln Depts, 89-90, chair, Radiation Biophysics Dept, 90-93, dep sci dir, 93-94, DIR, ARMED FORCES RADIOBIOL RES INST, USN, 95- *Educ:* Univ Tex, BS, 72; NTex State Univ, MS, 74; Univ Wis-Madison, PhD(radiol physics), 82; Am Bd Health Physics, cert. *Concurrent Pos:* Consult, Nat Vol Lab Accreditation Prog, 90-94, Plasma Physics Lab, Princeton Univ, 91, USN Bur Med & Surg Dosimetry Ctr, 92-94, Naval Sea Systs Command. *Mem:* Health Physics Soc; Am Asn Physicists Med; Radiation Res Soc; Am Acad Health Physics. *Res:* Author several publications in field. *Mailing Add:* AFRRI US Dept Defense Bldg 42 8901 Wisconsin Bethesda MD 20888

KEARLEY, FRANCIS JOSEPH, JR, ORGANIC CHEMISTRY. *Current Pos:* Assoc prof, 53-66, PROF CHEM & CHMN DEPT, SPRING HILL COL, 66- *Personal Data:* b Mobile, Ala, July 7, 21; m 54. *Educ:* Spring Hill Col, BS, 42; Vanderbilt Univ, MS, 44, PhD(org chem), 50. *Mailing Add:* 4121 Ursuline Dr Mobile AL 36608-2494

KEARNEY, JOHN F, IMMUNOBIOLOGY, MICROBIOLOGY. *Current Pos:* Res assoc, Dept Pediat, Univ Ala, Birmingham, 74-76, asst prof, Dept Microbiol, 76-80, assoc scientist, Comprehensive Cancer Ctr, 76-83, ASSOC PROF, CELLULAR IMMUNOBIOL UNIT, SR SCIENTIST, COMPREHENSIVE CANCER CTR & PROF, DIV DEVELOP & CLIN IMMUNOL, DEPT MICROBIOL, UNIV ALA, BIRMINGHAM, 83- *Personal Data:* b Orrorroo, SAustralia, Mar 30, 45. *Educ:* Univ Adelaide, SAustralia, BDS Hons, 69; Univ Melbourne, PhD, 73. *Concurrent Pos:* Vis foreign dent scientist, Dept Pediat, Univ Ala, Birmingham, 73-74; Europ Molecular Biol Orgn vis sr fel, Dept Genetics, Univ Cologne, WGer, 78; assoc scientist, Multipurpose Arthritis Ctr, Univ Ala, Birmingham, 79; consult, Becton-Dickinson, 79-84 & Idec Inc, Calif, 86-; mem adv bd, Am Type Cult Asn, 84-; Basel Inst Immunol, 85-86 & Allergy & Immunol Study Sect, 86-; Am Cancer Soc & Eleanor Roosevelt int cancer fels, 85-86. *Mem:* Am Asn Univ Prof; Am Asn Immunologists; Am Asn Pathologists; AAAS. *Mailing Add:* Dept Microbiol Univ Ala 378 Tumor Inst Birmingham AL 35294-3300. *Fax:* 205-934-1875

KEARNEY, JOSEPH K, COMPUTER SCIENCE. *Current Pos:* From asst prof to assoc prof, 83-96, PROF, DEPT COMPUT SCI, UNIV IOWA, 96- *Personal Data:* b Jan 2, 51. *Educ:* Univ Minn, BA, 75, MS, 81, PhD(comput sci), 83; Univ Tex, MA, 79. *Concurrent Pos:* Vis scientist, Robotics Lab, Dept Comput Sci, Cornell Univ, 86-87; grantee, NIH, 88, NSF, 88-89, 92-95, 94-97 & 95-98; assoc ed, Asn Comput Mach Comput Surveys, 90-94; chair, Dept Comput Sci, Univ Iowa, 93-96. *Mem:* Asn Comput Mach; Inst Elec & Electronics Engrs; Inst Elec & Electronics Engrs Comput Soc. *Res:* Author of several published articles. *Mailing Add:* Dept Comput Sci Univ Iowa Iowa City IA 52242

KEARNEY, JOSEPH W(ILLIAM), system engineering, microwave engineering, for more information see previous edition

KEARNEY, MICHAEL SEAN, COASTAL GEOMORPHOLOGY, PALYNOLOGY. *Current Pos:* Lectr, 80-81, asst prof, 81-87, ASSOC PROF, GEOMORPHOL, UNIV MD, COLLEGE PARK, 87- *Personal Data:* b Chicago, Ill, May 12, 47; m 80; c 1. *Educ:* Univ Ill, Urbana, AB, 73; Western Ill Univ, MA, 76; Univ Western Ont, PhD(geog), 81. *Concurrent Pos:* Consult, Environ Can, 77-78, US Fish & Wildlife Serv, 84-85 & Cult Triangle Proj, UNESCO, 84-; prin investr, US Environ Protection Agency, 83-84 & Off Water Policy, US Dept Interior, 83-85 US Fish & Wildlife Serv, 87- *Mem:* AAAS; Am Asn Geogr; Am Quaternary Asn; Am Asn Stratig Palynologists. *Res:* Coastal and quaternary geomorphology and paleoecology, with emphasis on the Holocene; coastal marshes; estuaries; sea-level rise. *Mailing Add:* Dept Geog Lab Coastal Res Univ Md College Park MD 20742-0001

KEARNEY, PHILIP C, BIOCHEMISTRY, AGRICULTURE. *Current Pos:* chief pesticide degradation lab, 72-88, BIOCHEMIST PESTICIDES, AGR RES CTR-WEST, USDA, 62-; DEP AREA DIR, NAT RESOURCES INST, 88- *Personal Data:* b Baltimore, Md, Dec 31, 32; m 55; c 2. *Educ:* Univ Md, BS, 55, MS, 57; Cornell Univ, PhD(agr), 60. *Honors & Awards:* Int Award Res Pesticide Chem, Am Chem Soc, 81. *Prof Exp:* NSF fel biochem, 60-62. *Concurrent Pos:* Unit leader, Pesticide Degradation Lab, 65-72; adj prof chem & biochem, Univ Md, 83. *Mem:* Am Chem Soc; Int Union Pure & Appl Chem; AAAS; Weed Sci Soc Am; Asn Off Anal Chemists. *Res:* Pesticides; metabolism of organic pesticides by soil microorganisms; enzymology of pesticides. *Mailing Add:* USDA Agr Res Serv Nat Res Bldg 3 Rm 108 10300 Baltimore Ave BARC W Beltsville MD 20705-2350

KEARNEY, PHILIP DANIEL, PHYSICS. *Current Pos:* Asst prof, 64-74, ASSOC PROF PHYSICS, COLO STATE UNIV, 74-, CONSULT, ARGONNE NAT LAB, 81-, CHEM-NUCLEAR CORP, 84-, CORE LAB, 87- *Personal Data:* b Detroit, Mich, Nov 21, 33; m 58, Elizebeth Davie; c 4. *Educ:* Univ Mich, BS, 58, MS, 60, PhD(physics), 64. *Concurrent Pos:* Sabbatical leave, Solar Particle Physics, Los Alamos Sci Lab, 71-72, Environ Radiation Measurements, Argonne Nat Lab, 80-81. *Mem:* Health Physics Soc. *Res:* Environmental radiation measurements, radon, radon flux density, soil radium measurements. *Mailing Add:* Dept Physics Colo State Univ Ft Collins CO 80523. *Fax:* 970-491-7947; *E-Mail:* kearneyp@lamar.colostate.edu

KEARNEY, ROBERT EDWARD, BIOMEDICAL ENGINEERING. *Current Pos:* res asst, Biomed Eng Unit, McGill Univ, 76-77, postdoctoral fel, Aviation Med Res Unit, 77-78, lectr, Biomed Eng Unit, 78, fac lectr, Dept Physiol, 78-79, asst prof Biomed Eng, 78-83 & Dept Physiol, 79-83, assoc prof, Biomed Eng & Dept Physiol, 83-90, PROF DEPT BIOMED ENG & PHYSIOL, MCGILL UNIV, 90-, CHMN BIOMED ENG, 90- *Personal Data:* b Montreal, Que, Jan 19, 47. *Educ:* McGill Univ, BEng, 68, MEng, 71, PhD(biomed eng), 76. *Honors & Awards:* Geddes Prize in Biomed Eng, 72. *Prof Exp:* Computer systs engr, Div Neurol, Montreal Gen Hosp, 74-77. *Concurrent Pos:* Assoc mem, Sch Phys & Occup Therapy, McGill Univ, 81-, dir, Biomed eng Unit, 85-89, assoc mem, Dept Mech Eng, 86-, Dept Elec Eng, 89, actg chmn, Dept Biomed Eng, 89-90; assoc ed, Inst Elec & Electronics Engrs Trans in Biomed Eng; mem Med Res Coun Grants Comt Biomed Eng, 89- *Mem:* Inst Elec & Electronics Engrs; Soc Neurosci; Biomed Eng Soc. *Res:* Biomedical engineering; medical imaging; human joint dynamics; motor control system; medical and biological engineering and computing; numerous technical publications. *Mailing Add:* Biomed Eng Dept McGill Univ Third Fl 3775 Univ St Montreal PQ H3A 2B4 Can. *Fax:* 514-398-7461

KEARNEY, ROBERT JAMES, SOLID STATE PHYSICS. *Current Pos:* from asst prof to assoc prof, 64-73, PROF PHYSICS, UNIV IDAHO, 73- *Personal Data:* b Manchester, NH, Oct 5, 35; m 61; c 4. *Educ:* Univ NH, BS, 57, MS, 59; Iowa State Univ, PhD(physics), 64. *Prof Exp:* Asst physics, Ames Lab, AEC, 60-64. *Concurrent Pos:* Vis prof, Univ Milan, Italy, 72-73. *Mem:* AAAS; Am Asn Physics Teachers; Am Phys Soc. *Res:* Electronic structure of metals and semi-conductors; optical spectroscopy of molecules. *Mailing Add:* 718 E Eighth St Moscow ID 83843

KEARNS, DAVID R, BIOPHYSICAL CHEMISTRY. *Current Pos:* chmn, Chem Dept, 88-89, PROF CHEM, UNIV CALIF, SAN DIEGO, 75- *Personal Data:* b Urbana, Ill, Mar 20, 35; m 58, Alice Chen; c 2. *Educ:* Univ Ill, BS, 56; Univ Calif, Berkeley, PhD(phys chem), 60. *Prof Exp:* Fel theoret chem, Univ Chicago, 60-61; fel, Mass Inst Technol, 61-62; from asst prof to prof phys chem, Univ Calif, Riverside, 62-75. *Concurrent Pos:* A P Sloan fel, 65-67; lectr comt biophys, Harvard Med Sch, 65; Guggenheim fel, 69-70; assoc ed, photochem & photobiol, 71-75, molecular photochem, 72-78, chem rev, Anal Biochem, 77-82; adv bd, Biopolymers, 74. *Mem:* Am Chem Soc; Am Photobiol Soc; Biophys Soc; Protein Soc. *Res:* Physical biochemistry; spectroscopy; nuclear magnetic resonance, protein and DNA. *Mailing Add:* Dept Chem 0342 Univ Calif San Diego La Jolla CA 92093-0342

KEARNS, DAVID TODD, FEDERAL AGENCY ADMINISTRATION. *Current Pos:* DEP SECY EDUC, US DEPT EDUC, 91- *Personal Data:* b Rochester, NY, Aug 11, 30; m 54, Shirley V Cox; c Katherine, Elizabeth, Anne, Susan, David T & Andrew. *Educ:* Univ Rochester, BS, 52. *Honors & Awards:* Chairman's Award, Am Asn Eng Soc, 92. *Prof Exp:* Staff, IBM, 54-71, vpres, Mkt Opers Data Processing Div, 71; staff, Xerox Corp, 71-72, group vpres info syst, 72-75, group vpres charge, Rank Xerox & Fuji Xerox, 75-77, exec vpres int opers, 77, pres & chief exec officer, Xerox Corp, 77-85, chief oper officer, 77-82, chmn & chief exec officer, 85-90, chmn, 90-91. *Concurrent Pos:* Mem, Pres Educ Policy Adv Comn. *Mem:* Am Philos Asn. *Mailing Add:* US Dept Educ 400 Maryland Ave SW No 4015 Washington DC 20202

KEARNS, DONALD ALLEN, MATHEMATICS. *Current Pos:* PROF MATH, MERRIMACK COL, 58- *Personal Data:* b New Bedford, Mass, Sept 10, 23; m 47; c 7. *Educ:* Boston Univ, AB, 47, PhD(math), 55; Brown Univ, MA, 50. *Prof Exp:* From instr to asst prof math, Merrimack Col, 48-53; asst prof math, Univ Maine, 53-58. *Mem:* Am Math Soc; Math Asn Am. *Res:* Differential equations. *Mailing Add:* 23 Pleasant St Andover MA 01810

KEARNS, LANCE EDWARD, GEOLOGY, MINERALOGY. *Current Pos:* ASSOC PROF TO PROF GEOL, JAMES MADISON UNIV, 76- *Personal Data:* b Greensburg, Pa, May 22, 49; m 91, Cynthia A; c Jessica C & Janel L. *Educ:* Waynesburg Col, BS, 71; Univ Del, MS, 73, PhD(mineral), 77. *Mem:* Am Mineral Soc. *Res:* Mineral chemistry, especially fluorine effects in high temperature metacarbonates; minerals of Amelia Pegmatite Dist, Va, USA. *Mailing Add:* Dept Geol & Geog James Madison Univ 800 S Main St Harrisonburg VA 22807-0001. *Fax:* 540-568-7938; *E-Mail:* fac__lkearns@vax1.acs.jmu.edu

KEARNS, ROBERT J, CELLULAR IMMUNOLOGY. *Current Pos:* asst prof, 84-90, ASSOC PROF BIOL, UNIV DAYTON, 90- *Personal Data:* b Feb 9, 46; m; c 3. *Educ:* Wash State Univ, PhD, 78. *Mem:* Am Soc Microbiologists; Am Asn Immunologists; Reticuloendothial Soc. *Res:* Cellular immunology. *Mailing Add:* Dept Biol Univ Dayton 300 College Park Dayton OH 45469-2320

KEARNS, ROBERT WILLIAM, MECHANICAL ENGINEERING. *Current Pos:* INVENTOR INTERMITTENT WINDSHIELD WIPER CONTROLS, KEARNS ENGRS, 62- *Personal Data:* b Gary, Ind, Mar 10, 27; m 53; c 6. *Educ:* Univ Detroit, BSME, 52; Wayne State Univ, MSEM, 57; Case Inst Technol, PhD(eng), 64. *Prof Exp:* Jr engr digital computers, Burroughs Corp Res Labs, 52-53; engr servo-mechanisms, Bendix Corp Res Labs, 53-57; from asst prof to assoc prof eng mech, Dept Eng Mech, Wayne State Univ, 57-67; comnr inspection bldg, Dept Bldg & Safety Eng, City Detroit, 67-71; prin investr, Bur Standards, US Dept Com, 71-76. *Concurrent Pos:* Mfr & partner, Kearns & Law Engrs, 57-61; prof engr, Kearns Engrs, 63-76; mfr, Computer Cent, 65-76; supvr, Wayne County, Mich Bd Supvr, 67-69; comnr, Comn Housing Law Rev, State Mich, 68-71. *Mem:* Sigma Xi; fel NSF. *Res:* Intermittent windshield wiper systems including those whose pause time varies automatically with the degree-of-dryness of the windshield-yet, no moisture sensor is utilized. *Mailing Add:* 301 Houghton Lab Lane Queenstown MD 77057

KEARNS, THOMAS J, ALGEBRA. *Current Pos:* asst prof, 75-77, ASSOC PROF MATH, NORTHERN KY UNIV, 77-, CHAIRPERSON DEPT, 81- *Personal Data:* b Evanston, Ill, June 1, 40; m 63; c 3. *Educ:* Univ Santa Clara, BS, 62; Univ Ill, MS, 64, PhD(math), 68. *Prof Exp:* From instr to asst prof math, Univ Del, 67-75. *Mem:* Am Math Soc; Math Asn Am. *Res:* Representation theory for Lie algebras of classical type. *Mailing Add:* Dept Math & Comput Sci Northern Ky Univ Highland Heights KY 41099-1700

KEARNS, THOMAS P, ophthalmology, for more information see previous edition

KEARSLEY, ELLIOT ARMSTRONG, RHEOLOGY, CONTINUUM MECHANICS. *Current Pos:* CONSULT, RHEOLOGY RES, 81- *Personal Data:* b Springfield, Mass, Jan 15, 27; m 57, 64; c 2. *Educ:* Harvard Univ, AB, 49, MA, 50; Brown Univ, PhD(physics), 55. *Prof Exp:* Physicist, Res Lab, Bendix Aviation Corp, Mich, 53-55; physicist, Nat Acad Sci-Nat Res Coun, 55-76; sr liaison scientist, Off Naval Res, Tokyo, 76-78; physicist, Polymers Div, Nat Bur Stand, 78-81. *Mem:* Fel Am Phys Soc; Soc Rheol. *Mailing Add:* 10413 Englishman Dr Rockville MD 20852-4663

KEAST, CRAIG LEWIS, ADVANCED MICROELECTRONICS RESEARCH IN SILICON TECHNOLOGIES, DEEP SUBMICRON LITHOGRAPHY. *Current Pos:* semiconductor process technician, Mass Inst Technol Lincoln Lab, 81-83, asst staff, 83-88, Kodak res fel, Mass Inst Technol, 88-92, mem tech staff, 92-94, DIR OPERS, MICROELECTRONIC LAB, MASS INST TECHNOL LINCOLN LAB, 94- *Personal Data:* b Los Angeles, Calif, Nov 6, 58; m, Rev Barbara Driver. *Educ:* Hamilton Col, BA, 80; Mass Inst Technol, SM, 89, Eng, 90, PhD(elec eng & comput sci), 92. *Prof Exp:* Math & sci teacher, Concord Pub Schs, 80-81. *Mem:* Inst Elec & Electronics Engrs; Sigma Xi; Int Soc Optical Eng. *Res:* Advanced optical lithography; three-dimensional silicon device fabrication and characterization; chemical-mechanical planarization; focal plane analog signal processing; advanced process development. *Mailing Add:* 650 Duck Pond Rd Groton MA 01450. *E-Mail:* keast@ll.mit.edu

KEAST, DAVID N(ORRIS), ENVIRONMENTAL NOISE, EMERGENCY WARNING. *Current Pos:* CONSULT, 88- *Personal Data:* b Pittsburgh, Pa, Jan 8, 31; m 55, Estelle Karvkas; c 4. *Educ:* Amherst Col, BA, 52; Mass Inst Technol, BS & MS, 54. *Prof Exp:* Engr acoust, Bolt Beranek & Newman, Inc, Los Angeles, 54-57, sr engr, 57-60, consult acoust & instrumentation, Calif, 60-64, supvr consult, 64-66, vpres Data Equip Div, 66-71; vpres develop, MFE Corp, Wilmington, 71-73; mgr, environ dept, Bolt Beranek & Newman, 73-83; vpres, HMM Assocs, Inc, 83-88. *Mem:* Fel Acoust Soc Am; sr mem Inst Elec & Electronics Engrs; Inst Noise Control Engrs. *Res:* Acoustic-meteorological interactions and processing techniques for high-frequency dynamic data; effects of sound on the human environment; community noise and emergency warning. *Mailing Add:* 657 Westford Rd Carlisle MA 01741-1542. *Fax:* 978-371-0840; *E-Mail:* dnk@world.std.com

KEASTER, ARMON JOSEPH, ENTOMOLOGY. *Current Pos:* From instr to assoc prof, 70-76, PROF ENTOM, UNIV MO-COLUMBIA, 76- *Personal Data:* b Lilbourn, Mo, Mar 12, 33; m 56; c 2. *Educ:* Univ Mo, BS, 59, MS, 61, PhD(entom), 65. *Mem:* Sigma Xi; Entom Soc Am. *Res:* Biology and management of soil and foliar pests attacking corn and other field crops; dispersal migration of Noctuidae. *Mailing Add:* Dept Entom Univ Mo Columbia MO 65211

KEAT, PAUL POWELL, ceramics, physical chemistry, for more information see previous edition

KEATING, BARBARA HELEN, PALEOMAGNETISM, ARCHAEOLOGY. *Current Pos:* RESEARCHER GEOPHYS, UNIV HAWAII, 76-, PROF OCEANOG, 81- *Personal Data:* b Brooksville, Fla, Dec 25, 50. *Educ:* Fla State Univ, BA, 71; Univ Tex, Dallas, MS, 75, PhD(geosci), 76. *Mem:* Geol Soc Am; Am Geophys Union; Int Asn Geomagnetism & Aeronomy; Soc Econ Paleontologist & Mineralogist. *Res:* Paleomagnetism and marine geology of the Pacific Ocean basin. *Mailing Add:* Hawaii Inst Geophys & Paleantol Univ Hawaii 2525 Correa Rd Honolulu HI 96822

KEATING, EUGENE KNEELAND, AGRICULTURAL BIOCHEMISTRY, NUTRITION. *Current Pos:* from asst prof to assoc prof, 64-71, chmn dept animal sci, 71-78, PROF RUMINANT NUTRIT, CALIF STATE POLYTECH UNIV, POMONA, 78- *Personal Data:* b Liberal, Kans, Feb 15, 28; m 51, Iris L Myers; c Denise L (Schnagl) & Kimberly A. *Educ:* Kans State Univ, BS, 53, MS, 54; Univ Ariz, PhD(ruminant nutrit), 64. *Prof Exp:* Instr animal sci, Midwestern Univ, 57-60, asst farm mgr, 57-59, farm mgr, 59-60. *Concurrent Pos:* mem coun, Agr Sci & Technol, Am Inst Chem. *Mem:* Am Soc Animal Sci; Brit Soc Animal Prod; fel Am Inst Chem. *Res:* Ruminant nutrition, particularly in cattle. *Mailing Add:* Dept Animal Sci Calif State Polytech Univ Pomona CA 91768

KEATING, JAMES T, ORGANIC CHEMISTRY, POLYMER CHEMISTRY. *Current Pos:* Res chemist, Plastic Prod & Resins Dept, Exp Sta, Wilmington, Del, 68-76, sr chemist, Seneca, Ill, 77-81, sr chemist, 81-83, res assoc, 83-89, SR RES ASSOC, E I DU PONT DE NEMOURS & CO, INC, WILMINGTON, DEL, 89- *Personal Data:* b Oak Park, Ill, Jan 21, 41; m 70, Mimi Liu; c 3. *Educ:* St Mary's Col, Minn, BA, 62; Pa State Univ, PhD(chem), 68. *Concurrent Pos:* NSF fel, 62-66. *Res:* Carbene chemistry; aliphatic carbonium ion reactions; fluorinated free radicals; electrochemistry; Friedel-Crafts-type polymerizations; organic and inorganic coatings; emulsion polymerization; occupational safety and health; ion exchange membranes; fluoropolymers chloralkali. *Mailing Add:* Du Pont Co Exp Sta PO Box 80-323 Wilmington DE 19880-0323

KEATING, JOHN JOSEPH, NUCLEAR REACTOR FUELS. *Current Pos:* RETIRED. *Personal Data:* b Montrose, SDak, Jan 17, 38; m 61; c 4. *Educ:* SDak State Col, BS, 60; Iowa State Univ, MS, 66, PhD(nuclear eng), 68. *Prof Exp:* Nuclear engr, Idaho Opers Off, US AEC 68-73, reactor fuels engr, Div Reactor Develop & Technol, 73-74, asst dir engr technol & fuels, Fast Flux Test Fac Proj Off, US Energy Res & Develop Agency, 74-78; dir, Reactor Technol Div, Fast Flux Test Fac Prog Off, US Dept Energy, 78-81, dir, Fuels Supply Div, Richland Opers Off, 81-89, asst mgr tech support, 89-94. *Mem:* Am Nuclear Soc. *Res:* Development and production of core components for liquid metal fast breeder reactors; core components include fuel, blanket, absorber and reflector assemblies. *Mailing Add:* 2611 Harris Ave Richland WA 99352

KEATING, KATHLEEN IRWIN, PLANKTON CULTURE, TRACE ELEMENT NUTRITION. *Current Pos:* PROF LIMNOL & ENVIRON SCI, DEPT ENVIRON SCI, RUTGERS UNIV, 74- *Personal Data:* b NJ, Mar 7, 38; m 62, Martin; c Sean Michael. *Educ:* Cornell Univ, BA, 60; William Patterson Col, MS, 70; Yale Univ, MPh, 72, PhD(limnol), 75. *Prof Exp:* Teacher sci & math, Dumont Pub Sch Syst, 62-68. *Concurrent Pos:* Prin investr, NJ Agr Exp Sta, 76-, NSF Ecol Prog, 79-82; consult, Dow Chem Co, 82- 89. *Mem:* AAAS; Am Soc Limnol & Oceanog; Crustacean Soc; Ecol Soc Am; Soc Environ Toxicol & Chem; Am Inst Nutrit. *Res:* Roles of trace element nutrition and allelochemistry in plankton (phytoplankton and zooplankton) community structure; use of highly controlled, defined cultures to isolate critical factors significant to in situ community structure; in vivo trace element interaction. *Mailing Add:* Dept Environ Sci Cook Rutgers Univ New Brunswick NJ 08903. *Fax:* 732-932-8644; *E-Mail:* kkeating@rci.rutgers.edu

KEATING, KENNETH L(EE), MATERIALS SCIENCE ENGINEERING. *Current Pos:* assoc prof, 61-67, prof, 67-90, EMER PROF METALL ENG, UNIV ARIZ, 90- *Personal Data:* b Chicago, Ill, May 19, 23; m 47, Charlotte Matthews; c Roger & Kevin. *Educ:* Mass Inst Technol, SB, 47; Univ Mo, MS, 50; Stanford Univ, PhD(metall), 54. *Prof Exp:* Metallurgist, Titanium Div, Nat Lead Co, 47-48; asst metall, Univ Mo, 48-49, instr, 49-50; instr, Stanford Univ, 51-54; metallurgist, Bell Tel Labs, Inc, 54-55; metallurgist, Semiconductor Prod Div, Motorola, Inc, Ariz, 55-61; consult, Cabot Corp, 78-86. *Mem:* Am Soc Metals; Electrochem Soc; Am Inst Mining, Metall & Petrol Engrs; Am Ceramic Soc; Nat Asn Corrosion Engrs. *Res:* Corrosion of metals; phase relations between materials; solid state metallurgy. *Mailing Add:* 5256 Camino de la Cumbre Tucson AZ 85715-1506. *E-Mail:* charken@azstarnet.com

KEATING, PATRICK NORMAN, APPLIED PHYSICS, ELECTRONICS ENGINEERING. *Current Pos:* proj physicist, Allied-Signal Aerospace Technol Ctr, 65-70, head Laser Optics & Acoustics Dept, 70-74, dir, Appl Physics Dept, Bendix Res Lab, 74-79, assoc dir res, Bendix Advan Technol Ctr, 80-83, DIR & GEN MGR, ALLIED-SIGNAL AEROSPACE TECHNOL CTR, 83- *Personal Data:* b Newcastle, UK, Feb 18, 39; div; c 2. *Educ:* Univ Nottingham, BSc, 59, MSc, 61; Univ Mich, PhD(physics), 69. *Prof Exp:* Physicist, Assoc Elec Industs, UK, 60-63; physicist, Tyco Labs, Inc, Waltham, Mass, 63-65. *Mem:* Am Mgt Asn; Inst Elec & Electronics Engrs. *Res:* Computer science, acoustics, underwater acoustics, and acoustic signal processing; sensors, optics; lattice dynamics; solid state physics. *Mailing Add:* 4240 Columbia Rd Ellicott City MD 21042

KEATING, RICHARD CLARK, SYSTEMATIC BOTANY. *Current Pos:* from asst prof to assoc prof, 66-75, PROF BIOL, SOUTHERN ILL UNIV, EDWARDSVILLE, 75-, ACTG COORDR, DEAN'S COL, 90- *Personal Data:* b St Paul, Minn, Aug 6, 37; m 61; c 2. *Educ:* Colgate Univ, AB, 59; Univ Cincinnati, MS, 62, PhD(bot), 65. *Prof Exp:* Asst prof biol, Wis State Univ, Platteville, 64-65; vis asst prof bot, Univ Cincinnati, 65-66. *Concurrent Pos:* Res assoc, Mo Bot Garden, St Louis, 69-; dir, Trop Biol Prog, Assoc Univs Int Educ, 70; res assoc, Marie Selby Bot Garden, Sarasota, 74-80; consult, Syst Panel, NSF, 82-84; elected fel, Ill State Acad Sci, 84. *Mem:* AAAS; Bot Soc Am; Int Asn Wood Anatomists; Int Asn Plant Taxon; Int Aroid Soc; Soc Conserv Biol; Am Soc Plant Taxon. *Res:* Anatomical investigations on the evolution and classification of vascular plants; Ranales, Solanaceae and Araceae. *Mailing Add:* PO Box 13 Edwardsville IL 62025-0013

KEATON, CLARK M, physical chemistry; deceased, see previous edition for last biography

KEATON, PAUL W, JR, nuclear physics, for more information see previous edition

KEATS, ARTHUR STANLEY, PHARMACOLOGY. *Current Pos:* CHIEF ANESTHESIA, DIV CARDIOVASC ANESTHESIA, TEX HEART INST, 74-; CLIN PROF ANESTHESIOL, UNIV TEX HEALTH SCI CTR HOUSTON, 78- *Personal Data:* b New Brunswick, NJ, May 31, 23; m 46; c 4. *Educ:* Rutgers Univ, BS, 43; Univ Pa, MD, 46. *Prof Exp:* Asst instr, Sch Med, Univ Pa, MD, 68; asst anesthetist, Mass Gen Hosp, 51; anesthesiologist, House Sisters Red Cross, Switz, 52-53 & Mary Imogene Bassett Hosp, 53-55; prof anesthesiol & chmn dept, Baylor Col Med, 55-74, clin prof, 74-75. *Concurrent Pos:* Assoc anesthesiol, Col Physicians & Surgeons, Columbia Univ, 53-55; dir anesthesiol, Ben Taub Gen Hosp, 55- *Mem:* AAAS; Am Soc Pharmacol & Exp Therapeut; Am Soc Anesthesiol. *Res:* Opiates; analgesics. *Mailing Add:* Div Cardiovasc Anesthesia Tex Heart Inst PO Box 20345 Houston TX 77225-0345. *Fax:* 713-791-2666

KEATS, JOHN BERT, INDUSTRIAL ENGINEERING, STATISTICS. *Current Pos:* AT ARIZ STATE UNIV, 83- *Personal Data:* b New York, NY, Sept 14, 36; m 68; c 2. *Educ:* Lehigh Univ, BS, 59; Fla State Univ, MS, 64, PhD(educ res), 70. *Prof Exp:* Indust engr, US Steel Corp, Ill, 59-61; asst prof indust eng, La Tech Univ, 64-66; assoc, Advan Proj Dept, Syst Develop Corp, Calif, 68; assoc prof, La Tech Univ, 69-80; mem fac, Sch Indust Eng & Mgt, Okla State Univ, 80-83. *Concurrent Pos:* Consult, Southern Regional Off, Col Entrance Exam Bd, Ga, 70- *Mem:* Sr mem Am Inst Indust Engrs; Am Statist Asn; Am Educ Res Asn. *Res:* Educational and operations research; computer assisted instruction. *Mailing Add:* Dept Indust Eng Mgt Systs Ariz State Univ PO Box 875906 Tempe AZ 85287-5906

KEATS, THEODORE ELIOT, RADIOLOGY. *Current Pos:* chmn dept, 64-91, PROF RADIOL, UNIV HOSP, UNIV VA SCH MED, 64- *Personal Data:* b New Brunswick, NJ, June 26, 24; m 74, Patricia Hart; c 2. *Educ:* Rutgers Univ, BS, 45; Univ Pa, MD, 47; Am Bd Radiol, dipl. *Honors & Awards:* Gold Medal, Am Col Radiol; Medal, Int Skeletal Soc. *Prof Exp:* Intern, Hosp Univ Pa, 47-48; resident radiol, Univ Mich Hosp, 48-51; from instr to asst prof, Sch Med, Univ Calif, 53-56; from assoc prof to prof, Sch Med, Univ Mo, 56-63; vis prof, Karolinska Inst, Sweden, 63-64. *Concurrent Pos:* Trustee, Am Bd Radiol, 73-85; ed, J Skeletal Radiol, J Appl Radiol, J Energy Radiol, J Current Prob Diag Radiol. *Mem:* Radiol Soc NAm; Roentgen Ray Soc; AMA; fel Am Col Radiol; Asn Univ Radiol; Int Skeletal Soc; Am Soc Energy Radiol; hon mem Soc Pediat Radiol. *Res:* Pediatric and skeletal radiology; name variants; musculo skeletal strain injury. *Mailing Add:* Dept Radiol Univ Va Hosp Charlottesville VA 22901

KEAVENEY, WILLIAM PATRICK, ORGANIC CHEMISTRY. *Current Pos:* SCIENTIST, SUN CHEM CORP, CARLSTADT, 91- *Personal Data:* b New York, Dec 25, 36; m 61; c 5. *Educ:* Manhattan Col, BS, 58; Fordham Univ, PhD(org chem), 64. *Prof Exp:* Res assoc, Inmont Corp, Clifton, 62-90. *Mem:* Am Chem Soc; affil Int Union Pure & Appl Chem. *Res:* Pyrodoxine determination; synthesis of dichloro-diphenyl-trichlorethane analogs; norbornylene polymerization; ozonolysis; radiation curing; polymer chemistry. *Mailing Add:* Sun Chem Corp Tech Ctr 631 Central Ave Carlstadt NJ 07072

KEAVENY, TONY M, BIO-MECHANICS. *Current Pos:* asst prof, 93-97, ASSOC PROF, DEPT MECH ENG, UNIV CALIF, BERKELEY, 97-, ASST PROF, DEPT ORTHOP SURG, UNIV CALIF, SAN FRANCISCO, 94- *Personal Data:* b Dublin, Ireland, June 14, 62. *Educ:* Univ Col Dublin, Ireland, BE, 84; Cornell Univ, MS, 88, PhD(mech eng), 91. *Honors & Awards:* Y C Fung Young Investr Award, Bioeng Div, Am Soc Mech Engrs, 96. *Prof Exp:* Asst lectr, Dublin Inst Technol, Ireland, 84-85; res asst, E I Dupont de Nemours & Co, Del, 87; Maurice E Muller Found postdoctoral fel orthop biomech, Orthop Biomech Lab, Dept Orthop Surg, Beth Israel Hosp, Mass, 90-91; sr res assoc, 91-93. *Concurrent Pos:* Instr, Dept Orthop Surg, Harvard Med Sch, 91-93; health sci & technol affil fac mem, Div Health Sci & Technol, Harvard Univ-Mass Inst Technol, 92-93; NIH First Award, 92-97; adj asst prof, Dept Ceramic Eng, Clemson Univ, 93-; fac mem, Joint Grad Group Bioeng, Univ Calif, Berkeley, 93-; NSF Career Award, 96- *Mem:* Orthop Res Soc; Am Soc Mech Engrs; Am Soc Biomech; Biomed Eng Soc; Am Soc Bone & Mineral Res. *Mailing Add:* Dept Mech Eng 6175 Etcheverry Hall Univ Calif Berkeley CA 94720-1740. *Fax:* 510-642-6163; *E-Mail:* tmk@euler.me.berkeley.edu

KEAY, LEONARD, ANIMAL CELL CULTURE FERMENTATION TECHNOLOGY. *Current Pos:* PRES, PIASA BIOTECHNOL INC, 88- *Personal Data:* b Crayford, Eng, Nov 26, 32; nat US; m 80; c 3. *Educ:* Univ London, BSc, 53, PhD(chem), 55, MSc, 56, Univ Mo, St Louis, MBA, 83. *Prof Exp:* Hon asst biochem, Univ Col, Univ London, 56-58; hon fel, Sch Advan Study & res fel enzymol, Mass Inst Technol, 58-60; res biochemist, Monsanto Co, 60-71; res biochemist, Sch Med, Washington Univ, 71-74, dir, Basic Cancer Res Ctr, 71-80; mem staff, McDonnell Douglas Astronaut Co, 80-89. *Concurrent Pos:* Salters Inst Indust Chem res fel, Univ Col, Univ London, 56-58; prog mgr, US Dept Energy, 88-95. *Mem:* Am Chem Soc. *Res:* Organo phosphorus chemistry and biochemistry; enzymology; applied biochemistry and microbiology; animal cell culture; tissue culture; fermentation technology. *Mailing Add:* 2055 Castle Dr Edwardsville IL 62025. *Fax:* 618-656-8279

KEBABIAN, JOHN WILLIS, ENDOCRINOLOGY, DOPAMINE RECEPTORS. *Current Pos:* VPRES RES & DEVELOP, RES BIOCHEM INT, 92- *Personal Data:* b New York, NY, Sept 20, 46; m 75, Procy R; c 2. *Educ:* Yale Univ, BS, 68, MPhil, 70, PhD(pharmacol), 73. *Prof Exp:* Res assoc, NIH, 74-76, sr staff fel, 76-78, pharmacologist, 78-81, sect chief, 81-86; from proj leader to sr proj leader neurosci, Abbott Labs, 86-92. *Concurrent Pos:* Bd dirs, Yale Alumni Fund, 83- *Mem:* Am Soc Biol Chemists; Am Soc Pharm & Exp Therapeut; Brit Pharmacol Soc; Endocrine Soc; AAAS. *Res:* Receptors for neurotransmitters; dopamine receptors; pituitary gland; author of 3 citation classics. *Mailing Add:* Res Biochem Int One Strathmore Rd Natick MA 01778

KEBARLE, PAUL, PHYSICAL CHEMISTRY. *Current Pos:* from asst prof to assoc prof, 58-68, PROF CHEM, UNIV ALTA, 68- *Personal Data:* b Sofia, Bulgaria, Sept 21, 26; m 55; c 1. *Educ:* Swiss Fed Inst Technol, Dipl Ing Chem, 52; Univ BC, PhD, 55. *Prof Exp:* Nat Res Coun Can fel, 55-58. *Mem:* Fel Royal Soc Can. *Res:* Application of mass spectrometry to reaction kinetics in the gas phase; ion-molecule interactions at high pressure; ionic solvation and ionic reactivity in the gas phase; ion-molecule equilibria. *Mailing Add:* Dept Chem Univ Alberta Edmonton AB T6G 2G2 Can. *Fax:* 403-492-8231

KEBLAWI, FEISAL SAID, COMMUNICATIONS SYSTEMS ENGINEERING. *Current Pos:* PROJ MGR, FED AVIATION AUTH, WASHINGTON, DC, 90- *Personal Data:* b Acre, Palestine, July 11, 35; US citizen; m 73; c 4. *Educ:* Am Univ Beirut, BS, 57; NC State Univ, MS, 62, PhD(elec eng), 65. *Prof Exp:* Mem tech staff satellite systs eng, RCA Corp, 65-68; satellite commun systs engr, Mitre Corp, 68-90. *Concurrent Pos:* US deleg, US/USSR Working Group on Air Traffic Control, Moscow, 78; cong fel, Inst Elec & Electronics Engrs, 81-82; staff asst defense, Senator Thurmond, 81-; US deleg, US/Ger group on air defense. *Mem:* Sr mem Inst Elec & Electronics Engrs; Planetary Soc. *Res:* Satellite communications deep space and tactical systems; tactical communications systems; air traffic control; forward air defense; control systems engineering; stabilization of heat transfer process in nuclear reactors; legislation in civil defense; researcher of major foreign policy and arms sales issues. *Mailing Add:* 2106 Freda Dr Vienna VA 22181

KEBLER, RICHARD WILLIAM, APPLIED PHYSICS. *Current Pos:* group leader, Union Carbide Res Inst, 60-66, mgr mat res & develop, Space Sci & Eng Lab, 66-68, sr res assoc, Linde Co Div, 68-70, PROG MGR COMPOSITES, LINDE CO DIV, UNION CARBIDE CORP, 70- *Personal Data:* b Owosso, Mich, Nov 25, 20; m 50; c 4. *Educ:* Univ Mich, BSE, 42, MS, 47, PhD(physics), 54. *Prof Exp:* Res assoc, Eng Res Inst, Univ Mich, 42; res physicist, Linde Co Div, Union Carbide Corp, 53-55, develop supvr, 56-59; res physicist, Gen Motors Res Lab, 59. *Mem:* Am Phys Soc; Optical Soc Am; Am Ceramic Soc; Metall Soc; Sigma Xi. *Res:* Spectro-chemical analysis; extreme ultraviolet spectroscopy; crystal growth; refractory and composite materials; turbine engine compressors. *Mailing Add:* 9785 E Skyview Dr Tucson AZ 85748-7507

KECECIOGLU, D(IMITRI) B(ASIL), ENGINEERING MECHANICS, RELIABILITY ENGINEERING. *Current Pos:* PROF AEROSPACE & MECH ENG, UNIV ARIZ, 63-, PROF, RELIABILITY ENG PROG, 69- *Personal Data:* b Istanbul, Turkey, Dec 26, 22; nat US; m 51; c 2. *Educ:* Robert Col, Istanbul, BS, 42; Purdue Univ, MS, 48, PhD(eng mech), 53. *Honors & Awards:* Ralph Teetor Award, Soc Automotive Engrs, 77; Allen Chop Award, Am Soc Qual Control, 81; Excellence Award, Soc Reliability Eng; Reliability Educ Advan Award, Am Soc Qual Control; Anderson Prize, Univ Ariz Col Eng & Mines. *Prof Exp:* Instr mech, Purdue Univ, 47, asst metal cutting, 49-52, asst instr eng drawing & descriptive geom, 50-52, asst instr mach tool lab, 51; eng scientist-in-chg mech lab, Res Labs, Allis-Chalmers Mfg Co, 52-57, asst to dir mech eng industs group, 57-63, dir reliability & corp consult, 60-63. *Concurrent Pos:* Fulbright scholar, Greece, 71-72; dir, Reliability Eng & Mgt Insts; consult reliability & maintainability eng, indust & govt; hon prof, Phi Kappa Phi, Shangai Univ Technol. *Mem:* AAAS; Am Soc Mech Engrs; Am Soc Eng Educ; Soc Exp Stress Anal; Inst Elec & Electronics Engrs; Sigma Xi; Soc Reliability Engrs; Inst Environ Sci; Soc Automotive Engrs. *Res:* System effectiveness, reliability, maintainability; quality control; statistics; probability; design; production engineering; design by reliability; tooling engineering; applied mathematics. *Mailing Add:* Dept Aerospace & Mech Eng Univ Ariz Bldg 16 Tucson AZ 85721

KECK, DONALD BRUCE, PHYSICS. *Current Pos:* Res physicist, Corning Glass Works, 68-74, res assoc physics, 74-76, mgr Appl Physics Dept, 76-86, DIR APPL PHYSICS RES, CORNING GLASS WORKS, 86-, DIR OPTICS & PHOTONICS RES, 86- *Personal Data:* b Lansing, Mich, Jan 2, 41; m 65, Ruth A Moilanen; c Lynne & Brian. *Educ:* Mich State Univ, BS, 62, MS, 64, PhD(physics), 67. *Honors & Awards:* Technol Achievement Award, Soc Photo-optical Instrumentation Engrs, 81; IR-100 Award, 81; Eng Achievement Award, Am Soc Metall, 83; John Tyndall Award, Inst Elec & Electronics Engrs/Optical Soc Am, 92, Nat Inventors Hall of Fame, 93; Nat Acad Eng, 93. *Mem:* Fel Optical Soc Am; fel Inst Elec & Electronics Engrs; Soc Photo-optical Instrumentation Engrs; Nat Acad Eng. *Res:* Near infrared molecular spectroscopy; magnetic rotation spectroscopy; fiber optics; propagation in fiber optic waveguides; gradient index imaging; guided wave optics; optical couplers; optical amplifiers; optical fiber sensors. *Mailing Add:* 2877 Chequers Circle Big Flats NY 14814. *Fax:* 607-974-3726; *E-Mail:* keck_db@corning.com

KECK, JAMES COLLYER, PHYSICS. *Current Pos:* Ford prof mech eng, 65-89, PROF EMER & SR LECTR, MASS INST TECHNOL, 89- *Personal Data:* b New York, NY, June 11, 24; m 47; c 2. *Educ:* Cornell Univ, BA, 47, PhD, 51. *Prof Exp:* Res assoc physics, Cornell Univ, 51-52; res fel, Calif Inst Technol, 52-55; prin scientist, Avco-Everett Res Lab, Mass, 55-65, dep dir, 60-64. *Mem:* Am Phys Soc; AAAS; Sigma Xi; fel Am Acad Arts & Sci; Combustion Inst. *Res:* Atomic and molecular kinetics; high temperature gas dynamics; combustion; nonequilibrium thermodynamics; high energy nuclear physics. *Mailing Add:* 52 Harold Parker Rd Andover MA 01810-5202

KECK, MAX HANS, POLYMER CHEMISTRY. *Current Pos:* RETIRED. *Personal Data:* b Konstanz, Ger, May 7, 19; US citizen; m 49; c 2. *Educ:* Col Wooster, BA, 41; Univ Akron, MSc, 45. *Prof Exp:* Sr res chemist polyester chem, Goodyear Tire & Rubber Co, 42-67, res scientist, Fiber Tech Ctr, 67-83. *Mem:* Am Chem Soc. *Res:* Linear polyester research, preparation of new linear polyesters and new monomers; catalysis studies; dyeable and specialty polyester fibers; cross-linkable polyesters for coatings. *Mailing Add:* 3117 Mayfield Rd Silver Lake Cuyahoga Falls OH 44224-3097

KECK, MAX JOHANN, VISUAL PSYCHOPHYSICS. *Current Pos:* From asst prof to assoc prof, 68-78, PROF PHYSICS, JOHN CARROLL UNIV, 78-, DEAN STUD DEVELOP. *Personal Data:* b Feb 22, 39; US citizen. *Educ:* Mass Inst Technol, BS, 61; Purdue Univ, MS, 64, PhD(physics), 68. *Concurrent Pos:* Adj staff mem ophthalmol, Cleveland Clin Found, Ohio, 78-; prin investr res grant, Nat Eye Inst, NIH, 79- *Mem:* Am Phys Soc; Asn Res Vision & Ophthal. *Res:* Binocular vision; spatial vision; amblyopia and strabismus. *Mailing Add:* Col Art & Sci Xavier Univ 3800 Victory Pkwy Cincinnati OH 45207

KECK, ROBERT WILLIAM, SCIENCE ADMINISTRATION, RESEARCH ADMINISTRATION. *Current Pos:* from asst to prof biol, Ind Univ-Purdue Univ, 72-82, asst dean, 82-84, assoc dean, 84-88, 87-90, actg dean, 88-89, PROF BIOL, IND UNIV-PURDUE UNIV, 90- *Personal Data:* b Manchester, Iowa, Jan 2, 41; m 64, Juanita F; c Robert A & Julie K. *Educ:* Univ Iowa, BS, 62, MS, 64; Ohio State Univ, PhD(plant physiol), 68. *Prof Exp:* Researcher photosynthesis, Charles F Kettering Res Lab, 68-70; researcher hort, Univ Ill, 70-71, researcher bot, 71-72, lectr bot, 72. *Mem:* Am Soc Plant Physiologists; Crop Sci Soc Am. *Res:* Photosynthesis, membrane physiology. *Mailing Add:* Dept Biol Ind Univ Purdue Univ 1100 W Michigan St Indianapolis IN 46202-2880

KECK, WINFIELD, PHYSICS. *Current Pos:* RETIRED. *Personal Data:* b Clifton Heights, Pa, Sept 15, 17; m 44, Margaret Yuza; c Peter, Lindsey, Jonathan & Timothy. *Educ:* Amherst Col, AB, 37; Univ Pa, MA, 38; Brown Univ, PhD(physics), 49. *Prof Exp:* Instr math, Franklin & Marshall Col, 39-40; instr physics, Muhlenberg Col, 41-46; instr, Brown Univ, 46-48; from asst prof to assoc prof, Lafayette Col, 49-61, prof physics, 61-83, chmn dept, 60-82. *Concurrent Pos:* Vis assoc prof, Brown Univ, 58-59. *Mem:* Am Asn Physics Teachers; Sigma Xi. *Res:* Acoustic wave propagation. *Mailing Add:* 127 S Sunrise Lane Box 124 Boyertown PA 19512-9417

KEDDY, JAMES RICHARD, COMPUTER SCIENCES. *Current Pos:* RETIRED. *Personal Data:* b Boston, Mass, Oct 18, 36; m 61; c 3. *Educ:* Colby Col, BA, 58. *Prof Exp:* Mem staff air defense, Syst Develop Corp, 60-62, sect mgr satellite control, 63-67; sect mgr oper systs, Sci Data Systs, 68-71, mem advan design staff, Xerox Data Systs, 72-73, prin engr off systs, Xerox Corp, 74-80; proj leader, Teradata Corp, 80-84, dir eng, 85-94. *Res:* Word processing systems; information storage and retrieval; operating systems; database management systems; communications. *Mailing Add:* 16331 Serenade Lane Huntington Beach CA 92647

KEDDY, PAUL ANTHONY, BOTANY, WETLAND ECOLOGY. *Current Pos:* from asst prof to assoc prof, 82-89, PROF ECOL, DEPT BIOL, UNIV OTTAWA, 89- *Personal Data:* b London, Ont, May 29, 53; c 2. *Educ:* York Univ, Toronto, BSc, 74; Dalhousie Univ, Halifax, PhD(ecol), 78. *Honors & Awards:* Gleason Prize, 90; Lawson Medal, 91. *Prof Exp:* Asst prof ecol, Dept Bot & Genetics, Univ Guelph, 78-82. *Concurrent Pos:* Vis lectr, Dept Bot & Microbiol, Univ London, 85-86 & Comp Plant Ecol Unit, Univ Sheffield, 86; mem, Subcomt Plants, Comt Status Endangered Wildlife Can, 85-91; chmn, Sci Comt, Can Coun Ecol Areas, 86-90; mem, Sci Adv Comt, World Wildlife Fund, Can, 86-90; grant comt, Population Biol Grant Selection Comt, Nat Sci & Eng Res Coun, Can, 86-89; coordr, Inst Res Environ & Econ, Univ Ottawa, 89-90. *Mem:* Ecol Soc Am; Brit Ecol Soc; Can Bot Asn; Int Asn Veg Sci. *Res:* Plant community ecology; competition and plant traits; assembly rules; wetland ecology; conservation of endangered wetland plants and habitats. *Mailing Add:* Dept Biol Univ Ottawa, Box 450, Station A Ottawa ON K1N 6N5 Can. *E-Mail:* pkeddy@uottawa.ca

KEDER, WILBERT EUGENE, GENERAL ENVIRONMENTAL SCIENCES. *Current Pos:* RETIRED. *Personal Data:* b Columbus, Nebr, July 29, 28; m 51, Janice Krenzer; c Nancy, John, Lisa & Martha. *Educ:* Doane Col, BA, 50; Univ Pittsburgh, PhD(chem), 56. *Prof Exp:* Asst, Univ Pittsburgh, 50-56; res chemist, Hanford Labs, Gen Elec Co, 56-64; sr res scientist, Pac Northwest Labs, Battelle-Northwest, 65-68; adj assoc prof, Wash State Univ, 68-69; res assoc, Battelle-Northwest, 69-71; from asst prof to prof chem, Univ Pittsburgh, Bradford, 71-86, dir, Petrol Technol Prog, 75-86, emer prof chem, 87- *Mem:* Am Chem Soc; Sigma Xi. *Res:* Solution chemistry; solvent extraction; chemistry of the actinide elements; petroleum technology; environmental effect of energy utilization. *Mailing Add:* 971 Terrace Circle Colorado Springs CO 80904-2841

KEDES, LAURENCE H, MOLECULAR GENETIC RESEARCH, GENE EXPRESSION. *Current Pos:* WILLIAM KECK PROF & CHMN, DEPT BIOCHEM & DIR, INST GENETIC MED, UNIV SOUTHERN CALIF, 88- *Personal Data:* b Hartford, Conn, July 19, 37; m 58; c 3. *Educ:* Stanford Univ, BS, 61, MD, 62. *Prof Exp:* Res assoc, Lab Biochem, Nat Cancer Inst, 64-66; biol, Mass Inst Technol, 67-69; from asst prof to prof med, Stanford Univ, 70-89. *Concurrent Pos:* Leukemia Soc Am scholar, 69-74; staff physician, Vet Admin Med Ctr, Palo Alto, 70-89; investr, Howard Hughes Med Inst, 74-82; vis scientist, Imp Cancer Res Fund, London, 76-77; assoc ed, J Biol Chem, Molecular & Cellular Biol, J Molecular Evolution & Oxford Surv Eukaryotic Genes; fel, John Simon Guggenheim Found, 76-77. *Mem:* Am Soc Microbiol; Am Soc Biochem & Molecular Biol; Int Soc Develop Biol; Am Soc Clin Invest; Asn Am Physicians; Am Soc Hemat. *Res:* Biotechnology; gene expression in animal cell differentiation. *Mailing Add:* Dept Biochem HMR No 413 Univ Southern Calif 2011 Zonal Ave Los Angeles CA 90033. *Fax:* 213-342-2764

KEDZIE, DONALD P, ENGINEERING ADMINISTRATION. *Prof Exp:* Prof mech eng, Ark State Univ, 84-96. *Mailing Add:* 17830 Desert Glen Dr Sun City West AZ 85375

KEDZIE, ROBERT WALTER, solid state physics, science education; deceased, see previous edition for last biography

KEE, DAVID THOMAS, ornithology; deceased, see previous edition for last biography

KEEDY, CURTIS RUSSELL, PHYSICAL CHEMISTRY, RADIOCHEMISTRY. *Current Pos:* asst prof, 72-75, assoc prof, 75-85, PROF CHEM, LEWIS & CLARK COL, 85-, CHMN DEPT, 82- *Personal Data:* b Selma, Calif, Sept 14, 38; m 76; c 3. *Educ:* Occidental Col, BA, 60; Univ Wis, PhD(phys chem), 65. *Prof Exp:* Resident res assoc nuclear chem, Chem Eng Div, Argonne Nat Lab, 64-66; asst prof chem, Reed Col, 66-70, reactor supvr, 68-72. *Concurrent Pos:* Vis lectr, Lewis & Clark Col, 71-72. *Mem:* Am Chem Soc; Sigma Xi; Am Asn Univ Prof. *Res:* Nuclear chemistry; neutron activation analysis as applied to geochemical systems and environmental areas. *Mailing Add:* 0666C SW Palatine Hill Rd Portland OR 97219-7831

KEEDY, HUGH F(ORREST), ENGINEERING MECHANICS. *Current Pos:* Asst prof appl math, Vanderbilt Univ, 51-68, assoc prof eng sci, 68-74, assoc dean instr, 69-71, PROF ENG SCI, VANDERBILT UNIV, 74- *Personal Data:* b Berkeley Springs, WVa, Sept 22, 26; m 48; c 2. *Educ:* George Peabody Col, BS, 51, MA, 52; Univ Mich, MSE, 62, PhD, 67. *Concurrent Pos:* Consult various industs, 54-; asst, Univ Mich, 62-63, instr, 63-65; tech ed & writer, Lawrence Livermore Nat Lab, 80-81; pres, Southeastern Sect, Am Soc Eng Educ, Zone II chmn, 88-90; author. *Mem:* Am Soc Eng Educ; Soc Tech Commun. *Res:* Fluid mechanics; engineering education; technical communication. *Mailing Add:* 6750 Lane Rd College Grove TN 37046

KEEFE, DEBORAH LYNN, CARDIOVASCULAR PHARMACOLOGY, NONINVASIVE CARDIOLOGY. *Current Pos:* assoc prof, 85-95, PROF MED, MED COL, CORNELL UNIV, 95-; ATTEND PHYSICIAN, MEM SLOAN-KETTERING HOSP, 94- *Personal Data:* b Oklahoma City, Okla, Nov 23, 50; m 71, Richard A; c Jennifer, Colin & Corwin. *Educ:* Rice Univ, BA, 73; NY Med Col, MD, 76; Columbia Univ, MPH, 90. *Prof Exp:* Resident internal med, St Vincents Hosp, NY, 76-79; fel cardiol, Stanford Univ, 79-81; asst prof med, Albert Einstein Col Med, 81-87; assoc dir clin invest, Am Cynamid Med Res, 87-88. *Concurrent Pos:* Dir coronary care, Bronx Munic Hosp Ctr, 81-87; attend physician, Hosp Albert Einstein Col Med, 81-87; assoc ed, J Clin Pharamacol, 85-; asst clin prof, Albert Einstein Col Med, 87-88; assoc mem & assoc attending physician, Mem Sloan Kettering Hosp, 88-94. *Mem:* Fel Am Col Cardiol; fel Am Col Chest Physicians; fel Am Heart Asn; fel Am Col Angiolog; fel Am Col Clin Pharmacol; fel Am Soc Clin Pharmacol & Therapeut; fel Am Col Critical Care Med. *Res:* Clinical investigation of cardiovascular therapeutic agents including clinical trials; pharmacokinetics and pharmacodynamics; epidemiology and the prevention of heart disease. *Mailing Add:* Sloan-Kettering Mem Hosp 1275 York Ave New York NY 10021-6094

KEEFE, THOMAS J, VETERINARY MEDICINE. *Current Pos:* DIR VET MED, BEECHAM LABS, 74- *Personal Data:* b Algona, Iowa, Dec 4, 37; m 65; c 4. *Educ:* Univ Mo, BS & DVM, 63. *Prof Exp:* Pvt vet pract, 66-67; livestock consult, Livestock Servs, Ralston Purina, 67-69; mgr clin res, Bristol Labs, 69-74. *Mem:* Am Vet Med Asn; Am Asn Swine Practitioners (pres, 71); Am Asn Bovine Practitioners; fel Am Col Pharmacol & Therapeut; Indust Vet Asn; Sigma Xi. *Res:* Pharmacology; pathology; diagnostic medicine. *Mailing Add:* 2431 Newport Ct Ft Collins CO 80526

KEEFE, THOMAS LEEVEN, BOTANY, BIOLOGY. *Current Pos:* ASST PROF BIOL, EASTERN KY UNIV, 66- *Personal Data:* b Columbia, SC, Jan 22, 37; m 64. *Educ:* Univ SC, BS, 59, MS, 61; Univ Ga, PhD(bot), 67. *Prof Exp:* Asst prof biol, Newberry Col, 62. *Mem:* Am Forestry Asn; Am Inst Biol Sci. *Res:* Shoot development in forest trees; radiation inducted mutations in insects. *Mailing Add:* Dept Biol Sci Eastern Ky Univ 521 Lancaster Ave Richmond KY 40475-3100

KEEFE, WILLIAM EDWARD, biophysics, crystallography, for more information see previous edition

KEEFER, CAROL LYNDON, IN VITRO FERTILIZATION, PREIMPLANTATION DEVELOPMENT. *Current Pos:* RES SCIENTIST, AM BREEDERS SERV SPECIALTY GENETICS, 89- *Personal Data:* b Columbia, SC, Jan 20, 53. *Educ:* Univ SC, BS, 74; Univ Del, PhD(biol sci), 81. *Prof Exp:* Postdoctoral fel reproductive physiol, Sch Hyg & Pub Health, Johns Hopkins, 81-82 & Sch Vet Med, Univ Pa, 82-83; reproductive biologist, Reproductive Biol Assocs, 83-86; asst physiologist reproductive physiol, Col Vet Med, Univ Ga, 84-85, asst prof, 85-89. *Mem:* Soc Develop Biol; Int Embryo Transfer Soc; Soc Study Reproduction; Am Soc Cell Biol. *Res:* Bovine oocyte maturation; in vitro fertilization and embryo culture; bovine embryo nuclear transfer; assisted fertilization. *Mailing Add:* 21111 Lakeshore Rd Box 183 St Anne de Bellevue PQ H9X 3V9 Can

KEEFER, DENNIS RALPH, AEROSPACE ENGINEERING, LASER PROPULSION. *Current Pos:* PROF ENG SCI & MECH, UNIV TENN, 78- *Personal Data:* b Winter Haven, Fla, Sept 22, 38; m 57; c 3. *Educ:* Univ Fla, BES, 62, MSE, 63, PhD(aerospace eng), 67. *Prof Exp:* Asst prof, 67-76, assoc prof aerospace eng, Univ Fla, 76-78. *Mem:* Am Phys Soc; Sigma Xi. *Res:* Electrodeless arcs and discharges; gas lasers; plasma spectroscopy. *Mailing Add:* Univ Tenn Space Inst Tullahoma TN 37388

KEEFER, DONALD WALKER, METALLURGY. *Current Pos:* mgr, Off Res Mgt, Fuels & Mat Div, 77-81, MGR MAT SCI BR, MAT TECH DIV, EG&G IDAHO INC, 81- *Personal Data:* b Idaho Falls, Idaho, Nov 7, 31; m 54; c 2. *Educ:* Univ Idaho, BS, 54; Univ Ill, MS, 57, PhD(metall), 61. *Prof Exp:* Mem tech staff, Atomics Int, 61-77. *Mem:* Am Asn Advan Sci; Am Soc Metals. *Res:* Studies of point defects in metals and alloys by means of anelastic techniques; studies of void formation in irradiated reactor cladding materials; environmental effects on materials. *Mailing Add:* 6731 E Lincoln Rd Idaho Falls ID 83401

KEEFER, LARRY KAY, NITROSAMINES, NITRIC OXIDE. *Current Pos:* head, Anal Chem Sect, Lab Carcinogen Metab, 71-83, CHIEF, CHEM SECT, LAB COMP CARCINOGENESIS, NAT CANCER INST, 83- *Personal Data:* b Akron, Ohio, Oct 28, 39; m 62, Julie A Klestadt; c Steven H & Simona N. *Educ:* Oberlin Col, BA, 61; Univ NH, PhD(org chem), 65. *Prof Exp:* Asst prof oncol, Inst Med Res, Chicago Med Sch, 65-68; asst prof biochem, Col Med, Univ Nebr, 68-71. *Mem:* Am Chem Soc; AAAS; Am Asn Cancer Res. *Res:* Chemistry and pharmacology of nitric oxide and its progenitors. *Mailing Add:* 7016 River Rd Bethesda MD 20817. *Fax:* 301-846-5946; *E-Mail:* keefer@ferfv1.nciferf.gov

KEEFER, RAYMOND MARSH, PHYSICAL ORGANIC CHEMISTRY, MOLECULAR COMPLEXES. *Current Pos:* From asst to assoc, 36-41, from instr to assoc prof, 41-56, chmn dept, 62-74, prof, 56-81, EMER PROF CHEM, UNIV CALIF, DAVIS, 81- *Personal Data:* b Twin Falls, Idaho, Apr 29, 13; m 43; c 3. *Educ:* Univ Calif, BS, 34, PhD(chem), 40. *Mem:* Am Chem Soc; Sigma Xi. *Res:* Molecular complexes; electrophilic aromatic halogenation; participation by ortho substituents in reactions at aromatic side chains; medium effects on nucleophilic solvolytic displacement reactions. *Mailing Add:* Dept Chem Univ Calif Davis CA 95616

KEEFER, ROBERT FARIS, SOIL SCIENCE. *Current Pos:* from asst prof to assoc prof soil sci, 65-74, assoc prof & assoc agronomist, 74-76, PROF AGRON & AGRONOMIST, WVA UNIV, 76- *Personal Data:* b Wheeling, WVa, May 27, 30; c 6. *Educ:* Cornell Univ, BS, 52; Ohio State Univ, MS, 61, PhD(agron), 63. *Prof Exp:* Res agronomist, Hercules Powder Co, 63-65. *Concurrent Pos:* HEW grant, 66-70. *Mem:* Am Soc Agron; Soil Sci Soc Am; Int Soil Sci Soc; Int Humic Sub Soc. *Res:* Soil organic matter; soil fertility, particularly micronutrient nutrition; sewage sludge, fly ash and strip mine reclamation. *Mailing Add:* Dept Plant Sci WVa Univ PO Box 6018 Morgantown WV 26506-0001

KEEFER, WILLIAM RICHARD, GEOLOGY. *Current Pos:* RETIRED. *Personal Data:* b Fayette, Ohio, June 7, 24; m 45; c 2. *Educ:* Univ Wyo, BA, 48, MA, 52, PhD, 57. *Prof Exp:* geologist, US Geol Surv, Denver, 48-81; explor adv, Mitchell Energy Corp, 81- *Mem:* Geol Soc Am; Am Asn Petrol Geologists. *Res:* Regional stratigraphy and structure, especially in sedimentary rocks. *Mailing Add:* 5693 Xeno Way Arvada CO 80002

KEEFFE, JAMES RICHARD, ORGANIC CHEMISTRY. *Current Pos:* from asst prof to assoc prof, 65-74, PROF CHEM, SAN FRANCISCO STATE UNIV, 74- *Personal Data:* b Visalia, Calif, Nov 13, 37; m 61; c 1. *Educ:* Univ Calif, Santa Barbara, BA, 59; Univ Wash, Seattle, PhD(chem), 64. *Prof Exp:* NIH res fel, 64-65. *Concurrent Pos:* Res grants, Petrol Res Fund, 65-66 & Res Corp, 66-68. *Res:* Kinetic hydrogen isotope effects; acid-base catalysis; organic reaction mechanisms. *Mailing Add:* Dept Chem San Francisco State Univ 1600 Holloway Ave San Francisco CA 94132-1722

KEEGAN, ACHSAH D, RESEARCH. *Current Pos:* RES ASSOC, NAT INST ALLERGY & INFECTIOUS DIS, NIH, 89- *Personal Data:* m 84, James P; c Simon H, Eleanore L & James D. *Educ:* Duke Univ, BS, 83; Johns Hopkins Univ, PhD(immunol), 89. *Mem:* Am Asn Immunologists. *Mailing Add:* Dept Immunol Holland Lab Am Red Cross 15601 Crabbs Br Rockville MD 20750

KEEGSTRA, KENNETH G, BIOMEMBRANES, CHLOROPLAST BIOGENESIS. *Current Pos:* DIR, PLANT RES LAB, MICH STATE UNIV, 93- *Personal Data:* b Grand Rapids, Mich, Aug 10, 45; m 65; c 3. *Educ:* Hope Col, BA, 67; Univ Colo, PhD(biochem), 71. *Honors & Awards:* George Olmsted Award, Am Paper Inst, 73. *Prof Exp:* Fel biochem, Mass Inst Technol, 71-73; asst prof microbiol, State Univ NY, 73-77; from asst prof to prof plant physiol, Univ Wis-Madison, 77-93. *Mem:* Am Soc Plant Physiologists; Int Soc Plant Molecular Biol. *Res:* Structure, function and biogenesis of plastid envelope membranes; import of cytoplasmically synthesized proteins into chloroplasts. *Mailing Add:* MSU-DOE Plant Res Lab Mich State Univ East Lansing MI 48824

KEEHN, PHILIP MOSES, ORGANIC CHEMISTRY, PHYSICAL-ORGANIC CHEMISTRY. *Current Pos:* asst prof, 71-78, Wolfson Professorship, 79-80, assoc prof chem, 78-86, PROF CHEM, BRANDEIS UNIV, 86- *Personal Data:* b Brooklyn, NY, Mar 22, 43. *Educ:* Yeshiva Col, BA, 64; Yale Univ, MA, 67, PhD(chem), 69. *Honors & Awards:* Alfred Bader Award, 80. *Prof Exp:* NIH res fel chem, Harvard Univ, 69-71. *Concurrent Pos:* Consult, Am Optical Corp, 76-, US Army, 79-80, Olive Corp, 82-85; Dreyfus teacher-scholar, 79-84; Nat Acad Sci E Europ Exchange fel, Yugoslavia, 85; Acad Sinica Lectureship, 87; Fulbright scholar, 88. *Mem:* Am Chem Soc; Sigma Xi. *Res:* Synthesis of strained rings and theoretically interesting molecules; synthetic methods; application of nuclear magnetic resonance spectroscopy to organic systems; photooxidation; thermal chemistry; pure and applied laser chemistry of organic systems; host-guest chemistry. *Mailing Add:* 121 Gibbs St Newton MA 02159-1927

KEELER, CALVIN LEE, JR, AVIAN VIROLOGY, RECOMBINANT VACCINE DEVELOPMENT. *Current Pos:* asst prof, 87-93, ASSOC PROF, DEPT ANIMAL SCI & AGR BIOCHEM, UNIV DEL, NEWARK, 93- *Personal Data:* b Boston, Mass, Nov 22, 54; m 87, Sharon J Brown; c Timothy L. *Educ:* Tufts Univ, BS, 76; Va Commonwealth Univ, Richmond, MS, 79; Univ Md, Baltimore Co, PhD(biol), 87. *Prof Exp:* Sr scientist, Igene Biotechnol, Inc, Columbia, Md, 81-85; assoc, E I du Pont de Nemours & Co, Wilmington, Del, 85-87. *Mem:* Am Soc Microbiol; assoc Am Soc Virol; Poultry Sci Asn; assoc Am Asn Avian Pathologists; AAAS. *Res:* Use an avian herpes virus as a model to study murosal cell-mediated immunity; molecular basis of viral pathogenesis and immunity; mucosal cell-mediated immunity. *Mailing Add:* Animal Sci Univ Del Newark DE 19717-0001. *Fax:* 302-831-3651; *E-Mail:* ckeeler@grahms.udel.edu

KEELER, CLYDE EDGAR, zoology; deceased, see previous edition for last biography

KEELER, EMMETT BROWN, SYSTEMS ANALYSIS. *Current Pos:* MEM STAFF, RAND CORP, 68-; FAC RAND GRAD SCH, 77- *Personal Data:* b West Point, NY, Sept 28, 41; m 75, Shan Cretin; c Mikala, Lauren & Alexis. *Educ:* Oberlin Col, BA, 62; Harvard Univ, MA, 67, PhD(math), 69. *Concurrent Pos:* Vis assoc prof econ, Univ Chicago, 73; vis res assoc, Sch Pub Health, Harvard Univ, 74-75 & 82. *Mem:* Math Asn Am; Asn Health Servs Res. *Res:* Utility theory; mathematical statistics; health economics; operations research; medical decision-making. *Mailing Add:* 1700 Main St Santa Monica CA 90401. *Fax:* 310-451-6930; *E-Mail:* emett_keeler@rand.org

KEELER, JOHN S(COTT), ELECTRICAL ENGINEERING. *Current Pos:* RETIRED. *Personal Data:* b Toronto, Ont, Can, Aug 12, 29; m 51; c 3. *Educ:* Univ Toronto, BASc, 51, MASc, 63. *Prof Exp:* Res officer, Nat Res Coun Can, 51-55; chief engr, Hallman Organs, Ont, 55-59; from lectr to assoc prof elec eng, Univ Waterloo, 60-90; consult, 90-97. *Concurrent Pos:* Acoust consult, 59- *Mem:* Sr mem Inst Elec & Electronics Engrs; Audio Eng Soc. *Res:* Numerical analysis and synthesis of sound particularly noise and music; effects of noise on man; acoustical instrumentation; environmental noise. *Mailing Add:* RR 8 Owen Sound ON N4K 5W4 Can

KEELER, JUDITH ADELE, ANIMAL BEHAVIOR, BIOLOGICAL RHYTHMS. *Current Pos:* Asst prof, 69-75, ASSOC PROF BIOL, CALIF STATE COL, STANISLAUS, 75- *Personal Data:* b Providence, RI, Dec 30, 44; m 73. *Educ:* Whittier Col, BA, 66; Northwestern Univ, MS, 69, PhD(biol), 73. *Concurrent Pos:* Res assoc, Inst Cult Resources, Calif State Col, Stanislaus, 73-; field res, Calif Fish & Wildlife Agency, 75- *Mem:* AAAS; Animal Behav Soc; Int Audio-Tutorial Cong. *Res:* Field research in animal behavior and laboratory research in patterns of biorhythmicity. *Mailing Add:* Dept Biol Sci Calif State Univ 801 W Monte Vista Stanislaus Turlock CA 95382-0299

KEELER, KATHLEEN HOWARD, PLANT POPULATION CYTOGENETICS, PLANT DEMOGRAPHY. *Current Pos:* From asst prof to assoc prof, 75-91, PROF BIOL SCI, UNIV NEBR, LINCOLN, 91- *Personal Data:* b Hackensack, NJ, Jan 17, 47; m 75, (Richard) Karl Anderson. *Educ:* Univ Mich, Ann Arbor, BS, 69; Univ Calif, Berkeley, PhD(genetics), 75. *Concurrent Pos:* Chair biol sci, Ecol Sect, Univ Nebr, Lincoln, 85-88, dir, Cedar Point Biol Sta, 92-94; prin investr, NSF, 87-; consult, Nat Audubon Soc, Calgene, 88-90; mem, Sci Adv Panel Biotechnol, US Environ Protection Agency, 92- *Mem:* Soc Study Evolution; Bot Soc Am; Ecol Soc Am; Am Soc Naturalists. *Res:* Function of polyploid variation with native plant populations, pioneering use of flow cytometry for population cytogenetics; longevity of prairie plants; role of extreme events (flood, drought) in evolution. *Mailing Add:* Sch Biol Scis Univ Nebr Lincoln NE 68588-0118. *Fax:* 402-472-2083; *E-Mail:* kkeeler@unlinfo.unl.edu

KEELER, MARTIN HARVEY, MEDICINE. *Current Pos:* DIR ALCOHOLIC TREAT PROG HOUSTON, VET ADMIN HOSP, 77- *Personal Data:* b New York, NY, June 16, 27; m 53; c 3. *Educ:* NY Univ, BA, 49; NY Med Col, MD, 53; Am Bd Psychiat & Neurol, dipl, 59. *Prof Exp:* Intern, State Univ NY Upstate Med Ctr, 53-54; from asst resident to resident psychiat, Sch Med, Univ NC, Chapel Hill, 54-57, from instr to assoc prof, 57-69; prof, NY Med Col, 69-70; prof psychiat, Med Univ, SC, 70-77; prof psychiat, Baylor Col Med, 77-92. *Concurrent Pos:* Res grants, 61 & 62- *Mem:* AMA; Am Psychoanal Asn; Am Med Soc Alcoholism; Am Psychiat Asn. *Res:* Defining of the psychological abnormalities in schizophrenia as specific to the individual or to the disease process and the pharmacological manipulation of these differences in schizophrenic and normal populations. *Mailing Add:* 5230 Ariel St Houston TX 77096

KEELER, RALPH, physiology, for more information see previous edition

KEELER, RICHARD FAIRBANKS, NATURAL PRODUCTS CHEMISTRY. *Current Pos:* RES CHEMIST BIOCHEM, USDA, UTAH STATE UNIV, 65- *Personal Data:* b Provo, Utah, Jan 24, 30; m 52; c 5. *Educ:* Brigham Young Univ, BS, 54; Ohio State Univ, MS, 55, PhD(biochem), 57. *Prof Exp:* Asst biochemist, Mont State Col, 57-61; res chemist biochem, Nat Animal Dis Lab, 61-65. *Mem:* Am Chem Soc; Soc Exp Biol & Med; AAAS; Teratol Soc. *Res:* Molybdenum-tungsten metabolism; silicon-mucoprotein interaction in urolithiasis; muscular dystrophy; cytochemistry of Listeria and Vibrio; products of Nocardia; steroidal, quinolizidine and piperidine alkaloid chemistry and metabolic effects; chemistry of poisonous and teratogenic plants. *Mailing Add:* 125 Quarter Circle 1150 E 14th N Logan UT 84321-6315

KEELER, ROBERT ADOLPH, PHYSICAL INORGANIC CHEMISTRY. *Current Pos:* RETIRED. *Personal Data:* b New York, NY, Feb 4, 20; m 49, Lillian Catricala; c Kathryn & Steven. *Educ:* Queens Col, NY, BS, 42. *Prof Exp:* Chief chemist, NY Testing Labs, 42-45 & Pub Serv Testing Labs, 45; supvr anal chem, Allied Chem & Dye Corp, 45-50; group leader nuclear chem, Vitro Labs Div, Vitro Corp, 50-63; prin supvr propellant chem, Reaction Motors Div, Thiokol Chem Corp, 63-68; sr res chemist, Radiation Safety Off, Syracuse Res Lab, Allied Signal Corp, 68-86. *Concurrent Pos:* Mem, Air Pollution Control Bd, Newark, NJ, 59-69. *Mem:* AAAS; Am Chem Soc. *Res:* Abatement of industrial atmospheric pollutants and recovery as useful materials. *Mailing Add:* 301 Oakridge Dr Camillus NY 13031

KEELER, ROGER NORRIS, SHOCK WAVE PHYSICAL & OPTICAL OCEANOGRAPHY, OCEAN LIDAR SYSTEMS. *Current Pos:* prin sci adv, 87-88, DIR TECH MKT, KAMAN DIVERSIFIED TECHNOL CORP, WASH, DC & BLOOMFIELD, CONN, 88- *Personal Data:* b Houston, Tex, Aug 12, 30; m 57, 87, Miriam S; c Catherine, John, Roger & Carolyn. *Educ:* Rice Univ, Houston, BA, BS, 47-51; Univ Colo, Boulder, MS, 57-58; Univ Calif, PhD(chem eng), 63. *Honors & Awards:* Ford Found Prof Chem Eng, Univ Mex City, Mex City, DF, 68; Gold Medal Eng, Am Soc Naval Engrs, Armed Forces Commun & Electronics Asn. *Prof Exp:* From staff mem to head, Physics Dept, Lawrence Livermore Lab, Livermore, Calif, 63-75; staff of dir, Lawrence Livermore Lab, Univ Calif, 78-80; dir technol, US Navy Dept. *Concurrent Pos:* Consult, Nat Tech & various orgns, 60-; lectr, Dept Applied Sci, Univ Calif, 67-75, Dept Chem Eng, 60-; lectr, Int Sch Physics, Enrico Fermi, Varenna, Italy, 68, 70, 7; adj prof, Physics & Chem, US Naval postgrad Sch, Calif, 79- 81; lectr, Nat Strategy Info Ctr, Wash, DC, 87. *Mem:* Sigma Xi; Res Soc Am; fel Am Inst Chemists; fel Am Phys Soc. *Res:* Turbulence, chemical kinetics, catalysis, cryogenics and cryogenic engineering; thermodynamics of Phase Equilibria; high pressure equation of state; optical and electronic properties of condensed media at high pressure; high pressure geophysics; high pressure fabrication of materials, anti-submarine warfare; advanced sensor technology; holds over 20 patents on submarine laser communications and ocean lidar systems. *Mailing Add:* 6652 Hampton Park Ct McLean VA 22101

KEELER, STUART P, MECHANICAL METALLURGY, SHEET METAL FORMABILITY. *Current Pos:* mgr metals, 87-96, MGR TECH DEVELOP, BUDD CO TECH CTR, 96- *Personal Data:* b Wausau, Wis, Sept 1, 34; m 61, Denise E Bradshaw; c Suzanne. *Educ:* Ripon Col, BA, 56; Mass Inst Technol, BS, 57, DSc(mech metal), 61. *Honors & Awards:* William Hunt Eisenman Award, Advan Semi Conductor Mat Int, 92. *Prof Exp:* Supvr Tech Develop, 63-72, Nat Steel Corp, Mgr Automotive res, 73-87. *Concurrent Pos:* Instr, Sheet Metal Formability, Univ Wis, 84- *Mem:* Fel Am Soc Metal; Fel Soc Automotive Engrs; Amer Inst Mining, Metal & Petrol Engrs; Int Deep Drawing Res Group (pres, 72-74 & 88-90). *Res:* Transforming sheet metal formability from an art to a science; discovered forming limit programs; developed circle grid analysis, statistical deformation control and other press shop analysis technologies. *Mailing Add:* Budd Co 1515 Alantic Blvd Auburn Hills MI 48326. *Fax:* 313-391-0325

KEELEY, DEAN FRANCIS, ANALYTICAL CHEMISTRY, HEADSPACE ANALYSIS. *Current Pos:* From asst prof to assoc prof, 57-77, PROF CHEM, UNIV SOUTHWESTERN LA, 77- *Personal Data:* b Chicago, Ill, Nov 16, 26; m 51; c 1. *Educ:* Univ Ill, BS, 52; Fla State Univ, PhD(chem), 57. *Mem:* Am Chem Soc; Am Asn Univ Prof. *Res:* Physical properties by headspace analysis. *Mailing Add:* Drawer 44250 Univ Southwestern La Lafayette LA 70504

KEELEY, FRED W, BIOCHEMISTRY. *Current Pos:* assoc prof, 83-90, PROF, RES INST, HOSP SICK CHILDREN, TORONTO, 90- *Personal Data:* b Winnipeg, Man, Mar 21, 44; m 66; c 3. *Educ:* Univ Man, BSc, 65, PhD(pharmacol), 70. *Prof Exp:* Med Res Coun Can fels, Agr Res Coun, Langford, Eng, 70-72 & Res Inst, Hosp Sick Children, Toronto, 72-73. *Concurrent Pos:* Med Res Coun Can scholarship, Res Inst, Hosp Sick Children, 73-; assoc prof 83-90, prof biochem, Univ Toronto, 90-, assoc prof, 87-90, prof clin biochem, 90- *Mem:* Can Biochem Soc; NY Acad Sci. *Res:* Biosynthesis of elastin; calcification of aortic tissue in atherosclerosis; effects of hypertension on vascular connective tissue. *Mailing Add:* Dept Biochem Univ Toronto Fac Med One Kings Col Cir Toronto ON M5S 1A8 Can

KEELEY, JON E, POPULATION ECOLOGY. *Current Pos:* asst prof, 77-83, assoc prof, 83-88, PROF BIOL, OCCIDENTAL COL, 88- *Personal Data:* b Chula Vista, Calif, Aug 11, 49; m 73, 90. *Educ:* San Diego State Univ, BS, 71, MS, 73; Univ Ga, PhD(bot), 77. *Prof Exp:* Lectr bot, Univ Ga, 76-77. *Concurrent Pos:* Res grants, NSF, 79-88; consult, EIRs Publ; Guggenheim fel, 85. *Mem:* Ecol Soc Am; Bot Soc Am; Am Soc Plant Physiologists; Am Soc Naturalists. *Res:* Aquatic plant photosynthesis; reproductive biology and demography of plants; fire ecology of mediterranean vegetation. *Mailing Add:* 1249 E Calaveras St Altadena CA 91001

KEELEY, LARRY LEE, INSECT PHYSIOLOGY & NEUROENDOCRINOLOGY. *Current Pos:* From asst prof to prof, 66-85, PROF ENTOM, TEX A&M UNIV, 85- *Personal Data:* b South Bend, Ind, Jan 3, 39; m 59; c 5. *Educ:* Univ Notre Dame, BS, 62; Purdue Univ, PhD(entom), 66. *Concurrent Pos:* NSF grants, 74-78, 81-83, 85-88, 91-94; NIH grant, 78-81, 84-87 & 93-97; Sea grant, 85-87, 87-89, 89-91 & 91-93 & 95-97. *Mem:* Fel AAAS; Entom Soc Am; Soc Integrative Comp Biol; Am Soc Biochem & Molecular Biol. *Res:* Hormonal regulation of metabolism; neuroendocrine regulation of mitochondrial development and functions; identification and action of neurohormones on physiological functions of insects and other invertebrates; neurohormone isolation; isolation, characterization and regulation of insect and shrimp reproduction; molecular biology of neurohormone genes. *Mailing Add:* Dept Entom Tex A&M Univ College Station TX 77843. *Fax:* 409-845-6305; *E-Mail:* llkeeley@tamu.edu

KEELEY, STERLING CARTER, SYSTEMATIC BOTANY, MOLECULAR SYSTEMATICS. *Current Pos:* PROF BOT, UNIV HAWAII, 91- *Personal Data:* b San Francisco, Calif, Oct 23, 48. *Educ:* Stanford Univ, AB, 70; San Diego State Univ, MS, 73; Univ Ga, PhD(bot), 77. *Prof Exp:* Res asst ecol, Int Biol Prog Struct Ecosyst, 70-73; lectr bot, Calif State Univ, Long Beach, 78-79; from assoc prof to prof biol, Whittier Col, 79-91. *Concurrent Pos:* NSF dissertation improv grant, 74-77; consult flora, Southern Calif Ocean Studies Consortium of Calif State Univ & Cols, 78-; res assoc, Los Angeles County Mus Natural Hist, 78-; consult salt marsh veg, Port of Los Angeles, 79-81; NSF grants, Systs Neotrop Vernonia, 79-81, 82-86; chloroplast DNA, Vernonia, NSF grant, 88-89; NSF vis prof biol, Univ Conn, 88-90. *Mem:* Soc Study Evolution; Am Soc Plant Taxonomists; Am Bot Soc; AAAS; Sigma Xi; Ecol Soc Am. *Res:* Systematics and biogeography of neotropical species of the genus Vernonia, Compositae, molecular systematics, genetic diversity in island ecosystems; ecology and reproductive biology of mediterranean climate plants in relation to fire. *Mailing Add:* Dept Bot Univ Hawaii 3190 Maile Way Honolulu HI 96822-2270. *Fax:* 808-956-3923; *E-Mail:* sterling@uhurix.uhcc.hawaii.edu

KEELING, BOBBIE LEE, PLANT PATHOLOGY. *Current Pos:* CONSULT, 92- *Personal Data:* b Durant, Okla, Apr 22, 31; div; c 2. *Educ:* Southeastern State Col, BS, 56; Okla State Univ, MS, 59; Univ Minn, Minneapolis, PhD(plant path), 66. *Prof Exp:* Res plant pathologist, Delta Br Exp Sta, USDA, Miss State Univ, 66-92. *Mem:* Am Phytopath Soc; Sigma Xi. *Res:* Diseases of soybeans with emphasis on pathogenic variation, nature of host resistance and host-parasite interaction. *Mailing Add:* PO Box 123 Stoneville MS 38776

KEELING, CHARLES DAVID, PHYSICAL CHEMISTRY, MARINE GEOCHEMISTRY. *Current Pos:* asst res chemist, 56-60, from assoc res chemist to assoc prof, 60-68, PROF OCEANOG, SCRIPPS INST OCEANOG, UNIV CALIF, SAN DIEGO, 68- *Personal Data:* b Scranton, Pa, Apr 20, 28; m 54; c 5. *Educ:* Univ Ill, BA, 48; Northwestern Univ, PhD(chem), 53. *Honors & Awards:* Second Half Century Award, Am Meteorol Soc, 80; Ewing Medal, Am Geophys Union, 91. *Prof Exp:* Fel geochem, Calif Inst Technol, 53-56. *Concurrent Pos:* Mem, Comn Atmospheric Chem & Global Pollution, Int Asn Meteorol & Atmospheric Physics, 67-85; guest prof oceanog, Univ Heidelberg, 69-70; mem, Panel on Energy & Climate of US, Nat Acad Sci, 74-77; dir, Cent Carbon Dioxide Lab, World Meteorol Orgn, 75-; mem, Interim Sci Directorate Carbon Dioxide Res Prog, US Dept Energy, 77-80; guest prof, Phys Inst, Univ Bern, Switz, 79-80; dir, Cent Carbon Dioxide Lab, World Meteorol Orgn, 75-; mem, CO_2 Panel, Ocean Sci Bd, Nat Acad Sci, 87-93; convenor carbon dioxide activ, Int Global Atmospheric Comt, 90- *Mem:* Nat Acad Sci; Am Geophys Union; fel Am Acad Arts & Sci; fel AAAS. *Res:* Marine chemistry; geochemistry of carbon and oxygen; atmospheric chemistry; influence of atmospheric carbon dioxide on carbon cycle and on world climate. *Mailing Add:* Scripps Inst Oceanog Mail Code A020 La Jolla CA 92037

KEELING, RICHARD PAIRE, MYCOLOGY. *Current Pos:* Asst prof microbiol, 63-70, assoc prof biol, 70-74, PROF BIOL, EMPORIA KANS STATE COL, 74- *Personal Data:* b Crawfordsville, Ind, Sept 17, 31; m 52; c 2. *Educ:* Wabash Col, AB, 57; Purdue Univ, MS, 60, PhD(bot), 63. *Mem:* AAAS; Mycol Soc Am; Am Soc Microbiol; Soc Indust Microbiol; Japanese Mycol Soc; Sigma Xi. *Res:* Fungus physiology; metabolism. *Mailing Add:* Div Biol Sci Emporia State Univ 1200 Commercial St Emporia KS 66801-5057

KEELING, ROLLAND OTIS, JR, PHYSICS. *Current Pos:* dept head, 80-84, prof physics, 61-84, EMER PROF PHYSICS, MICH TECHNOL UNIV, 84- *Personal Data:* b Hillsboro, Ind, Aug 13, 25; m 46, Esther E Glascock; c Stephen D & Cynthia S (Yotti). *Educ:* Wabash Col, AB, 50; Pa State Univ, MS, 52, PhD(physics), 54. *Prof Exp:* Instr physics, Pa State Univ, 53-54; physicist, Gulf Res & Develop Co, Pa, 54-61. *Mem:* AAAS; Am Phys Soc; Am Asn Physics Teachers; Am Crystallog Asn. *Res:* X-ray diffraction; crystallography; x-ray spectroscopy; magnetic structures. *Mailing Add:* RR 1 Box 61 Royalewood Houghton MI 49931

KEELUNG, HONG, membrane fusion, for more information see previous edition

KEEM, JOHN EDWARD, SOLID STATE PHYSICS. *Current Pos:* DIR RES & DEVELOP, OVONIC SYNTHETIC MAT CO, 84- *Personal Data:* b Buffalo, NY, May 31, 48; m 80. *Educ:* Syracuse Univ, BS, 70; Purdue Univ, PhD(physics), 76. *Prof Exp:* Fel Dept Physics, Purdue Univ, 76-77; Devices Phys Dept, Gen Motors Res, 77-80, mgr, Superconductivity Res, Energy Conversion, 80-83. *Concurrent Pos:* Mat res adv bd mat sub-micron struct, Nat Acad Sci. *Mem:* Am Phys Soc; Am Soc Metals; Mat Res Soc. *Res:* Synthesis of multilayer structures by sputtering and ion beam deposition; x-ray scattering from multilayer structures; melt spinning of Nd2 Fe14B permanent magnets; magnetic interactions between grains in Wd2 Fe14B materials; solid lubricating materials. *Mailing Add:* 1641 Lone Pine Rd Bloomfield Hills MI 48302

KEEN, CARL L, DEVELOPMENTAL NUTRITION, MINERALS. *Current Pos:* ASSOC PROF NUTRIT, UNIV CALIF, DAVIS, 84- *Educ:* Univ Calif, Davis, PhD, 79. *Mem:* Am Inst Nutrit; Teratology Soc; Soc Exp Biol & Med. *Mailing Add:* Dept Nutrit Univ Calif Davis CA 95616

KEEN, CHARLOTTE ELIZABETH, MARINE GEOPHYSICS. *Current Pos:* RES SCIENTIST MARINE GEOPHYS, ATLANTIC GEOSCI CENTRE, BEDFORD INST, 70- *Personal Data:* b Halifax, NS, June 22, 43; m 63. *Educ:* Dalhousie Univ, BSc, 64, MSc, 66; Cambridge Univ, PhD(geophys), 70. *Concurrent Pos:* Mem working group 8 of inter-union comn on geodynamics, Int Union Geod & Geophys & Int Union Geol Sci, 72-; chmn study group NW Atlantic Continental Margin, Inter-Union Comn Geodynamics; assoc ed, Can J of Earth Sci; chmn, Can Nat Lithosphere Comn, 81- *Mem:* Geol Asn Can; Royal Soc Can; Am Geophys Union. *Res:* Surface wave propagation in Canadian shield and along mid-ocean ridges; plate tectonics of Baffin Bay region; continental-oceanic transition in the North West Atlantic; application of Backus-Gilbert inversion to upper mantle properties at ocean-continent transition; subsidence and thermal history of continental margins. *Mailing Add:* Nine Wenlock Grove Halifax NS B3P 1P6 Can. *Fax:* 902-426-6152

KEEN, DOROTHY JEAN, PHYSICAL OCEANOGRAPHY. *Current Pos:* RETIRED. *Personal Data:* b Lancaster, Pa, June 19, 22. *Educ:* Swarthmore Col, BA, 44. *Prof Exp:* Res asst chem & phys oceanog, Woods Hole Oceanog Inst, 44-53; phys oceanogr mil appln, Hydrographic Off, US Naval Oceanog Off, 53-58, oceanogr ocean prediction, 58-66, head systs anal group, Ocean Prediction, 66-71, sci staff asst, Ocean Sci Dept, Plans & Requirements Off, 71-78; phys sci adminr, Naval Ocean Res & Develop Activ, 78-82. *Mem:* AAAS; Marine Tech Soc; Am Geophys Union. *Res:* Military oceanography, plans and analysis; ocean prediction; fleet environmental support programs; effects on acoustic systems and tactics; ocean and estuarine dynamics; chemical analyses of sea water. *Mailing Add:* 6 Kendal Dr Kennett Square PA 19348

KEEN, JAMES H, CELL BIOLOGY. *Current Pos:* PROF PHARMACOL, JEFFERSON CANCER INST, PHILADELPHIA, PA, 91- *Personal Data:* b New York, NY, Feb 14, 48; m 73; c 2. *Educ:* Cornell Univ, PhD, 76. *Prof Exp:* Assoc prof, Fels Res Inst, Sch Med, Temple Univ, 85-91. *Concurrent Pos:* Chmn grad studies, Prog Molecular Biol & Genetics, Sch Med, Temple Univ. *Mem:* AAAS; NY Acad Sci; Am Soc Cell Biol; Am Soc Biol Chem. *Res:* Structure and function of clathrin coated membranes; role in receptor-mediated endocytosis and membrane dynamics. *Mailing Add:* Jefferson Cancer Inst 915 BLSB 233 S Tenth St Philadelphia PA 19107-5541. *Fax:* 215-923-1098

KEEN, LINDA, MATHEMATICS. *Current Pos:* from asst prof to assoc prof, 67-74, PROF MATH, CUNY, LEHMAN COL, GRAD CTR, 74- *Personal Data:* b New York, NY, Aug 9, 40; m, Jonathan Brezin; c 2. *Educ:* City Col New York, BS, 60; NY Univ, MS, 62, PhD(math), 64. *Honors & Awards:* Abby Mauze Rockefeller Award, Mass Inst Technol, 90. *Prof Exp:* NSF fel math, Inst Advan Study, 64-65; asst prof, Hunter Col, 65-67. *Concurrent Pos:* Vis prof, 80-81, NSF partial res grant, 82-88, 89-92, 93-98, vis prof, Boston Univ, 87, vis scientist, IBM, 88, vis mem Nat Sci Res Inst, 86, Max Planck Inst, 88; vis prof, Princeton, 89-90, Mass Inst Technol, 91, SUNY, StonyBrook, 93. *Mem:* Am Math Soc (vpres 90-93); Asn Women Math (pres 85-86). *Res:* Complex analysis; Riemann surfaces; discontinuous groups; Teichmuller spaces; dynamical systems. *Mailing Add:* Dept Math City Univ NY Grad Ctr New York NY 10036. *E-Mail:* ljklc@cunyum.cuny.edu

KEEN, NOEL THOMAS, PLANT PATHOLOGY. *Current Pos:* PROF PLANT PATH, UNIV CALIF, RIVERSIDE, 68- *Personal Data:* b Marshalltown, Iowa, Aug 13, 40; m 86, Diane Ill. *Educ:* Iowa State Univ, BS, 63, MS, 65; Univ Wis-Madison, PhD(plant path), 68. *Honors & Awards:* Ruth Allen Award, Am Phytopath Soc; Award for Super Serv USDA. *Mem:* Nat Acad Sci; Am Phytopath Soc; Am Chem Soc; Am Soc Plant Physiologists; Int Soc Plant Path; Am Soc Microbiol; fel AAAS. *Res:* Mechanisms of pathogenesis by plant parasitic microorganisms; mechanisms of disease resistance. *Mailing Add:* Dept Plant Path Univ Calif Riverside CA 92521

KEEN, RAY ALBERT, ORNAMENTAL HORTICULTURE. *Current Pos:* From asst prof to prof, 47-81, res horticulturist, Agr Exp Sta, 72-81, EMER PROF HORT, KANS STATE UNIV, 81- *Personal Data:* b Valley Falls, Kans, Oct 9, 15; m 43; c Robert, Margaret (Cook), Kenneth & Catharine (Williams). *Educ:* Kans State Col, BS, 42; Ohio State Univ, MS, 47, PhD, 56. *Mem:* Am Soc Hort Sci; Am Soc Agron; Sigma Xi. *Res:* Turf grass genetics; shade trees; woody ornamentals; propagation; soils and mineral nutrition; granted 3 US patents. *Mailing Add:* 1916 Blue Hills Rd Manhattan KS 66502

KEEN, ROBERT ERIC, LIMNOLOGY, POPULATION ECOLOGY. *Current Pos:* asst prof, 77-81, ASSOC PROF BIOL, MICH TECHNOL UNIV, 81- *Personal Data:* b Oakland, Calif, May 29, 44; m 72; c 2. *Educ:* Kans State Univ, BS, 65; Mich State Univ, MS, 67, PhD(zool), 71. *Prof Exp:* Asst prof zool, Univ Vt, 71-76; vis asst prof biol, Kans State Univ, 76-77; vis asst prof zool, Ind Univ, 77. *Concurrent Pos:* Fel, Philadelphia Acad Natural Sci, 70-71; partic, Advan Inst Statist Ecol, Pa State Univ, 72; staff consult, Nat Comn Water Qual, 75; consult, Vt Inst Water Resources Res, 76-77. *Mem:* Am Soc Limnol & Oceanog; Ecol Soc Am; Int Soc Limnol; Soc Pop Ecol. *Res:* Population ecology of zooplankton; limnology of Lake Superior; toxicity tests with Ceriodaphnia. *Mailing Add:* Dept Biol Sci Mich Technol Univ Houghton MI 49931

KEEN, VERYL F, BIOLOGY. *Current Pos:* asst prof & coordr, 66-71, PROF BIOL & CHMN DEPT, ADAMS STATE COL, 71- *Personal Data:* b Stilwell, Okla, Jan 14, 23; m 59; c 2. *Educ:* Northeastern State Col, BS, 50; Okla State Univ, MS, 54; Univ Colo, MA, 62, PhD(zool), 65. *Prof Exp:* Teacher, Maramec Sch, Okla, 50-52; supt schs, 52-57; instr biol, Univ Colo, 59-60, vis lectr, 65-66; assoc prof, Northeastern Mo State Col, 63-65. *Mem:* AAAS; Am Soc Mammal; Nat Asn Biol Teachers. *Res:* Small mammal population ecology; rodent botflies of Colorado; ecology of small mammals of San Luis Valley in Colorado. *Mailing Add:* 12551 Chamisa Trail Alamosa CO 81101

KEEN, WILLIAM HUBERT, ECOLOGY, ZOOLOGY. *Current Pos:* VPRES ACAD AFFAIRS, YORK COL, CITY UNIV NY, 94- *Personal Data:* b Jewell Ridge, Va, Sept 2, 44; m 68; c 1. *Educ:* Pikeville Col, BA, 67; Eastern Ky Univ, MS, 71; Kent State Univ, PhD(ecol), 75. *Prof Exp:* Teacher biol & sci, Buchanan Co Pub Sch, Grundy, Va, 67-68; coordr interdisciplinary field studies, Pikeville Col, Ky, 68-69; teacher biol & sci, Jefferson Co Pub Sch, Louisville, Ky, 69-70; instr, Kent State Univ, Ohio, 75-76; from asst prof to prof biol, State Univ NY, Cortland, 76-94, chmn dept, 83-88, dean arts & sci, 88-94. *Concurrent Pos:* Lectr, Cuyahoga Community Col, Cleveland, Ohio, 75-76. *Mem:* Sigma Xi; AAAS; Am Asn Higher Educ; Soc Study Amphibians & Reptiles; Am Soc Ichthyologists & Herpetologists; Asn Gen & Lib Studies. *Res:* Population ecology and behavior of lower vertebrates; thermoregulation in amphibians; functions of fish schooling; interspecific interactions. *Mailing Add:* Vpres Acad Affairs York Col City Univ NY 94-20 Guy R Brewer Blvd Jamaica NY 11451. *Fax:* 607-753-5999

KEENAN, EDWARD JAMES, PHARMACOLOGY, ENDOCRINOLOGY. *Current Pos:* Res assoc, 75-76, ASST PROF SURG, UNIV ORE HEALTH SCI CTR, 76-, ASST PROF PHARMACOL, 78-, DEPT SURG. *Personal Data:* b Shelton, Wash, Sept 6, 48. *Educ:* Creighton Univ, BS, 70, MS, 72; WVa Univ, PhD(pharmacol), 75. *Concurrent Pos:* Dir, Clin Res Ctr Lab & Hormone Res Lab, Univ Ore Health Sci Ctr, 76-, instr pharmacol, 77-78. *Mem:* Am Soc Andrology; AAAS; Sigma Xi. *Res:* Significance of steroid hormones in cancer of the breast and prostate gland; mechanism of steroid hormone action; role of prolactin in male accessory sex organ function. *Mailing Add:* Dept Pharmacol Ore Health Sci Univ 3181 SW Sam Jackson Park Rd Portland OR 97201-3098

KEENAN, JOHN DOUGLAS, WATER & WASTEWATER TREATMENT, ALTERNATIVE ENERGY SOURCES. *Current Pos:* from asst prof to assoc prof civil eng, Univ Pa, 73-86, assoc prof, 86-90, prof civil eng systs & assoc dean undergrad educ, 90-94, DIR, RECRUITMENT, ADMIS & ADVS, UNIV PA, 94- *Personal Data:* b Sarnia, Ont, Mar 16, 44; US citizen; m 62, Martha; c Mark, Sean, Patrick & Matthew. *Educ:* State Univ NY, Buffalo, BA, 67; Syracuse Univ, MS, 70, PhD(civil eng), 72. *Hon Degrees:* MA, Univ Pa, 78. *Prof Exp:* Instr water & wastewater treat, Syracuse Univ, 70-72. *Concurrent Pos:* Vis asst prof civil eng, Univ Pa, 72-73. *Res:* Environmental systems engineering; water and wastewater engineering; biological and health effects of pollutants; alternative energy sources. *Mailing Add:* Dept Systs Eng Univ Pa Philadelphia PA 19104-6391. *Fax:* 215-898-1130; *E-Mail:* keenan@eniac.seas.upenn.edu

KEENAN, JOSEPH ALOYSIUS, NUCLEAR CHEMISTRY. *Current Pos:* mem res staff, 69-80, SR MEM TECH STAFF, MAT SCI LAB, TEX INSTRUMENTS INC, 80- *Personal Data:* b Washington, DC, Aug 5, 38; m 68; c 2. *Educ:* Spring Hill Col, BS, 64; Clark Univ, PhD(nuclear chem), 71. *Mem:* Am Chem Soc; Electro Chem Soc; Am Vacuum Soc. *Res:* Instrumental neutron activation analysis, radiotracer techniques and x-ray fluorescence analysis in materials characterization; design and building of mini computer systems for manufacturing and laboratory automation; auger spectroscopy; surface science ion backseat housing; nuclear reaction analysis. *Mailing Add:* 1214 Cherokee Dr Richardson TX 75080-3906

KEENAN, KATHLEEN MARGARET, BIOSTATISTICS. *Current Pos:* Asst prof, 64-69, ASSOC PROF ORAL SCI, SCH DENT, UNIV MINN, 69- *Personal Data:* b St Paul, Minn, May 24, 44. *Educ:* St Catherine Col, BA, 56; Univ Minn, MS, 58, PhD(biostatist), 64. *Mem:* AAAS; Am Statist Asn; Biom Soc; fel Am Pub Health Asn; Am Soc Human Genetics; Sigma Xi. *Res:* Biostatistical applications in dental research. *Mailing Add:* 1768 Field Ave St Paul MN 55116-2726

KEENAN, PHILIP CHILDS, SPECTRAL CLASSIFICATION. *Current Pos:* from asst prof to prof, 46-76, actg dir, 57-59, EMER PROF ASTRON, OHIO STATE UNIV, 76- *Personal Data:* b Bellevue, Pa, Mar 31, 08. *Educ:* Univ Ariz, BS, 29, MS, 30; Univ Chicago, PhD(astrophysics), 32. *Hon Degrees:* Dr, Univ Cordoba, 71. *Prof Exp:* Asst astron, Yerkes Observ, Univ Chicago, 29-35, instr, 36-42; instr Perkins Observ, Ohio State Univ & Ohio Wesleyan Univ, 35-36; physicist, Bur Ord, US Dept Navy, 42-46. *Mem:* Fel Royal Astron Soc. *Res:* Stellar spectroscopy; spectral classification; history of astronomy. *Mailing Add:* 35 Broadmeadows Blvd No 2A Columbus OH 43214

KEENAN, ROBERT GREGORY, ENVIRONMENTAL CHEMISTRY. *Current Pos:* RETIRED. *Personal Data:* b St Albans, Vt, Dec 19, 15; m 44, Yvonne Coutu; c Patricia, Richard & Eileen (Herzog). *Educ:* Catholic Univ, BS, 37; Univ Md, MS, 52; Am Bd Indust Hyg, cert indust hyg, 62. *Honors & Awards:* Moyer D Thomas Award, Am Soc Testing & Mat, 77. *Prof Exp:* Lab helper chem, Div Occup Health, USPHS, 38-40, from jr chemist to assoc chemist, 40-45, sr asst scientist, 45-49, scientist, 49-53, chief phys anal unit, 53-56, asst chief anal serv, 56-60, chief, 60-69, dep chief res & med affairs, 66-67, assoc chief div occup health, 67-69; vpres & dir lab serv, George D Clayton & Assocs, 69-76. *Concurrent Pos:* Guest worker, Anal Chem Div, Radiochem Anal Sect, Nat Bur Standards, 63-64. *Mem:* Emer mem Am Chem Soc; hon mem Am Indust Hyg Asn; Am Soc Testing & Mat. *Res:* Spectrography; determination of cobalt in dust samples; determination of iron in welding fume samples; quantitative analytical methods in emission spectroscopy and suppression of cyanogen bands in emission spectra; activation analysis; atomic absorption; beryllium in air; biological materials and ores; analytical techniques for industrial hygiene and air pollution; author or coauthor of over 75 scientific publications. *Mailing Add:* 122 Country Club Dr E South Burlington VT 05403-5838

KEENAN, ROBERT KENNETH, ELECTRONICS ENGINEERING. *Current Pos:* VPRES ENG, KEENAN CORP, 79- *Personal Data:* b Pueblo, Colo, Nov 29, 38; m 60, Jean Ellicott; c Megan, Kevin & Kerrick. *Educ:* Univ Calif, Los Angeles, BSc, 62; Calif Inst Technol, MSEE, 63; Monash Univ, Australia, PhD(elec eng), 67. *Prof Exp:* Staff engr, Commun Div, Hughes Aircraft Co, 62-64; lectr elec eng, Monash Univ, 64-67; eng specialist, Electronics Div, Gen Dynamics Corp, 67-68; mgr res & adv develop, Electronic Commun Inc, Nat Cash Register Co, 68-71; mem tech staff, Mitre Corp, 71-75, aerospace corp, 75-77; dir systs sci, BDM Corp, 77-78; sr prof eng, TRW Inc, 78-81. *Mem:* Inst Elec & Electronics Engrs; Am Inst Aeronaut & Astronaut; Sigma Xi. *Res:* Suppression of electromagnetic interference, as generated by digital electronic equipment. *Mailing Add:* TKC 8609 66th St Pinellas Park FL 33782. *Fax:* 813-544-2597

KEENAN, ROY W, metabolism, for more information see previous edition

KEENAN, THOMAS AQUINAS, COMPUTER SCIENCE. *Current Pos:* RETIRED. *Personal Data:* b Rochester, NY, Mar 8, 27; m 93, Marcelline Sweeney; c 3. *Educ:* Univ Rochester, BS, 47; Purdue Univ, MS, 50, PhD(physics), 55. *Prof Exp:* Instr physics, Purdue Univ, 50-55; dir comput ctr, Rochester Univ, 56-66, chmn prog appl math, 58-66, asst prof physics, 57-62; dir systs planning, Interuniv, Commun Coun, 66-68, exec dir educ info network, 68-69; prog dir software systs sci, NSF, 69-90. *Concurrent Pos:* Exec dir, comt on uses of comput, Nat Acad Sci-Nat Res Coun, 62-63; consult, Sch Math Study Group, 65-66. *Mem:* AAAS. *Res:* Computation; formal languages; symbol manipulation; information retrieval; data structure; phase transitions; combinatorial mathematics. *Mailing Add:* 12433 Over Ridge Rd Potomac MD 20854-3047

KEENAN, THOMAS K, INORGANIC CHEMISTRY. *Current Pos:* RETIRED. *Personal Data:* b Ft Dodge, Iowa, Oct 8, 24; m 52; c 4. *Educ:* SDak Sch Mines & Technol, BS, 48; Univ NMex, MS, 50, PhD(chem), 54. *Prof Exp:* Asst, Univ NMex, 49-53; mem staff, Los Alamos Nat Lab, 54-75, group leader waste mgt, 75-81, asst to dep assoc dir, 81-84, assoc group leader waste mgt, 84-86. *Mem:* Am Nuclear Soc. *Mailing Add:* 289 Venado Los Alamos NM 87544

KEENAN, THOMAS WILLIAM, FOOD SCIENCE. *Current Pos:* Assoc prof food sci, 67-73, PROF ANIMAL SCI, PURDUE UNIV, 73-, ASST DEAN GRAD SCH, 77- *Personal Data:* b Johnstown, Pa, May 12, 42; m 64; c 3. *Educ:* Pa State Univ, BS, 64; Ore State Univ, MS, 65, PhD(food sci), 67. *Mem:* Am Chem Soc; Am Dairy Sci Asn; Inst Food Technol. *Res:* Membrane function; microbial biochemistry; lipid metabolism. *Mailing Add:* Dept Biochem & Anaerobic Microbiol Va Polytech Inst & State Univ Blacksburg VA 24061-0308. *Fax:* 540-231-9070

KEENAN, WILLIAM JEROME, PEDIATRICS, NEONATAL-PERINATAL MEDICINE. *Current Pos:* PROF PEDIAT-OBSTET, ST LOUIS UNIV, 80- *Personal Data:* b Rawlins, Wyo, Sept 8, 39; m 65; c 7. *Educ:* Loyola-Stritch Sch Med, MD, 64. *Prof Exp:* Fel pediat, Univ Cincinnati, 67-69, from asst prof to prof, 69-80. *Concurrent Pos:* Dir neonatology, Cardinal Glennon Children's Hosp, 80-; dir pediat, St Mary's Health Ctr, 81-; dir, Southern Ill grant, 84-; consult, Mo Dept Health, 85. *Mem:* Soc Pediat Res; Am Fedn Clin Res; AAAS; Sigma Xi; Am Acad Pediat. *Res:* Neonatal hyperbilirubinemia; critical care of neonatal patients; developmental biology. *Mailing Add:* Dept Pediat St Louis Univ Med Sch 1465 S Grand Blvd St Louis MO 63104-1003

KEENE, CLIFFORD H, INTERNAL MEDICINE. *Current Pos:* MEM STAFF, COMMUNITY HOSP, MONTEREY, CALIF, 75- *Personal Data:* b Buffalo, NY, Jan 28, 10. *Educ:* Univ Mich, AB, 32, MD, 34, MSc, 38. *Hon Degrees:* DSc, Hannemann Med Col, 73; LLD, Goden Gate Univ, 74. *Prof Exp:* Intern, Univ Hosp, Ann Arbor, 34-36, teaching res, surg & path, 36-39; pres, Kaiser Found Hosp & Health Plan, 68-75. *Concurrent Pos:* Instr surg & path, Univ Mich, 36-39 & 46-54; dir, Sch Nursing, Kaiser Found Hosp & Health Plan, 60-80. *Mem:* Inst Med-Nat Acad Sci; AMA; Am Col Occup Med; fel Am Col Surgeons. *Mailing Add:* 3978 Ronda Rd PO Box 961 Pebble Beach CA 93953

KEENE, HARRIS J, oral pathology, for more information see previous edition

KEENE, JACK DONALD, MOLECULAR VIROLOGY, GENE EXPRESSION. *Current Pos:* from asst prof to assoc prof virol & molecular genetics, 79-88, ASST PROF RHEUMATOL & IMMUNOL, DEPT MED, DUKE UNIV MED CTR, DURHAM, 85-, PROF VIROL & MOLECULAR GENETICS, DEPT MICROBIOL & IMMUNOL, 88- *Personal Data:* b Jacksonville, Fla, June 21, 47; m 69; c 2. *Educ:* Univ Calif, Riverside, AB, 69; Univ Wash, Seattle, PhD(microbiol & immunol), 74. *Prof Exp:* Staff fel molecular virol, Lab Molecular Genetics, Nat Inst Neurol Dis & Stroke, NIH, 74-78. *Concurrent Pos:* Fac Res Award, Am Can Soc, 81-86; Assoc ed, Virol, 83-; spec reviewer, Virol Study Sect, NIH, 84-, mem, Exp Virol Study Sect, 85-88; Pew Scholar Biomed Sci, 86-90; mem, Molecular Biol Study Sect & Arthritis Found Study Sect, Fel Comn & Res Comn. *Mem:* Am Soc Microbiol; Am Soc Virol; Am Soc Biochem & Molecular Biol. *Res:* RNA metabolism and processing; nature of autoimmunity and genetic regulation; virus-host interactions as models of cellular gene expression. *Mailing Add:* Dept Microbiol Med Ctr Box 3020 Duke Univ 414 Jones Bldg Durham NC 27710-0001

KEENE, JAMES H, POULTRY NUTRITION. *Current Pos:* RETIRED. *Personal Data:* b Epps, La, May 8, 30; m 58; c 2. *Educ:* Univ Ark, BS, 57; La State Univ, MS, 59, PhD(poultry nutrit), 62. *Prof Exp:* Nutritionist, George B Matthews & Sons Inc, 62-64; from asst prof to prof poultry & dairying, Ark State Univ, 64-63. *Mem:* Poultry Sci Asn. *Res:* Poultry production and physiology. *Mailing Add:* 1103 Fernwood Cove Jonesboro AR 72401

KEENE, OWEN DAVID, POULTRY NUTRITION. *Current Pos:* POULTRY NUTRITIONIST, HERITAGE PMS INC, 90- *Personal Data:* b New Eagle, Pa, Apr 28, 34; m 57; c 1. *Educ:* Pa State Univ, BS, 55; Univ Md, MS, 59, PhD(poultry nutrit), 63. *Prof Exp:* Sr biochemist, Abbott Labs, 63-69; asst prof, Pa State Univ, 69-75, assoc prof poultry sci exten, 75-90. *Concurrent Pos:* Agr prog leader, Poultry Exten Prog, USDA/Exten Serv, Washington, DC, 84-85 & Residual Avoidance Prog, 85. *Mem:* Poultry Sci Asn; World Poultry Sci Asn. *Res:* Product development relating to the nutrition of poultry. *Mailing Add:* Heritage PMS Inc RD 1 Box 213 Annville PA 17003

KEENE, WILLIS RIGGS, INTERNAL MEDICINE, HEMATOLOGY. *Current Pos:* CLIN PRACTICE, 75- *Personal Data:* b Woodbine, Ga, Jan 30, 32; c 4. *Educ:* Emory Univ, BA, 53; Johns Hopkins Univ, MD, 57. *Prof Exp:* From intern to resident, Johns Hopkins Hosp, 57-59; with Nat Cancer Inst, 59-60 & USPHS Hosp, Boston, 60-61; fel med, Harvard Univ, 61-63, instr, 63-64; staff physician, Dept Internal Med, Lahey Clin, 64-68; prof med, Col Med, Univ Fla, 71-75, assoc chmn dept internal med, 74-75. *Mem:* Am Col Physicians; Am Soc Hemat. *Res:* Blood platelet physiology; iron metabolism. *Mailing Add:* 130 N Gross Rd No 205 Kingsland GA 31548

KEENER, CARL SAMUEL, BOTANY. *Current Pos:* from asst prof to assoc prof, 66-91, PROF BIOL, PA STATE UNIV, 91-, CUR SEED PLANTS HERBARIUM, 78- *Personal Data:* b Columbia, Pa, Apr 12, 31; m 55, Gladys E Swartz; c Carl, Dorothy & Joyce. *Educ:* Eastern Mennonite Col, AB, 57; Univ Pa, MS, 60; NC State Univ, PhD(bot), 66. *Honors & Awards:* Jesse M Greeman Award, 68; Henry Allan Gleason Award, 84. *Prof Exp:* Asst prof biol, Eastern Mennonite Col, 60-63. *Concurrent Pos:* Vis lectr, Univ Va, 66, 68, 72, 76 & 78; NFS grad fel bot, 63-66. *Mem:* Am Soc Plant Taxon; Int Asn Plant Taxon; Int Orgn Biosyst; Systs Asn; Sigma Xi. *Res:* Evolutionary patterns in the shale barren endemics of eastern US; floristics of Pennsylvania; Ranunculaceae of North America. *Mailing Add:* Biol Dept 208 Mueller Lab Pa State Univ University Park PA 16802-5301. *Fax:* 814-865-9193; *E-Mail:* kux@psuvm.psu.edu

KEENER, E(VERETT) L(EE), ELECTRICAL ENGINEERING. *Current Pos:* RETIRED. *Personal Data:* b Grafton, WVa, Jan 30, 22; m 42. *Educ:* Univ WVa, BSEE, 44; Purdue Univ, MSEE, 49. *Prof Exp:* Test engr, Gen Elec Co, 44; from instr to asst prof elec eng, Univ WVa, 46-55; instr, Purdue Univ, 47-48; sr res engr, Analog & Hybrid Comput, 55-66, US Steel Corp, 55-66, assoc res consult, Res Ctr, 66-82. *Concurrent Pos:* Sales, 87- *Mem:* Sr mem Inst Elec & Electronics Engrs; Soc Comput Simulation. *Res:* Instrumentation, control and electrical analogs for steel industry processes; develop micro-computers for data acquisition and control. *Mailing Add:* 303 McGraw Ave Grafton WV 26354

KEENER, HAROLD MARION, AGRICULTURAL ENGINEERING. *Current Pos:* From instr to asst prof, 68-80, ASSOC PROF AGR ENG, OHIO AGR RES & DEVELOP CTR, 80- *Personal Data:* b Ashland, Ohio, July 28, 43; m 65, Nancy Steward; c Kevin, Myra, Kathy & Clinton. *Educ:* Ohio State Univ, BS, 67, MS, 68, PhD(agr eng), 73. *Mem:* Am Soc Agr Engrs. *Res:* Biomass combustion systems; fluidized bed combustion applied to small scale energy systems; grain and solar grain drying; analysis of total energy consumption in crop production systems and livestock enterprises; composting agricultural and/or yard waste. *Mailing Add:* Dept Agr Eng Ohio Agr Res & Develop Ctr Wooster OH 44691. *Fax:* 330-263-3670; *E-Mail:* keener.3@osu.edu

KEENER, HARRY ALLAN, ANIMAL NUTRITION. *Current Pos:* from instr to asst prof animal & dairy husb, 41-45, assoc prof dairy husb, 45-50, prof animal sci, 50-78, dir agr exp sta, 58-78, dean, Col Life Sci & Agr, 61-78, EMER PROF ANIMAL SCI & EMER DEAN, COL LIFE SCI & AGR, UNIV NH, 78- *Personal Data:* b Greensboro, Pa, Dec 22, 13; m 41, Elizabeth Hartley; c Allan & William. *Educ:* Pa State Univ, BS, 36, PhD(animal nutrit, dairy husb), 41; WVa Univ, MS, 38. *Prof Exp:* Asst dairy husb, WVa Univ, 36-38 & Pa State Univ, 38-41. *Mem:* Am Soc Animal Sci; Am Dairy Sci Asn; NY Acad Sci. *Res:* Trace elements; cobalt; vitamin D; nitrogen and energy metabolism. *Mailing Add:* PO Box 165 Durham NH 03824-0165

KEENER, MARVIN STANFORD, MATHEMATICAL ANALYSIS. *Current Pos:* from asst prof to assoc prof, Okla State Univ, 70-79, head, Dept Maths, 87-90, assoc dean arts & sci, 90-93, interim provost & vpres acad affairs, 93-96, PROF MATH, OKLA STATE UNIV, 79-, EXEC VPRES, 96- *Personal Data:* b Birmingham, Ala, Oct 25, 43; m 65, Margaret Kidd; c Susan (Lavergne) & Ross S. *Educ:* Birmingham-Southern Col, BS, 65; Univ Mo-Columbia, MA, 67. PhD(math), 70. *Mem:* Am Math Soc; Sigma Xi; Soc Indust & Appl Math; Math Asn Am. *Res:* Ordinary differential equations. *Mailing Add:* 823 Ranch Dr Stillwater OK 74075. *E-Mail:* mkeener@okway. okstate.edu

KEENEY, ARTHUR HAIL, OPHTHALMOLOGY. *Current Pos:* dean, 73-80, EMER DEAN & DISTINGUISHED PROF OPHTHAL, SCH MED, UNIV LOUISVILLE, 80- *Personal Data:* b Louisville, Ky, Jan 20, 20; m 42, Virginia Tripp; c Steven, Douglas & Martha (Heyburn). *Educ:* Col William & Mary, BS, 41; Univ Louisville, MD, 44; Univ Pa, MS, 52, DSc(med), 55; Am Bd Ophthal, dipl, 51. *Hon Degrees:* Dr, Bellarmine Col, 96. *Honors & Awards:* Alvaro Lectr, SAm, 60; hom master, Opthal Optics, 93. *Prof Exp:* Res surgeon, Wills Eye Hosp, Philadelphia, Pa, 49-51; dir res, Sect Ophthal, Sch Med, Univ Louisville, 52-59, from asst prof to assoc prof ophthal, 59-65, ophthalmologist-in-chief, Wills Eye Hosp, Philadelphia, Pa, 65-74. *Concurrent Pos:* Area consult, US Vet Admin, 54-; consult ed, Am J Ophthal; mem sci adv comt, Nat Coun Combat Blindness; life trustee, J G Brown Found; ophthalmologist-in-chief, Wills Eye Hosp & Res Inst, 65-73; mem Nat Adv Coun to US Secy Transp, 67-71; prof & chmn dept, Sch Med, Temple Univ, 66-74; pres, Int Cong Ultrasound in Ophthal, 68; mem grants adv coun, The Seeing Eye, 68-71; vchmn, Residency Rev Comt Ophthal, 69-73; chmn Z80 comt on ophthal stand, Am Nat Stand Inst, 70-86; trustee, Med Found Jefferson Co Med Soc, 83-, pres, 87-89; med adv opthal, Off of Hearings & Appeals, Social Security Admin, 81-; mem, Nat Res Coun-Comt on Vision, Working Group on Mobility Aids for Visually Impaired, 85-86; mem, Joint Comn Allied Health Personnel Ophthal, pres, 87-88. *Mem:* Fel Am Ophthal Soc; AMA; fel Am Asn Hist Med; fel Am Acad Ophthal (pres, 84-86); Am Asn Automotive Med (pres, 67). *Res:* Light damage; ocular injuries; ultrasound; diabetic retinopathy; safety lens materials; macular disease; dyslexia; strabismus; ocular tumors; visual needs in transportation. *Mailing Add:* Off Dean Emer Univ Louisville Louisville KY 40292

KEENEY, CLIFFORD EMERSON, PHYSIOLOGY. *Current Pos:* asst prof physiol, 55-57, from asst prof to assoc prof biol, 57-65, dir Div Arts & Sci, 62-64, PROF BIOL, SPRINGFIELD COL, 65- *Personal Data:* b Springfield, Mass, June 28, 21; m 50; c 2. *Educ:* Springfield Col, BS, 48, MEd, 49; Rutgers Univ, MS, 51; NY UNiv, PhD(phys ed), 59. *Prof Exp:* Teacher high sch, Mass, 49-50; instr biol, Springfield Col, 51-52; biologist, Lederle Labs Div, Am Cyanamid Co, NY, 52-55. *Concurrent Pos:* NSF sci fac fel, 64-65. *Mem:* AAAS; Nat Asn Biol Teachers; NY Acad Sci. *Res:* Cytological changes induced by exercise. *Mailing Add:* 47 Old Coach Rd Hampden MA 01109

KEENEY, DENNIS RAYMOND, SOIL FERTILITY, BIOCHEMISTRY. *Current Pos:* DIR LEOPOLD CTR SUSTAINABLE AGR, IOWA STATE UNIV, 88-, PROF AGRON, 88-, DIR, IOWA STATE WATER RESOURCES RES INSTS, 92- *Personal Data:* b Osceola, Iowa, July 2, 37; m 59; c 2. *Educ:* Iowa State Univ, BS, 59, PhD(soil fertil), 65; Univ Wis, MS, 61. *Honors & Awards:* Soil Sci Res Award, Soil Sci Soc Am, 81, Soil Sci Prof Serv Award, 94; Environ Qual Res Award, Am Soc Agron, 86. *Prof Exp:* Fel soil biochem, Iowa State Univ, 65-66; from asst prof to prof soils, Univ Wis, 66-88, chmn dept, 79-84; chmn land resources, Inst Environ Sci, 85-88. *Concurrent Pos:* Romnes grad sch fel, Univ Wis Grad Sch, 75; sr res fel, Dept Sci & Indust Res, Grasslands, Palmerston N, NZ, 76-77; distinguished serv award, USDA. *Mem:* Fel Am Soc Agron (pres, 92-93); fel Soil Sci Soc Am (pres, 88); Soil Conserv Soc Am; fel AAAS. *Res:* Sustainable agriculture; agricultural systems; modeling of N cycle; elucidation of nitrogen transformation in soils and waters; sustainable agriculture; land application of solid and liquid municipal and industrial wastes. *Mailing Add:* Leopold Ctr Sustainable Agr 126 Soil Tilth Bldg Iowa State Univ Ames IA 50011. *Fax:* 515-294-9696

KEENEY, MARK, dairy science; deceased, see previous edition for last biography

KEENEY, NORWOOD HENRY, JR, CHEMICAL ENGINEERING, PULP AND PAPER-FOREST PRODUCTS. *Current Pos:* RETIRED. *Personal Data:* b Hartford, Conn, July 10, 24; m 46, Phyllis R Mottram; c Norwood H III. *Educ:* Trinity Col, Conn, BS, 48; Univ Maine, Orono, MS, 50; Victoria Univ, Manchester, PhD, 62. *Prof Exp:* Paper chemist, Fram Corp, 50-53; from asst prof to prof chem eng, Univ Lowell, 53-86, chmn dept, 76-83. *Mem:* Tech Asn Pulp & Paper Indust. *Res:* Chemical engineering applications to pulp and paper industry; porous media; filtration of compressibles; zeta potentials; stress-strain properties of fibers and fibrous structures. *Mailing Add:* Skyline Rd Unity NH 03773

KEENEY, PHILIP G, FOOD SCIENCE. *Current Pos:* Asst prof dairy sci, Pa State Univ, 55-63, assoc prof, 63-68, prof food sci, 68-85, EMER PROF, PA STATE UNIV, 68- *Personal Data:* b Caldwell, NJ, Feb 28, 25; m 57, Elsie Bamesberger; c Philip G II. *Educ:* Univ Nebr, BSc, 49; Ohio State Univ, MSc, 53; Pa State Univ, PhD(dairy sci), 55. *Concurrent Pos:* Consult, Sci & Technol Ice Cream & Chocolate. *Mem:* Fel AAAS; Am Chem Soc; Am Dairy Sci Asn; Inst Food Technol. *Res:* Food technology and chemistry; ice cream; chocolate products. *Mailing Add:* 1449 Curtin St State College PA 16803. *Fax:* 814-238-8157

KEENEY, RALPH LYONS, RISK ANALYSIS, DECISION ANALYSIS. *Current Pos:* PROF SYSTS SCI, UNIV SOUTHERN CALIF, 83- *Personal Data:* b Lewistown, Mont, Jan 29, 44. *Educ:* Univ Calif, Los Angeles, BS, 66; Mass Inst Technol, MS, 67, EE, 69, PhD(opers res), 69. *Prof Exp:* Engr, Bell Tel Labs, 66-69; asst prof civil eng & staff mem, Opers Res Ctr, Mass Inst Technol, 69-72, assoc prof mgt & opers res, 72-74; res scholar, Int Inst Appl Systs Anal, Laxenburg, Austria, 74-76; head, Decision Anal, Woodward-Cycle Consults, 76-83, vpres, 80-83. *Concurrent Pos:* Pvt consult, 69- *Mem:* Nat Acad Eng; Soc Risk Anal; Inst Opers Res & Mgt Sci. *Res:* Decision analysis, risk analysis; probabilistic models. *Mailing Add:* 101 Lombard St No 704W San Francisco CA 94111

KEENLEYSIDE, MILES HUGH ALSTON, FISH BEHAVIOR. *Current Pos:* from asst prof to assoc prof, 61-72, PROF ZOOL, UNIV WESTERN ONT, 72- *Personal Data:* b Ottawa, Ont, Apr 8, 29; m 51, Hilda A Alev; c Joel H & Eric M. *Educ:* Univ BC, BA, 52, MA, 53; Univ Groningen, PhD(zool), 55. *Prof Exp:* Asst scientist fisheries biol, Biol Sta, Fisheries Res Bd Can, 55-57, assoc scientist, 57-61. *Concurrent Pos:* Sr Queen's Fel Marine Sci, Australia, 83. *Mem:* Can Soc Zoologists; fel Animal Behav Soc; Int Soc Behav Ecol. *Res:* Social and reproductive behavior of fishes; parent-young interactions; social organization, mating systems and ecology; mate choice; correlates of reproductive success. *Mailing Add:* Dept Zool Univ Western Ont London ON N6A 5B7 Can. *Fax:* 519-661-2014

KEENLYNE, KENT DOUGLAS, WILDLIFE ECOLOGY, GEOLOGY. *Current Pos:* SR STAFF BIOLOGIST, OFFICE MGR, BLUESTEM, INC, 97- *Personal Data:* b Durand, Wis, May 28, 41; m 64; c 2. *Educ:* Univ Wis-River Falls, BS, 64; Univ Minn, MS, 68, MAPA, 71, PhD(wildlife ecol), 76. *Honors & Awards:* Spec Achievement Award, US Fish & Wildlife Serv, 89, 93, 94 & 95; Nat Wildlife Vol Award, 91, Star Award, 96. *Prof Exp:* Wildlife biologist river basin studies, US Fish & Wildlife Serv, Minneapolis, Minn, 70-72; coordr interagency coord, Upper Miss River Conserv Comt, 72-74; herpetologist herpetol studies & res, Fla Game & Fresh Water Fish Comn, 75-76; fish & wildlife biologist ecol serv & proj planning, US Fish Wildlife Serv, Rock Island, Ill, 76, coal coordr mineral develop, Casper, Wyo, 76-77, area supvr, Pierre, SD, 77-87, Mo River Natural Resources Comt, Coordr, 87-97. *Concurrent Pos:* Big game biologist, Minn Dept Natural Resources, 78; Interior Coal rep, Interior Task Force Strip Mine Legis Coal

Develop, 78; adj prof wildlife, SDak State Univ, Brookings, 87-, Pallid Sturgeon Recovery Team, 95-; Int Union Conserv, Nature & Natural Resources. *Mem:* Am Fisheries Soc. *Res:* Whitetailed deer reproduction; reproduction and life history of rattlesnakes; alligator attacks; physiology of whitetailed deer; sturgeon reproduction and life history; large river ecology. *Mailing Add:* Bluestem, Inc 105 S Euclid Suite D Pierre SD 57501. *Fax:* 701-223-4645; *E-Mail:* bluestem@tic.bisman.com

KEENMON, KENDALL ANDREWS, PETROLEUM GEOLOGY, REMOTE SENSING. *Current Pos:* OWNER & CONSULT, K-TECHNOL, 85- *Personal Data:* b Detroit, Mich, Sept 13, 20; m 42, Elizabeth A Pedersen; c Janet S (Gamble), John S, Joanne S (Parker) & Judith S (Janik). *Educ:* Univ Mich, BS, 47, MS, 48, PhD(geol), 50. *Prof Exp:* Div geologist, Shell Oil Co, 50-60, sr geologist, 60-61, sr res geologist, Shell Develop Co, 61-67, sr geologist, Shell Oil Co, 67-69 & Shell Develop Co, 69-72, sr geologist, Int Region, 72-77, staff geologist, Pecten Int Co, 78-85. *Mem:* Geol Soc Am; Am Asn Petrol Geol. *Res:* Structural geology; stratigraphy. *Mailing Add:* 5158 Imogene St Houston TX 77096

KEENS, THOMAS GEORGE, PEDIATRIC PULMONOLOGY, RESPIRATORY PHYSIOLOGY. *Current Pos:* from asst prof to assoc prof pediat pulmonol, 77-90, PROF PEDIAT, SCH MED, UNIV SOUTHERN CALIF & CHILDRENS HOSP, LOS ANGELES, 90- *Personal Data:* b Altadena, Calif, Nov 22, 46; m 72; c 2. *Educ:* St John's Col, Santa Fe, NMex, 68; Univ Calif, San Diego, MD, 72. *Honors & Awards:* Apnea of Infancy Award, Annenberg Ctr, 97. *Prof Exp:* Pediat intern & resident, Childrens Hosp Los Angeles, Calif, 72-75; res fel pediat respiratory physiol, Res Inst, Hosp Sick Children, Toronto, Ont, 75-77. *Concurrent Pos:* Pediat pulmonologist & neonatologist, Childrens Hosp Los Angeles, 77-; mem, Southern Adv Coun, Calif Sudden Infant Death Syndrome Info & Coun Proj, 79-, moderator, 84-85; pediat pulmonary consult, Kern Med Ctr, Bakersfield, Calif, 81-85. *Mem:* Am Physiol Soc; Soc Pediat Res; fel Am Acad Pediat; Am Thoracic Soc; Am Col Chest Physicians; Sleep Res Soc. *Res:* Sudden infant death syndrome; abnormal arousal responses in response to a hypoxic challenge in infants at high risk for sudden infant death syndrome; chronic lung disease; ventilatory muscle function; bronchopulmonary dysplasia; pediatric pulmonary function. *Mailing Add:* Univ Southern Calif Sch Med Children's Hosp Los Angeles 4650 Sunset Blvd Los Angeles CA 90027-6088

KEENY, SPURGEON MILTON, JR, PHYSICS. *Current Pos:* SCHOLAR-IN-RESIDENCE, NAT ACAD SCI, 81- *Personal Data:* b New York, NY, Oct 24, 24; m 52; c 3. *Educ:* Columbia Univ, BA, 44, MA, 46. *Prof Exp:* Asst physics, Columbia Univ, 44-46; intel analyst, Directorate of Intel Hq, US Air Force, 50-52, chief Spec Weapons Sect, 52-55; mem staff, Panel Peaceful Uses Atomic Energy, 55-56; chief atomic energy div, Off Asst Secy Defense Res & Eng, 56-57; mem, Gaither Security Resources Panel, 57; tech asst, President's Sci Adv, 58-69; sr staff mem, Nat Security Coun, 63-69; asst dir sci & technol, US Arms Control & Disarmament Agency, 69-73; dir policy & prog develop, Mitre Corp, 73-77; dep dir, US Arms Control & Disarmament Agency, 77-81. *Concurrent Pos:* Mem US del, Geneva Conf Experts Nuclear Test Detection, 58, Conf Discontinuance Nuclear Weapon Tests, 58-60;, Am Phys Soc Study Group Light-Water Reactor Safety, 74-75; dep chmn, Nat Acad Sci, Comt on Environ Decision Making, 74; chmn, Ford-Mitre Nuclear Energy Policy Study, 75-77; head US deleg, US/Soviet Theater Nuclear Force Talks, 80; mem Comt Int Security & Arms Control, Nat Acad Sci, 81- *Mem:* Fel Am Acad Arts & Sci; Coun Foreign Relations; Am Phys Soc. *Res:* Arms control and disarmament; defense policy; military and civilian applications of atomic energy; energy and environmental policy. *Mailing Add:* 3600 Albemarle St NW Washington DC 20008

KEEPIN, GEORGE ROBERT, JR, NUCLEAR PHYSICS, INSTRUMENTATION. *Current Pos:* sr adv, Los Alamos Safeguards & Security Prog, 85-90, FEL, LOS ALAMOS NAT LAB, 85- *Personal Data:* b Oak Park, Ill, Dec 5, 23; m 48, Madge M Twomey; c G Robert, William N, Ardis E (Davis), Mavis E & Denice C. *Educ:* Univ Chicago, PhB, 45; Mass Inst Technol, BS & MS, 47; Northwestern Univ, PhD(physics), 49. *Honors & Awards:* Am Nuclear Soc Spec Award, 73; Distinguished Serv Award, Inst Nuclear Mat Mgmt, 84. *Prof Exp:* Consult, Argonne Nat Lab, 48-49; AEC fel radiation lab, Univ Calif, 50; res physicist, Los Alamos Sci Lab, 52-62, group leader nuclear assay res, 66-75, prog dir nuclear safeguards, 75-79, prog mgr, nuclear safeguards affairs, 79-82; head physics sect, Int Atomic Energy Agency, Vienna, 63-65; spec adv dep dir gen, Int Atomic Energy Agency, 82-85. *Concurrent Pos:* Deleg, Atoms for Peace Conf, Geneva, 55, 64 & 71; tech adv, Int Atomic Energy Agency, Geneva, 64; nat prog chmn, Inst Nuclear Mat Mgt, 74-76, nat chmn, 78-80; app fel, Los Alamos Nat Lab, 85- *Mem:* NY Acad Sci; fel Am Phys Soc; fel Am Nuclear Soc; fel Inst Nuclear Mat Mgt. *Res:* Fission physics; reactor dynamics; pulsed neutron research, nuclear safeguards research and development; development of non-destructive assay techniques for domestic and international inspection and safeguards of fissionable materials; development and implementation of nondestructive assay technology for stringent nuclear safeguards and nonproliferation of nuclear weapons. *Mailing Add:* 600 La Bajada Los Alamos NM 87544

KEEPLER, MANUEL, RANDOM EVOLUTIONS, MARKOV PROCESSES. *Current Pos:* vis prof math & comput sci, 91-96, CHMN, DEPT MATH & COMPUT SCI, NC CENT UNIV, 96- *Personal Data:* b Atlanta, Ga, Nov 4, 44; m 66, Dannie L Hornsby; c Adriane K. *Educ:* Morehouse Col, BS, 65; Columbia Univ, MA, 67; Univ NMex, PhD(math), 73. *Prof Exp:* Asst prof math, Va State Univ, 70-71; assoc prof & chmn, Laugston Univ, 71-73; from assoc prof to prof math & comput sci, SC State Col, 73, chmn dept, 81-90; vis prof math, Cornell Univ, 89-91. *Concurrent Pos:* Vis prof, Dilliard Univ, 76; fel comput, Lawrence Livermore Lab, 77, comput sci, Langley Res Ctr, 81; SC rep, Nat Tech Asn, 80-89; mem, Comput Adv Comt, Comn Higher Educ State SC, 81-86; comt mem, Am Statist Asn, 87-89; exec bd, Pancomp, USA, 87-89; dir, Sloan Proj, 87-89; Pew vis prof, Pew Charitable Trusts, 89-90; pres, SC Acad Sci, 88-89. *Mem:* Consortium Comput Small Col; Am Statist Asn; Inst Math Statist; Math Assoc Am. *Res:* Random evolutions on Markov processes; mathematics; statistics; mathematics and statistical education; educational measurement; black mathematicians and their works; statistics and baseball. *Mailing Add:* Dept Math & Comput Sci NC Cent Univ Durham NC 14853-7901

KEEPORTS, DAVID, PHYSICS & CHEMISTRY EDUCATION, SOFTWARE DEVELOPMENT. *Current Pos:* from asst prof to assoc prof, 82-93, PROF PHYSICS/CHEM, MILLS COL, 93- *Personal Data:* b York, Pa, June 15, 51. *Educ:* Univ Del, BS, 73; Yale Univ, MS, 74; Univ Wash, PhD(phys chem), 82. *Prof Exp:* Lectr physics/chem/math, Quinnipiac Col, 75-79. *Concurrent Pos:* Lectr math, Southern Conn State Col, 76-78; lectr physics/math, Univ New Haven, 76-79. *Mem:* Am Chem Soc; Am Asn Physics Teachers; Sigma Xi. *Res:* Author of numerous publications on the practice and theory of molecular spectroscopy and numerous publications in physics, chemistry and math education journals; development of software for physics education. *Mailing Add:* Dept Chem & Physics Mills Col Oakland CA 94613

KEER, LEON M, CIVIL ENGINEERING, ENGINEERING MECHANICS. *Current Pos:* from asst prof to assoc prof, Northwestern Univ, 64-70, assoc dean grad studies & res, 85-92, chmn dept, 92-97, PROF CIVIL ENG, NORTHWESTERN UNIV, 70- *Personal Data:* b Los Angeles, Calif, Sept 13, 34; m 56, Barbara S Davis; c Patricia (Munro), Jacqueline, Harold & Michael. *Educ:* Calif Inst Technol, BS, 56, MS, 58; Univ Minn, PhD(eng mech), 62. *Prof Exp:* Mem tech staff, Hughes Aircraft Co, 56-59; NATO fel eng mech, Newcastle, 62-63; preceptor, Columbia Univ, 63-64. *Concurrent Pos:* NATO fel, 62-63; Guggenheim sr vis fel, Dept Math, Univ Glasgow, 72-73; fel, Japan Soc Prom Sci, 86; tech ed, J Appl Mech, ASME, 88-92. *Mem:* Fel Am Soc Mech Engrs; Acoust Soc Am; fel Am Soc Civil Engrs; fel Am Acad Mech (secy, 81-85, pres, 88-89). *Res:* Contact stress and fracture problems; contact mechanics; composite materials; wave propagation. *Mailing Add:* Dept Civil Eng Northwestern Univ Evanston IL 60201. *Fax:* 847-491-4011; *E-Mail:* l-keer@nwu.edu

KEES, KENNETH LEWIS, synthesis of non-insulin releasing antidiabetic agents & novel antiinflammatory agents, for more information see previous edition

KEESE, CHARLES RICHARD, CELL BEHAVIOR, CELL MOTILITY. *Current Pos:* SR RES SCIENTIST, RENSSELAER POLYTECH INST, 89-; VPRES, APPL BIOPHYSICS INC, 91- *Personal Data:* b Cooperstown, NY, Mar 4, 44; m 67; c 2. *Educ:* State Univ NY, Albany, BS, 67; Rensselaer Polytech Inst, PhD(biol), 71. *Honors & Awards:* IR-100 Award, 84, Sci Digest, Outstanding Investr, 84-85. *Prof Exp:* From asst prof to assoc prof physics, State Univ NY, Cobleskill, 71-79, prof biol, 71-83; staff scientist, Res & Develop, Gen Elec Corp, 83-89. *Concurrent Pos:* NSF fel sci fac prof develop award, Gen Elec Corp Res & Develop, 77-78; assoc investr, Nat Found Cancer Res, 81-82. *Mem:* Sigma Xi; AAAS; Soc In Vitro Biol. *Res:* Behavior of cells in culture; properties of proteins on surfaces; biosensors; electric cell-substrate impedance sensing. *Mailing Add:* Dept Biol Renesselaer Polytech Univ 110 Eighth St Troy NY 12180. *Fax:* 518-276-2825; *E-Mail:* usergapk@rpit.smts

KEESEE, ROBERT GEORGE, ION CHEMISTRY, AEROSOL SCIENCE. *Current Pos:* ASSOC PROF ATMOSPHERIC SCI, STATE UNIV NY, 91-, ASSOC PROF CHEM, 92- *Personal Data:* b Spokane, Wash, Nov 10, 53. *Educ:* Univ Ariz, BS, 75; Univ Colo, PhD(phys chem), 79. *Prof Exp:* Nat Res Coun res assoc, Space Sci Div, Ames Res Ctr, NASA, 79-81; res asst prof chem, Pa State Univ, 82-91. *Concurrent Pos:* Sr res assoc chem, Univ Colo, 82; assoc prog dir, Atmospheric Chem Prog, NSF, 88-89; res assoc, Atmospheric Sci Res Ctr, Albany, NY, 92- *Mem:* Am Chem Soc; Am Geophys Union; AAAS; Sigma Xi. *Res:* Chemistry of planetary atmospheres; nucleation phenomena; ion solvation; gas-surface interactions; ion-molecule and ion-aerosol interactions; chemical and physical properties of molecular clusters and aerosols. *Mailing Add:* Earth Sci 211 State Univ NY Albany NY 12222-0001. *Fax:* 518-442-5825; *E-Mail:* Bitnet: rgk@albnyvms

KEESEY, RICHARD E, NUTRITION. *Current Pos:* From asst prof to assoc prof, 62-69, PROF, UNIV WIS-MADISON, 69- *Personal Data:* b York, Pa, Oct 14, 34; c Ian. *Educ:* Dartmouth Col, AB, 56; Brown Univ, ScM, 58, PhD, 60. *Concurrent Pos:* Vis lectr, Sydney Univ, 74. *Mem:* Am Inst Nutrit; NAm Soc Study Obesity; Am Psychol Soc; Soc Study Ingestive Behav. *Res:* Physiology of body weight regulation; central nervous control of energy expenditure; obesity and other disorders of energy regulation. *Mailing Add:* Dept Psychol Univ Wis 1202 W Johnson St Madison WI 53706. *Fax:* 608-262-4029; *E-Mail:* rekeesey@macc.wisc.edu

KEESLING, JAMES EDGAR, TOPOLOGY, APPLIED MATHEMATICS. *Current Pos:* from asst prof to assoc prof, 67-75, PROF MATH, UNIV FLA, 75- *Personal Data:* b Indianapolis, Ind, June 26, 42; m 63, Marian E Calley; c James E Jr, Timothy C, Marian E & Ruth E. *Educ:* Univ Miami, Fla, BSIE, 64, MS, 66, PhD(math), 68. *Prof Exp:* Teaching asst, Univ Miami, Fla, 64-65; NASA fel, Univ Miami, 65-67. *Concurrent Pos:* Vis lectr, Univ Ga, 76-77; vis prof, Univ Utah, 91-92. *Mem:* AAAS; Am Math Soc; Math Asn Am; Soc Indust & Appl Math. *Res:* Topology; numerical analysis; biomathematics; over 60 professional publications; dynamical systems. *Mailing Add:* Dept Math Univ Fla PO Box 118105 Gainesville FL 32611-8105. *E-Mail:* jek@math.ufl.edu

KEESOM, PIETER HENDRIK, physics; deceased, see previous edition for last biography

KEETON, T KENT, ANTIHYPERTENSIVE DRUGS, CARDIOVASCULAR PHARMACOLOGY. *Current Pos:* ASSOC PROF PHARMACOL, UNIV TEX HEALTH SCI CTR, 83- *Educ:* Univ Tex, Dallas, PhD(pharmacol), 75. *Mem:* Am Fed Clin Res; Am Soc Pharmacol & Exp Therapeut. *Mailing Add:* Dept Pharmacol Univ Tex Health Sci Ctr 7703 Floyd Curl Dr San Antonio TX 78284-7764. *Fax:* 210-567-4303

KEEVER, CAROLYN ANNE, cellular immunology, immunogenetics, for more information see previous edition

KEEVER, DAVID BRUCE, SYSTEMS DESIGN & SYSTEMS SCIENCE. *Current Pos:* SR SYST ENGR, SCI APPLN INT ORGN, 90- *Personal Data:* b Oakland, Calif, June 29, 53; m 85, Deborah Atkins. *Educ:* Purdue Univ, BS, 75, MS, 76; Univ Va, PhD(syst eng), 84. *Prof Exp:* Res & develop engr, Aerojet Liquid Rocket Corp, 76-78; asst prof & assoc dir, Ctr Interactive Mgt, George Mason Univ, 84-89. *Concurrent Pos:* Vis prof, City Univ, London, Eng, 86- *Mem:* Inst Elec & Electronics Engrs. *Res:* Design theory and methodology using structure methods, group processes and selective computer assisted methodologies. *Mailing Add:* 11503 Hickory Cluster Preston VA 20190. *Fax:* 703-893-2187; *E-Mail:* keeverd@mcc.saic.com

KEEVIL, NORMAN BELL, MINING & METALLURGY. *Current Pos:* Vpres, explor, Teck Corp, Can, 62-68, exec vpres, 68-81, pres & chief exec officer, 81-89, chmn, pres & chief exec officer, 89-94, PRES & CHIEF EXEC OFFICER, TECK CORP, CAN, 94-; CHMN, COMINCO LTD, 86- *Personal Data:* b Cambridge, Mass, Feb 28, 38; m 90, Joan E Macdonald; c Scott, Laura, Jill & Norman B III. *Educ:* Univ Toronto, BA, 59; Univ Calif, Berkeley, PhD, 64. *Hon Degrees:* LLD, Univ BC, 93. *Honors & Awards:* Selwyn G Blaylock Medal, Can Inst Mining & Metall, 90. *Mem:* Can Inst Mining & Metall; Prospectors & Develop Asn; Soc Explor Geophysicists. *Mailing Add:* Teck Corp 200 Burrard St No 700 Vancouver BC V6C 3L9 Can

KEEVIL, THOMAS ALAN, ORGANIC CHEMISTRY, BIOCHEMISTRY. *Current Pos:* from asst prof to assoc prof, 74-86, PROF CHEM, SOUTHERN ORE STATE COL, 86. *Personal Data:* b Long Branch, NJ, Feb 11, 47; m 69, Jean Henderson; c Derek & Melissa. *Educ:* Bucknell Univ, BS, 68; Univ Calif, Berkeley, PhD(chem), 72. *Prof Exp:* Res assoc biochem, Med Sch, Univ Ore, 72-74. *Concurrent Pos:* Res Assoc, Univ Calif, San Diego, 82-83; vis scientist, Oxford Univ, 89-90. *Mem:* Am Chem Soc; AAAS. *Res:* Nickel biochemistry. *Mailing Add:* Dept Chem Southern Ore State Col Ashland OR 97520-5029. *Fax:* 541-552-6415

KEFALIDES, NICHOLAS ALEXANDER, BIOLOGICAL CHEMISTRY, INTERNAL MEDICINE. *Current Pos:* assoc prof, 70-74, assoc dean res, 94-95, PROF MED, UNIV PA, 74-, PROF BIOCHEM & BIOPHYSICS, 75-, DIR CONNECTIVE TISSUE RES INST, 77- *Personal Data:* b Alexandroupolis, Greece, Jan 17, 27; US citizen; m 49, Eugeia Kutsunis; c Alexandra (deceased), Patricia & Paul. *Educ:* Augustana Col, Ill, AB, 51; Univ Ill, BS, 54, MD & MS, 56, PhD(biochem), 65. *Hon Degrees:* MA, Univ Pa, 71; Dr, Univ Reims, France, 87. *Honors & Awards:* Borden Award, 56. *Prof Exp:* Intern med, Res & Educ Hosps, Univ Ill, 56-57; dir res proj in burns, USPHS, Peru, 57-60; resident internal med, Res & Educ Hosps, Univ Ill, 60-63, instr, Col Med, 64-65; from asst prof to assoc prof, La Rabida Inst & Dept Med, Univ Chicago, 65-70. *Concurrent Pos:* USPHS fel, 62-64; assoc attend physician, Cook County Hosp, Chicago, Ill, 62-65; chief infectious dis sect, Vet Admin Hosp, Hines, 64-65; chief infectious dis consult serv, Univ Chicago Hosp, 65-70; attend physician, Philadelphia Gen Hosp, 70-77, dir, Gen Clin Res Ctr, 72-76; dir, Connective Tissue Res Sect, Univ Pa, 75-; vis prof, Oxford Univ, Eng, 77-78 & 84-85; Guggenheim fel, 77-78; mem & chair NIH Pathobiochem Study Sect, 82-86; chair Gordon Res Conf Basement Membranes, 82. *Mem:* Int Soc Nephrology; Am Chem Soc; Am Soc Invest Path; AAAS; Sigma Xi. *Res:* Chemistry of glycoproteins and basement membranes; molecular biology of collagen; metabolism of endothelial cells. *Mailing Add:* Connective Tissue Res Inst Univ Pa 3624 Market St Philadelphia PA 19104-2614

KEFFER, CHARLES JOSEPH, SOLID STATE PHYSICS, CRYSTALLOGRAPHY. *Current Pos:* dean, 73-77, PROVOST, UNIV ST THOMAS, 77- *Personal Data:* b Philadelphia, Pa, Aug 7, 41; m 66, Barbara Franke; c Susan, David, Peter & Dennis. *Educ:* Univ Scranton, BS, 63; Harvard Univ, AM, 64, PhD(solid state physics), 69. *Prof Exp:* From instr to asst prof physics, Univ Scranton, 69-73. *Mem:* Am Phys Soc; Sigma Xi. *Mailing Add:* Univ St Thomas 2115 Summit Ave St Paul MN 55105

KEFFER, JAMES F, MECHANICAL ENGINEERING. *Current Pos:* from asst prof to assoc prof, 64-73, PROF MECH ENG & VPRES RES, UNIV TORONTO, 73- *Personal Data:* b Toronto, Ont, Dec 15, 33; m 55; c 2. *Educ:* Univ Toronto, BASc, 56, MASc, 58, PhD(mech eng), 62. *Prof Exp:* Nat Res Coun Can fel physics, Cambridge Univ, 62-64. *Concurrent Pos:* Consult, Pulp & Paper Res Co Can, 65-; vis prof, Inst Mechnique Statisique Turbulence, Marseille, France, 73-74, Univ Tarragova, Spain, 97- *Mem:* Sigma Xi. *Res:* Fluid mechanics; heat and mass transfer; turbulent flows; wind erosion, building aerodynamics turbulent combustion; environmental pollution. *Mailing Add:* Dept Mech Eng Kings Col Rd Toronto ON M5S 1A1 Can. *E-Mail:* jim.keffer@utoronto.ca

KEFFORD, NOEL PRICE, REGULATION OF GROWTH AND DEVELOPMENT. *Current Pos:* prof bot & chem dept, Univ Hawaii, 65-76, prof plant molecular physiol 82-95, dean & dir coop sci & educ, Col Trop Agr & Human Resources, 80-95, EMER PROF PLANT MOLECULAR PHYSIOL, UNIV HAWAII, 95- *Personal Data:* b Melbourne, Victoria, Australia, Feb 5, 27; m 50, Helen M Hanna; c 3. *Educ:* Univ Melbourne, BSc, 48, MSc, 50; Univ London, PhD(bot, plant physiol), 54. *Prof Exp:* Res officer, Australian Paper Mfrs, Ltd, 50-51; res officer, Div Plant Indust, Commonwealth Sci & Indust Res Orgn, 54-59, sr res officer, 59-64, prin res officer, 64-65. *Concurrent Pos:* Fulbright sr res fel & res assoc biol, Yale Univ, 62-63; res assoc, Univ Calif, Santa Cruz, 71; actg assoc dir, Hawaii Agr Exp Sta, 76-80; dir, Hawaii Inst Trop Agr & Human Resources, 80-82. *Mem:* Sigma Xi. *Res:* Plant growth and development; hormonal regulation; research management and administration. *Mailing Add:* Col Trop Agr & Human Resources 3050 Maile Way Honolulu HI 96822. *Fax:* 808-956-9105; *E-Mail:* keffordn@avax.ctahr.hawaii.edu

KEGEL, GUNTER HEINRICH REINHARD, NUCLEAR PHYSICS. *Current Pos:* prof physics, Univ Lowell, 64-66, prof nuclear eng, 66-71, chmn dept physics & appl physics, 71-81, PROF PHYSICS, UNIV LOWELL, 71- *Personal Data:* b Herborn, Ger, June 16, 29; m 57; c 2. *Educ:* Rio de Janeiro, BS, 51; Mass Inst Technol, PhD(physics), 61. *Prof Exp:* Engr, Nat Inst Technol, Brazil, 51-56; prof physics, Cath Univ, Rio de Janeiro, 61-64. *Concurrent Pos:* Prof, Rio de Janeiro, 52-56 & 61-64; res asst, Lab Nuclear Sci, Mass Inst Technol, 58-61; consult, Millipore Corp, Bedford, Mass, 69-70. *Mem:* Brazilian Acad Sci; Am Phys Soc; Electrochem Soc; Am Nuclear Soc; Inst Elec & Electronics Engrs; Am Vacuum Soc; Mat Res Soc. *Res:* Nuclear spectroscopy; Rutherford backscattering spectroscopy (RBS); proton induced x-ray emission (PIXE); neutron physics; neutron radiation damage. *Mailing Add:* 55 Williams Rd Lexington MA 02173

KEGELES, GERSON, BIOPHYSICAL CHEMISTRY. *Current Pos:* prof, 68-82, EMER PROF SECT BIOCHEM & BIOPHYS, UNIV CONN, 82- *Personal Data:* b New Haven, Conn, Apr 23, 17; m 44; c 5. *Educ:* Yale Univ, BS, 37, PhD(phys chem), 40. *Prof Exp:* Fel, Yale Univ, 40-41; fel, Univ Wis, 45-47; phys chemist, Nat Cancer Inst, 47-51; from assoc prof to prof chem, Clark Univ, 51-68, chmn, Chem Dept, 58-61. *Concurrent Pos:* Vis prof chem, Yale Univ, 68; mem, Study Sect Biophys Chem, NIH, 67-70. *Mem:* Am Chem Soc; Biophys Soc; Am Acad Arts & Sci. *Res:* Ultracentrifugation; countercurrent distribution; equilibria and kinetics of protein interactions; diffusion and optical methods for its study; pressure effects in protein transport experiments. *Mailing Add:* RFD 1 Box 156 Groveton NH 03582

KEGELES, LAWRENCE STEVEN, BRAIN IMAGING, THEORETICAL ASTROPHYSICS. *Current Pos:* RES PSYCHIATRIST, COLUMBIA PRESBY HOSP, 91- *Personal Data:* b Madison, Wis, Feb 9, 47; m 87, Wendy Winder; c Laura. *Educ:* Princeton Univ, AB, 69; Univ Pa, PhD(physics), 74, Mount Sinai Sch Med, MD, 91. *Prof Exp:* Res assoc physics, Univ Pa & Naval Res Lab, 74-76 & Univ Alta, 76-78; res assoc, Stevens Inst Technol, 78-80; mem tech staff, Bell Labs, 81-87. *Mem:* Sigma Xi; NY Acad Sci; Am Phys Soc. *Res:* Perturbations of spacetimes; equations of motion and radiation damping; tracer kinetics in nuclear medicine; functional brain imaging. *Mailing Add:* 127 W 96th St Apt 13D New York NY 10025-6430

KEGELMAN, MATTHEW ROLAND, ELECTROCHEMISTRY, POLYMER CHEMISTRY. *Current Pos:* RETIRED. *Personal Data:* b New York, NY, June 24, 28; m 53; c 10. *Educ:* Fordham Univ, BS, 48, MS, 49, PhD(org chem), 53. *Prof Exp:* From res chemist to sr res chemist, E I du Pont de Nemours & Co, 53-71, res assoc petrochem dept, 71-78, sr res assoc, 71-90. *Concurrent Pos:* Prin investr, Dielectric Gases Proj, Elec Power Res Inst. *Mem:* AAAS; Am Chem Soc; Sigma Xi. *Res:* Heterocyclics; pinacol rearrangement; petroleum chemicals; dielectric fluids; high-energy batteries; electro-organic synthesis; polymer intermediates; polyesters; polyamides. *Mailing Add:* 204 N Pembrey Dr Wilmington DE 19803-2005

KEGLEY, ELIZABETH BRIGHT, NUTRITIONAL MODIFICATION OF IMMUNE FUNCTION, BEEF CATTLE NUTRITION. *Current Pos:* ASST PROF, DEPT ANIMAL SCI, UNIV ARK, 96- *Personal Data:* b Staunton, Va, Oct 22, 63; m 95, Tim Johnson. *Educ:* Va Inst Technol, BS, 86; NC State Univ, MS, 89, PhD(nutrit), 96. *Mem:* Am Soc Animal Sci; Am Dairy Sci Asn. *Res:* Nutritional modification of the immune response of cattle. *Mailing Add:* 103 E Animal Sci Bldg Univ Ark Fayetteville AR 72701

KEHEW, ALAN EVERETT, HYDROGEOCHEMISTRY, CONTAMINANT HYDROGEOLOGY. *Current Pos:* ASSOC PROF GEOL, WESTERN MICH UNIV, 86- *Personal Data:* b Pittsburgh, Pa, Sept 17, 47; m 74; c 3. *Educ:* Bucknell Univ, BS, 69; Montana State Univ, MS, 71; Univ Idaho, PhD(geol), 77. *Prof Exp:* Geologist, NDak Geol Surv, 77-80; from asst prof to assoc prof geol, Univ NDak, 80-84. *Mem:* Geol Soc Am; Nat Water Well Asn; Am Geophys Union; Am Quaternary Asn. *Res:* Groundwater contamination by waste disposal; chemical evolution of groundwater in glacial terrains. *Mailing Add:* 1201 Oliver St Western Mich Univ Kalamazoo MI 49008-3804

KEHL, THEODORE H, COMPUTER SCIENCE, BIOPHYSICS. *Current Pos:* NIH fel, Sch Med, Univ Wash 61-63, from instr to assoc prof physiol & biophys, 63-73, assoc prof, 73-77, PROF PHYSIOL, BIOPHYS & COMPUT SCI, SCH MED, UNIV WASH, 77- *Personal Data:* b Racine, Wis, Apr 1, 33; m 54; c 2. *Educ:* Univ Wis, BS, 56, MS, 58, PhD(zool), 61. *Prof Exp:* Wis Alumni Res Found res assoc, Univ Wis, 56-61, NIH fel, 61. *Mem:* AAAS; Asn Comput Mach. *Res:* Implementation of computer science to quantitative physiology and biophysics. *Mailing Add:* 9116 20th Ave NE Seattle WA 98115

KEHL, WILLIAM BRUNNER, COMPUTER SCIENCE. *Current Pos:* RETIRED. *Personal Data:* b Pittsburgh, Pa, Apr 8, 19; m 44; c 2. *Educ:* Harvard Univ, SB, 40, AM, 42 & 48. *Prof Exp:* Instr math, Ga Inst Tech, 43-46; instr, Mass Inst Technol, 48-54, head anal group, Instrumentation Lab, 54-56; prof comput sci & dir comput & data processing ctr, Univ Pittsburgh, 56-66; assoc prof elec eng & assoc dir comput ctr, Mass Inst Technol, 66-67; dir academic computing, Univ Calif, Los Angeles, 67-93. *Concurrent Pos:* Consult, USAF, 57-59 & comt use of comput, Nat Acad Sci; consult, NSF & NIH; mem sci adv bd, Regional Indust Develop Corp. *Mem:* Asn Comput Mach. *Res:* Computers; applied mathematics. *Mailing Add:* 1201 Corsica Dr Pacific Palisades CA 90272

KEHLENBECK, MANFRED MAX, STRUCTURAL GEOLOGY, METAMORPHIC GEOLOGY. *Current Pos:* from asst prof to assoc prof, 71-86, PROF GEOL, LAKEHEAD UNIV, 86- *Personal Data:* b Bremen, Ger, Jan 16, 37; US citizen; m 68, Elenore E Kurz. *Educ:* Hofstra Univ, BA, 59; Syracuse Univ, MS, 64; Queen's Univ, PhD(geol), 71. *Prof Exp:* Vis prof geol, Univ NB, 69-70. *Concurrent Pos:* Nat Res Coun Can grant, 72-; dept chmn, Lakehead Univ, 76-82 & 91-97; Northern Ont Rural Develop Agreement grant, 83-85; Energy Mines & Resources grant, 86- *Mem:* Am Geol Inst; Geol Asn Can. *Res:* Structural evolution of Archean gneissic terrains; polyphase folding in volcano sedimentary belts in northwestern Ontario; archean subprovince margins and boundaries; transpressional basins. *Mailing Add:* Dept Geol Lakehead Univ Thunder Bay ON P7B 5E1 Can. *Fax:* 807-346-7853; *E-Mail:* mkehlenb@mist.lakeheadu.ca

KEHLER, PHILIP LEROY, STRATIGRAPHY, SEDIMENTOLOGY. *Current Pos:* chairperson, 73-78, ASSOC PROF EARTH SCI, UNIV ARK, LITTLE ROCK, 73-, CHAIRPERSON, 83- *Personal Data:* b Lyons, NY, June 15, 36; m 65; c 2. *Educ:* Purdue Univ, BS, 59, MS, 61; Southern Methodist Univ, PhD(geol), 70. *Prof Exp:* Asst, Southern Methodist Univ, 65-69; asst prof geol, ETex State Univ, 69-73, fac res grant, 71-72. *Concurrent Pos:* NSF student originated studies grant, 75; lignite consult, Shell Mining, 79-81; young scholar, NSF, 89-90. *Mem:* Geol Soc Am; Soc Econ Paleontologists & Mineralogists; Nat Asn Geol Teachers. *Res:* Regional studies of Jurassic and Cretaceous rocks in western North America; stratigraphic relationships associated with widespread unconformities within these rocks; statigraphic relationships, Ouachita Mountains of Arkansas and Oklahoma; earthquake mitigation in northeast Arkansas. *Mailing Add:* Twin Bluffs Loop Little Rock AR 72212

KEHOE, BRANDT, COMPUTATIONAL NEUROSCIENCE. *Current Pos:* dean, Sch Natural Sci, 72-83, dept chmn comput sci, 87-89, PROF PHYSICS, CALIF STATE UNIV, FRESNO, 72-, DEPT CHMN PHYSICS, 89- *Personal Data:* b Cleveland, Ohio, Nov 20, 33; m 61, Sandra K Robinson; c Noel E & Christopher J. *Educ:* Cornell Univ, BA, 56; Univ Wis, MS, 59, PhD(physics), 63. *Prof Exp:* Res asst physics, Los Alamos Sci Lab, 56-57; from asst prof to assoc prof, Univ Md, 62-72; pres, Deep Springs Col, 83-87. *Mem:* Am Asn Physics Teachers; AAAS. *Res:* Computational neuroscience; neural networks. *Mailing Add:* 4793 N Sunset Fresno CA 93704. *E-Mail:* brandtk@csufresno.edu

KEHOE, THOMAS J, ANALYTICAL CHEMISTRY, INORGANIC CHEMISTRY. *Current Pos:* appln engr, 54-61, MGR APPLN ENG, BECKMAN INSTRUMENTS, INC, 61- *Personal Data:* b Bisbee, Ariz, June 16, 19; m 50; c 6. *Educ:* Loyola Univ, BS, 41. *Prof Exp:* Res chemist, Am Potash & Chem Co, 42-48, lab supvr, 48-50; consult waste treatment, Pomeroy & Assocs, 50-54. *Mem:* Fel Instrument Soc Am (pres, 69-70); Am Inst Chem; Am Chem Soc; Am Inst Chem Eng. *Res:* Process analytical instrumentation; industrial waste treatment; phase rule studies in inorganic chemistry of Searles Lake brine. *Mailing Add:* 1506 Victoria Way Placentia CA 92670-2335

KEHR, AUGUST ERNEST, PLANT GENETICS. *Current Pos:* RETIRED. *Personal Data:* b Frankfort, Ky, Mar 2, 14; m 42, Mary L Coon; c Janet M (Flick). *Educ:* Cornell Univ, BS, 37, MS, 47, PhD, 50. *Honors & Awards:* Gold Medal, Rhododendron Soc, 77, Pioneer Award; B Y Morrison Lectr & Medal, 82; D Todd Gresham Award, Magnolia Soc, 92. *Prof Exp:* Assoc prof, La State Univ, Baton Rouge, 50-54; prof, Iowa State Univ, Ames, 54-58; br chief, Agr Res Serv, USDA, Beltsville, Md, 58-72, mem nat prog staff, 72-78. *Concurrent Pos:* Agr team mem, Egypt, 75 & 80, China, 77. *Mem:* Fel Am Soc Hort Sci; Am Genetics Asn (pres, 63-65); Magnolia Soc; Sigma Xi. *Res:* Plant physiology; development of azaleas, rhododendrons and magnolias. *Mailing Add:* 240 Tranquility Pl Hendersonville NC 28739-9336

KEHR, CLIFTON LEROY, ORGANIC CHEMISTRY, POLYMER CHEMISTRY. *Current Pos:* CONSULT POLYMER TECHNOL, 91- *Personal Data:* b Brodbecks, Pa, May 25, 26; m 48, Louise Walterick; c Alan D, David D & Alison J. *Educ:* Gettysburg Col, AB, 49; Univ Del, MS, 50, PhD(org chem), 52. *Prof Exp:* Res asst synthetic org chem, Forrestal Res Ctr, Princeton Univ, 52-53; res chemist, Org Chem Dept, E I du Pont de Nemours & Co, 53-57, elastomers chem dept, 57-59; res chemist, Res Div, Washington Res Ctr, W R Grace & Co, 59-91, res dir, 69-91. *Mem:* Am Chem Soc; Sigma Xi. *Res:* Mechanisms of organic reactions; polyurethanes; elastomers; polyolefins; isocyanate chemistry; polymers from chloroprene and related monomers; foam technology; radiation curable polymers; water based coatings; biocompatible polymers; medical polymers. *Mailing Add:* RR 1 Box 1639 Brodbecks PA 17329-9628. *Fax:* 717-227-0657; *E-Mail:* clkehr@worldnet.att.net

KEHRER, JAMES PAUL, PULMONARY TOXICOLOGY, CARDIAC TOXICOLOGY. *Current Pos:* from asst prof to assoc prof, 80-90, PROF PHARMACOL & TOXICOL, COL PHARM, UNIV TEX, AUSTIN, 90- *Personal Data:* b Watertown, Wis, Aug 25, 51; m 77; c 2. *Educ:* Purdue Univ, BS, 74; Univ Iowa, PhD(pharm), 78. *Honors & Awards:* Achievement Award, Soc Toxicol, 89. *Prof Exp:* Investr, Biol Div, Oak Ridge Nat Lab, 78-80. *Concurrent Pos:* Consult, Radian Corp, 82-84; res career develop award, NIH, 84-89; Gustavus Pfeiffer Centennial fel pharmocol, 85-; assoc ed rev, Toxicol Letters, 88- *Mem:* Soc Toxicol; AAAS; Am Soc Pharmacol & Theraput. *Res:* Collagen synthesis and degradation during the development of pulmonary fibrosis after acute lung damage; lung toxicity of anti-cancer drugs; oxidative stress in cardiac reperfusion injury. *Mailing Add:* Div Pharmacol & Toxicol Univ Tex Col Pharm Austin TX 78712-1074. *Fax:* 512-471-5002

KEHRES, PAUL W(ILLIAM), analytical chemistry, materials testing; deceased, see previous edition for last biography

KEHRL, HOWARD H, MECHANICAL ENGINEERING. *Current Pos:* RETIRED. *Personal Data:* b Detroit, Mich, Feb 2, 23. *Educ:* Ill Inst Technol, BS, 44; Univ Notre Dame, MS, 48; Mass Inst Technol, MS, 60. *Prof Exp:* Vpres & gen mgr, Oldsmobile Div, Gen Motors Corp, 72-73, vpres & group exec, 73-74, exec vpres, 74-81, vchmn, 81-91. *Mem:* Nat Acad Eng; Soc Automotive Engrs; Motor Vehicle Mfrs Asn US. *Mailing Add:* 5157 Country Club Shores Walloon Lake MI 49796

KEICHER, WILLIAM EUGENE, ELECTRO-OPTICAL SYSTEMS, LASER RADAR SYSTEMS. *Current Pos:* staff mem, Lincoln Labs, Mass Inst Technol, 75-83, asst group leader, 83-85, group leader, 85-93, ASSOC GROUP LEADER, LINCOLN LABS, MASS INST TECHNOL, 93- *Personal Data:* b Pittsburgh, Pa, Dec 28, 47; m 72, Barbara M Gurgacz; c Lisa A, Kathy M & William M. *Educ:* Carnegie-Mellon Univ, BS, 69, MS, 70, PhD(elec eng), 74. *Prof Exp:* Elec engr, Manned Spacecraft Ctr, NASA, 69; tech asst, Kodak Res Labs, 70; sr elec engr, CBS Labs, 73-75,. *Mem:* Sr mem Inst Elec & Electronics Engrs; Optical Soc Am. *Res:* Long range, high power laser radar systems; imaging radar; infrared detection systems; electro-optic modulators; atmospheric propagation; microwave radar. *Mailing Add:* 6 Winn Valley Dr Burlington MA 01803. *Fax:* 781-981-5359; *E-Mail:* keicher@ll.mit.edu

KEIDEL, FREDERICK ANDREW, PHYSICAL CHEMISTRY. *Current Pos:* CONSULT, 85- *Personal Data:* b New Brunswick, NJ, Feb 4, 26. *Educ:* Rutgers Univ, BS, 46; Cornell Univ, PhD(phys chem), 51. *Honors & Awards:* Longstreth Medal, Franklin Inst, 60. *Prof Exp:* Res engr phys chem, 51-56; res proj engr, E I du Pont de Nemours & Co, Inc, 56-60, sr res phys chemist, 61-80, res assoc, 80-85. *Mem:* Am Chem Soc; Sigma Xi; Mineral Soc Am; Am Inst Chemists. *Res:* Electron diffraction; electrochemical processes; chemical physics of surfaces; mineralogy. *Mailing Add:* 705 Prospect Ave Wilmington DE 19808

KEIDERLING, TIMOTHY ALLEN, SPECTROSCOPY, PROTEIN CONFORMATION. *Current Pos:* from asst prof to assoc prof, 76-85, PROF CHEM, UNIV ILL, CHICAGO, 85- *Personal Data:* b Waterloo, Iowa, June 22, 47; m 76, Candace R Crawford; c Michael. *Educ:* Loras Col, BS, 69; Princeton Univ, MA, 71, PhD(phys chem), 74. *Prof Exp:* Res assoc optical activity, Univ Southern Calif, 73-76. *Concurrent Pos:* Guest prof, Max Planck Inst Quantenoptik; Fulbright fel, WGer, 84; sr vis, Oxford Univ, 94. *Mem:* Am Chem Soc; Am Phys Soc; Biophys Soc; Soc Appl Spectros; Protein Soc. *Res:* Spectroscopic studies of protein and nucleic acid conformations; magnetic vibrational circular dichroism and associated vibronic coupling effects; experimental and theoretical studies of vibrational optical activity of small chiral molecules. *Mailing Add:* Univ Ill Dept Chem M/C 111 845 W Taylor Chicago IL 60607-7061. *Fax:* 312-996-0431; *E-Mail:* tak@uic.edu

KEIFFER, DAVID GOFORTH, PHYSICS. *Current Pos:* ASSOC PROF PHYSICS, LOYOLA UNIV, LA, 64-, CHMN DEPT, 73- *Personal Data:* b New Orleans, La, July 24, 31; m 56; c 6. *Educ:* Loyola Univ, La, BS, 52; Univ Notre Dame, MS, 54, PhD(physics), 56. *Prof Exp:* Asst prof physics, Canisius Col, 56-64. *Mem:* Am Phys Soc. *Res:* Radiation damage in glass. *Mailing Add:* Dept Physics Loyola Univ New Orleans LA 70118

KEIGHER, WILLIAM FRANCIS, ALGEBRA. *Current Pos:* ASST PROF MATH, RUTGERS UNIV, 78- *Personal Data:* b Montclair, NJ, Oct 28, 45; m 68; c 3. *Educ:* Montclair State Col, BA, 67; Univ Ill, AM, 69, PhD(math), 73. *Prof Exp:* Lectr math, Southern Ill Univ, Carbondale, 73-74; asst prof mat, Univ Tenn, Knoxville, 74-78. *Mem:* Am Math Soc; Math Asn Am. *Res:* Category theory and its applications to differential algebra. *Mailing Add:* Dept Math & Comput Sci Rutgers Univ 101 Warren St Newark NJ 07102-3105

KEIGHIN, CHARLES WILLIAM, GEOCHEMISTRY, ECONOMIC GEOLOGY. *Current Pos:* GEOLOGIST, US GEOL SURV, DENVER, 74- *Personal Data:* b Pontiac, Ill, Aug 29, 32; m 60; c 3. *Educ:* Oberlin Col, BA, 54; Univ Colo, MS, 60, PhD(geol), 66. *Prof Exp:* Res mineralogist, Cerro de Pasco Corp, La Oroya, Peru, SAm, 60-62, geologist, 62-63; asst prof geol, Northern Ill Univ, 66-72; vis asst prof geol & mineral, Ohio State Univ, 72-73; asst prof geosci, Northeastern La Univ, 73-74. *Mem:* Am Asn Petrol Geologists; Soc Econ Paleontologists & Mineralogists; Soc Petrol Engrs; Can Soc Petrol Geologists. *Res:* Trace element migration; diagenesis of clastic rocks; inorganic geochemistry; oil shale resource evaluation. *Mailing Add:* 1666 S Holland Ct Lakewood CO 80232

KEIGLER, JOHN EDWARD, aerospace engineering, electrical engineering; deceased, see previous edition for last biography

KEIHN, FREDERICK GEORGE, SOLID STATE CHEMISTRY. *Current Pos:* PROF CHEM, BRIDGEWATER COL, 67- *Personal Data:* b Scranton, Pa, Aug 29, 23; m 48; c 4. *Educ:* Randolph Macon Col, BS, 47; Lehigh Univ, MS, 49; Syracuse Univ, PhD(chem), 53. *Prof Exp:* Asst electrochem, Lehigh Univ, 48-49; asst chem, Syracuse Univ, 49-51; inorg chemist electronics lab, Gen Elec Co, 52-57; res chemist ceramics lab, Corning Glass Works, 57-59; mem staff, Union Carbide Res Inst, NY, 59-65; assoc prof chem, Presby Col, SC, 65-67. *Mem:* AAAS; Am Chem Soc; Am Crystallog Asn. *Res:* Double crystal x-ray diffractometry high temperature phase and mechanical properties studies; physical science curriculum development; applied ecology. *Mailing Add:* 1551 Central Ave Harrisonburg VA 22801-2808

KEIL, ALFRED ADOLF HEINRICH, ENGINEERING. *Current Pos:* prof & head, Dept Naval Archit & Marine Eng, Mass Inst Technol, 66-71, dean, Sch Eng, 71-77, Ford prof eng, 77-78, EMER PROF ENG, MASS INST TECHNOL, 78- *Personal Data:* b Kdhradswaldau, Ger, May 1, 13; c 2. *Educ:* Univ Breslau, GDr, 39. *Honors & Awards:* Gold Medal, Am Soc Naval Eng, 64; Gibbs Bros Gold Medal, Naval Archit-Nat Acad Sci, 67. *Prof Exp:* Chief scientist underwater explosive res, Norfolk Naval Shipyard, 47-59; tech dir, Struct Mech, 59-63, tech dir basin, David Taylor Model Basin, 63-66. *Mem:* Nat Acad Eng; Am Soc Naval Eng. *Mailing Add:* 39 Hillside Towers Belmont MA 02178

KEIL, DAVID JOHN, PLANT TAXONOMY. *Current Pos:* lectr, 76-78, from asst prof to assoc prof, 78-85, PROF BIOL, CALIF POLYTECH STATE UNIV, 85- *Personal Data:* b Elmhurst, Ill, Dec 13, 46; m 89, Kathleen A Faustini; c Michaela Alice & Kaitlyn Ruth. *Educ:* Ariz State Univ, BS, 68, MS, 70; Ohio State Univ, PhD(bot), 73. *Prof Exp:* Vis asst prof biol, Grand Valley State Col, 73-74; asst prof, Franklin Col, 75. *Concurrent Pos:* Vis assoc prof bot, Ohio State Univ, 80; ed, Madrono, 88-90. *Mem:* Bot Soc Am; Am Soc Plant Taxon; Int Asn Plant Taxon; Sigma Xi; Soc Syst Biologists. *Res:* Systematics of compositae; cytology, taxonomy, evolution and biogeography of genus Pectis; systematics of genus Cirsium; floristics. *Mailing Add:* Dept Biol Sci Calif Polytech State Univ San Luis Obispo CA 93407. *Fax:* 805-756-1419; *E-Mail:* dkeil@oboe.calpoly.edu

KEIL, JULIAN E, EPIDEMIOLOGY, CARDIOVASCULAR EPIDEMIOLOGY. *Current Pos:* instr, Sch Pub Health, Univ SC, 67-69, assoc, 70-72, asst prof prev med, 73-77, from assoc prof to prof, 77-92, EMER PROF EPIDEMIOL, SCH PUB HEALTH, UNIV SC, 93- *Personal Data:* b Charleston, SC, Oct 30, 26; m 48, Barbara Willis; c Barbara A (Burgis), Christopher & Jean M (Rigsby). *Educ:* Clemson Univ, BS, 49, MS, 68; Univ NC, Chapel Hill, PhD(epidemiol), 75. *Prof Exp:* Entomologist, W R Grace & Co, 49-55, mgr, Pesticide Dept, 56-67. *Concurrent Pos:* Coun epidemiol, Am Heart Asn. *Mem:* Am Pub Health Asn; Soc Epidemiol Res; Int Epidemiol Asn. *Res:* Cardiovascular epidemiology; environmental epidemiology; epidemiology of coronary disease in blacks and whites. *Mailing Add:* 16 Sheridan Rd Charleston SC 29407

KEIL, KLAUS, METEORITICS, PETROLOGY. *Current Pos:* HEAD & PROF, UNIV HAWAII, 90- *Personal Data:* b Hamburg, Ger, Nov 15, 34; US citizen; m 61, 84; c 2. *Educ:* Univ Jena, MSc, 58; Univ Mainz, PhD(mineral, meteoritics), 61. *Honors & Awards:* Apollo Achievement Award, NASA, 70; George P Merrill Award, Nat Acad Sci, 70; John Wesley Powell invited lectr, Ariz Acad Sci, 71; NASA Except Sci Achievement Medal, 77; Group Achievement Award, NASA, 84; Leonard Medal, Meteoritical Soc, 88. *Prof Exp:* Res assoc & instr mineral & meteoritics, Mineral Inst, Univ Jena, 58-60; res assoc, Meteoritics & Cosmochem, Max Planck Inst Chem, 61 & Univ Calif, San Diego, 61-63; Nat Acad Sci-Nat Res Coun resident res assoc, Space Sci Div, Ames Res Ctr, NASA, 63-64, staff res scientist, 64-68; lectr, Dept Geol, San Jose State Col, 66-67; prof geol & dir inst meteorites, Univ NMex, 68-90, Presidential prof, 85-90, chmn, Dept Geol, 86-89. *Concurrent Pos:* Mem, Nat Steering Comt, 66-68; prin investr, Electron Microprobe Study of Returned Lunar Sample, NASA, 67-68, mem planetology adv subcomt, space sci & applns steering comt, 68; US rep, Comt Cosmic Mineral, Int Mineral Asn, 67-70, secy, 70-; rep, Comt Meteorites, Int Union Geol Sci, 68-72; mem lunar sci review bd, 71-73; mem & chmn, US Nat Comt Geochem, Nat Acad Sci, 71-75; invited speaker, Int Geol Cong, 72; assoc ed, Chem Geol, 73-85 & J Geophys Res, 82-85, & J Earth Chem, 84-86; mem geophys res bd, Nat Acad Sci, 74-75; mem & chmn, Lunar Sample Anal Planning Team, 74-78 & chmn facil subcomt, 75-76; distinguished vis prof, Inst Earth Sci, 74, 76, 77 & 78 & Dept Astonomy & Geophys, Univ Sao Paulo, Brazil, 81; mem, Viking Mars Flight Team, 76-78; vis assoc geochem, Div Geol Planet Sci, Calif Inst Technol, 76-77; honorary res assoc, Dept Mineral Sci, Am Mus Natural Hist, 77-; mem, Lunar & Planet, Sci Coun, 77-79, 87-90, chmn, 80-84; mem, Antarctic Meteorite Working Group, NSF, 78-84; dir, Caswell Silver Found, Univ NMex, 80-90; distinguished vis scientist, Jet Propulsion Lab, Pasadena, 81; ann res lectr, Univ NMex, 81; mem adv comt, Comparative Planetology, Inst Geol Sci, 81-82, & Int Geophys, Planet, Physics, Univ Calif, Los Alamos Nat Lab, 84-90; mem, NASA adv comt, minority graduate researchers, 84; chmn rev panel, space sta planetology exp & Mars observer, NASA, 85; mem panel, Lunar & Planetology, Geoscience Review, 87-; assoc ed, Meteoritics. *Mem:* Fel AAAS; Geol Soc Brazil; Ger Mineral Soc; Microbeam Anal Soc; Int Asn Geochem & Cosmochem (secy, 72-76); Planetary Soc; fel Mineral Soc; Am Geophys Union; Geochemical Soc; fel Meteoritical Soc (pres, 68-70). *Res:* Lunar geology; chemistry, geology and mineralogy of extraterrestrial materials, such as meteorites, cosmic dust and lunar surface; application of electron microprobe, laser microprobe and ion microprobe to study of rocks and minerals; geology of Mars. *Mailing Add:* Dept Geol & Geophysics Univ Hawaii Honolulu HI 96822-2270. *Fax:* 808-956-6322; *E-Mail:* keil@baby.pgd.hawaii.edu

KEIL, LANNY CHARLES, PHYSIOLOGY, ENDOCRINOLOGY. *Current Pos:* RETIRED. *Personal Data:* b Elgin, Nebr, Apr 16, 36; m 66; c 3. *Educ:* Creighton Univ, BS, 63, MS, 66; Univ Calif, Davis, PhD(physiol), 73. *Prof Exp:* Res scientist, Physiol Br, Ames Res Ctr NASA, 67-72, res scientist endocrinol, Biomed Res Div, 72-92. *Mem:* Edocrine Soc; AAAS; Am Physiol Soc. *Res:* Hormonal control of water and electrolyte metabolism; gravitational biology; acceleration stress physiology. *Mailing Add:* 1637 Kennewick Dr Sunnyvale CA 94087-4129

KEIL, ROBERT GERALD, PHYSICAL CHEMISTRY. *Current Pos:* from asst prof to assoc prof, 69-84, chmn, 88-91, PROF CHEM, UNIV DAYTON, 84-, ASSOC DEAN, 91- *Personal Data:* b New Rochelle, NY, May 7, 41; m 82, Paula R Preskih; c 2. *Educ:* Villanova Univ, BS, 63; Temple Univ, PhD(phys chem), 67. *Prof Exp:* Res chemist, Org Chem Dept, E I du Pont de Nemours & Co, Inc, 67-69. *Concurrent Pos:* Alt counr, Dayton Sect, Am Chem Soc. *Mem:* Electrochem Soc; Am Chem Soc; Soc Electroanal Chem. *Res:* Anodic oxide films; voltammetry in aqueous and nonaqueous solutions; physical chemistry; infrared spectroscopy. *Mailing Add:* Dept Chem Univ Dayton 300 College Park Dayton OH 45469-2357. *Fax:* 513-229-2635

KEIL, STEPHEN LESLEY, SOLAR PHYSICS. *Current Pos:* Nat Acad Sci-Nat Res Coun res fel, Air Force Geophysics Lab, 78-80, scholar physicist, 80-83, RES ASSOC SOLAR PHYSICS, AIR FORCE CAMBRIDGE RES LAB, SACRAMENTO PEAK OBSERV, 75-, CHIEF, GEOPHYSICS DIR, SOLAR RES BR, 83- *Personal Data:* b Billings, Mont, Feb 21, 47; m 71; c 2. *Educ:* Univ Calif, Berkeley, AB, 69; Boston Univ, AM, 71, PhD(physics & astron), 75. *Concurrent Pos:* Res fel appl math, Univ Sydney, Australia, 76-77. *Mem:* Am Astron Soc; Int Astron Union. *Res:* Solar atmospheric inhomogenonities; multidimensional stellar atmospheres; high resolution solar observations; mathematical models of solar atmospheric structure. *Mailing Add:* Geophys Directurate Sacramento Peak Observ Sunspot NM 88349. *Fax:* 505-434-7029; *E-Mail:* skeil@sunspot.noao.edu

KEIL, THOMAS H, SOLID STATE PHYSICS. *Current Pos:* asst prof, 67-72, assoc prof & chmn dept physics, 72-78, PROF PHYSICS, WORCESTER POLYTECH INST, 78- *Personal Data:* b Philadelphia, Pa, July 24, 39; m 64. *Educ:* Calif Inst Technol, BS, 61; Univ Rochester, PhD(optics), 65. *Prof Exp:* Sloan fel solid state physics, Princeton Univ, 65-66, Sloan vis lectr, 66-67. *Mem:* Am Phys Soc; Sigma Xi. *Res:* Solid state theory; optics. *Mailing Add:* Dept Physics Worcester Polytech Inst Worcester MA 01609

KEILIN, BERTRAM, water chemistry, psychotherapy; deceased, see previous edition for last biography

KEILSON, JULIAN, MATHEMATICAL STATISTICS, OPERATIONS RESEARCH. *Current Pos:* prof statist & opers res, 66-87, EMER PROF & SR RES ASSOC, UNIV ROCHESTER, 92- *Personal Data:* b Brooklyn, NY, Nov 19, 24; m 54, Paula; c 2. *Educ:* Brooklyn Col, BS, 47; Harvard Univ, PhD(physics), 50. *Prof Exp:* Res fel electronics, Harvard Univ, 50-52; mem staff, Lincoln Lab, Mass Inst Technol, 52-56; staff consult & sr eng specialist, Gen Tel & Electronics Labs, Inc, 56-62, sr scientist, 62-66. *Concurrent Pos:* Lectr, Boston Univ, 56-; res fel, Univ Birmingham, 63; dir, Ctr Syst Sci; ed, Stochastic Processes & Their Appln, 73-79; sr scientist, GTE Labs, 87-92; adj prof opers res, Mass Inst Technol, 87-92, adj emer prof, 92- *Mem:* Am Phys Soc; sr mem Inst Elec & Electronics Engrs; fel Inst Math Statist; fel Royal Statist Soc; fel Int Statist Inst; Opers Res Soc Am; fel Japan Soc Prom Sci. *Res:* Semiconductor diffusion; electronic noise; Brownian motion; information theory; stochastic processes; electromagnetic propagation; probability theory; queuing theory; reliability theory; rarity and exponentiality. *Mailing Add:* William E Simon Grad Sch Bus Admin Univ Rochester Rochester NY 14627. *E-Mail:* keilson@mail.ssb.rochester.edu

KEILY, HUBERT JOSEPH, DRUG REGULATORY AFFAIRS & QUALITY OPERATIONS. *Current Pos:* CONSULT DRUG REGULATORY AFFAIRS, 93- *Personal Data:* b Worcester, Mass, Jan 29, 21; m 45, 71, Rosemary K Almer; c Mark & Lea. *Educ:* Niagra Univ, BS, 49; Union Col, MS, 51; Mass Inst Technol, PhD(anal chem), 56. *Prof Exp:* Lab asst, Res Lab, Linde Co, 40-43; asst, Union Col, 49-51 & Mass Inst Technol, 51-55; anal chemist, Gen Elec Co, 56-58; sect chief anal methods, Res Ctr, Lever Bros Co, 58-64; dept head anal chem, Merrell Dow Pharmaceut Inc, 64-82; mgr, Submissions & Develop Qual Control, Adria Lab Inc, 82- 84; rev chemist, Food & Drug Admin, 84-92. *Concurrent Pos:* Adj asst prof pharmaceut chem, Col Pharm, Univ Cincinnati, 82-83. *Mem:* Am Chem Soc; fel Am Inst Chem. *Res:* Evaluations of manufacturing and controls information submitted in support of investigational new drugs and new drug applications for drug products; analytical methods; packaging guidelines; computer assisted reviews. *Mailing Add:* 5052 S Ridge Dr Cincinnati OH 45224-5101. *Fax:* 513-853-2703

KEIM, BARBARA HOWELL, ECOLOGICAL GENETICS. *Current Pos:* DIR EXEC & PROF DEVELOP, BRADLEY UNIV, 91- *Personal Data:* b Detroit, Mich, Mar 9, 46; m 75, James A Kelni; c 2. *Educ:* Univ NC, Greensboro, BA, 67; Rutgers Univ, MS, 69; Univ Va, PhD(genetics), 76; Bradley Univ, MBA, 86. *Prof Exp:* Asst ed biol, Biol Sci Info Serv, Philadelphia, 69-70; instr, Dept Biol, Wheaton Col, Norton, Mass, 75-76; asst prof, Dept Biol, Bradley Univ, 76-77, asst prof, Dept Nursing, 77-78, adj prof, Dept Biol, 79-80; from asst prof to assoc prof biol, Eureka Col, Ill, 80-87; dir financial develop, Am Red Cross, 89-91. *Res:* Disruptive selection; speciation; polymorphisms. *Mailing Add:* 516 W Stratford Dr Peoria IL 61614

KEIM, CHRISTOPHER PETER, CHEMISTRY. *Current Pos:* RETIRED. *Personal Data:* b Tecumseh, Nebr, Apr 6, 06; m 29; c 2. *Educ:* Nebr Wesleyan Univ, AB, 27; Univ Nebr, MSc, 32, PhD(chem), 40. *Hon Degrees:* DSc, Nebr Wesleyan Univ, 59. *Prof Exp:* Head dept phys sci, York Col, 33-37; instr chem, Univ Tulsa, 40-41; res engr, Sylvania Corp, Mass, 41-42; res chemist & fel, Mellon Inst, 42-44; res physicist & adminr, Tenn Eastman Corp, 44-47; dir stable isotope res & prod div, Oak Ridge Nat Lab, 47-57, tech info div, 57-71; consult, Roane State Community Col, 71-81. *Concurrent Pos:* Pres & gen mgr, Mgt Servs, Inc, 73-75; consult, Hiwassee Col, 78-79; dir rowing, Spec Olympics Int, 86-89. *Mem:* Fel AAAS; Am Chem Soc; fel Am Phys Soc; Sigma Xi. *Res:* Isotope separations and properties; monomolecular surface films; electrical discharge in gases; surface chemistry; spreading of organic liquids and mixtures on water in the presence of monomolecular surface films; technical information. *Mailing Add:* 102 Orchard Lane Oak Ridge TN 37830-3803

KEIM, GERALD INMAN, paper chemistry, for more information see previous edition

KEIM, JOHN EUGENE, electronics engineering, for more information see previous edition

KEIM, KATHRYN SARAH, COOPERATIVE EXTENSION, NUTRITION EDUCATION. *Current Pos:* ASST EXTEN PROF, UNIV IDAHO, BOISE, 91-, PROG LEADER, NUTRIT, DIET & HEALTH, 91-, EXPANDED FOOD & NUTRIT EDUC PROG COORDR, 92-, PROG COORD, EXTEN WIC NUTRIT EDUC INITIATIVE, 93-, COORD PROG DIETETICS, CONSULT, 93- *Personal Data:* b Glencoe, Minn, Oct 20, 51; m 73, Kent Richard; c Lee R. *Educ:* Univ Minn, BS, 73; Univ Nebr, MS; Tex Tech Univ, PhD(nutrit), 83. *Honors & Awards:* Am Asn Diabetes Educators; Am Diabetes Asn; Am Dietetic Asn; Am Home Econs Asn; Am Inst Nutrit; Nat Asn Exten Home Econs; Sigma Xi. *Prof Exp:* Asst prof, Human Nutrit, Food & Food Syst Mgt, La State Univ, Baton Rouge, 83-84; asst prof & dir, Didactic Prog Dietetics, Dept Foods & Nutrit, Univ Ill, Urbana, 85-88. *Res:* Nutrition education methods that result in behavior change, determining which methods work with specific target groups. *Mailing Add:* 5595 Julian Ct Westminster CO 80030. *Fax:* 208-364-4035; *E-Mail:* kkheim@uidaho.edu

KEIM, LON WILLIAM, PULMONARY DISEASE. *Current Pos:* MEM MED STAFF, BISHOP CLARKSON MEM HOSP, 76- *Personal Data:* b Washington, DC, June 1, 43. *Educ:* Med Col Va, BS, 66, MD, 70. *Prof Exp:* Intern med, Univ Kans Med Ctr, Kansas City, 70-71; resident, Med Col Va, 71-73; fel, Col Med, Univ Iowa, 73-75, assoc pulmonary dis, 75-76; asst prof internal med, Univ Nebr, 76- *Mem:* Fel Am Col Physicians; fel Am Col Chest Physicians; Am Thoracic Soc; Undersea Med Soc; Int Union Aganist Tuberc; Am Med Asn. *Res:* Tuberculosis and atypical mycobacteria; pulmonary diagnostic techniques, fiberoptic bronchoscopy; hyperbaric oxygen therapy. *Mailing Add:* 4242 Farnham St Omaha NE 68131-2850

KEIM, ROBERT GERALD, ORTHODONTICS, CRANIOFACIAL ANOMALIES. *Current Pos:* ASSOC PROF ORTHOD, COL DENT, UNIV TENN, 90-, CLIN DIR, CRANIOFACIAL ANOMALIES CLIN, BOLING CTR DEVELOP DISABILITIES, 93- *Personal Data:* b Joplin, MO, Nov 19, 54; m 75, Cynthia Calahan; c Jason A, Eric R, Theresa R & Jennifer L. *Educ:* Univ NMex, BS, 77; Marquette, DDS, 81; Eastman Dent Ctr, Specialist Cert Orthod, 90. *Concurrent Pos:* Res award, Northeastern Soc Orthodontists, 90; Faustin Neff Weber fel, 92; assoc, Plastic Clin, Tenn Dept Health, 92- *Mem:* Am Asn Dent Schs; Am Asn Orthod; Am Dent Asn. *Res:* Developmental biology of craniofacial anomalies and histopathology in the temporomandibular joint; biological changes associated with orthodontic treatment. *Mailing Add:* 875 Union Ave Suite 301 Grad Orthodontic Clin Univ Tenn Memphis TN 38163. *Fax:* 901-448-7104; *E-Mail:* rkeim@utmeml.utmem.edu

KEIM, WAYNE FRANKLIN, PLANT BREEDING & GENETICS, GENETICS INSTRUCTION. *Current Pos:* head dept, 75-85, prof, 85-92, EMER PROF SOIL & CROP SCI, COLO STATE UNIV, 92- *Personal Data:* b Ithaca, NY, May 14, 23; m 47, Joyce Neumann; c Kathryn K (Logsdon), David W & Julie K (Hughes). *Educ:* Univ Nebr, BS, 47; Cornell Univ, MS, 49, PhD(plant genetics & breeding), 52. *Honors & Awards:* Agron Educ Award, Am Soc Agron, 71, Agron Serv Award, 91. *Prof Exp:* From instr to asst prof bot, Iowa State Col, 52-56; from asst prof to prof agron, Purdue Univ, 56-75. *Concurrent Pos:* NSF sci fac fel, Inst Genetics, Univ Lund, 62-63; bd dirs, Coun Agr Sci & Technol, 96- *Mem:* Fel AAAS; fel Am Soc Agron; Am Genetic Asn; fel Crop Sci Soc Am (pres, 83-84). *Res:* Breeding and genetics of forage and grain legumes. *Mailing Add:* Dept Soil & Crop Sci Colo State Univ Ft Collins CO 80523. *Fax:* 970-491-0564

KEINATH, GERALD E, MECHANICAL ENGINEERING. *Current Pos:* RETIRED. *Personal Data:* b Grand Rapids, Mich, May 1, 24; m 56; c 3. *Educ:* Northwestern Univ, BSME, 49. *Prof Exp:* Engr in training, Chicago & Northwestern RR, 46-49; res engr, Battelle Mem Inst, Ohio, 49-52, bus mgr Europ opers, Frankfurt & Geneva, 52-58, asst supvr contract prep, Ohio, 58-63; vpres, NStar Res & Develop Inst, 63-72; pres, Novus Inc, 72-93. *Mem:* Am Soc Mech Engrs; Am Soc Automotive Engrs. *Res:* Product development; glass repair; research management. *Mailing Add:* 5261 Lochloy Dr Minneapolis MN 55436-2023

KEINATH, JOHN ALLEN, MARINE VERTEBRATE BIOLOGY, HERPETOLOGY. *Current Pos:* ADJ PROF, THOMAS NELSON COMMUNITY COL, 95- *Personal Data:* b New London, Conn, Oct 6, 59; m 84, Debra Barnard. *Educ:* Univ RI, BS, 81, BA, 84, MS, 86; Col William & Mary, PhD(marine sci), 93. *Prof Exp:* Teaching asst intro zool & human anat, Univ RI, 81-84; fisheries tech, State Univ Col NY, Buffalo, 84-85; res asst, Va Inst Marine Sci, 86-93, postdoctoral assoc, 93-94. *Concurrent Pos:* mem, Marine Turtle Specialist Group, Int Union Conserv Nature & Natural Resources. *Mem:* Am Soc Ichtheyologists & Herpetologists; Ecol Soc Am; Herpet League; Soc Study Amphibians & Reptiles; Soc Conserv Biol. *Res:* Behavior, ecology and biology of marine vertebrates, primarily sea turtles, and how movements, distribution, ecology and behavior can be utilized for species conservation. *Mailing Add:* PO Box 310 Gloucester Point VA 23062. *Fax:* 804-642-7327; *E-Mail:* jak@vims.edu

KEINATH, STEVEN ERNEST, POLYMER SCIENCE. *Current Pos:* sr res asst, Mich Molecular Inst, 78-84, asst ed, MMI Press, 81-82, adminr grants & contracts, 83-84, independent researcher, 84-92, instr, 85-92, assoc res scientist, 92-94, ASST RES PROF, MICH MOLECULAR INST, 92-, SR ASSOC SCIENTIST, 94- *Personal Data:* b Saginaw, Mich, Sept 10, 54; m 87, Carol Elizabeth Keinath-Robinson. *Educ:* Saginaw Valley State Col, BS, 76, MBA, 81; Univ Mass, MS, 78; Cent Mich Univ, MA, 85; Mich Technol Univ, PhD(chem), 92. *Prof Exp:* Res asst, Chem Dept, Siginaw Valley State Col, Mich, 74-76; asst to dir instrumentation, Dept Polymer Sci & Eng, Univ Mass, 78. *Concurrent Pos:* Consult, 84-; ed, Midland Chemist, 84-87; adj asst res prof, Cent Mich Univ, 93- *Mem:* Am Chem Soc; Soc Advan Mat & Process Eng; NY Acad Sci; Sigma Xi; Soc Plastics Engrs; Internet Soc. *Res:* Thermal analysis; polymer transitions and relaxations; binary and ternary polymer blends; composites; effects of absorbed moisture on high performance organic fibers; molecular modeling; plastics recycling. *Mailing Add:* Mich Molecular Inst 1910 W St Andrews Rd Midland MI 48640-2696. *E-Mail:* skeinath@mmi.org

KEINATH, THOMAS M, ENVIRONMENTAL ENGINEERING. *Current Pos:* prof environ systs eng & head dept, 69-92, DEAN ENG & SCI, CLEMSON UNIV, 92- *Personal Data:* b Frankenmuth, Mich, Jan 5, 41; m 63; c 1. *Educ:* Univ Mich, Ann Arbor, BSE, 63, MSE, 64, PhD(water resources eng), 68. *Honors & Awards:* Huber Prize, Am Soc Civil Engrs, 86. *Prof Exp:* Inst Sci & Technol fel, Univ Mich, 68-69. *Concurrent Pos:* Consult, Waverly Assocs, 68-69; Westvaco Inc, 70-, Gaston Co, Dyeing Mach Co, 71-, Eng Sci, Inc, 74- & UNESCO, 80; expert sci adv, Environ Protection Agency, 75-76. *Mem:* Am Chem Soc; Am Inst Chem Engrs; Am Water Works Asn; Am Soc Civil Engrs; Asn Environ Eng Prof; Sigma Xi; Water Pollution Control Fedn; Int Asn Water Pollution Res & Control; Am Soc Engr Educ. *Res:* Physiochemical processes of water and wasterwaste treatment; automation and control of water and wastewater treatment systems. *Mailing Add:* Col Eng & Sci Clemson Univ PO Box 340901 Clemson SC 29634-0901

KEIPER, RONALD R, ANIMAL BEHAVIOR. *Current Pos:* Asst prof zool & biol, 68-73, assoc prof zool, 73-82, PROF ZOOL, PA STATE UNIV, 82-, DIR ACAD AFFAIRS & DISTINGUISHED PROF BIOL, 90- *Personal Data:* b Allentown, Pa, Sept 21, 41; m 64; c 2. *Educ:* Muhlenberg Col, BS, 63; Univ Mass, MS, 66, PhD(zool), 68. *Concurrent Pos:* Theodore Roosevelt Mem Fund-Am Mus Natural Hist grant, 68-69; Frank M Chapman Mem Fund-Am Mus Natural Hist grant, 68-70; Nat Park Serv study grants; Fulbright fel, 84-85. *Mem:* Animal Behav Soc; Lepidopterists Soc. *Res:* Causes and functions of the abnormal stereotyped behaviors shown by caged birds; effects of early experience on bird behavior; natural behavor of cryptic moths; studying the behavior, ecology and social organization of feral horses and Prezewalski horses. *Mailing Add:* 8141 St Andrew Circle Orlando FL 32835

KEIRANS, JAMES EDWARD, MEDICAL ENTOMOLOGY, ACAROLOGY. *Current Pos:* RES PROF & CUR, US NAT TICK COLLECTION, 90- *Personal Data:* b Worcester, Mass, Apr 4, 35; m 63; c 2. *Educ:* Boston Univ, AB, 60, AM, 63; Univ NH, PhD(zool), 66. *Prof Exp:* Res asst parasitol, Boston Univ, 60-63; res asst entom, Univ NH, 65-66; res entomologist, Commun Dis Ctr, USPHS, 66-69; res entomologist, NIH, 69-90. *Concurrent Pos:* Res entomologist, Brit Mus Nat Hist, 77-78. *Mem:* Am Soc Parasitol; Entom Soc Am; Acarological Soc Am. *Res:* Arthropods of public health significance; Ixodoidea taxonomy. *Mailing Add:* Inst Arthropodology & Parasitol Ga Southern Univ Statesboro GA 30460

KEIRNS, JAMES JEFFERY, BIOCHEMISTRY. *Current Pos:* dir, Dept Biochem, 79-88, DIR, DEPT DRUG METAB & PHARMACOKINETICS, BOEHRINGER INGELHEIM LTD, 88- *Personal Data:* b New Haven, Conn, July 1, 47; m 67, 75; c 3. *Educ:* Rice Univ, BA, 68; Yale Univ, MPhil, 70, PhD(molecular biophys & biochem), 72. *Prof Exp:* Jane Coffin Childs Mem Fund Med Res fel biochem, Dept Path, Sch Med, Yale Univ, 72-75; sr res biochemist & proj leader allergy res, Lederle Labs Div, Am Cyanamid Co, 75-79. *Mem:* Am Chem Soc; AAAS; NY Acad Sci; Am Acad Allergy; Health Physics Soc. *Res:* Biochemical aspects of metabolic, immunological and viral diseases; cyclic nucleotides; mechanism of enzyme reactions; inflammation; immediate hypersensitivity; pharmacokinetics and drug metabolism. *Mailing Add:* Boehringer Ingelheim Pharmaceut Inc 900 Ridgebury Rd PO Box 368 Ridgefield CT 06877-0368. *Fax:* 203-791-6003

KEIRS, RUSSELL JOHN, ANALYTICAL CHEMISTRY. *Current Pos:* RETIRED. *Personal Data:* b Springfield, Ill, Aug 27, 15; m 41; c 1. *Educ:* Univ Ill, BS, 37, MS, 38, PhD, 41. *Prof Exp:* Chemist, Continental Can Co, 41-42; assoc prof chem, Fla State Univ, 50-65, assoc dean, Grad Sch & dir res, 62-69, prof, 65-81. *Mem:* Am Chem Soc. *Res:* Molecular phosphorescence analysis at low temperatures; instrumental analysis. *Mailing Add:* 1506 Golf Terr Dr Tallahassee FL 32301-5604

KEISCH, BERNARD, RADIOCHEMISTRY. *Current Pos:* SCIENTIST, BROOKHAVEN NAT LAB, 78- *Personal Data:* b Brooklyn, NY, Aug 1, 32; m 54; c 3. *Educ:* Rensselaer Polytech Inst, BS, 53; Wash Univ, St Louis, PhD(chem), 57. *Prof Exp:* Res chemist, Idaho Chem Processing Plant, Phillips Petrol Co, 57-59, mat testing reactor, 59-62; sr scientist, Nuclear Sci & Eng Corp, 62-66; from fel to sr fel, Carnegie-Mellon Univ, 66-74, sr fel, Carnegie-Mellon Inst Res, 74-78. *Mem:* Sigma Xi; AAAS; Am Chem Soc. *Res:* Nuclear applications in art and archaeology; activation analysis; isotope mass spectrometry; carbon-14 dating; Mossbauer effect; nuclear safeguards. *Mailing Add:* 7112 Murray Park Dr San Diego CA 91221

KEISER, BERNHARD E(DWARD), TELECOMMUNICATIONS ENGINEERING, ELECTRICAL ENGINEERING. *Current Pos:* PRES, KEISER ENG, INC, 75- *Personal Data:* b Richmond Heights, Mo, Nov 14, 28; m 55, Evelyn Koenig; c Sandra, Carol, Nancy, Linda & Paul. *Educ:* Washington Univ, St Louis, BS, 50, MS, 51, DSc, 53. *Prof Exp:* Proj engr, White-Rodgers Elec Co, Mo, 53-56, Petrolite Corp, 56-57 & Mo Res Labs, 57-59; group leader new commun systs, RCA Corp, 59-64, mgr plans & prog sect, Kennedy Space Ctr Commun Proj, RCA Serv Co, Fla, 64-67, admin advan tech planning, RCA Missile & Surface Radar Div, NJ, 67-69; vpres systs res & eng, Page Commun Engrs, Va, 69-70; dir advan systs electronics & commun, Atlantic Res Corp, Alexandria, 71-72; dir anal, Fairchild Space & Electronics Co, 72-75. *Mem:* Fel Inst Elec & Electronics Engrs. *Res:* Telecommunications; electronic systems; engineering management and consulting. *Mailing Add:* 2046 Carrhill Rd Vienna VA 22181-2917. *Fax:* 703-281-9582; *E-Mail:* bekeiser@aol.com

KEISER, EDMUND DAVIS, JR, VERTEBRATE ZOOLOGY, WETLANDS ECOLOGY. *Current Pos:* assoc prof, 76, chmn dept, 76-87, PROF BIOL, UNIV MISS, 76- *Personal Data:* b Appalachia, Va, Feb 18, 34; m, Sue Tucker; c Marke E, Julie A, Louis A & Jenifer. *Educ:* Southern Ill Univ, BA, 56, MS, 61; La State Univ, PhD(vert zool), 67. *Prof Exp:* Teacher high sch, Ill, 56-57, pub schs, 57; sci instr & dist sci coordr, Dist 70, Freeburg, Ill, 58-62; instr zool & anat, La Salle-Peru-Oglesby Jr Col, 62-64; teaching asst zool, La State Univ, 64-66; from asst prof to prof comp anat & syst zool, Univ Southwestern La, 66-76; dir biol, Physics & Chem, NSF Coop Col-Sch Sci Prog biol, 69-70. *Concurrent Pos:* Teaching asst, Southern Ill Univ, 61; sci ed consult, Southwestern La Parish Schs, 66-71; res assoc, Gulf South Res Inst, Baton Rouge, 72-75; consult & proj dir, US Fish & Wildlife Serv, Atchafalaya Basin Surv, 73-76; dir, Lafayette Natural Hist Mus, 73; consult, La Chenier Plain Study, US Fish & Wildlife Serv, 78; comnr, Miss Dept Wildlife Conserv, 78-79 & 80-84, chmn, 83-84, mem, Miss Wildlife Heritage Comt, 80-84; mem, Governor's Select Comt Radioactive Waste & Waste Depository, 79; environ consult, Lockheed Eng, Abort Solid Rocket Motor Proj, NASA, 90-91 & 94-95, US Army Corps Engrs, 92-95 & NAA, 94-95. *Mem:* Am Soc Ichthyol & Herpet; Soc Study Amphibians & Reptiles; Herpetologist League. *Res:* Systematics, ecology and developmental morphology of vertebrates, especially amphibians and reptiles of the United States and the Neotropics; wetlands ecology and management; developmental embryology. *Mailing Add:* Dept Biol Univ Miss University MS 38677. *Fax:* 601-232-5144; *E-Mail:* bykeiser@olemiss.edu

KEISER, GEORGE MCCURRACH, GRAVITATIONAL & ATOMIC PHYSICS. *Current Pos:* MEM FAC, DEPT PHYSICS, STANFORD UNIV, 80- *Personal Data:* b Plainfield, NJ, July 21, 47. *Educ:* Middlebury Col, AB, 69; Duke Univ, PhD(physics), 76. *Prof Exp:* Res assoc, Joint Inst Lab Astrophys, 76-77; Nat Res Coun fel, Nat Bur Stand, 77-80. *Concurrent Pos:* Lectr, Univ Colo, 77-78. *Mem:* Am Phys Soc. *Res:* High precision measurements in gravitational and atomic physics. *Mailing Add:* Hansen Labs GP-B Stanford Univ Stanford CA 94305

KEISER, HAROLD D, RHEUMATOLOGY. *Current Pos:* PROF MED, ALBERT EINSTEIN COL MED, 83- *Educ:* New York Univ, MD, 64. *Mem:* Am Rheumatism Asn; Am Asn Immunologists; Am Asn Clin Res; Soc Complex Carbohydrates; Am Soc Clin Invest. *Mailing Add:* Dept Med Albert Einstein Col Med 1300 Morris Park Ave Bronx NY 10461-1975

KEISER, HARRY ROBERT, CLINICAL PHARMACOLOGY, HIGH BLOOD PRESSURE. *Current Pos:* CLIN DIR, NAT HEART, LUNG & BLOOD INST, NIH, 76-; CHIEF, HYPERTENSION-ENDOCRINE BR, 85- *Personal Data:* b Chicago, Ill, Aug 9, 33; m 65, 92, Phyllis E Swain; c Harry R II & Robert E. *Educ:* Northwestern Univ, BA, 55, MD, 58. *Concurrent Pos:* Clin prof med, Georgetown Univ, 91- *Mem:* Am Col Physicians; Am Fedn Clin Res; Am Heart Asn; Am Soc Pharmacol & Exp Therapeut; Am Soc Hypertension. *Res:* Etiology and therapy of high blood pressure. *Mailing Add:* Nat Heart Lung & Blood Inst NIH 10 Center Dr MSC 1754 Bethesda MD 20892-1754. *Fax:* 301-402-1679

KEISER, JEFFREY E, ORGANIC CHEMISTRY. *Current Pos:* SR RES ASSOC, PENFORD PROD CO, 88- *Personal Data:* b Kalamazoo, Mich, Feb 25, 41; m 88; c 5. *Educ:* Kalamazoo Col, AB, 62; Wayne State Univ, PhD(org chem), 66. *Prof Exp:* From asst prof to prof chem, Coe Col, 66-88, chmn dept, 76-88. *Mem:* Am Chem Soc; AAAS. *Res:* Organic analytical chemistry; starch chemistry. *Mailing Add:* PO Box 428 Penford Prod Co Cedar Rapids IA 52406-0428

KEISER, JOAN A, CARDIOVASCULAR RESEARCH. *Current Pos:* ASSOC RES FEL CARDIOVASC, PARKE-DAVIS PHARMACEUT, 88- *Personal Data:* b Muskegon, Mich, Oct 26, 53. *Educ:* Mich State Univ, BS, 76; Univ Mich, PhD(physiol), 82. *Prof Exp:* Res fel physiol, Mayo Clin, 82-85; res scientist cardiovasc, Ortho Pharmaceut, 85-88. *Concurrent Pos:* Mem, High Blood Pressure Coun, Am Heart Asn. *Mem:* Am Physiol Soc; Am Soc Exp Biol; Am Heart Asn; Am Soc Pharmacol & Exp Therapeut. *Mailing Add:* Dept Cardiovasc-Pharmacol Parke-Davis Pharmaceut Warner-Lambert 2800 Plymouth Rd Ann Arbor MI 48105. *Fax:* 313-996-1480

KEISER, TERRY DEAN, ICHTHYOLOGY, HERPETOLOGY. *Current Pos:* PROF & CHAIR, DEPT BIOL SCI, OHIO NORTHERN UNIV, 66- *Personal Data:* b Canton, Ohio, Oct 27, 42; m 84, Christine Provines. *Educ:* Ohio Northern Univ, BS, 64; Bowling Green State Univ, MA, 66. *Concurrent Pos:* Chair adv bd, Ohio Biol Surv. *Mem:* Am Fisheries Soc; Asian Fisheries Soc. *Res:* Stream fish distributions in Ohio; herptile populations-distributions in Hardin County Ohio. *Mailing Add:* Dept Biol Sci Ohio Northern Univ Ada OH 45810. *Fax:* 419-772-2330; *E-Mail:* t-keiser@onu.edu

KEISLER, HOWARD JEROME, MATHEMATICAL LOGIC. *Current Pos:* from asst prof to assoc prof, 62-67, PROF MATH, UNIV WIS, MADISON, 67- *Personal Data:* b Seattle, Wash, Dec 3, 36; m 59, Lois J Hoffman; c Randall B, Jeffrey M & Thomas D. *Educ:* Calif Inst Technol, BS, 59; Univ Calif, Berkeley, PhD(math), 61. *Prof Exp:* Mathematician, Commun Res Div, Inst Defense Anal, 61-62. *Concurrent Pos:* Vis res assoc, Princeton Univ, 61-62; Alfred P Sloan fel, 66-69; vis prof, Univ Calif, Los Angeles, 67-68; John S Guggenheim fel, 76-77; vis prof, Univ Colo, 85. *Mem:* Am Math Soc; Asn Symbolic Logic (vpres, 77-80). *Res:* Model theory; set theory; applications of model theory to probability theory and mathematical economics. *Mailing Add:* Univ Wis 480 Lincoln Dr Madison WI 53706-1313. *E-Mail:* keisler@math.wisc.edu

KEISLER, JAMES EDWIN, MATHEMATICS. *Current Pos:* from asst prof to assoc prof, 59-73, PROF MATH, LA STATE UNIV, BATON ROUGE, 73- *Personal Data:* b Spartanburg, SC, Aug 20, 29; m 50; c 3. *Educ:* Midland Col, BS, 49; Univ Mich, MA, 54, PhD(math), 59. *Prof Exp:* Teacher high sch, Nebr, 49-51. *Mem:* Am Math Soc; Math Asn Am. *Res:* Point-set topology; fixed point problems and characterizations of spaces. *Mailing Add:* 215 Stanford Ave Baton Rouge LA 70808-4666

KEISTER, DONALD LEE, PLANT-MICROBE INTERACTIONS. *Current Pos:* RES LEADER, SOYBEAN & ALFALFA RES LAB, USDA AGR RES SERV, 84- *Personal Data:* b Beckley, WVa, Dec 10, 33; m 62, Joyce E Diggs; c Alan, Julie & Cristyn. *Educ:* WVa Wesleyan Col, BS, 54; Univ Md, MS, 56, PhD, 59. *Prof Exp:* Fel, McCollum-Pratt Inst, Johns Hopkins Univ, 58-61; fel, Res Inst Adv Study, Md, 61-62; assoc prof biochem, Antioch Col, 62-80; sr investr, Charles F Kettering Res Lab, 62-84. *Concurrent Pos:* Nat Found fel, 58-60; chmn, Gordon Res Conf Photosynthesis, 69, Beltsville Symp Agr, 89; assoc prof, Wright State Univ, 80-84. *Mem:* Am Soc Biochem & Molecular Biol; Am Soc Plant Physiol; Am Soc Microbiol; Int Soc Molecular Plant-Microbe Interactions. *Res:* Mechanisms of pyridine nucleotide reduction in photosynthetic organisms; structure and function in photosynthetic organelles; control mechanisms in nitrogen fixation; symbiotic nitrogen fixation in legumes; author or co-author of over 100 publications. *Mailing Add:* Soybean & Alfalfa Res Lab USDA Agr Res Serv Bldg 011 HH19 BARC-W Beltsville MD 20705. *Fax:* 301-504-5728; *E-Mail:* jkeister@asrr.arsusda.gov

KEISTER, JAMES E, ELECTRICAL ENGINEERING, ELECTRONIC ENGINEERING. *Current Pos:* RETIRED. *Personal Data:* b Coburg, Iowa, July 11, 14; m 35, Ila MacLeod; c Jamieson C, Holly J (Crandall) & Bradley D. *Educ:* Cornell Univ, BS, 35. *Honors & Awards:* Apollo Achievement Award, NASA, 69. *Concurrent Pos:* Mem, Semiconductor Stand Comt, US Radio Tech Planning Bd & Nat TV Systs Comt. *Mem:* Fel Inst Elec & Electronics Engrs; Sigma Xi. *Res:* Development of television transmitters; radar counter measures, semiconductors; ground support equipment for Apollo & Skylab Prog. *Mailing Add:* 5566 Dry Ridge Rd Cincinnati OH 45252-1856

KEISTER, JAMIESON CHARLES, DIFFERENTIAL EQUATIONS. *Current Pos:* RES SPECIALIST, 3M PHARMACEUT, 92- *Personal Data:* b Schenectady, NY, Feb 28, 38; m 60; c 4. *Educ:* Cornell Univ, BS, 60; Georgetown Univ, MS, 67, PhD(physics), 70. *Prof Exp:* Engr, Nuclear Prop Div, Buships, 60-64; jr tech assoc, NUS Corp, 64-66; sr field res physicist, Melpar Div, West Airbrake Co, 66-67; prof physics & math, Covenant Col, 70-84; prin scientist basic res, Alcon Lab, 84-91. *Concurrent Pos:* Math consult, Miami Valley Labs, Procter & Gamble, Inc, 81- *Mem:* Electrochem Soc. *Res:* Tunneling in super conductors; mathematical modeling and experiments for diffusion problems; complex variables; conformal mapping; transdevual drug delivery systems. *Mailing Add:* 11518 172nd St W Lakeville MN 55044-9326

KEISTER, JEROME BAIRD, INORGANIC CHEMISTRY, ORGANOMETALLIC CHEMISTRY. *Current Pos:* from asst prof to assoc prof, 80-91, PROF INORG CHEM, STATE UNIV NY, BUFFALO, 91- *Personal Data:* b Baton Rouge, La, Mar 28, 53. *Educ:* La State Univ, Baton Rouge, BS, 73; Univ Ill, Urbana-Champaign, PhD(chem), 78. *Prof Exp:* Res chemist organometallic catalysis, Corp Pioneering Res, Exxon Res & Eng Co, 77-80. *Concurrent Pos:* Alfred P Sloan fel, 87-89. *Mem:* Am Chem Soc. *Res:* Homogeneous catalysis, organometallic chemistry; metal cluster chemistry. *Mailing Add:* Dept Chem State Univ NY 562 Natural Sci Complex Buffalo NY 14260-3000. *Fax:* 716-645-6963; *E-Mail:* keister@acsu.buffalo.edu

KEITEL, GLENN H(OWARD), ELECTRICAL ENGINEERING, OFFICE AUTOMATION. *Current Pos:* PRES, OFF AUTOMATION CONSULT, INC, 81- *Personal Data:* b Chicago, Ill, Feb 16, 30; m 53; c 2. *Educ:* Wash Univ, BS, 52, MS, 54; Stanford Univ, PhD(elec eng), 55. *Prof Exp:* Fulbright fel, Cavendish Lab, Cambridge Univ, 55-56; engr advan studies, Microwave Lab, Gen Elec Co, 56-59; eng dept mgr, Western Develop Lab, Philco Corp, Calif, 59-62; assoc prof elec eng, San Jose State Col, 62-66, prof & chmn dept, 66-69; prof elec eng & chmn elec eng curric, Drexel Univ, 69-71; prof elec eng & dean eng, Bucknell Univ, 71-79; dir eng & technol planning, CPT Corp, 80-81. *Concurrent Pos:* Consult, Stanford Res Inst, 62-63 & 64-69 & Western Develop Labs, Philco Corp, 62-63; electronics liaison scientist, Off Naval Res, Br Off, London, 63-64; adv scientist, Lockheed Missiles & Space Co, 65-69. *Res:* Functional and engineering design, selection and implementation of office automation systems, with training and applications development. *Mailing Add:* 510 Groveland Ave Minneapolis MN 55403

KEITER, ELLEN ANN, INORGANIC CHEMISTRY, PHYSICAL CHEMISTRY. *Current Pos:* From instr to assoc prof, 78-92, PROF CHEM EASTERN ILL UNIV, 92-, CHAIR, DEPT CHEM, 94- *Educ:* Augsburg Col, BA, 64; Univ Md, MS, 68; Univ Ill, PhD(inorg chem), 86. *Concurrent Pos:* Vis prof, Colo State Univ, 90. *Mem:* Am Chem Soc; AAAS. *Res:* Nuclear quadrupole double resonance spectroscopy; hydrogen bonds; metal hydrides; metal-protein complexes (model compounds); metal-nucleic acid complexes (model compounds). *Mailing Add:* Dept Chem Eastern Ill Univ Charleston IL 61920. *Fax:* 217-581-6613; *E-Mail:* cfeak@eiu.edu

KEITER, RICHARD LEE, INORGANIC CHEMISTRY. *Current Pos:* assoc prof, 69-79, PROF INORG CHEM, EASTERN ILL UNIV, 79-, DISTINGUISHED PROF, 88- *Personal Data:* b Winchester, Va, Jan 10, 39; m 66; c 2. *Educ:* Shepherd Col, BS, 61; WVa Univ, MS, 64; Univ Md, PhD(inorg chem), 67. *Prof Exp:* Assoc inorg chem, Iowa State Univ, 67-69. *Concurrent Pos:* Vis prof, Univ Wis, 72 & 77, Univ Exeter, Eng, 75, Univ Ill, 80 & Colo State Univ, 90. *Mem:* Am Chem Soc; AAAS. *Res:* Coordination chemistry of trivalent phosphorous ligands; transition metal carbonyls; polydentate phosphorus ligand control; synthetic inorganic and organometallic chemistry; phosphido-bridged complexes. *Mailing Add:* Dept Chem Eastern Ill Univ Charleston IL 61920. *E-Mail:* cfrlk@eiu.edu

KEITH, DAVID ALEXANDER, ORAL & MAXILLOFACIAL SURGERY. *Current Pos:* res fel, 75-77, asst prof, 78-84, ASSOC PROF ORAL SURG, HARVARD SCH DENT MED, 85-; CHIEF ORAL & MAXILLOFACIAL SURG, HARVARD COMMUNITY HEALTH PLAN, 83-, DENT DIR, HOWARD COMMUN HEALTH PLAN, 96- *Personal Data:* b Chelmsford, Essex, Eng, Aug 28, 44; m 76, Barbara Lewis; c Sean & Lisa. *Educ:* Univ London, BDS, 66; FDSRCS(Eng), 70; Harvard Univ, DMD, 83. *Honors & Awards:* Malleson Prize, 66; Brit Asn Oral Surgeons Award, 73. *Prof Exp:* Lectr oral surg, Hosp Dent Sch, Kings Col, London, 71-73; res fel, Mass Gen Hosp, Boston, 73-74. *Concurrent Pos:* Res assoc orthop surg, Children's Hosp Med Ctr, 77; clin assoc oral surg, Mass Gen Hosp, 78-84, asst surgeon, Oral & Maxillofacial Surg, 84- *Mem:* Brit Dent Asn; Brit Asn Oral Surgeons; Int Asn Dent Res; Am Dent Asn; Int Asn Oral Surgeons; Am Acad Orofacial Pain. *Res:* Craniofacial development; orofacial pain and temporo mandibular disorders. *Mailing Add:* Ambulatory Care Ctr No 230 Mass Gen Hosp Fruit St Boston MA 02114

KEITH, DAVID LEE, ENTOMOLOGY. *Current Pos:* EXTEN ENTOMOLOGIST, UNIV NEBR, LINCOLN, 67- *Personal Data:* b Mankato, Minn, Dec 7, 40; m 61; c 4. *Educ:* Gustavus Adolphus Col, BSc, 62; Univ Minn, MSc, 65; Univ Nebr, Lincoln, PhD(entom), 71. *Mem:* Sigma Xi; Entom Soc Am. *Res:* Biology, ecology and control of cutworms; development of integrated pest management projects on Nebraska field crops. *Mailing Add:* 210B Plant Indust Bldg IANR/UNL Lincoln NE 68583-0816

KEITH, DENNIS DALTON, ORGANIC SYNTHESIS, ANTIBIOTICS. *Current Pos:* sr res chemist, 71-76, res fel, 76-81, RES GROUP CHIEF, HOFFMANN-LA ROCHE INC, 81- *Personal Data:* b Hartford, Conn, July 11, 43; c 2. *Educ:* Bates Col, BS, 65; Yale Univ, MS, 67, MPh, 69, PhD(org chem), 69. *Prof Exp:* NIH fel, Harvard Univ, 69-71. *Mem:* Am Chem Soc; Am Soc Microbiol; Sigma Xi. *Res:* Synthesis of natural products; heterocyclic chemistry; synthetic methods. *Mailing Add:* Eight Mendl Terr Montclair NJ 07042-4108

KEITH, DONALD EDWARDS, INVERTEBRATE ECOLOGY. *Current Pos:* asst prof to assoc prof, 75-85, PROF ECOL TARLETON STATE UNIV, 85- *Personal Data:* b Ft Worth, Tex, Oct 7, 38; m 59. *Educ:* Tex Christian Univ, BA, 62, MS, 64; Univ Southern Calif, PhD(biol), 68. *Honors & Awards:* Tex Acad Sci fel, 77. *Prof Exp:* NSF res grant, summer, 61; asst prof biol, Tex Christian Univ, 68-75, dir environ sci prog, 69-71. *Concurrent Pos:* Consult, US Army CEngrs, Lake Proctor, 76-; res grant, Tarleton State Univ, 75-88; Tex Acad Sci fel, 77. *Mem:* AAAS; Sigma Xi. *Res:* Benthic ecology; substrate selection, feeding and functional digestive tract morphology of Caprellid amphipods; amphipod phylogeny; effects of industrial effluents on benthic invertebrate communities; corals of the Swan Islands, Honduras; brachyuran crabs of Roatan and The Swan Islands, Honduras; octocorals of Roatan. *Mailing Add:* Dept Biol Sci Tarleton State Univ Tarleton Sta Stephenville TX 76402-0001

KEITH, ERNEST ALEXANDER, RUMINANT NUTRITION. *Current Pos:* ASST PROF DAIRY NUTRIT, DEPT DAIRY SCI, LA STATE UNIV, 78- *Personal Data:* b Fayetteville, Tenn, Dec 19, 51; m 72. *Educ:* Univ Ark, BS, 73, MS, 74; Purdue Univ, PhD(ruminant nutrit), 78. *Mem:* Sigma Xi; Am Dairy Sci Asn; Am Soc Animal Sci; Am Forage & Grassland Coun. *Res:* Forage nutrition of dairy cattle. *Mailing Add:* 5015 S Rochelle Ct Springfield MO 65804

KEITH, FREDERICK W(ALTER), JR, CHEMICAL ENGINEERING. *Current Pos:* RETIRED. *Personal Data:* b Chicago, Ill, Jan 20, 21; m 43, Sidney Page; c 1. *Educ:* Yale Univ, BS, 42; Univ Pa, PhD(chem eng), 51. *Prof Exp:* Chem engr process develop, E I du Pont de Nemours & Co, 42-44; chem engr res & develop, Sharples Res Lab, 44-48; asst instr, Univ Pa, 49; chem engr process develop, Pennwalt Chem Equip Div, Sharples Corp, 50-71, dir environ technol, Sharples Div, Pennwalt Corp, Warminster, 71-79; consult, 79-88. *Mem:* Am Chem Soc; Am Inst Chem Engrs; Sigma Xi. *Res:* Development and evaluation of centrifuges; waste and sewage process development; separations in synfuel processing. *Mailing Add:* The Quadrangle Apt 5105 3300 Darby Rd Haverford PA 19041

KEITH, H(ARVEY) DOUGLAS, CRYSTALLINE MORPHOLOGY. *Current Pos:* res prof, 88-96, EMER PROF MAT SCI, UNIV CONN, 96- *Personal Data:* b Belfast, Northern Ireland, Mar 10, 27; US Citizen; m 53, 84, Gerhild Schmitt; c Sheela H & Brian. *Educ:* Queen's Univ, Belfast, BSc, 48; Univ Bristol, Eng, PhD(physics), 51. *Honors & Awards:* High-Polymer Physics Prize, Am Phys Soc, 73. *Prof Exp:* Lectr physics, Univ Bristol, 51-56; res physicist, Am Viscose Corp, 57-60; mem tech staff, Bell Tel Labs, 60-88. *Concurrent Pos:* Lectr physics, St Joseph's Col, Philadelphia, Pa, 58-60; div counr, Am Phys Soc, 77-85; consult, AT&T Bell Labs, 88-96. *Mem:* Fel Am Phys Soc. *Res:* Optical and electron microscopy; x-ray and electron diffraction of structure and morphology of crystalline polymers and relationships to properties. *Mailing Add:* 51 Gail Lane South Windsor CT 06074-4224

KEITH, JAMES OLIVER, WILDLIFE ECOLOGY, ECOTOXICOLOGY. *Current Pos:* CONSULT, 91- *Personal Data:* b Pasadena, Calif, Mar 20, 32; m 50, Berniece Schultz; c Edward, Paul, Joan, Ellen & Ann. *Educ:* Univ Calif, Berkeley, AB, 53; Univ Ariz, MS, 56; Ohio State Univ, PhD(ecol), 78. *Prof Exp:* Wildlife res biologist, Rocky Mt Forest & Range Exp Sta, US Forest Serv, 56-61; wildlife res biologist, Denver Wildlife Res Ctr, US Fish & Wildlife Serv, 61-76, chief, 69-73, wildlife res biologist environ contaminants, Patuxent Wildlife Res Ctr, 76-81, wildlife res biologist, Int Prog, Denver Wildlife Res Ctr, 81-90. *Concurrent Pos:* Res assoc, Agr Exp Sta, Univ Calif, 61-65; consult, World Wildlife Fund, Galapagos Islands, Food & Agr Orgn, Sudan, Kenya & Argentina, US Aid, Haiti, Sudan, Kenya, Senegal & Morocco, Nat Geog, Chile, govt Bahamas. *Mem:* Am Soc Mammalogists; Soc Conserv Biol; Wildlife Soc; Am Ornith Union; Soc Ecosyst Restoration & Mgt. *Res:* Ecological effects of land management practices; influence of logging, grazing, agriculture and pesticides on wildlife and their habitats; restoring altered ecosystems; control of introduced predators. *Mailing Add:* USDA Wildlife Res Ctr Bldg 16 Denver Fed Ctr Denver CO 80225

KEITH, JENNIE, GERONTOLOGY, ANTHROPOLOGY. *Current Pos:* From asst prof to prof, 70-90, CENTENNIAL PROF ANTHROP, SWARTHMORE COL, 90-, PROVOST, 92- *Personal Data:* b Carmel, Calif, Nov 15, 42; m 68, 80, Roy G Fitzgerald III; c Aaron & Kate. *Educ:* Pomona Col, BA, 64; Northwestern Univ, MA, 66, PhD(anthrop), 68. *Concurrent Pos:* Mem, Res Rev Comt, NIMH, 79-82; task group leader, Nat Res Plan Aging, 81; co-dir, Proj AGE, Nat Inst Aging, 82-90; mem, Aging & Human Develop Rev Panel, NIH, 85-90; exec comt Behav & Social Sci sect, Geront Soc Am, 85-87, prog chair, 89, chair, 90; assoc ed, J Gerontol, 86-92; sr adv coun, Brookdale Found, 89-92. *Mem:* Geront Soc Am; Am Anthrop Asn; Asn Anthrop & Geront. *Res:* Cross-cultural comparative research on social and cultural influences on aging and old age. *Mailing Add:* Swarthmore Col 500 College Ave Swarthmore PA 19081-1390. *E-Mail:* jkeithl@cc.swarthmore.edu

KEITH, JERRY M, ENZYMOLOGY, VIROLOGY. *Current Pos:* CHIEF, LAB MICROBIAL ECOL, NIH, BETHESDA, MD. *Personal Data:* b Salt Lake City, Utah, Oct 22, 40; m 92, Kim Y Green; c Stephanie D, Marlowe D & Jonathan K. *Educ:* Univ Calif, Berkeley, BA, 73, PhD(comp biochem), 76. *Prof Exp:* Staff fel, Lab Biol Viruses, Nat Inst Allergy & Infectious Dis, NIH, 76-78; asst prof biochem, Col Dent, NY Univ, 78-; sect chief, Dept Path, Rocky Mountain Labs, Nat Inst Allergy & Infectious Dis, NIH, Hamilton, Mont. *Concurrent Pos:* Adj asst prof biol doctoral fac, City Univ New York, 81-; prin investr, gen med-biochem, NIH, 81-84; indust consult, vaccine develop, Biotech. *Mem:* Sigma Xi; AAAS; Am Soc Microbiol; Am Soc Virol; Am Soc Biol Chem. *Res:* Molecular mechamisms of bacterial pathogens and the development of new generation vaccines; structure and function of biologically active nucleic acids and proteins, with a particular interest in the isolation and characerization of the enzymes related to the synthesis, processing and post-transcriptional modification of MRNA's. *Mailing Add:* NIDR/NIH Lab Microbiol Ecol Bldg 30 Rm 316 Bethesda MD 20892. *Fax:* 301-402-0396; *E-Mail:* keith@yoda.nidr.nih.gov

KEITH, LAWRENCE H, ENVIRONMENTAL CHEMISTRY, ELECTRONIC PUBLISHING. *Current Pos:* head, Org Chem Dept, Radian Corp, 77-78, mgr, Anal Chem Div, 79-81, chem develop coordr, 81-84, sr prog mgr, 85-92, PRIN SCIENTIST, RADIAN CORP, 85-, CORP FEL, RADIAN INT, 86- *Personal Data:* b Morris, Ill, Apr 5, 38; m 69; c Jack. *Educ:* Stetson Univ, BS, 60; Clemson Univ, MS, 63; Univ Ga, PhD(natural prod chem), 66. *Honors & Awards:* Chemist of the Year, Am Chem Soc, 75; Distinguished Serv Award, Am Chem Soc Div Environ Chem, 86. *Prof Exp:* Res chemist, Environ Protection Agency, 66-77. *Concurrent Pos:* Pres, KCP, 73-83; vchmn, Gordon Res Conf Environ Sci & Water, 73-; mem, Comt Mil Environ Res & Subcomt Indust Hyg, Nat Res Coun, 81; chmn, Am Chem Soc Div Environ Chem, 79, Am Chem Soc Subcomt on Environ Monitoring & Anal, 81-; adv bd, ES&T, 82-85, Environ Lab, 89-, Environ Protection, 90- *Mem:* Am Chem Soc; Sigma Xi; Am Soc Testing & Mat. *Res:* Chemical changes produced by pollution treatment; nuclear magnetic resonance of pesticides; mass spectrometry; identification of organic chemical pollutants;

computerized GC-MS analysis of pollutants; industrial pollutants; electronic book publishing; artificial intelligence. *Mailing Add:* Radian Int LLC PO Box 201088 Austin TX 78720-1088. *Fax:* 512-454-8807; *E-Mail:* larry_keith@radian.com

KEITH, LLOYD BURROWS, WILDLIFE MANAGEMENT. *Current Pos:* Asst forestry & wildlife mgt, 55-59, fel, 59-60, from instr to assoc prof, 60-70, PROF WILDLIFE ECOL, UNIV WIS-MADISON, 70- *Personal Data:* b Victoria, BC, Nov 29, 31; m 54; c 4. *Educ:* Univ Alta, BSc, 53, MSc, 55; Univ Wis, PhD(wildlife mgt), 59. *Mem:* Wildlife Soc; Am Soc Mammal; Ecol Soc Am. *Res:* Natural regulation of animal populations; ten-year cycle of northern fur-bearers and grouse. *Mailing Add:* 9344 Boxturtle Rd Mazomanie WI 53560

KEITH, MACKENZIE LAWRENCE, GEOCHEMISTRY, GEODYNAMICS. *Current Pos:* EMER PROF GEOCHEM, PA STATE UNIV. *Personal Data:* b Edmonton, Alta, Oct 12, 12; nat US; m 40, Mary E Skavlem; c 5. *Educ:* Univ Alta, BSc, 34; Queen's Univ, Can, MSc, 36; Mass Inst Technol, PhD(geol), 39. *Prof Exp:* Field geologist, Ventures, Ltd, 37, Geol Surv Can, 38 & US Smelting, Ref & Mining Co, 39-40; asst prof geol, Queen's Univ, Can, 40-47; petrologist, Geophys Lab, Carnegie Inst, 47-50. *Concurrent Pos:* Field geologist, McIntyre Mines, Ont, 41, Aluminum Co Can, Montreal, 42-43 & Ont Dept Mines, Toronto, 45-47. *Mem:* Fel Geol Soc Am; Mineral Soc Am; Geochem Soc; Geol Asn Can. *Res:* Petrology of alkaline rocks; staining methods for silicate minerals; mineral deposits; silicate chemistry, including system MgO-Cr2O3-SiO2; element distribution; geochemical prospecting; isotope ratios in limestone and fossils; geochemistry of sedimentary rocks; trace element and isotopic criteria for differentiating marine and fresh water sediments; global tectonics; evidence against plate tectonics. *Mailing Add:* Dept Geosci Pa State Univ 309 Deike Bldg University Park PA 16802

KEITH, ROBERT ALLEN, PSYCHOLOGY, MEDICAL REHABILITATION. *Current Pos:* From asst prof to prof, 53-89, EMER PROF PSYCHOL, CLAREMONT GRAD SCH, 89- *Personal Data:* b Brea, Calif, Mar 16, 24; m 49; c 2. *Educ:* Univ Calif, Los Angeles, BA, 48, MA, 51, PhD(psychol), 53; Am Bd Prof Psychol, dipl psychol. *Concurrent Pos:* Psychol consult, Casa Colina Hosp, 55-67, dir, Ctr Rehab Res & Planning, 65-95; res fel, Dept Nutrit, Sch Pub Health, Harvard Univ, 60-61; vis scholar, Dept Child Develop, Univ London, 67-68; fel, Div Rehab Psychol, Am Psychol Asn, 84, Int Exchange Experts & Info in Rehab, World Rehab Fund, 87. *Mem:* Am Psychol Asn; Am Congr Rehab Med. *Res:* Treatment effectiveness for brain injury, strokes, spinal cord injury; organizational analysis of operations of the rehabilitation hospital; market research and strategic planning. *Mailing Add:* Ctr Rehab Res & Planning Casa Colina Hosp 2850 N Garey Ave Pomona CA 91767

KEITH, TERRY EUGENE CLARK, HYDROTHERMAL ALTERATION, MINERALOGY. *Current Pos:* Assoc chief, Br Igneous & Geothermal Processes, 87-90, RES GEOLOGIST, US GEOL SURV, 64-, SCIENTIST-IN-CHG ALASKA VOLCANO OBSERV, 93- *Personal Data:* b Redlands, Calif, Jan 28, 40; m 66, William; c David & Caven. *Educ:* Univ Ariz, BS, 62; Univ Ore, MS, 64. *Mem:* Am Geophys Union; Geothermal Res Coun; Clay Mineral Soc. *Res:* Hydrothermal and fumarolic alteration mineralogy, primarily in Yellowstone National Park, the Pacific Northwest Cascade Range, and Alaskan volcanoes; field distribution and petrography of ultramafic rocks in the Yukon-Tanana Upland, Alaska. *Mailing Add:* US Geol Surv Alaska Volcano Observ 4200 University Dr Anchorage AK 99508-4667. *Fax:* 907-786-7450; *E-Mail:* tkeithetundra.wr.usgs.gov

KEITH, THEO GORDON, JR, THERMAL SCIENCES, NUMERICAL ANALYSIS. *Current Pos:* PROF & CHMN MECH ENG, UNIV TOLEDO, 71- *Personal Data:* b Cleveland, Ohio, July 2, 39; m 60; c 2. *Educ:* Fen Col, BME, 64; Univ Md, MSME, 68, PhD(mech eng). *Prof Exp:* Mech engr, Naval Ship Res & Develop Ctr, Annapolis, Md, 64-71. *Concurrent Pos:* Prin investr pumping ring seal grant, Lewis Res Ctr, NASA, 77-81 & wind energy grant, 79-, co-prin investr devicing grant, 80- *Mem:* Am Soc Mech Engrs; Am Soc Eng Educ; Am Inst Aeronaut & Astronaut; Soc Automotive Engrs; Sigma Xi. *Mailing Add:* 3866 Laplante Rd Monclova OH 43542-9728

KEITHLY, JANET SUE, MICROBIOLOGY. *Current Pos:* vis assoc prof microbiol, 79, res assoc med, 79-80, ASST PROF MICROBIOL MED, MED COL, CORNELL UNIV, 81- *Personal Data:* b Jefferson City, Mo, Nov 29, 41; m 73; c 2. *Educ:* Cent Mo State Univ, BSc, 63; Iowa State Univ, PhD(zool), 68. *Prof Exp:* Fel parasitol, Rutgers Univ, 68-70, Rockefeller Univ, 70-72; from asst prof to assoc prof biol, Herbert H Lehman Col, City Univ New York, 72-78. *Concurrent Pos:* Adj asst prof biochem cytol, Rockefeller Univ, 78-80; vis asst prof, Seattle Biomed Res Inst, 86-87. *Mem:* Am Soc Microbiol. *Res:* Chemotherapeutic strategies in treatment of leishmaniasis; drug mode of action against the human blood protozoa; factors influencing virulence of leishmania species; metabolic pathways of Leishmania as unique targets for chemotherapy; cloning the genes for and studying the expression of the rate-controlling enzymes in these pathways eg polyamine and trypanothione metabolism; ornithine decarboxylase and trypanothione reductase genes. *Mailing Add:* Biomed Sci State Univ NY-Albany 1400 Washington Ave Albany NY 12201-1000

KEITT, GEORGE WANNAMAKER, JR, PLANT PHYSIOLOGY, PESTICIDE REGULATION. *Current Pos:* PLANT PHYSIOLOGIST BIOL & ECON ANALYSIS DIV, PESTICIDE PROG, ENVIRON PROTECTION AGENCY, 75- *Personal Data:* b Madison, Wis, Sept 11, 28; m 57, Gretchen Pendill; c Anne L (Spell), Elizabeth P (Nowak), George W III & Edward N. *Educ:* Harvard Univ, AB, 50; Univ Wis, MS, 52, PhD(bot), 57. *Prof Exp:* Res assoc, Ford Agr Plant Nutrit Proj, Mich, 57-59; asst prof bot, Fla State Univ, 59-67; sr fel, Mackinac Col, 67-70; res dept, Brooklyn Botanic Garden, 70-75, chmn, 70-74. *Concurrent Pos:* Vis investr, Princeton Univ, 70. *Mem:* NY Acad Sci; Sigma Xi; Bot Soc Am; Am Inst Biol Sci; Scand Soc Plant Physiol; Am Soc Plant Physiol. *Res:* Chemical control of plant growth and differentiation. *Mailing Add:* Biol Anal Br BEAD 7503W EPA 401 M St SW Washington DC 20460. *E-Mail:* keitt.george@epamail.epa.gov

KEIZER, CLIFFORD RICHARD, PHYSICAL CHEMISTRY. *Current Pos:* head dept, NMex Inst Mining & Technol, 64-70, actg dean col, 66-67 & 74-75, actg vpres acad affairs, 76-77, PROF CHEM, NMEX INST MINING & TECHNOL, 64- *Personal Data:* b Hudsonville, Mich, Mar 19, 18; m 43; c 2. *Educ:* Hope Col, AB, 39; Univ Ill, MS, 41, PhD(phys chem), 43. *Prof Exp:* Jr res physicist, Monsanto Chem Co, 43-44; instr chem, Univ Ill, 44-46; from instr to asst prof chem, Western Reserve Univ, 46-48; prof chem & chmn Div Nat Sci, Cent Col Iowa, 48-57; prof chem, Ky Contract Team to Univ Indonesia, 57-62, from actg chief to chief, 58-62; prof chem, Lindenwood Col, 62-64. *Mem:* Am Chem Soc; Sigma Xi. *Res:* Electrochem. *Mailing Add:* 405 Col Ave Socorro NM 87801-4716

KEIZER, EUGENE O(RVILLE), VIDEO SYSTEMS, COLOR TELEVISION. *Current Pos:* RETIRED. *Personal Data:* b LeMars, Iowa, Sept 13, 18; m 41, Alice Schley; c 2. *Educ:* Iowa State Col, BS, 40. *Honors & Awards:* David Sarnoff Award, RCA Corp, 77 & 81; Edvard Rhein Award, 80; Vladimar K Zivoryki Award, Inst Elec & Electronics Engrs, 83. *Prof Exp:* Asst, Exp Sta, Iowa State Col, 37-40; res engr, RCA Labs, RCA Corp, 40-64, head, TV Res Group, Systs Res Lab, 64-67, head, Video Systs Res Group, Consumer Electronics Res Lab, 67-77, head microtopographics res, 77-78, head video recording res, Commun Res Labs, 78-79, staff scientist RCA selecta-vision video disc oper, 79-80, staff scientist, Video Disc Systems Res Lab, 80-84. *Concurrent Pos:* Instr war training prog, Rutgers Univ, 41-45. *Mem:* Inst Elec & Electronics Engrs; Sigma Xi. *Res:* Television; radar; microwave; radio frequency receivers and radio frequency circuits; color television; information storage and retrieval; video disc systems. *Mailing Add:* PO Box 125 Cornwall PA 17016-0125

KEIZER, JOEL EDWARD, PHYSICAL CHEMISTRY, STATISTICAL PHYSICS. *Current Pos:* from asst prof to prof chem, 71-93, DIR, INST THEORET DYNAMICS, UNIV CALIF, DAVIS, 85-, PROF BIOL SCIS, 93- *Personal Data:* b North Bend, Ore, Aug 31, 42; m 64, Susan J Swank; c Sidney J & Sarah R. *Educ:* Reed Col, BA, 64; Univ Ore, PhD(chem physics), 69. *Prof Exp:* Actg instr, Univ Calif, Santa Cruz, 69-71. *Concurrent Pos:* Battelle Mem Inst fel, 69-71; vis scientist, NIH, 78-79 & 86-87; assoc ed, Accounts Chem Res, 78-86; J S Guggenheim Mem fel, 86-87; guest researcher, NIH, 88-; assoc ed, modeling physiol, Am J Physiol. *Mem:* Fel AAAS; Biophys Soc; Am Diabetes Asn. *Res:* Molecular origins and nature of macroscopic dynamic phenomena in chemical, physical and biological systems; nonlinear, nonequilibrium thermodynamics; fluctuations and stochastic processes; cell biophysics. *Mailing Add:* Inst Theoret Dynamics Univ Calif Davis CA 95616. *Fax:* 530-752-7297

KELBER, CHARLES NORMAN, PHYSICS, MATHEMATICS. *Current Pos:* PHYSICIST & ADV REACTOR SAFETY RES, NUCLEAR REGULATORY COMN, 74- *Personal Data:* b Minneapolis, Minn, June 2, 28; m 50, Rhonda Joss; c Jeffrey A & Steven G. *Educ:* Univ Minn, BS, 47, MS, 48, PhD(physics), 51. *Prof Exp:* Physicist, Frankford Arsenal, Pa, 51-55 & Argonne Nat Lab, 55-74. *Mem:* Fel Am Phys Soc; Am Nuclear Soc. *Res:* Reactor physics and safety; reactor computation. *Mailing Add:* 11410 Strand Dr Rockville MD 20852. *Fax:* 301-492-7285; *E-Mail:* cnk@mnc.com

KELCH, ROBERT P, PEDIATRIC ENDOCRINOLOGY. *Current Pos:* PROF & DEAN, DEPT PEDIAT, UNIV IOWA COL MED, 94- *Educ:* Wayne State Univ, PhB, 63; Univ Mich, MD, 67. *Prof Exp:* From intern to resident pediat, Univ Hosp, Mich, 67-70; NIH trainee pediat endocrinol, Univ Calif, San Francisco, 70-72; from asst prof to prof pediat, Univ Mich, 72-94. *Concurrent Pos:* Res fel, Dept Obstet & Gynec, Univ Mich, 69-70, actg chmn, Dept Pediat, 79-80, chmn, 81-94; mem, Gen Clin Res Ctrs Comt, NIH, 87-89; chief clin affairs, Univ Mich Hosp, 89-92; asst dean clin affairs, Univ Mich Med Sch, 89-92; Univ Iowa distinguished fel, 94; chmn, Am Bd Pediat, 95. *Mem:* Inst Med-Nat Acad Sci; Soc Pediat Res (pres, 87). *Res:* Contributed numerous articles to professional publications. *Mailing Add:* Univ Iowa Col Med 212 CMAB Iowa City IA 52242-1101

KELCH, WALTER L, MANAGEMENT OF RESEARCH, ENGINEERING. *Current Pos:* ENGR & ANALYST, CENT INTEL AGENCY, LANGLEY, VA, 78- *Personal Data:* b Dayton, Ohio, Oct 27, 48; m 70, Tina Ziegler; c Matthew J. *Educ:* Miami Univ, AB, 70; Ind Univ, MA, 73, PhD(astrophys), 75. *Prof Exp:* Instr astron, Kean Col, NJ, 75-76; res assoc, Joint Inst Lab Astrophys, Univ Colo, 76-78. *Mem:* Am Astron Soc. *Res:* Spectral line formation in stellar atmospheres; solar and stellar atmosphere models; radiative transport; astrophysics. *Mailing Add:* 2103 Sugarloaf Ct Herndon VA 22070

KELCHNER, BURTON L(EWIS), chemical engineering, for more information see previous edition

KELDYSH, LEONID, THEORETICAL PHYSICS, CONDENSED MATTER PHYSICS. *Current Pos:* Sr sci researcher, P N Levedev Phys Inst Acad Sci, 65-68, head sector, 68-89, managing dir, 89-93, SR SCI RESEARCHER, PN LEBEDEV PHYS INST RUSS ACAD SCI, 94-; PROF, MOSCOW STATE UNIV, 65-, HEAD QUANTUM RADIOPHYSICS, CHAIR, PHYSICS DEPT, 78- *Personal Data:* b Moscow, Russia, July 4, 31. *Educ:* Moscow State Univ, MSc, 54; P N Lebedev Physics Inst Russ Acad Sci, PhD, 65. *Honors & Awards:* Lenin Prize, USSR, 74; Hewlett-Packard Prize, Europ Phys Soc, 75; Humboldt Res Award, 94. *Concurrent Pos:* Asst prof, Phys-Technol Inst, Moscow, 62-64; chmn, Gen Physics & Astron Sect, Russ Acad Sci; Roentgen prof, Univ Wuerzburg, 97. *Mem:* Foreign assoc Nat Acad Sci; Acad Sci USSR. *Res:* Many-body theory; semiconductors; superconductors; nonlinear optics; low-dimensional systems. *Mailing Add:* Lebedev Inst Physics Russ Acad Sci Leninskiy Prospect 53 117924GSP Moscow B-333 Russia

KELE, ROGER ALAN, INDUSTRIAL MICROBIOLOGY. *Current Pos:* RES MICROBIOLOGIST, LEDERLE LABS DIV, AM CYANAMID CO, 70- *Personal Data:* b Waterbury, Conn, Jan 24, 43; m 72; c 2. *Educ:* Clark Univ, BA, 64; Harvard Univ, MA, 66; Univ Wis, PhD(bact), 70. *Honors & Awards:* Am Cyanamid Sci Achievement Award, 80. *Mem:* Am Soc Microbiol; Soc Indust Microbiol. *Res:* Strain improvement work on the tetracycline antibiotics. *Mailing Add:* Lederle Labs Pearl River NY 10965

KELEHER, J J, ENVIRONMENTAL SCIENCES. *Current Pos:* RETIRED. *Personal Data:* b Winnipeg, Man, Feb 9, 26; m 53; c 3. *Educ:* Univ Man, BA, 48; Univ Toronto, MA, 50. *Prof Exp:* Biologist, Fisheries Res Bd Can, 50-68; chief fisheries biologist, Man Dept Mines & Natural Resources, 68-69, chief, Fisheries Opers, 70-71, spec asst, 72-82, environ officer, Man Dept Consumer, Corp Affairs & Environ, 83-85. *Concurrent Pos:* Exec secy, Man Environ Coun, 73-83. *Mem:* Am Fisheries Soc; Am Inst Fishery Res Biol. *Res:* Environmental management. *Mailing Add:* 10 Baldry Bay Winnipeg MB R3T 3C4 Can

KELEMEN, CHARLES F, MATHEMATICS, COMPUTER SCIENCE EDUCATION. *Current Pos:* PROF MATH & COMPUT SCI, DIR, COMPUT SCI PROG PROG, SWARTHMORE COL, 84- *Personal Data:* b Mt Vernon, NY, Jan 7, 43; m 75, Sylvia Brown; c Rebecca, Colin & Elizabeth. *Educ:* Valparaiso Univ, BA, 64; Pa State Univ, MA, 66, PhD(math), 69. *Prof Exp:* From asst prof to assoc prof math, Ithaca Col, 69-80; from assoc prof to prof comput sci, Lemoyne Col, 80-84. *Concurrent Pos:* Res assoc, Dept Comput Sci, Cornell Univ, 75-76, vis assoc prof, 77-81; NSF grant, 77-81. *Mem:* Inst Elec & Electronics Engrs; Math Asn Am; Asn Comput Mach; Soc Indust & Appl Math; Sigma Xi. *Res:* Computational complexity; analysis of algorithms; computer science education. *Mailing Add:* Comput Sci Prog Swarthmore Col 500 College Ave Swarthmore PA 19081-1397

KELEMEN, DENIS GEORGE, CHEMISTRY OF SOLIDS, ELECTRONIC MATERIALS. *Current Pos:* INDEPENDENT CONSULT, TECHNOL APPRAISALS, 88- *Personal Data:* b Budapest, Hungary, June 18, 25; nat US; m 94, Joanne Foulk; c Peter B. *Educ:* Princeton Univ, PhD(chem), 51. *Prof Exp:* Ed asst tables of chem kinetics, Nat Res Coun, 48-50; res chemist, E I du Pont de Nemours & Co, Inc, 50-57, res supvr, 57-68, res mgr electronic prod div, Electrochem Dept, 68-70, planning mgr, Photoprod Dept, 70-72, prod mgr, 72-78, develop mgr, Electronic Prod Div, Photoprod Dept, 78-80, prin consult, 80-84, sr consult, Electronic Mat Div, 84-87. *Mem:* Am Chem Soc; Am Solar Energy Soc; Inst Elec & Electronics Engrs. *Res:* Physical chemistry of solids. *Mailing Add:* 8 Smith Rd Hanover NH 03755

KELISKY, RICHARD PAUL, MATHEMATICS, DATA PROCESSING. *Current Pos:* RETIRED. *Personal Data:* b St Louis, Mo, Nov 27, 29; wid; c Jeffrey. *Educ:* Tex Tech Col, BS, 51; Univ Tex, MA, 53, PhD(math), 57. *Prof Exp:* Asst appl math, Univ Tex, 52-55, lectr, 55-57, asst prof, 57-58; dir, Comput Systs Dept, Thomas J Watson Res Ctr, IBM Corp, 71-82, dir lab opers, 82-86, res mathematician dir plan & qual, 86-91. *Concurrent Pos:* Adj prof, Grad Div, City Univ New York, 65-72. *Mem:* Math Asn Am. *Res:* Theory of numbers; numerical analysis; computing center management. *Mailing Add:* 24 Coolidge Ave White Plains NY 10606

KELKER, DOUGLAS, STATISTICS. *Current Pos:* vis asst prof, 73-76, asst prof math, 76-81, ASSOC PROF STATIST, UNIV ALTA, 81- *Personal Data:* b Logan, Utah, Mar 23, 40; m 75; c 2. *Educ:* Hiram Col, BA, 61; Univ Ore, MA, 63, PhD(math), 68. *Prof Exp:* Asst prof probability & statist, Mich State Univ, 68; asst prof math, Wash State Univ, 68-73. *Mem:* Inst Math Statist; Am Statist Asn; Can Statist Soc. *Res:* Characterization theorems; infinite divisibility; distributions on the unit sphere applied to geological data. *Mailing Add:* Math Scis Univ Alta Edmonton AB T6G 2G1 Can. *Fax:* 403-492-2927; *E-Mail:* kelk@fisher.stat.ualberta.ca

KELL, ROBERT M, EMULSION POLYMERIZATION, EXPERIMENTAL DESIGN. *Current Pos:* res chemist, 68-79, SR RES ASSOC, FRANKLIN INT, 79- *Personal Data:* b Piqua, Ohio, Nov 27, 22; m 49; c 3. *Educ:* Ohio State Univ, BChE, 47, MSc, 48. *Prof Exp:* Jr chem engr, Olin Corp, 48-52; res chemist, Battelle Mem Inst, 52-62, sr res chemist, 62-68. *Mem:* Am Chem Soc; Tech Asn Pulp & Paper Indust. *Res:* Adhesives; physical chemistry of polymers; plastics applications; vinyl polymerization. *Mailing Add:* 3848 Norbrook Dr Columbus OH 93220

KELLAND, DAVID ROSS, PHYSICS, MAGNETISM. *Current Pos:* staff mem, Mass Inst Technol, 67-77, asst group leader, 77-78, co-group leader, 78-80, group leader, Francis Bitter Nat Magnet Lab, 80-91, VIS SCIENTIST, MASS INST TECHNOL, 91- *Personal Data:* b East Orange, NJ, July 29, 35; m 89, Marjorie; c 3. *Educ:* Montclair State Col, BA, 57, MA, 60; Salford Univ, PhD, 89. *Prof Exp:* Instr physics, Simmons Col, 61-63; asst prof, Emmanuel Col, Mass, 63-67. *Concurrent Pos:* Prog mgr, NSF, 87-91; chmn, Forum Int Physics, Am Phys Soc, 94-96; chmn, Tech Comt Magnetic Separation, Inst Elec & Electronics Engrs. *Mem:* Am Phys Soc; Inst Elec & Electronics Engrs. *Res:* Applied magnetism and low temperature physics. *Mailing Add:* Mass Inst Technol 884 Massachusetts Ave Lexington MA 02173. *E-Mail:* kelland@mit.edu

KELLAR, KENNETH JON, NEUROPHARMACOLOGY, MOLECULAR PHARMACOLOGY. *Current Pos:* from asst prof to assoc prof, 76-85, PROF PHARMACOL, SCH MED, GEORGETOWN UNIV, 85- *Personal Data:* b Baltimore, Md, Feb 13, 45; m 72; c 2. *Educ:* Johns Hopkins Univ, BS, 66; Ohio State Univ, PhD(pharmacol), 74. *Honors & Awards:* Anna Monika Prize, Res Into Causes & Treatment of Depression. *Concurrent Pos:* Prof psychiat, Georgetown Univ Med Ctr. *Mem:* Soc Neurosci; Am Soc Pharmacol Exp Therapeut; Int Soc Neurochem. *Res:* Regulation of neurotransmission; signal transduction. *Mailing Add:* Dept Pharmacol Georgetown Univ Sch Med 3900 Reservoir Rd NW Washington DC 20007-2195. *Fax:* 202-687-6209

KELLAWAY, PETER, NEUROPHYSIOLOGY. *Current Pos:* from assoc prof to prof physiol, 48-77, CHIEF, SECT NEUROPHYSIOL, BAYLOR COL MED, 48-; PROF NEUROL, 77-, PROF, DIV NEUROSCI, 89- *Personal Data:* b Johannesburg, SAfrica, Oct 20, 20; nat US; m 58; c 5. *Educ:* Occidental Col, BA, 41, MA, 42; McGill Univ, PhD(physiol), 47, Am Bd Clin Neurophysiol, 52. *Hon Degrees:* MD, Gothenburg Univ, Sweden, 77. *Honors & Awards:* Sir William Osler Medal, Am Asn Hist Med, 46; Lennox lectr, Am Epilepsy Soc, 84, Lennox Award, 96; First Distinguished Clin Investr Award, Am Epilepsy Soc, 89; Jasper Award, Am Electroencephalog Soc, 91. *Prof Exp:* Demonstr physiol, McGill Univ, 44-46, lectr, 46-47, asst prof, 47-48. *Concurrent Pos:* Dir, Blue Bird Children's Epilepsy Clin, 49-60; dir, Dept Electroencephalog, Methodist Hosp, 49-71, chief & sr attend, Neurophysiol Serv, 71-; consult, US Vet Admin Hosp, 49-75, Hermann Hosp, 55-73 & St Luke's Hosp, 71-; dir, EEG Lab, Ben Taub Gen Hosp, 65-; ed, EEG & Clin Neurophysiol, 68-71, consult ed, 72-75; chief, Neurophysiol Serv, Dept Med, Tex Children's Hosp, 72- & St Luke's Hosp, 73-; dir, Epilepsy Res Ctr, Baylor Col Med & Methodist Hosp, 75-; hon pres, Int Soc Clin Neurophysiol, 93; ed, J Electroencephalo & Clin Neurophysiol. *Mem:* Am Physiol Soc; Am Electroencephalog Soc (treas, 56-58, pres elect, 62-63, pres, 63-64); Soc Neurosci; Am Neurol Asn; Int League Against Epilepsy (secy-treas, 55-58); Am Epilepsy Soc (pres, 60); hon fel Am Acad Pediat; Am Acad Neurol; Child Neurol Soc. *Res:* Genesis and ontogenesis of electrical activity of the brain and of the epileptic process; epilepsy. *Mailing Add:* Dept Neurol Sect Neurophysiol Baylor Col Med Houston TX 77030

KELLEHER, DENNIS L, ENVIRONMENTAL PHYSIOLOGY. *Current Pos:* HEAD TRAUMA RES, FAIRFAX HOSP, FALLS CHURCH, VA, 92- *Educ:* Univ Fla, PhD(physiol), 78. *Prof Exp:* Asst prof, Dept Physiol, Uniformed Serv Univ, Bethesda, 85-90. *Mem:* Am Physiol Soc; Aerospace Med Asn; Sigma Xi. *Mailing Add:* Antiviral Clin Res Glaxo Wellcome Inc 5 Moore Dr Research Triangle Park NC 27709

KELLEHER, HERBERT DAVID, AVIATION. *Current Pos:* FOUNDER, GEN COUNR, CHMN & DIR, SOUTHWEST AIRLINES, 67- *Personal Data:* b Camden, NJ, Mar 12, 31; m 55, Joan Negley; c Julie, Michael, Ruth & David. *Educ:* Wesleyan Univ, BA, 53; New York Univ, LLB, 56. *Honors & Awards:* Aircraft Opers Excellence Award, Am Inst Aeronaut & Astronaut, 94. *Mailing Add:* SW Airlines Co Box 36611 Love Field Dallas TX 75235-1611

KELLEHER, JAMES JOSEPH, MOLECULAR BIOLOGY, IMMUNOLOGY. *Current Pos:* from asst prof to assoc prof microbiol, 68-80, PROF MICROBIOL/IMMUNOL, SCH MED, UNIV NDAK, 80-, CHMN, 89- *Personal Data:* b Hudson, Mass, Sept, 12, 38; m 63; c 4. *Educ:* Boston Col, BS, 60, MS, 63; Rutgers Univ, PhD(microbiol), 66. *Prof Exp:* Instr microbiol, Rutgers Univ, 66-67; res asst, Woods Hole Oceanog Inst, 67-68. *Concurrent Pos:* Fel, Woods Hole Oceanog Inst, 67-68; consult diag virol, 72-, environ virol, 74-78. *Mem:* AAAS; Am Soc Microbiol; Sigma Xi; NY Acad Sci; Am Heart Asn. *Res:* Nutrition, viral infection and immune response; clinical diagnosis of viral infections; herpes virus latency in cell culture and animal model systems; virus transmission by the water route; virology; nucleic acid probes; immunological diagnosis. *Mailing Add:* Sch Med Univ NDak Grand Forks ND 58201

KELLEHER, MATTHEW D(ENNIS), MECHANICAL ENGINEERING, HEAT TRANSFER. *Current Pos:* from asst prof to assoc prof, 67-82, PROF MECH ENG, NAVAL POSTGRAD SCH, 82-, CHAIR DEPT, 92- *Personal Data:* b Flushing, NY, Feb 1, 39; m 69, Jean Jolliffe; c Genevieve & Veronica. *Educ:* Univ Notre Dame, BS, 61, MS, 63, PhD(mech eng), 66. *Prof Exp:* Asst prof mech eng, Univ Notre Dame, 65-66; Ford Found fel eng, Dartmouth Col, 66-67. *Concurrent Pos:* Consult, Apple Comput, 84 & Kaiser Engrs, 85; prog comt, Nat Heat Transfer Conf, 84-88; vis prof, Univ Notre Dame, 87; sr acad visitor, Oxford Univ, 88-89. *Mem:* Fel Am Soc Mech Engrs; Sigma Xi; Am Soc Eng Educ. *Res:* Heat transfer and fluid mechanics, specifically convection and radiation; heat pipes; electronics cooling. *Mailing Add:* Dept Mech Eng Naval Postgrad Sch Code ME Kk Monterey CA 93943. *Fax:* 408-656-2238; *E-Mail:* mkelleher@nps.navy.mil

KELLEHER, PHILIP CONBOY, TUMOR MARKERS, GLYCOCONJUGATES. *Current Pos:* from instr to asst prof, 63-68, ASSOC PROF MED, COL MED, UNIV VT, 69- *Personal Data:* b New Rochelle, NY, July 23, 28; m 55; c 3. *Educ:* Georgetown Univ, BS, 50, MD, 54. *Prof Exp:* Resident physician, State Univ NY Upstate Med Ctr, 55-58; res fel biochem, Harvard Med Sch, 60-63. *Concurrent Pos:* Tutor, Harvard Med Sch, 62-63; clin fel med, Mass Gen Hosp, 61-63. *Mem:* AAAS; Am Fedn Clin Res; Int Soc NCo-develop Mental Biol & Med; Am Asn Cancer Res. *Res:* Serum protein metabolism; glycoconjugates; specific fetal serum proteins; carcinoembryonic antigens; collagen metabolism. *Mailing Add:* Given Med Bldg Burlington VT 05405

KELLEHER, RAYMOND JOSEPH, JR, GENETICS, BIOCHEMISTRY. *Current Pos:* SR RES SCIENTIST, LEDERLE-PRAXIS BIOL, 93- *Personal Data:* b Fall River, Mass, Sept 27, 39; m 64; c 3. *Educ:* Col Holy Cross, AB, 61; Boston Col, MS, 64; Univ NC, Chapel Hill, PhD(genetics), 69. *Prof Exp:* NIH fel genetics & biochem, 69-73, res assoc, 73-75, sr res assoc, Salk Inst Biol Studies, 75-76; res fel, Univ Calif, San Diego, 76-77; asst prof, State Univ NY, Buffalo, 77-84, prof, Geneseo, 84-87; vpres res, T & B Bioclone Corp, 87-91; res scientist, Roswell Park Cancer Inst, 91-93. *Mem:* AAAS; Genetics Soc Am. *Res:* Somatic cell genetics; molecular endocrinology; eukaryotic gene regulation. *Mailing Add:* 97 Jeanmoor Dr Amherst NY 14228

KELLEHER, ROBERT NEAL, ASBESTOS REMEDIATION, HAZ-MAT REMEDIATION & INCIDENT RESPONSE. *Current Pos:* ENVIRON & CHEM CONSULT, CLEAN-AGRI FRUIT CHEM, 83- *Personal Data:* b Teaneck, NJ, June 26, 43; wid; c Scott & Kristen. *Educ:* Univ Eastern Fla, BS(chem eng), 65. *Prof Exp:* Pharmacist med supply, USAF, 65-67; asst res & develop chemist, Penetone Div, Amerace-Esna, 67-69; opers coodr, Jefferson Chem Co, 69-71; vpres & opers mgr, Ajax Div, Biscayne Chem, 71-79; opers mgr, Trojan Chem Co, 79-81; vpres opers mgr, Cyclo Chem Corp, 81-84. *Mem:* Am Chem Soc; AAAS; Am Inst Plant Engrs. *Res:* Agricultural/chemical formulation of environmentally safe products for the farm community and the development of non-toxic adjuvents and insecticides. *Mailing Add:* PO Box 2408 Fallon NV 89407-2408

KELLEHER, ROGER THOMSON, PHARMACOLOGY. *Current Pos:* from asst prof to assoc prof pharmacol, 61-72, PROF PSYCHOBIOL, HARVARD MED SCH, 72- *Personal Data:* b New Haven, Conn, Dec 28, 26; m 52; c 3. *Educ:* Univ Conn, BA, 50; NY Univ, MA, 53, PhD(exp psychol), 55. *Prof Exp:* Asst psychol, NY Univ, 52-55; asst exp psychol, Yerkes Labs Primate Biol, 55-56, res assoc, 56-57; sr pharmacologist, Smith Kline & French Labs, NJ, 57-61. *Concurrent Pos:* Specific field ed, J Am Soc Pharmacol & Exp Therapeut. *Mem:* AAAS; Am Soc Pharmacol & Exp Therapeut; Sigma Xi. *Res:* Behavioral pharmacology; behavioral physiology; effects of drugs on cardiovascular regulation. *Mailing Add:* Lab Psychobiol Harvard Med Sch Boston MA 02115-5701

KELLEHER, WILLIAM JOSEPH, BIOCHEMISTRY, PHARMACOGNOSY. *Current Pos:* RETIRED. *Personal Data:* b Hartford, Conn, July 18, 29. *Educ:* Univ Conn, BS, 51, MS, 53; Univ Wis, PhD(biochem), 60. *Prof Exp:* Asst pharm, Univ Conn, 51-53; asst biochem, Univ Wis, 56-60; from asst prof to assoc prof, Sch Pharm, Univ 60-70, prof pharmacog, 70-88, chmn, Med Chem & Pharmacog Sect, 71-76, asst dean, 76-81; consult, Vicks Res Ctr, 85-92; consult, Copley Pharmaceut, 92-95. *Concurrent Pos:* Mem, Nat Formulary Adv Panel Pharmacog, 64-71; guest prof, Univ Freiburg, 70-71 & 77-78; assoc ed, Lloydia, 71-76; vis scientist, Vicks Res Ctr, 84-85. *Mem:* Am Chem Soc; Am Soc Pharmacog; Brit Biochem Soc. *Res:* Microbial chemistry and the production and biosynthesis of alkaloids and other medicinal products by fermentation processes; formulation and dosage form development. *Mailing Add:* PO Box 205 Storrs CT 06268

KELLEMS, RODNEY E, MOLECULAR GENETICS. *Current Pos:* ASSOC PROF BIOCHEM, BAYLOR COL MED, 84- *Educ:* Princeton Univ, PhD(biochem), 75. *Mem:* Am Soc Biol Chem; Am Chem Soc; Am Soc Cell Biol; Am Soc Human Genetics. *Mailing Add:* Dept Biochem Baylor Col Med One Baylor Plaza Houston TX 77030-3498. *Fax:* 713-796-9438

KELLER, ANDREW, PHYSICS. *Personal Data:* b Budapest, Hungary, Aug 22, 25; m 51, Eva Bulhack; c Peter & Nicola. *Educ:* Univ Eotvos Lorant, Hungary, BS, 47; Univ Bristol, Eng, PhD(physics), 58. *Honors & Awards:* High Polymer Prize, Am Phys Soc, 64; Max Born Medal Physics, Inst Physics London, 83; Rumford Medal, Royal Soc, 94. *Prof Exp:* Tech officer, Imp Chem Indust, Eng, 48-55; res assoc, Univ Bristol, Eng, 55-62, lectr, 62-66, reader, 66-69, prof, 66-91, EMER PROF, UNIV BRISTOL, ENG, 91- *Concurrent Pos:* Vis prof, Case Western Res Univ, Cleveland, 69-; Clyde res prof, Univ Utah, 82-83; chmn, Macromolecular Sect, Europ Physicists Soc, 84-88; Morton res prof, Univ Akron, 93. *Mem:* Fel Royal Soc; Am Phys Soc; Acad Europaea; Europ Physicists Soc. *Res:* Contributed numerous articles to journals. *Mailing Add:* 41 Westbury Rd Bristol England

KELLER, ARTHUR CHARLES, electrical engineering, for more information see previous edition

KELLER, BARRY LEE, WILDLIFE ECOLOGY. *Current Pos:* from asst prof to assoc prof, 70-80, PROF POP ECOL, IDAHO STATE UNIV, 80- *Personal Data:* b Chicago, Ill, Nov 15, 37; m 62; c 2. *Educ:* Western Mich Univ, BA, 61, MA, 62; Ind Univ, PhD(ecol), 68. *Prof Exp:* Fel ecol, Ind Univ, 68-69; assoc prof biol, Keen State Col, 69-70. *Concurrent Pos:* prin investr, 65 grants, 70-; cur mammals, Idaho Mus Natural Hist, 79-; ed, Tebiwa, The J of Idaho Mus Nat Hist, 84-; vis scholar, Utah Mus Nat Hist, 87-88. *Mem:* Am Soc Mammalogists; Brit Ecol Soc; Ecol Soc Am; Soc Pop Ecol; Wildlife Soc; Sigma Xi. *Res:* Wildlife ecology, with emphasis on population ecology of non-game species; ecology of desert mammals, with emphasis on small mammals residing on radioactive waste disposal sites; powerline corridor analyses. *Mailing Add:* Dept Biol Sci Idaho State Univ 921 S Eighth Ave Pocatello ID 83209-0001

KELLER, BERNARD GERARD, JR, PHARMACY. *Current Pos:* from asst dean clin progs to dean, Okla State Univ, 72-87, prof pharmaceut & chmn dept, 69-81, chmn, Div Pharmaceut & Pharm Admin, 70-81, PROF PHARM ADMIN, SCH PHARM, SOUTHWESTERN OKLA STATE UNIV, 81- *Personal Data:* b New Orleans, La, Dec 18, 36. *Educ:* Loyola Univ, BS, 59; Univ Miss, MS, 64, PhD(pharm admin), 66. *Prof Exp:* Asst prof pharm & pharm admin, Southern Col Pharm, 65-67, assoc prof pharm admin, 67-69. *Mem:* Am Pharmaceut Asn; Am Soc Hosp Pharmacists; Am Col Apothecaries; Nat Asn Retail Druggists. *Res:* Pharmacy administration; motivation research; the pharmacist's relationship to the terminal patient; medical ethics. *Mailing Add:* 715 E Eureka Ave Weatherford OK 73096

KELLER, C KENT, HYDROGEOCHEMISTRY, VADOSE ZONE. *Current Pos:* ASSOC PROF HYDROGEOL, WASH STATE UNIV, 88- *Personal Data:* b Ashland, Ohio, Sept 6, 55; m 84, Teresa Harder. *Educ:* Stanford Univ, BS, 77; Univ Waterloo, Ont, MS, 85, PhD(earth sci), 87. *Prof Exp:* Res assoc, Sask Res Coun, 85-87. *Concurrent Pos:* Consult, USAID, 82-83; vis prof, NMex Inst Mining & Technol, 94-95. *Mem:* Am Geophys Union; Nat Ground Water Asn; Geol Soc Am; Am Chem Soc. *Res:* Carbon cycling in groundwater systems and the soil-vadose continuum; chemical weathering and the carbon cycle; groundwater chemical evolution. *Mailing Add:* Wash State Univ Dept Geol Pullman WA 99164

KELLER, CHARLES A(LBERT), chemical engineering; deceased, see previous edition for last biography

KELLER, D STEVEN, FINE PARTICLE & COLLOID SCIENCE, SUSPENSION RHEOLOGY. *Current Pos:* RES SPECIALIST PAPER CHEM, COL ENVIRON SCI & FORESTRY, STATE UNIV NY, 90-, ASST PROF, 97- *Personal Data:* b Syracuse, NY, July 15, 58; m 81; c 1. *Educ:* Syracuse Univ, BS, 80; State Univ NY, PhD, 96. *Prof Exp:* Asst chemist, Champion Chem, 80-81, regional tech serv coordr, 81-82; assoc res chemist, Otisca Industs, Ltd, 82-90. *Concurrent Pos:* Prin investr, SBIR Res Proj, Dept Energy, 89-90. *Mem:* Am Chem Soc; Soc Rheol; Technol Asn Pulp & Paper. *Res:* Investigation of surface properties of micron size precipitated and naturally occuring calcium carbonate compounds using inverse gas chromatography; kinetics of rheological instabilities in shear-thickening, non-Newtonian concentrated fine particle suspensions. *Mailing Add:* ESPRI State Univ NY One Forestry Dr Syracuse NY 13210-2778. *E-Mail:* dskeller@mailbox.syr.edu

KELLER, DOLORES ELAINE, REPRODUCTIVE PHYSIOLOGY, MICROBIOLOGY. *Current Pos:* PSYCHOTHER, PVT PRACT. *Personal Data:* b New York, NY, Oct 29, 26; m 46; c 3. *Educ:* Long Island Univ, BS, 45; NY Univ, MA, 47, PhD(sex educ), 56; Univ Hawaii, cert, 64; Univ Calif, Berkeley, cert, 66. *Prof Exp:* Teacher biol & chmn dept, NY Pub Sch, 49-52; instr biol, Fr& lang & asst dean women, Long Island Univ, 52-56; from instr to assoc prof & chmn, Dept Sci, Fairleigh Dickinson Univ, 56-65; chmn, Dept Biol, Pace Univ, Westchester Campus, 65-68, prof biol & dir allied health progs, 65-92, dir, NSF Inserv Inst Cell Physiol & Genetics, 66-92. *Concurrent Pos:* US deleg, Int Oceanog Conf, 59 & NSF grants, 63-; res assoc, Haskins Labs, Carnegie Found, 63-; consult, Rennselaer Polytech Prog Intgerdisciplinary Col Sci, Charles Kettering Found, 64-; curric chmn, Bergen Co Community Col, 64-; NSF-AEC grant marine & radiation biol, Univ Hawaii, 64-; res assoc, Lamont Geol Lab, Columbia Univ, Davis, 71; NSF partic, Conf Primate Behav, Univ Calif, Davis, 71; spec consult, UN Comt Human Environ, 71-72; clin asst prof biol psychiat, Dept Psychiat, Med Col, Cornell Univ, 74-; sr therapist, Payne Whitney Sexual Disorder Clin & pvt pract marriage counr sexual dysfunction, NJ, 74- *Mem:* Fel AAAS; Nat Sci Teachers Asn; Soc Protozool; Int Soc Clin & Exp Hypnosis; Am Sex Educ Counrs. *Res:* Protozoology; fresh water and marine microbiology; science curriculum and education; sex education; human sexuality. *Mailing Add:* 839 River Rd Piermont NY 10968

KELLER, DONALD V, EXPERIMENTAL PHYSICS. *Current Pos:* PRES, KTECH CORP, 71- *Personal Data:* b Centralia, Wash, Aug 17, 30; m 59; c 2. *Educ:* Harvard Univ, AB, 52; Univ Calif, Berkeley, PhD(physics), 57. *Prof Exp:* Chief shock dynamics, Boeing Co, 57-62; chief tech exp physics, Northrop Corp, Calif, 62-66; mem tech staff, Defense Res Corp, 66-69; pres, Effects Technol, Inc, 69-71. *Mem:* Am Phys Soc. *Res:* High energy nuclear physics; shock hydrodynamics; laser physics; dynamic mechanic and thermal properties of materials. *Mailing Add:* Ktech Corp 901 Pennsylvania St NE Albuquerque NM 87110

KELLER, DOUGLAS VERN, JR, PHYSICAL CHEMISTRY, MATERIAL SCIENCE. *Current Pos:* from asst prof to assoc prof metall eng, 59-69, prof, 69-78, ADJ PROF MATH SCI, SYRACUSE UNIV, 78-, RES PROF, 91- *Personal Data:* b Syracuse, NY, Feb 8, 28; m 53, Patricia S; c Brian A, Jennifer A, Douglas S & Diana L. *Educ:* Univ Buffalo, BA, 55; Syracuse Univ, PhD(chem), 58. *Prof Exp:* Asst prof metall, Mont Sch Mines, 58-59; vpres technol, Otisca Industs Ltd, 78-91. *Concurrent Pos:* Bd dirs, Otisca Industs Ltd, NY, 73-91. *Mem:* Am Chem Soc; Am Phys Soc; Am Soc Metals. *Res:* Physical chemistry of surfaces; coal physical chemistry and fuels benification. *Mailing Add:* Col Eng 409 Link Hall Syracuse Univ Syracuse NY 13244. *Fax:* 315-443-4936; *E-Mail:* dvkeller@mailbox.syr.edu

KELLER, EDWARD ANTHONY, GEOMORPHOLOGY. *Current Pos:* PROF ENVIRON STUDIES & GEOL SCI, UNIV CALIF, SANTA BARBARA, 76- *Personal Data:* b Los Angeles, Calif, June 6, 42; m 66; c 2. *Educ:* Calif State Univ, Fresno, BS, 65, BA, 68; Univ Calif, Davis, MS, 69; Purdue Univ, PhD(geol), 73. *Prof Exp:* Asst prof geol, Calif State Univ, Fresno, 69-70; instr, Purdue Univ, 70-73, res asst, 71-73; asst prof, Univ NC, Charlotte, 73-76. *Concurrent Pos:* Hartley vis prof, Southampton Univ, UK. *Mem:* Geol Soc Am; Sigma Xi. *Res:* Fluvial processes in geomorphology; environmental geology; tectonic geomorphology. *Mailing Add:* Environ Studies Univ Calif Santa Barbara CA 93106

KELLER, EDWARD CLARENCE, JR, ECOLOGY, BIOSTATISTICS. *Current Pos:* chmn dept, 69-74, PROF BIOL, WVA UNIV, 68- *Personal Data:* b Freehold, NJ, Oct 8, 32; c Edward C III & Kim L. *Educ:* Pa State Univ, BSc, 56, MSc, 59, PhD(genetics), 61. *Hon Degrees:* ScD, Salem Col, 78. *Prof Exp:* Asst genetics, Pa State Univ, 56-61; NIH trainee, Med Sch, Univ NC, 61-62, res assoc, 62, NIH fel, 62-64; asst prof zool, Univ Md, Col Park, 64-67; mgr biostatist, NUS Corp, 66-68. *Concurrent Pos:* Staff biologist, Comn Undergrad Educ Biol Sci, 65-66; pres, WVa Acad Sci, 75-76; vpres, Ecometrics Corp, 73-79; pres Found Sci & the Handicapped, 77; chmn, spec ed adv comt, Nat Sci Teachers Asn; expert, disabled affairs, EHR Directorate, NSF, 91-92; coordr equity & access, WVa Dept Educ, 95-. *Mem:* AAAS; Nat Sci Teachers Asn; Ecol Soc Am; Am Statist Asn; Am Inst Biol Sci; Found Sci & Disability; Asn Sci & Disabled Persons. *Res:* Aquatic ecology; quantitative inheritance of biochemical traits in Drosophila; vibration stress in organisms; ecosystem analysis and simulation; environmental influences on human health; disabled persons in science; science education; genetics. *Mailing Add:* Dept Biol WVa Univ Morgantown WV 26506-6057. *Fax:* 304-293-6363; *E-Mail:* u0072@wvnvm

KELLER, EDWARD LEE, APPLIED MATHEMATICS. *Current Pos:* from asst prof to assoc prof, 69-80, PROF MATH, CALIF STATE UNIV, HAYWARD, 80-, DEPT CHAIR, 89- *Personal Data:* b Glade Springs, Va, Nov 23, 41; m 68; c 2. *Educ:* Duke Univ, BS, 64; Univ Mich, Ann Arbor, MA, 66, PhD(math), 69. *Prof Exp:* Res asst, Univ Mich, Ann Arbor, 64-68. *Mem:* Am Math Soc; Math Asn Am; Soc Indust & Appl Math. *Res:* Mathematical programming, particularly quadratic programming; matrix theory; mathematics of population. *Mailing Add:* Math & Comput Sci Dept Calif State Univ Hayward CA 94542-3092. *Fax:* 510-727-2035; *E-Mail:* keller@csuhayward.edu

KELLER, EDWARD LOWELL, BIOMEDICAL ENGINEERING, NEUROBIOLOGY. *Current Pos:* From asst prof to assoc prof, 71-79, PROF ELEC ENG, UNIV CALIF, BERKELEY, 79- *Personal Data:* b Rapid City, SDak, Mar 6, 39; m 65; c 3. *Educ:* US Naval Acad, BS, 61; Johns Hopkins Univ, PhD(biomed eng), 71. *Concurrent Pos:* Dir, Smith-Kettlewell Ctr for Vision Res & sr scientist, Smith-Kettlewell Inst Visual Sci, 80. *Mem:* AAAS; Asn Res Vision & Ophthal; Inst Elec & Electronic Engrs; Soc Neurosci. *Res:* Neurophysiological studies of the central organization of the primate oculomotor system; mathematical modelling of neuromuscular control systems. *Mailing Add:* Smith-Kettlewell Inst Visual Sci 2232 Webster St San Francisco CA 94115. *Fax:* 415-561-1610; *E-Mail:* elk@skivs.ski.org

KELLER, ELDON LEWIS, NUCLEAR PHYSICS, RESEARCH ADMINISTRATION. *Current Pos:* From assoc scientist to sr scientist, 60-69, res prog adminr, 69-74, ASST TO RES DIR, WESTINGHOUSE RES & DEVELOP CTR, 74- *Personal Data:* b Tiffin, Ohio, Dec 25, 34; m 61; c 1. *Educ:* Heidelberg Col, BS, 56; Univ Pittsburgh, MS, 60. *Mem:* Am Phys Soc; Am Nuclear Soc. *Res:* Low-temperature radiation effects in superconductors; gamma-ray imaging using image intensifiers; semiconductor gamma-ray monitor; thickness gauging; gamma-ray spectrometry. *Mailing Add:* 629 Burden Lake Rd Aiken SC 29803

KELLER, ELIZABETH BEACH, BIOCHEMISTRY. *Current Pos:* res specialist, Cornell Univ, 62-65, asst prof, 65-71, assoc prof, 71-84, prof, 84-88, EMER PROF BIOCHEM, MOLECULAR & CELL BIOL, CORNELL UNIV, 88- *Personal Data:* b Diongloh, China, Dec 28, 17; US citizen; m 41, 84, Leonard B Spector. *Educ:* Univ Chicago, BS, 40; George Washington Univ, MS, 45; Cornell Univ, PhD(biochem), 48. *Prof Exp:* Asst, Med Col, Cornell Univ, 46-48; Atomic Energy Comn fel, Col Med, Ohio State Univ, 48-49; mem, Huntington Mem Lab, Mass Gen Hosp, 49-50, res fel, Harvard Univ, 50-52, res assoc, 52-58, USPHS spec fel & res fel, 58-60; res assoc, Mass Inst Technol, 60-62. *Mem:* Am Soc Biol Chem. *Res:* Mechanism of the biosynthesis and functions of nucleic acids. *Mailing Add:* Dept Biochem Molecular & Cell Biol Biotechnol Bldg Cornell Univ Ithaca NY 14853-0001. *Fax:* 607-255-2428

KELLER, EVELYN FOX, HISTORY & PHILOSOPHY OF SCIENCE, GENDER & SCIENCE. *Current Pos:* PROF HIST & PHILOS, MASS INST TECHNOL, 92- *Personal Data:* b New York, NY, Mar 20, 36; c Jeffrey & Sarah. *Educ:* Brandeis Univ, BA, 57; Harvard Univ, PhD(physics), 63. *Hon Degrees:* DHH, Mt Holyoke Col, 91; Dr, Amsterdam, 93, Tech Univ Lulea, Sweden, 96; LHD, Rensselaer Polytech Inst, 95; DSc, Simmons Col, 95. *Honors & Awards:* Welle K Lectr, Univ Calif, 93. *Prof Exp:* Instr, NY Univ, 62-63, asst res scientist, 63-66, from asst prof to assoc prof, Grad Sch Med Sci, Cornell Univ, 66-72; assoc prof, Col Purchase, State Univ NY, 72-81; vis prof math & humanites, Kreegerb Wolf distinguished prof, Nebr Univ, 81-82, prof, 82-88; prof, Univ Calif, Berkeley, 88-92. *Concurrent Pos:* Mem, Ctr for Policy Res, 76-; vis fel, Mass Inst Technol, 79-80, vis scholar, 80-84, vis prof, Prog Sci, 85-87; sr fel, Cornell Univ, 87; mem, Inst Advan Study, Princeton Univ, 87-88. *Mem:* Hist Sci Soc. *Res:* Meanings of explanation in developmental biology. *Mailing Add:* Sts E51-263B Mass Inst Technol 77 Massachusetts Ave Cambridge MA 02139-4307

KELLER, FREDERICK ALBERT, JR, BIOCHEMICAL ENGINEERING, BIOCHEMISTRY. *Current Pos:* TASK LEADER & SR BIOCHEM ENGR, NAT RENEWABLE ENERGY LAB, 91- *Personal Data:* b New York, NY; m 66, Judith A Paul; c 2. *Educ:* Stevens Inst Technol, BE, 61; Rutgers Univ, New Brunswick, MS, 67, PhD(microbial biochem eng), 68. *Prof Exp:* Chemist, Polymerization Develop Lab, Hercules Inc, 61-62; USPHS fel, 68-70; biochem engr, Biol & Med Sci Lab, Gen Elec Co, 70-75; sr biochem engr, Union Carbide Corp, 75-79; sect leader, CPC Int, 79-87, dir bioprocessing, Cambridge Biosci Corp, 87-90; sr consult, M G Pappas Co, 90-91. *Concurrent Pos:* Vis prof biochem eng, Ill Inst Technol, 85-87. *Mem:* Am Inst Chem Engrs; Am Chem Soc; Am Soc Microbiol; Soc Indust Microbiol. *Res:* Biosynthesis, bioregulation and biodegradation of structural and storage macromolecules, including cellulo-lignins, starch, hemicellulose, chitin, glycogen; biochemical engineering processing; separation processes; regenerable raw materials; SCP; commercialization of chemicals by fermentation processes; biotechnology process development. *Mailing Add:* Nat Renewable Energy Lab 1617 Cole Blvd Golden CO 80401-3305. *Fax:* 303-384-6877; *E-Mail:* kellerf@tcplink k.nrel.gov

KELLER, FREDERICK JACOB, EXPERIMENTAL SOLID STATE PHYSICS. *Current Pos:* from asst prof to assoc prof, 66-77, prof physics, 77-93, PROF EMER, CLEMSON UNIV, 93- *Personal Data:* b Huntington, WVa, May 10, 34; m 54; c 4. *Educ:* Marshall Univ, BS, 60; Univ Tenn, MS, 62, PhD(physics), 66. *Prof Exp:* Teaching asst physics, Univ Tenn, 63-64; physicist, Oak Ridge Nat Lab, 66. *Mem:* Am Phys Soc. *Res:* Color centers in alkali halides. *Mailing Add:* 140 McCracken Dr Seneca SC 29678

KELLER, GEOFFREY, ASTRONOMY. *Current Pos:* RETIRED. *Personal Data:* b New York, NY, June 12, 18; m 50; c 2. *Educ:* Swarthmore Col, BS, 38; Columbia Univ, PhD(astron), 48. *Prof Exp:* Asst physics, Columbia Univ, 38-41; assoc physicist, Bur Ord, USN, 41-45; from instr to prof physics & astron, Ohio State Univ, 48-59, dir Perkins Observ, 53-59; prog dir astron, NSF, 59-61, div dir math & phys sci, 61-66, dep planning dir, 66-68; dean, Col Math & Phys Sci, Ohio State Univ, 68-71, prof astron, 72-89. *Concurrent Pos:* Instr, Ohio Wesleyan Univ, 48-49. *Mem:* Am Astron Soc. *Res:* Internal constitution of stars; fluid turbulence. *Mailing Add:* 103 Abbey Cross Lane Westerville OH 43082-7309

KELLER, GEORGE E, II, ENGINEERING ADMINISTRATION, CHEMICAL ENGINEERING. *Current Pos:* Res assoc res & develop, 76-81, corp res fel, 81-87, SR CORP RES FEL, UNION CARBIDE CORP, 87- *Personal Data:* b Charleston, WVa, June 4, 33. *Educ:* Va Polytech Inst, BS, 55; Pa State Univ, MS, 58, PhD(chem eng), 64. *Honors & Awards:* Clarence Gerhold, Am Inst Chem Engrs, 95, Chem Pioneer Award, 96. *Concurrent Pos:* Adj assoc prof reaction eng, WVa Col Grad Studies, 63-; lectr, Am Chem Inst, 85; chair, Gordon Res Conf Separation & Purification, 85, Eng Found Int Conf Separation Technol, 91; adj prof, Dept Chem Eng, Univ WVa; regents prof eng, State Univ WVa. *Mem:* Nat Acad Eng; fel Am Inst Chem Engrs; Am Chem Soc. *Res:* Advanced technique hydrocarbon cracking; separation, process research and development; development of medical oxygen technology. *Mailing Add:* Union Carbide Corp PO Box 8361 South Charleston WV 25303

KELLER, GEORGE EARL, NUCLEAR PHYSICS. *Current Pos:* asst prof, 69-, ASSOC PROF PHYSICS, WGA COL. *Personal Data:* b Baton Rouge, La, Nov 6, 40; m 64. *Educ:* La State Univ, BS, 62, PhD(physics), 69. *Mem:* Am Phys Soc; Am Asn Physics Teachers; Am Inst Physics; Sigma Xi. *Res:* Gamma ray spectroscopy; determination of the properties of the excited states of the doubly even deformed nuclei. *Mailing Add:* Physics Dept WGa Col Carrollton GA 30118

KELLER, GEORGE H, MARINE GEOLOGY. *Current Pos:* assoc dean, sch oceanog, 75-81, dean res, 81-85, VPRES RES & GRAD STUDIES, ORE STATE UNIV, 85- *Personal Data:* b Hartford, Conn, Sept 9, 31; m 55; c 2. *Educ:* Univ Conn, AB, 54; Univ Utah, MS, 56; Univ Ill, PhD(marine geol), 66. *Prof Exp:* Geologist, Stand Oil Co Tex, 57-59; geol oceanogr, US Naval Oceanog Off, DC, 59-67; res oceanogr, Inst Oceanog, Md, 67-69, res oceanogr, Atlantic & Meteorol Oceanog Labs, Nat Oceanic & Atmospheric Admin, Fla, 69-75. *Concurrent Pos:* Mem Mid-Atlantic Ridge explor, Nat Oceanic & Atmospheric Admin & others, 74-77. *Mem:* Geol Soc Am; Int Asn Sedimentol; Am Geophys Union. *Res:* Marine geology and oceanography of the Malacca Strait, Malaysia; marine geotechnique, study of the mass physical and engineering properties of deep sea sediments and bottom material stability. *Mailing Add:* Res Off Ore State Univ Corvallis OR 97331

KELLER, GEORGE HENRY, BIOCHEMISTRY. *Current Pos:* TECHNOL LICENSING SPECIALIST, OFF TECHNOL TRANSFER, NIH, 95- *Personal Data:* b Harrisburg, Pa, Oct 21, 50; m 74, Nancy J Rossi; c Laura & Emily. *Educ:* Univ Md, BS, 72; Pa State Univ, PhD(biochem), 78. *Prof Exp:* Res assoc, M S Hershey Med Ctr, 78-81; staff fel, NIH, 81-83; consult biochemist, Keller Res Servs, 83-89; dir com develop, Biotech Res Labs Inc, 89-90; dir proj mgt, Cambridge Biotech Corp, 90-95. *Concurrent Pos:* Fel, Am Lung Asn, 79. *Mem:* Am Soc Microbiol; Asn Consult Chemists & Chem Engrs. *Res:* DNA probes. *Mailing Add:* 7504 Filbert Terr Gaithersburg MD 20879

KELLER, GEORGE MATTHEW, PETROLEUM ENGINEERING. *Current Pos:* RETIRED. *Personal Data:* b Kansas City, Mo, Dec 3, 23; m 46, Adelaide McCague; c William G, Robert A & Barry R. *Educ:* Mass Inst Technol, BS, 48. *Prof Exp:* Engr, Stand Oil, Calif, 48-63, foreign opers staff, 63-67, asst vpres, 67-69, vpres, 69-71, dir, 70-88, vchmn, 74-81, chmn & chief exec officer, 81-88. *Mailing Add:* Chevron Corp 555 Market St San Francisco CA 94105-2801

KELLER, GEORGE RANDY, JR, SEISMOLOGY. *Current Pos:* from asst prof to assoc prof, 76-82, PROF GEOPHYS, UNIV TEX, EL PASO, 82-, CHMN, 81- *Personal Data:* b Muskogee, Okla, Apr 17, 46; m 67; c William & Nicole. *Educ:* Tex Tech Univ, BS, 68, MS, 69, PhD(geophys), 73. *Prof Exp:* Instr geophys, Tex Tech Univ, 70-71; res asst prof, Univ Utah, 72-73; asst prof, Univ Ky, 73-76. *Mem:* Am Geophys Union; Am Asn Petrol Geologists; Geol Soc Am; Seismol Soc Am; Soc Explor Geophysicist; Royal Astron Soc. *Res:* Solid earth geophysics (seismology, gravity and geomagnetism); specifically the crustal structure, tectonics of North America and extensional terrains. *Mailing Add:* 6313 El Risco St El Paso TX 79912. *Fax:* 915-747-5073

KELLER, HAROLD WILLARD, MYCOLOGY. *Current Pos:* RES OFFICER, OFF RES & BIOTECHNOL, UNIV N TEX HEALTH SCI CTR, 90-; RES ASSOC, BOT RES INST TEX, 90- *Personal Data:* b Newton, Kans, Dec 10, 37; m 65, Brenda J Griffith; c David B & Brian L. *Educ:* Kans Wesleyan Col, BA, 60; Univ Kans, MA, 63; Univ Iowa, PhD(bot), 71. *Prof Exp:* Fel bot, Grad Sch, Univ Fla, 71-72; asst prof biol, Wright State Univ, Ohio, 72-78, from asst dir to assoc dir, Univ Res Serv, 78-82, adj assoc prof, Dept Microbiol & Immunol, 80-82; dir res & assoc prof biol, Univ NC, Wilmington, 82-83; dir off sponsored projs & assoc prof biol, Univ Tex, Arlington, 83-90. *Concurrent Pos:* Conf partic, Comn Undergrad Educ Biol Sci, 70; NSF fel, Summer Inst Systematics V, 71; Ohio Biol Surv, 74-75; NSF grants, 75-78 & 83-84; panel reviewer, Comprehensive Assistance Undergrad Sci Educ, NSF, 81 & Instrnl Sci Equip Prog, 80; gov's appointment, State NC Marine Res Ctr Admin Bd, 82-83; chmn planning team, Southeastern NC Regional Forum Sci & Technol, 83; mem, NC Bd Sci & Technol, 83; field reader & reviewer G-pop proposals, Dept Educ, 85-95; bd consult, N Tex Poison Ctr, 86-; bd trustess, Kans Wesleyan Univ, 92-; Living Sci Ctr trail guide, 94- *Mem:* Asn Southeastern Biologists; Mycol Soc Am; Sigma Xi; NAm Mycol Soc; Bot Soc Am; Nat Coun Univ Res Adminr; Soc Res Admin. *Res:* Systematics, floristics and ecology of coricolous myxomycetes; floristic studies-US southeastern Gulf states and middle latitude states and Myxomycetes from Mexico; systematic world monographs are in preparation for the genera Perichaena, Licea and related taxa; scanning and transmission electron microscopy and energy dispersive spectroscopy are being used to study the formation, deposition and composition of mineral deposits in the Myxomycetes; development and use of K-12 teaching materials for fungi and Myxomycetes represented by hands on laboratory exercises and videos. *Mailing Add:* 2228 Stafford Dr Arlington TX 76012-4141. *Fax:* 817-735-5485; *E-Mail:* keller@hsc.unt.edu

KELLER, HERBERT BISHOP, APPLIED MATHEMATICS, NUMERICAL ANALYSIS. *Current Pos:* PROF APPL MATH, CALIF INST TECHNOL, 67- *Personal Data:* b Paterson, NJ, June 19, 25; m 53; c 2. *Educ:* Ga Inst Technol, BEE, 45; NY Univ, MA, 48, PhD(math), 54. *Honors & Awards:* Theodore von Karman Prize, Soc Indust & Appl Math, 94. *Prof Exp:* Instr physics & math, Ga Inst Technol, 46-47; res scientist, Div Electromagnetic Res, Inst Math Sci, NY Univ, 48-53, lectr math, Washington Sq Col, 57-59, assoc prof, Univ, 59-61, prof appl math, Courant Inst Math Sci, 61-67, assoc dir, AEC Comput & Appl Math Ctr, 64-67. *Concurrent Pos:* Head dept math, Sarah Lawrence Col, 51-53; assoc ed, J Appl Math, Soc Indust & Appl Math, 61-66, J Comput & Systs Sci, 71-74, ed, 74- & Japan J Appl Math, 84-; ed, Monogr Ser, Asn Comput Mach, 63-65; J Numerical Anal, 64-71 & Numerical Math, 81-; vis prof, Calif Inst Technol, 65-66; mem math div, Nat Res Coun, 69-72; mem coun, Conf Bd Math Sci, 71-73; consult, var indust & govt concerns; Guggenheim fel, 79-80. *Mem:* Soc Indust & Appl Math (pres, 75-76); Asn Comput Mach; Am Math Soc; Math Asn Am; fel Am Acad Arts & Sci. *Res:* Numerical analysis; fluid mechanics; nuclear and chemical reactors; applied mechanics; computing machinery; bifurcation theory. *Mailing Add:* Dept Appl Math Calif Inst Technol 217-50 Pasadena CA 91125-0001

KELLER, JACK, AGRICULTURAL & IRRIGATION ENGINEERING. *Current Pos:* CHIEF EXEC OFFICER, KELLER-BLIESNER ENG, LOGAN, UTAH, 62- *Personal Data:* b Roanoke, Va, Jan 5, 28; m 54; c 3. *Educ:* Univ Colo, BS, 53; Colo State Univ, MS, 55; Utah State Univ, PhD(irrigation eng), 67. *Prof Exp:* Prof agr & irrigation eng, Utah State Univ, 60-90. *Concurrent Pos:* Sales engr, South Irrigation Co, Miss, 55-56; asst irrigation engr, indust sales mgr & eng coordr, WR Ames Co, Denver, Colo & San Jose, Calif, 56-60; chmn sprinkler irrigation comt, Soil & Water Br, Am Asn Agr Eng, 66-72, mem, 72-, mem comt consult eng, 76-; co-dir water mgt synthesis proj, Utah State Univ, 78-, head dept agr & irrigation eng, 79-85; mem tech control bd, Jordan Valley Irrigation Proj, Jordan, 78-80; mem comt water resources res, Water Sci Technol Bd, Nat Res Coun, 84-86; assoc ed, Irrigation & Drainage Systs J, Hague, Neth, 84-; vis prof, fac agr sci & fac appl sic, KU Leuven, Belg, 86, 90 & 91; mem Int Comn Irrigation & Drainage. *Mem:* Nat Acad Eng; Am Soc Agr Engrs; Am Soc Civil Engrs; Am Soc Eng Educ; AAAS; Irrigation Asn; Sigma Xi. *Res:* Sprinkle and trickle irrigation; socio-technical assistance for transferring irrigation technologies worldwide; improving irrigated agriculture in developing countries; author of 81 technical papers, 15 articles and 6 books. *Mailing Add:* Keller-Bliesner Eng 78 E Center St Logan UT 84321. *Fax:* 435-753-6139

KELLER, JAIME, MATERIALS SCIENCE, PHYSICS & CHEMISTRY. *Current Pos:* PROF THEORET PHYSICS, NAT AUTONOMOUS UNIV MEX, 72-, HEAD, DEPT THEORET CHEM, 74-, DEAN, HIGHER STUDIES FAC, 89- *Personal Data:* b Mexico, DF, Mex, Nov 10, 36; m 67; c 3. *Educ:* Nat Autonomous Univ Mex, Chem Eng, 59; Univ Bristol, UK, PhD(physics), 72. *Honors & Awards:* Nat Prize Chem, Chem Soc Mex, 80; Nat Award Chem Sci, Mex Fed Govt, 82; Jose Gomez-Ibanez Lectr, Wesleyan Univ, 82. *Prof Exp:* Res engr chem physics, Indust Chem Pennsalt, 59-63; tech dir chem process, Der Macrochem, 63-69; res fel physics, Univ Bristol, UK, 70-71. *Concurrent Pos:* Fac, IBM Res Lab, San Jose, Calif, 72; res visitor, Fed Polytech Inst, Zurich, 73- & Univ Geneve; mem vd, Mex Nat Res Syst & fel, 84-; dir, Fac Study, Super Cuauthlan, Nat Automous Univ Mex. *Mem:* Am Phys Soc; Chem Soc Mex; Mex Soc Physics; Ital Soc Physics; Mex Acad Sci Invest; Europ Acad Art & Sci. *Res:* Chemistry and physics of condensed matter especially of metals in the liquid, amorphous and crystalline state; fundamental theory behind chemistry and physics; foundations of quantum and elementary particles theory. *Mailing Add:* Col Fuente de la Juventud Mexico City DF 11000 Mexico

KELLER, JEFFREY THOMAS, NEUROANATOMY, NEUROSURGICAL RESEARCH. *Current Pos:* dir, Div Neurosurg Res, 84-89, DIR, DIV NEUROSURG EDUC, DEPT NEUROSURG, COL MED, UNIV CINCINNATI, 89-; DIR NEUROANAT RES, MAYFIELD NEUROL INST, 75- *Personal Data:* b Cincinnati, Ohio, Oct 17, 46; m 76, Adele M Beiting; c Jocelyn & Susan. *Educ:* Univ Cincinnati, BA, 69, MS, 72, PhD(anat), 75. *Prof Exp:* Asst biol, Univ Cincinnati, 69-71, asst anat, Col Med, 71-75. *Concurrent Pos:* Adj asst prof anat, Col Med, Univ Cincinnati, 75-79, fel, 78, 79-80, adj assoc prof, 75-79, res assoc prof neurosurg, 84-89, res prof neurosurg, 90-; NIH fel, Uniformed Serv Univ, 78-80. *Mem:* Sigma Xi; fel Am Heart Asn; Am Asn Anatomists; Soc Neurosci; NAm Skull Base Soc. *Res:* Post-operative cicatrix and the spinal dura; spinal dura repair; basal ganglia; trigeminal system; cephalgias; facial neuralgias; cranial nerves and their brainstem circuitry; applying state of the art neuroanatomical tract tracing techniques and immunocytochemistry to examine the neuronal circuitry of cranial nerves involved with cerebral vasculature including the dura mater and cephalgias; surgical anatomy of the skull base. *Mailing Add:* Dept Neurosurg ML515 Col Med Univ Cincinnati 231 Bethesda Awe Cincinnati OH 45267-0515. *Fax:* 513-558-7702

KELLER, JOSEPH BISHOP, MATHEMATICS. *Current Pos:* prof, 79-93, EMER PROF MATH, STANFORD UNIV, 93- *Personal Data:* b Paterson, NJ, July 31, 23; m 63; c 2. *Educ:* NY Univ, BA, 43, MS, 46, PhD(math), 48. *Hon Degrees:* Dr Tech, Tech Univ, Copenhagen; PhD, Univ Crete, 93, Northwestern Univ. *Honors & Awards:* Gibbs lectr, Am Math Soc; Von Karman Prize, Soc Ind Appl Math; Timoshenko Medal, Am Soc Mech Eng; Hedric lectr, Math Asn Am; Von Neuman lectr, Soc Ind Appl Math; Wolf Found Prize Math, 97. *Prof Exp:* Instr physics, Princeton Univ, 43-44; asst, Div War Res, Columbia Univ, 44-45; mathematician, Inst Math & Mech, 45-52; asst, Washington Sq Col, 46-47; asst prof, NY Univ, 48-52, assoc res prof, 52-56, prof, 56-79, chmn dept, 67-73, dir, Div Electromagnetic Res, Courant Inst Math Sci, 66-79. *Concurrent Pos:* Lectr, Grad Sch, Stevens Inst Technol, 48; head, Math Br, Off Naval Res, 53-54; vis prof, Stanford Univ, 69-70 & 76-78; res assoc, Woods Hole Oceanog Inst, 69-; vis scholar, Calif Inst Technol, 73-74; consult, var indust & govt concerns; hon prof math sci, Univ Cambridge. *Mem:* Nat Acad Sci; Am Phys Soc; Am Math Soc; Soc Indust & Appl Math (vpres, 78-79); Am Acad Arts & Sci; Royal Soc London. *Res:* Applied mathematics; acoustics; electromagnetic theory; fluid dynamics; geometrical optics. *Mailing Add:* Dept Math Stanford Univ Stanford CA 94303-2125

KELLER, JOSEPH EDWARD, JR, APPLIED MECHANICS & MECHANICAL ENGINEERING, RESEARCH ADMINISTRATION & TECHNICAL MANAGEMENT. *Current Pos:* RETIRED. *Personal Data:* b La Crosse, Wis, Mar 31, 36; m 74, Eleanor Bullock; c Lowrey Evan & Andrew Joseph. *Educ:* Swarthmore Col, BS, 58; Univ Kans, MS, 60, PhD(eng mech), 64. *Prof Exp:* Engr, Lawrence Livermore Nat Lab, 64-74, dep leader weapons prog, 74, dep div leader, 74-77, div leader, Lasers Prog, 77-87, proj mgr, SIS Prog, 86-89, asst assoc dir defense systs, 89-96. *Mem:* Am Soc Mech Engrs; Sigma Xi; AAAS. *Res:* Development and implementation of numerical techniques. *Mailing Add:* 786 Mirador Ct Pleasanton CA 94566

KELLER, JOSEPH HERBERT, PHYSICAL CHEMISTRY. *Current Pos:* INDEPENDENT CONSULT, CATALYSIS & PLATINUM METAL SALTS, 94- *Personal Data:* b Bristol, Va, Sept 25, 46; m 69; c 2. *Educ:* King Col, BS, 68; Univ Ill, Urbana, MS, 70, PhD(phys chem), 74. *Prof Exp:* Res assoc & NSF fel chem, Univ Tenn, Knoxville, 73-75; res assoc catalysis, Oxy-Catalyst, Inc, 75-77, sr res assoc, 77-80; mgr, Catalyst Dept, Met-Pro Corp, 80-85, mgr plant & Dept Catalysts, 85-92; mgr catalysts develop, Johnson Matthey, 92-95. *Mem:* Am Chem Soc; Sigma Xi; Catalysis Club; Org Reactions Catalysis Soc. *Res:* Heterogeneous catalysis; kinetic isotope effects of hydrogen and carbon; vapor pressure isotope effects; surface and media effect on reaction rates; wastewater analysis and treatment; catalyst manufacturing; nitrogen-oxygen catalyst; woodstove catalyst; volatile organic compound and polycyclic organic matter catalyst abatement, testing and manufacture; hydrogenation reactions involving supported catalysts phosphoglucomutase catalysts. *Mailing Add:* 522 N Maryland Ave West Chester PA 19380

KELLER, KENNETH F, MICROBIOLOGY. *Current Pos:* RETIRED. *Personal Data:* b Louisville, Ky, July 3, 21; m 46; c 7. *Educ:* Univ Louisville, BA, 43, MS, 57, PhD(microbiol), 65. *Prof Exp:* Inst, Univ Louisville, 61-66, from asst prof to assoc prof microbiol, Sch Med, 66-88, assoc prof path, 74-88. *Concurrent Pos:* Consult, Gen Elec Co, 60-63 & Stand Oil Co Ky, 63. *Mem:* Am Soc Microbiol. *Res:* Biological and antigenic properties of the inclusion conjunctivitis agent; adrenergic receptors of mouse adipose tissue; use of lectins in diagnostic microbiology. *Mailing Add:* 412 Cherry Lane Pewee Valley KY 40056-9051

KELLER, KENNETH H(ARRISON), science policy, for more information see previous edition

KELLER, LAURA R, CELL BIOLOGY, DEVELOPMENTAL BIOLOGY. *Current Pos:* ASST PROF BIOL, FLA STATE UNIV, 86- *Educ:* Univ Va, PhD, 80. *Mem:* Am Soc Cell Biol; Soc Develop Biol. *Mailing Add:* Dept Biol Sci Fla State Univ Unit 1 Tallahassee FL 32306-3050. *Fax:* 850-644-0481

KELLER, LELAND EDWARD, HISTORY OF MEDICINE, QUACKERY. *Current Pos:* From asst prof to prof anat & physiol, 57-74, prof, 74-87, EMER PROF BIOL, PITTSBURG STATE UNIV, 87- *Personal Data:* b Carnegie, Okla, Jan 21, 23; m 49, Eileen Ebel; c Charles, David & Margaret. *Educ:* Univ Wichita, BA, 50; Univ Kans, PhD(anat), 58. *Concurrent Pos:* Presents illus lectr-demonstrations, early med quack devices. *Mem:* Am Asn Hist Med. *Res:* Collecting, restoring and researching 19th and early 20th century medical quack and electrotherapeutic devices in private collection. *Mailing Add:* 1205 Imperial Dr Pittsburg KS 66762

KELLER, MARGARET AGNELLO, HEMATOLOGIC DISEASES RESEARCH, DNA ANALYSIS CORE FACILITY. *Current Pos:* RES SCIENTIST & CORE DIR, DUPONT HOSP CHILDREN, 96- *Personal Data:* b Rockville Center, NY, Aug 15, 66; m 90, Grant W. *Educ:* Rutgers State Univ, NJ, BA, 88; Univ Pa, PhD(molecular biol), 94. *Prof Exp:* Postdoctoral fel, DuPont Merck Pharm Co, 94-95; admin dir, Core Facil, Children's Hosp Philadelphia, 95-96. *Mem:* AAAS. *Res:* Molecular approaches to the treatment of sickle cell anemia and other hematologic disorders affecting children. *Mailing Add:* 118 Deschler Blvd Clayton NJ 08312

KELLER, MARGARET ANNE, INFECTIOUS DISEASES, PEDIATRIC AIDS. *Current Pos:* fel immunol & infectious dis, Dept Pediat, 76-78, asst prof, 78-85, ASSOC PROF PEDIAT, HARBOR-UNIV CALIF LOS ANGELES MED CTR, 85-, DIR, PROG PEDIAT ACQUIRED IMMUNE DEFICIENCY SYNDROME, 91- *Personal Data:* b Boston, Mass, May 29, 47; m 71, Robert A; c 2. *Educ:* Mass Inst Technol, SB, 68; Albert Einstein Col Med, MD, 72. *Prof Exp:* From intern to resident pediat, Med Ctr, Univ Calif, San Diego, 72-75; chief resident, 75, fel infectious dis, Dept Pediat, 75-76. *Mem:* Fel Am Acad Pediat; Am Fedn Clin Res; Soc Pediat Res; Am Phys Soc; Am Soc Microbiol; fel Infectious Dis Soc Am; Am Asn Immunol. *Res:* Pediatric AIDS; neonatal immunity; idiotypic networks. *Mailing Add:* 1000 W Carson St Box 468 Torrance CA 90509. *Fax:* 310-212-7440; *E-Mail:* keller@harbor2.bitnet

KELLER, MARION WILES, mathematics; deceased, see previous edition for last biography

KELLER, MARTIN DAVID, EPIDEMIOLOGY. *Current Pos:* assoc prof prev med, Ohio State Univ, 62-66, asst prof med, 62-66, head div epidemiol & biomet, 66-67, prof prev med, 66-84, head div community health, 67-92, PROF EMER, OHIO STATE UNIV, 92- *Personal Data:* b New York, NY, Apr 7, 23; m 53; c 3. *Educ:* Yeshiva Univ, AB, 44; NY Univ, MS, 46, PhD(biol), 53; Cornell Univ, MD, 52; Columbia Univ, MPH, 58. *Prof Exp:* Intern pediat, Ny Hosp-Cornell Med Ctr,52-53; med resident internal med, Vet Admin Hosp, Ny, 55-56; resident med serv, Columbia Univ, 57; actg dir chronic dis div, Ohio Dept Health, 57-58, dir res training, 58-60; dir clin serv, Beth Israel Hosp, Boston, Mass, 60-62. *Concurrent Pos:* Lectr, Harvard Med Sch, 60-62; consult, Ohio Dept Health, 64- *Mem:* Am Pub Health Asn; Am Col Prev Med; NY Acad Sci. *Res:* Environmental and host factors affecting distribution of human disease entities. *Mailing Add:* Dept Prev Med Ohio State Univ Med Ctr 320 W Tenth Ave Columbus OH 43210-1236

KELLER, OSWALD LEWIN, JR, PHYSICAL CHEMISTRY, RESEARCH ADMINISTRATION. *Current Pos:* RETIRED. *Personal Data:* b New York, NY, May 24, 30; m 53, Dona Guild; c Christopher, Claire (Ohshiro), Elaine (Roberts) & Elizabeth. *Educ:* Univ of the South, BS, 51; Mass Inst Technol, PhD(phys chem), 59. *Prof Exp:* USPHS res fel, 59-60; chemist, Oak Ridge Nat Lab, 60-67, dir, Transuranium Res Lab, 67-74 & 84-89 & Chem Div, 74-84. *Concurrent Pos:* Mem nuclear physics panel, Physics Surv Comt, Nat Acad Sci, 69-72. *Res:* Physical chemistry of proteins; chemistry of transuranium elements; molecular spectroscopy; preparation and characterization of compounds; heavy ion reactions; administration of nuclear research. *Mailing Add:* 734 Peachtree Hills Circle Atlanta GA 30305

KELLER, PATRICIA J, BIOCHEMISTRY. *Current Pos:* Res assoc biochem, Sch Med, 55-56, instr, 56-57, res asst prof, 57-62, assoc prof, Sch Dent, 62-87, assoc dean, Grad Sch, 74-77, PROF ORAL BIOL, SCH DENT, UNIV WASH, 67-, CHMN ORAL BIOL, 79- *Personal Data:* b Detroit, Mich, Nov 16, 23. *Educ:* Univ Detroit, BS, 45; Wash Univ, PhD(biochem), 53. *Concurrent Pos:* USPHS fels, Wash Univ, 53-54 & Univ Wash, 54-55; vis fel, Inst Marine Biochem, Aberdeen, Scotland, 78-79. *Mem:* AAAS; Am Soc Biol Chem; Am Soc Cell Biol; Am Chem Soc; Int Asn Dent Res. *Res:* Structure, function and biosynthesis of enzyme proteins. *Mailing Add:* Dept Oral Biol Univ Wash Sch Dent SB22 Seattle WA 98195-0001

KELLER, PHILIP CHARLES, INORGANIC CHEMISTRY. *Current Pos:* From asst prof to assoc prof, 66-75, PROF CHEM, UNIV ARIZ, 75- *Personal Data:* b San Francisco, Calif, Mar 10, 39; m 65. *Educ:* Univ Calif, Berkeley, BA, 61; Ind Univ, PhD(boron chem), 66. *Mem:* Am Chem Soc; Royal Soc Chem. *Res:* Boron hydride chemistry; chemistry of Group III elements. *Mailing Add:* Dept Chem Univ Ariz Tucson AZ 85721-0002

KELLER, PHILIP JOSEPH, PHYSICAL CHEMISTRY. *Current Pos:* res chemist, E I Du Pont de Nemours & Co, 69-72, develop rep, 71-72, prod technologist, 73-74, mkt res specialist, 75, planning specialist, Indust Chem Dept, 75-76, purchasing agt, 76-79, sr purchasing agt, 79-82, regional mgr, 82-84, mgr imaging med & electronics purchasing, Mat & Logistics Dept, 84-89, mgr eng procurement, 89-91, MGR PROCUREMENT PROCESS, SOURCING, E I DU PONT DE NEMOURS & CO, 91- *Personal Data:* b New Brunswick, NJ, Sept 21, 41; m 63; c 2. *Educ:* Temple Univ, AB, 64, PhD(phys chem), 70. *Prof Exp:* Sr anal chemist, Merck Sharp & Dohme Res Labs, Pa, 64-66. *Concurrent Pos:* Adj asst prof, Temple Univ, 69-70. *Mem:* Am Chem Soc. *Res:* Waste water chemistry; fused salts; electrochemistry; polyelectrolytes; surface chemistry. *Mailing Add:* E I du Pont de Nemours & Co Sourcing B-8342-5 Wilmington DE 19898-0001

KELLER, R KENNEDY, BIOCHEMISTRY. *Current Pos:* assoc prof 82-89, PROF CHEM, UNIV SFLA COL MED, 89- *Personal Data:* b New Rochelle, NY, Oct 15, 45. *Educ:* Fla Atlantic Univ, BS, 68; Vanderbilt Univ, PhD(biochem), 73. *Prof Exp:* Fel chem, Baylor Col Med, 75-80. *Concurrent Pos:* NIH Career Develop award. *Mem:* AAAS; Am Soc Biochem & Molecular Biol; NY Acad Sci. *Res:* Biochemistry. *Mailing Add:* Dept Biochem Univ SFla Col Med 12901 Bruce B Downs Blvd MDC 87 Box 7 Tampa FL 36612-4742. *Fax:* 813-974-5167

KELLER, RAYMOND E, DEVELOPMENTAL BIOLOGY, CELL BIOLOGY. *Current Pos:* ASSOC PROF, DEPT ZOOL, UNIV CALIF, BERKELEY, 80- *Personal Data:* b Cape Girardeau, Mo, May 25, 45; c 2. *Educ:* Southeast Mo State Univ, BS, 67; Univ Ill, Urbana, MS, 69, PhD(develop), 75. *Prof Exp:* Assoc, Lab of Prof J P Trinkaus, Dept Biol, Yale Univ, 75-76, Am Cancer Soc fel, 76-77; vis scientist, Ind Univ, 77-80. *Mem:* Soc Cell Biol; Soc Zool. *Res:* Analysis of the mechanisms of metazoan morphogenetic cell movements. *Mailing Add:* Univ Va Charlottesville VA 22903-2477. *Fax:* 510-643-6264

KELLER, REED THEODORE, gastroenterology, internal medicine, for more information see previous edition

KELLER, RICHARD ALAN, ANALYTICAL CHEMISTRY. *Current Pos:* STAFF MEM CHEM, LOS ALAMOS NAT LABS, 76- *Personal Data:* b Pittsburgh, Pa, Nov 28, 34; m 56, Mary; c Natalie, Bruce & Alan. *Educ:* Allegheny Col, BS, 56; Univ Calif, Berkeley, PhD(phys chem), 61. *Honors & Awards:* Anal Chem Award for Spectrochem Anal, Am Chem Soc, 93; Lester Strock Award, Soc Appl Spectros, 96. *Prof Exp:* Asst prof chem, Univ Ore, 59-63; staff mem, Div Phys Chem, Nat Bur Stand, 63-76. *Concurrent Pos:* fel, Los Alamos Nat Lab, 83- *Mem:* Am Chem Soc. *Res:* Laser induced chemistry; laser induced isotope enrichment; laser based analytical techniques. *Mailing Add:* CLS-2 MS M888 Los Alamos Nat Lab Los Alamos NM 87545

KELLER, ROBERT B, mechanical engineering, for more information see previous edition

KELLER, ROBERT ELLIS, ANALYTICAL INSTRUMENTATION, SPECTROSCOPY. *Current Pos:* RETIRED. *Personal Data:* b Marshalltown, Iowa, Jan 10, 23; wid; c James R & Karen L (Miller). *Educ:* Univ Iowa, BA, 47, MS, 49, PhD(anal chem), 51. *Prof Exp:* Res chemist anal chem, Smith, Kline & French Labs, 50-52; res chemist, Monsanto Co, 52-54, proj leader, 54-55, from group leader to sr res group leader, 55-67, sect mgr, 67-69, mgr appl sci, 69-82, mgr appl technol, 82-86, consult, 86-90; independent contractor/investr, St Louis Sci Ctr & NSF, 90-92. *Mem:* Am Chem Soc; Soc Appl Spectros. *Res:* Analytical and physical chemistry-separation; characterization and measurement of chemical species by chromatography, spectroscopy, general instrumental and chemical techniques; on line process; process monitoring and control, computerized data management. *Mailing Add:* 10142 Glenfield Terr St Louis MO 63126

KELLER, ROBERT H, HEMATOLOGY, IMMUNOLOGY. *Current Pos:* assoc dir clin diag lab & med dir hemat immunol res, 82-86, PRES & MED DIR, WILSON BODE CTR, 87-, BIODORON, 95-; CHMN, CHIEF EXEC OFFICER & DIR RES, IMMUNE BALANCE TECHNOL, 96- *Personal Data:* Brooklyn, NY, Oct 3, 45; div; c Stacie, Chiara, Magan & Robert. *Educ:* Fordham Univ, Bronx, BA, 66, MS, 66; Temple Univ, MD, 70; Mayo Grad Sch Med, Minn, MS, 76; Am Bd Internal Med, cert, 74. *Prof Exp:* Intern, resident & sr resident, Univ Rochester, 70-74; fel & sr res fel immunol, Mayo Sch Med, 74-77; asst prof, 77; asst prof hemat & oncol, Med Col Wis, 77-80, assoc prof, Dept Pediat, 80-82, assoc prof immunol & flow cytometry 82-86; res assoc & staff physician, Zablocki Bet Admin Med Ctr, 78-80, clin investr, 82-86; dir immunol, Midwest Children's Cancer Ctr, Milwaukee Children's Hosp, 80-82; assoc dir res develop, Coulter Immunol, 86-87; med dir & dir immune reconstitution prog, Ctr Spec Immunol, 92-95. *Concurrent Pos:* Mayo Found res fel, Mayo Grad Sch Med, 74-75; Nat Arthritis Found fel, 75-78; vet admin career develop award res assoc, 78-81, clin investr, 83-86; prin investr, Vet Admin Res, 78-80, Nat Cancer Inst, NIH, 81-86, NIH RR Shared Equip Prog, 84-86, Food & Drug Admin IND, 86-87; vis prof, Univ Miss, 80, Univ Calif, 81, Univ Tex Med Br, 82, Wilford Hall Air Force Res Ctr, 83, Max Plank Inst Biochemie, Munich, 84; co-prin investr, Nat Inst Allergy & Infectious Dis, NIH, 82-86, Hillman Found, 85-86; assoc dir res & develop Coulter Immunol, 86-87; consult immunol & hemat, Health Prof Inc & Ctr Spec Immunol, 94-95. *Mem:* Nat Acad Sci; Fel Am Col Physicians; Int Soc Hemat; Am Soc Hemat; Am Soc Immunol; AAAS; Soc Anal Cytol; Am Fed Clin Res; Am Soc Clin Path; NY Acad Sci. *Res:* Basic and clinical research in immune regulation, specifically the development of new testing modalities and new therapeutic strategies and agents using immunologic principles to heat human diseases. *Mailing Add:* Biodoron 5821 Hollywood Blvd Hollywood FL 33021. *Fax:* 305-672-7160

KELLER, ROY ALAN, analytical chemistry; deceased, see previous edition for last biography

KELLER, ROY FRED, MATHEMATICS, COMPUTER SCIENCE. *Current Pos:* prof & chmn dept, 81-90, EMER PROF, COMPUT SCI & ENG, UNIV NEBR, 90- *Personal Data:* b Cape Girardeau, Mo, Apr 3, 27; m 49, Eldora E Simpher; c Clifford & Jana. *Educ:* Southeast Mo State Univ, BS, 50; Univ Mo, AM, 58, PhD(math), 62. *Prof Exp:* Instr math, Univ Mo-Columbia, 56-57, actg dir Comput Res Ctr, 59-62, asst prof math & dir, Comput Ctr, 62-67; assoc prof math & comput sci, Iowa State Univ, 67-71, prof, 71-81. *Mem:* Asn Comput Mach; Inst Elec & Electronics Engrs. *Res:* Iterative methods for solving systems of equations; programming and programming languages. *Mailing Add:* 2307 Shepard Blvd Columbia MO 65201-6127. *E-Mail:* keller@unl.edu

KELLER, RUDOLF, ELECTROMETALLURGY, ELECTROCHEMISTRY. *Current Pos:* SOLE PROPRIETOR, EMEC CONSULT, 84-; PRES, ELECTROSTRIP CORP, 97- *Personal Data:* b Winterthur, Switz, Dec 27, 33; US citizn; m 62, Elisabeth Langhard; c Andrea K & Eva S. *Educ:* Kantonsschule Winterthur, Matura, 52; Swiss Fed Inst Technol, Zuerich, dipl, 56, DSc nat, 60. *Prof Exp:* Scientist, Stanford Res Inst, 61-63; mem tech staff, Rocketdyne Div, Rockwell Int, 63-70; group leader, Swiss Aluminium Ltd, 70-77, Argonne Nat Lab, 77-79; staff scientist, Alcoa Labs, 79-83. *Concurrent Pos:* Res assoc, Carnegie Mellon Univ, 88-91. *Mem:* Int Soc Electrochem (treas, 76-79); Electrochem Soc; Minerals, Metals & Mat Soc; Am Chem Soc; Space Studies Inst; Am Soc Metals Int. *Res:* Research and consulting in electrometallurgy, electrochemistry and related areas; principal investigator on government funded research, and development efforts on topics such as electrochemical processes to utilize lunar resources, neodymium oxide electrolysis; cyanide formation in Hall-Heroult cells; metal hydride battery electrodes and paint removal from steel structures. *Mailing Add:* 4221 Roundtop Rd Export PA 15632

KELLER, SEYMOUR PAUL, SOLID STATE PHYSICS. *Current Pos:* staff mem, 53-63, mgr solid state physics & chem, 62-64, dir tech planning res, 64-66, dir phys sci dept, 66-72, CONSULT TO DIR RES, THOMAS J WATSON RES CTR, IBM CORP, 72- *Personal Data:* b New York, NY, July 5, 22; m 49; c 4. *Educ:* Univ Chicago, BS, 47, MS, 48, PhD(chem, physics), 51. *Prof Exp:* Du Pont fel chem, Univ Wis, 51-52; res assoc, Columbia Univ, 52-53. *Mem:* Fel Am Phys Soc. *Res:* Optical and electrical properties of dielectric and semiconducting solids; luminescent materials; paramagnetic resonance of solids; wave function calculations. *Mailing Add:* 29 Gary Dr Chappaqua NY 10514

KELLER, STANLEY E, DENTISTRY. *Current Pos:* assoc prof dent, Sch Dent, Univ Ala, 57-61, chmn div restorative & prosthetic dent, 61-62, chmn, Dept Oral Diag, 62-74, prof, 61-82, dir clins, 62-82, EMER PROF, SCH DENT, UNIV ALA, 82- *Personal Data:* b Medford, Mass, Sept 9, 21; m 45; c 4. *Educ:* Tufts Univ, DMD, 44; Univ Ala, MS, 62. *Prof Exp:* Instr dent, Sch Dent Med, Tufts Univ, 47-48. *Concurrent Pos:* Consult, Vet Admin Hosp, Birmingham. *Mem:* Am Asn Dent Schs; Int Asn Dent Res; Sigma Xi; Am Dent Asn; fel Am Col Dentists. *Res:* Studies of the affect and removal of dental plaque. *Mailing Add:* 4266 Hoffman Rd Mobile AL 36619

KELLER, STEPHEN JAY, MOLECULAR BIOLOGY, BIOCHEMISTRY. *Current Pos:* asst prof, 69-75, ASSOC PROF BIOL, UNIV CINCINNATI, 75- *Personal Data:* b Philadelphia, Pa, July 30, 40; m 62, Ching Ho; c Lisa & Michelle. *Educ:* Univ Pa, AB, 63; State Univ NY Stony Brook, PhD(biol), 70. *Concurrent Pos:* Grantee, Am Cancer Soc, 69-71, NSF, 70-78, NIH, 75-77, Environ Protection Agency, 80-84; vis assoc prof microbiol, State Univ NY, Stony Brook, 78-79; consult biotechnol, Protatek Inc, Sperti Drug, MDH Labs, Arel Pharmaceut & Hy-Gene Inc, 84-, The Lotus-Group Inc & Promega Corp. *Mem:* Sigma Xi; Am Soc Virol; AAAS; Am Chem Soc. *Res:* Molecular biology of development and differentiation of animal cell cultures and viruses. *Mailing Add:* Dept Biol Univ Cincinnati Cincinnati OH 45221. *Fax:* 513-556-5299

KELLER, TEDDY MONROE, POLYMER & ORGANIC CHEMISTRY, SYNTHETIC INORGANIC & ORGANOMETALLIC CHEMISTRY. *Current Pos:* RES CHEMIST POLYMER CHEM, NAVAL RES LAB, 77- *Personal Data:* b Parrottsville, Tenn, Nov 20, 44; m 88, Molly O'Rear. *Educ:* ETenn State Univ, BS, 66; Univ SC, PhD(org chem), 72. *Prof Exp:* Nat Defense Educ Act fel, Univ SC, 66-69; fel, Univ Fla, 72-74; chief chemist leather, A C Lawrence Leather Co, 74-75. *Mem:* Am Chem Soc; Soc Aerospace Mat & Process Engrs. *Res:* Monomer synthesis, polymerization, and unusual polymer properties such as exceptional thermal and oxidative stability of phthalonitrile resins and polyamides; electrical conductivity of infinite network, fully conjugated polymers; fluoropolymers; inorganic-organic hybrid polymers; ceramics. *Mailing Add:* Dept Navy Naval Res Lab Code 6127 Washington DC 20375-5320

KELLER, THOMAS C S, CYTOSKELETON. *Current Pos:* asst prof, 86-92, ASSOC PROF BIOL SCI, FLA STATE UNIV, 93- *Personal Data:* b June 20, 50; m; c 1. *Educ:* Univ Va, PhD, 81. *Prof Exp:* Asst prof biol, Wesleyan Univ, Conn, 84-86. *Mem:* AAAS; Am Soc Cell Biol. *Res:* Cell and molecular biology of the cytoskeleton. *Mailing Add:* Dept Biol Sci Fla State Univ Unit 1 Tallahassee FL 32306-3050. *Fax:* 850-644-0481; *E-Mail:* tkeller@sb.fsu.edu

KELLER, THOMAS W, COMPUTER SCIENCE. *Current Pos:* sr scientist, 89-92, sr tech staff mem, AIX Performance, 92-96, SCIENTIST, RES AUSTIN LAB, IBM, 96- *Personal Data:* b 1949; c 3. *Educ:* Univ Tex, Austin, BS, 71, MA, 72, PhD(comput sci), 76. *Prof Exp:* Staff mem, Los Alamos Sci Lab, Comput Div, Los Alamos, NMex, 76-79; res assoc, Comput Ctr, Univ Tex, Austin, 79-81, assoc dir appln support, 81-84; sr mem tech staff, Advan Comput Archit Prog, Microelectronics & Comput Technol Corp, Austin, 84-89. *Concurrent Pos:* Vpres, Info Res Assoc, Austin, Tex, 79-84; secy, Spec Interest Group Measurement & Eval, Asn Comput Mach, 81-85, vchair, 85-89, chair, 89-91. *Mem:* Asn Comput Mech; Inst Elec & Electronics Engrs. *Res:* Computer performance measurement, analysis and modeling; computer systems design; numerous technical publications. *Mailing Add:* IBM 11400 Burnet Rd Austin TX 78758. *E-Mail:* keller@austin.ibm.com

KELLER, TONY S, BIOMECHANICS, ORTHOPAEDIC BIOMECHANICS. *Current Pos:* asst prof, 91-95, ASSOC PROF MECH ENG & ORTHOP & REHAB, 95-; CO-DIR, VT SPACE GRANT CONSORTIUM, 92- *Personal Data:* b Salzburg, Austria, Aug 13, 55; US citizen; m 83, Sally J Whitehead; c Jeffrey S, Sarah E & Erin L. *Educ:* Ore State Univ, BS(sci) & BS(eng), 78, Univ Wash, MS, 83; Vanderbilt Univ; PhD(mech eng), 88. *Honors & Awards:* Young Scientist Award, Am Soc Biomech, 87; Volvo Award Exp Studies, Int Soc Study Lumbar Spine, 90. *Prof Exp:* Res biomed engr, Veterans Admin Med Ctr, 83-91; dir orthop biomech, Vanderbilt Univ, 83-91, res asst prof orthop & mech eng, 88-91. *Concurrent Pos:* Vis scientist, Sahlgren Hosp, Sweden, 84; prin investr, Whitaker Found, 93-96, Nat Inst Chiropractic Res, 93-95. *Mem:* Inst Elec & Electronics Engrs; Am Soc Biomech; Am Soc Mech Engrs; Orthop Res Soc; Europ Soc Biomech. *Res:* Spine mechanics, material and structural properties of biologic tissues, orthopaedic implant-biomechanics and design, and skeletal growth and remodelling. *Mailing Add:* Dept Mech Eng Univ Vt Burlington VT 05405-0156. *Fax:* 802-656-1929; *E-Mail:* keller@emba.uvm.edu

KELLER, WALDO FRANK, VETERINARY SURGERY. *Current Pos:* RETIRED. *Personal Data:* b Hicksville, Ohio, Apr 13, 29; m 58; c 2. *Educ:* Ohio State Univ, DVM, 53; Mich State Univ, MS, 61; Am Col Vet Ophthal, dipl. *Prof Exp:* Instr, Mich State Univ, 53-55 & 57-61, univ clin res grant, 61-65, from asst prof to assoc prof vet surg & med, 61-70, assoc dean, 79-83 & 84-88, actg dean, 83-84, prof vet surg & med, 70-97, chmn, Dept Small Animal Surg & Med, 68-97, prof ophthal, 88-97. *Concurrent Pos:* Trainee, Div Ophthal, Sch Med, Stanford Univ, 65-66. *Mem:* Am Asn Vet Clinicians; Am Soc Vet Ophthal; Am Col Vet Ophthalmologists. *Res:* Veterinary ophthalmology; growth of cornea in tissue culture and pathology of eye tissues in evaluating surgical techniques. *Mailing Add:* 615 Baily St East Lansing MI 48823

KELLER, WALTER DAVID, GEOLOGY, CERAMICS. *Current Pos:* from asst prof to prof, 32-70, chmn dept, 42-45, EMER PROF GEOL, UNIV MO, COLUMBIA, 70- *Personal Data:* b North Kansas City, Mo, Mar 13, 00; m 36, Madge Jones; c David E & Dwight M. *Educ:* Univ Mo, AB, 25, AM, 26, BS, 30, PhD(geol), 33; Harvard Univ, AM, 32. *Hon Degrees:* DEngr, Univ Mo, Rolla, 88. *Honors & Awards:* Neil A Miner Award, Nat Asn Geol Teachers, 67; Hardinge Award, Am Inst Mining, Metall & Petrol Engrs, 79; William H Twenhofel Award, Soc Econ Paleontologists & Mineralogists. *Prof Exp:* Instr, Univ Mo, 26-29; ceramic technologist, A P Green Fire Brick Co, 29-31. *Concurrent Pos:* Chmn clay minerals comt, Nat Res Coun-Nat Acad Sci, 57-60; distinguished prof geol, Univ Mo; vis prof, Univ SFla, 70-73. *Mem:* Fel AAAS; Am Ceramic Soc; fel Geol Soc Am; fel Mineral Soc Am; Soc Econ Paleont & Mineral. *Res:* Clay mineralogy; fire clay; sedimentary petrology; optical mineralogy; mineral and rock soil amendments; lunar sample research. *Mailing Add:* 305 Geol Bldg Univ Mo Columbia MO 65211

KELLER, WILLIAM EDWARD, QUANTUM PHYSICS. *Current Pos:* RETIRED. *Personal Data:* b Cleveland, Ohio, Mar 11, 25; m 47, 61; c William Eric, Ann (Hinnen), Margaret & Amber (Archer). *Educ:* Harvard Univ, AB, 45, AM, 47, PhD(chem), 48. *Prof Exp:* Assoc supvr mil sponsored res, Res Found, Ohio State Univ, 48-50; mem staff, 50-70, group leader cryogenics, 70-83, asst div leader physics, Los Alamos Sci Lab, 83-87. *Concurrent Pos:* Vis scientist, Univ Sussex, England, 67-68; Nat Acad Sci/Nat Res Coun Panel to evaluate Nat Bur Standards, 70-76; chair, Appl Superconductivity Conf, 79-80; US/USSR comt superconducting power transmission, Pres Nixon's Sci Exchange Prog, 72-78. *Mem:* Am Chem Soc; fel Am Phys Soc; fel Am Inst Chemists; Sigma Xi. *Res:* Infrared spectroscopy; low temperature physics; liquid helium hydrodynamics; applications of superconductivity to electric power systems. *Mailing Add:* 1090 Old Taos Hwy Santa Fe NM 87501

KELLER, WILLIAM JOHN, ORGANIC CHEMISTRY. *Current Pos:* RETIRED. *Personal Data:* b Meridian, Miss, Sept 26, 20; m 46, Rosemary Kelsey; c Brian D & Janice K (Kent). *Educ:* Miss State Col, BS, 43; Mass Inst Technol, PhD(org chem), 51. *Prof Exp:* Chemist org res, E I Du Pont de Nemours & Co, Inc, 51-79. *Mem:* Fel AAAS; Am Chem Soc. *Res:* Synthetic rubber; noble metal catalysis. *Mailing Add:* 229 Afton Lane Branson MO 65616

KELLERHALS, GLEN E, PHYSICAL CHEMISTRY. *Current Pos:* Res chemist, 74-77, group leader, 77-80, strategic planner, 80-81, SPECIAL PROJ ENGR, CITIES SERV CO, 81- *Personal Data:* b Vinton, Iowa, Sept 29, 45; m 73; c 2. *Educ:* Upper Iowa Col, BS, 67; Okla State Univ, PhD(chem), 74; Tulsa Univ, MBA, 80. *Mem:* Am Chem Soc; Soc Petrol Engrs; Am Petrol Inst. *Res:* Enhanced oil recovery. *Mailing Add:* 4304 Valley Dr Midland TX 79707

KELLERMAN, KARL F(REDERIC), engineering; deceased, see previous edition for last biography

KELLERMAN, MARTIN, PHYSICAL CHEMISTRY. *Current Pos:* ASSOC PROF CHEM, CALIF POLYTECH STATE UNIV, SAN LUIS OBISPO, 68- *Personal Data:* b New York, NY, Feb 11, 32; m 63; c 2. *Educ:* Polytech Inst Brooklyn, BS, 53; Univ Wash, PhD(chem), 66. *Prof Exp:* Anal chemist, Continental Baking Co, 58-61; NIH res traineeship, Univ Calif, San Diego, 66-68. *Mem:* AAAS. *Res:* X-ray crystal structure analysis; structure of metal chelate compounds; circular dichroism studies on structure of molecules of biological interest. *Mailing Add:* Chem Dept Calif Polytech State Univ 1 Poly View Dr San Luis Obispo CA 93407-0001

KELLERMANN, KENNETH IRWIN, RADIO ASTRONOMY. *Current Pos:* from asst scientist to assoc scientist, Nat Radio Astron Observ, 65-69, scientist, 69-77, asst dir, 77, SR SCIENTIST, NAT RADIO ASTRON OBSERV, 78- *Personal Data:* b New York, NY, July 1, 37; wid; c 1. *Educ:* Mass Inst Technol, SB, 59; Calif Inst Technol, PhD(physics & astron), 63. *Honors & Awards:* Calif Inst Technol-Eastman Kodak Corp Eastman Kodak Prize, 63; Rumford Prize, Am Acad Arts & Sci, 70; Helen B Warner Prize, Am Astron Soc, 71; B A Gould Prize, Nat Acad Sci, 73. *Prof Exp:* Res scientist, Radiophys Lab, Commonwealth Sci & Indust Res Orgn, 63-65. *Concurrent Pos:* NSF fel, 65-66; lectr, Leiden Univ, 67; res assoc, Calif Inst Technol, 69; adj prof, Univ Ariz, 70-73; dir, Max Planck Inst Radio Astron, 77-79; vpres, Comn 40, Int Radio Sci Union, 79-82, pres, 82-85, chmn, Comn J, US Nat Comt. *Mem:* Nat Acad Sci; Am Astron Soc; Am Acad Arts & Sci; Int Astron Union; Int Radio Sci Union. *Res:* Extragalactic radio sources; galaxies; quasars; cosmology; instrumentation. *Mailing Add:* Nat Radio Astron Observ Edgemont Rd Charlottesville VA 22903. *Fax:* 804-296-0278; *E-Mail:* kkellerm@nrao.edu

KELLERS, CHARLES FREDERICK, PHYSICS. *Current Pos:* assoc prof, 68-70, chmn dept, 71-80, PROF PHYSICS, CALIF STATE UNIV, SAN BERNARDINO, 70- *Personal Data:* b Montclair, NJ, Sept 12, 30; m 58; c 2. *Educ:* Swarthmore Col, BA, 53; Duke Univ, PhD(physics), 60. *Prof Exp:* Engr, Gen Elec Co, 53-55; res assoc, Duke Univ, 60; asst prof physics, Wells Col, 61-65; sr res assoc, Cornell Univ, 65-68. *Mem:* Sigma Xi. *Mailing Add:* 694 E 39th St San Bernardino CA 92404

KELLERSTRASS, ERNST JUNIOR, CIVIL ENGINEERING, GEOPHYSICS. *Current Pos:* civil engr, Sanit Landfills, Bowse Morner Testing Lab, Systech Corp, 80-81, civil engr environ, 81-82, sr res scientist, Systs Res Lab, 82-97, CONSULT, SYSTECH CORP, 97- *Personal Data:* b Peoria, Ill, Jan 9, 33; m 54; c 5. *Educ:* Bradley Univ, BSCE, 54; St Louis Univ, MS, 62; George Washington Univ, MS, 67. *Prof Exp:* Engr, US Army Corps Engrs, 54, USAF, 54-, aeronaut meteorologist, 55-57, analyst & forecaster, Weather Cent Japan, 57-60, asst staff meteorologist for environ eng, 62-64, geophysicist, Electronic Syst Div, 64-66, geophysicist, VELA Prog, 67-71, chief planning, Remote Piloted Vehicle Syst Prog Off, Aeronaut Systs Div, 71-74, staff scientist, Advan Res Br, Foreign Technol Div, Wright-Patterson AFB, 74-79; Instr, Univ Dayton, 79-80. *Mem:* Am Meteorol Soc; Am Geophys Union; Am Soc Civil Engrs; Sigma Xi. *Res:* Meteorology, forecasting and environmental engineering; management of research in meteorological sensors, environmental effects, electric systems survivability-vulnerability, seismological instrumentation-field experiments and aeronautical systems; research and development management; geotechnical engineering; hydrology; environmental engineering. *Mailing Add:* 2547 Sugarloaf Ct Beavercreek OH 45434-6831

KELLETT, CLAUD MARVIN, RESEARCH ADMINISTRATION. *Current Pos:* RETIRED. *Personal Data:* b Memphis, Tenn, Sept 5, 28; m 48, Janice Jacobs; c Claudia, Richard, Daniel & Cynthia. *Educ:* Ga Inst Technol, BEE, 50; Purdue Univ, MS, 57. *Prof Exp:* Res test engr, Allison Div, Gen Motors Corp, 50-54; sr engr, Tex Instruments, Inc, 56-62; develop engr, Semiconductor Div, Raytheon Co, 62-63; prod eng supvr, Sperry Semiconductor Div, Sperry Rand Corp, 63-64; prod supvr transistor mfg, Crystalonics, Inc, 64-65; sr res physicist, Ion Physics Corp, 65-66; physicist, Electronics Res Ctr, NASA, 66-70; sr res scientist, Tyco Corp Technol Ctr, 71; prog mgt officer, NSF, 72-88. *Res:* Electrical measurements, especially Hall and photoelectromagnetic effects of semiconductor materials; modification of electrical properties of semiconductor materials by ion implantation. *Mailing Add:* 5203 Faraday Ct Fairfax VA 22032-2708

KELLEY, ALBERT J(OSEPH), STRATEGIC MANAGEMENT, TECHNOLOGY INVESTMENT. *Current Pos:* res dir, 94-96, RES AFFIL, DEPT AERONAUT & ASTRONAUT, MASS INST TECHNOL, 96- *Personal Data:* b Boston, Mass, July 27, 24; m 91, JoAnn Palmer; c Mark, Shaun & David. *Educ:* USN Acad, BS, 45; Mass Inst Technol, BS, 48, ScD(aeronaut & electronics eng), 56. *Honors & Awards:* Except Serv Medal, NASA, 67; Outstanding Serv Medal, Secy Defense, 92. *Prof Exp:* Exp test pilot & proj dir, USN Air Test Ctr, Patuxent River, Md, 51-53; asst head, Air-to-Air Missile Br, Navy Bur Aeronaut, Washington, DC, 56-57 & Guided Missile Guid Br, 57-58, proj mgr, Eagle Missile Syst, 58-60; proj mgr, Navy Bur Weapons, 60; prog mgr, Agena Launch Vehicle, NASA, Washington, DC, 60-61, dir electronics & control, 61-64, dep dir, Electronics Res Ctr, Cambridge, 64-67, consult, 67-77; pres, Arthur D Little Prog Systs Mgt Co, 77-85, chmn, 85-88, sr group vpres, Arthur D Little Inc, 85-88; sr vpres strategic planning, United Technol Corp, 88-90; dep undersecy defense, Int Progs, US Defense, Pentagon, 90-93; fel bus & govt, Kennedy Sch, Harvard Univ, 93-94. *Concurrent Pos:* Chmn, Bd Econ Adv, Mass, 70-75; consult, Dept Transp, 71-77; mem, Bd Vis, US Defense Systs Mgt Col, 74-78; mem, C S Draper Lab Corp, 75-90 & Space Appln Bd, Nat Acad Eng, 77-83; dir, State St Bank & Trust Co, State St Boston Corp, 75-93; dir, Mass Bus Develop Corp, 69-78, Mass Technol Develop Corp, 79-82. *Mem:* Assoc fel Am Inst Aeronaut & Astronaut; fel Inst Elec & Electronics Engrs; Int Acad Astronaut; Sigma Xi. *Res:* Guided missiles, space vehicles and aircraft; control systems engineering; electronics; strategic planning and management; project management; author of 3 books plus several articles & professional journals. *Mailing Add:* 11715 Arbor Glen Way Reston VA 20194-1577. *E-Mail:* ajkelley@mit.edu

KELLEY, ALLEN FREDERICK, JR, MATHEMATICS, FORESTRY. *Current Pos:* asst prof, 66-69, ASSOC PROF MATH, UNIV CALIF, SANTA CRUZ, 69- *Personal Data:* b Franklin, NH, July 1, 33. *Educ:* Mont State Univ, BS, 55; Univ Calif, Berkeley, PhD(math), 63. *Prof Exp:* Instr math, Univ Calif, Berkeley, 63-64; partic, Exchange Prog, US Nat Acad Sci-USSR Acad Sci, 64-65; mem fac, Inst Advan Study, 65-66. *Mem:* Soc Am Foresters; Am Math Soc. *Res:* Differential equations and celestial mechanics; wood technology and engineering. *Mailing Add:* Dept Math Univ Calif Santa Cruz CA 95064-1099

KELLEY, C STUART, NUCLEAR PHYSICS, COMPUTATIONAL PHYSICS. *Current Pos:* PROG MGR, DEFENSE SPEC WEAPONS AGENCY, 83- *Personal Data:* m 65, Melissa; c Brooks & Laura (Buell). *Educ:* Union Col, BS, 64; Univ Del, MS, 66, PhD(solid state physics), 70. *Prof Exp:* Physicist, Edgewood Arsenal, 70-73 & Harry Diamond Labs, 76-80; analyst, Gen Res Corp, 73-76; phys scientist, Defense Intel Agency, 80-83. *Res:* Optical properties of impurities in solids; combustion physics; optical properties of ocean layers; effects of nuclear weapons. *Mailing Add:* HQDSWA 6801 Telegraph Rd Alexandria VA 22310-3398

KELLEY, CHARLES JOSEPH, SYNTHESIS OF FLUORESCENT COMPOUNDS. *Current Pos:* asst prof, 77-83, ASSOC PROF CHEM, MASS COL PHARM, 83- *Personal Data:* b Akron, Ohio, Feb 2, 43; c Eurydice & Anthe. *Educ:* St Joseph's Col, Ind, BA, 64; Ind Univ, Bloomington, PhD(org chem), 70. *Prof Exp:* Res assoc org synthesis, Ind Univ, 70-75; asst prof chem, Ball State Univ, 75-76; res assoc natural prod, Northeastern Univ, 76-77. *Mem:* Am Chem Soc; Am Soc Pharmacog. *Res:* Isolation from plant sources of potential pharmaceutical agents; synthesis of oligophenylenes and proton-transfer fluors as laser dyes and scintillators. *Mailing Add:* Mass Col Pharm 179 Longwood Ave Boston MA 02115-5896. *Fax:* 617-732-2801

KELLEY, CHARLES THOMAS, JR, SYSTEMS ANALYSIS, PHYSICS. *Current Pos:* analyst, Washington Defense Res Div, Rand Corp, Washington, DC, 71-73, phys scientist, 73-77, dir, Ground Warfare Prog, 77-79, sr phys scientist, 79-94, DIR FORCE MODERIZATION & EMPLOYMENT PROG, RAND CORP, 94- *Personal Data:* b Boston, Mass, Feb 9, 40; m 64; c 3. *Educ:* Univ Notre Dame, BS, 61; Ind Univ, MS, 63; Ind Univ, PhD(nuclear physics), 67. *Prof Exp:* Res asst nuclear physics, Cyclotron Lab, Ind Univ, 65-67; physicist, Anal Serv Inc, Falls Church, Va, 67-71. *Mem:* Am Phys Soc; Opers Res Soc Am; Sigma Xi. *Res:* Weapon systems analysis; operations research; nuclear physics. *Mailing Add:* 909 Glenhaven Dr Pacific Palisades CA 90272

KELLEY, DARSHAN SINGH, DIET & IMMUNO-COMPETENCE, NUTRIENT REQUIREMENTS. *Current Pos:* RES CHEMIST, WESTERN HUMAN NUTRIT RES CTR, AGR RES SERV, USDA, 83- *Personal Data:* b Ludhiana, Punjab, India, Feb 5, 47; US citizen; m 80; c 2. *Educ:* Punjab Agr Univ Ludhiana, India, BSc, 67, MSc, 69 ; Okla Univ, PhD(biochem), 74. *Prof Exp:* Consult, res, Okla Med Res Found, 74-75; postdoctoral res assoc, McArdle Lab, Univ Wis, 75-80; asst prof, biochem, WVa Univ Med Ctr, 80-83. *Mem:* Am Instit Nutrit; Am Soc Biochem & Molecular Biol; AAAS; Sigma Xi. *Res:* Nutritional regulation of immune-status in humans and animals; nutritional and hormonal regulation of hepatic gene expression. *Mailing Add:* Nutrit Res Ctr ARS/USDA PO Box 29997 Presidio San Francisco CA 94129-0997. *Fax:* 415-556-1432

KELLEY, DONALD CLIFFORD, veterinary medicine; deceased, see previous edition for last biography

KELLEY, FENTON CROSLAND, MAMMALIAN PHYSIOLOGY, ENVIRONMENTAL PHYSIOLOGY. *Current Pos:* from asst prof to assoc prof zool, 76-88, EMER PROF ZOOL, BOISE STATE UNIV, 88-; AQUATIC CONSULT, US CENGRS, 73- *Personal Data:* b Chicago, Ill, Aug 24, 26. *Educ:* Univ NMex, BSc, 51, MSc, 54; Univ Calif, Berkeley, PhD(physiol), 67. *Prof Exp:* Fisheries biologist, Calif State Dept Fish & Game, 54-57; res assoc physiol, Inst Environ Stress, Univ Calif, Santa Barbara, 57-58, lectr, Dept Phys Educ & Ergonomics, 58-59. *Concurrent Pos:* consult fisheries, Stearns, Rogers, Inc, Denver, 75-, City of Boise, 80, 81 & 82 & M K Eng Co-Water Qual, Boise, 85-87; bd dirs, Fisheries West, Inc, 89-95. *Res:* Fresh water fisheries biology; aquatic ecology; various aspects of adaptation to environmental extremes in mammals; anatomy; physiological effects of selective pesticides; aquaculture and invertebrates. *Mailing Add:* 2260 Berkeley St Boise ID 83705

KELLEY, FRANK NICHOLAS, ADVANCED NON-METALLIC MATERIALS, SOLID ROCKET PROPELLANTS. *Current Pos:* DEAN DIR & PROF, INST POLYMER SCI, UNIV AKRON, 78- *Personal Data:* b Akron, Ohio, Jan 19, 35; m 60; c 3. *Educ:* Univ Akron, BS, 58, MS, 59, PhD(polymer chem), 61. *Honors & Awards:* Rubber Age Award; Outstanding Tech Contrib Award, Am Inst Aeronaut & Astronaut. *Prof Exp:* Res chemist, Air Force Rocket Propulsion Lab, 64-66, br chief solid rockets, 66-70, chief advan plans, 70-71, chief scientist, 71-73; chief scientist, Dept Defense, Wright-Patterson AFB, 73-76, dir, Air Force Mat Lab, 76-78. *Concurrent Pos:* Chmn, Interagency Working Group Mech Behav, 63-65; consult, NSF,

79- & Dept Energy Progs, Jet Propulsion Lab, Midwest Res Inst, Solar Energy Res Inst, 79- *Mem:* Assoc fel Am Inst Aeronaut & Astronaut; Am Chem Soc. *Res:* Polymer physics; structure-property relationships of elastomers and thermosetting resins; mechanical properties of solid propellants. *Mailing Add:* Inst Polymer Sci Univ Akron Akron OH 44325-3909

KELLEY, GAYNOR NATHANIEL, INSTRUMENTATION. *Current Pos:* Mgr, 51-85, pres & chief oper officer, 85-90, CHMN, PERKINS-ELMER CORP, 90- *Personal Data:* b New Canaan, Conn, May 12, 31; m 74, Diane Curio; c Gaynor Jr, Russell, Theodore, Ronald & Victoria. *Educ:* Delehanty Inst, BSME, 51. *Mailing Add:* Perkin-Elmer Corp 761 Main Ave Norwalk CT 06859

KELLEY, GEORGE G, plasma physics, electronic instrumentation; deceased, see previous edition for last biography

KELLEY, GEORGE GREENE, BIOLOGICAL CHEMISTRY. *Current Pos:* RETIRED. *Personal Data:* b Philadelphia, Pa, Nov 6, 18; m 47; c 4. *Educ:* Fla State Univ, BS, 50, MS, 51, PhD(biochem, food, nutrit), 56. *Prof Exp:* Tech res asst chem, Fla State Univ, 52-54; asst prof, Univ Mo, 56-57; instr pharmacol, Howard Col, 58-61; assoc prof chem, Jacksonville Univ, 63-67, chmn div sci & math, 64-73, prof chem, 67-88. *Concurrent Pos:* Sr biochemist, Southern Res Inst, 57-62; instr, Exten Ctr, Univ Ala, 59-62, guest lectr, Med & Dent Schs, 61. *Mem:* AAAS; Am Chem Soc; Am Soc Limnol & Oceanog; NY Acad Sci; fel Am Inst Chemists. *Res:* Study of the life cycle, the propagation and large scale cultivation of three species of the large fresh water shrimp, genus Macrobrachium. *Mailing Add:* 5332 Selton Ave Jacksonville FL 32277

KELLEY, GREGORY M, DESIGN ENGINEERING, VACUUM SYSTEM DESIGN. *Current Pos:* TECH LIAISON, ICON CORP, SHREVEPORT, LA, 95-96. *Personal Data:* b Boston, Mass, Nov 18, 33; m 96, Karen L Nix; c Michael R, Gregory M, & Alice A. *Educ:* Wentworth Inst Technol, Boston, AEng, 58 & 65; Col Santa Fe, BCS, 85. *Honors & Awards:* Award of Excellence, US Dept Energy, 89. *Prof Exp:* Sr technician, Avco Everett Res Lab, 61-66; sr technologist, Nuclear Weapons Diag, Los Alamos Nat Lab, 66-89, Nuclear Mat Mgt, 89-93, sr prod technologist, 89-94. *Concurrent Pos:* Group criticality safety officer, Los Alamos Nat Lab, 91-93; instr vacuum technol, Univ NMex, Los Alamos, 84- *Mem:* Soc Mfg Engrs. *Res:* Automated measurement of radioactive samples by gamma and neutron counting and calorimetry; robotic applications; nuclear shielding; ionsource design vacuum system design; weapons diagnostics; nuclear criticality safety. *Mailing Add:* 1710-37th St Los Alamos NM 87544-2152

KELLEY, JAMES CHARLES, OCEANOGRAPHY. *Current Pos:* DEAN SCI, SAN FRANCISCO STATE UNIV, 75- *Personal Data:* b Los Angeles, Calif, Oct 5, 40; m 63, Susan Cotner; c Jason & Megan. *Educ:* Pomona Col, BA, 63; Univ Wyo, PhD(geol), 66. *Prof Exp:* From asst prof to assoc prof oceanog, Biomath & Geol Sci, Univ Wash, 66-75. *Concurrent Pos:* Fulbright prof, Univ Athens, 71; pres, Calif Acad Sci, 86-93. *Mem:* AAAS; Am Geophys Union; Pac Sci Cong; Am Soc Limnology & Oceanog. *Res:* Coastal upwelling; structural petrology; statistics; computer science. *Mailing Add:* Sch Sci San Francisco State Univ San Francisco CA 94132. *E-Mail:* jkelley@sfsu.edu

KELLEY, JAMES LEROY, MEDICINAL CHEMISTRY. *Personal Data:* b San Diego, Calif, Nov 12, 43; m 67; c 3. *Educ:* Fresno State Col, BS, 67; Univ Calif, Santa Barbara, PhD(chem), 70. *Prof Exp:* Asst div dir, Burroughs Wellcome & Co, 70-90. *Mem:* Am Chem Soc; AAAS; NY Acad Sci. *Res:* Chemistry on purine, pyrimidine and imidazole heterocycles and antiviral agents especially acyclic nucleosides; design and synthesis of enzyme inhibitors and novel CNS active agents. *Mailing Add:* 10928 Raveu Rock Dr Raleigh NC 27614

KELLEY, JASON, CELL BIOLOGY. *Current Pos:* From asst prof to prof cell biol & med, 83-88, PROF, PULMONARY DIS SECT, UNIV VT, 88- *Personal Data:* b Buffalo, NY, Sept 8, 43; m 65; c 3. *Educ:* Harvard Univ, AB, 66; Univ Tex, Dallas, MD, 72. *Mem:* NY Acad Sci; Biochem Soc; Am Soc Cell Biol; Reticuloendothelial Soc; Am Thoracic Soc; AAAS. *Res:* Cellular and molecular mechanisms of tissue remodelling in growth and disease. *Mailing Add:* Pulmonary Unit Univ Vt Col Med Given C-305 Burlington VT 05405-0001. *Fax:* 802-656-3854

KELLEY, JAY HILARY, MINING ENGINEERING, COMPUTER SCIENCE. *Current Pos:* dean, 70-78, distinguisehd prof, 78-87, DISTINGUISHED EMER PROF, COL MINERAL & ENERGY RESOURCES, WVA UNIV, 87- *Personal Data:* b Greensburg, Pa, Mar 9, 20; m 49; c 9. *Educ:* Pa State Univ, BS, 42, MS, 47, PhD, 52. *Prof Exp:* Res asst, Pa State Univ, 46-49, instr, 49-52; sr res engr, Joy Mfg Co, Pa, 52-57; sr engr, Westinghouse Elec Corp, 57-62; staff scientist, Off Sci & Technol, Exec Off President, Washington, DC, 62-65; prof info sci & assoc dir, Bur Info Sci Res, Rutgers Univ, 65-66; mgr comput & asst instr, Philco-Ford Corp, Pa, 66-69; pres, Urbdata Inc, Pa, 69-80; pres, Kelastic Mine Beam Co, Greensburg, 69-86. *Concurrent Pos:* Vpres, Mammoth Coal & Coke Co, 46-54; dir, Leonard Express, Inc, 54-; exec secy panel sci info, President's Sci Adv Comt, 62-63, panel drug info, 64-66; comt sci & technol info, Fed Coun Sci & Technol, 62-65; trustee, Engrs Index, Inc, 67-80, dir, 69-78, pres, 76-78; ptnr, Mining Eng Consult, Greensburg, Pa; chmn, Coal Mining Sect, Nat Safety Coun, Chicago, 79-80; chmn proj comt, Eng Found, New York. *Mem:* AAAS; Inst Elec & Electronics Engrs; Opers Res Soc Am; Am Soc Info Sci; Am Inst Mining, Metall & Petrol Engrs; Am Mining Congress; Asn Comput Mach; Cosmos Club. *Res:* Mine design; mineral resource economics; entropic systems; computer science and applications; mine roof control; machinery design and development; bulk handling; spontaneous combustion. *Mailing Add:* 300 Maplewood Dr Greensburg PA 15601

KELLEY, JIM LEE, BIOCHEMISTRY, CHEMISTRY. *Current Pos:* ASSOC PROF, E TENN STATE UNIV, 94- *Personal Data:* b Ada, Okla, Oct 20, 47; m 68; c 3. *Educ:* Bethany Nazarene Col, BS, 69; Univ Okla, PhD(biochem), 73. *Prof Exp:* Fel, 73-76, staff scientist med res, Okla Med Res Found, 76-79; asst prof, Univ Tex Health Sci Ctr, San Antonio, 80-93. *Concurrent Pos:* Grants, Am Heart Asn, Okla Affil, Inc, 76-77 & 77-78 & HEW Pub Health Serv, 78- *Mem:* AAAS; Am Soc Cell Biol; Am Heart Asn; Am Soc Invest Path. *Res:* Metabolism of plasma lipoproteins by macrophages; role of antioxidants in atherosclerosis. *Mailing Add:* Dept Internal Med E Tenn State Univ Box 70622 Johnson City TN 37614. *Fax:* 423-929-6459

KELLEY, JOHN DANIEL, CHEMICAL PHYSICS. *Current Pos:* res scientist, McDonnell Douglas Res Labs, 67-70, assoc scientist, 70-73, sr scientist, 73-81, prin scientist, 81-89, CHIEF SCIENTIST, MCDONNELL DOUGLAS RES LABS, 89- *Personal Data:* b Chicago, Ill, July 30, 37; m 60, Elizabeth McDermott; c John, James & Ann. *Educ:* St Louis Univ, BS, 59; Georgetown Univ, PhD(phys chem), 64. *Prof Exp:* Res assoc theoret chem, Georgetown Univ, 63-64; res fel, Brookhaven Nat Lab, 64-67. *Concurrent Pos:* Adj prof, Dept Chem & Physics, Univ Mo, St Louis, 77- *Mem:* AAAS; Am Chem Soc; Sigma Xi. *Res:* Theoretical and experimental reaction kinetics; molecular quantum mechanics; inter-molecular energy transfer processes. *Mailing Add:* 13103 Gascogne Ct St Louis MO 63141. *Fax:* 314-232-0888; *E-Mail:* kelley@mdlgwy.mdl.com

KELLEY, JOHN ERNEST, MATHEMATICS. *Current Pos:* chmn dept, 66-69, ASSOC PROF MATH, UNIV SFLA, 64- *Personal Data:* b Milwaukee, Wis, June 27, 19; m 50; c 4. *Educ:* Univ Wis, BS, 41; Marquette Univ, MS, 48; Univ Mich, PhD(math), 60. *Prof Exp:* Instr math, Univ Miami, 49-51; analyst, US Dept Defense, 53-54; from instr to asst prof math & chmn dept, Marquette Univ, 54-64. *Mem:* Math Asn Am; Nat Coun Teachers of Math. *Res:* Mathematical logic. *Mailing Add:* 1120 Michigan Blvd Dunedin FL 34698-2711

KELLEY, JOHN FRANCIS, BIOCHEMISTRY, ACADEMIC ADMINISTRATON. *Current Pos:* from instr to prof chem, 47-93, from asst dean to assoc dean Acad Affairs, 68-93, EMER PROF CHEM, US NAVAL ACAD, 93- *Personal Data:* b Boston, Mass, July 10, 20; m 52; c 2. *Educ:* Boston Col, BS, 46, MS, 47; Georgetown Univ, PhD(chem), 52. *Prof Exp:* Asst chem, Boston Col, 46-47. *Res:* Organic iodine compounds; identification of organic compounds. *Mailing Add:* Off Acad Dean US Naval Acad Annapolis MD 21402-5000

KELLEY, JOHN FREDRIC, PSYCHIATRY. *Current Pos:* assoc prof, 68-74, dir child psychiat prog, Med Ctr, 68-83 & 87-90, PROF BEHAV MED, PSYCHIAT & PEDIAT, MED SCH, WVA UNIV, 74- *Personal Data:* b Gay, WVa, Sept 17, 31; m 60; c 3. *Educ:* Marietta Col, AB, 54; McGill Univ, MD, 58; Am Bd Psychiat & Neurol, cert psychiat, 66, cert child psychiat, 71. *Prof Exp:* Resident psychiat, Health Ctr, Ohio State Univ, 59-62; staff psychiatrist, Patuxent Inst, Md, 64-66; fel child psychiat, Worcester Youth Guid Ctr, Mass, 66-68. *Mem:* Am Psychiat Asn; AMA; Am Acad Child Psychiat. *Res:* Child psychiatry. *Mailing Add:* WVa Univ Med Ctr Morgantown WV 26506

KELLEY, JOHN JOSEPH, II, OCEANOGRAPHY, METEOROLOGY. *Current Pos:* oceanogr, Univ Alaska, 68-73, asst prof oceanog, 73-77, dir, Naval Arctic Res Lab, 77-80, assoc prof, 80-93, PROF MARINE SCI, UNIV ALASKA, 93- *Personal Data:* b Philadelphia, Pa, Jan 4, 33; m 70, Eleanor Johnson. *Educ:* Pa State Univ, BS, 58; Univ Nagoya, Japan, PhD(oceanog), 71. *Prof Exp:* Sr scientist meteorol, Univ Wash, 60-68. *Concurrent Pos:* Prog mgr, NSF Off Polar Prog, 74-76; chmn, Sci Adv Comt, Northslope Borough/Alaska Eskimo Whaling Comm, 80-; dir, NSF Polar Ice Coring Off, 89-; prog mgr, Ocean/Meteoro, Div Polar Prog, NSF, Washington, DC. *Mem:* Am Geophys Union; Am Soc Limnol & Oceanog; Am Polar Soc; Arctic Inst NAm; Sigma Xi. *Res:* Exchange processes; polar ecosystems; coastal upwelling phenomena; air-sea exchange processes; ice coring-drilling technology. *Mailing Add:* Inst Marine Sci Univ Alaska Fairbanks AK 99775-1080. *Fax:* 907-474-7204

KELLEY, JOHN LE ROY, MATHEMATICS. *Current Pos:* chmn dept, Univ Calif, Berkeley, 57-60 & 75-78, prof, 53-85, EMER PROF MATH, UNIV CALIF, BERKELEY, 85- *Personal Data:* b Kans, Dec 6, 16; m 38, 63; c 5. *Educ:* Univ Calif, Los Angeles, AB, 36, MA, 37; Univ Va, PhD(math), 40. *Prof Exp:* Asst prof math, Univ Notre Dame, 40-42; mathematician, Ballistic Res Lab, Aberdeen Proving Grounds, 42-45; asst prof math, Univ Chicago, 45-47; assoc prof, Univ Calif, 47-50; vis assoc prof, Tulane Univ, 50-52 & Univ Kans, 52-53. *Concurrent Pos:* Fel, Inst Advan Study, 45-46; NSF fel, 53-54; Fulbright res prof, Cambridge Univ, 57-58; Am-Kanpur Prog lectr, Indian Inst Technol, Kanpur, 64-65; nat teacher, Continental Classroom, NBC, 60. *Mem:* Fel AAAS; Nat Coun Teachers Math; Math Asn Am. *Res:* Topology; functional analysis. *Mailing Add:* Dept Math Univ Calif Berkeley CA 94720-0001

KELLEY, JOSEPH MATTHEW, POLYMER CHEMISTRY. *Current Pos:* VPRES, MOJAVE RES & DEVELOP CO, 84- *Personal Data:* b Baltimore, Md, Dec 10, 29; m 55; c 3. *Educ:* Loyola Col, Md, BS, 50; Fordham Univ, MS, 52, PhD(chem), 56; NY Univ, BSChE, 66. *Prof Exp:* Res chemist, Chem Res Div, Esso Res & Eng Co, NJ, 55-57, proj leader polyolefins, 57-61; suprv polyolefins res, Rexall Chem Co, Paramus, 61-63, mgr develop res, Dart Industs Chem Group, 63-65, mgr polymer res, 65-66, asst dir styrenic polymer develop, 66-67, dir, ABS res & develop, 67-69, dir mkt admin rexene polymers, 69-70, vpres res & develop, 70-79; vpres res & develop, El Paso Polyolefins Co, 79-84. *Mem:* Am Chem Soc; Sigma Xi. *Res:* Polymerization of olefins; stabilization of polymers; organic synthesis; enzyme chemistry; heterogeneous catalysis; styrene type polymers; chlorine oxide chemistry. *Mailing Add:* 1321 E Broad St Westfield NJ 07090-1105

KELLEY, KEITH WAYNE, IMMUNOPHYSIOLOGY. *Current Pos:* PROF, UNIV ILL, 84- *Personal Data:* b Bloomington, Ill, Nov 5, 47; m 78; c 1. *Educ:* Ill State Univ, BS, 69; Univ Ill, MS, 73, PhD(animal physiol), 76. *Honors & Awards:* Animal Mgt Award, Am Soc Animal Sci, 87. *Prof Exp:* From asst prof to assoc prof, Washington State Univ, 76-84. *Concurrent Pos:* Invited res scientist, Nat Inst Agron Res, Paris, France, 82-83, Nat Inst Med Res, Bordeaux, France, 87. *Mem:* Am Asn Immunologists; Am Soc Animal Sci; Soc Exp Biol & Med; AAAS; Am Asn Vet Immunologists. *Res:* Neuroimmunomodulation; influence of hormones and neurotransmitters on regulation of T and B cell function in young and aged mammals. *Mailing Add:* Dept Animal Sci Univ Ill 207 ERML 1201 W Gregory Dr Urbana IL 61801-3838. *Fax:* 217-333-8804, 244-5617

KELLEY, LEON A, biochemistry, for more information see previous edition

KELLEY, MAURICE JOSEPH, SURFACE ACTIVE CHEMICALS, PHOTOGRAPHIC AND GRAPHICS ARTS CHEMICALS. *Current Pos:* RETIRED. *Personal Data:* b Danielson, Conn, Aug 6, 16; m 45, Frances Sailsbery. *Educ:* La Salle Univ, AB, 36; Fordham Univ, MS, 40; Univ Pa, PhD(org chem), 42; NY Univ, MBA, 65. *Prof Exp:* Res chemist, Nopco Chem Co, 36-44, chief chemist in chg, Sales Develop Lab, 44-48, dir, Indust Develop Lab, 48-53, dir, Indust Specialties Lab, 53-58, dir, Proj Coord Dept, 58-61; dir res labs, Diversey Corp, Ill, 61-65; dir electrostatics res, Philip A Hunt Chem Corp, 66-69, dir res, 69-75, asst vpres & dir res, 75-82. *Mem:* AAAS; Am Chem Soc; Chem Mgt & Resources Asn; Soc Imaging Sci & Technol; fel Am Inst Chemists; fel Royal Soc Chem. *Res:* Management of research and development; surface active agents; nitrogen compounds oil and fat derivatives; emulsion polymers; plastics; metallic soaps; synthetic detergents; bactericides; metal processing chemicals; photographic and graphic arts chemicals. *Mailing Add:* 4709 N 76th Pl Scottsdale AZ 85251-1565

KELLEY, MAURICE LESLIE, JR, MEDICINE. *Current Pos:* assoc prof, 67-74, PROF CLIN MED, DARTMOUTH MED SCH, 74-; STAFF MEM, MARY HITCHCOCK MEM HOSP CLIN, 67- *Personal Data:* b Indianapolis, Ind, June 29, 24; m, Carol Povec; c Elizabeth & Mary. *Educ:* Univ Rochester, MD, 49. *Prof Exp:* From instr to assoc prof med, Univ Rochester, 55-67. *Concurrent Pos:* Fel, Mayo Clin, 57-59; from asst physician to assoc physician, Strong Mem Hosp, 55-59, sr assoc physician, 63-; consult, Vet Admin Hosp, Canandaigua, NY, Genesee Hosp & Rochester Gen Hosp. *Mem:* AMA; Am Gastroenterol Asn; Am Fedn Clin Res; Am Col Physicians; Am Physiol Soc. *Res:* Gastroenterology; motility of the esophagus. *Mailing Add:* Dept Med Dartmouth Hitchcock Med Ctr One Med Ctr Dr Lebanon NH 03756-0001. *Fax:* 603-650-8030

KELLEY, MICHAEL C, GEOPHYSICS. *Current Pos:* From asst prof to assoc prof, 75-82, PROF, SCH ELEC ENG, CORNELL UNIV, ITHACA, 82- *Personal Data:* b Toledo, Ohio, Dec 21, 43; m 66; c 3. *Educ:* Kent State Univ, Ohio, 64; Univ Calif, Berkeley, PhD(physics), 70. *Honors & Awards:* James MacElware Award, Am Geophys Union, 79. *Concurrent Pos:* Alexander von Humboldt fel, 74-75; mem, Nat Res Coun Comt on Jicamara Radar Observ, 76-79; assoc ed, J Geophys Res, 79-83; Nat Acad Sci Comt on Solar Space Plasmas, 80-83; proj scientist, NASA-Peru Rocket campaign, 81-83, NASA-Greenland I Rocket campaign, 84-85, Greenland II, 86-87; NSF Atmospheric Sic Adv Comt, 82-84; investr, NASA-CRRES satellite working group, 86- *Mem:* Fel Am Geophys Union. *Res:* AC-DC electrical field experiments in space; supplied electron and/or analyzing results for sixty rocket flights, four satellite missions and numerous balloon flights; author of two textbooks and over 100 articles. *Mailing Add:* Sch Elec Engr Cornell Univ 318 Rhodes Hall Ithaca NY 14853-3801

KELLEY, MICHAEL J, CHEMISTRY. *Current Pos:* RES SCIENTIST, AMGEN INC, THOUSAND OAKS, CALIF, 92- *Prof Exp:* Researcher, Dept Chem, Univ Calif, San Diego, 89-92. *Mailing Add:* Dept Protein Chem AMGEN Inc 1840 Oak Terrace Lane Thousand Oaks CA 91320-1789. *Fax:* 805-499-7464

KELLEY, MYRON TRUMAN, ANALYTICAL CHEMISTRY. *Current Pos:* Dir anal chem div, 48-72, CONSULT, OAK RIDGE NAT LAB, 73-; CONSULT, HARSHAW CHEMICAL CO, 81- *Personal Data:* b Allerton, Iowa, Mar 9, 12; m 37. *Educ:* Univ Nebr, BSc, 32, MSc, 33; Iowa State Univ, PhD(phys chem), 37. *Honors & Awards:* Chem Instrumentation Award, 73. *Prof Exp:* Asst chief anal chemist, Queeny Plant Monsanto Chem Co, Mo, 37-41, chief anal chemist, 41-45; asst sect chief chem process develop sect, Clinton Lab, 45-48. *Concurrent Pos:* Consult, Tennecomp Systs, Inc, 73-79. *Mem:* AAAS; Am Nuclear Soc; Am Chem Soc; Sigma Xi. *Res:* Analytical instrumentation; instrumental methods of analysis, especially applications of small computers; analysis of highly radioactive materials. *Mailing Add:* 1814 Village Lane Naples FL 33963

KELLEY, NEIL DAVIS, METEOROLOGICAL MEASUREMENTS, ACOUSTICS. *Current Pos:* br chief measurements, 77-80, PRIN SCIENTIST WIND ENERGY, SOLAR ENERGY RES INST, 80- *Personal Data:* b Clayton, Mo, Jan 8, 42. *Educ:* St Louis Univ, BS, 63; Pa State Univ, MS, 68. *Prof Exp:* Meteorologist, Meteorol Res Inc, 63-66; instr meteorol, Pa State Univ, 66-71; group chief airborne measurements, Nat Ctr Atmospheric Res, 72-77. *Concurrent Pos:* Prog supvr, ESSO (Exxon) Res & Eng Co, 67-68. *Mem:* Am Meteorol Soc; Instrument Soc Am; Am Inst Aeronaut & Astronaut; AAAS; Sigma Xi; Inst Environ Sci. *Res:* Developing a physical understanding of the role of atmospheric turbulence on the energy conversion efficiency and structural component lifetime of wind energy conversion systems. *Mailing Add:* 605 S 42nd St Boulder CO 80303-5908

KELLEY, PATRICIA HAGELIN, INVERTEBRATE PALEONTOLOGY, EVOLUTIONARY PALEONTOLOGY. *Current Pos:* PROF & CHAIR, DEPT GEOL & GEOL ENG, UNIV NDAKOTA, 92- *Personal Data:* b Cleveland, Ohio, Dec 8, 53; m 77; c Timothy D & Katherine L. *Educ:* Col Wooster, BA, 75; Harvard Univ, AM, 77, PhD(geol), 79. *Prof Exp:* Instr, New Eng Col, 79; from asst prof to prof geol, Univ Miss, 79-90; prog dir, geol & paleontol, NSF, 90-92. *Concurrent Pos:* Prin investr, NSF Grant. *Mem:* Paleont Soc; Geol Soc Am; AAAS; Sigma Xi; Paleont Res Inst. *Res:* Evolutionary patterns, including modes and rates of evolution; origin of macroevolutionary trends, particularly as exhibited by Miocene molluscs; gastropod predation and coevolution; sexual dimorphism; biometric analysis; coastal plain biostratigraphy; carboniferous biogeography. *Mailing Add:* Univ NDak PO Box 8358 Grand Forks ND 58202-8358. *Fax:* 701-777-4449; *E-Mail:* patricia___kelley@mail.und.nodak.edu

KELLEY, PAUL LEON, LASERS, NONLINEAR OPTICS. *Current Pos:* PROF ELEC ENG & COMPUT SCI & DIR, ELECTRO-OPTICS TECHNOL CTR, TUFTS UNIV, 92- *Personal Data:* b Philadelphia, Pa, Dec 8, 34; m 58, Patricia L Pieretti; c Matthew W & Diana R. *Educ:* Rutgers Univ, BA, 56; Cornell Univ, MS, 59; Mass Inst Technol, PhD(physics), 62. *Prof Exp:* Teaching asst physics, Cornell Univ, 56-58; staff assoc, Lincoln Lab, Mass Inst Technol, 58-62, staff mem, 62-69, asst group leader, 69-71, assoc group leader, 71-92. *Concurrent Pos:* Lectr, Northeastern Univ, 63-64, Mass Inst Technol, 66-67; vis lectr, Univ Calif, Berkeley, 68-69; ed, Optics Lett, Optical Soc Am, 84-89, chair bd ed, 90-; vis indust prof, Tufts Univ, 85- *Mem:* Am Phys Soc; Optical Soc Am; Sigma Xi. *Res:* Laser, nonlinear optics; ultrafast electro-optical devices. *Mailing Add:* 236 Varick Rd Waban MA 02168. *Fax:* 617-627-3151; *E-Mail:* pkelley@tufts.edu

KELLEY, RALPH EDWARD, ATOMIC PHYSICS, MOLECULAR PHYSICS. *Current Pos:* PROG MGR PHYSICS DIRECTORATE, OFF SCI RES, USAF, 66- *Personal Data:* b Greenville, SC, Mar 6, 30; m 68, Martha Griffith; c Mary, David & Robert. *Educ:* Furman Univ, BA, 51, BS, 55; Univ Va, MS, 57, PhD(physics), 60. *Prof Exp:* Sr scientist theoret anal, Res Labs Eng Sci, Univ Va, 60-66. *Mem:* Am Phys Soc; Sigma Xi. *Res:* Annihilation radiation of positrons in crystals; polarization effects in scattering. *Mailing Add:* 7551 Marshall Dr Annandale VA 22003

KELLEY, RAYMOND H, NUCLEAR PHYSICS. *Current Pos:* part-time instr math, 69-71, from assoc prof to prof, 71-83, EMER PROF PHYSICS & MATH, SOUTHWESTERN ORE COMMUNITY COL, 83- *Personal Data:* b Roscoe, Mont, July 10, 22; m 51; c 1. *Educ:* Mont State Col, BS, 50; Ohio State Univ, MS, 55, PhD(nuclear physics), 63. *Prof Exp:* Instr electronics, Ellington AFB, Tex, USAF, 51-54, nuclear res officer, Modern Physics Br, Wright-Patterson AFB, Ohio, 55 & Aeronaut Res Lab, 57-60, staff scientist, Brookhaven Nat Lab, 55-57, from instr to assoc prof physics, USAF Acad, 62-69. *Mem:* Am Phys Soc; Am Asn Physics Teachers. *Res:* Helium filled scintillation detectors; radiation damage to semiconductor materials; particle accelerators; gamma ray spectroscopy. *Mailing Add:* PO Box 335 Bandon OR 97411

KELLEY, ROBERT LEE, MATHEMATICAL PHYSICS. *Current Pos:* From instr to asst prof, 64-72, ASSOC PROF MATH, UNIV MIAMI, 72- *Personal Data:* b East St Louis, Ill, Mar 20, 37. *Educ:* Univ Ill, Urbana, BS, 58; Univ Miami, MS, 60; Univ Mich, PhD(math), 66. *Mem:* Am Math Soc; Math Asn Am; Sigma Xi; Soc Indust & Appl Math; Asn Comput Mach. *Res:* Mathematical physics; functional analysis; mathematical biology; theory of algorithms. *Mailing Add:* Dept Math Univ Miami PO Box 249085 Coral Gables FL 33124-4250

KELLEY, ROBERT OTIS, DEVELOPMENTAL BIOLOGY, CELL BIOLOGY. *Current Pos:* from instr to assoc prof, 69-79, PROF ANAT, SCH MED, UNIV NMEX, 79-, CHMN DEPT, 81- *Personal Data:* b Santa Monica, Calif, Apr 30, 44; m 94; c 2. *Educ:* Abilene Christian Col, BS, 65; Univ Calif, Berkeley, MA, 66, PhD(zool), 69. *Prof Exp:* Assoc zool, Univ Calif, Berkeley, 67-68, actg asst prof, 69. *Concurrent Pos:* NIH grant, 70- & res career develop award, 72; res fel, Hubrecht Lab, Utrecht, Neth, 72-73; distinguished res prof, Nat Inst Basic Biol, Okazaki Nat Res Inst, Japan, 85. *Mem:* Soc Develop biol; Am Soc Cell Biologists; Am Asn Anat; Electron Micros Soc Am; Biophys Soc. *Res:* Fine structural associations between interacting cell layers during early amphibian development; ultrastructure and cell biology of vertebrate limb mesenchyme and associated limb morphogenesis; biology of the aging cell surface; organization of the cytoskeleton, cell imaging. *Mailing Add:* Dept Anat Univ NMex Sch Med N Campus Albuquerque NM 87131. *Fax:* 505-277-1754

KELLEY, RUSSELL VICTOR, BIOLOGY, SCIENCE EDUCATION. *Current Pos:* ASSOC PROF BIOL SCI, MORGAN STATE UNIV, 66- *Personal Data:* b Norfolk, Va, Dec 21, 34; m 56; c 3. *Educ:* Va State Col, BS, 57; NY Univ, MA, 64; Purdue Univ, PhD(biol sci), 72. *Prof Exp:* Teacher chem & biol, Baltimore Pub Schs, 60-62; teacher biol, Plainview, Long Island Pub Schs, 62-66. *Concurrent Pos:* Consult, NASA, 67 & 68; lectr contemp biol, Towson State Univ, 72 & 75; lectr zool & biol, Community Col Baltimore, 74-; consult sci, Md State Dept Educ Bicentennial Comt, 76 & Sci Curric Adv Comt, Div Instr & Curric, Baltimore City Pub Sch Syst, 78-; chmn bd adv, Math Eng Sci Achievement, 77- *Mem:* Nat Sci Teachers Asn; AAAS. *Res:* Instructional strategies in science teaching and population genetics. *Mailing Add:* Dept Biol Morgan State Univ 1700 E Cold Spring Baltimore MD 21239-4001

KELLEY, THOMAS F, BIOMEDICAL ENGINEERING, CLINICAL CHEMISTRY. *Current Pos:* RETIRED. *Personal Data:* b Melrose, Mass, Mar 23, 32; m 56; c 3. *Educ:* Boston Univ, AB, 54, MA, 55; Brown Univ, PhD(biol), 59. *Prof Exp:* Sr res assoc, Bio-Res Inst, Inc, 58-68; prog mgr, Instrumentation Lab, Inc, 68-80, dir appl res, 80-92. *Mem:* Am Asn Clin Chemists; Am Soc Clin Path; Sigma Xi. *Res:* Development of hospital, medical and laboratory instrumentation. *Mailing Add:* 460 N Tenth St Albemarle NC 28001

KELLEY, VICKI E, AUTOIMMUNITY. *Current Pos:* ASSOC PROF MED, SCH MED, HARVARD UNIV, 81- *Educ:* Univ Pittsburgh, PhD, 77. *Mem:* Am Asn Immunologists; Am Asn Pathologists. *Mailing Add:* Dept Med Brigham & Women's Hosp 75 Francis St Boston MA 02115-6195. *Fax:* 617-732-6392

KELLEY, VINCENT CHARLES, PEDIATRICS. *Current Pos:* prof, 58-86, EMER PROF PEDIAT, SCH MED, UNIV WASH, 86- *Personal Data:* b Tyler, Minn, Jan 23, 16; m 42; c 7. *Educ:* Univ NDak, BA, 34, MS, 35; Univ Minn, MS, 36, PhD(biochem), 42, BS, 44, MB, 45, MD, 46. *Prof Exp:* Asst chem, Univ NDak, 34-35; asst biochem, Univ Minn, 40-41; asst prof org chem, Col St Thomas, 42-43; chief dept biophys, USAF Sch Aerospace Med, 46-47, res med, 47-48; instr pediat, Univ Minn, 49-50; from asst prof to assoc prof, Univ Utah, 50-58. *Concurrent Pos:* Swift fel pediat, Univ Minn, 48-50. *Mem:* AAAS; Am Chem Soc; Am Pediat Soc; Soc Pediat Res; Soc Exp Biol & Med. *Res:* Starch chemistry; renal and liver function; deceleration injuries; aviation medicine; protein chemistry; physiochemical studies of electrodialyzed starches; pituitary-adrenal function; endocrinology. *Mailing Add:* 8611 45th Ave NE Seattle WA 98115

KELLEY, WILLIAM NIMMONS, INTERNAL MEDICINE, RHEUMATOLOGY. *Current Pos:* EXEC VPRES, UNIV PA, 89-, CHIEF EXEC OFFICER, MED CTR & HEALTH SYST, 89-, DEAN, SCH MED & ROBERT G DUNLOP PROF MED, BIOCHEM & BIOPHYSICS, 89- *Personal Data:* b Atlanta, Ga, June 23, 39; m 59, Lois Faville; c Margaret P, Virginia L (Yost), Lori A & William M. *Educ:* Emory Univ, MD, 63. *Hon Degrees:* MA, Univ Pa, 89. *Honors & Awards:* John D Lane Award, USPHS, 69; Geigy Int Prize Rheumatology, 69; Heinz Karger Prize, 73; Numerous Named Lectr, US & Foreign Univs, 73-94; John Phillips Mem Award & Medal, Am Col Physicians, 90. *Prof Exp:* Intern med, Parkland Mem Hosp, 63-64, resident, 64-65; clin assoc, Nat Inst Arthritis & Metab Dis, 65-67; sr resident med, Mass Gen Hosp, 67-68; from asst prof to prof med, Med Ctr, Duke Univ, 68-75, from asst prof to assoc prof biochem, 68-75, chief div rheumatic & genetic dis, 70-75; John G Searle prof & chmn, Dept Internal Med & prof biol chem, Med Sch, Univ Mich, 75-89. *Concurrent Pos:* Mosby scholar award, 63-; Am Col Physicians Mead-Johnson scholar, 67-68; teaching fel med, Harvard Med Sch, 67-68; Am Rheumatism Asn clin scholar, 69-72; res career develop award, 72-75; Macy Fac scholar, Oxford Univ, 74-75; mem, numerous sci comts & councils, NIH, 74-; vis prof & lectr, numerous univs, 79-94; consult med, numerous univs & indust, 82-94; chmn, Am Bd Int Med, 85-86 & Sect 4, Inst Med Nat Acad Sci, 87-89; pres, Cent Soc Clin Res, 86-87; master, Am Col Physicians, 88; dir, Merck & Co Inc, 92-, Beckman Instruments, Inc, 94- *Mem:* Inst Med-Nat Acad Sci; Am Fedn Clin Res (pres, 79-80); Am Rheumatism Asn (pres, 86-87); Am Soc Biol Chemists; Am Soc Clin Invest (pres, 83-84); AAAS; Asn Am Physicians; Am Soc Human Genetics. *Res:* Human biochemical genetics; rheumatology; author of numerous articles and books. *Mailing Add:* Univ Pa Med Ctr 21 Penn Tower 34th St & Civic Ctr Blvd Philadelphia PA 19104-4385. *Fax:* 215-898-5607

KELLEY, WILLIAM RUSSELL, BOTANY. *Current Pos:* RETIRED. *Personal Data:* b Universal, Pa, Feb 3, 14; m 42, Beatrice L Koontz; c Carole L, David R, Beatrice R, Donald M & Kathryn A. *Educ:* Ind Univ Pa, BS, 39; Univ Pittsburgh, MLitt, 48; Cornell Univ, MS, 49, PhD(bot), 51. *Prof Exp:* Pub sch teacher, Pa, 39-41 & 45-48; asst bot, Cornell Univ, 49-51; from asst prof to assoc prof, Univ SC, 51-59; from assoc to prof bot, Shippensburg Univ, Pa, 61-77, prof biol, 77. *Mailing Add:* 9554 Forest Ridge Rd Shippensburg PA 17257

KELLEY, WILLIAM S, MICROBIAL GENETICS. *Current Pos:* sr scientist, 81-82, asst dir res for admin & molecular biol, 82-83, VPRES, PROD & PROCESS DEVELOP, BIOGEN RES CORP, CAMBRIDGE, MASS, 84- *Personal Data:* b Washington, Pa, Nov 30, 41; m 68; c 1. *Educ:* Haverford Col, BS, 63; Mass Inst Technol, MS; Tufts Univ, PhD(microbiol), 68. *Prof Exp:* From asst prof to assoc prof biol, Dept Biol Sci, Carnegie-Mellon Univ, Pittsburgh, Pa, 71-80. *Concurrent Pos:* US Pub Health Serv, postdoc fel, Dept Molecular Biol, Edinburgh Univ, Scotland, 68-70; dept fel, grad dept biochem, Brandeis Univ, Mass, 70-71. *Mem:* Am Chem Soc; Am Soc Microbiol; AAAS. *Res:* Responsible for transfer of projects from research into pharmaceutical development, overseeing the groups who devise the manufacturing processes and implement them at pilot scale sufficiently large to support clinical trials; head technology transfer teams for interaction with other companies. *Mailing Add:* Vertex Pharm 40 Allston St Cambridge MA 02139-4211. *Fax:* 617-499-2480

KELLGREN, JOHN, ORGANIC CHEMISTRY, RUBBER CHEMISTRY. *Current Pos:* PROCESS MGR, RHEIN-CHEMIE, 87- *Personal Data:* b New York, NY, Dec 26, 40; m 71, Joanne Selmasska; c Carl & Eric. *Educ:* Rutgers Univ, BS, 62; Columbia Univ, PhD(org chem), 66; Univ New Haven, MBA, 77 & MS, 84. *Prof Exp:* Res chemist, Uniroyal Res Ctr, 67-75, tech supt, Uniroyal Inc, 76-79, res scientist indust prod, 79-84; process mgr, Wyrough-Loser Inc, 84-87. *Mem:* Sigma Xi; Am Chem Soc. *Res:* Free radical reactions; polyurethane chemistry; oxidation of organic compounds; aging; vulcanization. *Mailing Add:* Rhein-Chemie 1008 Whitehead Rd Ext Trenton NJ 08638. *Fax:* 609-771-9539

KELLIHER, GERALD JAMES, PHARMACOLOGY. *Current Pos:* From asst prof to prof pharmacol, 70-78, ASSOC PROF MED, MED COL PA, 75-, ASSOC DEAN, MED EDUC. *Personal Data:* b Taunton, Mass, May 31, 42; m 65; c 2. *Educ:* Univ RI, BS, 65; Duquesne Univ, MS, 67; Univ Pittsburgh, PhD(pharmacol), 69. *Concurrent Pos:* Fel pharmacol, Sch Med, Univ Pittsburgh, 69-70; Southeast Pa Heart Asn, Del Heart Asn, Heart & Lung Found, Ayerst Co & Shering Co grants, Med Col Pa, 71-81; Whitehall Found grants, 71-77; Nat Heart & Lung Inst grants, 71-75 & 73-77, 76-80; Nat Inst Age grant, 76-80; Nat Inst Child Health & Human Develop grant, 72-76; consult, Vet Admin, 78-80; educ consult, Smith Kline Corp. *Mem:* Am Soc Pharmacol & Exp Therapeut; assoc fel Am Col Cardiol; Geront Soc; fel Am Col Clin Pharmacol; Am Fedn Clin Res. *Res:* Cardiovascular and autonomic pharmacology with emphasis on the mechanisms and treatment of cardiac arrhythmias and hypertension. *Mailing Add:* Dept Pharm Med Col Pa 3300 Henry Ave Philadelphia PA 19129-1121. *Fax:* 215-843-5495

KELLING, CLAYTON LYNN, VETERINARY VIROLOGY. *Current Pos:* asst prof, PROF, DEPT VET SCI, UNIV NEBR, LINCOLN. *Personal Data:* b Killdeer, NDak, Mar 26, 46; m 74. *Educ:* NDak State Univ, BS, 68, MS, 71, PhD(pharm chem), 75. *Prof Exp:* Technician vet virol, Dept Vet Sci, NDak State Univ, 68- *Mem:* Am Soc Microbiol; Sigma Xi. *Res:* Veterinary microbiology concerned with respiratory and reproductive diseases of animals; antiviral agents; virological diagnostic techniques. *Mailing Add:* PO Box 830905 Lincoln NE 68583-0905

KELLISON, ROBERT CLAY, FOREST GENETICS. *Current Pos:* liaison geneticist, 63-67, assoc dir coop prog, 66-77, DIR HARDWOOD COOP, NC STATE UNIV, 77- *Personal Data:* b Marlinton, WVa, Nov 20, 31; m 65; c 2. *Educ:* WVa Univ, BSF, 59; NC State Univ, MS, 66, PhD(forest genetics), 70. *Prof Exp:* Forest supt, WVa Univ, 59-61. *Concurrent Pos:* Fel, Am-Scand Found, 65; panel expert, Food & Agr Orgn-Int Breeding Prog for Preserv Forest Gene Resources, 68; scientist, NZ Forest Serv, 73-74; mem Panel Forest Tree Breeding, Peoples Repub China, 81, 83; adv forestry, Venezuela, 75, 77, Brazil, 80, Port, 83, 85, Taiwan, 85. *Res:* Selection and breeding of forest trees for improved volume yields, quality, adaptability and resistance to frost, drought and environmental pollution; preservation of forest gene resources. *Mailing Add:* Dept Forestry NC State Univ Box 8002 Raleigh NC 27695-0001

KELLMAN, RAYMOND, POLYMER CHEMISTRY, ORGANIC CHEMISTRY. *Current Pos:* PROG OFFICER, RES CORP, 92- *Personal Data:* b Staten Island, NY, Feb 27, 42; m 78, Kathryn J Schulze; c 2. *Educ:* St Peter's Col, NJ, BS, 63; Univ Colo, Boulder, PhD(org chem), 68. *Prof Exp:* Res assoc chem, Univ Wis-Madison, 67-69; res chemist, Uniroyal Inc, 69-72; res assoc, 72-75, lectr chem, Univ Ariz, 75-77; asst prof polymer chem, Univ Tex, 77-82; prof chem, San Jose State Univ, 82-92. *Concurrent Pos:* Fulbright res scholar, Univ Queensland, Australia, 88-89. *Mem:* AAAS; Am Chem Soc; Am Phys Soc. *Res:* Synthesis of new monomers; new methods of condensation polymerization; synthesis of thermally stable electroactive and biocompatable polymers; radiation effect on polymers. *Mailing Add:* Res Corp 101 N Wilmot Rd Suite 250 Tucson AZ 85711-3332. *E-Mail:* ray@rescorp.org

KELLMAN, SIMON, REACTOR PHYSICS. *Current Pos:* fel scientist, Westinghouse Elec Corp, 69-72, mgr math & programming, 72-76, acting mgr methods develop, 76-78, MGR, SAFEGUARDS RELIABILITY & APPLN, PWR SYSTS DIV, WESTINGHOUSE ELEC CORP, MONROEVILLE NUCLEAR CTR, 78- *Personal Data:* b Brooklyn, NY, July 26, 34; m 59; c 2. *Educ:* Carnegie Inst Technol, BS, 55, MS, 58, PhD(physics), 61. *Prof Exp:* Sr physicist, Lawrence Radiation Lab, Univ Calif, Livermore, 61-64 & United Nuclear Corp, 64-69. *Mem:* Am Nuclear Soc. *Res:* Depletion calculations; nuclear safety analysis; Monte Carlo techniques in neutron transport. *Mailing Add:* 5441 Fair Oaks St Pittsburgh PA 15217

KELLN, ELMER, ORAL PATHOLOGY, CANCER. *Current Pos:* prof oral med, Univ, 66-71, PROF ORAL MED, GRAD SCH & ASSOC DEAN SCH DENT, LOMA LINDA UNIV, 71- *Personal Data:* b Sask, Can, Nov 6, 26; m 51; c 3. *Educ:* Univ Nebr, BSc & DDS, 49; Univ Minn, MSD(path), 60. *Prof Exp:* Assoc prof path, Sch Med, WVa Univ, 60-66. *Concurrent Pos:* Grants wound healing, 60-63 & age studies, 61-; cancer coordr, Sch Dent, WVa Univ & mem tumor bd, WVa Univ Hosp, 63-66. *Mem:* Fel Am Acad Oral Path; Am Dent Asn; Int Asn Dent Res. *Res:* Cancer behavior; disease processes of oral diseases, particularly wound healing, cancer treatment and behavior, and vascular degeneration. *Mailing Add:* 25246 Lawton Ave Loma Linda CA 92354

KELLNER, HENRY L(OUIS), CHEMICAL ENGINEERING. *Current Pos:* RETIRED. *Personal Data:* b Philadelphia, Pa, Sept 18, 05; m 35; c 2. *Educ:* Pa State Col, BS, 26; Yale Univ, PhD(chem eng), 30. *Prof Exp:* Res chemist, Scovill Mfg Co, 27-29; chem engr, Doherty Res Co, 30-33 & Eastern Eng Co, 33-35; from chem engr to secy & tech dir, Lea Mfg Co, 35-56, vpres, 56-68, tech dir, 56-70, exec vpres, 68-76, mgr foreign opers, 70-80, pres, 76-78, vchmn, 78-82. *Concurrent Pos:* Pres & chmn, Lea Ronal Inc, 53-70. *Mem:* Am Chem Soc; Am Electroplaters Soc. *Res:* Buffing and polishing compositions; chemical and electroplating processes. *Mailing Add:* 3117 Ashlar Village Wallingford CT 06492

KELLNER, JORDAN DAVID, PHYSICAL CHEMISTRY. *Current Pos:* res assoc, 81-82, sr res assoc, 83-91, SR SCIENTIST, KENDALL RES LAB, 91- *Personal Data:* b New York, NY, Aug 25, 38; m 60; c 2. *Educ:* City Col New York, BS, 58; NY Univ, MS, 62, PhD(phys chem), 64; Rensselaer Polytech Inst, MS, 72. *Honors & Awards:* SAm Tour Award, Am Soc Testing & Mat. *Prof Exp:* Jr chemist, Kings County Hosp, 58-59; res asst biochem res, St Catherine's Hosp, 59-61; res asst phys chem, NY Univ, 61-64; sr chemist, Atomics Int Div, NAm Aviation, 64-68; res scientist, Hamilton Standard Div, United Technologies Corp, 68-71, sr res scientist, 71-78, supvr chem processes, Res Ctr, 78-80, supvr, 80-81. *Concurrent Pos:* Adj prof chem, Univ Hartford, 80-81; trustee, Boston sect, Nat Asn Corrosion Engrs, 87-90, career develop chmn, Northeast Region, 90- *Mem:* Sigma Xi; Am Chem Soc; Nat Asn Corrosion Engrs; Am Soc Testing & Mat. *Res:* Transport processes in fused salts and metal-metal salt mixtures; Soret effect and viscosity; electrodeposition of semi-metals and their compounds from fused fluorides; electrochemical techniques of corrosion measurement including electrochemical impedance spectroscopy. *Mailing Add:* 38 Grove St Wayland MA 01778

KELLNER, STEPHAN MARIA EDUARD, PHYSICAL CHEMISTRY. *Current Pos:* From asst prof to assoc prof, 59-69, chmn dept, 71-75, PROF CHEM, ST MICHAEL'S COL, VT, 69- *Personal Data:* b Friedberg, Ger, Feb 1, 33; US citizen; m 60; Jane Bogue; c Paul, Mark, Ted, Mary J, Elizabeth, Margaret, Bernard, Monica, Christine, Christopher, Julie & John. *Educ:* Univ Rochester, BS, 55, PhD(phys chem), 60. *Mem:* Am Chem Soc; Sigma Xi. *Res:* Rates and mechanisms of homogeneous gas phase reactions. *Mailing Add:* Dept Chem St Michael's Col Winsooki Park Colchester VT 05439

KELLOGG, CHARLES NATHANIEL, MATHEMATICS. *Current Pos:* ASSOC PROF MATH, TEX TECH UNIV, 70- *Personal Data:* b Albuquerque, NMex, June 29, 38; m 57; c 3. *Educ:* NMex Inst Mining & Technol, BS, 60; La State Univ, PhD(math), 64. *Prof Exp:* Teaching asst math, La State Univ, 63-64; asst prof, Univ Ky, 64-70. *Mem:* Am Math Soc; Math Asn Am. *Res:* Harmonic analysis; theory of multiplier operators; Banach algebras. *Mailing Add:* Dept Math Tex Tech Univ Lubbock TX 79409-1042

KELLOGG, CRAIG KENT, ORGANIC CHEMISTRY. *Current Pos:* asst prof, 66-70, ASSOC PROF CHEM, GA SOUTHERN COL, 70- *Personal Data:* b Westfield, Mass, Dec 3, 37; m 60; c 3. *Educ:* Ga Inst Technol, BS, 59, PhD(org chem), 63. *Prof Exp:* Res chemist, E I du Pont de Nemours & Co, Inc, 63-66. *Mem:* Am Chem Soc. *Res:* Natural products; dioxetanes. *Mailing Add:* 113 Herty Dr Statesboro GA 30458-5434

KELLOGG, DAVID WAYNE, NUTRITION, ANIMAL PHYSIOLOGY. *Current Pos:* head, Dept Animal Sci, 81-86, PROF, DEPT ANIMAL SCI, UNIV ARK, FAYETTEVILLE, 86- *Personal Data:* b Seymour, Mo, Aug 19, 41; m 64, Mary S Powell; c Kirk D, Susan J (Franz), Kimberley A (Vanvacter) & Gregory W. *Educ:* Univ Mo Columbia, BS, 63, MS, 64; Univ Nebr, Lincoln, PhD(nutrit), 68. *Prof Exp:* From asst prof to prof dairy sci, NMex State Univ, 67-81. *Mem:* Am Dairy Sci Asn; Am Regist Prof Animal Scientists. *Res:* Nutrition of dairy calves; nutritive value of alfalfa varieties; mineral nutrition; improvement of forage digestion by ruminants. *Mailing Add:* Dept Animal Sci Univ Ark Fayetteville AR 72701

KELLOGG, DOUGLAS SHELDON, JR, medical microbiology; deceased, see previous edition for last biography

KELLOGG, EDWIN M, ELECTRON & ION BEAM SYSTEMS, X-RAY DETECTION. *Current Pos:* astrophysicist, 73-79, ASTROPHYSICIST, SMITHSONIAN ASTROPHYS OBSERV, 88- *Personal Data:* b New York, NY, Feb 3, 39; m 60, 74, 81, Diane McKinney; c Andrew, Gregory, Russell, Amelia, Jeffrey & Bradford. *Educ:* Rensselaer Polytech Inst, BS, 60; Univ Pa, MS, 63, PhD(physics), 66. *Honors & Awards:* Newton Lacey Pierce Prize, Am Astron Soc, 74. *Prof Exp:* Physicist, Radiation Dynamics Inc, 61-62; sr scientist, Am Sci & Eng, Mass, 65-69, sr staff scientist, 69-73, mem, Inst Advan Study, 73; proj mgr, Micro-Bit Div, Control Data Corp, Mass, 80, software mgr, 81-82; staff scientist, Ion Beam Technol Inc, 82-83, vpres eng, 83-86, vpres develop, 86. *Concurrent Pos:* Lectr astron, Harvard Univ, 73-79. *Mem:* Fel Am Phys Soc; Inst Elec & Electronics Engrs; Am Vacuum Soc; Sigma Xi; Am Astron Soc. *Res:* Ion beam assisted surface phenomena; liquid metal ion sources; electron beam lithography; x-ray astronomy. *Mailing Add:* Ctr Astrophys 60 Garden St MS-27 Cambridge MA 02138

KELLOGG, GARY LEE, SURFACE SCIENCE, MICROSCOPY. *Current Pos:* SR MEM TECH STAFF, SANDIA NAT LABS, 76- *Personal Data:* b Meadville, Pa, Jan 16, 50; m 71, Susan J Lechefsky; c Brian & Justin. *Educ:* Pa State Univ, BS, 71, PhD(physics), 76. *Honors & Awards:* Award for Outstanding Accomplishment in Solid State Physics, Off Basic Energy Sci, Dept Energy, 91. *Concurrent Pos:* Chmn, Surface Sci Div, Am Vacuum Soc, 92-93. *Mem:* Fel Am Phys Soc; Am Vacuum Soc; Int Field Emission Soc (vpres, 92-93); Microbeam Anal Soc. *Res:* Application of field ion microscope, atom-probe mass spectrometer and low energy electron microscope to problems in surface physics and surface chemistry; single-atom surface diffusion, cluster nucleation, thin film growth and surface chemical reactions. *Mailing Add:* 917 La Charles Dr NE Albuquerque NM 87112. *Fax:* 505-844-5470; *E-Mail:* glkello@sandia.gov

KELLOGG, HERBERT H(UMPHREY), EXTRACTIVE METALLURGY. *Current Pos:* assoc prof extractive metall, Columbia Univ, 46-56, prof, 56-68, Stanley-Thompson prof chem metall, 68-90, EMER STANLEY-THOMPSON PROF, COLUMBIA UNIV, 90- *Personal Data:* b New York, NY, Feb 24, 20; c 4. *Educ:* Columbia Univ, BS, 41, MS, 43. *Honors & Awards:* James Douglas Gold Medal, Am Inst Mining, Metall & Petrol Engrs, 73. *Prof Exp:* Jr engr, Dorr Co, Conn, 41; asst mineral dressing, Columbia Univ, 41-42; instr, Pa State Col, 42-44, asst prof mineral preparation, 44-46. *Concurrent Pos:* Chmn titanium adv comt, Off Defense Mobilization, 54-58; consult, Int Nickel Co & Am Smelting & Refining Co, 69- *Mem:* Nat Acad Eng; Am Inst Mining, Metall & Petrol Engrs; fel Inst Mining & Metall, London. *Res:* Thermodynamics and kinetics of metallurgical reactions; high-temperature chemistry; equilibria in the systems Cu-S-O, Ni-Fe-S; slag chemistry; computer modeling of metallurgical processes. *Mailing Add:* 95 Closter Rd Palisades NY 10964

KELLOGG, LILLIAN MARIE, SOLID STATE CHEMISTRY. *Current Pos:* RES ASSOC RES LABS, EASTMAN KODAK CO, 68- *Personal Data:* b Detroit, Mich, Mar 6, 39. *Educ:* Ariz State Univ, BS, 61; Wayne State Univ, PhD(phys chem), 67. *Prof Exp:* Assoc scientist chem, Aeroneutronic Div, Ford Motor Co, 61-62. *Concurrent Pos:* Adj fac, Rochester Inst Technol, 70-75. *Mem:* AAAS; Am Chem Soc; Am Phys Soc; Soc Photog Scientists & Engrs; NY Acad Sci. *Res:* Solid state chemistry; light interactions in solids; photoconductivity, photochemical and photographic studies. *Mailing Add:* 1786 Lake Rd Webster NY 14580

KELLOGG, PAUL JESSE, PLASMA PHYSICS. *Current Pos:* res assoc, 56-57, from asst prof to assoc prof, 57-64, PROF PHYSICS, UNIV MINN, MINNEAPOLIS, 64- *Personal Data:* b Tacoma, Wash, Nov 6, 27; m 69, Janet Anderson; c 4. *Educ:* Mass Inst Technol, BS, 50; Cornell Univ, PhD(theoret physics), 55. *Prof Exp:* Nat Res Coun fel, Naval Res Lab, 55-56. *Concurrent Pos:* Guggenheim Mem Found fel, 62-63; NATO fel; fel, Minna-James-Heineman Stiftung, 73; res fel, Australian Nat Univ, 84 & 87. *Mem:* Fel Am Phys Soc. *Res:* Invented balloon measurements of electric fields, predicted earth's bow shock; plasma physics as applied to space; beam-plasma interaction, waves in plasma; antennas in flowing plasma. *Mailing Add:* Sch Physics & Astron Univ Minn Minneapolis MN 55455. *Fax:* 612-626-2029

KELLOGG, RALPH HENDERSON, PHYSIOLOGY. *Current Pos:* actg chmn dept physiol, 66-70, from asst prof to prof, Sch Med, 53-90, EMER PROF PHYSIOL, UNIV CALIF, SAN FRANCISCO, 90- *Personal Data:* b New London, Conn, June 7, 20. *Educ:* Univ Rochester, BA, 40, MD, 43; Harvard Med Sch, PhD(physiol), 53. *Prof Exp:* Intern med, Cleveland Univ Hosps, 44; investr physiol, Naval Med Res Inst, 46; instr, Harvard Med Sch, 47-53. *Concurrent Pos:* Sr res fel, Sch Pub Health, Harvard Univ, 62-63; mem physiol study sect, NIH, 66-70, physiol test comt, Nat Bd Med Examrs, 66-73 & chmn, 69-73; vis fel, Corpus Christi Col, Oxford Univ, 70-71; vis scientist, Lab Physiol Respiratory, Cent Nat Res Sci, Strasbourg, France, 77; adj lectr, Hist Health Sci Dept, Univ Calif, 78-93, actg chmn, 84-85. *Mem:* AAAS; Am Physiol Soc; Am Asn Hist Med; History Sci Soc; Sigma Xi. *Res:* Isotonic and osmotic diuresis in rats; respiration at altitude; history of physiology. *Mailing Add:* 601 Noriega St San Francisco CA 94122-4615

KELLOGG, RICHARD MORRISON, ORGANIC CHEMISTRY. *Current Pos:* res fel, 65-70, assoc prof, 70-75, PROF CHEM, STATE UNIV GRONINGEN, 75- *Personal Data:* b Los Angeles, Calif, Dec 24, 39; m 67; c 2. *Educ:* Kans State Teachers Col, AB, 61; Univ Kans, PhD(org chem), 65. *Prof Exp:* Res fel chem, Univ Kans, 65. *Mem:* Am Chem Soc; Royal Dutch Chem Soc. *Res:* Synthetic organic chemistry; photochemistry; bio-organic chemistry; synthesis of unusual organic molecules and models for mechanisms of enzymic reactions. *Mailing Add:* Dept Org Chem Nyenborgh 4 9747 A6 Groningen Netherlands

KELLOGG, ROYAL BRUCE, APPLIED MATHEMATICS. *Current Pos:* from assoc prof to prof math, 66-74, res prof, Inst Fluid Dynamics & Applied Math, 74-80, RES PROF MATH & INST PHYS SCI & TECHNOL, UNIV MD, COLLEGE PARK, 80- *Personal Data:* b Chicago, Ill, Dec 28, 30; m 56; c 3. *Educ:* Mass Inst Technol, BS, 52; Univ Chicago, MS, 53, PhD(math), 59. *Prof Exp:* Mathematician, Combustion Eng, Inc, 58-61; mathematician, Westinghouse Elec Corp, 61-66. *Mem:* Am Math Soc; Soc Indust & Appl Math. *Res:* Numerical analysis. *Mailing Add:* 7504 Hancock Ave Takoma Park MD 20912

KELLOGG, SPENCER, II, AERONAUTICAL ENGINEERING. *Current Pos:* RETIRED. *Personal Data:* b Buffalo, NY, Dec 9, 13; m 38; c 5. *Educ:* Cornell Univ, ME, 37; Polytech Inst Brooklyn, MSEE, 67. *Honors & Awards:* Pioneer Award, Inst Elec & Electronics Engrs Aerospace & Elec Systs Soc, 76. *Prof Exp:* Field serv engr, Sperry Gyroscope Co, 37-39, flight test engr, 39-40, from gyropilot eng to dept head, 40-50, dept head flight instrument eng, 50-59, asst chief engr, Aeronaut Equip Div, 59-67; independent aviation consult, 67-95. *Res:* Gyropilot and gyroscopic flight instruments; altitude control for aircraft; turn error control of gyroscopes; erection mechanism for gyroscopes; flight directors. *Mailing Add:* 25 Valentine Lane Glen Head NY 11545

KELLOGG, THOMAS B, PALEO-OCEANOGRAPHY, PALEO-CLIMATOLOGY. *Current Pos:* res assoc, 75-78, from asst prof to assoc prof, 78-89, PROF GEOL SCI & QUATERNARY STUDIES, UNIV MAINE, 89- *Personal Data:* b New York, NY, Apr 30, 42; m 67; c 3. *Educ:* Columbia Univ, BA, 68, PhD(geol), 73. *Honors & Awards:* Antarctic Serv Medal, US Congress, 79. *Prof Exp:* Res assoc, geol sci, Brown Univ, 73-75. *Concurrent Pos:* mem, Cushman Found Foraminiferal Res, Climap Long Range Invest, Mapping & Prediction, 71-80. *Mem:* Fel Geol Soc Am. *Res:* High latitude marine sediment & how it is used to determine the past extent of ice sheets, ice shelves & icebergs. *Mailing Add:* Geol Dept Univ Main Boardman Hall Orono ME 04469-0001

KELLOGG, THOMAS FLOYD, BIOCHEMISTRY. *Current Pos:* assoc prof, 70-78, PROF BIOCHEM, MISS STATE UNIV, 78- *Personal Data:* b Aurora, Ill, Apr 7, 34; m 82; c 3. *Educ:* Iowa State Univ, BS, 59, MS, 60; Univ Wis-Madison, PhD(biochem), 64. *Prof Exp:* Res asst biochem, Univ Wis, 60-64; fel microbiol, Lobund Lab, Univ Notre Dame, 64-65, res scientist, 65-68, asst prof, 68-70. *Concurrent Pos:* NIH Spec Res fel, 67-68. *Mem:* Am Physiol Soc; Asn Gnotobiotics (vpres & pres-elect, 81-82, pres, 82-83). *Res:* Cholesterol and bile acid metabolism; liquid scintillation counting. *Mailing Add:* Dept Biochem Miss State Univ Drawer BB Mississippi State MS 39762-9999. *Fax:* 601-325-8664

KELLOGG, WILLIAM WELCH, METEOROLOGY. *Current Pos:* RETIRED. *Personal Data:* b New York Mills, NY, Feb 14, 17; m 42, Elizabeth Thorson; c Karl, Judith, Joseph, Jane & Thomas. *Educ:* Yale Univ, AB, 39; Univ Calif, Los Angeles, MS, 42, PhD(meteorol), 49. *Honors & Awards:* Special Award, Am Meteorol Soc, 61; Decoration Except Civilian Serv, Dept Air Force, 66; Commemorative Medal, Soviet Geophys Comt, 85; Spec Citation, Garden Club Am, 88. *Prof Exp:* Teacher prep sch, Mass, 39-40; asst optics lab, Univ Calif, Berkeley, 40-41; instr meteorol, Univ Calif, Los Angeles, 42-43, res asst, 47-48, res assoc, Inst Geophys, 48-49, asst prof, 49-52; phys scientist & dept head, Rand Corp, Calif, 47-64; assoc dir, Nat Ctr Atmospheric Res, 64-73, sr scientist, 73-87, sr res assoc, 87- *Concurrent Pos:* Mem, Upper Atmosphere Comt, Nat Adv Comt Aeronaut, 53-55; mem, Comt Meteorol Aspects Effects Atomic Radiation, Nat Acad Sci, 56-64, Space Sci Bd, 59-66, Comt Atmospheric Sci, 63-67, Spec Comt Int Years Quiet Sun, 63-66 & Polar Res Bd, 75-78; Rocket & Satellite Res Panel, 57-62; chmn int comn meteorol upper atmosphere, Int Union Geod & Geophys, 60-75; mem tech panel, Earth Satellite Prog, Int Geophys Year, 57-58; consult & mem sci adv bd, US Air Force, 57-65, mem sci adv group, Off Aerospace Res, 65-70; chmn meteorol satellite comt, Adv Res Projs Agency, 58-59; mem planetary atmospheres subcomt, NASA, 61-65; chmn working group upper atmosphere, World Meteorol Orgn, 61-65; mem consult group potentially harmful effects of space exp, Comt Space Res, 62-68; mem tech adv bd, US Dept Com, 62-64; mem adv group supporting tech oper meteorol satellites, NASA-US Weather Bur, 64-75; mem panel on environ, President's Sci Adv Comt, 68-70; chmn meteorol adv comt, Environ Protection Agency, 70-74; chmn adv comt, Div Polar Progs, NSF, 82-85. *Mem:* Fel AAAS; fel Am Geophys Union; Sigma Xi; fel Am Meteorol Soc (pres, 73-74). *Res:* Physics of the atmosphere; turbulence and structure of the upper atmosphere; scientific uses of rockets, satellites and space probes; atmospheres of Mars and Venus; causes of climate change. *Mailing Add:* 445 College Ave Boulder CO 80302

KELLS, LYMAN FRANCIS, GENERAL SCIENCE, THEORY. *Current Pos:* INDEPENDENT THEORET RESEARCHER, 74- *Personal Data:* b Seattle, Wash, May 19, 17; div; c Leila (Newcomb) & Christina (Cohen). *Educ:* Univ Wash, BS, 38, PhD(phys chem), 44. *Prof Exp:* Teaching fel, Univ Wash, 38-44; res scientist, Manhattan Proj, Kellex Corp, Carbide & Carbon Corp & Columbia Univ, 44-46; res chemist, Stand Oil Develop Co, 46-48; mem fac, Hunter Col, 48-49; asst prof, Iona Col, 49-51; res chemist, Gen Chem Div, Allied Chem Corp, 51-61; spec lectr, Newark Col Eng, 61; assoc prof chem, E Tenn State Univ, 62-64; prof, Westmar Col, 64-74. *Mem:* Am Chem Soc; Am Astron Soc; Astron Soc Pac. *Res:* General astronomy and physics; variable stars, light, relativity, gravity and astrometry; philosophy of science; molecular and intermolecular structure, reaction kinetics and mechanisms, catalysis and non-ideality in solutions and chemical gases. *Mailing Add:* 13716 12th Ave SW Apt 47 Seattle WA 98166-1143

KELLS, MILTON CARLISLE, PHYSICAL CHEMISTRY. *Current Pos:* RETIRED. *Personal Data:* b Seattle, Wash, May 7, 20; m 49; c 3. *Educ:* Univ Wash, BS, 42; Mass Inst Technol, PhD(chem), 48. *Prof Exp:* Res scientist, Gaseous Diffusion Studies, Manhattan Proj, Kellex Corp, 44-46, Atomic Energy Process Develop, 48-51; contract adminr, Res Div, AEC, 51-54; atomic energy process develop, Sylvania Elec Co, 54-56; head detonations sect, Stanford Res Inst, 56-61; scientist, Ames Res Ctr, NASA, 61-66; prof phys sci, Calif Univ, Pa, 66-91. *Mem:* AAAS; Am Chem Soc; Sigma Xi. *Res:* Vacuum ultraviolet spectroscopy. *Mailing Add:* 11840 26th Ave S NO 211 Seattle WA 98168

KELLY, ALAN, DEVELOPMENTAL BIOLOGY. *Current Pos:* PROF PATH, SCH VET MED, UNIV PA, 80- *Educ:* Univ Pa, PhD(path), 68. *Mem:* Am Soc Cell Biol; Biophys Soc Am. *Mailing Add:* Dept Path Univ Pa Sch Vet Med Philadelphia PA 19104

KELLY, AMY SCHICK, NEUROBIOLOGY, NEUROPHYSIOLOGY. *Current Pos:* ASST PROF PHYSIOL, UNIV CALIF, SAN FRANCISCO, 78- *Personal Data:* b Rochester, NY, Nov 11, 40; m 71; c 2. *Educ:* Mt Holyoke Col, AB, 62; Brown Univ, MSc, 64, PhD(psychol), 67. *Prof Exp:* Fel psychol, Northeastern Univ, 67-68, asst prof, 68-71; fel neurobiol, Univ Calif, Berkeley, 72-74; fel neurobiol, Med Ctr, Stanford Univ, 74-78. *Concurrent Pos:* Fel, Northeastern Univ, 67-68; spec res fel, Med Sch, Stanford Univ, 74-77. *Mem:* Soc Neurosci; Asn Res Vision & Ophthal; AAAS. *Res:* Organization of the mammalian central visual system; development of the central visual pathways and visual centers; plasticity of central connections in the mammalian visual system. *Mailing Add:* 1315 Fourth Ave San Francisco CA 94122

KELLY, B(ERNARD) WAYNE, AGRICULTURAL ECONOMICS, HORTICULTURE PRODUCTION ECONOMICS. *Current Pos:* from asst prof to prof, 56-83, EMER PROF FARM MGT EXTEN, PA STATE UNIV, UNIV PARK, 83- *Personal Data:* b Corning, NY, Oct 7, 18; m 45; c Bruce W, Elizabeth A & Barbara L. *Educ:* Pa State Univ, BS, 49, MS, 50. *Prof Exp:* Instr & asst county agt, Agr Exten, Univ Md, 50-53, asst prof & county agt, 54-56. *Concurrent Pos:* Financial consult, 83- *Mem:* Am Agr Econ Asn; Am Soc Farm Mgrs & Rural Appraisors. *Res:* Cost of production; fruits and vegetable crops; taxation, insurance, investments and credits. *Mailing Add:* Dept Farm Mgt Exten 1427 S Pugh St State College PA 16801

KELLY, CLARK ANDREW, ANALYTICAL CHEMISTRY, PHARMACEUTICAL CHEMISTRY. *Current Pos:* RES ASSOC, CHEM DEPT, NMEX STATE UNIV, LAS CRUCES, 91- *Personal Data:* b Rocky Ford, Colo, Sept 14, 25; m 54, Ruth F Skinner; c Bret A. *Educ:* Univ Colo, BS, 46; Temple Univ, MS, 51; Univ Minn, PhD(anal pharm chem), 58. *Prof Exp:* Res asst, Sterling-Winthrop Res Inst, Rensselaer, 46-48 & summers, 51-54, res assoc, 56-63, res chemist, 63-68, sr res chemist & group leader, 68-88; sr res chemist & group leader, Sterling Res Group, 88-91. *Mem:* Am Chem Soc; Am Pharmaceut Asn; fel Acad Pharmaceut Sci. *Res:* Polarography of organic compounds; ion exchange separations of organic compounds; colorimetric and spectrophotometric studies. *Mailing Add:* 4024 Shadow Run Las Cruces NM 88011-7696

KELLY, CONRAD MICHAEL, CHEMICAL ENGINEERING. *Current Pos:* Asst prof, 69-75, assoc prof, 75-80, PROF CHEM ENG, VILLANOVA UNIV, 80- *Personal Data:* b Bradford, Pa, Nov 26, 44; m 66; c 1. *Educ:* Mich State Univ, BS, 66, MS, 67, PhD(chem eng), 70. *Concurrent Pos:* Assoc prof, Air Prod & Chem Inc, 80- *Mem:* Am Inst Chem Engrs; Am Soc Eng Educ; Sigma Xi. *Res:* Molecular diffusion; air and water pollution abatement; mathematical modeling. *Mailing Add:* Chem Eng Dept Villanova Univ Villanova PA 19085

KELLY, DONALD C, THEORETICAL PHYSICS. *Current Pos:* RETIRED. *Personal Data:* b Poland, Ohio, Aug 18, 33; m 55; c 4. *Educ:* Miami Univ, Ohio, AB, 55, MA, 56; Yale Univ, PhD(physics), 59. *Prof Exp:* Res assoc physics, Yale Lab Marine Physics, 59-60; from asst prof to prof physics, Miami Univ, Ohio, 60-93. *Concurrent Pos:* Nat Acad Sci sr res assoc, Inst Space Studies, 70-71. *Mem:* Am Phys Soc; Am Asn Physics Teachers. *Res:* Classical and quantum kinetic theory; scattering theory; theoretical plasma physics. *Mailing Add:* Dept Physics Miami Univ Oxford OH 45056-1618

KELLY, DONALD G, AERONAUTICAL & ASTRONAUTICAL ENGINEERING. *Current Pos:* exec asst to comnr patents & trademarks, 85-88, PATENT EXAM GROUP DIR, SR EXEC SERVS, US PATENT & TRADEMARK OFF, 88- *Educ:* Va Inst Technol, BS, 64. *Prof Exp:* Patent examr, US Patent & Trademark Off, 64-75; sci adv to US congressman, 75-76; Washington & Geneva coordr, Tokyo Round Gen Agreements Tariffs & Trade Negotiations, 76-78; patent info dir, Nat Tech Info Serv, 80-81; mktg dir, Pergamon Press, Ltd, 81-83. *Res:* Heat transfer; combustion engines; turbines; rocket propulsion systems; textile manufacturing; hydraulic/pneumatic engineering devices. *Mailing Add:* US Patent Office 2201 Jefferson Davis Hwy Bldg Crystal Plaza 4 Arlington VA 22202

KELLY, DONALD HORTON, VISION. *Current Pos:* INDEPENDENT CONSULT, 92- *Personal Data:* b Erie, Pa, May 6, 23; m 50, Jess Wells; c George B. *Educ:* Univ Rochester, BS, 44; Univ Calif, Los Angeles, PhD(eng), 60. *Honors & Awards:* Edgar B Tillyer Award, Optical Soc Am, 86. *Prof Exp:* Engr, Mitchell Camera Corp, 44; photog res engr, Technicolor Corp, 46-52, sr staff mem res, 53-61; sr staff mem, Optics Res Div, Itek Corp, Mass, 61-63, mgr, Info Systs Dept, Vidya Div, Calif, 63-66; staff scientist, Visual Sci Prog, SRI Int, 66-91. *Concurrent Pos:* Mem comt vision, Armed Forces-Nat Res Coun, 62-64; vis prof & NIH spec fel, Ctr Visual Sci, Univ Rochester, 71-72; mem visual sci B study sect, NIH, 73-77. *Mem:* AAAS; fel Optical Soc Am; Asn Res Vision & Ophthal. *Res:* Vision research; visual instruments; spatio-temporal interactions in the visual process; stabilized retinal images; afterimages; retinal inhomogeneity; automated psychophysical techniques. *Mailing Add:* 24143 Hillview Dr Los Altos Hills CA 94024. *Fax:* 650-949-1567; *E-Mail:* visionik@earthlink.net

KELLY, DOROTHY HELEN, PEDIATRICS, PULMONOLOGY. *Current Pos:* ASSOC PEDIATRICIAN, MASS GEN HOSP, 85- *Personal Data:* b Fitchburg, Mass, July 29, 44. *Educ:* Fitchburg State Col, BSN, 66; Wayne State Univ, BS, 68, MD, 72. *Prof Exp:* Intern, Dept Pediat, Mass Gen Hosp, 72-73, resident, 73-75; from instr to assoc prof pediat, Harvard Med Sch, 75-89. *Concurrent Pos:* Fel pediat pulmonary med, Mass Gen Hosp, 76-79, asst pediat, 75-79, co-dir, Pediat Pulmonary Lab, 77-86, asst pediatrician 79-84, assoc dir, Pediat Pulmonary Unit, 88; consult, Sudden Infant Death Syndrome Proj, Bur Commun Health Serv, Dept Health, Educ & Welfare, 79-80, prof, Orgn Soc Pediat Res, 85-, FDA, Health Devices, 85, ECRI, Apnea Monitoring Stand, 87-88, FDA, Health Devices, 88; chmn, Apnea Adv Comt, Nat Sudden Infant Death Syndrome Found, 79-81, mem, Sci Rev Comt, 81. *Mem:* Fel Am Acad Pediat; Asn Psychophysiol Study; Int Pediat Soc; Am Med Women's Asn; Am Thoracic Soc; Soc Pediat Res. *Res:* Control of ventilation; Sudden Infant Death Syndrome; sleep apnea. *Mailing Add:* Hermann Hosp SW SIDS Res Inst Fannin St Houston TX 77030. *Fax:* 617-726-1036

KELLY, DOUGLAS ELLIOTT, DEVELOPMENTAL ANATOMY, MICROSCOPIC ANATOMY. *Current Pos:* ASSOC VPRES BIOMED RES, ASN AM MED COLS, 89- *Personal Data:* b Cheyenne, Wyo, Nov 13, 32; m 54; c 5. *Educ:* Colo State Univ, BS, 54; Stanford Univ, PhD(biol sci), 58. *Honors & Awards:* Medal, Japan Asn Anat, 84. *Prof Exp:* From instr to asst prof biol, Univ Colo, 58-63; from asst prof to assoc prof biol struct, Sch Med, Univ Wash, 63-70; prof & chmn dept, Sch Med, Univ Miami, 70-74; prof anat & cell biol & chmn dept, Sch Med, Univ Southern Calif, 74-89. *Concurrent Pos:* USPHS res fel, Zool Lab, State Univ Utrecht, 59-60; NSF & NIH res grants, Univ Colo, 60-63, Univ Wash, 63-70, Univ Miami, 70-74, & Univ Southern Calif, 77-; Univ Colo fac res fel, Univ Wash, 62-63; mem anat comt, Nat Bd Med Exam, 70-74; NIH Human Embryol & Develop Study Sect, 78-82 & chmn, 83-85; pres, Asn Anat Chmn, 79-80 & Am Asn Anat, 86-87; mem admin bd, coun acad sci, Asn Am Med Col, 82-84 & 85-88, chmn, 87-88. *Mem:* Am Asn Anat; Soc Develop Biol; Am Soc Zool; Am Soc Cell Biol. *Res:* Electron microscopy; development and ultrastructure of junctional complexes; ultrastructure of muscle and eye. *Mailing Add:* Asn Am Med Cols 2540 N St NW Rm 529 Washington DC 20037-1126. *Fax:* 202-828-1125

KELLY, EDGAR PRESTON, JR, MATHEMATICS. *Current Pos:* prof math, 67-80, PROF MATH & STATIST, LA TECH UNIV, 80- *Personal Data:* b Beaumont, Tex, Aug 5, 33; m 54; c 3. *Educ:* Stephen F Austin State Col, BS, 55; Fla State Univ, MS, 56; Okla State Univ, PhD(math), 60. *Prof Exp:* Mathematician comput ctr, Socony Mobil Oil Co, 56-57; asst prof math, Stephen F Austin State Col, 60-62; prof & dir comput ctr & dean basic col, Univ Southern Miss, 62-64, chmn dept math, 64-67. *Mem:* Am Math Soc; Math Asn Am. *Res:* Infinite series and summability methods. *Mailing Add:* 605 University Dr Ruston LA 71272-0001

KELLY, EDWARD JOSEPH, PHYSICAL CHEMISTRY. *Current Pos:* asst prof, 75-80, ASSOC PROF CHEM, MARIAN COL, 80- *Personal Data:* b Baltimore, Md, Mar 4, 34; m 67; c 2. *Educ:* Johns Hopkins Univ, BES, 56, MAT, 62, MS, 68; Purdue Univ, MS, 67, PhD(chem, physics), 72. *Prof Exp:* Engr, Bendix Radio Corp, 60-61; teacher, Mt St Joseph High Sch, Md, 62-65; asst prof math & physics, Mt Marty Col, 72-75. *Mem:* AAAS; Am Chem Soc; Am Asn Physics Teachers; Sigma Xi. *Res:* Exploring alternatives in science teaching; quantum mechanics of small molecules. *Mailing Add:* 4440 Manning Rd Indianapolis IN 46208-2726

KELLY, ERNEST L, PHYSICAL PHARMACY, ANALYTICAL METHODS DEVELOPMENT. *Current Pos:* SR DIR QUAL ASSURANCE, RHORE-POULENC RORER, 90- *Personal Data:* b DuBois, Pa, Jan 6, 50; m 69, Glenna Crambaker; c Richard, David & Matthew. *Educ:* Millersville State Col, BA, 71; Villanova Univ, MS, 74, PhD(phys chem), 77. *Prof Exp:* Res asst, McNeil Labs, 72-74; sr anal chem, Merck Sharp & Dohme Res Labs, 74-79; sect head, Wm H Rorer, Inc, 79-81. *Concurrent Pos:* Adj prof pharmaceut, Temple Univ; panel mem, US Pharmacepol Aerosol. *Mem:* Am Chem Soc; Am Pharmaceut Asn; Acad Pharmaceut Sci; Am Asn Pharmaceut Soc. *Res:* Development of analytical and microscopic methods for the analysis of pharmaceutical drug substances and raw materials; evaluation of physical chemical properties of pharmaceutical drug substances in relationship to the formulation and stability of the drug; pharmaceutical quality assurance and compliance. *Mailing Add:* 159 Pine Lane Yardley PA 19067

KELLY, FLOYD W, JR, ORGANIC CHEMISTRY. *Current Pos:* INSTR CHEM, CASPER COL, 69- *Personal Data:* b Greeley, Colo, Dec 30, 41; m 65; c 2. *Educ:* Colo State Univ, BS, 63; Univ Ore, MS, 65; Univ Idaho, PhD(org chem), 68. *Prof Exp:* Fel chem, Utah State Univ, 68-69. *Concurrent Pos:* Adj prof chem, Univ Wyo. *Mem:* Am Chem Soc. *Res:* Organic synthesis; organic photochemistry; gas phase homolyses. *Mailing Add:* Dept Chem Casper Col Casper WY 82601

KELLY, FRANCIS JOSEPH, LONG WAVE PROPAGATION, MAGNETOSPHERIC PROPAGATION. *Current Pos:* SR RES ASSOC, CATH UNIV AM, 94- *Personal Data:* b Baltimore, Md, Oct 12, 40; m 64; c 3. *Educ:* Cath Univ Am, Washington, DC, BA, 62, PhD(physics), 66. *Prof Exp:* Physicist, Nat Bur Stand, Washington, DC, 62-65 & Naval Ord Lab, White Oak, Silver Spring, Md, 65-68; physicist, Naval Res Lab, Washington, DC, 68-94. *Concurrent Pos:* Lectr, Va Polytech Inst, 76-84. *Mem:* Am Phys Soc; Inst Elec & Electronics Engrs; Union Radio Sci Int. *Res:* Propagation of long electromagnetic waves and systems for transmitting and receiving them; constructed models of atmospheric noise and studied the propagation of such waves from a satellite to the earth; nuclear structure effects on electron and neutrino reactions; author of various publications. *Mailing Add:* Dept Physics Cath Univ Am Washington DC 20064. *Fax:* 301-422-9021

KELLY, GEORGE EUGENE, MECHANICAL ENGINEERING, STATISTICAL MECHANICS. *Current Pos:* MECH ENGR, NAT INST STANDARDS & TECHNOL, 72- *Personal Data:* b Brooklyn, NY, Mar 28, 44; m 70; c 3. *Educ:* State Univ NY, Stony Brook, BES, 65; Northwestern Univ, PhD(mech eng), 70. *Honors & Awards:* Silver Medal, Dept Commerce, 78. *Prof Exp:* Res assoc, Nat Res Coun, Nat Bur Standards 70-72. *Mem:* Am Phys Soc; Am Soc Heating, Refrig & Air-Conditioning Engrs. *Res:* Theoretical, laboratory and field research on the performance of heating and cooling equipment and systems, controls, and energy management systems in buildings and residences; thermodynamics, fluid mechanics, heat transfer and methods of numerical and analytical analysis. *Mailing Add:* Mech Systs Group Rm B114 Bldg 226 Nat Inst Standards & Technol Washington DC 20899

KELLY, GREGORY, CELL-CYCLE REGULATION, CARCINOGENESIS. *Current Pos:* PRES SW SCI RESOURCES, 95- *Personal Data:* b McKeesport, Pa, Dec 7, 54; m 76; c 2. *Educ:* Univ Pittsburgh, BS, 77; Purdue Univ, PhD(biochem), 83. *Prof Exp:* Fel, Dept Biochem, Univ Iowa, Sch Med, 83-86; staff scientist, Inhalation Toxicol Res Inst, 86-95. *Concurrent Pos:* Adj asst prof, Dept Vet Path, Purdue Univ, 89-92, adj prof exp path, 92-; clin asst prof, Toxicol Prog, Univ NMex, Sch Pharm, 90- *Mem:* Am Asn Cancer Res; Radiation Res Soc; AAAS. *Res:* Pulmonary carcinogenesis; development of the tracheo-bronchial epithelium; role of cell-cycle controlling genes in the development of neoplasia. *Mailing Add:* SW Sci Resources Inc 5300 Sequoia NW Suite 150 Albuquerque NM 87120. *Fax:* 505-845-1250

KELLY, GREGORY M, PHARMACOLOGY. *Current Pos:* ASST PROF ZOOL, UNIV WESTERN ONT, 94- *Prof Exp:* Sr fel, Dept Pharmacol, Univ Wash, 89-94. *Mailing Add:* Dept Zool Univ Western Ont London ON N6A 5B7 Can. *Fax:* 206-685-3822

KELLY, HENRY CHARLES, TECHNOLOGY & ECONOMIC GROWTH, ENERGY EFFICIENCY. *Current Pos:* SR ASSOC, OFF TECHNOL ASSESSMENT, 81- *Personal Data:* b Boston, Mass, July 10, 45; m 69; c 2. *Educ:* Cornell Univ, BA, 67; Harvard Univ, PhD(physics), 72. *Prof Exp:* Physicist, US Arms Control & Disarmament Agency, 71-74; tech adv to dir, Off Technol Assessment, 75-78, dir technol & int rels, 78-79; assoc dir, Solar Energy Res Inst, 79-81. *Concurrent Pos:* AAAS Cong Sci fel, 74-75; chmn, Lawrence Berkely Lab, Appl Sci Div Rev Comt, 89 & 90; mem sci adv bd, Risk Reduction Subcomt, Environ Protection Agency. *Mem:* Fel AAAS; fel Am Phys Soc; Fedn Am Specialists. *Res:* Theory and application of light scattering techniques; photovoltaic and other solar energy equipment; energy conservation technologies; international relations; policy, technology and structural economic change including publications on federal statistics, textiles and apparel, information technolgy, technology and education, energy efficiency technology, construction, and renewable energy; strategic arms control, nuclear effects, and quantumelectrodynamics. *Mailing Add:* 2210 N Nelson St Arlington VA 22207

KELLY, HENRY CURTIS, INORGANIC CHEMISTRY. *Current Pos:* from asst prof to assoc prof, 64-74, chmn, Dept Chem, 89-95, PROF CHEM, TEX CHRISTIAN UNIV, 74- *Personal Data:* b Providence, RI, May 17, 30; m 56, Lucille Mainland; c Luanne, Nancy & Curtis. *Educ:* Bates Col, BS, 51; Brown Univ, PhD(chem), 62. *Prof Exp:* Anal chemist, Metal Hydrides Inc, 51-52, res chemist, 52-58, sr res chemist, 62-64; from asst to instr chem, Brown Univ, 58-62. *Concurrent Pos:* Dir, honors prog, Tex Christian Univ, 81-87. *Mem:* AAAS; Am Chem Soc; Sigma Xi; Royal Soc Chem. *Res:* Chemistry of boron and silicon hydrides; boron-nitrogen compounds; kinetics and mechanisms of hydride reactions in solution; amineborane solvolysis and oxidation; kinetics of peroxidatic activity of metal-porphyrins and enzymes; cyclodextrin inclusion compound formation and function. *Mailing Add:* Dept Chem Tex Christian Univ Ft Worth TX 76129. *Fax:* 817-921-7110

KELLY, JAMES L(ESLIE), CHEMICAL ENGINEERING, MATERIALS SCIENCE ENGINEERING. *Current Pos:* assoc prof, 64-72, asst dean undergrad prog, 91-96, PROF NUCLEAR ENG, SCH ENG & APPL SCI, UNIV VA, 72- *Personal Data:* b New Orleans, La, Dec 20, 32; m 56, Aileen Wilson; c Kevin Wilson, Megan Elizabeth, Michael Wilson & Katherine (Wren). *Educ:* Tulane Univ, BS, 54; La State Univ, MS, 60, PhD(chem eng), 62. *Prof Exp:* Process engr, Kaiser Aluminum & Chem Corp, 56-57 & Ormet Corp, 57-59; chem tech div, Oak Ridge Nat Lab, 62-64. *Mem:* Am Inst Chem Engrs; Am Nuclear Soc; Nat Asn Corrosion Engrs. *Res:* Radiation processing; reactor materials; nuclear chemical engineering; radioactive waste disposal. *Mailing Add:* 2096 Stonemont Farm Keswick VA 22947

KELLY, JAMES MICHAEL, PLANT NUTRITION, FOREST SOILS. *Current Pos:* PROF & CHMN, DEPT FORESTRY, IOWA STATE UNIV, 95- *Personal Data:* b Knoxville, Tenn, Feb 2, 44; m 68, Susan Morris; c John K & Christopher K. *Educ:* ETenn State Univ, BS, 66; Univ Tenn, MS, 68, PhD(forest ecol), 73. *Prof Exp:* Asst prof biol, Ferrum Col, 69-70; postdoctoral res assoc, Purdue Univ, 74-76; tech specialist, Tenn Valley Authority, 76-78, sr tech specialist, 89-95. *Concurrent Pos:* Adj prof, Univ Tenn, 78-95, Purdue Univ, 87-95; vis prof agron, Purdue Univ, 88-89. *Mem:* Soil Sci Soc Am; Soc Am Foresters; Am Soc Agron; AAAS; Ecol Soc Am. *Res:* Cycling and availability of nutrients in forests, nutrient uptake by trees and the impacts of air pollution on forests and soils. *Mailing Add:* Forestry Dept Iowa State Univ 251 Bessey Hall Ames IA 50011-1021. *E-Mail:* jmkelly@iastate.edu

KELLY, JEFFREY JOHN, BIOCHEMISTRY, CHEMISTRY. *Current Pos:* FAC MEM, DEPT CHEM, EVERGREEN STATE COL, 72- *Personal Data:* b Portland, Ore, Nov 2, 42; m 66; c 3. *Educ:* Harvey Mudd Col, BS, 64; Univ Calif, Berkeley, PhD(chem), 68. *Prof Exp:* Asst prof chem, Reed Col, 68-72. *Concurrent Pos:* Vis prof chem, Harvey Mudd Col, 80-81; vis prof chem, Ctr Process Anal Chem, Univ Wash, 87-88. *Mem:* AAAS; Sigma Xi. *Res:* Physical and chemical processes of photosynthesis; biomedical spectroscopy; analytical near infrared spectroscopy. *Mailing Add:* 5735 Cedar Flats Rd SW Olympia WA 98512-9415

KELLY, JOHN BECKWITH, MATHEMATICS. *Current Pos:* assoc prof, 62-66, PROF MATH, ARIZ STATE UNIV, TEMPE, 66- *Personal Data:* b New York, NY, Aug 30, 21. *Educ:* Columbia Univ, AB, 42; Mass Inst Technol, PhD, 48. *Prof Exp:* Instr math, Univ Wis, 48-50; mem, Inst Advan Study, 50-51; from instr to assoc prof, Mich State Univ, 51-62. *Mem:* Sigma Xi. *Res:* Number theory; graph theory; combinatorial analysis. *Mailing Add:* Ariz State Univ Tempe AZ 85281

KELLY, JOHN FRANCIS, HORTICULTURE, OLERICULTURE. *Current Pos:* chmn dept, 78-90, PROF HORT, MICH STATE UNIV, 78- *Personal Data:* b Chicago, Ill, Nov 28, 31; m 59, Janet Wolf; c Marcia, Andrea, Shaun, Claudia, Daniel, Timothy, Michael, Kurt & Kristine. *Educ:* Mich State Univ, BS, 53, MS, 57; Univ Wis, PhD(hort, plant physiol), 60. *Hon Degrees:* Hon doctorate, Univ Hort & Food Indust, Budapest, Hungary, 88. *Prof Exp:* Agr res asst, Campbell Soup Co, 52-53; asst, Mich State Univ, 56 & Univ Wis, 57-59; asst prof veg crops & soils, Southern Ill Univ, 59-62; soils technologist, Campbell Soup Co, 62-64; dir pioneer plant res, 65-66, vpres pioneer res, Campbell Inst Agr Res, 66-72; prof veg crops & chmn dept, Univ Fla, 72-78. *Mem:* Fel AAAS; fel Am Soc Hort Sci (pres, 85-86); Int Soc Hort Sci. *Res:* Culture, physiology, nutrition and chemical composition of vegetable crops; quality of food crops. *Mailing Add:* Dept Hort Mich State Univ 428 Plant Sci Bldg East Lansing MI 48824-7325

KELLY, JOHN HENRY, DIFFRACTION, NON-LINEAR PROPAGATION. *Current Pos:* SEMICONDUCTOR RES CORP. *Personal Data:* b Tonawanda, NY, Sept 26, 52. *Educ:* Univ Buffalo, BS, 74; Univ Rochester, MS, 76, PhD(optics), 80. *Prof Exp:* Res assoc, Lab Laser Energetics, 80- *Mem:* Inst Elec & Electronics Engrs; Optical Soc Am; Sigma Xi. *Res:* Diffraction and the propagation of light in large laser systems; resonant energy transfer in both crystalline and amorphous materials. *Mailing Add:* 306 Rutherglen Dr Cary NC 27511-6439

KELLY, JOHN RUSSELL, OCEANOGRAPHY. *Current Pos:* RES ASSOC, ECOSYSTS RES CTR, CORNELL UNIV, 81- *Personal Data:* b Nashua, NH, Jan 25, 52. *Educ:* Univ NH, BA, 74; Univ RI, PhD(oceanog), 82. *Prof Exp:* Res asst, Grad Sch Oceanog, Univ RI, 75-81. *Mem:* Am Soc Limnol & Oceanog; Sigma Xi. *Res:* Elemental cycling in marine, aquatic and terrestrial systems. *Mailing Add:* 15 Alida Ave Hillcrest NY 13901

KELLY, JOHN V, OBSTETRICS, GYNECOLOGY. *Current Pos:* CHMN DEPT OBSTET & GYNEC, MARICOPA COUNTY HOSP, PHOENIX, 75- *Personal Data:* b London, Ont, Aug 21, 26; nat US. *Educ:* Wayne State Univ, BS, 48, MD, 51; Am Bd Obstet & Gynec, dipl, 61. *Prof Exp:* Intern, Metrop Hosp, NY Med Col, 51-52, resident obstet & gynec, 52-55; from instr to asst prof, Sch Med, Univ Calif, Los Angeles, 57-64; med missionary, St Luke's Hosp, Anua, ENigeria, 64-66; prof obstet & gynec, Sch Med, Univ Pa, 67-75. *Concurrent Pos:* Res fel, Harvard Med Sch, 55; Graves fel, Free Hosp Women, Brookline, Mass, 55; Fulbright fel, Stockholm, Sweden, 56; adj prof obstet & gynec, Sch Med, Univ Ariz, 75- *Mem:* Am Fertil Soc; Am Med Asn; Am Fedn Clin Res. *Res:* Dynamics of uterine muscle contraction. *Mailing Add:* Maricopa County Hosp Box 5099 Phoenix AZ 85010-5099

KELLY, KENNETH C, array antennas for microwaves, microwave filters, for more information see previous edition

KELLY, KENNETH WILLIAM, ORGANIC CHEMISTRY. *Current Pos:* DIR RES & DEVELOP, KAY-FRIES, INC, 69- *Personal Data:* b New York, NY. *Educ:* St John's Univ, NY, BS, 61, MS, 63; Rutgers Univ, PhD(chem), 69. *Prof Exp:* Chemist synthesis, Merck & Co, Rahway, NJ, 63-69. *Mem:* Am Chem Soc. *Res:* Organic synthesis; organic analysis. *Mailing Add:* PO Box 246 Tomkins Cove NY 10986-0246

KELLY, LEROY MILTON, mathematics, for more information see previous edition

KELLY, MAHLON GEORGE, JR, AQUATIC ECOLOGY, LIMNOLOGY. *Current Pos:* asst prof, 70-75, ASSOC PROF ENVIRON SCI, UNIV VA, 75- *Personal Data:* b Plymouth, NH, Mar 24, 39; m 70. *Educ:* Harvard Univ, AB, 60, PhD(biol), 68; Univ NH, MS, 62. *Prof Exp:* Sci staff, R/V Anton Bruun, 62-63; res asst biol, Woods Hole Oceanog Inst, 63 & Harvard Univ, 64-67; staff oceanogr, Mass Inst Technol, 68; vis asst prof environ biol, Univ Miami, 68-69; asst prof biol, Yale Univ, 69-70. *Concurrent Pos:* Vis scientist, Scottish Marine Biol Lab, 76, Danish Fresh Water Lab, 78 & 80-84, Freshwater Biol Asn, UK, 84, 85 & 88-90. *Mem:* AAAS; Am Soc Limnol & Oceanog; Ecol Soc Am; Sigma Xi; Freshwater Biol Asn UK; Scottish Marine Biol Asn. *Res:* Photosynthetic behavior of algae and aquatic macrophytes; marine bioluminescence; remote sensing of benthic communities; aquatic nutrient cycling. *Mailing Add:* 268 Turkey Ridge Rd Charlottesville VA 22901

KELLY, MARTIN JOSEPH, PHYSICS. *Current Pos:* RETIRED. *Personal Data:* b New York, NY, Sept 27, 24. *Educ:* St John's Univ, NY, BS, 49; NY Univ, PhD, 58. *Prof Exp:* Physicist, Naval Mat Lab, 51-53; assoc, Nucleonics, Inc, 54-59; assoc, Tech Res Group, Inc, 59; mem fac, Manhattan Col, 59-64; chmn dept, C W Post Col, Long Island Univ, 64-74, prof physics, 64-97. *Mem:* Am Phys Soc. *Res:* Neutron physics; reactors; shielding. *Mailing Add:* Dept Physics C W Post Col Greenvale NY 11548-1300

KELLY, MICHAEL DAVID, INTELLIGENT DATABASES, KNOWLEDGE-BASED SYSTEMS. *Current Pos:* PRES & CHIEF SCIENTIST, IKCS, 95- *Personal Data:* b Wis, Jan 26, 38; m 63; c 3. *Educ:* Ga Tech, BS, 64; Stanford Univ, MS, 67, PhD(computer sci), 70. *Prof Exp:* Asst prof comput sci, Ga Tech, 70-75; chief scientist, BDM Int Inc, 75-95. *Concurrent Pos:* Consult, IBM Corp, 68 & UNESCO, Caracas, Venezuela, 75; vis scientist, Carnegie-Mellon Univ, 73 & Centre Mondial, Paris, France, 83. *Mem:* Am Asn Artificial Intel; Asn Comput Mach; Inst Elec & Electronics Engrs. *Mailing Add:* 1670 Moorings Dr Reston VA 20190

KELLY, MICHAEL THOMAS, CLINICAL MICROBIOLOGY, IMMUNOLOGY. *Current Pos:* HEAD, MICROBIOL DEPT, METRO MCNAIR CLIN LAB. *Personal Data:* b Indianapolis, Ind, Mar 8, 43; m 65; c 4. *Educ:* Purdue Univ, BS, 65; Ind Univ, PhD(microbiol), 69, MD, 73. *Prof Exp:* Fel, Sch Med, Ind Univ, 69-71, res assoc infectious dis, 71-73; intern path, Scg Med, Univ Minn, 73-74; comn officer res, Rocky Mt Lab, NIH, USPHS, 74-76; asst prof path, Sch Med, Univ Utah, 76-78; assoc prof path, Univ Tex Med Br, Galveston, 78- *Mem:* AAAS; Reticuloendothelial Soc; Am Asn Immunologists; Am Soc Microbiol; Am Fedn Clin Res. *Res:* Host-parasite relationships; modulation of macrophage function by microbial agents; immunopotentiation by microbial agents; mechanism of macrophage activation; clinical microbiology; antimicrobial susceptibility testing; marine microbiology. *Mailing Add:* Metro McNair Clin Lab 660 W Seventh Ave Vancouver BC V5Z 1B5 Can

KELLY, MINTON J, HIGH TEMPERATURE CHEMISTRY. *Current Pos:* chemist, Reactor Chem Div, 63-74, RES ASSOC, CHEM TECHNOL DIV, OAK RIDGE NAT LAB, 74- *Personal Data:* b Liberty, Mo, Feb 14, 21; m 49; c 3. *Educ:* Tex A&M Univ, BS, 47, MS, 50, PhD(phys chem), 56. *Prof Exp:* Field party chief oceanog res found, Tex A&M Univ, 47-48, consult instrumentation, 50-54, teaching fel chem univ, 54-55; develop engr instrumentation & controls div, Oak Ridge Nat Lab, 55-59, group leader reactor chem div, 59-62; group supvr instrumentation, Aerospace Div, Boeing Co, 62-63. *Concurrent Pos:* Engr, Arabian-Am Oil Co, 48-49. *Mem:* AAAS; Sigma Xi; fel Am Inst Chemists. *Res:* Instrumental measurements under nuclear conditions. *Mailing Add:* 114 Lewis Lane Oak Ridge TN 37830

KELLY, NELSON ALLEN, PHOTOCHEMISTRY, ENVIRONMENTAL CHEMISTRY & AIR QUALITY. *Current Pos:* Sr res scientist, 77-82, STAFF RES SCIENTIST, GEN MOTORS RES LABS, 82- *Personal Data:* b Lakewood, Ohio, Aug 6, 51; m 82, Suzanne M Gerou; c Ben, Bryan & Dan. *Educ:* Miami Univ, Ohio, BS, 73; Pa State Univ, PhD(phys chem), 77. *Honors & Awards:* Joseph P Culler Prize. *Concurrent Pos:* Mem, Chem Comt, Air Pollution Control Asn, 82- *Mem:* Sigma Xi; Am Chem Soc; InterAm Photochem Soc; Air Pollution Control Asn. *Res:* The chemistry of ozone formation and transport in the atmosphere; the role of automobiles in the formation of photochemical smog; passenger-car cabin air quality. *Mailing Add:* 14004 Pernell Dr Sterling Heights MI 48313. *Fax:* 810-986-1910; *E-Mail:* nkelly@notes.gmr.com

KELLY, PATRICK JOSEPH, ORTHOPEDIC SURGERY. *Current Pos:* CONSULT, MAYO CLIN, 57- *Personal Data:* b Minneapolis, Minn, Feb 12, 26; m 50; c 8. *Educ:* St Lawrence Univ, BS, 45; St Louis Univ, MD, 49; Univ Minn, MS, 58. *Prof Exp:* Prof orthop surg, Mayo Grad Sch, 69-73; prof orthop surg, Mayo Med Sch, 73-90. *Concurrent Pos:* Am Orthop Asn Traveling Fel; pres, Bd Trustees, Orthopaedic Res & Educ Found; mem, Am Bd Orthop Surg; mem, Am Inst Biol Sci Adv Panel, NASA. *Mem:* Am Acad Orthop Surg; Am Orthop Asn; Orthop Res Soc (past pres); Am Physiol Soc. *Res:* Circulation and physiology of bone; bone metabolism. *Mailing Add:* Dept Orthop Surg Mayo Clin & Found 200 First St SW Rochester MN 55905

KELLY, PAUL ALAN, MEDICAL RESEARCH. *Current Pos:* PROF & DIR, INSERM UNITE 344, ENDOCRINOL MOLECULAR FAC MED NECKER, 91- *Personal Data:* b Washington, DC, June 3, 43; m 91; c Daniel. *Educ:* Western Mich Univ, BS, 66, MS, 68; Univ Wis, PhD(endocrinol & reprod physiol), 72. *Prof Exp:* Fel endocrinol, McGill Univ, 72-74, prof, Dept Med & Physiol, 83-91; res fel, 74-75, asst prof, 75-80, assoc prof physiol, Laval Univ, 80-82; dir, Lab Molecular Endocrinol, Royal Victoria Hosp, Montreal, 83-91. *Concurrent Pos:* Sr mem, Med Res Coun Group Molecular Endocrinol, 75-; Med Res Coun Can scholar, 75-80; dir, Lab Molecular Endocrinol, 83-91. *Mem:* Endocrine Soc; Can Soc Clin Invest; Int Soc Neuroendocrinol; Int Soc Neurodendocrinol; Am Soc Biochem & Molecular Biol. *Res:* signal transduction pathways of growth hormone and prolacton receptors; phenotypes associated with receptor knockouts. *Mailing Add:* INSERM UNITE 344 Endocrinologie Moleculaire Faculte de Medicine Necker Enfants Malades 156 rue de Vaugirard 75730 Paris Cedex 15 France. *Fax:* 331-430-60443; *E-Mail:* kelly@necker.fr

KELLY, PAUL J, MATHEMATICS. *Current Pos:* from asst prof to assoc prof, 49-59, PROF MATH, UNIV CALIF, SANTA BARBARA, 59- *Personal Data:* b Riverside, Calif, June 26, 16; m 46; c 2. *Educ:* Univ Calif, Los Angeles, AB, 37, MA, 39; Univ Wis, PhD(math), 42. *Prof Exp:* Instr math, Univ Southern Calif, 46-49. *Res:* Metric geometry. *Mailing Add:* 30 Winchester Canyon Rd Apt 68 Goleta CA 93117-1900

KELLY, PAUL JAMES, PHYSICS. *Current Pos:* From asst res officer to assoc res officer, 65-76, SR RES OFFICER PHYSICS, NAT RES COUN, 76- *Personal Data:* b Montreal, Que, July 19, 34; m 60; c 5. *Educ:* Sir George Williams Univ, BSc, 60; Carleton Univ, MSc, 62, PhD(physics), 65. *Concurrent Pos:* Asst invest officer, Energy Res & Develop Admin consult grant, Wash State Univ, 75-77; Air Force consult grant, Wash State Univ, 78- *Mem:* Am Phys Soc. *Res:* Thermally stimulated processes; interaction of high-intensity laser pulses with solids. *Mailing Add:* 310 Smyth Rd Ottawa ON K1H 5A3 Can

KELLY, PAUL SHERWOOD, ATOMIC PHYSICS, QUANTUM MECHANICS. *Current Pos:* RETIRED. *Personal Data:* b Erie, Pa, Dec 22, 27; m 56; c 3. *Educ:* Haverford Col, AB, 49; Yale Univ, MS, 50; Univ Calif, Los Angeles, PhD(physics), 61. *Prof Exp:* Physicist, US Naval Ord Lab, Md, 50-51; electronic scientist, Nat Bur Stand, Calif, 51-53; res scientist, Lockheed Missiles & Space Co, Palo Alto, 60-68; prof physics, Humboldt State Univ, 68-97. *Mem:* Am Phys Soc; Sigma Xi. *Res:* Calculation of atomic wave functions and related atomic parameters; nuclear structure calculations. *Mailing Add:* 2670 Kelly Ave McKinleyville CA 95519

KELLY, PETER MICHAEL, PHYSICS, ELECTRICAL ENGINEERING. *Current Pos:* RETIRED. *Personal Data:* b New York, NY, July 6, 22; m 46; c 3. *Educ:* Union Col, NY, BS, 50; Calif Inst Technol, MS, 52, PhD(physics) & PhD(elec eng), 60. *Prof Exp:* Design engr, Jet Propulsion Lab, Calif Inst Technol, 51-52; proj engr, Electronics Div, Century Metalcraft Co, 53-54; mem tech staff, Hughes Aircraft Co, 54-56; from design engr to prin scientist, Aeronutronic Div, Ford Motor Co, 56-61; mgr elec dept, Astropower, Douglas Aircraft Co, 61-62; from assoc dir res to chief engr, Systs Tech Ctr, Philco-Ford, 62-69; pres & chmn bd, Kelly Sci Corp, 69-80; consult, 93; prof elec eng & dir, Telecommun Ctr, George Washington Univ, Washington, DC, 80-93. *Concurrent Pos:* Consult, NSF, 60-61; consult, President's Crime Comn, 66 & President's Commun Task Force, 68. *Mem:* AAAS; Asn Comput Mach. *Res:* Radar; network synthesis; data processing. *Mailing Add:* 3431 Emerson St Arlington VA 22207

KELLY, RAYMOND CRAIN, ANALYTICAL TOXICOLOGY. *Current Pos:* DIR TOXICOL, ASSOC PATHOLOGISTS LABS, LAS VEGAS, 93-*Personal Data:* b Portland, Ore, Sept 4, 45; m 68, 94, Connie Brascia; c Leif, Nicole, Clinton & Joel. *Educ:* Wash State Univ, BS, 67; Univ Ore, PhD(chem), 75. *Prof Exp:* Develop chemist, Sacred Heart Gen Hosp, 69-71; assoc toxicologist, Cuyahoga Co Coroners Off, Ohio, 75-77; head toxicol, Lab Procedures, Upjohn Co, 77-78; asst dir, Dept Clin & Indust Toxicol, Bio-Sci Lab, Van Nuys, Calif, 78-83; lab & sci dir, Medtox Lab Inc, 89-93; chief toxicologist, Specialty Labs, 84; pres, Willow Toxicol Group, 85, State Toxicol Ctr, 85-89. *Concurrent Pos:* Nat Res Serv fel, Nat Inst Drug Abuse, NIH, 76; consult, Substance Abuse & Ment Health Serv Admin, 91-; mem, Subcomt Perinatal Substance Abuse, State Nev & lab dir, 97-; clin lab toxicologist, Calif, 89-; forensic toxicologist, NY, 95- *Mem:* Am Acad Forensic Sci; Am Asn Clin Chem; Soc Forensic Toxicologists; Col Am Pathologists. *Res:* Devising of novel methods for the analysis of drugs in biological samples, characterization of drug metabolites, mechanisms of drug toxicity and monitoring of therapeutic drug concentrations in man; pharmacology of drug abuse in man; laboratory automation; analysis for drugs in hair. *Mailing Add:* Assoc Pathologists Labs 4230 Burnham Ave Suite 250 Las Vegas NV 89119. *Fax:* 702-733-0318; *E-Mail:* rkelly@apllabs.com

KELLY, RAYMOND LEROY, ATOMIC SPECTROSCOPY. *Current Pos:* from assoc prof to prof, 60-83, EMER PROF PHYSICS, NAVAL POSTGRAD SCH, 83- *Personal Data:* b Rockford, Ill, Feb 2, 21; m 43, Ruth Garlock; c Peter & Katherine. *Educ:* Univ Wis, PhD(physics), 51. *Prof Exp:* Asst, Univ Wis, 47-51; res physicist, Stanford Res Inst, 51-60. *Concurrent Pos:* Mem, Comt Line Spectra Elements, Nat Res Coun, 71-78. *Mem:* Am Phys Soc; fel Optical Soc Am. *Res:* Infrared; spectroscopy of the ultraviolet. *Mailing Add:* Dept Physics Naval Postgrad Sch Monterey CA 93943

KELLY, REGIS BAKER, CELL BIOLOGY. *Current Pos:* from asst prof to assoc prof, 71-78, PROF BIOCHEM & BIOPHYS, UNIV CALIF, SAN FRANCISCO, 78-, DIR, CELL BIOL PROG, 88-, DIR, HORMONE RES INST, 92- *Personal Data:* b Edinburgh, Scotland, May 26, 40; m 92, Rae L Burke; c Gordon, Alison & Colin. *Educ:* Univ Edinburgh, BSc, 61, dipl, 62; Calif Inst Technol, PhD(biophys), 67. *Honors & Awards:* Javitz Investr Award, 85 & 92. *Prof Exp:* Instr neurobiol, Harvard Med Sch, 69-71. *Concurrent Pos:* Helen Hay Whitney Found fel, Sch Med, Stanford Univ, 67-69 & Harvard Med Sch, 69-70; Multi Sclerosis fel, 70-71; mem adv panel, NEI; mem, Study Sect, NIH; rev, Am Cancer Soc; vis prof, Mass Inst Technol, 86. *Mem:* Soc Neurosci; Am Soc Biol Chem; Am Soc Cell Biol. *Res:* Membrane traffice in cells; protein sorting; molecular events in nerve terminals; synaptic vesicles; development of the neuron. *Mailing Add:* Dept Biochem & Biophys Univ Calif San Francisco CA 94143-0448. *Fax:* 415-731-3612

KELLY, RICHARD DELMER, BIOLOGY, SCIENCE EDUCATION. *Current Pos:* PROF BIOL, STATE UNIV NY, ALBANY. *Personal Data:* b Kingston, NY, Aug 24, 35; m 54; c 4. *Educ:* State Univ NY Albany, BS, 55, MS, 56; Syracuse Univ, EdD(biol, sci educ), 65. *Prof Exp:* High sch teacher, NY, 56-63; prof biol, State Univ NY Albany, 63-; prof biol, Univ WFla, Pensacola. *Concurrent Pos:* Consult, NY State Educ Dept, 60- & NSF Summer Progs, 60-65; vis fel, Col Educ, Kingston Upon Hull, Eng, 73-74 & Rosentiel Inst, Univ Miami, 82. *Mem:* AAAS; Am Inst Biol Sci. *Res:* Instructional technology; television; audio-tutorial; cetaceans and whaling history. *Mailing Add:* Dept Biol State Univ NY 1400 Washington Ave Albany NY 12222

KELLY, RICHARD W(ALTER), ELECTRICAL ENGINEERING. *Current Pos:* assoc prof, 65-70, PROF ELEC ENG, ARIZ STATE UNIV, 70-, ASST DEAN, 80- *Personal Data:* b Iowa City, Iowa, Sept 6, 35; m 64. *Educ:* Univ Iowa, BSEE, 58, MS, 62, PhD(elec eng), 65. *Prof Exp:* From instr to asst prof elec eng, Univ Iowa, 58-65. *Concurrent Pos:* Sr Fulbright-Hays lectureship, Trinity Col, Dublin, 72-73. *Mem:* Inst Elec & Electronics Engrs; Am Soc Eng Educ. *Res:* Application of modern signal theory; detection and estimation theory. *Mailing Add:* Dept Elec Eng Ariz State Univ Tempe AZ 85281

KELLY, ROBERT CHARLES, ORGANIC CHEMISTRY. *Current Pos:* RES ASSOC ORG CHEM, UPJOHN CO, 65- *Personal Data:* b St Joseph, Mich, Nov 28, 39; m 60; c 2. *Educ:* Kalamazoo Col, BA, 61; Harvard Univ, MA, 63, PhD(chem), 66. *Mem:* Am Chem Soc. *Res:* Organic synthesis and structure determination, particularly of cyclic hydrocarbons; terpenes and oxygen heterocycles; natural products chemistry; prostaglandins. *Mailing Add:* Dept Chem 7246-209-6 Upjohn Co 301 Henrietta St Kalamazoo MI 49001-0199

KELLY, ROBERT EDWARD, FLUID MECHANICS, HEAT TRANSFER. *Current Pos:* from asst prof to assoc prof, 67-75, PROF ENG, UNIV CALIF, LOS ANGELES, 75- *Personal Data:* b Abington, Pa, Oct 20, 34; m 64, Karin E Lampert; c Nicholas & Jennifer. *Educ:* Franklin & Marshall Col, BA, 57; Rensselaer Polytech Inst, BS, 57; Mass Inst Technol, AE, 59, ScD(aeronaut eng), 64. *Prof Exp:* Guest scientist, Nat Phys Lab, UK, 60-61, UK Civil Serv sr res fel fluid mech, 64-66; res asst aeronaut eng, Mass Inst Technol, 61-64; asst res geophysicist, Inst Geophys & Planetary Physics, Univ Calif, San Diego, 66-67. *Concurrent Pos:* Sci Res Coun sr vis fel, Dept Math, Imp Col, London, 73-74; consult, Hughes Aircraft Co, 76-83; chmn, Div Fluid Dynamics, Am Phy Soc, 80-81; assoc ed, Physics Fluids, 81-83 & 92-; vis prof, Northwestern Univ, 85; vis scientist, Japan Atomic Res Inst, 91; vis prof, Manchester Univ, UK, 94. *Mem:* Fel Am Phys Soc; Am Inst Aeronaut & Aeronaut; fel Am Soc Mech Engrs; Sigma Xi; Am Acad Mech. *Res:* Viscous flow; flow instabilities; fluid wave motion; stratified and rotating flow phenomena; thermal convection; thermocapillary flow. *Mailing Add:* Dept Mech & Aeronaut Eng Engr IV Rm 46-147B Univ Calif Los Angeles CA 90095-1597. *Fax:* 310-206-4830

KELLY, ROBERT EMMETT, PHYSICS. *Current Pos:* PHYSICIST, LOS ALAMOS NAT LAB, 88- *Personal Data:* b Cape Girardeau, Mo, Nov 26, 29; m 62, Sarah Combs; c Katelyn, Frank & Tara. *Educ:* Southeast Mo State Univ, BS, 50; Univ Mo-Rolla, MS, 52; Univ Conn, PhD(physics), 59. *Prof Exp:* Prof physics, Univ Miss, 59-88. *Concurrent Pos:* Physicist, Gen Elec Co, 52 & Marshall Space Flight Ctr, NASA, 70 & 71; consult, Boeing Co, 54, E I du Pont de Nemours & Co, Inc, 57 & Am Optical Co, 59; Richland fac fel, Hanford Lab, 65; is investr oceanog, Woods Hole Oceanog Inst, 67; prof, NMex Highlands Univ, 68; consult, Los Alamos Sci Lab, 75-82 & Lawrence Livermore Lab, 75-79; vis scientist, Ctr d'Etudes Bruyeres-le-Chatel, Serv Physique Nucleaire, France, 81 & 82. *Mem:* Am Geophys Union; Acoust Soc Am; Int Soc Optical Eng. *Res:* Electromagnetic theory; physical optics; atmospheric and mathematical physics; mathematical approach to transient radiation damage in optical fibers; energy deposition and profiles of particle beams, plus topics in musical acoustics. *Mailing Add:* 75 Tesuque Los Alamos NM 87544

KELLY, ROBERT FRANK, BIOCHEMISTRY, ANIMAL HUSBANDRY. *Current Pos:* assoc prof, 55-58, PROF FOOD SCI & TECHNOL, VA POLYTECH INST & STATE UNIV, 58- *Personal Data:* b Fond du Lac, Wis, May 21, 19; m 44; c 6. *Educ:* Univ Wis, BS, 48, MS, 53, PhD(biochem, animal husb), 55. *Honors & Awards:* Signal Serv Award, Am Meat Sci Asn, 84. *Prof Exp:* Pub sch instr, Wis, 48-51; asst, Univ Wis, 51-55. *Concurrent Pos:* Williams-Waterman scientist, Haiti, 63; AED prof, Sri Lanka, 86. *Mem:* Fel AAAS; Am Meat Sci Asn; Am Soc Animal Sci; Am Inst Food Technologists; NY Acad Sci; Am Coun Sci & Health. *Res:* Food science and nutrition. *Mailing Add:* 2801 Shadowlake Rd Blacksburg VA 24060

KELLY, ROBERT JAMES, ORGANIC CHEMISTRY. *Current Pos:* res chemist, 51-62, sr res scientist, 62-65, mgr new fiber res & develop, Uniroyal Fiber & Textile Div, 65-69, mgr tire cord res & develop, 69-76, TECH DIR UNIROYAL FIBER & TEXTILE DIV, 76- *Personal Data:* b New York, NY, Dec 2, 23; m 52; c 7. *Educ:* Trinity Col, BS, 43; NY Univ, MS, 47, PhD(chem), 52. *Prof Exp:* Asst, NY Univ, 46-51. *Mem:* Am Chem Soc. *Res:* Synthetic rubber and fibers. *Mailing Add:* 4018 Sandwood Dr Columbia SC 29206-2222

KELLY, ROBERT P, cell physiology, for more information see previous edition

KELLY, ROBERT WITHERS, ZOOLOGY, ECOLOGY. *Current Pos:* RETIRED. *Personal Data:* b Stanford, Ky, Oct 20, 26; m 48; c 2. *Educ:* Centre Col, BA, 49; Univ Ore, MS, 50; Univ Mo, PhD(zool), 56. *Prof Exp:* Head sci dept, Campbellsville Jr Col, 51-53; assoc prof biol, Southeastern La Col, 56-63 & Ariz State Col, 63-64; prof biol, Furman Univ, 64-88, chmn dept, 74-85. *Mem:* Am Soc Zool. *Res:* Invertebrate ecology, especially freshwater forms. *Mailing Add:* 101 Redspire Dr Greenville SC 29617

KELLY, RONALD BURGER, ORGANIC CHEMISTRY. *Current Pos:* prof, 67-85, chmn Div Sci & Math, 73-79, EMER PROF CHEM, UNIV NB, 85- *Personal Data:* b Fairvale, NB, May 26, 20; m 45. *Educ:* Univ NB, MSc, 51, PhD(chem), 53. *Prof Exp:* Beaverbrook overseas scholar, Univ London, 53-54; Nat Res Coun Can fel, Queen's Univ, Ont, 54-55; sr res chemist, Merck & Co, Ltd, Can, 55-58; res assoc chem, Upjohn Co, 58-67. *Mem:* AAAS; Am Chem Soc; Royal Soc Chem; fel Chem Inst Can; NY Acad Sci. *Res:* Structure determination of organic molecules; synthesis of natural products. *Mailing Add:* 1029 Seawood Lane St John NB E2M 3G8 Can

KELLY, SALLY MARIE, CLINICAL PATHOLOGY, BIOCHEMICAL MEDICAL GENETICS. *Current Pos:* sr res scientist, 51-64, assoc res scientist, 64-67, RES PHYSICIAN, WADSWORTH CTR LABS & RES, NY STATE DEPT HEALTH, 67- *Personal Data:* b Bridgeport, Conn. *Educ:* Conn Col, AB, 43; Univ Wis, MA, 44, PhD(bot), 46; NY Univ, MD, 63; Am Bd Path, dipl, 71. *Prof Exp:* Instr, Simmons Col, 47-48; asst prof plant sci, Vassar Col, 48-51. *Concurrent Pos:* Fel, Brooklyn Bot Garden, 45-47; fel, Harvard Univ, 47-48; Brown-Hazen Fund fel, 58-59 & 60-63; res assoc prof pediat, Albany Med Col, 68- *Mem:* Col Am Pathologists; fel AAAS. *Res:* Cell physiology; enteroviruses; biochemical medical genetics; clincal pathology. *Mailing Add:* Wadsworth Ctr Labs & Res NY State Dept Health Albany NY 12201

KELLY, SUSAN JEAN, ENZYMOLOGY, BIOCHEMICAL ENGINEERING. *Current Pos:* BIOL, DURHAM NC, 90- *Personal Data:* b Cincinnati, Ohio, Oct 2, 47; div; c 2. *Educ:* Col Mt St Joseph, AB, 69; Purdue Univ, PhD(biochem), 74. *Prof Exp:* Res assoc enzyme eng, Dept Biochem, Purdue Univ, 74-80; res assoc, Univ NC, Chapel Hill, 80-84, workshop coordr, Carolina Workshop, 84-90. *Concurrent Pos:* Consult, 80-; lectr & lab mgr, Duke Univ, Howard Hughes Lab Molecular. *Mem:* Sigma Xi. *Res:* Enzyme-catalyzed synthesis of sucrose and other economically important physiological compounds; enzymic mechanism of phosphatases; phosphonate analogs of phosphatase substrates; relationship of phosphatases to developmental changes and to cancer. *Mailing Add:* 8104 Lair Ct Chapel Hill NC 27516

KELLY, THADDEUS ELLIOTT, MEDICAL GENETICS. *Current Pos:* assoc prof, 75-80, PROF PEDIAT, UNIV VA, 80- *Personal Data:* b New York, NY, Oct 7, 37; m 60; c 3. *Educ:* Davidson Col, BS, 59; Med Col SC, MD, 63; Johns Hopkins Univ, PhD(genetics), 75. *Prof Exp:* Asst prof med & pediat, Sch Med, Johns Hopkins Univ, 73-75. *Concurrent Pos:* Dir, Div Med Genetics, Univ Va, 75-; pres, Am Bd Med Genetics, 93-94. *Mem:* Soc Pediat Res; Am Pediat Soc; Am Soc Human Genetics; Am Col Med Genetics. *Res:* Biochemical genetic analysis of genetic heterogenity; genetic disorders in large family studies; molecular biology of X chromosome. *Mailing Add:* Univ Va Hosp Box 386 Charlottesville VA 22908-0001

KELLY, THOMAS J, MOLECULAR BIOLOGY. *Current Pos:* from asst prof to assoc prof microbiol, 72-79, PROF MOLECULAR BIOL & GENETICS, JOHNS HOPKINS UNIV, SCH MED, 81-, CHMN DEPT, 82- *Personal Data:* b Birmingham Al, Nov 21, 41; m 69; c 2. *Educ:* Johns Hopkins Univ, BA, 62, PhD(biophys), 68, MD, 69. *Prof Exp:* Staff assoc, NIH, 70-72. *Concurrent Pos:* Mem, Virol Study Sect, NIH, 80-84, chmn, 88-90; bd dirs, Passano Found, 87-; NIH career develop award, 72-77; mem, Awards Assembly, Gen Motors Cancer Prize, 86-89, Bd Sci Counr, Nat Ctr Biotechnol Info; Harvey Soc lectr, 90. *Mem:* Am Soc Microbiol; Am Soc Biol Chemists; Am Soc Virol; fel Am Acad Arts & Sci. *Res:* Molecular genetics of animal cells & viruses. *Mailing Add:* Dept Molecular Biol & Genetics Johns Hopkins Univ Sch Med 603 PCTB 725 N Wolfe St Baltimore MD 21205-2105. *Fax:* 410-955-0831

KELLY, THOMAS JOSEPH, AEROSPACE ENGINEERING, INFORMATION RESOURCE MANAGEMENT. *Current Pos:* RETIRED. *Personal Data:* b Brooklyn, NY, June 14, 29; m 51; c 6. *Educ:* Cornell Univ, BME, 51; Columbia Univ, MSME, 56; Mass Inst Technol, MS in IM, 70. *Hon Degrees:* DSc, State Univ NY, 83. *Honors & Awards:* Cert Appreciation, NASA, 69, Distinguished Pub Serv Medal, 73; Spacecraft Design Award, 73, fel, Am Inst Aeronaut & Astronaut. *Prof Exp:* Propulsion engr, Rigel Missile prog, Grumman Aerospace Corp, 51-53, group leader jet air induction, 53-56; performance engr, Wright Patterson AFB, 56-58; group leader rocket propulsion, Lockheed Aircraft Corp, 58-59; asst chief propulsion, Grumman Aeorspace Corp, 59-60, eng proj leader, Apollo & Lunar Module Studies & Proposals, 60-62, proj engr, eng mgr & dep prog mgr, Lunar Module Prog, 62-70, dep dir, Space Shuttle Prog, 70-72, dir space progs, 72-76, vpres eng, 76-81, vpres tech opers, 81-86, vpres IRM, Data Systs Div, 86- *Concurrent Pos:* Mem NASA panel on space vehicles, Res & Technol Adv Coun, 75-77; mem, Aeronaut & Space Eng Bd Ad Hoc Comt Technol Large Space Syst, Nat Res Coun, 78. *Mem:* Nat Acad Eng; Am Soc Mech Engrs; Am Inst Aeronaut & Astronaut. *Res:* Development of manned spacecraft; engineering effort of Project Apollo Lunar Module; development and production engineering of a variety of military aircraft; information systems planning. *Mailing Add:* 1050 W Cove Rd Cutchogue NY 11935

KELLY, THOMAS MICHAEL, PHYSICS, SOLID STATE SCIENCE. *Current Pos:* sr res physicist, Eastman Kodak Res Labs, 68-74, res assoc, 74-88, lab head, 82-84, asst div dir, 84-88, vpres & dir res develop, 88-93, DIR SPEC PROJ, DIGIT PROD CTR, EASTMAN KODAK RES LABS, 94- *Personal Data:* b Watertown, NY, May 16, 41; m 62, Ann Hanrattly; c Mary A, John & T Michael. *Educ:* Le Moyne Col, NY, BS, 62; Wayne State Univ, PhD(physics), 66. *Prof Exp:* AEC res assoc positron annihilation, New Eng Inst Med Res, 66-68. *Mem:* Inst Elec & Electronics Engrs. *Res:* Physics of solid state imaging; design and fabrication. *Mailing Add:* Eastman Kodak Co 901 Elmgrove Rd Rochester NY 14653-9053

KELLY, THOMAS ROSS, ORGANIC CHEMISTRY. *Current Pos:* from asst prof to prof, 69-89, VANDERSLICE PROF CHEM, BOSTON COL, 89- *Personal Data:* b New York, NY, Apr 26, 42; c 2. *Educ:* Col of the Holy Cross, BS, 64; Univ Calif, Berkeley, PhD(org chem), 68. *Honors & Awards:* Arthur C Cope Scholar Award, Am Chem Soc, 96. *Prof Exp:* NIH postdoctoral fel, 68-69. *Concurrent Pos:* Res career develop award, NIH, 75-80. *Res:* Organic synthesis; natural products. *Mailing Add:* Dept Chem Boston Col Chestnut Hill MA 02167-3800

KELLY, WALTER JAMES, ORGANIC CHEMISTRY, POLYMER CHEMISTRY. *Current Pos:* staff scientist, Polymer Technol, 78-80, proj engr, 80-81, PROJ MGR, FOIL DIV, GOULD INC, 81- *Personal Data:* b Cleveland, Ohio, Feb 25, 41; m 71. *Educ:* Case Inst Technol, BS, 63, Case Western Reserve Univ, PhD(phys org chem), 70. *Prof Exp:* Sr res chemist, Polymer Res, Goodyear Tire & Rubber Co, 69-78. *Mem:* Am Chem Soc; Electrochemical Soc. *Res:* Dynamic properties of elastomers; structure-property correlations; polymer rheology and processing; crosslinking mechanisms; post polymerization reactions; adhesion, polymer modification electrodeposition. *Mailing Add:* 1545 Forest Lane Marion IN 46952-9810

KELLY, WILLIAM ALBERT, NEUROSURGERY. *Current Pos:* resident, 57-59, chief resident & clin asst, 60-61, from instr to assoc prof, 61-77, PROF NEUROSURG, UNIV WASH, 77- *Personal Data:* b Cincinnati, Ohio, July 16, 27; m 52; c 2. *Educ:* Ohio Wesleyan Univ, BA, 50; Univ Cincinnati, MD, 54. *Prof Exp:* Res fel neurosurg, Univ Chicago Clins, 56-57. *Concurrent Pos:* Res fel, Univ Wash, 59-60. *Mem:* Am Asn Neurol Surg. *Res:* Pituitary tumors; medical education on student and resident level. *Mailing Add:* Dept Neurol Surg Univ Wash Sch Med R1-20 Seattle WA 98195

KELLY, WILLIAM ALVA, VETERINARY PATHOLOGY. *Current Pos:* SR VET PATHOLOGIST, BRISTOL MYERS SQUIBB, 87- *Personal Data:* b Cullman, Ala, Feb 24, 37; div; c 5. *Educ:* Auburn Univ, DVM, 62; Purdue Univ, PhD(vet path), 71. *Prof Exp:* Vet, pvt pract, 62-66; instr vet path, Purdue Univ, 66-70; vet pathologist, Mead Johnson & Co, 70-81. *Mem:* Am Col Vet Pathologists; Int Acad Path. *Res:* Experimental toxicologic pathology; pathology of laboratory animals; nutritionally-induced pathology; chemical carcinogenesis. *Mailing Add:* 3249 Lower New Harmony Rd Mt Vernon IN 47620

KELLY, WILLIAM CARY, VEGETABLE CROPS. *Current Pos:* assoc prof, 52-55, prof, Dept Veg Crops, 55-84, EMER PROF, CORNELL UNIV, 84- *Personal Data:* b Memphis, Tenn, June 14, 19; m 42; c 4. *Educ:* Univ Tenn, BS, 40; Ohio State Univ, MS, 41; Cornell Univ, PhD(veg crops), 45. *Prof Exp:* Asst, Ohio State Univ, 40-41 & Cornell Univ, 42-45; assoc agronomist, Plant Soil & Nutrit Lab, USDA, 45-46; horticulturist, 46-52. *Concurrent Pos:* Vis prof, Univ Philippines, 59-60. *Mem:* Fel AAAS; Am Soc Hort Sci; fel Am Soc Plant Physiol; Sigma Xi. *Res:* Plant growth and development; yield and composition of vegetables as influenced by environment and mineral nutrition. *Mailing Add:* 157 Plant Sci Cornell Univ Ithaca NY 14853

KELLY, WILLIAM CLARK, PHYSICS. *Current Pos:* RETIRED. *Personal Data:* b Braddock, Pa, Mar 18, 22; m 47, Gertrude C Blackwood; c Emily (Szumowski) & William B. *Educ:* Univ Pittsburgh, BS, 43, MS, 46, PhD(physics), 51. *Prof Exp:* From asst to assoc prof physics, Univ Pittsburgh, 46-58; dir dept educ & manpower, Am Inst Physics, 58-65; fel officer, Nat Acad Sci-Nat Res Coun, 65-67, dir off sci personnel, 67-74; exec dir comn human resources, Nat Res Coun, 74-83; spec asst, Am Assn Physics Teachers, 84-89. *Concurrent Pos:* Ford fac fel, 54-55; mem subcomt prof sci & technol manpower, Dept Labor, 71-72; secy comn physics educ, Int Union Pure & Appl Physics, 66-72, chmn, 72-75; mem coun on teaching sci, Int Coun Sci Unions, 75-78. *Mem:* AAAS; Am Asn Physics Teachers. *Res:* Measurement of spectral emissivities of metals; beta and gamma ray spectroscopy; improvements in the teaching of science; manpower studies; human-resource supply and demand, especially in science and engineering. *Mailing Add:* 9320 Renshaw Dr Bethesda MD 20817

KELLY, WILLIAM CROWLEY, ECONOMIC GEOLOGY. *Current Pos:* from instr to assoc prof geol, Univ Mich, Ann Arbor, 56-67, prof geol & mineral, 67-80, prof & chmn geol sci, 80-90, vpres res, 90-93, VPRES, DEPT GEOL, UNIV MICH, ANN ARBOR, 93- *Personal Data:* b Philadelphia, Pa, May 10, 29; m 59. *Educ:* Columbia Univ, AB, 51, MA, 53, PhD(geol), 54. *Prof Exp:* Asst econ geol, Columbia Univ, 51-53; instr geol, Hunter Col, 54; opers analyst, Opers Res Off, Johns Hopkins Univ, 54-56. *Concurrent Pos:* Ed, Geochem News, 61-63. *Mem:* Geol Soc Am; Geochem Soc; Mineral Soc Am; Soc Econ Geol; Geol Soc France. *Res:* Chemical weathering; telluride ore deposits; oxidation of lead-zinc ores; mineralogy of iron oxides; ore microscopy. *Mailing Add:* Dept Geol 1006 CC Little Univ Mich Main Campus 405 E University Ave Ann Arbor MI 48109-1063

KELLY, WILLIAM DANIEL, SURGERY. *Current Pos:* From instr to assoc prof, 53-61, prof surg, 61-80, mem surg staff, 62-80, CLIN PROF SURG, UNIV HOSPS, 80- *Personal Data:* b St Paul, Minn, Oct 28, 22; m 51; c 6. *Educ:* Univ Minn, BS, 43, MB, 45, MD, 46, PhD(surg), 55; Am Bd Surg, dipl, 55; Am Bd Thoracic Surg, dipl, 59. *Concurrent Pos:* Dir exp surg lab, Vet Admin Hosp, Minneapolis, 59-60, chief surg, 60-62. *Mem:* AAAS; Soc Exp Biol & Med; Soc Univ Surgeons; AMA; NY Acad Sci. *Res:* Homotransplantation; cardiovascular physiology and surgery. *Mailing Add:* 3838 Zenith Ave S Minneapolis MN 55410-1167

KELLY, WILLIAM H, EXPERIMENTAL NUCLEAR PHYSICS, PHYSICS PEDAGOGY. *Current Pos:* dean, Col Sci & Humanities, 83-89, PROF PHYSICS, IOWA STATE UNIV, AMES, 83- *Personal Data:* b Rich Hill, Mo, July 2, 26; m 50; c 3. *Educ:* Graceland Col, AA, 48; Univ Mich, BSE, 50, MS, 51, PhD(physics), 55. *Prof Exp:* Asst physics, Eng Res Inst, Univ Mich, 51-54; from asst prof to prof physics, Mich State Univ, 55-79, from assoc chmn to chmn dept, 68-79; prof physics, Mont State Univ, 79-83, dean col letters & sci, 79-83. *Concurrent Pos:* Physicist, Naval Res Lab, 56, Lawrence Radiation Lab, Univ Calif, 61-62, 67-68 & Oak Ridge Nat Lab, 64; mem bd trustees, Graceland Col, 78-90; mem, Spec Adv Comt on medium energy electron accelerator fac, Argonne Univ Asn, 81-83; mem bd trustees, Univ Res Asn; guest scientist, Lawrence Berkeley Lab, 89-90. *Mem:* AAAS; fel Am Phys Soc; Am Asn Physics Teachers (vpres, 79, pres elect, 80, pres, 81); Am Soc Eng Educ. *Res:* Nuclear spectroscopy; nuclear structure; gamma ray spectroscopy; physics pedagogy. *Mailing Add:* Dept Physics & Astron Physics Bldg Iowa State Univ Ames IA 50011

KELLY, WILLIAM ROBERT, GEOCHEMISTRY, ANALYTICAL CHEMISTRY. *Current Pos:* RES CHEMIST ANALYTICAL CHEM, NAT INST STAND & TECHNOL, 79- *Personal Data:* b Norfolk, Va, July 24, 44; m 69; c 1. *Educ:* Old Dominion Col, BS, 68; Ariz State Univ, PhD, 74. *Honors & Awards:* Nininger Meteorite Award, 74; IR100 Award, 84; Outstanding

Support Serv Award, Sigma Xi, 92. *Prof Exp:* Vis assoc geochem, Calif Inst Technol, 75-77, res fel, 77-79. *Mem:* Am Chem Soc; Meteoritical Soc; Geochem Soc; Sigma Xi. *Res:* Cosmochemistry; thermal ionization mass spectrometry; environmental chemistry; analytical chemistry. *Mailing Add:* Anal Chem Div Nat Inst Stand & Technol Gaithersburg MD 20899. *Fax:* 301-869-0413; *E-Mail:* william.kelly@nist.gov

KELLY-FRY, ELIZABETH, BIOACOUSTICS, MEDICAL ULTRASOUND. *Current Pos:* PROF RADIOL, SCH MED, IND UNIV, INDIANAPOLIS, 91-; RES SCIENTIST & PHYSICIST MED ULTRASOUND, INDIANAPOLIS BREAST CTR, 92- *Personal Data:* wid; c 2. *Educ:* Howard Univ, ScM, 53; Sarasota Univ, EdD(sci educ), 75. *Honors & Awards:* Japan Soc US Med Award, 76; Presidential Award, Am Inst Ultrasound Med, 80; World Fedn US Med Award, 88. *Prof Exp:* Biophys Res Lab, Univ Ill, 54-64; assoc dir res, Intersci Res Inst, 64-67, vpres, 68-71; assoc prof surg, Sch Med, Ind Univ, Indianapolis, 72-91, assoc prof radiol, 82-91; res scientist, Ind Ctr Advan Res, 72-92. *Concurrent Pos:* Consult, Bur Radiol Health, 73-81, Ultrasound Corp, 80-86; assoc ed, J Clin Ultrasound, 75-79; consult, Nat Heart, Lung & Blood Inst, NIH, 76-79, Med Physics Dept, Univ Wis, 83-87; mem, NIH Diag Res Adv Comt, 80-81. *Mem:* Am Phys Soc; Acoust Soc Am; Biophys Soc; fel Am Inst Ultrasound Med; Am Asn Univ Prof. *Res:* Ultrasound breast examination; design of ultrasound instrumentation for breast imaging; development of advanced ultrasound imaging techniques for detection of breast. *Mailing Add:* Indianapolis Breast Ctr 1950 W 86th St Indianapolis IN 46260. *Fax:* 317-872-9856

KELMAN, ARTHUR, PHYTOBACTERIOLOGY. *Current Pos:* UNIV DISTINGUISHED SCHOLAR, NC STATE UNIV, 90- *Personal Data:* b Providence, RI, Dec 11, 18; m 49; c 1. *Educ:* Univ RI, BS, 41; NC State Univ, MS, 46, PhD(plant path), 49. *Hon Degrees:* DSc, Univ RI, 77. *Honors & Awards:* Fel Award, Am Phytopath Soc, 69, Award of Distinction, 83; Stakman Award, 87. *Prof Exp:* From instr to prof plant path, NC State Univ, 48-62, Reynolds distinguished prof, 62-65; prof & chmn dept, Univ Wis-Madison, 65-75, L R Jones distinguished prof, 75-85, prof bact, 78-89, Wis Alumni Res Found sr distinguished prof plant path, 85-89. *Concurrent Pos:* Vis investr, Rockefeller Inst, 53-54; vis lectr, Am Inst Biol Sci, 58-60; NSF sr fel, Cambridge Univ, 71-72, vis prof, Dept Biochem, 71-72; mem US nat comt, Int Union Biol Sci; chmn, Sect Appl Biol & Agr Sci, Comn Life Sci, 81-83, Bd Basic Biol, 84-85; chmn, Div Biol Sci, Assembly Life Sci, Nat Res Coun, 81-84; coun, Nat Acad Sci, 86-89; chmn, Class VI, Appl Biol & Agr Sci, Nat Acad Sci, 88-91. *Mem:* Nat Acad Sci; Am Acad Arts & Sci; Am Inst Biol Sci; Soc Gen Microbiol; hon mem Int Soc Plant Path (vpres, 68-73, pres, 73-78); Am Phytopath Soc (vpres, 66, pres, 67); fel AAAS; Sigma Xi. *Res:* Physiology of parasitism; bacterial diseases of plants; nature of resistance to bacterial soft rot of potatoes. *Mailing Add:* Dept Plant Path NC State Univ PO Box 7616 Raleigh NC 27695-7616

KELMAN, BRUCE JERRY, TERATOLOGY, COMPARATIVE TOXICOLOGY. *Current Pos:* DEPT TOXICOL, FAILURE ANALYSIS ASSOC, 90- *Personal Data:* b Chicago, Ill, July 1, 47; m 72. *Educ:* Univ Ill, BS, 69, MS, 71, PhD(vet med sci); 75; Am Bd Toxicol, cert, 80, 85. *Prof Exp:* Res asst physiol, Univ Ill, 69-74; res assoc toxicol, Comp Animal Res Lab, Oak Ridge, Tenn, 74-76, asst prof prenatal toxicol, 76-79; sr res scientist develop toxicol, Pac Northwest Labs, Battelle Mem Inst, 79-80, assoc mgr, 80-81 & 83-84, mgr, 81-84, mgr biol & chem dept, 85-90. *Mem:* Soc Toxicol; Soc Exp Biol & Med; Teratol Soc; Am Soc Pharmacol & Exp Therapeut; Am Physiol Soc; Am Acad Vet & Comp Toxicol. *Res:* Toxicology of chemicals (including chemical mixtures and metals) and radiation; teratology and other developmental effects of toxic materials including radionuclides; transplacental movements of materials; toxicology of electrical and magnetic fields. *Mailing Add:* Dept Health & Environ Sci Golder Assoc Inc 4104 148th Ave NE Redmond WA 98052. *Fax:* 650-328-2981

KELMAN, CHARLES D, OPHTHALMOLOGY. *Current Pos:* OPHTHALMOLOGIST, MANHATTAN EYE, EAR, NOSE & THROAT, 67-; NY EYE & EAR INFIRMARY, 83-; CLIN PROF, NY MED COL, VALHALLA, 80- *Personal Data:* b Brooklyn, NY, May 23, 30; m, Ann Gur-Arie; c Evan A, David, Lesley & Jennifer. *Educ:* Tufts Univ, BS, 50; Univ Geneva, BMS, 52, MD, 56; Am Bd Ophthalmol, dipl. *Honors & Awards:* Outstanding Achievement Award, Am Soc Contemporary Ophthal, 81; Physicians Recognition Award, AMA; Can Implant Asn Award, 82; 1st Ann Innovators Award, Am Inst Intraocular Lens Cong, 85; Binkhorst Medal, Am Soc Cataract & Refractive Surg, 89; Ridley Medal, Int Congress Ophthal, 90; Special Recognition Award, Am Acad Ophthal; Arthur J Bedell Mem Lectr, 91; Nat Medal Technol, 92. *Prof Exp:* Intern, Kings Co Hosp, NY, 56-57; resident, Wills Eye Hosp, Pa, 56-60,. *Mem:* Fel Am Acad Ophthal; Am Med Asn; Int Asn Ocular Surg; Am Intraocular Implant Soc; Am Soc Contemporary Ophthal; Am Soc Cataracts & Refractive Surg (pres-elect). *Res:* Ophthalmology; author of 4 publications. *Mailing Add:* 220 Madison Ave New York NY 10016

KELMAN, L(EROY) R, ENGINEERING OF MATERIALS FOR NUCLEAR POWER. *Current Pos:* RETIRED. *Personal Data:* b Minneapolis, Minn, Aug 16, 19; m 84, Elizabeth Belk; c Bruce, Keith & Scott. *Educ:* Univ Minn, BS, 42. *Prof Exp:* Metallurgist, Caterpillar Tractor Co, 42-44; metallurgist anal, Argonne Nat Lab, 44-59, group leader, Metall Div, 47-66, mgr fuels & mat sect, Liquid Metal Fast Breeder Reactor Prog Off, 66-70, prog planner, Mat Sci Div, 70-73, proj leader & prog coodr, Safety of Light Water Reactor Fuels, 75-78, sr metallurgist, 59-89. *Mem:* Am Nuclear Soc; Am Soc Metals; Am Inst Mining, Metall & Petrol Engrs; Sigma Xi. *Res:* Metallurgy for nuclear reactors; fuels, structural materials and liquid metal coolants; behavior of nuclear fuels and structural materials under transient and hypothetical accident conditions; materials behavior in liquid metal coolants. *Mailing Add:* 1030 E Prairie Ave Naperville IL 60540

KELMAN, LORI MACELLARO, HISTONE GENE TRANSCRIPTION. *Current Pos:* Asst prof, 91-96, ASSOC PROF BIOL, IONA COL, 96- *Personal Data:* b New York, NY, May 16, 60; m 96, Zvi. *Educ:* Mt Holyoke Col, AB, 82; St Johns Univ, MS, 84; Cornell Univ, PhD(molecular biol), 94. *Concurrent Pos:* Sci writer, Online Mendelian Inheritance in Man, 96- *Mem:* AAAS; Asn Women Sci. *Res:* New developments in molecular biology that effect knowledge about human genes and diseases. *Mailing Add:* Iona Col 715 North Ave New Rochelle NY 10801. *Fax:* 914-633-2240

KELMAN, ROBERT BERNARD, MATHEMATICS, COMPUTER SCIENCE. *Current Pos:* DIR, KLMN CONSULT, 88-; OWNER, HEEL & TOE PUBL, 94- *Personal Data:* b Ansonia, Conn, Aug 12, 30; m 57; c Karl & Daniel. *Educ:* Univ Calif, Berkeley, AB, 53, MA, 55, PhD(math), 58. *Prof Exp:* Comput engr, NAm Aviation, Inc, 55-56; instr, Univ Ill, 57-58; mathematician, Int Bus Mach Corp, 58-61; mgr biomath res, Univac Div, Sperry Rand Corp, 61-63; res asst prof math, Univ Md, 63-66; assoc prof math, Colo State Univ, 66-68, prof comput sci, 72-88, chmn, 81-88; assoc prof prev med, Univ Colo Med Ctr, 67-72, prof, 72-80. *Concurrent Pos:* Lectr, Howard Univ, 61-65; consult, Exec Off President Eisenhower, 60-61. *Mem:* Fel AAAS; Math Asn Am; Soc Indust & Appl Math; Am Soc Nephrology. *Res:* Differential equations; theoretical renal physiology; computer modeling. *Mailing Add:* 1312 Robertson St Ft Collins CO 80524. *Fax:* 970-482-0974; *E-Mail:* klmn@compuserve.com

KELNER, ALBERT, biology; deceased, see previous edition for last biography

KELNHOFER, WILLIAM JOSEPH, MECHANICAL ENGINEERING, FLUID MECHANICS. *Current Pos:* from instr to assoc prof, 60-73, dept chmn, 83-92, ORD PROF MECH ENG, CATH UNIV AM, 73- *Personal Data:* b Manitowoc, Wis, Nov 24, 30. *Educ:* Marquette Univ, BME, 56; Cath Univ, MME, 60, DEng, 66. *Prof Exp:* Proj engr, US Navy Bur Ships, 56-59. *Concurrent Pos:* Prin investr, US Navy contract, 62-68; assoc, US Army contract, 63-64; prin investr, Off Naval Res contract, 66 & Nat Bur Stand contracts, 77-; res prof, Max Planck Inst, Goettingen, 66-67 & Munich Tech Univ, 69-70. *Mem:* Am Soc Mech Engrs; Nat Soc Prof Engrs; Am Soc Heating, Refrig & Air Conditioning Engrs; Sigma Xi. *Res:* Heat transfer; boundary layer theory; thermal systems; energy conservation; applied thermodynamics. *Mailing Add:* Dept Mech Eng Cath Univ Washington DC 20017

KELSAY, JUNE LAVELLE, NUTRITION. *Current Pos:* RETIRED. *Personal Data:* b Jacksboro, Tex, June 29, 25. *Educ:* NTex State Univ, BS, 46, MS, 47; Univ Wis, PhD(foods & nutrit), 67. *Honors & Awards:* Borden Award, Am Home Econ Asn, 82. *Prof Exp:* Instr nutrit, NTex State Univ, 47-50; technician nutrit res, Tex Agr Exp Sta, 51-52; nutrit specialist, USDA, 54-62, res nutritionist, Agr Res Serv, 67-87. *Mem:* Am Inst Nutrit; Am Soc Clin Nutrit; Am Home Econ Asn. *Res:* Preadolescent children; folic and pantothenic acid; vitamin B-6 deficiency in man; effect of protein level; forms of vitamin B-6; excretion of niacin metabolites; nutritional status; carbohydrate response in human subjects; effects of fiber in human subjects; mineral balances; oxalic acid and mineral bioavailability; fiber and nutrient intakes. *Mailing Add:* 10401 Grosvenor Pl No 1315 Rockville MD 20852

KELSEY, CHARLES ANDREW, MEDICAL PHYSICS. *Current Pos:* chief biomed physics, 75-80, PROF RADIOL, UNIV NMEX, 75- *Personal Data:* b Norfolk, Nebr, July 9, 35; m 60; c 4. *Educ:* St Edward's Col, BS, 57; Univ Notre Dame, PhD(physics), 62; Am Bd Radiol, dipl. *Prof Exp:* Res assoc physics, Univ Notre Dame, 62; res assoc, Univ Wis-Madison, 62-63, from instr to asst prof physics, 63-65, from asst prof to prof radiol, 65-75. *Mem:* AAAS; Am Phys Soc; Am Acad Phys Med & Rehab; Am Inst Ultrasonics in Med; Radiol Soc NAm; fel Am Col Radiol. *Res:* Application of physics technology to medical problems. *Mailing Add:* Dept Radiol Univ NMex Med Sch 1 Univ Campus Albuquerque NM 87131-0001

KELSEY, DONALD ROSS, HIGH PERFORMANCE POLYMERS, RING-OPENING METATHESIS POLYMERIZATIONS. *Current Pos:* sr res chemist, 87-95, STAFF RES CHEMIST, SHELL DEVELOP CO, 95- *Personal Data:* b Windsor, Mo, Sept 30, 45. *Educ:* Cent Mo State Univ, BS, 68; Calif Inst Technol, PhD(phys orgchem), 73. *Prof Exp:* Fel, Chem Dept, Yale Univ, 72-74; chemist, Union Carbide Corp, 74-77, proj scientist, 77-78, res scientist, 78-84, sr res scientist, 84-86; sr res scientist, Amoco Peformance Prod, Inc, 86-87. *Mem:* Am Chem Soc; Am Inst Chem. *Res:* Design and synthesis of polymers and polymerization catalysts; polyarylethers, ring-opening metathesis polymers, polyesters; mechanisms of nucleophilic displacement and aryl coupling reactions, orbital topology analysis of thermal reactions; granted 44 US patents and publications. *Mailing Add:* PO Box 1380 Houston TX 77441

KELSEY, EDWARD JOSEPH, SOFTWARE SYSTEMS, ATOMIC & MOLECULAR PHYSICS. *Current Pos:* MEM TECH STAFF COMPUT SCI, AT&T BELL LABS, 79- *Personal Data:* b Washington, DC, Dec 10, 48. *Educ:* Wesleyan Univ, BA, 70; Univ Md, MS, 72, PhD(physics), 74. *Prof Exp:* Res assoc physics, Univ Nebr, Lincoln, 74-76; assoc res scientist, NY Univ, 76-78. *Mem:* Am Phys Soc; Asn Comput Mach. *Res:* Quantum electrodynamic theory applied to problems concerning one and two electron systems; operation systems which maintain and test the telephone network. *Mailing Add:* 26 Malibu Dr Eatontown NJ 07724

KELSEY, EUGENE LLOYD, ELECTRICAL ENGINEERING, AERO-SPACE ENGINEERING. *Current Pos:* RETIRED. *Personal Data:* b Ponca City, Okla, May 10, 32; m 73; c 2. *Educ:* Okla State Univ, BSEE, 58; Va Polytech Inst, MSEE, 66. *Prof Exp:* Jr engr guidance, Autonetics-NAm Aviation, 56-57; test engr B-58 radar guidance, Gen Dynamics, Fort Worth, 58-62; aerospace technologist, NASA, 62-72, eng supvr systs develop-elec flight systs, 72-94. *Concurrent Pos:* Adj instr math, Christopher Newport Col, 76-79. *Mem:* Soc Automotive Engrs-Aerospace. *Res:* Design, development and analysis of aerospace stabilization control and pointing systems for aircraft, satellite and research projects; unique requirements-unique solutions. *Mailing Add:* 101 McClellan Ct Yorktown VA 23692

KELSEY, FRANCES OLDHAM, PHARMACOLOGY. *Current Pos:* DIR, DIV SCI INVEST, OFF SCI COMPLIANCE, CTR DRUG EVAL & RES, DEPT HEALTH & HUMAN SERV, FOOD & DRUG ADMIN, 60- *Personal Data:* b Cobble Hill, BC, Can, July 24, 14; nat US; m 43; c 2. *Educ:* McGill Univ, BSc, 34, MSc, 35; Univ Chicago, PhD(pharmacol), 38, MD, 50. *Hon Degrees:* DSc, Hood Col, 62, Univ NB, 64, Western Col Women, 64, Middlebury Col, 66, Wilson Col, 67, St Mary's Col, 69, Drexel Univ, 73, McGill Univ, 84 & Univ SDak, 82. *Prof Exp:* Asst prof pharmacol, Univ Chicago, 46; assoc prof med, Sch Med, Univ SDak, 54-57; pvt pract, 57-60. *Concurrent Pos:* Lederle award, 54-57. *Mem:* Am Soc Pharmacol & Exp Therapeut; Soc Exp Biol & Med; Teratol Soc; Am Women Sci; Am Med Writers' Asn; Sigma Xi. *Res:* Posterior pituitary; chemotherapy of malaria; radioisotopes. *Mailing Add:* 5811 Brookside Dr Chevy Chase MD 20815-6669

KELSEY, JOHN EDWARD, SCIENTIFIC INFORMATION, ENVIRONMENTAL HEALTH. *Current Pos:* RETIRED. *Personal Data:* b Beloit, Wis, Oct 28, 42; m 65; c 3. *Educ:* Univ Wis, BS, 65, PhD(pharm chem), 69. *Prof Exp:* Nat Cancer Inst overseas fel, 68-70; res chemist, Burroughs Wellcome Co, Inc, 70-74; sr res chemist, 75-78; dir occup health, 78-80; dir, Tech Serv Div, 81-84; dir tech & admin opers, 84-94. *Mem:* Am Chem Soc; Am Indust Health Coun. *Res:* Management of science information, automation, administration, radiation, and unit facilities services functions in the pharmaceutical research, development and manufacturing industry. *Mailing Add:* 106 Greenock Ct Cary NC 27511

KELSEY, MORRIS IRWIN, IMMUNOLOGY. *Current Pos:* sect head chem carcinogenesis prog, 75-80, exec secy, Exp Therapeut Study Sect, Div Res Grants, 85-89, ASST COORDR ENVIRON CANCER, NAT CANCER INST, NIH, 80-, PROG DIR, BIOL RESPONSE MODIFIERS PROG, 89- *Personal Data:* b Easton, Pa, Aug 14, 39; m 64; c 2. *Educ:* Lehigh Univ, BA, 61; Univ Mass, MS, 64; Univ Pittsburgh, PhD(biochem), 69. *Prof Exp:* Chemist starch chem, Nat Starch & Chem Corp, 63-65; asst prof biochem, Mo Inst Psychiat, 71-73; sr scientist, Frederick Cancer Res Ctr, 73-75. *Concurrent Pos:* Fel biochem, St Louis Univ, 69-71; adj asst prof, Univ Mo, 72-73; adj assoc prof agr biochem, WVa Univ, 77-79. *Mem:* Am Chem Soc; AAAS; Sigma Xi; Am Soc Biol Chemists. *Res:* Biotransformation of neutral sterols and bile acids by enterohepatic enzyme systems; effects of metabolism of endogenous steroid metabolites on the metabolic activation of chemical carcinogens; mechanism of action of chemotherapeutic agents. *Mailing Add:* NCI FCRDC Bldg 1052 Rm 253 Frederick MD 21702-1201. *Fax:* 301-846-5429

KELSEY, RICK G, PLANT CHEMISTRY, FOREST HEALTH. *Current Pos:* RES SCIENTIST, PNW RES STA, USDA FOREST SERV, 89- *Personal Data:* b Libby, Mont, Aug 14, 48; m 82; c 4. *Educ:* Univ Mont, BS, 70, PhD(forestry), 74. *Prof Exp:* res assoc plant chem, Wood Chem Lab, 74-80; from res asst prof to res assoc prof, Dept Chem, Univ Mont, 81-86; res assoc prof, Entomol Dept, Ore State Univ, 86-89. *Concurrent Pos:* Prin investr, McKnight Found Individual Award in plant biol, 83-86. *Mem:* NAm Phytochem Soc; AAAS. *Res:* Isolation and identification of plant allelochemicals, their physiological and ecological function in forest health and their potential use to man. *Mailing Add:* PNW Res Sta USDA Forest Serv 3200 Jefferson Way Corvallis OR 97331. *Fax:* 541-750-7329

KELSEY, RONALD A(LBERT), MATERIALS SCIENCE ENGINEERING. *Current Pos:* RETIRED. *Personal Data:* b Oakville, Conn, Mar 29, 23; m 47, Rita A Busch; c Mark C, David H & Peter A. *Educ:* Polytech Inst Brooklyn, BS, 49; Carnegie Inst Technol, MS, 52. *Prof Exp:* Res engr, Alcoa Res Labs, Aluminum Co Am, 49-55; nuclear engr, Gen Dynamics Corp, 49-55, sr res engr, 60-70, eng assoc, 70-74, sect head, 74-81, sr tech specialist, 81-83. *Concurrent Pos:* Chmn, Aluminum Alloys Comn, Welding Res Coun, 68-84; mem, Joint USA/USSR Comn on Properties of Welds for Low Temp Appln, 75-81; chmn, Int Comt Fatigue Data Exchange & Eval, 80-84; mem, Tech Adv Comt Metals Prop Coun, 80-83; pres, Seniors Helping Seniors, Inc, 90-95. *Mem:* Soc Exp Stress Anal; fel Am Soc Metals; Am Welding Soc. *Res:* Deformation and fracture mechanics of materials and structures; development of metal deformation process; armor development. *Mailing Add:* 27 Naushon N Rd Falmouth MA 02540

KELSEY, RUBEN CLIFFORD, COMPARATIVE ENDOCRINOLOGY. *Current Pos:* RETIRED. *Personal Data:* b Park Falls, Wis, May 26, 23; m 60, Margaret Doggett; c Janet I & Leonard D. *Educ:* Univ Wis, PhB, 49, MS, 50, PhD(zool), 59. *Prof Exp:* Sr res scientist biochem, Smith, Kline & French Labs, 59-63; asst prof biol sci, Drexel Inst Technol, 63-68; head dept, E Stroudsburg Univ, 68-74 & 80-83, prof biol, 68-88. *Mem:* AAAS; Am Soc Zool; Am Inst Biol Sci. *Res:* Physiology of mammalian reproduction; function. *Mailing Add:* 51 Club Ct Stroudsburg PA 18360

KELSEY, STEPHEN JORGENSEN, DESIGN & DEVELOPMENT, CONSTRUCTION OF CHEMICAL PLANTS. *Current Pos:* MGR ENG, THATCHER CO, SALT LAKE CITY, UTAH, 78- *Personal Data:* b Salt Lake City, Utah, Jan 15, 40; m 65, Justine Goddard; c Lydia K (Creager), Richard, Bruce, Mary & Julie. *Educ:* Univ Utah, BSChE, 65, MES, 69, PhD(chem eng), 71. *Prof Exp:* Process engr, Celanese Chem Co, Pampa, Tex, 65-66; GS-4, GS-9, US Bur Mines, Salt Lake City, Utah, 66-67; asst res prof, Div Mat Sci Mech Eng, Col Eng, Univ Utah, 71-76, asst res prof, Div Artificial Surg, Organs, Col Med, 71-76, assoc res prof, Computer Sci, Dept Elec Eng, Col Eng, 71-76; plant supt, Wasatch Chem Co, Salt Lake City, Utah, 76-78. *Mem:* Am Inst Chem Engrs. *Res:* Numerical analysis; chlorine and sulfur dioxide handling and facility design; sulfur dioxide manufacturing; plant design and construction. *Mailing Add:* 5368 Cottonwood Club Dr Salt Lake City UT 84117. *Fax:* 801-972-4606

KELSH, DENNIS J, PHYSICAL CHEMISTRY. *Current Pos:* from instr to assoc prof, Gonzaga Univ, 62-72, chmn dept, 68-74, 81-86 & 89-90, prof, 72-93, PROF CHEM & CHAIR, GONZAGA UNIV, 97- *Personal Data:* b Valley City, NDak, Dec 24, 36. *Educ:* St John's Univ, Minn, BA & BS, 58; Iowa State Univ, PhD(phys chem), 62. *Prof Exp:* Sr chemist, Sci Appl Int Corp, 93-96. *Concurrent Pos:* Res chemist, Spokane Mining Res Ctr, US Bur Mines, 65-93; assoc res scientist, NY Univ, 66-67; Am Coun Educ fel acad admin & spec asst to dean, Grad Sch, Wash State Univ, 74-75; coun mem, Am Chem Soc, 74-91; vis scientist, Univ Wash, 85; scientist in residence, US Dept Energy Hq, 91-92. *Mem:* Am Chem Soc; AAAS. *Res:* Electrical properties of surfaces; adsorption from solution; solid-liquid separations by electrokinetics; electrokinetic remediation of soils. *Mailing Add:* Dept Chem Gonzaga Univ E 502 Boone Ave Box 13 Spokane WA 99258. *E-Mail:* kelsh@barney.gonzaga.edu

KELSO, ALBERT FREDERICK, PHYSIOLOGY. *Current Pos:* RETIRED. *Personal Data:* b Ft Wayne, Ind, Nov 19, 17; m 43; c 3. *Educ:* George Williams Col, BA, 43, MS, 46; Loyola Univ, PhD, 59. *Hon Degrees:* DSc, Kirksville Col Osteop & Surg, 70. *Honors & Awards:* Louisa Burns Mem Lectr, 81; Guttensohn-Denslow Prize, 84; Phillips Medal Honor. *Prof Exp:* Instr physiol, George Williams Col, 46-47; from instr to prof physiol, Chicago Col Osteop Med, 46-90, actg chmn dept, 54-59, chmn dept, 58-90, dir res affairs, 76-90. *Concurrent Pos:* Consult, Nat Bd Osteopath Exam, 65-78; res consult, Am Acad Osteop; educ consult, Am Osteopath Asn. *Mem:* AAAS; Am Physiol Soc; Soc Exp Biol & Med; Am Heart Asn; Inst Elec & Electronics Eng; Sigma Xi. *Res:* Sensorimotor performance; circulation; tissue respiration; family medicine theory and practice. *Mailing Add:* Chicago Col Osteop Med 15443 University Dolton IL 60419-2728

KELSO, ALEC JOHN (JACK), PHYSICAL ANTHROPOLOGY. *Current Pos:* From instr to assoc prof anthrop, 58-75, chmn dept, 63-68 & 71-81, dir, Semester at Sea Prog, 78-79, PROF ANTHROP, UNIV COLO, BOULDER, 75- *Personal Data:* b Chicago, Ill, Dec 5, 30; m 51; c 2. *Educ:* Northern Ill Univ, BS, 52; Univ Mich, MA, 54, PhD, 58. *Concurrent Pos:* Consult, Coun Grad Schs US, 64-78; mem training comt, Nat Inst Child Health & Human Develop, 64-66; NIH spec fel, Univ Hawaii, 65-66; distinguished vis prof, Ore State Univ, 71; vchancellor acad affairs, Univ Colo, Colorado Springs, 75-77; dir, Farrand Hall Residential Acad Prog, 83-88; chmn biol unit, Am Anthrop Asn, 85-87; dir, Young Scholars Summer Session, 85-89, Honors Prog, 88-; Presidents Teaching Scholar, 90. *Mem:* Am Anthrop Asn; Am Asn Phys Anthropologists (vpres, 72-74). *Res:* Selection and blood groups; human sexuality; healthy people. *Mailing Add:* Dept Anthrop Univ Colo Box 233 Boulder CO 80309-0233

KELSO, DONALD PRESTON, MARINE ECOLOGY. *Current Pos:* Asst prof, 70-77, ASSOC PROF BIOL, GEORGE MASON UNIV, 77- *Personal Data:* b Pulaski, Va, Aug 12, 40; m 63; c 2. *Educ:* Univ Tenn, Knoxville, BS, 62; Univ Fla, MS, 65; Univ Hawaii, PhD(zool), 70. *Mem:* Am Inst Biol Sci; Am Soc Zool; Ecol Soc Am. *Res:* Inshore marine ecology; evolution of echinoderms; reproductive cycles of tropical animals. *Mailing Add:* Dept Biol George Mason Univ 4400 University Dr Fairfax VA 22030-4443

KELSO, EDWARD ALBERT, petroleum chemistry; deceased, see previous edition for last biography

KELSO, JOHN MORRIS, RADIO PHYSICS. *Current Pos:* RETIRED. *Personal Data:* b Punxsutawney, Pa, Mar 12, 22; m 45; c 1. *Educ:* Gettysburg Col, AB, 43; Pa State Univ, MS, 45, PhD(physics), 49. *Prof Exp:* Instr physics, Pa State Univ, 43-45, asst, 45-48, eng res assoc, 48-49, from asst prof to assoc prof eng res, 49-54; eval specialist, Martin Co, 54-55; mem tech staff, Ramo-Wooldridge, Inc, 55-58 & Space Tech Labs, 58-62; dir res, Electro-Physics Labs, ACF Indust, Inc, 62-66; dir res, ITT Electro-Physics Lab, Inc, 66-68, vpres & dir res, 68-75; consult, Off Telecommun Policy, Exec Off of the President, 76-78; chief scientist, Signal Anal Ctr, Honeywell Inc, Annapolis, MD, 78-87. *Concurrent Pos:* Vis observer, Chalmers Univ Technol, Sweden, 51-52; mem, Arecibo Eval Panel, 67-69; mem comn III & US del numerous Gen Assemblies, Int Union Radio Sci, chmn Comn G, 73-75; mem, US Nat Comt, 73-78. *Mem:* Am Geophys Union; Am Phys Soc; fel Inst Elec & Electronics Eng. *Res:* Radio wave propagation; ionospheric physics; space vehicle instrumentation; systems engineering; operational evaluation of weapon systems; space physics; electricity and magnetism. *Mailing Add:* 7801 Sylvan Dr Hudson FL 34667

KELSO, JOHN RICHARD MURRAY, ENVIRONMENTAL SCIENCE. *Current Pos:* RES SCIENTIST, CAN DEPT FISHERIES & OCEANS, 73- *Personal Data:* b Kingston, Ont, Feb 9, 45; m 66; c 2. *Educ:* Univ Guelph, BSc, 67, MSc, 69; Univ Man, PhD(zool), 71. *Honors & Awards:* Chandler-Misener Award, Int Asn Great Lakes Res, 82. *Prof Exp:* Dir, Nanticoke Proj, Ont Ministry Natural Resources, 71-73. *Concurrent Pos:* Assoc ed, Can J Fishery Aquatic Sci, 88- *Mem:* Can Soc Zoologists; Am Fisheries Soc; Int Asn Great Lakes Res. *Res:* Effects of environmental perturbations and natural factors on the community structure, biomass and production of freshwater fish communities. *Mailing Add:* Great Lakes Lab Fisheries & Aquatic Sci Can Dept Fisheries & Oceans One Canal Dr Sault St Marie ON P6A 6W4 Can

KELSO, RICHARD MILES, HEATING VENTILATION & AIR CONDITIONING, BUILDING SYSTEMS. *Current Pos:* mech engr, Facil Planning, 71-76, PROF ENVIRON CONTROLS, SCH ARCHIT, UNIV TENN, 76- *Personal Data:* b Knoxville, Tenn, Jan 20, 37; m 60; c Suzanne S (Logan), Richard A & Robert M. *Educ:* Univ Tenn, BS, 60, MS, 61. *Prof Exp:* Sales engr, Trane Corp, 60-68; vpres, George S Campbell & Assoc, 68-71. *Concurrent Pos:* Pres, Richard Kelso & Assoc, Consult Engrs, 74-89 & Kelso-Regen Assoc, Consult Engrs, 89-; coun mem, Am Soc Heating Refrig & Air Conditioning Engrs, 95-97; mem, Bd Assessment, Bldg & Fire Res Panel, Nat Inst Stand & Technol, 96-99. *Mem:* Fel Am Soc Heating Refrig & Air Conditioning Engrs; Am Soc Plumbing Engrs; Illum Eng Soc. *Res:* Thermal and moisture transfer in buildings; indoor air quality; energy consumption; numerical modeling of building systems. *Mailing Add:* Sch Archit Univ Tenn Knoxville TN 37996-2400. *Fax:* 423-974-0656; *E-Mail:* rkelso@utk.edu

KELTIE, RICHARD FRANCIS, STRUCTURAL DYNAMICS. *Current Pos:* from asst prof to assoc prof, 81-90, PROF MECH ENG, NC STATE UNIV, 90- *Personal Data:* b Alexandria, Va, Aug 1, 51; m 73; c 1. *Educ:* NC State Univ, BS, 73, MS, 75, PhD(mech eng), 78. *Prof Exp:* Engr, Appl Physics Lab, Johns Hopkins Univ, 78-81. *Mem:* Acoust Soc Am; Am Soc Mech Engrs. *Res:* Mechanical design; structural dynamics; forced acoustics radiation from large structures; structural acoustics; structural dynamics, acoustic radiation and acoustic emission. *Mailing Add:* 6336 Bayswater Trail Raleigh NC 27612. *Fax:* 919-515-7968; *E-Mail:* keltie@eos.ncsu.edu

KELTING, RALPH WALTER, plant ecology; deceased, see previous edition for last biography

KELTNER, LLEW, TECHNOLOGY ACQUISITION & MONITORING, CLINICAL DUE DILIGENCE. *Current Pos:* EXEC DIR, EPISTAT, 81- *Personal Data:* b Norman, Okla, Feb 5, 50; m 78, Leila Hocking; c Reed, Tiel, Mera & Case. *Educ:* Case Western Res Univ, MS, 82, PhD(med informatics), 83, MD, 84. *Concurrent Pos:* Vis prof, Univ Ore, 76-78; fel, Nat Libr Med, Case Western Res Univ, 81-83; chmn, Drilling Data Stand Comt, Int Asn Drilling Contractors, 85-88, Epistat Financial, 91-; dir, Infostat, 88-, Vital Choice, 90-93, Thesis Tech, 91-, Organ Life Sci, 93- *Mem:* Am Soc Clin Chem; AMA; Int Asn Tumor Marker Oncol. *Res:* Requirements for adequate clinical due diligence; implications of US health policy on the Japanese health care industry; biotechnology transfer; antimetastatic drugs; appropriate use of tumor markers. *Mailing Add:* PO Box 8229 Portland OR 97207. *Fax:* 503-233-0368

KELTON, DIANE ELIZABETH, GENETICS, CANCER. *Current Pos:* RETIRED. *Personal Data:* b Holden, Mass, Dec 4, 24. *Educ:* Univ Mass, BS, 45, PhD(zool), 61. *Prof Exp:* Res asst genetics, Jackson Lab, 47-50, sr res asst, 50-53; res asst cancer res, Univ Mass, Amherst, 53-56, histol, 56-58 & genetics, 58-61, res assoc genetics & neuropath, 61-74; staff scientist, Mason Res Inst, 74-83. *Mem:* AAAS; Am Inst Biol Sci; Am Genetic Asn; Genetics Soc Am; Environ Mutagen Soc; Sigma Xi. *Res:* Genetics; tumor biology; cancer chemotherapy. *Mailing Add:* 15 Heatherstone Rd Amherst MA 01002-1634

KELTS, LARRY JIM, MARINE BIOLOGY, ENTOMOLOGY. *Current Pos:* ASST PROF MARINE BIOL & ECOL, DEPT BIOL, MERRIMACK COL, 77- *Personal Data:* b Westfield, Pa, Aug 13, 37; m 67; c 2. *Educ:* Cornell Univ, BS, 59; Southeastern Mass Univ, MS, 71; Univ NH, PhD(zool), 77. *Prof Exp:* Res asst marine biol, Marine Lab, Duke Univ, 60-61; res asst plant path, Agr Exp Sta, Cornell Univ, 64-69. *Mem:* Am Inst Biol Sci; Ecol Soc Am; Nat Wildlife Fedn. *Res:* Faunal and floral community structure and composition in stressed aquatic environments, such as salt-marsh pannes, supratidal rock pools, mixohaline and oligohaline lotic systems, bogs, temporary woodland pools and creek beds; salt-marsh dragonfly ecology. *Mailing Add:* Dept Biol Merrimack Col Turnpike Rd North Andover MA 01845

KELTY, MIRIAM C FRIEDMAN, PSYCHOLOGY & PSYCHOBIOLOGY, AGING. *Current Pos:* exec secy, Human Develop Study Sect, Div Res Grants, 78-81, asst chief, Referral & Review, 81-86, ASSOC DIR, NAT INST AGING, NIH, 86- *Personal Data:* b New York, NY, Nov 4, 38; m 66, Edward J; c Joel P & Ruth A. *Educ:* City Col NY, BA, 60, MA, 62; Rutgers Univ, PhD(psychol & psychobiol), 65. *Prof Exp:* Lectr, City Col New York, 62-65; psychologist, Vet Admin Med Ctr, Boston, 66-68; res assoc, Sch Pub Health, Harvard Univ, 66-68; psychologist, NIMH, Bethesda, Md, 68-70; admin officer, Sci Affairs, Am Psychol Asn, Washington, DC, 70-74; psychologist, Nat Comn Protect Human Subj Res, Bethesda, Md, 74-78. *Concurrent Pos:* Ed, Contemp Psychol. *Mem:* Fel Am Psychol Asn; fel AAAS; World Future Soc; Geront Asn Am. *Res:* Aging, hormones and behavior; health research; ethics of research; science policy. *Mailing Add:* Off Extramural Affairs Nat Inst Aging NIH Gateway Bldg Rm 218 Bethesda MD 20892. *Fax:* 301-402-2945; *E-Mail:* kelty@nianihgw

KEMELHOR, ROBERT ELIAS, MECHANICAL ENGINEERING. *Current Pos:* CONSULT ENG MECH, 91- *Personal Data:* b New York, NY, May 19, 19; m 47, Shirley P Tennen; c Judy E, Joel M & Barry M. *Educ:* George Washington Univ, BSME, 49. *Prof Exp:* Design engr, Dept Navy, 39-52; chief engr, McLean Develop Lab, 52-57; dir res & develop, Pesco Div, Borg Warner Corp, 57-58, sect supvr, Polaris Prog, 58-62, proj engr, Landing Force Support Weapon, 62-66, prog mgr, Pershing Weapon Syst, 66-76, prog mgr, Ocean Data Acquisition Prog, 76-82, br supvr, Design & Fabrication Br, 82-85; chief engr, Appl Physics Lab, Tech Serv Dept, Johns Hopkins Univ, 86-91. *Concurrent Pos:* Consult, Thompson Ramo Wooldridge, Inc, 61-62, Cleveland Pneumatic, Inc, 62-63; US del, Int Stand Orgn Tech Comt; mem, Comput Automation Systs Asn Soc Mfg Engrs; chmn, DC Chap Soc Man Eng, Wash; consult, Nat Inst Stand & Technol & NASA. *Mem:* Assoc fel Am Inst Aeronaut & Astronaut; sr mem Soc Mfg Engrs; sr mem Am Astronaut Soc. *Res:* Magnetic fluids and mechanisms for use in shock and vibration absorbing devices; demonstrate the feasibility of electrically controlling spring rates and damping constants by electronically reactive fluids; methods of checking hazardous circuits, flow around pylons of sub and supersonic aircraft. *Mailing Add:* 6211 Redwing Ct Bethesda MD 20817-5914

KEMENY, GABOR, THEORETICAL PHYSICS. *Current Pos:* assoc prof elec eng, Mich State Univ, 68-70, assoc prof metall, mech & mat sci, 68-74, assoc prof, 70-74, PROF BIOPHYS, MICH STATE UNIV, 74- *Personal Data:* b Budapest, Hungary, Feb 6, 33; US citizen; m 58; c 2. *Educ:* Eotvos Lorand Univ, Budapest, dipl, 56; NY Univ, PhD(physics), 62. *Prof Exp:* Assoc scientist, Cent Res Inst Physics, Hungarian Acad Sci, 55-56; assoc scientist, Res Dept, Lamp Div, Westinghouse Elec Corp, 57-61; res scientist, Am-Stand, 61-62; res scientist, Ledgemont Lab, Kennecott Copper Corp, 63-68. *Concurrent Pos:* Sr vis, Cavendish Lab, Cambridge Univ, 66. *Mem:* AAAS; Am Phys Soc. *Res:* Quantum mechanics and electronics; many-body problem; solid state and mathematical physics; electrical conductivity in biomacromolecules; protein denaturation; microwave interactions with biological systems. *Mailing Add:* 3874 Sandelwood Dr Okemos MI 48864

KEMENY, LORANT, VETERINARY MICROBIOLOGY. *Current Pos:* RETIRED. *Personal Data:* b Abony, Hungary, May 28, 13; US citizen; m 50; c 1. *Educ:* Royal Hungarian Vet Col, dipl, 36, DVM, 39. *Prof Exp:* Head antisera prod dept, Phylaxia State Serum Inst, Budapest, 39-56; res fel virol, Rockefeller Found, 57-58; asst dir vet biol, Colo Serum Co, 58-63; res vet, Nat Animal Dis Ctr, USDA, 63-87. *Mem:* Am Vet Med Asn. *Res:* Virology and immunology; production, control testing and research of new veterinary biologicals; isolation and adaptation of new animal viruses to tissue culture systems; characterization of viruses. *Mailing Add:* 2017 Northwestern Ave Ames IA 50010

KEMENY, NANCY E, COLORECTAL CARCINOMA. *Current Pos:* Fel med oncol, 74-76, assoc attend physician, 83-91, ATTEND PHYSICIAN, MEM SLOAN-KETTERING CANCER CTR, 76-; PROF MED, CORNELL UNIV MED COL, 92- *Personal Data:* b Elizabeth, NJ, Jan 18, 45; m 77, Daniel Libby; c Jackie, Laura & Vicki. *Educ:* Univ Pa, BA, 67; NJ Col Med, MD, 71. *Honors & Awards:* Ancell Fund Award, 81. *Concurrent Pos:* Assoc prof, Clin Med, Cornell Univ Med Col, 82-92; chmn mem comt, Am Soc Clin Oncol, 87-, dir, 90-93, chairperson, Spec Awards, 91; mem, Oncol Drug Adv Comt, Food & Drug Admin, 90-94. *Mem:* Am Soc Clin Oncol; Am Asn Cancer Res. *Res:* Chemotherapeutic treatments for metastatic colorectal carcinoma; hepatic arterial infusion of hepatic metastases. *Mailing Add:* Mem Sloan-Kettering Cancer Ctr 1275 York Ave New York NY 10021

KEMIC, STEPHEN BRUCE, ASTROPHYSICS. *Current Pos:* STAFF MEM PHYSICS, LOS ALAMOS NAT LAB, 74- *Personal Data:* b Boston, Mass, Dec 31, 46. *Educ:* Univ NC, BS, 68; Univ Colo, MS, 70, PhD(astrophys), 73. *Mem:* Am Astron Soc. *Res:* Spectroscopy of magnetic white dwarfs; laser fusion. *Mailing Add:* 1213 San Ildefonso Rd Los Alamos NM 87544

KEMMERLY, JACK E(LLSWORTH), SYSTEMS ENGINEERING. *Current Pos:* assoc prof elec eng, 68-70, prof eng, 70-79 & 81-85, chmn elec eng fac, 72-77, chmn div eng, 77-79, EMER PROF ENG, CALIF STATE UNIV, FULLERTON, 85- *Personal Data:* b Marion, Ohio, Aug 19, 24; m 45; c 5. *Educ:* Cath Univ Am, BEE, 50; Univ Denver, MS, 52; Purdue Univ, PhD(elec eng), 58. *Prof Exp:* Asst res engr electronics, Denver Res Inst, Colo, 51-53; instr elec eng, Purdue Univ, 53-58; sr proj engr electronics, AC Spark Plug Div, Gen Motors Corp, 58-59; asst prof elec eng, Purdue Univ, 59-61; prin engr, Aeronutronic Div, Philco Corp, 61-68; sr staff engr, Ground Systs Group, Hughes Aircraft Co, 68. *Concurrent Pos:* Consult, AC Spark Plug Div, Gen Motors Corp; lectr, Univ Calif, Los Angeles; vis prof eng, Fort Lewis Col, Durango Colo, 80-81. *Mem:* Inst Elec & Electronics Engrs; Am Soc Eng Educ. *Res:* Systems analysis; applied probability; noise and circuit theory. *Mailing Add:* 323 Snowshoe Lane Durango CO 81301

KEMNITZ, JOSEPH WILLIAM, PHYSIOLOGICAL PSYCHOLOGY. *Current Pos:* res assoc, 77-79, asst scientist, 79-84, ASSOC SCIENTIST, WIS REGIONAL PRIMATE RES CTR, UNIV WIS, 84-, AFFIL SCIENTIST, INST AGING & ADULT LIFE, 89-, ASSOC SCIENTIST, DEPT MED, 90- *Personal Data:* b Baltimore, Md, Mar 15, 47; m 90, Amanda M Tuttle; c Julia E. *Educ:* Univ Wis, BA, 69, MS, 74, PhD(physiol psychol), 76. *Prof Exp:* Proj specialist psychol, Univ Wis, 69-71, teaching & res asst, 71-76. *Concurrent Pos:* Mem task force animal models in diabetes res, NIH, 80-81; vis scientist, Div Endocrinol, Med Ctr, Univ Calif, Los Angeles, 81; consult, Div Diabetes & Clin Nutrit, Univ Southern Calif Med Ctr, 84-, Div Comp Med, Caribbean Primate Res Ctr, 85-; mem, NIH Spec Study Sect, 87-; assoc ed, Hormones & Behav, 87- *Mem:* Am Diabetes Asn; Am Soc Primatologists; Int

Primatological Asn; NAm Asn Study Obesity; fel Gerontol Soc Am; Am Inst Nutrit; NY Acad Sci; Am Physiol Soc; Sigma Xi. *Res:* Regulation of energy balance, emphasizing obesity, diabetes, caloric restriction and aging, particularly in Rhesus monkeys. *Mailing Add:* Wis Regional Primate Res Ctr Univ Wis 1223 Capitol Ct Madison WI 53715-1299

KEMP, ARNE K, FOREST PRODUCTS. *Current Pos:* RETIRED. *Personal Data:* b Kajaani, Finland, Mar 5, 18; US citizen; m 43; c 2. *Educ:* Univ Ga, BSF, 48; Duke Univ, MF, 49; Univ Minn, PhD(wood tech), 57. *Prof Exp:* Instr wood tech, Sch Forestry, Univ Minn, 49-53; assoc prof, La State Univ, 53-55; head dept forestry, Stephen F Austin State Col, 55-63; chief div forest prod utilization, & mkt & eng res, Lake State Forest Exp Sta, US Forest Serv, 63-65, asst dir, 65-73, asst dir res, NCent Forest Exp Sta, 73-84. *Concurrent Pos:* NSF grant, 62. *Mem:* Forest Prod Res Soc; Soc Wood Sci & Technol; Int Union Forest Res Orgns. *Res:* Wood seasoning, preservation and anatomy; wood liquid relationships; forest products marketing. *Mailing Add:* 6 Captain Dunbar Lane Savannah GA 31411

KEMP, DANIEL SCHAEFFER, ORGANIC CHEMISTRY, PROTEIN SCIENCE. *Current Pos:* From asst prof to assoc prof, 64-72, PROF CHEM, MASS INST TECHNOL, 72- *Personal Data:* b Portland, Ore, Oct 20, 36. *Educ:* Reed Col, BA, 58; Harvard Univ, PhD(org chem), 64. *Concurrent Pos:* A P Sloan Found fel, 68-70; vis asst prof, Univ Calif, San Diego, 69; Camile & Henry Dreyfus fel, 70. *Mem:* Am Chem Soc. *Res:* Peptide chemistry. *Mailing Add:* Dept Chem 18-584 Mass Inst Technol 77 Mass Ave Cambridge MA 02139-4307

KEMP, EMORY LELAND, STRUCTURAL ENGINEERING. *Current Pos:* assoc prof, 62-65, chmn dept, 67-74, PROF CIVIL ENG, WVA UNIV, 65-, PROF HIST SCI & TECHNOL, 77- *Personal Data:* b Chicago, Ill, Oct 1, 31; m 58, Janet K Dodd; c Mark, Alison & Geoffrey. *Educ:* Univ Ill, BSc, 52, PhD(theoret & appl mech), 62; Univ London, DIC, 55, MSc, 58. *Honors & Awards:* Buxton Award, Inst Struct Engrs, 80; Hist & Heritage Award, Am Soc Civil Engrs, 81; Nat Inst Hist Preserv Honor Award, 91. *Prof Exp:* Asst engr, Ill State Water Surv, 52; struct engr, consult firms, London, 56-59; instr theoret & appl mech, Univ Ill, 59-62. *Concurrent Pos:* Fel, Am Coun Learned Socs, 75-76, regents fel, Smithsonian Inst, 83-84. *Mem:* Fel Am Soc Civil Engrs; fel Brit Inst Civil Engrs; fel Am Concrete Inst; Brit Inst Struct Engrs. *Res:* History of technology; industrial archeology; structural engineering. *Mailing Add:* Inst Hist Technol & Indust Archaeol WVa Univ 1535 Mileground Morgantown WV 26505

KEMP, GORDON ARTHUR, MICROBIOLOGY, RESEARCH ADMINISTRATION. *Current Pos:* PFIZER CENT RES, GROTON, 83- *Personal Data:* b Newark, NJ, Dec 12, 32; m 58; c 3. *Educ:* Lehigh Univ, AB, 54; Rutgers Univ, PhD(microbiol), 61. *Prof Exp:* Res scientist microbiol, 61-64, group leader chemother, 64-70, mgr chemother res, 70-73, mgr animal indust res, 73-76, dir, animal indust res & develop, Am Cyanamid Co, 76-82. *Mem:* Fel AAAS; Am Soc Microbiol; Sigma Xi. *Res:* Pathogenesis of disease; prophylaxis and therapy of experimental infections; veterinary microbiology and immunology; protozoal and helminth infections of domestic animals; non-medical uses of antibiotics. *Mailing Add:* Pfizer Cent Res Eastern Pt Rd Groton CT 06340

KEMP, GRAHAM ELMORE, VETERINARY PUBLIC HEALTH. *Current Pos:* RETIRED. *Personal Data:* b Alta, Can, Jan 8, 27; US citizen; m 48. *Educ:* Univ Toronto, DVM, 51; Univ Calif, Berkeley, MPH, 58. *Prof Exp:* Mem staff, Div Livestock Indust, Univ Ill, 51-52; pvt pract, Ill, 52-57; mem staff, Epidemiol Bur Commun Dis, Div Prev Med Serv, Calif State Dept Pub Health, 58-64; staff mem, Rockefeller Found, Virus Res Lab, Fac Med, Univ Ibadan, 64-72; chief virol unit, San Juan Trop Dis Labs, PR, 73-75; dir, Bur Labs, Vector-Borne Dis Div, Commun Dis Ctr, USPHS, 75-80. *Concurrent Pos:* Lectr, Sch Pub Health, Univ Calif, Berkeley & Sch Vet Med, Univ Calif, Davis, 57-64; consult zoonoses, State of Calif, 58-64; hon sr scientist, PR Nuclear Ctr, 73-74; mem animal res comt, San Juan Vet Admin Hosp, 73-74. *Mem:* Am Vet Med Asn; Am Pub Health Asn; Conf Pub Health Vets; Am Soc Trop Med & Hyg. *Res:* Arbovirus; food-borne disease and zoonoses. *Mailing Add:* 808 Inverness St Ft Collins CO 80524

KEMP, JAMES DILLON, ANIMAL SCIENCE. *Current Pos:* from asst prof to assoc prof animal husb, Univ Ky, 52-59, prof animal sci, 59-89, coord, food sci prog, 66-89, EMER PROF ANIMAL SCI, UNIV KY, 89- *Personal Data:* b Pickett, Ky, Feb 6, 23; m 47, Helen Walker; c Bonnie (Collins) & James W. *Educ:* Univ Ky, BS, 48, MS, 49; Univ Ill, PhD(animal sci), 52. *Honors & Awards:* Res Award, Am Soc Animal Sci, 71; Pollock Award, Am Meat Sci Asn, 88. *Prof Exp:* Asst animal sci, Univ Ill, 49-52. *Concurrent Pos:* Fulbright res scholar, NZ, 64; consult, Thailand, 74 & Italy, 85. *Mem:* Fel Am Soc Animal Sci; fel Inst Food Technologists; Sigma Xi; Am Meat Sci Asn (pres, 75-76). *Res:* Meats teaching and research; composition and processing characteristics of red meats. *Mailing Add:* 778 Hildeen Rd Lexington KY 40502

KEMP, JOHN DANIEL, MOLECULAR GENETICS. *Current Pos:* AT AGRIGENETICS CORP, MADISON, WIS. *Personal Data:* b Minneapolis, Minn, Jan 20, 40; m 75; c 3. *Educ:* Univ Calif, Los Angeles, BS, 62, PhD(biochem), 65. *Prof Exp:* NIH fel biochem, Univ Wash, 65-67, res assoc, 67-68; asst prof, Univ Wis-Madison, 68-72, assoc prof, 72-77, prof plant path, 77-85; res chemist, USDA, 68-81; prof plant path, NMex State Univ, Las Cruces, 85- *Mem:* Am Soc Plant Physiologists; Sigma Xi; Int Soc Molecular Plant-Microbe Interactions. *Res:* Molecular mechanisms of normal and abnormal plant growth and development; plant genetic engineering by novel approaches. *Mailing Add:* PGEL Box 3GL NMex State Univ Las Cruces NM 88003. *Fax:* 505-646-1302; *E-Mail:* jkemp@nmsu.edu

KEMP, JOHN WILMER, PHYSIOLOGICAL CHEMISTRY, PHARMACOLOGY. *Current Pos:* assoc prof pharmacol, 59-83, ASSOC PROF PHYSIOL, COL MED, UNIV UTAH, 83- *Personal Data:* b Midvale, Utah, July 28, 20; m 52; c 2. *Educ:* Westminster Col, AB, 50; Univ Calif, PhD(physiol chem), 57. *Prof Exp:* Res pharmacologist metab of heroin, Sch Med, Univ Calif, 57-59. *Mem:* Am Soc Pharmacol & Exp Therapeut. *Res:* Biochemistry and pharmacology of the central nervous system; nucleic acids; membrane transport; neuronal excitability; anticonvulsants; physiology. *Mailing Add:* Dept Physiol Sch Med Univ Utah 410 Chipeta Way 167 Stangl Salt Lake City UT 84108-1209

KEMP, KENNETH COURTNEY, PHYSICAL ORGANIC CHEMISTRY. *Current Pos:* vchmn dept, 76-80, from instr to prof, 55-90, EMER PROF CHEM, UNIV NEV, 90- *Personal Data:* b Chicago, Ill, Aug 7, 25. *Educ:* Northwestern Univ, BS, 50; Ill Inst Technol, PhD(chem), 56. *Prof Exp:* Asst chem, Ill Inst Technol, 50-55. *Mem:* Am Chem Soc; Chem Soc London; Sigma Xi. *Res:* Organic mechanisms; neighboring group reactions. *Mailing Add:* PO Box 8075 Reno NV 89557-8075

KEMP, KENNETH E, STATISTICS. *Current Pos:* asst prof, 68-71, assoc prof, 71-79, PROF STATIST, KANS STATE UNIV, 79- *Personal Data:* b Detroit, Mich, Aug 24, 41; m 64, 78; c 2. *Educ:* Mich State Univ, BS, 63, MS, 65, PhD(animal husb), 67. *Prof Exp:* Sr statist programmer, Biomet Serv, Agr Res Serv, USDA, 67-68. *Mem:* Biomet Soc; Am Statist Asn. *Res:* Algorithms and techniques for statistical analysis on the digital computer. *Mailing Add:* Dept Statist Dickens Hall Kans State Univ Manhattan KS 66506

KEMP, L(EBBEUS) C(OURTRIGHT), JR, CHEMICAL ENGINEERING. *Current Pos:* RETIRED. *Personal Data:* b Houston, Tex, Oct 8, 07; m 36; c 2. *Educ:* Rice Inst, BS, 29. *Prof Exp:* Res chemist, Texaco, Inc, Tex, 29-33, res supvr, 33-38, asst chief chemist, 38-40, asst supt res labs, NY, 40-41, dir res, 41-53, asst to vpres, 53-54, asst to sr vpres, 54-55, gen mgr petrochem, 55-57, vpres petrochem, 57-59, vpres res & technol, 59-68, vpres spec assignments, 68-71; vpres, Texaco, Inc, Houston Area, 71-72. *Concurrent Pos:* Mem indust adv comt, US Bur Mines, 44; trustee, United Eng Trustees, 58-60; dir, Am Inst Chem Engrs, 59-61; consult, 71- *Mem:* AAAS; Am Chem Soc; Am Inst Aeronaut & Astronaut; fel Am Inst Chem Engrs; Sigma Xi. *Res:* Petroleum refining including work on both product and process development; alkylation of isobutane with olefins; hydrocarbon synthesis from carbon monoxide and hydrogen; petrochemicals; synthetic liquid and gaseous fuels. *Mailing Add:* 12318 Huntingwick Dr Houston TX 77024-4905

KEMP, MARWIN K, PHYSICAL CHEMISTRY, GEOCHEMISTRY. *Current Pos:* sr res scientist, 81-85, staff res scientist, 85-88, RES SUPVR, AMOCO PROD CO, 88- *Personal Data:* b Strong, Ark, Nov 23, 42; m 61; c 2. *Educ:* Univ Ark, BS, 64; Univ Ill, MS, 65, PhD(phys chem), 68. *Honors & Awards:* Okla Chemist Award, 88. *Prof Exp:* From asst prof to assoc prof phys chem, Univ Tulsa, 68-81. *Mem:* Am Chem Soc; AAAS; Sigma Xi. *Res:* Geochemistry; statistical analysis of organic geochemistry data; thermodynamics; infrared spectroscopy. *Mailing Add:* 4335 S Allegheny Ave Tulsa OK 74135. *E-Mail:* mkemp@trc.amoco.com

KEMP, NORMAN EVERETT, DEVELOPMENTAL BIOLOGY. *Current Pos:* from instr to prof zool, 47-61, prof, 61-86, EMER PROF ZOOL, UNIV MICH, ANN ARBOR, 86- *Personal Data:* b Otisfield, Maine, June 20, 16; m 42, Ruth E Robinson. *Educ:* Bates Col, BS, 37; Univ Calif, PhD(zool), 41. *Prof Exp:* Asst zool, Univ Calif, 37-41; instr, Wayne Univ, 46-47. *Concurrent Pos:* Res assoc, Argonne Nat Lab, 54 & 55; vis investr, Rockefeller Inst, 58; vis colleague, Univ Hawaii, 65, 72; vis investr, Lab, Marine Biol Asn UK, Plymouth, Eng, 79. *Mem:* Am Soc Zool; Am Asn Anat; Electron Micros Soc Am; Am Soc Cell Biol; Soc Develop Biol. *Res:* Electron microscopy of differentiating cells; fertilization of amphibian eggs; differentiation of digestive tract and skin; calcification of calcified cartilage, bones, scales and teeth in aquatic vertebrates; fibrillogenesis of collagen; regeneration of fish fins. *Mailing Add:* Dept Biol Univ Mich Ann Arbor MI 48109-1048

KEMP, PAUL JAMES, IDENTIFICATION OF ODOPHORIC COMPOUNDS, DETOXIFICATION REACTIONS. *Current Pos:* INDUST APPLNS CHEMIST, INDUST CHEM DIV, BREWER ENVIRON INDUSTS, INC, 90- *Personal Data:* b Inglewood, Calif, June 26, 42; m 90, Hsu N Shieh; c James, Eran, Sean & Hong-ru. *Educ:* Iowa State Univ, BS, 65; Ore State Univ, MS, 69. *Prof Exp:* Grad teaching asst gen & anal chem, Ore State Univ, 65-69; gen mgr & chief exec officer food packaging prod, Outrite Plastics Inc, 69-74; grad teaching fel anal chem, Univ Hawaii, 75-77; dist mgr food processing & water treatment, Olin Water Serv, Olin Corp, 77-81; regional mgr food processing & water treatment, Assoc Chem & Serv, Inc, 81-89. *Concurrent Pos:* Tech Dir, Lens, Inc, Sunset Terr Wastewater Reclamation Facil. *Mem:* Am Chem Soc; Am Waterworks Asn; Water Environ Fedn; Sigma Xi. *Res:* Industrial odor control chemistry; non-halogen oxidative sterilants for industrial and potable water; industrial wastewater management. *Mailing Add:* 58110 Mamao St Apt 110 Haleiwa HI 96712. *Fax:* 808-532-7521

KEMP, PAULA ANN, MATHEMATICS, NUMBER THEORY. *Current Pos:* PROF MATH, SW MO STATE UNIV, 77- *Personal Data:* b Jonesbow, Ark, Aug 14, 47. *Educ:* Ark State Univ, BS, 68; Kans State Univ, MS, 70, PhD, 74. *Mem:* Am Math Soc; Mathh Asn Am. *Res:* Fix point theory; analysis; set theory; number theory. *Mailing Add:* Math Dept SW Mo State Univ Springfield MO 65804. *E-Mail:* pak170f@vma.smsu.edu

KEMP, ROBERT GRANT, BIOCHEMISTRY. *Current Pos:* chmn, 76-88, PROF BIOCHEM, UNIV HEALTH SCI, CHICAGO MED SCH, 76- *Personal Data:* b Massillon, Ohio, Feb 12, 37; m 67, 85; c 2. *Educ:* Col Wooster, BA, 59; Yale Univ, PhD(biochem), 64. *Prof Exp:* Res assoc biochem, Univ Wash, 64-66; from asst prof to prof biochem, Med Col Wis, 66-76. *Concurrent Pos:* Estab investr, Am Heart Asn, 68-73; Fulbright fel, 71. *Mem:* AAAS; Am Chem Soc; Am Soc Biol Chem; Sigma Xi; Protein Soc. *Res:* Control of carbohydrate metabolism; structure-activity relationships of enzymes. *Mailing Add:* Dept Biochem Univ Health Sci Chicago Med Sch 3333 Green Bay Rd North Chicago IL 60064-3095. *Fax:* 847-578-3240

KEMP, WALTER MICHAEL, IMMUNOBIOLOGY, PARASITOLOGY. *Current Pos:* from asst prof to assoc prof, 75-82, PROF BIOL, TEX A&M UNIV, 82-, ASSOC DEAN SCI, 89- *Personal Data:* b Big Spring, Tex, Aug 26, 44; m 83; c 4. *Educ:* Abilene Christian Col, BSE, 66; Tulane Univ, PhD(biol), 70. *Honors & Awards:* Henry Baldwin Ward Medal, Am Soc Parasitologists, 83. *Prof Exp:* Cell biol trainee biol, Tulane Univ, 68-70; asst prof, Abilene Christian Col, 70-75. *Concurrent Pos:* Res Corp res grant, 70-71; res assoc immunol, Southwest Found Res & Educ, 70-73 & Univ Ga, 74; NIH grants, 72-75, 78-83 & 86-89; Clark Found grants, 76-78, 78-82 & 82-85; mem, Study Sect Trop Med Parasitol, NIH, 81-85, chmn, 83-85. *Mem:* AAAS; Am Soc Parasitologists (pres, 89); Am Soc Trop Med & Hyg; Am Asn Immunologists. *Res:* Immune responses to parasites, particularly schistosomes and trypanosomes; host-parasite antigen sharing and parasite immune escape mechanisms. *Mailing Add:* Tex A&M Univ Col Sci 312 Admin Bldg College Station TX 77843-1112. *Fax:* 409-845-1855

KEMP, WILLIAM MICHAEL, ECOLOGY. *Current Pos:* SYSTS ECOLOGIST ENVIRON RES, CTR ENVIRON & ESTUARINE STUDIES, UNIV MD, 77- *Personal Data:* b Washington, DC, May 16, 47. *Educ:* Ga Inst Technol, BA, 69, MA, 71; Univ Fla, PhD(environ sci), 76. *Prof Exp:* Environ engr eval, US Environ Protection Agency, 71-72. *Mem:* Ecol Soc Am; Am Soc Limnol & Oceanog; AAAS; Sigma Xi. *Res:* Ecosystem modeling; productivity and nutrient dynamics of estuaries; structure of ecological trophic webs; economics and energetics of environment. *Mailing Add:* Univ Md PO Box 775 Cambridge MD 21613

KEMPE, LLOYD L(UTE), chemical engineering; deceased, see previous edition for last biography

KEMPE, LUDWIG GEORGE, NEUROSURGERY, NEUROANATOMY. *Current Pos:* PROF NEUROSURG & ANAT, MED UNIV SC, 73- *Personal Data:* b Brandenburg, Ger, Oct 16, 15; US citizen; m 55. *Educ:* Univ Berne, MD, 42. *Prof Exp:* Assoc clin prof neurosurg, George Washington Univ, 60-73. *Concurrent Pos:* Mem adv bd, Coun Neurosurg, 68- *Mem:* Am Asn Neurol Surgeons; Cong Neurol Surgeons; Soc Neurol Surgeons; Am Asn Anatomists; Am Col Surgeons. *Res:* Mesoscopic neuroanatomy. *Mailing Add:* 12 Valley View Dr Pisgah Forest NC 28768-9509

KEMPEN, RENE RICHARD, PHARMACOLOGY. *Current Pos:* ASST PROF, SCH MED, UNIV TEX MED BR GALVESTON, 63-, ASSOC DIR TOXICOL LAB, 73-, ASST PROF, SCH ALLIED HEALTH, 76- *Personal Data:* b Kankakee, Ill, Mar 24, 28; m 69; c 1. *Educ:* St Joseph's Col, Ind, BS, 50; Loyola Univ Chicago, MS, 55, PhD(pharmacol), 62. *Prof Exp:* Chemist, Chicago Biol Res Lab, 54-55; lab instr pharmacol, Stritch Sch Med, Loyola Univ Chicago, 56-59; instr, Col Med, Baylor Univ, 61-63. *Concurrent Pos:* Instr, St Anne's Hosp Sch Nursing, 55-57, Loyola Univ Sch Nursing, 56 & St Elizabeth's Hosp Sch Nursing, 57. *Mem:* AAAS; Am Asn Lab Animal Sci; Am Heart Asn; Sigma Xi. *Res:* Action of drugs on cardiac electrophysiological parameters; muscle contraction; toxicology; effect of drugs on endocrine pancrease. *Mailing Add:* Dept Pharmacol Univ Tex Med Sch 301 University Blvd Galveston TX 77550-2708

KEMPER, BYRON W, MOLECULAR BIOLOGY. *Current Pos:* From asst to assoc prof pharmacol/physiol, 74-86, PROF PHARMACOL, UNIV ILL, URBANA, 86-, PROF CELLULAR & STRUCT BIOL, 89-, DEPT HEAD PHARMACOL, 96- *Personal Data:* b Evansville, Ind, Oct 10, 43; m 92, Jonsook Kim; c Jason, Hanna & Esther. *Educ:* Wabash Col, BA, 65; Stanford Univ, PhD(pharmacol), 69. *Mem:* AAAS; Am Soc Biochem & Molecular Biol. *Mailing Add:* Dept Molecular & Integrative Physiol Univ Ill 524 Burrill 407 S Goodwin Urbana IL 61801-3704. *Fax:* 217-333-1133; *E-Mail:* byronkem@uiuc.edu

KEMPER, GENE ALLEN, NUMERICAL ANALYSIS, PERFORMANCE ANALYSIS. *Current Pos:* assoc prof, Univ NDak, 66-72, sr consult, Comput Ctr, 69-79, prof math, 72-96, dir, Inst Comput Use Educ, 74-81, assoc dir, Comput Ctr, 79-81, asst vpres acad affairs, 81-82, assoc vpres acad affairs, 82-96, vchancellor acad affairs, 93-96, EMER PROF MATH & EMER ASSOC VPRES ACAD AFFAIRS, UNIV NDAK, 96- *Personal Data:* b Drake, NDak, Apr 12, 33; m 69; c 1. *Educ:* Univ NDak, BS, 56, MS, 59; Iowa State Univ, PhD(appl math), 65. *Prof Exp:* Instr math, Univ NDak, 56-59; exten lectr math, Univ Wash, Seattle, 60-61 & 65-66; mathematician, Boeing Co, 60-61, sr res specialist & vis staff mem, Boeing Sci Res Labs, 65-66; instr math, Iowa State Univ, 61-65. *Concurrent Pos:* NSF Col Sci Improv Prog grant, Univ NDak, 68-71; vis soc indust & appl math lectr, 75-77, 79-80, 80-82; vis scientist, Atomic Energy Comn Lab, Iowa State Univ, Ames, Iowa. *Mem:* Soc Indust & Appl Math; Asn Comput Mach. *Res:* Numerical solution of functional differential equations and integral equations; mathematical modeling of biological systems. *Mailing Add:* 3130 Belmont Rd Grand Forks ND 58201

KEMPER, JOHN D(USTIN), MECHANICAL ENGINEERING. *Current Pos:* assoc prof, Univ Calif, Davis, 62-67, dean, Col Eng, 69-83, prof, 67-91, EMER PROF ENG, UNIV CALIF, DAVIS, 91- *Personal Data:* b Portland, Ore, May 29, 24; m 47, Barbara Lane; c Kathleen. *Educ:* Univ Calif, Los Angeles, BS, 49, MS, 59; Univ Colo, PhD(struct mech), 69. *Honors & Awards:* Alex Laurie Award, Am Soc Hort Sci, 74. *Prof Exp:* Engr, Telecomput Corp, Calif, 49-50, proj engr, 50-52, chief mech engr, 52-55; chief mech engr, H A Wagner Co, 55-56; asst to vpres eng, Marchant Calculators, Inc, 56-58, chief engr, Marchant Div, Smith-Corona Marchant Inc, 58-59, vpres eng, 59-62. *Concurrent Pos:* Chmn, Panel Grad Educ & Res, Nat Res Coun, 83-85, Task Force Prep Teaching Eng, Am Soc Eng Educ, 84-86; dir, Plantronics Inc, 83-86. *Mem:* Fel AAAS; fel Am Soc Mech Engrs; Am Soc Eng Educ. *Res:* Mechanical design; structural mechanics; writings on engineering profession, introduction to engineering profession, ethics, creativity, graduation education and research, preparation for teaching. *Mailing Add:* 1742 Midway Dr Woodland CA 95695. *E-Mail:* jdkemper@ucdavis.edu

KEMPER, JOHN THOMAS, INNOVATION IN THE MATHEMATICS & SCIENCE EDUCATION OF ELEMENTARY TEACHERS, DETERMINISTIC MODELS IN POPULATION BIOLOGY. *Current Pos:* fac mem, 78-87, dept chair, 87-94, PROF, DEPT MATH, UNIV ST THOMAS, 87- *Personal Data:* b San Francisco, Calif, Mar 7, 44. *Educ:* Rice Univ, BA, 66, PhD(math), 70. *Honors & Awards:* Nat Res Serv Award, Univ Minn, 76-78. *Prof Exp:* Asst prof math, NY Univ, 70-73; City Col, New York, 73-74, Univ Minn, 74-76; Nat Res Serv award, Univ Minn, 76-78. *Concurrent Pos:* Prin investr, NSF, 81-83; proj dir, Inst Sec Teachers, NSF, 84-85, Fund Improv Post Sec Educ, US Dept Educ, 95-97. *Mem:* Am Math Soc; Math Asn Am; Mathematicians Educ Reform; Nat Coun Teachers Math; Coun Undergrad Res. *Res:* Development and analysis of deterministic models in population biology and finance. *Mailing Add:* 221 Woodlawn Ave St Paul MN 55105

KEMPER, KIRBY WAYNE, NUCLEAR PHYSICS, ION SOURCE DEVELOPMENT. *Current Pos:* Res assoc nuclear physics, 68-71, from asst prof to assoc prof, 71-79, PROF PHYSICS, FLA STATE UNIV, 79- *Personal Data:* b New York, NY, Apr 13, 40; m 64, Margaret-Ray Thurman; c Margaret, Andrew & Ann. *Educ:* Va Polytech Inst, BS, 62; Ind Univ, MS, 64, PhD(physics), 68. *Mem:* Sigma Xi; Am Phys Soc. *Res:* Selective population of states with heavy ions; polarized ion source development; laser induced atomic polarizations; spin effects in nuclear reactions; implantation of heavy-ions; radiation damage. *Mailing Add:* Phys Dept Fla State Univ Tallahassee FL 32306. *Fax:* 850-644-9848; *E-Mail:* kirby@fsulcd.physics.fsu.edu

KEMPER, ROBERT SCHOOLEY, JR, MECHANICAL & METALLURGICAL ENGINEERING. *Current Pos:* res assoc, Battelle Mem Inst, 65-66, unit mgr, 66-69, mgr mat develop, 69-85, MGR RES OPERS, MAT SCI & TECHNOL DEPT, PAC NORTHWEST LABS, BATTELLE MEM INST, 85 -, SR PROG MGR, 92- *Personal Data:* b Oakland, Calif, Feb 20, 27; m 49, 66; c 4. *Educ:* Ore State Col, BS, 51, MS, 52. *Prof Exp:* Tech specialist, Hanford Atomic Prods Oper, Gen Elec Co, 52-64. *Mem:* Am Soc Metals; Soc Mfg Engrs; Am Defense Preparedness Asn; AAAS; Am Soc Testing & Mat. *Res:* Irradiation damage in fuel and structural materials; metallic fabrication development. *Mailing Add:* 1623 Alder Richland WA 99352

KEMPER, WILLIAM ALEXANDER, ENVIRONMENTAL CHEMISTRY, BALLISTICS. *Current Pos:* RETIRED. *Personal Data:* b Baltimore, Md, Jan 1, 11; m 56, 73, Marcia Berndt. *Educ:* Johns Hopkins Univ, PhD(phys chem), 34. *Prof Exp:* Chemist, Res Dept, Baltimore Gas & Elec Co, 34-43; physicist, US Naval Weapons Lab, 46-72; sci adv, Comdr Cruiser Destroyer Forces Atlantic Fleet, 72-73; sr ballistician, Navy Surface Warfare Ctr-Dahlgren Lab, 73-75; asst prof physics, Metrop State Col, 76-77. *Concurrent Pos:* Chmn, USN Aeroballistics Adv Comt, 67 & 68; US Nat Leader, US, Australia, Can & UK Coop Prog in Exterior Ballistics, 67-74. *Mem:* AAAS; Am Defense Prep Asn. *Res:* Ballistics; fire control; investigated sulphur and nitrogen compounds in heating gas; flight characteristics of missiles directed preparation of firecontrol data; radiologic measurements at crossroads (A-Bomb) tests (1946). *Mailing Add:* 7363 W 26th Pl Denver CO 80215

KEMPERMAN, JOHANNES HENRICUS BERNARDUS, PROBABILITY, MATHEMATICAL STATISTICS. *Current Pos:* prof statist, 86-95, EMER PROF STATIST, RUTGERS UNIV, 95- *Personal Data:* b Amsterdam, Neth, July 16, 24; wid; c Steven, Bruce, Hubert, Ingrid & Eric. *Educ:* Univ Amsterdam, BS, 45, MS, 48, PhD(math), 50. *Prof Exp:* Res assoc appl math, Math Ctr, Amsterdam, 48-51; from asst prof to prof math, Purdue Univ, 51-61; prof, Univ Rochester, 61-85. *Concurrent Pos:* On leave, Univ Amsterdam, 58-59 & 72-73, Univ Wis, 60-61, & Stanford Univ, 66-67 & Univ Tex, Austin, 77-78. *Mem:* Am Statist Asn; fel Inst Math Statist; Dutch Math Soc; Math Asn Am; fel Am Asn Advan Sci; corresp mem Royal Neth Acad Sci. *Res:* Analysis; probability; statistics. *Mailing Add:* Dept Statist Rutgers Univ New Brunswick NJ 08901

KEMPH, JOHN PATTERSON, PSYCHIATRY, PHYSIOLOGY. *Current Pos:* PROF PSYCHIAT, UNIV FLA, 86- *Personal Data:* b Lima, Ohio, Dec 17, 19; m 43; c 4. *Educ:* Ohio Northern Univ, AB, 47; Ohio State Univ, BSc, 47, MSc, 48, MD, 53; Am Bd Psychiat & Neurol, dipl psychiat, 60, dipl child psychiat, 62. *Prof Exp:* Res asst, Res Found, Ohio State Univ, 47-48, res assoc, 51-55; resident psychiat, Med Ctr, Univ Mich, 55-56, jr clin instr, 56-57; dir, Ohio Northwest Guid Ctr, 57-60; from instr to assoc prof psychiat, Univ Mich, 60-68; prof psychiat & dir child & adolescent psychiat, State Univ

NY Downstate Med Ctr, 68-72; prof psychiat & chmn dept, Med Col Ohio, 72-74, vpres acad affairs, dean med fac & prof psychiat, 74-86. *Concurrent Pos:* Res fel, Ohio State Univ, 48-51; fel child psychiat, Med Ctr, Univ Mich, Ann Arbor, 60-61; intern, Mt Carmel Hosp, Columbus, Ohio, 53-54; resident psychiat, Columbus State Hosp, 54-55; mem active staff, Mem Hosp, Lima, Ohio, 57-60; vice chief staff psychiat, St Rita's Hosp, 58-60; instr child psychiat, Med Ctr, Univ Mich, Ann Arbor, 60-61, infections control officer, 61-68, lectr human growth & behav, Sch Social Work & lectr psychosom med, Univ Hosp, 62-68, mem clin serv comt, 63-68; dir in-patient serv & coord res, Children's Psychiat Hosp, 61-65, clin dir, 65-68; consult, Cent Mich Coun Continuing Psychiat Educ, 64-68; chmn clin serv comt, Children's Psychiat Hosp, 65-68; emer prof & dean, Med Col Ohio, 86- *Mem:* Fel Am Psychiat Asn; AMA; Am Orthopsychiat Asn; Am Asn Ment Deficiency; Am Psychosom Soc; Sigma Xi. *Res:* Child psychiatry; applied cardiovascular and respiratory physiology; study of physiological and psychological correlates of behavior. *Mailing Add:* 3903 SW 77th St Gainesville FL 32608

KEMPHUES, KENNETH J, ANIMAL DEVELOPMENT. *Current Pos:* from asst prof to assoc prof, 84-96, PROF DEVELOP BIOL, CORNELL UNIV, 96- *Personal Data:* b Cincinnati, Ohio, July 3, 50; m 84, Diane Morton; c Zachary & Amanda. *Educ:* Univ Va, BA, 76; Ind Univ, PhD(genetics), 81. *Prof Exp:* Teaching fel, Univ Colo, 81-84. *Mem:* Genetics Soc Am; Soc Develop Am; AAAS. *Res:* The problem of determination in animal development; identification and characterization of gene encoding functions necessary for determination; the use of molecular, ultrastructural and biochemical techniques to exploit mutations in the genes. *Mailing Add:* Genetics & Develop Sect Cornell Univ 101 Biotech Bldg Ithaca NY 14853. *Fax:* 607-255-6249; *E-Mail:* kjk1@cornell.edu

KEMPLE, MARVIN DAVID, MAGNETIC RESONANCE. *Current Pos:* ASST PROF PHYSICS, IND UNIV-PURDUE UNIV, INDIANAPOLIS, 77- *Personal Data:* b Indianapolis, Ind, Sept 2, 42; m 64; c 2. *Educ:* Purdue Univ, BS, 64; Univ Ill, Urbana-Champaign, MS, 65, PhD(physics), 71. *Prof Exp:* Enrico Fermi fel chem & physics, Enrico Fermi Inst, Univ Chicago, 71-72, res assoc, Dept Chem, 72-76; Nat Res Coun res assoc, Nat Bur Standards, 76-77. *Mem:* Am Phys Soc; AAAS; Sigma Xi. *Res:* Application of electron paramagnetic resonance and electron nuclear double resonance to the study of ions and molecules in ionic crystals, organic crystals, protein crystals, and intact, live biological systems. *Mailing Add:* Dept Physics Ind Univ-Purdue Univ Indianapolis 402 N Blackford St Indianapolis IN 46205-3273

KEMPLER, WALTER, FAMILY COUNSELING. *Current Pos:* FOUNDER & DIR FAMILY COUN, KEMPLER INST, 60- *Personal Data:* b New York, NY, Sept 9, 23; c 5. *Educ:* Univ Tex, BS, 46, MD, 47. *Res:* The structure, dynamics and treatment of the family. *Mailing Add:* Kempler Inst PO Box 2185 Laguna Hills CA 92654

KEMPNER, DAVID H, IMMUNOCHEMISTRY, BIOCHEMISTRY. *Current Pos:* PRES, IMTA, INC, 92- *Educ:* Tufts Univ, PhD(chem), 75. *Prof Exp:* Prin consult, Bernard Wolnak & Assocs. 83-88; sr assoc, Strategic Tech Int, 88-92. *Mailing Add:* IMTA Inc 977 Lakeview Pkwy Suite 160 Vernon Hills IL 60061

KEMPNER, ELLIS STANLEY, RADIATION TARGET ANALYSIS. *Current Pos:* CHIEF, SECT MACROMOLECULAR BIOPHYSICS, NIAMS, 86- *Personal Data:* b New York, NY, Mar 20, 32; m 61; c 3. *Educ:* Brooklyn Col, BS, 53; Yale Univ, MS, 55, PhD(biophys), 59. *Prof Exp:* Asst scientist bionucleonics, 58-61, physicist, Nat Inst Arthritis, Diabetes & Digestive & Kidney Dis, NIH, 61-86. *Concurrent Pos:* Lectr, Univ Calif, Davis, 68-69. *Mem:* Biophys Soc. *Res:* Radiation effects on macromolecules; macromolecular synthesis; growth under extreme conditions; cellular organization. *Mailing Add:* NIAMS NIH Bethesda MD 20892

KEMPNER, JOSEPH, APPLIED MECHANICS, AEROSPACE ENGINEERING. *Current Pos:* from res asst to res assoc appl mech, Polytech Inst NY, 47-50, from instr to assoc prof, 50-57, head, Dept Aerospace & Appl Mech, 66-76, prof appl mech, 57-90, EMER PROF APPL MECH, POLYTECH INST NY, 90- *Personal Data:* b Brooklyn, NY, Apr 25, 23; m 47; c 2. *Educ:* Polytech Inst Brooklyn, BAeroE, 43, MAeroE, 47, PhD(appl mech), 50. *Honors & Awards:* Citation Distinguished Res, Sigma Xi, 73; Laskowitz Gold Medal Res Aerospace Eng, NY Acad Sci, 73. *Prof Exp:* Aeronaut engr struct res, Nat Adv Comt Aeronaut, 43-47. *Concurrent Pos:* Prin investr, Off Naval Res & Air Force Off Sci Res grants & contracts, 58-77; consult, USN, 70-; mem adv group, Ship Res Comt, Maritime Transp Res Bd, Nat Acad Sci, 73-76; mem comt basic res, Adv Army Res Off, 73-76 & 82-85. *Mem:* Assoc Fel Am Inst Aeronaut & Astronaut; Am Soc Mech Eng; fel Am Acad Mech; fel NY Acad Sci; Am Soc Eng Educ. *Res:* Structural research related to aerospace vehicles, submersible vessels and pressure vessels; statics and dynamics of plates and shells, including large deformation and elevated temperature effects; applied mechanics. *Mailing Add:* 82 Murray Hill Terr Marlboro NJ 07746

KEMPNER, WALTER, internal medicine, cell physiology, for more information see previous edition

KEMPSON, STEPHEN ALLAN, MEMBRANE & EPITHELIAL TRANSPORT. *Current Pos:* from asst prof to assoc prof, 82-93, PROF PHYSIOL, IND UNIV MED SCH, 93- *Personal Data:* b Walsall, Eng, July 2, 48; US citizen. *Educ:* Lancaster Univ, UK, BA, 70; Warwick Univ, MSc, 71; London Univ, PhD(biochem), 75. *Prof Exp:* Fel biochem, Univ Rochester, 75-77; fel physiol, Mayo Clinic Found, 77-80, asst prof, Mayo Med Sch, 79-80; asst prof med, Univ Pittsburgh, 80-82. *Mem:* Am Physiol Soc; Am Soc Renal Biochem & Metab; Am Soc Nephrol. *Res:* Biochemistry and physiology of the kidney, specifically the cellular control mechanisms which regulate the transport of inorganic phosphate by the kidney. *Mailing Add:* Dept Physiol & Biophys Ind Univ Sch Med 635 Barnhill Dr Indianapolis IN 46202-5120

KEMPTER, CHARLES PRENTISS, TOXICOLOGY. *Current Pos:* RETIRED. *Personal Data:* b Burlington, Vt, Feb 12, 25; m 77, Judith A Hardison; c Colin, Eric & Reid. *Educ:* Stanford Univ, BS, 49, MS, 50, PhD(chem), 56. *Prof Exp:* Asst phys sci, Stanford Univ, 49-50; phys chemist, Dow Chem Co, 50-53; staff mem, Los Alamos Sci Lab, Univ Calif, 56-71; sci consult, 71-73; tech dir, Kempter-Rossman Int, 73-75; sci adv, 75-93. *Concurrent Pos:* Vis scientist, Inst Phys Chem, Vienna, 63-64; thesis adv, Los Alamos Grad Ctr, Univ NMex, 59-71; gov's adv, NMex State Crime Lab, 71-73. *Mem:* Fel Inst Chemists; Am Chem Soc; AAAS; Sigma Xi. *Res:* Biomedical literature research primarily in toxicology. *Mailing Add:* 6202 Agee St San Diego CA 92122

KEMPTHORNE, OSCAR, STATISTICS, GENETICS. *Current Pos:* assoc prof, Iowa State Univ, 47-51, prof statist, 51-89, distinguished prof, 64-89, EMER DISTINGUISHED PROF STATIST & SCI & HUMANITIES, IOWA STATE UNIV, 89- *Personal Data:* b Cornwall, Eng, Jan 31, 19; nat US; m 49, Valda Scales; c Jill, Joan & Peter. *Educ:* Cambridge Univ, BA, 40, MA, 43, ScD, 60. *Hon Degrees:* DSc, Univ Ioannina, Greece, 93. *Prof Exp:* Statistician, Rothamsted Exp Sta, Eng, 41-46. *Mem:* Int Statist Inst; fel Am Statist Asn; fel Inst Math Statist; hon fel Royal Statist Soc; Biomet Soc (past pres); Inst Math Statist (pres, 84-85). *Res:* Design of experiments; statistical inference; genetic statistics. *Mailing Add:* 2020 Ashmore Dr Ames IA 50014

KEMPTON, JOHN P(AUL), GROUNDWATER GEOLOGY. *Current Pos:* from asst geologist to assoc geologist, Ill Geol Surv, 56-71, geologist, Hydrogeol & Geophys Sect, 71-84, SSC geol task force leader, 84-86, sr geologist & spec proj leader, 86-88, SR GEOLOGIST & HEAD, QUATERNARY FRAMEWORK STUDIES SECT, ILL GEOL SURV, 88- *Personal Data:* b Buffalo, NY, Aug 14, 32; m 54; c 2. *Educ:* Denison Univ, BS, 54; Ohio State Univ, MA, 56; Univ Ill, PhD, 62. *Prof Exp:* Asst, Ohio State Univ, 54-56; geologist, Ohio Div Water, 55-56. *Concurrent Pos:* Vis prof, Northern Ill Univ, 73. *Mem:* AAAS; Geol Soc Am; Asn Eng Geologists; Sigma Xi; Am Quaternary Asn. *Res:* Quaternary stratigraphy and mapping, environmental and groundwater geology; three-dimensional, lithostratigraphic stackunit geologic maps of quaternary sediments for direct interpretation for ground-water resources development and protection, siting, and other land uses. *Mailing Add:* 1007 W Church St Champaign IL 61821

KENAGA, CLARE BURTON, PLANT PATHOLOGY. *Current Pos:* vis assoc prof, 66-67, assoc prof, 67-77, prof plant path, 77-81, EDUC ADMIN, PURDUE UNIV, 81- *Personal Data:* b Cadillac, Mich, Jan 9, 27; m 52; c 4. *Educ:* Western Mich Col, BS, 50; Univ Mich, MS, 52; Mich State Univ, PhD(plant path), 57. *Prof Exp:* Plant pathologist, Morton Chem Co, 57-66. *Concurrent Pos:* Indust consult; mem, Coun Agr Sci & Technol. *Mem:* Fel Nat Asn Cols & Teachers Agr; Am Phytopath Soc; Soc Nematol. *Res:* Mechanisms of action of fungicides and soil fumigants; teaching. *Mailing Add:* 2850 Ashland St West Lafayette IN 47906

KENAGA, DUANE LEROY, WOOD TECHNOLOGY, PULP & PAPER TECHNOLOGY. *Current Pos:* RETIRED. *Personal Data:* b Midland, Mich, Mar 9, 20; m 83, E Donna Bailey; c Diane M, Lawrence J, Linda S & Charles G. *Educ:* Univ Mich, BSChe, 43, MWT, 48. *Prof Exp:* Asst, Univ Mich, 47-48; wood technologist, Wood & Paper Sect, Southern Res Inst, 48-51; wood technologist, biochem res lab, Dow Chem Co, 51-65, sr res wood chemist, 65-69, res specialist, 69-78, res assoc, Designed Prod Dept, 78-85. *Mem:* Forest Prod Res Soc; Soc Wood Sci & Tech; Tech Asn Pulp & Paper Indust. *Res:* Chemical utilization of wood; chemical modification of wood to promote dimensional stability; paper and fiber treatments; wet end additives in paper systems, including bulking aids, retention aids and high filler sheets. *Mailing Add:* 4622 Chatham Court Midland MI 48642. *E-Mail:* dlkenaga@aol.com

KENAGY, GEORGE JAMES, ECOLOGY & BEHAVIOR PHYSIOLOGY, EVOLUTION. *Current Pos:* from asst prof to assoc prof, 76-86, PROF, DEPT ZOOL, UNIV WASH, 86-, CUR MAMMALS, BURKE MUS, 94- *Personal Data:* b Los Angeles, Calif, July 9, 45; m 69; c 2. *Educ:* Pomona Col, BA, 67; Univ Calif, Los Angeles, PhD(zool), 72. *Prof Exp:* Fel, Max Planck Inst Behav Physiol, Ger, 72-73; res biologist, Univ Calif, Los Angeles, 74. *Concurrent Pos:* Vis scientist CSIRO Wildlife, Australia, 83-84; vis scholar, Univ Calif, Berkeley, 89-90; vis prof, Univ Catalica Chile, 96- *Mem:* AAAS; Animal Behav Soc; Am Soc Mammalogists; Soc Study Evolution. *Res:* Bahavior and population biology of small mammals; daily and seasonal rhythms; reproduction; hibernation; energetics. *Mailing Add:* Dept Zool NJ-15 Univ Wash Seattle WA 98195. *E-Mail:* kenagy@u.washington.edu

KENAN, RICHARD P, INTEGRATED OPTICS, FIBER & NONLINEAR OPTICS. *Current Pos:* PROF, ELEC ENG, GA INST TECHNOL, 86- *Personal Data:* b Waycross, Ga, Dec 25, 31; m 68, Jane Dodge; c Jeffrey C, Diane L & Richard A. *Educ:* Ga Inst Technol, BA, 55; Ohio State Univ, PhD(physics), 62. *Prof Exp:* Res physicist, 62-63, sr physicist, 63-69, fel, 69-75, prin res scientist, 75-81, assoc sect mgr, Battelle Mem Inst, 81-86. *Mem:* Am Phys Soc; Am Asn Physics Teachers; Soc Photo-Optical

Instrumentation Engrs; fel Optical Soc Am; sr mem Inst Elec & Electronics Engrs. *Res:* nonlinear optics; diffractive optics; integrated optics; optical processing. *Mailing Add:* Sch Elec & Comput Eng Ga Inst Technol 777 Atlantic Dr NW Atlanta GA 30332-0250. *E-Mail:* dick.kenan@ee.gatech.edu

KENAT, THOMAS ARTHUR, CHEMICAL ENGINEERING, POLYMER SCIENCE. *Current Pos:* PRIN CONSULT, KENA TECH PROCESS ENG, 92- *Personal Data:* b Cleveland, Ohio, Aug 6, 42; m 64, Wynne Kalvesmaki; c Steven T & Lisa M. *Educ:* Carnegie-Mellon Univ, BS, 64, MS, 65, PhD(chem eng), 68. *Prof Exp:* Res engr, Chemstrand Res Ctr, Inc, NC, 68-69; res engr, B F Goodrich Co, 69-74; sr res & develop engr, 74-80, sr eng scientist, 81-83, sr res & develop assoc, 83-88; sr res & develop assoc, Camet Co, 88-89; sr prog mgr, Quantum Technol Inc, 89-92. *Mem:* Am Inst Chem Engrs; Am Chem Soc; Nat Asn Corrosion Engrs; Nat Soc Prof Engrs. *Res:* Dynamics and control of polymerization reactions; design and development of chemical reaction systems; processing of polymer composites; corrosion testing to select materials of construction for chemical process applications; design and development of chemical process concepts; synthetic rubber research and development; paper pulp bleaching chemicals; process engineering. *Mailing Add:* 745 Falling Oaks Dr Medina OH 44256. *Fax:* 330-725-7091; *E-Mail:* kenatech@juno.com

KENDALL, BRUCE REGINALD FRANCIS, VACUUM TECHNOLOGY, SPACE PHYSICS. *Current Pos:* assoc prof, 64-69, prof, 69-91, EMER PROF PHYSICS, PA STATE UNIV, 91- *Personal Data:* b Guildford, Western Australia, July 23, 34; m 56, 88, Carolyn Ruwitch; c 3. *Educ:* Univ Western Australia, BSc, 54, PhD (physics), 60. *Prof Exp:* Nat Res Coun Can, 59-60, asst res officer, 60-61; sr res scientist, Nuclide Corp, 61-62, dir new prod develop, 62-64. *Concurrent Pos:* Consult, 64-; chmn, Vacuum Technol Div, Am Vacuum Soc, 88-89, trustee, 92-95, chmn, hist comt, 94- *Mem:* Am Phys Soc; Am Vacuum Soc. *Res:* Electron, vacuum and space physics; mass spectrometry; vacuum and electrical properties of spacecraft materials; measurement and production of high vacuum. *Mailing Add:* Dept Physics Pa State Univ University Park PA 16802

KENDALL, BURTON NATHANIEL, NETWORKS, DISTRIBUTED DATA BASES. *Current Pos:* CHIEF TECHNOL OFFICER, HILIFE INC, 96- *Personal Data:* b San Francisco, Calif, Dec 15, 40; m 63, 79, Sally J Towse; c Anne, James & Samuel. *Educ:* Stanford Univ, BS, 62; Brown Univ, PhD(physics), 69. *Prof Exp:* Res aide microwave design, Stanford Univ, 59-62; res asst physics, Brown Univ, 62-69; lectr, Univ Calif, Santa Barbara, 69-71, asst prof, 71-73; sr res scientist, Systs Control Inc, 73-78; sr staff scientist, Measurex Corp, 78-80, prin scientist, 80-89; syst archit, Octel Commun Corp, 89-93, dir technol, 93-96. *Concurrent Pos:* Consult, Libr Automation, 79-; pres, Delta Res Found, 80-; mem, NASA Adv Panel Knowledge Based Systs Verification & Validation, 87-89. *Mem:* AAAS; Am Phys Soc; Sigma Xi; Healthcare Info & Mgt Systs Soc. *Res:* Computer hardware and software design; large scale systems design and modelling; indust process control syst design; voice processing and multimedia system design; distributed medical information systems. *Mailing Add:* HiLife Inc 401 Marina Dr South San Francisco CA 94080. *Fax:* 650-873-6065; *E-Mail:* bkendall@hilife.com

KENDALL, DAVID NELSON, SPECTROSCOPY. *Current Pos:* CONSULT, DAVID KENDALL ASSOCS, 87- *Personal Data:* b Gardner, Mass, Oct 20, 16; m 42, Ruth Spencer; c Douglas, Bertrand & Katherine. *Educ:* Wesleyan Univ, BA, 38, MA, 39; Johns Hopkins Univ, PhD(chem, physics), 43. *Honors & Awards:* Gold Medal, Soc Appl Spectros, 73. *Prof Exp:* Res phys chemist, Titanium Div, Nat Lead Co, NJ, 43-44; res chem physicist, Calco Chem Div, Am Cyanamid Co, 44-46, head infrared spectros labs, 46-53; consult chemist & spectroscopist & infrared specialist, founder, Kendall Infrared Labs, 53-87. *Concurrent Pos:* Asst ed, Appl Spectros, Soc Appl Spectros, 46-48; ed, Your Consult, Newslett Asn Consult Chemists & Chem Engrs, Inc, 74-83. *Mem:* Am Chem Soc; Soc Appl Spectros (pres, 55-56); Coblentz Soc; Asn Consult Chemists & Chem Eng (pres, 64-66); fel Am Inst Chem; Sigma Xi. *Res:* Colloid chemistry; x-ray crystallography; pigment particle size determination; colored oil smokes; lightfastness of dyes and pigments; infrared, Raman, visual and ultraviolet spectroscopy; analytical chemistry; polymer chemistry. *Mailing Add:* Cypress Hilton Head SC 29926-1823

KENDALL, H(AROLD) B(ENNE), CHEMICAL ENGINEERING. *Current Pos:* chmn, Dept Chem Engr, Ohio Univ, 61-67, 71-72 & 82-83, PROF CHEM ENG, OHIO UNIV, 60- *Personal Data:* b Midland, Mich, Apr 27, 23; m 48; c 4. *Educ:* Grove City Col, BS, 48; Case Inst Technol, MS, 50, PhD(chem eng), 56. *Prof Exp:* Instr chem & metall eng, Univ Mich, 50-51; instr chem & chem eng, Case Inst Technol, 51-55, asst prof chem eng, 55-60. *Mem:* Am Chem Soc; Soc Hist Technol; Am Inst Chem Engrs. *Res:* Reaction kinetics in flow reactors; catalytic processing; heterogeneous catalysis; history of technology. *Mailing Add:* 69 Morris Ave Athens OH 45701

KENDALL, HARRY WHITE, PHYSICS. *Current Pos:* RETIRED. *Personal Data:* b Sopchoppy, Fla, Oct 9, 24; m 50; c 3. *Educ:* Tusculum Col, BA, 48; Fla State Univ, MS, 50; Univ Fla, PhD(electronics, physics), 61. *Prof Exp:* Instr physics, Chipola Jr Col, 50-51; asst prof, Emory & Henry Col, 51-54, assoc prof & head dept, 57-59; teaching asst, Univ Fla, 54-57, NSF fac fel, 59-60; assoc prof & chmn dept physics, Univ S Fla, 60-63, prof, 63-84, actg chmn dept, 78-84. *Mem:* Am Phys Soc; Am Asn Physics Teachers; Sigma Xi. *Res:* Electrical breakdown of gases. *Mailing Add:* Grand Ridge FL 32442

KENDALL, HENRY WAY, PHYSICS. *Current Pos:* from asst prof to prof, 61-91, J A SHATTON PROF PHYSICS, MASS INST TECHNOL, 91- *Personal Data:* b Boston, Mass, Dec 9, 26. *Educ:* Amherst Col, BA, 50; Mass Inst Technol, PhD(nuclear physics), 55. *Hon Degrees:* DSc, Amherst Col, 75. *Honors & Awards:* Nobel Prize Physics, 90; Leo Szilard Award, Am Phys Soc, 81; Bertrand Russell Soc Award, 82; WKH Panofsky Prize, 89. *Prof Exp:* NSF fel, Mass Inst Technol, 54-56; res assoc, High Energy Lab, Stanford Univ, 56-57, lectr physics, 57-58, asst prof, 58-61. *Concurrent Pos:* Chmn, Union Concerned Scientists, 75- *Mem:* Fel Nat Acad Sci; fel Am Acad Arts & Sci; fel AAAS; fel Am Phys Soc. *Res:* Nucleon structure; high energy electron scattering; meson and neutrino physics. *Mailing Add:* Mass Inst Technol 77 Massachusetts Ave Cambridge MA 02139. *Fax:* 617-253-1755

KENDALL, JOHN HUGH, FOOD SCIENCE, CEREAL CHEMISTRY. *Current Pos:* sr food technologist, 73-, DIR PROCESS DEVELOP, RIVIANA FOODS INC. *Personal Data:* b Mt Pleasant, Tex, Sept 30, 42; m 65; c 2. *Educ:* La State Univ, BS, 64, MS, 69, PhD(food sci), 73. *Prof Exp:* Qual control rep, Borden Inc, 71-73. *Concurrent Pos:* Adj asst prof, Univ Houston, 75- *Mem:* Inst Food Technologists; Am Asn Cereal Chemists; Int Asn Milk Food & Environ Sanitarians; Am Soc Microbiol. *Res:* Rice processing and by-product utilization. *Mailing Add:* Riviana Foods Inc 1702 Taylor Houston TX 77007

KENDALL, JOHN WALKER, JR, ENDOCRINOLOGY. *Current Pos:* from asst prof to assoc prof, Sch Med, Ore Health Sci Univ, 62-71, prof med & head, Div Metab, Med Sch, 71-80, prof med & asst dean res, 80-83, dean, 83-92 EMER DEAN, SCH MED, ORE HEALTH SCI UNIV, 92- *Personal Data:* b Bellingham, Wash, Mar 19, 29; m 54, Betty Meece; c John, Kay & Victoria. *Educ:* Yale Univ, BA, 52; Univ Wash, MD, 56. *Honors & Awards:* Mentor Award, Med Res Found Ore, 93. *Prof Exp:* USPHS trainee, 59-62. *Concurrent Pos:* Instr med, Sch Med, Vanderbilt Univ, 59-60; assoc chief of staff for res, Vet Admin Hosp, Portland, 71-83; chmn pro tem, Dept Med, Med Sch, Univ Ore, 75-76; mem, Vet Admin Res Adv Comt, 80-83; pres, Ore Found Med Excellence, 89-91; distinguished physician, Dept Vet Affairs, 93-96; acad affil liaison officer, Visn #20, Va, 96- *Mem:* Asn Am Physicians; Endocrine Soc; Am Soc Clin Invest; Am Fedn Clin Res. *Res:* Neural control of pituitary function. *Mailing Add:* Va Med Ctr PO Box 1034 Portland OR 97207

KENDALL, KATHERINE CLEMENT, GRIZZLY BEAR ECOLOGY, COMMUNITY ECOLOGY OF PLANTS & ANIMALS. *Current Pos:* RES ECOLOGIST, BIOL RESOURCES DIV, US GEOL SURV, 96- *Personal Data:* b Morristown, NJ, Dec 9, 51; m 82, George P Scherman; c Jack & Samuel. *Educ:* Univ Va, BA, 74; Mont State Univ, MS, 81. *Prof Exp:* Environ specialist, Nat Park Serv, DC, 74-77, res biologist, Bozeman, Mont, 77-82, res ecologist, W Glacier, Mont, 82-93; res ecologist, Nat Biol Serv, US Dept Interior, 93-96. *Concurrent Pos:* Adj prof, Univ Mont, 82-; rep, Interagency Grizzly Bear Res Subcomt, Nat Park Serv, 89-, chmn, 93- *Mem:* Int Bear Asn; Wildlife Soc; Sigma Xi; George Wright Soc. *Res:* Monitoring long-term population trends, community ecology and interaction between climate and community processes; focus on grizzly and black bears, huckleberry, whitebark pine; conservation biology. *Mailing Add:* Glacier Nat Park Sci Ctr West Glacier MT 59936. *Fax:* 406-888-7990; *E-Mail:* katherine_kendall@nbs.gov

KENDALL, MICHAEL WELT, GROSS ANATOMY, MICROSCOPIC ANATOMY. *Current Pos:* CONSULT, 84- *Personal Data:* b Glendale, Ariz, Jan 30, 43; m 65; c 1. *Educ:* Univ Northern Iowa, BA, 65; Univ Louisville, MS, 69, PhD(anat), 72. *Prof Exp:* Asst prof anat, Med Ctr, Univ Miss, 72-74; from asst prof to assoc prof anat, Sch Med Sci, Univ Nev, Reno, 74-84, chmn dept, 75-77. *Concurrent Pos:* Pesticide consult, Dept Agr, Univ Nev, 75-76; consult gross anat, Int Cong Col Physicians & Surgeons, 76- *Mem:* AAAS; Am Asn Anatomists; Am Heart Asn. *Res:* Ultrastructural descriptive analysis of carcinogenesis induced by aflatoxin-B, in rat liver; ultrastructural hepatotoxic effects of mirex in rats; scanning electron microscopy of human knee joints. *Mailing Add:* 4800 Olsen Blvd Amarillo TX 76106

KENDALL, NORMAN, pediatrics, for more information see previous edition

KENDALL, PERRY E(UGENE), ELECTRICAL ENGINEERING. *Current Pos:* RETIRED. *Personal Data:* b Paoli, Ind, July 27, 21; m 42; c 3. *Educ:* Purdue Univ, BS, 48, MS, 49, PhD(elec eng), 53. *Prof Exp:* Instr elec eng, Purdue Univ, 47-52; sr engr, res in servomechanisms, Cook Res Lab, 52-54; res proj engr, Capehart-Farnsworth Co Div, Int Tel & Tel Corp, 54-56, sr engr, Farnsworth Electronics Co, 56-58, head systs anal & design labs, 58-60, lab dir guidance & control lab, Astrionics Ctr, ITT Fed Labs, 60-63; mgr res & develop, Fed Systs Div, Indust Nucleonics Corp, 63-66; mgr guid & control, Missile Div, NAm Aviation Corp, 66-70; mgr advan develop, Indust Systs Res & Develop, Indust Nucleonics Corp, 70-74; mem sr tech staff, TRW Defense & Space Systs Group, 74-79, proj engr, 79-81. *Res:* Servomechanisms and electronics; circuits for photoemissive electron tubes and infrared cells; guidance for guided missiles and space vehicles; application of digital computers for process control; high energy laser systems. *Mailing Add:* RR 4 Mitchell IN 47446

KENDALL, PHILIP C, CHILD & ADOLESCENT CLINICAL PSYCHOLOGY. *Current Pos:* PROF PSYCHOL, TEMPLE UNIV, 84-, DIR CHILD & ADOLESCENT ANXIETY DISORDERS CLIN, 84- *Personal Data:* m 74; c 2. *Educ:* Old Dominion Univ, BS, 72; Va Commonwealth Univ, PhD(clin psychol), 77. *Prof Exp:* Prof psychol, Univ Minn, 77-84. *Concurrent Pos:* Fel, Ctr Advan Study Behav Sci, Stanford,

Calif, 77; head Div Psychol, Temple Univ, 84- *Mem:* Am Psychol Asn; Asn Advan Behav Ther (pres-elect, 88). *Res:* Child and adolescent clinical psychology with a special focus on the cognitive and behavioral aspects of psychopathology; design and evaluation of psychotherapeutic programs; self control, anxiety and depression. *Mailing Add:* Dept Psychol Temple Univ 1701 N Broad St Philadelphia PA 19122-2504

KENDALL, ROBERT MCCUTCHEON, CHEMICAL ENGINEERING. *Current Pos:* PRES, ALZETA CORP, 82- *Personal Data:* b Pasadena, Calif, Dec 29, 31; m 57, Angela Heine; c Thomas R, Kathleen K (Fitzgerald), John R & Paticia L. *Educ:* Stanford Univ, BS, 52, MS, 53; Mass Inst Technol, ScD, 59. *Prof Exp:* Thermodyn specialist, Calif Adv Propulsion Systs Oper, 56-60; sect mgr, Vidya Inc, 60-65; vpres & div mgr, Aerotherm Corp, 65-76, sr vpres, chief scientist & mgr combustion technol, Acurex Corp, 76-82. *Concurrent Pos:* Lectr, exten, Univ Calif, 59-62 & Stanford Univ, 63-64; consult prof, Stanford Univ, 78-84. *Mem:* Am Inst Chem Engrs; Combustion Inst. *Res:* Application of advanced experimental and computational techniques to the study of problems of mass, energy and momentum exchange in combusting or chemically active fluid dynamic systems. *Mailing Add:* 1097 Enderby Way Sunnyvale CA 94087

KENDALL, WILLIAM ANDERSON, PLANT PHYSIOLOGY. *Current Pos:* PLANT PHYSIOLOGIST, AGR RES SERV, USDA, 54- *Personal Data:* b Fitchburg, Mass, Sept 24, 24; m 52; c 3. *Educ:* Univ Maine, BS, 49; Ohio State Univ, PhD(bot), 54. *Prof Exp:* Asst, Ohio State Univ, 49-54. *Concurrent Pos:* Adj prof, Univ Ky, 54-70 & Pa State Univ, 70- *Mem:* Am Soc Agron; Am Soc Plant Physiol. *Res:* Interactions of genotypes and environments on growth and development of forage crops. *Mailing Add:* 714 Devonshire Dr State College PA 16803-3205

KENDE, ANDREW S, ORGANIC CHEMISTRY, ORGANIC SYNTHESIS. *Current Pos:* prof chem, 68-81, chmn, 79-83, CHARLES F HOUGHTON PROF CHEM, UNIV ROCHESTER, 81-; PRES, ORG SYNTHESES, INC, 91- *Personal Data:* b Budapest, Hungary, July 17, 32; nat US; m 54, Frances; c Mark. *Educ:* Univ Chicago, BA, 50; Harvard Univ, MA, 54, PhD, 57; Glasgow Univ, postdoc, 58; Univ Munchen, postdoc, 60. *Prof Exp:* Res chemist, Lederle Labs, Am Cyanamid Co, 57-62, res assoc, 63-67, res fel, 67-68. *Concurrent Pos:* Vis prof, Mich State Univ, 68 & Univ Geneve, 74; consult, Lederle Labs, 68-, Dow Chem Co, 74- & Eastman Kodak, 88-; consult, Med Chem Study Sect, NIH, 72-76 & 85-86, chmn, 74-76; Guggenheim fel, 78-79; chmn, Org Div, Am Chem Soc, 78-79; Japan Soc Prom Sci Award, 85-86. *Mem:* Am Chem Soc; Am Asn Univ Profs. *Res:* Thermal and photochemical rearrangements, total synthesis of alkaloids and antibiotics, synthetic methods; chemistry of antitumor compounds. *Mailing Add:* Dept Chem Univ Rochester Rochester NY 14627-0216. *Fax:* 716-473-6889

KENDE, HANS JANOS, PLANT HORMONE ACTION. *Current Pos:* dir, 85-88, from assoc prof to prof, 65-90, DISTINGUISHED UNIV PROF BOT & PLANT PATH, DEPT ENERGY PLANT RES LAB, MICH STATE UNIV, 90- *Personal Data:* b Szekesfehervar, Hungary, Jan 18, 37; US citizen; m 60, Gabriele Guggenheim; c Benjamin, Michael & Judith. *Educ:* Univ Zurich, PhD(bot), 60. *Hon Degrees:* DSc, Univ Fribourg, Switz. *Honors & Awards:* Medal Res Excellence, Int Plant Growth Substances Asn, 95. *Prof Exp:* Res fel, plant physiol, Nat Res Coun Can, 60-61; res fel, Div Biol, Calif Inst Technol, 61-63; plant physiologist, Negev Inst Arid Zone Res, Israel, 63-65. *Concurrent Pos:* Guggenheim Mem Found fel & vis prof, Swiss Fed Inst Technol, 72-73; vis prof, Swiss Fed Inst Technol, 79-80; vis scientist, Friedrich Miescher Inst Basel, Switz, 91. *Mem:* Nat Acad Sci; Am Soc Plant Physiol; fel AAAS; Ger Acad Sci. *Res:* Function, biosynthesis and action mechanism of plant growth regulators. *Mailing Add:* Dept Energy Plant Res Lab Mich State Univ East Lansing MI 48824-1312. *Fax:* 517-353-9168; *E-Mail:* hkende@msu.edu

KENDER, DONALD NICHOLAS, ANALYTICAL CHEMISTRY. *Current Pos:* MGR, CIBA-GEIGY CORP, 76- *Personal Data:* b Passaic, NJ, Aug 30, 48; m 71. *Educ:* Ohio State Univ, BA, 70; Georgetown Univ, PhD(chem), 75. *Prof Exp:* Chemist & Nat Res Coun assoc, Naval Surface Weapons Ctr, 75-76. *Mem:* Am Chem Soc; Soc Appl Spectros; Sigma Xi. *Res:* Isolation, identification and physical organic chemistry of pharmaceuticals. *Mailing Add:* CIBA-GEIGY Pharm 556 Morris Ave Summit NJ 07901-1330

KENDER, WALTER JOHN, AGRICULTURAL ADMINISTRATION, CITRUS. *Current Pos:* dir Citrus Res & Educ Ctr, Lake Alfred, 82-96, PROF, UNIV FLA, 82- *Personal Data:* b Camden, NJ, Dec 20, 35; m 57, Carole Kender Holm; c David & Lily. *Educ:* Del Valley Col, BS, 57; Rutgers Univ, MS, 59, PhD(plant nutrit), 62. *Hon Degrees:* DSc, Del Valley Col, 93. *Honors & Awards:* Darrow Award, Am Soc Hort Sci, 83. *Prof Exp:* From asst prof to assoc prof hort, Univ Maine, Orono, 62-69; assoc prof, 69-75, prof pomol & chmn dept, Cornell Univ, 75-82, head dept pomol & viticult, NY Agr Exp Sta 72-82. *Concurrent Pos:* Assoc ed, Am Soc Hort Sci, 72-76; distinguished scientist, ARIC Univ, Wageningen The Netherlands, 74; bd dir, Am Soc Hort Sci, 75-80, 82-85; adv comt, Farm Bur Citrus, 85-; consult, US-AID-Pakistan, 89; prin investor, ARS Coop Agreement Citrus Exotic Dis, 89-94; consult, World Bank, Indonesia, 91. *Mem:* Inst Food Technologists; Am Pomol Soc; fel Am Soc Hort Sci; Sigma Xi. *Res:* Physiology and culture of fruit crops; air pollution effects on agricultural crops; emphasis on impacts of fossil fuel effluents and acid rain on fruit crop productivity and economic assessment; citrus; agricultural administration; abscission chemicals for mechanically harvesting citrus fruit. *Mailing Add:* Citrus Res & Educ Ctr Univ Fla 700 Exp Sta Rd Lake Alfred FL 33850. *Fax:* 941-956-4631; *E-Mail:* kender@icon.lal.ufl.edu

KENDIG, EDWIN LAWRENCE, JR, PEDIATRICS, RESPIRATORY DISORDERS. *Current Pos:* dir, Child Chest Clin, Col Hosp, 44-54, assoc prof, 58-61, PROF PEDIAT, MED COL VA, VA COMMONWEALTH UNIV, 61- *Personal Data:* b Victoria, Va, Nov 12, 11; m 41; c Anne R (Young & Mary (Corb). *Educ:* Hampden-Sydney Col, BA, 32, BS, 33; Univ Va, MD, 36. *Hon Degrees:* DSc, Hampden-Sydney Col, 71. *Honors & Awards:* Abraham Jacabi Award, Am Acad Pediat & Am Med Asn; Int Medal, Int Pediat Asn. *Concurrent Pos:* Instr, Johns Hopkins Hosp, 44; mem, Comt Med Educ & founding mem, Sect Dis in Childhood, Am Thoracic Soc; mem bd visitors, Univ Va; mem Va steering comt, White House Conf, 60; chmn, Richmond City Bd Health; ed, Dis Respiratory Tract Children. *Mem:* Am Acad Pediat (pres, 78-79); Am Pediat Soc; Am Thoracic Soc; NY Acad Sci. *Res:* Pediatrics; sarcoidosis; unclassified mycobacteria; pediatric respiratory disease. *Mailing Add:* 4205 Dover Rd Richmond VA 23221. *Fax:* 804-355-6189

KENDIG, JOAN JOHNSTON, NEUROBIOLOGY. *Current Pos:* res assoc, 67-71, from asst prof to assoc prof, 71-86, PROF BIOL ANESTHESIA, SCH MED, STANFORD UNIV, 86- *Personal Data:* b Derby, Conn, May 1, 39; m 64; c Scott J & Leslie A. *Educ:* Smith Col, BA, 60; Stanford Univ, PhD(biol sci), 66. *Prof Exp:* NSF fel neurophysiol, Univ Calif, Berkeley, 65-67. *Concurrent Pos:* Mellon fac fel, Stanford Univ, 76; vis scientist, Clin Res Ctr, Northwick Park, UK, 84, vis prof, Ben Gurion Univ, Israel, 88; NIH physiol study sect, 81-85; Javits Neurosci Investr Award, 88-95; mem, Surg, Anethesia & Trauma Study Sect, NIH, 96- *Mem:* Soc Neurosci; Int Asn Study Pain; Am Pain Soc; Am Soc Anethesiologists. *Res:* Neuropharmacology of anesthetic and analgesic drugs; cellular effects of anesthetic and analgesic agents. *Mailing Add:* Dept Anesthesia Sch Med Stanford Univ Stanford CA 94305

KENDIG, MARTIN WILLIAM, PHYSICAL CHEMISTRY, CORROSION SCIENCE. *Current Pos:* SR SCIENTIST & MEM TECH STAFF, ROCKWELL INT SCI CTR, 80- *Personal Data:* b Danville, Pa, Oct 20, 45; m 69, Michele L Mulligan; c Rebecca L & Jamie A. *Educ:* Franklin & Marshall Col, AB, 67; Brown Univ, PhD(phys chem), 74. *Honors & Awards:* Melvin Romanoff Award, Nat Asn Corrosion Engrs. *Prof Exp:* Res assoc, Ctr Surface & Coatings Res, Lehigh Univ, 73-76; asst chemist, 76-78, assoc chemist corrosion sci, Brookhaven Nat Lab, 78-80. *Concurrent Pos:* Chmn, Corrosion Div, Electrochem Soc. *Mem:* Electrochem Soc; Am Chem Soc; Sigma Xi; Am Soc Testing & Mat; Nat Asn Corrosion Engrs. *Res:* Electrochemical aspects of surface energy, wetting wear and environmental fracture; the chemistry and physics of localized corrosion and corrosion protection; corrosion monitoring; polymer coatings. *Mailing Add:* Rockwell Sci Ctr Thousand Oaks CA 91360. *Fax:* 805-373-4383; *E-Mail:* mwkendig@scimail.risc.rockwell.com

KENDRICK, BRYCE, MYCOLOGY. *Current Pos:* from asst prof to prof biol, 65-94, assoc dean grad studies, 85-93, DISTINGUISHED EMER PROF, UNIV WATERLOO, 94- *Personal Data:* b Liverpool, Eng, Dec 3, 33; m 57, 77, Laureen A Carscadden; c Clinton & Kelly. *Educ:* Univ Liverpool, BSc, 55, PhD(mycol), 58. *Hon Degrees:* DSc, Univ Liverpool, 80. *Honors & Awards:* Distinguished Mycologist Award, Mycol Soc Am, 95. *Prof Exp:* Fel taxonomic mycol, Nat Res Coun Can, 58-59; mycologist, Plant Res Inst, Res Br, Can Dept Agr, 59-65. *Concurrent Pos:* Chmn, Plant Biol Grant Selection Comt, Nat Sci & Eng Res Coun, Can, 79; Guggenheim fel, 79-80; secy, Acad Sci, Royal Soc Can, 85-91; hon prof, Nanjing Forestry Univ, Nanjing, China, 88; distinguished res fel, Found Res Development, SAfrica, 90; Sir CV Raman fel, 93; adj prof, Univ Victoria, BC, 94- *Mem:* Mycol Soc Am; Brit Mycol Soc; fel Royal Soc Can; fel Brit Mycol Soc. *Res:* Computer simulations; systematics of hyphomycetes; development, ecology, karyology, and toxicology of microfungi; mycorrhizae; fungal biodiversity. *Mailing Add:* 8727 Lochside Dr Sidney BC V8L 1M8 Can. *Fax:* 250-655-0755; *E-Mail:* mycolog@pacificcoast.net, Internet: http://www.pacificcoast.net-mycolog

KENDRICK, FRANCIS JOSEPH, pathology, dentistry, for more information see previous edition

KENDRICK, HUGH, NUCLEAR ENGINEERING, SOLID STATE PHYSICS. *Current Pos:* vpres, 81-84, dep chief operating officer, 85-89, CORP VPRES, SCI APPLICATIONS INT CORP, 84-, ASST PRES, 89- *Personal Data:* b Ewell, Eng, Jan 25, 40; m 63, Diana W Adams; c Stuart & Amanda K. *Educ:* Univ London, BSc, 61; Calif Inst Technol, MS, 62; Univ Mich, PhD(nuclear eng), 68. *Prof Exp:* Teaching res asst mech eng, Calif Inst Technol, 61-62; scientist, Vickers Res Ltd, 62-63; sr physicist, Radiation Transport Group, Gulf Radiation Technol, 68-72; dep mgr, Div Environ & Safety, Sci Applns, Inc, 72-75, mgr, Div Safeguards & Nuclear Fuels, 75-77; spec asst, Off Fuel Cycle Eval, US Dept Energy, 77-79, dir, Off Plans & Anal, 79-81. *Mem:* Am Phys Soc; Inst Nuclear Mat Mgt; Am Nuclear Soc; Sigma Xi. *Res:* Investigation of magnetic materials through neutron diffraction; pulsed neutron investigation of radiation transport in shields; spectroscopy and unfolding techniques; nuclear materials assay; assessment of proliferation risks of nuclear technology; nuclear safeguards system effectiveness evaluation; environmental economic safety assessment of technology. *Mailing Add:* 13062 Caminito Pt Del Mar CA 92014-3853. *Fax:* 619-458-2739; *E-Mail:* hugh_kendrick@cpqm.saic.com

KENDRICK, JOHN EDSEL, PHYSIOLOGY. *Current Pos:* From instr to asst prof, 57-67, ASSOC PROF PHYSIOL, SCH MED, UNIV WIS-MADISON, 67- *Personal Data:* b Scott City, Kans, Dec 23, 28; m 54; c 3. *Educ:* Univ Kans, AB, 52, PhD(physiol), 57. *Mem:* Am Physiol Soc. *Res:* Cardiovascular physiology. *Mailing Add:* 3014 Shady Oak Lane Verona WI 53593

KENDZIORSKI, FRANCIS RICHARD, NUCLEAR PHYSICS. *Current Pos:* assoc prof, 67-77, chmn Dept Physics & Astron, 78-85, PROF PHYSICS, WESTERN CONN STATE COL, 77- *Personal Data:* b Alpena, Mich, Apr 2, 31; m 64; c 2. *Educ:* Univ Detroit, BS, 53; Cornell Univ, PhD(physics), 61. *Prof Exp:* Asst prof physics, Univ Detroit, 61-63; asst prof, Univ Dayton, 63-67. *Mem:* AAAS; Am Phys Soc; Am Asn Physics Teachers. *Res:* Low energy studies of nuclear structure in intermediate weight nuclei; extensive cosmic ray air showers; elementary education. *Mailing Add:* 37 Farview Ave Danbury CT 06810

KENEALY, MICHAEL DOUGLAS, ANIMAL NUTRITION, PHYSIOLOGY. *Current Pos:* from asst prof to assoc prof, 75-84, PROF ANIMAL SCI, IOWA STATE UNIV, 84- *Personal Data:* b Council Bluffs, Iowa, May 7, 47; m 69; c 2. *Educ:* Iowa State Univ, BS, 69, PhD(animal nutrit & physiol), 74. *Prof Exp:* Nutritionist, Dr Macdonalds Feed Co, 74-75. *Mem:* Sigma Xi; Am Dairy Sci Asn; Am Soc Animal Sci. *Res:* International work in China, Costa Rica, Taiwan, and the Soviet Union. *Mailing Add:* Dept Animal Sci Iowa State Univ Ames IA 50011-2010

KENEALY, PATRICK FRANCIS, MATHEMATICS EDUCATION. *Current Pos:* PROF PHYSICS & SCI EDUC, CALIF STATE UNIV, LONG BEACH, 88- *Personal Data:* b Chicago, Ill, Aug 4, 39. *Educ:* Loyola Univ, Ill, BS, 61; Univ Notre Dame, PhD(physics), 67. *Prof Exp:* From asst prof to assoc prof physics, Wayne State Univ, 67-88. *Concurrent Pos:* Vis assoc prof, Stanford Univ, 76-77; NSF fac fel visit, 76-77; vis scholar, grad group sci & math educ, Univ Calif, Berkeley; sr sci consult, Detroit Sci Ctr, 88. *Mem:* AAAS; Am Phys Soc; Am Asn Physics Teachers; Am Educ Res Asn. *Res:* Research on the role of language in science and mathematics learning; teacher training in science and mathematics; informal science and mathematics instruction in museum settings; use of computers in teaching physics; theoretical and experimental analysis of physics instruction and learning. *Mailing Add:* Dept Physics Sci Calif State Univ 1250 Bellflower Blvd Long Beach CA 90840-3901. *Fax:* 562-985-2315

KENEFICK, ROBERT ARTHUR, TRAPPED IONS. *Current Pos:* from asst prof to assoc prof, 65-74, PROF PHYSICS, TEX A&M UNIV, 74- *Personal Data:* b Syracuse, NY, Mar 9, 37; m 60, Kathleen Weeks; c 3. *Educ:* Mass Inst Technol, BS, 59; Fla State Univ, PhD(physics), 62. *Prof Exp:* Res assoc nuclear physics, Univ Colo, 62-63; asst prof, 63-64; asst prof, Univ Mich, 64-65. *Mem:* Am Phys Soc; AAAS; Am Asn Physics Teachers. *Res:* Atomic collisions; particle detectors; ion sources; musical acoustics. *Mailing Add:* Dept Physics Tex A&M Univ College Station TX 77843. *Fax:* 409-845-2590

KENELLY, JOHN WILLIS, JR, MATHEMATICS. *Current Pos:* head dept, 69-77, prof, 69-85, ALUMNI DISTINGUISHED PROF MATH SCI, CLEMSON UNIV, 85- *Personal Data:* b Bogalusa, La, Nov 22, 35; m 56, Charmaine; c Deidre & Trent. *Educ:* Southeastern La Col, BS, 57; Univ Miss, MS, 57; Univ Fla, PhD(math), 61. *Prof Exp:* Instr math, Univ Fla, 59-61; asst prof, Univ Southwestern La, 61-63; assoc prof, Clemson Univ, 63-68; prof & chmn dept, La State Univ, 68-69. *Concurrent Pos:* Vis lectr & curric consult, Math Asn Am, 70-, ed, Placement Test Newslett, 79-85; chief reader, Advan placement Prog Math, Educ Testing Serv, 75-79, dir advan placement reading, 85-; chmn, Advan Placement Math Comt, Col Bd, 79-83, Math Sci Adv Comt, 83- & coun acad affairs, 85-87; prog officer, NSF, 88; interim dir, Col & Advan Placement Prog, 89-90; chmn, Southeastern Sect, Math Asn Am, bd govs, 85-96. *Mem:* Am Math Soc; Math Asn Am; Nat Coun Teachers Math. *Res:* Geometry; convexity; operations research. *Mailing Add:* 327 Woodland Way Clemson SC 29631-1547. *Fax:* 864-656-5230; *E-Mail:* kenellj@clemson.edu

KENESHEA, FRANCIS JOSEPH, INORGANIC CHEMISTRY. *Current Pos:* RETIRED. *Personal Data:* b Providence, RI, June 25, 21; wid; c Ellen & Jane. *Educ:* RI State Col, BS, 43, MS, 48; Univ NMex, PhD(chem), 51. *Prof Exp:* Instr chem, RI State Col, 46-47; asst, Cornell Univ, 47-48; sr res engr, NAm Aviation, Inc, 51-55; sr chemist, Stanford Res Inst, 55-71; consult engr, Quadrex Corp, 74-80, sr consult, 80-85. *Concurrent Pos:* Sr res assoc, Ore State Univ, 63-64. *Mem:* Sigma Xi; Am Chem Soc. *Res:* Thermodynamics of vaporization; chemical diffusion; chemistry of molten salts and metal-salt solutions; nuclear and radiochemistry; nuclear technology. *Mailing Add:* 20 Bear Paw Portola Valley CA 94028-8014

KENETT, RON, statistical methods, design of experiments, for more information see previous edition

KENG, PETER C, CELL SEPARATION, RADIATION BIOLOGY. *Current Pos:* Asst prof, Dept Radiation Oncol, Univ Rochester, 80-85, asst prof, Dept Radiation Biol & Biophys, 81-85, assoc prof, Dept Radiation Oncol & Dept Radiation Biol & Biophys, 85-92, DIR RES, CELL SEPARATION & FLOW CYTOMETRY FACIL, UNIV ROCHESTER, 81-, PROF, DEPT RADIATION ONCOL & DEPT BIOPHYS, 93- *Personal Data:* b Kinagsu, China, Aug 12, 46; m 72, Suzan Lu; c 3. *Educ:* Tunghai Univ, BS, 69; Colo State Univ, PhD(radiation biol), 78. *Mem:* Radiation Res Soc; Anal Cytometry; Am Soc Cell Biol; AAAS. *Res:* Separation of cell subpopulations from solid tumors, bone marrow and tissue culture cells into various host cells; neoplastic cells and cells at different stages of the cell cycle to study the DNA damage of these cells. *Mailing Add:* Biophysics Univ Rochester Sch Med 601 Elmwood Ave Rochester NY 14642-0001

KENIG, MARVIN JERRY, APPLIED MECHANICS, MATERIALS SCIENCE. *Current Pos:* DEAN ENG & APPL SCI, UNIV NEW HAVEN, 89- *Personal Data:* b Philadelphia, Pa, Sept 20, 36; m 59; c 2. *Educ:* Drexel Univ, BSME, 59, MSME, 63; Princeton Univ, MA, 63, PhD(eng), 65. *Prof Exp:* From assoc prof to prof mech eng, Drexel Univ, 69-82, asst to pres, 74-83; prof & chmn, Dept Mech Eng, Western Mich Univ, 83-87, prof & chmn, Dept Aircraft & Automotive Eng, 87-89. *Concurrent Pos:* Consult, J P Oat & Sons, Inc, 68- & US Army Frankford Arsenal, 70-75. *Mem:* Am Soc Mech Engrs; Am Acad Mech; Am Soc Eng Educr; Am Defense Preparedness Asn; AAAS; Sigma Xi. *Res:* Effect Portevin-Le Chatalier phenomenon on plastic potential theory of yielding; implications with respect to propagation of small stress increments; creep; fatigue; quantum mechanics modeling of dislocation motion; response of orthotropic plates under lateral pressure pulse; inelastic buckling of non-prismatic columns; bending of prismatic unsymmetric eccentrically loaded columns; forensic engineering. *Mailing Add:* 380 Hitchcock Rd Unit 129 Waterbury CT 06705-3954. *Fax:* 203-932-7394; *E-Mail:* mjkenig@chager.newhaven.edu

KENK, VIDA CARMEN, INVERTEBRATE ZOOLOGY, BIVALVE MOLLUSKS. *Current Pos:* Asst prof, 66-70, assoc prof, 70-77, PROF BIOL, SAN JOSE STATE UNIV, 77- *Personal Data:* b San Juan, PR, Dec 24, 39; m 74, William J Minkel; c Chris & Lauren. *Educ:* Col William & Mary, BS, 61; Radcliffe Col, AM, 62; Harvard Univ, PhD(biol), 67. *Mem:* AAAS; Am Malacol Union; Western Soc Malacologists (pres, 80). *Res:* Systematics, ecology and functional anatomy of bivalve molluscs. *Mailing Add:* 18596 Paseo Pueblo Dr Saratoga CA 95070

KENKARE, DIVAKER B, BIOLOGICAL CHEMISTRY, PHYSICAL CHEMISTRY. *Current Pos:* res chemist, Colgate Palmolive Res Ctr, Piscataway, 68-71, sr res chemist, 71-78, res assoc, 78-85, sr assoc, 85-94, ASSOC DIR TECH, COLGATE PALMOLIVE RES CTR, 94- *Personal Data:* b Goa, India, May 25, 36; US citizen; m 66; c 2. *Educ:* Univ Poona, BSc, 59; Sardar Patel Univ, India, MSc, 61; Ohio State Univ, MSc, 63, PhD(food chem), 66. *Prof Exp:* Res assoc protein chem, Univ Ill, Urbana, 66-68. *Mem:* Am Chem Soc. *Res:* Changes of protein at elevated temperatures; characterization, physical chemical behavior, and modification of proteins. *Mailing Add:* Mountain View Rd Ashbury NJ 08802

KENKEL, JOHN V, ANALYTICAL CHEMISTRY. *Current Pos:* PROF SUPVR CHEM, SOUTHEAST COMMUNITY COL, 77- *Personal Data:* b Harlan, Iowa, Mar 20, 48; m 75; c 3. *Educ:* Iowa State Univ, BS, 70; Univ Tex, Austin, MA, 72. *Honors & Awards:* Gustav Ohans Award, Nat Sci Teachers Asn, 90. *Prof Exp:* Sr staff assoc, Sci Ctr, Rockwell Int, 73-77. *Concurrent Pos:* Mem, Comt Chem 2 Yr Col, Am Chem Soc, 82-, Comt Educ, Div Anal Chem, 88-; Burlington Northern Found fac achievement award, 85; Chem Mfg Asn regional catalyst award, 88. *Mem:* Am Chem Soc. *Res:* Analytical chemistry; author of 2 books and 2 publications. *Mailing Add:* Southeast Community Col 8800 O St Lincoln NE 68520-1227

KENKNIGHT, GLENN, plant pathology, for more information see previous edition

KENKRE, VASUDEV MANGESH, THEORETICAL SOLID STATE PHYSICS. *Current Pos:* res assoc, 72-74, asst prof, 74-79, ASSOC PROF PHYSICS, UNIV ROCHESTER, 79-, FEL, INST FUNDAMENTAL STUDIES, 72- *Personal Data:* b Panjim, India, Sept 21, 46; m 69; c 2. *Educ:* Indian Inst Technol, Bombay, BTech, 68; State Univ NY, Stony Brook, MA, 71, PhD(physics), 71. *Prof Exp:* Instr physics, State Univ NY, Stony Brook, 71-72. *Res:* Transport and response theories, master equations, random walks; charge, excitation and energy transfer in organic and amorphous solids; interaction of light with matter; polaron and exciton motion; size quantization effect; statistical mechanics. *Mailing Add:* 5312 Westwind NE Albuquerque NM 87111

KENLEY, RICHARD ALAN, organic chemistry, for more information see previous edition

KENNA, BERNARD THOMAS, nuclear chemistry, geochemistry; deceased, see previous edition for last biography

KENNAMER, JAMES EARL, WILDLIFE ECOLOGY. *Current Pos:* DIR RES & MGT, NAT WILD TURKEY FEDN, 80- *Personal Data:* b Fairfield, Ala, Aug 6, 42; m 67; c 2. *Educ:* Auburn Univ, BS, 64; Miss State Univ, MS, 67, PhD(wildlife mgt), 70. *Prof Exp:* Instr wildlife mgt, Miss State Univ, 69-70; from asst prof to assoc prof wild life ecol, Auburn Univ, 70-80. *Mem:* Wildlife Soc; Sigma Xi. *Res:* Wild turkey ecology and physiology; Canada goose, white-tailed deer and fallow deer ecology and physiology. *Mailing Add:* Hwy 23 Edgefield SC 29824

KENNARD, KENNETH CLAYTON, ORGANIC CHEMISTY, BIOCHEMISTY. *Current Pos:* RETIRED. *Personal Data:* b Battle Creek, Mich, Dec 18, 26; m 49, Albert A Wintz; c Norman J, Kathleen M (Hurst) & Elaine M (Schoch). *Educ:* Univ Notre Dame, BS, 49; Univ Nebr, MS, 52, PhD(org chem), 54; Mass Inst Technol, SM, 64. *Prof Exp:* Res chemist, Eastman Kodak Co, 54-65, asst div head, Emulsion Res Div, 65-69, staff asst to dir res, 69-75, dir, Biosci Div, Kodak Res Labs, 75-84, gen mgr & vpres, Bio-Prod Div, 84-87. *Mem:* Am Chem Soc; Am Asn Clin Chemists; AAAS. *Res:* Organic chemistry of phosphorous and sulfur compounds; preparation and properties of light sensitive materials; biotechnology. *Mailing Add:* 19 Veldor Park Rochester NY 14612

KENNARD, WILLIAM CRAWFORD, PLANT PHYSIOLOGY, HORTICULTURE. *Current Pos:* RETIRED. *Personal Data:* b Centreville, Md, Nov 29, 21; m 43; c 3. *Educ:* Univ Del, BS, 43; Pa State Univ, MS, 48, PhD(plant physiol, soils), 56; Oak Ridge Inst Nuclear Studies, cert, 60. *Prof Exp:* Res fel pomol, Pa State Univ, 46-48, instr, 48-52; horticulturist, Mayaguez Inst Trop Agr, Mayaguez, PR, 52-57; prin horticulturist & res adminr, US Off Exp Sta, Washington, DC, 57-62; prof hort & assoc dir res admin, Univ Conn, 62-74; prof plant physiol, 62-91, dir inst water resources, 65-74. *Concurrent Pos:* Vis prof, Univ PR, 56; actg dir, Inst Water Resources, Univ Conn, 64-65; assoc seminars, Columbia Univ, 69- *Mem:* Fel AAAS; Am Inst Biol Sci; Am Soc Hort Sci. *Res:* Physiology and culture of temperate zone fruit crops; physiology of flowering; growth and development of tropical plants, including fruits, drug crops, insecticidal crops and bamboo; remote sensing of the environment. *Mailing Add:* 70 Lynnwood Rd Storrs Mansfield CT 06268

KENNEDY, ALBERT JOSEPH, RADIOCHEMISTRY, CORROSION. *Current Pos:* prin chemist, 78-80, supvr chem, 80-89, CHEM ASSESSMENT ADMINR, COMMONWEALTH EDISON, 89- *Personal Data:* b Spring Valley, Ill, July 2, 43; m 67; c 4. *Educ:* Univ Ill, Champaign, BS, 66; Purdue Univ, PhD(nuclear chem), 72. *Prof Exp:* Fel nuclear chem, Lawrence Berkeley Lab, 72-73; sr res chemist, Babcock & Wilcox Co, 73-78. *Mem:* Am Chem Soc; Am Nuclear Soc. *Res:* Corrosion chemistry; corrosion product deposition; activation analysis, radiochemistry, quality control and nuclear fuel evaluation. *Mailing Add:* 415 Manor Hill Lane Lombard IL 60148-4437

KENNEDY, ANDREW JOHN, SOLID STATE PHYSICS, PHYSICAL ELECTRONICS. *Current Pos:* RES PHYSICIST, CTR NIGHT VISION & ELECTRO-OPTICS, 64- *Personal Data:* b Budapest, Hungary, May 16, 35; US citizen; m 58; c 2. *Educ:* Wash State Univ, BS, 61; Univ Wash, MS, 64. *Prof Exp:* Assoc res engr A, Boeing Co, 61-64. *Mem:* Inst Elec & Electronics Engrs; Am Inst Physics. *Res:* Solid state infrared detector physics and technology, intensified charge coupled devices; imaging focal plane technology. *Mailing Add:* US Army Res Lab AMSRL-SE-R 2800 Powder Mill Rd Adelphia MD 20783-1197

KENNEDY, ANN RANDTKE, CARCINOGENESIS. *Current Pos:* Res assoc, 73-75, asst prof, 76-80, ASSOC PROF RADIOBIOL, HARVARD UNIV, 80- *Personal Data:* b Rochester, NY, Dec 24, 46; m 73; c 2. *Educ:* Vassar Col, AB, 69; Harvard Univ, SM, 71, SD, 73. *Honors & Awards:* Outstanding Res Award, Radiation Res Soc, 84. *Concurrent Pos:* Comt mem, Nat Coun Radiation Protection Pub Educ, 80-; mem, chem pathol study sect, consult, workshops & prin investr grants, NIH, 81-88. *Mem:* Am Asn Cancer Res & Radiation Res; Sigma Xi; Free Radical Res Soc. *Res:* Radiobiology; mechanism of carcinogenesis with the ultimate aim of preventing cancer in human populations. *Mailing Add:* 1010 Indian Creek Lane Wynnewood PA 19096-3428

KENNEDY, ANTHONY JOHN, DIGITAL SIGNAL PROCESSING, ADOPTIVE CONTROL SYSTEMS. *Current Pos:* PRIN SCIENTIST, XYBION CORP, 77- *Personal Data:* b Brooklyn, NY, Dec 1, 32; m 60; c 6. *Educ:* Univ Notre Dame, BS, 54; Carnegie Inst Technol, MS, 56, PhD(physics), 62. *Prof Exp:* Scientist, Nuclear Div, Martin Marietta Corp, 60-65 & Space Div, Chrysler Corp, 65-70; consult, Boland & Boyce, Inc, 70-74; scientist, Space Sci Lab, Gen Elec Co, 74-77. *Res:* Design of signal processing systems for the detection of signals in ocean noise; computer systems for processing oceanographic information. *Mailing Add:* Xybion Corp 240 Cedar Knolls Rd Cedar Knolls NJ 07927

KENNEDY, BILL WADE, PLANT PATHOLOGY. *Current Pos:* RETIRED. *Personal Data:* b Dallas, Tex, Mar 21, 29; m 51; c 4. *Educ:* Southeastern State Col, BS, 51; Okla State Univ, MS, 55; Univ Minn, PhD(plant path), 61. *Prof Exp:* Asst plant path, Okla State Univ, 51-52 & 54-55; sr technician, Univ Calif, 55-58; res asst, Univ Minn, 58-59, res fel, 59-60, res assoc, 61-63, from asst prof to prof plant path, 63-93. *Concurrent Pos:* Res grants, Grad Sch, 64-66; coop, US Regional Soybean Lab, Ill, 64-; USDA grant, 67; leaves for advan study, Univ Calif, Berkeley, 67, Eng, 71 & Italy, 78; sr ed, Phytopath, 73-76. *Mem:* Am Phytopath Soc; Am Inst Biol Sci; Am Soybean Asn. *Res:* Chemical control of cotton seedling blight; root-rot studies; physiology of reproduction in Phytophthora, identity and epidemiology of bacterial blight on strawberry; seed pathology; ecology of bacteria associated with soybean. *Mailing Add:* 1987 E Singing Bow Way Tucson AZ 85737

KENNEDY, BURTON MACK, isotope geology, geochronology, for more information see previous edition

KENNEDY, BYRL JAMES, INTERNAL MEDICINE, ONCOLOGY. *Current Pos:* from asst prof to assoc prof, Med Ctr, Univ Minn, 52-67, prof med, Dept Med, Health Sci Ctr, 70-88, masonic prof oncol, 70-91, regents prof med, Sch Med, 88-91, EMER MASONIC PROF ONCOL, UNIV MINN, MINNEAPOLIS, 91- *Personal Data:* b Plainview, Minn, June 24, 21; m 50, Margaret Hood; c Sharon, Brad, Scott & Grant. *Educ:* Univ Minn, BA & BS, 43; BM, 45; MD, 46; McGill Univ, MSc, 51; Am Bd Internal Med, dipl, 58, Am Bd Med Oncol, cert, 79. *Honors & Awards:* Nat Div Award, Am Cancer Soc, 75, Distinguished Serv Award, 91, Medal of Honor Clin Res, 96; Margaret H Edwards Achievement Medal, Am Asn Cancer Educ, 90; Sci Achievement Award, AMA, 92; Laureate Award, Am Col Phys, Minn, 92; Charles Bolles Bolles-Roger Award, Hennepin Med Soc, 96. *Prof Exp:* Intern & asst resident med, Mass Gen Hosp, 45-46; fel, Mass Gen Hosp & Harvard Univ, 47-49, Med Sch, McGill Univ & Royal Victoria Hosp, 49-50, Med Sch, Cornell Univ, 50-51, NY Hosp, 50-51; resident, Mass Gen Hosp & Harvard Univ, 51-52. *Mem:* Master Am Col Phys; Am Asn Cancer Res; AMA; Am Asn Cancer Educ; Am Soc Clin Oncol. *Res:* Medical oncology, breast cancer, testis cancer, aging and cancer chemotherapy of cancer and clinical research. *Mailing Add:* Univ Hosps Box 286 Univ Minn 420 Delaware St SE Minneapolis MN 55455. *Fax:* 612-625-8966; *E-Mail:* kenne018@tc.umn.edu

KENNEDY, CHARLES, PEDIATRIC NEUROLOGY. *Current Pos:* prof, 71-90, EMER PROF PEDIAT, SCH MED, GEORGETOWN UNIV, 90-; MED OFFICER, LAB CEREBRAL METAB, NIMH, 90- *Personal Data:* b Buffalo, NY, Aug 27, 20; m 46; c 3. *Educ:* Princeton Univ, AB, 42; Univ Rochester, MD, 45. *Prof Exp:* Instr path, Sch Med, Yale Univ, 45-46; resident pediat, Children's Hosp, Buffalo, 48-51; resident neurol, Hosp Univ Pa, 53-54; asst neurologist, Children's Hosp, Philadelphia, 56-58, neurologist, 58-67; from asst prof to assoc prof neurol pediat, Sch Med, Univ Pa, 58-70. *Concurrent Pos:* Life Ins Med Res Fund Fel, 51-52; fel physiol, Grad Sch Med, Univ Pa, 51-53; vis fel, Neurol Inst, Columbia-Presby Med Ctr, 57-58; guest worker, Lab Cerebral Metab, NIMH, 68-; vis prof, Stanford Univ, 69; sr res scientist, NIMH, 79- *Mem:* AAAS; Soc Pediat Res; Am Neurol Asn; Am Pediat Soc; Soc Neurosci. *Res:* Cerebral circulation; developmental neurology; energy metabolism of developing brain. *Mailing Add:* HC71 Box 830 Machias ME 04654. *E-Mail:* charles@shiloh.nimh.nih.gov

KENNEDY, CHRISTOPHER JESSE, AQUATIC TOXICOLOGY, BIOCHEMICAL & PHYSIOLOGICAL TOXICOLOGY. *Current Pos:* res asst, 83-88, ASST PROF, DEPT BIOL SCI, SIMON FRASER UNIV, 91- *Personal Data:* b Las Vegas, Nev, Feb 6, 60. *Educ:* Simon Fraser Univ, BSc, 82, PhD(environ toxicol), 90. *Prof Exp:* Res assoc, Univ Miami, 87, fel, 89-90. *Mem:* AAAS; Am Fisheries Soc. *Res:* Environmental modulators of xenobiotic toxicity in aquatic organisms; life history modifications of xenobiotic toxicokinetics; biochemistry of toxicant metabolism; development of in vitro tests in toxicological research. *Mailing Add:* Dept Biol Sci Simon Fraser Univ Burnaby BC V5A 1S6 Can. *Fax:* 604-291-3496

KENNEDY, D J LAURIE, CIVIL ENGINEERING. *Current Pos:* EMER PROF CIVIL ENG, UNIV ALTA, CAN. *Honors & Awards:* Casimir Gzowski Medal, Can Soc Civil Eng, 80 & 92, Le Prix P L Pratley Award, 92; A B Sanderson Award, 89; Shortridge Hardesty Award, Am Soc Civil Engrs, 94; John Jenkins Award, Can Stand Asn, 95. *Mailing Add:* Dept Civil Eng Univ Alta Edmonton AB T6G 2G7 Can

KENNEDY, DAVID P, ELECTRICAL ENGINEERING. *Current Pos:* RETIRED. *Personal Data:* b Boston, Mass, Nov 15, 23. *Educ:* Mass Inst Technol, MA, 74. *Prof Exp:* Prof elec eng, Fla Univ; owner, D P Kennedy & Assoc Inc, 82-85. *Mem:* Fel Inst Elec & Electronics Engrs. *Mailing Add:* 2227 NW 16th Ave Gainesville FL 32605

KENNEDY, DIANE L, PHARMACOLOGY. *Current Pos:* Mgr, Ctr Drug Eval & Res, Div Epidemiol & Surveillance, DIR MEDWATCH, MED PROD REPORTING PROG, FOOD & DRUG ADMIN, 93- *Educ:* Purdue Univ, MS; Johns Hopkins Univ, MPH. *Mailing Add:* Off Oper HF-2 Food & Drug Admin 5600 Fishers Lane Rm 9-57 Rockville MD 20857. *Fax:* 301-443-5776

KENNEDY, DONALD, BIOLOGY, SCIENCE & PUBLIC POLICY. *Current Pos:* from asst prof to prof biol sci, Stanford Univ, 60-77, chmn dept, 65-72, vpres & provost, 79-80, pres, 80-92, BING PROF ENVIRON SCI, STANFORD UNIV, 92- *Personal Data:* b New York, NY, Aug 18, 31; m 53; c 2. *Educ:* Harvard Univ, AB, 52, AM, 54, PhD(biol sci), 56. *Hon Degrees:* DSc, Columbia Univ, 79, Williams Col, 80, Univ Mich, 82, Univ Rochester, 84, Univ Ariz, 85; LLD, Reed Col, 86, Whitman Col, 94. *Honors & Awards:* Bowditch Lectr, Am Physiol Soc, 70. *Prof Exp:* From asst prof to assoc prof zool, Syracuse Univ, 56-60; from asst prof to prof biol sci, Stanford Univ, 60-77, chmn dept, 65-72; comnr, Food & Drug Admin, 77-79. *Concurrent Pos:* Ed bd, J Exp Zool, 65-70, J Comp Physiol, 66-77, J Neurophysiol, 70-76, Science, 73-78; Nat lectr, Sigma Xi, 69-70. *Mem:* Nat Acad Sci; Inst Med-Nat Acad Sci; Am Soc Zool; Soc Gen Physiol; fel Am Acad Arts & Sci; Soc Exp Biol UK; Am Physiol Soc; Am Inst Biol Sci; fel AAAS; Marine Biol Asn UK. *Res:* Comparative physiology of sense organs, especially visual systems; central nervous system of crustacea; over 60 articles and publications; environmental policy studies. *Mailing Add:* Inst Int Studies Bldg 10 Stanford CA 94305-2060

KENNEDY, EDWARD EARL, ANALYTICAL CHEMISTRY. *Current Pos:* RETIRED. *Personal Data:* b Evansville, Ind, Jan 7, 25; m 50; c 2. *Educ:* Purdue Univ, BS, 45; Ind Univ, MA, 48. *Prof Exp:* Anal chemist, Eli Lilly & Co, 45-46; instr, Ind Univ, 47-48; anal chemist, Eli Lilly & Co, 48-50, head, Dept Assay Methods Develop, 50-52, head anal res & develop, 52-56, head anal develop & spec servs, 56-62, asst dir anal res & develop, 62-66, dir corp qual assurance, 66-69, dir, Park Fletcher Plant, 70, dir biochem mfg, 70-80, dir biosynthetic oper, 80-83, dir qual assurance, 83-85. *Mem:* AAAS; Am Pharmaceut Asn; Am Soc Qual Control; Am Chem Soc. *Res:* Instrumentation of analytical chemistry, particularly field of spectrophotometry. *Mailing Add:* 8305 Reef Ct Rd Indianapolis IN 46236-9539

KENNEDY, EDWARD FRANCIS, NUCLEAR PHYSICS. *Current Pos:* from asst prof to assoc prof physics, Holy Cross Col, 60-70, actg chmn dept, 63-64, chmn dept, 64-76, PROF PHYSICS, HOLY CROSS COL, 70- *Personal Data:* b Chicago, Ill, Jan 2, 32; m 56, Marcia Daly; c Kathryn, Edward III, Maribeth, Christopher, Marcia & John. *Educ:* Loyola Univ, Ill, BS, 54; Univ Notre Dame, PhD(nuclear physics), 60. *Prof Exp:* Technician,

Argonne Nat Lab, 52-54; asst physics, Univ Notre Dame, 54-58, res assoc, 58-60. Concurrent Pos: Consult, Air Force Cambridge Res Labs, 62-71; vis scientist, Cavendish Lab, Cambridge, 68-69, Fraunhofer-Inst, Munich, Ger, 82-83, Univ Aarhus, Denmark, 90; vis assoc, Calif Inst Technol, 75-76, 77 & 78; vis prof, Cornell Univ, 83, 84, 85; vis res physicist, Univ Calif, San Diego, 87. Mem: Am Phys Soc; Am Asn Physics Teachers; Sigma Xi. Res: Ion channeling in crystals; surface physics; nuclear fluorescence; radiation damage. Mailing Add: Physics Dept Holy Cross Col Worcester MA 01610. E-Mail: kennedy@hcacad.holycross.edu

KENNEDY, EDWIN RUSSELL, environmental chemistry, for more information see previous edition

KENNEDY, ELDREDGE JOHNSON, SOLID STATE ELECTRONICS, ELECTRICAL ENGINEERING. Current Pos: assoc prof, 69-75, PROF ELEC ENG, UNIV TENN, KNOXVILLE, 75- Personal Data: b Fayetteville, Tenn, Sept 19, 35; m 61; c 3. Educ: Univ Tenn, BS, 58, MS, 59, PhD(eng sci), 67. Prof Exp: Coop stud, Arnold Eng Develop Ctr, ARO Inc, Tenn, 53-57; asst elec eng, Univ Tenn, 58-59, instr, 59-63, res engr, Exp Sta, 60-63; design engr, Instrumentation & Controls Div, Oak Ridge Nat Lab, 63-70. Concurrent Pos: Ford Found assoc prof, 68-69; consult, Oak Ridge Nat Lab, 70- Mem: Inst Elec & Electronics Engrs; Sigma Xi; Int Soc Hybrid Microelectronics. Res: Electronic solid state circuit design; low-current meaurements; hybrid thick-film integrated circuits; high-speed pulse amplifiers, low-noise electronics; radiation effects in integrated circuits and devices. Mailing Add: Dept Elec Eng Univ Tenn Ferris Hall Knoxville TN 37996

KENNEDY, ELHART JAMES, AGRICULTURAL MICROBIOLOGY, BOTANY. Current Pos: RETIRED. Personal Data: b Lincoln, Nebr, Feb 15, 23; m 48; c 2. Educ: Colo Agr & Mech Col, BS, 50; Cornell Univ, PhD(veg crops), 53. Prof Exp: Dir res agr, Spud Chips, Inc, Colo, 53-59; chmn div sci & math, 68-81, dir continuing educ, 81-83, prof biol, N Park Col, 59-88. Concurrent Pos: Mem prod & tech div, Nat Potato Chip Inst, chmn potato div, 55-57; agr consult, Envirodyne, Inc, 74-88. Mem: AAAS; Am Sci Affiliation; Am Soc Microbiol; Am Inst Biol Sci. Res: Physiology of the potato, including tuberization, pathology and irradiation effects of clostridium botulinum; microbiology of surface waters. Mailing Add: 325 Kempton St No 656 Spring Valley CA 91977

KENNEDY, EUGENE P, BIOCHEMISTRY. Current Pos: Hamilton Kuhn prof, 90-91, EMER PROF BIOL, HARVARD MED SCH, 91- Personal Data: b Chicago, Ill, Sept 4, 19; m 43, Adelaide Majewski; c Lisa (Helprin), Sheila (Violich) & Katherine (Diller). Educ: Univ Chicago, PhD(biochem), 49. Hon Degrees: MA, Harvard Univ, 60; DSc, Univ Chicago, 77. Honors & Awards: Paul Lewis Award, Am Chem Soc, 58; Lipid Res Award, Am Oil Chem Soc, 70; Gairdner Found Award, 76; Ledlie Prize, 76; Passano Award, 86; Wieland Prize, 86. Prof Exp: From asst prof to prof, Dept Biochem & Ben May Lab, Univ Chicago, 51-60. Concurrent Pos: Am Cancer Soc fel, Univ Calif, 49-50; Am Chem Soc res award, 55; NSF fel, 59-60; von Humboldt sr fel, 84. Mem: Nat Acad Sci; Am Acad Arts & Sci; Am Chem Soc; Am Soc Biol Chemists (pres, 70-71); Am Philos Soc. Res: Metabolism and function of lipids; membrane function. Mailing Add: Dept Biol Chem Harvard Med Sch Boston MA 02115. E-Mail: ekennedy@warren.med.harvard.edu

KENNEDY, EUGENE RICHARD, BACTERIOLOGY. Current Pos: from instr to prof bact & immunol, 49-85, dean, Sch Arts & Sci, 73-85, EMER PROF BACT & IMMUNOL, CATH UNIV AM, 85- Personal Data: b Scranton, Pa, July 3, 19; m 45; c 3. Educ: Univ Scranton, BS, 41; Cath Univ Am, MS, 43; Brown Univ, PhD, 49; Am Bd Med Microbiol, dipl, 64. Prof Exp: Asst bact, Cath Univ Am, 41-43; instr, Brown Univ, 46-48. Concurrent Pos: Serologist, US Army Med Ctr, DC, 42; instr, RI Hosp, 46-48; bacteriologist, US Food & Drug Admin, 49; consult bacteriologist, Providence Hosp, DC, 54-58, staff microbiologist, 58-77, consult microbiologist, 81- Mem: AAAS; Am Soc Microbiol; Sigma Xi. Res: Vi antigen; quantitative dye adsorption; quantitative gram reaction; staphylococcus autogenous vaccine; in vivo and in vitro staphylococci. Mailing Add: Dept Biol Rm 103 McCort Ward Cath Univ Am 620 Michigan Ave NE Washington DC 20064

KENNEDY, FLYNT, ORGANIC CHEMISTRY. Current Pos: RETIRED. Personal Data: b Chillicothe, Tex, May 25, 31; m 57; c 1. Educ: Tex Christian Univ, BA, 52; Rice Univ, PhD(org chem), 56. Prof Exp: Res Corp fel, Calif Inst Technol, 56-57; res chemist, Conoco, Inc, 57-60, sr res chemist, 60-61, res group leader, 61-64, supv res scientist, 64-69, mgr, Chem Res Div, 69-82; gen mgr coal & chem res develop, Consol Coal Co, 84-87, vpres res & develop, 87-96. Mem: Am Chem Soc. Res: Investigation of reactions of organometallic compounds; synthesis of three and four membered compounds; upgrading of hydrocarbons; chemicals from coal, polyvinyl chloride and polyolefins; coal seam degasification; improved coal mining technology; coal processing and combustion; sulfurdioxide. Mailing Add: 110 Waterside Dr Canonsburg PA 15317

KENNEDY, FRANK SCOTT, METALLOENZYMES, TRACE METALS. Current Pos: asst prof, 76-78, ASSOC PROF BIOCHEM, SCH MED, LA STATE UNIV, SHREVEPORT, 78-, ASST DEAN STUDENT ADMIS, 88- Personal Data: b Washington, DC, Oct 16, 44; m 80; c 2. Educ: Washington & Lee Univ, BS, 66; Univ Ill, Urbana, PhD(biochem), 70. Prof Exp: Res assoc biochem, Harvard Med Sch, 74-76. Res: Intermediary metabolism in cardiac tissue; role of copper in normal iron metabolism. Mailing Add: PO Box 33932 Shreveport LA 71130-3932. E-Mail: fkenne@lsumc.edu

KENNEDY, FREDERICK JAMES, THEORETICAL PHYSICS. Current Pos: SCI LIBRN, KILLAM LIBR SCI, DALHOUSIE UNIV, 73- Personal Data: b Lowell, Mass, Mar 20, 37; m 67, Joyce Deveau; c Simon, David & Frederick. Educ: Lowell Tech Inst, BS, 60; Univ Del, MS, 65, PhD(physics), 67. Prof Exp: Asst prof physics, Univ Bridgeport, 67-68; fel, Theoret Physics Inst, Univ Alta, 68-73. Concurrent Pos: Lectr, Dept Math, Statist & Comput Sci, Dalhousie Univ, 82-86. Res: Classical mechanics and electrodynamics. Mailing Add: Killam Libr Sci Dalhousie Univ Halifax NS B3H 4M8 Can. E-Mail: frederick.kennedy@dal.ca

KENNEDY, GEORGE ARLIE, VETERINARY PATHOLOGY. Current Pos: instr vet path, Dept Path, Col Vet Med, 70-75, ASST PROF, VET DIAG LAB, KANS STATE UNIV, 72- Personal Data: b Chicago, Ill, Jan 11, 40; m 72. Educ: Univ NMex, BS, 62; Wast State Univ, DVM, 67; Kans State Univ, PhD(path), 75. Prof Exp: Res pathologist, US Army Med Res & Nutrit Lab, 67-70. Concurrent Pos: Clinician, Kans State Univ Vet Teaching Hosp, 70-72. Mem: Am Vet Med Asn; Am Col Vet Path; Sigma Xi. Res: Transmission and scanning electron microscipic study of swine enteric diseases, particularly swine dysentery and diseases of the large intestine. Mailing Add: 1029 Bertrand Manhattan KS 66502

KENNEDY, GEORGE GRADY, ECONOMIC ENTOMOLOGY, PEST MANAGEMENT & INSECT ECOLOGY. Current Pos: from asst prof to prof entom, 76-92, WILLIAM NEAL PROF, NC STATE UNIV, 92- Personal Data: b Amityville, NY, Mar 23, 48; m 73; c 2. Educ: Ore State Univ, BS, 70; Cornell Univ, PhD(entom), 74. Honors & Awards: L M Ware Res Award, Am Soc Hort Sci. Prof Exp: Asst prof entom, Univ Calif, Riverside, 74-75. Concurrent Pos: Prog mgr, USDA Competitive Grants Prog Entom/Nematol, 84-86; mem, assessment panel, US Off Technol, 85 & 90; external consult, Merck Sharp & Dohme, 90-94; mem, Sci Adv Subpanel Pesticidal Plants, US Environ Protection Agency, 93 & 94. Mem: Entom Soc Am; Am Inst Biol Sci. Res: Pest management; insect/plant interactions. Mailing Add: Dept Entom Box 7630 NC State Univ Raleigh NC 27695-7630. Fax: 919-515-3748

KENNEDY, GEORGE HUNT, SURFACE CHEMISTRY. Current Pos: from asst prof to assoc prof, 65-76, head dept chem & geochem, 76-88, PROF CHEM, COLO SCH MINES, 77- Personal Data: b Seattle, Wash, Apr 24, 36; m 61; c 2. Educ: Univ Ore, BS, 59; Ore State Univ, MS, 62, PhD(phys chem), 66. Prof Exp: Res chemist, Chevron Res Corp Div, Chevron Oil Co, 61-62. Mem: Am Chem Soc. Res: Physical adsorption of gases on solid adsorbents; gas chromatography; sorption of vapors on liquid coated adsorbents. Mailing Add: Dept Chem Colo Sch Mines Golden CO 80401

KENNEDY, HARVEY EDWARD, microbiology, information science, for more information see previous edition

KENNEDY, IAN MANNING, COMBUSTION. Current Pos: from asst prof to assoc prof, 86-93, PROF ENG, UNIV CALIF, DAVIS, 93- Personal Data: b Brisbane, Australia, Sept 11, 52; m 81; c 2. Educ: Sydney Univ, BEng, 75, PhD(mech eng), 80. Honors & Awards: Pres Young Investr Award, NSF, 88. Prof Exp: Mem res staff, Princeton Univ, 80-83; res scientist, Aeronaut Res Labs, 83-86. Mem: Am Inst Aeronaut & Astronaut; Combustion Inst; Am Asn Aerosol Res. Res: Fundamental combustion phenomena; turbulent reacting flows; formation of pollutants such as soot in flames; application of laser and optics to measurements in flames; dynamics of aerosol systems. Mailing Add: Mech & Aero Eng Univ Calif Davis CA 95616. Fax: 530-752-4158; E-Mail: imkennedy@ucdavis.edu

KENNEDY, J(OHN) R(OBERT), INDUSTRIAL & MANUFACTURING ENGINEERING. Current Pos: CONSULT ENGR, 79- Personal Data: b Frederick, Md, Mar 25, 25; m 45, MaryAnn Clery; c John Jr, Eileen, Katherine & Michael. Educ: Purdue Univ, BS, 49. Prof Exp: Aeronaut engr, Chem Corps, Ft Detrick, Md, 49-50, physicist, 50-51; biol test engr, 51-55, mech engr, 55-58; gen engr, Nat Animal Disease Ctr, USDA, 58-60, chief, Eng & Plant Mgt, 58-79, supvry gen engr, 60-79. Res: Maintenance engineering; design of containment laboratory facilities. Mailing Add: 510 Nicholas St Vincennes IN 47591-1057

KENNEDY, JAMES A, ENZYMOLOGY. Current Pos: assoc prof, 73-81, PROF MED, UNIV KANS MED CTR, 81- Personal Data: b Rochester, Minn, July 3, 35; m 65. Educ: Univ Notre Dame, BS, 57; St Louis Univ, MD, 61. Prof Exp: NIH fel med, Med Sch, Univ Kans, 63-65; assoc internal med, Col Physicians & Surgeons, Columbia Univ, 68-71; asst prof, 71-73. Concurrent Pos: Assoc Ed, J Lab Clin Med, 82-; mem, VA Res Adv Group A, 83-, chrmn, 85- Mem: Am Soc Biol Chemists. Res: Urea cycle; superoxide; regulation of pyrimidine biosynthesis in mammals; electron transport. Mailing Add: Res Serv Va Hosp 4801 Linwood Blvd Kansas City MO 64128-2295

KENNEDY, JAMES CECIL, EXPERIMENTAL CANCER THERAPIES. Current Pos: asst prof, 69-74, assoc prof radiation oncl, 77-91, ASSOC PROF PATH, QUEENS UNIV, ONT, 74-, PROF ONCOL, 91- Personal Data: b Toronto, Ont, Mar 14, 35; m 66, Ruth E Hermosa; c David, Andrew, Marta, Peter, Sara, Samuel & Joseph. Educ: Univ Toronto, BA, 57, MD, 61, PhD(biophys), 66. Prof Exp: Intern, Wellesley Hosp, Toronto, 61. Concurrent Pos: Res fel, Nat Cancer Inst Can, 66-68, res scholar, 69-72, res assoc, 72-77; res assoc, Ont Cancer Treat & Res Found, 77-83, career scientist, 83-; adj assoc prof chem & chem eng, Royal Mil Col, 89-91, adj prof, 91- Mem: Am Soc Photobiol; Europ Soc Photobiol; Am Asn Cancer Res. Res: Photoradiation therapy for cancer; fluorescence detection of cancer; chemistry and pharmacology of photosensitizing agents. Mailing Add: Dept Oncol Queen's Univ Kingston ON K7L 3N6 Can

KENNEDY, JAMES H, AQUATIC ECOSYSTEMS POLLUTANT EFFECTS, ECOLOGY. *Current Pos:* ASSOC PROF & DIR, WATER RES FIELD STA, UNIV NTEX, 87- *Personal Data:* b Garrett, Ind, May 20, 47; m 70, Virginia Tummon; c Amanda T. *Educ:* Mansfield State Col, BS, 69; Ind Univ Pa, MS, 73; Va Polytech Inst & State Univ, PhD(zool), 80. *Prof Exp:* Fisheries biologist, Pa Fish Comn, 72-73; res biologist, Ichthyol Assocs Inc, 73-75; sr ecologist, mgr aquatic toxicol, NUS Corp, 81-82; ecotoxicologist, Water Sci Assocs Inc, 82-87, pres. *Concurrent Pos:* Prin investr numerous grants, US Environ Protection Agency, 87-93, Bayer, 88-92, Hoechst-Roussel Agr-Vet, 89, CIBA, 92-97; consult, Zeneca, Intevep, Venezuela. *Mem:* Am Entom Soc; Entom Soc Am; Soc Environ Toxicol & Chem; NAm Benthological Soc; Sigma Xi. *Res:* Ecology of macroinvertebrates; pollution ecology of lakes, streams and estuaries; fate and effects of pesticides in aquatic ecosystems. *Mailing Add:* Dept Biol Sci Univ NTex Denton TX 76203-3078. *Fax:* 817-565-4297

KENNEDY, JAMES M, COMPUTER SCIENCE, ADMINISTRATION. *Current Pos:* RETIRED. *Personal Data:* b Ottawa, Ont, Apr 25, 28; m 50, Norah H Leake. *Educ:* Univ Toronto, BA, 49, MA, 50; Princeton Univ, PhD(physics), 53. *Prof Exp:* Res officer, Theoret Physics Br, Atomic Energy Can Ltd, 52-66, supvr, Comput Ctr, 56-66; dir, Comput Ctr, Univ BC, 66-80, vpres, 80-84, prof comput sci, 68-93. *Mem:* Can Math Soc; hon mem Can Info Processing Soc (pres, 71-72); Can Asn Physicists. *Res:* Numerical and non-numerical computer methods. *Mailing Add:* 1891 Acadia Rd Univ BC 2075 Wesbrook Pl Vancouver BC V6T 1R2 Can

KENNEDY, JAMES VERN, CHEMISTRY, RESEARCH ADMINISTRATION. *Current Pos:* SR RES ASSOC, CHEVRON RES CO, CHEVRON OIL CORP, 85- *Personal Data:* b Jessup, Pa, May 4, 34; m 62; c 2. *Educ:* Pa State Univ, BS, 55; Univ Pittsburgh, PhD(chem), 72. *Prof Exp:* Res assoc phys chem, Mellon Inst, 55-63; technologist, Baroid Div, Nat Lead Co, 63-69, sect leader catalysis sci, 70, supvr catalysis labs, 70-71, tech mgr mineral synthesis dept, NL Indusrs, Inc, 71-73, catalyst prod mgr, Baroid Div, 72-73; group leader petrol prod res, Engelhard Minerals & Chem Corp, 73-74, mgr prod res, Minerals & Chem Div, 74-78, dir res-existing bus, 78, dir res-new bus, 79-80; dir catalysis res, Chemicals & Minerals Div, Gulf Sci & Technol Co, 80-85. *Mem:* Am Chem Soc; fel Am Inst Chem; Catalysis Soc; Clay Minerals Soc; NY Acad Sci. *Res:* Fluidized cracking catalyst research and development for petroleum redefining; catalysis by layer-lattice silicates; alteration and synthesis of clay minerals; infrared characterization of synthetic clays; applications of minerals; new product development in catalyst, ceramic, industrial and paper products. *Mailing Add:* Chevron Res Co PO Box 1627 Richmond CA 94802-0627

KENNEDY, JERRY DEAN, PHYSICS. *Current Pos:* RETIRED. *Personal Data:* b Oklahoma City, Okla, June 23, 34; m 57; c 2. *Educ:* Univ Okla, BS, 56; Univ Calif, Berkeley, MA, 59; Lehigh Univ, PhD(physics), 63. *Prof Exp:* Adv study scientist, Lockheed Missile & Space Co, 56-59; engr, Autonetics Div, NAm Aviation, Inc, 59; mem tech staff physics, Sandia Labs, 63-69, supvr, Test Exp Div, 69-71, supvr, Exp Planning Div, 71-73, mgr, Eng Sci Dept, 73-93. *Mem:* Am Phys Soc. *Res:* Dynamic high pressure solid state physics in semiconductors; shock wave phenomena in solids. *Mailing Add:* 8904 Crestwood Ave NE Albuquerque NM 87112

KENNEDY, JOHN B, ENGINEERING MECHANICS, STRUCTURAL ENGINEERING. *Current Pos:* assoc prof, 63-66, head dept, 66-76, PROF CIVIL ENG, UNIV WINDSOR, 66- *Personal Data:* b Baghdad, Iraq, Jan 7, 32; m 57; c 3. *Educ:* Univ Wales, BSc, 55; Univ Toronto, PhD(civil eng), 61. *Hon Degrees:* DSc, Univ Wales, 84. *Honors & Awards:* T Y Lin Award, Am Soc Civil Engrs, 83; Duggan Medal, Eng Inst Can, 78. *Prof Exp:* Asst engr, Develop Bd Iraq, 55-57; res asst skewed bridges, Univ Toronto, 57-61; asst prof civil eng, Univ Sask, 61-63. *Concurrent Pos:* Consult engr, Ministry Transp & Commun, Ont. *Mem:* Am Soc Civil Engrs; Am Concrete Inst; Eng Inst Can. *Res:* Structural mechanics; skewed slab structures; waffle-slab bridges; cold-bending of HSS beams; reinforced-earth supporting soil-steel arch structures. *Mailing Add:* Dept Civil Eng Univ Windsor Windsor ON N9B 3P4 Can

KENNEDY, JOHN EDWARD, PHYSICS, ASTRONOMY. *Current Pos:* from assoc prof to prof physics, Univ Sask, 65-84, asst head dept, 66-67, asst dean, Col Arts & Sci, 67-81, EMER PROF PHYSICS, UNIV SASK, 84- *Personal Data:* b Kemptville, Ont, Sept 12, 16; m 41, 97, Virginia Blake; c David K, Barbara (Anderson) & Janet (MacLean). *Educ:* Queen's Univ, Ont, BA, 37; McGill Univ, MSc, 42. *Honors & Awards:* Serv Award, Royal Astron Soc Can, 70; Can Silver Jubilee Medal, 78. *Prof Exp:* Jr res physicist, Physics Div, Nat Res Coun Can, 41-45; from asst prof to prof physics, Univ NB, 45-56; sci serv officer, Defense Res Med Labs, Defense Res Bd, 56-65, head physics group, 61-65. *Concurrent Pos:* Consult physicist, NB Dept Health, 50-52; mem, Comn 41, Hist Astron, Comn 46, Teaching Astron, Int Astron Union, 70-; leave fel, Can Coun, 73-74; patron, Sask Libr Week, 79; hon pres, Saskatoon Centre Royal Astron Soc Can; Walter Murray fel, 95. *Mem:* Royal Astron Soc Can (nat secy, 58-64, 2nd vpres, 64-66, 1st vpres, 66-68, pres, 68-70); Can Astron Soc; fel Royal Astron Soc London; Can Soc Hist Philos Sci. *Res:* Spectroscopy; stellar physics; physics of clothing and footwear; history of early Canadian astronomy; history of early interest in solar-terrestrial interactions; history of the boundary survey Maine-New Brunswick of the 1840's. *Mailing Add:* 1902-315 Fifth Ave N Saskatoon SK Can

KENNEDY, JOHN ELMO, JR, MANUFACTURING TECHNOLOGY, ENVIRONMENTAL SCIENCE. *Current Pos:* PVT CONSULT, 77- *Personal Data:* b Louisville, Ky, June 21, 32; div; c Kevin, Eric, John III & Brian. *Educ:* Univ Louisville, BS, 59, PhD(org chem), 63. *Prof Exp:* Lab technician anal chem, Schenley Distillers, Inc, 55-56; chemist, Ky Color & Chem Co, 56-59; chemist, Dept Exp Med, Sch Med, Univ Louisville, 59-61; res chemist, Brown & Williamson Tobacco Corp, 63-64, group leader org chem, 64-67, sr group leader biol chem, 67-70, res area supvr, 70-76; instr org chem, Univ Louisville, 76-77. *Concurrent Pos:* Expert witness, Liability & Environ Litigation, Gen, Forensic & Environ Toxicol. *Mem:* AAAS; fel Am Inst Chem; NY Acad Sci; Am Chem Soc; Phytochem Soc NAm; Sigma Xi. *Res:* Biological chemistry; pharmacology; natural products; synthesis; steroids; alkaloids; alicyclics; biosynthetic routes; reaction mechanisms; psychopharmacology; information science; science writing; toxicology. *Mailing Add:* 3501 Pimlico Pkwy No 124 Lexington KY 40517

KENNEDY, JOHN HARVEY, ELECTROCHEMISTRY, ANALYTICAL CHEMISTRY. *Current Pos:* from asst prof to prof, 67-93, EMER PROF CHEM, UNIV CALIF, SANTA BARBARA, 93- *Personal Data:* b Oak Park, Ill, Apr 24, 33; m 56, 70, Victoria Matthew; c 5. *Educ:* Univ Calif, Los Angeles, BS, 54; Harvard Univ, PhD(anal chem), 57. *Prof Exp:* Res chemist, E I du Pont de Nemours & Co, Del, 57-61; asst prof, Univ Calif, Santa Barbara, 61-63; assoc prof, Boston Col, 63-64; head inorg chem, Gen Motors Defense Res Labs, 64-67. *Concurrent Pos:* Tech adv, Bissett-Berman Corp, 67-71, chmn dept, 82-85; Japan Soc Advan Sci, 74 & 75; vis prof, Japan Soc Prom Sci, 74 & 75, Univ NC, 81 & 82 & China Acad Sci, 90. *Mem:* Am Chem Soc; Electrochem Soc. *Res:* Solid electrolytes; fused salts; electrochemistry; instrumental methods of analysis; photoelectrochemistry. *Mailing Add:* Dept Chem Univ Calif Santa Barbara CA 93106. *Fax:* 805-893-4120; *E-Mail:* jvkennedy@aol.com

KENNEDY, JOHN HINES, THORACIC SURGERY, CARDIOVASCULAR SURGERY. *Current Pos:* VIS SCIENTIST, DEPT MOLECULAR PHYSIOL, BABRAHAM INST, CAMBRIDGE, ENG, 87- *Personal Data:* b Washington, DC, Nov 1, 25; m 47, 72, 77, Shirley A J Watson; c Anne, John, Mark & Joan. *Educ:* Harvard Med Sch, MD, 49; Am Bd Surg, dipl, 57; Am Bd Surg, 60; Imp Col, London, MPhil, 90. *Prof Exp:* Intern, Mass Gen Hosp, 49-50, asst resident, 50-51 & 53-54, resident, 54-55; sr registr, Thoracic Unit, Frenchay Hosp, Bristol, Eng, 59-60; asst prof thoracic surg, Sch Med, Case Western Res Univ, 62-69; prof surg, Baylor Col Med, 69-76, dir, Taub Labs Mech Circulatory Support, 70-76, mem, Admis Comt, 71-76; adj prof, Biomed Eng, Rice Univ, 75-76; fac mem, Dept Macro Molecular Sci, Case Western Res Univ, 76-77; consult surgeon, Middlesex Hosp Med Sch, Wembley & Cent Middlesex Hosps, London, 78-82; Physiol Flow Studies Unit, Imp Col, Univ London, 82-85; vis scientist, Nat Inst Health & Med Res, Paris, France, 86. *Concurrent Pos:* Clin asst, Bristol Royal Infirm, Bristol Univ, 59-60; dir, Div Thoracic Surg, Cleveland Metrop Gen Hosp, 62-69; res assoc, Eng Design Ctr, Case Western Res Univ, 66-69, vis prof, Dept Macromolecular Sci, 75-76; dir, Circulatory Assistance Prog Group, Artificial Heart-Myocardial Infarction Prog, NIH contract, Case Western Res Univ, 67-69 & Baylor Med Col, 69-71; mem, Coun Cardiovasc Surg & ed, Surg Supplement Circulation, Am Heart Asn, 68-70; mem, Tech Adv Group, Artificial Heart-Myocardial Infarction Prog, Nat Heart & Lung Inst, 68, consult site visitor prog proj grants, 70, prin investr grant, 70; adj prof, Rice Univ, 69-75; USPHS grant, Baylor Col Med, 69-72; consult, Pres Panel Biomed Res, 75-; med dir, Moat House Hosp, Gt Easton, Dunmow, Essex, 80-86. *Mem:* Am Asn Thoracic Surg; Soc Thoracic Surgeons; Western Surg Asn; fel Am Col Surg; Royal Soc Med. *Res:* Physiology; interstitium; physiology. *Mailing Add:* Dept Molecular Physiol Babraham Inst Cambridge CB2 4A5 England

KENNEDY, JOHN ROBERT, CELL BIOLOGY. *Current Pos:* from assoc prof to prof zool, 69-95, PROF BIOCHEM & CELLULAR & MOLECULAR BIOL, UNIV TENN, KNOXVILLE, 95- *Personal Data:* b Cleveland, Ohio, July 17, 37. *Educ:* Univ Mich, BS, 59, MS, 61; Univ Iowa, PhD(zool), 64. *Prof Exp:* From instr to asst prof anat, Bowman Gray Sch Med, 64-69. *Mem:* Am Soc Cell Biol; Electron Micros Soc Am. *Res:* Effect of physiological factors on tracheal cell fine structure and function; ciliary cell physiology; consulting in electron microscopy and toxicology. *Mailing Add:* Dept Biochem & Cellular & Molecular Biol Univ Tenn Knoxville TN 37996. *E-Mail:* njrkenad@utk.edu

KENNEDY, JOSEPH PATRICK, ANATOMY, ECOLOGY. *Current Pos:* from asst prof to assoc prof, Univ Tex, 60-68, prof animal ecol & chmn dept, Grad Sch Biomed Sci, 69-77, prof anat, Univ Tex Health Sci Ctr, Houston Med Sch, 76-77, PROF ANAT, BASIC SCI DENT BR, UNIV TEX, HOUSTON, 68- *Personal Data:* b Houston, Tex, Mar 9, 32; c Justice. *Educ:* Univ St Thomas, Tex, BA, 54; Univ Tex, MA, 55, PhD(zool), 58. *Honors & Awards:* Species named in hon, Hyla Kennedy, 73. *Prof Exp:* Chmn, Dept Biol, Univ St Thomas, Tex, 58-60. *Concurrent Pos:* Vis prof, Mt Lake Biol Sta, Univ Va, 62, Terra Alta Biol Sta, WVa Univ, 68; lectr, Univ Houston, 63; ed, J Herpet, 68-79; chmn, Adv Comt, Univ Tex Environ Sci Park, 69-71, chmn, 71-76; prof ecol, M D Anderson Hosp & Tumor Inst, 69-76; mem exec comt & bd trustees, Armand Bayou Nature Ctr, Inc, 74-77; mem, Coun Biol Eds. *Mem:* Soc Study Amphibians & Reptiles; Sigma Xi. *Res:* Ecology, evolution and behavior; herpetology; literary criticism. *Mailing Add:* Basic Sci Dent Br Health Sci Ctr Univ Tex PO Box 20068 Houston TX 77225-0068

KENNEDY, JOSEPH PAUL, POLYMER CHEMISTRY. *Current Pos:* DISTINGUISHED PROF POLYMER SCI & CHEM & RES ASSOC INST POLYMER SCI, UNIV AKRON, 70- *Personal Data:* b Budapest, Hungary, May 18, 28; US citizen; m 57, Igeborg; c Katherine, Cynthia & Julie. *Educ:* Univ Vienna, PhD(chem), 55; Rutgers Univ, MBA, 61. *Hon Degrees:* DHC,

Kossuth Sci Univ, Debrecen, Hungary, 89. *Honors & Awards:* Polymer Chem Award, Am Chem Soc, 85, Appl Polymr Sci, 95, G S Whitby Award, 96. *Prof Exp:* Fel biochem, Sorbonne, 55-56; res assoc, McGill Univ, 56-57; res chemist, Celanese Corp Am, 57-59; res chemist, Easso Res & Eng Co, 59-62, sr res chemist, 62-65, res assoc, 65-69, sr res assoc, 69-70. *Concurrent Pos:* Guest prof polymer chem, Kyoto Univ, Japan, 60. *Mem:* Am Chem Soc; Hungarian Acad Sci. *Res:* Cationic polymerizations; Friedel-Crafts chemistry; polymer synthesis; polymerization mechanisms; elastomer chemistry, particularly butyl rubber and polyisobutylene; blocks and grafts; terminally functional liquids; derivatization of polymers; living polymerizations; biomaterials. *Mailing Add:* Inst Polymer Sci Univ Akron Akron OH 44325-3909. *Fax:* 330-972-5290; *E-Mail:* kennedy@polymer.uakron.edu

KENNEDY, KATHERINE ASH, TOXICOLOGY, CANCER CHEMOTHERAPY. *Current Pos:* asst prof pharmacol, 81-87, ASSOC PROF, SCH MED, GEORGE WASHINGTON UNIV, 87- *Personal Data:* b Bryn Mawr, Pa, Mar 24, 50; m 87. *Educ:* Vanderbilt Univ, BA, 73; Univ Iowa, PhD(pharmacol), 77. *Prof Exp:* Fel, Sch Med, Yale Univ, 78-81. *Mem:* AAAS; Am Asn Cancer Res; NY Acad Sci; Radiation Res Soc; Am Soc Pharmacol & Exp Ther. *Res:* Role of biotransformation for drug activity and toxicity; mechanisms for antitumor agents in normally aerated and hypozic cells; mechanisms of drug induced cytotoxicity; tumor microenvironmental effects on drug induced toxcicity. *Mailing Add:* Dept Pharmacol George Washington Univ 2300 I St NW Washington DC 20037-2337. *Fax:* 202-994-2870

KENNEDY, KEN, SOFTWARE SYSTEMS, RESEARCH ADMINISTRATION. *Current Pos:* Noah Harding prof math sci, 80-84, NOAH HARDING PROF COMP SCI, RICE UNIV, HOUSTON, TEX, 84-, DIR, CTR RES PARALLEL COMPUT, 87- *Personal Data:* b Aug 12, 45. *Educ:* Rice Univ, BA, 67; NY Univ, MS, 69, PhD(comput sci), 71. *Honors & Awards:* W W McDowell Award, Inst Elec & Electronics Engrs Comput Soc, 95. *Prof Exp:* From asst prof to prof, Dept Math Sci, Rice Univ, 71-84, chmn, Dept Comput Sci, 84-88, dir, Comput & Info Tech Inst, 89-92, chair, Dept Comput Sci, 90-92. *Concurrent Pos:* Prin investr, numerous grants, 73-87; vpres, R M Thrall & Assoc, Inc, 74-81, pres, 81-; vis scientist, Space Shuttle Prog Lead Off, NASA, 75; mem, Panel Comput Sci & Eng Res, Div Comput Res, NSF, 75-77 & Adv Comt Comput Res, NSF, 84-; vis staff mem, comput Div, Los Alamos Sci Lab, 77; co-chair, White House Adv Comt, High Performance Comput & Commun Info Technol & Next Generation Internet, 97- *Mem:* Nat Acad Eng; fel Asn Comput Mach; Soc Indust & Appl Math; fel Inst Elec & Electronics Engrs; Sigma Xi; fel AAAS. *Res:* Numerous publications; computer science; theory and practice of programming language implementation, especially optimization of compiled code for scientific languages; programming systems for parallel computers. *Mailing Add:* Dept Comput Sci Rice Univ 6100 Main St Houston TX 77005. *Fax:* 713-285-5136; *E-Mail:* ken@rice.edu

KENNEDY, KENNETH ADRIAN RAINE, PHYSICAL & FORENSIC ANTHROPOLOGY, ARCHAEOLOGY. *Current Pos:* from asst prof to assoc prof anthrop, 64-81, assoc prof div biol sci, 69-81, PROF ECOL DIV BIOL SCI, ANTHROP & ASIAN STUDIES, CORNELL UNIV, 81- *Personal Data:* b Oakland, Calif, June 26, 30; m 61, 69, Margaret C Fairlie. *Educ:* Univ Calif, Berkeley, BA, 53, MA, 54, PhD(anthrop), 62; Am Acad Forensic Sci, dipl, 78. *Honors & Awards:* T Dale Stewart Award Forensic Anthrop, Am Acad Forensic Sci, 87. *Prof Exp:* Actg instr phys anthrop, Univ Calif, Berkeley, 62-63; vis prof, Deccan Col Post-Grad & Res Inst, 63-64. *Concurrent Pos:* NSF fels, Deccan Col Post-Grad & Res Inst, Univ Poona, India, 63-64 & 71, 80-81, Univ Calif, Berkeley, 68-69 & Cornell Univ, 72; Cornell Univ fac res grant, Brit Mus Natural Hist, London, 65-66; vis prof, Dept Anthropol, Univ Ariz, 79 & 85; vis fel, Kings Col, Cambridge Univ, 81; fel, Am Inst Indian Studies, 66, 71-72, & 80-88; actg ed-in-chief, Am J Phys Anthrop, 85; elected chmn, Biol Anthrop Unit, Am Anthrop Asn, 86-88; secy, Phys Anthrop Sect, Am Acad Forensic Sci, 93-94, chair, 94-95. *Mem:* Fel AAAS; fel Am Anthrop Asn; Am Asn Phys Anthrop (vpres, 94-96); fel Royal Anthrop Inst Gt Brit; Int Asn Human Biol. *Res:* Human evolution in South Asia, particularly the hominid osteological fossil record; history of biological sciences, especially human evolution and physical anthropology; palaeodemography of South Asia; forensic anthropology; paleoanthropology of South Asia (India, Pakistan, Sri Lanka); forensic anthropology with special emphasis on markers of occupational stress; human palaeontology; evolutionary biology. *Mailing Add:* Ecol & Systs E-231 Corson Hall Cornell Univ Ithaca NY 14853. *Fax:* 607-255-8088; *E-Mail:* kak10@cornell.edu

KENNEDY, KEVIN JOSEPH, ANAEROBIC TREATMENT PROCESS DESIGN, BIOREMEDIATION. *Current Pos:* ASSOC PROF CIVIL & CHEM ENG, UNIV OTTAWA, 91- *Personal Data:* b Clitheroe, UK, Dec 2, 54; Can citizen; m 80, Linda A Manila; c Erica, Jordan & Dean. *Educ:* Univ Western Ont, BSc, 77, MESc, 80; Univ Ottawa, PhD(civil & environ eng), 85. *Honors & Awards:* Innovative Wastewater Treatment Process Award, Que Ministry Environ, 86; Award Excellence Wastewater, Can Asn Environ Sci & Eng, 89. *Prof Exp:* Process engr, Eco-Res (CIL), 80-82; res officer, Nat Res Coun Can, 82-91. *Concurrent Pos:* Consult various cos, 91-; secy, Spec Group Anaerobic Digestion, Int Asn Water Qual, 91- *Mem:* Int Asn Water Qual; Water Pollution Control Fedn; Am Soc Microbiol; Can Asn Water Qual. *Res:* Biological treatment of industrial and municipal wastewater; advanced anaerobic process for treatment of recalcitrant toxic wastewaters. *Mailing Add:* 1040 Millburn Cumberland ON K4C 1C9 Can. *Fax:* 613-564-3432

KENNEDY, LAWRENCE A, FLUID MECHANICS, COMBUSTION. *Current Pos:* DEAN & PROF, COL ENG, UNIV ILL, CHICAGO, 94- *Personal Data:* b Detroit, Mich, May 31, 37; m 57; c 6. *Educ:* Univ Detroit, BS, 60; Northwestern Univ, MS, 62, PhD(mech eng), 64. *Honors & Awards:* AT&T Found Award, Am Soc Eng Educ; Ralph R Teetor Award, Soc Auto Engrs. *Prof Exp:* Res engr, Mech Res & Develop Div, Gen Am Transp Corp, Ill, 63-64; dir aerospace eng, State Univ NY, Buffalo, 69-71, prof mech eng, 64-83; dept mech eng, Ohio State Univ, Columbus, 83-94. *Concurrent Pos:* Consult, Cornell Aero Labs, 66-71, Adv Group Aerospace Res & Develop, NATO, 71, MGB Res Corp, 76- & Air Preheater Div, Combustion Eng Corp, 78-; NSF sci fac fel, 68-69, NATO sr fel sci, 71-72; ed, J Exp Methods in Thermal & Fluid Sci. *Mem:* Combustion Inst; assoc fel Am Inst Aeronaut & Astronaut; Am Phys Soc; fel Am Soc Mech Engrs; Soc Automotive Engrs; Am Soc Engr Educ. *Res:* High temperature gas dynamics; chemical reacting flow; magnetohydrodynamics and combustion; radiative transfer; combustion generated pollutants; manufacturing processes; extensive work in the areas of reacting flows and optical dragnistics; specific studies turbulent combustion, radiation transfer with application to coal combustion and catalytic combustion. *Mailing Add:* Univ Ill 851 S Morgan St M/C159 Chicago IL 60607-7043. *Fax:* 312-996-8664; *E-Mail:* lkennedy@ulc.edu

KENNEDY, M(ALDON) KEITH, ENTOMOLOGY. *Current Pos:* SECT MGR, ENTOM RES CTR, SC JOHNSON WAX CO, 84- *Personal Data:* b Little Rock, Ark, July 26, 47. *Educ:* Hendrix Col, BA, 69; Cornell Univ, MS, 71, PhD(insect ecol), 76. *Prof Exp:* asst prof entom, Mich State Univ, 75-81. *Mem:* Entom Soc Am; Ecol Soc Am; Acarological Soc Am. *Res:* Biology of the Sciaridae Diptera, especially those of economic importance. *Mailing Add:* 2 Lansdale Lane Racine WI 53402-3532

KENNEDY, MARGARET WIENER, TOXICOLOGY, ENDOCRINOLOGY. *Current Pos:* RETIRED. *Personal Data:* b Arlington, Mass, Dec 16, 29; wid. *Educ:* Jackson Col, BS, 50; Boston Univ, MA, 54; Albany Med Col, PhD(toxicol), 72. *Prof Exp:* Res asst biochem, Schering Corp, 54-57; res asst endocrinol, Children's Mem Hosp, Chicago, 57-58; res assoc, Dept Obstet & Gynec, Univ Chicago Clin, 59-63; res asst prof, Dept Obstet & Gynec, Albany Med Col, 63-68, res asst prof toxicol, Inst Exp Path & Toxicol, 68-76; res scientist toxicol, Health Res Inc, NY State Dept Health, 77-80; forensic toxicologist, NY State Police Crime Lab, 85-92. *Concurrent Pos:* Res assoc, NIH res grant, 64-67 & 72-76, prin investr, 72-75; prin investr, US AEC contract, 67-70. *Res:* Invitro metabolism of individual polychlorinated biphenyls; control of placental hormone synthesis. *Mailing Add:* 62 Touchstone Lake Oswego OR 97035. *E-Mail:* peggykennedy@worldnet.att.net

KENNEDY, MARY BERNADETTE, BRAIN BIOCHEMISTRY, LEARNING MECHANISMS. *Current Pos:* from asst prof to assoc prof, 81-92, PROF NEUROBIOL, CALIF INST TECHNOL, 92- *Personal Data:* b Pontiac, Mich, July 4, 47. *Educ:* St Mary's Col, BS, 69; Johns Hopkins Univ, PhD(biochem), 75. *Honors & Awards:* McKnight Neurosci Develop Award, 84; Fac Award, Women Scientist & Engrs, NSF, 91; Javits Neurosci Invest Award, NIH, 92. *Prof Exp:* Fel, Harvard Med Sch, 75-78, Yale Med Sch, 78-80. *Concurrent Pos:* Mem sci adv bd, Hereditary Dis Found, 84-87, chmn, 86-87; assoc ed, J Neurosci, 86-89; mem & consult, 1 study sect, NIH Neurol Sci, 90-93; vchmn, Gordon Conf Neural Plasticity, 91, chmn, 93. *Mem:* Soc Neurosci; Am Soc Biochem & Molecular Biol; Am Soc Cell Biol; fel AAAS. *Res:* Biochemical mechanisms by which calcium regulates neuronal function in the central nervous system; regulation of type II calcium/calmodulin-dependent protein kinase and the molecular structure of the postsynaptic density. *Mailing Add:* Div Biol 216-76 Calif Inst Technol Pasadena CA 91125-0001. *Fax:* 626-449-0679

KENNEDY, MAURICE VENSON, BIOCHEMISTRY. *Current Pos:* RETIRED. *Personal Data:* b Pontotoc, Miss, Nov 23, 25; m 48; c 2. *Educ:* Miss State Univ, BS, 49, MS, 54, PhD(biochem), 67. *Prof Exp:* Dir microbiol & chem, Miss Dept Agr Lab, 49-62; instr microbiol, 62-66, assoc prof biochem, 66-83, prof biochem, Miss State Univ, 84-86. *Concurrent Pos:* Consult, NATO Sponsored Symp Pesticides, Lethbridge, Can, 70. *Mem:* AAAS; Am Chem Soc; Am Soc Microbiol; Sigma Xi. *Res:* Biochemical mechanisms of toxic substances, metabolic pathways in food poisoning microorganisms, production of useful substances from animal waste, and degradation and disposal of waste pesticides. *Mailing Add:* 1027 Brandywine Rd Tuscaloosa AL 35406

KENNEDY, MICHAEL CRAIG, NEUROBIOLOGY. *Current Pos:* ASSOC PROF ANAT, HAHNEMANN UNIV, 81- *Personal Data:* b Buffalo, NY, Dec 5, 46; c 3. *Educ:* Rice Univ BA, 68; Univ Rochester, MS, 71, PhD(biol, neurobiol), 74. *Prof Exp:* Fel comp neuroanat, NY Univ Med Ctr, 74-76; asst prof biol, NY Univ, 76-81. *Mem:* AAAS; Am Asn Anatomists; Soc Neurosci. *Res:* Investigations of the anatomy and physiology of neural pathways in nonmammalian vertebrates; neural substrates of auditory communication in the Tokay Gecko; developmental neurobiology of the reptilian auditory system; the visual system in the sea lamprey, Petromyzon marinus; influence of norepinephrine on blood-forming cells in bone marrow. *Mailing Add:* Dept Anat MS 408 Hahnemann Univ Sch Med Broad & Vine Philadelphia PA 19102-1178

KENNEDY, MICHAEL JOHN, structural geology, tectonics, for more information see previous edition

KENNEDY, MICHAEL LYNN, VERTEBRATE ZOOLOGY. *Current Pos:* asst prof, 74-80, ASSOC PROF BIOL, MEMPHIS STATE UNIV, 80- *Personal Data:* b Scotts Hill, Tenn, Jan 31, 42. *Educ:* Memphis State Univ, BS, 66, MS, 68; Univ Okla, PhD(vert zool), 75. *Prof Exp:* Asst vert zool, Univ Okla, 69-74. *Mem:* Am Soc Mammalogists; Soc Syst Zool; Am Ornithologists Union. *Res:* Mammalian systematics; geographic variation studies with small mammals. *Mailing Add:* Life Sci 201 Memphis State Univ 3706 Alumni St Memphis TN 38152-0001

KENNEDY, PATRICK JAMES, meteorology, science education; deceased, see previous edition for last biography

KENNEDY, PETER CARLETON, VETERINARY PATHOLOGY. *Current Pos:* from lectr to prof, Univ Calif, Davis, 54-92, lectr path, Med Sch, 57-92, pathologist, Exp Sta, 70-92, EMER PROF VET PATH, UNIV CALIF, DAVIS, 92- *Personal Data:* b Berkeley, Calif, June 19, 23; m 46; c 4. *Educ:* Kans State Univ, DVM, 49; Cornell Univ, PhD(vet path), 54. *Prof Exp:* Intern, Angell Mem Animal Hosp, Mass, 50; asst large animal surg, Cornell Univ, 51, asst path, 52-53. *Mem:* Am Col Vet Path. *Res:* Pathology of infectious diseases and endocrinopathies of domestic animals. *Mailing Add:* Vet Med Haring Hall Univ Calif-Davis Davis CA 95616

KENNEDY, ROBERT ALAN, PLANT STRESS PHYSIOLOGY. *Current Pos:* VPRES RES & ASSOC PROVOST GRAD STUDIES, TEX A&M UNIV, 92- *Personal Data:* b Benson, Minn, Sept 29, 46; m 68, 84; c 4. *Educ:* Univ Minn, BS, 68; Univ Calif, Berkeley, PhD(bot), 74. *Honors & Awards:* Kenneth Post Award, Am Soc Hort Sci, 83. *Prof Exp:* Asst prof bot, Univ Iowa, 74-78; from assoc prof to prof plant physiol, Wash State Univ, 79-85, asst dir res, 84-85; prof hort & chair, Ohio State Univ, 85-87; prog dir, NSF, 87-89; assoc vchair & dir agr res, Univ Md, 89-92. *Concurrent Pos:* Res assoc, US Army Med Res & Nutrit Lab, 69-71; mem fac, Biotechnol Ctr, Ohio State Univ, 86-88; consult, NSF, 89-90. *Mem:* Am Soc Plant Physiologists; AAAS; Bot Soc Am; Sigma Xi; Am Inst Biol Sci. *Res:* Plant biochemistry and physiology, especially anaerobic or flooding metabolism; metabolic adaptation to flooding; induction and coordination of metabolic pathways during anoxia; energy relations and regulations of protein synthesis without oxygen. *Mailing Add:* Tex A&M Univ 312 Admin Bldg College Station TX 77843-1112

KENNEDY, ROBERT DELMONT, MECHANICAL ENGINEERING. *Current Pos:* RETIRED. *Personal Data:* b Pittsburgh, Pa, Nov 8, 32; m 56, Sally Duff; c Robert Boyd, Kathleen Tyson, Thomas Alexander & Melissa Kristine. *Educ:* Cornell Univ, BSME, 55. *Honors & Awards:* Palladium Medal, Soc Chem Indust, 91, Chem Indust Medal, 95. *Prof Exp:* Staff mem, Union Carbide Corp, 55-57, staff, Nat Carbon Div, 57-77, pres, Linde Div, 77-82, sr vpres corp & exec vpres, 82, pres & chief exec officer, Chem & Plastics, 85-86, pres, chief exec officer & chmn, 86-95. *Concurrent Pos:* Chmn, Inroads Inc. *Mem:* Hon Fel Am Inst Chem Engrs; Chem Mfr Asn. *Mailing Add:* Union Carbide Corp 39 Old Ridgebury Rd Danbury CT 06817

KENNEDY, ROBERT E, THEORETICAL PHYSICS, THERMAL PHYSICS. *Current Pos:* Asst prof, 66-72, chmn dept, 73-81, ASSOC PROF PHYSICS, CREIGHTON UNIV, 73- *Personal Data:* b Santa Monica, Calif, June 5, 39; m 61; c 5. *Educ:* Loyola Univ, BS, 61; Univ Notre Dame, PhD(physics), 66. *Mem:* Am Inst Physics; Am Phys Soc; Am Asn Physics Teachers. *Res:* Non-equilibrium thermodynamics; impact of Albert Einstein on modern physics. *Mailing Add:* Dept Physics Creighton Univ Omaha NE 68178-0001

KENNEDY, ROBERT P, SEISMIC LOADING. *Current Pos:* PRES, R P K STRUCT MECH CONSULT, 86- *Personal Data:* b Glendale, Calif, Apr 2, 39. *Educ:* Stamford Univ, BA, 60, MA, 61, PhD(struct eng), 67. *Honors & Awards:* Stephen Bechtel Energy Eng Award, Am Soc Civil Engrs, 92. *Prof Exp:* Res engr, Northrop Corp, 61-64; dir eng mech, Holmes & Narber, 66-76; vpres, Eng Div, Anal Corp, 76-80; pres, Struct Mech Assoc, 80-86. *Mem:* Nat Acad Eng; Am Concrete Inst; Earthquake Eng Res Inst; Am Soc Civil Engrs. *Mailing Add:* R P K Struct Mech Consult 18971 Villa Terr Yorba Linda CA 92686. *Fax:* 714-777-8299

KENNEDY, ROBERT SAMUEL, EXPERIMENTAL PSYCHOLOGY. *Current Pos:* FAC DIR, ESSEX CORP, COLUMBIA, MD, 81-, VPRES, ORLANDO, FLA, 87-; PROF, UNIV CENT FLA, 87- *Personal Data:* b Bronxville, NY, Jan 10, 36; div; c Kathryn J, Robert C, Richard M & Kristyne E. *Educ:* Iona Col, BA, 57; Fordham Univ, MA, 59; Univ Rochester, PhD(sensation & perception), 72. *Honors & Awards:* Raymond F Longacre Award, Aerospace Med Asn, 93; Franklin Taylor Award, Am Psychol Asn, 96. *Prof Exp:* Res psychologist, Psychol Div, Naval Sch Aviation Med, Pensacola, Fla, 59-65; head diver div eval, Naval Med Res Inst, Pensacola, 68-70; head, Br Human Factors Eng, Naval Missile Ctr, Pt Mugu, Calif, 72-76; head, Human Div Human Factors, Naval Air Develop Ctr, Warminster, Pa, 76; officer-in-charge, Dept Bioeng Sci, Naval Aerospace Med Res Lab Detachment, New Orleans, 76-79, head, Dept Human Performance, 77-79; head, Dept Human Performance, Naval Biomed Lab, New Orleans, 79-81. *Concurrent Pos:* Bd dirs, Aviation, Space & Environ Med; lectr grad, Psychol Dept, Laverne Col, Pt Mugu, 73-76; Syst Mgt Dept, Univ SCalif, 75-76; consult, NASA/Johnson Space Ctr, Houston, 85-, Systems Tech Inc, Univ Space Res Asn, Momterey Tech Inc, Battelle, Am Inst Biol Sci, Performance Metrics, Bolt, Beranek & Newman, NAS/Nat Sci Res Coun, NASA/Ames Res Ctr, US Navy Med Res & Develop Command; consult ed, Aviation, Space & Environ Med, Behav Res Methods, Instruments & Computers, J Exp Psychol. *Mem:* Fel Am Psychol Asn; fel Am Psychol Soc; Am Soc Safety Engrs; fel Aerospace Med Asn; AAAS; Am Soc Safety Engrs; Aerospace Human Factors Asn; Soc Neurosci; NY Acad Sci. *Res:* Development of microcomputer based test battery, motion sickness data base and prediction tools. *Mailing Add:* Essex Corp 1040 Woodcock Rd Suite 227 Orlando FL 32803

KENNEDY, ROBERT SPAYDE, ELECTRICAL ENGINEERING, COMMUNICATIONS. *Current Pos:* staff mem, Lincoln Lab, 63-64, from asst prof to assoc prof, 64-76, PROF ELEC ENG, MASS INST TECHNOL, 76- *Personal Data:* b Augusta, Kans, Dec 9, 33; m 55; c 3. *Educ:* Univ Kans, BS, 55; Mass Inst Technol, SM, 59, ScD(info theory), 63. *Prof Exp:* Nuclear engr, Naval Reactors Br, US AEC, 55-57; Ford Found grad fel, 59-60. *Concurrent Pos:* Ford fel, Mass Inst Technol, 64-65; dir, Commun Form, Mass Inst Technol, 84-88. *Mem:* Fel Inst Elec & Electronics Engrs; Optical Soc Am. *Res:* Extraordinary wide band fiber optic networks. *Mailing Add:* Dept Elect Eng Mass Inst Technol Cambridge MA 02139

KENNEDY, ROBERT WILLIAM, WOOD SCIENCE, TECHNOLOGY. *Current Pos:* RETIRED. *Personal Data:* b Syracuse, NY, Sept 13, 31; m 56; c 3. *Educ:* State Univ NY, BS, 53; Univ BC, MF, 55; Yale Univ, PhD(wood tech), 62. *Prof Exp:* Instr wood tech, Univ BC, 55-56 & 57-61; from asst prof to assoc prof, Univ Toronto, 62-66; head wood biol sect, Western Forest Prod Lab, 66-69, prog mgr, Protection & Prod Div, 69-71, from assoc dir to dir, 71-79; prof wood sci & indust, Univ BC, 79-83, dean, Fac Forestry, 83-90, prof wood sci, 90. *Concurrent Pos:* Consult, Forestry & Forest Prod Div, Food & Agr Orgn, UN, 64, 82. *Mem:* Forest Prod Res Soc; fel Int Acad Wood Sci (pres 87-); Can Inst Forestry; fel Inst Wood Sci. *Res:* Physiology of wood formation; wood structure and properties at micro level; wood utilization. *Mailing Add:* 6303 Salish Dr Vancouver BC V6N 4C2 Can

KENNEDY, ROBERT WILSON, ORGANIC CHEMISTRY. *Current Pos:* RETIRED. *Personal Data:* b Tampa, Fla, Sept 9, 27; div; c 1. *Educ:* Emory Univ, AB, 53, MS, 54, PhD(chem), 56. *Prof Exp:* Develop res chemist, Org Chem Div, Tenn Eastman Co, 56-58, sr chemist, 59-72, dept supt, Intermediates Dept, 72-73, asst div supt, Polymers Div, 73-74, asst to the works mgr, 74, proj mgr, New Prod Div, 74-79, proj mgr, 79-86. *Mem:* Am Chem Soc; Sigma Xi. *Res:* Developmental research in industrial organic chemistry; mechanisms of organic reactions; naturally occurring organic compounds, particularly pine resin acids; new products marketing aspects; new products development. *Mailing Add:* 3357 Ridgeview St Kingsport TN 37764-3467

KENNEDY, ROBIN JOHN, MATERIALS SCIENCE. *Current Pos:* PROF, DEPT PHYSICS, FLA A&M UNIV, 90- *Personal Data:* b NZ, May 12, 50. *Educ:* Univ Canterbury, BSc, 71, PhD(physics), 77. *Prof Exp:* Prof, Dept Physics, Fla State Univ, 68-90. *Mem:* Am Phys Soc. *Mailing Add:* Dept Physics Florida A&M Univ Tallahassee FL 32307

KENNEDY, RUSSELL JORDAN, CIVIL ENGINEERING, HYDRAULICS. *Current Pos:* RETIRED. *Personal Data:* b Dunrobin, Ont, Nov 23, 17; m 46, 68, Marjorie M Rice; c Ian, Robert, Nancy & Barbara. *Educ:* Queen's Univ, Ont, BSc, 41; Univ Iowa, MS, 49. *Hon Degrees:* DSc, Queen's Univ, 93. *Honors & Awards:* Angus Medal, Eng Inst Can, 58. *Prof Exp:* Lt, Royal Cdn Eng, Military Cross, 41-46; lectr, Queen's Univ, 46-48, from asst prof to prof civil eng, 49-84, assoc dean sch grad studies, 68-70, vprin admin, 70-76, exec dir, Alumni Asn, 81-86, emer prof, 83- *Concurrent Pos:* Consult, Ont Paper Co, 48-51, Pulp & Paper Res Inst Can, 51-64, Dept Energy, Mines & Resources, 68-71, Irving Pulp & Paper Ltd, St John, NB, 79-80 & NW Hydraul Consults, Vancouver, BC, 79-80. *Mem:* Eng Inst Can; Int Asn Hydraul Res. *Res:* Ice control; improvement of design criteria for air bubbler systems. *Mailing Add:* Ellis Hall Queen's Univ Kingston ON K7L 3N6 Can

KENNEDY, STEPHEN DANDRIDGE, ECONOMICS, STATISTICS. *Current Pos:* Analyst, 70-75, vpres, 75-88, CHIEF SCIENTIST, ABT ASSOCS INC, MASS, 88- *Personal Data:* b New York, NY, Feb 25, 42; m 65, Joanna Court Bartlett; c Julia (Paca) & Benjamin Bartlett. *Educ:* Harvard Univ, AB, 63; Mass Inst Technol, PhD, 72. *Concurrent Pos:* Adj lectr, John F Kennedy Sch Govt, Harvard Univ, 95. *Res:* Evaluation and research design. *Mailing Add:* 77 Marion Rd Watertown MA 02172-4734

KENNEDY, THELMA TEMY, NEUROPHYSIOLOGY. *Current Pos:* RETIRED. *Personal Data:* b Chicago, Ill, Oct 18, 25; m 64, Richard C Berner. *Educ:* Univ Chicago, PhB & BS, 47, MS, 49, PhD(biopsychol), 55. *Prof Exp:* Asst neurosurg, Univ Chicago, 51-56; from instr to prof, Univ Wash, 58-88, assoc dean grad sch, 69-72, emer prof physiol, 88. *Concurrent Pos:* USPHS fel neurophysiol, Univ Wash, 56-58. *Mem:* AAAS. *Res:* Cerebral cortex organization; unit activity; motor systems; sensory physiology. *Mailing Add:* Dept Physiol & Biophys SJ-40 Univ Wash MS357290 Seattle WA 98195

KENNEDY, THOMAS JAMES, JR, PHYSIOLOGY, NEPHROLOGY. *Current Pos:* RETIRED. *Personal Data:* b Washington, DC, June 24, 20; m 50, F Elaine Gedtfring; c Thomas J III, Ann E, Joan F, Paul E & Christopher A. *Educ:* Cath Univ, BS, 40; Johns Hopkins Univ, MD, 43; Am Bd Internal Med, dipl, 56. *Prof Exp:* Asst med, Col Med, NY Univ, 45-47 & Col Physicians & Surgeons, Columbia Univ, 47-50; investr, Lab Kidney & Electrolyte Physiol, Nat Heart Inst, 50-60, mem staff, Off of Dir, NIH, 60-65, chief, Div Res Facil & Resources, 65-68, assoc dir prog planning & eval, 68-74; exec dir assembly life sci, Nat Acad Sci-Nat Res Coun, 74-76; dir, Dept Planning & Policy Develop, Asn Am Med Col, 76-86, assoc vpres, 86-90, consult, 90-95. *Concurrent Pos:* Res assoc, Sch Med, George Washington Univ, 51-65. *Mem:* Am Physiol Soc; Am Fedn Clin Res. *Res:* Renal physiology, especially mechanisms for excretion of electrolytes; electrolyte physiology; clinical disorders of renal and electrolyte physiology; administration of research. *Mailing Add:* 10703 Weymouth St Box 427 Garrett Park MD 20896-0427

KENNEDY, THOMAS WILLIAM, CIVIL ENGINEERING. *Current Pos:* from asst prof to assoc prof, 65-74, dir, Coun Advan Transp Studies, 75-78, asst vpres res, 78-79, PROF CIVIL ENG, UNIV TEX, AUSTIN, 74-, ASSOC DEAN ENG RES PLANNING, 79-, ENG FOUND PROF, 85- *Personal Data:* b Danville, Ill, Jan 7, 38; div; c 2. *Educ:* Univ Ill, BS, 60, MS, 62, PhD(civil eng), 65. *Prof Exp:* From asst to instr civil eng, Univ Ill, 62-65. *Concurrent Pos:* Hwy Res Bd, Nat Acad Sci-Nat Res Coun, 65-; mem, Transp Res Bd. *Mem:* Am Soc Civil Engrs; Am Concrete Inst; Am Soc Testing & Mat; Asn Asphalt Paving Technologists. *Res:* Materials; pavements; transportation; civil engineering. *Mailing Add:* Dept Civil Eng Univ Tex Austin TX 78712-1076

KENNEDY, VANCE CLIFFORD, GEOCHEMISTRY, HYDROLOGY. *Current Pos:* Geologist geochem, 49-52 & 55-60, res geologist geochem & hydrol, 60-84, ANNUITANT, US GEOL SURV, 84- *Personal Data:* b Big Run, Pa, May 18, 23; m 48; c 4. *Educ:* Pa State Univ, BS, 48, MS, 49; Univ Colo, PhD(geol), 61. *Res:* Geochemical prospecting; uranium geology and geochemistry; transport of stream sediment; effects of stream sediment on the chemistry of water; chemistry of rainfall-runoff. *Mailing Add:* 5052 Tully Rd Modesto CA 95356

KENNEDY, W KEITH, JR, ELECTRICAL ENGINEERING, SOLID STATE PHYSICS. *Current Pos:* Mem tech staff, 68-69, mgr, Solid State Res & Develop Dept, 71-74, Solid State Div, 74-78, vpres, 77, vpres Devices Group, 78-86, Shareowner Relations & Planning Coord, 86-88, PRES & CHIEF EXEC OFFICER, WATKINS-JOHNSON CO, 88- *Personal Data:* b Phoenix, Ariz, Sept 19, 43; m 65; c 2. *Educ:* Cornell Univ, BEE & MS, 65, PhD(elec eng), 68. *Mem:* Inst Elec & Electronics Engrs. *Res:* Microwave power generation and amplication with semiconductor devices; microwave integrated circuits; microwave systems. *Mailing Add:* Watkins-Johnson Co 3333 Hillview Ave Palo Alto CA 94304

KENNEDY, WILBERT KEITH, AGRONOMY. *Current Pos:* assoc dir, Res & Agr Exp Sta, Col Agr, Cornell Univ, 59, dir, 59-65, assoc dean col, 65-67, vprovost univ, 67-72, dean col, 72-78, provost univ, 78-84, prof agron, NY State Col Agr & Life Sci, 49-84, EMER PROVOST, CORNELL UNIV, 84- *Personal Data:* b Vancouver, Wash, Jan 4, 19; m 41; c 2. *Educ:* State Col Wash, BS, 40; Cornell Univ, MSA, 41, PhD(agron), 47. *Prof Exp:* Asst, Cornell Univ, 40-42 & 46-47; asst prof & asst agronomist to assoc prof & assoc agronomist, exp sta, State Col, Wash, 47-49. *Concurrent Pos:* Fulbright res scholar & Guggenheim fel, 56-57. *Mem:* Fel AAAS; fel Am Soc Agron; Sigma Xi. *Res:* Chemistry; botany; factors influencing yield and nutritive value of farm crops; grazing management practices and their relationship to the behavior and grazing habits of cattle; measuring, harvesting and storage losses in hay and silage; accumulation of nitrates in forage plants; nitrate toxicity. *Mailing Add:* 410 Savage Farm Dr Ithaca NY 14850-6506

KENNEDY, WILLIAM ALEXANDER, FISH BIOLOGY. *Current Pos:* CO DIR, HAGENSBORG RESOURCES, 86- *Personal Data:* b Merlin, Ont, Can, Sept 28, 15; m 42, 89; c 5. *Educ:* Univ Toronto, BA, 37, PhD(ichthyol), 41. *Prof Exp:* Asst, Ont Fish Res Labs, 36-41; from asst scientist to dir, Cent Fish Res Sta, 45-56, dir biol sta, 57-66, res scientist, Fisheries Res Bd Can, Nanaimo Biol Sta, 66-76; consult, 77-85. *Concurrent Pos:* War res, Nat Res Coun Can, 41-45. *Mem:* Aquaculture Asn Can. *Res:* Fish farming and related fields. *Mailing Add:* 999 Beach Dr Nanaimo BC V9S 2Y4 Can

KENNEDY, WILLIAM ROBERT, NEUROLOGY. *Current Pos:* From asst prof to assoc prof, 64-71, PROF NEUROL, MED CTR, UNIV MINN, MINNEAPOLIS, 71- *Personal Data:* b Chicago, Ill, Nov 2, 27; m 57; c 5. *Educ:* Univ Ill, BS, 51; Univ Wis, MS, 52; Marquette Univ, MD, 58. *Concurrent Pos:* Fel internal med, Mayo Clin, 59-60, fel neurol, 60-64. *Mem:* AMA; Am Neurol Asn; Am Electroencephalog Soc; Am Asn Electromyog & Electrodiag (past pres); Am Acad Neurol. *Res:* Clinical-pathological-physiological research on neuromuscular disorders; patho-physiology of cutaneous nerves. *Mailing Add:* Box 187 UMHC 420 SE Delaware St Minneapolis MN 55455

KENNEL, CHARLES FREDERICK, PLASMA PHYSICS, SPACE PHYSICS. *Current Pos:* assoc prof, 67-71, chmn, 83-86, PROF PHYSICS, UNIV CALIF, LOS ANGELES, 71-, MEM, INST GEOPHYS & PLANETARY PHYSICS, 71-, EXEC VCHANCELLOR, 96- *Personal Data:* b Cambridge, Mass, Aug 20, 39; m 64; c 2. *Educ:* Harvard Univ, AB, 59; Princeton Univ, PhD(astrophys sci), 64. *Honors & Awards:* Fulbright Sr lectr, Brazil, 85. *Prof Exp:* Asst res scientist, Avco-Everett Res Lab, 60-61, staff mem, 64-65, prin res scientist, 66-67. *Concurrent Pos:* NSF fel, 65-66; vis scientist, Int Ctr Theoret Physics, Trieste, 65-66; consult, TRW Systs Group, Calif, 67-; Alfred P Sloan Found fac fel, 68-70; mem, Physics Res Eval Group, Air Force Off Sci Res, 70-78; mem sci adv group, NASA, 71-72; vis prof, Ctr Phys Theory, Polytech Sch, Paris, 74-75; mem, Space Sci Bd, Nat Acad Sci-Nat Res Coun, 77-80, chmn, Comt Space Physics, 77-80, Space & Earth Sci Adv Comt, NASA, 87-89; Fairchild prof, Calif Inst Tech, 87; Guggenheim fel, 88; vis scientist, Space Res Ctr, Moscow, 88-; vis scholar, Univ Alaska, 88, 89 & 90; mem, Fusion Policy Adv Comt, Dept Energy, 90; assoc dir, Inst Plasma Physics & Fusion Res, Univ Calif, Los Angeles; assoc adminr, Mission to Planet Earth, NASA, 94-96. *Mem:* Nat Acad Sci; fel Am Phys Soc; Int Union Radio Sci; Am Astron Soc; fel Am Geophys Union; fel AAAS; Int Acad Astronaut. *Res:* Plasma turbulence theory; solar system and astrophysical plasma physics. *Mailing Add:* Dept Physics Univ Calif 405 Hilgard Ave Los Angeles CA 90095-1450. *Fax:* 310-206-6030

KENNEL, JOHN MAURICE, AEROSPACE NAVIGATION & GUIDANCE SYSTEM DEVELOPMENT, STAR TRACKERS & INERTIAL INSTRUMENT DEVELOPMENT. *Current Pos:* RETIRED. *Personal Data:* b Sioux City, Iowa, Oct 7, 27; m 52, Clara J Whaley; c Susan J, Sandra L (Camp), John F & William P. *Educ:* Miami Univ, Ohio, AB, 48; Univ Tex, PhD(physics), 55. *Prof Exp:* Physicist, US Naval Ord Lab, Md, 49-51; res eng, Aerophys Lab, NAm Aviation, 51-52, res specialist inertial navig, Autonetics Div, 55-58, mgr gyro & accelerometer res, 58-60, mgr adv inertial navig & missile guid syst, 60-62, sr scientist navig req definition, 62-64, proj mgr N-40 navig syst develop, 64-67, proj mgr microelectronic process & device res & develop, 67-71; mgr liquid crystal display design & develop, Autonetics Div, Rockwell Int, 71-75, staff engr accuracy assurance, Peacekeeper (MX) ICBM missile guid inertial instrument and syst develop, 75-85; eng mgr, astro-inertial navigation res & develop, Northrop Corp, 85-89, res eng star trackers, 89-93. *Mem:* AAAS; Am Phys Soc; Am Inst Aeronaut & Astronaut; Astron Soc Pac; Int Soc Optical Eng; Inst Navig. *Res:* Precision measurement and the development of precision instruments; applications to navigation, missile guidance, attitude measurement and control; development of precision accelerometers, gyroscopes, star trackers and ancillary equipment. *Mailing Add:* 11591 Suburnas Way Santa Ana CA 92705

KENNEL, STEPHEN JOHN, TUMOR IMMUNOLOGY. *Current Pos:* staff mem, 76-81, SR STAFF SCIENTIST, BIOL DIV, OAK RIDGE NAT LAB, 81- *Personal Data:* b Peoria, Ill, Jan 15, 45; m 66, Ellen Builta; c Jennifer, Jill & Ted. *Educ:* Univ Ill, BS, 67; Univ Calif, San Diego, MS, 68, PhD(chem), 71. *Prof Exp:* USPHS Grad fel trainee fel, 67-71; res fel, Dept Exp Path, Scripps Clin & Res Found, 71-73, res asst, 73-74, res assoc, Dept Immunopath, 74-76. *Mem:* Am Asn Cancer Res. *Res:* Antibody directed specific chemotherapy and specific immunotherapy of malignancies; analysis of cell surface proteins; leukemia virus proteins and radioimmunoassay. *Mailing Add:* 126 Netherlands Rd Oak Ridge TN 37830. *Fax:* 423-574-1274; *E-Mail:* sj9@ornl.gov

KENNEL, WILLIAM E(LMER), CHEMICAL ENGINEERING. *Current Pos:* mgr tech develop, 57-60, dir chem res, 60-61, vpres res & develop & dir, 61-67, vpres & dir, 67-68, vpres plastics, 68-70, group vpres & dir, 70-72, vpres mkt & dir, 72-75, EXEC VPRES & DIR, AMOCO CHEM CORP, 75- *Personal Data:* b St Louis, Mo, Aug 11, 17; m 39; c 2. *Educ:* Univ Ill, BS, 40; Mass Inst Technol, MA, 47, DSc(chem eng), 49. *Prof Exp:* Chem engr, A E Staley Mfg Co, 39-41; chem engr, Stand Oil Co, Ind, 48-51, res group leader, 51-52, res sect leader, 52-57. *Mem:* Am Chem Soc; Am Inst Chem Engrs. *Res:* Technical development of petrochemicals. *Mailing Add:* 208 Inverness Lane Schererville IN 46375-2904

KENNELL, DAVID EPPERSON, MOLECULAR BIOLOGY. *Current Pos:* from instr to assoc prof, 61-73, PROF MICROBIOL, SCH MED, WASH UNIV, 73- *Personal Data:* b Syracuse, NY, May 23, 32; m 56, Tanner Wilma; c Charles, Frederick & Laura. *Educ:* Univ Calif, Berkeley, AB, 54, PhD(biophysics), 59. *Prof Exp:* Res eng mineral tech, Univ Calif, Berkeley, 56-57; res fel bact & immunol, Harvard Med Sch, 59-60; res assoc, Mass Inst Technol, 60-61. *Concurrent Pos:* Nat Cancer Inst fel, 67-61; NIH res career develop award, 69-74; mem, Microbial Physiol Study Sect, NIH, 81-85. *Mem:* Am Soc Microbiol; Am Soc Biol Chem; AAAS; Am Asn Univ Professors. *Res:* Ribonucleic acid metabolism in bacteria and reaction mechanisms of ribonucleases. *Mailing Add:* Dept Molecular Microbiol Box 8230 Wash Univ Sch Med St Louis MO 63110-1093. *Fax:* 314-362-1232; *E-Mail:* kennell@borcim.wustl.edu

KENNELL, JOHN HAWKS, PEDIATRICS, DEVELOPMENTAL-BEHAVIORAL PEDIATRICS. *Current Pos:* dir, Family Clin, Case Western Res Univ, 52-60, dir, Pediat Clin, 60-70, sr instr, 52-55, from asst prof to assoc prof, 55-73, PROF PEDIAT, CASE WESTERN RES UNIV, 73-, ASSOC PEDIATRICIAN, 56- *Personal Data:* b Reading, Pa, Jan 9, 22; m 49, Margaret Lloyd; c David, Susan & Jack. *Educ:* Univ Rochester, BS, 44, MD, 46. *Honors & Awards:* George Armstrong Award, Ambulatory Pediat Asn; Aldrich Award, Am Acad Pediat. *Prof Exp:* Intern pediat, Children's Hosp, Boston, 46-47; asst resident, Children's Hosp Med Ctr, 49-50, chief resident med out-patient dept, 50, dir dept, 52, chief med resident, 51. *Concurrent Pos:* Dir, Neonatal Nurseries, Univ Hosp, Cleveland, 82-67; Child Develop, Rainbow Babies & Childrens Hosp, 80-; Nat Inst Child Health & Human Develop spec res fel, Univ London, 66-67; consult, Headstart, 68- *Mem:* Am Acad Pediat; Am Pediat Soc; Asn Child Care Hosps (vpres, 73-75); Soc Res Child Develop; Ambulatory Pediat Asn (pres, 70); Soc Develop Behav Pediat (pres, 89). *Res:* Child development; medical education; social and psychological factors in medicine; effects of mother-infant separation on maternal attachment; effects of perinatal death on parents; effect of supportive companion during labor and delivery; parent to infant bonding for full term, premature, sick, malformed infants and stillborn and perinatal death; effects of continuous emotional support during labor. *Mailing Add:* Rainbow Babies & Childrens Hosp 2101 Adelbert Rd Cleveland OH 44106

KENNELLEY, JAMES A, METALLURGY, EXECUTIVE EDUCATION & DEVELOPMENT. *Current Pos:* CONSULT, 92- *Personal Data:* b Rochester, NY, Aug 23, 28; m 55, Sarah T Wade; c Kevin, Mark & Judith Ann. *Educ:* Col Wooster, BA, 45; Mich State Univ, PhD(chem), 55. *Prof Exp:* Res chemist uranium, Mallinckrodt, Inc, 55-57, group leader res, 57-59, mgr res, 59-62, tech dir div, 62-65; asst to pres, Que Iron & Titanium Corp, 65-73, vpres, 73-75, group vpres, 75-78; pres, Direct Reduction Corp, 78-83; assoc dir exec educ, Columbia Bus Sch, 83-92. *Mem:* Am Chem Soc; Am Soc Metals; Am Inst Mining, Metall & Petrol Engrs. *Res:* Rare earths; uranium chemistry and metallurgy; titanium; raw materials; ilmenite smelting; titanium dioxide pigments; direct reduction of iron ore. *Mailing Add:* 8774 SE Riverfront Terr Tequesta FL 33469-1813. *E-Mail:* jimkennel@jund.com

KENNELLEY, KEVIN JAMES, NONMETALLICS, ELASTOMERICS. *Current Pos:* Prin res engr, Mat Sect, Arco Explor & Prod Technol, 90-94, corrosion specialist, 94-95, MGR TECHNOL SUPPORT SERV, ARCO INDONESIA, 91- *Personal Data:* b St Louis, Mo, Aug 6, 58; m 82, Emily J Cromley; c Robert, Sarah & Natalie. *Educ:* Univ Okla, BS, 80, MS, 85, PhD(metall eng & mat sci), 86. *Honors & Awards:* AB Cambell Award, Nat Asn Corrosion Engrs, 93, 94. *Prof Exp:* Sr field engr, Duncan Dist, Schlumberger Well Serv, 80-82; res specialist, Mat Sect, Exxon Prod Res Co, 86-90. *Concurrent Pos:* Prog chmn, Ann Conf Nat Asn Corrosion Engrs, 88-89 & 89-90. *Mem:* Sigma Xi; Metall Soc; Am Soc Metals; Nat Asn Corrosion Engrs. *Res:* Controlling corrosion of materials in oil and gas production that are exposed to high temperature, high pressure sour hydrocarbon fluids; cathodic protection; nonmetallics. *Mailing Add:* ARCO Explor & Prod Technol 2300 W Plano Pkwy Plano TX 75075. *Fax:* 214-754-3565; *E-Mail:* kkennel@arco.fs.com

KENNELLY, MARY MARINA, INORGANIC CHEMISTRY, ORGANIC CHEMISTRY. *Current Pos:* RETIRED. *Personal Data:* b Chicago, Ill, Nov 12, 19. *Educ:* Mundelein Col, BS, 42; Univ Notre Dame, MS, 50, PhD(chem), 59. *Prof Exp:* Asst prof, Mundelein Col, 50-57, chmn dept, 59-69, prof chem, 59-74. *Concurrent Pos:* NSF sci fac summer fels, London, 60, Fla State, 61 & Seattle, 62. *Mem:* AAAS; Am Chem Soc; Nat Sci Teachers Asn; Sigma Xi. *Res:* Coordination chemistry; infrared studies of metal complexes of amino acids. *Mailing Add:* 1090 Hoagland Blvd Jacksonville IL 62650

KENNELLY, WILLIAM J, CHEMISTRY. *Current Pos:* sr res chemist, Amax Mat Res Ctr, 84-87, DIR, TECHNOL & OPERS, CYPRUS AMAX POLYMER ADDITIVES GROUP, ANN ARBOR, MICH, 87- *Personal Data:* b Cleveland, Ohio, Aug 22, 48; m 77; c 2. *Educ:* Mass Inst Technol, BS, 70; Northwestern Univ, PhD(chem), 75; Temple Univ, MBA, 86. *Prof Exp:* Fel, Univ NDak, Grand Forks, 75-76, Mass Inst Technol, 76-77; res scientist, Rohm & Haas Co, 77-84. *Mem:* Am Chem Soc; Soc Plastics Eng; Am Soc Testing & Mat. *Res:* Polymer additives especially flame retardants and smoke suppressants. *Mailing Add:* 2481 Windmill Way Saline MI 48176

KENNER, CHARLES THOMAS, analytical chemistry; deceased, see previous edition for last biography

KENNER, MORTON ROY, MATHEMATICS. *Current Pos:* PROF MATH & CHMN DEPT, NORTHWEST MO STATE UNIV, 70-, CHMN DIV MATH & COMPUT SCI, 78- *Personal Data:* b Rochester, NY, June 10, 25; m 54; c 2. *Educ:* Univ Rochester, AB, 49; Univ Minn, MA, 51; PhD(math, math ed), 58. *Prof Exp:* From asst prof to assoc prof math, Southern Ill Univ, 52-67; prof math & chmn dept, Stephens Col, 67-70. *Concurrent Pos:* Dir develop proj sec math, Southern Ill Univ, 58-67; consult, Opers Res Group, Ohio State Univ, 60-; dir Nairobi Math Ctr, Kenya, 64 & 65. *Mem:* Hist Sci Soc; Math Asn Am; Sigma Xi. *Res:* Foundations of mathematics; systems models; mathematical education; history of mathematics. *Mailing Add:* 4201 NW 74th St Kansas City MO 64151-1877

KENNERLY, GEORGE WARREN, INDUSTRIAL CHEMISTRY. *Current Pos:* RETIRED. *Personal Data:* b Boston, Mass, Mar 11, 22; m 49; c 2. *Educ:* Harvard Univ, BS, 44, MA, 47, PhD, 49. *Prof Exp:* Res chemist, 49-54, group leader, 54-59, mgr, 59-68, dir, Am Cyanamid Co, 68-84. *Mem:* AAAS; Am Chem Soc. *Res:* Auto-oxidation; peroxide chemistry; photochemistry; electrochemistry; luminescence; reaction kinetics. *Mailing Add:* 1072 Purdue Dr Longmont CO 80503-3655

KENNET, HAIM, AERONAUTICS, ASTRONAUTICS. *Current Pos:* Res engr gas dynamics, Aero-Space Div, Boeing Co, 61-63, sr group engr aerothermodyn, 63-65, sr supvr Mars Explor, 65-67, systs eng mgr, Space Div, 67-69, PROJ MGR SPACE EXPLOR SYSTS, AEROSPACE GROUP, BOEING CO, 69- *Personal Data:* b Jerusalem, Israel, Apr 20, 35; US citizen. *Educ:* Mass Inst Technol, SB & SM, 57, ScD(aeronaut & astronaut), 61. *Mem:* Am Inst Aeronaut & Astronaut. *Res:* Flight mechanics, flight control, propulsion and thermal control aspects of unmanned space probes. *Mailing Add:* 2040 43rd Seattle WA 98112

KENNETT, JAMES PETER, MICROPALEONTOLOGY, PALEOECOLOGY. *Current Pos:* assoc prof, 70-74, PROF, GRAD SCH OCEANOG, UNIV RI, 74- *Personal Data:* b Wellington, NZ, Sept 3, 40; m 64; c 2. *Educ:* New Zealand Univ, BSc, 62; Victoria Univ, Hons, 63, PhD(geol), 65, DSc, 76. *Honors & Awards:* McKay Hammer Award, Geol Soc NZ, 68. *Prof Exp:* Sci officer, NZ Oceanog Inst, 65-66; NSF fel micropaleont, Allan Hancock Found, Univ Southern Calif, 66-68; asst prof, Fla State Univ, 68-70. *Concurrent Pos:* Mem adv comt, Antarctic Deep-Sea Drilling. *Mem:* AAAS; Geol Soc Am; Am Asn Petrol Geol; Soc Econ Paleont & Mineral; Int Quaternary Asn; Sigma Xi. *Res:* Marine geology; foraminiferal ecology and paleoecology; stratigraphic paleontology and stratigraphy of the Cenozoic; geology of the Antarctic continent. *Mailing Add:* Dir Marine Sci Inst Univ Calif Santa Barbara CA 93106

KENNETT, ROGER H, GENETICS, IMMUNOLOGY. *Current Pos:* dir, Human Genetics Cell Ctr, 73-96, asst prof, 76-80, ASSOC PROF GENETICS, SCH MED, UNIV PA, 80-; STROSCHEIN PROF & CHAIR BIOL, WHEATON COL. *Personal Data:* b Lakewood, NJ, Dec 27, 40; m 66, Carol Lundberg; c Ted, David & Timothy. *Educ:* Eastern Col, AB, 64; Princeton Univ, PhD(biochem sci), 70; Univ Pa, MSEd, 86. *Prof Exp:* Demonstr, Genetics Lab, Oxford Univ, 72-73, res officer, 73-76. *Mem:* AAAS; Am Asn Immunologists; Am Soc Microbiol. *Res:* Use of combination of immunological, biochemical and molecular genetic techniques to study molecular changes related to oncogenesis, and to the growth and differentiation of human neuroblastoma cells. *Mailing Add:* Dept Biol Wheaton Col Wheaton IL 60187. *Fax:* 215-573-5892; *E-Mail:* kennett@pobox.upenn.edu

KENNETT, TERENCE JAMES, NUCLEAR PHYSICS. *Current Pos:* RETIRED. *Personal Data:* b Toronto, Ont, Aug 8, 27; m 49; c 2. *Educ:* McMaster Univ, BSc, 53, MSc, 54, PhD(physics), 56. *Prof Exp:* Fel physics, McMaster Univ, 56-57; assoc physicist, Argonne Nat Lab, 57-59; from asst prof to prof eng physics & physics, McMaster Univ, 59-76. *Mem:* Am Phys Soc. *Res:* Neutron physics; decay scheme studies; neutron capture gamma rays; instrumentation and detector development. *Mailing Add:* Dept Physics & Astron McMaster Univ 1280 Main St W Hamilton ON L8S 4K1 Can

KENNEY, DONALD J, PHYSICAL CHEMISTRY. *Current Pos:* RETIRED. *Personal Data:* b Chicago, Ill, Aug 26, 25; m 48; c 7. *Educ:* Loyola Univ, Ill, BS, 49; Iowa State Univ, PhD(phys chem), 53. *Prof Exp:* Res engr, Steel Div, Ford Motor Co, 53-54; prof chem, Univ Detroit, 54-94. *Concurrent Pos:* Dir govt projs, 54-65. *Mem:* Am Chem Soc. *Res:* Iron complexes; metallurgy. *Mailing Add:* 1840 E Morten Ave No 240 Phoenix AZ 85020

KENNEY, FRANCIS T, BIOCHEMISTRY. *Current Pos:* from biochemist to sr biochemist, 59-69, sci dir, Carcinogenesis Prog, 69-75, SR STAFF SCIENTIST, OAK RIDGE NAT LAB, 75- *Personal Data:* b Springfield, Mass, Mar 16, 28; m 51; c 2. *Educ:* St Michael's Col, BS, 50; Univ Notre Dame, MS, 53; Johns Hopkins Univ, PhD(biochem), 57. *Prof Exp:* Instr biol, St Michael's Col, 50-51; res assoc pediat, Med Col, Cornell Univ, 57-59. *Mem:* AAAS; Am Soc Biol Chemists; Am Chem Soc; Sigma Xi; Am Soc Cell Biol. *Res:* Mammalian biochemistry; regulation. *Mailing Add:* 919 W Outer Dr Oak Ridge TN 37830-8233

KENNEY, GERALD, SURGERY, MEDICINE. *Current Pos:* clin instr urol, 71-, ASST PROF, UNIV WASH; PVT PRACT, UROLOGY RESOURCE CTR, SEATTLE. *Personal Data:* b Seattle, Wash, Dec 14, 34; c 4. *Educ:* Notre Dame Univ, BS, 56; Northwestern Univ, MD, 60. *Prof Exp:* Gen med officer, Ft Sam Houston, 62 & Little Rock AFB, 62 & 64; fel, Inst Urol, Univ London, 67-68; priv pract, OA Nelson Med Group, 71-72, Belleuve Urol, Inc, 72-85, Overlake Urol, Inc, 85-; chief transplantation serv, Swed Hosp Med Ctr, 71-; secy-treas, NW Urol Soc, 80-83, pres, 84; Urol Adv Coun, Nat Kidney Found, 82-85; med rev bd, Nat Transplant Prog, 84-; bd dirs, NW Kidney Ctr, 85- & Lake Wash Kidney Ctr, 84-; treas, Seattle Surg Soc, 85-86. *Mem:* Am Med Asn; Am Urol Asn; Am Col Surgeons; Am Soc Transplant Surgens; Soc Univ Urol; Soc Acad Surg; Am Soc Clin Urologists; Int Urol Soc. *Res:* Evaluation of diagnostic modalities for urological cancer which includes transrectal prostatic ultrasound and serum blood studies; methods for early detection of organ transplantation rejection. *Mailing Add:* Urol Resource Ctr 1560 N 115th St Suite 106 Seattle WA 98133

KENNEY, JAMES FRANCIS, GEOPHYSICS. *Current Pos:* PROF, CITY UNIV, 93- *Personal Data:* b Buffalo, NY, Sept 3, 26; m 57; c 3. *Educ:* Union Col, NY, BS, 51; Univ NMex, MS, 53, PhD(physics), 57. *Prof Exp:* Res assoc physics, Univ NMex, 57-58, res fel, 58-59, instr, 59-60; staff mem geoastrophys res, Boeing Sci Res Lab, Boeing Aerospace Co, 60-69, head, Geoastrophys Dept, 69-70, head, Environ Sci Dept, 70-73, mgr, Laser & Environ Sci Lab, 73-75, resources develop mgr, 75-76, mgr, radiation physics, 76-79, chief scientist, 79-90, chief, Eng Missiles Systs, 90-93. *Concurrent Pos:* BSD technol mgr, Boeing Aerospace Co; res fel, Lab Cosmic Physics, La Paz, 58-59. *Mem:* Am Inst Aeronaut & Astronaut; AAAS; Am Geophys Union. *Res:* Cosmic rays; ionospheric properties and radio propagation; nuclear, space and solar physics; magnetic fields and micropulsations; environmental science, urban studies; remote sensing, laser physics; military sciences; radiation physics; countermeasures. *Mailing Add:* 26203 Marine View Dr SW Kent WA 98032

KENNEY, JAMES FRANKLIN, POLYMER SYNTHESIS. *Current Pos:* sr proj leader, 78-79, mgr polymers & mat sci, 79-90, MGR POLYMER & ANALYTICAL CHEM, VISTAKON DIV, JOHNSON & JOHNSON VISION PRODS, INC, 90- *Personal Data:* b Richmond, Va, Aug 4, 34; m 58; c 3. *Educ:* Howard Univ, BS, 56, MS, 58; Univ Akron, PhD(polymer chem), 64. *Prof Exp:* Res chemist, US Air Force Mat Lab, 58-61; res fel, Inst Rubber Res, Akron, 61-64; res chemist, Chemstrand Res Ctr, Inc, 64-68; res assoc, Plastics Div, Allied Chem Corp, 68-71 & M & T Chem, Inc, 71-78. *Mem:* Am Chem Soc. *Res:* Synthesis, structure, property and performance of polymers; adhesion to skin; adhesive tapes; emulsion, condensation and addition polymerization; graft and block copolymers; polyblends; impact modification;

processing characteristics of polymers; economic and technical evaluation of research; developing catalysts for polyesters and polyurethanes; emulsion and hot melt adhesives; hydrogel soft contact lens materials; synthesis and evaluation; acrylic adhesives. *Mailing Add:* 13153 Cricket Cove Rd N Jacksonville FL 32224

KENNEY, MALCOLM EDWARD, ORGANOSILICON CHEMISTRY. *Current Pos:* from instr to assoc prof, 56-66, PROF CHEM, CASE WESTERN RES UNIV, 66- *Personal Data:* b Berkeley, Calif, Oct 7, 28; m 51. *Educ:* Univ Redlands, BS, 50; Cornell Univ, PhD(chem), 54. *Prof Exp:* Asst, Cornell Univ, 50-52, fel, 54. *Concurrent Pos:* John Teagle prof fel, 64-66; Hurlbut prof chem, 91. *Mem:* Am Chem Soc. *Res:* Metal complexes and inorganic polymers. *Mailing Add:* Dept Chem Case Western Res Univ 2040 Adelbert Rd Cleveland OH 44106-7078

KENNEY, MARGARET JUNE, MATHEMATICS. *Current Pos:* From instr to assoc prof, 59-92, PROF MATH, BOSTON COL, 92- *Personal Data:* b Boston, Mass, June 7, 35. *Educ:* Boston Col, Chestnut Hill, BS, 57, MA, 59; Boston Univ, PhD(math), 77. *Concurrent Pos:* Asst dir, Math Inst, Boston Col, 57- *Mem:* Nat Coun Teachers Math; Math Asn Am; Am Math Soc; Nat Coun Supvrs Math; Asn Women Math. *Res:* Mathematics education at the pre-college level; number theoretic applications of mathematics to art; discrete mathematics for pre-college students. *Mailing Add:* Math Inst Boston Col Chestnut Hill MA 02167-3814. *Fax:* 617-552-3789; *E-Mail:* peg.kenney@bc.edu

KENNEY, MARY ALICE, NUTRITIONAL STATUS, NUTRITION & IMMUNOCOMPETENCE. *Current Pos:* PROF HOME ECON, UNIV ARK, 85- *Personal Data:* b Lubbock, Tex, May 16, 38. *Educ:* Tex Tech Univ, BS, 58; Iowa State Univ, MS, 60, PhD(nutrit), 63. *Prof Exp:* Instr nutrit, Purdue Univ, 60-61; from asst prof to assoc prof, Iowa State Univ, 63-73; prof food & nutrit, Tex Tech Univ, 73-78; prof food, nutrit & inst admin, Okla State Univ, 78-84. *Mem:* AAAS; Am Inst Nutrit; NY Acad Sci; Am Dietetic Asn; Am Pub Health Asn; Am Col Nutrit. *Res:* Immunoglobulin levels; assessment of nutritional status; magnesium nutrition. *Mailing Add:* Dept Home Econ Univ Ark 118 HOEC Bldg Fayetteville AR 72701. *Fax:* 501-575-7273

KENNEY, NANCY JANE, PSYCHOBIOLOGY, BEHAVIORAL ENDOCRINOLOGY. *Current Pos:* asst prof, 76-82, ASSOC PROF PSYCHOL & WOMEN STUDIES, UNIV WASH, 83- *Personal Data:* b Wilkes-Barre, Pa. *Educ:* Wilkes Col, BA, 70; Univ Va, MA, 72, PhD(psychol), 74. *Prof Exp:* Fel neurol sci, Univ Pa, 74-76. *Concurrent Pos:* NIH res fel, Nat Inst Child Health & Human Develop, 74-76; prin investr, Nat Inst Arthritis, Metab & Digestive Dis, 78-84. *Mem:* Soc Neurosci; Am Psychol Asn; Nat Women Studies Asn. *Res:* Neural, endocrine and behavioral control of food intake and body weight. *Mailing Add:* Women's Studies G N-45 Univ Wash 3900 Seventh Ave NE Seattle WA 98195-0001

KENNEY, RICHARD ALEC, medical physiology; deceased, see previous edition for last biography

KENNEY, ROBERT WARNER, HIGH ENERGY PHYSICS, PARTICLE PHYSICS. *Current Pos:* sr staff physicist, 53-90, EMER SR PHYSICIST, LAWRENCE BERKELEY LAB, UNIV CALIF, BERKELEY, 90- *Personal Data:* b Portland, Ore, Nov 9, 22; m 50, Alice Irish; c Jane & Wanda. *Educ:* Univ Calif, Los Angeles, BA, 44; Calif Inst Technol, BS, 47; Univ Calif, PhD(physics), 52. *Prof Exp:* Mem staff, Los Alamos Sci Lab, 52-53. *Concurrent Pos:* Lectr, Univ Calif, Berkeley; consult, Marquardt Corp; staff mem, NASA. *Mem:* Am Phys Soc; AAAS; Sigma Xi. *Res:* High energy particle physics; electromagnetic interactions at high energies; particle accelerators; pion nuclear interaction; weak interaction and symmetry principles; double beta decay and nature of the neutrino. *Mailing Add:* 122 Scenic Dr Orinda CA 94563. *Fax:* 510-486-5401; *E-Mail:* kenney@lbl.gov

KENNEY, T CAMERON, CIVIL & GEOTECHNICAL ENGINEERING. *Current Pos:* assoc prof civil eng, 67-68, chmn dept, 68-74, PROF CIVIL ENG, UNIV TORONTO, 68- *Personal Data:* b Montreal, Que, Mar 26, 31; m 60; c 4. *Educ:* McGill Univ, BEng, 53; Univ London, DIC, 54, MSc, 56, PhD(civil eng), 67. *Honors & Awards:* Walter L Huber Prize, Am Soc Civil Engrs, 67; First Bjerrum Lectr, Norweg Geotech Soc, 75; Silver Jubilee Medal, Govt Can, 77; Keefer Medal, Can Soc Civil Eng, 83; Can Geotech Prize, Can Geotech Soc, 85. *Prof Exp:* Geotech engr, Acres Ltd, Niagara Falls, Ont, 56-61; res engr, Norweg Geotech Inst, Oslo, 61-67. *Concurrent Pos:* Eng consult, 68- *Mem:* Fel Eng Inst Can; Can Geotech Soc (pres 74-76). *Res:* Engineering properties of natural soils; landslides; engineering geology; dams; tailings dams. *Mailing Add:* Dept Civil Eng Univ Toronto Toronto ON M5S 1A1 Can

KENNEY, VINCENT PAUL, PHYSICS, ELEMENTARY PARTICLE PHYSICS. *Current Pos:* assoc prof, 63-66, PROF PHYSICS, UNIV NOTRE DAME, 66- *Personal Data:* b New York, NY, Sept 15, 27; m 54, Margaret Dennison; c Ann, Charles, John & Mary E. *Educ:* Iona Col, AB, 48; Fordham Univ, MS, 50, PhD(physics), 56. *Prof Exp:* Res assoc, Brookhaven Nat Lab, 53-55; from prof to assoc prof physics, Univ Ky, 55-63. *Concurrent Pos:* Vis physicist, Brookhaven Nat Lab, 57-; Oak Ridge Inst Nuclear Studies, 58-64; European Organization for Nuclear Res, 61-62 & 82-85; Argonne Nat Lab, 65-82; Fermi Nat Accelerator Lab, 71-; fel, Max Planck Inst Physics & Astrophys, Munich, 61-62 & 72; sr vis fel, Cavendish Lab, Cambridge Univ, 82-83, life mem, Clare Hall, Cambridge Univ, 85-; sr physicist, Dept Energy, 86-88. *Mem:* Fel Am Phys Soc; AAAS; Sigma Xi. *Res:* High energy particle physics; energy studies. *Mailing Add:* Dept Physics Univ Notre Dame Notre Dame IN 46556. *Fax:* 219-631-5952; *E-Mail:* kenney@undhep

KENNEY, WILLIAM CLARK, BIOCHEMISTRY, PROTEIN SCIENCE. *Current Pos:* lab head, Protein Chem, 89-92, RES SCIENTIST, AMGEN, THOUSAND OAKS, CALIF, 84-, DIR, PROTEIN CHEM, 92- *Personal Data:* b Grand Forks, NDak, Feb 25, 40. *Educ:* Carleton Col, BA, 62; Univ Calif, Berkeley, PhD(biochem), 67. *Honors & Awards:* Alcoholism Res Award, Vet Admin, 79. *Prof Exp:* Teaching & res asst, Univ Calif, Berkeley, 63-67; asst & assoc res biochemist, Univ Calif, San Francisco, 70-79, res chemist, Vet Admin Med Ctr, 79-84. *Concurrent Pos:* Fel, Am Cancer Soc, 68-69; adj assoc prof biochem med, Univ Calif, San Francisco, 79-84. *Mem:* Am Soc Biochem & Molecular Biol; AAAS; Am Chem Soc; NY Acad Sci; Res Soc Alcoholism; Sigma Xi; Am Cancer Soc; Protein Soc. *Res:* Enzymology; protein biochemistry and biophysics; molecular biology; structure and function of enzymes; biological oxidations; biotechnology. *Mailing Add:* 2654 Castillo Circle Thousand Oaks CA 91360-1301

KENNEY, WILLIAM LAWRENCE, ENVIRONMENTAL PHYSIOLOGY, BIOPHYSICS OF HEAT EXCHANGE. *Current Pos:* Res assoc, 83, ASSOC PROF APPL PHYSIOL, PA STATE UNIV, 89- *Personal Data:* b Latrobe, Pa, Jan 3, 57; m 82, Patricia A McGuigan; c Matthew, Alex & Lauren. *Educ:* Indiana Univ Pa, BS, 78, MS, 80; Pa State Univ, PhD(physiol), 83. *Honors & Awards:* New Investr Award, NIH, 86, Am Col Sports Med, 87. *Concurrent Pos:* Assoc ed, J Appl Physiol. *Mem:* Fel Am Col Sports Med; Am Physiol Soc; Sigma Xi. *Res:* Effects of high heat and humidity on the human body with a special emphasis on age; biophysics of heat exchange. *Mailing Add:* 102 Noll Lab Pa State Univ University Park PA 16802-6900. *Fax:* 814-865-4602; *E-Mail:* w7k@psuvm.psu.edu

KENNEY-WALLACE, GERALDINE ANNE, CHEMICAL PHYSICS, CHEMICAL DYNAMICS OPTICS. *Current Pos:* from asst to assoc prof, 74-80, PROF CHEM & PHYSICS, UNIV TORONTO, 80- *Personal Data:* b London, Eng, Mar 29, 43. *Educ:* Royal Inst Chem, ARIC, 65; Univ BC, MS, 68, PhD(chem), 70. *Hon Degrees:* DSc, DLitt, Univ Toronto, 88. *Honors & Awards:* Corday-Morgan Medal, UK, 79; Noranda Award, 84; E W R Steacie Award, 84. *Prof Exp:* Res assoc biophys, Oxford Univ, 64-66; fel chem, Univ BC, 70-71; assoc, Radiation Lab, Univ Notre Dame, 71-72; from instr to asst prof, Yale Univ, 72-74. *Concurrent Pos:* Vis scientist chem, Argonne Nat Lab, 73-; Alfred P Sloan fel, 77-79; Killam Res fel, 79-81; vis scientist, Ecole Polytech Paris, 81; Guggenheim fel, 83; vis prof, Stanford Univ, 85-86; chmn, Res Bd, Univ Toronto, 85-87; chmn, Sci Coun Can, 87-92; pres, Univ MacMaster, 90-95. *Mem:* Royal Soc Chem; Am Chem Soc; Am Phys Soc; Sigma Xi; Optical Soc Am; InterAm Photochem Soc; Nat Adv Bd Sci & Technol. *Res:* Molecular photophysics, energy transfer and molecular dynamics studied via picosecond, femtosecond laser spectroscopy; electronic and molecular structure of electrons in fluids; laser-induced electron transfer; holography, picosecond non linear optics. *Mailing Add:* Univ Toronto Toronto ON M5S 1A1 Can

KENNICK, WALTER HERBERT, MEAT SCIENCE. *Current Pos:* RETIRED. *Personal Data:* b Hampton, Va, Aug 23, 20; m 43; c 3. *Educ:* Clemson Col, BS, 48; Ore State Col, MS, 58, PhD(animal husb, meats), 59. *Prof Exp:* Res fel, Ore State Univ, 56-59, from asst prof to prof animal husb, 59-84. *Concurrent Pos:* Res scientist, Agr Inst, 73; Fulbright-Hays, Animal Prod Res Ctr, Dublin, Ireland, 74. *Mem:* AAAS; Am Soc Animal Sci; Am Meat Sci Asn; Inst Food Technol. *Res:* Quantitative yield of lean tissue from meat animals, methods of evaluating quality and quantity of such tissue and factors contributing to their variation; post slaughter treatments to improve eating quality. *Mailing Add:* 3290 SW Chintimini Ave Corvallis OR 97333

KENNINGTON, GARTH STANFORD, ANIMAL ECOLOGY, ANIMAL PHYSIOLOGY. *Current Pos:* RETIRED. *Personal Data:* b Afton, Wyo, Apr 19, 15; m 43. *Educ:* Univ Wyo, BS, 40; Univ Chicago, MS, 48, PhD(zool), 52. *Prof Exp:* Instr biol, George Williams Col, 47-48; instr, Roosevelt Col, 48-49; from asst prof to assoc prof zool, Lawrence Col, 52-60; assoc prof zool, Univ Wyo, 60-62, prof, 62-81, prof physiol, 74-81. *Concurrent Pos:* Consult, Kimberly-Clark Corp, 58-; NSF fel, Donner Lab, Univ Calif, 59-60; Fulbright lectr, Aligarh Muslim Univ, India, 63-64; Assoc Rocky Mt Univs fac grant, Nat Reactor Testing Sta, Idaho Falls, Idaho, 65-67; Oak Ridge Assoc Univs res grant, Environ Sci Div, Oak Ridge Nat Lab, 72-73. *Mem:* Fel AAAS; Am Soc Zool; Ecol Soc Am; Sigma Xi. *Res:* Ecology and physiology of the high arid plains; assessment of effects of mining and milling on biological communities in Wyoming. *Mailing Add:* 1404 Bridger St Laramie WY 82070

KENNINGTON, MACK HUMPHERYS, animal science; deceased, see previous edition for last biography

KENNISH, JOHN M, ANALYTICAL CHEMISTRY. *Current Pos:* from asst prof to assoc prof, 79-88, PROF TEACHING & RES, UNIV ALASKA, ANCHORAGE, 88- *Personal Data:* b Vineland, NJ, Oct 6, 45; m 67; c 1. *Educ:* Rutgers Univ, AB, 67; Shippensburg Univ, MS, 73; Portland State Univ, PhD(environ chem), 78. *Prof Exp:* Res assoc res, Ore Health Sci Ctr, 77-79. *Concurrent Pos:* Vis fel res, Univ Colo, Boulder, 82-83; vis prof res, Ore State Univ, 88-89. *Mem:* Am Chem Soc; Sigma Xi. *Res:* Fish biochemistry related to evaluating the response of major hepatic enzymes to toxic agents; the biochemistry of post-mortem changes in fish tissue especially lipids and the application of analytical methods to environmental chemistry. *Mailing Add:* Dept Chem Univ Alaska Anchorage 3211 Providence Dr Anchorage AK 99508

KENNISH, MICHAEL JOSEPH, ECOLOGICAL RESEARCH ON ESTUARINE & COASTAL MARINE ECOSYSTEMS, GEOLOGICAL & BIOLOGICAL RESEARCH ON DEEP-SEA MID-OCEAN RIDGE SYSTEMS. *Current Pos:* Res asst, Geol Dept, Rutgers Univ, 74-77, vis prof, Inst Marine & Coastal Sci, 88-90, supv res scientist, 90-93, res marine scientist, 93-96, MGR, RES LABS, DEEP-SEA ECOL & BIOTECHNOL CTR, INST MARINE & COASTAL SCI, RUTGERS UNIV, 96- *Personal Data:* b Vineland, NJ, Apr, 1950; m 73, Jo-Ann C Castone; c Shawn M & Michael C. *Educ:* Rutgers Univ, BA, 72, MS, 74, PhD(geol), 77. *Prof Exp:* Environ scientist, Jersey Cent Power & Light Co, Morristown, 77-82; sr environ scientist, GPU Nuclear Corp, Forked River, 82-90. *Concurrent Pos:* Grad fac, Dept Geol Sci, Inst Marine & Coastal Sci, Rutgers Univ, 92-, grad fac, Dept Oceanog, 96- *Mem:* Sigma Xi; Am Geophys Union; Am Fisheries Soc; Atlantic Estuarine Res Soc. *Res:* Biological and geological investigations on estuarine and coastal marine ecosystems; pollution studies on these regions; assessment of fisheries and shellfisheries in coastal habitats; geological and biological research on deep-sea mid-ocean ridge systems. *Mailing Add:* Inst Marine & Coastal Sci Rutgers Univ New Brunswick NJ 08903. *Fax:* 732-932-6557; *E-Mail:* kennish@ahab.rutgers.edu

KENNISON, JOHN FREDERICK, MATHEMATICS. *Current Pos:* PROF MATH, CLARK UNIV, 63- *Personal Data:* b New York, NY, Oct 7, 38; m 64; c 2. *Educ:* Queens Col, NY, BS, 59; Harvard Univ, AM, 60, PhD(topology), 63. *Mem:* Am Math Soc. *Res:* Category theory. *Mailing Add:* Clark Univ Worcester MA 01610-1477

KENNY, ALEXANDER DONOVAN, endocrinology of calcium & bone metabolism; deceased, see previous edition for last biography

KENNY, ANDREW AUGUSTINE, AUTOMOTIVE CONTROL DESIGN & DEVELOPMENT, FACILITATE QUALITY FUNCTION DEPLOYMENT. *Personal Data:* b Chicago, Ill, July 21, 34; m 66; c 2. *Educ:* Univ Ill, BS, 61. *Prof Exp:* Proj engr, Bastian-Blessing, 63-70; proj engr, Controls Div, Eaton, 70-86, eng supvr, 81-86, chief engr, 86-89, qual assurance mgr, 89-91. *Mem:* Soc Automotive Engrs; Am Soc Qual Control. *Res:* Nineteen patents in a variety of automotive control fields; published many articles on engineering, management and quality control. *Mailing Add:* N 57 W 26515 Mt DuLac Dr Sussex WI 53089

KENNY, DAVID HERMAN, ORGANIC CHEMISTRY. *Current Pos:* chmn, Org Chem Dept, 74-81, assoc prof, 62-89, EMER PROF CHEM, MICH TECHNOL UNIV, 89- *Personal Data:* b Lake Linden, Mich, Oct 6, 27; m 76, Judith Archibald; c Melanie, Amber & Emily. *Educ:* Cornell Univ, AB, 49; Univ Mich, MS, 55, PhD, 59. *Prof Exp:* Asst prof chem, Eastern Mich Univ, 58-60; Smith-Mundt lectr, Baghdad, 60-62. *Mem:* AAAS; Am Chem Soc. *Res:* Organic nitrogen chemistry. *Mailing Add:* 1220 Military Rd Houghton MI 49931-1986

KENNY, GEORGE EDWARD, INFECTIOUS DISEASES. *Current Pos:* Res instr prev med, Univ Wash, 61-63, from asst prof to assoc prof, 63-71, chmn, Dept Pathobiol, 71-91, PROF, DEPT PATHOBIOL, UNIV WASH, 91- *Personal Data:* b Dickinson, NDak, Sept 23, 30; m 58, Mary Pearson; c Frank, Michael, John, Maureen & Edward. *Educ:* Fordham Univ, BS, 52; Univ NDak, MS, 57; Univ Minn, Minneapolis, PhD(microbiol), 61. *Honors & Awards:* Kimble Methodol Award, Am Pub Health Asn, 71. *Mem:* Am Soc Microbiol; Infectious Dis Soc Am; Int Orgn Mycoplasmol; Sigma Xi; fel Am Acad Microbiol. *Res:* Antigenic analysis of microorganisms; host-parasite relationships of animal cells and microorganisms; biology of the mycoplasmatales; human mycoplasmal diseases; blood borne viral diseases. *Mailing Add:* 1504 37th Ave Seattle WA 98122. *Fax:* 206-543-3873; *E-Mail:* kennyg@u.washington.edu

KENNY, JAMES JOSEPH, IMMUNE DEFICIENCY, B-LYMPHOCYTES. *Current Pos:* ASST PROF MICROBIOL & IMMUNOL, UNIFORMED SERV UNIV HEALTH SCI, 79- *Educ:* Univ Calif, Los Angeles, PhD(immunol), 77. *Mailing Add:* 4940 Eastern Ave NIA NIH Gerontol Res Ctr Baltimore MD 21224. *Fax:* 410-558-8137

KENNY, MICHAEL THOMAS, ANTIBIOTICS, ANTIVIRALS. *Current Pos:* Sr virologist, Biohazards Dept, Pitman-Moore Div, Marion Merrell Dow Pharmaceut Inc, 66-67, res virologist, Dow Human Health Res & Develop Labs, 67-71, sr res virologist, Dept Infectious Dis, 71-74, sr res immunologist, Dow Diag Res & Develop, 74-78, clin res assoc, Med Dept, 78-81, assoc scientist, Pharmacol Dept, 81-92, SR RES MICROBIOLOGIST & MICROBIOL DEPT HEAD, HOECHST MARION ROUSSEL, 92- *Personal Data:* b San Francisco, Calif, Oct 3, 38; m 63; c 1. *Educ:* Univ San Francisco, BS, 60; Univ Del, PhD(microbiol), 64. *Mem:* Am Soc Microbiol; Am Asn Immunologists; AAAS; Int Soc Antiviral Res; Soc Leukocyte Biol; Anaerobe Soc. *Res:* Invertebrate microbiology and invertebrate tissue culture; diagnostic virology; radioimmunoassay; laboratory safety; viral immunology; virus vaccine development; development of antibiotics and anti-viral compounds; immunomodulation and inflammatory disease. *Mailing Add:* Hoescht Marion Roussell Inc PO Box 9627 Kansas City MO 64134-0627

KENNY, RAY, STABLE ISOTOPE GEOCHEMISTRY, ENVIRONMENTAL GEOLOGY. *Current Pos:* ASST PROF GEOL, NMEX HIGHLANDS UNIV, 93- *Personal Data:* b Chicago, Ill, June 13, 55. *Educ:* Northeastern Ill Univ, BSc, 83; Ariz State Univ, MSc, 86, PhD(geochem), 91. *Prof Exp:* Prof res asst, Inst Arctic & Alpine Res, Univ Colo, 91-95. *Mem:* Nat Asn Geol Teachers; Geol Soc Am; Am Geophys Union; Am Quaternary Asn. *Res:* Paleotemperature determinations using stable isotope geochemistry on geologic materials and biological materials; estimating past carbon dioxide levels in the atmosphere; field geology studies on paleosols, carbonate sediments and sea level fluctuation studies (Caspian Sea). *Mailing Add:* Dept Life Sci NMex Highlands Univ Las Vegas NM 87701

KENSEK, RONALD P, nuclear engineering, computer simulation, for more information see previous edition

KENSHALO, DANIEL RALPH, PSYCHOPHYSIOLOGY. *Current Pos:* actg asst prof, 50-53, from asst prof to assoc prof, 53-59, PROF PSYCHOL, FLA STATE UNIV, 59- *Personal Data:* b West Frankfort, Ill, July 27, 22; m 70; c 4. *Educ:* Wash Univ, BA, 47, PhD(exp psychol), 53. *Prof Exp:* Instr psychol, Washington Univ, St Louis, 48-49. *Concurrent Pos:* Vis prof physiol, Univ Marburg, Ger, 69, Univ Claude Bernard, France, 73 & Peking Univ, People's Repub China. *Mem:* Soc Neurosci; Fel Am Psychol Asn; Fel AAAS; Fel NY Acad Sci; Am Physiol Soc. *Res:* Psychophysical and electrophysiological investigation of the skin senses. *Mailing Add:* 2414 Delgado Dr Tallahassee FL 32304-1304

KENSLER, CHARLES JOSEPH, PHARMACOLOGY, BIOCHEMISTRY. *Current Pos:* prof pharmacol & exp therapeut & chmn dept, 57-60, PROF PHARMACOL, SCH MED, BOSTON UNIV, 60- *Personal Data:* b New York, NY, Jan 21, 15; m 44; c 2. *Educ:* Columbia Univ, AB, 37, MA, 38; Cornell Univ, PhD(pharmacol), 48. *Prof Exp:* Chem asst, Rockefeller Inst, 38-39; res assoc biochem, Mem Hosp, NY, 39-43, researcher, Off Sci Res & Develop, 42-43; from instr to assoc prof, Med Col, Cornell Univ, 43-53; head biol labs, Arthur D Little, Inc, 54-57; prof & chief exec officer, Arthur D Little Int, Inc, 73-85. *Concurrent Pos:* Traveling fel, Oxford Univ, 49-50; Sloan scholar, 51-54; lectr, Harvard Med Sch, 54-57; mem drug evaluation panel & chmn pharmacol comt, Cancer Chemother Nat Serv Ctr, 57-61; mem sub-comt carcinogenesis, Nat Acad Sci-Nat Res Coun, 57-; consult, Food & Drug Admin, 57, 60 & 71- & Nat Cancer Inst, 62-70; sr vpres prof oper, Arthur D Little, Inc, 60-85; vis prof, Mass Inst Technol, 72-84; trustee, Gordon Res Conf Coun, 77-83, chmn, 79-80; pres, Mass Health Res Inst, 77-80, dir, 60-85. *Mem:* AAAS; Am Asn Cancer Res; Am Soc Pharmacol & Exp Therapeut. *Res:* Nutrition and cancer; tissue metabolism; mode of action of carcinogenic agents; activity and mode of action of cancer chemotherapeutic agents; biochemical aspects of pharmacology; industrial toxicology; research and development management. *Mailing Add:* Ryergate Box 612 North Hampton NH 03862-0612

KENSON, ROBERT EARL, PHYSICAL CHEMISTRY, AIR POLLUTION CONTROL. *Current Pos:* PRIN, KENSON ASSOC, 96- *Personal Data:* b Stoneham, Mass, Apr 15, 39; m 68; c Brian & Bruce. *Educ:* Boston Univ, AB, 61; Purdue Univ, PhD(phys chem), 65. *Prof Exp:* Sr res chemist, Olin Mathieson Chem Corp, 65-69 & Engelhard Minerals & Chem Corp, Newark, 69-74; sr proj scientist, TRC, The Res Corp New Eng, 74-78; mgr engineered systs div, Oxy-Catalyst Inc, 78-80; develop dir, Met-Pro Corp, 80-95; prin mclarenihart environ eng corp, 95-96. *Mem:* Am Chem Soc; Am Inst Chem Eng; Air Pollution Control Asn; Soc Mfg Engrs; Soc Pharml Engrs. *Res:* Catalysis; kinetics of gas and solution reactions; petroleum chemistry and petrochemicals; energy systems; environmental control. *Mailing Add:* 1126 E Cardinal Dr West Chester PA 19382. *Fax:* 610-399-1127

KENT, ALLEN, information science, for more information see previous edition

KENT, BARBARA, PHYSIOLOGY, GENERAL MEDICAL SCIENCES. *Current Pos:* ADMIN DIR, MT DESERT BIOL LAB, 91- *Personal Data:* b Decatur, Ill, July 29, 40. *Educ:* Emory Univ, BA, 62, MS, 64, PhD(physiol), 70. *Prof Exp:* Res physiologist, Bronx Vet Admin Hosp, 70-83, dir, surg res, 72-83; assoc prof geriat & adv develop, dept physiol, Mt Sinai Sch Med, New York, 83-91. *Concurrent Pos:* Investr, Mt Desert Island Biol Lab, 68-; res assoc prof surg, Mt Sinai Sch Med, NY, 71-, assoc prof physiol, 78; vis scientist, Jackson Lab, 82. *Mem:* Am Physiol Soc; NY Acad Sci. *Res:* Cardiovascular control systems; patho physiology of respiration; comparative cardiovascular physiology; aging. *Mailing Add:* Mt Desert Island Biol Lab PO Box 35 Salsbury Cove ME 04672-9999

KENT, BION H, STRATIGRAPHY, COAL GEOLOGY. *Current Pos:* RETIRED. *Personal Data:* b Utica, NY, Oct 19, 25. *Educ:* Cornell Univ, BA, 49; Stanford Univ, MS, 52. *Prof Exp:* Geologist, US Geol Surv, 49-86. *Mem:* Fel Geol Soc Am; Am Asn Petrol Geologists. *Mailing Add:* 13511 W Alaska Pl Denver CO 80228

KENT, CLAUDIA, BIOCHEMISTRY. *Current Pos:* PROF BIOCHEM, UNIV MICH, 91- *Personal Data:* b South Bend, Ind, Oct 6, 45; m 81; c 2. *Educ:* St Mary's Col, Ind, BS, 67; Johns Hopkins Univ, PhD(biochem), 72. *Prof Exp:* Am Cancer Soc fel biochem, Dept Biol Chem, Sch Med, Wash Univ, 72-75; NIH fel, 74-75; from asst prof to prof biochem, Purdue Univ, 75-91. *Concurrent Pos:* SAC Biochem & Carcinogenesis, Am Cancer Soc; Physiol Chem Study Sect, NIH; bd sci counrs, Nat Inst Heart Lungs & Blood; assoc ed, J Biol Chem. *Mem:* Am Soc Biochem Molecular Biol; Am Soc Cell Biol; fel AAAS. *Res:* Regulation of phospholipid metabolism. *Mailing Add:* Dept Biol Chem Univ Mich Sch Med Ann Arbor MI 48109-0606

KENT, CLEMENT F, THEORETICAL COMPUTER SCIENCE, LOGIC. *Current Pos:* chmn dept math, 68-72, 76-79 & 85-87, PROF MATH SCI, LAKEHEAD UNIV, 68- *Personal Data:* b Charleston, SC, Mar 15, 27; m 48; c 3. *Educ:* Ga Inst Technol, BS, 48, MS, 50; Mass Inst Technol, PhD(math), 60. *Prof Exp:* Instr physics, Ga Inst Technol, 48-50; sci staff mem, Opers Eval Group, Mass Inst Technol, 51-62; assoc prof math, Case Western Reserve Univ, 62-68. *Concurrent Pos:* Vis prof, Univ Bristol, 72-73, Univ Laval, 79-80. *Mem:* Math Asn Am; Am Math Soc; Asn Symbolic Logic; Can Math Cong; Asn Comput Mach. *Res:* Mathematical logic; theoretical computer science; proof theory; recursive functions. *Mailing Add:* 186 S High St Thunder Bay ON P7B 3K6 Can

KENT, CLIFFORD EUGENE, CHEMICAL ENGINEERING, ELECTROCHEMISTRY. *Current Pos:* RETIRED. *Personal Data:* b Butler Co, Kans, Oct 11, 20; m 42, Elizabeth Rue; c Jane, Peter & Richard. *Educ:* Purdue Univ, BSChE, 42, BA(Theol), 80. *Prof Exp:* Pilot plant supvr, Merck & Co, NJ, 42-45; develop engr, Western Prod, Inc, 45-46; develop engr, Gen Elec Co, 46-49, design engr, 49-52, prog planning supvr, 52-56, mgr proj eng, 56-61, prog mgr advan fuel cell technol, 61-65, prog mgr electrochem eng, 65-67, mgr chem systs design, Nuclear Energy Div, 67-82; priest assoc, 83-89; interim rector, St Patrick's, Kenwood, Calif, 89-90, asst rector, 92-97. *Concurrent Pos:* Prof placement counsellor, 81-82. *Mem:* Am Inst Chem Engrs; Am Chem Soc; Am Nuclear Soc; Electrochem Soc. *Res:* Fuel cells; radiochemical plants; equipment design; chemical and gas processes; nuclear plant effluent control; water treatment; personnel development; granted three US patents. *Mailing Add:* 5555 Montgomery Dr No 64 Santa Rosa CA 95409-8818

KENT, D RANDALL, ENGINEERING. *Current Pos:* VPRES, GEN DYNAMICS CORP, TEX. *Honors & Awards:* Aircraft Design Award, Am Inst Aeronaut & Astronaut, 92. *Mailing Add:* Ft Worth Div Gen Dynamics Corp PO Box 748 Ft Worth TX 76102

KENT, DENNIS V, PALEOMAGNETISM. *Current Pos:* Res assoc, Columbia Univ, 74-79, sr res scientist, 79-84, assoc dir, 87-89, interim dir, 89-90, DOHERTY SR SCIENTIST, LAMONT-DOHERTY EARTH OBSERV, COLUMBIA UNIV, 84-, DIR RES, 93- *Personal Data:* b Prague, Czech, Nov 4, 46; m 71, Carolyn A Cook; c Amanda Grace. *Educ:* City Col New York, BS, 68; Columbia Univ, PhD(geophys), 74. *Concurrent Pos:* Adj assoc prof geol sci, Dept Earth & Environ Sci, Columbia Univ, 81-86, adj prof, 87-; guest prof, Inst Geophys, ETH, Zurich, 82. *Mem:* Fel Am Geophys Union; fel Geol Soc Am; fel AAAS. *Res:* Paleomagnetism and rock magnetism and their application to the history of earth's magnetic field and geologic problems. *Mailing Add:* Lamont Doherty Earth Observ Columbia Univ Palisades NY 10964. *Fax:* 914-365-8158; *E-Mail:* dvk@ldgo.columbia.edu

KENT, DONALD MARTIN, SCANNING ELECTRON MICROSCOPE, CARBONATE ROCKS. *Current Pos:* assoc prof, Univ Regina, 71-77, head dept, 82-88, prof geol, 77-96, head dept, 91-96, EMER PROF GEOL, UNIV REGINA, 96-; CONSULT GEOL, 96- *Personal Data:* b Medicine Hat, Alta, Can, Jan 25, 33; m 87, Joyce Barton; c Mark, Christopher, Paul, Teresa, Carmel, Crystal, Terri & Doug. *Educ:* Univ Sask, BSc, 57, MSc, 59; Univ Alta, PhD(geol), 68. *Prof Exp:* Res geologist, Sask Dept Mineral Resources, 58-68, sr res geologist, 68-71. *Concurrent Pos:* Consult, Can Occidental Petrol, Union Oil Can, 76-81; pres, D M Kent Consult Geologist Ltd, 81-; assoc ed, Bull Can Petrol Geol, 86-88 & Geol Atlas of Western Can Sedimentary Basin, 89-93. *Mem:* Am Asn Petrol Geologists; Int Asn Sedimentologists; Can Soc Petrol Geologists; Geol Asn Can; Sask Geol Soc (pres, 65, 69 & 78); Soc Sedimentary Geol. *Res:* Microfacies, diagenesis and nature of pore systems in carbonate hydrocarbon reservoir rocks; depositional settings of mixed carbonate-siliciclastic and carbonate-evaporite sequences; application of scanning electron microscope to diagenetic studies of carbonate rocks; paleotectonic controls on sedimentation; application of cathodo luminescence to carbonate diagenesis. *Mailing Add:* 86 Metcalfe Rd Univ Regina Regina SK S4V 0H8 Can. *Fax:* 306-585-5205

KENT, DONALD WETHERALD, JR, PHYSICS. *Current Pos:* RETIRED. *Personal Data:* b Philadelphia, Pa, June 26, 26; m 58; c 3. *Educ:* Yale Univ, BSc, 49; Temple Univ, PhD(physics), 60. *Prof Exp:* Researcher cosmic radiation, H H Wills Lab, Eng, 49-52; res physicist, Bartol Res Found, Franklin Inst, 52- *Mem:* Am Phys Soc; Am Geophys Union; Sigma Xi. *Res:* Cosmic ray physics. *Mailing Add:* 510 Walnut Lane Swarthmore PA 19081

KENT, DOUGLAS CHARLES, GEOLOGY. *Current Pos:* asst prof, 69-72, ASSOC PROF GEOL, OKLA STATE UNIV, 72- *Personal Data:* b Hastings, Nebr, Sept 26, 39; m 62; c 2. *Educ:* Univ Nebr, BSc, 61, MSc, 63; Iowa State Univ, PhD(water resources, geol), 69. *Prof Exp:* Prod geologist, Gulf Oil Corp, 64-66; instr, Iowa State Univ, 67-68, res assoc, 68-69. *Concurrent Pos:* Groundwater consult, 71- *Mem:* Geol Soc Am; Am Geophys Union; Am Water Resources Asn; Nat Water Well Asn; Sigma Xi. *Res:* Application of remote sensing to groundwater exploration and water resources; geochemistry of aquifers; application of mathematical modeling to groundwater management; stratigraphy; groundwater geology; applied geophysics and water resources. *Mailing Add:* Dept Geol Main Campus Okla State Univ Stillwater OK 74078

KENT, EARLE LEWIS, acoustics, data processing; deceased, see previous edition for last biography

KENT, GEOFFREY, PATHOLOGY. *Current Pos:* from asst prof to prof, 60-84, chmn dept, 72-77, EMER PROF PATH, MED SCH, NORTHWESTERN UNIV, 84- *Personal Data:* b Amsterdam, Holland, Jan 30, 14; nat US; m 44; c 4. *Educ:* Univ Amsterdam, MD, 39; Univ Manchester, MSc, 44; Northwestern Univ, PhD(path), 57. *Prof Exp:* Chief asst hemat, Res Dept, Manchester Royal Infirmary, 40-43, asst dir, 43-44; pathologist, London Hosp, 47-50; sr pathologist, Cook County Hosp, Chicago, 53-56, assoc dir path, 56-57. *Concurrent Pos:* Chief pathologist, WSuburban Hosp, 58-69; chmn dept path, Chicago Wesley Mem Hosp, 69-72. *Mem:* AAAS; Am Soc Exp Path; Am Asn Pathologists; Col Am Path; Am Soc Cell Biol. *Res:* Iron metabolism; liver disease. *Mailing Add:* Dept Path Northwestern Univ Med Sch 303 E Chicago Ave Chicago IL 60611-3072

KENT, GEORGE CANTINE, JR, VERTEBRATE MORPHOLOGY. *Current Pos:* RETIRED. *Personal Data:* b Kingston, NY, July 25, 14; m 37; c 1. *Educ:* Maryville Col, AB, 37; Vanderbilt Univ, MA, 38, PhD(zool), 42. *Prof Exp:* From instr to prof comp anat, La State Univ, 42-67, chmn, Dept Zool, 60-63, alumni prof, 67-79, emer alumni prof zool, 79- *Concurrent Pos:* Consult, Consult Bur, Comn Undergrad Educ in Biol Sci, Southern Asn Cols & Schs, 70-79; vchmn, Ctr Res in Col Instruct in Sci & Math, Tallahassee, 66-67; ed, Proc La Acad Sci, 47-55. *Mem:* Am Soc Zool; Soc Exp Biol & Med; Endocrine Soc; Sigma Xi. *Mailing Add:* 87 Pine Hill Rd Stockton NJ 08559-1112

KENT, GORDON, ELECTRICAL ENGINEERING. *Current Pos:* CONSULT, 83- *Personal Data:* b Pittsfield, Mass, Oct 1, 20; m 57; c 1. *Educ:* Univ Wis, BS, 47; Stanford Univ, MS, 49, PhD(elec eng), 52. *Prof Exp:* Res engr comput design, Inst Adv Study, 51-53; res fel electronics, Gordon McKay Lab, Harvard Univ, 53-57; assoc prof elec eng, Syracuse Univ, 57-63, prof, 63-85. *Concurrent Pos:* Proprietor, GDK Prod. *Mem:* Inst Elec & Electronics Engrs. *Res:* Development of measuring techniques and hardware for microwave properties of materials. *Mailing Add:* 1995 Stanley Rd Cazenovia NY 13035

KENT, HARRY CHRISTISON, geology; deceased, see previous edition for last biography

KENT, HENRY JOHANN, ROBOTIC SYSTEMS FOR AUTOMATED PAPER PRODUCT QUALITY TESTING, PARTICLE MORPHOLOGY & SUSPENSION RHEOLOGY. *Current Pos:* PRIN SCIENTIST, INT PAPER, 86- *Personal Data:* b Plymouth, Eng, Feb 2, 53. *Educ:* Sussex Univ, Eng, BSc, 74, PhD(theoret phys), 79. *Prof Exp:* Head paper coating res, ECC Int, 77-86. *Concurrent Pos:* Chmn coating fundamentals comt, Tech Asn Pulp & Paper Indust, 91-92. *Mem:* Tech Asn Pulp & Paper Indust. *Res:* Equilibrium and stability of fluid bodies in gravitational fields; measurement and analysis of surface topography; characterization of physical systems by fractal descriptors; numerical modelling of capillary flow in complex pore systems. *Mailing Add:* 2 Wildwood Circle Bloomingburg NY 12721. *Fax:* 914-577-7307

KENT, JAMES RONALD FRASER, MATHEMATICAL ANALYSIS. *Current Pos:* from assoc prof to prof, 50-79, chmn dept, 50-64, EMER PROF MATH, STATE UNIV NY, BINGHAMTON, 79- *Personal Data:* b Halifax, NS, Feb 29, 12; nat US. *Educ:* Queen's Univ, Ont, BA, 33, MA, 34; Univ Ill, PhD(math), 47. *Prof Exp:* Asst math, Syracuse Univ, 34-35 & Univ Ill, 35-39; instr, Univ Ark, 39-42; asst prof math, Univ BC, 46-48; assoc prof in-charge, Dept Math, Triple Cities Col, Syracuse Univ, 48-50. *Mem:* Am Math Soc; Math Asn Am; Can Math Soc; Sigma Xi. *Res:* Differential equations. *Mailing Add:* 100 Martha Rd Vestal NY 13850

KENT, JOHN FRANKLIN, zoology, for more information see previous edition

KENT, JOSEPH C(HAN), CIVIL ENGINEERING. *Current Pos:* from instr to asst prof, 52-61, assoc prof, 61-90, EMER ASSOC PROF CIVIL ENG, UNIV WASH, 90- *Personal Data:* b Victoria, BC, Jan 16, 22; nat US; m 52; c 3. *Educ:* Univ BC, BS, 45; Stanford Univ, MS, 48; Univ Calif, PhD(fluid mech), 52. *Prof Exp:* Hydrographic surveyor, Dept Mines & Resources, Can, 45-47; asst civil eng, Univ Calif, 49-52. *Mem:* Am Soc Eng Educ. *Res:* Fluid mechanics specializing in waves; drag of submerged bodies and fluid flow. *Mailing Add:* 3600 Island Crest Way Mercer Island WA 98040-3529

KENT, JOSEPH FRANCIS, TOPOLOGY. *Current Pos:* asst prof, 73-80, ASSOC PROF MATH, UNIV RICHMOND, 80- *Personal Data:* b Richmond, Va, Feb 13, 44; m 70. *Educ:* Univ Va, BA, 66, MA, 67, PhD(math), 70. *Prof Exp:* Asst prof math, Univ Fla, 70-73. *Mem:* Am Math Soc; Math Asn Am; Sigma Xi. *Res:* Topological dynamics and the study of ergodic flows; differentiability of norms on Banach spaces. *Mailing Add:* 15 Quail Run Dr Manakin-Sabot VA 23103-2632

KENT, LOIS SCHOONOVER, GEOLOGY, PALEONTOLOGY. *Current Pos:* RETIRED. *Personal Data:* b Marietta, Ohio, Dec 1, 12; m 43, Louis R; c Katherine (Hanvey). *Educ:* Oberlin Col, AB, 34; Cornell Univ, AM, 36; Bryn Mawr Col, PhD, 40. *Prof Exp:* Demonstr geol, Bryn Mawr Col, 36-40; jr geologist, Sect Metalliferous Deposits, US Geol Surv, 41-43, asst geologist, 43-45; ed asst, Geol Soc Am, 46; instr geol, Univ Ill, 54-55; from asst geologist to assoc geologist, Ill State Geol Surv, 56-85, cur, 56-85. *Mem:* Paleont Res Inst; Paleont Soc; Geol Soc Am; Soc Econ Paleont & Mineral; Sigma Xi. *Res:* Miocene mollusks of Maryland; Pennsylvanian fossils of Illinois. *Mailing Add:* 1003 Lincolnshire Dr Champaign IL 61821

KENT, RAYMOND D, COMMUNICATIVE DISORDERS, SPEECH DEVELOPMENT. *Current Pos:* DEPT COMMUN DISORDERS, UNIV WIS-MADISON. *Personal Data:* b Red Lodge, Mont, Dec 21, 42. *Educ:* Univ Mont, BA, 65; Univ Iowa, MA, 69, PhD(speech path), 70. *Prof Exp:* Fel, Res Lab Electronics, Mass Inst Technol, 70-71; prof commun disorders, Univ Wis-Madison, 71-79; sr res assoc, Boys Town Inst Commun Disorders in Children, 79- *Concurrent Pos:* Ed, J Speech & Hearing Res, 77-81; prin investr, NIH grants, 73-; mem, Ad Hoc Adv Comt Commun Disorders Prog, Nat Inst Neurol & Commun Disorders & Stroke, 81- *Mem:* Am Speech-Language-Hearing Asn; Am Asn Phonetic Sci; Acoust Soc Am; Sigma Xi; NY Acad Sci. *Res:* Production and perception of speech, especially to speech development in children, neurologic speech and language disorders, and theories of speech production. *Mailing Add:* 1 Kingsbury Ct Madison WI 53711

KENT, RONALD ALLAN, CATALYSIS, INORGANIC CHEMISTRY. *Current Pos:* PRES, TECHNOL NETWORK, 87- *Personal Data:* b New York, NY, Feb 23, 35; m 60; c 2. *Educ:* Cornell Univ, AB, 54. *Prof Exp:* Develop chemist catalytic chlorination, Gen Chem Res Lab, Allied Chem, 55-57; res assoc inorg sulfur & nitrogen, Dept Chem, Univ Pa, 57-68; res chemist platinum metal catalysis, Matthey Bishop Inc, 68-71; prin chemist heterogeneous catalysis, Dart Industs, 71-75, sr res assoc catalysis, 75-78, dir systs technol res & appl catalytic chem, 78-81, dir tech & develop, 81-83; dir com develop, Phillips Petrol, 83-85; tech mgr, Process Develop, PQ Corp, 86-87. *Concurrent Pos:* Instr chem, Spring Garden Inst Technol, 60-61; chief chemist, Chem Info & Doc Serv, Univ Pa, 65-67. *Mem:* Am Chem Soc (secy treas, inorg sect, 70); NY Acad Sci; AAAS; Com Develop Asn; Catalysis Soc NAm. *Res:* Hydrogenation and isomerization catalysis; polymerization catalysis; oxide catalyst processes; ozone preparation and utilization; sulfur dioxide control; noble metal utilization and recovery; secondary copper recovery processes; polyolefins; silica products; composites for invivo use. *Mailing Add:* PO Box 23131 Federal Way WA 98093-0131

KENT, STEPHEN MATTHEW, EXTRAGALACTIC ASTRONOMY. *Current Pos:* SCIENTIST, FERMI NAT ACCELERATOR LAB, 91- *Personal Data:* b West Orange, NJ, Dec 2, 52. *Educ:* Mass Inst Technol, BS, 74; Calif Tech, PhD(astron), 80. *Prof Exp:* Res fel astron, Ctr Astrophys, 79-81; teaching fel astron, Mass Inst Technol, 81-83; asst prof astron, Harvard Univ, 83-91. *Mem:* Am Astron Soc; Int Astron Union. *Res:* Extragalactic astronomy; internal dynamics of galaxies and clusters of galaxies. *Mailing Add:* Fermi Lab MS 127 PO Box 500 Batavia IL 60510. *Fax:* 630-840-8274

KENT, THOMAS HUGH, pathology, for more information see previous edition

KENTFIELD, JOHN ALAN CHARLES, MECHANICAL ENGINEERING. *Current Pos:* assoc prof, 70-79, PROF ENG, UNIV CALGARY, 81- *Personal Data:* b Hitchin, Eng, Mar 4, 30; m 66, Amelia Emmerson. *Educ:* Univ Southampton, BSc, 59; Univ London, DIC & PhD(mech eng), 63. *Honors & Awards:* R J Templin Award, Can Wind Energy Asn, 92. *Prof Exp:* Trainee, C V A Kearney & Trecker Ltd, Eng, 50-52; asst tester, Ricardo & Co Ltd, 52-56; asst lectr res & educ, Imp Col, Univ London, 62-63; proj engr, Curtiss-Wright Corp, 63-66; lectr res & educ, Imp Col, Univ London, 66-70. *Concurrent Pos:* Nat Res Coun grant, Univ Calgary, 71-72, operating grant, 77 & 80 & Nat Sci & Eng Rec Coun Can grant, 83, 86, 89 & 93; Killam Resident fel, Univ Calgary, 80. *Mem:* Am Inst Aeronaut & Astronaut; Am Soc Mech Engrs; Brit Inst Mech Engrs; Am Wind Energy Asn; Can Wind Energy Asn. *Res:* Non-steady flow of compressible fluid and the application of non-steady flow phenomena in engineering equipment, such as pressure exchangers and pulsating combustors; wind-turbines and wind-energy systems; author of over 140 research publications plus a graduate level text/reference book. *Mailing Add:* 1222 Bowness Rd NW No 301 Calgary AB T2N 3J7 Can. *Fax:* 403-282-8406

KENTZER, CZESLAW P(AWEL), GAS DYNAMICS, COMPUTATIONAL FLUID MECHANICS. *Current Pos:* From asst prof to assoc prof aerodyn, 58-91, PROF EMER, PURDUE UNIV, 91- *Personal Data:* b Poland, June 29, 25; nat US; m 58; c 3. *Educ:* San Diego State Col, BS, 52; Purdue Univ, MS, 54, PhD(aerospace eng), 58. *Concurrent Pos:* Consult, Missiles & Space Systs Div, Douglas Aircraft Corp. *Mem:* Am Math Soc; Am Acad Mech; Am Inst Aeronaut & Astronaut. *Res:* Fluid mechanics; transonic aerodynamics; acoustics; nonlinear waves; turbulence theories; computational fluid mechanics; geophysical fluid mechanics. *Mailing Add:* 17714 W Windslow Dr Grayslake IL 60030

KENWORTHY, ALVIN LAWRENCE, horticulture; deceased, see previous edition for last biography

KENYON, ALAN J, BIOCHEMISTRY, IMMUNOLOGY. *Current Pos:* RETIRED. *Personal Data:* b Whitehall, Wis, Sept 10, 29; m 54; c 3. *Educ:* Univ Minn, BS, 54, DVM, 57, PhD(bact & biochem), 61. *Prof Exp:* From assoc prof to prof biochem, Univ Conn, 61-73; prof biol, Med Sch, Cornell Univ, 73-80; mem, Walker Lab, Sloan-Kettering Inst Cancer Res, 73-97. *Concurrent Pos:* NIH res grants, 63- & career develop award, 65-75; consult, Manned Spacecraft Ctr, Apollo Prog, NASA, 68-; Path Dept, Hartford Hosp, 70- & Res Inst, Ill Inst Technol, 71-; sabbatical leave pediat & path, Sch Med, Univ Minn, Minneapolis, 71-72. *Mem:* AAAS; NY Acad Sci; Am Soc Exp Path; Reticuloendothelial Soc; Am Asn Lab Animal Sci. *Res:* Immunochemistry as applied to lymphoproliferative diseases and neoplasias of man and animals; comparative biochemistry of Mustelidae; diseases of marine mammals; immunological deficiency. *Mailing Add:* Cross Link Technol 822 The Parkway Mamaroneck NY 10543

KENYON, ALLEN STEWART, POLYMER SCIENCE. *Current Pos:* CONSULT, PHARMACEUT ANALYSIS, FOOD & DRUG ADMIN, 89- *Personal Data:* b Constance, Ky, Mar 6, 16; m 42; c 4. *Educ:* Univ Ky, BS, 38, MS, 39; Columbia Univ, PhD(phys chem), 47. *Prof Exp:* Asst phys chem, Univ Ky, 38-39, instr chem, 39-40; asst, Columbia Univ, 40-42; res chemist, 47-58, group leader, 58-69, sr res specialist, 69-80, fel, Monsanto Co, 80-85; instr physics, St Louis Univ, 85-88. *Concurrent Pos:* Asst, Nat Defense Res Comt Proj, Columbia Univ, 41-42. *Mem:* Am Chem Soc; Sigma Xi. *Res:* Mechanical properties; light scattering on high polymers; nondispersed sulfur sols; higher order Tyndall spectra; physical chemistry, structure and property relations of polymers; polymer characterization; chemistry of interfaces in composite materials; separating of polymers; instrumental analysis; pharmaceutical analysis. *Mailing Add:* 1318 Lindgate Kirkwood MO 63122-2338

KENYON, GEORGE LOMMEL, BIOCHEMISTRY. *Current Pos:* asst prof pharm chem, 72-74, assoc prof, 74-77, Prof Pharm Chem, 77-, DEAN SCH PHARM, UNIV CALIF, SAN FRANCISCO, 93- *Personal Data:* b Wilmington, Del, Aug 29, 39; m 81; c 1. *Educ:* Bucknell Univ, BS, 61; Harvard Univ, MA, 63, PhD(org chem), 65. *Honors & Awards:* Merit Award, NIH, 86. *Prof Exp:* Fel biochem, Mass Inst Technol, 65-66; asst prof chem, Univ Calif, Berkeley, 66-72. *Mem:* Fel AAAS; Am Chem Soc; Am Soc Biol Chemists; fel NY Acad Sci. *Res:* Enzyme mechanisms; organophosphorus chemistry; bio-organic chemistry of nucleotides; application of nuclear magnetic resonance spectroscopy to biological problems; design of reagents for protein modification; design of specific enzyme inhibitors. *Mailing Add:* Dean's Off Sch Pharm Univ Calif San Francisco CA 94143-0446. *Fax:* 415-476-0688

KENYON, HEWITT, MATHEMATICS. *Current Pos:* from asst prof to assoc prof, 61-67, chmn dept, 67-71, PROF MATH, GEORGE WASHINGTON UNIV, 67- *Personal Data:* b Marysville, Calif, Aug 31, 20; m 47, 61; c 5. *Educ:* Univ Calif, BS, 42, PhD(math), 54. *Prof Exp:* From instr to asst prof math, Univ Rochester, 52-61. *Concurrent Pos:* Vis assoc prof, Univ Calif, Berkeley, 66-67. *Mem:* Am Math Soc; Math Asn Am; Sigma Xi. *Res:* Convergence in topology; differentiation of set functions. *Mailing Add:* 1611 Kennedy Pl NW Washington DC 20011-6826

KENYON, KAY A, ZOOLOGY. *Current Pos:* ref librarian, Smithsonian Inst Libr, 78-79, asst librarian, 79-81, actg chief librarian, 81, BR LIBRARIAN, NAT ZOOL PARK BR, SMITHSONIAN INST, 81- *Personal Data:* b Monterey Park, Calif, Mar 12, 55; m, Peregrine S Barboza. *Educ:* Cedar Crest Col, BA, 77; Univ Denver, MA, 78. *Prof Exp:* Libr intern, Denver Mus Natural Hist Libr, 78. *Mem:* Assoc mem Am Zoo & Aquarium Asn; Spec Libr Asn. *Res:* Author of numerous publications in field. *Mailing Add:* Nat Zool Park Br Smithsonian Inst Libr Washington DC 20008-2598. *Fax:* 202-673-4900; *E-Mail:* livem018@sivm.si.edu

KENYON, KERN ELLSWORTH, PHYSICAL OCEANOGRAPHY. *Current Pos:* ASST RES OCEANOGR, SCRIPPS INST OCEANOG, 73- *Personal Data:* b Kansas City, Mo, May 24, 38; m 66; c 2. *Educ:* Mass Inst Technol, BS & MS, 61; Scripps Inst Oceanog, PhD(oceanog), 66. *Prof Exp:* Asst prof, Grad Sch Oceanog, Univ RI, 67-73. *Mem:* Am Geophys Union; AAAS; Oceanog Soc Japan; Sigma Xi. *Res:* Large-scale ocean circulation and air sea interaction; wave-wave and wave-current interactions. *Mailing Add:* 4632 North Lane Del Mar CA 92014-4134

KENYON, PATRICIA MAY, TECTONICS & GEODYNAMICS, ENVIRONMENTAL GEOPHYSICS. *Current Pos:* ASSOC PROF, CITY COL NY, 94- *Personal Data:* b Binghamton, NY, Mar 16, 52. *Educ:* Rensselaer Polytech Inst, BS, 74; Cornell Univ, PhD(geophys), 86. *Prof Exp:* Res physicist, Eastman Kodak Co, 74-80; res assoc, Carnegie Inst Wash, 85-87; asst prof geol, Cent Conn State Univ, 87-88; asst prof geophys, Univ Ala, 88-94. *Concurrent Pos:* Mem, Basic Energy Sci Prog Rev Panel, Dept Energy, 93; mem, Marine Geol & Geophysics Proposal Rev Panel, Ocean Sci Div, NSF, 94. *Mem:* Am Geophys Union; Geol Soc Am; Sigma Xi; Environ & Eng Geophys Soc. *Res:* Magma migration and the influence of this migration on geochemistry, particularly on the midocean ridges; salt tectonics sediment deposition and mantle convection; resistivity and shallow seismic studies. *Mailing Add:* Earth & Atmospheric Sci Dept J-106 City Col NY Convent Ave 138th St New York NY 10031-0338

KENYON, RICHARD H, VIROLOGY, IMMUNOLOGY. *Current Pos:* Virologist-immunologist, US Army Biol Labs, Ft Detrick, 69-71, Virol Lab, US Army Med Res Inst Infectious Dis, 71, rickettsiologist-immunologist, Virol Lab, 71-77, ASST CHIEF, RICKETTSIOLOGY DIV, US ARMY MED RES INST INFECTIOUS DIS, 78-, VIROL DIV, 80- & DIS ASSESSMENT DIV, 88-, MED MAT DEVELOP, 88- *Personal Data:* b Blakely, Pa, Nov 22, 42; m 68. *Educ:* Bucknell Univ, BS, 64; Pa State Univ, MS, 66, PhD(microbiol), 68. *Res:* Vaccine development; Rocky Mountain spotted fever; Rickettsiae; Junn virus; Argentine hemorrliagic fever. *Mailing Add:* 3202 B Ward Kline Rd Myersville MD 21773

KENYON, RICHARD R(EID), ELECTRICAL ENGINEERING, COMPUTER SCIENCE. *Current Pos:* PVT CONSULT, 86- *Personal Data:* b Middletown, Ohio, Oct 6, 28. *Educ:* Purdue Univ, BS, 50, MS, 51, PhD(elec eng), 61. *Prof Exp:* Mem tech staff, Bell Tel Labs, NJ, 51-55; res asst comput sci, Purdue Univ, 55-58, instr, 58-61, asst prof, 61-65; consult comput sci, McDonnell Douglas Astronaut Co, 80-86. *Mem:* Asn Comput Mach; Inst Elec & Electronics Engrs; Sigma Xi. *Res:* Circuit theory; numerical methods of approximation; computer architecture, programming languages. *Mailing Add:* 17781 Crestmoor Lane Huntington Beach CA 92649

KENYON, STEPHEN C, DIGITAL SIGNAL PROCESSING, NEURAL NETWORKS. *Current Pos:* PRES, CREATIVE ENG CONCEPTS, INC, 90- *Personal Data:* b Coronado, Calif, May 9, 48; m 70; c 1. *Educ:* Va Polytech Inst, BS, 71. *Prof Exp:* Elec engr, US Army, 71-75; chief eng, Ensco Inc, 75-83; vpres eng, Digital Signal Corp, 83-90. *Mem:* Inst Elec & Electronics Engrs Systs Man & Cybernet Soc; Inst Elec & Electronics Engrs Control Systs Soc; Inst Elec & Electronics Engrs Acoust Speech & Signal Processing Soc; Inst Elec & Electronics Engrs Comput Soc; Inst Elec & Electronics Engrs Commun Soc; Int Neural Network Soc. *Res:* Research and Development in electronic, optical and software signal processing; intelligent sensors, pattern recognition and machine intelligence; adaptive control for autonomous systems; 3 US patents. *Mailing Add:* Creative Eng Concepts Inc 3545 Chain Bridge Rd Suite 6 Fairfax VA 22030

KEOGH, MICHAEL JOHN, ORGANIC CHEMISTRY, POLYMER CHEMISTRY. *Current Pos:* Chemist, Union Carbide Corp, 63-67, proj scientist, 67-70, res scientist, 70-78, sr res scientist, 78-82, res assoc, Polyolefins Div, 82-88, CORP RES FEL, UNION CARBIDE CORP, 88- *Personal Data:* b Bronx, NY, May 26, 37; m 75, Paula; c Michael, Laura & Christine. *Educ:* Manhattan Col, BS, 59; Purdue Univ, PhD(org chem), 63. *Mem:* Am Chem Soc; Fire Retardant Chem Asn; Soc Plastic Eng. *Res:* Synthetic, organic and polymer chemistry; fluorocarbons; condensation monomer synthesis; organometallic and anionic polymerization systems; epoxide and other thermosetting polymerization systems; polymers engineered for pollution control; wire and cable technology; flame retardant and polymer stabilization technology. *Mailing Add:* Res & Develop Dept Union Carbide Corp 1 Riverview Dr Somerset NJ 08873

KEOGH, RICHARD NEIL, CELL BIOLOGY. *Current Pos:* From asst prof to assoc prof, 67-77, PROF BIOL, RI COL, 77- *Personal Data:* b Nashua, NH, Apr 21, 40. *Educ:* Tufts Univ, BS, 62; Brown Univ, PhD(biol), 67. *Mem:* AAAS; Am Asn Biol Teachers; Am Inst Biol Sci; Sigma Xi. *Res:* Mammalian pigment cell biology; teaching of biology via television; multimedia methods of instruction. *Mailing Add:* Off Res & Grants Admin RI Col Providence RI 02908

KEON, WILBERT JOSEPH, CARDIOVASCULAR SURGERY, DISEASE COSTING. *Current Pos:* Assoc prof surg, Univ Ottawa, 69-76, dir, Cardiac Unit, 69-83, prof surg & chmn dept, 76-91, CHMN, DIV CARDIOVASC & THORACIC SURG, UNIV OTTAWA, 69-, DIR-GEN, HEART INST, 83-; CHIEF, DIV CARDIOTHORACIC SURG, OTTAWA CIVIC HOSP, 69- *Personal Data:* b Sheenboro, Que, May 17, 35; m 60; c 3. *Educ:* St Pat's Col, Ottawa, BSc, 57; Univ Ottawa, MD, 61; McGill Univ, MSc, 63; FRCPS(C), 66. *Honors & Awards:* Officer, Order of Can, Can Govt, 85; Hippocrates Award, Am Hellenic Educ Progressive Asn, 85. *Concurrent Pos:* Assoc prof surg, Univ Ottawa, 69-76, dir, Cardiac Unit, 69-83, prof surg & chmn dept, 76-91, chmn, Div Cardiovasc & Thoracic Surg, 69-, dir-gen, Heart Inst, 83-; sr fel, Ont Heart Found, 70-76; surg fel, James IV Asn Surgeons, 79; vchmn, med adv bd, Can Heart Found, 79-80, chmn, 80-83, med vpres, 83-85; assoc ed, Can J Cardiol, 84-; mem bd dirs, Transplant Int Inc; surgeon-in-chief, Ottawa Civic Hosp, 77-83; vpres, Med Res Coun Can, 85-90; sen, govt Can, 90. *Mem:* Am Surg Soc; Am Asn Thoracic Surg; Int Asn Cardiac Biol Implants; Int Cardiovasc Soc; Can Cardiovasc Soc (pres, 88-89); Soc Cardiothoracic Surgeons. *Res:* Surgical treatment in the presence of acute myocardial infarction; cardiac muscle mechanics; lasers for treatment of coronary artery disease; artificial heart as a bridge to transplantation. *Mailing Add:* Dept Surg Univ Ottawa Fac Med 451 Smyth Rd Ottawa ON K0A 2T0 Can

KEONJIAN, EDWARD, ELECTRONICS, SOLID STATE PHYSICS. *Current Pos:* ADJ PROF ELEC COMPUT ENG, UNIV ARIZ, 93- *Personal Data:* b Tiflis, Russia, Aug 14, 09; US citizen; m 36; c 1. *Educ:* Leningrad Inst, BS & MS, 32, PhD, 33. *Prof Exp:* Res engr electronics, Leningrad Cent Radio Lab, 32-36; scientist, Leningrad Res Inst Electronics, 36-40; asst prof elec commun, Leningrad Inst Elec Eng, 40-42; lectr elec commun, City Col NY, 49-51; electron develop engr, Gen Elec Co, Syracuse, NY, 51-57; solid circuit develop engr, Am Bosch Arma Corp, Garden City, NY, 57-63; staff scientist, Grumman Aircraft Corp, Bethpage, NY, 63-64; eng consult, 64-73; chief, Microelectronics Failure Anal, UN Develop Proj, India, 73-74; eng expert & chief tech adv, 75-76. *Concurrent Pos:* US mem & dir lectr series, Adv Group Aeronaut Res & Develop, NATO, 62-74; NSF vis prof, Carro Univ, 77; chmn var tech comts & distinguished colleague, Aerospace Indust Asn Am; eng consult, 77- *Mem:* Fel Inst Elec & Electronics Engrs; Explorers Club; Circumnavigators Club; Aerospace Inst Asn. *Res:* Research and development of solid state technology. *Mailing Add:* 981 W Camino Guarina Green Valley AZ 85614

KEOUGH, ALLEN HENRY, ORGANIC CHEMISTRY. *Current Pos:* TECH DIR, METALLIZED PRODS INC, 86- *Personal Data:* b Chelsea, Mass, Apr 24, 29; m 52; c 6. *Educ:* Univ Mass, BS, 50; Univ NH, MS, 52; Mass Inst Technol, PhD(org chem), 56. *Prof Exp:* Res chemist, Johnson & Johnson, 55-58; sr res engr, Explor Res Div, Norton Co, Worcester, 58-62, res assoc, 62, asst dir res & develop, 62-63; res assoc, Nat Res Corp, 63-66, asst dir res, 66-68; pres, Chem-Tech Assocs, Inc, Mass, 68-71; sect head, Res Div, 71-74, sect head advan develop div, Dennison Mfg Co, 74-78; pres, Design Cote Co, 78-81; tech dir, Metall Prods Div, Household Mfg, Inc, 81-86. *Concurrent Pos:* Chmn, Radiation Curing Div, Asn Finishing Processes, Soc Mfg Engrs, 85-86; bd dirs, Rad Tech Int, 86, 87-88, pres, 86; bd dir, Vitronics Corp, 89- *Mem:* AAAS; Am Chem Soc; Asn Finishing Processes Soc Mfg Engrs. *Res:* Synthetic organic chemistry; organometallic compounds; heterogeneous catalysis surface active agents; polymer chemistry; radiation curing printing inks and coatings. *Mailing Add:* 3 Elizabeth Dr Northborough MA 01532

KEOUGH, KEVIN MICHAEL WILLIAM, BIOCHEMISTRY. *Current Pos:* from asst prof to assoc prof biochem, Mem Univ Nfld, 72-82, assoc prof pediat, 80-82, head, Dept Biochem, 86-92, PROF BIOCHEM & PEDIAT, MEM UNIV NFLD, 82-, VPRES RES, 92- *Personal Data:* b St George's, Nfld, Aug 2, 43; m 67; c 2. *Educ:* Univ Toronto, BSc, 65, MSc, 67, PhD(biochem), 71. *Prof Exp:* Muscular Dystrophy Asn Can fel phys biochem, Univ Sheffield, 71-72. *Concurrent Pos:* Dir, Seabright Corp, Can Ctr Fisheries Innovation & Can Ctr Marine Commun, 92-; mem, Med Res Coun Can, 92- *Mem:* Can Biochem Soc (pres 88-89); Can Lung Asn; Biochem Soc; Am Soc Biol Chemists; Am Chem Soc; Biophys Soc; Sigma Xi; Biophys Soc Can; Am Oil Chem Soc. *Res:* Molecular organization in membranes and lung surfactant; synthetic lung surfactant; liposomal biotechnology. *Mailing Add:* Dept Biochem Mem Univ Nfld St John's NF A1B 3X9 Can. *Fax:* 709-737-2552; *E-Mail:* kkeough@kean.ucs.mun.ca

KEOWN, ERNEST RAY, APPLIED MATHEMATICS. *Current Pos:* RETIRED. *Personal Data:* b Thurber, Tex, Mar 17, 21; m 43, Ruby Jean Owens; c 2. *Educ:* Univ Tex, BS, 46; Mass Inst Technol, PhD(math), 50; Univ Ark, JD, 81. *Prof Exp:* Sr aerophysics engr, Consol Vultee Aircraft Co, 51-52; asst prof math, Tex A&M, 52-57; comput specialist, Douglas Aircraft Co, 57-59; tech specialist, Aerojet Gen Corp Div, Gen Tire & Rubber Co, 59-60; prof math, Tex A&M Univ, 60-67; prof math, Univ Ark, Fayetteville, 67-91; vis prof, Tex A&M Univ, 91-92. *Concurrent Pos:* Consult, AEC, Stand Oil Co, Tex & Magnolia Petrol Co; mem, Solid State & Molecular Theory Group, Mass Inst Technol, 63-64. *Mem:* Am Math Soc. *Res:* Group representation theory; applications of group representation theory in physics; numerical analysis; computers and law; gauge theory. *Mailing Add:* PO Box K-10 College Station TX 77844

KEOWN, ROBERT WILLIAM, PACKAGING CHEMISTRY, FOOD CHEMISTRY. *Current Pos:* prof, 85-87, prof & actg chair, 87-88, PROF & CHAIR, DEPT FOOD SCI, UNIV DEL, 88- *Personal Data:* b Louisville, Ky, Apr 23, 29; m 49, 93, Yan Shi; c 3. *Educ:* Univ Louisville, BS, 51, MS, 52, PhD(chem), 54. *Prof Exp:* Res chemist, E I du Pont de Nemours & Co, Inc, 54-71, tech assoc, 71-74, supvr, Adhesives & Fluids Div, 74-81, from res assoc to sr res assoc, 81-85. *Concurrent Pos:* Pres, Isomer Corp. *Mem:* Am Chem Soc; AAAS; Adhesion Soc; Inst Food Technologists; Soc Packaging Engrs. *Res:* Polymer chemistry; food interactions with polymeric packaging materials, specifically flavor loss and adhesion effects. *Mailing Add:* 724 Foulkslone Wilmington DE 19803-2226. *Fax:* 302-478-0809, 831-2822; *E-Mail:* meyer@brahms.udel.edu

KEPECS, JOSEPH GOODMAN, PSYCHIATRY, PSYCHOANALYSIS. *Current Pos:* PROF PSYCHIAT, MED SCH, UNIV WIS-MADISON, 65- *Personal Data:* b Philadelphia, Pa, Oct 8, 12; m 44; c 2. *Educ:* Univ Chicago, BS, 35, MD, 37; Chicago Inst Psychoanal, cert, 49. *Prof Exp:* Pvt practr, 46-65. *Concurrent Pos:* Vis lectr, Univ Cincinnati, 56; lectr, Chicago Inst Psychoanal, 57-60; prof lectr, Univ Chicago, 60-65; consult, Univ Wis, 60-65. *Mem:* Am Psychiat Asn; Am Psychoanal Asn; Am Psychosom Soc. *Res:* Applications of psychiatry to medicine; sociological studies of changes in therapists and patients; psychiatry in developing countries. *Mailing Add:* 3230 University Ave Madison WI 53705

KEPES, JOHN J, PATHOLOGY, NEUROPATHOLOGY. *Current Pos:* from asst prof to assoc prof, 60-68, PROF PATH, UNIV KANS MED CTR, KANSAS CITY, 68- *Personal Data:* b Budapest, Hungary, Mar 31, 28; US citizen; m 50; c 1. *Educ:* Univ Budapest, MD, 52. *Prof Exp:* Pathologist-in-chief, Nat Inst Neurosurg, 54-56. *Concurrent Pos:* Spec fel neuropath, Mayo Found, Univ Minn, 57-58; consult, Vet Admin Hosp, Kansas City, 60-; vis prof, Neurol Inst, Univ Vienna, 68-69. *Mem:* Am Acad Neurol; Am Asn Neuropathol (vpres, 78-79, pres, 84-85); Am Asn Neurol Surgeons. *Res:* Histological differential diagnosis of brain tumors; electron microscopic studies of meningiomas; spinal cord circulation; primary malignant lymphomas of central nervous system; histiocytosis and xanthosarcomas of central nervous system; pathogenesis of central pontine myelinolysis; etiology and pathogenesis of the Arnold-Chiari malformation. *Mailing Add:* Univ Kans Med Ctr 39th St & Rainbow Blvd Kansas City KS 66105-7410

KEPES, JOSEPH JOHN, NUCLEAR & REACTOR PHYSICS. *Current Pos:* assoc prof, 62-71, chmn dept, 62-75, PROF PHYSICS, UNIV DAYTON, 71- *Personal Data:* b Cleveland, Ohio, Jan 25, 31; m 54; c 6. *Educ:* Case Inst Technol, BS, 53; Univ Notre Dame, PhD(nuclear physics), 58. *Prof Exp:* Sr scientist, Bettis Atomic Power Lab, 57-62. *Mem:* Am Phys Soc; Am Asn Physics Teachers. *Res:* Electron-electron scattering at low energies; resonance escape probabilities in natural uranium plates. *Mailing Add:* Physics Dept Univ Dayton Dayton OH 45409

KEPHART, ROBERT DAVID, HIGH ENERGY PHYSICS, CRYOGENICS. *Current Pos:* staff physicist & group leader, 77-88, CDF DEPT HEAD, FERMI NAT ACCELERATOR LAB, 88- *Personal Data:* b Phillipsburg, Pa, Nov 27, 49; m 71; c 2. *Educ:* Va Polytech Inst & State Univ, BS, 71; State Univ NY, Stony Brook, MS, 73, PhD(physics), 75. *Prof Exp:* Res asst physics, Dept Physics, Va Polytech Inst & State Univ, 69-71; res asst, Dept Physics, State Univ NY, Stony Brook, 71-75, fel, 75-77. *Concurrent Pos:* Proj mgr, Chicago Cyclotron Super Conducting Magnet Proj & leader, Fermilab Superconducting Analysis Magnetic Group; proj physicist, Collider Defector Facil, 3M0X5M Superconditioning Solenoid Proj. *Mem:* Am Phys Soc. *Res:* Detector development; liquid argon calorimetry; super conducting magnet design and research and development; high purity gas systems; dimuon high energy physics; engineering physics; p collider physics; super conducting solenoid. *Mailing Add:* Fermilab MS 318 PO Box 500 Batavia IL 60510

KEPLER, CAROL R, LIPID CHEMISTRY. *Current Pos:* ASST PURCHASING ADMINR, STATE NC, 84- *Personal Data:* b Berea, Ohio, Oct 21, 37; m 59; c 2. *Educ:* Oberlin Col, AB, 59; Univ NC, PhD(zool), 65. *Prof Exp:* Asst prof nutrit, NC State Univ, 65-66, asst prof biochem, 66-81; asst prof, Meredith Col, 81-84. *Concurrent Pos:* NIH fel, 65-66. *Mem:* Sigma Xi; Am Soc Zoologists. *Res:* Rumen bacteria; hydrogenation and isomerization of unsaturated fatty acids; specificity of triglyceride synthesis. *Mailing Add:* Dept Admin State NC 116 W Jones St Raleigh NC 27603-8002

KEPLER, HAROLD B(ENTON), MECHANICAL ENGINEERING. *Current Pos:* from instr to assoc prof mech eng, 48-77, EMER PROF, USAF INST TECHNOL, 77- *Personal Data:* b Dayton, Ohio, Jan 3, 22; m 46; c 2. *Educ:* Sinclair Col, AEA, 53, BBA, 56; Xavier Univ, Ohio, MBA, 58. *Prof Exp:* Eng draftsman, Eng Div, Wright Field, Ohio, 40-42, design checker, Aircraft Lab, Wright-Patterson AFB, 46-47; prod designer, Ohmer Corp, 47-48. *Concurrent Pos:* Lectr, Sinclair Col, Ohio, 60- & Univ Dayton, 84- *Mem:* Am Soc Eng Educ. *Res:* Engineering graphics; mechanisms and reliability engineering. *Mailing Add:* 90 Sheldon Dr Dayton OH 45459

KEPLER, RAYMOND GLEN, EXPERIMENTAL SOLID STATE PHYSICS. *Current Pos:* RETIRED. *Personal Data:* b Long Beach, Calif, Sept 10, 28; m 53, Carol Flint; c Julianne, Linda, Russell & David. *Educ:* Stanford Univ, BS, 50; Univ Calif, MS, 55, PhD(physics), 57. *Prof Exp:* Res physicist, Cent Res Dept, E I du Pont de Nemours & Co, 57-64; div supvr, Sandia Nat Labs, 64-69, dept mgr, 69-89, res scientist, 89-95. *Concurrent Pos:* Mem, Solid State Sci Panel, Nat Acad Sci, 77-82; mem, Comt Educ, Am Phys Soc, 78-80, chmn, 79-80, Applns Physics Comt, 79-81; mem, Eval Panel Mat Sci, Nat Bur Stand, 82-88; vchmn, Panel 2 Comt Mat Sci & Eng, Nat Acad Sci-Nat Res Coun. *Mem:* AAAS; fel Am Phys Soc. *Res:* Photoconductivity; conductivity; excitons and other solid state properties, primarily of organic solids; piezoelectricity, pyroelectricity and ferroelectricity in polymers. *Mailing Add:* 404 Turner Dr NE Albuquerque NM 87123. *E-Mail:* glen.skepler@compuserve.com

KEPLINGER, MORENO LAVON, TOXICOLOGY. *Current Pos:* CONSULT TOXICOL, 78- *Personal Data:* b Ulysses, Kans, May 25, 29; m 50; c 3. *Educ:* Univ Kans, BS, 51, MS, 52; Northwestern Univ, PhD(pharmacol), 56; Am Bd Toxicol, dipl, 80. *Prof Exp:* Res instr pharmacol, Univ Miami, 56-59, asst prof, 59-60; toxicologist, Hercules Powder Co, 60-64; pharmacol, Univ Miami, 64-68; asst dir, Indust Bio-Test Labs, Inc, 68-70, mgr toxicol, 70-77. *Mem:* Europ Soc Toxicol; Soc Toxicol; Am Soc Pharmacol & Exp Therapeut; Am Indust Hyg Asn. *Res:* Experimental and industrial toxicology; pharmacology. *Mailing Add:* Keplinger PO Box 1299 Hilltop Lakes TX 77871-1299

KEPLINGER, ORIN CLAWSON, POLYMER CHEMISTRY, EXPLOSIVES. *Current Pos:* RETIRED. *Personal Data:* b Carlinville, Ill, Oct 7, 18; m 39; c 3. *Educ:* Southern Ill Univ, BEd, 40; Univ Ill, MS, 48, PhD(chem), 49. *Prof Exp:* From jr chemist to chemist explosives, Western Cartridge Co, 40-44; spec asst, Univ Ill, 46-49; sr res chemist, Polymers, Gen Tire & Rubber Co, 49-59; chem supvr, Sherwin-Williams Co, 59-64, dir varnish resin lab, 64-66, dir prod develop, 66-74, dir resin technol, 75-78; tech dir, Chem Coatings Div, Valspar, 79-81. *Concurrent Pos:* Pres, Paint Res Inst, 75-81. *Mem:* Am Chem Soc; Fedn Soc Coatings Technol; Soc Chem & Indust London. *Res:* Explosives process development; synthetic rubber and plastics preparation; resins and polymers for coatings; paint formulation. *Mailing Add:* 909 S 19th St Rogers AR 72756-4901

KEPNER, RICHARD EDWIN, ORGANIC CHEMISTRY. *Current Pos:* from asst prof to prof, 46-86, EMER PROF CHEM, UNIV CALIF, DAVIS, 86- *Personal Data:* b Los Angeles, Calif, July 27, 16; m 46, Beverly Bremster; c Elizabeth J & Douglas J. *Educ:* Univ Calif, BS, 38; Univ Calif, Los Angeles, MA, 42, PhD(org chem), 46. *Prof Exp:* Lab asst soil chem, Univ Calif, Los Angeles, 40-41, asst chem, 43-46. *Mem:* Am Chem Soc; Am Soc Enol; Phytochem Soc NAm. *Res:* Odor and flavor constituents of fruits and wines; grape pigments; volatile plant terpenes. *Mailing Add:* Dept Chem Univ Calif Davis CA 95616

KEPNER, ROBERT ALLEN, AGRICULTURAL ENGINEERING. *Current Pos:* EMER PROF, UNIV CALIF, DAVIS, 81- *Personal Data:* b Los Angeles, Calif, May 18, 15; m 41, Denzil McBride; c Gilbert, Dorothy, Ronald & Harold. *Educ:* Univ Calif, Davis, BS, 37. *Prof Exp:* Heater test engr, Stewart-Warner Corp, Chicago & Indianapolis, 42-47. *Mem:* Fel Am Soc Agr Engrs; Am Soc Eng Educ. *Res:* Agricultural engineering; co-author of three publications. *Mailing Add:* 630 Miller Dr Davis CA 95616-3619

KEPPEL, KENNETH G, PUBLIC HEALTH, EPIDEMIOLOGY. *Current Pos:* statistician, Maternal Child Health Bur, 79-90, CHIEF, STATE & LOCAL SUPPORT BR, DIV HEALTH PROM & STATIS, NAT CTR HEALTH STATIST, CTR DIS CONTROL, 92- *Personal Data:* b Somers Point, NJ, Jan 19, 49. *Educ:* Col William & Mary, 71, BA; Pa State Univ, MA, 80, PhD(sociol), 80. *Mem:* Am Pub Health Asn. *Mailing Add:* Nat Ctr Health Statist Ctr Dis Control 65-25 Belcrest Rd Rm 770 Hyattsville MD 20782. *Fax:* 301-436-3572; *E-Mail:* kgk1@nch07a.em.cdc.gov

KEPPEN, LAURA DAVIS, PEDIATRIC GENETICS, PEDIATRIC ENDOCRINOLOGY. *Current Pos:* assoc prof, 90-96, PROD PEDIAT, SCH MED, UNIV SDAK, 96- *Personal Data:* b Sioux Falls, SDak, Mar 13, 54; m 76, Michael; c David, Sarah, Thomas & Joseph. *Educ:* Cornell Univ, BS, 75; Univ SDak Sch Med, MD, 79. *Honors & Awards:* Janet M Glasgow Award, Am Med Women's Asn, 79. *Prof Exp:* Asst prof pediat, Univ Ark Med Sci, 84-90. *Concurrent Pos:* Ark Genetics Serv, 84-90; Young Investr Award, Southern Soc Pediat Res. *Mem:* Am Acad Pediat; Am Soc Human Genetics; Lawson Wilkins Pediat Endocrine Soc. *Res:* Clinical genetics; author of various publications. *Mailing Add:* 1100 S Euclid Ave Sioux Falls SD 57117-5039. *Fax:* 605-333-1585

KEPPER, ROBERT EDGAR, agricultural & food chemistry; deceased, see previous edition for last biography

KEPPIE, JOHN D, TECTONICS. *Current Pos:* CONSULT, 94- *Personal Data:* b Nakuru, Kenya, Oct 3, 42. *Educ:* Univ Glasgow, BSc, 64, PhD(geol), 67. *Prof Exp:* Asst prof geol, Bryn Mawr Col, 67-70; regional geologist, Geol Surv Zambia, 70-73; mgr, surv sect, Mineral Resources Div, NS Dept Mines & Energy, 74-94. *Concurrent Pos:* Co-leader, Terrains In Circum-Atlantic Paleozoic Orogens, Int Geol Correlation Prog, UNESCO. *Mem:* Fel Geol Soc Am; Geol Asn Can. *Res:* Tectonics of the circum-Atlantic area. *Mailing Add:* RR 3 Wolfville NS B0P 1X0 Can

KEPPLE, PAUL C, PHYSICS. *Current Pos:* RES PHYSICIST, NAVAL RES LAB, 69- *Personal Data:* b San Luis Potosi, Mex, Feb 6, 36; US citizen; m 62; c 2. *Educ:* Univ Okla, BS, 58, MS, 61; NMex State Univ, PhD(physics), 66. *Prof Exp:* Res assoc plasma physics, Univ Md, 66-69. *Mem:* Am Phys Soc. *Res:* Plasma physics; atomic physics. *Mailing Add:* Code 6720 Naval Res Lab 4555 Overlook Ave SW Washington DC 20375

KEPPLER, WILLIAM J, GENETICS, EVOLUTION. *Current Pos:* DEAN COL HEALTH & PROF GENETICS, FLA INT UNIV, 88- *Personal Data:* b Teaneck, NJ, Jan 20, 37; m 60; c 1. *Educ:* Univ Miami, Fla, BS, 59; Univ Ill, MS, 61, PhD(genetics), 65. *Prof Exp:* From asst prof to prof zool, Eastern Ill Univ, 65-76, asst provost, 73-76; dean arts & sch, Boise State Univ, 77-85; vchancellor, Univ Alaska, 85-88. *Mem:* Sigma Xi. *Res:* Cytochemistry of chromosomes. *Mailing Add:* Fla Int Univ Dept Pub Health AC1-394E 3000 NE 145th St North Miami FL 33181

KEPRON, MICHAEL RAYMOND, DIAGNOSTICS. *Current Pos:* RES SCIENTIST, IDEXX LABS, INC, 91- *Personal Data:* b Ann Arbor, Mich, Feb 15, 55; US & Can citizen; m 82, Ruth I Unrau; c Marla A, Nicole J & Jared M. *Educ:* McGill Univ, BSc, 77; Univ Man, PhD(immunol), 89. *Prof Exp:* Instr, Univ Tex Southwestern Med Ctr, 86-91. *Mem:* Am Asn Immunologists. *Res:* Development of diagnostic products for the veterinary market. *Mailing Add:* 1 Idexx Dr Westbrook ME 04092. *Fax:* 207-856-0474

KEPRON, WAYNE, IMMUNOLOGY, PHYSIOLOGY. *Current Pos:* ASSOC PROF INTERNAL MED, FAC MED, UNIV MAN, 75-, ASSOC PROF IMMUNOL, 78- *Personal Data:* b Winnipeg, Man, Mar 31, 42; m 66; c 3. *Educ:* Univ Man, BSc & MD, 67. *Concurrent Pos:* Attend physician, Respiratory Ctr, Health Sci Ctr; prin investr, Med Res Coun Group Allergy Res, Dept Immunol, Univ Man, 78- *Mem:* Am Acad Allergy; Am Thoracic Soc; Can Lung Asn. *Res:* Studies in the pathogenesis of Ige, Ige mediated asthma with specific reference to the role of local immune mechanisims in the lung; the modification of Ige metabolism with tolerogenic conjugates. *Mailing Add:* Dept Med Univ Man 753 McDermot Ave Winnipeg MB R3E 0W3 Can

KER, JOHN WILLIAM, FORESTRY. *Current Pos:* RETIRED. *Personal Data:* b Chilliwack, BC, Aug 27, 15; m 43, Marguerite F Witton; c John G, Kerry A (Markle) & Wendy R (Andrews). *Educ:* Univ BC, BASc, 47; Yale Univ, MF, 51, DF(forestry), 57. *Hon Degrees:* DSc, Univ BC, 71. *Prof Exp:* Forest ranger, BC Forest Serv, 41-45, asst forester, 45-48; asst prof forest mensuration, Univ BC, 48-53, assoc prof forest mensuration & econ, 53-61; prof forest mensuration & econ & dean, Fac Forestry, Univ NB, 61-82. *Concurrent Pos:* Consult, H G Acres & Agr Rehab & Develop Act, 64-65, Atlantic Develop Bd, 66-68, Royal Comn Econ State & Prospects of Nfld & Labrador, 66-67, Prov NB Land Compensation Bd, 70-71, Int Bank Reconstruct & Develop, 72-73, & Can Coun Rural Develop, 72-73; expert univ educ, Can Int Develop Agency, 73-74; Can deleg, Food & Agr Orgn, Adv Comt Forestry Educ, 75-78; chmn, Forest Mgt Task Force, NB Dept Natural Resources, 78-81; mem, Nat Sci & Eng Res Coun Can, 80-83; consult, Int Develop Res Ctr, People's Repub China, 87. *Mem:* Can Forestry Asn (vpres, 72-73); Can Inst Forestry (pres, 72-73). *Res:* Forest economics and valuation; forest measurements and biometry; university-level forestry education in both Canada and developing countries. *Mailing Add:* 760 Golf Club Rd RR3 Fredericton NB E3B 4X4 Can

KERAMIDAS, VASSILIS GEORGE, APPLIED PHYSICS, MATERIALS SCIENCE. *Current Pos:* mem tech staff optoelectronic mat & devices, Bellcore, 73-80, supvr III-V semiconductor mat devices & integrated circuits, Bell Lab, 80-83, dist res mgr, photonic & electronic mat res, 83-85, div mgr, Photonics & Electronics Mat Res, 85-91, EXEC DIR, INFO ACCESS & ENERGY STORAGE RES, BELLCORE, 91- *Personal Data:* b Moudros, Greece, June 27, 38; US citizen; m 67, Elaine Marikakis; c Jason & Kimon. *Educ:* Rockford Col, BA, 60; Univ Ill, BS, 62; John Carroll Univ, MS, 69; Pa State Univ, PhD(solid state sci), 73. *Prof Exp:* Res staff mem cadmium sulfide solar cells, Crystal Solid State Div, Harshaw Chem Co, 63-67. *Concurrent Pos:* Chmn, Electronic Mat Comt, Int Compound Semiconductor Comt, 91-94. *Mem:* Mat Res Soc; Electrochem Soc; Am Phys Soc; Am Asn Crystal Growth; sr mem Inst Elec & Electronics Engrs; Minerals, Metals & Mat Soc. *Res:* Leadership, technical management and personal research contributions in the fields of: optoelectronic materials research for fiber optic communications, novel materials and systems for information storage (memory research) and energy storage (rechargeable batteries). *Mailing Add:* 51 Brookside Dr Warren NJ 07059. *Fax:* 732-758-4372

KERANS, CHARLES, RESERVOIR CHARACTERIZATION, SEQUENCE STRATIGRAPHY. *Current Pos:* from res assoc to res scientist, 85-94, SR RES SCIENTIST, BUR ECON GEOL, UNIV TEX, AUSTIN, 93- *Personal Data:* b Boston, Mass, Oct 11, 54; m 83, Pamela D Soto; c Peter D & Graham M. *Educ:* St Lawrence Univ, BS, 77, PhD(geol). *Prof Exp:* Actg asst prof geol, Univ Kans, 81-82; sr res fel, Western Australian Mining & Petrol Res Inst, 82-85; sr geologist, Marathon Oil Co, 92. *Concurrent Pos:* Distinguished lectr, Am Asn Petrol Geologists, 90. *Mem:* Am Asn Petrol Geologists; Soc Sedimentary Geol. *Res:* Integrated reservoir characterization providing stratigraphic frameworks for quantification by engineers and petrophysicists; develop and test new concepts in the area of carbonate sequence stratigraphy. *Mailing Add:* 201 Laurelwood Trail Austin TX 78746. *Fax:* 512-471-0140; *E-Mail:* keransc@begv.beg.utexas.edu

KERBECEK, ARTHUR J(OSEPH), JR, CHEMICAL ENGINEERING. *Current Pos:* INDUST CONSULT, 68- *Personal Data:* b New York, NY, May 29, 26. *Educ:* Columbia Univ, BS, 47, MS, 48, PhD(chem eng), 51. *Prof Exp:* Res engr, Titanium Metal Div, E I du Pont de Nemours & Co, Del, 52; chief metallurgist, Terrebonne Titanium Co, Can, 52-53; res engr, Ord & Inorg Chem Div, Food Mach & Chem Corp, 53-58; engr, Res Dept, Bethlehem Steel Corp, Pa, 58-68. *Mem:* Am Chem Soc; Electrochem Soc; Am Inst Chem Engrs. *Res:* Chemical process technology; production metallurgy; corrosion; electrochemistry. *Mailing Add:* PO Box 1883 Chelan WA 98816

KERBEL, ROBERT STEPHEN, CANCER. *Current Pos:* DIR, CHAP RES DIV, SUNNY BROOK HEALTH SCI CTR, 91- *Personal Data:* b Toronto, Ont, Apr 5, 45; m 70; c 1. *Educ:* Univ Toronto, BS, 68; Queen's Univ, Ont, PhD(microbiol & immunol), 72. *Honors & Awards:* Wild Leitz Jr Sci Award, Exp Path, 80. *Prof Exp:* Res fel, Nat Cancer Inst Can, Chester Beatty Res Inst, London, 72-74; from asst prof to assoc prof, Dept Path, Queen's Univ, 80-91. *Concurrent Pos:* King George V Silver Jubilee Cancer Res fel, Nat Cancer Inst Can, 73-74; res scholar, 75-81, res assoc, 81-; mem, Grants Panel B, Nat Cancer Inst Can, 77-81; mem study sect B, NIH, 81-82; assoc ed, Inv & Metastasis, Cancer Metastasis Rev, 81- *Mem:* Brit Soc Immunol; Can Soc Immunol; Am Asn Immunologists; Can Assoc Pathol. *Res:* Cancer; tumor biology; immunology; cell biology of cancer metastasis studied using membrane mutant tumor sublines; tumor progression and heterogeneity; membrane biology of activated lymphocyte and macrophage cell populations. *Mailing Add:* Cancer Biol Res Sunnybrook Health Sci Ctr Rm S218 Res Bldg 2075 Bayview Ave Toronto ON M4N 3M5 Can. *Fax:* 416-480-5703

KERBER, ERICH RUDOLPH, CYTOGENETICS. *Current Pos:* Res officer, plant breeding, 56-60, WHEAT CYTOGENETICIST, RES STA, CAN DEPT AGR, 60- *Personal Data:* b Langham, Sask, Apr 2, 26; m 56; c 2. *Educ:* Univ Sask, BSA, 50, MSc, 53; Univ Alta, PhD(cytogenetics), 58. *Honors & Awards:* Gold Medal, Prof Inst Pub Serv Can, 83. *Mem:* AAAS; Genetics Soc Can; Am Soc Agron; Am Soc Crop Sci. *Res:* Plant cytology and genetics; cytogenetic investigations on the transfer of rust resistance to common wheat from related species and endosperm proteins of wheat related to baking quality. *Mailing Add:* 195 Dafoe Rd Winnipeg MB R3T 2M9 Can

KERBER, RICHARD E, CARDIOVASCULAR DISEASES. *Current Pos:* From asst prof to assoc prof, 71-78, PROF INT MED, COL MED, UNIV IOWA, 78- *Personal Data:* b New York, NY, May 10, 39; m; c Ross & Justin. *Educ:* Columbia Univ, AB, 60; NY Univ, MD, 64. *Honors & Awards:* Award Merit Achievement, Am Heart Asn. *Concurrent Pos:* Asn dir, Cardiol Div, Univ Iowa. *Mem:* Am Heart Asn; fel Am Col Cardiol; Am Physiol Soc; Am Soc Clin Invest; Asn Am Physicians; Asn Univ Cardiologists. *Res:* Echocardiography; resuscitation; defibrillation and cardioversion; cardiovascular pharmacology. *Mailing Add:* Dept Int Med Univ Iowa Hosps & Clins Iowa City IA 52242-0001. *Fax:* 319-356-4552; *E-Mail:* dick_kerber@uiowa.edu

KERBER, ROBERT CHARLES, CHEMICAL EDUCATION. *Current Pos:* from asst prof to assoc prof, 65-88, PROF CHEM, STATE UNIV NY, STONY BROOK, 88- *Personal Data:* b Hartford, Conn, Nov 29, 38. *Educ:* Mass Inst Technol, SB, 60; Purdue Univ, PhD(org chem), 65. *Prof Exp:* Fel org chem, Purdue Univ, 65. *Concurrent Pos:* Fel, Humboldt Found, WGer, 73-74; vis scientist, Brookhaven Nat Lab, 83. *Mem:* AAAS; Am Chem Soc; Royal Soc Chem; NY Acad Sci. *Res:* Organo transition metal chemistry; synthesis and structure of novel organometallics, stable complexes of unstable ligands. *Mailing Add:* Dept Chem State Univ NY Stony Brook NY 11794-3400. *Fax:* 516-632-7960; *E-Mail:* rkerber@ccmail.sunysb.edu

KERBER, RONALD LEE, MECHANICAL ENGINEERING, ELECTRICAL ENGINEERING. *Current Pos:* EXEC VPRES & CHIEF TECH OFFICER, WHIRLPOOL CORP, 91- *Personal Data:* b Lafayette, Ind, July 2, 43; m 63. *Educ:* Purdue Univ, BS, 65; Calif Inst Technol, MS, 66, PhD(eng sci), 70. *Prof Exp:* From asst prof to assoc prof mech eng, Mich State Univ, 69-78, assoc dir, Div Eng, 78-80, prof mech & elec eng, 78-85, assoc dean eng & dir, Div Eng Res, 80-83; dep undersecy, Dept Defense, 85-88; vpres tech bus develop, McDonnell Douglas Corp, 88-91. *Concurrent Pos:* Mem tech staff, Aerospace Corp, 70-72. *Mem:* Am Soc Mech Engrs; Inst Elec & Electronics Engrs. *Res:* Theory of phase transitions and liquids, gas-surface interaction, chemical and molecular lasers. *Mailing Add:* Whirlpool Corp R&E Ctr Monte Rd Benton Harbor MI 49022

KERBISPETERHANS, JULIAN C, DISTRIBUTION & SYSTEMATICS OF SMALL AFRICAN MAMMALS, TAPHONOMY IN AFRICAN SAVANNAH & RAIN FOREST CONTEXTS. *Current Pos:* collection mgr, 87-89, prog developer & coordr, Minority Undergrad Training Prog, 92-93, CURATORIAL ASSOC, FIELD MUS, 90-, RES ASSOC, COMT EVOLUTIONARY & ENVIRON BIOL, 93- *Personal Data:* b Chicago, IL, Dec 13, 52; m 93, Pamela K Austin. *Educ:* Beloit Col, Wis, BSc, 74; Univ Chicago, MA, 79, PhD(anthropol), 90. *Prof Exp:* Lectr, Loyola Univ Chicago, 81-82. *Concurrent Pos:* Co-prin investr, NSF, 89 & 92-93, consult, Forensic Lab, US Fish & Wildlife Serv, 92-; adj fac anthrop, Univ Chicago, 93- *Mem:* Am Soc Mammalogists. *Res:* Systematics and distribution of African mammals, especially those confined to the Albertine Rift mountaintops of central Africa; taphonomy of mammals in African contexts; establishing a suite of fingerprints necessary in identifying agents of predation; making inferences on the sociobiology of the prey species; taphonomy; paleoanthropology. *Mailing Add:* Field Mus Div Mammals Chicago IL 60605-2496. *Fax:* 312-663-5397; *E-Mail:* kerbis%fmnh785.fmnh.org@uicvm.uic.edu

KERCE, ROBERT H, MATHEMATICS. *Current Pos:* From instr to assoc prof, David Lipscomb Col, 46-66, chmn dept, 65-85, prof, 85-90, ADJ PROF MATH, DAVID LIPSCOMB COL, 90-, CHMN DEPT, 65- *Personal Data:* b Bartow, Fla, Nov 29, 25; m 46; c 3. *Educ:* Ga Inst Tech, BME, 46; Vanderbilt Univ, MS, 57; George Peabody Col, PhD(math), 65. *Mem:* Math Asn Am; Nat Coun Teachers Math. *Mailing Add:* 1193 Otter Creek Rd Nashville TN 37220

KERCHER, CONRAD J, ANIMAL NUTRITION. *Current Pos:* actg vpres, Acad Affairs, 75-76, head, Animal Sci Dept, 87-88, ANIMAL NUTRITIONIST, UNIV WYO, 54- *Personal Data:* b Yakima, Wash, June 17, 26; m 46, Lydia Zier; c Kathryn A, Nina L, Jane M & Kise S. *Educ:* Mont State Col, BS, 50; Cornell Univ, MS, 52, PhD(animal nutrit), 54. *Prof Exp:* Assoc animal nutrit, Cornell Univ, 50-54. *Concurrent Pos:* Consult, Agency Int Develop. *Mem:* AAAS; fel Am Soc Animal Sci; Am Dairy Sci Asn; Am Registry Prof Animal Scientists; Am Forage & Grassland Coun. *Res:* Forage harvesting systems; sources of dietary fat for ruminants; alternate crops for ruminants; feed additives for cattle; replacement value of feeds for ruminants. *Mailing Add:* Amimal Sci Dept Univ Wyo Box 3684 Laramie WY 82071

KERCHNER, HAROLD RICHARD, EXPERIMENTAL SOLID STATE PHYSICS. *Current Pos:* RES STAFF MEM, SOLID STATE PHYSICS, OAK RIDGE NAT LAB, 76- *Personal Data:* b Lewistown, Pa, Mar 5, 46; m 68, Ruth Fisher; c Geoffrey A & Nichole D. *Educ:* Harvard Univ, AB, 68; Univ Ill, MS, 70, PhD(physics), 74. *Prof Exp:* Res Assoc, Martin Marietta Energy Syst, 74-76. *Concurrent Pos:* Dir, Nat Low-Temp Neutron Irradiation Facil, Oak Ridge Nat Lab, 85-88. *Mem:* Am Phys Soc; Mat Res Soc. *Res:* Type II superconductivity; radiation effects in materials. *Mailing Add:* MS 061 Oak Ridge Nat Lab PO Box 2008 Bldg 3115 Oak Ridge TN 37831. *Fax:* 423-574-6270; *E-Mail:* hrk@ornl.gov

KERDESKY, FRANCIS A J, CHEMISTRY. *Current Pos:* RES INVESTR, ABBOTT LABS, NORTH CHICAGO, 81- *Personal Data:* b Wilkes-Barre, Pa, Mar 10, 53. *Educ:* Wilkes Col, BS, 75; Univ Pa, PhD(org chem), 79. *Prof Exp:* Res assoc, Mass Inst Technol, 80-81. *Mem:* Am Chem Soc; Sigma Xi. *Res:* Design and synthesis of drugs; process research; synthesis of natural products. *Mailing Add:* 207 Windjammer Lane Grayslake IL 60030-2625

KEREIAKES, JAMES GUS, PHYSICS. *Current Pos:* from asst prof to assoc prof, 59-68, prof, 68-91, EMER PROF RADIOL, COL MED, UNIV CINCINNATI, 91- *Personal Data:* b Columbus, Ohio, Aug 15, 24; m 50; c 4. *Educ:* Western Ky State Col, BS, 45; Univ Cincinnati, MS, 47, PhD(physics), 50; Am Bd Radiol, dipl radiol physics, 60. *Honors & Awards:* Coolidge Award, Am Asn Physicists in Med, 81, Gold Medal, 85; Gold Medal, Radiol Soc NAm, 88. *Prof Exp:* Res physicist, Environ Med Br, Med Res Lab, US Army, Ky, 50-53, supvy physicist, Radiobiol Dept, 53-57, dep dir, 57-59. *Mem:* AAAS; Am Soc Therapeut Radiol Oncol; Biophys Soc; Radiation Res Soc; Am Asn Physicists Med (pres, 69-70); Radiol Soc North Am (vpres, 81-82). *Res:* Radiation physics and biology; radiopharmaceutical dosimetry. *Mailing Add:* E555 Med Sci Bldg Univ Cincinnati PO Box 670579 Cincinnati OH 45267-0579. *Fax:* 513-558-0300

KEREKES, RICHARD JOSEPH, FLUID MECHANICS, SUSPENSIONS. *Current Pos:* DIR, PULP & PAPER CTR, UNIV BC, 83- *Personal Data:* b Welland, Ont, July 9, 40; m 78. *Educ:* Univ Toronto, BASc, 63, MASc, 65; McGill Univ, PhD(chem eng), 70. *Prof Exp:* Scientist, Pulp & Paper Res Inst Can, 71-77, sect head, 77-83. *Concurrent Pos:* Hon prof chem eng, Univ BC, 78- *Mem:* Can Soc Chem Eng; Can Pulp & Paper Asn. *Res:* Fibre flocculation; mixing in pulp suspensions; pulp screening. *Mailing Add:* Chem Eng Bldg Univ BC 2216 Main Mall Vancouver BC V6T 1Z2 Can

KEREN, JOSEPH, physics, for more information see previous edition

KERFOOT, BRANCH PRICE, COMPUTER SIMULATIONS. *Current Pos:* RETIRED. *Personal Data:* b New York, NY, May 9, 25; m 65; c 1. *Educ:* Yale Univ, BE, 45; Univ Mich, MSE, 47, PhD(electronics), 55; Western State Univ, JD, 87. *Prof Exp:* Ensign eng, US Navy, 45-46; AA engr, RCA Missile & Radar Dept, 49-57; prin eng, Ford Aeronutronic Div, 58-68; prin scientist, McDonnell Douglas Electronics, 68-90. *Concurrent Pos:* Teacher, Pasadena City Col, 58. *Mem:* Sr mem Inst Elec & Electronics Engrs; Sigma Xi; Naval Res Asn. *Res:* Electronic systems research and development, especially radar and communications technologies and equipment; analysis of performances. *Mailing Add:* 1420 Antigua Way Newport Beach CA 92660

KERFOOT, WILSON CHARLES, LIMNOLOGY, EVOLUTIONARY ECOLOGY. *Current Pos:* assoc prof, Mich State Technol Univ, 89-91, co-dir, Lake Superior Ecosyts Res Ctr, 90-92, PROF AQUATIC ECOL, DEPT BIOL SCI, MICH TECHNOL UNIV, 91-, DIR, LAKE SUPERIOR ECOSYSTS RES CTR, 92- *Personal Data:* b Staten Island, NY, Mar 13, 44; m 78, Lucille Zelazny; c Alex & Katherine. *Educ:* Univ Kans, BA(zool) & BA(geol), 66; Univ Mich, PhD(zool), 72. *Prof Exp:* NSF fel limnol, Dept Zool, Univ Wash, 72-73, res assoc, 73-76; asst prof aquatic ecol, Dept Biol Sci, Dartmouth Col, 75-82, assoc prof res ecol, 82-83; vis assoc res scientist, Great Lakes Res Div, Univ Mich, 83-84, assoc res scientist, 84-90. *Concurrent Pos:* Vis sr scientist, Ctr Ecosysts Studies, Cornell Univ, 81-83; adj assoc prof, Dept Biol, Sch Natural Resources, Univ Mich, 85-89, on leave assoc prof aquatic ecol, 89- *Mem:* Ecol Soc Am; Am Soc Limnol & Oceanog; Am Soc Naturalists; Int Asn Theoret & Appl Limnol; Int Asn Ecol. *Res:* Aquatic ecology of large and small lakes; zooplankton population biology and evolution; paleoecology of zooplankton; limnology; community ecology. *Mailing Add:* Dept Biol Sci Mich Technol Univ 1400 Townsend Dr Houghton MI 49931-1200. *Fax:* 906-487-3167

KERJASCHKI, DONTSCHO, IMMUNOPATHOLOGY. *Current Pos:* PROF PATH & CELL BIOL, DEPT PATH, UNIV VIENNA, 86-, DIR, DIV ULTRASTRUCT PATH & CELL BIOL, 90- *Personal Data:* b Vienna, Austria, Feb 8, 47; m 81; c 2. *Educ:* Albertus Magnus Sch, Vienna, Natura, 65; Univ Vienna, MD, 72. *Honors & Awards:* Vollhard Prize, Ger Nephrology Soc, 90. *Concurrent Pos:* Vis prof cell biol, Yale Univ Sch Med, 80-88; vis res scientist cell biol, Div Cellular & Molecular Med, Univ Calif, San Diego, 89-; mem, Comn Cell Biol, Int Soc Nephrology. *Mem:* Int Soc Nephrology. *Res:* Molecular aspects of autoimmune diseases, especially kidney. *Mailing Add:* Dept Clin Path Univ Vienna AKH Wahringer Gurtel 18-20 Vienna A-1090 Austria. *Fax:* 43-1-40400-5193

KERKA, WILLIAM (FRANK), MECHANICAL ENGINEERING. *Current Pos:* RETIRED. *Personal Data:* b Cleveland, Ohio, Apr 5, 21; m 53; c 1. *Educ:* Fenn Col, BS, 48; Case Inst Technol, MS, 52. *Prof Exp:* Instr graphics, Case Inst Technol, 51-52; instr mech eng, Ore State Col, 52-54; res engr res lab, Am Soc Heating, Refrig & Air-Conditioning Engrs, 54-61; assoc dean eng, Cleveland State Univ, 61-77, assoc prof mech eng, 77-81. *Res:* Odor control and acoustics as related to air conditioning. *Mailing Add:* 2913 Priscilla Ave Cleveland OH 44134

KERKAR, AWDHOOT VASANT, POLYMER ENGINEERING. *Current Pos:* RES ENGR, W R GRACE & CO, 90- *Personal Data:* b Bombay, India, Sept 20, 63; m 90. *Educ:* Univ Bombay, BChemE, 84; Univ Pittsburgh, MS, 86; Case Western Reserve Univ, PhD(chem eng), 90. *Prof Exp:* Res asst chem eng, Univ Pittsburgh, 84-86 & Case Western Reserve Univ, 86-90. *Mem:* Am Ceramic Soc. *Res:* Products and processes for materials application such as ceramics, polymers and their composites; chemical engineering, colloid science and polymer processing to develop novel processing strategies for materials. *Mailing Add:* 7042 Ivoryhand Pl Columbia MD 21045

KERKAY, JULIUS, CLINICAL CHEMISTRY. *Current Pos:* asst prof, 70-74, assoc prof & dir clin chem, 74-81, PROF CHEM & BIOL, CLEVELAND STATE UNIV, 81- *Personal Data:* b Sopron, Hungary, Apr 27, 34; US citizen; c 2. *Educ:* Veszprem Tech Univ, BS, 55, MS, 56; Univ Louisville, PhD(biochem), 69; Am Bd Clin Chem, dipl. *Honors & Awards:* Outstanding Contrib in Educ, Am Assoc Clin Chem, 88. *Prof Exp:* Chief chem engr, Alcohol Factory Gyor, Hungary, 56; technician, Alloys & Chem Mfg Co, Ohio, 57-58; asst in res, Cleveland Clin Found, 58-59; chief anal sect, US Army Res Inst Environ Med, 62-64; dir lab, Euclid Clin Found, 68-70. *Concurrent Pos:* Adj prof, Cleveland State Univ, 68-70; speaker, Health Careers Info, Cleveland Hosp Coun, 69-; adj consult, Cleveland Clin Found, 70-85; consult, Diamond Shamrock Health Sci Labs, 74-76. sci vpres, Euclid Clin Res Found, 69-86; affil staff, St Luke's Hosp Cleveland, 77-85. *Mem:* AAAS; fel Am Asn Clin Chem; fel Am Inst Chem; NY Acad Sci; Am Chem Soc; Sigma Xi; Nat Registry Clin Chem. *Res:* protein electrophoresis; protein and steroid hormone interactions; serum constituents of mothers of down syndrome children; clinical chemistry methodology, computerization in clinical chemistry; changes in body fluid constituents of hemodialysis patients; development of radiobioassays for vitamins and isoenzymes; plasticizers and their metabolites in human organs and body fluids; awarded one US patent. *Mailing Add:* Tatorjan U 11 Veszprem H-8200 Hungary

KERKER, MILTON, PHYSICAL CHEMISTRY, LIGHT SCATTERING. *Current Pos:* from instr to prof, Clarkson Univ, 49-60, chmn dept, 60-64, dean sch sci, 64-66 & 81-85, dean sch arts & sci, 66-74, Thomas S Clarkson prof, 74-91, EMER PROF, CLARKSON UNIV, 91- *Personal Data:* b Utica, NY, Sept 25, 20; m 46, Reva Stemerman; c Ruth A, Martin, Susan & Joel. *Educ:* Columbia Univ, AB, 41, MA, 47, PhD(chem), 49. *Hon Degrees:* DSc, Lehigh Univ, 75 & Clarkson Univ, 85. *Honors & Awards:* Kendall Award, Am Chem Soc, 71; Langmuir Lectr, Div Coloid Chem, Am Chem Soc, 81. *Prof Exp:* Asst chem, Columbia Univ, 46-49. *Concurrent Pos:* Ed-in-chief, J Colloid & Interface Sci, 65-93; fel, Ford Found, 52-53; Unilever prof, Univ Bristol, 67-68; chmn, Nat Acad Sci-Nat Res Coun Comt Colloids & Surface Chem, 70-74; vis prof, Hebrew Univ & Technion, 74-75; titular mem & secy comn on colloids & surfaces, Int Union Pure & Appl Chem, 78-83. *Mem:* Am Chem Soc; Hist Sci Soc; fel Optical Soc Am; Sigma Xi. *Res:* Light scattering; aerosols; history of science; surface enhanced; Raman scattering; heteropoly acids. *Mailing Add:* 7291 W Country Club Dr N 119 Sarasota FL 34243

KERKMAN, DANIEL JOSEPH, CHEMISTRY. *Current Pos:* MED CHEMIST, ABBOTT LABS, 80- *Personal Data:* b Milwaukee, Wis, Sept 17, 51; m 73; c 2. *Educ:* Johns Hopkins Univ, MA, 76; Mass Inst Technol, PhD(chem), 79. *Prof Exp:* Assoc fel, Mass Inst Technol, 79-80. *Mem:* Am Chem Soc. *Res:* Medicinal chemistry. *Mailing Add:* 21 Cremin Dr Lake Villa IL 60046-8864

KERKMAN, RUSSEL JOHN, ELECTRICAL ENGINEERING. *Current Pos:* sr proj engr, 80-86, PRIN ENGR, ALLEN-BRADLEY CO, 86- *Personal Data:* b Burlington, Wis, Aug 11, 48; m 71. *Educ:* Purdue Univ, BS, 71, MS, 73, PhD(elec eng), 76. *Prof Exp:* Elec engr mach anal, Gen Elec Co, 76-80. *Mem:* Inst Elec & Electronics Engrs. *Res:* Electric machine design and analysis; power systems; control systems; solid state power conditioning; AC motor drives. *Mailing Add:* 6815 W Howard Ave Milwaukee WI 53220

KERLAN, JOEL THOMAS, ENDOCRINOLOGY. *Current Pos:* Instr, 70-71, asst prof, 71-81, ASSOC PROF BIOL, HOBART & WILLIAM SMITH COLS, 81- *Personal Data:* b Minneapolis, Minn, Feb 23, 40. *Educ:* Col St Thomas, Minn, BS, 62; Univ Utah, MS, 65; Univ Mich, Ann Arbor, PhD(zool), 72. *Concurrent Pos:* Vis prof, Dept Obstet & Gynec, Univ Mich, 75. *Mem:* Sigma Xi; Am Soc Zoologists. *Res:* Regulation and biosynthesis of sex steroid hormones in vertebrate testes. *Mailing Add:* Dept Biol Hobart & William Smith Col Geneva NY 14456

KERLEE, DONALD D, NUCLEAR PHYSICS, MANAGEMENT INFORMATION. *Current Pos:* RETIRED. *Personal Data:* b Ryderwood, Wash, Dec 22, 26; m 50; c 4. *Educ:* Seattle Pac Col, BS, 51; Univ Wash, PhD(physics), 56. *Prof Exp:* Res instr physics, Univ Wash, 56; from asst prof to prof, Seattle Pac Col, 56-69, chmn dept, 62-69, dir inst res, 59-69; acad vpres, Roberts Wesleyan Col, 69-74; vpres admin, Seattle Pac Col, 74-76, dir res, 76-79, dir planning res, 79-84. *Concurrent Pos:* Sci fac fel, Univ Manchester, 63-64; Am Inst Physics & Am Asn Physics Teachers Regional Counsr, Washington State, 65-69. *Mem:* AAAS; Am Asn Physics Teachers; Am Phys Soc; Sigma Xi; Asn Comput Mach. *Res:* Heavy ion, nuclear and cosmic ray physics; institutional planning; forecasting models. *Mailing Add:* 20420 Marine Dr Apt O-3 Stanwood WA 98292-7805

KERLEY, GERALD IRWIN, STATISTICAL MECHANICS, EQUATIONS OF STATE. *Current Pos:* SCI TECH CONSULT, ALBUQUERQUE, NMEX, 95- *Personal Data:* b Houston, Tex, Mar 23, 41; m 90, Donna C Rice; c 3. *Educ:* Ohio Univ, BS, 63; Univ Ill, PhD(chem physics), 66. *Prof Exp:* Fel chem, Univ Ill, 66-67; US Army Officer, 67-69; staff mem phys chem, Los Alamos Nat Lab, Univ Calif, 69-84; sr mem tech staff, Computational Physics & Mech Dept, Saundia Nat Lab, 84-95. *Res:* Theory and calculation of equations of state of gases, liquids, and solids; statistical mechanics; theory of electrons in condensed matter; atomic physics; shock wave physics; theory of explosives. *Mailing Add:* PO Box 13835 Albuquerque NM 87192. *Fax:* 505-844-0918; *E-Mail:* 74140.700@compuserve.com

KERLEY, MICHAEL A, ANATOMY. *Current Pos:* ASSOC PROF BIOL, SOUTHWESTERN OKLA STATE UNIV, 71-, CHAIR, 93- *Personal Data:* b Crockett, Tex, Apr 17, 41; m 85, Jordana Dowell; c Timothy, Erin, Arista, Blayne & Graham. *Educ:* Stephen F Austin State Col, BS, 64; Tex A&M Univ, MS, 69, PhD(zool), 71. *Concurrent Pos:* Fel, Health Ctr, Univ Conn, 75-77. *Mem:* Am Asn Anatomists. *Res:* Embryonic development of mammalian dentitions. *Mailing Add:* Dept Biol Sci Southwestern Okla State Univ 100 Campus Dr Weatherford OK 73096

KERLEY, TROY LAMAR, PHARMACOLOGY. *Current Pos:* PHARMACEUT CONSULT, 92- *Personal Data:* b Allen, Okla, Aug 20, 29; m 50; c 1. *Educ:* Univ Okla, BS, 53, MS, 55; Purdue Univ, PhD(pharmacol), 58. *Prof Exp:* Pharmacologist, Dow Chem Co, 57-64, head biomed res dept, 64-66; dir biol sci sect, Riker Labs, Calif, 66-71; dir biol res, 3M Co, 71-73, tech dir, Riker Labs Res & Develop, 73-80, dir int new bus develop, 81-84, dir new bus develop, 3M Health Care Ltd, Tokyo, 84-89, dir tech eval-licensing, 3M Pharmaceut, 89-92. *Mem:* AAAS; Sigma Xi; Am Pharmaceut Asn; Am Found Pharmaceut Educ; Am Soc Pharmacol & Exp Therapeut. *Res:* Pharmacologic aspects of the blood-brain barrier; neuromuscular pharmacology; pharmacology and physiology of tremor and rigidity syndromes; asthmatic pharmacology. *Mailing Add:* 1926 Cypress Pt W Austin TX 78746

KERLICK, GEORGE DAVID, THEORETICAL PHYSICS. *Current Pos:* CONSULT, 90- *Personal Data:* b Sharon, Pa, June 24, 49. *Educ:* Rensselaer Polytech Inst, BS, 70; Princeton Univ, MA, 72, PhD(physics), 75. *Honors & Awards:* Siggraph Tutorial, Asn Comput Mach, 89. *Prof Exp:* Res assoc physics, Mont State Univ, 75; res fel physics, Alexander von Humboldt Found, Univ Cologne, 75-76 & Max-Planck Inst, Munich, 76-77; vis asst prof math, Ore State Univ, 77-78; adj asst prof physics, Univ San Francisco, 78-79; res scientist, Comput Fluid Dynamics Dept, Nielsen Eng & Res Inc, 79-83; res scientist Sterling Software, NASA Ames Res Ctr, 83-88, Comput Sci Coordr, 89; prin scientist, Tektronix Inc, 89-90. *Mem:* Am Phys Soc; Asn Comput Mach; Soc Indust & Appl Math; Sigma Xi. *Res:* Scientific visualization; computer graphics; computational geometry. *Mailing Add:* Boeing Corp Serv MS7L-43 PO Box 24346 Seattle WA 98124

KERLIN, THOMAS W, NUCLEAR ENGINEERING. *Current Pos:* assoc prof, 66-76, PROF NUCLEAR ENG, UNIV TENN, KNOXVILLE, 76- *Personal Data:* b Charlotte, NC, Apr 7, 36; m 54; c 3. *Educ:* Univ SC, BSChE, 58; Univ Tenn, MS, 59, PhD(eng sci), 65. *Honors & Awards:* Glenn Murphy Award, Am Soc Eng Educ, 78. *Prof Exp:* Res engr, Atomics Int Div, NAm Aviation, 59-61 & Oak Ridge Nat Lab, 61-66. *Concurrent Pos:* Consult, Oak Ridge Nat Lab, 66- *Mem:* Am Nuclear Soc; Instrument Soc Am; Am Soc Eng Educ. *Res:* Instrumentation, thermometry and process simulation. *Mailing Add:* Keltic Fla PO Box 2917 Ft Walton Beach FL 32549

KERMAN, ARTHUR KENT, THEORETICAL PHYSICS. *Current Pos:* from asst prof to assoc prof, 56-64, dir, Ctr Theoret Physics, 76-83, PROF PHYSICS, MASS INST TECHNOL, 64-, DIR, LAB NUCLEAR SCI, 83- *Personal Data:* b Montreal, Que, Can, May 3, 29; m 52; c 5. *Educ:* McGill Univ, BSc, 50; Mass Inst Technol, PhD, 53. *Honors & Awards:* Humboldt Sr US Scientist Award, Max Planck Inst, 85. *Prof Exp:* Nat Res Coun Can res fel theoret physics, Calif Inst Technol, 53-54 & Inst Theoret Physics, Copenhagen, 54-55, mem res staff, 55-56. *Concurrent Pos:* Consult, Educ Serv Inc, Shell Develop Co Div, Shell Oil Co, 53-58, Argonne Nat Lab, 61-83, Los Alamos Sci Lab, 61-, Lawrence Livermore Nat Lab, 64-, Brookhaven Nat Lab, 65-81, Lawrence Berkeley Nat Lab, 75-80, Oak Ridge Nat Lab, 79- & Nat Bur Standards, 80-81; exchange prof, Guggenheim mem fel, Univ Paris, 61-62; mem, physics surv comt, Panels Nuclear Data & Heavy Ion Physics, Nat Acad Sci; vis prof physics, State Univ NY, Stony Brook, 70-71; adj prof, Brooklyn Col, City Univ New York, 71-75 & Argonne Nat Lab; foreign mem, Sci Coun Nat Inst Nuclear & Particle Physics, Nat Ctr Sci Res, Paris, France, 72-76; mem adv comt high energy, Brookhaven Nat Lab, 75, Theory Div, Los Alamos Sci Lab, 77-85 & Physics Div, 84; mem, comt sci & acad, Lawrence Livermore Nat Lab & Los Alamos Sci Lab, 81-, comt sci & technol, Exec Off Pres, White House Sci Coun, 82-85 & Argonne Nat Lab, Univ Chicago, 84-, comt nuclear sci, Dept Energy & NSF, 82-85, comt sci, Nat Res Coun, 85; chmn, Lawrence Berkeley Nat Lab, 76-78 & 81; assoc prof, Inst Nuclear Physics, Univ Paris-South, 75- *Mem:* Fel Am Phys Soc; fel Am Acad Arts & Sci; fel NY Acad Sci. *Res:* Theoretical nuclear physics. *Mailing Add:* Dept Physics Rm 6-305 Mass Inst Technol Cambridge MA 02139

KERMAN, R A, ANALYSIS AND FUNCTIONAL ANALYSIS. *Current Pos:* From asst prof to assoc prof math, 70-85, PROF MATH, BROCK UNIV, 86- *Personal Data:* b Winnipeg, Manitoba, Can, May 31, 43; m 67; c 2. *Educ:* Univ Manitoba, BA, 65, MA, 66; Univ Toronto, PhD(math), 69. *Mem:* Am math soc. *Res:* Weighted norm inequalities with applications to differential equations; approximation theory in weighted lebesgue spaces; weighted convolution algebras. *Mailing Add:* Math Dept Brock Univ St Catharines ON L2S 3A1 Can

KERMANI-ARAB, VALI, REGULATION OF IMMUNE SYSTEM. *Current Pos:* RES SCIENTIST IMMUNOL. *Personal Data:* b Bombay, India, Jan 29, 39. *Educ:* Wash State Univ, PhD(immunol & microbiol), 75. *Mem:* Am Immunol Asn; Am Soc Microbiologist; AAAS. *Mailing Add:* Immunol-Biogene Inc 22030 Sherman Way Canoga Park CA 91303-1855. *Fax:* 310-470-2155

KERMICLE, JERRY LEE, CORN GENETICS, PLANT MOLECULAR GENETICS. *Current Pos:* Fel genetics & biochem, 63, from asst prof to assoc prof, 63-77, PROF GENETICS, UNIV WIS-MADISON, 77 - *Personal Data:* b Dundas, Ill, Mar 8, 36; m 57; c 5. *Educ:* Univ Ill, BS, 57; Univ Wis, MS, 59, PhD(genetics), 63. *Concurrent Pos:* NSF & Dept Energy grantee. *Mem:* AAAS; Genetics Soc Am. *Res:* Maize genetics, cytogenetics and development; analysis of spontaneous mutation, paramutation and complex loci. *Mailing Add:* Lab Genetics Univ Wis 445 Henry Mall Madison WI 53706-1577

KERMISCH, DORIAN, OPTICS, ELECTROMAGNETICS. *Current Pos:* SR SCIENTIST OPTICS, XEROX CORP, 68- *Personal Data:* b Bucharest, Romania, Nov 13, 31; m 62; c 2. *Educ:* Israel Inst Technol, BSc, 55; Polytech Inst Brooklyn, MS, 64, PhD(elec eng), 68. *Prof Exp:* Elec engr, Israeli Ministry Defense, 60-62; res fel, Polytech Inst Brooklyn, 62-66; lectr, City Col New York, 67-68. *Mem:* Optical Soc Am. *Res:* Theoretical investigations of blazed holograms, volume holograms and phase imaging; optical and computer image processing. *Mailing Add:* 329 Valley Green Dr Penfield NY 14526

KERN, BERNARD DONALD, NUCLEAR PHYSICS. *Current Pos:* from asst prof to prof, 50-85, chmn, dept physics & astron, 67-69, EMER PROF PHYSICS, UNIV KY, 85- *Personal Data:* b New Castle, Ind, Oct 31, 19; m 46, Nedda Wisler; c Richard B, Jonathan K & Arthur R. *Educ:* Univ Ind, BS, 42, MS, 47, PhD(physics), 49. *Prof Exp:* Jr physicist radar, Signal Corps, US Army, 42-43; asst nuclear physics, Metall Lab, Chicago, 43; physics, Ind Univ, 46-49; sr physicist, Nuclear Physics, Oak Ridge Nat Lab, 49-50. *Concurrent Pos:* Vis physicist, US Naval Radiol Defense Lab, 57-58; prof, Univ Ky Overseas Prog, Bandung Tech Inst, 61-62; vis, Stanford Univ, 71 & Inst Nuclear Physics, KFA WGer, 78. *Mem:* Am Phys Soc; Am Asn Physics Teachers. *Res:* Nuclear energy level studies with Van de Graaff accelerator; beta and gamma-ray spectroscopy; radioactive ion induced reactions; nuclear orientation. *Mailing Add:* Dept Physics & Astron Univ Ky Lexington KY 40506-0055. *E-Mail:* bdkern00@ukcc.uky.edu

KERN, CHARLES WILLIAM, THEORETICAL CHEMISTRY. *Current Pos:* VPRES RES & GRAD STUDIES, NORTHWESTERN UNIV, 92- *Personal Data:* b Middletown, Ohio, July 13, 35. *Educ:* Carnegie Inst Technol, BS, 57; Univ Minn, PhD(chem), 61. *Prof Exp:* Fel theoret chem, Dept Chem & IBM Watson Lab, Columbia Univ, 61-64; asst prof chem, State Univ NY Stony Brook, 64-66; res scientist, 66-72, mgr chem phys sect, Battelle Mem Inst, 72-76, dir Battelle Inst Prog, 74-76; prof chem, Ohio State Univ, 76-92; prog dir, NSF, 78-80 & 83-84, proj mgr, CSNET, 80-83, actg dir, Chem Div, 84-85; sect head phys chem & dynamics, Chem Div, 85-92. *Concurrent Pos:* Adj assoc prof, Ohio State Univ, 66-71, adj prof, 71-76, acad vchmn, Dept Chem, 72-73. *Mem:* Am Phys Soc; Am Chem Soc; Sigma Xi. *Res:* Theoretical chemistry; theory of molecular structure and spectra; quantum and computational chemistry. *Mailing Add:* Northwestern Univ 633 Clark St Crown 2-223 Evanston IL 60208-1108. *Fax:* 847-497-4620

KERN, CLIFFORD DALTON, METEOROLOGY. *Current Pos:* staff engr & group leader, Atmospheric Effects Group, 78-80, SR STAFF ENGR & GROUP LEADER, PROPAGATION SCI, LOCKHEED MISSILES & SPACE C0, 80- *Personal Data:* b Oakland, Calif, Jan 6, 28; m 51; c 3. *Educ:* Univ Calif, Berkeley, AB, 52; Univ Calif, Los Angeles, MA, 58; Univ Wash, Seattle, PhD(atmospheric sci), 65. *Prof Exp:* weather officer, USAF, 52-58, adv weather officer, Cambridge Res Lab & Electronics Systs Div, 58-65, tech serv officer, Southeast Asia, 65-67, adv weather officer, Satellite Control Facil, Calif, 67-69, chief spec proj br, Air Force Global Weather Ctr, Offutt AFB, Nebr, 69-70 & develop activ in sci & numerical area, 70-71, staff meteorologist, Space & Missile Systs Orgn, 71-72; res supvr, Environ Transp Div, Savannah River Lab, E I du Pont de Nemours & Co, Inc, 72-78. *Mem:* AAAS; Am Meteorol Soc; Am Geophys Union; Sigma Xi. *Res:* Infrared emission of the earth and its cloud fields as seen by weather satellites; satellites considering solar interactions with the earth, its upper atmosphere and geomagnetic field; propagation of electromagnetic radiation through the atmosphere and ionosphere. *Mailing Add:* 1879 Cole Rd Aromas CA 95004

KERN, CLIFFORD H, III, DEVELOPMENTAL GENETICS. *Current Pos:* PROG COORDR, DIABETES UNIV, LA DEPT HEALTH & HUMAN RESOURCES, 81- *Personal Data:* b New Orleans, La, Aug 30, 48; m 72; c 1. *Educ:* Washington & Lee Univ, BS, 70; Ind Univ, MA, 72, PhD(zool), 79. *Prof Exp:* Instr genetics & biochem, DePauw Univ, 76-79, asst prof, 79-81. *Concurrent Pos:* Vis asst prof, Ind Univ, Bloomington, 80 & 81; lectr, Ind Univ & Purdue Univ, 81. *Mem:* Soc Develop Biol; Genetics Soc Am; Sigma Xi; Am Diabetes Asn. *Res:* Diabetes; genetics and development of female-sterile mutants in Drosophila. *Mailing Add:* 1309 Richland Ave Metairie LA 70001-3634

KERN, FRANK HOWARD, PEDIATRIC CARDIAC ANESTHESIA, PEDIATRIC CRITICAL CARE MEDICINE. *Current Pos:* ASSOC PROF ANESTHESIOL, DUKE UNIV MED CTR, 88-, ASSOC PROF PEDIAT, 91-, ASSOC DIR PEDIAT INTENSIVE CARE UNIT, 91- & DIR PEDIAT CARDIAC ANESTHESIOL, 92-, CHIEF DIV PEDIAT ANESTHESIOL, 96- *Personal Data:* b Newark, NJ, July 24, 56; m, Sharon; c David & Aaron. *Educ:* George Washington Univ, BS, 78; Univ Pa, MD, 82. *Prof Exp:* Residency pediat, Baylor Col Med, 82-85; residency anesthesiol, Hosp Univ Pa, 85-87; fel pediat anesthesiol & critical care, Children's Hosp Philadelphia, 87-88. *Concurrent Pos:* Chmn, First George Washington Conf Biomed Ethics, 77-78; instr anesthesia, Children's Hosp & Harvard Med Sch, 90-91; lectr pediat crit care & cardiac anesthesiol, Duke Univ Med Ctr, 91-; Cecilie Grieg vis prof, Hammersmith Hosp, London, 92. *Mem:* Am Heart Asn; Am Acad Pediat; Am Soc Anesthesiologists; Soc Pediat Anesthesia; fel Soc Critical Care Med; Soc Cardiovascular Anesthesia. *Res:* Cerebral injury during cardiopulmonary bypass; cardiopulmonary effects of cardiopulmonary bypass; ventilatory strategies in patients with cardiac and/or respiratory disease. *Mailing Add:* Duke Univ Med Ctr PO Box 3046 Durham NC 27713. *Fax:* 919-681-8357

KERN, FRED, JR, INTERNAL MEDICINE, GASTROENTEROLOGY. *Current Pos:* from asst prof to prof, 52-92, head, Div Gastroenterol, 59-82, EMER PROF MED, UNIV COLO MED CTR, DENVER, 92- *Personal Data:* b Montgomery, Ala, Sept 9, 18; m 42, Bernie Cronheim; c 3. *Educ:* Univ Ala, BA, 39; Columbia Univ, MD, 43; Am Bd Internal Med, dipl, 52. *Prof Exp:* Asst, Sch Med, Emory Univ, 43, asst path, 44; asst med, Med Col, Cornell Univ, 47-48, instr, 51-92. *Concurrent Pos:* Res fel med, Med Col, Cornell Univ, 47-49, Ledyard Jr fel, 49-50; intern, Grady Hosp, Atlanta, 43, asst resident, 44; asst resident, NY Hosp, 47-48, provisional asst outpatients, 47 & 49; physician, Colo Gen Hosp, 52; assoc attend physician, Div Internal Med, Denver Gen Hosp, 52, chief, Div Prev Med & Pub Health, 52, dir, Gen Med Clin, 51-59; chmn, Am Bd Gastroenterol, 69-72; mem, Nat Arthritis, Metab & Digestive Dis Adv Coun, NIH, 78-81; pres, Digestive Dis Info Ctr, 78-80; mem, Sci Adv Bd, Nat Found Ileitis-Colitis, chmn, Grants Rev Comt, 78-81. *Mem:* AAAS; Am Inst Nutrit; Am Gastroenterol Asn (vpres, 73-74, pres-elect, 74-75, pres, 75-76); hon mem Gastroenterol Soc Australia; Asn Am Physicians; master Am Col Physicians. *Res:* Medical education and gastroenterology; bile acid metabolism; intestinal absorption; pathogenesis of gallstones; effect of female sex steroid hormones on bile acid and cholesterol metabolism. *Mailing Add:* 501 Madison St Denver CO 80206. *E-Mail:* 73514. 650@compuserve.com

KERN, JEROME, virology, for more information see previous edition

KERN, JOHN PHILIP, INVERTEBRATE PALEONTOLOGY. *Current Pos:* From asst prof to assoc prof, 68-77, PROF GEOL, SAN DIEGO STATE UNIV, 77- *Personal Data:* b Springfield, Mass, Jan 3, 39; m 69. *Educ:* Univ Calif, Los Angeles, AB, 63, PhD(geol), 68. *Mem:* Paleont Soc; Paleont Res Inst. *Res:* Paleoenvironmental studies of late Cenozoic marine invertebrates; trace fossils. *Mailing Add:* Dept Geol Sci San Diego State Univ San Diego CA 92182-1020

KERN, JOHN W, PETROLEUM ENGINEERING, SPACE RADIATION. *Current Pos:* TECH STAFF, DYNACS ENG, INC, 95- *Personal Data:* b Mansfield, Ohio, Dec 16, 30; m 62; c Wesley & Meredyth. *Educ:* Univ Calif, Berkeley, BS, 56, MA, 58, PhD(geophys), 60. *Prof Exp:* Phys scientist, Rand Corp, Calif, 60-64; from asst prof to prof physics, Univ Houston, 64-74, adj prof, 75-78; sr res specialist, Exxon Prod Res Co, Houston, 75-81; dir, Info & Interpretation Systs, Dresser Atlas, Houston, 81-84, staff petrophysicist, 84-87; dir training, Atlas Wireline Serv, 87-89, mgr Intepretational Support, 89-90; consult, petrophysics & reservoir eng, Rockwell Int, 91-95, tech staff, 91-95. *Concurrent Pos:* Mem comn 4, Int Sci Radio Union, 62; mem working group data anal, comn II, Int Union Geod & Geophys, 63-; consult phys scientist, Rand Corp, 64-75. *Res:* Rock magnetism; geomagnetism; auroral and magnetospheric physics; solar and planetary physics; well log analysis; well log methods development; well log instrument theory and applications; reservoir description; environment design verification for international space station; ionizing radiation. *Mailing Add:* 18307 Cape Bahamas Nassau Bay TX 77058. *E-Mail:* jkem@ssfg.jsc.nasa.gov

KERN, MICHAEL DON, AVIAN PHYSIOLOGY. *Current Pos:* asst prof animal physiol, 76-82, asst prof biol, 83-88, PROF BIOL, COL WOOSTER, 89- *Personal Data:* b Los Angeles, Calif, Nov 25, 38; m 61, Alice Platner; c Robert, Jeffrey & Sean. *Educ:* Whittier Col, BA, 62; Wash State Univ, MS, 65, PhD(zoophysiol), 70. *Prof Exp:* USPHS trainee avian reproductive physiol, Cornell Univ, 69-71; asst prof chordate morphogenesis, Fordham Univ, 71-75. *Mem:* Cooper Ornith Soc; Asn Field Ornithologists; Am Ornithologists Union; Sigma Xi. *Res:* Photoperiodism in birds; annual cycles of birds; avian reproductive physiology, particularly incubation, nests, eggs; alligator eggshells. *Mailing Add:* Dept Biol Col Wooster Wooster OH 44691. *Fax:* 216-263-2738; *E-Mail:* mkern@acs.wooster.edu

KERN, RALPH DONALD, JR, PHYSICAL CHEMISTRY. *Current Pos:* from asst prof to assoc prof, 67-77, PROF CHEM, UNIV NEW ORLEANS, LAKEFRONT, 77-, CHMN DEPT, 80- *Personal Data:* b New Orleans, La, Aug 8, 35; m 61; c 3. *Educ:* Univ Tex, Austin, BS, 57 & 60, PhD(chem), 65. *Prof Exp:* Res fel, Harvard Univ, 65-67. *Mem:* Am Chem Soc; Am Phys Soc; Combustion Inst. *Res:* Rates of gas phase reactions in shock tubes monitored by infrared emission and time-of-flight mass spectrometry. *Mailing Add:* Dept Chem Univ New Orleans Lakefront New Orleans LA 70122

KERN, ROLAND JAMES, CHEMISTRY. *Current Pos:* RES CHEMIST, MONSANTO CO, 52- *Personal Data:* b Bay City, Mich, Oct 29, 25; m 53; c 2. *Educ:* Univ Mich, BS, 48; Northwestern Univ, PhD(chem), 52. *Concurrent Pos:* Fac, Univ Col, Wash Univ. *Mem:* Am Chem Soc. *Res:* Polymerization; polymer technology. *Mailing Add:* 50 Forest Crest Dr Chesterfield MO 63017

KERN, ROY FREDRICK, METALLURGY, MECHANICAL ENGINEERING. *Current Pos:* OWNER, KERN ENG CO, 71- *Personal Data:* b Lewiston, Minn, Oct 25, 18; m 44; c 3. *Educ:* Macalester Col, BS, 39; Marquette Univ, BS, 43. *Prof Exp:* Chief metallurgist, Allis-Chalmers Mfg Co, 43-62; plant mgr, Knoxville Iron Co, 63-65; proj engr, Caterpillar Tractor Co, 65-71. *Mem:* Fel Am Soc Metals. *Res:* Development of boron and alloy boron steels, heat treating of steel parts, designing for heat treatment, selection of steel for heat treated parts; exclusive method developed for buying steels: cost reduction-works better-costs less; gear problems; gears of all kinds and sizes. *Mailing Add:* 818 E Euclid Peoria IL 61614

KERN, WERNER, CHEMICAL VAPOR DEPOSITION, SEMICONDUCTOR PROCESSING. *Current Pos:* PRES, WERNER KERN ASSOC, 87- *Personal Data:* b Basel, Switz, Mar 18, 25; US citizen; m 55, Mildred C Patti; c Jeffrey K, Vanessa A & Peter R. *Educ:* Univ Basel, Cert chem, 44; Polyglot Sch Lang, Switz, dipl lang, 47; Rutgers Univ, AB, 55. *Honors & Awards:* T C Callinan Award, Electrochem Soc Inc, 72. *Prof Exp:* Jr chemist, Hoffmann-LaRoche, Ltd, Switz, 42-48, anal res chemist, NJ, 48-55, Dept Radioisotope Biochem, 55-57; chief chemist & radiol safety off, Nuclear Corp Am, 58-59; engr & div health physicist, Electronics Component & Devices Div, Somerville, 59-64; fel tech staff, David Sarnoff Res Ctr, RCA Corp, 64-87 & Lam Res Corp, 88-92. *Concurrent Pos:* Safety coun rep, RCA Labs, RCA Corp, 70-87; chem vapor deposition course lectr, Am Vacuum Soc, 81- & Electrochem Soc, 85-; vchmn, Electrochem Soc, 81-82, chmn, 83-84, adv, 85-86, fel, 91-; sr scientist & tech consult, Teltech, Inc, Minneapolis, 88- *Mem:* Electrochem Soc; Am Vacuum Soc. *Res:* Semiconductor process research; chemical vapor deposition; silicon wafer cleaning technology; chemical etching of microelectronic materials; analytical process control methods; radioactive tracer applications; surface decontamination research; preparation and properties of dielectric films. *Mailing Add:* 22 Greeenways Lane Lakewood NJ 08701

KERN, WILLIAM H, pathology, cancer, for more information see previous edition

KERN, WOLFHARD, HIGH ENERGY PHYSICS. *Current Pos:* assoc prof, 64-65, PROF PHYSICS, UNIV MASS DARTMOUTH, 67- *Personal Data:* b Berlin, Ger, Feb 18, 27; m 52, Hille von Mengoden; c Rainer, Jurgen & Anne. *Educ:* Univ Frankfurt, BS, 48, MS, 51; Univ Bonn, PhD(physics), 58. *Prof Exp:* Asst prof physics, Univ Bonn, 58-60; res assoc, Deutsches Elektronen-Synchrotron, 60-63, scientist, 65-67; res assoc physics, Mass Inst Tech, 63-64. *Concurrent Pos:* Vis scientist, Max-Planck Inst, 75-76, Brookhave Nar Lab, 82-83 & 89-90. *Mem:* Am Phys Soc; Am Asn Physics Teachers; Sigma Xi; AAAS. *Res:* Experimental high energy physics; meson spectroscopy. *Mailing Add:* 139 Hancock St Auburndale MA 02166

KERNAGHAN, ROY PETER, BIOLOGY, GENETICS. *Current Pos:* PROF BIOL & CHMN DEPT, SALISBURY STATE COL, 74- *Personal Data:* b Schenectady, NY, Mar 26, 33; m 56. *Educ:* Dartmouth Univ, BA, MA, 57; Univ Conn, PhD(genetics), 63. *Prof Exp:* NIH trainee electron micros, Col Physicians & Surgeons, Columbia Univ, 63-65; asst prof biol sci, State Univ NY, Stony Brook, 65-74. *Mem:* Genetics Soc Am; Am Soc Cell Biol. *Res:* Developmental genetics. *Mailing Add:* Continuing Educ Salisbury State Univ 1101 Camden Ave Salisbury MD 21801-6800

KERNAN, ANNE, PHYSICS. *Current Pos:* assoc prof, 67-70, prof physics, 70-94, chmn dept, 73-76, dean, Grad Div & chancellor res, 91-94, EMER PROF PHYSICS, UNIV CALIF, RIVERSIDE, 94- *Personal Data:* b Dublin, Ireland, Jan 15, 33; US citizen. *Educ:* Univ Col, Dublin, BSc, 53, PhD(physics), 57. *Hon Degrees:* DSc, Nat Univ Ireland, 95. *Prof Exp:* Asst lectr physics, Univ Col, Dublin, 58-62; res physicist, Lawrence Berkeley Lab, 62-66 & Stanford Linear Accelerator Ctr, Stanford Univ, 66-67. *Concurrent Pos:* Prin investr, Dept Energy, res contract, 69-94; mem, Adv Comt Physics, NSF, 78-82, Sci & Educ Adv Comt, Lawrence Berkeley Lab, 83-87, Fermilab Prog Adv Comt, 86-90, Dept Energy, physics adv panel, 86-90, Users Orgn SSC, 89-92; councillor-at-large, Am Phys Soc, 85-; Am Phys Soc, 92-96. *Mem:* AAAS; Am Phys Soc. *Res:* Experimental high energy physics. *Mailing Add:* Dept Physics Univ Calif Riverside CA 92521. *Fax:* 714-488-7729; *E-Mail:* anne.kernan@ucr.edu

KERNAN, WILLIAM J, JR, PHYSICS. *Current Pos:* assoc prof, 63-66, PROF PHYSICS, IOWA STATE UNIV, 66-; SR PHYSICIST, AMES LAB, 66- *Personal Data:* b Baltimore, Md, Oct 18, 33; m 56; c 3. *Educ:* Loyola Col, Md, BS, 55; Univ Chicago, MS, 56, PhD(physics), 60. *Prof Exp:* Asst physicist, Argonne Nat Lab, 60-61; asst prof physics, NY Univ, 61-63. *Concurrent Pos:* Guest staff mem, Brookhaven Nat Lab, 60-65; physicist, Ames Lab, 63-66; prog dir high energy physics, Ames Labs, ERDA, 75-78, assoc dir opers, Dept Energy, 78- *Mem:* Fel Am Phys Soc. *Res:* Properties and interactions of elementary particles. *Mailing Add:* 2524 Eisenhower Ave Ames IA 50010

KERNBERG, OTTO F, PSYCHOANALYSIS. *Current Pos:* TRAINING & SUPV ANALYST, COLUMBIA UNIV CTR PSYCHOANALYTICAL TRAINING & RES, 74-; PROF PSYCHIAT, CORNELL UNIV MED COL, 76- *Personal Data:* b Vienna, Austria, Sept 10, 28; US citizen; m, Paulina Fischer; c Martin, Karen & Adine. *Educ:* Univ Chile, BS, 47, MD, 53. *Honors & Awards:* Heinz Hartman Award, 72; Edward A Strecker Award, 75; William F Schonfeld Award, 82; Van Geison Award, 86; Mary S Sigourney Award, 90. *Prof Exp:* Intern, Hosp J J Aquirre, Santiago, Chile, 53; resident psychiat, Psychiat Clin, Univ Chile, 54-57, staff mem, Dept Psychiat, 57-61, asst prof, 58-59; staff psychiatrist, C F Menninger Mem Hosp, Topeka, Kans, 61-62; staff psychiatrist, Res Dept, Menninger Found, 62-67, chief investr, Psychother Res Proj, 67-69; dir, C F Menninger Mem Hosp, 69-73; dir gen clin serv, NY State Psychiat Inst, 73-76; prof clin psychiat, Col Physicians & Surgeons, Columbia Univ, 73-76. *Concurrent Pos:* Prof psychopath, Sch Social Work, Nat Health Serv, Santiago, 57-59, prof ment health, 58-59; prof ment health & prof psychol diag, Sch Psychol, Cath Univ Chile, 58-61; Rockefeller Found fel psychiat, Henry Phipps Clin, Johns Hopkins Hosp, Baltimore, 59-60; consult, Topeka State Hosp, Kans, 64-68; fac mem, Menninger Sch Psychiat & Topeka Inst Psychoanal, 64-73; resident psychiat, C F Menninger Mem Hosp, Topeka, 65-68, consult, 68-69; training analyst, Topeka Inst Psychoanal, 66-73, treas, 68-73; staff psychiatrist, Adult Outpatient Serv, Menninger Found, 68-69; assoc clin prof psychiat, Univ Kans Med Ctr, Kansas City, Kans, 71-73; mem staff, A K Rice Inst, Group Rels Conf, Washington Sch Psychiat, 72-75; vis prof, Menninger Sch Psychiat & Mass Gen Hosp, Harvard Med Sch, 74-75 & Albert Einstein Col Med, 77-; attend psychiatrist, Serv Psychiat, Presby Hosp, NY, 74-76; asst ed, J Am Psychoanal Asn, 74-77, assoc ed, 77-93; fac mem, NY Psychoanal Inst, 74-81. *Mem:* Fel Am Psychiat Asn; AMA; fel Am Col Physicians; Sigma Xi; fel NY Acad Med; NY Acad Sci; AAAS; Int Psychoanal Asn (vpres, 83-); Cent Neuropsychiat Hosp Asn (pres, 88-); Asn Psychoanal Med (pres, 91-92). *Res:* Diagnosis of severe personality disorders with particular reference to borderline conditions and narcissistic pathology; the process and outcome of psychoanalytic psychotherapy with severe personality disorders; psychoanalytic object relations theory, institutional dynamics, psychopathology of love relations and psychoanalytic technique. *Mailing Add:* 21 Bloomingdale Rd White Plains NY 10605-1504. *Fax:* 914-997-5997

KERNELL, ROBERT LEE, SCIENCE EDUCATION. *Current Pos:* assoc prof, 67-79, PROF PHYSICS, OLD DOM UNIV, 79- *Personal Data:* b Greer, SC, Mar 24, 29; m 59; c 2. *Educ:* Wofford Col, AB, 50; Univ SC, MS, 58; Univ Tenn, PhD(physics), 68. *Prof Exp:* Asst prof physics, Col William & Mary, 58-62. *Mem:* Am Phys Soc; Am Asn Physics Teachers; NY Acad Sci; Sigma Xi. *Res:* Nuclear structure physics; radiation effects induced by charged particles. *Mailing Add:* 1725 W 49th St Norfolk VA 23508

KERNER, EDWARD HASKELL, THEORETICAL PHYSICS, THEORETICAL BIOLOGY. *Current Pos:* PROF PHYSICS, UNIV DEL, 62- *Personal Data:* b New York, NY, Apr 22, 74; m 48; c 3. *Educ:* Columbia Col, AB, 43; Cornell Univ, PhD(physics), 50. *Prof Exp:* Instr physics, Princeton Univ, 43-44; physicist, Manhattan eng dist, 44-45; asst prof physics, Wayne State Univ, 49-51; res assoc, Iowa State Univ, 51-53; from asst prof to assoc prof, Univ Buffalo, 53-62. *Mem:* Fel Am Phys Soc. *Res:* Relativistic particle dynamics; projective relativity; atomic and molecular collision theory; band structure of random lattices; theory of biological population fluctuations and of biochemical kinetics; non-linear dynamics. *Mailing Add:* Dept Physics Univ Del Newark DE 19711

KERNEY, PETER JOSEPH, MECHANICAL ENGINEERING. *Current Pos:* MGR ADVAN TECHNOL, CTI-CRYOGENICS, 77- *Personal Data:* b Philadelphia, Pa, Apr 7, 40; m 68; c 3. *Educ:* Univ Notre Dame, BS, 62, MS, 64; Pa State Univ, PhD(mech eng), 70. *Prof Exp:* Instr mech eng, Tri-State Col, 65-66 & Pa State Univ, 66-70; asst prof, Lafayette Col, 70-72; res staff engr, Draper Lab, Mass Inst Technol, 72-77. *Concurrent Pos:* Res asst, Ord Res Lab, 68-70; consult, US Army Frankford Arsenal, 71; adj prof mech eng, Tufts Univ, 77- *Mem:* Am Soc Mech Engrs; assoc mem Am Soc Eng Educ; Am Soc Heating, Refrig & Air Conditioning Engrs; Sigma Xi. *Res:* Two phase flow and turbulent jet mixing; jet penetration characteristics of a submerged steam jet; energy and momentum characteristics of liquid bath downstream of steam jet; convection and cryogenic heat transfer. *Mailing Add:* 7 Elwern Rd Arlington MA 02174

KERNIS, MARTEN MURRAY, ANATOMY, TERATOLOGY. *Current Pos:* assoc prof anat, Sch Basic Med Sci & dep exec dean, Univ Ill, 78-82, actg exec dean, 82-83, vdean, Col Med, 83-91, assoc vchancellor acad affairs, 91-93, ASSOC PROF HEALTH POLICY & ADMIN, SCH PUB HEALTH, UNIV ILL, CHICAGO, 93- *Personal Data:* b Chicago, Ill, Sept 21, 41; m 82, Janet Tockman; c Ariel. *Educ:* Roosevelt Univ, BS, 63; Univ Fla, PhD(anat sci), 68. *Prof Exp:* From asst prof to assoc prof anat, Sch Basic Med Sci, Univ Ill, 68-76; from asst prof to assoc prof anat obstet & gynec, Abraham Lincoln Sch Med, 68-76; from asst dean to assoc dean, Sch Basic Med Sci, Jefferson Med Col, 72-76, assoc prof anat & dean, Col Allied Health Sci, 76-78. *Mem:* Teratology Soc; Asn Am Med Cols. *Res:* Transport across the placenta during normal and abnormal embryogenesis; effects of teratogens on function; distribution of teratogens; mechanism of malformations. *Mailing Add:* Sch Pub Health Univ Ill 2035 W Taylor St Chicago IL 60612-7259. *Fax:* 312-996-5356; *E-Mail:* mmkernis@uic.edu

KERNS, DAVID MARLOW, ELECTROMAGNETICS. *Current Pos:* PHOTOG, 80- *Personal Data:* b Minneapolis, Minn, Oct 7, 13. *Educ:* Univ Minn, BEE, 35; Cath Univ Am, PhD(physics), 51. *Honors & Awards:* Silver Medal, US Dept Com, 60, Gold Medal, 73; Samuel Wesley Stratton Award, Nat Bur Standards, 81. *Prof Exp:* Asst, Univ Minn, 35-39; chief elec unit, Aerial Camera Lab, Air Mat Command, USAF, Ohio, 40-42; from proj leader to asst div chief, Radio Standards Lab & Electromagnetic Fields Div, 46-71, sr res scientist, Electromagnetic Fields Div, Nat Bur Standards, 71-80. *Concurrent Pos:* Adj prof, Univ Colo, 61-; mem US comn, Int Sci Radio Union, 58- *Res:* Electromagnetic theory of wave guides and wave guide junctions; scattering-matrix theory of antennas and antenna-antenna interactions. *Mailing Add:* 1365 Bear Mountain Dr Boulder CO 80303

KERNS, MICHAEL LESTER, ELASTOMER SYNTHESIS, FUNCTIONAL INITIATOR SYNTHESIS. *Current Pos:* SCIENTIST, BRIDGESTONE-FIRESTONE CENT RES, 95- *Personal Data:* m 91, Connie Elaine Emerson. *Educ:* Oberlin Col, BS, 91; Ohio State Univ, PhD(org chem), 95. *Mem:* Am Chem Soc. *Res:* Organic synthesis; national product synthesis, electrochemical organic synthesis methodology development; organic polymer synthesis including anionic and Ziegler-Natta systems. *Mailing Add:* 41869 Oberlin Rd Elyria OH 44035-7405. *E-Mail:* mkbuckeye@aol.com

KERNS, SHERRA E, ENGINEERING EDUCATION, RESEARCH CONSULTING. *Current Pos:* PROF COMPUT & ELEC ENG, VANDERBILT UNIV, 87-, CHAIR, 93- *Personal Data:* b Ann Arbor, Mich, May 27, 47; m, David V Jr; c Sara Horan (Lange), Melissa Caryl & David V III. *Educ:* Mt Holyoke Col, AB, 69; Univ Wis, MA, 71; Univ NC, PhD, 77. *Honors & Awards:* Res Achievement Award, Alcon Found, 86. *Prof Exp:* NIH postdoctoral biomed eng, Duke Univ, 77-79; asst prof elec eng, Auburn Univ, 79-82; assoc prof elec & comput eng, NC State Univ, 82-87. *Concurrent Pos:* Pres, Radiation Microsci Inc, 85-; mem, Comt Eng Accreditation Activ, 96- *Mem:* Fel Inst Elec & Electronics Engrs; Nat Asn Elec & Eng Dept Heads (pres, 95-); Am Asn Eng Educ. *Mailing Add:* Elec & Comput Eng Vanderbilt Univ Box 108 Sta B Nashville TN 37235

KERPER, MATTHEW J(ULIUS), CERAMICS. *Current Pos:* RETIRED. *Personal Data:* b St Louis, Mo, Apr 9, 22; m 48; c 1. *Educ:* Univ Mo, BS, 43, MS, 47; George Washington Univ, MS, 59; Am Univ, MPA. *Prof Exp:* Ceramic engr, Laclede Christy Co, Mo, 47-52, Nat Bur Standards, 52-66, Off Aerospace Res, 66-70 & Air Force Systs Command, 70-72, ceramic engr, Air Force Off Sci Res, 72-88. *Mem:* Am Ceramic Soc; Am Inst Ceramic Engrs. *Res:* Physical properties of ceramics and glass at elevated temperatures; science administration. *Mailing Add:* 4620 N Park Ave Chevy Chase MD 20815

KERR, ANDREW, JR, medicine, for more information see previous edition

KERR, ANTHONY ROBERT, MICROWAVE ELECTRONICS, RADIO ASTRONOMY. *Current Pos:* SCIENTIST, NAT RADIO ASTRON OBSERV, CHARLOTTESVILLE, VA, 84- *Personal Data:* b Farnborough, Eng, Aug 30, 41; US citizen; m 74, Tanya S Ross; c Tristan. *Educ:* Univ Melbourne, BE, 63, MESc, 67, PhD(elec eng), 69. *Honors & Awards:* The Microwave Prize, Inst Elec & Electronics Engrs, 78; Except Eng Achievement Medal, NASA, 83. *Prof Exp:* Res scientist radio astron, Div Radiophys, Commonwealth Sci & Indust Res Orgn, Sydney, Australia, 69-71; electronics engr millimeter-wave electronics, Nat Radio Astron Observ, Charlottesville, Va, 71-74; physicist millimeter-wave electronics, Goddard Inst Space Studies, NASA, 74-84. *Concurrent Pos:* Vis prof, Univ Va, 84-; consult, Macom Inc, 80-83 & NASA, 87-90. *Mem:* Fel Inst Elec & Electronics Engrs; Int Union Radio Sci; Astron Soc Australia; Sigma Xi; Am Phys Soc. *Res:* Development of low-noise receivers at millimeter and submillimeter wavelengths, and their application in radio astronomy, atmospheric physics, and space communications. *Mailing Add:* Nat Radio Astron Observ 2015 Ivy Rd Charlottesville VA 22903. *Fax:* 804-296-0324; *E-Mail:* akerr@nrao.edu

KERR, ARNOLD D, ENGINEERING MECHANICS & ICE COVER MECHANICS, RAILROAD ENGINEERING. *Current Pos:* PROF CIVIL ENG, UNIV DEL, 78- *Personal Data:* b Suwalki, Poland, Mar 9, 28; US citizen; m 66, Berta Borgenieht; c Regina & Orin. *Educ:* Tech Univ, Munich, Dipl Ing, 52; Northwestern Univ, MS, 56, PhD(theoret & appl mech), 58. *Prof Exp:* Engr design & anal, Hazelet & Erdal Consult Engrs, 55; asst res scientist mech solids, Courant Inst Math & Sci, NY Univ, 58-59, from asst prof aeronaut to assoc prof aeronaut & astronaut, 59-66, prof, 66-73, dir, Lab Mech Solids, 67-73; vis prof civil eng, Princeton Univ, 73-78. *Concurrent Pos:* Consult to US govt agencies & indust, 59-; pres, Inst Railroad Eng, 80-; fel, Ctr Advan Study, Univ Del, 89-90. *Mem:* Fel Am Soc Mech Engrs; Am Railway Eng Asn; Int Soc Interaction Mech & Math. *Res:* Structural mechanics; continuously supported structures; dynamics and stability of structures; bearing capacity and dynamics of floating ice covers; railroad track analyses and technology. *Mailing Add:* Dept Civil Eng Univ Del Newark DE 19716. *Fax:* 302-831-3640

KERR, CARL E, MATHEMATICS. *Current Pos:* prof math, 69-76, PROF MATH & COMPUT SCI, SHIPPENSBURG STATE COL, 76- *Personal Data:* b Corsicana, Tex, Sept 16, 26; m 50; c 1. *Educ:* La Salle Col, BA, 50; Univ Del, MA, 53; Lehigh Univ, PhD(math), 59. *Prof Exp:* Asst prof math, Lafayette Col, 53-59; asst prof, Dickinson Col, 59-69. *Concurrent Pos:* Mathematician, Frankford Arsenal, 52-54; mathematician, Convair Div, Gen Dynamics Corp, 56. *Mem:* Am Math Soc; Math Asn Am. *Res:* Linear spaces; summability. *Mailing Add:* 33 Oak Lane Shippensburg PA 17257-1641

KERR, DONALD L(AURENS), CHEMICAL ENGINEERING. *Current Pos:* Sr chemist, Photog Eng Lab, 69-75, RES ASSOC PHOTOG PROCESSES LAB, RES LABS, EASTMAN KODAK CO, 75- *Personal Data:* b Putnam, Conn, June 28, 43; m 66; c 1. *Educ:* Worcester Polytech Inst, BS, 65; Univ Del, MChE, 68, PhD(chem eng, phys chem), 70. *Mem:* Am Inst Chem Engrs. *Res:* Mass tranfer; chemical kinetics; drying; photographic processing. *Mailing Add:* 177 Long Pond Rd Rochester NY 14612

KERR, DONALD M, JR, TECHNICAL MANAGEMENT, GEOPHYSICS. *Current Pos:* DIR & EXEC VPRES, INFO SYSTS LABS, INC, SAN DIEGO, CALIF, 96- *Personal Data:* b Philadelphia, Pa, Apr 8, 39; m 61, Alison Kyle; c Margot K. *Educ:* Cornell Univ, BEE, 63, MS, 64, PhD(elec eng, physics), 66. *Honors & Awards:* Outstanding Serv Award, Dept Energy, 79. *Prof Exp:* Staff mem, Los Alamos Nat Lab, Univ Calif, 66-71, group leader, 71-73, asst, Dir Off, 73-75, alt energy div leader, 75-76, dir, 79-85; dep mgr, Nev Opers, Dept Energy, 76-77, dep & actg asst secy defense progs, 77-79, dep & actg asst secy energy technol, 79; from sr vpres to pres, EG&G Inc, Wellesley, Mass, 85-92; dir & corp exec vpres, Sci Applns Int Corp, San Diego, Calif, 93-96. *Concurrent Pos:* Consult, Navajo Sci Comt, 74-77, Los Alamos Nat Lab, 85, Lawrence Livermore Nat Lab, 92-; mem, US Army Sci Adv Panel, 75-78, Defense Sci Bd, 93-; chmn, Comt Res & Develop, Int Energy Agency, OECD, 79-85; mem, Joint Strategic Target Planning Staff, Sci Adv Group, 81-; mem corp, Charles Stark Draper Lab, 82-, SRI Nat Security Adv Coun, 80-89, Cornell Univ Eng Col Coun, 84-; dir, Nat Asn Mfrs, 87-92, Mirage Systs Inc, 88-91, Resources for the Future, 90-, Ktaadn Inc, 92- *Mem:* Fel AAAS; Am Phys Soc; Am Geophys Union. *Res:* Nuclear weapons research and development testing; laser, heavy ion, and electron beam fusion; nuclear safeguards and security; ionospheric physics; international activities relating to nuclear technology and political, military, economic and energy affairs. *Mailing Add:* 5861 Ravenswood Rd La Jolla CA 92037. *Fax:* 619-454-5903; *E-Mail:* donkerr@islinc.com

KERR, DONALD PHILIP, ATOMIC PHYSICS, MOLECULAR PHYSICS. *Current Pos:* from asst prof to assoc prof, 69-76, PROF PHYSICS, UNIV WINNIPEG, 76-; CONSULT, 79- *Personal Data:* b Winnipeg, Man, Oct 22, 38; m 62; c 2. *Educ:* Univ Man, BSc, 60, MSc, 61, PhD(physics), 65. *Prof Exp:* Nat Res Coun Can fel, Univ Giessen, 65-67; res assoc, Harvard Univ, 67-69. *Mem:* Can Asn Physicists. *Res:* Positron annihilation in organic liquids and solids; high resolution mass spectrometry; heavy ion scattering. *Mailing Add:* Dept Physics Univ Winnipeg 515 Portage Ave Winnipeg MB R3B 2E9 Can

KERR, DONALD R, MATHEMATICS. *Current Pos:* CLIN PSYCHOLOGIST, PSYCHOL ASSOCS TALLAHASSEE, 87- *Personal Data:* b Chicago, Ill, Mar 12, 38; m 60; c 1. *Educ:* Univ Ariz, BS, 60, MS, 62; Lehigh Univ, PhD(math), 67; Fla State Univ, PhD(clin psychol). *Prof Exp:* Instr math, Lafayette Col, 63-67; asst prof, State Univ NY Albany, 67-69; vis prof math, 69-71, assoc prof educ & asst dir math educ develop ctr, 71-78, acad officer & basic skills coordr math, Ind Univ, Bloomington, 78-82. *Mem:* Am Math Soc; Math Asn Am; Nat Coun Teachers Math. *Res:* Elementary education in mathematics and the mathematics training of elementary teachers; problem solving of children, grades 4, 5, 6; basic skills in mathematics for college students. *Mailing Add:* Psychol Assocs Tallahassee 130 Salem Ct Tallahassee FL 32301

KERR, DOUGLAS S, COMPUTER SCIENCES. *Current Pos:* Asst prof, 67-71, ASSOC PROF, COMPUT & INFO SCI, OHIO STATE UNIV, 71- *Personal Data:* b Washington, DC, Nov 19, 40; m 68. *Educ:* Yale Univ, BA, 62; Purdue Univ, MS, 64, PhD(computer sci), 67. *Mem:* Asn Comput Mach; Inst Elec & Electronics Engrs. *Res:* Data base systems; software engineering. *Mailing Add:* 2104 Iuka Ave Columbus OH 43201

KERR, ERIC DONALD, PHYTOPATHOLOGY. *Current Pos:* EXTEN PLANT PATHOLOGIST, PANHANDLE RES & EXT CTR, UNIV NEBR, 67- *Personal Data:* b Gipsy, Mo, Feb 21, 30; m 71, Joyce M Drury; c Robin E (Clark) & Joleanna M (Williams). *Educ:* Univ Mo, Columbia, BS, 51, MS, 60; Univ Nebr, Lincoln, PhD(plant path), 67. *Prof Exp:* Res plant pathologist, Agr Res Serv, 67. *Mem:* Soc Nematol; Am Phytopath Soc; Am Soc Sugar Beet Technol. *Res:* Control of Cercospora leaf spot on sugar beet; control of wheat disease; dry bean yield losses caused by white mold; control of nematodes on sugar beet. *Mailing Add:* 2460 Valencia Gering NE 69341

KERR, ERNEST ANDREW, PHYTOPATHOLOGY. *Current Pos:* RETIRED. *Personal Data:* b Guelph, Ont, Aug 24, 17; m 45, Olive L Gordon; c Gordon E, Douglas J & Elizabeth L (Simms). *Educ:* McMaster Univ, BA, 40; McGill Univ, MSc, 41; Univ Wis, PhD(genetics, plant path), 44. *Honors & Awards:* Award of Merit, Can Soc Hort Sci, 83; H R MacMillan Laureate Agr Award, 89 & 94. *Prof Exp:* Asst, Hort Exp Sta, Ont Ministry Agr & Food, 44-52, res assoc, 52-54, chief res scientist plant breeding, 54-70, res coordr prod systs, Hort Res Inst Ont, 70-72, res scientist, 72-82; dir plant breeding & res, Stokes Seeds, 83-94. *Mem:* fel Agr Inst Can; Can Soc Hort Sci; hon mem Can Phytopathological Soc. *Res:* Horticultural plant breeding, particularly tomatoes, sweet peppers and sweet corn; trilliums and rhododendrons. *Mailing Add:* 8 Eden Pl Simcoe ON N3Y 3K9 Can

KERR, FRANK JOHN, RADIO ASTRONOMY. *Current Pos:* vis prof, Univ Md, 66-68, dir, Astron Prog, 73-78, actg provost to provost, Div Math & Phys Sci & Eng, 78-85, prof astron, 68-87, EMER PROF ASTRON, UNIV MD, COLLEGE PARK, 87- *Personal Data:* b St Albans, Eng, Jan 8, 18; m 66; c 3. *Educ:* Univ Melbourne, BSc, 38, MSc, 40, DSc(astron), 62; Harvard Univ, MA, 51. *Prof Exp:* Res officer radiophysics, Div Radio Physics, Commonwealth Sci & Indust Res Orgn, Australia, 40-45, sr officer radio astron, 45-55, prin res officer, 60-68. *Concurrent Pos:* Res scholar, Harvard Univ, 51-52; vis scientist, Leiden Univ, 57-58; fel, Guggenheim Found, 75; prog dir, Univ Space Res Asn, 83- *Mem:* Int Astron Union; Am Astron Soc; Royal Astron Soc; Astron Soc Australia; Australian Inst Physics. *Res:* Galactic structure; tropospheric radio propagation; moon radar; radio studies of Galaxy and Magellanic Clouds. *Mailing Add:* Space Sci Bldg College Park MD 20742

KERR, GEORGE R, PUBLIC HEALTH NUTRITION, PEDIATRICS. *Current Pos:* PROF SCH PUB HEALTH, UNIV TEX HEALTH SCI CTR, 77- *Personal Data:* b Winnipeg, Man, May 15, 30; m 54; c 6. *Educ:* Dalhousie Univ, MD & CM, 55. *Prof Exp:* Intern med & surg, Victoria Gen Hosp, Halifax, NS, 54-55; gen pract, 55-56; resident pediat & orthop, Gen Hosp, St Johns, Nfld, 56-57; asst resident pediat, Vancouver Gen Hosp, BC, 57-58, asst resident med, 59; instr, Univ BC, 61-62; asst prof pediat, Med Sch, Univ Ore, 62-63; from asst prof to assoc prof, Sch Med, Univ Wis-Madison, 63-71; assoc prof nutrit, Sch Pub Health, Harvard Univ, 71-77. *Concurrent Pos:* Res fel, Vancouver Gen Hosp, BC, 59; R Samuel McLaughlin traveling fel, 59-60; res fel pediat endocrinol & metab, Med Sch, Univ Ore, 59-61; Queen Elizabeth II Can res fel, 60-61; asst dir, Ore Regional Primate Res Ctr, 62-63; res assoc, Joseph P Kennedy, Jr Mem Lab & Wis Regional Primate Res Ctr, 63-71; dir, Human Nutrit Ctr, Univ Tex, Health Sci Ctr, 77-88. *Res:* Public health maternal-child health program needs and effectiveness, nutrition and child development. *Mailing Add:* Univ Tex Health Sci Ctr Houston TX 77025

KERR, GEORGE THOMSON, SURFACE CHEMISTRY. *Current Pos:* RETIRED. *Personal Data:* b Baltimore, Md, May 7, 23; m 50, Lorraine Snyder; c Robert S & Joanna M (Harley). *Educ:* Pa State Univ, BS, 45, MS, 46, PhD(chem), 52. *Prof Exp:* Instr chem, Pa State Univ, 49-50; asst prof, Lebanon Valley Col, 50-52; res supvr, Res Div, AMP, Inc, 52-56; sr res chemist, Socony Mobil Labs, Mobil Res & Develop Corp, 56-62, res assoc, 62-75, sr res assoc, Cent Res Div Lab, 75-85. *Concurrent Pos:* Mem comt zeolite nomenclature, Int Union Pure & Appl Chem; mem organizing comt, Fourth Int Conf Molecular Sieves, 77. *Mem:* Int Zeolite Asn; Am Chem Soc; Int Zeolite Asn (pres, 80-83). *Res:* Synthesis and physical properties of high molecular weight hydrocarbons; kinetics of acid attack of clay minerals; synthesis and properties of crystalline zeolites. *Mailing Add:* 10 Pin Oak Dr Lawrenceville NJ 08648. *E-Mail:* zeolite@earthlink.net

KERR, HUGH BARKLEY, MECHANICAL ENGINEERING. *Current Pos:* ASSOC PROF ENG SCI & DIR, D W MATTSON COMPUT CTR, TENN TECHNOL UNIV, 62- *Personal Data:* b Maryville, Tenn, July 22, 22; m 51; c 2. *Educ:* Univ Tenn, BS, 47, MS, 51. *Prof Exp:* Mech engr res & develop, Combustion Eng Co, 47-48; instr mech eng, Clemson Col, 48-51; asst prof, Univ Ala, 51-54; gen engr, Mine Detection Lab, USN, Fla, 54-55; assoc prof mech eng, Univ Miss, 55-61 & Tex Western Col, 61-62. *Concurrent Pos:* Mech engr, Int Harvester Co, 57; plant engr, Western Elec Co, 59. *Mem:* Am Soc Eng Educ. *Res:* Heat power; refrigeration and air conditioning; photoelastic stress analysis; data processing; computer sciences. *Mailing Add:* 5390 Gainesboro Grade Cookeville TN 38501

KERR, I LAWRENCE, health administration; deceased, see previous edition for last biography

KERR, J(AMES) S(ANFORD) STEPHENSON, ELECTRICAL ENGINEERING, ELECTROMAGNETISM. *Current Pos:* RETIRED. *Personal Data:* b Vancouver, BC, Mar 9, 26; nat US; m 49, Jean A C McCulloch; c John S & Jane E. *Educ:* Univ BC, BASc, 48; Univ Ill, MS, 49, PhD, 51. *Prof Exp:* Eng analyst elec eng, Gen Elec Co, NY, 51-56; mgr guid, tracking & eval dept, TRW Space Technol Labs, 56-65, asst lab dir antisubmarine warfare, 65-66, asst mgr, Guid & Control Opers, TRW Systs Group, 66-67, sr staff engr to gen mgr electronics systs div, 67-71, sr staff engr, Ballistic Missile Defense Prog Off, Redondo Beach, 71-76, sr staff engr spec proj, TRW Defense & Space Systs Group, 76-80, sr staff engr, Space Commun Div, 80-86, sr staff engr, Appl Technol Div, TRW Electronics Systs Group, 86-90. *Mem:* Sr mem Inst Elec & Electronics Engrs. *Res:* Application of electromagnetic theory to space program: analysis of advanced radar systems and data therefrom; management of radio guidance system and radio guidance equation development for space programs such as Mercury, Ranger and Mariner. *Mailing Add:* 1564 Prospect Pl Victoria BC V8R 5X8 Can

KERR, JANET SPENCE, DEVELOPMENT NOVEL THERAPEUTICS. *Current Pos:* SR RES SCIENTIST, DUPONT MERCK PHARMACEUT CO, 85- *Personal Data:* b New Haven, Conn; m, Thomas A; c Sarah, Matthew & Timothy. *Educ:* Beaver Col, BA, 64; Rutgers State Univ, MS, 69, PhD(physiol), 73. *Prof Exp:* Asst prof physiol, Camden Col Arts & Sci, Rutgers Univ, 73-76; NIH trainee & res assoc physiol, Sch Med, Univ Pa, 76-79; asst prof med & physiol, Rutgers Med Sch, Univ Med & Dent NJ, 79-85. *Concurrent Pos:* Assoc mem, Grad Fac & Bur Biol Res, Rutgers Univ, 80-85; adj assoc prof, Sch Med, Univ Pa, 85-89, Philadelphia Sch Osteop Med, 94-; mem, Orgn Comt, Inflammatory Res Asn, 88-94. *Mem:* Am Physiol Soc; Am Thoracic Soc; Inflammatory Res Asn; AAAS; Am Soc Bone Mineral Res. *Res:* Modulators of tissue injury: including cytokires and oxygen- derived free radicals and their localization in the disease process. *Mailing Add:* Du Pont Merck Pharmaceut Co PO Box 80400 E400/4223 Wilmington DE 19880-0400. *Fax:* 302-695-7873; *E-Mail:* kerrjs@llcpmc.dnet.dupont.wm

KERR, JOHN (JACK) M(ARTIN), CERAMIC & CHEMICAL ENGINEERING. *Current Pos:* RETIRED. *Personal Data:* b Normal, Ill, Jan 31, 34; m 56; c 4. *Educ:* Univ Ill, BS, 56. *Prof Exp:* Metallurgist, Oak Ridge Nat Lab, 56-61; sr engr, Babcock & Wilcox Co, 61-66, supvr nuclear ceramics, 66-71, mgr, Ceramics Sect, 71-74, mgr, Nuclear Fuel Cycle Sect, 74-81, mgr, Systs Design & Eng Sect, 81-87, mgr, Fuels & Mat Unit, 87-94, adv engr, Advan Energy Components Eng, 94-95. *Mem:* Fel Am Ceramic Soc; Am Soc Testing & Mat. *Res:* Ceramic bodies for waste disposal; ceramic fuel-metal compatibility studies; ceramic fuels development and development of fuels fabrication methods; nuclear ceramics; nuclear fuel cycle studies. *Mailing Add:* 1425 Brookville Lane Lynchburg VA 24502

KERR, JOHN POLK, ZOOLOGY, AQUATIC BIOLOGY. *Current Pos:* ENVIRON MGR, DEPT ENVIRON REG, STATE FLA, 86- *Personal Data:* b Little Rock, Ark, July 14, 31; m 56; c 4. *Educ:* Rutgers Univ, BA, 56; Univ Calif, MS, 57; Univ Mich, PhD(zool), 62. *Prof Exp:* Asst biol, Rutgers Univ, 55-56; researcher animal behavior, CIBA Pharmaceut Co, 57-58; teaching asst zool, Univ Mich, 58-59; instr biol, Adrian Col, 61-62; res assoc fisheries, Univ Mich, 62-63; asst prof zool, Univ Ga, 63-69; assoc prof biol & marine sci, Univ WFla, 69-73, vpres & sr ecol consult, Baseline, Inc, 73-76, gen mgr & pres, 76-78; head, New South Ecosyst, Inc, 78-86; prof biol, Salem Col, 83-86. *Concurrent Pos:* Rackham fel fisheries, Univ Mich, 62-63; vis asst prof, Ore Inst Marine Biol, Univ Ore, 65; partic, Electronics for Scientists Prof, Univ Ill, 68; faculty fel, Systs Design Prog, NASA & Am Soc Eng Educ, Auburn Univ, 70. *Mem:* Am Soc Zool; Ecol Soc Am; Am Fisheries Soc; Am Soc Ichthyol & Herpet; Am Soc Limnol & Oceanog. *Res:* Aquatic ecology; biology of vertebrates, especially fishes; ichthyology and herpetology; fisheries; marine and freshwater ecosystems, especially rivers, estuaries, wetlands, and lakes; animal behavior, especially under field conditions. *Mailing Add:* 4770 Velasquez Pensacola FL 32504

KERR, KIRKLYN M, VETERINARY PATHOLOGY. *Current Pos:* DEAN & DIR, SCH AGR, UNIV CONN, 93- *Personal Data:* b Green Bank, WVa, May 1, 36; m 57; c 3. *Educ:* Univ WVa, BS, 61, MS, 66; Ohio State Univ, DVM, 61; Tex A&M Univ, PhD(vet path), 70; Am Col Vet Path, dipl, 68. *Prof Exp:* Vet practr, North Side Vet Clin, Carlisle, Pa, 61-62; res assoc vet microbiol & path, Univ WVa, 62-65; from instr to assoc prof vet path, Col Vet Med, Tex A&M Univ, 65-72; assoc prof vet pathobiol & dir div appl path, Col Vet Med, Ohio State Univ, 72-78; asst dean res & advan studies, Sch Vet Med & Head Vet Sci, La State Univ, 78-87; dir, Ohio Agr Res & Develop Ctr & prof poultry sci, Col Vet Med, Ohio State Univ, 87-90, Prof Vet Prev Med & Fac Mem, Dept Prev Med, 91-93. *Mem:* Am Vet Med Asn; Am Col Vet Path; Am Farm Bur; Am Asn Avian Path. *Res:* Veterinary pathology; mycoplasmatacea; cancer research in animals. *Mailing Add:* Col Agr & Natural Res Univ Conn 1376 Storrs Rd Storrs CT 06269-4066

KERR, MARILYN SUE, DEVELOPMENTAL BIOLOGY. *Current Pos:* ASST PROF BIOL, SYRACUSE UNIV, 70- *Personal Data:* b Sumner, Ill. *Educ:* Gettysburg Col, BA, 59; Duke Univ, MA, 61, PhD(zool), 66. *Prof Exp:* USPHS fel vitellogenesis, Biol Div, Oak Ridge Nat Lab, 66-69, Nat Inst Child Health & Human Develop trainee biophys, 69-70. *Mem:* Am Soc Zoologists; Soc Develop Biol; AAAS; Sigma Xi. *Res:* Vitellogenesis and limb regeneration correlated with studies of hemocyte origin, differentiation and functions in arthropods; hemocyanin synthesis, its isolation and characterization. *Mailing Add:* Biol Dept Syracuse Univ 214B Lyman Hall Syracuse NY 13244-0002

KERR, MILLER H, PUBLIC HEALTH. *Current Pos:* planning & eval officer, Nat Ctr Prev Serv, 71-84, pub health adv & asst dir pub health pract, 84-89, DEP DIR, DIV DIABETES TRANSLATION, CTR DIS CONTROL & PREV, 89- *Personal Data:* b St Augustine, Fla, Aug 3, 40. *Educ:* Univ Fla, BS, 62; Univ Ga, MPA, 71. *Prof Exp:* Pub health adv, State Health Dept, NC, 62-64, Mont, 64-66, NJ, 66-67, Ga, 67-71. *Mem:* Am Pub Health Asn. *Mailing Add:* Ctr Dis Control & Prev 4428 Nantucket Cove Stone Mountain GA 30083. *E-Mail:* kerr.4044@juno.com

KERR, NORMAN STORY, developmental biology; deceased, see previous edition for last biography

KERR, PETER DONALD, GEOGRAPHY. *Current Pos:* lectr, Univ Toronto, 46-51, from asst prof to prof, 51-85, chmn dept, 68-73, assoc dean, Sch Grad Studies, 76-79, EMER PROF GEOG, UNIV TORONTO, 85- *Personal Data:* b Toronto, Ont, Apr 19, 20. *Educ:* Univ BC, BA, 41; Univ Toronto, MA, 43, PhD(geog), 50;. *Prof Exp:* Meterol officer, RCAF, 43-45; teaching

Asst, Univ Calif, Berkeley, 45-46. *Concurrent Pos:* Grantee, Defense Res Bd, 46-49, Dept Mines & Tech Surveys, 55-61, Emergency Measures Org, 62-64, Dept Treas & Econ, 66-68, Can Coun, 73-75, Hist Atlas Can Proj, 80-89; partic, Pugwash Int Conf Chem & Biol Warfare, 59; mem, Nat Adv Comt Geog Res, 67-70, Publ Comt Social Sci Res Coun, Can, 74-77; mem exec comt, Hist Atlas Can, 80- *Mem:* Asn Am Geogr; Can Asn Geogr (vpres, 59, pres, 60); Int Geog Union; Sigma Xi. *Res:* Climatology of British Columbia; industrial and urban geography of southern Ontario, especially metro Ontario; land use and industrial change in Metropolitan Toronto; changing wholesale trade in Winnipeg; changing status in Canadian ports; various aspects of wholesale trade in Canada; resource development in Canada. *Mailing Add:* Dept Geog Univ Toronto 100 St George St Toronto ON M5S 1A1 Can

KERR, RALPH OLIVER, organic chemistry; deceased, see previous edition for last biography

KERR, ROBERT LOWELL, AIRBREATHING PROPULSION, ENERGY CONVERSION & AEROSPACE POWER. *Current Pos:* CONSULT, 92- *Personal Data:* b Dayton, Ohio, Mar 31, 36; m 91, Camille J Easton; c Mary, Donald, Brian, Kelly & Kendra. *Educ:* Ohio State Univ, BS, 59; Univ Dayton, MS, 70, PhD(mech eng), 86. *Prof Exp:* Apollo-LM subsyst mgr, NASA Manned Spacecraft Ctr, Tex, 64-65; fuel cell task mgr, Aero Propulsion Lab, Wright Patterson AFB, Ohio, 59-64, develop engr, Foreign Technol Div, 65-66, aerospace engr, 66-68 & 72-73, battery task mgr, 68-72, advan develop prog mgr, 73-78, electrochem res task mgr, 78-81, asst chief scientist, 81-91. *Concurrent Pos:* Instr physics, Wilberforce Univ, 62-64; adj assoc prof mech eng, Wright State Univ, 91-92. *Mem:* Am Phys Soc. *Res:* Investigation of the electrochemistry of batteries and fuel cells such as nickel-cadmium, nickel hydrogen and lithium rechargeable batteries along with hydrogen-oxygen fuel cells; heat transfer in cells and fundamental electrochemical studies of lithium couples. *Mailing Add:* 14236 Palm St Madeira Beach FL 33708

KERR, ROBERT MCDOUGALL, TURBULENCE, NUMERICAL METHODS. *Current Pos:* SCIENTIST, NAT CTR ATMOSPHERIC RES, 83- *Personal Data:* b Harvey, Ill, Mar 22, 54; m 84; c 2. *Educ:* Univ Chicago, BA, 75, MS, 75; Cornell Univ, PhD(physics), 81. *Prof Exp:* Postdoctoral, Ames Res Ctr, NASA, 81-83 & Lawrence Livermore Nat Lab, 83-86. *Mem:* Am Phys Soc; Soc Indust & Appl Math. *Res:* Three-dimensional direct simulations to study isotropic turbulence, convective turbulence and vortex interactions; produced numerical evidence for a singularity of the three-dimensional, incompressible, Euler equations. *Mailing Add:* Nat Ctr Atmospheric Res PO Box 3000 Boulder CO 80307. Fax: 303-497-8181; *E-Mail:* kerrrobt@ncar.ucar.edu

KERR, SANDRIA NEIDUS, SCIENTIFIC PROGRAMMING. *Current Pos:* from asst prof to assoc prof, 71-82, PROF MATH, WINSTON-SALEM STATE UNIV, 82- *Personal Data:* b Youngstown, Ohio, Oct 1, 40; m 63, William; c Tamara J & Elizabeth L. *Educ:* Col Wooster, BA, 62; Bryn Mawr Col, MA, 64; Cornell Univ, PhD(math), 71. *Prof Exp:* Instr math, Col Wooster, 63; teaching asst, Dept Math, Cornell Univ, 63-67; vis lectr, Chalmers Univ Technol, Sweden, 67. *Concurrent Pos:* Collabr, Los Alamos Nat Lab, 85-92; consult, 92- *Mem:* Am Math Soc; Asn Comput Mach; Inst Elec & Electronics Engrs Comput Soc. *Res:* Analysis on infinite-dimensional manifolds; studies involving placement of students in math courses; scientific programming. *Mailing Add:* Dept Comput Sci Winston Salem State Univ 601 Martin Luther King Jr Dr Comput Sci Winston-Salem NC 27110

KERR, STRATTON H, ENTOMOLOGY. *Current Pos:* From asst entomologist to assoc entomologist, 53-68, ENTOMOLOGIST, UNIV FLA, 68- *Personal Data:* b Springfield, Mass, May 17, 24; m 48; c 2. *Educ:* Univ Mass, BS, 49; Cornell Univ, PhD(entom), 53. *Mem:* AAAS; Entom Soc Am. *Res:* Insects of turfgrass, arthropod resistance to insecticides; applied entomology. *Mailing Add:* 936 NW 40th Terr Gainesville FL 32605

KERR, SYLVIA JEAN, BIOCHEMISTRY. *Current Pos:* Asst prof surg, 70-75, ASSOC PROF BIOCHEM, UNIV COLO MED CTR, DENVER, 76- *Personal Data:* b St Louis, Mo, July 2, 41. *Educ:* Smith Col, AB, 62; Columbia Univ, PhD, 67. *Concurrent Pos:* Nat Cancer Inst career develop award, 71- *Mem:* Am Chem Soc; Am Soc Biol Chemists; Am Asn Cancer Res. *Res:* Biochemical control mechanisms; transfer RNA metabolism. *Mailing Add:* 4200 E Ninth Univ Colo Health Sci Ctr Denver CO 80262-0001. Fax: 303-270-8215

KERR, SYLVIA JOANN, DEVELOPMENTAL BIOLOGY, MICROBIOLOGY. *Current Pos:* from asst prof to assoc prof, 76-89, PROF BIOL, HAMLINE UNIV, 89- *Personal Data:* b Detroit, Mich, June 19, 41; m 65; c David & Kathleen. *Educ:* Carleton Col, BA, 63; Univ Minn, Minneapolis, MS, 66, PhD(zool), 68. *Prof Exp:* Asst prof biol, Augsburg Col, 68-71; res fel pharmacog, Univ Minn, 72, med fel cell biol, 74-75; asst prof biol, Anoka-Ramsey Community Col, Augsburg Col & Hamline Univ, 72-74. *Mem:* Sigma Xi; AAAS; Soc Develop Biol. *Res:* Developmental biology-myxomycetes; planarian regeneration; population genetics-mutant allele frequencies in cats. *Mailing Add:* Dept Biol Hamline Univ St Paul MN 55104. Fax: 612-641-2620; *E-Mail:* skerr@piper.hamline.edu

KERR, THEODORE WILLIAM, JR, entomology; deceased, see previous edition for last biography

KERR, THOMAS JAMES, MICROBIOLOGY. *Current Pos:* RETIRED. *Personal Data:* b Muskogee, Okla, Oct 7, 27; m 51; c 7. *Educ:* Okla A&M Univ, BS, 50; Okla State Univ, MS, 63; Univ Ga, PhD(microbiol), 76. *Prof Exp:* Asst to dir biol res, US Biol Warfare Ctr, Frederick, Md, 58-60, dep dir med res, 63-64; proj officer, US Army Test & Eval Command, Aberdeen, Md, 67-70; res asst microbiol, Univ Ga, 71-76, dir lab studies, 76-90. *Mem:* Am Soc Microbiol; Sigma Xi. *Res:* Biological inhibition of fusarium moniliforme various subglutinans; the casual agent of pine pitch canker; production of single cell protein from agricultural waste products. *Mailing Add:* 430 Cherokee Ridge Athens GA 30606

KERR, WARWICK ESTEVAM, GENETICS, BEE BIOLOGY. *Current Pos:* PROF GENETICS, UNIV FED UBERLANDIA, 88- *Personal Data:* b Santana de Parnaiba, Brazil, Sept 9, 22; m 56; c 7. *Educ:* Univ Sao Paulo, MSc, 48, PhD(genetics), 50. *Hon Degrees:* Prof Hon Causa, Univ Fed Amazonas, 80, UNESP, Rio Claro, 92. *Honors & Awards:* Souzandrade Gold Medal, Univ Fed Maranhao. *Prof Exp:* Biologist genetics, Grad Sch Agr, 46-48, from asst prof to assoc prof, Univ Sao Paulo, 48-58; prof biol, Col Sci UNESP-Rio-Claro, 59-64; prof genetics, Col Med, Univ Sao Paulo, 64-75; dir, Nat Res Inst Amazon, 75-79; prof biol, Fed Univ Maranhao, Sao Luis, 81-88,. *Concurrent Pos:* Rockefeller Found Fel, 51-52; Brazilian Nat Res Coun grants, USDA, 61-66; State of Sao Paulo Res Found grants, 65-67; pres, State Univ Maranhao, 87-88; hon pres, Brazilian Asn Advan Sci. *Mem:* Foreign assoc Nat Acad Sci; Brazilian Genetics Soc (pres, 64-66 & 94-96); Brazilian Soc Advan Sci (pres, 69-73); Soc Study Evolution. *Res:* Bee genetics; cytology and evolution; plant breeding. *Mailing Add:* Dept Genetics & Biochem Univ Fed Uberlandia Uberlandia 38400-902 Brazil

KERR, WILLIAM, REACTOR SAFETY, REACTOR SHIELDING. *Current Pos:* RETIRED. *Personal Data:* b Sawyer, Kans, Aug 19, 19; m 45; c 3. *Educ:* Univ Tenn, BS, 42, MS, 47; Univ Mich, PhD(elec eng), 54. *Honors & Awards:* Arthur Holly Compton Award, Am Nuclear Soc, 74. *Prof Exp:* Asst prof elec eng, Univ Tenn, 47-48; asst prof elec eng, Univ Mich, Ann Arbor, 53-56, from assoc prof to prof nuclear eng, 56-89, from assoc dir to dir, Mich Mem Phoenix Proj, 60-89, chmn, Dept Nuclear Eng, 61-74, dir, Off Energy Res, 77-84. *Concurrent Pos:* Consult, Atomic Power Develop Assocs, 54-59, Union Carbide Nuclear Corp, 54 & USAID, 56-65; proj supvr nuclear energy proj, USAID, 56-65; pres bd dir, Assoc Midwest Univs, 65; mem adv comt reactor safeguards, US Nuclear Regulatory Comn, 72-92; mem gov task force on nuclear waste disposal, State of Mich, 76-84. *Mem:* Fel Am Nuclear Soc; sr mem Inst Elec & Electronics Engrs; Am Soc Eng Educ; Sigma Xi. *Res:* Application of telemetering to power systems; autoradiography; nuclear reactor system dynamics; reactor control; reactor shielding; reactor safety analysis. *Mailing Add:* 3034 Phoenix Mem Lab North Campus Univ Mich Ann Arbor MI 48109

KERR, WILLIAM B, HOSPITAL ADMINISTRATION. *Current Pos:* asst dir, 70-74, adminr, Inpatient Serv, 74-77, DIR MED CTR, UNIV CALIF, SAN FRANCISCO, 77- *Personal Data:* b Chicago, Ill, Dec 21, 43; c 3. *Educ:* Loyola Univ, BS, 64; Univ Minn, MS, 69. *Prof Exp:* US Army Mil Intel, 65-67; admin resident, Comnr Off, New York City Dept Hosps, 68-69, asst comnr, 69-70; exec asst hosp admin, New York City Health & Hosp Corp, 69-70. *Concurrent Pos:* Lectr, Inst Health Policy Studies, Univ Calif, San Francisco. *Mem:* Inst Med-Nat Acad Sci; Asn Am Med Col; Am Hosp Asn. *Mailing Add:* 825 Albatross Novato CA 94945

KERR, WILLIAM CLAYTON, COMPUTER SIMULATION. *Current Pos:* from asst prof to assoc prof, 70-83, PROF PHYSICS, WAKE FOREST UNIV, 83- *Personal Data:* b Steubenville, Ohio, Mar 8, 40; m 63, Sandria Neidus; c Tamara & Elizabeth. *Educ:* Col Wooster, BA, 62; Cornell Univ, PhD(theoret physics), 67. *Prof Exp:* Res assoc physics, Inst Theoret Physics, Chalmers Univ Technol, Sweden, 67-68 & Solid State Sci Div, Argonne Nat Lab, 68-70. *Concurrent Pos:* Vis scientist, Argonne Nat Lab, 71, 72 & 80, Chalmers Univ Technol, 74, Univ Paris, 76-77 & Los Alamos Nat Lab, 81, 86, 87, 88, 91, 92 & 94; collabr, Los Alamos Nat Lab, 84-85 & 95-96. *Mem:* Am Phys Soc; Am Asn Physics Teachers; Sigma Xi. *Res:* Theory of nonlinear systems; computer simulation of nonlinear, low dimensional systems of interest in statistical physics, including structural phase transitions, sine-Gordon chains and biological molecules. *Mailing Add:* Dept Physics Wake Forest Univ Box 7507 Winston-Salem NC 27109. Fax: 910-759-6142; *E-Mail:* wck@wfu.edu

KERREBROCK, JACK LEO, AERONAUTICS, ASTRONAUTICS. *Current Pos:* from asst prof to prof, Mass Inst Technol, 60-75, dir, Space Propulsion Lab, 62-76, Gas Turbine Lab, 68-78, head dept, 78-81 & 83-85, assoc dean eng, 85-90, Richard Cockburn Maclaurin prof aeronaut & astronaut, 75-, EMER PROF, MASS INST TECHNOL. *Personal Data:* b Los Angeles, Calif, Feb 6, 28; m 53; c 3. *Educ:* Ore State Col, BS, 50; Yale Univ, MS, 51; Calif Inst Technol, PhD(mech eng), 56. *Honors & Awards:* Dryden Lectr, Am Inst Aeronaut & Astronaut, 80. *Prof Exp:* Res engr, Oak Ridge Nat Lab, 56-58; sr res fel, Calif Inst Technol, 58-60. *Concurrent Pos:* Chmn, Sci & Technol Adv Group, USAF Sci Adv Bd; mem, Nat Res Coun Aeronaut & Space Eng Bd; mem, Am Soc Mech Engrs Turbomach Comt; NASA Adv Bd Aircraft Fuel Conserv Technol; hon prof, Beijing Inst Aeronaut & Astronaut, China, 80; assoc adminr, Off Aeronaut & Space Technol, NASA, 80; mem, Nat Comn Space, 85; Fairchild scholar, Calif Inst Tech, 90. *Mem:* Nat Acad Eng; fel Am Inst Aeronaut & Astronaut; fel Explorers Club; Am Phys Soc; sr mem Am Astronaut Soc; fel Am Acad Arts & Sci. *Res:* Aircraft propulsion; space propulsion and power generation systems; magnetohydrodynamics; nuclear rockets. *Mailing Add:* Prof Aeronaut & Astronaut Mass Inst Technol Rm 31-268 Cambridge MA 02139

KERRI, KENNETH D, CIVIL & SANITARY ENGINEERING. *Current Pos:* Assoc prof, 59-68, PROF CIVIL ENG, CALIF STATE UNIV, SACRAMENTO, 68- *Personal Data:* b Napa, Calif, Apr 25, 34; m 58, Judith Reeves; c Christopher & Kathleen. *Educ:* Ore State Univ, BS, 56, PhD(civil eng), 65; Univ Calif, Berkeley, MS, 59. *Honors & Awards:* Collection Syst Award, Water Pollution Control Fedn, 77. *Concurrent Pos:* Fac res award, Calif State Univ, Sacramento, 69; pres, Nat Environ Training Asn, 79-80, Asn Bds Cert, 83 & Calif Water Pollution Fedn, 83-84. *Mem:* Water Pollution Control Fedn; Am Soc Civil Engrs; Am Water Works Asn; Am Soc Eng Educ. *Res:* Water quality economics; training manuals for operators of water and wastewater facilities. *Mailing Add:* Dept Civil Eng Calif State Univ 6000 J St Sacramento CA 95819-6025

KERRICK, DERRILL M, PETROLOGY, GEOCHEMISTRY. *Current Pos:* from asst prof to assoc prof petrol, 69-79, chmn geochem & mineral grad prog, 78-83, PROF PETROL, PA STATE UNIV, 79-, PROF GEOPHYSICS, 92- *Personal Data:* b Santa Cruz, Calif, Dec 27, 40; m 61; c 3. *Educ:* San Jose State Col, BS, 63; Univ Calif, Berkeley, PhD(geol), 68. *Prof Exp:* Lectr geol, Victoria Univ Manchester, 67-69. *Concurrent Pos:* Assoc ed, Geochimica et Cosmochimica Acta. *Mem:* Fel Mineral Soc Am; Geochem Soc. *Res:* Laboratory and field investigations of metamorphic reactions and stability relations of metamorphic assemblages. *Mailing Add:* Dept Geophysics Pa State Univ University Park PA 16802-2713

KERRICK, WALLACE GLENN LEE, PHYSIOLOGY, BIOPHYSICS. *Current Pos:* assoc prof, 81-83, PROF PHYSIOL & BIOPHYS & MOLECULAR & CELLULAR PHARMACOL, UNIV MIAMI, 83- *Educ:* Univ Puget Sound, Tacoma, BS, 61; Univ Wash, Seattle, PhD(physiol & biophys), 71. *Prof Exp:* Postdoctoral fel, Dept Physiol & Biophys, Univ Wash, 71-72, actg asst prof, 72-74, from asst prof to assoc prof, 74-81. *Concurrent Pos:* Lectr, Univ Calif, San Diego, 76, Wash State Univ, 77, Univ Cincinnati, 80, Wash Univ, St Louis, 85 & Univ Calgary, 88; res grants, Muscular Dystrophy Asn, 82-91, Am Heart Asn, 82-92, NIH, 87; mem, Nat Peer Rev, Am Heart Asn, 86-. *Mem:* Fedn Am Socs Exp Biol; Biophys Soc; Am Heart Asn; Sigma Xi. *Res:* Mechanism of cardiac muscle regulation by troponin; effects of weightlessness on physiological and biochemical properties of single muscle cells; author of numerous technical publications. *Mailing Add:* Dept Physiol & Biophys Univ Miami Sch Med PO Box 016430 Miami FL 33136. *Fax:* 305-547-5931

KERRIDGE, KENNETH A, MEDICINAL CHEMISTRY, ORGANIC CHEMISTRY. *Current Pos:* ASSOC DIR LIT SERV, BRISTOL-MYERS SQUIBB CO, 71- *Personal Data:* b London, Eng, Mar 26, 28. *Educ:* Univ London, BPharm, 51, PhD(med chem), 55. *Prof Exp:* Res chemist, Smith & Nephew Res Ltd, 55-57; res chemist, Parke, Davis & Co, Eng, 57-60; sr org chemist, Arthur D Little, Inc, 60-61; sr res chemist, Armour Pharmaceut Co, 61-71. *Concurrent Pos:* Fel, Sch Pharm, Univ Md, 60. *Mem:* Am Chem Soc; Royal Inst Chem; fel Chem Soc; fel Pharmaceut Soc Gt Brit; Am Inst Chem. *Res:* Synthetic antibacterials, antitubercular, antifungal and antitumor agents; central nervous system stimulants and depressants; cardiovascular agents. *Mailing Add:* PO Box 69 Meriden CT 06450

KERSCHNER, JEAN, GENETICS. *Current Pos:* RETIRED. *Personal Data:* b Baltimore, Md, May 31, 22. *Educ:* Hood Col, AB, 43; Univ Pa, PhD(zool), 50. *Prof Exp:* Chemist, E I du Pont de Nemours & Co, 43-45; lab asst, Univ Pa, 45-46; asst prof biol, Elmira Col, 50-51; histologist, Army Chem Ctr, 51-52; from asst prof to assoc prof, Western Md Col, 52-68, prof biol, 68-80. *Concurrent Pos:* Fac fel, NSF, Columbia Univ, 60-61. *Mem:* Genetics Soc Am; Sigma Xi. *Res:* X-ray induced mutations in Drosophila. *Mailing Add:* 231 Geisky Creek Rd Hayesville NC 28904

KERSEY, JOHN H, LEUKEMIA. *Current Pos:* PROF LAB MED, PATH & PEDIAT, UNIV SCH MED, UNIV MINN, 77- *Personal Data:* b Apr 22, 38. *Educ:* Univ Minn, MD, 64. *Mem:* Am Asn Cancer Res; Am Soc Hemat; Am Soc Clin Investrs; Am Asn Pathologists. *Res:* Lymphoma. *Mailing Add:* Dept Cancer Ctr Univ Minn Health Ctr Box 86 420 Delaware St SE Minneapolis MN 55455-0392. *Fax:* 612-624-8965

KERSEY, ROBERT LEE, JR, ANALYTICAL CHEMISTRY. *Current Pos:* chemist, 53-65, spec asst to dir res, 65-70, mgr prod develop, 70-75, dir res, 75-78, chief res officer, 81-87, VPRES, LIGGETT & MYERS TOBACCO CO, 78-, CONSULT, 89- *Personal Data:* b Richmond, Va, Nov 6, 22; m 43. *Educ:* Univ Richmond, BS, 48. *Prof Exp:* Asst proj chemist, Standard Oil Co, Ind, 48-53. *Mem:* Am Chem Soc; Inst Food Technol. *Res:* Tobacco and tobacco products research and development. *Mailing Add:* 2520 Ross Rd Durham NC 27703

KERSHAW, DAVID STANLEY, THEORETICAL PHYSICS, COMPUTER SCIENCE. *Current Pos:* PHYSICIST LASER FUSION, LAWRENCE LIVERMORE LAB, UNIV CALIF, 74- *Personal Data:* b Missoula, Mont, May 20, 43; m 66, Winifred Shaw; c Miriam, Jeremy & Elizabeth. *Educ:* Harvard Univ, BA, 65; Univ Calif, Berkeley, PhD(physics), 70. *Prof Exp:* Fel theoret partical physics, Stanford Linear Accelerator Ctr, 70-72 & Dept Physics & Astron, Univ Md, College Park, 72-74. *Mem:* Am Phys Soc. *Res:* Computer simulation of the physics of laser fusion. *Mailing Add:* 1827 Newcastle Ct Walnut Creek CA 94595. *E-Mail:* dsk@icf.llnl.gov

KERSHAW, KENNETH ANDREW, PLANT ECOLOGY, LICHENOLOGY. *Current Pos:* PROF BIOL, MCMASTER UNIV, 69- *Personal Data:* b Morecambe, Eng, Sept 5, 30; m 67; c 3. *Educ:* Manchester Univ, BS, 52; Univ Wales, PhD(ecol), 57, DSc, 68. *Prof Exp:* Lectr, Imp Col, Univ London, 57-63; sr lectr, Secondment to Ahmadu Bell Univ, N Nigeria, 63-65; lectr, Imp Col, Univ London, 65-68. *Mem:* Brit Lichen Soc; fel Royal Soc Can. *Res:* Ecology of northern plant systems with special emphasis on the interaction of microclimate and plant physiology; lichen physiology. *Mailing Add:* 601 Old Dundas Rd Rm 3401 Ancaster ON L9G 3J3 Can

KERSHENBAUM, AARON, ALGORITHMS, NETWORK DESIGN. *Current Pos:* PROF COMPUT SCI, POLYTECH UNIV, BROOKLYN NY, 84- *Personal Data:* b Brooklyn, NY, Oct 9, 48; m 70; c 2. *Educ:* Polytech Inst NY, BS & MS, 70, PhD(elec eng), 76. *Prof Exp:* Vpres software, Network Anal Group, 69-78; from asst prof to prof elec & comput sci, Polytech Univ, 78-90; res mgr, IBM, 90-97. *Concurrent Pos:* Assoc ed, J Telecommun Networks, 83-85, Networks, 83-85; dir, Network Design Lab, Polytech Univ, 84- *Mem:* Asn Comput Mach; Inst Elec & Electronics Engrs. *Mailing Add:* Dept Comput Sci Polytech Univ 333 Jay St Brooklyn NY 11201

KERSHENSTEIN, JOHN CHARLES, PHYSICS, ELECTROOPTICS. *Current Pos:* Fel physics, 68-69, RES PHYSICIST, US NAVAL RES LAB, 69- *Personal Data:* b New York, NY, Sept 23, 41; m 68; c 1. *Educ:* Georgetown Univ, BS, 64, MS, 67, PhD(physics), 69. *Mailing Add:* 11842 Clara Way Fairfax Station VA 22039

KERSHNER, CARL JOHN, PHYSICAL CHEMISTRY, RADIOCHEMISTRY. *Current Pos:* VPRES, FEMTO-TECH, INC, 86- *Personal Data:* b Lima, Ohio, Dec 15, 34; m 58; c 2. *Educ:* Capital Univ, BS, 56; Univ Ohio, PhD(inorg chem), 61. *Prof Exp:* Sr res chemist, Monsanto Res Corp, 61-64, group leader radiochem res, 64-66, sect mgr, 66-68, sr res specialist, 68-70, sci fel, Mound Lab, 70-79, sr sci fel, 79-85. *Concurrent Pos:* Adj prof, Ohio State Univ, 80-81. *Mem:* Am Inst Physics; Am Chem Soc; Am Nuclear Soc; Sigma Xi. *Res:* High temperature radiochemical research; syntheses and physical property determinations; isotope separation; radioactive waste and emission control; laser photochemistry; radiation detection instrumentation. *Mailing Add:* 2123 Timberidge Circle Dayton OH 45459-1342

KERST, A(L) FRED, ORGANIC CHEMISTRY, PHYSICAL CHEMISTRY. *Current Pos:* vpres res & develop, 77-84, vpres mkt, 84-89, PRES, CALGON CORP, 89- *Personal Data:* b Greeley, Colo, June 3, 40; m 62; c 3. *Educ:* Colo State Univ, BS, 62, MS, 63; Harvard Univ, PhD(chem), 67. *Prof Exp:* Sr chemist, Monsanto Co, 67-68; mgr, Gates Rubber Co, 69-71; vpres res & develop, Mich Chem Corp, 71-76, Velsicol Chem Corp, 76-77. *Concurrent Pos:* Eval Panel, Nat Bur Standards Ctr Fire Res, 76-79. *Mem:* Am Chem Soc. *Res:* Chemistry of phosphorus compounds, flame retardants, polymers; agriculture pesticides and industrial biocides; water treatment chemicals. *Mailing Add:* 1042 Printers Pl Pittsburgh PA 15237

KERSTEIN, MORRIS D, VASCULAR TRAUMA. *Current Pos:* DEISSLER PROF & CHMN, DEPT SURG, HAHNEMANN UNIV, PHILADELPHIA, PA, 88- *Personal Data:* b Trenton, NJ, Jan 13, 38; m 80; c 1. *Educ:* Colgate Univ, AB, 59; Chicago Med Sch, 63. *Prof Exp:* Instr surg, Tufts Univ Sch Med, 70-71; from asst prof to assoc prof surg, Yale Univ Sch Med, 71-77; assoc prof, surg, Pritzker Sch Med, Univ Chicago, 77-79; prof surg, Tulane Univ Sch Med, 79-88, assoc dean, acad affairs & dir, grad & postgrad prog, 86-88. *Concurrent Pos:* Resident surg serv, Boston City Hosp, 69-70, chief resident, 70-71; staff surgeon, Vet Admin Hosp, West Haven, Conn, 71-77; chief, peripheral vascular surg, Michael Reese Hosp, Chicago, 77-79; surgeon, 81-; clin prof, surg, Tulane Univ Sch Med, 83- *Mem:* Am Col Surgeons; Am Heart Asn; AMA; Soc Vascular Surg; Am Surg Asn; Soc Univ Surgeons. *Res:* Prostoglandin metabolism in human vessels; vascular trauma; non-invasive laboratory. *Mailing Add:* Dept Surg Hahnemann Univ Broad & Vine Philadelphia PA 19102-1192

KERSTEN, MILES S(TOKES), ENGINEERING. *Current Pos:* from asst prof to prof, 45-78, EMER PROF SOIL MECH, HWYS & SOILS, UNIV MINN, MINNEAPOLIS, 78- *Personal Data:* b St Paul, Minn, Aug 12, 13; m 38; c Cynthia K (Doran) & Thomas L. *Educ:* Univ Minn, BCE, 34, MS, 36, PhD(hwys, soils), 45. *Honors & Awards:* Harold R Peyton Award, Am Soc Civil Eng, 89. *Prof Exp:* Soils engr, State Hwy Dept, Minn, 36-37; instr hwys & soils, Univ Minn, 37-44; spec investr, Hwy Res Bd, Washington, DC, 44-45. *Mem:* Hon mem Am Soc Civil Eng; Am Soc Eng Educ; Nat Asn Prof Engrs. *Res:* Thermal conductivity of soil; soil stabilization; sub-grade moisture conditions and their role in flexible pavement design; airport engineering; general civil engineering; surveying and mapping. *Mailing Add:* 4300 W River Pkwy Apt 619 Minneapolis MN 55406-3662

KERSTEN, ROBERT D(ONAVON), ENGINEERING EDUCATION & WATER RESOURCES. *Current Pos:* dir univ res, 68-69, dean, Col Eng, 68-87, PROF ENG, UNIV CENT FLA, 68- *Personal Data:* b Carlinville, Ill, Jan 30, 27; m 50; c Susan & John. *Educ:* Okla State Univ, BS, 49, MS, 56; Northwestern Univ, PhD(fluid mech), 61. *Prof Exp:* Hydraul engr, US Dept Interior, 49-53; res assoc civil eng, Okla State Univ, 53-56, asst prof, 56; res engr, Jersey Prod Res Co, Stand Oil NJ, 56-57; from asst prof to assoc prof eng, Ariz State Univ, 57-60, prof civil eng & chmn, 60-68. *Concurrent Pos:* Mem, NASA-NSF Conf Lunar Explor, 62, Flight Safety Found, 62, Col Bus Exchange Prog Found Econ Ed, 63 & NASA-Cambridge Conf Explor Mars & Venus, 65; vis scholar, Stanford Univ, 66; actg dir, Fla Solar Energy Ctr, 75; chmn bd trustees, Inst Cert Eng Technicians, 78-80; Fla Bd Prof Engrs,

80-86; mem, Eng Accreditation Comn, 82-89; mem, US Coun Int Eng Practice, 89-93; mem, Pan Am Union Eng Socs, Eng Educ Comt, 86-, vpres, 92- *Mem:* AAAS; Am Soc Eng Educ; Am Soc Civil Engrs; Nat Soc Prof Engrs (vpres, 84-85); Sigma Xi; Nat Coun Examr Eng & Surv; Fla Eng Soc (pres, 93-94). *Res:* Fluid mechanics, including fluid turbulence, turbulent diffusion, non-Newtonian flow, two phase flow; water resources engineering; applied mathematics. *Mailing Add:* 590 Demmerich Dr Maitland FL 32751. *Fax:* 407-823-3315

KERSTETTER, REX E, PLANT PHYSIOLOGY. *Current Pos:* from asst prof to assoc prof, 67-80, PROF BIOL, FURMAN UNIV, 80- *Personal Data:* b Ashland, Kans, Nov 22, 38; div; c Kelvin T & Derek E. *Educ:* Ft Hays Kans State Col, BS, 60, MS, 63; Fla State Univ, PhD(plant physiol), 67. *Prof Exp:* Instr biol, Fla State Univ, 67. *Mem:* AAAS; Am Soc Plant Physiologists; Bot Soc Am; Sigma Xi. *Res:* Plant hormone physiology; plant tissue culture; peroxidase isoenzymes. *Mailing Add:* Dept Biol Furman Univ Greenville SC 29613. *Fax:* 864-294-2058; *E-Mail:* kerstetter@furman.edu

KERSTETTER, THEODORE HARVEY, FISH PHYSIOLOGY, ELECTROLYTE BALANCE. *Current Pos:* dir, Marine Lab & Sea Grant Prog, 74-79, from asst prof to assoc prof, 70-79, PROF ZOOL, HUMBOLDT STATE UNIV, 79-, CHMN, DEPT FISHERIES, 92- *Personal Data:* b Milwaukee, Wis, Dec 16, 30; div; c 2. *Educ:* Univ Nev, Reno, BS, 59; Wash State Univ, MS, 62, PhD(zoo physiol), 69. *Prof Exp:* Instr biol, Peninsula Col, 63-64; NIH fel, Wash State Univ, 69-70. *Concurrent Pos:* Dir, Marine Lab & Sea Grant Prog, 74-79. *Mem:* Am Inst Fisheries Res Biologists. *Res:* Water and ion balance in lower vertebrates; mechanisms of ion transport through epithelia; fish physiology; heavy metal toxicity in fish. *Mailing Add:* PO Box 65259 Port Ludlow WA 98365. *E-Mail:* kerstettert@axe.humboldt.edu

KERTAMUS, NORBERT JOHN, FUEL & CHEMICAL ENGINEERING. *Current Pos:* SR RES SCIENTIST, SOUTHERN CALIF EDISON, 79- *Personal Data:* b Murray City, Utah, Oct 12, 32; m 56; c 3. *Educ:* Univ Utah, BS, 60, PhD(fuels eng), 64. *Prof Exp:* Res engr, Phillips Petrol Co, 64-66; sr res chemist nuclear fuels, Idaho Nuclear Co, 66-70; res specialist chem & combustion, Babcock & Wilcox Co, 70-75; sr process engr, C F Braun Engrs, 75-79. *Mem:* Am Chem Soc; Am Inst Chem Engrs. *Res:* Conversion of coal to gases and/or liquids; hydrogen processing and catalysis; combustion. *Mailing Add:* 1027 Entrada Way Glendora CA 91740-2227

KERTESZ, ANDREW (ENDRE), VISION, BIOMEDICAL ENGINEERING. *Current Pos:* PROF ELEC ENG, PSYCHOL & BIOMED ENG, NORTHWESTERN UNIV, EVANSTON, 72-, CHMN BIOMED ENG, 83- *Personal Data:* b Budapest, Hungary, Oct 10, 38; US citizen; m 63; c 2. *Educ:* McGill Univ, BEng, 63; Northwestern Univ, Evanston, MS, 66, PhD(bioeng), 69. *Prof Exp:* Asst prof elec eng, Univ Pittsburgh, 69-72. *Concurrent Pos:* Sr res fel appl sci, Calif Inst Technol & prin investr, USPHS res grant, 70-; NIH res career award, 74; clin assoc ophthal, Evanston Hosp, 77. *Mem:* Inst Elec & Electronics Engrs; Asn Res Vision & Ophthal; Biomed Eng Soc; Optical Soc Am. *Res:* Human binocular information processing; binocular vision. *Mailing Add:* Biomed Eng Dept Northwestern Univ 2145 Sheridan Rd Evanston IL 60208-3107

KERTESZ, JEAN CONSTANCE, PHARMACEUTICAL CHEMISTRY. *Current Pos:* Res asst biochem, Sch Med, 65-66, res assoc biomed chem, 68-77, ASST RES PROF, SCH PHARM, UNIV SOUTHERN CALIF, 77- *Personal Data:* b New York, NY, Sept 3, 43. *Educ:* Northwestern Univ, BA, 63; Univ Southern Calif, PhD(pharmaceut chem), 70. *Mem:* Am Chem Soc; Intra-Sci Res Found; Int Soc Magnetic Resonance; Sigma Xi. *Res:* Free radical intermediates in biological systems; utilization of electron spin resonance techniques for biomedical applications; molecular mechanisms of radiation damage; protection processes; carcinogenesis. *Mailing Add:* 2329 W Second St Apt 7 Los Angeles CA 90057

KERTESZ, MIKLOS, CHEMISTRY, QUANTUM CHEMISTRY OF SOLIDS & POLYMERS. *Current Pos:* PROF, DEPT CHEM, GEORGETOWN UNIV, 83- *Personal Data:* b Budapest, Hungary, July 15, 48; m 69, Eva Tarnok; c Anna & Kata. *Educ:* Eotvos L Univ, Budapest, dipl, 71, Dr rer nat, 79; Hungarian Acad Sci, Cand phys sci, 78. *Prof Exp:* Res scientist, Cent Res Inst, Hungarian Acad Sci, 71-79; res fel, Quantum Theory Proj, Univ Fla, 79-80 & Dept Chem, Cornell Univ, 80; sr scientist, Cent Res Inst, Hungarian Acad Sci, 81; res assoc, Dept Chem, Cornell Univ, 82-83. *Concurrent Pos:* Camille & Henry Dreyfus teacher-scholar, 84-89. *Mem:* Am Chem Soc; Am Phys Soc. *Res:* Theoretical solid state chemistry; structure and electronic structure of conducting polymers; vibrational spectrum of polymers. *Mailing Add:* Dept Chem Georgetown Univ Washington DC 20057-1227. *Fax:* 202-687-6209; *E-Mail:* kertesz@guvax.georgetown.edu

KERTH, LEROY THOMAS, PHYSICS. *Current Pos:* Asst, Lawrence Berkeley Lab, Univ Calif, 50-57, res physicist, 57-65, assoc dean, Col Lett & Sci, 66-70, prof, 65-93, EMER PROF PHYS, LAWRENCE BERKELEY LAB, UNIV CALIF, 93- *Personal Data:* b Visalia, Calif, Nov 23, 28; m 50, Ruth L Littlefield; c Norman L, Randall T, Christine G & Bradley N. *Educ:* Univ Calif, AB, 50, PhD, 57. *Concurrent Pos:* Assoc dir & div head comput sci, 86-87, assoc lab dir gen sci, 87-89; assoc lab dir, Sci & Tech Resources, 89-91. *Mem:* Fel Am Phys Soc. *Res:* High energy physics; weak interactions. *Mailing Add:* Dept Physics Lawrence Berkeley Lab Univ Calif Berkeley CA 94720

KERTZ, ALOIS FRANCIS, ANIMAL NUTRITION. *Current Pos:* res nutritionist, 73-75, mgr res, dairy res dept, 75-85, RES MGR, RUMINANT RES DEPT, PURINA MILLS INC, 85- *Personal Data:* b Bloomsdale, Mo, Sept 15, 45; m 69; c 4. *Educ:* Univ Mo-Columbia, BS, 67, MS, 68; Cornell Univ, PhD(animal nutrit), 74. *Prof Exp:* Nutrit officer, US Army Natick Labs, 68-69; food supply & mgt officer, US Army Depot, Sattahip, Thailand, 69-70; res asst animal nutrit, Cornell Univ, 70-73. *Mem:* Am Dairy Sci Asn; Am Soc Animal Sci; AAAS; Nutrit Today Soc; Am Inst Nutrit. *Res:* Efficiency of nitrogen and energy utilization by calves and dairy cattle; evaluation and utilization of common feedstuffs and other by-products. *Mailing Add:* Purina Mills Inc PO Box 66812 St Louis MO 63166-6812. *Fax:* 314-768-4433

KERTZ, GEORGE J, MATHEMATICS, COMPUTER SCIENCE. *Current Pos:* from asst prof to assoc prof, 66-78, PROF MATH, UNIV TOLEDO, 78- *Personal Data:* b Bloomsdale, Mo, Dec 10, 33; m 68. *Educ:* Cardinal Glennon Col, BA, 55; St Louis Univ, MA, 63, PhD(math), 66; Univ Mich, MSE, 78. *Prof Exp:* Mem staff, Int Bus Mach Corp, 58-60. *Mem:* Asn Comput Mach; Math Asn Am. *Res:* Database. *Mailing Add:* Univ Toledo Toledo OH 43606-3390

KERWAR, SURESH, molecular biology, for more information see previous edition

KERWIN, EDWARD MICHAEL, JR, ACOUSTICS. *Current Pos:* consult acoust, 54-67, SR CONSULT, INC, 67- *Personal Data:* b Oak Park, Ill, Apr 20, 27; m 53; c 9. *Educ:* Mass Inst Technol, SB & SM, 50, ScD(elec eng, acoustics), 54. *Prof Exp:* Consult acoustics, Bolt Beranek & Newman, Inc, 50-54; asst elec eng, Mass Inst Technol, 50-54. *Concurrent Pos:* Assoc staff, Peter Bent Brigham Hosp, Boston, 72-74. *Mem:* Fel Acoust Soc Am; Soc Indust & Appl Math; sr mem Inst Elec & Electronics Engrs. *Res:* Underwater sound; noise and vibration control; vibration damping; sound radiation and transmission. *Mailing Add:* 3 Legion Rd Weston MA 02193

KERWIN, JOHN LARKIN, PHYSICS. *Current Pos:* lectr, Laval Univ, 46, from asst prof to prof physics, 48-80, chmn dept, 61-67, vdean fac sci, 67-68, acad vrector, 69-71, rector, 72-77, EMER PROF, LAVAL UNIV, 92- *Personal Data:* b Quebec, Que, June 22, 24; m 50, Maria Guadalupe Turcot; c Lupita, Alan, Larkin, Terence, Rosa Maria, Gregory, Timothy & Guillermina. *Educ:* St Francis Xavier Univ, BSc, 44; Mass Inst Technol, MSc, 46; Laval Univ, DSc, 49. *Hon Degrees:* LLD, St Francis Xavier Univ, 70, Univ Toronto, 73, Concordia Univ, 79, Univ Alta, 83, Dalhousie Univ, 83; DSc, Univ BC, 73, McGill Univ, 74, Mem Univ & DCL, Bishops Univ, 78, Univ Ottawa, 81, Royal Mil Col, Kingston, 82, Univ Winnipeg, 83, Univ Windsor, 84, Univ Moncton, 85. *Honors & Awards:* Gov Gen Medal, 44; Laureate of Lit & Sci Competition of Prov of Que, 51; Pariseau Medal, Fr-Can Asn Advan Sci, 65; Centenary Medal, Romania, 67; Gold Medal, Can Asn Physicists, 69; Companion, Order Can, 80; Gold Medal, Can Coun Prof Engrs, 82; National Order Quebec, 88. *Prof Exp:* Pres, Nat Res Coun Can, 80-89; pres, Can Space Agency, 89-92. *Concurrent Pos:* Mem, Defence Res Bd Can, 71-77; mem standing comt int rels, Nat Res Coun Can, 72-80; pres, Int Union Pure & Appl Physics; mem bd dirs, Can-France-Hawaii Telescope Corp, Nat Res Coun Can, 73-78; pres, Asn Univs & Cols Can, 74; Can rep, working group res & develop, Int Econ Summit, 82- *Mem:* Am Phys Soc; Can Asn Physicists (vpres, 53, pres, 54); Fr-Can Asn Advan Sci; fel Royal Soc Can (pres, 76); Nat Sci & Eng Coun Can (vpres, 78-80); fel Royal Soc Arts; fel AAAS; fel Am Inst Physics; Can Acad Eng (vpres, 87, pres, 89). *Res:* Mass spectrometry; atomic and molecular structure. *Mailing Add:* 2166 Parc Bourbonniere Sillery PQ G1T 1B4 Can

KERWIN, JOSEPH PETER, ASTRONAUTICAL ENGINEERING, MEDICAL & HEALTH SCIENCES. *Current Pos:* astronaut, NASA, 65, mem, Skylab 2 Crew, 73, rep, Australia, 82-83, MGR, EVA SYSTS, LOCKHEED MISSILES & SPACE CO, NASA, 87-, MGR HOUSTON MANNED PROGS, 90- *Personal Data:* b Oak Park, Ill, Feb 19, 32; c 3. *Educ:* Col Holy Cross, BA, 53; Northwestern Univ, MD, 57. *Prof Exp:* Surgeon, USN, 59; aviator, 62. *Concurrent Pos:* Dir Space-Life Sci, 84-87. *Res:* Space exploration; medical sciences. *Mailing Add:* 1802 Royal Fern Ct Houston TX 77062

KERWIN, RICHARD MARTIN, BACTERIOLOGY. *Current Pos:* RETIRED. *Personal Data:* b West Chester, Pa, Apr 5, 22; m 57; c 3. *Educ:* Dartmouth Col, AB, 47; Univ NH, MS, 49; Pa State Univ, PhD(bact), 56. *Prof Exp:* Sr res scientist bact, Wyeth Labs Div, Am Home Prod Corp, 52-75; consult, 75-85; instr, Dublin Sch, Dublin, NH, 78-88, head Sci Dept, 83-86. *Mem:* Am Chem Soc; Am Soc Microbiologists; Soc Indust Microbiologists; Sigma Xi. *Res:* Antibiotics; screening new antibiotics; bacterial fermentation products; microbiological production of enzymes and steroids; anti-cancer research. *Mailing Add:* Box 117 Hancock NH 03449

KERWIN, WILLIAM J(AMES), ELECTRICAL ENGINEERING, PHYSICS. *Current Pos:* prof elec eng, 69-86, EMER PROF ELEC & COMPUT ENG, 86- *Personal Data:* b Portage, Wis, Sept 27, 22; m 47, Madolyn Lyons; c Dorothy, Deborah & David. *Educ:* Univ Redlands, BS, 48; Stanford Univ, MS, 54, PhD(elec eng), 67. *Honors & Awards:* Centennial Medal, Inst Elec & Electronics Engrs, 84. *Prof Exp:* Aeronaut res scientist, Nat Adv Comt Aeronaut & NASA, Ames Res Ctr, 48-62; head, Electronics Dept, Stanford Linear Accelerator Ctr, 62; chief, Space Tech Br, Ames Res Ctr, NASA, 62-64; chief, Electronics Res Br, 64-69. *Concurrent Pos:* Lectr, Stanford Univ, 56-61 & 68; asst prof, San Jose State Col, 63-68; NASA res awards, 70 & 75. *Mem:* Fel Inst Elec & Electronics Engrs; AAAS. *Res:* Network and circuit theory, especially synthesis of active resistance-capacitance networks; DC-DC power conversion; switched-mode converters. *Mailing Add:* 1981 W Shalimar Way Tucson AZ 85704

KERZMAN, NORBERTO LUIS MARIA, ANALYSIS, COMPLEX VARIABLES. *Current Pos:* assoc prof, 79-82, PROF MATH, UNIV NC, CHAPEL HILL, 82- *Personal Data:* b Buenos Aires, Arg, Feb 1, 43. *Educ:* Univ Buenos Aires, Lic, 66; NY Univ, PhD(math), 70. *Prof Exp:* Asst prof math, Princeton Univ, 70-73; asst prof, Mass Inst Technol, 73-76, assoc prof, 76-79. *Concurrent Pos:* Vis mem staff, Gottingen, Munster, Florence, Paris, Marseille, Grenoble, Stockholm, Amsterdam, Zurich, Buenes Aires, Mex; Sloan fel, 73-75. *Mem:* Am Math Soc. *Res:* Complex analysis in particular several complex variables, involving methods of partial differential equations and singular integrals; conformal mapping. *Mailing Add:* Dept Math Univ NC Chapel Hill NC 27599-3250. *E-Mail:* kerzman@math.umc.edu

KESARWANI, ROOP NARAIN, THEORETICAL PHYSICS. *Current Pos:* assoc prof, 64-70, PROF MATH, UNIV OTTAWA, ONT, 70- *Personal Data:* b Kanpur, India, July 6, 32; Can citizen; m 57; c 2. *Educ:* Univ Lucknow, BSc, 52, Hons, 53, MSc, 54, PhD(math), 57. *Honors & Awards:* Swami Rama Tirtha Gold Medal & Debi Sahai Misra Gold Medal, Univ Lucknow, 54. *Prof Exp:* Asst prof math, Univ Lucknow, 54-58; assoc prof, G S Tech Inst, Indore, 58-59; lectr, Punjab Univ, India, 59-61; asst prof, Wash Univ, 61-62; assoc prof, Wayne State Univ, 62-64. *Mem:* Am Math Soc; Math Asn Am; Indian Math Soc; Can Math Soc; Soc Indust & Appl Math; Can Appl Math Soc. *Res:* Theory of functions of a complex variable; special functions and applications to theoretical physics; integral transforms and equations; quantum mechanics. *Mailing Add:* Univ Ottawa Ottawa ON K1N 9B4 Can

KESAVAN, SUNIL KUMAR, REACTIVE POLYMERS, CHEMICAL ENGINEERING. *Current Pos:* prin engr, 90-93, MGR CORE TECHNOL, ALLIED SIGNAL FRICTION MAT, 93- *Personal Data:* b Kanpur, India, May 29, 61; US citizen; m 97, Rema P Menon. *Educ:* Univ Madras, India, BTech, 82; Univ Akron, Ohio, MSChE, 85, PhD(chem eng), 87. *Honors & Awards:* Soc Plastics Engrs Award, 94. *Prof Exp:* Res assoc, Chem Eng Dept, Univ Akron, 87-90. *Concurrent Pos:* Adj prof, Dept Chem Eng, Univ Akron, 90- *Mem:* Soc Plastics Engrs; Am Chem Soc; Am Inst Chem Engrs; Soc Automotive Engrs. *Res:* Reactive polymers; conductive plastics; friction materials,; biomaterials; slurry technologies,; process design. *Mailing Add:* Allied Signal 900 W Maple Troy MI 48084. *Fax:* 248-362-7228; *E-Mail:* sunil.kesavan@alliedsignal.com

KESHAVA, CHANNA K C, GENETIC TOXICOLOGY, CANCER BIOLOGY. *Current Pos:* RES FEL, FOX CHASE CANCER CTR, 97- *Personal Data:* b Kaiwara, India, May 5, 65; m 96, Nagalakshmi Ramachandra. *Educ:* Univ Agr Sci, Bangalore, India, BS, 89, MS, 91; WVa Univ, PhD(genetics & develop biol), 95. *Honors & Awards:* Nat Travel Award, Environ Mutagen Soc, 95, 96. *Prof Exp:* Postdoctoral fel, Sch Med, Emory Univ, 96-97. *Mem:* AAAS; Environ Mutagen Soc; Sigma Xi. *Res:* Radiation and chemically induced DNA damage and prevention of its damage by antigenotoxic agents; preneoplastic and neoplastic potential of morphologically distinct transformed foci. *Mailing Add:* 1135-E Clairmont Rd Decatur GA 30030-1227. *E-Mail:* ckeshav@emory.edu

KESHAVA, NAGALAKSHMI, CARCINOGENESIS & TUMOR BIOLOGY, ESTROGEN & BREAST CANCER. *Current Pos:* RES FEL, SCH MED, EMORY UNIV, 95- *Personal Data:* b Bangalore, India, Mar 30, 67; m 96, Channa. *Educ:* Univ Agr Sci, Bangalore, BS, 89, MS, 91; WVa Univ, PhD(genetics), 95. *Prof Exp:* Asst agr officer, Dept Agr, 89-90; sr res assoc, Univ Agr Sci, 91-92. *Concurrent Pos:* Nat travel award, Environ Mutagen Soc, 94, 95 & 96, int travel award, 97; mem, Publ Comt, Environ Mutagen Soc, 96-, Educ Comt, 96-, Spec Interest Group, 96. *Mem:* Environ Mutagen Soc; Am Asn Cancer Res; Sigma Xi. *Res:* Overexpression of int-5/aromatose in transgenic mice leads to preneoplastic and neoplastic lesions; increased in situ estrogen increases the risk for breast cancer. *Mailing Add:* 1135-E Clairmont Rd Decatur GA 30030-1227. *E-Mail:* rnagala@emory.edu

KESHAVAN, H R, GENERAL COMPUTER SCIENCES, ELECTRICAL ENGINEERING. *Current Pos:* MGR, AUTOMATION SCI LAB, NORTHROP RES, 85- *Personal Data:* b Bangalore, India, Apr 20, 49; US citizen; m 79; c 3. *Educ:* Bangalore Univ, BS, 69; Southern Methodist Univ, PhD(elec eng), 77. *Prof Exp:* Asst prof, Bangalore Univ, 71-74; scientist, Rockwell Int, 77-80; sr mem tech staff, Northrop Corp, 80-85. *Concurrent Pos:* Vis prof, Univ Southern Calif, 89- *Mem:* Sr mem Inst Elec & Electronics Engrs. *Res:* Computer science; intelligent systems; artificial intelligence; automation. *Mailing Add:* Automation Sci Lab Northrop Grumman 8900 E Washington Blvd Pico Rivera CA 90660

KESHAVAN, KRISHNASWAMIENGAR, CIVIL ENGINEERING, ENVIRONMENTAL ENGINEERING. *Current Pos:* assoc prof, 67-76, head dept, 76-86, PROF CIVIL ENG, WORCESTER POLYTECH INST, 76- *Personal Data:* b Hassan, India, June 5, 29; m 57, Sita; c Rangaswamy, Padma M & Leela. *Educ:* Univ Mysore, BSc, 50, BE, 55; Univ Iowa, MS, 60; Cornell Univ, PhD(sanit eng), 63. *Prof Exp:* Sect officer, Cent Pub Works Dept, Govt India, 55-58; asst civil eng, Cornell Univ, 60-63; assoc prof, Univ Maine, Orono, 63-67. *Concurrent Pos:* Water Resources Ctr res grant, Univ Maine, Orono, 65-67; Off Water Resources Res grant thermal pollution & NSF grant & chlorination, 71; co-dir, Environ Systs Study Prog, Sloan Found; sr adv, UNESCO, 75-76, consult, 76- *Mem:* Am Soc Civil Engrs; Am Soc Eng Educ; Water Pollution Control Fedn; Am Water Works Asn. *Res:* Kinetics of biological treatment of organic liquid wastes; nitrification of natural bodies of water and its effect on oxygen utilization; combined effects of thermal and organic pollution; hazardous chlorinated compounds due to chlorination. *Mailing Add:* Dept Civil & Environ Eng Worcester Polytech Inst Worcester MA 01609. *E-Mail:* keshavan@wpi.edu

KESHAVIAH, PRAKASH RAMNATHPUR, ARTIFICIAL ORGANS, END-STAGE RENAL DISEASE. *Current Pos:* DIR CLIN ONCOL, BAXTER HEALTH CARE CORP. *Personal Data:* b Bangalore, India, Feb 15, 45; c 2. *Educ:* Indian Inst Technol, Madras, BTech, 67; Univ Minn, MS, 70, PhD(mech eng), 74, MS, 80. *Prof Exp:* Process Planning Engr, Larsen & Toubro Ltd, India, 67-68; res asst, Dept Mech Eng, Univ Minn, 68-73; biomed engr, Regional Kidney Dis Ctr, 73-, mgr bioeng, 76- *Concurrent Pos:* Consult & mem, Artificial Kidney-Chronic Uremia Adv Comt, Nat Inst Arthritis, Metab & Digestive Dis, 78-79; prin investr, Dept Health Educ & Welfare, Food & Drug Admin, 77-81; res assoc, Dept Med, Hennepin County Med Ctr & Univ Minn, 77-81, sr res assoc, 81- *Mem:* Am Soc Artificial Internal Organs; Int Soc Artificial Organs. *Res:* Basic physiology, kinetic modeling and engineering design aspects of therapies for end-state renal disease and kinetic modeling of biological systems. *Mailing Add:* 10840 41st Ave N Minneapolis MN 55441

KESHGEGIAN, ALBERT ARAKEL, CLINICAL PATHOLOGY. *Current Pos:* Asst instr path, Univ Pa, 75-79, asst prof path, 79-81, adj asst prof path & lab med, 81-85, ADJ ASSOC PROF PATH & LAB MED, UNIV PA SCH MED, 85-; ASSOC PROF PATH, THOMAS JEFFERSON UNIV, 85-; ASSOC DIR PATH & CHIEF CLIN PATH, BRYN MAWR HOSP, 88- *Personal Data:* b Jan 22, 49; c 3. *Educ:* Univ Pa, BA, 69, PhD(biochem), 74, MD, 75. *Concurrent Pos:* Acting assoc dir, Protein Chem Div, William Pepper Lab, Hosp Univ Pa, 78-79, dir, 79-81; asst pathologist, Lankenau Hosp, 81-82, assoc pathologist, 81-87, dir immunopath & co-dir Clin Chem Sections, 81-87, dir Hemat Sect, 84-87; adj asst prof microbiol & cell biol, Pa State Univ, 82-87. *Mem:* Fel Col Am Pathologists; fel Am Soc Clin Pathologists; Am Asn Pathologists; Am Asn Clin Chem; Am & Can Acad Path. *Res:* Molecular markers detected by immunohistochemistry in cancer; clinical pathology. *Mailing Add:* Dept Path Bryn Mawr Hosp 130 S Bryn Mawr Ave Bryn Mawr PA 19010-3158

KESHOCK, EDWARD G, FLUID MECHANICS, THERMODYNAMICS. *Current Pos:* assoc prof, 77-80, PROF MECH & AEROSPACE ENG, UNIV TENN, 80- *Personal Data:* b Campbell, Ohio, Mar 2, 35; m 59; c 3. *Educ:* Univ Detroit, BME, 58; Okla State Univ, MS, 66, PhD(mech eng), 68. *Prof Exp:* Res engr, Lewis Res Ctr, NASA, 58-64; res asst film boiling heat transfer, Okla State Univ, 64-67; asst prof mech eng, Cleveland State Univ, 67-69; assoc prof thermal eng, Old Dominion Univ, 69-77. *Concurrent Pos:* Vis scientist, Nat Sci Coun, Repub China & Nat Tsing Hua Univ, Taiwan, 74-75; vis prof, Univ Petrol & Minerals, Saudi Arabia, 83-85. *Mem:* Am Soc Mech Engrs; Am Soc Eng Educ; Am Inst Chem Engrs. *Res:* Boiling heat transfer and two-phase flow; condensation heat transfer; thermophysical properties; phase change heat transfer; multiphase flow and heat transfer; energy systems; measurement techniques in heat transfer and fluid mechanics. *Mailing Add:* 1455 Windrow Lane Broadview Heights OH 44147

KESIK, ANDRZEJ B, PHYSICAL GEOGRAPHY, REMOTE SENSING. *Current Pos:* vis prof photo interpretation & geomorphol, 70-71, assoc prof photo interpretation, 71-81, PROF GEOG, UNIV WATERLOO, 76- *Personal Data:* b Warsaw, Poland, Oct 27, 30; m 64; c 2. *Educ:* Marie Curie-Sklodowska Univ, MSc, 51, PhD(geog), 59; Int Training Centre Aerial Surv, Holland, dipl geomorphol, 63. *Prof Exp:* Sr asst phys geog, Marie Curie-Sklodowska Univ, 55-60, lectr, 60-64; lectr cartog & photo interpretation, 64-70. *Concurrent Pos:* Govt training grant, Univ Amsterdam, 63; nat reporter, Comn VII, Int Soc Photogram, 68-70; Brit Coun scholar, 70. *Mem:* Can Inst Surveying; Am Soc Photogram; Can Asn Geogr; Am Asn Geogr. *Res:* Physical elements of the environment; application of remote sensing techniques to the land evaluation; geomorphological mapping. *Mailing Add:* Dept Geog Univ Waterloo Waterloo ON N2L 3G1 Can

KESKKULA, HENNO, MATERIAL SCIENCE. *Current Pos:* vis scholar, 82-83, RES FEL, UNIV TEX, 83- *Personal Data:* b Tartu, Estonia, Mar 25, 26; nat US; m 52, Carol L Tiemeyer; c Linda-Louise (Sorensen) & Lesli-Ann (Pitts). *Educ:* Davis & Elkins Col, BS, 49; Univ Cincinnati, MS, 51, PhD(org chem), 53. *Prof Exp:* Chemist, Dow Chem Co, 53-56, group leader, 56-68, assoc scientist, 68-82. *Concurrent Pos:* Sr vis res fel, Queen Mary Col, Univ London, 69-70. *Mem:* Am Chem Soc; Sigma Xi. *Res:* Elastomers; polymer chemistry; mechanical behavior of polymers; miscibility of polymers; toughened plastics. *Mailing Add:* 6205 Quail Hollow Austin TX 78750. *Fax:* 512-471-0542; *E-Mail:* keskkula@che.utexas.edu

KESLER, CLYDE E(RVIN), CONCRETE. *Current Pos:* res assoc, 47-48, from instr to prof, 48-82, EMER PROF CIVIL ENG, THEORET & APPL MECH, UNIV ILL, URBANA, 82- *Personal Data:* b Condit, Ill, May 7, 22; m 47, Mary A; c Philip R & David C. *Educ:* Univ Ill, BS, 43, MS, 46. *Honors & Awards:* Thompson Award, Am Soc Testing & Mat, 58; Lindau Award, Am Concrete Inst, 71. *Prof Exp:* Jr eng aide, 13th Cent RR, 46-47. *Concurrent Pos:* Prof civil eng, Univ Ill, Urbana, 63-82. *Mem:* Nat Acad Eng; fel Am Soc Civil Engrs; hon mem Am Concrete Inst (pres, 67-68); Am Soc Eng Educ; hon mem Wire Reinforcement Inst. *Res:* Plain and reinforced concrete; cracking and crack control; freeze-thaw durability; fracture; creeps; fiber reinforcement; diffusion; expansion; quick-setting; history and future; United States patentee. *Mailing Add:* Dept Civil Eng Univ Ill 205 N Mathews St Urbana IL 61801. *Fax:* 217-356-7808; *E-Mail:* cekes@prairienet.org

KESLER, DARREL J, REPRODUCTIVE BIOLOGY & PHARMACOLOGY. *Current Pos:* asst prof, 77-81, ASSOC PROF REPRODUCTIVE BIOL & BIOTECHNOL, DEPT ANIMAL SCI, UNIV ILL, URBANA, 81- *Personal Data:* b Portland, Ind, Sept 21, 49; m 73, Cheryl S; c Cheralyn E & D Phillip. *Educ:* Purdue Univ, BS, 71, MS, 74; Univ Mo, PhD, 77. *Honors & Awards:* Outstanding Young Scientist, Midwestern Am

Soc Animal Sci, 83. *Prof Exp:* Teaching asst acad coun & admin, Deans Off, Sch Agr, Purdue Univ, 71-74; res asst reprod & lactation physiol, Dept Dairy Husb, Univ Mo, 74-77. *Concurrent Pos:* Biochemist, Abbott Labs, Inc, 83-84; chmn, Antech Lab, Inc, 84-; consult, Sanoti Animal Health, 88-91 & Ballistivet, Inc, 89-92; dir, Enteron Inc, 92-93. *Mem:* AAAS; Am Soc Animal Sci; Controlled Release Soc; Sigma Xi. *Res:* Physiology and endocrinology; controlled release systems; industrial pharmacy and formulations; drug delivery systems; analytical chemisty. *Mailing Add:* 1207 W Gregory Dr Urbana IL 61801. *Fax:* 217-244-3169

KESLER, EARL MARSHALL, DAIRY SCIENCE. *Current Pos:* From instr to assoc prof, 48-64, PROF DAIRY SCI, PA STATE UNIV, UNIVERSITY PARK, 64- *Personal Data:* b Dunmore, WVa, Dec 3, 20; m 45; c 3. *Educ:* WVa Univ, BS, 43; Pa State Univ, MS, 48, PhD, 51. *Mem:* AAAS; Am Soc Animal Sci; Am Dairy Sci Asn; Sigma Xi. *Res:* Dairy cattle nutrition, physiology of digestion; calf nutrition rumen metabolism and intermediary metabolism of the bovine; forage production; physiology of milk secretion; management of cows. *Mailing Add:* 534 Beaumont Dr State College PA 16801

KESLER, G(EORGE) H(ENRY), HEAT TRANSFERS, METALS TECHNOLOGY. *Current Pos:* RETIRED. *Personal Data:* b West Terre Haute, Ind, Oct 29, 20; m 42, Wilma G Roush; c David (deceased), Deborah (deceased) & Sandra J (Hodge). *Educ:* Rose Polytech Inst, BS, 42; Mass Inst Technol, MS, 49, ScD, 52. *Prof Exp:* Chem engr distillation, Tex Co, 42-48; asst; prin chem engr, Battelle Mem Inst, 51-55, asst div chief, 55-59; assoc dir res, Nat Steel Corp, 59-65; dept mgr, Mat Lab Dept, McDonnell Aircraft Co, St Louis, 65-77; eng consult, 77-83. *Mem:* Am Soc Metals. *Res:* Mass transport in spray-laden turbulent air streams; titanium production; laboratory distillation column evaluation; heat and mass transfer; steelmaking fundamentals; materials testing. *Mailing Add:* Box 255 West Terre Haute IN 47885-0255. *E-Mail:* bigsquard@aol.com

KESLER, OREN BYRL, ELECTRICAL ENGINEERING, APPLIED ELECTROMAGNETIC THEORY. *Current Pos:* mem tech staff, 72-81, sr mem tech staff, 81-96, DISTINGUISHED MEM TECH STAFF, ANTENNA & MICROWAVE LAB, EQUIP GROUP, TEX INSTRUMENTS INC, 97- *Personal Data:* b Crawford Co, Ill, Aug 28, 39; m 67; c 1. *Educ:* Univ Ill, BS, 61, MS, 62, PhD(elec eng), 65; Univ Wis, MA, 68. *Prof Exp:* Asst prof elec eng, Univ Tex, Austin, 65-72. *Concurrent Pos:* NSF sci fac fel, 70-71. *Mem:* Sr mem Inst Elec & Electronics Engrs; Am Math Asn. *Res:* Electromagnetic field; antennas; microwaves; radar; information processing; mathematical and computational techniques for engineering analysis. *Mailing Add:* 3305 Dibrell Dr Plano TX 75023-5653. *Fax:* 972-952-3773; *E-Mail:* obk@timsg.csc.ti.com

KESLER, STEPHEN EDWARD, ECONOMIC GEOLOGY, EXPLORATION GEOCHEMISTRY. *Current Pos:* PROF GEOL, UNIV MICH, 77- *Personal Data:* b Washington, DC, Oct 5, 40; m 65; c 2. *Educ:* Univ NC, BS, 62; Stanford Univ, PhD(geol), 66. *Prof Exp:* Asst prof geol, La State Univ, Baton Rouge, 66-70; asst prof, 70-71, assoc prof geol, Univ Toronto, 71-77. *Concurrent Pos:* Vis scientist, Consejo de Recursos Minerales, Mex, 75-76; assoc ed, Econ Geol, 80-90, J Geochem Expl, 85-; Fulbright Panel, Coun Int Exchange Scholars, 84-87; int lectr, Soc Econ Geologists, 89-90. *Mem:* Geol Soc Am; Soc Econ Geologists (vpres, 90-91); Asn Explor Geochemists; Geochem Soc; fel Geol Soc Am. *Res:* Tectonic and petrologic framework of ore deposition; ore deposit and exploration geochemistry; geology of Central America, Mexico and West Indies. *Mailing Add:* Dept Geol 1006 CC Little Univ Mich 425 E University Ave Ann Arbor MI 48109-1063

KESLER, THOMAS L, GEOLOGY, MINERAL EXPLORATION. *Current Pos:* RETIRED. *Personal Data:* b Salisbury, NC, Dec 29, 08; m 32, Margaret Menges; c Stephen E & Susan (Porter). *Educ:* Univ NC, Chapel Hill, BS, 29, MS, 30. *Prof Exp:* Geologist, Shell Petrol Corp, 30-31, Soil Conserv Serv, 34-36, US Geol Surv, 36-46 & Thompson-Weinman & Co, 46-52; sr geologist, Tenn Coal & Iron Div, US Steel Corp, 52-53; chief geologist, Foote Mineral Co, 53-65 & Engelhard Minerals & Chemicals Corp, 65-68; consult geologist, domestic & foreign engagements, 68-74. *Concurrent Pos:* Counr, Soc Econ Geologists, 55-57; mem, Beryllium Panel, Mat Adv Bd, Nat Res Coun, 57-58 & Lithium Resources Group, Comt Nuclear & Alternative Energy Systs, 76; chmn, Indust Minerals Div, Soc Mining Engrs, 58 & Southeastern Sect, Geol Soc Am, 61; pres, Carolina Geol Soc, 58; mem, Forum Earth Resources, Voice of Am, 71. *Mem:* fel Soc Econ Geologists; fel Geol Soc Am; Soc Mining Engrs. *Res:* Southern Appalachian Stratigraphy, structure and mineral resources; geology of industrial mineral deposits; author of scientific and technical papers and reports published in professional media. *Mailing Add:* PO Box 3561 Bellevue WA 98009

KESLING, ROBERT VERNON, PALEONTOLOGY. *Current Pos:* From asst prof to assoc prof geol, 49-59, assoc cur micropaleont, Mus Paleont, 49-58, dir, 66-74, PROF GEOL, UNIV MICH, ANN ARBOR, 59-, CUR, MUS PALEONT, 58- *Personal Data:* b Cass Co, Ind, Sept 11, 17; m 42; c 3. *Educ:* DePauw Univ, AB, 39; Univ Ill, MS, 41, PhD(geol), 49. *Concurrent Pos:* Ed, J Paleont, 58-64. *Mem:* Paleont Soc; Sigma Xi; AAAS. *Res:* Living and fossil Ostracoda; middle Devonian stratigraphy; Paleozoic echinoderms. *Mailing Add:* 1941 Geddes Ave Ann Arbor MI 48104

KESMODEL, LARRY LEE, SOLID STATE PHYSICS, SURFACE SCIENCE. *Current Pos:* asst prof, 78-83, ASSOC PROF PHYSICS, IND UNIV, BLOOMINGTON, 83- *Personal Data:* b Ft Worth, Tex, Mar 5, 47; m 70; c 3. *Educ:* Calif Inst Technol, BS, 69; Univ Tex, Austin, PhD(physics), 74. *Prof Exp:* Fel phys chem, Univ Calif, Berkeley, 73-75, staff scientist surface physics, Mat & Molecular Res Div, Lawrence Berkeley Lab, 75-78. *Concurrent Pos:* prin investr, Off Naval Res Contract, 80- & US Dept Energy Grant, 84-; Pres, LK Technologies, 85- *Mem:* Am Phys Soc. *Res:* Experimental studies of solid surfaces and chemisorption; low-energy electron diffraction; high-resolution electron energy loss spectroscopy. *Mailing Add:* Dept Physics Swain Hall W Rm 117 Ind Univ Bloomington IN 47401

KESNER, JAY, PLASMA PHYSICS. *Current Pos:* SR RES SCIENTIST, PLASMA FUSION CTR, MASS INST TECHNOL, 81- *Personal Data:* b New York, NY, Mar 17, 43. *Educ:* Cornell Univ, BS, 65, MEng, 66; Columbia Univ, PhD(physics), 70. *Prof Exp:* Prof, Dept Physics, Univ Wis, 73-81. *Mem:* Am Phys Soc. *Mailing Add:* 167 Albany St Cambridge MA 02139

KESNER, LEO, BIOCHEMISTRY, ANALYTICAL CHEMISTRY. *Current Pos:* jr biochemist, 54-56, asst, 56-60, from instr to asst prof, 61-69, assoc prof, 69-89, PROF BIOCHEM, STATE UNIV NY, DOWNSTATE MED CTR, 69- *Personal Data:* b New York, NY, Feb 22, 31; m 54; c 3. *Educ:* City Col New York, BS, 54; State Univ NY, PhD(biochem), 61. *Prof Exp:* Sr technician biophys, Sloan-Kettering Inst, 54. *Mem:* AAAS; Am Asn Clin Chem; Am Chem Soc; NY Acad Sci; Am Soc Biol Chemists. *Res:* Relationship of acid-base balance to intermediary metabolism; nutrition; design of analytical techniques in biochemistry; protein chemistry; inborn errors of metabolism; membrane phospholipids; growth promotion; proteases; protease inhibitors. *Mailing Add:* Dept Biochem State Univ NY Health Sci Ctr 450 Clarkson Ave Box 8 Brooklyn NY 11203-2012. *Fax:* 718-270-3316

KESNER, MICHAEL H, SYSTEMATICS, MAMMALOGY. *Current Pos:* ASSOC PROF HUMAN ANAT & COMP ANAT, IND UNIV PA, 76- *Personal Data:* b Pawtucket, RI, Nov 30, 45; m 69; c 1. *Educ:* Northwestern Univ, BA, 69, MS, 72; Univ Mass, PhD(zool), 76. *Concurrent Pos:* Grant in aid, Sigma Xi, 76; Theodore Roosevelt Grant, Am Mus Natural Hist, 76 & Univ Res Grant, Ind Univ Pa, 77, 78 & 81. *Mem:* Am Soc Mammalogists; Soc Syst Zool. *Res:* Mammalian (Rodent) functional morphology and systematics primarily of the subfamily microtinae; biogeography and systematics of insular populations of the genus Microtus from off the coast of Northeastern North America. *Mailing Add:* Dept Biol Ind Univ Pa Main Campus Indiana PA 15705-0001

KESNER, RAYMOND PIERRE, PHYSIOLOGICAL PSYCHOLOGY, NEUROSCIENCE. *Current Pos:* from asst prof to assoc prof, 67-75, PROF PSYCHOL, UNIV UTAH, 75- *Personal Data:* b Oran, Algeria, Dec 19, 40; US citizen; m 65; c 2. *Educ:* Wayne State Univ, BS, 62; Univ Ill, MS, 64, PhD(psychol), 65. *Prof Exp:* Fel physiol, Ctr Brain Res, Rochester, NY, 65-67. *Concurrent Pos:* Fel, Ctr Advan Study Behav Sci, 71-72. *Mem:* Soc Neurosci; Psychonomic Soc. *Res:* Neurobiological mechanisms of memory. *Mailing Add:* Dept Psychol Univ Utah 502 Behav Sci Salt Lake City UT 84112-1107

KESSEL, BRINA, ORNITHOLOGY, VERTEBRATE ZOOLOGY. *Current Pos:* asst prof biol sci, Univ Alaska, 51-54, assoc prof zool, 54-59, head, Dept Biol Sci, 57-66, dean, Col Biol Sci & Renewable Resources, 61-72, PROF ZOOL, UNIV ALASKA, FAIRBANKS, 59- *Personal Data:* b Ithaca, NY, Nov 20, 25; wid. *Educ:* Cornell Univ, BS, 47, PhD(ornith), 51; Univ Wis, MS, 49. *Prof Exp:* Asst ornith & conserv, Cornell Univ, 47-48 & 49-51. *Concurrent Pos:* Proj dir, Ecol Invests, AEC Proj Chariot, Univ Alaska, 59-63, cur terrestrial vert mus collections, Univ Mus, 72-90, admin assoc, Acad Progs, Off Chancellor, 73-80, cur, Ornith Collection, Univ Mus, 90-95; ornithologist, invests NW Alaska pipeline, 76-81; ornithologist, Sustina Hydroelec Proj, Alaska, 80-83. *Mem:* Fel AAAS; fel Am Ornithologists' Union (pres-elect, 90-92, pres, 92-94); fel Arctic Inst NAm; Wilson Ornith Soc; Cooper Ornith Soc; Sigma Xi. *Res:* European starling in North America; biodiversity and natural history of Alaska birds; wildlife conservation management. *Mailing Add:* Univ Alaska Mus PO Box 80211 Fairbanks AK 99708. *Fax:* 907-474-5469; *E-Mail:* ffbxk@aurora.alaska.edu

KESSEL, CHARLES, PLASMA PHYSICS. *Current Pos:* PROJ SCIENTIST, PRINCETON PLASMA PHYSICS LAB, NJ, 88- *Educ:* Univ Calif, Los Angeles, PhD(fusion eng & appl plasma physics), 87. *Honors & Awards:* Fusion Eng Award, Fusion Power Assocs, 94. *Mailing Add:* James Forrestal Res Campus Plasma Physics Lab Princeton Univ PO Box 451 Princeton NJ 08543

KESSEL, DAVID HARRY, BIOCHEMISTRY. *Current Pos:* PROF PHARMACOL & MED, SCH MED, WAYNE STATE UNIV, 74- *Personal Data:* b Monroe, Mich, Jan 8, 31; c 2. *Educ:* Mass Inst Technol, BS, 52; Univ Mich, MS, 54, PhD(biochem), 59. *Prof Exp:* Res assoc, Children's Cancer Res Found & asst path, Harvard Med Sch, 65-68; from asst prof to assoc prof pharmacol, Sch Med, Univ Rochester, 69-73. *Concurrent Pos:* NIH fel, Harvard Univ, 59-63; res scientist, Mich Cancer Found, 74; secy-treas, Am Soc Photobiol, 88- *Mem:* AAAS; Biochem Soc; Am Asn Cancer Res; Am Soc Pharmacol & Exp Therapeut; Am Soc Biol Chemists. *Res:* Development of anti-tumor agents; mode of action of anti-neoplastic drugs and photosensitizing agents. *Mailing Add:* Pharmacol Dept Wayne State Univ Sch Med Detroit MI 48201

KESSEL, QUENTIN CATTELL, EXPERIMENTAL ATOMIC MOLECULAR & SURFACE PHYSICS, ACCELERATOR BASED MATERIALS SCIENCE. *Current Pos:* asst prof, 71-73, assoc prof, 73-78, PROF PHYSICS, UNIV CONN, 78- *Personal Data:* b Boston, Mass, Aug 15, 38; m 60, Margaret May; c Lori L & Scott M. *Educ:* Yale Univ, BS, 60; Univ Mich, MS, 62; Univ Conn, PhD(physics), 66. *Prof Exp:* Res asst physics, Univ Conn, 62-65, res assoc, 65-66; physicist, Robert J Van de Graaff Lab, High Voltage Eng Corp, 66-70; guest scientist, Inst Physics, Aarhus Univ, 70-71. *Concurrent Pos:* Guest prof, Univ Freiburg, Ger, 77-78. *Mem:* Fel Am Phys Soc; Europ Phys Soc; Mat Res Soc; Bohmische Phys Soc; Sigma Xi. *Res:* Interaction of accelerated ions and molecules with matter for the investigation and creation of new materials especially thin films and interfaces. *Mailing Add:* Dept Physics Univ Conn Storrs CT 06269. *Fax:* 860-486-3346; *E-Mail:* kessel@uconnvm.uconn.edu

KESSEL, RICHARD GLEN, ANATOMY, CELL BIOLOGY. *Current Pos:* from asst prof to assoc prof, 61-68, PROF BIOL, UNIV IOWA, 68- *Personal Data:* b Fairfield, Iowa, July 19, 31. *Educ:* Parsons Col, BS, 53; Univ Iowa, MS, 56, PhD(zool), 59. *Prof Exp:* From instr to asst prof anat, Bowman Gray Sch Med, 59-61. *Concurrent Pos:* NIH fel, 60-61; Nat Inst Gen Med Sci res grant, 60-65, career develop award, 64-69; Nat Inst Child Health & Human Develop res grant, 64-69; prog dir, NIH Training grant develop biol, 66-78; NSF res grant, 68-71; assoc ed, J Exp Zool, 78-82. *Mem:* Soc Study Reproduction; Am Asn Anat; Soc Develop Biologists; Am Soc Cell Biol; Am Phys Soc; Electron Micros Soc Am. *Res:* Electron microscopic, autoradiographic, cytochemical and freeze-fracture studies on oocyte growth and differentiation; origin, structure and function of cell organelles; mechanisms of secretion; scanning electron microscopy of tissues and organs; immunocytochemistry. *Mailing Add:* Dept Biol Scis Univ Iowa Iowa City IA 52242-1324. *Fax:* 319-335-1069

KESSEL, SAMUEL SHERWOOD, MATERNAL & CHILD HEALTH. *Current Pos:* spec asst to asst secy health & surgeon gen, Dept Health & Human Servs, USPHS, 79-81, med officer epidemiol & biomet res prog, Nat Inst Child Health & Human Develop, NIH, 81-83, chief, Res & Training Br, Div Maternal & Child Health, Bur Health Care & Delivery Assistance, Health Resources & Servs Admin, 83-87, dir, Div Maternal & Child Health Prog Coord & Systs Develop, Off Maternal & Child Health, Bur Maternal & Child Health & Resources Develop, 87-90, dir Div Systs, Educ & Sci, 90-95, DIR, DIV SCI, EDUC & ANALYSIS, MATERNAL & CHILD HEALTH BUR, HEALTH RESOURCES & SERVS ADMIN, DEPT HEALTH & HUMAN SERVS, USPHS, 95- *Personal Data:* b Philadelphia, Pa, Nov 30, 48; c 2. *Educ:* Drexel Univ, BS, 70; Yeshiva Univ, MD, 74; Johns Hopkins Univ, MPH, 82. *Honors & Awards:* Maternal & Child Health Young Prof Award, Am Pub Health Asn, 89; Job Lewis Smith Award, Am Acad Pediat, 96. *Prof Exp:* Intern, Dept Pediat, Boston City Hosp, Boston Univ Sch Med, 74-75, jr asst resident, 75-76, sr asst resident & fel, 76-77; spec fel ambulatory pediat, Dept Child Health & Develop, Childrens Hosp & Nat Med Ctr, George Washington Univ Sch Med, 77-79. *Concurrent Pos:* Consult, Off Comnr Health, City of Boston, 77; US Gen Accounting Off, 77-79; Bur Community Health Servs Admin, Dept Health & Human Servs, 77-78; Nat Capital Med Found Inc, 79; Expert Panel, USPHS, 87-94; clin instr, Dept Child Health & Develop, Children's Hosp & Nat Med Ctr, George Washington Sch Med, 78-; asst secy health's staff rep, USPHS, 79-81; asst clin prof, Dept Pediat, Uniformed Univ Health Sci, Md, 81-; liaison rep, Coun Pediat Res, Am Acad Pediat, 85-, Fedn Pediat Orgn, 88-; secy staff rep, Nat Comn to Prevent Infant Mortality, 88-92; staff dir, Task Force Infant Mortality, White House, 89-90. *Mem:* Am Pub Health Asn; Ambulatory Pediat Asn. *Res:* Hygiene and public health. *Mailing Add:* Maternal & Child Health Bur USPHS 5600 Fishers Lane Parklawn Bldg Rm 18A-55 Rockville MD 20857

KESSELMAN, WARREN ARTHUR, electromagnetic compatibility, communications security, for more information see previous edition

KESSELRING, JOHN PAUL, ENERGY ANALYSES, HVAC EQUIPMENT. *Current Pos:* sr proj mgr, 86-91, MGR, RESIDENTIAL SYSTS, ELEC POWER RES INST, 92- *Personal Data:* b Detroit, Mich, Mar 26, 40; m 66, Jane Edwards; c Joan P & Thomas M. *Educ:* Univ Mich, BS, 61; Stanford Univ, MS, 62, PhD(aeronaut & astronaut sci), 68. *Prof Exp:* Res engr, Rocketdyne Div, NAm Aviation, Inc, 62-63, mem tech staff, NAm Rockwell Corp, 67-69; asst prof mech & aerospace eng, Univ Tenn, Knoxville, 69-74; mgr catalytic combustion progs, Acurex Corp, 74-80, assoc mgr combustion technol, 81-82; vpres, Alzeta Corp, 82-86. *Concurrent Pos:* Instr aeronaut & astronaut, Stanford Univ, 77; lectr, Soviet Acad Sci, 86. *Mem:* Combustion Inst; Am Soc Mech Engrs; Sigma Xi. *Res:* Residential building energy analysis; HVAC equipment; heat pumps; residential appliances. *Mailing Add:* 279 Apricot Lane Mountain View CA 94040. *Fax:* 650-855-8576; *E-Mail:* jkesselr@eprinet.epri.com

KESSIN, RICHARD HARRY, DEVELOPMENTAL GENETICS, SIGNAL TRANSDUCTION. *Current Pos:* AT DEPT ANAT & CELL BIOL, COLUMBIA UNIV. *Personal Data:* b Bayonne, NJ, Feb 24, 44; c 2. *Educ:* Yale Univ, BA, 66; Brandeis Univ, PhD(biol), 71. *Prof Exp:* asst prof, 74-80, assoc prof biol, Harvard Univ, 80- *Res:* Development and regulation of signal transduction. *Mailing Add:* 560 Riverside Dr No 220L New York NY 10027

KESSINGER, MARGARET ANNE, MEDICINE. *Current Pos:* Asst prof to assoc prof med oncol, 72-90, PROF INTERNAL MED, UNIV NEBR MED CTR, 90-, CHIEF, SECT ONCOL/HEMATOL, 91- *Personal Data:* b Beckley, WVa, June 4, 41; m 71, Loyd Wegner. *Educ:* WVa Univ, BA, 63, MD, 67. *Concurrent Pos:* Assoc dep dir clin res, Univ Nebr Med Ctr/Eppley Cancer Ctr, 96- *Mem:* Am Col Physicians; Am Soc Clin Oncol; Am Asn Cancer Res; Am Asn Cancer Educ; Am Med Soc; Am Fedn Clin Res. *Res:* High dose therapy with autologous bone marrow transplantation for solid tumors; peripheral hematopietic stem cell transfusion. *Mailing Add:* 600 S 42nd St Omaha NE 68198-3330

KESSINGER, WALTER PAUL, JR, MICROPALEONTOLOGY. *Current Pos:* RETIRED. *Personal Data:* b Tex, July 9, 30; m 62, Dorothy Wallis; c Walter P III, Charles H & Linda K. *Educ:* Tex Technol Col, BS, 51, MS, 53; La State Univ, PhD(geol), 74. *Prof Exp:* From asst prof to prof, Univ Southwestern La, 53-86, head dept, 56-86. *Concurrent Pos:* ARCO, 66-69, Univ Ill, 62. *Mem:* Geol Soc Am; Am Asn Petrol Geologists; Paleont Soc; Soc Econ Paleontologists & Mineralogists; Nat Asn Geol Teachers; Sigma Xi. *Res:* Ostracoda of the Comanche Series of north Texas. *Mailing Add:* 406 Orangewood Dr Lafayette LA 70503-5228

KESSLER, ALEXANDER, MEDICINE, PUBLIC HEALTH. *Current Pos:* RETIRED. *Personal Data:* b Vienna, Austria, Mar 19, 31; Brit citizen; m 53, 92, Constance C Offen; c Daniel, Anne, David & Jonathan. *Educ:* NY Univ, BA, 51; Columbia Univ, MD, 55; Rockefeller Univ, PhD(pop biol), 66. *Prof Exp:* Physician, Bellevue Hosp Cornell Serv, 55-56; physician, Albert Einstein Med Ctr, NY, 56-57, Walter Reed Hosp & Res Inst, 57-60 & Georgetown Univ Hosp, 60-61; dir, Spec Prog Res Human Reprod, WHO, Geneva, 66-84, dir spec leave, 84-86. *Res:* International public health; family planning; reproductive biology and contraceptive technology; research administration. *Mailing Add:* 4 Ellerdale Close London NW3 6BE England

KESSLER, BERNARD V, LASERS, STOCK MARKET ANALYSES. *Current Pos:* RETIRED. *Personal Data:* b Brooklyn, NY, June 27, 28; wid; c Ellen (Chiniara) & Susan. *Educ:* NY Univ, BA, 59; Cath Univ Am, MS, 69, PhD(physics), 72. *Prof Exp:* Res physicist, Electro-optics Br, Naval Surface Warfare Ctr, 59-88. *Concurrent Pos:* Consult, pres & chief exec officer, Evgodic Processes, Ltd. *Mem:* Am Asn Physics Teachers. *Res:* Optics; adaptive optics for coherent optical systems; infrared search and surveillance; nonlinear dynamic (chaos) models of stock market price fluctuations. *Mailing Add:* 4505 S Hardy Dr Apt 2173 Tempe AZ 85282. *E-Mail:* kessler@primenet.com

KESSLER, DAN, HIGH ENERGY PHYSICS. *Current Pos:* RETIRED. *Personal Data:* b Vienna, Austria, May 23, 24; m 53; c 3. *Educ:* Hebrew Univ, Israel, MSc, 50; Sorbonne, DesSc(physics), 54. *Prof Exp:* Res physicist, Nat Ctr Sci Res, Fr Res Coun, 51-58; sr physicist, Israel Atomic Energy Comn, 58-64; res assoc high energy physics, Univ Chicago, 64-67; prof physics, Carleton Univ, 67-95. *Concurrent Pos:* Assoc prof, Tel-Aviv Univ, 62-64. *Mem:* Am Phys Soc; Can Asn Physicists. *Res:* Electromagnetic and nuclear interactions of cosmic-ray muons; interactions of K-mesons; mesic atoms; production of heavy mesons in P-P collisions. *Mailing Add:* 18 Pemberton Crescent Nepean ON K2G 4Y9 Can

KESSLER, DAVID, MEDICAL ADMINISTRATION. *Current Pos:* DEAN, MED SCH, YALE UNIV, 97- *Personal Data:* b New York, NY, May 31, 51. *Educ:* Amherst Col, BA, 73; Univ Chicago, JD, 78; Harvard Univ, MD, 79. *Honors & Awards:* Trumpeter Award, Nat Consumers League; Award Courage, Am Found AIDS Res. *Prof Exp:* Med dir, Hosp Albert Einstein Col Med, 84-90; comnr food & drug, Food & Drug Admin, 90-97. *Concurrent Pos:* Consult, Senate Labor & Human Resources Comt, 81-84; instr food & drug law, Columbia Univ, 86-90. *Mem:* Inst Med-Nat Acad Sci. *Mailing Add:* Food & Drug Admin 5600 Fishers Lane Rockville MD 20857. *Fax:* 202-785-7437

KESSLER, DAVID PHILLIP, CHEMICAL ENGINEERING, BIOENGINEERING. *Current Pos:* from asst prof to assoc prof chem eng, Purdue Univ, 64-73, asst provost, 76-80, dir, Acad Info Systs, 78-80, PROF CHEM ENG, PURDUE UNIV, 73-, HEAD, DIV INTERDISCIPLINARY ENG STUDIES, 82- *Personal Data:* b Anderson, Ind, Nov 1, 34; m 57; c 4. *Educ:* Purdue Univ, BS, 56; Univ Mich, MS, 59, PhD(chem eng), 62. *Prof Exp:* Mem res staff, Delco Remy Div, Gen Motors Corp, 52, 53, 55 & Dow Chem Co, 56-58; group leader explor develop, Procter & Gamble Co, 62-64. *Concurrent Pos:* Mem res staff, Humble Oil & Ref Co, 65 & Phillips Petrol Co, 66; consult, Great Lakes Chem Corp, 67; Midwest Appl Sci & D&M Corp, 68; Am Oil Co, Melnor Corp, Am Filters & Araneida Corp, 69; Roper Corp, 70; Westinghouse Corp, 71; Exxon Corp, 80; Howard W Sams Div MacMillan, 86 & Citizens Gas & Coke, 86; mediator/fact finder, Ind Educ Employ Rels Bd, 74-, Ind Better Bus Bur, 82-, Farm Debt Mediation, 88-; Barnes & Thornburg Law Firm, 96; Dynaclean Int, 96-97. *Mem:* Am Inst Chem Engrs; Am Soc Eng Educ; Soc Prof Dispute Resolution. *Res:* Multiphase flow; transport properties in disperse media. *Mailing Add:* Dept Chem Eng Purdue Univ Lafayette IN 47907

KESSLER, DIETRICH, CELL BIOLOGY, MOLECULAR BIOLOGY. *Current Pos:* head, Dept Biol, 84-90, PROF, DEPT BIOL, COLGATE UNIV, 84- *Personal Data:* b Hamilton, NY, May 28, 36; m 90, Johanna W Prins; c Jonathan F & Melissa B. *Educ:* Swarthmore Col, BA, 58; Univ Wis, MS, 60, PhD(zool), 64. *Prof Exp:* From asst prof to prof, Dept Biol, Haverford Col, 64-84. *Concurrent Pos:* Am Cancer Soc fel, Brandeis Univ, 66-67; NSF sci fac fel, Swiss Inst Exp Cancer Res, Lausanne, 71-72; Fulbright res grant, Bonn, Ger, 80-81; vis prof, McArdle Lab Cancer Res, Dept Oncol Med Sch, Univ Wis-Madison, 88; vis scientist, Genetics Dept, Univ Leicester, Eng, 90-91. *Mem:* AAAS; Am Soc Cell Biol. *Res:* Molecular mechanism of amoeboid movement in Physarum polycephalum using techniques of molecular and cell biology. *Mailing Add:* Dept Biol Colgate Univ Hamilton NY 13346-1398

KESSLER, EDWIN, 3RD, METEOROLOGY, SUSTAINABLE AGRICULTURE. *Current Pos:* adj prof & consult meteorol, 86-97, ADJ PROF GEOG, UNIV OKLA, 97- *Personal Data:* b New York, NY, Dec 2, 28; m 50, Lottie C Menger; c Austin R & Thomas R. *Educ:* Columbia Univ, AB, 50; Mass Inst Technol, SM, 52, ScD(meteorol), 57. *Honors & Awards:* Cleveland Abbe Award, Am Meteorol Soc, 89. *Prof Exp:* Chief synoptic sect, Weather Radar Br, Air Force Cambridge Res Ctr, 54-61; dir, Atmospheric Physics Div, Travelers Res Ctr, 61-64; dir, Nat Severe Storms Lab, US Weather Bur, 64-86. *Concurrent Pos:* Adj prof, Univ Okla, 64-; vis prof, Mass Inst Technol, 75-76; vis lectr, McGill Univ, 80; consult, Saudi Arabia, 87; chair, Common Cause Okla; mem, USDA Sustainable Agr, Res & Educ Prog. *Mem:* Fel AAAS; Am Geophys Union; fel Am Meteorol Soc; Royal Meteorol Soc; Sigma Xi; Am Inst Aeronaut & Astronaut. *Res:* Synthesis of varied observations and theory to improve understanding of meteorological phenomena and to develop and apply technology in the public interest; sustainable agriculture. *Mailing Add:* Depts Geog & Meteorol Univ Okla 100 E Boyd Energy Ctr Norman OK 73019. *Fax:* 405-360-3246; *E-Mail:* ekessler@metgem.gcn.uoknor.edu

KESSLER, ERNEST GEORGE, JR, PRECISION MEASUREMENTS, X-RAY SPECTROSCOPY. *Current Pos:* Nat Res Coun-Nat Bur Stand res assoc spectros, 69-71, PHYSICIST, CTR ATOMIC, MOLECULAR & OPTICAL PHYSICS, NAT INST STAND & TECHNOL, 71- *Personal Data:* b Hanover, Pa, Sept 12, 40; m 62; c 4. *Educ:* Shippensburg State Col, BS, 62; Univ Wis-Madison, MS, 64, PhD(physics), 69. *Mem:* Am Phys Soc. *Res:* High resolution studies of the ionized helium spectrum; determination of the Rydberg constant from wavelength measurements on ionized helium; precise x-ray and gamma ray wavelength measurements. *Mailing Add:* A-141 Physics Bldg Nat Inst Stand & Technol Gaithersburg MD 20899

KESSLER, FREDERICK MELVYN, ENGINEERING ACOUSTICS, ELECTROMECHANICAL ENGINEERING. *Current Pos:* CONSULT, 96- *Personal Data:* b Brooklyn, NY, May 15, 32; m 54; c 3. *Educ:* City Col NY, BME, 54; Rutgers Univ, MS, 67, PhD(elec eng), 71. *Prof Exp:* Jr test engr, Curtiss-Wr; sr proj mgr acoust, David Taylor Model Basin, Washington, DC, 59-61; sr develop engr eng acoust, Ingersoll-Rand Co, 61-68; fac mem elec eng, Rutgers Univ, 68-71; vpres eng acoust, Lewis S Goodfriend & Assoc, 71-73; partner, Dames & Moore, 73-80, managing partner eng acoust, 80-83; at TMK Technol Inc, Bound Brook. *Concurrent Pos:* Adj prof, Dept Mech Eng, Stevens Inst Technol, Hoboken, NJ, 78- *Mem:* Acoust Soc Am; Inst Elec & Electronics Engrs; Inst Noise Control Eng (pres, 88). *Res:* Optimization muffler design parameters using conjugate gradient search techniques. *Mailing Add:* 31 Shady Lane Bound Brook NJ 08805

KESSLER, GEORGE MORTON, HORTICULTURE. *Current Pos:* From instr to assoc prof, 47-82, EMER ASSOC PROF HORT, MICH STATE UNIV, 82- *Personal Data:* b Philadelphia, Pa, July 26, 17; m 43; c 2. *Educ:* Pa State Univ, BS, 46, MS, 47; Mich State Col, PhD(hort), 53. *Concurrent Pos:* Ed, Fruit Varieties & Hort Digest, Am Pomol Soc, 53-72. *Mem:* Am Soc Hort Sci; Am Pomol Soc (secy-treas, 57-64, pres, 67-68). *Res:* Teaching and evaluating of fruit varieties. *Mailing Add:* 1127 Lilac East Lansing MI 48823

KESSLER, GERALD, CLINICAL CHEMISTRY. *Current Pos:* DIR DIV BIOCHEM, JEWISH HOSP ST LOUIS, 67- *Personal Data:* b New York, NY, Mar 27, 30; m 52; c 4. *Educ:* City Col New York, BS, 50; Univ Md, MS, 52, PhD(biochem), 54. *Prof Exp:* Clin biochemist, Albert Einstein Med Ctr, 54-57; biochemist, Technicon Instruments Corp, NY, 57-61; head clin ctr core lab, Montefiore Hosp, NY, 61-64; chief automation div, Bio-Sci Labs, Los Angeles, 65-67. *Concurrent Pos:* Assoc scientist, Dept Biochem, Sloan-Kettering Inst Cancer Res, 59-61; consult automation res prog, Vet Admin Hosp, Bronx, NY, 63-64; assoc prof, Sch Med, Washington Univ, 67-82, prof, 82. *Mem:* AAAS; Am Chem Soc; Am Asn Clin Chem; NY Acad Sci; Acad Clin Lab Physicians & Scientists; Nat Acad Clin Biochem. *Res:* Clinical biochemistry; methodological instrumentation research as applied to automation of analytical procedures. *Mailing Add:* 2362 Claymoor Dr Chesterfield MO 63017-7834

KESSLER, HAROLD D, TITANIUM. *Current Pos:* CONSULT, 86- *Personal Data:* b Toledo, Ohio, Dec 28, 21. *Educ:* Case Inst Technol, BS, 42; Ill Inst Technol, MS, 49. *Honors & Awards:* Russ Ogden Award, Am Soc Testing & Mat, 85. *Prof Exp:* Mem staff, Nat Advan Comt Aeronaut, 43-44, Air Force, Wright Field, 44-45 & Armour Res Found, 45-54; mgr, Metall Res Lab, Titanium Metals Corp Am, 54-57 & Tech Develop Lab, 57-64; chief metallurgist, Reactive Metals Co, 64-69, vpres technol, 69-79; tech dir, DH Titanium, 79-81; mgr titanium opers, Cabot Corp, 81-86. *Concurrent Pos:* Mem bd dirs, Am Soc Metals. *Mem:* Am Inst Mining Metall & Petrol Engrs; Am Soc Metals. *Res:* Processes for manufacture of titanium; titanium alloys. *Mailing Add:* KesCo Inc 18010 Alyssum Dr Sun City West AZ 85375

KESSLER, IRVING ISAR, PREVENTIVE MEDICINE, EPIDEMIOLOGY. *Current Pos:* assoc prof prev med, 70-78, chmn epidemiol & prev med, 78-88, PROF DERMAT & MED, UNIV MD, 84- *Personal Data:* b Chelsea, Mass, Mar 22, 31; c 2. *Educ:* NY Univ, AB, 52; Harvard Univ, MA, 55, DrPH, 69; Stanford Univ, MD, 60; Columbia Univ, MPH, 62; Am Bd Prev Med, dipl. *Prof Exp:* Instr environ med, State Univ NY, 64-66; asst prof chronic dis, Johns Hopkins Univ, 66-69, assoc prof epidemiol, 70-72, prof, 73-78. *Concurrent Pos:* Fac res award, Am Cancer Soc, 72-77; med dir res, USPHS; mem exec comn, Gov Coun Toxic Substances, Md; exec dir, Md Cancer Registry, 82; scientific res bd, Ctr Indoor Dir Res; vpres health Sci, ECRI, 92-93. *Mem:* AAAS; Am Epidemiol Soc; Am Asn Cancer Res; Am Pub Health Asn; Asn Teachers Prev Med; Sigma Xi. *Res:* Epidemiological research in cancer, diabetes mellitus, birth defects and Parkinson's disease; epidemiological principles; community studies of health; gerontology; environmental and occupational health; health regulation. *Mailing Add:* Dept Epidemiol & Prev Med Sch Med Univ Md Baltimore MD 21201. *Fax:* 410-706-8013; *E-Mail:* ikessler@erin.ab.umd.edu

KESSLER, IRVING JACK, MATHEMATICS. *Current Pos:* RES STAFF MATH, INST DEFENSE ANALYSIS, 77-, PRES. *Personal Data:* b Brooklyn, NY, May 14, 40; c 2. *Educ:* Brooklyn Col, BA, 62; Univ Wis, MS, 63, PhD(math), 66. *Prof Exp:* Asst prof math, Univ Mich, 66-68; from asst prof to assoc prof, Southern Ill Univ, 68-78, prof math, 78-80. *Concurrent Pos:* Res staff math, Inst Defense Anal, 74-75 & 77- *Mem:* Am Math Soc; Math Asn Am. *Res:* Combinatorial mathematics; number theory; applying mathematics to problems in speech recognition. *Mailing Add:* Inst Defense Analysis Thanet Rd Princeton NJ 08540

KESSLER, JOHN OTTO, PHYCOLOGY, MICROBIOLOGY. *Current Pos:* PROF PHYSICS, UNIV ARIZ, 66- *Personal Data:* b Vienna, Austria, Nov 26, 28; nat US; m 50; c 2. *Educ:* Columbia Univ, AB, 49, MS, 50, PhD(physics), 53. *Prof Exp:* Asst physics, Columbia Univ, 48-52; physicist labs, Radio Corp Am, 52-62 & Princeton Univ, 63-65; mgr grad recruiting, RCA Corp, 65-66. *Concurrent Pos:* Vis prof physics, Univ Leeds, 72-73 & T H Delft, Neth, 79; Fulbright fel, Dept Appl Math & Theoret Phys, Cambridge Univ, 83-84, Cult Ctr Algae & Protozoa, 85-, Dept Appl Math, Univ Leeds, 90-91. *Mem:* Fel AAAS; Am Phys Soc; Phycol Soc Am. *Res:* Applied phycology; biophysics; plant physiology; fluid mechanics of microorganisms; concentrative and cooperative phenomena of microrganism populations for practical applications in cell separation and phycoculture and as a means for investigating self organizing systems. *Mailing Add:* Dept Physics Bldg 81 Univ Ariz Tucson AZ 85721

KESSLER, KARL GUNTHER, ATOMIC & MOLECULAR PHYSICS, OPTICS. *Current Pos:* div chief, 62-78, Dir, Ctr Basic Standards, 78-86, RES PHYSICIST, NAT BUR STANDARDS, 48-, ASSOC DIR INT AFFAIRS, 86- *Personal Data:* b Hamburg, Germany, Aug 21, 19; US citizen; m 41; c 2. *Educ:* Univ Mich, AB, 41, MS, 42, PhD(physics), 47. *Honors & Awards:* Gold Medal, Dept Com, 62; Dist Service Award, Optical Soc Am, 84. *Prof Exp:* Res physicist, Univ Mich, 41-48, instr, 43-48. *Mem:* Am Phys Soc; Optical Soc Am (pres, 69); Astron Soc Am; Int Astron Union; AAAS; Sigma Xi. *Res:* Atomic physics; atomic spectroscopy. *Mailing Add:* 5927 Anniston Rd Bethesda MD 20817

KESSLER, KENNETH J, JR, PLANT PATHOLOGY. *Current Pos:* PLANT PATHOLOGIST, NORTH CENT FOREST EXP STA, US FOREST SERV, 59- *Personal Data:* b Wheeling, WVa, Mar 15, 33; m 54; c 4. *Educ:* WVa Univ, BS, 55, MS, 57, PhD(plant path), 60. *Mem:* Am Phytopath Soc; Mycol Soc Am. *Res:* Hardwood tree diseases. *Mailing Add:* RR 2 No 254 Carbondale IL 62901

KESSLER, LAWRENCE W, ULTRASOUND, BIOENGINEERING. *Current Pos:* PRES ACOUST MICROS, SONOSCAN, INC, 74- *Personal Data:* b Chicago, Ill, Sept 26, 42; m 64, 85, Francesca Agramonte; c Jeffrey, Brett, Corey, Brandy, Lindsay, Bryan & Bradley. *Educ:* Purdue Univ, BS, 64; Univ Ill, Urbana-Champaign, MS, 65, PhD(elec eng), 68. *Prof Exp:* Mem res staff acoust visualization, Zenith Radio Corp, 68-74. *Concurrent Pos:* Mem adv panel, Tech Electronic Prod Radiation Safety Stand Comt, Dept Health, Educ & Welfare, 72-75; nat lectr, Inst Elec & Electronics Engrs, 81-82. *Mem:* Sr mem Inst Elec & Electronics Engrs; Am Inst Ultrasound Med; fel Acoust Soc Am; Am Soc Nondestructive Testing. *Res:* Acoustic microscopy and ultrasonic visualization applications in life and materials sciences; quality assurance inspection equipment; biomedical engineering; laser scanning systems. *Mailing Add:* Sonoscan Inc 530 E Green St Bensenville IL 60106

KESSLER, NATHAN, CHEMICAL ENGINEERING. *Current Pos:* CONSULT, TECHN INC, ST LOUIS, 85- *Personal Data:* b St Louis, Mo, Aug 19, 23; m 47; c 3. *Educ:* Washington Univ, BSChE & MS, 44. *Prof Exp:* Chem engr, A E Staley Mfg, Inc, 44-51, tech supvr, Ohio, 51-53, sr chem eng, Ill, 53-57, chief chem engr, 57-60, dir process eng, 60-61, plant supt, 61-62, gen supt, 62-67, mem bd dirs & tech group vpres, A E Staley Mfg Co, 67-85, pres, Staley Techventures, 64-86, technol consult, Biotech Resources, Inc, 85-87. *Concurrent Pos:* Mem eng adv bd, Rice Univ, 71 & Univ Ill, 82-87; mem bd dirs, Wastech, Inc, Tex, 70-76; mem, Jr Eng & Technol Soc Bd & pres, 82-85; mem, Biotechnical Resources Bd, 82-85; mem bd, Technol Transfer Soc, 83-; White-Rodgers fel; assoc dir, Biotech Resources, Inc, 85-89; chmn, Indust Adv Comt, Mich Biotechnol Inst, 87-; mem, Indust Adv Bd, Fed Lab Consortium, 87- *Mem:* Am Inst Chem Engrs; Am Chem Soc; Technol Transfer Soc (pres, 85-88, chmn, 88-90). *Res:* Engineering, research and development; food processes; biotechnology; technology transfer. *Mailing Add:* 232 N Kingshighway Blvd No 1114 St Louis MO 63108-1211

KESSLER, RICHARD HOWARD, MEDICINE, PHYSIOLOGY. *Current Pos:* RETIRED. *Personal Data:* b Paterson, NJ, Dec 15, 23; m 44; c 3. *Educ:* Rutgers Univ, BSc, 48; NY Univ, MD, 52. *Prof Exp:* Asst chem, Rutgers Univ, 47-48; asst med, NY Univ, 52-55; from instr to assoc prof physiol, Cornell Univ, 55-68; prof med, Med Sch Northwestern Univ, Chicago, 68-78, assoc dean, Med Sch, 70-78; prof med, Pritzker Sch Med, Univ Chicago, 78-83; sr vpres, Michael Reese Hosp & Med Ctr, 78-83; prof med, Mt Sinai Sch Med, NY, 84-88. *Concurrent Pos:* Life inst med res fel, 55-56; Hofheimer Found fel, 57-62; mem, Sect Renal Dis, Coun Circulation, Am Heart Asn; mem, Health Econ Adv Comt, Nat Bur Econ Res; consult, Educ Serv, Vet Admin; vpres, Kidney Found Ill; comnr, Health & Hosps Gov Comn Cook Co; fel, Hastings Inst Soc, Ethics & Life Sci; comnr, Chicago Health Systs

Agency. *Mem:* AAAS; Harvey Soc; Soc Exp Biol & Med; Am Physiol Soc; fel Am Col Physicians. *Res:* Cardiovascular and renal physiology; fluid balance; electrolyte transport; diuretics; renal disease; hypertension. *Mailing Add:* 349 S Wash Dr Sarasota FL 34236

KESSLER, SEYMOUR, GENETICS. *Current Pos:* CONSULT, 85- *Personal Data:* b New York, NY, Sept 3, 28; m 53; c 2. *Educ:* City Col New York, BS, 60; Columbia Univ, MA, 62, PhD(zool), 65; PhD(soc-clin psychol). *Prof Exp:* Fel psychiat, Sch Med, Stanford Univ, 65-67, asst prof, 67-73, sr scientist, 73-74, adj prof psychiat, 74-75; dir & sr lectr, Univ Calif, Berkeley, 75-85. *Concurrent Pos:* Assoc clin prof, Univ Calif, San Francisco. *Mem:* Am Soc Human Genetics; Sigma Xi; Am Psychol Asn; Nat Soc Genetic Counselors. *Res:* Behavior and psychiatric genetics; genetic counseling. *Mailing Add:* PO Box 7702 Berkeley CA 94707. *Fax:* 510-525-1996

KESSLER, WAYNE VINCENT, BIONUCLEONICS, ENVIRONMENTAL TOXICOLOGY. *Current Pos:* from asst prof to assoc prof, 60-68, PROF HEALTH SCI, PURDUE UNIV, WEST LAFAYETTE, 68- *Personal Data:* b Milo, Iowa, Jan 10, 33; m 53, Olive B Buremaster; c 2. *Educ:* NDak State Univ, BS, 55, MS, 56; Purdue Univ, PhD(pharmaceut chem), 59. *Prof Exp:* Asst pharmaceut chem, Purdue Univ, 56-57; asst prof, NDak State Univ, 59-60. *Concurrent Pos:* Lederle pharm fac award, 62; vis scientist, Am Asn Cols Pharm, 64-70; assoc prof, Sch Med, Ind Univ, 70-73. *Mem:* Fel AAAS; Am Pharmaceut Asn; Am Chem Soc; fel Acad Pharmaceut Sci; Health Physics Soc. *Res:* Inhalation toxicology of noxious substances; natural radioactivity in building materials. *Mailing Add:* Sch Health Sci 1338 CIVL Purdue Univ West Lafayette IN 47907-1968. *Fax:* 765-496-1377

KESSLER, WILLIAM J(OSEPH), COMMUNICATIONS ENGINEERING. *Current Pos:* OWNER, KESSLER & GEHMAN ASSOCS. *Personal Data:* b Roebling, NY, Feb 28, 17; c 4. *Honors & Awards:* Cert Off Sci & Res & Develop & Ord Develop Award, 45. *Prof Exp:* Lab instr elec eng, Univ Fla, 43-45, asst prof, 45-67, asst res engr, 45-53; owner, W J Kessler Assoc, 67- *Concurrent Pos:* Microwave, TV & commun consult, eng forensics. *Mem:* Nat Soc Prof Engrs; Am Electromagnetic Soc. *Res:* Thunderstorm electricity; propagation of low frequency electromagnetic radiations; special instrumentation for radio location of thunder-storms for meteorological forecasting purposes. *Mailing Add:* 1625 SW 35th Pl Gainesville FL 32608

KESSNER, DAVID MORTON, INTERNAL MEDICINE. *Current Pos:* PROF & VCHMN COMMUNITY & FAMILY MED, UNIV MASS MED CTR, 75- *Personal Data:* b New York, NY, Aug 23, 32; m 59; c 2. *Educ:* Univ Ariz, BS, 54; Washington Univ, MD, 58; Am Bd Internal Med, dipl, 67. *Prof Exp:* Intern med, Mary Imogene Bassett Hosp, 58-59, asst resident internal med, 59-60; jr attend physician, Med Clin, Univ Ill, 61-62; second year resident internal med, Sch Med, Yale Univ, 64-65, from instr to asst prof med & epidemiol, 65-69; study dir & res assoc, Inst Med, Nat Acad Sci, 69-73; dir, Health Serv Res Off & assoc prof community med & int health, Georgetown Univ, 73-75. *Concurrent Pos:* Fel prev med, Sch Med, Univ Ill, 60-62; fel med, Sch Med, Yale Univ, 62-64; Nat Inst Arthritis & Metab Dis fel, 63-64; attend physician, Metab Sect, Yale-New Haven Hosp, 65-69, assoc physician, Dept Med, 66-69, consult internist, Yale Psychiat Inst, 67-69; asst clin prof, Sch Med, George Washington Univ, 70-73, attend physician, Hosp, 70- *Mem:* Am Fedn Clin Res; Am Pub Health Asn; Int Epidemiol Asn; fel Am Col Physicians. *Res:* Chronic disease epidemiology; the use of epidemiology in health services research. *Mailing Add:* Coastal Couns Assoc 24 Front St Exeter NH 03833

KESTEN, ARTHUR S(IDNEY), RESEARCH ADMINISTRATION. *Current Pos:* res engr, United Technol Res Ctr, 63-65, sr res engr, 65-68, supvr kinetics & heat transfer, 68-72, prin scientist kinetics & environ sci, 72-76, mgr combustion sci, 76-77, mgr energy res, 77-81, asst dir res power indust systs technol, 81-90, asst dir, 90-92, assoc dir res, indust systs & technol, 92-93, assoc dir res, 93-95, DIR RES, PROGS UNITED TECHNOL RES CTR, 96- *Personal Data:* b New York, NY, Sept 10, 34; m 56, Hilda Rubenstein; c Ilene & Gwen. *Educ:* NY Univ, BS, 55; Univ Pittsburgh, MS, 58, PhD(chem eng), 61. *Prof Exp:* Assoc engr res & develop, Bettis Atomic Power Lab, Westinghouse Elec Corp, 55-57, engr, 57-61, sr engr, 61-63. *Concurrent Pos:* Adj assoc prof, Rensselaer Polytech Inst, 65-; chmn, Solar Energy Res Inst Adv Bd, 84- *Mem:* Fel Am Inst Chem; Sigma Xi; Am Inst Chem Engrs; Am Chem Soc; Combustion Inst; Res Soc Am. *Res:* Hydrogen energy systems, chemical reactors, transport processes, combustion; sixteen patents awarded in area of chemical heat pumps and gas transporting systems. *Mailing Add:* 17 Morning Crest Dr West Hartford CT 06117

KESTEN, HARRY, MATHEMATICS. *Current Pos:* from asst prof to assoc prof, 61-65, PROF MATH, CORNELL UNIV, 65- *Personal Data:* b Nov 19, 31. *Educ:* Cornell Univ, PhD, 58. *Honors & Awards:* Rietz Lectr, Inst Math Statist, 71; Wald Lectr, 86; Brouwer Mem Lectr & Medal, Dutch Math Soc, 81; George Polya Prize, Soc Indust & Appl Math, 94. *Prof Exp:* Instr, Princetown Univ, 58-59, Hebrew Univ, Jerusalem, 59-61. *Concurrent Pos:* Alfred P Sloan fel, 63-65; Guggenheim fel, 72-73. *Mem:* Nat Acad Sci; Am Math Soc; Inst Math Statist; corresp mem Royal Dutch Acad Sci. *Res:* Author of numerous publications. *Mailing Add:* Dept Math White Hall Cornell Univ Ithaca NY 14853. *Fax:* 607-255-7149; *E-Mail:* kesten@math.cornell.edu

KESTENBAUM, RICHARD CHARLES, BACTERIOLOGY. *Current Pos:* RETIRED. *Personal Data:* b New York, NY, Apr 3, 31; m 54, Rhoda Mutterperl; c Edward, Jeffrey & Roberta. *Educ:* City Col New York, BS, 52; Rutgers Univ, MS, 54, PhD(bact), 59. *Prof Exp:* Asst bact, Rutgers Univ, 52-54 & 56-59; bacteriologist, Colgate-Palmolive Co, Piscataway, 59-61, sr res microbiologist, 61-63, sect head microbiol, 63-66, sect head oral res, 66-69 & 71-75, sect head oral prod, 69-71, sr sect head oral prod & appl res, 77-78, mgr oral prod, 78-81, assoc dir personal care prod, 81-83, assoc dir res & develop planning, 83-88, assoc dir technol planning, 88-90. *Mem:* Am Soc Microbiol; Int Asn Dent Res. *Res:* Dental medicine; bacterial metabolism; microbial quality control; antimicrobial agents; oral and clinical research; oral products. *Mailing Add:* 18 Bradford Rd East Brunswick NJ 08816

KESTENBAUM, RICHARD STEVEN, NEUROPSYCHOPHARMACOLOGY, PSYCHOTHERAPY. *Current Pos:* ASSOC PROF PSYCHOL & CLIN SUPVR, TEACHER'S COL, COLUMBIA UNIV, 80-; PRES, PSYCHOL NETWORKS, 80- *Personal Data:* b New York, NY, Mar 20, 42; m 70; c 1. *Educ:* NY Univ, BA, 63, PhD(psychol), 68. *Prof Exp:* Res fel psychol, NIMH, 66-68; asst prof, State Univ NY Stony Brook, 68-73; assoc dir res, Dept Psychiat, NY Med Col, 74-79. *Concurrent Pos:* Fel, Nat Inst Psychother, 74-79. *Mem:* AAAS; Am Psychol Asn; NY Acad Sci. *Res:* Neural coding of pain and neuropsychopharmacology of pain perception; neuropsychopharmacology of opiates and implications for treatment; neuropsychopharmacology of cocaine in man; psychotherapy outcome evaluation. *Mailing Add:* 142 West End Ave New York NY 10023

KESTER, ANDREW STEPHEN, BACTERIOLOGY. *Current Pos:* asst prof, 67-74, ASSOC PROF BIOL, NTEX STATE UNIV, 74- *Personal Data:* b Abington, Pa, Sept 1, 32; m 60; c 2. *Educ:* Pa State Univ, BS, 54; Univ Tex, PhD(bact), 61. *Prof Exp:* Res microbiologist, Miles Chem Co, Ind, 61-67. *Mem:* Am Soc Microbiol; Am Chem Soc. *Res:* Microbial oxidation of hydrocarbons; industrial microbiology. *Mailing Add:* 387 7147 Kesterson Chad 619 Denton TX 76201

KESTER, DALE EMMERT, POMOLOGY. *Current Pos:* RETIRED. *Personal Data:* b Audubon, Iowa, July 28, 22; m 46; c 2. *Educ:* Iowa State Col, BS, 47; Univ Calif, MS, 49, PhD(plant physiol), 51. *Honors & Awards:* Stark Award, Am Soc Hort Sci, 80. *Prof Exp:* Res asst, Univ Calif, 48-50, jr specialist, 51, instr pomol, 51-53, lectr, 53, from asst prof to assoc prof, 54-69, from jr pomologist to assoc pomologist, 51-69, prof pomol & pomologist, Exp Sta, 69-91. *Mem:* AAAS; Fel Am Soc Hort Sci; Int Plant Propagators Soc; Genetics Soc Am; Int Asn Plant Tissue Cult; Am Pomol Soc; Int Hort Soc. *Res:* Plant breeding, almonds, rootstocks; tissue and embryo culture of prunus species; plant propagation; somatic variation. *Mailing Add:* 750 Anderson Rd Davis CA 95616

KESTER, DANA R, CHEMICAL OCEANOGRAPHY, PHYSICAL CHEMISTRY. *Current Pos:* From asst prof to assoc prof, 69-76, PROF OCEANOG, UNIV RI, 76- *Personal Data:* b Los Angeles, Calif, Jan 26, 43; m 63; c 1. *Educ:* Univ Wash, BS, 64; Ore State Univ, MS, 66, PhD(oceanog), 69. *Concurrent Pos:* Ed, Marine Chem, 73-78, J Marine Res, 73-80. *Mem:* Am Geophys Union; Sigma Xi; AAAS. *Res:* Physical chemistry of seawater; effects of temperature and pressure on ionic equilibria; transition metal marine chemistry; oceanic chemical distributions; waste disposal in the ocean. *Mailing Add:* Grad Sch Oceanog Univ RI S Ferry Rd Narragansett RI 02882

KESTER, DENNIS EARL, ORGANIC POLYMER CHEMISTRY. *Current Pos:* Res scientist polymers, coatings & eng, Am Nat Can Co, 74-80, supvr organic res & dir prod develop, 80-84, vpres res & develop, 84-91, SR VPRES, PLASTICS DIV, AM NAT CAN CO, 91- *Personal Data:* b Eureka, Kans, Aug 21, 47; m 68; c 1. *Educ:* Col Emporia, BS, 69; Univ Ark, PhD(org chem), 75. *Mem:* Am Chem Soc. *Res:* Polymer characterization and polymer synthesis; anionic, condensation and free radical polymerizations for the preparation of materials for specific coatings applications; radiation curable resins and coatings, adhesion; film and sheet laminating and extrusion, printing. *Mailing Add:* Am Nat Can Co MS 06K 8770 W Bryan Mawr Ave Chicago IL 60631-3542

KESTING, ROBERT E, POLYMER CHEMISTRY. *Current Pos:* vpres, 79-81, PRES, PURPORE INC, DIV GELMAN SCI, 82- *Personal Data:* b Jamaica, NY, Feb 8, 33; m 59; c 4. *Educ:* Manhattan Col, BS, 56; State Univ NY Col Forestry, Syracuse, MS, 59, PhD(chem), 61. *Prof Exp:* Res chemist, Heberlein & Co AG, Switz, 60-62 & Von Karman Ctr, Aerojet-Gen Corp Div, Gen Tire & Rubber Co, Calif, 62-65; sr scientist, Philco-Ford, 65-67; consult, 67-69; vpres polymer opers, Chem Systs, Inc, Santa Anna, 69-76, vpres, Irvine, 76-79. *Res:* Graft copolymerization on polymer substrates; structure and function of reverse osmosis membranes; new theory for the lyotropic swelling of polar polymers; developed Kesting process for the fabrication of wet-dry reversible reverse osmosis membranes; synthetic polymeric membranes. *Mailing Add:* 3220 199th Ave Ct E Sumner WA 98390

KESTNER, MARK OTTO, INORGANIC CHEMISTRY, DUST CONTROL. *Current Pos:* PRES, NATURAL ENVIRON SERV CO, 88- *Personal Data:* b Berea, Ohio, Dec 10, 47; m 71; c 1. *Educ:* Carnegie-Mellon Univ, BS, 69; Northwestern Univ, MS, 70, PhD(chem), 74. *Prof Exp:* Res chemist, Borg-Warner Corp, 74-78; group leader, Apollo Chem Corp, 78-80, mgr, prod develop, 80-83; pres, Chemicoal, Inc, 83-88. *Mem:* Am Chem Soc; NY Acad Sci; Sigma Xi. *Res:* Handling, storage and combustion of coal and other fossil fuel; air pollution control and chemical treatments for control of particulate and gaseous emissions; solid waste disposal. *Mailing Add:* 7 Hampshire Dr Mendham NJ 07945

KESTNER, MELVIN MICHAEL, ORGANIC CHEMISTRY. *Current Pos:* SR CHEMIST ORG CHEM, EASTMAN KODAK CO, 73- *Personal Data:* b Wooster, Ohio, Oct 20, 45; m 71. *Educ:* Heidelberg Col, BS, 67; Purdue Univ, PhD(org chem), 73. *Mem:* Am Chem Soc. *Res:* Synthesis of compounds used in photographic products. *Mailing Add:* 590 Parma Ctr Rd Hilton NY 14468

KESTNER, NEIL R, CHEMICAL PHYSICS. *Current Pos:* assoc prof, La State Univ, 66-72, chmn freshman chem, 73-76, chmn dept, 76-81, PROF CHEM, LA STATE UNIV, BATON ROUGE, 72- *Personal Data:* b Milwaukee, Wis, Dec 11, 37. *Educ:* Univ Wis-Milwaukee, BS, 60; Yale Univ, MS, 62, PhD(theoret chem), 64. *Prof Exp:* Res assoc, Inst Study Metals, Univ Chicago, 63-64; asst prof chem, Stanford Univ, 64-66. *Concurrent Pos:* A P Sloan fel, 67-69; vis prof, Tel-Aviv Univ, 72; res collabr, Brookhaven Nat Lab, 81. *Mem:* Am Chem Soc; Am Phys Soc; Sigma Xi; AAAS. *Res:* Quantum chemistry; intermolecular forces; electrons in disordered media; electron transfer reactions. *Mailing Add:* Dept Chem La State Univ Baton Rouge LA 70803-0001

KETCHA, DANIEL MICHAEL, HETEROCYCLIC CHEMISTRY. *Current Pos:* asst prof, 85-91, ASSOC PROF CHEM, WRIGHT STATE UNIV, DAYTON, OHIO, 91- *Personal Data:* b Newark, NJ, Jan 12, 56; c 1. *Educ:* King's Col, Wilkes-Barre, BS, 77; Temple Univ, Philadelphia, PhD(org chem), 84. *Prof Exp:* Res assoc, Dartmouth Col, Hanover, NH, 83-85, res instr chem, 85. *Mem:* Am Chem Soc. *Res:* Development of novel synthetic methodologies and their subsequent application towards the synthesis of molecules of biological importance. *Mailing Add:* Dept Chem Wright State Univ 3640 Colonel Glenn Dayton OH 45435-0001. *Fax:* 513-873-3301

KETCHAM, ALFRED SCHUTT, surgery, for more information see previous edition

KETCHAM, BRUCE V(ALENTINE), AEROSPACE ENGINEERING. *Current Pos:* head Dept Aerospace Eng, Univ Tulsa, 64-67, dir res & develop, 66-67, dir solar energy projs, 76-83, PROF MECH & AEROSPACE ENG, UNIV TULSA, 64-, EMER PROF, 83- *Personal Data:* b Wilmington, Del, Mar 17, 18; m 44. *Educ:* Yale Univ, BME, 40; Univ Okla, MAE, 56. *Prof Exp:* Designer aero engines, Pratt & Whitney Aircraft Div, United Aircraft Corp, 40-47; chmn sch aero eng, Univ Okla, 53-63, dir aero res, 57-64, mem fac, 47-64. *Concurrent Pos:* Consult, Aero Design & Eng Co, 56-58 & Todd Eng Co, 61-, Elec Peakload Probs, 84. *Mem:* Am Soc Eng Educ; Am Inst Aeronaut & Astronaut. *Res:* Space engineering; rocket propulsion; gas turbine. *Mailing Add:* 2956 E 47th St Tulsa OK 74105

KETCHAM, ROGER, ORGANIC CHEMISTRY, HETEROCYCLIC CHEMISTRY. *Current Pos:* RETIRED. *Personal Data:* b Berea, Ohio, Sept 2, 26; m 50; c 4. *Educ:* Antioch Col, BS, 51; Cornell Univ, PhD(chem), 56. *Prof Exp:* From instr to prof chem & pharmaceut chem, Sch Pharm, Univ Calif, San Francisco, 69-91. *Concurrent Pos:* Mem, Orgn Am States Prof, Monterrey Inst Technol & Higher Educ, 64-65; vis prof, Univ Graz, Austria, 71-72, Univ Hamburg, Ger, 79-80 & Univ Lund, Sweden, 83. *Mem:* Am Chem Soc; Am Pharmaceut Asn; Chem Soc; Sigma Xi. *Res:* Three-membered rings; nitrogen and sulfur heterocycles; reaction mechanisms; organo-sulfur chemistry. *Mailing Add:* Sch Pharm Univ Calif San Francisco CA 94143-0446

KETCHEL, MELVIN M, reproductive physiology, for more information see previous edition

KETCHEN, EUGENE EARL, PHYSICAL CHEMISTRY. *Current Pos:* chemist, Isotope Div, 51-74, INDUST HYG CHEMIST, OAK RIDGE NAT LAB, 74- *Personal Data:* b Miami, Fla, May 3, 21; m 51; c 3. *Educ:* Univ Miami, BS, 43; Univ Pittsburgh, PhD(phys chem), 50. *Prof Exp:* Asst, Univ Pittsburgh, 46-50; asst prof chem, Washington & Jefferson Col, 50-51. *Mem:* Am Chem Soc; Am Indust Hyg Asn; Am Acad Indust Hyg. *Res:* Radio-isotopes; industrial hygiene chemistry; industrial toxicology. *Mailing Add:* 654 Lakeshore Dr Kingston TN 37763-2010

KETCHEN, MARK B, CRYOGENIC DIGITAL DEVICES. *Current Pos:* RES STAFF MEM & MGR, THOMAS J WATSON RES CTR, IBM, 77- *Personal Data:* b St Stephens, Can, Sept 15, 48. *Educ:* Mass Inst Technol, BS, 70; Univ Calif, Berkeley, MA, 71, PhD(physics), 77. *Prof Exp:* Officer, Physics Thermodynamics Reactor Oper, US Naval Nuclear Power Prog, 72-76. *Mem:* Am Phys Soc; Inst Elec & Electronics Engrs. *Res:* Electrical design and evaluation of superconducting quantum interference devices for digital and analog applications; logic and power circuits for an ultra-high-speed cryogenic computer. *Mailing Add:* 6 Kosior Dr Hadley MA 01035

KETCHIE, DELMER O, PLANT PHYSIOLOGY, BIOCHEMISTRY. *Current Pos:* from asst horticulturist to assoc horticulturist, 67-80, HORTICULTURIST, TREE FRUIT RES CTR, WASH STATE UNIV, 80- *Personal Data:* b Salisbury, NC, July 7, 32; m 59, 79; c 4. *Educ:* Wash State Univ, BS, 59; Univ Idaho, MS, 61; Cornell Univ, PhD(pomol), 65. *Honors & Awards:* Stark Award, 73; Paul Howe Sheppard Award, 84. *Prof Exp:* Plant physiologist, Date & Citrus Sta, USDA, Calif, 65-67. *Mem:* Am Soc Hort Sci; Soc Cryobiol; Int Soc Hort Sci; Sigma Xi. *Res:* Winter hardiness of deciduous fruit trees, including biochemical and physical aspects; rest dormancy of deciduous fruit trees. *Mailing Add:* 1100 N Western Wenatchee WA 98801-1230

KETCHMAN, JEFFREY, MECHANICAL ENGINEERING, NEW PRODUCT DEVELOPMENT. *Current Pos:* DIR, MECH & SAFETY ENG, INTER-CITY TESTING & CONSULT INC, 87- *Personal Data:* b New York, NY, Nov 23, 42; m 62; c 2. *Educ:* City Col New York, BSME, 64; Ohio State Univ, MSME, 67; Columbia Univ, DrEngSci, 72. *Prof Exp:* Proj task leader, Battelle Mem Inst, 64-67; mem tech staff, Bell Labs, 67-76; dir, Eng & Res, AMF, Inc, 76-85; vpres design, eng & res, Lightolier Inc, 85-87; dir res & eng, Genlyte Group, 85. *Concurrent Pos:* Consult, new prod develop & eng mgt & forensic eng; adj prof, Cooper Union, New York. *Mem:* AAAS; NY Acad Sci; Asn Res Dirs; Am Soc Mech Eng; Am Soc Safety Eng; Syst Safety Soc; Soc Automotive Engrs. *Res:* Optimizing radioisotope thermoelectric generators; design and development of submarine sonar systems; exercise equipment; oil-field equipment; lighting systems; product safety; safety engineering and accident reconstruction. *Mailing Add:* 14 Caccamo Lane Westport CT 06880

KETCHUM, GARDNER M(ASON), fluid mechanics, heat transfer; deceased, see previous edition for last biography

KETCHUM, MILO S, STRUCTURAL ENGINEERING. *Current Pos:* EMER PROF CIVIL ENG, UNIV CONN, 78- *Personal Data:* b Denver, Colo, Mar 8, 10; wid; c David M, Marcia, Matthew P & Mark A. *Educ:* Univ Ill, BS, 31, MS, 32. *Hon Degrees:* DSc, Univ Colo, 76, Dr, 76. *Honors & Awards:* Turner Gold Medal, Am Concrete Inst, 72. *Prof Exp:* Founder & vpres, Kkbna Eng, 45-86. *Mem:* Nat Acad Eng; hon mem Am Concrete Inst; hon mem Am Soc Civil Engrs; Am Soc Eng Educ; fel Am Consult Eng Coun. *Mailing Add:* 111 Emerson St Apt 1523 Denver CO 80218-3791

KETCHUM, PAUL ABBOTT, MICROBIAL PHYSIOLOGY. *Current Pos:* DIR, RES ASSOCS CAPE COD INC, 94- *Personal Data:* b Hyannis, Mass, Aug 11, 42; m 63, 96, Robin Walder MacFarlin; c Geoffrey Stephen & Jennifer. *Educ:* Bates Col, BS, 64; Univ Mass, PhD(microbiol), 69. *Prof Exp:* NIH fel biochem, Johns Hopkins Univ, 68-70; from asst prof to assoc prof biol sci, Oakland Univ, 70-93, NSF grant, 71-77, prof, 93-95. *Concurrent Pos:* Guest scientist, Univ Ga, Athens, 89-90; Mem, Nat Coun & Comt A, Am Asn Univ Professors. *Mem:* AAAS; Am Soc Microbiol; Am Asn Univ Professors; Sigma Xi; Soc Indust Microbiol; Int Endotoxin Soc. *Res:* Inorganic nitrogen metabolism; biochemistry of nitrate reductase; role of molybdenum in inorganic nitrogen metabolism; biochemistry of limulus amebocyte lysate. *Mailing Add:* 31 Moorland Rd Falmouth MA 02540. *Fax:* 508-540-8680; *E-Mail:* pketchum@acciusa.com

KETELLAPPER, HENDRIK JAN, PLANT PHYSIOLOGY. *Current Pos:* lectr, Univ Calif, Davis, 64-65, assoc prof, 65-69, assoc dean, Col Lett & Sci, 67-83, prof, 69-91, EMER PROF BOT, UNIV CALIF, DAVIS, 91- *Personal Data:* b Ridderkerk, Neth, Dec 23, 25; nat US; m 51; c 3. *Educ:* Univ Utrecht, BSc, 47, PhC, 51, PhD(plant physiol), 53. *Prof Exp:* Instr gen bot, Univ Utrecht, 48-51; res officer, Div Plant Indust, Commonwealth Sci & Indust Res Orgn, Canberra, Australia, 54-57; res fel biol, Calif Inst Technol, 57-64. *Concurrent Pos:* Nat Acad Sci exchange scientist, USSR, 63. *Mem:* AAAS; Japanese Soc Plant Physiol; NY Acad Sci; Royal Neth Bot Soc; Sigma Xi. *Res:* Climate and plant growth and development; algal physiology; physiological ecology; environmental ethics. *Mailing Add:* 621 Francisco Pl Davis CA 95606

KETHLEY, JOHN BRYAN, ACAROLOGY. *Current Pos:* asst cur insects, 70-75, Head Div, 74-77 & 80-84, ASSOC CUR, FIELD MUS NATURAL HIST, 75- *Personal Data:* b Passaic, NJ, Oct 18, 42; m 68, Judith Townsend. *Educ:* Univ Ga, BS, 64, PhD(entom), 69. *Prof Exp:* NIH trainee acarol lab, Ohio State Univ, 69-70. *Concurrent Pos:* Lectr comt evolutionary biol, Univ Chicago, 71-72, 74-; instr biol sci, Northwestern Univ, 73-75; lectr acarology, Ohio State Univ, 74- *Mem:* Acarological Soc Am; Entom Soc Am; Sigma Xi. *Res:* Acarine systematics; deep soil arthropods; evolution of meiosis; arthropod terrestrialization; arthropod paleontology. *Mailing Add:* 533 Elgin Ave Forest Park IL 60130. *Fax:* 312-663-5397; *E-Mail:* kethley@fmnh785.fmnh.org

KETHLEY, THOMAS WILLIAM, BIOLOGY. *Current Pos:* from res asst prof to res assoc prof, Eng Exp Sta, Ga Inst Technol, 46-60, head bio-eng br, 60-77, res prof appl biol, 60-81, prof, 74-81, EMER PROF BIOL, GA INST TECHNOL, 81- *Personal Data:* b Crystal Springs, Miss, Apr 3, 13; wid; c T William Jr, John B & Dorothy A. *Educ:* Emory Univ, AB, 34, MS, 35. *Prof Exp:* Drug & insecticide chemist, State Chemist's Off, Ga, 37-41; mineral chemist, State Div Mines, 41; toxicologist, Med Div, US Army, Edgewood Arsenal, Md, 41-46. *Concurrent Pos:* Res biologist, Ga Inst Technol, 51-60; consult, Commun Dis Ctr, 54-55, 57-58 & Chem Corps, US Army, 58-62. *Mem:* AAAS; Am Pub Health Asn; Am Soc Microbiol; NY Acad Sci. *Res:* Effect of ice formation on living cells; thermal properties of frozen tissues; preservation of foods by freezing; instrumental methods of analysis; gas and aerosol chamber techniques; aerobiology; water content of bacterial aerosols; aerial disinfectants. *Mailing Add:* 514 Ponce de Leon Pl Decatur GA 30030

KETLEY, ARTHUR DONALD, PHOTOCHEMISTRY, POLYMER CHEMISTRY. *Current Pos:* MANAGING DIR, JAPAN RES CTR, 88- *Personal Data:* b London, Eng, Dec 27, 30; c 3. *Educ:* Univ London, BSc, 51, PhD(chem), 53. *Prof Exp:* Res assoc chem, Mass Inst Technol, 53-55; lectr, Univ Sydney, 56-57; res fel, Ga Inst Technol, 57-58; chemist, Esso Res & Eng Co, 58-59; chemist, W W Grace & Co, 59-73, mgr mat develop photopolymer systs, 73-79, dir technol prod res, 79-88. *Mem:* Am Chem Soc; Int Am Photochem Soc; Soc Photog Scientists & Engrs. *Res:* Mechanisms of organic reactions; organometallic chemistry; photochemistry; development and applications of photopolymerizable materials; imaging science. *Mailing Add:* 252 Whitmoor Terr Silver Spring MD 20901-1521

KETLEY, JEANNE NELSON, ENZYMOLOGY, DRUG METABOLISM. *Current Pos:* exec secy, Phys Biochem Study Sect, NIH, 79-85, chief, Spec Rev Sect, 85-89, chief, Phys Sci Rev Sect, Div Res Grants, 89-93, chief, Clin Sci Rev Sect, 94-96, COORDR, CARDIOVASC SCI IRG, DIV RES GRANTS, NIH, 96- *Personal Data:* b New York, NY; c Alex. *Educ:* Queens Col, NY, BS, 62; Cornell Univ, MS, 67; Johns Hopkins Univ, PhD(biochem), 73. *Prof Exp:* Res asst enzym & biochem, Med Col, Cornell Univ, 68-69; vis scientist develop biol, Nat Inst Dent Res, NIH, 73-74; staff fel enzyme biochem, lab biochem & metab, Nat Inst Arthritis, Metab & Digestive Dis, 74-76, sr staff fel, Nat Inst Aging, 76-77; chemist, Bur Foods, Food & Drug Admin, 77-79. *Concurrent Pos:* Muscular Dystrophy Asn Am fel, 73-74. *Mem:* AAAS; Am Chem Soc. *Res:* Drug metabolism; mammalian biochemical processes at the molecular level; changes in biological structure and function of proteins; physical biochemistry. *Mailing Add:* Cardivasc Sci IRG 6701 Rockledge Dr Rm 4100 Bethesda MD 20892-7814. *E-Mail:* jkc@drgpo.drg.nih.gov

KETNER, KEITH B, GEOLOGY OF NEVADA. *Current Pos:* Geologist & res geologist, 50-94, EMER GEOLOGIST, US GEOL SURV, 94- *Personal Data:* b Boscobel, Wis, Feb 5, 21. *Educ:* Univ Wis, BA, 47, MA, 52, PhD(geol), 68. *Mem:* AAAS; fel Geol Soc Am. *Mailing Add:* US Geol Surv MS 939 Box 25046 Fed Ctr Denver CO 80225. *E-Mail:* kketner@usgs.gov

KETOLA, H GEORGE, FISH NUTRITION. *Current Pos:* RES PHYSIOLOGIST, TUNISON LAB FISH NUTRIT, US FISH & WILDLIFE SERV, 73- *Educ:* Cornell Univ, BS, 65, MS, 67, PhD(nutrit), 73. *Concurrent Pos:* Adj asst prof, Dept Poultry & Avian Sci, Cornell Univ, 76-91; US Fish & Wildlife Serv res grant, 84-85 & Dept Natural Resources, 91-; consult fish nutrit, feed mfrs. *Mem:* Am Inst Nutrit; Poultry Sci Asn; Am Fisheries Soc; Am Soc Animal Sci; Sigma Xi; Animal Nutrit Res Coun. *Res:* Nutritional studies to reduce nutrient discharges in effluent waters from fish hatcheries; improvement of nutritional quality of diets for fry and fingerling salmon and trout. *Mailing Add:* Tunison Lab Fish Nutrit 3075 Gracie Rd Cortland NY 13045-9355

KETRING, DAROLD L, PLANT PHYSIOLOGY, BIOCHEMISTRY. *Current Pos:* PLANT PHYSIOLOGIST, USDA, 67- *Personal Data:* b Van Nuys, Calif, Mar 14, 30; m 50; c 2. *Educ:* Univ Calif, Los Angeles, BS, 63, PhD(plant sci), 67. *Mem:* Am Soc Plant Physiologists; Am Soc Agron; Am Peanut Res & Educ Asn; Plant Growth Regulator Soc Am; Sigma Xi. *Res:* Relation of ethylene and other plant hormones to plant growth, development, senescence and accompanying biochemistry; effect of environmental stress on plant growth and development. *Mailing Add:* 1933 Wildwood Dr Stillwater OK 74075

KETTELKAMP, DONALD B, orthopedic surgery, for more information see previous edition

KETTERER, JOHN JOSEPH, ZOOLOGY. *Current Pos:* from asst prof to prof, 53-73, head dept, 59-73, W P PRESSLY PROF BIOL, MONMOUTH COL, 73- *Personal Data:* b Philadelphia, Pa, Mar 12, 21; m 46; c 2. *Educ:* Dickinson Col, BS, 43; NY Univ, PhD(biol), 53. *Prof Exp:* Asst biol, NY Univ, 46-52, instr, 52-53. *Mem:* AAAS; Soc Protozool; Am Soc Zool. *Res:* Invertebrate zoology with special reference to protozoa. *Mailing Add:* 815 E Broadway Monmouth IL 61462

KETTERER, PAUL ANTHONY, ANALYSIS & CHARACTERIZATION OF POLYMERS, ADDITIVES & CATALYSTS. *Current Pos:* sr res chemist, 86-89, res scientist, 89-92, SR MGR CHARACTERIZATION & ANALYSIS, MONTELL INC, 92- *Personal Data:* b Warwick, NY, Aug 2, 41; m 62, Mary A Richiski; c Nancy & Paul. *Educ:* Syracuse Univ, AB, 64; Seton Hall Univ, MS, 73. *Prof Exp:* Chemist, Polaks Frutal Works Inc, 64-68; sr chemist, Tenneco Chem Inc, 68-73, group leader anal chem, 74-75, lab mgr polymer characterization & anal, 76-81, mgr anal serv, Tenneco Polymers Inc, 82-86. *Mem:* Am Chem Soc; Soc Appl Spectros; Soc Plastics Indust. *Res:* Polymer characterization and analysis, determination of structure-property relationships of polymers and additives; development of analytical methods for trace analysis of air and water pollutants; trace residual monomers in polymers. *Mailing Add:* 3308 Coachman Rd Wilmington DE 19803-1946

KETTERING, JAMES DAVID, MEDICAL MICROBIOLOGY, VIROLOGY, TUMOR IMMUNOLOGY. *Current Pos:* instr, 72-74, asst prof, 74-80, assoc prof microbiol, 80-89, PROF MICROBIOL, SCH MED, LOMA LINDA UNIV, 89- *Personal Data:* b Pekin, Ill, Mar 27, 42; m 63, Betty J Stevens; c Brian D, Pamela S & David E. *Educ:* Andrews Univ, BA, 64; Loma Linda Univ, MS, 68, PhD(microbiol), 74. *Prof Exp:* Microbiologist, Indust Bio-Test Labs, 64-66 & Abott Labs Inc, 66. *Concurrent Pos:* Fel microbiol, Calif State Dept Health, Berkeley, 75-77. *Mem:* Am Soc Microbiol; Sigma Xi; Am Asn Dent Schs; Am Asn Dent Res; Am Soc Virol. *Res:* diagnostic virology-clinical; tumor immunology; dental immunology; published in areas of tumor immunology, virology and dental microbiology and immunology research. *Mailing Add:* 11980 Canary Ct Grand Terrace CA 92313. *Fax:* 909-824-4035; *E-Mail:* jkettering@ccmail.llu.edu

KETTERSON, JOHN BOYD, PHYSICS. *Current Pos:* chmn dep, 85-90, FAYERWEATHER PROF PHYSICS, NORTHWESTERN UNIV, 74-; CONSULT, ARGONNE NAT LAB, 74- *Personal Data:* b Orange, NJ, Oct 2, 34; m 61; c 3. *Educ:* Univ Chicago, BS, 57, MS, 59, PhD(physics), 62. *Prof Exp:* Assoc physicist, Argonne Nat Lab, Ill, 62-72; sr physicist, 74. *Mem:* Fel Am Phys Soc. *Res:* Low and ultra low temperature technique; properties of monomolecular films; physics of liquid crystals; properties of composition modulated structures; properties of liquid and solid helium; electronic properties of metals and Fermi surfaces; semiconducting films; nonlinear optical films; thermoelectric materials. *Mailing Add:* 628 Garrett Pl Evanston IL 60201

KETTMAN, JOHN RUTHERFORD, JR, IMMUNOLOGY. *Current Pos:* asst prof, 73-75, assoc prof, 75-80, PROF MICROBIOL, SOUTHWESTERN MED SCH, SOUTHWESTERN MED CTR, UNIV TEX, DALLAS, 80- *Personal Data:* b Niles, Calif, Nov 29, 39; m 68; c 2. *Educ:* Univ Calif, Berkeley, BA, 61; Ore State Univ, PhD(biochem), 68. *Prof Exp:* Asst res biologist, Univ Calif, San Diego, 69-72. *Concurrent Pos:* NIH trainee immunochem, Kaiser Res Found, San Francisco, 67-69; mem, Immunol Sci Study Group, 80-83; Wellcome vis prof, 85. *Mem:* Am Chem Soc; Am Asn Immunologists; Soc Anal Cytol; AAAS. *Res:* Cellular immunology; cell cooperation in the immune response; development of lymphoid systems. *Mailing Add:* Microbiol Dept Southwestern Med Ctr Univ Tex Dallas TX 75235-9048

KETTNER, CHARLES ADRIAN, ENZYMOLOGY, PEPTIDE CHEMISTRY. *Current Pos:* prin investr biochem, CR&D Dept, 80-90, prin investr biochem, 91-92, RES FEL, DU PONT MERCK PHARMACEUT CO, 92- *Personal Data:* b Fredericksburg, Tex, Oct 27, 46; m 69; c 2. *Educ:* Southwest Tex State Univ, BSE, 69, MA, 71; Tex A&M Univ, PhD(biochem), 74. *Prof Exp:* Asst instr chem, Southwest Tex State Univ, 71; res asst, Tex A&M Univ, 71-74; res collabr biochem, Brookhaven Nat Lab, 74-77, sr res assoc biochem, 77-78, from asst biologist to assoc biologist biochem, 78-80. *Mem:* Am Soc Biochem & Molecular Biol; Am Chem Soc. *Res:* Design and synthesis of inhibitors of proteolytic enzymes; identification of target proteases where control of proteolysis can be theropeutically useful. *Mailing Add:* Du Pont Merck Pharmaceut E500/2464 Wilmington DE 19880-0500. *Fax:* 302-695-8168; *E-Mail:* kettneca@lldmpc.dnet.dupont.com

KETY, SEYMOUR S, NEUROSCIENCE, PSYCHOBIOLOGY. *Current Pos:* prof psychiat, 67-82, prof, EMER PROF NEUROSCI, HARVARD MED SCH, 83-, EMER SR SCIENTIST, NIMH, NIH, 96- *Personal Data:* b Philadelphia, Pa, Aug 25, 15; m 40, Josephine Gross; c Lawrence & Roberta. *Educ:* Univ Pa, AB, 36, MD, 40. *Hon Degrees:* ScD, Univ Pa, 65, Loyola Univ, 69, Univ Ill, 81, Mt Sinai Sch Med, 83, Med Col Pa, 85, Georgetown Univ, 87, Wash Univ, 89, Mich Univ, 91; MD, Univ Copenhagen, 79. *Honors & Awards:* Theobald Smith Award, AAAS, 49; Max Weinstein Award, United Cerebral Palsy Res Found, 54; McAlpin Medal & Res Achievement Award, Nat Asn Ment Health, 72; Paul Hoch Award, Am Psychopath Asn, 73; Kovalenko Award, Nat Acad Sci, 73, Neurosci Award, 88; Menninger Award, Am Col Physicians, 76; Fromm-Reichmann Award, Am Acad Psychoanal, 78; Passano Award, 80; FFRP Award Psychiat Res, 80; Res Award Asn Res Nerv & Ment Dis, 80; Thomas W Salmon Medal, NY Acad Med, 82; Emil Kraepelin Medal, Max Planck Inst, 84; Mihara Award, 84; Ralph Gerard Award, Soc Neurosci, 86, de Hevesy Nuclear Med Pioneer Award, Am Soc Nuclear Med,88; Sarnat Int Prize, Inst Med, 93; Lifetime Achievement Award, Int Soc Psychiat Genetics, 93, Soc Biol Psych, 96. *Prof Exp:* Nat Res Coun fel, Harvard Med Sch, 42-43; instr pharmacol, Sch Med, Univ Pa, 43-44, assoc, 44-46, asst prof, 46-48, prof clin physiol, Grad Sch Med, 48-61; sci dir, NIMH & Nat Inst Neurol Dis & Blindness, 51-56, chief lab clin sci, NIMH, 56-67; dir psychiat res lab, Mass Gen Hosp, 67-77; dir psychiat res labs, Mailman Res Ctr, McLean Hosp, 77-83. *Concurrent Pos:* Numerous hon lectureships, 51-; mem, Adv Bd Ment Health Res, Ford Found, 55-57; mem sci adv bd, Scottish Rite Found Res Schizophrenia, 57-, chmn, 61-; chmn biosci adv comt, NASA, 59-60; mem, President's Panel Ment Retardation, 61-62; Henry Phipps prof, Johns Hopkins Univ & psychiatrist-in-chief, Hosp, 61-62; assoc, Neurosci Res Found, 62-79; vis prof, Col France, 66-67; mem vis comt biol, Calif Inst Technol, 72-79; mem bd trustees, Rockefeller Univ, 77-85; founding ed, J Psychiat Res, 83-; sr scientist, NIMH, NIH, 83-96. *Mem:* Nat Acad Sci; Am Physiol Soc; Asn Res Nerv & Ment Dis (trustee, 63, pres, 65); Am Psychopath Asn (pres, 65); Am Acad Arts & Sci; Am Philos Soc. *Res:* Circulation and metabolism of the human brain; theory of capillary-tissue exchange of diffusible tracers; measurement of regional circulation of brain; genetics of schizophrenia; biological aspects of mental illness; basis of functional brain imaging in man. *Mailing Add:* 332 Samarpaway Apt 312 Boston MA 02130

KEUDELL, KENNETH CARSON, MICROBIOLOGY. *Current Pos:* ASSOC PROF MICROBIOL, WESTERN ILL UNIV, 78- *Personal Data:* b Oklahoma City, Okla, May 3, 41; m 67; c 2. *Educ:* Okla State Univ, BS, 63, MS, 67; Univ Mo, PhD(microbiol), 69. *Prof Exp:* Fel microbiol, Albert Einstein Col Med, 69-71; asst prof, Sch Dent Med, Wash Univ, 71-78. *Concurrent Pos:* Nat Inst Dent Res grant, 74-76. *Mem:* Am Soc Microbiol; Sigma Xi. *Res:* Medical microbiology, with emphasis on anaerobic microorganisms. *Mailing Add:* 40 Briarwood Pl Macomb IL 61455-1243

KEULKS, GEORGE WILLIAM, PHYSICAL CHEMISTRY. *Current Pos:* from asst prof to assoc prof chem, 66-74, assoc dean natural sci, 74-75, actg dean grad sch, 75-77, PROF CHEM, UNIV WIS-MILWAUKEE, 74-, DEAN, GRAD SCH, 77-, RESEARCHER, 86- *Personal Data:* b East St Louis, Ill, Apr 2, 38; m 60; c 4. *Educ:* Wash Univ, AB, 60; Univ Ark, MS, 62; Northwestern Univ, PhD(chem), 64. *Prof Exp:* Res chemist, Gulf Res & Develop Co, 64-65; res assoc, Johns Hopkins Univ, 65-66. *Concurrent Pos:* Consult, Nelson Industs, Inc, 74, Atlantic Richfield Co, 80- *Mem:* AAAS; Am Chem Soc; Catalysis Soc NAm. *Res:* Heterogeneous catalysis; catalytic kinetics; synthesis of new catalysts; mechanisms of catalytic oxidation; physical characteristics of catalysis. *Mailing Add:* Grad Sch Univ Wis-Milwaukee PO Box 340 Milwaukee WI 53201-0340

KEUPER, JEROME PENN, PHYSICS. *Current Pos:* PRES, FLA INST TECHNOL, 58- *Personal Data:* b Ft Thomas, Ky, Jan 12, 21; m 48; c 2. *Educ:* Mass Inst Technol, BS, 48; Stanford Univ, MS, 49; Univ Va, PhD, 52. *Prof Exp:* Res assoc, Carnegie Inst Technol, 49-50; sr res physicist, Remington Arms Co, Inc, 52-58; sr scientist, RCA Missile Test Proj, 58-60, mgr syst anal, 60-62. *Concurrent Pos:* Chmn math dept, Bridgeport Eng Inst, 54-58. *Mem:* Am Soc Eng Educ; Opers Res Soc Am; Asn Comput Mach; Sigma Xi. *Res:* Solid state, radiation and nuclear physics; computing machines; operations research; ballistics; error analysis; space technology. *Mailing Add:* PO Box 510394 Melbourne Beach FL 32951

KEUSCH, GERALD TILDEN, INFECTIOUS DISEASES. *Current Pos:* PROF MED, TUFTS-NEW ENG MED CTR, 78- *Personal Data:* b New York, NY, Apr 30, 38; m 62, 85; c 3. *Educ:* Columbia Col, AB, 58; Harvard Univ, MD, 63. *Honors & Awards:* Squibb Award, Infectious Dis Soc Am, 81. *Prof Exp:* Instr, Tufts-New Eng Med Ctr, 69-70; from asst prof to prof med, Mt Sinai Sch Med, 70-78. *Concurrent Pos:* Mem subcomt interactions nutrit & infection, Nat Acad Sci, 71-, chmn, 76-; mem comt int nutrit progs, 75- & comn int rels, 76- *Mem:* AAAS; Am Soc Microbiol; Am Fedn Clin Res; Infectious Dis Soc Am; NY Acad Sci; Asn Am Physicians. *Res:* Pathogenesis of enteric infections, particularly bacillary dysentery, giordiasis and cryptosporidiosis; effect of malnutrition on the immune response and host defenses. *Mailing Add:* 750 Washington St Box 041 Boston MA 02111

KEVAN, LARRY, PHYSICAL CHEMISTRY. *Current Pos:* CULLEN PROF CHEM, UNIV HOUSTON, 80- *Personal Data:* b Kansas City, Mo, Dec 12, 38. *Educ:* Univ Kans, BS, 60; Univ Calif, Los Angeles, PhD(chem), 63. *Honors & Awards:* Polish Soc Radiation Res Award, 79; Nat Honor Soc Res Award, 86; Am Chem Soc Tex Award, 86; Rector's Medal, Poland, 87; Sigma Xi Res Award, 89; Marie Curie Medal, 95. *Prof Exp:* Vis res assoc chem, Univ Newcastle, 63; instr, Univ Chicago, 63-65; from asst prof to assoc prof, Univ Kans, 65-69; prof chem, Wayne State Univ, 69- *Concurrent Pos:* Exchange fel, Czech, 69; vis scientist, Danish Atomic Energy Lab, 70; Guggenheim fel, 70-71; vis prof, Univ Utah, 71, Univ Nagoya, Japan, 76, Univ Paris, 77 & Armed Forces Tech Univ, Munich, 79, Hokkaido Univ, Japan, 87, Univ Florence, Italy, 87, 90; exchange fel USSR, Nat Acad Sci, 74, 75 & 77; vis comt chem, Brookhaven Nat Lab, 74-78, chmn, 78; chmn, Gordon Conf Radiation Chem, 75, Chem Div Rev Comt, Argonne Nat Lab, 80-86, chmn, 82; vis scientist, Japan Soc Prom Sci, 76; dir, Southwest Catalysis Soc, 82-84 & 96-98, chmn, 86-88. *Mem:* Fel AAAS; Am Chem Soc; fel Am Phys Soc; Int Soc Magnetic Resonance; fel Royal Soc Chem; Int Electron Paramagnetic Resonance Soc. *Res:* Electron magnetic resonance and relaxation; electron spin echo spectrometry; photoredox reactions in constrained media; electron localization and solvation; radiation damage in materials; synthesis and characterization of metal species in microporous oxide materials. *Mailing Add:* Dept Chem Univ Houston Houston TX 77204-5641. *Fax:* 713-743-2709; *E-Mail:* kevan@uh.edu

KEVAN, PETER GRAHAM, ENTOMOLOGY, BOTANY ECOLOGY EVOLUTION. *Current Pos:* PROF ECOL, ENTOM & APICULT, BOT UNIV GUELPH, CAN, 83-; VPRES, ENVIROQUEST LTD. *Personal Data:* b Edinburgh, Scotland, June 17, 44; Can citizen; m 84, Sherrene Kent; c Colin & Kayte. *Educ:* McGill Univ, BSc, 65; Univ Alta, PhD(entom), 70. *Prof Exp:* Nat coordr, Int Biol Prog, Univ Alta, Can, 69-70; contract biologist, Can Wildlife Serv, Inuvik, NT, Can, 70-71; fel, Plant Res Inst, Can Agr, Ottawa, Can, 71-72; proj mgr ecol, Mem Univ Nfld, Can, 72-75; asst prof biol, Univ Colo, Colo Springs, 75-82, grad fac asst prof biol & assoc, Inst Arctic & Alpine Res, Boulder, 75-83, prin investr NSF grants, Colo Springs, 76-82. *Concurrent Pos:* Consult, Can Wildlife Serv, 70-71; Palm Oil Res Inst Malaysia, 83-, Can Int Develop Agency, 83-, Can Int Develop Res Ctr, 83- & Food & Agr Orgn, Rome, 83-84 & 89-90; prin investr, Nat Sci & Eng Res Coun Grants, Univ Guelph, 83-; mem bd dirs & ed, Entom Soc Ont, 86-; mem bd dirs, Entom Soc Can, 90-; ed, Can Entomologist. *Mem:* Brit Ecol Soc; Bot Soc Am; Int Bee Res Asn; Entom Soc Can; Int Asn Ecol; Sigma Xi; fel Royal Entom Soc London. *Res:* Botanical and entomological research in co-evolutionary ecology; pollination biology; arctic and alpine ecology; apiculture and agriculture in developing countries; sustainable and ecological agriculture and development. *Mailing Add:* Dept Environ Biol Univ Guelph Guelph ON N1G 2W1 Can. *Fax:* 519-837-0442; *E-Mail:* pkevan@uoguelph.ca

KEVANE, CLEMENT JOSEPH, PHYSICS. *Current Pos:* assoc prof, 56-63, PROF PHYSICS, ARIZ STATE UNIV, 63- *Personal Data:* b Rembrandt, Iowa, May 17, 22; m 53; c 9. *Educ:* Iowa State Col, BS, 48, PhD(physics), 53. *Prof Exp:* Physicist, Motorola, Inc, 53-56. *Mem:* Am Phys Soc; Sigma Xi. *Res:* Physics of solid state, semiconductor properties; conduction of heat and electricity in refractory oxides. *Mailing Add:* 1714 S La Rosa Dr Tempe AZ 85281

KEVERN, NILES RUSSELL, AQUATIC ECOLOGY, FISHERIES SCIENCE. *Current Pos:* from asst prof to assoc prof, Mich State Univ, 66-69, chmn dept, 69-92, PROF FISHERIES & WILDLIFE, MICH STATE UNIV, 69-, ASSOC DIR, SEA GRANT PROG, 78- *Personal Data:* b Elizabeth, Ill, May 15, 31; m 55; c 3. *Educ:* Univ Mont, BS, 58; Mich State Univ, MS, 61, PhD(limnol), 63. *Prof Exp:* Limnologist, Oak Ridge Nat Lab, Union Carbide Corp, 63-66. *Concurrent Pos:* Asst dir, Inst Water Res, Mich State Univ, 67-69. *Mem:* Am Fisheries Soc; AAAS; Wildlife Soc. *Res:* Aquatic ecology, particularly bioenergetics and mineral cycling of flowing water ecosystems; fisheries. *Mailing Add:* Dept Fisheries & Wildlife Mich State Univ Nat Resources Bldg East Lansing MI 48824-1222. *Fax:* 517-336-1699

KEVILL, DENNIS NEIL, PHYSICAL ORGANIC CHEMISTRY. *Current Pos:* from asst prof to assoc prof, 63-70, presidential res prof, 85-89, PROF CHEM, NORTHERN ILL UNIV, 70-, UNIV RES PROF, 89- *Personal Data:* b Walton-le-Dale, Eng, May 27, 35. *Educ:* Univ Col London, BSc, 56, PhD(chem), 60. *Hon Degrees:* DSc, London Univ, 82. *Prof Exp:* Asst lectr chem, Univ Col London, 59-60; res assoc, Univ Nebr, 60-63. *Concurrent Pos:* Grants, Petrol Res Fund, 63-64 & 65-70, NSF, 67-71, 74-75 & 84-88, NIH, 75-76 & NASA, 82; consult, Carus Chem Co, Inc, 65-68; hon res fel, Univ Col London, 75-76; vis prof, Univ Tuebingen, 83, Univ Freiburg, 87, Univ Munich, 90 & Univ Wales, Swansea, 96; Nat Acad Sci Exchange Partic, Yugoslavia, 83. *Mem:* Am Chem Soc; The Chem Soc. *Res:* Organic reaction mechanisms; nucleophilicity; reaction mechanisms in solvents of low polarity; elimination reactions; electrophilic assistance to nucleophilic substitutions; perchlorate esters; adamantane derivatives; boron-carbon compounds; chemical vapor deposition. *Mailing Add:* Dept Chem Northern Ill Univ De Kalb IL 60115

KEVLES, DANIEL JEROME, HUMAN GENETICS, POLITICS OF SCIENCE. *Current Pos:* from assoc prof to prof hist, 64-86, chmn fac, 95-97, KOEPFLI PROF OF HUMANITIES, CALIF INST TECHNOL, 86- *Personal Data:* b Philadelphia, Pa, Mar 2, 39; m 61, Bettyann; c Beth & Jonathan. *Educ:* Princeton Univ, BA, 60, PhD(hist), 64. *Honors & Awards:* Nat Hist Soc Prize, 79. *Prof Exp:* Instr hist, Princeton Univ, 64. *Concurrent Pos:* Vis res fel, Univ Sussex, 76; exec officer humanities, Calif Inst Technol, 78-81; vis prof, Univ Pa, 79; mem, adv comt sci autobiog, Sloan Found, 80-90, adv comt, Harvard Univ, 81-82, Ctr Hist Physics, 84-, educ adv comt, Guggenheim Found, 86-95; fel, Ctr Adv Study Behav Sci, 86-87. *Mem:* Hist Sci Soc; Am Hist Asn; Am Acad Arts & Sci; Orgn Am Historians; fel AAAS; Am Philos Soc. *Res:* Social and political history of modern science, especially physics and genetics in the United States and Britain; environmentalism, scientific fraud and misconduct; intellectual property. *Mailing Add:* Humanities & Soc Sci Div Calif Inst Technol Pasadena CA 91125

KEVORKIAN, ARAM K, LARGE-SCALE SCIENTIFIC COMPUTATIONS, SPARSE MATRIX COMPUTATIONS. *Current Pos:* MEM TECH STAFF, NAVAL OCEAN SYSTS CTR, 89- *Personal Data:* b Aug 27, 42; US citizen; c 4. *Educ:* Univ London, BSc, 65, PhD(appl math), 68. *Prof Exp:* Sr mathematician, Royal Dutch Shell Res Lab, Amstead, 68-80; head comput, GA Technologies, 80-86; assoc dir, Cornell Nat Supercomputer Ctr, Cornell Univ, 88-89. *Concurrent Pos:* Vis scientist, T J Watson Res Ctr, IBM Corp, Yorktown Heights, NY, 86-87; adj prof, San Diego State Univ, 91-; sr fel, San Diego Supercomputer Ctr, 91- *Mem:* Soc Indust & Appl Math; Am Math Soc; Asn Comput Mach. *Res:* Large-scale scientific computations with emphasis on the use of graph theory to unearth structure out of large sparse matrix problems. *Mailing Add:* Pearl St La Jolla CA 92037

KEVORKIAN, JIRAIR, PERTURBATION METHODS, NONLINEAR WAVES. *Current Pos:* from asst prof to assoc prof, 64-71, PROF APPL MATH, AERONAUT & ASTRONAUT, UNIV WASH, 71- *Personal Data:* b Jerusalem, Palestine, May 14, 33; US citizen; m 80, Seta Tabourian. *Educ:* Ga Inst Technol, BS, 55, MS, 56; Calif Inst Technol, PhD(aeronaut, math), 61. *Prof Exp:* Aerodynamicist, Gen Dynamics/Convair, 56-57; res fel aeronaut, Calif Inst Technol, 61-64. *Concurrent Pos:* Vis prof, Univ Paris, 71-72; Fulbright-Hays Award, Coun Int Exchange of Scholars, 75. *Mem:* Soc Indust & Appl Math. *Res:* Development and application of perturbation techniques to problems in nonlinear systems. *Mailing Add:* Dept Appl Univ Wash Box 352420 Seattle WA 98195-2420. *Fax:* 206-685-1440; *E-Mail:* kevork@amath.washington.edu

KEW, DAVID, endocrinology, molecular biology, for more information see previous edition

KEY, ANTHONY W, PHYSICS EDUCATION, PARTICLE PHYSICS. *Current Pos:* Assoc chmn, Physics Dept & Undergrad Studies, Univ Toronto, 80-85 & Grad Studies, 86-92, actg chmn, 93, PROF PHYSICS, UNIV TORONTO, 73- *Personal Data:* b Edinburgh, Scotland, Mar 3, 39; m 63; c 2. *Educ:* Aberdeen Univ, MA, 60; Oxford Univ, DPhil(physics), 64. *Concurrent Pos:* Psychotherapist, Pvt Pract. *Mem:* Can Asn Physicists; Brit Inst Physics. *Res:* Experimental particle physics; high energy physics using the techniques of bubble or spark chambers; higher education. *Mailing Add:* Dept Physics Univ Toronto Sir George St Toronto ON M5S 1A7 Can. *E-Mail:* key@physics.utoronto.ca

KEY, CHARLES R, PATHOLOGY, CANCER EPIDEMIOLOGY. *Current Pos:* asst prof, 69-73, assoc path, 73-83, PROF PATH, SCH MED, UNIV NMEX, 83- *Personal Data:* b Oklahoma City, Okla, Aug 4, 34; m 58; c 3. *Educ:* Okla State Univ, BS, 56; Univ Okla, MD, 59, MS, 62, PhD(med sci), 66; Am Bd Path, dipl, 64. *Honors & Awards:* Div Ann Award, Am Cancer Soc, 85. *Prof Exp:* Intern path, Med Ctr, Univ Okla, 59-60, resident, 60-64; pathologist, Div Air Pollution, USPHS, 64-66; pathologist, Atomic Bomb Casualty Comn, Hiroshima, Japan, 66-69. *Concurrent Pos:* Med dir, NMex Tumor Registry, 69- *Mem:* Col Am Path; Int Acad Path; Am Asn Pathologists; Am Soc Prev Oncol. *Res:* Use of quantitative methods in morphology; pathology of radiation injury; epidemiological pathology of cancer; tumor registry. *Mailing Add:* Dept Path Univ NMex Sch Med 915 Stanford Dr NE Albuquerque NM 87131-0001

KEY, JOE LYNN, PLANT PHYSIOLOGY. *Current Pos:* RES PROF BOT, UNIV GA, 69- *Personal Data:* b Troy, Tenn, Sept 10, 33; m 56; c 2. *Educ:* Univ Tenn, BS, 55; Univ Ill, MS, 57, PhD(plant physiol), 59. *Prof Exp:* Asst agron, Univ Ill, 55-59, fel biochem, 59-60; NSF fel, Univ Calif, Davis, 60, asst prof, 60-62; from assoc prof to prof, plant physiol, Purdue Univ, 62-69. *Concurrent Pos:* Dir, Competitive Grants Prog, Sci & Educ Admin, USDA, 78-79; vpres res, Agrigenetics Corp, Boulder, CO, 84, 85. *Res:* Biochemistry of auxin action; nucleic acid metabolism; developmental regulation in plants; RNA metabolism; control of protein synthesis; stress-regulated RNA and protein synthesis. *Mailing Add:* Dept Bot Univ Ga Athens GA 30602

KEYES, DAVID ELLIOT, COMPUTATIONAL FLUID DYNAMICS, PARALLEL COMPUTATION. *Current Pos:* Res assoc comput sci, 84-85, asst prof, 86-90, ASSOC PROF MECH ENG, YALE UNIV, 90- *Personal Data:* b Brooklyn, NY, Dec 4, 56; m 80; c 2. *Educ:* Princeton Univ, BS, 78; Harvard Univ, MS, 79, PhD(appl math), 84. *Concurrent Pos:* NSF presidential young investr, 89; vis scientist, Inst Comput Appl Sci & Eng, NASA Langley Res Ctr, Hampton, Va, 90, 93-94, Maths & Comput Sci Div, Argonne Nat Lab, Argonne, Ill, 91. *Mem:* Am Inst Aeronaut & Astronaut; Am Soc Mech Engrs; Combustion Inst; Soc Indust & Appl Math; Int Asn Boundary Element Methods. *Res:* Numerical methods for partial differential equations; domain decomposition algorithms; parallel computation; computational modelling of combustion, heat transfer and aerodynamics. *Mailing Add:* NASA Langley Res Ctr ICASE M/S132C Hampton VA 23681-0001. *Fax:* 203-432-7654

KEYES, JACK LYNN, PHYSIOLOGY. *Current Pos:* assoc prof, 83-88, prof & chmnn sci, 88-94, PROF BIOL, LINFIELD COL, PORTLAND, 94- *Personal Data:* b St Johns, Mich, Nov 15, 41; m 68, Connie Gurney; c James & Tanya. *Educ:* Linfield Col, BA, 63; Univ Ore Med Sch, PhD(physiol), 70. *Prof Exp:* Instr physiol, Med Col, Cornell Univ, 70-71; from asst prof to assoc prof physiol, Med Sch, Ore Health Sci Univ, 71-83. *Mem:* Am Physiol Soc. *Res:* Renal physiology; acid-base regulation; venous blood-gas composition. *Mailing Add:* Linfield Col Portland Campus 2255 NW Northrup St Portland OR 97210-2952. *E-Mail:* jkeyes@linfield.edu

KEYES, MARION ALVAH, IV, REAL-TIME MISSION CRITICAL SYSTEMS, ARTIFICIAL INTELLIGENCE. *Current Pos:* PRES, TRICE ENGRS, 91-; SR VPRES TECHNOL & DEVELOP, EMERSON ELEC CO, 93- *Personal Data:* b Bellingham, Wash, May 11, 38; m 62; c 3. *Educ:* Stanford Univ, BS, 60; Univ Ill, MS, 68; Baldwin Wallace Col, MBA, 81. *Prof Exp:* Dir eng, Control Systs Div, Beloit Corp, 63-70; gen mgr digital systs, Div Taylor Instrument Co, 70-75; vpres eng, res & develop, Bailey Controls Co, 75-80, pres, 80-85, pres & chief exec officer, 89-90; sr vpres & group exec, McDermott Int Inc, 85-89; chmn, DCOM Corp, 90-93. *Concurrent Pos:* Mem, Automation Res Coun, NSF, 70-73; dir & secy, Am Automatic Control Coun, 72-80; trustee, Baldwin Wallace Col, 83-; dir, Fact Inc; bd dirs, Ohio Acad Scis, 91-; officer, Instrument Soc Am, 92- *Mem:* Fel Tech Asn Pulp & Paper Indust; fel Inst Elec & Electronics Engrs; fel Instrument Soc Am; Am Inst Chem Engrs; Soc Mfg Engrs; Soc Am Mil Engrs; Am Chem Soc. *Res:* Computers; process controls; information systems; electronics; process design and development automation; holder of over 50 US patents in these fields and have 17 patents pending. *Mailing Add:* 8 Washington Terr St Louis MO 63112. *Fax:* 314-746-9816

KEYES, PAUL HOLT, LIQUID CRYSTALS, PHASE TRANSITIONS. *Current Pos:* assoc prof, 87-91, PROF, WAYNE STATE UNIV, 91- *Personal Data:* b Hartford, Conn, Oct 23, 43; m 87, Mary E Jornlin; c Robert. *Educ:* Rensselaer Polytech Inst, BS, 65; Univ MD, PhD (physics), 72. *Prof Exp:* Fel physics, Univ Del, 72-75; asst prof physics, Univ Mass, Boston, 75-79; from asst prof to assoc prof, Bartol Res Found, Univ Del, 79-87. *Mem:* Am Phys Soc; Sigma Xi. *Res:* Critical phenomena; liquid crystals; phase transitions. *Mailing Add:* Dept Physics & Astron Wayne State Univ Detroit MI 48202. *Fax:* 313-577-3932; *E-Mail:* keyes@hal.physics.wayne.edu

KEYES, PAUL LANDIS, REPRODUCTIVE ENDOCRINOLOGY, PHYSIOLOGY. *Current Pos:* from asst prof to assoc prof path, 72-75, from asst prof to assoc prof physiol, 75-84, PROF PHYSIOL, UNIV MICH, ANN ARBOR, 84- *Personal Data:* b Thomasville, NC, July 7, 38; m 66, Sharon J Shull; c Jeffrey L & Christopher A. *Educ:* NC State Univ, BS, 60, MS, 62; Univ Ill, PhD(animal sci, physiol), 66. *Prof Exp:* Res asst prof, Dept Obstet & Gynec, Albany Med Col, 68-72. *Concurrent Pos:* NIH fel, Med Sch, Harvard Univ, 66-68; ed, Endocrinol, 79-82; mem, Clin Sci Study Sect, NIH, 85-89; dir, Soc Study Reproduction, 85-88. *Mem:* Endocrine Soc; Soc Study Reproduction; Am Physiol Soc; Soc Study Fertil. *Res:* Endocrine regulation of the ovary; regulation of the corpus luteum by growth factors and cytokines. *Mailing Add:* Dept Physiol 7637 Med Sci II Univ Mich Ann Arbor MI 48109-0622. *Fax:* 313-936-8813; *E-Mail:* landis.keyes@umich.edu

KEYES, ROBERT W, PHYSICS. *Current Pos:* physicist, 60-93, EMER RES STAFF MEM, IBM, 93- *Personal Data:* b Chicago, Ill, Dec 2, 21; m 66; c 2. *Educ:* Univ Chicago, BS, 42, MS, 49, PhD(physics), 53. *Honors & Awards:* WRG Baker Prize, Inst Elec & Electronics Engrs, 76. *Prof Exp:* Jr physicist, Argonne Nat Lab, 46-50; res physicist, Res Lab, Westinghouse Elec Corp, 53-56, adv physicist, 57-60, consult physicist, 60. *Concurrent Pos:* Corresp, Comments on Solid State Physics, 70-83; consult, Physics Surv Comt, Nat Acad Sci, 70-72; chmn, Comt Ion Implantation, Nat Mat Adv Bd, 79, Comt Applications Physics, Am Phys Soc, 76-78 & Int Conf Heavy Doping & Metal-Insulator Transition in Semiconductors, 84; assoc ed, Rev Mod Physics, 76-95; vis prof, Univ Sydney, 96. *Mem:* Nat Acad Eng; fel Am Phys Soc; fel Inst Elec & Electronics Engrs; AAAS; Sigma Xi. *Res:* Solid state physics and its applications to electronics. *Mailing Add:* T J Watson Res Ctr IBM Corp PO Box 218 Yorktown Heights NY 10598

KEYES, SUSAN RILEY, BIOCHEMISTRY, CELL BIOLOGY. *Current Pos:* dir cell biol, Primary Eval Unit, Biol Dept, 89-94, ASSOC DIR PROJ MGT, BIOMEASURE, INC, 94- *Educ:* Marymount Col, BS, 67; Univ Conn Health Ctr, 80. *Prof Exp:* Fel, Dept Pharmacol, Develop Therapeut Prog, Yale Univ Sch Med, 80-82, assoc, 82-83, assoc res scientist, 83-89. *Mem:* Am Asn Cancer Res; AAAS; Am Soc Biochem & Molecular Biol. *Res:* Cell biology; biochemistry; co-author of numerous scientific publications. *Mailing Add:* Bio Strategies 41 Pinckney St Boston MA 02114

KEYES, THOMAS FRANCIS, THEORETICAL CHEMISTRY. *Current Pos:* PROF CHEM, BOSTON UNIV. *Personal Data:* b New Haven, Conn, Sept 21, 45; m 68. *Educ:* Yale Univ, BS, 67; Univ Calif, Los Angeles, PhD(chem), 71. *Prof Exp:* NSF fel chem, Mass Inst Technol, 71-74; asst prof, Yale Univ, 74-81, assoc prof chem, 81- *Res:* Statistical mechanics, emphasizing theory of light scattering, dynamics of fluctuations in fluids and kinetic theory. *Mailing Add:* Dept Chem Boston Univ 685 Commonwealth Ave Boston MA 02215-1406

KEYNES, HARVEY BAYARD, ERGODIC THEORY & DYNAMICAL SYSTEMS, MATHEMATICS EDUCATION. *Current Pos:* vis asst prof, Univ Minn, Minneapolis, 68-69, from asst prof to assoc prof, 69-78, assoc head math, 79-82, assoc dir educ, geom ctr, 91-92, PROF MATH, UNIV MINN, MINNEAPOLIS, 78-, DIR, OUTREACH PROJS, 84- *Personal Data:* b Philadelphia, Pa, Dec 27, 40; m 64, Cheryl; c Davin, Michael & Alana. *Educ:* Univ Pa, BA, 62, MA, 63; Wesleyan Univ, PhD(math), 66. *Honors & Awards:* Distinguished Pub Ser Award, Am Math Soc; G Taylor Award, Distinguished Pub Serv Inst Tech. *Prof Exp:* Asst prof math, Univ Calif, Santa Barbara, 66-68. *Concurrent Pos:* Trainee math, US Naval Air Develop Ctr, Pa, 58-62; NSF grants, 67-; HEW grant, 73-75; vis prof math, Univ Witwatersrand, SAfrica, 77-96; prog dir, NSF, 82-83; proj dir, Math & Educ Reform Network, Minn Math Mobilization. *Mem:* Nat Coun Teachers Math; Am Math Soc; Asn Women Math; Math Asn Am. *Res:* Topological dynamics; dynamical systems; ergodic theory; mathematics education. *Mailing Add:* Dept Math Univ Minn 127 Vincent Hall Minneapolis MN 55455

KEYS, ANCEL (BENJAMIN), PHYSIOLOGY, NUTRITION. *Current Pos:* asst prof biochem, Mayo Found, 36-37, from assoc prof to prof physiol, 37-46, prof physiol hyg, 46-75, dir lab physiol hyg, 39-75, EMER PROF PHYSIOL HYG, UNIV MINN, MINNEAPOLIS, 75- *Personal Data:* b Colorado Springs, Colo, Jan 26, 04; m 39; c 3. *Educ:* Univ Calif, BA, 25, MS, 29, PhD(biol), 30; Cambridge Univ, PhD(physiol), 38. *Honors & Awards:* Medal Honor, Acad Finland; Medal Honor, Univ Belgrade. *Prof Exp:* Asst, Scripps Inst, Univ Calif, 27-30; Nat Res Coun fel, Copenhagen Univ, 30-31; Rockeffer Found Coun fel, Cambridge Univ, 31-32; lectr & demonstr physiol, 32-33; instr biochem sci, Harvard Univ, 33-36. *Concurrent Pos:* Res assoc, Oceanog Int, Woods Hole, 33-34; mgr, Int High Altitude Exped, Chile, 35; sr Fulbright fel, Oxford Univ, 51-52; USPHS spec fel, 63-64; consult, UN, WHO, Food & Agr Orgn & UNESCO, 50- *Mem:* AAAS; Am Physiol Soc; Am Inst Nutrit; Am Soc Clin Nutrit; Int Soc Cardiol. *Res:* Epidemiology; cardiology. *Mailing Add:* Sch Pub Health Univ Minn 1300 S Second St Suite 300 Minneapolis MN 55454

KEYS, CHARLES EVEREL, vertebrate embryology, for more information see previous edition

KEYS, JOHN DAVID, PHYSICS. *Current Pos:* CONSULT, 81- *Personal Data:* b Toronto, Ont, Sept 30, 22; m 45; c 2. *Educ:* McGill Univ, BSc, 47, MSc, 48, PhD(nuclear physics), 51. *Prof Exp:* From asst prof to prof physics, Can Serv Col, Royal Roads, 51-58, head dept, 57-58; sr sci off, Dept Energy, Mines & Resources, Ont, 58-67, head mineral physics sect, 63-67, chief hydrol sci div, Inland Waters Br, 67-70; sci adv, Treasury Bd Secretariat, 70-71; asst vpres, Nat Res Coun Can, 71-73, vpres, 73-76; asst dep minister, Sci & Technol Sector, Dept Energy, 76-81. *Mem:* AAAS; Am Phys Soc; Can Asn Physicists; Royal Astron Soc. *Res:* Application of radiotracers to industrial problems associated with mining; solid state physics studies applied to minerals and semiconductors. *Mailing Add:* 39 Ridean Terr Ottawa ON K1M 2A2 Can

KEYS, L KEN, MATERIALS SCIENCE ENGINEERING, CHEMISTRY. *Current Pos:* PROF & DEPT CHAIR INDUST & MFG SYSTS ENG, LA STATE UNIV, BATON ROUGE, 89- *Personal Data:* b Cincinnati, Ohio, Nov 6, 39; m 61, Carol J Waters; c Kevin J, Gian D & Perryn M. *Educ:* Univ Cincinnati, BS, 61; Pa State Univ, PhD(solid state sci), 65. *Prof Exp:* Res assoc, solid state sci, Pa State Univ, 65-66; prin engr, Nuclear Systs Progs Div, Gen Elec Co, 66-68; mgr advan microelectronics eng, Magnavox Co, 69-73; mgr microelectronics technol, Bell-Northern Res, 73-75; mgr, Advan Mfg Develop, Northern Telecom Ltd, 75-77; mgr, Advan Electronic Tel Develop, 77-78; mgr, Tel Progs, Stromberg-Carlson Corp, 77-78; prog mgr, DBX Progs & dir technol, United Technols Lexar Corp, 81-84; dir, Instrumentation Systs Ctr, Univ Wis-Madison, 84-87, assoc prof indust eng, 87-89. *Mem:* Sr mem Inst Elec & Electronics Engrs; sr mem Soc Mfg Engrs; Sigma Xi; sr mem Inst Indust Engrs; NY Acad Sci; Soc Eng & Mgt Systs. *Res:* New technology, product development and transfer into production-market place, including follow-up support (life cycle process); management of technology, intelligent, enterprise, virtual enterprise. *Mailing Add:* 5946 Hickory Ridge Blvd Baton Rouge LA 70817. *Fax:* 504-388-5990

KEYS, RICHARD TAYLOR, PHYSICAL CHEMISTRY. *Current Pos:* from asst prof to assoc prof, 59-72, PROF CHEM, CALIF STATE UNIV, LOS ANGELES, 72- *Personal Data:* b Salina, Kans, Feb 11, 31; m 55. *Educ:* Harvard Univ, AB, 53; Iowa State Col, PhD(chem), 58. *Prof Exp:* Asst chem, Iowa State Col, 53-58; res fel, Calif Inst Technol, 58-59. *Concurrent Pos:* NIH spec fel, Univ Calif, Riverside, 66-67; vis prof, Nat Auro Univ Mex, 75-76, Univ Southern Calif, 84-85. *Mem:* Am Chem Soc; Am Phys Soc. *Res:* Chemistry of free radicals; magnetic resonance. *Mailing Add:* Dept Chem Calif State Univ 5151 State University Dr Los Angeles CA 90032-8202

KEYS, THOMAS EDWARD, history of medicine; deceased, see previous edition for last biography

KEYSER, DAVID RICHARD, MECHANICAL ENGINEERING, AEROSPACE ENGINEERING. *Current Pos:* aerospace engr fluidic flight control, 80-96, AIRCRAFT SUBSYSTS, AIRCRAFT DIV PATUXENT RIVER, MD, 96- *Personal Data:* b Ft Wayne, Ind, Dec 5, 41; m 92, Eleanor A Diller; c Wendy & Orion. *Educ:* Swathmore Col, BS, 63; Univ Pa, MS, 65; Eurotech Res Univ, PhD, 91. *Honors & Awards:* Independent Eng Develop Award, USN, 84; Cert Award Code & Stands, Am Soc Mech Engrs, 91. *Prof Exp:* Res engr fluid dynamics & flow measurement, Naval Boiler & Turbine Lab, 65-68; res engr flow & temperature measurement, Naval Ship Eng Ctr, Philadelphia, 68-72, sr proj engr fluid dynamics & control systs, 72-80. *Concurrent Pos:* Secy, Res Comt Fluid Meters, Am Soc Mech Engrs, 78-; mem, Stand Comt, Measurement Fluid Flow, 78-, chmn, Fluid Power Control Systs Panel & vpres, Bd Performance Test Codes, Exec Comt, Fluid Power Syst & Technol Div; mem, Comn A-6D Flight Controls Panel, Soc Automotive Engrs. *Mem:* Fel Am Soc Mech Engrs; Soc Automotive Engrs. *Res:* Flight controls and flying qualities; fluidics; advanced actuation systems; unsteady flow measurements; new methods of flow measurement; Two US patents. *Mailing Add:* 185 Calvert Beach Rd St Leonard MD 20685. *Fax:* 301-342-9414; *E-Mail:* keyser_dave%pax5a@mr.nawcad.navy.mil

KEYSER, N(AAMAN) H(ENRY), METALLURGY. *Current Pos:* CONSULT, 80- *Personal Data:* b Philadelphia, Pa, Dec 5, 18; m 42; c 4. *Educ:* Antioch Col, BS, 41; Ohio State Univ, MS, 43. *Prof Exp:* Res engr process metall, Battelle Mem Inst, 41-47; asst group leader fabrication group, Los Alamos Sci Lab, Univ Calif, 47-48; asst chief process metall, Battelle Mem Inst, 48-62; dir res, Interlake Inc, 62-80. *Concurrent Pos:* Exec consult, Exec Serv Corps Chicago; master gardener, Coop Exten Serv, Univ Ill. *Mem:* Am Soc Metals; Am Foundrymen's Soc (secy, 48-60); Am Inst Mining, Metall & Petrol Engrs; Iron & Steel Soc. *Res:* Economic studies and new processes for metals and inorganic chemicals using elevated temperatures produced by electric and blast furnaces; making, forming and treating of steel and steel products especially in silicon and silicon alloys. *Mailing Add:* 122 W Walnut Hinsdale IL 60521-3350

KEYSER, PETER D, MEDICAL MICROBIOLOGY. *Current Pos:* PVT PRACT, 91- *Personal Data:* b Columbus, Ohio, Oct 26, 45; m 69; c 1. *Educ:* Ohio State Univ, BS, 68, MS, 70, PhD(microbiol), 72. *Prof Exp:* Res fel microbiol, Univ Ky & Fla State Univ, 72-73; asst prof microbiol, NTex State Univ Health Sci Ctr, 73-81, asst prof microbiol & immunol, Tex Col Osteop Med, 81-91, adj prof biol sci, 75-91. *Mem:* Sigma Xi; Am Soc Microbiol. *Res:* Role of lipases in pathogenicity of gram negative organisms, particularly those species isolated from burn wound sepsis. *Mailing Add:* 500 West Blvd Chesterfield SC 29709

KEYT, DONALD E, mechanical engineering, for more information see previous edition

KEYWORTH, DONALD ARTHUR, TECHNICAL MANAGEMENT, CATALYSIS. *Current Pos:* GROUP RES MGR, CATALYST DEVELOP, AKZO CHEM INC, 85- *Personal Data:* b Flint, Mich, Apr 21, 30; m 78, Dale Bowlen. *Educ:* Univ Mich, BS, 51; Mich State Univ, MS, 54; Wayne State Univ, PhD(chem), 58. *Honors & Awards:* Res Award, Sigma Xi, 68; Kirk-Patrick Award, 79. *Prof Exp:* Chief anal controls, Lapaco Chem Co, Mich, 51-52; anal chemist, Ethyl Corp, Mich, 54 & Wyandotte Chem Co, 58-60; asst res dir, Universal Oil Prod Co, 60-67, vpres & tech dir, Sci & Educ Serv, 67-68; mgr res, Tenneco Chem, Tenneco Inc, 68-80; mgr res, Petro-Tex Chem Corp, 80-85. *Concurrent Pos:* Instr, Wayne State Univ, 57-60. *Mem:* Am Soc Testing & Mat; Am Chem Soc; Soc Appl Spectros; NY Acad Sci; Sigma Xi. *Res:* Industrial research; methods and techniques of analysis of industrial products, acetylenics synthesis and manufacturing; industrial utilization of pi-complexes; industrial catalysis and catalyst evaluation. *Mailing Add:* 5320 Dora Houston TX 77005-1818. *Fax:* 281-474-0397

KEYWORTH, GEORGE A, II, EXPERIMENTAL NUCLEAR PHYSICS. *Current Pos:* DIR, OFF SCI & TECHNOL POLICY & SCI ADV TO PRES, 81- *Personal Data:* b Boston, Mass, Nov 30, 39; m 62; c 2. *Educ:* Yale Univ, BS, 63; Duke Univ, PhD(physics), 68. *Prof Exp:* Res assoc, Duke Univ, 68; staff mem, Los Alamos Sci Lab, 68-74, group leader, 74-78, alt physics div leader & physics div leader, 78-81, laser fusion div leader, 80-81. *Mem:* AAAS; Am Phys Soc; Sigma Xi. *Res:* Nuclear structure problems; isobaric analogue states; polarization experiments; fission physics; neutron physics; fusion physics; science policy. *Mailing Add:* 41 Avenida De Las Casos Santa Fe NM 87501-8604

KEYZER, HENDRIK, PHYSICAL CHEMISTRY, SOLID STATE CHEMISTRY. *Current Pos:* univ fel & NIH fel, Calif State Univ, Los Angeles, 67, res grant, 67-68, from asst prof to assoc prof, 67-79, PROF CHEM, CALIF STATE UNIV, LOS ANGELES, 79- *Personal Data:* b Djakarta, Indonesia, Dec 7, 31; m 54; c 7. *Educ:* Univ NSW, BS, 63, PhD(chem), 66. *Honors & Awards:* NASA Award, 71. *Prof Exp:* Res chemist, Mus Appl Arts & Sci, 62-63; lectr, Sydney Tech Col, 64-66. *Concurrent Pos:* NIMH res grant, 68-69 & 71-72; consult, Jet Propulsion Lab, 68-; reader, Victoria Univ, Wellington, 72-73; Health & Human Welfare, res grant, 76-80; Dept Educ, training grants, 81-86. *Mem:* Am Chem Soc. *Res:* Physical-organic chemistry of natural compounds and compounds of biological importance; psychotropic drugs; polymer chemistry; electrochemistry; micro-analysis; natural products. *Mailing Add:* Dept Chem Calif State Univ 5151 State University Dr Los Angeles CA 90032-8000

KEZDI, PAUL, CARDIOLOGY. *Current Pos:* assoc dean res affairs, 77-85, EMER PROF MED, WRIGHT STATE UNIV SCH MED, 86- *Personal Data:* b Hungary, Nov 13, 14; nat US; m 43, 65; c Melinda, Annie, Laura & Paula. *Educ:* Pazmany Peter Univ, Budapest, MD, 42; Am Bd Internal Med, dipl, 61. *Prof Exp:* Dir heart sta, Wesley Mem Hosp, Chicago, Ill, 54-65; assoc dean res affairs & prof med, Wright State Univ, 75-86; dir res, Cox Heart Inst, 65-67, dir, 87-86. *Concurrent Pos:* Am Heart Asn fel clin cardiol; assoc prof, Sch Med, Northwestern Univ, 62-65; mem, Med Adv Bd, Coun High Blood Pressue Res, Am Heart Asn, 63; prof med, Ind Univ, 65-72; clin prof, Ohio State Univ, 65-75; mem, Heart Prog Proj Comt, Nat Heart Lung & Blood Comn, 66-67. *Mem:* Fel Am Col Chest Physicians; Fel Am Col Cardiol; Am Physiol Soc; Am Fedn Clin Res; Am Heart Asn. *Res:* Cardiac physiology; coronary artery disease; hypertension; neurogenic control by baroreceptors of the ciruclation. *Mailing Add:* Cox Health Eval Serv 1712 Ladera Trail Dayton OH 45459

KEZDY, FERENC J, BIOCHEMISTRY. *Current Pos:* DISTINGUISHED SCIENTIST, UPJOHN CO, 88- *Personal Data:* b Budapest, Hungary, July 28, 29; m 58, Marie T Colas; c John F, Pierre G & Andre E. *Educ:* Univ Louvain, DrSci(phys org chem), 57. *Honors & Awards:* Stas-Spring Prize, Belg Royal Acad Sci, 58; Woutes Prize, Chem Soc Belg, 60. *Prof Exp:* Asst phys & org chem, Univ Louvain, 57-61; assoc biochem, Northwestern Univ, 61-65; from asst prof to prof biochem, Univ Chicago, 66-88. *Mem:* Am Chem Soc; AAAS; Sigma Xi. *Res:* Physical organic chemistry; surface biochemistry; enzymology. *Mailing Add:* 3805 Robin Lane Kalamazoo MI 49008-3148. *Fax:* 616-385-7373

KEZIOS, STOTHE PETER, THERMODYNAMICS. *Current Pos:* PROF MECH ENG & DIR, SCH MECH ENG, GA INST TECHNOL, 67- *Personal Data:* b Chicago, Ill, Apr 8, 21; m 52; c 1. *Educ:* Ill Inst Technol, BS, 42, MS, 48, PhD(mech eng), 55. *Honors & Awards:* Ralph Coates Roe award, Am Soc Eng Educ, 77. *Prof Exp:* Asst instr mech eng, Ill Inst Technol, 42-44, instr, 46-47, res engr, 47-49, from asst prof to prof, 49-67, dir heat transfer lab, 55-68. *Concurrent Pos:* Consult govt & indust, 48-; vchmn, Nat Heat Transfer Conf, 58; consult ed, J Heat Transfer, 58-63, tech ed, 63-; secy, Int Heat Transfer Conf, 61-62, adv orgn comt, 66; Am Soc Mech Eng rep, Comt Int Rels, Eng, Joint Coun, 62-; mem sci adv panel, Eng Sect, NSF, 63-66. *Mem:* Am Soc Mech Engrs (secy, 53-57, vpres, 73-77, pres, 77-78); Am Soc Eng Educ; Am Inst Chem Engrs; Sigma Xi. *Res:* Heat transfer; analogy between heat and mass transfer; forced convection heat transfer, especially with free jets; boiling in forced convection flow. *Mailing Add:* 1060 Winding Creek Trail NW Atlanta GA 30328-2854

KEZLAN, THOMAS PHILLIP, MATHEMATICS. *Current Pos:* ASSOC PROF MATH, UNIV MO, KANSAS CITY, 68- *Personal Data:* b Omaha, Nebr, Aug 6, 35. *Educ:* Univ Omaha, 57; Univ Kans, MA, 59, PhD(math), 64. *Prof Exp:* Asst prof math, Univ Mo, Kansas City, 63-64; asst prof, Univ Tex, Austin, 64-68. *Mem:* Math Asn Am; Am Math Soc. *Res:* Theory of rings. *Mailing Add:* Univ Mo Kansas City MO 64110-2499

KHABBAZ, SAMIR ANTON, MATHEMATICS. *Current Pos:* assoc prof, 64-68, PROF MATH, LEHIGH UNIV, 68- *Personal Data:* b Tel Aviv, Palestine, Mar 31, 32; US citizen; m 59; c 3. *Educ:* Bethel Col, BA, 54; Univ Kans, MA, 56, PhD, 60. *Prof Exp:* Instr math, Univ Mass, 60; asst prof, Lehigh Univ, 60-62; Off Naval Res res fel, Yale Univ, 62-63, univ res fel, 63-64. *Mem:* Am Math Soc. *Res:* Algebra and topology. *Mailing Add:* Dept Math Xmas-Saucon Hall 14 Lehigh Univ Bethlehem PA 18015

KHACHADURIAN, AVEDIS K, MEDICINE. *Current Pos:* PROF MED, UNIV MED & DENT NJ-R W JOHNSON MED SCH, 73-, CHIEF DIV ENDOCRINE, METAB DIS & NUTRIT, 73- *Personal Data:* b Aleppo, Syria, Jan 6, 26; m 61, Hadidian; c Cynthia & Linda. *Educ:* Am Univ Beirut, BA, 49, MD, 53. *Prof Exp:* Resident internal med, Am Univ Beirut, 53-56, fel biochem, 56-57, from asst prof to prof biochem & internal med, Sch Med, 59-71; lectr pediat, Northwestern Univ, Chicago, 65-66, prof, 71-73; dir, Clin Res Ctr, Children's Mem Hosp, 71-73. *Concurrent Pos:* Res fel, Harvard Med Sch & Joslin Clin, Mass, 57-59. *Mem:* Am Diabetes Asn; Endocrine Soc; Am Fedn Clin Res; Am Heart Asn; NY Acad Sci; Am Inst Nutrit. *Res:* Clinical and biochemical aspects of familial hypercholesterolemia; effect of excercise on metabolic parameters in diabetes mellitus. *Mailing Add:* Dept Med Univ Med & Dent NJ R W Johnson Med Sch C N 19 New Brunswick NJ 08903. *Fax:* 732-235-7096

KHACHATOURIANS, GEORGE G, TOXICOLOGY, BIOTECHNOLOGY. *Current Pos:* asst prof, 74-81, PROF APPL MICROBIOL, UNIV SASK, 81- *Personal Data:* b 1940; m 74; c 1. *Educ:* Calif State Univ, BA, 66, MA, 69; Univ British Columbia, PhD(Microbiol), 71. *Prof Exp:* Res assoc, Univ Mass, 73-74. *Concurrent Pos:* Chmn genetics, Univ Sask, 80-83, dir, Bioinsecticide Res Lab, 82-, Biotechnol, 84-86; mem, fed task force biotechnol, Govt Can, Ottawa, Ont, 80-81; vis prof, Univ BC, 92. *Mem:* Am Soc Microbiol; Can Soc Microbiol; Int Soc Toxins; Soc Invert Path; Am Entom Soc; Asn Integrative Studies; Am Soc Indust Microbiol. *Res:* Agricultural biotechnologies including microbial insect control system development and testing; microbial release and gene tracking in the environment; environmental toxicology and production of fungal toxins in agricultural products; effects of combination of food toxicants and additives; food biotechnology and transgeric plants; microbiology. *Mailing Add:* Univ Sask Dept Appl Microbiol & Food Sci Col Agr Biotechnol Lab Saskatoon SK S7N 5A8 Can. *Fax:* 306-966-8898; *E-Mail:* khachatouria@sask.usask.ca

KHACHATURIAN, NARBEY, CIVIL ENGINEERING, STRUCTURAL ENGINEERING. *Current Pos:* From instr to prof, 49-89, assoc head, Dept Civil Eng, 83-89, EMER PROF CIVIL ENG, UNIV ILL, URBANA, 89- *Personal Data:* b Teheran, Iran, Jan 12, 24; nat US; m 52, Margaret Miles; c Gregory M, Jon E, Mary D (Thrift) & Steven J. *Educ:* Univ Ill, BS, 47, MS, 48, PhD(eng), 52. *Honors & Awards:* Parmer Award, 86; Halliburton Award, 88. *Concurrent Pos:* NSF sr fel, Univ Calif, Los Angeles, 63-64; chmn, Ill Struct Engr Exam Comt, 71; pres, Struct Engrs Asn Ill, 89-90. *Mem:* Hon mem Am Soc Civil Engrs; Am Soc Eng Educ; Am Concrete Inst; Nat Soc Prof Engrs; Sigma Xi; Struct Engrs Asn. *Res:* Experimental and analytical structural engineering, especially reinforced and prestressed concrete; structural optimization; structural concrete. *Mailing Add:* PO Box 26 Philo IL 61864-0026

KHACHATURIAN, ZAVEN SETRAK, NEUROSCIENCE. *Current Pos:* DIR, RONALD & NANCY REAGAN RES INST, 95-; CONSULT ALZHEIMERS DIS, KR ASSOC INC, 95- *Personal Data:* b Alleppo, Syria, Apr 15, 37; US citizen; m 63; c 1. *Educ:* Yale Univ, BA, 61; Case Western Reserve Univ, PhD(neurobiol), 67. *Prof Exp:* Fel neurophysiol, Col Physicians & Surgeons, Columbia Univ, 67-69; asst prof develop neurobiol, Div Child Psychiat, Med Sch, Univ Pittsburgh, 69-72, prog dir neurophysiol, Dept Psychiat, 72-77; grants assoc, Div Res Grants, NIH, 77-78; prog dir, Neurosci Aging, Nat Inst Aging, NIH, 78-79; health policy coordr, Off Secy, Dept Health, Educ & Welfare, 79-80; spec asst dir, Nat Inst Aging, NIH, Physiol Aging Br, 80-81, chief, 81-85, assoc dir, Neurosci & Neuropsychol of Aging & dir, Off Alzheimer's Dis Res, 86-95. *Concurrent Pos:* Interim sci dir, Pittsburgh Biotechnol Ctr, 85-86; vpres res, Health Sci Univ Pittsburgh Med Ctr, 85; prof, Health Serv Admin, 86. *Mem:* Soc Neurosci. *Res:* Alzheimer's disease; neuroscience of aging; neural plasticity; science policy; calcium regulation in aging neurine. *Mailing Add:* 8912 Copenhaver Dr Potomac MD 20854

KHAIR, ABDUL WAHAB, ROCK MECHANICS, ACOUSTICS EMISSION. *Current Pos:* assoc prof mining eng, 81-86, PROF MINING ENG, WVA UNIV, 86- *Personal Data:* b Kabul, Afghanistan, March 20, 41; m 69. *Educ:* WVa Univ, BS, 67, MS, 68; Pa, State Univ, PhD(miningeng), 72. *Prof Exp:* Res assoc rock mech, Pa, State Univ, 72-75; pres, Ministry Mines & Ind, Afghanistan, 75-79; res assoc rock mech, Pa State Univ, 79-81. *Mem:* Soc Mining Eng; Int Soc Rock Mech. *Res:* Respirable dust generation in underground coal mines, coal bump and gas outburst; subsidence due to underground excavations, monitoring, and prediction; structural stability analysis of mines and design of mine layout and support system; rock mechanics and ground control relation problems, and physical and analytical modeling of geotechnical problems. *Mailing Add:* Dept Mining Eng Rm 359 M R WVa Univ PO Box 6070 Morgantown WV 26506-6070

KHAIRALLAH, EDWARD A, endocrinology, nutritional biochemistry & biochemical toxicology; deceased, see previous edition for last biography

KHAIRALLAH, PHILIP ASAD, PHYSIOLOGY, PHARMACOLOGY. *Current Pos:* Am Heart Asn estab investr, Found, 58-63, mem staff res div, 63-70, sci dir res div & head dept cardiovasc res, 70-80, staff res div, 80-86, DIR ANESTHESIA RES, CLEVELAND CLIN FOUND, 86- *Personal Data:* b New York, NY, Feb 3, 28; m 63; c 4. *Educ:* Am Univ Beirut, BA, 47; Columbia Univ, MD, 51. *Concurrent Pos:* Am Heart Asn fel, Duke Univ, 51-53, Cleveland Clin Found, 56-57 & Am Univ Beirut, 57-58; adj prof, John Carroll Univ & Cleveland State Univ; mem, Coun High Blood Pressure Res, Am Heart Asn. *Mem:* Am Soc Pharmacol & Exp Therapeut; Am Physiol Soc; Am Soc Nephrology; AMA; Int Anesthesia Res Soc. *Res:* Cardiovascular research in biochemistry, physiology and pharmacology; cardiac and blood vessel contraction; medical ethics; narcotic anesthetics. *Mailing Add:* Cleveland Clin Found 9500 Euclid Ave Cleveland OH 44195-0002

KHAKOO, MURTADHA A, ELECTRON SCATTERING, LASER EXCITED ATOMS. *Current Pos:* ASST PROF PHYSICS, CALIF STATE UNIV, FULLERTON, 89- *Personal Data:* b Zanzibar, Tanzania, Apr 29, 53; Brit citizen; m 83, Sherbanu S Rashid; c Naushad & Sabaha. *Educ:* Univ London, BSc Hons, 75, PhD(physics), 80. *Honors & Awards:* NASA Award, 88. *Prof Exp:* Postdoctoral fel, Univ Col London, 80-81 & Univ Windsor, Ont, 84-87; vis fel, Jet Propulsion Lab, NASA-Nat Res Coun, 81-84; res asst prof mech, Univ Mo, Rolla, 87-89. *Concurrent Pos:* Consult, Jet Propulsion Labs, Pasadena, 89-; reviewer, J Physics B, Phys Rev A & Phys Rev Lett. *Mem:* Am Phys Soc. *Res:* Electron impact studies of gaseous targets; elastic and inelastic electron scattering from atomic and molecular targets; electron-photon coincidence studies; fragmentation of molecules, lifetime studies; spin polarized electron scattering. *Mailing Add:* Dept Physics Calif State Univ Fullerton CA 92634-9480. *Fax:* 714-449-5810; *E-Mail:* mkhakoo@fullerton.edu

KHALAF, KAMEL T, ZOOLOGY, MEDICAL ENTOMOLOGY. *Current Pos:* RETIRED. *Personal Data:* b Mosul, Iraq, 1922; m 58, Layla H Haddo; c Suhad, Ramiz & Samir. *Educ:* Univ Baghdad, BS, 44; Univ Okla, MS, 50, PhD(zool), 52. *Prof Exp:* Instr high teachers col, Univ Baghdad, 53-56, from asst prof to prof, 56-62, res prof, Iraq Natural Hist Inst, 62-63; from asst prof to assoc prof, Loyola Univ, La, 63-69, prof entom, 69-86. *Concurrent Pos:* NIH res grant, 65-68; acad grant fund, Loyola Univ. *Res:* Surveys of biting gnats; biology of puss caterpillar and its parasites; animal surveys; micromorphology of Arthropods Integument. *Mailing Add:* 5811 S Claiborne Ave New Orleans LA 70125

KHALAFALLA, SANAA E, PHYSICAL CHEMISTRY, CHEMICAL METALLURGY. *Current Pos:* proj leader, 64-66, res supvr, Twin Cities Metall Res Ctr, Bur Mines, 66-87, CHIEF SCIENTIST, US DEPT INTERIOR, 87- *Personal Data:* b Mit Yaish, Egypt, July 1, 24; US citizen; m 57, Aida; c Ashraf & Sammy. *Educ:* Cairo Univ, BSc, 44; Univ Minn, Minneapolis, MS, 49, PhD(phys chem), 53. *Honors & Awards:* Spec Act of Serv Award, Twin Cities Metall Res Ctr, US Bur Mines, 66. *Prof Exp:* Demonstr chem fac sci, Cairo Univ, 44-48, from asst prof to assoc prof phys chem, 53-61; Hill Family Found res fel & res assoc, Univ Minn, 61-64. *Concurrent Pos:* Vis prof, Bristol Univ, 60-61. *Mem:* Am Inst Mining, Metall & Petrol Engrs; Am Inst Elec & Electronics Engrs. *Res:* Process and extractive metallurgy; kinetics and mechanisms of mineral reactions; electrochemistry and polarography; catalytic reactions; magneto chemistry; plasma chemistry; leaching processes; asbestos fibers; mine water and wastes; magnetic fluids; water conservation; minerals and mining. *Mailing Add:* 2551 37th Ave Minneapolis MN 55406-1745. *Fax:* 612-721-5542

KHALED, MOHAMMAD ABU, BIOPHYSICS, PHYSICAL CHEMISTRY & NUTRITIONAL BIOCHEMISTRY. *Current Pos:* fel, 75-77, from instr to asst prof biochem, 77-83, asst prof, 83-84, ASSOC PROF NUTRIT SCI, UNIV ALA, 84- *Personal Data:* b Murshidabad, India, Nov 1, 42; US citizen; m 76. *Educ:* Univ Calcutta, BSc, 61; Aligarh Muslim Univ, India, MSc, 64; Univ London, PhD(biophys, chem), 75. *Prof Exp:* Lectr chem, Polytech Inst, Chittagong, Bangladesh, 64-65; lectr, Cadet Col, Rajshahi, Bangladesh, 66-71. *Res:* Spectroscopic approach in determining biomolecular conformations and structure-function relationships; body composition measurements. *Mailing Add:* Dept Nutrit Sci Univ Ala-Birmingham Univ Sta Birmingham AL 35294. *Fax:* 205-934-7049

KHALIFA, RAMZI A, ACOUSTICS, METAL FABRICATING. *Current Pos:* DIR CORP MFG ACOUST, INDUST ACOUST CO, 85- *Personal Data:* b Cairo, Egypt, July 20, 40; US citizen; c 3. *Educ:* Cairo Univ, BSME, 64; NJ Inst Technol, MS, 74, MS, 89. *Prof Exp:* Mfg eng mgr, HVAC, Delta Indust Co, 64-69; dir eng electronics, Edson Tool & Mfg Co, 70-89. *Concurrent Pos:* Teacher, Cairo Univ, 64-69; prog chmn, Precision Metal Stamping Asn, 81-85. *Res:* Developed cable enclosures with patented self-locking devices; new metal stamping tooling concepts; universal mount dies; modular correctional security ceiling system; acoustical windows; modular track wall panels and highway barrier panels; five patents. *Mailing Add:* 448 Lincoln Ave Rutherford NJ 07070

KHALIFAH, RAJA GABRIEL, CHEMISTRY, BIOCHEMISTRY. *Current Pos:* MEM STAFF, VET ADMIN MED CTR, 80- *Personal Data:* b Tripoli, Lebanon, May 5, 42; nat US; m 71; c 2. *Educ:* Am Univ Beirut, BS, 62; Princeton Univ, PhD(phys chem), 69. *Prof Exp:* Res assoc biochem, Harvard Univ, 68-70; res assoc pharmacol, Sch Med, Stanford Univ, 70-73; asst prof chem, Univ Va, 73-80. *Concurrent Pos:* Res assoc prof biochem, sch med, Univ Kans, 79- *Mem:* Am Chem Soc; Am Soc Biol Chemists; Sigma Xi. *Res:* Biophysical chemistry; kinetics and thermodynamics of protein conformation changes; enzyme kinetics and mechanism; chemical modification of active sites; nuclear magnetic resonance applications to proteins and enzymes. *Mailing Add:* Dept Biochem Molecular Univ Kans Sch Med 3901 & Rainbow Blvd Kansas City MO 66103. *Fax:* 913-588-7440

KHALIL, M ASLAM KHAN, ATMOSPHERIC CHEMISTRY & PHYSICS. *Current Pos:* res asst, Inst Atmosphere Sci, Ore Grad Ctr, 77-79, sr res assoc, 79-80, from asst prof to assoc prof, environ sci, 80-84, prof chem, biol & environ sci, 84-87, PROF, DEPT ENVIRON SCI & ENG, ORE GRAD INST, 87-, DIR, GLOBAL CHANGE RES CTR, 90- *Personal Data:* b Jhansi, India, Jan 7, 50; US citizen; m 73, Giti Eshraghi; c Kathayoon & Kaviyaan. *Educ:* Univ Minn, BPhys, BA(math) & BA(psychol), 70; Va Polytech Inst & State Univ, MS, 72; Univ Tex, Austin, PhD(physics), 76; Ore Grad Ctr, MS & PhD(environ sci), 79. *Prof Exp:* Teach asst physics, Va Polytech Inst & State Univ, 70-71; grad asst math & physics, Univ Tex, Austin, 71-72, teaching asst physics, 72-73 & 76, res scientist asst, Ctr Particle Theory, 72-76. *Concurrent Pos:* Instr physics, Pac Univ, 77-78; prin investr, NSF, NASA, Environ Protection Agency & Dept Energy, 80-; owner, Andarz Co, 81- *Mem:* Am Phys Soc; Am Chem Soc; Am Geophys Union; Air & Waste Mgt Asn. *Res:* Elementary particles with spin (theoretical physics); author or co-author of 150 publications; atmospheric physics and chemistry; models for global dispersion of trace gases; effects of man-made trace gases; long-distance transport of pollution; receptor models for urban pollution; mathematical and statistical techniques in environmental sciences; biogeochemical cycles; climate models. *Mailing Add:* Dept Phys Portland State Univ PO Box 751 Portland OR 97207-0751. *Fax:* 503-690-1016

KHALIL, MICHEL, ORGANOHALOGENATED COMPOUNDS. *Current Pos:* PROF CHEM, UNIV QUEBEC, RIMOUSKI, 70- *Personal Data:* b Alexandria, Egypt, June 30, 35; Can citizen; m 67; c 3. *Educ:* Univ Alexandria, Egypt, BSc, 57, MSc, 64; Univ Laval, Can, PhD(chem), 70. *Prof Exp:* Chemist, El-Nasr Spinning, Egypt, 57-65 & Dionne Spinning, Can,

65-67. *Concurrent Pos:* Vis prof chem oceanog, Univ Marie Curie, Paris, 74 & Univ Miami, 77-78; consult, Provincial Dept Environ, 82, Provincial Dept Transports, 84-85 & PCB studies, Hydro-Quebec, 84-86. *Mem:* Am Chem Soc; Can Meterol & Oceanog Soc. *Res:* Bioconcentration and contamination studies in marine and estuarine ecosystems regarding halogenated and polyaromatic hydrocarbons. *Mailing Add:* UQAR 300 Ave Ursulines Rimouski PQ G5L 3A1 Can

KHALIL, MOHAMED THANAA, BIOPHYSICS, MATHEMATICS. *Current Pos:* from asst prof to prof phys sci, 69-74, dean int students, 74-77, PROF NATURAL SCI & ENG TECHNOL, POINT PARK COL, 74- *Personal Data:* b Al-Kosair, Egypt, Feb 8, 33; m 60; c 2. *Educ:* Cairo Univ, BSc, 53; Univ Pittsburgh, BS, 74, PhD(biophys), 66; Univ Alexandria, MSc, 61. *Prof Exp:* Instr & res asst physics, Univ Alexandria, 53-61; res assoc biophys, Univ Pittsburgh, 61-66, res prof biophys & microbiol, 66-71. *Mem:* AAAS; Biophys Soc; NY Acad Sci; Am Chem Soc; Am Inst Physics. *Res:* Effect of laser beam on the system of polymerization of virus protein; thermodynamics of the reconstitution of virus particles in deuterium; structure and function of tobacco mosaic virus interferon and plant viruses. *Mailing Add:* Dept Natural Sci Eng Tech Point Park Col 201 Wood St Rm 404 Acad Hall Pittsburgh PA 15222

KHALIL, SHOUKRY KHALIL WAHBA, pharmacognosy, for more information see previous edition

KHALILI, ALI A, REHABILITATION MEDICINE. *Current Pos:* asst prof, Med Ctr, 65-68, dir residency prog phys med & rehab, 67-69, ASSOC PROF PHYS MED & REHAB, MCGAW MED CTR, NORTHWESTERN UNIV, 68-; DIR REHAB MED, GRANT HOSP, CHICAGO, 68-, CHMN, DEPT REHAB MED, 77- *Personal Data:* b Ardebil, Iran, Feb 9, 32; US citizen; m 62; c 2. *Educ:* Tehran Univ, MD, 57. *Prof Exp:* Instr phys med & rehab, State Univ NY Downstate Med Ctr, 62-65. *Concurrent Pos:* Dir, Neuromuscular Diag & Res Dept, Rehab Inst Chicago, 68-70; consult physiatrist, Elmhust Mem Hosp, 68- & Rehab Inst Chicago, 70-; chmn, Comt Allied Health Professions, Grant Hosp, Chicago, 73-75; chmn med pract comt, Am Acad Phys Med & Rehab, 79-80. *Mem:* AMA; Am Acad Phys Med & Rehab; Am Cong Rehab Med; Am Asn Electromyography & Electrodiag. *Res:* Spasticity and peripheral phenol nerve block (clinical, physiological and histological aspects, including electromyographic changes); radio-linked bladder stimulation in neurogenic bladder; air splint in preprosthetic rehabilitation of lower extremity amputated limbs; sensory input discrimination in normal and hemiplegic subjects; burn rehabilitation. *Mailing Add:* 550 W Webster Ave Chicago IL 60614

KHALIMSKY, EFIM D, GENERAL TOPOLOGY, GENERALIZED HOMOLOGY & HOMOTOPY THEORY. *Current Pos:* PROF MATH, CENT STATE UNIV, 89- *Personal Data:* b Odessa, USSR, June 23, 38; US citizen; m 62, Elena Merems; c Olga. *Educ:* Pedagogical Inst, Odessa, MS, 60; Pedagogical Inst, Moscow, USSR, PhD(math), 69. *Prof Exp:* Teacher math & physics, MS, Odessa, USSR, 60-66; assoc prof math, Pedagogical Inst, Magnitogorsk, USSR, 69-72 & City Univ NY 79-80; sr res scientist, Opers Res Math Econ, Food Indust, Res & Prod Inst, 72-73; sr res scientist appl math & OS, Econ Inst, Acad Sci, Odessa, USSR, 73-77; assoc prof math & comput sci, Manhattan Col, Riverdale, NY, 80-85; assoc prof comput sci, Col Staten Island, City Univ NY, 85-89. *Concurrent Pos:* Postdoctoral studies, Pedagogical Inst, Moscow, USSR, 69; ed-at-large, Marcel Dekker Publ Co; assoc ed, J Appl Math & Stochastic Anal. *Mem:* Am Math Soc; Soc Indust & Appl Math; Asn Comput Mach; Inst Elec & Electronics Engrs Systs, Man & Cybernetics Soc. *Res:* Defined and investigated properties of ordered topological spaces and have used them in developing the generalized homotopy and homology groups, digital topology, topological cell complexes and used those theories in cmputer graphics, systems analysis and design. *Mailing Add:* 1260 Brentwood Dr Dayton OH 45406

KHALONA, RAMON ANTONIO, TELECOMMUNICATION SYSTEMS ENGINEERING, DIGITAL TRANSMISSION SYSTEMS. *Current Pos:* ASST PROF LECTR, GEORGE WASHINGTON UNIV, 91- *Personal Data:* b Managua, Nicaragua, Sept 14, 61. *Educ:* Ill Inst Technol, BS, 82, MS, 84, PhD(elec eng), 90. *Prof Exp:* Instr elec eng, Ill Inst Technol, 87-90. *Concurrent Pos:* Mem tech staff, Com Sat Lab, 90- *Mem:* Inst Elec & Electronics Engrs Commun Soc; Inst Elec & Electronics Engrs Info Theory Soc. *Res:* Digital transmission systems; modulation and coding techniques. *Mailing Add:* 2585 Jefferson St Carlsbad CA 92008

KHAMIS, HARRY JOSEPH, LOG-LINEAR MODEL THEORY. *Current Pos:* Assoc prof, 87-93, PROF MATH & STATIST, WRIGHT STATE UNIV, 93- *Personal Data:* b San Jose, Calif, Dec 20, 51. *Educ:* Santa Clara Univ, BS, 74; Va Tech, MS, 76, PhD(statist), 80. *Concurrent Pos:* Adj instr ethnic dance, Dept Health, Phys Educ & Recreation, consult, 82-90, Wright State Univ, dir, Statist Consult Ctr, 90-93, dir, 93-; prof, Dept Community health, Sch Med, 93- *Mem:* Am Statist Asn; Biomet Soc; Inst Math Statist. *Res:* Loglinear model analysis and applications to genetic data; goodness-of-fit tests. *Mailing Add:* 535 Green Tree Pl Fairborn OH 45324. *E-Mail:* hkhamis@desire.wright.edu

KHAN, ABDUL JAMIL, PEDIATRIC MEDICINE, PEDIATRIC NEPHROLOGY. *Current Pos:* fel, 71-73, chief Div Pediat Nephrol, 73-87, ASSOC DIR, DEPT PEDIAT, INTER FAITH MED CTR, BROOKLYN, 90-; CHMN & PROG DIR, MEHARRY MED COL, BROOKLYN, 92- *Personal Data:* b Allahabad, India, May 5, 40; m 68, Farida Ghani; c Faiz & Faiza. *Educ:* Univ Allahabad, BSc, 57; Univ Lucknow, MB & BS, 62; Agra Univ, DCH, 64; Panjab Univ, India, MD, 67; Am Bd Pediat, cert, 73, cert pediat nephrol, 85. *Prof Exp:* Intern, King George Med Col, Univ Lucknow, 62-63; physician med & pediat, Northern Railway Hosp, India, 64-65; teaching fel pediat, Inst Post-Grad Med, Panjab Univ, India, 66-67; registr pediat, Med Col, Aligarh Muslim Univ, India, 68-69; resident, Kings Co, State Univ Hosp, Brooklyn, 69-70; prof pediat, Meharry Med Col, 87-92. *Concurrent Pos:* From instr to asst prof clin pediat, State Univ NY Downstate Med Ctr, 73-78, assoc prof, 78-94, clin prof, Health Sci Ctr, 94- *Mem:* Am Fedn Clin Res; Soc Pediat Res; Am Soc Pediat Nephrol; Asn Ped Prog Dirs; fel Am Acad Pediat. *Res:* White blood cell functions including Chemotaxis; studies on efficacy and pharmacokinetics of newer antibiotics; renal diseases in infants and children; medical education. *Mailing Add:* 2 Bridle Path Ct Glen Head CT 11545-3303. *Fax:* 718-604-6630

KHAN, ABDUL WAHEED, BIOCHEMISTRY, MICROBIOLOGY. *Current Pos:* RETIRED. *Personal Data:* b Lahore, WPakistan, Apr 16, 28; Can citizen; m 60; c 2. *Educ:* Univ Panjab, Pakistan, MSc, 52, PhD(biochem), 56; Manchester Col Sci & Technol, Eng, PhD(microbiol), 58. *Prof Exp:* Res fel biochem, Univ Panjab, Pakistan, 52-54, lectr org chem, 54-55; res fel microbiol, Manchester Col Sci & Technol, Eng, 55-58; fel biophys, Div Biosci, Nat Res Coun Can, 58-60, from asst res officer to assoc res officer, 60-72, sr res officer, 72-89. *Mem:* Inst Food Technologists; Can Biochem Soc; Can Soc Microbiol; fel Royal Soc Chem. *Res:* Conversion of biomass to fuels and chemical feed stock; anaerobic degradation of cellulose; methanogensis; meat biochemistry; effect of freezing and storage on muscle proteins; biosynthesis of cellulose; studies in bacterial cell wall components; microbiological synthesis of fat from carbohydrates; nutritive values of foods and dietary standards. *Mailing Add:* 2155 Tawney Rd Ottawa ON K1G 1C2 Can

KHAN, ADAM, MICRONUTRIENTS, SORPTION OF ORGANIC POLLUTANTS. *Current Pos:* PROF AGRON, MO WESTERN STATE COL, 79- *Personal Data:* b Harrori, Pakistan, Jan 27, 46; US citizen; c Isaac A & David A. *Educ:* Peshawar Univ, Pakistan, BS, 67; Am Univ Beirut, MS, 72; Colo State Univ, PhD(agron), 77. *Prof Exp:* Postdoctoral soils, Univ Ill, 77-79. *Concurrent Pos:* Tech dir, Mey Soil Testing Lab. *Mem:* Am Soc Agron; Soil Sci Soc Am; Crop Sci Soc; Nat Asn Cols & Teachers Agr. *Res:* Sorption of organic pollutants on soil and sediments; zinc in soil; soil testing; teaching; maximum economic yield. *Mailing Add:* RR 2 Box 147 Hamilton NY 13346. *E-Mail:* khan@acad.mwsc.edu

KHAN, AKHTAR SALAMAT, SOLID MECHANICS, MECHANICAL ENGINEERING. *Current Pos:* PROF MECH & NUCLEAR ENG, UNIV MD, BALTIMORE, 94- *Personal Data:* b Aligarh, India, June 8, 44; m 72; c 2. *Educ:* Aligarh Univ, India, BS, 61, BS, 65; Johns Hopkins Univ, PhD(solid mech), 72. *Prof Exp:* Lectr mech eng, Aligarh Univ, India, 65-67; from res asst to res assoc mech, Johns Hopkins Univ, 67-73; staff engr stress anal, Arthur McKee, Cleveland, 73-74; sr staff engr, Bechtel Power Corp, 74-78; from asst prof to prof aerospace, Mech & Nuclear Eng, Univ Okla, 78-94. *Concurrent Pos:* Ed-in-chief, Int J Plasticity. *Mem:* Fel Am Soc Mech Engrs; Am Acad Mech; Soc Exp Mech; Soc Natural Philos. *Res:* Dynamic and quasi-static behavior of metallic solids; finite amplitude wave propagation in solids; use of finite element techniques to study stresses in shell-to-shell intersections; fracture mechanics; rock mechanics. *Mailing Add:* Dept Mech Eng Univ Md-Baltimore 1000 Hilltop Circle Catonsville MD 21250

KHAN, ALI ATHER, RESEARCH ADMINISTRATION, HEALTH SCIENCES. *Current Pos:* asst prof chem, 80-90, ASSOC PROF PHYS SCI, ELIZABETH CITY STATE UNIV, 90- *Personal Data:* b Dhaka, Bangladesh, Jan 31, 48; nat US; m, Sultana Ahmed; c Ahmed M. *Educ:* Dhaka Univ, Bangladlesh, BPharm. 69, MPharm, 72; Grenoble Univ, DPharm, 77. *Prof Exp:* Lectr chem, Dhaka Univ, Bangladesh, 73-74; pharm asst, Maryview Hosp, Va, 79-80. *Concurrent Pos:* extramural assoc, NIH, 91 & 96, trainee fel, 92 & prin investr, 96-; res fel, Nat Inst Drug Addiction, 92; prin investr, Dept Energy, 93- *Mem:* Am Chem Soc; Nat Coun Univ Res Adminrs; Nat Coun Undergrad Res; Soc Res Adminrs. *Res:* Undergradute research; extraction, purification and identification of natural products. *Mailing Add:* 94 Quail Run Elizabeth City NC 27909

KHAN, AMANULLAH RASHID, CHEMICAL ENGINEERING. *Current Pos:* mgr gas opers res, 62-70, PRES, GDC, INC, INST GAS TECHNOL, ILL INST TECHNOL, 70- *Personal Data:* b Bhavnagar, India, Mar 1, 27; US citizen; m 52; c 2. *Educ:* Univ Bombay, BS, 47; Ill Inst Technol, MS, 51. *Prof Exp:* Develop engr, Dry Freeze Corp, 51-52; res engr, Inst Gas Technol, Ill Inst Technol, 52-53; fel, French Petrol Inst, 53-54; supvr refinery processing, Attock Oil Co, 54-61; opers engr, Universal Oil Prod Co, 61-62. *Mem:* Am Chem Soc; Am Inst Chem Engrs; Am Gas Asn. *Res:* Liquefaction, storage and utilization of liquefied natural gas; gas distribution and transmission research; hydrocarbon processing. *Mailing Add:* 249 Westmoreland Dr Wilmette IL 60091-3059

KHAN, ANWAR AHMAD, PLANT PHYSIOLOGY, PLANT BIOCHEMISTRY. *Current Pos:* from asst prof to assoc prof, 65-80, PROF SEED PHYSIOL, NY STATE AGR EXP STA, CORNELL UNIV, 80- *Personal Data:* b Monghyr, India, Oct 16, 34; m 67, Tamken Ahmad; c Zeba & Karim. *Educ:* Univ Karachi, BS, 56, MS, 57; Univ Chicago, PhD(bot), 63. *Prof Exp:* Demonstr bot, Univ Karachi, 57-58; demonstr & lectr, Univ Sind, Pakistan, 58-60; res asst, Univ Chicago, 60-63; res assoc biochem, Mich State Univ, 63-65. *Concurrent Pos:* Am Seed Res Found res grants, 67-69 & 70-76; NSF traveling res fel, Univ Liege, Univ Ghent & Univ Clermont-Ferrand, 71-72; Herman Frasch Found grant agr chem, 72-76; Centre Nat de la Recherche res grant, Univ Clermont-Ferrand, France, 72; sr res fel, Agr Univ, Wageningen, Neth, 78; consult, Tenn Eastman Co, 80-81; UN Develop Prog,

Pakistan, 81-85; workshop on seed sci & technol, Zhongshan Univ, Guangzhou, China, 85; vis scientist, Int Rice Res Inst, Los Baenos, Philippines, 85-86. *Mem:* AAAS; Am Soc Plant Physiologists; Scand Soc Plant Physiologists; Am Soc Hort Sci; Int Plant Growth Substances Asn; Am Soc Agron; Crop Sci Soc Am. *Res:* Seed technology; seed physiology and biochemistry; molecular biology; growth regulators; stress physiology; hormone phyiology. *Mailing Add:* Dept Hort Cornell Univ State Agr Exp Sta Geneva NY 14456-0462. *Fax:* 315-787-2320; *E-Mail:* aaklnysaes.cornell.edu

KHAN, ATA M, TRANSPORTATION & TRAFFIC ENGINEERING. *Current Pos:* asst prof, 69-77, ASSOC PROF ENG, CARLETON UNIV, 77- *Personal Data:* b Khan, W Pakistan, Dec 15, 41; m 69. *Educ:* Am Univ Beirut, BEng, 63, MEng, 65; Univ Waterloo, PhD(transp planning), 70. *Prof Exp:* Asst civil eng, Am Univ Beirut, 63-65; engr, Trans Arabian Pipeline Co, 64; transp engr, De Leuw, Cather & Co, Chicago, 65-67; teaching asst transp eng, Univ Waterloo, 67-69. *Concurrent Pos:* Individual supporting mem, Hwy Res Bd, Nat Res Coun-Nat Acad Sci, 68-; spec consult, N D Lea & Assocs, 71; Nat Res Coun Can fel, 68-69. *Mem:* Assoc mem Am Soc Civil Engrs; jr mem Inst Traffic Eng. *Res:* Development of transport planning methodology for the evaluation of policy and investment alternatives and for the analysis of transport subsidy policy in Canada. *Mailing Add:* Carlton Univ 94-181 Forest Glade Ottawa ON K1S 5Z6 Can

KHAN, FAIZ MOHAMMAD, BIOPHYSICS, RADIOLOGICAL PHYSICS. *Current Pos:* instr radiol, 68-69, from asst prof to assoc prof, 69-79, HEAD SECT RADIATION PHYSICS, UNIV MINN, MINNEAPOLIS, 74-, PROF THERAPEUT RADIOL, 79- *Personal Data:* b Multan, Pakistan, Nov 1, 38; m 66; c 3. *Educ:* Emerson Col, Multan, Pakistan, BSc, 57; Govt Col Lahore, MSc, 59; Univ Minn, Minneapolis, PhD(biophys), 69. *Prof Exp:* Health physicist, Radiother Inst, Mayo Hosp, Lahore, Pakistan, 60-63. *Concurrent Pos:* Consult physicist, Vet Admin Hosp, Minneapolis, 71- *Mem:* Am Asn Physicists Med; Sigma Xi. *Res:* Radiation dosimetry and treatment techniques in radiation therapy; application of computers in radiotherapy; biological effects of radiation. *Mailing Add:* Univ Minn Med Sch Radiation Box 494 May Delaware St SE Minneapolis MN 55455-0374

KHAN, FAZAL R, ANALYTICAL CHEMISTRY, PROTEIN CHEMISTRY. *Current Pos:* Sr scientist, Hoffmann-La Roche, Inc, 84-86, res investr, 86-88, res leader, 88-90, dir, 90-95, DIR HUMAN GENOME SCI, HOFFMANN-LA ROCHE INC, 96- *Personal Data:* b Varanasi, India, Oct 30, 49; m, Fathun N; c Nareena, Abbasia & Asim. *Educ:* Aligarh Univ, BS, 69, MS, 71, MPh, 73, PhD(biochem), 76. *Mem:* Fedn Am Soc Exp Biol. *Res:* Heading a group of scientists involved in developing a process to produce proteins for clinical trials and market needs. *Mailing Add:* 318 Grant Ave Nutley NJ 07110. *Fax:* 973-235-4086

KHAN, HAMEED A, DNA BINDING AGENTS, HUMAN GENOME. *Current Pos:* HEALTH SCIENTIST ADMINR, NAT INST CHILD HEALTH & HUMAN DEVELOP, NIH, 89- *Personal Data:* b Hyerabad, Andhra Pradesh, India, Jan 3, 41; US citizen. *Educ:* Univ London, PhD(org chem), 69. *Prof Exp:* Univ London fel, Chester Beaty Cancer Res Inst, 69-71; vis fel, Nat Cancer Inst, 71-74; assoc found scientist, SW Res Found, San Antonio, 74-76; sr scientist, Microbiol Assocs, Md, 76-77; consumer safety officer, US Food & Drug Admin, Rockville, 78-89. *Mem:* Am Chem Soc; fel Am Inst Chem. *Res:* Synthesis of DNA-binding drugs for cancer treatment program; granted one patent. *Mailing Add:* NIH 11965 Old Columbia Pike Silver Spring MD 20904

KHAN, IQBAL M, TEACHING PHYSIOLOGY. *Current Pos:* ASSOC PROF & DIR IVF/ANDROLOGY LAB, DEPT OBSTET & GYNEC, MED COL GA, AUGUSTA, 90- *Personal Data:* b Karachi, Pakistan, Dec 27, 50; US citizen; m 80, Shahida; c Sohail, Imran, Nida & Adnan. *Educ:* Univ Karachi, BS, 69, MS, 70; Univ Göteborg, PhD(physiol), 80. *Prof Exp:* Postdoctoral fel physiol, Univ Ill, Urbana, 80-81; res assoc physiol, Univ Ill, Chicago, 81-82, res asst prof, 81-89. *Concurrent Pos:* Postdoctoral fel, Ford Found, 80-81. *Mem:* Soc Study Reproduction Fertil & Steril; Endocrine Soc. *Res:* Pituitary-ovarian axis; corpus luteum function; hormonal control of luteal steroidogenesis; in vitro fertilization. *Mailing Add:* Dept Obstet & Gynec Rm CK 159 Med Col Ga 1459 Laney Walker Blvd Augusta GA 30907

KHAN, ISHRAT MAHMOOD, POLYMER SYNTHESIS & CHARACTERIZATION, ELECTROACTIVE POLYMERS & SMART MATERIALS. *Current Pos:* ASST PROF CHEM, CLARK ATLANTA UNIV, 88- *Personal Data:* b Sylhet, Bangladesh, Feb 24, 56; m 90, Farhana Rahman; c Irfan. *Educ:* Susquehanna Univ, BA, 79; Univ Fla, PhD(org chem), 84. *Prof Exp:* Fel, Col Forestry, State Univ NY, Syracuse, 85-88. *Concurrent Pos:* Vis scientist, McGill Univ, 91-92. *Res:* Development of new electroactive polymers for sensors, nano-electronics, membranes for biological electron transfer processes; new methodologies for helix-sense selective polymerizations; chiral materials as smart materials. *Mailing Add:* 5649 Rodney Ct Stone Mountain GA 30087

KHAN, JAMIL AKBER, ORGANOMETALLIC CHEMISTRY. *Current Pos:* BUS MGR, ENICHEM AM, INC, 90- *Personal Data:* b Hyderabad, Pakistan, Mar 17, 52; m 81, Susan M; c Farooq J & Omar J. *Educ:* Univ Sind, Pakistan, BSc, 71, MSc, 73; Univ London, Eng, PhD(org chem), 79; Univ New Haven, MBA, 85. *Prof Exp:* Chemist qual control, Eastman Chem Co, 73-74; lectr chem, D J Sci Col, Pakistan, 74-76; demonstr chem, Univ Col London, Eng, 76-79; res assoc chem, Duke Univ, 79-81; res chemist, Uniroyal Inc, 81-84, res scientist, 84-85; dir mkt, Ausimont USA, 85-86, dir technol & mkt int, 86-87, prod mgr, Sales & Mkt Div, 87-90. *Concurrent Pos:* Secy gen, Inst Pub Affairs, Pakistan, 75-78; joint secy, Sind Lectr Asn, 76-77; mem, Presidential Task Force & Pub Educ Fund Comt, Am Inst Chemists; mem, Int Org Chem Sci Develop Network, UNESCO, bd educ, Mt Arlington, NJ; mem, Republican Presidential Task Force, Sen Inner Circle & Health Reforms Task Force; guest fac, Opers Enterprize, Am Mgt Asn. *Mem:* Am Chem Soc; Royal Soc Chem; Sigma Xi; Am Inst Chemists; Chem Mkt Res Asn; Am Mgt Asn. *Res:* Synthesis and development of activators and catalysts, which can be used in polymerization, autoxidation of unsaturated fatty acids; synthesis of antioxidants, which can be used to inhibit the autoxidation of phospholipid biomembranes; Ziegler-Natta catalysis; organometallic chemistry; free radical chemistry polymerization; polymerization kinetics; reaction mechanism; polypeptides; bio compatible polymers; synthetic lubricants; higher performance polymers and their application to high tech industry. *Mailing Add:* Enichem Am Inc 2000 W Loop St Suite 2210 Houston TX 77027. *Fax:* 212-382-6583

KHAN, MAHBUB R, MAGNETIC THIN FILMS, DIGITAL MAGNETIC RECORDING. *Current Pos:* SR SCIENTIST, IBM CORP, 96- *Personal Data:* b Dhaka, Bangladesh, Sept 11, 49, US citizen; m 76, Reena; c Madhury, Kamal, Jamal & Monika. *Educ:* Dhaka Univ, BSc, 69, MSc, 70; Boston Col, PhD(solid state physics), 79. *Prof Exp:* Lectr physics, Jahangirnagar Univ, Bangladesh, 72-74; grad asst, Boston Col, 74-79; teaching fel, Univ Nebr, Lincoln, 79-81; fel, Argonne Nat Lab, 81-83; sr scientist magnetic rec, Control Data Corp-MPI, 83-85, Alcoa-Stolie Corp, 85-86; mgr, Seagate Magnetics, 86-93; mem tech staff, Appl Mat, 94-96. *Mem:* Am Phys Soc; Inst Elec & Electronics Engrs. *Res:* Preparation, characterization, magnetic properties, anisotropy, surface analysis, electron microscopy of magnetic thin films; longitudinal and vertical high density digital magnetic recording; metallic superlattice; optical and electro-optical properties of layered materials. *Mailing Add:* 3463 Sagewood Lane San Jose CA 95132. *Fax:* 408-256-1522

KHAN, MAHMOOD AHMED, FOOD SCIENCE, HOTEL RESTAURANT & INSTITUTIONAL MANAGEMENT. *Current Pos:* asst head, 87-92, PROF, DEPT HOTEL & RESTAURANT, VA POLYYTECH & STATE UNIV, 87-, DEPT HEAD, 92- *Personal Data:* b Hyderabad, India, Sept 16, 45; US citizen; m 75; c Samala, Feras & Nufayl. *Educ:* Osmania Univ, BS, 66; Andhra Pradesh Agr Univ, BS, 69; La State Univ, MS, 72, PhD(food sci), 75. *Honors & Awards:* Donald K Tessler Res Award; Cesar Ritz Award. *Prof Exp:* Res asst food sci, La State Univ, 71-75; asst prof foods & nutrit, Albright Col, 75-78; asst prof, Univ Ill, Urbana, 78-84, assoc prof, 84-87. *Concurrent Pos:* Vis prof, Catering Res Ctr, Huddersfield Polytech, UK. *Mem:* Inst Food Technologists; Am Dietetic Asn; Coun Hotel, Restaurant & Inst Educ; Nat Restaurant Asn; Am Inst Nutrit; Int Nat Acad Hospitality Res. *Res:* Food quality in food service systems; concepts of nutrition and obesity; nutritional evaluation of food processing; international food patterns; food habits; food service consultant; food snacking and eating away from home; franchising in hospitality and tourism industry. *Mailing Add:* Va Tech Dept Hospitality & Tourism Mgt 362 Wallace Hall Blacksburg VA 24061-0429. *Fax:* 540-231-8313; *E-Mail:* khanma@utvm1

KHAN, MANZOOR M, IMMUNOPHARMACOLOGY, CELLULAR IMMUNOLOGY. *Current Pos:* ASSOC PROF, DEPT PHARMACEUT & PHARMACOL, CRIEGHTON UNIV, 90- *Personal Data:* b Karachi, Pakistan, July 3, 53; US citizen; m 85, Sadia Khanum; c Zoya & Taimoor. *Educ:* Univ Karachi, BSc & MSc, 72; Univ Bridgeport, MS, 75; Univ Ariz, PhD(pharmacol), 80. *Prof Exp:* Fel, Univ Colo, 80-82; fel, Stanford Univ, 82-83, from res assoc to sr res assoc, 83-90. *Concurrent Pos:* Arthritis Found res fel, 81; Am Heart Asn advan res fel, 83; res award, Health Future Found, 91 & 92. *Mem:* Am Asn Immunol; Am Soc Pharmacol & Exp Therapeut. *Res:* Regulation of helper T cell function by endogenous mediators; investigating the effects of histamine, prostaglandins and phosphodiesterase inhibitors on synthesis/secretion of interleukin-4 and interleukin-5; role of cytokines in allergic disease and asthma. *Mailing Add:* Dept Pharmaceut & Pharmacol Creighton Univ Health Sci Ctr Omaha NE 68178-0001. *Fax:* 402-280-2334

KHAN, MASOOD, BIOCHEMISTRY, INTERNAL MEDICINE. *Current Pos:* DIR, CHEM DEPT, PHOENIX INT, 91- *Personal Data:* b Amrobe, India, Aug 2, 48. *Educ:* Aligalgh Univ, India, BSc, 68, MSc, 70, PhD(biochem), 75. *Prof Exp:* Res fel chem, NIH, 76-79; fel chem, McGill Univ, 79-84, assoc prof med, 86-91. *Mem:* Am Soc Clin Chem; Am Soc Cell Biol; Biomed Mkt Asn; Am Endocrine Soc. *Mailing Add:* Phoenix Int 2330 Cohen St St Laurent PQ H4R 9Z7 Can

KHAN, MOHAMED SHAHEED, PLANT PATHOLOGY, AGRICULTURE. *Current Pos:* EXTEN SPECIALIST & PESTICIDE COORDR PATH, ENTOM PESTICIDES, UNIV DC & USDA, 72- *Personal Data:* b Bloomfield, Guyana, Dec 29, 33; US citizen; m 58; c 3. *Educ:* Eastern Caribbean Inst, Trinidad, diplom, 57; Iowa State Univ, BSc, 64, MSc, 66, PhD(plant path & hort), 68. *Prof Exp:* Agr ext agent agr educ, Govt Brit Guyana, 57-60; agr res asst, McGill Univ, 60-63; res asst, Iowa State Univ, 63-68; plant pathologist res, Ministry Agr Govt Guyana, 69-71; assoc prof biol & physical sci, Morris Col SC, 72. *Concurrent Pos:* Teacher hort & landscaping, Spingarn-Phelp's Voc Sch, Washington, DC, 73-77; teacher pesticide applicators, DC Coop Ext Serv, Washington, DC, 73-; coordr training, EPA grant, 74-; consult trop agr, Indonesia USAID, 77, consult res agronomist, JWK Int Corp, Govt Chad, Africa, 78-79, pest mgt specialist, Soma Lia, 79-80. *Mem:* Am Phytopath Soc; Am Hort Soc; Am Entom Soc; Am Chem Soc; Sigma Xi. *Res:* Mycorrhizal associates of Juglans Nigra with special emphasis on nitrogen and phosphorous uptake; pesticide screening; chemical and biological control of pests; environmental preservation. *Mailing Add:* Coop Exten Serv Univ DC 901 Newton St NE Washington DC 20017

KHAN, MOHAMMAD ASAD, GEODESY, RESEARCH ADMINISTRATION. *Current Pos:* from asst prof to assoc prof, 67-74, PROF GEOPHYS & GEOL, HAWAII INST GEOPHYS, UNIV HAWAII, 74- *Personal Data:* b Pakistan; m 74; c 1. *Educ:* Univ Panjab, WPakistan, BSc, 57, MSc, 63; Univ Hawaii, PhD(geophys), 67. *Prof Exp:* Lectr geophys, Univ Panjab, WPakistan, 63-64. *Concurrent Pos:* Sr vis scientist, Nat Acad Sci, Goddard Space Flight Ctr, NASA, 72-74; sr scientist, Comput Sci Corp, 74-76, sr consult, 76-77; adv resource surv, Gov of Pakistan, 74-76; mem, Hawaii State Environ Coun, 79-83, chmn, Environ Coun Exec Comn, 79-83 & vchmn, Environ Coun, 81-83; minister, Petrol & Natural Resources, Govt Pakistan, 83-86, chmn, Hydrocarbon Develop Inst, 84-86, chmn, Attock Oil Refinery, 84-86, cabinet mem, Nat Econ Coun, 83-86, senator, 85-86. *Mem:* Am Geophys Union; Am Geol Inst; Pakistan Asn Advan Sci. *Res:* Geophysics; Satellite altimetry; earth density modelling; geophysical, geodetic and geodynamical applications of satellites; plate tectonics; gravity and isostasy; geophysical exploration; resource surveys; geodesy; geodynamics; core-mantle boundary problems; technology transfer; technical management. *Mailing Add:* Hawaii Inst Geophys & Planetology Univ Hawaii 2525 Correa Rd Honolulu HI 96822

KHAN, MOHAMMAD IQBAL, ENDOCRINOLOGY, REPRODUCTIVE PHYSIOLOGY. *Current Pos:* ASSOC PROF & DIR IVF/ANDROLOGY LABS, MED COL GA, 89- *Personal Data:* b Karachi, Pakistan, Dec 27, 50; m 80; c 2. *Educ:* Univ Karachi, Pakistan, BSc Hons, 69, MSc, 70; Univ Goteborg, Sweden, PhD, 80. *Prof Exp:* Fel endocrinol, Dept Physiol, Univ Goteborg, Sweden, 80 & Dept Animal Sci, Univ Ill, Urbana-Champaign, 80-81; res asst & prof endocrinol, Dept Physiol & Biophys, Med Ctr, Univ Ill, Chicago, 81-89. *Concurrent Pos:* Asst lectr, Dept Physiol, Sch Med, Univ Goteborg, Swed, 76-79. *Mem:* Soc Study Reprod; Scand Soc Physiologists; Swed Med Asn; Endocrine Soc; Am Fertil Soc. *Res:* Mechanism of action of gonadotropins in the maintenance and function of the corpus luteum as well as the role of prostaglandins in the regression of the corpus luteum; endocrinology. *Mailing Add:* Dept Obstet & Gynec Rm CK 159 Med Col Ga 1459 Laney Walker Blvd Augusta GA 30912

KHAN, MOHAMMED ABDUL QUDDUS, BIOCHEMICAL & ENVIRONMENTAL TOXICOLOGY, INSECTICIDE TOXICOLOGY. *Current Pos:* assoc prof, 69-74, PROF BIOL SCI, UNIV ILL, CHICAGO, 74- *Personal Data:* b India, Mar 10, 39; m 74, Anwarun Nesa; c Sara, Samreen & Yaseen. *Educ:* Univ Karachi, BSc, 57, MSc, 59; Univ Western Ont, PhD(zool), 64; Univ Auto de Cd Juarez, MD, 84. *Prof Exp:* Fel entom, NC State Univ, 65-67, Ore State Univ, 67-68 & Rutgers Univ, 68-69. *Concurrent Pos:* Vis prof, Univ Wis, 70; consult, Velsicol Chem Corp, Chicago, 75, NSF, 77-78, Environ Protection Agency, 80, Eastern Res Group, 85 & Continental Chemists, 85; vis scientist, Nat Inst Environ Health Sci, NIH, 75-76; vis chemist, US Environ Protection Agency, Corvallis, 80; expert toxicol, UN Develop Prog, Pakistan, 80-81; ed, J Biochem Toxicol. *Mem:* AAAS; Soc Toxicol & Chem; Am Chem Soc; Sigma Xi; Soc Toxicol; Int Soc Study Xenobiotics. *Res:* Metabolism of insecticides, drugs and lipids; biochemistry and genetics of insecticide resistance; environmental toxicology; metabolism of xenobiotics including pesticides; in vitro detoxication and mechanisms; induction of drug metabolizing enzymes; effects on steriodogenesis. *Mailing Add:* Dept Bio-Sci, Univ Ill 845 W Taylor St Chicago IL 60607-7060. *Fax:* 312-413-2435

KHAN, MOHAMMED NASRULLAH, PHYSIOLOGY, VETERINARY SCIENCE. *Current Pos:* PROF ANAT & PHYSIOL, RAVENSWOOD HOSP, RADIOL SCH, 90- *Personal Data:* b Hyderabad, India, Oct 11, 33; c 2. *Educ:* Osmania Univ, India, BVSc, 55; La State Univ, Baton Rouge, MS, 63, PhD(environ physiol), 70. *Prof Exp:* Vet, Govts Hyderabad & Andhra Pradesh, India, 55-58; asst lectr anat, State Vet Sch, Hyderabad, India, 58-61; res asst, La State Univ, Baton Rouge, 61-63, & 67-70; asst lectr reproductive physiol, Tirupati & Hyderabad Vet Cols, India, 63-67; asst prof biol, City Cols Chicago, Mayfair Col & Southwest Col, 70-72; instr microbiol, Schs Nursing, Michael Reese Hosp & Med Ctr, Chicago, 73-74; instr anat, physiol & microbiol, South Chicago Community Hosp Schs Nursing & Radiol, 72-77; assoc prof anat, physiol, microbiol & chem, Little Co Mary Hosp Sch Nursing, 75-83; assoc prof, 77-87, prof biol, Truman Col, 87- *Concurrent Pos:* HEH Nizam fel; Ford Found res scholar. *Res:* Stress. *Mailing Add:* 2904 W Greenleaf Ave Chicago IL 60645-2916

KHAN, MUSHTAQ AHMAD, PERINATAL TOXICOLOGY, ENDOCRINOLOGY. *Current Pos:* physiologist food additives, Div Toxicol, Food & Drug Admin, 78-80, res physiologist perinatal toxicol, Metab Br, 80-81, supvry res physiologist & head, Perinatal Toxicol, Bur Foods, 81-88, HEALTH SCIENTIST ADMINR, GEN MED A-2 STUDY SECT, FOOD & DRUG ADMIN, 88- *Personal Data:* b Lyallpur, Pakistan, Dec 12, 39; US citizen; m 59, Jamila; c Shahid, Tahira, Zahid & Nasir. *Educ:* Univ Punjab, Pakistan, BSc, 60; Mont State Univ, MS, 62; Wash State Univ, PhD(vet sci & physiol), 68. *Prof Exp:* Chemist steroid biochem, Syntex Res Ctr, Calif, 64-65; asst prof vet physiol, Univ Agr, Pakistan, 65-72; res assoc pediat, Med Sch, Univ Md, Baltimore, 72-74, asst prof, 74-78, asst prof path, 77-78. *Concurrent Pos:* Prin investr, Sch Med, Univ Md, Baltimore, 72-78; adj asst prof, Univ RI, 80- *Mem:* Am Physiol Soc; Am Inst Nutrit; Am Col Toxicol; Am Soc Vet Physiologists & Pharmacologists; World Asn Physiol, Pharmacol & Biochem. *Res:* Endocrine and nutritional factors in obesity and atherosclerosis; perinatal toxicology; perinatal nutrition and delayed effects-imprinting; cholesterol metabolism; age and sex related changes in metabolic responses. *Mailing Add:* Adminr Div Res Grants NIH Gen Med A-2 Study Sect 3543 Westwood Bldg 6701 Rockledge Dr Bethesda MD 20892-7818

KHAN, NASIM A, GENE REGULATION, MITOCHONDRIAL GENETICS. *Current Pos:* fel gen biol, 62-64, lectr gen biol, 64-68, instr, Genetics Lab, 68-69, from asst prof to assoc prof, 70-84, PROF GENETICS, BROOKLYN COL, CITY UNIV NEW YORK, 85- *Personal Data:* b Benares, India, June 1, 38; US citizen; m 77. *Educ:* Univ Dacca, BSc, 58, MSc, 60; City Univ New York, PhD(genetics), 67. *Prof Exp:* Lectr bot, Univ Decca, 61-62. *Mem:* Sigma Xi; Am Soc Microbiol. *Res:* Construction of yeast strains exhibiting elevated levels of ethanol production using genetic selection procedures and certain recombinant DNA technique; interaction of nuclear and cytoplasmic genes in the utilization of fermentive sugars in yeast; regulation of maltase and alpha-methylglucosidose synthesis in yeast. *Mailing Add:* Dept Biol Brooklyn Col 2901 Bedford Ave Brooklyn NY 11210-2813

KHAN, PARWAIZ ASHRAF ALI, HIGH ENERGY LASER MATERIALS PROCESSING, SEMI SOLID METALWORKING. *Current Pos:* engr, 91-92, SR ENGR, CONCURRENT TECHNOL CORP, 92- *Personal Data:* b Hyderabad, Pakistan, Mar 4, 55; m 88, Ghazala; c Reema P & Bushra P. *Educ:* Nat Col Eng & Technol, BE, 78; Pa State Univ, MS, 83, PhD(metall-mat sci), 87. *Prof Exp:* Proj engr, Boomer Engrs & Technocrates Ltd, 78; metall engr, Resources Develop Corp, 78-81; res assoc laser processing, Mich State Univ, 87-91. *Concurrent Pos:* Lectr, Nat Col Eng & Technol, 80-81; res prof, Mich State Univ, 90-91. *Mem:* Laser Inst Am; Am Welding Soc; Am Soc Mat; Mining Metals & Mat Soc; Sigma Xi. *Res:* High energy laser welding, machining, surface treatment and laser fabrication of superconductors; characterization of thixtropic feed alloys and parts made by semi-solid metalworking. *Mailing Add:* C67 Block 4 Gulshan-E-Iobal Karachi Pakistan

KHAN, PAUL, FOOD SCIENCE, PRODUCT SAFETY. *Current Pos:* PRES, REGU-TECH ASSOCS, INC, 85- *Personal Data:* b Vienna, Austria, Nov 4, 23; nat US; m 50. *Educ:* NY Univ, BA, 48; Univ Chicago, MS, 49. *Honors & Awards:* Silver Medal of Honor, Pres Austria, 93. *Prof Exp:* Asst microbiol, Squibb Inst Med Res, Olin Mathieson Chem Co, 49-53; chief microbiologist, Food & Drug Res Lab, 53-55; dir, Frozen Food Prod Lab, DCA Food Industs, Inc, 55-60, mgr, Cent Res Labs, 60-62; mgr res admin, Continental Baking Co, 62-71; dir food protection, ITT Continental Baking Co, Inc, 71-80, vpres qual & food protection, 80-85. *Concurrent Pos:* Mem, Tech Comt Food Protection-Grocery Mfg; indust liaison panel, Food Protection Comt, Nat Acad Sci-Nat Res Coun; mem, Codex Alimentarius Comn, Food & Agr Orgn/WHO; contrib ed, Food Safety Notebook. *Mem:* Am Chem Soc; Am Asn Cereal Chemists; fel Inst Food Technologists; Asn Food & Drug Officials; Asn Res Dirs; Am Soc Qual Control. *Res:* Food preservation, technology, poisoning and protection; laboratory management; regulatory compliance; quality assurance; occupational safety and environment; nutrition. *Mailing Add:* Regu-Tech Assoc Inc 158 W Boston Post Rd PO Box 717 Mamaroneck NY 10543-0717

KHAN, RASUL AZIM, PARASITOLOGY. *Current Pos:* Asst prof, 69-74, assoc prof, 74-81, PROF BIOL, MEM UNIV NFLD, 82- *Personal Data:* b Port Mourant, Guyana, Oct 31, 34; Can citizen; m 66; c 3. *Educ:* Univ Toronto, Can, BSA, 64, MSc, 66, PhD(parasitol), 69. *Concurrent Pos:* Res scientist, Marine Sci Res Lab, 72- *Mem:* Am Soc Parasitilogists; Am Soc Protozoologists; Can Soc Zoologists. *Res:* Studies on the effects of parasites and pollutants as causative agents of disease in commercial fish in Eastern Canada; long term effects of petroleum on fish. *Mailing Add:* Marine Sci Res Lab Mem Univ Nfld St John's NF A1C 5S7 Can

KHAN, SEKENDER ALI, PLANT PATHOLOGY. *Current Pos:* actg chmn dept, 64-65, chmn dept, 65-78, PROF BIOL, ELIZABETH CITY STATE UNIV, 64- *Personal Data:* b Bogra, Bangladesh, Feb 1, 33; m 63; c 2. *Educ:* Univ Dacca, BArg, 53, MAgr, 54; La State Univ, PhD(plant path), 59. *Prof Exp:* Sect officer, EPakistan Indust Develop Corp, 55-57; asst cane develop officer, M/S Carew & Co, 57; prof biol, Tex Col, 59-63, chmn sci & math, 60-63. *Mem:* Phytochem Soc Nam; Phy & Chem Soc Nam; Helminthological Soc Wash DC. *Res:* Plant hormones; plant alkaloids extraction of active chemicals from Vitex negundo L; science education; tropical vegetable plants. *Mailing Add:* Dept Biol Elizabeth City State Univ Parkview Dr Elizabeth City NC 27909

KHAN, SHABBIR AHMED, MOLECULAR BIOLOGY, BIOCHEMISTRY. *Current Pos:* ASSOC PROF CHEM, WISTAR INST, 86- *Personal Data:* b Dec 24, 45; c 1. *Educ:* Bangalore Univ, India, PhD(peptide chem), 77. *Prof Exp:* Asst prof chem, Rockefeller Univ, 80-86. *Mem:* Am Soc Biochem & Molecular Biol; Am Chem Soc; AAAS. *Res:* Structure-function studies of the transacting proteins of HIV-1. *Mailing Add:* Infinity Biotech Res 610 Upland Ave Upland PA 19015. *Fax:* 610-499-8871

KHAN, SHAHAMAT ULLAH, ENVIRONMENTAL SCIENCES. *Current Pos:* res scientist org matter & environ sci, 68-82, PRIN RES SCIENTIST, CAN DEPT AGR, 82- *Personal Data:* b Rampur, India, Apr 25, 37; Can citizen; m 63; c 2. *Educ:* Agra Univ, BSc, 57; Aligarh Muslim Univ, India, MSc, 59; Univ Alta, MSc, 63, PhD(soil chem), 67. *Prof Exp:* Res asst soil chem, Univ Alta, 63-64. *Concurrent Pos:* Ed, J Environ Sci & Health, Part B. *Mem:* Fel Royal Soc Chem; Am Chem Soc; fel Chem Inst Can. *Res:* Chemistry and reactions of organic matter in soils and waters; soil and water pollution; pesticides in soils, plants and waters; pesticide toxicology. *Mailing Add:* 4 Barry Burn Ct Nepean ON K2R 1C5 Can

KHAN, SHAKIL AHMAD, PHYSICAL CHEMISTRY. *Current Pos:* fel, Fla State Univ, 77-78, RES SPECIALIST NUCLEAR MAGNETIC RENOSANCE SPECTROS & ANALYSIS, MOBAY CHEM CORP, 78- *Personal Data:* b Bareilly, India; US citizen; m 74; c 2. *Educ:* Univ Karachi, Pakistan, BS, 67, MS, 68; Univ Islamabad, MPhil, 69; Northwestern Univ, Evanston, Ill, PhD(phys org chem), 74. *Prof Exp:* Fel molecular orbital theory, Univ SC, 74; asst prof spectros quantum chem, Univ Islamabad, Pakistan, 74-77. *Mem:* Am Chem Soc; Soc Plastic Industs. *Res:* Use of nuclear magnetic renosance spectroscopy to study polymers especially polyurethanes, polycarbonates; laboratory and office automation; personal computer in chemistry. *Mailing Add:* Bayer Corp Bldg 8 Pittsburgh PA 15205-9741

KHAN, SULTANA, SOLID STATE PHYSICS, ASTRONOMY. *Current Pos:* assoc prof, 78-94, PROF PHYSICS, ELIZABETH CITY STATE UNIV, 94- *Personal Data:* b Dacca, Bangladesh, Dec 13, 47; m 74; c 1. *Educ:* Univ Dacca, BSc, 70, MSc, 72; Univ Grenoble, Doc(solid state physics), 77. *Concurrent Pos:* Planetarian. *Mem:* Bangladesh Phys Soc; Am Phys Soc. *Res:* Involved in a project to measure solar radiation in southeastern United States in cooperation with the Solar Energy Research Institute Department of Energy and National Oceanic and Atmospheric Administration since 1985. *Mailing Add:* Elizabeth City State Univ PO Box 845 Elizabeth City NC 27909

KHAN, WINSTON, APPLIED MATHEMATICS, MATHEMATICAL PHYSICS. *Current Pos:* from asst prof to assoc prof mat, Univ PR, Cayey, 70-74, assoc prof, 74-82, PROF PHYSICS, UNIV PR, MAYAQUEZ, 82- *Personal Data:* b San Fernando, Trinidad, Mar 12, 34; US citizen; m 61, Joan A Aziz; c Alima, Selina, Shereeza, Winston Jr & Alim. *Educ:* Univ London, BSc, 56, MSc, 58; Univ Birmingham, Eng, dipl, 61, PhD(mat Physics), 64. *Honors & Awards:* Commemorative Medal of Honor, ABI, 84. *Prof Exp:* Asst prof mat, Univ WI-London, 58-59; lectr & dir mat, Univ WI-Trinidad, 64-69. *Concurrent Pos:* Adv, Comn Educ Reform, NSF, 81-83; exec adv mem, Nat Sci Comn, 82-83; dir, US Army grants, 82-85; coordr, US Army Mat Command, Rep, Univ PR, 84-87. *Mem:* Am Mat Soc; Am Phys Soc; AAAS; Soc Inst & Appl Math; Int Asn Mat & Comput Modeling; Int Asn Math and Comput Simulation. *Res:* Fluid dynamics involving mathematics, physics and engineering sciences. *Mailing Add:* Univ PR Calle Uroyan AD4 Mayaquez PR 00680. *Fax:* 787-832-1135

KHANAL, PUNYA PRASAD, PAVEMENT DESIGN ANALYSIS & MANAGEMENT SYSTEMS, CONSTRUCTION MATERIALS. *Current Pos:* RES ENGR, REED & GRAHAM LAB SERV, 96- *Personal Data:* b Ilam, Nepal, Mar 29, 56; m 86, Saraswati Niroula; c Gaurav & Garima. *Educ:* Univ Rajasthan, BE, 80; Strathclyde Univ, MSc, 85; Ariz State Univ, PhD(civil eng), 95. *Prof Exp:* Civil engr, Dept Roads, Nepal, 80-89; transp engr assoc, Ariz Dept Transp, 93-95; proj engr, Appl Paving Technol, 95-96. *Mem:* Asn Asphalt Paving Technologist; Am Soc Testing & Mat; Am Soc Civil Engrs; Nat Soc Prof Engrs. *Res:* Design and analysis of pavements; use of available and innovative materials in highway and airport pavements; pavement management. *Mailing Add:* Reed & Graham Lab Serv 550 Sunol St San Jose CA 95126. *Fax:* 408-294-1959; *E-Mail:* ppkhanal@worldnet.att.net

KHANDAN, NIRMALA N, QUANTITATIVE STRUCTURE-ACTIVITY RELATIONSHIPS MODELING, REMEDIATION TECHNOLOGIES. *Current Pos:* ASSOC PROF CIVIL & ENVIRON ENG, NMEX STATE UNIV, 89- *Personal Data:* b Badulla, Sri Lanka, June 21, 47; m 75, Mary Thiruchelram; c Rajeer & Sanjeer. *Educ:* Univ Ceylon, BS, 70; Drexel Univ, MS, 85, PhD(environ eng), 88. *Prof Exp:* Mgr, Eng Dept, Hayleys Ltd, Sri Lanka, 75-83. *Concurrent Pos:* Res asst prof, Vanderbilt Univ, 88-; prin investr, NMex State Univ, 89-; consult, 89- *Mem:* Int Asn Water Qual; Asn Environ Eng Profs; Am Chem Soc. *Res:* Control and management of environmental hazards of organic chemicals; physical/biological processes. *Mailing Add:* Civil Eng Dept NMex State Univ Las Cruces NM 88003. *Fax:* 505-646-6049

KHANDEKAR, MADHAV LAXMAN, NUMERICAL MODELLING OF OCEAN SURFACE WAVES, LARGE SCALE ATMOSPHERIC CIRCULATION AND INDIAN MONSOON. *Current Pos:* RES SCIENTIST, ATMOSPHERIC ENVIRON SERV, ENVIRON CAN, 82- *Personal Data:* b Dohad, India, July 12, 35; Can citizen; m 68, Shalan Damle; c Nitin & Seema. *Educ:* Poona Univ, India, BSc, 55, MSc, 57; Fla State Univ, MS, 64, PhD(meterol), 68. *Honors & Awards:* Sci Contribution Award, Int Natural Hazards Soc, 93; Prize in Appl Oceanog, Can Meteorol & Oceanog Soc, 94. *Prof Exp:* Sci asst, India Meterol Dept, Poona, India, 57-62; fel, Nat Res Coun, Can, 69-70; res assoc, Univ Alta, Can, 71-74; lectr meteorol, World Meteorol Orgn, UN, 75-77; expert aeronaut meteorol, Int Civil Aviation Orgn, UN, 80-82. *Mem:* Can Meteorol & Oceanog Soc; Can Soc Agrometeorol; Am Meteorol Soc; Am Geophys Union. *Res:* Numerical modelling of ocean surface waves, impact of large-scale atmospheric and oceanic anomalies on Indian Monsoon droughts and floods and on world grain yields; statistical analysis of atmospheric and oceanic data. *Mailing Add:* Atmospheric Environ Serv 4905 Dufferin St Downsview ON M3H 5T4 Can. *Fax:* 416-739-4221

KHANDELWAL, RAMJI LAL, BIOCHEMISTRY OF DIABETES, SIGNAL TRANSDUCTION ENZYMES. *Current Pos:* assoc prof, 80-85, PROF BIOCHEM, UNIV SASK, 85- *Personal Data:* b Dausa, India, June 2, 44; Can citizen; m 62, Vimla Beemwal; c Deepak. *Educ:* Univ Udaipur, India, BSc, 63; Punjab, Agr Univ, India, MSc, 66; Univ Man, PhD(biochem), 72. *Prof Exp:* Demonstr agr, Univ Udaipur, India, 63-64; res asst, Govt Rajasthan, India, 66-68; teaching asst biochem, Univ Man, 69-70, res asst, 72-73; res biochem, Univ Calif, Davis, 73-75; asst prof oral biol, Univ Man, 75-80. *Concurrent Pos:* Med Res Coun Can scholar, 75-80, develop grant, 81-92. *Mem:* Can Biochem Soc; Am Soc Biochem & Molecular Biol. *Res:* Role of insulin and cyclic adenosine monophosphate in the regulation of glycogen metabolism in normal and diabetic animals; regulation of protein phosphorylation/dephosphorylation in biological systems. *Mailing Add:* Dept Biochem A10-1 Health Sci Bldg Univ Sask 107 Wiggins Rd Saskatoon SK S7N 5E5 Can. *Fax:* 306-966-4390; *E-Mail:* khandelw@sask.usask.ca

KHANDWALA, ATUL S, science, for more information see previous edition

KHANG, SOON-JAI, CHEMICAL ENGINEERING. *Current Pos:* asst prof, 75-79, ASSOC PROF CHEM ENG, UNIV CINCINNATI, 80- *Personal Data:* b Seoul, Korea, Feb 26, 44; m 73; c 2. *Educ:* Yonsei Univ, Korea, BE, 66; Ore State Univ, MS, 72, PhD(chem eng), 75. *Prof Exp:* Instr chem eng, Ore State Univ, 74-75. *Concurrent Pos:* Consult, Procter & Gamble Co, 78-80, Amoco Oil, 80- & Exxon, 81. *Mem:* Am Inst Chem Engrs; Sigma Xi. *Res:* Chemical reaction engineering, including residence time distribution, mixing and catalyst deactivation; energy conversion and coal gasification; application of statistical methods for process control; mathematical modeling. *Mailing Add:* 8040 Springvalley Dr Cincinnati OH 45236

KHANNA, FAQIR CHAND, NUCLEAR PHYSICS. *Current Pos:* Nat Res Coun Can fel, Univ Alta, 66-67, from assoc to sr res physicist, 67-84, AEC Labs, dir, Theoret Physics Inst, 86-93, PROF PHYSICS, UNIV ALTA, 84- *Personal Data:* b Lyallpur, India, Jan 23, 35; m 66, Swara J; c Shrawan F & Varun F. *Educ:* Univ Panjab, India, BSc, 55, MSc, 56; Fla State Univ, PhD(physics), 62. *Prof Exp:* Lectr physics, Univ Panjab, India, 56-58; fel, Univ Iowa, 61-63 & Rice Univ, 63-65. *Mem:* Fel Am Phys Soc; Can Asn Physics. *Res:* Nuclear physics, especially low and high energy physics; low energy physics study of the few nucleon problem, particularly the three nucleon system; many body problem with emphasis on nuclear physics and solid state physics; quantum liquids and solids; effective operators. *Mailing Add:* Univ Alta Theort Physics Inst Edmonton AB T6G 2J1 Can. *Fax:* 403-492-0714; *E-Mail:* khanna@phys.ualberta.ca

KHANNA, JATINDER MOHAN, BIOCHEMICAL PHARMACOLOGY. *Current Pos:* Res fel pharmacol, 64-65, lectr, 65-66, from asst prof to assoc prof, 66-77, PROF PHARMACOL, FAC MED, UNIV TORONTO, 77- *Personal Data:* b Amritsar, India, Apr 15, 36; m 66; c 2. *Educ:* Punjab Univ, India, BSc, 58, MSc, 60; Univ Conn, PhD(pharmacol), 64. *Concurrent Pos:* Scientist IV, Alcohol & Drug Addiction Res Found, 69-, head, Behav Pharmacol & Drug Anal Sect; mem ed bd, J Alcohol; Lederle Res fel, Univ Conn, Starrs. *Mem:* Soc Neurosci; Can Pharmacol Soc; Am Soc Pharmacol & Exp Therapeut; Res Soc Alcoholism; Int Soc Biomed Res Alcoholism; Sigma Xi. *Res:* Biochemical and behavioral mechanisms of alcohol and drug addiction. *Mailing Add:* Dept Pharmacol Univ Toronto Med Sci Bldg Toronto ON M5S 1A8 Can

KHANNA, KRISHAN L, PHYTOCHEMISTRY, PHARMACEUTICAL CHEMISTRY. *Current Pos:* CONSULT, 76- *Personal Data:* b Amritsar, India, Nov 19, 33; m 63; Urmilla Khurana; c Rajiv & Rayi. *Educ:* Univ Panjab, India, BPharm, 57, MPharm, 59; Univ Conn, PhD(pharm sci), 63. *Honors & Awards:* Gold Medal Except Serv, US Environ Protection Agency. *Prof Exp:* Lectr pharmacog, Univ Panjab, India, 59-60; asst instr org chem, Univ Conn, 62-63, instr, 63-64; lectr pharmacog, Univ Panjab, India, 64-68; res assoc, Col Pharm, Univ Mich, Ann Arbor, 68-70, NIH fel toxicol, 70-71; res assoc indust toxicol, 71-74; assoc prof, Col Pharm & Pharmacol Sci, Howard Univ, 74-76. *Mem:* AAAS; Soc Toxicol. *Res:* Toxicology; drug metabolism; metabolism of foreign compounds; risk assessment of drinking water contaminants. *Mailing Add:* 4203 Wynwood Dr Annandale VA 22003

KHANNA, PYARE LAL, BIO-ORGANIC CHEMISTRY, SYNTHETIC CHEMISTRY & IMMUNOCHEMISTRY. *Current Pos:* res group leader, Microgenics, 77-80, asst dir res, 80-86, vpres res & develop, 86-91, VPRES RES & DEVELOP, BOEHRINGER MANNHEIM, 92- *Personal Data:* b Lahore, Mar 28, 45; US citizen; m 73, Swatanter Kapour; c Sonia & Pavan. *Educ:* Univ Delhi, BSc, 65, MSc, 67, PhD(chem), 70. *Honors & Awards:* Syntex Sci Award, 84. *Prof Exp:* Res assoc natural prod, Indian Nat Sci Acad, 70-71; asst prof chem, Ramjas Col, Univ Delhi, 71-74; res assoc, Columbia Univ, 74-77. *Mem:* Am Chem Soc; Am Asn Clin Chem; NY Acad Sci; AAAS. *Res:* Natural products isolation and synthesis; steroids; small ring compounds; fluorescent dyes; protein modifications; development of new immunoassay techniques; dipstick immunoassays; homogenous and heterogenous immunoassays; future research and development strategy. *Mailing Add:* Boehringer Mannheim 2380 Bisso Lane Concord CA 94520. *Fax:* 510-490-1654; *E-Mail:* pyarekhanna@aol.com

KHANNA, RAVI, polymer chemistry, chemical engineering, for more information see previous edition

KHANNA, SARDARI LAL, PHYSICS. *Current Pos:* assoc prof, 70-78, PROF PHYSICS, YORK COL, PA, 78- *Personal Data:* b Amritsar, India, Apr 15, 37; m 63; c 2. *Educ:* Panjab Univ India, BA, 56; Univ Saugar, MSc, 59, PhD(physics), 63. *Prof Exp:* Lectr physics, DAV Col, Amritsar, India, 59-60; lectr, Panjab Univ, 62-64; from asst prof to assoc prof, York Jr Col, Pa, 65-68; sci pool off, Panjab Univ, 68-69. *Mem:* Am Phys Soc; Am Asn Physics Teachers. *Res:* Electrets; solid state physics; study of dielectrics subjected to electric and magnetic fields. *Mailing Add:* 159 Scott Rd York PA 17403. *Fax:* 717-849-1607

KHANNA, SHYAM MOHAN, PHYSIOLOGY, BIOPHYSICS. *Current Pos:* res assoc hearing, 64-70, from asst prof to assoc prof, 70-83, PROF OTOLARYNGOL, COL PHYSICIANS & SURGEONS, COLUMBIA UNIV, 83-, DIR RES, FOWLER MEM LABS, 83- *Personal Data:* b Agra, India, May 10, 32; m 59, Shirley E Leng; c Ravi & Shyama. *Educ:* Univ Lucknow, BS, 51; St Xavier's Col, India, DRE, 54; City Univ New York, PhD(hearing), 70. *Prof Exp:* Develop engr instrumentation, Pye Ltd, Eng, 54-55; design engr commun, Can Westinghouse Ltd, Ont, 55-58; sr engr avionics, Int Tel & Tel Labs, 58-61; adv engr commun, IBM Corp, 61-64. *Concurrent Pos:* NIH res grants, 64-, prin investr, 79-; res career develop award, NINCDS, 77-94, prin investr, Prog Proj grants, 85-, mem, Commun Disorders Rev Comt. *Mem:* Sr mem Inst Elec & Electronics Engrs; fel Acoust Soc Am; Sigma Xi; Asn Res Otolaryngol; AAAS; Int Soc Optics Life Sci (pres, 92-94). *Res:* Physics of hearing; mechanics of the middle and inner ear; transducer action and coding in the peripheral auditory system. *Mailing Add:* Col Physicians & Surgeons Rm 11-452 Columbia Univ 630 W 168th St New York NY 10032. *Fax:* 212-305-4045; *E-Mail:* smk3@columbia.edu

KHARAKA, YOUSIF KHOSHU, GEOCHEMISTRY, HYDROGEOLOGY. *Current Pos:* HYDROLOGIST WATER RESOURCES DIV, US GEOL SURV, 75- *Personal Data:* b Mosul, Iraq, May 15, 41; c 2. *Educ:* King's Col, Univ London, BSc, 63; Univ Calif, Berkeley, PhD(geol), 71. *Honors & Awards:* Spec Award, Soc Econ Paleontologists & Mineralogists, 85. *Prof Exp:* Asst geologist explor & res dept, Ministry of Oil, Baghdad, Iraq, 63-67; asst res geologist, Univ Calif. Berkeley, 71-75. *Concurrent Pos:* Asst geol, Univ Baghdad, 63-64; consult explor, Mining & Metals Div, Union Carbide Corp, 74-75. *Mem:* Int Asn Geochem & Cosmochem; Geochem Soc; Am Asn Petrol Geologists; Am Geophys Union; Geol Soc Am. *Res:* Geochemistry of sediments, sedimentary rocks and their associated fluids; computer modelling of water-rock interactions; membrane properties of fine grained sediments; stable isotopes. *Mailing Add:* 3385 St Michael Dr Palo Alto CA 94306

KHARAS, GREGORY B, BIODEGRADABLE POLYESTERS, POLYMERIC MATERIALS. *Current Pos:* ASST PROF ORG CHEM & POLYMER SCI, DEPAUL UNIV, 92- *Personal Data:* b Moscow, Russia, Sept 6, 46; US citizen; m 73, Cecilya; c Boris & Michael. *Educ:* Moscow Inst Petrochem & Gas Indust, BS & MS, 68; Technion-Israel Inst Technol, PhD(chem), 81. *Prof Exp:* Res assoc, Inst Petrochem Synthesis, Acad Sci USSR, 68-78; fel, Case Western Res Univ, 81-82, Univ Mass, Lowell, 82-83; res assoc, Albany Int, 83-85; assoc scientist, Novacor Chem Inc, 85-92. *Concurrent Pos:* Adj prof, Univ Mass, Lowell, 89-92. *Mem:* Am Chem Soc; Soc Biomat; Bio/Environmentally Degradable Polymer Soc; Coun Undergrad Educ. *Res:* Synthesis and characterization of copolymers of trisubstituted ethylenes; biodegradable polyesters for packaging and biomedical applications; analysis of microstructure of copolymers thermal and environmental degradation of polymeric materials. *Mailing Add:* Dept Chem DePaul Univ 25 E Jackson Blvd Chicago IL 60604-2218. *Fax:* 312-362-6636; *E-Mail:* chegbk@orion.depaul.edu

KHARASCH, NORMAN, chemistry; deceased, see previous edition for last biography

KHARE, ASHOK KUMAR, FORGINGS & EXTRUSIONS. *Current Pos:* sr prod metallurgist, Dept Metall, 75-82, SR DEVELOP METALLURGIST, RES & DEVELOP CORP, NAT FORGE CO, IRVINE, PA, 82- *Personal Data:* b Kanpur, India, Aug 7, 48; US citizen; m 74; c 2. *Educ:* Agra Univ, India, BSc, 64; Indian Inst Tech, BTech, 69; Stevens Institute Tech, MS, NJ, 71. *Mem:* AAAS; fel Am Soc Metals; Am Soc Mech Eng. *Res:* Product and process develpment for new and existing ferrous-non ferrous forgings and extrusions. *Mailing Add:* 5 Leslie Blvd Warren PA 16365

KHARE, BISHUN NARAIN, PHYSICS, PHYSICAL CHEMISTRY. *Current Pos:* NAT RES COUN SR RESIDENT RES ASSOC, AMES RES CTR, NASA, MOFFETT FIELD, CALIF, 96- *Personal Data:* b Varanasi, India, June 27, 33; m 62, Jyoti Rani; c Reena, Archana. *Educ:* Banaras Hindu Univ, BSc, 53, MSc, 55; Syracuse Univ, PhD(physics), 61. *Prof Exp:* Res assoc, Univ Toronto, 61-62 & State Univ NY, Stony Brook, 62-64; assoc res scientist, Ont Res Found, Can, 64-66; physicist, Smithsonian Astrophys Observ, Mass, 66-68; sr res physicist, Lab Planetary Studies, Ctr Radiophys & Space Res, Cornell Univ, 68-96. *Concurrent Pos:* Assoc, Harvard Observ, 66-68. *Mem:* AAAS; Am Phys Soc; Am Astron Soc; Int Soc Study Origin of Life; Astron Soc India; Am Chem Soc; Int Astron Union; Sigma Xi; Planetary Soc. *Res:* Interdisciplinary research; molecular structure and spectroscopy; synthesis of organic compounds in primitive terrestrial and contemporary planetary atmospheres by photochemical reaction; hydrogen bonding among molecules of biological interest; planetary surfaces and atmospheres; interstellar and cometary chemistry; optical constants of materials of astronomical interest. *Mailing Add:* NASA Moffett Field CA 94035-1000. *Fax:* 650-604-1088; *E-Mail:* khare@astronsun.tn.cornell.edu

KHARE, MOHAN, PHYSICAL CHEMISTRY, ENVIRONMENTAL CHEMISTRY. *Current Pos:* PRES & CHIEF EXEC OFFICER, ENVIROSYST, INC, 89- *Personal Data:* b Varanasi, India, May 15, 42; US citizen; m 73, Meena Srivastava; c Rohit. *Educ:* Banaras Hindu Univ, BSc, 61, MSc, 63 & PhD(chem), 67. *Prof Exp:* Lectr chem, Banaras Hindu Univ, 67; res assoc & fel, Univ Md, 67-69 & Radiation Ctr, Ore State Univ, 69-70; sr res assoc, Cornell Univ, 70-78; sr anal specialist & technologist, IT Corp, 78-82; res prof chem, Univ Nev, Las Vegas & mgr, Qual Assurance Lab, US Environ Protection Agency, 82-84; mgr, Environ Monitoring Servs Lab, Rockwell Int, 84-85; dir, Anal Chem Lab, EA Eng, Sci & Technol, Inc, 85-87; sr vpres, Recra Environ Inc, 87-89. *Mem:* Am Chem Soc; AAAS; Am Water Works Asn; Int Union Pure & Appl Chem. *Res:* Radiochemical separation of isotopes; kinetics of annealing of radiation damage; energy transfer in solids; photolysis and radiolysis of aqueous systems and interstellar molecules; water pollution characterization and environmental research; analytical methods development for trace and toxic materials, organic and inorganic, in diverse matrices; water quality and hazardous waste management; detoxification and disposal. *Mailing Add:* 10189 Maxine St Ellicott City MD 21042-6316. *Fax:* 410-740-9306

KHARGONEKAR, PRAMOD P, CONTROL THEORY, SYSTEM THEORY. *Current Pos:* PROF ELEC ENG & COMPUT SCI, UNIV MICH, ANN ARBOR, 89- *Personal Data:* b Indore, India, Aug 24, 56; India; m 83, Seema B Pai; c Aditya & Shivangi. *Educ:* Indian Inst Technol, Bombay, BTech, 77; Univ Fla, Gainesville, MS, 80, PhD(elec eng), 81. *Honors & Awards:* D Eckmann Award, 89; Axelby Award, Inst Elec & Electronics Engrs, 90, W R G Baker Prize, 91. *Prof Exp:* Asst prof elec eng, Univ Fla, Gainesville, 81-84; from assoc prof to prof elec eng, Univ Minn, Minneapolis, 84-89. *Concurrent Pos:* Prin investr, Air Force Off Sci Res, Army Res Off, NSF, 81-; vis asst prof, Tex Tech Univ, Lubbock, 82; vis prof, Swiss Fed Inst Technol, Zurich, 83; consult, Honeywell Corp, 84-; prin young investr award, NSF, 85; George Taylor res award, 87. *Mem:* Inst Elec & Electronics Engrs. *Res:* Control and systems theory; robust control, optimal control, infinite dimensional systems, adaptive control, algebraic system theory, control of electronics manufacturing. *Mailing Add:* 3620 Windmere Dr Ann Arbor MI 48105. *E-Mail:* pramod@eecs.umich.edu

KHASNABIS, SNEHAMAY, TRANSPORTATION ENGINEERING, SYSTEMS ANALYSIS. *Current Pos:* From asst prof to assoc prof, Wayne State Univ, Detroit, 75-82, actg chmn dept, 83-84, chmn dept, 84-87, PROF CIVIL ENG, WAYNE STATE UNIV, DETROIT, 82- *Personal Data:* b Dacca, India, Nov 4, 39; nat US; m 67; c 2. *Educ:* Univ Calcutta, India, BE, 62; NC State Univ, Raleigh, MCE, 70, PhD(civil eng), 73. *Concurrent Pos:* Transp engr, Barton-Aschman Assocs, Inc, Washington, DC, 74-75; prin investr, US Dept Transp Res Projs, Wayne State Univ, 77-91 & NSF Educ Proj, 83-86, chmn dept, 84-87; actg dir, Urban Transp Inst, Wayne State Univ, 85- *Mem:* Am Soc Civil Engrs; Inst Transp Engrs; Transp Res Bd. *Res:* Land-use models, simulation, transit station location, traffic safety and operation, transportation logistics; computer techniques for bus system planning and expansion, and financial strategies for transit system development; transit drivatization and intelligent vehicles highway systems. *Mailing Add:* 6195 Carriage Trail Dr Troy MI 48098

KHATAMI, MAHIN, protein chemistry, enzymology, for more information see previous edition

KHATIB, HISHAM M, ENERGY & ELECTRICITY GLOBAL IMPACT, ENVIRONMENTAL EFFECTS OF ENERGY. *Current Pos:* minister of planning, 93-95, CONSULT INT ORGN, 95- *Personal Data:* b Palestine, Jan 5, 36; Jordanian citizen; m 68, Maha; c Mohamed, Lynn & Issam. *Educ:* Univ Ain Shams, Cairo, BSc, 59; Univ Birmingham, MSc 62; Univ London, BSc, 67, PhD(elec eng), 74. *Prof Exp:* Asst engr, Jerusalem Dist Elec Co, 59-62, engr, 62-66, chief engr, 66-73; res fel elec eng, Univ London, 73-74; dep dir gen, Jordan Elec Authority, 74-76, dir gen, 80-84; energy adv, Arab Fund, Kuwait, 76-80; minister energy, Govt Jordan, 84-89. *Concurrent Pos:* Mem, Int Comt Availability Generating Plant, 82-; consult ed, Int J Elec & Energy Systs, 85- & Environ Policy, 90-; vchmn, World Energy Coun, 88-, hon vchmn, 93-; chmn, Inst Elec Engrs Ctr, Jordan, 89-; Bd World Energy Efficiency Asn. *Mem:* Fel Inst Elec & Electronics Engrs; World Energy Coun; fel Inst Elec Eng UK. *Res:* Global energy matters, demand and supply, effect on the environment; future of electrical energy and its environmental impact; human development and energy matters. *Mailing Add:* PO Box 925387 Amman Jordan. *Fax:* 698556

KHATIB-RAHBAR, MOHSEN, CHEMICAL ENGINEERING, NUCLEAR ENGINEERING. *Current Pos:* PRES, ENERGY RES, INC, 89- *Personal Data:* b Rafsandjan, Iran, Feb 21, 54; m 85, Maryam Amini; c Dara & Dina. *Educ:* Univ Minn, BChemEng, 74; Cornell Univ, PhD(nuclear eng), 78. *Prof Exp:* Mem sci staff, Brookhaven Nat Lab, 78-88, group leader accident anal group, 85-88. *Concurrent Pos:* Cornell McMullin fel, 75; vis scientist, Ger Res Satellite, WGerm, 82; prin investr, US Nuclear Regulatory Comn; consult, US Nuclear Regulatory Comm, US Dept Energy, Int Atomic Energy Lab, Los Alamos Nat Lab, Pac NW Lab, Swiss Nuclear Safety Inspecterate, Finnish Nuclear Safety Authority, Dutch Ministry Social Affairs & Swedish Nuclear Safety Inspectorate. *Mem:* Assoc mem Am Inst Chem Engrs; Am Nuclear Soc. *Res:* Nuclear reactor dynamics and safety; heat transfer; fluid dynamics; numerical methods; probabilistic risk assessment; severe nuclear reactor accident analysis; mathematical methods for propagation of stochastic and physical uncertainty. *Mailing Add:* Energy Res Inc 10711 Burbank Dr Potomac MD 20854

KHATRA, BALWANT SINGH, BIOCHEMISTRY. *Current Pos:* res assoc, 75-78, ASST PROF, DEPT PHYSIOL, VANDERBILT UNIV, 78- *Personal Data:* b Nabha, India, Feb 2, 45; US citizen; m 68; c 2. *Educ:* Punjab Univ, BSc Hons, 65, MSc, 67; Univ Leeds, PhD(biochem), 72. *Prof Exp:* Res fel, Clin Res Facil, Emory Univ, 72-75. *Mem:* Am Soc Biol Chemists. *Res:* Phosphoprotein phosphatases: isolation, characterization and their role in the regulation of glycogen metabolism. *Mailing Add:* Dept Biol Calif State Univ-Long Beach 1250 Bellflower Blvd Long Beach CA 90840-3702. *Fax:* 562-985-2315

KHATRI, HIRALAL C, MECHANICAL ENGINEERING. *Current Pos:* mech engr, 71-80, PHYS SCIENTIST, HARRY DIAMOND LABS, 80- *Personal Data:* b Navsari, India, Feb 6, 36; m 65; c 1. *Educ:* Imp Col Eng, Addis Ababa, Ethiopia, BS, 58; Purdue Univ, MS, 63, PhD(mech eng), 66. *Prof Exp:* Engr, Imp Hwy Authority, Ethiopia, 58-61; asst prof elec eng, Mont State Univ, 65-67; assoc prof mech eng, Cath Univ Am, 67-71. *Concurrent Pos:* NSF res grant, 66-68. *Mem:* Assoc mem Am Soc Mech Engrs; Inst Elec & Electronics Engrs. *Res:* Automatic control systems; optimal filter, identification and control of distributed systems; stability and sensitivity of distributed parameter systems; radar systems and signal processing. *Mailing Add:* US Army Res Lab 2800 Powder Mill Rd Adelphi MD 20783-1197

KHATTAB, GHAZI M A, polymer chemist, for more information see previous edition

KHATTAK, CHANDRA PRAKASH, SOLID STATE PHYSICS, MATERIALS SCIENCE. *Current Pos:* dir res & develop, Crystal Systs Inc, 77-80, vpres technol, 80-86, sr vpres, 87-89, EXEC VPRES, CRYSTAL SYSTS INC, 89- *Personal Data:* b Rawalpindi, Pakistan, May 19, 44; m 70, Veena Dhawan; c Payal & Gautam. *Educ:* Indian Inst Technol, Bombay, BTech, 65; State Univ NY, Stony Brook, MS, 71, PhD(mat sci), 73. *Honors & Awards:* IR-100 Award, 79. *Prof Exp:* Jr sci officer magnetism, DMR Lab, Hyderabad, India, 65-68; asst mat sci, State Univ NY, Stony Brook, 68-73; res assoc solid state physics, Brookhaven Nat Lab, 74-75, asst physicist, 75-77. *Mem:* Am Ceramic Soc; Am Phys Soc; Am Asn Crystal Growth; Electrochemical Soc; Am Soc Metals. *Res:* Growth of large diameter sapphire for optical application, directional solidification of silicon crystals for photovoltaic applications and laser crystals growth by heat exchanger method; low-cost slicing of silicon by multi-ware fixed abrasive slicing technique; characterization and evaluation of silicon material for solar cells; thermodynamic evaluation of vacuum processing of silicon; single crystal growth of compound semiconductors and non-linear crystals. *Mailing Add:* Crystal Systs Inc Shetland Indust Park 27 Congress St Salem MA 01970. *Fax:* 978-744-5059

KHAVKIN, THEODOR, HISTOLOGY, EXPERIMENTAL PATHOLOGY. *Current Pos:* sr scientist, 80-87, CONSULT, RES & DEVELOP LYMPHOKINE PROD, INTERFEROM SCI, INC, NEW BRUNSWICK, NJ, 88- *Personal Data:* b Kharkov, Ukraine, Feb 18, 19; US citizen; m 46, Leah Rabinov; c Misha & Vova. *Educ:* Kharkov Med Inst, Ukraine, Med Doct, 41; Mil Med Acad, St Petersburg, Russia, PhD cand(path), 49; USSR Acad Med Sci, SciD(path), 72. *Hon Degrees:* Med Doct Hons, Mil Med Acad, Bd, St Petersburg, Russia, 45. *Prof Exp:* Mil pathologist trauma, Soviet Army, World War II, 42-44; adj path & atherosclerosis, Mil Med Acad, St Petersburg, Russia, 44-49; chief pathologist, Mil Districts, USSR, 49-62; sr scientist path, Inst Exp Med, 62-79. *Concurrent Pos:* Vis prof & scientist, Rutgers State Univ, New Brunswick, NJ, 83-85; consult, Sci Testing, Inc, New Brunswick, 88-89. *Mem:* Am Asn Pathologists; hon mem Am Soc Rickettsiol & Rickettsial Dis; Am Soc Microbiol; Am Soc Exp Biol Med; Soc Leukocyte Biol. *Res:* Research and development of lymphokine production; pathology and immunomorphology of inflammatory and immune responses; pathology of infectious diseases; microscopy. *Mailing Add:* Interferon Sci Inc 783 Jersey Ave New Brunswick NJ 08901-3605. *Fax:* 732-249-6895

KHAW, BAN-AN, MODIFICATION OF ANTIBODIES, RADIOIMMUNOSCINTIGRAPHY. *Current Pos:* ASSOC RADIO CHEMIST, DEPT RADIOL, MASS GEN HOSP E, 90-; GEORGE D BEHRAKIS PROF PHARMACEUT SCI & DIR, CTR DRUG TARGETING & ANALYSIS, NORTHEASTERN UNIV, 91- *Personal Data:* b Bassein, Burma, July 25, 47; US citizen; m 76; c 4. *Educ:* State Univ NY, Oswego, BA, 69; Boston Col, MS, 70 & PhD(immunol), 73. *Honors & Awards:* Berson-Yalow Award, Soc Nuclear Med, 91. *Prof Exp:* Res fel, Mass Gen Hosp & Harvard Med Sch, 73-76; instr, Harvard Med Sch, 76-78; asst biochem, Mass Gen Hosp, 76-79; asst prof, dept path, Harvard Med Sch, 78-83, dept radiol, 83-84; asst biochemist, 80-81, assoc biochemist, Dept Med, Mass Inst Technol, 81-83, asst radio chemist, Dept Radiol, 83-89. *Concurrent Pos:* Consult, Centocor, 82-, Vasocor, 89-; assoc prof, Dept Radiol, Harvard Med Sch, 84- *Mem:* Soc Nuclear Med; Am Heart Asn Basic Sci; Chinese Am Soc Nuclear Med (pres, 90-); Am Chem Soc; Am Soc Nuclear Cardiol. *Res:* Application of antibodies in vivo diagnosis of cardiovascular diseases; modification of charge of proteins to affect changes in biodistribution and enhancement in vivo target localization; general application of radioimmunoscintigraphy; targeting with proteins, peptides and carbohydrates for diagnosis and therapy; autoimmune myocarditis; myocardial salvages, regeneration and genetherapy. *Mailing Add:* Bouve Col Pharm & Health Sci Northeastern Univ Boston MA 02115. *Fax:* 617-373-3663; *E-Mail:* bkwah@lynx.neu.edu

KHAWAJA, IKRAM ULLAH, ECONOMIC GEOLOGY. *Current Pos:* From asst prof to assoc prof, 68-81, PROF GEOL, YOUNGSTOWN STATE UNIV, 81- *Personal Data:* b Delhi, India, Dec 25, 42; m 68. *Educ:* Univ Karachi, BS, 62, MS, 63; Southern Ill Univ, MS, 68; Ind Univ, Bloomington, PhD(geol), 69. *Mem:* Geol Soc Am; Sigma Xi. *Res:* Coal geology; petrology; sulphides in coal. *Mailing Add:* Dept Geol Youngstown State Univ 410 Wick Ave Youngstown OH 44555-0001

KHAYAT, ALI, AGRICULTURAL CHEMISTRY, FOOD SCIENCE. *Current Pos:* ASSOC DIR RES, BEATRICE, 82- *Personal Data:* b Tehran, Iran, Feb 2, 38; US citizen; m 66; c 2. *Educ:* Univ Tehran, BS, 61; Univ Calif, Davis, MS, 64, PhD(agr chem), 68. *Prof Exp:* Res asst biochem, Univ Calif, Davis, 64-68; asst prof, Med Sch, Pahlavi Univ, Iran, 68-70; res biochemist, Ralston Purina Co, 70-72, assoc scientist, 72-77, sr scientist res dept, Van Camp Div, 77-82. *Mem:* Am Chem Soc; Sigma Xi; Inst Food Technologists; AAAS. *Res:* Chemical modification of proteins; flavor chemistry; studies on vegetable oils; food texture; sensory and microbiological evaluation of foods. *Mailing Add:* Hunt Wesson Food Inc 1645 W Valencia Dr Fullerton CA 92833

KHAZAN, NAIM, PHARMACOLOGY. *Current Pos:* prof pharmacol & toxicol, 74-80, chmn, Dept Pharmacol & Toxicol & dir, Grad Prog Pharmacol, 74-86, EMERSON PROF, PHARMACOL & TOXICOL, UNIV MD, 80- *Personal Data:* b Baghdad, Iraq, Feb 15, 21; US citizen; m 52; c 2. *Educ:* Col Pharm & Chem, Baghdad, PhC, 43; Hebrew Univ Jerusalem, PhD(pharmacol), 60. *Honors & Awards:* Ellis Grollman Lectr Award, 90. *Prof Exp:* Res assoc cent nerv syst pharmacol, Upjohn Co, 63-64; lectr, Hadassah Med Sch & Sch Pharm, Hebrew Univ, Jerusalem, 64, sr lectr, 66; asst prof, Med Sch, Univ Ore, 66-67; assoc prof, Columbia Univ, 67-68; assoc prof pharmacol, Mt Sinai Sch Med, 68-72; head dept pharmacol, Merrell Nat Labs, Cincinnati & assoc clin prof, Col Med, Univ Cincinnati, 72-74. *Concurrent Pos:* Mem, Grad Coun, Univ Md, Baltimore City, 78-; NIMH grants, 67, 68-72 & 72-75; Nat Inst Drug Abuse grants, 75-78, 78-88; USPHS int fel, 68. *Mem:* Am Pharmaceut Asn; Am Soc Pharmacol & Exp Therapeut; NY Acad Sci; Soc Neurosci; Sigma Xi. *Res:* Electroencephalographic and behavioral studies of experimental drug dependence on narcotics; electroencephalographic effects of cannabinoids; pharmacology of rapid eye movement sleep; opioid multiple receptors and electroencephalograph power spectra. *Mailing Add:* 2126 Caves Rd Owings Mills MD 21117. *Fax:* 410-363-0225

KHERA, KUNDAN SINGH, TOXICOLOGY, TERATOLOGY. *Current Pos:* sect head teratology, 64-79, sr scientist, 80-92, RES TERATOLOGIST, HEALTH PROTECTION BR, NAT HEALTH & WELFARE, CAN, 92- *Personal Data:* b Wadala Khurd, India, May 12, 22; Can citizen; m 86, Claire Paulin; c Surinder, Jagtar, Balbir, Autar, Paramjit & Rupinder. *Educ:* Punjab Univ, BSc, 44, DVM & BVSc, 52, MVSc & MSc, 56; Univ Paris, DSc, 58. *Honors & Awards:* Arnold J Lehmann Award, Soc Toxicol, 88. *Prof Exp:* Dis invest officer, Vet Dept, Punjab Govt, India, 58-61; prof vet path, Vet Col, Punjab Univ & Govt Punjab, 61-64. *Concurrent Pos:* Fel, Col Med, Baylor Univ, 62-63; mem, Coun Teratology Soc, 75-78; consult & adv, Int Agency Res on Cancer, 82, Int Programme Chem Safety, World Health Orgn, 81-83, Atomic Energy Control Bd, Can, 90, US Food & Drug Admin, 76 & 90. *Mem:* Soc Toxicol; Teratology Soc; Europe Teratology Soc. *Res:* Effects of drug-induced maternal and placental toxicity on fetal development. *Mailing Add:* 604-44 Emmerson Ave Ottawa ON K1Y 2L8 Can

KHESHGI, HAROON S, CLIMATE CHANGE, FLUID MECHANICS. *Current Pos:* STAFF ENGR CORP RES, EXXON RES & ENG CO, 86- *Personal Data:* b Bay Shore, NY, Sept 25, 57. *Educ:* Univ Ill, Champaign Urbana, BS, 78; Univ Minn, Minneapolis, PhD(chem eng), 84. *Prof Exp:* Engr laser isotope separating prog, Lawrence Livermore Nat Lab, 83-86. *Concurrent Pos:* Adj assoc prof dept earth sys sci, NY Univ, 93-; vis researcher climate change prog, Lawrence Livermore Nat Lab, 94. *Mem:* Am Inst Chem Eng; Am Phys Soc; Am Geophs Union. *Res:* Global climate change, mitigation of greenhouse gas emissions, fluid mechanics, coating operations and reaction engineering. *Mailing Add:* 251 Mountain Ave Somerville NJ 08876

KHO, BOEN TONG, ANALYTICAL CHEMISTRY. *Current Pos:* asst dir anal res & develop, 68-71, DIR ANAL RES & DEVELOP, AYERST LABS, INC, 71- *Personal Data:* b Tegal, Indonesia, Dec 3, 19; US citizen; m 60; c 4. *Educ:* Univ Utrecht, BS, 42; State Univ Leiden, Drs, 47, apotheker, 49; Philadelphia Col Pharm, MS, 52; Univ Wis, PhD(pharm), 57. *Prof Exp:* Res chemist, Cent Res Labs, Gen Aniline & Film Co, Pa, 57-60; head methods develop, Merck Sharp & Dohme, 60-64; head analytical res, Toms River Res Lab, Ciba Chem & Dye Co, 64-67; mgr analytical res, Ciba-Agrochem Co, 67-68. *Mem:* Am Chem Soc; Am Pharmaceut Asn; NY Acad Sci; Sigma Xi. *Mailing Add:* 37 Adirondack Lane Plattsburgh NY 12901-3213

KHODADAD, JENA KHADEM, ULTRASTRUCTURE, MEMBRANES. *Current Pos:* Fel membrane, 77-78, instr cell biol, Dept Path, 78-79, ASST PROF, DEPT ANAT & PATH, MED COL, RUSH UNIV, 79- *Personal Data:* b Tehran, Iran; US citizen; c 3. *Educ:* Mt Union Col, BS, 60; Northwestern Univ, MS, 71, PhD(biol sci), 75. *Mem:* Am Soc Cell Biol; Am Asn Anatomists; AAAS. *Res:* Membrane research; biological membranes and the correlationation of ultrastructure with biochemical studies; red blood cell is the model membrane system used. *Mailing Add:* Dept Anat Rush-Presby-St Luke's Med Ctr 600 S Paulina St Chicago IL 60612

KHONSARI, MICHAEL M, MECHANICAL ENGINEERING. *Current Pos:* asst prof, 88-90, ASSOC PROF, UNIV PITTSBURGH, 90-, MEM FAC, CTR MOTION CONTROL, 89- *Personal Data:* b Aug 17, 57; m 90, Karen S Troy. *Educ:* Univ Tex, BS, 78, MS, 79, PhD(mech eng), 83. *Honors & Awards:* Newark Award, Am Soc Mech Engrs, 90. *Prof Exp:* Res & teaching asst, Univ Tex, Austin, 78-83; asst prof, Ohio State Univ, Columbus, 84-87. *Concurrent Pos:* Fac res fel, NASA Lewis Res Ctr, 86, 87 & 88, Wright-Patterson AFB, 90 & US Dept Energy, 93; reviewer, NSF, NASA, Am Chem Soc Books, McGraw Hill Books, Addison Wesley Books, Prentice-Hall Books, Holt Rinehart & Winston books; William Whiteford fac fel, Univ Pittsburgh, 90-92; Found award, Alcoa, 90-91; assoc ed, J Tribology Trans, 90- *Mem:* Am Soc Mech Engrs; Soc Tribology & Lubrication Engrs. *Res:* Thermal effects in hydrodynamic bearings; multi-phase flows in bearings; friction associated with instrument pointing mechanisms operating under ultra low speeds; elastohydrodynamic lubrication; non-Newtonian fluid mechanics and heat transfer analysis. *Mailing Add:* 4305 Centre Ave Pittsburgh PA 15213. *Fax:* 412-624-1108; *E-Mail:* khonsari@vms.cis.pitt.edu

KHOO, MICHAEL C K, BIOMEDICAL ENGINEERING. Current Pos: asst prof, 83-90, ASSOC PROF BIOMED ENG, UNIV SOUTHERN CALIF, 90- Personal Data: b Kowloon, Hong Kong, Sept 15, 54; m 87; c 2. Educ: Univ London, BSc, 76; Harvard Univ, MS, 77, PhD(bioeng), 81. Prof Exp: Res assoc biomed eng, Vet Admin Med Ctr, West Roxbury & Brigham & Women's Hosp, Boston, 81-83. Concurrent Pos: NSF res initiation award, 85-87; biomed eng res award, Whitaker Found, 85-88; new investr award, NIH, 85-89, res career develop award, 90-96; career investr award, Am Lung Asn, 91-96. Mem: Biomed Eng Soc; Am Physiol Soc; Inst Elec & Electronics Engrs; Am Thoracic Soc; Am Sleep Disorders Asn. Res: Modeling of physiological control systems; cardiopulmonary physiology during sleep; biomedical signal processing. Mailing Add: Biomed Eng Dept Univ Southern Calif Los Angeles CA 90089-1451. Fax: 213-740-0343; E-Mail: khoo@bmsrs.usc.edu

KHOO, TENG LEK, NUCLEAR PHYSICS. Current Pos: from asst physicist to physicist, 77-85, SR PHYSICIST, NUCLEAR PHYSICS, ARGONNE NAT LAB, 79- Personal Data: b Penang, Malaysia, June 1, 43; m 72; c 2. Educ: Dalhousie Univ, BSc, 65, MSc, 67; McMaster Univ, PhD(physics), 72. Prof Exp: Res assoc nuclear physics, Mich State Univ, 72-74; asst prof, 74-77. Mem: Fel Am Phys Soc. Res: Experimental nuclear structure physics, especially properties of deformed nuclei, effective nucleon interaction and nuclei at high angular momentum and high temperature; formation and decay of compound nucleus. Mailing Add: Argonne Nat Lab Bldg 203 9700 S Cass Ave Argonne IL 60439

KHOOBYARIAN, NEWTON, VIROLOGY. Current Pos: actg head, Dept Microbiol & Immunol, 80-83, from asst prof to assoc prof, 60-72, PROF MICROBIOL, COL MED, UNIV ILL, CHICAGO, 72- Personal Data: b Tabriz, Iran, Oct 20, 24; US citizen; c 2. Educ: Lafayette Col, AB, 49; Univ Ill, MS, 50; Univ Wis, PhD(med microbiol), 54; Am Bd Microbiol, dipl. Prof Exp: Asst biol sci, Univ Ill, 49-50; asst med microbiol, Univ Wis, 50-54; res fel microbiol, Sch Med, Ind Univ, 54-55, res assoc, 55-56, instr pediat, 56-60. Concurrent Pos: Consult, Miles Labs, Inc, 70-80. Mem: AAAS; Am Soc Microbiol. Res: Mammalian cell-virus relationship; viral genetics; chemical and viral transformation. Mailing Add: Dept Microbiol & Immunol M/C 790 Univ Ill Col Med 901 S Wolcott Ave Chicago IL 60612-7340

KHORANA, BRIJ MOHAN, APPLIED OPTICS, RESEARCH & MANAGEMENT. Current Pos: assoc prof physics, 77-84, head, 80-91, PROF PHYSICS & APPL OPTICS, ROSE-HULMAN INST TECHNOL, 84-, DIR, CTR APPL OPTICS STUDIES, 85- Personal Data: b Multan, India, Apr 11, 39; m 67, Renu Sachdev; c 3. Educ: Univ Delhi, BSc, 58, MSc, 60; Indian Inst Technol, Kharagpur, MTech, 61; Univ Chicago, MS, 64; Case Western Res Univ, PhD(physics), 68. Prof Exp: Res assoc physics, James Franck Inst, Univ Chicago, 67-68 & Univ Rochester, 68-70; asst prof physics, Univ Notre Dame, 70-77. Concurrent Pos: Dir, Tech Assistance Servs Ctr, Rose-Hulman Inst Technol, 93- Mem: Sr mem Soc Mfg Engrs; fel Int Soc Optical Eng; Optical Soc Am; Machine Vision Asn. Res: Machine vision applications; quality inspection systems; design of automotive lighting (external); design of luminares; biomedical optic. Mailing Add: Ctr Appl Optics Studies Rose-Hulman Inst Technol Terre Haute IN 47803. E-Mail: brij.khorana@rose__hulman.edu

KHORANA, HAR GOBIND, ORGANIC CHEMISTRY. Current Pos: Alfred P Sloan prof, 70-, EMER ALFRED P SLOAN PROF BIOL & CHEM, MASS INST TECHNOL. Personal Data: b Raipur, India, Jan 9, 22; m 52; c 3. Educ: Punjab Univ, India, BSc, 43, MSc, 45; Univ Liverpool, PhD, 48. Hon Degrees: DSc, Univ Chicago, 66, Simon Fraser Univ, 69, Univ Liverpool, 71, Univ Wis, 76, Univ BC, 77, New Eng Col, 84, Hokkaido Univ, 93, Univ Miami, 94, Univ Bergen, 96; Dr, Adam Mickiewicz Univ, 94. Honors & Awards: Nobel Prize in Med, 68; Merck Award, Chem Inst Can, 58; Gold Medal, Prof Inst Can Pub Serv, 60; Dannie Heinneman Prize, 67; Lasker Found Award, 68; Louisa Gross Horwitz Prize, 68; Nat Medal of Sci; Paul Kayser Int Award of Merit in Retina Res, 87; Hans Neurath Lectr, Univ Wash; David E Green Lectr, Wis; First Phillip Handler Lectr, Duke Univ; John T Edsau Lectr, Harvard Univ. Prof Exp: Govt India fel, with Prof V Prelog, Swiss Fed Inst Technol, 48-49; Nuffield fel, with Prof Sir Alexander Todd, Cambridge Univ, 50-52; head org chem group, BC Res Coun & res prof fac grad studies, Univ BC, 52-60; prof & group leader, Inst Enzyme Res, Univ Wis-Madison, 60-62, prof, 62-71, Conrad A Elvejhem prof life sci, 64-71. Concurrent Pos: Vis prof, Rockefeller Inst, 59, Stanford Univ, 64, Harvard Med Sch, 66; Andrew D White prof, Cornell Univ, 74-80. Mem: Nat Acad Sci; fel AAAS; Am Chem Soc; Am Soc Biol Chem; fel Am Acad Arts & Sci; foreign mem Royal Soc; Am Philos Soc; Indian Acad Sci; Pontifical Acad Sci; Royal Soc Edinburgh; hon fel Indian Soc Genetics & Plant Breeding; hon mem Pharmaceut Soc Japan; hon mem Japanese Biochem Soc. Res: Peptides and proteins; chemistry of phosphate esters of biological interest; nucleic acids; chemical synthesis and structure; enzymes of nucleic acid metabolism; viruses and chemical genetics; chemistry and biochemistry of biological membranes; polynucleotide synthaes and the elucidation of the genetic code. Mailing Add: Dept Biol & Chem Mass Inst Technol 77 Massachusetts Ave Cambridge MA 02139

KHOSAH, ROBINSON PANGANAI, CHROMATOGRAPHY, MASS SPECTROMETRY. Current Pos: Scientist, Alcoa, 84-86, sr scientist, 86-87, staff scientist, 87-89, TECH SPECIALIST, ALCOA, 89- Personal Data: b Marondera, Zimbabwe, Jan 1, 54; US citizen. Educ: Univ Rhodesia, BS, 76; Univ Mass Amherst, MS, 81, PhD(chem), 85. Concurrent Pos: Pres & coatings consult, Diverse Technologies, Inc, 85- Mem: Am Chem Soc. Res: Separation mechanisms under supercritical fluids; analytical chromatography; preparative-scale supercritical fluid extraction. Mailing Add: 551 Larimer Ave Pittsburgh PA 15206

KHOSHNEVISAN, MOHSEN MONTE, ELECTROOPTICS, NONLINEAR OPTICS. Current Pos: mem tech staff, Electro-Optics Dept, 78-88, DIR OPTICS, SCI CTR, ROCKWELL INT, 88- Personal Data: b 1945; US citizen; m 70; c 2. Educ: Calif State Univ, San Jose, BS & BA, 68; Mich State Univ, MS, 71, PhD(physics), 73. Prof Exp: Asst prof physics, Arya-Mehr Univ Technol, Iran, 73-77; vis asst prof, Mich State Univ, Lansing, 77-78. Concurrent Pos: Mgr small tech groups, Infared Devices, Optical Devices & Appl Optics, dir, Optics. Mem: Am Phys Soc; Optical Soc Am; Soc Photo-Instrumentation Engrs. Res: Electro-optics; nonlinear optics; thin films. Mailing Add: Rockwell Int Sci Ctr 1049 Camino do Rios Thousand Oaks CA 91360

KHOSLA, MAHESH C, HYPERTENSION, NEUROSCIENCES. Current Pos: assoc staff, 71, STAFF, CLEVELAND CLIN FOUND, 71- Personal Data: b Rajoya, Hazara, India, July 6, 25; m 57, Santosh Bhandari; c Renu, Rajan & Rajesh. Educ: Panjab Univ, India, BS, 50, MS, 52, PhD, 57. Prof Exp: Sr sci officer, Cent Drug Res Inst, Lucknow, Uttar Pardesh, India, 57-69. Concurrent Pos: Fel med adv bd, Coun High Blood Pressure Res, Am Heart Asn, 71-; NIH grantee, 78- Mem: Am Chem Soc; Am Soc Biochem & Molecular Biol; Int Soc Hypertension; Am Soc Hypertension; AAAS; Am Heart Asn; NY Acad Sci; Inter-Am Soc Hypertension; Am Peptide Soc. Res: Synthesis of angiotensin II antagonists with minimum agonist activity; synthesis of tissue selective congeners of angiotensin II; hypertension; granted nine patents; author of various publications. Mailing Add: Health Sci Ctr REBV/NC3-147 Cleveland Clin Found 9500 Euclid Ave Cleveland OH 44195-5286

KHOSLA, RAJINDER PAUL, SOLID STATE PHYSICS. Current Pos: sr physicist, 66-70, res assoc, 71-76, group leader device technol, Solid State Lab, 75-76, lab head, 76-79, sr res lab head, 79-82, asst dir, Physics Div 82-85, DIR, MICROELECTRONICS TECHNOL DIV, EASTMAN KODAK CO, 85- Personal Data: b Phillaur, India, July 25, 33; m 66; c 3. Educ: Univ Delhi, BSc, 53; Benaras Hindu Univ, MSc, 55; Purdue Univ, PhD(physics), 66. Honors & Awards: Frederick Philips Award, Inst Elec & Electronics Engrs. Prof Exp: Lectr physics, Govt Col, Narnaul, India, 55-56; sci asst, Nat Phys Lab India, New Delhi, 56-59; teaching & res asst, Purdue Univ, 59-66. Concurrent Pos: Lectr, Eve Sch, Univ Rochester, 72-74; vis scholar, Dept Elec Eng & Comput Sci, Univ Calif, Santa Barbara, 74-75. Mem: AAAS; Am Phys Soc; fel Inst Elec & Electronics Engrs. Res: Transport and photoconductive properties of semiconductors and solid state devices; solid state imaging devices. Mailing Add: 9 Pine Cone Dr Pittsford NY 14534

KHOSRAVIYANI, FIROOZ, GROUP REPRESENTATION THEORY, ALGORITHMS. Current Pos: Asst prof, 92-95, ASSOC PROF MATH & COMPUT, TEX A&M INT UNIV, 95- Personal Data: b Tehran, Iran, Apr 21, 52; US citizen; m 75, Mahuash Bavafa; c Kourosh & Anahita. Educ: Tehran Univ, BSc, 74; Univ Col Wales, Eng, MSc, 77, PhD(math), 81. Prof Exp: Asst prof comput sci & math, Univ Gezira, Sudan, 81-84, Univ Tex, 85-92; adj fac res, San Diego State Univ, 84-85; adj fac res, San Diego State Univ, 84-85. Mem: Am Math Soc; Math Asn Am; Asn Comput Mach. Res: Group character tables over a finite field and the inter-relationship of group character tables over different fields; algorithms and data structures, e g extension of binary and fibonacci search to linear linked list. Mailing Add: 5201 University Blvd Laredo TX 78041-1990

KHRAIBI, ALI A, CARDIOVASCULAR PHYSIOLOGY, RENAL PHYSIOLOGY. Current Pos: sr res fel, 86-90, ASST PROF PHYSIOL, MAYO CLIN & FOUND, 90- Personal Data: b Sidon, Lebanon, Nov 21, 56; US citizen. Educ: Univ Miss Sch Med, BS, 78, MS, 88, PhD(physiol), 84. Prof Exp: Fel, Bowman Gray Sch Med, 84-86. Mem: Fel Am Heart Asn; Am Physiol Soc; Am Soc Nephrology. Res: Study the handling of regulation of sodium and water excretion by the kidneys in hypertension. Mailing Add: Dept Obstet & Gynec Univ Ill 820 S Wood St Chicago IL 60612-7313. Fax: 312-996-4238

KHURANA, KRISHAN KUMAR, SPACE PHYSICS, MAGNETOSPHERIC PHYSICS. Current Pos: ASST RES GEOPHYSICIST SPACE PHYSICS, UNIV CALIF, LOS ANGELES, 85- Personal Data: b New Delhi, India, June 1, 55. Educ: Delhi Univ, India, BSc, 74; Osmania Univ, India, MSc, 77, PhD(appl geophys), 81; Durham Univ, UK, PhD(pure geophys), 84. Concurrent Pos: Prin investr, NASA, 90- Mem: Am Geophys Soc; Am Phys Soc; Am Astron Soc. Res: Magnetospheres of Venus, Earth, Jupiter, Saturn and Uranus; structure and motion of Jupiter's magnetosphere; spherical harmonic models of planetary magnetic fields; data processing for the Galileo mission to Jupiter. Mailing Add: IGPP Slichter Hall Univ Calif Los Angeles CA 90035. Fax: 310-206-8042; E-Mail: kkhurana@igpp.ucla.edu

KHURANA, SURJIT SINGH, MATHEMATICS. Current Pos: asst prof, 68-74, assoc prof, 74-79, PROF MATH, UNIV IOWA, 79- Personal Data: b Tandlianwala, Pakistan, June 15, 31; m 62; c 3. Educ: Panjab Univ, India, BA, 53, MA, 55; Univ Ill, Urbana, PhD(math), 68. Prof Exp: Lectr math, Camp Col, Panjab Univ, India, 56-59 & Postgrad Inst, Univ Delhi, 59-64. Mem: Am Math Soc. Res: Measure theory; functional analysis; general topology; probability theory; topological vector spaces. Mailing Add: 2909 Raven St Iowa City IA 52242

KHURI, NICOLA NAJIB, THEORETICAL PHYSICS. Current Pos: assoc prof, 64-68, PROF PHYSICS, ROCKEFELLER UNIV, 68- Personal Data: b Beirut, Lebanon, May 27, 33; US citizen; m 55; c 2. Educ: Am Univ, Beirut, BA, 52; Princeton Univ, PhD(physics), 57. Prof Exp: Asst prof physics, Am

Univ, Beirut, 57-58; mem Inst Adv Study, 59-60; assoc prof physics, Am Univ, Beirut, 61-62; mem Inst Adv Study, 62-63; vis assoc prof, Columbia Univ, 63-64. *Concurrent Pos:* Brookhaven Nat Lab, 63-73; trustee, Am Univ Beirut, 69-; trustee, Brearley Sch, 70-79. *Mem:* Fel Am Phys Soc. *Res:* Quantum field theory; scattering theory; theory of dispersion relations and their applications; high energy particle physics. *Mailing Add:* Phys Dept Box 254 Rockefeller Univ New York NY 10021

KHUSH, GURDEV S, PLANT BREEDING, GENETICS. *Current Pos:* plant breeder, 67-72, head, Varietal Improv Dept, 72-85, PRIN PLANT BREEDER & HEAD, DIV PLANT BREEDING, GENETICS & BIOCHEM, INT RICE RES INST, 86- *Personal Data:* b Rurki, India, Aug 22, 35; m 61, Marwant K Grewal; c Ranjiv S, Manjeev K, Sonia K & Kiran K. *Educ:* Punjab Univ, India, BSc, 55; Univ Calif, Davis, PhD(genetics), 60. *Hon Degrees:* Dr, Punjab Agr Univ, India, 87, Tamil Nadu Agri Univ, 95, C S Azad Univ Agr Technol, 95, G B Pant Univ Agr & Technol, 96. *Honors & Awards:* Borlaung Award, 77; Japan Prize, 87; ASA Fel Award, 87; Int Agron Award, 89; Emil M Marak Int Award, 90; World Food Prize, 96. *Prof Exp:* Asst genetics, Univ Calif, Davis, 57-61, jr res geneticist, 61-62, asst res geneticist, 62-67. *Concurrent Pos:* Vis prof, Univ Philippines, Los Banos, 68- & Colo State Univ, 75-76. *Mem:* Foreign assoc Nat Acad Sci; Genetics Soc Am; Bot Soc Am; NY Acad Sci; Indian Nat Sci Acad; Third World Acad Sci. *Res:* Cytogenetic studies of genus Secale and origin of cultivated rye and genus Lycopersicon particularly gene location, chromosome mapping and centromere location in the cultivated tomato; rice genetics and breeding. *Mailing Add:* Int Rice Res Inst PO Box 933 Manila Philippines. *Fax:* 63-2-818-2087, 63-2-891-1292; *E-Mail:* g.khosh@cgnet.com

KHWAJA, TASNEEM AFZAL, CANCER, CHEMOTHERAPY. *Current Pos:* asst prof, 73-75, ASSOC PROF PATH, SCH MED, UNIV SOUTHERN CALIF, 76-, SR RES SCIENTIST & DIR ANIMAL TUMOR RESOURCE FACIL & PHARMACOANALYTIC FACIL, LOS ANGELES CO-UNIV SOUTHERN CALIF CANCER CTR, 73- *Personal Data:* b Pakistan, Apr 20, 36; m 65; c 2. *Educ:* Univ Panjab, WPakistan, BSc, 55, MSc, 57; Cambridge Univ, MA, 61, PhD(synthetic nucleic acid chem), 64. *Prof Exp:* NIH res assoc grant, Univ Utah, 65-66; NIH proj assoc grant, McArdle Lab Cancer Res, Univ Wis-Madison, 66-68; res asst, Max Planck Inst Exp Med, Ger, 69-70; head, Dept Cancer Chemother, ICN Nucleic Acid Res Inst, 70-73. *Mem:* Am Asn Cancer Res; fel Royal Chem Soc; Am Chem Soc. *Res:* Synthesis of nucleoside antimetabolites as antitumor agents; biochemical mechanisms of drug action; use of animal tumor models. *Mailing Add:* 1971 Port Albans Pl Newport Beach CA 92660

KIANG, CHIA SZU, ATMOSPHERIC SCIENCES, PHYSICS. *Current Pos:* dir, Sch Geophys Sci, 81-88, dir, Southern Oxidants Study, 88-92, dir, Off Environ Sci Technol & Policy, 91-92, PROF GEOPHYS SCI, GA INST TECHNOL, 78-, INST PROF, SCH EARTH & ATMOSPHERIC SCI, 88- *Personal Data:* b Shanghai, China, Sept 9, 39; US citizen; m 68, Marilyn Maisel; c Mia & Lara. *Educ:* Nat Taiwan Univ, BS, 62; Ga Inst Technol, MS, 64, PhD(physics), 70. *Honors & Awards:* Henry A Hill Distinguished Lectr Award, 86. *Prof Exp:* Assoc prof physics, Clark Col, 67-74; res scientist, Nat Ctr Atmospheric Res, 74-76, aerosol proj leader, 76-78. *Concurrent Pos:* Sr res assoc, Atmospheric Sci Res Ctr, State Univ NY, Albany, 71-; adj prof, Dept Chem, Atlanta Univ, 74-76 & Dept Atmospheric Sci, Colo State Univ, 74-78; adj prof physics, Ga Inst Technol, 76-77; nat lectr, Sigma Xi, 82-84. *Mem:* Am Chem Soc; Am Physics Soc; Am Meteorol Soc; AAAS. *Res:* Nucleation; aerosol physics; aerosol chemistry; atmospheric chemistry; surface science; phase transition; critical phenomena; statistical physics; planetary atmosphere; environmental science and planning; natural phenomena. *Mailing Add:* Sch Earth & Atmospheric Scis Ga Inst Technol Atlanta GA 30332. *Fax:* 404-894-1106

KIANG, DAVID TEH-MING, INTERNAL MEDICINE, ONCOLOGY. *Current Pos:* USPHS fel oncol, Univ Minn, Minneapolis, 68-70, instr, 70-73, asst prof, 73-81, assoc prof, 81-90, PROF MED, MED SCH, UNIV MINN, MINNEAPOLIS, 90- *Personal Data:* b Chekiang, China, Nov 13, 35; m 68; c 3. *Educ:* Nat Defense Med Ctr Taiwan, MB, 60; Columbia Univ, MS, 64; Univ Minn, PhD, 73. *Prof Exp:* Intern med, Beekman-Downtown Hosp, NY, 64-65, resident, 65-66; resident, Francis Delafield Hosp, 66-68. *Mem:* Soc Exp Biol & Med; Am Fedn Clin Res; Am Asn Cancer Res; Am Soc Clin Oncol; Sigma Xi. *Res:* Treatment of mammary cancer. *Mailing Add:* Dept Med Box 286 Mayo Univ Minn 420 Delaware St SE Minneapolis MN 55455-0392

KIANG, JULIANN G, SIGNAL TRANSDUCTION, HEAT SHOCK PROTEINS. *Current Pos:* res physiologist, 89-94, ASST CHIEF, DEPT CLIN PHYSIOL, WALTER REED ARMY INST RES, 94- *Personal Data:* b Taiwan, Dec 3, 52; US citizen; m 77, Peter M; c Sharon & Andrew. *Educ:* Fu-Jen Cath Univ, Taiwan, BS, 75; Univ Nebr, Omaha, MS, 77; Univ Calif, Berkely, PhD(toxicol), 83. *Honors & Awards:* Henry Christian Mem Award, Am Fedn Clin Res, 90 & 93. *Prof Exp:* Res technologist, Creighton Univ Hosp, Omaha, 77-78; asst toxicol specialist, Univ Calif, Berkeley, 84-88; res physiologist, Armed Forces Radiobiol Res Inst, 88-89. *Concurrent Pos:* Travel award, Nat Inst Drug Abuse, 82-87; jr investr travel award, Am Soc Gastroenterol, 92; asst prof pharmacol, Uniformed Serv Univ Health Sci, 92- *Mem:* Am Soc Cell Biol; Am Soc Pharmacol & Exp Therapeut; Soc Chinese Biologists Am. *Res:* Characterize heat shock proteins in cultured cell lines; investigate the relationship between heat shock protein and signal transduction; study the protective role of heat shock protein from environmental toxins toxicity. *Mailing Add:* Dept Clin Physiol Div Med Walter Reed Army Inst Res Bldg 40 Rm 3078 Washington DC 20307

KIANG, NELSON YUAN-SHENG, NEUROPHYSIOLOGY. *Current Pos:* RETIRED. *Personal Data:* b Wuxi, China, July 6, 29; m 57, 76, Barbara Norris; c Peter Nien-chu. *Educ:* Univ Chicago, PhB, 47, PhD(biopsychol), 55. *Hon Degrees:* MD, Univ Geneva, Switz, 81; MS, Harvard Univ. *Honors & Awards:* Beltone Award, Am Acad Arts & Sci, 68. *Prof Exp:* Dir, Eaton Peabody Lab, Mass Eye & Ear Infirmary, 62-96; neurophysiologist, Neurol Serv, Mass Gen Hosp, 77-96; prof, Dept Otol & Laryngol, Harvard Med Sch, 84-96. *Concurrent Pos:* Res asst otol, Harvard Med Sch, 57-61, res asst otolaryngol, 61-69, sr res assoc otolaryngol & physiol, 69-; mem, Commun Sci Study Sect, Div Res Grants, NIH, 68-72, Behav & Neurosci Study Sect, 85-89; mem, Comt Hearing Bioacoust & Biomech, Nat Acad Sci-Nat Res Coun, Collegium Otorhinol-Laryngol Amiticiam Sacrum, Deafness Res Found, & Int Brain Res Orgn; staff mem, Res Lab Electronics, Mass Inst Technol, 55-96, lectr elec eng, 68-83, Health Scis & Technol, Res Lab Electronics, 83-96; comn, Sci Freedom & Responsibility, AAAS, 95. *Mem:* AAAS; Soc Neurosci; Am Physiol Soc; fel Acoust Soc Am; Am Otol Soc; NY Acad Sci; Psychonomic Soc; Sigma Xi; Asn Res Otolaryngol; Royal Soc Med. *Res:* Physiology of auditory and other sensory systems; relation of brain to behavior. *Mailing Add:* Eaton-Peabody Lab Mass Eye & Ear Infirmary 243 Charles St Boston MA 02114-3004. *Fax:* 617-720-4408; *E-Mail:* bnk@epl.mcci.harvard.edu

KIANG, ROBERT L, MECHANICAL ENGINEERING, FLUID MECHANICS. *Current Pos:* MECH ENGR, DAVID TAYLOR RES CTR, 87- *Personal Data:* b Chungking, China, Nov 30, 39; US citizen; m 86; c 2. *Educ:* Nat Taiwan Univ, BS, 61; Stanford Univ, MS, 64, PhD(aeronaut eng), 70. *Prof Exp:* Res engr, Stanford Res Inst, 63-71, sr res engr, 71-87. *Concurrent Pos:* Teacher, USN Acad, Johns Hopkins Univ & San Jose State Univ. *Mem:* Am Soc Mech Engrs; Am Nuclear Soc. *Res:* Fluid dynamics; dynamic modeling; nuclear safety; heat transfer; noise and vibration; friction and lubrication. *Mailing Add:* 408 Hartman Dr Severna Park MD 21146

KIANG, YING CHAO, fiber optics, lasers, for more information see previous edition

KIANG, YUN-TZU, POPULATION GENETICS, PLANT BREEDING. *Current Pos:* from asst prof to assoc prof, 70-83, PROF PLANT SCI & GENETICS, UNIV NH, 83- *Personal Data:* b Taiwan, Feb 1, 32; US citizen; m 57; c 3. *Educ:* Taiwan Normal Univ, BS, 56; Ohio State Univ, MA, 62; Univ Calif, Berkeley, PhD(genetics), 70. *Prof Exp:* Res asst genetics, Univ Calif, Berkeley, 67-68, teaching asst, 68-69, teaching assoc, 69-70. *Concurrent Pos:* Vis prof, Taiwan Normal Univ, 78; vis scientist, Academia Sinica, 78 & 85; assoc ed, J Hered, 87- *Mem:* AAAS; Genetics Soc Am; Am Genetic Asn; Soc Study Evolution; Bot Soc Am; Am Soc Agron; Am Soc Naturalists; Genetics Soc Can. *Res:* Genetics and evolution of economic and natural plant populations. *Mailing Add:* 3 Magrath Rd Durham NH 03824

KIANI, MOHAMMAD F, BIOPHYSICS. *Current Pos:* NIH FEL, DEPT BIOPHYS, UNIV ROCHESTER, 90- *Educ:* Univ Okla, BSc, 83; La Tech Univ, MS, 87, PhD(biomed eng), 90. *Honors & Awards:* August Krough Young Investr Award, Am Microcirculatory Soc, 91, Young Investr Travel Award, 91. *Prof Exp:* Teaching asst, Dept Elec Eng, Univ Okla, 81-83; res teaching asst, Dept Biomed Eng, La Tech Univ, 84-90. *Mem:* Biomed Eng Soc; Microcirculatory Soc; Sigma Xi. *Res:* Mathematical modeling and simulation of network blood flow; microvascular growth and adaptation of hemodynamic factors; blood rheology and hemodynamics; in vitro cell culturing; in vivo hamster cremaster muscle preparations; high impedance instrumentation-microelectrode measurements; development of expert systems for biomedical applications; numerical methods, high performance computing and computer applications. *Mailing Add:* Dept Biomed Eng Univ Tenn 899 Madison Ave Suite 801 Memphis TN 38163

KIBBEL, WILLIAM H, JR, INORGANIC CHEMISTRY, PEROXYGEN CHEMICALS. *Current Pos:* RETIRED. *Personal Data:* b Buffalo, NY, Aug 31, 23; m 49, Anja T Inn; c Candace R & William H III. *Educ:* Case Inst Technol, BS, 44, MS, 48. *Prof Exp:* Chem eng reactor design, Buffalo Electro Chem Co, 47-52; sales mgr peroxy chem, Becco Sales Corp, 52-57, mgr mkt res, Becco Chem Div, 57-58; mgr indust appln develop, FMC Corp, 58-77, tech serv, 77-82 & tech admin, 82-85. *Mem:* Sigma Xi. *Res:* Pulp and paper; textiles; pollution control; metal surface treatments. *Mailing Add:* 24 Dublin Rd Pennington NJ 08534-2501

KIBBEY, MAURA CHRISTINE, EXTRACELLULAR MATRIX, METASTASIS. *Current Pos:* res biologist, 89-92, STAFF FEL, LAB DEVELOP BIOL, NAT INST DENT RES, NIH, 92- *Personal Data:* b Pittsburgh, Pa, Mar 13, 62; m 88, Timothy; c Siobhan. *Educ:* State Univ NY, Albany, BS, 83; Albany Med Col, PhD(anat & cell biol), 89. *Prof Exp:* Teaching asst gen biol, Va Polytech Inst & State Univ, 84, teaching asst histol, 85; teaching asst med gross anat & med histol, Albany Med Col, 87. *Concurrent Pos:* Inst med gross anat, Georgetown Univ Med Sch, 90. *Mem:* Am Soc Cell Biol; Sigma Xi. *Res:* Investigating the biological activity of laminin, as well as its receptors and proteases, with regard to tumor cell growth and metastasis and in the progression of Alzheimer's disease. *Mailing Add:* Igen Inc 16020 Industrial Dr Gaithersburg MD 20877. *Fax:* 301-230-0158

KIBBY, CHARLES LEONARD, CHEMICAL KINETICS, SURFACE CHEMISTRY. *Current Pos:* sr res assoc, 85-91, STAFF SCIENTIST, CHEVRON RES & TECHNOL CO, RICHMOND, CA, 91- *Personal Data:* b Wenatchee, Wash, Jan 2, 38; m 70, Diana; c Kenneth. *Educ:* Reed Col, BA, 59; Purdue Univ, PhD, 64. *Prof Exp:* Fel chem, Harvard Univ, 63-65; res assoc, Brookhaven Nat Lab, 65-67; fel catalysis, Mellon Inst Sci, Carnegie-Mellon Univ, 67-69; res chemist, Gulf Res & Develop Co, Pittsburgh, 70-75, res chemist, Pittsburgh Energy Res Ctr, 76-77, sr res chemist, 77-80, res assoc, 81-85. *Concurrent Pos:* Vis scientist catalysis, Inst Org Chem, Moscow, USSR, 74. *Mem:* Am Chem Soc; AAAS; Catalysis Soc. *Res:* Characterization of heterogeneous catalysts for hydrocarbon processing and chemicals production, by chemical and physical methods. *Mailing Add:* 846 Clifton Ct Benicia CA 94510. *E-Mail:* ckib@chevron.com

KIBENS, VALDIS, AEROACOUSTICS, TURBULENCE. *Current Pos:* sr scientist aeroacoust, 74-85, PRIN SCIENTIST, RES LABS, MCDONNELL DOUGLAS CORP, 85- *Personal Data:* b Riga, Latvia, Oct 22, 36; US citizen; m 58, 88; c 2. *Educ:* Yale Univ, BE, 57; Johns Hopkins Univ, PhD(mech), 68. *Prof Exp:* Res engr, Gen Dynamics Corp, Conn, 57-60; asst prof aerospace eng, Univ Mich, Ann Arbor, 68-74. *Concurrent Pos:* Consult & vis res scientist, Res Labs, Gen Motors Corp, Mich, 73. *Mem:* Am Phys Soc; assoc fel Am Inst Aeronaut & Astronaut; Sigma Xi. *Res:* Control of the development of turbulent structures in flow fields as the basis for technological devices to reduce aerodynamic noise, enhance mixing, and control buffeting. *Mailing Add:* 172 Hastings Way St Charles MO 63301-5506

KIBLER, KENNETH G, GEOPHYSICS, ENVIRONMENTAL SCIENCE. *Current Pos:* SR RES SCIENTIST, GEN DYNAMICS-CONVAIR AEROSPACE, 69-; ENG CHIEF STRUCT & MATS, LOCKHEED MARTIN, 95- *Personal Data:* b Peoria, Ill, Apr 15, 40; m 61; c 2. *Educ:* Univ Iowa, MS, 64, PhD(nuclear physics), 66. *Prof Exp:* Res asst nuclear physics, Univ Iowa, 62-66; res assoc, Case Western Res Univ, 66-69. *Concurrent Pos:* Asst prof, Tex Wesleyan Col, 69- *Mem:* AAAS; Am Phys Soc; Am Geophys Union. *Res:* Heavy-ion nuclear reactions; gravity measurement; remote sensing of earth resources; enhancement techniques for aerial or orbital images; physics of materials. *Mailing Add:* 8232 Saddlebrook Dr Ft Worth TX 76116-1417

KIBLER, RUTHANN, IMMUNOLOGY, VIROLOGY. *Current Pos:* ASST PROF BIOL, SAN JOSE STATE UNIV, 90- *Personal Data:* b Mansfield, Ohio, Dec 1, 42. *Educ:* Purdue Univ, BS, 64; Purdue Univ, MS, 67; Univ Calif, Berkeley, PhD(immunol), 73. *Prof Exp:* res scientist immmunol, Dept Microbiol, Col Med, Univ Ariz, 76-79, asst prof microbiol & immunol, 80-87; sr res scientist, Bio-Rad Lab, 87-89. *Concurrent Pos:* mem staff, Calif State Dept Health Serv, Berkeley, 79-80. *Mem:* Am Soc Microbiol; Sigma Xi; Am Asn Immunologists. *Res:* Flow cytometry-cell analysis. *Mailing Add:* Biol Dept San Jose State Univ San Jose CA 95192-0100. *Fax:* 408-446-0755; *E-Mail:* kibler@biomail.sjsu.edu

KIBRICK, ANNE K, EDUCATION. *Current Pos:* dean, 82-88, prof, 82-93, EMER PROF, UNIV MASS, 93- *Personal Data:* b Palmer, Mass, June 1, 19; m 49, Sidney; c Joan & John. *Educ:* Boston Univ, BS, 45; Columbia Teachers Col, 48; Harvard Univ, EdD, 58. *Hon Degrees:* DLitt, St Josephs Col. *Honors & Awards:* Nutting Award Leadership Nursing, Nat League Nursing, Stewart Award. *Prof Exp:* Asst educ dir, Cushing Mass Hosp, Framingham, 48-49; asst prof nursing, Simmons Col, 49-55; dir, Grad Div Nursing, Boston Univ Sch Nursing, 58-63, dean, 63-68, prof, 68-70; chmn, Dept Nursing, Boston Col Grad Sch Arts & Sci, 70-74 & Boston State Col, 74-82. *Concurrent Pos:* Mem staff, USPHS, NIH, 68-73; consult, Nat League Nursing, China, Soviet Union, Israel, Egypt, Australia & Africa; bd dir & exec comt, Post Grad Med Inst, Mass Med Soc. *Mem:* Nat Acad Sci; Inst Med; Nat League Nursing (pres, 71-73); fel Am Acad Nursing; Nat Acad Pract. *Res:* Self concept; role perception; occupational choice; minorities in nursing. *Mailing Add:* 381 Clinton Rd Brookline MA 02146. *Fax:* 617-265-7173

KIBRICK, SIDNEY, PEDIATRICS. *Current Pos:* assoc prof microbiol, Sch Med, Boston Univ, 61-67, chief, Sect Virol, Univ Hosp, 61-68, assoc prof med, 61-81, prof microbiol, 67-81, prof pediat, 72-81, EMER PROF PEDIAT & MICROBIOL & EMER ASSOC PROF MED, SCH MED, BOSTON UNIV, 82- *Personal Data:* b Boston, Mass, Apr 2, 16; m 49, Anne Karlon; c John D & Joan E. *Educ:* Harvard Univ, AB, 38; Mass Inst Technol, PhD(bact), 43; Boston Univ, MD, 46; Am Bd Pediat, dipl, 53; Am Bd Microbiol, dipl, 65. *Prof Exp:* Res assoc bact, Sch Med, Univ Boston, 43-44; intern med, Mass Mem Hosps, Boston, 46-47; jr asst resident med, Children's Hosp Med Ctr, 50-52; asst pediat, Harvard Med Sch, 52-53, instr, 53-56, res assoc, 56-57, assoc, 57-60, asst clin prof, 60-61. *Concurrent Pos:* USPHS res fel, Children's Hosp Med Ctr, Boston, 49-50, res assoc, 52-62, from asst physician to assoc physician, 52-61, consult, 61-; lectr microbiol, Sch Med, Boston Univ, 53-61; lectr pediat, Harvard Med Sch, 61-65; vis physician, Boston City Hosp & Boston Univ Hosp, 61-82; med consult, Disability Qual Br, Soc Sec Admin, HHS, 81- *Mem:* Soc Pediat Res; Infectious Dis Soc Am; Am Pediat Soc; Am Soc Microbiol; Nat Found Infectious Dis; Am Soc Virol. *Res:* Virology; infectious diseases. *Mailing Add:* Boston Univ Med Ctr 80 E Concord St Boston MA 02118

KICE, JOHN LORD, ORGANIC CHEMISTRY. *Current Pos:* prof & chmn dept, 85-88, dean, 88-95, EMER PROF SCI, MATH & ENG, UNIV DENVER, 95- *Personal Data:* b Colorado Springs, Colo, Feb 18, 30; m 53, Ellen Bass; c Virginia & Joanne. *Educ:* Harvard Univ, AB, 50, MA, 53, PhD(chem), 54. *Prof Exp:* Sr chemist, Rohm and Haas Co, 53-56; from asst prof to assoc prof chem, Univ SC, 56-60; from assoc prof to prof, Ore State Univ, 60-70; prof & chmn dept, Univ Vt, 70-75; chmn dept, chem, Tex Tech Univ, 75-85. *Concurrent Pos:* Fel, Japan Soc Prom Sci, 83; NIH spec fel, 68-69. *Mem:* Am Chem Soc; Sigma Xi. *Res:* Organic reaction mechanisms; free radical reactions; organic sulfur chemistry; organic selenium chemistry. *Mailing Add:* Dept Chem Univ Denver Denver CO 80208

KICHER, THOMAS PATRICK, ENGINEERING MECHANICS. *Current Pos:* asst prof eng, Case Western Res Univ, 65-68, assoc prof mech eng, 68-81, assoc dean sci & eng, 74-79, PROF MECH ENG, CASE WESTERN RES UNIV, 81-, CHMN DEPT MECH & AEROSPACE ENG, 85- *Personal Data:* b Johnsonburg, Pa, Oct 20, 37; m 62; c 3. *Educ:* Case West Res Univ, BS, 59, MS, 62, PhD(eng mech), 64. *Prof Exp:* Res engr, Aeronca Mfg Co, 59; res asst, Case Western Res Univ, 59-64; design engr, Douglas Aircraft Co, Inc, Calif, 64-65. *Concurrent Pos:* Consult, 65- *Mem:* Am Inst Aeronaut & Astronaut; Am Soc Mech Engrs; Soc Exp Mech. *Res:* Computer methods of optimum design; basic phenomena of buckling of elastic systems; analysis and testing of composite materials; analysis and testing of plates and shells; failure analysis and design. *Mailing Add:* Eng Case Western Res Univ Univ Circle Cleveland OH 44106-1749

KICKLER, THOMAS STEVEN, HEMATOLOGY. *Current Pos:* from asst prof to assoc prof, 80-96, PROF, JOHNS HOPKINS SCH MED, 96- *Personal Data:* b Pittsburgh, Pa, July 7, 47. *Educ:* W Va Univ, BA, 69, MD, 73. *Prof Exp:* Fel path, Johns Hopkins Univ, 74-76; fel med, Mayo Grad Sch, 76-78; fel hemat, Univ Rochester, 78-80. *Concurrent Pos:* Dir Hemat & Coagulation Lab, Dept Path. *Mem:* Am Soc Hemat; Am Asn Blood Banks; Col Am Path. *Res:* Platelet immunology; blood transfusion therapy; blood coagulation; laboratory testing for blood disorders. *Mailing Add:* Johns Hopkins Hosp Meyer B12 600 N Wolfe St Baltimore MD 21205. *Fax:* 410-955-0767; *E-Mail:* tkickler@uelchlink.welch.jhu.edu

KICLITER, ERNEST EARL, JR, NEUROANATOMY, COLOR VISION. *Current Pos:* assoc prof, 77-84, PROF ANAT, SCH MED, UNIV PR, 84- *Personal Data:* b Ft Pierce, Fla, June 19, 45; c Jennifer A. *Educ:* Univ Fla, BA, 68; State Univ NY Upstate Med Ctr, PhD(anat), 73. *Prof Exp:* Asst prof neuroanat, Col Med, Sch Basic Med Sci & asst prof physiol, Col Lib Arts & Sci, Univ Ill, Urbana-Champaign, 74-77. *Concurrent Pos:* NIH fel neurol surg, Sch Med, Univ Va, 72-74; vis prof, Univ Med Sch, Pecs, Hungary, 76. *Mem:* Fel AAAS; Soc Neurosci; Am Asn Anatomists; Cajal Club; J B Johnston Club. *Res:* Comparative studies of structure and function in vertebrate visual systems; color vision and neuronal plasticity in visual systems. *Mailing Add:* c/o Inst Neurobiol Blvd del Valle 201 San Juan PR 00901

KICSKA, PAUL A, PHYSICS. *Current Pos:* PROF PHYSICS, ESTROUDSBURG STATE COL, 67- *Personal Data:* b New York, NY, Nov 23, 32; m 60; c 3. *Educ:* Muhlenberg Col, BS, 58; Lehigh Univ, MS, 60, PhD(physics), 65. *Prof Exp:* Instr math, Lafayette Col, 58-60; engr, Bell Tel Labs, 60-61; instr physics, Lafayette Col, 61-63; engr, Gen Elec Co, 66-67. *Concurrent Pos:* Chief consult, Tech Consult Serv, 67- *Mem:* Am Phys Soc; Sigma Xi; Soc Physics Students; AAAS; Nat Fluid Power Asn. *Res:* Analytic description of vehicle collisions; accident reconstruction. *Mailing Add:* 2425 Norwood Ave Easton PA 18045

KIDAWA, ANTHONY STANLEY, PODIATRIC MEDICINE & SURGERY, ANGIOLOGY. *Current Pos:* chmn med, 74-84, PROF MED, PA COL PODIATRIC MED, 70-, DIR, VASCULAR LAB, 84- *Personal Data:* b Philadelphia, Pa, Apr 1, 42; m 69, Nancy A Skokowski; c Kevin & Lori. *Educ:* Villanova Univ, BS, 64, Pa Col Pediat Med, DPM, 69. *Honors & Awards:* William J Stickel Silver Medal, Am Podiatry Asn, 82, William J Stickel Bronze Medal, 85. *Prof Exp:* Resident podiatric med & surg, James C Guiffre Med Ctr, Philadelphia, 69-70. *Concurrent Pos:* Staff podiatrist, James C Guiuffre Med Ctr, Philadelphia, 71-82 & JFK Washington Div Hosp, Turnersville, 73-84; consult, Bionic Instruments, Bala Cynwyd, Pa, 72-74, Pa Blue Shield, 74, Sentry Instruments, Inc, Atlanta, Ga, 74-76, Vascular Diag Instruments, Cherry Hill, 76-82, NJ State Bd Med Examrs, 82 & Advan Diag, Inc, Oak Ridge, Tenn, 83-85; dir res educ podiatry, JFK Washington Div Hosp, Turnersville, 76-80; vis lectr podiatry, Ohio Col Podiatric Med, Cleveland, 80-81; vis lectr angiol, Logan Col Chiropractic, St Louis, 81-83; pres & dir angiol, Clindialab Inc, Cherry Hill, NJ, 84-; ed podiatry, J Am Podiatric Med Asn, 84- *Mem:* Am Podiatry Med Asn; Am Asn Hosp Podiatrists; Am Asn Col Podiatric Med; Am Soc Podiatric Angiol (pres, 83-); Am Diabetes Asn. *Res:* Effects of hypothermia and anesthetic blocks on the peripheral circulation; physiological studies for determining various parameters of circulation in the lower extremities; clinical trials for antifungal medication in the treatment of pedal fungus infections and vasodilators in the treatment of peripheral vascular diseases. *Mailing Add:* Pa Col Podiatric Med 810 Race St Philadelphia PA 19107

KIDD, BERNARD SEAN LANGFORD, CARDIOVASCULAR PHYSIOLOGY. *Current Pos:* RETIRED. *Personal Data:* b Belfast, Northern Ireland, July 7, 31; m 58; c 4. *Educ:* Queen's Univ Belfast, MB, BCh & BAO, 54, MD, 57. *Prof Exp:* Asst lectr physiol, Queen's Univ Belfast, 55-57; tutor & registr, Royal Victoria Hosp, Belfast, 57-60; physician & assoc scientist, Hosp for Sick Children, 61-67; assoc prof pediat physiol, Univ Toronto, 61-75; dep dir, Johns Hopkins Univ, 73-75, Harriet Lane Home prof pediat cardiol & dir div, Sch Med, 75-96, dir, Div Pediat Cardiol, 96. *Concurrent Pos:* Physician & assoc scientist, Hosp Sick Children, 67-75. *Mem:* Am Pediat Soc; Can Soc Clin Invest; Am Col Cardiol; Am Heart Asn; Soc Pediat Res. *Res:* Circulatory physiology, hemodynamics in congenital heart disease. *Mailing Add:* Helen B Taussig Children's Cardiac Ctr Johns Hopkins Univ Hosp 600 N Wolfe St Baltimore MD 21205

KIDD, DAVID EUGENE, PHYCOLOGY, RESERVOIR WATER QUALITY. *Current Pos:* from assoc prof to prof biol, 67-89, EMER PROF SCI EDUC & BIOL, UNIV NMEX, 89- *Personal Data:* b Evanston, Ill, Apr 13, 30; m 55, Dolores Dichtenmiller; c David, Dennis & Deborah. *Educ:* Ariz State Col, BS, 51; Northwestern Univ, MS, 52; Univ NH, MST, 60; Mich State Univ, PhD(bot), 63. *Prof Exp:* Sci teacher high sch, Ariz, 54-55; prof chem, Lindsey Wilson Col, 55-56; sci teacher high sch, Ariz, 56-60; asst prof natural sci, Mich State Univ, 60-67. *Concurrent Pos:* Grants, Am Philos Soc, 64-66; fel, Sigma Xi, 65-66; NSF Undergrad Equip, 69-71; Water Resources Inst, 69-72; NSF, 71-77; vol exec dir, Ajo Ariz Dist Chamber Com. *Mem:* Am Micros Soc; Am Chem Soc; Nat Sci Teachers Asn; Sigma Xi. *Res:* Taxonomy and ecology of algae in polluted ranch ponds in northern Arizona; carbon-14 primary productivity and population dynamics of phytoplankton in Elephant Butte Reservoir and Lake Powell; nutrient loading models and their modification as applied to Southwestern reservoirs. *Mailing Add:* 141 E Fifth St Ajo AZ 85321

KIDD, FRANK ALAN, PLANT PHYSIOLOGY. *Current Pos:* MEM STAFF, DOW CHEM USA. *Personal Data:* b Dodge City, Kans, July 24, 52; m 73. *Educ:* Ore State Univ, BS, 74; Colo State Univ, MS, 76, PhD(tree physiol), 82. *Prof Exp:* Teaching asst forestry, Ore State Univ, 73-74; teaching asst forest biomet, econ & physiol, Colo State Univ, 74-81, res asst forest tree physiol, 74-80, instr forest ecol, 80-81; res forester, Potlatch Corp, 81- *Concurrent Pos:* Consult, Repub Nat Bank, Dallas, Tex, 76-82; contributing researcher, Lightwood Res Coord Coun, US Forest Serv, 76-78. *Mem:* AAAS; Soc Am Foresters; Am Forestry Asn; Sigma Xi. *Res:* Forest tree physiology; mycorrhizal relationships; physiological consequences of silvicultural treatment of conifers. *Mailing Add:* 13916 Sandy Creek Ct Carmel IN 46032-8979

KIDD, GEORGE JOSEPH, JR, MECHANICAL ENGINEERING. *Current Pos:* Assoc engr, Y-12 Plant, Martin Marietta Energy Systs Inc, 57-58, res staff mem reactor develop, Oak Ridge Nat Lab, 58-68, develop engr, 68-77, DEPT SUPVR, OAK RIDGE GASEOUS DIFFUSION PLANT, MARTIN MARIETTA ENERGY SYSTS, INC, 77- *Personal Data:* b Grand Rapids, Mich, May 6, 34; m 56; c 3. *Educ:* Northwestern Univ, BS, 56, MS, 57; Univ Tenn, PhD(eng sci), 66. *Mem:* Am Soc Mech Engrs; Am Inst Chem Engrs; Nat Soc Prof Engrs. *Res:* Heat transfer; fluid mechanics. *Mailing Add:* 120 Windham Rd Oak Ridge TN 37830

KIDD, HAROLD J, CYTOGENETICS, PLANT MORPHOLOGY. *Current Pos:* RETIRED. *Personal Data:* b Billings, Okla, Jan 30, 24; m 55; c 2. *Educ:* Okla State Univ, BS, 49, MS, 51; Wash Univ, PhD(bot), 56. *Prof Exp:* Instr bot, Okla State Univ, 51-53; br plant mgr, Plant Breeding, Pioneer Hi-Bred Int, Inc, 55-83. *Mem:* Am Genetics Asn; Sigma Xi; AAAS; Bot Soc Am; Am Inst Biol Sci. *Res:* Cultivated sorghum; plant breeding; morphology. *Mailing Add:* 1617 Dallas St Plainview TX 79072

KIDD, KENNETH KAY, POPULATION GENETICS, HUMAN GENETICS. *Current Pos:* asst prof, 73-78, assoc prof human genetics, 78-81, assoc prof human genetics & psychiat, 81-86, PROF HUMAN GENETICS & PSYCHIATRY & BIOL, SCH MED, YALE UNIV, 86- *Personal Data:* b Bakersfield, Calif, Sept 5, 41; m 64. *Educ:* Univ Southern Calif, AB, 65; Univ Wis, MS, 67, PhD(genetics), 69; Am Bd Med Genetics, dipl, 82. *Prof Exp:* Res assoc genetics, Sch Med, Stanford Univ, 71-72; asst prof anthrop genetics, Sch Med, Washington Univ, 72-73. *Concurrent Pos:* NIH fel, Univ Pavia, 69-71 & Sch Med, Stanford Univ, 71; mem, NIH Study Sect, Mammalian Genetics, 79-83; vis assoc prof, Harvard Univ, 81-82; vis scientist, Mass Inst Technol, 82; bd dir, Am Bd Med Genetics, 82-84; ed bd, J Genetics, 86- & J Genomics, 87- *Mem:* Genetics Soc Am; Soc Study Evolution; Am Soc Human Genetics; Am Asn Phys Anthrop; Behav Genetics Asn; fel AAAS. *Res:* Genetics of human behavioral disorders; genetic relationships of human populations; human gene mapping. *Mailing Add:* 333 Cedar St Yale Univ Sch Med New Haven CT 06510-8005

KIDD, RICHARD WAYNE, PHYSICAL CHEMISTRY. *Current Pos:* STAFF MEM, HITCO INC, 97- *Personal Data:* b Westminster, Md, June 16, 47; m 69; c 1. *Educ:* Western Md Col, BA, 69; Univ Ill, MS, 71, PhD(chem), 75. *Prof Exp:* Teaching & res assoc, Univ Ill, Urbana, 69-75, res assoc chem, 75-77; res scientist, Mat Technol Sect, Battelle Mem Inst, 77-80, prin res scientist, Ceramics & Mat Processing Sect, Columbus Lab, 80-; staff mem, San Fernando Labs, Pacoima. *Mem:* Am Chem Soc; Sigma Xi. *Res:* Mathematical modeling and experimental determination of isotope effects in chemical reactions; mechanisms of reactions; chemical vapor deposition of coatings to enhance the properties of the substrate material. *Mailing Add:* 63 Rockinghorse Rd Rancho Palos Verde CA 90275-6569

KIDD, ROBERT GARTH, INORGANIC CHEMISTRY. *Current Pos:* Asst prof, 63-69, asst dean grad studies, 70-83, ASSOC PROF CHEM, UNIV WESTERN ONT, 69- *Personal Data:* b Stockton-on-Tees, Eng, July 19, 36; Can citizen; m 59, Edna Engen; c Jon, Dale & Warren. *Educ:* Univ Man, BSc, 58, MSc, 60; Univ London, PhD(chem), 62. *Mem:* Chem Inst Can; Am Chem Soc. *Res:* Nature of bonding in transition metal complexes; nuclear magnetic resonance spectroscopy of inorganic compounds; philosophy of science. *Mailing Add:* Dept Chem Univ Western Ont London ON N6A5B7 Can

KIDD, WILLIAM SPENCER FRANCIS, GEOLOGY. *Current Pos:* lectr, 74, asst prof, 75-81, ASSOC PROF GEOL, STATE UNIV NY, ALBANY, 81- *Personal Data:* b Shawford, Eng, Feb 23, 47; UK citizen; m 84; c 1. *Educ:* Univ Cambridge, Eng, BA, 69, PhD(geol), 74. *Prof Exp:* Vis lectr geol, Erindale Col, Univ Toronto, 72-73. *Mem:* Am Geophys Union; Geol Soc Am; AAAS. *Res:* Structural geology; tectonics; Appalachian geology; orogenic belts; Tibet. *Mailing Add:* Dept Geol Sci State Univ NY 1400 Washington Ave Albany NY 12222. *E-Mail:* wkidd@atmos.albany.edu

KIDDER, ERNEST H(IGLEY), engineering, for more information see previous edition

KIDDER, GEORGE WALLACE, JR, BIOLOGY, BIOCHEMISTRY. *Current Pos:* assoc prof, 46-49, Stone prof, 49-70, EMER PROF BIOL, AMHERST COL, 70- *Personal Data:* b Oregon City, Ore, Dec 29, 02; m 30; c 3. *Educ:* Univ Ore, AB, 26; Univ Calif, MA, 29; Columbia Univ, PhD(zool), 32. *Hon Degrees:* MA, Amherst Col, 49; ScD, Wesleyan Univ, 50. *Prof Exp:* Teacher pub sch, Ore, 26-28; instr biol, City Col New York, 29-37; asst prof, Brown Univ, 37-46. *Concurrent Pos:* Mem corp, Marine Biol Lab, Woods Hole, 43-47; chmn, vitamins & metab, Gordon Res Confs, 57; mem, Training Grant Comt, NIH, 60-64; vis prof biochem, Univ Calif, Santa Cruz, 68. *Mem:* Fel AAAS; fel Am Acad Microbiol; hon mem Am Soc Microbiol; fel Am Acad Arts & Sci; fel Am Soc Protozoologists. *Res:* Protozoan cytology and physiology; biochemistry of microorganisms; vitamins and amino acids; purine and pyrimidine metabolism in Trypanosomatid flagellates; metabolism; nutrition; chemotherapy of cancer. *Mailing Add:* Biol Lab Amherst Col Amherst MA 01002-5002

KIDDER, GEORGE WALLACE, III, PHYSIOLOGY, BIOPHYSICS. *Current Pos:* chmn, 84-91, PROF, DEPT BIOL SCI, ILL STATE UNIV, 84- *Personal Data:* b New York, NY, Sept 24, 34; m 57; c 2. *Educ:* Amherst Col, AB, 56; Univ Pa, PhD(bot), 61. *Prof Exp:* Res fel, Johnson Found, Univ Pa, 61-62; res fel biophys labs, Harvard Med Sch, 62-64; asst prof biol, Wesleyan Univ, 64-73; from assoc prof to prof physiol, Univ Md Sch Dent, 73-84. *Concurrent Pos:* USPHS fel, Harvard Univ, 64. *Mem:* AAAS; Am Physiol Soc; Biophys Soc. *Res:* Gastric acid secretion; electrophysiology; active transport of ions in relation to aerobic metabolism. *Mailing Add:* Ill State Univ Campus Box 4120 Ill State Univ Normal IL 61790. *Fax:* 309-438-3722; *E-Mail:* gkidder@llstu.edu

KIDDER, GERALD, SOIL FERTILITY, LAND APPLICATION OF NON-HAZARDOUS WASTES. *Current Pos:* asst prof agron, 75-80, assoc prof, 80-88, PROF SOIL SCI, INST FOOD & AGR SCI, UNIV FLA, 88- *Personal Data:* b Leonville, La, Jan 2, 40; m 66, Kathryn Larme; c Andrew W, Daniel P & Elizabeth Y. *Educ:* Univ Southwestern La, BS, 61; Univ Ill, MS, 64; Okla State Univ, PhD(soil sci), 69. *Prof Exp:* Lab asst soil nitrogen, Univ Ill, 63-64; vol, Papal Vol Latin Am, US Cath Bishops' Conf, 64-66; res agronomist, Standard Fruit Co, Castle & Cooke, Inc, 69-72, mgr agr serv, 72-75. *Mem:* Am Soc Agron; Int Soc Soil Sci; Soil Sci Soc Am; Sigma Xi. *Res:* Beneficial utilization of non-hazardous wastes through application to land. *Mailing Add:* Univ Fla PO Box 110290 Gainesville FL 32611-0290. *Fax:* 904-392-3902; *E-Mail:* kidder@gnv.ifas.ufl.edu

KIDDER, GERALD MARSHALL, DEVELOPMENTAL BIOLOGY, DEVELOPMENTAL GENETICS. *Current Pos:* from asst prof to assoc prof, 72-89, prof zool, 89-96, PROF PHYSIOL, UNIV WESTERN ONT, 96- *Personal Data:* b Harlingen, Tex, Dec 26, 44; m 83, Brigitte Moritz; c Joanna & Andrew. *Educ:* Hiram Col, BA, 66; Yale Univ, PhD(biol), 71. *Honors & Awards:* Millipore Can Res Team Award, 91. *Prof Exp:* Res fel biol sci, Reed Col, Ore, 71-72. *Concurrent Pos:* Res scientist, Alpha Helix Exped, Honduras Reef, 77; mem, bd trustees, Soc Develop Biol, 77-80 & 86-91; vis res assoc radiobiol, Med Sch, Univ Calif, San Francisco, 79-80; mem, Spec Study Sect, Nat Inst Child Health & Human Develop, 86; vis scientist, Mass Inst Technol, 86-87; distinguished res prof, Univ Western Ont, 90-91; mem sci officer, Pathol & Morphol Grants Comt, Med Res Coun Can, 95- *Mem:* Fel AAAS; Am Soc Cell Biol; Can Soc Biochem, Cellular & Molecular Biol; Soc Develop Biol; Can Fedn Biol Sci; Genetics Soc Am. *Res:* Developmental genetics of the early embryo: genetic control of morphogenesis and the early events of cell differentiation; control of gene expression in early mammalian development; development of the female gene line. *Mailing Add:* Dept Physiol Univ Western Ont London ON N6A 5C1 Can. *Fax:* 519-661-3827; *E-Mail:* gkidder@physiology.uwo.ca

KIDDER, JOHN NEWELL, PHYSICS, PHYSIOLOGICAL OPTICS. *Current Pos:* from asst prof to assoc prof, 62-74, chmn, dept physics, 84-90, PROF PHYSICS, DARTMOUTH COL, 74- *Personal Data:* b Boston, Mass, Apr 30, 32; m 60; c 3. *Educ:* Calif Inst Technol, BS, 54; Duke Univ, PhD(physics), 60. *Prof Exp:* Res assoc physics, Yale Univ, 60-62. *Concurrent Pos:* NSF fac fel, 71-72. *Mem:* Am Phys Soc; Am Asn Physics Teachers; Optical Soc Am; Inter-Soc Col Coun; Asn Res Vision & Ophthal; Sigma Xi. *Res:* Color science; vision; models of visual response. *Mailing Add:* Wilder Lab Dartmouth Col Hanover NH 03755

KIDDER, RAY EDWARD, APPLIED MATHEMATICS, PHYSICS. *Current Pos:* assoc div leader, Theoret Div, 56-90, ASSOC, LAWRENCE LIVERMORE LAB, UNIV CALIF, 90- *Personal Data:* b New York, NY, Nov 12, 23; m 47; c 3. *Educ:* Ohio State Univ, PhD(physics), 50. *Honors & Awards:* Alexander von Humboldt Award, 89. *Prof Exp:* Sr physicist, Calif Res Corp, 50-56. *Mem:* Fel Am Phys Soc. *Res:* Thermonuclear physics; astrophysics; quantum electronics. *Mailing Add:* 637 E Angela St Pleasanton CA 94566

KIDNAY, ARTHUR J, CHEMICAL ENGINEERING, PHYSICAL CHEMISTRY. *Current Pos:* from asst prof to assoc prof, Colo Sch Mines, 68-76, prof chem & petrol refining eng, 77-83, dept head Chem Eng, 83-90, DEAN GRAD STUDIES & RES, COLO SCH MINES, 90- *Personal Data:* b Milwaukee, Wis, Apr 4, 34; m 60; c 3. *Educ:* Colo Sch Mines, BS, 56, DSc(chem eng), 68; Univ Colo, MS, 61. *Prof Exp:* Proj engr, Monsanto Chem Co, Mass, 56-58; res engr, Cryogenics Div, Nat Bur Standards, Colo, 59-68. *Mem:* Am Inst Chem Engrs; Am Soc Eng Educ. *Res:* Solid-vapor and liquid vapor equilibria at cryogenic temperatures; physical adsorption at cryogenic temperatures. *Mailing Add:* 627 S Cole St Lakewood CO 80228

KIDWELL, ALBERT LAWS, PETROLEUM GEOLOGY. *Current Pos:* RETIRED. *Personal Data:* b Auxvasse, Mo, Jan 1, 19; m 43; c 4. *Educ:* Mo Sch Mines, BS, 40; Wash Univ, MS, 42; Univ Chicago, PhD(geol), 49. *Prof Exp:* Photogrammetric engr, US Coast & Geod Surv, 42-44; geologist, Mo Geol Surv, 44-47; res geologist, Carter Oil Co, 50-58; sect head, Jersey Prod Res Co, 58-65; res assoc, Esso Prod Res Co, 65-73, sr res assoc, Exxon Prod Res Co, 73-84. *Mem:* Geol Soc Am; Mineral Soc Am; Am Asn Petrol Geol; Soc Econ Geol. *Res:* Igneous and economic geology. *Mailing Add:* 14403 Carolcrest Dr Houston TX 77079

KIDWELL, MARGARET GALE, EVOLUTIONARY GENETICS, DROSOPHILA. *Current Pos:* prof ecol & evolutionary biol, 85-, head ecol & evolutionary biol, 92-96, REGENTS PROF ECOL EVOLUTION BIOL, UNIV ARIZ, 94- *Personal Data:* b Askham, Eng, Aug 17, 33; wid; c Mary R & Stella M. *Educ:* Nottingham Univ, BSc, 53; Iowa State Univ, MS, 62; Brown Univ, PhD(genetics), 73. *Prof Exp:* Adv officer agr, Ministry Agr, London, 55-60; assoc res, Brown Univ, 66-70, res fel, 73-74, res assoc, 74-75, investr, 75-77, from asst prof to prof biol, 77-85. *Mem:* Nat Acad Sci; Am Genetic Asn (pres, 91); Am Soc Naturalists (vpres, 84); Genetics Soc Am; Soc Study Evolution; Sigma Xi; fel AAAS; fel Am Acad Arts & Lett; Soc Molecular Biol & Evolution. *Res:* Drosophila genetics and evolution; recombination transposable elements; speciation. *Mailing Add:* Dept Ecol & Evolutionary Biol Univ Ariz Tucson AZ 85721-0001. *Fax:* 520-621-9190; *E-Mail:* mkidwell@ccit.arizona.edu

KIDWELL, ROGER LYNN, synthetic organic chemistry, for more information see previous edition

KIEBER, ROBERT JOHN, ENVIRONMENTAL CHEMISTRY. *Current Pos:* asst prof, 89-94, ASSOC PROF CHEM, UNIV NC, 94- *Personal Data:* b Red Bank, NJ, June 10, 60; m 85, Cecilia Baylouny; c Marissa & Robert. *Educ:* Rutgers Univ, BS, 82; Univ Md, PhD(environ chem), 87. *Prof Exp:* Postdoctoral fel, Rosenthiel Sch Marine & Atmospheric Sci, Univ Miami, 88-89. *Concurrent Pos:* Prin investr, NSF, 95- *Mem:* Am Chem Soc; Am Soc Limnol & Oceanog; Am Geophys Union. *Res:* Air-sea exchange processes including hydrogen ion and carbon deposition; trace metal photchemistry in seawater. *Mailing Add:* Dept Chem Univ NC Wilmington NC 28412. *Fax:* 910-962-3013; *E-Mail:* kieberr@uncwil.edu

KIEBLER, JOHN W(ILLIAM), COMMUNICATION SATELLITES, ORBIT & SPECTRUM UTILIZATION. *Current Pos:* CONSULT, 96- *Personal Data:* b Hershey, Pa, Apr 1, 28; m 81, Barbara Brunner; c Ruth K, Robert K, Jean (O'Donnell). *Educ:* Lafayette Col, BS, 50. *Honors & Awards:* Except Serv Medal, NASA, 85. *Prof Exp:* Electronic scientist, Nat Bur Stand, 51-52; proj engr, Off Chief Ord, 52-53; assoc engr, Appl Physics Lab, Johns Hopkins Univ, 53-58, sr engr, 58-59, prin engr, Emerson Res Labs, 59-60; head, Network Implementation Br, Goddard Space Flight Ctr, NASA, 60-65, actg chief, Proj Opers Support Div, 65-66, asst chief, 66-70, proj mgr, Satellite Tracking & Data Acquisition, 70-73, sr engr, Commun Div, 73-79, sr commun engr, NASA Hq, 79-85, head, Tech Consult Serv, 85-89, telecommun consult, 90-91, sr adv, Atlantic Res Corp, 91-92; lead engr, Mitre Corp, 96. *Concurrent Pos:* Mem, US Deleg World Admin Radio Conf, 79, 83, 85 & 88, Comt Radio Frequencies & Int Radio Consult Comt, Nat Acad Sci. *Mem:* Inst Elec & Electronics Engrs. *Res:* Communications systems; remote sensing; regulatory filings; radio wave propagation. *Mailing Add:* 14520 Dowling Dr Burtonsville MD 20866. *Fax:* 202-646-9109; *E-Mail:* jkiebler@mitre.org

KIEBURTZ, R(OBERT) BRUCE, ELECTRICAL ENGINEERING, TELECOMMUNICATIONS SYSTEM ENGINEERING. *Current Pos:* PRIN, KIEBURTZ ENG CONSULTS, 90- *Personal Data:* b Seattle, Wash, Mar 22, 31; m 54; c Geoffrey B & Karl D. *Educ:* Univ Wash, BSEE, 52, MSEE, 63, PhD(elec eng), 66. *Prof Exp:* Proj engr, Gen Elec Co, 54-57; res engr, Boeing Co, 57-65, supvr, 66-67; mem tech staff, Bell Tel Labs, 67-77, asst eng mgr, Network Planning & Bus Serv, AT&T Co, 77-83, mgr, AT&T Bell Labs, 88-89. *Mem:* AAAS; sr mem Inst Elec & Electronics Engrs; NY Acad Sci; Sigma Xi. *Res:* Ballistic missile defense; balanced magnetic circuits for logic and memory; digital processing of signals, including digital filtering. *Mailing Add:* 14 Cramer Dr Rm 1a12 Chester NJ 07930

KIEBURTZ, RICHARD B(RUCE), COMPUTER SCIENCE. *Current Pos:* mem tech staff, Prin Res Lab, Bell Labs, dist eng mgr prod planning & support, 77-80, dist mgr, 80-83, eng staff mgr info systs, 83-85, SUPVR DATA NETWORKING GROUP, AT&T BELL LABS, WHIPPANY, NJ, 85- *Personal Data:* b Spokane, Wash, Nov 28, 33; m 59; c 2. *Educ:* Univ Wash, BSEE, 55, MSEE, 57, PhD(elec eng), 61. *Prof Exp:* Develop engr, Gen Elec Co, 54-57; from res engr to group mgr ballistic missile defense, Boeing Co, 57-67. *Concurrent Pos:* Consult, CBS Labs, Conn, 62-63 & Rome Air Develop Ctr, USAF, 63-68; NSF sci fac fel, 68-69. *Mem:* AAAS; sr mem Inst Elec & Electronics Engrs; NY Acad Sci. *Res:* programming languages; distributed computing. *Mailing Add:* 515 NW 86th Ct Portland OR 97226

KIECH, EARL LOCKETT, ARTIFICIAL INTELLIGENCE. *Current Pos:* SCI PROGRAMMER, CALSPAN CORP, 73- *Personal Data:* b Jonesboro, Ark, Jan 29, 49. *Educ:* Southwestern Memphis, BS, 71; Memphis State Univ, MS, 73. *Concurrent Pos:* Sci programmer, Univ Tenn Space Inst, 87- *Mem:* Am Phys Soc; Sigma Xi. *Res:* Researching a program to diagnose mechanical problems or faults with the main engine in the space shuttle. *Mailing Add:* 306 Crosslake Dr Tullahoma TN 37388

KIECHLE, FREDERICK LEONARD, CLINICAL CHEMISTRY, INSULIN ACTION. *Current Pos:* CLIN ASSOC PROF PATH, WAYNE STATE UNIV SCH MED, 88-; CHMN DEPT CLIN PATH, WILLIAM BEAUMONT HOSP, 88- *Personal Data:* b Indianapolis, Ind, Mar 26, 46; m, Janet B Green; c Rachel, Elizabeth & Jonathan. *Educ:* Evansville Col, BA, 68; Ind Univ, PhD(chem), 73, MD, 75. *Honors & Awards:* Clin Scientist Year Award, Asn Clin Scientist, 96. *Prof Exp:* Resident path, William Beaumont Hosp, 75-79; res fel clin chem, Barnes Hosp, 79-80; asst prof path, Univ Pa Sch Med, 80-83; chief clin chem, Dept Clin Path, William Beaumont Hosp, 83-88; clin asst prof path, Wayne State Univ Sch Med, 84-88. *Concurrent Pos:* Vis lectr, Nat Univ Singapore, 84; adv & mem, subcomt, Nat Comt Clin Lab Stand, 87-94; mem coun spec topics, Am Soc Clin Path, 88-94; fel, Hartford Found, 82-83; chmn & adv, Patient Prep & Specimen Handling Comt, 89-96; mem, Therapeut Drug & Resource Comt, Col Am Pathologists, 90-95. *Mem:* Am Soc Clin Pathologists; Am Soc Invest Path; Am Asn Clin Chem; Am Diabetes Asn; Col Am Pathologists; Am Fedn Clin Res; Asn Clin Scientists; Am Med Asn; Am Chem Soc; Cliin Legend Assay Soc. *Res:* Unraveling the temporal sequence of rapid events which occur following the binding of insulin to its receptor; membrane polarization; phospholipid metabolism; fatty acid metabolism; redox potential and impedance changes induced by insulin; detection of nitric oxide; acyl-CoA metabolism in peroxisomal diseases, apoptosis, autoimmunity and endomitriosis. *Mailing Add:* William Beaumont Hosp 3601 W 13 Mile Rd Royal Oak MI 48073. *Fax:* 248-551-3694; *E-Mail:* fkiechle@beaumont.edu

KIECKHEFER, ROBERT WILLIAM, INSECT ECOLOGY. *Current Pos:* RES ENTOMOLOGIST, NORTHERN GRAIN INSECTS RES LAB, USDA, 63- *Personal Data:* b Milwaukee, Wis, Mar 13, 33; m 69, Janice A Kadlec; c Karla, Jon & Joel. *Educ:* Univ Wis, BS, 55, PhD(entom), 62; Univ Minn, MS, 58. *Mem:* Entom Soc Am; Ecol Soc Am; Int Orgn Biol Control. *Res:* Aphid biology and ecology; ecology and biological control of cereal insects. *Mailing Add:* Northern Grain Insects Res RR 3 Brookings SD 57006. *Fax:* 605-693-5240

KIEDA, DAVID BASIL, COSMIC RAY PHYSICS, INTERMEDIATE & ULTRA HIGH ENERGY GAMMA RAY ASTRONOMY. *Current Pos:* res assoc, 89, asst prof, 90-96, ASSOC PROF PHYSICS, UNIV UTAH, 96- *Personal Data:* b Johnson City, NY, Mar 22, 60; m 88, Lisa Goldstein; c Daniel J & Zachary A. *Educ:* Mass Inst Technol, SB, 82; Univ Pa, PhD(physics), 89. *Prof Exp:* Teaching asst physics, Univ Pa, 82-83, res asst, 83-88. *Concurrent Pos:* Lectr physics, SDak Sch Mines & Technol, 84; pres, Wildcat Sci Consult, 91-; prin investr, NASA, 93-96, NSF, 95- *Mem:* Sigma Xi; AAAS; Am Phys Soc. *Res:* High energy astrophysics; sources of ultra-high energy particles; experimental measurement of source spectra; high energy gamma ray astronomy; sources of gamma ray bursts; sources above one giga electron volt medical instrumentation; power conduction in electrosurgical environment; analysis of software/hardware. *Mailing Add:* Dept Physics 201 JFB Univ Utah Salt Lake City UT 84112. *Fax:* 801-581-4801; *E-Mail:* kieda@krusty.physics.utah.edu

KIEFER, BARRY IRWIN, DEVELOPMENTAL BIOLOGY. *Current Pos:* From asst prof to assoc prof, 65-77, PROF BIOL, WESLEYAN UNIV, 77- *Personal Data:* b Bayonne, NJ, May 16, 33; m 60. *Educ:* Univ Denver, BS, 60; Univ Calif, Berkeley, PhD(zool), 65. *Mem:* Am Soc Cell Biol. *Res:* Genetic regulation of spermiogenesis in Drosophila. *Mailing Add:* Box 8725 Reno NV 89507

KIEFER, CHARLES R(ANDOLPH), MONOCLONAL ANTIBODY PRODUCTION, CELL MEMBRANE SKELETAL STRUCTURE. *Current Pos:* Res fel, 81-87, asst res scientist, 87-91, ASST PROF IMMUNOL, MED COL GA, 91- *Personal Data:* b Minneapolis, Minn, Nov 24, 47; m 73, Samira El Gamal; c Alexandra. *Educ:* Univ Cincinnati, BS, 69; Med Col Ga, PhD(microbiol), 81. *Concurrent Pos:* Consult, Med Diag Technol, Inc, Augusta, Ga, 87-90; prin investr, Am Heart Asn, Ga Affil, 90-91. *Mem:* Am Asn Immunologists; Am Soc Hemat. *Res:* Immunology. *Mailing Add:* Hosp Labs Clin Path Univ Mass Med Ctr 55 Lake Ave N Worcester MA 01655-0220. *Fax:* 706-721-7507; *E-Mail:* ckiefer@uscn

KIEFER, DAVID JOHN, MICROBIOLOGY, IMMUNOLOGY. *Current Pos:* dir, 86-90, vpres, Prod Develop, 90-93, CHIEF OPERATING OFFICER, DIAMEDIX CORP, 93- *Personal Data:* b Sewickley, Pa, Oct 1, 38; m 62, Muriel Dooley. *Educ:* Univ Pittsburgh, BS, 68; Univ Miami, PhD(microbiol), 77. *Prof Exp:* Res technician immunol, Sch Med, Univ Miami, 68-77; staff immunologist, Cordis Labs, Inc, 77-80, sr staff immunologist, 80-83, prin immunologist, 83-86. *Mem:* Am Soc Microbiol; Nat Comt Clin Lab Standards. *Res:* Pregnancy associated plasma proteins; immunology of pregnancy; immunosuppressive properties of pregnancy serum; enzyme-labeled immunoassays for the detection and quantitation of humoral constituents, for example antibodies to rubella, herpes simplex virus, cytomegalovirus, Human T-Cell Leukemia/Lymphoma Virus I and HIV-1, Epstein Barr Virus and autoantigens in systemic rheumatic diseases. *Mailing Add:* Diamedix Corp 2140 N Miami Ave Miami FL 33127. *Fax:* 305-324-2378

KIEFER, EDGAR FRANCIS, ORGANIC CHEMISTRY. *Current Pos:* from asst prof to assoc prof, 62-72, PROF CHEM, UNIV HAWAII, 72-, CHAIR, CHEM DEPT, 95- *Personal Data:* b Qingdao, China, Sept 9, 34; US citizen; m 57, 74, Diane Dubois; c Nicholas, Lauren, Daniel, Miranda, Harrison & Britton. *Educ:* Stanford Univ, BS, 57; Calif Inst Technol, PhD(chem), 61. *Prof Exp:* Asst chem, Calif Inst Technol, 57-58; res assoc, Univ Ill, 60-61; res chemist, Chevron Res Corp, 61-62. *Concurrent Pos:* NSF sci fac fel, Stanford Univ, 68-69; vis scientist, Mass Inst Technol, 78, Oxford Univ, 85-86 & Univ Cambridge, 93-94. *Mem:* Am Chem Soc; AAAS. *Res:* Physical organic and bioorganic chemistry; stereochemistry. *Mailing Add:* Dept Chem Univ Hawaii Honolulu HI 96822-1888. *E-Mail:* kiefer@hawaii.edu

KIEFER, HAROLD MILTON, THEORETICAL PHYSICS. *Current Pos:* asst prof, 69-81, ASSOC PROF PHYSICS, NORFOLK STATE COL, 81- *Personal Data:* b Detroit, Mich, Mar 9, 33; m 66; c 1. *Educ:* Wayne State Univ, PhD(physics), 69. *Prof Exp:* Personnel exam, City of Detroit, 58-62. *Mem:* Am Phys Soc; Sigma Xi. *Res:* Applications of group theory to coulomb potential problems. *Mailing Add:* 116 W Government Ave Norfolk VA 23503

KIEFER, JOHN DAVID, GEOLOGIC HAZARDS, ENERGY RESOURCES. *Current Pos:* ASST STATE GEOLOGIST, KY GEOL SURV, UNIV KY, 81- *Personal Data:* b Evansville, Ind, Jan 2, 40; m 64; c 5. *Educ:* St Josephs Col, BA, 61; Univ Ill, MS, 65, PhD(eng geol), 70. *Prof Exp:* Instr geol, Univ Ill, 65-67; assoc prof, Eastern Ky Univ, 67-71; head, Eng Geol Div, Geotech Eng Assocs, 71-78; eng geologist, Geol Surv Ala, 78-79, head, Water Resources Div, 79-82. *Mem:* Geol Soc Am; Am Asn Petrol Geologists; Soc Econ Paleontologists & Mineralogists; AAAS; Sigma Xi. *Res:* Engineering geology and hydrogeology. *Mailing Add:* 228 Mining & Mineral Resources Bldg Univ Ky Lexington KY 40506

KIEFER, JOHN HAROLD, COMBUSTION, KINETICS. *Current Pos:* assoc prof, 67-72, actg head, 89-91, PROF CHEM ENG & CHEM, UNIV ILL, CHICAGO, 72- *Personal Data:* b New Ulm, Minn, Aug 27, 32; m 71, Barbara Berg; c Steven, Amy & Andrew. *Educ:* Univ Minn, BS, 54; Cornell Univ, PhD(phys chem), 61. *Prof Exp:* Fel, Cornell Univ, 59-60; res staff mem, Los Alamos Sci Lab, Univ Calif, 61-67. *Concurrent Pos:* Consult, Los Alamos Nat Lab, 67-, Ill Tool Works, 75-77; Shell res fel, Thorton, UK, 73-74; joint appointment, Argonne Nat Lab, 85-91. *Mem:* Combustion Inst; Am Inst Chem Eng; Am Chem Soc. *Res:* Shock tube studies of kinetics; energy transfer in high temperature gases; laser diagnostics; unimolecular rate theory. *Mailing Add:* Univ Ill 810 S Clinton Chicago IL 60607. *Fax:* 312-996-0808

KIEFER, RALPH W, CIVIL ENGINEERING, REMOTE SENSING & IMAGE INTERPRETATION. *Current Pos:* from asst prof to prof, 62-96, EMER PROF CIVIL ENG, UNIV WIS-MADISON, 96- *Personal Data:* b Somerville, NJ, Nov 28, 34; m 59, 83, Lois Argraves; c Hope, Joy, Lynn & Jennifer. *Educ:* Cornell Univ, BCE, 58, MS, 60, PhD(civil eng), 64. *Prof Exp:* Asst hwy engr, NJ State Hwy Dept, 58; asst civil eng, Cornell Univ, 58-62. *Concurrent Pos:* Vis prof, Univ Hawaii, 70-71. *Mem:* Am Soc Civil Engrs; Am Soc Photogram & Remote Sensing; Am Soc Eng Educ. *Res:* Remote sensing of the environment; engineering applications of airphoto interpretation; land use suitability evaluation. *Mailing Add:* 5 Preston Circle Madison WI 53719-1582. *E-Mail:* rwkiefer@facstaff.wisc.edu

KIEFER, RICHARD L, POLYMER CHEMISTRY. *Current Pos:* asst prof to assoc prof, 65-81, PROF CHEM, COL WILLIAM & MARY, 81- *Personal Data:* b Columbia, Pa, Dec 14, 37; m 62, Sharon E; c 3. *Educ:* Drew Univ, AB, 59; Univ Calif, Berkeley, PhD(nuclear chem), 64. *Prof Exp:* Res assoc, Brookhaven Nat Lab, 63-65. *Mem:* Am Chem Soc; Sigma Xi. *Res:* Space radiation effects on polymers. *Mailing Add:* Dept Chem Col William & Mary PO Box 8795 Williamsburg VA 23185-8795

KIEFF, ELLIOTT DAN, INFECTIOUS DISEASES, VIROLOGY. *Current Pos:* PROF MED, MICROBIOL & MOLECULAR GENETICS, HARVARD UNIV, 87- *Personal Data:* b Philadelphia, Pa, Feb 2, 43; m 65; c 2. *Educ:* Univ Pa, AB, 63; Johns Hopkins Univ, MD, 66; Univ Chicago, PhD(virol), 71. *Prof Exp:* Intern, Hosp, Sch Med, Univ Chicago, 66-67; from jr resident to sr asst resident, 67-69, resident, 69-70, chief, Sect Infectious Dis, 71-87, from asst prof to prof, Sch Med, 70-87. *Concurrent Pos:* Mem, Comt Virol, Univ Chicago, 70-; fac res award, Am Cancer Soc; Carl Hartford vis prof, Wash Univ. *Mem:* Nat Acad Sci; Infectious Dis Soc Am; Am Soc Clin Invest; Am Asn Cancer Res; Am Soc Microbiol. *Res:* Molecular biology of animal viruses, particularly herpes viruses. *Mailing Add:* Dept Med & Microbiol Harvard Univ Infectious Dis Div-Channing Lab 181 Longwood Ave Boston MA 02115. *Fax:* 617-525-4257; *E-Mail:* ekieff@rics.dwh.harvard.edu

KIEFFER, HUGH HARTMAN, PLANETARY SCIENCE, INFRARED INSTRUMENTATION. *Current Pos:* chief, 86-90, RES GEOPHYSICIST, BR ASTROGEOLOGY, GEOL DIV, US GEOL SURV, 78- *Personal Data:* b Norwich, Conn, Oct 31, 39; m 93, Victoria Fearheiley; c 1. *Educ:* Calif Inst Technol, BS, 61, PhD(planetary sci), 68. *Honors & Awards:* Sci Achievement Medal, NASA, 77; Antarctic Serv Medal, 68. *Prof Exp:* Res fel planetary sci, Calif Inst Technol, 68-69; asst prof, 69-75, assoc prof planetary sci, Univ Calif, Los Angeles, 75-77. *Concurrent Pos:* Vis assoc planetary physics, Calif Inst Technol, 75-77; prin investr, Viking Infrared Thermal Mapper; coinvestr, Mariner 6 & 7 Infrared Radiometer, Mariner 9 Infrared Radiometer, Galileo Near Infrared Mapping Spectrometer, Mars Observer Thermal Emission Spectrometer; US partic scientist, Soviet Mars-94 mission; team mem, Earth Observing Syst High Resolution Imaging Spectrometer; US team mem, Earth Observing Syst Advan Spaceborne Thermal Emission Radiometer (Japan); adj prof planetary sci, Univ Calif, Los Angeles, 78-81; Nat Acad Sci, Comt Lunar & Planetary Explor, 79-83; chmn, Fourth Int Conf Mars, 89. *Mem:* AAAS; Am Astron Soc; Am Meteorol Soc; Am Optical Soc; fel Am Geophys Union; Am Soc Photogram & Remote Sensing. *Res:* Planetary atmospheres and surfaces; spectra of the moon and planets; atmospheric condensation processes; infrared instrumentation, observations and thermal models; thermal infrared and radar observations of volcanos; remote sensing calibration. *Mailing Add:* Astrogeology 2255 N Gemini Dr Flagstaff AZ 86001. *Fax:* 602-556-7014; *E-Mail:* hkieffer@altair.wr.usgs.gov

KIEFFER, NAT, GENETICS. *Current Pos:* asst prof, Tex A&M Univ, 65-69, assoc prof mammalian cytogenetics, 69-77, prof, 77-87, EMER PROF GENETICS, ANIMAL & PLANT SCI, TEX A&M UNIV, 87- *Personal Data:* b Montgomery, La, July 13, 30; m 51; c 3. *Educ:* Univ Southwestern La, BS, 52; La State Univ, MS, 56; Okla State Univ, PhD(animal breeding), 59. *Prof Exp:* Animal geneticist, Range Livestock Exp Sta, USDA, 59-62, supt beef cattle res, 62-64; res assoc & fel molecular biol, Univ Calif, Berkeley, 64-65. *Mem:* Genetics Soc Am; Am Soc Animal Sci. *Res:* Population genetics; beef cattle breeding; molecular biology, gene action in bacteria on molecular level; mammalian cytogenetics, beef cattle. *Mailing Add:* 1212 Winding Rd College Station TX 77840

KIEFFER, STEPHEN A, RADIOLOGY, NEURORADIOLOGY. *Current Pos:* PROF RADIOL & CHMN DEPT, STATE UNIV NY HEALTH SCI CTR, SYRACUSE, 74- *Personal Data:* b Minneapolis, Minn, Dec 20, 35; m 58, Cyrille F Kaplan; c Alisa, Mitchell, Stuart & Paula. *Educ:* Univ Minn, BA, 56, BS, 57, MD, 59. *Prof Exp:* From instr to prof, Univ Minn, 66-74. *Concurrent Pos:* Nat Heart Inst cardiovasc trainee, Univ Minn, 61-62 & 64-65, Nat Inst Neurol Dis & Blindness fel neuroradiol, 66, James Picker Found scholar radiol res, 66-68; chief radiol, Minneapolis Vet Admin Hosp, 68-74; assoc ed, Year Book Diag Radiol, 81-87, Radiol, 86; panelist & subcomt chair, NIH Consensus Develop Conf Magnetic Resonance & Imaging, 87; consult to ed, Radiol, 87-93. *Mem:* Am Col Radiol; Am Soc Neuroradiol (pres, 78-79); Radiol Soc NAm; Am Roentgen Ray Soc; Asn Univ Radiologists. *Res:* Neuroradiology; utility of diagnostic imaging in evaluation and management of lowback pain; clinical outcomes research; MR engiography. *Mailing Add:* Dept Radiol Stat Univ NY Health Sci Ctr 750 E Adams St Syracuse NY 13210. *Fax:* 315-464-7458; *E-Mail:* kieffers@vax.cs.hscsyr.edu

KIEFFER, SUSAN WERNER, VOLCANOLOGY, MINERAL PHYSICS. *Current Pos:* CO FOUNDER, KIEFFER & WOO INC, 96- *Personal Data:* b Warren, Pa, Nov 17, 42; m 66; c 1. *Educ:* Allegheny Col, BSc, 64; Calif Inst Technol, MSc, 67, PhD(planetary sci), 71. *Hon Degrees:* DSc, Allegheny Col, 87. *Honors & Awards:* Mineral Soc Am Award, 80; W H Mendenhall Lectr, US Geol Surv, 80; Meritorious Serv Award, Dept Interior, 87; Int Geol Spendiarov Prize, 89; Day Medal, Geol Soc Am, 92; MacArthur Fel, John D & Catharine T MacArthur Found, 95. *Prof Exp:* Res geophysicist, Univ Calif, Los Angeles, 71-73, from asst prof to assoc prof geol, 73-79; geologist, US Geol Surv, 78-90; prof, Ariz State Univ, 89-93, regents prof, 91-93; prof & head, Dept Geol Sci, Univ BC, 93-95. *Concurrent Pos:* Alfred P Sloan res fel, 77-79. *Mem:* Nat Acad Sci; Am Geophys Union; Meteoritical Soc; Sigma Xi; Geol Soc Am; Am Acad Arts & Sci; Mineral Soc Am; Geol Asn Can. *Res:* Geological physics; high pressure geophysics and impact processes; shock metamorphism of natural materials; thermodynamic properties of minerals; mechanisms of geyser and volcano eruptions; river hydraulics. *Mailing Add:* Kieffer & Woo Inc PO Box 130 Palgrave ON L0N 1P0 Can. *Fax:* 905-857-5578; *E-Mail:* skieffer@geyser.com

KIEFFER, WILLIAM FRANKLIN, GENERAL CHEMISTRY. *Current Pos:* prof, 46-80, EMER PROF CHEM, COL WOOSTER, 80- *Personal Data:* b Trenton, NJ, Mar 16, 15; m 40, Elaine Steel; c Richard W & Lois J. *Educ:* Col Wooster, BA, 36; Ohio State Univ, MSc, 38; Brown Univ, PhD(photochem), 40. *Honors & Awards:* Award Chem Educ, Mfg Chem Asn, 65 & Am Chem Soc, 68. *Prof Exp:* Asst chem, Ohio State Univ, 36-38 & Brown Univ, 38-39; instr, Col Wooster, 40-42; from instr to asst prof, Western Reserve Univ, 42-46. *Concurrent Pos:* Res partic, Chem Div, Oak Ridge Nat Lab, 51-52; ed J Chem Educ, Am Chem Soc, 55-67; NSF fac fel, Mass Inst Technol, 63-64; vis scholar, Stanford Univ, 69-70 & Univ Calif, Santa Cruz, 74-75, vis prof, US Naval Acad, 81. *Mem:* AAAS; Am Chem Soc; Am Inst Chemists; NY Acad Sci. *Res:* Photochemistry; radiation chemistry; chemical education. *Mailing Add:* 1873 Golden Rain Rd 3 Walnut Creek CA 94595

KIEFL, ROBERT FRANCES, PHYSICS. *Current Pos:* Res assoc, Dept Physics, Univ BC, 82, Nat Sci & Eng Res Coun Can univ res fel, 87-90, asst prof, 90-92, PROF, DEPT PHYSICS, UNIV BC, 92- *Personal Data:* b Oct 28, 53. *Educ:* Carleton Univ, BASc, 76; Univ BC, MSc, 78, PhD, 82. *Honors & Awards:* Gerhard Herzberg Medal, Can Asn Physicists, 92; Killiam Res Prize, 92; McDowell Medal, 93. *Prof Exp:* Nat Sci & Eng Res Coun Can fel, Dept Physics, Univ Zurich, 82-84; res scientist II, Tri-Univ-Meson Facil, 84-87. *Concurrent Pos:* Grantee, Nat Sci & Eng Res Coun Can, 86, 90-91 & 92-, Univ BC, 87; assoc superconductivity, Can Inst Advan Res, 90. *Res:* Superconductivity. *Mailing Add:* Physics Dept Univ BC Vancouver BC V6T 1Z1 Can

KIEFT, JOHN A, PHYSICAL CHEMISTRY, INORGANIC CHEMISTRY. *Current Pos:* mgr regist, Zeneca, 87-91, mgr envirn sci, 91-93, mgr environ sci, 93-94, RES & DEVELOP OPERS LEAD, ZENECA, 94- *Personal Data:* b Oak Park, Ill, Feb 27, 41; m 65; c 1. *Educ:* Hope Col, BA, 63; Ill Inst Technol, PhD(chem), 68. *Prof Exp:* Chemist, Shell Chem Co, 67-70; res chemist anal chem, Stauffer Chem Co, 70-71, supvr prod develop, 72-74, sect mgr, 74-76, sr sect mgr anal, 76-79, dept mgr res serv, Western Res Lab, 79-85, dir, regulatory affairs, 85-87. *Mem:* Am Chem Soc. *Res:* New product development; analytical chemistry; agricultural chemicals; research administration. *Mailing Add:* 1200 S 47th St Richmond CA 94804-0023

KIEFT, LESTER, ANALYTICAL CHEMISTRY. *Current Pos:* from asst prof to prof, 42-81, head dept, 44-70, secy fac, 68-80, EMER PROF CHEM, BUCKNELL UNIV, 81- *Personal Data:* b Grand Haven, Mich, Sept 18, 12; m 41; c 3. *Educ:* Hope Col, AB, 34; Pa State Col, MS, 36, PhD(anal chem), 39. *Prof Exp:* Asst, Pa State Col, 34-37; asst prof chem, Pa State Jr Col, 37-42. *Mem:* AAAS; Am Chem Soc; Nat Sci Teachers Asn. *Res:* Analytical properties of salts of the iodometallic acids. *Mailing Add:* 319 Buffalo Rd Lewisburg PA 17837-1134

KIEFT, RICHARD LEONARD, INORGANIC CHEMISTRY, ANALYTICAL CHEMISTRY. *Current Pos:* from asst prof to assoc prof, 75-89, PROF CHEM, MONMOUTH COL, ILL, 89- *Personal Data:* b Lewisburg, Pa, Apr 27, 45. *Educ:* Dickinson Col, BS, 67; Univ Ill, Urbana, PhD(inorg chem), 73. *Honors & Awards:* Sears-Roebuck Found Award, 88. *Prof Exp:* Teaching res assoc chem, Tulane Univ, 73-75. *Mem:* Am Chem Soc. *Res:* Synthesis and identification of organometallic compounds; environmental analysis. *Mailing Add:* 520 E First Ave Monmouth IL 61462-1808

KIEHL, JEFFREY THEODORE, RADIATIVE TRANSFER, CLIMATE MODELING. *Current Pos:* Vis scientist, 81-82, fel adv studies, 82-84, RES SCIENTIST, ATMOSPHERIC SCI, NAT CTR ATMOSPHERIC RES, 84- *Personal Data:* b Harrisburg, Pa, June 10, 52; m 80; c 1. *Educ:* Elizabethtown Col, BS, 74; Ind Univ, MS, 77; State Univ NY, Albany, PhD(atmospheric sci), 81. *Mem:* Am Meteorol Soc; Am Geophys Union. *Res:* General circulation modeling, aerosols and climate; infrared transfer in the atmosphere with applications to the carbon dioxide climate problems. *Mailing Add:* Nat Ctr Atmospheric Res 1850 Table Mesa Dr Boulder CO 80303

KIEHL, RICHARD ARTHUR, physical electronics, for more information see previous edition

KIEHLMANN, EBERHARD, ORGANIC CHEMISTRY. *Current Pos:* asst prof, 66-72, ASSOC PROF CHEM, SIMON FRASER UNIV, 72- *Personal Data:* b Grosshartmannsdorf, Ger, Feb 9, 37. *Educ:* Univ Tuebingen, Vordiplom, 59; Univ Md, College Park, PhD(org chem), 64. *Prof Exp:* Res fel, Univ Calif, Berkeley, 64-65 & Dartmouth Col, 65-66. *Mem:* Am Chem Soc; Ger Soc Chem; Chem Inst Can. *Res:* Synthesis and reactions of flavanoids. *Mailing Add:* Dept Chem Simon Fraser Univ Burnaby BC V5A 1S6 Can. *Fax:* 604-291-3765; *E-Mail:* ekie@bohr.chem.sfu.ca

KIEHN, ROBERT MITCHELL, PHYSICS. *Current Pos:* assoc prof, 62-72, PROF PHYSICS, UNIV HOUSTON, 72- *Personal Data:* b Oak Park, Ill, Dec 29, 29; m 58. *Educ:* Mass Inst Technol, BS, 50, PhD, 54. *Prof Exp:* Staff physicist, Los Alamos Sci Lab, 54-62. *Mem:* Am Phys Soc; Am Nuclear Soc. *Res:* Neutron reactor physics; hydrodynamics; thermodynamics. *Mailing Add:* 7844 Kendelia Houston TX 77036

KIEL, JOHNATHAN LLOYD, BIOCHEMICAL IMMUNOLOGY, BACTERIOLOGY. *Current Pos:* vet, Vet Pub Health, Grissom AFB, Ind, 75-77, res immunol, Physics Br, Radiation Sci Div, Sch Aerospace Med, Brooks AFB, Tex, 81-91, CHIEF BIOPHYS MECHANISM FUNCTION RADIO FREQUENCY, RADIATION BR, ENERGY DIV, OCCUP & ENVIRON HEALTH DIRECTORATE, USAF, 91- *Personal Data:* b Houston, Tex, Sept 4, 49; m 73; c 2. *Educ:* Tex A&M Univ, BS, 73, DVM, 74, Health Sci Ctr, PhD(microbiol & biochem), 81. *Prof Exp:* Instr vet microbiol, Sch Vet Med, Tex A&M Univ, 74-75. *Mem:* Am Vet Med Asn; Bioelectromagnetics Soc; Am Col Vet Microbiologists, 84. *Res:* Oxidative metabolism of the various cells of the immune system and how it influences the immune response and cytotoxic mechanisms; influence of radiofrequency radiation on this metabolism. *Mailing Add:* USAF AL/OERT Brooks TX 78235-5301

KIEL, OTIS GERALD, ENGINEERING SCIENCES, MATHEMATICS. *Current Pos:* Sect supvr, Continental Oil Co, 59-80, CHIEF RESERVOIR ENGR, CONOCO, INC, 80- *Personal Data:* b Wichita Falls, Tex, Feb 10, 31; m 53; c 3. *Educ:* NTex State Univ, BS, 49; Univ Okla, BS, 56, MS, 57, PhD(eng sci), 63. *Honors & Awards:* C K Ferguson Award, Am Inst Mining, Metall & Petrol Engrs, 63. *Mem:* Am Inst Mining, Metall & Petrol Engrs; Soc Petrol Engrs. *Res:* Reservoir mechanics, mathematical modeling; reserve determination enhanced recovery projects. *Mailing Add:* 807 Soboda Ct Houston TX 77079

KIELKOPF, JOHN F, ATOMIC & MOLECULAR SPECTROSCOPY, ASTROPHYSICS. *Current Pos:* From asst prof to assoc prof, 69-77, PROF PHYSICS, UNIV LOUISVILLE, 77- *Personal Data:* b Louisville, Ky, Aug 1, 45; m 70, Helen Davidson; c Clara L. *Educ:* Univ Louisville, BS & MS, 66; Johns Hopkins Univ, PhD(physics), 69. *Concurrent Pos:* Assoc res scientist, Johns Hopkins Univ, 74; vis scientist, Argonne Nat Lab, 74-75; astron, Observ Paris, Meudon, 79-80; scientist in residence, Argonne Nat Lab, 81. *Mem:* Am Phys Soc; Optical Soc Am; Am Astron Soc. *Res:* Radiative processes in atomic and molecular collisions; physics of the interstellar medium. *Mailing Add:* Moore Observ Univ Louisville 8000 Old Zaring Rd Crestwood KY 40014. *E-Mail:* jfkiel01@nimbus.physics.louisville.edu

KIELY, DONALD EDWARD, SYNTHETIC ORGANIC CHEMISTRY. *Current Pos:* from asst prof to assoc prof, 68-77, PROF CHEM, UNIV ALA, BIRMINGHAM, 77- *Personal Data:* b Waterbury, Conn, Jan 5, 38; m 63; c 3. *Educ:* Fairfield Univ, BS, 60; Univ Conn, PhD(org chem), 65. *Prof Exp:* Vis asst prof org chem, Wofford Col, 65-66; staff fel, Nat Inst Arthritis & Metab Dis, 66-68. *Concurrent Pos:* Vis fel, Res Sch Chem, Australian Nat Univ, 74; resident prof, Staley Mfg Co, 81-82; ed, J Carbohydrate Chem, 81- *Mem:* Am Chem Soc; Sigma Xi. *Res:* Synthesis of biologically interesting carbohydrates, cyclitols and other carbocyclic and heterocyclic compounds; chemical studies related to cyclitol biosynthesis; synthetic carbohydrate chemistry; industrially related carbohydrate chemistry; synthetic carbohydrate based polymer synthesis. *Mailing Add:* 2521 Chatwood Rd Birmingham AL 35226-3503

KIELY, JOHN ROCHE, MECHANICAL ENGINEERING, MINING ENGINEERING. *Current Pos:* RETIRED. *Personal Data:* b Berkeley, Calif, Nov 8, 06; m 40; c 5. *Educ:* Univ Wash, BSCE, 31. *Prof Exp:* Construct engr, Rainier Pulp & Paper Co, 24-31, supt, 31-36; resident engr, Rayonier, Inc, 37-40, asst gen supt, 40-42; mgr outfitting, subassembly & transport, Calif Shipbldg Corp, 42-45; proj mgr, Bechtel Bros McCone Co, 45-48, mgr, Bechtel Corp, 48-51, vpres, 51-54, sr vpres, 57-67, exec vpres, 67-71, dir, 54-74, exec consult, 74-80, sr exec consult, Bechtel, Inc, 80-88. *Mem:* Nat Acad Eng; fel Am Inst Mech Engrs; Am Soc Civil Engrs; Am Soc Mech Eng; Sigma Xi. *Mailing Add:* PO Box 620303 Woodside CA 94062

KIELY, JOHN STEVEN, PHARMACOLOGY. *Current Pos:* DIR MED CHEM, ISIS PHARMACEUT, 93- *Personal Data:* b Missoula, Mont, Oct 11, 51; m 74; c 2. *Educ:* Mont State Univ, BSc, 74; NDak State Univ, PhD(organ chem), 79. *Prof Exp:* Assoc res fel, Lawrence Berkeley Lab, Univ Calif, 79-81; from scientist to sr scientist, Parke Davis/Warner Lambert Res, Warner Lambert Co, 81-87, from res assoc to sr res assoc, 87-93. *Mem:* Am Chem Soc; Sigma Xi; AAAS. *Res:* Quinolone antibacterials; cognition activators; peptide nucleic acid; antisense technology; oligonucleotide synthesis and sarcosine. *Mailing Add:* 12460 Saddle Rd Carmel Valley CA 93924. *E-Mail:* john_kiely@isisph.com

KIELY, LAWRENCE J, ANATOMY, PHYSIOLOGY. *Current Pos:* From instr to assoc prof biol, 49-60, prof sci educ, 60-74, prof biol, 60-75, CHMN BIOL, NIAGARA UNIV, 75- *Personal Data:* b Truxton, NY, Feb 26, 22; m 51; c 9. *Educ:* Niagara Univ, BS, 43, MA, 47; Columbia Univ, MA, 49, EdD(biol), 51. *Concurrent Pos:* Lectr, Rosary Hill Col, 55-, grant exp psychol, 64-65; res grant human physiol, Williams Col, 65; res grant marine biol & trop ecol, Univ PR, 67; res grant sci educ, Ithaca Col, 68; res grant hist biol, Ohio State Univ, 69. *Mem:* AAAS; Am Physiol Soc; Nat Sci Teachers Asn; Nat Asn Biol Teachers. *Res:* Human anatomy, physiology and biology; science education. *Mailing Add:* 3534 Ransomville Rd Ransomville NY 14131

KIELY, MICHAEL LAWRENCE, ANATOMY. *Current Pos:* PROF, NAT COL CHIROPRACTICS, 94- *Personal Data:* b Springfield, Ill, June 17, 38; m 67; c 2. *Educ:* Lewis Col, BS, 60; Loyola Univ Ill, MS, 64, PhD(anat), 67. *Prof Exp:* Res assoc, Stritch Sch Med, Loyola Univ, Chicago, 67, from asst prof to prof anat, Sch Dent, 67-94. *Mem:* Am Asn Anatomists; Int Asn Dent Res; Am Asn Dent Res; Am Asn Clin Anatomists. *Res:* Gross and oral anatomy; temporomandibulow joint; morphologic variations in the human skull and cranial soft tissue. *Mailing Add:* 200 E Roosevelt Rd Lombard IL 60148. *Fax:* 630-889-6554; *E-Mail:* mkiely@national.chiropractic.edu

KIEN, C LAWRENCE, STABLE ISOTOPIC TRACERS, CARBOHYDRATE & PROTEIN METABOLISM. *Current Pos:* PROF PEDIAT & DIR, DIV NUTRIT, OHIO STATE UNIV, 88- *Personal Data:* b Oct 5, 46; m, Patricia J Liddil; c 2. *Educ:* Duke Univ, BS, 68; Univ Cincinnati, MD, 72; Mass Inst Technol, PhD(nutrit & biochem), 77. *Honors & Awards:* Future Leaders Award, Nutrit Found. *Prof Exp:* From asst prof to assoc prof pediat & biochem, Med Col Wis, Milwaukee, 77-84; C E Compton prof nutrit, Sch Med, Univ WVa, 84-87. *Concurrent Pos:* Mem, Div Gastroenterol & Human Molecular Genetics, Ohio State Univ Hosp; assoc dir, Gen Clin Res Ctr; med consult, Amino Acid/Org Acid Lab, Children's Hosp. *Mem:* Am Physiol Soc; Am Soc Clin Nutrit; Am Inst Nutrit; Am Soc Parenteral & Enterol Nutrit; Am Soc Pediat Res; Am Pediat Soc; fel Am Acad Pediat; fel Am Col Nutrit; spec fel Leukemia Soc; Am Gastroenterol Asn. *Res:* Nutrition; study of protein and energy; use stable, non-radioactive isotopes to study lactose utilization, carbohydrate and amino acid metabolism, and energy expenditure in the newborn and in children with cystic fibrosis or obesity; effects of caloric fermentation on cell proliferation and apoptosis in colon and intestine; diagnosis and treatment of disorders of nutrition and inburn errors of metabolism. *Mailing Add:* Children's Hosp Rm W209 700 Children's Dr Columbus OH 43205

KIENHOLZ, ELDON W, animal nutrition; deceased, see previous edition for last biography

KIENTZ, MARVIN L, BIOCHEMISTRY. *Current Pos:* assoc prof, 67-74, PROF CHEM, SONOMA STATE UNIV, 74- *Personal Data:* b Clovis, Calif, Jan 28, 36; m 84, Sharon Steele; c Randal & Jane. *Educ:* Fresno State Col, BA, 58, MA, 61; Western Ont Univ, PhD(biochem), 66. *Prof Exp:* Teacher high sch, 59-63; res biochemist, Med Ctr, Univ Calif, San Francisco, 66-67. *Concurrent Pos:* Inst dir, NSF, 71-73. *Res:* Determination of the structure of proteins; protein polymorphism. *Mailing Add:* Dept Chem Sonoma State Univ 1801 E Cotati Ave Rohnert Park CA 94928-3613

KIER, ANN B, GENE TARGETING & COMPARATIVE PATHOLOGY. *Current Pos:* PROF & HEAD, DEPT PATHOBIOL, TEX A&M UNIV, 94- *Personal Data:* b Littlefield, Tex, June 26, 49; m 79, Friedhelm Schroeder; c Hilary. *Educ:* Univ Tex, Austin, BA, 71; Tex A&M Univ, BS, 73, DVM, 74; Univ Mo, Columbia, PhD(path), 79; Am Col Lab Animal Med, dipl. *Prof Exp:* NIH fel, Lab Animal Med & Comp Path, Univ Mo, Columbia, 76-79, from asst prof to assoc prof path & microbiol, 84-87; from assoc prof to prof path, Univ Cincinnati Med Sch, 87-93, head, Div Comparative Path, 90-93. *Concurrent Pos:* Dir, Histopath Lab, Vet Med Diag Lab, 80-87, Div Comparative Path, 91-93. *Mem:* Am Vet Med Asn; Am Asn Vet Med Col; Am Col Lab Animal Med; Am Soc Invest Path. *Res:* Immunpathology, histopathology and oncogenicity of tumors; interrelationships of coagulation, fibrinuolysis and inflammation; transgenic mice and gene targeting; genetics; neutrophil and macrophage chemotaxis. *Mailing Add:* Dept Pathobiol TVMC Tex A&M Univ College Station TX 77843-4467. *Fax:* 409-845-9231; *E-Mail:* akier@cum.tamu.edu

KIER, LEMONT BURWELL, MEDICINAL CHEMISTRY. *Current Pos:* chmn, 77-87, PROF, DEPT PHARMACEUT CHEM, MED COL VA, VA COMMONWEALTH UNIV, 77- *Personal Data:* b Cleveland, Ohio, Sept 13, 30; m 53; c 5. *Educ:* Ohio State Univ, BS, 54; Univ Minn, PhD(med chem), 58. *Prof Exp:* Asst prof pharmaceut chem, Univ Fla, 59-63; assoc prof, Ohio State Univ, 63-66; sr med chemist, Columbus Labs, Battelle Mem Inst, 66-69, assoc fel med chem, 69-72; prof chem, Mass Col Pharm, 72-77. *Concurrent Pos:* Adj prof, Univ Mich, 69-72; chmn, Dept Chem, Mass Col Pharm, 72-74; vis prof, Univ Lausanne, Switz, 92. *Mem:* Fel Am Asn Pharmaceut Scientists; Am Chem Soc; fel Acad Pharmaceut Sci; fel Am Pharmaceut Asn. *Res:* Theoretical approaches to drug structure activity relationships; topological structure indices; cellular automata models of dynamic solution phenomena. *Mailing Add:* Va Commonwealth Univ Box 980540 MCV SAS Richmond VA 23298. Fax: 804-371-7625; E-Mail: kier@vcuvax

KIERAS, FRED J, CONNECTIVE TISSUE BIOCHEMISTRY, GENETIC DISEASES. *Current Pos:* RES SCIENTIST, NY INST BASIC RES, 71- *Educ:* Univ Chicago, PhD(biochem), 68. *Mailing Add:* NY State Inst Basic Res 1050 Forest Hill Rd Staten Island NY 10314-6330. Fax: 718-698-3803

KIERBOW, JULIE VAN NOTE PARKER, PHYSICAL CHEMISTRY, RADIOCHEMISTRY. *Current Pos:* from asst prof to prof, 57-78, EMER PROF CHEM, CALIF STATE UNIV, LONG BEACH, 78- *Personal Data:* b Fayetteville, Tenn, Feb 13, 25; m 81, David C. *Educ:* Ohio State Univ, BS, 45; Univ Hawaii, MS, 48; Univ Colo, PhD(chem), 57. *Prof Exp:* Res engr, Battelle Mem Inst, 45-46 & 48-50; asst, Univ Hawaii, 46-48; phys chemist, Redstone Arsenal Res Div, Rohm & Haas Co, 51-54; asst chem, Univ Colo, 54-56, res fel, 56-57. *Mem:* AAAS; Am Chem Soc. *Res:* Scintillation properties of solutions, particularly as related to structure of metal-organic compounds; use of radiotracers in development of analytical techniques. *Mailing Add:* 19038 Sombrero Circle Sun City AZ 85373-1417

KIERNAN, JOHN ALAN, NEUROHISTOLOGY & HISTOCHEMISTRY. *Current Pos:* asst prof, 72-75, assoc prof, 75-81, PROF, DEPT ANAT, UNIV WESTERN ONT, 81- *Personal Data:* b Kidderminstar, Eng, 1942; m 67, Tessa Westcott; c Julia, Edward, Susan, Jeffrey & Philip. *Educ:* Univ Birmingham, BSc, 63, MB & ChB, 66, PhD(neuroanat), 69; DSc, (anat) Univ Birmingham, Eng, 79. *Prof Exp:* House surgeon, E Birmingham Hosp, 66-67, res fel, Dept Anat, Univ Birmingham, Eng, 67-69; fel, Sidney Sussex Col, Cambridge, Eng, 69-72. *Concurrent Pos:* House physician, Worcester Royal Infirmary, 67; sr res fel, Sidney Sussex Col, Cambridge, 69-71, dir studies med, 70-72; univ demonstr, Dept Anat, Univ Cambridge, 71-72; mem, Biol Stain Comn. *Mem:* Anat Soc Brit; Bot Soc Brit Isles; Histochem Soc; fel Royal Microscopical Soc. *Res:* Reactions of nervous tissue to injury and disease; histology and histochemistry; human neuroanatomy. *Mailing Add:* Dept Anat Univ Western Ont London ON N6A 5C1 Can

KIERSCH, GEORGE ALFRED, ENVIRONMENTAL ENGINEERING GEOLOGY RELATED TO CIVIL & MINING PROJECTS. *Current Pos:* chmn dept, 65-71, prof, 60-78, EMER PROF GEOL SCI, CORNELL UNIV, 78- *Personal Data:* b Lodi, Calif, Apr 15, 18; m 42, Jane K Keith; c George K, Dana E(Haycock), Mary A & Nancy M(Bohnett). *Educ:* Colo Sch Mines, GE, 42; Univ Ariz, PhD(geol), 47. *Honors & Awards:* Holdredge Award, Asn Eng Geol, 65 & 93; Distinguished Pract Award, Geol Soc Am, 86, E B Burwell Award, 92. *Prof Exp:* Geologist, 79 Mining Co, Ariz, 46-47; instr, Mont Sch Mines, 47; geologist eng geol, CEngr, 48 & Folsom Dam Proj, 49-50; supv geologist, Int Boundary & Water Comn, 50-51; asst prof geol, Univ Ariz, 51-55; asst chief explor, Southern Pac Co, 56-60. *Concurrent Pos:* Consult eng geologist, 53-; dir mineral resources surv, Navajo-Hopi Indian Reservations, 53-56; NSF sr fac fel, Tech Univ Vienna, 63-64; geol consult, 78- *Mem:* Fel Geol Soc Am; Soc Econ Geol; fel Am Soc Civil Eng; hon mem Asn Eng Geologists; Int Asn Eng Geologists. *Res:* Engineering geology; nonmetallic mineral deposits; environmental geology; geomechanics; forensic geology; application of geology to planning, design and operation engineering works. *Mailing Add:* 4750 N Camino Luz Tucson AZ 85718

KIERSTEAD, RICHARD WIGHTMAN, ORGANIC CHEMISTRY. *Current Pos:* RETIRED. *Personal Data:* b Fredericton, NB, Feb 17, 27; m 51, 64; c 3. *Educ:* Univ NB, BSc, 48, MSc, 50; Univ London, PhD(org chem), 52. *Prof Exp:* Res assoc, Univ Toronto, 52-53 & Univ Calif, Los Angeles, 53-54; res chemist, E I du Pont de Nemours & Co, 54-55 & Harvard Univ, 55-56; sr res chemist, Hoffman-La Roche, Inc, 56-63, group chief, 63-69, sect chief, 69-77, dir med chem, 78-92, dir, Chem Synthesis Dept, 93-94. *Mem:* Am Chem Soc. *Res:* Synthesis of medicinal compounds. *Mailing Add:* 30 Willowbrook Dr North Caldwell NJ 07006

KIES, CONSTANCE, nutrition science; deceased, see previous edition for last biography

KIESCHNICK, W(ILLIAM) F(REDERICK), CHEMICAL ENGINEERING. *Current Pos:* From jr engr to theoret oil reservoir engr, Atlantic Refining Co, Atlantic Richfield Co, 47-48, admin asst, Res Dept Admin, 48-49, sr chem engr, 49-51, supv engr, 51-54, head, Res Sect, 54-59, asst to gen mgr explor, 59-61, mgr explor prod dist, 61-63, div mgr dists, 63-66, vpres & mgr cent region, Tex, 66-69, vpres synthetic crude & mineral opers, 69-70, vpres chem opers, 70-72, vpres & head corp planning, 72-73, exec vpres, 73-79, vchmn, 79, pres & chief opers officer, 81, pres & chief exec officer, 82-85, DIR, EMER PRES & CHIEF OPERATING OFFICER, ARCO, 85- *Personal Data:* b Dallas, Tex, Jan 5, 23; m 48, 79; c 2. *Educ:* Rice Univ, BS, 47. *Concurrent Pos:* Mem bd dirs, Atlantic Richfield Co, 73-; vchmn bd trustees, Calif Inst Technol; trustee, Carnegie Inst Wash; dir, Atlantic Richfield, TRW, First Interstate Bancorp, Pac Mutual Life Ins; chmn bd, Coun Health, Safety & Environ; chmn, Biotech Group Inc. *Mem:* Am Inst Mining, Metall & Petrol Engrs; Am Inst Chem Engrs; Am Asn Petrol Geologists; Am Petrol Inst. *Mailing Add:* ARCO 515 S Flower MS AP 5099 Los Angeles CA 90071

KIESLING, ERNST W(ILLIE), STRUCTURAL MECHANICS. *Current Pos:* prof civil eng & chmn dept, 69-88, assoc dean res, 88-93, PROF CIVIL ENG, COL ENG, TEX TECH UNIV, 93- *Personal Data:* b Eola, Tex, Apr 8, 34; m 56, Joanita Haseloff; c Carol, Chris & Max. *Educ:* Tex Tech Col, BS, 55; Mich State Univ, MS, 58, PhD(appl mech), 66. *Prof Exp:* From instr to asst prof civil eng, Tex Tech Col, 56-63; sr res engr, Struct Res Dept, Southwest Res Inst, 66-69. *Concurrent Pos:* Dir, Ctr Advan Res & Eng Res Found, 88-93. *Mem:* Am Soc Eng Educ; Am Soc Civil Engrs; Nat Soc Prof Engrs; Sigma Xi. *Res:* Housing; earth sheltered buildings; occupant protection form serve winds. *Mailing Add:* Dept Civil Eng Tex Tech Univ Lubbock TX 79409

KIESS, EDWARD MARION, PHYSICS. *Current Pos:* ASSOC PROF PHYSICS, HAMPDEN-SYDNEY COL, 68- *Personal Data:* b Washington, DC, Mar 10, 33; m 59; c 3. *Educ:* Mass Inst Technol, 55; Pa State Univ, MS, 62, PhD(physics), 65. *Prof Exp:* Asst prof physics, Lycoming Col, 65; physicist, Battelle Mem Inst, 65-67. *Concurrent Pos:* Cotrell grant, 71- *Mem:* Optical Soc Am. *Res:* Brillouin scattering; Fourier spectroscopy. *Mailing Add:* Hwy 658 Hampden-Sydney VA 23943

KIESSLING, GEORGE ANTHONY, ELECTRICAL ENGINEERING. *Current Pos:* RETIRED. *Personal Data:* b New York, NY, Dec 2, 20; m 51; c 6. *Educ:* Manhattan Col, BSEE, 51; Stevens Inst Technol, MSIE, 53. *Prof Exp:* Mem tech staff, Physics Lab, Sylvania Electronics Prod, Inc, 51-54; adminr eng financial planning, RCA Corp, 54-55, mgr eng stand & serv, 56-61, staff engr, 61, mgr prod admin, 62-63, mgr prod eng prof develop, 63-69, dir prof eng serv, 69-70, dir prod safetyplans & progs, 70-85. *Mem:* Inst Elec & Electronics Engrs. *Res:* Product safety programs, including policy, management, systems, audit, standards, legislation and regulations; product ionizing and nonionizing radiation safety; laser safety including standards, legislation and regulations. *Mailing Add:* 421 Overhill Rd Haddonfield NJ 08033

KIESSLING, OSCAR EDWARD, mineralogy; deceased, see previous edition for last biography

KIEWIET DE JONGE, JOOST H A, ASTRONOMY. *Current Pos:* ALLEGHENY OBSERV, PITTSBURGH. *Personal Data:* b Leiden, Netherlands, Sept 4, 19; m 54; c 1. *Educ:* Harvard Univ, PhD(astron), 54. *Prof Exp:* Instr, 50-54, asst prof, 54-65, assoc prof astron, Univ Pittsburgh, 66-, actg chmn, 70-75. *Concurrent Pos:* Lectr, Chatham Col, 56-70; consult, J W Fecker Div, Am Optical, 60-70; actg dir, Allegheny Observ, 70-77, mem staff, 77- *Mem:* Am Astron Soc. *Res:* Astronomical navigation; stellar statistics; celestial mechanics; astronomical instrumentation. *Mailing Add:* 227 Forest Ave Pittsburgh PA 15202

KIEWIT, DAVID ARNOLD, APPLIED PHYSICS, MATERIALS SCIENCE. *Current Pos:* CONSULT & REGIST PATENT AGENT, 90- *Personal Data:* b Cincinnati, Ohio, Feb 25, 40; m 63; c 2. *Educ:* Northwestern Univ, Evanston, BA, 62, PhD(mat sci), 68. *Prof Exp:* Mem tech staff, Hughes Res Labs, Hughes Aircraft Co, 67-73; mgr device develop, Gould Lab, Elec & Electronic Res, Gould Inc, 73-81; dir eng & advan develop, A C Nielsen Co, 81-90. *Mem:* Am Phys Soc; Inst Elec & Electronics Engrs. *Res:* Development of intelligent instrumentation systems for statistical measurements; preparation and prosecution of patent applications. *Mailing Add:* 5901 Third St S St Petersburg FL 33705-5305. Fax: 813-866-0669; E-Mail: kiewit@compuserve.com

KIFER, EDWARD W, inorganic chemistry, physical chemistry, for more information see previous edition

KIFER, MICHAEL, MATHEMATICS, COMPUTER SCIENCE. *Current Pos:* ASSOC PROF COMPUT SCI, STATE UNIV NY, STONY BROOK, 84- *Educ:* Moscow Univ, Russia, MS, 76; Hebrew Univ Jerusalem, Israel, PhD (comput sci), 85. *Concurrent Pos:* Prof comput sci, Univ Toronto, Can, 91-92. *Res:* Declarative languages for data and knowledge manipulation; integration of object-oriented and deductive paradigms; object-oriented data bases; query optimization; logic programming; artificial intelligence. *Mailing Add:* Dept Comput Sci State Univ NY Stony Brook Long Island NY 11794-4400

KIFER, PAUL EDGAR, FOOD SCIENCE. *Current Pos:* head dept food sci & technol, 73-83, assoc dean, int agr, 83-85, EMER PROF FOOD SCI & TECHNOL, ORE STATE UNIV, 85- *Personal Data:* b Grove City, Pa, Aug 16, 24; m 50, D Joan; c 3. *Educ:* Mich State Univ, BS, 50, MS, 53, PhD(animal nutrit), 56. *Prof Exp:* Asst prof poultry, Univ Ga, 56-57; asst mgr poultry res div, Ralston Purina Co, 57-59, mgr, Spec Chows Res Div, 59-64, dir, Pet Food Res & Develop, 64-67, asst to vpres corp res, 67-69, asst dir corp res, 69-73. *Mem:* Poultry Sci Asn; Inst Food Technologists; Am Inst Nutrit. *Res:* Nutrition as related to food science, food safety. *Mailing Add:* 3950 NW Walnut Ct Corvallis OR 97330

KIGER, JOHN ANDREW, JR, DEVELOPMENTAL GENETICS, CYCLIC NUCLEOTIDE ACTION. *Current Pos:* from asst prof to assoc prof, 73-82, chair, Dept Genetics, 87-91, PROF GENETICS, UNIV CALIF, DAVIS, 82- *Personal Data:* b Dayton, Ohio, Feb 6, 41. *Educ:* Calif Inst Technol, BS, 63, PhD(biophys), 68. *Prof Exp:* Instr biol, Mass Inst Technol, 68-69; asst prof biochem, Ore State Univ, 69-73. *Concurrent Pos:* Am Cancer Soc fel, 69; NIH Fogarty fel, 93 & 94. *Mem:* AAAS; Genetics Soc Am; Soc Develop Biol. *Res:* Biochemical and developmental genetics of Drosophila; cyclic nucleotide metabolism and action. *Mailing Add:* Molecular & Cellular Biol Univ Calif Davis CA 95616

KIGER, ROBERT WILLIAM, SYSTEMATIC BOTANY, HISTORY OF BIOLOGY. *Current Pos:* asst dir & sr res scientist, 74-77, DIR & PRIN RES SCIENTIST, HUNT INST BOT DOC, CARNEGIE MELLON UNIV, 77- *Personal Data:* b Washington, DC, Oct 4, 40; m 68, Suellen Montgomery; c David & James. *Educ:* Tulane Univ, BA, 66; Univ Md, MA, 71, PhD(bot), 72. *Prof Exp:* Teacher elem schs, Montgomery Co, Md, 66-67; res botanist, Smithsonian Inst, 72-73; dir develop, Sea Kal Develop Cor, 73-74. *Concurrent Pos:* Res assoc, Bot Sect, Carnegie Mus Nat Hist, 78-; adj prof hist sci, Dept Hist, Carnegie Mellon Univ, 79-, adj prof, Dept Biol, 84-; secy gen, Int Cong Syst Evolution, 90-96; adj scientist, Pittsburgh Poison Ctr, 90- *Mem:* Bot Soc Am; Am Soc Plant Taxonomists; Soc Study Evolution; Int Asn Plant Taxon. *Res:* Floristic and monographic study of various New World angiosperms, especially Flacourtiaceae and Talinum; history, philosophy and theory of biological systematics; evolutionary philosophy, especially in relation to theory of evolutionary mechanism and change, and to systematics; Flora of North America project; botanical documentation and databanking. *Mailing Add:* Hunt Inst Carnegie Mellon Univ Pittsburgh PA 15213. Fax: 412-268-5677; E-Mail: rkiger@andrew.cmu.edu

KIGGINS, EDWARD M, MICROBIOLOGY. *Current Pos:* DIR RES, LUBRIZOL ENTERPRISES INC, 85- *Personal Data:* b Stamford, Conn, Mar 26, 29; m 58; c 2. *Educ:* Univ Conn, AB, 52, MS, 54, PhD(microbiol), 58. *Prof Exp:* Asst animal dis, Univ Conn, 52-57; mem staff microbiol, Abbott Labs, 58-60, group leader, 61-66, sect head, 66-67, mgr animal health res, Amdal Co Div, 67-70, dir res & develop, Agr & Vet Prod Div, 70-75, dir & prod develop, Rhodia, Hess & Clark Div, 75-80; with Diamond Shamrock Corp, 80-85. *Mem:* AAAS; Am Soc Microbiol; US Animal Health Asn; Sigma Xi; NY Acad Sci. *Res:* Veterinary microbiology. *Mailing Add:* 8950 Woodland Pl Mentor OH 44060

KIHARA, HAYATO, BIOCHEMISTRY, BIOCHEMICAL GENETICS. *Current Pos:* assoc res biochemist, 73-75, prof biochem, 75-87, EMER PROF BIOCHEM, UNIV CALIF, LOS ANGELES, 87-, CHIEF, BIOCHEM LAB, MENT RETARDATION RES CTR, UNIV CALIF, LOS ANGELES-LANTERMAN STATE HOSP, 73- *Personal Data:* b Oakland, Calif, Feb 28, 22; m 50; c 2. *Educ:* Univ Tex, BS, 44; Univ Wis, MS, 51, PhD(biochem), 51. *Prof Exp:* Chemist, US Army, 406th Med Gen Lab, Japan, 46-48; asst biochem, Univ Wis, 48-51; res scientist, Biochem Inst, Univ Tex, 51-56; asst res biochemist, Univ Calif, 56-60; res specialist, Sonoma State Hosp, Eldridge, Calif, 60-63; chief res biochemist, Pac State Hosp, 63-73. *Concurrent Pos:* Vis prof, Sch Med, Nihon Univ, Tokyo, 80. *Mem:* Am Chem Soc; Am Soc Biol Chem; Am Soc Human Genetics; Am Asn Ment Deficiency. *Res:* Biochemistry of inborn errors of metabolism; tissue culture; enzyme purification; diagnosis of genetic disorders; heterozygote identification; prenatal diagnosis. *Mailing Add:* Lanterman Develop Ctr 3530 W Pomona Blvd Pomona CA 91768

KIHLSTROM, KENNETH EDWARD, THIN FILM SUPERCONDUCTIVITY, SUPERCONDUCTING TUNNELING. *Current Pos:* from asst prof to assoc prof, 84-94, PHYSICS DEPT CHAIR, WESTMONT COL, 84-, PROF, 94- *Personal Data:* b Buffalo, NY, May 11, 54; m 78, Kim Potter; c Katherine, Karen & Kevin. *Educ:* Stanford Univ, BS, 76, MS, 79, PhD(physics), 82. *Prof Exp:* Res assoc, Nat Res Coun-Naval Res Lab, 82-84. *Concurrent Pos:* Prin investr, Off Naval Res, 85-87 & NSF, 87-; consult, R G Hansen & Assoc, 87-88, Santa Barbara Res Ctr, 89, Conductus, Inc, 92-93; vis scholar, Stanford Univ, 92-93. *Mem:* Am Phys Soc. *Res:* Thin film superconductivity; superconducting tunneling on high-core temperature materials. *Mailing Add:* Dept Physics Westmont Col 955 La Paz Rd Santa Barbara CA 93108. Fax: 805-565-6220; E-Mail: kihlstr@westmont.edu

KIHN, HARRY, ELECTRONICS. *Current Pos:* PRES, KIHN ASSOCS, INC, 77- *Personal Data:* b Tarnow, Austria, Jan 24, 12; nat US; m 37; c 2. *Educ:* Cooper Union, BSEE, 34; Univ Pa, MSEE, 52. *Honors & Awards:* Centennial Award, Inst Elec & Electronics Engr. *Prof Exp:* Res engr, Hygrade Sylvania Corp, 35-37; chief engr, Polytherm, Inc, 37-38; res engr, Ferris Instrument Co, 38-39; res engr, RCA Corp, Camden, 39-42 & Princeton, NJ, 42-58, group head major systs res, 58-60, staff engr to vpres res & eng, 60-70, staff tech adv corp licensing, 71-75, sr tech adv patent opers, 75-77. *Concurrent Pos:* Mem mat adv bd, Nat Acad Sci-Nat Res Coun, 60-; mem comm sr ed, Gov Comn Sci Technol. *Mem:* AAAS; Sigma Xi; fel Inst Elec & Electronics Engrs; NY Acad Sci; Am Defense Preparedness Asn; Am Mgt Asn; Nat Soc Prof Engrs. *Res:* Electronics and business research; television communication theory and devices; electromagnetics; radar; infrared; space physics and instrumentation; solid state circuits and devices; integrated circuits; computer design; information processing systems; medical electronics; nuclear energy and waste isolation; industrial electronics; robotics. *Mailing Add:* 30 Green Ave Lawrenceville NJ 08648

KIILSGAARD, THOR H, ECONOMIC GEOLOGY. *Current Pos:* RETIRED. *Personal Data:* b Honeyville, Utah, June 10, 19; m 46; c 3. *Educ:* Univ Idaho, BS, 42; Univ Calif, MA, 49. *Prof Exp:* Jr geologist, State Bur Mines & Geol, Idaho, 46-47, asst geologist, 48-49, assoc geologist, 49-51; proj geologist, US Geol Surv, 51-54, staff asst, 54-59, commodity geologist, 59-69, chief br resources res, 63-69, dep asst chief geologist, 69-72, US Geol Surv-Saudi Arabia Proj, 72-76, geologist-in-chg, US Geol Surv, Wash, 76-89. *Concurrent Pos:* Int Coop Admin consult, Peru, 58-59 & Bolivia, 59-60; US Geol Surv adv, Iran, 63, Sudan, 77 & Yemen, 79. *Mem:* Soc Econ Geol; Geol Soc Am; distinguished mem Am Inst Mining, Metall & Petrol Engrs; Northwest Mining Asn. *Res:* Challis 2 geologic map, Idaho; Hailey 2 geologic map, Idaho; trans-Challis fault system and its control on gold and silver deposits. *Mailing Add:* 4604 S Napa St Spokane WA 99223

KIJEWSKI, LOUIS JOSEPH, THEORETICAL PHYSICS. *Current Pos:* PROF PHYSICS, MONMOUTH COL, NJ, 68- *Personal Data:* b Philadelphia, Pa, Mar 20, 36; m 75; c 1. *Educ:* LaSalle Univ, BA, 58; Columbia Univ, MA, 61; NY Univ, PhD(physics), 67. *Prof Exp:* Asst physics, Columbia Univ, 58-61; physicist, RCA Corp, Moorestown & Princeton, 61-64; res asst atomic physics, NY Univ, 64-67, assoc res scientist, 67-68. *Mem:* Am Phys Soc; Math Asn Am. *Res:* Calculations for the energy of atomic systems using density matrices. *Mailing Add:* Dept Physics Monmouth Col West Long Branch NJ 07764

KIKKAWA, YUTAKA, PATHOLOGY. *Current Pos:* PROF & CHMN, DEPT PATH, UNIV CALIF, IRVINE, 88- *Personal Data:* b Jan 30, 32; c 4. *Educ:* Univ Tokyo, BS, 53, MD, 57. *Prof Exp:* From instr to prof, Dept Path, Albert Einstein Col Med, 63-76; prof, Dept Path, NY Med Col, 76-88. *Concurrent Pos:* Mem, Coun Acad Socs, Am Asn Med Cols. *Mem:* Fel Col Am Pathologists; fel Int Acad Path; Am Asn Pathologists & Bacteriologists; Am Thoracic Soc; Fedn Am Soc Exp Biol; Int Acad Path. *Res:* Pathology of pulmonary oxygen toxicity; pulmonary benzo(a)pyrene metabolism and tobacco smoking; tobacco related disease. *Mailing Add:* Dept Path Med Sci I D440 Univ Calif Irvine CA 92717-4800. Fax: 714-725-2160

KIKTA, EDWARD JOSEPH, JR, ANALYTICAL CHEMISTRY, CHROMATOGRAPHY. *Current Pos:* Anal res chemist & lab supvr, 76-80, MGR ANALYTICAL SERV, AGR CHEM GROUP, FMC CORP, 80- *Personal Data:* b Buffalo, NY, June 11, 48. *Educ:* State Univ NY, Buffalo, BA, 70, PhD(anal chem), 78; Canisius Col, MS, 72. *Honors & Awards:* Chromatography Award, Am Chem Soc, 81. *Mem:* Am Chem Soc; Am Inst Chemists; AAAS; Am Soc Testing & Mat; NY Acad Sci. *Res:* Chromagraphic methods and systems development; application of hplc to high resolution and high sensitivity analysis; optimization of hplc and gc systems; new hplc bonded phases. *Mailing Add:* Agr Chem Div FMC Corp US Hwy 1 PO Box 8 Princeton NJ 08543-0008

KIKUCHI, RYOICHI, STATISTICAL MECHANICS. *Current Pos:* ADJ PROF, MAT SCI & ENG DEPT, UNIV CALIF, LOS ANGELES, 87- *Personal Data:* b Osaka, Japan, Dec 25, 19; US citizen; m 43; c 2. *Educ:* Univ Tokyo, BS, 42, PhD(physics), 51. *Prof Exp:* Res assoc physics, Univ Tokyo, 45-50; res assoc, Div Indust Coop, Mass Inst Technol, 51-53; asst prof, Inst Study Metals, Univ Chicago, 53-55; res physicist, Armour Res Found, Ill Inst Technol, 55-56; assoc prof, Wayne State Univ, 56-58; mem tech staff, Hughes Res Labs, 58-59, sr staff physicist, 59-63, sr scientist, 63-85; res prof, Math Sci Dept, Univ Wash, 85-89. *Concurrent Pos:* Consult, Lawrence Radiation Lab, Univ Calif, 63-67; adj prof, Univ Calif, Los Angeles, 75-85; vis prof, Purdue Univ, 77-93, Delft Tech Univ, Neth, 80 & 81; research Alexander von Humboldt fel, Max-Planck-Inst, Dusseldorf, WGer, 85, 86 & 87. *Mem:* Am Phys Soc; Phys Soc Japan; Am Inst Mining, Metall & Petrol Engrs. *Res:* Statistical mechanics of cooperative phenomena, equilibrium, and irreversible solid state physics; physical metallurgy. *Mailing Add:* Mat Sci & Eng Dept Univ Calif Los Angelas Los Angeles CA 90095

KIKUCHI, SHINYA, FUZZY SET THEORY APPLICATION, LOGISTICS. *Current Pos:* from asst prof to assoc prof, 82-93, PROF, UNIV DEL, 93- *Personal Data:* b Kobe, Japan, May 5, 43; m 75, Laura Velasco. *Educ:* Hokkaido Univ, Japan, BS, 67, MS, 69; Univ Pa, PhD(transp), 74. *Prof Exp:* Assoc, Transp Develop Assocs, Seattle, Wash, 74-77; sr proj engr, Transp Systs Div, Gen Motors Corp, 77-79, staff asst, Logistics Opers, 79-82. *Concurrent Pos:* Dir, Del Transp Ctr, 89- *Mem:* Am Soc Civil Engrs; Inst Transp Engrs; Soc Logistics Engrs; Transp Res Bd. *Res:* Analysis of transportation systems and application of operations research; urban public transportation systems design and operation; application of fuzzy set theory; routing and scheduling of transportation system; traffic engineering; development of systems analysis methodologies. *Mailing Add:* 5423 Crestline Rd Wilmington DE 19808. E-Mail: kikuchi@ce.udel.edu

KIKUDOME, GARY YOSHINORI, cytogenetics; deceased, see previous edition for last biography

KILAMBI, RAJ VARAD, FISHERIES, ZOOLOGY. *Current Pos:* from asst prof to assoc prof, 66-71, PROF ZOOL, UNIV ARK, FAYETTEVILLE, 77- *Personal Data:* b India, Feb 1, 33; m 57; c 3. *Educ:* Univ Wash, PhD(fisheries), 65. *Mem:* Am Fisheries Soc; Sigma Xi. *Res:* Fish biology and population dynamics; reservoir fisheries. *Mailing Add:* Dept Biol Sci Univ Ark Fayetteville AR 72701

KILAMBI, SRINVASACHARYULU, BARACH ALGEBRA, TOPOLOGY OF COMPLEX MANIFOLDS. *Current Pos:* from asst prof to assoc prof, 65-84, PROF MATH, UNIV MONTREAL, 84- *Educ:* Univ Paris, DSc(math), 62. *Prof Exp:* Asst prof, math, Univ Md, 62-65. *Mem:* Am Math Soc. *Mailing Add:* Math Dept Univ Montreal Montreal PQ H3C 3J7 Can

KILB, RALPH WOLFGANG, PLASMA PHYSICS, IONOSPHERIC PHYSICS. *Current Pos:* physicist, 71-73, PLASMA PHYSICS GROUP LEADER, MISSION RES CORP, 73- *Personal Data:* b Chicago, Ill, Feb 7, 31; m 59, Elizabeth Lee; c Linda & Deborah. *Educ:* Univ Nebr, BS, 52; Harvard Univ, MA, 53, PhD(chem), 56. *Prof Exp:* Asst chem, Harvard Univ, 53; phys chemist, Res Labs, Gen Elec Co, 56-60, physicist, 60-69, Tech Mil Planning Opers, 69-71. *Concurrent Pos:* Fel, Am Phys Soc. *Mem:* Am Chem Soc; Am Phys Soc; Am Geophys Union; AAAS. *Res:* Microwave spectroscopy of gases; properties and structure of high polymers; thermonuclear fusion; atmospheric physics; nuclear burst effects at high altitudes; magnetohydrodynamic code simulation; collisionless magnetohydrodynamics; plasma structure in ionoshere. *Mailing Add:* Mission Res Corp PO Drawer 719 Santa Barbara CA 93102-0719

KILBERG, MICHAEL STEVEN, REGULATION OF NUTRIENT TRANSPORT. *Current Pos:* PROF BIOCHEM & MOLECULAR BIOL, UNIV FLA, 80- *Personal Data:* b Nov 21, 51; c 3. *Educ:* Univ SDak, PhD(biochem), 77. *Mem:* Am Phys Soc; Am Soc Biochem & Molecular Biol; Am Soc Cell Biol. *Res:* Regulation of hepatic amino acid transport and transcriptional control of gene expression by amino acids. *Mailing Add:* Dept Biochem & Molecular Biol Univ Fla Sch Med Box 1000245JHMHC Gainesville FL 32610-0245. *Fax:* 904-392-6511

KILBOURN, BARRY T, LANTHANIDE ELEMENTS. *Current Pos:* DEVELOP MAT, UNOCAL/MOLYCORP, WHITE PLAINS, NY, 81- *Personal Data:* b Burton-on-Trent, Eng, Jan 21, 39; m 64; c 2. *Educ:* Oxford Univ, BA, 63, PhD(chem), 65. *Prof Exp:* CIBA res fel, Eidg Tech Hochschule, Zurich, 66-67; researcher crystallog, Imperial Chem Indust, Runcorn, Eng, 67-73, develop mat, Belgium, 73-80. *Mem:* Royal Soc Chem; Am Chem Soc; Am Ceramic Soc; Metall Soc; Electrochem Soc. *Res:* Technology and industrial applications of yttrium and the Lanthanide elements (the Rare Earths). *Mailing Add:* 45 Alpine Dr Lincoln Park NJ 07035-2255

KILBOURN, JOAN PRISCILLA PAYNE, MEDICAL MICROBIOLOGY. *Current Pos:* PRES & LAB DIR, CONSULT CLIN & MICROBIOL LAB, INC, 84-, LAB DIR, TREATMENT ALTERNATIVES TO ST CRIME, 96- *Personal Data:* b Juneau, Alaska, June 15, 36; m 61, Lee Ferris; c Laurie J & Ellen M. *Educ:* Univ Ore, BS, 58, MS, 60; Ore State Univ, PhD(microbiol), 63. *Prof Exp:* Instr bact, Univ Ore, 63-66, pediat, Med Sch, 66-68; tutor sci & math, Portland Community Col, 68-71; microbiologist, Clin Path Lab, Vet Admin Hosp, 71-74; assoc dir, ICN Med Labs, 74-76; instr, Clackamas Community Col, 78; consult microbiologist, 78-84. *Concurrent Pos:* Am Cancer Soc res grant, 63-65; consult, Choice, Books for Col Libraries, 64-; tutor, Portland Community Col, 71-; instr, Med Sch, Univ Ore, 73-74; instr, Portland State Univ Cont Educ Div, 77; reviewer, AAAS Science Books & Films. *Mem:* Fel AAAS; Am Soc Clin Pathologists; Am Soc Microbiol; Nat Registry Microbiologist; Am Bd Bioanalysis. *Res:* Use of a radiation resistant microorganism as a protectant and therapeutic agent from the lethal effects of irradiation; automation of clinical medical microbiology; bacterial flora of chronic lung diseases; over the counter test for vaginal yeast infections. *Mailing Add:* 3178 SW Fairmount Blvd Portland OR 97201. *Fax:* 503-222-5279

KILBOURNE, EDWIN DENNIS, MEDICINE, PUBLIC HEALTH & EPIDEMIOLOGY. *Current Pos:* chmn, Dept Microbiol, 68-86, DISTINGUISHED SERV PROF, MT SINAI SCH MED, 86-; RES PROF, NY MED COL, 92- *Personal Data:* b Buffalo, NY, July 10, 20; m 52, Joy; c Edwin M, Richard S, Christopher N & Paul A. *Educ:* Cornell Univ, AB, 42, MD, 44. *Hon Degrees:* DSc, Rockefeller Univ, 86. *Honors & Awards:* R E Dyer Lectr Award, NIH, 73; Borden Award, Asn Am Med Cols, 74; Thomas Francis Jr Mem lectr, 76; Harry F Dowling Lect Award, 76; Henry Brainerd Mem lectr, 76; Bernard A Briody Mem lectr, 77; Harvey Soc lectr, 78; Harry M Rose Mem lectr, 80. *Prof Exp:* Intern med, NY Hosp, 44-45, asst resident, 45-46; asst resident physician, Hosp Rockefeller Inst, 48-51; assoc prof med & dir, Div Infectious Dis, Tulane Univ, 51-55; from assoc prof pub health to prof, Med Col, Cornell Univ, 55-69, dir, Div Virus Res, 55-69. *Concurrent Pos:* Asst, Rockefeller Inst, 48-51; mem, Comn Influenza, US Armed Forces Epidemiol Bd, 59-71; NIH res career award, 61-68; mem, Infectious Dis Adv Comt, Nat Inst Allergy & Infectious Dis, 69-73, chmn, Subcomt Influenza, 71-74; Virol Task Force chmn, NIH & mem, Adv Comt Immunization Pract, CDC, 76-80. *Mem:* Nat Acad Sci; Am Acad Microbiol; Asn Am Physicians; Am Asn Immunologists; Am Epidemiol Soc; Am Soc Clin Invest; fel NY Acad Sci. *Res:* Influenza virus genetics; host determinants of viral virulence; viral genetics and immunology; experimental epidemiology; vaccines; major research activities involve continuing studies of the genetics and virulence mechanisms of influenza viruses with special emphasis on the development of new vaccines. *Mailing Add:* Dept Microbiol & Immunol NY Med Col Basic Sci Bldg Rm 315 Valhalla NY 10595. *Fax:* 914-993-4176; *E-Mail:* kilbourn@ct1.nai.net

KILBOURNE, EDWIN MICHAEL, ENVIRONMENTAL EPIDEMIOLOGY, TOXICOLOGY & IMMUNIZATION INFORMATION SYSTEMS. *Current Pos:* epidemic intel serv officer, Ctr Dis Control, Atlanta, 80-82, chief, invests sect, Spec Studies Br, Ctr Environ Health, 83-85, med epidemiologist, Foreign Assignment, 85-87, med epidemiologist, Ctr Environ Health & Injury Control, 87-89, chief, Health Studies Br, Div Environ Hazards & Health Effects, Ctr Environ Health & Injury Control, 89-90, asst dir sci, epidemiol prog off, 90-96, DIR DATA MGT DIV, NAT IMMUNIZATION PROG, CTR DIS CONTROL & PREV, 96- *Personal Data:* b New Orleans, La, Oct 1, 53; m 82, Barbara K Williams; c David, Michael, Rebecca & Kate. *Educ:* Cornell Univ, AB, 74, MD, 78; Am Bd Internal Med, cert, 84; Am Bd Prev Med, cert, 88. *Honors & Awards:* Alexander D Longmuir Award, 82. *Prof Exp:* Resident internal med, Univ Ala Hosps, Birmingham, 78-80 & 82-83. *Mem:* Am Acad Clin Toxicol; Am Pub Health Asn; fel Am Col Physicians; fel Am Col Prev Med; Am Med Informatics Asn. *Res:* Epidemiologic research regarding the adverse effects on human health of physical and chemical environmental agents; effects of heat and cold, the newly discovered toxic-oil syndrome in Spain, and the eosinophilia-myalgia syndrome (EMS) in the United States; technical and logistical problems of implementing computerized registries of children to ensure that they are properly immunized. *Mailing Add:* Ctr Dis Control 1600 Clifton Rd NE Mailstop E-62 Atlanta GA 30333. *Fax:* 404-639-8171; *E-Mail:* emk1@cdc.gov

KILBURN, KAYE HATCH, INTERNAL & PREVENTIVE MEDICINE. *Current Pos:* RALPH EDGINTON PROF MED, UNIV SOUTHERN CALIF SCH MED, LOS ANGELES, 80-; DIR, SOUTHERN CALIF ENVIRON MED CLIN, LONG BEACH, 84-; PRES, NEURO INC, PASADENA, 94- *Personal Data:* b Logan, Utah, Sept 20, 31; m 54, Gerrie Griffin; c Ann L (Ingram), Scott K & Jean M. *Educ:* Univ Utah, BS, 51, MD, 54. *Prof Exp:* Intern med, Univ Hosps, Cleveland, 54-55; resident, Univ Utah Hosps, 55-57; asst prof med, Wash Univ, 61-62; from assoc prof to prof, Med Ctr, Duke Univ, 62-73, asst prof anat, 68-73, dir, Div Environ Med, 70-73; prof med, assoc prof anat & dir, Div Pulmonary & Environ Med, Med Ctr, Univ Mo-Columbia, 73-77; prof med & community Med, Mt Sinai Sch Med, City Univ New York, 77-80. *Concurrent Pos:* Fel cardiopulmonary physiol, Duke Univ, 57-58; Am Trudeau Soc fel, 58; USPHS fel cardiol, Brompton Hosp, Univ London, 60-61; Nat Heart Inst res grant & USPHS training grants, 62-; chief med serv, Durham Vet Admin Hosp, 63-68; consult, Vet Admin Hosps, Durham, Fayetteville & Oteen, 68-73; pres, Workers Dis Detection Serv, 86- *Mem:* Am Fedn Clin Res; Am Thoracic Soc; Am Phys Soc; AAP; ASCB. *Res:* Pulmonary structure and function, particularly pulmonary circulation; early detection of dysfunction; respiratory failure causing cerebral and circulatory dysfunction; pulmonary responses to environmental and occupational agents; alveolar surfactant; structure and function of cilia, mechanism of inflammation; proteolytic enzymes and antienzymes; mediators of leukocyte response; experimental pathology of lung; epidemiology of occupational diseases, byssinosis, asbestosis, and effects of exposure to formaldehyde, trichlorolthylene, welding gases and fumes; neurobehavioral toxicology of solvents, formaldehydes and PCB's; methods for measuring neurological functions in populations, toxic effects of chemicals associated with birth defects associated with metals, metal chelating agents and enzyme blockers, smoking cessation intervention in blue collar workers. *Mailing Add:* 3250 Mesaloa Lane Pasadena CA 91107. *Fax:* 213-342-1833

KILBY, JACK ST CLAIR, ELECTRICAL ENGINEERING. *Current Pos:* CONSULT, 70- *Personal Data:* b Jefferson City, Mo, Nov 8, 23; m 48; c 2. *Educ:* Univ Ill, BS, 47; Univ Wis, MS, 50. *Hon Degrees:* DSc, Univ Miami, 82, Rochester Inst Technol, 86, Univ Ill, 88, Rensselaer Polytech Inst, 89, Univ Wis, 90. *Honors & Awards:* Sarnoff Award, Inst Elec & Electronics Engrs, 66 & Brunetti Award, 80; Ballantine Medal, Franklin Inst, 66; Hall Minuteman Trophy, Order of Daedalians, 66; Nat Medal Sci, 70; Zworykwin Medal, Nat Acad Eng, 75; Holley Medal, Am Soc Mech Engrs, 82 & Charles Stark Draper Prize, 90; Medal Honor, Inst Elec & Electronics Engrs, 83; Nat Medal Technol, 90; Kyoto Prize for Tech Achievement, 93. *Prof Exp:* Engr, Globe-Union, Inc, Wis, 47-58; from engr to asst vpres, Tex Instruments Inc, 58-70. *Concurrent Pos:* Distinguished prof, Tex A&M Univ, 77-85. *Mem:* Nat Acad Eng; fel Inst Elec & Electronics Engrs. *Res:* Monolithic integrated circuits. *Mailing Add:* 6600 LBJ Freeway Suite 4155 Dallas TX 75240

KILDAL, HELGE, applied physics, for more information see previous edition

KILDAY, WARREN D, organic chemistry, for more information see previous edition

KILDSIG, DANE OLIN, PHYSICAL PHARMACY. *Current Pos:* from asst prof to assoc prof, 66-75, assoc head dept, 81-85, PROF PHYS PHARM, PURDUE UNIV, 85-, HEAD DEPT INDUST & PHYS PHARM, 85- *Personal Data:* b Oshkosh, Wis, Aug 3, 35; m 58; c 2. *Educ:* Univ Wis, Madison, BS, 57, PhD(phys pharm), 65. *Prof Exp:* Res scientist, Wyeth Labs, 65-66. *Mem:* Am Asn Pharmaceut Scientists; fel Am Asn Pharmaceut Scientists. *Res:* Mechanism of dissolution of solids and drug binding to protein; drug targeting; liposomes, pulmonary drug delivery. *Mailing Add:* 2526 Shagbark Lane West Lafayette IN 47906

KILEDJIAN, MEGERDITCH, REGULATION OF EUKARYOTIC GENE EXPRESSION, RNA-PROTEIN INTERACTIONS. *Current Pos:* ASST PROF, RUTGERS UNIV, 95- *Personal Data:* b Aleppo, Syria, Mar 24, 63; US citizen; m 96, Paneyiota Trifillis. *Educ:* Rutgers Univ, BA, 85; Univ Pa, PhD(molecular biol), 90. *Prof Exp:* Postdoctoral assoc, Univ Pa, 90-95. *Mem:* AAAS; Am Soc Biochem & Molecular Biol. *Res:* Structural and functional characterization of RNA-protein interactions in the regulation of RNA turnover and eukaryotic gene expression. *Mailing Add:* Dept Cell Develop & Neurobiol Rutgers Univ PO Box 1059 Piscataway NJ 08855. *E-Mail:* kiledjia@biology.rutgers.edu

KILEN, THOMAS CLARENCE, PLANT GENETICS, HOST PLANT RESISTANCE TO PESTS. *Current Pos:* PLANT RES GENETICIST, AGR RES SERV, USDA, 67- *Personal Data:* b Jackson, Minn, Jan 24, 33; m 65, Nancy A Kollath. *Educ:* Univ Wis, BS, 63, MS, 66, PhD(agron, genetics), 68. *Mem:* Am Soc Agron; Crop Sci Soc Am; Am Genetic Asn. *Res:* Inheritance of disease resistance in soybeans; inheritance of characters modifying plant type and their effect upon seed yield; genetics of resistance to foliar feeding insects of soybeans. *Mailing Add:* PO Box 196 Stoneville MS 38776-0196. *Fax:* 601-686-5465

KILEY, CHARLES WALTER, ICHTHYOLOGY. *Current Pos:* PVT PRACT DENT. *Personal Data:* b Staten Island, NY, Feb 25, 44; m 70; c 2. *Educ:* Wagner Col, BS, 66; NY Univ, MS, 69, PhD(biol, ichthyol), 73, DDS, 80. *Prof Exp:* Instr biol, Wagner Col, 69-74, asst prof biol, 74-, chmn dept, 75- *Concurrent Pos:* Adj asst prof, Staten Island Community Col, 74-75, St John's Univ, 76- & Int Med Educ, 76-; adj teaching staff, Staten Island Hosp, 81-; dir dent, NY Shipping-Port Police Union, 85- *Mem:* Am Inst Biol Sci; AAAS; Am Fisheries Soc; Am Soc Ichthyologists & Herpetologists; NY Acad Sci. *Res:* Histology and ultrastructure of immunocompetent organs in fishes; field collection and identification of fishes. *Mailing Add:* 2306 Redwood Rd Scotch Plains NJ 07076-2116

KILEY, JAMES P, RESPIRATORY PHYSIOLOGY, NEUROPHYSIOLOGY. *Current Pos:* CHIEF AIRWAYS DIS, NAT HEART, LUNG & BLOOD INST, NIH, 84- *Personal Data:* b Medford, Mass, Apr 16, 52; m 77, Randi Miller; c Lori, Karen & Steven. *Educ:* Kans State Univ, PhD(physiol), 82. *Prof Exp:* Fel physiol, Univ NC, Chapel Hill, 82-84. *Concurrent Pos:* Adj asst prof physiol, Georgetown Univ, Washington, DC. *Mem:* Am Physiol Soc; Sigma Xi. *Mailing Add:* 20124 Harron Valley Way Gaithersburg MD 20879

KILEY, JOHN EDMUND, MEDICINE. *Current Pos:* CONSULT, 85- *Personal Data:* b New York, NY, Mar 22, 20; m 45, Catherine Walsh; c Edmund, Elizabeth, Catherine, Mary & Abbie. *Educ:* Rennselaer Polytech Inst, BS, 42; Harvard Med Sch, MD, 45. *Prof Exp:* From instr to prof, Albany Med Col, 52-78; prof med nephrol, Med Ctr, Univ Miss, 78-85. *Concurrent Pos:* Fel physiol, Albany Med Col, 48-49. *Mem:* Fel Am Col Physicians. *Res:* Extracorporeal vividialysis and renal disease. *Mailing Add:* 27 Constitution Dr Glenmont NY 12077

KILEY, LEO AUSTIN, NUCLEAR CHEMISTRY, METEOROLOGY. *Current Pos:* RETIRED. *Personal Data:* b Boston, Mass, May 22, 18; m 44, Luna Hamilton; c 2. *Educ:* Mass Inst Technol, SB, 39; Ohio State Univ, PhD(chem), 52. *Hon Degrees:* LLD, NMex State Univ, 67. *Prof Exp:* Dep dir, Atomic Warfare Directorate, Air Force Cambridge Res Ctr, 53-54, dep chief biophys div, Spec Weapons Ctr, 55-56, chief, 57-58, tech dir, Weapons Effects Tests, Field Command, Defense Atomic Support Agency, 59-60, dir, 60-63, vcomdr, Air Force Cambridge Res Labs, 63-64, comdr, 64-65, Air Force Missile Develop Ctr, 65-68, Off Aerospace Res, 68-69; gen mgr, Neutron Devices Dept, Gen Elec Co, 69-78; vpres, Los Alamos Tech Assoc, Inc, 79-93. *Res:* Environmental and physical sciences; nuclear physics. *Mailing Add:* PO Box 1122 Santa Fe NM 87504

KILGORE, BRUCE MOODY, FOREST ECOLOGY, FIRE ECOLOGY. *Current Pos:* RETIRED. *Personal Data:* b Los Angeles, Calif, Mar 26, 30; m 52, A Elaine Grant; c David B & Steven P. *Educ:* Univ Calif, Berkeley, AB, 52, PhD(zool), 68; Univ Okla, MA, 54. *Prof Exp:* Info asst, Nature Conserv, DC, 56-57; ed, Nat Parks Mag, Nat Parks Asn, 57-60; managing ed, Sierra Club Pub & ed, Sierra Club Bull, Sierra Club, Calif, 60-65; teaching asst zool, Univ Calif, Berkeley, 63-68; res biologist, Off Chief Scientist, Nat Park Serv, 68-72, assoc regional dir prof serv, Western Region, 72-81; res proj leader, Northern Forest Fire Lab, Intermountain Forest & Range Exp Sta, US Forest Serv, Montana, 81-85; chief, Div Nat Res & Res, Western Region, Nat Park Serv, San Francisco, 85-93, assoc reg dir res mgt & planning, 93-96, assoc reg dir stewardship & sci, 96-97. *Res:* Fire ecology of giant sequoia-mixed conifer forests; crown fire potential; fire history frequency; impact of prescribed burning on vegetation, fuels, and breeding birds; role of fire in wilderness/ parks; understory burning in pine-larch-fir forests. *Mailing Add:* Nat Park Serv Western Reg 600 Harrison St Suite 600 San Francisco CA 94107. *Fax:* 650-427-1485

KILGORE, DELBERT LYLE, JR, ENVIRONMENTAL PHYSIOLOGY, RESPIRATORY PHYSIOLOGY. *Current Pos:* from asst prof to assoc prof, 73-83, PROF ZOOL, UNIV MONT, 83-, ASSOC DEAN, 91- *Personal Data:* b Hutchinson, Kans, Sept 28, 42; m 66, Judith Smith; c Alison & Trevor. *Educ:* Univ Kans, BA, 64, MA, 67, PhD(physiol, cell biol), 72. *Prof Exp:* Res assoc physiol, Duke Univ, 71-73. *Concurrent Pos:* Vis adj prof, Col Vet Med, Kans State Univ, 82-83 & 84; vis scholar, Dept Med, Univ Califm, San Diego, La Jolla, 90; res fel, Sch Biol Scis, Flinders Univ SAustralia, Adelaide, 92. *Mem:* Sigma Xi; Am Physiol Soc; Am Soc Zoologists. *Res:* Respiratory adaptations of birds to extreme environments; physiology of temperature regulation, control of respiration, acid-base balance and water balance. *Mailing Add:* Div Biol Sci Univ Mont Missoula MT 59812-1002. *Fax:* 406-243-4184

KILGORE, LEE A, ELECTRICAL ENGINEERING. *Current Pos:* RETIRED. *Personal Data:* b Levitt, Nebr, Aug, 05. *Educ:* Univ Nebr, BS, 27; Univ Pittsburgh, MS, 29. *Hon Degrees:* DEng, Univ Nebr, 56. *Honors & Awards:* Lamme Medal, Inst Elec & Electronics Engrs, 52. *Prof Exp:* Dir eng, Westinghouse Elec Co, 29-70; consult, 70-95. *Mem:* Nat Acad Eng; fel Inst Elec & Electronics Engrs. *Mailing Add:* 1470 W Tienken Rd Rochester MI 48306-4180

KILGORE, LOIS TAYLOR, NUTRITION. *Current Pos:* asst home economist, 55-69, prof, 69-84, EMER PROF HOME ECON, MISS STATE UNIV, 84- *Personal Data:* b Feb 9, 22; US citizen; wid; c Marcia K (Newsom) & Susan K (Booker). *Educ:* Miss State Univ, BS, 55, MS, 63, PhD(physiol), 68. *Prof Exp:* Med technologist, Vicksburg Hosp, 43-44 & Scales Clin, 44-46; med technologist with Dr Hunt Cleveland, 46-48; jr chemist, Petrol Prod Lab, Motor Vehicle Controller, 53-55. *Mem:* AAAS; Home Econ Asn Am; Am Soc Clin Path; Am Soc Nutrit; Am Dietetic Asn. *Res:* Nutrition of pre-school children; interrelationships of nutrients; international nutrition; breakdown of fats during cooking. *Mailing Add:* 1378 Kilgore Dr Starkville MS 39759

KILGORE, WENDELL WARREN, TOXICOLOGY. *Current Pos:* chmn dept, 70-77, dir Food Protection & Toxicol Ctr, 70-78, PROF ENVIRON TOXICOL, UNIV CALIF, DAVIS, 60-, PROF PHARMACOL, SCH MED, 78- *Personal Data:* b Greenfield, Mo, June 21, 29; m 52; c 3. *Educ:* Univ Calif, AB, 51, PhD(microbiol), 59. *Prof Exp:* Asst microbiol, Univ Calif, 55-58, microbiologist, 58-59; microbiologist, Stanford Res Inst, 59-60. *Concurrent Pos:* Chmn, Governor's Sci Adv Panel, 87- *Mem:* AAAS; Am Soc Microbiol; Am Chem Soc; Soc Toxicol. *Res:* Environmental toxicology; toxicology of pesticides; analysis and detection of pesticides; effect of pesticides on human health. *Mailing Add:* 1301 Cedar Pine Davis CA 95616

KILGOUR, GORDON LESLIE, BIOCHEMISTRY. *Current Pos:* head dept chem, 68-74, PROF CHEM, PORTLAND STATE COL, 68- *Personal Data:* b Vancouver, BC, Apr 24, 29; m 49; c 2. *Educ:* Univ BC, BA, 51, MSc, 53; Univ Wash, PhD(biochem), 56. *Prof Exp:* Jr res biochemist, Univ Calif, Berkeley, 56-57; asst prof biochem, Mich State Univ, 57-63; from assoc prof to prof, San Fernando Valley State Col, 63-68. *Mem:* Am Chem Soc. *Res:* Oxidative enzymes and coenzymes; chemistry and biochemistry of phosphorylated carbohydrate compounds. *Mailing Add:* 930 O'Brien St Lake Oswego OR 97034

KILHAM, SUSAN SOLTAU, ECOLOGY, AQUATIC BIOLOGY. *Current Pos:* ASSOC PROF, DREXEL UNIV, PHILADELPHIA, 91- *Personal Data:* b Duluth, Minn, Jan 22, 43; wid. *Educ:* Eckerd Col, BS, 65; Duke Univ, PhD(zool), 71. *Honors & Awards:* McArthur Alumnus Award, Eckerd Col, 77. *Prof Exp:* Res assoc microbiol, Duke Univ, 70-72; guest investr oceanog, Woods Hole Oceanog Inst, 72 & 79-80; lectr, Univ Mich, Ann Arbor, 73, asst res scientist natural resources, 73-75, asst res scientist, 75-78, assoc res scientist biol, 79-90. *Concurrent Pos:* NSF oceanog trainee, 67-70; nat lectr, Phycological Soc Am, 85-87; vis scientist, Max Planck Inst Limnol, 87-88; Max Panck Soc scholar, 88; vis assoc prof, Univ Wash, 90- *Mem:* Am Soc Limnol & Oceanog; Phycol Soc Am; AAAS; Int Soc Limnol; Int Asn Great Lakes Res; Ecol Soc Am. *Res:* Aquatic ecology; freshwater phytoplankton; algal physiology and ecology; population dynamics and competition. *Mailing Add:* Dept Biosci & Biotechnol Drexel Univ Philadelphia PA 19104. *Fax:* 215-895-1273; *E-Mail:* susan_kilham@coasmail.physics.drexel.edu

KILINC, ATTILA ISHAK, GEOCHEMISTRY. *Current Pos:* from asst prof to assoc prof, 70-79, head dept, 75-83, PROF GEOL, UNIV CINCINNATI, 79-, HEAD DEPT, 91- *Personal Data:* b Mersin, Turkey, Feb 15, 36; m 61; c 2. *Educ:* Istanbul Univ, BS, 60; Pa State Univ, MSc, 66, PhD(geol), 69. *Prof Exp:* Res assoc, Stanford Univ, 68-70. *Concurrent Pos:* Asst head, Dept Geol, Univ Cincinnati, 72-75. *Mem:* Am Geophys Union; Sigma Xi. *Res:* Geochemistry of magmatic and hydrothermal systems at high temperatures and pressures. *Mailing Add:* Geol Dept 13 Univ Cincinnati Cincinnati OH 45221-0001

KILKENNY, JOSEPH DAVID, PHYSICS. *Current Pos:* RES SCIENTIST, LAWRENCE LIVERMORE NAT LAB, 83- *Personal Data:* b Eng, July 7, 47. *Educ:* Imp Col, London, BS, 68, MS, 70, PhD(physics), 72. *Mem:* Am Phys Soc. *Mailing Add:* Lawrence Livermore Nat Lab Livermore CA 94550

KILKSON, HENN, CHEMICAL ENGINEERING, PHYSICAL CHEMISTRY. *Current Pos:* Res engr, Eastern Lab, E I DuPont de Nemours & Co, Inc, 57-59, res engr, Eng Res Lab, 60-65, sr res engr, Eng Tech Lab, 65-66, res assoc, 66-72, res fel, 72-55, sr res fel, 85-90, Fel, 90-96, CONSULT, E I DU PONT DE NEMOURS & CO, 96- *Personal Data:* b Tartu, Estonia, Dec 30, 30; nat US; m 63, Reet; c Tiia & Eero. *Educ:* Univ Colo, BS, 52, MS, 54; Cornell Univ, PhD(chem eng), 57. *Honors & Awards:* T H Chilton Award, Am Inst Chem Engrs, 89. *Concurrent Pos:* Ledership team mem, Eng Res & Develop, DuPont. *Mem:* Am Chem Soc; Am Inst Chem Engrs; NY Acad Sci. *Res:* Mathematical aspects of polymerizations; chemical kinetics; chemical reactor design and stability. *Mailing Add:* 5 Birch Knoll Rd Northminster Wilmington DE 19810

KILKSON, REIN, BIOPHYSICS. *Current Pos:* vis prof chem & physics, 70-72, PROF PHYSICS, UNIV ARIZ, 72-, PROF MICROBIOL & IMMUNOL, 76- *Personal Data:* b Tartu, Estonia, Aug 1, 27; nat US. *Educ:* Yale Univ, BS, 53, MS, 54, PhD(physics), 56. *Prof Exp:* Mem tech staff, Bell Tel Labs, Inc, 56-58; asst prof physics, Wayne State Univ, 58-59 & biophysics, Yale Univ, 59-66; guest researcher, Dept Med Physics, Karolinska Inst, Stockholm, 64-70. *Mem:* Biophys Soc; Am Soc Microbiol; Sigma Xi; Am Phys Soc; Int Soc Molecular Evolution. *Res:* Molecular biophysics; virus structure; macromolecular arrangements in cell organelles; molecular regulation; molecular evolution; theoretical biology and biophysics; biological systems; light scattering and nerve conduction; general laws of the biological state of matter. *Mailing Add:* Dept Physics Univ Ariz Tucson AZ 85721

KILLAM, ELEANOR, MATHEMATICS. *Current Pos:* from asst prof to assoc prof, 60-91, EMER PROF MATH, UNIV MASS, AMHERST, 91- *Personal Data:* b Whitefield, NH, May 18, 33. *Educ:* Univ NH, BS, 55, MS, 56; Yale Univ, PhD(math), 61. *Mem:* Am Math Soc; Math Asn Am. *Res:* Ring theory; banach algebras; locally m-convex algebras. *Mailing Add:* 26 Valley Lane Amherst MA 01002. *E-Mail:* killam@math.umass.edu

KILLAM, EVA KING, PHARMACOLOGY, NEUROPHARMACOLOGY. *Current Pos:* prof in residence, 68-78, PROF PHARMACOL, SCH MED, UNIV CALIF, DAVIS, 78- *Personal Data:* b New York, NY, Nov 16, 21; m 55; c 3. *Educ:* Sarah Lawrence Col, AB, 42; Mt Holyoke Col, AM, 44; Univ Ill, PhD(pharmacol), 53. *Honors & Awards:* Abel Award, Soc Pharm Exp

Therapist, 54. *Prof Exp:* Instr, Sarah Lawrence Col, 44-46; instr biol, Albertus Magnus Col, 46-47; asst therapeut, Col Med, NY Univ, 47-48; pharmacologist & toxicologist, Army Chem Ctr, Md, 48-51; instr pharmacol, Univ Ill, 52-53; res pharmacologist, Univ Cal, Los Angeles, 53-59; res assoc pharmacol, Sch Med, Stanford Univ, 59-68. *Concurrent Pos:* Ed-in-chief, J Pharmacol & Exp Therapeut, 78-; pres, Western Pharmacol Soc, 84. *Mem:* Am Soc Pharmacol & Exp Therapeut (pres 89-90); Am Col Neuropsychopharmacol (pres, 88); Soc Exp Biol & Med; Am Epilepsy Soc. *Res:* Neuropharmacology, especially central nervous system; influence of drugs on epilepsy; eletrophysiological correlates of behavior and influence of drugs thereon. *Mailing Add:* 2225 Anza Ave Davis CA 95616

KILLAM, EVERETT HERBERT, RESEARCH & DEVELOPMENT OF WASTE DISPOSAL METHODS. *Current Pos:* CONSULT, FORENSIC ENG, 90- *Personal Data:* b Whitefield, NH, Feb 2, 38; c 2. *Educ:* Univ NH, BS, 61; Univ Wyo, MS, 65, PhD(civil eng), 73. *Prof Exp:* Stress engr, Boeing Co, 67-68 & Earl & Wright, 73-74; instr mech, Univ Wyo, 68-72; asst prof mech, Rose-Hulman Inst Technol, 74-77; mgr res & develop, Custodis Construct Co, 77-82, engr mgr, Custodis-Cotrell, 83-88; consult, Waste Mgt, 88-90. *Concurrent Pos:* Eng mgr indust chimneys, Custodis Construct Co, 82. *Mem:* Am Soc Civil Engrs. *Res:* Dynamic and thermal effects on large industrial chimneys; new cooling tower designs using theoretical and experimental data; seperation of trash into useful end products. *Mailing Add:* 14 Fieldstone Pl Flemington NJ 08822

KILLAM, KEITH FENTON, JR, PHARMACOLOGY. *Current Pos:* chmn dept, 68-81, PROF PHARMACOL, SCH MED, UNIV CALIF, DAVIS, 68- *Personal Data:* b Hollywood, Fla, Mar 2, 27; m 55; c 3. *Educ:* Tufts Col, BS, 48; Univ Ill, MS, 53, PhD(pharm), 54. *Prof Exp:* Res pharmacologist, Smith Kline & French Labs, 48-50 & 54-55; NIH sr res fel, Univ Calif, Los Angeles, 55-59; prof pharmacol, Sch Med, Stanford Univ, 59-68. *Concurrent Pos:* Res fel neurophys, Mass Gen Hosp, 58; mem psychopharmacol study sect, NIH, 58-62; study sect, comput res, NIH, 62-65; mem, Int Brain Res Orgn, Drug Abuse Res Rev Comt, Nat Inst Drug Abuse, 82-85, chmn, 83-85. *Mem:* AAAS; Am Soc Pharmacol & Exp Therapeut; Am Col Neuropsychopharmacol; Int Soc Primatology. *Res:* Neuropharmacology; physiological mechanisms in brain; correlation between brain electrical activity and behavior and effects of psychotropic agents; substance abuse. *Mailing Add:* Dept Pharmacol Univ Calif Sch Med Davis CA 95616-8654. *Fax:* 530-752-7710

KILLEBREW, FLAVIUS CHARLES, MAMMALOGY. *Current Pos:* ASST PROF BIOL, WTEX STATE UNIV, 76- *Personal Data:* b Canadian, Tex, Apr 2, 49; m 78; c 1. *Educ:* WTex State Univ, BS, 70, MS, 72; PhD(zool), 76. *Prof Exp:* Instr zool, Univ Ark, 72-76. *Concurrent Pos:* Res asst grant, Killgore Comt, 71-72; res prof grant, 76-77; res asst grant-in-aid, Sigma Xi, 71-72; res asst, Univ Ark Mus, 74-76; res prof grant, US Dept Interior, 78-79. *Mem:* Sigma Xi (vpres, 77-78, pres, 78-79); Soc Study Amphibians & Reptiles; Herpetologists League; Am Soc Ichthyologists & Herpetologists. *Res:* Systematics and ecology of reptiles. *Mailing Add:* Dept Biol WTex State Univ 2501 Fourth Ave Canyon TX 79016-0001

KILLEEN, JOHN, PLASMA PHYSICS, MAGNETOHYDRODYNAMICS. *Current Pos:* RETIRED. *Personal Data:* b Guam, July 28, 25; m 50; c 6. *Educ:* Univ Calif, AB, 49, MA, 51, PhD(math), 55. *Prof Exp:* Mathematician, Radiation Lab, Univ Calif, 50-55, Bell Tel Labs, Inc, 55 & Inst Math Sci, NY Univ, 56; mathematician, Math Radiation Lab, Lawrence Livermore Lab, Univ Calif, 57-68, prof appl sci, 68-90, dir, Nat Magnetic Fusion Energy Comput Ctr, 74-90. *Concurrent Pos:* Ed, J Comput Physics, 68-90. *Mem:* Am Math Soc; Am Phys Soc; Sigma Xi. *Res:* Mathematical physics; computation; computer applications to controlled thermonuclear research. *Mailing Add:* 1528 Campus Dr Berkeley CA 94708

KILLEN, JOHN YOUNG, JR, MEDICAL RESEARCH. *Current Pos:* dep dir, 87-93, actg dir, 93-94, DIR, DIV AIDS, NAT INST ALLERGY & INFECTIOUS DIS, NIH, 94- *Personal Data:* b July 20, 49. *Educ:* Kenyon Col, AB, 71; Tufts Univ, MD, 75. *Prof Exp:* Physician, Moses Taylor Hosp, Scranton, 77-80; sr investr, Clin Invest Br, Cancer Ther Eval Prog, Div Cancer Treat, Nat Cancer Inst, 80-81, head, Med Sect, 81-84, dep chief, Clin Invest Br & prog dir, Coop Clin Trials Group, 84- 86; med dir, Whitman-Walker Clin, Washington, DC, 86-87. *Mem:* Am Col Physicians; Am Soc Clin Oncol; Int AIDS Soc; Am Asn Physicians Human Rights. *Res:* Medicine. *Mailing Add:* Div AIDS Nat Inst Allergy & Infectious Dis Solar Bldg Rm 2A18 6003 Exec Blvd Rockville MD 20892

KILLEN, ROSEMARY MARGARET, astronomy, physics, for more information see previous edition

KILLGOAR, PAUL CHARLES, JR, ELASTOMERS. *Current Pos:* MGR, FUELS & LUBRICANTS DEPT, FORD MOTOR CO, 90- *Personal Data:* b Boston, Mass, Aug 3, 46; m 69; c 2. *Educ:* State Col, Bridgewater, BA, 68; Mich State Univ, PhD(chem), 72. *Prof Exp:* Scientist, Cabot Corp, 68; res assoc, Mich State Univ, 72; scientist, 72-90. *Mem:* Am Chem Soc; Sigma Xi; Soc Plastic Engs. *Res:* Physical properties of elastomers; dynamic mechanical and fatigue properties; use of elastomers in automotive applications; polymer processing. *Mailing Add:* 15455 Ashurst Rd Livonia MI 48154-2603

KILLGORE, CHARLES A, MEDICAL PHYSICS & ENGINEERING. *Current Pos:* PRES, KILLGORE'S, INC, RADIATION & ENG CONSULTS, 76- *Personal Data:* b Lisbon, La, Aug 19, 34; m 54; c 3. *Educ:* La Polytech Inst, BS, 56, MS, 63. *Honors & Awards:* Am Soc Eng Educ Award, 70. *Prof Exp:* Chem engr, Am Oil Co, Ark, 56; chemist, Claiborne Gasoline Co, La, 59; from instr to prof chem eng, La Tech Univ, 59-76, dir, Nuclear Ctr, 63-76, assoc dean eng & dir eng res, 72-76. *Concurrent Pos:* NSF sci fac fel. *Mem:* Am Inst Chem Engrs; Am Soc Eng Educ; Am Nuclear Soc; Health Physics Soc; Am Asn Physicists Med; Am Col Radiol. *Res:* Industrial applications of radioactive isotopes. *Mailing Add:* 506-100 Oaks Dr Ruston LA 71270

KILLIAN, CARL STANLEY, chemical pathology, diagnostic immunology, for more information see previous edition

KILLIAN, FREDERICK LUTHER, POLYMER CHEMISTRY. *Current Pos:* from res chemist to sr res chemist, 67-81, sr financial adv, 81-92, PATENT ASSOC, E I DU PONT DE NEMOURS & CO, 92- *Personal Data:* b Lancaster, Pa, May 31, 42; m 63; c 2. *Educ:* Franklin & Marshall Col, AB, 63; Northwestern Univ, Ill, PhD(org chem), 67. *Mem:* Am Chem Soc. *Res:* Physical-organic chemistry; reaction mechanisms; polymer synthesis and conversion to synthetic fibers; fiber structure; organic polymer chemistry. *Mailing Add:* 1138 Elderon Dr Wilmington DE 19808. *Fax:* 302-892-7819

KILLIAN, GARY JOSEPH, REPRODUCTIVE PHYSIOLOGY. *Current Pos:* PROF ANIMAL SCI, PA STATE UNIV, 84- *Personal Data:* b Rockville Centre, NY, Dec 6, 45; m 65; c 3. *Educ:* Kans State Univ, BS, 67, MS, 69; Pa State Univ, PhD(reprod biol), 73. *Prof Exp:* Asst prof anat physiol, Dept Biol, Pa State Univ, 73-74, from res asst to res assoc, 72-75, asst prof reprod physiol, Dept Dairy & Animal Sci, 75-76; asst prof, 76-79, assoc prof reprod physiol, Dept Biol Sci, Kent State Univ, 79-84. *Mem:* Soc Study Reprod; AAAS. *Res:* Male reproductive physiology, endocrine regulation and effects of contraceptives on epididymal physiology and sperm maturation; biology of spermatozoa and sperm capacitation. *Mailing Add:* Dept Animal Sci Pa State Univ Dairy Breeding Res Ctr University Park PA 16802

KILLICK, KATHLEEN ANN, microbial biochemistry, for more information see previous edition

KILLINGBECK, STANLEY, PHYSICAL CHEMISTRY. *Current Pos:* asst prof, 63-71, ASSOC PROF CHEM, CENT MO STATE COL, 71- *Personal Data:* b Blackburn, Eng, May 20, 29; US citizen. *Educ:* Blackburn Tech Col, BS, 51; Cornell Univ, MS, 56, PhD(chem), Univ Kans, 64. *Prof Exp:* Lab asst, Walpamur Paint Co, Eng, 46-52; asst tech off, Imp Chem Indust, Eng, 52-54. *Res:* Analytical chemistry. *Mailing Add:* 623 Eusbus Hwy Warrensburg MO 64093

KILLINGER, DENNIS K, LASER REMOTE SENSING, QUANTUM OPTICS. *Current Pos:* PROF PHYSICS, UNIV SFLA, 87- *Personal Data:* b Boone, Iowa, Sept 23, 45; m 69; c 2. *Educ:* Univ Iowa, BA, 67; DePauw Univ, MA, 69; Univ Mich, PhD(physics), 78. *Prof Exp:* Res physicist, Naval Avionics Fac, 68-74; res assoc, physics, Univ Mich, 74-78; quantum electronics staff, Lincoln Lab, Mass Inst Technol, 79-81, prog mgr laser remote sensing, Lincoln Lab, 81-87. *Mem:* Am Phys Soc; Optical Soc Am. *Res:* Physics of new optical and laser sources, quantum electronics and non-linear optical techniques with applications toward laser remote sensing; lidar. *Mailing Add:* Dept Physics Univ SFla Tampa FL 33620

KILLINGSWORTH, LAWRENCE MADISON, CLINICAL CHEMISTRY, PATHOLOGY. *Current Pos:* DIR CLIN CHEM & IMMUNOL LABS, SACRED HEART MED CTR, 77- *Personal Data:* b Cuthbert, Ga, Mar 9, 46; m 66; c 1. *Educ:* Emory Univ, BS, 68; Univ Fla, PhD(path, clin chem), 73. *Prof Exp:* Asst prof med & path, Sch Med, Univ NC, Chapel Hill, 73-77, assoc dir clin chem, NC Mem Hosp, 73-77, assoc dir, Radioassay Lab, 74-76. *Mem:* Am Asn Clin Chem; Asn Clin Scientists. *Res:* Application of light-scattering techniques to the measurement of immunochemical reactions; application of immunochemical techniques to the clinical chemistry laboratory; study of protein physiology in health and disease. *Mailing Add:* 2704 E Player Dr Spokane WA 99223

KILLINGSWORTH, R(OY) W(ILLIAM), CIVIL ENGINEERING, ENGINEERING MECHANICS. *Current Pos:* asst dean, Col Eng, Univ Ala, 54-56, from asst prof to prof eng, 56-67, from asst dean to assoc dean, Col Eng, 63-70, dir phys planning & facil, 70-85 prof civil eng, 67-90, sr consult engr new proj, 85-80, EMER PROF CIVIL ENG, UNIV ALA, 90- *Personal Data:* b Headland, Ala, Apr 8, 25; m 50; c 2. *Educ:* Univ Ala, BS, 48, MS, 56. *Prof Exp:* Asst col eng, Univ Ala, 48-49; field engr, Pressure Concrete Co, 49-50, vpres, 50-52. *Concurrent Pos:* Gen contractor, Ala, 48-49; consult, US Army, 63- *Mem:* AAAS; Am Soc Civil Engrs; Am Soc Eng Educ; Nat Soc Prof Engrs. *Res:* Properties of materials; soil mechanics; hydrology. *Mailing Add:* 731 13th St Tuscaloosa AL 35401

KILLION, JERALD JAY, IMMUNOBIOLOGY, CANCER. *Current Pos:* ASSOC PROF DEPT CELL BIOL, MD ANDERSON CANCER CTR, UNIV TEX, 87- *Personal Data:* b Wichita, Kans, Oct 4, 42; c 2. *Educ:* Wichita State Univ, BS, 70, MS, 71; Univ Okla, PhD(biophys), 73. *Prof Exp:* Instr biophys, 73-74, asst prof, Dept Radiol Sci, Health Sci Ctr, Univ Okla, 74-78; mem fac, Sch Med, Oral Roberts Univ, 78-81, assoc prof, Dept Physiol, 81-87. *Concurrent Pos:* Affil instr, Cancer Res Prog, Okla Med Res Found,

73-74, staff scientist, 74-75, asst mem, 75- *Mem:* Sigma Xi; Am Asn Cancer Res; Am Soc Cell Biol; Biophys Soc; Tissue Cult Asn. *Res:* Membrane properties of tumor cells and tumor cell subpopulations; the influence of biological and biochemical properties of tumor on the tumor-host relationship; antigenic topography of tumor cell membranes. *Mailing Add:* M D Anderson Cancer Ctr Dept Cell Biol 1515 Holcombe Blvd Box 173 Houston TX 77030-4095. *Fax:* 713-792-8747

KILLION, LAWRENCE EUGENE, lasers, computer science, for more information see previous edition

KILLPATRICK, JOSEPH E, ELECTRICAL ENGINEERING, PHYSICS. *Current Pos:* Res engr, Aero Res, 55-59, sr res engr, MPG Res, 59-62, suprv optics, 62-67, sect head electro-optics, Systs & Res Ctr, 67-69, mem staff, Aeronaut Div, 69-74, RES MGR, SYSTS & RES CTR, HONEYWELL INC, 74- *Personal Data:* b Hillsboro, Ill, Feb 15, 33; m 55; c 3. *Educ:* Univ Ill, BS, 55. *Mem:* Optical Soc Am; Inst Elec & Electronics Engrs. *Res:* Electronic devices and circuitry; optical scanning and detection systems; horizon scanners; sun seekers; lasers; laser devices and systems; laser gyro; frequency stability and precision control of lasers. *Mailing Add:* Honeywell Inc Minneapolis MN 55413

KILMAN, JAMES WILLIAM, CARDIOVASCULAR SURGERY, THORACIC SURGERY. *Current Pos:* from asst prof to prof surg, 66-91, dir Thoracic Surg Div, 73-81, EMER PROF SURG, MED COL, OHIO STATE UNIV, 91- *Personal Data:* b Terre Haute, Ind, Jan 22, 31; m 68; c 3. *Educ:* Ind State Univ, BS, 56; Ind Univ, Indianapolis, MD, 60; Am Bd Surg, dipl 67; Am Bd Thoracic Surg, dipl, 67. *Prof Exp:* Intern, Med Ctr, Ind Univ, Indianapolis, 60-61, resident, 61-66. *Concurrent Pos:* USPHS fel cardiovasc surg, Med Ctr, Ind Univ, Indianapolis, 63-64; consult, Vet Admin Hosp, Dayton, Ohio, 66-; attend surgeon, Ohio State Univ & Children's Hosp, Columbus, 66- *Mem:* Am Col Surg; Am Acad Pediat; Am Col Chest Physicians; Am Col Cardiol; Am Surg Asn. *Res:* Infant cardiopulmonary bypass and peripheral blood flow. *Mailing Add:* Box 667 Grove City OH 43210

KILMER, LOUIS CHARLES, SOLAR CELLS, SEMICONDUCTOR PHYSICS. *Current Pos:* MEM TECH STAFF, AEROSPACE CORP, 92- *Personal Data:* b Baltimore, Md, Oct 5, 66; m 91, Krista L Santacroce. *Educ:* Univ Del, BEE, 87, MEE, 89, PhD(elec eng), 92. *Prof Exp:* Teaching asst, Dept Elec Eng, Univ Del, 87-89, res asst, 89-92. *Mem:* Inst Elec & Electronics Engrs; Optical Soc Am; Am Inst Aeronaut & Astronaut; The Planetary Soc. *Res:* Research and development of advanced technologies for satellite power systems, specifically concentrating in solar cells and battery subsystem components. *Mailing Add:* 3101 Plaza del Amo Torrance CA 90503. *Fax:* 310-336-5846; *E-Mail:* louis__kilmer@qmailz.aero.org

KILP, GERALD R, PHYSICAL METALLURGY, CERAMICS ENGINEERING. *Current Pos:* RETIRED. *Personal Data:* b Carrollton, Mo, Sept 16, 31; m 56, Cheryl Silverthorn; c Karen, Kevin & Brian. *Educ:* Mo Valley Col, BS, 52; Iowa State Univ, PhD(metall), 57. *Honors & Awards:* Harlan J Anderson Award, Am Soc Testing & Mat, Award of Merit. *Prof Exp:* Asst metall, Ames Lab, AEC, 52-57; sr engr, Atomic Power Dept, Westinghouse Elec Corp, 57-62, suprvy engr, Astro-Nuclear Lab, 62-68, mgr fuel eng, Nuclear Core Opers, 68-72 & Nuclear Fuel Div, 72-80, mgr mat interactions, 80-83, adv eng, Nuclear Fuel Div, 83-90. *Mem:* Am Soc Testing & Mat. *Res:* Thermoelectric and thermionic materials; graphite nuclear reactor fuels; light water reactor fuels development; nuclear waste disposal. *Mailing Add:* 890 Fredericka Dr Bethel Park PA 15102

KILP, TOOMAS, PHOTOPHYSICS, PHOTOCHEMISTRY. *Current Pos:* MGR POLYMER CHEM & MICROS, ORTECH INT, 88- *Personal Data:* b Charleroi, Belgium, Oct 24, 48; Can citizen. *Educ:* Univ Toronto, BSc, 74, MSc, 75, PhD(chem), 79. *Prof Exp:* Chemist, Inmont Can Ltd, 70-72; chemist, Lumonics Res Ltd, 78-79; asst prof, Univ Notre Dame, 79-83; consult, 83-88. *Mem:* Am Chem Soc; Can Thermal Anal Soc. *Res:* Polymer photochemistry; photophysics including degradation; polymerization; photoconductivity; intramolecular energy migration; excited state complex formation. *Mailing Add:* 23-3061 Sir Johns Homestead Mississauga ON L5K 1B3 Can

KILPATRICK, CHARLES WILLIAM, EVOLUTION, MOLECULAR SYSTEMATICS. *Current Pos:* asst prof, 74-80, ASSOC PROF, DEPT BIOL, UNIV VT, 80- *Personal Data:* b Wichita Falls, Tex, June 10, 44; wid; c 3. *Educ:* Midwestern Univ, BS, 68, MS, 69; NTex State Univ, PhD(zool), 73. *Prof Exp:* Instr human biol, Midwestern Univ, 69-70; vis asst prof, Dept Biol, St Lawrence Univ, 73-74. *Concurrent Pos:* Vis prof, Dept Zool, Univ Fla, 80-81; res assoc, Fla State Mus, Univ Fla, 80-81. *Mem:* Am Soc Mammalogists; Soc Study Evolution; Soc Syst Zoologists; Am Genetic Asn. *Res:* Genetic changes and evolutionary processes associated with speciation; effects of isolation on the genetic structure of populations; evolutionary relationships based upon analysis of morphology, protein electrophoresis, restriction fragments, DNA-DNA hybridization and karyology of vertebrates. *Mailing Add:* Dept Biol Univ Vt Marsh Life Sci Bldg Burlington VT 05405

KILPATRICK, DANIEL LEE, BIOCHEMISTRY. *Current Pos:* staff scientist, 84-89, SR SCIENTIST, WORCESTER FOUND EXP BIOL, 89- *Personal Data:* b Los Angeles, Calif, Apr 2, 51; m 79. *Educ:* Univ Calif, San Diego, BA, 74; Duke Univ PhD(biochem), 80. *Prof Exp:* Dept Physiol Chem & Pharmacol, Roche Inst Molecular Biol, 80-81, res assoc, 82-84; sr scientist, Unigene Labs, 81-82. *Concurrent Pos:* Lectr, Seventh Int Cong Endocrinol, Can, 84, Tufts Univ, 86 & 88, Univ Miami & Columbia Univ, 86, Harvard Univ, 87, Univ Mass, 87, 88 & 90 & Ore Regional Primate Ctr, 90; ad hoc reviewer, Biochem Endocrinol Study Sect, 89. *Mem:* AAAS; NY Acad Sci; Am Soc Neurochem; Am Soc Biol Chemists; Endocrine Soc. *Res:* Author of numerous publications in medical journals. *Mailing Add:* Worcester Found Biomed Res 222 Maple Ave Shrewsbury MA 01545. *Fax:* 508-842-9362

KILPATRICK, EARL BUDDY, FISH BIOLOGY. *Current Pos:* RETIRED. *Personal Data:* b Burkburnett, Tex, June 21, 20; m 56; c 6. *Educ:* Univ Okla, BS, 42, MS, 49, PhD(zool), 59. *Prof Exp:* Asst zool, Univ Okla, 46-49; from asst prof to assoc prof biol, Southeastern Okla State Univ, 49-62, prof & head dept, 62-83. *Concurrent Pos:* Dir, NSF res partic prog, 59-60. *Mem:* AAAS. *Res:* Cytology, seasonal gonadal cycles of the fresh-water fishes. *Mailing Add:* 1223 N Fifth Ave Durant OK 74701

KILPATRICK, JEREMY, MATHEMATICS EDUCATION RESEARCH, MATHEMATICS CURRICULUM. *Current Pos:* PROF MATH EDUC, UNIV GA, 75-, REGENTS PROF, 93- *Personal Data:* b Fairfield, Iowa, Sept 21, 35; m 62, Carlene J Friedrichsen; c Judson C & Barton P. *Educ:* Univ Calif, Berkeley, AB, 56, MA, 60; Stanford Univ MS, 62 PhD(educ), 67. *Honors & Awards:* Fulbright Sr Lectr, Spain, 89. *Prof Exp:* Teaching asst math educ, Sch Math Study Group, Stanford Univ, 61-63, res asst, 62-67; from asst prof to assoc prof math, Teachers Col, Columbia Univ, 67-75. *Concurrent Pos:* Suprv math interns, Sec Educ Proj, Stanford Univ, 62-63; res assoc, Sec Sch Math Curric Improv Study, Teachers Col, 69-75; vis lectr, Univ Cambridge, Eng, 73-74; guest prof, Institute Fr Didactik Der Mathematics, WGer, 76; distinguished visitor, NZ Asn Res Educ, 87; distinguished scholar, San Diego State Univ, 88; Fulbright res scholar, Sweden, 93. *Mem:* Nat Coun Teachers Math; Math Asn Am; Am Educ Res Asn; Nat Coun Measurement Educ. *Res:* Evaluations of math curricula; studies in testing and assessment; problem solving and mathematical abilities; editing translations of Soviet studies in mathematics education; surveys of research in mathematics education. *Mailing Add:* 227 Woodlawn Ave Athens GA 30606-4353. *Fax:* 706-542-5010; *E-Mail:* jkioprt@moe.cor.uga.edu

KILPATRICK, JOHN MICHAEL, CELL BIOLOGY & MOLECULAR BIOLOGY, STRUCTURE-BASED DRUG DESIGN & TRANSGENIC ANIMALS. *Current Pos:* SR SCIENTIST, BIOCRYST PHARMACEUT, INC, 93- *Personal Data:* b Feb 2, 53; c Alyson M, John M & Christopher M. *Educ:* Col Charleston, BS, 75; Med Univ SC, PhD(immunol & microbiol), 81. *Prof Exp:* Fel, Univ Ala, Birmingham, 81-84; asst prof microbiol & immunol, Med Univ SC, 85-87; lab dir, Biotherapeuts, Univ Ala, Birmingham, 87-89, asst prof rheumatol, 89-93. *Concurrent Pos:* Assoc scientist, Multipurpose Arthritis Ctr, Univ Ala, Birmingham, 89-93. *Mem:* AAAS; Am Asn Immunologists. *Res:* Development of drugs based on the three dimensional structure of proteins important for the development or exacerbation of diseases of the immune system. *Mailing Add:* Biocryst Pharmaceut Inc 2190 Pkwy Lake Dr Hoover AL 35244

KILPATRICK, KERRY EDWARDS, INDUSTRIAL ENGINEERING, OPERATIONS RESEARCH. *Current Pos:* PROF INDUST & SYSTS ENG, UNIV FLA, 70-, PROF HEALTH & HOSP ADMIN, COL BUS ADMIN, 71-, PROF COMMUNITY HEALTH & FAMILY MED, 72-, DIR, HEALTH SYSTS RES DIV, J HILLIS MILLER HEALTH CTR, 72-, DIR, CTR HEALTH POLICY RES, 81- *Personal Data:* b Baltimore, Md, Mar 17, 39; m 65; c 2. *Educ:* Univ Mich, Ann Arbor, BSE(mech eng) & BSE(eng math), 61, MS, 67, PhD(indust eng), 70; Harvard Univ, MBA, 63. *Prof Exp:* Methods engr, Buick Motor Div, Gen Motors Corp, 63-65; res asst indust eng, Univ Mich, Ann Arbor, 67-70. *Concurrent Pos:* Consult, World Health Orgn & Vet Admin, 77- *Mem:* Inst Mgt Sci; Opers Res Soc Am; Am Inst Indust Engrs. *Res:* Industrial and systems engineering, analysis of production and health service systems; analysis of extended function auxiliaries in health care delivery systems; evaluation of international health services delivery programs. *Mailing Add:* Dept Health Policy & Admin Sch Pub Health CB 7400 Univ NC Chapel Hill NC 27599-7400

KILPATRICK, LAURIE E, CELL BIOLOGY, IMMUNOLOGY. *Current Pos:* ASSOC MEM, JOSEPH STOKES JR RES INST CHILDREN'S HOSP, 93- *Personal Data:* b Philadelphia, Pa, Oct 1, 53; m 90, William Fox; c Lauren. *Educ:* Hampshire Col, BA, 76; Univ Pa, PhD(biochem), 83. *Prof Exp:* Res fel pharmacol, Univ Pa Med Sch, 83-86, res asst prof pediat, 86-93. *Concurrent Pos:* Med dent staff mem, Children's Hosp of Philadelphia, 87- *Mem:* Am Soc Cell Biol; Sigma Xi; Shock Soc. *Res:* Molecular mechanisms underlying cytokine; mediated cellular dysfunction in sepsis and host defense against infections; pharmacological approaches to protection in sepsis and inflammatory diseases. *Mailing Add:* Div Immunol & Infectious Dis 34th St & Civic Center Blvd Philadelphia PA 19104. *Fax:* 215-590-3044

KILPATRICK, S JAMES, JR, BIOSTATISTICS, EPIDEMIOLOGY. *Current Pos:* chmn biostatist, 65-83, prof family pract, 79-83, PROF BIOSTATIST, MED COL VA, 65- *Personal Data:* b Belfast, Northern Ireland, Apr 24, 31; nat US; m 56; c 2. *Educ:* Queen's Univ Belfast, BSc, 54, MSc, 57, PhD, 60. *Prof Exp:* Asst lectr med statist, Queen's Univ Belfast, 54-58, lectr, 58-61; lectr, Aberdeen Univ, 61-65; NIH fel statist, 62-63. *Concurrent Pos:* NIH fel statist, Iowa State Univ, 60-61; mem, Working Comt Drug Monitoring, Aberdeen Univ, 63-65; mem, Va Health Interview Coun, 77-79; chmn, Va Health Statist Adv Coun, 78-82; mem, Oral Biol Med Study Sect, NIH, 78-80, Indoor Air Pollution Adv Comt, 85- *Mem:* Biomet Soc; Int Epidemiol Asn; Royal Statist Soc. *Res:* Statistics of epidemiological studies; risk assessment methods. *Mailing Add:* Dept Biostatist Va Commonwealth Univ Sch Med Richmond VA 23298-1900

KILPPER, ROBERT WILLIAM, TOXICOLOGY, BIOMATHEMATICS. *Current Pos:* TOXICOLOGIST, XEROX CORP, 81- *Personal Data:* b Houston, Tex, Oct 21, 38; m 60; c 3. *Educ:* Univ Houston, BS, 61, MS, 63, PhD(biophys), 67. *Prof Exp:* Asst prof biomath, radiation biol & biophys, Sch Med & Dent, Univ Rochester, 67-75, assoc prof, 75-81. *Mem:* Soc Toxicol. *Res:* Mathematical model analysis of physiological systems, especially the mechanical behavior of some mammalian lung models and the compartmental distribution of various compounds. *Mailing Add:* 144 Branford Rd Rochester NY 14618

KILSHEIMER, JOHN ROBERT, AGRICULTURAL CHEMISTRY. *Current Pos:* CONSULT, 82- *Personal Data:* b Mt Vernon, NY, Sept 21, 23; m 46, Betty Carraher; c Joan, Jean, Kathleen, Mary, Elizabeth & Jacqueline. *Educ:* Col Holy Cross, BS, 44; Fordham Univ, MS, 48; Syracuse Univ, PhD(chem), 51. *Prof Exp:* Instr chem, Fordham prep sch, 46-47; asst, Syracuse Univ, 47-48; res chemist, Polymer Div, Union Carbide Chem Co, 50-54, org-agr, 54-61; supvr agr chem, Mobil Chem Co, 61-63, mgr org chem, 63-66; sr staff adv agr prods, Esso Res & Eng Co, 66-67, head pesticides res & develop, 67-71; vpres res & develop, O M Scott & Sons Co, 71-80, sr vpres res, mfg & sales, 80-82. *Concurrent Pos:* Mem bd dirs, Nat Agr Chem Asn, 72-81, Fertilizer Inst, 77-80. *Mem:* Am Chem Soc; Nat Agr Chem Asn; Fertil Inst. *Res:* Pesticides; fertilizers; oxidation reactions; synthetic organics; vinyl polymers; turf research. *Mailing Add:* 4141 S Atlantic Ave New Smyrna Beach FL 32169

KILSHEIMER, SIDNEY ARTHUR, ORGANIC CHEMISTRY. *Current Pos:* from asst prof to assoc prof, 58-72, PROF CHEM, BUTLER UNIV, 72- *Personal Data:* b New Rochelle, NY, Oct 19, 30; wid. *Educ:* Wagner Col, BS, 52; NC State Univ, MS, 54; Purdue Univ, PhD(chem), 59. *Prof Exp:* Asst chem, NC State Col, 52-54; asst, Purdue Univ, 54-56, instr, 56-58. *Mem:* Fel AAAS; Am Chem Soc; fel The Chem Soc; fel Am Inst Chemists. *Res:* Chemical reductions; natural products. *Mailing Add:* Dept Chem Butler Univ Indianapolis IN 46208

KIM, AGNES KYUNG-HEE, CLINICAL PATHOLOGY, HEMATOLOGY. *Current Pos:* ASSOC PATHOLOGIST, NEW ENG DEACONESS HOSP & NEW ENG BAPTIST HOSP, 73-; DEPT PATH, HARWARD MED SCH. *Personal Data:* b Seoul, Korea, May 17, 37; US citizen; m 65; c 3. *Educ:* Yonsei Univ, BS, 58, MD, 62. *Prof Exp:* Asst pathologist, St Barnabas Med Col, 69-70, Lenox Hill Hosp, 71; assoc pathologist, Vet Admin Hosp, WRoxbury, Mass, 71-73. *Mem:* Fel Col Am Pathologists; Am Soc Clin Pathologists. *Mailing Add:* New England Baptist Hosp 91 Parker Hill Ave Boston MA 02120-3215

KIM, BENJAMIN K, TRANSDERMAL DELIVERY SYSTEMS, CONTROLLED RELEASE DELIVERY SYSTEMS. *Current Pos:* RES & DEVELOP VPRES, PACO RES INC, 84- *Personal Data:* b Seoul, Korea, Apr, 27, 33; US citizen; m 59; c 4. *Educ:* Seoul Nat Univ, BS, 59; Kyung Hzz Univ, MS, 69; Univ Southern Calif, PhD(pharmaceut chem), 77. *Prof Exp:* Scientist, Nat Chem Lab, 59-61; dir res & develop, Seoul Pharmaceut Co, 61-65; sect head, NIH, 65-69; res scientist, Rochelle Labs, 70-76; tech dir, Rich Life Inc, 76-80; sr res scientist, G D Searle, 80-83; res & develop dir, Nelson Res, 83-84. *Mem:* Am Pharmaceut Asn; Am Pharmaceut Scientist Asn; Am Chem Soc. *Res:* New drug delivery systems; oral, transdermal implant and nasal delivery systems. *Mailing Add:* 226 Middle Dr Toms River NJ 08753

KIM, BORIS FINCANNON, MOLECULAR SPECTROSCOPY, LASERS. *Current Pos:* PRIN PROF STAFF PHYSICIST, JOHNS HOPKINS UNIV APPL PHYSICS LAB, 69- *Personal Data:* b Commerce, Ga, Nov 19, 38; m 62; c 2. *Educ:* Johns Hopkins Univ, BES, 60, PhD(physics), 67. *Concurrent Pos:* Instr physics, Evening Col, Johns Hopkins Univ, 70-; prin investr, Dept Health, Educ & Welfare Res Grant, 75-81. *Mem:* Am Phys Soc. *Res:* High resolution, low temperature optical spectroscopy, and electron spin resonance studies of the class of porphyrin compounds; high temperature superconductivity; computer vision. *Mailing Add:* Johns Hopkins Univ Appl Phys Lab Johns Hopkins Rd Laurel MD 20723

KIM, BYUNG CHO, PROCESS DEVELOPMENT, PROCESS DESIGN. *Current Pos:* Prin chem eng, Battelle Mem Inst, 61-66, sr chem engr, 66-79, assoc sect mgr, 79-82, proj mgr, 82-92, PROG MGR, BATTELLE MEM INST, 92- *Personal Data:* b Pyongyang, Korea, Nov 2, 34; US citizen; m 60, Dolores Carhrt; c Julian, Joseph, Ann, Helen & Robert. *Educ:* Ripon Col, AB, 56; Mass Inst Technol, BS, 58, MS, 61. *Honors & Awards:* R&D 100 Award, Res & Develop Mag, 92. *Mem:* Am Inst Chem Engrs; Sigma Xi; Am Chem Soc. *Res:* Fluidized bed combustion; biomass gasification; bioreactors; microencapsulation; hydrothermal process; separation processes; soil remediation; groundwater remediation; pollution prevention; waste minimization; solid waste management; hazardous waste management; radioactive waste management. *Mailing Add:* 55 W Livingston Ave Columbus OH 43215. *Fax:* 614-424-3321

KIM, BYUNG J, HAZARDOUS WASTE TREATMENT TECHNOLOGIES WASTEWATER TREATMENT TECHNOLOGIES. *Current Pos:* TEAM LEADER, CONSTRUCT ENG RES LAB, US ARMY, 87- *Personal Data:* b Seoul, Korea, Jan 25, 47; US citizen; m 74, Yangs Pyo; c Peter & NaYoung. *Educ:* Seoul Nat Univ, BS, 70; Polytech Univ, MS, 76, PhD(civil & environ eng), 80. *Prof Exp:* Civil engr, Korea Hwy Corp, 69-71, Seoul Metrop Transit Authority, 71-75; environ engr, NY State Environ Conserv Dept, 77-81; chief, Sanit Br, Eight US Army, Yongsan, 81-82; chief, Utilities Div, Facil Eng Activ, Korea, 82-87. *Concurrent Pos:* Lectr, Korea Univ, Seoul Nat Univ & City Col Seoul, 81-87. *Mem:* Water Environ Fedn; Am Water Works Asn; Soc Am Mil Engrs; Int Asn Water Qual; Am Soc Civil Engrs. *Res:* Army's effective hazardous waste management and wastewater treatment; domestic sludge dewatering using reed beds, energetic waste separation and treatment from munition production, and Army's industrial sludge treatment. *Mailing Add:* 2004 Mayfair Rd Champaign IL 61821. *Fax:* 217-373-3490; *E-Mail:* bkim@cecer.army.aol

KIM, BYUNG RO, TREATMENT OF MANUFACTURING WASTES & WASTEWATER, PROCESS & WATER QUALITY MODELING. *Current Pos:* PRIN STAFF ENGR, FORD RES LAB, 90- *Personal Data:* c Hahn & Hahna B. *Educ:* Seoul Nat Univ, CE, 71; Univ Ill, Urbana, MS, 74, PhD(environ eng), 76. *Honors & Awards:* Willem Rudolfs Medal, Water Environ Fedn, 90. *Prof Exp:* Environ engr, Tenn Valley Authority, 76-80; asst prof environ eng, Ga Inst Technol, 80-85; staff res engr, Gen Motors Res Labs, 85-90. *Concurrent Pos:* Assoc ed, J Environ Eng, Am Soc Civil Engrs, 90-; lectr environ eng, Wayne State Univ, 93- *Mem:* Am Soc Civil Engrs; Asn Environ Eng Profs; Am Water Works Asn; Int Asn Water Qual; Water Environ Fedn. *Res:* Industrial waste treatment, adsorption, mathematical modeling of treatment processes and natural water systems. *Mailing Add:* 2433 Wickfield St West Bloomfield MI 48323. *Fax:* 313-594-2923; *E-Mail:* bkim@mail.srl.ford.com

KIM, BYUNG SUK, IMMUNOLOGY. *Current Pos:* from asst prof to assoc prof, 76-91, PROF IMMUNOL, NORTHWESTERN UNIV, CHICAGO, 91- *Personal Data:* b Korea, Mar 20, 42; US citizen; m 67, Oak; c Peggy & Charles. *Educ:* Seoul Nat Univ, BS, 67; Va State Univ, MS, 69; Univ Ill, PhD(microbiol), 73. *Prof Exp:* Res assoc radiation biol, Atomic Energy Res Inst, Korea, 67-68; sr res technician genetics, Univ Chicago, 69-70; sr staff assoc, Columbia Univ, 73-74; res asst prof immunol, Univ Chicago, 74-76. *Concurrent Pos:* Mem, Study Sect, NIH, 85-89, 92-95. *Mem:* Am Soc Microbiol; Am Asn Immunol; Sigma Xi. *Res:* Effects of hapten on antigen presentation; expression of T-cell receptor genes; mouse model for multiple sclerosis. *Mailing Add:* Dept Microbiol & Immunol Med Sch Northwestern Univ Chicago IL 60611. *Fax:* 312-503-1339; *E-Mail:* bskim@casbah.acns.nwu.edu

KIM, CHANGHYUN, ULSI DESIGN, SOLID STATE SEMICONDUCTOR. *Current Pos:* RES ASST, UNIV MICH, ANN ARBOR, 89- *Personal Data:* b Seoul, Korea, Jan 1, 61; m 87; c 1. *Educ:* Seoul Nat Univ, Korea, BS, 82, MS, 84. *Prof Exp:* Researcher dynamic random access memory design, Samsung Semiconductor Tech Co, Ltd, 84-86, asst mgr, 86-88; mgr, MOS Device Develop, Samsung Electronics Co, Ltd, 89. *Mem:* Inst Elec & Electronics Engrs. *Res:* Dynamic random access memory from 64K bit to 16M bit dynamic random access memory; MOS device characterization for submicron devices and reliability problems; circuit design and BiCMOS process development for sensors. *Mailing Add:* Samsung Electronics Co San 24 Nogseo-R1 Kiheung Eup Kyungki-do 449-900 South Korea

KIM, CHANG-SIK, antennas, passive microwave components, for more information see previous edition

KIM, CHARLES WESLEY, IMMUNOLOGY, PARASITOLOGY. *Current Pos:* assoc prof microbiol, Health Sci Ctr, 70-87, assoc vprovost, Grad Sch, 81-83, PROF MICROBIOL & MED, HEALTH SCI CTR, STATE UNIV NY, STONY BROOK, 87-; RES COLLABR, MED DEPT, BROOKHAVEN NAT LAB, 70- *Personal Data:* b Nashville, Tenn, Mar 20, 26; m 56, Soo J; c Charles Jr. *Educ:* Univ Calif, BA, 49; Univ NC, MSPH, 52, PhD(parasitol, bact), 56. *Prof Exp:* Instr microbiol, NY Med Col, 56-59, asst prof, 59-64; assoc scientist, Brookhaven Nat Lab, 65-68, scientist, 68-70. *Concurrent Pos:* La State Univ Trop Med fel, Cent Am, 58; USPHS fel, Argonne Nat Lab & Univ Chicago, 64-65; assoc dean, Sch Basic Health Sci, Health Sci Ctr, State Univ NY Stony Brook, 72-74; assoc dean, Grad Sch, State Univ NY Stony Brook, 74-81; pres, Int Comn Trichinellosis, 88-92. *Mem:* Am Soc Parasitol; Am Soc Trop Med & Hyg; fel Royal Soc Trop Med & Hyg; Sigma Xi. *Res:* Immune response to parasites; mechanism of immunity to parasites, including Trichinella spiralis; Cryptosporiduim; pathogenesis and chemotherapy of cryptosporidiosis; chemotherapy of trichinellosis; complement activity of Trichinella spiralis. *Mailing Add:* Div Infectious Dis State Univ NY Health Sci Ctr Stony Brook NY 11794-8153. *Fax:* 516-444-7518

KIM, CHUNG SUL (SUE), POLYMER CONCRETES, PROPELLANT CHEMISTRY. *Current Pos:* from asst prof to assoc prof, 73-81, PROF CHEM, CALIF STATE UNIV, SACRAMENTO, 81- *Personal Data:* b Seoul, Korea, Dec 21, 32; US citizen; m 57; c 2. *Educ:* Univ Ill, BS, 55; Cornell Univ, PhD(org chem), 60. *Prof Exp:* Proj leader polymer chem, Stand Oil, Ohio, 59-62; res chemist, Ga Pac Corp, 63-65; sr chem specialist, Aerojet Solid Propulsion Co, 66-73. *Concurrent Pos:* Consult, Aerojet Solid Propulsion Co, 74-86; consult, unsaturated polyesters, vinyl esters & polymer concretes, 86- *Mem:* Am Chem Soc; Soc Advan Mat & Process Eng; Soc Plastics Engrs. *Res:* Chemistry and behavior of polymers in composite; propellant binders; polymer synthesis; bonding (coupling) agents; polymer concretes. *Mailing Add:* Dept Chem Calif State Univ 6000 J St Sacramento CA 95819-2605

KIM, CHUNG W, THEORETICAL HIGH ENERGY PHYSICS, THEORETICAL NUCLEAR PHYSICS. *Current Pos:* from asst prof to assoc prof, 66-73, PROF PHYSICS, JOHNS HOPKINS UNIV, 73- *Personal Data:* b Hiroshima, Japan, Jan 8, 34; m 60; c 1. *Educ:* Seoul Nat Univ, BS, 58; Univ

Ind, PhD(physics), 63. *Prof Exp:* Res assoc physics, Univ Pa, 63-66. *Mem:* Fel Am Phys Soc; Korean Acad Sci & Technol. *Res:* Nuclear and elementary particle physics; cosmology. *Mailing Add:* Dept Physics Astron Johns Hopkins Univ Baltimore MD 21218. *E-Mail:* kim@eta.pha.jhu.edu

KIM, DAE MANN, ATOMIC PHYSICS, QUANTUM ELECTRONICS. *Current Pos:* DEPT APPL PHYSICS & ELEC ENG, ORE GRAD CTR, BEAVERETON. *Personal Data:* b Seoul, Korea, Apr 22, 38; m 67; c 1. *Educ:* Seoul Nat Univ, BS, 60; Yale Univ, MS, 65, PhD(physics), 67. *Prof Exp:* Res assoc physics, Mass Inst Technol, 67-69, instr, 69-70; asst prof elec eng, Rice Univ, 70-74, assoc prof, 74-; Dept Elec-Comput Eng Rice Univ. *Mem:* Am Phys Soc. *Res:* Modelocked laser pulses and their detection processes; photorefractive phase holography, dye lasers, light scattering study. *Mailing Add:* Pohang Inst Sci & Technol PO Box 125 Pohang Kyungbuk 790-600 South Korea

KIM, DONG HAN, MOLECULAR RECOGNITION, ENZYME INHIBITOR DESIGN. *Current Pos:* PROF ORG CHEM & MED CHEM, POHANG UNIV SCI & TECHNOL, 86-, DIR, CTR BIOFUNCTIONAL MOLECULES, 91- *Personal Data:* b Korea, Aug 10, 34; US citizen; m 60, Yong N Yang; c Wook, Jean & John. *Educ:* Seoul Nat Univ, BS, 57; Univ NC, PhD(org chem), 65. *Honors & Awards:* Medal of Camellia, Pres Repub Korea, 88. *Prof Exp:* Sr res chemist, group leader & prin scientist, Res Div, Wyeth Labs, Inc, 65-86; vpres sci & eng, Res Inst Indust Sci & Technol, 87-88. *Mem:* Korean Scientists & Engrs Asn Am (pres, 85); Am Chem Soc; AAAS; Int Soc Heterocyclic Chem; Korean Chem Soc (vpres, 91); Korean Pharmacol Soc. *Res:* Novel types of enzyme inhibitor development; host-guest chemistry (chiral molecular recognition) and medicinal and heterocyclic chemistry (synthesis of structurally novel guinolone antibacterials). *Mailing Add:* Dept Chem Pohang Univ Sci & Technol San/31 Hyojatong Nampu Pohang 790-784 Pohang 790-600 South Korea. *Fax:* (82)-562-279-5877

KIM, DONG KWANG, TIRE REINFORCEMENT, STEEL TIRE CORD. *Current Pos:* sr metallurgist, 78-82, prin engr, 82-86, RES & DEVELOP ASSOC, GOODYEAR TIRE & RUBBER CO, 86- *Personal Data:* b Korea, Mar 18, 43; US citizen; m 72, Soojaa Lee; c Eugene & Norman. *Educ:* Seoul Nat Univ, Korea, BS, 67; NC State Univ, MS, 70, PhD(mat eng), 73. *Honors & Awards:* Arch T Colwell Award, Soc Automotive Engrs, 79. *Prof Exp:* Postdoctoral res assoc, Lehigh Univ, 73-76, res scientist, 76-78. *Concurrent Pos:* Steering comt, Edison Mats Technol Ctr, 91- *Mem:* Am Inst Mech Engrs; Am Soc Metal; Tire Soc. *Res:* Steel tire cords for tire reinforcing; ultra high strength steel cord development; steel cord process; adhesion between rubber and steel tire cord; cord mechanics and steel cord in tire or tire failure mechanisms. *Mailing Add:* 4194 Big Spruce Dr Akron OH 44333. *Fax:* 330-796-3947; *E-Mail:* dkkim@goodyear.com

KIM, DONG YUN, ELEMENTARY PARTICLE PHYSICS. *Current Pos:* assoc prof, 65-90, PROF PHYSICS, DEPT PHYSICS, UNIV REGINA, SASK, 90- *Personal Data:* b Korea, May 6, 29; Can citizen; m 62, Elisabeth Melech; c 3. *Educ:* Univ Seoul, Korea, BSc, 53; Aachen Tech Univ, Ger, PhD(theoret physics), 62. *Prof Exp:* Fel, Radiation Lab, New York Univ, 62-63; asst prof physics, Dept Physics, Mont State Univ, 63-65. *Concurrent Pos:* Vis scientist at var orgn including: Int Ctr Theoret Physics, Trieste, Italy; Inst Theoret Physics, Univ Heidelberg, Ger; Theory Group, Stanford Univ; Theory Group, Fermi Nat Lab; Dept Appl Math & Theoret Physics, Univ Cambridge, Eng & Bohr Inst, Denmark, 71-79. *Mem:* Can Asn Physicists; Am Phys Soc. *Res:* Theoretical nuclear and elementary particle physics. *Mailing Add:* Dept Physics & Astron Univ Regina Regina SK S4S 0A2 Can

KIM, GIHO, CLINICAL BIOCHEMISTRY. *Current Pos:* RES ASSOC MED RES, DOWNSTATE MED CTR, 73- *Personal Data:* b Seoul, Korea, May 15, 37; m 68; c 2. *Educ:* Simpson Col, BA, 63, Iowa State Univ, MS, 69, PhD(biochem), 71. *Prof Exp:* Res assoc biochem, Iowa State Univ, 71-72. *Concurrent Pos:* Clin instr, Downstate Med Ctr, 76- *Mem:* Am Chem Soc. *Res:* Biochemical effect of environmental pollutants on intestinal transport. *Mailing Add:* 81 Morewood Oaks Port Washington NY 11050

KIM, HAN JOONG, METALLURGY, CERAMICS ENGINEERING. *Personal Data:* b Seoul, Korea, Nov 3, 37; m 62; c 2. *Educ:* Seoul Nat Univ, BS, 60; San Jose State Col, MS, 66; Lehigh Univ, PhD(metall), 69. *Prof Exp:* Mem tech staff electronic mat, GTE Labs Inc, 69-76, mgr res & develop, Gibson Elec, Subsid GTE, 76-96. *Mem:* Am Ceramic Soc; Am Soc Metals; Am Inst Mining, Metall & Petrol Engrs. *Res:* Oxidation of metals; glass-metal sealing; crystal growth; electrical contact materials. *Mailing Add:* 342 Silver Hill Rd Concord MA 01742

KIM, HAN-SEOB, PATHOLOGY. *Current Pos:* from instr to asst prof path, 71-93, PROF CLIN PATH, BAYLOR COL MED, 93- *Personal Data:* b Seoul, Korea, Sept 5, 34; m 63; c 2. *Educ:* Seoul Nat Univ, MD, 59, MS, 62, PhD (biochem), 68. *Prof Exp:* Asst biochem, Col Med, Seoul Nat Univ, 63-67, from instr to asst prof, 67-69. *Concurrent Pos:* Dir cytopath, Ben Taub Gen Hosp. *Mem:* Am Asn Invest Path; Int Acad Path; Am Soc Cytol. *Res:* Anatomic pathology relating to cardiovascular and cytopathology. *Mailing Add:* Dept Path Baylor Col Med 1 Baylor Plaza Houston TX 77030-3498

KIM, HARRY HI-SOO, PATHOLOGY. *Current Pos:* asst prof, 61-67, ASSOC PROF PATH, NY MED COL, 67-, ASSOC PATHOLOGIST, FLOWER & FIFTH AVE HOSPS, 68- *Personal Data:* b Taegu, Korea, Jan 23, 22; US citizen; m 47; c 3. *Educ:* Yonsei Univ, Korea, MD, 45; Univ Pa, MSc, 59. *Prof Exp:* Res asst path, Children's Hosp, Philadelphia, Pa, 57-58; res assoc, Sch Med, Univ Wash & Children's Orthop Hosp, Philadelphia, Pa, 57-58; res assoc, Sch Med, Univ Wash & Children's Orthop Hosp, 58-59, clin instr, 60-61. *Concurrent Pos:* Fel, Grad Sch Med, Univ Pa, 56-58; assoc pathologist, Metrop Hosp, NY, 60-67; pathologist, NIH maternal & child health prog, NY Med Col Unit, 61-67, consult pathologist, 67- *Mem:* Int Acad Path; fel Am Soc Clin Path; fel Am Col Path. *Res:* Pediatric-pathology; genetics. *Mailing Add:* NYMC Metro Hosp 1901 First Ave Rm 2A47 New York NY 10029-7418

KIM, HEE JOONG, NUCLEAR PHYSICS. *Current Pos:* PHYSICIST, PHYSICS DIV, OAK RIDGE NAT LAB, 62- *Personal Data:* b Seoul, Korea, Feb 10, 34; US citizen; m 63; c 2. *Educ:* Case Inst Technol, MS, 59, PhD(physics), 62. *Mem:* Am Phys Soc. *Res:* Experimental nuclear physics. *Mailing Add:* MS 6368 Physics Div Oak Ridge Nat Lab Bldg 6000 PO Box 2008 Oak Ridge TN 37831

KIM, HEE YONG, BIOCHEMISTRY, BIOPHYSICS. *Current Pos:* SECTION CHIEF ALCOHOL ABUSE & ALCOHOLISM, LAB MEMBRANE BIOCHEM & BIOPHYSICS, NIH, 91- *Personal Data:* b Seoul, Korea, Feb 18, 56. *Educ:* Seoul Nat Univ, BS, 78, MS, 80; Univ Houston, PhD(chem), 84. *Mem:* Am Soc Mass Spectrometry; Am Soc Neurochem; Am Chem Soc. *Mailing Add:* Lab Membrane Biochem & Biophys NIH 12501 Washington Ave Rockville MD 20852. *Fax:* 301-594-0035; *E-Mail:* hykim@nih.gov

KIM, HONG C, PLASTICS & COMPOSITES, FATIGUE BEHAVIOR OF COMPOSITE MATERIALS. *Current Pos:* RES & DEVELOP LAB MGR, LNP ENG PLASTICS, 89- *Personal Data:* b Seoul, Korea, Mar 26, 49; US citizen; m 77; c 2. *Educ:* Seoul Nat Univ, BS, 71; Case Western Res Univ, MS, 76, PhD(metall & mat sci), 78. *Prof Exp:* Staff develop engr, Goodyear Tire & Rubber Co, 78-80; sr mat scientist, ICI Americas, 80-86, mat lab supvr advan mat, 86-89. *Mem:* Soc Plastics Engrs; Soc Advan Mat & Process Eng; Am Soc Testing & Mat. *Res:* Sheet molding compounds; reaction injection molding materials; advanced composites; filament wound composites; pultruded fiberglas-reinforced plastic; engineering plastics. *Mailing Add:* 1165 Arrowhead Dr West Chester PA 19382

KIM, HYEONG LAK, NATURAL PRODUCTS CHEMISTRY. *Current Pos:* Asst prof, 79-89, RES CHEMIST, TEX AGR STA, TEX, A&M UNIV, 69-, MEM GRAD FAC, DEPT VET PHYSIOL & PHARMACOL, 75-, ASSOC PROF, 89- *Personal Data:* b Korea, Jan 18, 33; nat US; m 67; c 5. *Educ:* Seoul Nat Univ, BS, 56; St Louis Univ, MS, 68; Tex A&M Univ, PhD(biochem), 70. *Mem:* Am Chem Soc; AAAS; NY Acad Sci. *Res:* Chemical constituents of poisonous plants; naturally occurring toxicants in food chain; metabolism of toxicants. *Mailing Add:* Dept Vet Physiol & Pharmacol Tex A&M Univ College Station TX 77840

KIM, HYUN DJU, PHYSIOLOGY, BIOCHEMISTRY. *Current Pos:* AT DEPT PHARMACOL, UNIV MO, COLUMBIA. *Personal Data:* b Ham Buk, Korea, Jan 4, 37; US citizen; m 69; c 2. *Educ:* Duke Univ, AB, 62, PhD(physiol), 68. *Prof Exp:* Muscular Dystrophy Asn of Am fel physiol, Univ Calif, Los Angeles, 69-71; Alexander von Humboldt fel, Div Med Physiol, Aachen Tech Univ, 71-72; assoc prof physiol, Univ Ariz, 72-80; prof pharmacol & physiol, Univ Ala, Birmingham, 80- *Mem:* Biophys Soc; Am Soc Cell Biol; Am Physiol Soc. *Res:* Membrane transport and energy metabolism in red blood cells; protein metabolism in muscle development. *Mailing Add:* Dept Pharmacol M-517 Med Sci Bldg Univ Mo-Columbia Columbia MO 65212. *Fax:* 573-884-4558

KIM, J JOHN, TURBULENCE, COMPUTATIONAL FLUID DYNAMICS. *Current Pos:* ROCKWELL INT PROF MECH ENG, UNIV CALIF, LOS ANGELES, 93- *Personal Data:* b Seoul, Korea, Oct 20, 47; US citizen; m 77, M Julie Kang; c June M. *Educ:* Seoul Nat Univ, BS, 70; Brown Univ, MS, 74; Stanford Univ, PhD(mech eng), 78. *Honors & Awards:* Except Sci Achievement Medal, NASA, 85. *Prof Exp:* Nat Res Coun fel, Ames Res Ctr, NASA, 78-80; res scientist, 82-87, head, Turbulence Physics Sect, 87-92, chief, Turbulence & Transition Physics Br, 92-93; actg asst prof, Stanford Univ, 80-82. *Concurrent Pos:* Consult, Nielson Eng, 80-85; consult prof, Stanford Univ, 87-93. *Mem:* Fel Am Phys Soc; assoc fel Inst Aeronaut & Astronaut; Am Soc Mech Engrs. *Res:* Investigate the fundamental physics of turbulence and transition to turbulence using large-scale computations on super computers. *Mailing Add:* 48-121 Eng IV Univ Calif Los Angeles CA 90095-1597. *Fax:* 310-206-4830; *E-Mail:* jkim@seas.ucla.edu

KIM, JAE HO, radiobiology, radiotherapy, for more information see previous edition

KIM, JAE HOON, phototonics & optoelectronics, compound semiconductor device & physics, for more information see previous edition

KIM, JAI BIN, CIVIL ENGINEERING. *Current Pos:* from asst prof to assoc prof civil eng, 66-77, PROF CIVIL ENG & CHMN DEPT, BUCKNELL UNIV, 77- *Personal Data:* b Seoul, Korea, May 17, 34; m 60; c 4. *Educ:* Ore State Univ, BS, 59, MS, 60; Univ Md, PhD(civil eng), 65. *Prof Exp:* Chief hwy res engr, DC Dept Transp, 64-66. *Concurrent Pos:* Res engr, Nat Bur Standards, 76-77. *Mem:* Am Soc Testing & Mat; Am Concrete Inst; Am Soc Civil Engrs; Sigma Xi. *Res:* Structural mechanics; engineering analysis; foundation engineering; nonlinear structural analysis; pile foundations; shallow excavations; pile caps. *Mailing Add:* Dept Civil Eng Bucknell Univ Lewisburg PA 17837

KIM, JAI SOO, ATMOSPHERIC PHYSICS. *Current Pos:* prof, 67-94, chmn dept, 69-76, EMER PROF ATMOSPHERIC SCI & PHYSICS, STATE UNIV NY, ALBANY, 94- *Personal Data:* b Korea, Nov 1, 25; nat US; m 52, Hai Kyou; c Kami, Tomi, Kihyun & Himi. *Educ:* Seoul Nat Univ, BSc, 49; Univ Sask, MSc, 57, PhD(physics), 58. *Prof Exp:* Instr physics, Tonga Col, Pusan, 52-53; instr, Sung Kyun Kwan Univ, Korea, 53-54; asst prof, Clarkson Univ, 58-59; from asst prof to prof, Univ Idaho, 59-67. *Concurrent Pos:* Rep, Univ Corp Atmospheric Res, State Univ NY, Albany, 71-76; consult, US Army Res Off, 78-80, Battelle Mem Inst, 77-80, NY State Environ Conserv Dept & Environ One Corp, 76-82, Norlite Corp, 82-84, Korean Studies Prog, State Univ NY, Stony Brook, 83-85 & Korean Antarctic Prog, 88-; investr grants, NSF, Air for Off Sci & Res, US Army Res Off, Off Naval Res, Environ Protection Agency & NY State Environ Conserv Dept, Korea Ocean Res & Develop Inst; vis prof, Advan Inst Sci & Tech, Seoul, Korea, 83. *Mem:* Am Asn Physics Teachers; Am Geophys Union. *Res:* Upper atmospheric physics; solar-terrestrial relations; plasma physics; magneto-hydrodynamics. *Mailing Add:* 22 Westover Rd Slingerlands NY 12159

KIM, JEAN BARTHOLOMEW, ORGANIC CHEMISTRY. *Current Pos:* EXEC DIR BD EDUC, AM BAPTIST CHURCHES, 89- *Personal Data:* b Philadelphia, Pa, Oct 12, 40; m 65; c 2. *Educ:* Eastern Baptist Col, BA, 61; Bryn Mawr Col, PhD(chem), 68. *Prof Exp:* Asst prof chem, Haverford Col, 67-68; res assoc chem, Drexel Univ, 68-70; prof chem & head dept, Eastern Co, 70, vpres & acad dean, 80-89. *Mem:* AAAS; Am Chem Soc; Sigma Xi; Nat Sci Teachers Asn. *Res:* Electrophilic substitution on electronic properties of porphin derivatives. *Mailing Add:* 131 Waterloo Ave Berwyn PA 19312

KIM, JIN BAI, ALGEBRA. *Current Pos:* PROF MATH, WVA UNIV, 76-, GRAD FAC, 89- *Personal Data:* b Sangju, Korea, June 23, 21; wid; c 1. *Educ:* Yonsei Univ, Korea, BS, 50; Univ Chicago, MS, 56; Va Polytech Inst, PhD(math), 65. *Prof Exp:* From instr to asst prof math, Yonsei Univ, Korea, 49-61; asst prof, Mich State Univ, 65-67, George Washington Univ, 69-71; Barnara Hindu Univ, India, 79-80. *Mem:* Am Math Soc; Math Asn Am. *Res:* Algebraic semigroups; linear algebra; matrices; tensors and differential manifolds. *Mailing Add:* Dept Math 311 Armstrong Hall WVa Univ Morgantown WV 26506. *E-Mail:* kim@mathwvu.edu

KIM, JINCHOON, NUCLEAR FUSION, PARTICLE ACCELERATOR. *Current Pos:* PRIN SCIENTIST, GEN ATOMICS, 80- *Personal Data:* b Choon-Chun, Korea, Mar 5, 43; US citizen; m 70, Yoonchung Park; c Nina, Margaret & Angela. *Educ:* Seoul Nat Univ, BS, 65; Univ Calif, Berkeley, MS, 68, PhD(plasma physics), 71. *Prof Exp:* Physicist, Cyclotron Corp, 71-74; res staff, Oak Ridge Nat Lab, 74-80. *Concurrent Pos:* Vis scientist, Jet Joint Undertaking, 88; adj fac, Mesa Col, 89-92. *Mem:* Am Phys Soc; Korean Nuclear Soc. *Res:* Thermonuclear fusion research, including tokamak plasma transport, spectroscopic diagnostics of plasma ions, neutral beam injection heating of plasma, particle accelerators, neutron dosimetry and shielding, and vacuum technology. *Mailing Add:* PO Box 85608 3550 Gen Atomics Ct San Diego CA 92138. *Fax:* 619-455-4156; *E-Mail:* kimj@gav.gat.com

KIM, JOHN K, ELECTRICAL ENGINEERING, MATERIAL SCIENCE. *Current Pos:* PRES, SUPERTEK CO, 75- *Personal Data:* b Seoul, Korea, Oct 26, 37; US citizen; m 61; c 2. *Educ:* Ohio Univ, BS, 63; Ohio State Univ, MS, 63, PhD(elec eng), 67. *Prof Exp:* Mem tech staff electronics, Lincoln Lab, Mass Inst Technol, 66-67; sr engr solid state, Semiconductor Group, Motorola, 67-68; head sect semiconductor eng, Micro State, 68-70; head dept semiconductor res & develop, Raytheon Co, 70-75. *Mem:* Sigma Xi; Inst Elec & Electronics Engrs; Korean Sci Eng Asn. *Res:* Analysis and development of solid state devices for high efficiency and high power generation of microwave energy. *Mailing Add:* 2231 Colby Ave Los Angeles CA 90064

KIM, JONATHAN JANG-HO, METALLURGICAL ENGINEERING. *Current Pos:* RETIRED. *Personal Data:* b Kwang-Ju, Korea, June 11, 32; m 58; c 1. *Educ:* Seoul Nat Univ, BS, 55; Carnegie-Mellon Univ, MS, 61: Univ Okla, PhD(metall eng), 65. *Prof Exp:* Res engr, Sci Res Lab, Ministry Nat Defense, Korea, 55-59; process design engr, Lummus Co, 65-67; sr proj engr, Ledgemont Lab, Kennecott Copper Corp, 67-75; staff metall engr, Lexington Develop Ctr, 75-80; mgr process technol, Carborundum Co, 80-91. *Mem:* Am Inst Mining, Metall & Petrol Engrs; Am Ceramic Soc. *Res:* Smelting and refining of nonferrous metals; extractive metallurgy; ceramic manufacturing processes via fusion and sintering; ceramic grains synthesis. *Mailing Add:* 79 Brandywine Dr Williamsville NY 14221

KIM, JUHEE, MICROBIOLOGY. *Current Pos:* from asst prof to assoc prof, 66-75, PROF MICROBIOL, CALIF STATE UNIV, LONG BEACH, 75- *Personal Data:* b Osan, Korea, Sept 13, 35; m 68; c 2. *Educ:* Seoul Nat Univ, BS, 58; Cornell Univ, MS, 62, PhD(food sci & microbiol), 66. *Prof Exp:* Researcher food & nutrit, Sci Res Inst, Ministry Defense, Seoul, Korea, 58-59. *Concurrent Pos:* Vis investr, Scripps Inst Oceanog, 70-71 & Wood Hole Oceanog Inst, 73; environ specialist, Southern Calif Coastal Water Res Proj, 74. *Mem:* AAAS; Am Soc Microbiol; Am Chem Soc; NY Acad Sci. *Res:* Food and industrial microbiology; public health. *Mailing Add:* Dept Biol Calif State Univ 3702 CSULB Long Beach CA 90840-0004

KIM, KE CHUNG, ENTOMOLOGY, SYSTEMATICS & COEVOLUTION. *Current Pos:* from asst prof to assoc prof, 68-79, CUR, FROST ENTOM MUS PA STATE UNIV, UNIVERSITY PARK, 68-, PROF ENTOM, 79-, DIR, CTR BIODIVERSITY RES, 88- *Personal Data:* b Seoul, Korea, Mar 7, 34; m 64, Young Hee; c Stuart & Sally. *Educ:* Seoul Nat Univ, BS, 56; Univ Mont, MA, 59; Univ Minn, PhD(entom), 64. *Honors & Awards:* Fulbright Lectr, Korea, 75; L O Howard Distinguished Achievement Award, Entom Soc Am, 88. *Prof Exp:* Res fel entom, Univ Minn, 64-67, res assoc, 67-68. *Concurrent Pos:* Consult, Smithsonian Inst, 64-67; Nat Inst Allergy & Infectious Dis res grants, 64-; vis scientist, Atomic Energy Res Inst, Seoul, 75-76; vis prof, Seoul Nat Univ, 75 & 93-94 & Univ Heidelberg, 76; Fulbright-Hays lectr & researcher award, 75-76; sr scholar, 93-94; chmn, Coun Syst & Soc, 81-87, Coun Appl Systs, Asn Systs Collections, 82-85, Sect A, Entom Soc Am, 85, Entom Col Network, 89-90 & Int Adv Coun Biosysts Serv in Entom, 85-86; pres, Pa Biol Surv, 96- *Mem:* Sigma Xi (pres, 92-95); Entom Soc Am; Soc Syst Biologists; Soc Conserv Biol; Korean Acad Sci & Technol. *Res:* Biosystematics of the dipterous family, Sphaeroceridae; systematics and ecology of sucking lice; ecology and evolution of ectoparasites-mammalian host relationships; biodiversity research, forensic entomology; contributed over 150 articles to professional journals. *Mailing Add:* Pa State Univ 116 Land & Water Res Bldg University Park PA 16802. *Fax:* 814-865-3048; *E-Mail:* kck1@ceres.enna.psu.edu

KIM, KENNETH, MICROBIOLOGY. *Current Pos:* asst prof, 71-80, ASSOC PROF CLIN PATH, BACT DIV, MED SCH, UNIV ORE, 80- *Personal Data:* b Honolulu, Hawaii, Dec 24, 31. *Educ:* Univ Hawaii, BA, 53; Wash Univ, MS, 60, PhD(microbiol), 64. *Prof Exp:* Instr prev med, Univ Wash, 64-71. *Mem:* Am Soc Microbiol; NY Acad Sci. *Res:* Relationship of diphtheria toxin to the diphtheria phage-bacterium relationship and the mode of action of toxin on cultured cells; biology of Rubella virus. *Mailing Add:* Dept Clin Path Sch Med Ore Health Sci Univ 3181 SW Sam Jackson Park Rd Portland OR 97201-3011

KIM, KEUN YOUNG, CHEMICAL ENGINEERING, INORGANIC CHEMISTRY. *Current Pos:* res chem engr, 62-66, res specialist, 66-70, FEL, DEPT RES & DEVELOP, DETERGENT & PHOSPHATE DIV, MONSANTO INDUST CHEM CO, 70- *Personal Data:* b Kaesong, Korea, May 29, 28; US citizen; m 58; c 2. *Educ:* Seoul Nat Univ, BS, 51; Univ Wis, MS, 56, PhD(chem eng), 59. *Prof Exp:* Res investr, Inst Sci Res & Technol, Korea, 50-53. *Mem:* Am Inst Chem Engrs; Am Chem Soc. *Res:* Phosphates product and process research; calcium phosphates, particularly dentifrices. *Mailing Add:* 237 Ladue Lake Dr St Louis MO 63141-7412

KIM, KI HANG, MATHEMATICS. *Current Pos:* prof, 74-87, DISTINGUISHED PROF MATH, ALA STATE UNIV, 88- *Personal Data:* b Mundok, Pyongando, Korea, Aug 5, 36; US citizen; m 63, Myong Ja Hwang; c John & Linda. *Educ:* Univ Southern Miss, BS, 60, MS, 61; George Washington Univ, MP, 70, PhD(math), 71. *Prof Exp:* Instr math, Univ Hartford, 61-66; lectr, George Washington Univ, 66-68; assoc prof, St Mary's Col, Md, 68-70 & Pembroke State Univ, 70-73. *Concurrent Pos:* Managing ed, Math Social Sci, 80-94; vis prof math, Portugal Inst Physics & Math, 71-74, Univ Stuttgart, 78-79, Chinese Acad Sci, 83-84, USSR Acad Scis, 90-91; grants, US Army Res Off, 72-76 & NSF, 83-; assoc ed, Future Generations Comput Systs, 83- & Pure Math & Applns, 90- *Mem:* Korean Acad Sci & Technol. *Res:* Diophantine decidability; symbolic dynamics; decision and game theory; elliptic curves; algebraic varieties; Boolean matrices. *Mailing Add:* Ala State Univ Box 69 Montgomery AL 36101-0271. *Fax:* 334-229-4982; *E-Mail:* kkim@asu.alasu.edu

KIM, KI HONG, ANALYTICAL CHEMISTRY. *Current Pos:* CONSULT, 85-; TECH DIR ELECTROMECH, SAMSUNG, 88- *Personal Data:* b Seoul, Korea; US citizen; m 68; c 3. *Educ:* Ohio State Univ, BS, 59; Ohio Univ, MS, 62; George Washington Univ, MPH, 73, PhD(chem), 76. *Prof Exp:* Res assoc biochem, Med Ctr, Univ Ky, 63-66; res chemist, Paktron Div, Ill Tool Works Inc, 66-73, proj leader, 73-78, mgr metal systs, 78-80; mat mgr, Kyocerra Int Inc, San Diego, 81-84, tech adv, 84-85. *Mem:* Am Chem Soc; Soc Appl Spectros; Am Ceramic Soc. *Res:* Spectrophotometric and photopolarographic studies of organo-metallic compounds; research and development of precious metal powder and electrode ink systems for ceramic chip capacitor. *Mailing Add:* 18195 Colonnades Pl San Diego CA 92128-1266

KIM, KI HWAN, COMPUTER ASSISTED MOLECULAR DESIGN, TWO-DIMENSIONAL & THREE-DIMENSIONAL QUANTITATIVE STRUCTURE-ACTIVITY RELATIONSHIP STUDY. *Current Pos:* RES INVESTR, ABBOTT LABS, 80- *Personal Data:* b Pyung-Yang, Korea, May 12, 46; US citizen; m 70, Esther K; c Daniel, Angela & Jane. *Educ:* Yonsei Univ, Seoul, Korea, BS, 69, MS, 71; Univ Kans, Lawrence, MS, 76, PhD(med chem), 81. *Prof Exp:* Res asst, Yonsei Univ, Seoul, Korea, 69-71; res asst, Chem Dept, Pomona Col, 71-73, res assoc, 76-80; res & teaching asst, Med Chem Dept, Univ Kans, 73-76. *Mem:* Am Chem Soc; Drug Inform Soc; Korean Scientists & Engrs Asn Am; Quant Struct Activ Relationships Soc. *Res:* Quantitative correlation of chemical structure and biological activity; conformational and quantum chemical calculations; application of computer graphics to drug design; mechanism of action of biologically active compounds; protein modeling and de novo drug design; over 80 research papers published in major scientific journals. *Mailing Add:* Abbott Labs D46Y AP10-2 100 Abbott Park Rd Abbott Park IL 60064. *Fax:* 847-937-2625; *E-Mail:* ki.h.kim@abbott.com

KIM, KI-HAN, BIOCHEMISTRY. *Current Pos:* from asst prof to assoc prof, 67-73, PROF BIOCHEM, PURDUE UNIV, 73- *Personal Data:* b Seoul, Korea, June 20, 32; US citizen; m 58, Lois N Magner; c Thomas, James & Oliver. *Educ:* Univ Calif, Berkeley, BA, 57; Wayne State Univ, PhD(chem), 61. *Prof Exp:* Res assoc biochem, Wayne State Univ, 61-65 & Univ Wis-Madison, 65-67. *Mem:* AAAS; Am Soc Biol Chem. *Res:* Mechanism of hormone action; biochemical basis of cellular differentiation. *Mailing Add:* Dept Biochem Purdue Univ West Lafayette IN 47907-1968. *Fax:* 765-494-7897

KIM, KI-HYON, MEDICAL PHYSICS, NUCLEAR MEDICINE. *Current Pos:* assoc prof nuclear physics, 68-72, PROF APPL PHYSICS, NC CENT UNIV, 72- *Personal Data:* b Ui ju City, Korea, Apr 20, 33; m 65; c 3. *Educ:* Seoul Nat Univ, BSc, 56; Univ Vienna, PhD(nuclear physics), 63. *Prof Exp:* Res off, Atomic Energy Res Inst, Seoul, 63-66. *Concurrent Pos:* Resident res assoc, NASA-Langley Res Ctr, 66-68, lectr-consult, 68-; consult, Oak Ridge Assoc Univs, 71- *Mem:* Am Phys Soc; Korean Phys Soc; Am Asn Physicists Med; Soc Nuclear Med; Korean Scientists & Engrs Am. *Res:* Nuclear spectrometry; high-flux pulsed neutron sources; biomedical applications of nuclear electronics; organ visualization by means of radiopharmaceuticals and computer based scanning. *Mailing Add:* Dept Physics NC Cent Univ 1805 Fayetteville St Durham NC 27707-3129

KIM, KIL CHOL, ANESTHESIOLOGY, PHARMACOLOGY. *Current Pos:* ASST PROF MED, MED CTR, IND UNIV, INDIANAPOLIS, 69- *Personal Data:* b Hyokyong Hampook, Korea, Apr 22, 19; US citizen; m 65; c 4. *Educ:* Kyung-Pook Nat Univ, Korea, MD, 44; Loyola Univ, PhD(pharm), 62. *Prof Exp:* Intern med, Edgewater Hosp, 56-57; resident, Univ Chicago Clin, 57-58; resident, Cook Co Hosp, 58-59; resident, Michael Reese Hosp, 59-60; sr investr pharm, Loyola Univ, 61-66; physician, Galesbury Res Hosp, 59-60; resident med, Albert Einstein Col Med, 68-69. *Mem:* AMA; assoc Am Soc Anesthesiol; Soc Neurosci. *Res:* Mechanism of contractility depression of cardiac muscle by anesthetics through interaction; investigation of drugs which reduce sleeping time of several anesthetics. *Mailing Add:* 1100 W Michigan St Indianapolis IN 46202-5208

KIM, KI-SOO, POLYMER CHEMISTRY. *Current Pos:* SCIENTIST, AKZO CHEM, 88- *Personal Data:* b Korea, Nov 6, 42; m 70, Cecilia Lee; c John, Julie & Peter. *Educ:* Seoul Nat Univ, BS, 65; City Univ New York, PhD(chem), 72. *Prof Exp:* Res asst chem, Atomic Energy Res Inst Korea, 66-68; assoc, Res Inst, City Univ New York, 72-74; res assoc, Eastern Res Ctr, Stauffer Chem Co, 74-87. *Concurrent Pos:* Adj fac, Mercy Coll, 94- *Mem:* Am Chem Soc; Korean Chem Soc. *Res:* Condensation and vinyl polymerization; synthesis of phosphorus and sulfur-containing polymers; engineering plastics; adhesive formulation, materials research for microelectronics, liquid crystalline polymers. *Mailing Add:* 104 Lily Pond Lane Katonah NY 10536-1814

KIM, KWANG SHIN, MEDICAL MICROBIOLOGY, HORTICULTURE. *Current Pos:* from asst res scientist to assoc res scientist microbiol, 67-71, asst prof, 71-75, ASSOC PROF MICROBIOL, SCH MED, MED CTR, NY UNIV, 75- *Personal Data:* b Seoul, Korea, Nov 15, 37; US citizen; m 65, Bu-Choon Chung; c Edwin C & Andrew K. *Educ:* Seoul Nat Univ, BS, 59; Rutgers Univ, NB, MS, 63, PhD(hort), 67. *Prof Exp:* Res asst hort, Rutgers Univ, NB, 65-66, res assoc, 66-67. *Concurrent Pos:* Mellon Found fel, 73-74; Merck Co Found grantee, 74-76. *Mem:* AAAS; Am Soc Microbiol; Sigma Xi; NY Acad Sci. *Res:* Ultrastructure and cytochemistry of bacteria, especially human pathogenes and their interactions with the host cells using immunoelectron-microscopy. *Mailing Add:* Dept Microbiol NY Univ Sch Med New York NY 10016

KIM, KWANG-JIN, ELECTROPHYSIOLOGY OF EPITHELIUM, PULMONARY DRUG DELIVERY. *Current Pos:* ASSOC PROF, UNIV SOUTHERN CALIF, 91- *Personal Data:* b Hamyang, Korea, Mar 22, 49; m 72, Soon-Ja Lee; c Min-Soo & Shirley. *Educ:* Seoul Nat Univ, BSEE, 71, MSEE, 73; Univ Pa, PhD(bioeng), 80. *Prof Exp:* Lectr electroncs, Korea Mil Acad, 73-76; res fel, Univ Pa, 76-80; fel, Univ Calif, Los Angeles, 80-82, asst res physiologist, 82-86; asst prof, Cornell Univ Med Col, 86-90. *Concurrent Pos:* Prin investr, Am Heart Asn, 80-85, NIH, 84-94, Nat Heart Lung & Blood Inst, 85-88, Am Lung Asn, 89-92. *Mem:* Biomed Soc; NY Acad Sci; Asn Res Vision & Ophthal; AAAS. *Res:* Study of the alveolar epithelial barrier properties in health and disease; mechanisms of injury and recovery of epithelial barrier. *Mailing Add:* HMR914 Univ Southern Calif Med Sch 2011 Zonla Ave Los Angeles CA 90033. *Fax:* 213-342-2611; *E-Mail:* kjkins@hsc.usc.edu

KIM, KYEKYOON K(EVIN), COMPOUND SEMICONDUCTOR MICROELECTRONICS, ELECTROHYDRODYNAMIC SPRAYING. *Current Pos:* fel phys chem, Univ Ill, 72-74, fel elec eng, 74-76, from asst prof to assoc prof, 76-85, PROF ELEC & COMPUT ENG, MECH & INDUST ENG & NUCLEAR ENG MAT SCI & ENG, UNIV ILL, 85- *Personal Data:* b Seoul, Korea, Oct 5, 41; US citizen; m 69; c 2. *Educ:* Seoul Nat Univ, BS, 66; Cornell Univ, MS, 68, PhD(appl physics), 71. *Prof Exp:* Res asst nuclear sci & appl physics, Cornell Univ, 66-71, fel appl physics, 71-72. *Concurrent Pos:* Consult, Y Div, Lawrence Livermore Lab, 78-, NASA, 80-86, Elec Power Res Inst, 81-86, Argonne Nat Lab, 86- & Lab Laser Energetics, Univ Rochester, 86-; chmn, Comt Fueling Plasma Devices, Am Vacuum Soc, 81-86. *Mem:* Am Phys Soc; Inst Elec & Electronics Engrs; Am Vacuum Soc. *Res:* Fusion technology; plasma engineering; cryogenic laser fusion targets; electrohydrodynamics; monodispersed micro-particle generation from insulators; polymers and metals; compound semiconductor microelectronics. *Mailing Add:* Dept Elec & Comput Eng Univ Ill 1406 W Green St 155 Everit Lab Urbana IL 61801

KIM, KYUNG SOO, PLANT CELL VIRUS INTERACTION, VIRUS-INDUCED INCLUSION. *Current Pos:* PROF PLANT PATH, UNIV ARK, 70- *Educ:* Univ Ark, PhD(plant path), 70. *Res:* Plant pathology; electron microscopy. *Mailing Add:* Dept Plant Pathol Plant Sci Bldg No 217 Univ Ark Fayetteville AR 72701. *Fax:* 501-575-7601

KIM, MATTHEW HIDONG, COMPOUND SEMICONDUCTOR HETEROJUNCTION ELECTRONIC DEVICES, VERTICAL CAVITY SURFACE EMITTING LASERS. *Current Pos:* SCIENTIST, MOTOROLA, 94- *Personal Data:* b Seoul, Korea, Sept 21, 58. *Educ:* Cornell Univ, BS, 80; Univ Ill, MS, 81, PhD(physics), 88. *Prof Exp:* Device scientist, Bandgap Technol, 89-93. *Mem:* Am Phys Soc; NY Acad Sci. *Res:* Electronic and opto-electronic properties of hetero-junction compound semiconductors. *Mailing Add:* Motorola Phoenix Corp Res Lab MD-EL703 2100 E Elliot Rd Tempe AZ 85284

KIM, MI JA, PHYSIOLOGY, NURSING. *Current Pos:* prof med surg nursing & dean, Col Nursing, 78-95, VCHANCELLOR RES, UNIV ILL, CHICAGO, 95- *Educ:* Univ Ill, PhD(physiol), 75. *Mem:* Fel Am Acad Nursing. *Res:* Respiratory muscle training. *Mailing Add:* Univ Ill Vchancellor Res 1737 W Polk M/C 672 Chicago IL 60612-7227. *Fax:* 312-996-8066

KIM, MOON W, MATHEMATICAL ANALYSIS. *Current Pos:* ASSOC PROF, SETON HALL UNIV, 69- *Personal Data:* b Seoul, Korea. *Educ:* Univ NH, BA, 64; Polytech Inst Brooklyn, MS, 68, PhD(math), 69. *Prof Exp:* Teaching fel math, Polytech Inst Brooklyn, 66-67, instr, 67-69. *Mem:* Am Math Soc; Math Asn Am. *Res:* Functional analysis; fixed points theorems in non-linear analysis; analytic sets in Banach spaces. *Mailing Add:* 584 White Oak Ridge Rd Short Hills NJ 07078-1368

KIM, MYUNGHWAN, electrical engineering; deceased, see previous edition for last biography

KIM, PETER S, BIOCHEMISTRY. *Current Pos:* from asst prof to assoc prof, 88-95, PROF BIOL, MASS INST TECHNOL, 95-; ASSOC INVESTR, HOWARD HUGHES MED INST, 93- *Personal Data:* b Atlanta, Ga, Apr 27, 58; m, Kathryn H Spitzer; c Michael, Jeremy & Alexander. *Educ:* Cornell Univ, AB, 79; Stanford Univ, PhD(biochem), 85. *Honors & Awards:* Excellence in Chem Award, ICI Pharmaceut Group, 89; Walter J Johnson Prize in Molecular Biol, J Molecular Biol, 89; Nat Acad Sci Award in Molecular Biol, Nat Acad Sci, 93; Eli Lilly Award in Biol Chem, Am Chem Soc, 94; Du Pont Merck Young Investr Award, Protein Soc, 94. *Prof Exp:* Whitehead fel, Whitehead Inst Biomed Res, 85-88, assoc mem, 88-92; asst investr, Howard Hughes Med Inst, 90-93. *Mem:* Nat Acad Sci. *Res:* Structural biology and physical biochemistry; mechanisms of protein folding, macromolecular recognition and protein-induced membrane fusion; peptide design and protein engineering; published over 80 publications. *Mailing Add:* Whitehead Inst Biomed Res 9 Cambridge Ctr Cambridge MA 02142. *Fax:* 617-258-5737

KIM, RHYN H(YUN), MECHANICAL & CHEMICAL ENGINEERING. *Current Pos:* PROF, COL ENG, UNIV NC, CHARLOTTE, 78- *Personal Data:* b Seoul, Korea, Feb 4, 36; m 66; c 3. *Educ:* Seoul Nat Univ, BSME, 58; Mich State Univ, MS, 61, PhD(mech eng), 65. *Prof Exp:* Assoc prof mech eng, Univ NC, Charlotte, 65-76; staff engr, Off Air Qual Planning & Stand, Environ Protection Agency, 76-77, mech engr, Indust Environ Res Lab, Off Res & Develop, 77-78. *Concurrent Pos:* Consult, Indust Environ Res Lab, Off Res & Develop, Environ Protection Agency, 78-; consult, Duke Power Co, NC, Westinghouse Steam Turbine Plant & Teledyne Allvac, 80; bd mem, NC State Bd Examiners, Plumbing, Heating & Sprinkler's Contractors, 88-91. *Mem:* Am Soc Mech Engrs; Am Soc Heating, Refrig & Air-Conditioning Engrs; Instrument Soc Am. *Res:* Combustion, energy conservation and utilization; environmental emission controls; mass transfer in porous media; thermal system optimization and simulations; computer aided heat exchanger design; flow phenomenon visualization; computational fluid mechanics. *Mailing Add:* 2726 Wamath Dr Charlotte NC 28210

KIM, SANG HYUNG, PHOTOGRAPHIC SCIENCE ENGINEERING, INTERFACIAL SCIENCE. *Current Pos:* res chemist, 74-78, sr res chemist, 79-85, RES ASSOC RES DEVELOP, RES LABS, EASTMAN KODAK CO, 86- *Personal Data:* b Kyunggi, Korea, Oct 18, 42; m 68; c 2. *Educ:* Seoul Nat Univ, BS, 64; Univ Utah, PhD(phys chem), 71. *Prof Exp:* Asst teaching & res, Seoul Nat Univ, 66-67; res asst, Univ Utah, 67-70; fel electrochem, Univ Pa, 70-71; fel membrane biophys, Northwestern Univ, 71-74. *Mem:* Am Chem Soc; Soc Imaging Sci Tech. *Res:* Ion-selective electrodes; solution and interfacial electrochemistry; membrane biophysics; electrochemistry applied to biological and medical sciences; emulsion and polymer coatings; photographic sciences. *Mailing Add:* 19 Sutton Pt Pittsford NY 14534-1729

KIM, SANG SOO, CIVIL ENGINEERING MATERIALS, TRANSPORTATION ENGINEERING. *Current Pos:* scientist, 91-92, RES ENGR, WESTERN RES INST, 92- *Personal Data:* b Chungsan, Chungbuk, Korea, Nov 28, 61; m 86, Hyunsun Min; c Dennis & Elliot. *Educ:* Hanyang Univ, Korea, BS, 84; Iowa State Univ, MS, 88, PhD(civil eng), 94. *Prof Exp:* Res asst, Iowa State Univ, 85-90. *Mem:* Asn Asphalt Paving Technologist; Am Soc Civil Engrs. *Res:* Characterizing asphalt properties for better use in highway construction; identifying chemical properties of asphalt which influence physical and engineering properties of asphalt. *Mailing Add:* 2638 Dover Dr Laramie WY 82070. *Fax:* 307-721-2300

KIM, SANGDUK, ENZYMOLOGY, NEUROCHEMISTRY. *Current Pos:* res assoc biochem, 65-78, assoc prof, 78-90, PROF BIOCHEM, FELS RES INST, SCH MED, TEMPLE UNIV, 90- *Personal Data:* b Seoul, Korea, June 15, 30; US citizen; m 59; c 3. *Educ:* Seoul Nat Univ Col Med, MD, 53; Univ Wis, PhD(biochem), 59. *Prof Exp:* Res assoc physiol chem, Univ Wis, 59-61; res assoc biochem, Univ Ottawa, 62-65. *Mem:* Am Soc Biol Chemist; Am Assn

Cancer Res; Am Soc Neurochem; Am Chem Soc. *Res:* Biochemistry of protein methylation; enzymatic modification of protein molecule, biology of myelination. *Mailing Add:* Fels Res Inst Temple Univ Sch Med Philadelphia PA 19140

KIM, SANGTAE, COMPUTER SCIENCE. *Current Pos:* from asst prof to prof, 83-90, PROF COMPUT SCI, DISTINGUISHED PROF CHEM ENG, UNIV WIS-MADISON, 91- *Personal Data:* b Seoul, Korea, Aug 2, 58; nat US; c 2. *Educ:* Calif Inst Technol, BS, 79, MS, 79; Princeton Univ, PhD, 83. *Honors & Awards:* Allan P Colburn Mem lectr, Univ Del, 89; Robert W Vaughan lectr, Calif Inst Technol, 91; Plenary lectr, Korean Inst Chem Engrs, 91; Award Initiatives Res, Nat Acad Sci, 92; Allan P Colburn Award, Am Inst Chem Engrs, 93. *Prof Exp:* Romnes fac fel, Univ Wis, 90; process engr, Intel Corp, Santa Clara, Calif. *Concurrent Pos:* Consult, Amoco Oil Corp, Ill, 83; pres young investr award, Nat Acad Sci, 85; George A Miller vis scholar, Univ Ill, Urbana-Champaign, 87; distinguished vis scholar, Univ Mass, Amherst, 89; vis prof, Pohang Inst Sci Tech, Korea, 91; prin invester, Am Chem Soc, 92-, Off Naval Res, 93-, NSF, 93- *Res:* Dynamics of particulate suspensions; protein dynamics & simulations; computational methods on high performance computers; author of 1 publication. *Mailing Add:* Dept Chem Eng Univ Wis 1415 Johnson Dr Madison WI 53706. *Fax:* 608-262-0832

KIM, SEUNG U, NEUROPATHOLOGY, NEUROBIOLOGY. *Current Pos:* from asst prof to assoc prof neuropath, 72-81, PROF NEUROL, UNIV HOSP, VANCOUVER, 81- *Personal Data:* b Osaka, Japan, Oct 28, 36; US citizen; m 62; c 2. *Educ:* Univ Seoul, Korea, MD, 60; Kyoto Univ, Japan, PhD(neurobiol), 65. *Prof Exp:* Multiple Sclerosis Soc fel, Col Physicians & Surgeons, Columbia Univ, 66-69; assoc prof neurobiol, Univ Sask, Saskatoon, 70-72. *Mem:* Tissue Cult Asn; Am Asn Neuropathologists; Histochem Soc; Soc Neurosci; Am Soc Cell Biol. *Res:* Experimental neurology; neural tissue culture. *Mailing Add:* Univ Hosp 2211 Wesbrook Mall Vancouver BC V6T 2B5 Can. *Fax:* 604-822-7897

KIM, SHOON KYUNG, THEORETICAL CHEMISTRY. *Current Pos:* PROF CHEM, TEMPLE UNIV, 69- *Personal Data:* b Ham Hun, Korea, Feb 29, 20; m 49; c 3. *Educ:* Osaka Univ, BS, 44; Yale Univ, PhD(phys chem), 56. *Honors & Awards:* Korean Nat Sci Award, 61. *Prof Exp:* Res chemist, Inst Chem, Kyoto Univ, 44-46; instr chem, Seoul Nat Univ, 46-47, from instr to prof phys chem, 49-62; res chemist, Cent Indust Res Inst, 47-49; vis prof phys chem, Brown Univ, 62-66; prof, Univ Louisville, 66-69. *Concurrent Pos:* Vis prof, phys chem lab, Oxford Univ, Eng, 80; vis prof, Fritz Harler Res Ctr Molecular Dynamics, Hebrew Univ, Jerusalem, Israel, 85. *Mem:* Korean Chem Soc (secy gen, 60-61); Am Chem Soc; Am Phys Soc; Am Vacuum Soc. *Res:* Statistical mechanical theory of classical and quantal systems; chemical kinetics; theory of optical activity; theory of light scattering; Representation theory of finite and continuous groups. *Mailing Add:* Dept Chem Temple Univ Philadelphia PA 19122-2585

KIM, SOO MYUNG, SOLID STATE PHYSICS. *Current Pos:* Nat Res Coun fel neutron physics br, 70-72, asst res officer, 72-76, assoc res officer, 77-84, RES OFFICER, ATOMIC ENERGY CAN RES CO, CHALK RIVER, 85- *Personal Data:* b Chaeryung, Korea, Oct 24, 36; m 70; c 1. *Educ:* Seoul Nat Univ, BS, 59; Univ NC, Chapel Hill, PhD(physics), 68. *Prof Exp:* Res assoc physics, Univ NC, Chapel Hill, 67-68; fel dept physics, Univ Guelph, 68-70. *Mem:* Am Phys Soc; Can Asn Physicists; Asn Korean Scientists & Engrs Am. *Res:* Positron annihilation in metals; defects in metals. *Mailing Add:* Neutron & Mat Sci Br Atomic Energy Can Res Co Chalk River ON K0J 1J0 Can

KIM, SOOJA K, EPIDEMIOLOGY, DIETETICS. *Current Pos:* prog dir nutrit, Nat Inst Aging, 85-86, HEALTH SCIENTIST ADMINR NUTRIT, DIV RES GRANT, NIH, 88- *Personal Data:* b Seoul, Korea; US citizen; m 85. *Educ:* Humboldt State Univ, BS, 67; Tex Woman's Univ, MS, 73, PhD(nutrit sci), 75. *Prof Exp:* Asst prof nutrit & food sci, Ga Col, 75-77; asst prof nutrit & dietetics, Bowling Green State Univ, Ohio, 77-80, from assoc prof to prof nutrit, 80-87. *Concurrent Pos:* Nutrit consult, Med Col Ohio, Toledo, 78-80, adj prof, 80-87; vis prof, Univ Mich, 81-83. *Mem:* Am Inst Nutrit; Am Dietetic Asn. *Res:* Dietary energy consumption in relation to longevity and health; age related metabolic changes during trauma and illness; nutritional status of elderly. *Mailing Add:* 4120 Rockledge II MSC 7818 Nutrit & Metab Sci IRG NIH 6701 Rockledge Dr Bethesda MD 20892-7818. *Fax:* 301-402-1349

KIM, SOON-KYU, MATHEMATICS. *Current Pos:* from asst prof to assoc prof, 69-83, assoc dept head, 85-88, PROF MATH, UNIV CONN, 83-, DEPT HEAD, 88- *Personal Data:* b Hadong, Korea, Oct 3, 32; US citizen; m 59, Kang-Un Seong; c Jin-Chul, Jin-Kyung & Jin-Wook. *Educ:* Seoul Nat Univ, BS, 57, MS, 59; Univ Mich, PhD(math), 67. *Prof Exp:* Instr math, Seoul Univ & Kunkook Univ, 59-62; instr, Univ Ill, Urbana, 66-69. *Concurrent Pos:* Vis assoc prof, Mich State Univ, 75-76; vis lectr, Seoul Nat Univ, Korea, 83; hon prof, Yanbian Univ, Jilin, People's Repub China, 92; vis prof, Pohang Univ Sci & Technol, 94. *Mem:* Am Math Soc; Korean Math Soc; Korean Scientists & Engrs Am (vpres, 84, pres, 87). *Res:* Fiberings and transformation groups; fixed point theory; infinite dimensional topology. *Mailing Add:* Dept Math Univ Conn Storrs CT 06269. *Fax:* 860-486-4238; *E-Mail:* kim@math.uconn.edu

KIM, SUKYOUNG, biomaterials-bioceramics, structural ceramics, for more information see previous edition

KIM, SUNG KYU, THEORETICAL PHYSICS. *Current Pos:* From asst prof to assoc prof, 65-75, PROF PHYSICS, MACALESTER COL, 75- *Personal Data:* b Chulla Namdo, Korea, Jan 12, 39; m 68, Sherry; c Robert, Jennifer, Alicia & Alexander. *Educ:* Davidson Col, BS, 60; Duke Univ, AM, 64, PhD(physics), 65. *Concurrent Pos:* Master teacher, Twin City Inst Talented Youth, 68-69, 83-; asst prof, Univ Calif, Irvine, 70-71; vis scholar, Fermi Inst, Univ Chicago, 80-81, Astron & Astrophys, Univ Chicago, 87-88 & 94-95. *Mem:* Am Phys Soc; Am Asn Physics Teachers. *Res:* Cosmology/astrophysics. *Mailing Add:* 1 Sparrow Lane St Paul MN 55127

KIM, SUNG WAN, BIOMATERIALS, PHARMACEUTICS. *Current Pos:* res asst chem, Univ Utah, 66-69, fel, 69, res assoc mat sci, 69-70, asst res assoc mat sci & eng, 70-73, from asst prof to assoc prof pharmaceut, 73-80, PROF PHARMACEUT, COL PHARM, UNIV UTAH, 80- *Personal Data:* b Pusan, Korea, Aug 21, 40; m 66; c 2. *Educ:* Seoul Nat Univ, BS, 63, MS, 65; Univ Utah, PhD, 69. *Prof Exp:* Res asst, Seoul Nat Univ, 63-65. *Concurrent Pos:* NIH res career develop award, 77-81. *Mem:* AAAS; Am Chem Soc; Korean Chem Soc; Am Soc Artificial Internal Organs; Am Pharm Asn. *Res:* Blood compatible polymers; membrane diffusion; interface induced thrombosis; polymeric drug delivery system. *Mailing Add:* Col Pharm Univ Utah 301 Skaggs Hall Salt Lake City UT 81412

KIM, SUNG-HOU, BIOPHYSICAL CHEMISTRY, STRUCTURAL MOLECULAR BIOLOGY. *Current Pos:* PROF BIOPHYS CHEM, UNIV CALIF, BERKELEY, 78-, FAC SR SCIENTIST, 79-, DIR, STRUCT BIOL LAB, LAWRENCE BERKELEY NAT LAB, 89- *Personal Data:* b Taegu, Korea, Dec 12, 37; US citizen; m 68; c 2. *Educ:* Seoul Nat Univ, Korea, BS, 60, MS, 62; Univ Pittsburgh, PhD(phys chem), 66. *Honors & Awards:* Pres Serv Merit Award, Repub Korea, 85; fel, Found Prom Cancer Res, Nat Cancer Ctr, Tokyo, Japan, 87; Ernest O Lawrence Award, Dept Energy, 87; Javits Neurosci Investr Award, Dept Health & Human Servs, 88; Princess Takamatsu Award, Princess Takamatsu Cancer Found, Tokyo, Japan, 89. *Prof Exp:* Res assoc biol, Mass Inst Tech, 66-70, sr res scientist, 70-72; asst prof biochem, Sch Med, Duke Univ, 72-73, assoc prof, 73-78. *Concurrent Pos:* Fulbright fel, Fulbright Found, 62; biophys, Dept Biol, Mass Inst Technol, Cambridge, Mass, 66-70, NIH consult, 76-80; ed bd, J Biol Chemistry, 79-83, Nucleic Acids Res, 83-; Lansdowne scholar, Univ Victoria, Can, 80; exchange prof, Peking Univ, Peking, China, 82; Miller res prof, Univ Calif, Berkleley, 83-84; mem, Sci Planning Comt, Nat Found Cancer Res, 83-; Guggenheim fel, NY, 85-86; vis prof, Univ Paris, France, 86; coun mem, Korean Scientists & Engrs Asn Am, 88-; chmn, Adv Comt, Ctr Korean Studies, Inst EAsian Studies, Univ Calif, Berkeley, 89-; mem, US Nat Comt Crystallog, Nat Res Coun, Nat Acad Sci, 90- *Mem:* Nat Acad Sci; Am Crystallog Asn; Am Chem Soc; AAAS; Korean Scientists & Engrs Am; Biophys Soc; Protein Soc; Am Soc Biochem & Molecular Biol. *Res:* Structure and function of DNA, RNA and proteins; reviewer for several scientific journals. *Mailing Add:* Calvin Lab Univ Calif Berkeley CA 94720. *Fax:* 510-486-5270; *E-Mail:* shkim@lbl.gov

KIM, SUN-KEE, CELL BIOLOGY, ANATOMY. *Current Pos:* RES BIOLOGIST, VET ADMIN MED CTR, 68-, COORDR ELECTRON MICROS, RES SERV, 73- *Personal Data:* b Seoul, Korea, Dec 11, 37; US citizen; m 63; c 2. *Educ:* Yon-sei Univ, Korea, BS, 60; Univ Rochester, MS, 64, PhD(biol), 70. *Prof Exp:* Asst cancer res scientist endocrinol, Rosewell Park Mem Inst, Buffalo, 64-65; pre-doctoral trainee, NIH, 65-68. *Concurrent Pos:* Co-dir, Advan Spec Training Dent Res, Vet Admin Med Ctr, 70-75; res assoc anat, Sch Med, Univ Mich, 70-74, asst prof anat & cell biol, 74-81, assoc prof, 81-, adj assoc prof oral biol, Sch Dent, 82-; proj dir aging studies salivary gland, Nat Inst Aging, NIH, 78-82, 87- *Mem:* Am Soc Cell Biol; Am Asn Anatomists; Int Asn Dent Res; AAAS; Sigma Xi. *Res:* Age-related changes in secretory function of exocrine glands; ultrastructure and protein synthesis in secretory cells of the salivary gland. *Mailing Add:* Res Serv Vet Admin Med Ctr 2215 Fuller Rd Ann Arbor MI 48105-2300. *Fax:* 313-761-7693

KIM, TAI KYUNG, PHYSICAL CHEMISTRY. *Current Pos:* Res chemist, 63-77, ENG SPECIALIST, CHEM & METALL DIV, GTE SYLVANIA INC, 77- *Personal Data:* b Pyungyang, Korea, June 19, 27; m 59; c 2. *Educ:* Seoul Nat Univ, BSE, 51; Adrian Col, BS, 55; Univ Detroit, MS, 60; Duquesne Univ, PhD(phys chem), 63. *Mem:* Am Chem Soc. *Res:* Metal complexation; solvent extraction; radiochemistry; molybdenum and tungsten chemistry. *Mailing Add:* RR 1 PO Box 84 Towanda PA 18848

KIM, THOMAS JOON-MOCK, MECHANICAL ENGINEERING, APPLIED MECHANICS. *Current Pos:* from asst prof to prof, 68-91, chmn mech eng, 79-91, DEAN ENG, UNIV RI, 91- *Personal Data:* b Seoul, Korea, Oct 13, 36; US citizen; m 67; c 2. *Educ:* Seoul Nat Univ, BS, 59; Villanova Univ, MS, 64; Univ Ill, PhD(mech), 67. *Honors & Awards:* Advan Technol Award, Am Waterjet Soc, 95. *Prof Exp:* Instr mech, Univ Ill, 65-67; asst prof math, Villanova Univ, 67-68. *Concurrent Pos:* Consult, US Naval Underwater Systs Ctr, 77-84. *Mem:* Am Soc Mech Engrs; Am Ceramic Soc; Soc Mfg Engrs. *Res:* Solid mechanics; ceramic processing; dynamic face seals; water jet machining. *Mailing Add:* Col Eng Univ RI 102 Bliss Hall Kingston RI 02881

KIM, UNTAE, CANCER RESEARCH, TUMOR IMMUNOLOGY. *Current Pos:* HEAD PATH RES, ROSWELL PARK MEM INST, 63- *Personal Data:* b Dec 16, 26. *Educ:* Seoul Univ, Korea, MD, 52. *Mem:* Am Asn Pathologists; Am Asn Immunologists; Am Asn Cancer Res; NY Acad Sci; Int Soc Differentiation; Int Soc Metastasis Res; Int Asn Breast Cancer Res. *Res:* Breast cancer research on carcinogenesis and evolution of neoplastic state; hormone dependency; immunology of tumor cells and acquisition of metastatic potential and its patterns; interaction between tumor and lymphoid cells. *Mailing Add:* Res Path 4720 Main St Snyder NY 14226. *Fax:* 716-845-8017

KIM, WON, DATABASE & DISTRIBUTED SYSTEMS. *Current Pos:* PRES, UNISQL INC, 90- *Personal Data:* b Korea, 1948. *Educ:* Mass Inst Technol, BS & MS, 71; Univ Ill, Urbana-Champaign, PhD(computer sci), 80. *Prof Exp:* Prin scientist, MCC, 84-90, dir, Object-Oriented Distrib Syst Lab, 87-90. *Concurrent Pos:* Chmn, Spec Interest Group Mgt Data, Asn Comput Mach, 89- *Mem:* Asn Comput Mach. *Mailing Add:* UniSQL 8911 N Capital Texas Hwy Suite 2300 Austin TX 78759

KIM, WOO JONG, MATHEMATICS. *Current Pos:* From asst prof to assoc prof appl math, 68-84, PROF APPL MATH & STATIST, STATE UNIV NY, STONY BROOK, 85- *Personal Data:* b Seoul, Korea, Jan 15, 37. *Educ:* Seoul Nat Univ, BS, 58; Okla State Univ, MS, 60; Carnegie-Mellon Univ, MS & PhD(chem eng), 64, PhD(math), 68. *Mem:* Am Math Soc. *Res:* Disconjugacy, oscillation and asymptotic behavior of ordinary differential equations. *Mailing Add:* Dept Math Educ & Statist Chungbak Nat Univ Cheongiu Chungbak 360-763 Korea

KIM, YEE SIK, BIOCHEMISTRY, PHARMACOLOGY. *Current Pos:* from asst prof to prof, 66-76, PROF PHARMACOL, ST LOUIS UNIV, 76- *Personal Data:* b Seoul, Korea, Apr 15, 28; US citizen; m 50, Young S Lee; c Karl, Ruth, Grace & Elizabeth. *Educ:* Kans State Univ, BS, 57, MS, 60; St Louis Univ, PhD(pharmacol), 65. *Prof Exp:* Instr chem, Kans State Univ, 60; res chemist, Union Starch & Refining Co, Ill, 60-63. *Concurrent Pos:* USPHS fel biochem, State Univ NY Buffalo, 65-66; Gen res support grant & Cancer Inst res grant, 66-; USPHS res grant, 67- *Mem:* AAAS; Am Soc Pharmacol & Exp Therapeut; Am Chem Soc; NY Acad Sci. *Res:* Molecular mechanism of hormone action; enzyme reaction mechanisms; metabolisms of macromolecules; diabetic pregnancy; mechanisms of vitamin D metabolites. *Mailing Add:* Dept Pharmacol St Louis Univ Sch Med 1402 S Grand St Louis MO 63104. *Fax:* 314-577-8554; *E-Mail:* kimy2@sluvca.slu.edu

KIM, YEONG ELL, THEORETICAL NUCLEAR PHYSICS. *Current Pos:* from asst prof to assoc prof, 67-77, PROF PHYSICS, PURDUE UNIV, 77- *Personal Data:* b S Korea; US citizen; m 61; c 2. *Educ:* Lincoln Mem Univ, BS, 59; Univ Calif, Berkeley, PhD, 63. *Honors & Awards:* US Sr Scientist Humboldt Award, 77. *Prof Exp:* Fel physics, Bell Tel Labs Inc, 63-65, Oak Ridge Nat Lab, 65-67. *Concurrent Pos:* Proj dir, Purdue Nuclear Theory Group, 71-; vis staff mem, Los Alamos Nat Lab, Univ Calif, 73-74, consult, 74-92; chmn, Gordon Res Conf, 77; vis prof, Seoul Nat Univ, 79 & 80. *Mem:* Korean Scientists & Engrs Asn Am; fel Korean Phys Soc; fel Am Phys Soc. *Res:* Quantum theory of scattering; theory of the three-nucleon systems; intermediate energy physics; theories of meson-exchange currents; parity violations in nuclear physics; photonuclear reactions; nuclear structure and reactions; quark degrees of freedom in nuclei; geodesy; geodynamics; gravitational theory; exploration geophysics; nuclear fusion; astrophysics. *Mailing Add:* Dept Physics Purdue Univ West Lafayette IN 47907-1396

KIM, YEONG WOOK, SOLID STATE PHYSICS, ATOMIC & MOLECULAR PHYSICS. *Current Pos:* PROF PHYSICS, WAYNE STATE UNIV, 60- *Personal Data:* b July 21, 25; c 3. *Educ:* Seoul Nat Univ, Korea, BS, 48, MS, 50; Brown Univ, Providence, RI, PhD(physics), 61. *Concurrent Pos:* Sigma Xi award, Wayne State Univ, 76; NIH cancer sci fel, 76-78. *Mem:* Fel Am Phys Soc; Am Asn Physics Teachers; Sigma Xi; Inst Elec & Electronics Engrs; Am Asn Univ Professors. *Res:* Solid State experiments; spatial pairing effects in high temperature superconductors. *Mailing Add:* Dept Physics & Astron Wayne State Univ Detroit MI 48202

KIM, YONG IL, BIOMEDICAL ENGINEERING, NEUROMUSCULAR TRANSMISSION. *Current Pos:* res assoc, Dept Neurol & Jerry Lewis Neuromuscular Ctr, 77-79, asst prof, 79-95, PROF BIOMED ENG & NEUROL, SCH MED, UNIV VA, 95- *Personal Data:* b Seoul, Korea, June 5, 45; m 75; c 3. *Educ:* Seoul Nat Univ, BS, 68; Cornell Univ, MS, 73, PhD(biomed eng), 77. *Prof Exp:* Systs analyst trainee, Korea Comput Ctr, 68; systs engr, Gadelius & Co, Ltd, 68-70; instr bioeng & elec systs, Cornell Univ, 77. *Concurrent Pos:* New investr res award, NIH, 82-85; vis scientist, Dept Pharmacol, Univ Lund, Sweden, 83-84. *Mem:* Inst Elec & Electronics Engrs; Biomed Eng Soc; AAAS; Soc Neurosci; Korean Scientists & Engrs Am. *Res:* Neuromuscular transmission in disease states; bioelectric systems; biomedical instrumentation. *Mailing Add:* Dept Biomed Eng Univ Va Box 377 Charlottesville VA 22908. *Fax:* 804-982-3870

KIM, YONG WOOK, ATOMIC PHYSICS, STATISTICAL PHYSICS. *Current Pos:* From asst prof to assoc prof, 68-77, chmn dept, 84-87, PROF PHYSICS, LEHIGH UNIV, 77- *Personal Data:* b Seoul, Korea, Sept 30, 38; nat US; m 66, Sook H; c Irene, Christopher & Michelle. *Educ:* Seoul Nat Univ, BS, 60, MS, 62; Univ Mich, PhD(physics), 68. *Concurrent Pos:* Lectr, USSR Acad Sci, 91. *Mem:* Fel Am Phys Soc; Sigma Xi; AAAS; Metall Soc; Electrochem Soc. *Res:* Non-linear phenomena in molecular and Brownian fluctuation; radiative transport in nonideal plasmas; spectroscopy of light scattering from small particle suspension and fractals; shock wave generation; laser-produced plasmas; nonlinear dynamics of interfaces. *Mailing Add:* Dept Physics Lehigh Univ Bldg 16 Bethlehem PA 18015. *Fax:* 610-758-5730; *E-Mail:* ywk0@ns1.cc.lehigh.edu

KIM, YONG-KI, ATOMIC PHYSICS. *Current Pos:* physicist, Nat Bur Stand, 83-87, supvry physicist, 87-96, PHYSICIST, NAT INST STAND & TECHNOL, 96- *Personal Data:* b Seoul, Korea, Feb 20, 32; m 63; c 2. *Educ:* Seoul Nat Univ, BS, 57; Univ Del, MS, 61; Univ Chicago, PhD(physics), 66. *Prof Exp:* Instr physics, Korean Air Force Acad, 57-59; res assoc, Argonne Nat Lab, 66-68, asst physicist, 68-72, physicist, 72-79, sr, physicist, 79-83. *Concurrent Pos:* Lectr, Univ Chicago, 67-68. *Mem:* Fel Am Phys Soc; Radiation Res Soc. *Res:* Atomic structure theory; atomic collision theory; radiation physics. *Mailing Add:* Nat Inst Stand & Technol Bldg 221 Rm A267 Gaithersburg MD 20899. *Fax:* 301-975-3038; *E-Mail:* kim@atm.phy.nist.gov

KIM, YOON BERM, IMMUNOLOGY. *Current Pos:* PROF BIOL & IMMUNOL, GRAD SCH MED SCI, CORNELL UNIV, 73-, CHMN, IMMUNOL UNIT, 80-; AT DEPT MICROBIOL & IMMUNOL, CHICAGO MED SCH, N CHICAGO. *Personal Data:* b Soon Chun, Korea, Apr 25, 29; m 59; c 3. *Educ:* Seoul Nat Univ, MD, 58; Univ Minn, PhD(microbiol), 65. *Prof Exp:* Intern med, Univ Hosp, Seoul Nat Univ, 58-59; from asst teaching & res to assoc teaching & res, 60-64, from instr to assoc prof microbiol, Med Sch, Univ Minn, Minneapolis, 65-73; head, lab ontogeny immune syst, Sloan-Kettering Inst Cancer Res, NY, 73- *Concurrent Pos:* Res fel, 60-64; USPHS career develop res award, 68-73. *Mem:* Asn Gnotobiotics (pres, 79-80); Am Asn Immunol; Am Soc Microbiol; Reticuloendothelial Soc; Am Asn Path. *Res:* Immunobiology and immunochemistry; ontogeny of the immune system; mechanism of the immune response, regulation of the immune system; tumor immunity; immunochemistry and biology of bacterial toxins and host-parasite relationships; gnotobiology. *Mailing Add:* Dept Microbiol & Immunol Finch Univ Health Sci Chicago Med Sch 3333 Green Bay Rd North Chicago IL 60064-3095. *Fax:* 847-578-3349

KIM, YOONKEE, MICROACOUSTICS, FREQUENCY CONTROL. *Current Pos:* ELECTRONICS ENGR, US ARMY RES LAB, 96- *Personal Data:* b Seoul, Korea, Apr 18, 58; m 87, Soae; c Junho & Jiho. *Educ:* Seoul Nat Univ, BS, 81; Korean Advan Inst Sci Technol, MS, 84, Ga Inst Technol, MS, 91, PhD(elec eng), 93. *Prof Exp:* Electronics engr, Goldstar Inc, 84-86; consult, Bon-oh Electronics, 87, Motorola, 92; postdoctoral fel, Ga Inst Technol, 93-94; res assoc, Nat Res Coun, 95-96. *Mem:* Inst Elec & Electronics Engrs. *Res:* High precision clocks and smart sensors based upon bulk acoustic wave devices and surface acoustic devices; author of more than 20 technical publications. *Mailing Add:* 117C White St Eatontown NJ 07724. *Fax:* 732-427-4805; *E-Mail:* ykim@arl.mil

KIM, YOUNG C, coastal engineering, hydraulic engineering, for more information see previous edition

KIM, YOUNG DUC, ELECTRICAL ENGINEERING. *Current Pos:* RES ELECTRONIC ENGR, US NAVAL AMMUNITION DEPOT, 68- *Personal Data:* b Korea, Oct 28, 32; m 65; c 1. *Educ:* Newark Col Eng, MSEE, 63, ScD, 68. *Mem:* Inst Elec & Electronics Engrs. *Res:* Investigation of noise spectral density observed in solid state devices. *Mailing Add:* 2922 N Ramble Rd W Bloomington IN 47408-1050

KIM, YOUNG JOO, BIOSEPARATION, SEPARATION PROCESS. *Current Pos:* ASST RESEARCHER CHEM ENG, RENSSELAER POLYTECH INST, 89- *Personal Data:* b Kwangju, Dec 12, 60; m 86; c 1. *Educ:* Chonnam Nat Univ, Korea, BE, 83; Seoul Nat Univ, Korea, ME, 85. *Prof Exp:* Res engr chem eng, Orient Chem Indust Res Ctr, 86, Ssangyong Oil Refinery, Korea, 87-89. *Mem:* Am Inst Chem Engrs. *Res:* Separation and purification of various pharmaceutical proteins and biochemicals by preparative chromatography; scale-up; mathematical modeling. *Mailing Add:* 400 McChesney Ave Bldg 6 No 3 Troy NY 12180

KIM, YOUNG NOK, THEORETICAL PHYSICS. *Current Pos:* prof physics, 64-92, EMER PROF, TEX TECH UNIV, 92- *Personal Data:* b Seoul, Korea, Jan 30, 21; m 60; c 3. *Educ:* Seoul Nat Univ, BS, 47, MS, 49; Univ Birmingham, PhD(math physics), 57. *Prof Exp:* Res grants, Inst Theoret Physics, Copenhagen, Denmark, 58-68, Heidelberg, Ger, 58, Edmonton, Can, 62-63, Inst Henri Poincare, Paris, France, 58-59 & Univ Wash, 60-62; prof physics, Mem Univ, 63-64. *Mem:* Am Phys Soc; Italian Phys Soc. *Res:* Nuclear structure; collision; mesonic atoms. *Mailing Add:* 8106 Elgin Ave Lubbock TX 79423

KIM, YOUNG SHIK, MEDICINE. *Current Pos:* from asst prof to assoc prof, 68-76, PROF MED, UNIV CALIF, SAN FRANCISCO, 76-; DIR, GI RES LAB, VET ADMIN HOSP, SAN FRANCISCO, 68- *Personal Data:* b Seoul, Korea, Feb 5, 33; US citizen; c 2. *Educ:* Stanford Univ, AB, 56; Cornell Univ, MD, 60. *Honors & Awards:* Western Gastroenterol Res Award, 78; Vet Admin Med Investr Award, 84-90; NIH Merit Award, 88. *Prof Exp:* Instr med, Med Col, Cornell Univ, 64-65; res assoc path, Stanford Univ, 65-66; asst prof biochem, New York Med Col, 67-68. *Concurrent Pos:* Am Cancer Soc res scholar, 65-68; mem gen med study sect A, NIH, 76-79; large bowel cancer working group, Nat Cancer Inst, 85-89; clin Sci I Study Sect, NIH, 89-; assoc ed, Gastroenterol, 81-86, cancer res, 87- *Mem:* Am Asn Cancer Res; Am Soc Clin Invest; Am Gastroenterol Asn; Biochem Soc; Asn Am Physicians. *Res:* Glycoprotein and glycolipid chemistry, immunochemistry and metabolism of the gastrointestinal tract; biology and molecular biology of gastrointestinal cancer. *Mailing Add:* GI Res Lab Vet Admin Ctr 4150 Clement St San Francisco CA 94121-1598. *Fax:* 415-750-6972

KIM, YOUNG TAI, biochemistry, immunology, for more information see previous edition

KIM, YOUNG-GIL, ALLOY DESIGN & DEVELOPMENT, HIGH TEMPERATURE ALLOYS. *Current Pos:* PROF MAT ENG, KOREA ADVAN INST SCI & TECHNOL, 78- *Personal Data:* b Andong, Korea, Oct 3, 39; m 70, Young-Ae; c James H & Joanne J. *Educ:* Seoul Nat Univ, BS, 64; Univ Mo, Rolla, 69; Rensselaer Polytech Inst, PhD(mat eng), 73. *Honors & Awards:* IR-100, Inco Alloys Int, 80; King Sejang Sci Award, Korea Govt, 86. *Prof Exp:* Res asst, Univ Mo, Rolla, 67-69; from res asst to res assoc, Mat Div, Rensselaer Polytech Inst, 69-73; res assoc, US Army Const Eng Res Lab, 73-74; Nat Res Coun res assoc, Lewis Res Ctr, NASA, 74-76; res metallurgist,

Inco Alloys Res & Develop Ctr, 76-78. *Concurrent Pos:* Vis prof, Dept Mat, Univ Calif, Los Angeles, 84-85; consult, Nickel Develop Inst, 90- *Mem:* Fel Am Soc Metals; Mineral Metals & Mat Soc; Korea Inst Metals. *Res:* Alloy development of oxide dispersion strengthened Nickel- base super alloys for gas turbine by mechanical alloying process; development of high strength automotive structural alloys and high strength-good electrical conductivity copper alloys for electronic applications. *Mailing Add:* Banpo Dong 7411 Kyungnam Apt Seochokuy Seoul 137047 South Korea. *Fax:* 82-42-869-3310

KIM, YUNG DAI, TUMOR IMMUNOLOGY, CLINICAL CHEMISTRY. *Current Pos:* sr scientist immunol, 74-88, assoc res fel, Cancer Res Lab, 88-92, PROBE DIAGS, RES & DEVELOP, ABBOTT LABS, 93- *Personal Data:* b Seoul, Korea, Mar 24, 36; US citizen; m 67, Young S Chyung; c Jean & Sue. *Educ:* Wash State Univ, BS, 61; Univ Idaho, MS, 63; Univ Minn, PhD(biophys chem), 68. *Prof Exp:* NIH fel, Northwestern Univ, 69-71; NIH res fel, Univ Pa, 71-73. *Concurrent Pos:* Vis scientist, C F Kettering Res Inst, 68-69. *Mem:* Am Asn Immunologists; Am Chem Soc; Sigma Xi; Am Asn Cancer Res. *Res:* Cancer research in immunology and immunochemistry; isolation and characterization of tumor-associated antigens; research and development of clinical diagnostic tests; DNA probe technology. *Mailing Add:* 1728 Virginia Ave Libertyville IL 60048

KIM, YUNGKI, ORGANIC CHEMISTRY, POLYMER CHEMISTRY. *Current Pos:* res chemist, Dow Corning Corp, 65-68, sr res chemist, 68-70, res group leader, Silicone Polymers & Intermediates, 70-77, process eng mgr, 77-83, res mgr, 83-84, develop mgr, 84-86, TS&D dir, 86-89, RES & DEVELOP DIR, FRPL, DOW CORNING CORP, 89- *Personal Data:* b Korea, Dec 11, 35; US citizen; m 61; c 2. *Educ:* Tex Christian Univ, BA, 59; Univ Colo, Boulder, MS, 61; Ariz State Univ, PhD(org chem), 65. *Prof Exp:* Fac res assoc chem, Ariz State Univ, 64-65. *Mem:* Am Chem Soc; Sigma Xi. *Res:* Synthetic organic and polymer chemistry; silicone fluorosilicone and hybrid of silicone and organic/fluoro-organic leading to sealants, rubbers, resins and fluids. *Mailing Add:* Mail Stop CO-2406 Dow Corning Corp Midland MI 48686-0994

KIM, ZAEZEUNG, IMMUNOLOGY, ALLERGY. *Current Pos:* from instr to assoc prof med, 72-80, CLIN ASSOC PROF, DEPT MED ALLERGY SECT, MED COL WIS, 80- *Personal Data:* b Hamhung, Korea, Feb 21, 29; US citizen; m 61; c 2. *Educ:* Seoul Nat Univ, MD, 60; Univ Cologne, PhD(immunol), 68. *Prof Exp:* Resident physician, Seoul Nat Univ Hosp, 61-63; resident physician, Heidelberg Univ Hosp, 63-64; res fel immunol, Max Planck Inst, 65-67; clin fel hematol, Univ Tex M D Anderson Hosp, 67-68; resident physician allergy-immunol, Temple Univ Hosp, 68-69; fel allergy-immunol, Col Med, Ohio State Univ, 69-71. *Concurrent Pos:* Travel grants, AAAS, 67 & Am Acad Allergy, 70; pvt pract. *Mem:* AAAS; Am Acad Allergy; AMA. *Res:* Modification (change) of cellular antigenicity by enzyme treatment. *Mailing Add:* 1300 Green Bay Rd Racine WI 53406-4469

KIMBALL, ALLYN WINTHROP, PUBLIC HEALTH & EPIDEMIOLOGY. *Current Pos:* prof, 60-94, EMER PROF BIOSTATIST, SCH HYG & PUB HEALTH, JOHNS HOPKINS UNIV, 94- *Personal Data:* b Buffalo, NY, Oct 2, 21; m 44; c 2. *Educ:* Univ Buffalo, BS, 43; NC State Univ, PhD(statist), 50. *Prof Exp:* Exp statistician aerospace med, USAF Sch Aviation Med, 48-50; chief statist sect, Math Panel, Oak Ridge Nat Lab, 50-60. *Concurrent Pos:* Chmn, Dept Biostatist, Johns Hopkins Univ, 60-66, prof, Sch Med, 60-, chmn, Dept Statist, 62-66, prof, Fac Arts & Sci, 62-, dean, Fac Arts & Sci, 66-70. *Mem:* Biomet Soc (treas, 55-60); Am Statist Asn. *Res:* Statistics and mathematics applied to biology and medicine. *Mailing Add:* 1106 Hampton Garth Baltimore MD 21286

KIMBALL, AMY SARAH, DNA REPLICATION, SITE-SPECIFIC RECOMBINATION. *Current Pos:* FEL, JOHNS HOPKINS UNIV, 91- *Personal Data:* b Palo Alto, Calif, Apr 25, 64; m 89, David B Schmickel. *Educ:* Univ Calif, Santa Cruz, BA, 85, Johns Hopkins Univ, PhD(biol), 90. *Mem:* AAAS. *Res:* Bactiophage and DNA replication. *Mailing Add:* 1325 Park Ave Baltimore MD 21217

KIMBALL, AUBREY PIERCE, drug metabolism, enzymology; deceased, see previous edition for last biography

KIMBALL, BRUCE ARNOLD, SOIL PHYSICS, MICROMETEOROLOGY. *Current Pos:* soil scientist, 70-90, RES LEADER, US WATER CONSERV LAB, AGR RES SERV, USDA, 90- *Personal Data:* b Aitkin, Minn, Sept 27, 41; m 66, Laurel Honway; c Britt, Rica & Megan. *Educ:* Univ Minn, St Paul, BS, 63; Iowa State Univ, MS, 65; Cornell Univ, PhD(soil physics), 70. *Concurrent Pos:* Adj prof, Dept Bot, Ariz State Univ, Tempe. *Mem:* Fel Am Soc Agron; fel Soil Sci Soc Am; Int Solar Energy Soc; AAAS; Int Soc Hort Sci; Int Soc Advan Indust Crops. *Res:* Carbon dioxide effects on plants; energy relationships of greenhouses; evaporation and transpiration; soil air movement. *Mailing Add:* US Water Conserv Lab 4331 E Broadway Rd Phoenix AZ 85040-8837

KIMBALL, CHARLES NEWTON, electrical engineering; deceased, see previous edition for last biography

KIMBALL, CHASE PATTERSON, PSYCHIATRY, INTERNAL MEDICINE. *Current Pos:* PROF PSYCHIAT & MED & BEHAV SCI, PRITZKER SCH MED, UNIV CHICAGO, 72- *Personal Data:* b Ware, Mass, July 21, 32; m 58; c 4. *Educ:* Brown Univ, AB, 54; State Univ NY, MD, 59. *Prof Exp:* Intern med, Univ Vt Hosps, 59-60, resident, 63-65; resident psychiat, NY Hosp, 60-61; instr psychiat med, Univ Rochester, 65-67; asst prof psychiat & med, Yale Univ, 67-72. *Concurrent Pos:* NIMH fel psychosom med, Univ Rochester, 65-67; lectr, Conn Acad Gen Pract, Conn Psychiat Asn, 67-; Am Heart Asn res grant, 68-71; consult, USPHS, 69-; chmn comt community health affairs & hosps, dir psychiat curric & chmn social med, Univ Chicago, 72-; lectr, Sch Med, Yale Univ, 72-; dir progs intercult med, Yale Univ & Univ Chicago, 72-; vpres, Int Col Psychosom Med, 77-79, pres-elect, 79- *Mem:* Am Psychosom Soc; Am Psychiat Soc; Am Heart Asn; NY Acad Sci; Soc Health & Human Values. *Res:* Investigation of psychosocial factors associated with illness and the adaptation of individuals to illness; medical education as a humanizing experience. *Mailing Add:* Univ Chicago Psychiat 950 E 59th St Chicago IL 60637-2602

KIMBALL, CLYDE WILLIAM, SOLID STATE PHYSICS. *Current Pos:* sci & technol adv to pres, Northern Ill Univ, 82-88, prof physics, 68-90, univ res prof, 86-90, DISTINGUISHED PROF, NORTHERN ILL UNIV, 90- *Personal Data:* b Laurium, Mich, Apr 20, 28; m 52; c 2. *Educ:* Mich Tech Univ, BS, 50, MS, 52; St Louis Univ, PhD(physics), 59. *Prof Exp:* Asst physicist, Argonne Nat Lab, 50-53, res assoc, 57-59; res physicist solid state physics, Autonetics Div, NAm Aviation, Inc, 59-60; mem res staff res opers, Aeronutronics Div, Ford Motor Co, Calif, 60-62; assoc physicist, Solid State Div, Argonne Nat Lab, 62-64; assoc prof physics, Northern Ill Univ, 64-68; prog dir low temperature physics, Div Mat Res, NSF, 77-78. *Concurrent Pos:* Consult, Argonne Nat Lab, 64- *Mem:* AAAS; fel Am Phys Soc; Sigma Xi; Am Asn Physics Teachers. *Res:* Experimental reactor physics; photodisintegration cross sections; neutron cross sections and nuclear reactions; magnetic and electronic properties of metals and alloys; Mossbauer effect; superconductivity; amorphous solids; lattice properties; optoelectronics. *Mailing Add:* Dept Physics Northern Ill Univ De Kalb IL 60115

KIMBALL, FRANCES ADRIENNE, REPRODUCTIVE ENDOCRINOLOGY. *Current Pos:* CONSULT DRUG DEVELOP, 96- *Personal Data:* b Oakland, Calif, May 2, 39. *Educ:* Univ Calif, Berkeley, BA, 61; Calif State Univ, Chico, MA, 70; Cornell Univ, PhD(physiol), 73. *Prof Exp:* Res asst endocrinol, Reed Col, 61-68; res technician, Med Sch, Univ Calif, San Francisco, 68; instr biol, Calif State Univ, Chico, 68-70; USPHS fel, Cornell Univ, 70-73; scientist, Upjohn Co, 74-75, res scientist II, 75-80, sr res scientist III reproductive endocrinol & fertil res, 80-85, sr proj mgr prod develop, 85-89, actg dir, 89-91, dir proj mgt, 91-95. *Concurrent Pos:* NIH fel, Upjohn Co, 73-74. *Mem:* Am Soc Zoologists; Soc Study Reproduction; Am Soc Microbiol; Drug Info Asn. *Res:* Mechanism of hormone action in the uterus and corpus luteum; action of prostaglandins in uterine contractility; physiology of antimicrobial agents. *Mailing Add:* 3602 Woodcliff Dr Kalamazoo MI 49008-2513

KIMBALL, JOHN WARD, BIOLOGY. *Current Pos:* RETIRED. *Personal Data:* b Portland, Maine, 1931; m 53, Margaret Wilkerson; c Christopher & Nicholas. *Educ:* Harvard Univ, AB, 53, AM, 70, PhD(biol), 72. *Prof Exp:* Assoc prof biol, Tufts Univ, 77-81; vis lectr biol, Harvard Univ, 82-86, 90-91; assoc prof biol, Bradford Col, 88-89. *Mem:* Fel AAAS; Am Asn Immunologists. *Res:* Author of biology textbooks. *Mailing Add:* 89 Prospect Rd Andover MA 01810. *E-Mail:* jkimball@ma.ultranet.com

KIMBALL, PAUL CLARK, MOLECULAR GENETICS, VIROLOGY. *Current Pos:* CONSULT, FOLEY & LORDNER, ALEXANDRIA, VA, 90- *Personal Data:* b New London, Conn, Jan 26, 46; m 85; c 1. *Educ:* Mass Inst Technol, BS, 68; Univ Calif, Berkeley, PhD(molecular biol), 72. *Prof Exp:* Instr microbiol, Univ Ill Med Ctr, 72-73; sr scientist tumor virol, Meloy Labs, Inc, 73-75; asst prof microbiol, Ohio State Univ & molecular virologist, Cancer Res Ctr, 75-81; prin res scientist, 81-82, sr res scientist, 83, res leader, Battelle, Columbus, 84-88; consult, Cushman, Darby & Cushman, Washington, DC, 88-90. *Mem:* AAAS; Am Soc Microbiol; Am Soc Virol. *Res:* Patenting of biotechnologies, especially genetic engineering products and processes; microbial production of biologicals with medical/veterinary/industrial import; use of microcomputers in biotechnology research; protein/peptide engineering. *Mailing Add:* 6908 Brierly Rd Chevy Chase MD 20815

KIMBELL, JULIA S, MATHEMATICS. *Current Pos:* APPL MATHEMATICIAN, CHEM INDUST INST TOXICOL, 92- *Personal Data:* b Waltham, Mass, Sept 11, 60. *Educ:* Middlebury Col, BA, 82; Duke Univ, MA, 84, PhD(math), 88. *Mem:* Am Math Soc; Biomed Eng Soc; Math Asn Am; Soc Risk Anal; Soc Indust & Appl Math. *Mailing Add:* 298 Jordan Hills Dr Chapel Hill NC 27514-8843

KIMBER, CLARISSA THERESE, GLOBAL CHANGE, ETHNO-MEDICINE. *Current Pos:* from asst prof to assoc prof, 68-81, PROF GEOG, TEX A&M UNIV, 81- *Personal Data:* b Merced, Calif, Feb 1, 29. *Educ:* Univ Calif, Berkeley, AB, 49; Univ Wis-Madison, MS, 62, PhD(geog), 69. *Prof Exp:* Teaching asst geog, Univ Wis-Madison, 61, res asst, 62-64; actg asst prof, Univ Calif, Riverside, 64-66, lectr, 66-67; asst prof, Calif State Col, Hayward, 67-68. *Concurrent Pos:* Pron investr, Res Coun Fiscal Grant, Tex A&M Univ, 71; HEW, NIH, 71-72; co-prin investr, Fish & Wildlife Serv, US Dept Interior, 78-82; mem bd gov, Orgn Trop Studies, 81-; Fulbright res scholar, 95-96. *Mem:* Sigma Xi; Soc Women Geogrs; AAAS; Asn Am Geogrs; Orgn Trop Studies; fel Royal Geog Soc. *Res:* Island biogeography; people-plant relations as in domestication of plants and ethno-medical systems; human impacts on isolated environments, sustainable strategie in context of global change. *Mailing Add:* Dept Geog Tex A&M Univ College Station TX 77843. *Fax:* 408-862-8847; *E-Mail:* ctk5617@venus.tamu.edu

KIMBER, GORDON, CYTOGENETICS. *Current Pos:* RETIRED. *Personal Data:* b Manchester, Eng, July 21, 32; m 57; c 1. *Educ:* Univ London, BSc, 54, DSc, 86; Univ Manchester, PhD(genetics), 61. *Prof Exp:* Res asst genetics, Univ Manchester, 54-58; sci officer, Plant Breeding Inst, 58-63, sr sci off, 63-67; assoc prof, Univ Mo, Columbia, 67-72, prof agron, 72-95. *Concurrent Pos:* Kellogg Found fel, 63-64; Int Atomic Energy Agency expert, Indian Agr Res Inst, New Delhi, 70-71. *Mem:* Genetics Soc Am; Brit Genetical Soc; Sigma Xi; Genetics Soc Can. *Res:* Wheat cytogenetics. *Mailing Add:* 12237 Alcosta Blvd San Ramon CA 94583

KIMBERLEY, JOHN A, MECHANICAL ENGINEERING. *Current Pos:* MGR ADVAN PROD GROUP, AM BOSCH, CONSULT, AMBAC, 86- *Educ:* Lehigh Univ, BS, 42. *Honors & Awards:* Internal combustion Engine Award, Am Soc Mech Engrs, 92. *Prof Exp:* Develop engr, Curtis Wright. *Mem:* Am Soc Mech Engrs; Soc Automotive Engrs. *Res:* Development of a gas carburetor, electric governor for generator sets, hydraulically-powered, electronically controlled unit injector research diesel fuel system, optical start to injection timing, automobile diesel injection pump with variable injection rate, system to control injection pressure in a pumpline-injection system independent of engine speed, fuel system for injecting a slurry of coal and water and a pilot diesel injector for gas/diesel engines; granted 15 patents. *Mailing Add:* 68 New Gate Rd East Granby CT 06026

KIMBERLING, WILLIAM J, GENE LINKAGE, COMMUNICATION DISORDERS. *Current Pos:* ASSOC PROF MED GENETICS, PROF OTOLARYNGOL & PATH, MED SCH, CREIGHTON UNIV, 79- *Personal Data:* b Logansport, Ind, Oct 16, 40; m 62, Rose M; c Susan E (Kannawin), Mary T (Dougherty), Patricia D, William J & Thomas D. *Educ:* Ind Univ Sch Med, PhD(med genetics), 67. *Prof Exp:* Fel, Med Sch, Univ Ore, 67-71, instr med genetics, 71-72; asst prof, Med Sch, Univ Colo, 72-79. *Concurrent Pos:* Res assoc, Boys Town Inst Hered Commun Dis, 79-, ctr dir, 90- *Mem:* AAAS; Am Soc Human Genetics. *Res:* Gene linkage and localization in humans. *Mailing Add:* 3338 S 107th St Omaha NE 68124. *Fax:* 402-498-6331; *E-Mail:* kimber@boystown.org

KIMBERLY, ROBERT PARKER, INTERNAL MEDICINE, RHEUMATOLOGY. *Current Pos:* PROF MED, MICROBIOL, SCH MED, UNIV ALA, 96-, DIR & SR SCIENTIST ARTHRITIS CTR, 96-, SR SCIENTIST, COMPREHENSIVE CANCER CTR, 96- *Personal Data:* b New Haven, Conn; m 72, Susan J Aleusburg; c Christopher, Taylor, Sarah, Michael & Thomas. *Educ:* Princeton Univ, BA, 68; Oxford Univ, BA & MA, 70; Harvard Univ, MD, 73. *Prof Exp:* Clin assoc, Nat Inst Arthritis, Metab & Digestive Dis, NIH, 75-77; fel, Hosp Spec Surg, NY Hosp, 77-79, asst prof, 79-84, assoc prof, 84-91; prof med, Cornell Univ Med Col, 91-96. *Concurrent Pos:* Attending physician, Hosp Spec Surg, NY Hosp; Howard L Holley Prof Med. *Mem:* Fel Am Col Physicians; fel Am Col Rheumatology; Am Asn Immunologists; Am Soc Clin Invest. *Res:* Immunology. *Mailing Add:* Univ Ala 1900 Univ Blvd Birmingham AL 35294-0006

KIMBLE, ALLAN WAYNE, IMAGE ANALYSIS, ANALYTICAL INSTRUMENTATION DESIGN. *Current Pos:* STAFF SCIENTIST NEW PROD RES & DEVELOP, VISTAKON, JOHNSON & JOHNSON VISION PRODS, 89- *Personal Data:* b Washington, DC, Jan 2, 60; m 86, Maura D Dennis; c Rebecca L & Rachel A. *Educ:* State Univ NY, Albany, BS, 89. *Concurrent Pos:* Anal instrumentation instr, 86- *Mem:* AAAS; Asn Off Anal Chemists; Coblentz Soc; Int Soc Optical Eng; Micros Soc Am. *Res:* Development of integrated image-spectral data analysis systems including ultraviolet, visible, near and mid infrared regions of the spectrum; functional analysis of polymers by spectral imaging techniques. *Mailing Add:* 7500 Powers Ave Jacksonville FL 32217. *Fax:* 904-443-3433

KIMBLE, GERALD WAYNE, NUMERICAL ANALYSIS. *Current Pos:* assoc prof, 67-75, prof, 75-88, EMER PROF MATH & COMPUT SCI, UNIV NEV, RENO, 88- *Personal Data:* b Bakersfield, Calif, Apr 24, 28; m 48, 65, Isabel Clemeshaw; c Craig L (Hill). *Educ:* Univ Calif, Berkeley, AB, 49, Univ Calif, Los Angeles, MA, 58, PhD(math), 62. *Prof Exp:* Mathematician, Nat Bur Stand Inst Numerical Anal, Univ Calif, Los Angeles, 49-51; engr, Hughes Aircraft Co, 55-58; res asst numerical anal, Univ Calif, Los Angeles, 59-61; asst prof math, Calif State Col, Long Beach, 61-63; assoc prof math & dir comput ctr, Univ Mont, 63; mathematician, TRW, Inc, Calif, 63-67. *Mem:* Math Asn Am. *Res:* Calculus of variations; computer science; random permutations; history of mathematics. *Mailing Add:* 12360 Big Blue Rd Nevada City CA 95959

KIMBLE, HARRY JEFFREY, PHYSICS. *Current Pos:* PROF PHYSICS, DEPT PHYSICS, CALIF INST TECHNOL, 89- *Personal Data:* b Floydada, Tex, Apr 23, 49. *Educ:* Abilene Christian Univ, BS, 71; Univ Rochester, MA, 73, PhD(physics), 78. *Prof Exp:* Assoc sr res physicist, Gen Motors Res Labs, 77-79; prof physics, Univ Tex, Austin, 79-85. *Mem:* Am Phys Soc; Optical Soc Am; AAAS. *Res:* Quantum optics; theory of coherence; atomic physics; infrared spectroscopy; semiconductor diode lasers; laser intracavity absorption spectroscopy; optoacoustic spectroscopy; theory of resonance fluorescence; photostatistics. *Mailing Add:* Div Physics Calif Tech MC 12-33 Pasadena CA 91125. *Fax:* 626-793-9506

KIMBLE, JUDITH E, MOLECULAR & CELLULAR BIOLOGY. *Current Pos:* PROF BIOCHEM & LAB MOLECULAR BIOL, HOWARD HUGHES MED INST, 92-, INVESTR MED GENETICS, 94- *Personal Data:* b Providence, RI, Apr 24, 49. *Educ:* Univ Calif, Berkeley, BA, 71; Univ Colo, Boulder, PhD(molecular, cellular & develop biol), 78. *Prof Exp:* Postdoctorate, Univ Wis, 78-82, from asst prof to assoc prof, 83-92. *Mem:* Nat Acad Sci; Am Acad Arts & Sci; Am Soc Cell Biol; Am Soc Biochem & Molecular Biol; Genetic Soc. *Mailing Add:* Dept Biochem Howard Hughes Med Inst 420 Henry Mall Madison WI 53706-1514. *Fax:* 608-265-5820

KIMBLER, DELBERT LEE, QUALITY ENGINEERING, TOTAL QUALITY MANAGEMENT. *Current Pos:* assoc prof, 86-90, PROF INDUST ENG, CLEMSON UNIV, 90-, CHAIR INDUST ENG, 95- *Personal Data:* b Whitman, WVa, Sept 8, 45; m 67, Elisabeth Davidson. *Educ:* Univ SFla, BSE, 76; Va Polytech Inst & State Univ, MS, 78, PhD(indust eng & opers res), 80. *Honors & Awards:* Mfg Systs Spec Citation, Inst Indust Engrs, 88. *Prof Exp:* Instr indust eng & opers res, Va Polytech Inst & State Univ, 78-80; from asst prof to assoc prof indust eng, Univ SFla, 80-86. *Concurrent Pos:* Actg dept head, Indust Eng, Clemson Univ, 89-90; consult engr, Ciba Viscon Corp, 92-93; coordr continuous qual improv, Col Eng, 93-94. *Mem:* Sr mem Inst Indust Engrs; sr mem Am Soc Qual Control; Soc Mfg Engrs; Sigma Xi; Nat Soc Prof Engrs. *Res:* Quality engineering and quality management; manufacturing modeling and analysis; research and development management. *Mailing Add:* Clemson Univ 110 Freeman Hall Clemson SC 29634-0920. *E-Mail:* delbert.kimbler@eng.clemson.edu

KIMBLIN, CLIVE WILLIAM, ARC & INTERRUPTION PHYSICS. *Current Pos:* DIR, TECHNOL DEVELOP, BEGEMANN, 90- *Personal Data:* b Stockport, Eng, Dec 25, 38; US Citizen; m 68; c 3. *Educ:* Univ Liverpool, BSc, 60, PhD(elec eng), 64, Univ Pittsburgh, MSIE, 76. *Prof Exp:* Res engr arch physics, Westinghouse Res & Develop Ctr, 64-65, sr engr, 65-74, fel engr, 74-75, mgr, Power Interruption Res, 75-86; dir, Prod Develop, Holec, 86-89. *Mem:* Am Phys Soc; sr mem Inst Elec & Electronics Engrs; Inst Elec Engrs. *Res:* Physics of arcing and interruption in vacuum and air with particular reference to electrode mechanisms, properties of the inter-electrode metallic plasma and development of high power switching devices. *Mailing Add:* 225 Tech Rd Pittsburgh PA 15205

KIMBRELL, DEBORAH ANN, INSECT IMMUNITY. *Current Pos:* ASST PROF, DEPT BIOL & INST MOLECULAR BIOL, UNIV HOUSTON, 91- *Personal Data:* b Goodfellow AFB, Tex, July 22, 50; m 91, S Ingemar Olsson. *Educ:* Mills Col, BA, 72; Univ Calif, Berkeley, PhD(genetics), 85. *Prof Exp:* Res technician, Dept Respiration Physiol, Max Planck Inst Exp Med, Ger, 73-74; Am Cancer Soc fel, Dept Genetics, Univ Cambridge, 85-88; Swed Med Res Coun vis scientist, Dept Microbiol, Univ Stockholm, Sweden 88-90. *Concurrent Pos:* Prin investr, Univ Houston, 92-93, Am Cancer Soc, 93- *Mem:* Genetics Soc Am; AAAS. *Res:* Immune response and regulation of tumor formation; author of several publications. *Mailing Add:* Dept Biol Univ Houston Houston TX 77204-5513. *Fax:* 713-742-2636; *E-Mail:* kimbrell@uh.edu

KIMBRELL, JACK T(HEODORE), mechanical engineering, for more information see previous edition

KIMBROUGH, DAVID L, GEOCHRONOLOGY, TECTONICS OF CIRCUM-PACIFIC OROGENIC BELTS. *Current Pos:* asst prof, 89-92, ASSOC PROF, DEPT GEOL SCI, SAN DIEGO STATE UNIV; 92- *Educ:* Univ Calif, Santa Cruz, BSc, 76; Univ Calif, Santa Barbara, PhD, 82. *Honors & Awards:* Antarctic Serv Medal, NSF, 90. *Prof Exp:* Geologist Ashland Explor Inc, Houston, 76; res assoc, Univ Calif, Santa Barbara, 83-88. *Concurrent Pos:* Sigma Xi res grantee, 78; Penrose grantee, 79; Geol Soc Am Harold T Stearns fel, 80; postdoctoral fel, Otago Univ, NZ, 82-83; William Evans Teaching fel, 87; dir, Baylor Brook Inst Isotope Geol, Col Sci, San Diego State Univ, 89-; J William Fulbright grantee, 95-96. *Mem:* Geol Soc Am; Am Geophys Union; Nat Asn Geosci Teachers. *Res:* Author of numerous publications. *Mailing Add:* Dept Geol Sci San Diego State Univ San Diego CA 92182-1020

KIMBROUGH, JAMES W, MYCOLOGY. *Current Pos:* from asst prof to assoc prof, Univ Fla, 64-76, assoc chmn dept, 74-75, prof bot, 76-87, actg chmn, 85-86, PROF PLANT PATH, UNIV FLA, 87- *Personal Data:* b Eupora, Miss, Nov 7, 34; m 61; c Virginia Dawn, John Jeffery & William Jay. *Educ:* Miss State Univ, BS, 57, MS, 60; Cornell Univ, PhD(mycol), 64. *Prof Exp:* Asst bacteriologist, Vet Sci Dept, Miss State Univ, 60-61; instr bot, 61-62; teaching asst mycol, Cornell Univ, 62-64. *Concurrent Pos:* Mem bd sci adv, Highlands Biol Sta; panelist, NSF, 82-85. *Mem:* Mycol Soc Am (secy-treas, 74-77, vpres, 77-78, pres elect, 78-79, pres, 79-80); Bot Soc Am; Int Asn Plant Taxon; Brit Mycol Soc; Linnean Soc. *Res:* Developmental and taxonomic studies in the powdery mildews; morphological, developmental and taxonomic studies of operculate Discomycetes; fungi as biocontrol agents of termites; fungi involved in indoor house pollution. *Mailing Add:* Dept Plant Path Univ Fla PO Box 110680 Gainesville FL 32611-2002. *Fax:* 352-392-2158; *E-Mail:* jwk@gnv.ifas.ufl.edu

KIMBROUGH, RENATE DORA, PATHOLOGY. *Current Pos:* SR MED ASSOC, INST EVALUATING HEALTH RISKS, 91- *Personal Data:* b Hannover, Ger, Jan 14, 33; US citizen; div; c Doris, Erich & Lucy. *Educ:* Univ Gottingen, MD, 57. *Honors & Awards:* Clinton H Thienes Award, Am Acad Clin Toxicol, 87; Herbert E Stockinger Award, Am Conf Govt & Indust Hygienists, 91. *Prof Exp:* Intern, Evanston Hosp, Ill, 58-59; resident path, St Joseph's Infirmary, Atlanta, Ga, 60-62; res pathologist, Pesticide Prog, Toxicol Lab, Nat Commun Dis Ctr, Ctr Dis Control, USPHS, 62-69, pathologist, Atlanta Toxicol Br, US Food & Drug Admin, 68-70 & Environ Protection Agency, 70-73, res med officer, Toxicol Br, Ctr Dis Control, 73-87. *Concurrent Pos:* Consult, St Joseph's Infirmary, 62-74; mem, Sci Adv Board, USAF, 92-94. *Mem:* Am Acad Clin Toxicol; fel Am Acad Pediat; Am Asn Clin Pathologists; Soc Toxicol. *Res:* Risk assessment; human exposure; human health effects of chemical exposure; extrapolating data on chemicals from laboratory animals to humans. *Mailing Add:* Inst Evaluating Health Risks 1629 K St NW Suite 402 Washington DC 20006

KIMBROUGH, THEO DANIEL, JR, PHYSIOLOGY, BIOCHEMISTRY. *Current Pos:* asst prof, 67-74, ASSOC PROF BIOL, VA COMMONWEALTH UNIV, 74- *Personal Data:* b Lafayette, Ala, Sept 17, 33; m 65; c 2. *Educ:* Univ Ala, BS, 55, MA, 59; Auburn Univ, PhD(zool), 65. *Prof Exp:* Teaching asst zool, Auburn Univ, 62-63, NIH fel physiol, 63-64; asst prof biol, Birmingham-Southern Col, 64-67. *Concurrent Pos:* NSF grant, Res Small Col Fac, Univ NC, 83. *Mem:* Fel Am Inst Chem; Soc Indust Microbiol; Sigma Xi; Am Entom Soc. *Res:* Physiology of intestinal serotonin; animal physiology; histology; physiology of intestinal serotonin; insect physiology, characterization of serotonin receptors in the cockroach digestive tract; neurophysiology, study of effects of aspartame on serotonin levels in brain and on behavior in mice. *Mailing Add:* 10300 Waltham Dr Richmond VA 23233-4823

KIMEL, JACOB DANIEL, JR, PARTICLE PHYSICS, THEORETICAL & COMPUTATIONAL PHYSICS. *Current Pos:* res assoc, Fla State Univ, 66-67, from asst prof to assoc prof, 67-88, dir grad affairs, Physics Dept, 89-91, PROF PHYSICS, FLA STATE UNIV, 88- *Personal Data:* b Winston-Salem, NC, Aug 11, 37; m 65, 91, Lauva G Gunter; c Leslie A, Kristine L, Jacob D III & Karen E. *Educ:* Univ NC, Chapel Hill, BS, 59; Univ Wis-Madison, MS, 60, PhD(physics), 66. *Prof Exp:* Res assoc physics, Univ Wis-Madison, 66. *Mem:* Sigma Xi; Am Phys Soc. *Res:* Theoretical physics with emphasis on studies of elementary particle properties and intearctions; computational and simulational physics. *Mailing Add:* Dept Physics Fla State Univ Tallahassee FL 32306. *Fax:* 850-644-6735; *E-Mail:* kimel@fsuheop.physics.fsu.edu

KIMEL, WILLIAM R(OBERT), MECHANICAL & NUCLEAR ENGINEERING. *Current Pos:* prof nuclear eng, dir Eng Exp Sta & dean Col Eng, 68-86, EMER DEAN & PROF COL ENG, UNIV MO, COLUMBIA, 86- *Personal Data:* b Cunningham, Kans, May 2, 22; m 52. *Educ:* Kans State Univ, BS, 44, MS, 49; Univ Wis, PhD(eng mech), 56. *Prof Exp:* Design engr, Goodyear Tire & Rubber Co, Ohio, 44-46; from instr to asst prof mech eng, Kans State Univ, 46-54; engr, US Forest Prod Lab, Univ Wis, 55-56; assoc prof mech eng, Kans State Univ, 54-59, prof nuclear eng & head dept, 58-68. *Concurrent Pos:* Mem, Kans Gov Atomic Energy Adv Coun, 61-68, chmn, 66-68; AEC observer, UN Atomics for Peace Conf, 64 & 71; mem, Adv Comt to Off Civil Defense, 64-70, chmn, 69-70; consult, Div Nuclear Educ & Training, AEC, 66-68; mem, fel rev panel, HEW, 66-68. *Mem:* AAAS; Am Soc Eng Educ; fel Am Soc Mech Engrs; Am Nuclear Soc (vpres & pres-elect, 77-78, pres, 78-79); Nat Soc Prof Engrs (vpres-elect, 85-86); Jr Eng Tech Soc (pres, 80-81). *Res:* Engineering mechanics composite structures; nuclear reactor and shielding analysis. *Mailing Add:* 900 Yale Columbia MO 65203

KIMELBERG, HAROLD KEITH, ASTROGLIA. *Current Pos:* res assoc prof neurosurg, Albany Med Col, Union Univ, 74-80, assoc prof biochem, 74-88, prof anat, 80-88, RES PROF NEUROSURG, 80-, PROF PHARMACOL & TOXICOL, ALBANY MED COL, UNION UNIV, 87- *Personal Data:* b Hertford, Eng, Dec 5, 41; nat US; div; c David & Michael. *Educ:* Univ London, BS, 63; State Univ NY, Buffalo, PhD(biochem), 68. *Prof Exp:* Fel, Johnson Res Found, Univ Pa, 68-69; NIH fel, Roswell Park Mem Inst, 69-70, sr cancer res scientist, 70-74; asst res prof, Roswell Park Div, Grad Sch, State Univ NY, 72-74. *Concurrent Pos:* Adj assoc prof biol, State Univ NY, Albany, 78-88; adj prof biol, State Univ NY, Albany; prof biochem, Albany Med Col, Union Univ, 88-; Fulbright grantee, Univ Heidelberg, Ger, 88. *Mem:* Am Soc Biol Chemists; Am Soc Neurochem; Soc Neurosci; AAAS. *Res:* Ion transport, electrical properties, transmitter responsiveness and uptake systems of astroglial cells; roles of astrocytes in trauma and ishemia especially in regard to cerebral cellular edema and excitotoxicity. *Mailing Add:* Div Neurosurg A-60 Albany Med Col Albany NY 12208. *Fax:* 518-262-6178; *E-Mail:* hkimelberg@ccgateway.amc.edu

KIMELDORF, GEORGE S, STATISTICS, MATHEMATICS. *Current Pos:* assoc prof, 75-76, PROF MATH SCI, UNIV TEX, DALLAS, 76- *Personal Data:* b New York, NY, Sept 3, 40; m 64, Carol Shulman; c Joyce & Joel. *Educ:* Univ Rochester, AB, 60; Univ Mich, MA, 61, PhD(math), 65. *Prof Exp:* From asst prof to assoc prof math, Calif State Univ, Hayward, 65-69; from asst prof to assoc prof statist, Fla State Univ, 69-75. *Concurrent Pos:* Vis asst prof, Math Res Ctr, Univ Wis, 67-68, vis assoc prof, 68-69. *Mem:* Inst Math Statist; Am Statist Asn. *Res:* Mathematical statistics; probability; operations research. *Mailing Add:* 7612 Queens Ferry Lane Dallas TX 75248. *E-Mail:* kmldorf@utdallas.edu

KIMERLING, LIONEL COOPER, SOLID STATE SCIENCE, PHYSICS. *Current Pos:* mem tech staff, 72-81, HEAD, MAT PHYSICS RES DEPT, BELL LABS, 81- *Personal Data:* b Birmingham, Ala, Dec 2, 43; m 66; c 2. *Educ:* Mass Inst Technol, SB, 65, PhD(mat sci), 69. *Prof Exp:* Res asst, Dept Metall & Mat Sci, Mass Inst Technol, 65-69; res physicist, Air Force Cambridge Res Labs, USAF, 69-72. *Concurrent Pos:* Vis fel, Inst Study Defects Solids, 75-; adj prof phys, Lehigh Univ, 77-; lectr, Welsh Found, 79. *Mem:* AAAS; Am Inst Mining, Metall & Petrol Engrs; Am Phys Soc; Electrochem Soc; Sigma Xi. *Res:* Defects in solids: structure, electrical properties and chemical reactions; elemental and III-V semiconductor systems. *Mailing Add:* Dept Mat Sci Rm 13-4118 Mass Inst Technol Cambridge MA 02139

KIMES, BRIAN WILLIAM, CANCER RESEARCH. *Current Pos:* grants assoc, Div Res Grants, NIH, 75-76, prog dir, Extramural Tumor Biol Prog, Div Cancer Resources Ctr & Div Cancer Biol & Diag, Nat Cancer Inst, 76-79, chief, Extramural Cancer Biol Br, 79-85, assoc dir, Extramural Res Prog, 82-88, ASSOC DIR, CENTERS, TRAINING & RESOURCE PROG, DIV CANCER BIOL & DIAG, NAT CANCER INST, NIH, 89- *Personal Data:* b Tampa, Fla, Sept 7, 43; m. *Educ:* Stanford Univ, BS, 66; Univ Wash, PhD(biochem), 71. *Prof Exp:* Am Cancer Soc fel, Salk Inst Biol Studies, San Diego, 71-73, res assoc, 73-75. *Concurrent Pos:* NIH grant & contract prog. *Res:* Structure and function of ribosomes; vitro protein synthesis; vitro macromolecular synthesis; tissue culture of nerve; muscle and fibroblast cell lines; electron microscopy; cell-cell communication. *Mailing Add:* 8201 Kentbury Dr Bethesda MD 20814

KIMES, THOMAS FREDRIC, NUMERICAL ANALYSIS, MATHEMATICAL ANALYSIS. *Current Pos:* from asst prof to prof math, Austin Col, 62-76, chmn dept, 62-73, dir interactive comput serv, 73-76, dir, Jan Term Prog, 81-90, Chadwick prof math, 76-90, chmn dept, 84-90, EMER PROF MATH, AUSTIN COL, 92- *Personal Data:* b Phoenixville, Pa, July 24, 28; m 52, 74, Kathleen Woods; c Christine & Thornton. *Educ:* Ursinus Col, BS, 49; Univ Tex, MA, 56; Carnegie Inst Technol, PhD, 62. *Prof Exp:* Asst math, Univ Tex, 54-56; asst, Carnegie Inst Technol, 56-58, proj mathematician, 58-59; mathematician, Bettis Atomic Power Lab, Westinghouse Elec Corp, 59-60, sr mathematician, 60-62. *Concurrent Pos:* Vis prof math, Furness Col, Univ Lancaster, 70; vis scholar, Cambridge Univ, 80, 87. *Mem:* Am Math Soc; Math Asn Am; Prehistoric Soc UK. *Res:* Ordinary and partial differential equations. *Mailing Add:* 2501 Turtle Creek Dr Sherman TX 75092-2232. *E-Mail:* tkimes.austinc.edu

KIMLER, BRUCE FRANKLIN, RADIATION BIOLOGY, CANCER BIOLOGY. *Current Pos:* from asst prof to assoc prof radiation ther, 77-84, PROF DEPT RADIATION ONCOL, UNIV KANS MED CTR, KANSAS CITY, 84- *Personal Data:* b St Paul, Minn, Sept 23, 48; m 75, Susan C Watson; c Laura J & Britton F. *Educ:* Univ Tex, Austin, BA, 70, MA, 71, PhD(radiation biol), 73. *Prof Exp:* Appointee radiation biol, Argonne Nat Lab, 73-75; fel, Thomas Jefferson Univ Hosp, 75-77. *Concurrent Pos:* Assoc scientist, Mid-Am Cancer Ctr Prog, 77-81; adj prof, Dept Radiation Biophys, Univ Kans, 77-82; adj prof, Dept Pharmacol, Toxicol & Therapeut, Univ Kans Med Ctr, 90-; councillor, Radiation Res Soc, 91-94. *Mem:* Radiation Res Soc; Am Asn Cancer Res; Cell Kinetics Soc (secy, 81-83, vpres, 91-92, pres, 92-93); Am Soc Therapeut Radiol & Oncol; Sigma Xi; Int Soc Anal Cytol. *Res:* Preclinical experimental radiation oncology; cancer chemotherapeutic agents; flow cytometry; in utero effects of radiation; brain tumor therapy; breast cancer prediction and chemoprevention. *Mailing Add:* Dept Radiation Oncol Univ Kans Med Ctr 3901 Rainbow Blvd Kansas City KS 66160-7321. *Fax:* 913-588-3663; *E-Mail:* bfkimler@kumc.edu

KIMLIN, MARY JAYNE, ANALYTICAL CHEMISTRY, PHYSICAL CHEMISTRY. *Current Pos:* from instr to assoc prof, 48-70, PROF CHEM, ST FRANCIS COL, PA, 70- *Personal Data:* b Cresson, Pa, July 4, 24. *Educ:* St Francis Col, Pa, BS, 48; Pa State Univ, MS, 58, PhD(anal chem), 69. *Prof Exp:* Lab asst chem, Kinetic Div, E I du Pont de Nemours & Co, 44-46. *Mem:* Sigma Xi; AAAS; Am Chem Soc. *Res:* Polarographic study of correlations between ionic diffusion coefficients and ionic strength; polarography in fused salts; polarography of copper hydroxo complexes. *Mailing Add:* 515 Ashcroft Ave Cresson PA 16630-1304

KIMME, ERNEST GODFREY, MATHEMATICS, ENGINEERING. *Current Pos:* PRIN ASSOC, AMETA, 74- *Personal Data:* b Long Beach, Calif, June 7, 29; m 78, Margaret J Bolen; c Ernest, Elizabeth & Karl. *Educ:* Pomona Col, BA, 52; Univ Minn, MA, 54, PhD(math), 56. *Prof Exp:* Instr math, Ore State Col, 55-57; mem tech staff, Bell Tel Labs, 57-63, supvr, 63-65; head appl sci dept, Collins Radio Co, 65-67, asst to vpres, 67-72; res engr, Northrop Electronics, 72-74; prin engr, Interstate Electronics, 74-79; dir spec commun prog, Gould Naval Commun Syst Div, 79-82; chief scientist & chief exec officer, Cobit, Inc, 82-84; tech staff, Gen Res Corp, 84-87; vpres eng, Starfind Inc, 87-89, dir eng res & develop, Unit Instruments, 89-90; res tech staff, Brunswick Defense Syst, 90-92. *Concurrent Pos:* Vpres & dir, A S Johnston Drilling Co, 68-; adj fac, Univ Redlands, 89- *Mem:* AAAS; Sigma Xi. *Res:* Analysis, particularly probability theory, mathematical statistics, information theory and operations research; communications sciences; quantitative management theory; experimental design; theoretical aerodynamics; published 121 papers. *Mailing Add:* 301 Starfire Anaheim CA 92807

KIMMEL, ALAN R, MOLECULAR BIOLOGY. *Current Pos:* sr investr molecular biol, 80-92, CHIEF SECT MOLECULAR METAB DEVELOP, NIH, 92- *Personal Data:* b New York, NY, Jan 22, 49. *Educ:* Rutgers Univ, BA, 70; Univ Rochester, PhD(biol), 77. *Prof Exp:* Am Chem Soc fel, 77-79, sr fel, 79-81. *Mem:* Fedn Am Socs Exp Biol; AAAS. *Mailing Add:* NIH Bldg 6 Rm B1-22 Bethesda MD 20892-2715

KIMMEL, BRUCE LEE, LIMNOLOGY, AQUATIC ECOLOGY. *Current Pos:* res staff mem & group leader ecosysts dynamics, Mat Transport & Fate, 80-90, PROG MGR, OFF-SITE ENVIRON RESTORATION PROG, ENVIRON SCI DIV, OAK RIDGE NAT LAB, 90- *Personal Data:* b Poplar Bluff, Mo, Nov 6, 45; m 67, 87; c 2. *Educ:* Baylor Univ, BS, 67, MS, 69; Univ Calif, Davis, PhD(ecol), 77. *Prof Exp:* Proj officer oceanic biol, Ocean Sci & Technol Group, Off Naval Res, 70-71; instr chem, Div Math Sci, US Naval Acad, 71-72; asst prof zool & asst dir, biol sta, Univ Okla, 77-80. *Concurrent Pos:* Prin investr res grant, Okla Water Resources Inst, Off Water Res & Technol, Dept Interior, 78-80; prin & co-prin investr res contracts, Dept Energy, US Army CEngrs & Tenn Valley Authority, NSF Ecosysts Progs, 80-; proj dir, RCRA Facil Invest, Environ Sci Div, Oak Ridge Nat Lab, 87- *Mem:* Am Soc Limnol & Oceanog; Int Asn Theoret & Appl Limnol; Ecol Soc Am; Am Inst Biol Sci; AAAS; Sigma Xi. *Res:* Biological productivity and foodweb interactions in lakes and reservoirs; energy flow and nutrient cycling in aquatic systems; contaminant transport, fate, and effects in river-reservoir ecosystems; reservoir and lake liminology and ecology; water resources management. *Mailing Add:* 24 Windhaven Rd Oak Ridge TN 37830

KIMMEL, CAROLE ANNE, DEVELOPMENTAL & REPRODUCTIVE TOXICOLOGY. *Current Pos:* develop toxicologist, 84-92, SR DEVELOP TOXICOLOGIST, ENVIRON PROTECTION AGENCY, 92- *Personal Data:* b Lexington, Ky, Apr 26, 44; m 70, Gary L; c Rebecca A. *Educ:* Georgetown Col, BS, 66; Univ Cincinnati, PhD(anat), 70. *Honors & Awards:* Commissioner's Commendable Serv Award, Food & Drug Admin, 83; Spec Achievement Award, US Environ Protection Agency, 85 & 86, Bronze Medals, 86, Sci Achievement Award Health Sci, 90 & 94, Sci Technol Achievement Award, 91. *Prof Exp:* Fel toxicol, Col Med, Univ Cincinnati, 70-72; sect head teratology, Environ Protection Agency, 72; instr anat, Sch Med, Harvard Univ, 72-73; sr staff fel teratology, Nat Inst Environ Health Sci, 73-77, chief, Perinatal & Postnatal Eval Br, 79-84; res pharmacologist, Div Teratogenesis Res, Nat Ctr Toxicol Res, NIH, 77-, chief, Perinatal & Postnatal Eval Br, 79-84. *Concurrent Pos:* Consult, Environ Protection Agency, 72-73; adj asst prof, Sch Med, Univ NC, 75-76; prog mgr, Reproductive & Develop Toxicol, Nat Toxicol Prog, 79-86; adj assoc prof, Interdis Toxicol Div, Univ Ark Med Sci, 82-89; guest worker, Food & Drug Admin, 84-; adj prof, Univ Md, 89- *Mem:* Soc Toxicol; Neurobehav Teratology Soc; Teratology Soc; Europ Teratology Soc; Int Fedn Teratology Socs; Soc Experimental Biol & Med. *Res:* The effects of developmental exposures to drugs and environmental agents on the behavior and function of offspring; test methodology in teratology; extrapolation of animal data for human risk assessment; Hyperthermia effects on developing enbryo; early molecular markers of heat stress and abnormal development; patterning of segmentation. *Mailing Add:* 401 M St SW Rm 3812A Mall USEPA 8623 Washington DC 20460

KIMMEL, CHARLES BROWN, DEVELOPMENTAL BIOLOGY. *Current Pos:* asst prof biol, 69-75, assoc prof, 75-83, PROF BIOL, UNIV ORE, 83-, MEM, INST NEUROSCI, 83- *Personal Data:* b New Orleans, La, May 3, 40; m 62, Reida Johnson; c Seth. *Educ:* Swarthmore Col, BA, 62; Johns Hopkins Univ, PhD(biol), 66. *Prof Exp:* NIH fel immunol, Salk Inst Biol Studies, 66-68. *Concurrent Pos:* Javits Investr Award, NIH, Nat Inst Neurol Dis & Stroke, 91- *Mem:* Fel AAAS; NY Acad Sci; Soc Develop Biol(pres, 93-94); Soc Neurosci. *Res:* Experimental neurogenesis; vertebrate neural development; cell lineage; developmental genetics. *Mailing Add:* Dept Biol Univ Ore Eugene OR 97403

KIMMEL, DONALD LORAINE, JR, DEVELOPMENTAL BIOLOGY. *Current Pos:* assoc prof & chmn dept, 71-78, PROF BIOL, DAVIDSON COL, 78- *Personal Data:* b Swedesboro, NJ, Apr 15, 35; m 83, Margaret Boykin; c 5. *Educ:* Swarthmore Col, BA, 56; Temple Univ, MD, 60, MSc, 62; Johns Hopkins Univ, PhD(developgenetics), 64. *Prof Exp:* Asst prof, Div Med Sci, Brown Univ, 64-71. *Concurrent Pos:* Res fel, Calif Inst Technol, 70-71; corp mem, Bermuda Biol Sta; res scientist, Div Res NC Dept Mental Health, 78-79. *Mem:* AAAS; Soc Develop Biol; Am Soc Cell Biol. *Res:* Web building behavior, neural control of web building and web geometry during development of orb weaving spiders. *Mailing Add:* Dept Biol Davidson Col Davidson NC 28036-1719. *Fax:* 704-892-2512; *E-Mail:* dokimmel@davidson.edu

KIMMEL, GARY LEWIS, BIOCHEMICAL TERATOLOGY. *Current Pos:* reproductive toxicologist, 77-84, DEVELOP TOXICOLOGIST, NAT CTR TOXICOL RES, ENVIRON PROTECTION AGENCY, 84- *Personal Data:* b Dayton, Ohio, Nov 20, 45; m 70, Carole Davis; c Rebecca. *Educ:* Miami Univ, AB, 67; Univ Cincinnati, MS, 69, PhD(physiol), 72. *Prof Exp:* Fel steroid biochem, Worcester Found Exp Biol, 72-73; reproduction biologist, Res Triangle Inst, 73-75. *Mem:* Teratology Soc. *Res:* Relationship of toxic exposures and developmental alterations in relation to risk assessment. *Mailing Add:* 401 M St SW Rm 3809 Mall USEPA Rd-689 Washington DC 20460. *Fax:* 202-260-8719

KIMMEL, HOWARD S, PHYSICAL CHEMISTRY. *Current Pos:* asst prof, 66-70, assoc prof, 70-80, PROF CHEM & ASSOC CHMN DEPT, NJ INST TECHNOL, 80- *Personal Data:* b Brooklyn, NY, Feb 2, 38; m 64; c 1. *Educ:* Brooklyn Col, BS, 59; WVa Univ, 61; City Univ New York, PhD(phys chem), 67. *Prof Exp:* Res assoc chem, Isaac Albert Res Inst, Jewish Chronic Dis Hosp, Brooklyn, NY, 62-63. *Mem:* Am Chem Soc. *Res:* Vibrational spectra of inorganic coordination compounds, tin compounds, olefinic compounds, monosubstituted benzene derivatives and biochemicals; kinetics studies using infrared spectroscopy. *Mailing Add:* Dept Chem Newark Col Eng Newark NJ 07102

KIMMEL, PAUL LAWRENCE, NEPHROLOGY. *Current Pos:* from asst prof to assoc prof, 83-92, PROF MED, GEORGE WASHINGTON UNIV MED CTR, 92- *Personal Data:* b New York, NY, Nov 12, 51. *Educ:* Yale Col, AB, 72; NY Univ, MD, 76. *Prof Exp:* Asst prof med, Sch Med, Univ Pa, 82-83. *Concurrent Pos:* Prin investr HIV & kidney, NIH, 89-94 & depression hemodialysis patients, 92- *Mem:* Am Soc Nephrology; fel Am Col Physicians. *Res:* Effect of HIV infection on kidney function; pathogenesis and treatment of HIV associated renal diseases; immune and psychologic adaptations to chronic renal diseases. *Mailing Add:* George Washington Univ Med Ctr 2150 Pennsylvania Ave NW Washington DC 20037

KIMMEL, ROBERT MICHAEL, MATERIALS ENGINEERING, POLYMER PHYSICS. *Current Pos:* INDUST MGR, AM HOECHST CORP, 80- *Personal Data:* b Beverly, Mass, Feb 6, 43; m 65; c 3. *Educ:* Mass Inst Technol, BS, 64, MS, 65, Mat Engr, 67, ScD(mat eng), 68. *Prof Exp:* Res chemist, Celanese Res Co, 68-71, sr res chemist, 71-73, group leader, Celanese Plastics Co, 73-75, prod supvr, 76-79. *Mem:* Am Phys Soc; Fiber Soc; Sigma Xi. *Res:* Fiber physics; physics of acrylic polymers; formation structure and properties of graphite fibers; effects of high pressure on materials; nature of the glassy state; structure properties of oriented films. *Mailing Add:* 116 Bridgeton Dr Greenville SC 29615

KIMMEL, WILLIAM GRIFFITHS, WATER POLLUTION BIOLOGY. *Current Pos:* From asst prof to assoc prof, 76-82, chmn, Dept Biol & Environ Sci, 87-93, PROF BIOL & ENVIRON SCI, CALIFORNIA UNIV, 82- *Personal Data:* b Scranton, Pa, Aug 27, 45; m 69, Janet Blair; c David & Christina. *Educ:* Wilkes Col, BA, 67; Pa State Univ, MS, 70, PhD(zool), 72. *Concurrent Pos:* Consult aquatic ecol. *Mem:* Sigma Xi; Am Fisheries Soc. *Res:* Responses of stream ecosystems to environmental stresses; aquatic macroinvertebrates and fishes as indicators of water quality. *Mailing Add:* Biol Dept Calif Univ Pa California PA 15419-1394

KIMMERER, ROBIN WALL, BRYOECOLOGY, DISTURBANCE ECOLOGY. *Current Pos:* ASST PROF BOT & ECOL, DEPT ENVIRON SCI & FORESTRY, STATE UNIV NY, SYRACUSE, 93- *Personal Data:* b Schenectady, NY, Sept 13, 53. *Educ:* State Univ NY, BS, 75; Univ Wis, MS, 78, PhD(bot), 83. *Prof Exp:* Asst prof bot & ecol, Centre Col, 85-93. *Res:* Community ecology of bryophytes; response of ecological communities to disturbance. *Mailing Add:* Dept Environ & Forest Biol CESF State Univ NY 320 Bray Hall Syracuse NY 13210-2723

KIMMERLE, FRANK, ELECTROCHEMISTRY. *Current Pos:* CHIEF ANALYTICAL CHEM, ALCAN INT LTD, 84- *Personal Data:* b Tuebingen, Ger, Mar 27, 40; Can citizen; m 63; c 3. *Educ:* Univ Toronto, BS, 63, MS, 64, PhD(electrochem), 67. *Prof Exp:* NATO fel, Free Univ Brussels, 67-68; from asst prof to assoc prof chem, Univ Sherbrooke, 68-84. *Concurrent Pos:* Can Res Coun fel, 67. *Mem:* Electrochem Soc. *Res:* Thermodynamics and kinetics of adsorption and reaction of organic compounds at the electrode-electrolyte interface; electro-organic synthesis; non-aqueous battery systems. *Mailing Add:* Res & Develop Ctr Alcan Int Ltd PO Box 1250 Jonquiere PQ G7S 4K8 Can

KIMMEY, JAMES WILLIAM, forest pathology, for more information see previous edition

KIMMICH, GEORGE ARTHUR, BIOCHEMISTRY, CELL PHYSIOLOGY. *Current Pos:* Nat Inst Dent Res fel biophys, 68-70, from asst prof to assoc prof radiation biol & biophys, 70-83, PROF BIOCHEM, RADIATION BIOL & BIOPHYS & ASSOC CHMN BIOCHEM, SCH MED & DENT, UNIV ROCHESTER, 83- *Personal Data:* b Cortland, NY, Dec 8, 41; m 63; c 2. *Educ:* Cornell Univ, BS, 63; Univ Wis-Madison, MS, 65; Univ Pa, PhD(biochem), 68. *Concurrent Pos:* Prin investr, NIH grant, 71; NIH Res Career Develop Award, 72-77; vis lectr biochem, Univ Manchester Inst Sci & Technol, Manchester, Eng, 75-76. *Mem:* Am Soc Biol Chemists; Am Physiol Soc. *Res:* Epithelial ion transport; metabolic regulation; sodium-dependent transport systems for sugars and amino acids; bioenergetics. *Mailing Add:* Dept Biochem Univ Rochester 601 Elmwood Ave Box 607 Rochester NY 14642-0001

KIMMINS, JAMES PETER (HAMISH), FOREST ECOLOGY, ENVIRONMENTAL SCIENCES. *Current Pos:* From asst prof to assoc prof, 69-79, PROF FOREST ECOL, DEPT FOREST SERV, UNIV BC, 79- *Personal Data:* b Jerusalem, Israel, July 31, 42; m 64, Ann Linnell; c Mark & Shaun. *Educ:* Univ Wales, BSc, 64; Univ Calif, MSc, 66; Yale Univ, MPhil, 68, PhD(ecol), 70. *Honors & Awards:* Gold Medal Sci Achievement, Int Union Forest Res Orgns, 86 & Can Inst Forestry, 87. *Concurrent Pos:* BC Govt Ecol Res Comt, 69-; consult, Environ Res Consults, 71-; chmn nat forest ecol working group, Can Inst Forestry, 74-76; Killam fel, Can Coun, 75-76; vis scientist, Kyoto, Japan, 82; moderator, Forestry Roundtable, Can Nat Roundtable Environ & Econ, 90-93. *Mem:* Commonwealth Forestry Asn; Can Inst Forestry. *Res:* Nutrient cycling in forest ecosystems; effects of forest management on ecosystem function; response of forest ecosystems to management-related and natural disturbance; forcyte, forecast, forcee, fortoon and horizon ecologically-based forest management computer simulation models. *Mailing Add:* Dept Forest Sci Univ BC 2357 Main Mall Vancouver BC V6T 1Z4 Can. *Fax:* 604-822-5744

KIMMINS, WARWICK CHARLES, MARINE MAMMALS. *Current Pos:* From asst prof to assoc prof, 65-74, chmn dept, 81-82 & 85-90, PROF BIOL, 74-, DEAN, FAC SCI, DALHOUSIE UNIV, 90- *Personal Data:* b London, Eng, July 20, 41; m 64; c 2. *Educ:* Univ London, BSc, 62, PhD, 65. *Concurrent Pos:* Consult res dept, Encyclop Britannica, 62-65; asst lectr, SE Essex Col Technol, Eng, 63-64. *Mem:* Soc Exp Biol & Med; Brit Asn Appl Biol; Can Soc Zool. *Res:* Marine mammals; large predator prey impact on fisheries; parasitology; population control. *Mailing Add:* Dept Biol Dalhousie Univ Halifax NS B3H 4H6 Can

KIMMONS, GEORGE H, ENGINEERING. *Current Pos:* RETIRED. *Personal Data:* b Oxford, Miss, 1919. *Educ:* Univ Miss, BS. *Prof Exp:* Mgr eng design & construct, Tenn Valley Authority, 84. *Mem:* Nat Acad Eng. *Mailing Add:* 2821 Williams Rd Knoxville TN 37932

KIMOTO, MASAO, IMMUNOLOGY, GENETICS. *Current Pos:* PROF IMMUNOL, SAGA MED SCH, 86- *Personal Data:* b Osaka, Japan, Aug 24, 47; m 74; c 3. *Educ:* Osaka Univ, MD, 72, PhD(med), 81. *Prof Exp:* Res assoc immunol, Osaka Univ, 72-78, asst prof internal med, 81-85; res fel immunol, Mayo Clin, 78-81. *Mem:* Am Asn Immunol. *Res:* Structure and function of major histocompatibility complex. *Mailing Add:* Dept Immunol Saga Med Sch 5-1-1 Nabeshima Saga 849 Japan. *Fax:* 81-952-332518

KIMOTO, WALTER IWAO, FOOD CHEMISTRY. *Current Pos:* RETIRED. *Personal Data:* b Honolulu, Hawaii, Mar 25, 32. *Educ:* Univ Hawaii, BA, 54; Univ Wis, PhD(org chem), 61. *Prof Exp:* Res chemist, Am Oil Co, 61-63; res chemist, Sci & Educ Admin-Agr Res, USDA, Beltsville, 63-71, res chemist, Eastern Regional Res Ctr, 71-85. *Mem:* Am Chem Soc; Sigma Xi. *Res:* Flavor and aroma of cured meat products. *Mailing Add:* 15790 E Alameda Pkwy Apt 4-210 Aurora CO 80017-2034

KIMPEL, JAMES FROOME, METEOROLOGY. *Current Pos:* asst prof, Univ Okla, 73-79, assoc dean eng, Col Eng, 78-81, dir, Sch Meteorol, 81-87, dean, Col Geosci, 87-92, sr vpres & provost, 92-95, PROF METEOROL, UNIV OKLA, 86-, DIR, NAT SEVERE STORMS LAB, 97- *Personal Data:* b Cincinnati, Ohio, Apr 18, 42; m 86, M'lou Smith; c J Andrew, Thomas J, Mollie A, Zoe A & Hanna A. *Educ:* Denison Univ, BS, 64; Univ Wis-Madison, MS, 70, PhD(meteorol), 73. *Prof Exp:* Weather officer meteorol, USAF, 64-68; res asst, Univ Wis-Madison, 68-73. *Concurrent Pos:* Prin investr, Nat Oceanic & Atmospheric Admin, NSF, 74-90; pres, Appl Systs Inst, Inc, 86-88; mem, Adv Comt Atmospheric Sci, NSF, 83-86, chair, 89-91; elected trustee, Univ Corp Atmospheric Res, 86-93, chair, bd trustees, 91-93; fel explor res, Elec Power Res Inst, 89-91; mem, Bd Natural Disasters, Nat Res Coun, 94- *Mem:* Fel Am Meteorol Soc; Nat Weather Asn; Am Asn Geog; Sigma Xi. *Res:* Synoptic and severe storms research for hydrometeorological applications. *Mailing Add:* Univ Okla 100 E Boyd Rm 1310 Norman OK 73019. *Fax:* 405-325-7689; *E-Mail:* jkimpel@ou.edu

KIMPEL, RICHARD R, METALLURGY. *Current Pos:* PRIN, R K ASSOCS, MICH, 95- *Personal Data:* b 1939; m 58; c Richard & Steven. *Educ:* NDak State Univ, BS, 61, MS, 62; Pa State Univ, PhD(mat sci), 64. *Honors & Awards:* Robert H Richards Award, Soc Mining, Metall & Explor, 88, Arthur F Taggart Award, 92 & Antoine M Gaudin Award, 94. *Prof Exp:* Mgr, Eng Anal Div, Dow Chem, 70-80, sr res scientist, 80-95. *Concurrent Pos:* Adj prof mat sci, Univ Fla, 96- *Mem:* Am Inst Chem Engrs; Am Chem Soc; Soc Mining, Metall & Explor (pres, 97). *Res:* Particle processing; mineral processing; froth flotation reagents and plant optimization; size reduction methodology. *Mailing Add:* R K Assocs 4805 Oak Ridge Dr Midland MI 48640-1917. *Fax:* 517-835-3141

KIMSEY, LYNN SIRI, SYSTEMATICS, FUNCTIONAL MORPHOLOGY EVOLUTION. *Current Pos:* res fel, 79-80 & 83-86, lectr, Dept Entom, 82-83, ASSOC PROF, UNIV CALIF, DAVIS, 89-; CONSULT, 83-; RES ASSOC, MUS COMP ZOOL, HARVARD UNIV, 89- *Personal Data:* b Oakland, Calif, Feb 1, 53; m 76, Robert; c Erin & Benjamin. *Educ:* Univ Calif, Davis, BS, 75, PhD(entomol), 79. *Prof Exp:* Res fel, Smithsonian Trop Res Inst, Panama, 81-82. *Concurrent Pos:* Dir, Bohart Mus Entom, 89- *Mem:* Asn Systs Collections; Int Hymenopterists Soc. *Res:* Systematics, biogeography and evolution of wasp families chrysididae, pompilidae, Tiphiidae and sphecidae. *Mailing Add:* Dept Entom Univ Calif Davis CA 95616-5200

KIMURA, DOREEN, NEUROPSYCHOLOGY, BEHAVIORAL ENDOCRINOLOGY. *Current Pos:* assoc prof, 67-74, PROF PSYCHOL, UNIV WESTERN ONT, 74- *Personal Data:* b Winnipeg, Man; c Charlotte Vanderwolf. *Educ:* McGill Univ, BA, 56, MA, 57, PhD(physiol & psychol), 61. *Hon Degrees:* LLD, Simon Fraser Univ, BC, 93. *Honors & Awards:* Distinguished Contrib to Can Psychol Sci Award, Can Psychol Asn, 85; Outstanding Sci Achievement Award, Can Asn Women Sci, 86; John Dewan Award, Ont Ment Health Found, 92. *Prof Exp:* Fel, Montreal Neurol Inst, 60-62; res assoc, Otologic Res Lab, Univ Calif, Los Angeles, 62-63; Geigy fel & res assoc, Neurochirurgische Klinik, Kantonsspital, Zurich, 63-64; res assoc II, Col Med, McMaster Univ, 64-67. *Concurrent Pos:* Supvr clin neuropsychol, Univ Hosp, London, 75-83; hon lectr, Dept Clin Neurol Sci, Univ Western Ont, 82-, coordr, Clin Neuropsychol, Dept Psychol, 84-; prin investr, Med Res Coun & Natural Sci & Eng Res Coun. *Mem:* Fel Am Psychol Soc; Int Soc Psychoneuroendocrinol; fel Can Psychol Asn; Can Soc Brain Behav & Cognitive Sci; Soc Neurosci; fel Royal Soc Can. *Res:* Research into the biological basis of human cognitive and motor function, including neural and hormonal mechanisms; emphasis on the neurobiology of brain asymmetry and sex differences in human problem-solving abilities. *Mailing Add:* Dept Psychol Univ Western Ont London ON N6A 5C2 Can. *Fax:* 519-661-3029; *E-Mail:* kimura@uwo.ca

KIMURA, EUGENE TATSURU, PHARMACOLOGY, TOXICOLOGY. *Current Pos:* res pharmacologist, Abbott Labs, 55-60, group leader, 60-62, sect head, 62-71, mgr fed autonomic pharmacol, Sci Div, 71-72, mgr corp res develop dept, Corp Res & Exp Ther, 72-76, SR TOXICOLOGIST, ABBOTT LABS, 76-, ASSOC RES FEL, 80- *Personal Data:* b Sheridan, Wyo, Sept 19, 22; m 50; c 3. *Educ:* Univ Nebr, BS, 44, MS, 46; Univ Chicago, PhD(pharmacol), 48. *Prof Exp:* Lab instr inorg chem & microbiol, Sch Nursing, St Elizabeth Hosp, Nebr, 45-46; res pharmacologist, Nepera Chem Co, NY, 49-55. *Concurrent Pos:* Fel pharmacol, Univ Chicago, 48-49; asst, Univ Nebr, 44-46. *Mem:* Am Soc Pharmacol & Exp Therapeut; Am Pharmaceut Asn; NY Acad Sci; Soc Exp Biol & Med; Soc Toxicol. *Res:* Pharmacology and toxicology of antihistamines and antiserotonins; bronchial asthma and allergy; drugs affecting ciliary motility; antiheparin agents; analeptics; antispasmodics; blood coagulants; anti-inflammatory compounds; toxicology and carcinogenicity of experimental drugs. *Mailing Add:* 4 Oak Brook Club Dr Oak Brook IL 60521-1314

KIMURA, HIDENORI, CONTROL ENGINEERING. *Current Pos:* PROF, DEPT MATH ENG & INFO PHYSICS, UNIV TOKYO, 97- *Personal Data:* b Tokyo, Japan, Nov 3, 41; m 71, Michiko; c Naofumi, Taeko & Kazufumi. *Educ:* Univ Tokyo, BEng, 65, MEng, 67, DEng, 70. *Honors & Awards:* George Axelby Awards, Inst Elec & Electronics Engrs, 85. *Prof Exp:* Res asst control eng, Osaka Univ, 70-71, lectr, 71-73, assoc prof, Dept Control Eng, 73-87, prof control eng, Dept Mech Eng, 87-97. *Mem:* Fel Soc Instrument & Control Engrs; fel Inst Elec & Electronics Engrs. *Res:* Control engineering; theory; mechanical control systems; robotics. *Mailing Add:* Dept Math Eng & Info Physics Univ Tokyo 7-3-1 Hongo Bunkyo-ku Tokyo 113 Japan

KIMURA, JAMES HIROSHI, BIOCHEMISTRY. *Current Pos:* SR STAFF, BONE & JOINT CTR, HENRY FORD HOSP, 90-, HEAD, DIV RES, 95- *Personal Data:* b Kona, Hawaii, Oct 29, 44; div; c Melissa H & Daniel T. *Educ:* Univ Hawaii, BS, 71; Case Western Res Univ, PhD(develop biol), 76. *Prof Exp:* Fel, Nat Inst Dent Res, NIH, 76-78, staff fel, 78-80, sr staff fel, 80-81; from asst prof to prof, Dept Biochem, Rush Presby St Luke's Med Ctr, 81-90, from asst prof to prof of biochem, Dept Ortho Surg, Rush Presby St Luke's Med Ctr, 81-90. *Mem:* Orthop Res Soc; Am Soc Biochem & Molecular Biol; AAAS; Soc Complex Carbohydrates. *Res:* Biochemistry of proteoglycans and mechanisms for the control of their synthesis; organization in cartilage. *Mailing Add:* Henry Ford Hosp 2799 W Grand Blvd Detroit MI 48202-2689. *Fax:* 313-876-8064; *E-Mail:* kimura@bjc.hfh.edu

KIMURA, KAZUO KAY, CLINICAL PHARMACOLOGY. *Current Pos:* MED DIR, WESTERN OHIO REGIONAL DRUG & POISON INFO SYST, CHILDRENS MED CTR, 80- *Personal Data:* b Sheridan, Wyo, Sept 16, 20; m 52; c 3. *Educ:* Univ Wash, BS, 42; Univ Nebr, MS, 44; Univ Ill, PhD(pharmacol), 49; St Louis Univ, MD, 53; Am Bd Med Toxicol, dipl, 75. *Honors & Awards:* Borden Award, 53. *Prof Exp:* Asst physiol & pharmacol, Univ Nebr, 43-44, instr, 44-45; asst pharmacol, Univ Ill, 45-46; from instr to asst prof, St Louis Univ, 49-54; intern, Children's Med Serv, Mass Gen Hosp, 54-55, asst resident, 55-56; from sr resident to chief resident pediat, Raymond Blank Mem Hosp Children, Des Moines, Iowa, 56-57; chief exp med br, Chem Res & Develop Labs, Army Chem Ctr, Md, 57-61; asst chief clin res div, 58-61, chief, 62; chief pharmacologist & mgr pharmacol sect, Atlas Chem Industs, Inc, 62-63; corp med dir & dir biomed res dept, 63-70; med dir & dir med res dept, ICI Am, Inc, Del, 70-73; vpres & res dir, Hazleton Labs Am, Inc, 73-75; exec vpres & med dir, Mediserve Int, Inc, 75-77; prof pharmacol & med, Sch Med, Wright State Univ, 77-88. *Concurrent Pos:* Teaching fel pediat, Harvard Med Sch, 55-56; founder & first dir, Iowa State Poison Info Ctr, 56-57; pvt pract, Md, 58-62; prof lectr, Univ Md, 60-62; consult pediat, Wilmington Med Ctr Hosps, 69-73; consult med, Vet Admin Hosp, 78-80; mem active staff, Childrens Med Ctr. *Mem:* Fel AAAS; fel Am Col Clin Pharmacol (secy, 85-, vpres, 87, pres, 88-90); fel Royal Soc Med; fel Am Col Physicians; Am Soc Pharmacol & Exp Therapeut. *Res:* Striated muscle paralyzing drugs; cardiac glycosides; medical toxicology; biochemophology of muscle paralyzants; dietary fiber and refined sugars; psychopharmacology; clinical pharmacology; poison control; pediatric and general toxicology. *Mailing Add:* 19 E Blossom Hill Rd Dayton OH 45449-2051. *Fax:* 937-859-4554

KIMURA, KEN-ICHI, NATURAL ENERGY UTILIZATION, DESICCANT COOLING & DEHUMIDIFICATION WITH SOLAR ENERGY. *Current Pos:* From asst prof to assoc prof, 64-73, PROF ENVIRON ENG & ARCHIT, WASEDA UNIV, 73- *Personal Data:* b Fushun, China, Mar 5, 33; Japan citizen; m 61, Aiko Takasaki; c Mari & Tomo. *Educ:* Waseda Univ, BArch, 57, MSc, 59, DEng, 64. *Hon Degrees:* DEng, Waseda Univ, 65. *Concurrent Pos:* Teaching asst, Mass Inst Technol, 60-62; fel, Nat Res Coun, 67-69; mem bd dirs, Int Solar Energy Soc, 73-79 & Archit Inst Japan, 80-82; pres, Japan Solar Energy Soc, 84-86. *Mem:* Int Solar Energy Soc; fel Am Soc Heating, Refrig & Air Conditioning Engrs; Archit Inst Japan; Soc Heating, Air Conditioning & Sanitary Engrs Japan (vpres, 80-82 & 92-94, pres, 94-96); Japan Solar Energy Soc; Int Soc Indoor Air Qual & Climate; Acad Indoor Air Sci. *Res:* Architectural utilization of solar energy; energy conservation in buildings; thermal comfort; indoor air quality; visual comfort in interiors; heat and moisture transfer in buildings; environmental engineering; architectural design; building science; vernacular architecture. *Mailing Add:* 13-21 Enoki-cho Tokorozawa Saitama 359 Japan. *Fax:* 81-3-3209-8316; *E-Mail:* kimura@kimura.arch.waseda.ac.jp

KIMURA, MINEO, chemical physics, condensed matter physics, for more information see previous edition

KIMURA, NAOKI, MATHEMATICS. *Current Pos:* PROF MATH, UNIV ARK, FAYETTEVILLE, 65- *Personal Data:* b Wakayama City, Japan, May 20, 22; m 47; c 3. *Educ:* Osaka Univ, DSc, 44; Tulane Univ, PhD, 57. *Prof Exp:* Lectr math, Tokyo Inst Technol, Japan, 49-55; asst prof, Univ Wash, 58-60 & Univ Sask, 60-62; assoc prof, Univ Okla, 62-65. *Mem:* Am Math Soc; Math Soc Japan; Swed Math Soc. *Res:* Functional analysis and general algebra. *Mailing Add:* Dept Math Univ Ark Fayetteville AR 72701

KIMURA, TOKUJI, ENZYMOLOGY, BIOPHYSICS. *Current Pos:* PROF CHEM, WAYNE STATE UNIV, 68- *Personal Data:* b Osaka, Japan, Nov 14, 25; m 51; c 2. *Educ:* Osaka Univ, BS, 50, PhD(chem), 60. *Prof Exp:* Prof chem, St Paul's Univ, Tokyo, 65-68. *Concurrent Pos:* NIH res grant, 65. *Mem:* Am Soc Biol Chemists; Am Soc Chem; Sigma Xi. *Res:* Adrenal cortex mitochondrial steroid hydroxylases. *Mailing Add:* Osaka Biosci Inst Fusuedai Osaka 565 Japan

KINARD, FRANK EFIRD, RESEARCH ADMINISTRATION. *Current Pos:* CONSULT, 90- *Personal Data:* b Newberry, SC, Jan 15, 24; m 52, Mary McNease; c Sally K (Bayless) & Anne D. *Educ:* Newberry Col, BS, 46, AB, 47; Univ NC, MS, 50, PhD(physics), 54. *Prof Exp:* Instr physics, Univ NC, 49-52; physicist tech div, Savannah River Lab, E I du Pont de Nemours & Co, 53-63, head univ rels off, 63-67; exec dir, SC Comn Higher Educ, 67-68, assoc dir, 68-87, sr assoc comnr, 87-90. *Mem:* Am Phys Soc. *Res:* Research in higher education generally; especially graduate education. *Mailing Add:* 801 Albion Rd Columbia SC 29205

KINARD, FREDRICK WILLIAM, PHYSIOLOGY, PHYSIOLOGICAL CHEMISTRY. *Current Pos:* from instr to assoc prof, Med Univ SC, 33-53, actg dir dept physiol, 44-46, chmn grad study comt, 49-65, prof, 53-78, dean, Col Grad Studies, 65-78, EMER PROF PHYSIOL, MED UNIV SC, 78- *Personal Data:* b Leesville, SC, Oct 14, 06; m 29, Betty Murray; c Anne & Frederick. *Educ:* Clemson Col, BS, 27; Univ Va, MS, 32, PhD(biochem), 33; Univ Tenn, MD, 45. *Honors & Awards:* Jefferson Res Medal, SC Acad Sci, 36. *Prof Exp:* Asst chem, Med Col SC, 27-30; instr biochem, Univ Va, 30-33. *Concurrent Pos:* Fac mem, Southeastern Sch Alcohol Studies, Athens, Ga. *Mem:* AAAS; Am Soc Zool; Am Physiol Soc; Soc Exp Biol & Med. *Res:* Creatine-creatinine metabolism; phosphatase; hemopoietine; ethanol metabolism. *Mailing Add:* Crescent Univ SC Med 2 Johnson Rd Charleston SC 29407-7515

KINARD, W FRANK, NUCLEAR CHEMISTRY. *Current Pos:* from asst prof to assoc prof, 72-83, PROF CHEM, COL CHARLESTON, 83- *Personal Data:* b Greenville, SC, Nov 16, 42. *Educ:* Duke Univ, BS, 64; Univ SC, PhD(anal chem), 68. *Prof Exp:* Nuclear chem, US AEC, Fla State Univ, 68-70; res assoc chem oceanog, Univ PR, 70-72. *Concurrent Pos:* Sr scientist, Oak Ridge Nat Lab, 78-79; guest scientist, Lawrence Livermore Nat Lab, 83-89; vis scientist, Westinghouse Savannah River Lab, 90-91. *Mem:* Am Chem Soc; AAAS; Sigma Xi. *Res:* Research in solution chemistry of lanthanide and actinide elements; applications of ICP-MS to radiochemical problems. *Mailing Add:* Dept Chem Col Charleston Charleston SC 29424

KINARIWALA, BHARAT K, ALGORITHMS, DATABASE SYSTEMS. *Current Pos:* chmn, Dept Elec Eng, 69-75 & 78-81, PROF ELEC ENG, UNIV HAWAII, 66- *Personal Data:* b Ahmedabad, India, Oct 14, 26; US citizen; m 53; c 2. *Educ:* Benares Hindu Univ, BS, 51; Univ Calif, Berkeley, MS, 54, PhD(elec eng), 57. *Prof Exp:* Actg asst prof elec eng, Univ Calif, Berkeley, 56-57; mem tech staff, Bell Tel Labs, 57-66. *Concurrent Pos:* Comput consult, Marchant, Inc, 56-57; prog chmn, Hawaiian Int Conf Systs Sci, 67; Inst Educ Exchange Serv deleg, Popov Soc Meeting, USSR, 67, prog chmn, Int Symp Circuit Theory, 68. *Mem:* Fel Inst Elec & Electronics Engrs. *Res:* System and computer sciences. *Mailing Add:* 581 Kamoku St Honolulu HI 96826

KINASEWITZ, GARY THEODORE, PULMONARY DISEASE, PULMONARY CIRCULATION. *Current Pos:* PROF MED & HEAD PULMONARY DIS & CRIT CARE MED, HEALTH SCI CTR, UNIV OKLA, OKLAHOMA CITY, OKLA, 88- *Personal Data:* b New York, NY, Aug 17, 46; m 69; c 3. *Educ:* Boston Col, BS, 68, MEd, 69; Wayne State Univ, MD, 73. *Prof Exp:* Resident med, Univ Pa Hosp, 73-76; fel pulmonary dis, Dept Med, Cardiovasc Pulmonary Div, Univ Pa, 76-78, res assoc med, 78-79, asst prof med, 79-80; from asst prof to assoc prof, 80-88, prof med & physiol & biophys, Med Ctr, La State Univ, Shreveport, 88- *Concurrent Pos:* Counr cardiopulmonary dis, Am Heart Asn; mem Okla Res Found, 94. *Mem:* Am Thoracic Soc; Am Col Chest Physicians; Am Fedn Clin Res; Am Col Physicians; Am Physiol Soc. *Res:* Quantitative analysis of fluid exchanges across the pulmonary capillaries of the visceral pleura; role of abnormal pulmonary vasomotor reactivity in the genesis of pulmonary hypertension; cardiopulmonary adjustments to exercise in patients with lung disease; mesothelial cell glycosaminoglycans. *Mailing Add:* Dept Med Univ Okla Health Sci Ctr PO Box 26901 Rm 35P-400 Oklahoma City OK 73190

KINBACHER, EDWARD JOHN, PLANT PHYSIOLOGY. *Current Pos:* assoc prof hort, 63-71, PROF HORT, UNIV NEBR, LINCOLN, 71- *Personal Data:* b Brooklyn, NY, Nov 19, 27; m 55; c 3. *Educ:* Cornell Univ, BS, 49; Purdue Univ, MS, 51; Univ Calif, PhD(plant physiol), 55. *Prof Exp:* Asst, Purdue Univ, 49-51 & Univ Calif, 51-55; assoc prof plant breeding & agron, Cornell Univ, 55-63. *Concurrent Pos:* Plant physiologist crops res div, Agr Res Serv, USDA, 55-62. *Mem:* Am Soc Plant Physiol; Am Soc Agron. *Res:* Heat, drought and cold resistance of horticultural crops and specifically turfgrasses. *Mailing Add:* 3816 Orchard St Lincoln NE 68503

KINCADE, PAUL W, IMMUNOBIOLOGY, MICROBIOLOGY. *Current Pos:* MEM & HEAD DEPT IMMUNOBIOL, OKLA MED RES FOUND, OKLAHOMA CITY, 82- *Personal Data:* b Moorhead, Miss, Oct 10, 44; div; c 1. *Educ:* Miss State Univ, BS, 66, MS, 68; Univ Ala, PhD(microbiol & immunol), 71. *Prof Exp:* Res asst, Lobund Lab, Univ Notre Dame, 68-69; fel, Univ Ala, 71-72, Walter & Eliza Hall Inst, Melbourne, 72-74; assoc, Sloan Kettering Inst, 74-79, assoc mem, 79-82; assoc prof, Grad Sch Med Sci, Cornell Univ, 80-82. *Concurrent Pos:* Mem, Immunobiol Study Sect, 84-88; mem, Prog Comt, Am Asn Immunologists, 89- *Mem:* Am Asn Immunologists; Am Soc Hematology; Sigma Xi; Am Soc Microbiologists; Int Soc Develop Comparative Immunologists; Am Soc Invest Pathol. *Res:* Humoral immune system with particular emphasis on relationships between stem cells and B lymphocytes and utilizing normal and genetically defective animal models. *Mailing Add:* Okla Med Res Found 825 NE 13th St Oklahoma City OK 73104-5097. *Fax:* 405-271-8568

KINCADE, ROBERT TYRUS, ENTOMOLOGY, WEED SCIENCE. *Current Pos:* FIELD RES SPECIALIST, BIOL RES INSECTICIDES, HERBICIDES, FUNGICIDES, VALENT USA, 77-; MGR, FIELD RES STAS. *Personal Data:* b Indianola, Miss, May 16, 41; m 68; c 3. *Educ:* Miss State Univ, BS, 63, MS, 66, PhD(entom), 70. *Prof Exp:* Field res specialist weed control, Chevron Chem Co, 69-75, supvr herbicides, fungicides & insecticides, 75-77. *Mem:* Sigma Xi. *Res:* Development of herbicides, fungicides and insecticides for agricultural use. *Mailing Add:* Box 5008 Valent USA Greenville MS 38704

KINCAID, DENNIS CAMPBELL, IRRIGATION SYSTEMS. *Current Pos:* AGR ENGR, AGR RES SERV, USDA, 70- *Personal Data:* b Deer Park, Wash, June 17, 44; m 75; c 3. *Educ:* Wash State Univ, BS, 66; Colo State Univ, MS, 68, PhD(agr eng), 70. *Concurrent Pos:* Affil prof, Univ Idaho, 79- *Mem:* Am Soc Agr Engrs; Am Soc Civil Engrs; Irrigation Asn; Sigma Xi. *Res:* Basic and applied research in irrigation system improvement and water management. *Mailing Add:* USDA-ARS 3793 N 3600 E Kimberly ID 83341

KINCAID, JAMES ROBERT, ANALYTICAL CHEMISTRY, BIOPHYSICAL CHEMISTRY. *Current Pos:* AT DEPT CHEM, MARQUETTE UNIV. *Personal Data:* b Covington, Ky, Feb 11, 45; m 68; c 1. *Educ:* Xavier Univ, Ohio, BS, 70; Marquette Univ, PhD(chem), 74. *Prof Exp:* Vis fel chem, Princeton Univ, 74-78; asst prof chem, Univ Ky, 78- *Concurrent Pos:* Nat res serv award, NIH, 75-77 & Nat Cancer Inst, 77-78. *Mem:* Am Chem Soc. *Res:* Applications of Raman spectroscopy to biologically significant systems; structure and function relationships in heme proteins; role of trace metals in biochemistry and medicine. *Mailing Add:* Dept Chem Marquette Univ 1515 W Wisc Ave Milwaukee WI 53233

KINCAID, RANDALL L, PHARMACOLOGY, CALMODULIN PHOSPHODIESTERASE. *Current Pos:* PRES, VERITAS INC, 94- *Educ:* Stanford Univ, PhD(pharmacol), 78. *Prof Exp:* Res pharmacologist, NIH, 79-94. *Mailing Add:* Veritas Inc 679 South Lawn Maine Rockville MD 20850. *Fax:* 301-838-8650

KINCAID, RONALD LEE, ANIMAL NUTRITION, BIOCHEMISTRY. *Current Pos:* PROF ANIMAL NUTRIT, WASH STATE UNIV, 77- *Personal Data:* b St Joseph, Mo, Oct 29, 50; m 70; c 4. *Educ:* Univ Mo, BS, 71, MS, 73; Univ Ga, PhD(animal nutrit), 76. *Prof Exp:* Lectr animal nutrit, Lincoln Col, Univ Canterbury, 76-77. *Mem:* Am Dairy Sci Asn; Am Soc Animal Sci; Am Inst Nutrit; Coun Agr Sci & Technol; Soc Exp Biol & Med. *Res:* Mineral metabolism in animals; phyto estrogens; dairy cattle nutrition. *Mailing Add:* Dept Animal Sci Wash State Univ 263 Clark Hall Pullman WA 99164-0001. *Fax:* 509-335-1082

KINCAID, STEVEN ALAN, ANATOMY. *Current Pos:* assoc prof anat, 89-96, PROF ANAT, AUBURN UNIV, 96- *Personal Data:* b Indianapolis, Ind, July 6, 43; m 77, Nancy Gail Hibbard; c Amy Elizabeth, Jeremy Brent, Cheryl Ann & Scott Alan. *Educ:* Purdue Univ, BS, 65, DVM, 69, MS, 71, PhD(anat), 77. *Prof Exp:* Veterinarian, South Bend, Ind, 72-73; asst prof anat, Univ Tenn, 77-81; assoc prof, Purdue Univ, 82-84; mgr physiol & sr scientist, Collagen Corp, Palo Alto, Calif, 84-89. *Concurrent Pos:* Seeing Eye Found, Inc grant, 69-71; NIH fel, 71-72. *Mem:* Sigma Xi; Am Asn Vet Anatomists; Am Vet Med Asn; Am Soc Animal Sci. *Res:* Pathobiology of articular cartilage; comparative arthrology; copper metabolism. *Mailing Add:* Dept Anat & Histol Auburn Univ Auburn AL 36849-5510

KINCAID, THOMAS GARDINER, NONDESTRUCTIVE EVALUATION. *Current Pos:* SYSTS ENGR, GEN ELEC CO, 65- *Personal Data:* b Hamilton, Ont, Sept 18, 37; m 62; c 3. *Educ:* Queens Univ Kingston, BSc, 59; Mass Inst Technol, SM, 61, PhD(elec eng), 65. *Mem:* Inst Elec & Electronics Engrs; Am Soc Nondestructive Testing. *Res:* Investigation of methods of evaluating materials for structural defects, including ultrasonic and electromagnetic techniques and x-ray. *Mailing Add:* Col Eng Boston Univ 44 Cummington St Boston MA 02215

KINCAID, WILFRED MACDONALD, STATISTICS, NUMERICAL ANALYSIS. *Current Pos:* instr math, Univ Mich, Ann Arbor, 46-51, res mathematician, Vision Res Lab, 50-58, lectr, 58-60, from asst prof to prof, 60-84, EMER PROF MATH, UNIV MICH, ANN ARBOR, 84- *Personal Data:* b Cornhill, Scotland, Sept 13, 18; US citizen; m 52, M Fay Allen; c William A, W James & David A. *Educ:* Univ Calif, AB, 40; Brown Univ, PhD(appl math), 46. *Prof Exp:* Instr math & eng, Brown Univ, 43-44; physicist, Nat Adv Comt Aeronaut, Langley Field, 44-46. *Mem:* AAAS; Am Math Soc; Math Asn Am; Asn Res Vision & Ophthal; Soc Sci Explor. *Res:* Numerical analysis; statistics; vision; psychophysics. *Mailing Add:* Dept Math Univ Mich Ann Arbor MI 48109-1109

KINCANNON, DONNY FRANK, BIOENVIRONMENTAL ENGINEERING. *Current Pos:* RETIRED. *Personal Data:* b Olustee, Okla, Jan 17, 33; m 57; c 2. *Educ:* Okla State Univ, BS, 59, MS, 60, PhD(bioeng), 66. *Prof Exp:* Sanit engr, Tex State Dept Health, 60-61; instr civil eng, Arlington State Col, 61-63; asst prof, Univ Mo, Rolla, 65-66; from asst prof to prof civil eng, Okla State Univ, 66-80. *Mem:* Am Soc Civil Engrs; Am Soc Eng Educ; Water Pollution Control Fedn. *Res:* Water pollution control; biological treatment; industrial wastes; solid wastes. *Mailing Add:* 4606 Fairfield Stillwater OK 74074

KINCH, MICHAEL ANTHONY, INFRARED DEVICES, SENSOR PHYSICS. *Current Pos:* mem tech staff, 66-78, sr mem, 78-85, RES FEL, TEX INSTRUMENTS INC, 85- *Personal Data:* b Northampton, Eng, Nov 14, 36; US citizen; wid; c Lisa Nicol & Mark Anthony. *Educ:* Oxford Univ, BA, 60, MA, 61, DPhil(solid state physics), 65. *Honors & Awards:* Jack A Morton Award, Inst Elec & Electronics Engrs, 87. *Prof Exp:* Postdoctoral fel, Oxford Univ, 64-66. *Mem:* Fel Am Phys Soc. *Res:* All aspects of the physics of infrared materials, devices and process development. *Mailing Add:* 7230 La Manga Dr Dallas TX 75248. *Fax:* 972-995-6558

KINCHEN, DAVID G, MATERIALS LABORATORY TESTING & CONSULTING, STATISTICAL ANALYSIS FOR PROCESS & PROBLEM EVALUATION. *Current Pos:* qual engr, Martin Marietta Qual Eval Lab, Martin Marietta Manned Space Systs, 83-85, sr qual engr, 85-91, group engr, Martin Marietta Qual Advan Technol, 91-92, chief process eval, 93-94, SR MAT ENGR, LOCKHEED MARTIN, 94- *Personal Data:* b Hammond, La, Mar 7, 53; m 79, Laurie Jones; c Adrianne, Travis & Lauren. *Educ:* La State Univ, BE, 80. *Prof Exp:* Tech mgr, Mat Eval Lab, Inc, 81-83. *Concurrent Pos:* Prin investr, Martin Marietta Qual Eval Lab, Qual Control Performance Criteria of Aerospace Aluminum Alloys, Martin Marietta Manned Space Systs, 84-85 & Eval of Straight Line X-Ray Radiographic Indications, 88. *Mem:* Am Soc Metals Int; Am Soc Qual Control. *Res:* Laboratory identification and investigation of unknown x-ray indications in aluminum alloy weldments; statistical study to characterise weld process performance; develop and train quality control weld inspectors to implement SPC based on study. *Mailing Add:* Lockheed Martin Manned Space Systs PO Box 29304 MS 3713 New Orleans LA 70189. *Fax:* 504-257-4403; *E-Mail:* davidkinchen@maf.nasa.gov

KIND, CHARLES ALBERT, BIOCHEMISTRY. *Current Pos:* CONSULT, 77- *Personal Data:* b Philadelphia, Pa, Apr 17, 17; m 44. *Educ:* Lafayette Col, BS, 39, Yale Univ, PhD(chem), 42. *Prof Exp:* Res chemist, Nat Defense Res Comt, Yale Univ, 42; from instr to asst prof chem, Univ Conn, 42-57, from assoc prof to prof zool, 57-67, asst dean, 63-67, prof biol & assoc dean Col Lib Arts & Sci, 67-77. *Concurrent Pos:* Lalor fel, Marine Biol Lab, Woods Hole, Mass, 49-50; Am Philos Soc fel, Bermuda Biol Sta, 51; mem corp, Marine Biol Lab, Woods Hole & Bermuda Biol Sta; actg dean, Col Lib Arts & Sci, Univ Conn, 70-71. *Mem:* AAAS; Am Chem Soc; Am Inst Chemists. *Res:* Lipids of marine invertebrate animals; sterols of vegetable oils; phosphatases. *Mailing Add:* 47 Willowbrook Rd Storrs CT 06268

KIND, LEON SAUL, MICROBIOLOGY. *Current Pos:* RETIRED. *Personal Data:* b Boston, Mass, Dec 26, 22. *Educ:* Harvard Univ, AB, 47; Yale Univ, PhD(microbiol), 51. *Prof Exp:* From asst prof to assoc prof, Med Col SC, 51-58; asst prof, Sch Med, Univ Calif, San Francisco, 58-70; assoc prof, Dalhousie Univ, 70-78, prof microbiol, 78- *Concurrent Pos:* Res grants, NIH, 53- *Mem:* Soc Exp Biol & Med; Am Soc Immunol. *Res:* Immunology; experimental allergy; sensitivity of pertussis inoculated mice to histamine; anaphylaxis. *Mailing Add:* Eight Heffler Bedford NS B4A 1N3 Can

KIND, PHYLLIS DAWN, CELLULAR IMMUNOLOGY. *Current Pos:* assoc prof microbiol, 74-79, PROF MICROBIOL & MED, GEORGE WASHINGTON UNIV, 79-, ASSOC DIR, TISSUE TYPING LAB, 78- *Personal Data:* b Sidney, Mont, July 31, 33. *Educ:* Univ Mont, BA, 55; Univ Mich, MS, 56, PhD(bact), 60. *Prof Exp:* Fel dermat, Univ Mich, 60-63; from instr to asst prof path, Univ Colo, 63-71; res microbiologist, Nat Cancer Inst, 71-74. *Concurrent Pos:* Chairperson, Immunol Div, Am Soc Microbiol, 75-76; fel mem, evauluation panel for NSF, 79-81; coun, immunol div, Am Soc Microbiol, 85-88; vis prof, Nat Cheng Kung Med Col, Tainan, Taiwan, 86; mem, Drug Abuse Biomed Res Review Comt, Nat Inst Drug Abuse, 86-88; fel, Prog Evaluation Panel, 88; mem, Drug Abuse Aids Res Comt, Nat Inst Drug Abuse, 88-90. *Mem:* AAAS; Am Asn Immunol; Am Soc Microbiol; Soc Exp Biol & Med; Sigma Xi; Am Soc Histol Compatability & Immunogenetics. *Res:* Regulation of antibody synthesis. *Mailing Add:* Microbiol 12941 Tower Rd Thurmond MD 21788. *Fax:* 202-223-3691

KIND, RICHARD JOHN, AERODYNAMICS OF AIRCRAFT & TURBOMACHINERY WIND ENGINEERING. *Current Pos:* From asst prof to assoc prof, 67-80, PROF ENG, CARLETON UNIV, 80- *Personal Data:* m 67, Lorraine F Burke; c David & Donna. *Educ:* Loyola Col, BSc, 62; McGill Univ, BEng, 64; Univ Cambridge, PhD (aerodyn), 67. *Honors & Awards:* Casey-Baldwin Award, Can Aeronaut & Space Inst, 93. *Concurrent Pos:* Vis asst prof, WVa Univ, 69; vis res officer, Nat Res Coun, 73-74; chmn, Dept Mech & Aerospace Eng, Carleton Univ, 86-92; mem, Fluid Dynamics Panel, NATO Adv Group Aerospace Res & Develop, 91- *Mem:* Fel Can Aeronaut & Space Inst; assoc fel Am Inst Aeronaut & Astronaut; Am Soc Mech Engrs. *Res:* Low speed aerodynamics with applications to aircraft, turbomachinery and wind engineering; boundary-layer flow, turbulence modelling, wind damage mechanisms, effects of surface roughness. *Mailing Add:* Dept Mach Carleton Univ Ottawa ON K1S 5B6 Can. *Fax:* 613-788-5715

KINDEL, JOSEPH MARTIN, PLASMA PHYSICS. *Current Pos:* mem staff controlled thermonuclear res group, Physics Div, Los Alamos Nat Lab, 71-72 & laser theory group, Theoret Div, 72-75, assoc group leader laser theory, Laser Div, 75-78, head, Plasma Theory Sect, 78-79, assoc group leader, 79-80, GROUP LEADER INERTIAL FUSION & PLASMA THEORY, APPL THEORET PHYSICS DVV, LOS ALAMOS NAT LAB, 80- *Personal Data:* b Barberton, Ohio, Mar 10, 43; c 2. *Educ:* Univ Akron, BS, 65; Univ Calif, Los Angeles, MS, 66, PhD(physics), 70. *Prof Exp:* Res assoc plasma physics, Princeton Univ, 70-71. *Mem:* Am Phys Soc. *Res:* Space plasma physics; radio frequency heating of plasmas; nonlinear theory; controlled thermonuclear fusion; laser plasma interaction; plasma simulation studies; hydrodynamics of laser fusion. *Mailing Add:* X-DO MS B218 Los Alamos Nat Lab PO Box 1663 Los Alamos NM 87545

KINDEL, PAUL KURT, BIOCHEMISTRY. *Current Pos:* from asst prof to assoc prof biochem, 63-77, PROF BIOCHEM, MICH STATE UNIV, 77- *Personal Data:* b Milwaukee, Wis, Sept 6, 34; m 61; c 3. *Educ:* Univ Wis, BS, 56; Cornell Univ, PhD(biochem), 61. *Prof Exp:* NIH fel, Max Planck Inst Cell Chem, Munich, 61-63. *Mem:* AAAS; Am Soc Biol Chemists; Am Soc Plant Physiol. *Res:* Isolation and structure of plant cell wall polysaccharides, particularly pectic polysaccharides; biosynthesis of pectic polysaccharides. *Mailing Add:* Dept Biochem Mich State Univ 212 Biol Chem East Lansing MI 48824-1319

KINDER, THOMAS HARTLEY, PHYSICAL OCEANOGRAPHY. *Current Pos:* oceanogr, Naval Ocean Res & Develop Activ, 78-87, MGR, COASTAL SCI PROG, OFF NAVAL RES, 87- *Personal Data:* b Riverside, Calif, Sept 6, 43; m 70. *Educ:* US Naval Acad, BS, 65; Univ Wash, MS, 74, PhD(phys oceanog), 76. *Prof Exp:* Res asst, Dept Oceanog, Univ Wash, 71-76, res assoc, 76-78. *Concurrent Pos:* Guest investr, Woods Hole Oceanog Inst, 84-85. *Mem:* Am Geophys Union; Am Meteorol Soc; AAAS; Sigma Xi. *Res:* Measurements of mesoscale features on shelves and in semi-enclosed seas (Bering, Caribbean, Mediterranean), especially fronts and eddies formed by flows exiting straits and flows within straits. *Mailing Add:* 5669 Ravenel Lane Springfield VA 22151-2427

KINDERLEHRER, DAVID (SAMUEL), MATHEMATICS. *Current Pos:* From instr to asst prof, 68-75, PROF MATH, UNIV MINN, MINNEAPOLIS, 75- *Personal Data:* b Allentown, Pa, Oct 23, 41. *Educ:* Mass Inst Technol, SB, 63; Univ Calif, Berkeley, PhD(math), 68. *Concurrent Pos:* Ital Govt researcher math, Advan Training Sch, Pisa, 71-72. *Res:* Partial differential equations; minimal surfaces; variational inequalities; mechanics. *Mailing Add:* Dept Math Carnegie Mellon Univ Pittsburgh PA 15213-3890

KINDERMAN, EDWIN MAX, ENERGY & ENVIRONMENTAL CONTROL TECHNOLOGIES, ENVIRONMENTAL REGULATION. *Current Pos:* INDEPENDANT CONSULT ENERGY & ENVIRON, 94- *Personal Data:* b Cincinnati, Ohio, Aug 21, 16; m, Jean M Rothchild; c Gibbs V, Albert J, Mary M & Joel F. *Educ:* Oberlin Col, AB, 37; Univ Notre Dame, MS, 38, PhD(phys chem), 41. *Prof Exp:* Instr chem, Univ Portland, 41-43; chemist, Radiation Lab, Univ Calif, 43-45; from asst prof to assoc prof chem, Univ Portland, 45-49; chemist, Gen Elec Co, Wash, 49-56; sr physicist, 56-57, mgr, Nuclear Physics Dept, 57-68, dir, Appl Physics Lab, 68-71, dir mkt, Phys Sci, 71-73; sr scientist, Sci Int, 73-75, mgr mkt Europe, 75-77, mgr nuclear & utility systs, mgr energy planning, 80-86, sr scientist, 86-94. *Concurrent Pos:* Chemist, Columbia Steel Casting Co, Ore, 43; res chemist, Res & Develop Div, H J Kaiser Co, Calif, 43. *Mem:* Am Chem Soc; Am Phys Soc; Am Nuclear Soc; Sigma Xi; Inst Nuclear Mat Mgt. *Res:* Analytical chemistry; radiation chemistry and radiation damage effect; nuclear materials management; energy economics and planning; non fossil energy technologies; nuclear energy and weapons proliferation; environmental regulation and techonologies. *Mailing Add:* 822 Marshall Dr Palo Alto CA 94303. *Fax:* 650-856-7414; *E-Mail:* ekinderman@aol.com

KINDERS, ROBERT JAMES, TUMOR MARKERS, BREAST CANCER. *Current Pos:* res scientist, Abbott Lab, 83-85, prof mgr, 85-89, proj mgr, 89-91, HEAD, MOLECULAR DIAG APPLN LAB, ABBOTT DIAG, ABBOTT LAB, 91- *Personal Data:* b Feb 12, 48; m 80, Patricia M Fogli. *Educ:* Loyola Univ, Chicago, BS, 70, MS, 76; Kans State Univ, PhD(biol), 80. *Prof Exp:* Res assoc, Div Biol, Kans State Univ, 80-83. *Concurrent Pos:* Staff, Dept Immunochem Res, Evanston Hosp, 76-77; mem adv coun, Ctr Basic Cancer Res, Kans State Univ, 90- *Mem:* Am Asn Cancer Res; Am Soc Cell Biol; Am Asn Clin Chem. *Res:* Application of monoclonal antibodies in cancer diagnosis and therapy; use of alternative binding agents in In Vitro Diagnostics; diagnostic immunoassays and their interferents; molecular diagnostics. *Mailing Add:* Bard Diag 12277 134th Ct NE Redmond WA 98052. *Fax:* 847-938-7996

KINDIG, DAVID A, PEDIATRICS, HEALTH POLICY. *Current Pos:* vchancellor health sci, Univ Wis-Madison, 80-85, dir progs health mgt, Sch Med, 85-94, PROF PREV MED, UNIV WIS-MADISON SCH MED, 80-, DIR WIS NETWORK HEALTH POLICY RES, 94- *Personal Data:* b May 19, 40; m 62, Mary Norton; c Mark, Laura Elizabeth & Brian David. *Educ:* Carleton Col, BA, 62; Univ Chicago, MD, 68, PhD(exp path), 68. *Prof Exp:* Intern, Dept Pediat, Univ Chicago, 68-69; from resident pediat to chief resident, Dept Pediat & Social Med, Montefiore Hosp & Med Ctr, NY, 69-71; dir, Div Prof Servs, Nat Health Servs Corp, HEW, 71-73; co-dir, Inst Health Team Develop, Montefiore Hosp & Med Ctr, 73-74; dep dir, Bur Health Manpower, HEW, 74-76; dir, Montefiore Hosp & Med Ctr, 76-80. *Concurrent Pos:* Prog coordr, Montefiore Hosp & Med Ctr, 69-70; instr, Dept Community Health, Albert Einstein Col Med, 70-71, assoc prof, 78-80; actg med dir, Martin Luther King Jr Neighborhood Health Ctr, 70-71; bd dirs, Rural Prod Proj, Robert Wood Johnson Found, 75-79, sr prog consult, 79-82; bd dirs, Am Med Student Asn Found, 84-86; chair, Wis Gov Task Force AIDS, 85-86; vis prof health mgt, Shanghi Second Med Univ, 87- & Beijing Med Univ, Sch Pub Health, 88- *Mem:* Inst Med-Nat Acad Sci; Asn Health Servs Res (treas, 93-96, pres-elect, 96); Am Col Physician Execs; Soc Med Adminr. *Mailing Add:* Wis Network Health Policy Res Univ Wis-Madison 229 Bradley Mem 1300 University Ave Madison WI 53706

KINDLER, SHARON DEAN, ENTOMOLOGY. *Current Pos:* RES ENTOMOLOGIST, AGR RES SERV, USDA, UNIV OKLAHOMA, 87- *Personal Data:* b Omaha, Nebr, Apr 27, 30; m 64; c 2. *Educ:* Univ Nebr, BSc, 59, PhD(entom), 67. *Prof Exp:* Res entomologist, Agr Res Serv, USDA, Univ Nebr, 64-87. *Mem:* Entom Soc Am; Sigma Xi. *Res:* Biology, ecology and control of sorghum and grass insects; plant resistance to sorghum and grass insects. *Mailing Add:* 5024 W Ninth Ave Stillwater OK 74074-1409

KINDT, GLENN W, NEUROSURGERY. *Current Pos:* MEM STAFF, DIV NEUROSURG, UNIV COLO MED CTR, 80- *Personal Data:* b Alpena, Mich, Sept 10, 30; m 60; c 4. *Educ:* Mich State Univ, BS, 51; Pa State Univ, BS, 52; Univ Mich, MD, 59. *Prof Exp:* Intern med, Univ Mich Hosp, 59-60, resident surg, 60-61, resident neurosurg, 62-65; resident, Harvard Med Sch & Peter Bent Brigham Hosp, Boston, 61-62; instr, Med Col SC, 65-66, assoc, 66-67; asst prof, Univ Calif, Davis, 67-69; from asst prof to assoc prof neurosurg, Univ Mich Med Ctr, Ann Arbor, 69-80. *Concurrent Pos:* Chief investr, US Vet Admin res grant, 66-; co-investr, NIH res grant, 67- Mem: AMA; Cong Neurol Surg. Res: Regional hypothermia and vascular insufficiency of the brain; intracerebral hematomas. Mailing Add: Univ Colo Health Sci 4200 E Ninth Ave C-307 Denver CO 80262-0001

KINDT, THOMAS JAMES, BIOCHEMISTRY, IMMUNOGENETICS. Current Pos: CHIEF LAB IMMUNOGENETICS, NAT INST ALLERGY & INFECTIOUS DIS, NIH, 77-, DIR, DIV INTRAMURAL RES, 95- Personal Data: b Cincinnati, Ohio, May 18, 39; m 64; c Rachel & James. Educ: Thomas More Col, AB, 63; Univ Ill, Urbana, PhD(biochem), 67. Prof Exp: NIH fel biol, City of Hope Nat Med Ctr, 67-69, asst res scientist, 69-70; fel, Rockefeller Univ, 70-71, asst prof, 71-73, assoc prof biol, 73-77. Concurrent Pos: Adj assoc prof med, Cornell Univ Med Col, 73-77; assoc ed, J Immunol, 73-; adv ed, J Exp Med, 77- & Immunochem, 77-; adj prof micro & pediatrics, Sch Med & Dent, Georgetown Univ, 81-; vis scientist, Inst Pasteur, Paris, 82-83. Mem: Am Heart Asn; Harvey Soc; Sigma Xi; Am Asn Immunol; Am Soc Biol Chemists. Res: Genetic determinants on immunoglobulins and histocompatibility antigens; protein and polysaccharide structure. Mailing Add: 8313 Still Spring Ct Bethesda MD 20817

KINEKE, J H, JR, TERMINAL BALLISTICS. Current Pos: RES PHYSICIST, US ARMY RES LAB, MD, 54- Personal Data: b Rockville Center, NY, Apr 27, 33. Educ: St Johns Univ, BS, 54; Univ Del, MS, 68. Mem: Am Phys Soc. Mailing Add: 3403 Crosswood Dr Aberdeen MD 21001

KINERSLY, THORN, DENTISTRY, DENTAL RESEARCH. Current Pos: res assoc, 64, asst prof, 64-67, ASSOC PROF DENT, DENT SCH, UNIV ORE HEALTH SCI CTR, 67- Personal Data: b The Dalles, Ore, Sept 15, 23; m 54; c 3. Educ: Univ Ore, DMD, 48. Prof Exp: Pvt pract, 48-49; intern children's dent, Forsyth Dent Infirmary, 49-50; asst resident, Sch Med, Yale Univ & Grace-New Haven Community Hosp, 50; res fel dent, Sch Med, Yale Univ, 52-56; pvt pract, 56-64. Concurrent Pos: Lectr, Forsyth Dent Infirmary, 52-56; res fel, Nobel Inst, 54; abstractor, Oral Res Abstr, 66-; prin investr, Educ & Res Found Prosthodont, 69; consult on-site invest res appl, Dent Sect, NIH, 70. Mem: Fel AAAS; Soc Exp Biol & Med; Int Asn Dent Res; Am Dent Asn; Sigma Xi. Res: Paper electrophoresis of saliva and salivary glands for identification of enzymes, blood group factors and anti-bacterial factors; track radioautography of teeth with Ca-45 isotopes; lasers and their relation to dentistry. Mailing Add: 10720 SW 30th Ave Portland OR 97219

KING, ALAN JONATHAN, OPTIMIZATION, STOCHASTIC PROGRAMMING. Current Pos: RES STAFF MEM, INT BUS MACH RES, 88- Personal Data: b Northampton, Eng, Oct 20, 54; Can citizen. Educ: Univ Wash, BS, 81, MS, 84, PhD(appl math), 86. Prof Exp: Postdoctoral fel math, Univ BC, 86-87; res scholar, Int Inst Appl Systs Anal, 87-88. Concurrent Pos: Actg asst prof, Dept Math, Univ Wash, 88, vis lectr, 89; assoc ed math, J Optimization, Soc Indust & Appl Math. Mem: Math Prog Soc; Opers Res Soc Am; Soc Indust & Appl Math. Res: Stochastic programming; applications to engineering and economic systems; optimization theory; statistical estimation; robustness and sensitivity analysis; large scale optimization. Mailing Add: IBM T J Watson Res Ctr PO Box 218 Yorktown Heights NY 10598

KING, ALBERT IGNATIUS, BIOENGINEERING. Current Pos: from instr to assoc prof, 60-76, ASSOC NEUROSURG, SCH MED, WAYNE STATE UNIV, 71-, PROF BIOENG, 76-, DISTINGUISHED PROF MECH ENG, 90- Personal Data: b Tokyo, Japan, June 12, 34; US citizen; m 60; c 2. Educ: Univ Hong Kong, BSc, 55; Wayne State Univ, MS, 60, PhD(eng mech), 66. Honors & Awards: Charles Russ Richards Mem Award, Am Soc Mech Engrs, 80; Volvo Award, 84. Prof Exp: Demonstr civil eng, Hong Kong, 55-58. Concurrent Pos: NIH Career develop award. Mem: Am Soc Eng Educ; Am Soc Mech Engrs; Am Acad Orthop Surg; Sigma Xi. Res: Human response to acceleration and vibration, automotive and aircraft safety; biomechanics of the spine; mathematical modelling of impact events; low back pain research. Mailing Add: Mech Eng Wayne State Univ 818 W Hancock Detroit MI 48202

KING, ALEXANDER HARVEY, ELECTRON MICROSCOPY, CRYSTALLOGRAPHY. Current Pos: from asst prof to assoc prof, Dept Mat Sci & Eng, State Univ NY, Stony Brook, 81-90, assoc vprovost grad studies, 87-90, vprovost grad studies , 90-92, PROF DEPT MAT SCI & ENG STATE UNIV NY, STONY BROOK, 90- Personal Data: b London, Eng, July 1, 54; m 77, Christine E Dring; c 2. Educ: Univ Sheffield, BMet, 75; Univ Oxford, DPhil(metall), 79. Prof Exp: Harwell fel, Dept Metall & Sci Mat, Univ Oxford, 79 & Dept Mat Sci & Eng, Mass Inst Technol, 79-81. Mem: Inst Metall; Am Inst Mining, Metall & Petrol Engrs; Electron Microscope Soc Am; Am Soc Metals; Mat Res Soc; Am Phys Soc. Res: Crystal lattice defects, particularly grain boundaries; electron microscopy, electron and x-ray diffraction. Mailing Add: Dept Mats Sci & Eng State Univ NY Stony Brook NY 11794-2275. Fax: 516-632-9528; E-Mail: aking@boundaries.eng.suntsb.edu

KING, ALFRED DOUGLAS, JR, FOOD MICROBIOLOGY. Current Pos: from assoc chemist to chemist, USDA, 61-65, microbiologist, 65-72, res leader microbiol, 73-77, RES MICROBIOLOGIST, WESTERN REGIONAL RES LAB, USDA, 78- Personal Data: b Portland, Ore, May 11, 33; m 59; c 2. Educ: Wash State Univ, BS, 55, PhD(food sci), 65; Univ Calif, Davis, MS, 61. Prof Exp: Food technologist, Nalley's Inc, 57-59. Concurrent Pos: Vis scientist, Commonwealth Sci & Indust Res Orgn Div Food Res, Sydney, Australia, 77-78, 89. Mem: Inst Food Technologists; Am Soc Microbiol; Asn Off Anal Chemists; Am Acad Microbiol; Int Comn Food Mycol (vpres). Res: Microbial physiology; food sanitation and public health; wine flavor; human and microbial nutrition; food mycology. Mailing Add: USDA Western Regional Res Lab 800 Buchanan St Albany CA 94710

KING, ALLEN LEWIS, HISTORY OF PHYSICS, BIOPHYSICS. Current Pos: from instr to prof, 42-75, EMER PROF PHYSICS, DARTMOUTH COL, 75-, CUR, HIST SCI APPARATUS, 71- Personal Data: b Rochester, NY, Mar 27, 10; m 37, Nancy T Form; c N Maribeth (Klobuchar), A Anthron & Fern T (Meyers). Educ: Univ Rochester, BA, 32, MA, 33, PhD(physics), 37. Hon Degrees: MA, Dartmouth Col, 48. Prof Exp: Instr physics, Univ Rochester, 36-37 & Rensselaer Polytech Inst, 37-42. Concurrent Pos: Consult, Behr-Manning Corp, NY, 41-42 & 48-57, Tougaloo Col, 57. Mem: Am Phys Soc; Biophys Soc; Am Asn Physics Teachers; Optical Soc Am. Res: Mechanical and hydrodynamical processes in biological systems; optical measurements; thermophysics; history of physics. Mailing Add: Dept Physics & Astron Dartmouth Col Hanover NH 03755

KING, AMY C P, ANALYSIS. Current Pos: from asst prof to assoc prof, 70-79, PROF MATH, EASTERN KY UNIV, 79- Personal Data: b Douglas, Wyo, Dec 30, 28; m 49. Educ: Univ Mo, BS, 49; Wichita State Univ, MA, 60; Univ Ky, PhD, 70. Prof Exp: Teacher pub schs, Goddard, Kans, 56-58; teaching fel, Wichita State Univ, 58-60, instr, 60-62; asst instr, Univ Kans, 62-65; instr math, Washburn Univ, 66-67; teaching asst, Univ Ky, 67-70. Concurrent Pos: Found Professorship, Eastern Ky Univ, Richmond, 93. Mem: Am Math Soc; Math Asn Am; Nat Coun Teachers Math. Res: Complex variables; mathematics education. Mailing Add: 1228 Tates Creek Rd Lexington KY 40502. Fax: 606-269-1362; E-Mail: matking@acs.eku.edu

KING, ANN CHRISTIE, biochemistry, molecular biology, for more information see previous edition

KING, ARTHUR FRANCIS, GEOLOGY. Current Pos: From asst prof to assoc prof, 67-80, dep head, Acad Earth Sci, 87-92, PROF GEOL MEM, UNIV NFLD, 80-, DEPT HEAD EARTH SCI, 87- Personal Data: b St John's, Nfld, Feb 11, 37; m 63, Muriel Noel; c Peter & Jennifer. Educ: Mem Univ, BSc, 61, MSc, 63; Univ Reading, PhD(geol), 67. Mem: Geol Asn Can. Res: Late precambrian clastic sequences in avalon zone of Newfoundland and the Appalachian-Caledonian Orogen. Mailing Add: Dept Earth Sci Mem Univ St John's NF A1C 5S7 Can

KING, B(ERNARD) G(EORGE), ELECTRICAL ENGINEERING. Current Pos: CONSULT, 89- Personal Data: b Kitchener, Ont, Can, Dec 22, 22; nat US; m 49, Joan Townsend; c Charles, Bernard, Adam, Philip & Quintas. Educ: Univ Southern Calif, BE, 44; Univ Wis, MS, 51, PhD(elec eng), 55. Prof Exp: Instr elec eng, Univ Southern Calif, 44-48 & Univ Wis, 48-55; mem tech staff, Bell Tel Labs, Inc, 55-88; prof, Stevens Inst Technol, 87-89. Concurrent Pos: Ed, Bell Syst Tech J, 81-84. Mem: Sigma Xi; Inst Elec & Electronics Engrs. Res: Atmospheric optical transmission; radio physics; microwave radio. Mailing Add: 5 Monmouth Ave Rumson NJ 07760

KING, BARRY FREDERICK, CELL BIOLOGY, DEVELOPMENTAL BIOLOGY. Current Pos: assoc prof anat, 78-82, actg chair, 87-89, PROF CELL BIOL & ANAT, MED SCH, UNIV CALIF, DAVIS, 82- Personal Data: b Perham, Minn, Sept 22, 42. Educ: Univ Minn, BA, 65; Univ Nev, MS, 67; Wash Univ, PhD(anat), 70. Prof Exp: Asst prof anat, Med Sch, Washington Univ, 71-77. Concurrent Pos: USPHS fel anat, Univ Wis-Madison, 70-71; human embryol & develop study sect, NIH, 85-89; res career develop award, NIH, 75-80. Mem: Am Asn Anat; Am Soc Cell Biol; Soc Gynecol Invest. Res: Cell biology of the female reproductive system, especially the functional cytology of the placenta and fetal membranes. Mailing Add: Dept Cell Biol & Human Anat Sch Med Univ Calif Davis CA 95616-8643. Fax: 530-752-8520

KING, BETTY LOUISE, METABOLISM. Current Pos: from asst prof to assoc prof, 78-84, asst div chmn nat sci, 83-85, PROF BIOL, NORTHERN VA COMMUNITY COL, 78- Personal Data: b Atlanta, Ga, Nov 26, 43; c 1. Educ: Brandeis Univ, BA, 65; Harvard Univ, PhD(microbiol, molecular genetics), 72. Prof Exp: Asst prof biol, Bard Col, 72-75; asst prof biol, Skidmore Col, 76-77. Res: Genetics and regulation of primary and secondary metabolism in bacteria, fungi and plants; chemical communication; biochemistry and ecology of alkaloids; drug use and abuse. Mailing Add: Div Sci & Appl Tech Northern Va Community Col 3001 N Beauregard St Alexandria VA 22311-5065. E-Mail: nvkingb@nv.cc.va.us

KING, BLAKE, MECHANICAL ENGINEERING, PHYSICAL METALLURGY. Current Pos: RETIRED. Personal Data: b Atlanta, Ga, Feb 4, 21; m 48; c 2. Educ: Univ Fla, BME, 48; Calif Inst Technol, MSME, 49. Prof Exp: Asst prof mech eng, Univ Miami, 49-51, 53-54; sr engr, Design Integration Dept, Martin Co, Md, 54-56, unit supvr, Nuclear Div, 56-58; from assoc prof to prof mech eng, Univ Miami, 58-87. Mem: Am Soc Metals; Metall Soc; Am Soc Mech Engrs. Res: Dispersion-strengthened high temperature alloys; creative mechanical design. Mailing Add: 4102 Alhambra Circle Miami FL 33146

KING, C(ARY) JUDSON, III, SEPARATION PROCESSES. Current Pos: from asst prof to assoc prof, Univ Calif, Berkeley, 63-69, vchmn dept, 67-72, chmn dept, 72-81, dean col chem, 81-87, provost, prof schs & cols, 87-94, vprovost res, 94-96, PROF CHEM ENG, 69-, PROVOST & SR VPRES ACAD AFFAIRS, UNIV CALIF, 96- Personal Data: b Ft Monmouth, NJ, Sept 27, 34; m 57, Jeanne A Yorke; c Mary E, Cary J IV & Catherine J. Educ: Yale Univ, BE, 56; Mass Inst Technol, SM, 58, ScD(chem eng), 60. Honors & Awards: 25th Ann Inst Lectr, 73; Food, Pharmaceut & Bioeng Div Award, 75; William H Walker Award, 76, Warren K Lewis Award, 90, Clarence Gerhold Award, 92, Am Inst Chem Engrs; George Westinghouse Award, 78,

Am Soc Eng Educ; Mac Pruitt Award, Coun Chem Res, 90; Award Separations Sci & Technol, Am Chem Soc, 97. *Prof Exp:* Asst prof chem eng, Mass Inst Technol, 59-63. *Concurrent Pos:* Dir Bayway Sta, Sch Chem Eng Pract, Mass Inst Technol, 59-61; consult, Procter & Gamble Co, 65-93. *Mem:* Nat Acad Eng; Am Chem Soc; fel Am Inst Chem Engrs; AAAS. *Res:* Synthesis and analysis of chemical processes; drying and concentration of foods; separation processes; water pollution abatement. *Mailing Add:* 7 Kensington Ct Kensington CA 94707-1009. *Fax:* 510-987-9209

KING, CALVIN ELIJAH, MATHEMATICS. *Current Pos:* RETIRED. *Personal Data:* b Chicago, Ill, June 5, 28. *Educ:* Morehouse Col, AB, 49; Atlanta Univ, MA, 50; Ohio State Univ, PhD(math educ), 59. *Prof Exp:* Instr math, Jackson Col, 53-55; asst instr, Ohio State Univ, 55-58; head, Dept Physics & Math, Tenn State Univ, 74-79, Prof Math, 58-88. *Concurrent Pos:* Specialist math & head dept, Fed Adv Teachers Col, Nigeria, 62-64. *Res:* Methods of teaching remedial mathematics; teaching elementary mathematics by television; the relation of modern mathematics to traditional mathematics. *Mailing Add:* 626 N Fifth St Nashville TN 37207

KING, CHARLES C, NATURAL HISTORY, NATURAL AREAS MANAGEMENT. *Current Pos:* exec dir, 72-92, EMER DIR, OHIO BIOL SURV, 93- *Personal Data:* b Kittanning, Pa, Jan 12, 33; m 56, 81, Anita Colton; c Connie, Jerry, Linda, Sylvia, Eric & Victor. *Educ:* Marietta Col, BS, 54; Ohio State Univ, MSc, 56, PhD(entom), 61. *Prof Exp:* Res technician entom, Ohio Agr Res & Develop, 56-61; from asst prof to prof biol, Malone Col, 61-72. *Concurrent Pos:* Consult radiation biol, Univ Wash, 62; consult, Dept Bot, Okla State Univ, 63, Dept Geol, Univ Calgary, 68 & Dept Geol, Univ Calgary, 68; coordr, Geobot Conf, Malone Col, 70, NAm Prairie Conf, Ohio State Univ, 78 & Ann Conf Lepidopterists Soc, 83; mem, Orgn Biol Field Sta, Ohio Acad Sci; mem, Ohio Natural Areas Coun, 84-90; coordr, 38th Meeting Am Inst Biol Sci, 87; mem, Ohio Acad Sci. *Mem:* Am Quaternary Asn; Am Inst Biol Sci; Ecol Soc Am; Nature Conserv. *Res:* Effects of herbicides and fungicides on honeybees, metabolism of 2, 4-D in blackjack oak; effects of 2, 4-D on nectar secretion; peat bog palynology; environmental analysis; distribution and ecology of prairies in central Ohio. *Mailing Add:* 483 Cliffside Pl Pagosa Springs CO 81147

KING, CHARLES EVERETT, POPULATION BIOLOGY. *Current Pos:* chmn dept, 77-86, PROF ZOOL, ORE STATE UNIV, 77- *Personal Data:* b Oak Park, Ill, May 8, 34; c 2. *Educ:* Emory Univ, AB, 58; Fla State Univ, MS, 60; Univ Wash, PhD(zool), 65. *Prof Exp:* Res assoc zool, Col Fisheries, Univ Wash, 65; instr biol, Yale Univ, 65-66; asst prof zool, Univ Ill, Urbana, 66-68; asst prof biol, Yale Univ, 68-72; from assoc prof to prof biol, Univ SFla, 72-77. *Concurrent Pos:* Vis prof, Shandong Col Oceanog, People's Repub China, 84-85 & Univ Valencia, Spain, 91-92; vis scholar, Univ Wash, 85, Univ Milan, Italy, 92. *Mem:* Fel AAAS; Soc Study Evolution; Sigma Xi. *Res:* Laboratory and field investigation of zooplankton population dynamics; interaction of genetical and ecological phenomena within populations; relation of life history characteristics to ecological adaptation. *Mailing Add:* Dept Zool Ore State Univ 3029 Cordley Hall Corvallis OR 97331-2914. *E-Mail:* kingc@ava.orst.edu

KING, CHARLES MILLER, BIOCHEMISTRY, ONCOLOGY. *Current Pos:* ADJ PROF CHEM, WAYNE STATE UNIV, 82- *Personal Data:* b West Salem, Ill, Oct 2, 32; m 54; c 2. *Educ:* Univ Ill, Urbana, BA, 54; Univ Minn, Minneapolis, PhD(biochem), 62. *Prof Exp:* Res assoc, Michael Reese Hosp & Med Ctr, 65-68, from actg dir to dir div cancer res, 65-75; asst prof med, Pritzker Sch Med, Univ Chicago, 73-75; expert, Nat Cancer Inst, Nat Ctr Toxicol Res, 75-77; assoc prof biochem, Univ Ark for Med Sci, 75-77; chmn Dept Chem Carcinogenisis, Mich Cancer Found, 77- *Concurrent Pos:* Res fel oncol, Med Sch, Univ Minn, Minneapolis, 62-63; Am Cancer Soc fel, Neth Cancer Inst, 63-65; mem, Nat Bladder Cancer Proj, Nat Cancer Inst, 73-78; mem, Amines Comt, Nat Res Coun, Nat Acad Sci, 79-80; mem, Chem Path Study Sect, NIH, 79-83; assoc ed, Cancer Res, 83-87; mem, Metab Path Study Sect, NIH, 86-90; mem, Coun Res & Clin Invest Awards, 88-91; dir carcinogenesis prog, Comprehensive Cancer Ctr Metrop Detroit, 77- *Mem:* Am Asn Cancer Res; Am Chem Soc; Am Soc Biochem & Molecular Biol; Japanese Cancer Soc; Environ Mutagen Soc. *Res:* Mechanism of action of chemical carcinogens; metabolism in covalent interaction with protein and nucleic acid. *Mailing Add:* Mich Cancer Found 110 E Warren Detroit MI 48201-1379

KING, CHARLES O(RRIN), CHEMICAL ENGINEERING. *Current Pos:* RETIRED. *Personal Data:* b Rochester, NY, Jan 9, 16; m 43, Mary L Stout; c Marilyn, Marjorie & Charles W. *Educ:* Univ Rochester, BS, 37; Univ Mich, MS, 39, ScD(chem eng), 43. *Prof Exp:* Asst chem eng, Univ Mich, 39-41; res engr, E I DuPont de Nemours & Co, Inc, 43-48, process develop supvr, Tenn, 48-52, asst to tech mgr, 52-56, planning engr, 56-60, process supvr, 60-61, sr engr, 61-67, asst to tech dir, Textile Fiber Dept, 67-82. *Mem:* Am Chem Soc; Am Inst Chem Engrs; Am Inst Chem; Sigma Xi. *Res:* Solvent extraction; polyamide textile fibers. *Mailing Add:* 1514 Woodsale Rd Wilmington DE 19809-2247

KING, CHERYL E, PHYSIOLOGY. *Current Pos:* fel, 83-86, ASST PROF PHYSIOL, QUEENS UNIV, 86- *Personal Data:* b Ont, Can, Sept 3, 54. *Educ:* Queens Univ, PhD(physiol), 83. *Honors & Awards:* Queen's Nat Scholar. *Mem:* Can Phys Soc; Am Phys Soc; Sigma Xi. *Res:* Oxygen transport during hypoxia. *Mailing Add:* Sch Rehab Ther Queens Univ Louise D Acton Bldg Kingston ON K7L 3N6 Can. *Fax:* 613-545-6776

KING, CHI-YU, GEOPHYSICS. *Current Pos:* GEOPHYSICIST, US GEOL SURV, 73- *Personal Data:* b Nanking, China, Aug 14, 34; m 62; c 3. *Educ:* Univ Taiwan, BEE, 56; Duke Univ, MS, 61; Cornell Univ, PhD(appl physics), 65. *Honors & Awards:* Spec Achievement Award, US Geol Surv, 70; Japanese Govt Res Award, 92. *Prof Exp:* Res fel geophys, Calif Inst Technol, 65-66; asst res geophysicist, Univ Calif, Los Angeles, 66-68; geophysicist, US Geol Surv, 68-70; geophysicist, US Earthquake Mechanism Lab, Nat Oceanic & Atmospheric Admin, 70-73. *Concurrent Pos:* Proj chief, Earthquake Mech & Chem. *Mem:* Am Geophys Union; Seismol Soc Am. *Res:* Earthquake source mechanisms and prediction; fracture of solids; heat transfer; geomagnetism; geophysical fracture phenomena. *Mailing Add:* 381 Hawthorne Ave Los Altos CA 94022. *Fax:* 650-329-5163; *E-Mail:* cking.wr.usgs.gov

KING, CRESTON ALEXANDER, JR, LOW TEMPERATURE PHYSICS. *Current Pos:* asst prof, 66-73, ASSOC PROF PHYSICS, 73-, CHMN DEPT, LOYOLA UNIV, LA, 80- *Personal Data:* b San Antonio, Tex, July 9, 35; m 62; c 3. *Educ:* Rice Univ, AB, 58, MA, 63, PhD(physics), 65; Duke Univ, MA, 62. *Prof Exp:* Asst physics, Rice Univ, 62-64. *Mem:* Am Phys Soc; Am Asn Physics Teachers. *Res:* Superconductivity; solid state physics. *Mailing Add:* Dept Physics Loyola Univ Box 74 New Orleans LA 70118

KING, DARRELL LEE, LIMNOLOGY. *Current Pos:* PROF FISHERIES & WILDLIFE, MICH STATE UNIV, 74-, ACTG DIR, INST WATER RES, 78- *Personal Data:* b Hall, Mont, Jan 10, 37; m 62; c 3. *Educ:* Mont State Col, BS, 59; Mich State Univ, MS, 62, PhD(limnol), 64. *Prof Exp:* From asst prof to prof civil eng, Univ Mo, Columbia, 64-74. *Concurrent Pos:* Consult, Ralston Purina, 64-65 & 72-73, St Louis Co Water Co, 67-69 & 73-74, Campbell Soup Co, 70-71, Harland Bartholomew & Assocs, 73-74 & A P Green Refractories Co, 75. *Mem:* AAAS; Am Soc Limnol & Oceanog; Am Fisheries Soc; Water Pollution Control Fedn. *Res:* Interrelationships between physical, chemical and biological factors with specific reference to detailing interacting mechanisms which govern aquatic ecosystems. *Mailing Add:* Dept Wildlife Mgmt Mich State Univ 13 Natural Resources East Lansing MI 48824-1222

KING, DAVID BEEMAN, ENDOCRINOLOGY, ANIMAL PHYSIOLOGY. *Current Pos:* From asst prof to prof, 65-88, DR E PAUL & FRANCES H REIFF PROF BIOL, FRANKLIN & MARSHALL COL, 88- *Personal Data:* b Ware, Mass, Mar 12, 37; m 61, Christine Ross; c Marcia & Linda. *Educ:* Univ Mass, BS, 59, MA, 61; Ind Univ, PhD(zool), 65. *Concurrent Pos:* Nat Inst Arthritis & Metab Dis res grant, 66-78. *Mem:* AAAS; Am Soc Zoologists; Sigma Xi. *Res:* Comparative endocrinology; hormonal regulation of growth in chickens; thyroidal influence on muscle growth and development. *Mailing Add:* Dept Biol Franklin & Marshall Col Lancaster PA 17604-3003. *E-Mail:* d__king@acad.fandm.edu

KING, DAVID GEORGE, NERVE CELLS, EVOLUTION. *Current Pos:* ASSOC PROF HISTOL, SOUTHERN ILL UNIV, 78- *Educ:* Univ Calif, PhD(neurosci), 75. *Res:* Neurobiology. *Mailing Add:* Dept Zool Southern Ill Univ Carbondale IL 62901

KING, DAVID S(COTT), PHOTO-DISSOCIATION. *Current Pos:* RES CHEMIST, NAT BUR STAND, 76- *Personal Data:* b Hartford, Conn, Nov 5, 49. *Educ:* Univ Pa, BA, 71, PhD(phys chem), 76. *Mem:* Am Chem Soc; Optical Soc Am. *Res:* State-resolved and time-resolved laser studies of the mechanisms and rates of energy flow within model molecular systems, including relaxation and bond rupture. *Mailing Add:* Nat Inst Stand & Technol Molecular Advanced Tech Program Gaithersburg MD 20899

KING, DAVID THANE, PHYSICS. *Current Pos:* RETIRED. *Personal Data:* b Wellington, NZ, Jan 16, 23; nat US; m 50; c 4. *Educ:* Univ NZ, BSc, 44, MSc, 47; Bristol Univ, PhD(physics), 51. *Prof Exp:* Physicist, US Naval Res Lab, 51-55; from asst prof to prof physics, Univ Tenn, Knoxville, 55-61. *Concurrent Pos:* Mem user's group zero gradient synchrotron, Argonne Nat Lab, 62-; consult, Oak Ridge Nat Lab, 65- *Mem:* Am Phys Soc; Italian Phys Soc. *Res:* High energy physics. *Mailing Add:* 117 Park Hill Circle Knoxville TN 37909

KING, DELBERT LEO, PHYSICAL CHEMISTRY. *Current Pos:* assoc prof, 65-72, chmn natural sci div, 70-76, PROF CHEM, 72-, DIR COMPUT CTR, DOANE COL, 76- *Personal Data:* b Kansas City, Mo, Jan 7, 34; m 57; c 7. *Educ:* Ariz State Col, BS, 56; Univ Nebr, MS, 59, PhD, 68. *Prof Exp:* Asst prof chem, Sterling Col, 59-62; asst prof, Nebr Wesleyan Univ, 62-65. *Res:* Solution colorimetry. *Mailing Add:* 613 Custer St Hemingford NE 69348

KING, DONALD M, ANALYTICAL CHEMISTRY. *Current Pos:* asst prof, 66-69, ASSOC PROF CHEM, 69-, CHMN DEPT, WESTERN WASH STATE COL, 74- *Personal Data:* b Seattle, Wash, June 5, 35; m 65; c 1. *Educ:* Wash State Univ, BS, 57; Calif Inst Technol, PhD(chem), 63. *Prof Exp:* Asst prof chem, Calif State Col Los Angeles, 61-63; Welsh fel, Univ Tex, 63-64; chemist, Org Chem Div, E I du Pont de Nemours & Co, 64-66. *Concurrent Pos:* NSF res grant, 68-70. *Mem:* Am Chem Soc. *Res:* Application of electroanalytical techniques to the study of reaction kinetics and mechanisms. *Mailing Add:* Dept Chem Western Wash Univ Bellingham WA 98225-5996

KING, DONALD WEST, JR, PATHOLOGY. *Current Pos:* CONSULT, 87- *Personal Data:* b Cochranton, Pa, June 30, 27; m 52; c 3. *Educ:* Syracuse Univ, MD, 49. *Prof Exp:* Resident & instr path, Col Physicians & Surgeons, Columbia Univ, 49-52; prof & chmn dept, Univ Colo, Denver, 61-67;

Delafield prof path & chmn dept, Col Physicians & Surgeons, Columbia Univ, 67-82. *Concurrent Pos:* USPHS fel, Univ Chicago, 54-55 & Carlsberg Lab, 55-56. *Mem:* Am Soc Exp Path; Am Soc Cell Biol; Human Genetics Soc; Am Asn Path; NY Acad Sci; AAAS. *Res:* Cell injury; membrane transport. *Mailing Add:* 2122 Massachusetts Ave NW Apt 501 Washington DC 20008

KING, DOROTHY WEI (CHENG), nutrition, physiology, for more information see previous edition

KING, EDGAR PEARCE, mathematical statistics; deceased, see previous edition for last biography

KING, EDWARD FRAZIER, INORGANIC CHEMISTRY. *Current Pos:* ASST PROF & CHMN SCI DEPT, S PLAINS COL, 89- *Personal Data:* b Lake Providence, La, Dec 3, 35; m 66; c 5. *Educ:* Gregorian Univ, BA, 58; Loyola Univ, BS, 65; La State Univ, New Orleans, PhD(chem), 69. *Prof Exp:* Instr, Tex Woman's Univ, 68-79, asst prof chem, 70-75; mem, fac chem & physics, Cent Tex Col, 75-89. *Res:* Complexes of the first row transition metals, particularly their preparation and visible infrared spectra; halogen complexes of vanadium and copper. *Mailing Add:* Sci Dept S Plains Col 1401 College Ave Levelland TX 79336-6503

KING, EDWARD LOUIS, INORGANIC CHEMISTRY. *Current Pos:* chmn dept, 70-72, prof chem, 63-86, EMER PROF, UNIV COLO, BOULDER, 86- *Personal Data:* b Grand Forks, NDak, Mar 15, 20; m 52; c 2. *Educ:* Univ Calif, Berkeley, BS, 43, PhD(chem), 45. *Prof Exp:* Asst chem, Univ Calif, 42-44; asst chem, Manhattan Dist Proj, 44-45, res assoc, 45-46, du Pont fel & lectr chem, Harvard Univ, 46-47, instr, 47-48; from asst prof to prof, Univ Wis, 48-63. *Concurrent Pos:* At Off Sci Res & Develop, 44; Guggenheim fel, Calif Inst Technol, 57-58; ed, Inorg Chem, Am Chem Soc, 64-68. *Mem:* Am Chem Soc. *Res:* Chemistry of chromium and other transition metals in solution; ion solvation in mixed solvents; mechanisms of reactions in solution. *Mailing Add:* Dept Chem Univ Colo Campus Box 215 Boulder CO 80309-0215

KING, ELBERT AUBREY, JR, PLANETOLOGY, SPACE GEOLOGY. *Current Pos:* chmn dept, 69-74, PROF GEOL, UNIV HOUSTON, 69- *Personal Data:* b Austin, Tex, Nov 12, 35; m 57; c 2. *Educ:* Univ Tex, BS, 57, MA, 61; Harvard Univ, PhD(geol), 65. *Prof Exp:* Geologist, Geol & Geochem Br, Manned Spacecraft Ctr, NASA, 63-67, cur, Lunar Receiving Lab, 67-69. *Mem:* Fel Meteoritical Soc. *Res:* Meteorites, planetary surfaces; geochemistry; mineralogy of pegmatites, petrography and composition of tektites; zoned ultramafic intrusive rocks; lunar samples. *Mailing Add:* Dept Geoscis Univ Houston 4800 Calhoun Rd Houston TX 77204-0001

KING, ELIZABETH NORFLEET, CELL PHYSIOLOGY. *Current Pos:* RETIRED. *Personal Data:* b Concord, NC, May 22, 25. *Educ:* Randolph-Macon Woman's Col, AB, 46; Wellesley Col, MA, 51; Duke Univ, PhD(cell physiol), 63. *Prof Exp:* Instr zool, Wellesley Col, 51-53; instr biol, Woman's Col, NC, 53-56 & Bucknell Univ, 60-61; instr physiol, Vassar Col, 61-63, asst prof biol, 63-69; assoc prof biol, Winthrop Col, 69-94. *Mem:* AAAS; Am Soc Zoologists; Nat Asn Biol Teachers. *Res:* Cellular physiology; separation of cellular organelles. *Mailing Add:* 1505 Estes Dr Rock Hill SC 29732

KING, ELIZABETH RAYMOND, GEOLOGY. *Current Pos:* Geologist, US Geol Surv, 48-51, geophysicist, 51-74, res geophysicist, 74-93, EMER SCIENTIST, US GEOL SURV, 93- *Personal Data:* b Halifax, NS, Dec 5, 23; US citizen. *Educ:* Smith Col, AB, 47. *Mem:* AAAS; Soc Explor Geophys; Am Geophys Union; fel Geol Soc Am. *Res:* Airborne magnetometer surveys; analysis of magnetic and gravity anomalies by modeling techniques; geologic interpretation of data from geophysical studies of continents and oceans. *Mailing Add:* US Geol Surv MS 927 Reston VA 22092. *E-Mail:* eking@usgs.gov

KING, FRANKLIN G, JR, CHEMICAL ENGINEERING, BIOCHEMICAL ENGINEERING. *Current Pos:* PROF CHEM ENG & DEPT CHMN, NC A&T STATE UNIV, 85- *Personal Data:* b Mahonoy City, Pa, Sept 23, 39; m 59, Phyllis M Tulin; c Jeffrey, Samantha & Timothy. *Educ:* Pa State Univ, BS, 61; Kans State Univ, MS, 62; Stevens Inst Technol, DSc, 66; Howard Univ, MEd, 76. *Prof Exp:* Res engr, Uniroyal Res Ctr, 62-65; process engr, Am Cyanamid Co, 65-66; asst prof chem eng, Lafayette Col, 66-72; from assoc prof to prof, Howard Univ, 72-85. *Mem:* Am Inst Chem Eng; Am Soc Eng Educ; Mat Res Soc. *Res:* Permeation and diffusion of gases through barriers, including volcanic tuff, food packaging materials and high temperature membranes; process control; physiological pharmacokinetic modeling of drug distribution in mammals. *Mailing Add:* Dept Chem Eng NC A&T State Univ Greensboro NC 27411. *Fax:* 910-834-7904; *E-Mail:* king@ncat.edu

KING, FREDERICK ALEXANDER, NEUROSCIENCE. *Current Pos:* dir & res emer prof neurobiol, Yerkes Regional Primate Res Ctr, 78-96, EMER PROF ANAT & CELL BIOL, SCH MED, EMORY UNIV, 78- *Personal Data:* b Paterson, NJ, Oct 3, 25; m 91, Sally Wolff; c Elizabeth G & Alexander K. *Educ:* Stanford Univ, AB, 53; Johns Hopkins Univ, MA, 55, PhD(psychol, med sci), 56. *Honors & Awards:* Spec Leadership & Serv Citation, Am Psychol Asn, 84 & 92; Pres Award, Soc Neurosci, 94; Commendation, AMA, 94, NIH, 94, Incurably Ill Animal Res, 94. *Prof Exp:* Instr psychol, Johns Hopkins Univ, 55-56; from instr to asst prof psychiat, Col Med, Ohio State Univ, 56-59; from asst prof to prof psychol & neurosurg, Col Med, Univ Fla, 59-69, prof neurosci & chmn dept, 69-78, dir ctr neurobiol, 68-78. *Concurrent Pos:* NIMH grant, 57-60, div biol sci training grant, 65-, Nat Inst Neurol Dis & Stroke grant, 59-71, NIMH fel & vis prof, Inst Physiol, Univ Pisa, 61-62; vis scientist, Am Psychol Asn-NSF prog, 62-67 & neuroanat prog, NIH, 63-70; scientist co-dir, Ctr Neurobiol Sci, Univ Fla, 64-68; consult, Battelle Mem Inst, 56-59 & res mem psychobiol adv panel, Biol & Med Sci Div, NSF, 63-67; mem adv comt, Primate Res Ctr, NIH, 69-73; mem ed adv bd, Behav Biol, 71-; ed, Physiol & Animal Psychol, 71- & J Suppl Abstr Serv; chmn comt commun & coord, Biol Sci Training Prog, NIMH, 72-78, mem & chmn res scientist develop rev comt, 74-78; mem bd sci adv, Yerkes Regional Primate Res Ctr, 74-78; mem Nat Res Coun-Nat Acad Sci brain sci comt, 74-; chmn & mem comt educ, Soc Neurosci, 74-77; adj prof psychol, Emory Univ, 78-; mem Int Adv Bd, Nat Mus Kenya & Kenyan Inst Primate Res, 83-; chair, Comn Animals Res & Experimentation, Am Psychol Asn, 83-85, bd sci affairs, 86-88; chair, Comn Animal Res, Soc Neurosci, 87, Govt & Pub Affairs Comn, 90-93; mem bd trustees, Am Asn Accreditation Lab Animal Care, 87-90; mem bd dir, Nat Asn Biomed Res, 87-90; mem adv bd & dir, NIH, 89-92. *Mem:* Fel AAAS; fel Am Psychol Asn; Am Physiol Soc; Soc Neurosci; Int Neuropsychol Soc (secy-treas, 69-73); Asn Clin Sci. *Res:* Effects of subcortical brain lesions on motivated behavior and learning in animals; analysis of cortical functions in infrahuman primates by use of ablation and brain stimulation techniques; electrophysiological and conditioning analysis of recovery of function in the isolated forebrain. *Mailing Add:* Yerkes Primate Ctr Emory Univ Atlanta GA 30322-1100. *Fax:* 404-634-6148; *E-Mail:* swolff@emory.edu

KING, FREDERICK JESSOP, FOOD SCIENCE. *Current Pos:* RETIRED. *Personal Data:* b Niagara Falls, NY, July 4, 28; m 56; c 3. *Educ:* Cornell Univ, BS, 51, MFS, 52; Mass Inst Technol, PhD, 60. *Prof Exp:* Biochemist, Northeast Utilization Res Ctr, Nat Marine Fisheries Serv, Nat Oceanic & Atmospheric Admin, 60-89. *Concurrent Pos:* Exec secy, New Eng Fisheries Inst, 70-89. *Mem:* Am Chem Soc; Inst Food Technologists; fel Am Inst Chemists; fel Asn Anal Chemists. *Res:* Denaturation of fish proteins; irradiation preservation of fish; flavor chemistry of fish; nutritive value; fishery technology; process and product improvements; quality assurance. *Mailing Add:* 84 Cherry St Wenham MA 01984

KING, FREDERICK WARREN, LOWER BOUNDS FOR ENERGY LEVELS, HIGH PRECISION CALCULATIONS ON THREE-ELECTRON SYSTEMS. *Current Pos:* PROF CHEM, UNIV WIS-EAU CLAIRE, 79- *Personal Data:* b Sydney, Australia, Apr 15, 47. *Educ:* Univ Sydney, BSc, 69; Univ Calgary, MSc, 71; Queen's Univ, PhD(chem), 75. *Honors & Awards:* Camille & Henry Dreyfus Teacher-Scholar Award, Dreyfus Found, 83, Camille & Henry Dreyfus Scholar Award, 91; Outstanding Contrib Chem Award, Am Chem Soc, Cent Wis Sect, 84. *Prof Exp:* Fel, Oxford Univ, 75-76 & Northwestern Univ, 77-78; fel Brock Univ, 78-79. *Res:* Efforts focus on problems in theoretical chemistry and atomic physics; bounds on the electronic density on the energy levels in three-electron systems and mathematical problems associated with these problems. *Mailing Add:* Dept Chem Univ Wis Eau Claire WI 54702. *E-Mail:* fking@uwec.edu

KING, GARY MICHAEL, MICROBIAL PHYSIOLOGICAL ECOLOGY, BIOGEOCHEMISTRY. *Current Pos:* from asst prof to assoc prof, 82-90, PROF MICROBIOL & OCEANOG, UNIV MAINE, 91- *Personal Data:* b Ft Walton Beach, Fla, Oct 30, 53. *Educ:* Univ Ga, BA, 74, PhD(microbiol), 78. *Prof Exp:* Res assoc, Mich State Univ, 78-81. *Concurrent Pos:* Vis asst prof, Mich State Univ, 81-82; prin investr, NSF, NASA & Nat Oceanic & Atmospheric Admin, 82-; Fulbright res scholar, Aarhus Univ, Denmark, 88-89, lecktor, 88-90; panelist, Div Environ Biol, NSF, 91-94. *Mem:* Am Soc Microbiol; Am Chem Soc; Am Soc Limnol & Oceanog. *Res:* Microbiology, ecology and marine science, especially those related to biogeochemical transformations of carbon, nitrogen and sulfur at regional and global scales. *Mailing Add:* Darling Marine Ctr Univ Maine Walpole ME 04573. *Fax:* 207-563-3119; *E-Mail:* gking@maine.maine.edu

KING, GAYLE NATHANIEL, PHYSICAL CHEMISTRY. *Current Pos:* CHIEF CHEMIST, KOCH MAT, 81- *Personal Data:* b Paulding, Ohio, July 17, 48; m 71, Helen Willis; c Daniel & Tisha. *Educ:* Heidelberg Col, BS, 70; Univ Pac, PhD(phys chem), 77. *Honors & Awards:* Emmon's Prize, Asn Asphal & Paving Technol. *Prof Exp:* Instr statist, USAF, 70-74; asst prof chem, Rose Hulman Inst Technol, 77-81. *Concurrent Pos:* Consult, Bituminous Mat Inc, 78- *Mem:* Am Chem Soc; Sigma Xi; Asn Asphalt Paving Technol. *Res:* Modified asphalt; asphalt and oil emulsions. *Mailing Add:* Koch Mat PO Box 1875 Wichita KS 67201

KING, GENERAL TYE, MEAT SCIENCE. *Current Pos:* from instr to asst prof meats, Tex A&M Univ, 53-60, assoc prof meats, 60-69, assoc prof animal sci, 69-76, prof animal sci, 76-89, asst head dept, 69-89, EMER PROF ANIMAL SCI, TEX A&M UNIV, 89- *Personal Data:* b King, Ky, Apr 7, 20; m 40. *Educ:* Union Col, Ky, BS, 48; Univ Ky, BS, 50, MS, 51; Tex A&M Univ, PhD(meats), 58. *Prof Exp:* Asst animal husbandman, SDak State Col, 51-53. *Mem:* Am Meat Sci Asn; Am Soc Animal Sci; Inst Food Technol. *Res:* Animal science; nutrition. *Mailing Add:* 1011 Walton Dr College Station TX 77840-2310

KING, GEORGE, III, EXPERIMENTAL NUCLEAR PHYSICS. *Current Pos:* MEM PROF STAFF, NUCLEAR DEPT, SCHLUMBERGER DOLL RES, 79- *Personal Data:* b Tampa, Fla, Nov 12, 46; m 68; c 2. *Educ:* Talladega Col, BA, 68; Stanford Univ, MS, 74, PhD(nuclear physics), 77. *Prof Exp:* Instr physics, Albany State Col, 69-71 & Col Notre Dame, 72-73; res asst nuclear physics, Stanford Univ, 73-77; res assoc nuclear physics, Lawrence Berkeley

Lab, 77-79. *Concurrent Pos:* Xerox Corp fel, 74-77. *Mem:* Am Phys Soc. *Res:* Giant resonance excitation for light nuclei; relativistic heavy ion central collisions. *Mailing Add:* Mary Wash Col 1301 College Ave Fredricksburg VA 22401

KING, GERALD WILFRID, CHEMICAL PHYSICS. *Current Pos:* from asst prof to prof, 57-89, EMER PROF CHEM, McMASTER UNIV, 89- *Personal Data:* b Eng, Jan 22, 28; m 54, Gwyneth Jones; c Richard J, Juliette M, Jennifer W & Gillian C. *Educ:* Univ London, BSc, 49, PhD(chem), 52. *Hon Degrees:* DSc, Univ London, 70. *Honors & Awards:* Gerhard Herzberg Award, Spectros Soc Can, 81. *Prof Exp:* Asst lectr, Univ Col, London, 54-56, lectr, 56-57. *Concurrent Pos:* Hon res assoc, Univ Col, London, 65; Ed, Can J Chem, 74-79; chmn, dept chem, McMaster Univ, 79-82; bd gov, McMaster Univ, 85-88. *Mem:* Fel Chem Inst Can; Optical Soc Am; fel Royal Soc Chem; fel Royal Soc Can. *Res:* Electronic states and structures of molecules; multi-photon laser spectroscopy; optical-optical double resonance; high resolution electronic molecular spectroscopy. *Mailing Add:* Dept Chem McMaster Univ Hamilton ON L8S 4M1 Can

KING, GORDON JAMES, REPRODUCTIVE PHYSIOLOGY, ENDOCRINOLOGY. *Current Pos:* asst prof, 68-70, assoc prof, 70-75, PROF ANIMAL SCI, UNIV GUELPH, 75- *Personal Data:* b Toronto, Ont, June 8, 32; m 57; c 2. *Educ:* Univ Toronto, DVM, 59; Univ Guelph, MS, 66, PhD(reproduction physiol), 68. *Prof Exp:* Pvt pract vet med, 59-60; field vet, Hamilton Dist Cattle Breeding Asn, 60-62, tech mgr, 62-65. *Concurrent Pos:* Can Dept Agr res grant, 76-78; Nat Res Coun Can res grant, 76-; consult, Food & Agr Asn, Can Int Develop Agency, Int Agr Exchange Asn, IFS. *Mem:* Am Soc Animal Sci; Soc Study Reprod; Soc Study Fertil; fel Inst Biol. *Res:* Reproductive biology. *Mailing Add:* Dept Animal & Poultry Sci Univ Guelph Guelph ON N1G 2W1 Can. *Fax:* 519-767-0573

KING, GREGORY L, NEUROSCIENCE, PHYSIOLOGY. *Current Pos:* RES PHYSIOLOGIST, ARMED FORCES RADIOBIOL RES INST, 84- *Personal Data:* b Plainsview, Tex, Mar 1, 48. *Educ:* Univ Houston, MA, 71; Baylor Col Med, PhD(physiol), 80. *Honors & Awards:* Minoru Susuki Award, 80. *Prof Exp:* Fel physiol, Univ NC, Chapel Hill, 80-84. *Mem:* Soc Neurosci; Am Physiol Soc. *Mailing Add:* Armed Forces Radiobiol Res Inst NNMC Bldg 42 8901 Wisconsin Ave Bethesda MD 20889-5603

KING, H(ENRY) E(UGENE), PSYCHOLOGY. *Current Pos:* PROF PSYCHOL, WASHINGTON & LEE UNIV, 80- *Personal Data:* b Wilmington, Va, Sept 24, 22; m 48; c 2. *Educ:* Univ Richmond, BA, 42; Columbia Univ, MA, 43, PhD, 48. *Prof Exp:* Asst psychologist, NY State Psychiat Inst, 42-43 & 46-48; sr res scientist, NY State Brain Res Proj, 48-49; assoc prof psychiat & neurol, Sch Med, Tulane Univ, 49-60; prof psychol, Sch Med & Chief Serv, Western Psychiat Inst, Univ Pittsburgh, 60-80. *Concurrent Pos:* Lectr, Columbia Univ, 46-49; vis scientist, Charity Hosp, New Orleans, 49-60. *Mem:* Fel AAAS; Am Physiol Soc; Soc Exp Biol & Med; fel Am Psychol Asn; Am Psychopath Asn. *Res:* Psychophysiology; experimental psychopathology; motor response systems; central nervous system stimulation and ablation. *Mailing Add:* Dept Psychol Washington & Lee Univ Lexington VA 24450. *Fax:* 540-463-8945

KING, HAROLD, SURGERY. *Current Pos:* From instr to assoc prof, 55-64, PROF SURG, MED CTR, 64-, DIR DIV THORACIC & CARDIOVASC SURG, IND UNIV, INDIANAPOLIS, 72- *Personal Data:* b Bedford, Ind, Aug 12, 22; m 52; c 2. *Educ:* Yale Univ, MD, 46. *Concurrent Pos:* Mem staff, Vet Admin Hosp & Indianapolis Gen Hosp. *Mem:* Soc Vascular Surg; Soc Univ Surg; Am Col Surg; Soc Thoracic Surg; Am Surg Asn. *Res:* Cardiovascular surgery. *Mailing Add:* Cardiothoracic Surg Inc 545 Barnhill Dr Indianapolis IN 46202-5112

KING, HARRISS THORNTON, NUCLEAR PHYSICS. *Current Pos:* MEM STAFF, MEASUREX CORP, 80- *Personal Data:* b Ames, Iowa, June 15, 47; m 76. *Educ:* Iowa State Univ, BS, 69; Stanford Univ, MS, 70, PhD(physics), 75. *Prof Exp:* Res assoc physics, Rutgers Univ, 74-77; asst prof physics, Stanford Univ, 77-80. *Mem:* Sigma Xi; Am Phys Soc. *Res:* Hyperfine interactions; nuclear electromagnetic moments; polarization phenomena. *Mailing Add:* 11171 Bobb Rd Cupertino CA 95014

KING, HARTLEY H(UGHES), AERONAUTICAL SCIENCES, MECHANICAL ENGINEERING. *Current Pos:* SR RES ENGR, EFFECTS TECHNOL, INC, 75- *Personal Data:* b Fresno, Calif, Apr 21, 36; m 62; c 2. *Educ:* Univ Calif, Berkeley, BS, 57, MS, 59, PhD(mech eng), 63. *Prof Exp:* Sr engr, Electrooptical Systs, 59-65; sr res engr, AC Electronics Defense Res Labs, Gen Motors Corp, 65-68; sr res engr, Gen Res Corp, 68-75. *Mem:* Am Inst Aeronaut & Astronaut; Inst Elec & Electronics Engrs. *Res:* Compressible fluid mechanics; wakes and separated flows; re-entry aerodynamics; flight mechanics. *Mailing Add:* Gen Res Corp 5383 Hollister Ave PO Box 6770 Santa Barbara CA 93111

KING, HENRY LEE, ORGANIC CHEMISTRY, POLYMER CHEMISTRY. *Current Pos:* RETIRED. *Personal Data:* b Muleshoe, Tex, Apr 12, 21; m 48; c 4. *Educ:* Tex Tech Col, BS, 52, MS, 54. *Prof Exp:* Res chemist, Chemstrand Res Ctr, Inc Monsanto Co, 54-65, sr res chemist, 65-70, res specialist, 70-76, sr res specialist, 76-81. *Mem:* Am Chem Soc. *Res:* Synthetic polymers and fibers; polymer processes; polymer modification for specific end uses; intermediate synthesis; condensation polymers, especially polyesters. *Mailing Add:* 102 Bogue Ct Cary NC 27511-5427

KING, HERMAN (LEE), ACADEMIC ADMINISTRATION. *Current Pos:* RETIRED. *Personal Data:* b Grand Ledge, Mich, Feb 24, 15; m 39, Alice Williams; c Judith & Margaret. *Educ:* Mich State Univ, BS, 39; Pa State Univ, MS, 41, PhD(biochem), 42. *Prof Exp:* Res fel, Reilly Tar & Chem Corp, Ind, 39-42; instr agr & biol chem, Pa State Univ, 43; orchard mgr, Mich, 44; exten entomologist, Mich State Univ, 45-46, from asst prof to assoc prof entom, 46-59, prof & asst dean, Col Arts & Sci, 59-62, dir, Div Biol Sci, 60-62, asst dean, Col Natural Sci, 62-63, asst provost, 63-74, dir acad serv, 74-81. *Res:* University administration. *Mailing Add:* 2700 Burcham Dr Apt 536 East Lansing MI 48823-3895

KING, HOWARD E, electrical engineering, for more information see previous edition

KING, HUBERT WYLAM, MATERIALS SCIENCE, ENGINEERING PHYSICS. *Current Pos:* PROF MAT ENG, UNIV WESTERN ONT, 91- *Personal Data:* b Cardiff, Wales, Jan 20, 30; Can citizen; m 57; c 4. *Educ:* Univ Birmingham, BSc, 54, PhD(metall), 56; Imp Col, London, DIC(metall), 71. *Prof Exp:* Fel metall, Univ Birmingham, 56-58; US AEC grant metal physics, Mellon Inst, 59-62; lectr phys metall, Imp Col, Univ London, 62-65, sr lectr, 65-67; vis prof metall, Univ Calif, Berkeley, 67; reader phys metall, Imp Col, Univ London, 67-70; prof eng physics, Dalhousie Univ, 71-83; prof eng physics, Tech Univ, NS, 83-91, head, Eng Physics Dept, 86-91. *Concurrent Pos:* UK Atomic Energy Authority & Sci Res Coun grant, Imp Col, Univ London, 62-70; co-ed comn struct reports, Int Union Crystallog, 66-; consult, US AEC, 67-69; Nat Res Coun Can grant, Dalhousie Univ, 71-83; nat sci eng res coun grant, Tech Univ NS, 83-91, Univ Western Ont, 91-; bd coun fed, Inf Space Univ, 87; mem, Am Bd of Engrs NS. *Mem:* Fel Brit Inst Metall; fel Brit Inst Physics; Can Inst Min Metall; Can Ceramic Soc; Am Ceramic Soc. *Res:* Structure and stability of oxide ceramic phases; effect of phase transformations on superconducting transition magnetic and ferroelectric properties of stainless steels; electronic properties of ceramics. *Mailing Add:* Mat Eng Univ Victoria PO Box 3055 MS 8895 Victoria BC N6A 5B9 Can

KING, IRENA B, NUTRITION, MOLECULAR BIOLOGY. *Current Pos:* Fel nutrit, 85-88, res fel nutrit, 88-92, STAFF SCIENTIST BIOCHEM, FRED HUTCHINSON CANCER RES CTR, 92- *Personal Data:* b Poland, June 22, 48. *Educ:* Univ Wash, BA, 76, MS, 81, PhD(molecular biol), 85. *Mem:* AAAS; Am Inst Nutrit; Am Asn Cancer Res. *Mailing Add:* Fred Hutchinson Cancer Res Ctr 1124 Columbia E601 Seattle WA 98104

KING, IVAN ROBERT, ASTRONOMY. *Current Pos:* from assoc prof to prof, 64-93, EMER PROF ASTRON, UNIV CALIF, BERKELEY, 93- *Personal Data:* b Far Rockaway, NY, June 25, 27; c 4. *Educ:* Hamilton Col, AB, 46; Harvard Univ, AM, 47, PhD(astron), 52. *Prof Exp:* Instr astron, Harvard Univ, 51-52; methods analyst, US Dept of Defense, 54-56; from asst prof to assoc prof, Univ Ill, 56-64. *Mem:* Nat Acad Sci; Am Astron Soc (pres, 78-80); Int Astron Union; Am Acad Arts & Sci. *Res:* Structure of stellar systems. *Mailing Add:* Dept Astron Univ Calif Berkeley CA 94720

KING, JAMES, JR, PHYSICAL CHEMISTRY, PHYSICS. *Current Pos:* mgr space physics, Jet Propulsion Lab, Calif Inst Technol, 79-80, mgr space sci & appln, 81-87, dept asst lab dir, 88-93, ASST LAB DIR, JET PROPULSION LAB, CALIF INST TECHNOL, 93- *Personal Data:* b Columbus, Ga, Apr 23, 33; div; c 2. *Educ:* Morehouse Col, BS, 53; Calif Inst Technol, MS, 55, PhD(chem, physics), 58. *Prof Exp:* Res engr electrochem, Jet Propulsion Lab, Calif Inst Technol, 56; sr res engr thermal properties, Atomics Int Div, NAm Aviation, Inc, 58-60; sr scientist, Electro-Optical Systs, Inc, 60-61; sr scientist, Jet Propulsion Lab, Calif Inst Technol, 61-69, sect mgr physics, 69-74; dir, Space Shuttle Environ Effects, Space Shuttle Prog, NASA, Washington, DC, 74-75 & Upper Atmospheric Sci Prog, 75-76; mgr, User Prog Develop Off, Jet Propulsion Lab, Calif Inst Technol, 76-78. *Mem:* Am Chem Soc; Am Phys Soc; Sigma Xi; AAAS; Am Geophys Union. *Res:* Nuclear and electron resonance; radiation chemistry. *Mailing Add:* 1135 Reunion Pl SW Atlanta GA 30331-6355

KING, JAMES CLAUDE, LOW TEMPERATURE PHYSICS, SOLID STATE PHYSICS. *Current Pos:* RETIRED. *Personal Data:* b St Joseph, Mo, Oct 2, 24; m 49, Martha H Dawson; c Elizabeth, Kathleen, Helen & Robert. *Educ:* Amherst Col, BA, 49; Yale Univ, MS, 50, PhD(physics), 53. *Honors & Awards:* C B Sawyer Award, Sawyer Res Prod, Inc, 73. *Prof Exp:* Instr physics, Yale Univ, 50, asst, 50-53; mem tech staff, Bell Tel Labs, 53-65, mgr thin film & acoust device dept, 62-65; mgr radiation physics dept, Sandia Labs, 65-68, dir appl res, 68-71, dir electrochem components & measurement systs, 71-77, dir weapons elec subsysts, 77-83, dir mats process eng & fabrication, 83-89. *Mem:* Fel Am Phys Soc; Sigma Xi. *Res:* Solid state physics; acoustic wave interactions with lattice defects; effects of radiation on the acoustic properties of alpha-quartz. *Mailing Add:* 7832 Academy Trail NE Albuquerque NM 87185

KING, JAMES DOUGLAS, NUCLEAR PHYSICS. *Current Pos:* asst prof, 65-67, assoc dean & registr, Scarborough Col, 71-74, assoc dean, 75-76, assoc prof, 67-80, PROF PHYSICS, UNIV TORONTO, 80- *Personal Data:* b Welland, Ont, May 28, 34; m 58. *Educ:* Univ Toronto, BA, 56; Univ Sask, PhD(nuclear physics), 60. *Prof Exp:* Fel, McMaster Univ, 60-61; asst prof physics, Univ Sask, 61-64. *Mem:* Am Asn Physics Teachers; Can Asn Physicists; Am Phys Soc; Am Astron Soc. *Res:* Nucleosynthesis; nuclear reactions; stellar reaction rates. *Mailing Add:* Dept Physics Univ Toronto Toronto ON M5S 1A7 Can. *Fax:* 416-978-2537

KING, JAMES EDWARD, PALYNOLOGY. Current Pos: DIR, CARNEGIE MUS, 87- Personal Data: b Escanaba, Mich, July 23, 40; m 73, Fronces Bartos; c Scott. Educ: Alma Col, BS, 62; Univ NMex, MS, 64; Univ Ariz, PhD(geosci), 72. Prof Exp: Res assoc geochronol, Univ Ariz, 71-72; cur paleobot, Ill State Mus, Springfield, 72-78, head sci sect, 78-85, asst dir sci, 85-87. Concurrent Pos: NSF res grants, 72, 74, 76 & 81; adj assoc prof geol, Univ Ill-Urbana, 78-88; res assoc, Hunt Bot Inst, Carnegie-Mellon Univ, Pittsburgh, 88-; adj prof geol, Univ Pittsburgh, 89- Mem: AAAS; Am Quaternary Asn (former treas); Am Asn Stratigraphic Palynologists; Ecol Soc Am; Asn Sci Mus Dirs (pres, 93-); Am Asn Mus. Res: Quaternary palynology, biogeography and paleoenvironments of North America; the ecology and extinction of the Pleistocene megafauna and the interaction of early man to his environments. Mailing Add: Cleveland Natural Hist Mus 1 Wade Oval Dr University Circle Cleveland OH 44106

KING, JAMES FREDERICK, ORGANIC CHEMISTRY. Current Pos: from asst prof to assoc prof, 59-67, PROF CHEM, UNIV WESTERN ONT, 67- Personal Data: b Moncton, NB, Apr 6, 34; m 65, Diane Metcalf; c Sarah, Peter & Thomas. Educ: Univ NB, BSc, 54, PhD(org chem), 57. Honors & Awards: Merck, Sharp & Dohme Lectr Award, 76. Prof Exp: Beaverbrook overseas scholar, Imp Col, London, 57-58; res fel chem, Harvard Univ, 58-59. Concurrent Pos: Alfred P Sloan res fel, 66-68. Mem: Am Chem Soc; Chem Inst Can; Royal Soc Chem. Res: Organic sulfur chemistry; reaction mechanisms; stereochemistry; organic reactions in water. Mailing Add: Dept Chem Univ Western Ont London ON N6A 5B7 Can. Fax: 519-661-3022; E-Mail: scijfk@uwoadmin.uwo.ca

KING, JAMES P, PHYSICAL INORGANIC CHEMISTRY. Current Pos: PROJ LEADER, PENNWALT CHEM CORP, 59- Personal Data: b Kiangsu, China, Nov 11, 33; m 61. Educ: Newberry Col, BS, 53; Loyola Univ, Ill, MS, 56; Purdue Univ, PhD(chem), 60. Concurrent Pos: Pres, Desilube Technol Inc, 89- Mem: Am Chem Soc; Am Soc Lubrication Eng. Res: Lubrication products on high temperature application; Thermochemistry of rhenium compounds; heats of formation of various rhenium compounds determined by solution calorimetry and electrochemical cell measurements; synthesis and characterization of coordination compounds and inorganic polymers. Mailing Add: 904 Breezewood Lane Lansdale PA 19446-5210. Fax: 610-948-0744

KING, JAMES S, NEUROANATOMY. Current Pos: From instr to assoc prof, 65-75, PROF ANAT, OHIO STATE UNIV, 75-, DIR, SPINAL CORD INJURY RES CTR, 77- Personal Data: b Painesville, Ohio, Nov 19, 38; m 61; c 2. Educ: Taylor Univ, BS, 60; Ohio State Univ, MSc, 62, PhD(anat), 65. Concurrent Pos: NIH gen res grant, 65-67; res fel neuroanat & electron micros, Wayne State Univ, 67-68; USPHS grant, 69-81. Mem: Am Asn Anat; Soc Neurosci; Sigma Xi; AAAS. Res: Synaptic organization and development of precerebellar nuclei. Mailing Add: Dept Anat 4072 Graves Hall Ohio State Univ Col Med 333 W Tenth Ave Columbus OH 43210. Fax: 614-292-7659

KING, JANET CARLSON, NUTRITION. Current Pos: fel, Univ Calif, Berkeley, 72, from asst prof to assoc prof, 72-83, chair, Dept Nutrit Sci, 88-94, PROF NUTRIT, UNIV CALIF, BERKELEY, 83-, WESTERN HUMAN NUTRIT RES CTR, 95- Personal Data: b Red Oak, Iowa, Oct 3, 41; m 67, Charles T; c Matthew & Samuel. Educ: Iowa State Univ, BS, 63; Univ Calif, Berkeley, PhD(nutrit), 72. Honors & Awards: Frances Fischer Mem Lectr, 85; Lederle Award Human Nutrit, 89; Agnes Higgins Award, Maternal Nutrit, 93; Int Award Human Nutrit, 96. Prof Exp: Dietitian, Fitzsimons Gen Hosp, Denver, 64-67. Concurrent Pos: Mem, Comt Nutrit Mother & Presch Child, Nat Acad Sci, Nat Res Coun, 74-80, Nutrit Study Sect, NIH, 81-85, Comt Mil Nutrit Res, Nat Acad Sci, Nat Res Coun, 85-90; consult, NIH, 79-80; mem, Comt Nutrit Status During Pregnancy & Lactation, Nat Res Coun, Nat Acad Sci, 88-92, Food & Nutrit Bd, Inst Med-Nat Acad Sci, 91-93; chair, Food & Nutrit Bd, Inst Med, Nat Acad Sci, 94- Mem: Inst Med Nat Acad Sci; Am Dietetic Asn; Sigma Xi; Soc Nutrit Educ; Am Inst Nutrit; AAAS; Am Soc Clin Nutrit. Res: Study of the nutritional requirements for protein, energy; calcium and zinc during pregnancy; zinc metabolism. Mailing Add: USDA western Human Nutrit Res Ctr PO Box 29997 San Francisco CA 94129

KING, JERRY PORTER, MATHEMATICS. Current Pos: Asst prof, Lehigh Univ, 62-68, assoc dean arts & sci, 79-81, dean grad sch, 81-87, PROF MATH, LEHIGH UNIV, 68- Personal Data: b Dyersburg, Tenn, July 9, 35; m 62; c 2. Educ: Univ Ky, BSEE, 58, MS, 59, PhD(math), 62. Mem: Math Asn Am; Am Math Soc. Res: Complex variables, summability. Mailing Add: Math Dept No 14 Lehigh Univ Bethlehem PA 18015

KING, JOE MACK, PHYCOLOGY. Current Pos: DEAN, COL SCI, UNIV NEW ORLEANS, 92- Personal Data: b Conroe, Tex, July 25, 44; m 67; c 1. Educ: Sam Houston State Univ, BS, 67, MA, 68; Univ Tex, Austin, PhD(bot), 71. Prof Exp: Res scientist aquatic ecol, Univ Tex, Austin, 68-70; asst prof biol, Univ Wis, La Crosse, 71-73; res assoc aquatic ecol, Rice Univ, 73-78; from asst prof to prof biol, Murray State Univ, 78-92. Concurrent Pos: Consult, Exxon Corp, Baytown, Tex, 73-74. Mem: Am Soc Limnol & Oceanog; Phycol Soc Am; Int Phycol Soc; Am Inst Biol Sci. Res: Phytoplankton ecology; impact of nutrient enrichment on aquatic ecosystems; aquatic phytotoxicity; algal taxonomy. Mailing Add: Col Sci Univ New Orleans Orleans LA 70148

KING, JOHN, PLANT PHYSIOLOGY. Current Pos: from asst prof to assoc prof, Univ Sask, 67-77, head, 81-87, actg head chem, 88-89, PROF BIOL, UNIV SASK, 77- Personal Data: b Darlington, Eng, Nov 4, 38; m 62, Myrna K Radcliffe; c Kate, Marie & Vicki. Educ: Univ Durham, BSc, 60; Univ Man, MSc, 62, PhD(bot), 66. Prof Exp: Asst prof biol, Bishops Univ, 64-67. Concurrent Pos: Natural Sci & Eng Res Coun Can res grant-in-aid, 64-; fel, Univ Man, 66; vis scientist, Univ Leicester, 73-74, Hawaiian Sugar Planter's Asn, 80-81, Max-Planck Inst, Cologne, 84 & Univ BC, Vancouver, 87-88, Natural Sci & Eng Res Coun Can URF Comt, 86-89, chair, 88-89 & Natural Sci & Eng Res Coun Can Plant Biol GSC, Natural Sci & Eng Res Coun Can, 89-92, chair, 90-91, group chair life sci, 93-96. Mem: Am Soc Plant Physiol; Can Soc Plant Physiol (pres, 83-84); Int Asn Plant Tissue Cult; Can Coun Univ Biol Chmn (pres, 82-83); Int Plant Molecular Biol Asn; Can Fedn Biol Socs Cell Cult. Res: Genetic transformation of plant cells; isolation and use of resistance mutants in cell culture; isolation of arabidopsis metabolic mutants; 1-carbon metabolism in higher plants. Mailing Add: Dept Biol Univ Sask 112 Science Pl Saskatoon SK S7N 5E2 Can. Fax: 306-966-4461; E-Mail: john.king@sask.usask.ca

KING, JOHN A(LBERT), RESEARCH ADMINISTRATION, NEW PRODUCT LICENSING. Current Pos: RETIRED. Personal Data: b Columbus, Ind, Sept 6, 16; m 41; c 4. Educ: Ind Univ, AB, 38; Univ Minn, MS, 40, PhD(org chem), 42. Prof Exp: Asst chem, Ind Univ, 37-38 & Univ Minn, 38-41; Merck fel, 42-43; sr chemist, Winthrop Chem Co Div, Sterling Drug, 43-46; dir chem res, Warner Lambert Pharmaceut Co, NJ, 46-57; dir res & gen mgr res div, Armour & Co, 57-60; mgr res & develop, Agr Div, Am Cyanamid Co, 60-69, assoc dir agr & pharmaceut res, 70-77, dir licensing agr prod, 78-85. Concurrent Pos: Civilian with Off Sci Res & Develop, 44. Mem: AAAS (vpres & chmn chem sect, 59-60); Am Chem Soc; fel Inst Chem; Sigma Xi; Soc Chem Indust. Res: Synthesized pharmacologically active organic compounds; mechanisms of chemical reactions; coordination of chemical research with evaluation of compounds produced; research management; research development and commercialization of pharmaceutical, nutritional and industrial chemical products; licensing of pharmaceutical and agricultural products. Mailing Add: 90 Battle Rd Princeton NJ 08540

KING, JOHN ARTHUR, ZOOLOGY. Current Pos: from assoc prof to prof, 61-86, EMER PROF ZOOL, MICH STATE UNIV, 86- Personal Data: b Detroit, Mich, June 22, 21; m 49, Joan McGinty; c Christopher L & Andrea J. Educ: Univ Mich, AB, 43, MS, 48, PhD, 51. Prof Exp: Asst genetics, Univ Mich, 47-51; USPHS fel, Jackson Mem Lab, 51-53, staff scientist, 53-60; Nat Acad Sci-Nat Res Coun fel, 60-61. Concurrent Pos: Develop res career award, USPHS, 64-70. Mem: Am Soc Mammal; Animal Behav Soc (secy, 62-65, pres, 70). Res: Sociobiology; mammalian behavior; effects of early experience; behavioral evolution. Mailing Add: 4619 Frost Rd Webberville MI 48892

KING, JOHN EDWARD, ANATOMY, HISTOLOGY. Current Pos: RETIRED. Personal Data: b Columbus, Ohio, Nov 16, 39. Educ: Ohio State Univ, BA, 61, PhD(anat), 65. Prof Exp: From instr to assoc prof anat, Ohio State Univ, 65-73, assoc prof physiol optics, Col Optom, 73-91. Concurrent Pos: Asst dean, Ohio State Univ. Mem: AAAS. Res: Hematology. Mailing Add: Col Optom Ohio State Univ 338 W Tenth Ave Columbus OH 43210

KING, JOHN GORDON, ATOMIC PHYSICS. Current Pos: From instr to prof physics, 53-74, FRANCIS L FRIEDMAN PROF PHYSICS, MASS INST TECHNOL, 74- Personal Data: b London, Eng, Aug 13, 25; nat US; m 49; c 8. Educ: Mass Inst Technol, SB, 50, PhD(physics), 53. Hon Degrees: ScD, Univ Hartford, 72. Honors & Awards: Millikan Award, 65; Harbison Award, 71. Mem: Am Phys Soc; Am Asn Physics Teachers. Res: Studies of biological surfaces; molecule microscopy. Mailing Add: Mass Inst Technol 26-457 Cambridge MA 02139

KING, JOHN MCKAIN, VETERINARY PATHOLOGY, WILDLIFE DISEASES. Current Pos: assoc prof, 69-80, PROF VET PATH, NY STATE COL, CORNELL UNIV, 80- Personal Data: b Boston, Mass, Jan 16, 27; m 47; c 1. Educ: Okla Agr & Mech Col, DVM, 55; Cornell Univ, PhD(path), 63. Prof Exp: Instr vet path, Cornell Univ, 59-60; asst prof, Wash State Univ, 60-62; fel path, Mellon Inst, 62-69. Concurrent Pos: USPHS res fel, 60; consult, Animal Med Ctr, NY, 62- Mem: Am Vet Med Asn; Am Col Vet Path; Brit Vet Asn. Res: Veterinary pathology, especially lung and liver diseases; wildlife pathology, both gross and micropathology. Mailing Add: Dept Vet Path NY State Vet Col Cornell Univ Ithaca NY 14853

KING, JOHN MATHEWS, ORGANIC CHEMISTRY. Current Pos: sr res assoc, 67-79, mgr, Lubricating Oil Additives Div, 79-82, MGR, COM ADDITIVE PROCESS DIV, CHEVRON RES CO, STAND OIL CO CALIF, 82- Personal Data: b New York, NY, Oct 25, 39; m 62; c 2. Educ: Cornell Univ, AB, 61; Univ Mich, MS, 63, PhD, 65. Prof Exp: NSF fel, Calif Inst Technol, 65-66, univ fel, 66-67. Mem: Am Chem Soc. Res: Synthesis of organic peroxides; organic photochemistry; radiation chemistry of organic compounds; lube oil additives; organic process development. Mailing Add: 1194 Idylberry Rd San Rafael CA 94903-1128

KING, JOHN PAUL, SOLID STATE PHYSICS. Current Pos: from asst prof to assoc prof, 68-77, PROF PHYSICS, CENT STATE UNIV, OKLA, 77- Personal Data: b Zena, Okla, Nov 23, 38; m 61; c 3. Educ: Cent State Col, Okla, BS, 61; Okla State Univ, PhD(solid state physics), 66. Prof Exp: Eng sci specialist, Missiles & Space Div, LTV Aerospace Corp, 66-68. Mem: Am Phys Soc; Sigma Xi. Res: Study of basic optics problems associated with imaging and interference. Mailing Add: 3420 Baird Dr Edmond OK 73013-6327

KING, JOHN STUART, GEOLOGY. *Current Pos:* from asst prof to assoc prof, 63-77, from actg chmn dept to chmn dept, 66-71, PROF GEOL, STATE UNIV NY, BUFFALO, 77-, ASSOC DEAN FAC NATURAL SCI & MATH, 90- *Personal Data:* b Buffalo, NY, Nov 12, 27. *Educ:* Univ Buffalo, BA, 55, MA, 57; Univ Wyo, PhD(geol), 63. *Prof Exp:* Res engr petrog, Res Div, Carborundum Co, 57-60. *Concurrent Pos:* Consult electro minerals div, Carborundum Co, 64-66. *Mem:* Fel Geol Soc Am; Am Asn Petrol Geologists. *Res:* Igneous and metamorphic petrology and structures; structural geology; field interpretations; planetology and analog studies. *Mailing Add:* Dept Geol State Univ NY PO Box 600001 Buffalo NY 14260-0001

KING, JOHN SWINTON, PHYSICS. *Current Pos:* assoc prof, 59-62, PROF NUCLEAR ENG, UNIV MICH, ANN ARBOR, 62-, CHMN DEPT, 74- *Personal Data:* b Detroit, Mich, Oct 31, 20; m 43; c 3. *Educ:* Univ Mich, PhD(nuclear physics). *Prof Exp:* Asst, Appl Physics Lab, Johns Hopkins Univ, 42-45; res assoc reactor physics, Knolls Atomic Power Lab, Gen Elec Co, 53-56, mgr submarine adv reactor physics sub-sect, 56-59. *Mem:* Am Nuclear Soc; Am Phys Soc. *Res:* Neutron physics as applied to reactor design and neutron optics. *Mailing Add:* 2311 Vinewood Ann Arbor MI 48104

KING, JOHN WILLIAM, AGRONOMY, CROP SCIENCE. *Current Pos:* ASSOC PROF AGRON, UNIV ARK, FAYETTEVILLE, 70- *Personal Data:* b Butler, Ind, Mar 31, 38; div; c 3. *Educ:* Purdue Univ, BS, 63; Univ RI, MS, 66; Mich State Univ, PhD(crop sci), 70. *Prof Exp:* Machinist, Gen Elec Co, Ind, 56-60. *Mem:* Am Soc Agron; Crop Sci Soc Am; Weed Sci Soc Am. *Res:* Turf grass soils fertilization, species and variety adaptation, cultural systems, weed control, irrigation management; shade and allelopathy. *Mailing Add:* Dept Agron Univ Ark Fayetteville AR 72701

KING, JONATHAN (ALAN), MOLECULAR BIOLOGY, BIOCHEMISTRY. *Current Pos:* from asst prof to assoc prof, 70-78, PROF MOLECULAR BIOL, MASS INST TECHNOL, 78-, DIR BIOL ELECTRON MICROSCOPE FACIL, 70- *Personal Data:* b Brooklyn, NY, Aug 20, 41; m 76; c 2. *Educ:* Yale Univ, BS, 62; Calif Inst Technol, PhD(genetics), 67. *Honors & Awards:* US Antarctic Serv Medal. *Prof Exp:* Assoc scientist microbial ecol, Jet Propulsion Lab, Calif Inst Technol, 67-68; fel molecular biol, Purdue Univ, 68-69; fel struct biol, Lab Molecular Biol, Brit Med Res Coun, 69-70. *Concurrent Pos:* Childs Mem Fund Med Res res fel, 68-70; Guggenheim fel, 87; counr, Am Soc Virol; chmn, Microbiol Physiol Study Sect & Genetic Based Dis Study Sect, NIH. *Mem:* Genetics Soc Am; Am Soc Microbiol; Biophys Soc; fel AAAS; Am Soc Virol; Am Soc Biochem & Molecular Biol. *Res:* Genetic control of morphogenesis; virus assembly; protein folding. *Mailing Add:* Dept Biol Bldg 68330 Mass Inst Technol 77 Massachusetts Ave Cambridge MA 02139-4307. *Fax:* 617-252-1843

KING, JONATHAN STANTON, CLINICAL CHEMISTRY. *Current Pos:* RETIRED. *Personal Data:* b Bristol, Tenn, Oct 30, 22; m 51, Betty Boyd; c Melissa & Robert. *Educ:* Univ Chicago, BS, 47; Univ Tenn, PhD(biochem), 54. *Honors & Awards:* Spec Area Award, Am Asn Clin Chem, 81, Miriam Reiner Award, 83 & Bernard F Gerulat Award, 86. *Prof Exp:* Control chemist, S E Massengill Co, 47; res chemist, 48-51, res biochemist, 54-56; res assoc, Bowman Gray Sch Med, Wake Forest Univ, 56-59, instr biochem & Whitney fel, 59-62, res asst prof, 62-65, res assoc prof, 65-70; exec dir, Am Asn Clin Chem, 71-73, exec ed, Clin Chem, 69-90. *Concurrent Pos:* NIH res career develop award, 65-70; guest investr, Rockefeller Univ, 68-69; emer ed, Clin Chem, 90. *Mem:* Am Asn Clin Chem. *Res:* Salicylate effect on pituitary-adrenal axis; function of adrenal ascorbic acid; enzyme adsorption by microcryst sulfas; colorimetric alkaloid estimation; metabolism of trimethylchromone; biochemistry of renal calculi; urinary macromolecular constituents; factors affecting calcium excretion; ninhydrin-positive substances in urine; taurine excretion in mongolism. *Mailing Add:* 2370 Lyndhurst Ave Winston-Salem NC 27103

KING, JOSEPH HERBERT, SPACE PHYSICS. *Current Pos:* Nat Acad Sci assoc fel, 67-69, HEAD, NAT SPACE SCI DATA CTR, NASA, 69- *Personal Data:* b Malden, Mass, Nov 16, 39; m 65; c 2. *Educ:* Boston Col, PhD(physics), 66. *Prof Exp:* Lectr physics, Regis Col, Mass, 63-64; staff scientist, Aerospace Corp, 65-67. *Concurrent Pos:* Proj scientist, Interplanetary Monitoring Platform Satellite, NASA, 74- *Mem:* Am Geophys Union. *Res:* Spacecraft plasma and field data concerning the mass and energy coupling between the solar wind and the earth's magnetosphere. *Mailing Add:* Code 633 NASA Goddard Space Flight Ctr Greenbelt MD 20771

KING, KATHERINE CHUNG-HO, PEDIATRICS, NEONATOLOGY. *Current Pos:* NEONATOLOGIST, SCHNEIDER CHILDREN'S HOSP, LONG ISLAND JEWISH HOSP, 85-; ASSOC PROF PEDIAT, ALBERT EINSTEIN SCH MED, 89- *Personal Data:* b Peiping, China, Aug 27, 37; US citizen; m 85, Louis H Li. *Educ:* Meredith Col, AB, 57; Bowman Gray Sch Med, MD, 62; Am Bd Pediat, dipl, 68, dipl, Neonatal & Perinatal Med, 77. *Prof Exp:* From intern pediat to resident pediat metab, Cleveland Metrop Gen Hosp, 62-66, actg dir, Newborn Serv, 74-75; from asst prof to assoc prof pediat, Sch Med, Case Western Res Univ, 71-85, assoc prof neonatology, Dept Reproductive Biol, 78-85; asst pediatrician, Cleveland Metrop Gen Hosp & co-dir, Perinatal Clin Res Ctr, 69-85, dir, Newborn Serv, 81-84; assoc prof pediat, State Univ NY, Stony Brook, 85-89. *Concurrent Pos:* USPHS trainee, 66-68; Cleveland Diabetes Found grant, Cleveland Metrop Gen Hosp, 69-70; sr instr, Case Western Reserve Univ, 69-71. *Mem:* Am Fedn Clin Res; Am Acad Pediat; fel Am Col Nutrit; Soc Pediat Res. *Res:* Carbohydrate metabolism of human fetus and neonatal; metabolism. *Mailing Add:* Long Island Jewish-Hillside Med Ctr Schneider Children's Hosp New Hyde Park NY 11042. *Fax:* 718-347-3850

KING, KENNETH, JR, BIOGEOCHEMISTRY. *Current Pos:* RES ASSOC BIOGEOCHEM, LAMONT-DOHERTY GEOL OBSERV, COLUMBIA UNIV, 72- *Personal Data:* b Philadelphia, Pa, Dec 27, 30; m 61; c 2. *Educ:* Mass Inst Technol, SB, 52, SM, 60; Columbia Univ, PhD(geol), 72. *Prof Exp:* Indust res & develop, Merck & Co, 55-64, dir res planning, 65-67; res asst, Columbia Univ, 67-72. *Concurrent Pos:* Fel, Carnegie Inst Wash, 72-74. *Mem:* Sigma Xi; AAAS; Am Chem Soc; Geol Soc Am; Geochem Soc. *Res:* Proteins of modern and fossil mineralized tissues; amino acid racemization; mechanism of biomineralization. *Mailing Add:* 275 Jones Rd Falmouth MA 02540-3338

KING, L D PERCIVAL, PHYSICS, MECHANICAL ENGINEERING. *Current Pos:* RETIRED. *Personal Data:* b Williamstown, Mass, Dec 29, 06; m 36, 70, 75, 79; c Nicholas S & Lidian. *Educ:* Univ Rochester, BS, 30; Univ Wis, PhD(exp nuclear physics), 37. *Prof Exp:* Asst physics, Univ Rochester, 30-31 & Mass Inst Technol, 31-33; asst, Univ Wis, 35-37; instr, Purdue Univ, 37-42, fel, Off Sci Res & Develop contract, 42-43; group leader, Manhattan Dist & AEC Projs, Los Alamos Sci Lab, 43-57; tech dir, US Atoms for Peace Conf, Atomic Energy Comn, Geneva, 57-58; asst div leader, Reactor Div, Los Alamos Sci Lab, 59, chmn, Rover Flight Safety Off, 60-69, res adv, 69-73; consult, 73-78. *Mem:* Fel AAAS; fel Am Phys Soc; fel Am Nuclear Soc. *Res:* Nuclear physics; artificial radioactivity; nuclear structure; design and construction of homogenous and fast nuclear research and test reactors; solution to flight safety problems in nuclear rocket reactors. *Mailing Add:* Rte 4 Box 16-B Santa Fe NM 87501

KING, L(EE) ELLIS, TRANSPORTATION ENGINEERING, ERGONOMICS. *Current Pos:* chmn & prof, 76-95, PROF DEPT CIVIL ENG, UNIV NC, CHARLOTTE, 95- *Personal Data:* b Jamestown, NC, Aug 21, 39; m 60, Rachel Garrett. *Educ:* NC State Univ, BS, 61; Univ Calif, Berkeley, DrEng, 67. *Honors & Awards:* Walter L Huber Civil Engr Res Prize, Am Soc Civil Engrs, 73. *Prof Exp:* From asst prof to assoc prof, WVa Univ, 67-73; assoc prof, Univ Colo, Denver Ctr, 73-75; prof, Wayne State Univ, 75-76. *Concurrent Pos:* Consult, various pvt & pub agencies. *Mem:* Am Soc Civil Engrs; Transp Res Bd; Am Soc Eng Educ; Human Factors & Ergonomics Soc; Nat Soc Prof Engrs; Inst Transp Engrs. *Res:* Traffic engineering problems; transportation planning; driver, vehicle and roadway interaction; driver behavior; reduced visibility performance; roadway lighting; roadway signing and marking; pedestrian behavior; traffic signals. *Mailing Add:* Dept Civil Eng Univ NC Charlotte NC 28223

KING, LAFAYETTE CARROLL, ORGANIC CHEMISTRY. *Current Pos:* res assoc, 42, from instr to prof chem, 42-85, EMER PROF CHEM, NORTHWESTERN UNIV, 85- *Personal Data:* b Marysvale, Utah, Sept 9, 14; m 37; c 5. *Educ:* Utah State Col, BS, 36; Mich State Col, MS, 38, PhD(chem), 42. *Honors & Awards:* Chem Educ Award, Am Chem Soc, 69. *Prof Exp:* Asst biol chem, Mich State Col, 36-42. *Concurrent Pos:* Indust consult, Food Chem, 50-; US-Japan Conf Chem Educ, Japan, 64; Berkeley, 68 & First Int Am Conf Chem Educ, Buenos Aires, 65; chmn adv coun col chem, 66-; chmn org comt, Indo-US Binat Conf Chem Educ, 69. *Mem:* Fel AAAS; Am Chem Soc; Oil Chem Soc; Royal Soc Chem. *Res:* Synthesis of quaternary salts, thiazoles and selenazoles; structures of sterols; mechanism of organic reactions. *Mailing Add:* Dept Chem Northwestern Univ Evanston IL 60201

KING, LARRY DEAN, SOIL SCIENCE. *Current Pos:* from asst prof to assoc prof, 74-88, PROF SOIL SCI, NC STATE UNIV, 88- *Personal Data:* b Atlanta, Ga, Mar 10, 39; div; c 2. *Educ:* Ga Inst Technol, BS, 62; Univ Ga, MS, 68, PhD(agron), 71. *Prof Exp:* Aircraft engr comput prog, Lockheed Aircraft, 62-65; fel soil sci, Univ Guelph, Ont, 71-72; agronomist agr develop, Tenn Valley Authority, 73-74. *Mem:* Am Soc Agron. *Res:* Alternative agricultural systems; land application of municipal and industrial wastes. *Mailing Add:* Dept Soil Sci NC State Univ Box 7619 Raleigh NC 27695-0001

KING, LARRY GENE, IRRIGATION & DRAINAGE ENGINEERING, GROUNDWATER HYDROLOGY. *Current Pos:* chmn, Agr Eng Dept, 79-87, PROF, BIOL SYSTS ENG DEPT, WASH STATE UNIV, 87- *Personal Data:* b Prosser, Wash, June 24, 36; m 56, Shirley Ruth Cobb; c Steven J, James P, Jani L (Rima) & Robert J. *Educ:* Wash State Univ, BS, 58; Colo State Univ, MS, 61, PhD(civil eng), 65. *Prof Exp:* Asst civil eng, Colo State Univ, 58-62, jr agr engr, 62; res engr hydrol, Gen Elec Co, 62-65; res scientist, Pac NW Labs, Battelle Mem Inst, 65, sr res engr, 65-68, res assoc, 68-69; assoc prof agr & irrig eng, Utah State Univ, 69-74. *Concurrent Pos:* Consult, Orchards Unlimited, 62-65; City Washington Terr, 73-75; Ken Earl, atty, 76, Paine, Hamblin, Coffin, Brooke & Miller, attys, 77, McCrosky Terr Trailer Park, 79, Wash State Dept Ecol, 75-81, USAID, 84, 86-90, Kenniwick Irrigation Dist, 84-86, Wash State Dept Transp, 87, Velikanje, Moore & Shore Inc, attys, 89-92, Culp, Guterson & Grader, attys, 93, Backman, Blumel & Reed, attys, 91-92, Gary J Libey, atty, 93-94, Westinghouse-Hanford Co, 94-95 & Off Atty Gen Wash, 95-96; mem, US Nat Comt, Int Comn Irrigation & Drainage. *Mem:* Am Soc Civil Engrs; Am Soc Agr Engrs. *Res:* Irrigation; drainage; water quality; salinity control; hydrology; groundwater hydrology; soil and water use and conservation; soil water movement; erosion control; wells; on-farm water management; irrigation system management; computer modeling. *Mailing Add:* Dept Biol Syst Eng Wash State Univ Pullman WA 99164-1620. *Fax:* 509-335-2722; *E-Mail:* king@wsu.edu

KING, LARRY MICHAEL, MATHEMATICS. *Current Pos:* asst prof, 74-79, ASSOC PROF MATH, UNIV MICH, FLINT, 79-, ASSOC DEAN, COL ARTS & SCI, 82- *Personal Data:* b Brooklyn, NY, Nov 29, 42; m 68. *Educ:* Brooklyn Col, BS, 63; Univ Md, College Park, MA, 66, PhD(math), 68. *Prof Exp:* Asst prof math, Univ Mass, Amherst, 68-74. *Mem:* Am Math Soc; Math

Asn Am. *Res:* Slices in transformation groups; topological dynamics and dynamical systems; R-isomorphisms of transformation groups; actions of non-compact semigroups; new ways of teaching calculus. *Mailing Add:* Dept Math Univ Mich Flint MI 48502-2186

KING, LEE CURTIS, FIBERGLASS COATINGS, TEST DEVELOPMENT. *Current Pos:* RES CHEMIST, CLARK-SCHWEBEL FIBER GLASS, 84- *Personal Data:* b Greenville, SC, Oct 20, 54. *Educ:* Univ SC, BS, 76, MEd, 80. *Prof Exp:* Technician, Cardinal Chem Co, 76-78; teacher math, chem & phys, Midlands Tech Col, 78-80; teacher chem, phys sci, Anderson Col, 80-82; teacher chem, phys sci & math, N Greenville Col, 82-83; instr chem, math, phys & astron, Tri Co Tech Col, 83-84. *Concurrent Pos:* Salesperson, Am Indust, Lumberton, NC, 83, Real Estate Assoc, Anderson, SC, 83- *Mem:* Am Soc Mat. *Res:* Development, evaluation, fiberglass coatings based on customer needs (market or applied orientation); polymer properties and processing characteristics; test development from size preparation to end product in many fields. *Mailing Add:* 2207 W North Ave Anderson SC 29621

KING, LEWIS H, MARINE GEOLOGY. *Current Pos:* GEOLOGIST, BEDFORD INST, DEPT ENERGY, MINES & RESOURCES. 63- *Personal Data:* b Lockeport, NS, Nov 10, 24; m 55; c 6. *Educ:* Acadia Univ, BSc, 49; Mass Inst Technol, PhD(geol), 55. *Prof Exp:* Geologist, Geol Surv Can, NS, 54-56; geochemist, Mines Br. Dept Mines & Tech Surv, Ont, 56-63. *Concurrent Pos:* Mem fac, Dalhousie Univ, 68- *Mem:* AAAS; fel Geol Soc Am; fel Geol Asn Can; Sigma Xi. *Res:* Geological mapping of the sea floor across the Scotian Shelf, eastern Gulf of Maine and the Grand Banks. *Mailing Add:* 50 Swanton Dr Dartmouth NS B2W 2C5 Can

KING, LLOYD ELIJAH, JR, DERMATOLOGY, ANATOMY. *Current Pos:* PROF MED & CHIEF DERMAT, VANDERBILT UNIV, 77- *Personal Data:* b Mayfield, Ky, Sept 10, 39; m 68; c 3. *Educ:* Vanderbilt Univ, BA, 61; Univ Tenn, Memphis, MD, 67, PhD(anat), 70. *Prof Exp:* Intern med, City of Memphis Hosps, 69-70; instr anat, Med Units, Univ Tenn, Memphis, 70-74, instr med, 73-76, asst prof dermat, 75-77. *Concurrent Pos:* NIH fel anat, Med Units, Univ Tenn, Memphis, 68-69; Vet Admin trainee dermat, Vet Admin Hosp, Memphis, 72-74, Vet Admin res & educ associateship, 75-; NIH spec fel, St Jude Children's Res Hosp, 74-76; resident internal med, City of Memphis Hosps, 70-71, resident dermat, 71-74; clin investr, Vet Admin Hosp, Nashville, Tenn, 77-80. *Mem:* AAAS; Am Acad Dermat; fel Am Col Physicians; Am Fedn Clin Res; AMA. *Res:* Skin diseases; cell membranes; growth factors; spider venom/bites. *Mailing Add:* Dermat Sect 1211 21st Ave S 620 Med Arts Bldg Nashville TN 37212

KING, LOWELL ALVIN, PHYSICAL PROPERTIES, ADA COMPUTER LANGUAGE. *Current Pos:* DISTINGUISHED VIS PROF, USAF ACAD, 96- *Personal Data:* b Spencer, Iowa, June 16, 32; m 54, Mary James; c 3. *Educ:* Iowa State Univ, BS, 53, PhD(inorg chem), 63; Wash Univ, AM, 55. *Honors & Awards:* Air Force Res & Develop Award, 70; Sci Eng Award, Air Force Asn, 71. *Prof Exp:* Group leader, Mat Lab, USAF, 56-59, instr chem, USAF Acad, 59-61, res assoc, Ames Lab, Iowa State Univ, 61-63, asst prof chem, USAF Acad, 63, assoc prof, 63-64, res assoc, F J Seiler Lab, Off Aerospace Res, 64-65, assoc prof chem, 65-71, prof chem, USAF Acad, 71-80, consult, F J Seiler Lab, Air Force Systs Command, USAF, 81-83; prof comput sci, Colo Tech Col, 83-96. *Concurrent Pos:* Dir, Chem Div, F J Seiler Lab, Off Aerospace Res, 66-68, dir, Chem Div, F J Seiler Lab, Air Force Systs Command, 74-75, sr scientist, 75-80; prof phys sci, Europ Christian Univ, Vienna, Austria, 81-86; lectr comput sci, Europ Div, Univ Md, 84-86. *Res:* Electrochemistry; molten salt chemistry; measurement of physical and electrochemical properties of molten salt mixtures containing complex halo-anions. *Mailing Add:* 3945 Hill Circle Colorado Springs CO 80904

KING, LOWELL RESTELL, UROLOGY, PEDIATRIC UROLOGY. *Current Pos:* chmn, Div Urol, 70-77, SURGEON-IN-CHIEF, CHILDREN'S MEM HOSP, 74-; PROF UROL, DUKE UNIV, 81-, HEAD, SECT PEDIAT UROL, 81- *Personal Data:* b Salem, Ohio, Feb 28, 32; div; c 2. *Educ:* Johns Hopkins Univ, BA, 52, MD, 56. *Honors & Awards:* Medal Urol Sect, Am Acad Pediat; Cancer Achievement Award, Am Urol Asn, 96. *Prof Exp:* Intern, Johns Hopkins Hosp, 56-57, resident, 57-61; asst prof urol, Med Sch, Johns Hopkins Univ, 63, from asst prof to assoc prof, Northwestern Univ, 63-68; prof, Univ Ill, 68-70; prof urol, Northwestern Univ, 70-81. *Concurrent Pos:* Am Cancer Soc fel, 58-59; chmn, Dept Urol, Presby-St Luke's Hosp, 68-70; mem, Am Bd Urol, 75-81, Emer trustee. *Mem:* Am Urol Asn; fel Am Acad Pediat; fel Am Col Surgeons; Soc Pediat Urol; Am Asn Genito-Urinary Surgeons; Clin Soc Genito Urinary Surgeons. *Res:* Pediatric urology; investigate causes/treatment of fetal/cogenital urinary obstruction; new types of treatment for high impalpable testis; new methods of continant urinary diversion. *Mailing Add:* Med Ctr Duke Univ PO Box 3831 Durham NC 27710. *Fax:* 919-684-4611

KING, LUCY JANE, PSYCHIATRY, ADDICTION PSYCHIATRY. *Current Pos:* PVT PRACT PSYCHIAT, ST VINCENT HOSP, INDIANAPOLIS, IND, 91-; ASSOC CLIN PROF PSYCHIAT, MED SCH, IND UNIV, 92- *Personal Data:* b Vandalia, Ill, Dec, 23, 32. *Educ:* Washington Univ, AB, 54, MD, 58; Am Bd Psychiat & Neurol, dipl psychiat, 66. *Prof Exp:* Intern, Butterworth Hosp, Grand Rapids, Mich, 58-59; asst resident psychiat, Renard Hosp, St Louis, Mo, 59-62, chief resident, 62-63; from instr to assoc prof, Sch Med, Washington Univ, 70-74; prof psychiat & pharmacol, Med Col Va, Va Commonwealth Univ, 74-79; med officer, Food & Drug Admin, 80-81; pvt pract psychiat, Prince William Hosp, Manassas, Va, 82-91. *Concurrent Pos:* NIMH res career develop awards neuropharmacol, 63-73. *Mem:* Fel Am Psychiat Asn; Sigma Xi; Am Soc Addiction Med; Am Acad Clin Psychiatrists; Am Acad Psychiatrist Alcoholism & Addiction. *Res:* Clinical and social psychiatry; neuropharmacology. *Mailing Add:* Midtown Comm Mental Health Ctr 1001 W 10th St Indianapolis IN 46202

KING, LUNSFORD RICHARDSON, mathematics, for more information see previous edition

KING, MALCOLM, MEDICINE, LUNG DISEASE. *Current Pos:* assoc prof, 85-90, PROF, DIV PULMONARY MED, UNIV ALTA, EDMONTON, 90-, CO-DIR, PULMONARY & CELL BIOL RES GROUP, 85- *Personal Data:* b Jan 24, 47. *Educ:* McMaster Univ, BSc, 68; McGill Univ, PhD(polymer chem), 73. *Prof Exp:* Fel, Weizmann Inst; centennial fel, Meakins-Christie Labs, McGill Univ, 74-78, asst prof, 79-85. *Concurrent Pos:* Guest prof, Robert Koch Clin, 86-87, Univ Freiburg, Ger, 91-92, Lab Atmospheric Pollution, Univ Sao Paulo, Brazil, 94, Dept Anat, Univ Bern, Switz; prin investr, Med Res Coun, Can Cystic Fibrosis Found, Alta Lung Asn, Galephar SA, Glaxo Inc. *Mem:* Chem Inst Can; Can Soc Clin Invest; Can Thoracic Soc; Am Physiol Soc; Am Thoracic Soc; Am Col Chest Physicians. *Res:* Epithelial defense mechanisms relating to lung disease involving mucociliary dysfunction; author of 36 publications. *Mailing Add:* Dept Med Univ Alta 173 Heritage Med Res Ctr Edmonton AB T6G 2S2 Can

KING, MARVIN, OPTICAL SYSTEMS, ELECTRONIC SYSTEMS. *Current Pos:* sr res engr, Riverside Res Inst, 67-68, asst head electrooptics lab, 68-69, mgr optics lab, 69-76, res dir, 77-81, exec dir prog develop, 81-82, vpres res, 82-88, exec vpres, 88-90, PRES, RIVERSIDE RES INST, 90- *Personal Data:* b New York, NY, Apr 23, 40; m 61, Carole Breindel; c Sarah M. *Educ:* City Col NY, BEE, 61; Polytech Inst Brooklyn, MSEE, 63; Columbia Univ, EngScD, 66. *Prof Exp:* Jr elec engr, ITT Fed Labs, 62-63, electrophysicist, 63-64; res asst, Electronics Res Labs, Columbia, 64-66, res engr, 66-67. *Concurrent Pos:* Consult, US Army Electronics Command, Ft Monmouth, NJ, 67-68, Adv Optics Ctr, Radiation, Inc, Mich, 69 & spec study sect on optics, NIH, 70; lectr, Columbia Univ Sci Honors Prog, 66-73; adj assoc prof, City Col NY 72-74. *Mem:* Inst Elec & Electronics Engrs; Optical Soc Am; Am Inst Physics; Quantum Electronics Soc. *Res:* Signal processing for radar and communications systems utilizing holography, photographic film, photonics and ultrasonics; atmospheric optics; optical oceanography; infrared holography; laser radar; laser signatures; infrared acquisition and tracking systems; image processing. *Mailing Add:* Riverside Res Inst 330 W 42nd St New York NY 10036. *Fax:* 212-502-1729; *E-Mail:* king@rringc.org

KING, MARY MARGARET, DRUG METABOLISM, NUTRITION. *Current Pos:* OWNER/PRES, ACRE VIEW PET HOSP, INC, 93- *Personal Data:* b Oklahoma City, Okla, May 26, 46. *Educ:* Cent State Univ, BS, 69; Univ Okla, PhD(med physiol & biophys), 75; Okla City Univ, MBA, 84; Okla State Univ, DVM, 93. *Honors & Awards:* Young Investr Award, NIH. *Prof Exp:* Instr physiol, Cent State Univ, 69; instr, Okla City Pub Schs, 69-71; fel, Okla Med Res Found, 75-76, res assoc biomembrane res, 76-77, staff scientist, 77-80; res asst prof biochem & molecular biol, Univ Okla Health Sci Ctr, 81-88, dir, Lab Animal Resources Ctr, 82-90, Sci Support Serv, 82-90, adj assoc prof biochem & molecular biol, 88-93, spec asst to pres, 90-93. *Concurrent Pos:* Young Investr Award, NIH/Nat Inst Environ Health Sci, 78-81; consult, Nat Cancer Inst, NIH, 83-, Grad Fac, Univ Okla, Health Sci Ctr, 83-; assoc mem, Okla Med Res Found, 86-93. *Mem:* NY Acad Sci; Am Asn Cancer Res; Am Inst Nutrit; Sigma Xi; Soc Exp Biol Med; Am Vet Med Asn. *Res:* Chemical carcinogens and dietary fat-antioxidant interactions as relates to mammary cancer; carcinogenesis; chemical carcinogens; dietary parameters; hormonal interactions in mammary gland, especially relating to the drug metabolizing system. *Mailing Add:* Acre View Pet Hosp Inc 1900 S Bryant Ave Edmond OK 73013. *Fax:* 405-271-3980

KING, MARY-CLAIRE, EPIDEMIOLOGY, HUMAN GENETICS. *Current Pos:* AM CANCER SOC RES PROF, DEPT MED & GENETICS, UNIV WASH, 95- *Personal Data:* b Evanston, Ill, Feb 27, 46; m 73; c 1. *Educ:* Carleton Col, BA, 66; Univ Calif, Berkeley, PhD(genetics), 73. *Honors & Awards:* Clowes Award Basic Res, Am Asn Cancer Res. *Prof Exp:* Asst prof, Univ Calif, Berkeley, 76-80, assoc prof epidemiol, 80-95. *Concurrent Pos:* Vis prof, Univ Chile, Santiago, 73; asst prof genetics, Univ Calif, San Francisco, 74-80, assoc prof epidemiol, 80-; prin investr, genetic epidemiol of breast cancer in families, NIH grant, 79- *Mem:* Inst Med-Nat Acad Sci; Soc Epidemiol Res; Am Epidemiol Soc; Sigma Xi; fel AAAS. *Res:* Genetics and epidemiology of breast cancer and other common chronic diseases, pedigree analysis, human and primate molecular evolution. *Mailing Add:* Div Med Genetics Univ Wash Seattle WA 98195-7720

KING, MERRILL KENNETH, combustion science, for more information see previous edition

KING, MICHAEL DUMONT, ATMOSPHERIC RADIATION, REMOTE SENSING. *Current Pos:* atmospheric scientist, 78-92, EARTH OBSERVING SYST SR PROJ SCIENTIST, GODDARD SPACE FLIGHT CTR, NASA, 92- *Personal Data:* b Kansas City, Mo, Oct 20, 49; m 72, Diana Goerner; c Jason & Hailey. *Educ:* Colo Col, BA, 71; Univ Ariz, MS, 73, PhD(atmospheric sci), 77. *Hon Degrees:* D Sc, Colo Col, 95. *Honors & Awards:* NASA Except Serv Medal, NASA Except Sci Achievement Medal. *Prof Exp:* Res asst, Univ Ariz, 71-77. *Concurrent Pos:* Prin investr, Earth Radiation Budget Exp Sci Team, 80-, proj scientist, 83-92; chmn, Comt Atmospheric Radiation, Am Meteorol Soc, 86-88; vis prof, Dept Atmospheric Sci, Univ Wash, 86-87; assoc ed, J Atmospheric Sci, 91-93; prin investr, Moderate Resolution Imaging Spectroradiometer Sci Team, 89-; mem, Clouds & Earth's Radiant Energy Syst Sci Team, 89-; adj prof atmospheric sci, Dept Oceanog, Dalhousie Univ, Halifax, NS, Can, 92-; scientist, Earth Radiation Budget Exp Proj, Goddard Space Flight Ctr, NASA, 83-92. *Mem:* Fel Am Meteorol Soc; Am Geophys Union. *Res:* Multiple light scattering and radiative transfer in cloud free and cloudy atmospheres; application of inversion methods to determination of aerosol size distributions; effect of clouds and aerosols on earth's radiation budget; determination of the optical thickness, particle radius and single scattering albedo of clouds from airborne and spaceborne measurements of scattered radiation. *Mailing Add:* 14613 Peach Orchard Rd Silver Spring MD 20905-4437. *E-Mail:* king@climate.gsfc.nasa.gov

KING, MICHAEL M, ORGANIC CHEMISTRY, ORGANIC SYNTHESIS. *Current Pos:* from asst prof to assoc prof, 73-84, PROF CHEM, GEORGE WASHINGTON UNIV, 84- *Personal Data:* b Chicago, Ill, May 10, 44; m 70, Linda; c Jacob. *Educ:* Ill Inst Technol, BS, 66; Harvard Univ, AM, 67, PhD(org chem), 70. *Prof Exp:* Asst prof chem, NY Univ, 70-73. *Mem:* Am Chem Soc. *Res:* Heterocycles, enzyme model systems, imidazoles and pyrroles, organofluorides. *Mailing Add:* Dept Chem George Washington Univ Washington DC 20052. *Fax:* 202-994-5873; *E-Mail:* kingm@gwis2.circ.gwu.edu

KING, MICHAEL STUART, GEOLOGICAL ENGINEERING, APPLIED GEOPHYSICS. *Current Pos:* MEM STAFF, DEPT ENG TECHNOL, CABOT INST ARTS & TECHNOL. *Personal Data:* b Brackley, Eng, June 2, 31; m 62; c 3. *Educ:* Univ Glasgow, BSc, 53; Univ Calif, Berkeley, MS, 61, PhD(eng sci), 64. *Prof Exp:* Design engr, John Brown & Co, Scotland, 52-54; field engr, Iraq Petrol Co, Kirkuk, 54-59; teaching asst mineral technol, Univ Calif, Berkeley, 59-64, lectr, 64-65; sr sci officer, Geotech Div, Ministry of Technol, Eng, 65-66; prof geol sci, Univ Sask, 66-81; staff scientist, Dept Mech Eng, Univ Calif, Berkeley, 81- *Concurrent Pos:* Mem Can Nat Comt Rock Mech. *Mem:* Assoc mem Am Geophys Union; Soc Explor Geophys; Am Inst Mining, Metall & Petrol Engrs; Brit Inst Mech Engrs; Can Inst Mining & Metall. *Res:* Geological sciences; application of ultrasonics in geology; rock mechanics; fluid flow in porous media. *Mailing Add:* Dept Eng Technol Cabot Inst Arts & Technol PO Box 1693 St John's NF A1C 5P7 Can

KING, NICHOLAS S P, NUCLEAR STRUCTURE. *Current Pos:* staff physicist, 78-80, assoc group leader, 81-84, GROUP LEADER, LOS ALAMOS NAT LAB, 84- *Personal Data:* b Lafayette, Ind, Dec 3, 40; m 66; c 2. *Educ:* Dartmouth Col, BA, 62; Univ NMex, MS, 64; Univ Colo, PhD(physics), 70. *Prof Exp:* Res physicist, Univ Calif, Davis, 71-77. *Mem:* Am Phys Soc; Inst Elec & Electronics Engrs; Soc Photo-Optical Instrumentation Engrs. *Res:* Investigation of the reaction mechanisms of nuclear particles with nuclei and the resultant excitation modes of the nucleus; determination of plasma properties via measurements of emitted radiation. *Mailing Add:* P23 D406 Los Alamos Nat Lab PO Box 1663 Los Alamos NM 87545

KING, NORVAL WILLIAM, JR, VETERINARY PATHOLOGY, COMPARATIVE PATHOLOGY. *Current Pos:* Res fel, Harvard Med Sch, 65-67, res assoc, 68-72, prin assoc, 72-76, assoc dir, New Eng Regional Primate Res Ctr, 80-97, ASSOC PROF COMP PATH, HARVARD MED SCH, 76- *Personal Data:* b Salisbury, Md, Apr 29, 38; m 64; c 2. *Educ:* Univ Ga, DVM, 62. *Concurrent Pos:* Lectr, Sch Med & Vet Med, Tufts Univ, 79-; consult, Pathobiol Inc, 74-; dir, NIH Training grant, vet & comparative path, NIH, 75-; Res Award, Am Asn Lab Animal Sci, 69. *Mem:* Int Acad Path; Am Asn Pathologists; Am Col Vet Pathologists; Am Vet Med Asn; New Eng Soc Pathologists; AAAS. *Res:* Ultrastructure of viruses and viral induced lesions; pathology of the reproductive tract; animal models for human diseases. *Mailing Add:* New Eng Regional Primate Res Ctr Harvard Med Sch 1 Pine Hill Dr Southborough MA 01772. *Fax:* 508-460-1209; *E-Mail:* nking@warren.med.harvard.edu

KING, PATRICIA ANN, ETHICS OF MEDICINE, BIOETHICS. *Current Pos:* prof law, 73, CARMACK WATERHOUSE PROF LAW, MED, ETHICS, & PUB POLICY, GEORGETOWN LAW CTR. *Personal Data:* b Norfolk, Va, June 12, 42. *Educ:* Wheaton Col, BA, 63; Harvard Univ, JD, 69. *Prof Exp:* dep dir, Civil Rights Off, HEW, 71-73. *Concurrent Pos:* Adj prof, Dept Health Policy & Mgt, Sch Hyg & Pub Health, Johns Hopkins Univ; bd mem, Hospice Found, Womens Legal Defense Fund, Wheaton Col; mem, Nat Res Coun Comt, Assessment Family Violence Interventions; dep asst atty gen, Civil Div Dept Justice. *Mem:* Inst Med-Nat Acad Sci; Am Soc Law & Med; Am Law Inst. *Mailing Add:* Georgetown Law Ctr 1507 Isherwood St NE 1 Washington DC 20002-5564

KING, PAUL HARVEY, BIOMEDICAL ENGINEERING, MECHANICAL ENGINEERING. *Current Pos:* asst prof eng, Vanderbilt Univ, 68-72, actg chmn dept biomed eng, 71-72, prog dir biomed eng, 72-75, asst prof, Ortho & Rehab, 73-81, chmn biomed eng, 75-77, ASSOC PROF BIOMED & MECH ENG, VANDERBILT UNIV, 72-, ASSOC PROF ANETHESIOL DEPT, 87- *Personal Data:* b Ft Wayne, Ind, Sept 4, 41; m 67, 78, 82, Betty S Freeman; c Paul E, Kelsey, Sarah M & Elizabeth. *Educ:* Case Inst Technol, BS, 63, MS, 65; Vanderbilt Univ, PhD(mech eng), 68. *Honors & Awards:* Skylab Awards. *Prof Exp:* Res asst eng, Case Inst Technol, 63-65. *Concurrent Pos:* Sr teaching fel mech eng, Vanderbilt Univ, 65-68; researcher, Oak Ridge Assoc Univ, Med & Health Sci Div, Radiopharmaceut Develop Group, 78-79. *Mem:* Biomed Eng Soc; Am Soc Eng Educ; Sigma Xi; Int Anesthesia Res Soc; Asn Advan Med Instrumentation; Inst Elec & Electronics Engrs. *Res:* Orthopedics research; computer analysis of electro-cardiograms; radioisotope scanning systems; biomedical data analysis; modelling and research; positron emission tomography; computer assisted monitoring in anesthesiology; instrumentation in anesthesiology. *Mailing Add:* Box 1631 Sta B Nashville TN 37235-1631. *Fax:* 615-343-7919; *E-Mail:* Kingpk@vuse.vanderbilt.edu

KING, PERRY, JR, radiochemistry; deceased, see previous edition for last biography

KING, PETER FOSTER, PHYSICAL CHEMISTRY. *Current Pos:* RETIRED. *Personal Data:* b New York, NY, Oct 7, 29; m 54, Ellen Cole; c Katherine, Kenneth & Karl. *Educ:* Ind Univ, BS, 51, MA, 52; Mass Inst Technol, DSc, 57. *Prof Exp:* Res & develop engr, Dow Chem Co, 57-65; chemist, Parker Chem Co,__65-67, group leader, 67-80, sr res chemist, res & develop, 80-87; res scientist, Parker & Amchem, 88-91. *Mem:* Electrochem Soc; Am Chem Soc; Nat Asn Corrosion Eng. *Res:* Electrochemistry; chemistry and electrochemistry of surfaces; corrosion, metal cleaning and conversion coating; cold forming lubricants. *Mailing Add:* 26500 Orchard Lake Rd Farmington Hills MI 48334

KING, PETER RAMSAY, COMPUTER SCIENCE. *Current Pos:* asst prof, 69-77, assoc prof, 77-80, PROF COMPUT SCI, UNIV MAN, 80- *Personal Data:* b Blackpool, UK, Nov 22, 43; m 70; c 1. *Educ:* Univ Nottingham, BSc, 65, PhD(comput sci), 69. *Prof Exp:* Lectr math & comput sci, Univ Nottingham, 67-69. *Concurrent Pos:* Nat Res Coun Can grants, 69-72. *Mem:* Asn Comput Mach; Brit Comput Soc; Brit Inst Math & Appln. *Res:* Compiler construction for high level languages, especially Algol 68; spline interpolation; interactive problem solving. *Mailing Add:* Dept Comput Sci Univ Man Winnipeg MB R3T 2N2 Can. *E-Mail:* prking@cs.umanitoba.ca

KING, RAY J(OHN), ELECTRICAL ENGINEERING, MATERIALS EVALUATION. *Current Pos:* VPRES, KDC TECHNOL CORP, 83- *Personal Data:* b Montrose, Colo, Jan 1, 33; m 64, Diane Henney; c Karl V & Kristin J. *Educ:* Ind Inst Technol, BS, 56 & 57; Univ Colo, Boulder, MS, 60, PhD(elec eng), 65. *Prof Exp:* Asst prof electronic eng, Ind Inst Technol, 60-61, asst prof elec eng & assoc chmn dept, 61-62; res assoc, Univ Colo, Boulder, 62-65; from assoc prof to prof elec eng, Univ Wis-Madison, 65-82; staff res engr, Lawrence Livermore Labs, 82-89. *Concurrent Pos:* vis lectr, Univ Colo, Boulder, 64-65; res assoc, Univ Ill, Urbana, 65; mem US nat comt, Int Sci Radio Union, Comns A, B & F, 67-; Fulbright guest prof, Tech Univ Denmark, 73-74; Erskine fel, Univ Canterbury, Christchurch, NZ, 77; prin investr, NSF, Air Force Off Sci Res grants; contracts, Naval Surface Warfare Ctr, Dept Com, Dept Agr, Naval Air Eng Ctr, Wright-Patterson AFB; admin comt mem, Antennas & Propagation Soc, 89-92. *Mem:* Fel Inst Elec & Electronics Engrs; Inst Elec & Electronics Engrs Soc Microwave Theory & Tech; Inst Elec & Electronics Engrs Antennas & Propagation; fel Inst Elec & Electronics Engrs Instrumentation & Measurement; Forest Prods Soc; Mat Res Soc. *Res:* Electromagnetic wave propagation over nonuniform surfaces; microwave surface and leaky wave antennas; microwave instrumentation and measurement systems; microwave nondestructive testing; environmental effects on antenna performance; high power microwave effects; microwave evaluation of materials; electromagnetism. *Mailing Add:* KDC Technol Corp 2011 Research Dr Livermore CA 94550. *Fax:* 510-449-4121; *E-Mail:* kdc@aimnet.com

KING, RAYMOND LEROY, FOOD SCIENCE. *Current Pos:* RETIRED. *Personal Data:* b Burbank, Calif, Oct 4, 22; m 47; c 6. *Educ:* Univ Calif, AB, 55, PhD(agr chem), 58. *Prof Exp:* Asst dairy prod, Univ Calif, 55-57, jr specialist, 57-58; asst prof daity technol, Univ Md, College Park, 58-62, from assoc prof to prof, 62-85, coordr & chmn, Food Sci Prog, 73-85. *Concurrent Pos:* Consult ice cream prod, Chile, 62; consult pesticide residues in milk, 60-61; consult milk packaging, 62. *Mem:* AAAS; Am Chem Soc; Am Dairy Sci Asn; Inst Food Technol. *Res:* Mechanism of lipid oxidation in milk; characterization of milk fat globule membrane; distribution and movement of pesticides in dairy cows; food chemistry. *Mailing Add:* 8424 Carrollton Pkwy Univ Md Col Agr New Carrollton MD 20784

KING, REATHA CLARK, INORGANIC CHEMISTRY, PHYSICAL CHEMISTRY. *Current Pos:* PRES, METROP STATE UNIV, ST PAUL, 77- *Personal Data:* b Pavo, Ga, Apr 11, 38; m 61; c 2. *Educ:* Clark Col, BS, 58; Univ Chicago, MS, 60, PhD(chem), 63; Columbia Univ, MBA, 77. *Prof Exp:* Chemist, Nat Bur Standards, 63-68; asst prof chem, 68-70, assoc prof chem & assoc dean div natural sci & math, 70-74, prof chem & assoc dean acad affairs, York Col, NY, 74-77. *Mem:* AAAS; Am Chem Soc; Nat Orgn Prof Advan Black Chemists & Black Engrs; Sigma Xi. *Res:* Experimental study on thermochemical properties of alloys using tin solution calorimetry; heats of formation of refractory compounds; fluorine flame calorimetry at room temperature. *Mailing Add:* 2138 Arcade St St Paul MN 55109

KING, RICHARD ALLEN, MEDICINE, GENETICS. *Current Pos:* from instr to assoc prof, 71-84, dir, Genetics Div, 85-90, PROF MED & PEDIAT, UNIV MINN, MINNEAPOLIS, 84-, DIR, DIV GENETICS & METAB, DEPT MED & PEDIAT & INST HUMAN GENETICS, 90-, ASSOC DIR CLIN RES, 96- *Personal Data:* b Fresno, Calif, Mar 20, 39; m 63; c 2. *Educ:* Pa State Univ, AB, 61; Jefferson Med Col, MD, 65; Univ Minn, PhD(genetics), 75. *Honors & Awards:* Seiji Award, Pigment Cell Soc, 96. *Prof Exp:* Intern med, Univ Minn, 65-66, resident, 66-69; USPHS surgeon, Atomic Bomb Casualty Comn, Hiroshima, Japan, 69-71. *Mem:* Am Soc Human Genetics; AAAS; Am Fedn Clin Res; fel Am Col Physicians; Pan Am Soc Pigment Cell (pres-elect); fel Am Col Med Genetics. *Res:* Gene mapping in common complex disease, cancer, SLE, asthma, diabetes; genetic regulation of melanin metabolism. *Mailing Add:* Box 485 UMHC Univ Hosp 420 Delaware St SE PO Box 485 Minneapolis MN 55455-0374. *Fax:* 612-624-6645; *E-Mail:* kingx002@maroon.tc.umn.edu

KING, RICHARD AUSTIN, PSYCHOPHYSIOLOGY, NEUROBIOLOGY. *Current Pos:* assoc prof, 65-71, assoc dir neurobiol, 73-90, PROF PSYCHOL, UNIV NC, CHAPEL HILL, 71- *Personal Data:* b Philadelphia, Pa, Mar 26, 29; m 56, Margy Skeel; c Richard, Gordon & Sarah. *Educ:* Univ Cincinnati, AB, 54, MA, 55; Duke Univ, PhD(psychol), 59. *Prof Exp:* From instr to asst prof psychol, Univ NC, Chapel Hill, 58-63; fel physiol, Univ Wash, 63-65. *Concurrent Pos:* Vis prof psychol, Brown Univ, 71. *Mem:* Soc Neurosci; Psychonomic Soc. *Res:* Biology of memory. *Mailing Add:* Dept Psychol Univ NC Chapel Hill NC 27599

KING, RICHARD JOE, ANIMAL PHYSIOLOGY. *Current Pos:* from asst prof to assoc prof, 74-80, PROF PHYSIOL, UNIV TEX HEALTH SCI CTR, SAN ANTONIO, 80- *Personal Data:* b Kansas City, Mo, Aug 30, 37; m 63, Leslie A; c Deborah A & David L. *Educ:* Univ Mo, Columbia, BA, 59; Univ Calif, Berkeley, PhD(biophys), 70. *Prof Exp:* Asst res biophysicist, Univ Calif, San Francisco, 71-74. *Concurrent Pos:* Consult, Review Comt, NIH, 75-76, 78-79 & 80-81; assoc ed, Am Rev Respiratory Dis, 88-89. *Mem:* Am Physiol Soc. *Res:* Composition and properties of pulmonary surfactant; metabolism and isolation of its associated apoproteins; interaction of lipids and proteins in pulmonary surfactant; correlation of structure function relationships; effects of nitrogens on lung cells; alterations in surfactant in chronic lung injury. *Mailing Add:* Dept Physiol Univ Tex Health Sci Ctr 7703 Floyd Curl Dr San Antonio TX 78284. *Fax:* 210-567-4410

KING, RICHARD WARREN, ANALYTICAL CHEMISTRY, PHYSICAL CHEMISTRY. *Current Pos:* RETIRED. *Personal Data:* b Philadelphia, Pa, Mar 25, 25; m 47, June Weigtind; c Linda B, Judith A, Andria J & Melissa (Buffington). *Educ:* Kenyon Col, AB, 47; Univ Del, MS, 59. *Honors & Awards:* Award of Merit, Am Soc Testing & Mat, 81. *Prof Exp:* Res chemist, Res & Develop Dept, Sun Oil Co, 47-59, sect chief, Anal Sect, 60-69, mgr res serv, Res & Develop Dept, 69-83. *Mem:* Am Chem Soc; fel Am Soc Testing & Mat. *Res:* Catalytic reactions of hydrocarbons; application of physical separation techniques to the study of high-boiling fractions from petroleum; gas chromatography of petroleum fractions. *Mailing Add:* 3031 Hermosa Lane Havertown PA 19083-1124

KING, ROBBINS SYDNEY, EMBRYOLOGY. *Current Pos:* RETIRED. *Personal Data:* b San Diego, Calif, Apr 23, 22; m 47; c 4. *Educ:* Stanford Univ, AB, 47, PhD(biol), 54. *Prof Exp:* Res assoc, Hopkins Marine Sta, Stanford Univ, 52-54, asst prof biol, Univ, 55; instr, Menlo Col, 54-55; asst prof, Wabash Col, 55-56; asst prof biol, Calif State Univ, Chico, 56-65, chmn dept, 65-69, prof biol sci, 65-89. *Mem:* AAAS; Am Soc Mammal; Nat Sci Teachers Asn. *Res:* Experimental embryology; regeneration. *Mailing Add:* 9 Calgary Lane Chico CA 95926

KING, ROBERT (BAINTON), NEUROSURGERY. *Current Pos:* chmn div & dept, 57-88, PROF NEUROSURG, COL MED, STATE UNIV NY HEALTH SCI CTR, 57-; MED DIR, STATE UNIV HOSP. *Personal Data:* b Pittsburgh, Pa, Aug 26, 22; m 51, Molly Gibbs; c 3. *Educ:* Rochester Univ, MD, 46; Am Bd Neurol Surg, dipl, 54. *Honors & Awards:* Cushing Medal, Am Asn Neurol Surgeons, 90. *Prof Exp:* Asst neuroanat, Med Sch, Wash Univ, 48; asst chief, Walter Reed Army Hosp, 49-51; from instr to asst prof neurosurg, Med Sch, Wash Univ, 51-57. *Concurrent Pos:* Markle scholar, 51-56; attend surg, Crouse-Irving Mem Hosp, 57 & State Univ Hosp, Syracuse, 57-; Consult, Vet Admin Hosp, 57; distinguished serv prof neurosurg, State Univ NY. *Mem:* Neurosurg Soc Am; Am Asn Neurol Surg; Am Col Surgeons; Am Acad Neurol Surg; Soc Neurol Surg; Sigma Xi; Am Neurol Asn. *Res:* Neurosurgery; neurophysiology/neur anatomy pain studies. *Mailing Add:* Dept Neurosurg Univ Hosp 750 E Adams St Syracuse NY 13210-2306

KING, ROBERT BRUCE, INORGANIC CHEMISTRY. *Current Pos:* res assoc prof chem, Univ Ga, 66-68, res prof, 68-73, actg head chem, 80-82, REGENTS' PROF CHEM, UNIV GA, 73- *Personal Data:* b Rochester, NH, Feb 27, 38; m 60, Jane Kempner; c Robert B II & David S. *Educ:* Oberlin Col, BA, 57; Harvard Univ, PhD(inorg chem), 61. *Honors & Awards:* Am Chem Soc Awards, 71, 91. *Prof Exp:* Res chemist, Explosives Dept, E I du Pont de Nemours, Del, 61-62; res fel, Mellon Inst, 62-64, sr res fel, 64-66. *Concurrent Pos:* Ed, Organometallic Syntheses, 63-94; tech adv, Pressure Chem Co, Pa, 64-75; ed, J Organometallic Chem, 64-; Sloan Found fel, 67-69; fel, Japan Soc Promotion Sci, 81; consult, Los Alamos Nat Lab, 79-83; consult, Westinghouse Savannah River Co, 96- *Mem:* Am Chem Soc; Chem Soc London; Mat Res Soc. *Res:* Synthetic and spectroscopic studies on organometallic compounds of transition metals; molecular catalysis; organophosphous chemistry; chemical applications of group theory and group theory; environmental inorganic chemistry. *Mailing Add:* Dept Chem Univ Ga Athens GA 30602. *Fax:* 706-542-9454

KING, ROBERT CHARLES, GENETICS. *Current Pos:* from asst prof to assoc prof, 56-63, PROF BIOL SCI, NORTHWESTERN UNIV, 64- *Personal Data:* b New York, NY, June 3, 28; m 79; c 2. *Educ:* Yale Univ, BS, 48, PhD(zool), 52. *Prof Exp:* Scientist, Brookhaven Nat Lab, 51-56. *Concurrent Pos:* NSF sr fels, Univ Edinburgh, 58, div entom, Commonwealth Sci & Indust Res Orgn, Canberra, Australia, 63 & sericulture exp sta, Tokyo, 70; Seoul Nat Univ, Seoul, Korea, 78 & Han Yang Univ, 79; vis investr & fel, Rockefeller Inst, 59. *Mem:* Fel AAAS; Genetics Soc Am; Am Soc Zool; Entom Soc Am; Am Soc Cell Biol (treas, 72, 73 & 74). *Res:* Developmental genetics; genetic control of oogenesis in Drosophila. *Mailing Add:* Biochem Molecular Biol & Cell Biol Dept Hogan Hall 5-130 Northwestern Univ Evanston IL 60208. *E-Mail:* r.king@nwu.edu

KING, ROBERT EDWARD, BIOLOGICAL CHEMISTRY, PHARMACEUTICAL CHEMISTRY. *Current Pos:* RETIRED. *Personal Data:* b Zanesville, Ohio, Dec 27, 23; m 50, Jane Klein; c Susan, Timothy, Peter, Christina & Jonathan. *Educ:* Ohio State Univ, BSc, 44; Univ Minn, PhD(pharmaceut chem), 48. *Prof Exp:* Res assoc, Merck Sharp & Dohme Res Labs, 48-61; emer prof indust pharm, Philadelphia Col Pharm, 61-86. *Concurrent Pos:* Ed, J Parenteral Drug Asn, 64-78. *Mem:* Am Pharmaceut Asn; Parenteral Drug Asn. *Res:* Pharmaceutical dosage forms. *Mailing Add:* 3475 Aquetong Rd Doylestown PA 18901

KING, ROBERT WILLIAM, MATHEMATICS. *Current Pos:* asst prof, 67-69, ASSOC PROF MATH, UNIV SOUTHERN MISS, 69- *Personal Data:* b Wesson, Miss, Nov 18, 29; m 59; c 2. *Educ:* Univ Southern Miss, BS, 51, MA, 56; Fla State Univ, MS, 65, PhD(math, educ), 67. *Prof Exp:* Instr math, Copiah-Lincoln Jr Col, 56-57; asst prof, Miss Col, 59-64. *Mem:* Math Asn Am; Nat Coun Teachers Math. *Res:* Use of various modifications of programmed instruction to investigate the effects of selected social and psychological factors in the teaching and learning of mathematics. *Mailing Add:* 829 Fourth St SE LeMars IA 51031

KING, ROBERT WILLIS, MOLECULAR BIOLOGY, MICROBIOLOGY. *Current Pos:* RES DIR, AVID THERAPEUT INC, PHILADELPHIA, PA, 94- *Personal Data:* b Grand Haven, Mich, June 9, 61; m 92, Emily S Shen. *Educ:* Mich State Univ, BS, 83; Purdue Univ, PhD(microbiol), 89. *Prof Exp:* Instr microbiol, Purdue Univ, 87-88, instr med microbiol, Ind Univ, Sch Med, 89; res assoc, Univ Chicago, 90-92; fel, DuPont Merck Pharmaceut Co, 93-94. *Mem:* Am Soc Microbiol; AAAS. *Res:* Designing infectivity and assay systems for the screening of potential therapeutic agents for antiviral activity. *Mailing Add:* Avid Therapeutics Inc 3401 Market St Suite 300 Philadelphia PA 19104

KING, ROBERT WILSON, JR, GEODESY. *Current Pos:* res assoc, 77-85, PRIN RES SCIENTIST, DEPT EARTH, ATMOS & PLANETARY SCI, MASS INST TECHNOL, 85- *Personal Data:* b Fayetteville, NC, Feb 8, 47; m 70, Mary E Eyler; c Elizabeth R & Leslie W. *Educ:* Davidson Col, BS, 70; NC State Univ, BS, 70; Mass Inst Technol, PhD(instrumentation), 75. *Prof Exp:* Res geodesist, Terrestrial Sci Div, Air Force Geophys Lab, 74-77. *Mem:* Am Geophys Union. *Res:* Use of precise extraterrestrial measurement techniques to monitor earth rotation, polar motion and crustal deformation. *Mailing Add:* 2 Pinewood St Lexington MA 02173

KING, ROGER HATTON, PEDOLOGY, PHYSICAL GEOGRAPHY. *Current Pos:* from asst prof to assoc prof, 70-88, PROF GEOG, UNIV WESTERN ONT, 88- *Personal Data:* b Barry, Wales, Dec 16, 41; m 65; c 2. *Educ:* Univ Wales, BSc, 63; Univ Aberdeen, MSc, 65; Univ Sask, PhD(geog), 69. *Prof Exp:* Tutor geog, Univ Wales, 69-70. *Concurrent Pos:* Vis prof, Inst Archaeol, Oxford Univ, Eng, 77-78; consult, Parks Can, 82-; vis prof, Dept Geog, Univ Canterbury, NZ, 85. *Mem:* Can Geog Soc; Int Quaternary Asn; Geol Asn Can; Can Quaternary Asn. *Res:* Persistence of chemical residues in archaeological soils and sediments; impact of environmental stress on soil development in arctic and alpine areas; palaeoenvironmental reconstruction in the Canadian Cordillera; archaeological pottery provenance; tephras; clay mineralogy and composition. *Mailing Add:* Dept Geog Univ Western Ont London ON N6A 5C2 Can

KING, RONALD PETER, MINERAL PROCESSING. *Current Pos:* PROF METALL ENG, UNIV UTAH, 90- *Personal Data:* b Springs, SAfrica, Mar 12, 38; m 61, Ellen A Courtenay; c Jeremy P, Andrew J & Janet M (Tyrrell-Ead). *Educ:* Univ Witwatersrand, BSc, 58, MSc, 62; Univ Manchester, PhD(chem eng), 63. *Honors & Awards:* Gold Medal, SAfrica Inst Mining & Metall, 91. *Prof Exp:* Lectr chem eng, Univ Witwatersrand, 63-65; sr lectr, Univ Natal, SAfrica, 66-67; chief scientist, Nat Inst Metall, SAfrica, 68-73 & 74; lectr, Univ Manchester, Eng, 73-74; prof extractive metall eng, Univ Witwatersrand, 74-90. *Concurrent Pos:* Vis fel, Camborne Sch Mines, 80; vis prof, Univ Utah, 87-88. *Mem:* SAfrican Inst Mining & Metall (pres); Soc Mining, Metall & Explor; Soc Indust & Appl Math. *Res:* Modeling and simulation of complex processing systems. *Mailing Add:* 306 Browning Bldg Salt Lake City UT 84112. *Fax:* 801-581-8119; *E-Mail:* rpking@mines.utah.edu

KING, RONOLD (WYETH PERCIVAL), PHYSICS & BIOPHYSICS, ELECTRICAL ENGINEERING. *Current Pos:* fac instr physics & commun eng, 38-39, from asst prof to prof, 39-72, EMER PROF APPL PHYSICS, HARVARD UNIV, 72- *Personal Data:* b Williamstown, Mass, Sept 19, 05; m 37, 91, Mary M Govoni; c Christopher M. *Educ:* Univ Rochester, AB, 27, SM, 29; Univ Wis, PhD(electrodyn), 32. *Hon Degrees:* AM, Harvard Univ, 42. *Honors & Awards:* Centennial Medal, Inst Elec & Electronics Engrs, 84; Distinguished Serv Award, Inst Elec & Electronics Engrs, Antennas & Propagation Soc, 91. *Prof Exp:* Asst physics, Univ Rochester, 28-29; asst elec eng, Univ Wis, 32-34, Alumni Res Found fel, 34; instr physics, Lafayette Col, 34-35, asst prof, 35-37; Guggenheim Mem Found fel, Berlin & Munich, 37-38. *Concurrent Pos:* Guggenheim Mem Found fel, 58; mem comn B, Int Sci Radio Union; consult, Raytheon Co, 74-75 & 87-93, Mitre Corp, 90; IBM distinguished scholar, Northeastern Univ, 85. *Mem:* AAAS; fel Inst Elec & Electronics Engrs; fel Am Phys Soc; fel Am Acad Arts & Sci; corresp mem Bavarian Acad Sci. *Res:* Electromagnetic theory, radiation and antennas; transmission-line theory; microwave circuits; insulated antennas, crossed antennas, antennas in dissipative media near surface; subsurface communication; electromagnetic pulses; electromagnetic surface waves; resonant antenna arrays; bioelectromagnetics. *Mailing Add:* 92 Hillcrest Pkwy Winchester MA 01890

KING, ROY WARBRICK, NUCLEAR MAGNETIC RESONANCE. *Current Pos:* res assoc chem, 69-84, ASST RES SCIENTIST, UNIV FLA, 84- *Personal Data:* b Liverpool, Eng, July 4, 33; US citizen; m 70. *Educ:* Cambridge Univ, BA, 54, MA & PhD(org chem), 58. *Prof Exp:* Norman fel org chem, Hickrill Chem Res Found, NY, 58; univ fel, Iowa State Univ, 58-60, supvr instrument serv, 60-66, asst prof chem, 66-69. *Mem:* Am Chem Soc; Sigma Xi; Royal Soc Chem. *Res:* Organic structure determination; organic analysis; applications of physical methods to organic chemistry. *Mailing Add:* Dept Chem Univ Fla PO Box 117200 Gainesville FL 32611-7200. *E-Mail:* rwking@chem.ufl.edu

KING, S(ANFORD) MACCALLUM, SOIL FERTILITY, CROP MANAGEMENT. *Current Pos:* PRES, KING INT, 90- *Personal Data:* b St Catharines, Ont, May 21, 26; US citizen; div, Iris Krueger; c Marilyn, Nancy, Gordon & Laura. *Educ:* Ont Agr Col, BSA, 48; Purdue Univ, MS, 50; Univ Wis, PhD(soil fertil), 56, Keller Grad Inst Mgt, MBA, 81. *Prof Exp:* Soil scientist, Stand Fruit & Steamship Co, 51-53; proj asst soil fertil, Univ Wis, 53-56; res asst, prof & sta supt, Mich State Univ, 56-61; mkt & tech serv specialist fertilizer, Int Minerals & Chem Corp, 62-70; dir agr, Develop & Resources Corp, 71-73; vpres, Taralan Corp, 73-87; vpres, Seed-Prep Corp & sr vpres, Competitive Edge Inc, 88-90. *Concurrent Pos:* Agr proj develop & mkt tasks 18 countries, Potash Corp, Saskatchewan; Consult, 80-83; instr mkt, Northern Ill Univ, 90-; Columbia Col, 97-; sr adv, Pro-Crop, Inc, 92-; consult, IMC Global, 95- *Mem:* Am Soc Agron; Soil Sci Soc Am. *Res:* Crop nutrition; crop management and production. *Mailing Add:* 36 Pine Ave Lake Zurich IL 60047-2326

KING, SHELDON SELIG, MEDICAL ADMINISTRATION. *Current Pos:* EXEC VPRES, SALICK HEALTH CARE, 94- *Personal Data:* b New York, NY, Aug 28, 31. *Educ:* NY Univ, AB, 52; Yale Univ, MS, 57. *Prof Exp:* Asst dir, Mt Sinai Hosp, 60-66, dir planning, 66-68; exec dir, Albert Einstein Col Med, Bronx Munic Hosp Ctr, 68-72; dir hosp & clin, Univ Hosp & assoc clin prof, Univ Calif, San Diego, 72-81; assoc vpres med affairs, exec vpres & dir, Stanford Univ Hosp, 81-85, pres, 86-89; pres, Cedars-Sinai Med Ctr, Los Angeles, 89-94. *Concurrent Pos:* Pres, Hosp Coun San Diego & Imp Co, 77; mem, Gov Coun, Sect Metrop Hosps, Am Hosp Asn, 84-89, Coun 2000 Comn, Am Podiatric Asn, 85-86, Accreditation Coun Grad Med Educ, 87-90, Bd Health Sci Policy, Inst Med & Health Leadership Coun, 89-, bd dirs, Nat Comt Qual Health Care & Vol Hosps Am, 90-; chmn, Bd Adv, Am Bd Internal Med, 85-91. *Mem:* Inst Med-Nat Acad Sci; fel Am Col Health Care Execs; fel Am Pub Health Asn; fel Royal Soc Health; Am Hosp Asn. *Res:* Author of publications in various medical journals. *Mailing Add:* Salick Health Care 111 8th Ave Suite 1510 New York NY 10011

KING, STANLEY SHIH-TUNG, PHYSICAL CHEMISTRY, MOLECULAR SPECTROSCOPY. *Current Pos:* ASSOC SCIENTIST, DOW CHEM USA, 80- *Personal Data:* b Liau-Ning, China, Nov 12, 34; m 66; c 3. *Educ:* Taiwan Normal Univ, BS, 57; Drexel Univ, MS, 62; Univ Minn, Minneapolis, PhD(phys chem), 66. *Mem:* Am Chem Soc; Am Catalypis Soc. *Res:* Vibrational spectroscopy; low temperature matrix isolation study; microsample analysis by vibrational spectroscopy; polymer analysis; chromatographic analysis; electromicroscopy; catalysis; analytical chemistry. *Mailing Add:* 1311 Kirkland Dr Midland MI 48640

KING, STEPHEN MURRAY, MONOCLONAL ANTIBODIES, PROTEIN SUBSTANCES. *Current Pos:* RES ASSOC, WORCESTER FOUND EXP BIOL, 83- *Educ:* Univ London, Eng, PhD(cell biol), 82. *Mailing Add:* Dept Biochem Univ Conn Health Ctr 263 Farmington Ave Farmington CT 06032-3305. *Fax:* 508-842-9632

KING, TALMADGE EVERETT, JR, INTERNAL MEDICINE, PULMONARY MEDICINE. *Current Pos:* sr staff mem, 90, EXEC VPRES CLIN AFFAIRS, NAT JEWISH CTR IMMUNOL & RESPIRATORY MED, 92- *Personal Data:* b Sumter, SC, Feb 24, 48; m 68, Mozelle Davis; c Consuelo & Malaika M. *Educ:* Gustavus Adolphus Col, BA, 70; Harvard Univ, MD, 74. *Prof Exp:* Prof med, Univ Colo Sch Med, 91, vchmn, Health Sci Ctr, 93. *Concurrent Pos:* Prin investr, Specialized Ctr Res, 81- *Mem:* Am Thoracic Soc; Am Lung Asn; fel Am Col Chest Physicians; fel Am Col Physicians; Am Fedn Clin Res; Nat Med Asn. *Res:* Pathogenesis, diagnosis and management of inflammatory and immunologic lung injury. *Mailing Add:* 1400 Jackson St Denver CO 80206

KING, TE PIAO, IMMUNOLOGY. *Current Pos:* Res assoc biochem, 53-57, asst prof, 57-63, ASSOC PROF BIOCHEM, ROCKEFELLER UNIV, 63- *Personal Data:* b Shanghai, China, Aug 21, 30; m; c 2. *Educ:* Univ Calif, AB, 50, MS, 51; Univ Mich, PhD, 53. *Mem:* Am Soc Biol Chemists; Am Acad Allergy. *Res:* Peptides; proteins. *Mailing Add:* Dept Bichem Rockefeller Univ 1230 York Ave New York NY 10021-6399. *Fax:* 212-327-8878

KING, TERRY LEE, ANALYSIS OF DATA, LINEAR MODELS. *Current Pos:* assoc prof, 81-88, chmn dept, 88-93, PROF MATH & STATIST, NW MO STATE UNIV, 89- *Personal Data:* b Akron, Iowa, Feb 24, 45; m 71, Carol E Glass; c Kevin, Shawn & Heather. *Educ:* Westmar Col, BA, 67; Univ Iowa, MS, 69; Pa State Univ, PhD(statist), 80. *Prof Exp:* Instr math, Thiel Col, 69-71; statistician, Desmatics, Inc, 75-79; instr, Dept Math, Frostburg State Col, 79-81; Prof, Math NW Sect, Math Asn Am, 90-91, chair, 91-92; vis prof, Dept Statist, Pa State Univ, 92. *Mem:* Am Statist Asn; Biometric Soc; Math Asn Am; Nat Coun Teachers Math. *Res:* Sample size determination; linear models; data analysis. *Mailing Add:* Dept Math & Statist NW Mo State Univ Maryville MO 64468. *Fax:* 660-562-1188; *E-Mail:* tlking@acad.nwmissouri.edu

KING, THEODORE MATTHEW, OBSTETRICS & GYNECOLOGY, PHYSIOLOGY. *Current Pos:* PROF OBSTET & GYNEC & DIR DEPT, SCH MED, JOHNS HOPKINS UNIV, 71- *Personal Data:* b Quincy, Ill, Feb 13, 31; m 54; c 2. *Educ:* Quincy Col, BS, 50; Univ Ill, Urbana, MS, 52, MD, 59; Mich State Univ, PhD(physiol), 59. *Prof Exp:* Lab asst physiol, Univ Ill, 55-59; intern surg, Presby Hosp, NY, 59-60; from resident to chief resident obstet & gynec, Sloane Hosp Women, 60-65; asst prof physiol, obstet & gynec, Sch Med, Univ Mo, 65-68, assoc prof, 68; prof & chmn dept, Albany Med Col, 68-71. *Concurrent Pos:* Macy fel, Sloane Hosp Women, 60-64, Macy fac fel obstet, 66-67; Nat Inst Child Health & Human Develop fel, 65-68. *Res:* Study of uterine contractile protein; influence of enzyme induction on animal reproduction. *Mailing Add:* Johns Hopkins Sch Med 600 N Wolfe St Baltimore MD 21205. *Fax:* 919-544-7261

KING, THEODORE OSCAR, TOXICOLOGY, PHARMACOLOGY. *Current Pos:* dir, 71-76, SR DIR SAFETY EVAL, PFIZER, INC, 76- *Personal Data:* b Portsmouth, Ohio, May 29, 22; m 52; c 2. *Educ:* Univ Mich, BS, 43; Georgetown Univ, PhD(pharmacol), 49; Univ Wyo, JD, 60; Am Bd Toxicol, dipl, 81. *Prof Exp:* Pharmaceut control chemist, Wm R Warner & Co, NY, 43-45; anal chemist, Res Div, Colgate-Palmolive-Peet Co, NJ, 46; from assoc prof to prof pharmacol, Col Pharm, Univ Wyo, 49-58; dir div pharmacol, Ortho Res Found, NJ, 59-65; vpres & dir res, Bio/Dynamics, Inc, 65-71. *Concurrent Pos:* WHO pub health fel, UK, 51; Fulbright res fel, State Univ Ghent, 55-56; sr pharmacologist, Johnson & Johnson Res Found, NJ, 57-59; lectr, Rutgers Univ, 58-65; assoc res prof, Col Pharmacol, Univ Conn, 80-; Intra-Acad (NAS-HAS) Exchange Scientist, Hungary, 85, 88. *Mem:* Soc Toxicol; Am Soc Pharmacol & Exp Ther; Am Chem Soc; NY Acad Sci; fel AAAS. *Res:* Drug safety evaluation; physiology of reproduction; endocrine pharmacology. *Mailing Add:* 185 Old Norwich Rd Quaker Hill CT 06375-1223. *Fax:* 860-441-5499

KING, THOMAS CREIGHTON, thoracic surgery, critical care, for more information see previous edition

KING, THOMAS K C, PULMONARY PHYSIOLOGY, PULMONARY DISEASES. *Current Pos:* asst prof, 70-73, ASSOC PROF MED, COL MED, CORNELL UNIV, 73-, ASSOC PROF BIOPHYS, 75- *Personal Data:* b Shanghai, China, June 1, 34; US citizen; m 59, Amy Penn; c Susan & Caroline. *Educ:* Univ Edinburgh, MB, ChB, 59, MD, 63; FRCP, 80. *Honors & Awards:* Pulmonary Acad Award, Nat Heart & Lung Inst, 72. *Prof Exp:* Eli Lilly Int fel, Bellevue Hosp, Columbia Univ, 65-66, Polachek Found Cardiopulmonary Lab fel, 66-67; lectr med, Sch Med, Univ Hong Kong, 67-70. *Concurrent Pos:* Vis prof, Univ Hong Kong, 81, Nat Defense Med Ctr, Taiwan, 87. *Mem:* Med Res Soc, UK; Am Fedn Clin Res; Am Physiol Soc; Am Thoracic Soc; Am Col Chest Physicians. *Res:* The mechanism and quantitation of impaired blood gas exchange in the lungs in disease. *Mailing Add:* Col Med Cornell Univ 1300 York Ave New York NY 10021. *Fax:* 212-746-8808

KING, THOMAS MORGAN, PHYSICAL INORGANIC CHEMISTRY, POLYMER CHEMISTRY. *Current Pos:* Res chemist, Monsanto, 66-68, sr res chemist, 68-69, res specialist, 69, res group leader, 69-72, com develop mgr, 72-76, dir planning & control, 77, com dir sorbates, 77-80, dir results mgt & personnel planning, 80-82, dir bus develop, 83-85, dir, Tech D&P Div, 86-92, dir, Tech Plastics Div, 92-96, TECH & MGT CONSULT, MONSANTO, 96- *Personal Data:* b Morristown, Tenn, Aug 28, 40; m 62, Judith; c Carole & Ashley. *Educ:* Carson-Newman Col, BS, 62; Univ Tenn, PhD(chem), 66. *Mem:* Am Chem Soc. *Res:* Coordination chemistry of Cobalt-II and Nickel-II compounds; basic and applied research on phosphonate compounds; precipitation inhibition and corrosion inhibition. *Mailing Add:* 639 Lampadaire Dr St Louis MO 63141

KING, THOMAS SCOTT, REPRODUCTIVE NEUROENDOCRINOLOGY, FEMALE REPRODUCTIVE HEALTH. *Current Pos:* Fel, Dept Obstet/Gynec, 80-82, asst prof, Dept Cellular & Struct Biol, 82-90, DIR NEUROENDOCRINE CORE, DEPT OBSTET-GYNEC, UNIV TEX HEALTH SCI CTR, SAN ANTONIO, 85-, ASSOC PROF, 90-, ASSOC PROF, DEPT CELLULAR & STRUCT BIOL, 90- *Personal Data:* b Ft Campbell, Ky, May 13, 53; m 85, Rita A Penshorn; c Matthew G & David R. *Educ:* Davidson Col, NC, BS, 75; Med Univ SC, Charleston, PhD(anat/path), 80. *Concurrent Pos:* Consult, West Brabant Polytech Inst, Ctr Med Biotechnol, Eiten-Leur, Neth, 92-, Univ Tex Health Sci Ctr, San Antonio Reproductive Health Ctr, 93-; prin investr, Nat Inst Drug Abuse, 90- *Mem:* Endocrine Soc; Soc Gynec Invest; Soc Neurosci; Soc Neuroendocrinol; Soc Neurochem. *Res:* Regulation of cyclic reproductive function in females and the adverse effects of drug abuse (cocaine, ethanol); human placental transport/metabolism of selected drugs of abuse and selected therapeutic drugs (acyclovir, AZT, pentamidine). *Mailing Add:* Dept Cellular & Struct Biol Univ Tex Health Sci Ctr 7703 Floyd Curl Dr San Antonio TX 78284-7762. *Fax:* 210-567-3803; *E-Mail:* kingt@uthscsa.edu

KING, WALTER BERNARD, inorganic chemistry; deceased, see previous edition for last biography

KING, WILLIAM CONNOR, RADAR SYSTEMS, COMMUNICATION SYSTEMS. *Current Pos:* RETIRED. *Personal Data:* b Newark, Ohio, Mar 10, 27; m 50; c 2. *Educ:* Denison Univ, BA, 49; Duke Univ, PhD(physics), 53. *Prof Exp:* Asst physics, Duke Univ, 49-53, res assoc, 53; res assoc, Radiation Lab, Johns Hopkins Univ, 53-56; commun physicist, Space Sci Lab, Missile & Space Div, Gen Elec Co, 56-62, mgr, Space Systs Anal Proj, 62-64, Commun Eng Spacecraft Dept, Pa, 64-67, data systs, 67-70; mgr, Hard Point Demonstration Array Radar Prog, RCA Corp, 71-74, leader tradex programming, Missile & Surface Radar Div, 74-77; mgr, Wayland Software Eng Dept, Raytheon Corp, 78-80, sr staff, Software Systs Lab, 81-89. *Mem:* Am Phys Soc; Asn Comput Mach; sr mem Inst Elec & Electronics Engrs; Am Inst Aeronaut & Astronaut. *Res:* Microwave spectroscopy and wave propagation in ionized media; design and development of real-time computer programs for radar, missile and communication systems; communications applications of computers. *Mailing Add:* 446 Hayward Mill Rd Concord MA 01742

KING, WILLIAM DAVID, CLINICAL TOXICOLOGY, INJURY EPIDEMIOLOGY. *Current Pos:* DIR TOXICOL, POISON CONTROL CTR, CHILDREN'S HOSP ALA, 83- *Personal Data:* b Owensboro, Ky, Apr 9, 53; m 78. *Educ:* Samford Univ, BS, 78; Univ Ala, Birmingham, MPH, 87, DrPH, 89. *Honors & Awards:* Child Advocacy Award, Am Acad Pediat. *Prof*

Exp: Assoc prof pediat, Univ Ala, Birmingham, 90. *Concurrent Pos:* Adj clin fac, Sch Pharm, Samford Univ, 79-; ed, Poison Info Bull, Children's Hosp, 79-; prin investr, prescription drug ingestions in preschool-aged children, US Consumer Prod Safety Comn, 83-84; div dir, SE Child Safety Inst, 87. *Mem:* Am Asn Poison Control Ctrs; Am Acad Clin Toxicol. *Res:* Childhood injury epidemiology; adolescent parasuicide by drug ingestion; epidemiology of poison exposures; development of a regional secondary prevention system for poison injuries. *Mailing Add:* Children's Hosp Ala 1600 Seventh Ave S Birmingham AL 35233-1711

KING, WILLIAM EMMETT, JR, CHEMICAL ENGINEERING. *Current Pos:* assoc prof, 83-89, DEPT CHAIR CHEM ENG, BUCKNELL UNIV, 86-, PROF, 89- *Personal Data:* b Pittsburgh, Pa, July 27, 43. *Educ:* Univ Pittsburgh, BS, 65; Carnegie-Mellon Univ, MS, 68; Univ Pa, PhD(chem eng), 76. *Prof Exp:* Chem engr, Esso Res & Eng Co, 66-68; engr mathematician, Cities Serv Res & Develop Co, 68-70; asst prof chem eng, Univ Md, 75-81; sr res engr, Gulf Res & Develop Co, 81-83. *Mem:* Am Inst Chem Engrs; Am Chem Soc; Am Soc Eng Educ. *Res:* Fluid-solid reactions; applied mathematics; biomedical engineering. *Mailing Add:* Dept Chem Eng Bucknell Univ Lewisburg PA 17837

KING, WILLIAM MATTERN, APPLIED CHEMISTRY. *Current Pos:* RETIRED. *Personal Data:* b Cando, NDak, Mar 12, 30; m 89, Linda Mott; c Julie K (Smith). *Educ:* NDak State Univ, BS, 57, MS, 58. *Prof Exp:* Chemist polymers, Hooker Chem Corp, 58-60; mgr develop membranes, Envirogenics Systs Co, 60-78; res dir, Spectrum Separations/Separex, 79-90. *Mem:* Am Chem Soc. *Res:* Asymmetric membranes for the separation of gases and organic liquids as well as the desalination of water by reverse osmosis. *Mailing Add:* 2830 Ithaca Dr Prescott AZ 86301

KING, WILLIAM ROBERT, JR, CHEMICAL METALLURGY. *Current Pos:* CHEM METALL CONSULT, 82- *Personal Data:* b Los Angeles, Calif, Aug 25, 24; m 50; c 3. *Educ:* Calif Inst Technol, BS, 47; Univ Calif, Los Angeles, PhD(chem), 52. *Prof Exp:* Res chemist, Univ Calif, Los Angeles, 47-50; res chemist, Filtrol Corp, 52-54 & Sierra Talc & Clay Co, 54-55; sect head, Kaiser Aluminum & Chem Corp, 55-77; sr staff res chemist, 77-82. *Concurrent Pos:* Writer, chem encyclopedias. *Mem:* Am Chem Soc. *Res:* Physical and inorganic chemistry; radiochemistry; molten salts; natural iron and aluminum minerals. *Mailing Add:* 875 Sunset Dr San Carlos CA 94070-3631

KING, WILLIAM STANELY, APPLIED PHYSICS, ENGINEERING. *Current Pos:* SYST ENGR, JPL, 91- *Personal Data:* b Monroe, La, June 16, 35; m 58, Velmo McGowan; c William Douglas & Vanessa Suzanne. *Educ:* Univ Calif, Berkeley, BSME, 57; Univ Calif, Los Angeles, MS, 60, PhD(appl math, physics), 66. *Prof Exp:* Res engr, Rocket Div, Rockwell Int Corp, 57-61; staff scientist, Aerospace Corp, 61-72; sr res scientist, Rand Corp, 72-83; res scientist, Rocketdyne Div, Rockwell Int Corp, 83-91. *Concurrent Pos:* Instr math, Santa Monica Col, 73-; instr eng, Univ Calif, Los Angeles, 77-; instr eng, Calif State Univ, Northridge, 85- *Mem:* Assoc fel Am Inst Aeronaut & Astronaut; Sigma Xi. *Res:* Fluid dynamics; numerical analysis; electromagnetic theory; laser physics; applied mathematics. *Mailing Add:* 4472 Don Milagro Dr Los Angeles CA 90008

KING, WILLIS KWONGTSU, COMPUTER SCIENCE, ELECTRICAL ENGINEERING. *Current Pos:* asst prof comput sci, 69-73, ASSOC PROF COMPUT SCI, UNIV HOUSTON, 73-, CHMN DEPT, 79- *Personal Data:* b Shanghai, China, Sept 23, 36; m 70. *Educ:* Darmstadt Tech Univ, Dipl Ing, 63; Univ Pa, PhD(elec eng), 69. *Prof Exp:* Res engr comput design, IBM Labs, 63-65. *Mem:* Asn Comput Mach; Sigma Xi; Inst Elec & Electronics Engrs. *Res:* Computer architecture; distributed computing; microprogramming. *Mailing Add:* Dept Comput Sci Univ Houston 3801 Cullen Blvd Houston TX 77204-0001

KING, WILTON W(AYT), ENGINEERING MECHANICS. *Current Pos:* from asst prof to assoc prof, 64-77, PROF ENG MECH, GA INST TECHNOL, 77- *Personal Data:* b Richmond, Va, Aug 11, 37; m 58; c 4. *Educ:* Univ Va, BME, 59, MME, 61; Va Polytech Inst, PhD(eng mech), 65. *Prof Exp:* Instr eng mech, Va Polytech Inst, 61-64. *Mem:* Am Soc Mech Engrs; Sigma Xi. *Res:* Vibrations; fracture mechanics. *Mailing Add:* 1865 Queen's Way Chamblee GA 30341-1021

KINGDON, HENRY SHANNON, BIOCHEMISTRY, HEMATOLOGY. *Current Pos:* vpres sci affairs & chief med officer, Blood Ther Group, 91-93, VPRES CLIN & REGULATORY AFFAIRS, GENE THER UNIT, BAXTER HEALTHCARE, 93- *Personal Data:* b Puunene, Hawaii, July 2, 34; m 57, 85, Jodi Kremiller; c Holly, Cathy & Henry C. *Educ:* Oberlin Col, AB, 56; Western Res Univ, MD & PhD(biochem), 63. *Prof Exp:* Intern & resident internal med, Univ Wash, 63-65; clin assoc, Nat Heart Inst, 65-67; from asst prof to assoc prof med & biochem, Univ Chicago, 67-73; prof med & biochem, Univ NC, Chapel Hill, 73-81; med dir, Hyland Therapeut, Glendale, Calif, 81-90, vpres, 84-90, vpres & gen mgr, Hyland Biotechnol, Hayward, Calif, 90-91. *Concurrent Pos:* Guggenheim fel, 72-73. *Mem:* Am Chem Soc; Am Fedn Clin Res; Int Soc Thrombosis & Haemostasis; Am Soc Hemat; Am Soc Biol Chem. *Res:* Hematology; enzymology of blood coagulation; regulation of nitrogen metabolism in microorganisms; primary structure of regulatory and coagulation enzymes; human immunodeficiency virus inactivation of blood products. *Mailing Add:* Gene Ther Unit Baxter Healthcare Baxter Technol Park 1627 Lake Cook Rd Deerfield IL 60015. *Fax:* 847-940-6271

KINGERY, BERNARD TROY, PHYSICS. *Current Pos:* ASST PROF PHYSICS, NJ INST TECHNOL, 52- *Personal Data:* b Metter, Ga, July 16, 20; m 59; c 2. *Educ:* Ga Southern Col, BS, 48; Columbia Univ, MA, 49. *Prof Exp:* Instr physics, Orange County Community Col, 50-52; supvr physics courses, Div Technol, Newark Col Eng. *Concurrent Pos:* Instr teaching of sci, Teachers Col, Columbia Univ, 57-58. *Mem:* AAAS; Am Soc Eng Educ; Am Asn Physics Teachers; Nat Sci Teachers Asn; Am Asn Univ Prof; Sigma Xi. *Res:* Science teacher education. *Mailing Add:* 92 Oak Ridge Ave Nutley NJ 07110

KINGERY, W DAVID, CERAMICS, MATERIALS SCIENCE. *Current Pos:* REGENTS PROF MAT SCI & ENG & REGENTS PROF ANTHROP, UNIV ARIZ, TUCSON, 92- *Personal Data:* b New York, NY, July 7, 26; m, Lily; c William, Rebekah & Andrew. *Educ:* Mass Inst Technol, SB, 48, ScD(ceramics), 50. *Hon Degrees:* PhD, Tokyo Inst Technol, 82; ScD, Ecole Polytechnique Federale de Lausanne, 88. *Honors & Awards:* Purdy Award, Am Ceramic soc, 54, John Jeppson Award, 58, Robert Sosman Mem Lectr, 73, Albert V Bleininger Award, 77, F H Norton Award, 77, Edward Orton Jr Mem Lectr, 80, Hobart M Kraner Award, 85; Wagener Lectr, Tokyo Inst Technol, 76; Kurtz Lectr, Technion, Haifa, 78; Centennial Award, Japanese Ceramic Soc, 91. *Prof Exp:* Res assoc, Mass Inst Technol, 49-50, from asst prof to prof, 50-88. *Concurrent Pos:* Foreign collabr, Comn Atomic Energy, France, 64-65; vis prof, Johns Hopkins Univ, 87-88; regents fel, Smithsonian Inst, 87-88; chmn, Comt Ceramic Hist & Archaeol, Am Ceramic Soc & bd trustees, Int Acad Ceramics; mem, Mat Educ Coun, Mat Res Soc; ed-in-chief, Ceramics Int. *Mem:* Nat Acad Eng; fel Am Ceramic Soc; fel AAAS; Am Acad Arts & Sci. *Res:* Archaeological ceramics; author of more than 200 technical publications. *Mailing Add:* Dept Mat Sci & Eng Univ Ariz Tucson AZ 85721. *Fax:* 520-621-8117

KINGHORN, ALAN DOUGLAS, PHARMACOGNOSY, PHYTOCHEMISTRY. *Current Pos:* res assoc, 76-77, from asst prof to assoc prof, 77-86, PROF PHARMACOG, UNIV ILL, CHICAGO, 86-, ASSOC DIR, PROG COLLAB RES PHARMACEUT SCI, 92-, ASST HEAD, DEPT MED CHEM & PHARMACOG, 95- *Personal Data:* b Newcastle-upon-Tyne, UK, Aug 31, 47; m 76, Helen M Bermudez. *Educ:* Univ Bradford, UK, BPharm, 69; Univ Strathclyde, Glasgow, UK, 70; Sch Pharm, Univ London, PhD(pharmacog), 75, DSc, 90. *Prof Exp:* Anal chemist, Burroughs Wellcome Co, Dartford, UK, 70-71; teaching fel pharmacog, Sch Pharm, Univ London, UK, 71-75; postdoctoral pharmacog, Univ Miss, 75-76. *Concurrent Pos:* Ed, Phytochem Anal, 89-93; guest prof pharmacog, ETH-Zentrum, Zurich, Switz, 90; B Kenneth West Univ Scholar, Univ Ill, 93-; mem, AIDS & Related Dis D Study Sect, NIH, 93-97; ed-in-chief, J Natural Prod, 94; vis prof, Univ Salerno Zlulu, 96. *Mem:* Am Chem Soc; Am Soc Pharmacog (pres, 90-91); fel Royal Pharmaceut Soc; Soc Econ Bot (pres, 91-92); fel Linean Soc London; fel Am Asn Pharmaceut Scientists. *Res:* Isolation, structure elucidation, semi-synthesis, chemical analysis, and bioassay of plant secondary metabolites with interesting biological activities, especially compounds that exhibit antineoplastic, antiviral bitter-tasting, cytotoxic, insecticidal, mutagenic, skin-irritant or sweet-tasting properties. *Mailing Add:* Dept Med Chem & Pharmacog Col Pharm Univ Il 833 S Wood St Chicago IL 60612. *E-Mail:* u1123a@ulcvm.ull.edu

KINGMAN, HARRY ELLIS, JR, VETERINARY MEDICINE. *Current Pos:* RETIRED. *Personal Data:* b Ft Collins, Colo, Sept 4, 11; m 36; c 1. *Educ:* Colo State Univ, DVM, 33. *Prof Exp:* Jr veterinarian, US Bur Animal Indust, 33-39; chief veterinarian, Wilson & Co, Inc, Ill, 39-53; asst exec secy, Am Vet Med Asn, 53-58, exec secy, 58-66; exec dir, Nat Soc Med Res, 66-78. *Concurrent Pos:* Mem, Nat Adv Food & Drug Coun, 65-69. *Mem:* Am Vet Med Asn (treas, 52-58). *Res:* Public health; food hygiene; physiology of reproduction of cattle. *Mailing Add:* 1707 Essex Dr Ft Collins CO 80526

KINGMAN, ROBERT EARL, PHYSICS. *Current Pos:* from asst prof to assoc prof, 71-79, PROF, ANDREWS UNIV, 79-, CHAIR, PHYSICS DEPT, 71- *Personal Data:* b Phoenix, Ariz, June 24, 38; m 59; c 4. *Educ:* Walla Walla Col, BS, 61; Univ Ariz, MS, 67, PhD(physics), 71. *Prof Exp:* Instr physics, Walla Walla Col, 63-66, asst prof, 66-67; instr physics, Univ Ariz, 71. *Mem:* Am Phys Soc; Am Asn Physics Teachers; Am Asn Univ Prof; Sigma Xi; Coun Undergrad Res. *Res:* Study of super clustering of galaxies; method of describing decay of unstable quatum states; study of cosmological models based on the Robertson-Walker metric. *Mailing Add:* Physics Dept Andrews Univ Berrien Springs MI 49104-0001

KINGREA, C(HARLES) L(EO), CHEMICAL ENGINEERING, PROGRAM MANAGEMENT. *Current Pos:* RETIRED. *Personal Data:* b Barren Springs, Va, Aug 17, 23; m 46, Margaret McCreary; c Richard Owen, David Leonard & Kay (Barnhill). *Educ:* Va Polytech Inst, BS, 43, MS, 51, PhD(chem eng), 53, Univ Houston, MBA, 81. *Prof Exp:* Owner-mgr, Kingrea Milling Co, Va, 46-53; process design engr, Ethyl Corp, 53-56, asst supt mfg tech serv, 56-58, econ anal engr, 58, proj mgr, 58-60, head eng & math sci, 60-63, head spec process design assignment, Ethyl Corp, La, 63-68, gen supt alcohol opers, Tex, 68-71, gen supt opers, 71-80, mgr tech planning & proj coordr, 80-87. *Concurrent Pos:* Prod engr, Dallas Chem Procurement Dist, 43-44, property disposal officer, 44-46; US Army Officer, 43-83. *Mem:* Am Inst Chem Engrs; Sigma Xi. *Res:* Mass transfer operations, particularly thermal diffusion; chemical process design; chemical project management. *Mailing Add:* 3737 Essen Lane No 16B Baton Rouge LA 70809

KINGREA, JAMES I, JR, QUALITY ASSURANCE MANAGEMENT, SUPPLIER SOURCE ASSURANCE MANAGEMENT. *Current Pos:* RETIRED. *Personal Data:* b Philadelphia, Pa, Mar 10, 28; m 47; c James I III & Kathleen V. *Educ:* Pa Mil Col, BSEE, 50. *Prof Exp:* Mgr, Qual Systs & Serv, Steam Div, Westinghouse Elec Corp, 69-86; mgr, Advan Develop & Eng Ctr, 86-89; dir qual, Eng Systs Co, Div Datron, 89-94. *Concurrent Pos:* Qual consult, 70-; weld inspector, Am Weld Soc, 82- *Mem:* Sr mem, Am Soc Qual Control; Am Soc Mech Engrs; Am Welding Soc. *Res:* Quality discipline relating to surface texture and lay; mathematical definition of finishes; equipment used to measure different finishes; specification of surface finish requirements; generation of specific finishes. *Mailing Add:* 65 Worrell Dr Springfield PA 19064

KINGSBURY, CHARLES ALVIN, ORGANIC CHEMISTRY. *Current Pos:* from asst prof to assoc prof, 67-72, PROF ORG CHEM, UNIV NEBR, LINCOLN, 72- *Personal Data:* b Louisville, Ky, Jan 12, 35; m 58; c 5. *Educ:* Iowa State Col, BS, 56; Univ Calif, Los Angeles, PhD(org chem), 60. *Prof Exp:* NSF fel, Harvard Univ, 62-63; instr org chem, Iowa State Univ, 63-67. *Mem:* Royal Soc Chem; Am Chem Soc. *Res:* Stereochemistry; reaction mechanisms. *Mailing Add:* 7327 York Lane Lincoln NE 68505-2149

KINGSBURY, DAVID THOMAS, VIROLOGY, MICROBIOLOGY. *Current Pos:* AT GEORGE WASHINGTON UNIV MED CTR, WASHINGTON, DC. *Personal Data:* b Seattle, Wash, Oct 24, 40; m 82. *Educ:* Univ Wash, BS, 62, MS, 64; Univ Calif, San Diego, PhD(biol), 71. *Prof Exp:* Microbiologist, Naval Med Res Inst, 64-67; res fel microbiol, Am Inst Biol Sci, 67-68; from asst prof to assoc prof microbiol, Univ Calif, Irvine, 72-81, prof med microbiol & virol, Berkeley, 81-86; asst dir biol, behav & social sci, NSF, 84-88. *Concurrent Pos:* Am Cancer Soc Dernham fel oncol, Univ Calif, San Diego, 71-72 & 77 & NIH, 78-79; vis scientist, Scripps Clin & Res Found, La Jolla, Calif, 73-80; dir, Naval Biosci Lab, Oakland, 81-84; mem, bd regents, Nat Libr Med, 84-; adj prof microbiol, George Washington Univ, 85- *Mem:* Fel AAAS; Am Soc Microbiol; Am Soc Virol; Soc Genetic Microbiol. *Res:* Oncogenic viruses; viral genetics; biochemistry of virus replication; techniques in diagnostic virology and microbiology; biochemistry and genetics of the unconventional viruses. *Mailing Add:* Dept Microbiol & Immunol George Washington Univ Med Ctr 2300 I St NW Washington DC 20037-2337

KINGSBURY, DAVID WILSON, VIROLOGY, MOLECULAR BIOLOGY. *Current Pos:* SR SCI OFFICER, HOWARD HUGHES MED INST, 88- *Personal Data:* b Jersey City, NJ, Apr 2, 33; m 57; c 7. *Educ:* Manhattan Col, BS, 55; Yale Univ, MD, 59. *Hon Degrees:* DSc, Manhattan Col, 90. *Prof Exp:* Intern path, Yale Univ, 59-60, asst resident, 60-61; from res fel to mem, 63-69, mem div virol, St Jude Hosp, Memphis, 69-88. *Concurrent Pos:* USPHS res fel, Yale Univ, 61-63, St Jude Hosp, Memphis, 63-64, career develop award, 64-73; adj prof microbiol, Univ Tenn, Memphis, 72-85. *Mem:* Am Asn Immunol; Am Soc Microbiol; Am Soc Virol. *Res:* Negative strand RNA viruses. *Mailing Add:* 4000 Cathedral Ave NW Washington DC 20016. *Fax:* 301-215-8828

KINGSBURY, ELIZABETH W, oncology, for more information see previous edition

KINGSBURY, HERBERT B, SOLID MECHANICS, BIOMECHANICS. *Current Pos:* RETIRED. *Personal Data:* b Pittsburgh, Pa, Feb 15, 34; m 56, 90, Ellen Fish; c 3. *Educ:* Univ Conn, BS, 58; Univ Pa, MS, 61, PhD(eng mech), 64. *Prof Exp:* Scientist, Dyna/Struct Inc, 61-64; engr, Missile & Space Div, Gen Elec Corp, 64-66; asst prof aerospace eng, Pa State Univ, 66-67; from asst prof to assoc prof aerospace eng, Univ Del, 67-80, prof mech eng, 80-96. *Concurrent Pos:* Eng consult, Scott Paper Co, 70-; adj assoc prof, Sch Vet Med, Univ Pa, 78-82. *Mem:* Am Soc Mech Engrs; Am Soc Biomech; Nat Soc Prof Engrs; Am Acad Mech. *Res:* Structural mechanics; mechanics of biological structures; mechanics of porous deformable solids; structural dynamics. *Mailing Add:* 87 Goodwin Rd Gerrish Island Kittery Point ME 03905

KINGSBURY, ROBERT FREEMAN, ATOMIC SPECTROSCOPY. *Current Pos:* prof, 64-78, EMER PROF PHYSICS, BATES COL, 78- *Personal Data:* b Ithaca, NY, June 26, 12; wid; c Robert A, Martha K (Bate), Mary K (Clark) & Rita K (Cassellins). *Educ:* Bowdoin Col, BS, 34; Cornell Univ, MS, 39; Univ Pa, PhD(physics), 56. *Prof Exp:* Teacher pub schs, NY; instr sci, Mass State Teachers Col, Westfield, 42-43; instr physics, Bowdoin Col, 43, Bates Col, 44 & Univ Maine, 44-47; from instr to assoc prof, Trinity Col, Conn, 50-64. *Mem:* AAAS; Am Phys Soc; Am Asn Physics Teachers; Am Optical Soc; Sigma Xi. *Res:* Atomic spectra. *Mailing Add:* 65 Vale St Lewiston ME 04240

KINGSBURY, WILLIAM DENNIS, ORGANIC CHEMISTRY, MEDICINAL CHEMISTRY. *Current Pos:* SR CHEMIST, SMITH KLINE & FRENCH LABS, 71- *Personal Data:* b Buffalo, NY, Nov 21, 41; m 67; c 3. *Educ:* State Univ NY, Buffalo, BA, 65; Wayne State Univ, PhD(chem), 70. *Prof Exp:* Chemist, Electro Refractories & Abrasives, 61-62; instr chem, Wayne State Univ, 65-67. *Concurrent Pos:* NIH fel, Univ Kans, 70-71. *Mem:* Am Chem Soc. *Res:* Anthelmintics; animal nutrition; heterocyclic chemistry; organo sulfur chemistry; immunochemistry; antimicrobial chemotherapy. *Mailing Add:* Smith Kline Pharm L421 709 Swedeland King of Prussia PA 19406-2711

KINGSLAKE, RUDOLF, OPTICS. *Current Pos:* from asst prof to assoc prof geom optics, 29-59, prof optics, 59-84, EMER PROF OPTICS, INST OPTICS, UNIV ROCHESTER, 84- *Personal Data:* b London, Eng, Aug 28, 03; US citizen; m 29, Hilda G Conrady; c David C & Alan H (deceased). *Educ:* Univ London, BSc, 24, Imp Col, MSc & dipl, 26, DSc, 50. *Hon Degrees:* DSc, Univ Rochester, 86. *Honors & Awards:* Progress Medal, Soc Motion Picture & TV Engrs, 64; Ives Medal, Optical Soc Am, 73; Gold Medal, Soc Photo-Optical Instrumentation Engrs, 80. *Prof Exp:* Optical designer, Sir Howard Grubb, Parsons & Co, Eng, 27-28; res engr, Int Stand Elec Corp, London, 28-29. *Concurrent Pos:* Exchange prof, Imp Col, Univ London, 36-37; optical designer, Eastman Kodak Co, 37-39, head, Optical Design Dept, 39-68. *Mem:* Fel & hon mem Optical Soc Am (vpres, 45-47, pres, 47-49); fel Soc Motion Picture & TV Engrs; fel Soc Photog Scientists & Engrs; fel Soc Photo-Optical Instrumentation Engrs. *Res:* Design of lenses and optical systems; measurement of aberrations; effect of aberrations on optical images; applied optics. *Mailing Add:* 1570 East Ave Rochester NY 14617

KINGSLAND, GRAYDON CHAPMAN, PLANT PATHOLOGY. *Current Pos:* asst prof bot & asst pathologist, 60-67, assoc prof, 67-84, PROF PLANT PATH & PHYSIOL, CLEMSON UNIV, 84- *Personal Data:* b Burlington, Vt, Aug 28, 28; m 50; c 4. *Educ:* Univ Vt, BA, 52; Univ NH, MS, 55; Pa State Univ, PhD(plant path), 58. *Prof Exp:* Res technician, Conn Tobacco Lab, 52-53; assoc pathologist, United Fruit Co, Honduras, 58-60. *Concurrent Pos:* Plant pathologist, USAID/SECID Seych Is food crop improv proj, 81-82 & 84. *Mem:* Am Phytopath Soc; Sierra Club; Wilderness Soc; Nat Audubon Soc; Sigma Xi. *Res:* Diseases of cereal grains; ecology of microflora of rhizospheres and seeds of cereal grains; chemical control of cereal grains diseases; teaching introductory and graduate phytopathology; tropical agriculture; mycology. *Mailing Add:* 209 Manley Dr Clemson SC 29631

KINGSLEY, HENRY A(DELBERT), CHEMICAL ENGINEERING, PROCESS ENGINEERING. *Current Pos:* PRES, COMTECH CONSULTS INC, 84- *Personal Data:* b Wakefield, RI, May 5, 21; m 43, Helen Polis; c John & Joyce. *Educ:* Univ RI, BS, 43; Yale Univ, DEng, 49. *Prof Exp:* Engr, Shell Develop Co, Calif, 49-59, supvr process eng, 59-63, dept head licensing & design eng, 64-65, dir res & develop lab, Indust Chem Div, Shell Chem Co, Tex, 65-67, mgr proj develop, Plastics & Resins Div, NY, 67-70, mgr chem & chem eng dept, Explor & Prod Res Ctr, Shell Develop Co, 70-72, mgr chem process eng, 72-74, mgr support process eng, Shell Oil Co, 74-82; consult, 82-97. *Mem:* Am Inst Chem Engrs; Am Chem Soc; Sigma Xi. *Mailing Add:* 411 W Fair Harbor Lane Houston TX 77079-2515. *E-Mail:* henrykingsley_houston@worldnet.att.net

KINGSLEY, JACK DEAN, SOLID STATE DEVICES, OPTOELECTRONICS. *Current Pos:* Physicist, Gen Elec Res & Develop Ctr, 60-71, mgr, Light Emitting Diode Array Prog, 71-72, mgr, Optoelectronics Br, 72-81, mgr, Electronic Mat Br, 81-83, mgr, Display Br, 83-85, PHYSICIST, GEN ELEC RES & DEVELOP CTR, 85- *Personal Data:* b Wonewoc, Wis, Aug 10, 34; m 62, Beverly; c Lawrence, Robert & Andrew. *Educ:* Univ Wis, BSEE, 56, MSEE, 57; Univ Ill, MS, 58, PhD(physics), 60. *Mem:* Am Phys Soc. *Res:* Optical spectroscopy of solids; quantum electronics; luminescence; point defects in solids; imaging and display devices. *Mailing Add:* 460 Tiara Vista Dr Grand Junction CO 81503-8700

KINGSLEY, MICHAEL CHARLES STEPHEN, ECOLOGY, BIOMETRICS. *Current Pos:* RES SCIENTIST, CAN DEPT FISHERIES & OCEANS, 83- *Personal Data:* b Harrow, UK, Oct 20, 41; Can citizen. *Educ:* Univ Cambridge, MA, 66; Lancaster Univ, MA, 68. *Prof Exp:* Statistician, Can Forestry Serv, 71-73; statistician, Can Wildlife Serv, 73-78, biologist, 78-83. *Mem:* Biomet Soc; Soc Marine Mammal; Arctic Inst NAm. *Res:* Ecology of marine mammals; behavior, vocalizations, population dynamics, population estimation, growth. *Mailing Add:* Inst Maurice LaMontague 850 Rte de la Mar PO Box 1000 Mont-Joli PQ G5H 3Z4 Can

KINGSOLVER, CHARLES H, PLANT PATHOLOGY. *Current Pos:* CONSULT PLANT DIS RES, 79- *Personal Data:* b Peru, Nebr, Aug 31, 14; wid; c Carolyn (Purvis), John G, Joel G & Cynthia (Gittinger). *Educ:* Nebr State Teachers Col, Peru, AB, 35; Iowa State Univ, MS, 39, PhD(plant path), 43. *Prof Exp:* Asst prof bot, Univ Mo, 46-51; sect chief, Biol Br, Chem Corps, Biol Warfare Labs, Md, 51-55, chief biol br II, 55-57; agr adminr, Mkt Qual Res Div, Agr Mkt Serv, USDA, 57-62; chief biol br, Crops Div, US Army Biol Labs, 62-68, chief biol br III, 68-71; dir, Plant Dis Res Lab, Northeast Region, Sci & Educ Admin-Agr Res, USDA, 71-79. *Concurrent Pos:* Adj prof plant path, Pa State Univ, 72- *Mem:* Sigma Xi; Am Phytopath Soc. *Res:* Plant disease epidemiology; quantitation of disease increase and spread; predictive systems; threat potential of foreign plant disease; biological control of weeds with plant pathogens. *Mailing Add:* PO Box 337 Braddock Heights MD 21714

KINGSOLVER, JOHN MARK, ENTOMOLOGY, TAXONOMY SEED BEETLES BRUCLIDAE. *Current Pos:* RETIRED. *Personal Data:* b Selma, Ind, Mar 20, 25; wid; c John M (deceased) & Rebecca D. *Educ:* Purdue Univ, BS, 51; Univ Ill, MS, 56, PhD(entom), 61. *Prof Exp:* Res asst entom, Univ Ill, 54-61; res assoc, Ill Natural Hist Surv, 61-62; res entomologist, Syst Entom Lab, USDA, 62-90. *Concurrent Pos:* Res assoc, USDA & Fla State Dept Agr. *Mem:* Am Entom Soc; Asn Trop Biol; Ctr Syst Entom; Coleop Soc. *Res:* Taxonomy of seed-beetles (Bruchidae) of Western Hemisphere. *Mailing Add:* 3035 SW First Ave Gainesville FL 32607

KINGSTON, CHARLES RICHARD, FORENSIC SCIENCE. *Current Pos:* PROF CRIMINALISTICS, JOHN JAY COL, CITY UNIV NY, 68- *Personal Data:* b San Diego, Calif, Apr 11, 31; m 69; c 1. *Educ:* Univ Calif, Berkeley, BS, 59, MCriminol, 61, Dr Criminol, 64. *Prof Exp:* Lab technician, Criminalistics Lab, Sch Criminol, Univ Calif, Berkeley, 58-63, res criminalist, 63-64, asst res criminalist, 64-65; consult, NY State Identification & Intel Syst, 65-66, chief criminalistics res bur, 66-68. *Mem:* Am Chem Soc; Am Statist Asn; Am Acad Forensic Sci. *Res:* Application of probability and statistics in criminalistics; computer applications in criminology and criminalistics. *Mailing Add:* 6 Surray Close White Plains NY 10607

KINGSTON, DAVID GEORGE IAN, NATURAL PRODUCTS CHEMISTRY. *Current Pos:* assoc prof, 71-77, PROF CHEM, VA POLYTECH INST & STATE UNIV, 77- *Personal Data:* b London, Eng, Nov 9, 38; m 66, Beverly Mark; c Joy, Christy, & Jonathan. *Educ:* Cambridge Univ, BA, 60, PhD(org chem), 63; dipl theol, Univ London, 62. *Prof Exp:* Res fel chem, Queens' Col, Cambridge Univ, 62-66, NATO fel, 64-66; asst prof chem, State Univ NY Albany, 66-71. *Concurrent Pos:* Res assoc, Mass Inst Technol, 63-64; mem, biomed sci study sect, NIH, 79-84; assoc ed, J Natural Prod, 83-; Div Cancer Treatment Contracts Rev Comm, NIH, 87-91; mem, Div Cancer Treatment Contracts Rev Comt, NIH, 87-92, Chmn, 89-92. *Mem:* Am Chem Soc; Royal Soc Chem; Am Soc Pharmacog (vpres, 87-88, pres, 88-89). *Res:* Natural products chemistry; structure and synthesis of biologically active natural products; chemistry of taxol. *Mailing Add:* Dept Chem Va Polytech Inst & State Univ Blacksburg VA 24061-0212. *Fax:* 540-231-7702; *E-Mail:* dkingston@chemserver.chem.vt.edu

KINGSTON, DAVID LYMAN, SOLID STATE PHYSICS, SEMICONDUCTOR MATERIAL CHARACTERIZATION. *Current Pos:* RETIRED. *Personal Data:* b Lansing, Mich, June 26, 30; m 54, Janice M Ebright; c Charlene R, Michelle M & David L Jr. *Educ:* Mich State Univ, BS, 53, MS, 55. *Prof Exp:* Res physicist, Aerospace Res Labs, Wright-Patterson AFB, Ohio, 55-75, res physicist solid state physics, Air Force Avionics Lab, 75-85, res physicist, Solid State Electronics Directorate, Wright Lab, 85-93. *Mem:* Am Phys Soc. *Res:* Conducting research on the characterization of III-V compound semiconductors such as GaAs and InP using the techniques of luminescence topography and x-ray photoemission spectroscopy. *Mailing Add:* 10 E Routzong Dr Fairborn OH 45324

KINGSTON, GEORGE C, POLYMER PROCESS DESIGN & DEVELOPMENT. *Current Pos:* Sr res engr, Monsanto Polymer Prod Co, 79-82, res specialist, 82-87, tech leader, 87-89, res & develop mgr, 89-93, applications develop mgr, 93-94, new prod develop process redesign leader, 94-96, RES & DEVELOP MGR, CHEM GROUP MONSANTO, 96- *Personal Data:* b New York, NY. *Educ:* Manhattan Col, BE, 70; Clarkson Col Tech, MS, 72, PhD(chem eng), 75. *Concurrent Pos:* Instr chem eng, Clarkson Col Tech, 74-75; adj chem eng, Univ Dayton, 78-79, Univ Mass, Amherst, 82. *Mem:* Am Inst Chem Engrs; Soc Plastics Engrs; Prod Develop Mgt Asn. *Res:* Design and development of polymer processes; polymerization; process effects on polymer structure and properties; oxidative stability of polymers. *Mailing Add:* Monsanto 730 Worcester St Springfield MA 01151. *E-Mail:* 72643.3640@compuserve.com

KINGSTON, H M, ANALYTICAL ENVIRONMENTAL CHEMISTRY, LABORATORY AUTOMATION. *Current Pos:* PROF ANALYTICAL & ENVIRON CHEM, DUQUESNE UNIV, 91- *Personal Data:* b Indiana, Pa, July 9, 49; m 76, Mary Lynn Mandigo. *Educ:* Indiana Univ Pa, BS, 73, MS, 75; Am Univ, PhD(anal chem), 78. *Honors & Awards:* Research & Develop 100 Award, 96. *Prof Exp:* Res chemist, Nat Inst Stand & Technol, 76-88, supvry res chemist & group leader, 88-91, proj mgr, Consortium Automated Lab Systs, 89-91. *Concurrent Pos:* Cong sci fel, US Cong, House Rep, 84-85. *Res:* Fundamental research in separation science, speciation, chromatography and microwave energy application, methods and instrument development, standard reference materials development and certification, environmental test method development, and automation including robotics. *Mailing Add:* Duquesne Univ 308 Mellon Pittsburgh PA 15282. *Fax:* 412-396-5359

KINGSTON, JOHN MAURICE, MATHEMATICS. *Current Pos:* assoc, 40-43, from instr to asst prof, 43-59, ASSOC PROF MATH, UNIV WASH, 59-, EXEC SECY DEPT, 52- *Personal Data:* b Joliet, Ill, May 25, 14; m 37; c 2. *Educ:* Univ Western Ont, BA, 35; Univ Toronto, MA, 36, PhD(theory, abstract groups), 39. *Prof Exp:* Lectr math, Univ BC, 39-40. *Concurrent Pos:* Fel, NSF, 59-60. *Mem:* Nat Coun Teachers Math; Math Asn Am. *Res:* Abstract group theory. *Mailing Add:* 3736 47th Pl NE Seattle WA 98105

KINGSTON, NEWTON, ZOOLOGY, PARASITOLOGY. *Current Pos:* assoc prof, 68-76, PROF PARASITOL, UNIV WYO, 76- *Personal Data:* b Akron, Ohio, June 6, 25; m 52; c 3. *Educ:* Wayne State Univ, BA, 54, MSc, 56; Univ Toronto, PhD(zool), 62. *Prof Exp:* Asst prof biol, Detroit Inst Technol, 59-62 & Geneva Col, 62-64; NIH fel, Nat Univ Mex, 64-65; assoc prof, Geneva Col, 65-68. *Mem:* Am Soc Parasitol; Am Micros Soc; Am Soc Protozoologists; Wildlife Dis Asn. *Res:* Morphology of the nervous system of trematodes; life history studies of monogenetic and digenetic trematodes, cestodes; systematics of spinturnicid mites from bats; protozoan parasites domestic and wild ungulate raptors. *Mailing Add:* 418 S 12th Ave Laramie WY 82070

KINGSTON, PAUL L, FINANCIAL MODELING, MARKETING STRATEGIES. *Current Pos:* Mem staff appl sci, Int Bus Mach Corp, 58-63, sr sci mkt, 63-74, consult power indust, 74-84, CONSULT ACAD MKT, IBM CORP, 84- *Personal Data:* b Rochester, NY, Feb 12, 32; m 62; c 6. *Educ:* Colgate Univ, BA, 54; Univ Rochester, MA, 57; Syracuse Univ, MS, 75. *Concurrent Pos:* Adj lectr, Syracuse Univ, 76-85. *Mem:* Am Math Soc; Math Asn Am; Opers Res Soc Am; Inst Mgt Sci; Soc Indust & Appl Math. *Res:* Mathematical programming and financial modeling for solving business and management problems. *Mailing Add:* 5490 Duguid Rd No 3A Fayetteville NY 13066-9508

KINGSTON, ROBERT HILDRETH, SOLID STATE DEVICES, OPTICS. *Current Pos:* RETIRED. *Personal Data:* b Somerville, Mass, Feb 13, 28; m 52; c 4. *Educ:* Mass Inst Technol, BS, 48, MS, 48, PhD(physics), 51. *Honors & Awards:* Centennial Medal, Inst Elec & Electronics Engrs, 84. *Prof Exp:* Mem staff, Transistor Res & Develop, Bell Labs, 51-52; mem, Solid State Physics Group, Mass Inst Technol, 52-61, leader, Optics & Infrared Group, 61-69, head, Optics Div, 69-72, leader, Infrared Radar Group, 72-77, sr staff, 77-84, assoc leader, Optical Communs Technol Group, 84-87, sr staff, Lincoln Lab, 87- 90. *Concurrent Pos:* Vis assoc prof, Stanford Univ, 64-65; ed, J Quantum Electronics, Inst Elec & Electronics Engrs, 65-70; adj prof, Mass Inst Technol, 85-90, sr lectr, 90-; auth, Detection Optical & Infrared Radiation, 78. *Mem:* Nat Acad Eng; fel Optical Soc Am; fel Inst Elec & Electronics Engrs; fel Am Phys Soc. *Res:* Physical principles of semiconductor devices; physics of semiconductor surfaces; magnetic resonance; solid state maser, parametric amplifiers; optical masers; non-linear optics; tuneable semiconductor lasers; infrared detectors. *Mailing Add:* 4 Field Rd Lexington MA 02173

KINI, ARAVINDA MATTAR, ORGANIC SOLID STATE CHEMISTRY & PHYSICS, ORGANIC SUPERCONDUCTORS. *Current Pos:* asst chemist, 86-91, CHEMIST, ARGONNE NAT LAB, 91- *Personal Data:* b Karkala, India, Jan 14, 51; US citizen; m 79, Mridula Sharma; c Rohini, Nutan, Seema & Ashvin. *Educ:* Univ Mysore, India, BSc, 70; Indian Inst Technol, Madras, MSc, 71; Univ Hawaii, Manoa, PhD(chem), 79. *Honors & Awards:* Outstanding Sci Accomplishment Award, Dept Energy, 90. *Prof Exp:* Lectr chem, Manipal Eng Col, India, 71-72; jr researcher, Univ Hawaii, 79; postdoctoral fel, Johns Hopkins Univ, Baltimore, 80-84; res scientist, LTV Aerospace & Defense Co, Dallas, 84-86. *Concurrent Pos:* Consult, Strem Chems Inc, 88-89; vis prof chem, Univ Angers, France, 95; prin investr, NATO, 95-96. *Mem:* Am Chem Soc; Am Phys Soc. *Res:* Design and synthesis of organic electrical conductors and superconductors; conducting polymers; organic synthesis; electrochemistry; crystal growth; organic thin films; isotope effect and superconductivity. *Mailing Add:* Argonne Nat Lab Bldg 200/A125 Argonne IL 60439-4831. *Fax:* 630-252-4470; *E-Mail:* amkini@anl.gov

KINKEL, ARLYN WALTER, PHARMACY. *Current Pos:* RETIRED. *Personal Data:* b Fond du Lac, Wis, Oct 15, 29; m 55; c 3. *Educ:* Univ Wis, BS, 52, MS, 57, PhD(pharm), 58. *Prof Exp:* From assoc res pharmacist to sr res pharmacist, Parke-Davis Res Div, Warner-Lambert Co, 58-70, sect dir pharmaceut res & develop, 70-80, dir clin pharmacokinetics, Pharmacokinetic-Drug Metab Dept, 81-92. *Mem:* Am Pharmaceut Asn; fel Acad Pharmaceut Sci; Am Col Clin Pharmacol; fel Am Asn Pharmaceut Sci. *Res:* Biopharmaceutics; assay of blood levels and drugs; pharmacokinetics. *Mailing Add:* 13966 N Buckingham Dr Oro Valley AZ 85737-5851

KINLOCH, BOHUN BAKER, JR, GENETICS, PLANT PATHOLOGY. *Current Pos:* GENETICIST, PAC SOUTHWEST FOREST & RANGE EXP STA, US FOREST SERV, 68- *Personal Data:* b Charleston, SC, July 21, 34; m 61, 69; c 4. *Educ:* Univ Va, BA, 56; NC State Univ, BS, 62, MS, 65, PhD(genetics), 68. *Prof Exp:* Res asst forest genetics & path, NC State Univ, 62-68. *Mem:* Am Phytopath Soc. *Res:* Genetics of disease resistance in forest trees; population genetics of forest trees. *Mailing Add:* 207 Scott St Mill Valley CA 94941

KINLOCH, ROBERT ARMSTRONG, NEMATOLOGY. *Current Pos:* Assoc nematologist, 68-80, ASSOC PROF AGRON, AGR EXP STA, UNIV FLA, 80- *Personal Data:* b Dumbarton, Scotland, Feb 15, 39; m 63; c 3. *Educ:* Glasgow Univ, BSc, 63; Univ Calif, Davis, PhD(entom, nematol), 68. *Concurrent Pos:* Ed, Ann of Appl Nematol. *Mem:* Soc Nematol; Orgn Trop Am Nematol. *Res:* Biology and host-parasite relationships of plant parasitic nematodes; economic control of plant parasitic nematodes affecting agronomic crops. *Mailing Add:* Agr Res Ctr Univ Fla PO Box Rte 3 Jay FL 32565. *E-Mail:* rakh@gnv.ifas.ufl.edu

KINLOUGH-RATHBONE, ROELENE L, HEMATOLOGY, ATHEROSCLEROSIS. *Current Pos:* lectr, 71-73, from asst prof to assoc prof, 73-82, PROF PATH, MCMASTER UNIV, 82- *Personal Data:* b Adelaide, SAustralia, Aug 20, 38. *Educ:* Univ Adelaide, MB & BS, 61, MD, 67; McMaster Univ, PhD(med sci), 71. *Prof Exp:* Res asst, Nat Heart Found, Australia, 64-67; fel, Med Res Coun Can, 67-71. *Concurrent Pos:* Sr res fel, Ont Heart Found, 75-80, res assoc, 80-83; consult, NIH, 77-79; mem, Sci Prog Comt, 8th Int Cong Haemostasis & Thrombosis, 79-81, Sci Rev Comt, Ont Heart Found, 81-84 & Coun Thrombosis, Am Heart Asn; prin investr,

Med Res Coun, Can, 74- & NATO res grant, 84; chmn grad prog med sci, McMaster Univ, 81-87, actg assoc dean educ, 87-88, assoc vpres fac health sci, 92- *Mem:* Int Soc Thrombosis & Haemostasis; Am Heart Asn; AAAS; Can Soc Clin Invest; Am Soc Hemat; Am Soc Invest Path; Can Atheroscal Soc; Sr Women's Acad Admin Can. *Res:* Mechanisms influencing hemostasis, thrombosis and the development of atherosclerosis; cellular and biochemical mechanisms in platelet response to stimuli; factors governing the response of blood and vessels to injury. *Mailing Add:* Dept Path McMaster Univ Med Ctr 1200 Main St W Rm 2E5C Hamilton ON L8N 3Z5 Can. *Fax:* 905-546-0800

KINMAN, RILEY NELSON, CIVIL & SANITARY ENGINEERING. *Current Pos:* assoc prof, 68-73, PROF CIVIL ENG, UNIV CINCINNATI, 73-; PRES, PRISTINE, INC, 74-; PRES, RNK ENVIRON, INC, 80- *Personal Data:* b Dry Ridge, Ky, Jan 25, 36; m 57, Barbara Brown; c Joe R & Kathy. *Educ:* Univ Ky, BS, 59; Univ Cincinnati, MS, 62; Univ Fla, PhD(sanit eng), 65. *Prof Exp:* Engr-in-training, Water Dept, City of Dayton, Ohio, 59-61, 62; res assoc chem & sanit sci, Univ Fla, 65-66; asst chief, Demonstration Grants Br, Fed Water Pollution Control Admin, 66-67, chief, 67-68. *Mem:* Am Soc Civil Engrs; Water Pollution Control Fedn; Am Water Works Asn; Am Chem Soc; Sigma Xi; Soc Prof Engrs. *Res:* Treatment and ultimate disposal of hazardous wastes; research and development for control of water pollution, especially the physical, chemical, biological, physiological, economic and political aspects of water pollution; solid and hazardous waste management. *Mailing Add:* 415 Stevenson Rd Erlanger KY 41018-2472

KINMAN, THOMAS DAVID, ASTRONOMY. *Current Pos:* astronr, 69-, EMER ASTRONR, KITT PEAK NAT OBSERV. *Personal Data:* b Rugby, Eng, Aug 10, 28; m 63; c 2. *Educ:* Oxford Univ, BA, 49, MA & DPhil(astron), 53. *Prof Exp:* Dept demonstr, Univ Observ, Oxford Univ, 49-53; sci officer physics, Admirality Res Lab, Teddington, 53-54; Radcliffe travelling fel astron, Univ Observ, Oxford Univ, 54-56 & Radcliffe Observ, Pretoria, 56-59; sr sci officer, Royal Observ, Cape Town, 59-60; from asst astronr to astronr, Lick Observ, Univ Calif, Santa Cruz, 60-69. *Concurrent Pos:* Mem comn, Int Astron Union, 58. *Mem:* Am Astron Soc. *Res:* Large scale structure of our own and other galaxies, particularly constitution and dynamics of older stars and star clusters; quasistellar objects. *Mailing Add:* Kitt Peak Nat Observ PO Box 26732 Tucson AZ 85726

KINN, DONALD NORMAN, ACAROLOGY, NEMATOLOGY. *Current Pos:* RETIRED. *Personal Data:* b Chicago, Ill. *Educ:* Lawrence Col, BS, 56; Univ Wyo, MS, 62; Univ Calif, Berkeley, PhD(entom), 69. *Prof Exp:* Assoc specialist, Div Biol Control, Univ Calif, 69-70, asst res entom, 71-73; res entomologist acarol, Southern Forest Exp Sta, 75- *Mem:* Entom Soc Am; Entom Soc Can; Int Orgn Biol Control; Acarol Soc Am; Soc Nematologists. *Res:* Natural control of forest insects, especially bark beetles, by mites and nematodes; control of the pine wood nematode in wood products. *Mailing Add:* Southern Forest Exp Sta 2500 Shreveport Hwy Pineville LA 71360

KINNAIRD, RICHARD FARRELL, ENGINEERING. *Current Pos:* RETIRED. *Personal Data:* b Des Moines, Iowa, Oct 21, 12; m 44; c 2. *Educ:* Millsaps Col, BS, 34; Univ Chicago, MS, 36. *Prof Exp:* Asst, Dearborn Observ, Northwestern Univ, 36-39; optical engr, Bell & Howell Co, Chicago, 39-40; optical engr, Perkin-Elmer Corp, 40-63, sr staff engr, 63-72. *Mem:* Am Phys Soc; Optical Soc Am. *Res:* Design and theory of optical instruments. *Mailing Add:* Oak Point Rd Ellsworth ME 04605

KINNAMON, KENNETH ELLIS, PHYSIOLOGY, RADIOBIOLOGY. *Current Pos:* assoc prof physiol & asst dean instrnl & res support, 75-80, PROF PHYSIOL & ASSOC DEAN OPERS, UNIFORMED SERV UNIV HEALTH SCI, 80- *Personal Data:* b Denison, Tex, May 28, 34; m 57; c 3. *Educ:* Okla State Univ, BS, 56; Tex A&M Univ, DVM, 59; Univ Rochester, MS, 61; Univ Tenn, PhD(physiol), 71. *Prof Exp:* Res investr radiation chem, Walter Reed Army Inst Res, 59-60, chief radioisotope lab, Army Nutrit Lab, Fitzsimons Gen Hosp, Colo, 61-65, chief dept surveillance inspection, Med Dept, US Army Vet Sch, 65-68, res investr biol, 71-75. *Mem:* Radiation Res Soc; Am Physiol Soc; Health Physics Soc; Am Vet Med Asn; Soc Exp Hemat; Sigma Xi. *Res:* Mineral metabolism; physiology of wound healing; bone marrow transplantation; secondary disease; immunology; cancer therapy; chemical radiation therapy; radiation injury therapy. *Mailing Add:* Uniformed Serv Univ Health Sci 4301 Jones Bridge Rd Bethesda MD 20814

KINNARD, MATTHEW ANDERSON, NEUROPHYSIOLOGY, DENTAL RESEARCH. *Current Pos:* biologist brain res, 63-67, scientist/admin, 72-79, HEALTH SCI ADMIN, NAT INST DENT RES, NIH, BETHESDA, 85- *Personal Data:* b Nashville, Tenn, April 12, 36; m 62; c 2. *Educ:* Tenn State Univ, BS, 57, MA, 60; Georgetown Univ, PhD(physiol), 70. *Prof Exp:* Biologist virol res, Walter Reed Army Med Ctr, 60-62; asst prof physiol, DC Teachers Col, 70-71; admin health sci specialist, Cent Off, Vet Admin, 79-85. *Concurrent Pos:* Consult, NIMH, 68-70, Physiol Dept, Howard Univ, 79-80; lectr, Univ DC, 71-79; physiologist, US Civil Serv Bd Examiners, 85- *Mem:* AAAS; Am Physiol Asn; Orgn Black Scientists; Int Asn Dent Res. *Res:* Oral soft tissue diseases (oral cancer, herpes, and AIDS). *Mailing Add:* 12903 Chathlake Lane Silver Spring MD 20904

KINNARD, WILLIAM J, JR, HIGHER EDUCATION ADMINISTRATION. *Current Pos:* RETIRED. *Personal Data:* b Wilmington, Del, Apr 18, 32; m 59. *Educ:* Univ Pittsburgh, BS, 53, MS, 55; Purdue Univ, PhD(pharmacol), 57. *Honors & Awards:* Honor Achievement Award, Angiol Res Found, 65. *Prof Exp:* From asst prof to prof pharmacol, Univ Pittsburgh, 58-68; prof pharmacol & dean, Sch Pharm, Univ Md, 68-90; actg dean, Grad Sch, 74-76, dean, 76-90, actg pres, 90-91, actg assoc chancellor, 91-97. *Concurrent Pos:* Chmn bd trustees, US Pharmacopoeial Conv, 74-85; consult pharm, Surgeon Gen USAF, 84-90. *Mem:* Inst Med-Nat Acad Sci; fel AAAS; Am Phys Soc; Am Pharmaceut Asn; Am Asn Pharmaceut Scientists; Am Asn Cols Pharm (pres, 76-77); Am Coun Pharm Educ (vpres, 86-). *Res:* Health care systems and education; higher education administration. *Mailing Add:* 4000 N Charles St Baltimore MD 21218

KINNAVY, M(ARTIN) G(ERALD), mechanical engineering, mechanics, for more information see previous edition

KINNEL, ROBIN BRYAN, ORGANIC CHEMISTRY. *Current Pos:* from asst prof to prof org chem, Hamilton Col, 66-78, assoc dean, 73-76, SILAS D CHILDS PROF CHEM, HAMILTON COL, 86-, CHMN DEPT, 82- *Personal Data:* b Milwaukee, Wis, Jan 18, 37; m 60, Anne E Lutton; c Timothy S & Geoffrey C. *Educ:* Harvard Univ, AB, 59; Mass Inst Technol, PhD(org chem), 65. *Prof Exp:* Asst chem, Hercules Powder Co, Del, 56-57; jr chemist, Merck, Sharp & Dohme, NJ, 59-60; res assoc org chem, Stanford Univ, 64-66. *Concurrent Pos:* Res assoc, Cornell Univ, 76-77, Univ Hawaii, 81-82, 86, 91-92; vis prof, Univ Wis-Madison, 79, Univ Hawaii, 90. *Mem:* Sigma Xi; AAAS; Am Chem Soc; Fedn Am Scientists; Union Concerned Scientists. *Res:* Organic reaction mechanisms; medium ring chemistry; chemistry of marine natural products; synthetic organic and natural products chemistry. *Mailing Add:* Dept Chem Hamilton Col Clinton NY 13323-1292. *Fax:* 315-859-4744; *E-Mail:* rkinnel@hamilton.edu

KINNEN, EDWIN, ELECTRICAL ENGINEERING. *Current Pos:* from assoc prof to prof, 63-92, chair, 89-92, EMER PROF ELEC ENG, UNIV ROCHESTER, 92-, SR SCIENTIST, 92- *Personal Data:* b Buffalo, NY, Mar 9, 25; m 52, Ellen S Underwood; c Susan, Janet, Peter & Andrew. *Educ:* Univ Buffalo, BS, 49; Yale Univ, ME, 50; Purdue Univ, PhD(elec eng), 58. *Prof Exp:* Res engr, Res Lab, Westinghouse Elec Corp, 50-55; asst prof elec eng, Purdue Univ, 58-59 & Univ Minn, 59-63. *Concurrent Pos:* Consult, Minneapolis-Honeywell, Wash Sci, Control Data Corp, Eastman Kodak; Westinghouse fel, 55-57, NIH spec fel, 71, sci res fel, Neth, 78, 81, Paul Harris fel, 90. *Mem:* Inst Elec & Electronics Engrs; Sigma Xi; Rehab Eng Soc NAm. *Res:* Computer aided design for integrated circuits; pediatric orthoses; dynamics of blood flow; computer aided design for floorplanning, placement and routing of custom integrated circuits, based on methods of analytic optimizations; design and development of lower body orthoses for paraplegic children. *Mailing Add:* Dept Elec Eng Univ Rochester Rochester NY 14627. *Fax:* 716-275-2073; *E-Mail:* kinnen@ee.rochester.edu

KINNEY, ANTHONY JOHN, PROTEIN PURIFICATION, LIPIDOLOGY. *Current Pos:* RES BIOCHEMIST BIOCHEM & BIOTECHNOL, DUPONT EXP STA, 89- *Personal Data:* b Ilkeston, Derbyshire, UK, Sept 9, 58; m 89. *Educ:* Sussex Univ, UK, BSc, 80; Oxford Univ, UK, DPhil, 85. *Prof Exp:* Res assoc bot, La State Univ, 83-87; res fel biochem & food sci, Rutgers Univ, 87-89. *Concurrent Pos:* Res student, Agr & Food Res Coun, Letcombe Lab, 80-83; mem, Univ Col, Oxford, 80-83. *Mem:* Am Soc Biochem & Molecular Biol; Biochem Soc; NY Acad Sci; Sigma Xi. *Res:* Biochemistry, molecular biology and genetics of membrane and storage lipid metabolism in plants and yeast; genetic engineering of crop plants; biotechnology of plant transformation. *Mailing Add:* Agr Exp Sta Agr Biotechnol PO Box 80402 Wilmington DE 19880-0402. *Fax:* 302-695-4296; *E-Mail:* kinneya@al.dupont.com

KINNEY, DOUGLAS MERRILL, GEOLOGY, MAPS & ILLUSTRATIONS. *Current Pos:* PRES, GEOL SURV ASSOC, INC, 80- *Personal Data:* b Los Angeles, Calif, Feb 24, 17; m 42, Jeanette Dawless; c Douglas, Frederick & Deborah. *Educ:* Occidental Col, BA, 37; Yale Univ, MS, 42, PhD(geol), 51. *Prof Exp:* Geologist, Union Oil Co, Calif, 37-40; asst, Yale Univ, 40-42; geologist, US Geol Surv, 42-56, geol map ed, 56-80. *Concurrent Pos:* Vpres NAm, Comn Geol Map of World, 66-80. *Mem:* Geol Soc Am. *Res:* Geologic map editing, cartography and printing of colored geologic maps; geologic mapping standards and symbols. *Mailing Add:* Geol Surv Assoc Inc 5221 Baltimore Ave Bethesda MD 20816-3003

KINNEY, GILBERT FORD, PHYSICAL CHEMISTRY, EXPLOSIONS. *Current Pos:* assoc prof thermodyn & phys chem, 46-50, prof chem eng, 50-71, chmn, Dept Mat Sci & Chem, 60-69, EMER PROF CHEM ENG, NAVAL POSTGRAD SCH, 71- *Personal Data:* b Judsonia, Ark, Dec 29, 07; m 34, Martha Stinson; c Gilbert F Jr & Albert H. *Educ:* Ark Col, AB, 28; Univ Tenn, MS, 30; NY Univ, PhD(phys chem), 35. *Prof Exp:* Radio engr, Radio Sta WNBZ, NY, 30-32; res chemist, Titanium Pigment Co, 35; instr chem, Pratt Inst, 35-39, head instr, 39-42; radiologist, US Navy Bikini, 46. *Concurrent Pos:* Consult, Naval Weapons Ctr, China Lake, Calif & Anamet Labs, Berkeley, Calif, 71- *Mem:* Am Chem Soc; Am Soc Eng Educ. *Res:* Explosive shocks; electroplating; chemical engineering thermodynamics; applications of thermodynamics to chemical equilibria problems; plastics. *Mailing Add:* 2000 Glenwood Circle #403 Monterey CA 93940

KINNEY, JOHN JAMES, SYMMETRIC FUNCTIONS IN STATISTICS, PROBABILITY. *Current Pos:* assoc prof, 74-79, PROF MATH, ROSE-HULMAN INST TECHNOL, 79- *Personal Data:* b Dansville, NY, Aug 2, 32; m 62, Cherry Carter; c Kaylyn. *Educ:* St Lawrence Univ, BS, 54; Harvard Univ, AMT, 56; Univ Mich, MS, 59; Iowa State Univ, PhD(statist), 71. *Prof Exp:* Instr, 55-58, asst prof math, St Lawrence Univ, 60-64; assoc prof, State Univ NY, Oneonta, 64-68; asst prof, Univ Nebr, 71-74. *Concurrent Pos:* Dupont fel, Harvard Univ, 54, Am Asn Qual Control, 58, NSF Sci Fac, 68; dir, Ind Quant Literacy Proj, 85-; chair, Joint Comt on Curric in Probability & Statist, Am Statist Asn-Nat Coun Teachers Math, 89-91. *Mem:* Am Statist Asn; Sigma Xi; Nat Counc Teachers Math; Am Soc Qual. *Res:* Multivariate polykays; simulation in probability theory; author of one publication. *Mailing Add:* 221 Highland Ct Terre Haute IN 47802-4957

KINNEY, JOHN MARTIN, SURGERY. *Current Pos:* DIR SURG METAB, PRESBY HOSP, 63- *Personal Data:* b Evanston, Ill, May 24, 21; m 44; c 3. *Educ:* Denison Univ, AB, 43; Harvard Univ, MD, 46; Am Bd Surg, dipl; Am Bd Nutrit, dipl. *Prof Exp:* Surg intern, Peter Bent Brigham Hosp, 46-47; AEC-Nat Res Coun fel, Med Sch, Univ Colo, 49-52; from asst resident surgeon to chief resident surgeon, Peter Bent Brigham Hosp, 52-57, jr assoc surgeon, 58-63; assoc prof, 63-67; prof surg, Col Physicians & Surgeons, Columbia Univ, 67- *Concurrent Pos:* Mead Johnson scholar, Am Col Surgeons, 56-59; Henry E Warren fel surg, Harvard Med Sch, 58-60 & 62-63; assoc attend surgeon, Presby Hosp, 63-67; attend surgeon, 67-; New York Health Res Coun career scientist award, 65; mem adv comt metabolism in trauma, US Army Med Res & Develop Command, 67; mem adv panel to comt on interplay of eng with biol & med, Nat Acad Eng, 68; chmn comt on shock, Comn Emergency Med Serv, Nat Res Coun, 69. *Mem:* Am Burn Asn; Am Asn Surg Trauma; Soc Univ Surg; fel Am Col Surgeons; Am Surg Asn. *Res:* Metabolic response to injury, burns, shock and peritonitis; gas exchange; calorimetry; energy balance; intensive care; patient monitoring; surgical nutrition. *Mailing Add:* 8 Harvard Lane Hastings on Hudson NY 10706. *Fax:* 914-478-5015

KINNEY, LARRY LEE, ELECTRICAL ENGINEERING. *Current Pos:* PROF ELEC ENG, UNIV MINN, MINNEAPOLIS, 68- *Personal Data:* b Salem, Iowa, Oct 26, 41; m 62; c 2. *Educ:* Univ Iowa, BS, 64, MS, 65, PhD(elec eng), 68. *Prof Exp:* Asst prof elec eng, Univ Iowa, 68. *Mem:* Inst Elec & Electronics Engrs; Asn Comput Mach. *Res:* Switching theory; computer systems. *Mailing Add:* Dept Elec Eng Univ Minn 200 Union St SE Minneapolis MN 55455

KINNEY, MICHAEL J, INTERNAL MEDICINE, NEPHROLOGY. *Current Pos:* MED DIR, FLA MED CARE CLIN, 89- *Personal Data:* b Chicago, Ill, July 9, 37; m 71; c 6. *Educ:* Univ Chicago, BS, 59, MD, 63. *Prof Exp:* Assoc chief, Renal Div Nephrol, US Pub Health Serv Hosp, 69-74; asst prof, State Univ NY, Downstate Med Ctr, 77-78; assoc prof med & chief nephrology sect, Marshall Univ, Sch Med, 78-80; med dir, Nephrol Res & Educ Found, 80-82. *Mem:* Fel Am Col Physicians; fel Am Col Clin Pharmacol; Am Soc Nephrology; Soc Exp Biol & Med; Am Physiol Soc. *Res:* Hypertension; nuclear medicine. *Mailing Add:* Fla Med Care Clin 333 S Tamiami Trail Suite 395 Venice FL 34285

KINNEY, RALPH A, ELECTRICAL ENGINEERING. *Current Pos:* assoc prof elec eng, 67-76, PROF ELEC ENG, LA STATE UNIV, BATON ROUGE, 76- *Personal Data:* b Frostproof, Fla, Nov 7, 30; m 60; c 3. *Educ:* Univ Fla, BEE, 56, MSE, 58, PhD(elec eng), 67. *Prof Exp:* Res asst elec eng, Univ Fla, 57-60; scientist, Northrop Space Labs, Calif, 60-62; asst res elec eng & aerospace, Univ Fla, 64-67. *Mem:* Inst Elec & Electronics Engrs. *Res:* Wave phenomena in homogeneous media; induction heating; computer applications; field theory. *Mailing Add:* Dept Elec Eng La State Univ Baton Rouge LA 70803

KINNEY, ROBERT BRUCE, MECHANICAL ENGINEERING. *Current Pos:* RETIRED. *Personal Data:* b Joplin, Mo, July 20, 37; m 61; Carol Stewart; c Rodney M, David S & Linda G. *Educ:* Univ Calif, Berkeley, BS, 59, MS, 61; Univ Minn, Minneapolis, PhD(mech eng), 65. *Prof Exp:* Sr res engr, United Aircraft Res Labs, 65-68; from assoc prof to prof aerospace & mech eng, Univ Ariz, 68-87, assoc head, 81-84. *Concurrent Pos:* Assoc tech ed, J Heat Transfer, Am Soc Mech Engrs, 73-76; Alexander von Humboldt Found vis scientist, Ger, 76; vis prof, US Mil Acad, West Point, NY, 84. *Mem:* Am Soc Mech Engrs. *Res:* Energy transport in gases and liquids; dynamics of fluid flow, including unsteady viscous aerodynamics; fluid flow analogies and experimental methods. *Mailing Add:* 456 22nd Ave SE St Petersburg FL 33705

KINNEY, TERRY B, JR, POPULATION GENETICS. *Current Pos:* RETIRED. *Personal Data:* b Norfolk, Mass, Sept 12, 25; m 46; c 2. *Educ:* Univ Mass, BS, 55, MS, 56; Univ Minn, PhD, 63. *Prof Exp:* Res asst poultry, Univ Mass, 55-56; geneticist, Hubbard Farms Inc, NH, 56-57; instr poultry, Univ Minn, 57-62; biometrician, USDA, Md, 63-65, res geneticist, Ind, 65-69; asst dir, Animal Sci Res Div, USDA,69-72, assoc dept adminr, NCent Region, 72-74, asst adminr livestock vet sci, 74-78, assoc adminr, 78-80, adminr, Sci & Educ Admin-Agr Res, 80-88. *Mem:* Poultry Sci Asn; Sigma Xi. *Res:* Statistics; population genetic studies; administration of research relating to livestock and veterinary sciences. *Mailing Add:* 4480 Partridge Pl York SC 29745

KINNIE, IRVIN GRAY, COMPUTER SYSTEM DESIGN. *Current Pos:* syst analyst & engr tech planning, IBM Corp, 74-76, engr software res, 76-77, engr mkt develop, 77-78, engr solar eng, 78-80, engr command, control & commun archit, 80-81, engr, comput systs design, command & space systs, Fed Systs Div, 81-82, nationwide network design, Entry Systs Div, 82-86, comput architect, 86-88, COMPUT ARCHITECT, PC TECHNOL FORECASTING, IBM CORP, 88- *Personal Data:* b Orlando, Fla, Apr 28, 32; m 68. *Educ:* US Mil Acad, BS, 53; Univ Ariz, MS, 60. *Prof Exp:* Res officer, E W Div, Army Proving Ground, Ariz, 56-58, area signal officer, Longlines Signal Battalion Pusan, Korea, 60-61, asst prof & info sci, US Mil Acad, 61-65, EDP specialist info sci, Allied Mil Commun Electronics Agency, Paris, 65-67, standards specialist, Mallard Proj, Ft Monmouth, NJ, 67-68, chief plans & opers, US Army Regional Commun Group, Saigon, 68-69, chief info sci, US Army Res & Develop Group, London, 69-73, dep dir res & develop, US Army Comput Systs Command, 73-74. *Mem:* Asn Comput Mach; Inst Elec & Electronics Engrs; Armed Forces Comn Electronics Asn. *Res:* Communications; electronics and information sciences; software engineering; computer systems architecture. *Mailing Add:* 10 Sugar Pine Lane Hilton Head Island SC 29926

KINNISON, GERALD LEE, PHYSIOLOGY. *Current Pos:* RETIRED. *Personal Data:* b San Diego, Calif, July 16, 31; m 50, 89; c Dana S, Susan K (Christiansen), Mark L & Leanne K (Peterson). *Educ:* Univ Calif, Los Angeles, BS, 58, MS, 60, PhD(physics), 63. *Honors & Awards:* Arthur S Fleming Award, 68. *Prof Exp:* Postdoctoral fel physics, Univ London, 63-64; res physicist, Electronics Lab, Ocean Systs Ctr, USN, 63-67, Undersea Ctr, 67-77, res physicist, 77-95. *Concurrent Pos:* Sonar adv panel, Navsea Explor Develop Panel, Passive Sonar, 67-86; master ASW study group, Chief Naval Opers, 84- *Mem:* Acoust Soc Am; Am Physics Teachers Soc. *Res:* Passive sonar arrays: design, instrumentation, beamforming (conventional and optimal), signal processing, display and performance prediction in various environmental noises (predicted and measured); recipient of one patent. *Mailing Add:* 3274 Trumbull St San Diego CA 92106-2421

KINNISON, ROBERT RAY, EXTREME VALUE & GEOGRAPHICAL STATISTICS, QUALITY ASSURANCE. *Current Pos:* PRIN STATISTICIAN, BECHTEL NEV CORP, LAS VEGAS, NEV, 89- *Personal Data:* b Los Angeles, Calif, Sept 10, 34; m 59, Karen Wingo; c 2. *Educ:* Pomona Col, BA, 56; Univ Calif Los Angeles, PhD(statist), 71. *Prof Exp:* Pharmacologist, Rexall Drug & Chem Co, 60-68; Statistician, Univ Calif, San Francisco, 71-72, US Environ Protection Agency, Las Vegas, 72-79, Battelle Pac NW Lab, 79-85 & Desert Res Inst, 85-89. *Concurrent Pos:* Assoc ed, J Simulation, 72- & Environ Monitoring & Assessment. *Mem:* Am Statist Asn; Biomet Soc; AAAS; Sigma Xi. *Res:* Extreme value statistics; bioassay statistics; exposure-dose assessment statistics for environmental pollutants; spatial and geographic statistics; quality assurance statistics. *Mailing Add:* 846 E Pescados Dr Las Vegas NV 89123-1359. *E-Mail:* kinnisrr@nv.doe.gov

KINNMARK, INGEMAR PER ERLAND, NUMERICAL METHODS OF DIFFERENTIAL, SCIENTIFIC & TECHNICAL TRASPORTATION. *Current Pos:* SWED SCI & TECH TRANSL, 89- *Personal Data:* b Sundbyberg, Sweden, Dec 8, 53; m 82; c 1. *Educ:* Royal Inst Technol, MS, 79; Princeton Univ, MA, 82 & PhD(water resources), 84. *Prof Exp:* Res assoc, 84-86, asst prof hydraul & numerical methods, Univ Notre Dame, 86-89. *Mem:* Am Translr Asn. *Res:* Mathematical modeling of flow in shallow seas, estuaries and rivers; design, analysis and application of numerical methods for the solution of ordinary and partial differential equations. *Mailing Add:* 2570 Beechwood Blvd Pittsburgh PA 15217-2509

KINO, GORDON STANLEY, ELECTRICAL ENGINEERING, ACOUSTICS. *Current Pos:* res assoc, Stanford Univ, 57-61, assoc prof, 61-65, assoc chmn, Elec Eng Dept, 85-88, assoc dean planning & facil, 87-92, dir, Ginzton Lab, 94-96, WM KECK PROF ELEC ENG, STANFORD UNIV, 65-, EMER PROF APPL PHYSICS, 76- *Personal Data:* b Melbourne, Australia, June 15, 28; nat US 67; m 57; c 1. *Educ:* Univ London, BSc, 48, MSc, 50; Stanford Univ, PhD(elec eng), 55. *Honors & Awards:* Centennial Medal, Inst Elec & Electronics Engrs, 84, Sonics & Ultrasonics Group Achievement, 84. *Prof Exp:* Jr scientist, Mullard Radio Valve Co, Eng, 47-51; res asst, Electronics Res Lab, Stanford Univ, 51-55, res assoc, Microwave Lab, 55; mem tech staff, Bell Tel Labs, NJ, 55-57. *Concurrent Pos:* Consult, Varian, Tex Instruments, Lockheed Aircraft Corp & Advan Res Projs Agency, 57-, Endosonics & Prometrix; Guggenheim fel, 67-68; chmn, Ultrasonics Group, Inst Elec & Electronics Engrs. *Mem:* Nat Acad Eng; fel Inst Elec & Electronics Engrs; fel Am Phys Soc; fel AAAS. *Res:* Electromagnetic theory; design of electron and ion guns; wave propagation in plasmas; microwave tubes; microwave acoustics; acoustic imaging; non-destructive testing; waves in solids; author of more than 460 technical publications; fiber optics, optical microscopy. *Mailing Add:* Rm 9 Ginzton Lab Mail Code 4085 Stanford Univ Stanford CA 94305

KINOSHITA, FLORENCE KEIKO, TOXICOLOGY, PHARMACOLOGY. *Current Pos:* sr toxicologist, 78-91, TOXICOL SCIENTIST, HERCULES, INC, 91- *Personal Data:* b Salem, Ore, Aug 6, 41. *Educ:* Univ Chicago, BS, 63, MS, 66, PhD(pharmacol), 69; Am Bd Toxicol, dipl. *Prof Exp:* From instr to asst prof pharmacol, Univ Chicago, 69-73; toxicologist, Indust Bio-Test Labs, Inc, 73-74, tech mgr toxicol, 74-77. *Concurrent Pos:* Consult, US Environ Protection Agency, 71-72, US Fed Drug Admin, 72-73; mem, Toxicol Study Sect, NIH, 79-83 & Toxicol Data Bank Peer Rev Comt, Nat Libr Med, 83-85; affil asst prof, Dept Pharmacol & Toxicol, Med Col Va, 84- *Mem:* Soc Toxicol; Am Indust Hyg Asn; Soc Exp Biol & Med; NY Acad Sci; Int Soc Ecotoxicol & Environ Safety; Int Soc Study Xenobiotics. *Res:* Interactions of drugs, pesticides and chemicals as inducers of hepatic microsomal enzyme systems; effects of organophosphorus compounds on cholinestrase and aliesterases; development of hepatic microsomal enzymes in fetal and neonatal animals. *Mailing Add:* Hercules Inc 1313 N Market St Wilmington DE 19894

KINOSHITA, JIN HAROLD, BIOLOGICAL CHEMISTRY, OPHTHALMIC RESEARCH. *Current Pos:* CLIN PROF OPHTHAL, UNIV CALIF, DAVIS, 90- *Personal Data:* b San Francisco, Calif, July 21, 22; m 48. *Educ:* Columbia Univ, AB, 44; Harvard Univ, PhD, 52. *Hon Degrees:* ScD, Bard Col, 67, Oakland Univ, 80. *Honors & Awards:* Friedenwald Award, Asn Res Vision & Ophthal, 65, Proctor Medal, 74. *Prof Exp:* Asst chem, Bard Col, 44-46; from instr to asst prof biochem, Harvard Med Sch, 52-64, from assoc prof to prof biochem ophthal, 64-73; chief, Lab Vision Res, Nat Eye Inst, 71-81, sci dir, 81-90. *Concurrent Pos:* Biochemist, Mass Eye & Ear Infirmary, 55-73; mem visual sci study sect, NIH, 65-69. *Mem:* AAAS; Am Chem Soc; Am Soc Biol Chemists; Asn Res Vision & Ophthal. *Res:* Chemistry and metabolism of ocular tissues. *Mailing Add:* 44269 Clubhouse Dr El Macero CA 95618. *Fax:* 530-753-1656

KINOSHITA, KAY, PHYSICS. *Current Pos:* PROF, VA POLYTECHNIC INST & STATE UNIV, 93- *Personal Data:* b Princeton, NJ, July 17, 54; m 89, Alan Schwartz. *Educ:* Harvard Univ, AB & AM, 76; Univ Calif, Berkeley, PhD(physics), 82. *Prof Exp:* Res assoc, Harvard Univ, 82-84, from asst prof to assoc prof physics, 84-93. *Concurrent Pos:* Sci scholar, Mary Ingraham Bunting Inst, 85-87. *Mem:* Am Phys Soc; Asn Women Sci. *Res:* Elementary particle physics; weak interactions of heavy quarks; exotic heavily ionizing particles. *Mailing Add:* Dept Physics Va Polytech Inst & State Univ Blacksburg VA 24061

KINOSHITA, KIMIO, ELECTROCHEMISTRY. *Current Pos:* MEM STAFF, SRI INT, 79- *Personal Data:* b Vancouver, BC, Aug 5, 42; m 65; c 2. *Educ:* Univ Alta, BSc, 64; Univ Calif, Berkeley, PhD(chem), 69. *Prof Exp:* Sr res assoc phys chem, Mat Eng Res Lab, Pratt & Whitney Aircraft, 69-76; mem staff, Chem Eng Div, Argonne Nat Lab, 76-79. *Mem:* Am Chem Soc; Electrochem Soc; Am Carbon Soc. *Res:* Corrosion; electrochemistry; carbon chemistry; catalysis. *Mailing Add:* 20644 Nancy Ct Cupertino CA 95014

KINOSHITA, SHIN'ICHI, topology, for more information see previous edition

KINOSHITA, TOICHIRO, THEORETICAL HIGH ENERGY PHYSICS. *Current Pos:* res assoc, 55-58, from asst prof to prof, 58-95, EMER PROF THEORET PHYSICS, CORNELL UNIV, 95- *Personal Data:* b Tokyo, Japan, Jan 23, 25; nat US; m 51, Magsako Matsuoka; c Kay, June & Ray. *Educ:* Univ Tokyo, BS, 47, PhD(physics), 52. *Honors & Awards:* J J Sakurai Prize, Am Phys Soc, 90. *Prof Exp:* Mem, Inst Adv Study, Princeton, NJ, 52-54; fel theoret physics, Columbia Univ, 54-55. *Concurrent Pos:* Ford fel, Europ Orgn Nuclear Res, Geneva, Switz, 62-63; Guggenheim Found fel, 73-74; tech adv panel univ progs, Dept Energy, 82-83; comt fundamental constants, Nat Res Coun, 84-86. *Mem:* Nat Acad Sci; fel AAAS; fel Am Phys Soc. *Res:* Quantum field theory; quantum theory of atoms; elementary particles; symmetry law. *Mailing Add:* Lab Nuclear Studies Cornell Univ Ithaca NY 14853-5001

KINRA, VIKRAM KUMAR, ENGINEERING MECHANICS, MATERIALS SCIENCE. *Current Pos:* assoc prof, 82-89, PROF AEROSPACE ENG & ASSOC DIR, CTR MECH COMPOSITES, TEX A&M UNIV, 89- *Personal Data:* b Lyallpur, India, Apr 3, 46; m 76, 88; c 1. *Educ:* Indian Inst Technol, Kanpur, BTech, 67; Utah State Univ, MSc, 68; Brown Univ, PhD(eng mech), 75. *Honors & Awards:* Dow Outstanding Young Fac Award, 80; Ralph R Teeter Award, 82. *Prof Exp:* Struct eng stress anal, Northrop Corp, Hawthorne, 68-70; proj engr mech eng, Ostgaard & Assocs, Inc, Gardena, 70-71; asst & res assoc, Brown Univ, 71-75; asst prof, Univ Colo, Boulder, 75-82. *Concurrent Pos:* Prin investr & proj dir, NSF grants, Univ Colo, Boulder, 76-81, Off naval Res, Air Force Off Sci Res, Tex adv tech prog grants, NASA grants, IBM grant & Martin-Marietta grant; consult, Willow Water Dist, Denver, 76-77, Ponderosa Asn, Louisville, 80 & Corning Glass, 80 & Martin-Marietta Corp, 88; Halliburton prof, 86. *Mem:* Soc Exp Mech; Am Acad Mech; Am Soc Eng Educ; Am Soc Mech Engrs; Sigma Xi; Acoust Soc Am. *Res:* Damping; wave propagation; nondestructive testing and evaluation; composite materials; ultrasonics. *Mailing Add:* Dept Aerospace Eng Tex A&M Univ College Station TX 77843

KINSBOURNE, MARCEL, PEDIATRIC NEUROLOGY, EXPERIMENTAL PSYCHOLOGY. *Current Pos:* RES PROF COGNITIVE STUDIES, TUFTS UNIV, 91-; PROF PSYCHOL, NEW SCH UNIV, 95- *Personal Data:* b Vienna, Austria, Nov 3, 31; m 65; c David, Daniel, Jeremy & Emily. *Educ:* Oxford Univ, BA, 52, MD, 55, MA, 56, DM(neuropsychol), 63. *Honors & Awards:* Queen Square Prize neurol, 61; J Arthur lectr, 74. *Prof Exp:* Lectr psychol, Oxford Univ, 64-67; assoc prof pediat & neurol & lectr psychol, Med Ctr, Duke Univ, 67-74; sr staff physician, Hosp Sick Children, Toronto, 74-80; prof psychol, Univ Waterloo, 74-79; prof pediat, Univ Toronto, 74-80, prof psychol, 75-80; dir, Behav Neurol Dept, Eunice Kennedy Shriver Ctr, 80-91; lectr neurol, Harvard Med Sch, 80-91. *Concurrent Pos:* Fel, New Col, Oxford Univ, 65-67; adj prof cognitive sci, Brandeis Univ, 83-; consult neurologist, Boston Vet Admin Med Ctr, 89- *Mem:* Fel Am Psychol Asn; Am Neurol Asn; fel Geront Soc; Int Neuropsychol Soc; Psychonomic Soc; Child Neurol Soc. *Res:* Human neuropsychology; developmental psychology; visual information processing; age-related changes in behavior. *Mailing Add:* 158 Cambridge St Winchester MA 01890. *Fax:* 781-729-8201

KINSEL, NORMA ANN, MICROBIOLOGY. *Current Pos:* SR MICROBIOLOGIST, ELI LILLY & CO, 74- *Personal Data:* b Boston, Mass, Feb 26, 29. *Educ:* Univ Va, BS, 49; Pittsburgh Univ, MS, 52, PhD(bact), 59. *Prof Exp:* Asst fel yeast chem, Mellon Inst, 52-53, asst, microbiol & micros sect, 53-56, assoc microbiologist, 56-62, fel petrol, 63-69; res biologist, Gulf Res & Develop Co, 69-73. *Concurrent Pos:* USPHS res fel, Rutgers Univ, 62-63. *Mem:* AAAS; Am Soc Microbiol; Soc Indust Microbiol. *Res:* Autotrophic iron and sulfur bacteria; petroleum microbiology; antibiotic fermentation technology. *Mailing Add:* 5258 Whisperwood Lane Indianapolis IN 46226

KINSELLA, JAMES L, PHARMACOLOGY. *Current Pos:* Sr staff fel, 83-88, RES CHEMIST PHARMACOL, GERONT RES CTR, NAT INST AGING, 88- *Personal Data:* b Oneida, NY, Mar 9, 50. *Educ:* Alfred Univ, BS, 72; Syracuse Univ, PhD(pharmacol), 78. *Honors & Awards:* Res Develop Award, US Fed Govt, 94. *Mem:* AAAS; NY Acad Sci; Am Soc Biochem & Molecular Biol. *Mailing Add:* Geront Res Ctr Nat Inst Aging NIH 4940 Eastern Ave Baltimore MD 21224-2735. *Fax:* 410-558-8150

KINSELLA, JOHN J, PHYSICS, SEMICONDUCTORS. *Current Pos:* CONSULT, RAVEN CONSULT, 86- *Personal Data:* b Seneca Falls, NY, Oct 15, 26; m 49, Lucille Taylor; c Susan, Daniel, Timothy, Thomas, Patricia, Elizabeth, James & Christopher. *Educ:* Univ Tex, BA, 49; Syracuse Univ, MS, 53. *Prof Exp:* Res physicist, Consol Vacuum Corp Div, Bell & Howell, 51-56; from physicist to sr physicist, Xerox Corp, 56-59, scientist, 59-62, res mgr, 62-65, mgr photoreceptor technol, 65-68, mgr xerographic consumables mfg, 68-70, mgr advan mfg eng, 70-73, mfg prog mgt, 73-78, mem res & eng tech staff, 78-81, strategic planning Corp Planning Consumables & Supplies, 81-86. *Mem:* Am Vacuum Soc; Inst Elec & Electronics Engrs; Optical Soc Am; Soc Photog Sci & Eng. *Res:* Vacuum pump and gauge design development; thin film microcircuit, resistors and capacitors; evaporated silver bromide research; xerographic photoconductors. *Mailing Add:* 2846 St Paul Blvd Rochester NY 14617. *Fax:* 716-266-2142; *E-Mail:* jackk2846@aol.com

KINSELLA, RALPH A, JR, INTERNAL MEDICINE. *Current Pos:* MED DIR, ST LOUIS UNIV HOSP, 85- *Personal Data:* b St Louis, Mo, June 4, 19; c 8. *Educ:* St Louis Univ, AB, 39, MD, 43. *Prof Exp:* From instr to assoc prof, 48-70, prof internal med, Sch Med, St Louis Univ, 70-; physician & chief unit 2, Med Serv, St Louis City Hosp, 57-80, med dir, 80-85. *Concurrent Pos:* Neilson fel, St Louis Univ, 47-48, Markle scholar, 48-53. *Mem:* AAAS; Endocrine Soc; NY Acad Sci; fel Am Col Physicians; Soc Exp Biol & Med; Sigma Xi. *Res:* Steroid hormone metabolism; endocrinology. *Mailing Add:* St Louis Univ Hosp 3635 Vista Ave St Louis MO 63110-2539

KINSER, DONALD LEROY, MATERIALS SCIENCE, ENGINEERING. *Current Pos:* From asst prof to assoc prof ceramic eng, 68-75, PROF MAT SCI, VANDERBILT UNIV, 75- *Personal Data:* b Loudon, Tenn, Sept 28, 41; m 61, Barbara Lange; c Elizabeth & Cynthia. *Educ:* Univ Fla, BS, 64, PhD(mat sci), 68. *Concurrent Pos:* Co-ed, J Non Crystalline Solids, 88- *Mem:* Am Ceramic Soc; Am Soc Metals; Am Inst Mining, Metall & Petrol Engrs; Soc Glass Technol UK; Mat Res Soc; Sigma Xi. *Res:* Electrical behavior of two-phase alkali-silicate glasses; semiconducting glasses; mechanical properties of glasses; electrical behavior of glasses; radiation damage and mechanical properties of materials. *Mailing Add:* 610 Olin Hall Vanderbilt Univ Nashville TN 37240

KINSEY, BERNARD BRUNO, physics; deceased, see previous edition for last biography

KINSEY, DAVID WEBSTER, MATHEMATICS. *Current Pos:* ASSOC PROF MATH, UNIV SOUTHERN IND, EVANSVILLE, 72- *Personal Data:* b Warsaw, Ind, Mar 11, 39; m 61; c 2. *Educ:* Manchester Col, BA, 61; Univ Ariz, MS, 64; Ind Univ, PhD(math), 72. *Prof Exp:* Instr math, Carthage Col, 63-64 & Millikin Univ, 64-68. *Mem:* Math Asn Am; Nat Coun Teachers Math; Am Math Soc. *Mailing Add:* Univ Southern Ind 8600 University Blvd Evansville IN 47712-3590

KINSEY, JAMES HUMPHREYS, APPLIED PHYSICS. *Current Pos:* SR SCIENTIST, APPL RES CORP, 88- *Personal Data:* b Xenia, Ohio, June 6, 32. *Educ:* Princeton Univ, AB, 60; Univ Md, College Park, PhD(physics), 70. *Prof Exp:* Aerospace technologist, NASA, 68-71; mem res staff x-ray diffraction, Princeton Univ, 71-73, lectr, 73-74; consult, Control Data Corp, 74-76; consult, Mayo Clinic, 76-82; asst prof biophys, 79-82, advan projs physicist, Space Telescope Sci Inst, 82-88. *Mem:* Am Phys Soc; Am Astron Soc; Am Geophys Union; Sigma Xi; Inst Elec & Electronics Engrs; Biomed Eng Soc; Optical Soc Am. *Res:* Optical aurora; low energy cosmic rays and energetic solar particles; x-ray diffraction studies of large biological molecules; computer analysis of radiographs; x-ray and optical detector systems for biomedical imaging, computer tomography; photo therapy of cancer; imaging instrumentation. *Mailing Add:* Appl Res Corp 8201 Corporate Dr Landover MD 20785

KINSEY, JAMES LLOYD, PHYSICAL CHEMISTRY. *Current Pos:* interim provost, 93-94, DEAN NAT SCI & D R BULLARD-WELCH FOUND PROF SCI, RICE UNIV, 88- *Personal Data:* b Paris, Tex, Oct 15, 34; m 62; c 3. *Educ:* Rice Univ, BA, 56, PhD(chem), 59. *Honors & Awards:* E O Lawrence Award, US Dept Energy, 87; Nobel Laureate Signature Award, Am Chem Soc, 90; Earle K Plyler Award, Am Phys Soc, 95. *Prof Exp:* NSF fel, Univ Uppsala, 59-60; Miller res fel, Univ Calif, Berkeley, 60-62; from asst prof to assoc prof, Mass Inst Technol, 62-74, chmn dept, 77-82, prof chem, 74-84. *Concurrent Pos:* Alfred P Sloan res fel, 63-67; Guggenheim fel, 69-70; vis assoc prof, Univ Wis, 69-70; consult, Los Alamos Nat Lab, 74-92; mem, Bd Chem Sci & Technol, Nat Acad Sci-Nat Res Coun, 80-83, co-chmn, 82-83; mem, Adv Comt, Army Res Off-Nat Res Coun, 81-86; assoc ed, J Chem Physics, 81-84; chmn, Am Chem Soc, Div Physics & Chemistry, 85, mem, Am Phys Soc, Div Chem, Phys Exec Comn, 86-89. *Mem:* Nat Acad Sci; Am Chem Soc; Sigma Xi; fel Am Acad Arts & Sci; fel AAAS; fel Am Phys Soc. *Res:* Chemical dynamics; spectroscopy; lasers; theoretical chemistry. *Mailing Add:* Wiess Sch Nat Sci Rice Univ 6100 S Main St, MS-102 Houston TX 77251. *Fax:* 713-285-5401; *E-Mail:* jlkinsey@rice.edu

KINSEY, JOHN AARON, JR, GENETICS. *Current Pos:* asst prof, 67-80, assoc prof microbiol, 80-, PROF, MED CTR, UNIV KANS. *Personal Data:* b Panama City, Fla, Mar 12, 39; m 62. *Educ:* Fla State Univ, BS, 61; Univ Tex, PhD(zool), 65. *Prof Exp:* NIH res fel genetics, Univ Wash, 65-67. *Mem:* Genetics Soc Am. *Res:* Biochemical aspects of Neurospora genetics. *Mailing Add:* Dept Microbiol Univ Kans Med Ctr 3901 Rainbow Blvd Kansas City KS 66160

KINSEY, KENNETH F, PHYSICS. *Current Pos:* PROF PHYSICS, STATE UNIV NY, COL GENESEO, 66- *Personal Data:* b Providence, RI, Sept 14, 33. *Educ:* Brown Univ, AB, 55; Univ Rochester, PhD(physics), 61. *Prof Exp:* Asst prof, Univ Rochester, 64-66. *Mem:* Am Phys Soc; Am Asn Physics Teachers. *Res:* Medium energy particle physics. *Mailing Add:* 3106 Avon Rd Geneseo NY 14454

KINSEY, PHILIP A, PHYSICAL CHEMISTRY. *Current Pos:* PROF CHEM, UNIV EVANSVILLE, 56- *Personal Data:* b Warsaw, Ind, Feb 10, 31; m 54; c 3. *Educ:* Manchester Col, AB, 53; Purdue Univ, PhD(chem), 57. *Concurrent Pos:* Sabbatical, Univ Calif, Santa Barbara, 69-70, Univ Ill, Urbana, 80-81. *Mem:* Am Chem Soc. *Res:* Uses of computers in chemical education. *Mailing Add:* 1612 Southeast Blvd Evansville IN 47714

KINSEY, WILLIAM HENDERSON, REPRODUCTION & FERTILIZATION, CELL BIOLOGY. *Current Pos:* ASSOC PROF GROSS ANAT & CELL BIOL, SCH MED, UNIV MIAMI, 85- *Educ:* Univ Wash, Seattle, PhD(anat & cell biol), 76. *Mailing Add:* Dept Anat & Cell Biol Kans Med Ctr 39th & Rainbow Blvd Kansas City KS 66103. *Fax:* 913-588-2710

KINSINGER, JACK BURL, HOSPITAL ADMINISTRATION. *Current Pos:* pres & chief exec officer, Chicago Osteop Health Syst, 87-93, PRES & CHIEF EXEC OFFICER, MIDWESTERN UNIV, 93- *Personal Data:* b Akron, Ohio, June 23, 25; m 47, 87, Addie Parker; c Paul & Amy. *Educ:* Hiram Col, BA, 48; Cornell Univ, MSc, 51; Univ Pa, PhD(phys chem), 58. *Prof Exp:* Group leader polymer chem, Rohm & Haas Co, 51-56; from asst prof to assoc prof phys chem, Mich State Univ, 57-66, prof chem, 66-75, from assoc chmn to chmn dept, 65-75; dir chem div, NSF, 75-77; asst vpres res, Mich State Univ, 77-82, assoc provost, 77-82; vpres acad affairs, Ariz State Univ, 82-87. *Concurrent Pos:* Consult, Union Carbide Chem Co, 58-80; mem bd, Kirksville Osteop Col, 86-87 & Ariz State Univ Res Park, 84-87. *Mem:* Fel AAAS; Am Chem Soc; Am Phys Soc; Am Osteop Asn. *Res:* Micro-structure of polymers; laser light scattering spectroscopy. *Mailing Add:* 680 N Lake Shore Dr Chicago IL 60611

KINSINGER, JAMES A, ANALYTICAL CHEMISTRY, MASS SPECTROMETRY. *Current Pos:* MANAGING DIR, INDUST LABS CO, 88- *Personal Data:* b Ottumwa, Iowa, Dec 6, 44; m 66; c 3. *Educ:* Wartburg Col, BA, 67; Univ Wis, PhD(anal chem), 72. *Prof Exp:* Asst prof chem, Tougaloo Col, 72-76; res assoc, Univ Wis, 76-77; res scientist, Warf Inst, Raltech Sci Serv & Hazelton Labs, 77-82; head, Appln & Training, Nicolet Instruments, 81-86; vpres mkt, Masstron, Inc, 87. *Concurrent Pos:* Head, Chem Dept, Tougaloo Col, 74-76. *Mem:* Am Chem Soc; Am Soc Mass Spectrometry; Asn Off Anal Chemists; Inst Food Technologists; Am Oil Chemists Soc; Asn Off Racing Chemists. *Mailing Add:* 1680 Oak Ave Boulder CO 80304

KINSINGER, RICHARD ESTYN, MEDICAL IMAGING PHYSICS. *Current Pos:* mgr, Appl Sci Lab, 82-96, MGR, GLOBAL ADVAN TECHNOL, GEN ELEC MED SYSTS, 96- *Personal Data:* b Wilmington, Del, July 23, 42; m 64, Barbara Naquin; c Lara & W Mark. *Educ:* Cornell Univ, BEngPhys, 64, MEng, 65, PhD(aerospace eng), 69. *Prof Exp:* Res physicist, Res & Develop Ctr, 68-76, mgr arc interruption res, 76-81, mgr plasma technol progs, 81-82. *Res:* Direct development of new concepts and technology for medical imaging. *Mailing Add:* W349 S4698 Kingdom Dr Dousman WI 53118. *Fax:* 414-521-6599; *E-Mail:* kinsingerr@med.ge.com

KINSKY, STEPHEN CHARLES, BIOCHEMISTRY. *Current Pos:* PROF BIOCHEM, NAT JEWISH HOSP, 78- *Personal Data:* b Berlin, Ger, Feb 9, 32; nat US; m 59; c 2. *Educ:* Univ Chicago, AB, 51; Johns Hopkins Univ, PhD(biochem), 57. *Prof Exp:* From instr to prof, Sch Med, Wash Univ, 59-78. *Concurrent Pos:* USPHS fel, 57-59, res career develop awards, 64-70. *Mem:* Am Soc Biol Chem; Am Asn Immunol. *Res:* Membrane biochemistry; immunology. *Mailing Add:* 5460 Patchwood Ct Las Vegas NV 89130

KINSLAND, GARY LYNN, GEOPHYSICS, MINERALOGY. *Current Pos:* asst prof, 77-80, ASSOC PROF GEOL, UNIV SOUTHWESTERN LA, 80- *Personal Data:* b Eugene, Ore, June 10, 47; div; c 1. *Educ:* Univ Rochester, BS, 69, MS, 71, PhD(geol), 74. *Honors & Awards:* A I Leversen Mem Award, Am Asn Petrol Geol, 84. *Prof Exp:* Res asst geol, Univ Rochester, 74-76; vis asst prof, Ariz State Univ, 76-77. *Concurrent Pos:* Prin investr, Dept Energy geopressure-geothermal energy grant, 78-79, high resolution 3-d seismic surv over geopressured resevoir, 82-85. *Mem:* Sigma Xi; Am Geophys Union; Soc Explor Geophysicists. *Res:* High pressure-high temperature simulation and study of earth mantle properties; geopressure-geothermal energy prospects; high pressure materials science; high-resolution 3-d seismic surveys; continental crustal structure deduced from potential field data. *Mailing Add:* Dept Geol Univ Southwestern La PO Box 44530 Lafayette LA 70504-4530

KINSLEY, HOMAN BENJAMIN, JR, WET LAID NONWOVEN ENGINEERING, FIBER PHYSICS. *Current Pos:* SR RES FEL, CUSTOM PAPERS GROUP INC, 91- *Personal Data:* b Baltimore, Md, Dec 31, 40; m 62; c 3. *Educ:* Western Md Col, BA, 63; Lawrence Univ, MS, 64, PhD(chem), 67. *Prof Exp:* Res assoc, Ethyl Corp, 67-74; res chemist, Du Pont, 74-75; res assoc, James River Corp, 75-78, tech dir, 78-82, dir technol, 82-86, sr res fel, 86-91. *Mem:* Am Chem Soc; Tech Asn Pulp & Paper Indust; AAAS; Filtration Soc. *Res:* Wet laid nonwovens; forming techniques; fibers and binders; physical properties of the resulting web structures. *Mailing Add:* Fiber Mark 110 Tredegar St Richmond VA 23219-4306

KINSMAN, DONALD MARKHAM, MEAT ANIMAL PRODUCTION & MEAT SCIENCE. *Current Pos:* from asst prof to prof, 56-88, EMER PROF ANIMAL SCI, UNIV CONN, 88- *Personal Data:* b Framingham, Mass, May 20, 23; m 49, Helen Bailey; c Elizabeth, David & Martha. *Educ:* Univ Mass, BS, 49; Univ NH, MS, 51; Okla State Univ, PhD, 64. *Honors & Awards:* Distinguished Serv Award, Am Soc Animal Sci, 78, Int Animal Agr Award, 92; Signal Serv Award, Am Meat Sci Asn, 75, R C Pollack Award, 85, Int Award, 96. *Prof Exp:* Instr animal sci, Univ NH, 49-51 & Univ Vt, 51-52; farm mgr, Univ Mass, 52-56. *Concurrent Pos:* Pres, New Eng Livestock Conserv, Inc, 66-78; dir, Am Soc Animal Sci, 72-74; dir, Am Meat Sci Asn, 76-78; Danforth Assoc, 79; mem, USDA Inspection Comt, Nat Acad Sci, 89-90; mem Nat Org Stands Bd, USDA, 92-96. *Mem:* Am Soc Animal Sci; Am Meat Sci Asn (pres, 78-79); Coun Agr Sci & Technol; Int Animal Agr. *Res:* Humane slaughter, reduced stress methods; evaluation and quality of meat and meat products; meat microbiology. *Mailing Add:* Dept Animal Sci Univ Conn Storrs CT 06269-4040. *Fax:* 860-486-4375

KINSMAN, DONALD VINCENT, ORGANIC CHEMISTRY. *Current Pos:* TECH DIR, HENKEL EMERY GROUP, 87- *Personal Data:* b Toledo, Ohio, July 16, 43; m 69; c 2. *Educ:* Univ Cincinnati, BS, 65; Pa State Univ, PhD(chem), 69. *Prof Exp:* Develop chemist household prod, Lever Bros, 69-71; group leader develop, 71-74; group leader oleo chem res, Emery Chem, 74-79, mgr, 79-87. *Mem:* Am Chem Soc; Am Oil Chemists Soc; Soc Automotive Engrs; Tech Asn Pulp & Paper Indust; Soc Tribologists & Lubrication Engrs. *Res:* Develop and administration of applications for oleo chemicals, synthetic lubricants, fatty alcohols, azelaic and pelargonic acids. *Mailing Add:* Henkel Emery Group 4900 Este Ave Cincinnati OH 45232-1491

KINSON, GORDON A, PHYSIOLOGY, ENDOCRINOLOGY. *Current Pos:* from asst prof to assoc prof, 68-79, PROF PHYSIOL, FAC MED, UNIV OTTAWA, 79- *Personal Data:* b Wood End, Eng, Sept 21, 35; m 60, 82; c 2. *Educ:* Univ Aston, BS, 57; Col Advan Technol, Birmingham, ARIC, 61; Univ Ala, Birmingham, MA, 62; Univ Birmingham, PhD(endocrinol), 67. *Hon Degrees:* FRSC (UK), London, 73. *Prof Exp:* Res asst endocrinol, Univ Ala, Birmingham, 59-63; sr res assoc, Med Sch, Birmingham Univ, 64-68. *Concurrent Pos:* Consult, Europ Orgn for Control of Circulatory Dis, 82, Comp Cancer Unit, UAB, USA, 83. *Mem:* Brit Soc Endocrinol; Royal Soc Chem; Can Physiol Soc; Am Physiol Soc. *Res:* Extrahepatic metabolism of androgen hormones; steroid hormone production by seminiferous tubules of the testis; chronic consequences of vasectomy; reninangiotensin and other factors influencing adrenocortical hormone secretion; pineal gland-adrenocortical hormone relationships; role of the pineal gland and indoles in testicular function and androgen biosynthesis; cardiac actions of anabolic androgens and estrogens; exercise and female reproductive function; steroids and Cyclosporin A in renal function. *Mailing Add:* Dept Physiol Univ Ottawa Fac Med 451 Smyth Rd Ottawa ON K1H 8M5 Can. *Fax:* 613-787-6718

KINSTLE, JAMES FRANCIS, POLYMER CHEMISTRY. *Current Pos:* MGR CORP CHEM & POLYMER RES & DEVELOP, JAMES RIVER CORP, 87- *Personal Data:* b Lima, Ohio, Nov 23, 38. *Educ:* Bowling Green State Univ, BS, 66, MA, 67; Univ Akron, PhD(polymer sci), 70. *Honors & Awards:* A K Doolittle Award, Am Chem Soc, 77. *Prof Exp:* Res & develop polymers, Wyandotte Chem Corp, 60-63; res & develop chemist, Allied Mat Corp, 63-65; sr res scientist, Ford Motor Co Sci Res Labs, 70-72; from asst prof to assoc prof chem, Univ Tenn, Knoxville, 72-83; sr res group leader, Polaroid, 83-87. *Concurrent Pos:* Ed-in-chief, J Radiation Curing, Technol Mkt Corp, 74-79; consult, 73-83. *Mem:* Am Chem Soc (treas, 85-87); Soc Petrol Engrs; Soc Vacuum Coaters. *Res:* Polymer synthesis and characterization; homogeneous and surface reactions on polymers; cellulose and paper chemistry; radiation chemistry in polymer sciences; polymer reuse and disposal. *Mailing Add:* James River Corp 1 Better Way Rd Milford OH 45150-2741. *Fax:* 513-576-7107

KINSTLE, THOMAS HERBERT, ORGANOFLUORINE CHEMISTRY, MASS SPECTROMETRY. *Current Pos:* assoc prof org chem, 70-74, PROF CHEM, BOWLING GREEN STATE UNIV, 74- *Personal Data:* b Lima, Ohio, Dec 18, 36; m 58. *Educ:* Bowling Green State Univ, BA, 58; Univ Ill, PhD(org chem), 63. *Prof Exp:* Res assoc org chem, Univ Ill, 63-64; from instr to asst prof org chem, Iowa State Univ, 64-70. *Concurrent Pos:* Am Chem Soc-Petrol Res Found grant, 64-; Res Corp grant, 65- *Mem:* Am Chem Soc; Am Acad Arts & Sci; Am Soc Mass Spectrometry. *Res:* Applications of mass spectrometry to organic chemical problems; synthesis and reactions of strained ring systems; structure determination; synthesis and biosynthesis of natural products; organofluorine chemistry. *Mailing Add:* 149 S Grove St Bowling Green OH 43402-2839

KINTANAR, AGUSTIN, NUCLEAR MAGNETIC RESONANCE SPECTROSCOPY, MACROMOLECULAR STRUCTURE. *Current Pos:* ASST PROF, IOWA STATE UNIV, 88- *Personal Data:* b New Haven, Conn, Apr 28, 58; m 89, Karen A Smith; c Ryan & Dylan. *Educ:* Univ Ill, Chicago, BS, 79; Univ Ill, Urbana, PhD(phys chem), 84. *Prof Exp:* Postdoctoral mem tech staff, AT&T Bell Labs, 84-85; postdoctoral, Univ Wash, 85-88. *Mem:* Am Chem Soc. *Res:* Nuclear magnetic resonance studies of protein and DNA structure and dynamics. *Mailing Add:* Dept Biochem & Biophys Iowa State Univ Ames IA 50011-2010. *Fax:* 515-294-0453; *E-Mail:* kintanar@iastate.edu

KINTER, LEWIS BOARDMAN, VASOPRESSIN, WHOLE ANIMAL MODELS. *Current Pos:* SCIENTIST, SMITH KLINE & FRENCH LABS, 81- *Personal Data:* b Exeter, NH, Aug 15, 50; m 73; c 3. *Educ:* Union Col, BS, 73; Harvard Univ, PhD(physiol), 78. *Prof Exp:* Asst dir pharmacol, 84-88, asst dir toxicol, 88-90, assoc dir toxicol, Smith Kline Beecham Pharmaceuticals, 90- *Concurrent Pos:* Adj asst prof physiol, Univ Pa. *Mem:* Am Physiol Soc; Am Soc Nephrology; Inst Soc Nephrology. *Res:* Homeostatic mechanisms involved in control of renal function and body fluid volume and body fluid composition. *Mailing Add:* Dept Biol Nycomed Inc 466 Devon Park Dr Box 6630 Wayne PA 19087-8630. *Fax:* 610-225-4416

KINTNER, EDWIN E, ENGINEERING. *Current Pos:* RETIRED. *Personal Data:* c 4. *Educ:* US Naval Acad, BS, 42; Mass Inst Technol, MA, 46, MA, 50. *Prof Exp:* Exec vpres, Gen Pub Utility, Nuclear Corp, 83-90. *Concurrent Pos:* Chmn, Re-conceptualize Utility Power Reactors Prog, Elec Power Res Inst Advan Light Water Reactors & Comt Environ Technol, Nat Res Coun; asst dir reactor eng & dep dir, Reactors Develop Div, AEC; mem bd dir, Brit Nuclear Fuels Inc; US rep, Int Fusion Res Coun. *Mem:* Nat Acad Eng; Am Nuclear Soc; Elec Power Res Inst. *Res:* Nuclear power. *Mailing Add:* Bradley Hill Rd PO Box 682 Norwich VT 05055

KINTNER, ROBERT ROY, ORGANIC CHEMISTRY. *Current Pos:* INSTR, CALIF LUTHERAN UNIV, 94- *Personal Data:* b Weeping Water, Nebr, Apr 3, 28; m 52, Helen R Remmers; c Timothy R, Melinda R (Hooper) & SueLynn R (Lautt). *Educ:* Iowa State Univ, BS, 53; Univ Wash, PhD(org chem), 57. *Prof Exp:* From asst prof to prof chem, Augustana Col, SDak, 57-94, chmn dept, 60-65 & 77-85. *Concurrent Pos:* Petrol res fund adv sci award, Univ Wash, Seattle, 64-65; NSF fac fel, Univ Calif, Santa Cruz, 71-72; vis prof chem, Univ Nebr, Lincoln, 80-81 & vis lectr chem, Munich, Ger Campus, Univ Md, 85-87; prin investr, Sioux Falls Refuse Derived Fuel Proj, 78-80; vis prof chem, Univ Calif, Santa Cruz, 87-88. *Mem:* Am Chem Soc. *Res:* Physical-organic chemistry, especially in reaction mechanisms; structure; investigation of the mechanism of the formation of 2, 3, 7, 8-tetrachlorodibenzodioxin. *Mailing Add:* Chem Dept Calif Lutheran Univ 60 W Olsen Rd Thousand Oaks CA 91360. *Fax:* 605-336-5299; *E-Mail:* Kintner@inst.augie.edu

KINYON, BRICE W(HITMAN), MECHANICAL ENGINEERING. *Current Pos:* RETIRED. *Personal Data:* b South Bend, Ind, May 1, 11; m 35; c 2. *Educ:* Purdue Univ, BSME, 33; Oak Ridge Sch Reactor Technol, cert, 55. *Honors & Awards:* Chattanooga Engr of the Year, 79. *Prof Exp:* Engr prod, Armstrong Cork Co, 35-37 & Hamilton Watch Co, 37-38; prod & design engr, Radio Corp Am, 38-44 & Elec Storage Battery Co, 44-47; sr design engr reactor design, Oak Ridge Nat Lab, 47-62; anal engr, Thermal Stress Consult, Combustion Eng, Inc, 62-76. *Mem:* Am Nuclear Soc; Sigma Xi; fel Am Soc Mech Engrs; Nat Soc Prof Engrs. *Res:* Fluid flow and heat transfer for power reactors and components. *Mailing Add:* 1312 N Shady Circle Chattanooga TN 37405

KINZEL, GARY LEE, COMPUTER-AIDED DESIGN, KINEMATICS. *Current Pos:* from asst prof to assoc prof, 78-87, PROF, OHIO STATE UNIV, 87- *Personal Data:* b Bremen, Ohio, Jan 18, 44; m 67; c 2. *Educ:* Ohio State Univ, BSME, 68, MS, 69; Purdue Univ, PhD(mech eng), 73. *Prof Exp:* Researcher, Batelle Mem Inst, 68-69; res eng, Batelle Columbus Labs, 68-69. *Mem:* Sigma Xi; Am Soc Mech Engrs. *Res:* Interactive computer graphics; machine element design; biomechanics; mechanism analysis and design; design and development of CAD software. *Mailing Add:* 3160 Caris Brook Rd Columbus OH 43221-2242

KINZEL, JERRY J, MICROBIAL PHYSIOLOGY, INTERMEDIATE METABOLISM. *Current Pos:* SR ASSOC RES SCIENTIST, 81-, SR RES SCIENTIST, INT MINERALS & CHEM CORP. *Personal Data:* b Avon, Ohio, Apr 24, 52; m 81. *Educ:* Cleveland State Univ, BS, 76; Miami Univ, MS, 78, PhD(microbiol), 81. *Mem:* Sigma Xi; Am Soc Microbiol. *Res:* Microbial physiology with special emphasis on genetics and enzymology. *Mailing Add:* 250 S 21st St Terre Haute IN 47803

KINZER, EARL T, JR, THEORETICAL PHYSICS, SOLID STATE PHYSICS. *Current Pos:* assoc prof, 67-93, actg head, Physics Dept, 86-89, EMER ASSOC PROF PHYSICS, AUBURN UNIV, 93- *Personal Data:* b Beckley, WVa, Apr 7, 31; m 57, Mary J Smith; c Charles & Kathleen. *Educ:* Auburn Univ, BEP, 58, MS, 60; Univ Va, PhD(physics), 62. *Prof Exp:* From asst prof to assoc prof physics, Univ Ala, Tuscaloosa, 61-67. *Concurrent Pos:* Adj assoc prof physics, LaGrange Col, 93- *Res:* Operational solution of partial difference equations; foundations of electromagnetic theory. *Mailing Add:* 317 Kimberly Dr Auburn AL 36832

KINZER, H GRANT, ENTOMOLOGY. *Current Pos:* From asst prof to assoc prof 64-76, PROF ENTOM, NMEX STATE UNIV, 76- *Personal Data:* b Grandfield, Okla, July 22, 37; m 57, 81; c 5. *Educ:* Okla State Univ, BS, 59, MS, 60, PhD(entom), 62. *Mem:* Entom Soc Am; Am Registery Prof Entomologists; Can Entom Soc; Am Mosquito Control Asn. *Res:* Biology, physiology and control of livestock insects; biology and physiology of bark beetles. *Mailing Add:* Dept Entom NMex State Univ PO Box 30003 Las Cruces NM 88003-8003

KINZER, ROBERT LEE, GAMMA RAY & X-RAY ASTRONOMY. *Current Pos:* Nat Acad Sci resident res fel cosmic ray physics, 67-69, RES PHYSICIST, US NAVAL RES LAB, 69- *Personal Data:* b Grandfield, Okla, June 23, 41; m 67; c 2. *Educ:* Univ Okla, BS, 62, MS, 66, PhD(elem particle physics), 67. *Mem:* Am Phys Soc; AAAS; Sigma Xi; Am Astron Soc. *Res:* Experimental elementary particle physics; experimental gamma-ray astronomy and x-ray astronomy. *Mailing Add:* Code 7653 Naval Res Lab C Washington DC 20375-0001. *E-Mail:* kinzer@osse.nrl.navy.mil

KINZEY, BERTRAM Y(ORK), JR, ARCHITECTURAL ACOUSTICS. *Current Pos:* from assoc prof to prof, 59-85, EMER PROF ARCHIT, UNIV FLA, 85- *Personal Data:* b Rutland, Mass, Sept 25, 21; m 44; c 2. *Educ:* Va Polytech Inst, BS, 42, MS, 43. *Prof Exp:* Naval architect, Norfolk Navy Yard, 43-45; archit draftsman & struct engr, Baskervill & Son, Va, 45-47; from asst prof to assoc prof archit eng, Va Polytech Inst, 47-59. *Concurrent Pos:* Mem comt archit & acoust, Am Guild Organists, 52-56; mem comn archit, Nat Coun Churches, 54-, chmn joint comt church archit & music, 56-; consult archit acoust, 60- *Mem:* Fel Acoust Soc Am; Am Inst Archit; Am Soc Heating, Refrig & Air-Conditioning Engrs; Nat Coun Acoust Consults. *Res:* Heating, lighting, acoustics and sanitation; tests on wood box columns to determine formulas for design; thermal performance of ventilated building skins. *Mailing Add:* 212 SW 42nd St Gainesville FL 32607-2769

KINZEY, WARREN GLENFORD, anatomy, physical anthropology; deceased, see previous edition for last biography

KINZIE, JEANNIE JONES, RADIATION, ONCOLOGY. *Current Pos:* dir radiation oncol, 85-91, prof radiol, 85-95, FEL NUCLEAR MED, UNIV COLO, 96- *Personal Data:* b Gt Falls, Mont, Mar 14, 40; m 91, Johnson Wachira; c Daniel. *Educ:* Mont State Univ, BS, 61; Washington Univ, MD, 65; Univ Phoenix, MBA, 97. *Prof Exp:* Intern surg, Univ NC, 65-66; resident therapeut radiol, Washington Univ, 68-71, instr radiol, 71-73; asst prof, Med Col Wis, 73-74; asst prof, Univ Chicago, 75-78, assoc prof, 78-80; assoc prof radiation oncol, Wayne State Univ, 80-85. *Concurrent Pos:* Am Cancer Soc advan clin fel, 71-74; consult radiol, Homer G Phillips Hosp, St Louis, 71-73, Vet Hosp, Wood, Wis & West Allis Mem Hosps, 73-74, Children's Hosp Mich, Detroit Receiving Hosp, Hutzel Hosp & Harper Grace Hosps, Detroit, 80-85; consult, Rose Med Ctr, Denver Gen Hosp & Denver Vet Hosp, 85- & Food & Drug Admin, 87. *Mem:* Fel Am Col Radiol; AMA; Am Soc Therapeut Radiol & Oncol; Am Soc Clin Oncol; Wilderness Med Soc; Soc Head & Neck Surgeons; Sigma Xi. *Res:* Patterns of care in Hodgkins disease and other cancers; combination treatment of head and neck cancer; combination radiation/chemotherapy studies for numerous types of cancer. *Mailing Add:* PO Box 2767 Evergreen CO 80439

KINZIE, ROBERT ALLEN, III, ZOOLOGY. *Current Pos:* asst prof, 71-79, ASSOC PROF ZOOL, UNIV HAWAII, 75- *Personal Data:* b Santa Cruz, Calif, June 7, 41. *Educ:* Univ Hawaii, MS, 66; Yale Univ, PhD(biol), 70. *Prof Exp:* Fel, Univ Ga, 70-71. *Concurrent Pos:* Consult, Upjohn Drug Co, 70- *Mem:* Ecol Soc Am; Soc Study Evolution; Soc Syst Zool; Am Soc Limnol & Oceanog. *Res:* Coral reef ecology; symbiosis. *Mailing Add:* Dept Zool Univ Hawaii Honolulu HI 96822

KINZLER, KENNETH W, ONCOLOGY. *Current Pos:* Postdoctoral fel, 88-90, asst prof, 90-94, ASSOC PROF ONCOL, JOHNS HOPKINS UNIV SCH MED, 94- *Personal Data:* b Philadelphia, PA, Jan 30, 62; m 84, Jacqueline; c Kathryn & William. *Educ:* Philadelphia Col Parm & Sci, BS, 83; Johns Hopkins Univ Sch Med, PhD, 88. *Concurrent Pos:* Assoc ed, Cancer Res, 93. *Mailing Add:* Johns Hopkins Oncol Ctr Res Lab Rm 111 424 N Bond St Baltimore MD 21231-1001

KINZLY, ROBERT EDWARD, ELECTROOPTICS, OPTICAL ENGINEERING. *Current Pos:* PRES, SCIPAR, INC, 75- *Personal Data:* b North Tonawanda, NY, July 4, 39; m 63; c 2. *Educ:* Univ Buffalo, BA, 61; Cornell Univ, MS, 64. *Prof Exp:* Physicist, Cornell Aeronaut Lab, Inc, 63-67, sect head & br head, Calspan Corp, 67-75. *Concurrent Pos:* Mem, Am Stand Inst working group microdensity. *Mem:* Optical Soc Am; Asn Old Crows. *Res:* Camouflage; image evaluation; atmospheric optics; remote sensing; visual perception; planetology; computer science; electro-optical warfare; optical countermeasures; target acquisition; image processing. *Mailing Add:* 45 Tartan Lane Buffalo NY 14221

KIP, ARTHUR F, SOLID STATE PHYSICS. *Current Pos:* RETIRED. *Personal Data:* b Los Angeles, Calif, Sept 27, 10. *Educ:* Univ Calif, BS, 35, PhD(physics), 39. *Prof Exp:* Dept Physics, Mass Inst Technol, 48-51 & Univ Calif, 51-65. *Mem:* Am Phys Soc. *Mailing Add:* 775 San Diego Rd Berkeley CA 94707

KIPHART, KERRY, INORGANIC TREATMENT, HAZARDOUS WASTE MANAGEMENT. *Current Pos:* Develop engr, Endicott, NY, 83-87, ENVIRON ENGR, IBM CORP, POUGHKEEPSIE, NY, 87- *Personal Data:* b South Haven, Mich, Apr 21, 49; m, Scott. *Educ:* Ill Wesleyan Univ, BA, 71; Univ Notre Dame, MS, 80, PhD(environ eng), 84. *Mem:* Am Chem Soc. *Res:* Physical and organizational structures ensuring responsible chemical and waste management; software development for chemical management data and product environmental assessment. *Mailing Add:* 121 Dusinberre Rd Gardiner NY 12525. *E-Mail:* kiphart@vnet.ibm.com

KIPLING, ARLIN LLOYD, SURFACE SCIENCE, BIOSENSORS. *Current Pos:* PROF PHYSICS, CONCORDIA UNIV, 67- *Personal Data:* b Melfort, Sask, Dec 15, 36; m 63, Joan Kalifey; c Caroline, Diane & Arlene. *Educ:* Univ Sask, BEng, 58; McGill Univ, MSc, 61; Univ Exeter, PhD(physics), 67. *Prof Exp:* Engr, Northern Elec Co, Que, 58-59; physicist, Noranda Res Ctr, Que,

63-64. *Res:* Sensing of biomolecules in a liquid using acoustic wave sensors, with applications in the medical field. *Mailing Add:* Dept Physics Concordia Univ Sir G Williams Campus Montreal PQ H3G 1M8 Can. *Fax:* 514-848-2828

KIPLINGER, GLENN FRANCIS, CLINICAL PHARMACOLOGY. *Current Pos:* CONSULT, 89- *Personal Data:* b Indianapolis, Ind, Sept 29, 30; m 53, Martha Peterson; c Jeffrey, Jonathan, Jason & Jennifer. *Educ:* Butler Univ, BS, 53; Univ Mich, PhD(pharmacol), 58; Univ Tex, Galveston, MD, 67. *Prof Exp:* Asst pharmacol, Boston Univ Sch Med, 58-62 & Univ Tex, Galveston, 62-67; clin pharmacologist, Eli Lilly & Co, Indianapolis, 67-72, dir toxicol, 72-75, vpres res, 75-77; managing dir, Lilly Res Ctr, UK, 77-80; vpres res & develop, Ortho Pharmaceut, Johnson & Johnson, 80-88 & R W Johnson Pharmaceut Res Inst, 88-89. *Concurrent Pos:* Trustee, Butler Univ, Indianapolis, 89- *Mem:* Am Soc Pharmacol & Exp Therapeut; Am Soc Clin Pharmacol & Therapeut. *Res:* Cardiovascular pharmacology; clinical pharmacology of analgesics and of marijuana; research and development management. *Mailing Add:* 1620 South Dr Sarasota FL 34239-5037. *Fax:* 941-957-0240

KIPNIS, DAVID MORRIS, INTERNAL MEDICINE, ENDOCRINOLOGY. *Current Pos:* asst prof biochem, Wash Univ, 57-62, dir, Clin Res Ctr, 60-87, from assoc prof to prof, 62-73, Busch prof med & chmn dept, 73-92, DISTINGUISHED UNIV PROF MED, WASH UNIV, 93- *Personal Data:* b Baltimore, Md, May 23, 27; m 53; c 3. *Educ:* Johns Hopkins Univ, AB, 45, MA, 49; Univ Md, MD, 51. *Hon Degrees:* ScD, Univ Md. *Honors & Awards:* Oppenheimer Award, Endocrine Soc. *Prof Exp:* Intern med, Johns Hopkins Hosp, 51-52; from jr asst resident to sr asst resident, Duke Univ Hosp, 52-54; chief resident, Univ Md Hosp, 54-55. *Concurrent Pos:* Am Col Physicians fel biochem, Sch Med, Wash Univ, 55-56; Markle scholar, 56-61; mem sci adv bd, USAF; mem Endocrinol Study Sect, NIH; mem, Nat Pituitary Agency; mem & chmn, Nat Diabetes Adv Bd, 77-81; mem, Fel Comt Burroughs Wellcome Fund. *Mem:* Nat Acad Sci; Inst Med-Nat Acad Sci; Asn Am Physicians; Endocrine Soc; Biochem Soc; Am Soc Clin Invest; Am Acad Arts & Sci. *Res:* Hormonal control of carbohydrate and protein metabolism. *Mailing Add:* Dept Med Wash Univ Sch Med St Louis MO 63110

KIPOUROS, GEORGES JOHN, LIGHT, REFRACTORY & RARE EARTH METALS. *Current Pos:* PROF & HEAD, DEPT MINING & METALL ENG, DALHOUSIE UNIV, 89- *Personal Data:* b Patras, Greece, July 17, 48; Can citizen; m 82, Matina Sarantopoulos; c Yiannis & Athanasios. *Educ:* Nat Tech Univ Athens, Dipl Eng, 71; Univ Toronto, MASc, 77, PhD(metall & mat sci), 82. *Prof Exp:* Actg head, permanent Comt Receiving Ammunition, Pyrkal, 72-74; postdoctoral assoc, Mass Inst Technol, 82-85; sr res scientist, Gen Motors Res & Develop Ctr, 85-89, fac consult, 95-96. *Concurrent Pos:* Vis prof, Norweg Inst Technol, 93, Univ Patras, Greece, 93, 94 & 96. *Mem:* Electrochem Soc; Can Inst Mining & Metall; Inst Soc Electrochem; Minerals, Metals & Mat Soc; Europ Rare Earth & Actinide Soc. *Res:* Chemical process metallurgy, both in fundamental and engineering applications of light, refractory, and rare earth metals; value-added metallurgy; materials science and engineeering; transfer of technology from laboratory to plant. *Mailing Add:* PO Box 1000 Halifax NS B3J 2X4 Can. *Fax:* 902-425-1037; *E-Mail:* kipouzgj@tuns.ca

KIPP, EGBERT MASON, RESEARCH ADMINISTRATION. *Current Pos:* INDEPENDENT CONSULT TECH MGT, 70- *Personal Data:* b Angola, Port WAfrica, Nov 27, 14; m 35; c 3. *Educ:* Iowa Wesleyan Col, BS, 34; Boston Univ, MS, 35; Pa State Univ, PhD(phys chem), 39. *Hon Degrees:* DSc, Iowa Wesleyan Col, 61. *Prof Exp:* Asst chem, Pa State Univ, 35-39; res chemist, Aluminum Co Am, 39-44, asst chief phys chem div, 44-47, exec secy oils & lubricants comt, 46-57, chief lubricants div, 47-57; dir res & develop, Foote Mineral Co, 57-59; asst to mgr prod develop, Sun Oil Co, 59-60, mgr basic res, 60-62, assoc dir res & develop, 62-70. *Concurrent Pos:* Consult, chem & metals indust, 71-; eval agent, Off Energy Related Inventions, Nat Bur Standards; chmn, tech comt K, Am Soc Test & Mat, vchmn, Pittsburgh dist; chmn, Am Inst Chemists, Philadelphia & pres-elect, Pa Inst Chemists; mem, Res Mgt Group Philadelphia, pres elect, 74 & pres, 75-76; plenary lectr, 3rd Int Conf Metal Working Lubricants, Esslingen, Ger, 82. *Mem:* Am Chem Soc; fel Am Soc Lubrication Eng (pres, 46); fel Am Inst Chemists (treas, 70); Sigma Xi; Am Soc Testing & Mat. *Res:* Lubrication engineering sciences; research and development management and organization; energy, market and commercial development; air, soil and water conservation; technology audits; author of one book and 16 publications; holder of 11 patents. *Mailing Add:* 745 Thomas St State College PA 16803

KIPP, JAMES EDWIN, CHEMICAL KINETICS, PHARMACEUTICAL FORMULATIONS. *Current Pos:* res scientist, 85-90, SR RES SCIENTIST, BAXTER HEALTHCARE CORP, 90- *Personal Data:* b Detroit, Mich, June 15, 53; m 86, Patricia Myers; c William R. *Educ:* Albion Col, BA, 75; Univ Mich, MS, PhD(chem), 83. *Honors & Awards:* Cert Recognition, Nat Aeronaut & Space Admin, 91. *Prof Exp:* Sr res assoc, Baxter Travenol, 83-85. *Mem:* Am Chem Soc; Am Asn Pharmaceut Scientist. *Res:* Mathematical modeling of nonisothermal decomposition of drugs in pharmaceutical formulations; prediction of pharmaceutical shelf life; variable pH experiments for rapid preformulation screening; development of parenteral drug formulations; pulmonary drug delivery; computer modeling of chemical equilibria. *Mailing Add:* Baxter Healthcare Corp Pharmaceut Res & Develop Rte 120 & Wilson Rd Round Lake IL 60073

KIPP, RAYMOND J, SANITARY ENGINEERING. *Current Pos:* from asst prof to prof civil eng, 57-90, dean, Col Eng, 57-87, RES PROF CIVIL ENVIRON ENG, MARQUETTE UNIV, 90- EMER DEAN, 90- *Personal Data:* b Ossian, Iowa, Dec 7, 22; m 49; c 2. *Educ:* Marquette Univ, BS, 51; Univ Wis, MS, 57, PhD(sanit eng, bact), 65. *Concurrent Pos:* Chmn, Milwaukee Metrop Sewerage Dist, 78-79. *Mem:* Water Pollution Control Fedn; Am Acad Environ Engrs; Am Soc Civil Engrs; Nat Soc Prof Engrs; Am Soc Eng Educ; Am Water Works Asn. *Res:* Industrial wastes; toxic and hazardous wastes. *Mailing Add:* Col Eng Marquette Univ 1515 W Wisconsin Ave Milwaukee WI 53201-1881

KIPPENBERGER, DONALD JUSTIN, physical chemistry, for more information see previous edition

KIPPENHAN, C(HARLES) J(ACOB), MECHANICAL ENGINEERING. *Current Pos:* chmn dept, 63-73, prof, 63-88, EMER PROF MECH ENG, UNIV WASH, SEATTLE, 88- *Personal Data:* b Middle Amana, Iowa, Nov 8, 19; m 41, Jane E Munsinger; c Kurt & Judith. *Educ:* Univ Iowa, BSME, 40, MSME, 46, PhD(mech eng), 48. *Prof Exp:* Jr mech engr, Stanley Eng Co, 40; instr mech eng, Univ Iowa, 41-42; from asst prof to assoc prof, Washington Univ, St Louis, 48-54, prof & head dept, 54-63. *Concurrent Pos:* Mech eng consult; adj prof archit, Univ Wash, Seattle. *Mem:* Am Soc Heating, Refrig & Air Conditioning Engrs; Am Soc Mech Engrs; Am Soc Eng Educ. *Res:* Building energy systems analysis, simulation; energy conservation and management; convective and radiation heat transfer; thermal properties; transient techniques. *Mailing Add:* 3908 Northeast 38th St Seattle WA 98105

KIPPS, THOMAS CHARLES, MATHEMATICS. *Current Pos:* from instr to assoc prof, 56-67, chmn dept, 69, PROF MATH, CALIF STATE UNIV, FRESNO, 67- *Personal Data:* b Eureka, Utah, Feb 28, 23; m 48; c 4. *Educ:* Univ Calif, Berkeley, AB, 49, MA, 50, PhD(math), 57. *Prof Exp:* Instr math & physics, Univ Santa Clara, 53-55; asst math, Univ Calif, Berkeley, 55-56. *Mem:* Am Math Soc; Math Asn Am; Sigma Xi. *Res:* Double integral problems in the calculus of variations; methods of linear algebra in numerical analysis. *Mailing Add:* 1459 E Portals Ave Fresno CA 93710-6423

KIPROV, DOBRI D, IMMUNOLOGY. *Current Pos:* clin res fel, 81-82, dir plasmapheresis, Dept Cellular Immunol, 82-, CHIEF, DIV IMMUNOL, CALIF PAC MED CTR, SAN FRANCISCO. *Personal Data:* b Sofia, Bulgaria, May 1, 49; US citizen; c 1. *Educ:* Med Acad, Bulgaria, MD, 74. *Prof Exp:* Instr path, Sackler Sch Med, Israel, 74-77; resident, Mt Sinai Hosp, Case Western Res Univ, 77-79; clin res fel, Mass Gen Hosp, Harvard Med Sch, 79-81. *Concurrent Pos:* Training & Res awardee, Nat Inst Allergies & Infectious Dis. *Mem:* AMA; Am Soc Clin Path; Am Col Pathologists; World Apheresis Asn; World Med Asn. *Res:* Basic immunologic defects in autoimmune diseases, including renal diseases; evaluation of lymphocyte subsets from peripheral blood and tissues using moncolonal antibodies; effect of plasmapheresis, lymphocytapheresis and immunosuppressive therapy on the immunologic system of patients with autoimmune diseases; clinical correlation with immunologic assays. *Mailing Add:* Calif Pac Med Ctr Rm 603 2351 Clay St San Francisco CA 94118

KIRBER, MARIA WIENER, MICROBIOLOGY, VIROLOGY. *Current Pos:* Asst bact, 41-43, from instr to prof, 43-72, prof microbiol, 62-72, EMER PROF VIROL & MICROBIOL, MED COL PA, 72- *Personal Data:* b Prague, Czech, Feb 19, 17; nat US; m 43; c 2. *Educ:* Univ Prague, MUC, 38; Univ Pa, MS, 41, PhD(bact), 42; Am Bd Microbiol, dipl. *Hon Degrees:* ScD, Med Col Pa, 73. *Honors & Awards:* Christian R & Mary E Lindback Award, 71. *Concurrent Pos:* Nat Coun Combat Blindness grant, Med Col Pa, 58-59, 62-63 & 66-67 & Nat Soc Prev Blindness grant, 68-70; mem res staff, Children's Hosp, Philadelphia, 51-52. *Mem:* Fel Am Acad Microbiol; Am Soc Microbiol. *Res:* Antigenic structure of hemolytic streptococci; complement fixing antigens of influenza viruses; mouse brain tissue culture; experimental viral infections and auto-immune reactions of the eye; experimental mycobacterial eye infection. *Mailing Add:* Juniper Dr Lakeville CT 06039

KIRBY, ALBERT CHARLES, PHYSIOLOGY. *Current Pos:* asst prof, 69-75, ASSOC PROF PHYSIOL, CASE WESTERN RES UNIV, 75-, ASSOC DEAN, 84- *Personal Data:* b Baton Rouge, La, Mar 31, 41; m 61; c 3. *Educ:* La State Univ, Baton Rouge, BS, 62, MS, 63; Univ Ill, Urbana, PhD(physiol), 67. *Prof Exp:* NIH sr fel physiol, Univ Wash, 67-69. *Concurrent Pos:* NIH res grants, Case Western Reserve Univ, 69- *Mem:* Soc Gen Physiol; Biophys Soc; Am Physiol Soc. *Res:* Excitation-contraction coupling and contractile proteins in denervated mammalian muscle. *Mailing Add:* 2119 Abington Rd Case Western Res Univ Sch Med Cleveland OH 44106-4920

KIRBY, ANDREW FULLER, SPECTROSCOPY, REMOTE SENSING. *Current Pos:* phys scientist, Off Sci & Weapons Res, CIA, 85-87, res scientist br chief, 87-90, div chief mat res, 91-93, SR PROG CHIEF, OFF RES & DEVELOP, CIA, 94- *Personal Data:* b Washington, DC, Feb 15, 55; m 81, Martha R Diaz; c Eleanor R & John R. *Educ:* Col Holy Cross, AB, 77; Duke Univ, PhD(phys chem), 81. *Prof Exp:* Fel assoc, Univ Va, 81-82. *Mem:* Am Chem Soc; Sigma Xi. *Res:* Detailed electronic and molecular structures of solid-state lanthanide complexes; advanced spectroscopic measurement techniques; remote sensing and geophysical techniques; technical research management. *Mailing Add:* PO Box 3313 Falls Church VA 22043-3313

KIRBY, BRUCE JOHN, APPLIED MATHEMATICS. *Current Pos:* lectr, Queen's Univ, Ont, 54-60, from asst prof to assoc prof, 60-69, prof, 69-, EMER PROF MATH, QUEEN'S UNIV, ONT. *Personal Data:* b Toronto, Ont, Nov 19, 28; m 58; c 2. *Educ:* Univ Toronto, BA, 50, MA, 51; Univ London, PhD, 67. *Prof Exp:* Teaching fel math, Univ Toronto, 51-53; lectr, Univ Liverpool, 53-54; asst dir serv, Skidaway Inst Oceanog, 67-95. *Mem:* Soc Indust & Appl Math. *Res:* Mathematics of control theory. *Mailing Add:* Dept Math & Statist Queen's Univ Kingston ON K7L 3N6 Can

KIRBY, CONRAD JOSEPH, JR, ecology, for more information see previous edition

KIRBY, EDWARD PAUL, biochemistry, hematology; deceased, see previous edition for last biography

KIRBY, HILLIARD WALKER, INTEGRATED PEST MANAGEMENT. *Current Pos:* ASST PROF PLANT PATH, COL AGR, UNIV ILL, 81- *Personal Data:* b Asheville, NC, June 12, 49; m 81. *Educ:* Univ NC, BS, 71; NC State Univ, MS, 74, PhD(plant path), 81. *Prof Exp:* Agr exten agent, NC Agr Exten Serv, 74-78. *Mem:* Am Phytopath Soc. *Res:* Effects of conservation tillage on plant disease development. *Mailing Add:* 1913 Galena St Urbana IL 61801

KIRBY, JAMES RAY, ANALYTICAL CHEMISTRY. *Current Pos:* MGR CHEM ANALYSIS, IBM, RESEARCH TRIANGLE PARK, 84- *Personal Data:* b Goldsboro, NC, Oct 22, 33; m 62; c 3. *Educ:* E Carolina Col, AB & BS, 55; Duke Univ, MA, 57, PhD(chem, physics), 60. *Prof Exp:* From res chemist to sr res chemist, 60-68, res specialist, 68-73, sr res specialist, Monsanto Co, 73- *Mem:* Am Chem Soc. *Res:* Chelate chemistry; polymer characterization. *Mailing Add:* IBM Dept E62 Bldg 061 PO Box 12195 Research Triangle Park NC 27709-2195

KIRBY, KATE PAGE, ATOMIC & MOLECULAR PROCESSES IN ASTROPHYSICS, ATMOSPHERIC PHYSICS. *Current Pos:* RES PHYSICIST, SMITHSONIAN ASTROPHYS OBSERV, 73-; ASSOC DIR, HARVARD-SMITHSONIAN CTR ASTROPHYS, ATOMIC & MOLECULAR PHYSICS DIV, 88-, DEP DIR HARVARD-SMITHSONIAN INST THEORET ATOMIC & MOLECULAR PHYSICS, 89- *Personal Data:* b Washington, DC, Dec 5, 45; m 77; c 4. *Educ:* Harvard, AB, 67; Univ Chicago, MS, 68, PhD(chem physics), 72. *Prof Exp:* Postdoctoral res fel astrophys, Harvard Col Observ, 72-73. *Concurrent Pos:* Lectr, Astron Dept, Harvard, 73-83 & 84-86; mem, Comt Atomic & Molecular Sci, Nat Acad Sci/Nat Res Coun, 82-85; mem, Comt Opportunities in Physics, Am Phys Soc, 87-89. *Mem:* Fel Am Phys Soc; Int Astron Union; Am Astron Soc; Am Geophys Union; fel AAAS. *Res:* Theoretical studies of atomic and molecular structure and processes; molecular excited states and transition probabilities; molecular photoionization; autoionization and photo dissociation; charge transfer; applications of atomic and molecular physics to astrophysics and atmospheric physics. *Mailing Add:* Ctr Astrophys 60 Garden St Cambridge MA 02138

KIRBY, MARGARET LOEWY, ANATOMY, PHARMACOLOGY. *Current Pos:* from asst prof to prof, 77-88, REGENTS PROF ANAT, MED COL GA, 88- *Personal Data:* b Ft Smith, Ark, June 5, 46; m 71; c 2. *Educ:* Manhattanville Col, AB, 68; Univ Ark, PhD(anat), 72. *Prof Exp:* Teaching asst anat, Univ Ark, 69-71; asst prof gross anat, Cent Univ Ark, 72-74. *Concurrent Pos:* Prin investr, Ga Heart Asn, 78-79, Nat Inst Drug Abuse, 79-81 & NIH, 81-89; Nat Heart, Lung & Blood Adv Coun, 85-91. *Mem:* Am Asn Anatomists; Sigma Xi; Soc Neurosci; Soc Develop Biol. *Res:* Effects of neurotransmitters on embryonic development; neural crest; heart development; molecular biology of development; pediatric cardiology. *Mailing Add:* Dept Anat Med Col Ga CB2930 Augusta GA 30912-2000. *Fax:* 706-721-6839

KIRBY, PAUL EDWARD, CELL BIOLOGY. *Current Pos:* VPRES, DIR OPER, SITEK RES LABS, 84- *Personal Data:* b Washington, DC, Mar 12, 49; m 71; c 4. *Educ:* Mt St Mary's Col, Md, BS, 71; Cath Univ Am, MS, 74, PhD(cell biol), 78. *Prof Exp:* Res scientist in vitro mutagenesis, EG&G Mason Res Inst, 78-80, chief, Mammalian Mutagenesis Sect, 80-82; dir oper, Microbiol Asn, 82-84. *Concurrent Pos:* Prin investr, Nat Cancer Inst; consult, 80- *Mem:* AAAS; Environ Mutagen Soc; Tissue Cult Asn; Genetic Toxicol Asn; Genetic & Environ Mutagen Soc. *Res:* In vitro carcinogenesis and mutagenesis in mammalian cells, especially the L5178Y mouse lymphoma mutagenesis assay as a tool for the screening of compounds for mutagenic potential; invitro toxicity test development. *Mailing Add:* 15235 Shady Grove Rd Sitek Corp Rockville MD 20850

KIRBY, RALPH C(LOUDSBERRY), EXTRACTIVE METALLURGY, MINERAL ENGINEERING. *Current Pos:* CONSULT, NETWORK CONSULT, 85- *Personal Data:* b Washington, DC, July 21, 25; m 50; c 1. *Educ:* Cath Univ Am, BChE, 50. *Honors & Awards:* Gold Medal, Am Inst Chem, 50; Invention Award, US Bur Mines. *Prof Exp:* Chem engr, Metall Res Ctr, US Bur Mines 50-54, metall engr, 55-58, proj leader, 59-65, staff metallurgist, Div Metall, 66-70, sr staff metallurgist, 71-72, chief, Div Metall, 72-76, asst dir metall, 76-79, dir, Min Resources Technol, 79-82, asst dir, 82-84, chief engr, 84-85. *Concurrent Pos:* Bd dirs, Metall Soc, 76- *Mem:* Am Inst Mining, Metall & Petrol Engrs; Am Inst Chem Engrs; AAAS; Am Soc Metals; Sigma Xi. *Res:* Metallurgical research; research and development management. *Mailing Add:* 15101 Interlachen Dr Apt 604 Silver Spring MD 20906-5617

KIRBY, RICHARD C(YRIL), electrical engineering, for more information see previous edition

KIRBY, ROBERT EMMET, ANALYTICAL CHEMISTRY. *Current Pos:* RETIRED. *Personal Data:* b Stowe Twp, Pa, Feb 27, 21; m 44; c 4. *Educ:* Univ Pittsburgh, BS, 49; Carnegie Inst Technol, MS, 52; Univ Ariz, PhD(anal chem), 61. *Prof Exp:* Res chemist, Shell Chem Co, 52-57; salesman, William C Buchanan Co, 57-58; instr, Tex Col Arts & Indust, 58-59; sr res chemist, Colgate-Palmolive Co, 62-63; from asst prof to assoc prof chem, Queens Col, NY, 63-83. *Mem:* Am Chem Soc; Royal Chem Soc. *Res:* Electroanalytical methods; chelate chemistry; photoelectron spectroscopy. *Mailing Add:* 5051 N Grey Mountain Trail Tucson AZ 85790

KIRBY, ROBERT F, CARTOGRAPHY, REMOTE SENSING & PHOTOGRAMMETRY. *Current Pos:* US Army, 68-, instr, Dept Topog, Engr Sch, VA, engr intel officer, Long Binh, 70, comdr, 69th Engr Battalion Vietnam, theatre mapping officer & detachment opers officer, 227th Engr Detachment Topog, Hq, Ger, 74-77, opers officer & exec officer, 30th Engr Battalion Topog Ft Belvoir, Va, 77-79, sr prog officer & test & eval officer, Directorate Combat Develop, Engr Sch, 79-81, topog prog officer, Off Asst Chief Staff Intel, Washington, DC, 81-85, battalion comdr, 29th Engr Battalion Topog, Ft Shafter, Hawaii, 85-88, dir, Dept Topog Eng, Engr Sch, Ft Leonard, Wood, Mo, 88-91, dir, Defense Mapping Agency, Hydrographic & Topog Ctr, Bethesda Md, 91-92, asst dep dir oper req, Plans & Req Directorate, Hq, Defense Mapping Agency, 92-94, dir, Defense Mapping Agency Combat Support Ctr, Bethesda, Md, 94-95, dir, Defense Mapping Agency, Dept Consumer Interface, 95-96, ACTG DIR, TOPOG ENG CTR, US ARMY, ALEXANDRIA, VA, 96- *Personal Data:* b Norfold, Va, Sept 1, 46; m, Angela Horsington; c Pamela, Brian & Jennifer. *Educ:* Univ Ill, BA, 68; Purdue Univ, MS, 74. *Res:* Geodetic science; topography. *Mailing Add:* US Army Corps Engrs Topog Eng Ctr 7701 Telegraph Rd Alexandria VA 22315-3864

KIRBY, ROBION C, MATHEMATICS. *Current Pos:* Asst prof, Univ Calif, Los Angeles, 65-69, PROF MATH, UNIV CALIF, BERKELEY, 71- *Personal Data:* b Chicago, Ill, Feb 25, 38; m 82; c 2. *Educ:* Univ Chicago, BS, 59, MS, 60, PhD(math), 65. *Honors & Awards:* Veblen Prize Geom, 71. *Concurrent Pos:* Dep dir, Math Sci Res Inst, 85- *Mem:* Am Math Soc. *Res:* Topology, specifically topology of manifolds, differential and combinatorial topology. *Mailing Add:* Dept Math Univ Calif Berkeley CA 94720-3840

KIRBY, ROGER D, PHYSICS. *Current Pos:* from asst prof to assoc prof, 71-81, PROF PHYSICS, UNIV NEBR, LINCOLN, 81-, CHAIR, DEPT PHYSICS & ASTRON, 95- *Personal Data:* b Lansing, Mich, June 1, 42; m 64, Suzanne Roesch; c Steven R. *Educ:* Mich State Univ, BS, 64; Cornell Univ, PhD(physics), 69. *Prof Exp:* Res assoc physics, Cornell Univ, 68-69 & Univ Ill, 69-71. *Mem:* Am Phys Soc; Am Asn Physics Teachers. *Res:* Magnetic and magneto optic properties of solids; thin film magnetism. *Mailing Add:* Behlen Lab Physics Univ Nebr Lincoln NE 68588. *Fax:* 402-472-2879; *E-Mail:* rdk@unlinfo.unl.edu

KIRBY, RONALD EUGENE, WILDLIFE BIOLOGY. *Current Pos:* DIR, US NAT BIOL SERV, N PRAIRIE SCI CTR, JAMESTOWN, 93- *Personal Data:* b Angola, Ind, Nov, 26, 47; m, Dona J; c Cyrus Robert, William Emil, Peter Waye, Joshua M, Emily A & Andrew J. *Educ:* Duke Univ, BS, 69, Southern Ill Univ, MA, 73; Univ Minn, PhD, 76. *Prof Exp:* Staff biologist, Coop Wildlife Res Lab, Southern Ill Univ, 69-72; NIH res trainee, Dept Ecol & Behav Biol, Univ Minn, 72-76; wildlife biologist, Patuxent Wildlife Res Ctr, US Fish & Wildlife Serv, Md, 76-80, pop mgt specialist, Div Refuge Mgt, Washington, 80-82, res coordr, Nat Wildlife Refuge Syst, 82-83, regional assistance biologist, Off Info Transfer, Ft Collins, 83-88, leader, Info Transfer Sect, 88-90; from asst dir to dir, N Prairie Wildlife Res Ctr, 91-93. *Concurrent Pos:* Collaborating biologist, US Forest Serv, Minn, 70-72; grantee, AEC, 72-76; res biologist, Antarctic Res Prog NSF, McMurdo Sta, 74. *Mem:* Wildlife Soc. *Res:* Contributed to numerous professional publications, science journals and professional reports. *Mailing Add:* N Prairie Sci Ctr US Nat Biol Serv 8711 37th St SE Jamestown ND 58401-9736

KIRBY, STEPHEN, ROCK MECHANICS. *Current Pos:* RES GEOPHYSICIST, WESTERN EARTHQUAKE HAZARD TEAM, US GEOL SURV, 68- *Personal Data:* b Ft Benning, Ga, May 5, 45; m 90, Lyle Rice; c Adam & Ben. *Educ:* Univ Ill, BS, 67; Univ Calif, Los Angeles, PhD(geol), 75. *Honors & Awards:* Richard Glen Award, Fuels Div, Am Chem Soc, 97. *Concurrent Pos:* Co-proj chief, China-US Coop Res, 79-85; co-prin investr, Planetary Geol & Geophysics Prog, NASA, 82-; mem, Int Comt Physics & Chem of Ice, 86-; staff specialist, Leg 118, Ocean Drilling Prog, SW Indian Ridge, 87; coordr, Nat Earthquake Hazard Reduction Prog, 90-93; chair, Mineral Physics Comt, Am Geophys Union, 91-93; mem, Sci Adv Comt, Geol Div, US Geol Surv, 92-95. *Mem:* Fel Am Geophys Union; fel Mineral Soc Am; Sigma Xi. *Res:* Investigate the properties of Earth and planetary materials, including ordinary rock-forming minerals and planetary ices; physics of earthquake sources in relation to mineralogical phase changes. *Mailing Add:* Western Earthquake Hazard Team US Geol Surv 345 Middlefield Rd MS977 Menlo Park CA 94025. *Fax:* 650-329-5163; *E-Mail:* skirby@lsdmnl.wr.usgs.gov

KIRCH, DARRELL G, PSYCHIATRY. *Current Pos:* DEAN SCH MED & GRAD STUDIES, MED COL GA, 94- *Personal Data:* b Denver, Colo, May 3, 49. *Educ:* Univ Colo, BA, 73, MD, 77. *Honors & Awards:* Commendation Award, USPHS, 89, Outstanding Serv Medal, 92; Exemplary Psychiatrist Award, Nat Alliance Ment Illness, 96. *Mem:* AAAS; Am Col Psychiatrists; AMA; Am Soc Clin Psychiat Pharmacol; Am Psychiat Asn. *Mailing Add:* Med Col Ga Sch Med Off of Dean Augusta GA 30912. *Fax:* 706-721-7035; *E-Mail:* dkirch.medicine@mailgw.mcg.edu

KIRCH, MURRAY R, PROGRAMMING METHODOLOGY. *Current Pos:* assoc prof math, 72-83, assoc prof info sci & math, 83-84, PROF COMPUT SCI & MATH, STOCKTON COL NJ, 84- *Personal Data:* b Philadelphia, Pa, Oct 11, 40; m 65; c 2. *Educ:* Temple Univ, AB, 62; Lehigh Univ, MS, 64, PhD(math), 68. *Prof Exp:* Opers analyst, Ctr Naval Anal, 65; instr math, Lehigh Univ, 65-68; asst prof, State Univ NY, Buffalo, 68-72. *Concurrent Pos:* MacArthur distinguished vis prof arts & sci, New Col, Univ SFla, 84-85; asst dir, Inst Retraining in Comput Sci, Clarkson Univ, 85-88; vis scientist, Software Eng Inst, Carnegie Mellon Univ, 89; vis prof & chair comput sci, Ind Univ Coop Prog, Malaysia, 90-91. *Mem:* Am Math Soc; Math Asn Am; Soc Indust & Appl Math; Am Statist Asn; Asn Comput Mach; Inst Elec & Electronics Engrs. *Res:* Point-set topology; functional analysis; numerical methods for nonlinear systems; mathematical analysis of gambling and risk taking; algorithms and data structure; programming methodology; computer science theory; computer science education; artificial intelligence and expert systems; software engineering; computational science. *Mailing Add:* Dept Comput Sci Stockton Col NJ Jim Leeds Rd Pomona NJ 08240-9988. *Fax:* 609-652-4858; *E-Mail:* mrk@vax002.stockton.edu

KIRCH, PATRICK VINTON, ARCHAEOLOGY, PALEOECOLOGY. *Current Pos:* RES ASSOC, BERNICE P BISHOP MUS, HAWAII, 84-; PROF ANTHROP, UNIV CALIF, BERKELEY, 87- *Personal Data:* b Honolulu, Hawaii, July 7, 50; div. *Educ:* Univ Pa, BA, 71; Yale Univ, MPhil, 74, PhD(anthrop), 75. *Honors & Awards:* John J Carty Award for Advan Sci, Nat Acad Sci, 97. *Prof Exp:* Assoc anthropologist, Bernice P Bishop Mus, Hawaii, 74-75, anthropologist, 73-85, head, Div Archaeol, 83-84; dir, Burke Mem Wash State Mus, Univ Wash, 85-87, from assoc prof to prof anthrop, 85-89. *Concurrent Pos:* Prin investr, NSF grants, Bernice P Bishop Mus, 76- & var other grants, 84-91; affil assoc prof, Univ Hawaii, 82-84. *Mem:* Nat Acad Sci; Sigma Xi; Asn Field Archaeol; Soc Am Archaeol; Am Anthrop Asn; Am Acad Arts & Sci; fel AAAS. *Res:* Archaeology, paleoecology and biogeography of the oceanic region. *Mailing Add:* Dept Anthrop Univ Calif Berkeley CA 94720. *Fax:* 510-643-9637; *E-Mail:* kirch@gal.berkeley.edu

KIRCHBERGER, MADELEINE, PHYSIOLOGY. *Current Pos:* instr physiol, 70-71, assoc, 71-74, asst prof, 74-78, ASSOC PROF PHYSIOL, BIOPHYS & MED, MT SINAI SCH MED, 78- *Personal Data:* b Buffalo, NY. *Educ:* Hunter Col, BA, 60; Columbia Univ, MA, 62, PhD(cell physiol), 66. *Prof Exp:* Res fel med, Mass Gen Hosp & Sch Med, Harvard Univ, 66-69. *Mem:* Am Physiol Soc; Biophys Soc; Am Soc Biol Chem; Int Soc Heart Res. *Res:* Regulation of cardiac contractility by catecholamines; calcium transport in biological membranes. *Mailing Add:* Dept Physiol & Biophys Mount Sinai Sch Med 1 Gustave L Levy Pl New York NY 10029. *Fax:* 212-860-3369

KIRCHER, JOHN FREDERICK, RADIATION CHEMISTRY, MATERIALS SCIENCES. *Current Pos:* proj leader, Battelle Mem Inst, 57-60, assoc div chief chem physics res, 60-65, fel chem physics res, 65-70, div chief chem physics res, 70-73, sr chemist, dept physics, 73-76, sr chemist, Energy & Environ Technol Dept, 76-78, prog mgr, 78-80, waste package dept mgr, 80-82, Syst Anal Dept Mgr, Off Nuclear Waste Isolation, 82-89, PROG MGR, ENERGY SYSTS GROUP, BATTELLE MEM INST, 89- *Personal Data:* b Athens, Ohio, Jan 31, 29; m 51; c 4. *Educ:* Ohio Univ, BS, 50, MS, 51; Syracuse Univ, PhD(chem), 56. *Prof Exp:* Design & develop engr, Radio Corp Am, 55-57. *Mem:* AAAS; Am Chem Soc; fel Am Inst Chem; Sigma Xi. *Res:* Radiation chemistry of inorganic gas phase reactions; polymers and other organic systems; radiation dosimetry; surface chemistry; vacuum techniques; gas kinetics and electrical discharges; flames; nuclear waste disposal. *Mailing Add:* 1174 Rockport Lane Columbus OH 43235

KIRCHER, MORTON S(UMMER), CHEMICAL ENGINEERING. *Current Pos:* INDUST CONSULT ELECTROCHEM, MORTON S KIRCHER, 71- *Personal Data:* b Rome, NY, May 3, 17; m 42; c 3. *Educ:* Univ Rochester, BS, 38. *Prof Exp:* Chem engr, Hooker Chem Corp, NY, 38-51, res supvr, 51-58, mgr electrochem & inorg res, 58-59, sr engr electrochem develop, 59-61; gen mgr, Dryden Chem Ltd, 61-71, pres, 67-71. *Concurrent Pos:* Civilian, Off Sci Res & Develop, AEC; gen mgr, BC Chem Ltd, 65-71. *Mem:* Electrochem Soc; Am Chem Soc; Am Inst Chem Eng. *Res:* Electrochemistry of caustic-chlorine cells, fluorine cells, chlorate, perchlorate and chloralkali cells including diaphragm type; development of membrane diaphragm, cells. *Mailing Add:* 1111 Granada St Clearwater FL 34615-1037

KIRCHGESSNER, JOSEPH L, PHYSICS, ELECTRICAL ENGINEERING. *Current Pos:* ACCELERATOR PHYSICIST, CORNELL ELECTRON SYNCHROTRON, 70- *Personal Data:* b Wheeling, WVa, June 23, 32; m 56; c 3. *Educ:* Le Moyne Col, NY, BS, 54; Cornell Univ, MS, 56. *Prof Exp:* Mem prof tech staff, Princeton Penn Accelerator, 56-65, sr tech staff, 65-70, div head, 68-70. *Concurrent Pos:* Del, Int Accelerator Conf, Italy, 65, Mass, 67 & USSR, 69; mem prog comm, US Nat Particle Accelerator Conf, 66 & 67; consult, Princeton Penn Accelerator, 71. *Mem:* Am Phys Soc. *Res:* Accelerator design and development. *Mailing Add:* 124 Newman Lab Cornell Univ Ithaca NY 14853

KIRCHHEIMER, WALDEMAR FRANZ, MICROBIOLOGY. *Current Pos:* RETIRED. *Personal Data:* b Schneidemuhl, Ger, Jan 11, 13; US citizen; m 45, Esther M Summerill. *Educ:* Univ Giessen, MD, 47; Univ Wash, PhD, 49. *Honors & Awards:* Medal Award Super Serv, Dept Health Educ & Welfare, 71, Medal Award Distinguished Serv, 77. *Prof Exp:* Res physician, King Co Tuberc Hosp, Seattle, Wash, 42-46; res assoc tuberc, Univ Wash, 46-47, instr microbiol, Sch Med, 48-49; from asst prof to assoc prof bact, Med Sch, Northwestern Univ, 49-56; dep safety dir & med bacteriologist, Ft Detrick, Md, 56-61; mem res staff, Inst Allergy & Infectious Dis, 61-62; chief, Microbiol Sect, USPHS Hosp, 62-64, Lab Br, 65-67 & Lab Res Dept, 67-71, chief, Lab Res Br, 71-83. *Concurrent Pos:* Clin prof bact trop dis & med parasitol, La State Univ Med Ctr, New Orleans. *Mem:* Am Soc Microbiol. *Res:* Immunology; mechanism of tuberculin-type sensitivity; medical bacteriology; cell culture of leprosy bacillus; animal transmission of leprosy. *Mailing Add:* 5631 California Ave SW No 204 Seattle WA 98136

KIRCHHOFF, WILLIAM HAYES, PHYSICAL CHEMISTRY. *Current Pos:* TECH MGR CHEM PHYSICS, CHEM SCI DIV, OFF ENERGY RES, US DEPT ENERGY, 87- *Personal Data:* b Chicago, Ill, Nov 27, 36; m 58, Ann Rogers; c Margaret A (Shearer), Daniel R, David P & Jennifer A. *Educ:* Univ Ill, BS, 58; Harvard Univ, MA, 61, PhD(chem physics), 63. *Prof Exp:* NATO fel phys chem, Inorg Chem Lab, Oxford Univ, 62-63; Nat Res Coun res assoc chem physics, Nat Bur Stand, 64-66, physicist, 66-72 & 83-87, phys sci adminr off air & water measurement, 72-78, dept dir, Ctr Thermodynamics & Molecular Sci, 78-80, chief off environ measurements, 80-82. *Mem:* AAAS; Am Phys Soc; Am Chem Soc. *Res:* Statistical analysis of physical chemistry data including spectroscopy and thermodynamics; computer modelling of physical chemical systems. *Mailing Add:* 14511 Woodcrest Dr Rockville MD 20853. *E-Mail:* william.kirchhoff@er.doe.gov

KIRCHMAYER, LEON K, electrical power engineering; deceased, see previous edition for last biography

KIRCHMEIER, ROBERT L, FLUORINE CHEMISTRY, SYNTHETIC CHEMISTRY. *Current Pos:* asst res prof, 87-92, ASSOC RES PROF CHEM, UNIV IDAHO, 92- *Personal Data:* b Portland, Ore, Apr 25, 42; m 70, Nancy S Bannon; c Benjamin R, Samuel Bannon & Katherine M. *Educ:* Univ Mont, BS, 68; Univ Idaho, PhD(chem), 75. *Prof Exp:* Chemist, US AEC, 68-71 & Univ Idaho, 71-75; res scientist qual control, Charles Pfizer, Inc, 75-79; chemist process develop, Parke-Davis Warner Lambert, 79-81; pres & founder, W Analytical Lab, 81-87. *Concurrent Pos:* Assoc mem, Women Chem Comt, Am Chem Soc, 91-92, exec comt, Fluorine Div, 93-; vis resaf fel, Japanese Agency Sci & Technol, 92. *Mem:* Am Chem Soc. *Res:* Synthesis and physical and chemical characterization of fluorine containing inorganic and organic compounds. *Mailing Add:* Dept Chem Univ Idaho Moscow ID 83844-2341. *Fax:* 208-885-6173; *E-Mail:* rlkirch@uidaho.edu

KIRCHNER, ERNST KARL, DESIGN & PRODUCTION OF BULK ACOUSTIC WAVE DEVICES. *Current Pos:* mem tech staff, Teledyne MEC, Palo Alto, Calif, 65-72, proj engr, 72-79, staff engr, 79-81, mgr, Mountain View Calif, 81-82, opers mgr, 82-83, sr mgr, 83-84, mgr eng, 84-87, dir eng, 87-88, vpres bus develop, Teledyne Microwave, 88-93, vpres, Delay Device Prod Line, 90-93, DIR MICROWAVE COMPONENT PROD, TELEDYNE ELECTRONIC TECHNOLOGIES, MOUNTAIN VIEW, CALIF, 93- *Personal Data:* b San Francisco, Calif, June 18, 37; m 60, Ursula Karmann; c Mark, Christi & Steven. *Educ:* Stanford Univ, BS, 59, MS, 60, PhD(elec eng), 63. *Prof Exp:* Res physicist, US Army Res & Develop Activ, Ft Huachuca, Ariz, 63-65. *Concurrent Pos:* Teacher physics, Univ Ariz, 63-65. *Mem:* Inst Elec & Electronics Engrs; Am Phys Soc. *Res:* Study of bulk acoustic waves in single crystals and their use as microwave delay devices and acousti-optic components. *Mailing Add:* 41 Ashfield Rd Atherton CA 94027. *Fax:* 650-962-6834; *E-Mail:* e.kirchner@mview.tet.com

KIRCHNER, FREDERICK KARL, organic chemistry, information science, for more information see previous edition

KIRCHNER, H(ENRY) P(AUL), CERAMICS. *Current Pos:* RETIRED. *Personal Data:* b Buffalo, NY, Sept 9, 23; m 50, Elizabeth Parson; c Peter D, James W & Robert L. *Educ:* Cornell Univ, BME, 47; Pa State Univ, PhD(ceramics), 55. *Prof Exp:* Prod engr, Carborundum Co, 47-51; proj engr, Corning Glass Works, 54-57; prin ceramic engr, Aeronaut Lab, Cornell Univ, 57-60, asst head, Mat Dept, 60-63; tech dir, Linden Labs, Inc, 63-66, vpres, 66-68; pres, Ceramic Finishing Co, 68-88; consult, 88-93. *Mem:* Fel Am Ceramic Soc; Nat Inst Ceramic Engrs. *Res:* Physical and chemical properties of ceramic materials, especially refractories, abrasives and dielectrics; processes to improve strength; fractography; failure analysis; fracture mechanics. *Mailing Add:* 700 S Sparks St State College PA 16801

KIRCHNER, JAMES GARY, IGNEOUS PETROLOGY, FIELD GEOLOGY. *Current Pos:* PROF GEOL, ILL STATE UNIV, 69- *Personal Data:* b Detroit, Mich, Sept 11, 38; m 76, Kathleen; c 5. *Educ:* Wayne State Univ, BS, 60, MS, 62; Univ Iowa, PhD(geol), 71. *Prof Exp:* Geologist petrol, Gulf Oil Corp, Libya & Nigeria, 62-66. *Mem:* Geol Soc Am; Nat Asn Geol Teachers; Sigma Xi; Am Geophys Union. *Res:* Igneous geology of the northern Black Hills in South Dakota. *Mailing Add:* Dept Geog & Geol Ill State Univ Campus Box 4400 Normal IL 61790-4400. *Fax:* 309-438-5310

KIRCHNER, JOHN ALBERT, OTOLARYNGOLOGY. *Current Pos:* from asst prof to prof, 51-85, EMER PROF OTOLARYNGOL, SCH MED, YALE UNIV, 85- *Personal Data:* b Waynesboro, Pa, Mar 27, 15; m 47, Aline Legault; c John C, Thomas L, Paul E, Marie C & Christine A. *Educ:* Univ Va, MD, 40. *Hon Degrees:* MS, Yale Univ, 52. *Honors & Awards:* Mosher Award, 58; Casselbery Award, Am Laryngol Asn, 66, Newcomb Award, 69, DeRoaldes Medal, 85; Semon lectr, Univ London, 81. *Prof Exp:* Instr otolaryngol, Johns Hopkins Hosp, 48-49, resident, 49. *Concurrent Pos:* Commonwealth Fund fel otolaryngol, Royal Col Surg, 63-64; jr attend otolaryngologist, Children's, Deaconess, Christ & Good Samaritan Hosps, 49-50; assoc surgeon, Grace-New Haven Community Hosp, 51-; mem, otolaryngol post-grad training comt, NIH, 56-59. *Mem:* Am Laryngol Asn (pres, 79); Am Laryngol, Rhinol & Otol Soc (pres, 81-82); Am Acad Ophthal

& Otolaryngol; Am Soc Head & Neck Surg (pres, 76); Ger Soc Otolaryngol; Ital Soc Otolaryngol. *Res:* Physiology of the larynx and pharynx; pathology of laryngeal cancer. *Mailing Add:* Yale-New Haven Med Ctr Box 3333 333 Cedar St New Haven CT 06510. *Fax:* 203-785-5269

KIRCHNER, RICHARD MARTIN, INORGANIC CHEMISTRY, STRUCTURAL CHEMISTRY. *Current Pos:* from asst prof to assoc prof, 73-87, PROF CHEM, MANHATTAN COL, 87- *Personal Data:* b San Francisco, Calif, Dec 1, 41; m 94, A'gota Fejes. *Educ:* Univ Calif, Berkeley, AB, 64; Calif State Univ, San Jose, MS, 66; Univ Wash, PhD(chem), 71. *Prof Exp:* Fel chem, Northwestern Univ, 71-73. *Concurrent Pos:* Consult, Tarrytown Tech Ctr, Union Carbide Corp, 74-93, UOP Res, 93-; res collabr chem, Brookhaven Nat Lab, 75-85. *Mem:* Am Crystallog Asn; Am Chem Soc; Am Phys Soc; Sigma Xi; Int Zeolite Asn. *Res:* Preparation and characterization of transition metal complexes with unusual ligands; x-ray crystallography; structural characterization of micro-crystaline molecular sieves. *Mailing Add:* Dept Chem Manhattan Col Bronx NY 10471. *Fax:* 718-862-7814; *E-Mail:* rkirchner@manvax.cc.manhattan.edu

KIRCHNER, ROBERT P, MECHANICAL ENGINEERING. *Current Pos:* From asst instr to assoc prof, Newark Col Eng, 62-76, PROF MECH ENG, NJ INST TECHNOL, 76- *Personal Data:* b Orange, NJ, Jan 21, 39; m 62; c 2. *Educ:* Newark Col Eng, BS, 62, MS, 64; Rutgers Univ, PhD(mech eng), 68. *Concurrent Pos:* Consult, Solar Energy Syst Design. *Mem:* Am Soc Mech Engrs; Int Solar Energy Soc. *Res:* Thermodynamics; fluid mechanics; heat transfer; solar energy; energy conservation. *Mailing Add:* Dept Mech Eng NJ Inst Technol 323 High St Newark NJ 07102-1824

KIRCHOFF, WILLIAM F, microbiology, for more information see previous edition

KIRCZENOW, GEORGE, THEORY OF SEMICONDUCTORS, THEORY OF INTERCALATION COMPOUNDS. *Current Pos:* assoc prof, 83-87, PROF PHYSICS, SIMON FRASER UNIV, 87- *Personal Data:* Australian citizen. *Educ:* Univ Western Australia, BSc, 70; Oxford Univ, DPhil(theoret physics), 74. *Prof Exp:* Asst prof physics, Boston Univ, 79-83. *Concurrent Pos:* Prin investr, NSF grant, 81-83, US Dept Energy, 83 & Natural Sci & Eng Res Coun, Can, 84- *Mem:* Fel Am Phys Soc; Can Asn Physicists. *Res:* Theoretical solid state physics; semiconductor nanostructures; superconductors; intercalation compounds; surface physics including scanning tunneling microscopy theory; mesoscopic persistent currents; optical properties of fullereness; composite fermions. *Mailing Add:* Dept Physics Simon Fraser Univ Burnaby BC V5A 1S6 Can. *Fax:* 604-291-3592; *E-Mail:* kirczeno@sfu.ca

KIRDANI, RASHAD Y, organic chemistry, biochemistry, for more information see previous edition

KIREMIDJIAN, ANNE SETIAN, EARTHQUAKES. *Current Pos:* From asst prof to assoc prof, 78-91, PROF STRUCT ENG, DEPT CIVIL ENG, STANFORD UNIV, 91- *Personal Data:* b Sofia, Bulgaria, Aug 11, 49; US citizen; m 72, Garo K; c Seta N. *Educ:* Columbia Univ, BS, 72; Stanford Univ, MS, 73, PhD(civil eng), 77. *Concurrent Pos:* Mem, Risk Comt, Am Soc Civil Engrs, 85-, Exp Comt, TELEE/Am Soc Civil Engrs, 92-; mem, Young Pres Investr Award, 93, chmn, 94. *Mem:* Am Soc Civil Engrs; Seismol Soc Am; Int Asn Struct Safety & Reliability; Earthquake Eng Res Inst. *Res:* Earthquake occurrence modelings for long term forecasting; ground motion characterization from earthquake vibrations; damage estimation and forecasting models; application of stochastic processes to earthquake engineering; structural reliability analysis models. *Mailing Add:* 14210 Berry Hill Ct Los Altos CA 94022. *Fax:* 650-725-8662

KIRK, ALEXANDER DAVID, INORGANIC CHEMISTRY, PHYSICAL CHEMISTRY. *Current Pos:* from asst prof to assoc prof, 61-71, chmn dept, 74-79, PROF CHEM, UNIV VICTORIA, BC, 71- *Personal Data:* b London, Eng, Apr 17, 34; Can citizen; m 80, Glenda S (Hawes); c Natalie S, Robin A & Madeleine R. *Educ:* Univ Edinburgh, BSc, 56, PhD(chem), 59. *Prof Exp:* Res fel chem, Univ BC, 59-61. *Concurrent Pos:* Humbolt fel, 68-69; vis prof, Sch Molecular Sci, Univ Sussex, 75-76; res assoc, Univ Southern Calif, Los Angeles, 80; actg dir, Can Ctr Picosecond Laser Flash Photolysis, Concordia Univ, Montreal, 83; NSERC/Swiss Nat Res Found Int Sci Exchange Award, Univ Bern, Switz, 91 & 95. *Mem:* Fel Chem Inst Can; Can Asn Univ Teachers; InterAm Photochemical Soc. *Res:* Photochemistry; inorganic photochemistry and luminescence; photochemistry and luminescence of coordination compounds. *Mailing Add:* Dept Chem Univ Victoria PO Box 3065 Victoria BC V8W 3V6 Can. *Fax:* 550-721-7147; *E-Mail:* kirkad@uvvm.uvic.ca

KIRK, BEN TRUETT, PLANT PATHOLOGY. *Current Pos:* From asst prof to assoc prof, 68-87, EMER PROF BOT, 89- *Personal Data:* b Natchitoches, La, Oct 1, 42; m 66. *Educ:* La Polytech Inst, BS, 64; La State Univ, MS, 66, PhD(plant path), 68. *Mem:* Am Phytopath Soc. *Res:* Fungal ultrastructure; systemic fungicides. *Mailing Add:* 80407 Meadow Lark Loop Bush LA 70431

KIRK, BILLY EDWARD, VIROLOGY. *Current Pos:* asst prof, 64-73, ASSOC PROF MICROBIOL, WVA UNIV, 73- *Personal Data:* b Robinson, Ill, May 5, 27; div; c 2. *Educ:* Univ Ill, BS, 49; Ohio State Univ, MSc, 55, PhD(microbiol), 57. *Prof Exp:* Sr bacteriologist, Eli Lilly & Co, Ind, 57-62; instr, Univ Mich, 62-64. *Mem:* AAAS; Am Soc Microbiol; Brit Soc Gen Microbiol; Tissue Cult Asn; Sigma Xi. *Res:* Virology; biology and pathogenic role of defective viruses; virus persistence. *Mailing Add:* 914 Guyasuta Lane Pittsburgh PA 15215-1650

KIRK, DALE E(ARL), AGRICULTURAL ENGINEERING. *Current Pos:* Asst, agr eng, Ore State Univ, 41-42, asst agr engr, 42-44 & 46-54, assoc prof agr eng, 54-63, actg head dept, 70-71 & 80-81, PROF AGR ENG & AGR ENGR, ORE STATE UNIV, 63-, EMER PROF, 83- *Personal Data:* b Payette, Idaho, July 2, 18; m 39; c 5. *Educ:* Ore State Univ, BS, 42; Mich State Univ, MS, 54. *Mem:* Fel Am Soc Agr Engrs; Sigma Xi. *Res:* Food engineering; processing and handling agricultural products; agricultural machine design. *Mailing Add:* 8150 NW Mitchell Dr Corvallis OR 97330-2823

KIRK, DANIEL EDDINS, BIOLOGY. *Current Pos:* PROF BIOL, CATAWBA COL, 57- *Personal Data:* b Rocky Mount, NC, Feb 19, 24; m 46; c 4. *Educ:* Furman Univ, BS, 48; Univ NC, MA, 50; Emory Univ, PhD, 57. *Prof Exp:* Asst prof biol, Furman Univ, 50-57. *Mem:* Am Soc Parasitol; Am Micros Soc. *Res:* Helminthology; reptilian blood flukes. *Mailing Add:* 40175 Palmerville Rd New London NC 28127

KIRK, DAVID BLACKBURN, MATHEMATICS. *Current Pos:* RETIRED. *Personal Data:* b Lock Haven, Pa, Nov 18, 21; m 44; c 2. *Educ:* Haverford Col, BS, 43; Univ Pa, MA, 48. *Prof Exp:* Instr statist, Univ Pa, 47-48; methods analyst electronics comt, Mutual Benefit Life Ins Co, NJ, 48-56; sr res mathematician, Res Div, Curtiss-Wright Corp, Pa, 56-59; res mathematician, Willow Run Labs, Univ Mich, 59-66; head statist & res prog, Data Processing Div, Educ Testing Serv, Princeton NJ, 66-67, opers res scientist, 67-74; dir statist serv, Univ City Sci Ctr, 74-77. *Concurrent Pos:* Part-time teaching comput sci & numerical anal, Rutgers Univ, 69-70 & quant methods & statist, Rider Col, 70-74. *Mem:* Am Math Soc; Math Asn Am; Am Statist Asn; Asn Comput Mach; Sigma Xi. *Res:* Application of digital computers to mathematical, engineering and statistical research problems. *Mailing Add:* 1914 Yardley Rd Yardley PA 19067-3208

KIRK, DAVID CLARK, PHYSICAL CHEMISTRY, PROTECTIVE COATINGS PIGMENT MANUFACTURING. *Current Pos:* TECH DIR, TULIP GAP TECHNOL, 89- *Personal Data:* b Newark, NJ, May 19, 24; m 53, Frances S Sutherland; c Winifred, Linda & Andrew. *Educ:* Lehigh Univ, BS, 44; Polytech Inst New York, MS, 51; Univ Iowa, PhD(chem), 53; Furman Univ, MBA, 79. *Prof Exp:* Chem engr, Am Dyewood Co 46-48; chemist, Merck & Co, 48-50; res chemist, Hercules Powder Co, 53-59; dir experimental res, Ecusta Paper Div, Olin Corp, 59-69, dir res & develop, 69-76; tech dir, Allied Paper Div, SCM Corp, 76-89. *Mem:* Am Chem Soc; Sigma Xi; Tech Asn Pulp & Paper Indust. *Res:* Organic chemistry; kinetics, photo and surface chemistry of protective coatings; elastomers and papers. *Mailing Add:* 114 River Ridge Rd Brevard NC 28712-9530

KIRK, DAVID LIVINGSTONE, DEVELOPMENTAL BIOLOGY, VOLVOCINE EVOLUTION. *Current Pos:* assoc prof, 69-79, PROF, BIOL, WASH UNIV, 79- *Personal Data:* b Clinton, Mass, Mar 19, 34; m 58, Marilyn Chaloupka; c 1. *Educ:* Northeastern Univ, AB, 56; Univ Wis, MS, 58, PhD(biochem), 60. *Prof Exp:* Res technician, Lovett Mem Lab, Mass Gen Hosp, Boston, 52-56; res asst biochem, Univ Wis, 56-60; sr res chemist, Biol Res Labs, Colgate-Palmolive Co, 60-62; res assoc develop biol, Univ Chicago, 62-65, asst prof, 65-69. *Concurrent Pos:* Dean Grad Sch, Wash Univ, 79. *Mem:* Fel AAAS; Am Chem Soc; Soc Develop Biol; Am Soc Cell Biol; Sigma Xi. *Res:* Developmental biochemistry and genetics; analysis of genetic, cytological and molecular basis of cell determination and cytodifferentiation in simple eukaryotes; evolution of multicellularity and germ/soma differentiation. *Mailing Add:* Dept Biol Campus Box 1229 Wash Univ St Louis MO 63130. *Fax:* 314-935-5125

KIRK, DONALD EVAN, ELECTRICAL ENGINEERING. *Current Pos:* assoc dean eng, 87-90, PROF ELEC ENG, SAN JOSE STATE UNIV, 90-, DEAN ENG, 94- *Personal Data:* b Baltimore, Md, Apr 4, 37; m 62, Judith Sand; c Kara, Valerie & Dana. *Educ:* Worcester Polytech Inst, BS, 59; Naval Postgrad Sch, MS, 61; Univ Ill, PhD(elec eng), 65. *Prof Exp:* Instr elec eng, Naval Postgrad Sch, 59-62; teaching asst, Univ Ill, 62-63, instr, 63-64; from asst prof to assoc prof, Naval Postgrad Sch, 65-76, chmn dept, 76-83, prof elec eng, 76-87. *Concurrent Pos:* Vis staff scientist, Lincoln Lab, Mass Inst Technol, 81-82; prog officer, Div Undergrad Studies, NSF, 93-94. *Mem:* Fel Inst Elec & Electronics Engrs; Am Soc Eng Educ; Sigma Xi; Soc Women Engrs. *Res:* Signal processing. *Mailing Add:* Col Eng San Jose State Univ San Jose CA 95192-0080. *Fax:* 408-924-3818; *E-Mail:* dkirk@email.sjsu.edu

KIRK, DONALD WAYNE, CIVIL ENGINEERING, RESEARCH ADMINISTRATION. *Current Pos:* from lectr to prof, 62-75, head, Dept Civil Eng, 77-84, PROF STRUCT, ROYAL MIL COL CAN, 75-, DEAN, ACAD SERV, 93- *Personal Data:* b Carleton Place, Ont, Aug 18, 34; m 58, Diane Varcoe; c Beth, Janice & David. *Educ:* Queen's Univ, BSc, 56, MSc, 65, PhD(struct eng), 69. *Honors & Awards:* Duggan Medal, Eng Inst Can, 65. *Prof Exp:* officer, Royal Can Engrs, Can Forces, 56-65; dean, Can Forces Mil Col, 84-93. *Mem:* Am Concrete Inst; Eng Inst Can; Am Soc Eng Educ. *Res:* Ultimate strength of reinforced concrete slab and girder systems; analysis and design of beams containing web openings; slab column connections. *Mailing Add:* Acad Serv Royal Mil Col Kingston ON K7K 5L0 Can. *Fax:* 613-545-3481

KIRK, HAROLD GLEN, HIGH ENERGY PHYSICS. *Current Pos:* STAFF SCIENTIST, BROOKHAVEN NAT LAB, 79- *Personal Data:* b Konawa, Okla, Dec 18, 41. *Educ:* Univ Okla, BS, 64, PhD(physics), 72. *Mem:* Am Phys Soc. *Mailing Add:* Dept Physics Brookhaven Nat Lab Upton NY 11973

KIRK, IVAN WAYNE, COTTON PRODUCTION, COTTON PROCESSING & APPLICATION TECHNOLOGY. *Current Pos:* Res agr engr, Agr Res Serv, USDA, Lubbock, 60-65 & 67-71, Auburn, 65-67, lab dir, NMex, 71-77, assoc dir, New Orleans, 77-80, actg dir, 80-82, dir, Southern Regional Res Ctr, 82-87, AGR ENGR, AERIAL APPLN UNIT, AGR RES SERV, USDA, COLLEGE STATION, TEX, 87- *Personal Data:* b Lark, Tex, Jan 25, 37; m 60, Latrelle Venable; c Kimberly (Westbrook) & Kendall W. *Educ:* Tex Tech Univ, BS, 59; Clemson Univ, MS, 61; Auburn Univ PhD(agr eng), 68. *Honors & Awards:* Arthur S Fleming Award, 75. *Concurrent Pos:* Instr & asst prof, Dept Agr Engr, Tex Tech Univ, 63-65; mem, Grad Fac, Tex A&M Univ, 94- *Mem:* AAAS; Am Soc Agr Engrs; Coun Agr Sci & Technol; Am Stand Testing Mat; Ecol Soc Am. *Res:* New and improved methods, and machinery for cotton production, harvesting, and ginning; improved technology for aerial application of pesticides. *Mailing Add:* 2771 F&B Rd Agr Res Serv USDA College Station TX 77845. *Fax:* 409-260-9386; *E-Mail:* i-kirk@tamu.edu

KIRK, JAMES CURTIS, ORGANIC CHEMISTRY. *Current Pos:* dir, Petrochem Res Div, Res & Develop Dept, Conoco Inc, 60-66, dir, Environ Conserv, Res & Eng Dept, 66-67, gen mgr, 67-75, VPRES RES & DEVELOP DEPT, CONOCO INC, 75- *Personal Data:* b Hubbard, Tex, May 10, 21; m 44; c 5. *Educ:* Baylor Univ, BS, 44; Ohio State Univ, PhD(chem), 49. *Prof Exp:* Analyst, Pan Am Ref Corp, 44-46; asst chem, Ohio State Univ, 46-49; from assoc res chemist to sr res chemist, Continental Oil Co, 49-53, res group leader, 53-55, supvry res chemist, 55-57; dir res, Petrol Chem, Inc, 57-60. *Mem:* Am Chem Soc; Soc Petrol Engrs. *Res:* Hydrocarbon oxidation; lubricating oil additives; surface active agents; reaction mechanisms; polymerization; research administration. *Mailing Add:* 1308 Arronimink Circle Austin TX 78746-6303

KIRK, JAMES ROBERT, FOOD SCIENCE & TECHNOL. *Current Pos:* SR VPRES RES & DEVELOP & QUALITY ASSURANCE, CAMPBELL SOUP CO, 83-; PRES, CAMPBELL INST RES & TECHNOL, 88- *Personal Data:* b Du Bois, Pa, Oct 30, 41; m 85, Paulette DeJong; c Leanne, James J & John D. *Educ:* Holy Cross Col, BS, 64; Mich State Univ, MS, 66, PhD(food sci & human nutrit), 71. *Honors & Awards:* Future Leader Award, Nutrit Found, 77; Babcock Hart Award, Inst Food Technol, 83. *Prof Exp:* from asst prof to assoc prof, Mich State Univ, 71-78, prof, 78; prof & chmn, Food Sci & Human Nutrit Dept, Univ Fla, 78. *Concurrent Pos:* Dir, Nat Nutrit Consort, 79-83, DNA Plant Technol Corp, 86-90. *Mem:* Joseph Stokes Jr Res Inst; Am Inst Nutrit; Nat Food Process Asn; Inst Food Technol; Int Life Sci Inst. *Res:* Effects of food processing on the stability and bioavailability of nutrients in foods. *Mailing Add:* Res & Develop Campbell Soup Co Campbell Pl Camden NJ 08103-1799

KIRK, JOE ECKLEY, JR, MATHEMATICS. *Current Pos:* assoc prof math, 80-88, PROF MATH, SAM HOUSTON STATE UNIV, 88- *Personal Data:* b Houston, Tex, May 17, 39; m 67; c 3. *Educ:* Sam Houston State Univ, BA, 60; Univ Tex, Austin, MA, 62, PhD(math), 67. *Prof Exp:* Opers res analyst, US Arms Control & Disarmament Agency, 67-69; asst prof math, Univ Wyo, 69-74; asst prof math, Univ Tenn, Chattanooga, 74-76, assoc prof, 76-80. *Mem:* Asn Comput Mach; Am Math Soc; Math Asn Am. *Res:* Complex analysis; function theory. *Mailing Add:* Dept Math Sam Houston Univ Huntsville TX 77341

KIRK, JOHN GALLATIN, SOLAR PHYSICS, AEROSPACE SCIENCES. *Current Pos:* MEM PROF STAFF, ILLGEN SIMULATION TECHNOL, INC, 95- *Personal Data:* b Wilmington, Ohio, Oct 21, 38. *Educ:* Amherst Col, AB, 60; Univ Mich, AM, 62, PhD(astron), 66. *Honors & Awards:* Tech Innovation Award, NASA, 81. *Prof Exp:* Jr astronr, Kitt Peak Nat Observ, 66-69; asst prof astron, Univ Toledo, 69-74; staff scientist, Comput Sci Corp, 74-79; sr analyst, Electronics Div, Gen Dynamics Corp, 79-80, mem prof staff, Geodynamics Corp, 80-95. *Mem:* Am Astron Soc; Sigma Xi; Am Geophys Union; Inst Navig. *Res:* Physics of the solar atmosphere; physical geodesy; satellite orbit management. *Mailing Add:* 325 Palisades Dr Santa Barbara CA 93109

KIRK, MARILYN M, DEVELOPMENTAL BIOLOGY. *Current Pos:* RETIRED. *Personal Data:* b Bridgeport, Nebr, May 8, 27; m 58; c 1. *Educ:* Univ Nebr, BS, 48; Univ Wis, MS, 54, PhD(nutrit, biochem), 56. *Prof Exp:* Asst nutrit, Univ Nebr, 48-52; asst prof foods & nutrit, Sch Home Econ, Univ Wis, 56-60; res assoc, Am Meat Inst Found, Ill, 63-64; res assoc, Dept Biol, Univ Chicago, 65-69; res assoc, Dept Biol, Wash Univ, 69-95. *Res:* Biochemical studies of development and cytodifferentiation in simple eukaryotes. *Mailing Add:* 7756 Burr Oak Lane University City MO 63130. *Fax:* 314-935-4432

KIRK, PAUL WHEELER, JR, MYCOLOGY, BACTERIOLOGY. *Current Pos:* RETIRED. *Personal Data:* b Jacksonville, Fla, Feb 23, 31; m 58; c 2. *Educ:* Univ Richmond, BS, 57, MS, 61; Duke Univ, PhD(bot), 66. *Prof Exp:* Asst prof biol, Western Carolina Col, 65-66; asst prof bot, Va Polytech Inst, 66-70; assoc prof biol, Old Dom Univ, 71-77, asst dean sci & health professions, 73-78, prof biol, 77-95. *Concurrent Pos:* Consult med microbiol & pre-health prof adv. *Mem:* Mycol Soc Am; Sigma Xi; Nat Asn Adv Health Prof. *Res:* Marine ascomycetes and deuteromycetes. *Mailing Add:* 1213 Kittery Dr Virginia Beach VA 23464

KIRK, R(OBERT) S(TEWART), CHEMICAL ENGINEERING. *Current Pos:* ASSOC PROF CHEM ENG, UNIV MASS, AMHERST, 66- *Personal Data:* b Chicago, Ill, Nov 2, 22; m 58; c 2. *Educ:* Ill Inst Technol, BS & MS, 43; Univ Wis, PhD(chem eng), 48. *Prof Exp:* Asst prof chem eng, Univ Wis, 48-55; res engr, Calif Res Corp, 55-58, group supvr thermal recovery, 58-64, sr res engr, Chevron Res Co, Standard Oil Co Calif, 64-66. *Mem:* Am Chem Soc; Am Inst Chem Engrs. *Res:* Process design and evaluation; chemical kinetics and reactor design; thermal methods of secondary recovery of crude oil. *Mailing Add:* PO Box 355 Leverett MA 01054-0355

KIRK, ROBERT WARREN, VETERINARY MEDICINE. *Current Pos:* RETIRED. *Personal Data:* b Stamford, Conn, May 20, 22; m 49; c 3. *Educ:* Univ Conn, BS, 43; Cornell Univ, DVM, 46; Am Col Vet Internal Med, dipl & cert internal med & dermat. *Honors & Awards:* Fido Award, Am Animal Hosp Asn, 64; Gaines Medal, 67. *Prof Exp:* Pvt pract, 46-50; from asst prof to prof med, Vet Col, State Univ NY, Cornell Univ, 52-85, chmn, Dept Small Animal Med & Surg & dir, Small Animal Hosp, 69-77. *Concurrent Pos:* Fel, Sch Med, Univ Colo, 60-61; NSF sci fac fel, Sch Med Stanford Univ, 67-69, vis prof, 75; mem Grants Adv Bd, Seeing Eye Found, NY, 70-73; Evelyn Williams fel & vis scholar, Univ Sydney, Australia, 74; pres, Am Col Vet Internal Med, 74-76; pres & chmn, Bd Regents, Am Col Vet Internal Med; trustee, Seeing Eye Found, 77- *Mem:* Am Vet Med Asn; Am Animal Hosp Asn; Am Col Vet Dermat (pres). *Res:* Clinical medicine and dermatology therapeutics. *Mailing Add:* 440 Savage Farm Rd Ithaca NY 14850-6507

KIRK, ROGER E, EXPERIMENTAL DESIGN. *Current Pos:* PRES, RES CONSULTS, 82- *Personal Data:* b Princeton, Ind, Feb 23, 30; m 83, Jane Abbott. *Educ:* Ohio State Univ, BS, 51, MA, 52, PhD(psychol), 55. *Prof Exp:* Sr psychoacoust engr, Baldwin Piano & Organ Co, 55-58; from asst prof to assoc prof, 58-64, prof psychol, Baylor Univ, 64-, dir, Inst Grad Statist, 91- *Concurrent Pos:* Postdoctoral statist, Univ Mich, 71; vis prof, Seinan Gaukin Univ, Fukuoka, Japan, 73-74; dir, Behav Statist Prog, Baylor Univ, 76-; assoc ed, J Educ Statist, 76-89; adv ed statist, Contemp Psychol, 81-85; mem-at-large div five exec coun, Am Psychol Asn, 89-91; Am Psych Assoc, pres, 92-93. *Mem:* Fel Am Psychol Asn; Am Statist Asn; Psychometric Soc; Human Factors Soc; fel Am Psychol Soc. *Res:* Statistical methodology; author of various publications; author of five textbooks on statistics and over 80 scientific papers. *Mailing Add:* Psychol Dept Baylor Univ Waco TX 76798-7334. *E-Mail:* rogerkirk@baylor.edu

KIRK, T KENT, MICROBIAL BIOCHEMISTRY, OXIDATIVE PROCESSES. *Current Pos:* USDA PROF, DEPT BACT, UNIV WIS-MADISON, 82- *Personal Data:* b 1940. *Educ:* La Polytech Inst, BS, 62; NC State Univ, MS, 64, PhD(biochem & plant path), 68. *Honors & Awards:* William H Aiken Prize, Tech Asn Pulp & Paper Indust, 86; Marcus Wallenberg Prize, Sweden, 85; Marvin Johnson Award, Am Chem Soc, 92. *Prof Exp:* Fel polymer chem, NC State Univ, 67-68; res assoc org chem, Chalmers Univ Technol, Sweden, 68-69; res microbiologist, Forest Prod Lab, Forest Serv, USDA, 70-80, supvry microbiologist, 80-85, dir, Inst Microbiol & Biochem Technol, 85-97. *Concurrent Pos:* Vis prof, Kyoto Univ, Japan, 79-80; chmn, Gordon Res Conf Chem & Mat Natural Resources, 82; co-organizer, Int Conf Biotechnol in Pulp & Paper Indust, 89; consult lignin biodegradation & applications of bio-ligninolytic systs, industs, univs & res insts. *Mem:* Nat Acad Sci; fel Int Acad Wood Sci (secy-treas, 85-90); Am Soc Microbiol; Am Chem Soc; Am Soc Biochem & Molecular Biol; Tech Asn Pulp & Paper Indust. *Res:* Biochemistry and physiology of wood decomposition by fungi, industrial application of fungi and enzymes; author of over 175 articles in scientific journals. *Mailing Add:* 3145 Timber Lane Verona WI 53593. *E-Mail:* tkkirk@facstaff.wisc.edu

KIRK, THOMAS BERNARD WALTER, HIGH ENERGY PHYSICS. *Current Pos:* ASSOC DIR HIGH ENERGY & NUCLEAR PHYSICS, BROOKHAVEN NAT LAB, 94- *Personal Data:* b Denver, Colo, June 13, 40; m 74; c 2. *Educ:* Univ Colo, Boulder, BS, 62; Univ Wash, MS, 64, PhD(physics), 67. *Prof Exp:* Fel physics, Harvard Univ, 67-69, from asst prof to assoc prof, 69-73; assoc prof physics, Univ Ill, Urbana, 73-76; head, Neutrino Dept, Fermi Nat Accelerator Lab, 76-81, Tev II proj mgr, physics res div head, 81-89; dir, Hep Div, Argonne Nat Lab, 89-94. *Concurrent Pos:* Mem, Prog Adv Comt, Fermilab, 70-72; consult, Dept Eng, Can Sci Coun, 84- *Mem:* Fel Am Phys Soc. *Res:* Experimental investigation of fundamental particle processes in strong, electromagnetic and weak interactions at high energies. *Mailing Add:* Brookhaven Nat Lab Bldg 510F Dallas TX 11973-5000

KIRK, WILBER WOLFE, MARINE CORROSION, CONSULTING. *Current Pos:* KIRK CORROSION CONSULT, 93- *Personal Data:* b Brownsville, Pa, Sept 21, 32; m 54, Dolores Tomer; c 4. *Educ:* Otterbein Col, BS, 54; Ohio State Univ, MS, 59. *Prof Exp:* Engr, Bettis Atomic Power Lab, Westinghouse Corp, 58-62; engr, Laque Ctr Corrosion Technol, Inco, Ltd, 62-67, pres, 68-90, sr tech adv, 91-92, consult, 92-93. *Concurrent Pos:* Chmn, Offshore Technol Conf, 77; chmn, Indust Panel, Nat Sea Grant Prog, 81-83 & Subcomt Atmospheric Corrosion, Am Soc Testing & Mat, 86-96. *Mem:* Nat Asn Corrosion Engrs; Am Soc Testing & Mat; fel Am Soc Metals Int. *Res:* Materials in marine environments, including steels, stainless steels, copper alloys, nickel alloys, aluminum and titanium alloys; corrosion and protection. *Mailing Add:* 1190 Eddie L Jones Rd Ivanhoe NC 28447

KIRK, WILEY PRICE, CONDENSED MATTER PHYSICS, NANOSTRUCTURES, LOW TEMPERATURE & MESOSCOPIC PHYSICS & NANOELECTRONIC SYSTEMS & DEVICES. *Current Pos:* from asst prof to prof physics, 78-84, PROF PHYSICS & ELEC ENG, TEX A&M UNIV, 86-, DIR, NANOFAB CTR, 90- *Personal Data:* b Joplin, Mo, July 24, 42; m 64, Sally A Stoots; c Alexander P & Camille M. *Educ:* Wash Univ, BA, 64; State Univ NY, Stony Brook, MS, 67, PhD(physics), 70. *Prof Exp:* Jr res assoc physics, Brookhaven Nat Lab, 67-69; instr, State Univ NY, Stony Brook, 69-70; fel, Univ Fla, 70-71, interim asst prof, 71-73, asst prof,

73-75. *Concurrent Pos:* Tech collabr, Brookhaven Nat Lab, 69-70; consult, Sci Instruments, Inc, 70-75, Nalorac Cryog Corp, 80-84, Tex Instruments, Inc, 83-; dir, Ctr Nanostruct Mat & Quantum Device Fabrication, 90-; assoc ed, Superlattices & Microstruct; adj prof elec eng, Erik Jonsson Sch Eng & Comput Sci, Univ Tex, Dallas, 95- *Mem:* AAAS; Am Phys Soc; Sigma Xi; Am Vacuum Soc; Mat Res Soc; Inst Elec & Electronics Engrs. *Res:* 2-D charge transport and magnetoconduction; quantum Hall effect; nanostructures and electron-beam patterning; transport in mesoscopic systems and superlattics; molecular beam epitaxy; quantum effect devices; thermodynamic, magnetic and nuclear magnetic resonance properties of materials; quantum crystals of helium; methods of low temperature thermometry; cryogenic and superconducting devices; low temperature thermoelectric studies; millikelvin-thermocouple-thermometry; superconducting quantum interference detector and pulsed nuclear magnetic resonance techniques; high temperature superconductivity; magnetic surface effects. *Mailing Add:* Eng-Physics Bldg Tex A&M Univ College Station TX 77843-4242. *Fax:* 409-845-2590; *E-Mail:* kirk@nanofab.tamu.edu

KIRK, WILLIAM ARTHUR, MATHEMATICS. *Current Pos:* assoc prof, 67-70, PROF MATH, UNIV IOWA, 70-, CHMN DEPT, 85- *Personal Data:* b Montour Falls, NY, Oct 3, 36; m 59; c 3. *Educ:* DePauw Univ, AB, 58; Univ Mo, MA, 60, PhD(math), 62. *Prof Exp:* Asst prof math, Univ Calif, Riverside, 62-67. *Mem:* Am Math Soc; Math Asn Am. *Res:* Metric and geodesic geometry; functional analysis. *Mailing Add:* Dept Math Univ Iowa Iowa City IA 52242-1419

KIRK, WILLIAM LEROY, NUCLEAR ENGINEERING. *Current Pos:* RETIRED. *Personal Data:* b Charleston, Miss, Aug 29, 30; m 53; c 3. *Educ:* US Naval Acad, BS, 52; Air Force Inst Technol, MS, 57. *Prof Exp:* Staff mem, Nuclear Rocket Div, Los Alamos Nat Lab, 61-67, asst div leader, 67-73, assoc div leader energy technol, 77-78, alt div leader, 78-81, prin asst div leader, 81-83, dep div leader, Energy Div, 83-87, dep div leader, Nuclear Technol & Eng Div, 87-91. *Res:* Energy research and development, including nuclear safeguards and safety, nuclear system development and other energy systems. *Mailing Add:* 3822 S Via Del Reyecuelo Green Valley AZ 85614-5416

KIRKALDY, J(OHN) S(AMUEL), PHYSICAL METALLURGY. *Current Pos:* from asst prof to assoc prof metall, 57-63, chmn dept, 62-66, PROF METALL, MCMASTER UNIV, 63-, STEEL CO CAN CHAIR METALL, 66- *Personal Data:* b Victoria, BC, May 13, 26; m 52; c 3. *Educ:* Univ BC, BASc, 49, MASc, 51; McGill Univ, PhD(physics), 53. *Prof Exp:* Res assoc physics, McGill Univ, 53-54, asst prof metall eng, 54-57. *Mem:* Am Soc Metals; Am Inst Mining, Metall & Petrol Engrs; Can Asn Physicists; Can Inst Mining & Metall; Sigma Xi. *Res:* Application of thermodynamics of irreversible processes to metallurgy. *Mailing Add:* Dept Metallurgy & Mat Sci McMaster Univ Hamilton ON L8S 4K1 Can. *Fax:* 905-521-2773

KIRKBRIDE, CHALMER GATLIN, CHEMICAL ENGINEERING IN PETROLEUM REFINING & CHEMICALS MANUFACTURING. *Current Pos:* RETIRED. *Personal Data:* b Tyrone, Okla, Dec 27, 06; wid; c Chalmer G Jr. *Educ:* Univ Mich, BSE & MSE, 30; Beaver Col, ScD, 59. *Hon Degrees:* DSc, Beaver Women's Col, 59; EngD, Drexel Univ, 60, Widner Univ, 70. *Honors & Awards:* Dedication Kirkbride Hall Sci & Eng, Widener Univ, 65; Fuels & Petrochem Award, Am Inst Chem Engrs, 76. *Prof Exp:* Chem engr, Stand Oil Co, 30-34; asst dir res, Amoco, 34-42; chief chem engr, Mobil Field Res Labs, 42-44; distinguished prof, Tex A&M Univ, 44-47; vpres res & develop, Houdry Process Corp, 47-52, bd dirs, 47-62, pres & chmn bd, 52-56; exec dir, Res, Eng & Patent Depts, 56-70, vpres, Sun Oil Co, 60-70; dir, Kirkbride Assocs, 63-70, pres, 77-89; consult engr, Gen elec, Inst Gas Technol, United Technol Inc, Elec Power Res Inst & Avco Corp, 70-74; petrol scientist, Fed Energy Off, 74-75; sci adv, Energy Res Develop Admin, 75-76. *Concurrent Pos:* Bd dirs, Houdry Process Corp, 47-62, Catalytic Co, 52-56, Sun Olin Chem Co, 58-68, Sun Oil Co, 63-70; pres, Avisun Corp, 59-60, bd dirs, 59-68; mem, Pres Nixon's Task Force Oceanog, 69. *Mem:* Nat Acad Eng; fel Am Inst Chem Engrs (vpres, 53, pres, 54); emer mem Am Chem Soc. *Res:* Energy use and conversion including catalytic and thermal processes; natural gas and petroleum production processes and high pressure gas wells; desulfuring of coal and oil; regeneration of catalysts; enhancement of catalytic reactions; recovery of oil from shale; granted 18 patents; author of numerous publications. *Mailing Add:* 4000 Massachusetts Ave NW Apt 1415 Washington DC 20016

KIRKBRIDE, CLYDE ARNOLD, VETERINARY BACTERIOLOGY. *Current Pos:* from instr to assoc prof, 67-82, PROF VET MED, ANIMAL DIS RES & DIAG LAB, SDAK STATE UNIV, 82- *Personal Data:* b Los Angeles, Calif, Mar 14, 24; m 44; c 5. *Educ:* Okla State Univ, DVM, 53; SDak State Univ, MS, 70. *Prof Exp:* Vet practr, 53-63; asst prof vet med, Col Vet Med, Kans State Univ, 63-67. *Concurrent Pos:* Vet investr officer, NZ Ministry Agr & Fisheries, 74-75; pres, Am Leptospirosis Res Conf, 81; pres-elect, Western Vet Conf, 88. *Mem:* Am Vet Med Asn; Am Asn Vet Lab Diagnosticians; US Animal Health Asn. *Res:* Water intoxication in cattle; relationship of milking machine function to mastitis in cattle; diseases affecting reproduction in animals; fetal serology in diagnosis of bovine abortion; swine tuberculosis; diagnosis of leptospirosis; nonclassified anaerobic bacterium that causes abortion in sheep. *Mailing Add:* 2015 Iowa St Brookings SD 57006

KIRKBRIDE, JOSEPH HAROLD, JR, TAXONOMIC BOTANY. *Current Pos:* Assoc cur bot, 75-79, RES ASSOC, SMITHSONIAN INST, 79-; BOTANIST, AGR RES SERV, USDA, 84- *Personal Data:* b St Louis, Mo, Feb 4, 43; m 75, Maria Cristina Garcia; c Joseph III & Tatiana. *Educ:* St Louis Univ, BA, 66, MS(R), 68; City Univ New York, PhD(biol), 75. *Prof Exp:* Prof, Univ Brazil, 79-84. *Concurrent Pos:* Consult, Interamer Inst Coop Agr, 83; mem bd adv, Int Ctr Trop Ecol, 85- *Mem:* Am Asn Plant Taxonomists; Int Asn Plant Taxon; Asn Trop Biol; Sigma Xi; Bot Soc Brasil. *Res:* Taxonomic revision of plants cultivated on American farms; taxonomic revision of selected neotropical Rubiaceae. *Mailing Add:* Agr Res Serv USDA Beltsville MD 20705. *Fax:* 301-504-5810; *E-Mail:* jkirkbride@asrr.arsusda.gov

KIRKBRIDE, L(OUIS) D(ALE), MEDICAL INSTRUMENTATION. *Current Pos:* VPRES, BIONETICS LAB PROD, ORGANON TEKNIKA CORP, 85-, VPRES, MKT. *Personal Data:* b Morris, Ill, Oct 18, 32; m 57; c 3. *Educ:* Carnegie Inst Technol, BS, 54, MS & PhD(metall), 57. *Prof Exp:* Develop engr nuclear mat, Knolls Atomic Power Lab, Gen Elec Co, 57-60, mgr core mat develop, 60-61; group leader power reactor mat, Los Alamos Sci Lab, 61-66; proj analyst, Gen Elec Res & Develop Ctr, Schenectady, 66-68, mgr clin equip develop, Med Develop Oper, 68-70, mgr bus develop & strategic planning, Med Systs Bus Div, Gen Elec Co, 70-71, mgr nuclear diag, Nat Systs Div, 71-74; gen mgr, Diag Div, J T Baker, 74-81; vpres & gen mgr, Lab Prod Div, Litton Bionetics, 81-85. *Mem:* Am Nuclear Soc; Instrument Soc Am; fel Am Inst Chemists. *Res:* Semiconductor materials; radioimmunoassay; clinical chemistry; hematology; immunology; enzyme immunoassay. *Mailing Add:* 12712 Waterman Dr Raleigh NC 27614

KIRKENDALL, ERNEST OLIVER, DIFFUSION IN SOLID STATE METALS. *Current Pos:* RETIRED. *Personal Data:* b East Jordon, Mich, July 6, 14; wid; c Carol (Leunk), Howard (deceased) & Barbara (Davis). *Educ:* Wayne State Univ, BS, 34; Univ Mich, MSE, 35, DSc(metall eng), 38. *Prof Exp:* From instr to asst prof chem eng, Wayne State Univ, 37-46; asst secy, Am Inst Mining & Metall Engrs, 46-55; gen secy, Am Inst Mining, Metall & Petrol Engrs, 55-63; secy & gen mgr, United Eng Trustees, 63-65; metall engr, Am Iron & Steel Inst, 65-66, asst secy, vpres, 66-68, vpres, 68-79. *Concurrent Pos:* Secy, Eng Found, 63-65; adj prof, Univ DC, 82-85. *Mem:* Iron & Steel Soc; Minerals Metals & Mat Soc; Am Soc Metals Int; hon mem Inst Metals. *Res:* Kirkendall Effect, difference in the diffusion rates of copper and zinc in copper plated alpha brass causing the interface to move. *Mailing Add:* 5100 Fillmore Ave No 909 Alexandria VA 22311-5047

KIRKENDALL, THOMAS DODGE, AEROSPACE MATERIALS & DEVICES. *Current Pos:* CONSULT, 93- *Personal Data:* b Columbus, Ohio, Sept 8, 37; m 61; c 3. *Educ:* Colby Col, BA, 61. *Honors & Awards:* NASA ATS-6 Propagation Exp Award, Commun Satellite Corp, 74 & Centimeter Wave Beacon Award, 76; Outstanding Mem of the Year, Soc Appl Spectros, 80. *Prof Exp:* Asst physics, Middlebury Col, 61-62; res scientist, Machlett Labs, Raytheon Co, 62-69; tech staff mem, Comsat Labs, 69-81, mgr, Dept Anal Chem & Failure Anal, 81-89, mgr, Dept Semiconductor Reliability & Qual Assurance, 89-93. *Concurrent Pos:* Consult, Commun Satellite Corp, Intelsat, JPL. *Mem:* Soc Appl Spectros (treas, 74-76, chmn, 77-78); Microbeam Anal Soc; Am Chem Soc; Electron Micros Soc Am. *Res:* Physics and failure mechanisms of solid state devices; energy conversion and storage; surface analysis and characterization. *Mailing Add:* 8610 Camille Dr Potomac MD 20854. *Fax:* 301-299-4395; *E-Mail:* tingkirk@aol.com

KIRKENDALL, WALTER MURRAY, internal medicine; deceased, see previous edition for last biography

KIRKHAM, DON, SOIL PHYSICS, LAND DRAINAGE. *Current Pos:* from assoc prof to prof, 46-59, CURTISS DISTINGUISHED PROF AGR, SOILS & PHYSICS, IOWA STATE UNIV, AMES, 59-, EMER PROF, 78- *Personal Data:* b Provo, Utah, Feb 11, 08; m 39, Mary E Erwin; c Victoria, Mary B & Don C. *Educ:* Columbia Univ, BA, 33, MA, 34, PhD(physics), 38. *Hon Degrees:* Dr Agr, Royal Agr Univ, Ghent, Belg, 63; DSc, Ohio State Univ, 93. *Honors & Awards:* Stevenson Award, Soil Sci Soc Am, 52; Wolf Prize Agr, 84. *Prof Exp:* Instr & asst prof math & physics, Utah State Univ, Logan, 37-40; civilian scientist, USN, 40-46. *Concurrent Pos:* Res prof, Fulbright-Hays grantee, Holland, 50-51 & Belg, 57-58, Guggenheim award, 57-58 & Ford Found appointee, Egypt, 61; consult, TAMS dam construct, eng co, Turkey, 59 & Orgn Am States, Arg, 65; dir, Iowa State Water Resources Inst Res, 64-73; vis prof, Hohenheim-Stuttgart Agr Univ, Ger, 82; lectr, People's Repub China, 85. *Mem:* Fel Am Phys Soc; fel Am Soc Agron; fel & hon mem Soil Sci Soc Am; hon mem Int Soil Tillage Res Orgn; Am Geophys Union; Math Asn Am; Int Soil Sci Soc. *Res:* Application of basic physics and mathematics to soil problems of agriculture, for the design of land drainage systems and other physical land management practices to increase soil fertility and maintain soil environment. *Mailing Add:* 2109 Clark Ave PO Box 827 Ames IA 50010. *Fax:* 515-294-3163

KIRKHAM, M B, SOIL-PLANT-WATER RELATIONSHIPS. *Current Pos:* assoc prof, PROF, KANS STATE UNIV, MANHATTAN. *Personal Data:* b Cedar Rapids, Iowa. *Educ:* Wellesley Col, BA; Univ Wis-Madison, MS, PhD(bot). *Honors & Awards:* Travel Award, Soil Sci Soc Am, 90. *Prof Exp:* NSF fel, Inst Environ Studies, Univ Wis-Madison; plant physiologist, US Environ Protection Agency, Cincinnati, Ohio; asst prof, Univ Mass, Amherst; asst prof, Okla State Univ, Stillwater. *Concurrent Pos:* Vis lectr evapotranspiration, China, 85, Italy, 89; vis scholar, Biol Labs, Harvard Univ, 90; vis scientist, Dept Sci Indust Res, Palmerston North, NZ, 91; prin investr, NSF, USDA & Dept Energy. *Mem:* Am Soc Plant Physiol; Am Meteorol Soc; fel Soil Sci Soc Am; fel Am Soc Agron; Bot Soc Am; fel AAAS; fel Crop Sci Soc Am. *Res:* Plant-soil-water relationships; uptake of trace elements by plants; effect on plants of elevated levels of carbon dioxide. *Mailing Add:* Dept Agron Throckmorton Hall Kans State Univ Manhattan KS 66506-5501. *Fax:* 785-532-6094, 539-1850; *E-Mail:* mbk@ksuvm.ksu.edu

KIRKIEN-RZESZOTARSKI, ALICJA M, CHEMICAL DYNAMICS. *Current Pos:* assoc prof, 65-69, prof & chair, 69-92, EMER PROF PHYS CHEM, TRINITY COL DC, 92- *Personal Data:* b Lodz, Poland; m 73, Waclaw Janusz. *Educ:* Polish Univ Col, London, MChEng, 51; Univ London, PhD(phys org chem), 55. *Prof Exp:* From asst prof to assoc prof phys chem, Univ Col West Indies, 56-61; assoc prof, Univ West Indies, 61-65. *Concurrent Pos:* Hon res fel, Univ Col, Univ London, 71-72; res assoc, George Washington Univ, 84. *Mem:* Royal Chem Soc; Royal Inst Chem; Am Chem Soc; Polish Acad Arts & Sci. *Res:* Physical organic chemistry; kinetics of reactions in solutions and in the gas-phase, kinetic isotope effects; organic mass spectrometry, effect of chemical structure on ionization potentials; fragmentation patterns; high performance liquid chromatography; history of science. *Mailing Add:* 407 Buckspur Ct Millersville MD 21108-1764

KIRKLAND, GORDON LAIDLAW, JR, MAMMALOGY, VERTEBRATE ECOLOGY. *Current Pos:* From asst prof to assoc prof, 69-78, cur, Vert Mus, 71-89, PROF BIOL, SHIPPENSBURG UNIV, 78-, DIR, VERT MUS, 89- *Personal Data:* b Troy, NY, June 4, 43; m 66, Carol A Jordon; c Stephen G. *Educ:* Cornell Univ, BS, 65; Mich State Univ, MS, 68, PhD(ornith), 69. *Concurrent Pos:* Res assoc, Sect Mammals, 73-90, Powdermill Biol, 96-; res collabr, Dept Vert Zool, Smithsonian Inst, 78-88; vis prof, Mountain Lake Biol Sta, Univ Va, 87; pres, P Biol Sur, 88-91. *Mem:* Am Soc Mammal (secy-treas, 80-86, dir, 86-89 & 94-97); Wildlife Soc; Am Soc Naturalists; Soc Syst Biologists; Ecol Soc Am; fel AAAS. *Res:* Systematics, ecology and zoogeography of north temperate small mammals; disturbance ecology of small mammals; ecology of shrews; conservation biology. *Mailing Add:* Vert Mus Shippensburg Univ 1871 Old Main Dr Shippensburg PA 17257. *Fax:* 717-530-4048; *E-Mail:* glkirk@ark.ship.edu

KIRKLAND, JAMES T, ENGINEERING GEOLOGY, GEOMORPHOLOGY. *Current Pos:* CONSULT GEOLOGIST, CHEVY CHASE, MD, 93- *Personal Data:* b Mt Kisco, NY, Mar 27, 43; m, Linda Hollar; c James Jr. *Educ:* Syracuse Univ, BA, 66; State Univ NY, MS, 69, PhD(geol), 73. *Prof Exp:* Asst prof geol, Univ Tex, Arlington, 75-79; asst prof, Univ Mo, Kansas City, 79-81; consult & sr geologist, Core Lab, Dallas, Tex, 81-83; consult geologist, 83-87; assoc, Schnabel Eng Assoc; proj mgr, SCS Engrs. *Concurrent Pos:* Pres & nat deleg, Capital Sect, Am Inst Prof Geologists. *Mem:* Am Inst Prof Geologists; fel Geol Soc Am; Sigma Xi; Asn Eng Geologists. *Res:* Expansive soils and geomorphology; Pleistocene geology; hydrogeology. *Mailing Add:* 11621 Brandy Hall Lane North Potomac MD 20878-2423

KIRKLAND, JERRY J, MICROBIOLOGY. *Current Pos:* SR RES SCIENTIST, SHARON WOODS BEAUTY CTR, 93- *Personal Data:* b Elk City, Okla, May 18, 36; m 57; c 4. *Educ:* Northwestern State Col, Okla, BS, 58; Okla State Univ, MS, 61, PhD(microbiol), 64. *Prof Exp:* Microbial physiologist, Procter & Gamble, 64-93. *Mem:* Am Soc Microbiol. *Res:* Inducible enzyme formation in microorganisms and their role in dental plaque; microbiology of skin; etiology of acne; toxic shock syndrome; etiology of acne and development of anti-acne products; quality control of manufacture of acne product and etiology of acne; the organisms of dental plaque and dental plaque formation; co-author of numerous articles. *Mailing Add:* Sharon Woods Health & Beauty Tech Ctr Procter & Gamble Co 11511 Reed Hartman Hwy Cincinnati OH 45241

KIRKLAND, JOSEPH JACK, ANALYTICAL CHEMISTRY. *Current Pos:* RETIRED. *Personal Data:* b Winter Garden, Fla, May 24, 25; m 49, 83, Karin Ruth Monson; c Kent Gordon, Kerry Lynn, Celeste Ann, Mark Robert & Holly Anne. *Educ:* Emory Univ, AB, 48, MS, 49; Univ Va, PhD(chem), 53. *Hon Degrees:* DSc, Emory Univ, 74. *Honors & Awards:* Chromatography Award, Am Chem Soc, 72; Stephen Dal Nogare Award in Chromatography, Chromatography Forum, 73; Anachem Award, 79; Torbern Bergman Medal, Anal Chem, Swed Chem Soc, 82; Delaware Sect Award, Am Chem Soc, 88; Eastern Analytic Symposium Award; Dupont Lavoisier Medal, 97; AJP Martin Gold Medal, 97. *Prof Exp:* Chemist, Exp Sta, Hercules Powder Co, 49-51; from res chemist to sr res chemist, E I Du Pont de Nemours & Co, Inc, 53-61, res assoc, 61-69, res fel, 69-82, Du Pont fel, 82-92; vpres, res & develop, Rockland Technol, 92-97; sect mgr, res & develop, Hewlett, Packard, 97- *Concurrent Pos:* Adj prof chem, Univ Del, 80, 82. *Mem:* Am Chem Soc. *Res:* Liquid chromatography; field flow fractionation; analytical separations. *Mailing Add:* 19 Kendall Ct Wilmington DE 19803

KIRKLAND, LARRY V, NEURAL NETWORKS, NEW TECHNOLOGY. *Current Pos:* Electronic technician, 66-80, electronic engr, 81-87, SR ELECTRONIC ENGR, OGDEN AIR LOGISTICS CTR, USAF, 88- *Personal Data:* b Ogden, Utah; m, Susan; c 3. *Educ:* Weber State Univ, BS, 76. *Honors & Awards:* ATE Neural Network Usage Award, Inst Elec & Electronics Engrs, 89, Walter E Peterson Award New Technol, 92, ATE Future COncepts Award, 94. *Concurrent Pos:* Chair, Artificial Intel Human Interface Group, Inst Elec & Electronics Engrs, 88-92, co-chair, Interoperability Stand for KB Systs, 94- *Mem:* Inst Elec & Electronics Engrs. *Res:* Testing utilizing alternative software technolgoies to improve test performance, accuracy and reliability; artificial intelligence and its inclusion into test and diagnosis. *Mailing Add:* OO-ALC/TISAC 7278 Fourth St Hill AFB UT 84056-5205

KIRKLAND, WILLIS L, CANCER RESEARCH. *Current Pos:* From asst prof to assoc prof, 80-92, PROF BIOL, MT MERCY COL, 92- *Personal Data:* b Galesburg, Ill, Aug 8, 44. *Educ:* Univ Kans, PhD(physiol & cell biol), 73. *Mem:* Am Soc Cell Biol; Am Soc Cl Sci Teachers. *Mailing Add:* 1929 B Ave NE Cedar Rapids IA 52402

KIRKLIN, JOHN W, CARDIOVASCULAR SURGERY. *Current Pos:* surgeon-in-chief, Hosps & Clin, 66-88, PROF SURG, MED COL, UNIV ALA, BIRMINGHAM, 66- *Personal Data:* b Muncie, Ind, Aug 5, 17; m; c 3. *Educ:* Univ Minn, BA, 38, Harvard Univ, MD, 42; Am Bd Surg, dipl, 50; Am Bd Thoracic Surg, dipl, 53. *Hon Degrees:* DMed, Univ Munich, 61; DSc, Hamline Univ, 66, Univ Ala, 78, Ind Univ, 83, Georgetown Univ, 84; Dr, Univ Bordeaux II, 82, Repub Oriental Uruguay Univ, 82, Univ Marseille, 88. *Honors & Awards:* Gold Medal Award, Am Roentgen Ray Soc, 67; Rene Leriche Prize, Soc Inst Surg, Buenos Aires, 69; Macewen Mem Lectr, Univ Glasgow, Scottland, 70; Moynihan Lectr, Royal Col Surgeons Eng, London, 70; Lister Medal, Royal Col Surgeons, Eng, 73; Res Achievement Award, Am Heart Asn, 76; Colles Medal, Royal Col Surgeons Ireland, Dublin, 79; Distinguished Serv Award, AMA, 80; Eugene H Drake Award, Am Heart Asn, 81. *Prof Exp:* Surgeon, Mayo Clin & Grad Sch Med, 50-66, from instr to assoc prof surg, 51-60, prof, 60-66, chmn dept, 64-66. *Concurrent Pos:* Mem surg study sect B, NIH, 64-67 & chmn Sect A, 68-70, mem comt stand of classification congenital heart dis, 67, mem adv comt artificial heart-myocardial infarction prog, 67-69 & adv comt crippled children serv regional prog; mem bd gov, Mayo Clin, 65-66; chmn ad hoc comt to consider appln for subspec bd pediat surg, Am Bd Surg, 66-73; chmn, Dept Surg, Univ Ala, Birmingham, 66-82, dir, Div Cardio Thoracic Surg, 66-84, assoc chief staff, 69-82, pres, Univ Health Servs, 75-88; dir, Ala Congenital Heart Dis Diag & Treatment Ctr, 82-85; ed, J Thoracic & Cardiovasc Surg, 87-94; mem, Comt Reg Health Data Networks, Inst Med-Nat Acad Sci, 92-94. *Mem:* Nat Acad Sci; Inst Med-Nat Acad Sci; Am Col Surgeons; Am Surg Asn; Am Asn Thoracic Surg; Am Col Cardiol; Am Soc Artficial Internal Organs; Am Soc Crit Care Med; hon mem Asn Med Argentina; hon fel Asn Surgeons Gt Brit & Ireland; hon mem Brazilian Soc Cardiol; Brit Cardiac Soc; corresp mem Cardiac Soc Australia & NZ; hon mem Ger Soc Thoracic & Cardiovasc Surg; hon mem Int Cardio-Thoracic Soc; hon mem Med Asn Argentina; hon mem Mex Soc Cardiol; Royal Co Surgeons Eng; NY Acad Sci; Soc Thoracic Surgeons. *Mailing Add:* Dept Surg Univ Ala Med Ctr Birmingham AL 35294

KIRKLIN, PERRY WILLIAM, PETROLEUM CHEMISTRY. *Current Pos:* ADJ PROF CHEM, CHEYNEY UNIV PA, 96- *Personal Data:* b Ellwood City, Pa, Feb 28, 35; m 56, Betty Lampkins; c 3. *Educ:* Westminster Col, BS, 57; Univ Minn, Minneapolis, PhD(phys chem), 64. *Prof Exp:* Group leader anal res, Rohm & Haas Co, Pa, 64-70; assoc chem & proj leader, Aviation Fuels, Mobil Oil Res & Develop, NJ, 70-91; assoc prof Bloomfield Col, 91-95. *Mem:* Am Chem Soc; Nat Orgn Black Chemists & Chem Engrs. *Res:* Electron nuclear double resonance studies of hole center in magnesium oxide single crystals; catalyst characterization, especially metal function of catalysts using x-ray and chemisorption techniques; exploratory process research; aviation fuels. *Mailing Add:* 1860 Hillside Rd Southampton PA 18966

KIRKMAN, HENRY NEIL, JR, MEDICINE, PEDIATRICS. *Current Pos:* PROF PEDIAT, SCH MED, UNIV NC, CHAPEL HILL, 65- *Personal Data:* b Jacksonville, Fla, Sept 14, 27; m 50; c 4. *Educ:* Ga Inst Technol, BS, 47; Emory Univ, MS, 50; Johns Hopkins Univ, MD, 52; Am Bd Pediat, dipl, 60. *Honors & Awards:* Mead Johnson Award, 67. *Prof Exp:* Intern pediat, Johns Hopkins Hosp, 52-53; resident, Vanderbilt Univ Hosp, 55-57; res investr, Nat Inst Arthritis & Metab Dis, 58-59; asst prof pediat, Sch Med, Univ Okla, 59-65. *Concurrent Pos:* Nat Inst Arthritis & Metab Dis fel metab enzymes, 57-58; Markle scholar, 61. *Mem:* Am Pediat Soc; Am Soc Biol Chem. *Res:* Metabolic and enzymatic disturbances in children; human biochemical genetics. *Mailing Add:* Dept Pediat Univ NC Sch Med Chapel Hill NC 27599-7487

KIRKPATRICK, CHARLES HARVEY, ALLERGY, IMMUNOLOGY. *Current Pos:* PROF, UNIV COLO, 79-; PRES, CYTOKINE SCI, 96- *Personal Data:* b Topeka, Kans, Nov 5, 31; m 59, Janice Fosha; c Heather, Michael & Brian. *Educ:* Univ Kans, BA, 54, MD, 58. *Honors & Awards:* Richard Farr lectr, Aspen Allergy Conf, 87; Stanislaus Jaros lectr, Am Col Allergy & Immunol, 87. *Prof Exp:* Asst med, Med Ctr, Univ Colo, 62-63, instr, 63-65; asst prof, Med Ctr, Univ Kans, 65-68, assoc prof, 68; sr investr & head, Sect Allergy & Hypersensitivity, Lab Clin Invest, Nat Inst Allergy & Infectious Dis, 68-79; dir, Div Allergy & Clinical Immunol, Dept Med, Nat Jewish Hosp, 79-93; pres, Innovative Therapeut, 93-96. *Concurrent Pos:* Fel allergy & immunol, Univ Colo, 62-65. *Mem:* AAAS; Am Acad Allergy; Am Soc Clin Invest; Am Asn Immunol; Am Col Physicians; Clin Immunol Soc; Molecular Med Soc. *Res:* Mechanisms of cellular immunity and the role of cellular immunity to resistance to infectious diseases and neoplasia; methods of correcting diseases associated with abnormal cellular immunity. *Mailing Add:* Cytokine Sci 1899 Gaylord St Denver CO 80206-1210. *Fax:* 303-333-9621

KIRKPATRICK, CHARLES MILTON, WILDLIFE ECOLOGY. *Current Pos:* RETIRED. *Personal Data:* b Greensburg, Ind, Jan 1, 15; m 39; c 2. *Educ:* Purdue Univ, BS, 38; Univ Wis, MA, 40, PhD(zool), 43. *Prof Exp:* Asst zool, Univ Wis, 38-41; from instr to prof wildlife mgt, Agr Exp Sta, Purdue Univ, 41-81. *Concurrent Pos:* Ed, J Wildlife Mgt, Wildlife Soc, 59-62. *Mem:* Wilson Ornith Soc; hon mem Wildlife Soc. *Res:* Wildlife physiology and ecology. *Mailing Add:* 2741 N Salisbury St Apt 2103 West Lafayette IN 47906

KIRKPATRICK, DIANA (RORABAUGH) M, QUALITY ASSURANCE AUDITING. *Current Pos:* CONSULT, 88- *Personal Data:* b Washington, DC, Mar 24, 44. *Educ:* George Washington Univ, BS, 67, PhD(phys chem), 72. *Prof Exp:* Forensic scientist chem, Bur Alcohol, Tobacco & Firearms, 72, res analyst, 73-74; res analyst, Consumer Prod Safety Comn, 74-77; prof leader thermal insulation & lab accreditation, Nat Bur Stand, 77-83; mgr, Prod Assurance Div Off Qual Assurance, Bur Engraving & Printing, Washington, DC, 83-85; res assoc, Paffenbarger Res Ctr, Am Dent Asn, Nat Bur Stand, Gaithersburg, Md, 85-88. *Res:* Quality assurance testing programs; dental composites and bonding materials. *Mailing Add:* 6706 NW 18th Ave Gainesville FL 32605

KIRKPATRICK, E(DWARD) T(HOMSON), MECHANICAL ENGINEERING. *Current Pos:* RETIRED. *Personal Data:* b Cranbrook, BC, Jan 15, 25; m 48, Barbara J Kelsberg; c Allan, Karen, Ann & Keith. *Educ:* Univ BC, BASc, 47; Carnegie Inst Technol, MS, 56, PhD, 58. *Prof Exp:* Test engr, Gen Elec Co, Can, 47; sales engr, F D Bolton, Ltd, 47-51, dist mgr, 51-53, sales mgr, 53-54; from instr to asst prof mech eng, Carnegie Inst Technol, 54-58; asst prof, Univ Pittsburgh, 58-59; prof & chmn dept, Univ Toledo, 59-64; dean, Col Appl Sci, Rochester Inst Technol, 64-71; pres, Wentworth Inst Technol, 71-90. *Mem:* Fel Am Soc Eng Educ; Am Soc Mech Engrs; Sigma Xi. *Res:* Conduction heat transfer; numerical analysis and digital computer technology. *Mailing Add:* 40 Radcliffe Rd Weston MA 02193

KIRKPATRICK, EDWARD SCOTT, SOLID STATE PHYSICS. *Current Pos:* STAFF MEM, RES DIV, IBM CORP, 71- *Personal Data:* b Wilmington, Del, Dec 12, 41. *Educ:* Princeton Univ, AB, 63; Harvard Univ, PhD(physics), 69. *Honors & Awards:* Am Phys Soc Prize Indust Appln Physics, 87. *Prof Exp:* Res assoc physics, James Franck Inst, Univ Chicago, 69-71. *Concurrent Pos:* Consult, Lincoln Labs, Mass Inst Technol, 65-66, Argonne Nat Labs, AEC, 69-71; vis assoc prof, State Univ NY, Stony Brook, 77; exchange prof, Ecole Normale Superieure, Paris, France, 78-; vis prof, Racah Inst Physics & Ctr Neural Comput, Hebrew Univ, Jerusalem, Israel, 93-94. *Mem:* Fel Am Phys Soc; fel AAAS. *Res:* Magnetic order and excitations in disordered materials, transport in low-mobility materials; optimization and pattern recognition using techniques of statistical physics, computer design and architecture for computers based around multimedia capabilities. *Mailing Add:* IBM Res Ctr Yorktown Heights NY 10598

KIRKPATRICK, FRANCIS HUBBARD, BIOTECHNOLOGY, SEPARATIONS TECHNOLOGY. *Current Pos:* ASSOC DIR, INTEL PROP, FOCAL, INC, 94- *Personal Data:* b Laurel Hill, NC, Nov 7, 43; m 69; c 1. *Educ:* Harvard Col, BA, 64; Stanford Univ, PhD(biophys), 70. *Prof Exp:* Postdoctoral fel, Wash State Univ, 69-71; postdoctoral fel, Sch Med, Univ Rochester, 72-74, asst prof biophys, 74-80; lab mgr, Pall Corp, 80-84; tech dir, Bioprod Dept, Marine Colloids Div, FMC Corp, 84-94. *Concurrent Pos:* SBIR study sect genetics, NIH, 87- *Mem:* Biophys Soc; Optical Soc Am; Am Soc Cell Biol; Am Chem Soc; Electrophoresis Soc; Am Soc Biochem & Molecular Biol. *Res:* Development of innovative products for research and analysis in biotechnology, life sciences and medicine. *Mailing Add:* Focal Inc 4 Maguire Rd Lexington MA 02173. *Fax:* 207-594-3426

KIRKPATRICK, JAY FRANKLIN, ANIMAL PHYSIOLOGY. *Current Pos:* DIR, SCI & CONSERV BIOL & ANIMAL CUR, ZOOMONTANA, 94- *Personal Data:* b Quakertown, Pa, Feb 24, 40; m 66. *Educ:* EStroudsburg State Col, BS, 62, MS, 64; Cornell Univ, PhD(physiol), 71. *Honors & Awards:* Burlington Northern Found Res Award, 86. *Prof Exp:* Teacher biol, Quakertown High Sch, Pa, 62-63 & Pennsburg High Sch, Yardley, Pa, 64-65; asst prof & chmn dept, Bucks Co Community Col, 65-67; assoc prof animal physiol, Eastern Mont Col, 70-76, dean, Sch Arts & Sci, 76-85, assoc prof physiol, 85-94. *Concurrent Pos:* Fel, Col Vet Med, Univ Pa, 73. *Mem:* Soc Study Reproduction; Soc Exp Biol & Med. *Res:* Comparative mammalian reproduction, especially species indigenous to hostile environments, such as the pika and wild horses; chemical fertility control in wild and feral species. *Mailing Add:* ZooMontana PO Box 80905 Billings MT 59108

KIRKPATRICK, JOEL BRIAN, NEUROPATHOLOGY. *Current Pos:* PROF PATH, BAYLOR COL MED, 81- *Personal Data:* b Odessa, Tex, Feb 19, 36; m 93, Elisabeth H Wolf; c Susan C, Andrew L, Katherine F & Patti J. *Educ:* Rice Univ, BA, 58; Wash Univ, MD, 62. *Prof Exp:* Instr path, Wash Univ, 65-67; asst prof pharmacol, Rutgers Univ, New Brunswick, 68-70; assoc prof path, Univ Ariz, 70-72, assoc prof path & neurol, Univ Tex Health Sci Ctr, Dallas, 72-78, prof, 78-80. *Concurrent Pos:* Am Cancer Soc fel, 64-65; NIH spec fel, 67-68; Nat Inst Neurol Dis & Stroke grantee, 70; staff, Vet Admin, NIH, 71-, mem, Study Sect Path A, 87-91. *Mem:* Am Asn Neuropath. *Res:* Video enhancement microscopy; quantitative analysis of cerebral cortex; dementia and trauma. *Mailing Add:* Dept Path Methodist Hosp MS 205 6565 Fannin Houston TX 77030. *Fax:* 713-793-1473; *E-Mail:* joelk@bcm.tmc.edu

KIRKPATRICK, JOEL LEE, ORGANIC & PROCESS CHEMISTRY, PESTICIDE CHEMISTRY. *Current Pos:* SR MGR, BASF, 96- *Personal Data:* b Abilene, Tex, June 21, 36; m 57, 91; c 2. *Educ:* Abilene Christian Col, BS, 58; Univ Tex, MS, 60; Univ Ill, PhD(org chem), 69. *Prof Exp:* Med chemist, Smith Kline & French Labs, 61-65; sr res chemist, Gulf Oil Chem Co, 69-79; res assoc, Mobil Chem Co, 79-81; sr scientist, Velsicol Chem Corp, 81-86; res mgr, Sardoz, Ltd, 86-89, sr mgr, Sardoz Agro Inc, 89-96. *Mem:* AAAS; Am Chem Soc. *Res:* Synthetic organic chemistry; nitrogen containing heterocycles; structure activity relationships, particularly pesticides; pheromones insect growth regulants; organophosphorus chemistry; process chemistry. *Mailing Add:* 4601 Sunken Ct Port Arthur TX 77642

KIRKPATRICK, LARRY DALE, PHYSICS, PHYSICS EDUCATION. *Current Pos:* from asst prof to assoc prof, 74-85, PROF PHYSICS, MONT STATE UNIV, 85- *Educ:* Wash State Univ, BS, 63, Mass Inst Technol, PhD(physics), 68. *Honors & Awards:* Distinguished Serv Citation, Am Asn Physics Teachers, 82. *Prof Exp:* Res assoc physics, Mass Inst Technol, 68-69; asst prof, Univ Wash, 69-74. *Concurrent Pos:* Vis assoc prof physics, Kans State Univ, 83-84; coach, US Physics Team, 88-95; field ed physics, Quantum Mag, 92- *Mem:* Am Asn Physics Teachers (vpres, 97); Nat Sci Teachers Asn; Am Phys Soc. *Res:* Physics education; use of computers in physics education; textbook writing for general physics. *Mailing Add:* Dept Physics Mont State Univ Bozeman MT 59717-3840. *Fax:* 406-994-4452

KIRKPATRICK, MARK ADAMS, ZOOLOGY. *Current Pos:* ASST PROF ZOOL, UNIV TEX, AUSTIN, 85- *Personal Data:* b New York, NY, Apr 20, 56. *Educ:* Harvard Univ, BA, 78; Univ Wash, PhD(zool), 83. *Prof Exp:* Miller fel zool, Miller Inst Basic Res Sci, Univ Calif, Berkeley, 83-85. *Mem:* Soc Study Evolution; Am Soc Naturalists; Ecol Soc Am. *Res:* Theoretical population genetics; evolution of mating systems; sexual selection; morphology; development. *Mailing Add:* Dept Zool Univ Tex Austin TX 78712-1026

KIRKPATRICK, RALPH DONALD, WILDLIFE ECOLOGY. *Current Pos:* from asst prof to prof, 67-93, EMER PROF BIOL, BALL STATE UNIV, 93- *Personal Data:* b Jonesboro, Ind, Feb 10, 30; m 67, Susan Clouse; c Maureen, Kathleen, Lindley S & Shane. *Educ:* Ball State Univ, BS, 53; Univ Ariz, MS, 57; Okla State Univ, PhD(zool), 64. *Prof Exp:* Game biologist, State Dept Conserv, Ind, 54-55, game res biologist, 56-59; asst prof biol, Taylor Univ, 59-60; res cur, Div Birds, Smithsonian Inst, 64-65; asst prof zool, Ind Univ, 65-67. *Concurrent Pos:* Consult, Pac Proj, Div Birds, Smithsonian Inst, 65-, Aquatic Control, Inc, Seymour, Ind, 71- & Upper Wabash Resource Ctr, Huntington Col, Huntington, Ind, 75- *Mem:* Wildlife Soc; Am Soc Mammal; Wilson Soc. *Res:* Ecology of Indiana wildlife; population dynamics of mammals, including rodents and house cats on coral atolls. *Mailing Add:* 7552 S 350 E Osage Farm Jonesboro IN 46938. *E-Mail:* osagekirk@aol.com

KIRKPATRICK, ROBERT JAMES, MINERALOGY-PETROLOGY, GEOCHEMISTRY. *Current Pos:* from asst prof to assoc prof, 78-83, dept head, 88-97, PROF GEOL, UNIV ILL, URBANA, 83- *Personal Data:* b Schenectady, NY, Dec 31, 46; m 68, 85, Carol Hanna; c Gregory R & Geoffry S. *Educ:* Cornell Univ, AB, 68; Univ Ill, PhD(geol), 72. *Prof Exp:* Sr res geologist, Exxon Prod Res Co, 72-73; res fel geophys, Harvard Univ, 73-76; asst res scientist, Deep Sea Drilling Proj, Scripps Inst Oceanog, Univ Calif, San Diego, 76-78. *Concurrent Pos:* Ed, Deep Sea Drilling Proj Initial Reports Legs, 46, 55 & 75-78; NSF & other grants, 77-; consult, 78-; US Rep Int Mineral Asn Crystal Growth Comn, 81-; fel, Churchill Col, Cambridge, Eng, 85; prog chmn, Int Mineral Asn Meeting, 86. *Mem:* Am Geophys Union; fel Am Mineral Soc; AAAS; Am Ceramic Soc; fel Geol Soc Am. *Res:* Geochemistry; nuclear magnetic resonance spectroscopy of solids, structure of amorphous materials, crystal physics and chemistry, rates and mechanisms of geologic processes, processes of crystallization of igneous rocks. *Mailing Add:* Dept Geol Univ Ill 254 Natural Hist Bldg 1301 W Green St Urbana IL 61801. *Fax:* 217-244-4996

KIRKPATRICK, ROY LEE, NUTRITIONAL ECOLOGY, REPRODUCTIVE PHYSIOLOGY. *Current Pos:* asst prof wildlife ecol, Va Polytech Inst & State Univ, 66-69, from asst prof to assoc prof, 72-77, prof wildlife sci, 77-89, T H JONES PROF FISHERIES & WILDLIFE, VA POLYTECH INST & STATE UNIV, 89- *Personal Data:* b Fairview, WVa, Apr 16, 40; m 61, Thelma Harris; c Tamra J (Kazmierczak) & Roy D II. *Educ:* WVa Univ, BS, 62; Univ Wis, MS, 64, PhD(reproductive physiol, endocrinol), 66. *Honors & Awards:* Wildlife Prof Award, Wildlife Soc, 93. *Prof Exp:* Res asst reproductive physiol, Univ Wis, 62-64, instr, 64-66, asst prof animal sci, 69-71. *Mem:* Wildlife Soc; Soc Conserv Biol; Wildlife Dis Asn. *Res:* Environmental influences on reproduction and mortality of wildlife, particularly effects of nutrition. *Mailing Add:* Dept Fisheries & Wildlife Va Polytech Inst & State Univ PO Box 0321 Blacksburg VA 24063-0001

KIRKPATRICK, THEODORE ROSS, STATISTICAL MECHANICS, CONDENSED MATTER THEORY. *Current Pos:* Res assoc, 81-83, PROF THEORET STATIST MECH, INST PHYS SCI & TECHNOL, UNIV MD, COLLEGE PARK, 83- *Personal Data:* b Kalispell, Mont, Aug 29, 53. *Educ:* Univ Calif, Los Angeles, BS, 77; Rockefeller Univ, PhD(theoret physics), 81. *Honors & Awards:* Pres Young Investr Award, NSF, 84. *Mem:* Am Phys Soc. *Res:* Condensed matter theory and statistical mechanics; physics of disordered solids and liquids. *Mailing Add:* Inst Phys Sci & Technol Univ Md College Park MD 20742-2431

KIRKSEY, AVANELLE, NUTRITION, BIOCHEMISTRY. *Current Pos:* from assoc prof to prof, 61-85, MEREDITH DISTINGUISHED PROF NUTRIT, PURDUE UNIV, 85- *Personal Data:* b Mulberry, Ark, Mar 23, 26. *Educ:* Univ Ark, BS, 47; Univ Tenn, MS, 50; Pa State Univ, PhD(nutrit), 61. *Hon Degrees:* DSc, Purdue Univ, 97. *Honors & Awards:* Borden Award; Lederle Award. *Prof Exp:* Assoc prof home econ, Ark Polytech Col, 50-55; res asst nutrit, Pa State Univ, 56-59. *Concurrent Pos:* Prog dir, Nutrit Collab Res Support Prog, Egypt, Kenya & Mex; nutrit prog coordr, Indonesian Second Univ develop proj. *Mem:* Fel Am Inst Nutrit; NY Acad Sci; Am Dietetic Asn; Am Home Econs Asn; Sigma Xi. *Res:* Vitamin B-6 metabolism; nutrition in pregnancy and development; human lactation; international nutrition. *Mailing Add:* 306 N 49th St Ft Smith AR 72903. *Fax:* 765-494-0674

KIRKSEY, DONNY FRANK, PHARMACOLOGY. *Current Pos:* assoc dir clin res, 87-91, DIR LICENSING & WORLDWIDE ALLIANCES, GLAXO, INC 91- *Personal Data:* b Aberdeen, Miss, Apr 13, 48; m 70. *Educ:* Delta State Univ, BS, 70; Univ Miss, PhD(pharmacol), 76. *Prof Exp:* Fel, Duke Univ, 76-78; asst prof biomed sci, Ohio Univ, 78-80; clin res scientist, Burroughs Wellcome, 80-86; pres, Clindar, Inc, Durham, NC, 86-87. *Concurrent Pos:* Neurosci fel, NIMH, 76-78; grant, NC Heart Asn, 77-78; NIH fel, Nat Inst Drug Abuse, 78. *Mem:* Sigma Xi. *Res:* Investigations of pre and postsynaptic neuronal mechanisms in the central monoaminergic systems and pharmacological manipulation of those systems by drugs of abuse. *Mailing Add:* Medco Res PO Box 13886 Research Triangle Park NC 27709. *Fax:* 919-248-7699

KIRKSEY, HOWARD GRADEN, JR, SCIENCE EDUCATION. *Current Pos:* Assoc prof, 69-79, PROF CHEM, MEMPHIS STATE UNIV, 79-, CHMN DEPT, 82- *Personal Data:* b Memphis, Tenn, June 19, 40; c 3. *Educ:* Mid Tenn State Univ, BS, 61; Auburn Univ, PhD(phys chem), 66. *Concurrent Pos:* Staff scientist phys sci group, Boston Univ, 70-72. *Mem:* AAAS; Am Chem Soc. *Res:* Chemical education, especially development of text and laboratory teaching materials. *Mailing Add:* 1140 Snowden Farm Rd Collierville TN 38017-8989

KIRKWOOD, CHARLES EDWARD, JR, MATHEMATICAL SCIENCES. *Current Pos:* RETIRED. *Personal Data:* b Richmond, Va, Oct 10, 13; m 42; c 2. *Educ:* Lynchburg Col, AB, 35; Univ Ga, MS, 37. *Prof Exp:* Teacher pub sch, Ga, 36-37; from instr to asst prof math, Clemson Univ, 37-48, assoc prof math sci, 48-79. *Concurrent Pos:* Assoc prof elec eng, Comput Ctr, Clemson Univ, 51-52, comput analyst, 64-70, mgr prog, 70-75; vis assoc prof comput sci & math sci, Clemson Univ, 79-86. *Res:* Dielectric properties of ceramic materials; electrical properties of cotton; thermoconductivity of felts. *Mailing Add:* Wren St Clemson SC 29631

KIRKWOOD, JAMES BENJAMINE, ZOOLOGY, RADIATION BIOLOGY. *Current Pos:* RETIRED. *Personal Data:* b Beulah, Ky, Jan 22, 24; m 53, Ola Hehl. *Educ:* West Ky State Col, 48; Univ Louisville, MS, 52, PhD(zool), 62. *Prof Exp:* Proj leader fishery biol, Ky Dept Fish & Wildlife Resources, 52-57; US Bur Com Fisheries, 57-60, prog supvr invert biol, 62-64, prog leader, 64-68; tech coordr bio-environ studies, Battelle-Columbus, 68-73, mgr, W F Clapp Labs, 73-75; coastal ecosysts activ leader, US Fish & Wildlife Serv, Region IV, 75-89. *Mem:* AAAS; Am Fisheries Soc; Sigma Xi; Nat Shellfish Asn; Int Acad Fishery Scientists. *Res:* Ecology and ichthyology of Kentucky teleost fishes; life history and ecology of Pacific salmon; biology and population dynamics of shellfish species in Gulf of Alaska and Bering Sea. *Mailing Add:* 34 N Country Club Dr Crystal River FL 32629-5358

KIRKWOOD, SAMUEL, BIOCHEMISTRY. *Current Pos:* assoc prof, 56-62, PROF BIOCHEM, COL BIOL SCI, UNIV MINN, ST PAUL, 62- *Personal Data:* b Edmonton, Alta, June 14, 20; US citizen; m 47; c 3. *Educ:* Univ Alta, BS, 42; Univ Wis, MS, 44, PhD(biochem), 47. *Prof Exp:* Biochemist, Camp Detrick, Md, 47; asst res officer, Nat Res Coun Can, 48; from assoc prof to prof chem, McMaster Univ, 50-56. *Mem:* Sigma Xi. *Res:* Intermediary metabolism; route of synthesis of thyroxin; enzymology of carbohydrates. *Mailing Add:* 9819 152nd St N Hugo MN 55038-9443

KIRMSE, DALE WILLIAM, COMPUTER AIDED DESIGN, ENERGY SYSTEMS. *Current Pos:* asst prof, 69-80, ASSOC PROF CHEM ENG, UNIV FLA, 80- *Personal Data:* b Alva, Okla, July 9, 38; m 79, Sue Highfield; c Kevin D, Karen H, Katherin M & Kristina J. *Educ:* Okla State Univ, BS, 60; Iowa State Univ, MS, 63, PhD(chem eng), 64. *Prof Exp:* Res assoc chem eng, Univ Fla, 64-65, asst prof, 65-67; mgr asst, Parma Tech Ctr, Union Carbide Corp, 67-69. *Concurrent Pos:* Reynolds Smith & Hill, 75-76. *Mem:* Am Soc Qual Control; Am Inst Chem Engrs. *Res:* Statistical process quality control and reliability; mathematical modeling and computer methods; stochastic systems and Monte Carlo techniques; knowledge base export systems; computer aided process design; energy systems analysis and design. *Mailing Add:* 2026 NW 35th St Gainesville FL 32605. *Fax:* 904-392-9513; *E-Mail:* kirmse@che.ufl.edu

KIRMSER, P(HILIP) G(EORGE), APPLIED MATHEMATICS, ENGINEERING. *Current Pos:* from assoc prof appl mech, Kans State Univ, 54-75, head dept, 62, prof, 75-90, EMER PROF ENG & MATH, KANS STATE UNIV, 90- *Personal Data:* b St Paul, Minn, Dec 17, 19; m 42, Jenne E Blomquist; c Sandra & Lawrence. *Educ:* Univ Minn, BChE, 39, MS, 44, PhD, 58. *Prof Exp:* Instr, Kans State Col, 42-44, Univ Minn, 49-54; mech engr, US Naval Ord Lab, 46-48. *Concurrent Pos:* Consult, Phillips Petrol Co, Bayer & McElrath & Boeing Co, Digital Equip Co; vis lect, Soc Indust & Appl Math, 74-75; vis prof, Ecole Polytech Federale, Lausanne, Switz, 78. *Mem:* Am Math Soc; Math Asn Am; Soc Indust & Appl Math; Neth Royal Inst Eng. *Res:* Partial differential equations of engineering dealing with heat flow, vibrations and stresses; dynamics and motion of artificial satellites; analog computers; simulation; approximation; automatic controls; industrial processes; analysis of data; co-inventor of Chinese word-processing and typing system; decoupler to protect buildings from earthquakes; co-inventor of expansion joint assembly having load transfer capability. *Mailing Add:* Dept Elec & Comput Eng Kans State Univ Manhattan KS 66506

KIRON, RAVI, PROTEIN PURIFICATION, RECEPTOROLOGY. *Current Pos:* SR RES SCIENTIST, PFIZER CENT RES, 91- *Personal Data:* b Shimoga, Karnataka, India, Mar 4, 59; m 89. *Educ:* Bombay Univ, India, BS, 79, MS, 81; Indian Inst Sci, Bangalore, India, PhD(biochem), 86. *Prof Exp:* Res fel, Cornell Univ Med Col, 82-86, postdoctoral, 86-89, asst prof med, 89-91, asst prof biochem, 90-91. *Concurrent Pos:* Sr res fel, US Dept Agr, 82-85, Indian Inst Sci, 85-86; young leadership award, Am Biograph Inst, 86; young investr award, Eastern Hypertension Soc, 88. *Mem:* AAAS; Harvey Soc; Am Soc Hypertension. *Res:* Biochemistry of renin angiotensin system; characterization of angiotensin II receptors; immunologic analysis and cloning of gene for receptor; renin and prorenin study and analysis. *Mailing Add:* 15 Obed Heights Rd Old Saybrook CT 06475

KIRPEKAR, ABHAY C, FERMENTATION-SCALE UP, OPTIMIZATION & DESIGN, MIXING-AGITATION. *Current Pos:* Staff engr, 85-87, sr engr, 87-91, FEL BIOCHEM ENGR, MERCK & CO INC, 91- *Personal Data:* b Nagpur, India, June 9, 56; m 86, Sadhana Tikekar; c Pooja. *Educ:* Indian Inst Technol, Bombay, BTech, 78; Univ RI, MS, 81; Univ Va, PhD(chem eng), 85. *Mem:* Am Inst Chem Engrs; Am Chem Soc. *Res:* Fermentor design, scale-up, optimization, on-line measurements, novel control strategies, agitation and aeration, mass transfer (gas liquid). *Mailing Add:* 2503 Brandermill Pl Charlottesville VA 22911

KIRSCH, DONALD R, MOLECULAR BIOLOGY. *Current Pos:* prin res scientist, Am Cyanamid Co, 88-89, res group leader, 89-91, res mgr, 92-95, assoc dir, 95-96, DIR, AGRIC RES DIV, AM CYANAMID CO, 97- *Personal Data:* b Newark, NJ, Apr 28, 50; m 74, Deana Mendelson; c Ingrid. *Educ:* Rutgers Col, BA, 72; Princeton Univ, MA, 74, PhD(biol), 78. *Prof Exp:* Instr pharmacol, Rutgers Med Sch, 78-81; res investr molecular biol, Squibb Inst Med Res, 81-82, sr res investr, 82-83, res group leader, 83-88. *Concurrent Pos:* Adj asst prof, Rutgers Med Sch, 82-83. *Mem:* Genetics Soc Am; Am Soc Microbiol; Sigma Xi. *Res:* Design of mechanism based screening assays utilizing genetically engineered microorganisms. *Mailing Add:* 152 Terhune Rd Princeton NJ 08540. *Fax:* 609-275-5233; *E-Mail:* kirshd@pt.cyanamid.com

KIRSCH, EDWIN JOSEPH, MICROBIOLOGY. *Current Pos:* assoc prof sanit eng microbiol, 63-70, PROF ENVIRON ENG, PURDUE UNIV, 70- *Personal Data:* b Hoboken, NJ, Aug 25, 24; m 45; c 3. *Educ:* Mich State Univ, BS, 49; Purdue Univ, MS, 55, PhD(microbiol), 58. *Prof Exp:* Biologist, Lederle Labs, Am Cyanamid Corp, 50-53, sr res scientist, 57-63. *Mem:* Am Soc Microbiol; Soc Indust Microbiol; Water Pollution Control Fedn. *Res:* Microbiology of wastewater purification; microbial interactions; environmental microbiology; biodegradation. *Mailing Add:* 1616 Sheridan Rd West Lafayette IN 47906

KIRSCH, FRANCIS WILLIAM, CHEMISTRY. *Current Pos:* DIR, CTR ENERGY MGT & ECON DEVELOP & VPRES, UNIV CITY SCI CTR, PHILADELPHIA, 73- *Personal Data:* b Wheeling, WVa, Aug 27, 25; m 61; c 2. *Educ:* Univ Del, BChE, 45, MChE, 47; Univ Pa, PhD(chem), 52. *Prof Exp:* Instr inorg qual anal, Univ Pa, 46-50; assoc res chemist, Houdry Process Corp, 50-59, proj dir, 59-64; proj dir, Sun Oil Co, 64-67, res assoc, Explor Res Div, 67-72. *Concurrent Pos:* Consult, Gov Energy Coun Pa, 79-, Pa Pub Util Comn, 77-78, World Bank, 80 & NMex State Govt. *Mem:* AAAS; Am Chem Soc. *Res:* Catalysis, heterogeneous and homogeneous; basic and process research and development: petroleum, chemicals, edible oils; industrial energy conservation; offshore oil and gas production; science policy; economic analysis and evaluation of manufacturing processes. *Mailing Add:* Univ City Sci Ctr 3624 Market St Philadelphia PA 19104

KIRSCH, JACK FREDERICK, BIOCHEMISTRY. *Current Pos:* from asst prof to prof biochem, 64-89, PROF BIOCHEM & MOLECULAR BIOL, UNIV CALIF, BERKELEY, 89- *Personal Data:* b Detroit, Mich, Aug 14, 34; m 62; c 2. *Educ:* Univ Mich, BS, 56; Rockefeller Inst, PhD(biochem, cytol), 61. *Prof Exp:* Jane Coffin Childs fel biochem, Brandeis Univ, 61-63; Helen Hay Whitney fel biophys, Weizmann Inst, 63-64. *Concurrent Pos:* Guggenheim fel, Max Planck Inst Biophys Chem, 71-72; vis prof, Univ Basel, 79-80. *Mem:* Am Chem Soc; Fedn Am Socs Exp Biol; AAAS. *Res:* Mechanism of enzyme action; genetic engineering. *Mailing Add:* Molecular Biol Dept Stanley Hall Univ Calif Berkeley CA 94720-3206. *Fax:* 510-642-6368

KIRSCH, JOSEPH LAWRENCE, JR, PHYSICAL CHEMISTRY. *Current Pos:* asst prof, 70-74, assoc prof, 74-81, PROF PHYS CHEM, BUTLER UNIV, 81-, HEAD DEPT CHEM, 87- *Personal Data:* b Indianapolis, Ind, Aug 20, 42; m 65, Linda K Biggs; c Traci M (Berns) & Joseph L III. *Educ:* Butler Univ, BS, 64; Univ Ill, MS, 66, PhD(phys chem), 68. *Prof Exp:* Asst prof inorg chem, Fairleigh Dickinson Univ, 68-70. *Mem:* Am Chem Soc; Sigma Xi. *Res:* Study of chemical bonding in molecules through the use of chemical spectroscopy. *Mailing Add:* Dept Chem Butler Univ 4600 Sunset Indianapolis IN 46208. *Fax:* 317-283-9519; *E-Mail:* kirsch@butler.edu, kirsch@butleru.bitnet

KIRSCH, LAWRENCE EDWARD, PHYSICS, COMPUTER SCIENCE. *Current Pos:* asst prof, 66-72, ASSOC PROF PHYSICS, BRANDEIS UNIV, 72-, DIR COMPUT CTR, 70- *Personal Data:* b Newark, NJ, Feb 24, 38. *Educ:* Columbia Univ, AB, 60; Rutgers Univ, MS, 62, PhD(physics), 65. *Prof Exp:* Res assoc physics, Nevis Labs, Columbia Univ, 64-66. *Mem:* Am Phys Soc; Inst Elec & Electronics Engrs; Asn Comput Mach. *Res:* High energy and particle physics. *Mailing Add:* Dept Physics Brandeis Univ 415 South St Waltham MA 02254

KIRSCH, MILTON, CHEMISTRY, ENVIRONMENTAL SYSTEMS. *Current Pos:* CONSULT, 85- *Personal Data:* b Montreal, Que, Jan 16, 23; nat US; m 47; c 3. *Educ:* McGill Univ, BSc, 42, PhD(chem), 45. *Prof Exp:* Res assoc rubber chem, McGill Univ, 45; asst prof chem, Univ Man, 46-49 & Univ BC, 49-56; sr res chemist, E I du Pont de Nemours & Co, 57-63; mem tech staff, Rocketdyne Div, Rockwell Inst, 63-78, sr res scientist, Environ Monitoring & Serv Ctr, 78-84, combustion engr, Environ Monitoring & Serv Inc, 84-85. *Mem:* Fel Am Inst Chem; Sigma Xi. *Res:* Detonation velocity; cross-section for absorption of thermal neutrons; radioactive tracers; chemical oceanography; colloid and surface chemistry; propellants; rheology; environmental chemistry; wastewater treatment; environmental technology. *Mailing Add:* 20414 Haynes St Winnetka CA 91306-4230

KIRSCH, NATHAN CARL, PHARMACEUTICAL MANUFACTURING, QUALITY ASSURANCE. *Current Pos:* VPRES & MEM BD DIRS, PARENTERAL DRUG ASN FOUND PHARMACEUT RES INC, 80- *Personal Data:* b New Brunswick, NJ, Oct 27, 18; m 46, Ida Bass; c Kenneth & Phillip. *Educ:* Rutgers Univ, BS, 40; Univ Ill, MS, 41. *Prof Exp:* Supvr res & develop projs, Schering Plough Corp, 42-51, actg mgr, Pharmaceut Develop Dept, 51-53, mgr, Sterile Prods Dept, 53- 68, mgr pharmaceut prod, 68-73, dir domestic mfg, 73-75, vpres qual control, 75-83. *Mem:* AAAS; Am Chem Soc; Am Pharmaceut Asn; Pharmaceut Fedn; Royal Soc Health. *Res:* Studied antibacterial action of oxidation products of adrenalin; methods of increasing yields of penecillin in submerged culture; selecting preservative for pharmaceutical products. *Mailing Add:* 93 Cedar St Millburn NJ 07041

KIRSCH, WOLFF M, NEUROSURGERY, BIOCHEMISTRY. *Current Pos:* AT DEPT SURG, UNIV NMEX, ALBUQUERQUE. *Personal Data:* b St Louis, Mo, Mar 2, 31; m 55; c 4. *Educ:* Wash Univ, BA, 51, MD, 55. *Prof Exp:* Intern med, NC Mem Hosp, Univ NC, 55-56; asst resident gen surg, Barnes Hosp, Wash Univ, 59-60 & neurosurg, 61-62, chief resident & instr, 64; asst prof neurosurg, Med Sch, Univ Colo, Denver, 65-68, assoc prof, 68-, dir & chmn training prog & chmn div, 71- *Concurrent Pos:* Fel neurol med, NC Mem Hosp, Univ NC, 56-57; fel neuroanat, Sch Med, Wash Univ, 60, res fel neuro-pharmacol, 63 & 65; attend, Vet Admin Hosp, Denver, 65-; consult, Fitzsimons Gen Hosp, Aurora, Colo, 69- *Mem:* Am Acad Neurol; Asn Acad Surg; Am Asn Neurol Surg; Int Soc Neurochem; Am Col Surg. *Res:* Experimental biology of brain tumors. *Mailing Add:* St Louis Univ Hosp 3635 Vista Ave Loma Linda CA 92357

KIRSCHBAUM, H(ERBERT) S(PENCER), ELECTRICAL ENGINEERING. *Current Pos:* RETIRED. *Personal Data:* b Cleveland, Ohio, Feb 6, 20; m 46; c 4. *Educ:* Cooper Union, BS, 42; Univ Pittsburgh, MS, 46; Carnegie Inst Technol, PhD(elec eng), 53. *Prof Exp:* Engr, Westinghouse Elec Corp, 42-46; assoc prof elec eng, Ohio State Univ, 47-57; div consult, Systs Div, Battelle Mem Inst, 57-59, consult, Dept Eng Physics, 59-69; mgr systs eng, Info Systs Lab, Westinghouse Elec Co, 69-82. *Mem:* Inst Elec & Electronics Engrs. *Res:* Systems engineering; control systems; process control. *Mailing Add:* 257 Shope Creek Rd Asheville NC 28805

KIRSCHBAUM, JOEL BRUCE, MOLECULAR BIOLOGY, GENETICS. *Current Pos:* INDEPENDENT CONSULT, BIOTECHNOL RES DEVELOP, 90-; SR LICENSING OFFICER, UNIV CALIF, SAN FRANCISCO, 96- *Personal Data:* b Palo Alto, Calif, Aug 29, 45; m 74, Felicity Russell; c Morgan & Ethan. *Educ:* Pomona Col, BA, 67; Harvard Univ, PhD(molecular biol), 72. *Prof Exp:* Fel molecular biol, H H Whitney Found, 73-75; sr researcher, Univ Geneva, 75-77; instr neuropath, Harvard Med Sch, 77-81; supvr, Genetic Eng Div, Stauffer Chem Co, 81-85; dir res & develop, Codon, 85-90; actg vpres res & develop, Octamer, Inc, 91; vpres res & develop, RiboGene, Inc, 92-93. *Concurrent Pos:* Teaching fel, Harvard Univ, 69; asst instr bact genetics, Cold Spring Harbor Lab, 71; res assoc, Children's Hosp Med Ctr, 77-81; res fel, Med Found Inc, 78-80; prin investr, Am Cancer Soc, 79-81; interim vpres res develop, Megabros Corp, 94. *Mem:* AAAS. *Res:* Discovery and development of biopharmaceuticals, small molecule therapeutic drugs, vaccines, and gene therapies. *Mailing Add:* 21 Knickerbocker Lane Orinda CA 94563. *E-Mail:* joelkirs@aol.com

KIRSCHBAUM, JOEL JEROME, ANALYTICAL CHEMISTRY, BIOCHEMISTRY. *Current Pos:* RES LEADER, ANALYTIC RES & DEVELOP DIV, BRISTOL-MYERS SQUIBB PHARM RES INST, 64- *Personal Data:* b New York, NY, Nov 23, 35; m 60, Marilyn Johnson; c Amy & Fredric. *Educ:* City Col New York, BS, 57; Rutgers Univ, PhD(biochem), 63. *Concurrent Pos:* Mem, Grants Comt, Am Found Scholarly Res; mem, Dir Inst Motivated Behav, Belle Mead, NJ. *Mem:* Am Chem Soc; Am Soc Biochem & Molecular Biol; Am Asn Pharm Scientists. *Res:* Analyses of drugs; lycanthropy; high pressure liquid chromatography; association and dissociation of proteins, enzymes and antibiotics. *Mailing Add:* Analytic Res & Develop Div Bristol-Myers Squibb Pharm Res Inst 1 Squibb Dr New Brunswick NJ 08903-0191

KIRSCHBAUM, THOMAS H, obstetrics & gynecology, for more information see previous edition

KIRSCHENBAUM, LOUIS JEAN, TRANSITION METAL SOLUTION CHEMISTRY, KINETICS & MECHANISMS. *Current Pos:* from asst prof to assoc prof, 70-83, PROF CHEM, UNIV RI, 83- *Personal Data:* b Washington, DC, Apr 17, 43; m 64; Susan Schulman; c Jay & Cynthia. *Educ:* Howard Univ, BS, 65; Brandeis Univ, MA, 67, PhD(chem), 68. *Prof Exp:* Lectr chem, Brandeis Univ, 68-69; Nat Res Coun fel, Naval Ord Lab, 69-70. *Concurrent Pos:* Vis prof, Ben Gurion Univ Negev, Israel, 78-79; vis scientist, Nat Cancer Inst, NIH, 91-92. *Mem:* Sigma Xi; Am Chem Soc. *Res:* Transition metals in uncommon oxidation states; kinetics and mechanisms of metal ion oxidation-reduction and complexation reactions; rapid reaction techniques; kinetics of chemical analysis; sonochemistry; hair chemistry; free radicals. *Mailing Add:* Dept Chem Univ RI Kingston RI 02881. *Fax:* 401-792-5072; *E-Mail:* kirschenbaum@chm.uri.edu

KIRSCHENBAUM, SUSAN S, ENGINEERING PSYCHOLOGY, HUMAN DECISION MAKING. *Current Pos:* ENG PSYCHOLOGIST, NAVAL UNDERWATER SYSTS CTR, 85- *Personal Data:* b Washington, DC, Sept 15, 43; m 64; c 2. *Educ:* George Washington Univ, BA, 65; Univ RI, MA, 75 & 83, PhD(exp psychol), 85. *Prof Exp:* Teacher, Boston Sch Dept, 65-67; dir, South Kingstown Orgn Laymen Educ, 74-77; dir educ serv, South Co Community Action, 77-78; lectr eng as foreign lang, Ben Gurion Univ, Negev, 78-79; spec instr psychol, Univ RI, 81-85. *Concurrent Pos:* Personnel psychologist, Naval Underwater Systs Ctr, 84-85; adj asst prof, Univ RI, 85- *Mem:* Am Psychol Asn; Asn Appl Exp & Eng Psychologists; Am Psychol Soc; Sigma Xi. *Res:* Information management for submarine combat control; human information gathering and usage for situation understanding and decision making in complex environments; apply findings to design of command decision aids. *Mailing Add:* 1783 South Rd Kingston RI 02881-1775

KIRSCHNER, LEONARD BURTON, PHYSIOLOGY. *Current Pos:* from instr to prof, 53-93, EMER PROF ZOOL, WASH STATE UNIV, 93- *Personal Data:* b Chicago, Ill, Nov 12, 23; m 50; c 4. *Educ:* Univ Ill, BS, 44, MS, 47; Univ Wis, PhD(physiol), 51. *Prof Exp:* Nat Found Infantile Paralysis res fel, Copenhagen Univ, 51-53. *Mem:* Am Physiol Soc; Soc Gen Physiol; Am Soc Zoologists; Sigma Xi. *Res:* Active transport of solutes and water; invertebrate excretory organs. *Mailing Add:* Dept Zool Wash State Univ Pullman WA 99164-4236

KIRSCHNER, MARC WALLACE, BIOCHEMISTRY, CELL BIOLOGY. *Current Pos:* PROF & CHAIR, DEPT CELL BIOL, HARVARD MED SCH, 93- *Personal Data:* b Chicago, Ill, Feb 28, 45; m 68; c 3. *Educ:* Northwestern Univ, BA, 66; Univ Calif, Berkeley, PhD(biochem), 71. *Honors & Awards:* J W Jenkinson Mem Lectr, Oxford Univ, 86; Howard Taylor Ricketts Award Lectr, Univ Chicago, 86; Harvey Lectr, 87; Stetten Lectr, 91; Richard Lounsberg Award, Nat Acad Sci, 91. *Prof Exp:* NSF fel develop biol, Univ Calif, Berkeley, 71-72; asst prof to assoc prof biochem sci, Princeton Univ, 72-78; prof biochem & biophys, Univ Calif, San Francisco, 78-93. *Concurrent Pos:* NIH res career develop award, 75 & 80; mem, Cell Biol Study Sect, 80-84. *Mem:* Nat Acad Sci; Am Soc Biol Chemists; Am Soc Cell Biol (pres-elect, 89, pres, 90-91); Am Acad Arts & Sci. *Res:* Mechanism of microtubule assembly, regulation of mitosis and regulation of cell division in amphibian eggs; biophysical studies of macromolecules; embryonic induction; granted one US patent. *Mailing Add:* Harvard Univ 1350 Massachusetts Ave Cambridge MA 02138

KIRSCHNER, MARVIN ABRAHAM, INTERNAL MEDICINE, ENDOCRINOLOGY. *Current Pos:* assoc prof, 69-72, PROF & VCHMN MED, UNIV MED & DENT NJ, NJ MED SCH, 73- *Personal Data:* b Brooklyn, NY, Mar 5, 35; m 57, Harriet Stock; c David, Lawrence & Kenneth. *Educ:* Albert Einstein Col Med, MD, 59. *Prof Exp:* Med intern, Bronx Munic Hosp Ctr, 59-60, asst resident, 60-61, resident med, 64-65; clin assoc endocrinol, Endocrine Br, Nat Cancer Inst, 61-64, fel reproductive endocrinol, Karolinska Inst, Stockholm, 65-66; sr investr, Endocrinol Br, 66-69; dir med, Newark Beth Israel Med Ctr, 69. *Concurrent Pos:* Consult, Res Comt, East Orange Vet Admin Hosp, 71-; mem, Breast Cancer Task Force-Epidemiol, Nat Cancer Inst, 74-78, prog proj comt, 80-84. *Mem:* Am Fedn Clin Res; Endocrine Soc; Am Asn Cancer Res; Am Diabetes Asn; Am Soc Clin Nutrit. *Res:* Androgen and estrogen metabolism; hirsutism; endocrine tumors; breast cancer; obesity management. *Mailing Add:* Newark Beth Israel Med Ctr 201 Lyons Ave Newark NJ 07112-2027. *Fax:* 973-926-0143

KIRSCHNER, ROBERT H, FORENSIC PATHOLOGY. *Current Pos:* asst prof path, 73-78, Ben Horwich scholar med sci, 75-78, ASSOC PROF PATH, UNIV CHICAGO, 78-, CLIN ASSOC, DEPT PATHOL & PEDIAT. *Personal Data:* b Philadelphia, Pa, Oct 30, 40; m 65, Barbara Starrels; c Joshua, Daniel & Benjamin. *Educ:* Washington & Jefferson Col, BA, 62; Jefferson Med Col, MD, 66. *Prof Exp:* Instr path, Univ Chicago, 69-71; asst chief, Path Dept, USPHS Hosp, 71-73. *Concurrent Pos:* Am Cancer Soc clin fel path, Univ Chicago, 69-70; dep med examr, 78-86; med adv comt, Lincoln Park Zoo, Chicago; AAAS forensic consult, Govt Arg, 85; mem, Comt Sci Freedom & Responsibility, AAAS, 87-93; comt mem, Child Abuse & Neglect, Am Acad Pediat; dep chief med examr, Cook Co, 87-95; dir, Int Forensic Prog, Physicians Human Rights, 95- *Mem:* AAAS; Am Soc Cell Biol; Sigma Xi; Am Acad Forensic Sci; NY Acad Sci; Nat Asn Med Examiners; Physicians Human Rights; Am Acad Pediat. *Res:* Sudden cardiac death; child abuse and neglect; trauma and injury; forensic documentation of human rights abuses. *Mailing Add:* Inst Forensic Med 2121 Harrison St Chicago IL 60612

KIRSCHNER, RONALD ALLEN, LASER-TISSUE INTERACTION, OPTICS & IMAGING. *Current Pos:* clin assoc prof head & neck, 75-85, clin prof, 85-89, PROF & CHMN HEAD & NECK & FACIAL SURG, PHILADELPHIA COL OSTEOPATH MED, 90-; PRES, KIRSCHNER DESIGN GROUP INC, 88- *Personal Data:* b New York, NY, Jan 18, 42; m 64; c 2. *Educ:* New York Univ, BA, 62; Philadelphia Col Osteopath Med, DO, 66, MSc, 72. *Prof Exp:* Dir head & neck serv, Main Navy Dispensary, 68-70, Neurosensory Unit, 73-76. *Concurrent Pos:* Pres, Suburban Ear, Nose & Throat Group Ltd, 76-; chmn head & neck, Suburban Gen Hosp, 76-, Div Surg, 83-89; vpres, Courtland Group Inc, 79-84, exec vpres, 84-85; exec dir, Inst Appl Laser Surg, 80-; design consult, Pilling Corp, 81-, Inframed Corp, 84-87, Sigma Dynamics, 87-; guest ed, Surg Clins NAm, 84; contrib ed, Photonics Spectra, 87- *Mem:* Laser Assoc Am; NY Acad Sci; Sigma Xi; Laser Inst Am; Am Soc Lasers Med Surv. *Res:* Laboratory and clinical research regarding lasers of various wavelengths and their interaction with tissue, delivery systems, related imaging systems and development of new instruments. *Mailing Add:* Kirschner Design Group Inc 2 Bala Plaza Suite Plaza 13 Bala Cynwyd PA 19004

KIRSCHNER, STANLEY, INORGANIC CHEMISTRY. *Current Pos:* from asst prof to assoc prof, Wayne State Univ, 54-60, vchmn dept, 61-64, actg chmn, 64-65, PROF CHEM, WAYNE STATE UNIV, 60- *Personal Data:* b Brooklyn, NY, Dec 17, 27; m 50; c 2. *Educ:* Brooklyn Col, BS, 50; Harvard Univ, AM, 52; Univ Ill, PhD(chem), 54. *Honors & Awards:* Fac Res Award, Sigma Xi, 74; Heyrovsky Medal, Czech Acad Sci, 78; Catalyst Award, Mfg Chem Asn, 84. *Prof Exp:* Res chemist inorg chem, Monsanto Chem Co, 51. *Concurrent Pos:* Res fels, Res Corp, 55-57, Chattanooga Med Co, 56, NSF, 58, 65-67 & 73-77, sr fel, 63-64 & Ford Found, 69; NIH grant, 62-65; Fulbright scholar, 63-64 & 84; perm secy, Int Conf Coord Chem, 66-89; vis prof, Univ London, 63-64, Univ Sao Paulo, Brazil, 69, Polytech Univ Timisoara, Romania, 73, Univ Florence, Italy, 76, Tohoku Univ, Sendai, Japan, Inst Chem, Cluj, Romania, 78, Polytech Inst, Lisbon, & Univ Porto, Portugal, 84; chmn, comt educ, 81-83, Div Chem Educ, Am Chem Soc, 86- & bd dirs, 88-92; ed, Inorg Synthesis, bd dirs, Am Chem Soc, 88-92; adv bd, Seaborg Ctr for Teaching & Learning of Sci & Math, 88-97. *Mem:* fel AAAS; Am Chem Soc; fel NY Acad Sci; Chem Soc; Brazilian Acad Sci; fel Indian Chem Soc; fel Japan Soc Prom Sci; fel Chilean Chem Soc. *Res:* Structure and stereochemistry of organosilicon and complex inorganic compounds; rotatory dispersion and circular dichroism of asymmetric coordination compounds; physiologically important complex inorganic compounds and their biological activity; application of computer techniques to the storage and retrieval of chemical literature references; optical properties of fast-racemizing complexes; the pfeiffer effect; chemistry education. *Mailing Add:* Dept Chem Wayne State Univ Detroit MI 48202

KIRSCHSTEIN, RUTH LILLIAN, PATHOLOGY. *Current Pos:* dir, Nat Inst Gen Med Sci, 74-93, actg dir, 93, DEP DIR, NIH, 93- *Personal Data:* b Brooklyn, NY, Oct 12, 26; m 50; c 1. *Educ:* Long Island Univ, AB, 47; Tulane Univ, MD, 51. *Hon Degrees:* DSc, Mt Sinai Sch Med, 84; LLD, Atlanta Univ, 85; DSc, Med Col Ohio, 86. *Prof Exp:* Pathologist, Div Biologics Stand, NIH, 57-60, chief, Sect Path, Lab Virol Immunol, 60-65 & asst chief, 62-65, chief, Lab Path, 65-72, asst dir, Div Biologics Stand, 71-72; dep dir, Bur Biologics, Food & Drug Admin, 72-73, dep assoc comnr sci, 73-74. *Concurrent Pos:* Mem,expert comt poliomyelitis, WHO, 65 & 67 & 71; chairperson, NIH Grants Peer Rev Study Team, 75-76, PHS Task Force Women's Health Issues, 83-84, PHS Coord, Comt Women's Health Issues, 85- *Mem:* Am Asn Pathologists; Am Asn Immunologists; Am Soc Microbiol. *Res:* Pathology and pathogenesis of viral diseases; poliomyelitis,; oncogenic viruses; viral vaccines; scientific peer review; scientific research administration; carcinogenesis. *Mailing Add:* Nat Inst Gen Med Sci NIH Shannon Bldg Rm 126 1 Center Dr Bethesda MD 20892-0148. *Fax:* 301-402-2700

KIRSHENBAUM, ABRAHAM DAVID, PHYSICAL INORGANIC CHEMISTRY, EXPLOSIVES. *Current Pos:* RETIRED. *Personal Data:* b New York, NY, July 8, 19; wid, Sarah Schrebrank (deceased); c 2. *Educ:* City Col New York, BS, 41; Polytech Inst Brooklyn, MS, 45. *Prof Exp:* Res scientist, S A M Labs, Columbia Univ, 41-46; res chemist, Houdry Process Corp, Pa, 46-48 & Standard Oil Develop Co, 48-49; res supvr, Res Inst, Temple Univ, 49-68; res chemist & proj leader, US Army Armament Munitions & Chem Command, 68-88. *Mem:* Am Chem Soc; Sci Res Soc Am; Sigma Xi; NAm Thermal Anal Soc. *Res:* Exchange reactions; lubrication oil additives; catalysis; inorganic fluorine chemistry; high vacuum techniques; gaseous burning velocity, calorimetric studies; high temperature physical measurements; rare gas chemistry; pyrotechnics and delays; propellants and explosives. *Mailing Add:* 7234 Fairfax Dr Tamarac FL 33321-4303

KIRSHENBAUM, GERALD STEVEN, POLYMER CHEMISTRY, PLASTICS RESEARCH. *Current Pos:* MGR PROD STEWARDSHIP, HOECHST CELANESE, 90- *Personal Data:* b New York, NY, Dec 6, 44; c Alan, Mark & Jeffrey. *Educ:* Case Inst Technol, BS, 66; Polytech Inst Brooklyn, MS, 70, PhD(polymer chem), 71. *Prof Exp:* Res chemist, Celanese Plastics Co, 71-74; sr res chemist, Soltex Polymer Corp, 74-75; sr chemist, Union Carbide Corp, Bound Brook, 76-78; develop assoc, supvr & mgr, Celanese Eng Resins Co, 78-89. *Concurrent Pos:* Asst ed, Polymer News, 72-75, ed, 75- *Mem:* Am Chem Soc; Soc Plastics Engrs. *Res:* Polyolefins; high-density polyethylene; polyethylene catalysis; polyethylene terephthalate for container application and plastics for packaging; regulatory affairs; author of several books; engineering plastics; product safety. *Mailing Add:* 10 Byron Lane Fanwood NJ 07023

KIRSHENBAUM, ISIDOR, CHEMISTRY. *Current Pos:* RETIRED. *Personal Data:* b New York, NY, June 22, 17; m 47; c 4. *Educ:* City Col New York, BS, 38; Columbia Univ, MA, 39, PhD(chem), 42. *Prof Exp:* Asst instr phys chem, Columbia Univ, 40-42, res scientist, 42-45; res assoc, 45-68, sr res assoc, 68-77, sci adv, Exxon Res & Eng Co, 77-85; pvt consult, 86-90. *Concurrent Pos:* Consult, AEC, 47-55. *Mem:* AAAS; Am Chem Soc. *Res:* Oxidation reactions; patents and research analysis; polymer properties; petrochemical petroleum processes; heterogeneous catalysis; separation and physical properties of isotopes. *Mailing Add:* 260 Garth Rd Apt 5J5 Scarsdale NY 10583

KIRSHNER, HOWARD STEPHEN, NEUROLOGY. *Current Pos:* from asst prof to assoc prof, 78-87, PROF NEUROL, SCH MED, VANDERBILT UNIV, 87-, VCHMN DEPT NEUROL, 93-; DIR NEUROL, VANDERBILT STALLWORTH REHAB HOSP, 93- *Personal Data:* b Bryn Mawr, Pa, July 11, 46; m 69, Carol Adams; c Joshua D & Jodie A. *Educ:* Williams Col, BA, 68; Harvard Med Sch, MD, 72. *Prof Exp:* Intern med, Mass Gen Hosp, 72-73; staff assoc lab perinatal physiol, Nat Inst Neurol & Commun Dis, 73-75; resident & clin instr, Mass Gen Hosp, 75-78. *Concurrent Pos:* Consult, Nashville Gen Hosp, 78- & Mid Tenn Ment Health Inst, 78-; mem, Stroke Coun, Am Heart Asn. *Mem:* Am Acad Neurol; Am Neurol Asn; Nat Aphasia Asn; Acad Aphasia; Am Bd Neurorehab; fel Am Heart Asn. *Res:* Aphasia; higher cortical functions; cerebrovascular disease; neurorehabilitation. *Mailing Add:* Dept Neurol Vanderbilt Univ Sch Med Nashville TN 37232. *Fax:* 615-936-0223

KIRSHNER, NORMAN, METABOLISM & CELL CULTURE PROTEIN SYNTHESIS. *Current Pos:* res asst, Duke Univ, 55-57, assoc biochem, 56-59, from asst prof to assoc prof, 59-70, prof, 70-93, chmn, Dept Pharmacol, 77-87, EMER PROF, DUKE UNIV, 93- *Personal Data:* b Wilkes-Barre, Pa, Sept 21, 23; m 61, Anette Grossman; c Naomi, Susan & Amy. *Educ:* Univ Scranton, BS, 47; Pa State Univ, MS, 51, PhD(biochem), 52. *Prof Exp:* Res asst physiol, Univ Rochester, 52-54; res asst, Yale Univ, 54. *Concurrent Pos:* USPHS sr res fel, 59-62, career develop award, 62-; mem, Prog Proj Rev Comt, Roche Inst Molecular Biol, 75-79, Coun Sci Adv, 79; ed, Molecular Pharmacol, 78-82; chmn, Neurol Sci Study Sect, 85-88. *Mem:* Am Soc Biol Chem; Am Soc Pharmacol & Exp Therapeut; Am Soc Neurochem. *Res:* Metabolism of Catecholamines; mechanism of storage and release of neurotransmitters. *Mailing Add:* Med Ctr Box 3813 Duke Univ Durham NC 27710-0001. *Fax:* 919-681-8609; *E-Mail:* nkirsh@acpub.duke.edu

KIRSHNER, ROBERT PAUL, ASTRONOMY. *Current Pos:* PROF ASTRON, HARVARD UNIV, 85- *Personal Data:* b Long Branch, NJ, Aug 15, 49; m, Lucy Herman; c Rebecca & Matthew. *Educ:* Harvard Col, AB, 70; Calif Inst Technol, PhD(astron), 75. *Honors & Awards:* Bowdoin Prize, Harvard Col, 70; Russel Award, Univ Mich, 80; Aaronson lectr, Univ Ariz, 89. *Prof Exp:* Res assoc astron, Kitt Peak Nat Observ, 74-76; from asst prof to prof astron, Univ Mich, 76-85, dir, McGraw Hill Observ, 80-85. *Concurrent Pos:* Users comt, Kitt Peak Nat Observ, 78-81, Cerro-Tololo Inter-Am Observ, 79-82; telescope allocation comt, Kitt Peak Nat Cerro-Tololo Inter Am Observ, 80-82; comt, Space Astron & Astrophys, 82-85; sci adv comt, Nat New Technol Telescope, 83-84; vis comt mem, Asn Univ Res Astron, 83-86; chmn, NSF subcomt Large Optical-IR Telescopes, 85-86; Alfred P Sloan fel, 79-82; coun mem, Am Astron Soc, 85-87; vis comt, Mt Wilson & Las Camponas Observ, 87-89 & Space Telescope Sci Inst, 88-89; bd dirs, Asn Univ Res Astron, 89- *Mem:* Am Astron Soc; Int Astron Union; Am Phys Soc; AAAS; fel Am Acad Arts & Scis. *Res:* Extragalactic supernovae and galactic supernova remnants; extragalactic distance scale; large scale structure. *Mailing Add:* Dept Astron Harvard Univ 60 Garden St Cambridge MA 02138. *Fax:* 617-495-7467; *E-Mail:* kirshnerd@cfa.harvard.edu

KIRSNER, JOSEPH BARNETT, INTERNAL MEDICINE, GASTROENTEROLOGY. *Current Pos:* From asst prof to prof med, 35-74, dean med affairs & chief staff, Univ Hosp, 71-76, LOUIS BLOCK DISTINGUISHED SERV PROF MED, UNIV CHICAGO, 74- *Personal Data:* b Boston, Mass, Sept 21, 09; m 34; c 1. *Educ:* Tufts Col, MD, 33; Univ Chicago, PhD(biol sci) & Am Bd Internal Med, dipl, 42. *Honors & Awards:* Friedenwald Medal, Am Gastroenterol Asn; John Phillips Mem Award, Am Col Physicians; George Howell Coleman Medal, Inst Med, Chicago; Rudolph Schindler Award, Am Soc Gastrointestinal Endoscopy. *Concurrent Pos:* Mem nat adv coun, Nat Inst Arthritis & Metab Dis; chmn, Adv Group, Nat Comn Digestive Dis, 78; assoc ed, Advances Internal Med, 70- *Mem:* Am Soc Clin Invest; Am Soc Gastrointestinal Endoscopy (secy-treas, Gastroscopic Soc, 42-48, pres, 49-50); fel AMA; Am Gastroenterol Asn (treas & pres, 65-66); mastership Am Col Physicians. *Res:* Gastroenterology, especially peptic ulcer, cancer, inflammatory diseases including regional enteritis and ulcerative colitis; protein metabolism; hepatic disease; immunological mechanisms in gastrointestinal disease. *Mailing Add:* Dept Med Univ Chicago 5841 S Maryland Ave MC 2100 Chicago IL 60637-1470

KIRST, HERBERT ANDREW, ORGANIC CHEMISTRY. *Current Pos:* sr chemist, Eli Lilly & Co, 73-77, res scientist, 78-83, sr res scientist, 84-91, RES ADV, ELI LILLY & CO, 92- *Personal Data:* b St Paul, Minn, Sept 22, 44; m 90, Peggy A Hillman. *Educ:* Univ Minn, BS, 66; Harvard Univ, PhD(org chem), 71. *Prof Exp:* Fel org chem, Calif Inst Technol, 71-73. *Concurrent Pos:* Ed, Antimicrobial Agents & Chemother, 91-96. *Mem:* Am Chem Soc; AAAS; Am Soc Microbiol; NY Acad Sci. *Res:* Structure determination and chemical modification of new antibiotics and other fermentation products. *Mailing Add:* Elanco Animal Health Res & Develop 2001 W Main St Greenfield IN 46140-0708. *Fax:* 317-276-4714

KIRSTEN, EDWARD BRUCE, NEUROPHARMACOLOGY, CLINICAL CARDIOLOGY. *Current Pos:* DIR CARDIO-RENAL, CNS & WOUND CARE, 91- *Personal Data:* b New York, NY, Jan 28, 42; m 63, Miriam Medina; c Suzanne & Eric. *Educ:* Fairleigh Dickinson Univ, BS, 62; NY Univ, MS, 66; City Univ New York, PhD(biol), 69. *Prof Exp:* Assoc, Col Physicians & Surgeons, Columbia Univ, 71-72, asst prof pharmacol, 72-77; dir clin pharmacol, Knoll Pharmaceut Co, 77-92. *Concurrent Pos:* NIH fel pharmacol, Col Physicians & Surgeons, Columbia Univ, 69-71, res career develop award, 72-77; adj asst prof pharmacol, Columbia Univ, 77- *Mem:* Am Soc Clin Pharmacol & Therapeut; Sigma Xi. *Res:* Clinical development of new cardiovascular and CNS drugs including compounds for arrlythmias, hypertension and stroke; pharmacokinetics. *Mailing Add:* Knoll Pharmaceut Co 3000 Continental Dr N Mt Olive NJ 07828-1234. *Fax:* 973-426-5593

KIRTLEY, JOHN ROBERT, SUPERCONDUCTIVITY, MICROSCOPY. *Current Pos:* RES STAFF MEM, IBM RES DIV, 78- *Personal Data:* b Palo Alto, Calif, Aug 27, 49; m 73; c 1. *Educ:* Univ Calif, Santa Barbara, BA, 71, PhD(physics), 76. *Prof Exp:* Post doctoral, Univ Pa, 76-77, res asst prof, 77-78. *Mem:* Fel Am Phys Soc. *Res:* Solid state physics in planar structures and using a scanning tunneling microscope; collective phenomena such as superconductivity, quantum hall effect at low temperatures. *Mailing Add:* T J Watson Res Ctr PO Box 218 Yorktown Heights NY 10598

KIRTLEY, MARY ELIZABETH, BIOCHEMISTRY. *Current Pos:* from asst prof to prof, 66-81, RES PROF BIOL CHEM, SCH MED, UNIV MD, BALTIMORE, 83-; DIR, GRAD & PROF STUDIES, DICKINSON COL, CARLISLE, PA. *Personal Data:* b Mansfield, Ohio, Aug 27, 35; m 93, Ted B Windsor. *Educ:* Univ Chicago, BA, 56; Smith Col, MA, 58; Western Res Univ, PhD(biochem), 64. *Prof Exp:* Lab instr chem, Smith Col, 58-59; res assoc biochem, Brookhaven Nat Lab, 64-65; res assoc, Univ Calif, Berkeley, 65-66. *Concurrent Pos:* Proj dir, Biochem Prog, NSF, 82-83; dir, Off Grad Studies, Dickinson Col, 83- *Mem:* Biophys Soc; Protein Soc; Am Soc Biochem & Molecular Biol; NY Acad Sci. *Res:* Enzyme mechanisms; biochemical regulation; enzyme structure and function; enzyme-membrane interactions. *Mailing Add:* 1118 Apple Dr Mechanicsburg PA 17055. *Fax:* 717-245-1989; *E-Mail:* kirtley@dickinson.edu

KIRTLEY, THOMAS L(LOYD), CHEMICAL ENGINEERING. *Current Pos:* RETIRED. *Personal Data:* b Salmon, Idaho, Nov 16, 18; m 43, Eugene Chappel; c Thomas L Jr & Frank C. *Educ:* San Jose State Col, AB(chem) & AB(physics & math), 40; Calif Inst Technol, MS, 42. *Prof Exp:* Tech shift supvr, Ammonia Prod, Hercules Powder Co, Hercules Inc, 42-44, shift supvr, Rocket Powder Prod, 44-45, serv supvr, Chem Cotton Prod, 45-56, asst chief chemist, 56-60, chem supvr, 60-65, chem cotton tech coordr, 65-69, chem cotton supt, 69-75, supt eng develop, 75-77, supt environ eng, 77-82. *Mem:* Am Chem Soc. *Res:* Cellulose chemistry; chemical cotton; cellulose ethers. *Mailing Add:* 306 Sherwood Dr Hopewell VA 23860. *E-Mail:* tom_kirtley@prodigy.com

KIRTLEY, WILLIAM RAYMOND, CLINICAL MEDICINE. *Current Pos:* RETIRED. *Personal Data:* b Crawfordsville, Ind, May 30, 14; m 40; c 2. *Educ:* Wabash Col, AB, 36; Northwestern Univ, MB, 40, MD, 41. *Honors & Awards:* Banting Medal, Am Diabetes Asn, 71. *Prof Exp:* Staff physician, Eli Lilly & Co, 47-56, physician in chg, Diabetes Res Lab Clin Res, 53-70, sr physician, 56-61, head, Clin Med Dept, 61-65, asst dir, Clin Res Div, 63-65, dir, Med Res Div, 65-72, dir, Lilly Lab Clin Res, 72-78; assoc prof med, Sch Med, Ind Univ, 73-78. *Concurrent Pos:* Assoc med, Wishard Mem Hosp, 49-, chief, Diabetes Clin, 53-70; abstr ed, Diabetes, Am Diabetes Asn, 50-68; assoc med, Sch Med, Ind Univ, 52-61, asst prof, 61-73. *Mem:* Am Soc Clin Pharmacol & Therapeut; Endocrine Soc; AMA; Am Diabetes Asn. *Res:* Insulin modifications; metabolism; diabetes mellitus; glucagon. *Mailing Add:* 33 Fairway Winds Pl Hilton Head Island SC 29928

KIRTMAN, BERNARD, PHYSICAL CHEMISTRY. *Current Pos:* asst prof chem, Univ Calif, Berkeley, 62-65, from asst prof to assoc prof chem, Santa Barbara, 65-68, PROF THEORET PHYS CHEM, UNIV CALIF, SANTA BARBARA, 72- *Personal Data:* b New York, NY, Mar 30, 35; m 58, Tybie Planzer; c Ann M & Benjamin P. *Educ:* Harvard Univ, PhD(phys chem), 61. *Prof Exp:* Fel chem, Univ Wash, 60-62. *Mem:* Am Chem Soc; Am Phy Soc. *Res:* Theoretical chemistry; application of quantum mechanics to electronic structure of atoms, molecules and extended systems. *Mailing Add:* Dept Chem Univ Calif Santa Barbara CA 93106

KIRWAN, ALBERT DENNIS, JR, PHYSICAL OCEANOGRAPHY. *Current Pos:* AT DEPT MARINE SCI, UNIV SFLA. *Personal Data:* b Louisville, Ky, Nov 29, 33; m 56; c 3. *Educ:* Princeton Univ, AB, 56; Tex A&M Univ, PhD(phys oceanog), 64. *Prof Exp:* Res asst oceanog, Tex A&M Univ, 59-64; from asst prof to assoc prof, NY Univ, 64-70; prog dir phys oceanog, Off Naval Res, 70-72. *Mem:* AAAS; Am Meteorol Soc; Am Geophys Union. *Res:* Air-sea interaction, general circulation of oceans; physics of fluids; engineering science. *Mailing Add:* Dept Oceanog Old Dom Univ Norfolk VA 23502

KIRWAN, DONALD FRAZIER, ENERGY, ENERGY EDUCATION. *Current Pos:* PROF PHYSICS, LA STATE UNIV, 95- *Personal Data:* b Oklahoma City, Okla, Nov 9, 37; m 59; c 5. *Educ:* Univ Mo, Columbia, BS, 63, MS, 64, PhD(physics), 69. *Prof Exp:* From instr to asst prof, Univ RI, 67-74, dir, Off Energy Educ, 79, prof physics, 81-88; mgr, Educ Div, Am Inst Physics, 88-95. *Concurrent Pos:* Consult, Fed Emergency Mgt Agency, 80-, Argonne Nat Labs, 82-, Int Atomic Energy Agency, 83-, Environ Protection Agency, 84-; ed, The Physics Teacher, 85-; at large mem exec bd, Soc Physics Students, 85-88, exec bd, Am Asn Physics Teachers, 85-; energy leader, Conf Sci & Technol Educ & Future Human Needs, 85; chmn, 81 Int Conf on Energy Educ. *Mem:* AAAS; Am Phys Soc; Am Asn Physics Teachers; Nat Sci Teachers Asn. *Res:* Fundamental interactions; few-nucleon systematics; excitation mechanisms of the nucleus; physics pedagogy; radiological accident assessment; radiological emergency preparedness. *Mailing Add:* Astron & Physics Dept 119 Nicholson Hall Baton Rouge LA 70803

KIRWAN, WILLIAM ENGLISH, MATHEMATICAL ANALYSIS. *Current Pos:* from asst prof to assoc prof math, 64-72, chmn dept, 77-81, vchancellor acad affairs, 81-88, actg pres, 88-89, PROF MATH, UNIV MD, COLLEGE PARK, 72-, PRES, 89- *Personal Data:* b Louisville, Ky, Apr 14, 38; m 60; c 2. *Educ:* Univ Ky, BA, 60; Rutgers Univ, MS, 62, PhD(math), 64. *Prof Exp:* Instr math, Rutgers Univ, 63-64. *Concurrent Pos:* Vis lectr, Royal Holloway Col, Univ London, 66-67; prog dir, NSF, 75-76. *Mem:* Math Asn Am; Am Math Soc; Sigma Xi. *Res:* Functions of one complex variable, particularly extremal properties of conformal and quasiconformal mappings of the unit disc. *Mailing Add:* President's Off Univ Md College Park MD 20742

KIRWIN, GERALD JAMES, ELECTRICAL ENGINEERING, APPLIED MATHEMATICS. *Current Pos:* RETIRED. *Personal Data:* b Lowell, Mass, Feb 11, 29; m 55; c 2. *Educ:* NE Univ, BSEE, 52; Mass Inst Technol, MSEE, 55; Syracuse Univ, PhD(elec eng), 68. *Prof Exp:* Mem tech staff, Bell Tel Labs, 55-56; assoc prof elec eng, Merrimack Col, 56-64; instr, Syracuse Univ, 64-68; prof, Univ Maine, Portland-Gorham, 68-73; prof elec eng, Sch Eng, Univ New Haven, 73-94. *Mem:* Inst Elec & Electronics Engrs. *Res:* Nonlinear systems; circuit theory and design; optimal network design, electrical engineering education. *Mailing Add:* PO Box 1412 Madison CT 06443

KIRZ, JANOS, SYNCHROTRON RADIATION, X-RAY OPTICS. *Current Pos:* assoc prof, State Univ NY, Stony Brook, 68-72, assoc chmn, 84-85, prof, 72-95, DISTINGUISHED PROF PHYSICS, STATE UNIV NY, STONY BROOK, 95- *Personal Data:* b Budapest, Hungary, Aug 11, 37; US citizen; m 88, Regina Moreno; c Steven. *Educ:* Univ Calif, Berkeley, BA, 59, PhD(physics), 63. *Prof Exp:* Nat Acad Sci-Nat Res Coun fel physics, Saclay Nuclear Res Ctr, France, 63-64; physicist, Lawrence Radiation Lab, Univ Calif, 64-68. *Concurrent Pos:* Lectr, Univ Calif, Berkeley, 67; Sloan Found fel, 70-72; visitor, Lab Molecular Biophys, Oxford Univ, 72-73; Guggenheim fel, 85-86. *Mem:* Fel AAAS; fel Am Phys Soc; Optical Soc Am; Micros Soc Am; Biophys Soc. *Res:* X-ray microscopy. *Mailing Add:* Dept Physics State Univ NY Stony Brook NY 11794-3800. *Fax:* 516-632-8101; *E-Mail:* kirz@sbhep.physics.sunysb.edu

KISCHER, CLAYTON WARD, EMBRYOLOGY, CELL BIOLOGY IN SURGICAL RESEARCH. *Current Pos:* vis prof surg biol, Univ Ariz Col Med, 76-77, dir, Sem Lab, 77-85, assoc prof, 77-93, EMER ASSOC PROF ANAT, UNIV ARIZ COL MED, 93- *Personal Data:* b Des Moines, Iowa, Mar 2, 30; m 64, Linda R Espejo; c Eric, Frank & Cynthia. *Educ:* Univ Omaha, BS, 53; Iowa State Univ, MS, 60, PhD(embryol), 62. *Prof Exp:* Cytologist, Col Med, Univ Nebr, 53-56; teacher high sch, Nebr, 56-58; asst prof zool, Ill State Univ, 62-63; resident res assoc biol & med, Argonne Nat Lab, 63; asst prof zool, Iowa State Univ, 63-64; chief sect electron micros, Southwest Found Res & Educ, 66-67; asst prof, 67-70, assoc prof, Univ Tex Med Br, 70-77. *Concurrent Pos:* Fel biochem, Univ Tex M D Anderson Hosp, 64-66; res consult to chief staff, Shriners Burns Inst, Galveston, 70-73. *Mem:* Am Asn Anat; Am Soc Cell Biol; Electron Micros Soc Am. *Res:* Ultrastructural changes during morphogenesis; electron microscopy; hypertrophic scarring and fibronectin; microvessels in wound healing; human embryology and public policy; analyses of public perception of human embryology through media sources. *Mailing Add:* 6249 N Camino Miraval Tucson AZ 85718-3024. *Fax:* 520-626-2097

KISER, DONALD LEE, ANALYTICAL CHEMISTRY, INTELLECTUAL PROPERTY. *Current Pos:* sr anal chemist, 64-73, mgr anal develop, 73-83, MGR INTELLECTUAL PROPERTY, GRAIN PROCESSING CORP, 83-, VPRES, 85- *Personal Data:* b Keokuk, Iowa, Jan 2, 33; m 53, Kathryn D McKay; c 3. *Educ:* Iowa State Univ, BS, 59; Ind State Univ, MS, 61; Univ Iowa, PhD(anal chem), 64. *Prof Exp:* Anal chemist, Com Solvents Corp, Ind, 59-61. *Concurrent Pos:* Coun mem, Am Chem Soc, 73-93; mem, Bd Trustees, Group Ins Plans, Am Chem Soc, 87-92; mem, Iowa State Univ Res Found, 92-, bd dirs, 93-, vpres, 93, pres, 94- *Mem:* Am Chem Soc; Asn Off Anal Chemists; Am Asn Cereal Chemists; Licensing Execs Soc. *Res:* Automated methods of analysis; exploratory research for new chemical and food business opportunities; alcohol congeners by gas chromatography; carbohydrate molecular weight profiles by liquid chromatography; food regulatory issues. *Mailing Add:* Grain Processing Corp 1600 Oregon Ave PO Box 349 Muscatine IA 52761. *Fax:* 319-264-4216

KISER, KENNETH M(AYNARD), CHEMICAL ENGINEERING. *Current Pos:* from asst prof to prof, 64-97, assoc dean eng, 78-97, EMER PROF CHEM ENG, STATE UNIV NY, BUFFALO, 97- *Personal Data:* b Detroit, Mich, Nov 28, 29; m 54; c 5. *Educ:* Lawrence Tech Univ, BS, 51; Univ Cincinnati, MS, 52; Johns Hopkins Univ, DS(chem eng), 56. *Prof Exp:* Asst, Univ Cincinnati, 51-52; res assoc, Inst Coop Res, Johns Hopkins Univ, 52-56; res assoc, Chem Dept, Res Lab, Gen Elec Co, 56-64; adj staff, Rensselaer Polytech Inst, 62-64. *Concurrent Pos:* Consult. *Mem:* Am Inst Chem Engrs; Am Soc Eng Educ; Sigma Xi. *Res:* Turbulent transport; non-Newtonian fluids; fluid mechanics in the human body; air and water pollution. *Mailing Add:* Dept Chem Eng State Univ NY 307 Furnas Hall Buffalo NY 14260

KISER, LOLA FRANCES, MATHEMATICS. *Current Pos:* from asst prof to prof, 55-96, EMER PROF MATH, BIRMINGHAM-SOUTHERN COL, 96- *Personal Data:* b Selmer, Tenn, Dec 6, 30. *Educ:* Memphis State Univ, BS, 52; Univ Ga, MA, 54; Univ Ala, Tuscaloosa, PhD(math), 71. *Prof Exp:* Instr math, Univ Ga, 54-55. *Mem:* Math Asn Am. *Res:* Complex analysis; differential equations. *Mailing Add:* Dept Math Box A-32 Birmingham-Southern Col Birmingham AL 35254

KISER, ROBERT WAYNE, INORGANIC CHEMISTRY, MASS SPECTROMETRY. *Current Pos:* dir, Mass Spectrometry Ctr, Univ Ky, 67-96, chmn chem dept, 68-72, dir gen chem, 88-95, PROF CHEM, UNIV KY, 67- *Personal Data:* b Rock Island, Ill, Apr 26, 32; m 54, Barbara M Hatje; c Mark D, Scott A & Ann M. *Educ:* St Ambrose Univ, BA, 53; Purdue Univ, MS, 55, PhD, 58. *Prof Exp:* From asst prof to prof inorg chem, Kans State Univ, 57-67. *Concurrent Pos:* Proj mgr, Student Info Syst, UK, 85-87. *Mem:* Am Soc Mass Spectrometry; Am Chem Soc. *Res:* Excited states of negative ions; energetics and thermochemistry of ionic species; artificial intelligence in mass spectrometry; mass spectrometry and molecular structures; multiply-charged ionic species. *Mailing Add:* Dept Chem CP-9 Univ Ky Lexington KY 40506-0055. *Fax:* 606-323-1069; *E-Mail:* kiser@pop.uky.edu

KISH, VALERIE MAYO, CELL BIOLOGY. *Current Pos:* PROF BIOL/ CLARENCE E DENOON PROF SCI, UNIV RICHMOND, VA, 93- *Personal Data:* b Paintsville, Ky, Nov 28, 44. *Educ:* Univ Ky, BS, 65; Ind Univ, MA, 66; Univ Mich, PhD(cell biol), 73. *Prof Exp:* Res asst, Inst Cancer Res, Philadelphia, 66-69; res assoc, Worcester Found Exp Biol, Shrewsbury, 73-76; prof biol, Hobart & William Smith Cols, 76-93. *Mem:* Am Soc Cell Biol; Am Soc Plant Physiol; Sigma Xi. *Res:* Interaction of proteins with RNA in eukaryotic cells and the role these interactions play in the regulation of gene expression. *Mailing Add:* Dept Biol Univ Richmond Gottwald Sci Bldg Richmond VA 23173. *Fax:* 315-781-3587

KISHEL, CHESTER JOSEPH, INDUSTRIAL & HUMAN FACTORS ENGINEERING. *Current Pos:* prof mech & indust eng, Cleveland State Univ, 65-70, dir Comput Ctr, 65-66, prof indust eng & actg chmn dept, 70-71, sr prof indust eng, 71-81, EMER PROF, CLEVELAND STATE UNIV, 81- *Personal Data:* b Cleveland, Ohio, Oct 12, 15; m 39; c 3. *Educ:* Fenn Col, BSME, 44, BSIE, 47; Case Inst Technol, MSIE, 54, PhD(eng admin), 59. *Prof Exp:* Asst chief prod eng, Iron Fireman Mfg Co, 43-45; prod mgr, A W Hecker Co, 45-46; vpres mfg, Kramic Corp, 46-48; from asst prof to assoc prof mech eng, Fenn Col, 48-57; spec lectr eng admin, Case Inst Technol, 57-59; assoc prof & dir, Comput Ctr, Fenn Col, 59-62; contract prof comput indust eng, Mich State Univ/USAID, Polytech Sch, Sao Paulo, Brazil, 62-64. *Concurrent Pos:* Polio Found grant, Highland View Hosp, 60-61. *Mem:* Am Inst Indust Engrs; Soc Mfg Eng; Asn Comput Mach; Am Arbit Asn. *Res:* Neuroanatomy and neurophysiology in desision making aspects of organization theory; electromyographical study-hypotheses of muscular control of human hand languages and techniques of digital computing; numerical controls. *Mailing Add:* 17512 Greenbrier Dr Strongsville OH 44136

KISHI, KEIJI, research administration & management, for more information see previous edition

KISHI, YOSHITO, MEDICINAL CHEMISTRY. *Current Pos:* prof, 74-82, MORRIS LOEB PROF CHEM, HARVARD UNIV, 82- *Personal Data:* b Nagoya, Japan, Apr 13, 37; m 63; c 2. *Educ:* Nagoya Univ, BS, 61; Harvard Univ, MA, 74 PhD(chem), 66. *Honors & Awards:* Japan Chem Soc Prize, 67; Am Chem Soc Award Creative Work Synthetic Org Chem, 80; Harrison Howe Award, 81. *Prof Exp:* Instr chem, Nagoya Univ, 66-69, assoc prof, 69-74. *Concurrent Pos:* Fel, Harvard Univ, 66-68, vis prof, 72-73; Arthur C Cope scholar award, 88, Javits neurosci invest award, 88. *Mem:* Am Chem Soc; Chem Soc Japan; Swiss Chem Soc; Am Acad Arts & Sci. *Res:* Total synthesis of complex natural products typified by the completed works of neurotoxins, metabolites of microorganisms and polyether, ansamycin and antitumor antibiotics. *Mailing Add:* Dept Chem Harvard Univ 12 Oxford St Cambridge MA 02138-2902

KISHIMOTO, TADAMITSU, PATHOLOGY IMMUNOLOGY. *Current Pos:* prof path, 79-83, prof immunol, 83-91, PROF & CHMN MED, MED SCH, OSAKA UNIV, 91-, DEAN, 95- *Personal Data:* b Tondabayashi, Japan, May 7, 39; m 67, Chizuko Tamura. *Educ:* Osaka Univ, Md, 64, PhD, 69. *Honors & Awards:* Imperial Prize, Japan Acad, 92; Sandoz Prize for Immunol, 92. *Prof Exp:* Res fel & asst prof, Med Sch, Johns Hopkins Univ, 70-74. *Mem:* Foreign assoc Nat Acad Sci; Japan Soc Immunbiol (pres, 91-92); Int Soc Immunopharmacol (pres, 91-94); foreign assoc Inst Med-Nat Acad Sci; hon mem Am Asn Immunologists; Japan Soc Immunobiol (pres, 91-92). *Res:* Discovery in interleukin six. *Mailing Add:* 3-5-31 Nakanocho Tonda Bayashi Osaka 584 Japan

KISHIMOTO, YASUO, MOLECULAR BIOLOGY, GENETICS. *Current Pos:* ADJ PROF, DEPT NEUROSCI SCH MED, UNIV CALIF, SAN DIEGO, 88- *Personal Data:* b Osaka-Shi, Japan, Apr 11, 25; m 49, Miyoko Nishikawa; c 4. *Educ:* Kyoto Univ, BS, 48, PhD(pharmaceut chem), 56. *Prof Exp:* Res chemist, Osaka Gas Co, 48-50; lectr pharm, Kyushu Univ, 50-54; asst prof, Shizuoka Col Pharm, 54-61; from asst to assoc res biochemist, Ment Health Res Inst, Univ Mich, Ann Arbor, 62-67; mem staff, Div Chem Res, G D Searle & Co, Ill, 67-69; asst biochemist, Mass Gen Hosp, 69-70, assoc biochemist neurol serv, 70-76; from assoc prof to prof, Sch Med, Johns Hopkins Univ, 76-88. *Concurrent Pos:* Res asst biochem, Med Sch, Northwestern Univ, 57-59; sr investr, Eunice Kennedy Shriver Ctr Ment Retardation, 69-76; assoc neurol, Harvard Med Sch, 69-76; dir biochem res, John F Kennedy Inst, 76-88. *Mem:* Am Soc Biochem & Molecular Biol; Int Soc Neurochem; AAAS; Am Soc Neurochem; Soc Glycobiol. *Res:* Structures and metabolism of brain lipids; myelination, demyelination; role of saposins (sphingolipid activator proteins) in glycolipid metabolism; Biochemistry. *Mailing Add:* 13771 Royal Melbourne Sq San Diego CA 92128. *Fax:* 619-534-1383

KISHK, AHMED A, APPLIED ELECTROMAGNETICS, NUMERICAL SOLUTIONS OF ELECROMAGNETIC PROBLEMS. *Current Pos:* asst prof, 86-90, ASSOC PROF ELEC ENG, UNIV MISS, 90- *Personal Data:* b Ashmoun, Egypt, Dec 9, 54; m 83, Iman M Gohav; c Mohammad, Omayma & Yassev. *Educ:* Cairo Univ, Egypt, BS, 77; Ain Shams Univ, Egypt, BS, 80; Univ Man, Can, MS, 83, PhD(elec eng), 86. *Prof Exp:* Teaching & res asst elec eng, Cairo Univ, 77-81; teaching & res asst elec eng, Univ Man, Can, 81-85, res assoc, 85-86. *Concurrent Pos:* Assoc ed, Antennas & Propagation Mag, Inst Elec & Electronics Engrs, 90-93, ed, 93-; mem, Comn B, US Nat Comt Int Union Radio Sci. *Mem:* Inst Elec & Electronics Engrs; Sigma Xi; Electromagnetic Acad. *Res:* Numerical solutions of electromagnetic problems and antenna design, especially antenna feeds, microstrip antennas, ground station antennas and mobile satellite antennas; antenna design; dielectric antenna. *Mailing Add:* Dept Elec Eng Univ Miss University MS 38677. *E-Mail:* eekishk@umsvm

KISHORE, GANESH M, PLANT GENETIC ENGINEERING, BIOCHEMISTRY. *Current Pos:* Sr res biochem, Monsanto Corp Res Labs, 80-82, res specialist, 82-86, assoc fel, 87-89, res mgr, 89-90, MGR, MONSANTO CORP RES LABS, 90- *Personal Data:* b Hunsur, India, Sept 26, 53; US citizen; m 76; c 2. *Educ:* Univ Mysore, BSc, 70, MSc, 72; Indian Inst Sci, PhD(biochem), 76. *Mem:* Am Soc Biochem & Molecular Biol; Am Soc Plant Physiol. *Res:* Plant biochemistry and plant genetics engineering; genetic engineering of herbicide tolerance, metabolism of herbicides and crop quality improvement. *Mailing Add:* 700 Chesterfield Village Pkwy St Louis MO 63198-0001. *Fax:* 314-537-6759

KISILEVSKY, ROBERT, BIOCHEMISTRY, PATHOLOGY. *Current Pos:* From asst prof to assoc prof, 70-79, head, 86-91, PROF PATH, QUEEN'S UNIV, 79- *Personal Data:* b Montreal, Can, Dec 19, 37; m 67, Barbara Smatsky; c David, Alexandra & Sarah. *Educ:* McGill Univ, BSc, 58, MD, CM, 62; Univ Pittsburgh, PhD(biochem), 69; FRCP(C), 72; Am Bd Path, dipl, 72. *Honors & Awards:* Boyd lectr, Can Asn Pathologists, 92; Claude P Beaubien Prize, Alzheimer Soc Can, 96. *Concurrent Pos:* Asst pathologist, Kingston Gen Hosp, 70-86, pathologist-in-chief, 86-91; from asst prof to assoc prof biochem, Queen's Univ, 71-90, prof, 90-; mem, Grant Comt, Med Res Coun, 74-77, sci officer, 77-83; mem, Nat Cancer Inst, 88-91. *Mem:* US-Can Acad Path; Am Soc Invest Path; Can Asn Pathologists; Can Biochem Soc. *Res:* Pathogenetic mechanisms of Amyloidosis and its relationship to Alzheimer's disease; serum amyloid A and its role in cholesterol metabolism during inflammation. *Mailing Add:* Dept Path Queen's Univ Kingston ON K7L 3N6 Can. *Fax:* 613-545-6411

KISKIS, JOSEPH EDWARD, JR, THEORETICAL PHYSICS, HIGH ENERGY PHYSICS. *Current Pos:* PROF PHYSICS, UNIV CALIF, DAVIS, 80-, VCHANCELLOR, DEPT PHYSICS. *Personal Data:* b Lynwood, Calif, Oct 2, 47. *Educ:* Univ Calif, Davis, BS, 69; Stanford Univ, MS, 71, PhD(physics), 74. *Prof Exp:* Fel, Mass Inst Technol, 74-76 & Los Alamos Sci Lab, 76-77; mem, Inst Advan Study, 77-78; Oppenheimer fel, Los Alamos Nat Lab, 78-80. *Res:* High energy physics; quantum field theory. *Mailing Add:* Dept Physics 443 Physics Univ Calif Davis CA 95616

KISLIUK, PAUL, PHYSICS. *Current Pos:* RETIRED. *Personal Data:* b Philadelphia, Pa, Feb 22, 22; m 50; c 4. *Educ:* Queen's Col, NY, BA, 43; Columbia Univ, MS, 47, PhD(physics), 52. *Prof Exp:* Mem tech staff, Bell Tel Labs, 52-62; dept head, Aerospace Corp, 62-66, sr scientist, 66-90. *Mem:* Am Phys Soc. *Res:* Microwave spectroscopy; contact physics; surface physics; lasers; solid state spectroscopy. *Mailing Add:* 2302 Veteran Ave Los Angeles CA 90064

KISLIUK, ROY LOUIS, BIOCHEMISTRY. *Current Pos:* from asst prof to assoc prof pharmacol, 60-71, assoc prof biochem, 71-72, PROF BIOCHEM, SCH MED, TUFTS UNIV, 72-, PROF PHARMACOL & EXP THERAPEUT, 92- *Personal Data:* b Philadelphia, Pa, Aug 4, 28; m 54, Ingrid Scheer; c Claudette (Beit-Aharon) & Michelle R. *Educ:* Queen's Col, NY, BS, 50; Yale Univ, MS, 52; Western Reserve Univ, PhD(biochem), 56. *Prof Exp:* Vis scientist, Nat Inst Arthritis & Metab Dis, 58-60. *Concurrent Pos:* Nat Found Infantile Paralysis fel biochem, Oxford Univ, 56-58; prog dir biochem, NSF, Washington, DC, 72-73. *Mem:* Am Soc Biol Chem; Am Chem Soc; Am Soc Pharmacol & Exp Therapeut; Am Soc Microbiol; Am Soc Cancer Res; AAAS. *Res:* Folate enzymes, coenzymes and antimetabolites. *Mailing Add:* Dept Biochem Tufts Univ Sch Med 136 Harrison Ave Boston MA 02111-1800

KISMAN, KENNETH EDWIN, PETROLEUM ENGINEERING. *Current Pos:* PRES, RANGEWEST RESOURCES, LTD, CALGARY, 96- *Personal Data:* b Sudbury, Ont, Nov 18, 46; m 70; c 2. *Educ:* Queens Univ, BS, 68; Univ Toronto, MS, 70, PhD(molecular physics), 74. *Prof Exp:* Res officer hyperbaric biophys, Defence & Civil Inst Environ Med, Can, 74-79, res supvr reservoir eng, 79-84, prin reservoir engr, 84-79; Alta Energy Dept, 84-96. *Mem:* Soc Petrol Eng; Can Inst Mining & Metall. *Res:* Engineering studies for heavy oil petroleum recovery processes, including field pilots, numerical simulation and direction of lab studies. *Mailing Add:* 5760 Buckboard Rd NW Calgary AB T3A 4R6 Can

KISPERT, LOWELL DONALD, SOLID STATE CHEMISTRY, RADIATION CHEMISTRY. *Current Pos:* from asst prof to prof, 68-80, RES PROF CHEM, UNIV ALA, 80-, CHMN, CHEM DEPT, 90- *Personal Data:* b Faribault, Minn, June 9, 40; m 89, Doris Lagrone; c 7. *Educ:* St Olaf Col, BA, 62; Mich State Univ, PhD(chem), 66. *Honors & Awards:* Burnum Award, 88. *Prof Exp:* Fel electron spin resonance, Varian Assocs, Calif, 66-67; radiation chem, Mellon Inst, 68. *Mem:* Am Chem Soc; Am Phys Soc; Sigma Xi; Int Soc Magnet Resonance; Int EPR Soc. *Res:* Free radicals as produced in irradiated organic single crystals by electron spin resonance; electron nuclear double resonance and electron-electron double resonance of paramagnetic single crystals, anions and cations in solution; radiation chemistry; conducting polymers; photosynthesis; solid-state photochemistry; polymer batteries, role of carotenoids in plant photosynthesis; coal porosity; materials for information technology. *Mailing Add:* Chem Dept Univ Ala Box 870336 Tuscaloosa AL 35487-0336. *Fax:* 205-348-9104; *E-Mail:* Bitnet: lkispert@ua1vm.ua.edu

KISS, KLARA, PHYSICAL CHEMISTRY, POLYMER CHEMISTRY. *Current Pos:* SR RES SCIENTIST, AKZO CHEMICALS INC, 87- *Personal Data:* b Budapest, Hungary, Aug 28, 30; m 51; c 2. *Educ:* Budapest Tech Univ, dipl Chemiker, 54, PhD, 82. *Prof Exp:* Jr chemist, Res Ctr Org & Polymer Chem, Budapest, 49-51; res chemist, Res Ctr Telecommun, 55-56; res &

develop chemist, Filmfabrik AGFA, EGer, 56; res chemist, Dom Dyeing & Printing Co, Can, 57-59; sr res assoc phys chem & polymer sci, Horizons, Inc, Ohio, 61-65; res assoc electron micros, Case Western Reserve Univ, 65-67; res chemist, GAF Corp, 67-70; sr res assoc, Stauffer Chem Co, 70-87. *Mem:* Soc Appl Spectros; Asn Hungarian Chemists; Ger Chem Soc; Am Crystallog Asn; Microbeam Analysis Soc. *Res:* Kinetics of redox bulk polymerization of acrylates; photopolymerization; controlled, ultrafine particle size ferroelectrics; epitaxial crystallization of polymers; identification of wairakite single crystals by electron diffraction; microbeam analysis; mechanical properties relationship in materials. *Mailing Add:* Akzo Chem Inc Livingstone Ave Dobbs Ferry NY 10522. *Fax:* 914-693-5780

KISS, LASZLO ISTVAN, heat transfer, thermophysical properties, for more information see previous edition

KISSA, ERIK, COLLOID CHEMISTRY, TEXTILE CHEMISTRY. *Current Pos:* CONSULT, 94- *Personal Data:* b Abja, Estonia, Apr 7, 23; nat US; m 52, Selma A Tamm; c Erik H & Karl M. *Educ:* Karlsruhe Univ, dipl, 51; Univ Del, PhD(chem), 56. *Prof Exp:* Analytical chemist, E I DuPont de Nemours & Co, Inc, 51-56, res chemist, 56-67, sr res chemist, 67-74, res assoc, 74-86, sr res assoc, Du Pont Chem Dept, 86-90, res fel, 90-93. *Concurrent Pos:* UN Indust Develop Orgn consult, Atira Textile Res Inst, Ahmedabad, India, 78 & 79, Shanghai Dye Res Inst, China, 82, Korea Res Inst Chem Technol, 86, 87 & 88. *Mem:* Am Chem Soc; fel Am Inst Chem; Int Asn Colloid & Interface Scientists; Fiber Soc; Am Oil Chemists Soc. *Res:* Colloid and surface chemistry; association colloids; dispersions; emulsions adsorption; detergency; surfactants, fluorinated surfactants dyes; textile chemicals; physical chemistry of dyeing and stain resistance; polymers; analytical chemistry; surface chemistry of fibers. *Mailing Add:* 1436 Fresno Rd Wilmington DE 19803. *E-Mail:* ekissa@aol.com

KISSA, KARL MARTIN, INTEGRATED OPTICS & FIBEROPTICS, OPTICAL COMMUNICATIONS. *Current Pos:* SR OPTICAL ENGR, UNIPHASE TELECOMMUN PROD, 94- *Educ:* Duke Univ, BS, 82; Univ Del, MS, 86, PhD(elec eng), 89. *Prof Exp:* Tech staff, Clark Stark Draper Lab, 89-94. *Mem:* Inst Elec & Electronics Engrs. *Res:* Computer modelling and simulation techniques for integrated and fiber-optics; conduct experiments and collect empirical data to validate and refine models. *Mailing Add:* 9 Rebecca Lane Simsbury CT 06070. *Fax:* 860-769-3007; *E-Mail:* karl.kissa@uniphase.com

KISSANE, JOHN M, MEDICINE. *Current Pos:* Asst path, 52-53, from instr to assoc prof, 53-68, PROF PATH & PROF PATH IN PEDIAT, SCH MED, WASHINGTON UNIV, 68- *Personal Data:* b Oxford, Ohio, Mar 30, 28; m 51; c 5. *Educ:* Univ Rochester, AB, 48; Washington Univ, MD, 52. *Concurrent Pos:* Intern, Barnes Hosp, 52-53, chief resident, 53-54, asst pathologist, Barnes & Assoc Hosps, 58-; Nat Found Infantile Paralysis res fel, Sch Med, Washington Univ, 54-55 & 57-58, med alumni scholar, 70-71; mem sect renal dis, Coun Circulation, Am Heart Asn. *Mem:* AMA; Am Asn Path & Bact; Am Soc Exp Path; Histochem Soc; Int Acad Path. *Res:* Pathology; pediatric pathology; quantitative histochemistry of nervous system; kidney. *Mailing Add:* Dept Path & Pediat Washington Univ Sch Med St Louis MO 63110-1010. *Fax:* 414-259-0319

KISSEL, CHARLES LOUIS, INDUSTRIAL ORGANIC CHEMISTRY. *Current Pos:* PRIN OWNER, CNC DEVELOP, 90- *Personal Data:* b Chicago, Ill, Aug 5, 47; m 70; c 2. *Educ:* Univ Calif, Irvine, BA, 69; Univ Calif, Santa Barbara, PhD(chem), 73. *Prof Exp:* Group leader chem res, 73-84, dir res, Magna Corp, 84-85; sr res chemist, Unocal Corp, 85-90. *Mem:* Am Chem Soc; Sigma Xi; AAAS; Nat Asn Corrosion Engrs; Tech Asn Pulp & Paper Indust. *Res:* Treating mechanisms and synthesis of industrial biocides, corrosion inhibitors, scale inhibitors, emulsion breakers and water clarifiers, zero formaldehyde textile binders for non-wovens, as well as specialty chemicals; special emphasis on acrolein chemistry; sol-gel chemistry; nonionic surfactants. *Mailing Add:* 2856 Skywood Circle Anaheim CA 92804-2061

KISSEL, DAVID E, SOIL CHEMISTRY, SOIL FERTILITY. *Current Pos:* head dept, 89-96, PROF, DEPT CROP & SOIL SCI, UNIV GA, 89- *Personal Data:* b Vanderburg Co, Ind, Aug 10, 43; m 66, Mary Seneker; c Eric, Laura & Anne. *Educ:* Purdue Univ, BS, 65; Univ Ky, MS, 67, PhD(soil acidity), 69. *Prof Exp:* From asst prof to assoc prof soil chem, Tex A&M Univ, 69-77, assoc prof & asst dir for res, Blackland Res Ctr, 77-78; prof agron, Kans State Univ, 78-88. *Concurrent Pos:* Assoc ed, J Environ Qual, 75-78; ed, Soil Sci Am J, 88-90. *Mem:* Fel Am Soc Agron; fel Soil Sci Soc Am (pres-elect, 94, pres, 95); Int Soc Soil Sci; fel AAAS; Soil & Water Conserv Soc. *Res:* Plant nutrition; soil acidity; movement of water and nitrate in soils; nitrogen and phosphorus fertilizer use efficiency; ammonia volatilization; nitrogen mineralization. *Mailing Add:* Dept Crop & Soil Sci 3111 Plant-Sci Bldg Univ Ga Athens GA 30602

KISSEL, JOHN WALTER, PHARMACOLOGY. *Current Pos:* RETIRED. *Personal Data:* b St Louis, Mo, Dec 12, 25; m 53, Jeanette Dehmer; c Carl, Catherine, Julia & John. *Educ:* Wash Univ, AB, 48; St Louis Col Pharm, BS, 51; St Louis Univ, MS, 55; Univ Mich, PhD(pharmacol), 58. *Prof Exp:* Asst prof pharmacog & pharmacol, Col Pharm, Univ Fla, 56-57; assoc sr pharmacologist, Mead Johnson & Co, 57-59, group leader cent nerv syst pharmacol, 59-62, sect leader, 62-69; from pharmacologist to sr pharmacologist, 69-71, Am Cyanamid Co, mgr drug eval, 71-73, clin res assoc med res dept, Cyanamid Int, 73-75, clin res assoc, clin res dept, Lederle Labs, 75-88, sr clin res assoc, 88-91. *Mem:* Fel AAAS; Am Soc Pharmacol & Exp Therapeut; NY Acad Sci; Am Soc Clin Pharmacol Therapeut. *Res:* Central nervous system pharmacology, especially opiate tolerance and addiction; spinal cord reflexes; muscle relaxants; effect of drugs on behavior; clinical evaluation of psychotherapeutic agents; antibiotics; anti-cancer therapy. *Mailing Add:* 115 Sherwood Dr Ramsey NJ 07446

KISSEL, THOMAS ROBERT, ANALYTICAL CHEMISTRY, CLINICAL ANALYSIS. *Current Pos:* PROG LEADER, JOHNSON & JOHNSON CLIN DIAG, 94- *Personal Data:* b Chicago, Ill, Sept 26, 47; m 72. *Educ:* Univ Notre Dame, BS, 69; Univ Wis, PhD(anal chem), 74. *Prof Exp:* Res Chemist, Eastman Kodak Co, 74-94. *Mem:* Sigma Xi; Am Asn Clin Chem. *Res:* Electrochemistry, specifically ion selective electrodes; immunol Assn; chemicuminescience; fluorescience; diagnostic systems design and performance. *Mailing Add:* 200 Willowood Dr Rochester NY 14612

KISSEL, WILLIAM JOHN, POLYMER PROPERTIES. *Current Pos:* SR RES CHEMIST, AMOCO CHEM CO, 67- *Personal Data:* b New York, NY, Mar 12, 41; m 66; c 2. *Educ:* City Col New York, BS, 62; State Univ NY, Buffalo, PhD(org chem), 68. *Mem:* Am Chem Soc; Am Soc Testing Mat. *Res:* Polymer evaluation; polymer stability. *Mailing Add:* Amoco Polymers Inc 4500 McGuinni's Ferry Rd Alpharetta GA 30005

KISSELL, FRED N, MINE ENGINEERING. *Current Pos:* MINING ENGR, US BUR MINES, PITTSBURGH. *Honors & Awards:* Howard N Eavenson Award, Soc Mining Metall & Explor, 93. *Mailing Add:* Pittsburgh Res Ctr US Bur Mines PO Box 18070 Pittsburgh PA 15236

KISSELL, KENNETH EUGENE, SPACE OBSERVATORIES, SPACE SURVEILLANCE. *Current Pos:* RES ASSOC PHYSICS, UNIV MD, 87-90 & 93-; CHIEF SCIENTIST, KISSELL CONSULT, ANNANDALE, VA. *Personal Data:* b Ohio, June 28, 28; m 88, Judith L Lee; c Kevin D & Bradley T. *Educ:* Ohio State Univ, BSc, 49, MSc, 58, PhD, 69. *Prof Exp:* Res assoc rocket res lab, Res Found, Ohio State Univ, 48-51; instrumentation physicist, Propulsion Br, Flight Res Lab, Wright-Patterson AFB, 51-57, physicist, Appl Math Lab, Aeronaut Res Lab, 58-59, chief, Gen Physics Res Lab, Aerospace Res Labs, Off Aerospace Res, 59-61, physicist, 61-66, dir, 66-72, br chief, Surveillance Br, Air Force Avionics Lab, 72-75, sr scientist, Reconnaissance & Weapon Delivery Div, Air Force Avionics Lab, 76-80; staff scientist laser syst anal, Rocketdyne Div, Rockwell Int, 80-83; prin staff mem, Optical Astron, BDM Corp, 83-87; chief scientist, AMOS Observ, Rockwell Power Systs, 90-93. *Concurrent Pos:* Solar eclipse experimenter, var expeds, 54-91; ed measurement applns, Trans, Instrument Soc Am, 62-68; vis prof, Arcetri Astrophys Observ, Italy, 69-70; lectr, Wright State Univ, 70-71; assoc dir, Aerospace Instrumentation Div, ISA, 78-83; instr physics, Sinclair Community Col, 80; vis astronr, Kitt Peak Nat Observ, 81; staff mem, Automatic Photoelec Telescope Serv, Mt Hopkins, Ariz, 85- *Mem:* Am Astron Soc; Am Geophys Union; Am Inst Aeronaut & Astronaut; Int Astron Union; fel Royal Astron Soc; Optical Soc Am. *Res:* Rocket exhaust temperature measurement; automated telescopes; satellite photometry; photoelectric imaging devices; stellar spectroscopy in near infrared; solar eclipse observation; optical scattering; super luminous stars; Cepheid variables; laser systems; space telescope optical systems and science instruments. *Mailing Add:* 8828 Burbank Rd Annadale VA 22003-3856

KISSEN, ABBOTT THEODORE, PHYSIOLOGY. *Current Pos:* RETIRED. *Personal Data:* b New York, NY, Nov 24, 22; m 46, Bette Elliot; c Christine & David. *Educ:* Brooklyn Col, BA, 50; Ohio State Univ, MA, 52, PhD(zool), 56. *Prof Exp:* Res assoc physiol, Ohio State Univ, 57-59, asst prof, 59-61; res physiologist, Aerospace Med Res Lab, Wright-Patterson AFB, 61-79. *Concurrent Pos:* Am Heart Asn fel, 57-58. *Mem:* Assoc fel Aerospace Med Asn; Am Physiol Soc; Sigma Xi. *Res:* Physiological effects of acceleration stresses encountered or anticipated in aerospace flight. *Mailing Add:* 311 Passage Way Osprey FL 34229

KISSICK, WILLIAM LEE, SCIENCE EDUCATION, MEDICINE. *Current Pos:* prof & chmn dept community med, 68-71, GEORGE S PEPPER PROF PUB HEALTH & PREVENT MED, SCH MED, UNIV PA, 69-, PROF HEALTH CARE SYSTS, WHARTON SCH, 71-, PROF HEALTH POLICY & MGT, SCH NURSING, 78-, DIR, CTR HEALTH POLICY, 81- *Personal Data:* b Detroit, Mich, July 29, 32; m 56, Priscilla Harriet Dillingham; c William, Robert-John, Jonathan & Elizabeth. *Educ:* Yale Univ, BA, 53, MD, 57, MPH, 59, DrPH, 61. *Prof Exp:* Intern, Yale-New Haven Med Ctr, 57-58; resident, Montefiore Hosp & Med Ctr, New York City, 61-62; Div Community Health Serv, 62-63; spec asst to asst secy health, US Dept HEW, 64-65; dir, Off Prog Planning Eval, Off Surgeon Gen, USPHS, 66-68; exec dir nat adv comn health facil, White House, Washington, 68. *Concurrent Pos:* Vis prof, community med, Guy's Hosp Med Sch, dept soc sci & admin, London Sch Econ & Polit Sci; vis prof, Inst European Health Serv Res, Leuven Univ, 74-75; fel mem exec comt, Nat Ctr Health Care Mgt; cons, Nat Ctr Health Serv Res, Health Resources Admin, Benedum Found, WHO, Appalachian Regional Commun, Smith Kline-Beckman, Pew Mem Trust, Colonial Penn group, Ctr Disease Control; mem, Accrediting Comn on Educ for Health Serv Admin, 80-86; mem, Mayor's Comn, 81-83, coun Col Physicians Pa, 83-88, coun med soc, Am Col Physicians, 83-88; chmn comn on med affairs coun, Yale Univ, 80-86, Yale Life Corp, 87-; dir, Health Policy, chmn bd govs Leonard Davis Inst Health Econ, 89- *Mem:* AAAS; Am Col Preventive Med; Am Pub Health Asn; Philadelphia Pa Col Physicians; Asn Health Serv Res; Asn Teachers Preventive Med; Am Col Physicians Exec; Physicians Soc Responsibility; Nat Asn Pub Health Policy. *Mailing Add:* 3400 Spruce St Philadelphia PA 19104

KISSILEFF, HARRY R, PHYSIOLOGICAL PSYCHOLOGY, INGESTIVE BEHAVIOR. *Current Pos:* asst prof, 76-88, ASSOC PROF CLIN PSYCHOL, PSYCHIAT & MED, COL PHYSICIANS & SURGEONS, COLUMBIA UNIV, 89- *Personal Data:* b Philadelphia, Pa, June 1, 40; m 63, Karen Stein; c Beth P & Eliot I. *Educ:* Univ Pa, BA, 62, PhD(zool), 66. *Prof Exp:* Guest investr, Rockefeller Univ, 66-69, asst prof, 69-71; asst prof, Univ Pa, 71-76. *Concurrent Pos:* Adj asst prof, NY Univ, 77-88. *Mem:* Soc Neurosci; Soc Study Ingestive Behav (pres, 87-89); Sigma Xi; Animal Behav Soc; Am Phys Soc. *Res:* Physiological and psychological control of human food consumption; demonstrated that equienergetic foods differ in satiating effectiveness and that the naturally occuring hormone, cholecystokinin, reduces food intake in humans. *Mailing Add:* St Luke's-Roosevelt Hosp 1111 Amsterdam Ave New York NY 10025. *Fax:* 212-523-4830; *E-Mail:* hrk2@columbia.edu

KISSIN, BENJAMIN, INTERNAL MEDICINE. *Current Pos:* Assoc prof, 60-68, dir div alcoholism & drug dependence, 70-81, PROF PSYCHIAT, STATE UNIV NY, DOWNSTATE MED CTR, 68- *Personal Data:* b Philadelphia, Pa, July 17, 17; m 50; c 1. *Educ:* Columbia Univ, BS, 38; Long Island Col Med, MD, 41; Am Bd Internal Med, dipl, 51. *Concurrent Pos:* Dir alcohol clin, Kings Co Hosp, 56-67, attend physician, 67-; dir psychosom clin & assoc physician med, Jewish Hosp, Brooklyn, 56-71, consult physician, 71-81. *Mem:* Fel Am Col Physicians; NY Acad Sci. *Res:* Psychosomatic medicine, especially alcoholism; autonomic nervous system and the endocrines. *Mailing Add:* 525 E 86th St New York NY 10028-7512

KISSIN, STEPHEN ALEXANDER, MINERALOGY, ECONOMIC GEOLOGY. *Current Pos:* from asst prof to assoc prof, 75-87, PROF GEOL, LAKEHEAD UNIV, 87- *Personal Data:* b Ithaca, NY, Apr 11, 42; m 71, Margaret Madigan; c Saul & Alexandra. *Educ:* Univ Wash, BS, 64; Pa State Univ, MS, 68; Univ Toronto, PhD(geol), 74. *Prof Exp:* Aerospace scientist, Goddard Space Flight Ctr, NASA, 67-68; engr, Siemens AG, WGer, 69; fel, McMaster Univ, Hamilton, 73; Nat Res Coun fel, Dept Energy, Mines & Resources, Ottawa, 74-75. *Concurrent Pos:* Vis Res prof, Dept Chem & Geol, Ariz State Univ, 81-82; assoc, Comt Meteorites, Nat Res Coun Can, 81-91. *Mem:* Geol Asn Can; Mineral Asn Can; Mineral Soc Am; Meteoritical Soc; Sigma Xi. *Res:* Mineralogy and crystal chemistry of sulfides; genesis of ore deposits; meteoritics. *Mailing Add:* 95 Regent St Thunder Bay ON P7A 5G8 Can

KISSIN, YURY VIKTOR, POLYMER CHEMISTRY. *Current Pos:* RES ASSOC, EDISON RES LAB, MOBIL CHEM CO, 85- *Personal Data:* b Moscow, Russia, Feb 17, 37; US citizen; m 60, Natalie Ziserson; c Anna. *Educ:* Lomonosov Inst Fine Chem Technol, MD, 60; Semenov Inst Chem Physics, PhD(polymer chem), 65. *Prof Exp:* Sr researcher, Semenov Inst Chem Physics, Russia, 72-80; res assoc, Gulf Res & Develop Co, 80-85. *Res:* Chemistry and kinetics of olefin homopolymerization and copolymerization reactions with transition metal-based catalysts (ziegler-natta and metallocene catalysts); chemistry and kinetics of alkane cracking over acidic catalysts; geochemistry: catagenesis of eight hydrocarbous in petroleum. *Mailing Add:* Edison Res Lab Mobil Chem Co PO Box 3029 Edison NJ 08818-3029

KISSINGER, DAVID GEORGE, TAXONOMY, DATABASE SYSTEMS. *Current Pos:* MGR DATABASE, LOMA LINDA UNIV, 86- *Personal Data:* b Reading, Pa, July 26, 33; m 55; c 2. *Educ:* Columbia Union Col, BA, 54; Univ Md, MS, 55, PhD(entom), 57; Univ Calif, MPH, 58. *Prof Exp:* Asst entom, Univ Md, 55-57; prof biol & head dept, Oakwood Col, 58-60; prof biol & head dept, Atlantic Union Col, 60-72; prof epidemiol, Loma Linda Univ, 72-83. *Concurrent Pos:* NIH fel, 74-75; consult. *Mem:* Asn Comput Mach. *Res:* Taxonomy of new world apionidae (coleoptera); application of computer techniques to taxonomic problems. *Mailing Add:* 24414 University Ave No 40 Loma Linda CA 92354

KISSINGER, HOMER EVERETT, METAL PHYSICS. *Current Pos:* RETIRED. *Personal Data:* b Ottawa, Kans, Aug 29, 23; m 48, Jane Stinebaugh; c Alan, Donald, Charles & Brian. *Educ:* Kans State Col, BS, 49, MS, 50. *Prof Exp:* Phys sci aide, Nat Bur Stand, 48, physicist, 50-60; asst physics, Kans State Col, 49-50; sr scientist, Gen Elec Co, 60-65; sr res scientist, Battelle-Northwest, 65-87. *Mem:* Am Crystallog Asn; Sigma Xi. *Res:* Crystallography of radiation damage, phase transformations and x-ray diffraction methods; crystal chemistry of solid nuclear waste forms and containments. *Mailing Add:* 1733 Horn Ave Richland WA 99352

KISSINGER, JOHN CALVIN, MICROBIOLOGY. *Current Pos:* RETIRED. *Personal Data:* b Shamokin, Pa, June 8, 25; m 50, Nancey Bezmer; c John A & George B. *Educ:* Bucknell Univ, BS, 49, MS, 50. *Honors & Awards:* Medal, Fedn Sewage & Indust Wastes Asn, 57. *Prof Exp:* Chemist, Campbell Soup Co, 50-51; asst mgr biol standards, Sharp & Dohme, 53-55; supvr fermentation, Grain Processing Corp, 55-56; res microbiologist, Eastern Regional Res Ctr, USDA, 57-83. *Concurrent Pos:* Assoc, Nat Maple Syrup Coun, 67-75. *Mem:* Fel Asn Off Anal Chem; Int Asn Milk, Food & Environ Sanit. *Res:* Industrial waste treatment; food microbiology; meat and meat products; maple products. *Mailing Add:* 1018 S Tenth St Emmaus PA 18049

KISSINGER, PAUL BERTRAM, MAGNETIC RESONANCE. *Current Pos:* from asst prof to assoc prof, 60-70, assoc dir, Develop Acad Progs, 73-74, chmn dept, 81-84, PROF PHYSICS & ASTRON, DEPAUW UNIV, 70- *Personal Data:* b New York, NY, Mar 30, 30; m 57; c 2. *Educ:* Albright Col, BS, 52; Northwestern Univ, MS, 54; Rutgers Univ, PhD(physics), 61. *Prof Exp:* Physicist, Gen Elec Co, 56; instr physics, Rutgers Univ, 59-60. *Concurrent Pos:* Vis lectr, Univ Colo, 64; vis investr, Woods Hole Oceanog Inst, 67-68; NSF lectr, Munich, Ger, 68-69 & Lima, Peru, 70; physicist, Biol Warfare Labs, 54-56, res, 56-62; consult, IBM Corp, 67, Dept State Schs Latin Am, 70 & 84, United Ministries Higher ed, 79-82, Dept Defense Schs Europe, 77- & Danforth Assocs, 81-87; res assoc, Univ Va, 82, Midwest Assoc in Higher Ed, 88-; solar ecplise exped, Nat Geog soc, 73, US Naval Obs, 83. *Mem:* AAAS; Am Asn Physics Teachers; Am Phys Soc; Sigma Xi; Nat Sci Teachers Asn. *Res:* Electron spin resonance. *Mailing Add:* Dept Physics DePauw Univ PO Box 37 Greencastle IN 46135

KISSINGER, PETER THOMAS, CHEMISTRY, NEUROCHEMISTRY. *Current Pos:* from asst prof to assoc prof, 75-82, PROF CHEM, PURDUE UNIV, 82- *Personal Data:* b Staten Island, NY, Dec 19, 44; m 78, Candice Briggs; c William H & Samuel T. *Educ:* Union Col, BS, 66; Univ NC, PhD(chem), 70. *Prof Exp:* Res assoc chem, Univ Kans, 70-72; asst prof chem, Mich State Univ, 72-75. *Concurrent Pos:* Pres, Bioanal Systs Inc, 74- *Mem:* Am Chem Soc; Am Asn Clin Chemists; AAAS; Am Asn Mass Spectrometry; Sigma Xi; Soc Electronanal Chem (pres, 87-89); Am Asn Pharm Scientists; Electrochem Soc. *Res:* Trace organic analysis using chromatographic and electrochemical techniques; metabolic pathways of aromatic compounds; neurochemistry; organic redox reactions; chemical instrumentation; electrochemistry; pharmaceutical analysis. *Mailing Add:* Bioanal Systs 2701 Kent Ave West Lafayette IN 47906-1350. *Fax:* 765-497-1102

KISSLING, DON LESTER, PALEOECOLOGY, SEDIMENTOLOGY. *Current Pos:* OWNER & PRES, JACKALOPE GEOLOGICAL LTD, 84- *Personal Data:* b St Louis, Mo, Jan 29, 34; m 59; c 2. *Educ:* Mo Sch Mines, BS, 58; Univ Wis, MS, 60; Ind Univ, PhD(geol), 67. *Prof Exp:* Res geologist, Superior Oil Co, 60-62; from instr to assoc prof paleont, State Univ NY, Binghamton, 65-74, assoc prof geol, 74-82. *Mem:* Geol Soc Am; Soc Econ Paleontologists & Mineralogists; Paleont Soc. *Res:* Paleoecology of Paleozoic corals and bioharmal fossil assemblages; ecology of modern corals; Paleozoic sedimentary environments and recent carbonate sediments. *Mailing Add:* 406 Welch Ave Berthoud CO 80513

KISSLINGER, CARL, SEISMOLOGY. *Current Pos:* prof geol sci, 72-94, dir, Coop Inst Res Environ Sci, 72-79 & 93-94, EMER PROF GEOL SCI, UNIV COLO, BOULDER, 94- *Personal Data:* b St Louis, Mo, Aug 30, 26; m 48, Millicent Thorson; c Susan, Karen, Ellen, Pamela & Jerome. *Educ:* St Louis Univ, BS, 47, MS, 49, PhD(geophys), 52. *Honors & Awards:* Alexander von Humboldt Found US Sr Scientist Award, 79; Commemorative Medal, USSR Acad Sci, 85; John Wesley Powell Award, US Geol Surv, 92. *Prof Exp:* From instr to prof geophys & geophys eng, St Louis Univ, 49-72, chmn dept earth & atmospheric sci, 63-72. *Concurrent Pos:* UNESCO expert in seismol & chief tech adv, Int Inst Seismol & Earthquake Eng, Tokyo, 66-67; consult, US Dept Energy, 69-78; chmn comt seismol, Nat Acad Sci-Nat Res Coun, 70-72, mem US Geodynamics Comt, 75-78; mem earth sci adv panel, NSF, 71-74; mem, US Nat Comt, Int Union Geod & Geophys, 74-92, mem bur, 75-83, vpres, 83-91; mem earthquake hazards reduction adv group, Off Sci Technol Policy, 77-78; mem earthquake studies adv panel, US Geol Surv, 77-82, chmn, 81-82; mem comt scholarly communication with People's Repub China, Nat Acad Sci, 78-81, chmn Subcomt on Earthquake Res, 84-88; fel, Univ Colo, Boulder, 79-; mem comt adv, US Geol Surv, 83-88; mem, Gov Bd, Am Inst Physics, 89-95; chmn, Panel Seismic Hazard Eval, Nat Res Coun, 93-96. *Mem:* Fel AAAS; Soc Explor Geophys; Seismol Soc Am (pres, 72-73); fel Am Geophys Union (foreign secy, 74-84); fel Geol Soc Am; corresp mem Austrian Acad Sci. *Res:* Generation of seismic waves by explosions and earthquakes; earthquake source physics; earthquake prediction. *Mailing Add:* Coop Inst Res Environ Sci Univ Colo Campus Box 216 Boulder CO 80309-0216. *Fax:* 303-492-1149; *E-Mail:* kissling@terra.colorado.edu

KISSLINGER, FRED, METALLURGICAL ENGINEERING. *Current Pos:* PARTNER, ASKELAND, KISSLINGER & WOLF, METALL ENG CONSULTS, 73- *Personal Data:* b St Louis, Mo, Nov 19, 19; m 45; c 3. *Educ:* Mo Sch Mines, BS, 42; Univ Cincinnati, MS, 45, PhD(metall eng), 47. *Prof Exp:* From instr to assoc prof metall eng, Ill Inst Technol, 47-64; assoc prof, 64-69, prof Metall Eng, Univ Mo-Rolla, 69-. *Mem:* Am Soc Metals; Am Inst Mining, Metall & Petrol Engrs. *Res:* Thermodynamics; heat treating. *Mailing Add:* 1108 Winchester Dr Rolla MO 65401

KISSLINGER, LEONARD SOL, THEORETICAL PHYSICS. *Current Pos:* PROF PHYSICS, CARNEGIE-MELLON UNIV, 68- *Personal Data:* b St Louis, Mo, Aug 15, 30; m 56. *Educ:* St Louis Univ, BS, 51; Ind Univ, MS, 52, PhD(physics), 56. *Prof Exp:* From instr to prof physics, Case Western Reserve Univ, 56-68. *Concurrent Pos:* Res Corp fel, Bohr Inst, Copenhagen, Denmark, 58-59; res assoc, Mass Inst Technol, 66-67; vis staff mem, Los Alamos Sci Lab, 69- *Mem:* Am Phys Soc; Sigma Xi. *Res:* Nuclear models and structure; many-body problem; particle physics. *Mailing Add:* Dept Physics Carnegie-Mellon Univ Pittsburgh PA 15213

KISSMAN, HENRY MARCEL, ORGANIC CHEMISTRY, COMPUTER SCIENCES. *Current Pos:* CONSULT, 92- *Personal Data:* b Graz, Austria, Sept 9, 22; nat US; m 56; c 2. *Educ:* Sterling Col, BS, 44; Univ Cincinnati, MS, 48; Univ Rochester, PhD(org chem), 50. *Honors & Awards:* Super Serv Award, US Dept Health, Educ & Welfare, 73; Dirs Award, NIH, 85. *Prof Exp:* Sr asst scientist org chem, NIH, 50-52; res chemist, Lederle Labs Div, Am Cyanamid Co, 52-62; dept head tech info, 62-67; dir sci info facil, US Food & Drug Admin, DC, 67-70; assoc dir specialized info servs, US Nat Libr Med, 70-92. *Concurrent Pos:* Chmn comt study environ qual info progs in fed govt, Off Sci & Technol; mem adv bd, Chem Abstr Serv, 74-77; chmn, Toxicol Info Subcomt, US Dept Health, Educ & Welfare, 73-; mem, Task Force, Environ Cancer & Heart & Lung Dis, 89-92; chmn, Sect Inform Comput & Commun, AAAS, 80-81. *Mem:* AAAS; Am Chem Soc; Am Soc Info Sci; Soc

Toxicol; hon mem Med Libr Asn. *Res:* Ethylenimine chemistry; amino acids; carbohydrates; nucleosides; steroids; tetracyclines; chemical documentation; development and national operation of online databases in toxicology such as toxline, chemline, hazardous substances data bank; AIDS drugs, AIDS trials. *Mailing Add:* 14809 Pennfield Circle Apt 404 Silver Spring MD 20906-1594. *Fax:* 301-460-0786; *E-Mail:* henryk@cpcug.org

KISSMEYER-NIELSEN, ERIK, FOOD SCIENCE, BOTANY. *Current Pos:* INT ADV, AGR & FOOD INDUST, 66- *Personal Data:* b Silkeborg, Denmark, Oct 22, 22; m 62; c 2. *Educ:* Royal Vet & Agr Col, Copenhagen, BS, 48; Cornell Univ, MS, 60; Univ Wis, PhD(food sci), 64. *Prof Exp:* Trainee food technol, Am Scand Soc, 48-50; inspector, R T French Co, NY, 50-53; asst mgr, Grimstrup Coop Starch & Dehydration Plant, Denmark, 53-58; asst food sci, Cornell Univ, 58-60 & Univ Wis, 60-63; asst prof biochem & food sci, Univ Del, 63-66. *Concurrent Pos:* Agr & food indust adv, UN Indust Develop Orgn & World Bank, 70-73; regional agr & food indust adv, UN Econ Comn for Africa, 73-75, Agr & Food Indust Adv Int, 75- *Mem:* Fel AAAS; Inst Food Technol. *Mailing Add:* 65 Crabtree Rd Concord MA 01742. *Fax:* 978-287-0181; *E-Mail:* kissmeyer@aol.com

KIST, JOSEPH EDMUND, MATHEMATICS. *Current Pos:* assoc prof, 66-67, PROF MATH, NMEX STATE UNIV, 67- *Personal Data:* b Buffalo, NY, Aug 11, 29; div; c 1. *Educ:* Univ Buffalo, BA, 52; Purdue Univ, MS, 54, PhD(math), 57. *Prof Exp:* Instr math, Purdue Univ, 57; asst prof, Wayne State Univ, 57-59 & Pa State Univ, 59-62; vis assoc prof, Purdue Univ, 62-63; assoc prof, Pa State Univ, 63-66. *Mem:* Fel AAAS; Am Math Soc; Math Asn Am; Sigma Xi. *Res:* Functional analysis; lattices; semigroups. *Mailing Add:* Dept Math NMex State Univ Las Cruces NM 88003

KISTER, JAMES MILTON, TOPOLOGY. *Current Pos:* from instr to assoc prof, 59-66, chmn dept, 71-73, PROF MATH, UNIV MICH, ANN ARBOR, 66- *Personal Data:* b Cleveland, Ohio, June 29, 30; m 56, 78, Jane Bridge; c Karen L. *Educ:* Wooster Col, AB, 52; Univ Wis, AM, 56, PhD, 59. *Prof Exp:* Res asst, Los Alamos Sci Lab, 53-55. *Concurrent Pos:* Fel, Off Naval Res, Univ Va, 60-61; mem, Inst Advan Study, 62-64; vis prof, Univ Calif, Los Angeles, 67; vis fel, Clare Hall, Cambridge Univ, Eng, 70; ed, Duke Math J, 72-75; vis mem, Institut des Hautes Etudes, France, 74; ed, Mich Math J, 76-78, managing ed, 77-78, 83-85 & 86-88; vis fel Wolfson Col, Oxford Univ, Eng, 77 & 85-86; hon res fel, Univ Col, London, 93. *Mem:* Am Math Soc; Math Asn Am. *Res:* Topology; isotopies; transformation groups; manifolds. *Mailing Add:* Dept Math Univ Mich Ann Arbor MI 48109. *Fax:* 313-763-0937

KISTIAKOWSKY, VERA, ELEMENTARY PARTICLE PHYSICS. *Current Pos:* scientist, Lab Nuclear Sci, 65-69, sr res scientist, Dept Physics, 69-72, prof, 72-94, EMER PROF PHYSICS, MASS INST TECHNOL, 94- *Personal Data:* b Princeton, NJ, Sept 9, 28; div; c Marc L & Karen M (Fischer). *Educ:* Mt Holyoke Col, AB, 48; Univ Calif, PhD(chem), 52. *Hon Degrees:* DSc, Mt Holyoke Col, 78. *Prof Exp:* Scientist, USN Radiol Defense Lab, 52-53; Berliner fel physics, Radiation Lab, Univ Calif, 53-54; res assoc, Columbia Univ, 54-57, instr, 57-59; from asst prof to adj assoc prof, Brandeis Univ, 59-65. *Mem:* Fel AAAS; fel Am Phys Soc; Asn Women Sci (pres, 82-84). *Res:* Observational astrophysics. *Mailing Add:* 29 Bellis Circle Cambridge MA 02140. *E-Mail:* verak@space.mit.edu

KISTLER, ALAN L(EE), FLUID DYNAMICS. *Current Pos:* PROF MECH ENG & ASTRONAUT, TECHNOL INST, NORTHWESTERN UNIV, EVANSTON, 69- *Personal Data:* b Laramie, Wyo, Nov 26, 28; m 55; c 3. *Educ:* Johns Hopkins Univ, BE, 50, MS, 52, PhD(aeronaut), 55. *Prof Exp:* Res group supvr, Jet Propulsion Lab, Calif Inst Technol, 57-61; assoc prof, Yale Univ, 61-65; fluid physics sect mgr, Jet Propulsion Lab, Calif Inst Technol, 65-69. *Mem:* Am Phys Soc; Am Soc Mech Engrs; AAAS. *Res:* Diffusion in turbulent flow fields; turbulence in compressible media; mechanics of wakes and separated flows. *Mailing Add:* 3241 Park Pl Evanston IL 60201

KISTLER, MALATHI K, CHEMISTRY. *Current Pos:* RES ASSOC PROF, DEPT CHEM, UNIV SC, 76- *Personal Data:* b India, Oct 29, 44. *Educ:* Indian Inst Sci, PhD(biochem), 70. *Mem:* Endocrine Soc; Cell Biol Soc. *Mailing Add:* Dept Chem Univ SC Columbia SC 29208-0001. *Fax:* 803-777-9521

KISTLER, RONALD WAYNE, GEOLOGY. *Current Pos:* GEOLOGIST, US GEOL SURV, 60- *Personal Data:* b Chicago, Ill, May 18, 31; m 57, Joyce F Lohr; c Julie & Bryan. *Educ:* Johns Hopkins Univ, BA, 53; Univ Calif, Berkeley, PhD(geol), 60. *Concurrent Pos:* Vis prof, Northwestern Univ, 71. *Mem:* Chinese Soc Mineral Petrol & Geochemistry; Geol Soc Am; Am Geophys Union. *Res:* Structural geology; geochronology. *Mailing Add:* US Geol Surv 345 Middlefield Rd MS 937 Menlo Park CA 94025. *Fax:* 650-329-4664

KISTLER, WILSON STEPHEN, JR, BIOCHEMISTRY, REPRODUCTIVE BIOLOGY. *Current Pos:* from asst prof to assoc prof, 75-86, PROF CHEM, UNIV SC, 86- *Personal Data:* b Newport News, Va, Mar 1, 42; m 76, Malathi Krishnamachari; c Mira & Lisa. *Educ:* Princeton Univ, AB, 64; Harvard Univ, PhD(biochem), 70. *Prof Exp:* Res assoc, Dept Microbiol & Molecular Genetics, Sch Med, Harvard Univ, 70-71; Ben May Lab Cancer Res, Univ Chicago, 71-75. *Mem:* Am Soc Biol Chemists; Am Chem Soc. *Res:* Study of changes in basic nuclear proteins accompanying mammalian spermatogenesis and the regulation of protein synthesis by androgenic steroid hormones; gene analysis using recombinant DNA. *Mailing Add:* Dept Chem Univ SC Columbia SC 29208-0001. *Fax:* 803-777-9521; *E-Mail:* kistler@chem.scarolina.edu

KISTNER, CLIFFORD RICHARD, INORGANIC CHEMISTRY. *Current Pos:* from asst prof to assoc prof, 64-68, PROF CHEM & CHMN DEPT, UNIV WIS, LA CROSSE, 68- *Personal Data:* b Cincinnati, Ohio, Dec 16, 36; m 61, Kathleen Shannow; c Amalia. *Educ:* Carthage Col, AB, 59; Univ Iowa, MS, 62, PhD(chem), 63. *Prof Exp:* Instr chem, Univ Iowa, 63, asst prof, 63-64. *Mem:* AAAS; Am Chem Soc; Sigma Xi. *Res:* Inorganic coordination chemistry. *Mailing Add:* N1596 Skyline Blvd La Crosse WI 54601-8439

KISTNER, DAVID HAROLD, ENTOMOLOGY. *Current Pos:* instr, 59-60, from asst prof to prof, 60-93, EMER PROF BIOL, CALIF STATE UNIV, 93- *Personal Data:* b Cincinnati, Ohio, July 30, 31; m 57; c 2. *Educ:* Univ Chicago, AB, 52, SB, 56, PhD(zool), 57. *Prof Exp:* Asst termites, Univ Chicago, 53-54, asst comp anat, 55, field zoologist comp anat & arthropods, 56-57; instr biol, Univ Rochester, 57-59. *Concurrent Pos:* NSF grants, 58-59, 60-71 & 72-88; Guggenheim Mem Found fel, 65-66; hon res assoc, Div Insects, Field Mus Natural Hist, Chicago, 67 & Atlantica Ecol Res Sta, Zimbabwe; dir, Shinner Inst Study Interrelated Insects, 68-72; consult developer, Dowtlanco, Indianapolis, Ind. *Mem:* AAAS; Entom Soc Am; Soc Study Evolution; Soc Syst Zool; Am Soc Zool; fel Explorers Club. *Res:* Systematics, evolution; zoogeography and behavior of myrmecophilous and termitophilous insects; systematics of Staphylinidae. *Mailing Add:* 3 Canterbury Circle Chico CA 95926-2411. *Fax:* 530-898-4363; *E-Mail:* dkistner@ougrp.csuchico.edu

KISTNER, OTTMAR CASPER, PHOTO NUCLEAR PHYSICS, HEAVY ION NUCLEAR REACTIONS. *Current Pos:* Asst physicist, 59-63, assoc physicist, 63-66, PHYSICIST, BROOKHAVEN NAT LAB, 66- *Personal Data:* b New York, NY, Mar 22, 30; m 59, Ann Ripoli; c Lisa, Dorothea & Regina. *Educ:* Polytech Inst Brooklyn, BS, 52; Columbia Univ, PhD(physics), 59. *Concurrent Pos:* Guest physicist, Max Planck Inst Nuclear Physics, 69-70, Weizmann Inst Sci, 80. *Mem:* Sigma Xi; fel Am Phys Soc. *Res:* Experimental nuclear physics; nuclear structure and hyperfine interactions by beta and gamma ray spectroscopy; on line spectroscopy with heavy ion reactions; Mossbauer effect; medium energy (350 MeV) photonuclear research and facility development of Laser-Electron-Gamma-Source at BNL NSLS. *Mailing Add:* Physics Dept 510A Brookhaven Nat Lab Upton NY 11973. *E-Mail:* kistner@legs4.phy.bnl.gov

KISVARSANYI, EVA BOGNAR, geology, petrology, for more information see previous edition

KISVARSANYI, GEZA, ECONOMIC GEOLOGY, ORE DEPOSITS. *Current Pos:* from instr to prof, 62-92, EMER PROF GEOL, UNIV MO, ROLLA, 92- *Personal Data:* b Tokay, Hungary, Feb 23, 26; US citizen; m 56, Eva Bognar; c Erika G. *Educ:* Eotvos Lorand, Budapest, MS, 52; Univ Mo, Rolla, PhD(geol), 66. *Prof Exp:* Asst prof geol, Eotvos Lorand, Budapest, 52-55; chief geologist, Ore Mining & Develop Co, Hungary, 55-56; explor geologist, Bear Creek Mining Co Div, Kennecott Copper Corp, 57-62. *Concurrent Pos:* Chmn, Int Geol Conf; consult, gold explor; mem, doctoral fac, Univ Mo, Rolla. *Mem:* Geol Soc Am; Soc Econ Geol. *Res:* Hydrothermal ore deposits; Mississippi Valley-type lead-zinc deposits; iron-titanium ore deposits; geotectonics of the midcontinent; remote sensing, radar, landsat, of geologic structures, precious and base metal deposits, prophyry copper and molybdenum deposits; author and editor of four books and over 160 papers and reports of investigations. *Mailing Add:* 2339 Cass St Sarasota FL 34231

KISZENICK, WALTER, PHYSICS, ELECTRICAL ENGINEERING. *Current Pos:* from instr to assoc prof physics, 53-64, ASSOC PROF PHYSICS & NUCLEAR ENG, POLYTECH INST NY, 62- *Personal Data:* b New York, NY, Apr 1, 18; m 43; c 2. *Educ:* Brooklyn Col, BA, 39; Polytech Inst Brooklyn, MS, 47, PhD(physics), 54. *Prof Exp:* Jr metallurgist, NY Naval Shipyard, 41-43; jr scientist, Los Alamos Sci Lab, 44-46; res asst phosphors, Polytech Inst Brooklyn, 46-52; physicist, Freed Radio Co, 52-53. *Mem:* Am Phys Soc; Electron Micros Soc Am; Sigma Xi. *Res:* Dielectric properties of phosphors; physical properties of ice. *Mailing Add:* Dept Physics 333 Jay St Brooklyn NY 11201

KIT, SAUL, BIOCHEMISTRY, CANCER. *Current Pos:* vis prof virol, 62, prof biochem & head, Div Biochem Virol, 62-93, EMER PROF BIOCHEM, BAYLOR COL MED, 93- *Personal Data:* b Passaic, NJ, Nov 25, 20; m 45, Dorothy Anken; c Sally, Malon & Gordon. *Educ:* Univ Calif, AB, 48, PhD(biochem), 51. *Prof Exp:* Nat Cancer Inst fel biochem, Chicago, 51-52, Nat Found Infantile Paralysis fel, 52; res biochemist, Univ Tex M D Anderson Hosp & Tumor Inst, 53-55; asst prof biochem, Col Med, Baylor Univ, 56-57; from asst prof to assoc prof, Post-Grad Sch Med, Univ Tex, 57-61. *Concurrent Pos:* Assoc biochemist, Univ Tex M D Anderson Hosp & Tumor Inst, 57-60, biochemist & chief Sect Nucleoprotein Metab, 61-62; mem Cancer Virol Panel, Nat Cancer Inst, USPHS, 61-62; mem cancer virol panel, USPHS, 61-62, consult, 71-; Nat Inst Arthritis & Infectious Dis res career award, 63-88; mem deleg, US-USSR exchange virol, 67; sci consult, molecular biol dept, Miles Lab, Elkhart, Ind, 69-72; vis prof, Inst Venezuela, Olano & Caracas, 71, Univ Buenos Aires, Argentina, 71 & Calouste Gulbenkian Found, Lisbon, Portugal, 73; chairperson, Pathobiol Chem Study Sect, NIH, 75-79; sci adv bd mem, Am Genetics Int, Inc, Denver, Colo, 81-84; distinguished vis prof, dept microbiol, La Trobe Univ, Australia, 82; chmn sci adv bd, Novagene, Inc, Houston, 82- *Mem:* Am Soc Biol Chemists; Am Cell Biol (treas, 65-67, pres, 71); Am Chem Soc; Am Soc Virol; Am Soc Microbiol; Am Asn Cancer Res; corresp mem Arg Soc Virol. *Res:* Molecular biology; biochemical virology; biochemistry of cancer; nucleic acids; genetically engineered vaccines; author of over 250 research publications; holder of 11 US patents and 13 foreign patents on vaccines. *Mailing Add:* 11935 Wink Rd Houston TX 77024. *Fax:* 713-781-6078; *E-Mail:* saulkit@hal-pc.org

KITABCHI, ABBAS E, INTERNAL MEDICINE, ENDOCRINOLOGY & DIABETES. *Current Pos:* from asst prof to assoc prof med, 68-73, assoc prof biochem, 68-73, PROF MED & BIOCHEM, CTR HEALTH SCI, UNIV TENN, 73-, CHIEF, DIV ENDOCRINOL & METAB & DIR, CLIN RES CTR, 73- *Personal Data:* b Tehran, Iran, Aug 28, 33; US citizen; c 4. *Educ:* Cornell Col, BA, 54; Univ Okla, MS, 56, PhD(med sci), 58, MD, 65. *Prof Exp:* Res assoc biochem, Okla Med Res Found, 60-61, biochemist, 61-65, sr investr, 65-66; instr med, Univ Wash, 66-68. *Concurrent Pos:* Fel biochem, Okla Med Res Found, 58-60; NIH spec fel endocrinol, Univ Wash, 66-68; assoc chief staff res & chief, Endocrinol & Metab Labs, Vet Admin Hosp, 68-73, assoc chief metab, Med Serv, 73-; chief, Diabetes & Endocrinol Clin, City of Memphis Hosp; consult, Baptist Hosp; chief endocrinol & attend physician, Univ Tenn Hosp; vis scientist, Va Mason Res Ctr & Univ Wash, Seattle, 90-91. *Mem:* Fel Am Col Physicians; Asn Am Physicians; Am Fedn Clin Res; Am Diabetes Asn; Endocrine Soc; Am Soc Biochem & Molecular Biol; Am Soc Clin Investrs; Am Inst Nutrit. *Res:* Mechanism of action of steroids and pancreatic hormones at molecular level; pathogenesis and treatment of diabetes; clinical diabetes and its acute complications. *Mailing Add:* Dept Med Univ Tenn Memphis Rm 335M 951 Court Ave Memphis TN 38163-0001. *Fax:* 901-577-4340

KITAHATA, LUKE MASAHIKO, ANESTHESIA, PAIN & NEUROSURGICAL ANESTHESIA. *Current Pos:* PROF ANESTHESIOL, SCH MED, YALE UNIV, 73- *Personal Data:* b Jan 12, 25; m; c 3. *Educ:* Tokyo Imperial Univ, Japan, MD, 47. *Mailing Add:* Dept Anesthesiol 789 Howard Ave New Haven CT 06504

KITAI, REUVEN, ELECTRICAL ENGINEERING. *Current Pos:* from assoc prof to prof, 65-88, EMER PROF ELEC ENG, MCMASTER UNIV, 88- *Personal Data:* b Johannesburg, SAfrica, Oct 4, 24; m 52; c 3. *Educ:* Univ Witwatersrand, BSc, 44, MSc, 48, DSc(elec eng), 62. *Prof Exp:* Lectr elec eng, Univ Witwatersrand, 47-55, sr lectr, 55-64. *Concurrent Pos:* Vis lectr, Eng Labs, Cambridge Univ, 53-54 & Dept Elec Eng, Imp Col, Univ London, 61-62; vis res officer, Stand Telecommun Labs, Ltd, Eng, 61 & Brown Boveri Co, Switz, 77; pres, Instrumentation & Measurement Soc, Inst Elec & Electronics Engrs, 82. *Mem:* Sr mem Inst Elec & Electronics Engrs. *Res:* Instrumentation. *Mailing Add:* Dept Elec Eng McMaster Univ Hamilton ON L8S 4L7 Can

KITAIGORODSKII, SERGEI ALEXANDER, PHYSICAL OCEANOGRAPHY. *Current Pos:* CHIEF SCIENTIST, INST OCEANOG, P P SHIRSOV, ACAD SCI, RUSSIA, 94- *Personal Data:* b Moscow, USSR, Sept 13, 34; m 69, Sisko-Kiuru; c Marins & Katarina. *Educ:* Inst Physics Atmosphere Acad Sci, USSR, PhD(geophys), 60; Inst Oceanology Acad Sci, DSc, 68. *Hon Degrees:* DSc, Univ Liege, Belfium, 94. *Honors & Awards:* Rosenstiel Gold Medal Award, 73. *Prof Exp:* Head lab res, Inst Oceanog Acad Sci, USSR, 68-78; lectr, Inst Phys Oceanog, Univ Copenhagen, 79-85; prof oceanog, Dept Earth & Planetary Sci, Johns Hopkins Univ, 80-92; foreign stypend, Finnish Acad Sci, 93. *Mem:* Foreign mem Danish Royal Acad Sci & Lett; hon mem Finnish Geophys Soc. *Res:* Oceanic turbulence and its modelling; physics of air-sea interaction; wave motions in the ocean; geophysical fluid dynamics; 120 papers in Russian and major western journals; 4 scientific monographs. *Mailing Add:* Krasikova St 23 Moscow 117218 Russia. *Fax:* 7-095-1245983

KITANI, OSAMU, AGRICULTURE. *Current Pos:* chmn, Dept Agr Eng, 80-88, dir libr fac, 91-93, PROF, UNIV TOKYO, 78- *Personal Data:* b Tokyo, Japan, Apr 1, 35; m 64, Shigeko Tanaka; c Yukiko & Mariko. *Educ:* Univ Tokyo, BAgr, 59, MAgr, 61, DAgr, 64; Mich State Univ, PhD, 66. *Prof Exp:* Assoc prof, Mie Univ, Japan, 66-78. *Concurrent Pos:* Fel, Alexander von Humboldt Found, Ger, 72; guest prof, Tech Univ Munich, 72-73; expert mem, Sci & Tech Agency, Tokyo, 76-87, Sci Coun, Ministry Educ, Tokyo, 79-89 & Coun Sci & Tech Prime Ministers Off, 81-; mem, Farm Mechanization Coun, Ministry Agr Forestry & Fishery, 93- *Mem:* Japan Fedn Agr Eng (vpres, 83-84); Japan Agr Systs Soc (vpres, 85-88, pres, 89-91); Am Japan Soc; Int Comn Agr Eng (secy, 90-, vpres, 94-); Japan Soc Energy & Resources; Japanese Soc Agr Mach (pres, 92-); Am Soc Agr Engrs; hon mem Ital Asn Agr Engrs. *Mailing Add:* Kataseyama 3-3-10 Kanagaw Fugisawa-shi 251 Japan

KITANIDIS, PETER K, CIVIL ENGINEERING. *Current Pos:* PROF CIVIL ENG, STANFORD UNIV. *Honors & Awards:* Walter L Huber Civil Eng Res Prize, Am Soc Civil Engrs, 94. *Mailing Add:* Dept Civil Eng Stanford Univ Stanford CA 94305

KITAY, JULIAN I, INTERNAL MEDICINE, ENDOCRINOLOGY. *Current Pos:* assoc dean curricular affairs, 78-84, Asst vpres & assoc dean acad affairs, 84-92, PROF INTERNAL MED, PHYSIOL & BIOPHYS, 78-, ASSOC VPRES & SR ASSOC DEAN ACAD & STUDENT AFFAIRS, UNIV TEX MED BR, GALVESTON, TEX, 92- *Personal Data:* b Kearny, NJ, Aug 29, 27; m 73; c 2. *Educ:* Princeton Univ, AB, 49; Harvard Med Sch, MD, 54. *Prof Exp:* Intern med, Grace-New Haven Hosp, Conn, 54-55; asst resident, Beth Israel Hosp, Mass, 55-56; instr, Col Physicians & Surgeons, Columbia Univ, 58-59; from asst prof to assoc prof internal med, Sch Med, Univ Va, 59-70, from asst prof to assoc prof physiol, 61-70, prof internal med & physiol, 70-78. *Concurrent Pos:* Commonwealth Fund fel, Col Physicians & Surgeons, Columbia Univ, 56-58; USPHS res career develop award, 61-70; asst physician, Med Serv, Presby Hosp, NY, 58-59; attend physician, Univ Hosp, Univ Va, 59-78, head div endocrinol & metab, Dept Internal Med, 70-78; mem neuroendocrinol panel, Int Brain Res Orgn. *Mem:* Endocrine Soc; Am Fedn Clin Res; Am Soc Clin Invest; Am Physiol Soc; Soc Exp Biol & Med. *Res:* Endocrine physiology; clinical aspects of endocrine disease. *Mailing Add:* Off Dean Med Univ Tex Med Br Galveston TX 77550

KITAZAWA, GEORGE, CHEMISTRY, WOOD SCIENCE. *Current Pos:* CONSULT & TECH INTERPRETER, 80- *Personal Data:* b San Jose, Calif, May 2, 17; m 43; c 3. *Educ:* Univ Calif, BS, 40; State Univ NY, MS, 44, PhD(wood technol), 47. *Prof Exp:* Technician, Guayule Rubber Res, War Relocation Auth, Calif, 42-43; indust res fel, State Univ NY Col Forestry, Syracuse, 44-47; res wood technologist, Casein Co Am, NY, 47; wood technologist, Timber Eng Co, 47-50; res assoc, State Univ NY Col Forestry, Syracuse, 50-53; res physicist, Gillette Safety Razor Co, 53-56; group leader, Cent Res Lab, Borden Chem Co, Philadelphia, 56-57, asst lab head, 57-59, lab head, 59-73; mgr, Wood Sci Group, Koppers Co, 73-78, forest prod res sect, 78-80. *Concurrent Pos:* Industrial liaison hydrostatic and ultrasonic pipe testers & coke oven mach for steel indust. *Mem:* AAAS; Am Chem Soc; Asn Asian Studies. *Res:* Wood preservatives and fire retardants; polymer characterization; analytical chemistry; adhesives; instrumentation; sonic and ultrasonic nondestructive testing; surface chemistry and physics; wood physics; steel industry machinery. *Mailing Add:* 926 Harvard Rd Monroeville PA 15146-4338

KITCHELL, JAMES FREDERICK, AQUATIC ECOLOGY, BIOENERGETICS. *Current Pos:* Proj assoc ecol, Inst Environ Studies, 70-72, asst scientist, 72-74, asst prof, 74-77, ASSOC PROF ZOOL, UNIV WIS-MADISON, 77- *Personal Data:* b Gary, Ind, July 20, 42; m 77; c 2. *Educ:* Ball State Teachers Col, BS, 64; Univ Colo, PhD(biol), 70. *Concurrent Pos:* Scientist, Smithsonian Inst Proj, Skadar Lake, Yugoslavia, 72-77; vis scientist, Nat Marine Fisheries Serv, Honolulu, 73-78. *Mem:* Am Fisheries Soc; Ecol Soc Am; Int Soc Limnol; AAAS; Am Inst Biol Sci. *Res:* Application of ecosystem models; predator-prey interactions; trophic ecology. *Mailing Add:* Dept Zool 145 Noland Hall Univ Wis 250 N Mills St Madison WI 53706-1794

KITCHELL, JENNIFER ANN, PALEOBIOLOGY, EVOLUTIONARY THEORY. *Current Pos:* res assoc, Univ Wis-Madison, 78-80, ASST SCIENTIST GEOL & ZOOL, 80- *Personal Data:* b Zanesville, Ohio, May 25, 45. *Educ:* Univ Wis, BS, 68, MS, 71, PhD(geol), 78. *Prof Exp:* at Mus Paleont, Univ Mich, Ann Arbor. *Mem:* Sigma Xi; Soc Econ Paleontol & Mineralogists; Soc Oceanog & Limnol; Paleont Soc; Geol Soc Am. *Res:* Paleobiology; coevolution; taxonomic diversification; predator-prey interactions; siliceous sedimentation; paleolimnological studies of predator-prey interactions. *Mailing Add:* 5706 Bittersweet Pl Madison WI 53705

KITCHELL, RALPH LLOYD, VETERINARY ANATOMY. *Current Pos:* prof vet anat, 72-90, EMER PROF, SCH VET MED, UNIV CALIF, DAVIS, 90- *Personal Data:* b Waukee, Iowa, July 9, 19; m 47; c 3. *Educ:* Iowa State Univ, DVM, 43; Univ Minn, PhD(human anat), 51. *Honors & Awards:* Small Animal Res Award, Rallston-Purina, 85. *Prof Exp:* Instr vet bact, Kans State Col, 43; instr vet med, Univ Minn, St Paul, 47-51, from assoc prof to prof vet anat, 51-64, head dept, 54; dean vet med, Kans State Univ, 64-66; prof vet anat, Iowa State Univ, 66-72, dean col vet med & dir vet med res inst, 66-71. *Concurrent Pos:* USPHS res fel, Swed & Eng, 57-58; vis prof, Sch Vet Med, Univ Calif, Davis, 71-72; res fel & vis prof, Royal Vet Col, Edinburgh, Scotland, 76; vis prof, Sch Vet Med, Massey Univ, Palmerstone North, New Zealand. *Mem:* NY Acad Sci; Am Vet Med Asn; Am Asn Vet Anat (secy, 51, pres, 54); Am Asn Anatomists; Am Vet Neurol Asn; Soc Neurosci. *Res:* Veterinary neuroanatomy; sexual and fetal physiology; somatosensory physiology. *Mailing Add:* Dept Anat Univ Calif Sch Vet Med Davis CA 95616-8762. *Fax:* 530-752-7690

KITCHEN, SUMNER WENDELL, NUCLEAR SCIENCE, NUCLEAR ENGINEERING. *Current Pos:* res assoc reactors physics, Knolls Atomic Power Lab, 54-56, mgr, 56-78, sr physicist, reactor physics, 78-79, mgr, Qual Assurance Eng, 79-90, CONSULT QUAL ASSURANCE, KNOLLS ATOMIC POWER LAB, 90- *Personal Data:* b Somerville, Mass, Sept 17, 21. *Educ:* Oberlin Col, BA, 43; NY Univ, PhD(physics), 51. *Prof Exp:* Physicist, physics of metals, Frankford Arsenal, 43-46; instr physics, NY Univ, 46-50; group leader accelerator design, E O Lawrence Radiation Lab, 50-54. *Concurrent Pos:* Consult, Dept Defense, 48-49. *Mem:* Am Phys Soc; Am Nuclear Soc; NY Acad Sci; Sr Mem Am Soc Qual Control. *Res:* Reactor and criticality safety; reactor physics; gas discharges; accelerators. *Mailing Add:* 1352 Stanley Lane Schenectady NY 12309

KITCHEN, W J, VERY LARGE SCALE INTEGRATION-ULTRA LARGE SCALE INTEGRATION RESEARCH, DEVELOPMENT & APPLICATIONS, SEMICONDUCTOR MANUFACTURING TECHNOLOGY. *Current Pos:* dir, Semiconductor Res & Develop Labs, Semiconductor Prods Sector, 82-86, vpres dir, Advan Tech Ctr, 86-91, vpres dir technol, 91-93, VPRES DIR TECHNOL & QUAL, MOTOROLA AUTOMOTIVE, ENERGY & CONTROLS GROUP, 93- *Personal Data:* b Colonial Heights, Va, Mar 20, 42; m 64, Maryellen Fuller; c Scott & Jeffrey. *Educ:* Va Mil Inst, BS, 64; Univ Va, MS, 66, ScD, 68; Indust Col Armed Forces, MBA, 81. *Prof Exp:* Tech mgr & sr technologist, Nat Security Agency, 68-82. *Concurrent Pos:* Mem, Sci Adv Bd, Motorola. *Mem:* Fel Inst Elec & Electronics Engrs; Electrochem Soc; Sigma Xi. *Res:* Semiconductor technology and ultra large scale intergration applications; cost effective semiconductor manufacturing facilities and factory of the future research; packaging and assembly. *Mailing Add:* 18 Lakeside Lane North Barrington IL 60010

KITCHENS, CLARENCE WESLEY, JR, armor-anti-armor mechanics, blast dynamics, for more information see previous edition

KITCHENS, THOMAS ADREN, CONDENSED MATTER PHYSICS. *Current Pos:* SCI COMPUT STAFF, DEPT ENERGY, 82- *Personal Data:* b Amarillo, Tex, Oct 31, 35; m 58; c 3. *Educ:* Rice Inst, BA, 58, Rice Univ, MA, 60, PhD(physics), 63. *Prof Exp:* Staff mem physics, Los Alamos Sci Lab, 63-65; physicist, Brookhaven Nat Lab, 65-75; liaison physicist, Off Naval Res, London, 75-76; alternate group leader, Los Alamos Sci Lab, 76-80, group leader physics, 78-80; staff assoc, Div Mat Res, NSF, 80-82. *Concurrent Pos:* Sr res fel, Univ Sussex, Gr Brit, 70-71. *Mem:* Fel Inst Physics UK; fel Am Inst Physics; Asn Comput Mach; AAAS. *Res:* Ultralow temperature physics and condensed matter research utilizing neutron and light scattering; high performance computing. *Mailing Add:* Dept Energy G-236 US Dept Eng-GTN Sci Comp ER-30 Washington DC 20585

KITCHENS, WILEY M, wetlands ecology, estuarine ecology, for more information see previous edition

KITCHIN, JOHN FRANCIS, RELIABILITY & LIFE TESTING. *Current Pos:* RES SCIENTIST, DIGITAL EQUIP CORP, 88- *Personal Data:* b Greenwood, Miss, May 6, 53. *Educ:* Univ Southern Miss, BS, 76; Fla State Univ, MS, 78, PhD(statist), 80. *Prof Exp:* Asst prof statist, Purdue Univ, 80-81; mem tech staff, Bell Labs, 81-84, mem tech staff, Commun Res, 84-85, tech mgr, Bell Commun Res, 85- *Mem:* Am Statist Asn; Inst Math Statist; Inst Elec & Electronics Engrs; Reliability Soc. *Res:* Development and comparison of statistical estimators of reliability; development of methods of reliability prediction for complex systems. *Mailing Add:* Digital Equip Corp HL02-3/J13 77 Reed Rd Hudson MA 01749

KITCHIN, ROBERT WALTER, PHYSICAL CHEMISTRY, INSTRUMENTAL ANALYSIS. *Current Pos:* PROF & CHMN, DEPT CHEM & PHYSICS, SOUTHWEST BAPTIST UNIV, 84- *Personal Data:* b Ft Sill, Okla, Jan 1, 45; m 71, Ann C Keen; c Jonathan W. *Educ:* Miss State Univ, BS, 68, PhD(phys chem), 76. *Prof Exp:* Res assoc, Pratt & Whitney Aircraft, 69-70; assoc chemist, Miss State Chem Lab, 70-71; instr chem & physics, Holmes Jr Col, 76-82; assoc prof, Graceland Col, 82-84. *Concurrent Pos:* Inst math, chem & physics, Miss Power Co, 77-78; temp assoc prof chem & physics, Miss State Univ, 79; vis prof chem, Univ Southern Miss, 80-91. *Res:* Basic chemistry, general physics, engineering physics and physical science. *Mailing Add:* 1912 S Hedgewood Dr Bolivar MO 65613

KITCHING, PETER, PARTICLE PHYSICS. *Current Pos:* res assoc, 69-71, from asst prof to assoc prof, 71-82, PROF, UNIV ALTA, EDMONTON, 82-, DIR, CTR SUBATOMIC RES, 88- *Personal Data:* b Leeds, Eng Apr 4, 38; m 64, Josephine M Rodgers; c John E, Andrew J & Matthew S. *Educ:* Oxford Univ, BA, 60; Yale Univ, MSc, 62, PhD, 66. *Prof Exp:* Res scientist, Nat Inst Res Nuclear Sci, Eng, 66-69. *Concurrent Pos:* Assoc dir, Triumf Lab, Vancouver, 83-88. *Mem:* Can Asn Physicists. *Res:* Physics. *Mailing Add:* Ctr Subatomic Res Univ Alta Edmonton AB Z6G 2H5 Can

KITE, FRANCIS ERVIN, CEREAL CHEMISTRY. *Current Pos:* RETIRED. *Personal Data:* b Galesburg, Ill, Dec 8, 18; m 42; c 2. *Educ:* Knox Col, AB, 40; Univ Iowa, MS, 42, PhD(phys chem), 48. *Prof Exp:* Res chemist, Corn Prods Co, 48-71; sr res chemist, CPC Int, 71-84. *Mem:* Am Chem Soc; Am Asn Cereal Chemists. *Res:* Raman spectroscopy; molecular structure; chemistry of corn sugar and its derivatives; starch and starch derivatives. *Mailing Add:* 332 Nuttall Rd Riverside IL 60546-1805

KITE, GEORGE FREDRICK, PHARMACEUTICAL DOSAGE FORM FORMULATION, PHARMACEUTICAL UNIT PROCESS. *Current Pos:* VPRES RES & DEVELOP, VESTA PHARMACEUT INC, 97- *Personal Data:* b Los Angeles, Calif, June 14, 37; div; c George F, Mary A, Philip C, Linda J, Richard E, Barbara A & Karen C. *Educ:* Calif State Univ, BA, 59; Purdue Univ, MS, 62; Carnegie Mellon Univ, PhD(org chem), 74. *Prof Exp:* Chemist, Gulf Res & Develop, 62-65 & Philip Morris, 72-79; dir mfg opers, Creative Lab Prods, 78-93; dir res & develop, Mfg Chemists, 94-97. *Mem:* Am Chem Soc. *Res:* Synthetic organic research and development; free radicals, petrochemicals, nitrite oxides, polyimides, tobacco flavor precursors; formulation and manufacture cleaning and personal care products, clinical diagnostic reagents, pharmaceutical dosage forms. *Mailing Add:* 8768 E 33rd St Indianapolis IN 46226. *Fax:* 317-895-9340

KITE, JOSEPH HIRAM, JR, TUBERCULOSIS, AUTOIMMUNE DISEASE. *Current Pos:* Res assoc, 58-59, from instr to assoc prof, 59-72, PROF MICROBIOL, SCH MED, STATE UNIV NY, BUFFALO, 72- *Personal Data:* b Decatur, Ga, Nov 11, 26; m 70, Jane Fay Pascale. *Educ:* Emory Univ, AB, 48; Univ Tenn, MS, 54; Univ Mich, PhD(bact), 59. *Concurrent Pos:* Principal investr res grant, teaching med, dental & grad students, scientific delegate, Citizen Ambassador Prog, People To People Intl. *Mem:* AAAS; Am Soc Microbiol; Tissue Cult Asn; Am Asn Immunol; NY Acad Sci. *Res:* Protective immunity to mycobacterium tuberculosis; autoimmune regulation in thyroiditis. *Mailing Add:* Dept Microbiol State Univ NY Sch Med Buffalo NY 14214-3078. *Fax:* 716-829-2158; *E-Mail:* jkite@ubmedb.buffalo.edu

KITHIER, KAREL, IMMUNOCHEMISTRY, COMPARATIVE PATHOLOGY. *Current Pos:* asst prof chem & immunochem, 74-78, ASSOC PROF PATH, DEPT PATH, SCH MED, WAYNE STATE UNIV, DETROIT, 78-; MED DIR, SPECIAL CHEM, DAMON CLIN LAB, DETROIT MED CTR, 89- *Personal Data:* b Prague, Czech, Dec 6, 30; m 61; c 1. *Educ:* Charles Univ, MD, 62, PhD(biochem), 67. *Prof Exp:* Res scientist immunochem, Res Inst Child Develop, Charles Univ, 67-68, Mich Cancer Found, Detroit, 72-74; res assoc, Child Res Ctr Mich, 68-71; assoc head, div clin chem, Detroit Res Hosp & Univ Health Ctr, 74-88, div head immunol, 80-88. *Concurrent Pos:* Staff pathologist immunol, Vet Admin Med Ctr, Allen Park, 78- *Mem:* Am Asn Cancer Res; Am Asn Immunol; Am Asn Clin Chem; Nat Acad Clin Biochem; NY Acad Sci. *Res:* Proteins of blood and tissues in health and disease; proteins of fetuses and cancer patients; development and pathology of proteins and related substances. *Mailing Add:* Dept Path 9374 Scott Hall Wayne State Univ Sch Med 540 E Canfield St Detroit MI 48201-1928

KITOS, PAUL ALAN, BIOCHEMISTRY. *Current Pos:* asst prof biochem, Univ Kans, 59-62, from asst prof to assoc prof comp biochem & physiol, 62-69, actg chmn dept, 69-71, PROF BIOCHEM, UNIV KANS, 69- *Personal Data:* b Saskatoon, Sask, May 31, 27; m 52; c 7. *Educ:* Univ BC, BSA, 50, MSA, 52; Ore State Univ, PhD(chem), 56. *Honors & Awards:* Amoco Award, 74. *Prof Exp:* Chemist, E I du Pont de Nemours & Co, 56-59. *Concurrent Pos:* NIH fel, dept microbiol, Harvard Med Sch, 71-72; sr scientist, Mid Am Cancer Ctr, 75-79; Fogarty fel, Inst d'Embryologie, Nogent-Sur-Marne, France, 83. *Mem:* AAAS; Am Chem Soc; Tissue Cult Asn; Am Soc Biol Chem & Mol Biol. *Res:* Metabolism in animal cells; developmental biology; effects of organophosphorus insecticides on avian embryos; biochemical basis of some birth defects; teratogenesis. *Mailing Add:* Dept Biochem Univ Kans Lawrence KS 66045. *Fax:* 785-864-5321

KITSON, JOHN AIDAN, FOOD SCIENCE. *Current Pos:* PRES & SR CONSULT, KITSON CONSULT LTD, 82- *Personal Data:* b Victoria, BC, Feb 14, 27; m 54; c 2. *Educ:* Univ BC, BA, 49; Ore State Univ, MSc, 54. *Honors & Awards:* Prix Industs Award, 68 & 70; W J Eva Award for Indust Serv, 77. *Prof Exp:* Food technologist, Sun Rype Prod Ltd, BC, 49-50; food technologist prod & process develop, Can Dept Agr, 50-64; food technologist & vis scientist, Eng & Develop Lab, USDA, Calif, 64-65; food technologist prod & process develop, Can Dept Agr, 65-71, head, Food Processing Sect, 71-80, assoc dir, Res Sta, Agr Can, 80-83. *Concurrent Pos:* Mem, Adv Comt Sci & Technol, BC Govt, 89-93. *Mem:* Inst Food Technologists; Can Inst Food Technologists; fel Inst Food Sci & Technol (UK). *Res:* Research and development of processes, products and equipment for fruit and vegetable processing industry. *Mailing Add:* RR 4 Site 104 Summerland BC V0H 1Z0 Can

KITSON, ROBERT EDWARD, POLYMER CHEMISTRY. *Current Pos:* RETIRED. *Personal Data:* b Ashtabula, Ohio, Aug 9, 18; m 42, Doris I Palmer; c James E & Richard P. *Educ:* Mt Union Col, BS, 40; Purdue Univ, MS, 42, PhD(anal chem), 44. *Prof Exp:* Res chemist, Rayon Tech Div, E I du Pont de Nemours & Co, Inc, 43-44, Ammonia Chem Div, 43-52 & Dacron Res Div, 52-64, supvr, Dacron Textile Res Div, 65-82. *Mem:* Am Chem Soc. *Res:* Texturing of textile fibers; physical chemistry of high polymers. *Mailing Add:* 322 Hampton Rd Wilmington DE 19803-2420

KITTAKA, ROBERT SHINNOSUKE, FOOD SCIENCE, MICROBIOLOGY. *Current Pos:* mgr microbiol, 69-71, MICROBIOL & QUAL ASSURANCE DIR, FOOD RES, CENT SOYA CO, INC, 71- *Personal Data:* b Los Angeles, Calif, Sept 23, 34; m 62; c 3. *Educ:* Univ Ill, BS, 57, MS, 59, PhD(food sci), 64. *Prof Exp:* Microbiologist, Swift & Co, 64-69. *Mem:* Inst Food Technol; Am Soc Microbiol; Asn Milk, Food & Environ Sanitarians; Soc Indust Microbiol; Brit Soc Appl Bact. *Res:* Food microbiology; public health and spoilage microbiology as related to food products and processes; development, implementation and auditing of quality assurance programs in food processing systems to assure compliance with governmental regulations and corporate standards for cost efficient operations. *Mailing Add:* 5231 Chippewa Trail Ft Wayne IN 46804

KITTEL, CHARLES, PHYSICS. *Current Pos:* vis assoc prof, 50, prof, 51-78, EMER PROF PHYSICS, UNIV CALIF, BERKELEY, 79- *Personal Data:* b New York, NY, July 18, 16; m 38, Muriel A Lister; c Peter, Timothy & Ruth. *Educ:* Cambridge Univ, BA, 38, MA, 93; Univ Wis, PhD(physics), 41. *Honors & Awards:* Buckley Prize, 57; Oersted Medal, 79. *Prof Exp:* Physicist, Naval Ord Lab, Washington, DC, 40-42; opers analyst, US Fleet, 43-45; res assoc physics, Mass Inst Technol, 45-46; res physicist, Bell Tel Labs, 47-50. *Concurrent Pos:* Guggenheim fel, 46, 57 & 64. *Mem:* Nat Acad Sci; Am Acad Arts & Sci. *Res:* Solid state physics; theory of ferromagnetism; extraterrestrial biogenics. *Mailing Add:* Dept Physics Univ Calif Berkeley CA 94720-7300

KITTEL, J HOWARD, TECHNOLOGY TRANSFER. *Current Pos:* RETIRED. *Personal Data:* b Ritzville, Wash, Oct 9, 19; m 43; c 4. *Educ:* Wash State Univ, BS, 43. *Honors & Awards:* Outstanding Achievement Award, Am Nuclear Soc, 79. *Prof Exp:* Aeronaut res scientist, NASA, 43-51; metal engr, Argonne Nat Lab, 51-61, sr metallurgist, 61-94, mgr adv fuels, 74-79, mgr nuclear waste res & develop, 79-85, technol transfer specialist, 89-94. *Concurrent Pos:* Mem, Mat Adv Bd, Nat Acad Sci, 56-58; US deleg, UN Geneva Conf, 58-64. *Mem:* Fel Am Nuclear Soc; Sigma Xi; Scientists & Engrs Secure Energy. *Res:* Technology transfer. *Mailing Add:* 1103 N Mill St No 103 Naperville IL 60563

KITTEL, PETER, PHYSICS, CRYOGENICS. *Current Pos:* Nat Res Coun assoc cryog, 78-80, RES SCIENTIST & TEAM LEADER, AMES RES CTR, NASA, 80- *Personal Data:* b Mt Vernon Dist, Va, Mar 23, 45; m 72, Mary E Murchio; c Katherine. *Educ:* Univ Calif, Berkeley, BS, 67; Univ Calif, San Diego, MS, 69; Univ Oxford, Eng, DPhil(physics), 74. *Honors & Awards:* Medal for Except Eng Achievement, NASA, 90. *Prof Exp:* Res assoc & adj asst prof physics, Univ Ore, 74-78; res assoc radiol, Stanford Univ, 78. *Concurrent Pos:* Bd dirs, Cryogenic Eng Conf, 83-89 & 92-; co-chmn, Int

Cryocooler Conf, 96- *Mem:* Am Phys Soc; AAAS. *Res:* Low temperature physics; far infrared spectroscopy; stocastic processes and applications of cryogenics in space. *Mailing Add:* MS 244-10 NASA-Ames Res Ctr Moffett Field CA 94035-1000

KITTELBERGER, JOHN STEPHEN, PHYSICAL CHEMISTRY. *Current Pos:* scientist, 73-81, MGR, XEROX CORP, 81- *Personal Data:* b Palmerton, Pa, Mar 14, 39; m 63. *Educ:* Hamilton Col, AB, 61; Princeton Univ, AM, 63, PhD(phys chem), 66. *Prof Exp:* res assoc, Mass Inst Technol, 66-68; asst prof, Amherst Col, 68-73. *Concurrent Pos:* Consult, surface sci & powder technol. *Mem:* Am Phys Soc; Tech Asn Pulp & Paper Indust. *Res:* Structural chemistry; surface science; reprographic science; materials science; powder technology; deinking technology, reactive extrusion. *Mailing Add:* Xerox Corp 800 Phillips Rd Webster NY 14580. *E-Mail:* stephen__kittelberger@wb.xerox.com

KITTELSON, DAVID BURNELLE, ENGINE EMISSIONS, PARTICLE MEASUREMENTS. *Current Pos:* asst prof, 70-76, assoc prof, 76-80, PROF MECH ENG, UNIV MINN, 80- *Personal Data:* b Pelican Rapids, Minn, Mar 12, 42; m 70, Vesna Krezich; c Andrei Karl. *Educ:* Univ Minn, Minneapolis, BSc, 64, MSc, 66; Cambridge Univ, PhD(chem eng), 72. *Honors & Awards:* Teeter Award, Soc Automotive Engrs, 73, Arch T Colwell Merit Award, 78, 83 & 95. *Concurrent Pos:* Overseas fel, Churchill Col, Cambridge Univ, Cambridge, England, 85-86. *Mem:* Sigma Xi; Am Chem Soc; Am Soc Mech Engrs; fel Soc Automotive Engrs. *Res:* Engine combustion and emissions; particle sampling and characterization; engine sensors; diagnostics and control. *Mailing Add:* Dept Mech Eng 111 Church St SE Minneapolis MN 55455

KITTILA, RICHARD SULO, organic chemistry; deceased, see previous edition for last biography

KITTING, CHRISTOPHER LEE, ECOLOGY OF MARINE POPULATIONS. *Current Pos:* AT DEPT MARINE BIOL, CALIF STATE UNIV, HAYWARD. *Personal Data:* b Monroe, Mich, May 23, 53. *Educ:* Univ Calif, Irvine, BS, 74; Stanford Univ, PhD(biol sci), 79. *Prof Exp:* Res assoc, Stanford Med Sch, Hopkins Marine Sta, 78-79; res biologist, Marine Sci Inst, Univ Calif, Santa Barbara, 79; asst prof, Marine Studies & Zool, Port Aransas Marine Lab, Univ Tex, Austin, 79- *Concurrent Pos:* Vis teaching asst, WI Lab, Fairleigh Dickinson Univ, 75, vis investr, 76; teaching asst, Dept Biol Sci, Hopkins Marine Sta, Stanford Univ, 77, fel, 74-79. *Mem:* Ecol Soc Am; Am Soc Limnol & Oceanog; Sigma Xi; NY Acad Sci. *Res:* Advancing ecological theory using specialized natural history studies, especially marine invertebrates, algae, foraging and competition; field experiments using close-up listening and visual records of activities on semi-isolated surfaces of shallow rocks, pilings, oyster reefs and seagrass blades. *Mailing Add:* Dept Biol Sci Calif State Univ Hayward CA 94542

KITTLE, CHARLES FREDERICK, surgery, for more information see previous edition

KITTLITZ, RUDOLF GOTTLIEB, JR CHEMICAL ENGINEERING. *Current Pos:* Engr, Du Pont Co, 57-62, res engr, 62-68, sr res engr, 68-87, res assoc, 87-92, SR RES ASSOC, DU PONT CO, 92- *Personal Data:* b Waco, Tex, Apr 19, 35; m 66, Linda W; c Lenell, Theresa, Liesel & Rolf. *Educ:* Univ Miss, BSChemE, 57. *Honors & Awards:* W G Hunter Award, Am Soc Qual Control, 89. *Concurrent Pos:* Adj prof, Univ Tenn, Chattanooga, 80-82; regional dir, Am Soc Qual Control, 86-91, exec regional dir, 87-91, dir at large, 91-93. *Mem:* Fel Am Soc Qual Control; Am Statist Asn. *Mailing Add:* Du Pont 4501 N Access Rd Chattanooga TN 37415-3899

KITTO, GEORGE BARRIE, BIOCHEMISTRY. *Current Pos:* asst prof, 66-71, PROF CHEM, UNIV TEX, AUSTIN, 71-; RES SCIENTIST, CLAYTON FOUND BIOCHEM INST, 66- *Personal Data:* b Wellington, NZ, July 31, 37; m 62, Mary B Scully; c David, Robyn & John. *Educ:* Victoria Univ, BSc, 61, MSc, 62; Brandeis Univ, PhD(biochem), 66. *Prof Exp:* Biochemist, Wellington Pub Hosp, 60-61. *Concurrent Pos:* Vis prof, Univ Calif, Berkeley, 78, Duke Univ, 86; consult, Am Cyanamid, Dell Corp, Aquanautics Corp, Whatman, Inc. *Mem:* AAAS; Am Chem Soc; Royal Soc Chem; assoc mem NZ Inst Chem; Royal Soc NZ; Am Soc Biochem Molecular Biol. *Res:* Enzyme structure and taxonomy; evolution of protein structure; multiple molecular forms of enzymes; immobilized enzymes. *Mailing Add:* Dept Chem Welch 4 260 Univ Tex Austin TX 78712. *Fax:* 512-471-8696

KITTO, JOHN BUCK, MECHANICAL ENGINEERING. *Current Pos:* Sr engr, Babcock & Wilcox Co, Ohio, 75-80, res engr, 80-81, prog mgr, 81-94, BUS DEVELOP SPECIALIST, BABCOCK & WILCOX CO, OHIO, 95- *Personal Data:* b Evanston, Ill, Dec 22, 52; m 74, Cecilia Higgins; c Christopher Daniel & Andrew Comstock. *Educ:* Lehigh Univ, BSME, 75; Univ Akron, MBA, 80. *Honors & Awards:* George Westinghouse Silver Medal, Am Soc Mech Engrs, 91, Prime Movers Award & Dedicated Serv Award, 92. *Mem:* Fel Am Soc Mech Engrs (sr vpres, 95-); Am Inst Chem Engrs. *Res:* Author and patentee in field. *Mailing Add:* Res & Develop Div Babcock & Wilcox Co 1562 Beeson St NE Alliance OH 44601-2165

KITTREDGE, CLIFFORD PROCTOR, engineering; deceased, see previous edition for last biography

KITTRELL, BENJAMIN UPCHURCH, TOBACCO, SOYBEANS. *Current Pos:* RESIDENT DIR, PEE DEE RES & EDUC CTR, 87- *Personal Data:* b Kittrell, NC, Oct 25, 37; m 58; c 2. *Educ:* NC State Univ, BS, 60, MEd, 69, PhD(crop sci), 75. *Prof Exp:* Teacher voc agr, Vance Co, NC, 60-63 & Wake Co, NC, 63-65; supt, res sta, NC State Univ, 65-68, agronomist tobacco, 68-75; asst prof agron, Univ Ga, 75-78; from assoc prof to prof agron, Clemson Univ, 78-87. *Mem:* Am Soc Agron. *Res:* Tobacco production management including plant density, leaf area index, fertilization, sucker control, harvest, curing, disease control; soybean production management. *Mailing Add:* 831 Wedgefield Rd Florence SC 29501

KITTRELL, JAMES RAYMOND, POLYMER CHEMISTRY. *Current Pos:* PRES, KSE, INC, 80- *Personal Data:* b Akransas City, Kans, Oct 28, 40; m 60; c 4. *Educ:* Okla State Univ, BS, 62; Univ Wis, MS, 63, PhD(chem eng), 66. *Prof Exp:* From res engr to sr res engr, Chevron Res Co, 66-69; oper asst, Stand Oil Co Calif, 69-70; prof chem eng, Univ Mass, Amherst, 70-80. *Concurrent Pos:* NSF fel & instr, Univ Wis, 66. *Mem:* Am Inst Chem Engrs; Am Chem Soc. *Res:* Petroleum refining; polymers; reactor design and analysis; catalyst deactivation; environmental processes; bioengineering. *Mailing Add:* KSE Inc PO Box 368 Amherst MA 01004-9974

KITTRICK, JAMES ALLEN, SOIL MINERALOGY. *Current Pos:* RETIRED. *Personal Data:* b Milwaukee, Wis, Aug 4, 29; m 53; c 2. *Educ:* Univ Wis, BS, 51, MS, 53, PhD, 55. *Honors & Awards:* Fel Am Soc Agron. *Prof Exp:* From asst prof to prof soils, Wash State Univ, 55-91. *Mem:* Soil Sci Soc; Clay Minerals Soc. *Res:* Mineral stability, weathering. *Mailing Add:* 160 Osborn Rd Port Angeles WA 98362

KITTS, DAVID BURLINGAME, VERTEBRATE PALEONTOLOGY, GEOLOGY. *Current Pos:* RETIRED. *Personal Data:* b Oswego, NY, Oct 27, 23; m 45; c 2. *Educ:* Univ Pa, AB, 49; Columbia Univ, PhD(zool), 53. *Prof Exp:* Instr biol, Amherst Col, 53-54; from asst prof to assoc prof geol, Univ Okla, 54-62, assoc prof geol & hist sci, 62-66, David Ross Boyd prof geol & hist sci, 66-80, head cur, Dept Geol, Stoval Mus, 68-80; at Dept Geol Physics, Univ Okla, Norman, 80-87. *Concurrent Pos:* Vis fel, Princeton Univ, 64-65. *Mem:* Soc Vert Paleontol; Philos Sci Asn. *Res:* Historical geology; Cenozoic mammals and stratigraphy; philosophy of geology and evolutionary theory. *Mailing Add:* 6559 Stonecroft Terr Santa Rosa CA 95409

KITTSLEY, SCOTT LOREN, CHEMICAL THERMODYNAMICS. *Current Pos:* from instr to prof, 45-81, chmn dept, 57-62, EMER PROF CHEM, MARQUETTE UNIV, 82- *Personal Data:* b Port Washington, Wis, Feb 17, 21; m 46, Helen Jung. *Educ:* Univ Wis, BS, 42; Case Western Reserve Univ, MS, 44, PhD(phys chem), 45. *Prof Exp:* Asst chem, Case Western Reserve Univ, 42-45. *Mem:* Sigma Xi; Am Chem Soc. *Res:* Chemical thermodynamics; solutions of nonelectrolytes. *Mailing Add:* 3838 N Oakland Apt 169 Shorewood WI 53211-2258

KITZ, RICHARD J, ANESTHESIOLOGY, ENZYMOLOGY. *Current Pos:* prof, 69-70, HENRY ISAIAH DORR PROF ANESTHESIA, HARVARD MED SCH, 70-, PROF RES & TRAINING ANAESTHETICS & ANAESTHESIA, HARVARD UNIV-MASS INST TECHNOL, 78-, FAC DEAN CLIN AFFAIRS, 94-; ANESTHETIST, MASS GEN HOSP, BOSTON, MASS, 94- *Personal Data:* b Oshkosh, Wis, Mar 25, 29; m 54; c 1. *Educ:* Marquette Univ, BS, 51, MD, 54; Harvard Univ, MA, 69; Am Bd Anesthesiol, cert, 62. *Honors & Awards:* Many named lectureships, 69-; Golden Emblem Award, Finnish Soc Anesthesiologists, 77. *Prof Exp:* Surg intern, Columbia-Presby Med Ctr, 54-55, surg resident, 56-57, resident anesthesiol, 58-60, instr, 60-61, from asst prof to assoc prof anesthesiol, 62-69. *Concurrent Pos:* NIH spec res fel, Columbia-Presby Med Ctr, 61-62 & Karolinska Inst, Stockholm, 68; NIH spec res fel, Karolinska Inst, Stockholm, 68; consult anesthesiol, Dept Navy, 69-71 & Surgeon Gen, USAF, 70-79; anesthetist-in-chief, Mass Gen Hosp, 69-94; consult, Air Force Surg Gen, 70-80, Brigham & Women's Hosp & Beth Israel Hosp, Boston, 70-94; ed-in-chief, J Clin Anesthesia; dir, Am Bd Anesthesiol, 74-, pres, 84-85; co-dir, Harvard-Mass Inst Technol Div Health Sci & Technol, 85-90. *Mem:* Inst Med-Nat Acad Sci; AMA; Am Soc Anesthesiologists; fel Am Col Anesthesiol; NY Acad Med; Am Chem Soc; Am Soc Pharmacol & Exp Therapeut; AAAS; fel Royal Col Anaesthesists Eng. *Res:* Basic sciences as related to anesthesiology with emphasis on uptake and distribution of anesthetic agents and enzymology; design, synthesis and testing of novel compounds used as molecular probes (active site investigations) and drugs (short-acting, non-depolarizing neuromuscular blocking agents, anticholinesterases); design, constructing and testing of new anesthesia delivery systems and monitoring devices for care of the critically ill patient in operating rooms and intensive care units; monitoring patient safety and standards of aestheticare; regulation and economics of medical care in the US; author of 2 books and numerous publications; granted 5 patents. *Mailing Add:* Dept Anesthesia Mass Gen Hosp Boston MA 02114. *Fax:* 617-726-5845; *E-Mail:* kitz@etherdume.mgh.harvard.edu

KITZEN, JAN MICHAEL, PHARMACOLOGY. *Current Pos:* Res assoc pharmacol, 80-90, SECT MGR, DEPT CARDIOVASC BIOL, RHONE-POULENC RORER, 90- *Personal Data:* b Philadelphia, Pa, Dec 23, 49. *Educ:* Temple Univ, BS, 72; Univ Iowa, PhD(pharmacol), 77. *Mem:* AAAS; Med Adv Serv; Int Soc Heart Res; Am Heart Asn. *Mailing Add:* Dept Cardiovasc Biol Rhone-Poulenc Rorer 500 Arcola Rd Collegeville PA 19426

KITZES, ARNOLD S(TANLEY), NUCLEAR ENGINEERING, CHEMICAL ENGINEERING. *Current Pos:* RETIRED. *Personal Data:* b Boston, Mass, Sept 21, 17; m 42, 78, Helen L Knox; c Judith A & David H. *Educ:* City Col New York, BChE, 39; Univ Minn, MChE, 41, PhD(chem eng), 47. *Prof Exp:* Instr chem eng, Univ Minn, 41-42, res assoc, 45-47, chief chemist, Sangamon Ord, Ill, 42-45; group leader, Oak Ridge Nat Lab, 48-57; mgr test eng, Atomic Power Div, Westinghouse Elec Corp, 57-72, adv engr, Nuclear Serv Div, 72-86. *Res:* Reactor technology; environment; spray drying and explosives; design of high pressure equipment; heat transfer; fluid flow; waste management; decontamination; technical administration. *Mailing Add:* 2740 Mount Royal Rd Pittsburgh PA 15217

KITZES, GEORGE, BIOCHEMISTRY, PHARMACOLOGY. *Current Pos:* SCI CONSULT, RES & RES TRAINING PROGS, CROHN'S & COLITIS FOUND AM, 81- *Personal Data:* b Denver, Colo, May 28, 19; m 42, Nettie Sherr; c Julie, Janet & Marjorie. *Educ:* City Col New York, BS, 41; Univ Wis, MS, 42, PhD(chem), 44. *Prof Exp:* Res biochemist, White Labs, NJ, 44-49 & Vet Admin, 49-51; res biochemist indust toxicol, USAF, 51-57, asst chief, Physiol Br, Aeromed Lab, 57-60, chief, Physiol Div, Aerospace Med Res Labs, Aero-Med Div, Wright-Patterson AFB, Ohio, 60-66; health sci adminr & gastroenterol prog dir, Extramural Prog, Nat Inst Arthritis, Metab & Digestive Dis, 66-81. *Mem:* Am Gastroenterol Asn. *Res:* Gastrointestinal physiology and biochemistry; nutrition; aviation physiology and toxicology; aero-space life support sciences; consultant to research and research manpower training programs for gastointestinal diseases, e.g., Crohn's Disease and alcerative colitis. *Mailing Add:* 10201 Grosvenor Pl Rockville MD 20852

KITZES, LEONARD MARTIN, NEUROPHYSIOLOGY. *Current Pos:* res neurophysiol neurol, 74-77, ASST PROF NEUROPHYSIOL, DEPT ANAT, UNIV CALIF, IRVINE, 77- *Personal Data:* b New York, NY, Apr 10, 41; m 67; c 2. *Educ:* Univ Calif, Los Angeles, BA, 62; Univ Calif, Irvine, PhD(psychobiol), 70. *Prof Exp:* Fel neurophysiol, Univ Wis, 70-73, res assoc, 73-74. *Concurrent Pos:* Nat Inst Neurol Dis & Stroke res grant, 78. *Res:* Auditory neurophysiology with primary interests in responses of single inferior colliculus neurons to binaural stimulation and functional and structural development of the brainstem audiroty system. *Mailing Add:* Dept Anat Univ Calif Sch Med Irvine CA 92717-0001

KITZKE, EUGENE DAVID, ENVIRONMENTAL HEALTH, TECHNICAL MANAGEMENT. *Current Pos:* OWNER, DANEL ENTERPRISES; PRES, OAK CRETE BLOCK CORP, 82- *Personal Data:* b Milwaukee, Wis, Sept 2, 23; m 46, Lorraine G Shummon; c Mary (Shummon), Paul, Patrice (Wessel) & Jerome. *Educ:* Marquette Univ, BS, 45, MS, 47. *Prof Exp:* From asst prof to assoc prof, St Thomas Aquinas Col, Grand Rapids, Mich, 47-51; res mgr biol, S C Johnson & Son, Inc, 57-76, vpres corp res & develop, 76-81. *Concurrent Pos:* Instr microbiol, St Mary's Nursing Sch, Grand Rapids, Mich, 47-51; asst clin prof environ med, Dept Environ Med, Med Col Wis, 73-82; distinguished scholar, Marquette Univ, 95. *Mem:* AAAS; Sigma Xi; Hist Sci Soc; Int Palm Soc. *Res:* Developer of wind crest, an environmentally integrated residential subdivision with boundaries coordinated along river frontage floodplain wetlands, and dedicated Department Natural Resources preservation lands. *Mailing Add:* 616 Aspen St South Milwaukee WI 53172

KITZMILLER, JAMES BLAINE, GENETICS, MEDICAL ENTOMOLOGY. *Current Pos:* from instr to prof, 48-74, EMER PROF ZOOL, UNIV ILL, URBANA, 74- *Personal Data:* b Toledo, Ohio, June 30, 18; m 74, Dorothy Meyer; c 4. *Educ:* De Sales Col, BS, 39; Univ Mich, MS, 41, PhD(genetics), 48. *Honors & Awards:* Meritorious Serv Award, Am Mosquito Control Asn, 78; John Belkin Mem Award, 86. *Prof Exp:* Entomologist, Toledo Mus Sci, 39-41; asst zool, Univ Mich, 41-42; vis prof, Fla Med Entomol Lab, 74-86. *Concurrent Pos:* Fulbright fel, Univ Pavia, Italy, 53; NIH fel, Univ Cagliari, Italy & Johannes Gutenberg Univ, Ger, 65-66; consult, WHO & Pan Am Health Orgn, 53-, NIH, 58- *Mem:* AAAS; Genetics Soc Am; Soc Study Evolution; Am Entom Soc; Am Mosquito Control Asn. *Res:* Genetics and cytogenetics of mosquitoes, especially Anophelines; evolutionary cytogenetics, polymorphism and cytotaxonomy. *Mailing Add:* Fla Med Entomol Lab 200 Ninth St SE Vero Beach FL 32962

KIUSALAAS, JAAN, MECHANICS. *Current Pos:* from asst prof to assoc prof, 63-74, PROF ENG MECH, PA STATE UNIV, 74- *Personal Data:* b Tartu, Estonia, June 23, 31; m 59; c 3. *Educ:* Univ Adelaide, BE, 56; Northwestern Univ, MS, 59, PhD(mech), 62. *Prof Exp:* Plant design engr, Chrysler Australia Ltd, 56-57, prod design & test engr, 57-58, prod develop engr, Eng Div, Chrysler Corp, 59-60; res fel, Mat Res Ctr, Northwestern Univ, 62-63. *Concurrent Pos:* Sr resident res assoc, Marshall Space Flight Ctr, NASA, 71-72. *Mem:* Am Soc Mech Engrs; Am Acad Mech. *Res:* Finite elements; optimal structural design; structural stability. *Mailing Add:* 104 Timber Lane State College PA 16801

KIVELSON, DANIEL, CHEMICAL PHYSICS. *Current Pos:* from asst prof to assoc prof chem, 55-63, chmn dept, 75-78, PROF CHEM, UNIV CALIF, LOS ANGELES, 63- *Personal Data:* b New York, NY, July 11, 29; m 49; c 2. *Educ:* Harvard Univ, AB, 49, MA, 50, PhD(chem physics), 53. *Prof Exp:* Instr physics, Mass Inst Technol, 53-55. *Concurrent Pos:* Guggenheim fel, 59; Res Corp spec grant, 59; Sloan fel, 61-65; NSF sr fel, 65-66; consult, NAm Sci Ctr, 63-64, Advan Res Projs Agency, 65-66 & NSF, 76-77; assoc ed, J Chem Phys, 68-71 & Molecular Physics, 75-85. *Mem:* Fel Am Phys Soc; Am Chem Soc. *Res:* Microwave spectroscopy; molecular structure; nuclear magnetic resonance; electron spin resonance; light scattering; theory of liquids; supercooled liquids and glasses. *Mailing Add:* Dept Chem Univ Calif Los Angeles CA 90024

KIVELSON, MARGARET GALLAND, SPACE PHYSICS. *Current Pos:* Adj asst prof physics, Univ Calif, 67-72, res geophysicist, Inst Geophys & Planetary Physics, 67-80, adj assoc prof, 72-73, assoc prof in residence, 75-77, prof geophys & space physics in residence, 77-80, chmn, Dept Earth & Space Sci, 84-87, PROF, UNIV CALIF, LOS ANGELES, 80- *Personal Data:* b New York, NY, Oct 21, 28; m 49, Daniel; c Steven & Valerie. *Educ:* Radcliffe Col, AB, 50, AM, 51, PhD(physics), 57. *Honors & Awards:* Group Achievement Awards, NASA. *Concurrent Pos:* Consult, Rand Corp, 55-71; scholar, Radcliffe Inst Independent Study, 65-66; fel, John Simon Guggenheim Mem Found, 73-74; overseer, Harvard Col, 77-83. *Mem:* Fel AAAS; fel Am Geophys Union; Am Phys Soc; Am Astron Soc; corresp mem Int Acad Astronaut. *Res:* Magnetospheric physics; plasma physics; particles and fields in the magnetospheres of Earth and Jupiter; interplanetary magnetic fields; magnetic fields of moons. *Mailing Add:* Inst Geophys & Planetary Physics Univ Calif Los Angeles CA 90024-1567. *Fax:* 310-206-8042; *E-Mail:* mkivelson@igpp.ucla.edu

KIVENSON, GILBERT, ENGINEERING INSTRUMENTATION. *Current Pos:* CONSULT, & PATENT AGENT, 75- *Personal Data:* b Pittsburgh, Pa, Dec 5, 20. *Educ:* Carnegie Inst Technol, BS, 42; Univ Pittsburgh, MS, 47. *Prof Exp:* Rubber Reserve Co fel fract distillation, Mellon Inst, 47-50, develop engr, 50-51; chem engr, US Steel Co, 51-53; consult instrumentation, 53-55; chem engr, Atomic Power Dept, Westinghouse Elec Corp, 55-62, sr engr, Res & Develop Ctr, 62-68; sr engr, Electro-Optical Systs Div, Xerox Corp, 68-70; sr engr, Liquid Metals Eng Ctr, Atomics Int, Chatsworth, 71-73; sr engr, Audio Instruments, C F Braun Co, Calif, 73-75, J B Lansing, Northridge, Calif, 80-81. *Concurrent Pos:* Lectr, Pa Technol Inst & Northrop Inst Technol. *Mem:* Am Chem Soc. *Res:* Electronic instruments; stroboscopes; control systems; transducers; process control instrumentation. *Mailing Add:* 22030 Wyandotte St Canoga Park CA 91303

KIVER, EUGENE P, GEOMORPHOLOGY. *Current Pos:* Chmn dept, 71-74, from asst prof to assoc prof, 71-77, PROF GEOL, 77-, CHMN DEPT, EASTERN WASH UNIV, 90- *Personal Data:* b Cleveland, Ohio, Feb 26, 37; m 64; c 3. *Educ:* Case Western Res Univ, BA, 64; Univ Wyo, PhD(glacial geol, geomorphol), 68. *Mem:* Am Quaternary Asn; Geol Soc Am; Nat Speleol Soc. *Res:* Pleistocene and neoglacial history of alpine regions of western US; general geomorphology; volcanism in the Cascade Mountains; geology of the national parks; quaternary geology of NE Washington. *Mailing Add:* Dept Geol Eastern Wash Univ Cheney WA 99004

KIVIAT, ERIK, WETLAND & HUMAN ECOLOGY. *Current Pos:* From instr to asst prof natural his, Bard Col, 73-78, dir, Field Sta, 72-78, asst prof environ studies, 88-91, RES ASSOC ECOL, 78-, ASSOC PROF ENVIRON STUDIES, GRAD SCH ENVIRON STUDIES, BARD COL, 91-; EXEC DIR, HUDSONIA LTD, 88- *Personal Data:* b New York, NY, June 9, 47; m 82, Elaine Colandrea. *Educ:* Bard Col, BS, 76; State Univ NY, New Paltz, MA, 79; Union Inst, PhD, 91. *Concurrent Pos:* Ecologist, Hudsonia Ltd, 81- *Mem:* Torrey Bot Soc; Ecol Soc Am; Estuarine Res Fedn; Soc Conserv Biol; Soc Wetland Scientists; Soc Study Amphibians & Reptiles. *Res:* Wetland ecology and management; vertebrates; insects vascular plants; vegetation change; habitat ecology; rare species conservation; introduced species ecology; cultural ecology. *Mailing Add:* Hudsonia Ltd Bard Col Field Sta Annandale NY 12504-0217

KIVIAT, FRED E, PROCESS & PRODUCT QUALITY MANAGEMENT SYSTEMS. *Current Pos:* RES ASSOC, DU PONT, 87- *Personal Data:* b New York, NY, May 16, 40. *Educ:* City Col, New York, BS, 62; Univ Pittsburgh, PhD(chem), 68, MS, 78. *Prof Exp:* Sr res chemist, Gulf Res & Develop Co, 68-83, dir, anal instrumentation & process comput, 83-85; automation consult, ICI Americas, 86. *Mem:* Am Chem Soc; Am Soc Qual Control. *Res:* Determination of properties of heterogeneous catalysts via spectroscopic techniques; mathematical modelling of physio-chemical processes; development and implementation of process control strategies in refining and chemical facilities; development and implementation of product quality management systems for chemical facilities and laboratories. *Mailing Add:* DuPont 400 Woodland Rd Seaford DE 19973

KIVILAAN, ALEKSANDER, PLANT PHYSIOLOGY. *Current Pos:* asst plant path, Mich State Univ, 54-56, res instr plant physiol, 57, from asst prof to assoc prof, 58-78, EMER ASSOC PROF PLANT PHYSIOL, MICH STATE UNIV, 78- *Personal Data:* b Jaarja, Estonia, July 20, 06; nat US; m 35; c 3. *Educ:* Univ Tartu, Estonia, BS, 32, MS, 35; Univ Berlin, dipl, 38; Mich State Univ, PhD(plant path, bot), 57. *Prof Exp:* Asst plant path, Univ Tartu, Estonia, 32-36, res instr pomol, 39-44; lectr dendrol, Baltic Univ, Ger, 48-50; plant propagator, Mt Arbor Nurseries, Iowa, 50-53. *Mem:* Am Phytopath Soc; Am Soc Plant Physiol. *Res:* Physiology of fungi, parasitism, plant growth and plant cell wall. *Mailing Add:* 1167 Marigold Ave East Lansing MI 48823

KIVIOJA, LASSI A, GEODESY. *Current Pos:* prof, 64-90, EMER PROF, PURDUE UNIV, 90- *Personal Data:* b Finland, Mar 29, 27; US citizen; m 64; c 2. *Educ:* Univ Helsinki, BS, 51, MS, 52; Ohio State Univ, PhD, 63. *Prof Exp:* Res asst, Int Isostatic Inst, Helsinki, Finland, 49-52; res assoc geod gravity, Ohio State Univ, 55-63. *Concurrent Pos:* Instr, Dept Geod Sci, Ohio State Univ, 59-62; geodesist, US Coast & Geod Surv, 70-71; res scientist, Defense Mapping Agency, 79-80 & 86-87. *Mem:* Am Geophys Union; Am Cong Surv & Mapping. *Res:* Gravity anomalies isostasy; geodetic and astro-geodetic instruments; geodesic lines on the ellipsoid; the vertical mirror and its applications; mean sea level; mercury leveling instruments; hydrostatic leveling on land; precise astro-azimuths by mercury leveling of a theodolite. *Mailing Add:* 60 Blackfoot Ct Lafayette IN 47905

KIVISILD, HANS R(OBERT), CIVIL ENGINEERING & OCEAN ENGINEERING. *Current Pos:* PRIN, HRK CONSULT INC, CALGARY, 87- *Personal Data:* b Tartu, Estonia, July 19, 22; m 47, Livia Martina; c Maria (Ogrydziak), Ann (Smith), Julia (Bailey) & Emma (Kivisild). *Educ:* Royal Inst Technol, Swed, CE, 46, DEng(hydraul eng), 54. *Honors & Awards:* Eng Medal, Asn Prof Engrs Ont, 76; Queen Elizabeth II Silver Jubilee Medal, 77; Award Merit Innovation, Manning Awards, 85; Alta Achievement Award For Excellence, 87; Frank Spragins Award, Asn Prof Engrs Geol Geophys Alta, 89. *Prof Exp:* engr, City of Stockholm, Swed, 46-48, VBB, Stockholm, Swed, 48-50; with Found Co Can, Ltd, Montreal, 50-53; designing engr, Found Can Eng Corp Ltd, Montreal, 54-56, dist engr, Vancouver, 57-63, chief hydraul engr, Toronto, 64-65, chief civil engr, 65-70, dir res & develop, 70-73, vpres, 73-75; vpres & mgr, western opers & dir, Fenco Consults Ltd, Calgary, 75-81; vpres, Lavalin Inc, Calgary, 82-87. *Concurrent Pos:* Consult, Belg Govt, 56, Tech Assistance Opers, UN, 61, Spec Fund, 63, Food & Agr Orgn, 64; mem snow & ice subcomt, Nat Res Coun Can, 65-75, mem cold regions res comt, 77-79; chmn working group design principles & safety considerations; mem tech comt, code for fixed offshore structs, Can Stands Asn, 83-91. *Mem:* Fel Can Soc Civil Eng; Int Asn Hydraul Res; Marine Technol Soc; fel Eng Inst Can. *Res:* storm surges in oceans and lakes; stratified flow; earthquake resistance of subaqueous structures; ice effects on northern marine structures and vessels; river ice jamming and resulting floods. *Mailing Add:* 1420 Premier Way SW Calgary AB T2T 1L9 Can. *Fax:* 403-244-0075

KIVLIGHN, HERBERT DANIEL, JR, physical chemistry, inorganic chemistry; deceased, see previous edition for last biography

KIVLIGHN, SALAH DEAN, DRUG DEVELOPMENT & DESIGN NOVEL THERAPEUTICS AGENTS. *Current Pos:* sr res pharmacologist, 90-93, res fel, 93-96, SR RES FEL, MERCK, SHARP & DOHME RES LABS, WEST POINT, PA, 96- *Personal Data:* b Iowa City, Iowa, July 12, 57; m 89, Jane Kersh. *Educ:* Iowa State Univ, BS, 79; Univ Houston, PhD(cardiovasc pharmacol), 89. *Prof Exp:* Fel physiol, Univ Miss Med Ctr, Jackson, 87-88, instr, 88-90. *Concurrent Pos:* Referee ed, Heart & Circulatory & Res & Integ, Am J Physiol, 88- *Mem:* Am Soc Hypertension; Am Physiol Soc; Am Soc Nephrol. *Res:* Design and development of novel therapeutic agents for the treatment of hypertension and heart failure. *Mailing Add:* Merck Sharp & Dohme Res Lab WP46-100 West Point PA 19486

KIVNICK, ARNOLD, CHEMICAL ENGINEERING, APPLIED MATH. *Current Pos:* RETIRED. *Personal Data:* b Philadelphia, Pa, June 30, 23; m 46, Stella Factor; c Helen, Eric & Seth. *Educ:* Univ Pa, BS, 43, PhD(chem eng), 51. *Prof Exp:* Asst, SAM Labs, Columbia Univ, 43-44; jr chem engr, Tenn Eastman Co, 44-46; res assoc chem eng, Univ Ill, 50-52; sr chem engr, Tech Div, Pennsalt Chem Corp, 52-60, group leader, 60-68, mgr, Process Develop Dept, 68-72; liaison engr, Cent Eng Dept, Pennwalt Corp, 72-88. *Concurrent Pos:* Adj prof chem eng, Univ Pa, 80- *Mem:* Am Inst Chem Engrs. *Res:* Process development; applied statistics; cost estimation; process economics. *Mailing Add:* 308 Glenway Rd Erdenheim PA 19038

KIYASU, JOHN YUTAKA, BIOCHEMISTRY. *Current Pos:* ASSOC CLIN PROF PATH, COL PHYSICIANS & SURGEONS, COLUMBIA UNIV, 72- *Personal Data:* b San Francisco, Calif, Dec 25, 27; m 54; c 4. *Educ:* Univ Calif, Berkeley, BA, 50, MA, 51, PhD(physiol), 55. *Prof Exp:* Fel biochem, Univ Chicago, 56-57, instr & res assoc, 57-60; asst prof biochem & asst res prof psychiat, Sch Med & Dent, Univ Rochester, 60-63; from asst prof to assoc prof chem, Adelphi Univ, 63-70; dir div biochem & asst dir lab, dept path, Roosevelt Hosp, 70-84. *Concurrent Pos:* USPHS fel, 55-57; NIH grant, Adelphi Univ; res biochemist & mem staff, Dept Path & Labs, Div Biochem, Meadowbrook Hosp, East Meadow, NY, 67-69, dir lab systs, 69-70. *Mem:* Am Oil Chem Soc; Am Chem Soc; fel Am Inst Chem; NY Acad Sci; Am Asn Clin Chem. *Res:* Biosynthesis of phospholipids and liponucleotides; lipid enzymology and control mechanisms. *Mailing Add:* 94 Meadow St Garden City NY 11530

KIYONO, HIROSHI, DENTISTRY. *Current Pos:* From asst prof to assoc prof, 84-91, SR SCIENTIST TO SCIENTIST, UNIV ALA, 88-, PROF, 91-, CO-DIR IMMUNOL CTR, 92- *Personal Data:* b Nagone, Japan, Mar 17, 53; m 86, Momoyo; c Erika. *Educ:* Univ Ala, PhD(immunopathol), 83. *Concurrent Pos:* Clin instr, Nikon Univ, 77; vis scientist, NIH, Tokyo, 84-85; vis sr scientist, May-Planick Inst, Ger, 86. *Mem:* Am Asn Immunologists; Soc Murosal Immunol; Int Asn Dent Res; Am Soc Investigative Path; Am Soc Microbiol. *Res:* Mucosal immunology; development of mucosal vaccine. *Mailing Add:* Dept Oral Biol BBRB761 Univ Ala Birmingham AL 35294-2170

KIZER, DONALD EARL, BIOCHEMISTRY. *Current Pos:* RETIRED. *Personal Data:* b Benton Co, Iowa, Oct 12, 21; m 42; c 6. *Educ:* Upper Iowa Univ, BS, 47; Purdue Univ, MS, 50; Univ NC, PhD(bact), 54. *Prof Exp:* Asst dairy, Purdue Univ, 48-50; asst animal indust, Univ NC, 52-54; res assoc, 64-60, head biochem pharmacol sect, Biomed Div, Samuel Roberts Noble Found, Inc, 60-85. *Mem:* AAAS; Am Chem Soc; Am Soc Microbiol; Soc Exp Biol & Med; Am Asn Cancer Res. *Res:* Biochemistry of carcinogenesis; biochemical changes in pre-cancerous tissues. *Mailing Add:* 825 H St NW Ardmore OK 73401

KIZER, JOHN STEPHEN, NEUROENDOCRINOLOGY. *Current Pos:* from asst prof to assoc prof, 75-85, PROF MED & PHARMACOL, SCH MED, UNIV NC, CHAPEL HILL, 86- *Personal Data:* b Charleston, WVa, Jan 8, 45; m 70; c 6. *Educ:* Princeton Univ, AB, 66; Duke Univ, MD, 70. *Prof Exp:* Intern med, Johns Hopkins Hosp, Baltimore, 70-71, resident, 71-72; res assoc neuroendocrinol, Lab Clin Sci, NIMH, 72-75. *Concurrent Pos:* Assoc dir, Biol Sci Res Ctr, 85-; res sci career develop award, 77-88. *Mem:* Am Soc Clin Invest. *Res:* Investigation of protein neurotransmitters; post-translational processing of protien neurotransmitters. *Mailing Add:* Biol Sci Res Ctr CB 7250 Sch Med Univ NC Chapel Hill NC 27599

KJAR, RAYMOND ARTHUR, ELECTRONICS ENGINEERING. *Current Pos:* res engr, R & E Div, Rockwell Int, 68-76, supvr, Electronics Div, IC Tech, 76-80, mgr, Mil IC Prod, 80-90, DIR ADVAN PROCESS TECHNOL, ROCKWELL DIGITAL COMMUN DIV, ROCKWELL INT, 90- *Personal Data:* b Farnam, Nebr, Feb 27, 38; m 67; c 1. *Educ:* Univ Nebr, BSEE, 60; Iowa State Univ, MS, 62, PhD, 64. *Prof Exp:* Res engr, Naval Res Lab, Off Naval Res, 64-68. *Mem:* Inst Elec & Electronics Engrs. *Res:* Semiconductor devices; integrated circuits; reliability physics; semiconductor surfaces. *Mailing Add:* Rockwell Int 4311 Jamboree Re 501-109 Newport Beach CA 92666

KJELDAAS, TERJE, JR, THEORETICAL PHYSICS. *Current Pos:* from asst prof to assoc prof, 59-63, head dept, 77-80, PROF PHYSICS, POLYTECH INST NY, 63- *Personal Data:* b Oslo, Norway, Oct 24, 24; US citizen; m 50; c 2. *Educ:* Polytech Inst Brooklyn, BS, 48; Columbia Univ, AM, 49; Univ Pittsburgh, PhD, 59. *Prof Exp:* Res engr, Res Labs, Westinghouse Elec Corp, 49-59. *Concurrent Pos:* Consult, indust labs. *Mem:* Am Phys Soc. *Res:* Solid state theory; atomic-molecule-electron interactions. *Mailing Add:* 50 Fort Pl Staten Island NY 10301

KJELDGAARD, EDWIN ANDREAS, APPLIED CHEMISTRY, METROLOGY. *Current Pos:* Staff mem, 66-70, div supvr, 70-84, SR MEM TECH STAFF, SANDIA LABS, 84- *Personal Data:* b Brush, Colo, Sept 14, 39; m 65; c 2. *Educ:* St Olaf Col, BA, 61; Univ Colo, PhD(chem), 66. *Res:* Organic fluorine chemistry; fluorinated cyclobutenes; explosive chemistry; coordination compounds; Risk analysis. *Mailing Add:* 2532 Harold Pl Albuquerque NM 87106

KJELDSEN, CHRIS KELVIN, PHYCOLOGY. *Current Pos:* from asst prof to assoc prof, 66-73, chmn dept, 72-75, PROF BIOL, SONOMA STATE UNIV, 73- *Personal Data:* b Stockton, Calif, Apr 26, 39; m 62; c 3. *Educ:* Univ of the Pac, BA, 60, MS, 62; Ore State Univ, PhD(bot), 66. *Honors & Awards:* Mosser Award, Ore State Univ, 66. *Prof Exp:* Instr bot, Ore State Univ, 62-66. *Concurrent Pos:* NSF, DOE, grants for sci educ, 69-; Sonoma Co Planning Comn, 74-76; Sabbatical leave, Univ NWales, 76; IPA assignment, US Dept Energy, Educ Progs, Washington, DC, 78-79; Sonoma Co Hazardous Mat Comn, 85- *Mem:* Sigma Xi (vpres, 67). *Res:* Marine algae; physiological ecology and taxonomy; Sacramento San Jouquin Delta habitar analysis. *Mailing Add:* Dept Biol Sonoma State Univ 1801 E Cotati Ave Rohnert Park CA 94928-3613

KJELGAARD, WILLIAM L, AGRICULTURAL ENGINEERING. *Current Pos:* RETIRED. *Personal Data:* b Lindley, NY, Aug 27, 20; m 50; c 5. *Educ:* Pa State Univ, BS, 50, MS, 53. *Prof Exp:* Instr agr eng, WVa Univ, 51-52; from instr to asst prof, 52-60, ASSOC PROF AGR ENG, PA STATE UNIV, 60- *Mem:* Am Soc Agr Engrs. *Res:* Mechanization and processing of forage crops. *Mailing Add:* 1311 Circleville Rd State College PA 16803

KJELSBERG, MARCUS OLAF, BIOSTATISTICS. *Current Pos:* assoc prof, 66-75, div head biomed, 72-87, PROF BIOSTATIST, SCH PUB HEALTH, UNIV MINN, MINNEAPOLIS, 75- *Personal Data:* b Mayville, NDak, Dec 27, 32; m 62; c 2. *Educ:* Concordia Col, Moorhead, Minn, BA, 52; Univ Minn, MA, 55, PhD(biostatist), 62. *Prof Exp:* Instr biostatist, Sch Med, Tulane Univ, 57-60; asst prof biostatist & res assoc epidemiol, Sch Pub Health, Univ Mich, Ann Arbor, 61-66. *Concurrent Pos:* Mem, US Nat Comt Vital & Health Statist, 73-77; prin investr, Mult Risk Factor Intervention Ctr, 72- *Mem:* Am Pub Health Asn; Am Statist Asn; Am Heart Asn; Biometric Soc; Pop Asn Am. *Res:* Statistical epidemiology; health statistics; clinical trials methodology. *Mailing Add:* Biostat Box 197 Mayo Bldg Univ Minn Minneapolis MN 55455

KJONAAS, RICHARD A, ORGANIC CHEMISTRY. *Current Pos:* from asst prof to assoc prof, 83-91, PROF CHEM, IND STATE UNIV, 91- *Personal Data:* b Minot, NDak, Mar 20, 49; m 79, Deborah Orth; c Michael & Tamara. *Educ:* Valley City State Col, BS, 71; Purdue Univ, PhD(chem), 78. *Prof Exp:* Teacher high sch, NDak, 71-73; fel, Ohio State Univ, 78-79; asst prof org chem, Ft Hays State Univ, 79-83. *Mem:* Am Chem Soc; Sigma Xi; Coun Undergrad Res. *Res:* Transition metals and carbanionic reagents in organic synthesis; identification of naturally occurring flavors and fragrances. *Mailing Add:* Dept Chem Ind State Univ Terre Haute IN 47809. *Fax:* 812-237-2232; *E-Mail:* chkjon@scifac.indstate.edu

KLAAS, ERWIN EUGENE, RESTORATION ECOLOGY. *Current Pos:* assoc prof, 75-80, PROF WILDLIFE BIOL, IOWA STATE UNIV, 80- *Personal Data:* b Batchtown, Ill, Aug 23, 35; m 69, Janet Engler; c Zachary, Abigail & Benjamin. *Educ:* Univ Mo, BS, 56; Univ Kans, MA, 63, PhD(zool), 70. *Prof Exp:* From asst prof to assoc prof biol, Rockhurst Col, 65-71. *Concurrent Pos:* Res biologist, US Fish & Wildlife Serv, 71-93, asst unit leader, 75-92, unit leader, 92-, res biologist, Nat Biol Surv, 93-96; leader, Iowa Coop Fish & Wildlife Res Unit, Biol Resources Div, US Geol Surv, 96- *Mem:* Am Ornith Union; Cooper Ornith Soc; Wilson Ornith Soc; Wildlife Soc; Soc Restoration Ecol. *Res:* Population ecology of birds; restoration of disturbed ecosystems; management of habitat for optimal utilization by game and non-game species; conservaton of biodiversity. *Mailing Add:* Iowa Coop Fish & Wildlife Res Unit Iowa State Univ Ames IA 50011. *Fax:* 515-294-5468; *E-Mail:* eklaas@iastate.edu

KLAAS, NICHOLAS PAUL, ORGANIC CHEMISTRY. *Current Pos:* PRES, KLAAS ASSOCS INC, 84-; PRES, INST INNOVATIVE ENTERPRISE, INC, 85-; ADJ PROF, SAN DIEGO STATE UNIV, 85- *Personal Data:* b Kieler, Wis, June 25, 25; m 49, Ruth Barry; c Paul, Patricia, Kathleen & James. *Educ:* Loras Col, BA, 45; Univ Notre Dame, PhD(org chem), 48. *Prof Exp:* Chemist, Rohm and Haas Co, 48, actg prod mgr, 49-51; tech asst to sales develop mgr, 3M Co, 52, mkt specialist, 52-53, mgr oil indust prod, 53-59, mgr res & develop, 60-65; exec vpres, Wyomissing Corp, Reading, 65-71, dir, 68-71, chief operating officer, 70-71; vpres com develop, GAF Corp, 71-74, group vpres chem group, 74-77; gen mgr spec chem div, Ga-Pac Corp, 77; from exec vpres to pres, 77-84, gen mgr, J T Baker Chem Co, 77-84. *Mem:* AAAS; Am Chem Soc. *Res:* Organic chemical intermediates and polymers; chemicals derived from acetylene; surfactants; dyes; pigments; carbonyl iron powders; textile auxiliaries; felts; filters; electronic, laboratory and agricultural chemicals; ceramics; materials science; roofing granules; building, photographic and quarry products; abrasives and adhesives; herbicides; ion exchange; soils and soil science; horticulture; natural products. *Mailing Add:* 51 Hoot Owl Terr Kinnelon NJ 07405-2409. *Fax:* 973-838-3426; *E-Mail:* npaulklaas@aol.com

KLAASEN, GENE ALLEN, mathematics, for more information see previous edition

KLAASSEN, CURTIS DEAN, PHARMACOLOGY, TOXICOLOGY. *Current Pos:* From instr to assoc prof, Univ Kans, 68-77, assoc dir, Environ Health & Occup Med Ctr, 86-89, interim dir, 89-91, PROF PHARMACOL & TOXICOL & HEAD SECT TOXICOL, MED CTR, UNIV KANS, 77- *Personal Data:* b Ft Dodge, Iowa, Nov 23, 42; m 64; c 2. *Educ:* Wartburg Col, BA, 64; Univ Iowa, MS, 66, PhD(pharmacol), 68. *Honors & Awards:* Achievement Award, Soc Toxicol, 76. *Concurrent Pos:* Guest prof clin pharmacol, Univ Bern, Swit, 75; mem comt, Toxicol Study Sect, NIH, 76-80; assoc ed, J Pharmacol & Toxicol Methods, 77-, Toxicol & Appl Pharmacol, 80-90; vis scientist, Dept Toxicol, Inst Radiation & Environ Res, Munich, Ger, 78; comt mem, Alkyl Benzenes, Nat Acad Sci, 79-81, Comt Toxicol, 88-91, Comt Storage & Disposal Chems Lab, 93-; Burroughs Wellcome scholar toxicol, 82-87; mem, Int Workshop Manpower Develop & Training in Toxicol & Chem Safety, WHO, 83-84; prof molecular cytol, Inst Invest Cytol, Valencia, Spain, 84-; distinguished vis prof, NMex State Univ, 85, Univ Toledo, 87; Coun Dent Therapeut, Am Dent Asn, 88-; trustee, Health & Environ Sci Inst, Int Life Sci Inst, 89- *Mem:* Soc Toxicol (vpres, 89-90, pres, 90-91); Am Soc Pharmacol & Exp Therapeut; Sigma Xi; AAAS; Am Asn Study Liver Dis; Soc Exp Biol & Med. *Res:* Biliary excretion of drugs and toxicants. *Mailing Add:* Dept Pharmacol Univ Kans Med Ctr Kansas City KS 66160-7417. *Fax:* 913-588-7501

KLAASSEN, DWIGHT HOMER, BIOCHEMISTRY. *Current Pos:* assoc prof, 64-67, PROF CHEM, UNIV WIS-PLATTEVILLE, 67- *Personal Data:* b Weatherford, Okla, Aug 15, 36; m 57; c 3. *Educ:* Tabor Col, BA, 58; Kans State Univ, MS, 61, PhD(biochem), 65. *Prof Exp:* Asst instr biochem, Kans State Univ, 63-64. *Concurrent Pos:* Coordr Coop Educ & Internships, 77-81; Assoc Dean, Student Affairs, 81-84, asst chancellor, Univ Relations, 84- *Mem:* Am Sci Affil; Sigma Xi. *Res:* Binding of sulfur-containing azo dyes related to dimethylaminoazobenzene to rat liver proteins; comparative study of mitochondrial proteins involving amino acid composition and solubility. *Mailing Add:* Dept Chem Univ Wis Platteville WI 53818

KLAASSEN, HAROLD EUGENE, ECOLOGY, FISH BIOLOGY. *Current Pos:* ASSOC PROF BIOL, KANS STATE UNIV, 67- *Personal Data:* b Hillsboro, Kans, Apr 18, 35; m 56; c 2. *Educ:* Tabor Col, BA, 57; Kans State Univ, MS, 59; Univ Wash, Seattle, PhD(aquatic ecol), 67. *Prof Exp:* Fishery biologist, Univ Wash, Seattle, 59. *Mem:* Am Fisheries Soc; Sigma Xi. *Res:* Fisheries management; fish distribution and production; aquaculture. *Mailing Add:* Div Biol Kans State Univ 232 Ackert Hall Manhattan KS 66506-4901

KLABUNDE, KENNETH JOHN, ORGANIC CHEMISTRY, INORGANIC CHEMISTRY. *Current Pos:* PROF CHEM & HEAD DEPT, KANS STATE UNIV, 79- *Personal Data:* b Madison, Wis, Aug 30, 43; m 67; c 3. *Educ:* Augustana Col, BA, 65; Univ Iowa, PhD(org chem), 69. *Honors & Awards:* Sigma Xi Res Award, 77, 87. *Prof Exp:* Res assoc org chem, Pa State Univ, 69-70; from asst prof to prof org chem, Univ NDak, 70-79. *Concurrent Pos:* Grants, Res Corp, 70-72, Univ NDak, 70-72, Petrol Res Fund, 71-74 & 79-85; grants from NSF, 72-91, US Dept Energy, 74-80, Indust, 79-85, Army Res Off, 84-91 & Naval Res Off, 85-88. *Mem:* Am Chem Soc; Sigma Xi. *Res:* Organic-Inorganic: reactive intermediates such as metal atom chemistry, carbonmonosulfide chemistry, organometallic synthesis, thin film materials; metal oxide chemistry; use of metal vapors and other reactive species as synthetic reagents; adsorbents. *Mailing Add:* Dept Chem Kans State Univ 111 Willard Hall Manhattan KS 66506-3701

KLABUNDE, RICHARD EDWIN, cardiovascular physiology, pharmacology, for more information see previous edition

KLACSMANN, JOHN ANTHONY, ORGANIC CHEMISTRY FINISHES, TOXIC WASTE CLEAN-UP. *Current Pos:* RETIRED. *Personal Data:* b West New York, NJ, Oct 6, 21; m 44, Bette Birdsey; c Steven B, Peter G & John A Jr. *Educ:* Yale Univ, BS, 42, MS, 44, PhD(org chem), 47. *Prof Exp:* Lab instr, Yale Univ, 42-44 & 46-47; dept supvr, Carbide & Carbon Chems Corp, Tenn, 44-46; res chemist, Fabrics & Finishes Dept, Newburgh Lab, E I du Pont de Nemours & Co, Inc, 47-49, supvr, 49-53, res mgr, 53-56, res mgr, Marshall Lab, 56-58, lab dir, Exp Sta, Del, 58-59, asst dir res, Fabrics & Finishes Dept, Res Div, 60-64, asst dir mkt, Automative & Indust Prods, 64-66, gen sales mgr consumer prods, 66-67, dir mkt, Consumer Prod Div, 67-69, dir, Finishes Mkt Div, Fabrics & Finishes Dept, 69-71, dir, Finishes Div, 71-73, vpres & gen mgr, Fabrics & Finishes Dept, 73-75, vpres & gen mgr, Int Dept, 75-78, vpres int, 78-81; exec vpres, Cleansites Inc, 85-86. *Mem:* Am Chem Soc; AAAS; Sigma Xi. *Res:* Finishes; coated fabrics; polymers. *Mailing Add:* 5160 Bridlewood Ct Marsh Landing Ponte Vedra Beach FL 32082

KLAFTER, RICHARD D(AVID), CONTROLS, ROBOTICS. *Current Pos:* PROF ELEC ENG, TEMPLE UNIV, 84- *Personal Data:* b New York, NY, Aug 5, 36; m 59, Marcia Balaban; c Leslie & Melissa. *Educ:* Mass Inst Technol, SB, 58; Columbia Univ, MSEE, 59, EE, 63; City Univ New York, PhD(optimal control), 69. *Prof Exp:* Lectr elec eng, City Col New York, 59-64 & 65-67; from asst prof to assoc prof elec eng, Drexel Univ, 67-84. *Concurrent Pos:* Assoc proj dir, NASA-Am Soc Eng Educ, 71; proj dir cardiac pacemakers, NSF, 73-75. *Mem:* Sigma Xi; Inst Elec & Electronics Engrs; Soc Mfg Engr; Robotics & Automation Soc (pres). *Res:* Mobile robots, optimal trajectory control of robots, tactile sensing, sensored and nonsensored robot navigation; motion control. *Mailing Add:* 607 Park Lane Wyncote PA 19095-1315. *Fax:* 215-204-6936; *E-Mail:* v5442e@vm.temple.edu

KLAGER, KARL, ORGANIC CHEMISTRY, PROPELLANTS & EXPLOSIVES. *Current Pos:* mgr solid propellant develop, Aerojet-Gen Corp, 50-67, mgr res & tech opers, 67-69, asst gen mgr, Solid Rocket Div, 69-71, vpres-dir opers, Aerojet Solid Propulsion Co, 71-73, TECH CONSULT, AEROJET-GEN CORP, 73- *Personal Data:* b Vienna, Austria, May 15, 08; nat US; m 38; c 1. *Educ:* Univ Vienna, PhD(chem), 34. *Honors & Awards:* James H Wyld Propulsion Award, Am Inst Aeronaut & Astronaut, 72; Chem Pioneer Award, Am Inst Chemists, 78; Austrian Honor Cross, Sci & Art Medal, 89. *Prof Exp:* Instr, Univ Vienna, 32-34; asst prod engr, Neuman Bros, Romania, 34-36; res chemist, Chinoin, AG, Hungary, 36-38 & I G Farben, Ger, 39-48; res & develop chemist, Off Naval Res, 49. *Concurrent Pos:* Tech consult, US govt, 73-, Cordova Chem Co, 80-85, Martin Marietta Aerospace, 75-79, Teledyne Coast Proseal, 73-76, Coalcon Co, NY, 78-79, Artek Burlin Game, Calif, 83, Brea Chem Co, 60-61, Ger Ministry Defense, 66-67, Aerochemie, Italy, 70, Dinippon Cellulose/Daicel, Japan, 64-86, Serv Poudre, France, 70, Australian Dept Defense Labs, Adelaide, 84, Essex Chem Co, 73-77. *Mem:* Fel Am Inst Aeronaut & Astronaut; fel Am Inst Chemists; Am Chem Soc; Sigma Xi. *Res:* Acetylene derivatives; hydrogenation; cyclooctatetraene; organic preparative and catalytic chemistry; rocket fuels; chemical rocket propellants; synthesis and composition; manufacturing methods; combustion properties; safety characteristics. *Mailing Add:* 4110 Riding Club Lane Sacramento CA 95864-1649

KLAGSBRUN, MICHAEL, CELL BIOLOGY, BIOMEDICAL RESEARCH. *Current Pos:* Assoc prof med res, 80-93, PROF, DEPT SURG, HARVARD MED SCH, 93- *Personal Data:* b Antwerp, Belg, Jan 16, 39. *Educ:* City Col New York, BS, 60; Univ Wis, PhD(biochem), 68. *Mem:* Am Soc Cell Biol; Am Soc Biol Chemists; NY Acad Sci. *Mailing Add:* Childrens Hosp Med Ctr Harvard Med Sch 300 Longwood Ave Boston MA 02115-5737

KLAHR, CARL NATHAN, APPLIED PHYSICS. *Current Pos:* sr assoc, 61-67, PRES, FUNDAMENTAL METHODS ASSOCS, INC, 67- *Personal Data:* b Pittsburgh, Pa, July 3, 27; m 53; c 3. *Educ:* Carnegie Inst Technol, BS & MS, 48, MS & DSc(physics), 50. *Prof Exp:* Physicist, Res Labs, Westinghouse Elec Corp, 50-52; physicist & proj mgr, Nuclear Develop Corp Am, 52-57; proj mgr & sr physicist, Tech Res Group, Inc, 57-61. *Concurrent Pos:* Lectr, Columbia Univ, 53-58. *Mem:* Am Phys Soc; Am Nuclear Soc; Opers Res Soc Am; Inst Mgt Sci; Inst Elec & Electronics Engrs. *Res:* Hypervelocity physics; space vehicle technology; semiconductor device design and technology; solid state physics; operations research; electromagnetic radiation and quantum electronics. *Mailing Add:* Fundamental Methods Assoc Inc 678 Cedar Lawn Ave Lawrence NY 11559

KLAHR, PHILIP, COMPUTER SCIENCE. *Current Pos:* VPRES PROF SERV, INFERENCE CORP, 86- *Personal Data:* b Mar 7, 46; US citizen. *Educ:* Univ Mich, BS, 67; Univ Wis, MS, 69, PhD(comput sci), 75. *Prof Exp:* Sr analyst, Syst Develop Corp, 72-78; dir, Info Processing Systs Prog, Rand Corp, 78-86. *Mem:* Asn Comput Mach; Cognitive Sci Soc; Am Asn Artificial Intel; Inst Elec & Electronics Engrs. *Res:* Artificial intelligence research in knowledge-based systems; rule-based modeling, simulation, languages; explanation techniques, man-machine interfaces,; deductive question-answering, problem solving, learning, planning; abstraction, data-base management and cognitive modeling. *Mailing Add:* 473 Live Oak Dr Mill Valley CA 94941

KLAHR, SAULO, NEPHROLOGY. *Current Pos:* USPHS trainee, Washington Univ, 61-63, from instr to assoc prof, 63-72, prof med & dir renal div, 72-91, co-chmn, Dept Med, 91-97, SIMON PROF MED, SCH MED, WASHINGTON UNIV, 91- *Personal Data:* b Santander, Colombia, June 8, 35; US citizen; m 65, Carol De Clue; c James & Robert. *Educ:* Col de Santa Librada, BS, 54; Nat Univ Colombia, MD, 59. *Honors & Awards:* Thomas Addis Award, Int Soc Renal Nutrit & Metab, 96; David M Hume Mem Award, 92. *Concurrent Pos:* Asst physician, Barnes Hosp, St Louis, Mo, 66-72, assoc physician, 72-75, physician, 75-; established investr, Am Heart Asn, 68-73; mem adv comt, Artificial Kidney, Chronic Uremia Prog, Nat Inst Arthritis & Metab Dis, 70-78; chmn med adv bd & mem bd dirs; Kidney Found Eastern Mo & Metro East, 73-74; mem fel comt, Nat Kidney Found, 77-81 & chmn, 80-81; assoc ed, J Clin Invest, 77-82; pres, Nate Kidney

Found, 88-90; ed, Am Kidney Dis, 91-96, Kidney Int, 97- *Mem:* NY Acad Sci; Am Physiol Soc; Biophys Soc; Am Soc Clin Invest; Asn Am Physicians. *Res:* Hormonal control of ion transport across isolated membranes; studies on the functional and metabolic alterations produced by kidney disease; intermediary metabolism of the kidney. *Mailing Add:* Dept Med Barnes Jewish Hosp 216 S Kingshighway Blvd St Louis MO 63110. *Fax:* 314-454-5110

KLAIBER, FRED WAYNE, STRUCTURAL ENGINEERING. *Current Pos:* assoc prof, 68-80, PROF CIVIL ENG, IOWA STATE UNIV, 68- *Personal Data:* b Lafayette, Ind, Oct 7, 40; m 64, Karen Reisen; c Brent & Kimberly K (Farmer). *Educ:* Purdue Univ, BSCE, 62, MSCE, 64, PhD(struct eng), 68. *Honors & Awards:* Raymond C Reese Res Prize, 78. *Prof Exp:* Res engr, Caterpillar Tractor Co, 68. *Concurrent Pos:* ACI fel, 87; Anson Marston Distinguished Prof, Col Eng, Iowa State Univ. *Mem:* Am Soc Civil Engrs; Am Railway Eng Asn; Am Concrete Inst; Can Soc Civil Eng. *Res:* Bridge rehabilitation and strengthening; prestressed folded plate theory; study of bridges behavior. *Mailing Add:* Dept Civil & Construct Eng Iowa State Univ Ames IA 50011

KLAIBER, GEORGE STANLEY, PHYSICS. *Current Pos:* RETIRED. *Personal Data:* b Toledo, Ohio, Nov 20, 16; m 44; c 2. *Educ:* Univ Buffalo, BA, 38; Univ Ill, MA, 41, PhD(physics), 43. *Prof Exp:* Asst physics, Univ Buffalo, 38-39; from asst to instr, Univ Ill, 39-44; res physicist, Gen Elec Co, 44-47; from asst prof to assoc prof physics, Univ Buffalo, 47-60; consult physicist, Wurlitzer Co, 60-67. *Concurrent Pos:* Independent consult physicist, 67- *Mem:* Am Phys Soc. *Res:* Acoustics and vibrations. *Mailing Add:* 2504 Colvin Blvd Tonawanda NY 14150

KLAIN, GEORGE J, toxicology, metabolism; deceased, see previous edition for last biography

KLAINER, ALBERT S, INTERNAL MEDICINE, INFECTIOUS DISEASES. *Current Pos:* PROF MED, MED SCH, RUTGERS UNIV, 75-; PROF CLIN MED, COL PHYSICIANS & SURGEONS, COLUMBIA UNIV, 80- *Personal Data:* b Chelsea, Mass, Oct 29, 35; m 57, Jo-Ann Showstack; c Peter, Lori & Traci. *Educ:* Mass Inst Technol, BSc, 57; Tufts Univ, MD, 61. *Honors & Awards:* Hull Award, AMA, 71, Morrissey Award, 72 & Bronze Medal, 72. *Prof Exp:* Assoc prof med, Col Med, Ohio State Univ, 71-72; prof med & infectious dis, Sch Med, WVa Univ, 72-75. *Concurrent Pos:* Grant infectious dis & internal med, New Eng Med Ctr Hosps, 63-64 &; chmn, Dept Med, Morristown Mem Hosp, 75- *Mem:* Infectious Dis Soc Am; fel Am Col Physicians; Am Fedn Clin Res. *Res:* Scanning electron microscopy; infectious diseases, antibiotic pharmacology and AIDS research. *Mailing Add:* 315 W 70th St New York NY 10023

KLAINER, STANLEY M, INSTRUMENTATION, PHYSICAL & ANALYTICAL CHEMISTRY. *Current Pos:* TECH CONSULT LASER SPECTROSCOPY, 78-; PRES, ST&E, INC, 82- *Personal Data:* b Chelsea, Mass, Apr 11, 30; m 52; c 6. *Educ:* Clark Univ, BA, 52, MA, 55, PhD, 59. *Prof Exp:* Res coordr qual control, Martin Div, Martin Marietta Corp, 57-59; chemist, Res Labs, Bendix Corp, 59-60; sr chemist, Nat Res Corp, 60-61; sr chemist, Tracerlab Div, Lab for Electronics, Inc, 61-63, spec projs mgr instruments, 63-64, from res & develop mgr to res mgr, 64-67; staff chemist, Block Eng, Inc, 67-70, mgr anal systs dept, 70-78; dep group leader geosci, Lawrence Berkeley Lab, 78-81, group mgr, 81-82. *Concurrent Pos:* Joseph F Donnelly fel, 55. *Mem:* Am Chem Soc; Soc Appl Spectros; Soc Photo-Optical Engrs; Combustion Inst. *Res:* Development of optical, RF and microwave spectrometers and nuclear instruments; analysis of trace atmospheric constituents, ablation, encapsulation, special quality control analytical techniques and ultracentrifugation; interferometry; Raman, remote Raman, micro Raman and infrared spectroscopy; nuclear quadrupole resonance; micro particle analysis; chemical transport in natural systems; fiber optical chemical sensors for environmental and chemical measurements; medical, biological diagnostics and process control; surface chemistry and structure studies. *Mailing Add:* 2063 Sutton Way Henderson NV 89014-4206

KLAMKIN, MURRAY S, MATHEMATICS. *Current Pos:* chmn dept, 76-81, prof, 76-90, EMER PROF MATH, UNIV ALTA, 90- *Personal Data:* b Brooklyn, NY, Mar 5, 21. *Educ:* Cooper Union, BChE, 42; Polytech Inst Brooklyn, MS, 47. *Hon Degrees:* DrMath, Univ Waterloo, 83. *Honors & Awards:* Distinguished Serv Math, Math Asn Am, 88; David Hilbert Award, World Fedn Nat Math Competitions, 92. *Prof Exp:* From instr to assoc prof math, Polytech Inst Brooklyn, 48-56; prin staff mathematician, Res & Adv Develop Div, Avco Corp, 56-62; prof interdisciplinary studies & res in eng, State Univ NY, Buffalo, 62-64; vis prof math, Univ Minn, 64-65; prin res scientist, Sci Lab, Ford Motor Co, 65-75; prof appl math, Univ Waterloo, 74-76. *Concurrent Pos:* Problem ed, Soc Indust & Appl Math Review, 59-94; vis lectr, Math Asn Am, 62-70, Soc Indust & Appl Math, 71-72; assoc problem ed, Math Mag, 70-71; mem, Nat High Sch Math Contest Comt, 72-85; mem, Can Olympiad Comt, 74-83; assoc ed, Comput & Math Applns, 74-, Math & Comput Modelling, 80; coach, US Int Math Olympiad Team, 75-84. *Mem:* Fel AAAS; Am Math Soc; Math Asn Am; Soc Indust & Appl Math; Sigma Xi; foreign mem Belg Acad Arts, Lett & Fine Arts. *Res:* Applied mathematics; geometry; heat conduction and radiation. *Mailing Add:* Dept Math Univ Alta Edmonton AB T6G 2G1 Can. *Fax:* 403-492-6826; *E-Mail:* mathdept@sirius.math.ualberta.ca

KLAND, MATHILDE JUNE, ENVIRONMENTAL CHEMISTRY, FOSSIL FUEL CHEMISTRY. *Current Pos:* CONSULT, HEALTH EFFECTS CHEMS, 82- *Personal Data:* b Chicago, Ill, June 6, 16; m 50; c 2. *Educ:* Univ Chicago, BS, 39; Northwestern Univ, PhD(org chem), 48. *Prof Exp:* Sr chemist, Distillation Prods, Inc, NY, 39-41; sr chemist, Revere & La Ord Divs, 41-43; asst prof chem, Goucher Col, 48-49; E I du Pont fel, Ohio State Univ, 49-51; res assoc, Boston Univ, 51-52; writer & abstractor, 52-54 & 56-58; res assoc, Med Sch, Tufts Univ, 54-56; staff scientist, Lawrence Berkeley Lab, Univ Calif, 58-82. *Concurrent Pos:* Univ fel, Northwestern Univ, 44-45, Allied chem & dye fel, 45-46; Dupont fel, Ohio State Univ, 49-51; writer, environ chem-toxicol, 86-; environ consult, Environ Asn. *Mem:* AAAS; Am Chem Soc; NY Acad Sci; Asn Women Sci. *Res:* Reactions of styrene oxide; structure of styrene oxide dimers; molecular structure and spectra of organic compounds; abnormal bimolecular reactions of furfuryl chloride; grignard reactions; radiation chemistry of peptides; water pollution monitoring of bio-parameters and organics; toxic effects of pollutants, food additives, pesticides and drugs; use of structure-toxicity/carcinogenicity relationships in prediction of health effects chemical teratogens/pesticedes; fossil fuel chemistry; teratogenicity of pesticides and other environmental pollutants. *Mailing Add:* 3678 Hastings Ct Lafayette CA 94549-3020

KLANDERMAN, BRUCE HOLMES, ORGANIC CHEMISTRY,ENVIRONMENTAL SCIENCES. *Current Pos:* SR PROG MGR, RADIAN CORP, 92- *Personal Data:* b Grand Rapids, Mich, Feb 27, 38; m 60, Alice E Bos; c Thomas J, David B & Paul W. *Educ:* Calvin Col, AB, 59; Univ Ill, MS, 61, PhD(org chem),63. *Prof Exp:* Res chemist, Eastman Kodak Co, 63-64; sr res chemist, 64-68, res assoc, 68-74, tech assoc, Synthetic Chem Div, 75, dept head, 76-77, govt regulations coordr, Gen Mgt, 78-80, dir, Environ Tech Serv, Kodak Park Div, 81-86, Occup Health Lab, 87, Health Environ Labs, 88-92. *Mem:* Soc Photog Scientists & Engrs; Am Chem Soc. *Res:* Benzyne chemistry; liquid crystals; organic semiconductors; aliphatic diazonium chemistry; anthracene and triptycene chemistry. *Mailing Add:* 31 Shadow Pines Dr Penfield NY 14526

KLANFER, KARL, CHEMICAL ENGINEERING. *Current Pos:* RETIRED. *Personal Data:* b Vienna, Austria, Oct 10, 04; m 46; c 1. *Educ:* Inst Technol, Vienna, Austria, ChemE, 27. *Prof Exp:* Chief chemist, Wiener Leather Indust, Vienna, Austria, 27-34; supt, E Traub Co, Prague, Czech, 35-39; res chemist, Beardmore & Co Ltd, Acton, Ont, Can, 40-46; res dir, Cortume Carioca, Brazil, 46-50; res dir, AR Clarke & Co Ltd, Toronto, Ont, Can, 50-56; tech dir, A C Lawrence Leather Co, Peabody, 56-61. *Concurrent Pos:* Lectr, Univ Exten, Vienna, 30-34; consult chem eng, 61- *Mem:* Sr mem Am Chem Soc; Am Leather Chem Asn; fel Chem Inst Can; Royal Soc Chem; Am Leather Chem Asn; Can Soc Chem Eng; Soc Leather Technologists, London. *Res:* Chemistry and technology of leather and tanning; author or coauthor of 40 publications; microanalysis; chemistry of chrom-complexes; chemistry of fats & oils; instrumental process control. *Mailing Add:* 18 Colgate Rd Marblehead MA 01945

KLAPMAN, SOLOMON JOEL, mathematical physics; deceased, see previous edition for last biography

KLAPPER, DAVID G, MICROBIOLOGY, IMMUNOLOGY. *Current Pos:* PROF MICROBIOL & IMMUNOL, MED SCH, UNIV NC. *Personal Data:* b New York, NY, Mar 15, 44. *Educ:* Tulane Univ, BS, 65; Univ Fla, PhD(microbiol & immunol), 72. *Prof Exp:* Prof microbiol & immunol, Rockefeller Univ, Univ Tex Southwestern Med Sch. *Mailing Add:* Dept Microbiol & Immunol Med Sch Univ NC CB No 7290 Chapel Hill NC 27599-7290

KLAPPER, GILBERT, PALEONTOLOGY. *Current Pos:* assoc prof, 68-73, PROF GEOL, UNIV IOWA, 73- *Personal Data:* b Wichita, Kans, Sept 29, 34; m 59; c 3. *Educ:* Stanford Univ, BS, 56; Univ Kans, MS, 58; Univ Iowa, PhD(geol), 62. *Prof Exp:* Paleontol, Shell Oil Co, La, 58-59; NSF fel & res assoc, Ill State Geol Surv, 62-63; res paleontol, Res Ctr, Pan Am Petrol Corp, 63-68. *Concurrent Pos:* Vis prof, Ore State Univ, 78. *Mem:* Paleont Res Inst; Paleont Soc; Soc Econ Paleont & Mineral; Brit Paleont Asn; Ger Paleont Soc. *Res:* Micropaleontology, especially research in conodonts; biostratigraphy, Silurian, Devonian and Mississippian. *Mailing Add:* Dept Geol Univ Iowa Iowa City IA 52242-1000

KLAPPER, JACOB, COMMUNICATIONS SYSTEMS, PHASE-LOCKED LOOPS. *Current Pos:* chmn dept, 86-92, PROF, ELEC ENG DEPT, NJ INST TECHNOL, NEWARK, 71- *Personal Data:* b Ulanow, Poland, Sept 17, 30; US citizen; m 58, Molly Teicher; c 2. *Educ:* City Col New York, BEE, 56; Columbia Univ, MS, 58; NY Univ, EngScD, 65. *Honors & Awards:* Region One Award, Inst Elec & Electronics Engrs, 86. *Prof Exp:* Elec engr, Columbia Broadcasting Syst, 52-56; lectr elec eng, City Col New York, 56-59; proj engr, Fed Sci Corp, 59-60; sr mem tech staff, Adv Commun Labs, Radio Corp Am, 60-65, sr proj mem tech staff, 65-67; assoc prof elec eng, Newark Col Eng, 67-71. *Concurrent Pos:* Consult, various orgn. *Mem:* Sr mem Inst Elec & Electronics Engrs; Commun Soc; Eng Med & Biol Soc. *Res:* Electrical communication; systems and techniques with emphasis on phase-locked loops and FM systems. *Mailing Add:* NJ Inst Technol 323 King Blvd Newark NJ 07102. *Fax:* 973-596-5680; *E-Mail:* klapper@admin.njit.edu

KLAPPER, MICHAEL H, BIOCHEMISTRY, BIOPHYSICS. *Current Pos:* from asst prof to assoc prof, 66-86, PROF CHEM, OHIO STATE UNIV, 86- *Personal Data:* b Berlin, Ger, June 10, 37; US citizen; m 60; c 2. *Educ:* Harvard Univ, AB, 58; Univ Rochester, MS, 59; Univ Calif, PhD(biochem), 64. *Prof Exp:* Fel chem, Northwestern Univ, 64-66. *Concurrent Pos:* Co-dir,

Nat Ctr Sci Teaching & Learning, 90. *Mem:* Biophys Soc; Am Soc Biol Chemists; Protein Soc; Am Chem Soc; AAAS. *Res:* Physical biochemistry of enzyme structure; theoretical and experimental studies of enzyme catalysis; long range electron transfer in polypeptides and proteins; fast radical reactions. *Mailing Add:* Chem Dept Ohio State Univ 120 W 18th Ave Columbus OH 43210-1328. *Fax:* 614-292-1585

KLAPPROTH, WILLIAM JACOB, JR, POLYMER CHEMISTRY. *Current Pos:* RETIRED. *Personal Data:* b Springfield, Ohio, Aug 2, 20; m 45; c 2. *Educ:* Wittenberg Col, AB, 42; Univ Chicago, MS & PhD(org chem), 49. *Prof Exp:* Res chemist, Stamford Res Labs, Am Cyanamid Co, 49-54, group leader, Warners Plant, 54-57, group leader catalytic & gen process improv, Bridgeville Plant, 57-59, mgr acids & miscellaneous chems develop, 59-63; tech dir, Bridgeville Plant, Koppers Co, Inc, 63-67, sr proj scientist, Monroeville Res Ctr, Arco Polymers Inc, 67-70, sr group mgr, 70-78, prin scientist, Arco Chem Co, 79-81. *Concurrent Pos:* Consult, 81-83. *Mem:* Am Chem Soc. *Res:* Research and development in polymers, especially polystyrene, high pressure polyethylene and related copolymers. *Mailing Add:* 3576 Logans Ferry Rd Murrysville PA 15668

KLARFELD, JOSEPH, THEORETICAL PHYSICS. *Current Pos:* ASSOC PROF, GRAD CTR, CITY UNIV NEW YORK, 80- *Personal Data:* b Poland, Dec 22, 35; c 2. *Educ:* Israel Inst Technol, BSc, 59, MSc, 62; Yeshiva Univ, PhD(physics), 69. *Prof Exp:* Instr physics, Israel Inst Technol, 58-61; res assoc, Israel Atomic Energy Comn, 61-63; asst prof, Queens Col, NY, 69-73, asst chmn dept, 69-76, dep chmn dept, 76-78, assoc prof physics, 74. *Concurrent Pos:* Vis assoc prof, Tel Aviv Univ, 78-79; res fel, City Univ New York, 78-79. *Mem:* Asn Math Physics; Am Phys Soc; NY Acad Sci; Int Soc Gen Relativity & Gravitation. *Res:* Quantization of general relativity; foundations of quantum field theory; relativistic astrophysics. *Mailing Add:* Queens Col Physics Dept 6530 Kissena Blvd Flushing NY 11367

KLARMAN, HERBERT E, MEDICAL ADMINISTRATION. *Current Pos:* RETIRED. *Personal Data:* b Chmielnick, Poland, Dec 21, 16. *Educ:* Columbia Univ, AB, 39; Univ Wis, MA, 46, PhD, 46. *Honors & Awards:* Norman A Welch Award, 65. *Prof Exp:* Asst dir, Hosp Coun Greater NY, 49-51, assoc dir, 52-62; mem, Health Serv Res Study Sect, NIH, 62-66; mem fac, Johns Hopkins Univ, 62-69, prof pub health admin & political econ, 65-69; prof environ med & commun health, Downstate Med Ctr, 69-70; prof pub admin, Grad Sch Pub Admin, NY Univ, 70-82; NY State Health Adv Coun, 76-83. *Concurrent Pos:* Asst dir, NY State Hosp Study, 48-49; Guggenheim fel, 48-49. *Mem:* Inst Med-Nat Acad Sci; fel AAAS; Pub Health Asn; Am Econ Asn. *Mailing Add:* 1 E University Pkwy Baltimore MD 21218

KLARMAN, KARL J(OSEPH), ELECTRICAL ENGINEERING. *Current Pos:* CONSULT, 74- *Personal Data:* b Scotia, NY, Mar 18, 22; c Nancy L & James D. *Educ:* Union Col, BS, 44; Columbia Univ, MS, 47. *Prof Exp:* Jr engr, Carl L Norden, Inc, 44; lectr elec eng, Union Univ, NY, 45-46; proj engr, Avion Instrument Corp, 46-47, Eclipse-Pioneer Div, Bendix Aviation Corp, 47-51; plant mgr, Electro Tec Corp, 51-53, dir eng, 53-55, vpres, 55-57; sect head, Sanders Assocs, 57-59; chief prod engr, Precision Prod Dept, Northrop, 59-61; eng scientist, Defense Electronic Prod Div, 61-74, eng scientist, Govt & Com Div, RCA Corp, 71-74. *Mem:* Sigma Xi; Nat Soc Prof Engrs; Inst Elec & Electronics Engrs. *Res:* Gyroscopic instruments, design, development and production; design, development, test and production of inertial and other electro-mechanical instruments and systems; granted two patents, gyroscopic devices. *Mailing Add:* 20 Kipling St Nashua NH 03062

KLARMAN, WILLIAM L, research administration, for more information see previous edition

KLARMANN, JOSEPH, PHYSICS. *Current Pos:* from asst prof to prof, 61-96, EMER PROF PHYSICS, WASHINGTON UNIV, 96- *Personal Data:* b Berlin, Ger, Jan 16, 28; m 57, Erika Muellers; c A Daniel & Peter R. *Educ:* Hebrew Univ, Israel, MSc, 54; Univ Rochester, PhD(physics), 58. *Prof Exp:* Res assoc & instr, Univ Rochester, 57-58, instr, 58-61. *Mem:* Int Astron Union; Am Phys Soc. *Res:* Cosmic ray astrophysics. *Mailing Add:* Dept Physics Washington Univ St Louis MO 63130. *E-Mail:* jkl@howdy.wustl.edu

KLASINC, LEO, MOLECULAR SPECTROSCOPY, ATMOSPHERIC CHEMISTRY. *Current Pos:* from asst prof to assoc prof, 71-79, PROF FAC SCI, UNIV ZAGREB, 79- *Personal Data:* b Zagreb, Croatia, May 20, 37; m 61, Darka Jerkovic; c Natasa & Anton-Jan. *Educ:* Univ Zagreb, dipl chem, 60, PhD(chem), 63. *Honors & Awards:* Ruder Boskovic Prize, Repub Croatia, 88. *Prof Exp:* Fel theoret & radiation chem, Nuclear Res Ctr, Karlsruhe, 66-68. *Concurrent Pos:* Res asst phys chem, Ruder Boskovic Inst, Zagreb, 61-63 & 64-68, res assoc, 68-72, sr res assoc, 72-77, sr scientist, 77-; vis prof, Dept Chem, La State Univ. *Mem:* Am Phys Soc; Int Soc Quantum Biol; World Asn Theoret Org Chemists; Am Chem Soc; Croatia Chem Soc; Croatia Acad Sci & Arts; NY Acad Sci. *Res:* Electronically excited states of molecules and ions, spectroscopy, quantum chemistry, photochemistry and chemical kinetics; chemical processes in the atmosphere, photosmog and troposphere ozone formation. *Mailing Add:* Dept Chem La State Univ Baton Rouge LA 70803. *E-Mail:* klasinc@olimp.irb.hr

KLASNER, JOHN SAMUEL, STRUCTURAL GEOLOGY, APPLIED GEOPHYSICS. *Current Pos:* from asst prof to assoc prof geol, Western Ill Univ, 74-79, chmn dept, 74-78, assoc dir hons prog, 90-93, PROF GEOL, 72-, DIR HONS PROG, WESTERN ILL UNIV, 94- *Personal Data:* b Flint, Mich, June 22, 35; m 64, Gretchen M Kolb; c Christopher J, Frederick L, Laura M & Paul H. *Educ:* Mich State Univ, BS, 57, MS, 64; Mich Technol Univ, PhD(geol), 72. *Prof Exp:* Geophys engr, Geophys Serv Inc, 57-62; geophysicist, Standard Oil Co Calif, 64-69. *Concurrent Pos:* Geologist econgeol, US Geol Surv, 92- *Mem:* Sigma Xi; fel Geol Soc Am; Soc Explor Geophysicists; fel Geol Asn Can; Am Geophys Union; Nat Asn Geol Teachers. *Res:* Economic and Precambrian geology of Northern Michigan; structural geology and tectonics of Northern Michigan and Wisconsin; geophysical archeology; regional geophysics Northern Michigan, Wisconsin, North and South Dakota. *Mailing Add:* Dept Geol Western Ill Univ 900 W Adams St Macomb IL 61455-1396. *Fax:* 309-298-2400; *E-Mail:* mfjsk@uxa.ecn.bgu.edu

KLASS, DONALD LEROY, ORGANIC CHEMISTRY, EDUCATOR, ENERGY & ENVIRONMENTAL SCIENTIST. *Current Pos:* DIR RES, ENTECH INT, INC, 92- *Personal Data:* b Waukegan, Ill, July 23, 26; m 49, Barbara A Boggess; c Richard R, Janet J (Grubbs) & Roger R. *Educ:* Univ Ill, BS, 51; Harvard Univ, AM, 52, PhD(org chem), 55. *Honors & Awards:* Nat Lubricating Grease Inst Award, 66; Mem Award, Foote Chem Co, 66; Clarence E Earl Mem Award, 66; Richard A Glenn Award, Bituminous Coal Res, Inc, 76. *Prof Exp:* Res chemist, Stand Oil Co, Ind, 54-55 & Am Can Co, 56-59; dir process & prod res div, Pure Oil Co, Ill, 59-65; asst dir basic res, Inst Gas Technol, Ill Inst Technol, 65-69, asst res dir, 69-76, dir basic res, 76-77, dir eng & sci res, 77-79, asst vpres, 79-80, vpres educ, 80-92. *Concurrent Pos:* Consult energy & chem prod; adj prof chem, Ill Inst Technol, 67-72; tech ed, J Solar Energy Eng, 83-89; bd mem, Biomass Energy Res Asn, 85-; vis prof, EChina Univ Chem Technol, 88. *Mem:* Am Chem Soc; Biomass Energy Res Asn; Am Inst Chem Eng. *Res:* Research and education administration; gas processing; petrochemicals; refining; catalysis; fermentation; waste treatment; pollution control; gasification-liquefaction of wastes, biomass and fossil fuels; energy supplies; environmental sciences and engineering; author of over 170 technical papers and granted numerous US and foreign patents. *Mailing Add:* 25543 W Scott Rd Barrington IL 60010. *Fax:* 847-382-5595

KLASS, MICHAEL R, EXPERIMENTAL BIOLOGY. *Current Pos:* lab head biochem genetics, 86-90, INTERIM DIR, CORP MOLECULAR BIOL, ABBOTT LABS, 90-, NEW BUS VENTURE. *Personal Data:* b July 31, 49. *Educ:* Univ Wis-Madison, BS, 71; Univ Wyo, Laramie, PhD(cell biol), 74. *Prof Exp:* Res asst, Dept Zool, Univ Wyo, 72-74; res assoc, Dept Molecular, Cellular & Develop Biol, Univ Colo, 74-79; from asst prof to assoc prof biol, Univ Houston, 79-86. *Concurrent Pos:* Res career develop award, NIH, 84; postdoctoral fel develop genetics, Univ Colo, 74-79. *Res:* Aging; numerous publications. *Mailing Add:* Dept Molecular Biol D9RB RIB/NC Bldg AP 20 Abbott Labs 100 Abbott Park Rd Abbott Park IL 60064

KLASSEN, DAVID MORRIS, INORGANIC CHEMISTRY, SPECTROSCOPY. *Current Pos:* from asst prof to assoc prof, 69-77, PROF CHEM, MCMURRY UNIV, 77- *Personal Data:* b Clovis, NMex, June 15, 39; m 65, Jan Overbury; c Kenneth & Christine. *Educ:* Univ Tex, El Paso, BS, 61; Univ NMex, PhD(phys chem), 67. *Prof Exp:* Teaching asst, Univ NMex, 61-62; NATO res fel, Inst Phys Chem, Frankfurt, WGer, 66-67; res assoc, Univ NC, Chapel Hill, 67-69. *Mem:* Am Chem Soc; Sigma Xi; Sci Res Soc Am. *Res:* Synthesis, bonding and electronic structure of transition-metal complexes; luminescence of ruthenium and osmium complexes. *Mailing Add:* Dept Chem McMurry Univ Abilene TX 79697

KLASSEN, J(OHN), chemical engineering, for more information see previous edition

KLASSEN, LYNELL W, RHEUMATOLOGY, TRANSPLANT IMMUNOLOGY. *Current Pos:* assoc prof rheumat & immunol, 82-90, PROF & VCHMN INTERNAL MED, UNIV NEBR MED CTR, 90-; CHIEF, ARTHRITIS SERV RHEUMAT, OMAHA VET ADMIN, 82- *Personal Data:* b Gossel, Kans, Jan 24, 47; m 67; c 4. *Educ:* Tabor Col, Hillsboro, Kans, AB, 69; Univ Kans, Kansas City, MD, 73. *Prof Exp:* Resident internal med, Univ Iowa Hosps & Clins, 73-75; res assoc immunol, Arthritis & Rheumatism Br, NIH, 75-77; chief resident internal med, Univ Iowa Hosps & Clins, 77-78, asst prof, 78-82. *Concurrent Pos:* Chmn, Sci Rev Comt, Nat Inst Alchol Abuse, Alcoholism, 89-; mem, Educ Coun, Am Col Rheumatology, 89- *Mem:* Am Col Physicians; Am Asn Immunol. *Res:* Mechanisms of hematopoietic allograft rejection; pathophysiology of graft-versus-host disease; use of cytotoxic therapy in non-malignant diseases. *Mailing Add:* Univ Nebr Med Ctr 600 S 42nd St Omaha NE 68198-3025. *Fax:* 402-559-6114

KLASSEN, NORMAN VICTOR, RADIATION CHEMISTRY, DOSIMETRY. *Current Pos:* MEM RES STAFF, INST NAT MEASUREMENT STAND, NAT RES COUN CAN, 66- *Personal Data:* b Winnipeg, Man, Nov 6, 33; m 61; c 3. *Educ:* McGill Univ, BSc, 54, PhD(chem), 57; Univ Col, London, PhD(chem), 61. *Prof Exp:* Fel, Nat Res Coun Can, 61-63; fel phys chem, Mellon Inst, 63-66. *Mem:* Fel Chem Inst Can; Radiation Res Soc. *Res:* Radiation chemistry; radiation biology; dosimetry. *Mailing Add:* Inst Nat Measurement Stand Nat Res Coun Can M-35 Ottawa ON K1A 0R6 Can

KLASSEN, RUDOLPH WALDEMAR, GEOLOGY. *Current Pos:* Res scientist quaternary geol, 65-94, EMER RES SCIENTIST, GEOL SURV CAN, 94- *Personal Data:* b Hanna, Alta, Sept 30, 28; m 67, Carmel Despins; c 4. *Educ:* Univ Alta, BSc, 59, MSc, 60; Univ Sask, PhD(geol), 65. *Concurrent Pos:* Lectr, Univ Calgary, 74-86. *Mem:* Geol Asn Can; Am Quaternary Asn; Can Quaternary Asn. *Res:* Quaternary stratigraphy and geomorphology;

reports and maps on Quaternary geology of Manitoba, Southern Saskatchewan, Northern Northwest Territories and Southern Yukon published mainly by Geological Survey of Canada; current studies of Tertiary and Quaternary geomorphology and stratigraphy of Cypress Lake and Wood Mountain areas Southwestern Saskatchewan. *Mailing Add:* Geol Surv Can 3303 33rd St NW Calgary AB T2L 2A7 Can

KLASSEN, WALDEMAR, entomology, genetics, for more information see previous edition

KLATT, ARTHUR RAYMOND, PLANT BREEDING. *Current Pos:* Plant breeder, 69-79, assoc dir, Wheat Prog Int Maize & Wheat Improv Ctr, 79-87, ASST DEAN, INT PROG, OKLA STATE UNIV, 88- *Personal Data:* b Hamilton, Tex, June 10, 43; m 80; c 5. *Educ:* Tex Tech Univ, BS, 66; Colo State Univ, MS, 68, PhD(plant breeding & genetics), 69. *Mem:* Am Soc Agron; Crop Sci Soc Am; Am Genetic Asn; AAAS; Weed Sci Soc Am. *Res:* Genetics and environmental factors affecting drought tolerance; genetics and environmental influence on dormancy, vernalization and winterhardiness; incorporation of horizontal resistance; breeding adapted high yielding winter and spring wheat varieties. *Mailing Add:* 505 W Hillcrest Ave Stillwater OK 74075

KLATT, GARY BRANDT, MATHEMATICS. *Current Pos:* from asst prof to assoc prof, 67-75, PROF MATH, UNIV WIS, WHITEWATER, 75- *Personal Data:* b Milwaukee, Wis, Nov 22, 39; m 64; c 2. *Educ:* Case Western Res Univ, BS, 61; Univ Wis, MS, 62, PhD(math), 69. *Prof Exp:* Instr math, Marquette Univ, 64-65. *Mem:* Math Asn Am; Nat Coun Teachers Math. *Res:* Theory of rings and modules. *Mailing Add:* 145 N Fremont St Whitewater WI 53190-1338

KLATT, LEON NICHOLAS, CHEMICAL INSTRUMENTATION. *Current Pos:* RES STAFF MEM, OAK RIDGE NAT LAB, 74- *Personal Data:* b Underhill, Wis, Aug 28, 40; m 61; c 2. *Educ:* Univ Wis, Oshkosh, BS, 62; Univ Wis-Madison, PhD(anal chem), 67. *Prof Exp:* Chemist, Dow Chem Co, Mich, 62-63; asst, Univ Wis-Madison, 63-66; asst prof chem, Southern Ill Univ, 67-69 & Univ Ga, 69-74. *Mem:* Am Chem Soc; Sigma Xi; AAAS; SAS. *Res:* Instrumentation for remote analyses; on-line control of instruments with small computers; multi variable data reduction systems; application of small computers to analytical problems; process monitor and control systems. *Mailing Add:* 111 Carnegie Dr Oak Ridge TN 37831-4898

KLATTE, EUGENE, RADIOLOGY. *Current Pos:* prof, 71-80, DISTINGUISHED PROF & CHMN DEPT, SCH MED, IND UNIV, INDIANAPOLIS, 80- *Personal Data:* b Indianapolis, Ind, Mar 19, 28; m 50; c 4. *Educ:* Ind Univ, AB, 49, MD, 52. *Prof Exp:* Resident radiol, Univ Calif, 55-57; from instr to assoc prof, Sch Med, Ind Univ, 58-62; prof & chmn dept, Sch Med, Vanderbilt Univ, 62-71. *Concurrent Pos:* Picker res scholar, Sch Med, Ind Univ, 57-58; consult, Vet Admin Hosp, Nashville, Tenn, 62-71; clin prof, Meharry Med Col, 64-71. *Mem:* Am Col Radiol; Asn Univ Radiol; Radiol Soc NAm; Soc Pediat Radiol; AMA. *Res:* Diagnostic radiology, especially cardiovascular radiology. *Mailing Add:* Riley Hosp Children Ind Univ Med Ctr 1053 702 Barnhill Dr Indianapolis IN 46202-5202

KLATZO, IGOR, neuropathology, for more information see previous edition

KLAUBER, MELVILLE ROBERTS, PUBLIC HEALTH & EPIDEMIOLOGY. *Current Pos:* prin statistician, 78-81, ADJ PROF FAMILY & PREVENTATIVE MED, SCH MED, UNIV CALIF, LA JOLLA, 81- *Personal Data:* b San Diego, Calif, Aug 9, 33; m 53, Sylvia Kenworthy; c 6. *Educ:* Stanford Univ, AB, 54, MS, 56, PhD(statist), 64. *Prof Exp:* From asst prof to prof family & community med & chief, Div Biostatist, Col Med, Univ Utah, 67-78. *Concurrent Pos:* Adj assoc prof math, Univ Utah, 72-76; adj prof math, 76-78. *Mem:* Am Statist Asn; Biomet Soc. *Res:* Biostatistics; statistical methods for the medical sciences, especially epidemiology. *Mailing Add:* Dept Family & Preventative Med Univ Calif Sch Med Code 0816 La Jolla CA 92093-0816. *E-Mail:* mklauber@ucsd.edu

KLAUBERT, DIETER HEINZ, MEDICINAL CHEMISTRY. *Current Pos:* RES CHEMIST, WYETH LABS INC, AM HOME PROD CORP, 73- *Personal Data:* b Ger, Dec 15, 44; Can citizen; m 69; c 2. *Educ:* Univ Alta, BSc, 67; Mass Inst Technol, PhD(org chem), 71. *Prof Exp:* Fel org chem, Univ Calif, Berkeley, 71-73. *Mem:* Am Chem Soc; The Chem Soc; Sigma Xi. *Res:* Synthesis of novel compounds of pharmaceutical interest. *Mailing Add:* Molecular Probes inc 4849 Pitchford Ave Eugene OR 97402

KLAUDER, JOHN RIDER, THEORETICAL PHYSICS, APPLIED MATHEMATICS. *Current Pos:* PROF, DEPTS PHYSICS & MATH, UNIV FLA, 88- *Personal Data:* b Reading, Pa, Jan 24, 32; m 53, 80; c 5. *Educ:* Univ Calif, Berkeley, BS, 53; Stevens Inst Technol, MS, 56; Princeton Univ, MA, 57, PhD(physics), 59. *Prof Exp:* Head theoret physics dept, Bell Tel Labs, 66-67 & 69-71, head solid state spectros dept, 71-76, mem tech staff, 53-88. *Concurrent Pos:* Vis assoc prof, Univ Bern, 61-62; adj prof, Rutgers Univ, 65; prof, Syracuse Univ, 67-68; vis prof, Univ Bern, 80, Gakushuin Univ, 82 & 84, Univ Trento, 88, Imperial Col, 88 & 90. *Mem:* Fel Am Phys Soc; fel AAAS. *Res:* Solid state physics; quantum optics; quantum field theory; fundamentals of quantum theory. *Mailing Add:* Dept Physics & Math Univ Fla Gainesville FL 32611

KLAUNIG, JAMES E, ENVIRONMENTAL TOXICOLOGY, CHEMICAL CARCINOGENESIS. *Current Pos:* PROF PHARMACOL, DIR TOXICOL, IND UNIV SCH MED, 91- *Personal Data:* b Newark, NJ, May 27, 51. *Educ:* Ursinus Col, BS, 73; Montclair State Col, MA, 76; Univ Md, PhD(path), 80. *Prof Exp:* Lab scientist, dept path, Univ Md, Baltimore, 76-80; from instr to asst prof, Dept Path, Med Col Ohio, Toledo, 80-86, assoc prof path, 86-91, assoc prof, Dept Pharmacol, 87-91. *Concurrent Pos:* Adj fac mem, W Alton Jones Cell Sci Ctr, Lake Placid, NY, 81; mem grad fac, Med Col, Ohio Grad Sch, 82-; prin investr on grants, US Environ Protection Agency, NIH & US Army, 82-; adj prof, Ctr Photochemical Sci, Dept Chem, Bowling Green State Univ, Ohio; vis scientist, Chem Indust Inst Toxicol, Res Triangle Park, NC, 90-91. *Mem:* Am Asn Cancer Res; Soc Toxicol Pathologists; Soc Toxicol; Sigma Xi; Tissue Cult Asn; Am Col Toxicol. *Res:* Environmental toxicology and carcinogenesis; liver tumor promotion; hepatic carcinogenesis; cell pathology; liver cell isolation and tissue culture; hepatotoxicology. *Mailing Add:* 135 Bennington Rd Indianapolis IN 46227

KLAUS, EWALD FRED, JR, ZOOLOGY, ENTOMOLOGY. *Current Pos:* From asst prof to assoc prof, 64-74, PROF BIOL, ETEX STATE UNIV, 74- *Personal Data:* b Needville, Tex, Oct 22, 28; m 64. *Educ:* Univ Tex, BA, 52, MA, 58; Tex A&M Univ, PhD(entom), 65. *Concurrent Pos:* Fac res grant, 67-68, NSF fel, Col Sci Improv Prog, 71-72. *Res:* Biology and taxonomy of mosquitoes; genetics of insecticide resistance in cotton insects; insecticide residue studies; food sanitation; aquatic ecology and water quality studies. *Mailing Add:* 1805 Jefferson St Commerce TX 75428

KLAUS, RONALD LOUIS, chemical engineering, for more information see previous edition

KLAUSMEIER, ROBERT EDWARD, MICROBIOLOGY, CHEMISTRY. *Current Pos:* RETIRED. *Personal Data:* b Evansville, Ind, June 6, 26; m 51; c 4. *Educ:* Univ Ind, AB, 51, MA, 53; La State Univ, PhD(bact), 58. *Prof Exp:* Asst bact, Univ Ind, 51-53; res bacteriologist, Army Chem Corps, Ft Detrick, Md, 53-55; asst prof bact, Southwestern La Inst, 55-57; asst, La State Univ, 57-58; microbiologist, Weapons Qual Eng Ctr, Naval Weapons Support Ctr, 58-80, chemist, 80-89. *Mem:* AAAS; Am Soc Microbiol; Soc Indust Microbiol. *Res:* Microbial deterioration of materials, particularly explosives and synthetic polymers; microbial physiology; enzymology; economically and environmentally effective demilitarization of ammunition. *Mailing Add:* 4111 Gran Haven Dr Bloomington IN 47401

KLAUSNER, JAMES FREDERICK, HEAT TRANSFER, FLUID MECHANICS. *Current Pos:* asst prof, 89-94, ASSOC PROF MECH ENG, UNIV FLA, 94- *Personal Data:* b Chicago, Ill, Dec 29, 61; m 87, Casey Swun; c Alexander & Jordan. *Educ:* US Merchant Marine Acad, BS, 84; Univ Ill, MS, 86, PhD(mech eng), 89. *Honors & Awards:* Tech Transfer Award, NASA, 92. *Prof Exp:* Res asst, Univ Ill, 84-89. *Mem:* Am Soc Mech Eng; Am Soc Eng Educ; Sigma Xi. *Res:* Fundamental mechanisms of flow boiling heat transfer and two phase flow, innovative instrumentation for multiphase flow research, particle science and technology, energy storage using phase change materials and solar photocatalytic oxidation. *Mailing Add:* 924 NW 51st Terr Gainesville FL 32605. *Fax:* 904-392-1071; *E-Mail:* klaus@nervm.nerdc.ufl.edu

KLAUSNER, RICHARD D, METABOLISM. *Current Pos:* res assoc, Nat Cancer Inst, NIH, 79-81, med officer, Nat Inst Arthritis, Diabetes & Digestive & Kidney Dis, 81-83, sr res investr, 83-84, CHIEF CELL BIOL & METAB BR, NAT INST CHILD HEALTH & HUMAN DEVELOP, NIH, 84-, DIR, NAT CANCER INST, 95- *Personal Data:* b New York, NY, Dec 22, 51; c 2. *Educ:* Yale Univ, BS, 73; Duke Med Sch, MD, 76. *Honors & Awards:* Young Investr Award, Am Fedn Clin Res, 88; William Castle Lectr, Harvard Univ, 90 & Kroc Lectr, 91; Marcel Piche Lectr, Univ Montreal, 91; Lamport Lectr, Columbia Univ, 91; Shannon Lectr, Mass Gen Hosp, 91; Damashek Prize, Am Soc Hemat, 92; Lederle Award, 92; 7th Nycomed Lectr, Norway; 5th Abelson Lectr, Washington Univ, St Louis, 92; Whitemore Lectr, Am Urol Asn, 97. *Prof Exp:* Fel internal med, Duke Med Ctr, 76-77; house officer internal med, Mass Gen Hosp, 77-78, clin fel, 78-79. *Concurrent Pos:* Attend physician, Acute Med Clin, Nat Naval Med Ctr, 81-85; instr, Dept Med, USUHS, 82-83, asst clin prof med, 83-85; Cartwright vis prof, Univ Utah, 96; var lect & keynote addresses. *Mem:* Nat Acad Sci; Inst Med-Nat Acad Sci; Am Soc Clin Invest (pres-elect, 93, pres, 94); Am Fedn Clin Res; Am Soc Cell Biol; Am Soc Hemat; Sigma Xi; fel Am Acad Arts & Sci; Am Asn Physicians; Am Asn Cancer Res; Am Asn Clin Oncol; Am Soc Endocrinol. *Res:* Molecular basis of normal and pathological states of iron metabolism in humans; mechanisms of post-transcriptional gene regulation; organelle cell biology; receptor biology; tumor suppressor genes. *Mailing Add:* Cell Biol & Metab Div NIH Child Health & Human Develop Bldg 18T Rockville Pike Bethesda MD 20892. *Fax:* 301-402-0338

KLAUSTERMEYER, WILLIAM BERNER, allergy, immunology, for more information see previous edition

KLAVANO, PAUL ARTHUR, PHARMACOLOGY. *Current Pos:* RETIRED. *Personal Data:* b Valley, Wash, Nov 30, 19; m 45; c 4. *Educ:* State Col Wash, BS, 41, DVM, 44. *Prof Exp:* Instr vet anat, Wash State Univ, 44-45, vet physiol & pharmacol, 45-48, from asst prof to prof vet pharmacol, 48-83, chmn dept, 52-72. *Concurrent Pos:* Chemist, Wash Horse Racing Comn, 42-46. *Mem:* Am Col Vet Pharmacol & Therapeut; Am Soc Vet Physiol & Pharmacol (secy, 53-54, pres, 64-65); NY Acad Sci; Am Soc Vet Anesthesiol. *Res:* Anesthesia of domestic animals. *Mailing Add:* 1125 SE Kamiaken St Pullman WA 99163

KLAVERKAMP, JOHN FREDERICK, pharmacology, toxicology, for more information see previous edition

KLAVINS, JANIS VILIBERTS, MEDICINE. *Current Pos:* DIR DEPT PATH, LONG ISLAND JEWISH MED CTR-QUEENS HOSP CTR, 70-; CHMN DEPT PATH, CATH MED CTR, 77- *Personal Data:* b Latvia, May 6, 21; nat US; m 50, Ilga M Krumins; c Ilze M, Lize K, Janis P & Filips K. *Educ:* Univ Kiel, MD, 48, PhD, 59; Am Bd Path, cert anal path, 57, cert clin path, 59; Am Bd Nutrit, cert, 68. *Hon Degrees:* Hon Dr Biol Sci, Univ Latvia, 91. *Honors & Awards:* Scientist of the Year, Asn Clin Scientists, 83. *Prof Exp:* Demonstr path, Sch Med, Western Res Univ, 54-55, from instr to sr instr, 55-60, asst prof, 60; from assoc prof to prof, Med Ctr, Duke Univ, 60-65, dir sch cytotech, 63-65; clin prof path, State Univ NY Downstate Med Ctr, 65-71; prof path, State Univ NY Stony Brook, 71-77. *Concurrent Pos:* Asst pathologist, Marymount Hosp, Garfield Heights, Ohio, 55-57; cytologist-in-chg, Cleveland Metrop Gen Hosp, 55-60, assoc pathologist, 58-60; chief lab serv, Vet Admin Hosp, Durham, NC, 61-63; pathologist-in-chief, Brooklyn-Cumberland Med Ctr, 65-70; adj prof biol, Fac Grad Arts, Long Island Univ, 68-; clin prof path, Col Physicians & Surgeons, Columbia Univ, 69-; prof lectr, State Univ NY Downstate Med Ctr, 71-77, prof path, 77-85; pres, Int Acad Tumor Marker Oncol, 84-; prof path, Med Col, Cornell Univ, 85-; ed-in-chief, J Tumor Marker Oncol, 87- *Mem:* Fel AAAS; Am Soc Cytol; Am Asn Pathologists; Col Am Path; Asn Clin Scientists; Int Acad Path; Biochem Soc; Col Am Path; Am Inst Nutrit; AMA; Int Acad Tumor Marker Oncol; hon mem Egypt Soc Tumor Marker Oncol; hon mem Nat Acad Eng Latvia; Nat Acad Med Venezuela. *Res:* Iron metabolism; pathology of iron excess; effects of antimetabolites, particularly entionine; embryonic and specific proteins in malignant neoplasms; pathology of amino acid excess; tumor markers. *Mailing Add:* 5 Broadmoor Rd Scarsdale NY 10583. *Fax:* 718-558-2166

KLAWE, MARIA, INTERACTIVE MULTI-MEDIA, EDUCATIONAL TECHNOLOGY. *Current Pos:* prof & head, 88-95, VPRES, STUDENT & ACAD SERV, UNIV BC, 95- *Personal Data:* b Toronto, Ont, July 5, 51; m 80, Nicholas Pippenger; c Janek & Sasha. *Educ:* Univ Alta, BSc, 73, PhD(math), 77. *Prof Exp:* Asst prof math, Oakland Univ, 77-78; asst prof comput sci, Univ Toronto, 79-80; res staff mem, Almaden Res Ctr, IBM, 80-84, mgr, Discrete Math Group, 84-88. *Concurrent Pos:* Ed, Combinatorica, 85-, Soc Indust & Appl Math J Computing, 86-93, Soc Indust & Appl Math J Discrete Math, 87-93, Electronic J Combinatorics, 94-; mem bd, Can Math Soc, 85-89, Comput Res Asn, 90-96; trustee, Am Math Soc, 92-97. *Mem:* Fel Asn Comput Math; Am Math Soc; Comput Res Asn; Soc Indust & Appl Math; Can Math Soc; Asn Women Math. *Res:* Interactive multi-media for mathematical education; computational geometry; complexity; data structures; graph theory; matrix searching. *Mailing Add:* Univ BC Old Admin Bldg Vancouver BC V6T 1Z2 Can

KLAWE, WITOLD L, FISH BIOLOGY. *Current Pos:* Jr scientist, 55-56, scientist, 56-61, SR SCIENTIST, INTER-AM TROP TUNA COMN, SCRIPPS INST OCEANOG, 61- *Personal Data:* b Piotrkow Trybunalski, Poland, June 9, 23; US citizen; m 55, Barbara Hillsdon; c David M. *Educ:* Univ Toronto, BA, 53, MA, 55. *Hon Degrees:* Dr hon causa, Acad Agr, Szczecin, Poland, 91. *Honors & Awards:* Gold Insignia of the Order of Merit Polish People's Repub, 88. *Concurrent Pos:* Mem working groups, Expert Panel Facilitation Tuna Res, Food & Agr Orgn, UN, 65, consult, Food & Agr Orgn, UN & SPacific Comn. *Mem:* Am Inst Fishery Res Biol; AAAS. *Res:* Early life history of scombroid fishes; general marine biology; fishery oceanography; statistics on global catches of tunas. *Mailing Add:* 6151 La Pintura Dr La Jolla CA 92037. *Fax:* 619-546-7133

KLAY, ROBERT FRANK, ANIMAL NUTRITION. *Current Pos:* NUTRITIONIST, MOORMAN MFG CO, 64- *Personal Data:* b Ft Benton, Mont, Jan 2, 30; m 59; c 3. *Educ:* Mont State Univ, BS, 52; Wash State Univ, MS, 58; Univ Minn, Minneapolis, PhD(nutrit), 64. *Prof Exp:* Asst animal sci, Wash State Univ, 56-58, asst prof, 61-64; res fel animal genetics, Commonwealth Sci & Indust Res Orgn, Australia, 58-59; res asst animal nutrit, Univ Minn, Minneapolis, 59-61. *Mem:* Am Soc Animal Sci; Sigma Xi; ARPAS. *Res:* Protein and amino acid digestion and availability; ruminant and nonruminant nutrition. *Mailing Add:* 1652 York St Quincy IL 62301

KLEBAN, MORTON H, SOCIAL GERONTOLOGY, STATISTICS & MEASUREMENT. *Current Pos:* SR RES PSYCHOLOGIST, PHILADELPHIA GERIAT CTR, 66-; MED RES SCIENTIST, NORRISTOWN STATE HOSP, 66- *Personal Data:* b Brooklyn, NY, Oct 23, 31; m 55; c 3. *Educ:* City Col New York, BBA, 53; State Univ Iowa, MA, 55; Univ NDak, PhD(exp psychol), 60. *Prof Exp:* Clin psychologist, Norristown State Hosp, Pa, 60-64; res psychologist, Off Ment Health, State of Pa, 64-66. *Mem:* Am Psychol Asn; Geront Soc. *Res:* Design, statistical applications and computer technology in applied gerontological research. *Mailing Add:* Polisher Res Inst Philadelphia Geriatric Ctr 5301 Old York Rd Philadelphia PA 19141

KLEBANOFF, SEYMOUR J, INFECTIOUS DISEASES, BIOCHEMISTRY. *Current Pos:* assoc prof, 62-68, head, Div Allergy & Infectious Dis, 76-94, PROF MED, SCH MED, UNIV WASH, 68- *Personal Data:* b Toronto, Ont, Feb 3, 27; m 51, Evelyn; c Carolyn & Mark. *Educ:* Univ Toronto, MD, 51; Univ London, PhD(biochem), 54. *Honors & Awards:* Marie T Bonazinga Annual Res Award, Soc Leukocyte Biol, 85; Mayo Soley Award, Western Soc Clin Invest, 91; Bristol Award, Infectious Dis Soc Am, 93; Bristol-Myers Squibb Award for Distinguished Achievement in Infectious Dis Res, 95. *Prof Exp:* Intern, Toronto Gen Hosp, 51-52; lectr path chem, Univ Toronto, 54-57; guest investr & asst physician, Rockefeller Univ, 57-59, res assoc, 59, asst prof, assoc physician & radiation protection officer, 59-62. *Concurrent Pos:* Res career develop award, NIH, 64-68, merit award, 88- *Mem:* Nat Acad Sci; Inst Med-Nat Acad Sci; Infectious Dis Soc Am; Asn Am Physicians; Am Soc Biol Chem; Am Soc Clin Invest. *Res:* Role of granulocytes in host defense; role of enzyme peroxidase in biological processes; microbicidal activity of peroxidases. *Mailing Add:* Dept Med Univ Wash Sch Med Seattle WA 98195

KLEBANOV, IGOR ROMANOVICH, STRING THEORY, QUANTUM GRAVITY. *Current Pos:* Asst prof, 89-95, ASSOC PROF PHYSICS, PRINCETON UNIV, 95- *Personal Data:* b Mar 29, 62; US citizen; m 91, Pamela Kato; c Rachel. *Educ:* Mass Inst Technol, SB, 82; Princeton Univ, PhD(physics), 86. *Prof Exp:* Res assoc, Linear Accelerator Ctr, Stanford Univ, 86-89. *Concurrent Pos:* Alfred P Sloan Res fel, 91-95; Presidential young investr, NSF, 91-; co-dir, Ann Int Ctr Theoret Physics Spring Sch, Trieste, Italy, 92-96. *Res:* Theoretical high energy physics; quantum field theory; string theory and quantum gravity. *Mailing Add:* Dept Physics Jadwin Hall Princeton Univ Princeton NJ 08544-0708

KLEBBA, PHILLIP E, MONOCLONAL ANTIBODIES, MEMBRANE BIOLOGY. *Current Pos:* ASSOC PROF CHEM, DEPT CHEM & BIOCHEM, UNIV OKLA, 95- *Personal Data:* b Ypsilanti, Mich, Dec 27, 51; m 82; c 3. *Educ:* Univ Notre Dame, BS, 75; Univ Calif, Berkeley, PhD(biochem), 81. *Prof Exp:* Postdoctoral fel med microbiol, Sch Med, Stanford Univ, 81-82; postdoctoral fel microbiol & immunol, Univ Calif, Berkeley, 82-84; asst prof microbiol, Univ Notre Dame, 84-88; asst prof microbiol, Med Col Wis, 86-93; CNRS vis assoc prof, Inst Pasteur, Paris France, 93-95. *Concurrent Pos:* Prin investr, USPHS, 86-90; consult, Chevron Chem Co, 86-89, Ensys, Inc, 88-90 & Thymax Corp, 90- *Mem:* Sigma Xi; Am Soc Microbiol; AAAS. *Res:* Bacterial pathogens shield themselves from the mammalian immune system by the barrier properties of molecules that reside in their outer membrane; structure of outer membrane proteins and lipopoly saccharide and the interactions of these two molecules with each other and the immune system. *Mailing Add:* Dept Chem & Biochem Univ Okla 620A Perrington Oval Suite 314 Norman OK 73019-0430

KLEBE, ROBERT JOHN, CELL ADHESION PROTEINS. *Current Pos:* assoc prof, 81-86, PROF ANAT, GRAD SCH BIOMED SCI, UNIV TEX HEALTH SCI CTR, 86- *Personal Data:* b Philadelphia, Pa, Oct 26, 43. *Educ:* Johns Hopkins Univ, BA, 65; Yale Univ, PhD(biol), 70. *Prof Exp:* From asst prof to assoc prof human genetics, Grad Sch Biomed Sci, Univ Tex Med Br, Galveston, 76-81. *Concurrent Pos:* Jane Coffin Child Mem Fund fel, Salk Inst, 70-72. *Mem:* Am Soc Human Genetics; Am Soc Cell Biol. *Res:* Somatic cell genetics; biochemistry of cell adhesion; developmental genetics; biochemical mechanism of cell adhesion: the analysis of the binding of fibronectin, laminim and other cell adhesion proteins to cell surface molecules. *Mailing Add:* Dept Cell & Struct Biol Univ Tex Health Sci Ctr San Antonio TX 78284-7762

KLEBER, EUGENE VICTOR, CHEMISTRY, ENVIRONMENTAL PROGRAMS. *Current Pos:* RETIRED. *Personal Data:* b Cleveland, Ohio, July 7, 20; m 42, 64, 78; c 5. *Educ:* Univ Calif, Los Angeles, AB, 40, MA, 41; Univ Wis, PhD(chem), 43. *Prof Exp:* Res chemist, Sharples Chem, Inc, Mich, 43-45, Golden Bear Oil Co, Calif, 45-46 & Lockheed Aircraft Corp, 46-47; pres, Res Chem, Inc, 47-59, gen mgr res chem div, Nuclear Corp Am, 59-62; staff asst, Atomics Int Div, Rockwell Int Corp, 62-78; phys scientist, Fed Energy Regulatory Comn, Dept Energy, 78-85. *Concurrent Pos:* Res chemist, Coast Paint & Chem Co, 47 & Lockheed Aircraft Corp, 51-56. *Mem:* Am Chem Soc. *Res:* Nuclear fuels and materials; organic synthesis; fine chemical manufacturing; production and use of purified rare earth oxides and metals; energy and environmental programs. *Mailing Add:* 406 Upper Wood Way Burnsville MN 55337-5728

KLEBER, HERBERT DAVID, PSYCHIATRY, DRUG ABUSE. *Current Pos:* PROF PSYCHIAT, SCH MED, COLUMBIA UNIV, 91-; DIR, DIV SUBSTANCE ABUSE RES, NY STATE PSYCHIAT INST, 91-; EXEC VPRES & MED DIR, NAT CTR ADDICTION & SUBSTANCE ABUSE, 92- *Personal Data:* b Pittsburgh, Pa, June 19, 34; div; c 3. *Educ:* Dartmouth Col, BA, 56; Jefferson Med Col, MD, 60. *Hon Degrees:* MA, Yale Univ, 75; PhD, NY Med Col, 91. *Honors & Awards:* Gold Medal, Am Psychiat Asn, 75; Nathan B Eddy Mem Award, 95. *Prof Exp:* Resident psychiat, Sch Med, Yale Univ, 61-64; chief receiving serv, USPHS Hosp, Lexington, Ky, 64-66; from asst prof to prof, psychiat, Sch Med, Yale Univ, 66-89; dep dir demand redction, Off Nat Drug Control Policy, Exec Off of the Pres, 89-91. *Concurrent Pos:* Consult, Nat Inst Drug Abuse, 71- & Nat Acad Sci, 73-; fund prize res psychiat, Am Psychiat Asn, 81. *Mem:* Inst Med-Nat Acad Sci; fel Am Col Neuropsychopharmacol; fel Am Acad Psychiat in Alcoholism & Addiction; fel Am Col Psychiat; fel Am Psychiat Asn; fel Col Prob Drug Dependence. *Res:* Treatment of drug dependence; etiological aspects of drug abuse; policy research in substance abuse. *Mailing Add:* Div Substance Abuse Columbia Univ Col Physicians & Surgeons 722 W 168th St New York NY 10032. *E-Mail:* hdk3@columbia.edu

KLEBER, JOHN WILLIAM, biopharmaceutics, for more information see previous edition

KLECK, ROBERT ELDON, PSYCHOLOGY, NONVERBAL BEHAVIOR. *Current Pos:* from asst to assoc prof, 66-75, John Sloan Dickey Third Century prof soc sci, 85-90, PROF PSYCHOL, DARTMOUTH COL, 75-, CHMN DEPT, 93- *Personal Data:* b Archbold, Ohio, Aug 3, 37; m 59, Jan Wyse; c Jennifer & Leslie (Bugbee). *Educ:* Denison Univ, AB, 59; Stanford Univ, PhD(social psychol), 63. *Prof Exp:* Fel, Stanford Univ, 63-64; asst prof, Williams Col, 64-66. *Concurrent Pos:* Consult, Crotchet Mountain Rehab Ctr, 73, Disadvantaged Children NH, 74, Bur Develop Disabilities, NH, 75-80, Abilities Inc, NY, 79-81, Vet Admin Stroke Proj, 83-, Can Res Coun, NSF & USPHS; vis res prof, Boy's Town Ctr Study Youth Develop, Stanford Univ, 74-75; assoc ed, J Personality & Social Psychol, 71-72, consult ed, 74-78; fel, USPHS, 77-78. *Mem:* Am Psychol Soc; Int Soc Res Emotion; Soc Exp Social Psychol; Sigma Xi. *Res:* Social psychological processes; interpersonal communication; nonverbal aspects of communication; stigmatization processes; emotional communications; contributed articles to professional journals. *Mailing Add:* Dept Psychol Dartmouth Col Hanover NH 03755. *Fax:* 603-646-1419; *E-Mail:* r.kleck@dartmouth.edu

KLECKA, MIROSLAV EZIDOR, CHEMICAL ENGINEERING. *Current Pos:* RETIRED. *Personal Data:* b Yoakum, Tex, Nov 9, 21; m 45. *Educ:* Univ Tex, BS, 43, MS, 46, PhD(chem eng), 48. *Prof Exp:* Res asst chem eng, Univ Tex, 45-46, res assoc, 46, instr, 46-47; sr res engr, Shell Oil Co Houston, 47-66, staff res engr, 66-77, staff res engr, 77-85. *Mem:* Am Inst Chem Engrs. *Res:* Petroleum refining design and evaluation; phase equilibria and separation processes; operations research and computer calculations systems design; process control systems. *Mailing Add:* 3908 Walnut Clay Dr Austin TX 78731

KLECKNER, NANCY E, GENETICS. *Current Pos:* from asst prof to assoc prof, 77-84, PROF, DEPT BIOCHEM & MOLECULAR BIOL, HARVARD UNIV, 84- *Personal Data:* b Santa Monica, Calif, Oct 16, 47. *Educ:* Harvard Univ, AB, 68; Mass Inst Technol, PhD(biol), 74. *Prof Exp:* NIH fel biol, Mass Inst Technol, 74-75. *Concurrent Pos:* Mem sci adv bd, New Eng Biolabs, 82-; bd dirs, Genetics Soc Am, 86-88. *Mem:* Nat Acad Sci Inst Med; fel AAAS; fel Am Acad Arts & Sci; fel Am Acad Microbiol. *Res:* Numerous publications. *Mailing Add:* Dept Molecular & Cellular Biol Harvard Univ 7 Divinity Ave Cambridge MA 02138

KLECKNER, WILLARD R, ELECTRICAL ENGINEERING, ENVIRONMENTAL ENGINEERING. *Current Pos:* ELEC, ENVIRON & SAFETY ENGR, KLECKNER ENTERPRISES INC. *Personal Data:* b Plainfield, NJ, Sept 29, 37; m 93, Linda Re; c Tamara L. *Educ:* Pa State Univ, BS(elec eng) & BS(bus admin), 59; MBA, 76; LaSalle Univ, LLB, 65; Calif Western Univ, PhD(bus admin & eng), 80. *Mem:* Am Arbit Asn; sr mem Am Eng Asn; Am Psychol Asn; Am Soc Safety Engrs; sr mem Asn Energy Engrs; sr mem Inst Elec & Electronics Engrs; Nat Aeronaut & Space Admin; Nat Registry Environ Professionals; Nat Safety Coun. *Res:* Low frequency electromagnetic field radiation pertaining to high voltage electrical transmission lines; osmosis technology for water purification; ozone technology for air, soil, and water applications; published one book and numerous technical articles; granted one patent and assisted in numerous others. *Mailing Add:* 34 Glen Ridge Dr Long Valley NJ 07853. *Fax:* 908-813-8872

KLEE, CLAUDE BLENC, CALMODULIN, PROTEIN-PROTEIN INTERACTION. *Current Pos:* Head macromolecular interactions, 74-87, actg chief, 87-89, CHIEF, LAB BIOCHEM, NAT CANCER INST, 89- *Educ:* Univ Marsailles, France, MD, 59. *Mem:* Inst Med-Nat Acad Sci. *Mailing Add:* Nat Cancer Inst NIH Bldg 37 Rm 4E28 Bethesda MD 20892. *Fax:* 301-402-3095; *E-Mail:* ckl@helix@nih.gov

KLEE, GERALD D'ARCY, PSYCHIATRY, MEDICINE. *Current Pos:* LECTR PSYCHIAT, SCH MED, JOHNS HOPKINS UNIV, 76- *Personal Data:* b New York, NY, Jan 29, 27; m 50; c 5. *Educ:* Harvard Med Sch, MD, 52; Am Bd Psychiat & Neurol, dipl, 59. *Prof Exp:* Sr asst surgeon, USPHS, 53-54; res assoc psychiat, Sch Med, Univ Md, 56-58, from asst prof to assoc prof, 58-67, dir div outpatient psychiat, Psychiat Inst, 58-67; prof psychiat, Sch Med, Temple Univ, 67-70. *Concurrent Pos:* Pvt pract, psychiat, 71-; med dir, USPHS. *Mem:* AMA; fel Am Psychiat Asn. *Res:* Psychopharmacology; psychotherapy; community psychiatry; epidemiology. *Mailing Add:* 28 Allegheny Ave Towson MD 21204-3909

KLEE, VICTOR LA RUE, JR, MATHEMATICS. *Current Pos:* from asst prof to assoc prof math, 53-57, prof appl math, 76-84, PROF MATH, UNIV WASH, 57-, ADJ PROF COMPUT SCI, 76- *Personal Data:* b San Francisco, Calif, Sept 18, 25; m 45, 85, Joann Polack; c Wendy, Barbara, Lisette & Heidi. *Educ:* Pomona Col, BA, 45, Univ Va, PhD(math), 49. *Hon Degrees:* DSc, Pomona Col, 65; Dr, Univ Liege, 84 & Univ Trier, 95. *Honors & Awards:* Pres & Visitor's Res Prize, Univ Va, 52; L R Ford Award, 72; C B Allendoerfer Award, Math Asn Am, 80; Vollum Award, Reed Col, 82; Barrows Award, Pomona Col, 88. *Prof Exp:* Instr math, Univ Va, 47-48, asst prof, 49-53. *Concurrent Pos:* Nat Res Coun fel, Inst Advan Study, 51-52; vis assoc prof, Univ Calif, Los Angeles, 55-56 & Univ Western Australia, 79; Sloan res fel, Univ Wash, 56-58 & 60-61; NSF sr fel, Copenhagen Univ, 58-59, Sloan res fel, 59-60; consult, Boeing Sci Res Labs, 63-69, Rand Corp, 66-69, Holt, Rinehart & Winston, 66-76, E I du Pont de Nemours & Co, Inc, 68-72, IBM Corp, 72 & W H Freeman, 76-96; Sigma Xi nat lectr, 69; vis prof, Univ Colo, 71; adj prof comput sci, Univ Wash, 74-; vis prof, Univ Victoria, 75; fel, Ctr Advan Study Behav Sci, 75-76; trustee, Conf Bd Math Sci, 72-73; Guggenheim fel & Von Humboldt awardee, Univ Erlangen-Nurnberg, 80-81; mem, Math Sci Res Inst, 85-86; sr fel, Inst Math & Its Applns, 87; Fulbright fel, Univ Trier, 92; Max Planck res prixe, von Humboldt Found, 92. *Mem:* Fel AAAS; Am Math Soc (assoc secy, 55-58); Math Asn Am (1st vpres, 68-69, pres-elect, 70, pres, 71-72); Soc Indust & Appl Math; Math Prog Soc; Asn Comput Mach. *Res:* Convex sets; mathematical programming; combinatorial mathematics; design and analysis of algorithms; functional analysis; point-set topology. *Mailing Add:* Dept Math Univ Wash Box 4350 Seattle WA 98195-4350. *Fax:* 206-543-0397; *E-Mail:* klee@math.washington.edu

KLEE, WERNER A, MOLECULAR BIOLOGY. *Current Pos:* Res chemist, Ment Health Dept, 62-82, sect chief chem, 82-92, CHIEF MOLECULAR BIOL LAB, NIMH, NIH, 92- *Personal Data:* b Ger, Aug 6, 33. *Educ:* Yale Univ, BS, 54, PhD(biochem), 58. *Mem:* Cell Biol Soc; Soc Biochem & Molecular Biol. *Mailing Add:* NIMH Bldg 36 Rm ID-08 Bethesda MD 20892-0001

KLEEMAN, CHARLES RICHARD, PHYSIOLOGY, METABOLISM. *Current Pos:* from prof & chief to emer prof & emer chief, Div Nephrol, Sch Med, 75-94, dir, Ctr Health Enhancement, 81-86, FACTOR FOUND EMER PROF MED & NEPHROL, SCH MED, UNIV CALIF, LOS ANGELES, 94-; SCI DIR, RES INST, 83-; NEPHROLOGIST, VET ADMIN MED CTR, WEST LOS ANGELES, 93- *Personal Data:* b Los Angeles, Calif, Aug 19, 23; m 45; c 3. *Educ:* Univ Calif, BS, 44, MD, 47. *Prof Exp:* Rotating internship, San Francisco City Hosp, 47-48; asst resident path, Mallory Inst, Boston City Hosp, 48-49; from intermediate resident to sr resident med, Newington Vet Admin Hosp, 49-51; from instr to asst prof, Metab Sect, Sch Med, Yale Univ, 53-56; from assoc clin prof to assoc prof, Sch Med, Univ Calif, Los Angeles, 56-64, prof, Sch Med & dir, Div Med, Cedars-Sinai Med Ctr, 64-74; prof med & chief dept, Hadassah Med Sch, Hebrew Univ, Israel, 72-75. *Concurrent Pos:* Fel metab, Newington Vet Admin Hosp, 50-51; Upjohn-Endocrine Soc scholar, Univ Col, Univ London, 60-61; chief metab sect, Vet Admin Hosp, Los Angeles, 56-60, consult, 62-; dir, Div Med, Mt Sinai Hosp, Los Angeles, 61-78; mem sci adv bd, Nat Kidney Dis Found; vis prof, Univ Queensland, 66; consult artificial kidney, Chronic Uremia Prog & Kidney Dis Control Prog, NIH, 67-72; vis prof, Beilinson Hosp, Tel-Aviv Univ & Med Sch, Hadassah-Hebrew Univ, 68; vis prof, St Francis Hosp, Honolulu, 69; chmn, Internal Med Sect, Nat Bd Med Examr, 71; dir, Ctr Health Enhancement Educ & Res, Cedar Sinai Med Ctr, 71-86, dir, Div Nephrol, 75-81. *Mem:* Inst Med-Nat Acad Sci; AMA; Am Physiol Soc; Am Soc Clin Invest; Endocrine Soc. *Res:* Renal physiology; electrolyte and water metabolism; nephrology. *Mailing Add:* Dept Med Div Nephrol W111L West LA VA Med Ctr Wilshire & Sawtelle Blvds Los Angeles CA 90073. *Fax:* 310-268-4653

KLEEN, HAROLD J, GEOLOGY. *Current Pos:* RETIRED. *Personal Data:* b Nebr, July 2, 11; m 34; c Roger H & Karen (Inman). *Educ:* Univ Nebr, BSc, 33. *Prof Exp:* Geologist, Skelly Oil Co, 37-44, dist geologist, Okla, 44-49; div mgr, Cent US, Kerr-McGee Oil Industs, Inc, 49-53, chief geologist, 53-58, explor mgr, 58-61, geol adv to pres, 61-67, mgr mineral explor, 67-68, explor asst to chief exec off, Kerr-McGee Corp, 68-69, vpres minerals explor, 69-74; consult, 74-92. *Mem:* Sigma Xi. *Res:* Investment economics (applied to minerals). *Mailing Add:* 6229 Smith Blvd Oklahoma City OK 73112-4119

KLEGERMAN, MELVIN EARL, IMMUNOBIOLOGY & IMMUNOTHERAPY OF CANCER, BACTERIAL IMMUNOMODULATORS & VACCINES. *Current Pos:* PRES & CHIEF EXEC OFFICER, MID-ATLANTIC BIOMED RES LAB, INC, SILVER SPRING, MD, 96- *Personal Data:* b Chicago, Ill, Aug 30, 45; div; c Melanie & Jessica. *Educ:* Univ Ill, Chicago, BA, 68; Loyola Univ Chicago, PhD(biochem), 84. *Prof Exp:* Asst ed, Encycl Britannica, 70-73; res assoc, Loyola Univ Med Ctr, 73-78, Evanston Hosp, 79, Rush Presby-St Luke Med Ctr, 86-87; res investr, Michael Reese Hosp & Med Ctr, 80-86; assoc dir, Inst Tuberculosis Res, Univ Ill, Chicago, 87-96, asst prof pharmaceut, 88-95. *Concurrent Pos:* Adj res assoc, Univ Chicago, 85-86 & 95-; adj asst prof, Univ Ill, Chicago, 87-88. *Mem:* Am Asn Pharmaceut Scientists. *Res:* Identification, purification and formulation of bacterial immunomodulators for cancer treatment; development of technology for rapid evaluation of anti-cancer immunotherapeutic drugs; ultrasonic diagnosis of atherosclerosis. *Mailing Add:* 11215 Oak Leaf Dr No 212 Silver Spring MD 20901

KLEI, HERBERT EDWARD, JR, CHEMICAL ENGINEERING. *Current Pos:* RETIRED. *Personal Data:* b Detroit, Mich, May 5, 35; m 59; c 5. *Educ:* Mass Inst Technol, BS, 57; Univ Mich, MS, 58 & 59; Univ Conn, PhD(chem eng), 65. *Honors & Awards:* Ralph Teetor Award, Soc Automotive Engrs, 78. *Prof Exp:* Res engr, Chas Pfizer & Co, 59-63; instr, Sch Eng, Univ Conn, 64-65, from asst prof to prof chem eng, 65-93- *Concurrent Pos:* Vis prof, US Military Acad, 85. *Mem:* Am Inst Chem Eng; Am Chem Soc; Catalysis Soc NAm. *Res:* Water pollution control, including biological kinetics and reactor design, membrane polarization and process control. *Mailing Add:* Bristol-Myers Squibb Pharm Res PO Box 4000 Princeton NJ 08543-4000. *Fax:* 609-252-6030

KLEI, THOMAS RAY, PARASITOLOGY, IMMUNOLOGY. *Current Pos:* from asst prof to assoc prof, 77-82, PROF PARASITOL, SCH VET MED, LA STATE UNIV, 82- *Personal Data:* b Detroit, Mich, Dec 11, 42; m 65; c 1. *Educ:* Northern Mich Univ, BS, 65; Wayne State Univ, PhD(biol & parasitol), 71. *Prof Exp:* NIH fel parasitol, Sch Vet Med, Univ Ga, 71-73; asst prof biol & zool, Millersville State Col, 73-75. *Concurrent Pos:* Prin investr, WHO & USDA Coop States Res Study grants, 77-; consult vet parasitol. *Mem:* Am Soc Parasitologists; Am Soc Trop Med & Hyg; AAAS; Am Asn Vet Parasitol, (pres, 87); Wildlife Dis Asn. *Res:* Immunologic and pathologic responses of vertebrate hosts to parasitic animals; parasitic diseases of horses. *Mailing Add:* Dept Vet Med La State Univ Baton Rouge LA 70803-0001

KLEIER, DANIEL ANTHONY, PHYSICAL CHEMISTRY, THEORETICAL CHEMISTRY. *Current Pos:* SR RES ASSOC, DU PONT CO, 86- *Personal Data:* b Louisville, Ky, Aug 19, 45; m 68, Catherine Boone; c Heidi & Curt. *Educ:* Bellarmine Col, Ky, BA, 67; Univ Notre Dame, PhD(chem), 71. *Prof Exp:* Woodrow Wilson teaching intern & asst prof chem, Va State Col, 70-72; res fel, Harvard Univ, 72-75; asst prof chem, Williams Col, 75-81; chemist, Shell Develop Co, 81-86. *Concurrent Pos:* NSF fel, Harvard Univ, 72-73, Am Cancer Soc fel, 74-75; vis staff mem, Los Alamos Nat Lab, 78-79. *Mem:* Am Chem Soc; Sigma Xi. *Res:* Theoretical investigations of chemical bonding and potential energy surfaces; nuclear magnetic resonance studies of stereodynamic processes; computer aided design of crop protection chemicals. *Mailing Add:* 31 Johnston Dr Elkton MD 21921

KLEIMAN, DEVRA GAIL, ETHOLOGY, REPRODUCTIVE & CONSERVATION BIOLOGY. *Current Pos:* reproduction zoologist, Nat Zool Park, Smithsonian Inst, 72-79, head zool res, 79-83, asst dir animal progs, 83-84, ASST DIR RES, NAT ZOOL PARK, SMITHSONIAN INST, 84- *Personal Data:* b New York, NY, Nov 15, 42; m 88, Ian Yeomans; c 2. *Educ:* Univ Chicago, BS, 64; Univ London, PhD(zool), 69. *Honors & Awards:* Ann Wise Award, NSF, 87; Distinguished Achievement Award, Soc Conserve Biol, 88. *Prof Exp:* Res asst biopsychol, Univ Chicago, 64-65; res asst reproductive biol, Wellcome Inst Comp Physiol, Zool Soc London, 65-69; NIH fel develop, Inst Animal Behav, Rutgers Univ, 69-71. *Concurrent Pos:* Adj asst prof psychol, Rutgers Univ, 70-71; res assoc, Smithsonian Inst, 70-72; adj assoc prof, George Washington Univ, 73-76 & Univ Md, 79-81; adj prof, George Mason Univ, 80- & Univ Md, 82-; coordr, Golden Lion Tamarin Conserv Prog, Brazil; grantee, Nat Geog Soc, Smithsonian Inst, World Wildlife Fund, Friends Nat Zoo, NIMH, Wildlife Preserve Trust Int & Am Zoo & Aquarium Asn. *Mem:* Fel Animal Behav Soc (secy, 77-81 & pres, 81-82); Am Asn Zool Parks & Aquariums; Am Soc Mammalogists; Sigma Xi; Am Inst Biol Sci; fel AAAS. *Res:* Social behavior and social organization of mammals; mammalian reproductive strategies; conservation and reintroduction of endangered species in the wild and in zoos; application of behavior techniques to management and breeding of endangered species in captivity. *Mailing Add:* Zool Res Nat Zool Park Smithsonian Inst Washington DC 20008. *E-Mail:* sivh@si.edu

KLEIMAN, HERBERT, PHYSICS. *Current Pos:* MEM STAFF, LINCOLN LAB, MASS INST TECHNOL, 66- *Personal Data:* b New York, NY, Oct 1, 33; m 60; c 1. *Educ:* Mass Inst Technol, BS, 54; Purdue Univ, MS, 57, PhD(physics), 61. *Prof Exp:* NSF fel physics, Univ Calif, Berkeley, 61-63, asst prof, 63-66. *Res:* High resolution spectroscopy; atomic structure and atomic spectra; quantum optics and photon correlation studies; physical optics. *Mailing Add:* 16 Reed Lane Bedford MA 01730

KLEIMAN, HOWARD, ALGEBRA, NUMBER THEORY. *Current Pos:* from asst prof to prof, 67-91, EMER PROF MATH, QUEENSBOROUGH COMMUNITY COL, 91- *Personal Data:* b New York, NY, Apr 15, 29; m 56, Edna M Benjamin; c Michele, Jeffrey & Daniel. *Educ:* NY Univ, BA, 50, MS, 61; Columbia Univ, MA, 54; King's Col, Univ London, PhD(math), 69. *Prof Exp:* Teacher, New York City Bd Educ, 55-56 & Bur Educ Physically Handicapped, 56-67. *Mem:* Am Math Soc. *Res:* Investigation of ordinary arithmetic function fields which contain non-trivial units; improvement of running times for algorithms used to obtain Hamilton cycles in random graphs. *Mailing Add:* 188-83 85th Rd Hollis NY 11423. *Fax:* 718-776-8478; *E-Mail:* rorryroon@aol.com

KLEIMAN, MORTON, ORGANIC CHEMISTRY. *Current Pos:* PRES & TECH DIR, M KLEIMAN ASSOCS, 53- *Personal Data:* b Kansas City, Mo, Mar 8, 16; m 40; c 2. *Educ:* Univ Mich, BS, 37, MS, 38; Univ Chicago, PhD, 42. *Prof Exp:* DuPont fel, Univ Chicago, 41-42, Coman fel, 42-43; res chemist, Velsicol Corp, 43-46, head org res dept, 46-51, dir res, 51-53; pres & tech dir, Chemley Prods co, 53-82. *Mem:* Sigma Xi; Am Chem Soc. *Res:* Syntheses of various medicinals; insecticides and fungicides; reactions such as liquid ammonia, Grignard, elimination, carboxylation, chlorination, Diels-Alder and redistribution; structure proofs; ionic and free radical mechanisms; synthetic resins; organo-metallics; industrial organic chemicals. *Mailing Add:* 2827 W Catalpa Ave Chicago IL 60625-3211

KLEIN, ABEL, MATHEMATICAL PHYSICS. *Current Pos:* from asst prof to assoc prof, 74-82, PROF MATH, UNIV CALIF, IRVINE, 82- *Personal Data:* b Rio de Janeiro, Brazil, Jan 16, 45; m 83; c 2. *Educ:* Univ Brazil, BS, 67; Inst Pure & Appl Math, MS, 68; Mass Inst Technol, PhD(math), 71. *Prof Exp:* Instr math, Inst Pure & Appl Math, 67; teaching asst, Mass Inst Technol, 68-71; actg asst prof, Univ Calif, Los Angeles, 71-72; instr, Princeton Univ, 72-74. *Mem:* Am Math Soc; Int Asn Math Physics. *Res:* mathematical physics; functional analysis. *Mailing Add:* Dept Math Univ Calif Irvine CA 92717-3875

KLEIN, ABRAHAM, THEORETICAL PHYSICS. *Current Pos:* assoc prof, 55-58, PROF PHYSICS, UNIV PA, 58- *Personal Data:* b Brooklyn, NY, Jan 10, 27; m 50, Murielle Pollack; c Julia M & Hilary B. *Educ:* Brooklyn Col, BA, 47; Harvard Univ, MA, 48, PhD(physics), 50. *Hon Degrees:* Dr, Univ Frankfurt, 96. *Prof Exp:* Asst physics, Harvard Univ, 47-49, instr, 50-52, jr fel, 52. *Concurrent Pos:* Consult, Res Inst Advan Study, Martin Marietta, 59 & Gen Dynamics-Convair, 60; NSF sr fel, 61-62; Alfred P Sloan Found fel, 61-63; vis prof, Univ Paris, 61-62, Princeton Univ, 69-70, Univ Tsukuba, Japan, 81, Yale Univ, 83, Tech Univ, Munich, 84 & Univ Frankfurt, 87 & 88; Guggenheim fel, 75; vis scientist, Ctr Theoret Physics, Mass Inst Technol, 75-76; assoc, Nat Ctr Sci Res, France, 84; Alexander von Humboldt sr scientist award, 87. *Mem:* Fel Am Phys Soc; Am Asn Physics Teachers. *Res:* Quantum electrodynamics; meson theory of nuclear forces; theory of scattering; many body problem; quantum field theory; theory of nuclear structure. *Mailing Add:* Dept Physics Univ Pa Philadelphia PA 19104-6396

KLEIN, ALBERT JONATHAN, topology, for more information see previous edition

KLEIN, ANDREW JOHN, TRACE ORGANIC ANALYSIS, ENVIRONMENTAL ANALYSIS. *Current Pos:* sr res chemist, Monsanto Co, 80-82, res specialist, 82, res group leader, 82-85, sr group leader, 85-86, MGR, REGULATORY AFFAIRS, MONSANTO CO, 86- *Personal Data:* b Wilkes-Barre, Pa, Dec 31, 51; m 78. *Educ:* King's Col, BS, 73; Univ Wis, PhD(chem), 78. *Prof Exp:* Res assoc, Univ Wis, 78-80. *Mem:* Am Chem Soc; AAAS; Asn Ground Water Scientists & Engrs. *Res:* Trace organic analysis in environmental matrices and natural water; analysis of xenobiotics in animal tissues. *Mailing Add:* 12917 Topping Estates Dr 800 N Lindbergh Blvd C3NA St Louis MO 63131

KLEIN, ATTILA OTTO, PLANT PHYSIOLOGY. *Current Pos:* asst prof, 62-67, chmn dept, 68-70, ASSOC PROF BIOL, BRANDEIS UNIV, 67- *Personal Data:* b Subotica, Yugoslavia, July 10, 30; nat US; m 52; c 3. *Educ:* Brooklyn Col, BA, 53; Ind Univ, PhD(plant physiol), 59. *Prof Exp:* USPHS fel biochem, Yale Univ, 59-61; asst biochemist, Conn Agr Exp Sta, 61-62. *Res:* Cellular and plant physiology; developmental biochemistry of leaves; light-induced metabolic oscillations. *Mailing Add:* Dept Biol Brandeis Univ 415 South St Waltham MA 02154-2700

KLEIN, AUGUST S, PHYSICS, CHEMISTRY. *Current Pos:* CONSULT, 92- *Personal Data:* b Newton, Mass, Aug 31, 24; m 67; c 3. *Educ:* Williams Col, BA, 48; Harvard Univ, MS, 50. *Prof Exp:* Physicist, Atomic Power Div, Westinghouse, 50-58; west coast mgr, High Voltage Eng Corp, 59-64; gen mgr, spec prod div, Tech Measurement Corp, 64-67; pres, Nuclear Equip Corp, 67-84; pres, Ion Implantation Corp, 85-90, pres Saval Circuits, 90-92. *Concurrent Pos:* Chmn, Greater Silicon Valley Implant Users Group; bd dir, Northern Calif Sect, Am Vacuum Soc. *Mem:* Electron Micros Soc Am; Am Inst Mining Engrs. *Res:* Energy dispersive x-ray fluorescent analysis; x-ray crystallography; ion implantation. *Mailing Add:* 160 La Questa Way Woodside CA 94062

KLEIN, BARBARA P, FOOD CHEMISTRY, NUTRITIONAL SCIENCE. *Current Pos:* res asst, Col Agr, Univ Ill, Urbana, 66-68, teaching asst, 69-72, from asst prof to assoc prof, 74-85, div chair, 85-90, PROF FOOD SCI & HUMAN NUTRIT, COL AGR, CONSUMER & ENVIRON SCI, UNIV ILL, URBANA, 85- *Personal Data:* b New York, NY, Dec 30, 36; m 56, Miles V; c Cynthia (Banai) & Gail Isabel. *Educ:* Cornell Univ, BS, 57, MS, 59; Univ Ill, PhD(foods & nutrit), 74. *Honors & Awards:* Borden Award, Am Home Econ Asn, 88. *Prof Exp:* Res asst food chem, Col Home Econ, Cornell Univ, 57-58. *Mem:* Inst Food Technologists; Am Soc Nutrit Sci; Am Chem Soc; Am Dietetics Asn; Am Asn Cereal Chemists; fel Inst Food Technologists. *Res:* Nutritional and sensory alterations in food quality during processing, particularly vegetables and soy products. *Mailing Add:* Food & Nutrit 274 Bevier Hall Univ Ill 905 S Goodwin Urbana IL 61801. *Fax:* 217-333-9368; *E-Mail:* b-klein@uiuc.edu

KLEIN, BENJAMIN GARRETT, MATHEMATICAL ANALYSIS. *Current Pos:* from asst prof to prof, 71-92, JOLAN PROF MATH, DAVIDSON COL, 92-, CHAIR, DEPT MATH, 94- *Personal Data:* b Durham, NC, Jan 24, 42; m 71, Rosemary McAndrew; c David G & Peter R. *Educ:* Univ Rochester, BA, 63; Yale Univ, MA, 65, PhD(Ergodic theory), 68. *Honors & Awards:* Thomas Jefferson Award, 90. *Prof Exp:* Lectr math, NY Univ, 67-68, asst prof, 69-71. *Concurrent Pos:* Consult, NC Dept Public Instr; vpres, Col Western Region NC, Coun Teachers Math, 89-90; chair, Southeastern Sect, Math Asn, 92-96. *Mem:* Am Math Soc; Math Asn Am; Nat Coun Teachers Math. *Res:* General mathematics. *Mailing Add:* Dept Math Davidson Col PO Box 1719 Davidson NC 28036. *Fax:* 704-892-2005; *E-Mail:* beklein@davidson.edu

KLEIN, BERNARD, ORGANIC CHEMISTRY. *Current Pos:* prof, 81-85, EMER PROF, DEPT LAB MED, EINSTEIN COL MED, BRONX, NY, 85- *Personal Data:* b New York, NY, Sept 16, 14; m 42, Rose Shweitzer; c David Andrew & Peter Alan. *Educ:* Brooklyn Col, BS, 34; Polytech Inst Brooklyn, PhD(chem), 50. *Honors & Awards:* Van Slyke Award, Am Asn Clin Chemists, 69, Ames Award, 75. *Prof Exp:* Chemist, Bethel Hosp, NY, 36-41; biochemist, Jewish Sanitarium & Hosp Chronic Dis, 41-42; res chemist, Warner Inst, NY, 46-48 & Harlem Hosp Cancer Found, 48; biochemist, US Vet Admin Hosp, Bronx, 48-67; biochemist, Res Div, Hoffmann-La Roche, Inc, 67, group chief clin chem, 67-71, asst dir, Dept Diag Res, 71-80. *Concurrent Pos:* Consult chemist, Area Reference Lab. *Mem:* Am Chem Soc; Am Asn Clin Chem. *Res:* Pyrazine chemistry; automated biochemical analyses. *Mailing Add:* 129 Patton Blvd New Hyde Park NY 11040-1726

KLEIN, CARL FREDERICK, MANUFACTURING RESEARCH, SENSORS ACTUATORS & DIAGNOSTIC SYSTEMS. *Current Pos:* res scientist, 72-77, mgr tech forecasting, 77-80, res group mgr, 80-90, MGR NEW TECHNOL, JOHNSON CONTROLS INC, 92- *Personal Data:* m 69, Mary J Uschan; c Christine, Mathew, John & James. *Educ:* Univ Wis, Madison, BS, 65, MS, 67. *Prof Exp:* Res engr, Johnson Serv Co, 67-72. *Concurrent Pos:* Instr physics semiconductor devices, Marquette Univ, 67-72. *Mem:* Inst Elec & Electronics Engrs; Soc Mfg Engrs; Soc Automotive Engrs; Am Welding Soc. *Res:* Enhanced profitability of manufacturing plants by accelerating the integration of new technology onto the factory floors; author/co-author of sixteen technical papers; inventor/co-inventor of eighteen US patents. *Mailing Add:* 5740 S Lochleven Lane New Berlin WI 53146. *Fax:* 414-228-2446

KLEIN, CERRY M, OPTIMIZATION, COMPUTER-AIDED DESIGN & MANUFACTURING. *Current Pos:* PROF INDUST ENG, UNIV MO, COLUMBIA, 84-, DIR GRAD STUDIES, 92- *Personal Data:* b Kansas City, Mo, Dec 11, 55; m 80, Debra A Baker; c Corey, Jonathan, Trevor, Nicolas, Breanna & Zachary. *Educ:* NW Mo State Univ, BS, 77; Purdue Univ, MS, 80, PhD(indust eng), 83. *Honors & Awards:* Ralph R Teetor Award, 89. *Prof Exp:* Teacher math, Consol Sch Dist No 1, Kansas City, Mo, 77-78; systs analyst, Nisus Corp, Indianapolis, Ind, 80-83. *Concurrent Pos:* Consult, 3M Co, 86 &

McDonnell Douglas Corp, 87; prin investr, Off Naval Res, 88 & McDonnell Douglas Corp, 88, Soc Mech Engrs, 89, 90, Eisenhower grant, 92, 94, 95 & 96, NSF, 96; vis prof, Monteray Technol Univ, 94. *Mem:* Inst Opers Res & Mgt Sci; Soc Indust & Appl Math; Math Prog Soc; Inst Indust Eng; Sigma Xi. *Res:* Dynamic programming; combinatorial optimization; design and analysis of heuristics; submodular functions; manufacturing processes; decision analysis; applications of operations research techniques and interior methods for mathematical programming; fuzzy set methodology. *Mailing Add:* Indust Eng E3437 Eng Bldg E Univ Mo Columbia MO 65211. *Fax:* 573-882-2693; *E-Mail:* Klein@risc1.ecn.missouri.edu

KLEIN, CHRISTOPHER FRANCIS, LASERS, ELECTRO-OPTICS. *Current Pos:* RES LASER SPECTROSCOPY, LASER SYSTS DESIGN & ANALYSIS, AEROSPACE CORP, 75- *Personal Data:* b Los Angeles, Calif, Sept 11, 43; m 73; c 2. *Educ:* Calif State Univ, Long Beach, BS, 67, MS, 72. *Prof Exp:* Mem res & develop staff electro-optic design, Autonetics Div, NAm Rockwell, 67-72; mem res & develop staff laser design, Hughes Aircraft Co, 72-75. *Concurrent Pos:* Instr physics, El Camino Col, 76-77. *Mem:* Soc Photo-Optical Instrumentation Engrs. *Res:* Laser spectroscopy; laser design; laser damage to optical materials. *Mailing Add:* Aerospace Corp M4-980 PO Box 92957 El Segundo CA 99009-2957

KLEIN, CLAUDE A, PHYSICS. *Current Pos:* CONSULT SCIENTIST, 89- *Personal Data:* b Strasbourg, France, Nov 4, 25; nat US; m 50; c 1. *Educ:* Univ Paris, EE, 51, PhD(physics), 55. *Prof Exp:* Asst to mgr, Mil Dept, French AEC, 55-57; prin scientist, Res Div, Raytheon Co, 57-88. *Concurrent Pos:* Vis lectr, Univ Lyons, 53-54, Univ Paris, 54-56 & Univ Lowell, 62-63. *Mem:* Fel Am Phys Soc; Inst Elec & Electronics Engrs. *Res:* Solid state physics; lasers and infrared; systems engineering. *Mailing Add:* 9 Churchill Lane Lexington MA 02173

KLEIN, CORNELIS, MINERALOGY, PETROLOGY. *Current Pos:* chmn, Dept Geol, 84-86, PROF EARTH & PLANETARY SCI, UNIV NMEX, 84- *Personal Data:* b Haarlem, Holland, Sept 4, 37; US citizen; wid; c Stephanie W (Peponis) & Marc A. *Educ:* McGill Univ, BSc, 58, MSc, 60; Harvard Univ, PhD(geol), 65. *Honors & Awards:* Carnegie Mineral Award for Int Recognized Achievements in Mineral, 97. *Prof Exp:* Res assoc geol, Harvard Univ, 63-65, lectr, 65-69, assoc prof mineral, 69-72; prof mineral, Ind Univ, Bloomington, 72-84. *Concurrent Pos:* Allston Burr sr tutor & asst dean, Harvard Col, 66-70; assoc ed, Am Mineralogist, 77-82, Precambrian Res, 83-, & Can Mineralogist, 89-91; Guggenheim fel, 78; John Simon Guggenheim fel, 78; mem, Precambrian Paleobiol Res Group, Univ Calif Los Angeles, 79- *Mem:* Fel Mineral Soc Am; fel Geol Soc Am; Mineral Asn Can; fel AAAS. *Res:* Precambrian iron formation; chemical, optical and x-ray properties of amphiboles; minerals in meteorites; mineralogy and petrology of lunar rocks; electron probe analysis of minerals; natural dust and asbestos. *Mailing Add:* Dept Earth & Planetary Sci Univ NMex Albuquerque NM 87131

KLEIN, DALE EDWARD, NUCLEAR ENGINEERING. *Current Pos:* asst prof, 77-82, DIR, NUCLEAR ENG TEACHING PROG, UNIV TEX, AUSTIN, 78-, ASSOC PROF MECH ENG, 82-, ASSOC CHANCELLOR, UNIV TEX SYST, 95- *Personal Data:* b Cooper Co, Mo, July 6, 47; m 71. *Educ:* Univ Mo, Columbia, BS, 70, MS, 71, PhD(nuclear eng), 77. *Honors & Awards:* Eng Found Award, Univ Tex, Austin, 79 & 82. *Prof Exp:* Design engr, Procter & Gamble Co, 70-72; teaching & res asst nuclear eng, Univ Mo, Columbia, 73-77. *Concurrent Pos:* Engr, Gen Atomic Co, 74; dep dir, Ctr Energy Studies, 86- *Mem:* Am Soc Mech Engrs; Am Nuclear Soc; Nat Soc Prof Engrs. *Res:* Thermal analysis of nuclear shipping containers; heat transfer augmentation for flow over rough surfaces; liquid metal flows through a packed bed under the influence of a transverse magnetic field. *Mailing Add:* Dept Mech Eng Univ Tex Austin TX 78712-1063

KLEIN, DAVID C, NEUROENDOCRINOLOGY. *Current Pos:* sr staff fel, Sect Physiol Controls, Lab Biomed Sci, 71-73, physiologist, 73-77, CHIEF NEUROENDOCRINOL SECT, LAB DEVELOP NEUROBIOL, NAT INST CHILD HEALTH & HUMAN DEVELOP, NIH, 77- *Personal Data:* b New York, NY, May 11, 40. *Educ:* Cornell Univ, AB, 62; Rice Univ, PhD(biol), 68. *Prof Exp:* Res asst endocrinol, Cornell Univ, 61 & phys biol, 62; res asst biophys cytol, Rockefeller Univ, 62-64; lab instr gen biol, endocrinol & radioisotope methodology, Rice Univ, 64-66; fel pharmacol, Univ Rochester Sch Med & Dent, 67-69. *Concurrent Pos:* Rice fel biol, 64; Nat Inst Dent Res trainee, 65-67; pres, Nat Inst Child Health & Human Develop Assembly Scientists, 74-75; chmn, Nat Inst Health Child Care Adv Comt, 75-76. *Mem:* AAAS; Sigma Xi; Tissue Cult Soc; Endocrine Soc; Am Soc Pharmacol & Exp Therapeut; Int Soc Neurochem; Am Soc Neurochem. *Res:* Biochemical signal transduction, using pinealocyte as an experimental model; the neural regulation of gene expression; the molecular basis of the biochemical "AND" gate. *Mailing Add:* Lab Develop Neurobiol Nat Inst Child Health & Human Develop NIH Bldg 49 Rm A82 MSC4480 Bethesda MD 20892-4480. *Fax:* 301-480-3526

KLEIN, DAVID HENRY, ANALYTICAL METHODS DEVELOPMENT. *Current Pos:* dir analytical chem, 89-90, div dir pharmaceut res & develop, 90-94, DISTINGUISHED RES FEL ALLIANCE PHARMACEUT CORP, 94- *Personal Data:* b Milwaukee, Wis, May 28, 33; m 54; c 2. *Educ:* Albion Col, BA, 54; Case Western Res Univ, PhD, 59. *Prof Exp:* Instr chem, Calif Inst Technol, 59-60; asst prof, Los Angeles State Col, 60-64; from assoc prof to prof chem, Hope Col, 64-81, chmn dept, 69-73; proj scientist, Parke Davis Co, 81-85; analytical group leader, Adamantech Inc. *Concurrent Pos:* NSF fel, Scripps Inst Onceanog, 68-69; vis scientist, Oak Ridge Nat Lab, 73-74. *Mem:* AAAS; Am Chem Soc. *Res:* Kinetics of nucleation; precipitation and co-precipitation; mercury and other heavy metals in the environment; geochemistry and marine chemistry; analysis of pharmaceutical materials; analysis of perfluorocarbons particle size measurements; pharmacokinetics of perfluorocarbons. *Mailing Add:* 920 East Bay Dr NE 3C-301 Olympia WA 98506

KLEIN, DAVID JOSEPH, RADIOLOGICAL PHYSICS. *Current Pos:* ASST CLIN PROF RADIOL, MED SCH, UNIV SOUTHERN CALIF, 74- *Personal Data:* b Los Angeles, Calif, Aug 3, 22; m 45, Ruth F; c 2. *Educ:* Calif Inst Technol, BS, 43, PhD(physics), 51. *Concurrent Pos:* Asst, Calif Inst Technol, 46-51; res engr, NAm Aviation, Inc, 51-52, sr engr, 53-58, sr physicist, 59-63, mem tech staff, Autonetics Div, NAm Rockwell Corp, 63-71; consult, Advan Info Methods, Inc, 71-72; health physicist, Los Angeles Co-Univ Southern Calif Med Ctr, 72-88. *Mem:* Am Asn Physicists Med; Am Phys Soc. *Res:* Solid state physics; reactor fuels; X-ray diffraction; electron diffraction and microscopy; radiation effects; semiconductors; dosimetry; diagnostic radiological physics; image quality; resolution; modulation transfer function; diagnostic quality assurance. *Mailing Add:* 2339 Kenilworth Ave Los Angeles CA 90039-3041

KLEIN, DAVID L, GEOPHYSICS. *Current Pos:* PRIN SCIENTIST & OWNER, IMAGE TOOLS, 89- *Educ:* Case Western Res Univ, BS, 73; Univ Ill, MS, 75, PhD(physics), 78. *Prof Exp:* Res staff geophysicist, Cogniseis Develop, 88-89. *Mem:* Am Phys Soc. *Mailing Add:* Image Tools 5814 Braesheather Houston TX 77096

KLEIN, DAVID M, ENVIRONMENTAL ANALYSIS, ORGANIC CHEMISTRY. *Current Pos:* LAB MGR, TEX PARKS & WILDLIFE, 93- *Personal Data:* b Ft Worth, Tex, Oct 31, 56. *Educ:* Univ Tex, BS, 78; Tex Christian Univ, MA, 80; Univ Hawaii, PhD(chem), 86. *Prof Exp:* Postdoctoral, Univ Hawaii, 86-88; chem instr, Kapiolani Community Col, 88-90; lab mgr, Hawaii Dept Agr, 90-93. *Concurrent Pos:* Adj fac, Southwest Tex State Univ, 95. *Mem:* Am Chem Soc (pres-elect, 93); Asn Off Anal Chemists (pres-elect, 97-). *Res:* Environmental analysis; tissue matrices for residue analysis. *Mailing Add:* PO Box 947 San Marcos TX 78667-0947. *Fax:* 512-353-7329; *E-Mail:* dk02@admin.swti.edu

KLEIN, DAVID ROBERT, MAMMALIAN ECOLOGY. *Current Pos:* SR SCIENTIST, ALASKA COOP FISH & WILDLIFE RES UNIT & PROF WILDLIFE ECOL, UNIV ALASKA, 62- *Personal Data:* b Fitchburg, Mass, May 18, 27; m 88, Lou A Maxwell; c 3. *Educ:* Univ Conn, BS, 51; Univ Alaska, MS, 53; Univ BC, PhD(zool), 63. *Honors & Awards:* Spec Recognition Serv Award, Wildlife Soc, 91; Meritorius Serv Honor Award, Dept Interior, 92. *Prof Exp:* Biologist, US Fish & Wildlife Serv, 55-59; biologist, Alaska Dept Fish & Game, 59-61, res dir, 61-62. *Concurrent Pos:* NSF instr grant, 63-64; Bur Sport Fisheries & Wildlife grant, 64-65 & Bur Land Mgr, 65-67; vis res biologist, Kalo Game Biol Sta, Denmark, 67; vis prof, Univ Oslo, 71-72, Univ Pretoria, 83. *Mem:* AAAS; Wildlife Soc; Arctic Inst NAm; Soc Range Mgt; Am Soc Mammalogists. *Res:* Foraging dynamics of arctic ungulates, artic herbivory; man's impact on the environment. *Mailing Add:* Wildlife & Biol Univ Alaska Fairbanks AK 99775-0990

KLEIN, DEANA TARSON, MYCOLOGY. *Current Pos:* from assoc prof to prof, 67-91, EMER PROF BIOL, ST MICHAEL'S COL, VT, 91- *Personal Data:* b Chicago, Ill, Jan 7, 25; m 47. *Educ:* Univ Chicago, BS, 47, MS, 48, PhD(bot), 52. *Prof Exp:* Res asst, Food Res Inst, Univ Chicago, 52-53; res asst chem embryol, Columbia Univ, 54-55, USPHS res fel, Dept Zool, 55-57; USPHS res fel microbiol & immunol, Albert Einstein Col Med, 57-58, from instr to asst prof, 58-66; asst prof biol sci, Hunter Col, 66-67. *Mem:* Am Soc Plant Physiologists; Bot Soc Am. *Res:* Physiology microorganisms and stress in angiosperm. *Mailing Add:* Dept Biol St Michael's Col Colchester VT 05439

KLEIN, DIANE M, CIRCULATORY SHOCK. *Current Pos:* Asst prof, 78-83, ASSOC PROF PHYSIOL, LOYOLA UNIV, 83- *Personal Data:* b Chicago, Ill, Mar 21, 48. *Educ:* Univ Ill, PhD(physiol), 78. *Mem:* Am Physiol Soc; Circulatory Shock Soc. *Mailing Add:* Nursing/Grad Prog Loyola Univ Lake Shore Campus 6525 N Sheridan Rd Chicago IL 60626-5311

KLEIN, DOLPH, CLINICAL MICROBIOLOGY. *Current Pos:* dir, Clin Microbiol Lab, Dulce Hosp, 74-89, ASSOC PROF MICROBIOL, MED CTR, DUKE UNIV, 74- *Personal Data:* b New York, NY, May 2, 28; m 56; c 4. *Educ:* City Col New York, BS, 50; Rutgers Univ, PhD(microbiol), 61; Am Bd Med Microbiol, dipl, 77. *Prof Exp:* Med technologist, Manhattan Gen Hosp, 50-51; lab asst microbiol, New York City Dept Health, 51-53; bacteriologist, Beth Israel Hosp, NY, 53-54; chief med technologist, Lakeside Hosp, Copiague, 54-57; res asst biophys, Sloan-Kettering Inst Cancer Res, 57-58; res asst agr microbiol, Rutgers Univ, 58-61; res microbiologist, Monsanto Co, Mo, 61-62; sr res microbiologist, Monsanto Res Corp, Mass, 62-63; res assoc biophys chem, Purdue Univ, 63-67; asst prof biochem, Univ Minn, Minneapolis, 67-71; asst prof microbiol & asst dir, Diag Microbiol Lab, Med Ctr, 72-74. *Concurrent Pos:* Vis prof, Univ Groningen, Neth, 82-83 & Univ Amsterdam, Neth, 91. *Mem:* Am Soc Microbiol. *Res:* Applications of biotechnology for rapid detection and identification of pathogenic bacteria; bacterial dissimilation of streptomycin; evaluation of antimicrobial agents and their modes of action; physicochemical basis of biological stability in structural proteins. *Mailing Add:* Dept Microbiol & Immunol Duke Univ Med Ctr PO Box 3322 Durham NC 27710-7599

KLEIN, DONALD ALBERT, MICROBIOLOGY. *Current Pos:* from asst prof to assoc prof, 70-78, PROF MICROBIOL, COLO STATE UNIV, 78- *Personal Data:* b Bridgeport, Conn, Sept 11, 35; m 56; c 4. *Educ:* Univ Vt, BS, 57, MS, 61; Pa State Univ, PhD(microbiol), 66. *Prof Exp:* Asst qual control, Nat Dairy Prod Corp, Vt, 57-58; instr food microbiol, Univ Vt, 58-61; res asst microbiol, Pa State Univ, 62-66; asst prof, Ore State Univ, 67-70. *Concurrent Pos:* Vis prof, Univ Kiel, 75 & Univ Copenhagen, 78. *Mem:* Am Soc Microbiol; Am Soc Agron. *Res:* Mined land reclamation microbiology; rhizosphere microbiology; microbial transformation of hydrocarbons and pesticides; soil ecology. *Mailing Add:* Dept Microbiol Colo State Univ Ft Collins CO 80523-0001

KLEIN, DONALD FRANKLIN, PSYCHIATRY, PSYCHOPHARMACOLOGY. *Current Pos:* DIR RES & DEPT THERAPEUTICS, NY STATE PSYCHIAT INST, 76-, DIR, MENT HEALTH CLIN RES CTR, 78-; PROF PSYCHIAT, COL PHYSICIANS & SURGEONS, COLUMBIA UNIV, 78- *Personal Data:* b New York, NY, Sept 4, 28; c 5. *Educ:* Colby Col, BA, 47; State Univ NY, MD, 52; Am Bd Psychiat & Neurol, dipl psychiat, 59. *Honors & Awards:* A E Bennett Neuropsychiat Res Award, 64; Res Award, Nat Asn Pvt Psychiat Hosps, 65 & 71; Samuel W Hamilton Award, Am Psychopath Asn, 80; William R McAlpin Award, Res Achievement, 88; Gold Medal Award, Soc Biol Psychiat, 90; Paul Hoch Distinguished Serv Award, Am Col Nuclear Physicians, 91; Thomas W Salmon Medal, Distinguished Serv Psychiat, NY Acad Med, 93. *Prof Exp:* Intern, USPHS Hosp, Staten Island, NY, 52-53; resident, Creedmoor State Hosp, 53-54 & 56-58; sr asst surg & staff psychiatrist, USPHS Hosp, Lexington, Ky, 54-56; res assoc psychiat, Creedmoor Inst Psychobiol Studies, 57-59; res assoc, Hillside Hosp, 59-64, dir res, 65-70, med dir eval, 70-71, dir, Dept Psychiat Res & Eval, Long Island Jewish-Hillside Med Ctr, 72-76; prof psychiat, Col Med, State Univ NY, Stony Brook, 72-76. *Concurrent Pos:* Pvt pract, 56-; cand, NY Psychoanal Inst, 57-61; USPHS ment health career investr, 61-64, sr staff psychiatrist, 65; NIMH grants, 61-; mem, Hofheimer Prize Bd, Am Psychiat Asn, 69-75 & task force methadone & narcotic antagonist eval, 71-73; adj prof psychol, Queens Col, City Univ New York, 69-; psychiatrist-in-chief, Queen Hosp Ctr, 70-71, full attend psychiatrist, 72-85; mem, Clin Pharmacol Study Sect, NIMH, 71-75 & Neuropharmacol Adv Comt, Food & Drug Admin, 71; chmn, Comt Res & Pub, Long Island Jewish-Hillside Med Ctr, 72-75, consult, 76-85; vis prof psychiat, Univ Auckland, NZ, 75, Albert Einstein Col Med, 76-77; lectr, Columbia Univ, 76-78; chmn, Res Adv Coun, Tex Dept Ment Health & Ment Retardation, 83-85; pres, Nat Found Depressive Illness, 83-; mem, Sci Adv Bd, Nat Depressive & Manic Depressive Asn, 86-, chmn, Clin Comt, 88-; consult, Alcohol Drug Abuse & Ment Health Admin, 88-89, sr sci adv, 89-90; consult, Nat Inst Drug Admin, 90-; mem, Bd Sci Counr, Nat Inst Alcohol Abuse & Alcoholism, 96- *Mem:* Fel Am Col Neuropsychopharmacol (pres, 81); fel Am Psychiat Asn; Am Psychopath Asn (treas, 72, pres, 78); Int Neuropsychol Soc; fel Royal Col Psychiat; Am Soc Clin Psychopharmacol (pres). *Res:* Diagnosis and drug treatment of psychiatric disorders; psychiatric case studies, treatment, drugs and outcome; age of onset of drug abuse in psychiatric inpatients; phobic anxiety syndrome complicated by drug dependence and addiction; physiology of panic attack. *Mailing Add:* NY State Psychiat Inst 722 W 168 New York NY 10032. *Fax:* 212-795-5886

KLEIN, DONALD LEE, INORGANIC CHEMISTRY SEMICONDUCTOR MATERIALS & PROCESSING. *Current Pos:* CONSULT, 87- *Personal Data:* b Brooklyn, NY, Dec 19, 30; m 52, Ruth; c Emilie H (Packer), Lynn M (Wiener), Sandra A (Worona), Jeffrey D, Robin D (Schwartz) & Gail B (Buiumsohn). *Educ:* Polytech Inst Brooklyn, BSCh, 52; Univ Conn, MS, 56, PhD(chem), 59. *Honors & Awards:* Jack A Morton Award, Inst Elec & Electronics Engrs, 94. *Prof Exp:* Engr, Sylvania Elec Prod, Inc, 52-54; asst, Univ Conn, 54-55, asst instr, 55-58; mem tech staff, Bell Tel Labs, Inc, 58-67; sr engr, Gen Technol Div, IBM Corp, 67-87. *Concurrent Pos:* Adj prof, Rensselaer Polytech Inst, 86; adj lectr, Rochester Inst Technol, 87-92; Lectr, Dutches Comm Unity Col, 87-93, Ctr Lifetime Study, Marist Col, 94- *Mem:* Am Chem Soc; Sigma Xi. *Res:* Electrochemistry; photochemistry; semiconductor materials and processing. *Mailing Add:* 4 Carnelli Ct Poughkeepsie NY 12603

KLEIN, DOUGLAS J, THEORETICAL CHEMISTRY, MOLECULAR PHYSICS. *Current Pos:* from asst prof to assoc prof, 79-87, PROF CHEM, TEX A&M UNIV, GALVESTON, 88- *Personal Data:* b Portland, Ore, Nov 8, 42; m 66, Janet C Goodrich; c 2. *Educ:* Ore State Univ, BSc, 64; Univ Tex, Austin, MA, 67, PhD(chem), 69. *Prof Exp:* Instr chem, Univ Tex, Austin, 69; Air Force Off Sci Res-Nat Res Coun fel, Princeton Univ, 69-70, univ fel, 70-71; asst prof physics, Univ Tex, Austin, 71-78. *Concurrent Pos:* Vis asst prof, Rice Univ, Houston, 79; vis sci officer, Off Naval Res, 84; Fulbright fel, 94. *Mem:* Am Chem Soc; Am Phys Soc; AAAS; Math Asn Am. *Res:* Theoretical models for molecules, polymers, and solids, with special emphasis on correlation effects and group-theoretic methods; eco-environmental modelling. *Mailing Add:* Dept Marine Sci Tex A&M Univ Galveston TX 77553-1675. *Fax:* 409-740-4429

KLEIN, EDMUND, medicine, dermatology, for more information see previous edition

KLEIN, EDWARD LAWRENCE, WOOD ENERGY, FOREST PRODUCTS. *Current Pos:* VPRES, CAPITAL RESOURCES EAST, 94- *Personal Data:* b Roscoe, Pa, Feb 17, 36; m 63; c 4. *Educ:* Pa State Univ, BS, 58, MS, 61; Baylor Univ, MBA, 63; La State Univ, PhD(forestry mkt), 68. *Prof Exp:* Asst dist forester, Md Dept of Forestry, 58-60; instr in charge mkt res, La State Univ, 65-68; mkt analyst, US Forest Serv, Princeton, WVa, 68-69; supvr econ sect, Tenn Valley Auth, 69-73; mfg mgr, Indust Wood & Pallet Co, 73-75; staff asst to dir, Div Forestry, Tenn Valley Auth, Norris, 75-77, proj leader wood energy, 77-79; dir mkt, Enerco Assocs, Langhorne, PA, 79-86; dir timber opers, Brooke Int, 91-94. *Mem:* Soc Am Foresters; Forest Prod Res Soc. *Res:* Economics of new plant sites and construction; production of saw mills and pallet plants; utilization of biomass as an energy source. *Mailing Add:* 1022 Olive St Coatesville PA 19320

KLEIN, ELENA BUIMOVICI, MICROBIOLOGY, INFECTIOUS DISEASES. *Current Pos:* CONSULT, VIROLOGY LAB, ROOSEVELT HOSP, 94- *Personal Data:* b Bucharest, Romania, Nov 12, 30; m 62; c 1. *Educ:* Univ Bucharest, MD, 53. *Prof Exp:* Sr res scientist microbiol, Cantacuzino Inst, Bucharest, 53-72; res scientist virol, Bellevue Hosp, NY Univ, 72-73; asst prof pediat, Roosevelt Hosp, Columbia Univ, 73-; dir, Virus Lab, St Luke's-Roosevelt Hosp Ctr, 80-94. *Mem:* Romanian Soc Infectious Path; Am Soc Microbiol; fel Soc Infectious Dis. *Res:* Epidemiology of diptheria; genetics of enteroviruses; epidemiology of poliomyelities; congenital rubella; cell mediated immunity in viral infections; viral vaccines. *Mailing Add:* 27 Nob Ct New Rochelle NY 10804

KLEIN, ELIAS, PHYSICAL CHEMISTRY. *Current Pos:* ASSOC PROF ENG, SCH CHEM ENG, UNIV LOUISVILLE, 82-, PROF MED, SCH MED, 84- *Personal Data:* b Leipzig, Ger, Oct 26, 24; m 48; c 3. *Educ:* Tulane Univ, MS, 52, PhD(phys chem), 54. *Prof Exp:* Res chemist, Southern Regional Res Lab, USDA, 54-55, invest head, 55-58; res chemist phys chem, Courtaulds, Inc, Ala, 58-60, sect head, 60-62, mgr res dept, 62-64, dir res & develop, 64-67; dir phys chem, Gulf Southern Res Inst, 67, dir Lake Pontchartrain Lab, 67-81. *Concurrent Pos:* Consult, Kalvar Corp, 52-55; adj prof, Loyola Univ, La, 69-; founder & pres, NAm Membrane Soc. *Mem:* Am Chem Soc; Sci Res Soc Am; Am Soc Artificial Internal Organs. *Res:* Kinetics; cellulose and fiber chemistry; membrane transport; hemodialysis; reverse osmosis. *Mailing Add:* 5517 Hempstead Rd Louisville KY 40207-1207

KLEIN, FRANCIS MICHAEL, ORGANIC CHEMISTRY. *Current Pos:* asst prof, 68-73, asst dean, 78-79, chmn dept, 87-93, ASSOC PROF CHEM, CREIGHTON UNIV, 73- *Personal Data:* b Wilkes Barre, Pa, Nov 1, 41; m 64, Janet Bauman; c Kathleen (Murray), Kristin (Pluhacek), Mark, Matthew & Rachel. *Educ:* King's Col, Pa, BS, 63; Univ Notre Dame, PhD(org chem), 67. *Prof Exp:* NIH fel, Iowa State Univ, 67-68. *Mem:* Int Union Pure & Appl Chem; Am Chem Soc. *Res:* Organic photochemistry; reaction mechanisms, especially stereochemical factors; molecular orbital calculations of reaction energetics; electrophilic addition reactions. *Mailing Add:* Dept Chem Creighton Univ Omaha NE 68178-0104. *Fax:* 402-280-5737; *E-Mail:* fklein@creighton.edu

KLEIN, GEORGE D, SEDIMENTOLOGY, MARINE GEOLOGY. *Current Pos:* PRES, NJ MARINE SCI CONSORTIUM, 93- *Personal Data:* b s'Gravenhage, Neth, Jan 21, 33; US citizen. *Educ:* Wesleyan Univ, BA, 54; Univ Kans, MA, 57; Yale Univ, PhD(geol), 60. *Prof Exp:* Part-time geologist, State Geol Surv, Kans, 55-56; res geologist, Sinclair Res, Inc, 60-61; asst prof geol, Univ Pittsburgh, 61-63; from asst prof to assoc prof, Univ Pa, 63-69; assoc prof geol, Univ Ill, Urbana, 70-72, prof, 72-93. *Concurrent Pos:* Vis fel, Oxford Univ, 69; vis assoc prof geol & geophys, Univ Calif, Berkeley; vis prof oceanog, Ore State Univ, 74, Seoul Nat Univ, 80, Univ Tokyo, 83; assoc, Ctr Adv Study, Univ Ill, 74 & 83; vis exchange prof geophys sci, Univ Chicago, 79-80; sr res fel, Japan Soc Prom Sci, 83; sr Fulbright res fel, Vrije Univ, Amsterdam, 89. *Mem:* Geol Soc Am; Am Asn Petrol Geol; Int Asn Sedimentology; Am Geophys Union; Soc Econ Paleontologists & Mineralogists. *Res:* Recent sediments; sedimentary and sandstone petrology; basin analysis; marine geology; turbidites; sedimentation on tidal flats; tidalites; back arc and cratonic basins; Deep-ocean sediment transport; petroleum sandstone reservoir prediction and diagenesis; beach erosion. *Mailing Add:* PO Box 944 Matawan NJ 07747. *Fax:* 732-291-4483

KLEIN, GERALD I(RWIN), ELECTRICAL ENGINEERING. *Current Pos:* ADV ENGR, HERLEY INDUST, 88- *Personal Data:* b Brooklyn, NY, Sept 22, 28; m 48; c 4. *Educ:* Cooper Union, BEE, 48; Polytech Inst Brooklyn, MEE, 53. *Prof Exp:* Asst head, Radar & Microwave Electronics Sect, Naval Mat Lab, NY, 48-55; chief, Oscillators & Amplifiers Sect, Evans Signal Lab, NJ, 55-58; mgr, Microwave Tubes Sect, Electronic Tube Div, Westinghouse Elec Corp, 58-65, mgr microwave tech lab, Aerospace Div, Md, 65-68; vpres eng & mfg, Solitron Microwave, 68-70; adv engr, Westinghouse Elec Corp, 70-88. *Mem:* Sr mem Inst Elec & Electronics Engrs. *Res:* Microwave electronics; electromagnetic theory; microwave plasmas; electron tubes. *Mailing Add:* Herley Indust 10 Industry Dr Lancaster PA 17603

KLEIN, GORDON LESLIE, GASTROENTEROLOGY, PEDIATRICS. *Current Pos:* PROF PEDIAT & NUTRIT, UNIV TEX MED BR, GALVESTON, 86-, PROF PEDIAT & PREV MED. *Personal Data:* b New York, NY, Aug 26, 46; m 73, Joann P Schulz; c Adrienne L. *Educ:* Columbia Univ, BA, 67; Albert Einstein Col Med, MD, 71; Univ Calif, Los Angeles, MPH, 80. *Prof Exp:* Postgrad student, investigative med, Univ Cambridge, UK, 70-71; intern & resident pediat, Stanford Univ Med Ctr, Calif, 71-74; fel nutrit, Sch Med, Johns Hopkins Univ, 76-78; fel gastroenterol, Med Ctr, Univ Calif, Los Angeles, 78-80, adj asst prof pediat, 80-82; asst prof pediat, Med Ctr, & adj asst prof nutrit, Sch Pub Health, Tulane Univ, 82-84; chief serv, Pediat Gastroenterol & Nutrit, City Hope Nat Med Ctr, 84-86. *Concurrent Pos:* Res affil, Wadsworth Med Ctr, Vet Admin, Calif, 80-82; clin assoc prof pediat, Sch Med, Univ Southern Calif, 84-; US Pharmacopeia Gen Comt of Rev, 90-95; Am Soc Parenteral & Enteral Nutrit Tech Adv Group on Parenteral Nutrit, 90- *Mem:* Am Soc Bone & Mineral Res; Am Soc Clin Nutrit; Am Gastroenterol Asn; Am Fedn Med Res; Soc Pediat Res; Am Acad Pediat. *Res:* Investigation of abnormalities in calcium and bone metabolism; aluminum contamination of parenteral solution and toxicity to bone and other organs; characterization of metabolic bone disease and its consequences following burn injury. *Mailing Add:* Univ Tex Med Br 301 University Blvd Galveston TX 77555-0352. *Fax:* 409-772-4599; *E-Mail:* gklein@edi.utmb.edu

KLEIN, HAROLD GEORGE, VERTEBRATE ZOOLOGY. *Current Pos:* from asst prof to assoc prof, 62-91, EMER PROF BIOL, STATE UNIV NY COL PLATTSBURGH, 91. *Personal Data:* b Jersey City, NJ, Mar 14, 29; m 65. *Educ:* Cornell Univ, BS, 53, MS, 54, PhD(vert zool), 58. *Prof Exp:* Instr biol, Swarthmore Col, 57-58; asst prof zool, Pa State Univ, 59-62. *Mem:* Ecol Soc Am; Am Soc Mammal; Animal Behav Soc. *Res:* Ecological research on vertebrate animals, particularly mammals. *Mailing Add:* 5 Haynes Rd Plattsburgh NY 12901

KLEIN, HAROLD PAUL, MICROBIAL PHYSIOLOGY, EXOBIOLOGY. *Current Pos:* SCIENTIST-IN-RESIDENCE, SANTA CLARA UNIV, 84-; RES SCIENTIST, SETI INST, 85- *Personal Data:* b New York, NY, Apr 1, 21; m 42, Gloria Dolgov; c Susan A & Judith E. *Educ:* Brooklyn Col, BA, 42; Univ Calif, Berkeley, PhD(bact, biochem), 50. *Honors & Awards:* NASA Medal Except Sci Achievement, 77; Co-recipient, Cleveland-Newcomb Award, AAAS, 77. *Prof Exp:* Chemist, US Civil Serv, 42-43; instr bact, Armstrong Jr Col, 46-47; asst, Univ Calif, 47-50; res fel, Am Cancer Soc, Mass Gen Hosp, 50-51; from asst prof to prof biol, Brandeis Univ, 55-63, chmn dept, 56-63; chief exobiol div, Ames Res Ctr, NASA, 63-64, dir life sci, 64-84. *Concurrent Pos:* Am Cancer Soc fel, 50; vis prof, Univ Calif, 60-61; NSF sr fel, 63; mem, Joint US-USSR Space Med & Biol Working Group, 71-; leader biol team, Viking Mission Mars, 75-77; investr, US-USSR Cosmos Flights, 75 & 79; mem space sci bd, Nat Acad Sci, 84-89. *Mem:* Int Soc Study Origin Life; Am Soc Biol Chem; Int Acad Astronaut. *Res:* Microbial metabolism; formation of adaptive enzymes; lipid synthesis; space biology; exobiology. *Mailing Add:* Biol Dept Santa Clara Univ Santa Clara CA 95053. *Fax:* 650-961-7099

KLEIN, HARVEY G, TRANSFUSION MEDICINE. *Current Pos:* CHIEF DEP TRANSFUSION MED, CLIN CTR, NIH, 75- *Personal Data:* b Boston, Mass, May 8, 43. *Educ:* Harvard Univ, AB, 65; Johns Hopkins Univ, MD, 69. *Honors & Awards:* Cohn Delavel Award, World Apheresis Asn, 96. *Prof Exp:* Spec asst to dir, Blood Div, Nat Heart Lung Blood Inst, 73-75. *Mem:* Am Asn Blood Bank; Soc Hemat; Fedn Clin Res. *Mailing Add:* Clin Ctr - NIH Bldg 10 Rm 1C711 Bethesda MD 20892. *Fax:* 301-402-1981

KLEIN, HARVEY GERALD, PHARMACEUTICS, MEDICAL INSTRUMENTATION. *Current Pos:* pres, Klein Assocs, 73-80, PRES, KLEIN BIOMED CONSULTS, 81- *Personal Data:* b New York, NY, Oct 22, 30; m 83, Lesli Dworkin; c Zoe. *Educ:* City Col New York, BS, 53; NY Univ, MS, 57; Purdue Univ, PhD(chem), 61. *Prof Exp:* Chemist plastic additives res, Cent Res Div, Am Cyanamid Co, Stamford, Conn, 61-63, sr mkt analyst, Com Develop Div, Wayne, NJ, 63-66, tech rep & liaison, Washington, DC, 66-67; drug & health care financial analyst, R W Pressprich & Co, 67-69, Wertheim & Co, 69-70 & Andresen & Co, 71-72. *Mem:* Am Chem Soc; Am Inst Ultrasound Med; Inst Elec & Electronics Engrs; Am Soc Echocardiography; Am Heart Asn. *Res:* Medical diagnostic instrumentation and pharmaceutical development. *Mailing Add:* 215 W 90th St New York NY 10024

KLEIN, HERBERT A, NUCLEAR MEDICINE. *Current Pos:* Dir, Nuclear Med Educ, 84-91, assoc dir, Div Nuclear Med, Dept Radiol, Sch Med, Univ Pittsburgh, 80-96, MEM, MED STAFF, PRESBY-UNIV HOSP, PITTSBURGH, 80-; CHIEF NUCLEAR MED SERV, VET ADMIN MED CTR, PITTSBURGH, 91-, INTERIM CHIEF, NUCLEAR MED & RADIOL SERV, 96- *Personal Data:* b Milwaukee, Wis, Mar 28, 36; m 73, Inara Berzins; c Benjamin & Alexandra. *Educ:* Columbia Univ, AB, 56, MD, 60; Harvard Univ, MA, 68, PhD(biochem), 75; Am Bd Nuclear Med, cert, 74. *Concurrent Pos:* Prin investr, Wechsler Res Found Grant, 84-85. *Mem:* Soc Nuclear Med. *Res:* Computer analysis of radionuclide studies of esophageal function; use of radioiodine in the diagnosis and treatment of thyroid carcinoma. *Mailing Add:* Nuclear Med 115 Vet Admin Pittsburgh Health Care Syst University Dr Pittsburgh PA 15240

KLEIN, HOWARD JOSEPH, METALLURGICAL ENGINEERING. *Current Pos:* VPRES, HAYNES INT INC, 87- *Personal Data:* b Kokomo, Ind, July 5, 41; m 64; c 5. *Educ:* Purdue Univ, BS, 63; Univ Ala, MS, 65; Univ Tenn, PhD(metall eng), 69. *Honors & Awards:* Von Karman Award, Theodore Von Karman Mem Found, 74; IR 100, Indust Res, 75 & 77. *Prof Exp:* Engr, Haynes Stellite Div, Cabot Corp, 69-71, sr engr process metall, 72-73, group leader process metall & ceramics, 73-75, sect mgr, 75-77, dir technol, 77-79, oper mgr high technol, 79-82, dir inventory mgt & qual control, CWP Div, 82-83, dir opers, 83-85, dir & gen mgr technol, Cabot Corp, 85-86. *Concurrent Pos:* Mem, Comt Electroslag Remelting & Plasma Melting Technol, Nat Mat Adv Bd, 74-75 & Comt Joint Coop Electro Metall, US State Dept, 76-; mem comt review US-USSR Agreement Coop Fields Sci & Technol, Nat Acad Sci, 77; chmn tech bd, Am Soc Metals, 85-87; dir, Metals Property Coun, 87. *Mem:* Fel Am Soc Metals Int; Am Inst Mining, Metall & Petrol Engrs; Am Vaccum Soc. *Res:* Development and processing of nickel and cobolt base alloys for application in the aerospace corrosion and wear resistant areas; primary and secondary processing technologies. *Mailing Add:* 2227 S Wabash Ave Kokomo IN 46902

KLEIN, IMRICH, plastics & chemical engineering; deceased, see previous edition for last biography

KLEIN, JACOB, PHYSICS OF MATERIALS. *Current Pos:* PROF, WEIZMAN INST SCI, ISRAEL, 87- *Personal Data:* b Tel Aviv, Israel, Aug 20, 49; m 74, Michele Castle; c 4. *Educ:* Univ Cambridge, Eng, BA, 73, MA & PhD, 77. *Honors & Awards:* Charles Vernon Boys Prize, Brit Inst Physics, 84; High Polymer Physics Prize, Am Phys Soc, 95. *Prof Exp:* Staff, Univ Cambridge, 80-84. *Concurrent Pos:* Kao fel, Japan, 94. *Res:* Contributed over 120 papers to scientific journals in areas of polymer physics. *Mailing Add:* Fac Chem Weizman Inst Sci PO Box 26 Rehovot 76100 Israel

KLEIN, JAN, BIOLOGY, IMMUNOGENETICS. *Current Pos:* DIR DEPT IMMUNOGENETICS, MAX PLANCK INST BIOL, 78-; DISTINGUISHED RES PROF, DEPT MICROBIOL & IMMUNOL, SCH MED, UNIV MIAMI, FLA, 87- *Personal Data:* b Opava, Czech, Jan 18, 36; m 69, Dagmar; c Norman A, Daniel K & Pavel J. *Educ:* Charles Univ, Prague, BS, 55, MS, 58; Czech Acad Sci, PhD(genetics), 64. *Honors & Awards:* Elisabeth Goldschmidt Mem lectr; Rabbi Schacknai Mem Prize, Transplantation Soc. *Prof Exp:* Res assoc genetics, Inst Exp Biol & Genetics, Prague, 64-65; res assoc, Sch Med, Stanford Univ, 68-69; from asst prof to assoc prof, Univ Mich, Ann Arbor, 69-74; from assoc prof to prof microbiol, Univ Tex Health Sci Ctr, Dallas, 74-78. *Concurrent Pos:* Managing ed, Immunogenetics; mem, Immunobiol Study Sect, NIH. *Mem:* Am Asn Immunol; Transplantation Soc; Scand Soc Immunol; Fr Soc Immunol. *Res:* Immunogenetics; cellular immunology; molecular biology. *Mailing Add:* Max-Planck Inst fuer Biol Dept Immunogenetics Corrensstr 42 72076 Tuebingen Germany. *Fax:* 49-7071-600437; *E-Mail:* klein@mpib-tuebingen.mpg.de

KLEIN, JERRY ALAN, CHEMICAL ENGINEERING. *Current Pos:* Develop engr, 72-78, group leader environ control technol, Chem Technol Div, 78-96, PROG MGR ISOTOPE PROG, OAK RIDGE NAT LAB, 97- *Personal Data:* b Neenah, Wis, Apr 19, 45; m 66; c 2. *Educ:* Univ Wis, BS, 67; Princeton Univ, PhD(chem eng), 72. *Res:* Environmental control technology for coal conversion processes. *Mailing Add:* 135 Danbury Dr Oak Ridge TN 37830

KLEIN, JOHN PETER, SURVIVAL ANALYSIS. *Current Pos:* PROF & HEAD BIOSTATIST, MED COL WIS, 93- *Personal Data:* b Milwaukee, Wis, Dec 30, 50. *Educ:* Univ Wis, Milwaukee, BA, MS, 75; Univ Mo, PhD(statist), 80. *Prof Exp:* Asst math, Univ Wis-Milwaukee, 74-75; statistitian, Univ Mo, 75-80; from asst prof to prof statist, Ohio State Univ, 80-93. *Concurrent Pos:* Researcher, Oak Ridge Nat Labs, 76-77; biostatistician, Ohio State Comprehensive Cancer Ctr, 81-93; statist dir, IBM, 93- *Mem:* Biomet Soc; Am Statist Asn; Inst Mat Statist; Soc Clin Trials; Int Statist Inst. *Res:* Survival analysis. *Mailing Add:* Dept Biostatist Med Col Wis 8701 Watertown Plank Rd Milwaukee WI 53226. *Fax:* 414-266-8481; *E-Mail:* klein@biostat.mcw.edu

KLEIN, JOHN ROBERT, MUCOSAL IMMUNOLOGY, EXTRATHYMIC T CELL DEVELOPMENT. *Current Pos:* asst prof, 87-89, ASSOC PROF, DEPT BIOL SCI, UNIV TULSA, 89- *Personal Data:* b Detroit, Mich, Aug 27, 47. *Educ:* Elmhurst Col, BA, 71; Johns Hopkins Univ, PhD, 80. *Prof Exp:* Fel, Univ Pa, 80-81, Mass Inst Technol, 81-82; Scripps Clin & Res Found, 82-83; asst res immunologist, Univ Calif, San Diego, 83-87. *Concurrent Pos:* Res career develop award, Crohiss & Coltis Found, 86-87; study sect mem, NIH, NSF & Am Cancer Soc, 92-93. *Mem:* Soc Mucosal Immunol. *Res:* Studies of T cell development within the intestine; extrathymic nature of intestinal T cells. *Mailing Add:* Dept Biol Sci Univ Tulsa 600 S College Ave Tulsa OK 74104. *Fax:* 918-631-5005

KLEIN, JOHN SHARPLESS, applied mathematics, for more information see previous edition

KLEIN, LARRY L, ORGANIC CONDUCTORS, CARBOHYDRATE CHEMISTRY. *Current Pos:* ASST PROF CHEM, TEX A&M UNIV, 82- *Personal Data:* b Chicago, Ill, Jan 24, 53. *Educ:* Ill Inst Technol, BS, 75; Mich State Univ, PhD(chem), 80. *Prof Exp:* NIH fel chem, Harvard Univ, 80-82. *Mem:* Am Chem Soc. *Res:* Organic synthesis of natural products. *Mailing Add:* Abbott Labs Dept 47M AP9A 100 Abbott Park Rd Abbott Park IL 60064-3500

KLEIN, LAWRENCE ROBERT, ECONOMICS. *Current Pos:* prof, 58-64, univ prof, 64-68, BENJAMIN FRANKLIN PROF, UNIV PA, 68- *Personal Data:* b Omaha, Nebr, Sept 14, 20; m 47, Sonia Adelson; c Hannah, Rebecca, Rachel & Jonathan. *Educ:* Univ Calif, Berkeley, BA, 42; Mass Inst Technol, PhD, 44. *Hon Degrees:* Numerous from US & foreign univs. *Honors & Awards:* Nobel Prize in Econ, 80; John Bates Clark Medal, Am Econ Asn, 59. *Prof Exp:* Fac, Univ Chicago, 44-47; res assoc, Nat Bur Econ Res, 48-50; res assoc, Surv Res Ctr, 49-54, Oxford Inst Statist, 54-58. *Concurrent Pos:* Consult numerous orgns, 47-; ed, Int Econ Rev, 59-65, assoc ed, 65-; vis prof, Univ Osaka, Japan, 60, Univ Colo, 62, City Univ NY, 62-63 & 82, Hebrew Univ, 64, Princeton Univ, 66, Stanford Univ, 68 & Univ Copenhagen, 74; Ford vis prof, Univ Calif, Berkeley, 68 & Inst Advan Sci, Vienna, 70 & 74; coordr, Jimmy Carter's Econ Task Force, 76. *Mem:* Nat Acad Sci; fel Econometric Soc; fel Am Acad Arts & Sci; Am Econ Asn; Am Philos Soc. *Mailing Add:* Univ Pa McNeil Bldg Rm 335 3718 Locust Walk Philadelphia PA 19104-6297

KLEIN, LEONARD C, CHEMISTRY. *Current Pos:* SECY, AM MICROCHEM SOC; SR RES CHEMIST, ANALYTICAL DEPT, AGR CHEM GROUP, FORD MOTOR CO. *Mem:* Am Microchem Soc. *Mailing Add:* c/o FMC Corp PO Box 8 Princeton NJ 08543

KLEIN, LEROY, BIOCHEMISTRY, MEDICAL RESEARCH. *Current Pos:* From instr to assoc prof biochem in orthop surg, 63-77, from sr instr to asst prof biochem, 65-71, PROF BIOCHEM IN ORTHOP & MACROMOLECULAR SCI, 77-, ASSOC PROF BIOCHEM, CASE WESTERN RES UNIV, 71- *Personal Data:* b Newark, NJ, Oct 1, 26; m 58; c 3. *Educ:* Syracuse Univ, BA, 50; Boston Univ, MA, 52, PhD(biochem), 58; Case Western Res Univ, MD, 65. *Concurrent Pos:* Res fel biochem, Case Western Res Univ, 58-60, res fel orthop, 60-63, instr orthop surg, 63-65; Kappa Delta res award, 63, res grants, 63- *Mem:* Am Fedn Clin Res; Am Soc Biol Chem; Orthop Res Soc; Geront Soc; Am Soc Bone & Mineral Res; Sigma Xi. *Res:* Connective tissue metabolism and diseases; collagen and mineral turnover in experimental and metabolic bone diseases, aging, wound healing. *Mailing Add:* 511 Wearn Bldg Case Western Med 11100 Euclid Ave Cleveland OH 44106-5043. *Fax:* 216-844-5970

KLEIN, LEWIS S, THEORETICAL PHYSICS. *Current Pos:* assoc prof, 65-70, PROF PHYSICS, HOWARD UNIV, 70- *Personal Data:* b Youngstown, Ohio, Sept 2, 32; m 60. *Educ:* Union Col, NY, BS, 54; Yale Univ, MS, 55, PhD(physics), 58. *Prof Exp:* Fulbright fel & res physicist, Nat Ctr Sci Res, France, 58-59; instr physics, Northwestern Univ, 59-60; sr res staff, Nat Bur Stand, 60-65. *Mem:* Am Phys Soc. *Res:* Field theory; statistical mechanics; plasma physics. *Mailing Add:* Dept Physics & Astron Howard Univ 2355 Sixth St NW Washington DC 20059-0001

KLEIN, LUELLA, GYNECOLOGY, MATERNAL FETAL MEDICINE. *Current Pos:* clin instr, Emory Univ, 56-67, assoc prof, 67-73, chmn, 86-93, PROF GYNEC & OBSTET, EMORY UNIV, 73- *Personal Data:* b Walker, Iowa, 1924. *Educ:* Univ Iowa Sch Med, MD, 49. *Prof Exp:* Rotating intern, 49-50, jr asst resident med, 50-51, jr asst resident surg, 51-52, asst resident obstet- gynec, 52-54, resident obstet-gynec, 54-55; instr, Western Residency, 55. *Concurrent Pos:* Sr Fulbright Res Scholar, Univ London, 56; consult, Ga Dept Pub Health, 58-62; staff, Piedmont Hosp, Ga Byst Hosp, Crawford Hosp, Atlanta, 60- *Mem:* Inst Med-Nat Acad Sci; AMA; Am Col Obstet & Gynecol; Am Med Women's Asn. *Mailing Add:* Dept Gynec & Obstet Emory Univ 69 Butler St SE Atlanta GA 30303. *Fax:* 404-521-3589

KLEIN, MARSHALL S, OPHTHALMOLOGY. *Current Pos:* ADMINR, EYE INST NJ, NEWARK, 72- *Personal Data:* b New York, NY, Mar 19, 26; m; Barbara Janet Cohen; c Marcia Jill & Geoffrey Lee. *Educ:* Fairleigh Dickinson Univ, BS, 66, MBA, 80. *Prof Exp:* Owner & dir, Styertowne Youth Ctr, 52-72. *Mem:* Eye Bank Asn Am. *Mailing Add:* Eye Inst NJ 90 Bergen St Newark NJ 07103-2425

KLEIN, MARTIN J(ESSE), HISTORY OF PHYSICS. *Current Pos:* Guggenheim fel, 67-68, prof, 67-73, EUGENE HIGGINS PROF PHYSICS & HIST SCI, YALE UNIV, 73- *Personal Data:* b New York, NY, June 25, 24; m 80; c 4. *Educ:* Columbia Univ, AB, 42, AM, 44; Mass Inst Technol, PhD(physics), 48. *Prof Exp:* Asst physics, Columbia Univ, 42-44, physicist, Underwater Sound Ref Lab, 44-45; mem, Opers Res Group, Washington, DC, 45-46; res assoc physics, Mass Inst Technol, 46-49; from instr to prof, Case Inst Technol, 49-67. *Concurrent Pos:* Nat Res fel, Dublin Inst Advan Studies, 52-53; Guggenheim fel, Inst Lorentz, Leiden, 58-59; mem, Inst Advan Study, 72; Van der Waals prof, Univ Amsterdam, 74; vis prof, Rockefeller Univ, 75 & Harvard, 89-90. *Mem:* Nat Acad Sci; fel AAAS; fel Am Phys Soc; Hist Sci Soc; Acad Int Hist Sci; Am Acad Arts & Sci. *Res:* History of modern physics; statistical mechanics. *Mailing Add:* Dept Physics Yale Univ PO Box 208120 New Haven CT 06520-8120. *Fax:* 203-432-6175

KLEIN, MAX, CHEMICAL PHYSICS, THERMODYNAMICS. *Current Pos:* CONSULT, 91- *Personal Data:* b New Bedford, Mass, Feb 5, 25; m 85, Suzette Aldon; c Nehemiah D, David N & Sara H (Glashofer). *Educ:* Univ Mass, BS, 48; Univ Md, PhD(physics), 62. *Honors & Awards:* Dept Silver Medal, US Dept Com. *Prof Exp:* Electronics engr comput memory, Nat Bur Stand, 50-55, physicist thermodyn, 55-63; physicist chem physics, Weizmann Inst Sci, 63-65; physicist thermodyn, Nat Bur Stand, 65-67, sect chief, 67-77, supvry physicist, 77-81; sr scientist thermodyn, Gas Res Inst, 81-91. *Concurrent Pos:* Mem fac grad sch, NIH, 66-76; mem adv comt grad sch, Dept Agr, 67-72. *Mem:* Am Phys Soc; Am Inst Chem Engrs; AAAS; Sigma Xi; Am Chem Soc; Am Ceramic Soc; Mat Res Soc. *Res:* Theory brittle fracture in polyethyene; accelerated testing measurement and fatigue behavior of polyethylene; thermodynamic properties of fluids. *Mailing Add:* 900 24th St NW Unit No G Washington DC 20037

KLEIN, MELVIN PHILLIP, BIOPHYSICS, BIOPHYSICAL SPECTROSCOPY. *Current Pos:* Physicist, Radiation Lab, 52-59, biophysicist, Lawrence Radiation Lab, 59-69, BIOPHYSICIST & ASSOC DIR, CHEM BIODYN LAB, SR SCIENTIST, LAWRENCE BERKELEY LAB, UNIV CALIF, 69- *Personal Data:* b Denver, Colo, July 27, 21; m 60, Margaret Dearey; c Peter, Adrienne & Mark. *Educ:* Univ Calif, Berkeley, AB, 52, PhD(biophys), 59. *Concurrent Pos:* Vis mem tech staff, Bell Tel Labs, Murray Hill, NJ, 60-61; mem biophys & biophys chem study sect, Div Res Grants, NIH, 69-74; mem adv comt, Stable Isotopes Resource, Los Alamos Sci Labs, 75; mem exec comt, Stanford Magnetic Resonsance Lab, Stanford Univ, 76; sabbatical vis, Biophys Group, Ecole Polytech, Palaiseau & Synchrotron Radiation Lab, Univ Paris, 76-77; John Simon Guggenheim Mem Found, 76-77; chmn, Gordon Res Conf Magnetic Resonance, 77; mem/chmn, Users Org, Stanford Synchrotron Radiation Lab, 80-82; Alexander von Humboldt Sr Scientist Award, Free Univ, Hahn-Meitner Inst Berlin, 88-89; mem, Users Exec Comt/Advan Light Source, 89-92. *Mem:* Biophys Soc; Am Phys Soc. *Res:* Photosynthesis; magnetic resonance spectroscopy; x-ray spectroscopy with synchrotron radiation; photosynthetic oxygen evolution/ water splitting; electron spin resonance; electron spin echo envelope modulation. *Mailing Add:* Lawrence Berkeley Lab Univ Calif 1 Cyclotron Rd Bldg 3 Rm 130 Berkeley CA 94720

KLEIN, MICHAEL GARDNER, BIOLOGICAL CONTROL, INSECT PATHOLOGY. *Current Pos:* RES ENTOMOLOGIST, HORT INSECTS RES LAB, APPLN TECHNOL RES UNITS, AGR RES SERV, USDA, 69- *Personal Data:* b Rockford, Ill, Jan 14, 41; m 64, Pauline R Knieff; c Mary R & Steven M. *Educ:* Univ Wis-Madison, BS, 63, MS, 65, PhD(entom), 72. *Concurrent Pos:* Adj assoc prof entom, Ohio State Univ, 73- *Mem:* Entom Soc Am; Soc Invert Path; Soc Nematologists; Soil Ecology Soc; Int Oregn Biol Control. *Res:* Biological control of turf and ornamental insect pests such as the Japanese Beetle; finding new pathogens, demonstrating their effectiveness, and developing application techniques. *Mailing Add:* USDA-ARS Hort Insects Res Lab 1680 Madison Ave Wooster OH 44691. *E-Mail:* klein.10@osu.edu

KLEIN, MICHAEL JOHN, RADIO ASTRONOMY. *Current Pos:* Nat Res Coun-NASA resident res assoc, 68-69, sr scientist radio astron, Space Sci Div, 69-73, MEM TECH STAFF, SPACE SCI DIV, JET PROPULSION LAB, CALIF INST TECHNOL, 73-, PROJ MGR SEARCH EXTRA-TERRESTRIAL INTEL, 81-, MGR, DEEP SPACE NETWORK SCI OFF. *Personal Data:* b Ames, Iowa, Jan 19, 40; m 62; c 3. *Educ:* Iowa State Univ, BS, 62; Univ Mich, MS, 66, PhD(astron), 68. *Prof Exp:* Asst res engr, Radio Astron Lab, Univ Mich, 63-64. *Mem:* Am Inst Elec & Electronics Engrs; Am Astron Soc; Int Astron Union; Int Union Radio Sci; Am Inst Aeronaut & Astronaut. *Res:* Measuring and interpretating radio frequency emission of galactic and extragalactic radio sources and solar system planets and satellites; apply radio astronomy techniques to the Search for Extraterrestrial Intelligence (SETI). *Mailing Add:* Jet Propulsion Lab MS 303-402 Pasadena CA 91109-8099

KLEIN, MICHAEL LAWRENCE, BIOPHYSICS. *Current Pos:* PROF CHEM, UNIV PA, 87-, HEPBURN PROF PHYS SCI, 93-, DIR, LAB RES STRUCT MATTER, 93- *Personal Data:* b London, Eng, Mar 13, 40; m 62; c 2. *Educ:* Bristol Univ, BSc, 61, PhD(theoret chem), 64. *Prof Exp:* Ciba Found fel physics, Univ Genoa, 64-65; Imp Chem Industs fel theoret chem, Bristol Univ, 65-67; res assoc physics, Rutgers Univ, 67-68; pr res off chem, Nat Res Coun Can, 68-87. *Concurrent Pos:* Fel World Trade, IBM, San Jose, 70; prof, Univ Paris, 75; prof chem, McMaster Univ, Hamilton, Ont, 77; fel, Japan Soc Prom Sci, 82, Commoner Trinity Col, Cambridge, UK, 85; Louis Neel prof, Ecole Normale Superierre, Lyon, France, 88; Guggenheim fel, 89-90; prof, Univ Firenze, 93; Humboldt Fel, 96; Miller Prof, Univ Calif, Berkeley, 97. *Mem:* Am Phys Soc; Royal Soc Chem; Can Inst Physics; fel Chem Inst Can; fel Royal Soc Can. *Res:* Computer simulation studies in physical chemistry; solid state physics and biophysics. *Mailing Add:* Dept Chem Univ Pa Philadelphia PA 19104-6323

KLEIN, MICHAEL TULLY, MODELLING, APPLIED & INDUSTRIAL CHEMISTRY. *Current Pos:* from asst prof to assoc prof chem eng, Univ Del, 81-89, assoc dean, Col Eng, 87-88, dept chair, 90-96, DIR, CTR CATALYTIC SCI & TECHNOL, UNIV DEL, 88-, PROF CHEM ENG, 89-, ELIZABETH INEL KELLEY PROF, 94- *Personal Data:* b Wilmington, Del, Mar 15, 55; m, Elizabeth; c Jennifer, Michael & Lisa. *Educ:* Univ Del, BChE, 77; Mass Inst Technol, ScD, 81. *Prof Exp:* Instr chem eng, Mass Inst Technol, 80. *Concurrent Pos:* Consult, var oil & chem cos; lectr, var univ & orgn, 82-91; prin young investr, Outstanding Young Men Am, NSF, 85 & 88. *Mem:* Am Inst Chem Engrs; Am Chem Soc. *Res:* Chemical reaction engineering of complex mixtures, including resid upgrading, hydroprocessing, and applied catalysis; author of over 150 technical papers. *Mailing Add:* Dept Chem Eng Univ Del Newark DE 19716. *Fax:* 302-831-1810; *E-Mail:* klein@che.udel.edu

KLEIN, MICHAEL W, SOLID STATE PHYSICS, STATISTICAL MECHANICS. *Current Pos:* head dept, 79-84, PROF PHYSICS, WORCESTER POLYTECH INST, 79- *Personal Data:* b Teglas, Hungary, Mar 29, 31; US citizen; m 55, Lida Rosenfeld; c Ira J & David H. *Educ:* Univ Colo, BS, 56; Cornell Univ, PhD(physics), 62. *Prof Exp:* Asst physics, Cornell Univ, 56-61; res physicist, Lincoln Labs, Mass Inst Technol, 61-62 & Sperry Rand Res Ctr, Mass, 62-68; assoc prof physics, Wesleyan Univ, 68-71; assoc prof physics, Bar-Ilan Univ, Israel, 71-77; vis prof, Physics Dept, Univ Ill, 77-79. *Concurrent Pos:* Vis assoc prof, Brandeis Univ, 67-68. *Mem:* Am Phys Soc. *Res:* Theory of magnetism; solid state physics; statistical mechanics; plasma physics; glassy and amorphous systems; superconductivity. *Mailing Add:* Dept Physics Worcester Polytech Inst Worcester MA 01609

KLEIN, MILES VINCENT, PHYSICS. *Current Pos:* from asst prof to assoc prof, 62-69, PROF PHYSICS, UNIV ILL, URBANA, 69-, DIR, SCI & TECHNOL CTR SUPERCONDUCTIVITY, 89- *Personal Data:* b Cleveland, Ohio, Mar 9, 33; m 56, Barbara Pincus; c Cynthia (Banai) & Gail K. *Educ:* Northwestern Univ, BS, 54; Cornell Univ, PhD(physics), 61. *Honors & Awards:* Frank Isakson Prize, Am Phys Soc, 90. *Prof Exp:* NSF fel physics, Stuttgart Tech Univ, 61-62. *Mem:* Sr mem Inst Elec & Electronics Engrs; fel Am Phys Soc; Mat Res Soc; fel AAAS. *Res:* Raman scattering in solids; optical properties of solids. *Mailing Add:* Loomis Lab Univ Ill 1110 W Green Urbana IL 61801

KLEIN, MILTON M, FLUID DYNAMICS. *Current Pos:* RES PHYSICIST, AIR FORCE CAMBRIDGE RES LABS, BEDFORD, 67- *Personal Data:* b New York, NY, Apr 19, 17; m 51; c 1. *Educ:* NY Univ, MS, 50, PhD(physics), 56. *Prof Exp:* Physicist aerodyn, Nat Adv Comt Aeronaut, 42-47, aeronaut res scientist, 48-50; instr physics, NY Univ, 50-55; physicist, Gen Elec Co, 55-61; physicist nuclear debris studies, Geophys Corp Am, 61-63, re-entry physics, Lincoln Lab, 63-64 & plasma physics & hydrodyn, GCA Corp, 64-67. *Concurrent Pos:* Lectr, Grad Sch, Univ Pa, 57-58. *Mem:* Am Phys Soc. *Res:* Fluid dynamics; diffusion; turbulence; heat transfer; interaction of buoyant turbulent jets with air; dissipation of fog by heat; cloud physics; meteorology. *Mailing Add:* 54 Burlington St Lexington MA 02173

KLEIN, MORTON, INDUSTRIAL ENGINEERING, OPERATIONS RESEARCH. *Current Pos:* from instr to assoc prof, Sch Eng & Appl Sci, 56-69, chmn dept, 82-85 & 94-95, PROF INDUST ENG & OPERS RES, COLUMBIA UNIV, 69- *Personal Data:* b New York, NY, Aug 9, 25; m 49, Gloria Ritterband; c Lisa & Melanie. *Educ:* Duke Univ, BS, 46; Columbia Univ, MS, 52, EngScD, 57. *Prof Exp:* Ord engr, Picatinny Arsenal, US Army, 50-54. *Concurrent Pos:* Consult indust & govt; ed, Mgt Sci, 70-77. *Mem:* Opers Res Soc Am; Inst Mgt Sci; Am Inst Indust Engrs. *Res:* Network flows; production planning; research and publications on production planning; scheduling early cancer detection examinations, network flows and statistical quality control; author of numerous publications. *Mailing Add:* Dept Indust Eng Columbia Univ Main Div New York NY 10027

KLEIN, MORTON JOSEPH, INORGANIC CHEMISTRY. *Current Pos:* RETIRED. *Personal Data:* b Chicago, Ill, Feb 26, 28; m 53; c 3. *Educ:* Univ Ill, BS, 48; Ill Inst Technol, PhD(chem), 53. *Prof Exp:* Assoc chemist catlysis, IIT Res Inst, 53-54, res chemist org chem, 54-56, asst supvr propellant res, 56-59, supvr, 59-62, asst dir chem res, 62-65, dir appl chem, 65-69, dir chem res, 69-75, dir chem & chem eng res, 75-77, vpres res opers, 77-91. *Mem:* Am Chem Soc; Am Inst Aeronaut & Astronaut; Am Inst Chem; Int Ozone Asn (pres, 75-79). *Res:* Synthesis and evaluation of new high energy materials; research management. *Mailing Add:* 7608 Tucson Rd Scottsdale AZ 85258

KLEIN, NATHAN, PHYSICAL CHEMISTRY. *Current Pos:* AT US ARMY RES LAB, ABERDEEN PROVING GROUND, MD. *Personal Data:* b New York, NY, July 29, 31; m 52; c 5. *Educ:* City Col New York, BS, 51; Columbia Univ, MA, 52; Univ Del, PhD(chem), 67. *Prof Exp:* Res asst biochem, Sloan-Kettering Inst Cancer Res, 52; chemist, Edgewood Arsenal, 55-66, group leader radiation chem, US Army Nuclear Defense Lab, 66-74, group leader, US Army Ballistic Res Labs, 74-93. *Mem:* Am Chem Soc; Sigma Xi; fel Am Inst Chem. *Res:* Physical chemistry of aqueous solutions; reactions rates of high energy compounds; chemical kinetics of propellants and explosives; high temperature, high pressure reaction studies. *Mailing Add:* 6813 Fox Meadow Rd Baltimore MD 21207-5628. *Fax:* 410-278-6159; *E-Mail:* klein@arl.army.mil

KLEIN, NELSON HAROLD, PHYSICS. *Current Pos:* Assoc prof physics, 72-78, chmn, Dept Sci, 78-85, PROF ENG & PHYSICS, BUCKS COUNTY COMMUN COL, COORDR PHYSICS DEPT, 80- *Personal Data:* b New York, NY, Mar 6, 42; m 66; c 2. *Educ:* Drexel Univ, BS, 64, MS, 68, PhD(physics), 72. *Mem:* Am Asn Physics Teachers. *Mailing Add:* Dept Sci Bucks County Commun Col Swamp Rd Newtown PA 18940

KLEIN, NORMAN W, REPRODUCTIVE TOXICOLOGY. *Current Pos:* PROF ANIMAL GENETICS & NUTRIT & MOLECULAR CELL BIOL, UNIV CONN, 76- *Personal Data:* b San Francisco, Calif, Feb 6, 31. *Educ:* Univ Calif, PhD(nutrit), 60. *Mailing Add:* Ctr Environ Health Univ Conn Storrs CT 06268. *Fax:* 860-486-5067

KLEIN, PAUL ALVIN, VIROLOGY, IMMUNOLOGY. *Current Pos:* PROF PATH, COL MED, UNIV FLA, 69- *Personal Data:* b Weehawken, NJ, Feb 1, 41; m 63; c 2. *Educ:* Rutgers Univ, New Brunswick, BA, 63; Univ Fla, PhD(med sci), 67. *Mem:* AAAS; Am Asn Immunol; Reticuloendothelial Soc; Sigma Xi. *Res:* Viral immunology; autoimmunity; diabetes; cancer biology. *Mailing Add:* Dept Path Univ Fla Col Med Box 100275 Gainesville FL 32610-0275. *Fax:* 352-392-1619

KLEIN, PETER DOUGLAS, ANALYTICAL CHEMISTRY, BIOCHEMISTRY. *Current Pos:* prof pediat, 80-95, prof med, 86-95, EMER PROF PEDIAT & MED BAYLOR COL MED, 95- *Personal Data:* b Elmhurst, Ill, Nov 30, 27; m 50, 68, E Roseland Purcell; c 3. *Educ:* Antioch Col, BS, 48; Wayne State Univ, MS, 50, PhD(physiol chem), 54. *Prof Exp:* From asst biochemist to sr biochemist, Div Biol Med Res, Argonne Nat Lab, 69-72; prof med, Univ Chicago, 72-80; mem staff, Div Biol & Med Res, Argonne Nat Lab, 76-80; dir, Stable Isotope Lab, Childrens Nutrit Res Ctr, 80-93. *Concurrent Pos:* Vpres res & div, Meretek Diag Inc, Houston, Tex, 93- *Mem:* Am Soc Mass Spectrometry; Am Asn Study Liver Dis; Am Soc Biol Chemists; Am Gastroenterol Asn; Am Soc Clin Nutrit; Am Pediat Asn. *Res:* Application of stable isotope tracer methodology and mass spectrometry to clinical research in gastroenterology; development of non-invasive diagnostic and functional assessments in disease processes, metabolic and genetic disorders. *Mailing Add:* Med Towers Bldg 1709 Dryden Rd, Suite 1513 Houston TX 77030. *Fax:* 713-664-1735; *E-Mail:* pklein@eatsbcm.tmc.edu

KLEIN, PHILIPP HILLEL, MATERIALS PURIFICATION & CRYSTAL GROWTH. *Current Pos:* CONSULT, PHILIPP KLEIN CONSULT, 90- *Personal Data:* b New York, NY, Sept 14, 26; m 53, Charlotte Feuerstein; c Joshua D, Daniel W & Jonathan H. *Educ:* Syracuse Univ, BS, 48, MS, 51, PhD(phys chem), 53. *Prof Exp:* Asst chem, Syracuse Univ, 48-49, res asst, 51-52; res assoc, Knolls Atomic Power Lab, Gen Elec Co, 52-56, phys chemist, Electronics Lab, 56-61; mem sci staff, Sperry Rand Res Ctr, 61-66; head dielec mat sect, Electronics Res Ctr, NASA, Mass, 66-70; head, Crystals & Pure Mat Sect, USN Res Lab, 70-73, Dielec Mat Sect, 73-87, res consult electronic mat, 87-90. *Mem:* Fel Am Inst Chem; Sigma Xi; Inst Elec & Electronics Engrs; Mat Res Soc; Am Phys Soc; Am Asn Crystal Growth. *Res:* Effects of nuclear radiation on gases and dielectric solids; thermoelectricity; compound semiconductors; thermal properties of solids; electronically and optically active solids; crystal growth. *Mailing Add:* 2017 Hillyer Pl NW Washington DC 20009-1005. *Fax:* 202-462-4493; *E-Mail:* nielkhp@aol.com

KLEIN, RALPH, physical chemistry, for more information see previous edition

KLEIN, RICHARD, PUBLIC HEALTH & EPIDEMIOLOGY, HEALTH STATISTICS. *Current Pos:* CHIEF, DATA MONITORING & ANALYSIS BR, DIV HEALTH PROMOTIONS & STATIST, CTR DIS CONTROL, 92- *Personal Data:* b Baltimore, Md, Aug 26, 48. *Educ:* Univ Md, BA, 86; Johns Hopkins Univ, MA, 88. *Prof Exp:* Statistician, Div Vital Statist, 92. *Mem:* Am Pub Health Asn. *Mailing Add:* 6525 Belcrest Rd Hyattsville MD 20782. *Fax:* 301-436-8459; *E-Mail:* rjk6@cdc.gov

KLEIN, RICHARD JOSEPH, microbiology, experimental medicine, for more information see previous edition

KLEIN, RICHARD LESTER, PHARMACOLOGY, CELL PHYSIOLOGY. *Current Pos:* from asst prof to assoc prof, 59-66, prof pharmacol, 66-81, PROF PHARMACOL & TOXICOL, MED CTR, UNIV MISS, 81- *Personal Data:* b Hempstead, NY, Nov 6, 29; m 53; c 2. *Educ:* Hofstra Univ, BA, 51, MA, 52; Vanderbilt Univ, PhD(biol, chem), 57. *Prof Exp:* Instr pharmacol, Vanderbilt Univ, 58-59. *Concurrent Pos:* Nat Heart Inst fel pharmacol, Vanderbilt Univ, 57-59; NIH career prog award, 62-72; vis prof, Biophys Lab, Wenner-Gren Inst, 63-64; vis prof, Karolinska Inst, 69-70. *Mem:* Am Soc Pharmacol & Exp Therapeut; Electron Micros Soc Am; Soc Neurosci; Sigma Xi. *Res:* Sympathetic nerve and catecholamine storage vislcles, including permeability, enzyme activity, composition, histochemistry and ultrastructure; human serum dopamine beta-hydroxylase and sympathetic homeostasis. *Mailing Add:* 706 Shore Dr Destin FL 32541-5276. *Fax:* 850-837-9041

KLEIN, RICHARD M, INORGANIC CHEMISTRY, ORGANIC CHEMISTRY. *Current Pos:* group vpres chem, 78-84, PRES & CHIEF EXEC OFFICER, SYBRON CHEM, INC, 84- *Personal Data:* b Philadelphia, Pa, Nov 10, 37. *Educ:* Williams Col, BA, 59; Univ Ill, MS, 62, PhD(polymer chem), 63. *Prof Exp:* Mem staff sales develop spec prod, Rohm and Haas Co, 63-65, mgr sales develop, Pa, 65-66, mgr int opers sales develop, 66-68; asst managing dir, Triton Chem SAfrica, 68-69; asst to pres int opers, Tanatex Chem Corp, NJ, 69-70; pres, Ionac Chem Co, 70-78. *Concurrent Pos:* Pres, Gamlen Chem Co NAm, 75-78. *Mem:* Am Chem Soc. *Res:* Chemical management and development. *Mailing Add:* Sybron Chem Inc Birmingham Rd PO Box 66 Birmingham NJ 08011

KLEIN, RICHARD M, PLANT PHYSIOLOGY. *Current Pos:* prof, 67-92, EMER PROF BOT, UNIV VT, 92- *Personal Data:* b Chicago, Ill, Mar 17, 23; m 47. *Educ:* Univ Chicago, BS, 47, MS, 48, PhD(bot), 51. *Honors & Awards:* UVM Biol Sci Univ Scholar. *Prof Exp:* Am Cancer Soc fel bot, Univ Chicago, 51-53; res assoc, NY Bot Garden, 53-55, assoc cur, 55-57, Alfred H Caspary cur plant physiol, 57-67. *Mem:* Am Soc Plant Physiol; Bot Soc Am; Am Soc Photobiol. *Res:* Growth and development of plants; photobiology; physiological ecology of forest decline. *Mailing Add:* Dept Bot Univ Vt Burlington VT 05405

KLEIN, RICHARD MORRIS, MATERIALS SCIENCE, GLASS SCIENCE. *Current Pos:* actg res mgr, 81-82, MEM TECH STAFF, 66-, PRIN INVESTR, 75-, DEPT MGR, 82-, DIR, NETWORK TECH, GTE LABS, INC, 88- *Personal Data:* b Brooklyn, NY, Apr 26, 42; m 64, Ronnie Suchman; c Michael & Jennifer. *Educ:* State Univ NY Col Ceramics, Alfred, BS, 63, PhD(ceramic sci), 67. *Concurrent Pos:* Mem Nat Bd Adv, Rose-Hulman Inst Technol, Terre-Haute, Ind, 87- *Mem:* Am Ceramic Soc; Nat Inst Ceramic Engrs; Soc Glass Technol; Sigma Xi; Inst Elec & Electronics Engrs. *Res:* Management of research and development on the physical elements that comprise communication networks. *Mailing Add:* GTE Labs Inc 40 Sylvan Rd Waltham MA 02154-1120. *E-Mail:* rmk0@gte.com

KLEIN, ROBERT HERBERT, PHYSICS. *Current Pos:* dir First Col, 75-78, 84-90, ASSOC PROF PHYSICS, CLEVELAND STATE UNIV, 67- *Personal Data:* b New York, NY, Dec 5, 32; m 61; c 3. *Educ:* Columbia Univ, AB, 53; Carnegie Inst Technol, PhD(physics), 63. *Prof Exp:* Asst physics, Carnegie Inst Technol, 53-55; assoc scientist, Avco Res & Adv Develop Corp, 56-57; solid state physicist, Electronic Res Directorate, Air Force Cambridge Res Ctr, Mass, 57-59; asst theoret physics, Carnegie Inst Technol, 59-63; res scientist, Courant Inst, NY Univ, 63-65; res assoc physics, Case Inst Technol, 65-67. *Mem:* Am Phys Soc. *Res:* Theoretical physics. *Mailing Add:* First Col Dept Physics Cleveland State Univ Cleveland OH 44115

KLEIN, ROBERT L, PROCESS DEVELOPMENT & SCALE-UP, PRODUCT DEVELOPMENT. *Current Pos:* VPRES RES & DEVELOP, ANGUS CHEM CO, 90- *Personal Data:* m 77, Mary L Nagel; c Andrew, Lawrence & William. *Educ:* Case Western Res Univ, BS, 75; Univ Wis, MS, 79; Univ Minn, PhD(chem eng), 83. *Prof Exp:* Group leader, UOP, 83-87; dir res & develop, Henkel Corp, 87-90. *Mem:* Am Inst Chem Engrs; Am Chem Soc. *Res:* Product and process development of nitroparaffins and their derivatives. *Mailing Add:* 705 Arthur Ave Libertyville IL 60048. *Fax:* 847-808-3704

KLEIN, ROBERT MELVIN, ANATOMY, CELL BIOLOGY. *Current Pos:* from asst prof to assoc prof, 81-86, PROF & CHMN DEPT ANAT, MED CTR, UNIV KANS, 87- *Personal Data:* b New York, NY, Dec 17, 49; m 75; c 3. *Educ:* Queens Col, City Univ New York, BA, 70; NY Univ, MS, 73, PhD(anat), 74. *Concurrent Pos:* Assoc scientist, Mid-Am Cancer Ctr, 75-; NIH Travel Awards, 77-; fel, Marquette Univ, 74-75; prin investr grants, NIH, 78-88 & Am Heart Asn 80-82. *Mem:* Am Asn Anatomists; Cell Kinetics Soc; Soc Develop Biol; NY Acad Sci; Am Soc Cell Biol; Sigma Xi. *Res:* Influence of growth factors on tooth eruption and development; influences of autonomic nervous system on growth and differentiation of neonatal digestive system. *Mailing Add:* Dept Anat Univ Kans Med Ctr 3901 Rainbow Blvd Kansas City KS 66160-7400. *Fax:* 913-588-2710

KLEIN, RONALD, OPHTHALMOLOGY. *Current Pos:* From asst prof to assoc prof, 78-85, PROF OPHTHAL, SCH MED, UNIV WIS-MADISON, 85- *Personal Data:* b New York, NY, July 25, 43; m 65; c 1. *Educ:* Brooklyn Col, BS, 65; NY Univ, MD, 69; Univ NC, MPH, 73. *Mem:* Am Epidemiol Soc; Soc Epidemiol Res; Am Col Epidemiol; Asn Res Vision & Ophthal; AMA; Am Diabetes Asn. *Res:* Epidemiological studies on ocular and systemic complications of diabetes mellitus; age-related ocular diseases, macular degeneration and cataract. *Mailing Add:* Dept Ophthal Univ Wis 600 Highland Ave Madison WI 53792

KLEIN, RONALD DON, BIOTECHNOLOGY. *Current Pos:* CONSULT, 84- *Personal Data:* b Mt Clemens, Mich, July 30, 48; m 68; c 2. *Educ:* Western Mich Univ, BA, 70, MA, 71; Univ Wis-Madison, PhD(molecular biol), 81. *Prof Exp:* Instr, Western Mich Univ, 70-72; grad res fel, Biochem Dept, Wayne State Univ, 75-76; res asst, Biochem Dept, Univ Wis-Madison, 76-81; fel, Chem Dept, Mass Inst Technol, 81-82; res scientist, Res & Develop Div, Phillips Petrol Co, 82-84. *Concurrent Pos:* Assoc ed, Madison Rev Books, 78-80. *Mem:* AAAS; Am Chem Soc; Am Soc Microbiol; Sigma Xi; assoc Hastings Inst. *Res:* Relationship of DNA sequence and structure to gene regulation by the analysis of DNA/protein interactions; physical properties of defined DNA molecules; plasmid vectors for the expression of cloned genes; large scale isolation of gene products. *Mailing Add:* 9721 S Sixth St Schoolcraft MI 49087

KLEIN, SHERWIN JARED, psychophysiology, for more information see previous edition

KLEIN, SIGRID MARTA, MICROBIOLOGY, BIOCHEMISTRY. *Current Pos:* TRANSLR, SCI MAT-GERMAN TO ENGLISH, SIGRID, 94- *Personal Data:* b Koenigsberg, Ger, May 1, 32. *Educ:* Univ Kiel, Staatsexamen, 57; Brigham Young Univ, MS, 61, PhD(microbiol), 64. *Prof Exp:* Res asst biochem, Sloan-Kettering Lab, 58-59; res assoc microbiol, Brigham Young Univ, 64-67; fel, Charles F Kettering Labs, 67-70; res assoc biochem, Brigham Young Univ, 70-81; chemist, Becton Dickinson, 82-87; qual assusrance mgr, Murdock Int, Springville, 87-94. *Mem:* Am Soc Microbiol. *Res:* Organization of photosynthetic membranes; intermediary metabolism in blue-green algae; immunodiagnostics. *Mailing Add:* 39 N Valley View Dr No 99 St George UT 84770

KLEIN, TERRY ALLEN, MALARIA EPIDEMIOLOGY & VECTOR STUDIES, NEW REPPELLENTS-REPELLENT FORMULATIONS. *Current Pos:* CHIEF, VECTER ASSESSMENT BR, VIROL DIV, US ARMY MED RES INST INFECTIOUS DIS, 95- *Personal Data:* m 67, Jacqueline L McEachran; c Kevin D, Aaron R, Michelle R & Robert A. *Educ:* Ore Col Educ, BS, 68; Ore State Univ, MS, 75; Univ Fla, PhD(entom), 85. *Prof Exp:* Teacher biol/earth sci, Cascade Union High Sch, 68-73; entomologist, US Army Environ Hyg Agency, 76-78 & 80; entomologist & asst chief, US Army Med Component, Bangkok, 78-80; chief, Entom Sect, US Army Med Res Unit, Brazil, 86-90; mgr, Malaria Sect, Walter Reed Army Inst Res, 90-93, repellent sect, Dept Entom, Div CD&I, 93-94; comdr, 5th Med Detachment, Ento, Korea, 95. *Concurrent Pos:* Vis prof, Univ Brasilia, 86-88; adj prof, Univ Para, Belem, 89-90, Uniformed Serv Univ Health Scis, 90- *Mem:* Am Entom Soc; Am Mosquito Control Asn; Am Soc Trop Med & Hyg. *Res:* Field and laboratory malaria vector studies in Thailand and Brazil; research on dengue and evaluated arthropod repellents/ repellent formulations against biting flies; arbounus epidemiology studies in Peru. *Mailing Add:* US Army Med Res Inst Infectious Dis Attn: MCMR-UIV-V LTC Terry Kein 1425 Porter St Ft Detrick MD 21702-5011. *Fax:* 301-619-2492; *E-Mail:* ltc__terry__klein@ftdetrck-ccmail.army.mil

KLEIN, V(ERNON) A(LFRED), CHEMICAL ENGINEERING. *Current Pos:* RETIRED. *Personal Data:* b Marion, Tex, Sept 10, 18; m 50; c 2. *Educ:* Univ Tex, BSChE, 40, MSChE, 42. *Prof Exp:* Instr chem eng, Univ Tex, 41-42; asst supt org chem prod, Dow Chem Co, 42-44, res & develop engr & group leader org res, 44-51, tech specialist, 51-56, sr tech specialist, 56-60, consult, 60-63, systs specialist, 63-68, sr process specialist, 68-81. *Mem:* Am Chem Soc; Am Inst Chem Engrs; Sigma Xi. *Res:* High pressure vapor-liquid equilibrium; physical chemistry. *Mailing Add:* 63 Plantation Ct Lake Jackson TX 77566-5865

KLEIN, WILLIAM, STATISTICAL MECHANICS. *Current Pos:* from asst prof to assoc prof, 76-84, PROF PHYSICS, BOSTON UNIV, 84- *Personal Data:* b Philadelphia, Pa, Apr 1, 43; m 67; c 2. *Educ:* Temple Univ, BS, 65, PhD(physics), 72. *Prof Exp:* Res scientist physics, Univ Cologne, 74-76. *Res:* Mathematics and physics of phase transitions. *Mailing Add:* Dept Physics Rm 319 Boston Univ 590 Commonwealth Boston MA 02215

KLEINBERG, ISRAEL, ORAL BIOLOGY. *Current Pos:* PROF & CHMN, DEPT ORAL BIOL & PATH, STATE UNIV NY, STONY BROOK, 73- *Personal Data:* b Toronto, Ont, May 1, 30; m 55, Constance L Sfreddo; c Michael E, Brian D, Alan J & Rochelle L. *Educ:* Univ Toronto, DDS, 54; Univ Durham, PhD(physiol & biochem), 58; Royal Co Dentists Can, FRCD(C), 69. *Hon Degrees:* DSc, Univ Man, 83. *Honors & Awards:* Can Centennial Medal, Govt Can, 67. *Prof Exp:* Demonstr, Univ Durham, 55-58; from asst prof to prof biochem, Univ Man, 58-73. *Concurrent Pos:* Mem assoc comt dent res, Nat Res Coun Can, 59-60, exec mem, 60-65; consult, Nat Inst Dent Res, NIH, 74-81; mem, NY State Health Res Coun, 81-87. *Mem:* Int Asn Dent Res; Am Asn Dental Res; Am Soc Microbiol; Am Asn Oral Biol (pres, 91-92). *Res:* Metabolism of the dental bacterial plaque; plaque formation; peptide growth factors in plaque and other microbial flora control, saliva composition and its oral microbial effects; microchemical and oral diagnostic techniques; biomedical instrumentation development; gingival crevice fluid and its relation to oral and systemic disease. *Mailing Add:* 14 Three Pond Rd Smithtown NY 11787. *Fax:* 516-632-7130

KLEINBERG, JACOB, INORGANIC CHEMISTRY. *Current Pos:* from asst prof to assoc prof, 46-51, chmn dept, 63-70, PROF CHEM, UNIV KANS, 51- *Personal Data:* b Passaic, NJ, Feb 14, 14; m 42; c 2. *Educ:* Randolph-Macon Col, BS, 34; Univ Ill, MS, 37, PhD(chem), 39. *Prof Exp:* Asst chem, Univ Ill, 37-39; asst prof, James Millikin Univ, 40-43; assoc prof, Col Pharm, Univ Ill, 43-46. *Mem:* Am Chem Soc. *Res:* Reactions in non-aqueous solvents; unfamiliar oxidation states of the elements. *Mailing Add:* Dept Chem Univ Kans Lawrence KS 66044

KLEINBERG, ROBERT LEONARD, GEOPHYSICAL INSTRUMENTATION, PHYSICS OF POROUS MEDIA. *Current Pos:* res physicist, 80-85, prog leader electromagnetics, 85-88, SR RES SCIENTIST, SCHLUMBERGER-DOLL RES, 88- *Personal Data:* b San Francisco, Calif, Aug 3, 49. *Educ:* Univ Calif, Berkeley, BS, 71; Univ Calif, San Diego, PhD(physics), 78. *Prof Exp:* Postdoctoral fel, Exxon Res & Eng Co, 78-80. *Mem:* Am Phys Soc. *Res:* Ultrasonic, electromagnetic, nuclear magnetic resonance, and gravimetric instrumentation for in situ characterization of subsurface geologic formations; physics of porous media. *Mailing Add:* Schlumberger-Doll Res Old Quarry Rd Ridgefield CT 06877. *E-Mail:* kleinberg@sdr.slb.com

KLEINBERG, WILLIAM, PHYSIOLOGY. *Current Pos:* RETIRED. *Personal Data:* b New York, NY, Jan 24, 11; m 41; c 3. *Educ:* NY Univ, BS, 32, MS, 35; Princeton Univ, PhD(physiol, endocrinol), 43. *Prof Exp:* Asst biol, NY Univ, 32-33, teaching fel, 33-36, asst, 36-41; instr biol, Princeton Univ, 41-44; instr pharmacol, Col Physicians & Surgeons, Columbia Univ, 44-45; asst prof & Upjohn fel, Princeton Univ, 45-46; dir, Princeton Labs, Inc, 47-74, consult, Princeton Lab Prod Co, 74-77. *Concurrent Pos:* Res assoc, Princeton Univ, 46-50, vis biologist, 50-65, sr vis biologist, 65-76. *Mem:* Endocrine Soc; NY Acad Sci; Reticuloendothelial Soc. *Res:* Blood; protein hormones; enzymes; immunological diagnostics; development of diagnostic tests. *Mailing Add:* 50 Woodland Dr Princeton NJ 08540

KLEINER, ALEXANDER F, JR, MATHEMATICS. *Current Pos:* from asst prof to assoc prof, 69-79, PROF MATH, DRAKE UNIV, 79-, CHMN, DEPT MATH & COMPUT SCI, 84- *Personal Data:* b New York, NY, June 18, 42; m 65; c 2. *Educ:* Univ St Thomas, Tex, BA, 64; Tex A&M Univ, MS, 66, PhD(math), 69. *Prof Exp:* Instr math, Tex A&M Univ, 66-69. *Mem:* Math Asn Am; Am Math Soc; Asn Comput Mach. *Res:* Summability theory; mathematics of political processes; graph theory. *Mailing Add:* Math & Comput Sci Dept Drake Univ Des Moines IA 50311-4505

KLEINER, SUSAN MALA, SPORTS NUTRITION, CARDIOVASCULAR NUTRITION. *Current Pos:* SPORTS NUTRITIONIST, HIGH PERFORMANCE NUTRIT. *Personal Data:* b Cleveland, Ohio, Oct 17, 57; m 81. *Educ:* Hiram Col, BA, 79; Case Western Res Univ, MS, 82, PhD(nutrit), 87. *Prof Exp:* Vis prof nutrit, Univ NC, Greensboro, 87-88; asst res prof nutrit, Dept Med, Div Nutrit, Prev Approach Cardiol & assoc dir, Sarah W Stedman Ctr Nutrit Studies, Dept Med, Duke Univ Med Ctr, 88-91; sports nutrit consult, Cleveland Browns/Cleveland Cavaliers, 91- *Concurrent Pos:* Young investr award, Am Col Nutrit, 87; columnist, Physician & Sportsmed J, 88- & Exec Health Report Newslett, 89-; adj prof, Dept Nutrit, Sch Med, Case Western Res Univ, 91- *Mem:* Am Dietetic Asn; Am Col Sports Med; fel Am Col Nutrit; Nat Strength & Conditioning Asn. *Res:* Nutritional requirements of strength training and muscle building and bodybuilding; writings on nutrition and health. *Mailing Add:* 7683 SE 27th St NE No 167 Mercer Island WA 98040

KLEINER, WALTER BERNHARD, ELECTROCHEMISTRY. *Current Pos:* RES DIR & CONSULT, KLEINER ELECTROCHEM CO, 52- *Personal Data:* b Plainfield, NJ, Mar 1, 18; m 44, Emily Meek; c Paula (Vuckovich), Tim, Diana (Scocchio) & Kim. *Educ:* Rutgers Univ, BS, 39; Ohio State Univ, PhD(electrochem), 46. *Prof Exp:* Anat & control chemist, Calco Chem Div, Am Cyanamid Co, NJ, 39-40; asst chem, Ohio State Univ, 40-43; res engr, Battelle Mem Inst, 44; res & develop electrochemist, Manhattan Proj, Dayton, 45; res electrochemist, Am Smelting & Refining Co, 47-52; from asst prof to prof chem, Essex County Col, 68-85. *Concurrent Pos:* Instr chem, Rutgers Univ, 51-52; res dir, Spiral Glass Pipe Co, 53-55; res electrochemists, Hanson-Van Winkle-Munning Co, 58-61, res dir, Electrochem Mach Div, 61-63; mem, Am Electroplaters Soc Res Comt, Nat Bur Stand; res dir, Ionic Mach Co, 63-65; asst prof chem, Upsala Col, 65-66; lectr chem, Newark Col Eng, 66-67; res dir, View-Formall Co, BC, 67. *Mem:* AAAS; Am Chem Soc; Electrochem Soc; Am Electroplaters Soc; emer mem Am Soc Metals; Sigma Xi. *Res:* Electrochemical machining; electroplating-electrodeposition. *Mailing Add:* 1845 First St Dunellen NJ 08812-1340

KLEINERMAN, JEROME, PATHOLOGY, PHYSIOLOGY. *Current Pos:* DIR, DEPT PATH, METRO HEALTH MED CTR, 86- *Personal Data:* b Pittsburgh, Pa, July 7, 24; m 44; c 3. *Educ:* Univ Pittsburgh, BS, 43, MD, 46; Am Bd Path, dipl, 52. *Prof Exp:* Demonstr path, Sch Med, Case Western Reserve Univ, 51-52, from instr to assoc prof, 52-72; assoc dir, St Luke's

Hosp, 57-64, head, Dept Path Res & Clin Path, 65-70, assoc dir med res, 70-80, dir, Div Path Res, 76-80; prof path, Sch Med, Case Western Reserve Univ, 72-80, dir dept, 76-80; prof & chmn, Dept Path, Mt Sinai Med Sch, 80-86. *Concurrent Pos:* Res fel physiol, Grad Sch Med, Univ Pa, 50-51; Am Heart Asn res fel, Cleveland Metrop Gen Hosp, 52-54, asst path, 52-63, vis assoc path, 62; lectr, Sch Med, Univ Pittsburgh, 63-; attend pulmonary dis, Vet Admin Hosp, 65-; consult path, Saranac Lab, Trudeau Found; mem path B study sect NIH, 65- *Mem:* Am Soc Exp Path; fel Am Soc Clin Path; Am Asn Path & Bacteriologists; Am Heart Asn; Col Am Path. *Res:* Experimental pathology; pulmonary emphysema and physiology; cerrbral blood flow; experimental renal disease; electron microscopy. *Mailing Add:* 6164 Cleadon Circle Palm Beach Gardens FL 33418. *Fax:* 216-459-5463

KLEINFELD, A M, MEMBRANE BIOPHYSICS. *Current Pos:* MEM, MED BIOL INST, CALIF, 87- *Personal Data:* b New York, NY, Feb 6, 41. *Educ:* Univ Wis, BA, 63; Rutgers Univ, PhD(nuclear physics), 68. *Prof Exp:* Privat dozent physics, Univ Cologne, Ger, 68-76, consult physics, Weiman Inst, 70, Yale Univ, 72; assoc prof physiol & biophys, Harvard Univ, 76-87. *Concurrent Pos:* Consult, Lidak Pharmaceut, La Jolla, Calif. *Mem:* Am Phys Soc; Biophys Soc; AAAS; Am Chem Soc. *Res:* Research in fatty acids transport and interaction with immune cells. *Mailing Add:* Med Bio Inst 11077 N Torrey Pines Rd La Jolla CA 92037. *Fax:* 619-554-0614; *E-Mail:* kleinfeld@axp1.salk.edu

KLEINFELD, ERWIN, ALGEBRA, COMBINATORICS & FINITE MATHEMATICS. *Current Pos:* PROF MATH, UNIV IOWA, 68- *Personal Data:* b Vienna, Austria, Apr 19, 27; nat US; m 68, Margaret A Morgan. *Educ:* City Col New York, BS, 48; Univ Pa, MA, 49; Univ Wis, PhD(math), 51. *Prof Exp:* Instr math, Univ Chicago, 51-53; from asst prof to prof, Ohio State Univ, 53-62; prof, Syracuse Univ, 62-68. *Concurrent Pos:* Vis lectr, Yale Univ, 56-57; partic conf algebra, Bowdoin Col, 57; res assoc, Cornell Univ, 58; vis lectr, Univ Calif, Los Angeles, 59, Stanford Univ, 60, Inst Defense Anal, 61-62 & Agency Int Develop Educ, India, 64-65; consult ed, Charles E Merrill Publ Co, 63-; vis prof, Emory Univ, 76-77, Univ Hawaii, 67-68; mucia consult, Univ Indonesia, Jakarta, 85-86; ed, J Algebra, 64-; prof, ITM/Mucia, Prog Malaysia, 88-89; visitor, Univ New Eng Armidale, Australia, 92. *Mem:* Am Math Soc. *Res:* Algebra and the foundations of projective geometry. *Mailing Add:* Dept Math Univ Iowa Iowa City IA 52242. *Fax:* 319-335-0627

KLEINFELD, IRA H, ENGINEERING ECONOMY. *Current Pos:* from asst prof to assoc prof, 76-83, PROF INDUST ENG & CHMN, DEPT INDUST ENG & COMPUT SCI, SCH ENG, UNIV NEW HAVEN, 83- *Personal Data:* b New York, NY, Apr 5, 47; m 71; c 2. *Educ:* Columbia Univ, BS, 67, MS, 69, Eng ScD(indust eng), 74. *Prof Exp:* Instr math, John Jay Col Criminal Justice, City Univ New York, 70-72; from instr to asst prof quant methods, Sch Bus, Hofstra Univ, 72-76. *Mem:* Inst Indust Engrs; Inst Mgt Sci; Soc Mfg Engrs; Am Soc Eng Educ. *Res:* Engineering economy; use of computers in industrial engineering. *Mailing Add:* 93 Melrose Dr Hamden CT 06518

KLEINFELD, MARGARET HUMM, MATHEMATICS, ALGEBRA. *Current Pos:* asst prof, 68-75, ASSOC PROF MATH, UNIV IOWA, 76- *Personal Data:* b St Louis, Mo, Apr 7, 38; m 59, 68, Erwin; c Barbara (Kenny) & David. *Educ:* Univ Rochester, BA, 60; Syracuse Univ, MS, 63, PhD(math), 65. *Prof Exp:* Asst prof math, Syracuse Univ, 65-68. *Concurrent Pos:* consult MUCIA, Univ Indonesia, 85-86; vis fel, Univ New Eng, Armidale, NSW Australia, 92. *Mem:* Am Math Soc; Asn Women in Math. *Res:* Non associative ring theory; algebra. *Mailing Add:* Dept Math Univ Iowa Iowa City IA 52242-0001

KLEINFELD, RUTH GRAFMAN, CELL BIOLOGY, REPRODUCTIVE BIOLOGY. *Current Pos:* assoc prof anat, 70-72, chmn, 80-83, PROF ANAT & REPRODUCTIVE BIOL, UNIV HAWAII, MANOA, 72- *Personal Data:* b New York, NY, Feb 9, 28; m 48, 73, James F Lenney. *Educ:* Brooklyn Col, BS, 49; Univ Wis, MA, 51; Univ Chicago, PhD(cell biol), 53. *Prof Exp:* Res assoc prev med, Yale Univ, 56-57; res assoc path, Ohio State Univ, 57-62; assoc prof pharmacol, State Univ NY Syracuse, 62-70. *Concurrent Pos:* USPHS fel physiol, Ohio State Univ, 53-55, Mary S Muellhaupt scholar, 55-56; USPHS res career develop award pharmacol, State Univ NY Syracuse, 62-70; mem NIH Reproductive Biol Study Sect. *Mem:* Histochem Soc; Am Soc Cell Biol; Am Asn Anat; Soc Develop Biol. *Res:* cell replication and cytodifferentiation; decidualization and placentation in pregnancy; cytochemistry and cell-fine structure. *Mailing Add:* Dept Anat & Reproductive Biol Univ Hawaii 1960 East-West Rd Honolulu HI 96822-2319. *Fax:* 808-956-9481

KLEINHOFS, ANDRIS, GENETICS, AGRONOMY. *Current Pos:* from asst prof to assoc prof, 67-77, chair, Genetics & Cell Biol, 83-87, PROF GENETICS, WASH STATE UNIV, 77- *Personal Data:* b Dobele, Latvia, Dec 25, 37; US citizen; m 65, Jolanta Smeils; c Laura & Anita. *Educ:* Univ Nebr, Lincoln, BS, 58, MS, 64, PhD(genetics), 67. *Prof Exp:* Instr genetics, Univ Nebr, Lincoln, 65-67. *Mem:* AAAS; Genetics Soc Am; Sigma Xi. *Res:* Genetics and biochemistry of nitrate reduction in plants; mechanisms of chemical mutagenesis; plant genome mapping. *Mailing Add:* 605 NW Polaris St Wash State Univ Pullman WA 99163. *Fax:* 509-335-8674; *E-Mail:* coleco@jaguar.csc.wsu.edu

KLEINHOLZ, LEWIS HERMANN, physiology, for more information see previous edition

KLEINKOPF, GALE EUGENE, PLANT PHYSIOLOGY, POTATO SCIENCE. *Current Pos:* assoc prof, 75-82, PROF CROP PHYSIOL, UNIV IDAHO, 82- *Personal Data:* b Twin Falls, Idaho, Oct 2, 40; c 1. *Educ:* Univ Idaho, BS, 63; Univ Calif, Davis, PhD(plant physiol), 70. *Prof Exp:* Chemist, Aerojet Gen Corp, 63-64; res assoc agron, Univ Calif, Davis, 64-70, fel plant sci, 70-72; asst prof plant ecol, Univ Calif, Los Angeles, 72-75. *Mem:* Potato Asn Am; Crop Sci Soc Am; Am Soc Plant Physiol. *Res:* Carbon and nitrogen cycling in some crop species as affected by environmental stress. *Mailing Add:* 3793 N 3600 E Univ Idaho Kimberly ID 83341. *Fax:* 208-423-6555

KLEINKOPF, MERLIN DEAN, GEOPHYSICS. *Current Pos:* res geophysicist, Br Regional Geophys, 66-70, dep asst to chief geologist, 70-72, RES GEOPHYSICIST, US GEOL SURV, 72- *Personal Data:* b Macomb, Ill, Feb 1, 26; div; c 4. *Educ:* Monmouth Col, Ill, BS, 49; Univ Mo-Rolla, BS, 51; Columbia Univ, PhD(geol), 55. *Prof Exp:* Seismic comput geologist, Atlantic Refining Co, 51-52; geologist-geophysicist, Standard Oil Co Calif, 55-57, geologist, 57-58, lead geophysicist gravity & magnetics, 58-62 & 64-65, dist explor geologist, 62-64, prof specialist gravity & magnetics, 65-66. *Concurrent Pos:* Leader, US Deleg Geophysicists to USSR, 71. *Mem:* Geol Soc Am; Am Inst Mining, Metall & Petrol Engrs; Soc Explor Geophysicists; Am Asn Petrol Geologists; Soc Econ Geologists; Sigma Xi. *Res:* Gravity and magnetic model studies using electronic computer; regional geophysical studies of Belt Basin, Northwestern Montana; geophysical studies of porphyry copper, Sonora, Mexico; geophysical studies of Arabian Shield, Saudi Arabia; geophysical studies of the Idaho batholith and associated mineral deposits; geological survey of Bangladesh. *Mailing Add:* US Geol Surv MS 964 Box 25046 Denver CO 80225

KLEINMAN, ARTHUR MICHAEL, PSYCHIATRY, MEDICAL ANTHROPOLOGY. *Current Pos:* PROF MED ANTHROP & PSYCHIAT, MED SCH & FAC ARTS & SCI, HARVARD UNIV, 82-, CHMN, DEPT SOCIAL MED, 93- *Personal Data:* b New York, NY, Mar 11, 41; m 65; c 2. *Educ:* Stanford Univ, AB, 62, MD, 67; Harvard Univ, MA, 74. *Honors & Awards:* Wellcome Medal Med Anthrop, Royal Anthrop Inst, 80. *Prof Exp:* Lectr anthrop, Harvard Univ, 74-76; clin instr psychiat, Mass Gen Hosp & Harvard Med Sch, 75-76; assoc prof & adj assoc prof, Univ Wash, 76-79, prof psychiat & adj prof anthrop, 79-82. *Concurrent Pos:* Intern med, Yale-New Haven Hosp, Yale Univ, 67-68; resident psychiat, Mass Gen Hosp, 72-75; Dupont Warren fel, Harvard Med Sch, 74-75 & Milton Fund fel, 75-76; Found Fund Res Psychiat fel, 74-76; ed-in-chief, Cult, Med & Psychiat, 76-86; prin investr, NIMH res grant, Univ Wash, 78-79, NSF res grant, 83-86; Rockefeller Found grant, 83-86; NIMH training grant, 84-; Carnegie Corp grant, 89- *Mem:* Inst Med-Nat Acad Sci; fel AAAS; fel Am Anthrop Asn; Soc Med Anthrop; fel Am Psychiat Asn. *Res:* Medical anthropology; depression; cross cultural psychiatry; pain and disability; therapeutic relationships and indigenous healing; China; anthropology of suffering. *Mailing Add:* 330 William James Hall Harvard Univ Cambridge MA 02138. *E-Mail:* gillestie@wjh.harvard.edu

KLEINMAN, CHEMIA JACOB, PHYSICS. *Current Pos:* PROF PHYSICS, LONG ISLAND UNIV, 64-, CHMN DEPT, 80- *Personal Data:* b Sandomierz, Poland, Feb 1, 32; US citizen; m 55; c 2. *Educ:* Yeshiva Univ, BA, 53; NY Univ, MS, 56, PhD(physics), 65. *Prof Exp:* Physicist, Mat Lab, Brooklyn Naval Shipyard, 56-57; engr microwave res, Ford Instrument Co, 57-60; lectr physics, City Col New York, 60-64. *Concurrent Pos:* Instr, Yeshiva Univ, 54-55, 58-60; consult, Budd-Lewyt Corp, 56-57; res fel, NY Univ, 65; NASA fel, Goddard Space Flight Ctr, 66; NSF fel, Univ Colo, Boulder, 67; assoc res scientist, NY Univ, 69, consult, 71. *Mem:* Am Phys Soc. *Res:* Atomic and electromagnetic scattering and bound state problems. *Mailing Add:* Dept Physics Long Island Univ Brooklyn NY 11201

KLEINMAN, HYNDA KAREN, CELL BIOLOGY, CONNECTIVE TISSUE RESEARCH. *Current Pos:* res chemist, 75-85, CHIEF CELL BIOL SECT, NAT INST DENT RES, NIH, 85- *Personal Data:* b Boston, Mass, May 20, 47; m 68; c 2. *Educ:* Simmons Col, BS, 69; Mass Inst Technol, MS, 71, PhD(nutrit biochem), 73. *Honors & Awards:* Dirs Award, NIH, 85; Doren Kamp-Zbinden Award, 87. *Prof Exp:* Res fel, Med Sch, Tufts Univ & Vet Admin Hosp, 73-75. *Mem:* Soc Biol Chemists; AM Soc Cell Biol; Soc Complex Carbohydrates; Tissue Cult Asn; Am Asn Cancer Res; Wound Healing Soc; AAAS; Asn Women Sci. *Res:* Structure and function of extracellular matrices and their role in development and in diseases. *Mailing Add:* Nat Inst Dent Res NIH Bldg 30 Rm 433 Bethesda MD 20892-4370. *Fax:* 301-402-0897; *E-Mail:* kleinman@yoda.nidr.nih.gov

KLEINMAN, JACK G, ACID-BASE PHYSIOLOGY, RENAL DISEASES. *Current Pos:* assoc prof, 80-89, PROF MED, MED COL, UNIV WIS, 89-; CHIEF, RENAL DIS SECT, ZABLOSKI VET ADMIN MED CTR, 86- *Personal Data:* b New York, NY, Feb 8, 44; m 66; c 2. *Educ:* NY Univ, MD, 68. *Prof Exp:* Asst chief, Renal Dis Sect, Zabloski Vet Admin Med Ctr, 76-86. *Mem:* Am Physiol Soc; Am Fedn Clin Res; Am Soc Nephrology. *Res:* Cell biology of renal transport mechanisms involved in cell pH regulation and acid-base transport, intestinal acid-base transport; pathophysiology of kidney stone disease. *Mailing Add:* Dept Internal Med Med Col Wis Vet Admin Med Ctr 5000 W National Ave Milwaukee WI 53226-0001. *Fax:* 414-382-5319

KLEINMAN, KENNETH MARTIN, PSYCHOPHYSIOLOGY, BIOPSYCHOLOGY. *Current Pos:* from asst prof to assoc prof, 69-78, PROF PSYCHOL, SOUTHERN ILL UNIV, EDWARDSVILLE, 78-, CHMN DEPT, 79- *Personal Data:* b Brooklyn, NY, Aug 10, 41; m 82, Sheila L O'Brien; c Seth M & Scott E. *Educ:* Grinnell Col, BA, 62; Wash Univ, St Louis, MA, 64, PhD(psychol), 67. *Prof Exp:* Res fel, Dept Psychiat, Washington Univ Sch Med, 62-66; Instr, Dept Psychiat, Univ Mo Sch Med,

67-69. *Concurrent Pos:* Res consult, St Louis Vet Admin Med Ctr, 69-; res fel psychiat, Charing Cross Hosp Med Sch, London, Eng, 77. *Mem:* Sigma Xi; Soc Psychophysiol Res; Am Psychol Soc. *Res:* Brain-behavior relationships; behavioral med; effects of stress on physiology and behavior; research design and statistical analysis; program evaluation. *Mailing Add:* Dept Psychol Southern Ill Univ Edwardsville IL 62026-1121

KLEINMAN, LEONARD, SOLID STATE PHYSICS. *Current Pos:* PROF PHYSICS, UNIV TEX, AUSTIN, 67- *Personal Data:* b New York, NY, July 25, 33; m 57, Faye Millar; c Paul & Julie A (Martin). *Educ:* Univ Calif, Los Angeles, BA, 55, MA, 56; Univ Calif, Berkeley, PhD(physics), 60. *Prof Exp:* Res assoc physics, Univ Chicago, 60-61; asst prof, Univ Pa, 61-64; assoc prof, Univ Southern Calif, 64-67. *Mem:* Fel Am Phys Soc. *Res:* Energy band theory; pseudopotential and density functional theory; semiconductor superlattices; covalent bonding and theory of cohesive energies; electron gas theory; theory of metal surfaces. *Mailing Add:* Dept Physics Univ Tex Austin TX 78712. *Fax:* 512-471-6518; *E-Mail:* kleinman@mail.utexas.edu

KLEINMAN, LEONARD I, PHYSIOLOGY, NEONATOLOGY. *Current Pos:* PROF PEDIAT, STATE UNIV NY, STONY BROOK, 83- *Personal Data:* b Brooklyn, NY, June 29, 35; m 61, Yorkette Solomon; c Jonathan, David & Miriam. *Educ:* Columbia Col, AB, 56; State Univ NY, MD, 60. *Prof Exp:* From intern to resident pediat, Mass Gen Hosp, 60-62; from asst prof to prof physiol & pediat, Col Med, Univ Cincinnati, 66-83. *Concurrent Pos:* Res fel physiol, Harvard Univ, 62-65; Fulbright res scholar, Univ Milan, 65-66. *Mem:* Am Physiol Soc; Soc Pediat Res; Am Pediat Soc; Am Soc Nephrology; AAAS; Am Acad Pediat. *Res:* Respiratory, renal and neonatal physiology. *Mailing Add:* Dept Pediat State Univ NY Health Sci Ctr Stony Brook NY 11794-8111. *Fax:* 516-444-2894

KLEINMAN, MICHAEL THOMAS, ENVIRONMENTAL & OCCUPATIONAL HEALTH, TOXICOLOGY EXPOSURE & RISK ASSESSMENT. *Current Pos:* PROF COMMUNITY & ENVIRON MED, UNIV CALIF, IRVINE, 82- *Personal Data:* b Brooklyn, NY, Mar 8, 42; m 65; c 2. *Educ:* City Univ NY, BS, 65; Polytech Inst Brooklyn, MS, 71; NY Univ, PhD(environ health), 77. *Prof Exp:* Radiochemist, US AEC, 63-65, phys scientist, 65-72; asst res scientist, NY Univ Med Ctr, 72-77; dir Aerosol Lab, Rancho Los Amigos Hosp, 77-82. *Concurrent Pos:* Consult, environ health & toxicology. *Mem:* Air Pollution Control Asn; AAAS; Sigma Xi; Am Asn Aerosol Res; NY Acad Sci. *Res:* Health effects of pollutant aerosols and gases in humans and animals; chemical alterations of airborne pollutants; development of methods for the generation and characterizations of air pollutants; industrial hygiene toxicology. *Mailing Add:* 3492 Lotus St Irvine CA 92714. *Fax:* 714-824-4763; *E-Mail:* mtkleinm@uci.edu

KLEINMAN, RALPH ELLIS, APPLIED MATHEMATICS. *Current Pos:* assoc prof, 68-72, PROF MATH, UNIV DEL, 72- *Personal Data:* b New York, NY, July 27, 29; m 55; c 2. *Educ:* NY Univ, BA, 50; Univ Mich, MA, 51; Delft Univ Technol, PhD(appl math), 61. *Prof Exp:* Res asst math, Univ Mich, Ann Arbor, 51-53, res assoc, 55-58, from assoc res mathematician to res mathematician, 59-68. *Concurrent Pos:* Danish Nat Found Tech Sci grant, Lab Electromagnetic Theory, Tech Univ Denmark, 65-66; vis prof math, Univ Strathclyde, 72 & 82; Nat Res Coun sr resident res assoc, Air Force Cambridge Res Labs, 74-75; vis scientist, David Taylor Naval Ship Res & Develop Ctr, 82 & Naval Res Lab, 86; vis prof, Delft Univ Technol, 87. *Mem:* Am Math Soc; Edinburgh Math Soc; Gesellschaft Angewandte Math & Mech; Soc Indust & Appl Math; Inst Elec & Electronics Engrs; Int Sci Radio Union. *Res:* Classical electromagnetic theory; propagation and scattering of electromagnetic and acoustic waves; boundary value problems; integral equations; partial differential equations; special functions. *Mailing Add:* Math Sci Dept Univ Del Newark DE 19716-0001

KLEINMAN, ROBERT L P, geomicrobiology, biogeochemistry, for more information see previous edition

KLEINMAN, ROBERTA WILMA, ORGANIC CHEMISTRY, CONSERVATION CHEMISTRY. *Current Pos:* CONSERV CHEMIST, PANHANDLE-PLAINS HIST MUS, TEX, 82- *Personal Data:* b New York, NY, Oct 10, 42. *Educ:* Barnard Col, Columbia Univ, AB, 64; Rutgers Univ, NB, PhD(org chem), 69. *Prof Exp:* NIH fel chem, Rutgers Univ, NB, 69-70, instr, 70-71, fel, 71-72; asst prof chem, Univ Mich, Dearborn, 72-79, lectr, Ann Arbor, 79-82. *Concurrent Pos:* Consult, Henry Ford Mus, Dearborn, 79-80. *Mem:* Am Chem Soc; AAAS. *Res:* Carbene additions to steroid analogues; micelle formation and catalysis; synthetic polynucleotides as catalysts of enzymatic ractions; nucleic acid interactions; identification of natural dyes on textiles; stability studies of natural dyes. *Mailing Add:* Dept Chem Lock Haven Univ Lock Haven PA 17745

KLEINMANN, DOUGLAS ERWIN, ASTRONOMY, PHYSICS. *Current Pos:* PROG MGR, LORAL INFRARED & IMAGING SYSTS, 80- *Personal Data:* b Chicago, Ill, July 11, 42; m 70, Susan Geisel; c 1. *Educ:* Rice Univ, BA, 64, PhD(space sci), 69; Mass Inst Technol, SM, 80. *Prof Exp:* Fel astron, Rice Univ, 68-70, astronr, Smithsonian Astrophys Observ, Smithsonian Inst, 70-79. *Concurrent Pos:* Lectr, Harvard Col Observ, Harvard Univ, 71-79; res affil, Mass Inst Technol, 73-79; mem infrared instrument development team, Space Telescope, NASA, 73-77. *Mem:* Am Astron Soc; Int Astrophys Union; Am Optical Soc; fel Explorers Club. *Res:* Infrared devices, infrared astronomy; instrumentation using infrared devices. *Mailing Add:* 15 Hastings Rd Lexington MA 02173. *E-Mail:* doug.dkleinmann@imco.com

KLEINROCK, LEONARD, COMPUTER NETWORKS & COMPUTER SCIENCE. *Current Pos:* from asst prof to assoc prof, 63-70, PROF COMPUT SCI, UNIV CALIF, LOS ANGELES, 70- *Personal Data:* b New York, NY, June 13, 34; m 71, Stella Schuler; c Martin C, Nancy S (Schneider), Robin (Schorr) & Lynn (Hirschberg). *Educ:* City Col New York, BEE, 57; Mass Inst Technol, SMEE, 59, PhD(elec eng), 63. *Honors & Awards:* Lanchester Prize, 76; L M Ericsson Prize, 82; Marconi Int Fel, 86; Sigcomm Award, Asn Comput Mach, 90; Harry H Goode Award, 96. *Prof Exp:* Asst engr, Photobell Co, NY, 51-57; res asst, Servomechanism Lab, Mass Inst Technol, 57-58, res asst, Electronics Res Lab, 58-61, staff mem, Lincoln Lab, 63. *Concurrent Pos:* Prin investr, Advan Res Projs Agency, Dept Defense Contract, 69-; pres, Linkabit Corp, 68-69; Guggenheim fel, 71-72; chief exec officer, Technol Transfer Inst, 76-; mem adv coun sci & eng, City Col New York; mem, sci adv comt, IBM, Comput Sci & Technol Bd, Nat Res Coun, 86-93; pres, Nomadix, LLC, 95- *Mem:* Nat Acad Eng; Opers Res Soc Am; fel Inst Elec & Electronics Engrs. *Res:* Design of advanced packet switching networks; wireless packet radio networks to fiber-based to gigabit networks; queueing theory; distributed systems; pioneer in nomadic computing. *Mailing Add:* Comput Sci Dept 3732 Boelter Hall Univ Calif Los Angeles CA 90095-1596. *Fax:* 310-825-2273; *E-Mail:* lk@cs.ucla.edu

KLEINROCK, MARTIN CHARLES, CRUSTAL GENERATION & DEFORMATION, MARINE GEOLOGY & GEOPHYSICS. *Current Pos:* investr, 88-89, ASST ASST SCIENTIST MARINE GEOL & GEOPHYS, WOODS HOLE OCEANOG INST, 89- *Personal Data:* b Boston, Mass, Aug 21, 58; m 86, Cynthia Mable; c Jacob & Jennifer. *Educ:* Univ Calif, Santa Barbara, BA, 81; Univ Calif, San Diego, MS, 84, PhD(earth sci), 88. *Prof Exp:* Teaching asst field geol & optical mineral, Scripps Inst Oceanog, 82-83, res asst marine geol & geophys, 81-86; vis prof colleague marine geol & geophys, Hawaii Inst Geophys, 86-87, asst geophysicist, 88. *Concurrent Pos:* Earle C Anthony fel, Univ Calif, San Diego, 85-86; W M Keck scholar, 88. *Mem:* Am Geophys Union; Geol Soc Am; Oceanog Soc; Sigma Xi. *Res:* Plate tectonics; plate boundary processes; generation and deformation of lithosphere; mid-ocean ridge tectonics; evolution of seafloor morphology; hydrothermal processes; seafloor survey instruments; author of various publications. *Mailing Add:* Box 1805 Sta B Vanderbilt Univ Nashville TN 37235. *Fax:* 508-457-2187; *E-Mail:* mkleinrock@whoi.edu

KLEINSCHMIDT, ALBERT WILLOUGHBY, ORGANIC CHEMISTRY. *Current Pos:* RETIRED. *Personal Data:* b Clinton, Iowa, Mar 20, 13; m 43; c 3. *Educ:* Iowa State Univ, BS, 35; Purdue Univ, PhD(org chem), 41. *Prof Exp:* Res chemist, Cent Soya Co, In, 40-44, Beatrice Foods Inc, Ill, 44-47 & Am Maize Prod Co, Inc, 47-58; res chemist, J R Short Milling Co, 58-63, lab mgr, 63-67, tech dir, 67-69, vpres, 69-79. *Mem:* Am Chem Soc; Am Oil Chem Soc; Am Asn Cereal Chem; Inst Food Technol; Am Soc Brewing Chem. *Res:* Oil; fats; carbohydrates. *Mailing Add:* 452 King St Oviedo FL 32765-9711

KLEINSCHMIDT, R STEVENS, CIVIL ENGINEERING, WATER POWER ENGINEERING. *Current Pos:* partner, Kleinschmidt & Dutting Consult Engrs, 70-80, chmn bd & sr vpres, 80-85, pres, 85-, VPRES, KLEINSCHMIDT ASSOCS. *Personal Data:* b Boston, Mass, Oct 8, 25; wid; c 4. *Educ:* Harvard Univ, AB, 49, SM, 51, ScD(civil eng), 58. *Hon Degrees:* Dr Community Develop, Unity Col, Maine, 76. *Honors & Awards:* Herschel Prize, 51. *Prof Exp:* Res engr, Harvard Univ, 50-58; asst engr water supply & sewage disposal, Camp Dresser & McKee, Mass, 58-59; asst prof hydraul & sanit eng, Northeastern Univ, 59-62; hydraul engr, Great Northern Paper Co, Maine, 62-66; independent consult engr, 66-70. *Mem:* Am Soc Civil Engrs; Am Consult Engrs Coun; Sigma Xi. *Res:* Hydraulics as applied to sanitary engineering. *Mailing Add:* 202 Beckwith Woods RR 4 Ellsworth ME 04605

KLEINSCHMIDT, ROGER FREDERICK, ORGANIC CHEMISTRY, PETROLEUM TECHNOLOGY. *Current Pos:* RETIRED. *Personal Data:* b New York, NY, May 12, 19; m 45; c 3. *Educ:* Lehigh Univ, BS, 40; Columbia Univ, PhD(org chem), 44. *Prof Exp:* Asst chem, Columbia Univ, 41-44; res chemist, Interchem Corp, NY, 44 & Gen Aniline & Film Corp, 46-52; group leader org chem, Phillips Petrol Co, 52-57, sr group supvr, 57-59, sect mgr org chem synthesis, 59-65, mgr, Hydrocarbon Chem Br, 65-68, vpres res & develop, Phillips Sci Corp, 68-71, licensing rep, Phillips Petrol Co, 71-74, planning consult natural resources, 74-97, prog mgr tertiary recovery petrol, Energy Res & Develop Admin-Phillips Petrol Co Proj, 75-97, mem staff corp planning, Norweg Indust Develop, 81-97. *Concurrent Pos:* Instr, Exten, Okla State Univ, 53- *Mem:* Soc Petrol Engrs. *Res:* Synthetic organic chemicals; acetylene chemistry; polymerization; pressure reactions; petrochemicals from olefins and diolefins; naphthenes; non-aromatic cyclics; organometallic catalysts and intermediates; industrial organic chemistry; enhanced recovery of oil; micellar/polymer recovery methods; exploration and production planning, economics and budgets. *Mailing Add:* 1827 SE Hampden Rd Bartlesville OK 74006

KLEINSCHMIDT, WALTER JOHN, BIOCHEMISTRY. *Current Pos:* RETIRED. *Personal Data:* b Wabash Co, Ill, Apr 11, 18; m 42; c 1. *Educ:* Ind Univ, BS, 40; Univ Minn, MS, 49, PhD(biochem), 50. *Prof Exp:* Sr res biochemist cell & molecular biol, Lilly Res Labs, 50-66, res scientist, Biol Res Div, 66-83. *Mem:* AAAS; Am Chem Soc; Am Soc Biol Chem. *Res:* Antiviral agents; interferon; viruses; virus inhibition; aging; nucleic acids. *Mailing Add:* 5444 Steinmeier Dr N Indianapolis IN 46220-3973

KLEINSCHUSTER, JACOB JOHN, ORGANIC POLYMER CHEMISTRY. *Current Pos:* Res chemist, E I du Pont de Nemours & Co, Inc, 72-74, sr res chemist, 74-75, supvr org polymer chem, 75-78, sr supvr, 79-82, tech supt, 82-83, mfg supt, 83-84, tech mgr, 84-85, worldwide tech mgr, 85-89, TECH DIR, E I DU PONT DE NEMOURS & CO, INC, 89- *Personal Data:* b Northampton, Pa, July 5, 43; m 70; c 3. *Educ:* Va Mil Inst, BS, 64; Pa State Univ, MS, 66, PhD(chem), 72. *Mem:* Am Chem Soc. *Res:* High performance organic industrial fibers, and apparel and spandex fibers. *Mailing Add:* 6 Twin Turns Lane Chadds Ford PA 19317-9347

KLEINSCHUSTER, STEPHEN J, III, DEVELOPMENTAL BIOLOGY, IMMUNOTHERAPY. *Current Pos:* dean agr & nat resources, 85-89, PROF MARINE & COASTAL SCI, RUTGERS UNIV, 89- *Personal Data:* b Bath, Pa, June 3, 39; m 66; c 2. *Educ:* Colo State Univ, BS, 63, MS, 66; Ore State Univ, PhD(zool), 70. *Prof Exp:* Fel develop biol, Univ Chicago, 71; asst prof biol, Metrop State Col, Denver, 71-73; affil prof bot & plant path, Colo State Univ, 73, assoc prof anat, 75-77, chmn exec comt anat, 76-77; actg head, Utah State Univ, 80-81, dir, Animal Tumor Prog, Animal, Dairy & Vet Sci, 77-85, prof & head, Animal, Dairy & Vet Sci Dept, 81-85. *Concurrent Pos:* Consult, NASA, 71-77; prin investr, NIH, Cancer Immunoprophylaxis Contracts, 77-81 & Immunother Procurement Contracts, 75-81; Impact Rev Group, Dept Agr, State Utah, 77; surg oncol res group, LDS Hosp, Salt Lake City, Utah, 79-; organizer & dir, Vet Sci Tissue Cult Facil, Utah State Univ, 79- *Mem:* AAAS; Am Asn Anatomists; Am Asn Vet Anatomists; NY Acad Sci; Am Soc Animal Sci. *Res:* Cancer biology; immunotherapy and immunoprophylaxis; molecular biology of development and morphogenesis. *Mailing Add:* Marine Sci Rutgers Univ New Brunswick NJ 08903

KLEINSMITH, LEWIS JOEL, CELL BIOLOGY, BIOCHEMISTRY. *Current Pos:* from asst prof to assoc prof zool, 68-74, PROF BIOL SCI, UNIV MICH, ANN ARBOR, 75- *Personal Data:* b Detroit, Mich, Apr 13, 42; m 64, Cynthia Weinstein; c 2. *Educ:* Univ Mich, BS, 64; Rockefeller Univ, PhD(life sci), 68. *Honors & Awards:* Henry Russel Award, 71. *Concurrent Pos:* Vis prof biochem, Univ Fla, Gainesville, 74-75; Guggenheim fel, 74-75; Arthur Thurnau prof, 88-91. *Mem:* Am Soc Cell Biol; Am Soc Biol Chemists. *Res:* Biochemistry of cell nucleus; role of nuclear proteins in regulating gene function; nucleoprotein chemistry and function; biochemical regulatory mechanisms; regulation of normal and malignant cell growth. *Mailing Add:* Dept Biol 2056 Kraus Nat Sci Bldg Univ Mich Ann Arbor MI 48109-1048. *E-Mail:* lewis.kleinsmith@umich.edu

KLEINSPEHN, GEORGE GEHRET, ORGANIC CHEMISTRY. *Current Pos:* prof, 67-83, dept chair, 79-82, Whitaker prof, 83-93, WHITAKER EMER PROF CHEM, HOOD COL, 93- *Personal Data:* b Middlebury, Vt, Mar 27, 24; div; c 2. *Educ:* Colgate Univ, AB, 44; Johns Hopkins Univ, AM, 47, PhD(chem), 51. *Prof Exp:* Jr chemist, Clinton Eng Works-Tenn Eastman Corp, 44-46; jr instr, Johns Hopkins Univ, 46-49, res assoc & univ fel, 51-56; sr res assoc & treas, Monadnock Res Inst, 56-59; res assoc, Johns Hopkins Univ, 60; chemist, US Army Ballistic Res Labs, 60-63, chief, Org Chem Sect, Chem Br, 63-67. *Concurrent Pos:* USPHS fel, NIH, 51-52; consult, US Army Ballistic Res Labs, 68; fel, DuPont, 50 & Beneficial-Hodson, 84. *Mem:* Am Chem Soc; Sigma Xi. *Res:* Nitrogenous heterocyclic compounds, especially pyrroles and porphyrins; organic substances of high nitrogen content. *Mailing Add:* 6419 S Clifton Rd Frederick MD 21702

KLEINSTEUBER, TILMANN CHRISTOPH WERNER, PHYSICS, PHYSICAL CHEMISTRY. *Current Pos:* RETIRED. *Personal Data:* b Berlin, Ger, July 16, 34. *Educ:* Univ Hamburg, BSc, 56; Univ Munich, PhD(phys chem), 61. *Prof Exp:* Res assoc phys chem, Univ Munich, 61-63; res assoc, Amherst Col, 63-64, asst prof chem, 64-65; from asst prof to prof physics & chmn, King's Col, Pa, 65-96, chmn dept, 65-96, assoc prof, 68-96. *Mem:* Am Asn Physics Teachers; Sigma Xi. *Res:* Calorimetry at high and low temperatures; thermodynamics of metals and alloys; surface chemistry; gas chromatography. *Mailing Add:* 1646 E 1185 N King's Col Wilkes-Barre PA 84341-3036

KLEINZELLER, ARNOST, CELL PHYSIOLOGY. *Current Pos:* prof, 67-85, EMER PROF PHYSIOL, SCH MED, UNIV PA, 85- *Personal Data:* b Ostrava, Czech, Dec 6, 14; m 43, Lotte Reuter; c 2. *Educ:* Univ Brno, Czech, MD, 38; Univ Sheffield, PhD(biochem), 42. *Hon Degrees:* DSc, Czech Acad Sci, 59; MA, Univ Pa, 73. *Prof Exp:* Med Res Coun grant biochem, Cambridge Univ, 43-44; head lab cell metab, Czech Inst Health, 46-48; assoc prof fermentation chem & head dept, Prague Tech Univ, 48-52; assoc prof biochem, Charles Univ, Prague, 52-55; head lab cell metab, Czech Acad Sci, 56-66; vis prof physiol, Univ Rochester, 66-67. *Concurrent Pos:* Rockefeller fel, Cambridge Univ, 41-42; ed, Biochem Biophys Acta & Current Topics in Membranes & Transport, 69-; mem & secy, US Nat Comt Physiol Sci, 76-; Fogarty Sr Int Fel, 80. *Mem:* Biophys Soc; Am Physiol Soc; Am Soc Cell Biol; Soc Gen Physiol; Brit Biochem Soc; Ger Acad Sci; Physiol Soc UK. *Res:* Intermediate metabolism; transport of electrolytes and sugars across cell membranes. *Mailing Add:* Dept Physiol Univ Pa Sch Med B704 Richards Bldg Philadelphia PA 19104-6085. *Fax:* 215-573-5851

KLEIS, JOHN DIEFFENBACH, ELECTRONIC GRADE BONDING WIRE, ELECTRICAL CONTACTS. *Current Pos:* vpres res elec contacts, Sterndent Corp, 69-70, pres, Cooper Div, 70-78, vpres & technol dir precious metals group, 78-82, CONSULT, STERN METALS, 83-; TECH DIR, POLYMETALL CORP, 89- *Personal Data:* b Hamburg, NY, Feb 1, 12; m 49, Marie E Dahl; c Cheryl, Lynn & John. *Educ:* Univ Buffalo, BA, 32, MA, 33; Yale Univ, PhD(physics), 36; Harvard Bus Sch, AMP, 57. *Prof Exp:* Physicist elec contacts, Fansteel, Inc, 36-57, vpres res refractory metals, 57-63, vpres & gen mgr elec & electronic prod, 63-69. *Concurrent Pos:* Electronics consult, 83- *Mem:* Soc Automotive Engrs; fel Am Soc Testing & Mat; Inst Elec & Electronics Engrs; Am Soc Qual Control. *Res:* Solid state, areas relating to bonding procedures and bonding, interconnect materials; precious metals, metallurgy of Al and AliSi materials. *Mailing Add:* 161 Clapboard Ridge Rd Greenwich CT 06831

KLEIS, ROBERT W(ILLIAM), AGRICULTURAL ENGINEERING. *Current Pos:* RETIRED. *Personal Data:* b Martin, Mich, Nov 30, 25; m 49, Beatrice Heinze; c Cinthia Lee (Johnson) & Pamela Sue (Trimmer). *Educ:* Mich State Univ, BS, 49, MS, 51, PhD(agr eng), 57. *Prof Exp:* Instr agr eng, Mich State Univ, 49-51; instr, Univ Ill, 51-53, asst prof, 53-56; prof & head dept, Univ Nebr, Lincoln, 66-67, assoc dir, Agr Exp Sta, 67-83, dean int progs, 76-84, exec dean int affairs, 84-90. *Concurrent Pos:* Dir, MidAM Int Agr Consortium, Inc, 76-; consult, Indust, 50- & Int Agr Develop, 75-; dir, Int Collab Res Support Prog, 78-; exec dir, Bd Int Food & Agr, Washington, DC, 85-87; mem bd dir, Self Help Found. *Mem:* Fel Am Soc Agr Engrs; Am Soc Eng Educ; Nat Asn Univ Dirs Int Progs; Agr Exp Sta Dir Asn; Sigma Xi; Soc Int Develop. *Res:* Materials handling systems for agriculture; product processing; food and feed preservation; farm operations mechanization; international food production systems development. *Mailing Add:* 6520 Sumner Lincoln NE 68506

KLEITMAN, DANIEL J, MATHEMATICS. *Current Pos:* assoc prof, 66-69, head dept, 79-84, PROF MATH, MASS INST TECHNOL, 69- *Personal Data:* b New York, NY, Oct 4, 34; m 64; c 3. *Educ:* Cornell Univ, AB, 54; Harvard Univ, AM, 55, PhD, 58. *Prof Exp:* NSF fel physics, Copenhagen Univ, 58-59 & Harvard Univ, 59-60; asst prof, Brandeis Univ, 60-66. *Concurrent Pos:* Consult, Nuclear Regulatory Comn, Gen Acct Off, 73-81; managing ed, Soc Indust & Appl Math J Algebraic & Discrete Methods, 75-82; ed, J Networks. *Mem:* Am Math Soc; Oper Res Soc Am; Soc Indust & Appl Math; Am Acad Arts & Sci; NY Acad Sci. *Res:* Combinatorial mathematics; graph theory; numeration and optimization; applications to operations research. *Mailing Add:* 74 Kenwood Ave Newton MA 02159

KLEITMAN, DAVID, SOLID STATE PHYSICS. *Current Pos:* RETIRED. *Personal Data:* b New York, NY, June 28, 31; m 52; c 3. *Educ:* Cornell Univ, BA, 52; Purdue Univ, MS, 53, PhD(physics), 58. *Prof Exp:* Group head labs & head display res, David Sarnoff Res Ctr, RCA, 57-67; vpres & dir res & develop, Signetics Corp, 67-78, vpres res, 78-80; pres, Protracoa, 80-91; dir technol, Branson-IPC, 81-82. *Mem:* Inst Elec & Electronics Engrs; AAAS. *Res:* Semiconductors; radiation damage; luminescence; optical amplification; color television system and display system management; integrated circuits, their materials, processing devices, circuits design and applications in computers, communications and consumer and industrial systems; semiconductor devices for integrated circuits, microwave, power, computer, instrumentation, optical and novel applications and systems; computer software; plasma processing. *Mailing Add:* 12387 Stonebrook Dr Los Altos CA 94022

KLEKOWSKI, EDWARD JOSEPH, JR, BOTANY, GENETICS. *Current Pos:* Asst prof, 68-73, ASSOC PROF BOT, UNIV MASS, AMHERST, 73- *Personal Data:* b Brooklyn, NY, Oct 24, 40. *Educ:* NC State Univ, BS, 62, MS, 64; Univ Calif, Berkeley, PhD(bot), 68. *Mem:* Bot Soc Am. *Res:* Pteridology; genetic and evolutionary studies of homosporous ferns. *Mailing Add:* Biol Univ Mass Amherst MA 01003-0002

KLEMA, ERNEST DONALD, NUCLEAR PHYSICS. *Current Pos:* dean col eng, 68-73, prof, 68-88, EMER PROF ENG SCI, TUFTS UNIV, 88-, EMER DEAN, COL ENG, 88- *Personal Data:* b Wilson, Kans, Oct 4, 20; m 53, Virginia Carlock; c Donald & Catherine. *Educ:* Univ Kans, AB, 41, AM, 42; Rice Univ, PhD(physics), 51. *Prof Exp:* Jr scientist, Los Alamos Sci Lab, 43-46; sr physicist nuclear physics, Oak Ridge Nat Lab, 50-56; assoc prof nuclear eng, Univ Mich, 56-58; prof nuclear & sci eng, Northwestern Univ, 58-68, chmn dept eng sci, 60-67. *Concurrent Pos:* Adj prof int politics, Fletcher Sch Law & Diplomacy, 73-83. *Mem:* Fel Am Phys Soc; fel Am Nuclear Soc; sr mem Inst Elec & Electronics Engrs. *Res:* Angular correlations of gamma rays; fission cross sections; empirical nuclear models; semiconductor detectors; science and technology policy. *Mailing Add:* 105 Anderson Hall Tufts Univ Medford MA 02155. *Fax:* 617-627-3819

KLEMANN, LAWRENCE PAUL, LIPIDS TECHNOLOGY, EDIBLE OILS PROCESSING. *Current Pos:* SR PRIN SCIENTIST, NABISCO BRANDS, INC, 86- *Personal Data:* b Cincinnati, Ohio, Aug 13, 43; m 63, Diane Wirsing; c Eric & Lauren. *Educ:* Univ Mass, BS, 65, MS, 68, PhD(org chem), 69. *Prof Exp:* Res assoc, Exxon Res & Eng Co, 69-86. *Mem:* Am Chem Soc. *Res:* Organic and organometallic synthesis; lipid chemistry; reduced calorie fats and oils; catalysis; coordination chemistry; lithium organic electrolytes and batteries; separation science and surfactant chemistry; author of 30 publications; granted 45 US patents. *Mailing Add:* 6 Cobblestone Lane Annandale NJ 08801. *Fax:* 973-503-2967

KLEMARCZYK, PHILIP THADDEUS, ORGANIC & POLYMER CHEMISTRY. *Current Pos:* sr chemist, 82-87, scientist, 87-96, SR SCIENTIST, LOCTITE CORP, 96- *Personal Data:* b Exeter, NH, Oct 10, 51. *Educ:* Holy Cross Col, BA, 73; Brandeis Univ, PhD(chem), 79. *Prof Exp:* Res chemist, Int Flowers & Fragrances, 79-82. *Mem:* Am Chem Soc; Sigma Xi. *Res:* Synthesis and evaluation of new monomers and polymers for use in adhesives and sealants; investigation of new processes for existing materials; exploration of new technologies. *Mailing Add:* Loctite Corp 1001 Trout Brook Crossing Rocky Hill CT 06067

KLEMAS, VICTOR V, OPTICAL PHYSICS, MARINE STUDIES. *Current Pos:* assoc prof, 71-80, PROF MARINE STUDIES, UNIV DEL, 80-, DIR REMOTE SENSING CTR, 75-, DIR APPL OCEAN SCI PROG, 81- *Personal Data:* b Klaipeda, Lithuania, Nov 29, 34; US citizen; m 60; c 3. *Educ:* Mass Inst Technol, BS, 57, MS, 59; Univ Brunswick, PhD(optical physics), 65. *Honors & Awards:* Achievement Medal, Korean Advan Inst Sci & Merit Award, India Remote Sensing Agency, 78. *Prof Exp:* Mgr optical physics & space explor, Space Div, Gen Elec Co, 59-71. *Concurrent Pos:* Fel, Gen Elec Co, 63; consult, Environ Protection Agency, NASA, NSF & AID, UNESCO, United Nations, Ecuador, Peru, Costa Rica, Panama, India, Sri Lanka, Egypt, Korea, France & Ger; mem Comn Natural Resources, Nat Acad Sci, 75-78; mem, Ocean Policy Comt, Nat Acad Sci; mem adv comts, NASA, 75-; prog mgr, Scientists & Engrs Econ Develop, NSF, 77-78; mem, Man & the Biosphere, UNESCO, 77-; mem, Comt Earth Studies, Nat Acad Sci, 88- *Mem:* Inst Elec & Electronics Engrs; Asn Am Geographers; Am Geophys Union; Am Soc Photogram. *Res:* Management of coastal resources; remote sensing of environment, especially physical and biological coastal processes; third world resources development; geographic information systems. *Mailing Add:* Col Marine Studies Univ Del Newark DE 19716

KLEMCHUK, PETER PAUL, ORGANIC CHEMISTRY, POLYMER CHEMISTRY. *Current Pos:* CONSULT & PROF-IN-RES, INST MAT SCI, UNIV CONN, 93- *Personal Data:* b Oakville, Conn, Oct 31, 28; m 49; c 5. *Educ:* Mass Inst Technol, BS, 50; Rutgers Univ, MS, 56, PhD(org chem), 57. *Prof Exp:* Chemist, Merck & Co Inc, 50-56, Esso Res & Eng Co, 57-59, Stauffer Chem Co, 59-60; sr res fel, Ciba-Geigy Corp, 60-92. *Mem:* Am Chem Soc; Soc Plastics Engrs; Am Soc Testing Mat. *Res:* Polymer stabilization; polymer additives; polymer degradation; polymers recycling; photochemistry, reaction mechanisms. *Mailing Add:* Plastics Stabilization Plus 903 Buckingham St Watertown CT 06795-1630. *Fax:* 860-274-7561

KLEMCKE, HAROLD G, ENDOCRINOLOGY. *Current Pos:* RES PHYSIOLOGIST ENDOCRINOL, USDA, 84- *Personal Data:* b San Antonio, Tex, Oct 10, 45. *Educ:* Univ Md, BS, 67, MS, 73, PhD(endocrinol), 78. *Prof Exp:* Fel endocrinol, Univ Tex Health Sci Ctr, 78-82, res asst, 82-84. *Mem:* Am Soc Reprod; Am Endocrinol Soc; Am Physiol Soc; Am Soc Exp Biol & Med; Sigma Xi. *Mailing Add:* USDA Meat Animal Res Ctr PO Box 166 Clay Center NE 68933-0166

KLEMENS, PAUL GUSTAV, PHYSICS, THERMAL CONDUCTIVITY. *Current Pos:* chmn dept, 67-74, prof physics, 67-91, EMER PROF PHYSICS, UNIV CONN, 91- *Personal Data:* b Vienna, Austria, May 24, 25; m 50, Ruth Wiener; c Michael W & Susan M. *Educ:* Univ Sydney, BSc, 46, MSc, 48; Oxford Univ, DPhil(theoret physics), 50. *Honors & Awards:* Y S Touloukian Award, Am Soc Mech Engrs, 88. *Prof Exp:* Prin res officer, Nat Standards Lab, Sydney, Australia, 50-59; physicist, Westinghouse Res Labs, 59-64, mgr transport properties, Solids Dept, 64-67. *Concurrent Pos:* Consult, Los Alamos Nat Lab, 70- *Mem:* Mat Res Soc. *Res:* Theoretical solid state and low temperature physics, particularly thermal conductivity of solids and other non-equilibrium and transport properties; ultrasonic attenuation, properties of composites; laser welding and surface modification; thermal conductivity of ceramics at high temperatures. *Mailing Add:* Dept Physics Univ Conn 2152 Hillside Rd Storrs CT 06269. *Fax:* 860-486-3346; *E-Mail:* klemens@uconnvm.uconn.edu

KLEMENT, VACLAV, RADIATION ONCOLOGY, MICROBIOLOGY. *Current Pos:* res fel pediat, 68-69, ASSOC PROF RADIATION ONCOL & MICROBIOL, SCH MED, UNIV SOUTHERN CALIF, 79- *Personal Data:* b Pilsen, Czech, May 7, 35; m 67; c 2. *Educ:* Charles Univ, Prague, MD, 59; Czech Acad Sci, Prague, PhD(biol), 64. *Prof Exp:* Vis scientist viral oncol, Nat Inst Allergy & Infectious Dis, NIH, 67-68. *Mem:* Am Endocurieth Soc; Am Soc Therapeut Radiol & Oncol. *Res:* Viral carcinogensis and tumor biology; radiation oncology; oncogenes. *Mailing Add:* Sch Med LAC-Univ Southern Calif Med Ctr 1200 N State St Los Angeles CA 90033

KLEMENT, WILLIAM, JR, MATERIALS SCIENCE. *Current Pos:* CONSULT, 94- *Personal Data:* b Chicago, Ill, Sept 30, 37; m 91, Susan M Colby. *Educ:* Calif Inst Technol, BS, 58, PhD(eng sci), 62. *Honors & Awards:* co-recipient, Int Prize New Ma, 80. *Prof Exp:* Asst res geophysicist, Inst Geophys & Planetary Physics, Univ Calif, Los Angeles, 62-64; Miller res fel physics, Univ Calif, Berkeley, 64-66; from asst prof to assoc prof eng, Univ Calif, Los Angeles, 66-94. *Concurrent Pos:* NATO fel, Royal Inst Technol, Sweden, 63; Guggenheim Mem Found fel, Australian Nat Univ, 68-69; Ford Found Prog, Univ Chile, 73; vis scientist, Nat Phys Res Lab, Pretoria, SAfrica, 74-76 & Inorg Chem Lab, Oxford Univ, 79. *Res:* Phase transformations; archaeological, ethnographic and historical materials. *Mailing Add:* PO Box 5153 Vancouver WA 98668

KLEMER, ANDREW ROBERT, PHYSIOLOGICAL ECOLOGY, LIMNOLOGY. *Current Pos:* ASST PROF BIOL & ENVIRON SCI, STATE UNIV NY, PURCHASE, 76- *Personal Data:* b St Clair, Pa, June 4, 42; m 63; c 4. *Educ:* La Salle Col, BA, 64; Univ Minn, PhD(ecol), 73. *Prof Exp:* Consult limnol, Dept Sci & Indust Res, NZ, 73-74; vis scientist algal physiol, Cawthron Inst, 74-75. *Concurrent Pos:* Nat Res Adv Coun NZ, res fel, 73-75; State Univ NY Res Found fac res fel, 77 & 79. *Mem:* Phycol Soc Am; Am Soc Limnol & Oceanog; Int Asn Theoret & Appl Limnol; AAAS; Sigma Xi. *Res:* Factors that limit the distribution and affect the community structure of phytoplankton; physiological mechanisms involved in responses to those factors. *Mailing Add:* Dept Biol Univ Minn Duluth MN 55812-2496

KLEMES, VIT, HYDROLOGY, WATER RESOURCES. *Current Pos:* RETIRED. *Personal Data:* b Podivin, Czech, Apr 30, 32; m 57, Marie Radetzki; c Marek & Ivo. *Educ:* Tech Univ-Brno, Czech, Dipl Eng; Tech Univ, Bratislava, Slovakia PhD(hydrol & water resources), 64; Tech Univ-Prague, Czech, DrSc. *Honors & Awards:* Gold Medal, Slovak Acad Sci, 93; Int Hydrol Prize, Int Asn Hydrol Sci, 94; Ray K Linsley Award, Am Inst Hydrol, 95. *Prof Exp:* Assoc prof mech eng, Univ Toronto, 68-72; res hydrologist, Nat Hydrol Res Inst, Ottawa, 72-80, chief scientist, Saskatoon, 80-89. *Concurrent Pos:* Vis prof, Nat Inst Sci Res-Eau, Univ Que, Ste-Foy, 94- *Mem:* Fel Am Geophys Union; Int Asn Hydrol Sci. *Res:* Water resources; waste storage theory; stochastic hydrology. *Mailing Add:* 3460 Fulton Rd Victoria BC V9C 3N2 Can

KLEMM, DONALD J, AQUATIC BIOLOGY, AQUATIC ECOLOGY & TOXICOLOGY. *Current Pos:* RES AQUATIC BIOLOGIST, ENVIRON MONITORING & SUPPORT LAB, US ENVIRON PROTECTION AGENCY, 74- *Personal Data:* b Detroit, Mich, Jan 13, 38. *Educ:* Valley City State Col, BS, 63; Eastern Mich Univ, MS & SpecS, 70; Univ Mich, Ann Arbor, PhD(fisheries), 74. *Prof Exp:* Res assoc malacol, Mollusk Div, Mus Zool, Univ Mich, Ann Arbor, 72-74. *Mem:* Soc Environ Toxicol & Chem; Int Asn Theoret & Appl Limnol; Am Soc Testing & Mat; NAm Benthol Soc; Brit Freshwater Biol Asn; Am Fisheries Soc. *Res:* Stream and lake ecology; ecology of polluted waters; invertebrate and fish zoology; macroinvertebrates and fish methodology, parasitology and toxicology; systematics and ecology of freshwater fish, macroparasites, insects, mollusks, annelids, aquatic oligochaetes and Hirudinea of the world. *Mailing Add:* PO Box 44090 Cincinnati OH 45244-0090

KLEMM, JAMES L, APPLIED MATHEMATICS, COMPUTER SCIENCE. *Current Pos:* sr publ, NCR Corp, 77-80, sr systs analyst, 80-82, consult analyst, 82-91, CONSULT ENG, QUAL ASSURANCE, NCR CORP, 91- *Personal Data:* b South Bend, Ind, Oct 30, 39; m 81; c 2. *Educ:* Univ Chicago, BS, 61; Purdue Univ, MS, 63; Mich State Univ, PhD(eng mech), 70. *Prof Exp:* Asst math, Purdue Univ, 61-65; asst prof, Ind Univ Pa, 65-67; asst, Dept Metall, Mech & Mat Sci, Mich State Univ, 67-69, res assoc, 70; asst prof eng sci, Univ Cincinnati, 70-77. *Concurrent Pos:* Partic, NSF Inst Appl Math & Mech, Mich State Univ, 67. *Mem:* Sigma Xi; AAAS. *Res:* St Venant boundary value problems in 2 and 3 dimensional theories of classical elasticity; computer applications in manufacturing. *Mailing Add:* 136 Woodale Dr Lexington SC 29169-9581

KLEMM, LEROY HENRY, ORGANIC CHEMISTRY. *Current Pos:* RESEARCHER, 90- *Personal Data:* b Maple Park, Ill, July 31, 19; m 45, Christine Jones; c Richard A, Rebecca J & Ann C. *Educ:* Univ Ill, BS, 41; Univ Mich, MS, 43, PhD(org chem), 45. *Prof Exp:* Res chemist, Am Oil Co, Tex, 44-45; fel, Univ Res Found, Ohio State Univ, 46; instr chem, Harvard Univ, 46-47; from instr to asst prof, Ind Univ, 47-52; from asst prof to prof chem, Univ Ore, 52-90. *Concurrent Pos:* Fel, Guggenheim Mem Found, Med Res Coun Labs, London & Swiss Fed Inst Tech, Zurich, 58-59; vis prof, Univ Cincinnati, 65-66; Fulbright-Hays res fel & NATO res grant, Aarhus Univ, Denmark & Univ Groningen, Neth, 72-73; vis prof, La Trobe Univ & sr assoc, Univ Melbourne, Australia, 79-80; vis prof, Univ Queensland, Australia, 86. *Mem:* Fel AAAS; Am Chem Soc; Int Soc Heterocyclic Chem. *Res:* Synthesis of carbocyclic and heterocyclic compounds; organic reactions; biologically active compounds; chromatography; heterogeneous catalysis; thienopyridines; condensed thiophenes. *Mailing Add:* Dept Chem Univ Ore Eugene OR 97403. *Fax:* 541-346-0487; *E-Mail:* lklemm@oregon.uoregon.edu

KLEMM, REBECCA JANE, STATISTICS, OPERATIONS RESEARCH. *Current Pos:* PRES, KLEMM ANALYSIS, 87- *Personal Data:* b Bloomington, Ind, Feb 21, 50. *Educ:* Miami Univ, BS, 71, Iowa State Univ, MS, 73, PhD(statist), 76. *Prof Exp:* Asst prof statist, Temple Univ, 76-80; mem fac statist, Sch Bus Admin, Georgetown Univ, 80- *Concurrent Pos:* US Dept Energy fac fel, Sch Bus, Am Assembly Col, 78-79. *Mem:* Am Statist Asn; Opers Res Soc Am; Inst Mgt Sci. *Res:* Statistical education; constrained least squares, econometric model building. *Mailing Add:* 7926 W Beach Dr NW Washington DC 20012

KLEMM, RICHARD ANDREW, THEORETICAL SOLID STATE PHYSICS, SUPERCONDUCTIVITY. *Current Pos:* tech staff mem & vis scientist, 90-92, TECH STAFF SCIENTIST, ARGONNE NAT LAB, 92- *Personal Data:* b Bloomington, Ind, Mar 13, 48; m 80, Dwaraka S Rao; c Amitabh R & Siddhartha R. *Educ:* Stanford Univ, BS, 69; Harvard Univ, MA, 72, PhD(physics), 74. *Prof Exp:* Fel, Stanford Univ, 74-76; asst prof physics, Ames Lab, Iowa State Univ, 76-81, assoc prof, 81, vis scientist, 88-89; staff physicist, 82-84, sr staff physicist, Exxon Res & Eng Co, 84-86; vis prof physics, Univ Calif San Diego, La Jolla, 86-88; vis scientist, Oak Ridge Nat Lab, 89-90. *Concurrent Pos:* Vis scientist, AT&T Bell Labs, 75-76, Univ Koln, Ger, 76, Univ, BC, 78, Univ Fraser Univ, 79, Univ Hamburg, Ger, 80, 81 & 87, Univ Calif, La Jolla, 86 & Argonne Nat Lab, 89. *Mem:* Fel Am Phys Soc. *Res:* Theory of condensed matter involving superconductivity; p-wave superconductivity; lower dimensional conductors; charge-density waves and spin-glasses; high temperature superconductors. *Mailing Add:* Mat Sci Div Bldg 223 Rm D-209 Argonne Nat Lab 9700 S Cass Ave Argonne IL 60439. *Fax:* 630-252-7777

KLEMM, ROBERT DAVID, VERTEBRATE MORPHOLOGY, WILDLIFE CONSERVATION. *Current Pos:* DIR, CONSERV & RES, SUNSET ZOO PARK; CHAIR AM ZOO & AQUARIUM ASN, PARAGUAY FAUNA INTEREST GROUP. *Personal Data:* b Youngstown, Ohio, Sept 13, 29; div; c 1. *Educ:* Capital Univ, BS, 57; Ohio Univ, MS, 59;

Southern Ill Univ, PhD(vert zool), 64. *Prof Exp:* Asst prof biol, Capital Univ, 64-67; asst prof anat, Col Vet Med, Kans State Univ, 67-70; asst prof, Mich State Univ, 70-72, invests leader, Avian Anat Invests, USDA, 70-72; assoc prof anat, Dept Anat & Physiol, Col Vet Med, Kans State Univ, 72-79, prof, 79-91. *Concurrent Pos:* Guest prof, Institut fur Anat u Cytobiol Der Justus-Liebig Univ Giessen WGer, 79-80. *Mem:* Am Asn Anatomists; Am Asn Vet Anatomists; emer mem Am Soc Zoologists; Am Zoo & Aquarium Asn. *Res:* Gross, light and electron microscopy studies of vertebrate structure with special reference to normal and diseased lungs of domestic animals. *Mailing Add:* 411 Timberwick Pl Manhattan KS 66502. *Fax:* 785-587-2730; *E-Mail:* morphol@ksu.edu

KLEMM, WALDEMAR ARTHUR, JR, SILICATE CHEMISTRY. *Current Pos:* SR PRIN SCIENTIST & MGR, MATS RES GROUP, CONSTRUCT TECHNOL LABS, PORTLAND CEMENT ASN, 93- *Personal Data:* b Elgin, Ill, July 10, 34; m 59; c 3. *Educ:* Univ Calif, Riverside, BA, 56; Ore State Univ, MS, 67. *Prof Exp:* Res chemist propellant chem, Lockheed Propulsion Co, 59-66; group leader cement chem, Tech Ctr, Am Cement Corp, 66-70; assoc specialist geochem, Inst Geophys & Planetary Physics, Univ Calif, 70-72; sr res scientist, Gen Portland Inc, 72-75; sr scientist, Martin Marietta Labs, 75-83; mgr, Cent Process Lab, Southdown, Inc, 83-93. *Concurrent Pos:* Vchmn solid-liquid interactions cement hydration, Gordon Res Conf, 75-76; trustee, Cements Div, Am Ceramic Soc, 87-90. *Mem:* Fel Am Ceramic Soc; Am Chem Soc. *Res:* High-temperature silicate chemistry; cement clinkering reactions; admixture interactions; expansive cements; cement hydration. *Mailing Add:* 5420 Old Orchard Rd Skokie IL 60077-1030

KLEMM, WILLIAM ROBERT, ANIMAL PHYSIOLOGY. *Current Pos:* assoc prof, 66-70, PROF, TEX A&M UNIV, 70- *Personal Data:* b South Bend, Ind, July 24, 34; m 57, Doris Mewha; c Mark & Laura. *Educ:* Auburn Univ, DVM, 58; Univ Notre Dame, PhD(biol), 63. *Prof Exp:* NIH fel, 60-63; assoc prof physiol & pharmacol, Iowa State Univ, 63-66. *Concurrent Pos:* Retired colonel, USAF, 58-88. *Mem:* Sigma Xi; Soc Neurosci; AAAS; Amer Vet Med Assoc. *Res:* Animal hypnosis; theta rhythm; brain stem functions; animal electroencephalography; psychopharmacology; chemical senses; alcohol; educational software. *Mailing Add:* Dept Vet Anat & Pub Health Tex A&M Univ College Station TX 77843. *Fax:* 409-847-8981; *E-Mail:* wklemm@cvm.tamu.edu

KLEMME, HUGH DOUGLAS, PETROLEUM GEOLOGY. *Current Pos:* PRES, GEO BASINS LTD, 80-; CONSULT PETROL GEOLOGIST, 82- *Personal Data:* b Belmond, Iowa, Jan 24, 21; m 43; c 3. *Educ:* Coe Col, AB, 42; Princeton Univ, MA, 48, PhD(geol), 49. *Prof Exp:* Regional geologist, Standard Oil Co, 49-51; staff geologist, Am Overseas Petrol, Ltd, 51-58, mgr explor, 58-63, asst chief geologist, 63-69; vpres explor, Lewis G Weeks Assocs, Ltd, Westport, 69-76; sr vpres, Weeks Petrol Corp, Westport, 76-79. *Mem:* Geol Soc Am; hon mem Am Asn Petrol Geologists; AAAS; Am Geophys Union; Am Petrol Inst. *Res:* Regional petroleum geology; regional tectonics; basin studies; petroleum formation, migration and accumulation. *Mailing Add:* RR 1 Box 179-B Bondville VT 05340

KLEMMEDSON, JAMES OTTO, SOIL SCIENCE, FOREST & RANGE ECOLOGY. *Current Pos:* prof range & forestry, 66-88, PROF RANGE & WATERSHED MGT, UNIV ARIZ, 66-, RES SCIENTIST, AGR EXP STA, 80- *Personal Data:* b Ft Collins, Colo, Aug 20, 27; m 52; c 4. *Educ:* Univ Calif, Berkeley, BS, 50, PhD(soil sci), 59; Colo State Univ, MS, 53. *Prof Exp:* Soil conservationist, Soil Conserv Serv, USDA, 50-51; instr forestry, Colo State Univ, 51-52, res asst range mgt, 52-53; instr, Mont State Univ, 53-55; res asst forestry, Univ Calif, Berkeley, 55-56, soils & plant nutrit, 56-59; range scientist, Int Forest & Range Exp Sta, USDA, 59-66. *Concurrent Pos:* Charles Bullard forest res fel, Harvard Univ, 74-75; Vis scientist, Swiss Fed Inst Forest, Snow & Landscape Res, Bermensdorf, Switz, 82-83 & 89-90; NATO/Hienemann Found grant, study vis chair soil sci, Univ Munich, Ger, 83. *Mem:* Soc Am Foresters; Soc Range Mgt; Soil Sci Soc Am; Am Soc Agron. *Res:* Soil-plant-nutrient relations in forest, range and shrub ecosystems; ecology of forest and range ecosystems. *Mailing Add:* 7551 N Palm Circle Tucson AZ 85704

KLEMOLA, ARNOLD R, ASTRONOMY. *Current Pos:* from asst res astronr to assoc res astronr, 67-84, RES ASTRONR, LICK OBSERV, UNIV CALIF, SANTA CRUZ, 84- *Personal Data:* b Pomfret, Conn, Feb 20, 31. *Educ:* Ind Univ, AB, 53; Univ Calif, Berkeley, PhD(astron), 62. *Prof Exp:* Res asst astron, Yale Univ, 61-63, res staff astronr, 63-67. *Mem:* Am Astron Soc; Int Astron Union; Astron Soc Pac. *Res:* Photographic astrometry. *Mailing Add:* UCO/Lick Observ Univ Calif Santa Cruz CA 95064. *E-Mail:* klemola@ucolick.org

KLEMOLA, TAPIO, mathematics, for more information see previous edition

KLEMPERER, FRIEDRICH W, RHEUMATOLOGY. *Current Pos:* RETIRED. *Educ:* Harvard Univ, MD, 37. *Prof Exp:* Prof med, Sch Med, Syracuse Univ, 65-78. *Mailing Add:* 37 Minuteman Rd Acton MA 01720

KLEMPERER, MARTIN R, HEMATOLOGY, ONCOLOGY. *Current Pos:* PROF, DEPT PEDIAT, COL MED, UNIV SFLA, 87- *Personal Data:* b New York, NY, June 26, 31; m 59, Helen R Mitlof; c John, Thomas & Sally. *Educ:* Dartmouth Col, AB, 53; NY Univ, MD, 57. *Prof Exp:* Instr pediat, Harvard Med Sch, 65-67, assoc, 67-69, asst prof, 69-70, tutor med sci, 67-70; assoc pediat, Sch Med, Univ Rochester, 70-74, prof med, 71-74, prof pediat & med, 74-81; prof & chmn, Dept Pediat, Marshall Univ, 81-87. *Concurrent Pos:* Res fel pediat, Harvard Med Sch, 63-65; fel hemat & med, Children's Hosp Med Ctr, Boston, Mass, 63-65, asst med, 65-66, res assoc immunol & hemat, 66-68, assoc med, immunol & hemat, 68-70; sr assoc pediatrician, Strong Mem Hosp, Med Ctr, Univ Rochester, 70-74, pediatrician & physician, 74-81; dir, Bone Marrow Transplant Serv, All Children's Hosp, St Petersburg, Fla, 87- *Mem:* Soc Pediat Res; Am Fedn Clin Res; Int Soc Exp Hemat; Am Soc Hemat; NY Acad Sci; Am Pediat Soc. *Res:* Hereditary and acquired defects of the serum complement system; role of the complement system in inflammation; therapy of childhood malignancies; bone marrow transplantation. *Mailing Add:* All Childrens Hosp 801 Sixth St S St Petersburg FL 33701-4816. *Fax:* 813-892-8619

KLEMPERER, SIMON LOUIS, REFLECTION SEISMOLOGY. *Current Pos:* ASSOC PROF GEOPHYS, STANFORD UNIV, 90- *Personal Data:* b London, Eng, Feb 24, 58. *Educ:* Cambridge Univ, BA, 80; Cornell Univ, PhD(geophys), 85. *Prof Exp:* Royal Soc res fel, Cambridge Univ, 85-90. *Mem:* Fel Geol Soc Am; Am Geophys Union; Geol Soc Am; Soc Explor Geophysicists; Sigma Xi. *Res:* Crustal structure of active tectonic areas-California, Tibet, Alaska; regional tectonics; precursors to earthquakes. *Mailing Add:* Mitchell Bldg Stanford Univ Stanford CA 94305-2215. *Fax:* 650-725-7344; *E-Mail:* klemp@geo.stanford.edu

KLEMPERER, WALTER GEORGE, MATERIALS CHEMISTRY. *Current Pos:* PROF CHEM, UNIV ILL, URBANA-CHAMPAIGN, 81- *Personal Data:* b Saranac Lake, NY, Apr 2, 47; m 77; c 2. *Educ:* Harvard Univ, BA, 68; Mass Inst Technol, PhD(chem), 73. *Prof Exp:* From asst prof to prof chem, Columbia Univ, 73-81. *Concurrent Pos:* Alfred P Sloan Found fel, 76; Camille & Henry Dreyfus Found grant, 78; Guggenheim fel, 80. *Mem:* Am Chem Soc; The Chem Soc. *Res:* Inorganic chemistry; materials chemistry of oxides; polyoxuanion chemistry; sul-gel chemistry; cement chemistry; zeolite chemistry. *Mailing Add:* Dept Mat Chem Univ Ill 405 N Mathews Ave Urbana IL 61801-2325

KLEMPERER, WILLIAM, PHYSICAL CHEMISTRY. *Current Pos:* from instr to assoc prof, 54-65, PROF CHEM, HARVARD UNIV, 65- *Personal Data:* b New York, NY, Oct 6, 27; m 49, Elizabeth Cole; c Joyce Hillary, Paul & Wendy Judith. *Educ:* Harvard Univ, AB, 50; Univ Calif, PhD, 54. *Hon Degrees:* DSc, Univ Chicago, 96. *Honors & Awards:* John Price Wetherill Medal, Franklin Inst, 78; The Irving Langmuir Award in Chem Physics, Am Soc Phys, 80; Evans lectr, Ohio State Univ, 81; Pratt lectr, Univ Va, 84; Rollefson lectr, Univ Calif, Berkeley; Flygare Mem lectr, Univ Ill, Urbana, 85; Oesper lectr, Univ Cincinnati, 87; Kolthoff lectr, Univ Minn, 87; Mary E Kapp lectr, Va Commonwealth Univ, 87; Linus Pauling Distinguished lectr, Ore State Univ, 88; Harry Emmett Gunning lectr, Univ Alta, 88; Fritz London Mem lectr, Duke Univ, 89; Hinshelwood lectr, Oxford Univ, Eng, 89; Bomem Michelson Award, Coblentz Soc, 90; Neckers lectr, Southern Ill Univ, 90. *Prof Exp:* Instr chem, Univ Calif, 54. *Concurrent Pos:* Asst dir, NSF, 79-81. *Mem:* Nat Acad Sci; fel Am Chem Soc; Am Acad Arts & Sci; Am Phys Soc. *Res:* Molecular structure; molecular spectroscopy; energy transfer and intermolecular forces; modelling molecule formation and detection in the interstellar medium. *Mailing Add:* Dept Chem Harvard Univ Cambridge MA 02138. *Fax:* 617-495-1792

KLEMPNER, DANIEL, PHYSICAL POLYMER CHEMISTRY & ENGINEERING, ENVIRONMENTAL STUDIES. *Current Pos:* MEM FAC, POLYMER INST, UNIV DETROIT MERCY, 72-, PROF POLYMER CHEM & ENG, 74-, ASSOC DIR, POLYMER TECHNOL, INC & DIR, CTR EXCELLENCE ENVIRON ENG & SCI, 92- *Personal Data:* b Brooklyn, NY, June 4, 43; m 82, Lois Grodan; c Jessica, Stephanie & Rebecca. *Educ:* Rensselaer Polytech Inst, BS, 64; Williams Col, MS, 68; State Univ NY, Albany, PhD(phys chem), 70. *Prof Exp:* Engr, Sprague Elec Co, Mass, 64-68; vis scientist, Univ Mass, Amherst, 70-72. *Concurrent Pos:* Int consult, 73-; prin investr numerous indust & govt sponsored res proj. *Mem:* AAAS; Am Chem Soc; Am Inst Chem Engrs; Am Phys Soc; Am Inst Chem; Soc Plastics Engrs; Fedn Coatings Socs; Nat Forensic Ctr. *Res:* Electrical properties of materials; inter-penetrating polymer networks; high pressure effects on polymers; x-ray diffraction studies of polymers; morphological and viscoelastic studies on polymers; theories of fusion and blending of polymers; polyurethanes of all types; flammability; environmental studies; polymer recycling; hazardous waste treatment. *Mailing Add:* Ctr Excellence Environ Eng & Sci Univ Detroit Mercy PO Box 19900 Detroit MI 48219-0900. *Fax:* 313-993-1409

KLEMPNER, MARK STEVEN, INFECTIOUS DISEASES. *Current Pos:* assoc prof med, 83-88, PROF MED, NEW ENG MED CTR, 89- *Personal Data:* b Utica, NY, Jan 18, 49; m 79; c 3. *Educ:* Cornell Univ, MD, 73. *Prof Exp:* Intern med, Mass Gen Hosp, 73-74, resident, 74-75; clin assoc, NIH, 75-78; asst prof med, Tufts Univ, 78-82. *Concurrent Pos:* Prin investr, NIH, Nat Inst Allergy & Infectious Dis & US Army Res Command, 79-; mem, NIH study sect, Nat Inst Allergy & Infectious Dis study sect & sub-spec Bd, Am Bd Internal Med, 88-; vis lectr, Brazil, Austria, Italy, Sweden, Switz, UK & Denmark; vis prof, Boston Univ, 87. *Mem:* Am Fedn Clin Res; Am Soc Clin Invest; Infectious Dis Soc Am; AAAS. *Res:* Interactions of infectious agents with host cells; cell activation for eradicating pathogens. *Mailing Add:* Dept Med Div Exp Med Infectious Dis Tufts New England Med Ctr 750 Washington St Box 236 Boston MA 02111-1854

KLEMS, GEORGE J, METALLURGY, SHEET STEEL FORMABILITY. *Current Pos:* div metallurgist, Flat Rolled Div, 84-85, staff metallurgist, Flat Rolled & Coated Prods, Prod Develop Div, Res Ctr, 85-86, MARKET DEVELOP ENGR, AUTOMOTIVE DEVELOP GROUP, LTV STEEL CO, 86- *Personal Data:* b Brno, Czech, May 4, 36; US citizen; m 68, Judith

L Kyle; c G Kyle & Ryan R. *Educ:* Harvard Univ, AB, 58; Ill Inst Technol, MS, 61; Case Western Res Univ, PhD(metall & mat sci), 71. *Prof Exp:* Res asst solid state physics & mat sci, Ill Inst Technol, 58-61 & x-ray crystallog, 61-64; res metallurgist, Res Ctr, Repub Steel Corp, 64-73; mkt develop metallurgist, Molycorp, Inc, 73-76; prod metallurgist high strength steels, Steel Group, Flat Rolled Div, Repub Steel Corp, 76-84. *Mem:* Am Soc Metals Int; Metall Soc Am Inst Mining & Metall Engrs; Soc Automotive Engrs; Sigma Xi; Am Soc Testing & Mat; Am Welding Soc; Soc Mfg Engrs. *Res:* Phase transformations; alloy development; sheet steel formability. *Mailing Add:* 32840 Ledge Hill Dr Solon OH 44139-1917. *Fax:* 440-248-9499; *E-Mail:* 70253.1064@compuserve.com

KLEMS, JOSEPH HENRY, ENERGY CONSERVATION. *Current Pos:* STAFF SCIENTIST, LAWRENCE BERKELEY LAB, UNIV CALIF, 78-, DEP GROUP LEADER, 89- *Personal Data:* b Cincinnati, Ohio, July 14, 42; m 67, Jeanne E Weinhold; c Julia A & Steven J. *Educ:* Univ Chicago, SB, 64, SM, 65, PhD(physics), 70. *Prof Exp:* Res assoc physics, Lab Nuclear Studies, Cornell Univ, 70-73; asst res physicist, Univ Calif, Davis, 73-78. *Mem:* Am Phys Soc; AAAS; Sigma Xi. *Res:* Energy-efficient windows and lighting systems; solar energy; measurement of energy flows through architectural windows under realistic conditions; contrast mechanisms for X-ray microscopy; optical measurements. *Mailing Add:* Appl Sci Div Lawrence Berkeley Lab Univ Calif 90-3111 1 Cyclotron Rd Berkeley CA 94720. *Fax:* 510-486-4089; *E-Mail:* jhklems@lbl.gov

KLENIN, MARJORIE A, MECHANICS. *Current Pos:* asst prof, 77-80, ASSOC PROF SOLID STATE PHYSICS, NC STATE UNIV, 80- *Personal Data:* b Lancaster, Pa. *Educ:* Swarthmore Col, BA, 65; Univ Pa, MS, 66, PhD(physics), 70. *Prof Exp:* Res assoc solid state physics, Inst Max von Lane-Paul Langevin, 70-72 & Univ Saarlandes, 72-74; guest scientist, Brookhaven Nat Lab, 74-76, sr res assoc reactor safety, 76-77. *Concurrent Pos:* Vis asst prof solid state physics, State Univ NY, Stony Brook, 74-76; guest scientist, Max Plank Inst Solid State Physics Res, 85- *Mem:* Am Phys Soc; Sigma Xi. *Res:* Structural modeling and growth dynamics of bond-directed disordered compounds; covalent semiconductors; equilibrium dynamic properties; complex orientational ordering as mediated by quadrupolar couplings. *Mailing Add:* Dept Physics NC State Univ Box 8202 Raleigh NC 27695

KLENKE, EDWARD FREDERICK, JR, CHEMICAL ENGINEERING. *Current Pos:* MEM, INT EXEC SERV CORPS, 85- *Personal Data:* b New York, NY, May 22, 16; m 38; c 2. *Educ:* Newark Col Eng, BS, 40. *Prof Exp:* Sr supvr, Kankakee Ord Works, 41-44; chem engr, Manhattan Proj, Univ Chicago, Hanford, Wash, 44-45; res chem & engr, Pigments Dept, E I du Pont de Nemours & Co, Inc, 45-64; sr res engr, 64-69, res supvr, 69-74, coordr new facil, 74-77, safety, health & environ coord, 77-81. *Concurrent Pos:* Eng consult, 46-51 & 81- *Mem:* Am Inst Chem Engrs. *Res:* Colored pigments research; process design and development. *Mailing Add:* 7200 Third Ave Sykesville MD 21784

KLENKNECHT, KENNETH S(AMUEL), AEROSPACE & AERONAUTICAL ENGINEERING, TECHNICAL MANAGEMENT. *Current Pos:* RETIRED. *Personal Data:* b Washington, DC, July 24, 19; m 47, Patricia Todd; c Linda (May), Patricia A & Frederick W. *Educ:* Purdue Univ, BS, 42. *Honors & Awards:* John J Montgomery Award, Nat Soc Aerospace Prof, 63; W Randolph Lovelace, II Award, Am Astronaut Soc, Inc, 75. *Prof Exp:* Proj engr, NASA Lewis Res Ctr, 42-51, head opers eng sect & aeronaut res scientist, NASA Flight Res Ctr, Calif, 51-59, mem, Space Task Group, Langley Field, Va, 59-61, tech asst to dir, NASA Johnson Space Ctr, 61-62, mgr, Proj Mercury, 62-63, dep mgr, Gemini Prog, 63-67, mgr, Command & Serv Modules, Apollo Spacecraft Prog, 67-70, mgr, Skylab Prog, 70-74, dir flight opers, 74-76, asst mgr, Orbiter Proj, 76-77, dep assoc admin space transp systs, Europ Opers, NASA HQ, Washington, DC, 77-79, asst mgr, Orbiter Proj & vehicle mgr, Orbiter 102, NASA Johnson Space Ctr, 79-81; sr space transport syst tech adv, Martin Marietta Denver Aerospace, Colo, 81-84, dir, design-to-cost productivity, Space Sta Proj, 84-88, dir, Zenith Star Proj, Laser Payload Element, 88-90. *Mem:* Fel Am Astronaut Soc; Int Acad Astronaut; assoc fel Am Inst Aeronaut & Astronaut. *Res:* Aircraft icing research during 1950's; development of the X-15 research aircraft and implementation of scientific and medical experiments on the Mercury, Gemini, Apollo and Skylab space flight programs. *Mailing Add:* 825 Front Range Rd Littleton CO 80120

KLENS, PAUL FRANK, MICROBIOLOGY. *Current Pos:* from assoc prof to prof, 58-86, dean arts & sci, 66-74, EMER PROF BIOL, LOCK HAVEN UNIV, 86- *Personal Data:* b Scranton, Pa, July 21, 18; m 47; c 4. *Educ:* Syracuse Univ, AB, 40, MS, 42, PhD(microbiol), 51. *Prof Exp:* Asst bot, Syracuse Univ, 40-42, instr bact & mycol, 45-51; chemist & mat engr, Carrier Corp, NY, 42-45; chief germicides unit, QM Res & Develop, US Dept Army, 51-53; chief microbiol lab, Nuodex Prods Co, NJ, 54-58. *Mem:* Am Soc Microbiol; Soc Indust Microbiol. *Res:* Physiology of fungi; microbiological deterioration; industrial microbiology; water pollution studies. *Mailing Add:* Box 405 RD 3 Mill Hall PA 17751

KLENSIN, JOHN, COMPUTER SCIENCE. *Current Pos:* PRIN RES SCIENTIST ARCHIT, MASS INST TECHNOL, 78- *Personal Data:* b Tucson, Ariz, Feb 1, 45. *Educ:* Mass Inst Technol, BS, 67, PhD(comput appln & use polit sci), 79. *Concurrent Pos:* Lectr, Dept Polit Sci, Mass Inst Technol, 80-; chmn, Comt X3J1, Am Nat Stand, 84-; dir secretariat, Int Network Food Data Syst, 89- *Mem:* Am Comput Mach; Inst Elec & Electronics Engrs Comput Soc; Am Statist Asn; Int Asn Statist Comput. *Mailing Add:* PO Box 197 Cambridge MA 02140

KLEPCZYNSKI, WILLIAM J(OHN), ASTRONOMY. *Current Pos:* Astronr, Nautical Almanac Off, 61-71, ASTRONR, TIME SERV DIV, US NAVAL OBSERV, 71- *Personal Data:* b Philadelphia, Pa, Apr 16, 39; m 61; c 2. *Educ:* Univ Pa, AB, 61; Georgetown Col, MA, 64; Yale Univ, PhD(astron), 69. *Concurrent Pos:* Pres, Inst Navig, 88-89. *Mem:* AAAS; Am Astron Soc; Am Inst Navig; Int Astron Union. *Res:* Planetary motion; masses of the planets; motion of minor planets; observations of minor planets; eclipsing variable stars. *Mailing Add:* 2303 Yvonnes Way Dunn Loring VA 22027

KLEPINGER, LINDA LEHMAN, BIOLOGICAL ANTHROPOLOGY. *Current Pos:* From asst prof to assoc prof, 72-92, PROF ANTHROP, UNIV ILL, URBANA, 92- *Personal Data:* b Hammond, Ind, Mar 27, 41. *Educ:* Ind Univ, AB, 63; Univ Kans, MPhil, 71, PhD(anthrop), 72. *Mem:* Am Asn Phys Anthropologists; AAAS; Paleopath Asn; Am Acad Forensic Sci. *Res:* Biological relationships of prehistoric populations; paleopathology of New and Old World populations; forensic anthropology; chemical analyses of archaeological bone; bone biology. *Mailing Add:* Dept Anthrop Univ Ill 607 S Matthews Ave Urbana IL 60801. *E-Mail:* klepinge@uiuc.edu

KLEPPA, OLE JAKOB, PHYSICAL CHEMISTRY. *Current Pos:* asst prof chem, Inst Study Metals, Univ Chicago, 52-57, assoc prof, Inst Study Metals & Dept Chem, 58-62, chmn calorimetry conf, 66-67, assoc dir, James Franck Inst, 68-71, dir, 71-77, prof, Dept Chem, 62-90, prof, Dept Geophys Sci, 68-90, dir, Mat Res Lab, 84-87, EMER PROF, UNIV CHICAGO, 90- *Personal Data:* b Oslo, Norway, Feb 4, 20; m 48, Joy Stodder; c Karen J & Abbie L. *Educ:* Norwegian Tech Univ, ChE, 46, Dr techn(chem), 56. *Honors & Awards:* Huffman Mem Award, 82; Hume-Rothery Mem Award, 94. *Prof Exp:* Instr, Inst Study Metals, Univ Chicago, 49-50; res supvr, Dept Chem & Metall, Norweg Defense Res Estab, 50-51. *Concurrent Pos:* Consult, Argonne Nat Lab; Alexander von Humboldt Award, 83-84; vis prof, Japan Soc Prom Sci, 75, Univ Paris, Orsay, 77. *Mem:* Am Chem Soc; Am Inst Mining, Metall & Petrol Eng; Am Ceramic Soc; Norweg Chem Soc; fel AAAS; Am Soc Metals; Soc Norweg Engrs; Norweg Acad Tech Sci; Royal Norweg Soc Sci & Letters. *Res:* Thermodynamics; thermochemistry; electrochemistry; chemical and physical metallurgy; solid state chemistry; fused salts. *Mailing Add:* James Franck Inst Univ Chicago 5640 Ellis Ave Chicago IL 60637-1433. *Fax:* 773-702-5863

KLEPPER, DAVID LLOYD, architectural acoustics, electroacoustics, for more information see previous edition

KLEPPER, ELIZABETH LEE (BETTY), PLANT PHYSIOLOGY. *Current Pos:* mem staff & supvry plant physiologist, 76-85, RES LEADER, AGR RES SERV, USDA, 85- *Personal Data:* b Memphis, Tenn, Mar 8, 36. *Educ:* Vanderbilt Univ, BA, 58; Duke Univ, AM, 63, PhD(bot), 66. *Honors & Awards:* Wise Award. *Prof Exp:* Teacher high sch, Tenn, 60-61; teaching asst bot, Duke Univ, 63-64; res scientist, Div Irrig Res, Commonwealth Sci & Indust Res Orgn Griffith, Australia, 66-68; asst prof bot, Auburn Univ, 68-72; res scientist, Battelle NW Labs, 72-74, sr res scientist, Ecosysts Dept, 74-76. *Concurrent Pos:* Tech ed, Crop Sci, 90-92, ed, 92-; adv ed, Irrig Sci, 87-92. *Mem:* AAAS; fel Soil Sci Soc Am; Bot Soc Am; Am Soc Plant Physiol; fel Am Soc Agron; Sigma Xi; fel Crop Sci Soc Am. *Res:* Environmental plant physiology including water relations and stress; root growth and uptake of water; cereal developmental history and modelling of cereal yield. *Mailing Add:* 1454 SW 45th Pendleton OR 98701

KLEPPER, JOHN RICHARD, ULTRASONIC IMAGING, PATTERN RECOGNITION. *Current Pos:* STAFF MEM, SIEMENS ULTRASOUND, 95- *Personal Data:* b Dayton, Ohio, Sept 20, 47; m 69; c 1. *Educ:* Ohio State Univ, BS, 69; Wash Univ, MA, 75, PhD(physics), 80. *Prof Exp:* Res asst, Biomed Comput Lab, Wash Univ, 77-80; res bioengr, Inst Appl Physiol & Med, 80-81, dir, Dept Phys Sci, 81-95, exec dir, 87-95. *Concurrent Pos:* Affil asst prof elec eng, Univ Wash, 82-87. *Mem:* Inst Elec & Electronics Engrs; Eng Med & Biol Soc; Am Inst Ultrasound Med. *Res:* Development of computer aided ultrasonic imaging systems for use in medical diagnosis; ultrasonic tissue characterization, through application of computed tomographic techniques; blood flow analysis, through Doppler shift measurements. *Mailing Add:* Siemens Ultrasound PO Box 7002 Issaquah WA 98027-7002

KLEPPNER, ADAM, MATHEMATICAL ANALYSIS. *Current Pos:* From asst prof to assoc prof, 61-68, PROF MATH, UNIV MD, COLLEGE PARK, 68- *Personal Data:* b New York, NY, June 5, 31; m 58. *Educ:* Yale Univ, BS, 53; Univ Mich, MA, 54; Harvard Univ, PhD(math), 60. *Concurrent Pos:* Vis prof, Univ Colo, 70-71 & Univ Calif, Berkeley, 75. *Mem:* Am Math Soc. *Res:* Group representations; functional analysis. *Mailing Add:* Dept Math Univ Md College Park MD 20742

KLEPPNER, DANIEL, PHYSICS. *Current Pos:* assoc prof, 66-73, head, Dept Physics, Div Atomic, Plasma & Condensed Matter Physics, 76-79, PROF PHYSICS, MASS INST TECHNOL, 74-, LESTER WOLFE PROF, 85-, ASSOC DIR, RES LAB ELECTRONICS, 87- *Personal Data:* b New York, NY, Dec 16, 32; m 58, Beatrice Spencer; c Paul S, Sofie R & Andrew N. *Educ:* Williams Col, BS, 53; Cambridge Univ, BA, 55; Harvard Univ, PhD(physics), 59. *Honors & Awards:* Davisson-Germer Prize, Am Phys Soc, 85; Julius Edgar Lilienfeld Prize, 90; Morris Loeb Lectr Physics, Harvard Univ, 87; Starley H Klosk Vis Lectr, NY Univ, 90; William F Meggers Award, Optical Soc Am, 91; Houston Lectr, Rice Univ, 92; Russel Marker Lectr, Pa State Univ, 92; Edwin Yunker Lectr, Ore State Univ, 93; Kay Malmstron Lectr, Hamline Univ, 94; Donald R Hamilton Lectr, Princeton Univ, 95; Dersted

Medal, Am Asn Physics Teachers, 97. *Prof Exp:* Res fel physics, Harvard Univ, 59-60, from instr to asst prof, 60-66. *Concurrent Pos:* Alfred P Sloan Found fel, 62-64; mem, Comt Atomic, Molecular & Optical Physics, Nat Res Coun, 73-76 & 80-85; chmn, Div Atomic, Molecular & Optical Physics, Am Phys Soc, 83-84; mem, Bd Physics & Astron, Nat Acad Sci, 87-90; chair, Physics Planning Comt, Am Phys Soc. *Mem:* Nat Acad Sci; fel AAAS; fel Am Phys Soc; fel Am Acad Arts & Sci; Optical Soc Am; Int Union Pure & Appl Physics (secy, 88-90); Japan Asn Math Sci. *Res:* Atomic physics; redetermination of the Rydberg constant; quantum chaos; studies of hydrogen in the microkelvin regime; ultra precise laser spectroscopy. *Mailing Add:* Dept Physics Mass Inst Technol 77 Massachusetts Ave Rm 26-237 Cambridge MA 02139-4307. *Fax:* 617-253-4876; *E-Mail:* dk@ano.mit.edu

KLERER, JULIUS, PHYSICAL CHEMISTRY, SOLID STATE CHEMISTRY. *Current Pos:* from assoc prof to prof, 80-92, EMER PROF CHEM ENG, COOPER UNION, 92- *Personal Data:* b New York, NY, July 19, 28; m 61. *Educ:* NY Univ, BA, 49, MS, 55, PhD(phys chem), 58. *Prof Exp:* Instr phys chem, Brooklyn Col, 57-58; group leader, Radio Corp Am, 58-60; supvry mem tech staff, Bell Tel Labs, 60-67. *Mem:* Electrochem Soc; Royal Soc Chem; NY Acad Sci; Sigma Xi. *Res:* Solid state chemistry concerned with thin films of oxides and metals, their preparation and properties both on semiconductors and semiconducting oxides. *Mailing Add:* 29 Grove St New York NY 10014-5357

KLERER, MELVIN, COMPUTER SCIENCE. *Current Pos:* PROF COMPUT SCI, POLYTECH INST NY, 74- *Personal Data:* b New York, NY, Feb 17, 26; m 51; c 2. *Educ:* NY Univ, BA, 48, MS, 50, PhD(theoret physics), 54. *Prof Exp:* Tutor physics, City Col New York, 52-53, instr, 54-57; sr res assoc, dir comput & data processing facil & head, Comput Sci Prog, Hudson Labs, Columbia Univ, 57-67; prof indust eng, NY Univ, 67-73; vis scientist, Weizman Inst Sci, 73-74. *Concurrent Pos:* Nat lectr, Asn Comput Mach, 67; chmn, sci comput, Hudson Labs Columbia Univ, 57-67; Joint Users Group, Asn Comput Mach, 66-68, comt social implications, Inst Elec & Electronics Engrs, 70-71, Eval Panel, Nat Res Coun, 76; reviewer comput res, Int Fedn Info Processing Soc & Am Fedn Info Processing Soc; ed, Asn Comput Mach Comput Reviews. *Mem:* AAAS; Asn Comput Mach; Inst Elec & Electronics Engrs; Am Asn Artificial Intel; Am Asn Ling. *Res:* Automating the programming process for scientific-engineering-mathematical application programming and in user-oriented computer languages and terminal design. *Mailing Add:* 79 Lakeview Ave Scarsdale NY 10583

KLERLEIN, JOSEPH BALLARD, FINITE MATHEMATICS. *Current Pos:* Instr, 74-75, from asst prof to assoc prof, 75-85, PROF MATH, WESTERN CAROLINA UNIV, 85-, DEPT HEAD, 90- *Personal Data:* b Baltimore, Md, Dec 16, 48; m 70; c 4. *Educ:* Furman Univ, BS, 70; Vanderbilt Univ, PhD(math), 75. *Mem:* Am Math Soc; Math Asn Am; Sigma Xi. *Res:* Graph theory especially the study of traversability in cayley color graphs; line graphs for directed graphs. *Mailing Add:* Rte 3 PO Box 365-L Sylvia NC 28779-9803

KLERMAN, LORRAINE VOGEL, MATERNAL & CHILD HEALTH. *Current Pos:* PROF & DEPT CHAIR, UNIV ALA, BIRMINGHAM. *Personal Data:* b New York, NY, July 10, 29; div; c 4. *Educ:* Cornell Univ, BA, 50; Harvard Univ, MPH, 53, DrPH, 62. *Honors & Awards:* Martha May Eliot Award, Am Pub Health Asn. *Prof Exp:* From assoc prof to prof pub health, Florence Heller Grad Sch Advan Studies Social Welfare, Brandeis Univ, 73-84; prof, Dept Epidemiol & Pub Health, Yale Sch Med. *Concurrent Pos:* Mem, Res Rev Comt, Nat Inst Alcohol Abuse & Alcoholism, 73-76, Health Serv Res Rev Subcomt, Nat Ctr Health Serv Res & Health Care Technol Assessment, 86-90, Expert Panel Content Prenatal Care, Pub Health Serv, 86-89, Priority Expert Panel A (Low Birthweight), Nat Ctr Nursing Res, 88-89, Prog Develop Bd, Am Pub Health Asn, 90-; mem ed adv comt, Family Planning Perspectives, 90-94; chairperson, Maternal & Child Health Sect, Am Pub Health Asn, 86-88, New Haven Family Alliance; consult, Comt Study Prev Low Birthweight, Inst med; mem, Comt Study Outreach Prenatal Care, Inst Med, sci adv panel & bd dirs, Alan Guttmacher Inst, coun adv, Nat Ctr Children in Poverty, tech adv comt, Community Childhood Hunger Identification Proj, adv comt, Primary Care Asst & Accountability Proj, Maternal & Child Health Progs, prof adv comt, Conn Child Health Access Proj. *Mem:* Fel Am Pub Health Asn. *Res:* Maternal and child health; prenatal care; adolescent parenting. *Mailing Add:* Sch Pub Health Univ Ala 1825 Univ Blvd Birmingham AL 35294-2010

KLESIUS, PHILLIP HARRY, IMMUNOLOGICAL RESEARCH. *Current Pos:* RES LEADER & MICROBIOLOGIST, FISH DIS & PARASITES RES LAB, AUBURN, AGR RES SERV, US DEPT AGR, 73- *Personal Data:* b Bryn Mawr, Pa, Mar 1, 38; m 70; c 2. *Educ:* Fla Southern Col, BS, 61; Northwestern State Univ, MS, 63; Univ Tex, Austin, PhD(microbiol), 66. *Prof Exp:* Asst prof, microbiol, Univ Tex, Austin, 68-69; asst prof, microbiol, Univ Ariz, 69-72; asst chief, Ctr Dis Control, Ft Collins, Colo, 72-73. *Concurrent Pos:* Adj prof, Dept Pathobiol, Col Vet Med, Auburn Univ, 73-; vis prof vet microbiol, Col Vet Med, Tuskegee Univ, 74-; assoc prof, Med Univ SC, 76-; comn mem patent biotech, Agr Res Serv, 88- *Mem:* Am Asn Vet Immunologists (secy-treas, 88-91); Am Asn Immunologists; Am Soc Microbiologists; fel Am Acad Microbiol. *Res:* Immunological and parasitological research on control of internal parasites of fish; immune system of cultured catfish. *Mailing Add:* Fish Dis & Parasites Res Lab USDA Agr Res Serv PO Box 952 Auburn AL 36830. *Fax:* 334-887-2983; *E-Mail:* kles.ph@vermed.auburn.edu

KLESSIG, DANIEL FREDERICK, MOLECULAR BIOLOGY, BIOCHEMISTRY. *Current Pos:* PROF MOLECULAR BIOL & ASSOC DIR WAKSMAN INST, 85- *Personal Data:* b Fond du Lac, Wis, Feb 24, 49; m, Judith Hope. *Educ:* Univ Wis-Madison, BS, 71; Univ Edinburgh, BSc (hons), 73; Harvard Univ, PhD(molecular biol, biochem), 78. *Prof Exp:* Fel, Cold Spring Harbor Lab, 78, staff scientist tumor virol, 79-80; mem fac, Dept Cell & Molecular Biol, Univ Utah, 80-85. *Concurrent Pos:* Marshall scholar, 71-73, Searle scholar, 82-85; McKnight scholar, 83-86. *Mem:* Am Soc Plant Physiologist; Am Phytopath Soc; Am Soc Microbiologists; AAAS; Plant Molecular Biol Soc. *Res:* Control of gene expression in plants and in animal cells and their viruses; molecular and cellular biology; virus research; salicylic acid signal transduction pathway. *Mailing Add:* Waksman Inst Rutgers Univ PO Box 759 Piscataway NJ 08855. *Fax:* 732-932-5735

KLESTADT, BERNARD, ELECTROMECHANICAL-ELECTRONIC DEVICES & SYSTEMS, MEDICAL ELECTRONICS. *Current Pos:* TECH CONSULT, 90- *Personal Data:* b Buren, Ger, Jan 31, 25; nat US; m 56, Bernice F Hersch; c Ralph H. *Educ:* Columbia Univ, BS, 49, MS, 50; Univ Southern Calif, PhD(elec eng), 58. *Prof Exp:* Elec engr, Aircraft Radiation Lab, Wright Air Develop Ctr, 49; asst proj engr, Sperry Gyroscope Co, 50; mem tech staff, Systs Develop Labs, Hughes Aircraft Co, 50-58, sr staff eng, 58-62, sr scientist, 62-63, asst mgr flight control systs dept, 63-66, mgr missile control systs dept, 66-69, sr scientist, Space & Commun Group, 69-76, sr scientist, Missiles Systs Group, 76-81, mgr, Control Systs Dept, 81-86, chief scientist, 87-88, prog mgr, Automotive Controls Eng, 88-89. *Concurrent Pos:* Lectr, Univ Southern Calif, 56-58. *Mem:* Sigma Xi; Inst Elec & Electronics Engrs; NY Acad Sci. *Res:* Servomechanisms; circuit theory; guidance and control systems; automatic computation; space flight development. *Mailing Add:* 56-845 Merion La Quinta CA 92253. *Fax:* 760-771-1304; *E-Mail:* bkeng@aol.com

KLETSKY, EARL J(USTIN), ELECTRICAL ENGINEERING. *Current Pos:* from instr to prof elec eng, 57-82, asst dir, Lab Sensory Commun, 64-74, coordr bioeng prog, 73-82, ASST DEAN, COL ENG, SYRACUSE UNIV, 82- *Personal Data:* b Springfield, Mass, July 22, 30; m 58; c 1. *Educ:* Mass Inst Technol, BS, 51, MS, 53; Syracuse Univ, PhD(elec eng), 61. *Prof Exp:* Torchiana fel & res engr elec eng, Univ Delft, 55-56; elec engr, Gen Electronics Labs, 56-57. *Concurrent Pos:* Admin dir, Inst Sensory Res, Syracuse Univ, 74-80. *Mem:* Inst Elec & Electronics Engrs; Am Soc Eng Educ. *Res:* Biosimulation; analog and digital simulation of sensory systems; modeling of sensory information processing. *Mailing Add:* 113 Humbert Ave Syracuse NY 13224

KLETT, JAMES ELMER, LANDSCAPE HORTICULTURE, NURSERY PRODUCTION. *Current Pos:* ASSOC PROF ORNAMENTAL HORT, COLO STATE UNIV, 79- *Personal Data:* b Cincinnati, Ohio, May 20, 47. *Educ:* Ohio State Univ, BS, 69; Univ Ill, MS, 71, PhD(hort), 74. *Prof Exp:* Res asst ornamental hort, Univ Ill, 69-72, teaching asst, 72-74; asst prof, ornamental hort, SDak State Univ 74-77, assoc prof, 77-79. *Concurrent Pos:* Water Qual Inst grant, SDak State Univ, 76, new chem prod grants; numerous nat & indust res grants, landscape hort. *Mem:* Am Soc Hort Sci; Am Hort Soc; Int Plant Propagators Soc; Sigma Xi; Int Soc Arboriculture. *Res:* Herbaceous and woody ornamental plant evaluation research; water utilization studies with landscape plants; herbicide research with container nursery crops and landscape management studies. *Mailing Add:* Dept Hort Colo State Univ Ft Collins CO 80523-0001

KLETZIEN, ROLF FREDERICK, BIOCHEMISTRY. *Current Pos:* SR SCIENTIST, UPJOHN CO, 89- *Personal Data:* b Beloit, Wis, Dec 15, 46; m 69; c 2. *Educ:* Univ Wis, BS, 70, PhD(oncol), 74. *Prof Exp:* Fel biochem, Princeton Univ, 74-75, Harvard Univ, 75-77; assoc prof biochem, WVa Univ, 77-89. *Mem:* Am Soc Cellular Biol. *Res:* Regulation of cellular function and metabolism. *Mailing Add:* Upjohn Co 7250-126-327 Kalamazoo MI 49001. *Fax:* 616-384-9763

KLEVANS, EDWARD HARRIS, PLASMA PHYSICS, NUCLEAR ENGINEERING. *Current Pos:* from asst prof to assoc prof, 66-76, assoc dean res, 80-84, PROF NUCLEAR ENG, PA STATE UNIV, 76-, DEPT HEAD, 87- *Personal Data:* b Roaring Spring, Pa, Oct 13, 35; m 59, Deborah Rosen; c Linda & Jennifer H. *Educ:* Pa State Univ, BS, 57; Univ Mich, MS, 58, PhD(nuclear eng), 62. *Prof Exp:* Sr scientist, Jet Propulsion Lab, Calif Inst Technol, 62-66. *Concurrent Pos:* Physicist, Off Fusion Energy, US Dept Energy, 84-85. *Mem:* Am Phys Soc; Am Nuclear Soc; fel AAAS; Am Soc Eng Educ. *Res:* Plasma physics; thermonuclear engineering. *Mailing Add:* 103 W Marylyn Ave State College PA 16801. *Fax:* 814-865-8499; *E-Mail:* ehknuc@engr.psu.edu

KLEVATT, STEVE, SOFTWARE SYSTEMS. *Current Pos:* MGR, PROD SOFTWARE, METROLIGHT STUDIOS, LOS ANGELES. *Educ:* Univ Calif, Los Angeles, MBA, 90. *Prof Exp:* Staff mem, Robert Abel & Assocs; staff mem, Wavefront Tech. *Mailing Add:* Metrolight Studios 5724 W Third St Suite 400 Los Angeles CA 90036-3078

KLEVAY, LESLIE MICHAEL, NUTRITION MEDICAL & HEALTH SCIENCES, ENVIRONMENTAL & PUBLIC HEALTH & EPIDEMIOLOGY. *Current Pos:* RES MED OFFICER, HUMAN NUTRIT RES CTR, AGR RES SERV, USDA, 72- *Personal Data:* b Chicago, Ill. *Educ:* Univ Wis-Madison, BS, 56, MD, 60; Harvard Univ, MS, 62. *Hon Degrees:* DSc, Harvard Univ, 65. *Prof Exp:* Teaching asst chem, Univ Wis-Madison, 55-57; intern med, St Louis City Hosp, Mo, 60-61; from instr to asst prof internal med, Col Med, Univ Cincinnati, 65-72, from asst prof to assoc prof environ health, 65-72. *Concurrent Pos:* Asst, Wash Univ, 60-61; consult, Off Int Res, NIH, 67, Ky Dept Health, 68-69, Div Chronic Dis Progs, Health Serv & Ment Health Admin, 69- & Nat Ctr Health Statist, 70; assoc prof & prof internal med, Univ NDak, 72, mem, attending med staff, 76-; Joseph Goldberger vis prof clin nutrit, 76; consult, Nat Heart & Lung Inst, 76; adv, Scientific Rev Comt, Human Nutrit Res Coun, Ont, 80; adv, Nutrit Comt, Am Acad Pediat, 81; mem Comt Clin Issues Health Dis, Am Soc Clin Nutrit; tech adv, Comt Sci & Educ Res Grants Prog, USDA, 83; chmn, Spec Study Sect, USPH, NIH & DHHS, 86. *Mem:* AAAS; Am Fedn Clin Res; Soc Exp Biol & Med; Am Inst Nutrit; Am Soc Clin Nutrit. *Res:* Experimental atherosclerosis; epidemiology of ischemic heart disease; metabolism of metallic trace elements; definition of nutritional requirement; interrelationships of nutrients; nutritional aspects of the human environment; mammalian metabolism of insecticides; nutritional problems of underdeveloped countries. *Mailing Add:* USDA ARS Human Nutrit Res Ctr PO Box 9034 Univ Sta Grand Forks ND 58202-9034. *Fax:* 701-795-8395

KLEVECZ, ROBERT RAYMOND, CELL BIOLOGY, MOLECULAR BIOLOGY. *Current Pos:* SR RES SCIENTIST, CITY OF HOPE MED CTR, 67- *Personal Data:* b Stratford, Conn, Feb 8, 39; m 61; c 2. *Educ:* Ga Inst Technol, BS, 62; Univ Tex, PhD(cell biol), 66. *Concurrent Pos:* Fel, Yale Univ, 66, Nat Cancer Inst res fel enzyme chem, 66-67. *Mem:* AAAS; Am Soc Cell Biol. *Res:* Cellular regulatory mechanisms; cellular clocks and oscillators; control of growth and division in mammalian cells in culture; periodic gene function and the temporal organization of RNA and enzyme synthesis. *Mailing Add:* 1821 La Cresta Dr Pasadena CA 91103

KLEVEN, STANLEY H, VETERINARY MICROBIOLOGY, AVIAN MEDICINE. *Current Pos:* from asst prof to assoc prof med microbiol, 70-78, head dept Avian Med, 73-82, PROF AVIAN MED & MED MICROBIOL, POULTRY DIS RES CTR, UNIV GA, 78- *Personal Data:* b Dawson, Minn, June 24, 40; m 60; c 3. *Educ:* Univ Minn, St Paul, BS, 63, DVM, 65, PhD(microbiol), 70. *Honors & Awards:* Upjohn Achievement Award, Am Asn Avian Pathologists,80; Am Feed Indust Award, Am Vet Med Asn, 85. *Prof Exp:* Pvt pract, 65-66; instr vet microbiol, Univ Minn, 66-67, res fel, 67-70. *Mem:* AAAS; Am Vet Med Asn; Am Asn Avian Path; World Vet Poultry Asn; Poultry Sci Asn. *Res:* Respiratory infections of poultry; avian mycoplasmosis. *Mailing Add:* 172 Hickory Pointe Dr Athens GA 30605

KLIBANOV, ALEXANDER M, APPLIED ENZYMOLOGY, BIOTECHNOLOGY. *Current Pos:* asst prof appl biochem & Henry L Doherty prof, 79-83, from assoc prof to prof appl biochem, 83-88, PROF CHEM, MASS INST TECHNOL, 88- *Personal Data:* b Moscow, USSR, July 15, 49; US citizen; m 72, Margarita Romanycheva; c Tatyana. *Educ:* Moscow Univ, MS, 71, PhD(chem enzym), 74. *Honors & Awards:* Leo Friend Award, Am Chem Soc, Ipatieff Prize, Marvin J Johnson Award, Int Enzyme Eng Prize, Arthur C Cope Scholar Award. *Prof Exp:* Res chemist, Moscow Univ, 74-77; res assoc, Univ Calif, San Diego, 78-79. *Mem:* Nat Acad Sci; Nat Acad Eng; Am Chem Soc; Am Soc Biochem & Molecular Biol; Am Inst Med & Biol Eng. *Res:* Mechanisms of protein inactivation; stabilization of proteins; immobilized enzymes and cells; enzymes as catalysts in organic syntheses; biocatalysis in extreme environments. *Mailing Add:* 61 W Boulevard Rd Newton MA 02159-1218. *Fax:* 617-252-1609; *E-Mail:* klibanov@mit.edu

KLICH, MAREN ALICE, MYCOLOGY, MYCOTOXICOLOGY. *Current Pos:* RES MICROBIOLOGIST, SOUTHERN REGIONAL RES CTR, AGR RES SERV, USDA, 80- *Personal Data:* b Chicago, Ill, Apr 12, 52; m 89, Edward J Mullaney; c Gwen K Mullaney. *Educ:* St Olaf Col, BA, 74; Iowa State Univ, MS, 78, PhD(bot), 80. *Mem:* Mycol Soc Am; Am Soc Microbiol; Am Phytopath Soc. *Res:* Ecology and taxanomy of hyphomycetous fungi with emphasis on mycotoxigenic fungi in Aspergillus and Penicillium. *Mailing Add:* Res Suc US Dept Agr PO Box 19687 New Orleans LA 70179-0687. *Fax:* 504-286-4419

KLICK, CLIFFORD C, SOLID STATE PHYSICS. *Current Pos:* RETIRED. *Personal Data:* b Strausstown, Pa, Aug 31, 18; m 47; c 6. *Educ:* Muhlenberg Col, AB, 39; Harvard Univ, MA, 47; Carnegie Inst Technol, ScD(physics), 49. *Prof Exp:* Asst elec eng, Mass Inst Technol, 41-42; assoc physicist, Radiation Lab, Johns Hopkins Univ, 42-45; physicist, Naval Res Lab, 49-52, head luminescent mat sect, 53-67, supt mat sci div, 67-77; mem staff, Off Naval Res, London, 77-79. *Concurrent Pos:* Consult, US Army, 45. *Mem:* Fel Am Phys Soc; Sigma Xi. *Res:* Color centers and luminescent centers in solids. *Mailing Add:* 7200 Third Ave C-059 Sykesville MD 21784-5201

KLICKA, JOHN KENNETH, COMPARATIVE ENDOCRINOLOGY. *Current Pos:* RETIRED. *Personal Data:* b Chicago, Ill, Dec 9, 33; m 54; c 7. *Educ:* Northern Ill Univ, BS, 57, MS, 58; Univ Ill, Urbana, PhD(physiol & endocrinol), 62. *Prof Exp:* From instr to prof physiol & biochem, Wis State Univ, Oshkosh, 62-79; res assoc, Vet Admin Hosp, Univ Minn, 79-89. *Concurrent Pos:* NIH training prog fel, Med Sch, Univ Minn, 65-67; career develop award environ toxicol, Nat Inst Environ Health Sci, NIH, 81-84. *Mem:* AAAS; Am Soc Zool; Am Physiol Soc; NY Acad Sci; Sigma Xi. *Res:* Mechanism by which estrogens act to induce renal tumors in Syrian golden hamsters; chemical carcinogenesis. *Mailing Add:* 15017 Stevens Ave Burnsville MN 55306

KLIEBENSTEIN, JAMES BERNARD, ECONOMICS OF LIVESTOCK PRODUCTION, ANIMAL HEALTH MANAGEMENT. *Current Pos:* PROF, IOWA STATE UNIV, 86- *Personal Data:* b Dodgeville, Wis, June 1, 47; m 67; c 3. *Educ:* Univ Wis-Platteville, BS, 69; Univ Ill, MS, 70, PhD(agr econ), 72. *Prof Exp:* Asst prof, NW Mo State Univ, 72-74; from asst prof to prof, Univ Mo, 74-86. *Concurrent Pos:* Vis prof, Univ Wis-Madison, 82-83; mem eval comt, Nat Animal Health Monitoring Syst, 87-88; respondent, Off Technol Assessment, US Cong, 89-90, consult, 90-91. *Mem:* Am Agr Econ Asn; Am Soc Farm Managers & Rural Appraisers; Nat Asn Cols & Teachers Agri. *Res:* Economics of livestock production; economics of animal health management and food safety, primary focus at the product production level. *Mailing Add:* Dept Econ Iowa State Univ 266 Heady Hall Ames IA 50011-1321

KLIEFORTH, HAROLD ERNEST, METEOROLOGY. *Current Pos:* RES PROF ATMOSPHERIC SCI, DESERT RES INST, UNIV NEV, RENO, 65- *Personal Data:* b San Francisco, Calif, July 6, 27; m 54; c 2. *Educ:* Univ Calif, Los Angeles, BA, 49, MA, 51. *Honors & Awards:* Paul Tuntland Mem Res Award, Soaring Soc Am, 54. *Prof Exp:* Res meteorologist, Univ Calif, Los Angeles, 51-56; field dir flight group meteorol, Air Force Cambridge Res Labs, Edwards AFB, Calif, 58-61, chief, Exp Meterol Br, 61-65. *Mem:* AAAS; Am Meteorol Soc; Royal Meteorol Soc; Sigma Xi. *Res:* Mountain meteorology; air flow over mountains; mountain lee waves; meso-scale meteorology; synoptic meteorology and climatology; severe storms; snow water resources; macrophysics of clouds. *Mailing Add:* Desert Res Inst Lab Atmo Stead Facil PO Box 60221 Reno NV 89506

KLIEGER, PAUL, CIVIL ENGINEERING, CONCRETE DURABILITY. *Current Pos:* CONSULT, CONCRETE & CONCRETE MAT, 86- *Personal Data:* b Milwaukee, Wis, Oct 26, 16; m 42; c 1. *Educ:* Univ Wis, BS, 39. *Honors & Awards:* Award of Merit, Am Soc Testing & Mat, 75, Frank Richart Award, 77; Hon Mem, Am Concrete Inst. *Prof Exp:* Mat inspector & state engr, Wis, 39; engr farm planning, Soil Conserv Serv, 39-41; sr res engr, 41-60, mgr field res sect, 60-63 & concrete res sect, Portland Cement Asn, 63-71, dir, concrete mat res dept, 71-86. *Concurrent Pos:* Mem, Hwy Res Bd & US Comt on Large Dams, Am Concrete Inst. *Mem:* Am Soc Testing & Mat; Am Concrete Inst. *Res:* cement and concrete technology; materials testing. *Mailing Add:* 3908 Dundee Rd Northbrook IL 60062

KLIEJUNAS, JOHN THOMAS, PLANT PATHOLOGY. *Current Pos:* plant pathologist, 79-87, SUPVR PLANT PATHOLOGIST, PAC SOUTHWEST REGION, US FOREST SERV, 87- *Personal Data:* b Sheboygan, Wis, May 4, 43; m 68, Barbara; c Trina & Mary. *Educ:* Univ Wis-Stevens Point, BS, 65; Univ Minn, MF, 67; Univ Wis-Madison, PhD(plant path), 71. *Prof Exp:* Fel plant path, Univ Wis-Madison, 71-72; jr plant pathologist, Univ Hawaii, Hilo, 72-75, asst plant pathologist, 75-79. *Mem:* Am Phytopath Soc. *Res:* Epidemiology and control of forest nursery disease and other diseases of Californian forest trees. *Mailing Add:* Forest Pest Mgt 630 Sansome St San Francisco CA 94111

KLIEM, PETER O, ANALYTICAL CHEMISTRY, PHOTOGRAPHIC CHEMISTRY. *Current Pos:* asst scientist to sr scientist, 60-66, Polaroid Corp, dept mgr to sr develop mgr, 66-75, div vpres negative res & develop, 75-77, asst corp vpres res, 77-80, vpres res, 80-, SR VPRES, POLAROID CORP. *Personal Data:* b Berlin, Ger, May 13, 38; US citizen; m 62; c 3. *Educ:* Bates Col, BS, 60; Northeastern Univ, MS, 65. *Concurrent Pos:* Sr vpres & dir res & eng, Polaroid Corp. *Mem:* Nat Acad Sci; Soc Photog Sci & Eng; Indust Res Inst; Am Chem Soc. *Res:* Electronic imaging, medical diagnostic research and development; general management, photographic research and development. *Mailing Add:* 75 Grove St Wellesley MA 02181

KLIER, KAMIL, PHYSICAL CHEMISTRY. *Current Pos:* vis prof physics & chem of solids & surfaces, 67-68, res assoc prof, 68-73, PROF CHEM, LEHIGH UNIV, 73-, DIR, CATALYSIS LAB, 75-, ASSOC DIR, CTR SURFACE RES, 78- *Personal Data:* b Prague, Czech, Mar 21, 32; m 61; c 2. *Educ:* Charles Univ, Prague, dipl chem, 54; Czech Acad Sci, CSc(phys chem), 61. *Prof Exp:* Res fel surface phys chem, Inst Phys Chem, Czech Acad Sci, 54-57, asst, 57-61, res scientist, 61-67. *Concurrent Pos:* Int Atomic Energy Agency fel radiation chem surfaces, Wantage Res Labs, Eng, 59-60; consult catalysis, spectros & separation processes. *Mem:* Am Chem Soc; Sigma Xi. *Res:* Physics and chemistry of solids; surface chemistry; chemisorption; catalysis. *Mailing Add:* Ctr Surface Coatings Lehigh Univ Bethlehem PA 18015

KLIEWER, JOHN WALLACE, MEDICAL ENTOMOLOGY, ENVIRONMENTAL PROTECTION. *Current Pos:* CONSULT, 90- *Personal Data:* b Lanigan, Sask, Jan 20, 24; US citizen; m 54; c 4. *Educ:* Bethel Col, Kans, BA(biol), 50; Univ Utah, MS(Invert Zool), 52; Univ Kans, PhD(entom), 62. *Honors & Awards:* Spec Achievement Awards, Environ Protection Agency, 87 & 88. *Prof Exp:* Asst prof biol sci, Bethel Col, Kans, 53-56; sr vector control specialist & proj leader, Calif State Dept Pub Health, 60-67; proj officer, Aedes Aegypti Eradication Prog, 67-69, sr res entomologist, Malaria Prog, Ctr Dis Control, USPHS, 69-72; pesticides specialist, Pesticide Prog, Environ Protection Agency, 72-90. *Concurrent Pos:* Consult, WHO, 66-, AID, 83; adj prof prev med, Med Univ SC, 74-83. *Mem:* Entom Soc Am; Am Mosquito Control Asn; Am Registry Prof Entomologists; Soc Vector Ecologists. *Res:* Ecology and behavior of insects, mites and ticks; public health and agricultural uses of pesticides; environmental aspects of pest control. *Mailing Add:* 9805 Meadow Knoll Ct Vienna VA 22181

KLIEWER, KENNETH L, THEORETICAL SOLID STATE PHYSICS, COMPUTATIONAL SCIENCE. *Current Pos:* DIR, CTR COMPUT & SCI, OAK RIDGE NAT LAB, 92- *Personal Data:* b Mountain Lake, Minn, Dec 31, 35; m 59, Kathleen Kay Zimmermann; c Steven Anthony, Lisa Jo & Christopher Lee. *Educ:* Univ Minn, BS, 57, MSEE, 59; Univ Ill,

PhD(physics), 64. *Prof Exp:* From asst prof to assoc prof, Iowa State Univ, 63-69, prof physics, 69-81; assoc dir phys res, Argonne Nat Lab, 81-86; dean, Sch Sci, Purdue Univ, 86-91, asst vpres res, 91-92. *Concurrent Pos:* From assoc physicist to sr physicist, Ames Lab, US Dept Energy, 63-81, prog dir solid state physics, 74-78, assoc dir sci & technol, 78-81, mem staff, Off Basic Eng Sci, Off Energy Res, 79-80; guest prof, Univ Hamburg, Ger, 72-73, Free Univ, Berlin, 74 & Fritz-Haber Inst, Berlin, 75; vis scientist, Rockwell Int Sci Ctr, Thousand Oaks, Calif, 76. *Mem:* Fel Am Phys Soc; AAAS; Sigma Xi. *Res:* Optical properties of solids, particularly metals; lattice dynamics; surface physics; photoemission; optics; electro chemistry; data storage systems and strategies for high performance computing environments. *Mailing Add:* Oak Ridge Nat Lab Bldg 4500N PO Box 2008 MS 6203 Oak Ridge TN 37831. *Fax:* 423-241-2850; *E-Mail:* kliewer@ccs.ornl.gov

KLIEWER, WALTER MARK, BIOCHEMISTRY, PLANT PHYSIOLOGY. *Current Pos:* asst biochemist, 63-68, assoc biochemist, 68-74, BIOCHEMIST, UNIV CALIF, DAVIS, 74- *Personal Data:* b Escondido, Calif, Dec 10, 33; m 62, Helga E Bedacht; c 1. *Educ:* Calif State Polytech Col, BS, 55; Cornell Univ, MS, 58, PhD(agron), 61. *Prof Exp:* Scientist, Soil Conserv Serv, USDA, 55; fel, Ore State Univ, 61-63. *Concurrent Pos:* Pres, Am Soc Viticult & Enol, 82. *Mem:* Am Soc Plant Physiol; Am Soc Enol; Am Soc Hort Sci; Sigma Xi. *Res:* Effect of environment on fruit quality and growth and development of grapevines; organic acid, amino acid and carbohydrate metabolism of grapevines; translocation; photosynthesis; plant growth regulators; fruit coloration; mineral nutrition; vineyard canopy management. *Mailing Add:* 615 Coolidge St Davis CA 95616

KLIGER, DAVID SAUL, PHYSICAL CHEMISTRY, BIOPHYSICS. *Current Pos:* PROF CHEM, UNIV CALIF, SANTA CRUZ, 71-, DEAN NATURAL SCI, 90- *Personal Data:* b Newark, NJ, Nov 3, 43; m 79. *Educ:* Rutgers Univ, BS, 65; Cornell Univ, PhD(phys chem), 70. *Prof Exp:* NIH res fel phys chem, Harvard Univ, 70-71. *Concurrent Pos:* Petro Res Fund-Am Chem Soc res grant, Univ Calif, Santa Cruz, 71-74; NIH res grant, 73-; NSF res grant, 76- *Mem:* Am Soc Photobiol; Biophys Soc; Am Chem Soc. *Res:* Molecular spectroscopy; spectroscopic and photochemical studies of visual pigments; photochemistry; biophysics. *Mailing Add:* Div Natural Sci Univ Calif Santa Cruz CA 95064

KLIGMAN, ALBERT MONTGOMERY, DERMATOLOGY. *Current Pos:* resident dermat, Univ Hosp, 48-51, prof, Div Grad Med, Hosp Univ Pa, 58-72, from instr to assoc prof, 48-57, PROF DERMAT, SCH MED, UNIV PA, 57- *Personal Data:* b Philadelphia, Pa, Mar 17, 16; m 42; c 3. *Educ:* Pa State Univ, BS, 39; Univ Pa, PhD(bot), 42, MD, 47; Am Bd Dermat & Syphilol, dipl, 51. *Prof Exp:* Dir res, J B Swayne Co, Pa, 39-44; intern, N Div, Albert Einstein Med Ctr, 47-48. *Mem:* AAAS; Soc Invest Dermat; Soc Exp Biol & Med; AMA; Am Acad Dermat; Sigma Xi. *Res:* Medical mycology; dermatologic allergy. *Mailing Add:* Dermat Dept Univ Pa Clin Res Bldg 219 Philadelphia PA 19104

KLIGMAN, RONALD LEE, STATISTICAL MECHANICS, ACOUSTICS. *Current Pos:* RES PHYSICIST STATIST MECH & ACOUST, NAVAL SURFACE WEAPONS CTR, 72- *Personal Data:* b Philadelphia, Pa, Aug 20, 40; m 68; c 2. *Educ:* Temple Univ, BA, 62; Am Univ, MS, 67, PhD(physics), 68. *Prof Exp:* asst prof physics, Sweetbriar Col, 68-69; physicist acoust, Naval Ship Res & Develop Ctr, 69-71; asst prof physics, Robert Col, 71-72. *Mem:* Am Phys Soc. *Res:* Statistical mechanics applied to phase transitions in solids; transport theory in ionized media; wave propagation and scattering, acoustic and electromagnetic. *Mailing Add:* 1394 Canterbury Way Rockville MD 20854

KLIJANOWICZ, JAMES EDWARD, ORGANIC CHEMISTRY. *Current Pos:* Sr res chemist, 70-78, res lab head, Chemiphotog Systs Lab, 78-81, RES LAB HEAD, PHOTOG MECHANISMS LAB, EASTMAN KODAK CO, 81- *Personal Data:* b Baltimore, Md, Sept 24, 44; m 75; c 1. *Educ:* Loyola Col, Md, BS, 66; Carnegie-Mellon Univ, MS, 69, PhD(org chem), 71. *Mem:* AAAS; Am Chem Soc; Sigma Xi. *Res:* Mechanisms of photographic chemical reactions. *Mailing Add:* 7 Millstone Ct Pittsford NY 14534-3238

KLIMAN, ALLAN, INTERNAL MEDICINE. *Current Pos:* instr, 61-71, ASST CLIN PROF MED, HARVARD MED SCH, 71-; CHIEF, HEMAT-ONCOL DEPT, SPAULDING REHAB HOSP, 74- *Personal Data:* b Boston, Mass, Dec 20, 33; m 56; c 2. *Educ:* Harvard Univ, AB, 54, MD, 58. *Prof Exp:* Res assoc org chem, Harvard Univ, 53-54, res assoc endocrinol, 55; intern, Beth Israel Hosp, 58-59; chief, Clin Ctr Blood Bank, NIH, 59-61. *Concurrent Pos:* Med dir, Mass Red Cross Blood Prog, 64-74; clin assoc med, Mass Gen Hosp. *Mem:* Am Fedn Clin Res; Am Soc Hemat. *Res:* Hematology; blood transfusion; serum hepatitis; automation of laboratory procedures; plasmapheresis; cancer chemotherapy; clinical pharmacology. *Mailing Add:* 40 Newton St Brookline MA 02146

KLIMAN, GERALD BURT, ROTATING & LINEAR ELECTRIC MACHINES, RECIPIENTS FAILURE DIAGNOSTICS. *Current Pos:* electromagnetic engr advan propulsion equip prog, Transp Technol Ctr, 71-75, prin engr, Fast Breeder Reactor Dept, 75-77, ELEC ENGR, CORP RES & DEVELOP, GEN ELEC CO, 77- *Personal Data:* b Boston, Mass, July 28, 31; m 60, Edith Moses; c Jonathan & Daniel. *Educ:* Mass Inst Technol, SB, 55, SM, 59, ScD(elec eng), 65. *Prof Exp:* Armaments & electronics officer, USAF, 55-57; teaching asst elec eng, Mass Inst Technol, 57-61, instr, 61-65; asst prof, Rensselaer Polytech Inst, 65-71. *Mem:* Fel Inst Elec & Electronics Engrs; Am Phys Soc; Int Conf Elec Mach. *Res:* Magnetohydrodynamics; Alfven waves in wave guides; electromagnetic pumps; electrical machines, magnetic materials and electronic drive systems; fecipient failure diagnostics. *Mailing Add:* Corp Res & Develop Gen Elec Co Schenectady NY 12301-0008. *Fax:* 518-387-6675; *E-Mail:* kliman@crd.ge.com

KLIMAN, HARVEY LOUIS, PHYSICAL CHEMISTRY, POLYMER PHYSICS. *Current Pos:* SR RES CHEMIST POLYMER CHEM & PHYSICS, FIBERS DEPT, FIBERS & COMPOSITES DEVELOP CTRS, E I DU PONT DE NEMOURS & CO, INC, 69- *Personal Data:* b Boston, Mass, May 28, 42; m 66. *Educ:* Boston Univ, AB, 63; Princeton Univ, MA, 66, PhD(phys chem), 70. *Mem:* AAAS; Am Chem Soc; Sigma Xi. *Res:* High pressure physical chemistry of solutions; hydrophobic interactions in biochemical macromolecules; physical chemistry and physics of fiber forming polymers; textile yarn process engineering; computer modelling; composites. *Mailing Add:* 48 H Webb Rd Chadds Ford PA 19317-9125

KLIMAS-TAVANTZIS, DOROTHY J, CLINICAL NUTRITION. *Current Pos:* instr, 81, asst prof, 88-94, ASSOC PROF CLIN NUTRIT, UNIV MAINE, 94- *Personal Data:* b Greece, Nov 19, 52; US citizen. *Educ:* Beaver Col, Pa, BA, 74; Pa State Univ, MS, 78, PhD(nutrit), 82. *Prof Exp:* Lab asst, Dept Biol, Beaver Col, 73-74; res asst, Dept Physiol, NO11 Lab Human Performance, Pa State Univ, 75-77 & Nutrit Prog, 78-80; asst prof sci, Husson Col, 83-85; vis scientist, Dept Physiol Chem & Dept Clin Chem, Univ Cologne, WGer, 86-87. *Concurrent Pos:* Invited speaker, Am Heart Asn, 91; Fulbright fel, 95-96. *Mem:* Sigma Xi. *Res:* Assessment and nutritional intervention in reducing cardiovascular risk factors in children and adolescents; lipid and lipoprotein metabolism as related to heart disease/diabetes; trace element metabolism and nutriture as related to atherosclerosis/osteoporosis; obesity and its effects on lipid metabolism. *Mailing Add:* Univ Maine Merrill Hall Rm 20 Food Sci Orono ME 04469

KLIMEK, JOSEPH JOHN, INFECTIOUS DISEASES, HOSPITAL EPIDEMIOLOGY. *Current Pos:* Intern & resident med, Hartford Hosp, 72-74, fel infectious dis, 74-76, chief epidemiol, 76-88, assoc dir infectious dis & asst dir med, 76-88, assoc dir med, 88-90, dir, Aids Prog, 85-90, DIR DEPT MED, HARTFORD HOSP, CONN, 90-; ASSOC DIR, DEPT MED, UNIV CONN SCH MED, 90-, PROF MED, 90- *Personal Data:* b Wilkes-Barre, Pa, Sept 14, 46; m 71, Jane Stout; c Adam. *Educ:* Princeton Univ, AB, 68; Pa State Univ, MD, 72. *Honors & Awards:* Lange Award, Pa State Univ Col Med, 72; Am Red Cross Commun Award, 88. *Concurrent Pos:* From asst prof to assoc prof med, Sch Med, Univ Conn, 77-90; sr ed, Am J Infection Control, 82-; lectr, Merck Sharpe & Dohme Vaccine, 82-; med ed, Asepsis, Infection Control Forum, 83-; bd dir, Asn Practr Infection Control, 78-82. *Mem:* Fel Am Col Physicians; fel Infectious Dis Soc Am; Am Soc Microbiol; Soc Hosp Epidemiologists Am; Am Pub Health Asn; AAAS; Asn Practr Infection Control. *Res:* Hospital epidemiology and infection control; antibiotic pharmacokinetics; acquired immunodeficiency syndrome. *Mailing Add:* Hartford Hosp 80 Seymour St Hartford CT 06102-5037. *Fax:* 860-545-5057

KLIMISCH, RICHARD L, CATALYSIS, ENVIRONMENTAL HEALTH. *Current Pos:* sr res chemist, 67-71, supvry res chemist, Fuels & Lubrication Dept, 71-73, asst dept head, Phys Chem Dept, 73-75, DEPT HEAD, ENVIRON SCI DEPT, GEN MOTORS RES LABS, 75- *Personal Data:* b Yankton, SDak, Jan 1, 38; m 62; c 2. *Educ:* Loras Col, BS, 60; Purdue Univ, PhD(org chem), 64. *Prof Exp:* Res chemist, Explosives Dept, Exp Sta, E I du Pont de Nemours & Co, Inc, 64-67. *Mem:* Am Chem Soc; Sigma Xi. *Res:* Catalysis; air pollution; surface chemistry; atmospheric chemistry. *Mailing Add:* 43 Fairford Rd Grosse Pointe Shores MI 48236-2617

KLIMKO, EUGENE M, MATHEMATICS. *Current Pos:* MEM FAC, DEPT MATH, STATE UNIV NY, BINGHAMTON, 73- *Personal Data:* b Youngstown, Ohio, Mar 13, 39. *Educ:* Ohio State Univ, BS, 61, MS, 64, PhD(math), 67. *Prof Exp:* Sr res eng, NAm Aviation, Inc, 62-65; asst prof math, 67-75. *Mem:* Am Math Soc; Inst Math Statist. *Res:* Application of ratio ergodic theorems to Glivenko-Cantelli theorem and to convergence of information ratios. *Mailing Add:* Dept Math Sci State Univ NY Binghamton NY 13901

KLIMPEL, GARY R, INTERFERON, CYTOTOXIC EFFECTOR CELLS. *Current Pos:* ASSOC PROF MICROBIOL & IMMUNOL, MED BR, UNIV TEX, 80- *Educ:* Univ Ariz, PhD(microbiol), 76. *Mailing Add:* Dept Microbiol Univ Tex Med Br Galveston TX 77555-1019. *Fax:* 409-772-5065

KLIMPEL, RICHARD ROBERT, MINERAL PROCESSING, PARTICLE TECHNOLOGY. *Current Pos:* PRES RK ASSOC, 95- *Personal Data:* b Billings, Mont, Sept 23, 39; c 2. *Educ:* NDak State Univ, BS, 61, MS, 62; Pa State Univ, PhD(mat sci), 64. *Honors & Awards:* Robert H Richards Award, Am Inst Mining Engrs, 88; Arthur F Taggert Award, Soc Mining, Metall & Explor, 92, Antoine M Gaudin Award, 95. *Prof Exp:* Teaching asst math, NDak State Univ, 61-62; res assoc fuel sci, Pa State Univ, 62-64; res mgr math, 64-77; sr res scientist eng, Dow Chem Co, 77-95. *Concurrent Pos:* Lectr math, Saginaw Valley State Col, 65-75; adj prof mineral eng, Pa State Univ, 78-95, mat sci, Univ Fla, 95- *Mem:* Sigma Xi; Am Inst Mining Engrs; Am Inst Chem Engrs; Am Chem Soc; Soc Mining, Metall & Explor (pres, 97). *Res:* Mining chemicals; math modeling of engineering processes; operations research; engineering research in grinding, flotation, solids separation and other related particulate handling processes. *Mailing Add:* 4805 Oakridge Dr Midland MI 48640. *Fax:* 517-835-3141

KLIMSTRA, PAUL D, MEDICINAL CHEMISTRY, PROJECT MANAGEMENT. *Current Pos:* MGT-TECHNOL CONSULT, 93- *Personal Data:* b Erie, Ill, Aug 25, 33; m 57; c David & Jonathan. *Educ:* Augustana Col, BA, 55; Univ Iowa, MS, 57, PhD, 59. *Prof Exp:* Res chemist, G D Searle & Co, 59-70, from asst dir to dir chem res, 70-73, dir preclin res & develop, 73-74, vpres NAm Preclin Res & Develop, 74-86, sr vpres, World-Wide Preclin Develop, 86-89, exec vpres, Sci & Technol, 89-93. *Concurrent Pos:* Mem, Intra-Sci Res Found & Indust Res Inst. *Mem:* Sigma Xi; fel Indust Res Inst; Am Chem Soc; Am Soc Pharmacol & Exp Therapeut. *Res:* Steroids; heterocyclics; science management; pharmaceutical research and development-business management. *Mailing Add:* 1670 Chapel Ct Northbrook IL 60062. *Fax:* 847-272-4690

KLINCK, JOHN MICHAEL, PHYSICAL OCEANOGRAPHY. *Current Pos:* assoc prof, 89-96, PROF OCEANOG, CTR COASTAL PHYS OCEANOG, OLD DOMINION UNIV, 96- *Personal Data:* b Ft Monmouth, NJ, May 15, 50; m 79, Eileen E Hofman; c Julian Michael. *Educ:* Clemson Univ, BS, 72; Univ NC, MS, 75; NC State Univ, PhD(marine sci), 80. *Prof Exp:* Postdoctoral res assoc, Fla State Univ, 79-81; asst res scientist, Tex A&M Univ, 81-83, asst prof, 83-89. *Mem:* Am Geophys Union; Am Meteorol Soc; Europ Geophys Soc; AAAS; Nat Shellfisheries Asn. *Res:* Analytical and numerical modelling of physical and biological processes in oceanic, coastal and estuarine environments; analysis of marine observations. *Mailing Add:* CCPO Crittenton Hall Old Dominion Univ Norfolk VA 23529. *E-Mail:* klinck@ccpo.odu.edu

KLINCK, ROSS EDWARD, PHYSICAL & ORGANIC CHEMISTRY. *Current Pos:* assoc prof & chmn, Sci Div, Adirondack Community Col, 78-83, asst dean, 84-86, exec asst to pres, 89-94, PROF CHEM, ADIRONDACK COMMUNITY COL, 79- *Personal Data:* b Kitchener, Ont, Dec 1, 38; m 63, Joyce Kennedy; c Bryan. *Educ:* Univ Western Ont, BSc, 60, PhD(chem), 65. *Prof Exp:* Res assoc physics, Duke Univ, 64-66; asst prof chem, Univ Conn, 66-71; assoc prof chem, Urbana Col, 71-76, coordr sci, 74-76. *Concurrent Pos:* Vis researcher chem, Univ Western Ont, 72-77 & 86-87. *Mem:* Am Chem Soc; Chem Inst Can. *Res:* High resolution nuclear magnetic resonance spectroscopy related to conformational studies and barriers to rotation; homoenolization of cyclic ketones; MNDO and molecular mechanics calculations. *Mailing Add:* Adirondack Community Col Glens Falls NY 12801. *E-Mail:* klinckr@acc.sunyacc.edu

KLINE, BERRY JAMES, CHROMATOGRAPHY. *Current Pos:* asst dir, 83-90, DIR, ANALYTICAL RES & DEVELOP, BRISTOL-MYERS SQUIBB PHARM RES INST, 90- *Personal Data:* b Mont Alto, Pa, Jan 9, 41; m 63, Darlene Baranowske; c Michele & Danielle. *Educ:* Philadelphia Col Pharm, BS, 62; Temple Univ, MS, 65; Univ Wis, PhD(pharm), 68. *Prof Exp:* Sr analyst, Vick Divisions Res, Richardson-Merrell, Inc, 68-69; Sr scientist, CIBA Pharmaceut Co, 69-72, sr staff scientist, CIBA-Geigy Pharmaceut, 72-76; assoc prof & dir, anal serv, Sch Pharm, Med Col Va, 76-83. *Concurrent Pos:* Consult, NIH-Nat Cancer Inst. *Mem:* Am Pharmaceut Asn; Am Asn Pharmaceut Scientists; Am Chem Soc; fel Am Found, Pharmaceut Educ; Sigma Xi. *Res:* Homogeneous solution kinetics; complexation interactions; pharmaceutical analysis, especially gas and high performance liquid chromatography. *Mailing Add:* Bristol-Myers Squibb PO Box 191 New Brunswick NJ 08903-0191

KLINE, BRUCE CLAYTON, MOLECULAR BIOLOGY, MICROBIOLOGY. *Current Pos:* assoc prof microbiol, 84-87, PROF BIOCHEM & MOLECULAR BIOL, GRAD SCH MED, MAYO CLIN, ROCHESTER, MINN, 87-; CONSULT, 75- *Personal Data:* b Grand Rapids, Mich, June 22, 37; m 63; c 3. *Educ:* Aquinas Col, BS, 59; Mich State Univ, MS, 66, PhD(microbiol), 68. *Prof Exp:* Microbiologist, Mich Dept Health, 60-63; instr microbial genetics, Mich State Univ, 68; asst prof biochem, Univ Tenn, Knoxville, 71-75. *Concurrent Pos:* NIH fel, Univ Calif, San Diego, 68-70; assoc prof microbiol, Univ Minn, 80-84. *Mem:* Am Soc Microbiol; fel Am Acad Microbiol. *Res:* Mechanism and control of plasmid maintenance in procaryotic organisms; control DNA replication, Domain analysis in proteins. *Mailing Add:* Dept Molecular Biol & Med Mayo Med Sch 200 First St SW Rochester MN 55905-0001

KLINE, DANIEL LOUIS, PHYSIOLOGY. *Current Pos:* from chmn dept to prof, 66-88, EMER PROF PHYSIOL, COL MED, UNIV CINCINNATI, 88- *Personal Data:* b Philadelphia, Pa, Dec 25, 17; m 45; c 3. *Educ:* Purdue Univ, BS, 42; Columbia Univ, PhD(physiol), 46. *Honors & Awards:* Harold Lamport Award, NY Acad Sci, 79. *Prof Exp:* Instr physiol, Col Physicians & Surgeons, Columbia Univ, 45; instr, Long Island Col Med, 46-47; nat res coun fel physiol chem, Sch Med, Yale Univ, 47-49, asst prof, 49-52, from asst prof to assoc prof physiol, 52-66. *Concurrent Pos:* Guggenheim fel, 58-59. *Mem:* AAAS; Sigma Xi; Soc Exp Biol & Med; Int Soc Thrombosis & Haemostasis; Am Physiol Soc. *Res:* Purification of plasminogen and plasmin; mechanism of activation. *Mailing Add:* Dept Physiol Univ Cincinnati Col Med ML 576 Cincinnati OH 45267-0001

KLINE, DAVID G, NEUROSURGERY. *Current Pos:* instr surg & neurosurg, La State Univ, New Orleans, 67-68; asst prof neurosurg, 68-70; assoc prof surg & neurosurg, 70-71, prof neurosurg, 71-73, prof surg & neurosurg, 73-76, chmn div, 71-76, PROF NEUROSURG & CHMN DEPT, SCH MED, LA STATE UNIV, NEW ORLEANS, 76- *Personal Data:* b Philadelphia, Pa, Oct 13, 34; m 58; c 3. *Educ:* Univ Pa, AB, 56, MD, 60. *Honors & Awards:* Frederick A Coller Award, Am Col Surgeons, 67. *Prof Exp:* From intern to resident surg, Univ Mich, Ann Arbor, 60-62; res investr neurosurg, Walter Reed Gen Hosp & Inst Res, 62-64; teaching assoc, Univ Mich & res investr, Kresge Neurosurg Labs, 64-67. *Concurrent Pos:* Vis investr, Delta Regional Primate Ctr, 67-; vis surgeon, Charity Hosp, New Orleans, 67-; mem staff, Southern Baptist Hosp, Hotel Dieu, Touro Infirmary & Ochsner Clin & Found, 67-; consult, Keesler AFB, 69-, USPHS Hosp, 71- & Vet Admin Hosp, 74; secy, Am Bd Neurol Surg. *Mem:* Cong Neurol Surg; Asn Acad Surg; Am Asn Neurol Surg; Soc Univ Surgeons; Res Soc Neurosurgeons; Soc Neurol Surg (treas, 87-92); Am Bd Neurol Surg (secy, 78-83, chmn, 83-84); Southern Neurol Surg Soc (secy, 75-78, pres, 85-86). *Res:* Peripheral nerve injuries and their repair; computer utilization for neurosurgical research; hepatic encephalopathy. *Mailing Add:* Dept Neurosurg La State Univ Sch Med 1542 Tulane Ave New Orleans LA 70112-2865

KLINE, DONALD EDGAR, PHYSICS. *Current Pos:* from assoc prof to prof nuclear eng, 61-68, prof mat sci, 68-, EMER PROF MAT SCI, PA STATE UNIV. *Personal Data:* b DuBois, Pa, Aug 28, 28; m 49; c 3. *Educ:* Pa State Univ, BS, 51, MS, 53, PhD(physics), 55. *Prof Exp:* Instr eng mech, Pa State Univ, 54-55, asst prof physics, 55-56, vis physicist, Nuclear Reactor Facil, 56-57; staff res physicist, HRB-Singer, Inc, 57-61. *Concurrent Pos:* Consult, Jet Propulsion Lab, Calif Inst Technol, NASA, HRB-Singer, Inc, Avco Corp, Pfaudler, Hershey Med Ctr & NETCO. *Mem:* Am Phys Soc; Am Nuclear Soc; Am Soc Eng Educ. *Res:* Radiation effects; dosimetry; polymer physics; polymer impregnated concrete, wood, biomaterials; composite polymer systems. *Mailing Add:* 1210 E Branch Rd State College PA 16801

KLINE, FRANK MENEFEE, PSYCHIATRY. *Current Pos:* prof psychiat & vchmn dept, 78-92, EMER CLIN PROF PSYCHIAT, UNIV CALIF, IRVINE, 92-; EMER PROF, UNIV SOUTHERN CALIF. *Personal Data:* b Cumberland, Md, May 14, 28; m 53; c 2. *Educ:* Univ Md, BS, 50, MD, 52. *Prof Exp:* Intern med, Cincinnati Gen Hosp, 52-53; psychiat resident, Brentwood Vet Admin Hosp, Los Angeles, 55-58; consult, E Los Angeles Probation Off, 60-63; psychiat consult, Univ High Sch & Francis Blend Sch Blind, Los Angeles, 64-67; regional chief, W Cent Ment Health Serv, Los Angeles Co, 67-68; assoc dir, Psychiat Outpatient Dept, Los Angeles Co-Univ Southern Calif Med Ctr, 68-77; chief psychiat, Long Beach Vet Med Ctr, 77-92. *Concurrent Pos:* Pvt pract, 58-; instr, Exten Div, Southern Calif Psychoanal Inst, 64-67; instr, Inst, 67-79; fac mem, Psychother Group, Los Angeles Ctr, 67-69; reviewer, JAPA & J Neuropsychiat; assoc prof psychiat, Sch Med, Univ Southern Calif, 74-78; consult, Los Angeles Co Ment Health, 92-; staff physician, Martin Luther King Hosp, 92- *Res:* Evaluation of psychotropic drugs; training of psychiatric residents and evaluation of the best methods for accomplishing this; group psychotherapy, particularly as a device for maintaining competence in practicing psychotherapists; historical evolution of psychoanalytic and psychodynamic theory. *Mailing Add:* 24 Sorrel Lane Rolling Hills CA 90274-4226

KLINE, GORDON MABEY, PLASTICS CHEMISTRY, POLYMER ENGINEERING. *Current Pos:* RETIRED. *Personal Data:* b Trenton, NJ, Feb 9, 03; wid; c 1. *Educ:* Colgate Univ, AB, 25; George Washington Univ, MS, 26; Univ Md, PhD(chem), 34. *Honors & Awards:* Gold Medal, Dept Com, 53; Am Soc Testing & Mat Award, 54; Rosa Award, Nat Bur Standards, 65; Am Nat Standards Inst Award, 87; Plastics Hall of Fame, 73. *Prof Exp:* Res chemist, State Dept Health, NY, 26-28 & Picatinny Arsenal, Dept of War, 28-29; chief plastics sect, Nat Bur Standards, 29-52, chief, Div Polymers, 52-63; consult, 64-69; sci editor, 69-90. *Concurrent Pos:* Tech ed, Mod Plastics, 36-90; ed dir & consult, Mod Plastics Encycl, 36-60; chmn, Fed Specifications Plastics Tech Comt, 41-54; tech investr, US Army, Europe, 45; chmn tech comt plastics & US deleg, Int Standardization Orgn, var US & foreign countries, 51-90; hon secy, Plastics & High Polymers Sect, Int Union Pure & Appl Chem, 51-59, from vpres to pres, 59-67. *Mem:* Am Chem Soc; Am Soc Testing & Mat; Soc Plastics Eng; Soc Plastics Indust; fel Am Inst Chem. *Res:* Plastics; adhesives; polymers; pioneer in research on testing methods and properties of polymers and plastics and in the preparation and adoption of engineering standards for polymeric materials and products. *Mailing Add:* 3063 Donnelly Dr Apt C-318 Lantana FL 33462-6405

KLINE, IRA, cancer; deceased, see previous edition for last biography

KLINE, IRWIN KAVEN, MEDICINE, PATHOLOGY. *Current Pos:* CHMN PATH, LANKENAU HOSP, 69-; PROF PATH, JEFFERSON MED COL, THOMAS JEFFERSON UNIV, PA, 79- *Personal Data:* b Canton, Ohio, Mar 18, 31; m 56, Tilde Saphir; c 4. *Educ:* Columbia Univ, AB, 53; Western Res Univ, MD, 57; Am Bd Path, dipl, 62. *Prof Exp:* Intern, Mt Sinai Hosp, Cleveland, 57-58; resident path, Michael Reese Hosp, Chicago, 58-63; USPHS trainee, 60-63; instr, Univ Ill Col Med, 63-64; asst prof, Sch Med & assoc pathologist, Hosp, Boston Univ, 64-66; clin assoc path, Harvard Med Sch, 66-68; asst pathologist, Mass Gen Hosp, 68-69; from clin assoc prof to clin prof path, Sch Med, Temple Univ, 69-79. *Concurrent Pos:* Pathologist & chief anat path, Cambridge City Hosp, 66-68. *Mem:* Int Soc Lymphology; fel Col Am Pathologists; Am Soc Clin Path; Am Asn Path; fel Am Col Cardiologists; AMA. *Res:* Cardiac disease, principally infections and immunologic myocarditis and the effect of the obstructed cardiac lymphatics. *Mailing Add:* Dept Path Lankenau Hosp 100 E Lancaster Ave Wynnewood PA 19096-1419. *Fax:* 610-645-8456

KLINE, JACOB, biomedical engineering, for more information see previous edition

KLINE, JENNIE KATHERINE, EPIDEMIOLOGY. *Current Pos:* SR RES SCIENTIST, NY STATE PSYCHIAT INST, 75- *Personal Data:* b Boston, Mass, Jan 15, 50. *Educ:* Univ Chicago, BA, 72; Columbia Univ, MS, 74, PhD(epidemiol), 77. *Concurrent Pos:* Adj assoc prof public health, Sch Pub

Health & Gertrude H Sergievsky Ctr, Columbia Univ, 85- *Mem:* Soc Epidemiol Res; Int Epidemiol Asn; Am Pub Health Asn; Am Epidemiol Soc. *Res:* Epidemiology of fetal defects and spontaneous abortions; mental retardation; prenatal HIV infection. *Mailing Add:* 722 W 168th St Unit 53 New York NY 10032. *Fax:* 212-795-5886

KLINE, JERRY ROBERT, SOIL CHEMISTRY, ANALYTICAL CHEMISTRY. *Current Pos:* ADMIN JUDGE, ATOMIC SAFETY & LICENSING BD, US NUCLEAR REGULATORY COMN, 80- *Personal Data:* b Minneapolis, Minn, May 20, 32; m 54; c 5. *Educ:* Univ Minn, BS, 57, MS, 60; Univ Minn, PhD(soil sci), 64. *Prof Exp:* Res assoc neutron activation appl to soils, Argonne Nat Lab, 64-65; assoc scientist, PR Nuclear Ctr, 65-66, dir terrestrial ecol proj, 66-68; ecologist, Radiol & Environ Res Div, Argonne Nat Lab, 68-74; sr land use analyst, US Nuclear Regulatory Comn, 74-76, sect leader, 76-80. *Concurrent Pos:* Adj prof, Univ Ill, Chicago Circle, 72-76. *Mem:* AAAS; Sigma Xi; Nature Conservancy. *Res:* Terrestrial ecology; trace elements in environmental systems; water relationships in soil-plant systems. *Mailing Add:* 13624 Middlevale Lane Silver Spring MD 20906

KLINE, KENNETH A(LAN), ENGINEERING MECHANICS, MECHANICAL ENGINEERING. *Current Pos:* assoc prof, 66-73, PROF MECH ENG, 73-, CHMN MECH ENG, WAYNE STATE UNIV, 86- *Personal Data:* b Chicago, Ill, July 11, 39; m 60; c 4. *Educ:* Univ Minn, BS, 61, PhD(eng mech), 65. *Prof Exp:* Sr res engr, Esso Prod Res Co, Stand Oil Co, NJ, 65-66. *Concurrent Pos:* Prin investr, NSF res grants, 67-68, 69-71, 72-75, 76-78 & 80-82; Sr US Scientist Award, Alexander von Humboldt-Stiftung, 72-73; co-prin investr, Dept Energy res grant, 77-79; prin investr, Glm res grant, 80-81, Ford res grants, 84, TACOM res grant, 84-86. *Mem:* Soc Rheology; Soc Automotive Engrs; Am Soc Mech Engrs; Sigma Xi; Am Inst Astronaut & Aeronaut. *Res:* Computer-aided structural analysis; boundary integral method of structural analysis; optimal design; structural dynamics, system identification. *Mailing Add:* Mech Eng Dept Wayne State Univ 5050 Anthony Wayne Dr Detroit MI 48202-4095

KLINE, LARRY KEITH, MOLECULAR BIOLOGY. *Current Pos:* asst prof, 71-74, ASSOC PROF BIOL SCI, STATE UNIV NY COL BROCKPORT, 74- *Personal Data:* b Buffalo, NY, Oct 20, 39; m 61; c 3. *Educ:* Valparaiso Univ, BS, 61; Pa State Univ, MS, 65; State Univ NY, Buffalo, PhD(biochem), 70. *Prof Exp:* Asst cancer res scientist, Roswell Park Mem Inst, 65-67; NIH fel, Yale Univ, 69-71. *Mem:* AAAS; Sigma Xi. *Res:* Nucleic acid biosynthesis and function in mammalian cells. *Mailing Add:* Dept Biol Sci State Univ NY 350 New Campus Dr Brockport NY 14420-2915

KLINE, LOREN W, NEUROPHYSICS. *Current Pos:* Asst prof med, 73-83, PROF ORAL BIOL, UNIV ALTA, 83- *Personal Data:* b Bethlehem, Pa, July 18, 46. *Educ:* Buena Vista Col, BS, 68; Okla State Univ, MS, 69; Univ Alta, PhD(neurophys), 73. *Mem:* Am Physiol Soc; Am Soc Zoologists; Can Physiol Soc; Am Endocrinol Soc. *Mailing Add:* Dept Oral Biol Univ Alta Fac Dent Edmonton AB T6G 2N8 Can

KLINE, RALPH WILLARD, FOOD SCIENCE. *Current Pos:* RETIRED. *Personal Data:* b Omaha, Nebr, Sept 23, 17; m 46; c 2. *Educ:* Univ Omaha, AB, 39; Iowa State Univ, PhD(poultry prod technol), 45. *Prof Exp:* Mem staff, Food Res Div, Armour & Co, 42-80. *Concurrent Pos:* Consult, 80- *Mem:* Am Chem Soc; Poultry Sci Asn; Inst Food Technologists. *Res:* Technology of egg and poultry products. *Mailing Add:* 4940 E Laurel Lane Phoenix AZ 85254-4641

KLINE, RAYMOND MILTON, ELECTRICAL ENGINEERING. *Current Pos:* from asst prof to assoc prof, 62-77, PROF ELEC ENG, WASH UNIV, 77- *Personal Data:* b St Louis, Mo, Feb 25, 29; m 51; c 4. *Educ:* Univ Mo-Rolla, BS, 51; Iowa State Univ, MS, 54; Purdue Univ, PhD(elec eng), 62. *Prof Exp:* Systs engr, Sperry Gyroscope Co, NY, 54-57; sr systs engr, Aircraft Div, McDonnell Aircraft Co, Mo, 57-59; instr elec eng, Purdue Univ, 59-62. *Mem:* Inst Elec & Electronics Engrs; Am Soc Eng Educ; Asn Comput Mach; Sigma Xi. *Res:* Design and application of information processing systems including digital computers, switching theory, especially areas in the field of artificial intelligence, pattern recognition and learning machines; image processing. *Mailing Add:* 14824 Ralls Dr Bridgeton MO 63044-1936

KLINE, RICHARD WILLIAM, POLYMER RHEOLOGY, ENERGY ENGINEERING. *Current Pos:* SR DEVELOP ENGR, CRYOVAC DIV, W R GRACE & CO, 76- *Personal Data:* b Philadelphia, Pa, Dec 33, 42. *Educ:* Mass Inst Technol, SB, 64, SM, 65, PhD(chem eng), 70. *Prof Exp:* Res engr, Milliken, Inc, 70-75; group leader, Lockwood Greene Engrs, 75-76. *Concurrent Pos:* Consult, Am Hoechst, 78-79, Batchelder-Blasius, Inc, 77-81, City Landrum, 80. *Mem:* Am Inst Chem Engrs; Soc Plastics Engrs; Sigma Xi. *Res:* Simulation and modelling of plasticating extrusion, including extruder screws and dies; development of rheological theory. *Mailing Add:* 711 Stallion Dr Auburn PA 17922

KLINE, ROBERT JOSEPH, inorganic chemistry; deceased, see previous edition for last biography

KLINE, RONALD ALAN, ENGINEERING. *Current Pos:* ASSOC PROF MECH ENG, UNIV OKLA, 82- *Personal Data:* b Wilkes-Barre, Pa, June 28, 52. *Educ:* Johns Hopkins Univ, BES, 74, MSE, 75, PhD(mech & mat sci), 78. *Prof Exp:* Res asst, Johns Hopkins Univ, 72-78; sr res scientist, Gen Dynamics Corp, 78-79; sr res engr, Gen Motors Res Labs, 79-82. *Mem:* Adhesion Soc Am; Am Soc Nondestructive Testing. *Res:* Mechanical behavior of fiber reinforced composite materials and adhesively bonded composite joints. *Mailing Add:* Dept Aerospace & Mech Eng Univ Okla 900 Asp Blvd Norman OK 73069-4857. *Fax:* 405-325-1088; *E-Mail:* rkline@ou.edu

KLINE, STEPHEN JAY, MECHANICAL ENGINEERING, FLUID MECHANICS. *Current Pos:* RETIRED. *Personal Data:* b Los Angeles, Calif, Feb 25, 22; c 3. *Educ:* Stanford Univ, BS, 43, MS, 49; Mass Inst Technol, ScD, 52. *Honors & Awards:* Melville Medal, Am Soc Mech Engrs, 59, Fluids Eng Award, 75; George Stephenson Medal, Brit Inst Mech Engrs, 66. *Prof Exp:* Res analyst turbomach, Aerophys Lab, NAm Aviation, Inc, 46-48; asst mech eng, Stanford Univ, 48-50; from instr to asst prof, Mass Inst Technol, 50-52; from asst prof to prof, Stanford Univ, 52-92, dir, Thermosci Div, 61-73. *Mem:* Nat Acad Eng; Am Soc Mech Engrs; AAAS; Nat Asn Sci Technol & Soc. *Res:* Internal flow; thermodynamics; industrial innovation; multidisciplinary thinking; international reassessment on knowledge of coherent structures which produce turbulence on boundary layers; zonal modeling of turbulent flows; uncertainty analysis; similitude and approximation theory. *Mailing Add:* Dept Mech Eng Rm 500V Stanford Univ Stanford CA 94305-3030

KLINE, TONI BETH, neurosciences, pharmacy, for more information see previous edition

KLINE, VIRGINIA MARCH, PLANT ECOLOGY, VEGETATION MANAGEMENT. *Current Pos:* STAFF ECOLOGIST, UNIV WIS ARBORETUM & LECTR BOT, UNIV WIS, 76- *Personal Data:* b Cleveland, Ohio, Jan 26, 26. *Educ:* Univ Wis, BS, 47, MS, 75, PhD(bot), 76. *Mem:* Am Inst Biol Sci; Ecol Soc Am; Sigma Xi. *Res:* Community ecology; prairie, temperate forest, wetland; relationship of climate and geology to vegetation; succession; management of natural vegetation. *Mailing Add:* Arboretum Univ Wis 1207 Seminole Hwy Madison WI 53711

KLINEBERG, JOHN MICHAEL, AEROSPACE ENGINEERING. *Current Pos:* aerospace engr, Ames Res Ctr, NASA, 70-74, Hq, 74-78, dep assoc adminr, aeronaut & space technol, 78-79, dep dir, 79-86, actg dir, 86-87, DIR, LEWIS RES CTR, NASA, 87- *Personal Data:* b New York City, NY, Oct 16, 38; m 67, Anne-Marie M Mellet; c Eric, Arnaud & Logan. *Educ:* Princeton Univ, BS, 60; Calif Inst Technol, MS, 62, PhD, 68. *Honors & Awards:* Meritorious Exec, US Gov, 86. *Prof Exp:* Engr, Douglas Aircraft Co, Santa Monica, 60-62; res engr, Calif Inst Technol, 68-70. *Concurrent Pos:* Bd govs, Nat Space Club, 87- *Mem:* Fel Am Inst Aeronaut & Astronaut; Nat Space Club; Sigma Xi. *Res:* Aerospace engineering. *Mailing Add:* Space Systems Loral 3825 Fabian Way Palo Alto CA 94303

KLINEDINST, KEITH ALLEN, CHEMICAL VAPOR DEPOSITION, ELECTROCHEMISTRY. *Current Pos:* MEM TECH STAFF MAT SCI LAB, GTE LABS INC, GEN TEL & ELECTRONICS CORP, 76- *Personal Data:* b York, Pa, Nov 8, 44; m 74; c 2. *Educ:* Franklin & Marshall Col, BA, 66; Stanford Univ, MS, 70, PhD(chem), 72. *Prof Exp:* Res assoc, Advan Fuel Cell Res Lab, Pratt & Whitney Aircraft, United Technol Corp, 72-76. *Concurrent Pos:* Woodrow Wilson fel,. *Mem:* Sigma Xi; Am Chem Soc; Electrochem Soc. *Res:* Fuel cell electrochemistry; lithium batteries; heterogeneous catalysis; porous electrode research and development; luminescence; chemical vapor deposition. *Mailing Add:* PO Box 796 Marlborough MA 01752-0796

KLINEDINST, PAUL EDWARD, JR, ORGANIC CHEMISTRY. *Current Pos:* from asst prof to assoc prof, 60-69, chair chem, 83-88, PROF CHEM, CALIF STATE UNIV, NORTHRIDGE, 69-, ASSOC DEAN SCI & MATH, 88- *Personal Data:* b York, Pa, Dec 29, 33; m 67; c 2. *Educ:* Lehigh Univ, BS, 55; Univ Calif, Los Angeles, PhD(chem), 59. *Prof Exp:* NSF fel chem, Harvard Univ, 59-60. *Mem:* Am Chem Soc; Sigma Xi. *Res:* Organic reaction mechanisms; salt effects and ion pairs in solvolysis and related reactions. *Mailing Add:* Dept Sci & Math Calif State Univ 18111 Nordhoff St Northridge CA 91330-8238

KLINENBERG, JAMES ROBERT, INTERNAL MEDICINE, RHEUMATOLOGY. *Current Pos:* SR VPRES MED AFFAIRS, CEDARS-SINAI MED CTR, 85- *Personal Data:* b Chicago, Ill, June 17, 34; m 59; c 4. *Educ:* Johns Hopkins Univ, AB & AM, 55; George Washington Univ, MD, 59. *Prof Exp:* From asst prof to assoc prof, Univ Calif, Los Angeles, 66-73, vchmn dept, 72-, prof med, 73-, asst dean, Sch Med, 80- *Concurrent Pos:* Consult, Wadsworth Vet Admin Hosp & Sepulveda Vet Admin Hosp; consult, Calif Regional Med Progs, Inland Area VI, 66-72; chmn, Calif State Arthritis Coun, 74-78; fel, Arthritis Found, 66-70, clin scholar; attend physician, Cedars-Sinai Med Ctr, 72-, dir, Dept Med, 72-85; mem, US Pharmacopeia Adv Panel Number 1 Allergy, Immunol & Connective Tissue Dis, 75-; mem bd trustees, Arthritis Found, 78-; chmn, Nat Arthritis Adv Bd, 81-87, Arthritis Found, 91- *Mem:* Fel Am Col Physicians; Am Rheumatism Asn; Am Fedn Clin Res; Asn Prog Dirs in Internal Med; Am Fedn Clin Res. *Res:* Clinical investigation in purine metabolism and gout. *Mailing Add:* Cedars-Sinai Med Ctr 8700 Beverly Blvd Los Angeles CA 90048-1804

KLING, GERALD FAIRCHILD, SOIL SCIENCE. *Current Pos:* ASST PROF SOIL SCI, ORE STATE UNIV, 74- *Personal Data:* b Lewisburg, Pa, Dec 12, 41; m 64; c 1. *Educ:* Purdue Univ, BS, 68; Cornell Univ, MS, 73, PhD(soil sci), 74. *Mem:* Am Soc Agron; Soil Sci Soc Am; Int Soc Soil Sci; Sigma Xi. *Res:* Quantification of the dynamic soil system so that predictions can be made regarding the probable effects of various land use changes on the system. *Mailing Add:* Dept Crop Sci Ore State Univ 3017 Agr Life Sci Corvallis OR 97331-7306

KLING, O(ZRO) RAY, REPRODUCTIVE ENDOCRINOLOGY, BIOLOGY. *Current Pos:* from asst prof to assoc prof gynec & obstet, Sci Med, Univ Okla, 70-84, from adj asst prof to adj assoc prof physiol & biophys, 70-84, assoc dean, Grad Col & vprovost acad affairs & grad prof, 87-90, dean, Grad Col, 90-95, PROF GYNEC & OBSTET, PHYSIOL & BIOPHYS & ZOOL, HEALTH SCI CTR, UNIV OKLA, 84-, VPROVOST ACAD AFFAIRS & DEAN, 93- *Personal Data:* b Peru, Ind, May 3, 42; m 66; c 2. *Educ:* Butler Univ, BS, 65; Ind Univ, Bloomington, PhD(zool), 69. *Prof Exp:* NIH fel, Div Steroid Res, Ohio State Univ, 69-70. *Concurrent Pos:* Ford Found res fel, Human Reproductive Endocrinol Res Unit, Karolinska Inst, Stockholm, 74-75. *Mem:* Endocrine Soc; Am Soc Primatologists; Soc Study Reproduction; Soc Gynec Invest; Am Soc Zool. *Res:* Reproductive biology and physiology; factors regulating ovarian function; endocrine regulation of pregnancy and fetal development. *Mailing Add:* Off Acad Affairs & Grad Col Univ Okla Health Sci Ctr PO Box 26901 Oklahoma City OK 73190-3046. *Fax:* 405-271-1155

KLINGBEIL, WERNER WALTER, APPLIED MECHANICS, APPLIED MATHEMATICS. *Current Pos:* res scientist, 66-71, sr res scientist, 71-82, RES ASSOC, RES CTR, UNIROYAL, INC, 82- *Personal Data:* b Onoway, Alta, June 19, 32; m 66; c 2. *Educ:* Univ Alta, BSc, 54; Col Aeronaut, Eng, dipl, 56; Brown Univ, SM, 64, PhD(appl math), 66. *Prof Exp:* Stress engr, Avro Aircraft Ltd, Can, 56-59; res engr, Allied Res Assocs, Inc, 59-61. *Mem:* Sigma Xi. *Res:* Stress analysis and design of engineering structures; deformation and flow behavior of polymeric materials; finite elasticity; viscoelasticity; composite materials; tire mechanics. *Mailing Add:* 9744 Shenandoah Dr Brecksville OH 44141

KLINGBERG, WILLIAM GENE, pediatrics, hematology; deceased, see previous edition for last biography

KLINGE, ALBERT FREDERICK, AGRICULTURAL ENGINEERING. *Current Pos:* from assoc prof to prof, 65-88, EMER PROF AGR ENG, UNIV MAINE, ORONO. *Personal Data:* b Dudleytown, Ind, May 8, 23; m 53, Catherine V Werner; c Alice D & Sidney W. *Educ:* Purdue Univ, BS, 52, MS, 55; Univ Calif, Los Angeles, PhD(eng hydraul), 66. *Prof Exp:* Asst eng, Purdue Univ, 52-55; assoc, Univ Calif, Los Angeles, 55-65, lectr, 62-63. *Mem:* Am Soc Agr Engrs; Am Soc Eng Educ. *Res:* Hydraulics, water and soil resource management; waste management. *Mailing Add:* 108 Forest Ave Orono ME 04473

KLINGE, CAROLYN M, MOLECULAR ENDOCRINOLOGY, ESTROGEN RECEPTOR. *Current Pos:* ASST PROF BIOCHEM, SCH MED, UNIV LOUISVILLE, 96- *Personal Data:* b Utica, NY, May 20, 57. *Educ:* Keuka Col, BA, 79; Pa State Univ, MS, 81, PhD(pharmacol), 84. *Honors & Awards:* Nichols Inst New Investr Award, Endocrine Soc, 90. *Prof Exp:* Fel biochemn & oncol, Dept Biochem & Cancer Ctr, Sch Med & Dent, Univ Rochester, 84-89, asst res prof, 89-95, assoc res prof, 96. *Concurrent Pos:* Adj asst prof biol, Monroe Community Col, 87-88. *Mem:* AAAS; Am Asn Cancer Res; NY Acad Sci; Endocline Soc; Fedn Am Soc Exp Biol. *Res:* Molecular mechanisms regulating the transcription of steroid hormone-responsive genes in target tissues; role of the ligand, hormone agonist or antagonist, on estrogen receptor DNA binding and transactivation. *Mailing Add:* Dept Biochem Univ Louisville Sch Med Louisville KY 40292. *Fax:* 502-852-6222; *E-Mail:* cmklin01@ulkyvm.louisville.edu

KLINGEBIEL, ALBERT ARNOLD, SOIL SCIENCE. *Current Pos:* RETIRED. *Personal Data:* b Hinton, Iowa, Oct 1, 10; m 37; c 4. *Educ:* Iowa State Univ, BS, 36, MS, 37. *Prof Exp:* Res asst range reseeding, Intermt Forest & Range Exp Sta, US Forest Serv, 37-38; guest lectr, Univ Ill, 60; pres, Salut Corp, 76-84; soil scientist, Soil Conserv Serv, USDA, 38-42, dir training, 42-46, state soil scientist, 46-52, Ill State dir soil & water mgt res, Agr Res Serv, 52-54, from asst dir to dir soil surv interpretations, Soil Conserv Serv, 54-73, consult, Agr Res Serv, USDA, 86-87. *Concurrent Pos:* Soils consult, Int Bank Reconstruct & Develop, Mex, 73-75; Econ Res Serv, USDA, DC, 75-76, Nat Res Coun, DC, 75, Remote Sensing Inst, SDak State Univ, 77-81, Mexico DF, 78-79, Soil Conserv Serv, 82-89 & World Bank, 83. *Mem:* Fel Am Soc Agron; fel Soil Sci Soc Am; Am Soc Planning Off; Int Soc Soil Sci; Soil Conserv Soc Am. *Res:* Soil classification and interpretation; soil and water management; land use planning; remote sensing; author of over 50 scientific articles. *Mailing Add:* 2413 Countryside Dr Silver Spring MD 20905

KLINGELE, HAROLD OTTO, INFORMATION SCIENCE, BIOCHEMISTRY. *Current Pos:* PRES, AURORA CONSULT SERVS, 91- *Personal Data:* b Niagara Falls, NY, Aug 4, 37. *Educ:* Mass Inst Technol, BSc, 59; Yale Univ, MS, 61; Cornell Univ, PhD(org chem), 65. *Prof Exp:* Instr pharmacol, Univ Louisville, 65-66, asst prof, 66-71; pres, HOK Assocs, 71-92. *Concurrent Pos:* Chem consult & chem anal, HOK Assoc, 71-92; sr res assoc, Dept Chem, Ctr Environ Educ & Res, State Univ NY, Buffalo, 73-75 & 82-90, lectr, 91-92; mgr, treas & chem consult, Peninsula Chem Anal Ltd, 76-78; vis indust chemist, Chem Dept, Canisius Col, Buffalo, NY, 80-82; pres, Soap Factory Stores, Inc, 80-91. *Mem:* Am Chem Soc; Royal Soc Chem. *Res:* Forensics; analytical method development; industrial problems involving chemistry; carcinogens; toxicology; environmental chemistry; organic synthesis; electronics-radiowave propagation; atmospheric chemical reactions; photo oxidation of organic pollutants. *Mailing Add:* 505 Meadowbrook Dr Lewiston NY 14092-1936

KLINGEMAN, PETER C, HYDRAULIC ENGINEERING, HYDROLOGY. *Current Pos:* from asst prof to assoc prof, 66-68, from assoc prof to prof 68-76, PROF CIVIL ENG, ORE STATE UNIV, 76- *Personal Data:* b Evanston, Ill, May 31, 34; m 57; c 2. *Educ:* Northwestern Univ, BS, 57, MS, 59; Univ Calif, Berkeley, PhD(civil eng), 65. *Honors & Awards:* Hilgard Hydraul Prize, Am Soc Civil Eng, 83. *Prof Exp:* Asst prof civil eng, NDak State Univ, 59; res engr, Univ Calif, Berkeley, 62-64; Ford Found Prog vis prof hydraul eng, Cath Univ Chile, 64-66. *Concurrent Pos:* Dir, Ore Water Resources Res Inst, 75-89, actg dept head civil eng, 89-91. *Mem:* Am Soc Civil Eng; Am Geophys Union; Int Asn Hydraul Res. *Res:* Planning development and management of river basins and estuaries, including hydraulics, hydrology, sediment transport, problem analysis, impact assessment and related aspects of water resources development. *Mailing Add:* 3225 NW Elmwood Dr Corvallis OR 97330

KLINGEN, THEODORE JAMES, PHYSICAL INORGANIC CHEMISTRY. *Current Pos:* from asst prof to assoc prof, Univ Miss, 64-70, dir, Ctr Radiation Res, 72-74, dir, Off Environ Safety, 85-95, PROF CHEM, UNIV MISS, 70-, DIR, DEPT HEALTH & SAFETY. *Personal Data:* b St Louis, Mo, Oct 7, 31; m 58, Maura E Downey; c Joseph & Anne. *Educ:* St Louis Univ, BS, 53, MS, 55; Fla State Univ, PhD(chem), 62. *Prof Exp:* Nuclear res officer, Res Div, Spec Weapons Ctr, USAF, NMex, 55-57; analyst chem, McDonnell Aircraft Corp, 57-58; fel, Fla State Univ, 58-60, asst, 60-62; res scientist, Res Div, McDonnell Aircraft Corp, 62-64. *Concurrent Pos:* Grants, US Dept Energy & NSF; Am conf govt indust hygienists, Am Biol Safety Asn. *Mem:* Am Chem Soc; Am Phys Soc; Am Nuclear Soc; Health Physics Soc; Sigma Xi. *Res:* Radiation chemistry of plastic crystals; radiation induced polymerization of organo-substituted carboranes; environmental chemistry. *Mailing Add:* Health & Safety Dept Univ Miss University MS 38677-9701. *E-Mail:* gstjk@vm.cc.olemiss.edu

KLINGENBERG, JOSEPH JOHN, ANALYTICAL CHEMISTRY, MANDELIC ACIDS OF ZIRCONIUM. *Current Pos:* From instr to prof, 49-86, EMER PROF CHEM, XAVIER UNIV, OHIO, 86- *Personal Data:* b Bellevue, Ky, Nov 16, 19; wid; c 5. *Educ:* Xavier Univ, Ohio, BS, 41; Univ Cincinnati, MS, 47, PhD(chem), 49. *Concurrent Pos:* Vis lectr, Univ Cincinnati, 66, 69 & 75; sci adv, Food & Drug Admin, 67-72; vis lectr, Univ Ky, 76 & 77; vis scientist, Va Polytech Inst & State Univ, 81-82. *Mem:* Am Chem Soc. *Res:* Chemistry of zirconium; mandelic acid derivatives. *Mailing Add:* 51 Pleasant Ridge Ave Ft Mitchell KY 41017-2811

KLINGENER, DAVID JOHN, zoology; deceased, see previous edition for last biography

KLINGENSMITH, GEORGE BRUCE, PHYSICAL & ORGANIC CHEMISTRY, POLYMER CHEMISTRY & ENGINEERING. *Current Pos:* DIR RES & DEVELOP, HUNTSMAN POLYPROPYLENE CORP, 90- *Personal Data:* b Pittsburgh, Pa, Dec 6, 34; m 60; c 2. *Educ:* Univ Pittsburgh, BSc, 59, PhD(phys-org chem), 63. *Prof Exp:* Fel phys & org chem, Pa State Univ, 63-64; res supvr, Shell Chem Co Woodbury, 66-74, sr staff res chemist, Shell Develop Co, 74-90. *Mem:* Am Chem Soc; Sigma Xi; Soc Advan Mat & Process Eng. *Res:* Reactions and physical properties of aromatic systems; solvent effects; crystallization and crystal structure of polymers; nuclear magnetic resonance spectroscopy. *Mailing Add:* 1222 N Bay Shore Dr Virginia Beach VA 23451-3763

KLINGENSMITH, MERLE JOSEPH, PLANT PHYSIOLOGY. *Current Pos:* from asst prof to assoc prof, 65-76, PROF BIOL, ROCHESTER INST TECHNOL, 76- *Personal Data:* b Grenora, NDak, Mar 27, 32; m 59, Maree McGauhey; c Wesley J & Peter G. *Educ:* Wheaton Col, Ill, BS, 54; Univ Mich, MS, 56, PhD(bot), 59. *Prof Exp:* Lab asst bact, Fla State Univ, 54-55; asst bot, Univ Mich, 55-56; vis asst prof bot & bact, Ohio Wesleyan Univ, 59-60; asst prof bot, Colgate Univ, 60-65. *Mem:* Fel AAAS; Sigma Xi; Am Sci Affiliation. *Res:* Plant tissue culture; exogenous growth regulators; radiation effects on plant growth. *Mailing Add:* 2281 North Rd Scottsville NY 14546

KLINGENSMITH, RAYMOND W, NUCLEAR PHYSICS. *Current Pos:* RETIRED. *Personal Data:* b Pittsburgh, Pa, Mar 21, 31; m 53, 84, 93, Janet Shaffer; c 2. *Educ:* Hanover Col, AB, 53; Miami Univ, MA, 55; Ohio State Univ, PhD(elastic scattering), 63. *Prof Exp:* Physicist, Westinghouse Elec Corp, 56-57; prin physicist, Battelle Mem Inst, 57-63, proj leader nuclear physics, 63-68, prog mgr strategic technol, 68-74, supvr, Hot Lab, 74-77, mgr & assoc sect mgr nuclear mat technol, Battelle-Columbus, 77-81, proj mgr, Off Nuclear Waste Isolation, 81-88, proj mgr, Battelle Columbus, 88-93. *Res:* Low energy scattering as related to nuclear structure physics; nuclear weapons effects; strategic technology; nuclear materials technology; hot cell technology and operations; research management; nuclear waste repository development; licensing; technology transfer. *Mailing Add:* 3134 Mt Holyoke Rd Columbus OH 43221

KLINGER, ALLEN, PATTERN ANALYSIS, ENGINEERING ELECTRONICS. *Current Pos:* PROF COMPUT SCI & ENG, UNIV CALIF, LOS ANGELES, 67- *Personal Data:* b New York, NY, Apr 2, 37; m 88, Dorothy J Fisher; c Deborah & Richard. *Educ:* Cooper Union, BEE, 57; Calif Inst Technol, MS, 58; Univ Calif, Berkeley, PhD(elec eng), 66. *Prof Exp:* Mem tech staff electronics, Hughes Aircraft Co, 57; electronics engr elec systs, ITT Labs, 58-59; electronics engr comput systs, Syst Develop Corp, 59-62, consult, 67 & 78; sr res engr electronics systs, Jet Propulsion Lab, 64-65, consult, 78; researcher math, Rand Corp, 65-67, consult, 67-69 & 72-73. *Concurrent Pos:* Sr radar systs specialist, Litton Industs, 68-69; prin investr, NSF, 68-71 & Air Force Off Sci Res, 70-77; chmn, Conf Data Struct

Pattern Recognition & Comput Graphics, 74-75; consult, Los Angeles Unified Sch Dist, 76-78, Radiol Dept, Long Beach Mem Hosp, 77-78, IBM Los Angeles Sci Ctr, 78-79, US Army Eng Topogr Labs, 78-80, Aerospace Corp, 80-87; res travel fel, USSR, Nat Acad Sci, 82-83 & 85-86; SAIC chmn, Panel Soviet Image Pattern Recognition; Fulbright fel, 90-91. *Mem:* Fel Inst Elec & Electronics Engrs; Classification Soc. *Res:* Computer vision and neural networks; image data bases; human computer interaction; allocation of unreliable units; composite views from tomography; biomedical wave forms; data analysis. *Mailing Add:* 3531-H Boelter Hall Univ Calif Los Angeles CA 90095-1596. *Fax:* 310-825-7578; *E-Mail:* klinger@cs.ucla.edu

KLINGER, HAROLD P, GENETICS. *Current Pos:* from asst prof to assoc prof anat & genetics, 63-72, PROF GENETICS, ALBERT EINSTEIN COL MED, 72- *Personal Data:* b Brooklyn, NY, July 20, 29; m 59. *Educ:* Harvard Univ, BA, 52; Univ Basel, MD, 59, PhD, 63. *Prof Exp:* Demonstr anat, Univ Basel, 55-57, from second asst to first asst, 59-61, dir cytogenetics res unit, 61-63. *Concurrent Pos:* Ed, Cytogenetics & Cell Genetics, 60-; NIH career develop award, 65-74; mem adv comt, Pop Coun, Rockefeller Univ, 71- *Mem:* Genetics Soc Am; Am Soc Human Genetics; Am Asn Phys Anthrop; NY Acad Sci; Swiss Anat Soc. *Res:* Cytogenetics; role of chromosomal aberrations in human development; somatic cell genetics; gene regulation and interaction in normal and malignant cells. *Mailing Add:* Dept Genetics Albert Einstein Col Med 1300 Morris Park Ave Bronx NY 10461-1926

KLINGER, LAWRENCE EDWARD, FOOD ENGINEERING. *Current Pos:* RETIRED. *Personal Data:* b Chicago, Ill, Nov 18, 29; m 53, Ellen Reidy; c Patricia, Therese, Robert & Edward. *Educ:* Loyola Univ, Ill, BS, 51; Ill Inst Technol, MS, 53. *Prof Exp:* Res chemist, Swift & Co, 52-54, asst to dir labs, 54-55, div head, Res Labs, 55-59, asst to vpres res, 59-61, div head, Res Labs, 61-62, gen mgr new prod develop dept, 62-68, dir planning & acquisitions, Swift Chem Co, 68-69, plant mgr, 69-70, sr admin asst, 70-71, dir pub responsibility, 71-77, dir qual assurance, 78-84; mgr qual & assurance/regulatory, Beatrice Refrig Foods, 84-85, vpres, Beatrice Meats Inc, 85-86; dir qual assurance/regulatory affairs, Swift-Eckrich, Inc, 86-89. *Concurrent Pos:* Dir, Food Update, 75-79; steering comt, Nutrit Planning Conf, Food & Drug Admin, 75-76; mem, Coun Agr Sci & Technol. *Mem:* Inst Food Technol (treas, 57 & 58); Am Soc Qual Control. *Res:* New products development; nutrition education; food safety. *Mailing Add:* 1218 Indian Trail Hinsdale IL 60521

KLINGER, THOMAS SCOTT, MARINE BIOLOGY, PHYSIOLOGICAL ECOLOGY. *Current Pos:* asst prof, 85-90, assoc prof, 90-96, PROF BIOL, BLOOMSBURG UNIV, 96- *Personal Data:* b Kalamazoo, Mich, May 5, 55; m 87, Signe Dolloff; c Austin T & Pepin S. *Educ:* Macalester Col, BA, 75; Univ SFla, MA, 79, PhD(biol), 84. *Prof Exp:* Teaching asst biol, Univ SFla, 76-83, adj lectr, 83-84; instr biol, Pasco-Hernando Community Col, 84; adj prof biol, St Leo Col, 84-85. *Concurrent Pos:* Dir, Marine Sci Consortium, 86-, vpres acad affairs, 88- *Mem:* AAAS; Sigma Xi; Am Micros Soc; Soc Integrative & Comp Biol. *Res:* Physiological ecology and nutritional physiology of marine invertebrate animals, primarily echinoderms; feeding, digestion, and energetics. *Mailing Add:* Dept Biol & Allied Health Sci Bloomsburg Univ 400 E Second St Bloomsburg PA 17815-1301. *Fax:* 717-389-3028; *E-Mail:* tklinger@bloomu.edu

KLINGER, WILLIAM RUSSELL, MATHEMATICS. *Current Pos:* asst prof, 73-74, ASSOC PROF MATH, MARION COL, 74-, HEAD DEPT, 73- *Personal Data:* b Columbia City, Ind, Feb 9, 39; m 60; c 1. *Educ:* Taylor Univ, BS in Ed, 61; Ohio State Univ, MSc, 67, PhD(math, educ), 73. *Prof Exp:* Teacher math, Marion Community Schs, Ind, 61-68; instr, Ohio State Univ, 68-73. *Concurrent Pos:* Mem assoc fac, Ind Univ, Kokomo, 73- *Mem:* Math Asn Am. *Res:* Necessary and sufficient conditions for continuity in metric spaces and topological spaces. *Mailing Add:* Taylor Univ Upland IN 46989

KLINGHAMMER, ERICH, ETHOLOGY, PSYCHOLOGY. *Current Pos:* DIR & FOUNDER, WOLF PARK, 72- *Personal Data:* b Kassel, Ger, Feb 28, 30; m 58; c 1. *Educ:* Univ Chicago, AB, 58, PhD(psychol), 62. *Prof Exp:* From instr to asst prof psychol, Univ Chicago, 63-68; assoc prof, Purdue Univ, Lafayette, 68-95. *Concurrent Pos:* Pres, NAm Wildlife Park Found, 72-; sci ed, Grzimek's Animal Life Encycl; consult, animal behavior. *Mem:* AAAS; Am Ornith Union; Animal Behav Soc. *Res:* Ethology; imprinting; effects of early experience on adult behavior; behavior mechanisms in canids development and motivation; predator-prey interactions in wolves and bison; applied ethology. *Mailing Add:* Wolf Park RR 1 Battleground IN 47920

KLINGHOFFER, JUNE F, INTERNAL MEDICINE. *Current Pos:* fel path, Med Col Pa, 47-48, clin asst med, 48-50, dir student health serv, 48-51, from instr to prof, 50-87, ETHEL RUSSELL MORRIS PROF MED, MED COL PA, 87- *Personal Data:* b Philadelphia, Pa, Feb 12, 21; m 47, Sidney U Wenger; c Robert Wenger. *Educ:* Univ Pa, BA, 41; Woman's Med Col Pa, MD, 45; Am Bd Internal Med, cert, 51; Spec Bd Rheumatology, cert, 76. *Honors & Awards:* Commonwealth Citation, Commonwealth Bd of Med Col Pa, 73. *Prof Exp:* Intern, Albert Einstein Med Ctr, 45, resident internal med, 45-47. *Mem:* Am Med Women's Asn; Asn Women Sci; fel Am Col Physicians; AMA; Am Col Rheumatology; Asn Am Med Col. *Mailing Add:* Med Col Pa 3300 Henry Ave Philadelphia PA 19129-1121

KLINGLER, EUGENE H(ERMAN), ELECTROMECHANICAL ENGINEERING. *Current Pos:* PRES & CHMN BD, EUGENE KLINGLER INC, 70- *Personal Data:* b Ft Wayne, Ind, Sept 3, 32; m 54; c 6. *Educ:* Ind Inst Technol, BSEE, 53; NMex State Univ, MSEE, 57; Carnegie Inst Technol, PhD(elec eng), 61. *Prof Exp:* Servomech engr, Bell Aircraft Corp, 53-55; instr, NMex State Univ, 57; proj engr, Carnegie Inst Technol, 57-61; staff engr, Space Tech Labs, 61-62; chief electronics engr, Fairchild Camera & Instrument Corp, 62; sr mem tech staff, Northrop Space Labs, 62-63; mgr eng res lab, NAm Aviation Inc, Okla, 63-65; chmn, Dept Elec Eng, Ind Inst Technol, 65-69; prof & chmn dept, Univ Detroit, 69-70. *Concurrent Pos:* Instr, Ind Inst Technol, 58. *Mem:* Inst Elec & Electronics Engrs. *Res:* Synthesis of artificial dielectric materials by means of control of electric and magnetic losses as a function of frequency. *Mailing Add:* 5045 Charing Cross Rd Bloomfield Hills MI 48304

KLINGMAN, DAYTON L, AGRONOMY. *Current Pos:* RETIRED. *Personal Data:* b Neosho Falls, Kans, Feb 10, 13; m 41; c 4. *Educ:* Univ Nebr, BSc, 38, PhD(agron), 54; Purdue Univ, MSc, 42. *Prof Exp:* Asst agronomist & asst prof agron, Univ Wyo, 42-48; agronomist, Crops Res Div, USDA, 48-52, sr agronomist & coordr weed invests, 53-56, leader weed invests-grazing lands, 57-72, chief, Turfgrass Lab, 72-74, chief, Field Crops Lab, 74-76 & Weed Sci Lab, 76-83. *Mem:* AAAS; Am Soc Agron; Weed Sci Soc Am; Soc Range Mgt. *Res:* Technique study of use of cages in pasture research; small grain improvement; weed control in pastures and field crops. *Mailing Add:* 407 Russell Ave No 204 Gaithersburg MD 20877

KLINGMAN, GERDA ISOLDE, PHARMACOLOGY. *Current Pos:* from instr to assoc prof, 61-73, PROF BIOCHEM PHARMACOL, STATE UNIV NY, BUFFALO, 73- *Personal Data:* b Berlin, Ger, May 6, 24; US citizen; m 53; c 1. *Educ:* Fordham Univ, BS, 52; Med Col Va, PhD(pharmacol), 56. *Prof Exp:* Res assoc, Dept Pharmacol & Physiol, Med Sch, Duke Univ, 55-57; instr, Dept Pharmacol & Exp Therapeut, Sch Med, Johns Hopkins Univ, 57-61. *Concurrent Pos:* Career develop award, NIH, 62-67. *Mem:* Am Soc Pharmacol & Exp Therapeut. *Res:* Neuropharmacology; neurochemistry; adrenergic nervous system and catecholamine metabolism; acute and chronic tolerance; drug dependence; nerve growth factor and nerve growth factor antiserum. *Mailing Add:* Dept Biochem Pharmacol State Univ NY Buffalo N Campus 447 Hochstetter Hall Buffalo NY 14260-0001

KLINGMAN, JACK DENNIS, BIOCHEMISTRY, NEUROSCIENCES. *Current Pos:* from instr to prof, 61-95, EMER PROF BIOCHEM, STATE UNIV NY, BUFFALO, 95- *Personal Data:* b Johnson City, NY, Apr 21, 27; m 53, Gerda I Schultz; c Karin L. *Educ:* Syracuse Univ, BA, 51; Med Col Va, MS, 53; Duke Univ, PhD(biochem), 58. *Prof Exp:* Res assoc pharmacol, Med Col Va, 53; asst biochem, Duke Univ, 54-55; res assoc neurochem, Johns Hopkins Univ, 58-61. *Concurrent Pos:* Mem fac, Dept Biochem, Sch Med, Monash Univ, Australia, 71-72; Hayes-Fulbright fel, 71-72. *Mem:* AAAS; Am Chem Soc; Neurochem Soc; Am Soc Biol Chem; Sigma Xi; Int Neurochem Soc. *Res:* N15-ethanolamine metabolism; purification and mechanism of renal glutaminase; C14-glucose metabolism in surviving superior cervical ganglion; biochemical events in excitation; phospholipid and amino acid metabolism. *Mailing Add:* Dept Biochem State Univ NY Buffalo NY 14214

KLINGSBERG, CYRUS, SOLID STATE CHEMISTRY, CERAMICS. *Current Pos:* RETIRED. *Personal Data:* b Philadelphia, Pa, Nov 12, 24; m 50, Vera Ichelson. *Educ:* Univ Pa, BA, 48; Bryn Mawr Col, MA, 49; Pa State Univ, PhD(geo chem), 58. *Prof Exp:* Res mgr, G F Pettinos Inc, 50-51; petrologist, Simonds Abrasive Co, 51-54; asst geochem, Pa State Univ, 54-57; res chemist, Corning Glass Works, NY, 57-59; ceramist, Off Naval Res, 59-63, liaison scientist ceramics, London, 63-64, ceramist, 64-66; exec secy, Comt Radioactive Waste Mgt, Nat Acad Sci-Nat Res Coun, 68-75; sr res assoc, Arhco, 76-77; geologist, US Dept Energy, 77-87. *Concurrent Pos:* Vis prof, Japan Soc Prom Sci, 75. *Mem:* Fel Am Ceramic Soc; Mineral Soc Am; Sigma Xi; AAAS. *Res:* Solid state chemistry of ceramics, minerals and ionic solids; synthesis and characterization of crystalline phases; management of radioactive wastes. *Mailing Add:* 1318 Deerfield Dr State College PA 16803-2208

KLINK, JOEL RICHARD, ORGANIC CHEMISTRY. *Current Pos:* from asst prof to assoc prof, 63-71, PROF CHEM, UNIV WIS-EAU CLAIRE, 71-, CHMN DEPT, 78-83, 91- *Personal Data:* b Nevada, Ohio, June 28, 35; m 59; c 2. *Educ:* Ohio State Univ, BS, 57, PhD(chem), 64. *Prof Exp:* Instr chem, Ohio Northern Univ, 61-63. *Mem:* Am Chem Soc. *Res:* Reactions of diazoalkenes. *Mailing Add:* Dept Chem Univ Wis Eau Claire WI 54701

KLINK, WILLIAM H, THEORETICAL PHYSICS. *Current Pos:* From asst prof to assoc prof, 65-77, PROF PHYSICS & ASTRON, UNIV IOWA, 77- *Personal Data:* b Chicago, Ill, Sept 29, 37; m 59. *Educ:* Univ Mich, BA, 59; Johns Hopkins Univ, PhD(physics), 64. *Concurrent Pos:* Fulbright grant, Univ Heidelberg, 64-65. *Mem:* Am Phys Soc. *Res:* Elementary particle physics, primarily using group theory. *Mailing Add:* Dept Physics & Astron Univ Iowa Iowa City IA 52240

KLINKE, DAVID J, ORGANIC CHEMISTRY. *Current Pos:* res chemist petrol additives, Jackson Lab, E I du Pont de Nemours & Co, Inc, 63-66, prod supvr miscellaneous org intermediates, Chambers Works, 66-68, supvr mgt training & personnel develop, 68-71, prod supvr dyes, 71-74, sr supvr mat distrib, 74-80, supt safety, Environment, Protection, 80-86, SR QUAL MGR, E I DU PONT DE NEMOURS & CO, Inc, 86- *Personal Data:* b Detroit, Mich, Feb 27, 32; m 64; c 3. *Educ:* Mich State Univ, BS, 54, PhD(org chem), 63. *Prof Exp:* Teacher jr high sch, Mich, 54-55 & high sch, 55-59. *Mem:* Am Chem Soc. *Res:* Thiophene chemistry; organo-metallics. *Mailing Add:* 44 Laurel Lane Woodstown NJ 08098-9638

KLINMAN, DENNIS M, MEDICAL RESEARCH. *Current Pos:* med officer, Div Virol, 89-91, tenured sr invstr, Div Viral Prod, 91-93, CHIEF SECT RETROVIRAL IMMUNOL, DIV VIRAL PROD, CBER/FDA, 93- *Personal Data:* b Philadelphia, Pa, Oct 9, 54. *Educ:* St Joseph's Univ, BS, 76; Univ Pa, MA & PhD, 82. *Honors & Awards:* Regional & Sr Rheumatology Awards, Am Rheumatology Asn, 87. *Prof Exp:* Med internship, Faulkner Hosp, 82-83; med & sr staff fel, NIADDK & NINDS, NIH, 83-89. *Concurrent Pos:* Vis scientist, Inst Animal Physiol, ARC, 78-79; fel, Arthritis Found, 85-87. *Mem:* Am Soc Clin Invest; Am Soc Immunologists; AAAS; Am Rheumatology Asn. *Res:* Radioiodination of monoclonal antibodies; dialyzable serum components support the growth of hybridoma cell lines in vitro; analysis of non-dominaur idio types during alloimmune responses; suppression of autoantibody production with anti-class II antibodies; idiotypy and autoimmunity. *Mailing Add:* Div Virol FDA Bldg 29A Rm 3D16 Bethesda MD 20892-4555

KLINMAN, JUDITH POLLOCK, BIOCHEMISTRY, PHYSICAL ORGANIC CHEMISTRY. *Current Pos:* assoc prof, 78-82, CHANCELLORS PROF CHEM & MOLECULAR & CELL BIOL, UNIV CALIF, BERKELEY, 82- *Personal Data:* b Philadelphia, Pa, Apr 17, 41; div; c 2. *Educ:* Univ Pa, AB, 62, PhD(org chem), 66. *Honors & Awards:* Repligen Award, Am Chem Soc, 94. *Prof Exp:* Fel phys org chem, Isotopes Dept, Weizmann Inst, 66-67; assoc, Inst Cancer Res, 68-70, res assoc biochem, 70-72, asst mem, 72-77, assoc mem, 77-78. *Concurrent Pos:* Asst prof med biophys, Univ Pa, 74-78; Guggenheim fel, 88. *Mem:* Nat Acad Sci; Am Soc Biochem & Molecular Biol; Am Acad Arts & Sci; Am Chem Soc. *Res:* Mechanism and regulation of enzyme action. *Mailing Add:* Dept Chem Univ Calif Berkeley CA 94720

KLINMAN, NORMAN RALPH, IMMUNOLOGY. *Current Pos:* MEM STAFF, SCRIPPS CLIN & RES FOUND, 78- *Personal Data:* b Philadelphia, Pa, Mar 23, 37; m 78; c 2. *Educ:* Haverford Col, AB, 58; Jefferson Med Col, MD, 62; Univ Pa, PhD(microbiol), 65. *Prof Exp:* Fel immunol, Univ Pa, 62-66, Weizmann Inst, 66-67 & Nat Inst Med Res, London, 67-68; from asst prof to assoc prof microbiol, Sch Med, Univ Pa, 68-75, prof path, 75-78. *Concurrent Pos:* NIH res fel, 62-63; Helen Hay Whitney Found res fel, 63-66; Am Cancer Soc res scholar, 66-68; adj prof, Univ Calif, San Diego, 79- *Mem:* Am Asn Immunol; Am Asn Exp Pathologists; Sigma Xi; Am Asn Exp Pathologists. *Res:* Structure, activity and synthesis of antibody. *Mailing Add:* Dept Immunol IMM-16 Scripps Clin & Res Found 10666 N Torrey Pines Rd La Jolla CA 92037-1092. *Fax:* 619-554-6298

KLINTWORTH, GORDON K, PATHOLOGY, ANATOMY. *Current Pos:* assoc, 64-66, from asst prof to assoc prof, 66-73, PROF PATH, MED CTR, DUKE UNIV, 73- PROF OPHTHAL, 81- A C JOSEPH RES PROF OPHTHAL, 86- *Personal Data:* b Ft Victoria, Rhodesia, Aug 4, 32; US citizen; m 57, Felicity Tait; c 3. *Educ:* Univ Witwatersrand, BSc, 54, MB, BCh, 57, BSc(Hons), 61, PhD(anat), 66. *Honors & Awards:* Zimmerman Award; Acad Res Award. *Prof Exp:* Intern med & surg, Johannesburg Hosp, 58-59, sr house physician, psychiat, 59-60, registr, Neurol & Neurosurg, 60-61. *Concurrent Pos:* Louis B Mayer scholar, 72; distinguished prof, Duke Univ. *Mem:* AAAS; Am Asn Pathologists; Sigma Xi; Int Soc Neuropath; Tissue Cult Asn; NY Acad Sci; Int Acad Path; Am Acad Ophthal. *Res:* Diseases of the eye and nervous system; infectious diseases; secondary effects of increased intracranial pressure; human genetics and diseases of the cornea. *Mailing Add:* Dept Path Duke Univ Med Ctr Durham NC 27710-0001. *Fax:* 919-684-8983; *E-Mail:* klint001@dukemc.bitnet

KLINZING, GEORGE ENGELBERT, CHEMICAL ENGINEERING. *Current Pos:* From asst prof to assoc prof, 63-81, PROF CHEM ENG, UNIV PITTSBURGH, 81-, ASSOC DEAN RES, 87- *Personal Data:* b Natrona Heights, Pa, Mar 22, 38; m 69; c 2. *Educ:* Univ Pittsburgh, BS, 59; Carnegie Inst Technol, MS, 61, PhD(chem eng), 63. *Concurrent Pos:* Consult, Univ Develop Proj, Ecuador, 63-66; hon prof, Cent Univ Ecuador, 66; continuing ed lectr, Prev Transport, Am Inst Chem Engrs. *Mem:* Fel Am Inst Chem Engrs; Am Soc Eng Educ. *Res:* Solid/gas flow systems; electrostatics; mass transfer in partially miscible systems; molecular hydrogen permeation; micrographic analysis of particles. *Mailing Add:* 5121 Beeler St Pittsburgh PA 15217-1001

KLIONSKY, BERNARD LEON, MEDICINE, PATHOLOGY. *Current Pos:* assoc prof, 61-70, PROF PATH, SCH MED, UNIV PITTSBURGH, 71- *Personal Data:* b Binghamton, NY, Oct 8, 25; m 50; c 4. *Educ:* Harvard Univ, AB, 47; Hahnemann Med Col, MD, 52; Am Bd Path, dipl, 57. *Prof Exp:* Nat Cancer Inst trainee path, Med Ctr, Univ Kans, 53-55, Am Cancer Soc clin fel, 55-57, fel path, 56-57, from instr to assoc prof, 56-61. *Mem:* Am Cancer Soc. *Res:* Intrauterine fetal growth retardation; yellow hyaline membranes. *Mailing Add:* Dept Path Rm 708 Scaife Univ Pittsburgh Sch Med Pittsburgh PA 15261-0001. *Fax:* 412-648-1916

KLIORE, ARVYDAS J(OSEPH), PLANETARY SCIENCE, ATMOSPHERIC PHYSICS. *Current Pos:* sr res engr, Jet Propulsion Lab, Calif Inst Technol, 62-64, res specialist, 64-66, res scientist, 66-87, SR RES SCIENTIST, JET PROPULSION LAB, CALIF INST TECHNOL, 87- *Personal Data:* b Kaunas, Lithuania, Aug 5, 35; US citizen; m 60; c 2. *Educ:* Univ Ill, BS, 56; Univ Mich, MS, 57; Mich State Univ, PhD(elec eng), 62. *Honors & Awards:* Exceptional Sci Achievement Medal, NASA, 72. *Prof Exp:* Engr, Armour Res Found, Ill Inst Technol, 57-59; instr elec eng, Mich State Univ, 61-62. *Concurrent Pos:* Lectr, Univ Calif, Los Angeles, 63-64. *Mem:* AAAS; Am Astron Soc; Am Geophys Union; Comt Space Res; Int Astron Union. *Res:* Space astronomy; radio propagation experiments to study planetary atmospheres; spacecraft radio propagation experiments to study the atmospheres and ionospheres of planets and their satellites. *Mailing Add:* Jet Propulsion Lab 4800 Oak Grove Dr Pasadena CA 91109

KLIOZE, OSCAR, PHARMACEUTICAL CHEMISTRY. *Current Pos:* RETIRED. *Personal Data:* b Baltimore, Md, Jan 2, 19; m 43, Olive Berman; c Solomon S, Susanne B (Edelson) & Lawrence H. *Educ:* George Washington Univ, BS, 40; Va Polytech Inst, BS, 44; Univ Md, PhD(pharmaceut chem), 49. *Prof Exp:* Jr chemist, Baltimore Paint & Color Works, Inc, 40-41 & Bur Plant Indust, USDA, 41-42 & 46; jr biochemist, Manhattan Proj, US Army Engrs, 44-46; res assoc biochem, Northwestern Univ, 49-50; res chemist pharmaceut chem, Chas Pfizer & Co, Inc, 50-54, res supvr, 54-58; dir prod develop, A H Robins Co, Inc, 58-60 & prod develop & qual control, 60-64, dir, 65-81, vpres pharm res & anal serv, 81-84. *Concurrent Pos:* Lectr, Med Col Va, 66-75. *Mem:* Am Chem Soc; Am Pharmaceut Asn; Am Inst Chem; Parenteral Drug Asn. *Res:* Relationship of chemical structure to biological activity; pharmaceutical research and development; physiological effects of radiant energy; plant biochemistry; protein synthesis. *Mailing Add:* 2 High Stepper Ct Apt 203 Baltimore MD 21208

KLIOZE, SOLOMON S, DIABETES & METABOLISM, ENDOCRINOLOGY. *Current Pos:* ASSOC DIR CLIN RES, PFIZER CENT RES, 92- *Personal Data:* b Baltimore, Md, Mar 17, 46; m 69, Trudy Genderson Klioze; c Jason D. *Educ:* Univ NC, BS, 68; Columbia Univ, PhD(org chem), 72. *Prof Exp:* Postdoctoral res fel, Yale Univ, 72-73; sr res chemist, Hoechst-Roussel Pharmaceut, 73-79, res assoc, 79-82, clin res assoc, 82-83, sr clin res assoc, 84-85, asst dir clin res, 85-87, assoc dir, 88-92. *Mem:* Am Diabetes Asn; Endocrine Soc; Am Soc Microbiol; Am Chem Soc. *Res:* Clinical trials of new drugs on humans, primarily in the areas of diabetes, diabetes complications and metabolism; oncology, reproductive endocrinology and infectious diseases. *Mailing Add:* Pfizer Cent Res Eastern Point Rd Groton CT 06340. *Fax:* 860-441-8466; *E-Mail:* kliozs@pfizer.com

KLIP, DOROTHEA A, FUNCTIONAL ANALYSIS, APPLIED MATHEMATICS. *Current Pos:* Asst prof, physiol, 63-73, ASSOC PROF PHYSIOL & BIOPHYS, UNIV ALA, BIRMINGHAM, 73-, ASST PROF INFO SCI, 71- *Personal Data:* b Hague, Neth, Sept 27, 21; m 55; c 4. *Educ:* State Univ Utrecht, Dr(theoret physics), 62. *Concurrent Pos:* Reviewer, NSF, Inst Elec & Electronics Engrs & J Comput Appl Math. *Mem:* AAAS; Asn Comput Mach; Sigma Xi; Soc Indust & Appl Math; Math Asn Am. *Res:* Design and implementation of algorithms for the solution of nonlinear (polynomial) equations; symbolic algebraic manipulation by computer. *Mailing Add:* 3137 Dolly Ridge Dr Birmingham AL 35243-5705

KLIP, WILLEM, BIOPHYSICS. *Current Pos:* prof med physics, Dept Physiol Med & Physics, 58-88, EMER PROF PHYSICS, UNIV ALA, BIRMINGHAM, 88- *Personal Data:* b Rotterdam, Neth, Nov 26, 17; US citizen; m 55; c 4. *Educ:* Univ Utrecht, MD, 45, PhD(bact), 51, PhD(theoret physics), 55, DSc(physics), 62. *Prof Exp:* Staff mem of Dr H C Burger, Dept Med Physics, Univ Utrecht, 53-58. *Res:* Medical and theoretical physics. *Mailing Add:* 3137 Dolly Ridge Dr Birmingham AL 35243

KLIPHARDT, RAYMOND A(DOLPH), ENGINEERING SCIENCES. *Current Pos:* asst civil eng, Northwestern Univ, 45-46, from asst prof to assoc prof eng graphics, 46-58, from assoc prof to prof eng sci, 58-70, prof, 70-87, chmn dept, 78-87, EMER PROF ENG SCI & APPL MATH, NORTHWESTERN UNIV, 87- *Personal Data:* b Chicago, Ill, Mar 18, 17; m 45, Rhoda Joan Anderson; c Janis (Emery), Judith (Ecklund), Jill (White), Joan (Quinn) & Jennifer (Miller). *Educ:* Ill Inst Technol, BS, 38, MS, 48. *Prof Exp:* Instr graphics & math, NPark Col, 38-43; asst math, Ill Inst Technol, 43-44. *Concurrent Pos:* Campus coordr, Khartoum Proj, USAID; consult, Appl Math Div, Argonne Nat Lab. *Mem:* AAAS; Am Soc Eng Educ; Asn Comput Mach; Am Acad Mech. *Res:* Abstract geometry; computer automation. *Mailing Add:* 6619 Palma Lane Morton Grove IL 60053

KLIPPEL, JOHN HOWARD, MEDICAL RESEARCH. *Current Pos:* Sr investr, Arthritis & Rheumatism Br, 76-87, CLIN DIR, NAT INST ARTHRITIS & MUSCULOSKELETAL & SKIN DIS, BETHESDA, 87- *Personal Data:* b Warren, Ohio, Oct 15, 44; m 67; c 2. *Educ:* Univ Cincinnati, MD, 70; Bowling Green State Univ, BA, 66; Am Bd Internal Med, cert, 74. *Concurrent Pos:* Borden res award, Univ Cincinnati, 70; clin asst prof med, Med Ctr, Georgetown Univ, 85- *Mem:* Am Col Physicians; Am Col Rheumatology. *Res:* Numerous publications; medicine. *Mailing Add:* NIH Bldg 10 Rm 9N240 Bethesda MD 20892-0001

KLIPPLE, EDMUND CHESTER, mathematical analysis; deceased, see previous edition for last biography

KLIPSCH, PAUL W, ELECTRICAL ENGINEERING. *Current Pos:* RETIRED. *Personal Data:* b Elkhart, Ind. *Educ:* NMex State Univ, BSEE, 26. *Hon Degrees:* LLD, NMex State Univ, 81; DSc, Ark State Univ, 95. *Prof Exp:* Geophysicist, 34-41; founder, Klipsch & Assocs, 46-88. *Mem:* Fel Inst Elec & Electronics Engrs; Acoust Soc Am. *Res:* Patents on firearms, geophysics and audio loudspeakers; contributed articles to professional journals. *Mailing Add:* Klipsch & Assocs PO Box 688 Hope AR 71802

KLIPSTEIN, DAVID HAMPTON, ENGINEERING MANAGEMENT, ALTERNATIVE ENERGY UTILIZATION. *Current Pos:* VPRES CORP DEVELOP, BIOSYM TECHNOL. *Personal Data:* b New York, NY, July 25, 30; m 55, 72; c 8. *Educ:* Princeton Univ, BSE, 52; Mass Inst Technol, SM, 56, ScD, 63. *Prof Exp:* Res engr, Am Cyanamid Corp, 51-54; dir, Bound Brook Sta, Sch Chem Eng Practice, Mass Inst Technol, 58-60; mkt rep, Union Carbide Chem Corp, 62-69, mkt develop mgr, Develop Div, 69-70, prod mgr acrylate monomers & polymers, 70-71, mkt mgr, Trade Paint Intermediates,

71-72; bus develop mgr, Res Cottrell Inc, 72-73, vpres planning & develop oper, Air Pollution Control Group, 73-74, vpres particulate opers, 74-76, dir advan technol corp develop, Res Cottrell Inc, 76-80, dir biphase energy systs, 80- *Concurrent Pos:* Mem, Environ Adv Comt, Fed Energy Admin, 74-76. *Mem:* Am Chem Soc; Am Inst Chem Eng; Geothermal Resources Coun. *Res:* Commercial development; optimization of combustion processes, precombustion fuel cleaning, high efficiency energy conversion systems, load leveling controls. *Mailing Add:* Reaction Design 11436 Sorrento Valley Rd San Diego CA 92121

KLIPSTEIN, FREDERICK AUGUST, MEDICINE. *Current Pos:* assoc prof, 68-72, PROF MED & MICROBIOL, SCH MED & DENT, UNIV ROCHESTER, 72- *Personal Data:* b Greenwich, Conn, June 5, 28; m 65; c 3. *Educ:* Williams Col, BA, 50; Columbia Univ, MD, 54; Am Bd Internal Med, dipl, 63; Am Bd Clin Nutrit, dipl, 67. *Prof Exp:* From intern to asst resident, Med Serv, Presby Hosp, NY, 54-56; NIH trainee, Col Physicians & Surgeons, Columbia Univ, 58-59, instr med, 61-63, from asst prof to assoc prof, 63-68; Postgrad Med Sch, London, Eng, 59-60; chief med resident, Francis Delafield Hosp, New York, 60-61. *Concurrent Pos:* Asst physician, Presby Hosp, NY, 60-68; Am Cancer Soc advan clin fel, 61-63; clin asst vis physician, First Med Div, Bellevue Hosp, 63-68; consult, Greenwich Hosp, Conn, 63-68 & Harlem Hosp, 66-68; vis physician, Francis Delafield Hosp, 66-68; physician, Strong Mem Hosp, Med Ctr, Univ Rochester; dir trop malabsorption unit, Univ Rochester-Univ PR, San Juan, 70-73; assoc prof, Sch Med, Univ PR, San Juan, 70-73. *Mem:* Am Gastroenterol Asn; Am Soc Hemat; Am Soc Clin Nutrit; fel Am Col Gastroenterol; Am Soc Microbiol; fel Am Col Med. *Res:* Diarrheal disorders; tropical malabsorption. *Mailing Add:* 601 Elmwood Ave Univ Rochester Med Ctr New York NY 14642-0001. *Fax:* 716-273-1055

KLIR, GEORGE JIRI, HISTORY & PHILOSOPHY OF SCIENCE, MATHEMATICS GENERAL. *Current Pos:* from assoc prof to prof systs sci, 69-84, CHMN DEPT, SCH ADVAN TECHNOL, STATE UNIV NY, BINGHAMTON, 76-, DISTINGUISHED PROF, T J WATSON SCH, 84- *Personal Data:* b Prague, Czech, Apr 22, 32; m 62, Milena Reholova; c John & Jane. *Educ:* Tech Univ, Prague, MSEE, 57; Czech Acad Sci, PhD(comput sci), 64. *Hon Degrees:* Dr, Univ Econs, Czech, 94. *Honors & Awards:* Advancing Gen Systs Res Award, Neth Soc Systs Res, 76; Outstanding Contribution to Systs Res & Cybernet Award, Austrian Soc Cybernet Studies; Gold Medal of Bernard Bolzano, Czech Acad Sci, 94; Distinguished Leadership Award, Int Soc Syst, Sci, 96. *Prof Exp:* Res asst, Res Inst Telecommun, Prague, 51-52; lectr, Charles Univ, 62-64; lectr elec eng, Univ Baghdad, 64-66; lectr comput sci, Univ Calif, Los Angeles, 66-68; assoc prof elec eng, Fairleigh Dickinson Univ, 68-69. *Concurrent Pos:* Ed, Czech Acad Sci, Prague, 62-63; IBM Systs Res Inst fel, 69; Ed-in-chief, Int J Gen Systs, 74; Neth Inst Advan Studies fel, 75-76 & 82-83; Japan Soc Prom Sci fel, 80. *Mem:* Fel Inst Elec & Electronics Engrs (pres); Philos Sci Asn; Soc Gen Systs Res (pres, 81); Cognitive Sci Soc; Int Fed Systs Res (pres, 80-84); Am Fuzzy Info Processing Soc (pres, 88-91); Intern Fuzzy Syst Asn (pres, 93-95). *Res:* Switching and automata theory; logical design of digital computers; general systems theory and methodology; computer architecture; discrete mathematics; generalized information theory; intelligent systems. *Mailing Add:* Dept Systs Sci & Indust Eng TJ Watson Sch State Univ NY Binghamton NY 13902. *Fax:* 607-777-2577

KLITGAARD, HOWARD MAYNARD, PHYSIOLOGY, ENDOCRINOLOGY. *Current Pos:* from instr to prof, Med Col Wis, 53-78, asst chmn dept, 61-66, vchmn dept, 67-78, ADJ PROF, MED COL WIS, 78- *Personal Data:* b Harlan, Iowa, Oct 16, 24; m 45, Anna Plazova; c Andrew G, Margaret A, Patricia B, Michael L & Diana C. *Educ:* Univ Iowa, BA, 49, MS, 50, PhD(physiol), 53. *Prof Exp:* Instr physiol, Univ Iowa, 51-53. *Concurrent Pos:* Consult, Vet Admin Hosp, Wood, Wis, 57-89; chmn basic sci, Marquette Univ Sch Dent, 78-90, emer prof, 90- *Mem:* AAAS; Endocrine Soc; Am Physiol Soc; Soc Exp Biol & Med; Int Asn Dent Res. *Res:* Physiology and biochemistry of the thyroid hormone, endocrines and metabolism; radioisotope methodology. *Mailing Add:* 9073 N Silver Brook Lane Milwaukee WI 53223-2209

KLITZMAN, BRUCE, MICROCIRCULATION, PLASTIC & RECONSTRUCTIVE SURGERY. *Current Pos:* ASST MED RES PROF PLASTIC SURG & PHYSIOL (CELL BIOL), DUKE UNIV MED CTR, 85-, DIR, PLASTIC SURG RES LABS, 85-, ASSOC PROF BIOCHEM ENG, 93- *Personal Data:* b Dayton, Ohio, Nov 4, 51; m 80, Hardee Brown; c Rachel & Page. *Educ:* Duke Univ, BSE, 74; Univ Va, PhD(physiol), 79. *Honors & Awards:* First Prize Invest, Plastic Surg Educ Found, 88. *Prof Exp:* Res assoc microcirculation, Univ Ariz, 79-81; from asst prof to assoc prof physiol, La State Univ Med Ctr, Shreveport, 82-85. *Concurrent Pos:* Young investr award, European Soc Microcirculation, 80; mem, Mem Comt, Microcirculatory Soc, 82-85; vis prof, Univ Manchester, UK, 85; vis scientist, Burroughs-Wellcome Found, 85; study sect reviewer, NIH, 85-; assoc ed, J Reconstructive Microsurg, 88- *Mem:* Microcirculatory Soc (secy, 93-); Am Physiol Soc; Plastic Surg Res Coun; Am Heart Asn; European Soc Microcirculation; Soc Biomat. *Res:* Regulation of microcirculation and oxygenation of tissue; adaptation of microcirculation to different environments; hyperbaric physiol; biomaterials; microvascular prostheses; soft tissue implants; pressure sore prevention. *Mailing Add:* Duke Univ Med Ctr Box 3906 Durham NC 27710. *Fax:* 919-681-2670; *E-Mail:* klitz@acpud.duke.edu

KLIVINGTON, KENNETH ALBERT, NEUROSCIENCE, COGNITIVE SCIENCE. *Current Pos:* vpres sci, 93-96, SR SCI ADV, FETZER INST, 96- *Personal Data:* b Cleveland, Ohio, Sept 23, 40; m 76, Marie Rose Lopez; c Jason. *Educ:* Mass Inst Technol, SB, 62; Columbia Univ, MS, 64; Yale Univ, PhD(neurosci), 67. *Prof Exp:* Res engr, Electronics Res Lab, Columbia Univ, 62-64; asst res neuroscientist, Univ Calif, San Diego, 64-67; dir res urban design, Fisher-Jackson Assocs, 68-69; prog officer sci, Alfred P Sloan Found, 69-81; vpres res & develop, Electro-Biol Inc, 81-84; asst pres sci planning, Salk Inst, La Jolla, Calif, 84-93. *Concurrent Pos:* Vis scientist, Univ Calif, San Diego, 73; consult, Nat Res Coun, 75-77; vis comt, Dept Psychol, Mass Inst Technol, 81-86; fel, Fetzer Inst, 90- *Mem:* AAAS; Soc Neurosci; Bioelectromagnetics Soc; Cognitive Sci Soc. *Res:* Electromagnetic properties of biological tissues; neural correlates of behavior; neural information processing. *Mailing Add:* Fetzer Inst 9292 W K'L Ave Kalamazoo MI 49009. *Fax:* 616-372-2163; *E-Mail:* kklivington@fetzer.org

KLIWER, JAMES KARL, PHYSICS. *Current Pos:* res assoc, Univ Nev, Reno, 63-65, from asst prof to assoc prof, 65-75, prof, 75-, EMER PROF PHYSICS, UNIV NEV, RENO. *Personal Data:* b Abilene, Kans, Dec 17, 28; m 63. *Educ:* Univ Colo, BS, 57, MS, 59, PhD, 63. *Prof Exp:* Asst, Nuclear Physics Lab, Univ Colo, 57-63. *Mem:* Sigma Xi. *Res:* Atomic and nuclear spectroscopy. *Mailing Add:* Dept Physics Univ Nev Reno NV 89507

KLOBUCAR, WILLIAM DIRK, ORGANOPHOSPHORUS CHEMISTRY. *Current Pos:* SR RES & DEVELOP SPECIALIST, ALBEMARLE CORP, 81- *Personal Data:* b Highland Park, Mich, Mar 16, 53; m 75, Judith M Plotkowski; c Megan S & Adam D. *Educ:* Univ Detroit, BS, 75; Ohio State Univ, PhD(chem), 81. *Mem:* Am Chem Soc. *Res:* Synthesis-organic, organometallic, organophosphorus, orthoalkylation of phenols and aromatic amines. *Mailing Add:* 5154 Sandy Ridge Baton Rouge LA 70817. *Fax:* 504-768-5970

KLOBUCHAR, RICHARD LOUIS, NAVAL ANALYSIS. *Current Pos:* DIR ADV TECHNOL, INC, 81- *Personal Data:* b Chicago, Ill, Oct 15, 48; m 71. *Educ:* Univ Ill, BS, 70; Carnegie-Mellon Univ, MS, 72, PhD(chem), 75. *Prof Exp:* Res assoc nuclear chem, Brookhaven Nat Lab, 75-77; mem prof staff, Ctr Naval Analyses, 77-81. *Mem:* Am Chem Soc; Am Nuclear Soc; Am Phys Soc; Sigma Xi. *Res:* Scientific analysis of naval weapons systems; analytical support of fleet activities; applications of positronium chemistry; high energy nuclear reactions. *Mailing Add:* 758 Suffolk Lane Virginia Beach VA 23452

KLOBUKOWSKI, MARIUSZ ANDRZEJ, MOLECULAR STRUCTURES & PROPERTIES. *Current Pos:* I W Killam fel, Univ Alta, 80-83, res assoc, 83-88, programmer analyst comput sci, 88-89, asst prof chem, 89-94, ASSOC PROF CHEM, UNIV ALTA, 94- *Personal Data:* b Wroclaw, Poland, Mar 6, 48; Can citizen; m 84; c Anna & Emily. *Educ:* NCopernicus Univ, Torun, Poland, BSc, 71, PhD(physics), 78. *Prof Exp:* Asst prof chem, NCopernicus Univ, Poland, 78-81. *Mem:* Chem Inst Can. *Res:* Development and use of accurate Gaussian basis sets for the studies of molecular structure and properties; calculations of the molecular structure and properties of molecules in their excited electronic states; development of parallel algorithms. *Mailing Add:* Dept Chem Univ Alta Edmonton AB T6G 2G2 Can. *Fax:* 403-492-8231; *E-Mail:* mariusz@qc.chem.ualberta.ca

KLOCK, BENNY LEROY, DIGITAL MAPPING, RESEARCH ADMINISTRATION. *Current Pos:* SR CONSULT, ADV MAPPING CONCEPTS, 89- *Personal Data:* b Wash, DC, Oct 29, 34; m 57, 76, Millie Burgess; c Mark S, Lorri & Brian L. *Educ:* Cornell Univ, BA, 56, MS, 60; Georgetown Univ, PhD(astron), 64. *Honors & Awards:* NSF int grant, 74; Distinguished Civilian Serv Award, 89. *Prof Exp:* Tech asst dir six-inch transit circle div, 60-69, dir, Northern Transit Circle Div, 69-76, chief instrumentation br, US Naval Observ, 76-84; geodist, Defense Mapping Agency, 84-85, phys scientist, 85-89. *Mem:* Am Astron Soc; Int Astron Union. *Res:* Design and development of transit circle instrumentation; microcomputer systems; determination of star positions; automation of telescopes; electro-optics system design; advanced weapon system requirements for digital mapping data; digital mapping. *Mailing Add:* 4509 Bayside Dr Milton FL 32583-8423. *E-Mail:* blklock@msn.com

KLOCK, GLEN ORVAL, FOREST SOILS. *Current Pos:* PRIN SCIENTIST, WESTERN RESOURCES ANALYSIS, 82- *Personal Data:* b Portland, Ore, Aug 26, 37; m 58; c 4. *Educ:* Ore State Univ, BS, 59, PhD(soil physics), 68; Iowa State Univ, MS, 63. *Prof Exp:* Res assoc soil physics, Ore State Univ, 64-67; prin res soil scientist, Pac Northwest Forest & Range Exp Sta, USDA Forest Serv, 68-82. *Concurrent Pos:* Pres, Western Resources Anal Inc. *Mem:* Am Soc Agron; Soil Sci Soc Am; Soil Conserv Soc Am; Int Soil Sci Soc; Am Forestry Assoc. *Res:* Water resource and plant nutrient management for maintaining and enhancing the productivity of forest ecosystems in the western United States; use of image processing for development of geographic information system data bases for natural resources management. *Mailing Add:* Western Resources Analysis 2113 Sunrise Circle Wenatchee WA 98801

KLOCK, HAROLD F(RANCIS), ELECTRICAL ENGINEERING. *Current Pos:* prof elec eng, 66-94, EMER PROF ELEC ENG, OHIO UNIV, 94- *Personal Data:* b Miami Beach, Fla, Mar 21, 29; m 55; c 3. *Educ:* Northwestern Univ, BS, 52, MS, 54, PhD(elec eng), 56. *Prof Exp:* Lectr elec eng, Northwestern Univ, 56; asst prof, Case Western Res Univ, 56-62, prof lectr, 62-64; systs engr, Bailey Meter Co, Ohio, 64-66. *Concurrent Pos:* Consult, Reliance Elec & Mfg Co, Nat Cash Register Co & Curtiss-Wright Corp. *Mem:* Inst Elec & Electronics Engrs; Asn Comput Mach; Soc Indust & Appl Math. *Res:* Feedback control systems; switching theory. *Mailing Add:* 2 Strouds Run Rd Athens OH 45701-2979

KLOCK, JOHN W, SANITARY & CIVIL ENGINEERING. *Current Pos:* PROF ENG, ARIZ STATE UNIV, 60- *Personal Data:* b Orange, NJ, Nov 12, 28; m 53; c 2. *Educ:* Southern Calif Univ, BE, 51; Univ Calif, Berkeley, MS, 56, PhD(sanit eng), 60. *Concurrent Pos:* Consult, Ariz Health Planning Authority, USPHS, 51-55, Commun Dis Ctr, 60-, Off Surgeon Gen, 61- & Honeywell Corp, 80-84. *Mem:* Am Water Works Asn; Water Pollution Control Fedn. *Res:* Communicable disease control; water pollution; waste water reclamation. *Mailing Add:* 2626 N 58th Pl Scottsdale AZ 85257-1010

KLOCKE, FRANCIS J, CARDIOLOGY. *Current Pos:* DIR, FEINBERG CARDIOVASC RES INST & PROF MED, MED CTR, NORTHWESTERN UNIV, 91- *Mailing Add:* Northwestern Univ 303 E Chicago Ave Tarry 12-703 Chicago IL 60611-3008. Fax: 312-503-0137

KLOCKE, ROBERT ALBERT, PULMONARY DISEASES, PULMONARY PHYSIOLOGY. *Current Pos:* Res asst prof med, State Univ NY, Buffalo, 70-71, from asst prof to assoc prof med, 71-78, from asst prof to assoc prof physiol, 76-81, PROF MED, STATE UNIV NY, BUFFALO, 78-, PROF PHYSIOL, 81-, CHAIR, DEPT MED, 96- *Personal Data:* b Buffalo, NY, Oct 4, 36; c 3. *Educ:* Manhattan Col, BS, 58; State Univ NY, Buffalo, MD, 62. *Concurrent Pos:* Chief pulmonary lab, Walter Reed Gen Hosp, Washington, DC, 63-66; mem attend staff, E J Meyer Mem Hosp, Buffalo, 70-; chief pulmonary div, dept med, 77-95. *Mem:* Am Physiol Soc; Am Thoracic Soc. *Res:* Pulmonary gas exchange, particularly the rates of chemical reactions of carbon dioxide and oxygen in blood. *Mailing Add:* Dept Med & Physiol State Univ NY 462 Grider St Buffalo NY 14215. Fax: 716-898-5063

KLOET, WILLEM M, NUCLEAR PHYSICS. *Current Pos:* asst prof, 77-82, ASSOC PROF THEORET PHYSICS, RUTGERS UNIV, 82- *Personal Data:* b Neth. *Educ:* Univ Utrecht, PhD(theoret physics), 73. *Prof Exp:* Res assoc theoret physics, Inst Fisica Teorica, Sao Paulo, 68-70, Univ Md, 73-75 & Los Alamos Sci Lab, 75-77. *Mem:* Am Phys Soc; AAAS. *Res:* Theoretical nuclear physics. *Mailing Add:* Dept Physics Rutgers Univ Serin Physics Lab Frelinghuysen Rd Piscataway NJ 08854

KLOETZEL, JOHN ARTHUR, CELL BIOLOGY, PROTOZOOLOGY. *Current Pos:* asst prof, 70-75, ASSOC PROF BIOL, UNIV MD, BALTIMORE CO, 75- *Personal Data:* b Cambridge, Mass, Mar 21, 41; m 62, Judith Nattress; c Jeffrey, Steven, Jennifer & Melanie. *Educ:* Univ Southern Calif, BA, 62; Johns Hopkins Univ, PhD(biol), 67. *Prof Exp:* NIH fel biol, Univ Colo, 67-70. *Concurrent Pos:* Fel, Alexander von Humboldt Found, WGer, 78; pres, Chesapeake Soc Electron Micros, 80-81; vis assoc prof biochem, Johns Hopkins Univ Sch Med, 87; mem exec comt, Soc Protozool, 94- *Mem:* Soc Protozool; Am Soc Cell Biol; Micros Soc Am. *Res:* Fine-structural aspects of cellular function, development and differentiation; Morphogenesis and post-conjugant development in ciliated protozoans, form and function of the ciliate cytoskeleton. *Mailing Add:* Dept Biol Sci Univ Md Baltimore Co Catonsville MD 21228. E-Mail: kloetzel@umbc7.umbc.edu

KLOETZEL, MILTON CARL, ORGANIC CHEMISTRY. *Current Pos:* from asst prof to prof, Univ Southern Calif, 45-58, dean, Grad Sch, 58-68, vpres res & grad affairs, 67-70, acad vpres, 70-75, EMER ACAD VPRES, UNIV SOUTHERN CALIF, 75- *Personal Data:* b Detroit, Mich, Aug 28, 13; m 38, Elizabeth Gorder; c John, James, Paul & Mark. *Educ:* Univ Mich, BS, 34, PhD(org chem), 37. *Prof Exp:* Du Pont fel chem, Univ Mich, 37-38; instr, Harvard Univ, 38-41; from asst prof to assoc prof, DePauw Univ, 41-45. *Mem:* Am Chem Soc. *Res:* Chemistry of polycyclic and heterocyclic compounds; Diels-Alder reaction; chemistry of nitroparaffins. *Mailing Add:* 45090 Namoku St Apt 1313 Apt 1106A Kaneohe HI 96744

KLOHS, WAYNE D, BIOCHEMISTRY, CELL BIOLOGY. *Current Pos:* SR SCIENTIST, WARNER-LAMBERT CO, 83- *Educ:* Ind State Univ, PhD(cell biol), 77. *Mailing Add:* Dept Cancer Res Warner-Lambert Co 2800 Plymouth Rd Ann Arbor MI 48105-2430. Fax: 313-996-1480

KLOKHOLM, ERIK, SOLID STATE PHYSICS. *Current Pos:* res staff mem, Thomas J Watson Res Ctr, 62-73, RES PROJ MGR, MFR RES LABS, DATA SYSTS DIV, IBM CORP, 73- *Personal Data:* b Nykobing, Denmark, Mar 13, 22; US citizen; m 43. *Educ:* Mass Inst Technol, BS, 51; Temple Univ, PhD(physics), 60. *Prof Exp:* From res asst to head struct & metals div, Labs Res & Develop, Franklin Inst, 51-59; res physicist, Moorehead Patterson Res Ctr, Am Mach & Foundry Co, 59-61; assoc prof physics, State Univ NY Col Ceramics, Alfred Univ, 61-62. *Mem:* NY Acad Sci. *Res:* Structure and properties of solids, particularly thin metallic films; crystallographic aspects of solid state physics. *Mailing Add:* 64 Willard Terr Stamford CT 06903

KLOMBERS, NORMAN, ADMINISTRATION. *Current Pos:* RETIRED. *Personal Data:* b New York, NY, Jan 28, 23; m 55, Gloria Eve Piatek; c 2. *Educ:* New York Col Podiat Med, DPM, 44. *Prof Exp:* Fac mem & clin instr, New York Col Podiat Med, 44-78; dir div sci affairs, 78-80, exec dir, Am Podiatric Med Asn, 80-90; exec dir, Anxiety Dis Asn, 91-93. *Concurrent Pos:* Practr podiatric med, New York, NY, 44-68; dir peer rev activ & dir prof serv, Podiatry Soc State NY, 69-78; mem, adv comm Health & Hosp Corp, New York, 70-77 & Health Comt, City Long Beach, NY, 76. *Mem:* Am Col Foot Orthopedists; Am Bd Podiatric Orthopedics; Nat Acad Pract; Acad Podiatric Med. *Mailing Add:* 11213 Joshua Tree Pl North Potomac MD 20878

KLOMP, EDWARD, MECHANICAL ENGINEERING, FLUID MECHANICS. *Current Pos:* Res engr, Gen Motors Corp, 53-59, assoc sr res engr, 59-65, sr res engr, 65-77, staff res engr, 77-80, SR STAFF RES ENGR, RES LABS, GEN MOTORS CORP, WARREN, 80- *Personal Data:* b Detroit, Mich, Oct 18, 30; m 59, Hildegard Schuchardt; c Eric, Kurt & Karl. *Educ:* Wayne State Univ, BS, 52, MS, 53. *Concurrent Pos:* Instr, Wayne State Univ, 55-65. *Mem:* Am Soc Mech Engrs; Soc Automotive Engrs; Sigma Xi. *Res:* Fluid mechanics relating to turbomachinery and internal combustion engines; author of 7 publications; 46 US patents. *Mailing Add:* 36237 Acton Dr Clinton Township MI 48035

KLOMPARENS, KAREN L, PLANT SCIENCE, ELECTRON OPTICS. *Current Pos:* Asst prof, 80-85, PROF ELECTRON OPTICS, DEPTS BOT & PLANT PATH ENTOM, MICH STATE UNIV, 85-, DIR, CTR ELECTRON OPTICS, 80- *Personal Data:* b East Lansing, Mich, Sept 17, 50. *Educ:* Mich State Univ, BS, 72, MS, 74, PhD(bot & electron optics), 77. *Concurrent Pos:* Fulbright fel, Cambridge Univ, 94. *Mem:* Electron Micros Soc Am; Am Phytopath Soc; AAAS; Am Inst Biol Sci; Mycol Soc Am. *Res:* Ultrastructural and analytical electron microscopy methods relevant to plant science; applications to plant host-pathogen-vector relationships, fungal morphology and spore development. *Mailing Add:* Entomol Mich State Univ 243 Nat Sci East Lansing MI 48824-1115. E-Mail: kklompar@msu.bitnet

KLOMPEN, J S H, systematics, parasitology, for more information see previous edition

KLONER, ROBERT A, CARDIOLOGY, HYPERTENSION. *Current Pos:* PROF MED, UNIV SOUTHERN CALIF, 88-; DIR RES, HEART INST & HOSP GOOD SAMARITAN, 88- *Personal Data:* b Buffalo, NY, Oct 8, 49; m 77, Judith; c Alissa & Susan. *Educ:* Northwestern Univ, BS, 71, PhD(exp path), 74, MD, 75. *Honors & Awards:* Sheard-Sanford Award, Am Soc Clin Pathologists, 76; Continuing Serv Award, Am Heart Asn, 91. *Prof Exp:* Med intern, resident & cardiol fel, Brigham & Women's Hosp, Harvard Med Sch, 75-79, asst prof to assoc prof, 79-86; prof med, Wayne State Univ Med Sch, 85-88. *Concurrent Pos:* Jr assoc physician, Brigham & Women's Hosp, 79-82, assoc physician, 82-84; estab investr award, Am Heart Asn, 86, fel, Coun Clin Cardiol, 91-; mem, Cardiovasc Study Sect A, NIH, 95- *Mem:* Am Heart Asn; Am Soc Clin Invest; fel Am Col Cardiol. *Res:* Pathophysiology of heart during is chemial/reperfusion; studies of stunned myocardrion, no-reflow phenomenon, hibernating myocardium, preconditioning phenomenon; studies of gene therapy of the heart; clinical studies involving thrombolysis, hypertension and triggers of heart disease. *Mailing Add:* Heart Inst Good Samaritan Hosp 1225 Wilshire Blvd Los Angeles CA 90017. Fax: 213-977-4107

KLONTZ, EVERETT EARL, PHYSICS. *Current Pos:* RETIRED. *Personal Data:* b Akron, Ohio, Sept 28, 21; m 42; c 3. *Educ:* Kent State Univ, BS, 42; Univ Ill, MS, 43; Purdue Univ, PhD(physics), 52. *Prof Exp:* Asst physics, Univ Ill, 42-44; instr, Bowling Green State Univ, 44; asst, Purdue Univ, West Lafayette, 46-52, res assoc & asst prof, 52-62, assoc prof physics, 62-92. *Mem:* Am Phys Soc; Am Asn Physics Teachers. *Res:* Effects of high energy particle irradiations on physical properties of crystals. *Mailing Add:* Dept Physics Purdue Univ West Lafayette IN 47907-1396

KLOPATEK, JEFFREY MATTHEW, ECOLOGY, BOTANY. *Current Pos:* PROF & RES ECOLOGIST, DEPT BOT, ARIZ STATE UNIV, 81- *Personal Data:* b Milwaukee, Wis, Dec 5, 44; m 84; c 2. *Educ:* Univ Wis, Milwaukee, BS, 71, MS, 74; Univ Okla, PhD(bot), 78. *Prof Exp:* Res assoc ecol, Okla Biol Surv, 73-76; res ecologist, Environ Sci Div, Oak Ridge Nat Lab, 76-81. *Concurrent Pos:* Consult, Elec Power Res Inst, AEC-Energy Res & Develop Admin, 73-74 & Forest Serv, USDA, 81-; lectr, Univ Tenn, 80-81; chmn, Munic Planning Comn, Farragut, Tenn, 80-81; vis scientist, US Environ Protection Assoc, 90; Fulbright scholar, 90-91; bd mem-prof cert, Ecol Soc Am, 92- *Mem:* Ecol Soc Am; Int Asn Ecol; Am Inst Biol Sci; Soc Wetland Sci; Soil Sci Soc Am; Int Soc Ecol Model. *Res:* Nutrient cycling; ecosystem analysis; ecosystem restoration; wetland ecology; landscape ecology; microbial processes; succession and disturbance in arid and semi-arid environments. *Mailing Add:* Dept Bot Ariz State Univ Tempe AZ 85287-0002

KLOPFENSTEIN, CHARLES E, PHYSICAL ORGANIC CHEMISTRY, CHEMICAL INSTRUMENTATION. *Current Pos:* Asst prof, 66-80, DIR LABS, UNIV ORE, 66-, ASSOC PROF CHEM, 80- *Personal Data:* b Los Angeles, Calif, July 6, 40; m 63. *Educ:* Univ Ore, BA, 62, PhD(chem), 66. *Concurrent Pos:* NATO res fel, Lab Org Chem, Swiss Fed Inst Technol, 66-67. *Mem:* Am Chem Soc. *Res:* Synthesis of aromatic heterocyclic compounds; calculation of physical properties of aromatic compounds; computer analysis of physical data. *Mailing Add:* 3650 Glen Oak Dr Eugene OR 97405-4737

KLOPFENSTEIN, KENNETH F, MATHEMATICS. *Current Pos:* asst prof, 67-73, ASSOC PROF MATH, COLO STATE UNIV, 73- *Personal Data:* b Mt Pleasant, Iowa, Mar 13, 40; m 61; c 3. *Educ:* Iowa Wesleyan Col, BA, 61; Colo State Univ, MS, 63; Purdue Univ, PhD(math), 67. *Prof Exp:* Instr math, Wabash Col, 66-67. *Mem:* Math Asn Am; Am Math Soc. *Res:* Hilbert space; operator theory; mathematics education. *Mailing Add:* Dept Math Colo State Univ Ft Collins CO 80523

KLOPFENSTEIN, WILLIAM ELMER, BIOCHEMISTRY. *Current Pos:* PROF BIOCHEM & CHMN CHEM DEPT, WESTERN ILL UNIV, 88- *Personal Data:* b Paris, Ohio, Dec 23, 35; m 59; c 3. *Educ:* Pa State Univ, BS, 58, MS, 61, PhD(biochem), 64. *Prof Exp:* Asst technologist food res, Gen Foods Corp, 58; instr biochem, Pa State Univ, 60-64; from asst prof to prof biochem, Kans State Univ, 64-88, assoc biochemist, Agr Exp Sta, 72-88, chmn, grad biochem group, 77-86. *Mem:* Am Chem Soc; Sigma Xi; Am Soc Biol Chemists; Am Oil Chem Soc. *Res:* Structure and function of lipids; physical properties of lipids; binding of lipids to proteins; use of lipids as alternative fuels. *Mailing Add:* Dept Chem Western Ill Univ Macomb IL 61455

KLOPFER, PETER HUBERT, ZOOLOGY & ANIMAL BEHAVIOR, ECOLOGY. *Current Pos:* DEPT ZOOL, DUKE UNIV. *Personal Data:* b Berlin, Ger, Aug 9, 30; m 55, Martha Smith; c 3. *Educ:* Univ Calif, Los Angeles, AB, 52; Yale Univ, PhD(zool), 57. *Honors & Awards:* NIMH Res Scientist Award, 70; Humboldt Prize, Fed Repub Ger, 79. *Prof Exp:* Head, Sci Dept, Windsor Mountain Sch, Mass, 52-53 & 55-56; USPHS fel, Cambridge Univ, 57-58; from asst prof to prof zool, Duke Univ, 58-81, dir, Field Sta Animal Behav, 68-81. *Concurrent Pos:* NIMH career develop award, 65; Alexander von Humboldt Prize, 79-80. *Mem:* Fel AAAS; Ecol Soc Am; fel Animal Behav Soc; Int Soc Res Aggression. *Res:* Behavior and ecology, especially analysis of the development of species-specific behavior in birds and mammals; maternal-filial relations and aggression. *Mailing Add:* Duke Univ Dept Zool Box 90325 Durham NC 27708-0325. *Fax:* 919-684-6168; *E-Mail:* phk@acpub.duke.edu

KLOPMAN, GILLES, CHEMISTRY. *Current Pos:* assoc prof chem, Case Western Res Univ, 67-69, dean, math & sci, 86-88, prof chem, 69-86 CHMN, CHEM DEPT, CASE WESTERN RES UNIV, 81-, CHARLES S MABERY PROF RES, 86- *Personal Data:* b Brussels, Belg, Feb 24, 33; m 57. *Educ:* Free Univ Brussels, Lic es Sci, 56, Dr es Sci, 60. *Honors & Awards:* Stas-Spring Award, Belg Chem Soc; Morley Award, Am Chem Soc, 93. *Prof Exp:* Res assoc org chem, Cyanamid Europ Res Inst, 60-67. *Concurrent Pos:* Welch fel, Univ Tex, 65-66; vpres, Biofor Inc. *Mem:* Am Chem Soc; The Chem Soc; Swiss Chem Soc; Belg Chem Soc; Am Asn Univ Professors; Sigma Xi. *Res:* Applied theoretical organic chemistry; chemical reactivity; nucleophilic reactivity; quantum mechanical calculation of large organic molecules; quantitative structure activity relationship of pharmacological and of carcinogenic molecules. *Mailing Add:* Dept Chem Case Western Res Univ Cleveland OH 44106-7078

KLOPOTEK, DAVID L, ORGANIC CHEMISTRY. *Current Pos:* from asst prof to assoc prof, 68-82, PROF CHEM, ST NORBERT COL, 83- *Personal Data:* b Green Bay, Wis, Jan 11, 42; m 63; c 2. *Educ:* St Norbert Col, BA, 64; Utah State Univ, PhD(chem), 68. *Prof Exp:* Res assoc chem, E I Du Pont de Nemours & Co Inc, 67-68. *Concurrent Pos:* NSF grant, 71-73; Res Corp grant, 72-74; vis prof, Dartmouth Univ, 83; summer fac fel, Lewis Res Ctr, Cleveland, Ohio, 85, 86 & 92, NASA, Am Soc Environ Educ; NASA grants, polyimide res, 86- *Mem:* Am Chem Soc. *Res:* Chemistry of compounds containing nitrogen-fluorine bonds; reactivity of fluoronitrene with nucleophiles; diamines for polyimide composites. *Mailing Add:* 8066 KK Lane Sobieski WI 54171

KLOPP, CALVIN TREXLER, SURGERY. *Current Pos:* from asst clin prof to assoc prof, George Washington Univ, 46-60, Warwick prof surg, Sch Med, 60-76, med dir, Univ Clin, 68-76, EMER PROF SURG, SCH MED, GEORGE WASHINGTON UNIV, 76- *Personal Data:* b Atlantic City, NJ, Dec 7, 12; c 3. *Educ:* Swarthmore Col, BA, 34; Harvard Univ, MD, 38. *Prof Exp:* Intern surg, Boston City Hosp, Mass, 39-40; rotating intern med, Reading Hosp, Pa, 40-41; resident, Mem Hosp, New York, 41-44. *Concurrent Pos:* Consult, var hosps, 46- *Mem:* Am Radium Soc; Am Asn Cancer Res; Am Col Surgeons; James Ewing Soc; Am Thyroid Asn; Sch Head & Neck Surg; Southern Surg Asn. *Res:* Cancer. *Mailing Add:* 4443 64th Ave Dr W Bradenton FL 34210-4014

KLOPPEL, THOMAS MATHEW, CELL BIOLOGY. *Current Pos:* sr res scientist, 88-92, BIOANAL GROUP LEADER, CORTECH, INC, 93- *Personal Data:* b Denver, Colo, Oct 27, 50; m 76, Myra Nugent; c Erika & Seth. *Educ:* Colo State Univ, BS, 72, MS, 74; Purdue Univ, PhD(cell biol), 79. *Prof Exp:* Res biologist, Vet Admin Med Ctr, Denver, 81-88; asst prof biochem, Univ Colo Sch Med, 81-88. *Concurrent Pos:* Fel, Am Cancer Soc, 80. *Mem:* Am Soc Cell Biol. *Res:* Examination of potential anti-inflammatory drugs for clinical use; role of membrane receptors in intracellular vesicle trafficking. *Mailing Add:* 35353 Whetstone Ct Elizabeth CO 80107

KLOS, EDWARD JOHN, PLANT PATHOLOGY. *Current Pos:* from asst prof to assoc prof, 54-67, PROF PLANT PATH, MICH STATE UNIV, 67-, CHMN DEPT, 80- *Personal Data:* b Hamilton, Ont, June 27, 25; m 49; c 2. *Educ:* Ont Agr Col, BSAg, 50; Cornell Univ, PhD(plant path), 54. *Prof Exp:* Asst plant path, Cornell Univ, 50-54. *Mem:* Am Phytopath Soc. *Res:* Effect of Erwinia herbicola on fire blight of pome fruits; population studies of Erwinia amylovora; resistance or tolerance of Venturia inaequalis to fungicides; control of tree fruit diseases by chemicals and other means. *Mailing Add:* 2791 Southwood Dr East Lansing MI 48823

KLOS, WILLIAM ANTON, ELECTRICAL ENGINEERING. *Current Pos:* STAFF MEM, VECTOR GRAPHICS, 83- *Personal Data:* b Houston, Tex, Aug 14, 36; m 63; c 1. *Educ:* Univ Houston, BS, 63 & 64, PhD(elec eng), 69. *Prof Exp:* Res asst elec eng, Univ Houston, 66-69; prin engr, Lockheed Electronics Co, Tex, 69-70; from assoc prof to prof, Univ Southwestern La, 70-83, head dept, 70-83. *Mem:* Nat Soc Prof Engrs; Acoust Soc Am; Am Soc Eng Educ; Am Geophys Union; Inst Elec & Electronics Engrs; Sigma Xi. *Res:* Electromagnetic wave propagation; radar cross-section and radar systems. *Mailing Add:* Vector Graphics 410 Audubon Blvd Lafayette LA 70503

KLOSE, JULES ZEISER, ATOMIC PHYSICS, VACUUM ULTRAVIOLET RADIOMETRY. *Current Pos:* physicist, Nat Bur Stand, 61-88, GUEST SCIENTIST, NAT INST STAND & TECHNOL, 89- *Personal Data:* b St Louis, Mo, Aug 7, 27; m 58, Evelyn Y Brady; c Linda M, Jules S, Charles D & James M. *Educ:* Wash Univ, St Louis, AB, 49; Univ Rochester, MS, 53; Cath Univ Am, PhD(physics), 58. *Prof Exp:* Physics aid, US Naval Gun Factory, 48; instr, Dunford Sch, Mo, 49; asst physics, Univ Rochester, 49-53; from asst prof to assoc prof, US Naval Acad, 53-61. *Concurrent Pos:* Res assoc & lectr, Univ Mich, 60-61. *Mem:* Am Phys Soc; Optical Soc Am; Sigma Xi; Coun Optical Radiation Measurements. *Res:* Vacuum ultraviolet radiometry; measurement of atomic lifetimes and transition probabilities; ultrasonics; thermal relaxation in gases; cosmic rays; calibration of space instrumentation. *Mailing Add:* Nat Inst Stand & Technol Gaithersburg MD 20899

KLOSE, THOMAS RICHARD, ORGANIC CHEMISTRY. *Current Pos:* RES CHEMIST ORG CHEM, EASTMAN KODAK CO RES LABS, 75- *Personal Data:* b Adelaide, Australia, Apr 20, 46; m 74; c 2. *Educ:* Univ Adelaide, BSc, 67, Hons, 68, PhD(org chem), 72. *Prof Exp:* Fel org chem, Res Inst Med & Chem, 72-74 & Mass Inst Technol, 74-75. *Mem:* Am Chem Soc. *Res:* Synthesis of novel dyes and pigments for use in non-silver imaging systems. *Mailing Add:* 19 Sandpiper Hill Fairport NY 14450-9306

KLOSEK, RICHARD C, MICROBIOLOGY. *Current Pos:* From asst prof to assoc prof, 60-74, PROF MICROBIOL, FAIRLEIGH DICKINSON UNIV, 74- *Personal Data:* b Olyphant, Pa, Feb 18, 33; m 56; c 3. *Educ:* Univ Scranton, BS, 54; St John's Univ, MS, 56, PhD(microbiol), 60. *Concurrent Pos:* Res grants, Fairleigh Dickinson Univ, 61-62 & 71; res grant, Jomol Pharmaceut Corp, 63-64, consult, 65; mem, Smithsonian Inst, 74. *Mem:* Fel AAAS; Am Acad Microbiol; Soc Protozool; Sigma Xi. *Res:* Protozooan nutrition and cellular chemistry, especially pathways associated with carbohydrate, protein and lipid metabolism; isolation and functional aspects of chemotherapeutic agents utilized in bacterial, fungal and viral diseases. *Mailing Add:* 25 Palmer Dr Wayne NJ 07470-2627

KLOSNER, JEROME M, APPLIED MECHANICS, STRUCTURAL DYNAMICS. *Current Pos:* from res assoc to assoc prof, 56-67, PROF APPL MECH, POLYTECH INST NY, 67- *Personal Data:* b New York, NY, Mar 23, 28; m 65, Naomi Certner; c Michael, Lise & Marc. *Educ:* City Col New York, BCE, 48; Columbia Univ, MS, 50; Polytech Inst Brooklyn, PhD(appl mech), 59. *Prof Exp:* Sr stress analyst, Repub Aviation Corp, 52-56; sr scientist appl mech, Res & Advan Develop Div, Avco Corp, 56. *Concurrent Pos:* Consult, Res & Advan Develop Div, Avco Corp, Gen Appl Sci Labs, Fed Trade Comn, Res Ctr, Hazeltine Corp, Ingersoll-Rand Corp & Technautics Corp; consult, Weidlinger Assocs, Consult Engrs, 76-; mem comt on recommendations US Army basic sci res, Nat Res Coun, 76-79, & 85-88. *Mem:* Am Soc Mech Engrs; assoc fel Am Inst Aeronaut & Astronaut; Soc Rheol; fel Am Soc Civil Engrs. *Res:* Structural dynamics; hydroelasticity; acoustic radiation; elastodynamics. *Mailing Add:* Prof Appl Mech Polytech Univ Rte 110 Farmingdale NY 11735. *Fax:* 516-755-4404; *E-Mail:* jklosner@duke.poly.edu

KLOSTERMAN, ALBERT LEONARD, SOLID GEOMETRIC MODELING, PRODUCT DEFINITION DATA BASE. *Current Pos:* proj mgr, Stuct Dynamics Res Corp, 70-72, mem tech staff, 72-73, dir tech staff, 73-78, vpres & gen mgr, 78-83, sr vpres, chief tech officer & gen mgr, 83-95, SR VPRES & CHIEF SCIENTIST, STRUCT DYNAMICS RES CORP, 95- *Personal Data:* b Cincinnati, Ohio, Oct 22, 42; m 64; c Scott, Lance, Kimberly & Brad. *Educ:* Univ Cincinnati, BSME, 65, MSME, 68, PhD(mech eng), 71. *Prof Exp:* Instr mech eng, Univ Cincinnati, 65-70. *Concurrent Pos:* Adj assoc prof, Univ Cincinnati, 72- *Mem:* Am Soc Mech Engrs; Asn Comput Mach. *Res:* System dynamics; experimental modal analysis; solid geometric modeling; product definition data base for mechanical design; mechanical computer aided engineering (MCAE) technology. *Mailing Add:* 5444 Forest Ridge Circle Milford OH 45150

KLOSTERMAN, HAROLD J, BIOCHEMISTRY. *Current Pos:* From asst to assoc chemist, 46-57, prof biochem & chmn dept, 57-88, EMER PROF, NDAK STATE UNIV, 88- *Personal Data:* b Mooreton, NDak, Jan 11, 24; m 46; c 7. *Educ:* NDak State Univ, BS, 46, MS, 49; Univ Minn, PhD(biochem), 55. *Hon Degrees:* DSc, NDak State Univ, 90. *Mem:* Am Chem Soc. *Res:* Isolation and characterization of natural products. *Mailing Add:* 1437 12th St N Fargo ND 58102-2529

KLOSTERMEYER, EDWARD CHARLES, ENTOMOLOGY. *Current Pos:* asst entomologist, Irrig Exp Sta, 47-58, assoc entomologist, 58-62, entomologist, 62-81, prof, 75-81, EMER PROF ENTOM, WASH STATE UNIV, 81- *Personal Data:* b Omaha, Nebr, Feb 25, 19; m 41; c 2. *Educ:* Univ Nebr, BSc, 40, MSc, 42; State Col Wash, PhD, 52. *Prof Exp:* Asst entom, Univ Nebr, 40-42; asst, Univ Calif, 46-47. *Mem:* Entom Soc Am. *Res:* Field crop insect control; insect pollination; bee behavior. *Mailing Add:* 1915 Benson Ave Prosser WA 99350-1543

KLOSTERMEYER, LYLE EDWARD, ENTOMOLOGY. *Current Pos:* OWNER, LYLE'S PEST CONTROL & ENTOM SERV, 85- *Personal Data:* b Oakland, Calif, Dec 4, 44. *Educ:* Wash State Univ, BS, 68; NDak State Univ, MS, 74; Univ Nebr, PhD(entom), 78. *Prof Exp:* Res asst, Dept Entom, NDak State Univ, 70-73 & Univ Nebr, 73-78; asst prof entom, Dept Agr Biol, Univ Tenn, 78-80, asst prof entom, Dept Entom & Plant Path, 80-85. *Mem:* Entom Soc Am; Sigma Xi. *Mailing Add:* 550 Wine Country Rd Apt 11 Prosser WA 99350

KLOTMAN, PAUL, nephrology, cardiology, for more information see previous edition

KLOTS, CORNELIUS E, UNIMOLECULAR REACTIONS, VAN DER WAALS MOLECULES. *Current Pos:* STAFF SCIENTIST CHEM PHYSICS, OAK RIDGE NAT LAB, 64- *Personal Data:* b Rochester, NY, Oct 19, 33; m 59; c 4. *Educ:* Haverford Col, BS, 55; Harvard Univ, PhD(phys chem), 59. *Prof Exp:* Res assoc chem, Fla State Univ, 61-64. *Concurrent Pos:* Ford Found prof, Physics Dept, Univ Tenn, 66-69; vis prof, Univ Paris-Sud, 81-82. *Mem:* Fel Am Phys Soc; Sigma Xi. *Res:* Properties of reactions in small isolated aggregates of matter. *Mailing Add:* Oak Ridge Nat Lab MS 6125 Oak Ridge TN 37831

KLOTZ, ARTHUR PAUL, CLINICAL MEDICINE. *Current Pos:* RETIRED. *Personal Data:* b Milwaukee, Wis, Sept 28, 13; m 41, Margaret Pollard; c Stephen, Suzanne, John & Peter. *Educ:* Univ Chicago, SB & MD, 38. *Prof Exp:* Asst in med, Univ Chicago, 49-51, instr, 51-54; from asst prof to prof med, Med Ctr, Univ Kans, 54-75, dir, Div Gastroenterol, 54-75; dir gastrointestinal lab, Boswell Mem Hosp, Sun City, 75-86, dir res Biogerontol Res Inst, 86-88. *Concurrent Pos:* Consult, Menorah Hosp, Vet Hosp, Kansas City, Mo & Wadsworth, Kans; mem, Gastroenterol Res Group; res collabr, Brookhaven Nat Lab, NY; pvt pract clin gastroenterol, 75-82; ed, Boswell Hosp Proc, 80-88. *Mem:* Am Soc Gastrointestinal Endoscopy; Soc Nuclear Med; Am Gastroenterol Asn; Am Physiol Soc; Am Col Physicians; Am Geriat Soc. *Res:* Gastric secretions; pancreatic function; liver disease; ulcerative colitis; small bowel absorption in humans by perfusion technique. *Mailing Add:* 5642 N Mina Vista Dr Tucson AZ 85718-4122

KLOTZ, EDWARD SEYMOUR, LINEAR & INTEGER PROGRAMMING. *Current Pos:* MATH PROG SPECIALIST, CPLEX OPTIMIZATION, INC, 91- *Educ:* Oberlin Col, BA, 82; Stanford Univ, MS, 88; Stanford Univ, PhD(opers res), 88. *Prof Exp:* Analyst, Ketron Mgt Sci, 88-90; assoc, Stanford Bus Software, 90-91. *Mem:* Soc Indust & Appl Math. *Mailing Add:* PO Box 4670 Incline Village NV 89450. *Fax:* 702-831-7755; *E-mail:* ed@cplex.com

KLOTZ, EUGENE ARTHUR, MATHEMATICS. *Current Pos:* instr, 63-69, assoc prof, 69-77, PROF MATH, SWARTHMORE COL, 77- *Personal Data:* b Fredericksburg, Iowa, June 25, 35; m 57; c 2. *Educ:* Antioch Col, BS, 58; Yale Univ, PhD(math), 65. *Prof Exp:* Actg instr math, Yale Univ, 62-63. *Concurrent Pos:* NSF sci fac fel, 74; prin investr, prog math educ using info technol, NSF-Nat Inst Educ, 81-82. *Mem:* Am Math Soc; Math Asn Am; Asn Comput Mach; Asn Develop Comput Based Instrnl Systs; Sigma Xi. *Res:* Real-time microcomputer color graphics units for mathematics instruction, using video arcade technology; social science mathematics. *Mailing Add:* Dept Math Swarthmore Col Swarthmore PA 19081

KLOTZ, IRVING MYRON, PHYSICAL BIOCHEMISTRY. *Current Pos:* Abbott res assoc, Northwestern Univ, 40, Nat Defense Res Comt assoc, 41-42, from instr to prof, 42-50, Morrison prof, 63-86, EMER PROF CHEM & BIOCHEM MOLECULAR BIOL & CELL BIOL, NORTHWESTERN UNIV, EVANSTON, 86- *Personal Data:* b Chicago, Ill, Jan 22, 16; m 47, 66, Mary S Hanlon; c Edward, Audie & David. *Educ:* Univ Chicago, SB, 37, PhD(chem), 40. *Honors & Awards:* Eli Lilly Award, Am Chem Soc, 49; Reilly lectr, Univ Notre Dame; Mack lectr, Ohio State Univ; Barton lectr, Univ Okla; Gooch-Stephens lectr, Baylor Univ; Midwest Award, Am Chem Soc, 70; Welch lectr, Univ Tex, 73; Winzler lectr, Fla State Univ, 77; Steiner lectr, Oberlin, 81; Shaw lectr, Univ SDak, 82; Watkins lectr, Wichita State Univ, 83; Bull lectr, Iowa, 85; Shrage lectr, Univ Ill, 88; W C Rose Award, Am Soc Biochem & Molecular Biol, 93; Heritage lectr, Univ Alta. *Prof Exp:* Asst chem, Univ Chicago, 37-39; Winzler prof biochem, Univ Ill Med Sch, 88-91. *Concurrent Pos:* Lalor fel, 47-48; chmn biophys & biophys chem, Study Sect, NIH, 63-66; mem corp & trustee, Marine Biol Lab, Woods Hole; distinguished vis prof, Univ Buffalo, 67, Univ Calif, Davis, 82, Ohio State Univ, 89. *Mem:* Nat Acad Sci; fel Am Acad Arts & Sci; Am Chem Soc; Am Soc Biochem & Molecular Biol; fel AAAS; fel Roy Soc Med. *Res:* Structure and function of proteins and polymers; spectroscopy; biochemical energetics; thermodynamics. *Mailing Add:* 2515 Pioneer Rd Evanston IL 60201-2203. *Fax:* 847-491-7713; *E-Mail:* chemdept@chem.nwu.edu

KLOTZ, JEROME HAMILTON, BIOSTATISTICS. *Current Pos:* assoc prof, 65-69, PROF STATIST, UNIV WIS-MADISON, 69- *Personal Data:* b Loma Linda, Calif, June 21, 34; m 56; c 2. *Educ:* Univ Calif, Berkeley, AB, 56, PhD(statist), 60. *Prof Exp:* Lectr math & statist, McGill Univ, 60-61; asst prof statist, Univ Calif, Berkeley, 61-62; asst prof, Harvard Univ, 62-65. *Concurrent Pos:* Consult statistician clin oncol, Univ Wis, 72-; prof statist, Cent Oncol Group, 72- & Wis Clin Cancer Ctr, 73-; prof, Ohio State Univ, 81-82. *Mem:* Fel Inst Math Statist; Am Statist Asn; Biomet Soc. *Res:* Nonparametric methods; computer techniques; components of variance; biostatistical methods. *Mailing Add:* Dept Statist Univ Wis 1210 W Dayton St Madison WI 53706-1685

KLOTZ, JOHN WILLIAM, genetics, philosophy of science; deceased, see previous edition for last biography

KLOTZ, LOUIS HERMAN, STRUCTURAL ENGINEERING, GEOTECHNICAL ENGINEERING. *Current Pos:* asst prof, Univ NH, 65-69, assoc prof, 69-86, actg chmn dept, 69-71, chmn dept, 71-73, EMER ASSOC PROF CIVIL ENG, UNIV NH, 86-; EXEC DIR, NEW ENG STATES EARTHQUAKE CONSORTIUM, 91-; PRES KLOTZ CONSULT GROUP INC, 94- *Personal Data:* b Elizabeth, NJ, May 21, 28; m 66, Virginia H Roll; c Emily L & Jennifer C. *Educ:* Pa State Univ, BSCE, 51; NY Univ, MCE, 56; Rutgers Univ, NB, PhD(civil eng), 67. *Prof Exp:* Struct engr, firms, NY & NJ metrop area, 51-56; civil engr, Ebasco Int Corp, New York, 56-58, construct proj engr defense electronic prod, Missile & Surface Radar Div, Radio Corp Am, NJ, 58-59; res assoc civil eng, Univ Ill, Urbana, 59-61; consult engr, Ohio & NJ, 61-65. *Concurrent Pos:* Ed, Energy Sources, Promises & Probs, 80; pres, Durham Inst, 80-85; consult engr, 85-, Univ NH, 87-; spec proj dir, ASCE Hq, NY, 86-87. *Mem:* AAAS; Am Soc Civil Engrs; Am Soc Eng Educ; NY Acad Sci. *Res:* Applications of linear graph system; mathematical models and computer applications in structures, manufacturing processes and soil mechanics; seismic analysis, design and rehabilitation of structures and life-lines; forensic analysis of structural problems. *Mailing Add:* 90 Mainmast Circle New Castle NH 03854-0204. *Fax:* 603-430-4041; *E-Mail:* ihk@star.net

KLOTZ, LYNN CHARLES, PHYSICAL BIOCHEMISTRY. *Current Pos:* CONSULT, BIOTECHNOL STRATEGY, 89- *Personal Data:* b Trenton, NJ, Nov 25, 40; c 1. *Educ:* Princeton Univ, AB, 65; Univ Calif, San Diego, PhD(chem), 71. *Prof Exp:* Res asst molecular biol, Princeton Univ, 61-62; asst prof biochem, Harvard Univ, 71-74, assoc prof, 74-79; staff mem, Biotechnica Int, 81-89. *Concurrent Pos:* Vis lectr, Princeton Univ, 79-81. *Mem:* AAAS; Sigma Xi; Am Chem Soc. *Res:* Physical studies of DNA and chromosomes; evolution of DNA and chromosomes; triplex physical chemistry. *Mailing Add:* 71 Winslow Ave Somerville MA 02144-2502

KLOTZ, RICHARD LAWRENCE, BIOLOGY. *Current Pos:* From asst prof to assoc prof, 79-89, PROF BIOL, STATE UNIV NY, CORTLAND, 89- *Personal Data:* b Philadelphia, Pa, Jan 4, 50; m 75, Laurie Kraft; c Leidy, Carrie & Rick. *Educ:* Denison Univ, BS, 72; Univ Conn, MS, 75, PhD(bot), 79. *Mem:* Am Soc Limnol & Oceanog; AAAS; Sigma Xi; NAm Benthol Soc. *Res:* Phosphorus influence on stream ecosystems. *Mailing Add:* Dept Biol Sci State Univ NY Box 2000 Cortland NY 13045-0900

KLOTZBACH, ROBERT J(AMES), CHEMICAL ENGINEERING. *Current Pos:* RETIRED. *Personal Data:* b New York, NY, Aug 27, 22; m 46, Myrtle Byrd; c Robert B. *Educ:* Fordham Univ, BS, 43; NY Univ, ASTP, 44. *Prof Exp:* Develop engr, Oak Ridge Nat Lab, 46-48, design engr, 48-53, design problem leader, 53, proj engr, Union Carbide Nuclear Div, 55-57, mgr eng dept, 57-65, mgr, Union Carbide Mining & Metals Div, 65-69, asst dir eng, 69, dir eng, 69-72, dir technol, Union Carbide Metals Div Union Carbide Corp, 73-85, Union Carbide Corp Res Comt, 73-83; dir technol, Umetco Minerals Corp, 83-85. *Mem:* AAAS. *Res:* Solvent extraction; power reactor fuel reprocessing; mining and milling; ion exchange. *Mailing Add:* 5140 Dana Dr Lewiston NY 14092

KLOUDA, MARY ANN ABERLE, PHYSIOLOGY. *Current Pos:* INSTR BIOL SCI, CALIF STATE UNIV, SACRAMENTO, 87- *Personal Data:* b Peoria, Ill, Jan 8, 37; m 62; c 4. *Educ:* Col Notre Dame, Calif, BA, 58; Loyola Univ, Ill, PhD(physiol), 64. *Prof Exp:* Res assoc physiol, Loyola Univ, Ill, 64-65; from instr to asst prof, Univ Mass, Amherst, 65-71; lectr, Col of Our Lady of the Elms, 74-79, from asst prof to assoc prof biol, 79-87. *Res:* Cardiac response to sympathetic stimulation; effects of cardiac sympathectomy. *Mailing Add:* 8539 Story Ridge Way Antelope CA 95843-5321

KLOWDEN, MARC JEFFREY, MEDICAL ENTOMOLOGY. *Current Pos:* PROF ENTOM, UNIV IDAHO, MOSCOW, 81- *Personal Data:* b Chicago, Ill, June 6, 48; m 70, Anne J Weitzman; c Daniel & Amanda. *Educ:* Univ Ill, Chicago Circle, BS, 70, MS, 73, PhD(biol), 76. *Honors & Awards:* Sigma Xi Res Awards, 80, 82 & 88. *Prof Exp:* Res asst biol, Univ Ill, Chicago Circle, 70-73, teaching asst biol, 73-76; res assoc, Dept Entom, Univ Ga, 76-81. *Mem:* AAAS; Entom Soc Am; Sigma Xi; Soc Vector Ecologists; Am Mosquito Control Asn; Am Soc Zool. *Res:* Physiology of mosquito behavior. *Mailing Add:* Dept Entom Univ Idaho Moscow ID 83843-2339. *E-Mail:* mklowden@marvin.ag.uidaho.edu

KLUBA, RICHARD MICHAEL, FOOD SCIENCE, ANALYTICAL CHEMISTRY. *Current Pos:* Res assoc, 77-80, DIR RES, TAYLOR WINE CO INC, 80- *Personal Data:* b Altoona, Pa, July 16, 47; m 81. *Educ:* Pa State Univ, BS, 69, MS, 73; Cornell Univ, PhD(food sci), 77. *Mem:* Inst Food Technol; Am Soc Enologists; Sigma Xi. *Res:* Wine chemistry; analytical instrumentation. *Mailing Add:* 78 Edward Dr Eureka MO 63025

KLUBEK, BRIAN PAUL, SOIL MICROBIOLOGY, MICROBIAL ECOLOGY. *Current Pos:* from asst prof to assoc prof, 78-91, PROF SOIL MICROBIOL, SOUTHERN ILL UNIV, CARBONDALE, 91-, ASST CHMN, DEPT PLANT & SOIL SCI, 91- *Personal Data:* b Buffalo, NY, Apr 21, 48; m 72; c 3. *Educ:* Colo State Univ, BS, 71; Ore State Univ, MS, 74; Utah State Univ, PhD(microbiol ecol), 77. *Prof Exp:* Res assoc microbiol, NC State Univ, 77-78. *Concurrent Pos:* Adv, Southern Ill Fertilizer & Pest Conf com, 78-; co-investr, Ctr Res on High Sulfur Coal, Ill Dept Energy & Natural Resources, 86-91, Ill Groundwater Symp, USDA, Nat Mineland Reclamation Ctr, US Bur Mines, 90-95, Ill Coun Food & Agr Res, 96-; assoc ed, J Arid Soil Rest Rehab, 92- *Mem:* Am Soc Microbiol; Am Soc Agron; Soil Sci Soc Am; Sigma Xi. *Res:* Biological sulfur oxidation; disposal of waste pesticide solutions; pesticide decomposition; microbial desulfurization of coal; pesticide movement in soil; reclamation of mine lands; biological nitrogen fixation. *Mailing Add:* Dept Plant, Soil & Gen Agr Southern Ill Univ Carbondale IL 62901-4415. *Fax:* 618-453-7457

KLUBES, PHILIP, PHARMACOLOGY. *Current Pos:* asst res prof, 65-70, from asst prof to assoc prof, 70-79, PROF PHARMACOL, MED CTR, GEORGE WASHINGTON UNIV, 79- *Personal Data:* b Brooklyn, NY, June 23, 35; m 64, Jane Ballantine; c Benjamin & David. *Educ:* Queens Col, NY, BS, 56; Univ Minn, MS, 59, PhD(biochem), 62. *Prof Exp:* Res fel bact, Harvard Med Sch, 62-63; res assoc microbiol, Sch Med, Univ Southern Calif, 63-64, instr, 64-65. *Concurrent Pos:* Res fel, USPHS, 62-63 & Bank Am-Giannini Med Found, 63-64. *Mem:* Am Asn Cancer Res; Am Soc Pharmacol & Exp Therapeut; AAAS. *Res:* Studies on the mechanism of action and metabolism of drugs. *Mailing Add:* Dept Pharmacol George Washington Univ Med Ctr Washington DC 20037. *Fax:* 202-994-2870; *E-Mail:* klubes@gwis2.circ.gwu.edu

KLUCAS, ROBERT VERNON, MICROBIAL BIOCHEMISTRY, PLANT BIOCHEMISTRY. *Current Pos:* from asst prof to assoc prof, 69-81, PROF BIOCHEM, UNIV NEBR, LINCOLN, 81- *Personal Data:* b Montevideo, Minn, Oct 19, 40; m 66; c 2. *Educ:* SDak State Col, BS, 62; Univ Wis, MS, 64, PhD(biochem), 67. *Prof Exp:* Res asst biochem, Univ Wis, 62-67; res assoc plant physiol, Ore State Univ, 67-69. *Concurrent Pos:* NIH fel, Ore State Univ, 67-68. *Mem:* Am Soc Plant Physiol; Am Soc Microbiol. *Res:* Biological nitrogen fixation. *Mailing Add:* Sch Biol Sci 345 Manter Univ Nebr PO Box 880118 Lincoln NE 68588-0118

KLUEH, RONALD LLOYD, ALLOY DEVELOPMENT, MECHANICAL PROPERTIES STUDIES. *Current Pos:* Res staff corrosion, 66-71, sr res staff mech properties, 71-80, SR RES STAFF, ALLOY DEVELOP, OAK RIDGE NAT LAB, 80- *Personal Data:* b Ferdinand, Ind, Oct 23, 36; m 59, Helen Kays; c Rona A & Kevin G. *Educ:* Purdue Univ, BS, 61; Carnegie-Mellon Univ, MS, 64, PhD(metall), 66. *Mem:* Fel Am Soc Metals; Mat Soc. *Res:* New steels for fusion-reactor applications; published over 160 papers. *Mailing Add:* Oak Ridge Nat Lab PO Box 2008 MS 6376 Oak Ridge TN 37831-6376. *Fax:* 423-574-0641; *E-Mail:* ku2@ornl.gov

KLUENDER, HAROLD CLINTON, ORGANIC CHEMISTRY, MEDICINAL CHEMISTRY. *Current Pos:* RES SCIENTIST & SUPVR MED CHEM, NATURAL PROD LAB, 73-, MILES DELEG, MILES LABS, INC. *Personal Data:* b Baraboo, Wis, Jan 28, 44; m 69; c 2. *Educ:* Univ Wis, Stevens Point, BS, 66; Univ Wis-Madison, MS, 68; Wesleyan Univ, PhD(org chem), 71. *Prof Exp:* Res assoc org chem, Pharmaceut Dept, Univ Wis, 72-73. *Concurrent Pos:* NIH fel org chem, Harvard Univ, 70-72. *Mem:* Am Chem Soc; AAAS. *Res:* Prostanoids, chemistry and biological activity. *Mailing Add:* 27 Academy Rd Trumbull CT 06611-1401

KLUEPFEL, DIETER, MICROBIOLOGY, BIOCHEMISTRY. *Current Pos:* RES PROF, INST A FRAPPIER, UNIV QUE, MONTREAL, 75-, DIR, APPL MICROBIOL, RES CTR, 89- *Personal Data:* b Zurich, Switz, Oct 7, 30; Can & Swiss citizen; m 59; c 2. *Educ:* Swiss Fed Inst Technol, Dipl Sc nat, 54, Dr Sc nat, 56. *Prof Exp:* Res asst microbiol, Swiss Fed Inst Technol, 54-56, res assoc biochem, 56-57; Nat Res Coun Can postdoctoral fel, 57-58; res scientist microbiol, Lepetit SPA, Milan, Italy, 59-61, head, Lab Biochem, 61-65; sr res scientist microbiol, Ayerst Labs, 65-70, res assoc, 70-75. *Concurrent Pos:* Lectr, Univ Montreal, 70-78; adj prof, Univ Concordia, Montreal, 78-87. *Mem:* Am Soc Indust Microbiol; Am Soc Microbiol; Can Soc Microbiol. *Res:* Microbial metabolism; biosynthesis of natural products; biodegradation and bioconversion; isolation of secondary metabolites and antibiotics; cellulases and hemicellulases from streptosrycetes; structure function of entyries; molecular biology of actinouycetes. *Mailing Add:* 2314 Grand Blvd Montreal PQ H4B 2W9 Can. *Fax:* 514-686-5501; *E-Mail:* dieter_kluepfel@iaf.uquebec.ca

KLUESSENDORF, JOANNE, PALEONTOLOGY. *Current Pos:* Curator, Mus Natural Hist, 90-93, RES ASST & TEACHING ASST, DEPT GEOL, UNIV ILL, 83-; CUR, GREENE GEOL MUS, UNIV WIS-MILWAUKEE, 84- *Personal Data:* b Milwaukee, Wis, Apr, 8, 49. *Educ:* Univ Ill, Urbana-Champaign, BS, 83, MS, 86. *Concurrent Pos:* Sci consult, Milwaukee Pub Mus, 80-83. *Mem:* Geol Soc Am; Paleont Soc; Sigma Xi; Soc Sedimentary Geol; Soc Preserv Natural Hist Cols. *Res:* Preservation of lagerstatten; genesis of oolitic iron stones; evolution and depositional environment of Silurian reefs; gastropod and polyplacophoran systematics and paleoecology. *Mailing Add:* Univ Ill Dept Geol 245 Nat Hist Bldg 1301 W Greene St Urbana IL 61801

KLUETZ, MICHAEL DAVID, BIOPHYSICAL CHEMISTRY. *Current Pos:* MEM STAFF, CARGILL INC. *Personal Data:* b Wausau, Wis, June 20, 48. *Educ:* Univ Wis-Madison, BS, 71; Univ Ill, Urbana, PhD(phys chem), 75. *Prof Exp:* Asst prof chem, Univ Idaho, 75-, asst prof biochem, 80- *Mem:* Am Chem Soc; Biophys Soc. *Res:* Biophysical, particularly magnetic resonance, studies of enzyme systems which are responsible for the degradation of several physiologically important polyamines and histamine in both plant and animal systems. *Mailing Add:* 5435 Joyce St Maple Plain MN 55359

KLUG, AARON, BIOLOGICAL CHEMISTRY, STRUCTURAL BIOCHEMISTRY. *Current Pos:* RETIRED. *Personal Data:* b Aug 11, 26; c 2. *Educ:* Univ Wit Watersrand, Cape Town & Cambridge. *Hon Degrees:* Numerous from US & foreign univs, 78-94. *Honors & Awards:* Nobel Prize Chem, 82; Heineken Prize, Royal Neth Acad Sci, 79; Copley Medal, Royal Soc, 85; Harden Medal, Biochem Soc, 85. *Prof Exp:* Dir, Virus Struct Res Group, Birkbeck Col, 58-61; dir studies, Peterhouse Col, Univ Cambridge, 62-86; dir, Lab Molecular Biol, Med Res Coun, 86-96. *Mem:* Foreign assoc Nat Acad Sci; Am Acad Arts & Sci; fel AAAS; fel Royal Soc (pres, 95-). *Res:* Protein-nucleic acid interactions and proteins involved in gene regulation. *Mailing Add:* Lab Molecular Biol Med Res Coun Cambridge CB2 2QH England

KLUG, DENNIS DWAYNE, PHYSICAL & THEORETICAL CHEMISTRY, SPECTROSCOPY. *Current Pos:* Fel, 68-70, RES CHEMIST, NAT RES COUN CAN, 70- *Personal Data:* b Milwaukee, Wis, Aug 22, 42; m 62, Joan G Doperalski; c Christopher A. *Educ:* Univ Wis-Milwaukee, BS, 64; Univ Wis-Madison, PhD(phys chem), 68. *Mem:* Sigma Xi; Am Phys Soc. *Res:* Experimental and theoretical studies of phase transformations and structures of crystalline and disordered solids; raman and infrared spectroscopy, high pressure techniques and instrumentation. *Mailing Add:* Steacie Inst Molecular Sci Nat Res Coun Can Ottawa ON K1A 0R6 Can. *Fax:* 613-954-5242

KLUG, MICHAEL J, MICROBIOLOGY, ECOLOGY. *Current Pos:* mem staff, 70-80, ASSOC PROF, W K KELLOGG BIOL STA, MICH STATE UNIV, 80- *Personal Data:* b Milwaukee, Wis, Mar 7, 41; m 69. *Educ:* SDak State Univ, BS, 63; Univ Iowa, MS, 66, PhD(microbiol), 69. *Prof Exp:* NIH res fel microbiol, Univ Ill, Urbana, 69-70. *Mem:* AAAS; Am Chem Soc; Am Soc Microbiol; Am Inst Biol Sci. *Res:* Ecology and metabolism of heterotrophic bacteria in natural waters and insects. *Mailing Add:* Dept Microbiol Mich State Univ 178 Giltner Hall East Lansing MI 48824-1101

KLUG, WILLIAM STEPHEN, BIOLOGY, MOLECULAR BIOLOGY. *Current Pos:* assoc prof biol & chmn dept, 73-78, chmn dept, 81-93, PROF BIOL, TRENTON STATE COL, 79- *Personal Data:* b Parkersburg, WVa, Sept 2, 41; div; c Cynthia, Braden & Dori. *Educ:* Wabash Col, BA, 63; Northwestern Univ, PhD(develop genetics), 68. *Prof Exp:* Instr biol, Wabash Col, 63-65, asst prof, 68-73. *Mem:* AAAS; Sigma Xi. *Res:* Developmental genetics in the ovarian system of Drosophila melanogaster; co-author two books on genetics. *Mailing Add:* Dept Biol Col NJ Trenton NJ 08650. *Fax:* 609-771-2674

KLUGE, ARNOLD GIRARD, VERTEBRATE ZOOLOGY. *Current Pos:* asst prof comp anat & embryol, 65-66, assoc prof biol, 74-76, UNIV MICH, ANN ARBOR, 66-, PROF BIOL, 76- *Personal Data:* b Glendale, Calif, July 27, 35; m 59; c 2. *Educ:* Univ Southern Calif, BA, 57, MS, 60, PhD(biol), 64. *Prof Exp:* Lectr embryol, Univ Southern Calif, 64; asst prof comp anat, San Fernando Valley State Col, 64-65. *Concurrent Pos:* Res asst, Los Angeles Ment Health Asn grant, 58; NSF grants, 59 & 69-71, USPHS grant, 60-61; Fulbright scholar, Australia, 61-62; Am Philos Soc grant, 69; Guggenheim fel, 71-72; NSF fel, 60, Sigma Xi & Sci Res Soc Am fel, 63. *Mem:* AAAS; Am Soc Ichthyol & Herpet; Soc Study Evolution; Soc Syst Zool. *Res:* Evolution; numerical taxonomy; herpetology. *Mailing Add:* 1121 Nat Sci Biol Univ Mich 830 N University Ave Ann Arbor MI 48109-1048

KLUGE, JOHN PAUL, VETERINARY PATHOLOGY, COMPARATIVE PATHOLOGY. *Current Pos:* from assoc prof to prof path, 68-75, chmn dept, 75-90, PROF VET PATH, IOWA STATE UNIV, 75- *Personal Data:* b St Louis, Mo, July 7, 37; m 58, Joan D Kwentus; c Paula M (Johnson), Janna Marie (Morrison), Thomas J & Erika J. *Educ:* Univ Mo, BS & DVM, 62; Iowa State Univ, MS, 65; George Washington Univ, PhD(comp path), 68; Am Col Vet Path, dipl, 70. *Prof Exp:* Res vet, Nat Animal Dis Lab, 62-68. *Concurrent Pos:* Consult, Agr Res Serv & Animal & Plant Health Inspection Serv, USDA; mem bd dirs, Bethesda Lutheran Homes & Serv, Inc. *Mem:* Am Asn Vet Lab Diagnosticians; Am Vet Med Asn; US Animal Health Asn; Conf Res Workers Animal Dis; Am Col Vet Path. *Res:* Comparative pathology of infectious diseases and neoplasms. *Mailing Add:* RR 2 Ames IA 50010. *Fax:* 515-294-5423; *E-Mail:* jkluge@iastate.edu

KLUGER, MATTHEW JAY, PHYSIOLOGY. *Current Pos:* DIR & SR SCIENTIST, INST BASIC & APPL MED RES, THE LOVELACE INSTS, ALBUQUERQUE, NM, 93- *Personal Data:* b Brooklyn, NY, Dec 14, 46; m 67; c Sharon & Hilary. *Educ:* Cornell Univ, BS, 67; Univ Ill, MS, 69, PhD(zool), 70. *Honors & Awards:* Paul Levy Mem lectr, Univ Witwatersrand, 91; Napolean Cybulski's Medal, Polish Physiol Soc, 93. *Prof Exp:* NIH fel, Yale Univ & J B Pierce Found Lab, 70-72; from asst prof to prof physiol, Med Sch, Univ Mich, Ann Arbor, 72-93. *Concurrent Pos:* Vis prof med, St Thomas's Hosp Med Sch, London, Eng, 79; vis scientist, Cetus Immune Corp, Palo Alto, Calif, 86-87, Univ Witwatersrand, SAfrica, 91- *Mem:* Am Physiol Soc; Am Soc Zoologists; Am Asn Immunologists; Int Soc Neuroimmunomodulation; Soc Neurosci; Am Col Sports Med. *Res:* Temperature regulation and bioenergetics; evolution and adaptive value of fever; host responses to infection; role of monokines and cytokines in regulation of body temperature and food intake. *Mailing Add:* Lovelace Inst 2425 Ridge Crest Dr SE Albuquerque NM 87108. *Fax:* 505-262-7043; *E-Mail:* kluger@audrey.lmf.org.

KLUGER, RONALD H, ORGANIC CHEMISTRY, BIOCHEMISTRY. *Current Pos:* from asst prof to assoc prof, 74-81, assoc chair, 89-92, PROF CHEM, UNIV TORONTO, 81- *Personal Data:* b Newark, NJ, Dec 22, 43; m 69, Ronna Yosim; c Melissa & Jennifer. *Educ:* Columbia Univ, AB, 65; Harvard Univ, AM, 66, PhD(chem), 69. *Honors & Awards:* Merck Sharp & Dohme lectr, Chem Inst Can, 83; Labatt Award, Can Soc Chem, 90, Syntex lectr, 94, Bader Award, 96; Dales Award Med Res, Univ Toronto, 93. *Prof*

Exp: NIH fel biochem, Brandeis Univ, 69-70; asst prof chem, Univ Chicago, 70-74. *Concurrent Pos:* Sloan Found fel, 73. *Mem:* Can Soc Chem; Am Chem Soc; fel AAAS. *Res:* Mechanisms of biochemical catalysis and related organic reaction mechanisms; thiamin, biotin and enzymes; enzyme inhibitors based on mechanistic analysis; functional group interactions and reactive intermediates; drug design; blood substitutes; protein modification. *Mailing Add:* Dept Chem Univ Toronto Toronto ON M5S 3H6 Can. *E-Mail:* rkluger@chem.utoronto.ca

KLUGHERZ, PETER D(AVID), CHEMICAL REACTION ENGINEERING, CATALYSIS. *Current Pos:* SR CHEMIST, RES LABS, ROHM AND HAAS CO, SPRING HOUSE, PA, 68- *Personal Data:* b Brooklyn, NY, Feb 25, 42; m 62, Joyce Barnett; c 4. *Educ:* Cornell Univ, BChE, 63, PhD(chem eng), 69. *Mem:* Am Chem Soc; Am Inst Chem Engrs; Catalysis Soc. *Res:* Heterogeneous catalytic oxidation; monomer process research. *Mailing Add:* 760 Killdeer Lane Huntingdon Valley PA 19006. *E-Mail:* rsepdk@rohmhaas.com

KLUIBER, RUDOLPH W, INORGANIC CHEMISTRY. *Current Pos:* from asst prof to assoc prof, 66-71, PROF CHEM, RUTGERS UNIV, NEWARK, 71- *Personal Data:* b Chicago, Ill, Feb 20, 30; m 55. *Educ:* Univ Ill, BS, 50; Columbia Univ, AM, 52; Univ Wis, PhD(chem), 54. *Prof Exp:* Chemist, Plastics Div, Union Carbide Corp, 54-64; res assoc, Princeton Univ, 64-66. *Mem:* Am Chem Soc. *Res:* Metal chelate compounds. *Mailing Add:* Dept Chem Rutgers Univ Newark NJ 07102-1897

KLUK, EDWARD, APPLICATION OF COMPUTERS IN TEACHING PHYSICS. *Current Pos:* PROF PHYSICS, DICKINSON STATE UNIV, 84- *Personal Data:* b Warsaw, Poland, June 31, 36; US citizen; m 58, Herminia Szalapieta; c Dorota Kolinska. *Educ:* Adam Mickiwicz Univ, Poland, MSc, 58, DrSc, 63; Jagiellonian Univ, Poland, Dr HabSc, 78. *Honors & Awards:* Award of Polish Acad Sci, Polish Acad Scis, 79. *Prof Exp:* Lectr, Dept Physics, Adam Mickiewicz Univ, Poland, 63-67; assoc prof, Dept Physics, Silesian Univ, Poland, 68-82, chmn, 79-82. *Mem:* Am Asn Physics Teachers. *Res:* Molecular motion liquids; application of computers in teaching physics and physics labs on introductory level. *Mailing Add:* 1156 21 St W Dickinson ND 58601. *E-Mail:* ed_kluk@dsu1.nodak.edu

KLUKSDAHL, HARRIS EUDELL, CHEMISTRY, HETEROGENEOUS CATALYSIS. *Current Pos:* res chemist, Chevron Res Co, 60-67, sr res chemist, 67-70, sr res assoc, 70-89, res scientist, 89-91, CONSULT SCIENTIST, CHEVRON RES & TECHNOL CO, 92- *Personal Data:* b Bismarck, NDak, Mar 4, 33; m 89, Jacqueline Bailey; c James H, Scott N & Thomas R. *Educ:* Western Wash Univ, BA, 54; Univ Wash, PhD(inorg chem), 58. *Prof Exp:* Res chemist, E I du Pont de Nemours & Co, 58-60. *Mem:* AAAS. *Res:* Catalytic reforming; petroleum refining processes; bimetallic catalysts and processes; heterogeneous catalysis; extractive metallurgy of platinum group metals. *Mailing Add:* 871 Tamarack Dr San Rafael CA 94903

KLUMPAR, DAVID MICHAEL, SPACE PHYSICS. *Current Pos:* res scientist, Ctr Space Sci, 78-84, res scientist, 84-90, STAFF SCIENTIST, LOCKHEED PALO ALTO RES LABS, 90- *Personal Data:* b Jacksonville, Fla, Apr 14, 43; m 64; c 2. *Educ:* Univ Iowa, BA, 65, MS, 68; Univ NH, PhD(physics), 73. *Prof Exp:* Res assoc physics, Univ NH, 72-74; res assoc space physics, Inst Phys Sci, Univ Tex, Dallas, 74-77,. *Mem:* Am Geophys Union; assoc mem Sigma Xi; Am Phys Soc. *Res:* Investigations of the low energy charged particle environment in the earth's near magnetosphere and interactions between the magnetosphere and ionosphere, especially at high latitudes in the auroral region. *Mailing Add:* Dept 91-20 Bldg 255 Lockheed Palo Alto Res Labs 3251 Hanover Palo Alto CA 94304

KLUMPP, THEODORE GEORGE, INTERNAL MEDICINE. *Current Pos:* RETIRED. *Personal Data:* b New York, NY, May 15, 03; m 34; c 6. *Educ:* Princeton Univ, BS, 24; Harvard Univ, MD, 28. *Hon Degrees:* DSc, Philadelphia Col Pharm, 43, New Eng Col Pharm, 61 & Albany Med Col, 64; LLD, Univ Chattanooga, 60. *Prof Exp:* Intern, Peter Bent Brigham Hosp, 29-30; asst resident physician, Lakeside Hosp, Cleveland, 30-32; instr & asst clin prof internal med, Med Sch, Yale Univ, 32-36; chief drug div, Food & Drug Admin, Fed Security Agency, Washington, DC, 36-41; dir drugs, food & phys ther & secy coun pharm & chem, AMA, Ill, 41-42; pres, Winthrop Labs Div, Sterling Drug, Inc, 42-70, chmn, 70-73, mem bd dirs & vpres, Sterling Drug, Inc, 60-73. *Concurrent Pos:* Assoc physician, New Haven Hosp, 32-36; chief hemat clin & dir med lab, 33-36; adj clin prof, Med Sch, George Washington Univ, 40-41; attend physician, Gallinger Munic Hosp, 41; mem pharmaceut mfrs indust adv comt & penicillin producers indust adv comt, War Prod Bd, 42-47; chmn bd gov, Nat Vitamin Found, 47-56; dir, Sterwin Chem, Inc, 49-70; chmn task force on handicapped, Off Defense Mobilization, Washington, DC, 51-52; pres, Nat Pharmaceut Coun, Inc, 53-55; chmn med serv task force, Hoover Comn on Orgn Exec Br Govt, 53-55; mem study comt fed aid to pub health, Comn Inter-Govt Rels, Washington, DC, 54; mem, Nat Adv Coun Voc Rehab, 55-59; consult surgeon, Chesapeake & Ohio RR, 56-; mem bd vis, Sch Pub Health, Harvard Univ, 58-64 & Med & Dent Schs, 64-70; mem med adv comt, Off Voc Rehab, 60-62; mem health resources adv comt, Off Emergency Planning, Exec Off of President, 62-69; mem, NY State Voc Rehab Coun, 67-73; secy, Nat Fund Med Educ, 68-69, pres, 69-71, chmn, 71-75, vpres, 75-80; mem bd trustees, Brooklyn Col Pharm, Long Island Univ, 68-77, chmn, 74-77; mem comt on aging, Coun Med Serv, AMA; mem, Gov Coun Rehab, NY & Found Trop Med; mem bd trustees, Affil Cols & Univs, Inc, 72-; med consult, President's Coun Phys Fitness & Sports, 73-; assoc ed, Med Times, 73-; mem bd trustees, Human Resources Sch, NY, 74- & Arnold & Marie Schwartz Col Pharm & Health Sci, Long Island Univ, 77-; chmn bd dirs, Nat Asn Human Develop, 74-80. *Mem:* AAAS; fel Am Soc Clin Invest; fel Am Col Physicians; fel AMA. *Res:* Therapeutics; materia medica; medical pharmacology; hematology; physiological chemistry. *Mailing Add:* Keelona Charlottsville VA 22902

KLUN, JEROME ANTHONY, ENTOMOLOGY. *Current Pos:* RES SCIENTIST, EDUC ADMIN & RES LEADER, INSECT CHEM ECOL LAB, AGR RES SERV, USDA, 65- *Personal Data:* b Ely, Minn, May 4, 39; m 93, Harriet Rosenfeld; c Curt, Eric, Toinette, Karen & Greg. *Educ:* Univ Minn, Duluth, BS, 61; Iowa State Univ, PhD(entom), 65. *Prof Exp:* Res asst, Iowa State Univ, 61-65. *Concurrent Pos:* Assoc prof entom, Iowa State Univ, 69-77. *Mem:* AAAS; Am Chem Soc; Entom Soc Am. *Res:* Insect sex pheromone chemistry, behavior, biosynthesis, and deertick kairomones and pheromone. *Mailing Add:* 11621 Spring Ridge Rd Potomac MD 20854. *Fax:* 301-504-6580; *E-Mail:* jklun@asrr.arsusda.gov

KLUNDT, IRWIN LEE, ORGANIC CHEMISTRY. *Current Pos:* ADJ & VIS PROF CHEM, FT LEWIS COL, DURANGO, COLO, 91- *Personal Data:* b Pasco, Wash, Aug 7, 36; m 59; c 3. *Educ:* State Col Wash, BS, 58; Mont State Univ, MS, 59; Wayne State Univ, PhD(org chem), 63. *Prof Exp:* Chemist, Detroit Inst Cancer Res, 63; sr res scientist, Pac Northwest Labs, Battelle Mem Inst, 65-66; proj leader, Aldrich Chem Co, 66, group leader, 66-71, biochem tech mgr, 71-73, tech serv mgr, 73-74, vpres, Aldrich Chem Co Inc, 74-90, vpres, Sigma-Aldrich Corp, 75-83, dir, Aldrich Chem Co Inc, 78-90, dir, Sigma Chem Co, 78-90; mem staff, Earth Technol Corp, 90-91. *Mem:* Am Chem Soc; NY Acad Sci. *Res:* Aliphatic and alicyclic chemistry; small ring compounds; carbohydrates. *Mailing Add:* 250 Skyline Dr Bayfield CO 81122. *E-Mail:* klundt_i@fortlewis.edu

KLURFELD, DAVID MICHAEL, ATHEROSCLEROSIS, TUMOR PROMOTION. *Current Pos:* PROF & CHMN, DEPT NUTRIT & FOOD SCI, WAYNE STATE UNIV, DETROIT, 92- *Personal Data:* b New York, NY Feb 22, 51; m 73; c 2. *Educ:* Cornell Univ, BS, 72; Med Col Va, MS, 75, PhD(path), 77. *Honors & Awards:* Nutrit Res Award, J Nutrit Res, 82. *Prof Exp:* Res fel, Wistar Inst Anat & Biol, 77-79, res assoc, 79-82, asst prof, 82-87, assoc prof, 87-92. *Concurrent Pos:* USPHS fel, 77-79; Univ Pa Sch Med, assoc prof, nutrit surg, 89- *Mem:* Fel Am Col Nutrit; Am Heart Asn; Am Soc Nutri Sci; NY Acad Sci; Soc Exp Biol & Med; Sigma Xi; Am Asn Pathologists. *Res:* Relationship of atherosclerosis to immune system, macrophages and nutrition; nutrition and tumor promotion; dietary fiber; Lipid metabolism. *Mailing Add:* Dept Nutrit & Food Sci 3009 Sci Hall Wayne State Univ Detroit MI 48202. *Fax:* 313-577-8616; *E-Mail:* kdlurfe@lifesci.wayne.edu

KLUS, JOHN P, NEW PRODUCT DEVELOPMENT. *Current Pos:* from instr to assoc prof struct, 62-70, chmn dept eng & prof struct, 70-80, PROF DEVELOP, UNIV WIS-MADISON, 80- *Personal Data:* b Goodman, Wis, June 13, 35; m 61; c 4. *Educ:* Mich Technol Univ, BS, 57, MS, 61; Univ Wis, PhD(civil eng), 65. *Honors & Awards:* Leonardo da Vinci Medal, 87. *Prof Exp:* Appraiser, Am Appraisal Co, 57-58; res engr designer, Eng & Res Develop Labs, Va, 58-59; instr, Mich Technol Univ, 60-61; instr drawing, Univ Wis, 61-62; struct designer, Warzyn Eng Co, 62. *Concurrent Pos:* Fulbright scholar, Finland, 66-67; chmn, Working Group Continuing Educ Engrs, UNESCO, 73-; gen chmn, 1st World Conf Continuing Eng Educ, 79; Fulbright Researcher, Finland, 85. *Mem:* AAAS; Am Soc Civil Engrs; Am Soc Eng Educ; Nat Soc Prof Engrs. *Res:* Continuing education research; new product development. *Mailing Add:* 3409 Kingston Dr Madison WI 53713

KLUSKENS, LARRY F, PATHOLOGY, CYTOPATHOLOGY. *Current Pos:* AT RUSH-PRESBY-ST LUKES MED CTR. *Educ:* Univ Chicago, PhD(path), 75, MD, 76, Am Bd Path, cert. *Prof Exp:* Resident, Univ Chicago, dir, cellular immunol; dir cytol, Univ Iowa. *Mem:* Fedn Am Soc Exp Biol; Am Soc Psychol. *Mailing Add:* 10155 W Ivanhoe Schiller Park IL 60176. *Fax:* 847-942-4228

KLUSMAN, RONALD WILLIAM, GEOCHEMISTRY. *Current Pos:* assoc prof, 72-77, PROF GEOCHEM, COLO SCH MINES, 77-, PROF CHEM, 80- *Personal Data:* b Batesville, Ind, June 16, 41; m 64; c 2. *Educ:* Ind Univ, Bloomington, BS, 64, MS, 67, PhD(geochem), 69. *Prof Exp:* Instrumental analyst geochem, Ind Geol Surv, 64-67; asst prof, Purdue Univ, 69-72. *Mem:* Geol Soc Am; Soc Environ Geochem & Health. *Res:* Trace elements in geological and environmental systems; instrumental analysis; computer applications in geology. *Mailing Add:* Dept Chem & Geochem Colo Sch Mines 1500 Illinois St Golden CO 80401-1887

KLUSS, BYRON CURTIS, CELL BIOLOGY. *Current Pos:* from asst prof to assoc prof biol, 59-66, dir spec progs, 70-75, prof biol, 66-80, PROF ZOOL, CALIF STATE UNIV, LONG BEACH, 80- *Personal Data:* b Luzerne, Iowa, May 25, 28. *Educ:* Univ Iowa, BA, 49, MS, 55, PhD(zool), 57. *Prof Exp:* Asst zool, Univ Iowa, 53-57; instr, Albion Col, 57-59. *Concurrent Pos:* Lalor Found fel, 58; Fulbright fel, Assiut, 65-66. *Mem:* Am Soc Zool; Am Soc Cell Biol; Electron Micros Soc Am. *Res:* Cytology; bioluminescence; electron microscopy. *Mailing Add:* 4864 Ironwood Ave Seal Beach CA 90740

KLUTCHKO, SYLVESTER, SYNTHETIC ORGANIC CHEMISTRY, MEDICINAL CHEMISTRY. *Current Pos:* From asst scientist to sr scientist org chem, 55-93, RES ASSOC MED CHEM, WARNER-LAMBERT CO, INC, ANN ARBOR, 93- *Personal Data:* b Wilkes-Barre, Pa, Sept 2, 33; m 62, Carolyn Balchus; c Mark, Carole L & Melissa A. *Educ:* Pa State Univ, BS, 55. *Concurrent Pos:* Excellence Indust Chem res award, Am Chem Soc. *Mem:* Am Chem Soc. *Res:* Synthesis of agents that affect the renin-angiotensin system, ie angiotensin converting enzyme (ACE) inhibitors and renin inhibitors; invention of marketed antihypertensive ACE inhibitor quinapril (accupril); preparation of antiallergy chromones by novel synthetic procedure; study of a general rearrangement of 3-substituted chromones; synthesis of nonpeptide endothelin antagonists. *Mailing Add:* 5143 Pratt Rd Scio Twp Ann Arbor MI 48103

KLUTE, ARNOLD, AGRONOMY. *Current Pos:* RETIRED. *Personal Data:* b Galein, Mich, Sept 24, 21; m 48; c 4. *Educ:* Mich State Col, BS, 47, MS, 48; Cornell Univ, PhD(soil physics), 51. *Honors & Awards:* Soil Sci Award, Am Soc Agron, 65. *Prof Exp:* Res engr, Schlumberger Well Surv Corp, 51-53; from asst prof to prof agron, Univ Ill, 53-70; prof soils, Colo State Univ, 70-87; res leader, Irrig & Soil-Plant-Water Rels, Agr Res Serv, USDA, Ft Collins, 78-82. *Concurrent Pos:* US Salinity Lab, Riverside, Calif, 60; soil scientist, Sci & Educ Admin-Agr Res, USDA, 70-78. *Mem:* Am Soc Agron; Soil Sci Soc Am; Am Geophys Union; Sigma Xi. *Res:* Investigations of the transport of water, gases, heat, and solutes in soils. *Mailing Add:* 3469 Fogle Cliff Dr Estes Park CO 80517

KLUVER, J(OHAN) W(ILHELM), COMMUNICATIONS. *Current Pos:* PRES, EXPS IN ART & TECHNOL, INC, 68- *Personal Data:* b Monaco, Nov 13, 27; m 64; c 2. *Educ:* Royal Inst Technol, Sweden, Engr, 51; Univ Calif, MS, 55, PhD, 57. *Prof Exp:* Engr TV develop, Thomson-Houston Co, France, 53-54; asst prof elec eng, Univ Calif, 57-58; mem tech staff, Bell Tel Labs, 58-68. *Mem:* Assoc Am Phys Soc; Assoc Inst Elec & Electronics Engrs; Optic Soc Am; Soc Info Display. *Res:* Microwave electronics; electron dynamics; electron devices; microwave tubes; gas lasers; optics. *Mailing Add:* 69 Apple Tree Row Berkeley Heights NJ 07922

KLYCE, STEPHEN DOWNING, PHYSIOLOGY. *Current Pos:* PROF OPHTHAL, LA STATE UNIV MED CTR SCH MED, NEW ORLEANS, 79-, ADJ FAC, DEPT ANAT, 92- *Personal Data:* b Arlington, Mass, Oct 30, 42; m 64; c 3. *Educ:* Univ Mass, BS, 64; Yale Univ, PhD(physiol), 71. *Honors & Awards:* Recognition Award Ophthalmic Res, Alcon Res Inst, 86; Broadhurst lectr, Eye Res Inst, Boston, 89; Everett Kinsey lectr, Contact Lens Asn Ophthal, 90; Lans lectr, Int Soc Refractive Keratoplasty, 91; Spec Recognition Award, Asn Res Vision & Ophthal, 91; Max Schapero Mem lectr, Am Acad Optometry, 91; Honor Award, Am Acad Ophthal, 92; Holland Guest lectr, Europ Contact Lens Asn Ophthalmologists, 93. *Prof Exp:* Res assoc ocular physiol, Yale Univ, 71-72; res assoc, 72-75, sr res assoc ocular physiol, Stanford Univ, 75-79. *Concurrent Pos:* Prog comt mem, Physiol & Pharmacol Sect, Asn Res Vision & Ophthal, 76-80, prog chmn, Southern Sect Meeting, 80, trustee, Physiol & Pharmacol Sect, 85-90, vpres, 88-90, pres, 90; spec reviewer, NIH DRG Visual Sci A1 Study Sect, NIH DRG Spec Study Sections, NSF, 79-, mem, 88-91; prin investr, Nat Eye Inst Res Grant, 80-; mem, Corneal Dis Panel, Nat Adv Eye Coun, 80-81 & 84-85; ad hoc consult, Prospective Eval Radial Keratotomy Study, Nat Eye Inst, 84-; mem coun, Int Soc Contact Lens Res, 86-90, vpres, 90-; grad fac mem, Med Ctr Grad Coun, La State Univ, 87-, dir, Training Prog Vision Res, 90-; consult, Comt on Vision on Use of Contact Lenses Adverse Conditions, Nat Res Coun, 88; sr sci consult, Computed Anat, Inc, New York, NY, 88-; mem, Tech Adv Panel, La State Univ Technol Transfer Prog, 88-, Ophthal & Visual Optics Organizing Comt, Optical Soc Am, 91-92; guest ed, Refractive & Corneal Surg, 89; invited participant, Meeting on Policy Issues, Vision Res Prog Planning Subcomt, Nat Adv Eye Counb, 90; prog comt, Tenth Int Cong Eye Res, 90-92; adj prof biomed eng, Tulane Univ, New Orleans, La, 90-; exec ed, Exp Eye Res, 91-; counr, Int Soc Eye Res, 92- *Mem:* Asn Res Vision & Ophthal; Biophys Soc; Am Physiol Soc; Int Soc Eye Res; Int Soc Contact Lens Res; Contact Lens Asn Ophthalmologists. *Res:* Physiology and biophysics of membrane transport and permeability in epithelial tissues; corneal retractive surgery research. *Mailing Add:* Dept Ophthal La State Univ Sch Med Eye Ctr 2020 Gravier St Suite B New Orleans LA 70112

KLYMENKO, VICTOR, ELECTRO-OPTICAL DISPLAY, SCIENTIFIC DATA VISUALIZATION. *Current Pos:* SR SCIENTIST, UES, INC, US ARMY AEROMED RES LAB, 91- *Personal Data:* b New York, NY, Nov 4, 51. *Educ:* Univ Buffalo, PhD(cognitive psychol), 84. *Prof Exp:* Vis asst prof psychol, Univ Buffalo, 84-87; res asst prof radiol, Univ NC, Chapel Hill, 87-91. *Res:* Visual perception and visual psychophysics; identifying and characterizing the optical invariants to which the human visual system is tuned to present visual information efficaciously. *Mailing Add:* 505 Briarwood Dr No J3 Enterprise AL 36330

KLYMKOWSKY, MICHAEL W, CELL BIOLOGY. *Current Pos:* ASST PROF CELL BIOL, UNIV COLO, 83- *Educ:* Calif Inst Technol, PhD(biophysics), 80. *Res:* Intermediate filaments; early xenopus development. *Mailing Add:* Dept Molecular, Cellular & Develop Biol Univ Colo Campus Box 347 Boulder CO 80309-0347. *Fax:* 303-492-7744

KMAK, WALTER S(TEVEN), chemical engineering; deceased, see previous edition for last biography

KMETEC, EMIL PHILIP, EXTRACELLULAR BASEMENT MEMBRANES, KIDNEY COLLAGEN & GLYCOPROTEIN. *Current Pos:* from assoc prof to prof biol, Wright State Univ, 64-75, asst vpres acad affairs, 79-84, prof, 75-88, EMER PROF BIOL CHEM, SCH MED & COL SCI & MATH, WRIGHT STATE UNIV, 88- *Personal Data:* b Carlinville, Ill, Sept 29, 27; m 55, Jean Maize; c 5. *Educ:* Univ Chicago, MS, 53; Univ Wis, PhD(plant physiol), 57. *Prof Exp:* Asst bot, Univ Chicago, 50-52; asst plant physiol, Iowa State Univ, 52-53; asst, Univ Wis, 53-57, res assoc, 57; res assoc biochem, Sch Med, La State Univ, 57-60; sr instr biochem & pediat, Sch Med, Case-Western Res Univ, 60-61, asst prof, 61-64. *Concurrent Pos:* Vis prof, Okayama Univ of Sci, Japan, 84, St George's Univ, Sch Med, Grenada, 89-93; adj biol, Edison State Community Col, 93-96, Self Health Sch Med Massage, 96- *Mem:* AAAS; Am Chem Soc; Sigma Xi. *Res:* RNA metabolism and protein synthesis; extracellular Matrix and basement membranes. *Mailing Add:* 2172 Crabtree Dr Dayton OH 45431. *E-Mail:* ekmetec@desire.wright.edu

KMETZ, JOHN MICHAEL, HISTOLOGY, CYTOCHEMISTRY. *Current Pos:* ASST PROF BIOL SCI, KEAN COL NJ, 78- *Personal Data:* b Johnstown, Pa, Jan 14, 43; m 66; c 3. *Educ:* Pa State Univ, BS, 64, PhD(physiol), 68. *Prof Exp:* Asst prof biol, Pa State Univ, 68-73; res dir, Sci Unlimited Res Found, 73-78. *Mem:* NY Acad Sci; Am Inst Biol Sci. *Res:* Quantitative histochemistry and cytophotometry. *Mailing Add:* Dept Biol Kean Col NJ 1000 Morris Ave Union NJ 07083-7133

KMIECIK, JAMES EDWARD, ORGANIC CHEMISTRY. *Current Pos:* BUS MGR, TEXACO CHEM CO, 80- *Personal Data:* b New Waverly, Tex, Feb 11, 36; m 59; c 1. *Educ:* St Edwards Univ, BS, 56; Univ Tex, MA, 60, PhD(chem), 61. *Prof Exp:* Res chemist, Cities Serv Res & Develop Co, 61-64; sr res chemist, Columbia Carbon Co, 64-66; sr res chemist, Com Develop Div, Jefferson Chem Co, 66-68, proj chemist, 68-70, mgr amine prod develop, Mkt Dept, 70-77, mgr new prod develop, 77-80. *Mem:* Soc Aerospace Mat & Process Engrs; Am Chem Soc. *Res:* Synthesis of organic nitrogen heterocyclic compounds; reactions of carbon monoxide with organic compounds; reactions of aliphatic and aromatic nitro compounds. *Mailing Add:* 5807 Boyce Springs Dr Houston TX 77066

KNAAK, JAMES BRUCE, BIOCHEMISTRY, TOXICOLOGY. *Current Pos:* PROD STEWARDSHIP SCIENTIST, OCCIDENTAL CHEM CORP, 90- *Personal Data:* b Milwaukee, Wis, Aug 20, 32; m 58, Scinta; c James R, Julie A & Robert B. *Educ:* Univ Wis, BS, 54, MS, 57, PhD(biochem, dairy husb), 62. *Prof Exp:* Res asst dairy husb, biochem & entom, Univ Wis, 56-61; fel biochem, Union Carbide Indust, Mellon Inst, 61-66, sr fel, 67; sr res chemist, Niagara Chem Div, FMC Corp, 67-71; group leader agr chem, CIBA-Geigy Corp, 71-73; staff toxicologist, Calif Dept Food & Agr, 73-85, Calif Dept Health Serv, 86-89. *Concurrent Pos:* Asst adj prof, Dept Molecular Biosci, Sch Vet Med, Univ Calif, Davis, 89- *Mem:* AAAS; Am Chem Soc; Soc Toxicol; NY Acad Sci; fel Am Inst Chem. *Res:* Toxicology and metabolism of organophosphate and carbamate insecticides; urea and s-triazine herbicides; metabolism of industrial chemicals; biochemical pharmacology; dermal dose response and dermal absorption studies; environmental monitoring; behavioral and biochemical pharmacology; risk assessment; PBPK modeling; agricultural field worker safety studies; indoor safety studies; inhalation neurotoxicology. *Mailing Add:* Occidental Chem Corp 5005 LBJ Freeway Dallas TX 75244. *Fax:* 972-404-3287

KNABE, GEORGE W, JR, PATHOLOGY. *Current Pos:* assoc dean clin affairs, 72-75, PROF PATH, SCH MED, UNIV MINN, DULUTH, 72- *Personal Data:* b Grand Rapids, Mich, June 29, 24; m 54, L Jeanette Moffit; c Katharine, Elizabeth, Ann & Dorothy. *Educ:* Univ Md, MD, 49. *Prof Exp:* Fel path, Cleveland Clin Found, 50-51; resident path, Henry Ford Hosp, Detroit, 53-54; chief lab serv, Vet Admin Ctr, Dayton, Ohio, 55-57; med ed adv, Int Coop Admin, 57-59; asst prof path & chief clin lab, Sch Med, PR, 59-60; prof path & chmn dept, Sch Med, Univ SDak, 60-72, dean sch med, 67-72. *Concurrent Pos:* Mem staff, Univ Med Ctr-Mesabi, Hibbing, Minn, 86- *Mem:* AMA; Am Soc Clin Pathologists; Col Am Pathologists; Int Acad Pathologists. *Res:* Infectious disease; insect vectors of disease. *Mailing Add:* 1008 Seventh Ave S Virginia MN 55792-3151

KNACKE, ROGER FRITZ, ASTROPHYSICS, ASTRONOMY. *Current Pos:* HEAD, DIV SCI & PROF PHYSICS, PA STATE ERIE, 92- *Personal Data:* b Stuttgart, Ger, June 22, 41; US citizen; m 72, Nancy Jones; c Zachary & Elizabeth. *Educ:* Univ Calif, Berkeley, BA, 63, PhD(physics), 69. *Prof Exp:* Fel astron, Lick Observ, Univ Calif, 70-71; from asst prof to prof astron, Dept Earth Sci, State Univ NY, Stony Brook, 71-92. *Concurrent Pos:* Vis scientist, Max Plank Inst Nuclear Physics, Heidelberg, Ger, 78-85; scientist, Marshall Space Flight Ctr, NASA, Huntsville, Ala, 89-90. *Mem:* Am Astron Soc; Int Astron Union. *Res:* Interstellar matter; infrared astronomy; planetary atmospheres; comets. *Mailing Add:* Pa State Erie Div Sci Station Rd Erie PA 16563. *Fax:* 814-898-6213; *E-Mail:* rfk2@psuvm.psu.edu

KNAEBEL, KENT SCHOFIELD, CHEMICAL ENGINEERING. *Current Pos:* asst prof, 80-86, ASSOC PROF CHEM ENG, OHIO STATE UNIV, 86- *Personal Data:* b Cincinnati, Ohio, Aug 20, 51; m 73; c 3. *Educ:* Univ Ky, BSChE, 73; Univ Del, MChE, 78, PhD(chem eng), 80. *Prof Exp:* Chem engr, Tenn Eastman Co; instr chem eng, Univ Del, 79-80. *Concurrent Pos:* Vis scientist, Brookhaven Nat Lab, 81, Sch Areospace Med, 84. *Mem:* Am Chem Soc; Am Inst Chem Engrs. *Res:* Separation process: cyclic sorption, including both gas and liquid phase versions. *Mailing Add:* Adsorption Res Inc 6185 D Shamrock Ct Dublin OH 43017-1275

KNAFF, DAVID BARRY, PHOTOBIOLOGY. *Current Pos:* assoc prof chem, 76-80, PROF CHEM, TEX TECH UNIV, 80- *Personal Data:* b New York, NY, June 5, 41; m 62; c 1. *Educ:* Mass Inst Technol, BS, 62; Yale Univ, MS, 63, PhD(chem), 66. *Prof Exp:* Biochemist, Dept Cell Physiol, Univ Calif, Berkeley, 66-76. *Mem:* Biophys Soc; Am Soc Photobiol; Am Soc Plant Physiol; AAAS; Am Soc Biol Chemists; Sigma Xi. *Res:* Electron transport in plants and photosynthetic bacteria with emphasis on the roles of cytochromes and iron-sulfur proteins. *Mailing Add:* Dept Chem & Biochem Tex Tech Univ Lubbock TX 79409-1061. *Fax:* 806-742-1289

KNAGGS, EDWARD ANDREW, ORGANIC CHEMISTRY. *Current Pos:* RETIRED. *Personal Data:* b Oak Park, Ill, July 28, 22; m 47, Pearl M Bonouich; c Kathleen L & Thomas E. *Educ:* YMCA Col, BS, 45; Ill Inst Technol, MS, 53. *Prof Exp:* Pilot plant technician, Glue Div, Swift & Co, 42; asst chemist, Inst Gas Technol, 42-45; res chemist, Ninol Labs, Inc, 45-49, chief chemist & plant engr, 49-58; assoc tech dir, Stepan Chem Co, 58-62, asst to gen mgr, 65-69, dir res & develop, 62-87, tech dir, Indust Chem Div, 69-74, corp dir com develop, 75-76, corp vpres & gen mgr, Petrol Prod Dept, 77-87. *Concurrent Pos:* Consult tech auth lectr, Ctr Prof Advan. *Mem:* AAAS; Am Chem Soc; Am Oil Chemists' Soc; Water Pollution Control Fedn; Am Water Works Asn. *Res:* Organic synthesis; organic sulfur compounds; desulfurization of gas and petroleum; SO3 sulfation and sulfonation; surface-active agents; author of 30 technical articles; granted 46 US and foreign patents. *Mailing Add:* 715 Colwyn Terr Deerfield IL 60015-3111

KNAKE, ELLERY LOUIS, WEED SCIENCE, AGRONOMY. *Current Pos:* instr plant sci, Voc Agr Serv, 56-60, from asst prof to assoc prof agron, 60-64, PROF WEED SCI AGRON, UNIV ILL, URBANA, 69- *Personal Data:* b Gibson City, Ill, Aug 26, 27; m 51, Colleen M Wilken; c Gary L & Kim P. *Educ:* Univ Ill, BS, 49, MS, 50, PhD(agron), 60. *Honors & Awards:* Crops & Soils Mag Award, Am Soc Agron, 67, Exten Educ Award, 78; Outstanding Exten Worker Award, Weed Sci Soc Am, 72; Ciba-Geigy Award for Outstanding Contrib to Agr, 72; Educr Award, Midwest Agr Chem Asn, 75; Sustained Excellence Award, Ill Coop Exten Serv, 83; Super Serv Award, US Dept Agr, 83. *Prof Exp:* Teacher, High Sch, Barrington, Ill, 50-56. *Concurrent Pos:* Bd dirs, N Cent Weed Control conference, 68-72 & 85-88, pres, 71, Weed Sci Soc Am, 72-75 & 86-89; UNDP consult Yugoslavia, 76; partic, East-West Center Confs, Honolulu, 76 & 77; assoc ed, Agron J, 76-78; ed, Weeds Today Mag, 78-82; mem, Comt Integrated Pest Mgt, Off Technol Assessment, 79; weed sci rep, People to People Prog, Peoples Rep China, 83; mem bd dirs, Coun Agr Sci & Technol, 84-, task force, Ecol Impacts Fed Conserv & Cropland Reduction Progs, 88-90; mem bd dirs, Coun Agr Sci & Technol, 84-93; mem, First Int Weed Control Cong, Australia, 92. *Mem:* Fel Weed Sci Soc Am (pres, 74); fel Am Soc Agron; Crop Sci Soc Am; Int Weed Sci Soc. *Res:* Competitive effects of giant foxtail; cultivation versus chemical weed control; herbicide incorporation; improving effectiveness of pre-emergence herbicides; site of herbicide uptake; weed control for conservation tillage and conservation acreage reserve; herbicide performance; effect of herbicides on crops. *Mailing Add:* N323 Turner Hall Univ Ill 1102 S Goodwin Ave Urbana IL 61801

KNAP, JAMES E(LI), INVESTMENT RECOVERY, CHEMICAL ENGINEERING. *Current Pos:* EMER PRES, 87- *Personal Data:* b Denver, Colo, Oct 5, 26; m 49; c 6. *Educ:* Univ Colo, BS, 49; Univ Ill, MS, 51, PhD(chem eng), 53. *Honors & Awards:* Bronze Medal & Chromium Plating Award, Am Electroplaters Soc, 67. *Prof Exp:* Asst chem eng, Ill, 49-50; chem engr, Process Develop Lab, Carbide & Carbon Chem Co, 52-55; group leader, Res & Develop Dept, Union Carbide Chem Div, 55-68, asst mgr, Invest Recovery Dept, 68-74, gen mgr, Invest Recovery Dept, 74-86, pres, Invest Recovery Asn, 83-85; Union Carbide Corp; invest recovery asn consult, 86-92. *Concurrent Pos:* Pres, Invest Recovery Asn, 83-85. *Mem:* Am Chem Soc; Am Inst Chem Engrs; Am Electroplaters Soc; Nat Soc Prof Engrs. *Res:* High pressure reactions; reaction kinetics; reactions of carbon monoxide; organometallic reactions; vapor plating; unit operations. *Mailing Add:* 120 Pine Cone Dr Huddleston VA 24104-2824

KNAPCZYK, JEROME WALTER, ADHESION, COATINGS. *Current Pos:* SCI FEL, MONSANTO CHEM CO. *Personal Data:* b Chicago, Ill, Sept 3, 38; m 86, Satsuki Oshiro; c Jason, Sarah & Jeremy. *Educ:* Benedictine Col, BS, 60; Univ Mass, PhD(chem), 64. *Honors & Awards:* Roon Award, Fedn Socs Coatings Technol, 87. *Prof Exp:* Res assoc, Univ NC, 69, Duke Univ, 70, Univ Mass, 71 & 72; prof chem, Johnson State Col, 74-78, chmn, Div Sci & Math, 74-79; fel chem, Univ Mass, Amherst, 79-80. *Concurrent Pos:* Vis prof chem, Univ Mass, Amherst, 74-77. *Mem:* Am Chem Soc; Sigma Xi; Mat Res Soc; Am Vacuum Soc. *Res:* Design of transparent, infrared reflecting films for glazing applications; mechanism of corrosion and transmission loss in optical stacks containing silver; adhesion modification of plastic substrates; photochemistry of onium compounds; polymer material science; adhesion of polymers to various substrates. *Mailing Add:* Monsanto Co 730 Worcester St Springfield MA 01151

KNAPHUS, GEORGE, BOTANY PLANT PATHOLOGY, SCIENCE EDUCATION. *Current Pos:* from instr to assoc prof, 62-72, PROF BOT, IOWA STATE UNIV, 72-, PROF SEC EDUC, 80- *Personal Data:* b McCallsburg, Iowa, Aug 31, 24; m 47, Marie Gjenvick; c Kristopher, Deborah (Raines), Dawn (Bovenmyer) & Daniel. *Educ:* Univ Northern Iowa, BA, 49; Iowa State Univ, MS, 51, PhD(plant path), 64. *Honors & Awards:* Gov Sci Medal, 86. *Prof Exp:* Prin & teacher, High Sch, Iowa, 58-62. *Mem:* Am Phytopath Soc; Bot Am; Am Inst Biol Sci; Nat Sci Teacher Asn. *Res:* Fungistasis of soil fungi, taxonomy and physiology of mushrooms; prairie plant diseases. *Mailing Add:* Dept Bot Iowa State Univ 353 Bessay Ames IA 50011. *Fax:* 515-294-1337

KNAPKA, JOSEPH J, PHYSIOLOGY. *Current Pos:* NUTRITIONIST, DIV RES SERV, NIH, 67- *Personal Data:* b Benton Pa, Jan 27, 35. *Educ:* Univ Tenn, PhD(animal sci), 67. *Mem:* Am Inst Nutrit; NY Acad Sci; Am Asn Lab Sci. *Res:* Animal nutrition. *Mailing Add:* 19725 Olney Mill Rd Brookeville MD 20833. *Fax:* 301-774-2956

KNAPP, ANTHONY WILLIAM, LIE GROUPS, REPRESENTATION THEORY. *Current Pos:* PROF MATH, STATE UNIV NY, STONY BROOK, 86- *Personal Data:* b Morristown, NJ, Dec 2, 41; m 63; c 2. *Educ:* Dartmouth Col, BA, 62; Princeton Univ, MA, 64, PhD(math), 65. *Prof Exp:* C L E Moore instr math, Mass Inst Technol, 65-67; from asst prof to prof math, Cornell Univ, 67-90. *Concurrent Pos:* Mem, Inst Advan Study, NJ, 68-69, 75-76 & 82-83; invited address, Int Congress Math, 74; res assoc, Princeton Univ, 71; prof d'echange, Univ de Paris-Sud, Orsay, 72; vis assoc prof, Rice Univ, 73; vis scholar, Univ Chicago, 81 & 83; prof associe, 82, prof invite, Univ Paris Seventh, 87; vis prof, Univ di Trento, Italy, 84, Tata Inst, Bombay, India, 88, Univ NSW, Australia, 89, Univ Montreal, 90; foreign expert, Hunan Normal Univ, Changsha, PR China, 88. *Mem:* Am Math Soc. *Res:* Representations of semi-simple Lie groups. *Mailing Add:* Dept Math State Univ NY Stony Brook NY 11794-3651

KNAPP, CHARLES FRANCIS, BIOENGINEERING. *Current Pos:* From asst prof to prof mech eng, 68-85, PROF, BIOMED ENG CTR, UNIV KY, 85-, DIR, 90- *Personal Data:* b Evansville, Ind, Mar 28, 40; m 68, Ann Konzen; c 3. *Educ:* St Procopius Col, BA, 62; Univ Notre Dame, BS, 63, MS, 65, PhD(aerospace eng), 68. *Concurrent Pos:* Prin investr grants, NIH, NASA, Air Force Off Sci Res; co-investr, NIH grants. *Mem:* Inst Elec & Electronics Engrs; Biomed Eng Soc. *Res:* Frequency response characteristics of cardiovascular regulation; cardiovascular changes during oscillatory lower-body negative pressure; custom designed surgical implants and aids from CT scans; blood rheology. *Mailing Add:* Wenner-Gren Biomed Eng Ctr Univ Ky Lexington KY 40506

KNAPP, CHARLES H, ELECTRICAL ENGINEERING. *Current Pos:* from instr to assoc prof, 57-74, PROF ELEC ENG, UNIV CONN, 74- *Personal Data:* b New York, NY, June 8, 31; m 55; c 4. *Educ:* Univ Conn, BSEE, 53, PhD(elec eng), 62; Yale Univ, ME, 56. *Prof Exp:* Eng trainee, RCA Victor Div, Radio Corp Am, 53; assoc engr, Res Div, Int Bus Mach Corp, 56-57. *Concurrent Pos:* Consult, Elec Boat Div, Gen Dynamics Corp, 61-78, Unimation Inc, 80, US Navy Underwater Systs Ctr, 84- *Mem:* Inst Elec & Electronics Engrs. *Res:* Automatic control; estimation and identification; communications and signal processing. *Mailing Add:* Dept Elec Eng Box U-157 Univ Conn Rm 312 260 Glenbrook Rd Storrs CT 06269

KNAPP, DANIEL ROGER, PHARMACOLOGY. *Current Pos:* from asst prof to assoc prof, 72-84, PROF PHARMACOL, MED UNIV SC, 84- *Personal Data:* b Evansville, Ind, July 29, 43; c 2. *Educ:* Univ Evansville, BA, 65; Ind Univ, Bloomington, PhD(org chem), 69. *Prof Exp:* NIH fel, Univ Calif, Berkeley, 69-70; asst prof exp med, Col Med, Univ Cincinnati, 71-72. *Mem:* Am Chem Soc; Am Soc Mass Spectrometry; Am Soc Pharmacol & Exp Therapeut; The Protein Soc. *Res:* Organoanalytical chemistry; mass spectrometry; protein structure. *Mailing Add:* Med Univ SC 171 Ashley Ave Charleston SC 29425. *E-Mail:* knappdr@musc.edu

KNAPP, DAVID ALLAN, PHARMACY, DRUGS & PUBLIC POLICY. *Current Pos:* assoc prof, Sch Pharm, Univ Md, 71-72, chmn, 73-79, dir grad studies, 79-81, assoc dean, 81-83, chmn pharm pract admin, 87-91, dir, Ctr Drugs & Pub Policy, Grad Sch, 87-96, PROF PHARM ADMIN, SCH PHARM, UNIV MD, 72-, DEAN, 91- *Personal Data:* b Cleveland, Ohio, Feb 25, 38; m 62, Deanne; c Wendy K (Steagall). *Educ:* Purdue Univ, BS, 60, MS, 62, PhD(pharm admin), 65. *Honors & Awards:* E H Volwiler Res Award, Am Asn Col Pharm, 86. *Prof Exp:* From asst prof to assoc prof pharm admin, Col Pharm, Ohio State Univ, 64-71. *Concurrent Pos:* Vis scholar, Sch Pub Health, Univ Mich, 70-71; researcher, Nat Ctr Health Serv Res, Dept Health & Human Serv, 78; consult, Am Pharm Asn, 84-85; Schering-Plough scholar in residence, Am Asn Col Pharm, 86-87. *Mem:* Fel AAAS; fel Am Pharmaceut Asn; fel Am Pub Health Asn; Am Asn Col Pharm; Am Soc Hosp Pharm (pres elect, 93-). *Res:* Applications of the social and administrative sciences to the drug component of medical care; cost and quality control methods in third party drug programs; drugs and public policy. *Mailing Add:* 11318 Cushman Rd Rockville MD 20852. *E-Mail:* knapp@pharmacy.ab.umd.ed

KNAPP, DAVID EDWIN, NUCLEAR PHYSICS. *Current Pos:* Res scientist, Long Beach Div, Douglas Aircraft Co, Inc, 54-55, consult, 55-57, res scientist, 57-58, res scientist, Missile & Space Systs Div, 61-62, chief nuclear res br, 62-64, asst chief scientist, Nuclear Dept, 64-69, chief scientist, Donald W Douglas Labs, Richland, Wash, 69-74, chief scientist, 74-76, PRIN STAFF ENGR, MCDONNELL DOUGLAS ASTRONAUT CO, 76- *Personal Data:* b El Paso, Tex, July 9, 32; m 54; c 4. *Educ:* Calif Inst Technol, BS, 53; Univ Rochester, MA, 59, PhD(physics), 61. *Mem:* AAAS; Am Phys Soc; Sigma Xi. *Res:* Elementary particle physics; energy conversion; nuclear power sources and propulsion. *Mailing Add:* 814 Market St Emporia KS 66801-2947

KNAPP, EDWARD ALAN, PHYSICS. *Current Pos:* pres, 90-95, EMER PRES, SANTA FE INST, 96- *Personal Data:* b Salem, Ore, Mar 7, 32; m 54; c Sandra K, David, Robert & Mary F (Parlange). *Educ:* Pomona Col, BA, 54; Univ Calif, PhD(physics), 58. *Hon Degrees:* DSc, Pomona Col, 84, Bucknell Univ, 84. *Honors & Awards:* David Barrows Awards, Pomona Col, 88. *Prof Exp:* Group leader, Los Alamos Sci Lab, Univ Calif, 59-68, asst div leader, 68-72, assoc div lab, Medium Engery Physics Div, 72-76, alt div leader, Physics Div, 76-77, div leader, Accelerator Technol Div, 78-82; dir, NSF, Washington, DC, 82-84; pres, Univs Res Asn, Washington, DC, 85-89. *Concurrent Pos:* Mem bd dir, ABC Inc, K/P Co, Inc. *Mem:* Fel AAAS; fel Am Phys Soc; Sigma Xi; Inst Elec & Electronics Engrs. *Res:* Medical application of accelerators and accelerator produced particles to cancer therapy; application of particle accelerators; high energy nuclear physics; photomeson processes and pi meson interactions; high energy linear accelerators, microwave cavities and related electromagnetic phenomena; applied physics; scientific administration. *Mailing Add:* 19 Bishop's Trail Sante Fe NM 87501. *Fax:* 505-982-0565; *E-Mail:* eak@santafe.edu

KNAPP, FRANCIS MARION, CARDIOVASCULAR PHYSIOLOGY, NEUROPHYSIOLOGY. *Current Pos:* chmn, Dept Biol, 83-91, PROF BIOL, STETSON UNIV, 91- *Personal Data:* b Caldwell, Idaho, Oct 17, 24; div; c 3. *Educ:* Col Idaho, AB, 49; Univ Southern Calif, MS, 55, PhD(physiol), 60. *Prof Exp:* Asst physiol, Sch Med, Univ Southern Calif, 54-59; res assoc, Thudichum Lab, State Res Hosp, Galesburg, Ill, 61-64; from asst prof to assoc prof physiol & biol, Duquesne Univ, 64-70; chmn, Dept Biol, Stetson Univ, 70-77; dir acad affairs, Pa State Univ, New Kensington, 78-83. *Concurrent Pos:* NIH fel, Karolinska Inst, Sweden, 60-61. *Mem:* AAAS; Am Physiol Soc; Am Inst Biol Sci; Microcirc Soc; Am Soc Zool; Sigma Xi. *Res:* Cerebro-vascular and peripheral blood flow problems; neurophysiology and central nervous system; behavioral studies and drug action. *Mailing Add:* 1001 Genter St Apt 8I La Jolla CA 92037-5526

KNAPP, FRED WILLIAM, ENTOMOLOGY. *Current Pos:* from asst prof to assoc prof, 61-71, PROF ENTOM, UNIV KY, 71- *Personal Data:* b Princeton, Ill, Oct 14, 28; m 58; c 2. *Educ:* Univ Ill, BS, 56; Kans State Univ, MS, 58, PhD(entom), 61. *Honors & Awards:* Distinguished Med Vet Entomologist, 86; C V Riley Award, Entom Soc Am. *Prof Exp:* Asst entom, Kans State Univ, 56-58, asst instr, 58-60, instr, 60-61. *Concurrent Pos:* Consult, USAID, pub health & indust, 61-85; entom adv, Agr Ctr NE, Thailand, 68-70; consult pesticide indust, 71-; pres, Am Registry Prof Entomologist, 87; pres, Ky Vector Control Asn & NCent Br, Entom Soc Am. *Mem:* Entom Soc Am; Am Mosquito Control Asn; Thailand Agr Soc; Sigma Xi. *Res:* Medical and veterinary entomology; insecticides; application methods and residues; pest management; integrated control of insects affecting man and animals. *Mailing Add:* Dept Entom Univ Ky Lexington KY 40506-0001

KNAPP, GAYLE, MOLECULAR BIOLOGY, BIOTECHNOLOGY. *Current Pos:* MKT DIR & RES SCIENTIST, CYBERSYM, PROVIDENCE, UTAH, 95- *Personal Data:* b Norwich, NY, July 31, 49; m 90, Bruce R Copeland. *Educ:* Barnard Col, AB, 71; Univ Ill, PhD(biochem), 77. *Prof Exp:* Fel molecular biol, Dept Chem, Univ Calif, San Diego, 77-81; asst prof micro-molecular biol, Dept Microbiol, Univ Ala, Birmingham, 81-88; asst prof, Dept Chem & Biochem, Utah State Univ, 88-93, sr res scientist, Nat Ctr Design Molecular Function, 93-95. *Mem:* Am Chem Soc; Sigma Xi; Am Soc Microbiol; NY Acad Sci; AAAS. *Res:* Biosynthesis of eukaryotic (yeast) tRNA's, in particular those which arise through splicing of intron-containing RNA precursors; nucleic acid structure and how altering structure affects the biological activity of the nucleic acid. *Mailing Add:* CyberSym Technol PO Box 127 Providence UT 84332. *Fax:* 435-750-3328; *E-Mail:* gayle@cybersym.com

KNAPP, GORDON GRAYSON, ORGANIC CHEMISTRY. *Current Pos:* Res chemist, Ethyl Corp, 56-63, res supvr, 66-69, res assoc, 70-85, sr res assoc, 85-89, RES ADV, ETHYL CORP, 89- *Personal Data:* b Miami, Ariz, Nov 26, 30; m 55; c 4. *Educ:* Ore State Col, BS, 52; Univ Wis, MS, 53, PhD(chem), 57. *Mem:* Am Chem Soc. *Res:* Polymer research, especially epoxies and polyurethanes; hydrometallurgy; industrial organic chemicals. *Mailing Add:* 2096 Highbury Dr Troy MI 48098

KNAPP, JOAN S, MICROBIOLOGY. *Current Pos:* chief, Bact Res Br, Neisseria Res Lab, 85-87, CHIEF GONNERHEA, CHLAMYDIA & CHANCHROID BR, DIV AIDS, TB, LAB RES, NAT CTR INFECTIOUS DIS, 87- *Personal Data:* b Dayleford, Victoria, Australia, Apr 12, 46. *Educ:* Univ Queenland, Brisbane, Australia, BA, 70, PhD(microbiol), 72. *Prof Exp:* Res assoc prof, Dept Med, Univ Wash, 73-85. *Mem:* Am Soc Microbiol; Int Soc Sexually Transmitted Dis Res. *Mailing Add:* Gonnerhea Chlamydia & Chancroid Br Div AIDS TB Lab Res Nat Ctr Infectious Dis G-39 Ctr Dis Control & Prev Atlanta GA 30333. *Fax:* 404-639-3976; *E-Mail:* jska@cdc.gov

KNAPP, JOHN WILLIAMS, CIVIL & SANITARY ENGINEERING. *Current Pos:* RETIRED. *Personal Data:* b Huntington, WVa, Dec 9, 32; m 57; c 3. *Educ:* Va Mil Inst, BS, 54; Johns Hopkins Univ, MSE, 62, PhD(sanit eng, water resources), 65. *Prof Exp:* Admin asst, Chesapeake & Potomac Tel Co, 54; off engr, Concrete Pipe & Prod Co, 58-59; instr civil eng, Va Mil Inst, 59-61; res asst sanit eng, Johns Hopkins Univ, 61-64; from asst prof to prof civil eng, Va Mil Inst, 64-95, head dept, 66-71. *Mem:* Am Soc Civil Engrs; Am Water Works Asn; Water Pollution Control Fedn; Nat Soc Prof Engrs. *Res:* Urban hydrology; economics and systems analysis; water supply and treatment; waste treatment and disposal; radioactive waste disposal. *Mailing Add:* 212 Barclay Lane Lexington VA 24450

KNAPP, JOSEPH LEONCE, JR, AGRICULTURAL CHEMISTRY, INTEGRATED PEST MANAGEMENT. *Current Pos:* mem staff, 77-80, PROF ENTOM & NEMATOL, UNIV FLA, 80- *Personal Data:* b New Boston, Tex, Nov 6, 37; m 57; c 2. *Educ:* Miss State Univ, BS, 60, PhD(entom), 65; Kans State Univ, MS, 62. *Prof Exp:* Scientist host plant resistance entom, USDA, 62-65; supvr field entom, Int Minerals & Chem Co, 65; entomologist, Upjohn Co, 69-70, plant scientist, 70-77. *Concurrent Pos:* consult, IPM, Grenada, Honduras, Egypt, Israel. *Mem:* Entom Soc Am; Am Registry Prof Entom. *Res:* Field research and development of insecticides, fungicides, herbicides and plant growth regulators for use on a wide range of agronomic crops. *Mailing Add:* 391 Escambia Dr Winter Haven FL 33884

KNAPP, KENNETH T, ENVIRONMENTAL CHEMISTRY. *Current Pos:* chief non-metal sect, Div Atmos Surveillance, US Environ Protection Agency, 71-73, chief, Particulate Emissions Res Sect, 73-80, chief, Stationary Sources Emissions Res Br, 80-88, CHIEF, MOBILE SOURCES EMISSIONS RES BR, ATMOSPHERIC RES & EXPOSURE ASSESSMENT LAB, US ENVIRON PROTECTION AGENCY, RESEARCH TRIANGLE PARK, NC, 88- *Personal Data:* b Jacksonville, Fla, June 9, 30; m 54; c 3. *Educ:* Univ Fla, BS, 54, PhD(chem), 60. *Prof Exp:* Chemist, Res Div, Procter & Gamble Co, 60-63, chemist, Foods Div, 63-65; chemist, Int Latex & Chem Corp, 65-67; chemist, Southern Res Inst, 67-70; head anal sect, Vick Chem Co, Mt Vernon, NY, 70-71. *Mem:* Am Chem Soc. *Res:* Instrumental analysis, especially gas chromatography, x-ray analysis; infrared spectroscopy, ultraviolet and visible spectroscopy, isolation and identification of naturally occurring compounds; measurement and characterization of air pollutants from source emissions. *Mailing Add:* Environ Protection Agency Research Triangle Park NC 27711

KNAPP, LESLIE W, ICHTHYOLOGY. *Current Pos:* dep dir, 68-72, dir, 81-88, SUPVR VERT, OCEANOG SORTING CTR, SMITHSONIAN INST, 63-68, 72-81 & 88- *Personal Data:* b Port Byron, NY, Nov 17, 29; m 57; c 2. *Educ:* Cornell Univ, BS, 52, PhD(vert zool), 64; Univ Mo, MA, 58. *Mem:* Am Soc Ichthyol & Herpet; Soc Syst Zool. *Res:* Systematic ichthyology, particularly the families Percidae and Platycephalidae. *Mailing Add:* Oceanog Sorting Ctr Smithsonian Inst Washington DC 20560

KNAPP, MALCOLM HAMMOND, INDUSTRIAL ORGANIC CHEMISTRY. *Current Pos:* CONSULT, 91- *Personal Data:* b Orange, NJ, Sept 20, 39; m 70; c 2. *Educ:* Rutgers Univ, BS, 61. *Prof Exp:* Chemist electrochem, Nuodex Div, Heyden Newport Corp, 64-66, sr chemist organometallics synthesis, Nuodex Div, Tenneco Chem, Inc, 67-70, lab mgr, 71-80, mgr lubricants, Res & Develop Dept, Tenneco Chem, Inc, 80-82 & Nuodex Inc, 83-85; mgr, Lubricants Res & Develop, Huls Am, 85-94. *Mem:* Soc Automotive Engrs; Am Soc Testing & Mat; Soc Tribologists & Lubrication Engrs. *Res:* Development of synthetic lubricants, novel base fluids, additives; test development. *Mailing Add:* 316 Raymond Ct Bridgewater NJ 08807. *Fax:* 732-981-5033

KNAPP, RICHARD MAITLAND, HEALTH ADMINISTRATION. *Current Pos:* proj dir, Teaching Hosp Info Ctr, Coun Teaching Hosps, Asn Am Med Cols, 68-69, dir, Div Teaching Hosps, 69-73, dir, Dept Teaching Hosps, 73-87, sr vpres, 87-93, EXEC VPRES, ASN AM MED COLS, WASHINGTON, 94- *Personal Data:* b Hartford, Conn, July 23, 41; m 69, Elizabeth Burgoyne; c Heather & Peter. *Educ:* Marietta Col, Ohio, BA, 63; Univ Iowa, MA, 65, PhD(hosp & health admin), 68. *Prof Exp:* Trainee, USPHS, 64-65. *Concurrent Pos:* Mem, Adv Comt Ambulatory Dent Servs Prog, Robert Wood Johnson Hosp, 78-83; bd dirs, Nat Asn Biomed Res & Hosp Fund Inc, 84- *Mem:* Inst Med-Nat Acad Sci; Am Hosp Asn. *Res:* Contributed articles to professional journals. *Mailing Add:* 2037 Durand Dr Reston VA 20191-1340

KNAPP, ROBERT HAZARD, JR, THEORETICAL PHYSICS, TECHNOLOGY STUDIES. *Current Pos:* CONSULT, 80-; MEM FAC, EVERGREEN STATE COL. *Personal Data:* b Boston, Mass, May 18, 44; c 3. *Educ:* Harvard Col, BA, 65; Oxford Univ, PhD(theoret physics), 68. *Honors & Awards:* Burlington Northern Award, 86. *Prof Exp:* Res physicist, Carnegie-Mellon Univ, 68-70; lectr, Calif State Polytech Col, 70-72; mem fac physics, Evergreen State Col, 72- & asst acad dean, 76-79; res asst, Univ Col, London, 80. *Concurrent Pos:* Mem, Nat Fac Humanities Arts & Sci, 87- *Mem:* Am Phys Soc; Soc Values Higher Educ; AAAS. *Res:* Philosophy of education; energy and transportation; design of college-level interdisciplinary studies; physics and natural history. *Mailing Add:* Evergreen State Col MS Lab 1 2700 Evergreen Pkwy NW Olympia WA 98505-0002

KNAPP, ROBERT LESTER, ORGANIC CHEMISTRY. *Current Pos:* RETIRED. *Personal Data:* b Keokuk, Iowa, Nov 17, 21; m 42; c 4. *Educ:* Brown Univ, ScB, 43. *Prof Exp:* Jr res chemist, Naugatuck Chem Div, US Rubber Co, 46-48, sr res chemist plastics, 48-52, sr group leader, 52-57, sect mgr Kralastic res & develop, 57-60, prod supt; Synthetic Rubber Plant, 60-63, sales mgr Kralastic, 64-66; dir mkt, Uniroyal Inc, 66-69, group mgr plastics res & develop, Uniroyal Chem Div, 69-76, dir bus develop & planning, 77-81, dir, Int Bus Develop, 81. *Concurrent Pos:* Consult, 81- *Mem:* Am Chem Soc; Soc Plastics Eng. *Res:* High polymers, both synthesis and physical behavior, particularly polyesters and gum plastics. *Mailing Add:* 189 Alder Lane PO Box 65 North Falmouth MA 02556-2936

KNAPP, ROGER DALE, NUCLEAR MAGNETIC RESONANCE SPECTROSCOPY. *Current Pos:* ASST PROF, BAYLOR COL MED, 81- *Personal Data:* b Natchez, Miss, Sept 6, 43. *Educ:* Miss State Univ, BS, 65; Univ Houston, PhD(chem), 74. *Mem:* Am Soc Biochem & Molecular Biol. *Res:* Biopolymer structure by nuclear magnetic resonance; computer, instrument interface. *Mailing Add:* Dept Med Baylor Col Med 6535 Fannin A 601 Houston TX 77030-2705. *Fax:* 713-798-4888

KNAPP, ROY M, PETROLEUM RESERVOIR ENGINEERING, MATHEMATICAL SIMULATION OF PETROLEUM PRODUCTION PROCESSES. *Current Pos:* assoc prof, 79-83, dir, Sch Petrol & Geol Eng, 79-88, PROF PETROL ENG, UNIV OKLA, 83- *Personal Data:* b Gridley, Kans, May 20, 40; m 62, Judith A Young; c Charles F, Michael K & Richard W. *Educ:* Univ Kans, BS, 63, MS, 69, DEng, 73. *Prof Exp:* Dir opers res, Northern Nat Gas Co, 64-71; res asst, Ctr for Res Inc, 71-73; from asst prof to assoc prof petrol eng, Univ Tex, Austin, 73-78. *Concurrent Pos:* Distinguished lectr, Soc Petrol Engrs, 80-81. *Mem:* Soc Petrol Inst; Am Soc Eng Educ; Am Petrol Inst; Int Asn Math & Comput Simulation; Am Gas Asn; Soc Hist Technol. *Res:* Development and application of computer simulators for petroleum reservoirs and ground water hydrology; use of microorganisms for enhanced oil recovery. *Mailing Add:* Dept Petrol Eng Univ Okla Main Campus Norman OK 73019-0628. *Fax:* 405-325-7477

KNAPP, WILLIAM ARNOLD, JR, VETERINARY PHARMACOLOGY, TOXICOLOGY. *Current Pos:* CONSULT VET PHARMACEUT, AGRICHEM & RELATED INDUST, W A KNAPP ASSOC, 83- *Personal Data:* b Atlanta, Ga, Oct 4, 25; m 50; c 3. *Educ:* Univ Ga, DVM, 51, MS, 64. *Prof Exp:* Asst prof vet med & surg, Univ Ga, 51-52; pvt practice, 52-54; asst prof physiol & pharmacol, Sch Vet Med, Univ Ga, 54-62; dir res, Morris Res Labs, Inc, 62-65; assoc dir & res coordr, Toxicol Div, Hazleton Labs, Inc, 65-68, pres, Hazleton Res Animals, Inc, 68-71; dir, Animal Sci-Prod Div, Flow Labs Inc, Rockville, Md, 71-78, pres, Flow Res Animals Inc, 71-77; vpres, Flow Labs Inc, McLean, Va, 76-83. *Mem:* Am Soc Vet Physiol & Pharmacol; Vet Med Asn; Am Asn Lab Animal Sci; Indust Vet Asn (pres, 69-70); Am Col Vet Toxicologists. *Res:* Veterinary pharmacology; drug evaluations; toxicology; nutrition; research administration and general management. *Mailing Add:* 3212 Queens Rd Raleigh NC 27612-6233

KNAPPE, LAVERNE F, MECHANICAL ENGINEERING, APPLIED MECHANICS. *Current Pos:* mgr mech analysis lab, 57-70, SR ENGR, IBM CORP, 70- *Personal Data:* b Ellsworth, Wis, Jan 8, 22; m 44; c 3. *Educ:* Univ Minn, BME, 44, MSME, 47, PhD(mech eng), 53. *Prof Exp:* Mech engr, Barber Colman Co, 47-50; instr mech eng, Univ Minn, 50-53; res engr, Am Mach & Foundry Co, 53-55; consult, Booz, Allen & Hamilton, Inc, 55-57. *Concurrent Pos:* Consult, Gen Mills, Inc, 51-53. *Mem:* Am Soc Mech Engrs; Soc Exp Stress Anal; NY Acad Sci. *Res:* Research and development of computer-aided mechanical design systems, including engineer-computer communication, analytical design procedures, system modeling and design optimization. *Mailing Add:* 501 17th St SW Rochester MN 55902

KNAPPENBERGER, HERBERT ALLAN, INDUSTRIAL ENGINEERING, APPLIED STATISTICS. *Current Pos:* MEM STAFF, DEPT INDUST ENG, WAYNE STATE UNIV, 77-, CHMN OPERS RES, 81-, ASSOC DEAN, SCH ENG. *Personal Data:* b Reading, Pa, May 24, 32; m 57; c 3. *Educ:* Pa State Univ, BS, 57, MS, 60; NC State Univ, PhD(exp statist), 66. *Prof Exp:* Apprentice draftsman, Textile Mach Works, Pa, 50-54; instr indust eng, Pa State Univ, 58-60; from instr to asst prof, NC State Univ, 60-68; from assoc prof to prof, Univ Mo-Columbia, 68-77. *Concurrent Pos:* Mem health serv res training comt, Nat Ctr Health Serv Res & Develop. *Mem:* Am Inst Indust Engrs; Am Statist Asn; Opers Res Soc Am; Am Soc Eng Educ. *Res:* Health care systems design; patient scheduling systems design; automated radiology systems design; resource allocation on large systems. *Mailing Add:* Dept Indust Mfg Eng Wayne State Univ 5050 Anthony Wayne Dr Detroit MI 48202

KNAPPENBERGER, PAUL HENRY, JR, SCIENCE ADMINISTRATION, ASTRONOMY. *Current Pos:* PRES, ADLER PLANETARIUM, 91- *Personal Data:* b Reading, Pa, Sept 5, 42; m 63; c 2. *Educ:* Franklin & Marshall Col, AB, 64; Univ Va, MA, 66, PhD(astron), 68. *Prof Exp:* Chmn dept astron, Fernbank Sci Ctr, Atlanta, 68-72; dir, Sci Mus Va, 73-91. *Concurrent Pos:* Instr astron, Emory Univ & adj prof, Ga State Univ, 70-72; asst prof, Va Commonwealth Univ, 73-; adj assoc prof, Univ Richmond, 74-81; pres, Asn Sci & Technol Ctrs, 85; councilman, Nat Mus Act. *Mem:* Am Astron Soc; AAAS; Am Asn Mus; Int Coun Mus. *Res:* Astronomical interferometry; astronomical applications of image converters and intensifiers; development of educational activities in astronomy; design and evaluation of interactive exhibits in science; education in science museums. *Mailing Add:* Alder Planetarium 1300 S Lake Shore Dr Chicago IL 60605

KNASTER, TATYANA, durability of concrete, structural design, for more information see previous edition

KNATTERUD, GENELL LAVONNE, BIOSTATISTICS. *Current Pos:* asst prof epidemiol & biostatist, Pakistan Med Res Ctr, Univ Md, 66-67; from asst prof to assoc prof, Inst Int Med, 67-72, from assoc prof to prof, 72-84, RES PROF EPIDEMIOL & PREV MED, UNIV MD, BALTIMORE, 85- *Personal Data:* b Minot, NDak. *Educ:* Macalester Col, BA, 52; Univ Minn, MS, 59, PhD(biostatist), 63. *Prof Exp:* Asst biochemist, Pillsbury Mills Res Labs, 52-53; teaching asst anat, Univ Minn, 54-56, statistician, Biostatist Div, 56-57, sr statistician, 58-60, instr, Sch Pub Health, 60-62; anal statistician, Off Biomet, Consult Sect, NIMH, 63-64. *Concurrent Pos:* Mem nat cancer adv comt, Nat Bladder-Prostate Cancer Projs, 72-74; vpres, Md Med Res Inst, 74-; mem lipid metab adv comt, Nat Heart & Lung Inst, 75-83. *Mem:* AAAS; Am Diabetes Asn; Am Pub Health Asn; Am Statist Asn; Biomet Soc. *Res:* Design, methods and applications of clinical trials; epidemiology of cardiovascular disease and diabetes. *Mailing Add:* 40 Bouton Green Baltimore MD 21210-1503

KNAUER, BRUCE RICHARD, PHYSICAL-ORGANIC CHEMISTRY. *Current Pos:* from asst prof to assoc prof, 70-91, chmn, Chem Dept, 82-85, PROF ORG CHEM, STATE UNIV NY COL, ONEONTA, 91- *Personal Data:* b New York, NY, Nov 24, 42. *Educ:* Cooper Union, BChE, 63; Cornell Univ, MS, 65, PhD(chem), 69. *Prof Exp:* USAF Off Aerospace Res fel, Univ Ga, 68-70. *Mem:* Am Chem Soc. *Res:* Electron spin resonance; nitroxide free radicals; reaction mechanisms. *Mailing Add:* Dept Chem State Univ NY Col Oneonta NY 13820-4015. *Fax:* 607-436-2654; *E-Mail:* knauerbr@oneonta.edu

KNAUER, JAMES PHILIP, PLASMA PHYSICS. *Current Pos:* SCIENTIST MGR, LAB LASER ENERGETICS, UNIV ROCHESTER, NY, 86- *Personal Data:* b Sandusky, Ohio, May 12, 50; m 74, Susan Diana Holmes. *Educ:* Mass Inst Technol, BS, 72; Univ Hawaii, MS, 74, PhD, 77. *Honors & Awards:* Excellence Plasma Physics Res Award, Am Phys Soc, 95. *Prof Exp:* Res investr, Univ Pa, 77-78; jr researcher, Univ Hawaii, 78-79; assoc res scientist, Lockheed Missiles & Space Co, 79-86, res scientist, 79-86. *Concurrent Pos:* Mgr, Nat Laser Users Facil, Rochester, 86- *Mem:* Am Phys Soc; Sigma Xi. *Mailing Add:* Nat Laser Users Facil Univ Rochester 250 E River Rd Rochester NY 14623-1212

KNAUER, THOMAS E, EXPERIMENTAL BIOLOGY. *Current Pos:* ATTY ENVIRON LAW, MCSWEENEY, BURTCH & CRUMP, 90- *Mailing Add:* McSweeney Burtch & Crump 11 S 12th St Richmond VA 23219. *Fax:* 804-782-2130

KNAUF, PHILIP A, BIOPHYSICS. *Current Pos:* PROF BIOPHYS, UNIV ROCHESTER, 80- *Personal Data:* b Rochester, NY, Mar 25, 42. *Educ:* Boston Col, BA, 63; Univ Rochester, PhD(biophys), 70. *Honors & Awards:* K S Collinswood Award, Biophys Soc, 87. *Prof Exp:* Prof biophys, Univ Toronto & Hosp Sick Children, 72-80. *Mem:* Am Physiol Soc; Biophys Soc; Soc Gen Psychologists; Sigma Xi. *Res:* Biophysics. *Mailing Add:* Dept Biophys Univ Rochester Med Ctr Box BPHYS 601 Elmwood Ave Rochester NY 14642-8408

KNAUFF, RAYMOND EUGENE, ENDOCRINE BIOCHEMISTRY. *Current Pos:* prof biochem & chmn dept, 74-89, EMER PROF & CHMN, PHILADELPHIA COL OSTEOP MED, 89- *Personal Data:* b Venus, Pa, July 22, 25; m 49, Helen M Rengert; c Patricia A. *Educ:* Capital Univ, BS, 47; Univ Mich, MS, 49, PhD(biol chem), 52. *Prof Exp:* Chem technician, Barneby-Cheney Eng Co, 44; org chemist, Dow Chem Co, 45, anal chemist, 46, biochemist toxicol, 47; biochemist, Univ Mich Hosp, 47-49, asst biol chem, Med Sch, 49-50; endocrinologist, Upjohn Co, 51-55; head bioanal dept, G D Searle Co, 56-57; asst prof biochem, Univ Mich, 57-61; assoc prof biochem, Sch Med, Temple Univ, 61-74. *Concurrent Pos:* Dir res, Cystic Fibrosis Res Inst, 61-67. *Mem:* AAAS; Am Chem Soc; Am Inst Chemists; NY Acad Sci. *Res:* Biological chemistry; endocrine biochemistry; bioanalytical chemistry; protein and amino acid chemistry and metabolism; cystic fibrosis; nutritional biochemistry; eicosanoid biochemistry. *Mailing Add:* 37 Meade Rd Ambler PA 19002-5122

KNAUFT, DAVID A, PLANT BREEDING, FARMING SYSTEMS. *Current Pos:* PROF & HEAD DEPT, CROP SCI DEPT, NC STATE UNIV. *Personal Data:* b Evergreen Park, Ill, May 10, 51; m 78; c 1. *Educ:* Univ Wis-Madison, BS, 73; Cornell Univ, PhD(plant breeding), 77. *Prof Exp:* Vis instr genetics, Agron & Soils Dept, Clemson Univ, 77-78; from asst prof to prof plant breeding & genetics, Agron Dept, Univ Fla, 78-93. *Mem:* Am Soc Agron; Am Genetic Asn; Crop Sci Soc Am; AAAS. *Res:* Genetic factors important in the improvement of cultivated peanuts, including genetic stability, response to stress environments, disease resistance and intercropping. *Mailing Add:* NC State Univ Dept Crop Sci PO Box 7620 Raleigh NC 27695-0001. *Fax:* 919-515-7959

KNAUS, EDWARD ELMER, MEDICINAL CHEMISTRY. *Current Pos:* asst prof, 72-80, PROF MED CHEM, UNIV ALTA, 80- *Personal Data:* b Leroy, Sask, Jan 7, 43; m 74, Alexis Haryett; c Valerie, Joanne & Gordon. *Educ:* Univ Sask, BSP, 65, MSc, 67, PhD(pharmaceut chem), 70. *Honors & Awards:* McNeill Res Award. *Prof Exp:* Med Res Coun Can fel chem, Tex A&M Univ, 70-71 & Univ BC, 71-72. *Mem:* Am Chem Soc; Can Pharmaceut Asn; Chem Inst Can. *Res:* Synthesis of new nitrogen heterocycles and diagnostic agents; structure-activity studies; drug design. *Mailing Add:* Fac Pharm & Pharmaceut Sci Univ Alta Edmonton AB T6G 2N8 Can. *Fax:* 403-492-1217; *E-Mail:* eknaus@pharmacy.ualberta.ca

KNAUS, RONALD MALLEN, RADIOECOLOGY, RADIOBIOLOGY. *Current Pos:* PROF & RESEARCHER RADIOECOL & RADIOBIOL, LA STATE UNIV, 75- *Personal Data:* b San Jose, Calif, June 9, 37; m 60, Nancy Walsh; c Christopher & Scott. *Educ:* San Jose State Univ, AB, 60, MA, 62; Ore State Univ, PhD(radiation biol), 71. *Prof Exp:* Teacher, Fremont Union High Sch Dist, 60-65 & Fresno City Col, 65-68; researcher biochem, Ore State Univ, 68-71; prof biol, Univ Tex, Arlington, 71-75. *Concurrent Pos:* Consult, Comp Planning Inst, Dallas, 76- & City & Parish, East Baton Rouge, 77-81; prin investr, Lake Restoration Proj, City Baton Rouge, 77-, study marsh sediments, US Dept Interior & US Geol Surv; neutron activation anal biol sci, US Dept Energy; southeast regional dir, Sigma Xi. *Mem:* AAAS; Sigma Xi. *Res:* Investigation into the behavior of stable metal and rare earth tracers in the lotic environment; establish stable, activable tracers as soil horizon markers in fresh, brackish, and saltwater wetlands. *Mailing Add:* Nuclear Sci Ctr La State Univ Baton Rouge LA 70803-0001. *Fax:* 504-388-2094

KNAUSENBERGER, WULF H, ELECTRONICS ENGINEERING. *Current Pos:* mem tech staff, 70-78, TECH SUPVR, BELL LABS, 78- *Personal Data:* b Vienna, Austria, May 3, 43; US citizen; m 67; c 4. *Educ:* Pa State Univ, BS, 65, PhD(solid state sci), 69. *Prof Exp:* Res assoc, Pa State Univ, 69-70. *Concurrent Pos:* Chair, Comput Packaging Tech Comt, Inst Elec & Electronics Engrs, 84-85; assoc ed, CHMT trans, Inst Elec & Electronics Engrs, 85- *Mem:* Inst Elec & Electronics Engrs; Int Electronics Packaging Soc (pres, 94). *Res:* Analysis of electronic system design, electronic packaging and interconnection system design; history of computer packaging. *Mailing Add:* 88 Hainesburg River Rd Columbia NJ 07832. *Fax:* 973-386-2084; *E-Mail:* knausenberger@att.com

KNAUSS, JOHN ATKINSON, OCEANOGRAPHY, OCEAN POLICY. *Current Pos:* prof oceanog, Univ RI, 62-90, dean, Grad Sch Oceanog, 62-87, provost marine affairs, 69-82, vpres marine progs, 82-87, DEAN & EMER PROF, UNIV RI, 90-; RES ASSOC, SCRIPPS INST OCEANOG, UNIV CALIF, SAN DIEGO, 94- *Personal Data:* b Detroit, Mich, Sept 1, 25; m 54, Lynne; c Karl & William. *Educ:* Mass Inst Technol, BS, 46; Univ Mich, MA, 49; Univ Calif, Los Angeles, PhD(oceanog), 59. *Hon Degrees:* DSc, Univ RI, 92. *Honors & Awards:* Sea Grant Asn Award, 74; Ocean Sci Award, Ocean Sci Sect, Am Geophys Union, 88. *Prof Exp:* Physicist, Navy Electronics Lab, 47-48; oceanogr, Off Naval Res, 50-51 & 53-54; res staff, Scripps Inst Oceanog, 51-52, oceanogr, 55-62; adminr, Nat Oceanic & Atmospheric Admin, US Dept Com, 89-93. *Concurrent Pos:* Comt Oceanog, Nat Acad Sci, 66-70, chmn, Ocean Sci Comt, 71-73, Ocean Policy Comt, 72-82, Univ Nat Oceanog Lab Syst, 74-75; mem, Pres Comn Marine Sci, Eng & Resources, 67-68; chair, comt Oceanog, Nat Res Coun, 70-73, Ocean Policy Comt, 73-82; first vchair, Int Oceanog Comm, 91-93. *Mem:* Fel Am Geophys Union (pres elect, 96-98); fel AAAS; fel Am Meteorol Soc; Sigma Xi; fel Marine Technol Soc; Oceanog Soc. *Res:* Ocean circulation; law of the sea; marine affairs. *Mailing Add:* 2634 Ellentown Rd La Jolla CA 92037. *E-Mail:* jknauss@gso.uri.edu

KNAVEL, DEAN EDGAR, HORTICULTURE. *Current Pos:* From asst prof to assoc prof, 59-78, PROF HORT, UNIV KY, 78- *Personal Data:* b Windber, Pa, Sept 5, 24; m 47; c 3. *Educ:* Pa State Univ, BS, 54; Univ Del, MS, 56; Mich State Univ, PhD(hort), 59. *Mem:* Fel Am Soc Hort Sci. *Res:* Breeding, nutrition and minimum tillage of vegetable crops. *Mailing Add:* 1112 Meridian Dr Lexington KY 40504

KNAZEK, RICHARD ALLAN, MEDICINE, ENGINEERING. *Current Pos:* INVESTR MED, NIH, 71- *Personal Data:* b Cleveland, Ohio, Mar 23, 42; m 67; c 2. *Educ:* Case Inst Technol, BS, 62; Lehigh Univ, MS, 64; Ohio State Univ, MD, 69; Am Bd Internal Med, dipl, 74. *Prof Exp:* Engr cryogenic res, Air Prod & Chem, 62-63; engr plastics develop, E I du Pont de Nemours & Co, Inc, 63-65; intern med, Duke Hosp, 69-70, resident, 70-71. *Concurrent Pos:* Vis fac, W A Jones Cell Sci Ctr, 73-76; vis lectr, Univ Toronto & Mass Gen Hosp, 74; contract officer, Breast Cancer Task Force, Nat Cancer Inst, 74-80; PhD thesis adv, Univ Del, 76-77. *Mem:* Endocrine Soc; Am Asn Cancer Res; Soc Exp Biol Med. *Res:* Developer of artificial capillary cell culture technique to grow solid organs in vitro; study of the control of prolactin receptors in liver and mammary cancer. *Mailing Add:* Nat Ctr Res Resources 6705 Rockledge Dr Rm 6030 Bethesda MD 20892-7965

KNEALE, SAMUEL GEORGE, MATHEMATICS. *Current Pos:* RETIRED. *Personal Data:* b Tulsa, Okla, Dec 13, 21; m 45, Marian Rickards; c Andrew & Elizabeth. *Educ:* Univ Kans, AB, 47, MA, 48; Harvard Univ, PhD(math), 53. *Prof Exp:* Consult math, Philco Corp, Pa, 51-56, Gen Elec Co, 56-59 & Avco Corp, Ohio, 59-61; prin scientist math, Opers Res Inc, 61-85. *Mem:* Math Asn Am. *Res:* Applied mathematics, including probability theory and statistics, game theory, systems analysis, and other aspects of operations research. *Mailing Add:* 4111 Cheney Pl Wilmington NC 28412

KNEBEL, HARLEY JOHN, GEOLOGICAL OCEANOGRAPHY, MARINE GEOLOGY. *Current Pos:* assoc br chief, 85-93, OCEANOGR, CTR COASTAL & MARINE GEOL, US GEOL SURV, 73-, SUPVR ENVIRON STUDIES, 96- *Personal Data:* b Iowa City, Iowa, Nov 10, 41; m 69, Carole J Marciniak; c Paula T & Ellen J. *Educ:* Univ Iowa, BA, 65; Univ Wash, MS, 67, PhD(oceanog), 72. *Prof Exp:* Res asst oceanog, Univ Wash, 65-67; oceanogr, Nat Oceanic & Atmospheric Admin, Atlantic Oceanog & Meteorol Labs, 67-69; res assoc, Univ Wash, 69-73. *Concurrent Pos:* Texaco fel oceanog, Univ Wash, 71-72; mem adv bd, Geol Dept, Univ Iowa, 88- *Mem:* Am Geophys Union; fel Geol Soc Am; Sigma Xi. *Res:* Sedimentology; estuarine, nearshore, and continental shelf sedimentary processes and stratigraphy; statistics applied to geological oceanography; mass movements of sediments on continental slopes; clay mineralogy; submarine canyon development; coastal environments. *Mailing Add:* Ctr Coastal & Marine Geol US Geol Surv 384 Woods Hole Rd Woods Hole MA 02543-1598

KNECHT, CHARLES DANIEL, VETERINARY SURGERY, NEUROLOGY. *Current Pos:* PROF & HEAD, DEPT SMALL ANIMAL SURG & MED, COL VET MED, AUBURN UNIV, 79- *Personal Data:* b Halethorpe, Md, Mar 22, 32; wid; c Charles M & Thomas R. *Educ:* Univ Pa, VMD, 56; Univ Md, College Park, BS, 60; Univ Ill, Urbana, MS, 66; Am Col Vet Surgeons, dipl, 68; Am Col Vet Internal Med, dipl & cert neurol, 74. *Honors & Awards:* Norden Award, 76; Gaines Award, 82. *Prof Exp:* Assoc vet, Broad St Vet Hosp, Richmond, Va, 56; assoc vet, Wertz Mem Animal Hosp, Pittsburgh, 58-59; assoc vet, Towson Vet Hosp, Md, 59-64; from instr to asst prof vet med & surg, Col Vet Med, Univ Ill, Urbana, 64-68, assoc prof vet surg, 68-70; prof med & surg, Col Vet Med, Univ Ga, 70-72; prof & chief of surg, Sch Vet Sci & Med, Purdue Univ, West Lafayette, 72-79. *Concurrent Pos:* Abstractor, Chirurgia Veterinaria, WGer, 66-68 & Auburn Univ, 79-; mem grad fac, Univ Ill, Urbana, 68-70, Univ Ga, 71-72, Purdue Univ, 72-79, Auburn Univ, 80-; abstractor, J World & Europ Vet Surgeons, 68-72; pres neurol specialty, Am Col Vet Internal Med, 83-86; pres & chmn bd, Am Col Vet Surg, 88-90; assoc ed, Vet Med Report, 87-90. *Mem:* Am Vet Med Asn; Am Col Vet Surg (pres, 88-89); Am Asn Vet Neurol (pres, 74-75); Am Asn Vet Clinicians (pres, 91-92); Am Animal Hosp Asn; Am Col Vet Internal Med; Nat Acad Vet Pract. *Res:* Orthopedic surgery; neurosurgery; electrodiagnostics. *Mailing Add:* Dept Small Animal Surg & Med Col Vet Med Auburn Univ Auburn AL 36849-5523

KNECHT, DAVID JORDAN, MAGNETOSPHERIC PHYSICS. *Current Pos:* PHYSICIST, SPACECRAFT INTERACTIONS BR, PHILLIPS LAB, MASS, HANSCOM AFB, 91- *Personal Data:* b Elgin, Ill, June 2, 30; m 57, Dzidra Jirgensons; c 1. *Educ:* Univ Ill, BS, 51, MS, 52; Univ Wis, PhD(physics), 58. *Prof Exp:* Proj assoc nuclear physics, Univ Wis, 58-59; proj officer physics div, Air Force Spec Weapons Ctr, 59-61, res physicist spec proj div, 61-63; sci dir, Space Physics Br, Air Force Weapons Lab, 63-64; res physicist, Space Physics Lab, Air Force Cambridge Res Labs, 64-75; physicist, Space Physics Div, Geophys Lab, 75-91. *Mem:* Am Geophys Union. *Res:* Magnetospheric substorms and other disturbances using magnetic measurements made by ground networks and spacecraft; interactions of orbiting vehicles with space plasmas using spectroscopic observations made on space shuttle. *Mailing Add:* 56 South Rd Bedford MA 01730. *Fax:* 781-377-5571

KNECHT, LAURANCE A, ANALYTICAL CHEMISTRY, PHYSICAL CHEMISTRY. *Current Pos:* AT NC SCH SCI & MATH, 85- *Personal Data:* b Elgin, Ill, Mar 16, 32; m 66; c 1. *Educ:* Univ Ill, BS, 53; Univ Minn, PhD(anal chem), 59. *Prof Exp:* Instr chem, Iowa State Univ, 60-63; asst prof, Univ Cincinnati, 63-68; from assoc prof to prof chem, Marietta Col, 68-84. *Mem:* AAAS; Am Chem Soc. *Res:* Electroanalytical techniques. *Mailing Add:* 1303 Willow Dr Chapel Hill NC 27514-2607

KNECHT, WILLIAM G, MECHANICAL ENGINEERING, NUCLEAR ENGINEERING. *Honors & Awards:* Bernard F Langer Nuclear Codes & Stand Award, Am Soc Mech Engrs, 95. *Mailing Add:* 1330 Campbell St Williamsport PA 17701

KNECHTLI, RONALD (C), PHYSICS. *Current Pos:* RETIRED. *Personal Data:* b Geneva, Switz, Aug 14, 27; nat US; m 53, Diane Weisul; c Alain, Bernard & Daniel. *Educ:* Swiss Fed Inst Technol, Dipl, 50, PhD(elec eng), 55. *Honors & Awards:* Outstanding Work Res Award, RCA Lab; L A Hyland Patent Award. *Prof Exp:* Res engr, Brown Boveri & Co, Switz, 50-51; asst, Mass Inst Technol, 51-52; res engr, Brown Boveri & Co, 52-53; res engr, Res Labs, Radio Corp Am, 53-58; sr scientist, Res Labs, Hughes Aircraft Co, 58-86. *Mem:* Am Inst Aeronaut & Astronaut; Am Phys Soc; Sigma Xi; Inst Elec & Electronics Engrs. *Res:* Photovoltaic and electrochemical devices. *Mailing Add:* 22929 Ardwick St Woodland Hills CA 91364

KNEE, DAVID ISAAC, TEACHING, TEACHER TRAINING. *Current Pos:* asst prof, 65-69, ASSOC PROF MATH, HOFSTRA UNIV, 69- *Personal Data:* b New York, NY, July 13, 34; m 83; c 2. *Educ:* City Col New York, BS, 56; Mass Inst Technol, PhD(math), 62. *Prof Exp:* Mathematician, Arde Assocs, NJ, 56; instr math, Columbia Univ, 62-65. *Concurrent Pos:* Dir, Teacher Training Inst, Hofstra, 86- *Mem:* Math Asn Am; Nat Coun Teachers Math. *Res:* Algebra; mathematics education; representation theory; mathematical linguistics. *Mailing Add:* Dept Math Hofstra Univ Adams Hall Hempstead Turnpike Hempstead NY 11550-1090

KNEE, TERENCE EDWARD CREASEY, SYNTHETIC TEXTILE FIBERS. *Current Pos:* RETIRED. *Personal Data:* b Brussels, Belg, Apr 20, 32; m 56, Martha McManamy; c Christine & Michael. *Educ:* Trinity Col, Dublin, BASc, 53; Mass Inst Technol, PhD(chem), 56. *Prof Exp:* Instr chem, Franklin Tech Inst, 55-56; res chemist, DuPont Co Can, 57-60, res supvr, E I du Pont de Nemours & Co, Inc, 60-70, tech supvr, 70-72, tech supt, 72-76, tech supt, Chattanooga Res & Develop Sect, 76-85; consult, 85-96. *Mem:* Am Chem Soc. *Res:* Synthetic textile fibers; polymer chemistry; reaction mechanisms. *Mailing Add:* 228 Masters Rd Hixson TN 37343

KNEEBONE, LEON RUSSELL, MYCOLOGY. *Current Pos:* Asst bot, 47-50, from asst prof to prof, 50-78, EMER PROF BOT & PLANT PATH, PA STATE UNIV, 78- *Personal Data:* b Bangor, Pa, May 28, 20; m 45, Elizabeth C Morgan; c Patricia A, Stephen B & Eileen E. *Educ:* Pa State Univ, BS, 42, PhD(bot), 50. *Concurrent Pos:* Consult mushroom indust, int consult, nat govt Australia, Jamaica, Haiti & Dominican Repub; founder & gen chmn, mushroom indust short course, Pa State Univ, 56-78. *Mem:* AAAS; Bot Soc Am; Mycol Soc Am; Am Phytopath Soc; Am Inst Biol Sci; Am Mushroom Inst; Mushroom Grower Asn UK; Mushroom Grower Asn Can; Mushroom Grower Asn Australia; Int Soc Mushroom Sci; Sigma Xi. *Res:* Mushroom culture, especially spawn and strain development, diseases; edible fungi. *Mailing Add:* 628 Fairway Rd State College University Park PA 16803

KNEEBONE, WILLIAM ROBERT, AGRONOMY, PLANT BREEDING. *Current Pos:* PROF AGRON, UNIV ARIZ, 63- *Personal Data:* b Eveleth, Minn, July 11, 22; m 48; c 3. *Educ:* Univ Minn, BS, 47, MS, 50, PhD(plant genetics), 51. *Prof Exp:* Asst grass breeding, Univ Minn, 47-50; res agronomist, Okla Agr Exp Sta & Crop Res Div Agr Res Serv, USDA, 51-63. *Concurrent Pos:* Consult revegetation & golf course maintanience. *Mem:* Fel AAAS; Am Soc Agron; Coun Agr Sci & Technol; Soc Econ Bot; Sigma Xi. *Res:* Breeding; genetics; seed production; factors involved in stand establishment, vigor and spread of forage and turf grasses; water use by grasses. *Mailing Add:* 2491 N Camino de Oeste Tucson AZ 85745

KNEECE, ROLAND ROYCE, JR, MATHEMATICS, OPERATIONS RESEARCH. *Current Pos:* MEM STAFF, ACQUISITION & LOGISTICS, OFF SECY DEFENSE, 74-, OPER RES ANALYST, DEFENSE DEPT. *Personal Data:* b Tifton, Ga, Oct 15, 39; m 63. *Educ:* Ga Inst Technol, BS, 61, MS, 62; Univ Md, PhD(math), 70. *Prof Exp:* Mem staff opers res, Inst Defense Anal, Arlington, 67-74. *Concurrent Pos:* Prof lectr, Am Univ, 69- *Mem:* Am Math Soc; Asn Comput Mach. *Res:* Operator theory; functional analysis; strictly singular operators; computer technology. *Mailing Add:* 7406 Colshire Dr 3 McLean VA 22102

KNEIB, RONALD THOMAS, ECOLOGY. *Current Pos:* Res assoc, Univ Ga Marine Inst, 81-83, asst res scientist, 84-86, assoc res scientist, 86-93, SR RES SCIENTIST, UNIV GA MARINE INST, 94-, ADJ ASSOC PROF, DEPT MARINE SCI, UNIV GA, 92- *Personal Data:* b Pittsburgh, Pa, Jan 29, 51. *Educ:* Pa State Univ, BS, 72; Univ NC, Chapel Hill, MA, 76, PhD(ecol), 80. *Concurrent Pos:* Adj asst prof, Zool Dept, Univ Ga, 85-86, adj assoc res scientist, 86-; vis assoc prof, Col Marine Studies, Univ Del, 86. *Mem:* Ecol Soc Am; Am Fisheries Soc; Estuarine Res Fedn; Am Soc Zoologists; Am Soc Ichthyologists & Herpetologists; Sigma Xi; Soc Wetland Scientists. *Res:* Ecological interactions within and between populations of estuarine fishes and invertebrates; processes affecting recruitment and population dynamics in salt marshes. *Mailing Add:* Univ Ga Marine Inst Sapelo Island GA 31327-9999. Fax: 912-485-2133; E-Mail: rtkneib@uga.cc.uga.edu

KNEIP, G(EORGE) D(EWEY), JR, metallurgy; deceased, see previous edition for last biography

KNEIP, THEODORE JOSEPH, ANALYTICAL CHEMISTRY, ENVIRONMENTAL CHEMISTRY. *Current Pos:* RETIRED. *Personal Data:* b St Paul, Minn, Dec 20, 26; div; c 6. *Educ:* Univ Minn, BCh, 50; Univ Ill, MS, 52, PhD, 54. *Prof Exp:* Chemist, Mallinckrodt Chem Works, 54-58, head, Anal Res Lab, 59-61, asst mgr, Uranium Div, Anal Lab, 61-63, mgr, Lab Supply Res, 63-66; asst dir, Lab Environ Studies, NY Univ Med Ctr, 71-83, dir, 84-91. *Concurrent Pos:* Mem, Environ Health Subcomt, NY Acad Med, 84-; chmn & ed, CLSP Subcomt Biol Monitoring-Manual Method, Am Pub Health Asn, 86-88; consult, US NIH, US Environ Protection Agency, Off Tech Assessment-Cong, Nat Oceanic & Atmospheric Admin, State NY & NJ, NY City Dept Health & var industs; mem, Intersoc Comt Methods Air Sampling & Anal, 87- *Mem:* Fel NY Acad Sci; AAAS; Inst Stand Orgn (secy, 75-83); Am Chem Soc; Am Pub Health Asn; Am Indust Hyg Asn; Sigma Xi. *Res:* Analysis, wet and instrumental; sampling and evaluation of natural and polluted environmental systems, air, water, biota, hazardous wastes; toxicological studies in aquatic and mammalian species. *Mailing Add:* Rte 1 Box 1836 Manchester Center VT 05255

KNELLER, ROBERT WILLIAM, LAW BIOMEDICAL RESEARCH & TECHNOLOGY TRANSFER, JAPANESE BIOMEDICAL SCIENCE & SCIENCE POLICY. *Current Pos:* cancer epidemiologist, Nat Cancer Inst, 88-91, PROG OFFICER JAPAN, FOGARTY INT CTR, NIH, 92- *Personal Data:* b Chicago, Ill, Feb 7, 54; m 91, Sachiko Shudo. *Educ:* Swarthmore Col, BA, 75; Harvard Univ, JD, 80; Mayo Med Sch, MD, 84; Johns Hopkins Univ, MPH, 86. *Prof Exp:* Prev med resident, Johns Hopkins Univ, 91-92. *Concurrent Pos:* Pediat resident, Univ Hawaii, 84-85; physician & pub health teacher, China, 86-87; disaster relief Turkey & China, Red Cross, 91; med officer, WHO, 91-92; resident physician, Occup Safety & Health Admin, 92. *Res:* Epidemiology of stomach and other cancers; refugee health; protein engineering and environmental biotechnology in Japan. *Mailing Add:* 4709 Edgefield Rd Bethesda MD 20814. Fax: 301-480-3414; E-Mail: rwk@cu.nih.gov

KNELLER, WILLIAM ARTHUR, ORGANIC PETROLOGY, ECONOMIC GEOLOGY. *Current Pos:* prof geol & chmn dept, 61-85, dir Eitel Inst Silicate Res, 76-85, EMER PROF GEOL, UNIV TOLEDO, 89-, EMER DIR, EITEL INST SILICATE RES, 89- *Personal Data:* b Cleveland, Ohio, Apr 7, 29; m 51; c 2 Karinlee, Gregory, John, Ellen K, Kurt & Tihon. *Educ:* Miami Univ, AB, 51, MS, 55; Univ Mich, PhD(econ geol), 64. *Prof Exp:* Asst prof geol, Eastern Mich Univ, 56-59. *Concurrent Pos:* Adj prof civil eng, Univ Toledo, 92- *Mem:* Fel Geol Soc Am; Soc Mining Eng; NAm Soc Thermal Anal. *Res:* Coal characterization for industrial use, coal petrology and petrography; industrial mineralogy; economic geology of industrial rocks and minerals; characterization of waste materials for industrial use; geochemistry of chert; concrete petrology. *Mailing Add:* 7027 Hickory Ridge Rd Sylvania OH 43560-1108

KNEPPER, MARK A, ELECTROLYTE METABOLISM. *Current Pos:* CHIEF, RENAL MECH SECT, NAT HEART LUNG & BLOOD INST, NIH. *Personal Data:* b Ohio, Apr 23, 48. *Res:* Electrolyte metabolism. *Mailing Add:* Nat Heart Lung & Blood Inst Bldg 10 Rm 6N307 NIH Bethesda MD 20892-1598. Fax: 301-402-1443

KNEPPER, SHEILA M, PHARMACOLOGY. *Current Pos:* SR RES PHARMACOLOGIST, ABBOTT LABS, 88- *Personal Data:* b SDak, Feb 27, 53. *Educ:* Univ Nebr, BS, 75; Univ Kans, MS, 84, PhD(pharmacol), 85. *Prof Exp:* Sr res pharmacologist, Monsanto Labs, 85-88. *Mem:* Am Soc Cell Biol; Am Soc Pharmacol. *Res:* Pharmacology. *Mailing Add:* 573 Pine Grove St Gurnee IL 60031

KNERR, REINHARD H, MICROWAVES, LIGHTWAVE. *Current Pos:* Mem tech staff, 68-79, SUPVR, AT&T BELL LABS, 79- *Personal Data:* b Pirmasens, Ger, Feb 18, 39; m 68; c 4. *Educ:* Tech Univ Aachen, BS, 60; Enseeht, Toulouse France, dipl eng, 62; Lehigh Univ, MS, 64, PhD(elec eng), 68. *Concurrent Pos:* Mem tech staff microwave, 68-79, supvr fiber optic components, 79-81, supvr integrated optics, 81-84, supvr lightwave technol; mem admin comt, Inst Elec & Electronics Engrs-Microwave Theory & Tech Soc, 80-, pres, 86, lectr, 88- *Mem:* Fel Inst Elec & Electronics Engrs. *Res:* Fiber optics; lightwaves; microwave circulators; power amps; integrated optics; local area networks; data interfaces. *Mailing Add:* 1330 Wasba Dr Orefield PA 18069

KNESEL, JOHN ARTHUR, REPRODUCTIVE PHYSIOLOGY, CHELONIAN REPRODUCTION. *Current Pos:* asst prof, 85-90, ASSOC PROF BIOL, NE LA UNIV, 90- *Personal Data:* b Ferriday, La, Jan 20, 49; m 72, Patricia Louise Pope; c Martha K. *Educ:* NE La Univ, BS, 71, MS, 74; Purdue Univ, PhD(reproductive physiol), 83. *Prof Exp:* Grad student, Purdue Univ, 75-78, David Ross fel, 78-81, vis lectr biol, 81-84, asst prof, 84-85. *Mem:* Sigma Xi; Soc Study Reproduction; Soc Study Reptiles & Amphibians; Am Soc Animal Sci; Human Anat & Physiol Soc. *Res:* Reproductive physiology in macroclemys temmincki & other turtles; physiology of the oviduct and the effects of elevated temperature on reproduction in the female. *Mailing Add:* Dept Biol NE La Univ Monroe LA 71209. E-Mail: biknesel@alpha.nlu.edu

KNEVEL, ADELBERT MICHAEL, MEDICINAL CHEMISTRY. *Current Pos:* from instr to assoc prof med chem, 54-65, asst dean, Sch Pharm & Pharm Sci, 68-75, PROF MED CHEM, SCH PHARM & PHARM SCI, PURDUE UNIV, WEST LAFAYETTE, 65-, ASSOC DEAN, 75- *Personal Data:* b St Joseph, Minn, Oct 20, 22; m 50; c 5. *Educ:* NDak State Univ, BS, 52, MS, 53; Purdue Univ, PhD(med chem), 57. *Prof Exp:* Instr pharmaceut chem, NDak State Univ, 53-54. *Mem:* AAAS; Am Chem Soc; Am Asn Pharm Scientists; fel Am Asn Pharm Sci. *Res:* Methods development for drugs; drug metabolites in biological systems; studies of mechanism of drug action. *Mailing Add:* Sch Pharm Purdue Univ Lafayette IN 47907-9980

KNIAZUK, MICHAEL, ELECTRONICS. *Current Pos:* RETIRED. *Personal Data:* b Wilkes-Barre, Pa, June 12, 14; m 36. *Educ:* NY Univ, BEE, 41. *Prof Exp:* Lab asst, Res Labs, Merck Inst Therapeut Res, 32-33, technician, 33-37, res assoc, 37-43, asst dir, 46-60, mgr bioelectronics lab, 60-83. *Mem:* AAAS; Am Phys Soc; Inst Elec & Electronics Engrs. *Res:* Design and development of electronic instruments for biological research. *Mailing Add:* 1349 Birch Hill Rd Mountainside NJ 07098

KNIAZZEH, ALFREDO G(IOVANNI) F(RANCESCO), MECHANICAL ENGINEERING, PHYSICAL CHEMISTRY. *Current Pos:* from scientist to sr scientist, 70-78, asst lab mgr, 78-84, PROD DEVELOP MGR, POLAROID CORP, 84- *Personal Data:* b New York, NY, July 31, 38; m 68; c 2. *Educ:* Mass Inst Technol, BS, 59, MS, 61, PhD(mech eng), 66. *Prof Exp:* Physicist, Electronics Res Ctr, NASA, 66-70. *Mem:* Am Phys Soc; Am Vacuum Soc; Electrochem Soc; Mat Res Soc. *Res:* Thin films; physical electronics; mechanics of materials; photochemistry; chemical kinetics; thermodynamics; radiation transport; fluid mechanics; direct energy conversion; electrochemistry; optics; solid state physics; electronics engineering. *Mailing Add:* 1265 Main St W4 4H Waltham MA 02154

KNICKLE, HAROLD NORMAN, CHEMICAL ENGINEERING. *Current Pos:* ASSOC PROF CHEM ENG, UNIV RI, 69- *Personal Data:* b Boston, Mass, Jan 6, 36; m 63; c 2. *Educ:* Univ Mass, BSME, 62; Rensselaer Polytech Inst, MS, 65, PhD(nuclear eng), 69. *Prof Exp:* Engr nuclear eng, Knolls Atomic Power Lab, Gen Elec Co, 62-66. *Concurrent Pos:* Res prof, Pittsburgh Energy Technol Ctr, 77-80. *Mem:* Am Chem Soc; Am Inst Chem Engrs; Am Soc Eng Educ; Sigma Xi. *Res:* Mass transfer including azeotropic and extractive distillation, gas absorption, and leaching; heat transfer including single and two phase flow and insulation properties; design including mass transfer and heat transfer equipment; multiphase flow. *Mailing Add:* 99 Vaughn Ave Warwick RI 02886

KNIEBES, DUANE VAN, ANALYTICAL CHEMISTRY, RESEARCH ADMINISTRATION. *Current Pos:* CONSULT, 84- *Personal Data:* b Marquette, Mich, May 17, 26; m 50; c 3. *Educ:* Mich State Univ, BS, 48; Ill Inst Technol, MS, 54. *Honors & Awards:* Merit Award, Am Soc Testing & Mat; Gold Merit Award, Am Gas Asn. *Prof Exp:* Asst chemist, 49-51, supvr, Instrumental Anal Lab, Inst Gas Technol, 51-54, head Anal Div, 54-57, asst res dir, 57-62, assoc dir, 62-69, dir opers, 69-75, asst vpres educ serv, 75-84. *Mem:* Am Chem Soc; Am Soc Testing & Mat; Am Gas Asn. *Res:* Odorization of natural and liquid propane gases; analysis of gaseous fuels; management of research and research facilities; design and operation of engineering education and technician training programs in natural gas technology. *Mailing Add:* 4612 Hampshire St Boulder CO 80301-4211

KNIEF, RONALD ALLEN, REACTOR & FUEL FACILITY SAFETY, EDUCATION & TRAINING & RISK MANAGEMENT. *Current Pos:* PRIN CONSULT, OGDEN ENVIRON & ENERGY SERV CO, 90- *Personal Data:* b Hinsdale, Ill, Oct 8, 44; m 83, Pamela Hurd; c Kyle A. *Educ:* Albion Col, BA, 67; Univ Ill, PhD(nuclear eng), 72. *Honors & Awards:* Achievement Award, Am Nuclear Soc, Nuclear Criticality Safety Div, 83. *Prof Exp:* Sr physicist, Combustion Eng, Inc, 72-74; from asst to assoc prof nuclear eng, Univ NMex, 74-80; mgr plant training, Three Mile Island, GPU Nuclear Corp, 80-83, mgr educ develop, 83-85, co-chair, prog safety comn, 85-86, mgr corp training, 86-87, staff consult, 87-90. *Concurrent Pos:* Adj prof, Univ Hartford, 72-74; consult, Sandia Nat Lab, 74-81, Babcock & Wilcox Naval Nuclear Fuel Div & Westinghouse Goco Nuclear Safety Comt, 88-93; adj prof, Univ NMex & Pa State Univ, 80- & Pa State Univ, 80-93. *Mem:* Am Nuclear Soc; Sigma Xi; Inst Nuclear Mat Mgt; AAAS. *Res:* Nuclear reactor technology and safety; nuclear fuel facility safety and risk management; education and training development. *Mailing Add:* PO Box 90818 Albuquerque NM 87199-0818. Fax: 505-881-9357

KNIEVEL, DANIEL PAUL, CROP PHYSIOLOGY, STRESS PHYSIOLOGY. *Current Pos:* asst prof, 72-75, ASSOC PROF CROP PHYSIOL, PA STATE UNIV, UNIVERSITY PARK, 75- *Personal Data:* b West Point, Nebr, Jan 29, 43; m 65; c Jason & Ann. *Educ:* Univ Nebr,

Lincoln, BS, 65; Univ Wis-Madison, MS, 67, PhD(agron, biochem), 68. *Prof Exp:* Crop physiologist plant sci, Univ Wyo, 68-72. *Concurrent Pos:* NSF grant, 69-72; crop sci adv, Pa State Univ-USAID, Grad Sch Develop Proj Arg, 72-74, Postgrad Develop Proj Sri Lanka, 85; assoc ed, Agron J, 78-83; vis scientist, Sea Educ Admin, USDA, 80-81; bd dirs, Coun Agr Sci & Technol, 87-90; mem, Rev Panel, USDA-SBIR Grant Prog, 88, topic mgr, 89. *Mem:* Am Soc Agron; Crop Sci Soc Am; Am Soc Plant Physiol; Coun Agr Sci & Technol; Soil Sci Soc Am; Nat Asn Col Teachers Agr. *Res:* Physiology of assimilate transport in plants; physiology of crop response to environmental stress; computer simulation of crop growth and development; phloem unloading and sink metabolism. *Mailing Add:* Dept Agron 116ASI Bldg Pa State Univ University Park PA 16802-3504. Fax: 814-863-7043; E-Mail: dpk@psuvm.psu.edu

KNIFFEN, DONALD AVERY, ASTROPHYSICS, GAMMA-RAY ASTRONOMY. *Current Pos:* WILLIAM W ELLIOTT PROF & CHMN, DEPT PHYSICS & ASTRON, HAMPTON-SYDNEY COL, 92- *Personal Data:* b Kalamazoo, Mich, Apr 27, 33; m 52, Janis K Nesom; c Karyol (Poole), Donald Jr & Kimberley. *Educ:* La State Univ, BS, 59; Washington Univ, St Louis, MA, 60; Cath Univ Am, PhD, 67. *Concurrent Pos:* Astrophysicist & proj scientist, Compton Observ, Goddard Space Flight Ctr, NASA, 60-91, consult, 91- *Mem:* Royal Astron Soc; Am Astron Soc; Am Phys Soc; Am Asn Univ Profs; Sigma Xi; Int Astron Union. *Res:* Galactic and solar cosmic rays, including both charged particles and gamma rays; trapped radiation, pulsars; historic research includes pioneering work in the study of trapped radiation (Von Allen belts), galactic and solar cosmic rays and space instrumentation; gamma-ray astronomy. *Mailing Add:* Dept Physics & Astron Hampden Sydney Col PO Box 862 Hampden Sydney VA 23943-0862. Fax: 804-223-6374; E-Mail: donk@pulsar.hsc.edu

KNIGGE, KARL MAX, NEUROENDOCRINOLOGY. *Current Pos:* prof anat & chmn dept, Sch Med & Dent, 65-79, PROF & DIR, NEUROENDOCRINE UNIT, UNIV ROCHESTER, 80- *Personal Data:* b Brooklyn, NY, July 17, 26; m 48; c 3. *Educ:* Rutgers Univ, BS, 50; Univ Mich, PhD(anat), 53. *Prof Exp:* Instr anat, Univ Pittsburgh, 53-55; asst prof, Univ Calif, Los Angeles, 55-59; from assoc prof to prof, Univ Cincinnati, 59-65. *Mem:* Endocrine Soc; Am Physiol Soc; Am Asn Anatomists; Int Soc Neuroendocrinol; Soc Neurosci. *Res:* Neuroendocrinology. *Mailing Add:* 2561 Clover St Rochester NY 14618

KNIGHT, ALAN CAMPBELL, POLYMER SCIENCE. *Current Pos:* RETIRED. *Personal Data:* b Hartford, Conn, Nov 2, 22; m 48; c 2. *Educ:* Ore State Col, BS, 48; Univ Calif, Berkeley, PhD(chem), 50. *Prof Exp:* Chemist, E I du Pont de Nemours & Co, Inc, Wilmington, 50-55, asst tech supt mfg, 55-56, tech supt, 56-58, sr supvr res & develop, 58-67, res assoc, 67-73, res assoc, Polymer Prod Dept, Wash Lab, 73-86. *Mem:* Am Chem Soc. *Res:* Reaction kinetics and mechanisms; polymer synthesis; degradation mechanisms; stabilization; relation of structure to properties; manufacture of heavy organic chemicals; applied mathematics; computer applications; applied physical theory. *Mailing Add:* Rte 1 Box 231 Parkersburg WV 26101

KNIGHT, ALLEN WARNER, AQUATIC ECOLOGY, WATER POLLUTION. *Current Pos:* from asst prof to prof hydrobiol, 68-94, EMER PROF HYDROBIOL, UNIV CALIF, DAVIS, 94- *Personal Data:* b Grand Rapids, Mich, Feb 7, 32; m 55, Barbara A Clark; c Valerie L, Kimberly S, Pamala A & Richard A. *Educ:* Western Mich Univ, BS, 59; Mich State Univ, MS, 61; Univ Utah, PhD(zool), 65. *Prof Exp:* Asst prof entom & zool, Mich State Univ, 65-68. *Concurrent Pos:* Consult, EBASCO Environ, Inc. *Mem:* AAAS; Ecol Soc Am; Am Soc Limnol & Oceanog; Inst Soc Limnol; Entom Soc Am. *Res:* Pollution ecology; effect of environmental factors and pollutants on aquatic life; aquaculture, culture of freshwater organisms; growth metabolism studies of aquatic life; hydrobiology; trace element (Se) bioaccumulation and toxicity. *Mailing Add:* Dept Hydrol Univ Calif 113 Veihmeyer Hall Davis CA 95616

KNIGHT, ARTHUR ROBERT, PHOTOCHEMISTRY. *Current Pos:* from asst prof to assoc prof, Univ Sask, 64-76, head dept, 76-81, dean, Col Arts & Sci, 81-90, PROF CHEM, UNIV SASK, 76-, ACTG ASSOC VPRES ACAD, 90- *Personal Data:* b St John's, Nfld, Feb 24, 38; m 59, 86; c 8. *Educ:* Mem Univ Nfld, BSc, 58, MSc, 60; Univ Alta, PhD(chem), 62. *Prof Exp:* Fel chem, Univ Alta, 62-64. *Mem:* Fel Can Inst Chem. *Res:* Reactions of radicals produced in photolytic decompositions; primary process studies in photolyses; photochemistry and photophysics of sulfur containing compounds. *Mailing Add:* 354 Balfour St Saskatoon SK S7H 3Z5 Can

KNIGHT, BRUCE L, CHEMICAL & PETROLEUM ENGINEERING. *Current Pos:* Res engr, Denver Res Ctr, 69-75, sr petrol engr, 75-77, environ coordr, 77-81, SR RES ENGR, MARATHON OIL CO, 81- *Personal Data:* b Kansas City, Mo, Jan 4, 42; m 64; c 2. *Educ:* Univ Kans, BS, 64; Univ Colo, MS, 65, PhD(chem eng), 69. *Mem:* Am Inst Chem Engrs; Soc Petrol Engrs; Am Petrol Inst; Sigma Xi. *Res:* Cryogenic heat transfer through porous media; tertiary oil recovery processes; production logging. *Mailing Add:* Marathon Oil Co PO Box 269 Littleton CO 80160

KNIGHT, BRUCE WINTON, (JR), BIOPHYSICS, APPLIED MATHEMATICS. *Current Pos:* MEM FAC, ROCKFELLER UNIV, 61- *Personal Data:* b Milwaukee, Wis, Dec 4, 30; m 73, Catherine Mytilineou; c Bruce & Ian. *Educ:* Dartmouth Col, BS, 52. *Prof Exp:* Staff mem, Los Alamos Sci Lab, 55-61. *Res:* Neurophysiology of vision; applied theoretical physics. *Mailing Add:* Dept Biophys Rockefeller Univ 1230 York Ave New York NY 10021

KNIGHT, CHARLES ALFRED, CLOUD PHYSICS, ICE PHYSICS. *Current Pos:* prog scientist cloud physics, Lab Atmospheric Sci, 62-74, SR SCIENTIST, NAT CTR ATMOSPHERIC RES, 76- *Personal Data:* b Chicago, Ill, Mar 28, 36; m 62, Nancy Chase. *Educ:* Univ Chicago, MS, 57, PhD(geol), 59. *Honors & Awards:* Publications Prize, Nat Ctr Atmospheric Res, 70. *Prof Exp:* Res scientist arctic ice, Univ Wash, 59-61. *Concurrent Pos:* Mem fac, Univ Wyo, 77- & Univ Okla, 95- *Mem:* Am Meteorol Soc; Am Geophys Union; Am Asn Crystal Growth; Soc Cryobiology; Glaciol Soc. *Res:* Structure of hail; formation of rain; biological antifreezes; ice crystal nucleation and growth. *Mailing Add:* Nat Ctr Atmospheric Res Boulder CO 80307. Fax: 303-497-8171; E-Mail: knightc@ncar.ucar.edu

KNIGHT, CLIFFORD BURNHAM, INSECT ECOLOGY. *Current Pos:* Instr biol, East Carolina Univ, 56-57, from asst prof to assoc prof zool, 57-64, dir grad studies biol, PROF ZOOL, EAST CAROLINA UNIV, 64-, DIR UNDERGRAD STUDIES BIOL, 89- *Personal Data:* b Rockville, Conn, Jan 6, 26; m 56, 80; c 2. *Educ:* Univ Conn, BA, 50, MA, 52; Duke Univ, PhD(invert ecol), 57. *Mem:* Ecol Soc Am; Nat Audubon Soc; Am Inst Biol Sci; Nat Wildlife Fed; Am Entom Soc. *Res:* Ecology of Collembola in forest communities of North Carolina; benthic invertebrate estuarine ecology. *Mailing Add:* Dept Biol ECarolina Univ 1000 W Fifth St Greenville NC 27834-3006

KNIGHT, DAVID BATES, ORGANIC CHEMISTRY. *Current Pos:* from asst prof to assoc prof, 67-82, PROF CHEM, UNIV NC, GREENSBORO, 82- *Personal Data:* b Louisville, Ky, Sept 23, 39; m 65; c 2. *Educ:* Univ Louisville, BS, 61; Duke Univ, MA, 63, PhD(org chem), 66. *Prof Exp:* Vis res assoc chem, Ohio State Univ, 66-67 & 77-78. *Mem:* AAAS; Am Chem Soc. *Res:* Protium-deuterium exchange in hydrocarbons; chemistry of fulvenes. *Mailing Add:* 701 Sussex Ct Univ NC Greensboro NC 27410-5433

KNIGHT, DENNIS HAL, PLANT ECOLOGY. *Current Pos:* from asst prof to assoc prof, 66-79, PROF BOT, UNIV WYO, 79- *Personal Data:* b Clear Lake, SDak, Dec 24, 37; m 67; c 2. *Educ:* Augustana Col, SDak, BA, 59; Univ Wis-Madison, MS, 61, PhD(bot), 64. *Prof Exp:* Instr bot, with Peace Corps, Loja, Ecuador, 64-66. *Mem:* AAAS; Ecol Soc Am; Am Inst Biol Sci; Soc Range Mgt; Sigma Xi. *Res:* Ecology of Great Plains and Rocky Mountain vegetation; tropical plant ecology; impact of vegetation structure on ecosystem function. *Mailing Add:* Dept Bot Univ Wyo PO Box 3165 Laramie WY 82071-3165

KNIGHT, DOUGLAS MAITLAND, EDUCATIONAL ADMINISTRATION. *Current Pos:* PRES, QUESTAR CORP, 76- *Personal Data:* b Cambridge, Mass, June 8, 21; m 42, Grace Wallace Nichols; c Christopher, Douglas, Thomas & Stephen. *Educ:* Yale Univ, BA, 42, MA, 44, PhD(comp lit), 46. *Hon Degrees:* LLD, Ripon Col, Knox Col, Davidson Col, 63, Univ Col, 65, Emory Univ, 65, Ohio Wesleyan Univ, 70, Centre Col, 73; LHD, Lawrence Univ, 64. *Prof Exp:* Instr english, Yale Univ, 46-47, asst prof, 46-53; pres, Laurence Col, Appleton, Wis, 53-62 & Duke Univ, Durham, NC, 62-69; div vpres educ develop, RCA, New York, 69-73; pres soc, econ & educ develop, 73-76. *Concurrent Pos:* Morse res fel, 51-52; bd dirs, Woodrow Wilson Nat Fel Found, 59-, chmn, 82; US deleg, SEATO Conf Asian Univ, Pres, Pakistan, 61, Nat Comn Sci & Eng Manpower, 65 & Nat Comn, UNESCO, 65-67; mem, Corp Mass Inst Technol, 65-70; chmn, Nat Adv Comn Libr, 66-68; adv, Imp Orgn Social Serv Govt Iran, 70-77; chmn, Near East Found, 75-, Int Sch Serv, 75-81, Solebury Sch, 75-83, Nat Comn Higher Educ Issues, 81-; trustee, Questar Libr Sci & Art, 81- *Res:* Comparative literature; optical systems design; author and editor of seven books and over 100 articles; uses of unique microscope designs with emphasis on industrial and biomedical applications. *Mailing Add:* 68 Upper Creek Rd Stockton NJ 08559. Fax: 215-862-0512

KNIGHT, DOUGLAS WAYNE, COMPUTER SCIENCE, ASSEMBLER. *Current Pos:* dept chmn, 80-90, assoc prof, Comput Sci Technol Fac, 91-93, PROF, DEPT COMPUT ENG TECHNOL FAC, UNIV SOUTHERN COLO, 93- *Personal Data:* b Batavia, NY, Oct 7, 38; m 61; c 3. *Educ:* Ariz State Univ, BS, 61, MS, 69, PhD(elec eng), 75. *Prof Exp:* Geophysicist seismol, Shell Oil Co, 61-67; fac assoc prog, Ariz State Univ, 71-73; contractor, Govt Electronics Div, Motorola, 73-74; prog supvr, Trans Test Ctr, Dynalectron Corp, 74-79; prog mgr, Kentron Int, 79. *Concurrent Pos:* Referee, Fed Info Processing Stand, 73; owner, Computerland, Colorado Springs, 78-81. *Mem:* Data Processing Mgt Asn; Asn Comput Mach. *Res:* Microprocessing operating systems; real-time dynamic structures; role playing simulations; gaming strategies. *Mailing Add:* Dept Comput Sci 2200 N Bonforte Blvd Pueblo CO 81001. E-Mail: knight@meteor.uscolo.edu

KNIGHT, FRANK B, MATHEMATICS, MATHEMATICAL STATISTICS. *Current Pos:* from asst prof to assoc prof, 63-69, prof, 69-91, EMER PROF MATH & STATIST, UNIV ILL, URBANA, 91- *Personal Data:* b Chicago, Ill, Oct 11, 33; m 70, Ingeberg G Belz; c Marion A, Marc A & Ellen D. *Educ:* Cornell Univ, BA, 55; Princeton Univ, PhD(math), 59. *Prof Exp:* Res asst math, Univ Minn, 59-60, from instr to asst prof, 60-63. *Mem:* Am Math Soc; Inst Math Statist. *Res:* Probability theory; continuous time stochastic processes. *Mailing Add:* Dept Math Univ Ill Urbana IL 61801. E-Mail: f-knight@math.uiuc.edu

KNIGHT, FRED BARROWS, FOREST ENTOMOLOGY. *Current Pos:* dir, Sch Forest Resources, Univ Maine, Orono, 72-83, assoc dean, 83-86, prof, 72-90, dean, 86-90, EMER PROF & DEAN, FOREST RESOURCES, UNIV MAINE, ORONO, 91- *Personal Data:* b Waterville, Maine, Dec 12, 25; m 45; c 3. *Educ:* Univ Maine, BSF, 49; Duke Univ, MF, 50, DF(forest entom),

56. *Prof Exp:* Entomologist, Bur Entom & Plant Quarantine, NC, 50-51 & Colo, 51-54; entomologist, Forest Insect & Dis Lab, US Forest Serv, Colo, 54-60; from assoc prof to prof forestry, Univ Mich, 60-72, chmn dept, 66-70. *Concurrent Pos:* Vis prof, Sch Forestry, Univ Canterbury, 70; from vpres to pres, Forestry Res Orgn, Asn State Col & Univ, 76-80; assoc dir, Maine Agr Exp Sta, Univ Maine, Orono, 76-83 & 86-90. *Mem:* Fel AAAS; fel Soc Am Foresters; Entom Soc Am; Soil & Water Conserv Soc; Ecol Soc Am; Forestry Hist Soc. *Res:* Forest insect population, biological and silvicultural control; silviculture; forest ecology. *Mailing Add:* 395 Main St Orono ME 04473-1322

KNIGHT, FRED G, EARTH SCIENCES. *Current Pos:* geophysicist, 47-53, dist geologist, Gulf & West Coasts, 53-61, adv sr staff geologist, 61-65, div explor mgr, 65-67, coord mgr explor, US & Can, 67-72, ASSOC RES DIR EXPLOR, MARATHON OIL CO, 72- *Personal Data:* b Fargo, NDak, May 23, 20; div; c 2. *Educ:* Colo Sch Mines, Geol Engr, 42. *Prof Exp:* Computer-party chief, Seismograph Serv Corp, 42-46. *Mem:* Am Asn Petrol Geologists; Soc Explor Geophysicists; Sigma Xi. *Mailing Add:* 6624 S Prescott Way Littleton CO 80120

KNIGHT, GLENN B, MOLECULAR BIOLOGY. *Current Pos:* STAFF RESEARCHER, LAHEY CLIN MED CTR, 88- *Educ:* Univ Mass, Amherst, BS, 75; Ohio State Univ, MS, 77; Boston Univ, PhD(biochem), 85. *Prof Exp:* Post doctoral fel, Dana Farber Cancer Inst, Harvard Med Sch, 84-88. *Mem:* Am Soc Microbiol; Am Soc Biol & Molecular Biol. *Mailing Add:* Dept Immunol Res & Molecular Biol Lahey Clin Med Ctr 41 Mall Rd Burlington MA 01805-0001. *E-Mail:* glenn.knight@lahey.hitchcock.org

KNIGHT, HOMER TALCOTT, ANALYTICAL CHEMISTRY. *Current Pos:* asst prof, 69-74, ASSOC PROF ANALYTICAL CHEM, UNIV WIS-PARKSIDE, 74- *Personal Data:* b Rochelle, Ill, June 2, 23; m 48; c 2. *Educ:* Northern Ill State Teachers Col, BS, 47; Colo State Col, MA, 48; Univ Ill, MS, 50; Univ Wis, PhD(chem), 52. *Prof Exp:* Chemist, Fansteel Metall Corp, Ill, 52-57, asst dir res, 57-63, tech dir, 63-65; tech asst to gen mgr, Gen Instruments Corp, SC, 65; mgr, Newport Facil, Elpac, Inc, 65-68. *Mem:* Am Chem Soc; Soc Appl Spectros. *Mailing Add:* 6712 Third Ave Kenosha WI 53140-5114

KNIGHT, JAMES ALBERT, JR, RADIATION CHEMISTRY OF HYDROCARBONS, PYROLYSIS OF CELLULOSIC MATERIALS. *Current Pos:* RETIRED. *Personal Data:* b La Grange, Ga, Oct 16, 20; m 48; Marian Krape; c Marcia (Orr), James K & John C. *Educ:* Wofford Col, BS, 42; Ga Inst Technol, MS, 44; Pa State Univ, PhD(chem), 50. *Prof Exp:* From assoc prof to assoc prof chem, Ga Tech Res Inst, Ga Inst Technol, 50-58, from res assoc prof to res prof, 58-85. *Concurrent Pos:* Consult, Indust Firms, 70-90, Nat Bur Stand, 80-81 & UNFAD, 84-85. *Mem:* AAAS; Am Chem Soc. *Res:* Pyrolytic and carbon technologies utilizing agricultural and forestry materials; radiation chemistry of organic systems; synthetic organic chemistry; gas and liquid chromatography. *Mailing Add:* 2117 Kodiak Dr NE Altanta GA 30345-4149

KNIGHT, JAMES ALLEN, PSYCHIATRY. *Current Pos:* PROF PSYCHIAT & MED ETHICS, TEX A&M UNIV COL MED, COLLEGE STATION, 91- *Personal Data:* b St George, SC, Oct 20, 18; m 63, Sally Templeman; c Steven A. *Educ:* Wofford Col, AB, 41; Duke Univ, BD, 44; Vanderbilt Univ, MD, 52; Tulane Univ, MPH, 62. *Honors & Awards:* Annual Award, Soc Health & Human Values, 86; Michael J McCulloch Mem Award, Delta Soc, 87. *Prof Exp:* Intern, Grady Mem Hosp, Atlanta, Ga, 52-53; asst resident pediat & obstet, Duke Univ Hosp, 53-54; instr psychiat, Sch Med, Tulane Univ, 55-58; asst prof, Col Med, Baylor Univ, 58-61, asst dean, 60-61; assoc prof psychiat, Sch Med, Tulane Univ, 61-63, prof & assoc dean, 64-74; prof psychiat, Union Theol Sem, NY, 63-64; dean, Col Med, Tex A&M Univ, 74-77; prof psychiat & med ethics, La State Univ Sch Med, 78-91. *Concurrent Pos:* Resident, Tulane Serv, Charity Hosp, New Orleans, 55-58, chief resident, 57-58. *Mem:* Am Psychiat Asn; Acad Psychoanal; Group Advan Psychiat; Am Osler Soc; Soc Health & Human Values; Soc Sci Study Relig. *Res:* Interrelationships of religion and psychiatry; suicide; motivation; psychosomatic medicine; ethics and human values; medical student maturation. *Mailing Add:* Tex A&M Univ Col Med 113 Reynolds Med Bldg College Station TX 77843-1114. *Fax:* 409-845-6509

KNIGHT, JAMES MILTON, THEORETICAL PHYSICS. *Current Pos:* assoc prof physics, 65-77, PROF PHYSICS & ASTRON, UNIV SC, 77- *Personal Data:* b Jacksonville, Fla, Feb 20, 33; m 67; c 2. *Educ:* Spring Hill Col, BS, 54; Univ Md, PhD(physics), 60. *Prof Exp:* Res assoc & instr physics, Univ Md, 60-61; res assoc, Duke Univ, 63-65. *Mem:* Am Phys Soc. *Res:* Quantum optics; chaotic dynamics; symmetry properties; phase transitions. *Mailing Add:* Dept Physics Univ SC Columbia SC 29208

KNIGHT, JAMES WILLIAM, REPRODUCTIVE PHYSIOLOGY. *Current Pos:* PROF REPROD PHYSIOL, VA POLYTECH INST & STATE UNIV, 76- *Personal Data:* b Alexandria, La, Nov 27, 48. *Educ:* Univ Southwestern La, BS, 70; Univ Fla, MS, 72, PhD(reprod physiol), 75. *Prof Exp:* Fel reprod physiol, Univ Mo, 75-76. *Concurrent Pos:* Sabbatical, Fed Repub Ger, 88-89. *Mem:* Am Soc Animal Sci; Soc Study Reprod; AAAS. *Res:* Conceptus-maternal interrelationships; uterine protein secretions; placental function; endocrinology of gestation. *Mailing Add:* Dept Animal Sci Va Polytech Inst & State Univ 3160 Animal Sci Bldg Blacksburg VA 24061-0306

KNIGHT, JERE DONALD, PHYSICAL CHEMISTRY. *Current Pos:* CONSULT, 82- *Personal Data:* b Deer River, Minn, July 2, 16; m 81, Sylvia DeVilliers. *Educ:* St John's Univ, Minn, BS, 38; Univ Minn, PhD(phys chem), 48. *Honors & Awards:* Clark Medal, Am Chem Soc, 80. *Prof Exp:* Instr, St John's Prep Sch, Minn, 38-40; asst chem, Univ Minn, 41-42; asst, Nat Defense Res Comt Chicago, 42-43, jr chemist, Metall Lab, 43; assoc chemist, Clinton Labs, Tenn, 43-45; instr chem, Univ Ill, 48, res assoc physics, 48-49; mem staff, 49-80, fel, Los Alamos Nat Lab, 81-82. *Concurrent Pos:* Vis researcher, Brookhaven Nat Lab, 54-55. *Mem:* Am Chem Soc; fel Am Phys Soc. *Res:* Nuclear chemistry; nuclear structure and reactions; chemical and nuclear studies with mesons. *Mailing Add:* 6404 Merrill Rd Columbia SC 29209

KNIGHT, JOHN C (IAN), UNDERWATER ACOUSTICS, OPERATIONS RESEARCH. *Current Pos:* RETIRED. *Personal Data:* b Musselburgh, Scotland, June 16, 26; US citizen; m 63, Rita Hartlieb Latifullah; c Riaz Latifullah. *Educ:* Univ Edinburgh, BSc, 50, PhD(physics), 53. *Prof Exp:* Asst physics, Univ Edinburgh, 52-54; sr sci officer, Admiralty, Eng, 54-58, prin sci officer, Home Fleet, 58-59; mem staff opers res, Saclant Anti-Submarine Warfare Res Ctr, Italy, 59-63; prin sci officer, Ministry of Defence, Eng, 63-65; sr staff mem, Opers Res Inc, Md, 65-68; sr staff & dep dir, John D Kettelle Corp, Va, 68-70; head, Systs Anal Group, Acoust Div, Naval Res Lab, 70-80; prin scientist, EG & G Washington Anal Serv Ctr, 80; mem prin staff, Summit Res Corp, 80-88. *Concurrent Pos:* Sci asst to chief scientist, Royal Navy, 63-65; consult, Comt Undersea Warfare, Nat Acad Sci, 67-70; staff scientist, Comdr Oceanog Syst Atlantic, 74-77; tactical analyst, Staff Comdr ASW Forces, Sixth Fleet, Naples, Italy, 83-87; consult, Saclant ASW Res Ctr, La Spezia, Italy, 87; asst tech dir oper, Security Prog, Off Chief Naval Opers, 88-93. *Mem:* Acoust Soc Am; Opers Res Soc Am; Sigma Xi. *Res:* Beta and gamma ray spectroscopy; military operations research; analysis of naval system performance; naval tactics development and evaluation. *Mailing Add:* 3403 Fessenden St NW Washington DC 20008

KNIGHT, KATHERINE LATHROP, BIOCHEMISTRY, IMMUNOLOGY. *Current Pos:* Res assoc, 66-68, from asst prof to assoc prof, 68-75, PROF MICROBIOL, UNIV ILL MED CTR, CHICAGO, 75- *Personal Data:* b Jackson, Mich, May 13, 41. *Educ:* Elmira Col, BA, 62; Ind Univ, PhD(chem), 66. *Concurrent Pos:* NIH res career develop award, 70-75. *Mem:* AAAS; Am Chem Soc; Am Asn Immunologists. *Res:* Immunochemistry; immunogenetics; protein chemistry. *Mailing Add:* Dept Microbiol Loyola Univ Chicago Stritch Sch Med 2160 S First Ave Bldg 105-3846 Maywood IL 60153. *Fax:* 708-216-9574

KNIGHT, KATHY B, TEACHING UNDERGRADUATE & GRADUATE NUTRITION & FOODS COURSES, CALCIUM & HYPERTENSION. *Current Pos:* actg asst prof, 85-89, ASST PROF NUTRIT, UNIV MISS, 89- *Personal Data:* b Memphis, Tenn, June 20, 57; m 79, Scott S; c Bradley S & Anna B. *Educ:* Univ Miss, BA, 79; Miss State Univ, MS, 81; Auburn Univ, PhD(nutrit), 89. *Honors & Awards:* Miss Recognized Young Dietitian, Am Dietetic Asn, 90. *Prof Exp:* Nutrit educ specialist, Miss State Dept Health, 84-85. *Mem:* Am Dietetics Asn; Am Home Econ Asn. *Res:* Calcium and hypertension, eating behavior in children and feeding children in a day care setting. *Mailing Add:* Dept Home Econ Univ Miss Gen Delivery University MS 38677-9999

KNIGHT, LARRY V, PHYSICS. *Current Pos:* from asst prof to assoc prof, 69-80, PROF PHYSICS & ASTRON, BRIGHAM YOUNG UNIV, 80- *Personal Data:* b Pocatello, Idaho, Mar 13, 35; m 58, Jewel O; c 8. *Educ:* Brigham Young Univ, BS, 58, MS, 59; Stanford Univ, PhD(physics), 65. *Prof Exp:* Res assoc physics, Stanford Univ, 65-69. *Concurrent Pos:* Mem tech staff, Hewlett-Packard Co, 64-69; vpres, Holograf Corp, 70-72; consult, Lawrence Livermore Lab, 75-; pres, Moxtek Corp, 86-; ed, J X-ray Sci & Technol, 87- *Mem:* Am Phys Soc. *Res:* Low temperature physics; fundamental constants; magnetic resonance; electron spectroscopy; quantum electronics; holography; laser fusion; plasma and x-ray physics. *Mailing Add:* 1476 Oak Lane Provo UT 84604

KNIGHT, LEE H, JR, MECHANICAL ENGINEERING. *Current Pos:* CONSULT, 95- *Personal Data:* b Westville, Fla, July 8, 28; m 60; c 1. *Educ:* Univ SC, BS, 57; Ga Inst Technol, MS, 62. *Prof Exp:* Res asst, Ga Inst Technol, 57-69, asst res engr, 60-62; sr engr, Lockheed Ga Co, 62-64; br head mech eng, Ga Inst Technol, 64-67; asst dir serv, Skidaway Inst Oceanog, 67-95. *Mem:* Oceanog Soc. *Res:* Heat and mass transfer; underwater propulsion systems; electromechanical equipment for oceanographic research. *Mailing Add:* Skidaway Inst Oceanog 10 Ocean Science Circle Savannah GA 31411

KNIGHT, LON BISHOP, JR, PHYSICAL CHEMISTRY. *Current Pos:* asst prof, 71-75, ASSOC PROF CHEM, FURMAN UNIV, 75- *Personal Data:* b Milledgeville, Ga, Apr 24, 44; m 66; c 2. *Educ:* Mercer Univ, BS, 66; Univ Fla, PhD(chem), 70. *Prof Exp:* Res assoc phys chem, Univ Fla, 70-71. *Mem:* Am Chem Soc. *Res:* Study of reactions of metal atoms in the gas phase at low temperatures; metallic transport mechanisms; ESR matrix isolation of high temperature species. *Mailing Add:* Dept Chem Furman Univ 3300 Poinsett Hwy Greenville SC 29613-0420

KNIGHT, LYMAN COLEMAN, mathematics; deceased, see previous edition for last biography

KNIGHT, PATRICIA MARIE, MEDICAL DEVICE RESEARCH & DEVELOPMENT, BIOMATERIALS. *Current Pos:* dir mat res, 87-88, dir res, 88-91, VPRES RES & DEVELOP, ALLERGAN MED OPTICS, 91- *Personal Data:* b Schnectady, NY, Jan 25, 52. *Educ:* Ariz State Univ, BS, 74, MS, 76; Univ Utah, PhD(biomed eng), 83. *Prof Exp:* Teaching & res asst, Ariz State Univ, 74-76; proj engr, Am Med Optics, 76-77; res asst & PhD cand, Univ Utah, 79-83; mgr mat res, Am Med Optics, 83-87. *Mem:* Soc Biomat; Asn Res in Vision & Ophthal; Am Chem Soc; Biomed Eng Soc; Soc Women Engrs. *Res:* Develop products for ophthalmic surgery; polymer research; optical and mechanical engineering; biological science. *Mailing Add:* Allergan Inc 2525 Dupont Dr PO Box 19534 Irvine CA 92623-9534. *Fax:* 714-246-2230

KNIGHT, PAUL R, ANESTHESIOLOGY. *Current Pos:* HEAD, DEPT ANESTHESIA, STATE UNIV NY MED SCH, 92- *Personal Data:* b Mechanicsburg, Pa, June 27, 47; m; c 2. *Educ:* Pa State Univ, MD & PhD(med microbiol), 73. *Prof Exp:* Assoc prof anesthesia, Univ Mich Hosps, 82-86, prof, 86-92. *Mem:* Am Soc Microbiol; Asn Univ Anesthesiologists; Am Soc Anesthesiol. *Res:* Anesthetic action and its effects and on cellular function and viral replication. *Mailing Add:* State Univ NY Anesthesiol Buffalo Gen Hosp Hamlin House 100 High St Buffalo NY 14203. *Fax:* 716-859-4529

KNIGHT, STEPHEN, EXPERIMENTAL PHYSICS. *Current Pos:* Mem tech staff, Bell Tel Labs, 64-68, supvr explor device tech group, 68-71, supvr optical mat properties group, 71-72, supvr displays group, 72-73, supvr opto-isolators group, 73-78, supvr govt systs support, 78-80, supvr technol options, 80-81, head electronics technol planning, 81-84, div mgr, AT&T Corp Hq, 83-86, dir, AT&T Bell Labs, Kelly Educ & Training Ctr, 86-90, DIR, SEMATECH TECHNOL TRANSFER, AT&T BELL LABS, 90- *Personal Data:* b San Mateo, Calif, Feb 24, 38; m 59; c 3. *Educ:* Beloit Col, BS, 59; Yale Univ, MS, 60, PhD(physics), 64. *Concurrent Pos:* Assoc ed, Inst Elec & Electronics Engrs Trans Electron Devices, 68-79, ed, 79-83, pub chmn, 83-86. *Mem:* Am Phys Soc; sr mem Inst Elec & Electronics Engrs; Electron Devices Soc. *Res:* Low temperature physics, turbulent superfluid helium; semiconductor physics, bulk negative resistance; light emitting diodes; magnetic bubble materials; integrated circuit planning; high performance technology evaluation. *Mailing Add:* 117 Treehaven St Gaithersburg MD 20878

KNIGHT, VERNON, MEDICINE. *Current Pos:* dir, Ctr Biotechnol & prof biotechnol, med, microbiol & immunol, 66-95, PROF MED & CHMN, DEPT MICROBIOL & IMMUNOL, BAYLOR COL MED, 66-, ACTG CHMN, DEPT MOLECULAR PHYSIOL & BIOPHYS, 95- *Personal Data:* b Osceola, Mo, Sept 6, 17; m 46; c 4. *Educ:* William Jewell Col, AB, 39; Harvard Univ, MD, 43; Am Bd Internal Med, dipl. *Hon Degrees:* ScD, William Jewell Col. *Prof Exp:* Asst prof med, Med Col, Cornell Univ, 53-54; assoc prof, Sch Med, Vanderbilt Univ, 54-59; clin dir, Nat Inst Allergy & Infectious Dis, Md, 59-66. *Mem:* Soc Exp Biol & Med; Am Soc Clin Invest; Am Clin & Climat Asn; Am Col Physicians. *Res:* Infectious disease and allergy. *Mailing Add:* Dept Physiol Baylor Col Med 1 Baylor Plaza Houston TX 77030

KNIGHT, WALTER DAVID, SOLID STATE PHYSICS, ATOMIC & MOLECULAR & CLUSTER PHYSICS. *Current Pos:* from asst prof to assoc prof, Univ Calif, Berkeley, 50-61, asst dean col lett & sci, 59-61, assoc dean, 61-63, dean, 67-72, PROF PHYSICS, 61-90, EMER PROF, UNIV CALIF, BERKELEY, 90- *Personal Data:* b New York, NY, Oct 14, 19; m 72, Sara Pattershall; c Margaret, Jonathan & Nathaniel. *Educ:* Middlebury Col, AB, 41; Duke Univ, MA, 43, PhD(physics), 50. *Hon Degrees:* DSc, Middlebury Col, 76, Fed Polytech Sch, Lausanne, Switz, 83. *Honors & Awards:* Sackler Distinguished Lectr Chem, Univ Tel Aviv, 89. *Prof Exp:* Instr physics, Duke Univ, 43-44; instr, Trinity Col, 46-50. *Concurrent Pos:* Alfred P Sloan fel, 56-59; Guggenheim fel, 61; Miller fel, 79; vis res fel, Clarendon Lab, Oxford, UK, 83-84; Christensen fel, St Catherine's Col, Oxford, 83; vis distinguished prof, Niels Bohr Inst, 88; vis prof, Fed Polytech Sch, Lausanne, Switz, 80. *Mem:* Nat Acad Sci; fel AAAS; fel Am Phys Soc; fel Am Acad Arts & Sci; Sigma Xi. *Res:* Study of metal microclusters by molecular beam methods; nuclear magnetic resonance shift in metals; relative abundance, stability, and photo-absorption crossection of free metal clusters in molecular beam. *Mailing Add:* Dept Physics Univ Calif Berkeley CA 94720

KNIGHT, WALTER REA, PSYCHOBIOLOGY. *Current Pos:* Instr psychol, Hiram Col, 56-57, asst prof, 57-58, 60-65, assoc prof, 65-68, PROF PSYCHOL & BIOL, HIRAM COL, 68- *Personal Data:* b Cortland, Ohio, Apr 25, 32; m 54; c 3. *Educ:* Baldwin-Wallace Col, AB, 54; Pa State Univ, MS, 56, PhD(psychol), 61. *Concurrent Pos:* NIMH spec res training fel, Univ Fla, 64-66. *Mem:* AAAS; Animal Behav Soc; Psychonomic Soc; Sigma Xi. *Res:* Neural, hormonal and early experience factors in animal social behavior and social stress. *Mailing Add:* Hiram Col Box 165 Hiram OH 44234-0165

KNIGHT, WILBUR HALL, OIL & GAS EXPLORATION & DEVELOPMENT. *Current Pos:* CONSULT GEOLOGIST, 59- *Personal Data:* b Denver, Colo, May 8, 21; m 41; c 1. *Educ:* Univ Wyo, BA, 40, MA, 41. *Prof Exp:* Geologist oil & gas, Union Prod Co, 41-48, dist geologist, 41-55; chief geologist oil & gas, Larco Drilling Co, 55-59. *Concurrent Pos:* Mem, div prof affairs cert bd, Am Assoc Petrol Geol, 75-; instr, Millsaps Col, 79-81. *Mem:* Fel Geol Soc Am; Am Asn Petrol Geologists; Soc Petrol Engr; Soc Independent Prof Earth Scientists; Am Inst Prof Geologists; Soc Explor Geophysicists. *Res:* Oil and gas exploration and development. *Mailing Add:* 2030 Southwood Rd Jackson MS 39211

KNIGHT, WILLIAM ALLEN, JR, GASTROENTEROLOGY. *Current Pos:* Asst int med, St Louis Univ, 47-48, instr, 48-49, sr instr, 49-51, asst prof med, 51-55, dir int med, Housestaff & Residency Training Prog, 50-59, DIR, DIV GASTROENTEROL, SCH MED, ST LOUIS UNIV, 54-, ASSOC PROF MED, 55- *Personal Data:* b St Louis, Mo, Oct 5, 14; m 41; c 3. *Educ:* Drury Col, AB, 36; St Louis Univ, MD, 40; Am Bd Int Med cert, 51. *Concurrent Pos:* Area consult int med, US Vet Admin, 56-60; dir int med, St Louis City Hosp, St Louis Univ Med Serv, 48-55 & Firmin Desloge Hosp, 55-58; dir, Dept Internal Med, St Mary's Health Ctr, 65-80, emer dir, Cancer Res & Treatment Ctr, 81- *Mem:* Am Col Gastroenterol; Am Soc Gastrointestinal Endoscopy; Am Gastroenterol Asn; Am Asn Study Liver Dis; fel Am Col Phys; Sigma Xi. *Res:* Qualitative and quantitative analysis of pancreatic secretions, proteins and electrolytes in the normal and diseased pancreas to aid in the diagnosis of pancreatic disease. *Mailing Add:* Knight Int Inc 1035 Bellevue Suite 503 St Louis MO 63117-1854

KNIGHT, WILLIAM GLENN, BIOGEOCHEMISTRY, RHIZOSPHERE CHEMISTRY-MYCORRHIZAE. *Current Pos:* SCI CHAIR & ASSOC PROF CHEM, FRONT RANGE COMMUNITY COL, 92- *Personal Data:* b Greenville, SC, July 4, 52; m 85, Lorie Federman; c Elijah & Maya. *Educ:* Utah State Univ, BS, 74, MS, 78, PhD(soil chem), 87. *Prof Exp:* Sr soil scientist, Nerco, Inc, 78-82; environ scientist, T W Mann & Co, 82-84; res & teaching asst soil chem, Utah State Univ, 84-87; res assoc soil biochem, USDA-Agr Res Serv, 87-89. *Concurrent Pos:* Dir & environ geochemist, Earth Sci Group, 89-; consult, Belize Citrus Growers Asn, 90-; co-dir, Ecol Sta, DESSED-Belize, 91-; co-prin investr, USDA-Coop State Res Serv, 92- *Res:* Investigations of rhizosphere biochemistry of desert and rangeland plants including influence of mycorrhizae, exudates (oxalic acid and carbon dioxide) on mineral stability in soils; effects of elevated atmospheric carbon dioxide on biogeochemistry of soils. *Mailing Add:* Sci Chair Front Range Community Col PO Box 270490 Ft Collins CO 80527-0490

KNIGHT, WILSON BLAINE, PROTEIN CHEMISTRY, ENZYMOLOGY. *Current Pos:* sr biochemist, 87-89, RES FEL, MERCK, SHARPE & DOHME RES LAB, 89- *Personal Data:* b Aug 20, 55. *Educ:* Univ Va, BA; Univ Md, College Park, PhD(biochem), 83. *Prof Exp:* Res assoc, Univ Wis, 83-87. *Mem:* AAAS; NY Acad Sci; Sigma Xi. *Res:* Enzyme mechanisms; mechanism of inhibition of elastoses; mechanism of signal peptidase; enzyme inhibitors. *Mailing Add:* Biochem Dept Res Lab Bldg V248 Glaxo Wellcome Inc 5 Moore Dr Research Triangle Park NC 27709. *Fax:* 919-483-4320

KNIGHTEN, JAMES LEO, ELECTROMAGNETICS, ELECTROMAGNETIC PULSE ENGINEERING. *Current Pos:* VPRES & MGR, DEFENSE ELECTRONICS, MAXWELL LABS, 89- *Personal Data:* b Lafayette, La, Apr 1, 43; m 70; c 2. *Educ:* La State Univ, BS, 65, MS, 68; Iowa State Univ, PhD(elec eng), 76. *Prof Exp:* Asst prof electromagnetics, Iowa State Univ, Ames, 76-77; staff engr, IRT Corp, 77-80, mgr electromagnetics, 80-89. *Mem:* Inst Elec & Electronics Engrs. *Res:* Nuclear electromagnetic pulse effects on systems; numerical methods; nuclear electromagnetic pulse hardening of ground launched Cruise missile; assessment of electromagnetic pulse coupling to ground based command, control and communications facilities, tactical systems, aircraft and missiles. *Mailing Add:* 13248 Poway Hills Dr Poway CA 92064

KNIGHTS, JOHN CHRISTOPHER, physics, for more information see previous edition

KNIKER, WILLIAM THEODORE, ALLERGY, IMMUNOLOGY. *Current Pos:* from assoc prof to prof pediat & microbiol, 69-88, PROF PEDIAT, MICROBIOL & INTERNAL MED, UNIV TEX MED SCH, SAN ANTONIO, 88- *Personal Data:* b Seguin, Tex, Aug 30, 29; div; c 4. *Educ:* Univ Tex, BA, 50, MD, 53; Am Bd Pediat, dipl, 59; Conjoint Bd Allergy & Immunol, dipl, 74. *Honors & Awards:* Stanley Jaros Lectr, Am Asn Clin Immunol & Allergy, 77; Bela Schick Award & Lectr, Am Col Allergy & Immunol, 84. *Prof Exp:* Intern, Henry Ford Hosp, Detroit, 53-54; resident pediat, Univ Tex Med Br, 56-58; chief resident, Med Ctr, Univ Ark, 58-59, from instr to asst prof pediat, 59-62, from asst prof to assoc prof pediat & path, 65-69. *Concurrent Pos:* Res fel infectious dis, Am Thoracic Soc, 59-62; res fel, Div Exp Path, Scripps Clin & Res Found, Calif, 62-65; asst dir clin res unit, Univ Ark Med Ctr, 65-69; dir sect immunol-allergy, 69-; NIH res career develop award, 68-69; mem bd regents, Am Col Allergy & Immunol, 81-84. *Mem:* Am Asn Path; Am Asn Immunologists; Am Col Allergy & Immunol; Am In Vitro Allergy & Immunol Soc (vpres); Am Acad Allergy & Immunol. *Res:* Immunopathology, mechanisms of hypersensitivity and immunological diseases; immunochemistry of mycobacterial antigens; primate immunology; pediatrics. *Mailing Add:* Dept Pediat Univ Tex Health Sci Ctr 7703 Floyd Curl Dr San Antonio TX 78284-6200

KNILL, RONALD JOHN, GEOMETRIC TOPOLOGY. *Current Pos:* from asst prof to prof, 63-96, EMER PROF MATH, TULANE UNIV, 96- *Personal Data:* b Chicago, Ill, Feb 20, 35; m 58, Barbara Bauman; c Joseph, David & Mary. *Educ:* Marquette Univ, BS, 56; Univ Notre Dame, MS, 60, PhD(math), 62. *Prof Exp:* NSF fel, Univ Calif, Berkeley, 62-63. *Concurrent Pos:* Res assoc, Col France, 69-70; vis fel, Univ Warwick, 78; vis scholar, Specola Vaticana, 84; Univ Md, Col Park; vis prof, Col Holy Cross, 85-86. *Mem:* Am Math Soc; Math Asn Am; Math Soc France; Sigma Xi. *Res:* Low dimensional topology; knot theory and applications; fixed point theory. *Mailing Add:* Dept Math Tulane Univ New Orleans LA 70118. *Fax:* 504-891-9273; *E-Mail:* rjk@math.tulane.edu

KNIPE, DAVID MAHAN, VIROLOGY, CELL BIOLOGY. *Current Pos:* Fel, 76-79, from asst prof to assoc prof, 79-89, PROF VIROL, DEPT MICROBIOL & MOLECULAR GENETICS, HARVARD MED SCH, 89- *Personal Data:* b Lancaster, Ohio, Aug 6, 50; m 73, Suzanne Maloof; c Rachel & Jennifer. *Educ:* Case Western Res Univ, BA, 72; Mass Inst Technol, PhD(cell biol), 76. *Concurrent Pos:* Fac res award, Am Cancer Soc, 84-; mem, Clin Sci Study Sect, NIH, 85-89 & Virol Study Sect, 90- *Mem:* Am Soc Microbiol; Am Soc Virol; AAAS. *Res:* How herpes simplex virus replicates in and interacts with its host cell; molecular biological and genetic approaches to study how viral and cellular proteins function within the cell nucleus; regulation of herpes simplex virus gene expression; mechanism of infection of the nervous system; host immune response, vaccines and vaccine vectors. *Mailing Add:* 58 Auburn St Auburndale MA 02166. *Fax:* 617-432-0223; *E-Mail:* dknipe@warren.med.harvard.edu

KNIPE, RICHARD HUBERT, CHEMICAL PHYSICS. *Current Pos:* RETIRED. *Personal Data:* b Salmon, Idaho, Sept 12, 27; m 57, Teresa Herrera; c Krina, Kevin & Kurt. *Educ:* Calif Inst Technol, BS, 50; Duke Univ, PhD(physics), 54. *Prof Exp:* Physicist, Naval Weapons Ctr, 54-57, aeronaut power plant res engr, 57-62, phys chemist, 62, res physicist, 62-89. *Mem:* Am Phys Soc; Am Chem Soc. *Res:* Quantum theory of molecules; gas phase chemical kinetics and mechanism; performance analysis of flash lamps pumped dye lasers. *Mailing Add:* 1121 Lucille Ct Ridgecrest CA 93555-5901

KNIPFEL, JERRY EARL, NUTRITION & BIOCHEMISTRY, RESEARCH ADMINISTRATION. *Current Pos:* prog specialist, Forage Prod & Utilization Sect, 84-87, prog dir Prarie Region Res Br, 84-87, RES SCIENTIST, FORAGE PROD & UTILIZATION SECT, RES STA, AGR CAN, 73-84, 87-, SECT HEAD, 89- *Personal Data:* b Calgary, Alta, June 30, 41; m 66; c 2. *Educ:* Univ Sask, BSA, 65, MSc, 67; McGill Univ, PhD(nutrit), 73. *Prof Exp:* Chemist, Health Protection Br, Nutrit Res Div, Health & Welfare Can, 67-69, res scientist, 69-73. *Concurrent Pos:* Asst ed, Can J Animal Sci, 77-80, assoc ed, 80-83; lectr, Dept Biol, Univ Regina, 78; consult, Topline Feeds, Inc, Swift Current, 74; mem, Exp Comt Animal Nutrit, 81-91, Exp Comt Forage Crops, 79-82, prog rev comt, Agr Can Western Region, 80; sci authority, Res Br, Agr Can, Contract Res Progs, 79-; asst prof biol, Univ Regina, 81 & 90, lectr & dept chmn, 91; adj prof, Univ Sask, 87-92; dir & rep, Can Feed Info Ctr, 86-, chmn exec comt, Int Network Feed Info Ctrs, 88-; mgr, Res Br Prarie Region Contract Res & ERDA progs, 85-90; coordr, Forage Commodity Coord Directorate Agr Can, 86; mem Nat Res Coun task force on feed composition, 89- *Mem:* Can Soc Animal Sci; Nutrit Soc Can; Can Asn Lab Animal Sci; Am Chem Soc; Inst Food Technologists; NY Acad Sci. *Res:* Nutrition in relation to fetal development and post partum performance; nitrogen metabolism in ruminants; evaluation of nutritional quality and nutrient availability; improvement in nutritional value of roughage. *Mailing Add:* Forage Prod & Utilization Sect Res Sta Agr Can Swift Current SK S9H 3X2 Can

KNIPLING, EDWARD FRED, ENTOMOLOGY. *Current Pos:* COLLABR, USDA, 73- *Personal Data:* b Port Lavaca, Tex, Mar 20, 09; m 34; c 5. *Educ:* Tex A&M Univ, BS, 30; Iowa State Univ, MS, 32, PhD(entom), 47. *Hon Degrees:* DSc, Catawba Col, 62, NDak State Univ, 70, Clemson Univ, 70 & Fla State Univ, 75. *Honors & Awards:* Medal, Typhus Comn; Hoblitzelle Nat Award, 60; Nat Medal Sci, 66; Agr Res Serv, Scientist Hall of Fame, 85. *Prof Exp:* Field asst, Bur Entom & Plant Quarantine, USDA, 30, from jr entomologist to assoc entomologist, 31-42, sr entomologist, Off Sci Res & Develop Contract, 42-46, prin entomologist, 46-53, dir, Entom Res Div, Agr Res Serv, 53-71, sci adv, 71-73. *Mem:* Nat Acad Sci; Entom Soc Am. *Res:* Biology, ecology, population dynamics and control of insects. *Mailing Add:* 2623 N Military Rd Arlington VA 22207

KNIPMEYER, HUBERT ELMER, ORGANIC CHEMISTRY, RESEARCH ADMINISTRATION. *Current Pos:* RETIRED. *Personal Data:* b Sharon, Conn, Nov 7, 29; m 52; c 4. *Educ:* Mass Inst Technol, SB, 51; Univ Ill, PhD(chem), 57. *Prof Exp:* Res chemist, Cent Res Dept, E I Du Pont de Nemours & Co, Inc, 56-60, tech investr, Film Dept, 60-61, res chemist, 61-62, staff scientist, 62-63, tech rep, 64-65, group mgr, 65-69, res mgr, Ohio, 69-71, prod mgr, 71-74, tech mgr, Film Dept, 74-75, mgr mkt develop & customer serv, 76, lab supt, 77, res mgr, Plastic Prod & Resins Dept & mgr corp automotive develop, Corp Plans Dept, 78-82, mgr membranes, 83-84, tech mgr, Polymers Prod Dept, 85-92. *Mem:* Am Chem Soc; NAm Membrane Soc. *Res:* Physical organic chemistry; organic synthesis; heterocyclic organic chemistry; polyimide, polyester and polyolefin chemistry; membranes. *Mailing Add:* 1017 Weldin Circle Wilmington DE 19803

KNIPP, ERNEST A, (JR), COMPUTER SCIENCES, GENERAL. *Current Pos:* CONSULT, 71- *Personal Data:* b Houston, Tex, Oct 10, 29; m 79. *Educ:* Rice Univ, BS, 50, MS, 52; Yale Univ, PhD(chem eng), 58. *Prof Exp:* Fel chem, Univ NC, 57-59, Rice Univ, 60; asst prof chem eng, Mich Col Mining & Technol, 59; res chem engr, Humble Oil & Ref Co, 61-63; sr res chem engr, Esso Res & Eng Co, 63-65, res specialist, 68-71. *Mem:* Am Chem Soc; Am Inst Chem Engrs; Asn Comput Mach; Royal Soc Chem. *Res:* Computer applications. *Mailing Add:* PO Box 3041 Houston TX 77001

KNIPPING, HANS D, PETROLEUM ENGINEERING. *Honors & Awards:* Michel T Halbouty Human Needs Award, Am Asn Petrol Geologists, 90. *Mailing Add:* 40 Lafferty St Etobicoke ON M9C 5B6 Can

KNIPPLE, DOUGLAS CHARLES, MOLECULAR BIOLOGY OF INSECTICIDE TARGET SITES, MOLECULAR BIOLOGY OF PHEROMONE BIOSYNTHESIS. *Current Pos:* ASSOC PROF, CORNELL UNIV, 85- *Personal Data:* b Johnstown, Pa, Mar 17, 53. *Educ:* Hobart Col, BS, 76; Cornell Univ, PhD(genetics), 83. *Prof Exp:* Europ Molecular Biol Orgn fel, Max-Planck Inst Evolutionary Biol, Tubingen, Ger, 83-84, NATO/ NSF fel, 84-85. *Mem:* AAAS; Am Chem Soc; Genetics Soc Am; Entom Soc Am. *Res:* Investigations of structure and function of key molecules mediating excitatory and inhibitory neurotransmission and sex pheromone biosynthesis of insects, which are current or potential targets for disruption in insect control strategies. *Mailing Add:* 109 Maxwell Ave Geneva NY 14456. *Fax:* 315-787-2326; *E-Mail:* doug_knipple@cornell.edu

KNIPPLE, WARREN RUSSELL, INDUSTRIAL & PETROLEUM CHEMISTRY, REFRACTORY METALS. *Current Pos:* REGIONAL SALES MGR, CLIMAX SPECIALTY METALS, 86- *Personal Data:* b Johnstown, Pa, May 28, 34; m 59; c 2. *Educ:* Univ Pittsburgh, BS, 59; Case Western Reserve Univ, MS, 61, PhD(chem), 68. *Prof Exp:* Sr chemist, Res Dept, Standard Oil Co (Ohio), 59-68; sr res chemist, Chase Brass & Copper Co, Inc, 68-69, prod mgr chem, 69-70, chem opers mgr, 70-72, gen mgr, Cleveland Refractory Metals Div, 72-85. *Mem:* Am Chem Soc; AAAS; Am Mgt Asn. *Res:* Organic synthesis; organometallic research; heterogeneous catalysis; peroxide chemistry; aromatic substitution; rhenium chemistry; ion exchange and solvent extraction technology; molybdenum; tungsten chemistry. *Mailing Add:* 872 Wellmon St Bedford OH 44146-3877

KNISELY, WILLIAM HAGERMAN, ANATOMY. *Current Pos:* vpres acad affairs, 75, PRES, MED UNIV SC, 75-, PROF ANAT, 75- *Personal Data:* b Houghton, Mich, Feb 3, 22; m 47; c 5. *Educ:* Univ Chicago, PhB, 47, BS, 50; Med Col SC, MS, 52, PhD, 54. *Prof Exp:* Asst anat, Med Col SC, 49-50 & 51-54; from instr to asst prof med & from instr to assoc prof anat, Duke Univ, 54-59; prof anat & chmn dept, Univ Ky, 59-63; dir, Inst Biol & Med, Mich State Univ, 63-70; vchancellor health affairs, Univ Tex Syst, 70-73, prof anat & cell biol, 70-75, asst to chancellor health affairs, 73-75. *Concurrent Pos:* Univ res fel med, Duke Univ, 54-57, Am Heart Asn fel, 55-57, USPHS sr res fel, 57-59; mem, Nat Adv Coun Educ for Health Prof, 68-71, chmn policy plan comn, 69-71, vchmn, Study Comn on Dietetics, 69-71; comnr, Navajo Health Authority, 72-76; mem adv comt, Regional Health Serv Res Inst, Univ Tex Health Sci Ctr San Antonio, 73-75 & Univ Tex Austin Ctr Social Work, 74-75; mem bd dirs, Holy Cross Hosp, 73-75; consult, Regions IX & X, Dept HEW, 73-79 & Dept Med & Surg, Vet Admin, 74-; assoc mem, Inst Soc, Ethics & Life Sci, 74-75; gen adj prof, Union Grad Sch, Yellow Springs, Ohio, 74- *Mem:* AAAS; Geront Soc; Am Heart Asn; Am Asn Anatomists; Microcirc Soc. *Res:* Anatomy, physiology, pharmacology and pathology of small blood vessels, especially the lung. *Mailing Add:* Health Sci Ctr BMSB Univ Okla PO Box 26901 Oklahoma City OK 73190

KNISKERN, VERNE BURTON, PARASITOLOGY. *Current Pos:* RETIRED. *Personal Data:* b Negaunee, Mich, Oct 16, 21; m 42; c 3. *Educ:* Univ Mich, BS, 47, MS, 48, PhD(zool), 50. *Prof Exp:* From assoc prof to prof, Eastern Ill Univ, 50-86. *Mem:* Am Micros Soc; Am Soc Parasitol; Wildlife Dis Asn. *Res:* Parasitology; protozoology; genetics; histology; malacology; medical biology. *Mailing Add:* 1531 Division St Charleston IL 61920

KNISLEY, STEPHEN, electrophysiology, biomedical engineering, for more information see previous edition

KNITTEL, MARTIN DEAN, MICROBIOLOGY. *Current Pos:* RETIRED. *Personal Data:* b Torrington, Wyo, Dec 19, 32; m 56; c 3. *Educ:* Willamette Univ, BS, 55; Ore State Univ, MS, 62, PhD(microbiol), 65. *Honors & Awards:* Gold Medal For Res, Environ Protection Agency, 78. *Prof Exp:* Bacteriologist, Ore Agr Div, 55-56; med technologist, Doctors' Clin, 58-59; aquatic biologist, Ore Fish Comn, 62-63; sr res microbiologist, Norwich Pharmacal Co, 65-66; microbiologist, Pac Northwest Water Lab, Fed Water Pollution Control Admin, 66-69; sr engr, Jet Propulsion Lab, 69-71; res microbiologist, Pac Northwest Water Lab, Environ Protection Agency, 71-74, Western Fish Toxicol Sta, 74-88. *Mem:* AAAS; Am Soc Microbiol. *Res:* Physiology of the bacterium Sphaerotilus natans as is related to its growth in polluted streams; microbiology of waste treatment; detection of pathogenic organisms in waste water; biochemistry of waste water treatment; effect of stress on disease in fish. *Mailing Add:* 2244 Kiger Island Dr Corvallis OR 97333

KNIZE, RANDALL JAMES, LASER COOLING, OPTICAL COMPUTING. *Current Pos:* ASST PROF, UNIV SOUTHERN CALIF, 88- *Personal Data:* b Tacoma, Wash, Feb 4, 53. *Educ:* Univ Chicago, BA & MS, 75; Harvard Univ, MA, 76, PhD(physics), 81. *Prof Exp:* Res asst, Harvard Univ, 76-81; res physicist, Princeton Univ, 80-88. *Mem:* Am Phys Soc; Am Vacuum Soc. *Res:* Fundamental atomic physics; optical pumping. *Mailing Add:* Dept Physics Univ Southern Calif Los Angeles CA 90089. *Fax:* 213-740-6653

KNOBEL, LEROY LYLE, GROUND WATER, WATER-ROCK INTERACTION. *Current Pos:* HYDROLOGIST, US GEOL SURV, 77- *Personal Data:* b Valley City, NDak, July 10, 45. *Educ:* Univ Wash, BS, 72; George Washington Univ, MS, 79. *Honors & Awards:* Presidential Citation, Dominican Repub, 75; Serv Award, Peace Corps, 75. *Prof Exp:* Hydrologist, Peace Corps, 73-75. *Concurrent Pos:* Chairperson, Group Saltwater Intrusion, Am Soc Testing & Mat, 96- *Mem:* Geochem Soc; Am Geophys Union; Am Soc Testing & Mat. *Res:* Geochemical, microbial and physical processes controlling the carbon dioxide cycle and water-rock interactions in the Snake River Plain aquifer, Idaho. *Mailing Add:* PO Box 2230 MS 4148 Idaho Falls ID 83403-2230. *Fax:* 208-526-2548; *E-Mail:* llknobel@usgs.gov

KNOBELOCH, F X CALVIN, SPEECH PATHOLOGY, AUDIOLOGY. *Current Pos:* ASSOC PROF, DIV SPEECH, HEARING & LANG, NC CENT UNIV, DURHAM, 90- *Personal Data:* b Tell City, Ind, Aug 5, 25; m 53; c 3. *Educ:* Ind Univ, BSEd, 49; Univ Fla, PhD(speech path, audiol), 59. *Honors & Awards:* Hons, NC Speech-Hearing-Lang Asn, 83. *Prof Exp:* Assoc prof speech & dir, Speech & Hearing Clin, Univ Miss, 59-60; asst chief speech path & audiol, Vet Admin Regional Off, Louisville, Ky, 60-62, chief speech path & audiol, Winston-Salem, NC, 62-66 & Durham, NC, 66-69; assoc dir, Biol Sci Res Ctr, Univ NC, Chapel Hill, 69-85, co-dir interdisciplinary training & head, Commun Disorders Ctr Develop & Learning, 69-90. *Concurrent Pos:* Clin assoc prof, 77-85, clin prof, Inst Speech & Hearing Sci & Dept Pediat, Univ NC, Chapel Hill, 85-90; assoc prof, Shaw Univ, 72-79; adj assoc prof, Speech, Lang & Auditory Path Prog, East Carolina Univ, 72-80. *Mem:* Am Speech, Language & Hearing Asn; fel Am Speech & Hearing Asn. *Res:* Hearing and language development in high risk and normal infants. *Mailing Add:* Educ NC Cent Univ 1801 Fayetteville St Durham NC 27707-3129

KNOBIL, ERNST, ENDOCRINOLOGY, PHYSIOLOGY. *Current Pos:* dean, Med Sch, 81-84, H WAYNE HIGHTOWER PROF MED SCI & DIR, LAB NEUROENDOCRINOL, UNIV TEX HEALTH SCI CTR, HOUSTON, 81-, ASHBEL SMITH PROF, 89- *Personal Data:* b Berlin, Ger, Sept 20, 26; nat US. *Educ:* Cornell Univ, BS, 48, PhD(zool), 51. *Hon Degrees:* Dr, Univ Bordeaux, France, 80; ScD, Med Col Wis, 83; Univ Liege, 94. *Honors & Awards:* Ciba Award, Endocrine Soc, 61; Carl G Hartman Award, Soc Study Reproduction, 83; Axel Munthe Award Field Reproduction, 85; Officer des Palmes Academiques, France, 89; Ray C Daggis Award, 94; Transatlantic Lectr, Soc Endocrinol Gt Brit, 79; Lawson Wilkins Lectr, Endocrine Soc, 80; Bard Lectr, Sch Med, Johns Hopkins Univ, 81; Herbert M Evans Mem Lectr, Univ Calif, 81; Carl Gemzell Lectr, Univ Uppsala, 81; Fred Conrad Koch Award, Endocrine Soc, 82; James Leathem Lectr, Rutgers Med Sch, 82; var lectr, 82-95. *Prof Exp:* Milton res fel, Biol Res Lab, Sch Dent Med, Harvard Univ, 51-53, instr physiol, Med Sch, 53-55, assoc, 55-57, Markle scholar acad med, 56-61, asst prof, 57-61; Richard Beatty Mellon prof physiol & chmn dept, Sch Med, Univ Pittsburgh, 61-81, dir, Ctr Res Primate Reproduction, 74-81. *Concurrent Pos:* Mem, Human Growth & Develop Study Sect, NIH, 64-66, chmn, Reproductive Biol Study Sect, 66-68, mem, Primate Res Ctr Adv Comt, 69-73 & Corpus Luteum Panel, Contraceptive Develop Br, 69-71; mem, Adv Coun, Inst Lab Animal Resources, Nat Acad Sci, 66-69; mem, Physiol Test Comt, Nat Bd Med Examr, 70-74; mem, Liaison Comt Med Educ, AMA-Am Asn Med Cols, 71-74; consult, Pop Off, Ford Found, 74-75, Uniformed Serv Univ Health Sci, 75 & Human Reproduction Unit, WHO, 76-82; mem, Pop Res Comt, Ctr Pop Res, Nat Inst Child Health & Human Develop, 74-77; mem, Med Adv Bd, Nat Hormone Pituitary Prog, 80-83; ed-in-chief, Ann Rev Physiol, 74-77, Sect Endocrinol & Metab, Am J Physiol, 79-82; mem adv comt, Searle Scholars Prog, 81-82; mem, Planning Comt Develop Endocrinol & Phys Growth, Nat Inst Child Health & Human Develop, 84-86; panel chairperson biol II, Int Sci Found, 93-94; chair, Int Physiol Comt, Am Physiol Soc, 96- *Mem:* Nat Acad Sci; sr mem Inst Med-Nat Acad Sci; Int Soc Endocrinol (pres, 84-88); Endocrine Soc (pres, 76-77); Am Acad Arts & Sci; hon mem Hungarian Acad Sci; foreign mem Fr Acad Sci; Fel AAAS; Am Asn Med Cols; hon fel Am Asn Obstetricians & Gynecologists; fel Am Gynec & Obstet Soc; Asn Chmn Departments Physiol (pres, 69-70); Fedn Am Socs Exp Biol; Nat Soc Med Res; Am Physiol Soc (pres, 78-80); Soc Neurosci; Soc Res Biol Rhythms; Soc Study Reproduction; Int Soc Neuroendocrinol; hon mem Japan Endocrine Soc. *Res:* Physiology of the pituitary gland; reproductive physiology. *Mailing Add:* Lab Neuroendocrinol Univ Tex Med Sch PO Box 20708 Houston TX 77225. *Fax:* 713-500-0655; *E-Mail:* eknobil@girchlmed.uth.tmc.edu

KNOBLER, CAROLYN BERK, STRUCTURAL CHEMISTRY, INORGANIC CHEMISTRY. *Current Pos:* from asst res chemist to assoc res chemist, Dept Chem & Biochem, 64-90, RES CHEMIST, DEPT CHEM & BIOCHEM, UNIV CALIF, LOS ANGELES, 90- *Personal Data:* b New Brunswick, NJ, Jan 6, 34; m, Charles M. *Educ:* George Washington Univ, BS, 55; Pa State Univ, PhD(inorg chem), 59. *Prof Exp:* Res asst geol, Calif Inst Technol, 62-64. *Concurrent Pos:* Res chemist, Pierre & Marie Curie Univ, 83-84 & 87, Univ Canterbury, 78-79, Univ Leiden, 70-71 & 60-61; vis lectr dept chem, Univ Calif, Los Angeles, 75; Nat Sci Found fel chem, Univ Amsterdam, 59-60. *Mem:* Am Crystallog Asn. *Res:* Structural characterization (single crystal x-ray crystallography) of metal clusters, organometallic compounds and metallacarboranes; conformational changes in uncomplexed host and in host-guest complexes. *Mailing Add:* Dept Chem & Biochem Univ Calif 405 Hilgard Ave Los Angeles CA 90095. *Fax:* 310-825-5490; *E-Mail:* knoblerh@chem.ucla.edu

KNOBLER, CHARLES MARTIN, PHYSICAL CHEMISTRY. *Current Pos:* from asst prof to assoc prof, 64-77, PROF CHEM, UNIV CALIF, LOS ANGELES, 77- *Personal Data:* b Newark, NJ, June 1, 34; m 57; c Daniel A & Michael D. *Educ:* NY Univ, BA, 55; Leiden Univ, Neth, PhD(molecular physics), 61. *Honors & Awards:* Herbert Newby McCoy Award. *Prof Exp:* Res assoc phys chem, Ohio State Univ, 61-62; fel chem eng, Calif Inst Technol, 62-64. *Concurrent Pos:* Ed, Physica A; vchmn, Univ Calif, Los Angeles, 75-78, chmn, 84-87 & 94-97; Fulbright scholar; Alexander von Humboldt sr res award. *Mem:* Am Chem Soc; fel Am Phys Soc; Sigma Xi. *Res:* kinetics of phase transitions; statistical mechanics of complex fluids; organic thin films. *Mailing Add:* Dept Chem Univ Calif Los Angeles CA 90095-1569. *Fax:* 310-206-5381; *E-Mail:* knobler@chem.ucla.edu

KNOBLER, ROBERT LEONARD, NEUROIMMUNOLOGY, NEUROVIROLOGY. *Current Pos:* MEM STAFF, DEPT NEUROL, JEFFERSON MED COL, PHILADELPHIA; FEL IMMUNOPATH, SCRIPPS CLIN & RES FOUND, 79- *Personal Data:* b New York, NY, Nov 10, 48; m 79; c Adam, Jonathan & Cory. *Educ:* City Col New York, BS, 69; State Univ NY, Brooklyn, MD & PhD(anat), 75. *Honors & Awards:* Roland P Mackay Award, Am Acad Neurol. *Prof Exp:* Intern med & psychiat, Kings County Hosp Ctr, State Univ NY, 75-76, resident neurol, 76-79; clin coordr, Multiple Sclerosis Clin, Gen Clin Res Ctr, 81-84. *Concurrent Pos:* Co-dir, Multiple Sclerosis Comprehensive Clin Ctr; dir, Reflex Sympathetic Dystrophy Clin. *Mem:* Am Acad Neurol; Am Asn Anatomists; Sigma Xi; Soc Neurosci; Am Asn Neuropathologists. *Res:* Viral and immune mechanisms of multiple sclerosis and reflex sympathetic dystrophy; ultrastructure of neurocellular relationships; clinical neurophysiology. *Mailing Add:* Dept Neurol Jefferson Med Col 1025 Walnut St Philadelphia PA 19107-5083. *Fax:* 215-923-6792

KNOBLOCH, EDGAR, STABILITY THEORY, NONLINEAR DYNAMICS. *Current Pos:* from asst prof to assoc prof, 78-87, PROF PHYSICS, UNIV CALIF, BERKELEY, 87- *Personal Data:* b Praha, Czech, Mar 30, 53; UK citizen; m 87. *Educ:* Cambridge Univ, BA, 74, ScD, 94; Harvard Univ, AM, 75, PhD(astron), 78. *Prof Exp:* Res asst astron, Harvard Univ, 76-78. *Concurrent Pos:* Jr fel, Harvard Soc Fels, 78-80; Alfred P Sloan res fel, 80-84. *Mem:* Am Phys Soc. *Res:* Astrophysical fluid dynamics; magnetohydrodynamics (dynamo theory); stochastic processes; stellar dynamics; bifurcation theory; nonlinear dynamics. *Mailing Add:* Dept Physics Univ Calif Berkeley CA 94720

KNOBLOCH, HILDA, PEDIATRICS, DEVELOPMENTAL DISABILITIES. *Current Pos:* RETIRED. *Personal Data:* b New York, NY, Dec 14, 15; div. *Educ:* Barnard Col, Columbia Univ, BA, 36; NY Univ, MD, 40; Johns Hopkins Univ, MPH, 51, DrPH, 55; Am Bd Pediat, dipl, 47; Am Bd Prev Med, dipl, 54. *Prof Exp:* Asst clin child develop, Sch Med, Yale Univ, 45-46; clin asst child guid clin, Mt Sinai Hosp, NY, 47-49; pediat consult, Maternity & Newborn Div, New York City Health Dept, 49-50; res assoc, Maternal & Child Health Div, Sch Hyg & Pub Health, Johns Hopkins Univ, 51-55, asst prof, 55; from assoc prof to prof pediat, Col Med, Ohio State Univ, 55-66, asst prof psychiat, 58-66; prof pediat, Univ Ill Col Med, 66-67; prof, Mt Sinai Sch Med, 67-70; prof, Albany Med Col, 70-82, emer prof pediat, 82. *Concurrent Pos:* Pvt pract, NY, 47-49; asst clin vis pediatrician, Bellevue Hosp, NY, 47-49; dir clin child develop, Children's Hosp, Colo, 56-64, dir div child develop, 64-66; dir, Child Develop Div, Dept Pediat, Mt Sinai Hosp, NY, 67-70, med specialist, NY State Off Ment Retardation & Develop Disabilities, 70-81. *Mem:* Fel Soc Res Child Develop; fel Am Acad Pediat; Am Pediat Soc; Am Acad Cerebral Palsy; Sigma Xi. *Res:* Developmental assessment and infant neurology, especially etiologic factors in neuropsychiatric disabilities of childhood. *Mailing Add:* 230 E Oglethorpe Ave Savannah GA 31401

KNOBLOCH, IRVING WILLIAM, BOTANY. *Current Pos:* from asst prof to prof natural sci, 45-59, prof bot, 59-76, EMER PROF BOT, MICH STATE UNIV, 76- *Personal Data:* b Buffalo, NY, Mar 1, 07; m 34, Natalie N Mueller; c Karen, Keith & Craig. *Educ:* Univ Buffalo, BA, 30, MA, 32; Iowa State Univ, PhD(bot), 42. *Prof Exp:* Asst, Univ Buffalo, 28-30; dir bot gardens, City of Buffalo, 31-33; wildlife technician, US Fish & Wildlife Serv, 33-37; instr bot, Iowa State Univ, 42-43; asst prof bot, Univ Buffalo, 43-45. *Mem:* Bot Soc Am; Am Fern Soc(vpres, 65-66, pres, 66-69); Am Inst Biol Sci; Am Asn Univ Professors. *Res:* Structure of economic plants; cytology of plants; morphology; agrostology; hybrids and evolution; pteridophytes. *Mailing Add:* 6104 Brookhaven Lane East Lansing MI 48823-2216

KNOBLOCH, JAMES OTIS, ORGANIC CHEMISTRY. *Current Pos:* CONSULT, 82- *Personal Data:* b Thibodaux, La, Jan 9, 20; m 50, Kathleen Breed; c John, Timothy & Susan. *Educ:* La State Univ, BS, 41; Univ Notre Dame, MS, 47, PhD(chem), 49. *Prof Exp:* Inspector, Radford Ord Works, 41-42; shift supvr acid plant, Pa Ord Works, US Rubber Co, 42-43; chem engr, Magnesium Plant, Mathieson Alkali Works, 43-44; chemist, Synthetic Rubber Plant, Firestone Tire & Rubber Co, 44-45; chemist, Whiting Res Labs, Standard Oil Co, Ind, Amoco Chem Corp, 49-59, sr res scientist, 59-70, sr res chemist, 70-82. *Concurrent Pos:* Adj prof, Ill Benedictine Col, 82-88. *Mem:* Am Chem Soc. *Res:* Structure of petroleum sulfonic acids; reactions of ozonides; synthesis of trifluoromethyl olefins; reduction of acetylenic glycols; oxidation studies; aromatic acid halogenations; polyanhydrides; fire retardants; catalytic hydrogenation of aromatic polycarboxylic acids. *Mailing Add:* 242 Green Acres Dr 7S Naperville IL 60540

KNOBLOCK, CRAIG, COMPUTER SCIENCE. *Current Pos:* SR RES SCIENTIST, INFO SCI INST & RES ASST PROF COMPUT SCI, UNIV SOUTHERN CALIF, 91- *Educ:* Syracuse Univ, BS, 84; Carnegie Mellon Univ, BS, 84, MS, 88, PhD (comput sci), 91. *Res:* Developing and applying planning, machine learning and knowledge representation techniques to the problem of providing access to distributed, heterogeneous information sources. *Mailing Add:* Info Sci Inst Univ Southern Calif 4676 Admiralty Way Marina del Ray CA 90292

KNOCHE, HERMAN WILLIAM, PHYTOPATHOLOGY. *Current Pos:* From instr to assoc prof biochem & nutrit, 62-73, PROF, DEPT BIOCHEM, UNIV NEBR, 73- *Personal Data:* b Stafford, Kans, Nov 15, 34; m 55; c 2. *Educ:* Kans State Univ, BS, 59, PhD(biochem), 63. *Concurrent Pos:* Consult, Physicians Path Lab, Univ Nebr, 66-70; hon res assoc & NIH fel, Harvard Univ, 71-72; consult, Smith Klein Beecham, 73- & Vet Hosp, Lincoln Nebr, 75-. *Mem:* Sigma Xi; Am Chem Soc; Am Soc Biol Chemists. *Res:* Biochemistry and structure of lipids; structures and activity of plant toxins; radioactive tracer methodology. *Mailing Add:* Dept Biochem Univ Nebr Lincoln NE 68583-0664. *Fax:* 402-472-7842

KNOCKEMUS, WARD WILBUR, INORGANIC CHEMISTRY. *Current Pos:* PROF CHEM & CHMN DEPT, HUNTINGDON COL, 74- *Personal Data:* b Des Plaines, Ill, Jan 29, 34; m 64; c 3. *Educ:* Knox Col, BA, 55; Pa State Univ, MS, 58; Univ Nebr, PhD, 69. *Prof Exp:* From asst prof to assoc prof chem, Morningside Col, 61-70; asst prof chem, Behrend Campus, Pa State Univ, 70-74. *Concurrent Pos:* Consult, Great Lakes Res Inst, Pa, 70-; res consult, Wesley Indust Inc, Mobile Ala, 87-, electrochem corrosion res, NASA, Marshall Space Flight Ctr, 85, 86. *Mem:* Am Chem Soc; Space Studies Inst. *Res:* Chemistry of metal-organic chelates; hydrolysis of oxymolybdenum chelates; adduct type compounds of octamolybdic acid; elecrochemical corrosion studies. *Mailing Add:* 5749 Carriage Barn Lane Montgomery AL 36116-1535

KNODEL, ELINOR LIVINGSTON, BIOCHEMISTRY, CELLCULTURE TECHNOLOGY. *Current Pos:* process chemist, 80-85, res & develop chemist, 86-90, SR INFO DESIGNER, CLIN SYSTS DIV, E I DU PONT DE NEMOURS & CO, 90- *Personal Data:* b New York, NY, Jan 25, 47; m 80; c 2. *Educ:* Columbia Univ, AB, 69; Yale Univ, MS, 72; Univ Conn, PhD(biochem), 76. *Prof Exp:* Res fel, Univ Conn, 74-76; res fel neuroendocrinol, Rockefeller Univ, 76-77; res fel neurochem, Mayo Clin, 78-80. *Mem:* Am Chem Soc; Soc Tech Commun. *Res:* Communications research into cognitive processes used in understanding online information; biochemistry of neural transmission in the brain and its regulation by hormones and drugs; automated clinical chemistry test development; cellculture technology; monoclonal antibody production. *Mailing Add:* 2518 Duncan Rd Wilmington DE 19808-4647. *E-Mail:* elinor.l.knodel@usa.dupont.com

KNODEL, RAYMOND WILLARD, MATHEMATICS EDUCATION. *Current Pos:* RETIRED. *Personal Data:* b Butte, NDak, June 10, 32; m 59; c 3. *Educ:* Minot State Col, BS, 55; Univ Northern Colo, MA, 60, DEduc(math educ), 70. *Prof Exp:* Instr sci, Ashley High Sch, NDak, 55-56; instr math, Mandan Sr High Sch, 56-59 & Anaconda Sr High Sch, Mont, 60-61; prof, Bemidji State Col, 61-96. *Res:* Team teaching mathematics and arithmetic methods to prospective elementary school teachers. *Mailing Add:* Rte 7 Box 79 Bemidji MN 56601

KNODT, CLOY BERNARD, dairy science; deceased, see previous edition for last biography

KNOEBEL, LEON KENNETH, physiology; deceased, see previous edition for last biography

KNOEBEL, SUZANNE BUCKNER, INTERNAL MEDICINE, CARDIOLOGY. *Current Pos:* From asst prof to prof, 66-77, HERMAN C & ELLNORA D KRANNERT PROF MED, SCH MED, IND UNIV, INDIANAPOLIS, 77- *Personal Data:* b Ft Wayne, Ind, Dec 13, 26. *Educ:* Goucher Col, AB, 48; Ind Univ, Indianapolis, MD, 60. *Mem:* Fel Am Col Cardiol; Asn Univ Cardiologists; Am Fedn Clin Res; Am Heart Asn. *Res:* Myocardial blood flow; arrhythmias in coronary artery disease; computer analysis of cardiovascular data. *Mailing Add:* Krannert Inst Med Dept Ind Univ Med Ctr 1111 W Tenth St Indianapolis IN 46202

KNOECHEL, EDWIN LEWIS, PHARMACY. *Current Pos:* CONSULT, 90- *Personal Data:* b Milwaukee, Wis, June 15, 31; m 53; c 2. *Educ:* Univ Wis, BS, 53, MS, 55, PhD(pharm), 58. *Prof Exp:* Res assoc prod res & develop, Upjohn Co, 58-65, head mat inspection, Control Div, 65-90. *Mem:* Am Pharmaceut Asn; Am Acad Pharmaceut Scientists. *Res:* Control activities associated with Food and Drug Administration, especially good manufacturing practices, self inspection, raw material evaluation, contract processor inspections, determination of mesh analysis, bulk volume, dissolution rates, surface area and particle size distributions, solids technology and in-process testing. *Mailing Add:* 12290 Pineridge Trail Eastport MI 49627-0446

KNOEDLER, ELMER L, CHEMICAL ENGINEERING. *Current Pos:* sr proj engr, Sheppad T Powell, 41-58, SR PROJ ENGR & PARTNER, SHEPPAD T POWELL ASSOCS, 58- *Personal Data:* b Gloucester, NJ, Feb 12, 12; m 41. *Educ:* Cornell Univ, ME, 34; Columbia Univ, MS, 36, PhD(chem eng), 52. *Prof Exp:* Mem tech staff, Atlantic Refining Co, Pa, 34-35; asst supt, Davis Emergency Equip Co, NJ, 36-37; develop engr & supt iron powder prod, Metals Disintegrating Co, 39-41. *Mem:* Am Chem Soc; Am Soc Mech Eng; Inst Elec & Electronics Engrs; Am Inst Chemists; Am Inst Chem Eng. *Res:* Industrial water; boiler feedwater; corrosion; industrial waste waters. *Mailing Add:* 513 Little John Hill Sherwood Forest MD 21405

KNOEFEL, PETER KLERNER, HISTORY & PHILOSOPHY OF SCIENCE, PHARMACOLOGY. *Current Pos:* from asst prof to prof, 35-68, chmn dept, 41-66, EMER PROF PHARMACOL, UNIV LOUISVILLE, 69- *Personal Data:* b New Albany, Ind, Aug 4, 06; m 53, Francesia Spina. *Educ:* Univ Wis, BA, 27, MA, 28; Harvard Univ, MD, 31. *Prof Exp:* Res fel pharmacol, Nat Res Coun, 31-33; assoc pharmacol, Vanderbilt Univ, 33-35. *Concurrent Pos:* Vis prof, Inst & Mus Hist & Sci Firenze, Florence, Italy, 68-81. *Mem:* Emer mem Am Chem Soc. *Res:* Classical studies of venomous serpents. *Mailing Add:* 211 W Oak St Apt 921 Louisville KY 40203-5402. *Fax:* 713-794-7853

KNOEPFLER, NESTOR B(EYER), CHEMICAL ENGINEERING, CHEMISTRY. *Current Pos:* fel, Nat Cottonseed Prod Asn, Southern Regional Res Lab, USDA, 50-52, asst chem engr, 52-55, assoc chem engr, 55-56, tech asst to dir, 56-58, asst to dir, 58-60, res chem engr, 60-66, head, Cotton Prod Invests Eng & Develop Lab, 66-73, res leader textile chem eng, eng & develop, 73-79, CONSULT CHEM ENGR, USDA, 79- *Personal Data:* b New Orleans, La, Oct 1, 18; m 43; c 3. *Educ:* Tulane Univ, BE, 40. *Prof Exp:* Lab asst, Southern Cotton Oil Co, 40-41; asst mgr, Southern Photocraft, 45-50. *Mem:* Am Oil Chem Soc; Sigma Xi; Am Asn Textile Chem & Colorists. *Res:* Processing of Southern grown agricultural products, especially oilseeds, fruits, vegetables, pine gum; mechanical processing and chemical finishing of cotton; author of 129 technical articles and granted nine patents. *Mailing Add:* 17 Jennifer Ct Mandeville LA 70448-6321

KNOERR, KENNETH RICHARD, FORESTRY. *Current Pos:* asst prof forest climat, 61-67, assoc prof forest meteorol, 67-72, assoc prof biometeorol, 67-81, prof forest meteorol, 72-81, assoc prof bot, 76-81, PROF FORESTRY & ENVIRON STUDIES, SCH FORESTRY, DUKE UNIV, 81- *Personal Data:* b Milwaukee, Wis, Sept 2, 27; m 52; c 3. *Educ:* Univ Idaho, BS, 52; Yale Univ, MF, 55, PhD, 61. *Prof Exp:* Res forester meteorol & asst proj leader snow physics studies, Pac Southwest Forest & Range Exp Sta, US Forest Serv, 56-61, proj leader forest microclimate studies, Cent States Forest Exp Sta, 61. *Concurrent Pos:* Mem, Nat Acad Sci Adv Comt Climat, US Weather Bur, 65- *Mem:* AAAS; Soc Am Foresters; Am Meteorol Soc; Am Geophys Union; Int Asn Sci Hydrol; Sigma Xi. *Res:* Micrometeorology and microclimatology of forests related to surface energy balance; evapotranspiration and watershed management. *Mailing Add:* Sch Forestry Duke Univ Durham NC 27706

KNOKE, JAMES DEAN, biostatistics, for more information see previous edition

KNOKE, JOHN KEITH, VIROLOGY, EPIPHYTOLOGY. *Current Pos:* RETIRED. *Personal Data:* b Detroit, Mich, Mar 31, 30; m 56; c 2. *Educ:* Univ Wis, BS, 52, MS, 59, PhD(entom), 62. *Prof Exp:* Entomologist, Cacao Entom, Inter-Am Inst Agr Sci, 60-63; proj assoc, Univ Wis-Madison, 63, asst prof, 63-67; res entomologist, Agr Res Serv, USDA, Ohio Agr Res & Develop Ctr, 67-89. *Concurrent Pos:* Collab, Univ Wis-Madison, 60-63; adj assoc prof entom, Ohio Agr Res & Develop Ctr & Ohio State Univ, 67- *Mem:* Entom Soc Am; Am Phytopath Soc. *Res:* Control of insects attacking vegetables, especially through the use of systemic insecticides; study of all phases of entomology relative to production of Theobroma cacao L; epidemiology of virus diseases of corn; vectors of maize viruses. *Mailing Add:* 550 Beechwood St Wooster OH 44691

KNOLL, ALAN HOWARD, CIVIL ENGINEERING, SOFTWARE SYSTEMS. *Current Pos:* INDEPENDENT CONSULT, 86- *Personal Data:* b St Joseph, Mich, Apr 16, 31; m 52, Ruth Klammer; c David A, Deborah A, Stephen R, Mark W, Rebecca M & Andrew A. *Educ:* Univ Mich, BSc, 52, MSc, 56. *Prof Exp:* Res engr, Alcoa Labs, 56-67, group leader, 67-70, sect head, 70-75, mgr sci & bus systs, 75-77 & mgr elec prods div, 77-80; gen mgr, REA Magnet Wire Co, 80-82, vpres technol, 82-86. *Mem:* Sigma Xi; Am Soc Civil Engrs. *Res:* Structural use of aluminum; application of digital computation to structural and other engineering problems; new products and test methods for overhead electrical transmission and magnet wire. *Mailing Add:* 15 Cambridge Dr Frankenmuth MI 48734-9779

KNOLL, ANDREW HERBERT, PALEONTOLOGY, GEOLOGY. *Current Pos:* assoc prof biol, 82-85, PROF BIOL & CUR BOT MUS, HARVARD UNIV, 85-, PROF EARTH & PLANETARY SCI, 85-, CHMN, DEPT ORGANISMIC & EVOLUTIONARY BIOL, 92- *Personal Data:* b West Reading, Pa, Apr 23, 51; m 74; c 2. *Educ:* Lehigh Univ, BA, 73; Harvard Univ, AM, 74, PhD(geol), 77. *Hon Degrees:* PhD, Uppsak Univ, Sweden, 96. *Honors & Awards:* Walcott Medal, NAS, 87; Schuchert Award, Paleontol Soc, 87. *Prof Exp:* Asst prof, Oberlin Col, 77-81. *Concurrent Pos:* Assoc ed, Palebiol, 80-90, Precambrian Res, Rev Paleobot Palynology, 87-, Trends in Ecol & Evolution, 87-92, Am J Sci, 91-, Palaios, 97-; mem, Comt Planetary Biol & Chem Evolution, US Space Sci Bd, 80-88, 97-, Space Sci Bd Task Group, Major Directions in Space Sci: 1995-2015, 85-88; prin investr, NSF, 80-; mem, NRC Bd Earth Sci, 87-89, NASA Exobiol Adv Comt, 88-96, chmn, Terminal Precambrian Syst, Int Stratig Comn Working Group, 88-; Guggenheim fel, 87; vis fel, Australian Nat Univ, 87-, Gonville & Caius Col, Cambridge, 91-92; vis scientist, Australian Bur Mineral Resources, 87-; mem, Nat Bd US Nat Mus Natural Hist, 92-, Nat Res Ctr, Bd Earth Scis & Resources, 92- *Mem:* Nat Acad Sci; Bot Soc Am; Soc Econ Paleontologists & Mineralogists; Sigma Xi; Paleont Soc; fel Am Acad Arts & Sci; fel Geol Soc Am. *Res:* Precambrian biological evolution; evolution of land plants; Precambrian sedimentary geology. *Mailing Add:* Bot Mus Harvard Univ Cambridge MA 02138

KNOLL, GLENN F, NUCLEAR ENGINEERING. *Current Pos:* From asst prof to assoc prof, Univ Mich, Ann Arbor, 62-72, chmn dept, 79-90, interim dean eng, 95-96, PROF NUCLEAR ENG, UNIV MICH, ANN ARBOR, 72- *Personal Data:* b St Joseph, Mich, Aug 3, 35; m 57; c 3. *Educ:* Case Western Res Univ, BS, 57; Stanford Univ, MS, 59; Univ Mich, PhD(nuclear eng), 63. *Honors & Awards:* Glenn Murphy Award, Am Soc Eng Educ, 79; Arthur Holly Compton Award, Am Nuclear Soc, 91; Ann Merit Award, Inst Elec & Electronics Mgrs, 96. *Concurrent Pos:* Fulbright travel grant & vis scientist, Nuclear Res Ctr, Karlsruhe, Ger, 65-66; consult to var indust orgn, 82- *Mem:* Fel Am Nuclear Soc; Am Phys Soc; fel Inst Elec & Electronics Engrs; Am Soc Eng Educ; fel Am Inst Med Biol Eng. *Res:* Neutron spectroscopy; radiation detection and measurements; radioisotope imaging; medical instrumentation; neutron cross sections. *Mailing Add:* 3891 Waldenwood Ann Arbor MI 48105

KNOLL, JACK, ANIMAL PHYSIOLOGY. *Current Pos:* from asst prof to assoc prof, 62-76, prof, 76-81, EMER PROF BIOL, UNIV NEV, RENO, 81- *Personal Data:* b Ashland, Wis, Feb 17, 24; m 48, Ella Kripli; c Robert. *Educ:* Mich State Univ, BS, 50, MS, 59, PhD(physiol), 62. *Prof Exp:* Asst physiol, Mich State Univ, 57-61. *Mem:* AAAS; Sigma Xi. *Res:* Ion transport across natural biological membranes; fish physiology. *Mailing Add:* Rte 2 Box 271 Mason WI 54856

KNOLLENBERG, ROBERT GEORGE, INSTRUMENTATION. *Current Pos:* PRES, PARTICLE MEASURING SYSTS, INC, 72-, CHIEF RES EXEC, 76- *Personal Data:* b Mattoon, Ill, Aug 28, 39; m 66; c 3. *Educ:* Eastern Ill Univ, BS, 61; Univ Wis-Madison, MS, 64, PhD(cloud physics), 67. *Prof Exp:* Res asst, Univ Wis-Madison, 64-66; scientist, NCAR Res Aviation, Colo, 67-69; asst prof geophys sci, Univ Chicago, 69-72; vis prof atmospheric sci, Colo State Univ, 73-75. *Mem:* Am Meteorol Soc; Am Chem Soc; Am Inst Physics; Inst Elec & Electronics Engrs; Optical Soc Am. *Res:* Particle physics research and instrumentation development applied to the development of particle size spectrometers. *Mailing Add:* 1855 S 57th Ct Boulder CO 80301

KNOLLMAN, GILBERT CARL, MATERIAL SCIENCE, ULTRASONICS. *Current Pos:* res scientist, Res Labs, Lockheed Missiles & Space Co, 62-63, head, Hydrospace Physics Lab, 64-70, staff scientist, 63-64, dir, Adv Acoust Lab, 71-76, head, Ultrasonics Lab, 76-84, SR STAFF SCIENTIST, LOCKHEED PALO ALTO RES LABS, 64-, SR MEM, 66-, HEAD, LOCKHEED ACOUST IMAGING PROG, 84- *Personal Data:* b Cleveland, Ohio, Mar 14, 28; m 59, Lorraine Gordon; c Katrina (Jaquette), Kristi (Barnes), Tom Jenkins & Scott Jenkins. *Educ:* Ga Inst Technol, BS, 49, MS, 50, PhD(physics), 61. *Prof Exp:* Instr physics, Ga Inst Technol, 49-50, res physicist, Eng Exp Sta, 50-62, asst prof math, Inst, 52-60. *Concurrent Pos:* NSF grant, 60-61; consult, Ga Tech Res Inst, 62-65 & Lockheed Calif Co, 64-67; fel, Stanford Univ, 65-66; consult, Saratoga Systs, 70-76; mem Lockheed Res Comt, 70-71, chmn, 72-73; staff, Lockheed Eng Sci, 72-74; consult, Naval Weapons Lab, 73-; staff, Lockheed Mat Sci, 74-; consult, Air Force Astronaut Lab, 86-, Nat Res Coun Can, 88-, Analitic Eng Co, 90- *Mem:* Fel AAAS; fel Am Phys Soc; fel Am Inst Physics; fel NY Acad Sci; Res Soc Am; Acoust Soc Am; Sigma Xi. *Res:* Quantum field theory; quantum and statistical mechanics; many-body theory; superconductivity and superfluidity; liquid state physics; theoretical acoustics and hydrodynamics; orbital and wave mechanics; electromagnetic theory; viscoelasticity; ultrasonics; underwater acoustics and electronics; material sciences; nondestructive test and evaluation; ocean science; granted one US patent. *Mailing Add:* 705 Charleston Ct Palo Alto CA 94303

KNOLLMUELLER, KARL OTTO, INDUSTRIAL ORGANIC CHEMISTRY. *Current Pos:* from res chemist to sr res chemist, 60-74, res assoc, 74-84, SR RES ASSOC, OLIN CORP, CONN, 78- *Personal Data:* b Regensburg, Ger, July 12, 31; US citizen; m 68, Ruth Nelson; c Linnea E & Marit R. *Educ:* Univ Munich, MS, 57, PhD(chem), 60.. *Prof Exp:* Res chemist, Diversey Corp, Ill, 60. *Mem:* Am Chem Soc; AAAS; Sigma Xi. *Res:* Inorganic and organic phosphorus compounds; sequestration agents; metal treatment chemicals; high temperature stable polymers; functional fluids; chemicals for electronics; photoresists; chlorine/hypochlorites; sulfur chemistry; hydrosulfite bleaching/reductions; pulp & paper chemistry; propellants. *Mailing Add:* 28 Apple Tree Lane Hamden CT 06518

KNOOP, FLOYD C, INFECTIOUS DISEASES, MEDICAL MICROBIOLOGY & IMMUNOLOGY. *Current Pos:* from asst prof to assoc prof, 75-93, PROF MED MICROBIOL, CREIGHTON UNIV SCH MED, 93-, COMPONENT I DIR, 96- *Personal Data:* b Troy, Ohio, Nov 11, 44; m 67, Pamela Johnson; c Tiffany N. *Educ:* Defiance Col, BS, 66; Univ Dayton, MS, 69; Univ Tenn Med Ctr, PhD(medmicrobiol), 74. *Prof Exp:* Instr microbiol, Univ Tenn Med Ctr, 74-75. *Concurrent Pos:* Fel, Univ Tenn Med Ctr, 74-75; consult, Burns-Biotec Labs, 78-82, Dellen Labs, 80-83, Norden Labs, 82-85, Fermenta Animal Health, 85-90, Omaha-Douglas Co Health Dept, 78-; numerous grants from private, state & nat orgns, 76- *Mem:* Am Soc Microbiol; AAAS; NY Acad Sci; Sigma Xi; Am Soc Biochem & Molecular Biol; Int Ctr Diarrheal Dis; Col Am Pathologists; Int Soc Toxinology. *Res:* Structure and biological function of microbial toxins; effects of pharmacologic agents on the secretory activity induced by bacterial enterotoxins; transmembrane receptor-mediated signalling; microbial vaccine production; monoclonal antibodies; technology assessment and transfer. *Mailing Add:* 208 Bellevue Blvd S Bellevue NE 68005. *Fax:* 402-280-1875

KNOP, CHARLES M(ILTON), ELECTROMAGNETIC ENGINEERING, ELECTRICAL ENGINEERING. *Current Pos:* mgr res & develop, 70-76, dir res & develop, 76-80, CHIEF SCIENTIST & DIR, ANTENNA RES, ANDREW CORP, 80- *Personal Data:* b Chicago, Ill, Feb 18, 31; m 77. *Educ:* Ill Inst Technol, BSEE, 54, MSEE, 60, PhD(elec eng), 63. *Prof Exp:* Mem tech staff antenna res, Hughes Aircraft Co, 54-55; res asst, Princeton Univ, 55-56; asst engr, Armour Res Found, Ill, 56-58, assoc engr, 58-60; sr engr, Res Lab, Systs Div, Bendix Corp, 60-61; asst dir res & develop, Hallicrafters Co, 61-64; mem sr staff, Nat Eng Sci Co, Calif, 64-65; assoc dir antenna design, Andrew Corp, 65-67, res consult, 67-68; independent consult electrodyn, 68-70. *Concurrent Pos:* Lectr, Dept Elec Eng, Ill Inst Technol, 66-72. *Mem:* fel Inst Elec & Electronics Engrs; Am Phys Soc. *Res:* Electromagnetic wave radiation, propagation, scattering and diffraction as related to antennas and communication systems; waveguiding systems. *Mailing Add:* Andrew Corp 10500 W 153rd St Orland Park IL 60462

KNOP, CHARLES PHILIP, INORGANIC CHEMISTRY. *Current Pos:* res asst prof, 65-70, chmn dept, 69, assoc prof, 70-76, PROF CHEM, GRAND VALLEY STATE COL, 76-, CHMN DEPT, 74- *Personal Data:* b Detroit, Mich, May 23, 27; m 52; c 9. *Educ:* Aquinas Col, BS, 52; Mich State Univ, PhD(chem), 58. *Prof Exp:* Chemist, Haviland Prod Co, 52-53; asst, Mich State Univ, 53-58. *Mem:* Am Chem Soc; Sigma Xi. *Res:* Pollution abatement; plating wastes recovery. *Mailing Add:* Dept Chem Grand Valley State Univ Allendale MI 49401

KNOP, HARRY WILLIAM, JR, PHYSICS. *Current Pos:* RETIRED. *Personal Data:* b Chicago, Ill, June 20, 20; m 50. *Educ:* Ripon Col, BA, 42; Univ Wis, PhD(physics), 48. *Prof Exp:* Res physicist, Photo Prods Dept, E I DuPont De Nemours & Co, 49-56, res supvr, 56-60, sales tech supvr, 60-65, field sales mgr, 65-66, mgr, Rochester Res & Develop, 66-69, res mgr, Exp Sta Lab, 69-73, dir Du Pont Photo Prods, Japan, 73-75, Lab dir, Exp Sta Lab, 76-83. *Mem:* Am Phys Soc; Soc Motion Picture & TV Eng; Sigma Xi. *Res:* Physics of photography, solid state physics. *Mailing Add:* PO Box 791 Wilmington DE 19899-0791

KNOP, OSVALD, CRYSTALLOGRAPHY, SOLID STATE CHEMISTRY. *Current Pos:* from assoc prof to prof, 64-90, Harry Shirreff prof chem res, 81-90, EMER PROF CHEM, DALHOUSIE UNIV, 90- *Personal Data:* b Kurim, Czech, July 11, 22; nat Can; m 51, Helga Norregaard; c 1. *Educ:* Masaryk Univ, Czech, BS, 46; Laval Univ, DSc(phys chem), 57. *Prof Exp:* Asst, Calif Inst Technol, 49; lectr indust chem, Dept Chem Eng, NS Tech Col, 50-53, from asst prof to assoc prof chem, 53-64. *Mem:* Fel Chem Inst Can; Royal Soc Chem. *Res:* Structural inorganic and solid state chemistry; computer-simulation methods; application of combinatorial analysis and graph theory to chemistry and physics; Structura; inorganic and solid-state chemistry; hydrogen bonding in solids; ab initio and semiempirical calculations. *Mailing Add:* Dept Chem Dalhousie Univ Halifax NS B3H 4J3 Can. *Fax:* 902-494-1310

KNOPF, DANIEL PETER, chemistry; deceased, see previous edition for last biography

KNOPF, FRITZ L, WILDLIFE ECOLOGY, ORNITHOLOGY. *Current Pos:* proj leader, 93-96, SR SCIENTIST, US NAT BIOL SURV, 96- *Personal Data:* b Aurora, Ohio, June 6, 45; c 3. *Educ:* Hiram Col, Ohio, BA, 67; Utah State Univ, MS, 73, PhD(wildlife ecol), 75. *Honors & Awards:* Douglas L Gilbert Award for Outstanding Prof Achievement. *Prof Exp:* Instr, Utah State Univ, 75-76; asst prof wildlife ecol, Okla State Univ, 76-79; res wildlife biologist, US Fish & Wildlife Serv, 80-81, proj leader, 82-93, sect leader, 93-96. *Concurrent Pos:* Ed, Wildlife Soc Bull, vols 11-13, 83-85. *Mem:* Wildlife Soc; Cooper Ornith Union; Am Ornithologists Union; Wilson Ornith Soc; Soc Conserv Biol. *Res:* Habitat preference and utilization by wild birds; landscape ecology, management of landscapes; conservation of biodiversity. *Mailing Add:* Nat Biol Surv US Fish & Wildlife Serv 4512 McMurray Ave Ft Collins CO 80525-3400. *E-Mail:* fritz_knopf@nbs.gov

KNOPF, PAUL M, BIOLOGY. *Current Pos:* assoc prof, 72-77, CHARLES A & HELEN B STUART PROF MED SCI, BROWN UNIV, 77- *Personal Data:* b Trenton, NJ, Apr 4, 36; m 58, Carol L Harrison; c Jeffrey W, Steven H & Rachel A. *Educ:* Mass Inst Technol, PhD(molecular biol), 62. *Prof Exp:* Res assoc, Salk Inst, 64-72. *Concurrent Pos:* Fulbright fel, 78-79 & Fogarty fel, 86-87; chmn, Dept Molecular Microbiol & Immunol, Brown Univ. *Mem:* AAAS; Am Asn Immunologists; Am Soc Trop Med & Hyg; Soc Neurosci; Am Soc Microbiol. *Res:* Development of vaccine against human schistosomiasis; central nervous system/immune system interactions. *Mailing Add:* Div Biol & Med Brown Univ PO Box G-B413 Providence RI 02912. *Fax:* 401-863-1971; *E-Mail:* paul_knopf@brown.edu

KNOPF, RALPH FRED, INTERNAL MEDICINE. *Current Pos:* resident internal med, Univ Mich, Ann Arbor, 56-58, resident ophthal, 58-59, fel internal med, 59-62, from instr to assoc prof, 62-73, PROF INTERNAL MED, MED CTR, UNIV MICH, ANN ARBOR, 73- *Personal Data:* b Muskegon, Mich, Mar 26, 26; m 54; c 3. *Educ:* Univ Mich, BS, 51, MD, 54; Am Bd Internal Med, dipl, 63. *Prof Exp:* Intern med, Virginia Mason Hosp, Seattle, Wash, 54-55; resident internal med, 55-56. *Mem:* Am Fedn Clin Res; Am Diabetes Asn; Endocrine Soc. *Res:* Diabetes mellitus; inter-relationship between carbohydrate, protein and lipid metabolism and insulin glucagon and growth hormone secretion. *Mailing Add:* 3820 Taubman Ctr Univ Mich Hosps Univ Mich Ann Arbor MI 48109

KNOPF, ROBERT JOHN, ORGANIC CHEMISTRY, POLYMER CHEMISTRY. *Current Pos:* RETIRED. *Personal Data:* b West New York, NJ, Apr 18, 32; m 83, Mary J Kuhl; c Kenneth, Kim & Katherine. *Educ:* Gettysburg Col, BA, 54; Princeton Univ, MA, 56, PhD(org chem), 57. *Prof Exp:* Chemist, Union Carbide Corp, SCharleston, 57-66, group leader res & develop, 66-70, res scientist, 70-75, prod develop mgr, 74-76, sr develop scientist, Ethylene Oxide-Glycol Div, 75-86. *Concurrent Pos:* Consult alkoxylation chem, Union Carbide, 86-90. *Mem:* Am Chem Soc. *Res:* Flame retardants for plastics; chemistry of isocyanates; polyurethane foams, coatings and elastic fibers; aldol condensation chemistry; condensation polymerizations in solution; polyethers; hydrogel polymers; photocure coatings intermediates; surfactant intermediates; ethylene oxide derivatives; catalysis of ethoxylation reactions. *Mailing Add:* 2657 Lakeview Dr St Albans WV 25177

KNOPKA, W N, FIBER TECHNOLOGY, WATER TREATMENT. *Current Pos:* PRES, QUORUM ASSOC INC, 90- *Personal Data:* b Buffalo, NY, Dec 1, 38; m 65, Carol Gold; c 3. *Educ:* Canisius Col, BS, 61; Seton Hall Univ, MS, 63, PhD(org chem), 65. *Prof Exp:* Sr res chemist, Cent Res & Develop, FMC Corp, NJ, 65-69, group leader, Fiber Div, Pa, 69-73, prod mgr, 73-76, agr chem, 76-77; dir fabric develop, Goodyear Tire & Rubber Co, 77-79, dir elastomer & chem res, 79-83; vpres corp develop, Interchem Inc, 86-88; pres, Interchem Develop Co, 88-90. *Mem:* Am Chem Soc; Com Develop Asn. *Res:* Specialty organic chemical intermediates; fiber processing; wire process technology; condensation and addition polymers; synthetic rubbers; rubber chemicals; specialty monomers, coatings and adhesives radiation curable chemicals. *Mailing Add:* 5300 Woodridge Forest Trail NW Atlanta GA 30327

KNOPMAN, DEBRA SARA, HYDROLOGY & WATER RESOURCES, OPERATIONS RESEARCH. *Current Pos:* DIR, CTR INNOVATION & ENVIRON, PROGRESSIVE FOUND, 95- *Personal Data:* b Philadelphia, Pa, Aug 13, 53; m 85, Donald Weightman; c Leah & David. *Educ:* Wellesley Col, BA, 75; Mass Inst Technol, MSCE, 78; Johns Hopkins Univ, PhD(hydrol), 86. *Prof Exp:* Prof staff mem, US Sen Comt Environ & Pub Works, 80-83; hydrologist, Off Groundwater, US Geol Surv, 84-86, res hydrologist, Nat Res Prog, 86-87, hydrologist, Br Systs Anal, 87-92, chief, Br Systs Anal, 92-93; dep asst secy water & sci, Dept Interior, 93-95. *Concurrent Pos:* Teaching asst hydrol & fluid dynamics, Dept Civil Eng, Mass Inst Technol, 77-78; Luce scholar, Henry R Luce Found, 78-79; teaching asst water resources systs design, Johns Hopkins Univ, 83-85; chair, Pub Info Comt, Am Geophys Union, 90-92. *Mem:* Am Geophys Union. *Res:* Design of sampling strategies for model discrimination and parameter estimation in subsurface solute transport studies; use of water quality and other hydrologic information in the development of national water policy. *Mailing Add:* 518 C St NE Washington DC 20002. *E-Mail:* dknopman@pf.org

KNOPOFF, LEON, GEOPHYSICS, PHYSICS. *Current Pos:* from res assoc to assoc res geophysicist, Inst Geophys, Univ Calif, Los Angeles, 50-56, assoc prof geophys, 56-57, assoc dir, Inst Geophys & Planetary Physics, 72-86, PROF GEOPHYS, UNIV CALIF, LOS ANGELES, 57-, PROF PHYSICS, 59-, RES MUSICOLOGIST, 61- *Personal Data:* b Los Angeles, Calif, July 1, 25; m 61, Joanne Van Cleef; c Katherine, Rachel & Michael. *Educ:* Calif Inst Technol, BS, 44, MS, 46, PhD(physics), 49. *Honors & Awards:* Harold Jeffreys Lectr, Royal Astron Soc, 77; Emil Wiechert Medal, Ger Geophys Soc, 78; Gold Medal, Royal Astron Soc, 79; Sidney Chapman Mem Lectr, Univ Alaska, 88; Medal, Seismol Soc Am, 90. *Prof Exp:* From asst prof to assoc prof physics, Miami Univ, 48-50. *Concurrent Pos:* Mem earth sci panel, NSF, 59-62; NSF sr fel, Cambridge Univ, 60-61; prof, Calif Inst Technol, 62-63; secy gen, Int Upper Mantle Comt & chmn, US Comt, 63-71; vis prof, Technische Hochschule, Karlsruhe, Ger, 66, Harvard Univ, 72 & Univ Chile, Santiago, 73; chmn, Comt Math Geophys, Int Union Geophys & Geophysicists, 71-82, mem, US Nat Comt; Guggenheim fel, 76-77; mem, Educ Adv Bd, Guggenheim Found, 89-; distinguished geophys lectr, Tex A&M Univ, 90. *Mem:* Nat Acad Sci; fel Am Acad Arts & Sci; Am Phys Soc; hon mem Seismol Soc Am; fel Am Geophys Union; fel AAAS; Royal Astron Soc; Am Philos Soc. *Res:* Theory of earthquakes; self-organizing systems; acoustics of solids; physics and chemistry of deep interior of earth; elastic wave propagation; systematic musicology; author or co-author of over 300 scientific papers and publications; theoretical and observational seismology. *Mailing Add:* Inst Geophys & Planetary Physics Univ Calif Los Angeles CA 90024. *Fax:* 310-206-3051; *E-Mail:* knopoff@physics.ucla.edu

KNOPP, JAMES A, BIOPHYSICAL CHEMISTRY. *Current Pos:* asst prof, 69-74, ASSOC PROF BIOCHEM, NC STATE UNIV, 74-, UNDERGRAD COORDR BIOCHEM, 95- *Personal Data:* b Grand Rapids, Mich, Oct 26, 40; m 62; c 2. *Educ:* Carleton Col, BA, 62; Univ Ill, PhD(biophys chem), 67. *Prof Exp:* Investr biol div, Oak Ridge Nat Lab, 67-69, biophysicist, 67-69. *Mem:* Am Chem Soc; Am Soc Biol Chemists. *Res:* Physical chemistry of proteins; fluorescence techniques in biochemistry; video image microscopy; plant pathogen interactions. *Mailing Add:* Dept Biochem NC State Univ PO Box 7622 Raleigh NC 27695-0001. *Fax:* 919-515-2047; *E-Mail:* jaknopp@ncsu.edu

KNOPP, MARVIN ISADORE, MODULAR FORMS, ANALYTIC NUMBER THEORY. *Current Pos:* PROF MATH, TEMPLE UNIV, 76- *Personal Data:* b Chicago, Ill, Jan 4, 33; m 57; c Seth, Yudah, Abby & Elana. *Educ:* Univ Ill, BS, 54, AM, 55, PhD(math), 58. *Prof Exp:* Asst math, Univ Ill, 54-58; res mathematician, Space Tech Labs, 58-59; fel, NSF Inst Advan Study, 59-60; from asst prof to prof, Univ Wis-Madison, 60-70; prof, Univ Ill, Chicago Circle, 70-76, Bryn Mawr Col, 88-89. *Concurrent Pos:* Res grants, NSF, 60-89, NASA, 90-; mathematician, Nat Bur Stand, 63-64; vis prof, Math Inst, Univ Basel, Switz, 68-69, Ohio State Univ, 79; visitor, Inst Advan Study, 75, 78, mem, 88. *Mem:* Am Math Soc. *Res:* Construction of automorphic forms; uniformization and Riemann surfaces; Eichler cohomology of automorphic forms; rational period functions of automorphic integrals and quadratic forms; Fourier coefficients of modular forms of small weight; Mellin transforms of modular integrals. *Mailing Add:* Temple Univ Philadelphia PA 19122

KNOPP, ROBERT H, medicine, for more information see previous edition

KNOPP, WALTER, PSYCHIATRY. *Current Pos:* from instr to prof, 85, EMER PROF PSYCHIAT, COL MED, OHIO STATE UNIV, 85- *Personal Data:* b Ostrava, Czech, Oct 22, 22; US citizen; m 51; c 2. *Educ:* Univ Heidelberg, MD, 50; Am Bd Psychiat & Neurol, dipl, 61. *Prof Exp:* Intern med, Univ Heidelberg Hosp, 50, resident pediat, 51; toxicologist, Europ Lab, US Army Med Ctr, Ger, 52-54; intern, Glens Falls Hosp, NY, 54-55; psychiat resident, Springfield State Hosp, Sykesville, Md, 55-58, chief serv, Men's Group, 58-60. *Concurrent Pos:* Attend staff physician, Ohio State Univ Hosps, 60-85, coordr preclin educ, 66-85, premed educ, 73-85, asst prof, Sch Soc Work, 64-67, adv, Grad Sch, 65-85, asst prof phys med, Univ, 66-67; consult, Vet Admin Hosp, Chillicothe, Ohio, 61-85, Vet Admin Ment Hyg Clin, Columbus, 65-76 & Athens Ment Health Ctr, 79-85; dipl mem psychiat Pan-Am Med Asn, 65-75. *Mem:* Fel Am Psychiat Asn; Soc Neurosci; NY Acad Sci; Int Col Neuropsychopharmacol. *Res:* Bridging the gaps between neuro-sciences, human behavior and patient oriented therapeutic research and between behavioral sciences, biological sciences and educational technology and research. *Mailing Add:* 4829 Sherry Lane Ft Myers FL 33908-2025

KNOPPERS, ANTONIE THEODOOR, PHARMACOLOGY. *Current Pos:* RETIRED. *Personal Data:* b Kapelle, Neth, Feb 27, 15; nat US; m 39; c 4. *Educ:* Univ Amsterdam, MD, 39; Univ Leyden, PharD, 41. *Hon Degrees:* DSc, Worcester Polytech Inst, 65. *Prof Exp:* First asst, Pharmacol Inst, Univ Amsterdam, 40-43; dir pharmacol, Amsterdamsche Chininefabriek, 43-49; mem managing bd combination Amsterdamsche, Bandoengsche en Nederlandsche Kininefabrieken, 50-52; mgr med serv, Merck-NAm, Inc, 52-53, dir med serv, Merck Sharp & Dohme Int Div, 53-55, dir sci activities, 55, vpres & gen mgr, 55-57, pres, 57-67, from sr vpres to pres, Merck & Co, 67-74, vchmn, 74-75. *Concurrent Pos:* Mem, Malaria Comn Neth, 51-53; mem, Coun Foreign Rels; dir, Centucor Inc; mem bd dirs, Neth-Am Found; vchmn, Salk Inst. *Mem:* Fel NY Acad Sci. *Res:* Physiology and pharmacology of the regulation of the body temperature; chemotherapy of malaria, especially chemoresistance; cardiovascular pharmacology. *Mailing Add:* 7 Oxbow Lane Summit NJ 07901

KNORR, DIETRICH W, food technology, for more information see previous edition

KNORR, GEORGE E, PLASMA PHYSICS. *Current Pos:* assoc prof physics & astron, 67-74, PROF PHYSICS, UNIV IOWA, 74- *Personal Data:* b Munich, Ger, Jan 29, 29; m 60, Christiane Bliersbach; c 4. *Educ:* Munich Tech Univ, Vordiplom, 51, dipl, 54; Univ Munich, PhD(physics), 63. *Prof Exp:* Physicist, Philips Corp, C H F Mueller AG, 55-58; res asst, Max Planck Inst Physics, 58-65; res fel plasma physics, Princeton Univ, 63-64; res assoc, Inst Plasma Physics, Garching, Ger, 65-66; asst prof & res assoc physics, Univ Calif, Los Angeles, 66-67. *Mem:* Am Phys Soc. *Res:* Radiation from plasmas; confinement and instabilities of plasmas; wave propagation, non-linear effects, numerical methods and computer simulation of plasmas; turbulence in fluids. *Mailing Add:* 330 Kimball Rd Iowa City IA 52242. *Fax:* 319-335-1753; *E-Mail:* knorr@iowa.physics.uiowa.edy

KNORR, PHILIP NOEL, FOREST ECONOMICS, RESOURCE MANAGEMENT. *Current Pos:* assoc prof forestry, 59-66, PROF FORESTRY, UNIV ARIZ, 66-; RES SCIENTIST, AGR RES STA, 76- *Personal Data:* b Mitchell, Nebr, Apr 9, 16; m 64. *Educ:* Univ Calif, BS, 38; Duke Univ, MF, 40; Univ Minn, PhD(forest econ), 63. *Honors & Awards:* Ford-Bartlett Award, Am Soc Photogram, 66. *Prof Exp:* Timber supvr & mapper, US Forest Serv, 38-39, jr forester, Southern Forest Exp Sta, New Orleans, 41; asst res forester, Weyerhaeuser Co, 46-48; asst prof forest mgt, Ore State Univ, 48-51; from asst to instr forest mgt, Univ Minn, 54-59. *Mem:* Fel AAAS; Soc Am Foresters; Am Econ Asn; Am Agr Econ Asn; Am Soc Photogram; Sigma Xi. *Res:* Decision making in forest management; remote sensing, including photo-interpretation; decision making in renewable resources policy. *Mailing Add:* 1333 E Indian Wells Rd Tucson AZ 85718-1184

KNORR, THOMAS GEORGE, SOLID STATE PHYSICS. *Current Pos:* assoc prof, 65-77, PROF PHYSICS, WHEELING COL, 77- *Personal Data:* b Buffalo, NY, Apr 14, 32; m 56; c 5. *Educ:* Canisius Col, BS, 53; Case Inst Technol, MS, 55, PhD(physics), 58; Univ Detroit, MA, 78. *Prof Exp:* Asst, Case Inst Technol, 53-58; from instr to asst prof physics, Univ Dayton, 58-60; sr physicist, Battelle Mem Inst, 60-65. *Mem:* Am Phys Soc; Am Inst Physics; Am Asn Physics Teachers. *Res:* Thin films; defect properties and structure; radiation damage; linguistics; surface structures. *Mailing Add:* 18 Bae Mar Pl Wheeling WV 26003

KNOSPE, WILLIAM H, HEMATOLOGY. *Current Pos:* PROF MED, RUSH MED COL, 74- *Personal Data:* b Oak Park, Ill, May 26, 29; m 54; c 3. *Educ:* Univ Ill, Urbana, AB, 51, BS, 52; Univ Ill Med Ctr, MD, 54; Univ Rochester, MS, 62. *Prof Exp:* Chief med serv, US Army Hosp, Berlin, Ger, 58-61; attend physician, Walter Reed Gen Hosp, Washington, DC, 63-64, asst chief hemat serv, 64-66; assoc prof med, Univ Ill Col Med, 69-72; assoc dir hemat sect & chief radio hemat lab, Presby-St Luke's Hosp, 67-74, dir clin hemat sect, 74-82, elodia kehn prog & dir hemat, Rush Presby St Luke's Med Ctr, 86-93. *Concurrent Pos:* Investr radiation biol, Walter Reed Army Inst Res, Washington, DC, 62-64 & investr hemat, 64-66; asst prof med, Col Med, Univ Ill, 67-69 & assoc prof med, Rush Med Col, 71-74; attend staff & attend physician, Presby-St Luke's Hosp, 67-; prin investr, Southeastern Cancer Study Group, 69-80 & Polycythemia Vera Study Group, 78-; vis prof med, Dept Hematol, Univ Basel, Switz, 80-81, Free Univ Berlin, WGer, 81, Nat Taiwan Univ Sch Med, Taipei, Taiwan, 85 & McGill Cancer Ctr, McGill Univ, Montreal, 87; vis prof med, McGill Cancer Ctr, McGill Univ, Montreal, 87; vis prof, Cancer Ctr, Univ NMex, 92-93. *Mem:* Fel Am Col Physicians; Am Soc Hemat; Am Fedn Clin Res; Radiation Res Soc; Sigma Xi; Int Soc Exp Hemat. *Res:* Radiation effects upon bone marrow; role of sinusoidal microcirculation in aplastic anemias; regulation of hematopoietic stem cells; clinical investigation of leukemia and lymphomas; role of hematopoietic stroma in hematopoieisis. *Mailing Add:* 310 Big Horn Ridge Dr Albuquerque NM 87122

KNOTEK, MICHAEL LOUIS, SOLID STATE PHYSICS, SURFACE PHYSICS. *Current Pos:* SR SCI DIR, PAC NORTHWEST LABS, 89-, DIR, MOLECULAR SCI RES CTR & ENVIRON & MOLECULAR SCI LAB, 89- *Personal Data:* b Norfolk, Nebr, Nov 23, 43; m 69; c 3. *Educ:* Iowa State Univ, BS, 66; Univ Calif, Riverside, MS, 69, PhD(physics), 72. *Honors & Awards:* Distinguished Assoc Award, Dept Energy, 93. *Prof Exp:* Physicist amorphous semiconductors, Naval Weapons Ctr, 70-72; mem tech staff superionic conductors & surface physics, Sandia Lab, 73-85, supvr, Surface Physics Div, 79-85; chmn, Nat Synchrotron Light Source, Brookhaven Nat Lab, 85-89. *Concurrent Pos:* Consult, Bourns Inc, 70. *Mem:* Am Vacuum Soc; Sigma Xi; Am Phys Soc; Am Chem Soc; Coun Chem Res. *Res:* Transport properties of amorphous and disordered semiconductors; transport properties of superionic conductors, especially related to surface and interface properties; surface studies of photocatalytic properties of rutile and related materials; surface science; electron and photon stimulated desorption. *Mailing Add:* KA-48 Battelle Pacific NW Labs Richland WA 99352

KNOTH, WALTER HENRY, JR, HETEROPOLYANIONS, BORON HYDRIDES. *Current Pos:* RETIRED. *Personal Data:* b New York, NY, Feb 18, 30; m 53; c 2. *Educ:* Syracuse Univ, BS, 50; Pa State Univ, PhD(chem), 54. *Prof Exp:* Res chemist, E I du Pont de Nemours & Co, Inc, 53-85. *Mem:* Sigma Xi. *Res:* Organo-silicon and organoboron chemistry; boron hydrides; nitrogen complexes; transition metal chemistry. *Mailing Add:* PO Box 6 Mendenhall PA 19357

KNOTT, DONALD MACMILLAN, INDUSTRIAL ORGANIC CHEMISTRY. *Current Pos:* PRES, KNOTT ASSOCS, 88- *Personal Data:* b Boston, Mass, Oct 20, 19; m 43; c 4. *Educ:* Mass Inst Technol, SB, 41, PhD(org Chem), 47. *Prof Exp:* With Gen Elec Co, 47-54; with Chas Pfizer & Co, 54-63, chem consult, 63-68; pres, Chemconsul Inc, 68-88. *Mem:* Am Chem Soc; Com Develop Asn; Tech Asn Pulp & Paper Indust. *Res:* Commercial chemical development; pulp and paper technology; wood science and technology. *Mailing Add:* 9790 NE Denton Newport OR 97365-9532

KNOTT, DOUGLAS RONALD, CYTOLOGY. *Current Pos:* prof & head dept, Univ Sask, 65-75, prof, 75-88, assoc dean res, 88-93, EMER PROF CROP SCI, UNIV SASK, 93- *Personal Data:* b New Westminster, BC, Nov 10, 27; m 50, Joan M Hollinshead; c Holly A, Heather, Ronald & Douglas (deceased). *Educ:* Univ BC, BSA, 48; Univ Wis, MS, 49, PhD, 52. *Prof Exp:* From asst prof to assoc prof, 52-65. *Concurrent Pos:* Res Adv, Zambia-Can Wheat Proj, 86-91. *Mem:* Fel Am Soc Agron; Genetics Soc Can; fel Agr Inst Can; Can Soc Agron; Crop Sci Soc Am; Sigma Xi. *Res:* Genetics and cytogenetics of rust resistance in wheat; transfer of resistance to wheat from its relatives; wheat breeding. *Mailing Add:* Dept Crop Sci & Plant Ecol Univ Sask Saskatoon SK S7N 5A8 Can. Fax: 306-966-5015

KNOTT, FRED NELSON, ANIMAL NUTRITION. *Current Pos:* RETIRED. *Personal Data:* b NC, July 18, 33; m 55; c 4. *Educ:* NC State Col, BS, 55; NC State Univ, MS, 62; Va Polytech Inst, PhD(animal nutrit), 68. *Prof Exp:* Res asst, NC State Univ, 55-56, agr exten agent, 56-67, exten dairy specialist, 57-65, exten dairy specialist dairy husb, 67-92, from assoc prof to prof, 72-92, specialist in chg exten dairy husb, 82. *Concurrent Pos:* Mem, Exten Serv Team, VI, 78. *Mem:* Am Dairy Sci Asn; Sigma Xi. *Res:* Utilization of urea by dairy cattle as a supplement to protein nutrition. *Mailing Add:* 2132 US Hwy 158 Oxford NC 27565

KNOTT, GARY DON, MATHEMATICAL & STATISTICAL MODELING SOFTWARE. *Current Pos:* CHIEF EXEC OFFICER, CIVILIZED SOFTWARE INC, 85- *Personal Data:* b Colfax, Wash, Aug 5, 40. *Educ:* Am Univ, BA, 65; Calif Inst Technol, MS, 69; Stanford Univ, PhD(comput sci), 75. *Prof Exp:* Res comput scientist, NIH, 61-85. *Res:* Mathematical and statistical modeling software. *Mailing Add:* 3310 Pendleton Dr Silver Spring MD 20902. *E-Mail:* knott@civilized.com

KNOTT, JOHN RUSSELL, neurophysiology, for more information see previous edition

KNOUS, TED R, FUNGAL PHYSIOLOGY & TOXINS, PLANT TISSUE CULTURE. *Current Pos:* asst dean res, Res Promo Serv, 89-93, ASSOC DEAN RES & GRAD STUDIES, UNIV WIS-STOUT, 93- *Personal Data:* b Ely, Nev, May 11, 49; m 69; c Taryn & Kristae. *Educ:* Univ Nev, BS, 72, MS, 74; Univ Minn, PhD(plant path), 79. *Prof Exp:* Teaching fel plant path, Univ Minn, 79; asst prof dis physiol, Dept Plant Sci, Univ Nev, 79-88; dir, Grants & Sponsored Progs, Winona State Univ, 88-89. *Concurrent Pos:* Consult, Sierra Biotechnol, 82-; mem, Admin Comt, Nat Plant Pest Surv & Detection Prog, 83-88 & Dis & Pathogen Physiol Comt, Am Phytopath Soc, 84-87; assoc ed, Plant Dis, Am Phytopath Soc, 84-87; mem, Nat Coun Univ Res Admin. *Mem:* Am Phytopath Soc; Am Soc Plant Physiologists; AAAS; Sigma Xi. *Res:* Plant disease physiology. *Mailing Add:* Res Promo Serv 410 Bowman Hall Univ Wis-Stout Menomonie WI 54751-0790. Fax: 715-232-1749; *E-Mail:* tknoys@uwstout.edu

KNOWLES, AILEEN FOUNG, BIOCHEMISTRY. *Current Pos:* ASSOC PROF BIOL, NORTHEASTERN UNIV, 87- *Personal Data:* b China, Aug 9, 42; US citizen; m 69; c 2. *Educ:* Nat Taiwan Univ, BS, 63; Univ Calif, Riverside, PhD(biochem), 68. *Prof Exp:* Fel biochem, Cornell Univ, 68-70, res assoc, 72-77; scientist, Pub Health Res Inst, New York, 70-72; from res biochemist to assoc prof, Biochem, Cancer Ctr, Univ Calif, 77-87. *Mem:* Am Soc Biochem & Molecular Biol. *Res:* Biophysics and biochemsitry of membrane-bound enzymes; ATP hydrolyzing enzymes of tumor membranes. *Mailing Add:* PO Box 22129 San Diego CA 92192

KNOWLES, BARBARA B, GENETICS, CELL BIOLOGY. *Current Pos:* ASSOC DIR, DIR RES & SR STAFF SCIENTIST, JACKSON LAB, BAR HARBOR, MAINE. *Personal Data:* b New York, NY, Feb 27, 37; div; c Amanda (Gay-Lord) & Jared Appleten. *Educ:* Middlebury Col, AB, 58, Ariz State Univ, MS, 63, PhD(dev biol), 65. *Prof Exp:* Res asst drosophila genetics, Ariz State Univ, 62-65; res fel genetics, Univ Calif, Berkeley, 65-66; from res asst to res assoc, Univ Pa, 67-76, assoc prof, 77-83, prof, Wistar Inst Anat & Biol, 83-, Wistar prof path, Lab Med & Microbiol, 84- *Concurrent Pos:* Career develop award, Nat Inst Allergy & Infectious Dis, 75; mem, Univ Pa Immunol Grad Group, 77-; consult, Can Info Dissemination Serv, Am Can Soc; mem, Can Res Manpower Review Bd, 80-83; vis sr scientist, Cold Spring Harbor Lab, 87-88; mem, Grad Fac, Univ Maine; bd mem, Maine Math & Sci Alliance. *Mem:* Am Soc Human Genetics; Genetics Soc Am; Am Soc Immunol; Humane Genome Org. *Res:* Immunogenetics; genetic control of human cell surface molecules; murine immune response genes to tumor specific antigens; cell surface molecules of preimplantation stage mouse embryos; HBV and hepatocellular carcinoma; molecular control of preimplantation embryogenesis, translational control of material MRNAS and definition of new genes and molecules that control the activation of the embryonic genome; development biology. *Mailing Add:* Jackson Lab 600 Main St Bar Harbor ME 04609. *Fax:* 207-288-6071; *E-Mail:* bbk@jax.org

KNOWLES, CECIL MARTIN, ORGANIC CHEMISTRY. *Current Pos:* RETIRED. *Personal Data:* b Newton, Miss, Jan 6, 18; m 48; c 2. *Educ:* Miss Col, BA, 39; Univ Tex, MA, 41, PhD(org chem), 43. *Prof Exp:* Instr chem, Univ Tex, 39-42; chemist, GAF Corp, NY, 43-51, mgr tech serv & com develop, 51-67; vpres & dir res, Trylon Chem, Inc, 68-72; vpres & tech dir, chem specialties groups, Emery Indust, Inc, 72-83. *Res:* Surface active agents; organic chemical specialties. *Mailing Add:* 1204 Edwards Rd Greenville SC 29615

KNOWLES, CHARLES ERNEST, PHYSICAL OCEANOGRAPHY. *Current Pos:* asst prof, 70-76, ASSOC PROF PHYS OCEANOG, NC STATE UNIV, 76- *Personal Data:* b Ogden, Utah, Mar 7, 37; m 76; c 6. *Educ:* Univ Utah, BS, 60; Tex A&M Univ, MS, 67, PhD(phys oceanog), 70. *Prof Exp:* Res scientist phys oceanog, Tex A&M Univ, 69-70. *Concurrent Pos:* Consult, NUC Corp, 75. *Mem:* Am Geophys Union. *Res:* Wind wave generation and dissipation in deep and finite depth water; wave current interaction; non-ideal wind wave generation and parametergation of directional wave spectrum; tributary esturarine circulation dynamics. *Mailing Add:* 1222 Currituck Dr Raleigh NC 27609

KNOWLES, CHARLES OTIS, ENTOMOLOGY, PESTICIDE TOXICOLOGY. *Current Pos:* From asst prof to prof, 65-74, PROF ENTOM, UNIV MO, COLUMBIA, 74- *Personal Data:* b Tallassee, Ala, Feb 1, 38; m 59, Marie Wells; c Kathy K (Dowd), Lauri K (Hamilton) & Jeffrey C. *Educ:* Auburn Univ, BS, 60, MS, 62; Univ Wis, PhD(entom), 65. *Concurrent Pos:* Vis sr scientist, Commonwealth Sci & Indust Res Orgn, Long Pocket Labs, Brisbane, Australia, 72. *Mem:* Entom Soc Am; Am Chem Soc. *Res:* Toxicology of insecticides; comparative insect and mite biochemistry; mode of action and metabolism of acaricides; environmental impact of pesticides. *Mailing Add:* Dept Entom 1-87 Agr Bldg Univ Mo Columbia MO 65211. Fax: 573-882-1469; *E-Mail:* agcknowl@muccmail.missouri.edu

KNOWLES, DANIEL M, HEMATOPATHOLOGY, IMMUNOPATHOLOGY. *Current Pos:* DAVID D THOMPSON PROF PATH, CORNELL UNIV, 94-; CHMN PATH, NY HOSP-CORNELL MED CTR, 94- *Personal Data:* b Brooklyn, NY, Aug 21, 47; m 80, Marian Limberg; c Tyler. *Educ:* Univ Bridgeport, BA, 69; Univ Chicago, MD, 73. *Honors & Awards:* Arthur Purdy Stout Prize, 87. *Prof Exp:* USPHS fel, 76-77; asst prof path, Col Physicians & Surgeons, Columbia Univ, New York, 78-81, assoc prof, 82-83, prof, 87-93; assoc prof path, Sch Med, NY Univ, 83-87. *Concurrent Pos:* Asst attend pathologist, Presby Hosp, 78-81, assoc atten pathologist, 82-83; dir, Lymphocyte Marker Lab, Columbia Presby Med Ctr, 81-83, Div Surg Path, 87-93, attend pathologist, 87-93; dir, Immunopath Lab, NY Univ Med Ctr, 83-87; assoc atten pathologist, Univ Hosp, 83-87; pathologist in chief, NY Hosp, 94-; adj prof path, Col Physicians & Surgeons, Columbia Univ, New York, 95-96. *Mem:* Am Asn Pathologists; Am Soc Clin Pathologists; Asn Res Vision & Opthal. *Res:* Correlative, clinical, morphologic, immunologic and molecular analysis of lymphoproliferative disorders to gain understanding of the clinical and biological aspects of lymphomagenesis; molecular biological analysis of the kaposis sarcoma associated herpesvirus. *Mailing Add:* Cornell Univ Med Col 1300 York Ave New York NY 10021

KNOWLES, DAVID M, GEOLOGY. *Current Pos:* ASSOC PROF GEOL, LAKE SUPERIOR STATE COL, 69- *Personal Data:* b Saginaw, Mich, July 22, 27; m 45; c 2. *Educ:* Mich Technol Univ, BS, 54, MS, 55; Columbia Univ, PhD(geol), 67. *Prof Exp:* Chief geologist, Can Javelin Ltd, 54-69. *Mem:* Geol Soc Am; Geol Asn Can; Can Inst Mining & Metall; Sigma Xi. *Res:* Structural geology of Labrador Trough formations near Wabush Lake; superposed folds, Hudsonian events and Grenville Province events. *Mailing Add:* 1212 Davitt St Sault Ste Marie MI 49783-2726

KNOWLES, FRANCIS CHARLES, BIOPHYSICAL CHEMISTRY. *Current Pos:* SCIENTIST BIOCHEM, SCRIPPS INST OCEANOG, 77- *Personal Data:* b Akron, Ohio, Sept 11, 41; m 69; c 2. *Educ:* Univ Southern Calif, BA, 63; Univ Calif, Riverside, PhD(biochem), 68. *Prof Exp:* Lectr physiol & biochem, Mt Sinai Sch Med, New York, 68-72; res fel biochem, Cornell Univ, 72-77. *Mem:* Am Soc Plant Physiol; Am Chem Soc; Scand Soc Plant Physiol. *Res:* Biophysical chemistry; evolution of cooperative mechanisms of dioxygen transport proteins; arsenic biochemistry and mechanisms of arsenic toxicity; regulation of photosynthetic carbon dioxide fixation; pathways of photorespiration. *Mailing Add:* Phys Sci Dept 2022 Nicholls State Univ Thibodaux LA 70310

KNOWLES, HAROLD LORAINE, PHYSICS. *Current Pos:* from instr to prof physics, Univ Fla, 31-54, prof phys sci, 54-72, head dept, 54-67, EMER PROF PHYS SCI, UNIV FLA, 72- *Personal Data:* b Chicago, Ill, Aug 21, 05; wid; c Carolyn (Eubank). *Educ:* Phillips Univ, BA, 26; Univ Kans, PhD(physics), 31. *Prof Exp:* Asst instr physics, Univ Kans, 27-31. *Concurrent Pos:* Supvr sig corps contract proj, War Res Lab, Fla Eng & Indust Exp Sta, 44-45. *Mem:* Am Phys Soc; Am Asn Physics Teachers. *Res:* Dielectric constant measurements; direction finder for atmospherics; physical sciences in general education. *Mailing Add:* 2805 NW 83rd St Apt C-104 Gainesville FL 32606

KNOWLES, HARROLD B, DESIGN RADIATION SHIELDING, ACCELERATOR HEALTH PHYSICS. *Current Pos:* PHYSICS CONSULT, 90- *Personal Data:* b Berkeley, Calif, July 28, 25; m 49, Geraldine Lore; c William B & Laura E. *Educ:* Univ Calif, Berkeley, AB, 47, MA, 51, PhD(physics), 57. *Prof Exp:* Res asst oceanog, Univ Wash, 48-50; res asst physics, Univ Calif, Berkeley, 51-57; sr exp physicist, Lawrence Radiation Lab, Univ Calif, Livermore, 57-61; res assoc, Yale Univ, 61-64; from assoc prof to prof physics, Wash State Univ, 64-80; prin staff mem, BDM Corp, 80-83; mem tech staff VI, Rocketdyne, 84-90. *Concurrent Pos:* Vis scientist, Los Alamos Sci Lab, 73-74, vis staff mem, 74-80; consult, Lawrence Berkeley Lab, 78 & 92-93; BDM Corp, 83-84; Los Alamos Sci Lab, 83-85; Rensselaer Polytech Inst, 83-85, Dept Energy, 92, Univ Calif Los Angeles, 92, Mass Gen Hosp, 95, Johns Hopkins Univ, 96-97; res assoc, Air Force Weapon Lab, 80. *Mem:* Am Phys Soc; Health Phys Soc. *Res:* Nuclear physics; accelerator physics; radiation protection; radiological physics; charged particle optics; dosimetry. *Mailing Add:* 4030 Hillcrest Rd El Sobrante CA 94803. *Fax:* 510-758-5449; *E-Mail:* hbknowls@ix.netcom.com

KNOWLES, JAMES KENYON, APPLIED MATHEMATICS & MECHANICS. *Current Pos:* from asst prof to W M R Kenan prof, 58-96, EMER PROF APPL MECH, CALIF INST TECHNOL, 96- *Personal Data:* b Cleveland, Ohio, Apr 14, 31; m 52, Jacqueline Debolt; c John, Jeffrey & James. *Educ:* Mass Inst Technol, SB, 52, PhD(math), 57. *Hon Degrees:* DSc, Nat Univ Ireland, 85. *Honors & Awards:* Eringen Medal, Soc Eng Sci. *Prof Exp:* Instr math, Mass Inst Technol, 57-58. *Mem:* Fel Am Soc Mech Engrs; fel Am Acad Mech; Soc Indust & Appl Math; fel AAAS. *Res:* Mathematical problems in continuum mechanics. *Mailing Add:* 522 N Michillinda Sierra Madre CA 91024

KNOWLES, JEREMY RANDALL, CHEMISTRY. *Current Pos:* AMORY HOUGHTON PROF CHEM & BIOCHEM, HARVARD UNIV, 79-, DEAN, FAC ARTS & SCI, 91- *Personal Data:* b Rugby, UK, Apr 28, 35; m 60; c 3. *Educ:* Magdalen Col, MA. *Hon Degrees:* Dr, Univ Edinburgh, 92. *Honors & Awards:* Charmian Medal, Royal Soc Chem, 81; Prelog Medal, 89; Alfred Bader Award, Am Chem Soc, 89, Arthur Cope Scholar Award, 89; Davy Medal, Royal Soc, 91; Repligen Award, 93; var named lectr, 78-90. *Prof Exp:* Res assoc, Calif Inst Technol, 61-62; fel & tutor, Wadham Col, Oxford, 62-74; lectr chem, Univ Oxford, 66-74. *Concurrent Pos:* Vis prof, Yale Univ, 69, 71; Sloan vis prof, Harvard Univ, 73; Newton-Abraham vis prof, Oxford Univ, 83-84. *Mem:* Foreign assoc Nat Acad Sci; fel Am Acad Arts & Sci; Am Philos Soc; fel Royal Soc Chem. *Res:* Bioorganic chemistry. *Mailing Add:* Dept Chem Harvard Univ 12 Oxford St Cambridge MA 02138. *Fax:* 617-495-8208; *E-Mail:* jeremy_knowles@harvard.edu

KNOWLES, JOHN APPLETON, III, DRUG METABOLISM. *Current Pos:* res scientist, 68-78, MGR DRUG KINETICS SECT, WYETH LABS, AM HOME PROD CORP, 78- *Personal Data:* b Portchester, NY, Nov 20, 35; m 84; c 2. *Educ:* Middlebury Col, AB, 58; Ariz State Univ, PhD(anal chem), 66. *Prof Exp:* Res chemist, Orchem Dept, Chambers Works, E I du Pont de Nemours & Co, 66-68. *Mem:* AAAS; Am Chem Soc. *Res:* Analysis of drugs and their metabolites. *Mailing Add:* 402 Herritage Dr Harleysville PA 19438-3958

KNOWLES, JOHN WARWICK, NUCLEAR PHYSICS. *Current Pos:* RETIRED. *Personal Data:* b Toronto, Ont, Dec 9, 20; m 43; c 5. *Educ:* Univ Toronto, BA, 43; McGill Univ, PhD(physics), 47. *Prof Exp:* Res physicist nuclear physics, Nat Res Coun, 43-45; from asst res officer to assoc res officer gen physics, Atomic Energy Can Ltd, 47-58, sr res officer nuclear physics, 58-85. *Mem:* Fel Am Phys Soc; Can Asn Physicists. *Res:* Low energy nuclear physics; crystal diffraction of neutron capture x-rays; precision measurements of reference x-rays; photo fission and related photo nuclear reactions. *Mailing Add:* 2 Alexander Pl Box 736 Deep River ON K0J 1P0 Can

KNOWLES, RICHARD JAMES ROBERT, BIOPHYSICS. *Current Pos:* SR MED PHYSICIST, NY HOSP-CORNELL MED CTR, 82- *Personal Data:* b McPherson, Kans, Aug 2, 43; m 70, Stephanie R Closter; c Guenevere R. *Educ:* St Louis Univ, HBS, 65; Cornell Univ, MS, 69; Polytechnic Univ, PhD(physics), 79. *Prof Exp:* Chief med physicist, Long Island Col Hosp, 77-81; dir, Radiation Physics Lab, Downstate Med Ctr, 81-82. *Concurrent Pos:* Clin asst prof radiol, Col Med, State Univ NY Downstate Med Ctr, 80-82; adj asst prof physics, Dept Natural Sci, York Col, City Univ NY, 82; asst prof, 82-89, ASSOC PROF PHYSICS IN RADIOL, CORNELL UNIV MED COL, 89- *Mem:* Am Phys Soc; Soc Nuclear Med; Health Physics Soc; Am Asn Physicists Med; Soc Magnetic Resonance Med; Soc Photo-Optical Instrumentation Engrs. *Res:* Medical image formation including MRI, CT, radioisotopes, and ultrasound; computerized image processing and analysis; data processing including artificial intelligence; data communications including PACS. *Mailing Add:* Dept Radiol NY Hosp Cornell Med Ctr 525 E 68th St New York NY 10021

KNOWLES, RICHARD N, ORGANIC CHEMISTRY, MANUFACTURING. *Current Pos:* Res chemist, E I Dupont De Nemours & Co, 60-73, res supvr, 73, develop supvr, Indust Chem Dept, 73-75; tech supt, 75, prod supt, 76-77, mfg mgr, 78-80, asst plant mgr, 80-83, Niagara, 83-87, PLANT MGR, E I DU PONT DE NEMOURS & CO, INC, BELLE, WVA, 87- *Personal Data:* b Wilmington, Del, Aug 8, 35; m 88, Claire E Frerichs; c Elizabeth, Dorothy, Cynthia & Christine (Stoelting). *Educ:* Oberlin Col, BA, 57; Univ Rochester, PhD(chem), 60. *Honors & Awards:* Crystal Award, DuPont Agr Prods, 91. *Concurrent Pos:* Bd mem, Nat Inst Chem Studies & WVa Manufacturer's Asn. *Mem:* Am Chem Soc; Sierra Club; Nat Audubon Soc; Nature Conserv. *Res:* Herbicides, fungicides, insecticides, pharmaceutical agents, azo catalysts and flame retardants; colloidal silica; production of organic and inorganic chemicals in volumes ranging from lab scale to bulk commodities; granted 40 US patents. *Mailing Add:* 1303 Delaware Ave Apt 1312 Wilmington WV 19806

KNOWLES, ROGER, MICROBIOLOGY. *Current Pos:* From asst prof to prof, 57-71, PROF MICROBIOL, MACDONALD COL, MCGILL UNIV, 71- *Personal Data:* b Halifax, Eng, July 7, 29; m 63; c 2. *Educ:* Univ Birmingham, BSc, 53; Univ London, PhD, 57. *Hon Degrees:* DSc, Univ London, 86. *Honors & Awards:* Can Soc Microbiol Award, 82. *Concurrent Pos:* Dept chmn, Macdonald Col, McGill Univ, 70-74 & 79-87. *Mem:* Soil Sci Soc Am; Am Soc Microbiol; Can Soc Microbiol; fel Royal Soc Can. *Res:* Soil and aquatic microbiology; forest soils; nitrogen fixation; denitrification; nitrification; methane metabolism. *Mailing Add:* Dept Natural Resource Sci Macdonald Campus McGill Univ 21111 Lakeshore Rd Ste Anne de Bellevue Quebec PQ H9X 3V9 Can

KNOWLES, STEPHEN H, IONOSPHERIC PHYSICS, RADIO ASTRONOMY. *Current Pos:* Astronr, US Naval Observ, 61, ASTRONOMER, US NAVAL RES LAB, 61- *Personal Data:* b New York, NY, Feb 28, 40; m 65; c 2. *Educ:* Amherst Col, BA, 61; Yale Univ, PhD(astron), 68. *Mem:* AAAS; Int Union Radio Sci; Am Astron Soc; Int Astron Union; Am Geophys Union. *Res:* Radar astronomy; celestial mechanics; radio spectroscopy; very long baseline interferometry; ionospheric physics. *Mailing Add:* 9455 Deramus Farm Ct Vienna VA 22182

KNOWLTON, DAVID A, CHEMISTRY. *Current Pos:* MGR RES & DEVELOP, QUIGLEY CO, INC, 84- *Personal Data:* b Washington, DC, June 20, 38; m 83; c 2. *Educ:* Capital Univ, BS, 61; Ohio State Univ, MSc, 67, PhD(biochem), 69. *Prof Exp:* Instr, Ohio State Univ, 70-71, asst prof, 71-73; researcher, Battelle Mem Inst, 73-76; res chemist, Gunning Refractories Inv, 77-81, dir new prof develop, 82-83. *Concurrent Pos:* Consult, Cent Labs, State Ohio & Consolidated Biomed Labs, 71-73. *Mem:* Sigma Xi; Am Chem Soc; Am Ceramic Soc. *Res:* Development of carbon-bonded refractory, especially products for use in the manufacture of iron and steel. *Mailing Add:* BMI Refractories Inc PO Box 267 South Webster OH 45682-0267

KNOWLTON, FLOYD M(ARION), CHEMICAL ENGINEERING. *Current Pos:* RETIRED. *Personal Data:* b Milan, Ind, Jan 18, 18; m 41; c 3. *Educ:* Purdue Univ, 39. *Prof Exp:* From process operator to res chemist, Joseph E Seagram & Sons, Inc, 39-42; supvr, Chem Control Div, Pa Ord Works, 42-43; develop engr, Naugatuck Chem Div, US Rubber Co, 43-45; develop engr, Bristol Labs Div, Bristol-Myers Co, 45-50, dept head, Chem Develop Pilot Plant, 50-58, mgr chem develop, 58-67, dir develop, 67-75, dir develop spec projs, Indust Div, 75-81. *Mem:* Am Chem Soc; Am Inst Chem Engrs. *Res:* Industrial fermentations; recovery processes; organic syntheses. *Mailing Add:* 2857 Ptarmigan Dr Walnut Creek CA 94595

KNOWLTON, FREDERICK FRANK, WILDLIFE RESEARCH. *Current Pos:* BIOLOGIST, ANIMAL & PLANT HEALTH INSPECTION SERV, USDA, DENVER WILDLIFE RES CTR. *Personal Data:* b Springville, NY, Nov 24, 34; c 4. *Educ:* Cornell Univ, BS, 57; Mont Stat Col, MS, 59; Purdue Univ, PhD(ecol, physiol), 64. *Prof Exp:* Proj biologist, Mont Fish & Game Dept, 59; lectr biol, Univ Mo, Kansas City, 64; Wildlife biologist, US Fish & Wildlife Serv, 64- *Concurrent Pos:* Vis assoc prof, Cornell Univ, 71; assoc prof wildlife sci, Utah State Univ, 72- *Mem:* Wildlife Soc; Am Soc Mammal; Wildlife Dis Asn; Nat Audubon Soc. *Res:* Dynamics and mechanisms of natural vertebrate populations; especially mammalian physiology and phenomenon of predation; ungulates; the larger carnivores. *Mailing Add:* 4420 W North Cornish UT 84308

KNOWLTON, GREGORY DEAN, CHEMISTRY OF PROPELLANTS, PYROTECHNICS & EXPLOSIVES. *Current Pos:* sr chemist & prin investr, 80-83, MGR PYROTECHNICS & EXPLOSIVES, TALLY DEFENSE SYSTS, 94. *Personal Data:* b Santa Barbara, Calif, Jan 6, 46; m 83, Wlatka Peric; c Ryan. *Educ:* San Jose State Univ, BS, 74, MS, 76; Ariz State Univ, PhD(chem), 82. *Prof Exp:* Res geochemist, Lawrence Livermore Nat Lab, 75 & 76; res assoc, Ariz State Univ, 76-79; anal lab mgr, Commerce Metal Refiners, 79-80. *Concurrent Pos:* Instr chem, Phoenix Col, 78-80. *Mem:* Am Chem Soc; fel Am Inst Chemists; Int Pyrotechnics Soc; Sigma Xi; Am Defense Preparedness Asn; Soc Automotive Engrs. *Res:* Pyrolysis of complex salts and organometallics; adsorption and desorption of gases and liquids inzeolites; determination of light elements in refractory materials; inorganic azide research; development, analysis and testing of propellants, pyrotechnics and explosives. *Mailing Add:* 615 W Summit Circle Chandler AZ 85224. *Fax:* 602-898-2402; *E-Mail:* gknowlton@talleyds.com

KNOWLTON, ROBERT CHARLES, CHEMICAL ENGINEERING. *Current Pos:* CONSULT, 88- *Personal Data:* b Gardner, Mass, Aug 3, 29; m 52, Edith Lind; c Alison. *Educ:* Northeastern Univ, BS, 52; Newark Col Eng, MS, 58. *Prof Exp:* Appl Engr, Worthington Corp, 52-55; serv engr, Eng Dept, E I du Pont de Nemours & Co, Inc, 55-58, res engr, Textile Fibers Dept, 58-65, sr res engr, 65-75, sr res assoc, 75-87. *Mem:* Am Inst Chem Engrs; Textured Yarn Asn Am. *Res:* Synthetic fibers; spinning, drawing, and processing of polyester fibers; texturing of continuous filament yarns. *Mailing Add:* 1940 Hampton Rd Kinston NC 28504

KNOWLTON, ROBERT EARLE, INVERTEBRATE ZOOLOGY, MARINE BIOLOGY. *Current Pos:* asst prof, 72-75, asst dean, 80-85, ASSOC PROF BIOL, GEORGE WASHINGTON UNIV, 75- *Personal Data:* b Summit, NJ, Oct 14, 39; m 63, Dorothy Smith; c Julia & Kathryn. *Educ:* Bowdoin Col, AB, 60; Univ NC, Chapel Hill, PhD(zool), 70. *Prof Exp:* Asst zool, Univ NC, Chapel Hill, 60-64; res asst fisheries, Inst Marine Sci, 64-65; from instr to asst prof biol, Bowdoin Col, 65-72. *Concurrent Pos:* Teaching fel zool, Univ NC, Chapel Hill, 62-63; vis lectr biol, Univ Southern Maine, 72-80. *Mem:* AAAS; Am Inst Biol Sci; Am Soc Zool; Sigma Xi. *Res:* Autecology of decapod larvae; effects of eyestalk extirpation on snapping shrimp larvae; distribution, life history, and behavior of grass shrimp. *Mailing Add:* Dept Biol Sci George Washington Univ Washington DC 20052. *Fax:* 202-994-6100

KNOX, ARTHUR STEWART, geology, palynology; deceased, see previous edition for last biography

KNOX, BRUCE E, MATERIALS SCIENCE, SCIENCE TECHNOLOGY & SOCIETY. *Current Pos:* RETIRED. *Personal Data:* b Binghamton, NY, Aug 4, 31; m 53, Susan Marshall; c Mark A, Kathern A & John M. *Educ:* Rensselaer Polytech Inst, BS, 53; Syracuse Univ, MS, 58; Pa State Univ, PhD(fuel technol), 63. *Prof Exp:* Res asst, Syracuse Univ, 56-57; res asst shock tube chem, Pa State Univ, 57-59 & 60-62, instr geochem, 63, asst prof solid state technol, 63-67, solid state sci, 67-68 & mat sci, 68-69, assoc prof mat sci, 69-91, asst dir, Mat Res Lab, 75-91, adj assoc prof sci, technol & soc, 92- *Concurrent Pos:* Vis prof, Pohang Inst Sci & Eng, Pohang, Korea, 88. *Mem:* AAAS; fel Am Inst Chemists; Am Chem Soc; Am Soc Eng Educ; Am Phys Soc; Am Vacuum Soc; NY Acad Sci; Sigma Xi; Nat Asn Sci; Technol & Soc. *Res:* Mass spectrometry; vapor species of solid materials; laser-solid interaction; thin films; characterization of materials; chemical kinetics; trace elements in disease; materials science and engineering education; auger electron spectrometry; ion scattering spectrometry. *Mailing Add:* West Crestview Ave Boalsburg PA 16827

KNOX, BURNAL RAY, FLUVIAL GEOMORPHOLOGY, SPELEOLOGY. *Current Pos:* from asst prof to assoc prof, 65-76, PROF GEOL SCI, SE MO UNIV, 76- *Personal Data:* b Pineville, Mo, Mar 29, 31; m 55; c 3. *Educ:* Univ Ark, BS, 53, MS, 57; Univ Iowa, PhD(geol), 66. *Prof Exp:* Explor geologist, Gulf Oil Corp, 56-58; teacher high sch, Kans, 59-62. *Mem:* Geol Soc Am; Nat Asn Geol Teachers; Am Sci Affil; Sigma Xi. *Res:* Geomorphic evolution of Ozarks and Mississippi-Ohio rivers confluence area; Karst geomorphology and speleology of southeast Missouri; correlation of landforms with quaternary events, particularly climatic changes as controls of landscape evolution. *Mailing Add:* 5 Camellia Dr Cape Girardeau MO 63703

KNOX, CHARLES KENNETH, NEUROPHYSIOLOGY, ENGINEERING. *Current Pos:* Asst prof, 69-76, ASSOC PROF PHYSIOL, UNIV MINN, MINNEAPOLIS, 76- *Personal Data:* b Minneapolis, Minn, Nov 19, 38. *Educ:* Univ Minn, Minneapolis, BS, 61, MS, 62, PhD(physiol), 69. *Concurrent Pos:* NIH res fel, Nobel Inst Neurophysiol, Stockholm, 69-70; NIH res grant, 73-76 & 76-79. *Mem:* Am Physiol Soc; Soc Neurosci; NY Acad Sci. *Res:* Neural control of respiration. *Mailing Add:* 1000 Ingerson Rd St Paul MN 55126

KNOX, DAVID LALONDE, NEURO-MEDICAL OPHTHALMOLOGY, OCULAR INFLAMMATION. *Current Pos:* ASSOC PROF OPHTHAL, SCH MED, JOHNS HOPKINS UNIV, 62-, ASST DEAN ADMIS, 76- *Personal Data:* b Chicago, Ill, Sept 3, 30; m 58; c 3. *Educ:* Baylor Univ, MD, 55. *Res:* Neuro-medical ophthalmology; ocular inflammation; clinical investigations identifying etiologic factors, especially gastrointestinal food & allergies. *Mailing Add:* Dept Ophthal Johns Hopkins Univ Baltimore MD 21287-9013

KNOX, ELLIS GILBERT, NEW CROP INTRODUCTION. *Current Pos:* RETIRED. *Personal Data:* b Sterling, Ill, Mar 25, 28; m 48; c 2. *Educ:* Univ Ill, BS, 49, MS, 50; Cornell Univ, PhD(soils), 54. *Prof Exp:* From asst prof to prof soils, Ore State Univ, 54-73; pedologist, Aero Serv Corp, Bogota, Colombia, 73-75; exec officer, Soil & Land Use Technol, Inc, 75-85; soil scientist, Soil Conserv Serv, USDA, 85-96. *Concurrent Pos:* Soil scientist, Soil Conserv Serv, USDA, 62-63; consult, InterAm Inst Agr Sci, Turrialba, Costa Rica, 66; tech officer, Food & Agr Orgn UN, Turrialba, Costa Rica, 69-70. *Mem:* AAAS; Soil Sci Soc Am; Sigma Xi; Soil & Water Conserv Soc; Am Soc Agron. *Res:* Soil classification and mapping; soil survey interpretations; land resource and land use evaluation; analysis of crop production-marketing-consumption systems; biomass crops; development of crop systems. *Mailing Add:* 7011 Lincolnshire Rd Lincoln NE 68506

KNOX, ERIC, BOTANY. *Current Pos:* PROF, DEPT BOT, UNIV MICH, ANN ARBOR. *Honors & Awards:* George R Cooley Award, Am Soc Plant Taxonomists, 92. *Mailing Add:* Dept Bot Univ Mich Ann Arbor MI 48108

KNOX, ERICK H, RESEARCH & DEVELOPMENT PROSTHETIC DEVICES, IMPACT BIOMECHANICS. *Current Pos:* STAFF ENGR, ENG SYSTS INC, 96- *Personal Data:* b Oak Park, Ill, May 10, 65. *Educ:* Marquette Univ, BS, 87; Northwestern Univ, MS, 90, PhD(biomed eng), 96. *Mem:* Am Soc Mech Engrs; Inst Elec & Electronics Engrs; Eng Med & Biol; Am Soc Biomech; Soc Automotive Engrs. *Res:* Analysis of human locomotion, particularly as it relates to persons with disabilities; design and development of prosthetic and orthotic devices; human factors, impact biomechanics and injury causation related to workplace and motor vehicle accidents. *Mailing Add:* 3851 Exchange Ave Aurora IL 60504. *Fax:* 630-851-4870

KNOX, FRANCIS STRATTON, III, PHYSIOLOGY, BIOMEDICAL ENGINEERING. *Current Pos:* res physiologist & chief crew biotechnol br, Biomed Appln Res Div, Aeromed Res Lab, 80-86, supvry res physiologist, spec proj, 87-88, supvry res physiologist & chief crew, 88-89, CHIEF, ESCAPE & IMPACT PROTECTION BR, USAF, ARMSTRONG LAB, 89- *Personal Data:* b Wilmington, Del, Jan 28, 41; m 65; c 2. *Educ:* Brown Univ, BA, 63; Iowa State Univ, MS, 66; Univ Ill, PhD(physiol & biomed eng), 71. *Prof Exp:* Grad teaching asst zool, Iowa State Univ, 63-66; USPHS trainee biomed eng, Med Ctr, Univ Ill, 66-70; chief bioinstrumentation br, US Army Aeromed Res Lab, 70-73; asst prof, Med Ctr, La State Univ, Shreveport, 73-76, mem Grad Fac, 74-80, assoc prof physiol & biophys, 76-80. *Concurrent Pos:* Consult physiol & bioeng, US Army Aeromed Res Lab, Ft Rucker, Ala, 73-80; affil asst prof bioeng, La Tech Univ, 75-; assoc prof, Community Med Dept, Wright State Sch Med. *Mem:* Sigma Xi; Am Burn Asn; Inst Elec & Electronics Engrs; Soc Neurosci; Aerospace Med Asn; assoc fel, Aerospace Med Asn. *Res:* Quantitative physiology; systems analysis of physiological systems; use of biomedical instrumentation and computers to study physiological systems and to create economical, comprehensive diagnostic and patient monitoring systems; physiological effects of protective clothing under operational conditions. *Mailing Add:* AL/CFBE 2800 Q St Wright Patterson AFB OH 45433-7901. *E-Mail:* tknox@falcon.al.wpafb.af.mil

KNOX, FRANKLYN G, RENAL PHYSIOLOGY. *Current Pos:* dean, Mayo Med Sch, 82-90, DISTINGUISHED INVESTR, MAYO FOUND, 91-, CHAIR, STRATEGIC ALLIANCES & HEAD, NEPHROLOGY RES UNIT. *Personal Data:* b Rochester, NY, Dec 20, 37; m 60, Anne Mitchell; c Michael, Sally, David & Susan. *Educ:* State Univ NY, Buffalo, MD & PhD(physiol), 65. *Hon Degrees:* DSc, State Univ NY, 97. *Honors & Awards:* Daggs Award, Am Physiol Soc, 96, Berliner Award, 97. *Prof Exp:* Chair, Dept Physiol & Biophys, Mayo Clinc, 74-83. *Mem:* Am Physiol Soc (pres, 86-87); Am Soc Nephrol; Am Heart Asn; Am Asn Physicians; Am Soc Clin Invest; Am Fedn Clin Res. *Res:* Regulation of renal sodium and phosphate transport. *Mailing Add:* Dept Med & Physiol Mayo Med Sch Rochester MN 55905. *Fax:* 507-266-4710; *E-Mail:* knox.franklyn@mayo.edu

KNOX, GAYLORD SHEARER, MEDICINE, RADIOLOGY. *Current Pos:* RADIOLOGIST, GREATER LAUREL BELTSVILLE HOSP, 79- *Personal Data:* b Bangkok, Thailand, Oct 18, 23; US citizen; m 46; c 3. *Educ:* Tulane Univ, MD, 51; Am Bd Radiol, cert, 58. *Prof Exp:* Intern gen med, Charity Hosp, New Orleans, 51-52; pvt pract, La, 52-53; physician, US Army, Ft Bliss, Tex, 53-55, resident radiol, Walter Reed Army Hosp, 55-58, chief radiol serv, Hosp, Bad Canstatt, Ger, 58-61; assoc prof radiol, Univ Okla, 61-65; chief, Dept Radiol, Baltimore City Hosps, 65-79. *Concurrent Pos:* Consult, Vet Admin Hosp, Oklahoma City, 61-65 & Perry Point, Md, 65-; asst prof, Sch Med, Johns Hopkins Univ, 65-; assoc prof, Sch Med, Univ Md, Baltimore City, 65-; active consult, Sinai Hosp Baltimore, 66-; pres, Chesapeake Physicians, 73-78, Chesapeake Casualty Ins Co, Denver, 74-78. *Mem:* Radiol Soc NAm; fel Am Col Radiol; AMA; Soc Nuclear Med; Am Inst Ultrasound Med. *Res:* Clinical radiology, particularly skeletal and visceral changes in the aging process and vascular changes in aging. *Mailing Add:* 12340 Shadetree Lane Laurel MD 20708

KNOX, JACK ROWLES, polymer science; deceased, see previous edition for last biography

KNOX, JAMES CLARENCE, GEOMORPHOLOGY, PHYSICAL GEOGRAPHY. *Current Pos:* From asst prof to assoc prof geog, Univ Wis-Madison, 68-76, chmn dept, 83-86, dir, Ctr Geol Anal, Inst Environ Studies, 73-78, PROF GEOG, UNIV WIS-MADISON, 77- *Personal Data:* b Platteville, Wis, Nov 29, 41; m 64, Kathleen A McCabe; c Lezlie S & Sara E. *Educ:* Univ Wis, Platteville, BS, 63; Univ Iowa, PhD(geog), 70. *Honors & Awards:* Honors Award, Asn Am Geogr, 90, GK Gilbert Award, 96. *Concurrent Pos:* Assoc ed, Geog Annals, 78-81, 93-96, Coun Am Quaternary Asn, 76-80,; mem, US Nat Comt Int Quaternary Union, 82-91, secy, 86-91, vchmn & chmn, Quaternary Geol & Geomorphol Div, Geol Soc Am, 85-88; US deleg & corresp mem, Int Geomorphol Assoc, 86-90; Geog & Regional Sci Panel, NSF, 88-90, Continental Hydrol Panel, 91-93; assoc ed, Geol Soc Am Bull, 91-; adj res assoc, Wis Geol & Nat Hist Surv, 95- *Mem:* Am Quaternary Asn; fel AAAS; fel Geol Soc Am; Soil Conserv Soc Am; Asn Am Geogr; Am Geophys Union. *Res:* Fluvial geomorphology; paleoclimatology and paleohydrology of the Quaternary; effects of present-day climate variation and land use on stream flow characteristics and sedimentation problems; Quaternary landscape evolution of upper Miss Valley; erosion, transportation and storage of sediment in river systems; hydrology and water resources. *Mailing Add:* Dept Geog 234 Sci Hall Univ Wis 550 N Park St Madison WI 53706-1491. *Fax:* 608-265-3991; *E-Mail:* knox@geography.wisc.edu

KNOX, JAMES L(ESTER), ELECTROMAGNETICS, INSTRUMENTATION. *Current Pos:* RETIRED. *Personal Data:* b Youngstown, Ohio, July 30, 19; m 46; c 5. *Educ:* Univ Tenn, BS, 42; Univ Mich, MSE, 54; Ohio State Univ, PhD(elec eng), 62. *Prof Exp:* Instr elec eng, Univ Tenn, 42-43; engr, Gen Elec Co, 43-46; Am Baptist For Mission Soc Missionary instr physics, Univ Shanghai, 47-48; asst prof eng, Cent Philippine Univ, 48-50; tech dir eng, Radio Sta DYSR, 50-51; assoc prof, Cent Philippine Univ, 51-59; prof & dean, 62-65; instr elec eng, Ohio State Univ, 60-61, res assoc, Res Found, 61-62; assoc prof chem, Mont State Univ, 65-69, prof, 69-; staff mem, Dept Elec Eng, Univ Petrol & Minerals, Saudi Arabia. *Concurrent Pos:* Prof elec eng, Univ Petrol & Minerals, Dhahran, Saudi Arabia, 73-75 & 76-78. *Mem:* Inst Elec & Electronics Engrs; Instrument Soc; Am Soc Eng Educ; Sigma Xi. *Res:* Electromagnetics; electric power; instrumentation; community acoustics; remote sensing. *Mailing Add:* 1331 Robin Lane Bozeman MT 59715

KNOX, JAMES RUSSELL, JR, PHYSICAL BIOCHEMISTRY, X-RAY CRYSTALLOGRAPHY. *Current Pos:* from asst to assoc prof, 70-80, PROF BIOPHYS, DEPT MOLECULAR & CELL BIOL, UNIV CONN, 80- *Personal Data:* b Bonne Terre, Mo, May 28, 41; m 65, Jane Levitas; c Craig P & Clara R. *Educ:* Univ Mo, Rolla, BS, 63; Boston Univ, PhD(phys chem), 67. *Honors & Awards:* Author Award, Am Chem Soc, 82. *Prof Exp:* NIH fel, Oxford Univ, 66-69; res assoc biophys, Dept Molecular Biophysics, Yale Univ, 69-70. *Concurrent Pos:* Vis prof, Harvard Biol Labs, 77; NIH Study Sect, biophys Chem, 78, Spec Study Sect, 87-88, 94; consult, Hoffman-LaRoche Co, 85-87 & Eli Lilly & Co, 88-90; external adv comt, Crystallographic Data Anal Ctr, Purdue Univ, 88-90, Univ 90-97. *Mem:* AAAS; Am Chem Soc; Am Crystallog Asn (secy-treas, 92-94); Sigma Xi; Biophys Soc; Protein Soc. *Res:* Enzyme structure and function by means of x-ray analysis; penicillin-binding proteins; beta-lactamases and bacterial cell-wall synthesizing enzymes; molecular modelling, energetics and dynamics; bacterial resistance to beta-lactams and vancomycin. *Mailing Add:* Molecular & Cell Biol Dept Univ Conn U-125 Storrs CT 06269. *Fax:* 860-486-4745; *E-Mail:* knox@uconnvm.uconn.edu

KNOX, JOHN MACMURRAY, PHYSICS. *Current Pos:* Res fel & asst prof, Inst Paper Chem, 81-84, ASSOC PROF PHYSICS, IDAHO UNIV, 84- *Personal Data:* b Sheboygan, Wis, Nov 21, 46; m 69; c 2. *Educ:* Gustavus Adolphus Col, BA, 68; Univ Wyo, MS, 77, PhD(physics), 81. *Mem:* Am Phys Soc; Am Vac Soc; Am Asn Physics Teachers; Health Physics Soc. *Res:* Interaction of 2 Mev ion beams with materials, analysis, primarily using particle induced x-ray emission and backscattered ion spectroscopy; gas phase electron capture; negative ion and optically modified mass spectra. *Mailing Add:* Physics Dept Idaho State Univ Box 8106 Pocatello ID 83209

KNOX, KENNETH L, CHEMICAL ENGINEERING. *Current Pos:* RETIRED. *Personal Data:* b Winnipeg, Man, Sept 18, 20; US citizen; m 51, Margaret; c 3. *Educ:* Univ Saskatchewan, BE, 42, MSc, 46; Columbia Univ, PhD(chem eng), 49. *Prof Exp:* Res engr, Yerkes Res & Develop Lab, E I Du Pont de Nemours & Co Inc, NY, 48-52, develop supvr, Cellophane Plants, NY, Iowa & Kans, 52-60, tech supt, Cellophane Lab, Kans, 60-63, res assoc, Circleville Res & Develop Lab, 63-82. *Mem:* Am Chem Soc; Am Inst Chem Engrs; Soc Plastics Engrs. *Res:* Industrial research on polyester film. *Mailing Add:* 327 Meadow Lane Circleville OH 43113-1436

KNOX, KERRO, INORGANIC CHEMISTRY. *Current Pos:* VIS PROF, UNIV MASS, 89- *Personal Data:* b Philadelphia, Pa, June 17, 24; m 49; c 4. *Educ:* Yale Univ, BS, 45, PhD(phys chem), 50; Cambridge Univ, PhD(phys chem), 52. *Prof Exp:* From instr to assoc prof chem, Univ NC, 51-56; mem tech staff, Bell Tel Labs, 56-63; assoc prof chem, Case Western Reserve Univ, 63-69; prof chem, Cleveland State Univ, 69-85. *Mem:* Am Crystallog Asn. *Res:* X-ray crystallography. *Mailing Add:* 11 Wildwood Lane Amherst MA 01002

KNOX, KIRVIN L, NUTRITION. *Current Pos:* PROF NUTRIT SCI & HEAD DEPT, UNIV CONN, 72- *Personal Data:* b Sayre, Okla, Aug 9, 36; m 58; c 3. *Educ:* Fresno State Col, BS, 58; Colo State Univ, MS, 60; Univ Calif, PhD(physiol, nutrit), 64. *Prof Exp:* Lab supt, Escalon Packers Inc, 60; asst prof animal sci, Colo State Univ, 64-65, from asst prof to assoc prof animal sci & physiol, 65-72, dir metab lab, 65-72. *Concurrent Pos:* Co-investr, NIH res grant, 65-68 & prin investr, 66-69; Am Cancer Soc res grant, 66-68; sabbatical leave, Univ Calif, Berkeley, 78-79. *Mem:* Am Dairy Sci Asn; Am Soc Animal Sci; Am Inst Nutrit; NY Acad Sci; AAAS. *Res:* Comparative nutrition as related to energy and vitamin metabolism; behavioral response to nutrition. *Mailing Add:* Colo State Univ 108 Admin Ft Collins CO 80523. *Fax:* 970-491-0215

KNOX, LARRY WILLIAM, PALEONTOLOGY. *Current Pos:* From asst prof to assoc prof, 74-83, PROF GEOL, TENN TECHNOL UNIV, 83- *Personal Data:* b Mishawaka, Ind, Nov 10, 42; m 64; c 2. *Educ:* Ind Univ, AB, 65, AM, 71, PhD(geol), 74. *Mem:* Geol Soc Am; Paleont Soc; Paleont Asn; Soc Econ Paleontologists & Mineralogists. *Res:* Paleoecology and biostratigraphy of paleozoic ostracodes. *Mailing Add:* Dept Earth Sci Tenn Technol Univ 900 N Dixie Ave Cookeville TN 38501-2684

KNOX, ROBERT ARTHUR, PHYSICAL OCEANOGRAPHY. *Current Pos:* res asst oceanogr, Scripps Inst Oceanog, 73-81, assoc res oceanogr, 81-86, acad adminr, 80-90, RES OCEANOGR, SCRIPPS INST OCEANOG, 86-, ASSOC DIR, 92- *Personal Data:* b Washington, DC, Jan 15, 43; m 66; c 2. *Educ:* Amherst Col, AB, 64; Mass Inst Technol-Woods Hole Oceanog Inst, PhD(oceanog), 71. *Prof Exp:* Res assoc, Mass Inst Technol, 71-73. *Mem:* Sigma Xi; Am Meteorol Soc; Am Geophys Union; Oceanog Soc. *Res:* Equatorial ocean dynamics and circulation; structure and dynamics of oceanic mixed layer; acoustic sensing of ocean circulation. *Mailing Add:* Scripps Inst Oceanog 0230 Univ Calif at San Diego La Jolla CA 92093-0230

KNOX, ROBERT GAYLORD, QUANTITATIVE FOREST ECOLOGY, ECOLOGICAL MODELING. *Current Pos:* Huxley res instr evolution, Dept Biol, 87-90, vis lectr, Dept Ecol & Evolutionary Biol, 90, SR RES ASSOC, RICE UNIV, 90-; RES SCIENTIST FOREST ECOL, BIOSPHERIC SCI BR, GODDARD SPACE FLIGHT CTR, NASA, 91- *Personal Data:* b Washington, DC, Oct 24, 56; m 78, Julie Johnson. *Educ:* Princeton Univ, AB, 78; Univ NC, PhD(bot), 87. *Prof Exp:* Comput programmer cancer epidemiol, Syst Cancer Ctr, Univ Tex, 78-82. *Mem:* Ecol Soc Am; Int Asn Veg Sci; Am Inst Biol Sci; Sigma Xi; Torrey Bot Soc. *Res:* Plant community structure and distribution; methods of vegetation analysis; ecological theory; physiological ecology of resource capture and limitation; computer modeling of individuals, communities and ecosystems; inference from long term studies and from spatial pattern; philosophy of biology. *Mailing Add:* Biospheric Sci Br NASA-Goddard Space Flight Ctr Code 923 Greenbelt MD 20771

KNOX, ROBERT SEIPLE, BIOPHYSICS, CONDENSED MATTER. *Current Pos:* from asst prof to assoc prof, 60-68, chmn dept, 69-74, PROF PHYSICS, UNIV ROCHESTER, 68- *Personal Data:* b Franklin, NJ, July 13, 31; m 54, Myrta Borges; c Bruce, Wayne & Lee. *Educ:* Lehigh Univ, BS, 53; Univ Rochester, PhD(physics, optics), 58. *Honors & Awards:* Biol Physics Prize, Am Phys Soc, 94. *Prof Exp:* Res assoc physics, Univ Ill, 58-59, res asst prof, 59-60. *Concurrent Pos:* Consult, Solid State Sci Div, Argonne Nat Lab, 59-69, Naval Res Lab, 60-70; NSF sr fel, Univ Leiden, 67-68; fel, Japanese Soc Prom Sci, Kyoto, Japan, 79; dean, Univ Col, Univ Rochester, 82-85; UK Fulbright scholar, 93. *Mem:* Fel Am Phys Soc; Am Soc Photobiol; Am Asn Physics Teachers; Biophys Soc. *Res:* Optical and electrical properties of ionic and molecular crystals; theory of photosynthesis, picosecond spectroscopy. *Mailing Add:* Dept Physics & Astron Univ Rochester Rochester NY 14627-0171. *Fax:* 716-242-0851; *E-Mail:* knox@pas.rochester.edu

KNOX, WALTER ROBERT, ORGANIC CHEMISTRY, PETROCHEMISTRY. *Current Pos:* chemist, Hydrocarbons & Polymers Div, Monsanto Co, 52-54, sr res chemist, 54-56, group leader, 56-62, mgr res, 62-70, dir res, Petrochem Div, Monsanto Polymers & Petrochem Co, 70-80, TECHNOL DIR SPEC ASST, MONSANTO INT CO, 80- *Personal Data:* b Childress, Tex, July 18, 26; m 48; c 3. *Educ:* Baylor Univ, BS, 47; Univ Iowa, MS, 49, PhD(org chem), 50. *Prof Exp:* Control chemist, Fibreboard Prod, Inc, 47; res chemist, Gen Aniline & Film Corp, 50-52. *Mem:* Am Chem Soc; Catalysis Soc. *Res:* Catalysts and catalytic interconversions, especially with hydrocarbons; monomer synthesis; surfactant synthesis; general organic synthesis. *Mailing Add:* 2118 Babler Ridge Lane Glencoe MO 63038-1178

KNOX, WAYNE H, ATOMIC & MOLECULAR PHYSICS. *Current Pos:* RES SCIENTIST, AT&T BELL LABS, 84- *Personal Data:* b Nov 8, 57. *Educ:* Univ Rochester, BS, 79, PhD(physics), 83. *Mem:* Am Phys Soc. *Mailing Add:* AT&T Bell Labs 413-415 Crawfords Corner Rd Holmdel NJ 07733

KNOX, WILLIAM JORDAN, NUCLEAR PHYSICS. *Current Pos:* chmn dept, 71-75 & 80-83, PROF PHYSICS, UNIV CALIF, DAVIS, 66- *Personal Data:* b Pomona, Calif, Mar 21, 21; m 48; c 4. *Educ:* Univ Calif, BS, 42, PhD(physics), 51. *Prof Exp:* Asst chem, Metall Lab, Univ Chicago, 42-43; from jr chemist to chemist, Clinton Labs, Oak Ridge, 43-46; jr technologist, Hanford Eng Works, 44-45; chemist, Radiation Lab, Univ Calif, 46, physicist, 47-51; asst prof physics, Yale Univ, 51-53; physicist, AEC, Washington, DC, 53-55 & consult, 55-56; asst prof physics, Yale Univ, 55-59; assoc prof physics, Univ Calif, Davis, 60-66, chmn dept, 63-66; actg dir Crocker Nuclear Lab, 66-67 & 78-79. *Concurrent Pos:* Vis sci, Cambridge Univ, 67-68, Europ Ctr Nuclear Res, 73-74; sr Fulbright Hayes Prog res fel France, Comt Int Exchange Persons, 73-74; vis scientist, Lawrence Berkeley Lab, 81-86. *Mem:* Fel Am Phys Soc; Am Asn Physics Teachers. *Res:* Nuclear reactions; nuclear structure; plutonium and fission product chemistry; particle production. *Mailing Add:* Dept Physics Univ Calif Davis CA 95616

KNUCKLES, JOSEPH LEWIS, PARASITOLOGY. *Current Pos:* instr biol & math, Fayetteville State Univ, 56-59, coordr biol, 59-67, asst to acad dean, 71, dir summer sch, 71, actg head, Div Sci & Math, 73-75, actg head, Div Arts Scis, 75-76, chmn, Dept Biol & Phys Sci, 67-78, coordr, Area Biol, 78-80, PROF BIOL, FAYETTEVILLE STATE UNIV, 59- *Personal Data:* b Lumberton, NC, Mar 17, 24. *Educ:* NC Cent Univ, BS, 48, MS, 50; Univ Conn, PhD(parasitol), 59. *Prof Exp:* Instr biol, Bishop Col, 50-52, chmn dept sci, 51-52. *Concurrent Pos:* Sigma Xi grant, 58; consult, NC Teachers Asn, 59; NC Acad Sci grant, 60; NSF stipend, 64; dir coop prog, Fayetteville State Univ, 70, dir consortium prom acad excellence & dir sci improv & exp biol prog; Title III grants, 72-76; NIH res grant, 82-86. *Mem:* AAAS; Am Entom Soc; Am Soc Parasitol; Am Asn Univ Professors; Am Pub Health Asn; Am Inst Biol Sci. *Res:* Transmission of disease agents by flies; general parasitology. *Mailing Add:* Nat Sci Fayetteville State Univ 1200 Murchison Rd Fayetteville NC 28301-4252

KNUDSEN, DENNIS RALPH, PHYSICAL CHEMISTRY. *Current Pos:* Res chemist, 70-86, PHYS SCIENTIST, US NAVAL SURFACE WARFARE CTR, 86- *Personal Data:* b Warren, Minn, July 22, 43; m 65, Bonita Peterson; c Sara & Rachel. *Educ:* NDak State Univ, BS, 65, PhD(phys chem), 70. *Res:* Thermodynamics of solutions; determination of chemical compounds in air; chemical instrument development; combustion; fiber optics in adverse environments. *Mailing Add:* US Naval Surface Warfare Ctr Dahlgren VA 22448-5000

KNUDSEN, ERIC INGVALD, NEUROSCIENCE, BIOLOGY. *Current Pos:* MEM FAC, DEPT NEUROSCI, STANFORD SCH MED, 80- *Personal Data:* b Palo Alto, Calif, Oct 7, 49; m 75. *Educ:* Univ Calif, Santa Barbara, BA, 71, MA, 73; Univ Calif, San Diego, PhD(neurosci), 76. *Prof Exp:* Res fel neurosci, Calif Inst Technol, 76-80. *Mem:* Acoust Soc Am; AAAS; Soc Neurosci; Sigma Xi. *Res:* Neurophysiology, anatomy and ethology related to the evolution of the auditory system, specifically encoding of space by the auditory system. *Mailing Add:* Dept Neurobiol Stanford Univ Sch Med Stanford CA 94305-9991

KNUDSEN, HAROLD KNUD, ELECTRICAL ENGINEERING. *Current Pos:* assoc prof, 66-74, prof, 74-, EMER PROF ELEC ENG, UNIV NMEX. *Personal Data:* b San Francisco, Calif, Aug 6, 36; m 58; c 2. *Educ:* Univ Calif, Berkeley, BS, 58, MS, 60, PhD(elec eng), 62. *Prof Exp:* Staff mem data systs anal, Lincoln Lab, Mass Inst Technol, 62-66. *Mem:* Inst Elec & Electronics Engrs; Sigma Xi. *Res:* Data systems analysis; system theory, especially the application of theories of optimization. *Mailing Add:* Dept Comput Sci Univ NMex Rm 313 Albuquerque NM 87131

KNUDSEN, J(AMES) G(EORGE), CHEMICAL ENGINEERING. *Current Pos:* From asst prof to assoc prof, Ore State Univ, 49-57, asst dean, 59-71, assoc dean, 71-81, PROF CHEM ENG, ORE STATE UNIV, 57- *Personal Data:* b Youngstown, Alta, Mar 27, 20; nat US; m 47; c 2. *Educ:* Univ Alta, BS, 43, MS, 44; Univ Mich, PhD(chem eng), 50. *Honors & Awards:* Founders Award, Am Inst Chem Engrs, 77. *Concurrent Pos:* Nat Sci sr fel, Cambridge Univ, 61-62; eng consult. *Mem:* Am Inst Chem Engrs (pres, 81); Am Chem Soc; Sigma Xi. *Res:* Fluid mechanics; heat transfer; relationship between these processes; applied mathematics. *Mailing Add:* Dept Chem Eng Ore State Univ Corvallis OR 97331

KNUDSEN, JOHN R, APPLIED MATHEMATICS. *Current Pos:* RETIRED. *Personal Data:* b Brooklyn, NY, July 12, 16; m 42, Ruth I Strube; c John K & Thomas P. *Educ:* NY Univ, BS, 37, PhD(math), 51. *Prof Exp:* Instr math, NY Univ, 39-51, from asst prof to prof, 51-72, asst dean & budget officer, 66-72; mem tech staff, Educ Ctr, Bell Tel Labs, 72-83. *Concurrent Pos:* Consult, Bell Tel Labs, NJ, 57-72, 83-87 & Univ Bangalore, India, 68. *Mem:* Am Math Soc; Math Asn Am; NY Acad Sci. *Res:* Self-study instructional techniques. *Mailing Add:* 10105 Jupiter Hills Dr Austin TX 78747-1322

KNUDSEN, KAREN ANN, CELL ADHESION, MYOGENESIS. *Current Pos:* SR SCIENTIST, LANKENAU MED RES CTR, 85- *Personal Data:* b June 30, 43; c 1. *Educ:* Univ Pa, PhD(biochem), 77. *Mem:* AAAS; Am Women sci; Am Soc Cell Biol. *Mailing Add:* Dept Cell Biol 234 Lankenau Med Res Ctr West City Line 100 Lancaster Ave Wynnewood PA 19096. *Fax:* 610-645-2205

KNUDSEN, RICHARD CARL, VIROLOGY, IMMUNOLOGY. *Current Pos:* CHIEF, BIOSAFETY BR, OFF HEALTH & SAFETY, CTR DIS CONTROL, 92- *Educ:* Univ Ariz, PhD(microbiol), 71. *Prof Exp:* Lead scientist, Plum Island Animal Dis Ctr, 76-91, chief, 91-92. *Mailing Add:* Biosafety Br Off Health & Safety MS F05 Ctr Dis Control 1600 Clifton Rd NE Atlanta GA 30333

KNUDSEN, WILLIAM CLAIRE, PHYSICS. *Current Pos:* ADJ PROF GEOPHYS, BRIGHAM YOUNG UNIV, 96- *Personal Data:* b Provo, Utah, Dec 12, 25; m 48; c 4. *Educ:* Brigham Young Univ, BS, 50; Univ Wis, MS, 52, PhD(physics), 54. *Prof Exp:* Res physicist geophys, Calif Res Corp Div, Standard Oil Co, 54-62; res physicist geophys, Lockheed Aircraft Corp, Lockheed Res Lab, 62-67, staff scientist, 67-84; pres, Knudsen Geophys Res, 84-95. *Mem:* Am Geophys Union. *Res:* Low temperature physics; exploration geophysics; ground water hydrology; planetary atmospheres; planetary ionospheres. *Mailing Add:* 942 E 1420 N American Fork UT 84003. *E-Mail:* knudsen@earthlink.net

KNUDSON, ALFRED GEORGE, JR, MEDICINE, GENETICS. *Current Pos:* dir, 76-83, SR MEM, INST CANCER RES, FOX CHASE CANCER CTR, 76- *Personal Data:* b Los Angeles, Calif, Aug 9, 22; m 76, Anna Taback; c Linda (Butler), Nancy & Dorene. *Educ:* Calif Inst Technol, BS, 44, PhD(biochem, genetics), 56; Columbia Univ, MD, 47. *Hon Degrees:* DSc, Thomas Jefferson Univ, 93. *Honors & Awards:* Mott Prize, Gen Motors Cancer Res Found, 88; Medal of Hon, Am Cancer Soc, 89; William Allan Award, Am Soc Human Genetics, 91. *Prof Exp:* Chmn, Dept Pediat, City of Hope Med Ctr, Calif, 56-62, chmn, Dept Biol, 62-66; prof pediat & assoc dean, Health Sci Ctr, State Univ NY, Stony Brook, 66-69; prof biol & pediat & assoc dir educ, M D Anderson Hosp & Tumor Inst, Univ Tex, Houston, 69-70, prof med genetics & dean, Grad Sch Biomed Sci, 70-76. *Mem:* Nat Acad Sci; fel AAAS; Am Asn Cancer Res; Am Pediat Soc; Am Soc Human Genetics (pres, 78); Asn Am Physicians; Int Soc Pediat Oncol; Am Philos Soc; Am Acad Arts & Sci. *Res:* Cancer genetics; medical genetics; tumor suppressor genes. *Mailing Add:* 2034 Locust St Philadelphia PA 19103-5614. *Fax:* 215-728-3105

KNUDSON, ALVIN RICHARD, RADIATION EFFECTS. *Current Pos:* CONSULT, 93- *Personal Data:* b Minneapolis, Minn, Aug 17, 34; m 60, Christine Wilson; c Joann M, Cynthia E (Estienne) & Patricia R. *Educ:* Cath Univ, AB, 54; Johns Hopkins Univ, PhD(physics), 60. *Prof Exp:* Res physicist, US Naval Res Lab, 60-67, head, Charged Particle Reactions Sect, 67-70, head, Mat Anal Sect, 70-85, head, Radiation Effects Sect, 85-88, head, Van de Graaff Applns Sect, 88-92. *Mem:* Am Phys Soc. *Res:* Study of charged particle radiation effects in microelectronics; use of high energy ion beams for materials analysis. *Mailing Add:* US Naval Res Lab Code 6613 Washington DC 20375-5000. *E-Mail:* knudson@radef.nvl.navy.mil

KNUDSON, DOUGLAS MARVIN, FOREST RECREATION, TROPICAL SILVICULTURE. *Current Pos:* assoc prof, 69-82, PROF FORESTRY, PURDUE UNIV, WEST LAFAYETTE, 82- *Personal Data:* b Anoka, Minn, June 11, 36; m 57, Deloris J Streeb; c Cynthia J & Scott D. *Educ:* Colo State Univ, BS, 59, MS, 60; Purdue Univ, PhD(forest econ), 65. *Prof Exp:* Forester, Purdue Univ-Agr Univ Brazil, 60-62, asst prof forestry, 65-67. *Concurrent Pos:* Hon prof, Fed Univ Vicosa, Brazil, 68; Wilderness planner, Nat Park Serv, 70; res assoc, US Forest Serv, 79; consult corp engrs, US Forest Serv, 80-81; vis scientist, Bogor Agr Univ, Indonesia, 88; resident adv, Fuelwood Res Prog, Dominican Repub, 83-87. *Mem:* Soc Am Foresters; Int Asn Torch Clubs (pres, 78-79); Nat Asn Interpretation. *Res:* Outdoor recreation economics and planning, including interpretive services evaluation. *Mailing Add:* Dept Forestry & Natural Resources Purdue Univ West Lafayette IN 47907

KNUDSON, RONALD JOEL, PULMONARY PHYSIOLOGY. *Current Pos:* assoc prof internal med, 70-75, PROF INTERNAL MED, COL MED, UNIV ARIZ, 75-, ASSOC DIR DIV RESPIRATORY SCI, 74- *Personal Data:* b Chicago, Ill, Feb 22, 32; m 71. *Educ:* Yale Univ, BS, 53; Northwestern Univ, MD, 57. *Prof Exp:* Intern, Chicago Wesley Mem Hosp, 57-58; fel surg, Ochsner Found Hosp, New Orleans, 59-63; fel thoracic surg, Overholt Thoracic Clin, Boston, 63-64; res fel pulmonary physiol, Boston Univ Med Ctr, 64-66 & Sch Pub Health, Harvard Univ, 66-68; asst prof physiol & med, Sch Med, Yale Univ, 68-70. *Concurrent Pos:* Dir respiratory serv, Ariz Med Ctr, Tucson, 74- *Mem:* Am Physiol Soc; Am Thoracic Soc; AAAS; Am Col Chest Physicians. *Res:* Respiratory mechanics; airway dynamics; respiratory structure and function relationships. *Mailing Add:* Div Respiratory Sci Univ Ariz Med Col 3593 N Bear Canyon Rd Tucson AZ 85749

KNUDSON, VERNIE ANTON, LIMNOLOGY. *Current Pos:* asst prof biol sci, 71-77, asst prof, 77-80, ASSOC PROF NATURAL RESOURCES TECHNOL, LAKE SUPERIOR STATE COL, 80- *Personal Data:* b Olsburg, Kans, Sept 18, 32; m 54; c 3. *Educ:* Bethany Col, BS, 54; Ft Hays Kans State Col, MS, 59; Okla State Univ, PhD(zool), 70. *Prof Exp:* Instr biol, Bethany Col, 59-60; instr, Dodge City Col, 60-63; partic, Acad Yr Inst, Univ Ore, 64-65; asst prof fisheries & wildlife, Mich State Univ, 66-69. *Mem:* Am Inst Biol Sci; Am Chem Soc. *Res:* Water quality; eutrophication; nutrient removal by algae. *Mailing Add:* 508 Dillon St Sault Ste Marie MI 49783

KNUDTSON, JOHN THOMAS, PHYSICAL CHEMISTRY. *Current Pos:* MEM TECH STAFF, AEROSPACE CORP, 85- *Personal Data:* b Charleston, SC, July 3, 45; m 84; c 2. *Educ:* Colo Col, BS, 67; Columbia Univ, MS, 69, PhD(chem), 72. *Prof Exp:* Res assoc chem, Univ Utah, 72-74 & Univ Wis, 74-75; from asst prof to assoc prof chem, Northern Ill Univ, 75-85. *Mem:* Am Phys Soc; Am Chem Soc. *Res:* Laser spectroscopy; spectral radiometery. *Mailing Add:* Aerospace Corp M5/747 PO Box 92957 Los Angeles CA 90009-2957

KNULL, HARVEY ROBERT, BIOCHEMISTRY. *Current Pos:* assoc prof, 80-87, PROF BIOCHEM, UNIV NDAK, 87-, DEAN, GRAD SCH, 90- *Personal Data:* b Thorsby, Alta, Sept 15, 41; m 65, Diane Zessin; c Tania & Tami. *Educ:* Univ Alta, BSc, 63; Univ Nebr, MS, 65; Pa State Univ, PhD(biochem), 70. *Prof Exp:* Fel neurochem, Dept Biochem, Mich State Univ, 70-73; asst prof oral biol, Univ Man, 73-78, assoc prof, 78-80. *Mem:* Int Soc Neurochem; Am Soc Neurochem; Soc Complex Carbohydrates; Can Biochem Soc; Can Fedn Biol Sci; Am Soc Biol Chemists; Sigma Xi. *Res:* Neurochemistry; axonal transport; brain energy metabolism; compartmentation of glycolytic enzymes; carbohydrate metabolism, tubulin, microtubules, actin and cytoskeleton. *Mailing Add:* Dept Biochem Univ NDak Sch Med Grand Forks ND 58202. *Fax:* 701-777-3916; *E-Mail:* hknull@mail.med.und.nokak.edu

KNUTH, DONALD ERVIN, ALGORITHMS, DIGITAL TYPOGRAPHY. *Current Pos:* prof, Stanford Univ, 68-77, Fletcher Jones prof comput sci & elec eng, 77-91, prof, 90-92, EMER PROF ART COMPUT PROG, STANFORD UNIV, 93- *Personal Data:* b Milwaukee, Wis, Jan 10, 38; m 61, Nancy J Carter; c John & Jennifer. *Educ:* Case Inst Technol, BS & MS, 60; Calif Inst Technol, PhD(math), 63. *Hon Degrees:* Numerous from US & foreign univs, 80-96. *Honors & Awards:* G M Hopper Award, 71; A M Turing Award, Asn Comput Mach, 74, Software Systs Award, 86; Nat Medal of Sci, 79; W McDowell Award, Inst Elec & Electronics Engrs, 80; Comput Pioneer Award, 82, John von Neumann Medal, 95; J B Priestley Award, 81; Steele Prize, Am Math Soc, 86; NY Acad of Sci Award, 87; Franklin Medal, 88; J D Warnier Prize, 89; Adelskold Medal, Swed Acad Sci, 94; Harvey Prize, Technion, 95; Kyoto Prize, Inamori Found, 96. *Prof Exp:* From asst prof to prof math, Calif Inst Technol, 63-68. *Concurrent Pos:* Consult, Burroughs Corp, 60-68; staff mathematician, Commun Res Div, Inst Defense Anal, 68-69; Guggenheim Found fel, 72. *Mem:* Nat Acad Sci; Nat Acad Eng; Norweg Acad Sci; fel Asn Comput Mach; hon mem Inst Elec & Electronics Engrs; Fr Acad Sci. *Res:* Analysis of algorithms; combinatorial theory; programming languages; history of computer science; typography. *Mailing Add:* Comput Sci Dept Stanford Univ Stanford CA 94305-9045

KNUTH, ELDON L(UVERNE), MOLECULAR DYNAMICS, COMBUSTION. *Current Pos:* assoc res engr, Univ Calif, 56-68, assoc prof, 59-65, gen chmn, Heat Transfer & Fluid Mech Inst, 59, head molecular-beam lab, 61-88, head, Chem, Nuclear & Thermal Div, 63-65, chmn, Dept Energy & Kinetics, 69-75, prof eng, 65-91, EMER PROF, UNIV CALIF, LOS ANGELES, 91- *Personal Data:* b Luana, Iowa, May 10, 25; m 73, Margaret I Simko; c Stephen, Dale, Margot & Lynette. *Educ:* Purdue Univ, BS, 49, MS, 50; Calif Inst Technol, PhD(aeronaut eng), 53. *Honors & Awards:* Award, Am Inst Aeronaut & Astronaut, 50; Alexander von Humboldt Found Award, 75.

Prof Exp: Group leader aerothermodyn, Aerophys Develop Corp, 53-56. *Concurrent Pos:* Consult, Marquadt Aircraft Corp, 58-60, Jet Propulsion Lab, 79-81, TRW Inc, 79-84. *Mem:* Am Phys Soc; Am Inst Aeronaut & Astronaut; Am Inst Chem Engrs; Combustion Inst; Am Vacuum Soc. *Res:* Combustion; thermodynamics and statistical mechanics; transport phenomena and properties; free-molecule flows and molecular beams. *Mailing Add:* Dept Chem Eng 5531 Boelter Hall Univ Calif Los Angeles CA 90024. *E-Mail:* elknuth@ucla.edu

KNUTSON, CARROLL FIELD, GEOSCIENCES SCIENCE. *Current Pos:* PRES & BD DIRS, C K M RESOURCES, 75-; SR SCIENTIST, EG&G IDAHO, INC. *Personal Data:* b Santa Monica, Calif, Mar 14, 24; m 48; c 4. *Educ:* Stanford Univ, BS, 50, MS, 51; Univ Calif, Los Angeles, PhD(geol), 59. *Prof Exp:* Reservoir engr, Continental Oil Co, 51-54, from prod engr to sr prod engr, 54-58, sr res engr, 58-61, res group leader, 61-66, res assoc, 66-67; chief geologist, Cer Geonuclear Corp, 67-74; consult geologist, C F Knutson & Assocs, 74-76; vpres, C K Geoenergy, 76. *Concurrent Pos:* Environ dir, Western Oil Shale Corp, 75-76. *Mem:* Geol Soc Am; Am Asn Petrol Geol; Soc Petrol Engrs; Am Geophys Union; Soc Independent Prof Earth Scientists; Sigma Xi. *Res:* Formation evaluation; rock mechanics; subsurface nuclear engineering geology; hydrology, environmental geology; development of energy with minimum adverse environmental impact. *Mailing Add:* 2817 S Higbee Ave Idaho Falls ID 83404-7140

KNUTSON, CLARENCE ARTHUR, JR, ORGANIC CHEMISTRY, CARBOHYDRATE ANALYSIS. *Current Pos:* RES CHEMIST, NORTHERN REGIONAL RES CTR, AGR RES SERV, USDA, 61- *Personal Data:* b Minot, NDak, June 18, 37; m 59, Lois Stevenson; c Debra & David. *Educ:* Concordia Col, Moorhead, Minn, BA, 59; NDak State Univ, MS, 61. *Concurrent Pos:* Consult dir, Mericon Industs, 78-96; assoc ed, Cereal Chem, 89-93. *Mem:* Am Chem Soc; Am Asn Cereal Chemists. *Res:* Carbohydrate chemistry; composition structure and properties of cereal polysaccharides; quantitative analytical methods; starch-hydrolyzing enzymes. *Mailing Add:* 5927 Tampico Dr Peoria IL 61614-3861. *Fax:* 309-681-6685; *E-Mail:* knutsoca@ncaur1.ncaur.gov

KNUTSON, DAVID W, NEPHROLOGY. *Current Pos:* PROF NEPHROLOGY & CHIEF, MILTON S HERSHEY MED CTR, PA STATE UNIV, 85- *Personal Data:* b Minneapolis, Minn, Feb 12, 41; c 4. *Educ:* Univ Minn, MD, 67. *Mem:* Am Soc Nephrology; Int Soc Nephrology; Nat Kidney Found; Am Asn Immunol. *Res:* Immunology. *Mailing Add:* Hershey Med Ctr PO Box 850 Hershey PA 17033-0850

KNUTSON, KENNETH WAYNE, PLANT PATHOLOGY, POTATO CROP MANAGEMENT. *Current Pos:* RETIRED. *Personal Data:* b Williams, Minn, Feb 11, 32; m 57, Audrey Tostenson; c 2. *Educ:* Univ Minn, BS, 54, MS, 56, PhD(plant path), 60. *Prof Exp:* Asst plant pathologist, Univ Idaho, 60-64; mgr, Colo Potato Cert Serv, 64-89. *Concurrent Pos:* Exten assoc prof, Colo State Univ, 64-93. *Mem:* Potato Asn Am; Sigma Xi. *Res:* Potato diseases and other cultural problems; soil-borne fungi; viruses; seed potato improvement; potato variety development; growth analysis. *Mailing Add:* 1116 Morgan St Ft Collins CO 80524. *Fax:* 970-491-7745

KNUTSON, LLOYD VERNON, BIOLOGICAL CONTROL, TAXONOMY. *Current Pos:* DIR, EUROP BIOL CONTROL LAB. *Personal Data:* b Ottawa, Ill, July 4, 34; m 57; c David S Kari. *Educ:* Macalester Col, BA, 57; Cornell Univ, MS, 59, PhD(limnol), 63. *Prof Exp:* Res assoc entom, Cornell Univ, 63-68; res entomologist, USDA, Beltsville, Syst Entom Lab, USDA, Beltsville, 68-73, dir, Biosystematics & Beneficial Insects Inst, 73-88, spec asst, biosyst & biocontrol, Plant Sci Inst, Agr Res Ctr, Agr Res Serv, 88- *Concurrent Pos:* Sci cooperator, Royal Inst Natural Sci, Belg, 65-; resident ecologist, Smithsonian Inst, 71-72; dir, Systematic Biol Prog, NSF, 83-84. *Mem:* Hon mem, Entom Soc Am (pres, 88); Int Orgn Biol Control (vpres, 96-); Soc Syst Zool (treas, 71-74); AAAS; Am Registry Prof Entomologist (pres, 87); hon mem Russian Entomol Soc. *Res:* Taxonomy and biology of Diptera, especially malacophagous and entomophagous groups; phylogeny of Sciomyzoidea; biological control of pest molluscs; taxonomic services; immigrant anthropods; computer applications to taxonomy and biocontrol. *Mailing Add:* Europ Biol Control Lab USDA ARS Parc Sci Agropolis II Montpellier Cedex 34397 France. *Fax:* 33-4-67045620; *E-Mail:* ebch@cirad.fr

KNUTSON, LYNN D, POLARIZATION PHENOMENA IN NUCLEAR REACTIONS, FEW-BODY SYSTEMS. *Current Pos:* From asst prof to assoc prof, 77-85, PROF PHYSICS, UNIV WIS-MADISON, 85- *Personal Data:* b Red Wing, Minn, Aug 22, 46; m 68. *Educ:* St Olaf Col, BA, 68; Univ Wis-Madison, MA, 70, PhD(physics), 73. *Mem:* Fel Am Phys Soc. *Res:* Polarization effects in nuclear reactions and scattering at low and intermediate energies with emphasis on few-body systems; wave functions of A-2 and 3 nuclei; tests of charge symmetry; production of polarized beams and targets. *Mailing Add:* Physics Dept Univ Wis Madison WI 53706

KNUTSON, ROGER M, BOTANY, PLANT LIFE HISTORIES & THERMOGENESIS. *Current Pos:* RETIRED. *Personal Data:* b Montevideo, Minn, Jan 3, 33; m 57, Sharon Belding; c Karin, Anne, Benjamin, Steven & Samuel. *Educ:* St Olaf Col, BA, 57; Mich State Univ, MS, 61, PhD(plant path), 65. *Prof Exp:* From asst prof to assoc prof, Luther Col, Iowa, 64-74, prof biol, 74. *Concurrent Pos:* NSF sci fac fel, Univ Ga, 71-72; vis researcher, Selby Bot Gardens, Sarasota, Fla. *Mem:* AAAS; Am Inst Biol Sci. *Res:* Plant thermoregulation in members of the araceae, especially symplocarpus factidus. *Mailing Add:* 408 Burns St Charlevoix MN 49720

KNUTSON, VICTORIA P, BIOCHEMISTRY, ENDOCRINOLOGY. *Current Pos:* ASST PROF PHARMACOL, SCH MED, HEALTH & SCI CTR, UNIV TEX, 83- *Educ:* Univ Minn, PhD(biochem), 81. *Mailing Add:* Dept Pharmacol Univ Tex Med Sch 6431 Fannin Houston TX 77030-1501

KNUTTGEN, HOWARD G, APPLIED PHYSIOLOGY. *Current Pos:* asst prof anat & physiol, Boston Univ, 61-65, assoc prof physiol, 65-71, assoc dean, 75-80, PROF PHYSIOL, COL ALLIED HEALTH PROFESSIONS, BOSTON UNIV, 71-, CHMN, DEPT HEALTH SCI, 80- *Personal Data:* b Yonkers, NY, May 5, 31; m 61; c 2. *Educ:* Springfield Col, BS, 52; Pa State Univ, MS, 53; Ohio State Univ, PhD(phys educ), 59. *Prof Exp:* Instr phys educ, Ohio State Univ, 54-59. *Concurrent Pos:* Ed-in-chief, Med & Sci in Sports, 74- *Mem:* AAAS; Am Col Sports Med; Am Physiol Soc. *Res:* Human performance; exercise physiology; muscle metabolism. *Mailing Add:* Ctr Sports Med Pa State Univ 146 Rec Bldg University Park PA 16802-0001

KNYCH, EDWARD THOMAS, PHARMACOLOGY. *Current Pos:* ASST PROF PHARMACOL, UNIV MINN, 72- *Personal Data:* b Chicago, Ill, Oct 8, 42; m 65; c 3. *Educ:* Loyola Univ, Chicago, BS, 64; Creighton Univ, MS, 66; WVa Univ, PhD(pharmacol), 70. *Prof Exp:* Fel pharmacol, Univ Wis, 70-72. *Mem:* AAAS; Sigma Xi. *Res:* Mechanism of polypeptide hormone action and effect of drugs of abuse on hormone release. *Mailing Add:* Dept Pharmacol Univ Minn Sch Med Duluth MN 55812-2403. *Fax:* 218-726-6235

KNYSTAUTAS, EMILE J, ATOMIC PHYSICS, MATERIALS SCIENCE. *Current Pos:* From asst prof to assoc prof, 71-82, PROF PHYSICS, LAVAL UNIV, 82- *Personal Data:* Can citizen. *Educ:* Univ Montreal, BSc, 65; Univ Conn, MS, 67, PhD(physics), 69. *Concurrent Pos:* Foreign guest worker, Nat Bur Stand, Washington, DC, 78-79. *Mem:* Can Asn Physicists; Mat Res Soc. *Res:* Atomic spectroscopy; ion implantation; accelerator technology; advanced materials. *Mailing Add:* Dept Phys Laval Univ Quebec PQ G1K 7P4 Can. *Fax:* 418-656-2040; *E-Mail:* ejknyst@phy.ulaval.ca

KO, CHE MING, THEORETICAL NUCLEAR PHYSICS. *Current Pos:* from asst prof to assoc prof, 80-88, PROF PHYSICS, TEX A&M UNIV, 88- *Personal Data:* b Szechuan, China, Jan 7, 43; US citizen; m 73, Shiao-Yen Chou; c Kevin & Shan-Wei. *Educ:* Tunghai Univ, Taiwan, BSc, 65; McMaster Univ, Can, MSc, 68; State Univ NY, Stony Brook, PhD(physics), 73. *Honors & Awards:* Humboldt Res Award, for Sr US Scientists, 95. *Prof Exp:* Res assoc, McMaster Univ, 73-74; vis scientist, Max Planck Inst, 74-77; res assoc, Mich State Univ, 77-78; staff physicist, Lawrence Berkeley Lab, 78-80. *Concurrent Pos:* Vis scientist, Oak Ridge Nat Lab, 84-85. *Mem:* Fel Am Phys Soc. *Res:* Transport processes and particle productions in heavy-ion reactions; hadronic matter; quark-gluon plasma. *Mailing Add:* Physic Dept Tex A&M Univ Col Sta TX 77843-3366. *Fax:* 409-845-1899; *E-Mail:* ko@comp.tamu.edu

KO, CHIEN-PING, DEVELOPMENTAL NEUROBIOLOGY. *Current Pos:* asst prof, 81-87, ASSOC PROF, DEPT BIOL SCI, UNIV SOUTHERN CALIF, 87- *Personal Data:* b Taipei, Taiwan, July 5, 48; US citizen; m 75; c 2. *Educ:* Nat Taiwan Univ, BS, 70; Washington Univ, PhD(physiol & biophys), 75. *Honors & Awards:* Res Career Develop Award, NIH, 83-87. *Prof Exp:* Res fel, dept anat, Univ Colo, 75-78, Nat Inst Neurol & Commun Dis & Stroke, NIH, 78-81. *Mem:* Soc Neurosci; Am Soc Cell Biol. *Res:* Membrane structure and function of synapses; development and plasticity of synaptic connections; freeze-fracture electron microscopy. *Mailing Add:* Dept Biol Sci Univ Southern Calif Los Angeles CA 90089-2520

KO, EDMOND INQ-MING, CHEMICAL CATALYSIS, SOLID STATE CHEMISTY. *Current Pos:* From asst prof to assoc prof, 80-88, PROF CHEM ENG, CARNEGIE-MELLON UNIV, 88-, VICE PROVOST EDUC, 96- *Personal Data:* b Hong Kong, July 8, 52. *Educ:* Univ Wis-Madison, BS, 74; Stanford Univ, MS, 75, PhD(chem eng), 80. *Honors & Awards:* Award Catalysis, Pittsburgh-Cleveland Catalysis Soc, 92; Nat Catalyst Award, Chem Manufacturers Asn, 92. *Concurrent Pos:* Vis assoc prof, Univ Calif, Berkeley, 87-88; vis prof, Hong Kong Univ Sci & Technol, 95 & Calif Inst Technol, 96. *Mem:* AAAS; Am Inst Chem Engrs; Am Chem Soc; Sigma Xi; Am Soc Eng Educ; Am Asn Higher Educ; Mat Res Soc; Catalysis Soc. *Res:* Synthesis and characterization of sol-gel catalytic materials; solid acids. *Mailing Add:* Dept Chem Eng Carnegie-Mellon Univ Pittsburgh PA 15213

KO, FRANK K, TEXTILE MATERIALS ENGINEERING, TEXTILE STRUCTURAL COMPOSITES. *Current Pos:* assoc prof, 84-90, PROF MAT ENG, DREXEL UNIV, 90-, DIR FIBROUS MAT RES LAB, 84- *Personal Data:* b Canton, China, Aug 5, 47; c 2. *Educ:* Philadelphia Col Textiles & Sci, BS, 70; Ga Inst Technol, MS, 71, PhD(textile engr), 77. *Honors & Awards:* Distinguished Achievement Award, Fiber Soc. *Prof Exp:* Asst res engr, textile engr, Ga Inst Technol, 72-73; from asst prof to assoc prof textile eng, Philadelphia Col Textile & Sci, 76-84. *Concurrent Pos:* Adj prof, Temple Univ, 80, chmn, student chapters comt, Soc Advan Mat & Processing Eng, 85-; advan composites roadmap team mem, Aerospace Indust Asn, 88; comt mem, Soc Advan Mat & Process Eng, 88-; mem, sci bd Am Composites Technol Inc, 88- *Mem:* Fel Soc Advan Mat & Process Eng; Am Ceramic Soc; AAAS; Am Soc Mech Eng. *Res:* Fibrous materials ranging from textile surgical implants to textile structural composites; textile structural mechanics; 3-D composites. *Mailing Add:* Hershey Chocolate USA 19E Chocolate Ave PO Box 819 Hershey PA 17033

KO, H(SIEN) C(HING), ELECTRICAL ENGINEERING, RADIO ASTRONOMY. *Current Pos:* res asst, Radio Observ, Ohio State Univ, 52-55, from instr to assoc prof elec eng, 55-63, asst dir, Radio Observ, 57-66, chmn, Dept Elec Eng, 77-89, PROF ELEC ENG & ASTRON, OHIO STATE UNIV, 63-, EMER CHMN, 89- *Personal Data:* b Formosa, Apr 28, 28; m 55; c 3. *Educ:* Nat Taiwan Univ, BS, 51; Ohio State Univ, MSc, 53, PhD(elec eng), 55. *Prof Exp:* Asst, Radio Wave Res Labs, Formosa, 51-52. *Mem:* Int Union Radio Sci; fel Inst Elec & Electronics Engrs; Am Asn Eng Educ. *Res:* Space physics; electromagnetic theory and antennas; electronics and communications. *Mailing Add:* Dept Elec Eng Ohio State Univ 2015 Neil Ave Columbus OH 43210. *E-Mail:* ko.3@osu.edu

KO, HON-CHUNG, ATOMIC ABSORPTION SPECTROSCOPY, ELEMENTAL ANALYSIS. *Current Pos:* RES CHEMIST, ALBANY RES CTR, BUR MINES, 74- *Personal Data:* b Canton, China, June 27, 37; m 68, Erh-Mei Chou; c Benjamin. *Educ:* Chung Chi Col, BS, 59; Univ Va, MS, 62; Carnegie Inst Technol, PhD(phys chem), 64. *Prof Exp:* Res chemist, Rocket Power Res Lab, Maremont Corp, 63-67 & Space Sci Inc, 67-68; res assoc chem, Univ Chicago, 69-70, Univ Pittsburgh, 70-72 & Univ Lethbridge, 72-74. *Mem:* Sigma Xi; Am Chem Soc. *Res:* Thermochemistry; thermodynamics; calorimetry; molten salts; solvent effects; high temperature chemistry; low-temperature heat capacities; chlorination of metals; vapor-liquid equilibria; instrumental analysis. *Mailing Add:* Albany Res Ctr Dept Energy Albany OR 97321-3554

KO, HON-YIM, SOIL & ROCK MECHANICS. *Current Pos:* from asst prof to assoc prof, 67-75, dept chmn, 83-90, PROF CIVIL ENG, UNIV COLO, BOULDER, 75- *Personal Data:* b Hong Kong, China, Jan 18, 40; m 64; c 2. *Educ:* Univ Hong Kong, BSc, 62; Calif Inst Technol, MS, 63, PhD(civil eng), 66. *Honors & Awards:* Huber Res Prize, Am Soc Civil Engrs, 79. *Prof Exp:* Res fel eng, Calif Inst Technol, 66-67. *Concurrent Pos:* Consult, Jet Propulsion Lab, Calif Inst Technol, 67-69, prin investr, NSF, Air Force Off Sci Res, US Bur Reclamation & US Bur Mines res grants, 67-; consult, Martin Marietta Corp, 70-, Sandia Corp, 75-81, Exxon Prod Res, 81-, Earth Technol Corp, 84- *Mem:* Am Soc Civil Engrs; Am Soc Eng Educ; Soc Exp Stress Anal. *Res:* Fundamental mechanical properties of soil, rock and other geological materials, and the analysis of engineering problems in geotechnics; centrifugal modeling of geotechnical structures; geotechnical engineering. *Mailing Add:* Dept Civil & Environ Eng Univ Colo Campus Box 428 Boulder CO 80309-0428

KO, LI-WEN, EXPERIMENTAL BIOLOGY. *Current Pos:* RES SCIENTIST, BURKE MED RES INST, WHITE PLAINS, NY; ASST PROF PATH, MED SCH, CORNELL UNIV. *Personal Data:* b Taipei, Taiwan, Jan 31, 49. *Educ:* Taiwan Univ, Vet Med; Univ Wash, MS; Ohio State Univ, PhD(exp path). *Concurrent Pos:* Vis scientist, Univ Miss, Kansas City; assoc prof, Nat Yeng-Ming Med, Taipei. *Mem:* Am Soc Path Biol; Soc Exp Biol & Med. *Mailing Add:* Dept Path Albert Einstein Col Med 1300 Morris Park Ave Bronx NY 10461-1975. *Fax:* 718-597-7508

KO, PAK LIM, TRIBOLOGY. *Current Pos:* RES ENGR, NAT RES COUN CAN, 84- *Personal Data:* b Hong Kong, Mar 4, 37; Can citizen; m 64; c 2. *Educ:* Univ Strathclyde, BSc, 63; Univ BC, MASc, 65, PhD(tribology), 70. *Prof Exp:* Fel mech eng, Univ BC, 69-70; res engr, Chalk River Nuclear Labs, Atomic Energy Can Ltd, 70-84. *Concurrent Pos:* Adj prof, dept mech eng, Univ BC, 84- *Mem:* Inst Mech Engrs; Eng; Inst Mech Engrs; Am Soc Mech Eng. *Res:* Friction and friction-induced vibration mechanisms; impact and fretting wear studies; flow-induced vibration and tube fretting wear in steam generators and heat exchangers. *Mailing Add:* Nat Res Coun Can 3250 East Mall Vancouver BC V6T 1W5 Can. *Fax:* 604-221-3088; *E-Mail:* pak.ko@nrc.ca

KO, WEN HSIUNG, BIONICS, IMPLANT INSTRUMENTATIONS. *Current Pos:* from asst prof to assoc prof elec eng, Case Western Res Univ, 59-67, assoc prof surg, Sch Med, 64-70, actg dir, Eng Design Ctr, 70-71, dir, Electronics Design Ctr, 71-83, prof, 67-93, EMER PROF, ELEC BIOCHEM ENG DEPT, CASE WESTERN RES UNIV, 93- *Personal Data:* b Fukien, China, Apr 12, 23; US citizen; m 57, Christina H F Chem; c Kathleen, Janet, Linda & Alexander. *Educ:* Nat Amoy Univ, BS, 46; Case Inst Technol, MS, 56, PhD(elec eng), 59. *Honors & Awards:* Cecon Award, Electronics Rep Asn, 70; Achievement Award, Inst Chinese Am Elec Engrs, 77. *Prof Exp:* Engr, Taiwan Telecommun Admin, 46-54. *Concurrent Pos:* Mem biomed eng training comt, NIH, 66-70, mem oviduct panel, Contraceptive Develop Br, Ctr Pop Res, 71; NIH fel, Sch Med, Stanford Univ, 67-68; mem, NASA Life Sci Prog Space Sci Bd, Nat Acad Sci, 69-70; reviewer, NIH, NASA, NSF & Inst Elec & Electronics Engrs; pres, Transducer Res Found. *Mem:* Fel Inst Elec & Electronics Engrs; Electronics & Biol Eng; Int Soc Biotelemetry; Biomed Eng Soc; Int Soc Hybrid Microelectronics; fel Int Asn Med & Biol Environ. *Res:* Microelectronic instrumentation and technology; medical instrumentation; implant electronic transducers, telemetry and stimulators; solid state sensors and actuators; bulk and surface micromachining technol; micro sensors and actuators; micro-electro mechanical systems. *Mailing Add:* 1356 Forest Hills Blvd Cleveland OH 44118. *E-Mail:* whk-@po.cwru.edu

KO, WEN-HSIUNG, PLANT PATHOLOGY, SOIL MICROBIOLOGY. *Current Pos:* From res assoc to assoc prof, 66-76, PROF PLANT PATH, UNIV HAWAII MANOA, HILO, 76- *Personal Data:* b Chao Chow, Taiwan, May 14, 39; m 68, Sachi Su; c Subo & Supin. *Educ:* Nat Taiwan Univ, BS, 62; Mich State Univ, PhD(plant path), 66. *Honors & Awards:* Ruth Allen Award, Am Phytopath Soc, 84. *Mem:* Fel Am Phytopath Soc; Mycol Soc Am. *Res:* Ecology of soil-borne diseases; general soil microbiology; fungal physiology. *Mailing Add:* Agr Exp Sta Univ Hawaii 461 Lanikaula St Hilo HI 96720

KO, WINSTON TAI-KAN, HIGH ENERGY PHYSICS. *Current Pos:* Asst res physicist, 70-72, from asst prof to assoc prof, 72-82, PROF PHYSICS, UNIV CALIF, DAVIS, 82- *Personal Data:* b Shanghai, China, Apr 5, 43; m 70, Katy; c 2. *Educ:* Carnegie Inst Technol, BS, 65; Univ Pa, MS, 66, PhD(physics), 71. *Concurrent Pos:* Assoc, Europ Coun Nuclear Res, 85-86; Fulbright sr fel (Ger), 92-93. *Mem:* Am Phys Soc. *Res:* Experimental high energy physics; elementary particle physics; computer application to physics experiments. *Mailing Add:* Dept Physics Univ Calif Davis CA 95616

KOBALLA, THOMAS RAYMOND, JR, ATTITUDE CHANGE. *Current Pos:* Dept Currie & Inst, Univ Tex, 82-90, UNIV GA DEPT OF SCI EDU, 90- *Personal Data:* b Manchester, NH, June 28, 54. *Educ:* East Carolina Univ, BS, 76, MA, 78; Pa State Univ, PhD, 81. *Prof Exp:* Asst prof, Pikeville Col, 81-82. *Res:* Systematic design of attitude change paradigms in changing attitudes toward science. *Mailing Add:* 200 Tanglewood Dr Athens GA 30606

KOBATA, AKIRA, SYNTHETIC ORGANIC & NATURAL PRODUCTS CHEMISTRY, MEDICAL SCIENCE. *Current Pos:* PROF, INST MED SCI, UNIV TOKYO, 82-, DIR MGT, 90- *Personal Data:* b Nemuro, Japan, Mar 17, 33; m 60; c 3. *Educ:* Univ Tokyo, BS, 56, MS, 58, PhD(biochem), 62. *Prof Exp:* Staff mem, Res Inst, Takeda Chem Indust Co, 58-67; prof, Kobe Univ Sch Med, 71-83. *Concurrent Pos:* Vis assoc, Nat Inst Arthritis & Metab Dis, NIH, 67-69, vis scientist, 69-71; Fogarty scholar-in-residence, Fogarty Int Ctr, 85-87; nat rep, Int Glycoconjugata Asn, 87-; dir, Japanese Soc Protein Eng, 88- & Japanese biochem Soc, 89- *Mem:* Am Soc Biol Chemists; AAAS. *Res:* Structure and function of the sugar chains of glycoprotein; clinical application of glycoconjugate research. *Mailing Add:* Tokyo Metro Inst Geront 35-2 Sakae-cho Itabashi-ku Tokyo 173 Japan. *Fax:* 81-3-3579-4776

KOBAYASHI, ALBERT S(ATOSHI), SOLID MECHANICS. *Current Pos:* from asst prof to prof, 58-88, BOEING PENNELL PROF STRUCT ANALYSIS, UNIV WASH, 95- *Personal Data:* b Chicago, Ill, Dec 9, 24; c Dori K (Ogami), Tina & Laura. *Educ:* Univ Tokyo, BS, 47; Univ Wash, MS, 52; Ill Inst Technol, PhD(mech eng), 58. *Honors & Awards:* F G Tatnall Award, Soc Exp Stress Anal, 73, B J Lazan Award, 81, R E Peterson Award & William Murray Medal, 83; Mech & Mat Div Award, Japan Soc Mech Engrs, 91; M M Frocht Award, 95. *Prof Exp:* Tool engr, Konishiroku Photo Indust, Japan, 47-50, design engr, Ill Tool Works, 53-55; res engr exp stress anal, Armour Res Found, Ill Inst Technol, 55-58. *Concurrent Pos:* Mem staff, Boeing Co, Wash, 58-75; assoc ed, J Appl Mech, 77-84, Trans Japan Soc Composite Mats, 74-; honoree, Int Conf Dynamic Fracture Mech, San Antonio, Tex, 84; res fel, Japan Soc Prom Sci, 96. *Mem:* Nat Acad Eng; fel Am Soc Mech Engrs; fel Soc Exp Mech; Am Ceramic Soc; Am Soc Testing & Mat; hon mem, Soc Exp Mech; fel Japan Soc Prom Sci. *Res:* Fracture mechanics; experimental stress analysis; theories of elasticity; theory of structures and dynamic response of structures; author of over 390 publications. *Mailing Add:* Dept Mech Eng Univ Wash Seattle WA 98195. *Fax:* 206-685-8047; *E-Mail:* ask@u.washington.edu

KOBAYASHI, F(RANCIS) M(ASAO), ENGINEERING MECHANICS. *Current Pos:* Asst prof eng mech, Univ Notre Dame, 48-58, assoc prof eng sci, 58-64, asst vpres advan studies res, 71-95, PROF ENG SCI, UNIV NOTRE DAME, 64- *Personal Data:* b Seattle, Wash, Nov 19, 25; m 63, Monique H Nquyen; c John F, Yvonne M & Robert F. *Educ:* Univ Notre Dame, BS, 47, MS, 48, ScD(eng mech), 53. *Concurrent Pos:* Asst dir eng sci prog, NSF, 59-60. *Res:* Fluid mechanics; wave resistance; systems engineering; operations research. *Mailing Add:* Univ Notre Dame Notre Dame IN 46556. *Fax:* 219-631-8335; *E-Mail:* kobayashi.1@nd.edu

KOBAYASHI, GEORGE S, MYCOLOGY, BIOCHEMISTRY. *Current Pos:* from instr to prof, 64-77, PROF MYCOL, SCH MED, WASHINGTON UNIV, 77- *Personal Data:* b San Francisco, Calif, Nov 25, 27; m 56; c 4. *Educ:* Univ Calif, Berkeley, BS, 52; Tulane Univ, PhD(microbiol), 63. *Prof Exp:* Chemist enol, Roma Wine Co, Calif, 52; sr lab technician mycol, Sch Pub Health, Univ Calif, Berkeley, 52-59. *Concurrent Pos:* Assoc dir, Microbiol Labs, Barnes Hosp, St Louis, 65-; assoc ed, Cutaneous Path, 74-; consult, Bur of Biologics, Food & Drug Admin, 74-76; mem NIH study sect, Nat Inst Allergy & Infectious Dis, 78-84. *Mem:* AAAS; Int Soc Human & Animal Mycol; NY Acad Sci; Med Mycol Soc Am; Infectious Dis Soc; Am Soc Microbiol. *Res:* Immunology and biochemistry of medically important fungi. *Mailing Add:* Dermat Div Box 8123 Washington Univ St Louis MO 63110

KOBAYASHI, HISASHI, RESEARCH & UNIVERSITY EDUCATION. *Current Pos:* dean eng & appl sci, 86-91, SHERMAN FAIRCHILD PROF ELEC ENG & COMPUT SCI, PRINCETON UNIV, 86- *Personal Data:* b Tokyo, Japan, June 13, 38; m 63, Masae Okubo. *Educ:* Univ Tokyo, BS, 61, MS, 63; Princeton Univ, MA, 66, PhD(elec eng) 67. *Honors & Awards:* Humboldt Prize, 79; Silver Core, Int Fed Info Processing, 80. *Prof Exp:* Res staff mem, IBM T J Watson Res Ctr, 67-71, mgr syst measurement-modeling, 71-73, sr mgr syst anal, 75-75, 77-79, dept mgr, VLSI design, 81-82; dir, IBM Japan Sci Inst, 82-86. *Concurrent Pos:* vis asst prof, Syst Sci Dept, Univ Calif, Los Angeles, 69-70, vis prof, Info Sci Dept, Univ Hawaii, 75, Technische Hochschule Darmstadt, WGer, 79-80 & int prof comput sci, Free Univ Brussells, Belgium, 80; consult, ALOHA systs proj, 75; consult prof, Comput Systs Lab, Stanford Univ, 76; prof, Univ Tokyo, 91-92; consult, AT&T Bell Labs, 93- *Mem:* Fel Inst Elec & Electronics Engrs; Asn Comput Mach; Eng Acad Japan. *Res:* Radar signal design; detection and estimation theory; data transmission theory; seismic signal processing; image date compression; magnetic recording theory; optical networks; high-speed networks; queueing theory. *Mailing Add:* 21 Russell Rd Princeton NJ 08540

KOBAYASHI, KAZUMI, PHARMACEUTICAL SCIENCE. *Current Pos:* PROCESS SCIENTIST II, BIOGEN, CAMBRIDGE, 93- *Personal Data:* b Fukuyama-City, Japan, Feb 16, 52. *Educ:* Kyoto Univ, Japan, BS, 74, MS, PhD(pharmaceut sci), 83. *Prof Exp:* Asst lectr & instr, Dept Biochem, Niigata Col Pharm, Japan, 79-83; assoc, Dept Chem, Mass Inst Technol, 83-85; res fel, Dept Molecular Biol, Mass Gen Hosp & Dept Genetics, Med Sch, Harvard Univ, 85-87; staff scientist II & group leader protein chem, Cambridge Neurosci, Inc, 87-93. *Concurrent Pos:* Prin investr, NIH, 88-89 & 90-92. *Mem:* Am Soc Biochem & Molecular Biol; Am Chem Soc; Protein Soc; AAAS. *Res:* Isolation of novel neuroactive compounds from natural products; author of 11 technical publications. *Mailing Add:* BioGen 14 Cambridge Ctr Cambridge MA 02142. *Fax:* 617-679-2296

KOBAYASHI, NOBUHISA, COASTAL ENGINEERING, HYDRODYNAMICS. *Current Pos:* from asst prof to assoc prof, 81-91, PROF COASTAL ENG, UNIV DEL, 91- *Personal Data:* b Osaka, Japan, May 4, 50; m 96, Yoko Iwasa; c Sachi C & Orion A. *Educ:* Kyoto Univ, Japan, BCE, 74, MCE, 76; Mass Inst Technol, PhD(civil eng), 79. *Prof Exp:* Res asst coastal eng, Mass Inst Technol, 78-79; sr engr ocean eng, Brian Watt Assocs, Inc, Houston, 79-81. *Concurrent Pos:* Chmn, Tidal Hydraul Comt, Am Soc Civil Eng, 86-87 & Task Comt Sea Level Rise & Its Effects, 87-90; mem, Waves & Wave Forces Comt, Am Soc Civil Engrs, 87-; assoc dir, Ctr Appl Coastal Res, Univ Del, 89-; ed, J Waterway, Port, Coastal & Ocean Eng, Am Soc Civil Engrs, 92-94; mem, Waterway, Port, Coastal & Ocean Eng Exec comt, 95-, Coastal Eng Res Coun, 95- *Mem:* Am Soc Civil Engrs; Am Geophys Union; Int Asn Hydraul Res; Japan Soc Civil Engrs. *Res:* Interaction of wind waves with coastal structures; wave mechanics in surf and swash zones; sediment transport mechanics in nearshore region; transport and mixing processes; numerical prediction of tsunami run-up. *Mailing Add:* Ctr Appl Coastal Res Ocean Eng Lab Univ Del Newark DE 19716. *Fax:* 302-831-1228; *E-Mail:* nK@coastal.udel.edu

KOBAYASHI, RIKI, CHEMICAL PHYSICS. *Current Pos:* From asst prof to prof, 51-67, LOUIS CALDER PROF CHEM ENG, RICE UNIV, 67- *Personal Data:* b Webster, Tex, May 13, 24; m, Lee M Parker; c James B, Alec S, Anne W & Susan W. *Educ:* Rice Inst, BS, 44; Univ Mich, MSE, 47, PhD(chem eng), 51. *Honors & Awards:* Katz Lectr, Univ Mich, 75; Katz Award, Gas Processor Asn, 85. *Concurrent Pos:* Res engr, Continental Oil Co, Okla; consult, appl thermodyn, gas transmission & gas processing, 52. *Mem:* Nat Acad Eng; fel Am Inst Chemists; Am Inst Physics; Am Chem Soc; Am Inst Mining & Metal Engrs; hon mem Inst Chem Engrs Japan; fel Japan Soc Prom Sci; fel Am Inst Chem Engrs. *Res:* Thermodynamic and transport properties of fluids and solids, particularly at advanced pressures; cryogenic temperatures to moderately high temperatures; kinetics; phase and volumetric behavior of mixtures at high pressures and low temperatures; approx 200 papers in learned journals. *Mailing Add:* Rice Univ Dept Chem Eng 6100 Main St Houston TX 77005

KOBAYASHI, ROGER HIDEO, PEDIATRIC IMMUNOLOGY & ALLERGY, PEDIATRIC RHEUMATOLOGY. *Current Pos:* Assoc prof, 88-90, assoc clin prof, 90-95, CLIN PROF PEDIAT, UNIV CALIF, LOS ANGELES CTR HEALTH SCI, 88- *Personal Data:* b Honolulu, Hawaii, May 21, 47; m 74, Ai Lan Doan; c Lisa & Timothy. *Educ:* Univ Nebr, Lincoln, BA, 69, MD, 75; Univ Hawaii, MS, 75; Am Bd Pediat, cert pediat, 80; Am Bd Allergy & Immunol, cert allergy & immunonol, 81. *Prof Exp:* Resident pediat, Sch Med, Univ Southern Calif, 75-77; clin fel pediat immunol, Sch Med, Univ Calif, Los Angeles, 77-78, res fel immunol, 78-80; asst prof pediat & microbiol, Univ Nebr Med Ctr, 80-84, assoc prof pediat, path & microbiol, 84-88. *Concurrent Pos:* Vis prof, Univ Hawaii, 82, 87, Univ Kansas, 90, Tripler Army Hosp, Hawaii, 90; gen partner, Allergy Asthma & Immunol Assoc PC Omaha, 90-; Lee Hill Prof Iowa, 91-; Consult, Quantum Inc, 91-92, Rare Antibody Inc, Shanghai China, 92-95, Bayer Pharm, 96-97. *Mem:* Am Soc Microbiol; Am Fedn Clin Res; Am Acad Pediat; Am Acad Allergy & Immunol; Clin Immunol Soc. *Res:* Antimicrobiol treatment of respiratory infections adverse effects on viral infections of neutrophil function; treatment of asthma in infants and young children; use of intravenous gammaglobulin in children. *Mailing Add:* 2808 S 80th St Suite 210 Omaha NE 68124. *E-Mail:* rhkobaya@unmc.edu

KOBAYASHI, SHIRO, mechanical engineering; deceased, see previous edition for last biography

KOBAYASHI, SHOSHICHI, MATHEMATICS. *Current Pos:* from asst prof to assoc prof, 62-66, chmn dept, 78-81, PROF MATH, UNIV CALIF, BERKELEY, 66- *Personal Data:* b Kofu, Japan, Jan 4, 32; m 57; c 2. *Educ:* Univ Tokyo, BS, 53; Univ Wash, PhD(math), 56. *Honors & Awards:* Geom Prize, Math Soc Japan, 87. *Prof Exp:* Mem staff, Inst Advan Study, 56-58; res assoc math, Mass Inst Technol, 58-60; asst prof, Univ BC, 60-62. *Concurrent Pos:* A P Sloan fel, 64-66; lectr, Univ Tokyo, 65; vis prof, Univ Mainz, 66, Univ Bonn, 69 & 78 & Mass Inst Technol, 70; assoc ed, Duke J Math, 70-80; ed, J Differential Geometry, 73-85; Guggenheim fel, 77-78; vis prof, Univ Tokyo, 81; ed, Int J Math, 90- *Mem:* Am Math Soc; Math Soc Japan; Math Soc France; Swiss Math Soc. *Res:* Differential geometry and functions of several complex variables. *Mailing Add:* Dept Math Univ Calif Berkeley CA 94720-0001

KOBAYASHI, YUTAKA, BIOCHEMISTRY. *Current Pos:* RETIRED. *Personal Data:* b San Francisco, Calif, Mar 11, 24; m 54, 82, E Maureen Byrne; c Andrew Y, David H & Thomas S. *Educ:* Iowa State Col, BS, 46, MS, 50; Univ Iowa, PhD(biochem), 53. *Prof Exp:* Res assoc, Rheumatic Fever Res Inst, Chicago, Ill, 53-57; sr scientist, Worcester Found Exp Biol, Inc, 57-74; mgr, Appln Lab, New Eng Nuclear Corp, 74-82; staff mem, DuPont, 82-85. *Concurrent Pos:* Consult biotechnol, 85- *Mem:* Am Chem Soc; Am Soc Pharmacol & Exp Therapeut; Am Soc Biol Chemists; Sigma Xi. *Res:* Intermediary metabolism of amino acids and biogenic amines; amine oxidases. *Mailing Add:* 60 Audubon Rd Wellesley MA 02181

KOBE, DONALD HOLM, QUANTUM PHYSICS. *Current Pos:* assoc prof, 68-75, PROF PHYSICS, UNIV NTEX, 75- *Personal Data:* b Seattle, Wash, Jan 13, 34; m 92, Sonia Maria Couri. *Educ:* Univ Tex, Austin, BS, 56; Univ Minn, Minneapolis, MS, 59, PhD(physics), 61. *Prof Exp:* Vis asst prof physics, Ohio State Univ, 61-63; Fulbright lectr, Nat Taiwan Univ & Taiwan Norm Univ, 63-64; vis scientist, Quantum Chem Inst, Univ Uppsala, 64-66; vis asst prof physics, H C Oersted Inst, Copenhagen Univ, 66-67 & Northeastern Univ, 67-68. *Concurrent Pos:* Fulbright lectr/researcher, Instituto de Fisica Teorica, Sao Paulo, Brazil, 88-89. *Mem:* AAAS; Am Phys Soc; fel Am Sci Affil; Am Asn Physics Teachers; Sigma Xi. *Res:* Quantum theory of many-particle systems; applications to superfluid helium; quantum theory of radiation; interaction of electromagnetic radiation and matter; geometrical phase in quantum theory; geometrical angle in classical mechanics. *Mailing Add:* Dept Physics Univ NTex PO Box 5368 Denton TX 76203. *E-Mail:* kobe@jove.acs.unt.edu

KOBER, C(ARL) L(EOPOLD), MECHANICAL ENGINEERING. *Current Pos:* PRES, DENVER MINERAL EXPLOR CORP, 73- *Personal Data:* b Vienna, Austria, Nov 22, 13; nat US; m 42; c 2. *Educ:* Vienna Univ, PhD, 35; Vienna Tech Univ, Dr phil habil, 38. *Prof Exp:* From tech asst to vpres prod, Elin, Inc, Austria, 36-40; chief radar dept, GEMA GmbH, Ger, 40-45; mgr, Secowerk, 48-49; consult, Wright Air Develop Ctr, Wright-Patterson Air Force Base, Ohio, 49-55; tech dir, Tech Div, Gen Mills, Inc, Minn, 55-58; vpres ord opers, Crosley Div, Avco Corp, 58-61; dir manned space opers, Denver Div, Martin Marietta Corp, 61-73. *Concurrent Pos:* Prof, Colo State Univ, 68-79. *Mem:* Inst Elec & Electronics Engrs; AAAS. *Res:* Ordnance; missile detection; plasma physics; data processing; remote sensing geology. *Mailing Add:* 605 Front Range Rd Littleton CO 80120

KOBERNICK, SIDNEY D, PATHOLOGY. *Current Pos:* RETIRED. *Personal Data:* b Montreal, Que, May 7, 19; nat US; m 41, Gail Green; c Allan, Michael K & Joan. *Educ:* McGill Univ, BSc, 41, MD, CM, 43, MSc, 49, PhD(exp path), 51; Am Bd Path, cert path anat, 53, cert clin path, 59. *Prof Exp:* Asst prof path, McGill Univ, 51-52; dir labs, Sinai Hosp, Detroit, 52-82; clin prof path, Wayne State Univ, 53-82. *Concurrent Pos:* Adj prof med technol, Wayne State Univ, 53-82. *Mem:* Am Soc Exp Biol & Med; Am Asn Path & Bact; fel Am Soc Clin Path; fel Col Am Pathologists; Electron Micros Soc Am; Sigma Xi. *Res:* Experimental atherosclerosis; tissue hypersensitivity; morphological pathology. *Mailing Add:* 5627 County Lakes Dr Sarasota FL 34243. *Fax:* 941-355-9221

KOBERSTEIN, JEFFREY THOMAS, POLYMER CHEMISTRY, CHEMICAL ENGINEERING. *Current Pos:* assoc prof, 86-89, PROF CHEM ENG, UNIV CONN, 89- *Personal Data:* b Milwaukee, Wis, Sept 27, 52; m 75; c 2. *Educ:* Univ Wis, BS, 74; Univ Mass, PhD(chem eng), 79. *Honors & Awards:* Doolittle Award, Am Chem Soc, 84. *Prof Exp:* Fel, Ctr Res Macromolecules, 79-80; asst prof chem eng, Princeton Univ, 80-86. *Concurrent Pos:* Vis asst prof, Univ Wis, 81; vis res scientist, IBM, 85. *Mem:* Am Chem Soc; Am Phys Soc; NAm Thermal Anal Soc; Soc Plastics Engrs. *Res:* Polymer morphology; structure property relationships in block copolymers; polymer-polymer interfaces; microphase separation; small angle x-ray, neutron and light scattering; polymer blends; compatibility. *Mailing Add:* Inst Mat Sci Univ Conn U-136 Storrs CT 06269

KOBILINSKY, LAWRENCE, BIOCHEMISTRY, MOLECULAR BIOLOGY. *Current Pos:* prof biol & immunol, 89-95, ASSOC PROVOST, JOHN JAY COL, 95- *Personal Data:* b New York, NY, Nov 7, 46; m 71, Estelle Kartagener; c Hayley. *Educ:* City Univ NY, BS, 69, MA, 71, PhD(biol), 77. *Prof Exp:* Res asst biophys, Columbia Presby Med Ctr, 69-70; lectr biol, City Univ NY, 70-71, Brooklyn Col, 72-74, Hunter Col, 74-75 & John Jay Col Criminal Justice, 75-77; res fel immunol, Sloan Kettering Inst Cancer Res, 77-80. *Concurrent Pos:* Mem, Doctoral Fac Biochem Grad Ctr, City Univ NY. *Mem:* Sigma Xi; AAAS; NY Acad Sci; Am Chem Soc; Am Acad Forensic Sci; Am Col Forensic Examrs. *Res:* Indentification of individuals by DNA profiling analysis. *Mailing Add:* Dept Forensic Sci John Jay Col Criminal Justice 445 W 59th St New York NY 10019. *Fax:* 212-237-8901; *E-Mail:* lkjjj@cunyvm.cuny.edu

KOBISKE, RONALD ALBERT, ADMINISTRATION, PHYSICS LABORATORY DEVELOPMENT IN NUCLEAR SPECTROSCOPY. *Current Pos:* PROF & CHMN, PHYSICS DEPT, MILWAUKEE SCH ENG, 63- *Personal Data:* b New London, Wis, Feb 2, 38; m 58, Ann M Lutz; c Bret R, Mark D & Suzanne. *Educ:* Ind Inst Technol, BS(physics) & BS(math), 62; Highlands Univ, MS, 64; Univ Wis Milwaukee, PhD(physics), 76. *Mem:* Am Asn Physics Teachers. *Res:* General relativity; teaching and laboratory development efforts. *Mailing Add:* Dept Physics Milwaukee Sch Eng PO Box 644 Milwaukee WI 53201-0644

KOBLICK, DANIEL CECIL, PHYSIOLOGY. *Current Pos:* ASSOC PROF PHYSIOL, ILL INST TECHNOL, 63- *Personal Data:* b San Francisco, Calif, May 13, 22; m 60; c 2. *Educ:* Univ Calif, AB, 44; Univ Ore, PhD(biol), 57. *Prof Exp:* Instr biol, Univ Ore, 57-58; asst prof zool, Univ Mo, 58-59; USPHS fel, Univ Calif, Berkeley, 59-60; asst res physiologist, 60-63. *Concurrent Pos:* Lectr physiol, Univ Calif, 60-61. *Mem:* Fel AAAS; Am Physiol Soc; Biophys Soc; Soc Gen Physiol; Sigma Xi. *Res:* Ion transport; bioelectricity; invertebrate physiology. *Mailing Add:* Dept Biol Ill Inst Technol 3300 S Federal St Chicago IL 60616-3793

KOBLICK, IAN, DIVING TECHNOLOGY, UNDERSEA LIVING TECHNOLOGY. *Current Pos:* PRES, MARINE EDUC, MARINE RESOURCES DEVELOP FOUND, 84-, VPRES, SEALODGE INT, 86-; PRES & CO-OWNER, KEY LARGO UNDERSEA PARK, 89- *Personal Data:* b San Francisco, Calif, July 12, 39; m 62, Tonya Smithousen; c Tav & Toren. *Educ:* Calif State Univ, BA, 64. *Honors & Awards:* Lowell Thomas Award, Underwater Explor, 86. *Prof Exp:* spec asst, Govt VI, 69-71; consult, US Dept Com, 79; Port Everglades Environ consults, 79-80. *Concurrent Pos:* Bd dirs, Int Defense Equip Exhibitors Asn. *Res:* Undersea living, man-in-sea technology and diving physiology; natural resource management; environmental education. *Mailing Add:* PO Box 787 Key Largo FL 33037. *Fax:* 305-451-3909

KOBLINSKY, CHESTER JOHN, SATELLITE REMOTE SENSING, OCEANOGRAPHY. *Current Pos:* oceanogr, Goddard Space Flight Ctr, 83-91, HEAD, OCEANS & ICE BR, NASA, 91- *Personal Data:* b Hartford, Conn, March 25, 48; m 77; c 1. *Educ:* Reed Col, BA, 71; Ore State Univ, PhD(oceanog), 79. *Honors & Awards:* Spec Achievement Award, NASA, 85, Except Sci Achievement Medal, 90. *Prof Exp:* Oceanogr, US Environ Protection Agency, 75-76; res assoc, Ore State Univ, 79; res fel, Scripps Inst Oceanog, 79-81, res assoc oceanogr, 82-83. *Concurrent Pos:* Adj assoc prof, Univ Colo, 87- *Mem:* Am Geophys Union; Inst Elec & Electronics Engrs; Am Meteorol Soc; Oceanog Soc. *Res:* Physical oceanography: general ocean circulation, models, observations; satellite remote sensing; airborne remote sensing. *Mailing Add:* Goddard Space Flight Ctr NASA 971 Greenbelt Rd Greenbelt MD 20771. *E-Mail:* chet@neptune.gstc.nasa.gov

KOBRIN, ROBERT JAY, CHEMICAL INSTRUMENTATION. *Current Pos:* sr chem, 61-73, res assoc, 74-84, RES CONSULT, ADV AUTOMATION & DATA SYSTS, MOBIL RES & DEVELOP CORP, 84- *Personal Data:* b New York, NY, Nov 4, 37; m 69, Eileen Raden; c Michael, David & Daniel. *Educ:* City Col New York, BS, 60; Univ Del, PhD(phys chem), 69. *Honors & Awards:* IR 100 Award, Indust Res Mag, 76. *Prof Exp:* Jr chemist anal chem, Sonneborn Chem & Refining Co, 60-61. *Mem:* Asn Comput Mach; Sigma Xi; Am Chem Soc. *Res:* Laboratory automation; information systems and computer networks; analytical instrumentation. *Mailing Add:* 16 Tracey Terr Cherry Hill NJ 08003. *E-Mail:* 70252.3014@compuserve.com

KOBRINE, ARTHUR, NEUROSURGERY. *Current Pos:* from asst prof to assoc prof, 75-79, PROF NEUROSURG, GEORGE WASHINGTON UNIV, 79- *Personal Data:* b Chicago, Ill, Oct 9, 43; m 69; c 2. *Educ:* Northwestern Univ, BS, 64, MD, 68; George Washington Univ, PhD(physiol), 79. *Prof Exp:* Resident neurosurg, Walter Reed Hosp, 70-73, asst chief, 73-75. *Mem:* Soc Neurol Surgeons; Am Phys Soc; Am Bd Neurol Surg. *Mailing Add:* 2440 M St NW Washington DC 20037-1404

KOBSA, HENRY, PHYSICAL CHEMISTRY. *Current Pos:* Res chemist, Dacron Res Lab, E I Du Pont de Nemours & Co, Del, 56-58, res chemist, Pioneering Res Lab, 58-61, sr res chemist, 61, res assoc, 61-62, res supvr, 62-64, res supvr, Benger Res Lab, Va, 64-65, tech supvr, Lycra Tech Sect, Va, 65-66, sr supvr, 66-68, sr supvr, May Plant Tech Sect, 68-69, res mgr, Dacron Res Lab, 69-73, tech supt, Indust Tech Sect, Kinston plant, NC, 73-77, res fel, Pioneering Res Lab, 77-81, sr res fel, 81-89, FEL, E I DU PONT DE NEMOURS & CO, DEL, 89- *Personal Data:* b Vienna, Austria, May 4, 29; nat US; m 80, Mary J Liston; c 2. *Educ:* Univ Vienna, PhD(chem), 56. *Mem:* Am Chem Soc; Am Inst Chem Engrs; AAAS; Am Asn Textile Chemists & Colorists; Int Soc Optical Eng; Am Optical Soc. *Res:* Photochemistry of polymers and dyes; energy transfer phenomena; polymer physics; polymerization kinetics; diffusion; laser materials processing; laser micromachining; solid state lasers. *Mailing Add:* 111 Greenspring Rd Greenville DE 19807. *Fax:* 302-999-4541; *E-Mail:* kobsah@csoc.dnet.dupont.com

KOBURGER, JOHN ALFRED, FOOD MICROBIOLOGY. *Current Pos:* prof food microbiol, Dept Food Sci, Univ Fla, 69-86. *Personal Data:* b Queens, NY, Apr 20, 31; m 52; c 4. *Educ:* Kans State Univ, BS, 59, MS, 60; NC State Col, PhD(food microbiol), 62. *Prof Exp:* Res asst, Res Labs, Nat Dairy Prod Corp, 56-57; from asst prof to assoc prof food microbiol, WVa Univ, 62-69. *Mem:* Am Chem Soc; Am Dairy Sci Asn; Am Soc Microbiol; Inst Food Technol. *Res:* Physiology of microorganisms important to the food industry. *Mailing Add:* PO Box 58 Suwannee FL 32692

KOBYLARZ, ERIK J, neurology, for more information see previous edition

KOBYLNYK, RONALD WILLIAM, LASER ENTOMOLOGY. *Current Pos:* MEM STAFF, PESTICIDE MGT SECT, MINISTRY ENVIRON, VICTORIA, 80- *Personal Data:* b Calgary, Alta, Aug 19, 42. *Educ:* Univ Calgary, BSc, 63; Univ Guelph, Ont, MSc, 65, PhD(entom), 72. *Prof Exp:* Eval officer insecticides, Agr Can, 70-80. *Mem:* Entom Soc Can. *Res:* Effects of laser radiation on insects. *Mailing Add:* Pesticide Mgt Sect Ministry Environ 4th Floor 737 Courtnay St Victoria BC V8V 1X4 Can

KOCAN, KATHERINE M, TICK BORNE DISEASES OF CATTLE, VECTOR-BORNE HEMOPARASITES OF DOMESTIC & WILD ANIMALS. *Current Pos:* Res assoc & mgr electron micros, Okla State Univ, 75-80, adj asst prof, 80-83, from asst prof to assoc prof path, 83-93, PROF PATH, COL VET MED, OKLA STATE UNIV, 93-, ENDOWED CHAIR, FOOD ANIMAL RES, 96- *Personal Data:* b Cleveland, Ohio, Mar 27, 46; m, Andrew A; c Jonathan M & Andrew J. *Educ:* Hiram Col, BA, 68; Univ NC, Chapel Hill, 71; Okla State Univ, PhD(vet parasitol), 79. *Honors & Awards:* Phizer Res Award, 86 & 96. *Concurrent Pos:* Vis scientist, Int Lab Res Animal Dis, Kenya, 84-85, Vet Res Inst, Onderstepoort, Repub S Africa, 86. *Mem:* Sigma Xi (treas, 88-90, pres elect, 95-96, pres, 96-97); Soc Trop Vet Med (pres-elect, 91-93, pres, 93-95); Soc Vector Ecologists; Electron Micros Am; Am Soc Vet Parasitol. *Res:* Tick-borne diseases of cattle; Anaplasma marginale in ticks. *Mailing Add:* Dept Anat, Path & Pharmacol Okla State Univ Stillwater OK 74078. *Fax:* 405-744-5275

KOCAOGLU, DUNDAR F, ENGINEERING MANAGEMENT, MULTICRITERIA DECISION MAKING. *Current Pos:* PRES, TECHNOL MGT ASSOCS, 73-; PROF & DIR, ENG MGT PROG, PORTLAND STATE UNIV, 87- *Personal Data:* b Turkey, June 1, 39; US citizen; m 68, Alev Baysak; c Timur. *Educ:* Robert Col, Turkey, BS, 60; Lehigh Univ, MS, 62; Univ Pittsburgh, MS, 72, PhD(opers res), 76. *Honors & Awards:* Centennial Medal, Inst Elec & Electronics Engrs, 84. *Prof Exp:* Struct engr, Modjeski & Masters, 62-63; proj engr, United Engrs & Constructors, 63-66, consult proj engr, 69-71; partner, Tekser Consult Co, 66-69; res asst indust eng, Univ Pittsburgh, 71-74, vis asst prof mgt, 74-76, assoc prof opers res, Indust Eng & Eng mgt & dir eng mgt proj, 76-87. *Concurrent Pos:* Consult, Tokten Prog, UN, 79-80, 87; pres, Col Eng Mgt, Inst Mgt Sci, 79-81; publ dir, Eng Mgt Soc, Inst Elec & Electronics Engrs, 82-85, ed-in-chief, Trans Eng Mgt, 85-; pres, Portlant Int Conf Mgt Eng & Technol, 90- *Mem:* Am Soc Eng Educ; fel Inst Elec & Electronics Engrs; Am Soc Civil Engrs; Am Soc Eng Mgt; Inst Opers Res & Mgt Sci; hon mem Soc Turkish Scientists, Engrs & Architects. *Res:* Engineering management; hierarchical decision modeling; multicriteria decisions, project management, strategic planning, manpower analysis and strategic management; operations research; resource optimization; quantification of expert judgments; technological innovations; risk assessment; technology management; conflict resolution. *Mailing Add:* Portland State Univ PO Box 751 Portland OR 97207-0751. *Fax:* 503-725-4667; *E-Mail:* kocaoglu@emp.pdx.edu

KOCATAS, BABUR M(EHMET), CHEMICAL ENGINEERING. *Current Pos:* CONSULT, 85- *Personal Data:* b Istanbul, Turkey, Apr 7, 27; m 55, Semra Ozsoydan; c Reha. *Educ:* Robert Col, Istanbul, BS, 47; Univ Tex, MS, 53, PhD(chem eng), 62. *Prof Exp:* Design engr, Union Carbide Chem Co, 56-57; lectr math, Univ Tex, 57-62; sr res engr, Monsanto Co, 62-76, sr res group leader, 76-85. *Mem:* Am Chem Soc; Am Inst Chem Engrs; Sigma Xi. *Res:* Process design and development; micro pilot planting; distillation; fuel cells; mathematical modeling; systems engineering; air pollution control. *Mailing Add:* Dilhayat Sok 22 13 Camlik Etiler Istanbul Turkey. *Fax:* 90-212-2933082

KOCH, ALAN R, PHYSIOLOGY. *Current Pos:* ASSOC PROF ZOOPHYSIOL, MED SCH, WASH STATE UNIV, 66- *Personal Data:* b St Louis, Mo, Oct 6, 30; m 56; c 3. *Educ:* Univ Mich, BS, 51; Columbia Univ, PhD(pharmacol), 55. *Prof Exp:* Asst pharmacol, Columbia Univ, 53-55; res instr, Col Med, Univ Utah, 55-57; from res instr to res asst prof to asst prof physiol, Univ Wash, 59-65. *Concurrent Pos:* USPHS fel, 55-58. *Mem:* Biophys Soc; Am Physiol Soc. *Res:* Renal physiology; ion transport in brain; active ion transport. *Mailing Add:* Dept Zool Wash State Univ One SE Stadium Way Pullman WA 99163

KOCH, ALISA ERIKA, IMMUNOLOGY. *Current Pos:* assoc prof rheumatology, 92-95, CHIEF, SECT RHEUMATOLOGY, VET ADMIN LAKESIDE MED CTR, 91-, PROF RHEUMATOLOGY, 95- *Personal Data:* b Jerusalem, Israel, Feb 26, 56; US citizen; m 88, Howard Stein; c Joshua W Stein. *Educ:* Northwestern Univ, BS, 78, MD, 80. *Honors & Awards:* Henry Christian Award, Am Fedn Clin Res, 92, Am Asn Clin Invest, 94. *Prof Exp:* Clin instr, Northwestern Univ Med Sch, 83-86, asst prof med, Sect Arthritis Connective Tissue Dis, 86-92. *Concurrent Pos:* Assoc investr, Vet Admin Lakeside Med Ctr, 86-89, staff physician, 89-; staff physician, Northwestern Mem Hosp, 86-; consult physician, Rehab Inst Chicago, 88-; vis scholar, Univ Mich, Ann Arbor, 90-91; mem, Spec Study Sect 7, NIH, 91, prin investr, 92- *Mem:* Am Fedn Clin Res; Am Soc Clin Invest; fel Am Col Physicians; Am Col Rheumatology; Am Asn Immunologists; Sigma Xi. *Res:* Immunopathogenesis of rheumatoid arthritis as regards to macrophage and endothelial interactions; macrophage production of cytokines and angiogenic factors. *Mailing Add:* Ward 3-315 303 E Chicago Ave Chicago IL 60611. *Fax:* 312-503-0994; *E-Mail:* ae_koch@nwu.edu

KOCH, ARTHUR LOUIS, THEORETICAL BIOLOGY, BACTERIAL PHYSIOLOGY. *Current Pos:* PROF MICROBIOL, IND UNIV, BLOOMINGTON, 67- *Personal Data:* b St Paul, Minn, Oct 25, 25; m 47, 83; c 2. *Educ:* Calif Inst Technol, BS, 48; Univ Chicago, PhD(biochem), 51. *Prof Exp:* Res assoc & instr, Univ Chicago, 51-52 & 53-56; from asst prof to assoc prof biochem, Col Med, Univ Fla, 56-63, prof biochem & microbiol, 63-67. *Concurrent Pos:* Assoc scientist, Argonne Nat Lab, 52-56; Guggenheim fel, 60-61 & 81-82. *Mem:* Am Soc Microbiol; Am Soc Biol Chemists. *Res:* Enzyme and haploid evolution; active transport systems; microbial growth physiology; microbial response to toxic and antibiotic substances. *Mailing Add:* Dept Biol Ind Univ Bloomington IN 47405-6801. *Fax:* 812-855-6705

KOCH, BRUCE D, NEUROPHARMACOLOGY. *Current Pos:* STAFF RESEARCHER, SYNTEX DISCOVERY RES, 91- *Personal Data:* b Dayton, Ohio, Nov 27, 57. *Educ:* Bates Col, BS, 79; Harvard Univ, PhD(cell & develop biol), 86. *Prof Exp:* Res asst, Tufts New Eng Med Ctr, 79-80; fel, Univ Calif Berkeley, 86-91. *Concurrent Pos:* Fel, Jane Coffin Childs Mem Fund Med Res, 86-89; sr fel, Calif Am Cancer Soc, 89-91. *Mem:* Soc Neurosci; Am Soc Cell Biol. *Res:* Neuropharmacology of pain; intracellular calcium homeostasis. *Mailing Add:* Roche Bio Sci 3401 Hillview Ave Palo Alto CA 94304. *Fax:* 650-354-7400; *E-Mail:* bruce.koch@syntex.com

KOCH, CARL CONRAD, RAPID SOLIDIFICATION, ALLOY BEHAVIOR. *Current Pos:* PROF MAT SCI & ENG, NC STATE UNIV, 83- *Personal Data:* b Cleveland, Ohio, Oct 19, 37; m 65, Evelyn Windridge; c Paul & Alexander. *Educ:* Case Inst Technol, BS, 59, MS, 61, PhD(metall), 64. *Honors & Awards:* Metall & Ceramics Award, US Dept Energy, 80; IR 100 Award, Indus Res & Develop Mag, 83; Award for Spec Creativity, NSF, 90-92. *Prof Exp:* NSF fel metall, Univ Birmingham, Eng, 64-65; staff scientist superconducting mat, Oak Ridge Nat Lab, 65-70, group leader, 70-83. *Concurrent Pos:* Vis scientist, AERE, Harwell, Eng, 71-72; lectr, Univ Tenn, Knoxville, 71; secy, Alloy-phases Comt, Metall Soc, 81-83, chmn, 83-85. *Mem:* Fel Am Phys Soc; fel AAAS; Mat Res Soc; fel Am Soc Metals Int; Am Inst Mining, Metall & Petrol Engrs. *Res:* Materials science; rare earth alloy behavior; superconducting materials; fluxoid pinning; amorphous superconductors; non-equilibrium processing; rapid solidification; vapor deposition; mechanical alloying; intermetallic compounds; solid state amorphization; nanocrystalline materials. *Mailing Add:* 1713 Lookout Point Ct Raleigh NC 27612. *Fax:* 919-515-7724; *E-Mail:* koch@mte.ncsu.edu

KOCH, CARL FRED, PALEOECOLOGY, BIOSTRATIGRAPHY. *Current Pos:* from asst prof to assoc prof, 78-89, PROF GEOL, OLD DOM UNIV, 89- *Personal Data:* b Washington, DC, July 13, 32; m 88, Joyce Paul; c Carla. *Educ:* Univ Md, BS, 57, MS, 61; George Washington Univ, PhD(geol), 77. *Prof Exp:* Engr, Appl Physics Lab, Johns Hopkins Univ, 58-61, Rixon Electronics Inc, 62-67 & Seismic Data Anal Ctr, 68-77. *Concurrent Pos:* Geologist, US Geol Surv, 77-92; res assoc, Smithsonian Inst, 81- *Mem:* Geol Soc Am; Paleont Soc; Int Paleont Inst. *Res:* Geologic data for restricted time intervals of large geographic extent; biosphere history; quantitative paleoecology and biostatigraphy using upper cretaceous molluscs. *Mailing Add:* Dept Geosci Old Dom Univ 5215 Hampton Blvd Norfolk VA 23508

KOCH, CARL MARK, SLUDGE MANAGEMENT. *Current Pos:* ENVIRON ENGR, GREELEY & HANSEN, 76-, ASSOC, 80- *Personal Data:* b Orefield, Pa, Apr 29, 44; m 66, Nancy Varady; c Carcy, Roger & Janine. *Educ:* Univ Del, BSCE, 66; Univ Pa, MSCE, 67, PhD(water resources), 72. *Prof Exp:* Environ engr, Reentry & Environ Syst Div, Gen Elec Corp, 70-74; consult engr, United Engrs & Constructors, 74-76. *Concurrent Pos:* Hydraul engr, US Army CEngr, 66; lectr water resources, Univ Del, 73 & 92; chmn, Gen Elec Corp Int-Div Panel Waste Disposal & Pollution Control, 73-74; consult, Engrs Energy & Environ, 74-77; co-chair, Sludge Comt, Am Soc Civil Engrs. *Mem:* Water Pollution Control Fedn; Am Soc Civil Engrs; Am Acad Environ Engrs. *Res:* Biological treatment of municipal and industrial wastewaters and sludge residues; water resources, hydrological investigations and water quality modeling; environmental assessment and impact evaluations; sludge processing and management. *Mailing Add:* 1919 Gravers Lane Wilmington DE 19810. *Fax:* 215-563-1139

KOCH, CHARLES FREDERICK, MATHEMATICS. *Current Pos:* RETIRED. *Personal Data:* b Tarrytown, NY, Mar 23, 32. *Educ:* Union Col, BS, 53; Univ Ill, MS, 57, PhD(math), 61. *Prof Exp:* Instr math, Univ Minn, 61-64; asst prof math, Kans State Univ, 64-66; asst prof math, Southern Ill Univ, Carbondale, 66-91. *Mem:* Am Math Soc; Math Asn Am; Sigma Xi. *Res:* Summability of sequences and series. *Mailing Add:* RR1 PO Box 125 Grand Forks ND 58201

KOCH, DAVID GILBERT, INFRARED ASTRONOMY, EXTRA-SOLAR PLANET DETECTION. *Current Pos:* ASTROPHYSICIST, AMES RES CTR, NASA, 88- *Personal Data:* b Milwaukee, Wis, Aug 6, 45; m 74; c 3. *Educ:* Univ Wis-Madison, BS, 67; Cornell Univ, MS, 71, PhD(physics), 72. *Prof Exp:* Sr scientist x-ray astron, Am Sci & Eng, 72-76, staff scientist, 76-77; astrophysicist infrared astron, Smithsonian Astrophys Observ, 77-89. *Concurrent Pos:* Assoc, Harvard Col Observ, 77-89. *Mem:* AAAS; Am Astron Soc; Int Astron Union. *Res:* Search for other planetary systems using photometry; infrared, x-ray and gamma-ray astrophysics with particular emphasis on spaceborne instrumentation and computer aided data reduction. *Mailing Add:* NASA Ames Res Ctr MS 245-6 Moffett Field CA 94035

KOCH, DAVID WILLIAM, AGRONOMY. *Current Pos:* PROF, CROP PHYSIOL, UNIV WYO, 85- *Personal Data:* b Frankfort, Kans, Nov 22, 42; m 66. *Educ:* Kans State Univ, BS, 64, MS, 66; Colo State Univ, PhD(agron), 71. *Prof Exp:* Asst prof, Univ NH, 71-77, assoc prof crop physiol, 77-85. *Mem:* Am Soc Agron. *Res:* Minimum tillage establishment of forage crops; forage crop management; methods of forage conservation. *Mailing Add:* Dept Plant Sci Univ Wyo PO Box 3354 Laramie WY 82071-3354

KOCH, DONALD LEROY, STRATIGRAPHY, GROUNDWATER GEOLOGY. *Current Pos:* Res geologist, Geol Surv Bur, 59-71, chief subsurface geol, 71-75, asst state geologist, 75-80, state geologist & dir, Iowa Geol Surv, 80-86, STATE GEOLOGIST & BUR CHIEF, GEOL SURV BUR, 86- *Personal Data:* b Dubuque, Iowa, June 3, 37; m 62, C Jean Swede; c Kyle, Amy & Nathan. *Educ:* State Univ Iowa, BS, 59, MS, 67. *Mem:* Sigma Xi. *Res:* Carbonate petrology and carbonate hydrology, defining the relationship of primary and secondary porosity to parameters of water availability and water quality. *Mailing Add:* 109 Trowbridge Hall Geol Surv Bur/IDNR Iowa City IA 52242-1319. *Fax:* 319-335-2754; *E-Mail:* dkoch@gsbth_poigsb.uiowa.edu

KOCH, ELIZABETH ANNE, BIOCHEMICAL GENETICS, ELECTRON MICROSCOPY. *Current Pos:* asst prof, 69-74, ASSOC PROF BIOCHEM & GENETICS, CHICAGO MED SCH, 74- *Personal Data:* b Toronto, Ohio, Oct 8, 36; m 73. *Educ:* Mt Union Col, BS, 58; Northwestern Univ, PhD(genetics), 64. *Prof Exp:* Teacher gen sci & eng, Ely Jr High Sch, Elyria, Ohio, 58-59; instr gen biol & genetics, Hope Col, 63-64; res assoc electron microscopy & genetics, Northwestern Univ, 64-69. *Concurrent Pos:* Fel, Cancer Inst, NIH, 64-66; lectr, Eve Div, Northwestern Univ, 65-72. *Mem:* Am Soc Cell Biol; Genetics Soc Am; AAAS; Sigma Xi; Am Asn Univ Prof. *Res:* Ultrastructural localization of proteins using immune chemical methods; oogenesis. *Mailing Add:* Dept Biol Chem Chicago Med Sch 3333 Greenbay Rd North Chicago IL 60064-3095. *Fax:* 847-578-3240

KOCH, FREDERICK BAYARD, PHYSICAL METALLURGY. *Current Pos:* RETIRED. *Personal Data:* b St Paul, Minn, Aug 15, 35; m 63; c 3. *Educ:* Carleton Col, BA, 57; Univ Minn, Minneapolis, MS, 62; Northwestern Univ, PhD(mat sci), 67. *Prof Exp:* Mem staff, Sci Lab, Ford Motor Co, 60-62; mem tech staff, Bell Tel Labs, 67-90; mem tech staff, Bellcore, 97. *Mem:* Am Inst Metall Engrs; Electrochem Soc. *Res:* Discrete wiring methods for circuit board development. *Mailing Add:* 92 Highland Ave Highlands NJ 07732

KOCH, GARY MARLIN, ORNAMENTAL HORTICULTURE. *Current Pos:* Asst prof ornamental hort, 70, assoc prof plant sci, 70-77, PROF PLANT SCI, CALIF STATE UNIV, FRESNO, 77- *Personal Data:* b Pottsville, Pa, Nov 7, 41. *Educ:* Pa State Univ, BS, 63, MS, 65, PhD(hort), 70. *Mem:* Am Soc Hort Sci. *Res:* Plant materials and usage; commercial floriculture; floral design; turfgrass production. *Mailing Add:* Dept Plant Sci Calif State Univ 2415 E San Ramon Fresno CA 93740-8033

KOCH, GEORGE SCHNEIDER, JR, ECONOMIC GEOLOGY, STATISTICS. *Current Pos:* PROF GEOL, UNIV GA, 71- *Personal Data:* b Washington, DC, Oct 30, 26; m 73; c 3. *Educ:* Harvard Univ, SB, 48, PhD(econ geol), 55; Johns Hopkins Univ, MA, 49. *Prof Exp:* Geologist, US Geol Surv, 48-52; chief geologist, Minera Frisco, SA, Mex, 52-56; asst prof geol, Ore State Univ, 56-62; res geologist, US Bur Mines, 62-71. *Concurrent Pos:* Consult, firms in mineral indust & US govt. *Mem:* Soc Econ Geol; Am Inst Mining, Metall & Petrol Eng; Int Asn Math Geol. *Res:* Statistical analysis of geological data; exploration for and evaluation of mineral deposits; precious and nonferrous metal and uranium deposits. *Mailing Add:* 385 Springdale St Athens GA 30606

KOCH, HEINZ FRANK, PHYSICAL ORGANIC CHEMISTRY, FLUORINE CHEMISTRY. *Current Pos:* from asst prof to assoc prof, Ithace Col, 65-70, chmn, Dept Chem, 67-79, Div Fluorine Chem, 77, PROF ORG CHEM, ITHACA COL, 70- *Personal Data:* b Berlin, Ger, June 21, 32; US citizen; m 58; c 2. *Educ:* Haverford Col, BS, 54, MS, 56; Cornell Univ, PhD(org chem), 60. *Prof Exp:* Res chemist, Univ Calif, Berkeley, 60-62; res chemist, Plastics Dept, E I Du Pont de Nemours & Co, Inc, 62-65. *Concurrent Pos:* NSF fac fel, Univ Calif, Berkeley, 71-72, vis prof, 72-73; vis prof, Univ Grenoble, France, 79 & Univ Auckland, NZ, 79-80. *Mem:* Am Chem Soc (secy-treas, Div Fluorine Chem, 74-75); Royal Chem Soc; NY Acad Sci; Sigma Xi. *Res:* Physical organic studies of reaction mechanisms, particularly fluorohalocarbon chemistry; studies of 1, 2 elimination reactions, carbanions and isotope effects. *Mailing Add:* Dept Chem Ithaca Col Ithaca NY 14850

KOCH, HENRY GEORGE, medical entomology, for more information see previous edition

KOCH, HERMAN WILLIAM, PHYSICS. *Current Pos:* RETIRED. *Personal Data:* b New York, NY, Sept 28, 20; m 45; c 5. *Educ:* Queens Col, NY, BS, 41; Univ Ill, MS & PhD(physics), 44. *Prof Exp:* Res physicist, Univ Ill, 44-45 & Clinton Labs, Oak Ridge, 45-46; asst prof res nuclear physics, Univ Ill, 46-49; physicist, High Energy Radiation Sect, Nat Bur Stand, 49-62, chief, Radiation Physics Div, 62-66; dir, Am Inst Physics, 66-67. *Concurrent Pos:* Chmn, US Nat Comt, Comt Data Sci & Technol, past-chmn, Copy Clearance Ctr; past-pres, Nat Fedn Abstracting & Indexing Serv. *Mem:* Fel Am Phys Soc; fel Optical Soc Am; Am Asn Physics Teachers; fel AAAS; Acoust Soc Am. *Res:* Nuclear physics research on 20 million electron volt, 50 million electron volt and 180 million electron volt electron accelerator; development of high-energy x-ray spectrometer; Bremsstrahlung production; radiation physics research from 50 kiloelectron volts to 180 million electron volts; studies of science information flow. *Mailing Add:* 2105 Ambassador Dr 106 Colorado Springs CO 30921

KOCH, HOWARD A(LEXANDER), CHEMICAL ENGINEERING. *Current Pos:* RETIRED. *Personal Data:* b Evanston, Ill, June 15, 22; m 43; c 2. *Educ:* Northwestern Univ, BS, 43, MS, 46, PhD(chem eng), 49. *Prof Exp:* Asst chem engr, Northwestern Univ, 46, res supvr, 46-49; proj leader, Reservoir Mechs, Atlantic Refining Co, 49-59, sr reservoir engr, 59-61, div reservoir engr, 61-63, mgr, Block 31 Unit Opers, 63-67, dist mgr, Rocky Mt-Mid Continent Dist, 67-69; res eng mgr, Atlantic Richfield Co, 69-73; vpres eng, Arco Oil & Gas Co, 73-84. *Mem:* Am Inst Chem Engrs; Am Inst Mining, Metall & Petrol Engrs. *Res:* Unit operations; gas absorption; reservoir mechanics; fluid flow and mass transfer. *Mailing Add:* 4529 Crooked Lane Dallas TX 75229

KOCH, J FREDERICK, SEMICONDUCTOR PHYSICS. *Current Pos:* PROF PHYSICS, TECH UNIV MUNCHEN, 73- *Personal Data:* b Berlin, Ger, June 1, 37; US citizen; m 85; c 4. *Educ:* NY Univ, BA, 58; Univ Calif, Berkeley, PhD(physics), 62. *Prof Exp:* Asst prof physics, Univ Calif, Berkeley, 62-63; from asst prof to prof physics, Univ Md, College Park, 63-73. *Mem:* Fel Am Phys Soc; Deutsche Phys Gesellschaft. *Mailing Add:* Dept Physics Tech Univ Munchen 85747 Garching Germany

KOCH, KAY FRANCES, ORGANIC CHEMISTRY. *Current Pos:* RETIRED. *Personal Data:* b Tremont, Ill, June 18, 36; m 71. *Educ:* Univ Ill, BS, 58; Univ Calif, Berkeley, PhD(org chem), 62. *Prof Exp:* Instr chem, Wellesley Col, 61-63, asst prof, 63-66; sr org chemist, Res Labs, Eli Lilly Co, 66-77, head microbiol & fermentation res, 77-80, head phys chem res, 80-88, mgr sci info serv, 88-93. *Concurrent Pos:* Nat Inst Gen Med Sci spec fel, 64-65. *Mem:* Am Chem Soc. *Res:* Photochemistry of highly conjugated cyclic organic and other organic compounds; biosynthesis of quinones in insects and study of defensive secretions of insects; fermentation products chemistry; antibiotics, especially amino glycosides. *Mailing Add:* 8518 Hughes Rd North Salem IN 46165

KOCH, LEONARD JOHN, NUCLEAR POWER. *Current Pos:* RETIRED. *Personal Data:* b Chicago, Ill, Mar 30, 20; c 1. *Educ:* Ill Inst Technol, BS, 43; Univ Chicago, MBA, 68. *Prof Exp:* Var mgt positions, Argonne Nat Lab, 48-72; mgr nuclear projs, Ill Power Co, 72-76, vpres, 76-83. *Mem:* Nat Acad Eng; fel Am Nuclear Soc. *Mailing Add:* 1 E Desert Sky Rd No 16 Tucson AZ 85737

KOCH, MELVIN VERNON, pharmaceutical chemistry, for more information see previous edition

KOCH, PETER, WOOD SCIENCE & TECHNOLOGY. *Current Pos:* PRES, WOOD SCI LABS INC, CORVALLIS, MONT, 84- *Personal Data:* b Missoula, Mont, Oct 15, 20; m 50, Doris Hagen. *Educ:* Mont State Univ, BS, 42; Univ Wash, PhD(wood sci), 54. *Hon Degrees:* DSc, Univ Maine, 80. *Honors & Awards:* John Scott Award, 73; Distinguished Serv Award, Soc Wood Sci & Technol, 87; Forest Indust Award, 87. *Prof Exp:* Asst to pres, Stetson-Ross Mach Co, Wash, 46-52; consult engr, 52-55; assoc prof wood sci, Mich State Univ, 55-57; vpres & dir, Champlin Co, NH, 57-62; res & writing, 62-63; chief wood scientist & proj leader, Southern Forest Exp Sta, Forest Serv, USDA, Pineville, 63-82, res scientist, Intermountain Res Sta, Missoula, 82-84. *Concurrent Pos:* Adj prof wood & paper sci, NC State Univ, 73-; mem, Comt Renewable Resources for Indust Mat, Nat Res Coun, 75; adj prof, Wood Sci, Univ Mont, 83-; distinguished affil prof, Wood Sci, Univ Idaho, 83; concurrent prof, Univ Nanjing, 86- *Mem:* Am Soc Mech Engrs; Nat Soc Prof Engrs; Wood Sci & Technol; Forest Prod Res Soc (pres, 72-73); fel Int Acad Wood Sci; fel Soc Am Foresters. *Res:* Wood machining processes, wood conversion processes; improved utilization of southern pines, southern hardwoods and lodgepole pine; author of more than 200 papers and four major texts. *Mailing Add:* Wood Sci Lab Inc 942 Little Willow Creek Rd Corvallis MT 59828

KOCH, PETER M, ATOMIC PHYSICS, DYNAMICS. *Current Pos:* from asst prof to assoc prof, 82-89, PROF PHYSICS, STATE UNIV NY, STONY BROOK, 89- *Personal Data:* b Washington, DC, Feb 11, 45; m; c 2. *Educ:* Univ Mich, BS, 66; Yale Univ, MP, 69, PhD(physics), 74. *Prof Exp:* Asst prof physics, Yale Univ, 76-82. *Concurrent Pos:* A P Sloan Found fel, 78-82; Alexander von Humboldt Found Sr US Scientist Award, 89-90. *Mem:* Am Inst Physics; Am Phys Soc; Sigma Xi. *Res:* Experimental study of highly excited simple atoms (hydrogen and helium) in intense electromagnetic fields for understanding quantum dynamics in classically chaotic systems, ie, quantum chaology; atomic laser and synchrotron radiation spectroscopy; rf electric discharges. *Mailing Add:* Dept Physics State Univ NY Stony Brook NY 11794

KOCH, RICHARD, PEDIATRICS, PHENYLKETONMIA. *Current Pos:* From instr to prof pediat, 55-75, head, Div Child Develop, 65-75, PROF CLIN PEDIAT, SCH MED, UNIV SOUTHERN CALIF, 76-; DIR, MATERNAL PKU NAT COL LAB STUDY, 84- *Personal Data:* b NDak, Nov 24, 21; m 43, Kathryn J Holt; c Jill, Thomas, Christine, Martin & Leslie. *Educ:* Univ Rochester, MD, 51; Univ Calif, AB, 58. *Concurrent Pos:* Dir, Child Develop Clin, Los Angeles Children's Hosp, 55-75, mem, Div Med Genetics, 76-80, actg head, 80-86; dir, Regional Ctr Developmentally Disabled; dep dir chg ment health, develop, disabilities & drug abuse, Calif State Dept Health, 75-76. *Mem:* Acad Pediat; Am Asn Ment Deficiency; Soc Inherited Metab Dis. *Res:* Mental retardation in children; metabolic diseases; clinical genetics. *Mailing Add:* Children's Hosp 4614 Sunset Blvd Los Angeles CA 90027. *Fax:* 213-663-8446

KOCH, RICHARD CARL, MEDICINAL CHEMISTRY. *Current Pos:* chemist, Pfizer Inc, 59-66, proj leader, 66-68, sect mgr, 68-72, asst dir, 72-76, DIR, CENT RES DIV, PFIZER, INC, 76- *Personal Data:* b Pittsburgh, Pa, Aug 10, 30; m 47; c 4. *Educ:* Cornell Univ, BA, 52; Yale Univ, PhD(org chem), 57. *Prof Exp:* Res chemist, Res & Eng Div, Monsanto Chem Co, 57-59. *Mem:* Am Chem Soc; Sigma Xi; Soc Environ Toxicol & Chem. *Res:* Discovery and development of animal health drugs. *Mailing Add:* 22 Laurel Hill Dr S Niantic CT 06357-1508

KOCH, RICHARD MONCRIEF, GEOMETRY. *Current Pos:* from asst prof to assoc prof, 66-84, PROF MATH, UNIV ORE, 84- *Personal Data:* b Hutchinson, Kans, Jan 29, 39. *Educ:* Harvard Univ, AB, 61; Princeton Univ, PhD(math), 64. *Prof Exp:* Instr math, Univ Calif, 64-66. *Mem:* Am Math Soc; Math Asn Am. *Res:* Differential geometry, particularly pseudogroups. *Mailing Add:* Dept Math Univ Ore Eugene OR 97403-1222

KOCH, ROBERT B, biochemistry; deceased, see previous edition for last biography

KOCH, ROBERT HARRY, ASTRONOMY. *Current Pos:* assoc prof, Univ Pa, 67-69, actg chmn dept, 68-73, prof, 69-96, EMER PROF ASTRON, UNIV PA, 96- *Personal Data:* b York, Pa, Dec 19, 29; m 59; c 4. *Educ:* Univ Pa, AB, 51, MA, 55 & PhD(astron), 59. *Prof Exp:* Instr astron, Amherst & Mt Holyoke Cols, 59-60, from asst prof to assoc prof, Joint Dept Astron, Amherst, Mt Holyoke & Smith Cols & Univ Mass, 60-66; assoc prof astron, Univ NMex, 66-67. *Mem:* AAAS; Am Astron Soc; Int Astron Union. *Res:* Photoelectric photometry, polarimetry, visible band and ultraviolet spectroscopy and evolution of eclipsing variable stars. *Mailing Add:* Dept Physics & Astron Univ Pa 209 S 33rd St Philadelphia PA 19104-6394

KOCH, ROBERT JACOB, MATHEMATICS. *Current Pos:* From asst prof to assoc prof, 53-62, PROF MATH, LA STATE UNIV, BATON ROUGE, 62- *Personal Data:* b Chicago, Ill, Apr 17, 26; m 57; c 2. *Educ:* Tulane Univ, La, PhD(math), 53. *Mem:* Am Math Soc. *Res:* Topological semigroups. *Mailing Add:* Dept Math La State Univ Baton Rouge LA 70803-0001

KOCH, ROBERT MICHAEL, STRUCTURAL DYNAMICS & ACOUSTICS OF ADVANCED MARINE VEHICLES, STATE-OF-THE-ART FINITE ELEMENT ANALYSIS & UNDERWATER SHOCK ANALYSIS. *Current Pos:* RES SCIENTIST APPL MECH, NAVAL UNDERSEA WARFARE CTR, 91- *Personal Data:* b Mineola, NY, Apr 19, 64; m 91, Laureen Chase. *Educ:* Polytech Univ, BS, 86, MS, 88, PhD(appl mech), 91. *Prof Exp:* Engr, Vernitron Corp, 83-85; teaching fel, Polytech Univ, 86-91. *Concurrent Pos:* Consult, Beltran Inc, 88-91; adj prof eng, Roger Williams Univ, 93- *Mem:* Am Soc Mech Engrs; Am Inst Aeronaut & Astronaut; Sigma Xi; NY Acad Sci. *Res:* Underwater structural acoustics; adaptive procedures in h-, p- and hp-version finite element analysis; rapid prototyping with stereolithography; probabilistic structural mechanics; ultrasonic wave propagation in elastic solids. *Mailing Add:* 18 McIntosh Dr Portsmouth RI 02871. *Fax:* 401-841-6202; *E-Mail:* koch@caspr5.npt.nuwc.navy.mil

KOCH, ROBERT MILTON, ANIMAL BREEDING. *Current Pos:* From asst prof to assoc prof animal husb, 50-59, chmn dept, 59-66, PROF ANIMAL SCI, UNIV NEBR, 59- *Personal Data:* b Sioux City, Iowa, May 15, 24; wid; c William, James & Richard. *Educ:* Mont State Univ, BS, 48; Iowa State Univ, MS, 50, PhD(animal breeding, genetics), 53. *Honors & Awards:* Animal Breeding & Genetics Award, Am Soc Animal Sci, 76; Pioneer Award, Beef Improvement Fed, 79. *Concurrent Pos:* Supt, Ft Robinson Beef Cattle Res Sta, 54-57. *Mem:* Fel AAAS; fel Am Soc Animal Sci. *Res:* Beef cattle breeding; population genetics. *Mailing Add:* Animal Sci Dept Lincoln NE 68583-0908. *Fax:* 402-472-6362

KOCH, RONALD JOSEPH, PHYSICS, MATERIALS SCIENCE. *Current Pos:* From res spectrochemist to sr res spectrochemist, Armco Inc, 69-75, sr res chemist, 75-78, sr res physicist, 78-83, RADIATION SAFETY OFFICER, ARMCO INC, 78-, SR STAFF PHYSICIST, 83- *Personal Data:* b Cincinnati, Ohio, June 30, 39; m 61; c 4. *Educ:* Xavier Univ, Ohio, BS, 61; Johns Hopkins Univ, PhD(physics), 69. *Mem:* Am Iron & Steel Inst; Am Soc for Testing & Mat. *Res:* X-ray physics and diffraction; auger spectroscopy; surface analysis; radiation safety. *Mailing Add:* Armco Inc 705 Curtis St Middletown OH 45043

KOCH, RONALD N, FLOW MEASUREMENT. *Current Pos:* OWNER, RONCOKE ASSOC, 89- *Personal Data:* b Pittsburgh, Pa, Aug 19, 41; m 63; c 3. *Educ:* Carnegie-Mellon Univ, BSME, 63; Univ Pittsburgh, MBA, 83. *Honors & Awards:* Indust Prod Award, Soc Petrol Engrs, 84. *Prof Exp:* Develop engr, Rockwell Int, 63-76, mgr eng, 76-85, dir technol, 85-89. *Mem:* Am Water Works Asn; Am Soc Sanit Engrs; Asn Mech Engrs; Int Water Supply Asn. *Res:* New product development activities for equipment in the field of flow measurement. *Mailing Add:* 112 Deer Valley Dr Sewickley PA 15143

KOCH, RUDY G, science education, plant taxonomy; deceased, see previous edition for last biography

KOCH, STANLEY D, ORGANIC CHEMISTRY, POLYMER CHEMISTRY. *Current Pos:* MGR POLYMERIC COATINGS RES, ENTHONE, INC, 79- *Personal Data:* b Cleveland, Ohio, Feb 10, 24; m 58; c 3. *Educ:* Univ Ill, BA, 47; Cornell Univ, PhD(org chem), 50. *Prof Exp:* Fel, Univ Chicago, 50-51; res chemist, Jackson Lab, E I Du Pont de Nemours & Co, 51-54 & Glendale Plaskon Lab, Barrett Div, Allied Chem Corp, 54-57; sr res chemist, Boston Lab, Monsanto Res Corp, 57-59, group leader, 59-64, res mgr, 64, Dayton Lab, 65-69; dept head, Horizons Res, Inc, 69-73; sec head, photo cure, Dwight P Joyce Res Ctr, Glidden-Durkee Div, SCM Corp, 74-77; develop assoc, Washington Res Ctr, W R Grace & Co, 77-78. *Mem:* Am Chem Soc; Inst Interconnecting & Packaging Electronic Circuits. *Res:* UV-curable coatings, including those used in the electronics industry; radiation curing; herbicides. *Mailing Add:* 118 Briarwood Dr Guilford CT 06437-1806

KOCH, STEPHEN ANDREW, INORGANIC CHEMISTRY. *Current Pos:* from asst prof to assoc prof, 78-93, PROF CHEM, STATE UNIV NY, 93- *Personal Data:* b Jamaica, NY, Nov 19, 48; m 75, Michelle Millar. *Educ:* Fordham Univ, BS, 70; Mass Inst Technol, PhD(chem), 75. *Prof Exp:* Assoc inorg chem, Tex A&M Univ, 75-77 & Cornell Univ, 78. *Mem:* Am Chem Soc. *Res:* Structural, electronic and reactivity properties of transition metal compound; bioinorganic chemistry; catalysis. *Mailing Add:* Dept Chem State Univ NY Stony Brook NY 11794-3400. *Fax:* 516-632-7960; *E-Mail:* skoch@ccmail.sunysb.edu

KOCH, STEPHEN DOUGLAS, PLANT TAXONOMY. *Current Pos:* PROF-INVESTR BOT, POSTGRAD COL, CHAPINGO, MEX, 73- *Personal Data:* b New York, NY, Dec 16, 40; m 68, Carol A Patrick; c Nicholas & Oliver. *Educ:* Swarthmore Col, BA, 62; Univ Mich, MS, 64, PhD(plant taxon), 69. *Honors & Awards:* Sistema Nacional de Investigadores, 84- *Prof Exp:* Instr bot, Duke Univ, 67-68; asst prof, NC State Univ, 68-73. *Mem:* Fel AAAS; Am Soc Plant Taxonomists; Int Asn Plant Taxonomists; Mex Bot Soc; Sigma Xi; Torrey Bot Club. *Res:* Grass systematics. *Mailing Add:* Centro Botanica Colegio de Postgraduados Chapingo Edo 56230 Mexico. *Fax:* 52-545-45077

KOCH, TAD H, ORGANIC CHEMISTRY. *Current Pos:* from asst prof to assoc prof, 68-80, chair, 83-86, PROF ORG CHEM, UNIV COLO, BOULDER, 80- *Personal Data:* b Mt Vernon, Ohio, Jan 1, 43; m 76, Carol A Kuban. *Educ:* Ohio State Univ, BS, 64, Iowa State Univ, PhD(org photochem), 68. *Concurrent Pos:* Grants, Petrol Res Fund, 68-72, 77-79, 83-86 & 97-, Res Corp, 69- 70, Gen Med Sci Inst, 71-77, Nat Cancer Inst, 78-91 & 93-, Army Res Off, 80-88, NSF, 86-91, Nat Heart Lung Blood Inst, 87-89, Coun Tobacco Res, 92- *Mem:* Am Chem Soc; Am Asn Cancer Res; Am Soc Photobiol; AAAS. *Res:* Mechanistic and synthetic photochemistry; free radical chemistry; bioorganic chemistry; lasers. *Mailing Add:* Dept Chem & Biochem Univ Colo Boulder CO 80309-0215

KOCH, THEODORE AUGUR, PHYSICAL CHEMISTRY, CATALYSIS. *Current Pos:* CHEMIST, PETROCHEM DEPT, E I DU PONT DE NEMOURS & CO, INC, 52- *Personal Data:* b Schenectady, NY, Oct 21, 25; m 52; c 5. *Educ:* St Michael's Col, BS, 46, MS, 47; Univ Pa, PhD(chem), 52. *Prof Exp:* Instr chem, Univ Vt, 46 & Drexel Inst, 47-51. *Mailing Add:* 600 Cheltenham Rd Wilmington DE 19808

KOCH, THOMAS L, OPTOELECTRONICS, OPTICAL FIBER COMMUNICATIONS. *Current Pos:* Mem tech staff, Electronic Device Res Dept, 82-87, supvr, Photonic Circuits Res Dept, 87-89, HEAD, OPTOELECTRONICS RES DEPT, AT&T BELL LABS, 89- *Personal Data:* b Boston, Mass, July 13, 55; m 79; c 2. *Educ:* Princeton Univ, AB, 77; Calif Inst Technol, PhD(appl physics), 82. *Concurrent Pos:* Mem prog comts for numerous int & nat conf, 85-; distinguished lectr award, Laser & Electroptics Soc, Inst Elec & Electronics Engrs, 90, mem bd gov, 91-93. *Mem:* Sr mem Inst Elec & Electronics Engrs Laser & Electroptics Soc; fel Optical Soc Am. *Res:* Semiconductor lasers and optical fiber communications; single-frequency and tunable lasers; device fabrication, dynamic characteristics for high speed transmission; integration of semiconductor guided-wave optoelectronic components to form photonic integrated circuits. *Mailing Add:* Lucent Technols Rm 4E-338 101 Crawfords Corner Rd Holmdel NJ 07733

KOCH, THOMAS RICHARD, CLINICAL CHEMISTRY, ANALYTICAL CHEMISTRY. *Current Pos:* LAB DIR, MD MED LAB, 92- *Personal Data:* b Strasburg, Pa, Oct 9, 44; m 68; c 3. *Educ:* Lebanon Valley Col, BS, 66; Univ Md, PhD(anal chem), 70. *Prof Exp:* Trainee clin chem, State Univ NY, Buffalo, 70-72; clin chemist, St Joseph Hosp, 72-75; asst prof path & assoc dir clin chem, Sch Med, Univ Md, 75-82, assoc prof path & dir clin chem, 82-92. *Concurrent Pos:* Consult, Vet Admin Hosp, 76-80 & Food & Drug Admin, USPHS, 77- *Mem:* Am Asn Clin Chem. *Res:* Trace elements in human disease; bilirubin measurement. *Mailing Add:* 1117 Chatterleigh Circle Baltimore MD 21204

KOCH, WALTER THEODORE, ORGANIC CHEMISTRY. *Current Pos:* RETIRED. *Personal Data:* b Orwigsburg, Pa, Jan 4, 23; m 46; c 3. *Educ:* Albright Col, BS, 44; Rutgers Univ, MS, 50, PhD(org chem), 51. *Prof Exp:* Asst gen chem, Rutgers Univ, 47-50; res chemist, Merck & Co, Inc, 51-53 & Am Viscose Corp, 53-63; res chemist, 63-66, sect leader, FMC Corp, 66-78. *Mem:* Am Chem Soc. *Res:* High polymers; cellophane, coatings; thermoplastic films. *Mailing Add:* 4 E Langhorne Ave Havertown PA 19083-4707

KOCH, WILLIAM EDWARD, ANATOMY. *Current Pos:* assoc prof, 68-75, PROF ANAT, SCH MED, UNIV NC, CHAPEL HILL, 68-, ADJ PROF ZOOL, 77- *Personal Data:* b York, Pa, Nov 22, 33; m 61; c 2. *Educ:* Univ Pa, AB, 56, AM, 59; Stanford Univ, PhD(biol), 62. *Prof Exp:* From instr to asst prof anat, Sch Med, Yale Univ, 62-68. *Mem:* AAAS; Am Soc Zoologists; Am Asn Anatomists; Soc Develop Biol. *Res:* Study of embryonic tissue interacting and differentiating in vitro. *Mailing Add:* Cell Biol & Anat Univ NC 108 Taylor Bldg CB 7090 Chapel Hill NC 27599

KOCH, WILLIAM FREDERICK, PH MEASUREMENTS, ION CHROMATOGRAPHY RESEARCH. *Current Pos:* Res fel, Nat Inst Stand & Technol, 75-77, res chemist, 77-79, group leader, 79-88, dep div chief, 88-93, DIV CHIEF, INORG ANALYTICAL RES DIV, NAT INST STAND & TECHNOL, 94-, DEP DIR, CHEM SCI & TECHNOL LAB, 95- *Personal Data:* b Oak Park, Ill, Mar 11, 50; m 75, Paula A Budewitz; c William H & Benjamin J. *Educ:* Loyola Univ, Chicago, BS, 72; Iowa State Univ, MS, 74, PhD(anal chem), 75. *Concurrent Pos:* Lectr chem, Montgomery Col, Rockville, Md, 83-88; bd dirs, Nat Comt Clin Lab Stand, 90- *Mem:* Am Chem Soc; Soc Electroanal Chem; Sigma Xi; Am Soc Testing & Mat; Nat Comt Clin Lab Stand (pres-elect, 96-); Am Asn Clin Chem. *Res:* Responsible for the nations reference standards, measurements and data for chemistry, chemical engineering and biotechnology; ion chromatography; pH conductivity; coulometry; standard reference materials; clinical chemistry; electrolytic conductivity. *Mailing Add:* 20468 Watkins Meadow Dr Germantown MD 20876. *Fax:* 301-975-3845; *E-Mail:* william.koch@nist.gov

KOCH, WILLIAM GEORGE, PHYSICAL CHEMISTRY. *Current Pos:* from asst prof to assoc prof, 55-59, chmn dept, 74-77, PROF CHEM, UNIV NORTHERN COLO, 59- *Personal Data:* b Forsyth, Mont, May 16, 24; m 51; c 1. *Educ:* Univ Notre Dame, BS, 47; Mont State Univ, MA, 53. *Prof Exp:* Asst chemist, Great Western Sugar Co, Colo, 54-55. *Mem:* AAAS; Am Chem Soc. *Res:* Carbon isotope effects in decarboxylation reactions; effect of deuterium on carbon isotope effects; kinetics in the reaction between organolithium compounds and ether. *Mailing Add:* 2602 16th Ave Greeley CO 80631-8204

KOCH, WILLIAM JULIAN, MYCOLOGY. *Current Pos:* RETIRED. *Personal Data:* b Durham, NC, May 17, 24; m 47; c 4. *Educ:* Univ NC, MA, 50, PhD(bot, plant physiol, zool), 55. *Prof Exp:* From asst to prof bot, Univ NC, Chapel Hill, 47-86. *Concurrent Pos:* Vis investr, Mich Biol Sta, 56, Highlands Biol Sta, 57, 58 & Int Bot Cong, Can, 59. *Mem:* AAAS; Bot Soc Am; Mycol Soc Am; Am Soc Plant Taxon; Electron Micros Soc Am. *Res:* Culture, comparative morphology, sexuality and mobility of fungus of reproductive cells; fungi parasitic on algae. *Mailing Add:* 10610 NW 22nd St Univ NC Pembroke FL 33026

KOCHAKIAN, CHARLES DANIEL, ENDOCRINOLOGY, BIOCHEMISTRY. *Current Pos:* prof physiol & biophys, Univ Ala, Birmingham, 57-61, prof biochem & prof & dir exp endocrinol, 61-79, prof physiol & biophys, 64-75, EMER PROF BIOCHEM, MED & DENT SCHS, UNIV ALA, BIRMINGHAM, 79- *Personal Data:* b Haverhill, Mass, Nov 18, 08; m 40; c 1. *Educ:* Boston Univ, AB, 30, AM, 31; Univ Rochester, PhD(physiol chem), 36. *Honors & Awards:* Claude Bernard Medal, Univ Montreal, 50; Medal, Osaka Endocrine Soc, 62; Charles D Kochakian Award, Endocrinol & Nutrit, Sch Med & Dent, Univ Rochester, 85. *Prof Exp:* Instr physiol, Sch Med & Dent, Univ Rochester, 36-40, assoc, 40-44, from asst prof to assoc prof endocrinol, 44-51; prof res biochem, Sch Med, Univ Okla, 51-57. *Concurrent Pos:* Assoc, Jackson Mem Lab, 46-49; mem panel hormones, Comt Growth, Nat Res Coun, 49-51 mem panel appraisers handbk biol data, 49-52; vis Claude Bernard prof, Inst Exp Med Surg, Univ Montreal, 50; assoc dir, Okla Med Res Found, 51-53, head dept biochem & endocrinol, 51-57, coordr res, 53-55; consult, Dent Sch Comt, Okla Dent Asn, 54-57; consult, Univ Tex M D Anderson Hosp & Tumor Inst Houston, 56, drug evaluations, AMA, 93; actg coordr res, Univ Ala, Birmingham, 60-61; consult, Div Int Med Educ, Asn Am Med Cols, 64-70; mem panel drugs for metab disturbances, Drug Efficacy Study, Nat Acad Sci-Nat Res Coun, 67-69; mem metab & endocrine eval comt, Vet Admin Hosp, 69-72; mem nomenclature comt, Int Union Physiol Sci, 69-73. *Mem:* AAAS; Am Chem Soc; Am Physiol Soc; Am Soc Biol Chemists; Endocrine Soc. *Res:* Steroid biochemistry; protein; carbohydrate and fat metabolism; enzymes; hormones; nucleic acids; mechanisms of anabolic action of steroid hormones. *Mailing Add:* 3617 Oakdale Rd Birmingham AL 35223

KOCHAN, IVAN, IMMUNOLOGY. *Current Pos:* prof microbiol, 67-89, EMER PROF MICROBIOL, MIAMI UNIV, 89- *Personal Data:* b Ukraine, Aug 20, 23; nat US; m 49; c 3. *Educ:* Univ Man, BSc, 53, MSc, 55; Stanford Univ, PhD(med microbiol), 58; Am Bd Med Microbiol, dipl. *Prof Exp:* Res assoc, Stanford Univ, 58-59; assoc prof microbiol, Baylor Univ, 59-61, prof & chmn deptof, 61-67. *Concurrent Pos:* Prof microbiol, Sch Med, Wright State Univ, 74-77. *Mem:* AAAS; Am Asn Immunologists; Reticuloendothelial Soc; Am Soc Microbiol; Am Thoracic Soc; fel Am Trudeau Soc; Am Acad Microbiol. *Res:* Study of transferrin-iron-mycobactin interplay in host-parasite relationship; nutritional immunity; role of fatty acids in cellular immunity and immunological diseases. *Mailing Add:* 121 Carriage Lane Grass Valley CA 95949

KOCHAN, ROBERT GEORGE, EXERCISE PHYSIOLOGY, BIOCHEMISTRY. *Personal Data:* b Prince Albert, Sask, Oct 25, 49; m 72; c 4. *Educ:* Univ Sask, BA, 71; Univ Toledo, PhD(exercise physiol), 78. *Prof Exp:* Teaching asst, Univ Sask, 71-73 & Univ Toledo, 73-77; fel biochem, Med Col Ohio, 77-79, res assoc, 79-80; asst prof exercise physiol, Univ Wis-Madison, 80-87. *Concurrent Pos:* Res fel, Juvenile Diabetes Found, 77-79. *Mem:* Am Col Sports Med. *Res:* Exercise metabolism; glycogen synthesis; insulin action mechanism; diabetes control. *Mailing Add:* 814 Lewis Ct Madison WI 53711

KOCHAN, WALTER J, PLANT PHYSIOLOGY. *Current Pos:* from asst horticulturist to assoc horticulturist, 57-70, res prof hort, Exp Sta, 70-87, PROF EMER, UNIV IDAHO, 87- *Personal Data:* b Plainfield, NJ, July 15, 22; m 48; c 1. *Educ:* Utah State Univ, BS, 50, MS, 52; Rutgers Univ, PhD(plant physiol), 55. *Prof Exp:* Asst horticulturist, Univ Idaho, 55-57; asst plant biochemist, Div Indust Res, Wash State Univ, 57. *Mem:* Am Soc Plant Physiologists; Sigma Xi. *Res:* Mineral nutrition of plants; post-harvest physiology of tree fruits. *Mailing Add:* 1107 Virginia Ave Moscow ID 83843

KOCHANOWSKI, BARBARA ANN, EXPERIMENTAL BIOLOGY. *Current Pos:* Res scientist health care, 85-90, SECT HEAD, HEALTH CARE, PROCTER & GAMBLE CO, 91- *Personal Data:* b Beaver, Pa, 1957. *Educ:* Pa State Univ, BS, 79; Univ Ill, Champaign, MS, 81, PhD(nutrit), 84. *Mem:* Am Inst Nutrit. *Mailing Add:* Procter & Gamble Co PO Box 8006 Mason OH 45040-8006

KOCHANSKY, JAN PETER, INSECT PHEROMONES & HORMONES, PESTICIDE SYNTHESIS. *Current Pos:* RES CHEMIST, AGR RES SERV, USDA, 76- *Personal Data:* b New York, NY, June 21, 44; m 69, Mary McCutchen Cooper; c Alice Amanda & Justina Janet. *Educ:* Harvard Col, AB, 66; Stanford Univ, MS, 67; Univ Colo, PhD(chem), 71. *Prof Exp:* Res assoc, NY Agr Exp Sta, 72-76. *Mem:* Am Chem Soc; Entom Soc Am; Int Soc Chem Ecol; Am Peptide Soc; Sigma Xi. *Res:* Biology and control of diseases and pests or bees; insect neurohomones, phermones and their analogs; pesticide synthesis and structure-activity studies. *Mailing Add:* Agr Res Serv US Dept Agr Bldg 476 Beltsville MD 20705-2350

KOCHAR, HARVINDER K, muscle diseases, for more information see previous edition

KOCHEN, MANFRED, INFORMATION SCIENCE, COGNITIVE SCIENCE. *Current Pos:* assoc prof math biol, 65-69, PROF INFO SCI & URBAN/REGIONAL PLANNING & RES MATHEMATICIAN, MENT HEALTH RES INST, 69-, ADJ PROF COMPUT INFO SYSTS, GRAD SCH BUS ADMIN, 82- *Personal Data:* b Vienna, Austria, July 4, 28; nat US; m 54; c 2. *Educ:* Mass Inst Technol, BS, 50; Columbia Univ, MA, 51, PhD(appl math), 55. *Prof Exp:* Asst, Spectros Lab, Mass Inst Technol, 49-50; mathematician aeroelasticity res, Biot & Arnold Co, 50-52; lectr math, Columbia Univ, 52-53; mem staff, Electronic Comput Proj, Inst Advan Study, 53-55; Ford fel math models in behav sci, Princeton Univ & Harvard Univ, 55-56; staff mathematician, Thomas J Watson Res Ctr, Int Bus Mach Corp, 56-58, mem res tech staff, 58-60, mgr info retrieval proj, 60-63, exchange vis expert at Euratom, Italy, 63-64. *Concurrent Pos:* Consult, Paul Rosenberg Assocs, 53-55, RCA Res Lab, 65, United Aircraft Corp, 66-69, Rand Corp, 68- & Sci Ctr Berlin, 78-; assoc ed, Behav Sci, 68-70, J Asn Comput Mach, 72- & managing ed, Human Systs Mgt, 79-; vis lectr, Asn Comput Mach, 69; hon res assoc, Harvard Univ, 73-74; pres, Wise Found, 75-; vis prof, Rockefeller Univ, 80-81; chmn, sociotechnol systs area in planning PhD prog, UTEP, Ment Health Res Inst, 83-; prin investr grants, NIH & NSF, 85- *Mem:* Am Math Soc; Am Soc Info Sci; Fedn Am Scientists; Am Phys Soc; fel AAAS; NY Acad Sci; Inst Elec & Electronics Engrs. *Res:* Information systems and organization of knowledge; models for information-seeking behavior, problem representation solving, cognitive learning processes; decentralization theory; science of science; social planning; artificial intelligence; decision support systems. *Mailing Add:* 2026 Devonshire Rd Ann Arbor MI 48104

KOCHEN, SIMON BERNARD, MATHEMATICS. *Current Pos:* PROF MATH, PRINCETON UNIV, 67- *Personal Data:* b Antwerp, Belg, Aug 14, 34; nat US. *Educ:* McGill Univ, BSc, 54, MSc, 55; Princeton Univ, MA, 56, PhD(math), 58. *Honors & Awards:* Cole Prize, Am Math Soc, 67. *Prof Exp:* Asst lectr math, Princeton Univ, 57-58; Nat Res Coun Can res assoc & asst prof, Univ Montreal, 58-59; from asst prof to prof, Cornell Univ, 59-67. *Concurrent Pos:* Guggenheim fel, 62-63; mem, Inst Advan Study, 66-67. *Mem:* Am Math Soc; Asn Symbolic Logic. *Res:* Mathematical logic. *Mailing Add:* Dept Math Princeton Univ Fine Hall Washington Rd Princeton NJ 08544-1000

KOCHER, BRYAN S, COMPUTER SCIENCE. *Current Pos:* PRES, G&E SYSTS, 92- *Personal Data:* b July 3, 48; m 71, Sandra Wagner; c Dana & Whitney. *Educ:* Moravian Col, AB, 70; Univ Mass, MS, 75; Wang Inst, PhD, 81. *Prof Exp:* Proj leader, Com Union, 75-77; syst mgr, Raytheon Data Systs, 77-80; sr software eng, Cullinane, 80-82; prod mgr, Interactive Data Corp, 82-85; dept mgr, Data Resources Inc, 85-86; consult proj mgr, Consults Mgt Decisions, Inc, 86-92. *Concurrent Pos:* Chmn, Boston Chap, Asn Comput Mach, 78-80, regional vpres, 80-88. *Mem:* Asn Comput Mach (pres, 88-90, past pres, 90-92). *Mailing Add:* G&E Systs 250 Edge Hill Rd Sharon MA 02067

KOCHER, CARL A, EXPERIMENTAL ATOMIC PHYSICS. *Current Pos:* from asst prof to assoc prof, PROF PHYSICS, ORE STATE UNIV, 73- *Personal Data:* b Seattle, Wash, Feb 14, 42; m 68, Marilyn Tennant; c Suzanne, Paul & Scott. *Educ:* Univ Calif, Berkeley, AB, 63, PhD(physics), 67. *Prof Exp:* Fel, Oxford Univ, 67-68; vis scientist, Mass Inst Technol, 68-69; lectr, Columbia Univ, 69-73. *Concurrent Pos:* Fel, NSF, 76-77. *Mem:* Am Phys Soc; Am Asn Physics Teachers; Fedn Am Scientists; Union Concerned Scientists. *Res:* Atomic collisions; radiative and autoionization processes; high Rydberg states; surface physics; analytical and computer instrumentation. *Mailing Add:* Dept Physics Ore State Univ Corvallis OR 97331-6507. *Fax:* 541-737-1683; *E-Mail:* kocher@physics.orst.edu

KOCHER, CHARLES WILLIAM, NUCLEAR PHYSICS. *Current Pos:* scientist, 65-67, SR RES PHYSICIST, ANALYSIS LAB, DOW CHEM USA, 67- *Personal Data:* b Johnson City, NY, May 16, 32; m 54; c 3. *Educ:* Harpur Col, BA, 54; NC State Col, MS, 56; Ind Univ, PhD(nuclear physics), 61. *Prof Exp:* Res assoc physics, Solid State Physics Group, Brookhaven Nat Lab, 61-62; sr staff scientist, Phys Res Lab, Budd Co, 62-65. *Mem:* AAAS; Am Chem Soc; Am Phys Soc; Sigma Xi. *Res:* Nuclear research reactors and decay schemes; Mossbauer effect; solid state physics, corrosion testing; metalorganic chemistry. *Mailing Add:* 907 Deerfield Ct Midland MI 48640-2708

KOCHER, DAVID CHARLES, PHYSICS, ENVIRONMENTAL SCIENCES. *Current Pos:* res assoc, 71-76, RES SCIENTIST PHYSICS & ENVIRON SCI, OAK RIDGE NAT LAB, 76- *Personal Data:* b Washington, DC, Nov 9, 41; m 77. *Educ:* Univ Md, BS, 63; Univ Wis-Madison, MS, 65, PhD(physics), 70. *Prof Exp:* Res assoc physics, Univ Birmingham, 70-71. *Mem:* Am Phys Soc; Am Nuclear Soc; Health Physics Soc. *Res:* Development of models and data bases for the assessment of health and safety impacts on man from energy production technologies. *Mailing Add:* Oak Ridge Nat Lab 1060 Commerce Park Oak Ridge TN 37830-6480. *Fax:* 423-574-1778

KOCHER, HARIBHAJAN S(INGH), FLUID MECHANICS. *Current Pos:* RES ASSOC, EASTMAN KODAK CO, ROCHESTER, NY, 82- *Personal Data:* b Lyall Pur, WPakistan, Sept 29, 34; m 63; c 2. *Educ:* Okla State Univ, BS, 57; Purdue Univ, MS, 59; Mich State Univ, PhD(fluid mech), 63. *Prof Exp:* Lectr mech eng, Indian Inst Technol, New Delhi, 62-63; develop engr, Civilian Atomic Power Dept, Can Gen Elec Co, 63-64; sr res physicist, Delco Prod Div, Gen Motors Corp, NY, 64-66; scientist, Xerox Corp, 66-82. *Concurrent Pos:* Adj asst prof, Univ Rochester, 76- *Mem:* Am Soc Mech Engrs; Inst Elec & Electronics Engrs. *Res:* Thermal properties of metals; heat transfer in nuclear reactors and electrical motors; boundary layer studies; fluid flow instability; air bearing technology; heat transfer in xerographic systems; photographic film process fluid mechanics. *Mailing Add:* 56 Leonard Crest Penfield NY 14526

KOCHERLAKOTA, KATHLEEN, STATISTICS. *Current Pos:* sessional lectr statist, 67-69, from asst prof to assoc prof, 69-87, PROF, UNIV MAN, 87- *Personal Data:* b Pittsburgh, Pa, Mar 31, 38; m 62, Subrahmaniam; c 2. *Educ:* Muskingum Col, BS, 60; Johns Hopkins Univ, MS, 63, DSc(statist), 69. *Prof Exp:* Lectr math, Muskingum Col, 62-63; consult statist, Dept Community Med, Univ Western Ont, 65-70. *Mem:* Biomet Soc; Am Statist Asn. *Res:* Applied multivariate analysis and analysis of discrete data. *Mailing Add:* Dept Statist Univ Man Winnipeg MB R3T 2N2 Can. *Fax:* 204-275-5011; *E-Mail:* kocherl@ccu.umanitoba.ca

KOCHERLAKOTA, SUBRAHMANIAM, MATHEMATICAL STATISTICS. *Current Pos:* assoc prof, 66-70, PROF STATIST, UNIV MAN, 70- *Personal Data:* b Bangalore, India, Feb 3, 35; m 62, Kathleen Jackson; c 2. *Educ:* Univ Col Sci, Benares, India, BSc, 54, MSc, 57; Inst Agr Res Statist, dipl, 63; ScD, Johns Hopkins, 64. *Prof Exp:* Jr res fel statist, Inst Agr Res Statist, 57-58, sr res fel, 58-59; investr, Rockefeller Found, India, 59-60; asst prof math, Univ Western Ont, 64-66. *Concurrent Pos:* Nat Res Coun operating grants pure & appl math, 66- *Mem:* Inst Math Statist; Am Statist Asn; fel Royal Statist Soc; Int Statist Inst. *Res:* Multivariate analysis; distribution theory; statistical tests of significance; applied probability theory; non-normality. *Mailing Add:* Dept Statist Univ Man Winnipeg MB R3T 2N2 Can. *Fax:* 204-275-5011; *E-Mail:* kocherl@cc.umanitoba.ca

KOCHERT, GARY DEAN, BOTANY. *Current Pos:* From asst prof to assoc prof, 67-78, PROF BOT & CHMN DEPT, UNIV GA, 78- *Personal Data:* b Louisville, Ky, Oct 12, 39; m 63; c 2. *Educ:* Ind Univ, AB, 63, PhD(microbiol), 67. *Res:* Molecular genetics and systematics of rice, peanuts, and bamboo. *Mailing Add:* Bot Dept Univ Ga Rm 4512 Plant Sci Blvd Athens GA 30602

KOCHHAR, DEVENDRA M, ANATOMY, EMBRYOLOGY. *Current Pos:* PROF ANAT, JEFFERSON MED COL, 76- *Personal Data:* b Sailkot, India, Mar 10, 38; wid; c Vineet S & Romeen. *Educ:* Punjab Univ, India, BSc, 58, MSc, 59; Univ Fla, PhD(anat), 64. *Honors & Awards:* Warkany Award, 90. *Prof Exp:* Instr anat, Univ Fla, 64-65; vis scientist, Karolinska & Wenner-Grens Insts, Stockholm, Sweden, 65-66; vis scientist, Strangeways Res Lab, Cambridge, 66-67; guest investr, Rockefeller Univ, 67-68; from asst prof to assoc prof anat, Univ Iowa, 68-71; from assoc prof to prof, Univ Va, 71-76. *Concurrent Pos:* Consult pharmaceut indust, Environ Protection Agency & Food & Drug Admin. *Mem:* Am Soc Cell Biol; Am Asn Anatomists; Teratology Soc (pres, 82-83); Soc Develop Biol. *Res:* Experimental teratology; development of skeletal system; congenital abnormalities of limb; collagen genes in development; retinoids in health and disease. *Mailing Add:* Dept Anat Jefferson Col Med 1020 Locust St Philadelphia PA 19107-6799. *Fax:* 215-923-3808

KOCHHAR, MAN MOHAN, MEDICINAL CHEMISTRY, BIOCHEMICAL TOXICOLOGY. *Current Pos:* RES SCI, OFF STAND-FDA, 83- *Personal Data:* b Lahore, Pakistan, Sept 14, 32; US citizen; m 54; c 3. *Educ:* Punjab Univ, India, BS, 53; Univ Tex, Austin, MS, 61, PhD(med chem), 64. *Prof Exp:* Chief chemist, Dr Nayer Chem Works, India, 54-55; med rep, Geigy Pharmaceut, India, 55-58; asst med chem, Univ Tex, Austin, 59-63; spec instr, Col Pharm, 63-64; from asst prof to assoc prof pharm & pharmaceut chem, Auburn Univ, 64-75, prof toxicol, 75-81, prof pharmacol & toxicol, 81-83. *Concurrent Pos:* Lederle fac awards, 64 & 65; grant-in-aid, Auburn Univ, 65-68; Nat Inst Drug Abuse award, 73; Dept Ment Health award, State of Ala, 74; dir, Drug Screening Training Prog, Auburn Univ & Drug Anal Lab, 73- *Mem:* Am Acad Clin Toxicol; Am Asn Clin Chem; Am Pub Health Asn; Can Acad Clin Anal Toxicol. *Res:* Structure-activity relationships among psychotropic and antineoplastic agents; biochemical approach to toxicology including analytical toxicology. *Mailing Add:* 9458 Macomber Lane Columbia MD 21045

KOCHHAR, RAJINDAR KUMAR, POLYMER CHEMISTRY. *Current Pos:* CHEM CONSULT, 83- *Personal Data:* b Nurmahal, India, Aug 1, 22; US citizen; m 54; c 2. *Educ:* Panjab Univ, India, BS, 45; Univ Delhi, MS, 48; Univ Tex, Austin, PhD(phys org chem), 65; Univ Mo-Kansas City, MBA, 69. *Prof Exp:* Asst med res, Lady Hardinge Med Col, Delhi, 55-58; res chemist, Gulf Res & Develop Co, 64-68, sr res chemist, 68-77, mgr polymerization res, 77-81, dir process chem, plastics div, 81-83. *Res:* Color and chemical constitution; dyes for nylon; research on medicinal plants; fixed oils; polymer synthesis and characterization; polyolefin development; polypropylene catalysts. *Mailing Add:* 610 Brenwick Ct Katy TX 77450

KOCHI, JAY KAZUO, ORGANIC CHEMISTRY. *Current Pos:* ROBERT WELCH DISTINGUISHED PROF CHEM, UNIV HOUSTON, UNIV PARK, 84- *Personal Data:* b Los Angeles, Calif, May 17, 27; m 59; c Sims, Ariel & Julia. *Educ:* Univ Calif, Los Angeles, BS, 49; Iowa State Univ, PhD(chem), 52. *Honors & Awards:* James Flack Norris Award, Am Chem Soc, 81; A C Cope Scholar Award, Am Chem Soc, 88; A V Humboldt Sr Scientist Award, 87. *Prof Exp:* Instr org chem, Harvard Univ, 52-55; NIH fel, Cambridge Univ, 55-56; vis asst prof, Iowa State Univ, 56; chemist, Shell Develop Co, 57-62; from assoc prof to prof chem, Case Western Res Univ, 62-69; prof chem, Ind Univ, Bloomington, 69-74, Earl Blough prof chem, 74-84. *Mem:* Nat Acad Sci; Am Chem Soc; Royal Soc Chem. *Res:* Mechanisms of organic reactions catalyzed by metal complexes; application of metal complexes to organic synthesis; electron-transfer and charge-transfer processes in organic chemistry; photochemistry of organometallic compounds; application of electron spin resonance spectroscopy to organic and organometallic free radicals and to the mechanism of homolytic reactions; time-resolved spectroscopy of inactive intermediates. *Mailing Add:* 4372 Faculty Lane Houston TX 77004-6601. *Fax:* 713-743-2709; *E-Mail:* cjulian@pop.uh.edu

KOCHMAN, RONALD LAWRENCE, DRUG SURVEILLANCE & LABELING, CLINICAL RESEARCH. *Current Pos:* Res biologist, G D Searle & Co, 75-79, res assoc, 79-82, res investr, 82-86, sr res assoc, 86-88, from asst dir to assoc dir, 88-93, DIR LABELING & OPERS, WORLDWIDE SAFETY & LABELING, G D SEARLE & CO, SUBSID MONSANTO CO, 93- *Personal Data:* b Rome, NY, Apr, 7, 46; m 68; c 2. *Educ:* Pa State Univ, BS, 68; Northeastern Univ, MS, 74. *Mem:* Drug Info Asn; Am Soc Pharmacol & Exp Therapeut; Am Soc Neurochem. *Res:* Clinical trails of anti-ulcer, analgesic and anxiolytic medications; neurochemistry of memory and learning; neuro-transmitters and drug receptors. *Mailing Add:* G D Searle & Co 4901 Searle Pkwy Skokie IL 60077. *Fax:* 847-982-7715; *E-Mail:* rlkoch@searle.monsanto.com

KOCHMAN, STANLEY OSCAR, ALGEBRAIC TOPOLOGY. *Current Pos:* PROF MATH, YORK UNIV, 85- *Personal Data:* b New York, NY, July 18, 46; m 69, Ann Whitney Gardiner; c Shoshanah, Leah, Sarah, Israel Zvi, Ruchama, Yehuda Leib & Chaim Ezra. *Educ:* Kenyon Col, AB, 66; Univ Chicago, MS, 67, PhD(math), 70. *Prof Exp:* Gibbs instr math, Yale Univ, 70-72; asst prof, Purdue Univ, West Lafayette, 72-77; from asst prof to assoc prof, Univ Western Ont, 77-85. *Concurrent Pos:* Lectr, Mass Inst Technol, 73-74; ed-in-chief, Can Math Bulletin, 89-95. *Mem:* Am Math Soc; Can Math Soc; Math Asn Am. *Res:* Algebraic topology, especially homology operations, Cobordism theory and stable homology. *Mailing Add:* York Univ 4700 Keele St Downsview ON M3J 1P3 Can

KOCHTANEK, THOMAS RICHARD, INFORMATION STORAGE & RETRIEVAL, INFORMATION SYSTEMS. *Current Pos:* From asst prof to assoc prof, 77-83, CHAIR, DEPT INFO SCI, UNIV MO, COLUMBIA, 83- *Personal Data:* b Cleveland, Ohio, Jan 21, 51; m 79, Barbara Brandt; c Jeffrey T & Kyle B. *Educ:* Case Inst Technol, BS, 73; Case Western Res Univ, PhD(info sci), 78. *Concurrent Pos:* Fel, Nat Libr Med, 83-84, co-prin investr, 84-86; fel, Med Informatics, Univ Mo, Columbia, 84; vis prof, Sch Info & Libr Sci, Univ NC, Chapel Hill, 89-93. *Mem:* Am Soc Info Sci; Asn Libr & Info Sci Educators. *Res:* Information storage and retrieval systems focusing on text-based information sources; address both the information technology component of open systems design and the end user/evaluative portion of applied information systems. *Mailing Add:* Sch Info Sci & Learning Technol Univ Mo 201 F Townsend Hall Columbia MO 65211

KOCHWA, SHAUL, BIOCHEMISTRY, IMMUNOCHEMISTRY. *Current Pos:* assoc prof med, Mt Sinai Sch Med, 66-72, prof path, 72-85, prof med, 79-83, EMER PROF MED, MT SINAI SCH MED, 85- *Personal Data:* b Vienna, Austria, Apr 30, 15; nat US; m 40, Hadasa Margolis; c Varda. *Educ:* Hebrew Univ Jerusalem, MSc, 40, PhD(immunol), 49; Harvard Univ, MPH, 53. *Prof Exp:* Chief chemist, Gordon Co, Israel, 43-45; med lab dir, Bikur Cholim Hosp, Jerusalem, 45-47; assoc dir immunochem, Rogoff Med Res Inst, Beilinson Hosp, 55-58; sr res assoc, Mt Sinai Hosp, 59-66. *Mem:* Am Asn Immunologists; Am Chem Soc; Harvey Soc; Am Soc Hemat; NY Acad Sci. *Res:* Physicochemistry and purification of proteins, toxins, antibodies and enzymes; protein-protein interaction and complex formation. *Mailing Add:* Mt Sinai Sch Med 67-22 Harrow St Forest Hills NY 11375

KOCH-WESER, DIETER, EXPERIMENTAL PATHOLOGY, PREVENTIVE MEDICINE. *Current Pos:* RETIRED. *Personal Data:* b Kassel, Ger, July 13, 16; nat US; m 50; c 2. *Educ:* Univ Sao Paulo, MD, 43; Northwestern Univ, MS, 50, PhD, 56. *Honors & Awards:* Couto Prize, Acad Med, Brazil, 45. *Prof Exp:* Asst med, Hosps & Clin, Sao Paulo, Brazil, 44-47; asst path, Hektoen Inst Med Res, Cook Co Hosp, Chicago, 49-51; from instr to asst prof med, Grad Sch Med, Univ Chicago, 51-56; assoc prof, Sch Med, Western Res Univ, 57-62; chief, Latin-Am Off, NIH, Brazil, 62-64; assoc prof, Sch Pub Health, Harvard Univ, 64-71, assoc dean int progs, 67-84, prof prev & social med, Med Sch, 71-84. *Mem:* Am Soc Clin Invest; Am Thoracic Soc; AMA; Am Col Chest Physicians; Sigma Xi. *Res:* Isotope and biochemical studies in tuberculosis, hypersensitivity and liver diseases. *Mailing Add:* 19 Standish Rd Wellesley MA 02181

KOCH-WESER, JAN, INTERNAL MEDICINE, CLINICAL PHARMACOLOGY. *Current Pos:* AT F HOFFMANN LA ROCHE & CO, SWITZ. *Personal Data:* b Berlin, Ger, Oct 30, 30; US citizen. *Educ:* Univ Chicago, AB, 50; Harvard Med Sch, MD, 54. *Prof Exp:* Intern med, Mass Gen Hosp, 54-55, asst resident, 55-56, resident, 59; from instr to assoc prof pharmacol, Harvard Med Sch, 62-75; assoc dir res ctr & chief med res, 75-76, dir res ctr & vpres res, Merrell Int, 76- *Concurrent Pos:* Assoc physician & chief hypertension & clin pharmacol unit, Mass Gen Hosp, 66-75; mem med adv bd, Coun High Blood Pressure Res, Am Heart Asn; mem sci adv bd, Pan Am Health Orgn; mem pharmacol-toxicol rev comt & prog comt, Nat Inst Gen Med Sci; mem bd trustees, US Pharmacopeial Coun; USPHS res fel pharmacol, Harvard Med Sch, 60-61, Burroughs Wellcome scholar clin pharmacol, 66-71; USPHS spec res fel, 62 & grant, 64-75. *Mem:* Am Col Cardiol; Am Fedn Clin Res; Am Soc Clin Pharmacol & Therapeut; Am Soc Pharmacol & Exp Therapeut; Cardiac Muscle Soc. *Res:* Cardiovascular physiology and pharmacology; clinical pharmacology and human therapeutics; adverse drug reactions; drug metabolism and pharmacokinetics; antiarrhythmic, antihypertensive and anticoagulant drugs. *Mailing Add:* 3930 Swenson St Apt 704 Las Vegas NV 89119-7270. *Fax:* 41-61-691-9391

KOCIBA, RICHARD JOSEPH, VETERINARY PATHOLOGY, TOXICOLOGY. *Current Pos:* res pathologist, 70-80, SR ASSOC SCIENTIST, TOXICOL RES LAB, DOW CHEM CO, 80- *Personal Data:* b Harbor Beach, Mich, Apr 8, 39; m 66; c 2. *Educ:* Mich State Univ, BS, 64, DVM, 66, MS, 69, PhD(path), 70. *Prof Exp:* Practr, Milford Vet Clin, 66-67; instr anat, Mich State Univ, 67-68, NIH fel path, 68-70. *Concurrent Pos:* Adj asst prof path, Mich State Univ, 81- *Mem:* Am Vet Med Asn; Am Col Vet Pathologists; Soc Toxicol; Soc Pharmacol & Environ Pathologists; Am Bd Toxicol. *Res:* Design, conduction, evaluation and interpretation of research in the area of acute and chronic toxicity, with special emphasis on carcinogenesis and pathology. *Mailing Add:* Toxicol Res Lab 1803 Bldg Dow Chem Co Midland MI 48640

KOCKS, U(LRICH) FRED, MATERIALS SCIENCE. *Current Pos:* FEL, LOS ALAMOS NAT LAB, 83- *Personal Data:* b Dusseldorf, Ger, Nov 25, 29; nat US; m 54; c 4. *Educ:* Univ Gottingen, dipl physics, 54; Harvard Univ, PhD(appl physics), 59. *Hon Degrees:* DrTech, Tampere Univ Tech, 82. *Honors & Awards:* Japan Soc Promotion Sci Sr Award, 85. *Prof Exp:* Lectr & res fel, Harvard Univ, 59-61, asst prof, 61-65; sr scientist, Argonne Nat Lab, 65-83. *Concurrent Pos:* Vis prof, Munich Tech Univ, 64, Aachen Tech Univ, 71-72 & McMaster Univ, 78; Humboldt award, Fed Repub Ger, 79. *Mem:* The Metall Soc; Am Soc Mat; Int Soc Mat; fel Am Inst Mining Eng. *Res:* Mechanics and thermodynamics of solids; defects in crystals; strengthening mechanisms; kinetics of plasticity and creep; textures, constitutive relations. *Mailing Add:* 902 Paseo Del Sur Santa Fe NM 87501

KOCOL, HENRY, HEALTH PHYSICS. *Current Pos:* ASSOC HEALTH PHYSICIST, RADIOL HEALTH BR, CALIF DEPT HEALTH SERVS, 90- *Personal Data:* b Chicago, Ill, July 16, 37; m 71, Cleo; c Henry. *Educ:* Loyola Univ, Chicago, BS, 58; Purdue Univ, Lafayette, MS, 61. *Prof Exp:* Radiochemist, Nat Bur Stand, 61-64 & USPHS, 64-71; res chemist, Food & Drug Admin, Rockville, Md, 71-73, regional radiation control, Philadelphia, 73-77, regional radiol health rep, 77-79, fed-state liaison, 82-90; mgr x-ray control & regulation, Wash State Dept Social & Health Serv, Seattle, 79-82. *Mem:* Health Physics Soc. *Res:* The explanation of scientific concepts and facts, especially in the field of radiation safety, to lay audiences, to enable societal decisions to be based on fact rather than hype. *Mailing Add:* Radiol Health Br PO Box 942732 Sacramento CA 94234. *Fax:* 916-324-3610; *E-Mail:* ckocol@lx.netcom.com

KOCON, RICHARD WILLIAM, CLINICAL CHEMISTRY, MEDICAL LABORATORY SCIENCE. *Current Pos:* LAB DIR, DAMON MED LAB, INC, 79- *Personal Data:* b Fall River, Mass, Apr 18, 42; m 68; c 2. *Educ:* Southeastern Mass Univ, BS, 70; Providence Col, PhD(chem), 73. *Prof Exp:* Org Chem, Rhode Island Hosp, 74-77. *Mem:* Am Asn Clin Chem. *Res:* Clinical chemistry, specifically clinical application of radioimmunoassay procedures and enzyme-linked immunosorbent blocking assay techniques. *Mailing Add:* 408 Oakland Pkwy Franklin MA 02038

KOCSIS, JAMES JOSEPH, PHARMACOLOGY, TOXICOLOGY. *Current Pos:* From instr to assoc prof, 56-74, PROF PHARMACOL, JEFFERSON MED COL, 74- *Personal Data:* b Barberton, Ohio, Aug 13, 20; m 52, Grace Herzog; c Rosemary, Elizabeth & Joan. *Educ:* Ohio State Univ, BA, 43; Univ Chicago, MS, 52, PhD(pharmacol), 56. *Mem:* Am Chem Soc; Am Soc Pharmacol & Exp Therapeut; Soc Toxicol; Sigma Xi. *Res:* Bioassay; drug metabolism. *Mailing Add:* 306 N Woodstock Dr Cherry Hill NJ 08034

KOCUREK, MICHAEL JOSEPH, PAPER SCIENCE, ENGINEERING. *Current Pos:* DIR, HEARTY FOUND, 86- *Personal Data:* b New York, NY, Jan 6, 43; m 67; c 2. *Educ:* State Univ NY, BS, 64, MS, 67; Syracuse Univ, PhD(paper sci & eng), 71. *Prof Exp:* Assoc prof paper sci, Univ Wis-Stevens Point, 70-80, chmn dept, 76-80, prof paper sci & eng, 80-86. *Concurrent Pos:* Mem acad adv coun, Tech Asn Pulp & Paper Indust, 71-, mem prof develop oper coun, 76-, chmn continuing educ div, 76-78, mem US-Can joint textbook comt, 78-, instr intro to pulp & paper tech, 75- *Mem:* Tech Asn Pulp & Paper Indust. *Res:* Wood and pulping chemistry; paper and fiber physics. *Mailing Add:* Dept Wood & Paper Sci NC State Univ Box 8005 Raleigh NC 27695

KOCURKO, MICHAEL JOHN, GEOLOGY, SEDIMENTOLOGY. *Current Pos:* PROF GEOL, MIDWESTERN STATE UNIV, WICHITA FALLS, TEX, 79- *Personal Data:* b Orange, Calif, Jan 28, 45; m 88, Debra J Lindsay. *Educ:* Midwestern Univ, BS, 66; Univ Wis-Milwaukee, MS, 68; Tex Tech Univ, PhD(geol), 72. *Prof Exp:* Explor geologist, Union Oil Co Calif, 68-69 & 72-75; asst prof geol, Tulane Univ, 75-79. *Concurrent Pos:* Chmn, Geol Dept, Midwestern State; Charles and Elizabeth Prothro distinguished prof geol sci. *Mem:* Soc Econ Paleontologists & Mineralogists; Geol Soc Am; Paleont Soc. *Res:* Application of modern carbonate depositional environments and post-depositional history to the paragenesis of carbonate rocks; taxonomy of fossil Octocorallia. *Mailing Add:* Dept Geol Midwestern State Univ Wichita Falls TX 76308. *E-Mail:* fkocurkj@nexus.mwsu.edu

KOCZAK, MICHAEL JULIUS, composite materials, materials processing; deceased, see previous edition for last biography

KODA, ROBERT T, PHARMACOLOGY. *Current Pos:* Asst prof, Univ Southern Calif, 68-74, fel, 69, assoc prof pharmaceut chem & assoc dean, 75-85, assoc prof pharmaceut, 85-94, PROF PHARMACEUT SCI, UNIV SOUTHERN CALIF, 94- *Personal Data:* b Watsonville, Calif, June 18, 33; m 59; c 2. *Educ:* Univ Southern Calif, PharmD, 61, PhD(pharmaceut chem), 68. *Concurrent Pos:* Fel acad admin internship prog, Am Coun Educ, 71; consult, Allergan, 73- *Mem:* Am Pharmaceut Asn; Sigma Xi; Am Asn Cols Pharm. *Res:* Pharmacokinetics of drugs of current clinical interest; percutaneous absorption. *Mailing Add:* Sch Pharm Univ Southern Calif 1985 Zonal Ave Los Angeles CA 90033. *E-Mail:* rtkoda@hsc.usc.edu

KODALI, DHARMA RAO, NEW & VALUE ADDED PRODUCT DEVELOPMENT, SYNTHESIS & PHYSICAL PROPERTIES PROCESS IMPROVEMENTS BY-PRODUCT UTILIZATION OF FATS & OILS. *Current Pos:* STAFF SCIENTIST, CENT RES, CARGILL INC, 91- *Personal Data:* b Gudavalli, India, July 31, 51; m 82, Suseela Karlapudi; c Harsha S & Sithara. *Educ:* Andhra Univ, India, BSc, 73; Kurukshetra Univ, MSc, 76, PhD(synthetic med chem), 80. *Prof Exp:* Postdoctoral fel, Chem Dept, Polytech Inst NY, 80-81; res assoc, Biophys Inst, Sch Med, Boston Univ, 81-84, res scientist, 84-88, instr biophys, 89-90, asst prof, Biophys Dept, 90-91. *Concurrent Pos:* Invited lectr, Nara Workshop Functional Fats & Lipids, Japan, 88; Whitaker res grant, Whitaker Health Sci Fund, Mass, 89-90; lectr phys chem fats & oils applns to prod develop, Am Oil Chemists Soc, Calif, 91, Ill, 93; tech chair indust uses fats & oils, Ann Meeting, Am Oil Chemists Soc, Tex, 94, Ind, 95; circuit speaker, Fedn Socs Coating Technol, 95. *Mem:* Am Oil Chemists Soc; fel Am Inst Chemists; Am Chem Soc; Indian Sci Cong Asn; Fedn Soc Coatings Technol. *Res:* Development of new and value added products from agricultural raw materials, fats, oils and their byproducts for industrial and food uses; investigation of lipid oxidation, technical problem solving and process improvement. *Mailing Add:* 710 Olive Lane N Plymouth MN 55447. *Fax:* 612-742-5639; *E-Mail:* dharma_kodali@cargill.com

KODALI, V PRASAD, RADAR, AEROSPACE ELECTRONICS & ELECTROMAGNETIC COMPATIBILITY. *Current Pos:* from dir to sr dir, 73-84, ADV, DEPT ELEC, GOVT INDIA, 86- *Personal Data:* b Guntar, India, Nov 1, 39; m 87, Arati; c Mitul & Tara. *Educ:* Univ Madras, BE, 61; Case Inst Technol, MS, 63; Univ Leeds, PhD(elec eng), 67. *Honors & Awards:* Centennial Medal, Inst Elec & Electronics Engrs, 84; Vasvik Res Award for Electronics, 89. *Prof Exp:* Res scientist, Tata Inst Fundamental Res, 68-73; dir elec & instrumentation, Defense Res & Develop Org, 84-86. *Concurrent Pos:* Vis scholar, Case Western Res Univ, 83; distinguished visitor, Univ Victoria, 91-92; nat proj dir, UN Develop Prog, UN Indust Develop Orgn, 89-93. *Mem:* Fel Inst Engrs; fel Inst Elec & Telecommun Engrs; fel Inst Elec & Electronics Engrs. *Res:* Research and technology planning in radar and navigational aids; research in electromagnetic compatibility; author of two books on electromagnetic compatability. *Mailing Add:* Govt India Dept Elec Electronics Niketan 6 CGO Complex Lodi Rd New Delhi 110 003 India. *Fax:* 91-11-4363079; *E-Mail:* kodalivp@xm.doe.ernet.in

KODAMA, ARTHUR MASAYOSHI, INDUSTRIAL HYGIENE. *Current Pos:* from asst prof to assoc prof, 78-89, PROF, ENVIRON & OCCUP HEALTH PROG, PUB HEALTH SCIS DEPT, SCH PUB HEALTH, UNIV HAWAII, 90- *Personal Data:* b Honolulu, Hawaii, Dec 17, 31; m 59, Laura Ketchum; c Sharon & Richard. *Educ:* Wash Univ, BA, 54; Univ Calif, Berkeley, PhD(physiol), 63, MPH, 78. *Prof Exp:* Res physiologist, Univ Calif, Berkeley, 63-77. *Mem:* AAAS; Am Physiol Soc; Am Pub Health Asn; Am Indust Hyg Asn. *Res:* Environmental physiology; environmental toxicology; occupational health and safety. *Mailing Add:* Dept Pub Health Sci Sch Pub Health Univ Hawaii 1960 East-West Rd Honolulu HI 96822. *Fax:* 808-956-4585; *E-Mail:* akodama@uhunix.uhcc.hawaii.edu

KODAMA, GOJI, BORON HYDRIDE CHEMISTRY, METALLABORANE CHEMISTRY. *Current Pos:* assoc res prof, 69-80, RES PROF CHEM, UNIV UTAH, 80- *Personal Data:* b Sakai City, Japan, Dec 2, 27; m 57; c 2. *Educ:* Tokyo Inst Technol, BE, 51; Univ Mich, Ann Arbor, MS, 52, PhD(chem), 58. *Prof Exp:* From res assoc to instr chem, Univ Mich, 58-60; res fel, Harvard Univ, 60-61; from asst prof to prof, Tokyo Sci Univ, 61-69. *Mem:* Am Chem Soc. *Res:* Reactions of boron hydrides with various bases; transition metal-boron hydride complexes. *Mailing Add:* Dept Chem Univ Utah 2020 H Eyring Bldg Salt Lake City UT 84112-1194

KODAMA, HIDEOMI, CRYSTAL CHEMISTRY, STRUCTURAL CHEMISTRY. *Current Pos:* res scientist, Soil Res Inst, Can Dept Agr, Agr Can, 64-77, sr res scientist, Chem & Biol Res Inst & head, Mineral Anal Serv, 78-86, res scientist & proj leader, Land Resource Res Ctr, 86-90, sr res scientist & study leader, 91-97, HON RES ASSOC, CTR LAND & BIOL RESOURCES RES, AGR CAN, 97- *Personal Data:* b Tokyo, Japan, Oct 9, 31; Can citizen; m 59, Tomoko Maekawa; c Sakie F, Tohru M & Jun M. *Educ:* Tokyo Univ Educ, BSc, 56, MSc, 58, DSc(mineral), 61. *Prof Exp:* Japan Soc Promoting Sci fel & lectr, Int Christian Univ, Tokyo, 61-62; Nat Res Coun Can fel, 62-64. *Concurrent Pos:* Vis scientist, Nat Ctr Sci Res, Orleans, France, 69-70; vis res fel, Japan Soc Prom Sci, 84; assoc ed, Mineral Asn Can, 83-86, Clay Minerals Soc, 86-92, consult ed, Soil Sci, 90-96; vis prof, Grad Sch Sci & Eng Kanazawa. *Mem:* Mineral Soc Am; Clay Minerals Soc; fel Can Soc Soil Sci; Int Asn Study Clay (treas, 78-85); Mineral Soc Japan; Mineral Soc UK; fel Am Soc Soil Sci; Clay Sci Soc Japan. *Res:* Structure and genesis of interstratified clay minerals; fine structure analysis of layer silicates; crystal chemistry of silicate minerals; interactions between clay minerals and soil organic matter; intercalations of clay materials; characterization of non-crystalline inorganic soil components; non-crystalline inorganic soil components. *Mailing Add:* 1251 Southwood Dr Ottawa ON K2C 3C4 Can. *Fax:* 613-759-1926; *E-Mail:* kodamae@ncccot.agr.ca

KODAMA, JIRO KENNETH, PHARMACOLOGY, TOXICOLOGY. *Current Pos:* staff toxicologist, 77-80, TECH LIAISON REP, CHEVRON CORP, CALIF, 81- *Personal Data:* b Reedley, Calif, Mar 4, 24; m 51; c 5. *Educ:* Univ Calif, AB, 51, MS, 55, PhD(pharmacol), 57. *Prof Exp:* Instr pharmacol, Med Sch & toxicol, Sch Pub Health, Univ Calif, 57-59; from asst dept chief toxicol & pharmacol to sr pharmacologist, Hazleton Labs, Inc, 59-63; pharmacologist, Shell Develop Co, 63-66, supvr pharmacol dept, 66-68, vis Shell scientist, Tunstall Lab, Shell Res Ltd, Eng, 69-70, staff toxicologist, Agr Div, Shell Chem Co, 70-77. *Mem:* AAAS; Am Soc Pharmacol & Exp Therapeut; Soc Toxicol. *Res:* Drug research and development; pharmacotoxic characterization of chemical warfare agents; mechanisms of toxic actions of organophosphorus chemicals and cytotoxic alkylating agents; toxicology and safety evaluation of industrial and agricultural chemicals; preclinical evaluation of pharmaceuticals; forensic toxicology; technical management. *Mailing Add:* 3 Corwin Dr Alamo CA 94507-2103

KODAMA, KENNETH PHILIP, PALEOMAGNETISM, ROCK MAGNETISM. *Current Pos:* From asst prof to assoc prof geol, 78-88, PROF EARTH & ENVIRON SCI, LEHIGH UNIV, 88-, CHMN DEPT, 91- *Personal Data:* m 80, Anna; c Emily, Alice & Peterson. *Educ:* Univ Pa, BA, 73; Stanford Univ, MS & PhD(geophysics), 77. *Concurrent Pos:* Assoc ed, J Geophys Res, Am Geophys Union, 90-93, secy, Geomagnatism & Paleomagnatism Sect. *Mem:* Am Geophys Union; Geol Soc Am; Sigma Xi. *Res:* Effects of rock or sediment deformation on the accuracy of the paleomagnetic signal. *Mailing Add:* Geol Dept Lehigh Univ 27 Memorial Dr West Bethelem PA 18015-3044

KODAMA, ROBERT MAKOTO, CELL PHYSIOLOGY. *Current Pos:* from asst prof to assoc prof, 67-76, PROF BIOL, DRAKE UNIV, 76- *Personal Data:* b Kauai, Hawaii, May 30, 32; m 64; c 2. *Educ:* Univ Hawaii, BA, 55; Univ Ill, PhD(physiol), 67. *Prof Exp:* Phys sci aide, US Fish & Wildlife Serv, 55-56; med technologist, Mt Sinai Hosp, Chicago, Ill, 59; asst cell physiol, Med Ctr, Univ Ill, 60-62, physiol, 66-67. *Mem:* Sigma Xi. *Res:* Biological transport; endocrinology; electron microscopy. *Mailing Add:* 3830 Twana Dr Des Moines IA 50310-4231

KODAVANTI, PRASADA RAO S, TOXICOLOGY, NEUROSCIENCES. *Current Pos:* TOXICOLOGIST, NEUROTOXICOL, HEALTH EFFECTS RES LAB, US ENVIRON PROTECTION AGENCY, NC, 91- *Personal Data:* b Dharmavaram, AP, India, Aug 1, 54; m 89, Urmila M Joshi; c Preeti & Pooja. *Educ:* Andhra Univ, India, BS, 74, MS, 76; SV Univ, India, PhD(toxicol), 81. *Prof Exp:* Scientist off, Dept Zool, SV Univ PG Ctr, India, 82-83; fel, Dept Neurol, Univ Miss Med Ctr, Jackson, 83-84, res assoc, Dept Pharmacol & Toxicol, 84-89, res asst prof, Dept Neurol, 89-91. *Mem:* Sigma Xi; Soc Toxicol. *Res:* Neuro, hepato and pulmonary toxicity by chemicals and drugs. *Mailing Add:* Neurotoxicol Div Nat Health & Environ Effects Res Lab US Environ Protection Agency MD 74B Research Triangle Park NC 27711. *Fax:* 919-541-4849

KODAVANTI, URMILA P, MOLECULAR BIOLOGY OF LUNG DISEASES, ENVIRONMENTAL AIR POLLUTANTS & LUNG TOXICITY. *Current Pos:* RES FEL TOXICOL, UNIV NC, 92-; RES BIOLOGIST, US ENVIRON PROTECTION AGENCY. *Personal Data:* b Malpara, Gujarat, India, Jan 26, 56; m, Prasada Rao; c Preeti & Pooja. *Educ:* Univ India, BSc, 77; MS Univ Baroda, India, MSci, 79, PhD(toxicol), 83. *Prof Exp:* Teaching asst, Dept Zool, MS Univ Baroda, India, 82-83, lectr, Dept Foods & Nutrit, 83-84; res fel, Dept Pharmacol & Toxicol, Mich State Univ, 84-85, Univ Miss Med Ctr, 85-91. *Res:* Cell and molecular biology of cardiopulmonary diseases. *Mailing Add:* MD 82 Health Effects Res Lab US Environ Protection Agency Research Triangle Park NC 27711. *Fax:* 919-541-0026

KODIRA, UMESH CHENGAPPA, NEMATOLOGY. *Current Pos:* res asst, 88-93, POST-DOCTORAL RESEARCHER, UNIV CALIF, DAVIS, 93- *Personal Data:* m 88, Kaveramma S Mukkatira; c Chengappa U. *Educ:* Univ Agr Sci, India, BSc, 84, MSc, 86; Univ Calif, Davis, PhD(plant path), 93. *Prof Exp:* Jr merit teaching fel plant path, Univ Agr Sci India, 87; res assoc, Int Crops Res Inst Semi-Arid Tropics, 87-88. *Mem:* Am Phytopath Soc; Soc Nematal. *Res:* Interactions between plant parasitic nematodes, population biology and nematode management; epidemiology of viruses affecting melons in California; developing DNA-based detection methods for pathogenic bacteria on carrots and lettuce. *Mailing Add:* Dept Plant Path Univ Calif Davis CA 95616. *Fax:* 530-752-5674; *E-Mail:* uckodira@ucdavis.edu

KODRICH, WILLIAM RALPH, ECOLOGY. *Current Pos:* Assoc prof, 67-74, PROF BIOL, CLARION STATE COL, 74- *Personal Data:* b Cooperstown, NY, Aug 26, 33; m 60. *Educ:* Hartwick Col, BA, 55; Univ Pittsburgh, PhD(biol), 67. *Mem:* Ecol Soc Am; Am Soc Mammalogists. *Res:*

Physiological rates of small mammals living freely in their natural environments; relative thyroid release rates of 131-I of mammals living at different altitudes; bioenergetics of mammals in natural environments. *Mailing Add:* RR1 Box 186 Clarion PA 16214

KOE, B KENNETH, NEUROCHEMISTRY. *Current Pos:* RETIRED. *Personal Data:* b Astoria, Ore, Apr 15, 25; wid; c Karen E & Kristin M. *Educ:* Reed Col, BA, 45; Univ Wash, MS, 48; Calif Inst Technol, PhD(chem), 52. *Prof Exp:* Res fel chem, Calif Inst Technol, 52-54; assoc org chemist, Southwest Res Inst, 54-55; res chemist, Pfizer Inc, 55-74, sr res investr, 74-79, res adv, 79-95,. *Mem:* Am Soc Pharmacol & Exp Therapeut; Soc Neurosci; Am Col Neuropsychopharmacol. *Res:* Discovery of new psychotherapeutic drugs (antidepressants, antipsychotics, anxiolytics); psychopharmacology; neurotransmitters; receptor binding. *Mailing Add:* 41 Woodridge Circle Gales Ferry CT 06335-1137

KOEDERITZ, LEONARD FREDERICK, RESERVOIR SIMULATION & EVALUATION, TRANSIENT PRESSURE ANALYSIS. *Current Pos:* from assoc prof to prof petrol eng, 75-92, DISTINGUISHED TEACHING PROF, UNIV MO-ROLLA, 92- *Personal Data:* b St Louis, Mo, Aug 21, 46; m 68, Cheryl Lemp; c 3. *Educ:* Univ Mo, BS, 68, MS, 69, PhD(petrol eng), 70. *Prof Exp:* Sr engr, Atlantic Richfield, 70-74, proj dir, 74-75. *Concurrent Pos:* Head petrol eng dept, Univ Mo, Rolla, 79-80 & 89-94, dept chmn, 80-81. *Mem:* Soc Petrol Engrs. *Res:* Reservoir simulation; transient pressure analysis; advanced reservoir applications in petroleum engineering; reservoir valuation. *Mailing Add:* 1610 Lincoln Lane Rolla MO 65401. *Fax:* 573-341-6935; *E-Mail:* koe@umvvmb.umr.edu

KOEGLE, JOHN S(TUART), chemical engineering, for more information see previous edition

KOEHL, WILLIAM JOHN, JR, FUEL SCIENCE, AIR POLLUTION. *Current Pos:* sr res chemist, Mobil Res & Develop Corp, 68-76, supv chemist, 76-83, sr res assoc, Prod Res & Technol Serv Di,, 83-88, SCIENTIST, MOBIL RES & DEVELOP CORP, 88-, RES SCIENTIST, 92- *Personal Data:* b Newport, Ky, July 27, 35; m 60. *Educ:* Xavier Univ, Ohio, BS, 55, MS, 57; Univ Ill, PhD(org chem), 60. *Prof Exp:* Sr res chemist, Cent Res Div Lab, Socony Mobil Oil Co Inc, NJ, 60-68. *Mem:* Am Chem Soc; Soc Automotive Engrs; Air & Waste Mgt Asn. *Res:* Automotive fuels and exhaust emissions. *Mailing Add:* 6 Mimosa Lane Woodstown NJ 08098

KOEHLER, ANDREAS MARTIN, MEDICAL PHYSICS, ACCELERATOR PHYSICS. *Current Pos:* tech assoc accelerator physics, 53-61, asst dir, 61-77, DIR ACCELERATOR MED PHYSICS, CYCLOTRON LAB, HARVARD UNIV, 77- *Personal Data:* b Weimar, Ger, Jan 21, 30; US citizen; m 52; c 3. *Educ:* Harvard Univ, BS, 50. *Prof Exp:* Proj engr mech design, Hesse-Eastern Corp, 51-53. *Res:* Radiation therapy using beams of charged particles; radiation physics and dosimetry of protons; radiography using protons and alpha particles; proton activation analysis; accelerator designs for medical applications. *Mailing Add:* 306 Beacon St Somerville MA 02143

KOEHLER, DALE ROLAND, RADIATION EFFECTS ON QUARTZ. *Current Pos:* RETIRED. *Personal Data:* b Milwaukee, Wis, Oct 13, 32; m 55; c 4. *Educ:* Auburn Univ, BS, 54, MS, 55; Univ Ala, PhD(physics), 64. *Prof Exp:* Physicist, Signal Eng Labs, NJ, 55 & Army Ballistic Missile Agency, Ala, 57-58; physicist, Phys Sci Lab, Army Missile Command, 58-64, chief, Radiation Physics Br, 64-67; mgr, Advan Res Lab, Bulova Watch Co, 67-77; physicist, Sandia Labs, 77-97. *Res:* Ionizing radiation effects on quartz crystal resonators, primarily on frequency and acoustic loss changes; development of quartz purification and radiation hardness assurance technologies; quartz transducer development. *Mailing Add:* 1516 La Charles NE Albuquerque NM 87112

KOEHLER, DON EDWARD, PLANT PHYSIOLOGY. *Current Pos:* PLANT PHYSIOLOGIST, DEPT PESTICIDE REGULATION, CALIF ENVIRON PROTECTION AGENCY, 82- *Personal Data:* b Urbana, Ill, May 10, 42. *Educ:* Univ Ill, BS, 64; Purdue Univ, MS, 67; Mich State Univ, PhD(biochem), 72. *Prof Exp:* Fel develop biol, Univ Chicago, 72-74; fel plant physiol, Univ Calif, Riverside, 74-77; asst prof plant sci, Tex A&M Univ, 77-82. *Mem:* Am Soc Plant Physiologists; AAAS; Western Soc Weed Sci; Western Plant Growth Regulator Soc. *Res:* Hormonal control of enzyme induction and developmental processes in plants. *Mailing Add:* Dept Pesticide Regulation Calif Environ Protection Agency 1020 N St Rm 332 Sacramento CA 95814

KOEHLER, FRED EUGENE, SOIL FERTILITY. *Current Pos:* assoc soil scientist, 58-66, soil scientist & prof, 66-88, EMER PROF SOILS, WASH STATE UNIV, 88- *Personal Data:* b Naylor, Mo, Jan 25, 23; m 47; c 4. *Educ:* Univ Mo, BS, 43, MS, 50, PhD(soils), 51. *Prof Exp:* Soil scientist, USDA & asst agronomist, Univ Nebr, 51-57. *Mem:* Am Soc Agron; Soil Sci Soc Am; Sigma Xi. *Res:* Soil fertility and soil chemistry. *Mailing Add:* 1140 SE Spring St Pullman WA 99163

KOEHLER, HENRY MAX, SCIENTIFIC INFORMATION, TRANSLATION. *Current Pos:* CONSULT ED, 80- *Personal Data:* b Offenbach, Ger, Oct 13, 31; nat US; m 57. *Educ:* Roosevelt Univ, BS, 52, MS, 57, MBA, 62. *Prof Exp:* Sr water chemist, Water Bur, Chicago, 53-54; asst biochem, Med Sch, Northwestern Univ, 54-55; asst chem, Roosevelt Univ, 55-56, sr chemist, Div Chem, 56-64; ed supvr, Oral Res Abstr, Am Dent Asn, 64-72, ed updates, 70-79, ed, Oral Res Abstr, 74-79. *Concurrent Pos:* Mem, State of Ill Weather Modification Bd, 74-77. *Mem:* Fel AAAS; Am Asn Dent Ed; Am Chem Soc; Am Med Writers' Asn; Int Asn Dent Res. *Res:* Abstract preparation; editing; translation. *Mailing Add:* 211 E Chicago Ave No 1200 Chicago IL 60611. *Fax:* 773-288-5700

KOEHLER, JAMES K, CELL BIOLOGY. *Current Pos:* from asst prof to assoc prof, 63-75, PROF BIOL STRUCT, UNIV WASH, 75- *Personal Data:* b Darmstadt, Ger, June 7, 33; US citizen; m 94, Alberta May; c 5. *Educ:* Univ Ill, BS, 55; Univ Calif, Berkeley, MS, 58, PhD(biophys), 61. *Prof Exp:* Asst prof physics, NMex Highlands Univ, 62-63. *Concurrent Pos:* NIH fel, Swiss Fed Inst Technol, 61-62; vis lectr, Dept Anat, Univ Malaya, 71-72; mem exec coun, Electron Micros Soc Am, 91-93. *Mem:* Electron Micros Soc Am; Am Asn Anat; Am Soc Cell Biologists; Am Soc Study Reproduction. *Res:* Fine structure of cells and tissues; cryobiology; gamete biology. *Mailing Add:* Dept Biol Struct Univ Wash Seattle WA 98195. *Fax:* 206-543-1524

KOEHLER, JAMES STARK, PHYSICS. *Current Pos:* assoc prof, 50-53, PROF PHYSICS, UNIV ILL, URBANA, 53- *Personal Data:* b Oshkosh, Wis, Nov 10, 14; m 40; c 2. *Educ:* Wis State Teachers Col, BEd, 35; Univ Mich, PhD, 40. *Prof Exp:* Rackham fel, Univ Mich, 40-41, Westinghouse res fel, 41-42; instr physics, Carnegie Inst Technol, 42-46, assoc prof, 46-50. *Concurrent Pos:* Guggenheim fel, 57; mem solid state adv comt, Oak Ridge Nat Lab. *Mem:* Fel Am Phys Soc. *Res:* Effects of internal rotation on molecular spectra; plastic deformation of solids; radiation damage; point defects produced by quenching, irradiation and ion bombardment. *Mailing Add:* 101 W Winsdor Rd Urbana IL 61801

KOEHLER, KENNETH JOSEPH, APPLICATIONS OF SURVIVAL ANALYSIS & STATISTICAL MODELING IN ECOLOGY & HUMAN HEALTH RESEARCH. *Current Pos:* PROF STATIST, IOWA STATE UNIV, 77- *Personal Data:* m 78, Susan; c Kristine, John, Robert & Sarah. *Educ:* Univ Wis, BS, 72; Univ Minn, PhD(statist), 77. *Mem:* Am Statist Asn; Royal Statist Soc; Biomet Soc; Inst Math Statist. *Res:* Development of statistical methods and models for the analysis of data from studies of ecology, the environment, and human and animal health. *Mailing Add:* Iowa State Univ 120 Snedecor Hall Ames IA 50011. *E-Mail:* kkoehler@iastate.edu

KOEHLER, LAWRENCE D, DEVELOPMENTAL BIOLOGY, CELL BIOLOGY. *Current Pos:* From asst prof to assoc prof, 60-68, chmn dept, 75-93, PROF BIOL, CENT MICH UNIV, 68- *Personal Data:* b Grand Rapids, Mich, Feb 19, 32; m 60, Evelyn M Zirk; c Daniel L, David L & Deborah L (Conner). *Educ:* Otterbein Col, BS, 54; Mich State Univ, PhD(zool), 60. *Concurrent Pos:* NIH spec res fel, Inst Molecular Evolution, Univ Miami, 68-69; vis scientist, Statzione Zoologica, Napoli, Italy, 85; vis researcher, Univ Queensland, Brisbane, Australia, 92. *Mem:* Soc Develop Biol; Am Soc Cell Biologists; Int Soc Develop Biol. *Res:* Gametogenesis and fertilization, including ultrastructural changes in gametes and early zygotes. *Mailing Add:* Dept Biol Cent Mich Univ Mt Pleasant MI 48859. *Fax:* 517-774-3462; *E-Mail:* l.koehler@cmich.edu

KOEHLER, MARK E, INSTRUMENTATION. *Current Pos:* GROUP LEADER, GLIDDEN CO-ICI, 77- *Personal Data:* b Dayton, Ohio, July 6, 49; m 70; c 1. *Educ:* Univ Dayton, BS, 71; Wright State Univ, MS, 73; Case Western Res Univ, PhD(chem), 78. *Prof Exp:* Chemist, Glidden Coatings & Resins, Div SCM Corp, 77-80, sect leader, 80-83. *Mem:* Am Chem Soc. *Res:* Development and computer interfacing of laboratory instrumentation; areas of computer applications in chemistry; scientific computing and analog and digital electronics. *Mailing Add:* 6715 Winona Circle Cleveland OH 44130-4894

KOEHLER, P RUBEN, RADIOLOGY. *Current Pos:* chief, Div Diag Radiol, 80-83, PROF RADIOL, COL MED, UNIV UTAH, 70-; MED DIR, DEPT RADIOL, MERCY HOSP, 83- *Personal Data:* b Berlin, Ger, Apr 29, 31; US citizen; c 2. *Educ:* Univ Bern, MD, 56. *Prof Exp:* Assoc radiol, Albert Einstein Med Ctr, Philadelphia, Pa, 61-62; instr, Sch Med, Temple Univ, 62-64; from asst prof to prof, Sch Med, Washington Univ, 64-70. *Mem:* Am Col Radiol; Am Roentgen Ray Soc; Radiol Soc NAm; Asn Univ Radiologists; Int Soc Lymphology. *Res:* Lymphology; visceral arteriography. *Mailing Add:* 3930 Grand Ave No 306 Des Moines IA 50312

KOEHLER, PHILIP EDWARD, FOOD SCIENCE. *Current Pos:* From asst prof to assoc prof, 69-80, PROF FOOD SCI, UNIV GA, 80- *Personal Data:* b Kansas City, Mo, Mar 30, 43; m 66, Linda Hamilton; c Brian & Warren. *Educ:* Emporia Kans State Col, BS, 65; Okla State Univ, PhD(biochem), 69. *Mem:* Am Chem Soc; Inst Food Technologists; Sigma Xi. *Res:* Food safety and toxicology; food colorants; flavor chemistry. *Mailing Add:* Dept Food Sci Univ Ga Athens GA 30601. *Fax:* 706-542-1050; *E-Mail:* pkoehler@uga.cc.uga.edu

KOEHLER, PHILIP GENE, URBAN ENTOMOLOGY, HOUSEHOLD INSECTS. *Current Pos:* From asst prof to assoc prof exten entom, 75-84, PROF ENTOM, UNIV FLA, 84- *Personal Data:* b Doylestown, Pa, July 21, 47; m 74. *Educ:* Catawba Col, AB, 69; Cornell Univ, PhD(entom), 72. *Honors & Awards:* Award for Technol Transfer, Fed Lab Consortium, 89; Distinguished Achievement Award in Exten, Entom Soc Am, 93. *Concurrent Pos:* Proj leader, USDA Household Insect Res Proj. *Mem:* Entom Soc Am; Sigma Xi. *Res:* Cockroach and flea research; household and structural pest management. *Mailing Add:* Bldg 970 Univ Fla Gainesville FL 32611

KOEHLER, RAYMOND CHARLES, BRAIN BLOOD FLOW. *Current Pos:* ASST PROF ANESTHESIOL, JOHNS HOPKINS HOSP, 80- *Educ:* State Univ NY, Buffalo, PhD(physiol), 78. *Mailing Add:* Dept Anesthesiol/Critical Care Med Blalock 1404 Johns Hopkins Hosp 601 N Wolfe St Baltimore MD 21287-4961

KOEHLER, RICHARD FREDERICK, JR, PHYSICS, ELECTRICAL ENGINEERING. *Current Pos:* Assoc scientist, Xerox Corp, 72-75, scientist, 75-78, sr scientist, 78-80, AREA MGR, XEROX CORP, 80- *Personal Data:* b New York, NY, Mar 27, 45; m 69; c 2. *Educ:* Mass Inst Technol, BS, 67; Stanford Univ, MS, 68, PhD(elec eng), 72. *Mem:* Soc Photog Scientists & Engrs. *Res:* Physics and materials of the xerographic system. *Mailing Add:* 15 Woodrose Dr Webster NY 14580

KOEHLER, THOMAS RICHARD, PHYSICS. *Current Pos:* STAFF PHYSICIST, SAN JOSE RES LAB, IBM CORP, 60- *Personal Data:* b Toledo, Ohio, Aug 8, 32; m 61. *Educ:* Seattle Univ, BS, 54; Calif Inst Technol, PhD(physics), 60. *Prof Exp:* Physicist, Aeronutronic Div, Ford Motor Co, 59-60. *Mem:* Am Phys Soc. *Res:* Theoretical solid state and low temperature physics. *Mailing Add:* K66-803 IBM Almaden Res Ctr 650 Harry Rd San Jose CA 95120

KOEHLER, TRUMAN L, JR, STATISTICS. *Current Pos:* DIR, MASTER BUILDERS INC, 96- *Personal Data:* b Allentown, Pa, Apr 9, 31; m 54; c 3. *Educ:* Muhlenberg Col, BS, 52; Rutgers Univ, MS, 57. *Prof Exp:* Engr qual control, Sylvania Elec Prod Inc, 52-57; statistician, Am Cyanamid Co, 57, head qual control sect, Org Chem Div, 57-62, mgr systs anal, 62-66, mfg mgr, Org Pigments Dept, 66-68, dir mkt, Pigments Div, 68-70, mgr titanium dioxide dept, 70-77, dir planning, 77-79, gen mgr, Spec Prods Dept, 79-80; exec vpres & chief oper officer, Sodyeco Div, Martin Marietta Chem, 81-84; pres & chief exec officer, Sandoz Corp, 84-87, group vpres chem, 87-96. *Concurrent Pos:* Lectr, Rutgers Univ, 57-; partic, NSF TV Prog, Pursuit of Perfection, 65-; dir, Nat Asn Mfrs & Chem Mfrs Asn; chmn, Finance Comt, Muhlenberg Col. *Mem:* Fel Am Soc Qual Control; Am Statist Asn; Am Inst Chem Engrs; Nat Asn Mfrs; Chem Mfrs Asn. *Res:* Design and analysis of experimental programs; numerical analysis and computing. *Mailing Add:* 5222 Winding Brook Rd Charlotte NC 28226

KOEHLER, WILBERT FREDERICK, OPTICAL PHYSICS, HUMAN RESOURCE MANAGEMENT. *Current Pos:* asst dean, 61-62, dean progs, 62-76, EMER DEAN & DISTINGUISHED EMER PROF PHYSICS, NAVAL POSTGRAD SCH, 76- *Personal Data:* b Braddock, Pa, Feb 20, 13; m 36, Gearhart; c Gary & Robert. *Educ:* Allegheny Col, BS, 33; Cornell Univ, MA, 34; Johns Hopkins Univ, PhD(physics), 49. *Prof Exp:* Pub sch instr, Pa, 34-36; instr, Punahou Acad, Hawaii, 36-43; instr physics, Johns Hopkins Univ, 46-48; assoc prof, Naval Postgrad Sch, 48-51; sect head phys optics, Naval Ord Test Sta, 51-54, res scientist, 54-58, head physics div, 58-61. *Concurrent Pos:* Mem, Naval Officer Prof Develop Study Group, 74. *Mem:* Am Phys Soc; fel Optical Soc Am; Am Asn Physics Teachers; Sigma Xi. *Res:* Multiple-beam interferometry; optical constants; surface smoothness; specific heats of gases; solid state physics; developed a salary-growth model for professionals in the academic and industrial sectors. *Mailing Add:* 52 Alta Mesa Circle Monterey CA 93940-4610

KOEHLER, WILLIAM HENRY, INORGANIC CHEMISTRY. *Current Pos:* asst prof, 69-74, ASSOC PROF CHEM, TEX CHRISTIAN UNIV, 74-, ACTG DEAN GRAD SCH, 78-, VCHANCELLOR ACAD AFFAIRS, 80- *Personal Data:* b Houston, Tex, Feb 17, 39. *Educ:* Southern Methodist Univ, BS, 60, MS, 62; Univ Tex, Austin, PhD(chem), 69. *Prof Exp:* Instr chem, Southern Methodist Univ, 61-63; res scientist, Tracor, Inc, Tex, 68-69. *Concurrent Pos:* Vpres, Tex Christian Univ Res Found. *Mem:* Nat Coun Univ Res Adminr; Am Chem Soc. *Res:* Raman spectroscopy; reflection and transmission spectroscopy; characterization of metal-ammonia solutions; synthesis and reaction mechanisms in nonaqueous solvents. *Mailing Add:* Tex Christian Univ Ft Worth TX 76129-0001

KOEHMSTEDT, PAUL LEON, INJECTION ELECTRICAL GROUNDING, CHEMICAL AGENT DECONTAMINATION. *Current Pos:* RETIRED. *Personal Data:* b Seattle, Wash, Sept 21, 23; m 56; c 3. *Educ:* Ore State Univ, BS, 49, MS, 51. *Prof Exp:* Chemist, Gen Elec Co, 50-53; res engr mat, Boeing Airplane Co, 53-67; res scientist mat, Battelle Pac Northwest Labs, 67-93. *Mem:* Am Chem Soc; Nat Asn Corrosion Engrs. *Res:* Innovative applications towards solving material and methods problems involving chemical processes, corrosion, chemical and radiochemical decontamination, preparation and testing. *Mailing Add:* 24410 Mt Washington View Lane NW Poulsbo WA 98370

KOEHN, ENNO, PROJECT MANAGEMENT SYSTEMS, OPTIMAL PRODUCTIVITY & COST FACTORS. *Current Pos:* CHAIR, DEPT CIVIL ENG, LAMAR UNIV, 84- *Personal Data:* b Flushing, NY, April 29, 36; m 67, Carol Butcher; c William & James. *Educ:* City Univ NY, BCE, 58; Columbia Univ, MS, 60; NY Univ, MCE, 65; Wayne State Univ, PhD(civil eng), 75. *Honors & Awards:* Pres citation, Am Soc Civil Engrs, 83. *Prof Exp:* Res engr struct eng, NAm Rockwell, 58-59; asst prof eng, Long Island Univ, 60-66; educ specialist continuing educ, IBM, 66-67; from assoc prof to prof civil eng, Ohio Northern Univ, 67-79; assoc prof, Purdue Univ, 79-84. *Concurrent Pos:* Prin investr, Stanford Univ/NSF grants, 64-66, NSF grants, 70-72, US Army Construct Eng Res Lab, 83-88; fel, Mass Inst Technol, 72, Univ Mich/NSF Construct Res Sem, 72 & 82, Pa State Univ, Dept Energy Sem, 76, NASA-Am Soc Eng Educ & Stanford Univ Inst, 77; sr civil engr, Bechtel Corp, 78-81; chmn, Social & Environ Concerns Comt, Am Soc Civil Engrs, 79-87. *Mem:* Fel Am Soc Civil Engrs; Sigma Xi; Am Asn Cost Engrs; Nat Soc Prof Engrs; Am Soc Eng Educ. *Res:* International productivity in design and construction systems; probabilistic and pre-design cost estimating; optimal productivity and project management systems; weather related productivity factors in construction; national infrastructure/rehabilitation costs; engineering education, ethics and professionalism. *Mailing Add:* Civil Eng Dept Lamar Univ PO Box 10024 Beaumont TX 77710. *Fax:* 409-880-8121; *E-Mail:* koehneu@hal.lamar.edu

KOEHN, PAUL V, BIOCHEMISTRY. *Current Pos:* assoc prof biochem, State Univ NY, Oneonta, 67-70, head dept, 69-70, fac res grant, 71, chmn dept, 70-82, PROF BIOCHEM, STATE UNIV NY, ONEONTA, 69- *Personal Data:* b Bristol, Conn, Jan 10, 31; m 63; c 3. *Educ:* Bates Col, BS, 52; Cent Mo State Col, MSEd, 58; Univ Conn, PhD(biochem), 64. *Prof Exp:* Jr chemist, Am Cyanamid Co, 52-55; instr gen chem, Cent Mo State Col, 56-58; instr biochem, Univ Conn, 63-64. *Concurrent Pos:* NY State Res Found grant, 68-70; fac grants, State Univ NY, 74 & 77. *Mem:* Am Chem Soc; Sigma Xi; NY Acad Sci. *Res:* Synthesis of phosphopeptides and structural studies of proteins. *Mailing Add:* Dept Chem State Univ NY Oneonta NY 13820

KOEHN, RICHARD KARL, POPULATION GENETICS. *Current Pos:* VPRES RES, UNIV UTAH, 92-, PRES, RES FOUND & RES INST, 92- *Personal Data:* b Niles, Mich, Aug 25, 40; m 83, Sheryl A Scott; c Rachel, Christopher & Kathryn. *Educ:* Western Mich Univ, BA, 63; Ariz State Univ, PhD(genetics), 67. *Honors & Awards:* Stoye Prize, Am Soc Ichthyol & Herpet, 65. *Prof Exp:* Trainee immunol, Univ Kans, 67, asst prof zool, 67-70; vis scientist genetics, Aarhus Univ, 70-71 & 76-77; assoc prof ecol & evolution & provost biol sci, State Univ NY, Stony Brook, 71-80, dean biol sci, 78-88, prof ecol & evolution, 78-92, dir, Ctr Biotechnol, 83-92. *Concurrent Pos:* NSF & NIH grants; NATO sr sci fel, 75; assoc ed, J Soc Study Evolution, 75-77, Molecular Biol Evolution, 83-92 & J Exp Marine Biol Ecol, 84-92; George C Marshall fel, Denmark, 76-77; ed, Marine Biol Lett, 78-85; Guggenheim fel, 88-89; bd dirs, Boyce Thompson Inst Plant Res, 88-93, Long Island Forum Technol, 88-92, Asn Biotechnol Co, 91-90; vpres develop, Orgn Trop Studies, 88-92; chmn, Coun Biotechnol Ctrs, 89-91; dir, Utah Res Inst, 92- & Utah Life Sci Asn, 95- *Mem:* AAAS; Am Soc Naturalists; Genetics Soc Am; Soc Study Evolution (vpres, 83-84, pres, 85); Linnean Soc. *Res:* Evolutionary genetics and physiological energetics of natural populations, particularly marine invertebrates; protein function, structure and adaptation. *Mailing Add:* 210 Park Bldg Univ Utah Salt Lake City UT 84112. *Fax:* 801-585-6212; *E-Mail:* richard.koehn@vpres.adm.utah.edu

KOEHN, UWE, STATISTICAL CONSULTING, APPLIED STATISTICS. *Current Pos:* from asst prof to assoc prof, 68-83, PROF, DEPT STATIST, UNIV CONN, 84- *Personal Data:* b Brooklyn, NY, Mar 25, 40; m 96, Helen Fiala; c John & Eric. *Educ:* Queens Col, BS, 61; Univ Ill, MS, 62, PhD(statist), 68. *Prof Exp:* Asst prof, Butler Univ, 66-68. *Concurrent Pos:* Statist consult, 66- *Mem:* Am Statist Asn; Am Soc Qual; Inst Math Statist. *Res:* Application of statistics to industrial problems, biology, legal problems and pay equity. *Mailing Add:* 1 Eastwood Rd Storrs CT 06268-2401. *Fax:* 860-486-4113; *E-Mail:* qqqq@uconnvm.uconn.edu

KOELLA, WERNER PAUL, NEUROPHYSIOLOGY. *Current Pos:* RETIRED. *Personal Data:* b Zurich, Switz, Apr 13, 17; nat US; m 55; c 3. *Educ:* Univ Zurich, MD, 42. *Prof Exp:* Resident neurosurg, Univ Zurich, 43-45, resident physiol, 45-48, head asst dept, 48-51; res assoc neurophysiol, Univ Minn, 51-52, assoc prof, 52-55; mem staff, Worcester Found Exp Biol, 57-68; chmn dept pharmacol & med, Robapharm Ag, 68-70; sr mem staff, Lab Neurophysiol, Ciba-Geigy Ltd, 70-82. *Concurrent Pos:* Prof affil, Clark Univ, 57-, Boston Univ, 59 & Univ Berne, 70. *Mem:* AAAS; Am Physiol Soc; Am Soc Pharmacol & Exp Therapeut; fel Am Col Neuropsychopharmacol; NY Acad Sci. *Res:* Cerebellum; vestibular apparatus; subcortical-cortical relationships; sleep; organization of autonomic functions; neuropharmacology. *Mailing Add:* Buchenstrasse 1 CH-4104 Oberwil CH4104 Switzerland

KOELLE, GEORGE BRAMPTON, histochemistry, anticholinesterase agents; deceased, see previous edition for last biography

KOELLE, WINIFRED ANGENENT, ESSENTIAL HYPERTENSION, CARDIAC DRUGS. *Current Pos:* Teaching assoc pharmacol, Grad Sch Med & Sch Med, 56-72, teaching assoc med, Sch Med, 70-76, ASST PROF PHARMACOL, SCH MED, UNIV PA, 72-, ASST PROF MED, 76- *Personal Data:* b Soerakarta, Indonesia, Mar 26, 26; m 54; c 3. *Educ:* Wellesley Col, BA, 48; Columbia Univ, MD, 52; Am Bd Internal Med, cert, 79. *Concurrent Pos:* Chief, Intensive Care Unit, Taylor Hosp, Ridley Park, Pa, 67-69; asst prof pharmacol, Pahlavi Univ, Shiraz, Iran, 69-70; co-chief & chief, med clin, Philadelphia Gen Hosp, Univ Pa Serv, 73-77; vis prof, Sch Med, Free Univ, Lille, France, 76-, Mahidol Univ, Bangkok, Thailand, 78 & St George's Univ, St Vincent, WI, 84; deleg, US Pharmacopeia, Univ Pa, 80-85. *Mem:* Am Soc Pharmacol & Exp Therapeut; fel Am Col Clin Pharmacol; Sigma Xi. *Res:* Metabolism of catecholamines by ocular tissue; histochemistry and life cycles of cholinesterases; anticholinesterase agents; mechanisms of release of acetylcholine; neurotrophic factors. *Mailing Add:* Dept Pharmacol & Med Univ Pa Sch Med 114 Med Labs G3 Philadelphia PA 19104

KOELLER, RALPH CARL, MECHANICAL ENGINEERING, CONTINUUM MECHANICS. *Current Pos:* PRES, MECH DESIGN GROUP, 89- *Personal Data:* b Chicago, Ill, Aug 9, 33; div; c 3. *Educ:* Ill Inst Technol, BS, 57, MS, 59, PhD(mech), 63. *Prof Exp:* Res & teaching asst mech eng, Ill Inst Technol, 59-62; from instr to prof, Univ Colo, 62-84; prof mech eng, Univ Wis, 84-89. *Concurrent Pos:* Univ Colo Fac fel, Univ Calif, Berkeley, 65-66; consult, Colo Instruments Inc, 69, Dow Chem Co, 70-71, Dieterich Stand Corp, 73 & Hewlett-Packard Co, 74; resident fac fel, Am Soc Eng Educrs, 74-75; vis asst prof, Cornell Univ, 76-77; consult, Ponderosa Assoc, 78-88. *Mem:* Am Soc Mech Engrs; Sigma Xi. *Res:* Engineering consulting; design analysis; scale models; product liability. *Mailing Add:* 960 Stonebridge No 6 Platteville WI 53818-2078

KOELLING, DALE DEAN, SOLID STATE SCIENCE, ELECTRONIC STRUCTURE CALCULATIONS. *Current Pos:* physicist, 72-87, SR PHYSICIST MAT SCI DIV, ARGONNE NAT LAB, 87- *Personal Data:* b Great Bend, Kans, May 8, 41; m 68, Maria Vellini; c Melinda & Alexia. *Educ:* Kans State Univ, BS, 63; Mass Inst Technol, PhD(physics), 68. *Prof Exp:* Res assoc, Northwestern Univ, 68-72. *Concurrent Pos:* Vis prof, Northern Ill Univ, 85-87; Full Admin training, Div Mat Sci, Off Basic Energy Sci, Off Energy Res, Dept Energy, Germantown, Md, 94-96. *Mem:* Fel Am Phys Soc; Mat Res Soc; Soc Indust & Appl Math. *Res:* Electronic structure and resulting properties primarily in metallic or semiconducting actinide, rare-earth, or transition element materials. *Mailing Add:* Mat Sci Div Argonne Nat Lab Argonne IL 60439-4845. *Fax:* 630-252-7777; *E-Mail:* koelling@anl.gov

KOELLING, MELVIN R, FORESTRY. *Current Pos:* from asst prof to assoc prof, 67-77, PROF FORESTRY & EXTEN SPECIALIST, MICH STATE UNIV, 77- *Personal Data:* b Sullivan, Mo, July 18, 37; m 59. *Educ:* Univ Mo, BS, 59, MS, 61, PhD(bot), 64. *Prof Exp:* Assoc plant physiol, NE Forest Exp Sta, USDA, 64-67. *Mem:* AAAS; Am Inst Biol Sci; Ecol Soc Am; Soc Am Foresters. *Res:* Botany; improvement of sugar maple with respect to sap production; maple sap physiology. *Mailing Add:* 126 Nat Resources Forestry Mich State Univ East Lansing MI 48824-1222

KOELSCHE, CHARLES L, INORGANIC CHEMISTRY, ANALYTICAL CHEMISTRY. *Current Pos:* RETIRED. *Personal Data:* b Seattle, Wash, Sept 23, 06; m 44. *Educ:* Univ Southern Calif, AB, 28, MS, 30; Ind Univ, EdD(sci educ), 53. *Prof Exp:* Pub sch teacher sci & math, 29-42; Fed Security Agency inspector, US Food & Drug Admin, 42-44; assoc prof chem & chmn dept, Univ Alaska, 44-47; assoc prof, Ariz State Univ, 47-52; assoc prof phys sci, Wis State Col, Eau Claire, 52-57; prof sci educ & chem, Univ Toledo, 57-58; specialist for sci, US Off Educ, 58-59; spec asst to dir off sci personnel, Nat Acad Sci-Nat Res Coun, 59-60; prof sci educ, Univ Ga, 60-74; consult sci educ, 74-75; chmn dept sci, Athens Acad, 75-81. *Concurrent Pos:* NSF Summer & In-serv Insts Sci Teachers, Univ Ga, 61-73; vis prof chem, Embry-Riddle Aeronaut Univ, Prescott, Ariz, 82, 83 & 85- *Res:* Chemistry; physics; physical science; science education. *Mailing Add:* 116 Cedar Ct Forsyth GA 31029

KOELSCHE, GILES ALEXANDER, INTERNAL MEDICINE. *Current Pos:* RETIRED. *Personal Data:* b Ashland, Ore, Sept 3, 08; m 30; c 2. *Educ:* Pac Union Col, BS, 30; Loma Linda Univ, MD, 31; Univ Minn, MS & PhD(med), 35. *Prof Exp:* Fel, Mayo Found, Univ Minn, 31-35; asst, Mayo Grad Sch Med, Univ Minn, 35-37, from instr to assoc prof, 37-74, consult, Div Med, Mayo Clin, 37-74, emer assoc prof clin med, 74,84. *Mem:* Emer fel Am Acad Allergy; emer fel Am Col Allergists (pres, 60-61). *Res:* Newer therapy for asthma, hay fever and perennial allergic rhinitis; management of chronic urticaria; problems of immunologic tolerance and organ transplantation; auto-immune diseases; immunology in relation to cancer. *Mailing Add:* 13825 Crown Point Sun City AZ 85351-2308

KOELTZOW, DONALD EARL, BIOCHEMISTRY, ORGANIC CHEMISTRY. *Current Pos:* asst prof, 71-77, ASSOC PROF CHEM, LUTHER COL, 77-, CHMN DEPT, 78- *Personal Data:* b Clovis, NMex, May 9, 44; m 65; c 3. *Educ:* NMex Inst Mining & Technol, BS, 66; Univ Ill, MS, 68, PhD(biochem), 70. *Prof Exp:* Fel med microbiol, Stanford Univ, 70-71; assoc res scientist pharmacol, Univ Iowa, 77-78. *Concurrent Pos:* US Army med res grant, 73-75. *Mem:* Am Chem Soc; Am Soc Microbiol; AAAS; Midwest Asn Chem Teachers Lib Arts Cols. *Res:* Structure and function of membrane components, particularly carbohydrates and lipids. *Mailing Add:* 8335 N Overland Dr Kansas City MO 64151

KOELZER, VICTOR A, hydraulic engineering; deceased, see previous edition for last biography

KOEMTZOPOULOS, C ROBERT, DIAMOND FILM TECHNOLOGY. *Current Pos:* RES ASST, CHEM ENG DEPT, UNIV HOUSTON, 89- *Personal Data:* b New York, NY, Dec 20, 67. *Educ:* Johns Hopkins Univ, BSc, 89; Univ Houston, PhD, 94. *Mem:* Am Inst Chem Engrs; Electrochem Soc. *Res:* Designed and used two experimental configurations of a microwave plasma CVD reactor to produce diamond films; developed mathematical models to simulate a hydrogen glow discharge and determine the gas phase composition in a remote plasma CVD reactor for diamond film growth. *Mailing Add:* 25200 Carlos Bee Blvd Apt 553 Hayward CA 94542. *Fax:* 713-743-4323; *E-Mail:* chee1la@jetson.uh.edu

KOEN, BILLY VAUGHN, NUCLEAR ENGINEERING. *Current Pos:* From asst prof to assoc prof, 68-82, PROF MECH ENG, UNIV TEX, AUSTIN, 82- *Personal Data:* b Graham, Tex, May 2, 38; m 67, Deanne Rollins; c Kent V & Douglas B. *Educ:* Univ Tex, Austin, BA, 60, BS, 61; Mass Inst Technol, SM, 62, ScD(nuclear eng), 68; Saclay Nuclear Res Ctr, France, dipl eng, 63. *Honors & Awards:* Chester F Carlson Award, Am Soc Eng Educ, 80, W Leighton Collins Award, 92 & Centennial Medallion Award, 93. *Concurrent Pos:* Foreign collabr, Fr Atomic Energy Comn, 71-72 & 76-77; mem Acad Educ Develop, Tunisian Technol Transfer Proj, 84. *Mem:* Am Nuclear Soc; Am Soc Eng Educ; Am Soc Mech Engrs. *Res:* Nuclear reactor kinetics; engineering education. *Mailing Add:* Dept Mech Eng Univ Tex ETC 5160 Austin TX 78712-1063

KOENEMAN, JAMES BRYANT, ORTHOPEDIC BIOMECHANICS, BIOMATERIALS. *Current Pos:* DIR BIOENG, HARRINGTON ARTHRITIS RES CTR, 84- *Personal Data:* m 64, Mary A Endecavegeh; c Edward, Paul & Brian. *Educ:* Univ Minn, BSME, 59; Case Western Res Univ, MS, 66, PhD(mech eng), 69. *Prof Exp:* Reactor engr, Argonne Nat Labs, 59-60, US AEC, 60-64; mem tech staff, Bell Tel Labs, 70-74; dir, Bioeng Div, Lord Corp, 74-81; pres, Paulson Med Devices, 81-83. *Concurrent Pos:* Instr biomech & biomat, Orthop Res Prog, Erie, 75-81; sect chmn, Am Soc Mech Engrs, 77-79; dir res, Shrine Hosp, Erie, 77-82; adj fac, Case Western Res Univ, 81-83; adj prof bioeng, Ariz State Univ, 84-; prog chmn, Soc Biomat, 87. *Mem:* Fel Soc Advan Mat & Process Engrs; Am Soc Mech Engrs; Orthop Res Soc; Soc Biomat; Am Soc Testing & Mat. *Res:* Development of orthopedic medical devices; evaluation of implant materials including composites, characterization of stress related bone changes, and the study of human and animal biomechanics. *Mailing Add:* 1760 E Hale Mesa AZ 85203. *Fax:* 602-253-4817

KOENG, FRED R, ORGANIC CHEMISTRY. *Current Pos:* sr res chemist, 70-80, RES ASSOC, EASTMAN KODAK CO, 80- *Personal Data:* b Wilmington, Del, Aug 6, 41; m 63; c 1. *Educ:* Franklin & Marshall Col, AB, 63; Northwestern Univ, PhD(org chem), 70. *Prof Exp:* Chemist, Rohm and Haas Co, 65-67. *Mem:* AAAS; Soc Photog Scientists & Engrs; Sigma Xi. *Res:* Photographic systems research. *Mailing Add:* 93 Damsen Rd Rochester NY 14612-3637

KOENIG, CHARLES LOUIS, PHYSICAL CHEMISTRY. *Current Pos:* RETIRED. *Personal Data:* b Yonkers, NY, Oct 11, 11; m 52, Jamie R Shofner; c 4. *Educ:* NY Univ, BS, 32, PhD(chem), 36. *Prof Exp:* Sr chemist, Solvay Process Co, NY, 36-45; res chemist, Lithaloys Corp, 45-46; chief res br, AEC, 46-47; chmn dept chem & chem eng res, Armour Res Found, 47-49; asst dir res, Stanford Res Inst, 50-51; vpres, Southwest Res Inst, 51-56; owner, Louis Koenig Res, 56- *Concurrent Pos:* Sect ed, Chem Abstr, 49-; adv, Saline Water Conservation Prog, Secy Interior, 52-56; adv, Advan Waste Treatment Prog, USPHS, 60-63. *Mem:* Sigma Xi; Am Chem Soc. *Res:* Phase relations of aqueous systems; water resources; waste disposal; cost engineering; market research; economics. *Mailing Add:* 26890 Sherwood Forest San Antonio TX 78258

KOENIG, DANIEL RENE, nuclear engineering, computer graphics, for more information see previous edition

KOENIG, EDWARD, NEUROBIOLOGY, NEUROCHEMISTRY. *Current Pos:* From asst prof to assoc prof, 63-75, PROF PHYSIOL, STATE UNIV NY BUFFALO, 75- *Personal Data:* b New York, NY, Nov 10, 28; m 53; c 3. *Educ:* Franklin & Marshall Col, BA, 56; Univ Pa, PhD(physiol), 61. *Concurrent Pos:* Res career prog award, Nat Inst Neurol Dis & Stroke, 68-73. *Mem:* AAAS; Am Physiol Soc; Am Soc Neurochem; Int Soc Neurochem; Soc Neurosci. *Res:* Cellular biology of the neuron as related to central and local regulation of synthesis of axonal proteins and structure, function and organizational regulation of axonal cytoskeleton; microchemistry; microanalysis. *Mailing Add:* Dept Physiol 321 Cary Hall State Univ NY Buffalo NY 14214-3078

KOENIG, ELDO C(LYDE), ELECTRICAL ENGINEERING. *Current Pos:* RETIRED. *Personal Data:* b Randolph Co, Ill, Oct 17, 19; m 50, Gloria J Houting; c Lloyd W, Evan F, Eva L & Beth E. *Educ:* Washington Univ, St Louis, BS, 43; Ill Inst Technol, MS, 49; Univ Wis, MS, 51, PhD, 56. *Honors & Awards:* Alfred Nobel Prize. *Prof Exp:* Engr, Manhattan Proj, 44-46; engr, Allis-Chalmers Mfg Co, 46-52, supvr comput lab, 54-57, engr in chg eng anal, 57-62; fac, Univ Wis-Madison, 62-83. *Mem:* Fel AAAS; Asn Comput Mach; sr mem Inst Elec & Electronics Engrs. *Res:* Engineering and mathematical analysis and research for computers; systems and design; intelligent properties of systems. *Mailing Add:* 35005 W Fairview Rd Oconomowoc WI 53066

KOENIG, HEIDI M, neuroanesthesiology, neuroscience research-cerebral vascular reactivity & brain protection, for more information see previous edition

KOENIG, HERMAN E, electrical engineering, for more information see previous edition

KOENIG, JACK L, POLYMER CHEMISTRY, PHYSICAL CHEMISTRY. *Current Pos:* from asst prof to assoc prof chem, 63-70, PROF MACROMOLECULAR SCI, CASE WESTERN RES UNIV, 70- *Personal Data:* b Cody, Nebr, Feb 12, 33; m 53; c 4. *Educ:* Yankton Col, BA, 56; Univ Nebr, MS, 58, PhD(chem), 60. *Honors & Awards:* Res Award, Sigma Xi. *Prof Exp:* Mem staff, Plastics Dept, E I du Pont de Nemours & Co, 59-63. *Concurrent Pos:* Consult, El Tech, Charden, Ohio & 3M Co, 59-63; NSF, US Army, US Navy res grants, 65-88. *Mem:* Am Chem Soc; Am Phys Soc; Soc Appl Spectros. *Res:* Spectroscopy of polymeric materials. *Mailing Add:* Dept Macro Sci Case Western Res Univ Cleveland OH 44106-7202

KOENIG, JAMES BENNETT, STRUCTURAL GEOLOGY. *Current Pos:* PRES, GEOTHERMEX INC, 73- *Personal Data:* b New York, NY, Nov 25, 32; c 3. *Educ:* Brooklyn Col, BS, 54, Ind Univ, MA, 56; USN Postgrad Sch, dipl meteorol, 58. *Prof Exp:* Ground water geologist, US Geol Surv, St Paul, Minn, 55-56; jr mining geologist, Calif Div Mines, San Francisco, 56-57, asst geologist, 60-63, supvry geologist, 65-72; ensign & lt, USN Postgrad Sch, Monterey & USN Weather Res Facil, Norfolk, 57-60; asst geologist, Calif Div Mines & Geol, 60-63, supvry geologist, 65-72. *Concurrent Pos:* Instr econ geog, Col William & Mary, 59-60; student geol & seismol, Univ Nev, 63-65; instr geol, Univ Calif, Berkeley, 68-70; consult, UN Geothermal Explor, Ethiopia & El Salvador, 71, Weyerhaeuser Co & Pac Power & Light Co, 71-72; mem bd dir, Geothermal Resource Coun, 75-, pres-elect, 87; mem int working group, Int Geothermal Asn, 86- *Mem:* Fel Geol Soc Am; Am Geophys Union; Int Asn Volcanology. *Res:* Exploration, drilling and development of geothermal resources as energy source, on behalf of electric utilities, international lender and donor agencies, major and independent oil/gas/mining companies, landowners, turbine manufacturers, government agencies in US and abroad (Japan, Costa Rica, Kenya, Philippines, etc); exploration for geothermal energy; feasibility assessments of energy resources. *Mailing Add:* Geothermex Inc 5221 Central Ave Suite 201 Richmond CA 94804

KOENIG, JAMES J(ACOB), CHEMICAL ENGINEERING. *Current Pos:* RETIRED. *Personal Data:* b Le Mars, Iowa, Sept 4, 18; m 51, Eva M Sprakties; c James G, Eva J, Donald M & Kenneth B. *Educ:* Iowa State Col, BS, 39. *Prof Exp:* Foreman, Procter & Gamble Mfg Co, Kans, 40-41, gen foreman & tech supvr, Tenn, 41-44; asst dir prod div, NY Opers Off, USAEC, 46-47, asst area mgr, Mo, 47-52, chief, Fla Field Off, 52-56; res engr, Aluminum Co Am, 56-67, sr res engr, 67-77; mem staff, James J Koenig consult, Inc, 81- *Mem:* Sigma Xi. *Res:* Explosives loading; uranium extraction and metallurgy; alumina chemicals. *Mailing Add:* 129 Country Club Acres Belleville IL 62223-3609

KOENIG, JANE QUINN, RESPIRATORY PHYSIOLOGY. *Current Pos:* asst prof, Med Sch, Univ Wash, 66-70, vis scientist, 70-71, actg asst prof physiol, Dept Zool, 72-73, ASSOC PROF, DEPT ENVIRON HEALTH, SCH PUB HEALTH & COMMUNITY MED, UNIV WASH, 74- *Personal Data:* b Seattle, Wash, Sept 16, 35; c 2. *Educ:* Univ Wash, BS, 59, MS, 61, PhD(physiol psychol), 63. *Prof Exp:* Fel neurophysiol, Med Sch, Stanford Univ, 63-65. *Concurrent Pos:* Consult, Clear Air Sci Adv Comt, Environ Protection Agency. *Mem:* AAAS; Fedn Am Scientists; Union Concerned Scientists; Am Thoracic Soc; Air Pollution Control Asn; Am Pub Health Asn. *Res:* Effects of acute exposures to air pollutants upon respiratory physiology in human volunteers especially susceptible individuals. *Mailing Add:* Dept Environ Health SC034 Univ Wash 3900 Seventh Ave NE Seattle WA 98195-0001

KOENIG, JOHN WALDO, INVERTEBRATE. *Current Pos:* RETIRED. *Personal Data:* b Newark, NJ, July 19, 20; m 50, Paula J Parks; c Karl E. *Educ:* Columbia Univ, BS, 47; Univ Kans, MS, 51. *Prof Exp:* Sci illusr, Kans State Geol Surv, 47-51; geol engr, Phillips Petrol Co, 51-54; geologist, Mo Geol Surv & Water Resources, 54-65, Continental Oil Co, 65-66 & Mo Geol Surv, 66-67; tech ed, Univ Mo, Rolla, 67-85. *Concurrent Pos:* Lectr art, Univ Mo-Rolla, 74-80. *Mem:* Asn Earth Sci Ed. *Res:* Invertebrate paleontology; Bryozoa and Crinoidea; Mississippian stratigraphy. *Mailing Add:* 1319 Woodlawn Dr Rolla MO 65401

KOENIG, KARL E, AMINO ACID SYNTHESIS, HERBICIDE SYNTHESIS. *Current Pos:* Sr res chemist asymmetric catalysis, Monsanto Corp Res Labs, 76-79, res specialist, Corp Res & Develop Biomed Prog, 79-81, sr res specialist, Nutrit Chem Div, 81-86, res group leader, 86-89, MGR PROCESS DEVELOP, NEW PROD DIV, MONSANTO AGR GROUP, 89- *Personal Data:* b Washington, DC, Dec 27, 47; m. *Educ:* Univ Tex, Austin, BS, 70; Univ Southern Calif, PhD(chem), 74. *Prof Exp:* Fel chem, Univ Calif, Los Angeles, 74-76. *Mem:* Am Chem Soc; AAAS; Org Reactions Catalysis Soc; Am Inst Chemists. *Res:* Homogeneous catalysis; drugs based on low molecular weight polyelectrolytes; asymmetric synthesis; nutritional chemicals; selective complexation of transition metals; organosilicon chemistry; growth promotants; weed control agents; strategic planning for product development. *Mailing Add:* 1912 Gastorf Pointe Ct Ballwin MO 63011

KOENIG, KARL JOSEPH, GEOLOGY. *Current Pos:* ASSOC PROF GEOL, TEX A&M UNIV, 55- *Personal Data:* b Milwaukee, Wis, Jan 9, 20; m 59; c 1. *Educ:* Univ Ill, BS, 41, MS, 46, PhD, 49. *Prof Exp:* Stratigrapher, Shell Oil Co, Tex, 49-55. *Mem:* Soc Econ Paleont & Mineral; Geol Soc Am; Am Asn Petrol Geol. *Res:* Miocene stratigraphy and paleontology; sedimentation and clay mineralogy. *Mailing Add:* Dept Geol Tex A&M Univ College Station TX 77843-0100

KOENIG, LLOYD RANDALL, METEOROLOGY. *Current Pos:* SR SCI OFFICER, WORLD METEOROL ORG, GENEVA, SWITZ, 80- *Personal Data:* b St Louis, Mo, July 17, 29; m 55; c 2. *Educ:* Washington Univ, BSChE, 50; Univ Chicago, MS, 59, PhD(meteorol), 62. *Prof Exp:* Instr chem eng, USN Postgrad Sch, 50-53; res asst meteorol, Univ Chicago, 57-59, res assoc, 60-62; chief atmospheric sci br, Missile & Space Systs Div, Douglas Aircraft Co, 62-66; phys scientist, Rand Corp, Santa Monica, 66-79; assoc prog dir meteorol, NSF, 79-80. *Mem:* Am Geophys Union; Am Meteorol Soc; Sigma Xi. *Res:* Cloud physics, including natural and artificial precipitation mechanisms, scavenging, effects of atmospheric processes on the atmosphere. *Mailing Add:* 258 Nottearegenta Rd Pacific Palisades CA 90272-3110

KOENIG, MICHAEL EDWARD DAVISON, INFORMATION MANAGEMENT. *Current Pos:* dean & prof grad sch libr & info sci & prof grad sch bus, Rosary Col, 88-95, EMER DEAN & PROF, DOMINICAN UNIV, 95- *Personal Data:* b Rochester, NY, Nov 1, 41; m 80, Luciana Marulli; c Christopher & Davison. *Educ:* Yale Univ, BA, 63; Univ Chicago, MS, 68, MBA, 70; Drexel Univ, PhD(info sci), 82. *Prof Exp:* Mgr info serv, Pfizer, Inc, Groton, Conn, 70-74; dir prod opers, Inst Sci Info, Philadelphia, Pa, 74-77, dir develop, 77-78; vpres opers, Swets NAm, Berwyn, Pa, 78-80; assoc prof info systs, Sch Libr Serv, Columbia Univ, 80-85; vpres info mgt, Tradenet Inc, 85-88. *Concurrent Pos:* Adj fac, Grad Sch Bus, Columbia Univ, 83-88, Sch Libr Serv, 85-88. *Mem:* Am Soc Info Sci; Asn Comput Mach; AAAS; Spec Libr Asn; Soc Social Study Sci; Int Soc Scientometrics & Informetrics (pres, 95-97). *Res:* Bibliometrics and scientometrics; relationship between information technology and productivity; research productivity and the information environment. *Mailing Add:* 1018 Randolph St Oak Park IL 60302. *Fax:* 847-524-6849; *E-Mail:* koenigmd@email.rosary.edu

KOENIG, MILTON G, THERMODYNAMICS. *Current Pos:* From instr to assoc prof, 56-89, EMER PROF MECH ENG, WAYNE STATE UNIV, 89- *Personal Data:* b Moberly, Mo, Aug 23, 27; m 56; c 3. *Educ:* Wayne State Univ, BSME, 56, MSME, 57. *Mem:* Soc Automotive Eng. *Res:* Thermodynamics and its applications; automotive design; vehicle dynamics and handling. *Mailing Add:* 46266 Pickford St Northville MI 48167

KOENIG, PAUL EDWARD, ORGANIC CHEMISTRY. *Current Pos:* from asst prof to prof chem, La State Univ, 58-83, asst head dept, 63-67, assoc dean grad sch, 67-70, vchancellor acad affairs, 70-81, CONSULT CHEMIST, RUNNELS SCH, LA STATE UNIV, BATON ROUGE, 83-, DEAN, 84- *Personal Data:* b Gallup, NMex, May 30, 29; m 50, Norma Putnam; c Michael, Lawrence, Karen, Thomas, Paula, Thecla, Gretchen & Monica. *Educ:* Univ Ariz, BS, 50, MS, 52; Univ Iowa, PhD(chem), 55. *Prof Exp:* Chemist, Ethyl Corp, 55-58. *Mem:* Am Chem Soc. *Res:* Organic reaction mechanisms; physical organic chemistry; organic synthesis; reactions of metal nitrides with organic compounds; structure of tertiary amides. *Mailing Add:* 2006 Cherrydale Ave Baton Rouge LA 70808-2817

KOENIG, SEYMOUR HILLEL, BIOPHYSICS. *Current Pos:* PRES, RELAXOMETRY INC, 93- *Personal Data:* b Manchester, NH, July 16, 27; m 47; c 2. *Educ:* Columbia Univ, BS, 49, MA, 50, PhD, 52. *Prof Exp:* Asst physics, Columbia Univ, 49-51; mem staff, Watson Res Lab, IBM Corp, 52-64, from asst dir to dir, 64-70, dir gen sci, Res Ctr, 70-71, staff mem, Phys Sci Dept, 71-93. *Concurrent Pos:* From adj asst prof to adj prof, Dept Elec Eng, Columbia Univ, 57-68, lectr, Dept Art Hist & Archeol, 70-76, adj prof, 76- consult, Physics Div, Los Alamos Sci Lab, 59-; mem gov coun, Am Phys Soc, 70-74. *Mem:* Fel Am Phys Soc; Biophys Soc; Sigma Xi; Am Soc Biol Chemists; NY Acad Sci. *Res:* Low temperature electrical transport in semiconductors and semi-metals; inelastic neutron scattering by solids; biophysics of proteins; nuclear magnetic relaxation in protein solutions; protein-water interactions; laser light scattering from macromolecule and virus solutions. *Mailing Add:* Relaxometry Inc PO BOX 760 Mahopac NY 10541

KOENIG, THOMAS W, ORGANIC CHEMISTRY. *Current Pos:* RETIRED. *Personal Data:* b Kansas City, Mo, Feb 11, 38; m 61; c 2. *Educ:* Southern Methodist Univ, BS, 59; Univ Ill, MS, 61, PhD(chem), 63. *Prof Exp:* From asst prof to assoc prof, Univ Ore, 63-74, prof chem, 74-92. *Mem:* Am Chem Soc. *Res:* Mechanisms of organic reactions. *Mailing Add:* 739 Edgemont Way Springfield OR 97403

KOENIGSBERG, ERNEST, OPERATIONS RESEARCH, MANAGEMENT SCIENCE. *Current Pos:* EMER PROF, UNIV CALIF, SAN FRANCISCO, 93- *Personal Data:* b New York, NY, Apr 15, 23; m 55; c 2. *Educ:* NY Univ, BA, 48; Iowa State Univ, PhD(theoret physics), 53. *Prof Exp:* Sr physicist, Midwest Res Inst, 53-55; group leader, EMI Eng Develop, 55-57; sect head opers res, Midwest Res Inst, 57-58; mgr mgt serv, Touche, Ross, Bailey & Smart, 58-61; mgr tech serv, CEIR Inc, 61-64; prof indust, Univ Pa, 64-65; vpres, Matson Res Corp, 65-69; sr vpres & tech dir, Manalytics Inc, 69-72; sr lectr, Schs Bus Admin, Univ Calif, Berkeley, 72-93. *Concurrent Pos:* Vis lectr, Stanford Univ, 60; vis lectr, Univ Calif, Berkeley, 61-63, grad sch bus admin, 91-96, 66-72; mem comt future port develop, Maritime Transp Res Bd, Nat Acad Eng, 74-75. *Mem:* Fel Royal Statist Soc; Opers Res Soc; Inst Mgt Sci (vpres, 61-65). *Res:* Application of operations research to business, commercial and non-military government problems; queue theory; inventory theory; linear programming; transportation, distribution and energy development. *Mailing Add:* 2345 Divisadero St Univ Calif San Francisco CA 94115

KOEPF, ERNEST HENRY, CHEMICAL ENGINEERING. *Current Pos:* RETIRED. *Personal Data:* b Bruceville, Tex, Jan 23, 12; m 38; c 2. *Educ:* Univ Tex, BS, 34, MS, 36, PhD(chem eng), 39. *Prof Exp:* Chem engr, Atlantic Refining Co, 39-52; vpres & gen mgr, Texas City Chem, Inc, 52-54; admin coordr, Crude Oil Producing Dept, Atlantic Refining Co, 54-55; mgr res & tech servs, Core Labs, Inc, 55-65, gen mgr, Francolerab, 65-68, vpres res & tech servs, 68-78, vpres res & develop, 78-82. *Concurrent Pos:* Engr, AAAS, Interstate Oil Compact Comn Res Comt & Am Petrol Inst; pres, Ocean Pollution Control, Inc, 71-72, Ecol Audits, Inc, 72-78, P-V-T, Inc, 75-78 & Syndrill Carbide Diamond Co, 80-82; consult, 82-90. *Mem:* Am Chem Soc; Am Inst Mining, Metall & Petrol Engrs; Soc Independent Prof Earth Scientists. *Res:* High pressure phase behavior of hydrocarbons; petroleum reservoir operation; physical properties of oil reservoir rock and their contained fluids; distribution and flow of hydrocarbons in porous media; environmental protection. *Mailing Add:* 3607 Greenbrier Dr Dallas TX 75225

KOEPFINGER, J L, ELECTRICAL ENGINEERING. *Current Pos:* DIR, SYST & RES ELEC UTILITIES, DUQUESNE LIGHT CO, 85- *Personal Data:* b Sewickley, Pa, May 6, 25; c 6. *Educ:* Univ Pittsburgh, BS, 49, MS, 53. *Honors & Awards:* Steinmetz Award. *Prof Exp:* Dir, Commun & Protective Relaying, 64-85. *Concurrent Pos:* Dir, Maglev Inc & Mehtu Tech, Inc. *Mem:* Fel Inst Elec & Electronics Engrs. *Res:* Development of technology for operation of electronic utility. *Mailing Add:* Duquesne Light Co 301 Grant St 19-5 Pittsburgh PA 15279

KOEPFLI, JOSEPH B, ORGANIC CHEMISTRY. *Current Pos:* res assoc chem, 32-72, EMER SR RES ASSOC, CALIF INST TECHNOL, PASADENA, 72- *Personal Data:* b Los Angeles, Calif, Feb 5, 04; m 35; c 2. *Educ:* Stanford Univ, BA, 24, MA, 25; Oxford Univ, DPhil(chem), 28. *Prof Exp:* Instr pharmacol, Sch Med, Johns Hopkins Univ, 30-32. *Res:* Alkaloids; phytohormones; antimalarials. *Mailing Add:* 580 Freehaven Dr Santa Barbara CA 93108

KOEPKE, BARRY GEORGE, CERAMICS. *Current Pos:* MKT MGR, DESPATCH INDUST. 95- *Personal Data:* b Detroit, Mich, Oct 27, 37. *Educ:* Univ Ill, BS, 60, MS, 62; Iowa State Univ, PhD(metall), 68. *Prof Exp:* Res engr metall, Rocketdyne Div, NAm Aviation, 62-64; ceramics prog dir, NSF, 79-81; scientist, Honeywell Corp Res Ctr, Honeywell Inc, 64-79, prog mgr, syst & Res Ctr, 81-83, res & develop, Ceramics Ctr, 83-85, opers mgr, 85-88, opers mgr & components, 88-93, environ eng mgr, Alliant Tech Systs, 93-95. *Concurrent Pos:* Adj prof mat sci, Univ Minn, 76-; dir Ceramics Prog Div Mat Res, NSF, 80-81. *Mem:* fel Am Ceramic Soc; Am Soc Metals; Sigma Xi. *Res:* Studies of the mechanical properties and fracture behavior of ceramic materials, the nature and extent of surface damage introduced into dielectrics by machining and polishing; piezo electric ceramics; production of ceramics with tailored microstructures by unique processing techniques. *Mailing Add:* 2122 Noble Lane Mound MN 55364

KOEPKE, GEORGE HENRY, MEDICINE, ELECTRODIAGNOSTIC MEDICINE. *Current Pos:* RETIRED. *Personal Data:* b Toledo, Ohio, Jan 1, 16; m 40; c Susan (Healy) & Sandra (Bunting). *Educ:* Univ Toledo, BS, 45; Univ Cincinnati, MD, 49; Am Bd Phys Med & Rehab, dipl, 55. *Prof Exp:* Intern, Toledo Hosp, 49-50; resident, Univ Mich Hosp, 50-52, instr phys med & rehab, Med Sch, 52-53; pvt pract, 53-54; from asst prof to prof phys med & rehab, Med Ctr, Univ Mich, Ann Arbor, 54-76. *Concurrent Pos:* Consult, Vet Admin Hosp, Ann Arbor, 55-75, Lapeer State Home & Training Sch, 64- & Mary Free Bed Hosp, Grand Rapids, 71-76; mem staff, Saginaw Community Hosp, St Mary's Hosp, Saginaw Gen Hosp & St Luke's Hosp; chmn, Am Bd Phys Med & Rehab, 76; emer mem prof adv coun, United Cerebral Palsy Asn; Am Bd Electrodiag Med, 90. *Mem:* Fel Am Acad Phys Med & Rehab; Am Asn Electromyog & Electrodiag; Am Acad Orthop Surg; Am Cong Rehab Med; AMA. *Res:* Physical medicine and rehabilitation; electromyography and prosthetics. *Mailing Add:* 2222 S Main St Findlay OH 45840

KOEPKE, JOHN ARTHUR, CLINICAL PATHOLOGY, HEMATOLOGY. *Current Pos:* prof & med dir, Clin Hemat Labs, 80-94, EMER PROF PATH, MED CTR, DUKE UNIV, 94- *Personal Data:* b Milwaukee, Wis, Mar 25, 29; m 55, Evelyn M Lovekamp; c Mary, John, Mark & James. *Educ:* Valparaiso Univ, BA, 51; Univ Wis, MD, 56; Marquette Univ, MS, 64. *Prof Exp:* Instr path, Marquette Univ, 58-60; from asst prof to assoc prof, Univ Ky, 61-70; assoc clin prof med technol, Col Med, Univ Iowa, 70-71, prof path & vchmn dept, 72-79. *Concurrent Pos:* From asst pathologist to assoc pathologist, Univ Ky Hosp, 61-71; attend pathologist & consult, USPHS, 63-71; vis scientist, Karolinska Inst, Sweden, 67-68; dir lab, Lexington Clin, 71-72; chief lab serv, Vet Admin Hosp, Iowa City, 72-78; attend pathologist, Univ Iowa Hosp & Clins, 72-; vis colleague, Royal Postgrad Med Sch, London, Eng, 78. *Mem:* Col Am Path; Am Soc Clin Path; AMA. *Res:* Blood coagulation; flow cytometry; hematology instrumentation; quality assurance systems. *Mailing Add:* Duke Univ Med Ctr PO Box 2929 Durham NC 27710-2929. *E-Mail:* nckoepke@mindspring.com

KOEPKE, MARK E, EXPERIMENTAL, WAVES & INSTABILITIES. *Current Pos:* asst prof, 87-93, ASSOC PROF PHYSICS, WVA UNIV, 93- *Personal Data:* b Camp Pendleton, Calif, May 13, 56. *Educ:* Univ Md, BS, 78, MS, 80, PhD(physics), 84. *Prof Exp:* Res assoc, Univ Wash, Seattle, 84-86, res asst prof, 86-87. *Concurrent Pos:* Young investr award, Off Naval Res, 87; vis scientist, Univ Kiev, Ger, 93, 94; guest prof, Univ Innsbruck, Austria, 96. *Mem:* Am Phys Soc; Am Geophys Union. *Res:* Plasma waves and instabilities in a laboratory device known as a Q machine; both linear and nonlinear phenomena are investigated, the results are applicable to space plasmas. *Mailing Add:* Physics Dept WVa Univ Morgantown WV 26506-6315. *Fax:* 304-293-5732; *E-Mail:* koepke@wvnvms.wvnet.edu

KOEPNICK, RICHARD BORLAND, SEDIMENTARY PETROLOGY. *Current Pos:* res geologist, Mobil Field Res Lab, 77-84, res assoc geol res, 85-86, res assoc geol, Dallas Res Lab, 86-92, SR GEOL RES ADV, EXPLOR & PRODUCING TECH CTR, MOBIL RES DEVELOP CORP, 92- *Personal Data:* b Dayton, Ohio, Feb 5, 44. *Educ:* Univ Colo, BA, 67; Univ Kans, MS, 69, PhD(geol), 76. *Prof Exp:* Asst prof, Dept Geol, Williams Col, 75-77. *Mem:* Soc Econ Paleontologists & Mineralogists; Am Asn Petrol Geologists; Sigma Xi. *Res:* Application of strontium isotope analysis to stratigraphic and diagenetic studies; diagenesis of carbonate rocks and sandstones; temporal controls on carbonate reservoir development; carbonate reservoir characterization. *Mailing Add:* 4249 Southcrest Rd Dallas TX 75229-6357

KOEPP, LEILA H, SCIENCE EDUCATION. *Current Pos:* ASSOC PROF BIOL, ANAT & PHYSIOL, BLOOMFIELD COL, NJ, 81- *Personal Data:* b Haifa, Israel, July 7, 45; US citizen; m 69; c 2. *Educ:* Messiah Col, BA, 68; NTex State Univ, MS, 70; Univ Med & Dent NJ, PhD(microbiol), 81. *Prof Exp:* Instr microbiol, Montclair State Col, 74-76, instr biol, anat & physiol, Fairleigh Dickson Univ, Madison, 76-77; asst med microbiol & researcher microbiol, Univ Med & Dent NJ, 78-81. *Concurrent Pos:* Bacteriologist clin microbiol, genetics, immunol & gen biol, Overlook Hosp, Summit, NJ, 75-81. *Mem:* Am Soc Microbiol. *Res:* Molecular basis for the biological activity of the slime glycolipoprotein of Pseudomonas aeruginosa; isolation and identification of fungi from stone monuments of the New York Metropolitan Art Museum. *Mailing Add:* Dept Math & Natural Sci Bloomfield Col 467 Franklin St Bloomfield NJ 07003-3425

KOEPP, STEPHEN JOHN, ZOOLOGY, CYTOPATHOLOGY. *Current Pos:* Asst prof, 73-78, assoc prof biol, 79-85, PROF BIOL, MONTCLAIR STATE COL, 85- *Personal Data:* b Los Angeles, Calif, Apr 24, 46; m 69; c 2. *Educ:* Messiah Col, BA, 68; NTex State Univ, MS, 70, PhD(biol), 73. *Concurrent Pos:* Environ consult. *Mem:* Electron Micros Soc Am; Am Col Toxicol, 80- *Res:* Histopathologic and cytopathologic response of aquatic fauna following toxic exposure to heavy metals; electron microscopy. *Mailing Add:* Dept Biol Monclair State Col 1 Normal Ave Upper Montclair NJ 07043-1624

KOEPPE, MARY KOLEAN, ENVIRONMENTAL TOXICOLOGY, HERBICIDE METABOLISM IN PLANTS. *Current Pos:* Sect res chemist, 83-94, SR RES CHEMIST, E I DU PONT NEMOURS & CO INC, 94- *Personal Data:* b Holland, Mich, July 7, 55; m 78, John F. *Educ:* Hope Col, BA, 77; Univ Wis, Madison, MS, 79, PhD(entomol), 83. *Mem:* Am Chem Soc; Weed Sci Soc. *Res:* Optimization of herbicide lead areas via a biokinetic approach; understanding rates of metabolism in plants as well as a high throughput screening approach. *Mailing Add:* Agr Dept Dupont Stine-Haskell PO Box 30 Newark DE 19714-0030. *Fax:* 302-451-4863; *E-Mail:* koeppe@a1.esvax.umc.dupont.com

KOEPPE, OWEN JOHN, BIOCHEMISTRY. *Current Pos:* RETIRED. *Personal Data:* b Cedar Grove, Wis, May 29, 26; m 50; c 3. *Educ:* Hope Col, AB, 49; Univ Ill, MS, 51, PhD(biochem), 53. *Prof Exp:* Asst chem, Univ Ill, 49-51, asst biochem, 51-52; USPHS res fel, Univ Minn, 53-55; from asst prof to assoc prof biochem, Sch Med, Univ Mo, Columbia, 55-61, chmn dept, 68-73, prof, 61-, provost acad affairs, 73-80; provost, Kans State Univ, 80-87, prof biochem, 80-90. *Mem:* Am Chem Soc; Am Soc Biochem & Molecular Biol. *Res:* Mechanism of enzyme action; peptide bond synthesis. *Mailing Add:* 3009 Crawford St Columbia MO 65203

KOEPPE, ROGER E, II, CHEMISTRY, BIOCHEMISTRY. *Current Pos:* from asst prof to prof, 79-96, UNIV PROF, DEPT CHEM & BIOCHEM, UNIV ARK, 96- *Personal Data:* b Champaign, Ill, July 1, 49; m 71, Jessie L Smith; c Matthew, Julia, Franklin, Jason & Joshua. *Educ:* Haverford Col, BA, 71; Calif Inst Technol, PhD(chem & biochem), 76. *Honors & Awards:* Harold Lamport Lectr, Cornell Univ, 87. *Prof Exp:* NIH postdoctoral fel struct biol, Sch Med, Stanford Univ, 76-79. *Concurrent Pos:* Guest asst scientist, Brookhaven Nat Lab, 80-86; vis assoc, Calif Inst Technol, 85-86; Fulbright fel, Neth, 92; vis prof, Univ Utrecht, Neth, 92. *Mem:* Fedn Am Socs Exp Biol; Biophys Soc; Am Chem Soc; Sigma Xi; Fulbright Asn. *Res:* Mechanism of ion transport through membrane channels; physico-chemical studies of proteins and nucleic acids; author of 65 technical publications. *Mailing Add:* Dept Chem & Biochem 103 Chem Bldg Univ Ark Fayetteville AR 72701. *Fax:* 501-575-4049

KOEPPE, ROGER ERDMAN, BIOCHEMISTRY. *Current Pos:* from assoc prof to prof, 59-90, head dept, 63-90, EMER PROF & HEAD BIOCHEM, OKLA STATE UNIV, 90- *Personal Data:* b Amoy, China, May 2, 22; m 47, Norma Lemmer; c Roger III, Mary, Sarah, Edwin & Peter. *Educ:* Hope Col, AB, 44; Univ Ill, MS, 47, PhD(biochem), 50. *Prof Exp:* Asst, Univ Ill, 46-48 & 50-51; res assoc, Univ Tenn, 51-52, from instr to assoc prof chem, 52-59. *Concurrent Pos:* NIH sr fel, Univ Pa, 66-67; Sigma Xi lectr, 74. *Mem:* AAAS; Am Chem Soc; Am Soc Biol Chemists; Brit Biochem Soc. *Res:* Metabolism, including enzymology, of acetate, mannose, pyruvate and glutamate in mammalian brain and liver. *Mailing Add:* Dept Biochem & Molecular Biol 246 Nat Res Coun Okla State Univ Stillwater OK 74078

KOEPPEN, BRUCE MICHAEL, ELECTROPHYSIOLOGY, ION TRANSPORT. *Current Pos:* ASSOC PROF MED & PHYSIOL, HEALTH CTR, UNIV CONN, 82- *Personal Data:* b Oct 7, 51; m; c 2. *Educ:* Univ Chicago, MD, 77; Univ Ill, PhD(physiol), 80. *Mem:* Am Soc Nephrology; Am Physiol Soc; Am Biophys Soc; Int Soc Nephrol; Soc Gen Physiol. *Mailing Add:* Dept Med Sch Med Univ Conn Health Ctr MC-1920 Farmington CT 06030-0001

KOEPPL, GERALD WALTER, CHEMICAL PHYSICS. *Current Pos:* from instr to assoc prof, 71-88, PROF CHEM, QUEENS COL, NY, 89- *Personal Data:* b Chicago, Ill, Dec 4, 42; m 78, Karen Kitfield; c Jacob & Rebecca. *Educ:* Ill Inst Technol, BSc, 65, PhD(chem), 69. *Prof Exp:* NIH res fel chem, Harvard Univ, 69-70, res fel, 70. *Concurrent Pos:* Proj dir res grant, Res Found City Univ New York, 71-97; Sloan Found fel, 75-79; vis assoc prof, Harvard Univ, 75 & Univ Vt, 78. *Mem:* Am Chem Soc; Sigma Xi; Am Phys Soc. *Res:* Classical mechanical trajectory studies of the statistical theories of chemical reaction dynamics. *Mailing Add:* Dept Chem & Biochem Queens Col City Univ NY Flushing NY 11367. *Fax:* 718-997-5531

KOEPSEL, WELLINGTON WESLEY, ELECTRICAL ENGINEERING, MICROWAVE MEASUREMENTS ELECTROMAGNETIC SYSTEMS. *Current Pos:* CHIEF ENGR & OWNER, MUTRONIC SYSTS. *Personal Data:* b McQueeney, Tex, Dec 5, 21; m 50, Dorothy Adams; c Kirsten, Gretchen & Lief. *Educ:* Univ Tex, BS, 44, MS, 51; Okla State Univ, PhD(elec eng), 60. *Prof Exp:* Res scientist elec eng, Univ Tex, 48-51; res engr aerophys lab, NAm Aviation, Inc, 51; asst prof, Southern Methodist Univ, 51-56 & Okla State Univ, 56-58; assoc prof, Southern Methodist Univ, 58-59, Univ NMex, 60-63 & Duke Univ, 63-64; head dept, Kans State Univ, 64-76, prof, 64-84, emer prof elec eng, 84- *Concurrent Pos:* Vis prof, Tex A&M Univ. *Mem:* Sr mem Inst Elec & Electronics Engrs; Sigma Xi. *Res:* Feedback control systems; microcomputer and digital control systems; electro-magnetic techniques to measure fuel consumption in zero gravity environment. *Mailing Add:* 6506 Marblewood Dr Austin TX 78731

KOEPSELL, PAUL L(OEL), CIVIL ENGINEERING. *Current Pos:* asst prof civil eng, SDak State Univ, 58, assoc prof, 59-65, dir res & data processing, 65-76, PROF CIVIL ENG, SDAK STATE UNIV, 67-, DIR COMPUT CTR, 76-, HEAD, DEPT COMPUT SCI, 81- *Personal Data:* b Canova, SDak, June 17, 30; m 52, Delores Johnson; c Steven, Royal & Pamela. *Educ:* SDak State Univ, BS, 52; Univ Wash, Seattle, MS, 54; Okla State Univ, PhD, 65. *Prof Exp:* Stress analyst, Aircraft Struct, Boeing Airplane Co, 52-57. *Mem:* Am Soc Civil Engrs; Am Concrete Inst; Nat Soc Prof Engrs (vpres, 79-81); Asn Comput Mach. *Res:* Structural components; approximate analysis of structures; application of matrix methods to structural analysis. *Mailing Add:* Box 2219 Univ Sta 100 University Dr Brookings SD 57007-0495. *Fax:* 605-688-5878

KOERBER, GEORGE G(REGORY), ELECTRICAL ENGINEERING. *Current Pos:* RETIRED. *Personal Data:* b Akron, Ohio, Aug 30, 24; m 51, Barbara Jackson; c Anne (Koerber-Schwab), Laura (Farrington) & Gregory. *Educ:* Hiram Col, BA, 48; Purdue Univ, MS, 50, PhD(phys chem), 52. *Prof Exp:* Mem tech staff component develop, Bell Tel Labs, Inc, 52-56; assoc prof mech, Rensselaer Polytech Inst, 56-58; assoc prof eng mech, Mich Col Mining & Technol, 58-59; assoc prof theoret & appl mech, Iowa State Univ, 60-61, from assoc prof to prof elec eng, 61-84. *Mem:* Inst Elec & Electronics Engrs. *Res:* Applied mathematics; properties of solids; propagating disturbances, particularly piezo electric surface waves. *Mailing Add:* 510 Ridge View Dr Sequim WA 98382-9589

KOERING, MARILYN JEAN, ANATOMY, REPRODUCTIVE BIOLOGY. *Current Pos:* from asst prof to assoc prof, 69-79, PROF ANAT, MED CTR, GEORGE WASHINGTON UNIV, 79-, DIR MICROS ANAT, 82-, DIR NEUROSCI PROG, 90- *Personal Data:* b Brainerd, Minn, Jan 7, 38. *Educ:* Col St Scholastica, BA, 60; Univ Wis-Madison, MS, 63, PhD(anat), 67. *Prof Exp:* Res asst chem, Col St Scholastica, 60-61; instr anat, Univ Wis, 63-64; res trainee reproductive physiol, Ore Primate Res Ctr, 66-67; NIH fel, Primate Res Ctr, 67-68, proj assoc, Univ Wis-Madison, 68-69. *Concurrent Pos:* Consult, Primate Res Ctr, Univ Wis, 75-78; vis scientist, du Pont, Calif Inst Technol, 76, Jones Inst Reproductive Med, E Va Med Sch, Norfolk, 85-92; guest worker, Pregnancy Res Br, Nat Inst Child Health & Human Develop, 77-85; mem primate res adv bd, NIH, 78-82. *Mem:* AAAS; Am Asn Anatomists; Soc Study Reproduction. *Res:* Cyclic changes in ovarian morphology as observed in light and electron microscopy; correlation of reproductive morphology with physiology. *Mailing Add:* Dept Anat George Washington Univ Med Ctr Washington DC 20037

KOERKER, FREDERICK WILLIAM, INORGANIC CHEMISTRY. *Current Pos:* RETIRED. *Personal Data:* b Milwaukee, Wis, June 9, 13; m 37; c 3. *Educ:* Univ Wis, BS, 34, MS, 36. *Prof Exp:* Asst chem, Univ Wis, 34-36; analyst, Main Lab, 36-37, chemist, Chlorine Dept, 37-41, asst supt, 41-53, tech expert electrochem planning, 53-62, tech expert, Chem Dept, 62-68, mgr qual standards, 68-78, consult, Dow Chem Co, 78-82. *Mem:* Am Chem Soc; Electrochem Soc. *Res:* Electrolytic production of chlorine, caustic and allied products; specifications and methods of analysis for general chemicals. *Mailing Add:* Judson Park Retirement Community 23600 Marine View Dr S Apt 233 Des Moines WA 98198-7396

KOERKER, ROBERT LELAND, PHARMACOLOGY. *Current Pos:* ASSOC PROF PHARMACOL, MED SCH, WRIGHT STATE UNIV, 80- *Personal Data:* b Saginaw, Mich, Jan 10, 43. *Educ:* Kalamazoo Col, BA, 65; Emory Univ, PhD(pharmacol), 70. *Prof Exp:* Asst biologist microbiol, Biochem Res Lab, Dow Chem Co, 63-64, asst chemist, Dept Chem Res Lab, 65; NIH res fel pharmacol, Univ Colo Med Ctr, 70-73; USPHS res fel, Emory Univ, 73-74; asst prof pharmacol, La State Univ Med Ctr, 74-80. *Mem:* Sigma Xi; AAAS; Am Soc Pharmacol & Exp Therapeut; Soc Toxicol. *Res:* Toxicity of aldehydes, alcohols, organo-mercurials and other agents in cultured mouse neuroblastoma cells; characterization of uptake and storage mechanisms in cultured mouse neuroblastoma cells. *Mailing Add:* Dept Pharmacol/Toxicol Wright State Univ PO Box 927 Dayton OH 45401-0927. *Fax:* 937-775-7221; *E-Mail:* rkoerker@discover.wright.edu

KOERNER, E(RNEST) L(EE), CHEMICAL ENGINEERING. *Current Pos:* PRES, TECHRAD INC, 83- *Personal Data:* b Cleveland, Ohio, Mar 17, 31; m 53; c 6. *Educ:* Univ Dayton, BChE, 53; Iowa State Col, MS, 55, PhD(chem eng), 56. *Prof Exp:* Asst chem eng, Ames Lab, AEC, Iowa State Col, 53-56; res engr & sect leader extractive processes, Union Carbide Metals Co, 57-59; res specialist, Monsanto Co, 59-67; sr res specialist, Kerr-McGee Corp, 67, sr res group leader, 67-70; pres, Technol Res & Develop Inc, 70-83. *Mem:* Am Inst Chem Engrs; Am Inst Mining, Metall & Petrol Engrs; Nat Soc Prof Engrs. *Res:* Extractive metallurgical processes; liquid-liquid extraction; hazard wastes treatment; energy recovery from solid wastes; biological and enzyme treatment of waste waters. *Mailing Add:* 12721 St Andrews Terr Oklahoma City OK 73120-8807

KOERNER, JAMES FREDERICK, BIOCHEMISTRY, NEUROSCIENCE. *Current Pos:* from asst prof to assoc prof, 61-72, PROF BIOCHEM, SCH MED, UNIV MINN, MINNEAPOLIS, 72- *Personal Data:* b Charles City, Iowa, June 30, 29; m 58; c 2. *Educ:* Iowa State Col, BS, 50, PhD(biochem), 56. *Prof Exp:* Res assoc biochem, Iowa State Col, 50-52, asst, 52-56; USPHS fel, Mass Inst Technol, 56-58, res assoc, 58-61. *Mem:* AAAS; Am Soc Biol Chemists; Soc Neurosci; Am Soc Neurochem. *Res:* Neurochemistry; acidic amino acids as excitatory neurotransmitters; glutamate metabolism. *Mailing Add:* Dept Biochem Univ Minn Med Sch 435 Delaware St S E Minneapolis MN 55455

KOERNER, ROBERT M, SOIL MECHANICS. *Current Pos:* from asst prof to assoc prof, 68-76, PROF CIVIL ENG, DREXEL UNIV, 76- *Personal Data:* b Philadelphia, Pa, Dec 2, 33; m 59; c 3. *Educ:* Drexel Inst Technol, BSCE, 56, MSCE, 63; Duke Univ, PhD(soil mech), 68. *Prof Exp:* Engr & supt, Conduit & Found Corp, 56-60; engr analyst, Dames & Moore, 60-62; engr & supt, J J Skelly, Inc, 62-63; instr, Pa Mil Col, 64-65; NSF teaching intern, Duke Univ, 65-67, instr, part-time, 67-68. *Mem:* Am Soc Civil Engrs; Am Soc Eng Educ. *Res:* Foundation engineering; particle mechanics; powder metallurgy. *Mailing Add:* 130 Wood Rd Springfield PA 19064

KOERNER, T J, FACILITATE PEER REVIEW. *Current Pos:* SCI PROG DIR, AM CANCER SOC, 88- *Personal Data:* b Rochester, NY, June 15, 54; m 78; c 3. *Educ:* Univ Toronto, Ont, Can, BSc, 76; Univ Cincinnati, PhD(develop biol), 85. *Prof Exp:* Postdoctoral researcher, Columbia Univ, New York, 82-85; asst med res prof, Duke Univ Med Ctr, 85-88. *Mem:* Am Soc Biochem & Molecular Biol; Genetics Soc Am; Am Asn Cancer Res; Am Soc Microbiol; AAAS. *Res:* Administration of the peer review of applications and oversight of awards in the areas of molecular biology, immunology, and virology. *Mailing Add:* Res Dept Am Cancer Soc 1599 Clifton Rd NE Atlanta GA 30329-4251. *Fax:* 404-321-4669

KOERNER, THEODORE ALFRED WILLIAM, JR, BLOOD TRANSFUSION MEDICINE, CELL MEMBRANE BIOCHEMISTRY. *Current Pos:* asst prof, 86-88, ASSOC PROF PATH, UNIV IOWA COL MED, 88-, ASSOC PROF BIOCHEM, 90- *Personal Data:* b Waco, Tex, July 30, 47; m 71; c 2. *Educ:* La State Univ, BS, 70, PhD(biochem), 75; Tulane Univ, MD, 78. *Prof Exp:* Intern path, Yale-New Haven Hosp, 78-79, resident physician, 79-81; fel lab med, Yale Univ Sch Med, 81-82; asst prof path, Tulane Univ Sch Med, 82-86. *Concurrent Pos:* Acad Clin Lab Physicians & Scientists young investr award, 82; adj asst prof, Dept Biochem, Tulane Univ Sch Med & med dir, Blood Ctr & Apheresis Serv, Tulane Univ Hosp, 82-86; asst med dir, DeGowin Blood Ctr, Univ Iowa Hosp & Clins, 86-88, assoc med dir, 88-; legal expert, blood-borne acquired immune deficiency syndrome, Law Off Meis & Waite, San Francisco, 89- *Mem:* Am Chem Soc; Am Asn Blood Banks; Am Soc Biochem & Molecular Biol; Am Asn Pathologists; Am Soc Hemat; Am Soc Apheresis. *Res:* Structure, function, immunology and pathophysiology of blood platelet membrane glycoproteins, glycolipids and phospholipids; oligosaccharide and lipid chemistry; high pressure liquid chromatography and multidimensional nuclear magnetic resonance spectroscopy; transfusion medicine; storage and survival of platelets; transfusion-transmitted acquired immune deficiency syndrome and other infectious diseases. *Mailing Add:* Dept Path Med Res Ctr 143 Univ Iowa Col Med Iowa City IA 52242-1087. *Fax:* 319-335-8348

KOERNER, WILLIAM ELMER, PHYSICAL CHEMISTRY, ANALYTICAL CHEMISTRY. *Current Pos:* RETIRED. *Personal Data:* b Neenah, Wis, Nov 3, 23; m 47, Anita Ziegenhagen; c Pamela & Janet. *Educ:* Univ Wis, BS, 46, PhD(phys chem), 49. *Prof Exp:* Res phys chemist, Monsanto Co, 49-54, group leader phys chem, 54-64, mgr, Phys Sci Ctr, 64-80, dir phys sci, 80-86, fel prog coordr, 86-95. *Concurrent Pos:* Dual tech ladder consult & coordr, 80-95. *Mem:* AAAS; Soc Appl Spectros; Am Chem Soc; Sigma Xi. *Res:* Chemical reaction kinetics; thermochemistry; physical analytical chemistry. *Mailing Add:* 5642 Murdoch Ave St Louis MO 63109

KOERTING, LOLA ELISABETH, GENETICS, CYTOLOGY. *Current Pos:* CONSULT GENETICIST, KITCHAWAN RES LAB, BROOKLYN BOT GARDEN, NY, 75- *Personal Data:* b Munich, Ger, Jan 31, 24; US citizen; m 53; c 2. *Educ:* Munich Tech Univ, BS, 47, MS, 49, PhD(biol, agr), 53. *Prof Exp:* Res asst plant genetics, Munich Tech Univ, 48-53; chief histol & ultrasonics, New Eng Inst Med Res, 54-55; res assoc forest genetics, Sch Forestry, Yale Univ, 55-58; res fel cytogenetics, New Eng Inst Med Res, 65-73. *Mem:* AAAS; Environ Mutagen Soc; Bot Soc Am; Sigma Xi; Tissue Cult Asn. *Res:* Cytogenetics; induced chromosome abnormalities and mutations; tissue culture. *Mailing Add:* PO Box 551 Ridgefield CT 06877-0551

KOESTEL, MARK ALFRED, FIELD GEOLOGY & GEOCHEMISTRY. *Current Pos:* GEOLOGIST & PHOTOGRAPHER, 90- *Personal Data:* b Cleveland, Ohio, Jan 1, 51; c Bonnie & Jennifer. *Educ:* Univ Ariz, BS, 78. *Prof Exp:* Field geologist, Falconbridge Nickel Mines/Superior Oil Co, 77; sr geologist-proj mgr, Union Oil Calif, 78-86; mgr geol serv-hydrogeologist, Harmsworth Assocs, 86-88; proj mgr-sr geologist, Appl Geosysts, 88-90. *Concurrent Pos:* NMex state rep, Minerals Explor Coalition, 82. *Mem:* Am Inst Prof Geologists; Geol Soc Am; Nat Geog Soc; Soc Mining Engrs. *Res:* Environmental, economic and general education geology; base, precious and strategic metal exploration; subsurface investigation and interpretation; geochemistry. *Mailing Add:* 45 Brownfield Lane Phillips Ranch CA 91766

KOESTER, CHARLES JOHN, OPHTHALMIC OPTICS, MICROSCOPY. *Current Pos:* RETIRED. *Personal Data:* b Niagara Falls, NY, Jan 26, 29; m 53; c 4. *Educ:* Carnegie Inst Technol, BS, 50; Univ Rochester, PhD(physics, optics), 55. *Prof Exp:* Asst, Univ Rochester, 50-55; physicist, Am Optical Co, 55-58; res assoc, Nat Bur Standards, 58-59; physicist, Am Optical Corp, 59-65, appl res mgr, 65-75, dir res, Sci Instrument Div, 75-77; asst prof biophys ophthal, Columbia Univ Col Physicians & Surgeons, 78-84, assoc prof clin biophys ophthal, 84-91. *Concurrent Pos:* Lectr ophthal, Columbia Univ, 70-; indust rep, Food & Drug Admin Ophthalmic Device Classification Panel, 74-78; mem bd dirs, Optical Soc Am, 74-76. *Mem:* Optical Soc Am; Asn Res Vision & Ophthal; Am Acad Ophthal; Am Soc Cataract Refractive Surg; Am Acad Optom. *Res:* Ophthalmic instruments and microscopes; interference, polarizing, and confocal microscopes; image enhancement in fiber optics; laser photocoagulation; microscopy of the cornea; intraocular lenses. *Mailing Add:* 60 Kent Rd Glen Rock NJ 07452

KOESTER, JOHN D, BEHAVIOR, BIOPHYSIOLOGY. *Current Pos:* ACTG DIR, CTR NEURO-BIOL & BEHAV, SCH MED, COLUMBIA UNIV, 74- *Educ:* Columbia Univ, PhD(physiol), 71. *Mailing Add:* 205 W 19th St Apt 5R New York NY 10011

KOESTER, MARTHA K, PULP & PAPER INCLUDING ADDITIVES, BIOCHEMISTRY OF SOFTWOOD EMBRYOLOGY. *Current Pos:* SCIENTIST, WEYERHAEUSER CO, 88- *Personal Data:* b Chicago, Ill, Nov, 24, 46; m 70, Kurt Cockram. *Educ:* Knox Col, BA, 68; Univ Calif, PhD(biochem), 79. *Prof Exp:* Postdoctoral assoc, Boston Biomed Res, 80-82; sci writer, 82-88. *Mem:* Am Chem Soc; Asn Women Sci. *Res:* Proprietary research in pulp and paper process characterization; biochemical characterization of softwood embryos. *Mailing Add:* WTC 2F25 Tacoma WA 98477. *Fax:* 253-924-6654

KOESTERER, MARTIN GEORGE, MICROBIOLOGY. *Current Pos:* PRIVATE CONSULT, 93- *Personal Data:* b Rochester, NY, July 2, 33; m 58; c 4. *Educ:* Univ Rochester, AB, 55; Syracuse Univ, MS, 57. *Honors & Awards:* NASA Tech Brief, 72. *Prof Exp:* Res supvr sterilization, Wilmot Castle Co, 59-64; sr microbiologist & prog mgr sterilization & planetary quarantine, Valley Forge Space Technol Ctr, Gen Elec Co, 65-75; mgr microbiol res, Ethicon Inc, 75-77; CONSULT INDUST, 77-; mem staff microbiol & sterilization technol, Wyeth Labs, Inc, 78-93. *Concurrent Pos:* Spec lectr, Grad Sch Environ Sci, Drexel Univ, 69-70; guest lectr, Contamination Control Sem, Rochester Inst Technol, 71-75; consult microbial contamination control & sterilization, 69- *Mem:* Am Soc Microbiol; Inst Environ Sci; Soc Indust Microbiol; Am Soc Testing & Mat. *Res:* Resistance of bacterial spores to dry heat, moist heat, irradiation, various chemical agents; bioburden and microbial contamination control as it pertains to good manufacturing practices on pharmaceutical, biomedical devices and products; biological indicator development; sterilization development and validation. *Mailing Add:* 572 Charles Dr King of Prussia PA 19406

KOESTLER, ROBERT CHARLES, PESTICIDE CHEMISTRY. *Current Pos:* RETIRED. *Personal Data:* b Elizabeth, NJ, Oct 31, 32; m 58, Sally Moore; c Jane, Julia & David. *Educ:* Cornell Univ, BA, 54; Univ NC, Chapel Hill, PhD(org chem), 61. *Prof Exp:* Res chemist, Am Viscose Div, FMC Corp, 61-65; sr res chemist, Pennwalt Corp, 65-77, proj leader, 77-83, res scientist, 83-86; sr res scientist, Atochem Nam, 86-95. *Concurrent Pos:* Financial mgr, Controlled Release Soc. *Mem:* Am Chem Soc; Int Controlled Release Soc. *Res:* Organometallics; films and coatings; organic synthesis; microencapsulation and controlled release technology. *Mailing Add:* 2004 Pebblestone Ct College Station TX 77845. *Fax:* 409-823-1544

KOESTNER, ADALBERT, VETERINARY PATHOLOGY. *Current Pos:* chmn path, 81-91, EMER PROF, MICH STATE UNIV, 91- *Personal Data:* b Hatzfeld, Rumania, Sept 10, 20; US citizen; m 51; c 2. *Educ:* Univ Munich, DMV, 51; Ohio State Univ, MSc, 57, PhD, 59. *Prof Exp:* Res assoc bact, Vet Col, Univ Munich, 51-52; from instr to assoc prof, Vet Path, Ohio State Univ, 55-64, chmn, Dept Vet Pathobiol, 72-81, prof, 64-71. *Mem:* AAAS; Am Asn Pathologists; Soc Neurosci; Am Vet Med Asn; Am Asn Cancer Res; Am Asn Neuropath; Am Col Vet Path. *Res:* Comparative neuropathology; comparative and experimental oncology. *Mailing Add:* Dept Pathobiol Ohio State Univ 1925 Coffey Rd Columbus OH 43210. *Fax:* 614-292-6473

KOETHE, SUSAN M, IMMUNOLOGY. *Current Pos:* NIH fel, 74-76, asst prof, 76-81, ASSOC PROF PATH, MED COL WIS, 81- *Personal Data:* b San Diego, Calif, Sept 4, 45; m 68; c 1. *Educ:* San Diego State Col, BS, 67; Harvard Univ, PhD(immunol), 74. *Concurrent Pos:* Chmn, Milwaukee Immunol Group, 78-82. *Mem:* Am Asn Immunol. *Res:* Immunoregulation in myasthenia gravis and multiple sclerosis. *Mailing Add:* Dept Path Med Col Wis 8700 W Wisconsin Ave Milwaukee WI 53226-3512

KOETKE, DONALD D, NUCLEAR STRUCTURE. *Current Pos:* PROF PHYSICS, VALPARAISO UNIV, 77- *Personal Data:* b Chicago, Ill, Dec 12, 37; m 59; c 3. *Educ:* Concordia Col, Ill, BS, 59; Northwestern Univ, MS, 63, PhD(physics), 68. *Prof Exp:* Assoc prof physics, Concordia Col, Ill, 67-77. *Concurrent Pos:* Vis scientist, Argonne Nat Lab, 69 & 71-82, Los Alamos Nat Lab, 82-; consult, Int Atomic Energy Agency, 80- *Mem:* Am Phys Soc; Am Asn Physics Teachers; Sigma Xi. *Res:* Experiments in muon and neutrino physics done at Los Alamos; low energy nuclear cross-section measurements relative to solar neutrino production. *Mailing Add:* Niels Sci Ctr Valparaiso Univ Valparaiso IN 46383

KOETZLE, THOMAS F, CHEMICAL CRYSTALLOGRAPHY, NEUTRON AND X-RAY DIFFRACTION. *Current Pos:* Res assoc chem, Brookhaven Nat Lab, 70-73, assoc chemist, 73-75, chemist, 75-89, SR CHEMIST, BROOKHAVEN NAT LAB, 89- *Personal Data:* b Brooklyn, NY, Oct 15, 43; m 67, Carole E Peltz; c Laura E & John H. *Educ:* Harvard Univ, BA, 64, MA, 65, PhD(chem), 70. *Concurrent Pos:* AEC fel, 70-71; NIH fel, 71-73; prin investr, Protein Data Bank, 73-93; mem, Int Union Crystallog Comn, Crystallog Data, 81-93; mem, US Nat Comt Crystallog, 84-86 & 88-90; chmn, Neutron Scattering Spec Interest Group, Am Crystallog Asn, 83-84; mem, Am Chem Soc Task Force Sci Numerical Data, 87-; ed, Molecular Struct Biol, 88-92; mem ed bd, J Phys Chem Ref Data, 91-93; mem, US Nat Comt Codata, 92-94. *Mem:* AAAS; NY Acad Sci; Am Chem Soc; Am Crystallog Asn; Mats Res Soc; Neutron Scattering Soc Am. *Res:* Applications of neutron and x-ray diffraction to the analysis of molecular structure and chemical bonding; transition metal hydride and molecular hydrogen complexes and related organometallic systems important in catalysis site-specific isotope labeling. *Mailing Add:* Dept Chem Brookhaven Nat Lab PO Box 5000 Upton NY 11973-5000. *Fax:* 516-344-5815; *E-Mail:* koetzle@chm.chm.bnl.gov

KOEVENIG, JAMES L, BOTANY, BIOLOGY. *Current Pos:* RETIRED. *Personal Data:* b Postville, Iowa, Mar 18, 31; wid; c Kimberly K & Kurt L. *Educ:* Univ Iowa, BA, 55, PhD(sci educ & bot), 61; State Col Iowa, MA, 57. *Prof Exp:* Elem sch teacher, 55-56; res assoc, Univ Iowa, 61; asst prof zool, San Diego State Col, 61-62; res consult, Biol Sci Curric Study, Univ Colo, 62-64; from assoc prof to prof bot & biol, Univ Kans, 64-72; prof biol, Univ Cent Fla, 72-95. *Concurrent Pos:* Vis lectr, Univ Colo, 63-64; mem eval panel, Comn Undergrad Educ in Biol, 65; NSF sci fac fel, Princeton Univ, 67-68; United Nations Educ Sci & Cult Orgn Panel on Short Biol Films, 64; Fac Res Partic, Savannah River Ecol Lab, 78. *Mem:* AAAS; Bot Soc Am; Nat Asn Biol Teachers; Am Inst Biol Sci; Sigma Xi. *Res:* Myxomycete taxonomy; plant growth and development; science visual aid and evaluation. *Mailing Add:* Dept Biol Univ Cent Fla Box 25000 Orlando FL 32816

KOFF, BERNARD LOUIS, MILITARY & COMMERCIAL AIRCRAFT & ROCKET PROPULSION. *Current Pos:* RETIRED. *Personal Data:* b Huntington, NY, Mar 24, 27. *Educ:* Clarkson Univ, BS, 51; NY Univ, MS, 58. *Hon Degrees:* DSc, Clarkson Univ, 93. *Honors & Awards:* Air Breathing Propulsion Award, Am Indust Arts Asn, 84; Theodore von Karman Award, Air Force Asn, 88; R Tom Sawyer Award, Am Soc Mech Engr, 88; George Mead Medal, United Technologies Corp, 88; Reed Aeronaut Award, 90; Daniel Guggenheim Award, Am Indust Arts Asn, Am Soc Mech Engrs, Soc Automotive Engrs, 92; Franklin W Kolk Award, Soc Automotive Engrs, 93. *Prof Exp:* Test engr, Gen Elec, 51-52; design engr, Fairchild, 52-56; design engr, Curtis Wright, 56-58; design engr, Gen Elec, 58-62, sr engr, 62-64, mgr to gen mgr, 65-75, chief engr, 75-80; sr vpres, Govt Prod Div, Pratt & Whitney, 80-83, Eng Div, 83-87 & Govt Eng Bus, 87-90, exec vpres eng & technol, 90-97. *Concurrent Pos:* Mem, Sci Adv Bd, USAF, 86-90, Space Div Adv Bd, 88- *Mem:* Nat Acad Eng; Am Soc Mech Engrs; fel Am Inst Aeronaut & Astronaut; fel Soc Automotive Engrs. *Res:* Aircraft and spacecraft engine industry; author of 16 technical publications; awarded 13 patents. *Mailing Add:* 8 Cambria Rd E Palm Beach Gardens FL 33418. *Fax:* 561-626-9434

KOFF, RAYMOND STEVEN, INTERNAL MEDICINE, GASTROENTEROLOGY. *Current Pos:* PROF, SCH MED, UNIV MASS, 91- *Personal Data:* b Brooklyn, NY, June 11, 39; m 60; c 2. *Educ:* Adelphi Col, BA, 58; Albert Einstein Col Med, MD, 62; Am Bd Internal Med, dipl. *Prof Exp:* Intern med, Barnes Hosp, Washington Univ, 62-63, asst resident, 63-64; teaching fel, Tufts Univ & Lemuel Shattuck Hosp, 64-65, res fel, 65-66; clin & res fel, Mass Gen Hosp, Harvard Med Sch, 66-68, res fel, 68-69; from asst prof to prof, Sch Med, Boston Univ, 69-91. *Concurrent Pos:* NIH trainee gastroenterol, Mass Gen Hosp, 66-69; clin investr, Vet Admin, 69-72, chief hepatology sect, 73-86, chmn med, Columbia MetroWest Med Ctr, 86- *Mem:* Soc Epidemiol Res; Am Asn Study Liver Dis; fel Am Col Physicians; Am Gastroenterol Asn; Int Asn Study Liver; fel Am Col Gastroenterol. *Res:* Viral hepatitis; drug hepatotoxicity; chronic hepatitis. *Mailing Add:* Columbia Metro West Med Ctr 115 Lincoln St Framingham MA 01702

KOFFLER, HENRY, MICROBIOLOGY. *Current Pos:* PROF BIOCHEM & MICROBIOL & PRESIDENT, UNIV ARIZ, 82- *Personal Data:* b Vienna, Austria, Sept 17, 22; nat US; m 49. *Educ:* Univ Ariz, BS, 43; Univ Wis, MS, 44,PhD(bact), 47. *Honors & Awards:* Eli Lilly & Co Award, 57. *Prof Exp:* From asst prof to assoc prof bact, Purdue Univ, West Lafayette, 47-52, coordr res, 49-59, prof biol, 52-74, asst to dean grad sch, 57-59, asst dean, 59-60, head dept biol sci, 59-75, F L Hovde Distinguished prof, 74-75; prof biochem & microbiol & vpres acad affairs, Univ Minn, Minneapolis, 75-79; prof biochem & microbiol, Univ Mass, Amherst, 79-82. *Concurrent Pos:* Guggenheim fel, Sch Med, Case Western Reserve Univ, 53-54; mem, Comn Undergrad Educ in Biol Sci, 66-69, vchmn, 66-67; chmn, 67-69; mem, Purdue Res Found, 67-; consult-examr, NCent Asn Cols, 67-; mem, 2nd-7th Int Cong Biochem, Paris, Brussels, Vienna, Moscow & Tokyo; mem, 6th-8th & 10th Int Cong Microbiol, Rome, Stockholm, Montreal & Mexico City; mem, 9th & 11th Int Bot Cong, Montreal & Seattle; mem, 1st-3rd Int Biophys Cong, Stockholm, Vienna & Boston; mem, 5th Int Cong Electron Micros, Philadelphia, 16th Int Zool Cong, Washington, DC, 4th Int Cong Chemother, Washington, DC, 24th Int Cong Physiol Sci, 1st Int Cong Bact, Jerusalem & 1st Int Cong Int Asn Microbiol Soc, Tokyo. *Mem:* Am Soc Biol Chemists; Biophys Soc; Am Soc Microbiol; fel Am Acad Microbiol; Am Soc Cell Biologists. *Res:* Biosynthesis of carbohydrates; chemistry, biosynthesis and mechanism of action of antibiological peptides; structure and biosynthesis of flagellin and bacterial flagella; self-assembly of macromolecular structures; molecular bases for biological stability. *Mailing Add:* 312 Univ Ariz M D Johnson Bldg 1111 N Cherry Tucson AZ 85721-0001. *Fax:* 520-626-7800

KOFFMAN, ELLIOT B, COMPUTER SCIENCE EDUCATION, ARTIFICIAL INTELLIGENCE. *Current Pos:* Assoc prof, 74-77, PROF COMPUT SCI, TEMPLE UNIV, 77- *Personal Data:* b Boston, Mass, May 7, 42. *Educ:* Mass Inst Technol, SBEE & SMEE, 64, PhD(eng), 67. *Mem:* Asn Comput Mach. *Mailing Add:* Dept Comput & Info Sci Temple Univ 038-24 Broad & Montgomery Philadelphia PA 19122-2585

KOFFYBERG, FRANCOIS PIERRE, SOLID STATE SCIENCE. *Current Pos:* assoc prof chem, Brock Univ, 65-67, actg head physics, 67-68, assoc prof, 68-74, PROF PHYSICS, BROCK UNIV, 74- *Personal Data:* b Eindhoven, Neth, Nov 17, 34; m 59; c 3. *Educ:* Free Univ, Amsterdam, Drs, 59. *Prof Exp:* Nat Res Coun Can fel, 59-62; res chemist, Corning Glass Works, NY, 62-65. *Mem:* AAAS; Am Asn Physics Teachers; Can Asn Physicists. *Res:* Semiconductivity of oxides and glasses; photo-electronic properties. *Mailing Add:* Dept Physics Brock Univ St Catharines ON L2S 3A1 Can

KOFLER, RICHARD ROBERT, PHYSICS. *Current Pos:* asst prof, 65-69, ASSOC PROF PHYSICS, UNIV MASS, AMHERST, 69-; AT LAWRENCE BERKELEY LAB. *Personal Data:* b Milwaukee, Wis, July 4, 35; m 59; c 3. *Educ:* Marquette Univ, BS, 58; Univ Wis, MS, 60, PhD(elem particle physics), 64. *Prof Exp:* Res assoc physics, Univ Wis, 64-65. *Mem:* Am Inst Physics; Am Phys Soc. *Res:* High energy elementary particle physics. *Mailing Add:* MS67 SLAC Stanford Univ PO Box 4349 Stanford CA 94309

KOFOID, MELVIN J(ULIUS), electrical engineering; deceased, see previous edition for last biography

KOFORD, JAMES SHINGLE, VLSI COMPUTER AIDED DESIGN. *Current Pos:* VPRES COMPUT AIDED DESIGN, LSI LOGIC INC, 81- *Personal Data:* b Cheyenne, Wyo, July 26, 38. *Educ:* Stanford Univ, BS, 59, MS, 60, PhD(elec eng), 64. *Prof Exp:* Res asst mem tech staff, Stanford Electronics Lab, 60-64; proj engr, IBM Components Div, 64-66; mem tech staff, Fairchild Semiconductor Corp, 66-69, sr mem tech staff, 69-73; vpres develop, Packet Commun, Inc, 73-75; mgr, Network Develop Lab, Boeing Comput Servs, 75-81. *Mem:* Inst Elec & Electronics Engrs. *Res:* Adaptive pattern-recognition systems, speech recognition, threshold elements, adaptation algorithms; computer-aided design for microelectronic circuits, logic simulation, graphic data processing. *Mailing Add:* 11538 Saddle Rd Monterey CA 93940

KOFRON, JAMES THOMAS, JR, PHOTOGRAPHIC CHEMISTRY. *Current Pos:* RETIRED. *Personal Data:* b Petersburg, Va, Mar 11, 28; m 60; c 4. *Educ:* Univ Notre Dame, BS, 52; Mass Inst Technol, PhD(org chem), 56. *Honors & Awards:* Progress Medal, Photog Soc Am, 88. *Prof Exp:* Res assoc chem, Res Labs, Eastman Kodak Co, 76-75, sr res assoc, 75-92. *Mem:* AAAS; Am Chem Soc. *Res:* Reaction mechanisms in chemistry of photographic processes. *Mailing Add:* 123 El Mar Dr Rochester NY 14616

KOFRON, WILLIAM G, ORGANIC CHEMISTRY. *Current Pos:* from asst prof to prof, 65-96, EMER PROF CHEM, UNIV AKRON, 96- *Personal Data:* b Petersburg, Va, Aug 9, 34. *Educ:* Univ Notre Dame, BS, 56; Univ Rochester, PhD(chem), 61. *Prof Exp:* Res assoc chem, Duke Univ, 60-62; fel, Columbia Univ, 62-63; sr chemist, Med Chem Dept, Geigy Res Labs, NY, 63-65. *Mem:* Am Chem Soc. *Res:* Chemistry of carbanions; heterocyclic chemistry. *Mailing Add:* Dept Chem Univ Akron Akron OH 44325-3601. *E-Mail:* wkofron@atlas.chemistry.uakron.edu

KOFSKY, IRVING LOUIS, PHYSICS. *Current Pos:* PRES & TECH DIR, PHOTOMETRICS INC, 68- *Personal Data:* b New York, NY,; m 69; c 3. *Educ:* Syracuse Univ, BA, 45, PhD(physics), 52. *Prof Exp:* Instr physics, Syracuse Univ, 47-51; asst prof, Smith Col, 52-56; physicist, Tech Opers, Inc, 57-68. *Mem:* Am Phys Soc; Am Asn Physics Teachers. *Res:* Extensive showers in cosmic radiation; weapons effects; gaseous electronics; atmospheric optics; photometry, image analysis and scanning theory. *Mailing Add:* PhotoMetrics Inc 4 Arrow Dr Woburn MA 01801. *Fax:* 781-935-0747

KOFT, BERNARD WALDEMAR, BACTERIOLOGY. *Current Pos:* from asst prof to prof, 57-87, EMER PROF MICROBIOL, RUTGERS UNIV, 87- *Personal Data:* b Hammonton, NJ, Nov 21, 21; m 44, Betty J Ward; c Susan, Helen, David, Daniel & Paul. *Educ:* Rutgers Univ, BS, 43; Univ Pa, MS, 47, PhD(bact), 50. *Prof Exp:* From instr to asst prof bact, Jefferson Med Col, 50-57. *Mem:* Am Soc Microbiol; fel NY Acad Sci; Sigma Xi. *Res:* Bacterial nutrition; metabolism; vitamin synthesis; cellulose degradation. *Mailing Add:* 196 Hardenburg Lane East Brunswick NJ 08816

KOGA, PHILIP G, CYTOKINES, BIOSENSORS. *Current Pos:* DIR, CEL-SCI CORP, 94- *Personal Data:* b Fresno, Calif, Aug 15, 50; m 94, Lori. *Educ:* Univ Calif, BS, 72, PhD(molecular biol), 78. *Prof Exp:* Postdoctoral biochem, State Univ NY Upstate Med Ctr, 79; NIH fel immunochem, Johns Hopkins Sch Med, 80-83; sr scientist, Becton-Dickinson, 83-84; group leader, US Army Chem & Eng Ctr, 84-87; prog mgr & prin engr, Allied Signal, 87-89. *Concurrent Pos:* Int deleg biodefense, 85; mem, Tech Adv Comt, Univ Wash, 89-90; team leader, Indust Adv Group Biosensors, NATO, 92; consult, Biogencontronix Corp, Sci Applns Int Corp, 92- *Mem:* Am Chem Soc; AAAS; Sigma Xi; Am Soc Microbiol. *Res:* Application of cytokine mixtures to stimulate immune response in test subjects for treatment of various forms of cancer and AIDS. *Mailing Add:* 4820-C Seton Dr Baltimore MD 21215-3210. *Fax:* 410-358-1647

KOGA, ROKUTARO, ASTROPHYSICS. *Current Pos:* RES PHYSICIST SPACE & ASTROPHYS, AEROSPACE CORP, 81- *Personal Data:* b Nagoya, Japan, Aug 18, 42; US citizen; m 81, Cordula Rosow; c Evan A & Nicole A. *Educ:* Univ Calif, Berkeley, BA, 66; Univ Calif, Riverside, PhD(physics), 74. *Prof Exp:* Physicist, Berkeley Sci Labs, 66-69; fel, Univ Calif, Riverside, 74; res assoc astrophys, Case Western Reserve Univ, 74-76, sr res assoc astrophys, 77-78, asst prof physics, 79-80. *Mem:* Am Phys Soc; Sigma Xi; NY Acad Sci; Am Geophys Union. *Res:* Measurements of heavy ions in space using satellite based sensors; the effects of cosmic rays on microcircuits in space; gamma-ray astronomy. *Mailing Add:* Space Sci Lab Aerospace Corp PO Box 92957 M2-259 Los Angeles CA 90009-2957

KOGA, TOYOKI, FOUNDATIONS OF QUANTUM PHYSICS. *Current Pos:* RES & WRITING, 69- *Personal Data:* b Japan, Apr 1, 12; div; c Rokutaro & Akiya. *Educ:* Univ Tokyo, MS, 37. *Hon Degrees:* DSc, Univ Tokyo, 48. *Prof Exp:* Asst prof aeronaut, Nagoya Univ, 40-48; prof mech eng & appl physics, 48-59; res scientist, Eng Ctr, Univ Southern Calif, 59-63; prof mech eng, Univ NC, 63-64; mem prof staff, TRW Systs, Inc, 67-69. *Concurrent Pos:* Fulbright sr res fel, Calif Inst Technol, 55-56; vis prof, Univ Calif, 56-59 & Grad Ctr, Polytech Inst Brooklyn, 64-67. *Mem:* Am Phys Soc. *Res:* Gas dynamics; kinetic theory of gases; plasma physics; kinetic theory of quantum mechanical systems; revision of quantum mechanics; theory of elementary particles; superconductivity. *Mailing Add:* 3061 Ewing Ave Altadena CA 91001

KOGAN, MARCOS, ENTOMOLOGY, ECOLOGY. *Current Pos:* PROF ENTOM & DIR, INTEGRATED PLANT PROTECTION CTR, ORE STATE UNIV, CORVALLIS, 91. *Personal Data:* b Rio de Janeiro, Brazil, June 9, 33; m 53; c 2. *Educ:* Univ Rural do Rio de Janeiro, BS, 61; Univ Calif, Riverside, PhD(entom), 69. *Honors & Awards:* ASA/ICI-Am Soybean Res Award, 86. *Prof Exp:* Entomologist res, SCent Inst Agr Res, Rio de Janeiro, 61-63; biologist res, Inst Oswaldo Cruz, Rio de Janeiro, 63-66; res fel entom, Univ Calif, Riverside, 66-69, res assoc, 69; assoc entomologist res, Ill Natural Hist Surv, Urbana, 69-76; assoc prof agr entom, Univ Ill, Urbana, 73-77, prof entom & agr entom, 77-90; entomologist, Ill Natural Hist Surv, Urbana, 76-90. *Concurrent Pos:* Consult soybean entom Brazil, 74-78, Korea, 78-79; mem sci deleg Repub China, 81; ed comt, Ann Rev Entom, 84-88, Entomologia Experimentalis et Applicata, 85-90, Thomas Say Pub Entom Soc Am, 88-91. *Mem:* Entom Soc Am; Brazilian Entom Soc; Sigma Xi; Am Chem Soc. *Res:* Management of soybean insect pests; soybean resistance to insects; insect plant interactions; nutrition of phytophagous insects; bionomics of Strepsiptera; international cooperation in soybean entomology and crop protection; chemical ecology. *Mailing Add:* 2305 NW Maser Dr Corvallis OR 97330-2219

KOGELNIK, H W, LASERS, COMMUNICATIONS. *Current Pos:* mem staff electronics res, Bell Labs, 61-67, head coherent optics, Res Dept, 67-76, dir, Electronics Res Lab, 76-83, DIR, PHOTONICS SYSTS RES LAB, LUCENT TECHNOLS, 83- *Personal Data:* b Graz, Austria, June 2, 32; m 64; c 3. *Educ:* Vienna Tech Univ, Dipl Ing, 55, Dr Tech, 58; Oxford Univ, DPhil(electromagnetic theory), 60. *Honors & Awards:* Frederic Ives Medal, Optical Soc, 84; David Sarnoff Award, Inst Elec & Electronics Engrs, 89; Quantum Electronics Award, Lasers & Electro Optics Soc, 91. *Prof Exp:* Asst prof electronics, Inst High Frequency Electronics, Vienna, Austria, 55-58; Brit Coun scholar, Oxford Univ, 58-60. *Mem:* Nat Acad Sci; Nat Acad Eng; fel Inst Elec & Electronics Engrs; fel Optical Soc Am; AAAS; Am Phys Soc. *Res:* Lasers; integrated optics; optical communication. *Mailing Add:* Lucent Technols 791 Holmdel Keyport Rd Holmdel NJ 07733. *Fax:* 732-888-7013; *E-Mail:* herwig@bell.labs.com

KOGER, JOHN W, PHYSICAL METALLURGY. *Current Pos:* PROG MGR WASTE MINIMALIZATION, MARTIN MARIETTA ENERGY SYSTS INC, 90- *Personal Data:* b Florence, Ala, Aug 20, 40. *Mailing Add:* 9924 Rainbow Dr Knoxville TN 37922-5107

KOGER, MARVIN, ANIMAL BREEDING, GENETICS. *Current Pos:* prof animal husb & animal geneticist, 51-80, PROF ANIMAL SCI, AGR EXP STA, UNIV FLA, 80- *Personal Data:* b Colgate, Okla; m 38; c 4. *Educ:* NMex Col, BS, 39; Kans State Univ, MS, 41; Univ Mo, PhD(physiol), 43. *Prof Exp:* From instr to assoc prof animal husb, NMex Col, 43-51. *Mem:* Am Soc Animal Sci; Am Dairy Sci Asn. *Res:* Nutritional deficiencies of sorghums; effects of hyperthyroidism; genetics of cattle and sheep; physiology of reproduction. *Mailing Add:* 1764 NW 17th Lane Gainesville FL 32605

KOGGE, PETER MICHAEL, COMPUTER ARCHITECTURE. *Current Pos:* MCCOURTNEY PROF COMPUT SCI, UNIV NOTRE DAME, 94- *Personal Data:* b Washington, DC, Dec 3, 46; m 71, Mary E Clarke; c Peter M, Mary E & Timothy M. *Educ:* Univ Notre Dame, BSEE, 68; Syracuse Univ, MS, 70; Stanford Univ, PhD(elec eng), 73. *Prof Exp:* From jr engr to sr engr, IBM, 68-81, mem sr tech staff, 81-93, fel, 93. *Concurrent Pos:* Adj prof comput sci, State Univ NY, Binghamton, 77-94; distinguished vis scientist, Jet Propulsion Lab, 97. *Mem:* Fel Inst Elec & Electronics Engrs; Asn Comput Mach; Am Asn Artificial Intel. *Res:* Massively parallel computing using integrated memory and logic very large scale integration. *Mailing Add:* Dept Comput Sci & Eng Univ Notre Dame 384 Fitzpatrick Hall Notre Dame IN 46556. *Fax:* 219-631-9260; *E-Mail:* kogge@cse.nd.edu

KOGON, IRVING CHARLES, POLYMER CHEMISTRY. *Current Pos:* RETIRED. *Personal Data:* b Brooklyn, NY, Aug 8, 23; m 48; c 2. *Educ:* Brooklyn Col, BA, 48, MA, 51; Polytech Inst Brooklyn, PhD(chem), 54; Univ Wis, PhD, 54. *Prof Exp:* Asst org chem, Brooklyn Col, 49-51; res assoc, Univ

Wis, 53-54; res assoc, Polymer Prod Dept, Exp Sta, E I Du Pont De Nemours & Co, Inc, 54-82. *Concurrent Pos:* Consult, polyurethane indust, 82- *Mem:* AAAS; Am Chem Soc; Polyurethane Mfg Asn; Soc Plastics Indust. *Res:* Synthesis of antispasmodics, antihistamines and local anesthetics; heterocyclic vinyl monomers; mechanism of organic reactions; chemistry of isocyanates and polyurethanes; new urethane curatives and synthetic rubbers; polymer chemistry. *Mailing Add:* 1420 Drake Rd Wilmington DE 19803

KOGOS, L(AURENCE), CHEMICAL ENGINEERING. *Current Pos:* CONSULT, 90- *Personal Data:* b Boston, Mass, July 24, 29; m 51; c 2. *Educ:* Northeastern Univ, BS, 51. *Prof Exp:* Chem engr, Sawyer-Tower, Inc, 51-52; chief res engr, 52-53, dir tech sales, 55, tech dir, 56-58, gen mgr, 58-59; exec vpres, Farrington Texol Corp, 59-63; gen mgr, Dynamic Coaters, Inc, 63-70; dir opers, Plymouth Rubber Co, Inc, 70-72; pres, Polymeric Fabricants Div, Whittaker Corp, 72-73; pres, Plastics Div, W R Grace & Co, 73-79; vpres & gen mgr, Roper Plastics, Inc, NY, 80-82, TLB Plastics, Brewster, NY, 82-84; chief exec officer, Ouimet group, Brockton, Mass, 84-90. *Mem:* Am Chem Soc; Am Soc Plastics Engrs; Am Inst Chem Engrs. *Res:* Application of protective and decorative coatings to fabrics; plastics molding, extrusion and forming. *Mailing Add:* 9 Pioneer Circle Sharon MA 02067

KOGUT, JOHN BENJAMIN, THEORETICAL PHYSICS. *Current Pos:* PROF PHYSICS, UNIV ILL, 78- *Personal Data:* b Brooklyn, NY, Mar 6, 45; m 85; c 1. *Educ:* Princeton Univ, BA, 67; Stanford Univ, MS, 68, PhD(physics), 71. *Prof Exp:* Assoc physics, Inst Advan Study, 71-73 & Tel Aviv Univ, 73; res assoc, Cornell Univ, 73-74, from asst prof to assoc prof, 74-78. *Concurrent Pos:* Sloan Found fel & NSF grant, Cornell Univ, 76-78; NSF grant, Univ Ill, 78-; Guggenheim fel, 88-89. *Mem:* Fel Am Phys Soc; Comt Concerned Scientists. *Res:* Theory of elementary particles; field theory and statistical mechanics. *Mailing Add:* Dept Phys Loomis Lab Univ Ill 1110 W Green St Urbana IL 61801

KOGUT, MAURICE D, PEDIATRICS, ENDOCRINOLOGY. *Current Pos:* AT DEPT PEDIAT, WRIGHT STATE UNIV, DAYTON, OHIO. *Personal Data:* b Brooklyn, NY, July 7, 30; m 59; c 3. *Educ:* NY Univ, BA, 51, MD, 55. *Prof Exp:* Intern pediat, Bellevue Hosp, NY, 55-56, resident, 56-57; chief resident, Children's Hosp, Los Angeles, 59-60, USPHS fel endocrinol, 60-62; from instr to assoc prof, Sch Med, Univ Southern Calif, 62-73, prof pediat, 73-80, assoc head dept, 75-80, clin prof med, 80-; head div endocrinol & metab & prog dir, Clin Res Ctr, Children's Hosp, 71- *Mem:* Endocrine Soc; Am Diabetes Asn; Am Acad Pediat; Soc Pediat Res; Am Pediat Soc. *Res:* Carbohydrate metabolism in idiopathic hypoglycemia; growth hormone and insulin metabolism in hypopituitarism; the role of circulating insulin and glucagon in children with genetic predisposition to diabetes mellitus; uric acid metabolism. *Mailing Add:* Childrens Med Ctr One Childrens Plaza Dayton OH 45404-1815

KOH, EUNSOOK TAK, NUTRITIONAL SCIENCE. *Current Pos:* PROF, DEPT NUTRIT SCI, COL ALLIED HEALTH, UNIV OKLA, OKLAHOMA CITY, 89- *Personal Data:* b Seoul, Korea, May 3, 36; US citizen; m 61; c Kyung-Ho, Kyung-Run & Lucy. *Educ:* Seoul Nat Univ, Korea, BS, 58; Univ Md, MS, 70, PhD(nutrit sci), 73. *Prof Exp:* Res asst, Univ Md, College Park, 68-70; res asst, Agr Res Serv, Nutrit Inst, USDA, 70-73, res assoc, 73-74; assoc prof, Alcorn State Univ, Miss, 74-81; prof, Univ Okla, Norman, 81-89. *Concurrent Pos:* Prin investr, Alcorn State Univ, 74-81, Univ Okla, 81-91, USDA, Agr Res Serv, Nutrit Inst, 87-88 & Hallym Univ, 87; vis prof, Hallym Univ, Kangwon Do, Korea, 87 & USDA, Agr Res Serv, Nutrit Inst, Beltsville, 87-88. *Mem:* Am Inst Nutrit; Am Dietetic Asn; Nutrit Educ Soc; Am Col Nutrit; Sigma Xi. *Res:* Nutrition survey; carbohydrates and lipid metabolism; copper and fructose interaction; interaction of fructose, magnesium deficiency and sex hormone on nephrocalcinosis; mechanism of the interaction on nephrocalcinosis; fructose, Magnesium and bone. *Mailing Add:* Dept Nutrit Sci Col Allied Health Rm 465 Univ Okla PO Box 26901 Oklahoma City OK 73104. *Fax:* 405-271-3120; *E-Mail:* eunsook-koh@uokhsc.edu

KOH, EUSEBIO LEGARDA, DISTRIBUTION THEORY, INTEGRAL TRANSFORMATIONS & OPERATIONAL CALCULUS. *Current Pos:* assoc prof, 70-75, dept head, 77-79, PROF MATH & STATIST, UNIV REGINA, 75- *Personal Data:* b Manila, Philippines, Oct 4, 31; Can citizen; m 58, Donelita Viardo; c Monette, Elizabeth, Ethel & Denise. *Educ:* Univ Philippines, BS, 54; Purdue Univ, Ind, MS, 56; Univ Birmingham, UK, MSc, 61; State Univ NY, Stony Brook, PhD(appl math), 67. *Prof Exp:* Res engr, Int Harvester Co, Ill, 56-57; asst prof, 59-64, dept head mech eng, Univ Philippines, 63-64; asst prof math, Univ SC, 67-68, Univ Sask, 68-70. *Concurrent Pos:* Dir, DCCD Eng Corp, Philippines, 62-64; Nat Sci Eng Res Coun res grant, Can, 71-; guest prof,Technische Hochschule Dermstadt, Ger, 75-76; travel fel, Nat Sci Eng Res Coun, Ger, 75-76; prof, Univ Petrol & Minerals, Saudi Arabia, 79-82. *Mem:* Am Math Soc; Math Asn Am; Soc Indust & Appl Math; Can Math Soc; Can Appl Math Soc. *Res:* Extension of integral transformations to generalized functions; development of operational calculus by algebraic approach; association of variables technique; functional equations in distributions. *Mailing Add:* Dept Math & Statist Univ Regina Regina SK S4S 0A2 Can. *Fax:* 306-585-4020; *E-Mail:* elkoh@max.cc.uregina.ca

KOH, JOHN TZE-TZUN, BIOORGANIC CHEMISTRY, PROTEIN-LIGAND & PROTEIN DNA INTERACTIONS. *Current Pos:* ASST PROF BIOORG CHEM, DEPT CHEM & BIOCHEM, UNIV DEL, 96- *Personal Data:* b St Louis, Mo, Apr 3, 67. *Educ:* West Chester Univ, Pa, Bs, 89; Columbia Univ, MS, 90, MPhil, 93, PhD(org chem), 94. *Prof Exp:* Am Cancer Soc postdoctoral fel, Univ Calif, Berkeley, 94-96. *Mem:* Am Chem Soc. *Mailing Add:* Dept Chem & Biochem Univ Del Newark DE 19716. *E-Mail:* johnkoh@udel.edu

KOH, KWANGIL, MATHEMATICS, MATHEMATICAL PHYSICS. *Current Pos:* From instr to assoc prof, 64-68, PROF MATH, NC STATE UNIV, 68- *Personal Data:* b Seoul, Korea, July 8, 31; m 58, Toni L; c Debra, James & Patricia. *Educ:* Auburn Univ, BS, 59, MS, 60; Univ NC, PhD(math), 64. *Mem:* Am Math Soc; Math Asn Am. *Res:* Algebra; theory of rings. *Mailing Add:* 4812 Metcalf Dr Raleigh NC 27612

KOH, P(UN) K(IEN), physical metallurgy; deceased, see previous edition for last biography

KOH, ROBERT CY, FLUID MECHANICS, APPLIED MATHEMATICS. *Current Pos:* MEM STAFF, CALIF INST TECH, 72- *Personal Data:* b Shanghai, China, May 23, 38; m 61; c 1. *Educ:* Calif Inst Technol, BS, 60, MS, 61, PhD(appl mech, math), 64. *Prof Exp:* Res fel eng, Calif Inst Technol, 64-65; mem tech staff, Nat Eng Sci Co, 65-66; sr scientist, Tetra Tech Inc, 66-72. *Mem:* Int Asn Hydraul Res. *Res:* Fluid mechanics; applied mathematics. *Mailing Add:* 212 S Marengo Ave Pasadena CA 91101

KOH, SEVERINO LEGARDA, THEORETICAL & APPLIED MECHANICS, COMPOSITE MATERIALS. *Current Pos:* assoc dean, 85-91, PROF MECH ENG, UNIV MD, 85-, DIR, INT ENG PROGS, 91- *Personal Data:* b Manila, Philippines, Jan 8, 27; m 52, Paz Ongjoco; c Amelita P, Bernadette P, Cynthia P (Knox), Dorothy P (deceased) & Evangeline P (Brown). *Educ:* NY Univ, BS, 50; Nat Univ, Manila, BS, 52; Pa State Univ, MS, 57; Purdue Univ, PhD(eng sci), 62. *Honors & Awards:* Cert Appreciation, Soc Eng Sci, 74; Balik Scientist Award, Nat Sci Develop Bd, Philippines, 76; Meritorious Serv Award, Nat Soc Prof Engrs, 91. *Prof Exp:* Meteorologist-in-chg marine unit, Weather Bur, Manila, 48-54; res asst hydrodyn lab, Johns Hopkins Univ, 54-55; instr eng mech, Pa State Univ, 55-57; instr eng sci, Purdue Univ, 57-59; res assoc viscoelasticity, Gen Tech Corp, 59-61; mech engr, Major Appliance Lab, Gen Elec Co, 61-62; from asst prof to prof aeronaut & eng sci, Purdue Univ, 62-73, prof mech eng, 73-80, asst head, Div Interdisciplinary Eng Studies, 77-80, head, Dept Eng, 80-81; chmn mech & aerospace eng, WVa Univ, 81-83, prof, 81-85. *Concurrent Pos:* Mem, Pres Fact-Finding Comt, Philippines, 53-54; res assoc, B G Bantegui & Assocs, Manila, 53-54; scientist-consult, Gen Tech Corp, 62-; Stand Oil Co (Ind) Found teaching award, 67; vis prof & res assoc, Clausthal Tech Univ, 68-69; vis prof, Univ Karlsruhe, 69; Humboldt vis prof, Univ Bonn, 74-75; consult, 3IE, Inc, 77- & Batelle Northwest, 78; dir, Eng Sci Perspective, 70-73 & 78-80, ed-in-chief, 76-81 & 85-93; prog mgr eng res, Dept Energy, 83-85. *Mem:* Soc Eng Sci (secy, 63-68); Am Acad Mech; Am Soc Eng Educ; Am Soc Mech Engrs; Soc Rheology; Sigma Xi; Philippine-Am Acad Sci & Eng (pres, 80); AAAS; NY Acad Sci; Philippine Meteorol Soc. *Res:* Elasticity; viscoelasticity; fluid dynamics; rheology of nonlinear materials; composite materials; testing of materials; sandwich structures; micromechanics; solar energy systems; geotechnical engineering problems; heat and mass transfer; smart structures. *Mailing Add:* 12116 Blue Paper Trail Columbia MD 21044. *Fax:* 410-455-3559

KOH, SUNG-CHEOL, xenobiotics degradation by methanotrophs, industrial enzyme production & utilization, for more information see previous edition

KOHAN, MELVIN IRA, POLYMER CHEMISTRY & ENGINEERING. *Current Pos:* RETIRED. *Personal Data:* b Boston, Mass, Mar 11, 21; m 43, Beatrice Nesson; c Stanford P, Allen M, Donald E & James M. *Educ:* Harvard Univ, AB, 42; Univ Ill, PhD(chem), 50. *Prof Exp:* Chemist, Dept Electrochem, E I Du Pont de Nemours & Co Inc, 42-44 & 46-47, chemist, Dept Plastics, 50-62, sr res chemist, 62-74, res assoc, Dept Plastics, 74-80, res assoc, Polymer Products Dept, Exp Sta, 80-82. *Concurrent Pos:* Consult, Eng Thermoplastics, 83-; adj prof, Drexel Univ, 83-85. *Mem:* Am Chem Soc; Soc Plastic Engrs; Sigma Xi. *Res:* Polymer chemistry; plastics engineering; nylon plastics technology; publications, patents and books. *Mailing Add:* 1913 Longcome Dr Wilmington DE 19810

KOHANE, THEODORE, PHYSICS. *Current Pos:* RETIRED. *Personal Data:* b New York, NY, Apr 20, 23; m 55; c 2. *Educ:* City Col New York, BS, 44; Rutgers Univ, PhD(physics), 53. *Prof Exp:* Physicist, Nat Adv Comt Aeronaut, 44-46; asst physics & instr, NY Univ, 46-48; asst & fel, Rutgers Univ, 48-53; mem res staff, Raytheon Res Div, 53-89. *Mem:* Am Phys Soc; Optical Soc Am. *Res:* Nuclear magnetic resonance; magnetic and electrical properties of ferrites; microwaves; optical properties of solids. *Mailing Add:* 8277 Springtree Rd Boca Raton FL 33496

KOHEL, RUSSELL JAMES, PLANT GENETICS. *Current Pos:* RES GENETICIST COTTON, AGR RES SERV, USDA, 59- *Personal Data:* b Omaha, Nebr, Nov 30, 34; m 57; c 3. *Educ:* Iowa State Univ, BS, 56; Purdue Univ, MS, 58, PhD(plant breeding), 59. *Mem:* Am Soc Plant Physiologists; fel Am Soc Agron; Am Genetic Asn; Genetics Soc Am. *Res:* Qualitative and quantitative genetics of the cotton plant. *Mailing Add:* 2765 F & B Rd College Station TX 77845

KOHIN, BARBARA CASTLE, MOLECULAR PHYSICS. *Current Pos:* EXEC DIR, ACCORD, 93- *Personal Data:* b Providence, RI, Dec 11, 32; m 59, Roger P; c 3. *Educ:* Col William & Mary, BS, 53; Univ Md, MS, 56, PhD(physics), 60. *Prof Exp:* Res assoc molecular physics, Cath Univ Am, 59-61; physicist theoret physics, Inst Battelle, Geneva, Switz, 61-62; instr physics, Mass State Col Worcester, 64-67; asst prof physics, Clark Univ, 67-68; assoc dir, Off Spec Studies, Col of the Holy Cross, 78-85 & 86-87, actg dir, 85-86. *Concurrent Pos:* Res assoc, Mass Inst Technol, 73-74. *Res:* Quantum chemistry; solid state physics; elementary and atomic physics. *Mailing Add:* 11 Berwick St Worcester MA 01602

KOHIN, ROGER P(ATRICK), PHYSICS. *Current Pos:* asst prof, Clark Univ, 62-67, chmn dept, 74-76 & 85-87, assoc prof physics, 67-94, EMER PROF, CLARK UNIV, 94- *Personal Data:* b Chicago, Ill, Mar 2, 31; m 59, Barbara Castle; c Margaret (Nitschelm), Judith A & Suzanne. *Educ:* Univ Notre Dame, BSEE, 53; Univ Md, PhD(physics), 61. *Prof Exp:* Scientist physics, Battelle Mem Inst, Geneva, Switz, 61-62. *Concurrent Pos:* Vis scientist, Inst J Stefan, Ljubljana, Yugoslavia, 68-69; Indo-Am fel, Indian Inst Tech-Kanpur, 76-77; vis prof, Univ Nairobi, Kenya, 87-88. *Mem:* Am Phys Soc. *Res:* Electron-spin resonance spectroscopy; radiation damage of solids; experimental ferroelectric materials; organic and inorganic free radicals; computer simulation. *Mailing Add:* Dept Physics Clark Univ Worcester MA 01610. *E-Mail:* rkohin@black.clarku.edu

KOHL, A(RTHUR) L(IONEL), GAS PURIFICATION, NUCLEAR ENGINEERING. *Current Pos:* CONSULT ENGR, 89- *Personal Data:* b Ont, Can, Aug 21, 19; nat US; m 43, Evelyn Belinsky; c Jeffrey, Martin & Donald. *Educ:* Univ Southern Calif, BE, 43, MS, 47. *Honors & Awards:* Outstanding Achievement Award, Am Inst Chem Engrs, 66; Tech Achievement Award, Engrs Joint Coun, 67. *Prof Exp:* Res engr, Turco Prod, Inc, 42-44 & 46-47; chief chem eng res, Fluor Corp Ltd, 47-60; group leader process develop, Atomics Int, 60-68, proj engr & proj mgr advan develop, 68-78, prog mgr fossil energy, Rocketdyne Div, Rockwell Int, 78-89. *Concurrent Pos:* Author of technical books & papers. *Mem:* Am Inst Chem Engrs. *Res:* Gas purification; process equipment; saline water conversion; chemical process development; nuclear reactor fuels and materials; nuclear reactor component development; coal conversion; paper mill black liquor gasification. *Mailing Add:* 22555 Tiara St Woodland Hills CA 91367

KOHL, DANIEL HOWARD, PLANT PHYSIOLOGY. *Current Pos:* Asst prof bot, Washington Univ, 65-70, assoc prof, 70-79, sr fel, Ctr Biol Natural Systs, 71-81, PROF BIOL, WASHINGTON UNIV, 79- *Personal Data:* b Cleveland, Ohio, July 30, 28; m 50; c 4. *Educ:* Univ Calif, Berkeley, BS, 60; Washington Univ, PhD(molecular biol), 65. *Mem:* Am Soc Plant Physiol; Soil Sci Soc Am. *Res:* N isotope distribution in various components of N cycle; N fixation biochemistry. *Mailing Add:* Dept Biol Campus Box 1137 Wash Univ 1 Brookings Dr St Louis MO 63130-4862

KOHL, FRED JOHN, PHYSICAL CHEMISTRY. *Current Pos:* RES CHEMIST & MGR, MAT SCI SPACE PROJ, LEWIS RES CTR, NASA, 68-, BR CHIEF. *Personal Data:* b Cleveland, Ohio, Jan 1, 42. *Educ:* Case Inst Technol, BS, 63; Case Western Reserve Univ, PhD(chem), 68. *Mem:* Am Chem Soc; Am Soc Mass Spectrometry; Combustion Inst. *Res:* Hot corrosion of superalloys; oxidation of metals; high temperature vaporization and thermodynamics; mass spectrometry; oxidation/vaporization processes; high temperature chemistry; vaporization of refractories; materials science experiments in space; combustion process related to corrosion; microgravity science and applications. *Mailing Add:* 4829 S Park Dr Cleveland OH 44126-2613

KOHL, HARRY CHARLES, JR, FLORICULTURE, PLANT PHYSIOLOGY. *Current Pos:* prof floricult & plant physiologist, 62-77, prof & chairperson, Plant Phys Grad Group, 77-80, EMER PROF ENVIRON HORT, UNIV CALIF, DAVIS, 80- *Personal Data:* b St Louis, Mo, Aug 6, 19; m 41; c 2. *Educ:* Univ Ill, BS, 40, MS, 48; Cornell Univ, PhD(hort), 50. *Prof Exp:* Assoc exten specialist floricult, Rutgers Univ, 50-53; asst prof, Univ Calif, Los Angeles & asst plant physiologist, 57-62. *Mem:* Am Soc Plant Physiol; Am Soc Hort Sci; Bot Soc Am; Int Soc Soil Sci. *Res:* Control of plant growth and differentiation; preharvest and post-harvest physiology of flowers; mineral translocation; root aeration; salinity tolerance. *Mailing Add:* 1113 Halifax Ave Davis CA 95618

KOHL, JEROME, MANAGEMENT & MINIMIZATION OF HAZARDOUS WASTES. *Current Pos:* sr nuclear eng exten specialist & lectr nuclear eng, 69-88, EMER NUCLEAR ENG SPECIALIST & LECTR, NC STATE UNIV, 88- *Personal Data:* b Montreal, Que, Mar 13, 18; nat US; m 45, Freeke von Novhuys; c Joyce E & Adelle P. *Educ:* Calif Inst Technol, BS, 40; NC State Univ, MS, 75. *Prof Exp:* Chem & proj engr, Avon Refinery, Tidewater Assoc Oil Co, Calif, 43-46, asst supt, 46-48; chem engr, Tracerlab, Inc, 48-51, sect leader, Mobile Radiochem Lab, 51-53, chief engr, 53-58, mgr eng & develop, 58-60; coordr spec prod, Gen Atomic Div, Gen Dynamics Corp, 60-64; mkt mgr, Oak Ridge Tech Enterprises, 65-69. *Concurrent Pos:* Instr & lectr, Univ Calif, Berkeley & San Diego, 47-64; lectr, Univ Delft, 56 & int lectr on waste reduction, mgt & minimization hazardous waste, NC State Univ. *Mem:* Am Nuclear Soc; Am Inst Chem Engrs; Soc Photog Educ. *Res:* Radiation monitoring instrumentation; industrial applications of radioisotopes; measurement of nuclear radiations; energy conservation; co-generation; measurement and minimization of hazardous waste. *Mailing Add:* Dept Nuclear Eng NC State Univ Box 7909 Raleigh NC 27695-7909. *Fax:* 919-515-5115

KOHL, JOHN C(LAYTON), civil engineering; deceased, see previous edition for last biography

KOHL, JOHN LESLIE, EXPERIMENTAL ATOMIC PHYSICS, SOLAR PHYSICS. *Current Pos:* Res fel physics, 69-72, res assoc physics, Harvard Col Observ, 72-76, ASTROPHYSICIST & LECTR, SMITHSONIAN ASTROPHYS OBSERV, HARVARD UNIV, 76- *Personal Data:* b Zanesville, Ohio, Apr 27, 41; m 65; c 2. *Educ:* Muskingum Col, BS, 63; Univ Toledo, MS, 66, PhD(physics), 69. *Concurrent Pos:* NSF fel. *Mem:* Am Phys Soc; Am Astron Soc; Int Astron Union; Am Geophys Union. *Res:* Experimental studies of atomic and molecular processes needed to understand astrophysical and laboratory plasmas; experimental studies of solar wind generation using space instrumentation. *Mailing Add:* 160 Lawsbrook Rd Concord MA 01742

KOHL, PAUL ALBERT, ELECTROCHEMISTRY, PHYSICAL CHEMISTRY. *Current Pos:* CHEMIST, AT&T BELL LABS, 78- *Personal Data:* b Buffalo, NY, Aug 6, 52; m 74; c 2. *Educ:* Bethany Col, BS, 74; Univ Tex, PhD(chem), 78. *Honors & Awards:* Weston Award, Electrochem Soc, 77; Ayres Award, Univ Tex, 78. *Prof Exp:* Chemist, Nuclear Radiation Develop, 74. *Mem:* Am Chem Soc; Electrochem Soc. *Res:* Chemical and electrochemical reactions involved in the processing of semiconductor materials for the development of microelectronic devices. *Mailing Add:* 130 Cameron Glen Dr Atlanta GA 30328-4707

KOHL, ROBERT A, SOIL PHYSICS, IRRIGATION. *Current Pos:* assoc prof, 75-87, PROF PLANT SCI, SDAK STATE UNIV, 87- *Personal Data:* b Harvey, Ill, Jan 22, 36; m 57; c 4. *Educ:* Purdue Univ, BS, 58; Utah State Univ, MS, 60, PhD(soils, irrig), 63. *Prof Exp:* Agr missionary, Lutheran Mission, Nigeria, 63-66; res soil scientist, Snake River Conserv Res Ctr, Agr Res Serv, USDA, Idaho, 67-74. *Mem:* Soil Sci Soc Am; Am Soc Agron. *Res:* Water management; sprinkler irrigation. *Mailing Add:* Dept Plant Sci SDak State Univ PO Box 2207a Brookings SD 57007-0001

KOHL, SCHUYLER G, OBSTETRICS & GYNECOLOGY. *Current Pos:* RETIRED. *Personal Data:* b Philadelphia, Pa, Feb 22, 13; m 43, Blossim Schultz; c Eileen Kaufman. *Educ:* Univ Md, BS, 36, MD, 40; Columbia Univ, MS, 52, PhD, 54; Am Bd Obstet & Gynec, dipl, 51. *Prof Exp:* Asst obstet, Univ Md, 42-49, instr, 49-50; res assoc obstet & gynec, Health Sci Ctr, State Univ NY, Brooklyn, 50-51, from asst prof to assoc prof, 51-62, from asst dean to assoc dean, 58-71, distinguished serv prof, 62-90. *Concurrent Pos:* Consult, Nat Inst Neurol Dis & Stroke, mem, Hosp Facil Res Study Sect, 58-60 & Human Ecol Study Sect, 60-65; lectr, Columbia Univ, 59-84; consult, Pan Am Health Orgn, 60-80. *Mem:* Asn Planned Parenthood Physicians; Soc Gynec Invest; Am Pub Health Asn; AMA. *Res:* Application of statistical methods to clinical practice. *Mailing Add:* Dept Obstet & Gynec State Univ NY Health Sci Ctr 450 Clarkson Ave Brooklyn NY 11203-2102. *Fax:* 718-270-4711

KOHLAND, WILLIAM FRANCIS, PETROLOGY, ATMOSPHERIC SCIENCE. *Current Pos:* PROF GEOL & EARTH SCI, MID TENN STATE UNIV, 67- *Personal Data:* b Chester, Pa, May 13, 25; m 56, Sylvia R Hurlock; c Louis. *Educ:* Bucknell Univ, AB, 51; Univ Tenn, Knoxville, MS, 52, PhD(earth sci), 69. *Prof Exp:* Asst prof geol & earth sci, Edinboro State Col, 59-67. *Concurrent Pos:* Consult & field geologist; consult geologist, Deltacon Consults. *Mem:* Geol Soc Am; Nat Asn Geol Teachers; Soil Sci Soc Am. *Res:* Petrology of St Francois NIT; metasomatic changes in rocks; mineral identification; minerology of Unakite. *Mailing Add:* Dept Geol & Geog Geol Mid Tenn State Univ Box 416 Murfreesboro TN 37132-0002

KOHLBRENNER, PHILIP JOHN, TECHNICAL REGULATORY AFFAIRS. *Current Pos:* RETIRED. *Personal Data:* b South Bend, Ind, Nov 17, 31; m 57, Ann E Cahoon; c Michael, Kathleen, Matthew, Linda, Andrew & Elizabeth. *Educ:* Purdue Univ, BS, 53; State Univ NY Col Forestry, Syracuse Univ, PhD(org chem), 58. *Prof Exp:* Res chemist synthetic org chem, Cowles Chem Co, 57-58; res chemist, Am Cyanamid, 58-64, group leader synthetic org chem, 64-76, dept head basic pharmaceut, Lederle Labs Div, 76-80, assoc dir, 80-87, dir, Regulatory Affairs-Global Tech Support, Med Res Div, 87-89, dir, Regulatory Affairs Int, 89-90, sr dir, Int Regulatory Affairs, 90-93. *Mem:* Am Chem Soc; Am Asn Pharm Scientists. *Res:* Synthetic organic chemistry. *Mailing Add:* Outlet Rd Piseco NY 12139

KOHLER, BRYAN EARL, PHYSICAL CHEMISTRY. *Current Pos:* AT DEPT CHEM, UNIV CALIF, RIVERSIDE. *Personal Data:* b Heber City, Utah, June 9, 40; m 60; c 3. *Educ:* Univ Utah, BA, 62; Univ Chicago, PhD(chem), 67. *Prof Exp:* Fermi Inst res fel chem, Univ Chicago, 67; NSF fel, Calif Inst Technol, 67-68; from asst prof to assoc prof, Harvard Univ, 69-75; assoc prof, Wesleyan Univ, 75-77, prof chem, 77-, chmn dept, 80- *Concurrent Pos:* Grants, Am Chem Soc, Harvard Univ, 69-70, Advan Res Proj Agency, 69-, NIH, 69- & NSF, 72-; Sloan Found fel, 74-76; Alfred P Sloan Found fel, 74; vis fel, Joint Inst Lab Astrophysics, 78; Alexander von Humboldt fel, 79. *Mem:* Am Phys Soc; NIH; Am Phys Soc; NY Acad Sci; Biophys Soc; Sigma Xi. *Res:* Investigation of the electronic structure of molecules and molecular crystals using the techniques of magnetic resonance and optical spectroscopy; electronic properties of biomolecules; dynamics of excitation. *Mailing Add:* Dept Chem Univ Calif Riverside CA 92521

KOHLER, CARL, MARINE BIOLOGY, ICHTHYOPLANKTON. *Current Pos:* RETIRED. *Personal Data:* b Hamilton, Ont, June 24, 30; m 50, Claire Jebb; c Michael, Brian, Christopher & Erik. *Educ:* McMaster Univ, BA, 53; McGill Univ, MSc, 56, PhD(zool), 60. *Prof Exp:* Asst conservationist, Royal Bot Gardens, Ont, 51-53; technician to technician, Biol Sta, Fisheries Res Bd Can, 53-56, sr scientist, 56-67, head groundfish prog, 67-73, head fishery biol sect, 73-85, Kohler Guiding, 86-97. *Concurrent Pos:* Demonstr, McGill Univ, 55-56 & 58-59; prof hunting, fishing guide & outfitter, 86- *Mem:* Am Fisheries Soc. *Res:* Fishery biology and biostatistics; fishery management; wildlife biology. *Mailing Add:* 316 Prince of Wales St Andrews NB E0G 2X0 Can

KOHLER, CONSTANCE ANNE, PHARMACOLOGY, BIOCHEMISTRY. *Current Pos:* res pharmacologist, 74-80, SR RES SCIENTIST, LEDERLE LABS, DIV AM CYANAMID, NY, 80- *Personal Data:* b Flushing, NY, Jan 9, 43; m 80; c 2. *Educ:* St John's Univ, NY, BS, 65; Univ Calif, San Francisco, PhD(pharmacol), 73. *Prof Exp:* Fel pharmacol, Roche Inst Molecular Biol, NJ, 72-74. *Mem:* AAAS; Am Heart Asn; Am Chem Soc; NY Acad Sci; Sigma Xi; Soc Exp Biol & Med. *Res:* Allergy and asthma; platelet biochemistry; phospholipid, platelet-activating factor, arachidonic acid metabolism and pharmacology; mammalian cell culture; growth factors; hormones, drugs and signal transduction. *Mailing Add:* Wyeth Ayerst 401 N Middletown Rd Bldg 200 Pearl River NY 10965

KOHLER, DONALD ALVIN, X-RAY PHYSICS, PLASMA PHYSICS. *Current Pos:* res scientist, 65-73, staff scientist, 73-79, SR STAFF SCIENTIST, LOCKHEED PALO ALTO RES LAB, 79- *Personal Data:* b Rainier, Ore, Oct 29, 28; m 59; c 2. *Educ:* Univ Ore, BS, 51, MS, 52; Calif Inst Technol, PhD(physics), 59. *Prof Exp:* Res assoc nuclear physics, Stanford Univ, 59-62, res assoc, 62-63, lectr, 62-65. *Mem:* AAAS; Am Phys Soc; Inst Elec & Electronics Engrs. *Res:* X-ray physics and instrumentation; laser-plasma interaction; experimental low-energy nuclear physics, particularly of the light nuclei; cosmology and astrophysics; elementary particle physics; weak interactions. *Mailing Add:* 10481 Baywood Dr Cupertino CA 95014

KOHLER, ERWIN MILLER, VETERINARY MICROBIOLOGY. *Current Pos:* from asst prof to assoc prof, 65-73, PROF INFECTIOUS DIS DOMESTIC ANIMALS, VET SCI DEPT, OHIO AGR RES & DEVELOP CTR, 73-, CHMN DEPT, 76- *Personal Data:* b Cincinnati, Ohio, June 24, 30; m 54; c 2. *Educ:* Ohio State Univ, DVM, 55, MS, 63, PhD(microbiol, immunol), 65. *Prof Exp:* Vet, Winchester Animal Hosp, Va, 55-62. *Mem:* Am Vet Med Asn; Am Soc Microbiol; Conf Res Workers Animal Diseases; Am Asn Swine Practitioners. *Res:* Studies of colibacillosis of gnotobiotic and conventional swine; studies of the oral immunization of sows as an aid in the prevention of neonatal enteric colibacillosis of pigs. *Mailing Add:* 2853 Mara Loma Circle Wooster OH 44691

KOHLER, GEORGE OSCAR, BIOCHEMISTRY, PROCESS ENGINEERING. *Current Pos:* OWNER, G O KOHLER & ASSOC, CONSULT, 72- *Personal Data:* b Milwaukee, Wis, Apr 9, 13; m 40, Christie Gilchrist; c Cynthia (Castner), William M & Sylvia (Luftig). *Educ:* Univ Wis, BS, 34, MS, 36, PhD(biochem), 38. *Prof Exp:* Asst, Univ Wis, 34-39, Cerophyl Labs grant, 38-39; assoc dir res, Cerophyl Labs, Inc, 39-50, vpres & dir res, 50-54, dir res, Alfalfa Dehydration & Milling Co, 54-55; pres, Cerophyl Labs, Inc, 55-56; sr exec serv res leader, Western Regional Res Ctr, Sci & Educ Admin-Agr Res, USDA, 56-81. *Concurrent Pos:* Sr Exec Serv, USDA, 79-82. *Mem:* Am Inst Nutrit; Am Chem Soc; Inst Food Technologists; Am Asn Cereal Chemists; Poultry Sci Asn. *Res:* Chicken and guinea pig nutrition; hormone assay and synthesis; vitamin assay; isolation of compounds from natural materials; process development; amino acid analysis; protein isolates from leaves and oilseeds for foods and feeds. *Mailing Add:* PO Box 454 Inverness CA 94937-0454. *Fax:* 415-669-7147; *E-Mail:* gkohl@aol

KOHLER, HEINZ, PROTEIN CHEMISTRY; IMMUNOLOGY. *Current Pos:* PROF, DEPT MICROBIOL & IMMUNOL & DIR RES, LUCILLE P MARKEY CANCER CTR, 93- *Personal Data:* b Duisburg, Ger, Sept 11, 39; m 65; c 2. *Educ:* Univ Munich, MD, 65. *Prof Exp:* Res fel, Max Planck Inst Biochem, 65-67; res assoc, Div Biol Sci, Ind Univ, 67-70; asst prof, Dept Path, 70-74, assoc prof, depts path & biochem, Univ Chicago, 74-81; Dept Molecular Immunol, Roswell Park Mem Inst, Buffalo, NY, 81-87; dir res, Idec Pharmaceut Corp, La Jolla, Calif, 87-89, sr sci fel, 89-93. *Concurrent Pos:* Res career develop award, USPHS, 73; adj prof, Dept Path, Univ Calif, San Diego, 87-90; adj mem, San Diego Regional Cancer Ctr, La Jolla, 90- *Mem:* Fedn Am Soc Exp Biol. *Res:* Relationship of function and structure of proteins; regulation of immune response. *Mailing Add:* Univ Ky Med Ctr Lucille P Markey Cancer Ctr 800 Rose St 205 Combs Res Bldg Lexington KY 40536-0096. *Fax:* 606-257-8940

KOHLER, MAX A, HYDROLOGY, GEOPHYSICS. *Current Pos:* RETIRED. *Personal Data:* b Lincolnville, Kans, Sept 6, 15; m 39, Estella Anna Pospisil; c Donna, Max II & Kathryn. *Educ:* Univ NMex, BS, 39. *Honors & Awards:* Hydrol Prize, Int Am Hydrol Sci, 86. *Prof Exp:* Hydrologist, Nat Weather Serv, 41-51, chief hydrologist, 51-71, assoc dir, 71-73. *Concurrent Pos:* Consult, UN, Yugoslavia, 53, SAfrica, 62 & 72, World Met Orgn, NY, Geneva, Switz, 74-75; pres, Comn Hydrol, World Meteorol Orgn, 60-68; coun mem, Am Meteorol Soc, 72-75. *Mem:* Nat Acad Eng; fel Am Geophys Union; fel Am Meteorol Soc; Am Soc Chem Engrs. *Mailing Add:* 3530 Twin Branches Dr Silver Spring MD 20906

KOHLER, PETER, ENDOCRINOLOGY, CELL CULTURE. *Current Pos:* PRES, ORE HEALTH SCI UNIV, 88- *Personal Data:* b Brooklyn, NY, July 18, 38; m 59; c 4. *Educ:* Univ Va, Charlottesville, BA, 59; Duke Univ, MD, 63. *Honors & Awards:* Qual Award, NIH, 69, 71. *Prof Exp:* Intern med, Duke Hosp, 63-64, fel endocrinol, 64-65; clin assoc, Nat Cancer Inst, NIH, 65-67, sr investr, Nat Inst Child Health & Develop, 68-73; prof med & cell biol & chief endocrinol, Baylor Col Med, 73-77; prof & chmn med, Univ Ark, Little Rock, 77-86, interim dean, Col Med, 86; dean, Sch Med, Health Sci Ctr, Univ Tex, 86-88. *Concurrent Pos:* Head endocrinol serv, Nat Inst Child Health & Develop, NIH, 72-73; prof med & cell biol & chief endocrinol, Baylor Col Med, 73-77; mem, NIH Endocrinol Study Sect, 81-85, chmn, 84-85; mem, Endocrinol Bd, Am Bd Internal Med, 83-; mem, Bd Sci Counrs, Nat Inst Child Health & Develop, 86- *Mem:* Inst Med-Nat Acad Sci; Am Soc Clin Invest; Asn Am Physicians; Am Diabetes Asn; Endocrine Soc; Sigma Xi; Am Soc Cell Biol; Am Fedn Clin Res. *Res:* Regulation of cell function and pituitary pathophysiology. *Mailing Add:* Ore Health Sci Univ L101 3181 SW Sam Jackson Park Rd Portland OR 97201-3098. *Fax:* 503-494-8935

KOHLER, PETER FRANCIS, IMMUNOLOGY. *Current Pos:* CHIEF, CHARITY HOSP, LA, 85- *Personal Data:* b Milwaukee, Wis, Apr 14, 35; m 62; c 3. *Educ:* Princeton Univ, AB, 57; Columbia Univ, MD, 61. *Prof Exp:* From asst prof to prof med, Univ Colo Med Ctr, 67-81, head div clin immunol, 75-81; PROF MED, SCH MED, TULANE UNIV, 85- *Mem:* Am Soc Clin Invest; Am Asn Immunologists; Am Acad Allergy. *Res:* Immunopathogenic mechanisms in disease; complement; immunology of hepatitis B virus infection. *Mailing Add:* Dept Med Tulane Univ Med Sch 1430 Tulane Ave New Orleans LA 70112-9826. *Fax:* 504-585-4045

KOHLER, ROBERT HENRY, PHYSICS. *Current Pos:* PROF PHYSICS, STATE UNIV NY COL BUFFALO, 66- *Personal Data:* b Philadelphia, Pa, Apr 25, 33. *Educ:* Mass Inst Technol, BS, 55, PhD(physics), 60. *Prof Exp:* Res assoc exp physics, Columbia Univ, 60-63; asst prof physics, NY Univ, 63-65; vis asst prof, Rutgers Univ, 65-66. *Mem:* Am Phys Soc; Am Asn Physics Teachers. *Res:* Lasers and quantum electronics; optical pumping. *Mailing Add:* Dept Physics State Univ Col Buffalo 1300 Elmwood Ave Buffalo NY 14222

KOHLER, SIGURD H, NUCLEAR PHYSICS. *Current Pos:* PROF PHYSICS, UNIV ARIZ, 68- *Personal Data:* b Uppsala, Sweden, Dec 1, 28; wid. *Educ:* Univ Uppsala, Fil Kand, 51, Fil Mag, 52, Fil Lic, 56, Fil Dr(theoret physics), 59. *Prof Exp:* Asst, Inst Meteorol, Univ Uppsala, 50-53 & Inst Theoret Physics, 53-57; fel theoret physics, Cern, Geneva, Switz, 57-59; res assoc, Cornell Univ, 59-60; asst res physicist, Univ Calif, Los Angeles, 60-61; spec res, AEC Sweden, Uppsala, 61-63; asst res physicist, Univ Calif, San Diego, 63-65; vis assoc prof physics, Rice Univ, 65-68. *Mem:* Am Phys Soc. *Res:* Nuclear theory; many body problems; properties of nuclear matter. *Mailing Add:* Dept Physics Univ Ariz 1600 E U BI Tucson AZ 85721-0001. *Fax:* 520-621-4721

KOHLHAW, GUNTER B, BIOCHEMISTRY. *Current Pos:* NATO fel intracellular regulation, 64-66, from asst prof to assoc prof, 66-73, PROF BIOCHEM, PURDUE UNIV, WEST LAFAYETTE, 73- *Personal Data:* b Elbing, Ger, May 5, 31; m 59, Ellen. *Educ:* Univ Freiburg, MS, 59, PhD(biochem), 62. *Prof Exp:* Res asst gen biochem, Univ Freiburg, 62-64. *Mem:* Genetics Soc Am; Am Soc Biol Chemists; Ger Soc Biol Chem. *Res:* Gene structure function; metabolic regulation; analysis of the structure-function relationship of structural and regulatory genes in yeast; with special attention to the regulation of gene expression by upstream elements. *Mailing Add:* Dept Biochem Purdue Univ West Lafayette IN 47907. *Fax:* 765-494-7897; *E-Mail:* kohlhaw@biochem.purdue.edu

KOHLHEPP, SUE JOANNE, ANALYTICAL BIOCHEMISTRY. *Current Pos:* RES ASSOC, GILBERT RES LAB, PROVIDENCE MED CTR, PORTLAND, 77- *Personal Data:* b Kittanning, Pa, July 15, 39. *Educ:* WVa Wesleyan Col, BS, 61; Pa State Univ, MS, 63, PhD(biophys), 69. *Prof Exp:* Teacher physics & phys sci, Marple-Newtown Sch Dist, Pa, 63-66; res assoc clin chem, St Anthony Hosp, Louisville, Ky, 69-74; res assoc biochem, Ore State Univ, 75-77. *Concurrent Pos:* Assoc prof biochem, Catherine Spalding Col, 71. *Mem:* AAAS; Biophys Soc; Am Soc Microbiol; NY Acad Sci. *Res:* Identification and quantitation of metabolic products of the anti-tumor agent 1-2-chloroethyl-3-cyclohexyl-1-nitrosourea in rats, monkeys and humans as a means of deducing the mechanisms of action of the drug and decreasing its toxicity; infectious diseases such as molecular mechanism of aminoglycoside renal toxicity and subcellular distribution of gentamicin in renal cortical tissue; mechanism of action of toxins from Clostridium difficila. *Mailing Add:* 11704 NE 70th Ave Vancouver WA 98686. *E-Mail:* sue_kohlhepp@phsor.org

KOHLI, DILIP, MECHANICAL ENGINEERING. *Current Pos:* asst prof, 76-79, assoc prof 79-, PROF MECH ENG, UNIV WIS-MILWAUKEE. *Personal Data:* b Kanpur, India, July 22, 47; m 77. *Educ:* Indian Inst Technol, Kanpur, BS, 69, MS, 71; Okla State Univ, PhD(mech eng), 73. *Prof Exp:* Res asst mech eng, Okla State Univ, 71-73, assoc, 74; assoc & instr, Rensselaer Polytech Inst, 74-75. *Concurrent Pos:* Consult, Procter & Gamble, 76-, Burroughs Corp, 77- & Control Data Corp, 78-; vis scientist, Univ Fla, Gainesville, 78- *Mem:* Am Soc Mech Engrs; Am Soc Eng Educ. *Res:* Kinematics and dynamics of machinery, vibrations, rotor dynamics and machine elements; robotics and manipulators. *Mailing Add:* Dept Mech Eng Univ Wis PO Box 784 Milwaukee WI 53201

KOHLMAN, DAVID L(ESLIE), AERODYNAMICS, AIRCRAFT DESIGN. *Current Pos:* vpres & dir aeronaut eng, 93-96, PRIN ENGR, ENG SYST INC, 96-; PRES, KOHLMAN AVIATION CORP, 77- *Personal Data:* b Houston, Tex, Oct 13, 37; m 59, Linda Norris; c Bradley D & Jeffrey A. *Educ:* Univ Kans, BS, 59, MS, 60; Mass Inst Technol, PhD(aeronaut, astronaut), 63. *Prof Exp:* Res engr, Boeing Co, 63-64; from asst prof to assoc prof, Univ Kans, 64-70, chmn dept, 67-72, prof aerospace eng, 70-81, dir, flight res lab, 81-82. *Concurrent Pos:* Consult, Centron Corp, 66-75, Beech Aircraft Corp, 69-70, Bell Helicopter Co, 70, Cessna Aircraft Co, 74 & 78-, NASA, 75-77, Gates Learjet, 78-, Piaggio, 78 & Singer-Link, 81-88; mem, Flight Mech Panel, NAtlantic Treat Org-Adv Group Aeronaut Res & Develop, 81-85; distinguished vis prof, USAF Acad, 76-77; pres, Kohlman Syst Res Inc, 82-88, chmn bd, 88- *Mem:* Fel Am Inst Aeronaut & Astronaut; Soc Automotive Engrs. *Res:* Aerodynamic design of aircraft; aircraft stability and control; flight simulation; aircraft ice protection systems; flight testing. *Mailing Add:* 4775 Centennial Blvd Suite 106 Colorado Springs CO 80919

KOHLMAYR, GERHARD FRANZ, MATHEMATICAL PHYSICS, APPLIED MATHEMATICS. *Current Pos:* staff scientist, 61-71, sr appl mathematician, Pratt & Whitney Aircraft, 71-74, FOUNDER, MATHMODEL CONSULT BUR, 74-, FOUNDER, MATHMODEL PRESS, 79- *Personal Data:* b Klagenfurt, Austria, Nov 30, 30; m 63. *Educ:* Graz Tech Univ, BS, 51, PhD(theoret physics), 59. *Prof Exp:* Sci asst, Darmstadt Tech Univ, 59-60; fel, Von Humboldt Found, 60-61. *Concurrent Pos:* Adj asst prof, Rensselaer Polytech Inst, 61-66. *Mem:* Am Math Soc. *Res:* Acoustical duct lining theory; inconsistency of Zermelo-Fraenkel set theory; neutron transport theory; mathematical foundation of electrodynamic theory; elementary particle theory; negative solution of Hilbert's second problem; absolute invalidity of Hilbert's program; transient heat transfer; numerical operational calculus; generalized functions. *Mailing Add:* 80 Founders Rd Glastonbury CT 06033

KOHLMEIER, RONALD HAROLD, VETERINARY PHYSIOLOGY, NUTRITIONAL PHYSIOLOGY. *Current Pos:* Tech dir animal nutrit, 88-92, ANIMAL NUTRIT CONSULT, SOYBEAN ASN, 92- *Personal Data:* b Craig, Nebr, Oct 16, 36; m 63, 92, Lan L Zhad; c Debora L (Crull), Pamela & Douglas. *Educ:* Univ Nebr, BS, 59; Iowa State Univ, PhD(ruminant nutrit), 66, DVM, 68. *Prof Exp:* Farmer, 59; eng change notice coordr, RCA Missile Div, 60; asst nutritionist, Iowa State Univ, 60-66, res assoc nutrit & physiol, 66-68, asst prof, 68-70, assoc prof nutrit & physiol, 70-73; res ruminant nutritionist & vet, Agr Res Serv, USDA & assoc prof animal sci, Univ Nebr, 73-75; mgr tech serv processing group, 75-80, mgr feed sci servs, The Andersons, 80-84; technical sales mgr, Nutrius Inc, 84-87. *Concurrent Pos:* Nutrit consult for Dr Richard Hubbard, Gowrie Vet Serv, 68-73, Doane Marketing Res Inc, 93- *Mem:* Am Soc Animal Sci; Am Asn Bovine Practioners; Am Vet Med Asn; Am Asn Swine Practitioners; Sigma Xi; Am Dairy Sci Asn. *Res:* Animal nutrition and usage of feed additives; animal nutrition and disease interrelationships. *Mailing Add:* 15622 Century Lake Dr Chesterfield MO 63017-4912. *Fax:* 314-576-2786

KOHLMEYER, JAN JUSTUS, MYCOLOGY. *Current Pos:* assoc prof, 69-74, PROF INST MARINE SCI, UNIV NC, 74- *Personal Data:* b Berlin, Ger, Mar 15, 28; US citizen; m, Brigitte Volkmann. *Educ:* Free Univ Berlin, Dr rer nat(bot), 55. *Prof Exp:* Res asst mycol, Fed Inst Mat Testing, Berlin-Dahlem, Ger, 56-59 & Bot Mus, 60-64; asst prof, Inst Fisheries Res, 64-69. *Concurrent Pos:* Res assoc, Univ Wash, 59-60 & Duke Univ, 63-64. *Mem:* Mycol Soc Am; hon mem Brit Mycol Soc; Am Inst Biol Sci; Sigma Xi. *Res:* Marine mycology; taxonomy of fungi; animal-fungus relationships; phytopathology. *Mailing Add:* Inst Marine Sci Univ NC Morehead City NC 28557. *Fax:* 919-726-2426

KOHLS, CARL WILLIAM, DISCRETE APPLIED MATHEMATICS. *Current Pos:* from asst prof to prof, 61-91, EMER PROF MATH, SYRACUSE UNIV, 91- *Personal Data:* b Rochester, NY, Mar 14, 31. *Educ:* Univ Rochester, AB, 53; Purdue Univ, MS, 55, PhD(math), 57. *Prof Exp:* Res asst math, Purdue Univ, 57; instr, Columbia Univ, 57-58; asst prof, Univ Ill, 58-61. *Concurrent Pos:* Res assoc & vis asst prof, Univ Rochester, 60-61; translr, Am Math Soc Russian Transl Proj, 68-91. *Mem:* Am Math Soc; Math Asn Am. *Res:* The study of regulatory systems using Boolean methods. *Mailing Add:* Syracuse Univ Syracuse NY 13244-1150

KOHLS, DONALD W, EXPLORATION GEOLOGY. *Current Pos:* PRES, KOHLS EXPLORATION LTD, 91- *Personal Data:* b Minneapolis, Minn, Oct 21, 34; m 62; c 2. *Educ:* Carleton Col, BA, 56; Univ Minn, MS, 58, PhD(geol), 61. *Prof Exp:* Res scientist, NJ Zinc Co, 64-74, gen mgr & asst to pres, NJ Zinc Explor Co, 74-76; vpres explor, Golf Fields Mining Corp, 76-91, Mem Bd Dirs, 79-89. *Mem:* Am Asn Petrol Geologists; Am Inst Mining, Metall & Petrol Engrs; Geol Soc Am; Soc Econ Paleont & Mineral; Soc Econ Geologists. *Res:* Economic geology; petrology; mineralogy; geochemistry; field mapping. *Mailing Add:* 1792 S Beech St Lakewood CO 80228-2009

KOHLS, ROBERT E, VETERINARY PARASITOLOGY, ENTOMOLOGY. *Current Pos:* ANIMAL HEALTH CONSULT, 85- *Personal Data:* b Portage, Wis, Mar 15, 31; m 54, Patricia A Allin; c 4. *Educ:* Univ Wis, BS, 53, MS, 55, PhD, 58. *Prof Exp:* Proj asst, Dept Vet Sci, Univ Wis, 58; dir res, Specifide, Inc, Ind, 58-59; vet parasitologist, Upjohn Co, 59-68; chief parasitol, Norwich Pharmacol Co, 68-73, chief avian prod develop, 73-75, chief feed additives, 75-77; chief parasitol, W Agro Chem Inc, 77-84; prod mgr, Bristol Labs, 84-85. *Concurrent Pos:* Consult & pres animal health, Grey Fox Ltd, 85- *Mem:* Am Soc Parasitol. *Res:* Insect taxonomy; Diptera and Coleoptera; prophylactic worm control in cattle and sheep using phenothiazine; internal parasite control, especially prophylaxis. *Mailing Add:* 1627 County Rd 36 Norwich NY 13815

KOHLSTAEDT, KENNETH GEORGE, medicine; deceased, see previous edition for last biography

KOHLSTEDT, DAVID L, GEOLOGIC & CERAMIC MATERIALS. *Current Pos:* PROF, DEPT GEOL & GEOPHYS, UNIV MINN, 89- *Personal Data:* m 66, Sally Gregory; c Kristian Gregory & Kurt Frederick. *Educ:* Valparaiso Univ, BS, 65; Univ Ill, MS, 67, PhD(physics), 70. *Prof Exp:* Res assoc, Cavendish Lab, Cambridge Univ, 70-71, Dept Earth & Planetary Sci, Mich Technol Univ, 71-75; from asst prof to prof, Dept Mat Sci & Eng, Cornell Univ, 75-89. *Concurrent Pos:* Vis scientist, Dept Earth Sci, Mich Technol Univ, 82, Australian Nat Univ, 83, Hannover Univ Physics, 84, Bayerisches Geoinst, Univ Bayreuth, 93-94; Alexander von Humboldt award, 93-94. *Mem:* Fel Am Geophys Union; Am Ceramic Soc; Mat Res Soc. *Res:* Physical and chemical properties of rocks and minerals; high temperature, high pressure experimental research kinetics of solid state reactions; role of water on kinetic properties of silicates; effects of small amount of melt on strength of rocks. *Mailing Add:* Dept Geol & Geophys Pillsbury Hall Univ Minn Minneapolis MN 55455. *Fax:* 612-625-3819; *E-Mail:* dlkohl@maroon.tc.umn.edu

KOHLSTEDT, SALLY GREGORY, HISTORY OF SCIENCE. *Current Pos:* assoc dean acad affairs, 89-95, PROF HIST SCI, UNIV MINN, 89-, DIR, CTR ADVAN FEMINIST STUDIES, 97- *Personal Data:* b Ypsilanti, Mich, Jan 30, 43; m 66, David L; c Kris & Kurt. *Educ:* Valparaiso Univ, BA, 65; Mich State Univ, MA, 66; Univ Ill, PhD(Am hist), 72. *Prof Exp:* Asst prof hist, Simmons Col, 71-75; from asst prof to prof hist, Syracuse Univ, 75-89. *Concurrent Pos:* Fel, Smithsonian Inst, 70-71; mem, US Nat Comt Int Union Hist & Philos Sci, 78-81; mem, Adv Comt, US Nat Archive Records Serv, 79-81; Fulbright vis prof, Univ Melbourne, Australia, 83; NASA Hist Adv Comt, 84-87; consult, NY Acad Sci, 86-; res fel, Woodrow Wilson Int Ctr, 86; chair, Sect L, AAAS, 86-87; Smithsonian Inst Sr Fel, 87; vis prof, Cornell Univ, 89, Am-Inst, Univ Munich, 97; assoc ed, Am Nat Biography, 89-98. *Mem:* Hist Sci Soc (secy, 78-81, vpres, 90-91, pres, 92-93); AAAS; Orgn Am Historians; Am Hist Asn. *Res:* History of the institutional development of scientific activity in the United States; professional origins of scientific societies; inclusion of women in scientific organizations; role of museums in connecting science and the public. *Mailing Add:* Univ Minn 123 Pillsbury Hall Minneapolis MN 55406. *E-Mail:* sgk@mailbox.mail.umn.edu

KOHMAN, TRUMAN PAUL, ASTRONOMY. *Current Pos:* from asst prof to prof, 48-81, EMER PROF CHEM, CARNEGIE-MELLON UNIV, 81- *Personal Data:* b Champaign, Ill, Mar 8, 16; m 45, Jane Sierers; c Leslie, Paulette & Steven. *Educ:* Harvard Univ, AB, 38; Univ Wis, PhD(inorg & anal chem), 43. *Honors & Awards:* Am Chem Soc Award, 62. *Prof Exp:* Asst chem, Univ Wis, 38-42; res assoc metall lab, Univ Chicago, 42-44 & 45-46; chemist, Hanford Eng Works, Wash, 44-45; res assoc, Argonne Nat Lab, 46; fel chem, Inst Nuclear Studies, Univ Chicago, 46-48. *Concurrent Pos:* NSF fel, Max-Planck Inst Chem, 57-58; vis prof, Indian Inst Technol, Kanpur, 62-63. *Mem:* Fel AAAS; Am Chem Soc; fel Am Phys Soc; Am Astron Soc; Meteoritical Soc. *Res:* Artificial and natural radioactivity; nuclear reactions; geochronometry; meteorites; high-energy astronomy instrumenutation. *Mailing Add:* Dept Chem Carnegie-Mellon Univ Schenley Park Pittsburgh PA 15213. *Fax:* 412-681-0648; *E-Mail:* tk11@andrew.cmu.edu

KOHN, ALAN JACOBS, ZOOLOGY. *Current Pos:* from asst prof to assoc prof, 61-67, PROF ZOOL, UNIV WASH, 67- *Personal Data:* b New Haven, Conn, July 15, 31; m 59; c 4. *Educ:* Princeton Univ, AB, 53; Yale Univ, PhD(zool), 57. *Prof Exp:* Res assoc zool, Marine Lab, Univ Hawaii, 54-56; Anderson fel, Bingham Oceanog Lab, Yale Univ, 58; asst prof zool, Fla State Univ, 58-61. *Concurrent Pos:* Biologist, Yale Exped to Seychelles Islands, 57-58; partic, Int Indian Ocean Exped, 63; sr vis res assoc, Smithsonian Inst, 67, res assoc, 85-; sr post-doctorial fel, 90; vis prof, Univ Hawaii, 68; Guggenheim Found fel, 74; adj cur malacol, Thomas Burke Mem Wash State Mus, 71-; adj prof, Inst Environ Studies, Quaternary Res Inst, 78-; prog officer, NSF, 85-86. *Mem:* Fel AAAS; Ecol Soc Am; Am Soc Zool (treas, 71-73); Am Soc Naturalists; Soc Syst Zool; Am Malacological Union (pres, 83); Am Soc Limnol & Oceanog; Brit Ecol Soc; Int Soc Reef Studies. *Res:* Ecology, systematics and paleobiology of marine mollusks; coral reefs. *Mailing Add:* Dept Zool NJ-15 Univ Wash 3900 Seventh Ave NE Seattle WA 98195-0001. *E-Mail:* kohn@u.washington.edu

KOHN, DAVID H, BIOMECHANICS, BIOMATERIALS. *Current Pos:* asst prof, Dept Biol & Mat Sci, Sch Dent, Univ Mich, 89-96, grad prog bioeng, Horace Rackham Sch Grad Studies, 90-96, FAC MEM & ADV ORAL HEALTH SCI, UNIV MICH, 93-, ASSOC PROF, DEPT BIOL & MAT SCI, SCH DENT & BIOMED COL ENG, 96- *Personal Data:* b Sept 9, 61; m 96, Lisa Kozak. *Educ:* Tulane Univ, BSE, 83; Univ Pa, MSE, 85, PhD(bioeng), 89. *Honors & Awards:* Res Initiation Award, NSF, 94. *Prof Exp:* Res asst, Biomech Lab, Tulane Univ, 82-83, Hosp Spec Surg, 83; teaching asst, Dept Bioeng, Univ Pa, 83, res fel, 84-89. *Concurrent Pos:* Lectr, Dept Bioeng, Univ Pa, 86; health sci specialist, Vet Admin, Pa, 87-89; consult, Med Device Co, Labs & Individuals, 88-; prin invest, Univ Mich, 90-92, 90-92, 91-92 & 93, Delta Dent Fund, 91-92; co-investr, Nat Inst Dent Res, 90-, NSF & Whitaker Found, 94-, NIH, 91-92; mem, Study Sect & Reviewer, NIH, 89- *Mem:* Am Soc Testing & Mat; Biomed Eng Soc; Int Asn Dent Res; Soc Biomat; Sigma Xi; Mat Res Soc; Am Soc Mech Engrs; Am Asn Dent Res. *Res:* Biomechanics & biomaterials for hand tissue replacement and regeneration; smart materials bioninetics structure function relations in tissue; contributed over 100 papers, chapters, articles; granted 1 patent. *Mailing Add:* Dept Biol & Mat Sci 2213 Sch Dent Univ Mich Ann Arbor MI 48109-1078. *Fax:* 313-764-7406; *E-Mail:* dhkohn@umich.edu

KOHN, ERWIN, PHYSICAL CHEMISTRY, POLYMER CHEMISTRY. *Current Pos:* SR PROJ SCIENTIST, APPL TECHNOL DIV, MASON & HANGER CO, 72- *Personal Data:* b Vienna, Austria, Aug 23, 23; nat US; m 49, Henrietta L Klapman; c Joseph H, Michael D, Daniel R, Benjamin, Samuel L & Susan M (Shay). *Educ:* Univ Ill, BS, 48; Univ Notre Dame, MS, 50; Univ Tex, PhD(chem), 56. *Prof Exp:* From res chemist to sr res chemist, Monsanto Co, Tex, 55-62, res specialist, 62-66; assoc prof chem, Southwestern Okla State Univ, 66-68; assoc prof polymer chem, NDak State Univ, 68-72, dir NSF prog, 71-72. *Mem:* Fel Am Inst Chemists; Am Chem Soc; Am Phys Soc; AAAS. *Res:* Physical and physical-organic chemistry; analytical chemistry; liquid and gel permeation chromatography; explosives analysis; kinetics and mechanisms; Ziegler-Natta polymerization; structure of polyolefins; polymer characterization; organometallic chemistry; kinetic isotope effects; supercritical fluid chromatography. *Mailing Add:* 3613 Nebraska Amarillo TX 79109. *E-Mail:* hapyfins@arn.net

KOHN, FRANK S, ORGANIZATIONAL BEHAVIOR SCIENCES. *Current Pos:* DIR MFG, WYETH-LEDERLE VACCINES & PEDIAT, WYETH-AYERST LABS, 92- *Personal Data:* b Bristol, Pa, June 21, 42; m 82, Marge; c Frank A & David G. *Educ:* NJ State Col Trenton, BA, 69; Drexel Univ, Philadelphia, Pa, MS, 72; Univ Wis-Madison, PDD, 79. *Honors & Awards:* H Burrows Award, Franklin Sch Sci, 61. *Prof Exp:* Virologist, NJ Dept Health, 63-69; from asst microbiologist to assoc microbiological pharmaceut, Schering Plough Corp, 69-72; scientist, 76-78; dir oper pharm & biol, 78-82; dir mfg pharm & biol, Am Home Prod, Ft Dodge Labs, 82-86; dir mfg pharm, Sanofi Animal Health, Sanofi Inc, 86-91. *Concurrent Pos:* Consult, Bristol Sanitation Co; instr org behavior, Iowa Cent Community Col, 82-87; consult org development, Mussic & Assoc; instr clearing validation & barrier technol, Inst Appl Pharmaceut Sci, 92-; adj prof, Campbell Univ, 95.

Mem: Am Soc Microbiologists; Parenteral Drug Asn; Am Soc Pharmaceut Engrs; AAAS; Am Acad Microbiol. *Res:* Pharmaceutical microbiology; environmental microbiology in clean rooms; infectious diseases; leptospirosis lab methods development; management to technical staff; interpersonal relationship; value engineering as applied to the pharmaceutical industry. *Mailing Add:* 113 Cumberland Greens Dr Cary NC 27513

KOHN, FRED R, experimental biology, for more information see previous edition

KOHN, GUSTAVE K, CHEMISTRY. *Current Pos:* RETIRED. *Personal Data:* b Syracuse, NY, Feb 12, 10; m 50; c 3. *Educ:* NY Univ, BS, 30. *Prof Exp:* Control chemist, Ortho Div, Chevron Chem Co, Standard Oil Co, Calif, 46-51, res chemist, 51-54, group leader org synthesis, 54-56, chief res chemist, 56-62, mgr cent res labs, 62-70, sr res scientist, 70-75; pesticide prod adv to govt India, UN Indust Develop Orgn, New Delhi, 75-76; res dir, Zoecon Corp, 76-78, sr scientist, 79-90, mgr licensing & technol, Sandor Corp, 84-90. *Concurrent Pos:* Coun, Am Chem Soc, 79-, immediate past chmn, agrochem div. *Mem:* AAAS; Am Chem Soc; Entom Soc Am; Am Inst Biol Sci; Sigma Xi. *Res:* Synthesis of biologically active and agriculturally useful compounds; organophosphate insecticides; halo-organic fungicides; plant and insect growth regulators. *Mailing Add:* 198 Pine Lane Los Altos CA 94022

KOHN, HAROLD LEWIS, MECHANISM OF DRUG ACTION, SYNTHETIC METHODS. *Current Pos:* PROF CHEM, UNIV HOUSTON, 73-; PROF CHEM, M D ANDERSON CANCER CTR, UNIV TEX. *Personal Data:* b New York, NY, Apr 1, 45; m 91, Carol A Kakalec; c Jeffrey S & Nicholas W. *Educ:* Univ Mich, BS, 66; Pa State Univ, PhD(chem), 71. *Concurrent Pos:* Dreyfus scholar, Dreyfus Found, 77; Sloan scholar, A P Sloan Found, 77. *Mem:* Am Chem Soc; Sigma Xi. *Res:* Determining the mechanism of drug action and the elucidation of the site of drug function. *Mailing Add:* Dept Chem Univ Houston Houston TX 77204-5641. *Fax:* 713-743-2709; *E-Mail:* chemag@jetson.uh.edu

KOHN, HAROLD WILLIAM, ENVIRONMENTAL SCIENCE. *Current Pos:* RETIRED. *Personal Data:* b Newark, NJ, Nov 9, 20; m 57, Janet Mitchell; c Frederick J, Marilyn L (Sims), Andrew D & Matthew J. *Educ:* Univ Mich, Ann Arbor, BS, 43; Syracuse Univ, PhD(chem), 53. *Prof Exp:* Chemist, Oak Ridge Nat Labs, 47-48 & 54-73; asst chem, Syracuse Univ, 48-53; res engr, Battelle Mem Inst, 52-53; staff scientist environ, Ohio Environ Protection Agency, 73-86. *Concurrent Pos:* Vis lectr, Univ Calif, Berkeley, 63-64; vis prof, Dickinson Col, 71-72. *Mem:* Am Chem Soc; Health Physics Soc; Am Nuclear Soc. *Res:* Effects of ionizing radiations on heterogeneous catalysts; radiation chemistry of surfaces; molten salt chemistry; power plant siting and productivity; environmental impacts. *Mailing Add:* 147 Chatham Rd Columbus OH 43214

KOHN, HENRY IRVING, RADIATION EPIDEMIOLOGY, RADIATION BIOLOGY. *Current Pos:* Fuller-Am Cancer Soc prof radiol, 63-68, Gaiser prof, 68-76, EMER PROF RADIATION BIOL, SCH MED, HARVARD UNIV, 76- *Personal Data:* b New York, NY, Aug 19, 09; m 61, Linda Hansen; c Hari A (Munyan) & Lars S. *Educ:* Dartmouth Col, AB, 30; Harvard Univ, PhD(physiol), 35, MD, 46. *Prof Exp:* Gen Educ Bd fel, cell biol, Univ Stockholm, 35-36, Univ Cambridge, 36-37; instr & asst prof physiol & pharmacol, Med Sch, Duke Univ, 37-43; clin prof exp radiol, Univ Calif, San Francisco, 53-63. *Concurrent Pos:* Sci secy, adv comt biol & med, US AEC, 57-61; dir, Shields Warren Radiation Lab, New Eng Deaconess Hosp, Boston, 64-79, Ctr Human Genetics, Med Sch, Harvard Univ, 71-76; chair, Bikini Atoll Rehab Comt, US Dept Interior, 84-88; referee, Rongelap Reassessment Proj, Repub Marshall Islands, 88-90. *Mem:* Am Physiol Soc; Radiation Res Soc. *Res:* Radiation biology: epidemiology, toxicology, environmental. *Mailing Add:* Harvard Med Sch 1203 Shattuck Ave Berkeley CA 94709-1412. *Fax:* 510-548-0313

KOHN, HERBERT MYRON, NEUROPSYCHOLOGY, ELECTROENCEPHALOGRAPHY. *Current Pos:* asst prof, 72-75, ASSOC PROF PSYCHIAT, RUTGERS MED SCH, COL MED & DENT NJ, 75-, CHIEF NEURODIAG LAB, 72- *Personal Data:* b Chicago, Ill, Feb 24, 35; m 57; c 2. *Educ:* Univ Ill, BA, 58; Roosevelt Univ, MA, 60; Ill Inst Technol, PhD(psychol), 65. *Prof Exp:* Med res assoc, Ill State Psychiat Inst, 60-67; dir, Darrow Mem Lab, Inst Juv Res, 68-70; res scientist, Ill State Pediat Inst, 71-72. *Concurrent Pos:* Lectr, Roosevelt Univ, 65-72; asst prof, Ill Inst Technol, 67-72 & Abraham Lincoln Sch Med, Univ Ill, 68-72; lectr, Northeastern Ill State Univ, 70-72 & Univ Ill, Chicago Circle, 72; assoc psychobiol, Grad Fac, Rutgers Univ, 72-78; adj assoc prof, Grad Sch of Appl & Prof Psychol, Rutgers Univ, 76-. *Mem:* Am Psychol Asn; Psychonomic Soc; Int Neuropsychol Soc. *Res:* Neural bases of human behavior; primate behavior; vision and effects of early brain damage. *Mailing Add:* Dept Psychiat Univ Med & Dent Robert Wood Johnson Sch 675 Hoes Lane Piscataway NJ 08854-5635

KOHN, JACK ARNOLD, MATERIALS RESEARCH, CRYSTALLOGRAPHY. *Current Pos:* physicist & dep dir solid state sci div, US Army Electronics Res & Develop Command, Ft Monmouth, 55-69, dep dir inst explor res, 69-71, dep dir technol, 71-73, dir electronic mat res, Electronics Technol & Devices Lab, 74-85. *Personal Data:* b Trenton, NJ, July 17, 25; m 51, Norma Bialy; c Steven B & Martha (Wurzel). *Educ:* Univ Mich, BS, 47, MS, 48, PhD(mineral), 50. *Honors & Awards:* Prize, Army Sci Conf, 59, 62 & 70. *Prof Exp:* Asst mineral, Univ Mich, 48-50, res assoc, 50-51; mineralogist, Electrotech Lab, US Bur Mines, 51-55. *Concurrent Pos:* Consult mineralogist, US Bur Mines, 50-51. *Mem:* Fel AAAS; fel Mineral Soc Am; Am Crystallog Asn. *Res:* Crystallography of electronic and magnetic materials; twinning; polymorphism; polytypism; general x-ray crystallography. *Mailing Add:* 65 Wigwam Rd Locust NJ 07760

KOHN, JAMES P(AUL), CHEMICAL ENGINEERING. *Current Pos:* from asst prof to assoc prof, 55-64, PROF CHEM ENG, UNIV NOTRE DAME, 64- *Personal Data:* b Dubuque, Iowa, Oct 31, 24; m 58; c 3. *Educ:* Univ Notre Dame, BS, 51; Univ Mich, MSE, 52; Univ Kans, PhD, 56. *Honors & Awards:* D L Katz Award, Gas Processors Asn, 88. *Prof Exp:* Chem engr, Reilly Tar & Chem Corp, 46-51. *Concurrent Pos:* Consult, Eng Enterprises; dir, Solar Lab for Thermal Appln, 74- *Mem:* AAAS; Am Chem Soc; fel Am Inst Chem Engrs. *Res:* Heterogeneous phase equilibrium; applied thermodynamics; unsteady state diffusion; physical properties; molecular transport. *Mailing Add:* Dept Chem Eng Univ Notre Dame Notre Dame IN 46556

KOHN, JOSEPH JOHN, MATHEMATICS. *Current Pos:* chmn dept, 73-76 & 93-96, PROF MATH, PRINCETON UNIV, 68- *Personal Data:* b Prague, Czech, May 18, 32; nat US; m 66; c 3. *Educ:* Mass Inst Technol, BS, 53; Princeton Univ, MA, 54, PhD(math), 56. *Honors & Awards:* Steele Prize, Am Math Soc, 79; Czech Math & Physics Union Award, 90 & 93. *Prof Exp:* Instr math, Princeton Univ, 56-57; mem, Inst Advan Study, 57-58; from asst prof to prof math, Brandeis Univ, 58-68. *Concurrent Pos:* Ed, Transactions Am Math Soc, Advances Math & Annals Math. *Mem:* Nat Acad Sci; Am Acad Arts & Sci; Am Math Soc. *Res:* Several complex variables; partial differential equations. *Mailing Add:* Dept Math Princeton Univ Princeton NJ 08540. *Fax:* 609-258-1367; *E-Mail:* kohn@math.princeton.edu

KOHN, KURT WILLIAM, CHEMICAL PHARMACOLOGY. *Current Pos:* Clin assoc, Nat Cancer Inst, 57-59, SR INVESTR, NAT CANCER INST, 59-, CHIEF LAB MOLECULAR PHARMACOL, 68- *Personal Data:* b Austria, Sept 14, 30; nat US; m 56; c 2. *Educ:* Harvard Univ, AB, 52, PhD(biochem), 66; Columbia Univ, MD, 56. *Mem:* Am Chem Soc; Am Asn Cancer Res; Am Asn Biol Chemists. *Res:* Effects of chemotherapeutic agents on structure and function of deoxyribonucleic acid. *Mailing Add:* Nat Cancer Inst NIH Bldg 37 Rm 5C27 Bethesda MD 20892-0001

KOHN, LEONARD DAVID, BIOCHEMICAL PHARMACOLOGY. *Current Pos:* res assoc, Lab Biochem & Metab, Nat Inst Arthritis, Metab & Digestive Dis, 64-66, med res officer, Lab Biochem Pharmacol, 66-74, chief, Sect Biochem of Cell Regulation, Lab Biochem Pharmacol, 74-95, CHIEF, BELL REGULATION SECT, METAB DIS BR, NAT INST ARTHRITIS, METAB & DIGESTIVE DIS, 95- *Personal Data:* b New York, NY, Aug 1, 35; m 62; c 2. *Educ:* Columbia Univ, BA, 57, MD, 61. *Prof Exp:* Intern med, Columbia Presby Med Ctr, 61-62, asst resident, 62-63, sr resident, 63-64. *Concurrent Pos:* Vis prof, Dept Med, Univ Liege, Belg, 70-71. *Mem:* Am Soc Biol Chemists; Am Endocrinol Soc; Am Thyroid Asn. *Res:* Mechanism by which hormones interact with membrane components to elicit functional responses and growth; enzymatic conversion of precursors of collagen to collagen; enzymes concerned with solute transport across membranes; autoimmunity. *Mailing Add:* Sect Cell Regul NIDDK Bldg 10 Rm 9C101B NIH Bethesda MD 20892-0001. *Fax:* 301-496-0200; *E-Mail:* lenk@bdg10.niddk.nih.gov

KOHN, MICHAEL, BIOMEDICAL ENGINEERING, NEUROPHYSIOLOGY. *Current Pos:* Res engr, 57-68, DIR, BIOENG DEPT, ROCKLAND RES INST, 68- *Personal Data:* b Budapest, Hungary, June 18, 34; US citizen; m 55; c 1. *Educ:* City Univ New York, BEE, 60, MEE, 68; NY Univ, PhD(elec eng), 74. *Concurrent Pos:* Consult, Mnemotron Corp, 61-62. *Res:* Development of biomedical instrumentation; analysis of electrophysiological data. *Mailing Add:* Nathan Kline Inst 140 Old Orangeburg Rd Orangeburg NY 10962

KOHN, MICHAEL CHARLES, BIOMATHEMATICS, BIOCHEMISTRY. *Current Pos:* expert, 91-96, STAFF SCIENTIST, NAT INST ENVIRON SCI, RESEARCH TRIANGLE PARK, NC, 96- *Personal Data:* b Brooklyn, NY, July 29, 41; m 71, Lynn Mitchell. *Educ:* Mass Inst Technol, BS, 64; Univ SC, PhD(chem), 70. *Prof Exp:* Technician chem, Gen Latex & Chem Co, 62; consult, BB Chem Co, 62-63; fel, Univ Tex, Austin, 69-71; chemist, Naval Undersea Res & Develop Ctr, 71-73; sr res investr & adj assoc prof, Univ, Pa, 74-84; assoc med res prof, Depts Physiol & Cell Biol, Duke Med Ctr, 84-91. *Concurrent Pos:* Nat Res Coun fel, Naval Undersea Res & Develop Ctr, 71-73. *Mem:* AAAS; Sigma Xi; Soc Comput Simulation; Soc Math Biol. *Res:* Valence force field calculations of strain energy; molecular orbital theory; statistical mechanics of polymer solutions; biomedical computer models; sensitivity analysis; graph-theoretical analysis of metabolic networks; computer modeling of responses to toxins. *Mailing Add:* 1014 Shepherd St Durham NC 27707. *Fax:* 919-541-1479; *E-Mail:* kohn@valiant.niehs.nih.gov

KOHN, WALTER, THEORETICAL PHYSICS. *Current Pos:* prof, Univ Calif, 60-79, chmn dept, San Diego, 61-63, dir, Inst Theoret Physics, Santa Barbara, 79-84, prof, 84-91, EMER PROF PHYSICS, UNIV CALIF, SANTA BARBARA, 91- *Personal Data:* b Vienna, Austria, Mar 9, 23; nat US; m 78; c J Marilyn, Ingrid E (Katz) & E Rosalind. *Educ:* Univ Toronto, BA, 45, MA, 46; Harvard Univ, PhD(physics), 48. *Hon Degrees:* LLD, Univ Toronto, 67; DSC, Univ Paris, 80, Brandeis Univ, 81; DPhil, Hebrew Univ, Jerusalem, 81; DSc, Queens Univ, Can, 86, Tech Univ Vienna, 96; DNatSci, Fed Inst Technol, Zurich, 94; Drerum naturalium, Univ Wuerzburg, Ger, 95. *Honors & Awards:* Oliver E Buckley Prize, 60; Davisson Germer Prize, 77; Nat Medal Sci, President US, 88; Feenberg Medal, 91. *Prof Exp:* Instr physics, Harvard Univ, Cambridge, Mass, 48-50; prof, Carnegie-Mellon Inst, Pittsburgh Pa, 50-60. *Concurrent Pos:* Nat Res Coun fel, Copenhaagen, 50-51, Oersted fel, 51-52, sr NSF fel, Imperial Col, 58; NSF sr fel, Univ Paris, 67; Guggenheim fel, 63; vis prof, Superior Normal School, Paris, 63-64 & Hebrew Univ, Jerusalem, 70; Battelle distinguished vis prof, Univ Wash, 74; mem solid state sci panel, Nat Acad Sci; ed, J Non-Metals & J Physics & Chem of Solids; vis scholar, Univ Pa, Univ Mich, Univ Wash, Seattle, Univ

Paris, Univ Copenhaagen, Univ Jerusalem, Imp Col, London, ETH, Zurich, 58-85; consult, Westinghouse Res Lab, 53-57, Bell Tel Labs, 53-66, Gen Atomic, 60-72, IBM, 78; mem, Brookhaven Nat Labs, Argonne Nat Labs, Oak Ridge Nat Labs, Int Adv Comt Strongly Interacting Plasmas. *Mem:* Nat Acad Sci; fel Am Acad Arts & Sci; fel Am Phys Soc; Int Acad Quantum Molecular Sci. *Res:* Theory of solids; surface physics; collision theory; theory of surfaces, chemisorption, physisorption, electron theory of metals, density functional theory. *Mailing Add:* Dept Physics Univ Calif Santa Barbara CA 93106. *Fax:* 805-893-3307; *E-Mail:* kohn@physics.ucsb.edu

KOHNHORST, EARL EUGENE, MANUFACTURING RESEARCH DEVELOPMENT & ENGINEERING, PURCHASING & LOGISTICS. *Current Pos:* OPERS DIR, BRIT AM TOBACCO HOLDINGS LTD, 95- *Personal Data:* b Louisville, Ky, Apr, 15, 47; m 72, Mary L Pierce; c 1. *Educ:* Univ Louisville, BChE, 70, MSChE, 71. *Prof Exp:* Process engr, Brown & Williamson Tobacco Corp, 71-76, mgr, Develop Ctr, 76-79, dir mfg planning & eng, 80-87, vpres planning, Batus, 87-89, exec vpres, 89-93, exec vpres & chief operating officer, 93-95. *Concurrent Pos:* Bd mem, Coop Ctr Sci Res Rel Tobacco. *Mem:* Am Inst Chem Engrs. *Res:* Catalytic conversion of nitric oxides using rare earth catalysts; determining mechanisms and kinetic rate equations. *Mailing Add:* Brit Am Tobacco Holdings Ltd Millbank Knowle Green Staines Middlesex TW18 1DY England

KOHONEN, TEUVO KALEVI, INTERDISCIPLINARY SCIENCE. *Current Pos:* res prof, 75-78, RES PROF, ACAD FINLAND, 80- *Personal Data:* b Lauritsala, Finland, July 11, 34; m 59, Elvi A Trast; c Virpi, Eevi, Jussi & Jukka. *Educ:* Helsinki Univ Technol, dipl, 57, licentiate tech, 60, DEng(physics), 62. *Hon Degrees:* PhD, Univ York, Eng, 92, Abo Acad, Finland, 93. *Honors & Awards:* Knight First Class, White Rose of Finland, 76; Comdr, Lion of Finland, 87; Neural Networks Pioneer Award, Inst Elec & Electronics Engrs, 91; Tech Achievement Award, Inst Elec & Electronics Engrs Signal Processing Soc, 95; Centennial Prize, Finnish Asn Grad Engrs, 96; King Sun Fu Prize, 96. *Prof Exp:* Teaching asst physics, Helsinki Univ Technol, 57-59, asst prof physics, 63-65, prof tech physics, 65-93; res assoc, Finnish Atomic Energy Comn, 59-62. *Concurrent Pos:* Vis prof, Univ Wash, 68-69. *Mem:* Fel Inst Elec & Electronics Engrs; Europ Neural Network Soc (pres, 91-92); Int Asn Pattern Recognition; Int Neural Network Soc; Europ Acad Sci; Finnish Acad Sci; Finnish Acad Eng Sci; hon mem Pattern Recognition Soc Finland; Finnish Soc Med Physics & Med Eng; Brain Res Soc Finland. *Mailing Add:* Lab Comput & Info Sci Helsinki Univ Tech Rakentajanaukio 2 C Espoo FIN-02150 Finland

KOHOUT, FREDERICK CHARLES, III, LUBRICATION SCIENCE, ENVIRONMENTAL SCIENCE. *Current Pos:* Mem staff, Mobil Res & Develop, Cent Res Div, 66-73, mem staff, Prod Res Div, 73-81, mgr comp res & environ serv, 81-88, mgr, Res Ser Div, 88-93, RES CONSULT, RES SER DIV, MOBIL RES & DEVELOP, PAULSBORO LAB, 88- *Personal Data:* b Flint, Mich, June 19, 40; m 61; c 3. *Educ:* Mich State Univ, BS, 62; Pa State Univ, PhD(phys chem), 66. *Mem:* Am Chem Soc; Am Soc Lubrication Engrs. *Res:* Development of marine diesel lubricants, gear lubricants and greases; analytical chemistry of petroleum streams and products; environmental science; groundwater. *Mailing Add:* 305 Seneca Dr Wenonah NJ 08090

KOHRMAN, ARTHUR FISHER, PEDIATRICS. *Current Pos:* PROF PEDIAT, CHILDREN'S MEM HOSP, NORTHWESTERN UNIV, 97- *Personal Data:* b Cleveland, Ohio, Dec 19, 34; m 55, Claire; c Deborah, Benjamin, Ellen & Rachel. *Educ:* Univ Chicago, BA & BS, 55; Western Res Univ, MD, 59. *Prof Exp:* NIH trainee & spec fel pediat, Stanford Univ, 65-68; from asst prof to prof, Col Human Med, Mich State Univ, 68- 81, assoc dean educ prog & prof med educ res & develop, 77-80; prof & assoc chmn, Dept Pediat, Pritzker Sch Med, Univ Chicago, 81-96; pres, La Rabida Children's Hosp & Res Ctr, 81- 96. *Concurrent Pos:* Prof biol sci, Col Div, Univ Chicago, 85-97. *Mem:* Lawson Wilkins Pediat Endocrinol Soc; Am Acad Pediat; Am Pediat Soc; Soc Pediat Res; Soc Health & Human Values. *Res:* Childhood chronic disease and health policy; developmental endocrinology and biochemistry; effects of environmental agents on human development. *Mailing Add:* Children's Mem Hosp 2300 Childrens Plaza Chicago IL 60614

KOHRT, CARL FREDRICK, SURFACE SCIENCE, PHOTOGRAPHIC IMAGING SCIENCES. *Current Pos:* sr scientist, Res Labs, Eastman Kodak Co, 71-76, lab head, Color-Photog Res Div, 76-82, asst div dir, Instant Photog Res Div, 82-83, analyst, Corp Strategic Planning Off, 83, asst exec vpres, Corp Staff, 84-85, div dir, Hybrid Imaging Systs Div, 85-87, group lab dir, Photog Res Labs, 87-90, VPRES & GEN MGR, HEALTH SCI DIV, EASTMAN KODAK CO, 91- *Personal Data:* b Normal, Ill, Dec 18, 43; m 62, Lynne McCartney; c Kristopher, Brian & Jason. *Educ:* Furman Univ, BS, 65; Univ Chicago, PhD(phys chem), 71; Mass Inst Technol, MS, 91. *Prof Exp:* Fel, James Frank Inst, Univ Chicago, 70-71; Sloan fel, Sloan Sch Mgt, Mass Inst Technol, 90-91. *Res:* Focus on heterogeneous catalysis or thermal catalysis to generate dyes or other photographically useful species; developed photographic quality sublimation thermal imaging systems and other digital imaging systems. *Mailing Add:* 45 Hilltop Dr Pittsford NY 14534. *Fax:* 716-724-6505

KOHUT, ROBERT JOHN, POLLUTION EFFECTS ON VEGETATION, VEGETATION STRESS. *Current Pos:* RES ASSOC, BOYCE THOMPSON INST, CORNELL UNIV, 80- *Personal Data:* b Cannonsburg, Pa, Nov 19, 43. *Educ:* Pa State Univ, BS, 65, MS, 72, PhD(plant path), 75. *Prof Exp:* Res fel, Dept Plant Path, Univ Minn, 75-77; plant pathologist, Environ Res & Technol, 77-80. *Concurrent Pos:* Affil fac, Dept Plant Path, Colo State Univ, 78-80; comt mem, Colo Gov Air Pollution Tech Working Comt, 79-80, Toxic Substances Subcomt, Environ Protection Agency Sci Adv Bd, 80- *Mem:* Am Phytopath Soc; Air Pollution Control Asn; Sigma Xi. *Res:* Field and laboratory research evaluating the effects of air pollutants on growth and yield of agricultural crops, trees and on native plants and plant communities. *Mailing Add:* 214 Eastern Heights Dr Ithaca NY 14850-6304

KOIDE, FRANK T, BIOMEDICAL & ELECTRONICS ENGINEERING. *Current Pos:* assoc prof elec eng, 69-74, assoc prof physiol, 72-74, PROF ELEC ENG & PHYSIOL, UNIV HAWAII, 74- *Personal Data:* b Honolulu, Hawaii, Dec 25, 35; c Julie & Cheryl. *Educ:* Univ Ill, BSEE, 58; Clarkson Univ, MS, 61; Univ Iowa, PhD(physiol), 66. *Prof Exp:* Engr res div, Collins Radio Co, 59-61; asst prof elec eng, physiol & biomed eng, Iowa State Univ, 66-68; prin res scientist, Life Sci Div, Technol Inc, Tex, 68-69. *Concurrent Pos:* Instr, Cedar Rapids Adult Educ, 60-61; consult, Collins Radio Co, 61-63; NASA-Am Soc Eng Educ fac fel, 67; consult, Shared Clin Eng Servs Hawaii & Acupuncture Asn Hawaii, 74-; external examr, Chinese Univ Hong Kong, 77- *Mem:* Inst Elec & Electronics Engrs; Sigma Xi. *Res:* Application of engineering techniques in solution of biomedical problems; membrane physiology; electrophysiology; nerve; bioinstrumentation; operational amplifiers; electronic circuits. *Mailing Add:* Dept Elec Eng Univ Hawaii 2540 Dole St Honolulu HI 96822. *Fax:* 808-956-3427; *E-Mail:* koide@spactra.eng.hawaii.edu

KOIDE, ROGER TAI, PLANT PHYSIOLOGICAL ECOLOGY. *Current Pos:* from asst prof to assoc prof, 86-96, PROF PLANT ECOL, PA STATE UNIV, 96- *Personal Data:* b Berkeley, Calif, Dec 14, 57; m 79; c 2. *Educ:* Pomona Col, BA, 80; Univ Calif, Berkeley, PhD(bot), 84. *Prof Exp:* Postdoctoral res affil plant ecol, Stanford Univ, 84-86. *Concurrent Pos:* NSF presidential young investr award, 87; Fulbright sr scholar. *Mem:* Ecol Soc Am; Bot Soc Am; Am Soc Plant Physiologists; AAAS. *Res:* Plant physiological ecology; nutrient ecology; reproductive biology; mycorrhizal symbiosis. *Mailing Add:* 285 Leawood Lane State College PA 16803. *Fax:* 814-863-6139; *E-Mail:* rxk13@psu.edu

KOIDE, SAMUEL SABURO, BIOCHEMISTRY, INTERNAL MEDICINE. *Current Pos:* asst dir biomed div, 65-70, ASSOC DIR & SR SCIENTIST, CTR FOR BIOMED RES, POP COUN, ROCKEFELLER UNIV, 70- *Personal Data:* b Honolulu, Hawaii, Oct 6, 23; m 60; c 3. *Educ:* Univ Hawaii, BS, 45; Northwestern Univ, MD, 53, MS, 54, PhD(biochem), 60. *Honors & Awards:* Joseph A Capps Prize Med Res, 58. *Prof Exp:* Assoc, Sloan-Kettering Inst, 60-65, asst prof biochem, 64-65. *Concurrent Pos:* Asst prof, Cornell Univ, 61-65; Nat Inst Arthritis & Metab Dis career develop award, 63-65. *Mem:* Biochem Soc; Endocrine Soc; Am Col Physicians; Am Soc Biol Chemists; Soc Exp Biol & Med; Am Col Physicians. *Res:* Signal transduction system in genetics; immunobiology of sperm; causation of unexplained infertility; reproductive biology. *Mailing Add:* Biomed Div Pop Coun Rockefeller Univ 1230 York Ave New York NY 10021-6399

KOIKE, HIDEO, PHYTOPATHOLOGY, SUGARCANE DISEASES. *Current Pos:* CONSULT, SUGARCANE PATH, 84- *Personal Data:* b Hilo, Hawaii, Mar 10, 21; m 48, Takeko Iida; c Donna Y (Bourg), Edgar H & Kevin H. *Educ:* Univ Hawaii, BA, 44; Kans State Univ, MS, 51, PhD(bact), 56. *Prof Exp:* Asst pathologist, Exp Sta, Hawaiian Sugar Planters Asn, 52-54; asst, Kans State Univ, 54-56; assoc pathologist, Exp Sta, Hawaiian Sugar Planters Asn, 57-66; res microbiologist sugarcane & sweet sorghum invest, Tobacco & Sugar Crops Res Br, Crops Res Div, Agr Res Serv, Univ PR, Gurabo, 66-69; res plant pathologist, US Sugarcane Field Lab, USDA, 69-83. *Mem:* Fel AAAS; Am Phytopath Soc; Int Soc Plant Path; Sigma Xi; Int Soc Sugarcane Technol. *Res:* Sugarcane pathology. *Mailing Add:* 43 Alamo Dr Houma LA 70360

KOIKE, THOMAS ISAO, PHYSIOLOGY. *Current Pos:* from asst prof to assoc prof, 65-78, PROF PHYSIOL, MED CTR, UNIV ARK, LITTLE ROCK, 78- *Personal Data:* b Watsonville, Calif, July 27, 27; m 55; c 2. *Educ:* Univ Calif, Berkeley, AB, 51, PhD(physiol), 58. *Prof Exp:* Jr res physiologist, Univ Calif, Berkeley, 58-61; USPHS fel animal physiol, Univ Calif, Davis, 61-63, asst specialist physiol, 63-64, asst res physiologist, 64-65. *Concurrent Pos:* Co-prin investr grants, Nat Inst Arthritis & Metab Dis, 63-65; NIH grant, 66-72. *Mem:* AAAS; Am Physiol Soc; Soc Exp Biol & Med; NY Acad Sci; Am Asn Univ Professors; Sigma Xi. *Res:* Regulation of body fluids. *Mailing Add:* Dept Physiol Biophys Univ Ark Med Ctr 4301 W Markham Slot 505 Little Rock AR 72205-7101

KOIRTYOHANN, SAMUEL ROY, ANALYTICAL CHEMISTRY. *Current Pos:* from instr to asst prof, Univ Mo, Columbia, 63-70, assoc prof agr chem, 70-80, chmn chem dept, 84-90, PROF CHEM, UNIV MO, COLUMBIA, 80- *Personal Data:* b Washington, Mo, Sept 11, 30; m 52; c 3. *Educ:* Univ Mo, BS, 53, MS, 58, PhD(agr chem), 66. *Prof Exp:* Chemist, Oak Ridge Nat Lab, 59-63. *Mem:* Am Chem Soc; hon mem Soc Appl Spectros. *Res:* Determination of trace elements in biological and agricultural materials using spectroscopic and other instrumental methods. *Mailing Add:* 123 Chem Univ Mo Columbia MO 65211

KOISTINEN, DONALD PETER, METAL PHYSICS. *Current Pos:* RETIRED. *Personal Data:* b Lake Norden, SDak, Nov 19, 27; m 59; c 3. *Educ:* Univ Mich, BS, 52; Wayne State Univ, MS, 58. *Prof Exp:* Res physicist, Res Labs, Gen Motors Corp, 52-58, sr res physicist, 58-69, supvry res physicist metal physics, 69-82, sr staff res scientist, Res Labs, 82-89. *Mem:* Am Phys Soc; Sigma Xi; Metall Soc; Am Inst Mining, Metall & Petrol Engrs. *Res:* Mechanics of large-scale plasticity in metals; strain hardening; precipitation; crystalline deformation mechanisms and transformations; fatigue in metals; surface hardening techniques. *Mailing Add:* 16172 Knobill Dr Linden MI 48451

KOIVO, ANTTI J, ELECTRICAL ENGINEERING, ROBOTICS BIOENGINEERING. *Current Pos:* from asst prof to assoc prof, 64-78, PROF ELEC ENG, PURDUE UNIV, WEST LAFAYETTE, 78- *Personal Data:* b Vaasa, Finland, Apr 9, 32; div; c Lilli S & Allan T. *Educ:* Inst Technol, Finland, dipl eng, 56; Indiana Univ, MS; Cornell Univ, PhD(elec eng), 63. *Prof Exp:* Design engr, Oy Stroemberg Ab, Finland, 57-59. *Concurrent Pos:* Sr researcher, Finnish Acad Sci & Technol, 73-74, MEL, Ministry Int Trade & Indust, Tsukuba, Japan, 91, Armstrong Lab, Wright-Patterson AFB, Ohio, 92-96, Wright Lab, Tyndall AFB, Tyndall, Fla, 95. *Mem:* Fel Inst Elec & Electronics Engrs; Sigma Xi. *Res:* Robotics, control of sensor-based robots, multiple robotic manipulators, fuzzy systems, artificial neural network; application of system theory and pattern recognition to biomedical problems. *Mailing Add:* Elec & Comput Eng Purdue Univ West Lafayette IN 47907. *Fax:* 765-494-0880; *E-Mail:* koivo@ecn.purdue.edu

KOIZUMI, CARL JAN, NUCLEAR GEOPHYSICS, ENVIRONMENTAL SCIENCES. *Current Pos:* PRIN SCIENTIST, RUST GEOTECH, 93- *Personal Data:* b Reno, Nev, Jan 7, 43; m 68, Jean Edman; c Emi M. *Educ:* Univ Nev, Reno, BS, 65, MS, 73, PhD(physics), 77; Ariz State Univ, MS, 67. *Prof Exp:* Res geophysicist, Bendix Field Eng Corp, 77-81; res physicist, Austin Res Ctr, Gearhart Indust, 82-86; staff scientist, Rockwell Hanford, 86-87; prin scientist, Westinghouse Hanford, 87-93. *Concurrent Pos:* Mem, Borehole Sensors Task Group, Am Soc Testing & Mat, 79-86; mem, Spectral Gamma-Ray Calibration Comt, Am Petrol Inst, 82-90. *Mem:* Am Phys Soc; Soc Prof Well Log Analysts; Minerals & Geotech Logging Soc. *Res:* Calibration of devices used for uranium detection; gamma-ray logging theory; neutron logging theory; Mossbauer spectroscopic studies of hydrides of intermetallic compounds; modeling responses of nuclear logging tools with radiation transport calculations; characterization of nuclear waste disposal sites by nuclear logging; radiation measurements to characterize contaminated sites. *Mailing Add:* 3954 N Seville Circle Grand Junction CO 81506

KOIZUMI, KIYOMI, AUTONOMIC NERVOUS SYSTEM, NEUROENDOCRINOLOGY. *Current Pos:* assoc prof, 63-70, PROF PHYSIOL, STATE UNIV NY, DOWNSTATE MED CTR, 70-, INTERIM CHAIR, DEPT PHYSIOL, 91- *Personal Data:* b Kobe, Japan, Sept 4, 24; m 54, Morimichi Watanabe; c Tsugumichi. *Educ:* Tokyo Women's Med Col, MD, 47; Wayne State Univ, MS, 51; Kobe Univ Med Col, PhD(physiol), 57. *Honors & Awards:* Medal Hon, Semmelweis Med Univ, Hungary, 79. *Prof Exp:* Fel physiol, State Univ NY, Downstate Med Ctr, 51-52, from instr to asst prof, 52-60; vis lectr, Kobe Med Col, 60-61. *Concurrent Pos:* NIH res grants, 55-90; hon res fel, Aberdeen Univ, 62; vis scientist, Univ Heidelberg, WGer, 71, Tokyo Metrop Inst Geront, 76, Semmelweis Med Univ, Hungary, 79-80 & vis prof, Univ Occup Health, Japan, 84, 89-90, 91, 93; NSF grants, 74-78; assoc ed, J Autonomic Nerv Syst, 79-; sr int fel, Fogarty Ctr, NIH, 79-80; mem, Comt Antonomic Nerv Syst, Int Union Physiol Soc, 91-96. *Mem:* Soc Neurosci; Int Brain Res Orgn; Am Physiol Soc; Harvey Soc; fel NY Acad Sci; Sigma Xi; Int Behav Neurosci Soc. *Res:* Neurophysiology; neuroendocrinology. *Mailing Add:* Dept Physiol State Univ NY Health Sci Ctr Brooklyn NY 11203. *Fax:* 718-270-3103

KOJIMA, HARUO, LOW TEMPERATURE PHYSICS. *Current Pos:* from asst prof to assoc prof, 75-87, PROF PHYSICS, RUTGERS UNIV, 87- *Personal Data:* b Japan, May 18, 45; m 70; c 2. *Educ:* Univ Calif, Los Angeles, BS, 68, MS, 70, PhD(physics), 72. *Prof Exp:* Adj asst prof, Univ Calif, Los Angeles, 72-73; res assoc, Univ Calif, San Diego, 73-75. *Mem:* Am Phys Soc. *Res:* Experimental investigation of superfluid phases of helium at ultra low temperatures. *Mailing Add:* Dept Physics Rutgers Univ Piscataway NJ 08854

KOJOIAN, GABRIEL, ASTRONOMY, RADIO ASTRONOMY. *Current Pos:* vis assoc prof, 76-80, ADJ ASSOC PROF PHYSICS & ASTRON, UNIV WIS-EAU CLAIRE, 80- *Personal Data:* b Providence, RI, Dec 11, 27; m 53; c 2. *Educ:* Brown Univ, BSc, 52; Univ Calif, Berkeley, DPhil(physics), 66. *Prof Exp:* Head theoret div physics, Div Lab Electronics, Tracerlab, 66-67; Nat Acad Sci res fel, NASA-Ames Res Ctr, 67-69; lectr, Dept Physics, Univ Mass, Amherst, 69-71; staff scientist astron, Northeast Radio Observ, Mass Inst Technol, 72-73; assoc prof, Pahlavi Univ, Shiraz, Iran, 75-76. *Concurrent Pos:* Invited guest, Am Acad Sci, Soviet Socialist Repub, 76; exchange scientist, Nat Acad Sci & Soviet Acad Sci, 78. *Mem:* Am Astron Soc; AAAS; Sigma Xi. *Res:* Radio-continuum measurements of galactic and extragalactic objects. *Mailing Add:* Dept Physics & Astron Univ Wis Eau Claire WI 54702-4004

KOK, LOKE-TUCK, ENTOMOLOGY, BIOLOGICAL CONTROL. *Current Pos:* from asst prof to assoc prof, 78-82, PROF ENTOM, VA POLYTECH INST & STATE UNIV, 82- *Personal Data:* b Ipoh, Malaysia, Nov 10, 39; m 66; c 1. *Educ:* Univ Malaya, BAgrSc Hons, 63, MAgrSc, 65; Univ Wis-Madison, PhD(entom), 71. *Honors & Awards:* Nat Agr Recognition Award, Outstanding Contrib to Agr, Entom Soc Am, 88. *Prof Exp:* Tutor, Univ Malaya, 63-65, from asst lectr to lectr, 65-71. *Concurrent Pos:* Res scholar, Int Rice Res Inst, Philippines, 64; from res asst to res assoc, Univ Wis-Madison, 68-71. *Mem:* Entom Soc Can; Entom Soc Am; Weed Sci Soc Am; Int Orgn Biol Control. *Res:* Biological control of insect and weed pests of forage and field crops in Virginia, with special emphasis on the control of Carduus thistles using introduced beneficial insects; pest management of cruciferous crop pests. *Mailing Add:* Dept Entom Va Polytech Inst & State Univ PO Box 0319 Blacksburg VA 24063-0001

KOKA, MOHAN, PATHOLOGY. *Current Pos:* SR SCIENTIST PATH, HAZLETON LABS AM INC, 78- *Personal Data:* b India, Oct 16, 38. *Educ:* Madias Univ, India, BVM, 60; RI Univ, MS, 63; Ohio State Univ, PhD(microbiol), 67. *Prof Exp:* Researcher pharmacol, Searle Labs, 74-78. *Mem:* Int Soc Vet Path. *Mailing Add:* Dept Path Hazleton Washington Inc 9200 Leesburg Turnpike Vienna VA 22182-1699. *Fax:* 703-759-6947

KOKALIS, SOTER GEORGE, INORGANIC CHEMISTRY. *Current Pos:* RETIREED. *Personal Data:* b E Chicago, Ind, Jan 29, 36. *Educ:* Purdue Univ, BSc, 58; Univ Ill, MSc, 60, PhD(inorg chem), 62. *Prof Exp:* Asst inorg chem, Univ Ill, 59-62; asst prof, Wash Univ, 62-64 & Univ Ill, Chicago Circle, 64-67; assoc prof, Chicago State Col, 67-69; assoc prof inorg chem, William Rainey Harper Col, 69-91. *Concurrent Pos:* Consult, Col Bd Advan Placement Chem Exam, Income Tax Planning. *Mem:* AAAS; Am Chem Soc; Royal Soc Chem; Am Col Sports Med. *Res:* Synthesis and chemical properties of inorganic ring structures; analysis of electron delocalization in heterocyclic compounds; phosphonitrilic compounds and their applications. *Mailing Add:* 1476 Dennison Rd Schaumburg IL 60195

KOKAME, GLENN MEGUMI, SURGERY, THORACIC SURGERY. *Current Pos:* asst prof, 67-71, ASSOC PROF SURG, SCH MED, UNIV HAWAII, 71- *Personal Data:* b Waimea, Hawaii, July 7, 26; m 53; c 2. *Educ:* Univ Hawaii, BA, 50; Tulane Univ, BS, 52, MD, 55; Am Bd Surg, dipl, 62; Am Bd Thoracic Surg, dipl, 63. *Prof Exp:* From instr to asst prof surg, Sch Med, Tulane Univ, 55-67. *Concurrent Pos:* Am Cancer Soc adv clin fel, 64-66. *Mem:* Fel Am Col Surgeons; AMA; Am Asn Cancer Res; Am Soc Clin Oncol. *Res:* Regional chemotherapy of cancer; hyperbaric oxygenation in medicine; immunology of cancer; vascular surgery; heterotransplantation of human cancer and tissue culture; transplantation of organs. *Mailing Add:* 321 Kuakini St Suite 307 Honolulu HI 96817-2360

KOKATNUR, MOHAN GUNDO, CLINICAL BIOCHEMISTRY, NUTRITION. *Current Pos:* from asst to assoc prof, 66-93, PROF PATH, LA STATE UNIV MED CTR, NEW ORLEANS, 93-; DIR, CLIN CHEM LAB, CHARITY HOSP, NEW ORLEANS, 95- *Personal Data:* b Belgaum, India, Mar 19, 30; m 63, Saroj Saraf; c Sharmila & Vinita. *Educ:* Univ Poona, BS, 51; Univ Nagpur, BS, 53; Univ Ill, Urbana, PhD(food sci, biochem, nutrit), 59. *Prof Exp:* Res assoc food sci & lipids, Univ Ill, Urbana, 59-61; Coun Sci & Indust Res Pool fel biochem & nutrit, Cent Food Res Inst, Mysore, India, 61-63; res assoc nutrit biochem, Univ Ill, Urbana, 63-66. *Concurrent Pos:* La Heart Asn sr res grant-in-aid, 67-69; Mem, Coun Arteriosclerosis, Am Heart Asn, 68. *Mem:* Am Soc Clin Nutrit; Am Inst Nutrit; Am Asn Clin Chemists; Soc Exp Biol Med. *Res:* Lipid chemistry, biochemistry and metabolism; importance of lipids and nutrition in atherosclerosis; lipids and atherosclerosis; clinical chemistry methodology; vitamin E deficiency and fat oxidation; prostate lipids; prostate specific antigen. *Mailing Add:* Dept Path La State Univ Med Ctr New Orleans LA 70112. *Fax:* 504-568-6037

KOKE, JOSEPH R, CYTOSKELETON, MOLECULAR BIOLOGY & CARDIOVASCULAR PHYSIOLOGY. *Current Pos:* from asst prof to assoc prof biol, 78-88, PROF BIOL, SW TEX STATE UNIV, 88-; VIS PROF MED, UNIV WIS, 89- *Educ:* Univ Ore, BS, 66, MS, 68; Univ Alta, PhD(cell biol), 71. *Honors & Awards:* Am Physiol Soc; Am Soc Cell Biol. *Prof Exp:* Fel biol, Univ Alta, 71-72; fel med, Univ Wis, 72-74, instr med, 74-78. *Res:* Cytoskeleton in muscle and nervous system disorders; cardiac renin-angiotensin system as an autocrine system that regulates left ventricular growth; mechanism by which striated myocytes take up naked DNA from their immediate environment; mechanism of nerve growth. *Mailing Add:* Dept Biol SW Tex State Univ San Marcos TX 78666

KOKENGE, BERNARD RUSSELL, INORGANIC CHEMISTRY. *Current Pos:* CONSULT, EG&G ROCKY FLATS, INC, 90-; PRES, TECH & MGT CONSULT, BRK ASSOCS, INC, 90- *Personal Data:* b Dayton, Ohio, Dec 7, 39; m 59, Joy C Grooms; c Dawn J & Todd R. *Educ:* Univ Dayton, BS, 61; Ohio Univ, PhD(inorg chem), 66. *Prof Exp:* Lab technician, Wright-Patterson AFB, summers 60 & 61; sr res chemist, Mound Lab, Monsanto Res Corp, Miamisburg, Ohio, 65-66, group leader inorg chem & isotopic fuels, 66-72, plutonium processing mgr, 72-77, mgr nuclear technol, 77-82, dir, Nuclear Oper Dept, 82-85, assoc dir & mound dir, Advan Devices Dept, 85-86; chmn, Gen Studies Dept, Ky Christian Col, Grayson, Ky, 86-88, vpres, Strategic Planning & Prog Develop, 88-90. *Concurrent Pos:* Chmn, Dept Energy Mgt Team for Galileo & Ulysses RTG space mission progs; Achievement Awards, Significant Overall Prog Contrib, Dept Energy. *Mem:* Am Chem Soc. *Res:* Synthesis of various compounds of plutonium for use as isotopic fuels; high temperature vapor pressure of various plutonium-oxide compounds; management of plutonium fuel fabrication and nuclear waste treatment facilities; patent on plutonium-238 isotopic fuels. *Mailing Add:* 5233 S Clayton Rd Farmersville OH 45325-9211

KOKESH, FRITZ CARL, POLYMER CHARACTERIZATION, ORGANIC CHEMISTRY. *Current Pos:* res chemist, Phillips Petrol Co, 77-86, supvr, 86-90, technol planner, 90-92, technol transfer, 92-96, CONTRACT RES, PHILLIPS PETROL CO, 96- *Personal Data:* b Minneapolis, Minn, Jan 12, 43; m 69, Judith Hanna; c Timothy & Christine. *Educ:* Lewis Univ, BSc, 65; Ohio State Univ, PhD(org chem), 69. *Prof Exp:* NIH fel, Harvard Univ, 69-71; asst prof biochem, Univ Guelph, 72-77. *Mem:* Am Chem Soc; Asn Univ Technol Managers. *Res:* Collaborations with universities, federal laboratories and other companies; coordination of work-for-others. *Mailing Add:* Res Ctr Phillips Petrol Co Bartlesville OK 74004

KOKJER, KENNETH JORDAN, ELECTRICAL ENGINEERING, COMPUTER SCIENCE. *Current Pos:* TECH SYSTS BR CHIEF, ALASKA FIRE SERV, BUR LAND MGT, 91- *Personal Data:* b Beatrice, Nebr, Feb 27, 41; m 92, Nikki Kinne; c Joshua, Angela, Quin O'Brien, Clare O'Brien & Kevin O'Brien. *Educ:* Nebr Wesleyan Univ, BS, 63; Univ Ill, Urbana-Champaign, MS, 67, PhD(biophys), 70. *Prof Exp:* From asst prof to assoc prof elec eng, Univ Alaska, Fairbanks, 70-87; comput consult, Cognitech, 88-90. *Concurrent Pos:* Vis scientist, Tohoku Univ, Sendai, Japan,

81. *Mem:* Inst Elec & Electronics Engrs; Comput Soc. *Res:* Applications of computers to real time support of biological research laboratories; computer based instrumentation. *Mailing Add:* Cognitech PO Box 80907 Fairbanks AK 99708-0907. *E-Mail:* kkokjer@ak.blm.gov

KOKKINAKIS, DEMETRIUS MICHAEL, CARCINOGENESIS, DNA REPAIR & DAMAGE. *Current Pos:* ASST PROF NEUROL, SW MED CTR, UNIV TEX, 93- *Personal Data:* b Heraklion, Crete, Mar 5, 50; m; c 2. *Educ:* Nat Univ Athens, BS, 73; Pa State Univ, MS, 75; WVa Univ, PhD(biochem), 77. *Prof Exp:* Fel med biochem, Sch Med, Tex Tech Univ, 78-80; fel, Med Sch, Northwestern Univ, 80-81, assoc path, 81-85, res asst prof, 85-93. *Concurrent Pos:* Chairman, IACUC, 90- *Mem:* Am Asn Cancer Res; NY Acad Sci; AAAS. *Res:* Chemistry of carcinogens; metabolism of carcinogens by target organs; carcinogen mediated DNA damage and cellular mechanisms of its repair. *Mailing Add:* 5320 Harry Hines Blvd Dallas TX 75235

KOKKO, JUHA PEKKA, NEPHROLOGY. *Current Pos:* ASA G CANDLER PROF & CHMN, DEPT MED, EMORY UNIV SCH MED, ATLANTA, GA, 86- *Personal Data:* b Mar 26, 37; m 61, Nancy Radford; c Ken & Karl. *Educ:* Emory Univ, MD & PhD(phys chem), 64. *Prof Exp:* Chief nephrology, Univ Tex Southwestern Med Ctr, Dallas. *Mem:* Am Soc Clin Invest; Am Asn Physicians; Am Fedn Clin Res; Am Soc Nephrology (pres, 84); Am Physiol Soc; Asn Prof Med. *Res:* Salt, water and acid-base homeostasis as examined by in vitro perfusion of isolated kidney tubules. *Mailing Add:* Dept Med 1364 Clifton Rd NE Suite F410 Atlanta GA 30322-0001. *Fax:* 404-727-3099

KOKNAT, FRIEDRICH WILHELM, INORGANIC ANALYSIS, X-RAY CRYSTALLOGRAPHY. *Current Pos:* asst prof, 69-74, assoc prof, 74-80, PROF CHEM, YOUNGSTOWN STATE UNIV, 80- *Personal Data:* b Muenster, Ger, Feb 19, 38; m 64; c 2. *Educ:* Univ Giessen, BS, 59, MS, 63, PhD(chem), 65. *Prof Exp:* Instr chem, Univ Giessen, 64-66; fel, Iowa State Univ, 66-69; instr, Boone Jr Col, 68-69. *Concurrent Pos:* Consult, Tri-State Labs, Inc, 83- *Mem:* Am Chem Soc; Am Crystallog Asn; Sigma Xi. *Res:* Structural inorganic chemistry; transition metal cluster compounds; phase relationships and stabilization of low oxidation states by formation of complexes and double salts. *Mailing Add:* Dept Chem Youngstown State Univ Youngstown OH 44555-0001

KOKOSKI, CHARLES JOSEPH, PHARMACY. *Current Pos:* RETIRED. *Personal Data:* b Chicopee Falls, Mass, June 2, 27; m 52, Catherine L Langhirt; c Mary F, Charles L & John D. *Educ:* Univ Md, BS, 51, MS, 53, PhD(pharm), 56. *Prof Exp:* From asst prof to assoc prof pharm, George Washington Univ, 56-64; biochemist, Dept Health & Human Serv, Food & Drug Admin, Washington, DC, 64-77, chief, Div Toxicol, Stand & Monitoring Br, 77-92. *Mem:* AAAS; Am Pharmaceut Asn; Soc Toxicol; Sigma Xi. *Res:* Toxicology; pharmaceutical and cosmetic product development; food additive and contaminants toxicology and safety assessment. *Mailing Add:* 4504 Maple Ave Halethorpe MD 21227

KOKOSZKA, GERALD FRANCIS, PHYSICAL INORGANIC CHEMISTRY. *Current Pos:* from asst prof to assoc prof, 68-73, PROF CHEM, STATE UNIV NY COL PLATTSBURGH, 73- *Personal Data:* b Meriden, Conn, Sept 26, 38; m 61; c 3. *Educ:* Univ Conn, BA, 60; Univ Md, MS, 64, PhD(phys chem), 66. *Prof Exp:* Res scientist, Inorg Chem Sect, Nat Bur Stand, 61-68; bd dirs, State Univ NY, Res Found, 84-91. *Concurrent Pos:* State Univ NY Res Found grants, 68 & 70; Res Corp grant, 69; Petrol Res Found grants, 70, 71-73 & 74-90. *Mem:* Am Chem Soc; Am Phys Soc; Royal Chem Soc. *Res:* Electron spin resonance of metal complexes, free radicals, minerals, low-dimensional systems and biochemical systems. *Mailing Add:* Dept Chem State Univ NY Plattsburgh NY 12901

KOKOTAILO, GEORGE T, SOLID STATE PHYSICS. *Current Pos:* VIS PROF PHYSICS, UNIV GUELPH, 83- *Personal Data:* b Willingdon, Alta, June 21, 19; US citizen; m 53; c 2. *Educ:* Univ Alta, BSc, 41, MSc, 48; Temple Univ, PhD(physics), 55. *Honors & Awards:* Sci Award, Am Chem Soc, 76; Alexander von Humboldt Sr US Scientist Award, 85. *Prof Exp:* Physicist, Ont Res Found, 41-42 & Defense Indust Ltd, 42-44; physicist, Nat Res Coun Can, 44-45, sr res physicist, Socony Mobil Oil Co, 48-60, res assoc, Mobil Res & Develop Corp, 60-82. *Concurrent Pos:* Adj prof physics, Drexel Inst Technol, 58- *Mem:* Fel Am Phys Soc; Am Chem Soc; Electron Micros Soc Am; Am Crystallog Asn; AAAS. *Res:* Radiowave propagation; cloud chamber physics; rubber physics; x-ray spectroscopy; x-ray absorption fine structure; crystal structure; anomalous transmission of x-rays and electrons; chemistry and structure of zeolites; solid state nuclear magnetic resonance. *Mailing Add:* 98 N American St Woodbury NJ 08096

KOKOTOVIC, PETAR V, ELECTRICAL & COMPUTER ENGINEERING. *Current Pos:* PROF, DEPT ELEC & COMPUT ENG, UNIV CALIF, SANTA BARBARA, RES PROF & DIR, CTR CONTROL ENG & COMPUT, 91- *Educ:* Univ Belgrade, BS, 58, MS, 63; USSR Acad Sci, PhD, 65. *Honors & Awards:* Bode Prize Lectr, Inst Elec & Electronic Engrs, 91, Outstanding Transactions Award, 93, Control Systs Field Award, 95; Quazza Medal Highest Trienial Award, Int Fedn Automatic Control, 90. *Prof Exp:* Res engr, Nuclear Sci Inst, Yugoslavia, 58-62; asst, Dept Elec Eng, Univ Belgrade, Yugoslavia, 60-64; head process analysis & control sect, M Pupin Inst, Yugoslavia, 62-66; vis assoc prof, Dept Elec Eng, vis res assoc & prof coordr sci lab, Univ Ill, 66-69, prof, Dept Elec & Comput Eng, res prof coordr sci libr, 70-91. *Concurrent Pos:* Consult, Ford Motor Co, 70-, Systs Control Inc, Palo Alto, Calif, Eused & Gen Elec Co, NY, 77-86; vis prof, Swiss Fed Inst Technol, Zurich & Univ Brazil, Rio & San Paolo Campus, 73, Stanford Univ & Systems Control Inc, Palo Alto, 78, Swiss Fed Inst Technol, Zurich & Inst Nat Info & Automation, Paris, 81, Univ Notre Dame, 84, Res Sch Physics, Australian Nat Univ, 85, Univ Rome Tor Vegata, 87, Univ Calif, Berkeley, 88, Univ Southern Calif, Los Angeles, 89 & Univ Calif, Santa Barbara, 88-89; lectr, Nat Ctr Sci Res, Paris, 82; distinguished lectr, Inst Elec & Electronic Engrs Control Systs Soc, 87; assoc ed, Int J Adaptive Control & Signal Processing, 87- & Math Control, Signals & Systs, 90-; co-dir, Ctr Control Eng & Comput, 91-95, dir, 91-95. *Mem:* Nat Acad Eng; fel Inst Elec & Electronics Engrs; Int Fedn Automatic Control. *Mailing Add:* Dept Elec & Comput Eng Univ Calif Santa Barbara CA 93106-9560

KOKTA, BOHUSLAV VACLAV, COMPOSITES OF THERMOPLASTICS, EXPLOSION PULPING. *Current Pos:* res assoc, polymers, 71-72, PROF, WOOD CHEM, QUEBEC UNIV, 72- *Personal Data:* b Brno, Czech, Apr 15, 40. *Educ:* Univ Chem Technol, Pardubice, BS, 60, MSc, 62, Acad Sci, Prague, PhD, 67. *Honors & Awards:* Bates Prizes, Can Pulp & Paper Asn, 83 & 88. *Prof Exp:* Sr res chemist, Res Inst of Macromolecular Chem, Brand, Czech, 62-67; fel, reverse osmosis, Syracuse Univ, 67-71; sr res chemist, wood fibers, polymers, Consolidated Bathhurst Ltd, Grand Mere, Que, 69-71. *Mem:* Can Inst Can; Am Chem Soc; Can Pulp & Paper Asn. *Res:* Composites of thermoplastics reinforced with wood fibers; grafting of thermoplastics with lignocellulosic materials; explosion pulping (ultra high yield pulp for paper); bleaching of ultra-high yield pulps. *Mailing Add:* Univ Quebec Pates & Papiers Recherche Ctr CP 500 Trois Rivieres PQ G9A 5H7 Can

KOKTA, MILAN RASTISLAV, SOLID STATE CHEMISTRY. *Current Pos:* STAFF SCIENTIST, UNION CARBIDE CORP, 77- *Personal Data:* b Brno, Czech, Mar 22, 41; m 70, Elena Tauc; c Robert & Theresa. *Educ:* Inst Chem Technol, Pardubice, MS, 68; Newark Col Eng, DESc, 72. *Prof Exp:* Staff chemist inorg chem res, Lachema, Czech, 65-68; mem tech staff, Bell Labs, 72-73; staff chemist res, Allied Chem Corp, 73-77. *Mem:* Am Chem Soc; Sigma Xi; Am Asn Crystal Growth; Am Optical Soc; Int Soc Optical Eng. *Res:* Liquid phase epitaxy; crystal chemistry of oxide and chalcogenide compounds; relation between structure and physical properties; magnetism; phase relations in oxide systems with respect to crystal growth; crystal growth of electro-optical materials. *Mailing Add:* 1906 SE 331st Ave Washougal WA 98671-9777. *Fax:* 253-835-8792

KOLADE, ALABI E, SPECTROSCOPY, LABORATORY AUTOMATION. *Current Pos:* TEAM MEM/SR PHARMACEUT ANALYST, NOVARTIS CONSUMER HEALTH INC, 97- *Personal Data:* b Nigeria, Feb, 52; m 77, Christianah; c 3. *Educ:* Univ Nebr, BS, 76, MS, 81, PhD(soil sci agron), 83. *Prof Exp:* Technician, MidAm Webpress Inc, 74-76; human servs instr II, Region V, Lancaster Co, 76-78; chemist, Dorsey Labs, 77-78, scientist A, 79-83; sr scientist A, Sandoz Pharmaceuts, 87-96. *Concurrent Pos:* Youth leader, Cent States Conf, 87-90; managing dir, Ataba Inc, 88-92. *Mem:* Am Chem Soc; Sigma Xi. *Res:* Instrument design; automate, validate and evaluate automation technologies for data acquisitions and processing in a pharmaceutical quality control laboratory; laboratory electronic troubleshooting; team design member. *Mailing Add:* Sandoz Pharmaceut PO Box 83288 Lincoln NE 68501

KOLAIAN, JACK H, colloid chemistry, coal gasification, for more information see previous edition

KOLAKOWSKI, DONALD LOUIS, psychometrics, human quantitative genetics, for more information see previous edition

KOLAR, JOHN JOSEPH, PLANT BREEDING. *Current Pos:* Asst agronomist, Univ Idaho, 56-69, assoc prof agron & assoc agronomist, 69-77, res prof, 77-86, EMER PROF AGRON, UNIV IDAHO, 86- *Personal Data:* b Raynesford, Mont, June 14, 22; m 55; c 2. *Educ:* Mont State Col, BS, 50, MS, 52; Iowa State Col, PhD(plant breeding), 55. *Mem:* Crop Sci Soc Am; Am Soc Agron; Sigma Xi; Coun Agr Sci & Technol. *Res:* Bean breeding and production. *Mailing Add:* 892 Sunrise Blvd N Twin Falls ID 83301

KOLAR, JOSEPH ROBERT, JR, VETERINARY VIROLOGY. *Current Pos:* CONSULT, VET VIROL, 96- *Personal Data:* b Chicago, Ill, Sept 26, 38; m 72, Carol Hoffman; c Christina R. *Educ:* Southern Ill Univ, Carbondale, BA, 65, MA, 68, PhD(microbiol), 72. *Prof Exp:* Res assoc dent med, Dent Res Ctr, Univ NC, 72-73; prod mgr virus, Armour-Baldwin Labs, 73-74; res scientist vet virol, 74-77, res dir, Fromm Labs, Inc, Salisbury Labs, 77-84; virus group leader, Beecham Labs, 84-85; virus prod mgr, Biologics Corp, 86-87, virus res mgr, Fermenta Animal Health, 87-91; virus res mgr, Biocor, Inc, 91-95; virus prod mgr, Schering-Plouott Animal Health, 95. *Concurrent Pos:* Consult com poultry oper, 84. *Mem:* Am Tissue Cult Asn; US Animal Health Asn. *Res:* Applied in development of veterinary viral vaccines for domestic and international sales. *Mailing Add:* 5642 Blackwell Dr Omaha NE 68137-2471. *Fax:* 507-392-2957

KOLAR, MICHAEL JOSEPH, DESIGN, MANUFACTURING. *Current Pos:* PROF & CHMN MECH ENG, UNIV PITTSBURGH, 87- *Personal Data:* b Cleveland, Ohio, Apr 8, 39; m 61, Anne Baldus; c Marguerite, Michael, Joseph, David & Timothy. *Educ:* John Carroll Univ, BS, 61, MS, 63; Case Western Res Univ, PhD(eng), 68. *Prof Exp:* Res engr thermal sci, Am Gas Asn, 61-62; aerospace engr, NASA, 62-69; asst prof math, Cleveland State Univ, 69-73; mgr eng analysis, Gilbert/Commonwealth, 73-78; sr prog mgr, Elect Power Res Inst, 78-84; asst vpres, Sci Applns Int Corp, 84-87. *Concurrent Pos:* Chair, Math Div, Am Soc Eng Educ, 71, Radiation Protection & Shielding Div, Am Nuclear Soc, 82. *Mem:* Am Nuclear Soc; Am

Soc Eng Educ; Am Soc Mech Engrs. *Res:* Relation between culture and success in manufacturing; new product development and commercialization; design education. *Mailing Add:* 104 Maple Heights Rd Pittsburgh PA 15232. *Fax:* 412-624-1108; *E-Mail:* majak@polar.me.edu

KOLAR, OSCAR CLINTON, NUCLEAR CRITICALITY SAFETY, PHYSICS. *Current Pos:* Sr physicist, Lawrence Livermore Lab, Univ Calif, 55-87. *Personal Data:* b Los Angeles, Calif, Sept 26, 28; m 82, Ingeborg A Brautingam; c Elizabeth L, John C & Walter M. *Educ:* Univ Calif, Los Angeles, BA, 49; Univ Calif, PhD(physics), 55. *Concurrent Pos:* Priv consult, US Dept Energy, 87-92; courtesy prof, Ore State Univ. *Mem:* Am Phys Soc; Sigma Xi; Am Nuclear Soc; Am Asn Physics Teachers; Am Soc Safety Engrs. *Res:* Nuclear physics, especially nuclear reactions; reactor physics, including criticality hazards evaluation; geophysics; seismology. *Mailing Add:* 7595 NW McDonald Pl Corvallis OR 97330

KOLASA, KATHRYN MARIANNE, NUTRITION, ANTHROPOLOGY. *Current Pos:* prof & chairperson food & nutrit, 83-86, PROF & SECT HEAD, NUTRIT EDUC & SERV SECT, DEPT FAMILY MED, SCH MED, E CAROLINA UNIV, 86-, SECT HEAD RESIDENT EDUC, 95- *Personal Data:* b Detroit, Mich, July 26, 49; m 83, Patrick Kelly. *Educ:* Mich State Univ, BS, 70; Univ Tenn, Knoxville, PhD(food sci), 74. *Honors & Awards:* Career Achievement, Soc Nutrit Educ, 95. *Prof Exp:* Test kitchen home economist, Kellogg Co, 71; res assoc, Home Learning Ctr Res Proj, Off Educ, 74-75; from asst prof to assoc prof community nutrit, Mich State Univ, 80-82. *Concurrent Pos:* Kellogg Nat Leadership fel, 85-88. *Mem:* Am Inst Nutrit; Soc Nutrit Educ (pres, 84-85); Am Dietetic Asn; Soc Teachers Family Med; Am Soc Clin Nutrit. *Res:* Interactions of nutrition and culture upon the health of the individual and family in the US and the developing world; nutrition in medicine; methods to teach nutrition to medical students, residents especially multimedia. *Mailing Add:* Family Med Dept E Carolina Univ Greenville NC 27858-4354. *Fax:* 919-816-4614

KOLAT, ROBERT S, ANALYTICAL CHEMISTRY. *Current Pos:* res chemist, 65-73, RES MGR, DOW CHEM CO, MIDLAND, 73- *Personal Data:* b Bay City, Mich, May 8, 31; m 54; c 4. *Educ:* Mich State Univ, BS, 58; Iowa State Univ, PhD(phys chem), 61. *Prof Exp:* Res chemist, Am Cyanamid Co, 61-65. *Mem:* AAAS; Am Chem Soc. *Res:* Chelation; bomb calorimetry; aerosol research. *Mailing Add:* 3370 Parkway Dr Bay City MI 48706-3338

KOLATA, DENNIS ROBERT, STRATIGRAPHY, INVERTEBRATE PALEONTOLOGY. *Current Pos:* assoc geologist, 74-80, GEOLOGIST, ILL STATE GEOL SURV, 80- *Personal Data:* b Rockford, Ill, June 9, 42; m 63; c 2. *Educ:* Northern Ill Univ, BS, 68, MS, 70; Univ Ill, PhD(geol), 73. *Prof Exp:* Geologist explor & develop, Texaco Inc, 73-74. *Mem:* Paleontol Soc; Paleont Asn; Geol Soc Am. *Res:* Stratigraphy and paleontology of Paleozoic rocks in the Eastern Interior of North America. *Mailing Add:* 614 Pittsfield Dr Champaign IL 61821

KOLATA, JAMES JOHN, HEAVY-ION REACTION MECHANISMS. *Current Pos:* assoc prof, 77-84, PROF PHYSICS, UNIV NOTRE DAME, 84- *Personal Data:* b Milwaukee, Wis, Dec 26, 42; m 67, Ann Roberts; c David & Kathryn. *Educ:* Marquette Univ, BS, 64; Mich State Univ, MS, 66, PhD(physics), 69. *Prof Exp:* Res assoc physics, US Naval Res Lab, 69-70 & Univ Pittsburgh, 70-72; asst physicist, Brookhaven Nat Lab, 72-73, assoc physicist, 73-76, physicist, 76-77. *Concurrent Pos:* Vis prof, Ctr Nuclear Res, Strasbourg, France, 78; chmn, Steering Comt, Nat Superconducting Cyclotron Facil, Mich State Univ, 78-79 & 90-91, chmn, User's Group Exec Comt, 92-93; vis scientist, Argonne Nat Lab, 83-84 & chmn, User's Group Exec Comt, Atlas facil, 86-87. *Mem:* AAAS; fel Am Phys Soc; Sigma Xi. *Res:* Nuclear reaction mechanisms; nuclear fusion of heavy ions; reactions with exotic nuclear beams. *Mailing Add:* Dept Physics Univ Notre Dame PO Box 0338 Notre Dame IN 46556-0338. *Fax:* 219-631-5952; *E-Mail:* kolata.1@nd.edu

KOLATTUKUDY, P E, GENE EXPRESSION, RESEARCH ADMINISTRATION. *Current Pos:* DIR & PROF, OHIO STATE BIOTECHNOL CTR, OHIO STATE UNIV, 86- *Personal Data:* b Kerala, India Aug 27, 37; US citizen; m, Marie M Paul; c Sunny. *Educ:* Univ Madras, BSc, 57; Univ Kerala, BEd, 59; Ore State Univ, PhD(chem), 64. *Prof Exp:* Asst biochemist, Conn Agr Exp Sta, 64-69; from assoc prof to prof biochem, Wash State Univ, 69-80, dir, fel & prof, Inst Biochem, 80-86. *Concurrent Pos:* Mem, Physiol Chem Study Sect, NIH, 84-88. *Mem:* Am Soc Plant Physiologists; Am Soc Biochem & Molecular Biol; Am Soc Advan Sci. *Res:* Structure and function of genes and enzymes involved in lipid metabolism; gene expression in fungal interaction with plant and animal hosts; plant genes involved in defense against pathogens; gene expression in differentiation and genetic deficiency diseases. *Mailing Add:* Ohio State Neurol Biotechnol Ctr 206 Rightmire Hall 1060 Carmack Rd Columbus OH 43210-1002. *Fax:* 614-292-5379; *E-Mail:* Kolattukudy.2@osu.edu

KOLB, ALAN CHARLES, PHYSICS. *Current Pos:* Supt plasma physics div, Naval Res Lab, 55-70, pres & chief exec officer, 70-78, CHMN & CHIEF EXEC OFFICER, MAXWELL LABS INC, 78- *Personal Data:* b Hoboken, NJ, Dec 14, 28. *Educ:* Ga Inst Technol, BS, 49; Univ Mich, MS, 50, PhD(theoret physics), 55. *Concurrent Pos:* Adj prof, Univ Md, College Park, 68-70; vis prof, Cath Univ Am, 65-68. *Mem:* Fel Am Phys Soc; NY Acad Sci. *Res:* Plasma physics and controlled thermonuclear research; theoretical and experimental spectroscopy; hydrodynamics and very high Mach number shock waves; electron beam research; high voltage engineering; laser development. *Mailing Add:* 8888 Balboa Ave San Diego CA 92123

KOLB, BRYAN EDWARD, NEUROPSYCHOLOGY, BEHAVIORAL NEUROSCIENCE. *Current Pos:* from asst prof to assoc prof, 76-83, PROF PSYCHOL, UNIV LETHBRIDGE, 83- *Personal Data:* b Calgary, Alta, Nov 10, 47. *Educ:* Univ Calgary, BSc, 68, MSc, 70; Pa State Univ, PhD(psychol), 73. *Prof Exp:* Fel psychol, Univ Western Ont, 73-75; med res coun fel, Montreal Neurol Inst, 75-76. *Concurrent Pos:* Dept chair, Univ Lethbridge, 87-90. *Mem:* Soc Neurosci; fel Am Psychol Asn; fel Can Psychol Asn; Am Psychol Soc. *Res:* Frontal lobe function in mammals; recovery of function following brain damage. *Mailing Add:* Dept Psychol Univ Lethbridge Lethbridge AB T1K 3M4 Can. *Fax:* 403-329-2555; *E-Mail:* kolb@hg.uleth.ca

KOLB, CHARLES EUGENE, JR, CHEMICAL KINETICS, ATMOSPHERIC CHEMISTRY. *Current Pos:* Sr res scientist, Aerodyne Res Inc, 71-75, dir, Ctr Chem & Environ Physics, 77-80, tech dir, Appl Sci Div, 80-81, vpres & dir, Appl Sci Div, 81-85, PRIN RES SCIENTIST, AERODYNE RES INC, 75-, PRES & CHIEF EXEC OFFICER, 85- *Personal Data:* b Cumberland, Md, May 21, 45; m 65, Susan Foote; c 2. *Educ:* Mass Inst Technol, SB, 67; Princeton Univ, MA, 68, PhD(phys chem), 71. *Honors & Awards:* Award Creative Adv Environ Sci & Technol, Am Chem Soc, 97. *Concurrent Pos:* Hon res fel atmospheric chem, Ctr Earth & Planetary Physics, Harvard Univ, 76-85; res affil, Spectros Lab, Mass Inst Technol, 81-92, Dept Aeronaut & Astronaut, 93; mem, Nat Acad Sci-Nat Res Coun Comt, Atmospheric Chem, 87-89, chair, 90-93, Disposal Chem Weapons Stockpile, 93-; chmn-elect, Northeastern Sect, Am Chem Soc, 90, chair, 91, trustee, 94-96; mem, Nat Res Coun Comt Tropospheric Ozone Formation Measures, Nat Acad Sci, 89-91, Comt Res Opportunities & Priorities Environ Protection Agency, 95-97; ed, Geophys Res Lett, 96-. *Mem:* Combustion Inst; Am Chem Soc; Am Phys Soc; fel Optical Soc Am; Am Geophys Union; AAAS. *Res:* Experimental and theoretical studies of inelastic energy exchange in hyperthermal molecular collisions; chemistry and physics of trace atmospheric species; chemical kinetics and spectroscopy of combustion and gas lasers; laser and spectroscopic trace gas sensors for environmental and industrial applications. *Mailing Add:* Aerodyne Res Inc 45 Manning Rd Billerica MA 01821. *Fax:* 978-663-4918

KOLB, DORIS KASEY, ORGANIC CHEMISTRY, CHEMICAL EDUCATION. *Current Pos:* PROF CHEM, BRADLEY UNIV, 86- *Personal Data:* b Louisville, Ky, Aug 4, 27; m 48, Kenneth E; c Kenneth E Jr, Ronald F & Jerome W. *Educ:* Univ Louisville, BS, 48; Ohio State Univ, MSc, 50, PhD(chem), 53. *Honors & Awards:* Chem Mfrs Award, 81. *Prof Exp:* Chemist info res, Standard Oil Co, (Ind), 53-57; assoc prof chem & head dept, Corning Community Col, 59-62; prof chem, Ill Cent Col, 67-86; dir, Prog Elementary Teachers, 89-94. *Concurrent Pos:* TV lectr, WTTW, Chicago, 57. *Mem:* Am Chem Soc; Sigma Xi. *Res:* Sugars; fatty acid solubility; petroleum chemistry; plastics; chemical education. *Mailing Add:* 7309 N Edgewild Dr Peoria IL 61614-2113. *Fax:* 309-677-3023; *E-Mail:* dkkolb@bumail.bradley.edu

KOLB, EDWARD WILLIAM, COSMOLOGY. *Current Pos:* HEAD, FERMILAB ASTROPHYS, 83- *Personal Data:* b New Orleans, La, Oct 2, 51; m 72, Adrienne Wild; c Christine, Jeffrey & Karen. *Educ:* Univ New Orleans, BS, 73; Univ Tex, PhD(physics), 78. *Honors & Awards:* Quantrell Award, 93. *Prof Exp:* Fel astrophys, Calif Inst Technol, 78-80; J Robert Opphenheimer res fel, Los Alamos Nat Lab, 80-81, mem staff astrophys, 80-82. *Concurrent Pos:* Prof, Dept Astron & Astrophys, Enrico Fermi Inst, Univ Chicago, 83- *Mem:* Fel Am Phys Soc; Am Astron Soc; Int Astron Union. *Res:* Application of particle physics to the study of the early universe; cosmology; neutrino processes in supernovae; weak interactions. *Mailing Add:* Theoret Astrophys Fermilab Batavia IL 60510. *Fax:* 630-840-8231; *E-Mail:* rocky@fnal.gov

KOLB, FELIX OSCAR, MEDICINE, ENDOCRINOLOGY. *Current Pos:* asst, Univ Calif, 51-53, from clin instr to asst clin prof, 52-59, assoc clin prof & assoc res physician, 59-68, res physician, Metab Unit, 53-59 & 68-81, CLIN PROF MED, SCH MED, UNIV CALIF, SAN FRANCISCO, 68- *Personal Data:* b Vienna, Austria, Nov 12, 21; nat US; m 68, Susan Goldberger; c Lisa & Marc. *Educ:* Univ Calif, AB, 41, MD, 43; Am Bd Internal Med, 52, cert endocrinol & metab, 73. *Prof Exp:* Asst med, Univ Calif, 46-49; asst, Mass Gen Hosp, 50-51. *Concurrent Pos:* Consult endocrinol, Calif Pac Med Ctr, San Francisco; assoc chief med, Mt Zion Univ Calif Med Ctr, San Francisco. *Mem:* Endocrine Soc; AMA; Am Diabetes Asn; fel Am Col Physicians; Am Fedn Clin Res; Am Soc Bone & Mineral Res. *Res:* Metabolic bone disease; renal tubular disorders and renal stones, including cystinuria. *Mailing Add:* 9 Starboard Ct Mill Valley CA 94941

KOLB, FREDERICK J(OHN), JR, RECORDING MEDIA, IMAGE & DATA RECORDING & REPRODUCTION. *Current Pos:* RETIRED. *Personal Data:* b Rochester, NY, May 7, 17; m 42, Priscilla P Pollock; c Carolyn K (Grafton-Pearson), Katharine K (Zwemke), Frederick J III & Merribeth K (Advocate). *Educ:* Mass Inst Technol, SB, 38, SM, 39, ScD(chem eng), 47. *Honors & Awards:* Samuel L Warner Medal, Soc Motion Picture & TV Engrs, 88; Tech Achievement Award, Acad Motion Picture Arts & Sci, 91, Technicolor/Herbert T Kalmus Gold Medal, 95. *Prof Exp:* Chem engr, Eastman Kodak Co, 42-50, sr sect supvr, 54-67, tech assoc, 67-74, proj coordr, 73-82, res assoc, 82-86. *Concurrent Pos:* Instr, Univ Rochester, 45; mem, Comt TC36, Deleg Int Stand Orgn, 58-87. *Mem:* AAAS; Am Chem Soc; fel Soc Motion Picture & TV Engrs; Am Inst Chem Engrs; sr mem Inst Elec & Electronics Engrs; Soc Photog Scientists & Eng; Brit Kinematograph Sound & TV Soc; Sigma Xi. *Res:* Physical and chemical properties of photographic and magnetic media; theory and practice of magnetic and photographic recording systems, especially from the viewpoint of information theory; production of cellulose ester and polyester films; cine film manufacture and applications; effects of radiation on motion-picture films; development, manufacture and applications of magnetic recording media; storage and retrieval of audio and visual information; international standardization; image recording and processing in film and video systems. *Mailing Add:* 211 Oakridge Dr Rochester NY 14617-2511

KOLB, JAMES A, ENVIRONMENT, MARINE SCIENCE. *Current Pos:* EXEC DIR, MARINE SCI SOC PAC NW, POULSBO, WASH, 92- *Personal Data:* b Berkeley, Calif, May 31, 47; m; c 2. *Educ:* Univ Calif, Berkeley, BA(zool) & BA(biosci), 70, MS, 72. *Prof Exp:* Res asst, Sagehen Creek Res Sta, Univ Calif, Berkeley, 70, teaching asst, Dept Wildlife & Fisheries, 70-71, res assoc, Air Pollution Resource Ctr, 71; teaching secondary sci, Hayward Unified Sch Dist, Calif, 72-77; dir, Marine Sci Ctr, Poulsbo, Wash, 81-92. *Concurrent Pos:* Proj dir, Marine Sci Proj Sea, 78-81; mem, Wash State Environ Educ Task Force, Olympia, 86-, Puget Sound Water Qual Authority Educ & Pub Involvement, 87-91, Marine Plastics Debris Task Force, 87; consult, Hood Canal Wetlands Proj, Hoodsport, Wash, 90. *Mem:* Nat Sci Teachers Asn; Asn Supvr & Curric Develop; Int Reading Asn; Nat Marine Educr(pres); Wildlife Soc. *Res:* Marine science. *Mailing Add:* PO Box 188 Indianola WA 98342

KOLB, KENNETH EMIL, ORGANIC CHEMISTRY. *Current Pos:* CHEMIST, BRADLEY UNIV, 65- *Personal Data:* b Louisville, Ky, Jan 21, 28; m 48; c 3. *Educ:* Univ Louisville, BS, 48; Ohio State Univ, PhD(chem), 53. *Prof Exp:* Chemist, Nat Distillers, 48, Stand Oil Co, Ind, 53-58 & Corning Glass Works, 58-65. *Mem:* Am Chem Soc; Soc Plastics Eng; Royal Soc Chem. *Res:* Electro-organic chemistry; electrophilic bromination and aklylation; iodine organic complexes; furan chemistry. *Mailing Add:* 7309 N Edgewild Dr Bradley Univ Peoria IL 61614-2113

KOLB, LAWRENCE COLEMAN, PSYCHIATRY. *Current Pos:* prof, 54-75, EMER PROF PSYCHIAT, COL PHYSICIANS & SURGEONS, COLUMBIA UNIV, 76-; PROF PSYCHIAT, ALBANY MED COL, 78- *Personal Data:* b Baltimore, Md, June 16, 11; wid; c Pamela, Mary (Clarke) & Richards J. *Educ:* Trinity Col, Dublin, BA, 32; Johns Hopkins Univ, MD, 34; Am Bd Psychiat & Neurol, dipl, 42. *Honors & Awards:* Henry Wisner Miller Mem Award; Joan Plehn Award Humane Serv, Ment Health Asn New York & Bronx Counties, 72; Distinguished Serv Award, Am Psychiat Asn, 83; Pioneer Award, Int Soc Traumatic Stress, 91. *Prof Exp:* Intern med, Strong Mem Hosp, NY, 34-35, intern surg, 35-36; asst dispensary neurologist, Sch Med, Johns Hopkins Univ, 36-38, instr neurol, 39-41; resident psychiatrist, Milwaukee Sanitarium, 41-42; dir res, Div Ment Hyg, USPHS, 46-49; consult, Mayo Clin, 49-54; comnr, NY State Dept Ment Hyg, 75-77; distinguished physician, US Vet Admin, 78-90. *Concurrent Pos:* Fel, Sch Med, Johns Hopkins Univ, 36-38; Markle Found fel, Nat Hosp, London, 38; consult, USN, Washington, DC, 46-49, USPHS, 54-62 & NIMH; res assoc, Wash Sch Psychiat, 47-49; assoc prof, Univ Minn, 49-53; chmn dept psychiat & dir psychiat serv, Presby Hosp, New York, 54-74, pres med bd, 62-64, trustee, 71-73; dir, NY State Psychiat Inst, New York, 54-74; dir & mem bd dirs, Res Fedn Ment Hyg Inc, 54-75, pres & chmn bd, 60-75; mem comt, Navy Med Res, Nat Res Coun, 56-59; dir, Am Bd Psychiat & Neurol, 60-68, pres, 68; assoc comnr res, NY State Dept Ment Hyg, 68-69; ed, Yearbk Psychiat & Appl Ment Health, 71-; pres adv bd, PR Inst Psychiat, 72. *Mem:* Am Psychoanal Asn; Am Neurol Asn; hon fel Royal Col Psychiat; Asn Res Nerv & Ment Dis (pres, 59; Am Psychiat Asn (pres, 68). *Res:* Psychiatry and psychoanalysis; neurology; post traumatic stress. *Mailing Add:* 232 Van Wies Pt Rd Glenmont NY 12077. *E-Mail:* lck1@columbia.edu

KOLB, VERA, ORGANIC CHEMISTRY, MEDICINAL CHEMISTRY. *Current Pos:* assoc prof, 85-90, PROF CHEM, UNIV WIS, PARKSIDE, 90- *Personal Data:* b Belgrade, Yugoslavia, Feb 5, 48; div. *Educ:* Univ Belgrade, BS, 71, MS, 73; Southern Ill Univ, Carbondale, PhD(org chem), 76. *Prof Exp:* Fel, Univ Res Found, La Jolla, Calif, 77-78; res assoc & instr chem, Southern Ill Univ, Carbondale, 78-81, adj asst prof, 81-85. *Concurrent Pos:* Fulbright travel grant, 73-76; tour speaker, Am Chem Soc, 80; mem, task force occup safety & health, Am Chem Soc, 80-; NIH/Nat Inst Drug Abuse grant, 84-85; vis scientist, Salk Inst, San Diego, Calif, 92-94; vis scholar, Univ Calif, San Diego, 92-94. *Mem:* Am Chem Soc; Sigma Xi; Serbian Chem Soc; fel Am Soc Biochem & Molecular Biol; Int Soc Study Origins of Life. *Res:* Reaction mechanisms; steroid chemistry; carbanion chemistry; electron transfer reactions; conformational analysis; mechanism of action of morphine agonists and antagonists; intra-red frequencies of semicarbazones; urazole based RNA precursors; polymerization reactions under prebiotic conditions. *Mailing Add:* Dept Chem Univ Wis Parkside Kenosha WI 53141

KOLBE, LLOYD J, ADOLESCENT HEALTH. *Current Pos:* chief, Off Sch Health & Spec Proj, Ctr Health Prom & Educ, 86-87, DIR, DIV ADOLESCENT & SCH HEALTH, NAT CTR CHRONIC DIS PREV & HEALTH PROM, CTR DIS CONTROL & PREV, ATLANTA, 88- *Educ:* Towson State Univ, BS, 73; Univ Toledo, MS, 75, PhD(health educ), 78. *Honors & Awards:* Presidential Citation, Asn Advan Health Educ, 88; Milton J E Senn Mem Award, Am Acad Pediat, 92; Freedom Award, Nat Sch Health Educ Coalition, 94; William A Howe Award, Am Sch Health Asn, 95. *Prof Exp:* Health educ teacher, Mt Airy High Sch, Sheppard-Pratt Ment Hosp, Towson, Md, 73; health educ instr, Towson State Univ, Md, 73; asst prof health sci, Univ Northern Colo, 77-78; dir eval, Sch Health Educ Proj, Nat Ctr Health Educ, San Francisco, 79-80, dir, 81; chief, Eval Sect, US Off Dis Prev & Health Prom, Off Asst Secy Health, Washington, DC, 82; assoc dir, Ctr Health Prom Res & Develop & assoc prof behav sci & health educ, Sch Pub Health, Univ Tex Health Sci Ctr, Houston, 83-85. *Concurrent Pos:* Res coun, Am Sch Health Asn, 73-; assoc ed, J Sch Health, 84-85, J Appl Social Res, 86-89, Prev Pediat, 88-90, AIDS Educ & Prev, 88-; chair, Task Force AIDS Educ, Int Union Health Prom & Educ, 87-90; chairperson, USPHS Liaison Comt, Nat Acad Sci & Comt AIDS Res & Behav, Soc & Statist Sci, 87-89; dir, Collaborating Ctr Health Educ & Prom Sch-Age Children & Youth, WHO, 91-; adj prof behav sci & health educ, Emory Univ Sch Pub Health & Ctr Int Health, 92-; US sr biomed res serv, 96- *Mem:* Fel Am Public Health Asn; Am Sch Health Asn (vpres, 88, pres elect, 89, pres, 90); Asn Advan Health Educ; Soc Adolescent Med; Int Union Health Prom & Educ; Soc Pub Health Educ. *Res:* Published over 70 articles. *Mailing Add:* Div Adolescent & Sch Health Nat Ctr Chronic Dis Prev & Health Prom US Ctr Dis Control & Prev 4770 Buford Hwy NE (k32) Atlanta GA 30341-3724

KOLBECK, RALPH CARL, PHYSIOLOGY, BIOPHYSICS. *Current Pos:* instr med, Med Col Ga, 73-77, asst prof med & asst dir hemodynamic res, 77-80, lectr physiol, 77-89, ASSOC PROF MED & DIR PULMONARY RES, MED COL GA, 80-, ASSOC PROF PHYSIOL, 89- *Personal Data:* b Wausau, Wis, Sept 2, 44; m 66, Donna Jean Belling; c Lisa Jean & John Carl. *Educ:* Univ Minn, BA, 66, PhD(physiol, biochem), 70. *Prof Exp:* NIH Res fel cardiac physiol, Univ Minn, Minneapolis, 70-73. *Concurrent Pos:* Fel, NIH, 70-73; Ga Heart Asn grant, 74-76; Gen Res Support grant, 74-76, 80-82, 84-85, 88-89 & 93-94; NIH grant, 75-78, 87-90 & 93-97; Am Heart Asn grant, 76-78, 77-82 & 87-88; Ga Heart Asn investr, 77-81; Am Lung Asn grant, 82-83, 87-91 & 94-97. *Mem:* Am Thoracic Soc; Am Physiol Soc; Biophys Soc; Am Col Sports Med. *Res:* Fatigue of skeletal muscle; fatigue of diaphragm; calcium uptake by mammalian myocardium; subcellular calcium localization in mammalian myocardium; smooth muscle contractility. *Mailing Add:* 1120 15th St Med Col Georgia Augusta GA 30912. *Fax:* 706-721-7299; *E-Mail:* rkolbeck@peachnet.campus.mci.net

KOLBER, HARRY JOHN, CHEMISTRY. *Current Pos:* res chemist, NY, 45-50, res supvr, Del, 50-66, TECH SERV MGR, E I DU PONT DE NEMOURS & CO, INC, 66- *Personal Data:* b Buffalo, NY, June 5, 18; c 2. *Educ:* Hamilton Col, BS, 40; Haverford Col, MS, 41; Northwestern Univ, PhD(chem), 43. *Prof Exp:* Proj engr, Naval Res Lab, Washington, DC, 43-44. *Concurrent Pos:* Mem body armour comt, Nat Res Coun. *Mem:* Sigma Xi. *Res:* Thermodynamics of dehydration of alcohols; crystallography; corrosion chemistry; polymer chemistry; textile research. *Mailing Add:* 807 W 22nd St Wilmington DE 19802

KOLBEZEN, MARTIN (JOSEPH), PESTICIDE CHEMISTRY, GAS DIFFUSION IN SOILS & PLASTICS. *Current Pos:* asst insect toxicologist, Univ Calif, Riverside, 50-56, from asst chemist to assoc chemist plant path, 56-64, chemist & lectr, 64-81, EMER CHEMIST & LECTR PLANT PATH, CITRUS EXP STA, UNIV CALIF, RIVERSIDE, 81- *Personal Data:* b Pueblo, Colo, Apr 16, 14; m 53, Fredrica R Jones. *Educ:* Colo State Univ, BS, 39; Univ Utah, MS, 41, PhD(org chem), 50. *Prof Exp:* Nat Defense Res Coun fel, Iowa State Univ, 41-42; asst, Univ Utah, 39-41, 47-48; anal chemist, US Bur Mines, Utah, 42-44. *Mem:* Am Chem Soc; Am Phytopath Soc. *Res:* Chemistry and mode of action of pesticides; residue analysis and development of methods of analysis; climatic and biological breakdown of pesticides; soil fumigation measurements and techniques. *Mailing Add:* 4721 Monroe St Riverside CA 92504-2327

KOLBYE, ALBERT CHRISTIAN, JR, PUBLIC HEALTH. *Current Pos:* RETIRED. *Personal Data:* b Philadelphia, Pa, Feb 15, 35. *Educ:* Harvard Col, AB, 57; Temple Univ, MD, 61; Johns Hopkins Univ, MPH, 65; Univ Md, JD, 66. *Prof Exp:* Intern med, Univ Hosps, Madison, Wis, 62; resident physician, Div Chronic Dis, USPHS, 62-65, chief field staff, Heart Dis Control Prog, 65-67, assoc dir sci, Nat Ctr Smoking & Health, 67-68, staff dir & exec secy, Comn Pesticides & Environ Health, Dept Health, Educ & Welfare, 69, dir off stand & compliance, Consumer Protection & Environ Health Serv, USPHS, 69-70, dep dir, Bur Foods, 70-72, assoc dir sci, Food & Drug Admin, 72-82, asst surgeon gen, USPHS, 71-82. *Concurrent Pos:* Consult. *Mem:* Fel Am Pub Health Asn; fel Am Col Prev Med; fel Am Col Legal Med; fel Am Acad Clin Toxicol; Am Acad Forensic Med. *Res:* Epidemiology of heavy metal toxicity, halogenated hydrocarbons; environmental contaminants; epidemiology of cancer and carcinogenesis; medicolegal aspects of clinical and epidemiological research; medicolegal aspects of malpractice. *Mailing Add:* 7313 Helmsdale Rd Bethesda MD 20817-4625

KOLC, JAROSLAV JERRY F, REACTIVE MACROMOLECULES, APPLIED MACROMOLECULAR CHEMISTRY. *Current Pos:* res chemist, Allied Signal Inc, 77-85, sr res chemist, 85-89, res scientist res & technol, 89-93, RES SCIENTIST, PERFORMANCE ADDITIVES, ALLIED SIGNAL INC, 94- *Personal Data:* b Hradec Kralove, Czech, Apr 27, 37; US citizen; c Mark. *Educ:* Charles Univ, Prague, BS, 61; Czech Acad Sci, Prague, PhD(org chem), 66. *Honors & Awards:* Czechoslovakian Acad Sci Award, 67. *Prof Exp:* Res scientist, Inst Org Chem & Biochem, Czech Acad Sci, Prague, 66-68; fel, Univ Houston, 69-70; fac intern, Univ Utah, 70-73; vis scholar, Dept Chem, Univ Geneva, Switz, 74; res fel, Chem Dept, Univ Calif, Los Angeles, 75; res chemist, Vertac, Inc, 76-77. *Mem:* Am Chem Soc; Int Union Pure & Appl Chem. *Res:* Broad-based industrial research involving synthetic organic chemistry, in particular of carboxy, amino, amido, ester and similar functionalities, biological molecules and macromolecules, intermolecular interactions, separation science, and performance materials; published 40 publications and granted 14 patents. *Mailing Add:* TPL Bldg Allied Signal Inc Morristown NJ 07962-1039. *Fax:* 973-455-2551; *E-Mail:* jerry.kole@alliedsignal.com

KOLDER, HANSJOERG E, OPHTHALMOLOGY, PHYSIOLOGY. *Current Pos:* assoc prof, 68-73, PROF OPHTHAL, UNIV IOWA, 73- *Personal Data:* b Vienna, Austria, Nov 29, 26; c 3. *Educ:* Univ Vienna, MD, 50. *Prof Exp:* Asst physiol, Univ Vienna, 51-59, docent, 59; vis asst prof, Emory Univ, 59-63, assoc prof, 63-68. *Concurrent Pos:* Europ Coun res fel aviation med, Karolinska Inst, Sweden, 58 & 61. *Mem:* AAAS; Am Acad Ophthal & Otolaryngol; Am Physiol Soc. *Res:* Aviation and sensory physiology; ophthalmic electrodiagnosis; cataract management. *Mailing Add:* Dept Ophthal Univ Iowa Iowa City IA 52242-0001

KOLDEWYN, WILLIAM A, PHYSICS, SYSTEM DESIGN MANAGEMENT. *Current Pos:* sr mem tech staff, Ball Aerospace Div, 75-78, prin mem staff, 80-83, SR SYST MGR, BALL CORP, 88-, STAFF CONSULT & PROG MGR, 91- *Personal Data:* b Ogden, Utah, Apr 23, 42; m 67, Katherine S Trapp; c Kennis & Kami. *Educ:* Weber State Col, BS, 67;

Wesleyan Univ, PhD(physics), 76. *Prof Exp:* Electro-mech engr, Xytex Corp, 74-75; staff physicist, Off Prod Div, IBM, 78-80; dir eng, Scientech Inc, 83-87. *Concurrent Pos:* Consult syst design, 82- *Mem:* Am Phys Soc; Laser Inst Am. *Res:* Remote sensing; high precision control systems; high accuracy measurements of physical constants; laser power and energy measurements. *Mailing Add:* 933 Columbia Pl Boulder CO 80303. *E-Mail:* wkoldcwyn@ball.com

KOLDOVSKY, OTAKAR, DEVELOPMENTAL PHYSIOLOGY, GASTROENTEROLOGY. *Current Pos:* PROF PEDIAT & PHYSIOL, UNIV ARIZ, 80- *Personal Data:* b Olomouc, Czech, Mar 31, 30; m 71, Eva Libicka. *Educ:* Charles Univ, Prague, MD, 55; Czech Acad Sci, Prague, PhD(develop physiol), 62. *Hon Degrees:* MA, Univ Pa, 74. *Honors & Awards:* Spec Award, Czech Acad Sci, 67; Nutrit Award, Am Acad Pediat, 86; Harry Shwachman Award Pediat Gastroenterol & Nutrit, 91. *Prof Exp:* Scientist nutrit biochem & develop physiol, Inst Physiol, Czech Acad Sci, 56-68; res assoc, Dept Pediat, Stanford Univ, 68-69; from asst prof to prof pediat, Univ Pa, 69-79. *Concurrent Pos:* Vis scientist, Dept Pediat, Stanford Univ, 65 & Dept Biochem, Univ Lund, Sweden, 67-68; prin investr, NIH prog proj, 96- *Mem:* Am Inst Nutrit; Am Physiol Soc; Am Pediat Soc; Am Gastroenterol Soc. *Res:* Role of hormonal and dietary factors in expression of normal developmental patterns of gastrointestinal functions; milk-borne hormones and their role for the neonate. *Mailing Add:* Dept Pediat Univ Ariz PO Box 24-5073 1501 N Campbell St Tucson AZ 85724-5073. *Fax:* 520-626-5009; *E-Mail:* otakar@ccit.arizona.edu

KOLE, HEMANTA KUMAR, INSULIN RESISTANT TYPE II DIABETES, CANCER BIOLOGY. *Current Pos:* SR STAFF FEL, NAT INST AGING, NIH, 92-; ASST PROF, JOHNS HOPKINS UNIV, 92- *Personal Data:* b Calcutta, India, Jan 1, 55; m 83, Sutapa K Rang; c Abhisake & Ayeeshik. *Educ:* Calcutta Univ, BA, 74, MS, 76, PhD(biochem), 85. *Prof Exp:* Indian Coun Med Res fel award, 83-85; assoc, Cornell Univ, 85-88; res assoc, Univ Med & Dent NJ, Robert Wood Johnson Med Sch, 88-92. *Mem:* Am Soc Cell Biol; AAAS. *Res:* Insulin resistant type II diabetes is common for older people; studying to design a drug which can inhibit tyrogene phosphatase, as a result insulin-receptor will stay active for a longer period and cure type II diabetes. *Mailing Add:* Nat Inst Aging 4940 Eastern Ave Baltimore MD 21224-2735. *Fax:* 410-558-8381

KOLEGA, JOHN PATRICK, BIOLOGICAL IMAGING, CELL MOTILITY & CYTOSKELETON. *Current Pos:* ASST PROF, SCH MED & BIOMED SCI, STATE UNIV NY, BUFFALO, 93- *Personal Data:* m, Wendy L Kinsey; c Kinsey & Hayley. *Educ:* Mass Inst Technol, BS(chem) & BS(life sci), 78; Yale Univ, MPhil, 81, PhD(biol), 84. *Prof Exp:* Postdoctoral res fel, NIH, 84-85; NY Univ Med Ctr, 85-89; postdoctoral res fel, Carnegie Mellon Univ, 89-92, spec res fac, 92-93. *Concurrent Pos:* Prin investr, NSF, 95-98. *Mem:* AAAS; Am Soc Cell Biol; Am Soc Develop Biol; Union Concerned Scientists. *Res:* Cytoskeletal mechanisms underlying cell migration, particularly the movements of endothelial cells during wound healing and angiogenesis; regulation and intracellular dynamics of actin-myosin interactions in non-muscle cells. *Mailing Add:* Dept Anat & Cell Biol Sch Med State Univ NY 3435 Main St Buffalo NY 14214. *Fax:* 716-829-2915; *E-Mail:* jkolega@ubmedb.buffalo.edu

KOLEK, ROBERT LOUIS, plastics technology, materials science, for more information see previous edition

KOLENBRANDER, HAROLD MARK, METABOLISM, ENZYMOLOGY. *Current Pos:* PRES, MT UNION COL, 86- *Personal Data:* b Sibley, Iowa, Oct 7, 38; m 58; c 3. *Educ:* Cent Col, Iowa, BA, 60; Univ Iowa, PhD(biochem), 64. *Prof Exp:* From asst prof to prof chem, Cent Col, Iowa, 64-71; asst to pres, Grand Valley State Col, 71-72, dean, Col Planning, 72-75; prof chem, provost & dean, Cent Col, Iowa, 75-86. *Concurrent Pos:* USPHS grant amino acid metab, 65-68, spec fel, 69-70; vis scientist, Case Western Reserve Univ, 70. *Mem:* Royal Soc Chem; Biochem Soc; Sigma Xi. *Res:* Histidine metabolism and the associated enzymes. *Mailing Add:* Mt Union Col 1972 Clark Ave Alliance OH 44601-3929

KOLENBRANDER, LAWRENCE GENE, GEOGRAPHIC INFORMATION SYSTEMS. *Current Pos:* ASSOC PROF & PROG COORDR, NAT RESOURCES MGT PROG, WESTERN CAROLINA UNIV, 85- *Personal Data:* b Holland, Mich, July 9, 43. *Educ:* Grand Valley State Univ, BS, 73; Colo State Univ, MS, 75, PhD(resource planning & admin), 81. *Prof Exp:* Owner-mgr, Natural Resource Consults, 81-85. *Mem:* Am Soc Photogram & Remote Sensing; Am Water Resources Asn. *Res:* Applications of geographic information systems to problems in natural resources planning, management and administration. *Mailing Add:* Nat Resources Mgt Prog Western Carolina Univ Cullowhee NC 28723. *Fax:* 704-227-7647; *E-Mail:* lkolenb@wcu.edu

KOLER, ROBERT DONALD, MEDICAL GENETICS, HEMATOLOGY. *Current Pos:* resident med, Med Sch, Univ Ore, 51-53, clin assoc med & hemat, 53-56, from asst prof to assoc prof, 56-64, head div hemat & exp med, 64-67, head div med genetics, 67-81, chmn dept med genetics, 81-87, EMER PROF MED & HEMAT, MED SCH, UNIV ORE, 64-, ASSOC VPRES ACAD AFFAIRS, 88- *Personal Data:* b Casper, Wyo, Feb 14, 24; m 45; c 2. *Educ:* Univ Ore, Md, 47; Am Bd Internal Med, dipl, 55. *Prof Exp:* Intern, Med Sch, Univ Ore, 47-48, resident hemat, 48-49; instr basic sci, Med Dept Res & Grad Sch, US Army, 49-50, chief gen med, 181st Gen Hosp, 50-51. *Concurrent Pos:* USPHS res fel & hon res asst, Univ Col, Univ London, 60-61. *Mem:* Am Soc Hemat; Am Fedn Clin Res; fel Am Col Physicians; Am Soc Human Genetics; Int Soc Hemat. *Res:* Medical and human genetics; characterization of hemoglobin and red cell enzymes. *Mailing Add:* Ore Health Sci Univ Ore Med Portland OR 97201

KOLESAR, EDWARD S, MICROELECTRONICS, SOLID STATE PHYSICS. *Current Pos:* W A MONCRIEF PROF ENG, DEPT ENG, ELEC ENG LABS, TEX CHRISTIAN UNIV, FT WORTH, TEX, 93- *Personal Data:* b Canton, Ohio, June 24, 50; m 76, Llinor Kropac; c Lauren M, Elizabeth A & Gregory E. *Educ:* Univ Akron, BSEE, 73; Midwestern Univ, MBA, 76, Air Force Inst Technol, MSEE, 78; Univ Tex, Austin, PhD(elec eng), 85. *Honors & Awards:* H V Nobel Award, Inst Elec & Electronics Engrs, 88; Res & Develop Award, USAF, Chief Staff Res & Develop, Washington, DC, 88; Charles A Stone Award, Air Force Asn, Wright Mem Chap, Dayton, Ohio, 89; Outstanding Engr & Scientist Award, Eng & Sci Found, E W Kettering Ctr, Dayton, Ohio, 90. *Prof Exp:* Elec engr, USAF Elec Syst Div, Hanscom AFB, Mass, 73-77, elec engr, Sch Aerospace Med, Brooks AFB, Tex, 78-82; prof elec eng, Air Force Inst Tech, Wright Patterson AFB, 85-93. *Concurrent Pos:* Co-op eng student, Hoover Co, N Canton, Ohio, 71-72; consult, USAF Sci Adv Bd, Washington, DC, 81, Johns Hopkins Univ, Sch Hyg & Pub Health, Baltimore, MD, 83, Ardex Inc, Austin Tex, 85, Foreign Technol Div, Wright-Patterson AFB, Ohio, 86- & EG&G Mound Appl Technol Lab, Mat Div, Miamisburgh, OH, 88-, Lockheed-Martin Corp, 95, Technispan LLC, Lutherville, Md, 95- *Mem:* Sr mem, Inst Elec & Electronics Engrs; Am Soc Eng Educ; Sigma Xi. *Res:* Design and development of microelectronic sensors to detect environmentally sensitive chemical compounds and to facilitate robotics potential, such as sensors having a tactile sense; microelectromechanical systems. *Mailing Add:* 4801 River View Dr Ft Worth TX 76132-1147. *Fax:* 817-921-7704; *E-Mail:* kolesar@zeta.is.tcu.edu

KOLESAR, PETER JOHN, OPERATIONS RESEARCH, STATISTICAL ANALYSIS. *Current Pos:* assoc prof, 75-77, PROF MGT SCI, COLUMBIA UNIV, 77- *Personal Data:* b New York, NY, Nov 25, 36; m, Miriam Larsson; c Alex, Lara & Angelica. *Educ:* Queens Col, NY, BA, 59; Columbia Univ, BSIE, 59, MS, 61, PhD(opers res), 64. *Honors & Awards:* Lanchester Prize, Opers Res Soc Am, 75; NATO Syst Sci Prize, 76. *Prof Exp:* Systs analyst appl statist, Procter & Gamble Co, 59-61; lectr opers res, Imp Col, Univ London, 64-65; asst prof, Columbia Univ, 65-70; assoc prof, Univ Montreal, 70-71; sr analyst, Rand Corp, 71-72; assoc prof comput sci, City Col New York, 72-75. *Concurrent Pos:* Consult, Rand Corp, 72-, NY State, 73-, Mt Sinai Hosp, 74-80, New York, 80-81; Citibank, 81-84, Int Paper, 84 & Alcoa, 88 & Merck, 90. *Mem:* Opers Res Soc Am; Inst Mgt Sci; fel AAAS; Am Statist Assoc; Am Soc Qual Control. *Res:* Quality management and control application of operations researches; applied optimization; probability and statistics particularly in litigation, clinical trial and public systems analysis. *Mailing Add:* Grad Sch Bus Uris Hall Rm 408 Columbia Univ 3022 Broadway Ave New York NY 10027-6902

KOLESAR, PETER THOMAS, GEOCHEMISTRY, PETROLOGY. *Current Pos:* asst prof, 74-80, ASSOC PROF GEOL, UTAH STATE UNIV, 80- *Personal Data:* b Bridgeport, Conn, Oct 14, 42; m 65, Mary V Mason; c Michael & Matthew. *Educ:* Rensselaer Polytech Inst, BS, 66, MS, 68; Univ Calif, Riverside, PhD(geol), 73. *Prof Exp:* Fel isotope geochem, Inst Geophys & Planetary Physics, Univ Calif, Riverside, 73-74. *Concurrent Pos:* Fel, US Geol Surv, Water Resources Div, 83-93. *Mem:* Sigma Xi; Soc Econ Paleontologists & Mineralogists; Geochem Soc; Nat Asn Geol Teachers; Int Asn Geochem & Cosmochem. *Res:* Deciphering carbonate rocks; their original depositional environments, the changes which they have undergone (diagenesis) and the chemistry of fluids responsible for those changes; investigation of groundwater resources. *Mailing Add:* Dept Geol Utah State Univ Logan UT 84322-4505. *Fax:* 435-750-1588; *E-Mail:* petes@cc.usu.edu

KOLESARI, GARY LEE, TERATOLOGY. *Current Pos:* Asst prof anat & teratology, 78-81, asst adj prof, Dept Anat, 81-86, ASSOC PROF CELLULAR BIOL & FAMILY & COMMUNITY MED, MED COL WIS, 86- *Personal Data:* b Milwaukee, Wis, Aug 5, 48; m 73. *Educ:* Univ Wis, Milwaukee, BS, 71; Med Col Wis, MS, 73, PhD(anat), 76, MD, 77. *Mem:* Teratology Soc; AMA. *Res:* Teratology, environmental and abuse drug related. *Mailing Add:* Dept Anat Med Col Wis 8701 Waterton Plank Rd Milwaukee WI 53226

KOLESKE, JOSEPH VICTOR, POLYMER CHEMISTRY, RADIATION CHEMISTRY & MATERIAL SCIENCE. *Current Pos:* CONSULT, CONSOL RES INC, 88- *Personal Data:* b Stratford, Wis, Jan 23, 30; m 51, Mary A Casey; c Robert C & Krista K. *Educ:* Univ Wis, BS, 58; Inst of Paper Chem, MS, 60, PhD, 63. *Prof Exp:* Sr res scientist, Union Carbide Corp, 63-77, res assoc, chemicals & plastics, 77-83, corp res fel, polymer sci, solvents & coatings mat, 83-88. *Mem:* Am Chem Soc; Am Soc Testing & Mats; Fedn Soc Coating Technol. *Res:* Polymer physical chemistry; high solids; polyurethane; powder; water-borne and cationic free radical radiation cure coatings. *Mailing Add:* 1513 Brentwood Rd Charleston WV 25314

KOLFF, WILLEM JOHAN, EXPERIMENTAL MEDICINE, CLINICAL MEDICINE. *Current Pos:* RETIRED. *Personal Data:* b Leiden, Holland, Feb 14, 11; nat US; m 37, Janke Huldekoper; c Jack, Adriana, Kees, Albert & Therus. *Educ:* Univ Leiden, MD, 38; Univ Groningen, PhD, 46. *Hon Degrees:* DSc, Allegheny Col, 60, Tulane Univ, 75, Univ L'Aquila, Italy, 81, Temple Univ, 83, Univ Utah, 83, Univ Twente, Neth, 86; MD, Univ Turin, 69, Univ Rostock, 75, Univ Bologna, 77 & Univ Athens, 88, Univ d'Aix-Marseille II, France, 93. *Honors & Awards:* Landsteiner Silver Medal, Neth Red Cross, 42; Frances Amory Award, Am Acad Arts & Sci, 48; Addingham Gold Medal, Univ Leeds, 62; K Award, Nat Kidney Dis Found, 63; Oliver Sharpey Prize, Royal Col Physicians, 63; Cameron Prize, Univ Edinburgh, 64; Gairdner Found Prize, Can, 66; 1st Gold Medal, Neth Surg Soc, 70; Leo Harvey Prize, 72; Austrian Gewerbeverein's Wilhelm-Exner Award, 80; Jean Hamburger Award, Int Soc Nephrol, 87; Christopher Columbus Discovery Award for Biomed Res, 91. *Prof Exp:* Asst path anat,

State Univ Leiden, 34-36; asst med, State Univ Groningen, 38-41; head dept, Munic Hosp, Kampen, 41-50; prof clin invest, Educ Found, Cleveland Clin Found, 50-67, mem staff, Res Div, 50-63, mem, Surg Div & head, Dept Artificial Organs, 58-67; dir, Inst Biomed Eng & Dept Artifical Organs, Univ Utah, 67-86, distinguished prof med & surg & res prof, Col Med, 67-97, dir, Kolff's Lab, 86-97. *Concurrent Pos:* Pvt docent, Med Sch, State Univ Leiden, 49-51; hon mem, Europ Dialysis & Transplant Asn, Europ Renal Asn & Europ Soc Artificial Organs, 86. *Mem:* Nat Acad Eng; fel Am Col Physicians; Am Heart Asn; hon fel AMA; Am Physiol Soc; hon mem Austrian Soc Nephrol; AAAS; Am Soc Artificial Internal Organs; European Soc Internal Organs; Int Soc Internal Organs. *Res:* Kidney transplantation; application of heart-lung machines; development of artificial heart inside the chest; avoidance of thrombiosis on plastics; development of blood oxygenators; new types of artificial kidneys and dialysis techniques; development of techniques for organ preservation for transplantation and visual prosthesis; development of artificial hearts, valves and cardiac assist devices. *Mailing Add:* Kolff's Lab Dept Bioeng 2460a Merrill Eng Bldg Univ Utah Salt Lake City UT 84112

KOLHOFF, M(ARVIN) J(OSEPH), ENGINEERING. *Current Pos:* RETIRED. *Personal Data:* b Goodland, Ind, Oct 22, 15; m 37, Ardis Prouty; c James A & Mark A. *Educ:* Purdue Univ, BSEE, 39. *Prof Exp:* Mem staff, Gen Elec Co, NY, 39-42, requisition engr control eng div, Locomotive & Car Equip Dept, Pa, 42-46, admin asst, 46-51, proj engr, 51, asst mgr lab, 51-53, mgr, 53-56, chmn opers res & synthesis study, 56-59, prog planning engr gen eng lab, NY, 59-60, consult eng applns, 60-63, mgr design eval, Gen Purpose Control Dept, 63-66, adminr modern eng course, NY, 66-71, staff assoc tech res, Corp Tech Staff, Gen Elec Co, Conn, 71-79; sr partner, Kolhoff Assocs, Fla, 80-88. *Mem:* Inst Elec & Electronics Engrs. *Res:* Technical resources and technological implications of legislative and regulatory issues related to environment, safety and other protection of consumers and public. *Mailing Add:* 2373 Carefree Cave Tallahassee FL 32308

KOLI, ANDREW KAITAN, ORGANIC CHEMISTRY. *Current Pos:* PROF CHEM, SC STATE COL, 68- *Personal Data:* b Bombay, India, Aug 1, 25; US citizen; m 58; c 2. *Educ:* Univ Bombay, BSc, 55; Howard Univ, MS, 64, PhD(chem), 68. *Prof Exp:* Develop chemist res, Dow Chem Co, 55-61; res asst, Howard Univ, 61-66, res assoc, 66-67, instr, Dept Pharm, 67-68. *Mem:* Am Chem Soc; Sigma Xi; Indian Chem Soc; Am Soc Microbiol. *Res:* Organic synthesis and environmental pollution. *Mailing Add:* SC State Univ PO Box 7133 Orangeburg SC 29117-0001

KOLIN, ALEXANDER, BIOPHYSICS. *Current Pos:* assoc res biophysicist, 56-57, from assoc prof to prof, 57-76, EMER PROF BIOPHYS, SCH MED, UNIV CALIF, LOS ANGELES, 77- *Personal Data:* b Odessa, Russia, Mar 12, 10; nat US; m 51, Renee Bourcier. *Educ:* Prague Ger Univ, PhD(physics), 34. *Honors & Awards:* John Scott Medal, 65; Albert F Sperry Medal, 67; Humboldt Award, 77; Founders Award, Electrophoresis Soc, 80. *Prof Exp:* Res fel biophys, Reese Hosp, Chicago, 35-37; physicist, Mt Sinai Hosp, NY, 38-41; res assoc sch eng, Columbia Univ, 41-46, instr physics, 44-45; asst prof, NY Univ, 45-46; asst prof, Univ Chicago, 46, actg chmn col physics, 47-50, chmn, 50-53, assoc prof, 53-55. *Concurrent Pos:* Res fel, Med Sch, NY Univ, 41-42; instr physics, City Col NY, 41-44. *Mem:* AAAS; Biophys Soc; Am Phys Soc; Sigma Xi; Am Physiol Soc; hon mem Electrophoresis Soc. *Res:* Photoelectric effects; Geiger counters; gas discharges; biophysics of circulation of blood; electromagnetic measurement of fluid flow and turbulence; isoelectric focusing; electromagnetophoresis; electrophoresis; cell electrophoresis; studies of vasomotion and blood flow. *Mailing Add:* Jules Stein Inst Dept Ophthal Rm 2-132 Univ Calif 1000 Stein Pl Los Angeles CA 90024. *Fax:* 310-472-0335

KOLINER, RALPH, CIVIL ENGINEERING. *Current Pos:* RETIRED. *Personal Data:* b New York, NY, Mar 20, 17; m 42, Selma Kirsch; c Charles. *Educ:* Cooper Union, BChE, 39; Univ Pa, MS, 48, PhD(civil eng), 56. *Hon Degrees:* DSc, Villanova Univ, 85. *Honors & Awards:* Lindback Award, Villanova Univ, 69 & Farrell Award, 81. *Prof Exp:* Naval architect, Philadelphia Naval Shipyard, 40-46; instr mech eng, Drexel Inst, 46-49; instr & asst prof civil eng, Univ Pa, 46-57; from assoc prof to prof civil eng, Villanova Univ, 57-83. *Concurrent Pos:* Consult, 46-; lectr & coordr, Rutgers Univ, 53-67. *Mem:* Am Soc Eng Educ; Am Soc Civil Engrs; Am Concrete Inst. *Res:* Reinforced concrete; fluid and applied mechanics; engineering materials. *Mailing Add:* 1290 Boyce Rd Apt C-230 Pittsburgh PA 15241-3912

KOLIS, STANLEY JOSEPH, DRUG METABOLISM. *Current Pos:* Sr scientist, 80-86, RES SCIENTIST, HOFFMAN-LA ROCHE INC, 86- *Educ:* St Peter's Col, BS, 67; Rutgers Univ, MS, 70. *Mem:* Am Chem Soc; Am Soc Pharmacol & Exp Therapeut. *Res:* Drug metabolism. *Mailing Add:* Hoffman-La Roche Inc 340 Kingsland St Bldg 86 Rm 814 Nutley NJ 07110-1150. *Fax:* 973-235-4795

KOLIWAD, KRISHNA M, MICROELECTRONICS, SEMICONDUCTORS. *Current Pos:* MEM TECH STAFF, JET PROPULSION LAB, CALIF INST TECHNOL, 75- *Personal Data:* b Byadgi, India, Feb 27, 38; m 67; c 2. *Educ:* Karnatak Univ, India, BSc, 58, MSc, 60; Rensselaer Polytech Inst, MS, 64; Cornell Univ, PhD(mat sci), 67. *Prof Exp:* Res assoc mat sci, Cornell Univ, 67; res assoc solid state physics, Univ Md, College Park, 67-68; res assoc mat sci, Cornell Univ, 68; mem tech staff semiconductor, Tex Instruments, Inc, 70-75. *Res:* Development of low cost silicon crystal growth technology for terrestrial solar energy application; photovoltaic devices. *Mailing Add:* 429 Paulette Pl La Canada Flintridge CA 91011

KOLKA, MARGARET A, TEMPERATURE REGULATION. *Current Pos:* RES PHYSIOLOGIST, INST ENVIRON, US ARMY RES LABS, 83- *Personal Data:* b Bay City, Mich, Aug 19, 52. *Educ:* Ind Univ, PhD(exercise physiol), 80. *Prof Exp:* Fel physiol, Ind Univ, 80-83. *Mem:* Am Physiol Soc; Sigma Xi; AAAS. *Res:* Evaluation of environmental shessors on the physiological and biophysical properties of heat exchange in humans; skin blood flow; local sweating. *Mailing Add:* Dept Thermals & Altitude USARIEM Natick MA 01760-5007

KOLLAR, EDWARD JAMES, ORAL BIOLOGY, EMBRYOLOGY. *Current Pos:* assoc prof, 71-75, actg head dept, 85-86, PROF ORAL BIOL, SCH DENT MED, UNIV CONN, FARMINGTON, 76-, ASSOC DEAN ACAD AFFAIRS, 88- *Personal Data:* b Forest City, Pa, Mar 3, 34; m 63; c 5. *Educ:* Univ Scranton, BS, 55; Syracuse Univ, MS, 59, PhD(zool), 63. *Honors & Awards:* Quantrell Teaching Award, Univ Chicago, 68, Ryerson Fac Fel, 69; Fogerty Int Fel, 78, Nat Acad Sci Exchange Fel, 78; Isaac Schour Mem Award, Int Asn Dent Res, 81; City Medal, Paris, 86. *Prof Exp:* Instr zool, Univ Chicago, 63-66, asst prof biol, 66-67, asst prof anat, 67-71. *Concurrent Pos:* Vis fac, W Alton Jones Cell Sci Ctr, Lake Placid, NY, 71-75; mem educ comt, Tissue Cult Asn, 74-78; bd dir, cranio-facial group, Int Asn Dent Res, 78-81; nat bd exam comt, Am Dent Asn, 78-83; ed-in-chief, Arch Oral Biol, 80-96; vpres & prog dir, Craniofacial Group, Asn Dent Res, 81-82. *Mem:* Int Asn Develop Biol; Soc Develop Biol; Am Asn Anatomists; Int Soc Differentiation; Am Asn Dent Res. *Res:* Experimental studies of tooth and skin development with special reference to the etiology of craniofacial defects. *Mailing Add:* Dept Bio Struct & Function Univ Conn Health Ctr Farmington CT 06032-9984

KOLLEN, WENDELL JAMES, SURFACE PHYSICS, POLYMER SCIENCE. *Current Pos:* adj res prof, 87-95, RES PROF, UNIV TOLEDO, 95- *Personal Data:* b Adrian, Mich, Feb 22, 35; m 55; c 4. *Educ:* Hope Col, AB, 64; Clarkson Col Technol, MS, 67, PhD(physics), 69. *Prof Exp:* Res physicist, 69-74, sr physicist, Tech Ctr, Owens-Ill, Inc, 74-87. *Mem:* Am Phys Soc; Am Vacuum Soc; Am Chem Soc; NY Acad Sci; Sigma Xi; Soc Automotive Eng. *Res:* Vacuum ultramicrogravimetry; gas-solid interactions; chemical physics; high temperature corrosion; catalysis; gas and vapor transport in polymers; plastic barrier packaging, surface properties of plastics; solvent sorption and permeation of plastics. *Mailing Add:* Univ Toledo Polymer Inst Toledo OH 43606-3390. *Fax:* 419-537-5019

KOLLER, CHARLES RICHARD, TEXTILE FIBERS, NONWOVEN FABRICS. *Current Pos:* CONSULT, C R KOLLER ASSOC, 82- *Personal Data:* b North Manchester, Ind, Nov 16, 20; m 44, Joan Lautzenhiger; c James, John, William, Robert & David. *Educ:* Manchester Col, AB, 43; Purdue Univ, MS, 48, PhD(chem), 50. *Prof Exp:* Asst, Purdue Univ, 46-49; from res chemist to sr res chemist, E I du Pont de Nemours & Co, 50-62, res supvr, 62-67, res assoc, 67-82. *Concurrent Pos:* Consult, Int Exec Serv Corp, 89. *Mem:* Am Chem Soc; Sigma Xi; fel Am Inst Chem; Fiber Soc. *Res:* Textile and inorganic fibers; nonwoven fabrics; condensation and vinyl polymerization; nitroparaffins; polymer and textile chemistry; fiber and textile engineering; fiber reinforced composites; engineered fabrics design and evaluation; biopolymers. *Mailing Add:* 317 Cecil St North Manchester IN 46962

KOLLER, EARL LEONARD, PHYSICS. *Current Pos:* from instr to assoc prof, 59-69, PROF PHYSICS, STEVENS INST TECHNOL, 69- *Personal Data:* b Brooklyn, NY, Dec 8, 31; m 56; c 2. *Educ:* Columbia Univ, AB, 52, MA, 58, PhD(physics), 58. *Hon Degrees:* MEng, Stevens Inst Technol, 73. *Honors & Awards:* Ottens Res Award, 63. *Prof Exp:* Asst physics, Columbia Univ, 52-59. *Mem:* Am Phys Soc; Sigma Xi; Am Asn Univ Prof. *Res:* High energy nuclear physics, especially particle physics; investigation of strange particle and pi meson properties; K meson decays; pi-p, K-p, p-p and p-d interactions using the Fermilab 30 inch bubble chamber hybrid system; neutronino interactions using bubble chamber techniques. *Mailing Add:* 19 Bernard Rd East Brunswick NJ 08816

KOLLER, GLENN R, GEOSTATISTICS. *Current Pos:* MATH GEOLOGIST, AMOCO PROD RES, 80- *Personal Data:* b Buffalo, NY, Nov 25, 51; m; c 3. *Educ:* State Univ NY, Buffalo, BA, 73; Syracuse Univ, MS, 76, PhD(geol), 78. *Prof Exp:* Geologist, Savannah River Lab, Dept Energy, 78-80. *Mem:* Sigma Xi. *Res:* Mathematical and statistical manipulation of geologic data in the area of petroleum exploration; numerous patents. *Mailing Add:* 6642 S 67 E Ave Tulsa OK 74133-1721

KOLLER, LOREN D, NUTRITION, VETERINARY MEDICINE. *Current Pos:* dean, 85-95, PROF, COL VET MED, ORE STATE UNIV, CORVALLIS, 85- *Personal Data:* b Pomeroy, Wash, June 16, 40; m 63, Kathleen Ringness; c Susan E, Michael D & Christopher L. *Educ:* Wash State Univ, DVM, 65; Univ Wis, MS, 69, PhD(path), 71. *Prof Exp:* Pvt vet pract, 65-66; capt, US Army Med Univ, 66-68; res assoc path, Vet Sci Dept, Univ Wis, 68-71; head diag & comt path, Animal Sci & Technol Br, Nat Inst Environ Health Sci, Research Triangle Park, NC, 71-72; res assoc, Sch Vet Med, Ore State Univ, 72-76, assoc prof, 76-78; asst dean, Vet Med, Univ Idaho, 78-81, from assoc prof to prof, 78-85, assoc dean, 81-85. *Concurrent Pos:* Prin investr & co-investr numerous grants, NIH, Environ Protection Agency, Health, Educ & Welfare Dept, US Dept Agr, Food & Drug Admin, 75-90; ed, Am J Vet Res, 76, 86, 87 & 89; J Am Vet Med Asn, 80-81 & 84-86; J Reticuloendothelial Soc, 82-85, Can J Comp Med, 84-85, J Toxicol & Environ Health, 84-85, J Clin Toxicol, 91; grants, Dow Chem, 80-81, Merck, Sharp & Dohme, 81-82, Idaho Beef Coun, 84-85, Warner Lambert Co, 87 & Pew Found, 88-89; mem, Pub Relations & Stand, Soc Toxicol, 81-84, Prog Comt, 84-87, Immunotoxicol Steering Comt, 84-85, vpres, Immunotoxicol

Spec Sect, 85, pres, 86, chmn, Animals in Res, 89-91, pres, Vet Spec Sect, 93-95; adm adv, WRCC-46 Ram Epididymitis Regional Res Prog, 82-; adv ed, Int J Immunopharmacol, 87-89; mem, Subcomt Immunotoxicol, Nat Acad Sci, 89-90, Comt Toxicol, Nat Res Coun, 90-96. *Mem:* Soc Toxicol; Soc Toxicol Pathologists; Am Vet Med Assoc; Am Asn Vet Immunolgists; Acad Vet & Comp Toxicologists; Soc Risk Analysis; fel Acad Toxicol Sci. *Res:* Effect of drugs and chemicals on immunity; toxicological, pathological and immunological studies of toxic substances; effect of environmental contaminants on tumor growth and immunity; development of immunopharmacology/toxicology procedures; selenium responsive diseases in livestock; pathology service; extensive publications. *Mailing Add:* Col Vet Med Ore State Univ Corvallis OR 97331-4801. *Fax:* 541-737-0502

KOLLER, NOEMIE, NUCLEAR PHYSICS, SOLID STATE PHYSICS. *Current Pos:* from asst prof to assoc prof, 60-70, PROF PHYSICS, RUTGERS UNIV, NEW BRUNSWICK, 70-, ASSOC DEAN, NATURAL SCIS, FAC ARTS & SCIS, 92- *Personal Data:* b Vienna, Austria, Aug 21, 33; US citizen; m 56; c 2. *Educ:* Columbia Univ, BA, 53, MA, 55, PhD(physics), 58. *Prof Exp:* Fel physics, Columbia Univ, 58-60. *Concurrent Pos:* Chairperson, Div Nuclear Physics, Am Phys Soc, 93-94. *Mem:* Fel Am Phys Soc; fel AAAS. *Res:* Study of hyperfine interactions at nuclei in ionized atoms or in solids; nuclear spectroscopy; nuclear magnetic moments. *Mailing Add:* Dept Physics Rutgers Univ New Brunswick NJ 08903

KOLLER, ROBERT DENE, PHYSICAL CHEMISTRY, STATISTICS. *Current Pos:* SR SCIENTIST CHEM, ROHM & HAAS CO, 73- *Personal Data:* b Sidney, Nebr, Mar 7, 45; m 66; c 1. *Educ:* Univ Nebr, BS, 67, PhD(theoret chem), 72. *Prof Exp:* Anal chemist, Com Solvents Corp, 67 & 68; fel theoret chem, Mellon Inst, Carnegie Mellon Univ, 72-73. *Mem:* Am Chem Soc; Soc Automotive Engrs. *Res:* The application of computer and statistical techniques for analysis of chemical problems arising in industrial research; research and development of oil additives. *Mailing Add:* 668 Sourwood Dr Hatfield PA 19440-3548

KOLLIG, HEINZ PHILIPP, ANALYTICAL & CLINICAL CHEMISTRY, ENVIRONMENTAL FATE DATA OF ORGANIC COMPOUNDS. *Current Pos:* RETIRED. *Personal Data:* b Bonn, Ger, 28; US citizen; m 51, Hannelore Giessen; c Monika & Frank. *Educ:* Univ Bonn, Ger, BS, 50; Fla Inst Technol, BS, 69. *Prof Exp:* Chemist clin chem, Univ Bonn, Ger, 51-57; chemist power plant chem, City Bonn, Ger, 57-59; res chemist, Univ Ala, 59-60; anal chemist microanal, Southern Res Inst, 60-68; anal chemist environ health, TWA Kennedy Space Ctr, Fla, 68-71; res chemist water, US Environ Protection Agency, 71- *Mem:* Am Chem Soc. *Res:* Ecology; experimental and computational rate and equilibrium constants for organic chemicals. *Mailing Add:* 1050 Dogwood Hill NW Watkinsville GA 30677. *Fax:* 706-546-3636

KOLLMAN, PETER ANDREW, THEORETICAL CHEMISTRY, BIOPHYSICAL CHEMISTRY. *Current Pos:* asst prof, 71-76, assoc prof, 76-80, PROF CHEM & PHARMACEUT CHEM, SCH PHARM, UNIV CALIF, SAN FRANCISCO, 80- *Personal Data:* b Iowa City, Iowa, July 24, 44; m 70; c 2. *Educ:* Grinnell Col, BA, 66; Princeton Univ, PhD(chem), 70. *Prof Exp:* NATO fel theoret chem, Cambridge Univ, 70-71. *Concurrent Pos:* Career develop award, Nat Inst Gen Med Sci, 74. *Mem:* Am Chem Soc; Am Phys Soc; Sigma Xi. *Res:* Application of quantum mechanics and molecular mechanics to intermolecular interactions and to structure activity relationships in biological systems. *Mailing Add:* Dept Pharm/Chem 926S Univ Calif San Francisco CA 94143

KOLLMORGEN, G MARK, CELL BIOLOGY, IMMUNOLOGY. *Current Pos:* from asst prof to assoc prof, 66-74, PROF RADIOL, SCH MED, UNIV OKLA, 74-; MEM, OKLA MED RES FOUND, 76- *Personal Data:* b Bancroft, Nebr, June 23, 32; m 54; c 4. *Educ:* Univ Iowa, BA, 57, MA, 60, PhD(radiation biol), 63. *Prof Exp:* Instr biol sci, Univ Iowa, 58-60, instr radiation biol, 61-63; resident res assoc, Argonne Nat Lab, 63-65, asst biologist, 65-66; asst mem, Okla Med Res Found, 66-69, assoc mem, 69-76. *Mem:* Am Asn Cancer Res; Am Soc Cell Biol; Soc Exp Biol & Med; Tissue Cult Asn; Sigma Xi. *Res:* Effects of dietary fat on tumor incidence and immune responses; serum factors which inhibit immune responses; influence of prostaglandins on tumor growth and transplantability; effects of products derived from cyclooxygenase and lipoxygenase pathways on function of natural killer cells. *Mailing Add:* 6425 W Kensington Rd Oklahoma City OK 73132

KOLLROS, JERRY JOHN, EMBRYOLOGY, CELL BIOLOGY. *Current Pos:* assoc, Univ Iowa, 46-47, from asst prof to prof, 47-88, actg chmn, 54-55, chmn dept, 55-77, EMER PROF ZOOL, UNIV IOWA, 88- *Personal Data:* b Vienna, Austria, Dec 29, 17; nat US; m 42, Catharine Lutherman; c James C & Peter R. *Educ:* Univ Chicago, SB, 38, PhD(zool), 42. *Prof Exp:* Asst zool, Univ Chicago, 40-42, neurosurg, 43-45, Toxicity Lab, 45, instr zool, Col, 45-46. *Concurrent Pos:* Consult, Am Col Dict & Random House Dict of Eng Lang; Mem, Cell Biol Study Sect, NIH, 60-64; Biol Sci Training Rev Comt, NIMH, 62-70; consult, Div Inst Progs, NSF, 64-66; Comn Undergrad Educ Biol Sci, 67-71, chmn, 69-71. *Mem:* AAAS; Am Soc Cell Biol; Soc Develop Biol; Am Asn Anat; Am Soc Zool (treas, 59-62). *Res:* Control of skin gland development and segregation of skin regions; development of behavior in Amphibia; experimental embryology of amphibian central nervous system; amphibian metamorphosis; regeneration of Amphibia; neuroscience. *Mailing Add:* Dept Biol Sci Univ Iowa Iowa City IA 52242

KOLM, HENRY HERBERT, MAGNETISM. *Current Pos:* PRES, MAGNEPLANE INT INC, 89-; VPRES, PARAMAG CORP, 89- *Personal Data:* b Vienna, Austria, Sept 10, 24; nat US; m 53, Elizabeth Cushing; c Margaret, Juliet (Gibbs), Edna (Dripps) & Cornelia (Cesari). *Educ:* Mass Inst Technol, SB, 50, PhD(physics), 55. *Honors & Awards:* Peter Mark Medal, Dept Defense, 83. *Prof Exp:* Asst low temperature physics, Mass Inst Technol, 50-54, mem res staff, Lincoln Lab, 54-60, sr scientist & lectr, Dept Aeronaut & Astronaut, Nat Magnet Lab, 60-82; pres, Electromagnetic Launch Res Inc, 82-89; dir, Piezo Elec Prod Inc, 81-93. *Mem:* Am Phys Soc; Am Inst Aeronaut & Astronaut; Inst Elec & Electronics Engrs. *Res:* Hydrodynamics of liquid helium; semiconductor surface physics; cyclotron resonance in solids; design of pulsed and continous high-field solenoid magnets; superconductivity; magnetic separation; magnetic levitation and propulsion of high speed vehicles; applications of magnetism; piezoelectricity; electromagnetic launch technology. *Mailing Add:* One Weir Meadow Path Wayland MA 01778. *Fax:* 508-358-2175

KOLMAN, BERNARD, MATHEMATICS. *Current Pos:* from asst prof to prof, 64-76, PROF MATH, DREXEL UNIV, 76- *Personal Data:* b Havana, Cuba, July 4, 32; US citizen; m 86; c 2. *Educ:* Brooklyn Col, BS, 54; Brown Univ, ScM, 56; Univ Pa, PhD(math), 65. *Prof Exp:* Prin mathematician, Univac Div, Sperry Rand Corp, 57-64. *Mem:* Am Math Soc; Math Asn Am; Soc Indust & Appl Math; Asn Comput Mach. *Res:* Lie algebras; operations research. *Mailing Add:* Dept Math Drexel Univ 32nd & Chestnut St Philadelphia PA 19104

KOLMEN, SAMUEL NORMAN, PHYSIOLOGY. *Current Pos:* DIR MED EDUC & RES, MERCY HOSP PITTSBURGH, 89- *Personal Data:* b Brownsville, Tex, Mar 20, 30; m 54, Barbara Kass; c Benita (Solomon) & Jeanette (Rosato). *Educ:* Univ Tex, BA, 54, PhD(physiol), 57. *Prof Exp:* From asst prof to prof physiol, Univ Tex Med Br, Galveston, 58-75, head, Div Physiol, Shriners Burns Inst, 68-70, res coordr, 70-75; prof physiol & chmn dept, Sch Med, Wright State Univ, 75-84, asst dean sci & eng med, 80-84; prof physiol & assoc dean acad affairs, Sch Med, Hahnemann Univ, 84-89. *Concurrent Pos:* Kempner fel med, London Hosp Med Col, Univ London, 57-58; mem, Coun Thrombosis, Am Heart Asn, res & rev comt, Ohio affil, 81-84; consult, Nat Bd Med Examr, Philadelphia, 89. *Mem:* AAAS; Soc Exp Biol & Med; Am Physiol Soc; Brit Biochem Soc; Microcirculatory Soc; Sigma Xi. *Res:* Adsorptive phenomena related to biological processes; fibrinogen metabolism, storage and distribution; lymphatic circulation; microcirculation; burn physiopathology. *Mailing Add:* 256 Sweet Gum Rd Pittsburgh PA 15238

KOLMES, STEVEN ALBERT, ERGONOMIC EFFICIENCY, BEHAVIORAL TOXICOLOGY. *Personal Data:* b Poughkeepsie, NY, Sept 17, 54; m 87, Linda Fergussan; c Sara K & Elijah J. *Educ:* Ohio Univ, BS, 76; Univ Wis, MS, 78, PhD(zool), 84. *Prof Exp:* Lectr, Univ Wis-Madison, 83-84; asst prof, Hobart & William Smith Cols, 84-89, assoc prof biol, 89-94. *Concurrent Pos:* Vis scientist, Univ Col, Cardiff, UK, 87; assoc ed, J Apicult Res, 89-91; Fulbright res scholar, Utrecht Univ, Neth, 91. *Mem:* Animal Behav Soc; Entom Soc Am; Acarological Soc Am; Int Union Study Social Insects; AAAS. *Res:* Ethology of invertebrates, specifically how ecological considerations have evolutionary shaped different aspects of behavior; concentrations are social insect division of labor, and behavioral aspects of pesticide resistance in spider mites. *Mailing Add:* 5000 N Willamette Blvd Portland OR 97023. *Fax:* 315-781-3587; *E-Mail:* kolmes@hws.bitnet

KOLOBIELSKI, MARJAN, PETROLEUM CHEMISTRY, FUEL SCIENCE. *Current Pos:* res chemist, Coating & Chem Lab, Aberdeen Proving Ground, 64-74, RES CHEMIST, US ARMY MOBILITY EQUIP RES & DEVELOP CTR, 74- *Personal Data:* b Warsaw, Poland, Aug 17, 15; nat US; m 48; c 1. *Educ:* Univ Lodz, MPhil, 48; Univ Paris, PhD(phys sci), 54. *Prof Exp:* Mem res staff, French Nat Ctr Sci Res, Normal Sch, Paris, 49-55; fel org chem, Northwestern Univ, 55-56; res fel, Mellon Inst, 56-63; res chemist, Borden Chem Co, 63-64. *Mem:* Am Chem Soc; Combustion Inst; Chem Soc Fr; Am Inst Chemists; Am Soc Testing & Mat; Sigma Xi. *Res:* Development of new products, fuels and lubricants. *Mailing Add:* 6710 Sherwood Rd Baltimore MD 21239

KOLODNER, IGNACE I(ZAAK), MATHEMATICS, NONLINEAR PROBLEMS. *Current Pos:* head dept, 64-71, prof, 64-90, EMER PROF MATH, CARNEGIE-MELLON UNIV, 90- *Personal Data:* b Warsaw, Poland, Apr 12, 20; nat US; div; c Richard D, Paul R & Eva M. *Educ:* Gymnasium Ascola, Warsaw, BA, 37; Univ Grenoble, Dipl, 40; NY Univ, PhD(math), 50. *Honors & Awards:* Fulbright lectr, Rep Univ, Montevideo, Uruguay, 67. *Prof Exp:* Asst, Col Eng, NY Univ, 47-48, asst, Inst Math Sci, 48-51, res assoc, 51-53, sr scientist, 53-56; prof math, Univ NMex, 56-64. *Concurrent Pos:* Instr, Wash Sq Col, NY Univ, 48-51; lectr, Stevens Inst Tech, 50-53, nat lectr, Soc Indust & Appl Math, 60-61 & 80-83; consult, Underwater Mine Comt, Nat Res Coun, 55; Courant Inst Math Sci, 56-60, 69; Sandia Corp, 56-68 & Lawrence Radiation Lab, 60-67; vis mem, Math Res Ctr, Univ Wis-Madison, 62; sch math study group, Stanford Univ, 65; Sussman vis prof, Israel Inst Technol, Haifa, 72-73; adj prof, Univ Pittsburgh, 76-77 & 78-79; grants, NSF, 57-60, 62-65, 71-78, OOR, 57-61, NONR, 65-69. *Mem:* Am Asn Univ Profs; Am Math Soc; Math Asn Am; Soc Indust & Appl Math; Soc Natural Philos. *Res:* Differential equations; integral equations; mathematical physics. *Mailing Add:* Dept Math Carnegie-Mellon Univ Pittsburgh PA 15213-3890

KOLODNER, PAUL R, NONLINEAR DYNAMICS & PATTERN FORMATION. *Current Pos:* MEM TECH STAFF, AT&T BELL LABS, 80- *Personal Data:* b Morristown, NJ, Dec 16, 53; m 80, Joan C Borod. *Educ:* Princeton Univ, AB, 75; Harvard Univ, AM, 77, PhD(physics), 80. *Honors & Awards:* 1-R100 Award, 85. *Mem:* Am Phys Soc. *Res:* Nonlinear dynamics and pattern formation, specifically, convection in binary fluids. *Mailing Add:* AT&T Bell Labs Rm 1E-446 600 Mountain Ave Murray Hill NJ 07974-0636

KOLODNER, RICHARD DAVID, MOLECULAR BIOLOGY. *Current Pos:* Res fel molecular biol, 75-78, from asst prof to assoc prof, 79-88, PROF BIOCHEM & MOLECULAR PHARMACOL, SCH MED & DANA-FARBER CANCER INST, HARVARD UNIV, 88- *Personal Data:* b Morristown, NJ, Apr 3, 51. *Educ:* Univ Calif, Irvine, BS, 71, PhD(biol), 75. *Hon Degrees:* BSc, Harvard Univ, 88. *Concurrent Pos:* Fel, Cystic Fibrosis Found, 75-76 & NIH, 76-78; jr fac res award, Am Cancer Soc, 81-83, fac res award, 88-89. *Mem:* Am Soc Biol Chemists; Am Soc Microbiol; Genetics Soc Am. *Res:* Enzymatic and molecular mechanism of genetic recombination in procaryotes and eucaryotes; DNA structure; cancer genetics. *Mailing Add:* Dept Cell Molecular Biol Dana 830 Dana-Farber Cancer Inst 44 Binney St Boston MA 02215-6084

KOLODNY, GERALD MORDECAI, RADIOLOGY. *Current Pos:* DIR, DIV NUCLEAR MED, BETH ISRAEL HOSP, 79- *Personal Data:* b Brookline, Mass, Apr 22, 37; m 64; c 3. *Educ:* Harvard Univ, AB, 58; Northwestern Univ, Chicago, MD, 62; Am Bd Radiol, dipl, 67; Am Bd Nuclear Med, dipl, 74. *Prof Exp:* Intern med, Stanford Univ Med Ctr, 62-63; resident radiol, Mass Gen Hosp, 63-66; Picker Found fel biol, Mass Inst Technol, 66-69; asst radiologist, Mass Gen Hosp, 69-75, assoc radiologist & dir, Radiol Res Lab, 75-79; from instr to asst prof, 69-75, ASSOC PROF RADIOL, HARVARD MED SCH, 75- *Concurrent Pos:* Picker Found grant, 69-71; res assoc biochem, Huntington Labs, Harvard Univ, 69-70, assoc chmn curric, Div Med Sci, 74- *Mem:* Am Soc Cell Biol; Tissue Cult Asn; Inst Elec & Electronics Engrs; Soc Nuclear Med; Radiol Soc NAm. *Res:* Gene regulation; RNA biochemistry; cell to cell communication; contact inhibition; electronics and computers in medicine; nuclear medicine; cellular radiation biology. *Mailing Add:* Div Nuclear Med Beth Israel Hosp 330 Brookline Ave Boston MA 02215-5491

KOLODNY, NANCY HARRISON, PHYSICAL BIOCHEMISTRY. *Current Pos:* Dean, Class of 76, Wellesley Col, 72-74, dir, Sci Ctr, 74-77, from asst prof to assoc prof, 69-85, PROF CHEM, WELLESLEY COL, 85- *Personal Data:* b Brooklyn, NY, Mar 30, 44; m 64; c 3. *Educ:* Wellesley Col, BA, 64; Mass Inst Technol, PhD(phys chem), 69. *Concurrent Pos:* Radcliffe Inst scholar, 70-72; res fel med, Mass Gen Hosp, Boston, 71-72; res assoc & lectr ophthal, Mass Eye & Ear Infirmary, Harvard Med Sch, Boston, 84- *Mem:* Am Chem Soc; Sigma Xi. *Res:* Electron spin resonance spectroscopy of charge transfer complexes in solution; nuclear magnetic resonance spectroscopy of protein-nucleic acid interactions; magnetic resonance imaging and spectroscopy of ocular disorders. *Mailing Add:* 124 Dartmouth St West Newton MA 02165-2839

KOLODZIEJ, BRUNO J, MICROBIOLOGY, MICROBIAL PHYSIOLOGY. *Personal Data:* b Chicago, Ill, Aug 27, 34; wid; c B Allen, John A & Joy A. *Educ:* Northern Ill Univ, BSEd, 58; Northwestern Univ, MS, 60, PhD(biol), 63. *Prof Exp:* NIH fel microbial physiol, Univ Chicago, 63-65; res assoc, Albert Einstein Med Ctr, Pa, 65-66; from asst prof to assoc prof microbiol, Ohio State Univ, 66-93. *Mem:* AAAS; Am Soc Microbiol; Sigma Xi. *Res:* Elucidation and characterization of bacterial cell surface components with emphasis on membrane binding-transport proteins associated with sugar and amino acid transport and structure and function of exocellular capsule material. *Mailing Add:* 3816 Longton Dr Columbus OH 43221. *Fax:* 614-292-1538

KOLODZIEJSKI, LESLIE ANN, ELECTRONIC MATERIALS, OPTOELECTRONIC DEVICES. *Current Pos:* asst prof elec eng, 88-93, ASSOC PROF ELEC ENG, MASS INST TECHNOL, 93- *Personal Data:* b Ft Leonard Wood, Mo, July 31, 58; m 79. *Educ:* Purdue Univ, BSc, 83, MS, 84, PhD(elec eng), 86. *Prof Exp:* Asst prof elec eng, Purdue Univ, 86-88. *Concurrent Pos:* NSF presidential young investr & Off Naval Res young investr, 87. *Mem:* Am Phys Soc; Mat Res Soc; Optical Soc Am; Inst Elec & Electronics Engrs. *Res:* Fabrication of thin film semiconductors, such as zine-selenium and gallium-arsenic, which are layered to form sophisticated heterostructures. *Mailing Add:* Mass Inst Technol Rm 13-3065 77 Massachusetts Ave Cambridge MA 02139

KOLODZY, PAUL JOHN, NEURAL NETWORKS, SMART SENSORS. *Current Pos:* Staff mem, opto-radar systs, 86-89, ASST GROUP LEADER, NEURAL NETWORKS, MASS INST TECHNOL LINCOLN LAB, 89- *Personal Data:* b Akron, Ohio, Aug, 1959; m 86; c 1. *Educ:* Purdue Univ, BS, 83; Case Western Res Univ, MS, 84, PhD(chem eng), 86. *Concurrent Pos:* Co-chair, Simulation Panel, DARPA Neural Network Study, 88-89. *Res:* Develop and exploit neural network techniques for active and passive optical sensors; design and model optical sensor systems; advanced simulation technology. *Mailing Add:* 25 Deerhaven Dr Nashua NH 03060

KOLOPAJLO, LAWRENCE HUGH, PHYSICAL-ANALYTICAL CHEMISTRY, CHEMICAL KINETICS. *Current Pos:* STAFF MEM, ST MARY'S COL, ORCHARD LAKE, MICH, 94- *Personal Data:* b Steubenville, Ohio, Dec 27, 50; m 80; c 1. *Educ:* Muskingum Col, BS, 74; Pa State Univ, MS, 78; Wester Mich Univ, PhD(chem), 82. *Prof Exp:* Chemist, Dow Chem Co, 76-77; qual control, Allied Paper Co, SCM, 78-80; res assoc, State Univ NY, Buffalo, 82-84; asst prof phys chem, Claflin Col, 84-85; asst prof phys & analytical chem, Marietta Col, 85-88; team leader, oh mat, Environ Qual Labs, 88-92, supvr, 92-94. *Concurrent Pos:* Instr, Univ SC, 85. *Mem:* Am Chem Soc. *Res:* Coordination chemistry; kinetics and mechanisms of complex formation and ligand exchange reactions carried out in solution. *Mailing Add:* 347 Yorkshire Newport MI 48166

KOLP, BERNARD J, AGRONOMY, PLANT BREEDING. *Current Pos:* RETIRED. *Personal Data:* b Caroll, Iowa, Oct 20, 28; m 52; c 3. *Educ:* Iowa State Univ, BS, 54; Kans State Univ, MS, 55, PhD, 58. *Prof Exp:* Asst prof agron, Univ Wyo, 57-70, prof plant breeding, 70-86. *Res:* Drought resistance and emergence of wheat; nitrate content in oats; winter hardiness in wheat. *Mailing Add:* 1808 Ord St Laramie WY 82070

KOLSKI, THADDEUS L(EONARD), INORGANIC CHEMISTRY. *Current Pos:* RETIRED. *Personal Data:* b Chicago, Ill, Nov 29, 28; m 55, Ann Miller; c Lynda & Patricia. *Educ:* Ill Inst Technol, BS, 50; St Louis Univ, MS, 54, PhD(inorg chem), 57. *Prof Exp:* Res chemist, E I du Pont de Nemours Co, Inc, 56-85. *Concurrent Pos:* Ed, High-Solids Coatings, 79-81. *Res:* Oxidation of niobium and niobium alloys; anodic characteristics of tantalum and niobium; electrolytic capacitators; surface and boron chemistry; white and colored pigments. *Mailing Add:* 1116 Graylyn Rd Chatham Wilmington DE 19803

KOLSKY, HARWOOD GEORGE, PHYSICS, COMPUTER ENGINEERING. *Current Pos:* prof, 85-91, EMER PROF COMPUT ENG, UNIV CALIF, SANTA CRUZ, 91- *Personal Data:* b Portland, Ore, Jan 18, 21; m 42, Frances G Cilek; c Barbara, Franklin, Alan & Douglas. *Educ:* Univ Kans, BS, 43, MS, 47; Harvard Univ, PhD(physics), 50. *Prof Exp:* Asst instr physics, Univ Kans, 46-47; mem staff, Weapons Div & Theoret Div, Los Alamos Sci Lab, 50-52; assoc group leader, Hydrodyn Group, Theoret Div, 52-57; sr planning rep prod planning, IBM Sci Ctr, 57-59, proj coordr stretch comput, 59, asst mgr, 438 L Proj, Omaha, 59-60, mgr, Systs Sci Res Lab, San Jose, 61-62, spec proj, Adv Systs Develop Lab, 62-64, univ prog, Palo Alto, 64-66, mgr, atmospheric physics dept, 66-69, IBM fel, 69-86. *Mem:* Am Phys Soc; Inst Elec & Electronics Engrs; Sigma Xi. *Res:* Digital computer application and design; compressible fluid hydrodynamics; nuclear moments by molecular beam technique; numerical meteorology. *Mailing Add:* 18950 Lynbrook Ct Saratoga CA 95070

KOLSRUD, GRETCHEN SCHABTACH, TECHNOLOGY ASSESSMENT, DEMOGRAPHY. *Current Pos:* INDEPENDENT CONSULT, 94- *Personal Data:* b Schenectady, NY, Jan 9, 39. *Educ:* McGill Univ, BSc, 60; Johns Hopkins Univ, MA, 63, PhD(psychol), 66. *Prof Exp:* Prin res scientist physiol psychol, Systs & Res Ctr, Honeywell Inc, 66-67; sr syst scientist human factors eng, Serendipity Inc, 67-71; staff scientist, BioTechnol Inc, 71-73; prog mgr, NASA, 73-74; prog mgr, Transp Prog, US Cong, 74-76, asst to dir, New & Emerging Technol, 76-78, acting group mgr, Health Group, prog mgr, biol appl, 79-89, sr assoc, Off Technol Assessment, 78-94. *Concurrent Pos:* Consult, Flight Mgt Systs, 67 & Nat Hwy Traffic Safety Admin, 71; bd trustees, Pop Ref Bur, 92-; fel, Green Ctr Study Sci & Soc, 94. *Mem:* Fel AAAS; Human Factors Soc (secy & treas, 74-75); NY Acad Sci; Sigma Xi. *Res:* Science policy; demography; relationships between society and technology. *Mailing Add:* 114 Roberts Ct Alexandria VA 22314

KOLSTAD, GEORGE ANDREW, NUCLEAR PHYSICS, EARTH SCIENCES. *Current Pos:* RETIRED. *Personal Data:* b Elmira, NY, Dec 10, 19; m 44, Christine J Stillman; c Charles D, Martha (Rae) & Peter K. *Educ:* Bates Col, BS, 43; Yale Univ, PhD(physics), 48. *Honors & Awards:* DOSECC Award Outstanding Contrib Continental Sci Drilling, 90. *Prof Exp:* Asst physics, Wesleyan Univ, 43-44; res assoc radar, Harvard Univ, 44-45; spec asst physics, Yale Univ, 45-46, asst, 46-47, instr, 48-50; with physics & math prog, Div Res, US Atomic Energy Comn, 50-52, head, 52-73; sr physicist & head geosci prog, Div Phys Res, US Energy Res & Develop Admin, 73-77, sr physicist & head geosci prog, Off Energy Res, Div Eng & Geosci, US Dept Energy, 77-90. *Concurrent Pos:* Guest staff mem, Inst Theoret Physics, Copenhagen, 56-57; trustee, Bates Col, 58-64 & Laytonsville Elem Sch, 66-71; mem bd dirs, Sandy Springs Friends Sch, 71-77 & Friends House Retirement & Nursing Home; mem, European-Am Nuclear Data Comt, 60-73; US del, Int Nuclear Data Comt, Int Atomic Energy Agency, 63-73, chmn, 70-72; mem, Fed Coun Sci & Technol, Ad Hoc Comt Int Geodyn Proj, 73-78; liaison mem, Geophys Res Bd, Nat Acad Sci, 79-82; Geophysics Study Comn, 78-90; liaison mem, Bd Earth Sci, 78-86; mem, Interagency Coord Group Continental Sci Drilling, USDOE, NSF & US Geol Surv, 84-90; liaison mem, US Geodynamics Comt, 73-90; mem, Bd Energy & Natural Resources, Nat Acad Sci, 87-90. *Mem:* Fel Am Phys Soc; Am Geophys Union; Sigma Xi. *Res:* Mass spectroscopy; radar countermeasures; a linear accelerator for the production of high intensity gamma rays and neutrons; earth sciences and solar-terrestrial physics; study of state of physics in European universities, post-war. *Mailing Add:* Oak Hill Farm 7920 Brink Rd Laytonsville MD 20882

KOLTUN, DANIEL S, THEORETICAL PHYSICS, NUCLEAR PHYSICS. *Current Pos:* res assoc physics, 62-63, from asst prof to assoc prof, 63-74, PROF PHYSICS, UNIV ROCHESTER, 74- *Personal Data:* b Brooklyn, NY, Dec 7, 33; m 56; c 2. *Educ:* Harvard Col, AB, 55; Princeton Univ, PhD(physics), 61. *Prof Exp:* Res assoc physics, Princeton Univ, 60-61; NSF vis fel nuclear physics, Weizmann Inst, 61-62 & Inst Theoret Phys, Copenhagen, 62. *Concurrent Pos:* Res assoc ctr theoret physics, Mass Inst Technol, 69-70; Alfred P Sloan res fel, 69-71; vis prof, Tel Aviv Univ, 76-77 & J S Guggenheim fel, 76-77, Lady Davis vis prof, Hebrew Univ, 85; vis scientist, Mass Inst Technol, 84; assoc ed, Phys Rev C, 78-80, Phys Rev

Letters, 79-81. *Mem:* Fel Am Phys Soc. *Res:* Theoretical nuclear spectroscopy; many-body theory; interaction of nuclei with mesons; scattering theory; quarks in nuclei. *Mailing Add:* Dept Physics & Astron Univ Rochester Rochester NY 14627

KOLTUN, STANLEY PHELPS, CHEMICAL ENGINEERING. *Current Pos:* Chem engr, Proc Design Unit, USDA, 56-59, cost engr, Cost & Design Unit, 59-63, proj leader, Food Prod Invests, 63-70, res chem engr, 70-76, actg res leader, Oilseed Prod Res, 76-82, RES LEADER, FOOD & FEED ENGR RES UNIT, SOUTHERN REGIONAL RES CTR, USDA, 82- *Personal Data:* b Bogalusa, La, Mar 5, 25; wid; c Karen (Lovett), Ellen K & Patricia (Calamari). *Educ:* La State Univ, BSChE, 48. *Mem:* Am Inst Chem Engrs; Nat Soc Prof Engrs; Am Oil Chemists' Soc; Sigma Xi; Inst Food Technologists. *Res:* Detoxification and inactivation of aflatoxin contaminated oilseeds; oilseed solvent extraction; food dehydration; utilization of oilseed proteins as human food; oilseed meals; cottonseed; peanuts; sweetpotatoes; human nutrition; food safety. *Mailing Add:* 5601 Avron Blvd Metairie LA 70003-1011

KOLTUN, WALTER LANG, BIOPHYSICAL CHEMISTRY. *Current Pos:* CONSULT, 94- *Personal Data:* b New York, NY, Apr 23, 28; m 62; c 2. *Educ:* Mass Inst Technol, BS, 48, PhD(biochem), 52. *Prof Exp:* Asst biol, Mass Inst Technol, 51-52, res assoc, 52-53; asst prof biochem, Sch Med, Univ Va, 55-56; res assoc, Med Col, Cornell Univ, 56-59; consult biophys, Univ Calif, Berkeley, 59-61; staff mem, Sci Resources Planning Off, NSF, 61-64, prog dir molecular biol, 64-65; spec asst, Off Vpres & Secy & Inst Secy for Found, Mass Inst Technol, 65-68; dir prog advan study, Bolt, Beranek & Newman, 68-70; asst dir resources, Harvard-Mass Int Technol Health Prog, 70-93. *Mem:* AAAS; Fedn Am Sci; Am Soc Biol Chem; Sigma Xi. *Res:* Structure, function and interaction of macromolecules, particularly proteins. *Mailing Add:* 76 Goodnough Rd Brookline MA 02167

KOLYER, JOHN M, ORGANIC CHEMISTRY, POLYMER CHEMISTRY. *Current Pos:* SR ENG SPECIALIST, AUTONETICS DIV, ROCKWELL INT CORP, 73- *Personal Data:* b East Williston, NY, June 30, 33; m 60; c 4. *Educ:* Hofstra Col, BA, 55; Univ Pa, PhD(org chem), 60. *Prof Exp:* Technician pesticides, Olin Mathieson Chem Corp, NY, 55-56; res chemist, FMC Corp, NJ, 60-62, Thompson Chem Co, Mass, 62-63; sr res chemist, Plastics Div, Allied Chem Corp, 64-65, group leader, 65-67, tech supvr, Morristown, 67-71. *Concurrent Pos:* Mem, Lepidoptera Found, 65-73. *Mem:* Am Chem Soc; NY Acad Sci; EOS/ESD Asn. *Res:* Preparation processes for plastics additives and monomers; polymerization processes and fabrication methods; polymer modifications; lepidopterological research; ESD (electrostatic discharge) control; author of one book and 70 technical publications; granted 16 patents; materials science engineering. *Mailing Add:* 885 Sea Gull Lane Apt B-311 Newport Beach CA 92663. *Fax:* 714-762-6222

KOMAI, HIROCHIKA, ANESTHESIOLOGY. *Current Pos:* ASSOC SCIENTIST, UNIV WIS, 80- *Educ:* Univ Calif, Berkeley, PhD(biochem), 67. *Mailing Add:* Dept Anesthesiol Univ Wis Health Sci Ctr 600 Highland Ave Madison WI 53792-3272

KOMAR, ARTHUR BARAWAY, THEORETICAL PHYSICS. *Current Pos:* assoc prof, 63-66, chmn, Div Mat Sci, 83-86, PROF PHYSICS, YESHIVA UNIV, 66-, CHMN, DEPT PHYSICS, 78-82 & 92- *Personal Data:* b Brooklyn, NY, Mar 26, 31; m 52; c 2. *Educ:* Princeton Univ, AB, 52, PhD(physics), 56. *Prof Exp:* Fel, Scandinavian-Am Found, Inst Theoret Physics, Denmark, 56-57; asst prof physics, Syracuse Univ, 58-60, assoc prof, 60-63; dean, Belfer Grad Sch Sci, 69-78. *Concurrent Pos:* Prog dir, Gravitational Physics, NSF, 82-83, 86-87 & 91-92; adj prof physics, NY Univ, 85- *Res:* General relativity and quantum field theory. *Mailing Add:* 2621 Palisade Ave Apt 7C New York NY 10463

KOMAR, PAUL D, OCEANOGRAPHY, MARINE GEOLOGY. *Current Pos:* asst prof, 70, assoc prof, 70-78, PROF OCEANOG, ORE STATE UNIV, 78- *Personal Data:* b Grand Rapids, Mich, Dec 2, 39; m 62; c 1. *Educ:* Univ Mich, BA, 61, MS, 62 & 65; Univ Calif, San Diego, PhD(oceanog), 69. *Prof Exp:* NATO fel, St Andrews Univ, Scotland, 69-70. *Concurrent Pos:* Kajima Found fel, Japan, 87. *Mem:* Soc Econ Paleont & Mineral; Am Geophys Union; Int Asn Sedimentologists. *Res:* Coastal process of waves, currents, sediment transport and changes in the morphology of beaches; mechanics of sediment transport. *Mailing Add:* Col Oceanog Ore State Univ Corvallis OR 97331-5503

KOMARKOVA, VERA, PLANT ECOLOGY. *Current Pos:* RES ASSOC, INST ARCTIC & ALPINE RES, UNIV COLO, BOULDER, 76-; ASST PROF, DEPT ENVIRON POP & ORGANISMIC BIOL, 79- *Personal Data:* b Pisek, Czech, Dec, 25, 42. *Educ:* Charles Univ, Czech, MSc, 64; Univ Colo, PhD(biol), 76. *Concurrent Pos:* Prin investr, 79- *Mem:* AAAS; Am Inst Biol Sci; Ecol Soc Am; Int Soc Veg Sci. *Res:* Phytosociology; photogeography; vegetation mapping; methods of vegetation analysis; environment-vegetation relationship; community development; vegetation and environmental data management; effects of perturbation. *Mailing Add:* Villa Elisabeth 5 CH1854 Leysin Switzerland

KOMARMY, JULIUS MICHAEL, PHYSICAL CHEMISTRY, ORGANIC CHEMISTRY. *Current Pos:* CATALYTIC CONVERTER COLLETORS INC, 87- *Personal Data:* b Franklin, NJ, Oct 19, 26; m 52; c 4. *Educ:* SW Mo State Col, BS, 49; Univ Ark, MS, 52, PhD, 58. *Prof Exp:* Asst chem, Univ Ark, 49-52, instr, 52-54, 56-67; instr, Flint Jr Col, 57-61; Supvr chem, Res Dept,

AC Spark Plug Div, Gen Motors Corp, 61-65, Supvr chem res, 65-66, sr staff res scientist, 66-86. *Mem:* AAAS; Am Chem Soc; Soc Automotive Eng; Am Soc Testing & Mat; Soc Info Displays. *Res:* Automotive applications of plastics and elastomers; fuels and lubricants and filtration processes; catalyst development for automotive exhaust environmental controls; materials development for fabrication of large liquid crystal displays. *Mailing Add:* 8521 Pepper Ridge Dr Grand Blanc Flint MI 48439-7959

KOMARNENI, SRIDHAR, MATERIALS RESEARCH, CLAY MINERALOGY. *Current Pos:* proj assoc solid state sci, Pa State Univ, 76-78, res assoc, 78-81, sr res assoc, 81-84, assoc prof, 84-87, PROF CLAY MINERAL, PA STATE UNIV, 87- *Personal Data:* b Komarneni Varipalem, India, Sept 26, 44; US citizen; m 79, Sreedevi Nagabhairu; c Jayanth. *Educ:* Andhra Pradesh Agr Univ, India, BSc, 68; Indian Agr Res Inst, MSc, 70; Univ Wis-Madison, PhD(soils), 73. *Honors & Awards:* Fedn Mat Soc Award, 94. *Prof Exp:* Proj assoc, Univ Wis-Madison, 73-76. *Mem:* Fel AAAS; fel Am Soc Agron; fel Soil Sci Soc Am; Clay Minerals Soc; fel Am Ceramic Soc; Sigma Xi. *Res:* Crystal chemistry of clay minerals and zeolites; new materials preparation and characterization; sol-gel chemistry; nuclear and hazardous waste disposal; nanocomposites; porous materials. *Mailing Add:* Mat Res Lab Pa State Univ University Park PA 16802. *Fax:* 814-865-2326; *E-Mail:* sxk1@alpha.mrl.psu.edu

KOMERS, PETR E, behavioral ecology, for more information see previous edition

KOMIAK, JAMES JOSEPH, mmic & mic technology-circuit design, t-r module & system architectures, for more information see previous edition

KOMINEK, LEO ALOYSIUS, MICROBIOLOGY & BIOCHEMISTRY, PSYCHOLOGY. *Current Pos:* PSYCHOLOGIST, BORJESS BEHAV MED, 96- *Personal Data:* b Chicago, Ill, Apr 11, 37; m 59, Anita Mars; c Stephen, Laura, Mary & Leo. *Educ:* St Joseph's Col, Ind, BS, 59; Univ Ill, PhD(microbiol), 64; Western Mich Univ, MA, 95. *Prof Exp:* Res assoc, 64-72, Upjohn Co, sr scientist microbiol, 72-78, res mgr, 78-79, sr scientist, 79-96. *Mem:* Am Soc Microbiol; Am Chem Soc; Sigma Xi; Am Acad Microbiol; NY Acad Sci. *Res:* Biochemical aspects of bacterial sporulation; microbial metabolism; antibiotic biosynthesis; steroid and sterol bioconversions. *Mailing Add:* 2209 Hickory Point Dr Portage MI 49024

KOMINZ, DAVID RICHARD, PROTEIN CHEMISTRY. *Current Pos:* RES PROF PHYSIOL, UNIV MASS MED SCH, 78- *Personal Data:* b Rochester, NY, Apr 2, 24; m 88, Phyllis Damon; c 3. *Educ:* Univ Rochester, MD, 47; Harvard Univ, BA, 50. *Prof Exp:* Intern, Gorgas Hosp, CZ, 47-48; res fel phys chem lab, Harvard Univ, 50-51; from sr asst surgeon to med dir, Nat Inst Arthritis & Metab Dis, 51-65, chief, NIH Pac Off, Tokyo, 66-68, med dir, Nat Inst Arthritis, Metab & Digestive Dis, 68-76, chief sect bioenergetics, Lab Biophys Chem, 70-76; assoc dir, Nat Bladder Cancer Proj, 76-78. *Mem:* AAAS; Am Chem Soc; Am Soc Biol Chem; Biophys Soc. *Res:* Amino acid analysis; comparative biochemistry of muscle proteins; protein modifications; interactions of muscle proteins. *Mailing Add:* Dept Physiol Univ Mass Med Sch 55 N Lake Ave Worcester MA 01655-0001. *Fax:* 781-235-6263

KOMISARUK, BARRY RICHARD, PSYCHOBIOLOGY, NEUROPHYSIOLOGY. *Current Pos:* asst prof zool, Rutgers Univ, 66-68, assoc prof, 68-72, prof zool, 72-84, PROF II PSYCHOL, RUTGERS UNIV, NEWARK, 84- *Personal Data:* b New York, NY, Apr 4, 41; wid; c Adam C & Kevin M. *Educ:* City Univ New York, BS, 61; Rutgers Univ, PhD(neuroendocrinol), 65. *Honors & Awards:* Hugo F Beigel Award Res, Soc Sci Study Sex, 89. *Prof Exp:* NIMH fel neuroendocrinol, Univ Calif, Los Angeles, 65-66. *Concurrent Pos:* NIMH res grant, Rutgers Univ, Newark, 66-79; NIMH Res Scientist Develop Award, 69-79; NSF res grant, Rutgers Univ, Newark, 79-; MBRS-NIH grant, 87-; NIH res grant, 92-95. *Mem:* Int Behav Neurosci Soc; Soc Neurosci; Soc Sci Study Sex. *Res:* Neurophysiological bases of species characteristic, hormonally influenced behavior, analgesic mechanisms; sexual response in laboratory species and humans; neutral pathways and brain activity in humans and sub species. *Mailing Add:* Dept Psychol 101 Warren St Newark NJ 07102-1814. *Fax:* 973-648-1102; *E-Mail:* brk@andromeda.rutgers.edu

KOMISKEY, HAROLD LOUIS, TOXICOLOGY. *Current Pos:* ASSOC PROF, TOXICOL, COL PHARM, XAVIER UNIV, 89- *Personal Data:* b Oct 21, 48; m 70, Judy A; c 2. *Educ:* Univ Wis, PhD(pharmacol), 75; Am Bd Toxicol, dipl, 81. *Prof Exp:* Assist prof pharmacol, Col Pharm, Wash State Univ, 77-83 & Col Med, Univ Ill, 83-89. *Mem:* Soc Toxicol; Soc Neurosci; Am Soc Pharmacol & Exp Therapeut. *Res:* Isolation and characterization of the actions of an endogenous substance with a high affinity for benzodiazepine receptors; determination of the subchronic neurotoxicity of various zinc salts. *Mailing Add:* Col Pharm Xavier Univ 7325 Palmetto St New Orleans LA 70125. *Fax:* 504-488-3108

KOMKOV, VADIM, OPTIMIZATION, CONTROL OF NONLINEAR SYSTEMS. *Current Pos:* RETIRED. *Personal Data:* b Moscow, USSR, Aug 18, 19; US citizen; m 46; c 5. *Educ:* Warsaw Polytech Inst, dipl mech eng, 48; Univ Utah, PhD(math), 64. *Prof Exp:* Asst prof mech eng, Univ Utah, 57-64; vis assoc prof math, Med Res Coun, Univ Wis, 64-65; assoc prof, Fla State, 65-69; prof, Tex Tech, 69-77; ed, Math Rev, 77-80; prof & head math, WVa Univ, 80-83, Winthrop Col, 83-87 & Air Force Inst Technol, 87-93; vis prof, Mercer Univ, Macon, Ga 93-96. *Concurrent Pos:* Consult, Southwest Res Inst, 70-75, US Army Arm Com, 72-77 & Univ Cincinnati, 80-82; vis prof,

Polish Acad Sci, Warsaw, 80. *Mem:* Soc Indust & Appl Math; Math Asn Am; Am Math Soc. *Res:* Applied mathematics-variational methods; theoretical classical mechanics; continuum mechanics; engineering optimization, sensitivity of mechanical and structural systems to design changes. *Mailing Add:* 205 Leeward Lane Roswell GA 30076

KOMM, HORACE, MATHEMATICS. *Current Pos:* assoc prof, 63-71, chmn dept, 71-77, PROF MATH, HOWARD UNIV, 71- *Personal Data:* b Russia, Dec 30, 16; nat US; m 47; c 3. *Educ:* Univ Buffalo, BA, 37; Univ Mich, MA, 38, PhD(math), 42. *Prof Exp:* Structures engr, Curtiss-Wright Corp, 42-44, asst to chief mathematician, Res Lab, 44-46; instr math, Univ Rochester, 46-48, asst prof, 48-52; assoc prof, Univ of the South, 52-53; asst prof, Rensselaer Polytech Inst, 53-62. *Mem:* Am Math Soc; Math Asn Am. *Res:* Dimension of partially ordered sets; general and algebraic topology. *Mailing Add:* 5130 Wickett Terr Bethesda MD 20814-5715

KOMMA, DONALD JERRY, DROSOPHILA GENETICS, CHROMOSOME SEGREGATION. *Current Pos:* res assoc, 84-93, ASSOC, DUKE UNIV, MED CTR, 93- *Personal Data:* b Aug 14, 34. *Educ:* Univ Col, BA, 57; Ind Univ, MA, 59; Univ Mich, PhD(human genetics), 64. *Prof Exp:* Fel, Columbia Univ, 65-67, Univ Ill, 67-72; res assoc, Columbia Univ, 72-84. *Mem:* Genetics Soc Am; Planetary Soc. *Res:* Non-claret disjunctional motor protein in Drosophila, which plays a major role in chromosome disjunction during meiosis in females. *Mailing Add:* Dept Microbiol & Immunol Duke Univ Med Ctr 437 Jones Bldg Box 3020 Durham NC 27710

KOMMEDAHL, THOR, PLANT PATHOLOGY. *Current Pos:* from asst prof to prof, 53-90, EMER PROF PLANT PATH, UNIV MINN, ST PAUL, 90-, PROF CONTINUING EDUC & EXTEN, 90- *Personal Data:* b Minneapolis, Minn, Apr 1, 20; m 51, Faye Jensen; c Kris, Siri & Lori. *Educ:* Univ Minn, BS, 45, MS, 47, PhD(plant path), 51. *Honors & Awards:* Award of Excellence, Weed Sci Soc Am, 66; Distinguished Serv Award, Nat Am Phytopath Soc, 84; E C Stakman Award, 90; Distinguished Serv Award, Regional Am Phytopath Soc, 93. *Prof Exp:* Instr, Agr Exp Sta, Univ Minn, 46-51; asst prof, Agr Exp Sta, Ohio State Univ, 51-53. *Concurrent Pos:* Consult botanist & taxonomist, Div Plant Indust, State Dept Agr, Dairy & Food, Minn, 54-60; Guggenheim fel, Waite Agr Res Inst, Australia, 61-62; Fulbright fel, Iceland, 68; consult, McGraw-Hill Co; counr, Int Soc Plant Path, 72-78, secy gen & treas, 83-88; consult, Sci Mus Minn, 90-; external assessor, Univ Pertanian, Malaysia, 94- *Mem:* Fel AAAS; Am Inst Biol Sci; fel Am Phytopath Soc (vpres, 69, pres, 71); Mycol Soc Am; Int Soc Plant Path (treas, 83-93); Bot Soc Am; NY Acad Sci; Weed Sci Soc Am; Coun Biol Ed. *Res:* Flax and corn diseases; weed ecology; root diseases and ecology of root-infecting fungi; biological control root diseases; Fusarium species. *Mailing Add:* Dept Plant Path 495 Borlaug Hall Univ Minn St Paul MN 55108-6030. *Fax:* 612-625-9728; *E-Mail:* thork@puccini.crl.umn.edu

KOMOREK, MICHAEL JOESPH, JR, NUCLEAR MEDICINE, RADIATION SAFETY. *Current Pos:* RADIATION SAFETY OFFICER, ROSWELL PARK CANCER INST, 88- *Personal Data:* b Buffalo, NY, July 14, 52; m 82. *Educ:* State Univ NY, Buffalo, BA, 74, BS, 77. *Prof Exp:* Res radioactive gases, Nuclear Sci & Technol Ctr, State Univ NY, Buffalo, 72-77, asst health physicist, 78-82; health physicist/nuclear engr, West Valley Demonstration Proj, 83; corp health physicist, Syncor Int Radiopharm, 83-84; PRES & RADIATION SAFETY OFFICER, ALARA MGT CO, 79- *Concurrent Pos:* Health physicist, bd dirs, Elma Nuclear Consults, 84- *Mem:* Health Physics Soc; Am Asn Physicists in Med; Laser Inst Am; Soc Nuclear Med; Am Indust Hyg Asn. *Res:* Nuclear medicine related research for new imaging compounds which may be used for imaging of diseases related to cancer. *Mailing Add:* 80 Pinewood Trail East Aurora NY 14052

KOMORIYA, AKIRA, STRUCTURE-FUNCTION OF GROWTH FACTORS & THEIR RECEPTORS. *Current Pos:* SR STAFF FEL, DIV CYTOKINE BIOL, FOOD & DRUG ADMIN, BETHESDA, MD, 88- *Educ:* Duke Univ, PhD(phys chem), 77. *Prof Exp:* Prin investr, Biotechnol Res Ctr, Meloy Lab, Inc, 84-88. *Mailing Add:* Onco Immunin Inc PO Box 2155 Kensington MD 20891

KOMORNICKI, ANDREW, theoretical chemistry, for more information see previous edition

KOMOROSKI, RICHARD ANDREW, ANALYTICAL CHEMISTRY, PSYCHIATRY. *Current Pos:* PROF RADIO, PATH & PSYCHIAT & PROF BIOCHEM, UNIV ARK MED SCI, 86- *Personal Data:* b St Louis, Mo, Feb 4, 47; m 79, Eva Marczewski; c Elizabeth, Christopher & Laura. *Educ:* St Louis Univ, BS, 69; Ind Univ, PhD(phys chem), 73. *Prof Exp:* Fel chem, Fla State Univ, 73-76; sr res chemist, Diamond Shamrock Corp, 76-79; Res & Develop Ctr, B F Goodrich Co, 79-85. *Concurrent Pos:* Affil prof staff, Ark Children's Hosp, 89- *Mem:* Am Chem Soc; AAAS; Int Soc Magnetic Resonance Med; Sigma Xi; Soc Biol Psychiat; Soc Neurosci. *Res:* Nuclear magnetic resonance spectroscopy; nuclear magnetic resonance imaging; in vivo nuclear magnetic resonance spectroscopy; applications of nuclear magnetic resonance in psychiatry. *Mailing Add:* Radiol Dept Slot 582 Univ Ark Med 4301 W Markham Little Rock AR 72205. *Fax:* 501-686-5406

KOMP, RICHARD JOSEPH, SOLAR ENERGY, ENERGY ENGINEERING. *Current Pos:* vpres res & develop, 81-88, PRES, SUNWATT CORP, 88- *Personal Data:* b Chicago, Ill, Aug 7, 38; m 83, Mirdza Leskov. *Educ:* Loras Col, BS, 60; Wayne State Univ, PhD(phys chem), 64. *Prof Exp:* Sr scientist, Xerox Corp, Webster, NY, 64-68; assoc prof physics & astron, Western Ky Univ, 68-73; vpres, Zip Serv, Educ Activ Inc, 73-75; res assoc, Wayne State Univ, 75-81. *Concurrent Pos:* Dir, Skyheat Asn, 73-; NATO fel, Univ Louis Pasteur, Strasbourg, France, 80; pres, Maine Solar Energy Asn, 89-92, 95-; adj prof physics & renewable energy, Col Atlantic, Bar Harbor, Maine, 91, 97- *Mem:* Int Solar Energy Soc; AAAS; Sigma Xi. *Res:* Development of new photovoltaic cells and systems including hybrid systems that distill or heat while producing electricity; new thin film solar cells. *Mailing Add:* RR1 Box 7751 Jonesport ME 04649. *E-Mail:* sunwatt@juno.com

KOMPALA, DHINAKAR S, BIOPROCESS ENGINEERING, RECOMBINANT MICROBIAL & MAMMALIAN CELL CULTURE. *Current Pos:* asst prof, 85-91, ASSOC PROF CHEM ENG, UNIV COLO, BOULDER, 91- *Personal Data:* b Madras, India, Nov 20, 58; US citizen; m 83, Sushila R Viswamurthy; c Tejaswi D & Chytanya R. *Educ:* Indian Inst Technol, Madras, BTech, 79; Purdue Univ, MS, 82, PhD(chem eng), 84. *Concurrent Pos:* Presidential young investr, NSF, 88-93; vis assoc, Calif Inst Technol, 91-92. *Mem:* Am Inst Chem Engrs; Am Chem Soc; Am Soc Eng Educ; Soc Indust Microbiol; Int Soc Anal Cytometry. *Res:* Development of optimal operating strategies and novel bioreactor designs for maximizing bioprocesses or heterologous protein expressions in recombinant microbial and mammalian cultures; metabolic modeling; recombinant DNA; biotechnology. *Mailing Add:* Dept Chem Eng Univ Colo Boulder CO 80309-0424. *Fax:* 303-492-4341; *E-Mail:* dhinakar.kompala@colorado.edu

KON, MARK A, PARTIAL DIFFERENTIAL OPERATIONS, WAVELET THEORY. *Current Pos:* asst prof, 81-88, ASSOC PROF MATH, BOSTON UNIV, 88- *Educ:* Cornell Univ, BA, 74; Mass Inst Technol, PhD(math), 79. *Prof Exp:* Irvine lectr, Univ Calif, Irvine, 80; assoc prof, Columbia Univ. *Concurrent Pos:* Vis asst prof math & comput sci, Columbia Univ, 85-87 & 89-; Fulbright fel, 96-97. *Mem:* Am Math Soc; Int Asn Math Physics; AAAS; Int Neural Network Soc; Math Asn Am. *Res:* Mathematical physics, primarily in quantum statistical mechanics; partial differential equations, primarily the Schrodinger equation; complexity of approximately solved problems; wavelet theory. *Mailing Add:* Dept Math Boston Univ Boston MA 02215. *Fax:* 617-353-8100; *E-Mail:* mkon@math.bu.edu

KONARSKA, MARIA MAGDA, NUCLEIC ACID BIOCHEMISTRY, RNA PROCESSING & REPLICATION. *Current Pos:* ASST PROF & HEAD LAB, ROCKEFELLER UNIV, 89- *Personal Data:* b Bukowina, Tatrz, Poland, Aug 22, 55. *Educ:* Univ Warsaw, MSc, 79; Polish Acad Sci, PhD(biochem), 83. *Honors & Awards:* Jakub Karol Parnas Award, Polish Biochem Soc, 85. *Prof Exp:* Res fel, Max-Planck Inst Biochem, 79, Inst Biochem, Univ Wuerzburg, 81-83; fel, Ctr Cancer Res, Mass Inst Technol, 84-86, res assoc, 87-89. *Concurrent Pos:* Fel, Jane Coffin Childs Mem Fund, 83-86; prin investr, Lucille P Markey Charitable Trust, 87-, NIH, 93-; career scientist award, Monique Weill-Caulier Award, 92- *Mem:* Am Soc Microbiol; AAAS. *Res:* Mechanism of MRNA splicing, assembly of snRNP particles into spliceosome complex; replication of RNA by DNA-dependent RNA polymerases, specifically replication of hepatitis delta virus by RNA polymerase II. *Mailing Add:* 504 E 63rd St New York NY 10021

KONAT, GREGORY W, GENE EXPRESSION, NEURAL DEGENERATION & REGENERATION. *Current Pos:* PROF MOLECULAR NEUROBIOL, DEPT ANAT, SCH MED, WVA UNIV, MORGANTOWN, 89- *Personal Data:* b Mar 6, 47; Danish citizen. *Educ:* Univ Warsaw, MSc, 69; Univ Odense Med Sch, PhD(med sci/biochem), 75. *Honors & Awards:* Gold Medal, Univ Odense Med Sch, 76. *Prof Exp:* Res teaching asst biochem, Dept Neurochem, Med Res Ctr, Polish Acad Sci, Warsaw, 69-71; res scientist biochem-neurochem, Neurochem Inst, Copenhagen, 71-81; res assoc prof neurochem, Inst Med Physiol & Neuropath, Univ Copenhagen, 81-83; res scientist neurochem, Dept Neurobiol & Anat, Med Sch, Univ Tex, Houston, 83-84; asst prof neurochem, dept neurol med, Univ SC, Charleston, 84-87, assoc prof neurochem & molecular biol, 87-90. *Concurrent Pos:* Adj prof molecular neurobiol, Dept Pediat, Sch Med, WVa Univ, Morgantown, 90-, adj prof neurosurg, 96- *Mem:* Int Soc Neurochem; Int Soc Develop Neurosci; Soc Complex Carbohydrates; Am Soc Neurochem; Am Soc Biochem & Molecular Biol; Fedn Europ Biochem Soc. *Res:* Mechanisms of myelin gene expression; spinal cord degeneration and regeneration; chromatin structure and function. *Mailing Add:* Dept Anat Sch Med WVa Univ 4052 HSN PO Box 9128 Morgantown WV 26506. *Fax:* 304-293-8159; *E-Mail:* gkonat@wvu.edu

KONDE, ANTHONY JOSEPH, physical chemistry; deceased, see previous edition for last biography

KONDO, EDWARD SHINICHI, FOREST PATHOLOGY. *Current Pos:* Res officer, Can Forestry Serv, Dept Environ, 69-71, res scientist forest path, 71-82, dir, Forest Insect & Dis Surv, 83-88 & Biorational Control Agents Prog, 88-90, DIR GEN, FOREST PEST MGT INST, CAN FORESTRY SERV, 90- *Personal Data:* b Victoria, BC, Sept 5, 39; m 70, Jeanne D Sabourin; c Christine & Michelle. *Educ:* Univ Toronto, BScF, 64, MScF, 66, PhD(plant path), 70. *Concurrent Pos:* Adj prof, Forestry Fac, Univ Toronto, 72-74. *Res:* Vascular wilt tree diseases; Dutch elm disease; urban forestry; tree and fungus physiology, mycology, chemotherapy of tree diseases. *Mailing Add:* Can Forestry Serv Box 490 Sault Ste Marie ON P6A 5M7 Can. *Fax:* 705-759-5714

KONDO, NORMAN SHIGERU, ORGANIC CHEMISTRY. *Current Pos:* ASSOC PROF CHEM, UNIV DC, 77- *Personal Data:* b Honolulu, Hawaii, Oct 30, 41; m 71; c 1. *Educ:* Univ Hawaii, BA, 63; Univ Calif, Riverside, PhD(chem), 67. *Prof Exp:* Res assoc biophys, Argonne Nat Lab, 71-73; asst prof chem, Fed City Col, 73-77. *Concurrent Pos:* NIH fel, Johns Hopkins Univ, 67-69 & fel, 69-71; NIH grant, Fed City Col, Univ DC, 75- *Mem:* Am Chem Soc; Biophys Soc. *Res:* Synthesis and conformational studies on nucleic acid constituents. *Mailing Add:* 7135 Red Horse Tavern Lane Springfield VA 22153-1406

KONDO, YOJI, ASTRONOMY, ASTROPHYSICS. *Current Pos:* Nat Acad Sci res assoc, Astron & Space Lab, Goddard Space Flight Ctr, NASA, 65-68, astronr, 68-69, chief, Astrophys Sect, Johnson Space Ctr, 69-77, ASTROPHYSICIST, GODDARD SPACE FLIGHT CTR, NASA, 78-, PROJ SCIENTIST, INT ULTRAVIOLET EXPLORER SATELLITE OBSERV, 82-, PROJ SCIENTIST, EXTREME ULTRAVIOLET EXPLORER, 88-, SPEC ADV TO ADMINR, 95- *Personal Data:* b Hitachi, Japan, May 26, 33; US citizen; m 65; Ursula; c Beatrice, Cynthia & Angela. *Educ:* Tokyo Univ Foreign Studies, BA, 58; Univ Pa, MS, 63, PhD(astron), 65. *Honors & Awards:* Fed Design Achievement Award, 88; Except Achievement Medal, NASA, 90; Sci Award, Nat Space Club, 95. *Concurrent Pos:* Mem adj grad fac, Univ Houston, 68-74, adj prof, 74-77; from adj assoc prof to adj prof, Univ Okla, 71-77; ed, Earth & Extraterrestrial Sci, 74-79 & Comments Astrophys, 79-; adj prof, Univ Pa, 78-; consult, NASA Hq, 81-82; vis prof, Inst Space & Astronaut Sci, Tokyo, 83; pres comt 44 astron from space, Int Astron Union, 85-88 & comt 42 close binary stars, 91-94; prof, George Mason Univ, 89-; prof, Catholic Univ Am, 96- *Mem:* AAAS; Am Astron Soc; Int Astron Union; Int Astron Union Div V (pres 94-97). *Res:* Astronomical observations from space; interacting close binary stars; interstellar medium; active galactic nuclei. *Mailing Add:* Lab Astron & Solar Physics Code 680 Goddard Space Flight Ctr Greenbelt MD 20771. *Fax:* 301-286-1573; *E-Mail:* kondo@iue.gsfc.nasa.gov

KONDRA, PETER ALEXANDER, POULTRY GENETICS. *Current Pos:* from asst prof to prof, 46-78, EMER PROF, UNIV MAN, 78- *Personal Data:* b Mikado, Sask, July 30, 11; m 39; c 3. *Educ:* Univ Man, BSA, 34, MSc, 43; Univ Minn, PhD(poultry genetics), 53. *Prof Exp:* Poultry inspector, Man Dept Agr, 36-40; asst poultry, Univ Man, 40-43, mgr hatchery, 44-45; asst poultry specialist, Man Dept Agr, 45-46. *Concurrent Pos:* Mem poultry breeding comt, Can Dept Agr, 53-; exchange scientist, Acad Sci, USSR, 64, adv, Thailand 68-69, Brazil, 74 & Costa Rica, 78. *Mem:* Poultry Sci Asn; World Poultry Sci Asn; Genetics Soc Can; Agr Inst Can. *Res:* Poultry breeding biology; incubation; housing. *Mailing Add:* 60 Purdue Winnipeg MB R3T 3C7 Can

KONECKY, MILTON STUART, ORGANIC CHEMISTRY. *Current Pos:* PRES, KONECKY ASSOCS ENTERPRISES, POTTERSVILLE, NJ. *Personal Data:* b Omaha, Nebr, July 29, 22; m 48; Naomi M Schipporeit; c Mark & Chad. *Educ:* Creighton Univ, BS, 44, MS, 48; Univ Ill, PhD(chem), 58. *Prof Exp:* Chemist, Omaha Grain Exchange Labs, Nebr, 47-50; chemist pesticide chem res br, Entom Res Div, USDA, Md, 50-54; sr chemist, Exxon Res & Eng Co, 57-60, res assoc, 61-63, sect head, 63-69, sr staff adv, 69-87, sr res assoc, 88-91. *Mem:* AAAS; Sigma Xi; Am Chem Soc; NY Acad Sci. *Res:* Agricultural chemicals; petrochemicals; biodegradation methods for and synthesis of detergents; industrial, trade sales and specialty resins for surface coatings; heterogeneous catalysis; information research and analysis; consulting industrial research. *Mailing Add:* Konecky Assocs Enterprises Dryden Rd PO Box 307 Pottersville NJ 07979

KONEN, HARRY P, NUMERICAL ANALYSIS. *Current Pos:* from asst prof to assoc prof, 69-83, PROF MATH, SAM HOUSTON STATE UNIV, 83- *Personal Data:* b Dayton, Ky, Sept 18, 40; m 71; c 2. *Educ:* St Thomas Univ, BA, 62; Tex A&M Univ, MS, 65, PhD(math), 67. *Prof Exp:* Instr math, San Jacinto Col, 66-69. *Mem:* Soc Indust & Appl Math; Math Asn Am; Asn Comput Mach; Sigma Xi. *Res:* Fifth-order Runge-Kutta methods for the numerical solution of differential equations. *Mailing Add:* Math & Info Sci Dept Sam Houston State Univ PO Box 2206 Huntsville TX 77341-2206

KONG, ERIC SIU-WAI, MATERIALS SCIENCE, POLYMER PHYSICS. *Current Pos:* RES DIR, MAT SCI & TECHNOL INST, 92- *Personal Data:* b Hong Kong, Jan 14, 53; US citizen. *Educ:* Univ Calif, Berkeley, BA, 74; Rensselaer Polytech Inst, MSc, 76, PhD(polymer chem), 78. *Prof Exp:* Res assoc, Va Polytech Inst, 78-79; res scientist, Ames Res Ctr, NASA, 79-83; mem tech staff, Sandia Nat Labs, 83-84 & Hewlett Packard Labs, 84-86; sr res specialist, Swedlow Inc, 86-87; biomat tech adv, Mentor Corp, 87-89; fac med chem, Univ Calif, San Francisco, 89-90; sr res chemist, Becton Dickinson, 91-92. *Concurrent Pos:* Chmn, San Francisco Chap, Soc Plastics Engrs, 83-84; consult, Elec Power Res Inst, Palo Alto, 91- *Mem:* Fel Am Inst Chemists; fel NY Acad Sci; Am Chem Soc; Am Phys Soc; Soc Polymer Sci Japan; Soc Biomat. *Res:* Polymer chemistry research and development where there is a close tie between basic science and applied engineering. *Mailing Add:* 4250 El Camino Real Suite A206 Palo Alto CA 94306. *Fax:* 408-739-8236

KONG, JIN AU, ELECTRICAL ENGINEERING. *Current Pos:* asst prof, 69-73, assoc prof, 73-80, PROF ELEC ENG, MASS INST TECHNOL, 80- *Personal Data:* b Kiangsu, China, Dec 27, 42; US citizen; m 70; c 2. *Educ:* Nat Taiwan Univ, BS, 62; Chiao Tung Univ, MS, 65; Syracuse Univ, PhD(elec eng), 68. *Prof Exp:* Res engr elec eng, Syracuse Univ, 68-69. *Concurrent Pos:* Vinton Hayes fel eng, Mass Inst Technol, 69-71; consult remote sensing technol, Off Tech Coop, UN, 77-79; Raytheon Co, Lincoln Lab & Hughes Aircraft Co, 80. *Mem:* Inst Elec & Electronics Engrs; Am Phys Soc; Optical Soc Am; Am Geophys Union; Am Soc Eng Educ; Int Union Radio Sci; Sigma Xi. *Res:* Electromagnetic Wave Theory; author of 8 books, 178 refereed journal articles and 245 conference papers. *Mailing Add:* 26-305 Mass Inst Technol Cambridge MA 02139

KONG, SIOW-KEE, BIOCHEMISTRY, PHYSIOLOGY. *Current Pos:* VIS ASSOC & SCIENTIST, NIH, 90- *Personal Data:* b Singapore, Feb 8, 53; Can citizen; m 82; Peng-Suat; c Hai-Yin & Hai-Li. *Educ:* Nanyang Univ, BSc, 77; Univ Man, MSc, 81, PhD(physiol), 85. *Prof Exp:* Postdoctoral fel, Univ Calgary, 85-87; res assoc med physiol & cell biol, Univ Man, 88-90. *Concurrent Pos:* Postdoctoral fel, Alta Heritage Found Med Res, 85-86, Med Res Coun Can, 86-88. *Mem:* Am Soc Biochem & Molecular Biol; NY Acad Sci. *Res:* Protein phosphorylation and cell regulation; smooth muscle physiology and biochemistry. *Mailing Add:* NIH Bldg 3 Rm 203 Bethesda MD 20892-0001. *Fax:* 301-496-0599

KONG, YI-CHI MEI, IMMUNOLOGY, MICROBIOLOGY. *Current Pos:* from asst prof to assoc prof, 66-77, PROF IMMUNOL & MICROBIOL, SCH MED, WAYNE STATE UNIV, 77- *Personal Data:* b Boston, Mass, Feb 2, 34; c 2. *Educ:* Wellesley Col, BA, 55; Univ Mich, MS, 57, PhD(microbiol), 61. *Prof Exp:* Res assoc, Univ Mich, 60-61; asst res bacteriologist, Naval Biol Lab, Univ Calif, Berkeley, 61-66. *Concurrent Pos:* Mem immunol sci study sect, NIH, 74-77 & bacteriol mycol study sect, 81-84; ed, Infection & Immunity, 78-83, Clin Immunol & Immunopath, 87-98; Found Lectr, Am Soc Microbiol, 87; Fogarty Int Sr Fel, NIH, 88; vis fel, Cambridge Univ, Eng, 88, life mem, Clare Hall, 90, bd govs distinguished fac fel, 90-92. *Mem:* AAAS; Transplantation Am Soc Microbiol; Am Asn Immunologists; Am Thyroid Asn. *Res:* Mechanisms of immunologic tolerance; transplantation antigens and immunity; immunogenetic and cellular control of autoimmunity; effect of adjuvants. *Mailing Add:* Dept Immunol & Microbiol Wayne State Univ Sch Med 540 E Canfield Ave Detroit MI 48201-1908

KONGSAMUT, SATHAPANA, REGULATION INTRACELLULAR CALCIUM, NEUROTRANSMITTER & RECEPTOR FUNCTION. *Current Pos:* sr res biochemist, 91-93, RES ASSOC, HOECHST-ROUSSEL PHARMACEUT, 93- *Personal Data:* b Saigon, Vietnam, July 6, 56; Thailand citizen; m 85, Siribhan Singhaviroj; c Narissa & Tira W. *Educ:* Univ Ottawa, BSc, 79; Univ Ill, Chicago, MS, 82; Univ Chicago, PhD(neuropharmacol), 86. *Prof Exp:* Fel, Cornell Univ, 86-87; assoc, Yale Univ, 87-91. *Concurrent Pos:* Assoc ed, Thai Jour Physiol Sci, 91-; adj asst prof physiol, Univ Med & Dent NJ, 93- *Mem:* AAAS; NY Acad Sci; Soc Neurosci. *Res:* Regulation in neutrons by various mechanisms and its effects on neurotransmitter release; neurotransmitter receptors that can contribute to the treatment of schizophrenia. *Mailing Add:* 14 Coursen Way Madison NJ 07940. *Fax:* 908-231-2413; *E-Mail:* kongsam1@hrpi6.enet.hcc.com

KONHAUSER, JOSEPH DANIEL EDWARD, mathematics; deceased, see previous edition for last biography

KONHEIM, ALAN G, MATHEMATICS. *Current Pos:* PROF COMPUT SCI, UNIV CALIF, SANTA BARBARA, 82- *Personal Data:* b Brooklyn, NY, Oct 17, 34; m 57; c 2. *Educ:* Polytech Inst Brooklyn, BEE, 55, MS, 57; Cornell Univ, PhD(math), 60. *Prof Exp:* Res staff mem math, Thomas J Watson Res Lab, IBM Corp, 60-82, res staff mem, IBM Res Lab, Switz, 70-71. *Mem:* Am Math Soc; Math Asn Am; Soc Indust & Appl Math; Asn Comput Mach. *Res:* Probability theory; harmonic analysis. *Mailing Add:* 3735 Essex Dr Santa Barbara CA 93105

KONIECZNY, STEPHEN FRANCIS, GENE EXPRESSION, DIFFERENTIATION. *Current Pos:* SYST PROF BIOL, PURDUE UNIV, 84- *Educ:* Brown Univ, PhD(biol), 82. *Mailing Add:* Dept Biol Sci Purdue Univ West Lafayette IN 47907-1392

KONIG, RONALD H, STRUCTURAL GEOLOGY, ECONOMIC GEOLOGY. *Current Pos:* From asst prof to assoc prof, 59-71, chmn Dept Geol, 71-80, PROF, UNIV ARK, FAYETTEVILLE, 71- *Personal Data:* b Albany, NY, Aug 12, 32; m 76, Janet; c Elizabeth & Mary. *Educ:* St Lawrence Univ, BS, 54; Cornell Univ, MS, 56, PhD(geol), 59. *Mem:* Geol Soc Am; Soc Econ Geol. *Res:* Areal geologic mapping; geologic investigation of mineral deposits. *Mailing Add:* Dept Geol Univ Ark Fayetteville AR 72701. *Fax:* 501-575-3846

KONIGSBACHER, KURT S, ORGANIC CHEMISTRY, BIOCHEMISTRY. *Current Pos:* PRES, K-BACH CONSULTS, INC, 89- *Personal Data:* b Switz, Sept 15, 23; nat US; m 45, Renee Kaliski; c Susan & Peter. *Educ:* Dartmouth Col, BA, 44; Swiss Fed Inst Technol, DrSc Tech, 49. *Prof Exp:* Group leader org chem, Foster D Snell, Inc, 49-50; group leader, Evans Res & Develop Corp, 50-57, assoc develop mgr, 57-60, develop mgr, 60-63, vpres, 63-68, sr vpres, 68-69; vpres, Foster D Snell, Inc, Booz, Allen & Hamilton, Inc, 69-74; vpres opers, William T Thompson Co, 74-75; vpres, Herbert V Shuster, Inc, 75-89. *Concurrent Pos:* Guest lectr, NY Univ, 55. *Mem:* Am Chem Soc; Am Inst Chem; Inst Food Technol; NY Acad Sci; Am Soc Testing & Mat. *Res:* Biochemistry of foods and food products; product development; pharmaceuticals; market research; enzymes; dehydrated and intermediate moisture compressed foods; canless sterilization of foods; performance testing; cosmetics; health and beauty aids. *Mailing Add:* 128 Dogwood Lane Stamford CT 06903. *Fax:* 203-329-0229

KONIGSBERG, ALVIN STUART, ATMOSPHERIC SCIENCE, BIOMETEOROLOGY. *Current Pos:* from asst prof to assoc prof physics, 68-77, chmn dept, 77-79, dir innovative studies, 79-82, ASSOC PROF GEOL SCI, STATE UNIV NY COL NEW PALTZ, 82- *Personal Data:* b New York, NY, Apr 28, 43; m 94, Kathleen McCue; c Laura & Amy. *Educ:* City Col New York, BS, 63; Syracuse Univ, MS, 65, PhD(physics), 69. *Prof Exp:* Res assoc physics, Atmospheric Sci Res Ctr, State Univ NY, Albany, 65; teaching asst, Syracuse Univ, 63-68. *Concurrent Pos:* Aeronaut & Space res fel, NASA & Am Asn Eng Educ, 73 & 74; NY State Col teaching fel. *Mem:* AAAS; Am Water Resources Asn; Sigma Xi; Am Meteorol Soc. *Res:* Oxidant pollution; condensation nuclei studies; light scattering instrumentation; alternate energy systems. *Mailing Add:* Dept Geol Sci State Univ NY Col New Paltz NY 12561. *Fax:* 914-257-3791; *E-Mail:* konigsba@matrix.newpaltz.edu

KONIGSBERG, MOSES, ORGANIC CHEMISTRY. *Current Pos:* CONSULT, 84- *Personal Data:* b Montreal, Que, Can, Sept 21, 12; nat US; m 39; c 2. *Educ:* Ohio State Univ, AB, 35, PhD(org chem), 39. *Prof Exp:* Atlas Powder Co fel, Ohio State Univ, 39-40; res chemist, Nat Starch Prod, Inc, NY, 40-46; res chemist & vpres, Polymer Industs, Inc, 46-54, vpres res & develop, 54-58, commercial develop, 58-61; vpres & tech dir, Hudson Industs Corp, 61-84. *Mem:* AAAS; Am Chem Soc; NY Acad Sci. *Res:* Natural and synthetic polymers; industrial adhesives. *Mailing Add:* 40019 Village Apt 40 Camarillo CA 93010

KONIGSBERG, WILLIAM HENRY, BIOCHEMISTRY. *Current Pos:* assoc prof biochem, 64-74, assoc prof molecular biophys & biochem & human genetics, 74-77, PROF MOLECULAR BIOPHYS & BIOCHEM & HUMAN GENETICS, YALE UNIV, 77- *Personal Data:* b New York, NY, Apr 5, 30; m 56; c 1. *Educ:* Rensselaer Polytech Inst, BSc, 52; Columbia Univ, PhD(chem), 56. *Prof Exp:* Asst prof biochem, Rockefeller Inst, 58-64. *Res:* Protein chemistry; structure of hemoglobin; structure and function of proteins, peptides and natural products; antibodies; virus proteins; mechanism of T4 DNA replication. *Mailing Add:* Dept Biochem & Molecular Biophys C-113 Sterling Hall Yale Univ Sch Med 333 Cedar St New Haven CT 06510-3219

KONIJN, HENDRIK SALOMON, ECONOMICS. *Current Pos:* PROF STATIST, TEL-AVIV UNIV, 65- *Personal Data:* b Amsterdam, Netherlands, Mar 17, 18; nat US. *Educ:* Columbia Univ, MA, 42; Univ Calif, PhD(statist), 54. *Prof Exp:* Jr staff mem, Nat Bur Econ Res, NY, 41-42; statistician, Combined Shipping Adj Bd, DC, 42-45; res analyst, Off Strategic Servs, 45, Off Far Eastern Affairs, US Dept State, 45-47, statist consult econ res, Univ Calif, 53-54; lectr agr econ, Univ Calif, Berkeley, 54-56; sr lectr econ statist, Sydney, 56-61; prof, City Col New York, 63-65. *Concurrent Pos:* Vis assoc prof, Cowles Found, Yale Univ, 61-62; vis prof statist, Univ Minn, 62-63 & Univ BC, 88. *Mem:* Fel AAAS; fel Am Statist Asn; Am Econ Asn; Inst Math Statist; Royal Statist Soc. *Res:* Statistical methodology; econometric studies. *Mailing Add:* Rehov Hahaganall Apt 12 Jerusalem 97851 Israel

KONIKOW, LEONARD FRANKLIN, HYDROLOGY & GEOLOGY, GROUND-WATER MODELING. *Current Pos:* HYDROLOGIST, US GEOL SURV, 72- *Personal Data:* b Far Rockaway, NY, Jan 26, 46; m 66; c 2. *Educ:* Hofstra Univ, BA, 66; Pa State Univ, MS, 69, PhD(geol), 73. *Honors & Awards:* Birdsall Distinguished Lectr, Geol Soc Am, 86; Sci Award, Nat Groundwater Asn, 89. *Prof Exp:* Geologist, Geraghty & Miller Inc, 66; instr geol, Hofstra Univ, 66. *Concurrent Pos:* Assoc ed, Water Resource Res, 81-84; chmn, hydrol prog, Am Geophys Union; lectr, Univ Va, 91-92; chmn, Hydrogeol Div, Geol Soc Am, 93-94. *Mem:* Fel Geol Soc Am; Am Geophys Union; Int Asn Hydrogeol; Nat Groundwater Asn. *Res:* Transport and dispersion of solutes in flowing ground water. *Mailing Add:* 11316 Myrtle Lane Reston VA 20191

KONING, ROSS E, PLANT GROWTH REGULATION, FLOWER PHYSIOLOGY. *Current Pos:* from asst prof to assoc prof, 87-93, PROF BOT, EASTERN CONN STATE UNIV, 94- *Personal Data:* b Adrian, Mich, Oct 5, 53; m 81, Christine E Steeb; c Hans, Katje & Kurt. *Educ:* Univ Mich, BS, 75, MS, 76, PhD(bot), 81. *Prof Exp:* Asst prof bot, Rutgers Univ, 81-87. *Concurrent Pos:* Spec ed, Am Jour Bot, 83-86; ed, Physiol Sect, Bot Soc Am, 85- *Mem:* Bot Soc Am; Am Soc Plant Physiologist; Plant Growth Regulators Soc Am. *Res:* Developmental physiology of flowering, particularly growth of flower parts and hormonal and environmental cues involved in the timing mechanisms. *Mailing Add:* Dept Biol Sci Eastern Conn State Univ 83 Windham St Willimantic CT 06226-2211. *Fax:* 860-465-5213; *E-Mail:* koning@ecsu.ctstateu.edu

KONINGSTEIN, JOHANNES A, CHEMISTRY, CHEMICAL PHYSICS. *Current Pos:* RETIRED. *Personal Data:* b Velsen, Netherlands, Nov 30, 33; Can citizen; m 59; c 2. *Educ:* Univ Amsterdam, Drs & Dr(chem), 59. *Prof Exp:* Fel, Nat Res Coun Can, 59-61; mem res staff, Bell Tel Labs, 62-65; from asst prof to prof chem, Carleton Univ, 65-95. *Concurrent Pos:* Vis prof, Nat Res Coun Can, 69-; Isac Walton Killam res fel, 85-87. *Mem:* Am Phys Soc; Chem Inst Can. *Res:* Molecular and atomic research; electronic Raman spectroscopy. *Mailing Add:* 728 Eastbourne Ave Ottawa ON K1K 0H7 Can

KONISHI, FRANK, NUTRITION. *Current Pos:* RETIRED. *Personal Data:* b Ft Lupton, Colo, Dec 2, 28; m 50, Gladys Koshio; c Gayle, Greg & Laura. *Educ:* Colo State Univ, BS, 50, MS, 52; Cornell Univ, PhD(animal nutrit), 58. *Prof Exp:* Asst, Colo State Univ, 50-52 & Cornell Univ, 52-54, 57-58; radiobiologist, US Naval Radiol Defense Lab, 58-61; assoc prof nutrit, Southern Ill Univ, Carbondale, 61-65, chmn dept, 65-77, prof sch med, 74-83, prof nutrit, 66-83. *Concurrent Pos:* Adj prof, Univ Colo, Boulder, 84- *Mem:* Am Inst Nutrit; Am Dietetic Asn; NY Acad Sci; Sigma Xi. *Res:* Nutritional dietary surveys; obesity; energy metabolism. *Mailing Add:* Univ Colo 2736 Winding Trail Pl Boulder CO 80304-1412

KONISHI, MASAKAZU, NEUROBIOLOGY. *Current Pos:* prof, 75-79, BING PROF BEHAV BIOL, CALIF INST TECHNOL, 79- *Personal Data:* b Kyoto, Japan, Feb 17, 33. *Educ:* Hokkaido Univ, BS, 56, MS, 58; Univ Calif, Berkeley, PhD(zool), 63. *Honors & Awards:* Newcomb Cleveland Prize, AAAS, 78; Elliot Couse Award, Am Ornithol Union, 83; F O Schmitt Prize, 87; Int Prize, Biol, Japanese Asn Prom Sci, 90. *Prof Exp:* Alexander von Humboldt Found fel, 63-64; Int Brain Res Orgn-UNESCO fel, 64-65; asst prof zool, Univ Wis, 65-66; from asst prof to assoc prof biol, Princeton Univ, 70-75. *Mem:* Nat Acad Sci; AAAS; Am Soc Zoologistss; Am Soc Naturalists; Acoust Soc Am; Soc Neurosci; Am Acad Arts & Sci; Int Soc Neuroethology (pres, 87-89). *Res:* Behavior and neurobiology. *Mailing Add:* Calif Inst Technol Div Biol 216-76 Pasadena CA 91125. *Fax:* 626-459-0879

KONISHI, YASUO, PROTEIN SCIENCE, PEPTIDE CHEMISTRY. *Current Pos:* SR RES OFFICER, NAT RES COUN CAN, 89- *Personal Data:* m 76, Mamiko Nawamoto; c Akira, Misato & Kyoko. *Educ:* Shizuoka Univ, BSc, 71; Tohoku Univ, MSc, 73, PhD(chem), 76. *Prof Exp:* Postdoctoral assoc, Cornell Univ, 76-80, res assoc, 81-84; shorei-kenkyu-in, Kyoto Univ, 80-81; res specialist, Monsanto Co, 84-89. *Concurrent Pos:* Adj prof, McGill Univ, 93- *Mem:* Am Peptide Soc; Protein Soc; Biophys Soc; Am Soc Mass Spectrometry. *Res:* Structure and function of protein-ligand interactions; design of peptides and peptidomimetics as protease inhibitors; characterization of proteins by mass spectrometry. *Mailing Add:* Biotechnol Res Inst 6100 Royalmount Ave Montreal PQ H4P 2R2 Can. *Fax:* 514-496-5143; *E-Mail:* yasuo.konishi@nrc.ca

KONISKY, JORDAN, MICROBIAL PHYSIOLOGY. *Current Pos:* from asst prof to assoc prof, 70-81, head, Dept Microbiol, 84-89, PROF MICROBIOL, UNIV ILL, URBANA, 81-; DIR, SCH LIFE SCI, 89- *Personal Data:* b Providence, RI, Apr 8, 41; m 67; c 2. *Educ:* Providence Col, BA, 63; Univ Wis, Madison, PhD(genetics), 68. *Prof Exp:* Res assoc genetics, Univ Wis, Madison, 68; NIH fel molecular biophys & biochem, Yale Univ, 68-70. *Concurrent Pos:* Career develop award, NIH, 75. *Mem:* Am Soc Microbiol; AAAS; fel AAAS; fel Am Acad Microbiol. *Res:* regulation of gene expression in bacteria; functions of bacterial membrane; physiology and molecular biology of methanogenic bacteria. *Mailing Add:* Dept Microbiol Univ Ill 131 Burrill Hall 407 S Goodwin Ave Urbana IL 61801

KONIZER, GEORGE BURR, PHYSICAL ORGANIC CHEMISTRY, SYNTHETIC FIBERS. *Current Pos:* RETIRED. *Personal Data:* b Wilmington, Del, Dec 24, 42; m 66, Virginia Jones; c Christopher G & Eric D. *Educ:* Univ Del, BA, 64, MBA, 76; Univ SC, PhD(chem), 68. *Prof Exp:* Res chemist, Dacron Res Lab, E I Du Pont de Nemours & Co Inc, 69-71 & Textile Res Lab, 71-75, sr res chemist, Textile Res Lab, 75-78, supvr res & develop orlon, 78-81, supvr res & develop nylon, 81-83, tech group mgr, Lycra, 83-94, strategic planning, 94-96. *Concurrent Pos:* Fel, State Univ NY Col Forestry, Syracuse Univ, 68-69. *Mem:* Am Chem Soc; Sigma Xi. *Res:* Fiber research. *Mailing Add:* PO Box 11541 Prescott AZ 80304-1541. *Fax:* 520-445-1693; *E-Mail:* konizerg@northlink.com

KONKEL, DAVID ANTHONY, MOLECULAR GENETICS, CELL BIOLOGY. *Current Pos:* ASST PROF CELL BIOL, DEPT HUMAN GENETICS & CELL BIOL, UNIV TEX MED BR GALVESTON, 80- *Personal Data:* b Washington, DC, Feb 20, 48; m 70. *Educ:* Boston Col, BS, 70; Mass Inst Technol, PhD(biochem), 77. *Prof Exp:* Asst biochem, Dept Biol, Mass Inst Technol, 70-77; staff fel, Lab Molecular Genetics, Nat Inst Child & Human Develop, 77-80. *Concurrent Pos:* Prin investr grants, NSF, 80-83, NIH, 82-85 & Tex Heart Asn, 85-86. *Mem:* AAAS; Sigma Xi; Am Soc Cell Biol. *Res:* Recombinant DNA technology to study the structure and regulation of genes encoding mouse and chicken myoglobin; characterization of a new gene family related to ras oncogenes. *Mailing Add:* Dept Human Biol Chem & Genetics Univ Tex Med Br 111-B Galveston TX 77550-0643

KONKEL, PHILIP M, PETROLEUM GEOLOGY. *Current Pos:* Geologist, Ohio, 40-55, asst chief geologist, 55-61, geologist, Tulsa Div, 61-65, explor mgr, 65-74, EXPLOR CONSULT, 74- *Personal Data:* b Brush, Colo, May 5, 12; m 36. *Educ:* Univ Wyo, BA, 34, MA, 35. *Mem:* Am Asn Petrol Geologists; Soc Explor Geophys. *Res:* Petroleum exploration. *Mailing Add:* 3227 S Quebec Ave Tulsa OK 74135

KONKOWSKI, DEBORAH ANN, GENERAL RELATIVITY THEORY, NATURE OF SINGULARITIES. *Current Pos:* PROF MATH, US NAVAL ACAD, 87- *Personal Data:* b Akron, Ohio, Mar 3, 55. *Educ:* Harvey Mudd Col, BS, 77; Univ Tex, Austin, PhD(physics), 83. *Prof Exp:* Res fel, Univ Md, Col Park, 83-85; Queen Mary Col, Univ London, 85-87. *Concurrent Pos:* Prin investr, NSF, 89- *Mem:* Am Phys Soc; Soc Gen Relativity & Gravitation; Am Math Soc; Math Asn Am; AAAS. *Res:* Mathematical physics and theoretical physics; general theory of relativity; nature and stability of space time singularities; mild quasiregular and non-scalar curvature singularities and cauchy horizons. *Mailing Add:* 514 Andrew Hill Ct Arnold MD 21012. *E-Mail:* dak@nadn.navy.mil

KONNERTH, KARL LOUIS, MEDICAL ELECTRONICS, BIO-MEDICAL ENGINEERING. *Current Pos:* staff res engr, Thomas J Watson Res Ctr, 64-74, mgr, I/O Systs, IBM Res Div, 74-77, MGR ADVAN TECHNOL, IBM BIOMED SYSTS, IBM CORP, 77- *Personal Data:* b Mt Pleasant, Pa, Aug 15, 32. *Educ:* Carnegie Inst Technol, BS, 54, MS, 55, PhD(elec eng), 61. *Honors & Awards:* Outstanding Innovation Award, IBM Corp, 76. *Prof Exp:* Asst prof elec eng, Carnegie Inst Technol, 61-64. *Mem:* Sr mem Inst Elec & Electronics Engrs; Asn Advan Med Instrumentation. *Res:* Investigation of new types of bio-medical instrumentation. *Mailing Add:* Quincy Rd Putnam Valley NY 10579

KONO, TETSURO, PHYSIOLOGY, BIOCHEMISTRY. *Current Pos:* from asst prof to prof physiol, 63-85, prof, 85-92, EMER PROF MOLECULAR PHYSIOL & BIOPHYS, SCH MED, VANDERBILT UNIV, 92- *Personal Data:* b Tokyo, Japan, May 17, 25; m 61, Seiko Kanda; c Michiko, Masahiro & Kenji. *Educ:* Univ Tokyo, BA, 47, PhD(anal chem), 58. *Prof Exp:* Instr agr chem, Univ Tokyo, 47-58 & 60-63. *Mem:* Am Soc Biochem; Am Diabetes Asn. *Res:* Mechanism of insulin action. *Mailing Add:* Dept Molecular Physiol & Biophys Vanderbilt Univ Sch Med 209 Oxford House 21st Ave S Nashville TN 37232-4245

KONOPINSKI, VIRGIL J, SAFETY, INDUSTRIAL HYGIENE. *Current Pos:* regional safety engr, 91-93, HUMAN RESOURCE ANALYST-SAFETY, US POSTAL SERV, CHICAGO, 93- *Personal Data:* b Toledo, Ohio, July 11, 35; m 64, Joan M Wielinski; c Ann M, Carol S & Peter J. *Educ:* Univ Toledo, BS, 56; Pratt Inst, MS, 60; Bowling Green State Univ, MBA, 71. *Prof Exp:* Asst to dir environ control, Owens Corning Fiberglass, Toledo, 67-72; chief exec officer, Midwest Environ Mgt, 72-73; staff specialist, Williams Brothers Waste Control, Tulsa, 73-75; dir IH & RH, Ind State Bd Health, Indianapolis, 75-87; exec vpres, Asbestos Technol, Indianapolis, 87-89; consult pvt pract, Zionsville, 89-90; sr consult, Occusafe, Wheeling, 90-91. *Concurrent Pos:* Consult pvt pract, 75- *Mem:* Am Soc Safety Engrs; Am Indust Hyg Asn; Am Conf Govt Indust Hygienists. *Res:* Occupational health and safety; formaldehyde; carbon monoxide; carbon dioxide; pesticides; indoor air; mercury; sampling strategies and techniques; long range planning and forecasting; lead; herbicides. *Mailing Add:* 14 Fairfield Lane Cary IL 60013-1946

KONOPKA, ALLAN EUGENE, MICROBIOLOGY. *Current Pos:* from asst prof to assoc prof, 77-83, PROF BIOL, PURDUE UNIV, 92- *Personal Data:* b Chicago, Ill, Feb 26, 50; m 73; c 3. *Educ:* Univ Ill, Urbana, BS, 71; Univ Wash, MS, 73, PhD(microbiol), 75. *Prof Exp:* Res assoc microbiol, Univ Wis-Madison, 75-77. *Concurrent Pos:* Fulbright fel, 84; Fogarty fel, 92; chair, Microbiol Ecol Div, Am Soc Microbiol, 94. *Mem:* Am Soc Microbiol; Sigma Xi. *Res:* Microbial ecology; microbial growth kinetics; microbial biodegradation. *Mailing Add:* Dept Biol Sci Purdue Univ West Lafayette IN 47907. *E-Mail:* akonopka@bilbo.bio.purdue.edu

KONOPKA, RONALD J, NEUROGENETICS. *Current Pos:* BIOTECHNOL CONSULT, 90- *Personal Data:* b Cleveland, Ohio, Oct 19, 47. *Educ:* Univ Dayton, BS, 67; Calif Inst Technol, PhD(biochem), 72. *Prof Exp:* Fel biol, Stanford Univ, 72-74; asst prof biol, Calif Inst Technol, 74-82; assoc prof biol, Clarkson Univ, 83-90. *Concurrent Pos:* NSF fel, 72-73; mem sci adv bd, Found Res Hereditary Dis, 72-81; Helen Hay Whitney fel, 73-74; mem, Biol Sci Study Sect, NIH, 90-94. *Res:* Circadian rhythm; behavior genetics of Drosophila; genetic engineering. *Mailing Add:* 430 S Santa Anita Ave Pasadena CA 91107

KONORT, MARK D, ORGANIC CHEMISTRY. *Current Pos:* RETIRED. *Personal Data:* b Sliven, Bulgaria, Nov 20, 18; nat US; m 52, Marliese C Ambach; c Paul F & Philip A. *Educ:* Univ Toulouse, Dipl Ing Chim, 40; Rutgers Univ, MS, 50, PhD(org chem), 52. *Prof Exp:* Chemist, Matam Corp, 42-44; develop chemist, R J Prentiss & Co, 47; asst, Rutgers Univ, 48-52; sr res chemist, Lever Bros Co, 52-56, prin res chemist, 56-59, res assoc, 59-63, sr res assoc, 63-72, res scientist, 72-81, sr res scientist, 81-84. *Mem:* Am Chem Soc; Sigma Xi. *Res:* Lubricating and cutting oils; insecticides; substituted phenanthrenes and hydrophenanthrenes; detergents; edible products; organic synthesis. *Mailing Add:* 90 Morris Ave Haworth NJ 07641

KONOWALOW, DANIEL DIMITRI, theoretical chemistry, for more information see previous edition

KONRAD, DUSAN, ELECTROCHEMISTRY. *Current Pos:* MEM TECH STAFF, TEX INSTRUMENTS, INC, DALLAS, 78- *Personal Data:* b Brno, Czech, Jan 7, 35; US citizen; m 72, Yitka Svachova; c Peter & Martin. *Educ:* Masaryk Univ, Czech, MS, 57; Czech Acad Sci, PhD(chem), 62. *Prof Exp:* Instr inorg chem, Masaryk Univ, Czech, 57-62; res scientist phys chem, J Heyrovsky Inst Polarography, Czech Acad Sci, 63-66; res chemist, Govt Assay Off, Czech, 67-68; sr res fel, Rudjer Boskovic Inst, Yugoslavia, 68-69; res fel chem, Calif Inst Technol, 70-71; sr scientist electrochem, Technol Ctr, ESB Inc, Yardley, Pa, 71-78. *Mem:* Electrochem Soc. *Res:* Electrochemical instrumentation; automatized data taking and processing; electrode impedance in Laplace plane analysis; electrochemistry of lead-acid cell; non-stoichiometric oxide electrodes; porous electrodes; computer software systems. *Mailing Add:* 13450 Maham Rd No 932 Dallas TX 75240. *E-Mail:* dusankonrad@juno.com

KONRAD, GERHARD T(HIES), ELECTRICAL ENGINEERING. *Current Pos:* MGR, PHYSICS/MICROWAVE ENG, SIEMONS MED SYSTS, CONCORD, CALIF. *Personal Data:* b Konigsberg, Ger, Feb 23, 35; US citizen; m 64, Martha Kespohl; c Matthew Nathan. *Educ:* Univ Mich, BSE, 57, MSE, 60, PhD(elec eng), 69. *Prof Exp:* Asst res engr, Univ Mich, 60-61, assoc res engr, 61-69; staff mem, Lincoln Lab, Mass Inst Technol, 69-72; staff mem, Stanford Linear Accelerator Ctr, 72-77, head, Klystron Dept, 77-86. *Concurrent Pos:* Consult, Litton Indust, 79-89 & Valvo, Ger, 78-82 & Los Alamos Nat Lab, 88- *Mem:* Inst Elec & Electronics Engrs; Am Phys Soc; Nat Soc Prof Engrs; Sigma Xi. *Res:* Electron devices; microwave circuits; electron optics; high-voltage techniques; vacuum techniques; plasma physics; electromagnetic theory; medical physics. *Mailing Add:* 787 Kirkcrest Rd Danville CA 94526. *Fax:* 510-246-8370; *E-Mail:* gkonrad@smsocs.com

KONRAD, MICHAEL WARREN, PHYSICAL CHEMISTRY OF NUCLEIC ACIDS, SIMULATIONS OF MOLECULAR DYNAMICS. *Current Pos:* PRES, GENE VUE, INC, 93- *Personal Data:* b San Diego, Calif, Dec 20, 36; m 69, 84, Wanda deVlaninck; c Robin (Dederich), Hans & Michel. *Educ:* Calif Inst Technol, BS, 58; Univ Calif, Berkeley, PhD(biophys), 64. *Prof Exp:* NSF res fel biochem, Harvard Univ, 64-66; asst prof chem, Univ Calif, Los Angeles, 66-74; assoc res scientist, Univ Calif, Berkeley, 74-80; sr scientist, Cetus Corp, 80-90; dir, de Vlaminck Inst, 90-93. *Mem:* AAAS; Am Soc Biochem & Molecular Biol. *Res:* Development of DNA diagnostics; computer simulations of the response of macromolecules to distorting forces. *Mailing Add:* 1199 Camino Vallecito Lafayette CA 94549. *Fax:* 510-295-9809; *E-Mail:* genevue@ccnet.com

KONRADI, ANDREI, SPACE PHYSICS. *Current Pos:* Aero space technologist, Goddard Space Flight Ctr, NASA, 61-70, AERO SPACE TECHNOLOGIST, JOHNSON SPACE CTR, NASA, 70- *Personal Data:* b Prague, Czech, July 22, 31; US citizen; m 57; c 5. *Educ:* Franklin & Marshall Col, BS, 54; Univ Rochester, PhD(nuclear physics), 62. *Mem:* Am Geophys Union; Am Inst Aeronaut & Astronaut; Am Phys Soc; NY Acad Sci; AAAS. *Res:* Study of dynamic processes in the magnetosphere; space plasma simulation; magnetospheric physics; solar-terrestrial interations. *Mailing Add:* 430 Hickory Ridge Dr Seabrook TX 77586-6009

KONSLER, THOMAS RHINEHART, HORTICULTURE. *Current Pos:* From asst prof to prof, 61-88, EMER PROF HORT SCI, MOUNTAIN HORT CROPS RES, NC STATE UNIV, 88- *Personal Data:* b Henderson, Ky, Apr 17, 25; m 54; c 9. *Educ:* Univ Ky, BS, 55; NC State Univ, MS, 57, PhD(exp statist), 61. *Mem:* Am Soc Hort Sci. *Res:* Cultural practices and plant breeding with vegetable crops and American Ginseng. *Mailing Add:* 805 Oakland St Hendersonville NC 28791

KONSTAM, AARON HARRY, PROGRAMMING LANGUAGES, EXPERT SYSTEMS. *Current Pos:* assoc prof, 72-86, PROF COMPUT SCI, TRINITY UNIV, 86- *Personal Data:* b Bronx, NY, Aug 11, 36; m 61, Patricia Smuthers; c David. *Educ:* Polytech Inst Brooklyn, BS, 57; Pa State Univ, PhD(phys org chem), 61. *Prof Exp:* Instr chem, Brooklyn Col, 61-62; fel & res assoc phys org chem, Israel Inst Technol, 62-64; sr res chemist, Monsanto Res Corp, 65-69; dir comput ctr & assoc prof math, Lindenwood Cols, 69-72. *Concurrent Pos:* Treas, 77-80, vpres, Vanguard Systs Corp, 80-83. *Mem:* Asn Comput Mach; Inst Elec & Electronics Engrs. *Res:* Artificial intelligence, genetic algorithims and programming languages. *Mailing Add:* Trinity Univ 715 Stadium Dr San Antonio TX 78212. *Fax:* 210-736-7477; *E-Mail:* akonstam@trinity.edu

KONSTAN, JOSEPH A, COMPUTER SCIENCE. *Current Pos:* Instr, 92-93, ASST PROF, UNIV MINN, 93- *Personal Data:* b New York, NY, May 10, 66; m, Ellen Kletzman. *Educ:* Harvard Univ, AB, 87; Univ Calif, Berkeley, MS, 90, PhD(comput sci), 93. *Concurrent Pos:* NSF grantee, 94-; lectr, Asn Comput Mach, 97-98. *Mem:* Asn Comput Mach. *Res:* Graphical user-interface toolkits and frameworks; human computer interaction; multimedia systems; collaborative filtering; internet tools and applications. *Mailing Add:* Dept Comput Sci & Eng Univ Minn Minneapolis MN 55455. *E-Mail:* konstan@cs.umn.edu

KONSTANTOPOULOS, TAKIS, APPLIED PROBABILITY & STOCHASTIC NETWORKS, STATIONARY & ERGODIC STOCHASTIC PROCESSES & SYSTEMS. *Current Pos:* asst prof, 92-96, ASSOC PROF, UNIV TEX, AUSTIN, 97- *Personal Data:* b Patras, Greece, May 29, 61. *Educ:* Nat Tech Univ Athens, dipl, 83; Univ Calif, Berkeley, MSc, 85, PhD(elec eng), 89. *Prof Exp:* Sr researcher, Nat Res Inst, France, 89-91; lectr, Univ Calif, Berkeley, 91-92. *Concurrent Pos:* Vis prof, Cornell Univ, 92. *Mem:* Inst Math Statist; Inst Elec & Electronics Engrs; Math Asn Am. *Res:* Stochastic networks in the presence of long-range dependent data; macroscopic approximations of complex stochastic systems; stationarity and stability of stochastic networks; stochastic control and optimization of telecommunication systems; performance analysis of high speed networks. *Mailing Add:* Elec & Comput Eng Dept Univ Tex Austin TX 78712. *E-Mail:* takis@alea.ece.utexas.edu

KONTNY, VINCENT L, MINING ENGINEERING. *Current Pos:* managing dir, Fluor Australia, Melbourne, 79-82, group vpres, Fluor Engrs, Inc, 82-85, pres & chief exec officer, 85-87, group pres, Fluor Daniel, 87-88, pres, Fluor Corp, 90-94, vchmn, 94, PRES, FLUOR DANIEL, 88- *Personal Data:* b Chappell, Nebr, July 19, 37; m 70, Joan D FitzGibbon; c Natascha M, Michael C & Amber B. *Educ:* Univ Colo, BSCE, 58. *Hon Degrees:* DSc, Univ Colo, 91. *Prof Exp:* Proj mgr, Utah Construct & Mining Co, Western Australia, 65-69; proj mgr, Fluor Australia, Queensland, Australia, 69-72; sr proj mgr, Fluor Utah, 72-73; sr vpres, Holmes & Narver, Inc, 73-79. *Concurrent Pos:* Mem eng develop coun, Univ Colo, 59-65; mem eng adv coun, Stanford Univ, 59-65. *Mem:* Am Asn Cost Engrs; Australian Asn Engrs; Am Petrol Inst. *Res:* Author of numerous articles. *Mailing Add:* 601 Lido Park Dr 2AB Newport Beach CA 92663

KONTOS, EMMANUEL G, NEW POLYMER SYNTHESIS, MANAGEMENT OF TECHNOLOGY. *Current Pos:* res scientist elastomers prod develop mgr, Uniroyal Chem Co, 59-63, group leader colloidal prod, 63-66, res assoc new prod, 76-79, mgr thermoplastic elastomers, 79-84, MGR ELASTOMERS TECHNOL, UNIROYAL CHEM CO, 84-, MGR, TECHNOL LIC, 97- *Personal Data:* b Mar 23, 32; m 58, Clare Wright; c Nina J & Leila M. *Educ:* Nadunal Tech Univ, Greece, BS, 55; Columbia Univ, NY, MS, 57, PhD(chem), 59. *Prof Exp:* Mgr polymer physics, Uniroyal Res & Develop Ctr, 66-73; mgr compounds processing tires, Uniroyal Tire Co, 73-76. *Concurrent Pos:* Adj assoc prof phys & polymer chem, Southern Conn State Col, 60-62; vchmn, Rubber Div, Am Chem Soc, 89 & 91. *Mem:* Am Chem Soc; Sigma Xi. *Res:* Development of improved ethylene-propylene-diene and nitrile-butadiene synthetic rubbers, new catalyst and process improvement; development of new applications for ethylene-propylene-diene and nitrile-butadiene rubbers in thermoset and thermoplastic elastomeric applications. *Mailing Add:* Uniroyal Chem Co Inc World Hq Middlebury CT 06749. *Fax:* 203-573-3393; *E-Mail:* kontos@uniroyal.geis.com

KONTOS, HERMES A, MEDICINE, PHYSIOLOGY. *Current Pos:* From instr to assoc prof, 64-72, PROF MED, MED COL VA, 72-, CHMN DIV CARDIO PULMONARY MED, 81- *Personal Data:* b Lefka, Cyprus, Dec 13, 33; US citizen; m 60; c 2. *Educ:* Nat Univ Athens, MD, 58; Med Col Va, PhD(physiol), 67; Am Col Physicians, dipl, 69. *Concurrent Pos:* USPHS res career develop award, 67-72; Markle scholar acad med, 69-74. *Mem:* Am Fedn Clin Res; Am Heart Asn; Am Physiol Soc; Am Soc Clin Invest; Sigma Xi. *Res:* Circulatory physiology and pathophysiology. *Mailing Add:* Dept Med Med Col Va Va Commonwealth Univ Box 980565 Richmond VA 23298-0565. *Fax:* 804-828-7628

KONTRAS, STELLA B, PEDIATRICS, GENETICS. *Current Pos:* Intern med, Ohio State Univ, 54, instr pediat, 54-60, asst prof pediat & anat, 60-66, assoc prof pediat, 66-69, PROF PEDIAT, COL MED, OHIO STATE UNIV, 69- *Personal Data:* b Newport News, Va, June 28, 28; m 47; c 3. *Educ:* Ohio State Univ, BA, 48, MA, 49, MD, 53. *Concurrent Pos:* Resident pediat, Ohio State Univ, 55 56, resident path, 57-58; consult, Ohio Dept Health, 62-70; NIH spec fel cancer, Ohio State Univ, 63-64; dir, Med Genetics Ctr, Children's Hosp, Columbus, 65-71, vchmn, Dept Pediat, 80. *Mem:* Soc Pediat Res; Am Soc Hemat; Am Soc Human Genetics. *Res:* Hematology. *Mailing Add:* Children's Hosp 700 Children's Dr Columbus OH 43205-2696

KONYA, CALVIN JOSEPH, MINING ENGINEERING, BLASTING. *Current Pos:* assoc prof, Ohio State Univ, 78-81, chmn dept, 81-85, prof mining eng, 81-88, ADJ PROF, OHIO STATE UNIV, 88- *Personal Data:* b Cleveland, Ohio, June 23, 43. *Educ:* Mo Sch Mines, BS, 66; Univ Mo-Rolla, MS, 68 & 70, PhD(mining eng), 72. *Hon Degrees:* Dr, Univ Miskolc, Hungary. *Prof Exp:* From asst prof to assoc prof mining eng, WVa Univ, 71-78. *Concurrent Pos:* Mgr tech servs, Precision Blasting Servs, 73-; exchange scientist, Nat Acad Sci, 75; pres, Hydrocarbon Fuels, 83-87; dir, Ohio Mining & Mineral Resources Res Inst; pres, Precision Blasting Syst, 87; adj prof, Ohio Univ, 88-; adj prof, John Caroll Univ, 88- & Univ Miskolc, 88- *Mem:* Soc Explosives Engrs (pres, 75-77, exec dir, 74-87); Am Inst Mining, Metall & Petrol Engrs. *Res:* Rock mechanics; explosives engineering; definition of mechanisms of rock fragmentation by blasting both for production rounds and for controlled blasting techniques; development of practical equations for prediction of blast design variables in the field. *Mailing Add:* 11783 Clay Huntsburg OH 44064

KONZ, STEPHAN A, ERGONOMICS. *Current Pos:* from asst prof to assoc prof, 64-69, PROF INDUST ENG, KANS STATE UNIV, 69- *Personal Data:* b Milwaukee, Wis, Nov 25, 33; m 58; c 5. *Educ:* Univ Mich, BS, 56, MBA, 56; Univ Iowa, MS, 60; Univ Ill, PhD(indust eng), 64. *Honors & Awards:* Fitts Award, Human Factors Soc. *Prof Exp:* Indust engr, Westinghouse Elec Corp, 56-57 & Collins Radio Co, 58-60; instr mech & indust eng, Univ Ill, 60-64. *Mem:* Inst Indust Engrs; Human Factors Soc; Am Indust Hyg Asn; Am Soc Heat, Refrig & Air-Conditioning Engrs. *Res:* Ergonomics, especially design of industrial jobs; heat stress; Inspection; hand tools. *Mailing Add:* Dept Indust Eng Kans State Univ Durland Hall Rm 237 Manhattan KS 66502-5101

KONZAK, CALVIN FRANCIS, INDUCED MUTATIONS IN PLANTS, GENETICS. *Current Pos:* PROPRIETOR, NW PLANT BREEDING CO, INC, 82-, SCIENTIST DIR, 94- *Personal Data:* b Devils Lake, NDak, Oct 17, 24; div; c Kenneth & Gary James. *Educ:* NDak Agr Col, BS, 48; Cornell Univ, PhD, 52. *Prof Exp:* Assoc geneticist, Dept Biol, Brookhaven Nat Lab, 52-57; from assoc prof to prof & assoc agronomist to agronomist, Wash State Univ, 57-63, prof genetics, 63-94. *Concurrent Pos:* USPHS sr fel, 65-66; spec adv, Plant Breeding & Genetics Sect, Jt Food & Agr Orgn-Int Atomic Energy Agency Div Food & Agr, Vienna, 65-67; food & agr consult, Crop Res & Introd Ctr, Izmir, Turkey, 71; sci adv, Plant Breeding & Genetics Sect, Jt Food & Agr Orgn-Int Atomic Energy Agency Div Atomic Energy Food & Agr, 73-74 & 82-83; pres & prop, Northwest Plant Breeding Co, 94- *Mem:* Fel AAAS; Genetics Soc Am; fel Am Soc Agron; fel Crop Sci Soc Am. *Res:* Breeding semidwarf, hard red and soft white spring wheat, durum wheat oats for improved yield, and tolerance in semidwarf oats to barley yellow dwarf virus; genetics of reduced height and other traits in wheat and oats; induction of useful mutations in wheat and oats; development and application of electronic data capture and management systems for plant breeding; agronomic crop research. *Mailing Add:* 2001 Country Club Rd Pullman WA 99163

KONZELMAN, LEROY MICHAEL, ORGANIC CHEMISTRY. *Current Pos:* DIR BUS DEVELOP, CHEM DYNAMICS CORP, SOUTH PLAINFIELD, NJ, 84- *Personal Data:* b Jersey City, NJ, May 27, 36; m 60, Mercedes D Franz; c Michael L, Patricia A & Christine. *Educ:* St Peter's Col, NJ, BSc, 58; Seton Hall Univ, MSc, 64, PhD(org chem), 66. *Prof Exp:* Chemist, Schering Corp, NJ, 60-65; res chemist, 66-72, group leader dyes & intermediates dept, 72-74, chief chemist dyes & intermediates mfg dept, 74-79, chief chemist pharmaceut mfg dept, Am Cyanamid Co, Bound Brook, 79-82; mgr, color res & develop, Inmont Corp, Hawthorne, NJ, 82-83. *Mem:* Am Chem Soc; NY Acad Sci; Sigma Xi; AAAS. *Res:* Process and product development of organic intermediates for pharmaceutical and agricultural products and a variety of specialty organic intermediates; marketing and product development for organic intermediates for use in the pharmaceutical, agricultural and specialty fields. *Mailing Add:* 61 Elm St Madison NJ 07940. *Fax:* 732-981-8282

KOO, BENJAMIN, STRUCTURAL ENGINEERING, APPLIED MECHANICS. *Current Pos:* prof civil eng, 65-90, EMER PROF ENG, UNIV TOLEDO, 90- *Personal Data:* b Shanghai, China, Apr 4, 20; US citizen; wid. *Educ:* St John's Univ, BS, 41; Cornell Univ, MS, 42, PhD(struct eng), 46. *Prof Exp:* Struct engr, 42-55; engr concrete & found sect, M H Treadwell Co, 56-61; proj engr, Am Car & Foundry Div, ACF Industs, 61-65. *Concurrent Pos:* NSF, NASA & Dept Transp Res Awards. *Mem:* Am Soc Civil Engrs; Am Soc Eng Educ; Am Concrete Inst; Sigma Xi. *Res:* Structural reliability in reinforced concrete members and frames; trailer train freight car patent; cushioned underframe system patent; structural stability; structural analysis and design; structural reliability. *Mailing Add:* Dept Civil Eng Univ Toledo Toledo OH 43606

KOO, DAVID CHIH-YUEN, OBSERVATIONAL COSMOLOGY, EVOLUTION OF GALAXIES. *Current Pos:* asst astronr/asst prof astron, 88-91, ASSOC ASTRON/ASSOC PROF ASTRON, LICK OBSERV, UNIV CA OBSERV, 91- *Personal Data:* b Bangkok, Thailand, Jan 1, 51. *Educ:* Cornell Univ, AB, 72; Univ Calif, Berkeley, MA, 74, PhD(astron), 81. *Prof Exp:* Fel, Dept Terrestrial Magnetism, Carnegie Inst Wash, 81-83, sr res fel, 83-84; fel, Space Telescope Sci Inst, 84-86, asst astronr, 86-87; asst astronr/asst prof astron, Lick Observ, Univ Calif, Santa Cruz, 88-91. *Concurrent Pos:* Vis fel, Sci & Eng Res Coun, UK, 83; NSF presidential young investr award, 88- *Mem:* Int Astron Union; Am Astron Soc; Astron Soc Pac; Int Asn Pattern Recognition. *Res:* Faint optical imaging and spectroscopy of distant galaxies, quasars, and radio sources; examination of the age, size, texture, and shape of the universe; probe very large-scale distributions of galaxies. *Mailing Add:* Lick Observ Kerr Hall Santa Cruz CA 95064

KOO, DELIA WEI, MATHEMATICS, STATISTICS. *Current Pos:* RETIRED. *Personal Data:* b Hankow, China, May 14, 21; US citizen; m 43, Anthony; c Victoria (Hitchins), Margery (Bussey) & Emily. *Educ:* St John's Univ, China, BA, 41; Radcliffe Col, AM, 42, PhD(eng philol), 47; Mich State Univ, MA, 54. *Prof Exp:* Instr math, Mich State Univ, 55-56; lectr, Douglass Col, Rutgers Univ, 56-57; instr, Mich State Univ, 57-58; from asst prof to prof math, Eastern Mich Univ, 65-83. *Mem:* Math Asn Am; Inst Math Statist; Economet Soc. *Res:* Author of 2 books. *Mailing Add:* 4554 Sequoia Trail Okemos MI 48864

KOO, GLORIA C, IMMUNOLOGY, CELL BIOLOGY. *Current Pos:* sr res fel, Merck Sharp & Dohme Res Labs, 84-91, SR INVESTR, MERCK RES LAB, NJ, 91- *Personal Data:* b Chunking, China, Nov 22, 44; US citizen. *Educ:* Goshen Col, BA, 65; Temple Sch Med, PhD(immunol), 70. *Prof Exp:* Med technologist, Clin Microbiol, Rhode Island Hosp, 65-66; med technologist clin microbiol, Temple Univ Hosp, Pa, 66-67; fel, Dept Microbiol, Temple Univ Sch Med, Pa, 67-70; fel, Sloan-Kettering Inst, NY, 70-72, res assoc, 72-74, assoc, 74-81; asst prof, Sloan-Kettering Div, Cornell Univ Med Col, 75-84. *Concurrent Pos:* NIH RO1 Awards, 74-86; vis inbestr, Univ Helsinki, Finland, 77 & Univ Calif, San Francisco Med Ctr, 83; asst mem, Sloan-Kettering Inst, 81-84; vis assoc prof, Dept biol, Rutgers Univ, 85-88; spec reviewer, NIH Exp Immunol Study Sect, 89-90, mem, 91-94. *Mem:* Sigma Xi; Am Asn Immunologists. *Res:* Immune modulation and transplantation. *Mailing Add:* Dept Immunol & Inflammation Merck Res Lab 115-80 W PO Box 2000 Rahway NJ 07065-0900

KOO, KEE P, FIBER-OPTIC SENSORS, LASER PHYSICS. *Current Pos:* RES PHYSICIST, NAVAL RES LAB, 80- *Personal Data:* b Hong Kong, Mar 30, 49; UK citizen; m 87. *Educ:* Univ Ill, Chicago, BS, 71; Case Western Res Univ, MS, 75, PhD(elec eng), 77. *Prof Exp:* Res assoc, Brookhaven Nat Lab, 77-78 & John Carroll Univ, 78-80. *Mem:* Inst Elec & Electronics Engrs; Optical Soc Am. *Res:* Fiber-optic sensors research with emphasis in interferometric sensors, especially in magnetic field sensing; fiber-optic magnetometer, gradiometer. *Mailing Add:* 807 N Howard St Apt 124 Alexandria VA 22304

KOO, PETER H, CANCER IMMUNOLOGY & BIOLOGY, NEURO-IMMUNO-REGULATION OF ALPHA-TWO-MACROGLOBULIN. *Current Pos:* from asst prof to assoc prof, 77-93, PROF IMMUNOL & MICROBIOL, COL MED, NORTHEASTERN OHIO UNIV, 94- *Personal Data:* b Shanghai, China; US citizen; m 67, S Alice; c David & Christopher. *Educ:* Univ Wash, BA, 64; Univ Md, PhD(biochem), 70. *Prof Exp:* Fel immunol, Johns Hopkins Univ, 71-74; staff fel, NIH, 74-75; asst prof oncol, Johns Hopkins Univ, 75-77. *Concurrent Pos:* Prin investr & grantee, Am Cancer Soc, 78-79 & 81-82, bd dirs, Portage Co, 81-89, chmn, Prof Educ Comt, 85-89, vpres, 87-89; prin investr & grantee, Cystic Fibrosis Care Fund & Pediat Akron, Inc, 78-79, 81-82, NSF, 84-87, Mefcom Found Funds, 82-, United Way, 82-83 & 89-90, Oncol Fund Akron Gen Develop Fund, 90-93, Ric-Man Fund, 93-94; prin investr, Nat Cancer Inst, NIH, 78-82, grantee, 92-96; grad fac, Neurosci Prog, Cellular & Molecular Biol Prog, Sch Biomed Sci, Kent State Univ, OH. *Mem:* Soc Neurosc; NY Acad Sci; Am Asn Immunologist; Am Soc Biochem & Molecular Biol. *Res:* Structure and function of Alpha-2 macroglobulins; neuroimmunology of alpha-2-macroglobulin; alpha-2-macroglobulin in regulating neurotrophins, nerve growth and repair; nerve growth factor regulation and catabolism. *Mailing Add:* Dept Microbiol & Immunol Col Med Northeastern Ohio Univ 4209 St Rte 44 PO Box 95 Rootstown OH 44272. *Fax:* 330-325-2524; *E-Mail:* prog@neoucom.edu

KOO, ROBERT CHUNG JEN, POMOLOGY. *Current Pos:* Interim asst biochemist, Citrus Exp Sta, Univ Fla, 53-57, from asst horticulturist to assoc horticulturist, 57-68, prof & horticulturist, Agr Res & Educ Ctr, 69-90, EMER PROF, CITRUS RES & EDUC CTR, UNIV FLA, 90- *Personal Data:* b Shanghai, China, Mar 20, 21; nat US; m 49; c 3. *Educ:* Cornell Univ, BS, 44; Univ Fla, MS, 50, PhD(fruit crops), 53. *Honors & Awards:* Presidential Gold Medal Award, Fla State Horticult Soc, 65; Res Award, Fla Fruit & Vegetable Asn, 75. *Mem:* Am Soc Hort Sci; Am Agron Soc. *Res:* Plant nutrition of citrus; irrigation and water management. *Mailing Add:* 2223 12th St NW Winter Haven FL 33881

KOO, SUNG IL, NUTRITION, LIPID BIOCHEMISTRY. *Current Pos:* PROF FOODS & NUTRIT, KANS STATE UNIV, 90- *Educ:* Clemson Univ, PhD(nutrit), 76. *Prof Exp:* Assoc prof, 78-88, PROF BIOCHEM, ORAL ROBERTS UNIV, 89- *Mailing Add:* Dept Foods/Nutrit Kans State Univ Justin Hall Manhattan KS 66506

KOOB, ROBERT DUANE, PHYSICAL CHEMISTRY. *Current Pos:* PRES, UNIV NORTHERN IOWA. *Personal Data:* b Graettinger, Iowa, Oct 14, 41; m 60; c 7. *Educ:* Univ Northern Iowa, BA, 62; Univ Kans, PhD(chem), 67. *Prof Exp:* Instr high sch, Iowa, 63-64; res assoc chem, Univ Kans, 67; from asst prof to prof chem, NDak State Univ 67-90, chmn dept, 73-77, dir, Water Resources Res Inst, 74-85, dean, Col Sci & Math, 81-84, vpres acad affairs, 85-90, interim pres, 87-88; vpres acad affairs & sr vpres, Calif Polytech Univ, 90- *Mem:* Am Chem Soc; Sigma Xi. *Res:* Radiation chemistry; photochemistry; mass spectrometry. *Mailing Add:* Pres Univ Northern Iowa 1222 W 27th St Cedar Falls IA 50614

KOOB, ROBERT PHILIP, PHOTOCHEMISTRY, PHYSICAL CHEMISTRY. *Current Pos:* from asst prof to assoc prof, 55-59, PROF CHEM, ST JOSEPH'S COL, PA, 59- *Personal Data:* b Philadelphia, Pa, Jan 3, 22; m 54; c 3. *Educ:* Villanova Col, BS, 43; Univ Pa, MS, 47, PhD(chem), 49. *Prof Exp:* Asst instr, Univ Pa, 43-44, 46-49; asst prof chem, Villanova Col, 49-55. *Concurrent Pos:* Res chemist, E I du Pont de Nemours & Co, 47 & Eastern Lab, Dept Agr, 59, 60, 62 & 63; asst prof, Rosemont Col, 51-52. *Mem:* Am Chem Soc; Sigma Xi. *Res:* Phase and reaction rate studies; effects of solvent on reaction; extensions of the Fries Rearrangement; organic photochemistry. *Mailing Add:* 600 Turner Ave Drexel Hill PA 19026-2435

KOOBS, DICK HERMAN, PATHOLOGY, BIOLOGICAL CHEMISTRY. *Current Pos:* asst prof, 65-78, ASSOC PROF PATH, SCH MED, LOMA LINDA UNIV, 78- *Personal Data:* b Hinsdale, Ill, July 22, 28; m 55, Ardyce Hanson. *Educ:* Andrews Univ, BA, 50; Loma Linda Univ, MD, 55; Univ Calif, Los Angeles, PhD(biol chem), 65; Am Bd Path, dipl, 66. *Prof Exp:* Intern, Robert B Green Mem Hosp, San Antonio, Tex, 55-56; resident physician path, White Mem Hosp, Los Angeles, 56-59. *Mem:* Int Acad Path. *Res:* Experimental and molecular pathology, related to genetically acquired defective enzymes. *Mailing Add:* Dept Path Univ Sch Med Loma Linda CA 92354

KOOH, SANG WHAY, PEDIATRICS. *Current Pos:* ASSOC PROF, DEPT PHYSIOL & DEPT PEDIAT, UNIV TORONTO, 68- *Personal Data:* b Seoul, Korea, Oct 5, 30; m 56, Rak-Hay Kim; c Nancy (Zipple), Pamela J (Burtzlaff) & Michael. *Educ:* Yan-Sei Univ, MD, 55; Univ Toronto, PhD(physiol), 67; Am Acad Pediat, dipl, 61; FRCP, 68. *Prof Exp:* Fel pediat, Michael Reese Hosp & Med Ctr, 60-62; sr res fel, Res Inst, Hosp Sick Children, Toronto, 62-67. *Concurrent Pos:* Sr staff physician, Hosp Sick Children, 68- *Mem:* Soc Pediat Res; Can Soc Clin Investigation; Am Soc Bone & Mineral Res. *Res:* Metabolism bone diseases in children; metabolism of vitamin D in human and in experimental animals; regulation of bone mineralization. *Mailing Add:* Hosp Sick Children 555 University Ave Toronto ON M5G 1X8 Can

KOOHMARAIE, MOHAMMAD, BIOCHEMISTRY, MICROBIOLOGY, FOOD SCIENCE TECHNOLOGY. *Current Pos:* res fel, 84-86, res physiologist, 87-91, SUPVR RES PHYSIOLOGIST, USDA-ARS, 91- *Educ:* Pahlavi Univ, BS, 78; Tex A&I Univ, MS, 80; Ore State Univ, PhD(muscle biol), 84. *Honors & Awards:* Am Meat Asn; Am Soc Animal Sci; Sigma Xi; Fedn Am Soc Exp Biol. *Prof Exp:* Res asst animal sci, Ore State Univ, 80-84. *Concurrent Pos:* Res fel food sci & human nutrit, Mich State Univ, 86-87. *Mailing Add:* 521 N Brown Ave USDA ARS Clay Center NE 68933

KOOIJ, THEO, ACOUSTIC SIGNAL PROCESSING, ELECTRONICS ENGINEERING. *Current Pos:* tech dir, Acoust Res Ctr, 76-78, PROG MGR, TACTICAL TECHNOL OFF, DEFENSE ADVAN RES PROJS AGENCY, 78- *Personal Data:* b Dordrecht, Neth, Nov 29, 33; m 56; c 3. *Educ:* Delft Univ Technol, BSc, 58, MSc, 61; Cath Univ Am, PhD(elec eng), 77. *Prof Exp:* Jr res scientist, Saclant ASW Res Ctr, La Spezia, Italy, 61-65, sr res scientist & teamleader underwater acoustics, 65-68; sci adv sonar interpretation, US Naval Ship Res & Develop Ctr, Washington, DC, 68-74, head, Target Physics Br, Ocean Sci Dept, Naval Underwater Systs Ctr, New London, Conn, 74-76. *Concurrent Pos:* Lectr, Am Univ, 68-69. *Mem:* Acoust Soc Am; Netherlands Royal Inst Eng; Am Soc Cybernet; Inst Elec & Electronics Engrs. *Res:* Theoretical, model and computer simulated, and full scale experimental research in detection and classification of underwater targets; design and development of digital sonar signal processing systems. *Mailing Add:* 7103 Tyndale St McLean VA 22101

KOOMEN, MARTIN J, SOLAR PHYSICS. *Current Pos:* RES PHYSICIST, US NAVAL RES LAB & SACHS/FREEMAN INC, 82- *Personal Data:* b Bristol, NY, Dec 30, 17; wid; c Stephen D (deceased) & William N. *Educ:* Univ Rochester, BS, 40, MS, 43. *Prof Exp:* Instrument inspector, Bausch & Lomb Optical Co, 41-42; res physicist, Univ Rochester, 42-46; res physicist, US Naval Res Lab, 46-82. *Mem:* Optical Soc Am; Am Astron Soc; Am Geophys Union; AAAS. *Res:* Night vision; light emission from the upper atmosphere (night airglow); solar physics; design of rocket and satellite-borne instrumentation for study of the night airglow and the sun. *Mailing Add:* 5194 Dungannon RD Fairfax VA 22030

KOON, NORMAN C, CONDENSED MATTER PHYSICS. *Current Pos:* RES PHYSICIST, NAVAL RES LAB, 69- *Personal Data:* b Malvern, Ark, June 19, 38. *Educ:* Ga Inst Technol, BS, 60, MS, 66, PhD(physics), 70. *Mem:* Am Phys Soc. *Mailing Add:* 634 N Payne St Alexandria VA 22314. *Fax:* 202-404-8933

KOONCE, ANDREA LAVENDER, FOREST PATHOLOGY, TROPICAL FORESTRY. *Current Pos:* At DEPT FORESTRY, UNIV WIS, STEVENS POINT. *Personal Data:* b Denver, Colo, Dec 31, 51. *Prof Exp:* Researcher, US Forest Serv, 78; teacher pathol & ecol, Ore State Univ, 75-78, res asst, 75-81; prof ecol, bot, pathol & head genetic res, Nat Sch Forestry Sci, 81- *Concurrent Pos:* Consult, Lew Roth Forest, 80-81. *Mem:* Soc Am Foresters; Soc Trop Foresters. *Res:* Tree improvement of tropical pines, hardwoods and legumes; tree disease-fire interactions; tree physiology. *Mailing Add:* 11516 Spyglass Circle Moreno Valley CA 92557

KOONCE, KENNETH LOWELL, EXPERIMENTAL STATISTICS. *Current Pos:* from asst prof to assoc prof, 67-76, head dept, exp statist, 82-89, PROF EXP STATIST, LA STATE UNIV, BATON ROUGE, 76-, ASST DIR, AGR EXP STA, 89- *Personal Data:* b Lake Charles, La, Sept 6, 39; m 62; c 3. *Educ:* Univ Southwestern La, BS, 61; La State Univ, MS, 63; NC State Univ, PhD(animal genetics), 68. *Prof Exp:* Instr animal sci, NC State Univ, 67. *Mem:* Biomet Soc; Am Soc Animal Sci; Am Soc Info Sci; Am Statist Asn. *Mailing Add:* Dept Exp Statist La State Univ PO Box 25055 Baton Rouge LA 70803-5055

KOONCE, SAMUEL DAVID, technical intelligence; deceased, see previous edition for last biography

KOONG, LING-JUNG, EXPERIMENTAL BIOLOGY. *Current Pos:* ASSOC DEAN, COL AGR SCI, ORE STATE UNIV, 94- *Prof Exp:* Dept head animal sci, Ore State Univ, 91-94. *Mailing Add:* 3106 NW Huckleberry Pl Corvallis OR 97330

KOONIN, STEVEN ELLIOT, THEORETICAL NUCLEAR PHYSICS. *Current Pos:* Asst prof theoret physics, 75-78, assoc prof physics, 78-81, PROF THEORET PHYSICS, CALIF INST TECHNOL, 81- *Personal Data:* b Brooklyn, NY, Dec 12, 51; m 75; c 3. *Educ:* Calif Inst Tech, BS, 72; Mass Inst Technol, PhD(physics), 75. *Honors & Awards:* Humboldt Sr Scientist Award, 85. *Concurrent Pos:* Consult, Lawrence Berkeley Lab, Lawrence Livermore Lab, Los Alamos Sci Lab & Oak Ridge Nat Lab, 77-; res fel, Niels Bohr Inst, 76-77; Alfred P Sloan Found res fel, 77-79. *Mem:* Fel Am Phys Soc; fel AAAS. *Res:* Nuclear reaction models; heavy ion physics. *Mailing Add:* Calif Inst Technol 106-38 Pasadena CA 91125

KOONS, CHARLES BRUCE, ORGANIC CHEMISTRY. *Current Pos:* CONSULT, 89- *Personal Data:* b Oklahoma City, Okla, Nov 14, 29; m 56, Margaret C Suter; c Robert, David & Steven. *Educ:* Southern Ill Univ, BS, 51; Univ Minn, PhD(org chem), 58. *Prof Exp:* Res chemist, Jersey Prod Res Co, Div Standard Oil Co, NJ, Exxon Prod Res Co, 58-64, sr res chemist, 64-75, res assoc, 75-83, res adv, 83-89. *Mem:* Am Chem Soc. *Res:* Kinetics of aromatic substitution reactions; organic geochemistry, involving studies of the origin, migration and accumulation of petroleum; environmental chemistry, involving the fate of petroleum in the marine environment. *Mailing Add:* 10835 Saint Marys Lane Houston TX 77079-3619. *E-Mail:* hxpr79a@prodigy.com

KOONS, DAVID SWARNER, CHEMICAL ENGINEERING, PETROLEUM ENGINEERING. *Current Pos:* RETIRED. *Personal Data:* b Fresno, Calif, June 17, 30; div; c 2. *Educ:* Calif Inst Technol, BS, 52, MS, 55; Univ Colo, PhD(chem eng), 60. *Prof Exp:* Process engr, Texaco Inc, 52-54; res asst, Exp Sta, Univ Colo, 60; sr res technologist, Mobil Oil Co Inc, 60-77; staff engr, Mobil Corp, 77-86. *Mem:* Am Chem Soc; Am Inst Chem Engrs; Am Inst Mining, Metall & Petrol Engrs. *Res:* Simultaneous fluid flow; heat transfer and reaction kinetics of processes for recovering oil from underground reservoirs; pneumatic conveying of solids and petroleum refining. *Mailing Add:* 30343 Arena Dr Evergreen CO 80439

KOONS, DONALDSON, GEOMORPHOLOGY. *Current Pos:* RETIRED. *Personal Data:* b Seoul, Korea, Aug 23, 17; US citizen; m 44; c 4. *Educ:* Columbia Univ, AB, 39, AM, 41, PhD(geol), 45. *Hon Degrees:* DSc, Col of Wooster, 74, Unity Col, 76. *Honors & Awards:* Huddleston Medal. *Prof Exp:* Instr geol & geog, Carleton Col, 42-43; lectr geol, Columbia Univ, 46; asst prof, WVa Univ, 46-47; from asst prof to prof geol, Colby Col, 47-75, Dana prof, 75-82, head dept, 47-82. *Concurrent Pos:* Comnr, Maine Dept of Conserv, 73-75. *Mem:* Fel AAAS; fel Geol Soc Am. *Res:* Areal geology; dynamic geomorphology; geology of Colorado Plateau; Pleistocene Glaciation of Maine. *Mailing Add:* Pond Rd Augusta ME 04330

KOONS, STEPHEN J, BIOPHYSICS. *Current Pos:* SR BIOMED ENG, VISX, INC, 90- *Personal Data:* b Washington, DC, Oct 26, 51. *Educ:* Brandeis Univ, BA, 73; State Univ NY, Buffalo, PhD(biophysics), 81. *Prof Exp:* Develop mgr physics, Lacktos Sigmor Labs, 86-90. *Mem:* Am Biophys Soc; Am Soc Cell Biol; AAAS. *Res:* Biophysics. *Mailing Add:* VISX Inc 3400 Central Expressway Santa Clara CA 95051-0703

KOONTZ, FRANK P, CLINICAL MICROBIOLOGY, PARASITOLOGY. *Current Pos:* asst prof prev med, Univ Iowa, 64-70, asst dir, State Hygenic Lab, 67-77, prin bacteriologist, 73-76, assoc prof, dept path, 76-79, ASSOC PROF PREV MED & ENVIRON HEALTH, UNIV IOWA, 70-, PROF, DEPT PATH, 80-; DIR CLIN MICROBIOL, UNIV HOSP, 76- *Personal Data:* b Baltimore, Md, Nov 13, 32; m 60; c 3. *Educ:* Univ Md, BS, 58, MS, 60, PhD(biochem, microbiol), 62; Am Bd Med Microbiol, dipl. *Prof Exp:* NIH fel, Oxford Univ, 62-64. *Mem:* Am Soc Microbiol; fel Am Pub Health Asn. *Res:* Automation and rapid methods in clinical microbiology; blood culture techniques; evaluation of antimicrobial agents. *Mailing Add:* Dept Path Univ Iowa Col Med Iowa City IA 52242-1000

KOONTZ, JAMES L, RESEARCH ADMINISTRATION. *Current Pos:* exec vpres, 78-82, PRES & CHIEF EXEC OFFICER, KINGSBURY CORP, KEENE, NH, 82- *Personal Data:* b Dayton, Ohio, 1934. *Honors & Awards:* Gold Medal, Soc Mfg Engrs, 90. *Prof Exp:* Staff mfg & eng, Gen Motors, Chrysler & Bendix Corp; staff, Micromatic Inc, subsid, Ex-Cell-O Corp, Detroit, Mich, 66-68; gen mgr, XLO Parker, subsid, Ex-Cell-O Corp, Div Mach Tools, Ex-Cell-O Corp, 68; group vpres, Ex-Cell-O Corp, 69-78. *Concurrent Pos:* Emer chmn, Nat Ctr Mfg Sci; mem, Mfg Sci Bd, Dept Defense. *Mem:* Nat Mach Builders Asn. *Mailing Add:* Kingsbury Corp 80 Laurel St Keene NH 03431

KOONTZ, WARREN WOODSON, JR, UROLOGY. *Current Pos:* PROF UROL & CHMN DEPT, MED COL VA, 70-; AT DEPT SURG, VA COMMONWEALTH UNIV. *Personal Data:* b Lynchburg, Va, June 10, 32; m 57; c 2. *Educ:* Va Mil Inst, BA, 53; Univ Va, MD, 57. *Prof Exp:* From intern to resident surg, Ny Hosp, 57-62, resident urol, 62-66; from instr to asst prof, Med Col Va, 66-69; asst prof, Harvard Univ, 69-70. *Concurrent Pos:* Asst urologist, Mass Gen Hosp, 69-70; consult, McGuire Vet Admin Hosp, 70- & Portsmouth Naval Hosp, 71- *Mem:* Am Col Surgeons; Am Urol Asn; Soc Pediat Urol; Soc Univ Urol. *Res:* Pediatric urology; urinary tract cancer. *Mailing Add:* Dept Surg Med Col Va PO Box 118 Richmond VA 23201-0118

KOOP, CHARLES EVERETT, SURGERY. *Current Pos:* CHMN, NAT SAFE KIDS CAMPAIGN, WASHINGTON, DC, 89- *Personal Data:* b Brooklyn, NY, Oct 14, 16; wid; c 3. *Educ:* Dartmouth Col, AB, 37; Cornell Univ, MD, 41; Univ Pa, ScD(med), 47. *Hon Degrees:* LLD, Eastern Baptist Col, 60; MD, Univ Liverpool, 68; LHD, Wheaton Col, 73. *Honors & Awards:* Denis Brown Gold Medal, Brit Asn Pediat Surgeons; William E Ladd Gold Medal, Am Acad Pediat; Order of Duarte, Sanchez & Mella; Medal, Legion of Hon, France, 80. *Prof Exp:* From asst instr to instr surg, Univ Pa, 42-47, assoc, 47-48, from asst prof to assoc prof, 48-59, prof pediat surg, 59-89, prof pediat, 71-89. *Concurrent Pos:* Surgeon-in-chief, Children's Hosp, Philadelphia, 48-81; consult, US Naval Hosp, 64-; ed, J Pediat Surg; dep asst secy health, USPHS, 80-89; surg gen, 81-89 & dir, Off Int Health, 82; chmn, Bd Trustees, Nat Mus Health & Med Found & Bd Int Health, Inst Med. *Mem:* Inst Med-Nat Acad Sci; Am Surg Asn; fel Am Col Surgeons; Brit Asn Pediat Surg; Am Pediat Surg Asn; fel Am Acad Pediat; Royal Col Surgeons Eng; Soc Univ Surgeons. *Res:* Pediatric surgical techniques; neo-natalogy; childhood tumors. *Mailing Add:* Nat Safe Kids Campaign 111 Michigan Ave NW Washington DC 20010-2970

KOOP, DENNIS RAY, ENZYMOLOGY, METABOLISM. *Current Pos:* ASSOC PROF, DEPT PHARMACOL, OREGON HEALTH SCIENCES UNIV, 91- *Educ:* Northwestern Univ, PhD(biochem), 79. *Prof Exp:* Asst prof biochem, Univ Mich, 83-86, assoc prof, Environ Health Sci & Pharmacology Case West, 86-91. *Mailing Add:* Dept Pharmacol Ore Health Sciences Univ 3181 SW Sam Jackson Park Rd Portland OR 97201-3098. *Fax:* 503-494-5786

KOOP, JOHN C, STATISTICS. *Current Pos:* CONSULT, 82- *Personal Data:* b Myitkyina, Burma, Mar 6, 19; US citizen; m 43, Elsie E Ure; c Wilfred, Rachel, Elizabeth, Helen, Thomas, Paul, Arthur & George. *Educ:* Univ Rangoon, BSc, 42; NC State Univ, PhD(statist), 58. *Prof Exp:* Chief labor statist, Directorate Labour, Govt Burma, 48-58; mem, Int Labour Off, Switz, 59-60; vis asst prof exp statist, NC State Univ, 60-61, vis assoc prof, 61-65, assoc prof, 65-66; sr adv sampling agr & head res training, Dom Bur Statist, Can, 66-70; sr appln scientist, statist sci admin, Res Triangle Inst, 70-81. *Mem:* Fel Am Statist Asn; Royal Statist Soc; Burma Res Soc; Int Asn Survey Statisticians; Int Statist Inst. *Res:* Sampling theory for finite universes derived on basis of axioms; theory of ratio estimation; unified theory of estimation for sample surveys taking into account response and measurement errors; statistical inference; demographic study of minority community in Burma. *Mailing Add:* 3201 Clark Ave Raleigh NC 27607

KOOPMAN, KARL FRIEDRICH, MAMMALOGY. *Current Pos:* from asst cur to cur, 61-85, EMER CUR, AM MUS NATURAL HIST, 85- *Personal Data:* b Honolulu, Hawaii, Apr 1, 20. *Educ:* Columbia Univ, BA, 43, MA, 45, PhD(zool), 50. *Honors & Awards:* Newberry Prize, 49; Gerrit S Miller Jr Award, 77; Hartley H T Jackson Award, 88. *Prof Exp:* Instr biol, Middletown Collegiate Ctr, 49-58 & Queens Col, NY, 52-58; asst cur, Acad Natural Sci, Philadelphia, 58-59 & Chicago Natural Hist Mus, 59-61. *Mem:* Am Soc Mammal; Nature Conservancy. *Res:* Systematic mammalogy; taxonomy and zoogeography of bats; paleontology and zoogeography of West Indian mammals. *Mailing Add:* Dept Mammal Am Mus Natural Hist New York NY 10024-5192

KOOPMAN, RONALD P, APPLIED PHYSICS. *Current Pos:* PROG LEADER, LAWRENCE LIVERMORE NAT LAB, 68- *Personal Data:* b Grand Rapids, Mich, Mar 15, 43. *Educ:* Univ Mich, BS, 65, MS, 67; Univ Calif, PhD(appl physics), 77. *Mem:* Am Phys Soc. *Mailing Add:* Lawrence Livermore Nat Lab 4673 Almond Ctr Livermore CA 94550

KOOPMAN, WILLIAM JAMES, IMMUNOLOGY. *Current Pos:* from asst prof to assoc prof, PROF MED RHEUMATOLOGY & CLIN IMMUNOL, UNIV ALA, 77-, DIR MULTIPURPOSE ARTHRITIS CTR, 83-, CHMN, DEPT MED, 95- *Personal Data:* b Lafayette, Ind, Aug 19, 45; m 68, Lilliane Kathryn Desimone; c Benjamin, Anna, Rebecca & Steven. *Educ:* Washington & Jefferson Univ, BA, 67; Harvard Univ, MD, 72; Am Bd Internal Med, dipl. *Honors & Awards:* Carol Nachman Res Prize, Fed Repub Ger, 82. *Prof Exp:* Intern/resident med, Mass Gen Hosp, 72-74; res fel, NIH, 74-77, chmn bd sci counselors, 91-95; Howard L Holley prof med, Univ Ala, 88-95. *Concurrent Pos:* Ed, Arthritis & Rheumatism J, 85-90; chmn bd sci counselors, Nat Inst Arthritis, Metab & Digestive Dis, 91-95. *Mem:* Inst Med-Nat Acad Sci; fel Am Col Rheumatology (treas, 92-94, pres elect, 95-96, pres, 96-); Am Soc Clin Invest (pres, 90-91); Asn Am Physicians; Am Asn Immunologists; fel Am Col Physicians. *Res:* Contributed over 245 articles to professional journals. *Mailing Add:* Diabetes Hosp 420 University Sta Birmingham AL 35294

KOOPMANN, GARY HUGO, MECHANICAL ENGINEERING. *Current Pos:* PROF MECH ENG & DIR, CTR ACOUST & VIBRATIONS, PA STATE UNIV, 88- *Personal Data:* b Howells, Nebr, May 8, 39; m 72, Barbara Bogue; c Hannah & Eve. *Educ:* Univ Nebr, BS, 62; Cath Univ, MS, 66, PhD, 69. *Prof Exp:* Res scientist, US Naval Res Lab, 62-66; fel, Inst Sound & Vibration, Southampton, Eng, 69-70, Univ lectr, 70-76; prof, Univ Houston, 76-87. *Mem:* Fel Am Soc Mech Engrs; fel Acoust Soc Am. *Res:* Noise reduction; granted several patents. *Mailing Add:* 220 Kennedy St State College PA 16801

KOOPMANS, HENRY SJOERD, NUTRITION, ENERGY BALANCE. *Current Pos:* assoc prof, 83-86, PROF MED PHYSIOL, UNIV CALGARY, 86- *Personal Data:* b Washington, DC, Jan 28, 44; m 90, Jan Robertson; c Robert, Lisa & Mark. *Educ:* Harvard Col, BA, 66; Univ Calif, San Diego, PhD(physiol psychol), 72. *Honors & Awards:* Future Leader Award, Nutrit Found. *Prof Exp:* Res prof psychol, Univ Calif, San Diego, 72-73; from asst prof to assoc prof, Columbia Univ, 73-83. *Concurrent Pos:* Res assoc, Obesity Ctr, St Luke's-Roosevelt Hosp, 73-83; NIH career develop award, 75-86; adj prof, Rockefeller Univ, 78-79; vis colleague, Hammersmith Hosp, London, 79-81; Alta Heritage med res scholar, 83-95. *Mem:* Neurosci Soc; Int Union Physiol Sci; NAm Asn Study Obesity; Soc Study Ingestive Behav; Inst Asn Study Obesity. *Res:* Internal control of food intake, energy expenditure and body weight; obesity. *Mailing Add:* Dept Physiol & Biophys Univ Calgary Calgary AB T2N 4N1 Can

KOOPMANS, LAMBERT HERMAN, MATHEMATICAL STATISTICS. *Current Pos:* RETIRED. *Personal Data:* b Chicago, Ill, July 23, 30; m 55; c 4. *Educ:* San Diego State Col, AB, 52; Univ Calif, PhD, 58. *Prof Exp:* Asst statist, Univ Calif, 52-56, assoc biostatist, 75-; mem staff, Sandia Corp, 58-64; assoc prof, Univ NMex, 64-68, chmn dept, 69-74, prof math & statist, 68-89. *Concurrent Pos:* Consult, Sandia Corp, 64-72, Westinghouse Corp, 65-67, civil eng fac & dept path, Univ NMex, 76-77, diabetes proj, 78-82 & Vet Admin Hosp, Albuquerque, 78-79; sabbatical leave fac math, Univ Calif, Santa Cruz, 71-72; vis prof statist, Princeton Univ, 75. *Mem:* Fel Am Statist Asn; Biomet Soc; fel Inst Math Statist. *Res:* Data analysis; time series analysis. *Mailing Add:* 7312 Marilyn Ave Albuquerque NM 87109

KOOPOWITZ, HAROLD, NEUROPHYSIOLOGY, INVERTEBRATE ZOOLOGY. *Current Pos:* Asst prof, 68-75, ASSOC PROF BIOL, UNIV CALIF, IRVINE, 75- *Personal Data:* b East London, SAfrica, Sept 10, 40; m 69; c 1. *Educ:* Rhodes Univ, SAfrica, BSc, 62, MSc, 64; Univ Calif, Los Angeles, PhD(zool), 68. *Mem:* Brit Soc Exp Biol; Am Soc Zool; Soc Gen Physiol; Soc Neurosci. *Res:* Organization of flatworm nervous systems; electrophysiology of vision in insect eyes. *Mailing Add:* Dept Ecol Univ Calif Irvine CA 92717-0001

KOOSER, ROBERT GALEN, PHYSICAL CHEMISTRY. *Current Pos:* From asst prof to assoc prof, 68-84, PROF CHEM, KNOX COL, ILL, 84- *Personal Data:* b Mankato, Minn, July 23, 41; div; c Ara & Amanda. *Educ:* St Olaf Col, BA, 63; Cornell Univ, PhD(chem), 68. *Concurrent Pos:* Vis assoc prof, Dartmouth Col, 83-84. *Mem:* Am Chem Soc; Am Phys Soc; Sigma Xi. *Res:* Electron spin resonance, primarily spin relaxation processes of organic and inorganic singlet systems in solution. *Mailing Add:* O E South St-46 Knox Col Galesburg IL 61401. *Fax:* 309-341-7718; *E-Mail:* rkooser@knox.knox.edu

KOOSIS, PAUL, MATHEMATICAL ANALYSIS. *Current Pos:* from asst prof to assoc prof, 63-70, PROF MATH, UNIV CALIF, LOS ANGELES, 70- *Personal Data:* b Los Angeles, Calif, Apr 20, 29. *Educ:* Univ Calif, Berkeley, BA, 50, PhD(math), 54. *Prof Exp:* Instr math, Univ Mich, 54-55; asst instr math sci, NY Univ, 55-57, 59-60; Fulbright fel to France, 57-58; NSF fels, 58-59, 60-61; from asst prof to assoc prof, Fordham Univ, 62-63. *Mem:* Am Math Soc; Math Soc France. *Res:* Classical harmonic analysis; complex variable theory; theory of approximation. *Mailing Add:* Dept Math 805 Sherbrooke St W Montreal PQ H3A 2K6 Can

KOOTSEY, JOSEPH MAILEN, COMPUTER SIMULATION. *Current Pos:* prof biophys, Andrews Univ, 76-79, dean, Col Arts & Sci, 91-94, vpres acad, 94-97, CHIEF INFO OFFICER, ANDREWS UNIV, 97- *Personal Data:* b Houston, Tex, Sept 3, 39; m 61, Lynne D Wiles; c Brenden & Sean. *Educ:* Pac Union Col, BA, 60; Brown Univ, ScM, 64, PhD(physics), 66. *Prof Exp:* Asst prof physiol & biophys, Loma Linda Univ, 67-69; asst prof physiol & pharmacol, Duke Univ, 71-76, res assoc prof physiol, 79-84, assoc prof physiol, 82-89, res assoc prof comput sci, 82-91, dir, Nat Biomed Simulation Resource, 83-91, assoc prof cell biol, 89-91. *Concurrent Pos:* Bank Am-Giannini Found grant, Loma Linda Univ, 65-67; NIH spec fel, Duke Univ, 69-71; pres, Simulation Resources, Inc, 91-; adj assoc prof cell biol & comput sci, Duke Univ, 91-93. *Mem:* AAAS; Am Physiol Soc; Biophys Soc; Asn Comput Mach; Soc Comput Simulations; Inst Elec & Electronics Engrs. *Res:* Cardiac electrophysiology; computer simulation in physiology; medical education; utilization of computer simulation to reassemble complex biological systems; ion regulation and electrical activity in cardiac muscle cells; computer software for simulations. *Mailing Add:* Admin 322 Andrews Univ Berrien Springs MI 49104

KOOYMAN, GERALD LEE, COMPARATIVE PHYSIOLOGY. *Current Pos:* res physiologist, 67-68, from asst res physiologist to res physiologist, 68-91, PROF, SCRIPPS INST OCEANOG, UNIV CALIF, SAN DIEGO, 91- *Personal Data:* b Salt Lake City, Utah, June 16, 34; m 62, Melba Bingham; c Carstem & Tory. *Educ:* Univ Calif, Los Angeles, AB, 57; Univ Ariz, PhD(zool), 66. *Honors & Awards:* AAAS; Creative Scientist Award, NSF, 91. *Prof Exp:* Res asst Antarctic seal studies, Univ Ariz, 63-66; NSF fel, Anat & Physiol of Marine Mammals, London Hosp Med Col, Eng, 66-67. *Concurrent Pos:* Sci fel Zool Soc London. *Mem:* AAAS; Am Soc Zool; Am Physiol Soc; Sigma Xi; Explorers Club. *Res:* Behavior and physiology of diving in aquatic birds and mammals, especially pressure effects; comparative respiratory physiology and anatomy of vertebrates; conservation of marine birds and mammals. *Mailing Add:* CMBB-0204 Scripps Inst Oceanog La Jolla CA 92093. Fax: 619-534-1305; *E-Mail:* kooyman@uesd.edu

KOOZEKANAI, SAID H, ELECTRICAL ENGINEERING, BIOMEDICAL ENGINEERING. *Current Pos:* from asst prof to assoc prof, 66-76, PROF ELEC ENG, OHIO STATE UNIV, 76- *Personal Data:* b Mash-had, Iran, Mar 15, 33; m 65. *Educ:* Univ Tehran, Electro-Mech Eng, 56; Brown Univ, PhD(elec eng), 61; Univ Dayton, MS, 69. *Prof Exp:* Sr res scientist, Raytheon Res Div, Mass, 61-65. *Mem:* Am Inst Physics; Am Phys Soc; Inst Elec & Electronics Engrs. *Res:* Quantum electronics; lasers; antennas and propagation. *Mailing Add:* 1271 Camelot Dr Columbus OH 43220

KOPANSKI, JOSEPH J, INTEGRATED CIRCUIT ENGINEERING, SCANNING PROBE MICROSCOPY. *Current Pos:* ELEC ENGR, NAT INST STAND & TECHNOL, 85- *Personal Data:* b Cleveland, OH, Feb 8, 60. *Educ:* Case Western Reserve Univ, BS, 82, MS, 85. *Mem:* Inst Elec & Electronics Engrs; Electrochem Soc. *Res:* Electrical characterization of semiconductor materials, processes and circuits; developing scanning probe microscope based methods for semiconductor characterization. *Mailing Add:* Bldg 225 Rm A305 Nat Inst Stand & Technol Gaithersburg MD 20899. Fax: 301-948-4081; *E-Mail:* kopanski@sed.eeel.nist.gov

KOPASKA-MERKEL, DAVID CRISPIN, GROUND WATER RESOURCES, EDUCATIONAL TECHNOLOGY TRANSFER. *Current Pos:* geologist, 89-94, HEAD, GROUND WATER SECT, GEOL SURV ALA, 94- *Personal Data:* b Charlottesville, Va, Jan 11, 57; m 79; c 2. *Educ:* Col William & Mary, BS, 78; Univ Kans, PhD(geol), 83. *Prof Exp:* Petrol geologist, Shell Oil Co, 82-86; post doctoral, Univ Toronto, 86-87; res assoc, Northeastern Sci Found, 87-89. *Concurrent Pos:* Ed, Ala Geol Soc Newslettt, 92-96; corresp ed, J Sedimentary Res, 93-96; chair, Geol Sect, Ala Acad Sci, 94-96; mem, K12 Earth Sci Educ Comt, Soc Sedimentary Res, 94- *Mem:* Soc Sedimentary Geol. *Res:* Responsible for preparing annual reports summarizing Alabama's water resources; write educational materials for all levels from Kindergarten through adult on earth science in Alabama; participate in diverse water-related research projects. *Mailing Add:* Geol Surv Ala PO Box O Tuscaloosa AL 35486. *E-Mail:* davidkm@ogb.gsa.tuscaloosa.al.us

KOPCHICK, JOHN J, MOLECULAR BIOLOGY, ZOOLOGY. *Current Pos:* PROF MOLECULAR BIOL, ZOOL & BIOMED SCI & DIR, MOLECULAR BIOL DEPT, EDISON ANIMAL BIOTECHNOL CTR, OHIO UNIV, 87- *Personal Data:* b Punxsutawney, Pa, Nov 2, 50; m. *Educ:* Ind Univ Pa, BS, 72, MS, 75; Univ Tex, PhD(virol-biomed sci), 80. *Prof Exp:* Teaching asst microbiol, genetics & gen biol, Ind Univ Pa, 72-75; med technologist, Bellaire Gen Hosp, 76-80; Am Cancer Soc postdoctoral fel, Roche Inst Molecular Biol, 80-82; sr res biochemist, Dept Biochem Genetics, Merck Inst Therapeut Res, Merck Sharp & Dohme Res Labs, 82-84, res fel, 84-85, group leader molecular biol, Dept Animal Drug Discovery, 85-86. *Concurrent Pos:* Milton & Lawrence H Goll eminent scholar endowed prof molecular & cellular biol, Ohio Univ, 87-; mem, Child Health & Human Develop Grant Rev Comt, NIH, 88 & 91, Adv Comt Emerging Agr Technologies, Off Technol Assessment, 89-90, Competitive Res Grants Prog, USDA, 90-91; sci adv, DNX, Princeton, NJ. *Mem:* Sigma Xi; Am Soc Microbiol; AAAS; Am Soc Biochem & Molecular Biol. *Res:* Molecular cloning of DNA molecules encoding wildtype and in vitro mutated growth hormones, growth hormone receptors, hypothalmic regulatory proteins and neuropeptides; cloning of efficient eucaryotic expression vectors for the production of proteins in cultured mammalian cells; structure-function studies of growth hormone employing transgenic animals; author of more than 60 publications. *Mailing Add:* Molecular Biol Edison Biotech Inst Athens OH 45701

KOPCHIK, RICHARD MICHAEL, POLYMER PRODUCT & PROCESS DEVELOPMENT, POLYMER MORPHOLOGY & MICROSTRUCTURE. *Current Pos:* PROJ MGR, CATALYST GROUP, 95- *Personal Data:* b Punxsutawney, Pa, Apr 29, 41; m 64, Joan L Sabo; c David & Ann. *Educ:* Carnegie-Mellon Univ, BS, 63; Univ Rochester, PhD(org chem), 68. *Prof Exp:* Res chemist polymers, Rohm & Haas Co, 69-80, sr res assoc, 80-86, tech mgr, 86-89, sect mgr, 89-94. *Mem:* Am Chem Soc; Sigma Xi; Soc Plastics Eng; NY Acad Sci. *Res:* Organic chemistry; free radical reactions; chemical modification of polymers; continuous preparation and processing of polymers; polymer chemistry; polymeric sorbents; engineering plastics; elastomers; polymer morphology and microstructure. *Mailing Add:* 1335 Stephen Way Southampton PA 18966-4349. *E-Mail:* rkopchik@voicenet.com

KOPE, ROBERT GLENN, STOCK ASSESSMENT, OPTIMAL MANAGEMENT. *Current Pos:* FISHERY BIOLOGIST, NAT MARINE FISHERIES SERV, 89- *Personal Data:* b Reedley, Calif, Aug 5, 53; m 76, Mary S Scott; c Laura & Rachel. *Educ:* Calif State Univ, BA, 80; Univ Calif, Davis, PhD(ecol), 87. *Prof Exp:* Postgrad researcher, Univ Calif, Davis, 87-89. *Concurrent Pos:* Lectr, Univ Calif, Davis, 89. *Mem:* Resource Modeling Asn; Pac Fisheries Biologists. *Res:* Optimal management of renewable resources; stock assessment; spatial population modeling. *Mailing Add:* F/NWC1 2725 Mount Lake Blvd E Seattle WA 98122

KOPECEK, JINDRICH, POLYMERIC DRUG DELIVERY SYSTEMS, BIOCOMPATIBILITY OF POLYMERS. *Current Pos:* PROF BIOENG & PHARMACEUT, UNIV UTAH, 89- *Personal Data:* b Strakonice, Czech, Jan 27, 40; m 85, Pavla Hruskova; c Jana. *Educ:* Inst Chem Technol, Prague, MS, 61; Czech Acad Sci, Prague, PhD(polymer chem), 65, DSc, 90. *Honors & Awards:* Sci Award, Chem Sect, Czech Chem Soc, 72, 75, 77, 78 & 85; Sci Award, Presidiums Czech & USSR Acad Sci, 77; Barre's Lectr, Univ Montreal, 90. *Prof Exp:* Res sci officer, Czech Acad Sci, Inst Macromolecular Chem, 65-72, head lab med polymers, 72-88; fel chem eng, Nat Res Coun Can, 67-68. *Concurrent Pos:* Prin investr numerous grants, 69-; mem, Comt New Polymers, Ministry Health, Czech, 76-86; vis prof, Univ Paris-Nord, 83 & Univ Utah, 86-88; co-dir, Ctr Controlled Chem Delivery, Univ Utah, 86-; bd gov, Controlled Release Soc, 88-91. *Mem:* Am Chem Soc; Biomat Soc; AAAS; fel Am Asn Pharmaceut Scientists; Am Asn Cancer Res; Controlled Release Soc (pres, 95-96); fel Am Inst Med Biomed Eng. *Res:* Biocompatibility and biodegradation of polymers; tailor-made synthesis of bioactive, biorecognizable polymers; targetable polymeric anticancer drug carriers; hydrogels for oral delivery of peptides and proteins; genetically engineered biomaterials. *Mailing Add:* Dept Bioeng BPRB Rm 205 Univ Utah Salt Lake City UT 84112. Fax: 801-581-7848; *E-Mail:* jindrich.kopecek@m.cc.utah.edu

KOPECKY, KARL RUDOLPH, ORGANIC CHEMISTRY. *Current Pos:* from asst prof to assoc prof, 61-77, PROF CHEM, UNIV ALTA, 77- *Personal Data:* b Hradec Kralove, Czech, Oct 5, 32; US citizen; m 63; c 2. *Educ:* Iowa State Col, BS, 54; Univ Calif, Los Angeles, PhD, 59. *Prof Exp:* Instr chem, Univ Calif, Los Angeles, 59; NIH fel, Calif Inst Technol, 59-61. *Mem:* Am Chem Soc; Chem Inst Can. *Res:* Thermal reactions of styrene; radicals from chiral sources; peroxide reactions; chemiluminescent compounds; reactions of stable radicals. *Mailing Add:* 11914 87th Ave Edmonton AB T6G 0Y6 Can

KOPELL, NANCY J, DYNAMICAL SYSTEMS. *Current Pos:* PROF MATH, BOSTON UNIV, 86- *Personal Data:* b New York, NY, Nov 8, 42. *Educ:* Cornell Univ, AB, 63; Univ Calif, Berkeley, MA, 65, PhD(dynamical systs), 67. *Honors & Awards:* R Bowen Mem Lectr, Berkeley, 86; Vollmer Fries Mem Lectr, Rensselaer Polytech Inst, 91; Emmy Noether Lectr, Am Math Soc, Baltimore, 92; KAC Mem Lectrs, Los Alamos Nat Lab, 92; Matthew Vassar Lectr, Vassar Col, 94. *Prof Exp:* From asst dir to dir, High Sch Students & Teachers Regional Prog, NSF, 65-67; CLE Moore instr math, Mass Inst Technol, 67-69; asst prof, Northeastern Univ, 69-72, assoc prof, 72-78, prof, 78-86. *Concurrent Pos:* Fel, Nat Ctr Sci Res, 70; vis assoc prof appl math, Mass Inst Technol, 75; vis scholar, 76-77; Alfred P Sloan fel, 75-77; vis scholar, Calif Inst Technol, 76; vis sr res scientist, Sci Res Coun, Eng, 76; consult, Math Res Ctr, Madison, 79 & Sci Systs Inc, 80-84; J S Guggenheim fel, 84-85; John D & Catherine T MacArthur fel, 90-95; Ordway vis prof, Univ Minn, 92. *Mem:* Nat Acad Sci; Am Acad Arts & Sci. *Res:* Contributed over 60 articles to professional publications. *Mailing Add:* Dept Math Col Arts & Sci Boston Univ 111 Cummington St Boston MA 02215

KOPELMAN, JAY B, INTERNATIONAL ENERGY SCIENCES. *Current Pos:* RETIRED. *Personal Data:* b New York, NY, Feb 24, 39; m 90. *Educ:* Rensselaer Polytech Inst, BS, 60; Northwestern Univ, PhD(physics), 65. *Prof Exp:* Res assoc physics, Univ Colo, Boulder, 64-66, asst prof, 66-74, asst dean grad sch, 68-74, mgr, Energy Modeling Prog, Stanford Res Inst, 74-78; mgr spec studies, Elec Power Res Inst, 78-82, mgr int activities & exec asst vpres, 82-94. *Mem:* AAAS; Am Phys Soc. *Res:* Energy technology; energy economics; modelling. *Mailing Add:* Elec Power Res Inst PO Box 10412 Palo Alto CA 94303

KOPELMAN, RAOUL, PHYSICAL CHEMISTRY, ANALYTICAL CHEMISTRY. *Current Pos:* from asst prof to prof chem, 66-94, prof physics, 91-94, FAJANS PROF CHEM, PHYSICS & APPL PHYSICS, UNIV MICH, ANN ARBOR, 94- *Personal Data:* b Vienna, Austria, Oct 21, 33; US citizen; m 55, Chava Blodek; c Orion, Leeron & Shirli. *Educ:* Israel Inst Technol, BS, 55, dipl eng, 56, MSc, 57; Columbia Univ, PhD(chem), 60. *Honors & Awards:* Sokol Award; Creativity Award, NSF. *Prof Exp:* Res assoc chem, Harvard Univ, 60-62; lectr, Israel Inst Technol, 62-64; res fel, Calif Inst Technol, 64-65, sr res fel, 65-66. *Concurrent Pos:* Fulbright award, 57; spec res fel, NIH, 72-73, Fogarty int fel, 79; sr fel, NATO, 76; nat res serv award, NIH, 87-88; Fulbright fel, 87-88. *Mem:* Fel Am Phys Soc; Am Chem Soc; Biophys Soc; Mat Res Soc; fel AAAS. *Res:* Excitation dynamics in molecular and biomimetic aggregates, excitons and phonons in disordered materials, membranes and photosynthetic units; 1.5 K time-resolved high-resolution tunable-laser microspectroscopy; supercomputer simulations of critical phenomena, transport and chemical kinetics; heterogeneous kinetics in low-dimensional and fractal domains; near-field optical microscopy and chemical nano-sensors. *Mailing Add:* Dept Chem Univ Mich Ann Arbor MI 48109-1055. *E-Mail:* kopelman@umich.edu

KOPELOVE, ALAN BRIAN, ANALYTICAL INSTRUMENTATION DESIGN & DEVELOPMENT, CUSTOM SENSOR DESIGN & DEVELOPMENT. *Current Pos:* RES & DEVELOP MGR, ELECTROCHEM PRODS, DENVER INSTRUMENT CO, 93- *Personal Data:* b Norfolk, Va, Feb 22, 54; m 75, Merry Gutzler; c Katherine & Daniel. *Educ:* Va Polytech Inst, BS, 76; Colo State Univ, MS, 81. *Prof Exp:* Grad res asst, Colo State Univ, 76-79, res asst, 88-92; adj instr, Hunter Col, 79-81; sr res chemist, Hach Co, 81-88. *Concurrent Pos:* Consult, Clear Creek Chem, 89-92, pres, 96- *Res:* Development of new analytical methodologies and instrumentation using electroanalytical techniques; study of conducting polymers and small molecule analogs of the active site of hemoglobin and cytochrome proteins. *Mailing Add:* 7024 Blue Creek Rd Evergreen CO 80439. *Fax:* 303-423-4831; *E-Mail:* akopelove@aol.com

KOPELOVICH, LEVY, ONCOLOGY, MEDICAL SCIENCES. *Current Pos:* dir res & develop, 86-92, SR SCIENTIST, VET ADMIN MED CTR, BAY PINES, 84-; PROF PATH & BIOCHEM, UNIV SFLA COL MED, 84- *Personal Data:* b Vilna, Poland, Aug 13, 34; US citizen; m 75, Lenore R Stess; c Rachel, Jonathan & Sarah. *Educ:* Hebrew Univ Jerusalem, BSc, 58; Univ Calif, Berkeley, PhD(toxicol), 62. *Prof Exp:* Fel physiol chem, Univ Calif, Berkeley, 62-65; fel, Dept Biochem, Brandeis Univ, 65-66; asst prof biochem physiol & dir cancer res unit, Univ Tel-Aviv Med Sch, 66-68; asst mem, Mem Sloan Kettering Cancer Ctr, 69-77, assoc mem, 77-83; asst prof biochem, Cornell Univ Grad Sch Med Sci, 69-77, assoc prof, 77-83. *Concurrent Pos:* Edith Wolfson cancer res award, 66; distinguished scientist, Ford Found, 67; vis prof, Ger Cancer Ctr, Heidelberg, 78, Norweg Nat Cancer Ctr, Oslo, 81, French Nat Cancer Inst, Ville Juiff, 88 & 90; mem, Molecular Biol Ctr, Univ SFla, 84-; consult, Sci Panel Comt Interagency Radiation, Washington, 84-; charter mem, Tampa Bay Sci Consortium, 87- *Mem:* Sigma Xi; AAAS; Am Soc Biol Chem; Am Asn Cancer Res; NY Acad Sci. *Res:* Genetic determinants of cancer predisposition in humans; systemic effects, biomarkers in cancer and the role of oncogenes in normal differentiation, including potential therapy. *Mailing Add:* Dept Med Res, Lab Cancer Genetics Univ SFla Col Med, Vet Admin Med Ctr Bay Pines FL 33504-9999. *Fax:* 813-398-9549; *E-Mail:* kopelovichlevy@baypines.va.gov

KOPF, ALFRED WALTER, ONCOLOGY. *Current Pos:* asst dermat, Post Grad Med Sch, NY Univ, 54-55, instr, 57-59, asst clin prof, 59-61, from asst prof to prof, 61-83, assoc dir serv, Dept Dermat, 68, CLIN PROF DERMAT, SCH MED, NY UNIV, 83-; ATTEND PHYSICIAN, UNIV HOSP, 65- *Personal Data:* b Buffalo, NY, June 21, 26; m 49, Dorothy M Dows; c Christopher J, Katherine A, Cynthia J & Timothy D. *Educ:* Cornell Univ, BA, 48, MD, 51; NY Univ, MS, 55; Am Bd Dermat, dipl, 57. *Honors & Awards:* Wershaw Lectr Israel, Am Acad Dermat, 71; Dohi Lectureship, Japan, 79; Louis A Duhring Lectr, Penn Acad Dermat, 92. *Prof Exp:* Intern, Cleveland City Hosp, Ohio, 51-52; clin res dermat, Skin & Cancer Unit, Univ Hosp, NY Univ Med Ctr, 53-54, organizer, Oncol Sect, 54, asst attend med staff, 58-62, assoc attend dermat, 62-65. *Concurrent Pos:* Pvt pract dermat, Ny, 55-; from co-ed to sr ed, Yearbook Dermat, 63-70; mem bd dirs, Inst Dermat Commun & Educ, 63-87; mem bd dirs, Am Acad Dermat, 66, Rudolf L Baer Found Skin Dis, Inc, 76, Am Dermat Asn, 81; med adv bd, Skin Cancer Found, 82; chmn bd dirs, Int Found Dermat, 87. *Mem:* AAAS; Soc Invest Dermat; Am Acad Dermat (pres, 80); Am Dermat Asn (treas, 72); AMA; NY Acad Sci; fel NY Acad Med; Int Soc Trop Dermat; Am Asn Cancer Surg; Am Soc Dermat Surg. *Res:* Cutaneous oncology, especially neoplasms of the melanocyte including clinical studies on pigmented nevi and malignant melanoma. *Mailing Add:* 350 Fifth Ave New York NY 10018-0189

KOPF, PETER W, PHYSICAL CHEMISTRY, POLYMER CHEMISTRY. *Current Pos:* sr consult, 85-89, DIR, ARTHUR D LITTLE INC, 90- *Personal Data:* b Philadelphia, Pa, Apr 23, 44; m 70; c 2. *Educ:* Rutgers Col, AB, 65; Univ Rochester, PhD(phys chem), 70. *Prof Exp:* Group leader & technol mgr, Res & Develop Dept, Union Carbide Corp, Bound Brook, 70-85. *Mem:* Am Chem Soc; Sigma Xi; Soc Advan Mat & Process Eng. *Res:* Polymer physical chemistry; polymer microstructural analysis; stable and transient free radicals; engineering thermoplastics; computer assisted calculations and simulations; polymer synthesis; thermoset reaction mechanisms; surface chemistry; dynamic mechanical analysis; polymers in coatings and adhesives applications; new specialty chemicals. *Mailing Add:* Arthur D Little Inc Acorn Park Cambridge MA 02140. *Fax:* 617-498-7250; *E-Mail:* kopf.p@adlittle.com

KOPF, RUDOLPH WILLIAM, STRATIGRAPHY, STRUCTURAL GEOLOGY. *Current Pos:* CONSULT GEOLOGIST, 84- *Personal Data:* b Munich, Ger, Sept 10, 22; US citizen; m 49; c Eric C & Wendy S (Caufield). *Educ:* Univ Buffalo, BA, 50, MA, 52. *Prof Exp:* Instr geol, Univ Buffalo, 50-51; oceanogr, US Navy Hydrographic Off, 52; geologist, US Geol Surv, 52-56; geol engr, USAEC, 56-61; geologist, US Geol Surv, 61-82, 84. *Concurrent Pos:* WCoast rep & ed, Geol Names Comt, US Geol Surv, 61-80, lectr, 82- *Mem:* fel Geol Soc Am. *Res:* Mechanics of thrust faulting; development of fault breccia, clastic pipes and dikes, cryptoexplosion structures, diatremes and mud volcanoes; uranium-vanadium deposits, stratigraphy, and structure of parts of Colorado plateaus, and basin and range province; origin of auriferous placers in California; source of diamonds in California. *Mailing Add:* 129 E Empire St Grass Valley CA 95945

KOPFLER, FREDERICK CHARLES, ENVIRONMENTAL CHEMISTRY. *Current Pos:* supvry chemist, Water Supply Progs Div, US Environ Protection Agency, 71-79, chief, Chem & Statist Support Br, 79-87, coordr, Exposure Assessment & Pharmacokinetics Sect, Health Effects Res Lab, 87-89, SR ENVIRON SCIENTIST, GULF MEX PROG, US ENVIRON PROTECTION AGENCY, 89- *Personal Data:* b New Orleans, La, Aug 14, 38; m 61, Eliska Lawrence; c Eliska, Gretchen, Frederick III & John. *Educ:* Southeastern La Col, BS, 60; La State Univ, MS, 62, PhD(food sci), 64. *Prof Exp:* Res chemist milk proteins, Agr Res Serv, USDA, 64-66, supvry chemist, 66-71. *Concurrent Pos:* Adj asst prof, Univ Ala, 68-73. *Mem:* Sigma Xi; Estuarine Res Fedn; Soc Environ Toxicol & Chem. *Res:* Bioassay directed isolation, fractionation and identification of mutagenic organic chemicals from water; effects of toxic substances on estuarine ecosystems. *Mailing Add:* Gulf Mex Prog US Environ Protection Agency Bldg No 1103 Rm 202 Stennis Space Ctr MS 39529. *Fax:* 228-688-2709

KOPIA, GREGORY A, PHARMACOLOGY. *Current Pos:* Dir cardiovasc pharmacol, 86-90, DIR PHARMACOL, ZYNAXIS CELL SCI INC, 90- *Personal Data:* b Montclair, NJ, Feb 16, 49. *Educ:* Gettysburg Col, BA, 71; Univ Med & Dent NJ, PhD(pharmacol), 80. *Mem:* Heart Res Inst; Am Heart Asn; NY Acad Sci; AAAS; Am Soc Pharmacol & Exp Therapeut. *Mailing Add:* 6 Oakwood Lane Phoenixville PA 19460

KOPIN, IRWIN J, INTERNAL MEDICINE, PHARMACOLOGY. *Current Pos:* actg chief, Sect Med, Lab Clin Sci, NIH, 61-63, actg chief, Lab Clin Sci, 68-69, chief, sect med, 63-83, chief, Lab Clin Sci, 69-83, assoc dir, clin res, NIMH, 82-83, DIR, IRP, NAT INST NEUROL & COMMUN DIS & STROKE, NIH, 83- *Personal Data:* b New York, NY, Mar 27, 29; m 52; c 3. *Educ:* McGill Univ, BSc, 51, MD, 55. *Prof Exp:* Intern med, Boston City Hosp, 55-56, resident, 56-57; res assoc, NIH, 57-60; resident med, Columbia-Presby Med Ctr, 60-61. *Mem:* AAAS; Asn Am Physicians; Am Soc Biol Chemists; Am Soc Clin Invest; Am Soc Pharmacol & Exp Therapeut. *Res:* Biochemical pharmacology. *Mailing Add:* IRP Nat Inst Neurol & Commun Dis & Stroke Bldg 10 5N-214 Bethesda MD 20892-0001

KOPITO, RON RIEGER, BIOCHEMISTRY, NEUROSCIENCES. *Current Pos:* ASST PROF BIOL SCI, STANFORD UNIV, 87- *Personal Data:* b Haifa, Israel, Dec 21, 54; US citizen; m 87; c 2. *Educ:* Bowdoin Col, AB, 76; Mass Inst Technol, PhD(biochem), 82. *Prof Exp:* NIH postdoctoral fel, Mass Inst Technol & Whitehead Inst, 82-86. *Concurrent Pos:* Lucille P Markey scholar biomed sci, 85; Basil O'Connor starter scholar res award, 89; NSF presidential young investr award, 89; asst prof, Dept Molecular & Cell Physiol, Stanford Univ Sch Med, 91- *Mem:* Soc Gen Physiologists; Am Soc Cell Biol; Sigma Xi. *Res:* Molecular physiology; membrane transport; cytoskeleton-membrane interactions. *Mailing Add:* Dept Biol Sci Stanford Univ Stanford CA 94305-5020

KOPLIK, JOEL, THEORETICAL PHYSICS, FLUID MECHANICS. *Current Pos:* PROF PHYSICS, CITY COL NY, 89- *Personal Data:* b Brooklyn, NY, Oct 31, 48. *Educ:* Cooper Union, BS, 69; Univ Calif, Berkeley, PhD(physics), 74. *Prof Exp:* Res assoc physics, Columbia Univ, 74-76; mem, Inst Advan Study, 76-79; researcher, Ecole Normal Sup, Paris, France, 77-78; mem prof staff, Schlumberger-Doll Res, 79-88. *Concurrent Pos:* Resident assoc ed, Physics of Fluids. *Mem:* Fel Am Phys Soc. *Res:* Theoretical physics of transport in random systems, particularly fluid flow, diffusive properties and electrical properties of porous media; pattern selection in non-equilibrium growth processes; molecular dynamics of fluid flow; superfluidity. *Mailing Add:* Levich Inst City Col NY Steinman 1-M New York NY 10031

KOPLOW, JANE, MICROBIOLOGY, MOLECULAR BIOLOGY. *Current Pos:* CONSULT, 84- *Personal Data:* b Ulm, Germany, Mar 15, 48; US citizen. *Educ:* Univ Wis, BA, 70; Univ Pa, MS, 73, PhD(molecular biol), 77. *Prof Exp:* Fel virol, Sch Med, Washington Univ, 78-79, fel immunol & membranes, 79-81, fel plasmids, Dept Biol, 82-84. *Res:* Synthesis of microbial membranes; defense mechanisms of pathogens. *Mailing Add:* 7146 Tulane St University City MO 63130. *Fax:* 314-727-8206

KOPLOWITZ, JACK, PATTERN RECOGNITION, IMAGE ANALYSIS. *Current Pos:* ASSOC PROF ELEC & COMPUT ENG, CLARKSON UNIV, 73- *Personal Data:* b Lenger, USSR, Mar 12, 44; US citizen; m 82; c Abraham. *Educ:* City Col New York, BEE, 67; Stanford Univ, MEE, 68; Univ Colo, PhD(elec eng), 73. *Prof Exp:* Mem tech staff Elec Eng, Bell Tele Labs, 67-70. *Concurrent Pos:* Secy, Info Theory Group, Inst Elec & Electronics Engrs, 81-83; assoc ed, Inst Elec & Electronics Engrs Trans Info Theory, 83-87 & Pattern Recognition, 90-; consult, Teltech, Inc, 89- *Mem:* Sigma Xi; sr mem Inst Elec & Electronics Engrs. *Res:* Pattern recognition; image analysis; graphics; information theory; digital encoding of bilevel images; subpixel reconstruction of image edge information; estimation of shape characteristics of digitized shapes. *Mailing Add:* Elec & Comput Eng Dept Clarkson Univ Box 5720 Potsdam NY 13699-5720

KOPLYAY, JANOS BERNATH, applied mathematics, computer science, for more information see previous edition

KOPP, EUGENE H(OWARD), ELECTRICAL ENGINEERING. *Current Pos:* sr scientist, 80-85, MGR RES & DEVELOP, HUGHES AIRCRAFT CO, 85- *Personal Data:* b New York, NY, Oct 1, 29; m 50; c 3. *Educ:* City Col New York, BEE, 50, MEE, 53; Univ Calif, Los Angeles, PhD(eng), 65. *Honors & Awards:* Excellence in Eng Educ Award, Western Elec Co, Inc, 67. *Prof Exp:* Proj engr, Polarad Electronics Corp, 50-53 & Kaye-Halbert Corp,

53-54; proj engr, Precision Radiation Instruments, Inc, 54-56, chief engr, 56-58; from asst prof to prof eng, Calif State Col, Los Angeles, 58-73, dean sch eng, 67-73; vpres acad affairs, West Coast Univ, 73-79. *Concurrent Pos:* Res fel, Univ Leeds, 66-67; adj fac, Univ Calif, Los Angeles, 79- *Mem:* Sr mem Inst Elec & Electronics Engrs. *Res:* Microwave components and antennas; satellite communications. *Mailing Add:* 483 W Avenue 46 Los Angeles CA 90019

KOPP, JAY PATRICK, PHYSICS. *Current Pos:* ASST PROF PHYSICS, LORAS COL, 69- *Personal Data:* b Buffalo Center, Iowa, 38. *Educ:* Loras Col, BS, 59; Univ Wis, MS, 61; Northwestern Univ, PhD(physics), 68. *Prof Exp:* Instr physics, Loras Col, 61-64; res assoc, Solid State Physics Lab, Swiss Fed Inst Technol, 67-69. *Mem:* Am Phys Soc; Am Asn Physics Teachers; Swiss Phys Soc. *Res:* Experimental solid state physics using nuclear magnetic resonance and magnetization measurements to study magnetic properties of rare earth systems, principally indirect exchange mechanisms. *Mailing Add:* Dept Physics & Eng Loras Col Dubuque IA 52001

KOPP, MANFRED KURT, INSTRUMENTATION. *Current Pos:* PRES, ORDELA, INC. *Personal Data:* b Koenigsberg, Ger, Mar 8, 32; US citizen; m 58; c 1. *Educ:* Univ Buenos Aires, Arg, BSEE, 62; Univ Tenn, BSEE, 70, MSEE, 75. *Prof Exp:* Develop engr nuclear instrumentation, Comision Nac de Energia Atomica, Buenos Aires, Arg, 56-67; res engr instrumentation, Oak Ridge Nat Lab, 67- *Mem:* Inst Elec & Electronics Engrs; Sigma Xi. *Res:* Low noise electronics; position sensitive proportional counters; radiation detectors, and basic measurement science. *Mailing Add:* Ordela Inc 1009 Alvin Weinberg Dr Oak Ridge TN 37830

KOPP, OTTO CHARLES, GEOLOGY. *Current Pos:* RETIRED. *Personal Data:* b Brooklyn, NY, July 22, 29; m 54, Helen S Shotkowski; c Michael A, Patricia A, Mary B & Paul B. *Educ:* Univ Notre Dame, BS, 51; Columbia Univ, MA, 55, PhD(geol), 58. *Honors & Awards:* Centennial of Sci Award, Univ Notre Dame, 65; Distinguished Prof Award, Am Fedn of Mineral Soc, 76. *Prof Exp:* Res asst, Columbia Univ, 55-58; from asst prof to prof geol, Univ Tenn, Knoxvill, 58-96. *Concurrent Pos:* Consult, Oak Ridge Nat Lab, 59-77, res partic, 77- *Mem:* Fel Geol Soc Am; Soc Appl Coal Sci; Sigma Xi; Soc Sedimentary Geol; Soc Luminescent Micros & Spectros; Nat Asn Geol Teachers (exec secy, 82-84). *Res:* Mineralogy; cathodoluminescence microscopy; petrology; coal geology; thermal analysis. *Mailing Add:* 5808 Meadow Glen Dr Knoxville TN 37919. *Fax:* 423-974-2368; *E-Mail:* otto_kopp.rocks@freddy.gg.utk.edu

KOPP, RICHARD E, systems analysis, control theory, for more information see previous edition

KOPP, ROGER ALAN, SOLAR PHYSICS, LASER FUSION. *Current Pos:* TECH STAFF MEM, LOS ALAMOS NAT LAB, 76- *Personal Data:* b Detroit, Mich, Feb 17, 40; m 62, Joyce E Schrage; c Gregory, Lori & Duane. *Educ:* Univ Mich, BS, 61; Harvard Univ, MA, 63, PhD(astron), 68. *Honors & Awards:* Award of Excellence, US Nuclear Weapons Prog, Dept Energy, 93. *Prof Exp:* Staff scientist, High Altitude Observ, Nat Ctr Atmospheric Res, 66-76. *Concurrent Pos:* Vis scientist, Max Planck Inst Physics & Astrophys, 71-72, 79-80; guest prof, Univ Florence, 88; full astronomer, Astrophys Observ Catania, 96. *Mem:* Am Astron Soc; Am Geophys Union; Int Astron Union; Am Phys Soc. *Res:* Heating of the solar corona; origin and dynamics of the solar wind; structure of the chromosphere-corona transition region; laser fusion target design and experiments; laser-plasma interactions. *Mailing Add:* Los Alamos Nat Lab MS B259 PO Box 1663 Los Alamos NM 87545. *Fax:* 505-665-7725; *E-Mail:* rak@lanl.gov

KOPPA, RODGER J, HUMAN FACTORS, REHABILITATIVE ENGINEERING. *Current Pos:* asst res psychologist, 73-79, ASSOC RES ENGR, TEX TRANSP INST, 79-; ASSOC PROF INDUST ENG, DEPT INDUST ENG, TEX A&M UNIV, 82- *Personal Data:* b Oak Park, Ill, June 23, 36; m 57; c Virginia K (Tipton) & Cynthia A (Grimes). *Educ:* Univ Tex, Austin, BA, 58, MA, 60; Tex A&M Univ, PhD(indust eng), 79. *Prof Exp:* Engr, LTV Aerospace Corp, 61-67; specialist, Gen Elec Co, 67-72. *Concurrent Pos:* Lectr, Dept Indust Eng, Tex A&M Univ, 79-82; chair spec task force, Transp Vehicle Res, Transp Res Bd Nat Res Coun-Nat Acad Sci, 80-81; mem, Adaptive Devices Stand Comt, Soc Automotive Engrs, 88-; chair, Educr Prof Group, Human Factors Soc, 89-91. *Mem:* Fel Human Factors Soc; Inst Indust Engrs; Soc Automotive Engrs. *Res:* Design and evaluation of automotive adaptive equipment for disabled drivers; transportation human factors; highway safety; visibility and driver information presentation; job performance aid design. *Mailing Add:* 1214 N Ridgefield Circle College Station TX 77840. *Fax:* 409-845-4872; *E-Mail:* rjk3686@acs.tamu.edu

KOPPEL, GARY ALLEN, ORGANIC CHEMISTRY, IMMUNOLOGY. *Current Pos:* res scientist org chem, 70-80, RES ASSOC, ELI LILLY & CO, 80- *Personal Data:* b Cleveland, Ohio, Aug 8, 43; m 66; c 2. *Educ:* Case Western Res Univ, 65; Univ Pittsburgh, PhD(org chem), 69. *Prof Exp:* NIH fel org chem, Columbia Univ, 69-70. *Concurrent Pos:* Mobay fel, 66-68; Nat Cancer Inst fel, 69-70. *Mem:* Sigma Xi; AAAS; Am Asn Immunologist; Am Chem Soc; NY Acad Sci; Clin Immunol Soc. *Res:* Synthesis of natural products; development of new cephalosporins; new synthetic methods in the synthesis of penicillins and cephalosporins; biochemistry; molecular biology. *Mailing Add:* 7823 Sunset Lane Indianapolis IN 46260-3575

KOPPEL, LOWELL B, CHEMICAL ENGINEERING. *Current Pos:* dir & sr consult, 85-, VPRES, PROF MGT DIV, ASPEN TECH INC. *Personal Data:* b Chicago, Ill, Sept 13, 35; m 57; c 2. *Educ:* Northwestern Univ, BS, 57, PhD(chem eng), 60; Univ Mich, MSE, 58. *Prof Exp:* Instr chem eng, Calif Inst Technol, 60-61; from asst prof to prof, Purdue Univ, 61-85. *Concurrent Pos:* Consult, Argonne Nat Lab, 62- *Mem:* Am Chem Soc; Am Inst Chem Engrs. *Res:* Process control; transport phenomena; applied mathematics; process simulation and optimization. *Mailing Add:* Aspen Tech Inc 14701 St Mary's Lane Houston TX 77079

KOPPELMAN, ELAINE, MATHEMATICS. *Current Pos:* From instr to asst prof, 61-74, ASSOC PROF MATH, GOUCHER COL, 74- *Personal Data:* b Brooklyn, NY, Mar 28, 37; m 70. *Educ:* Brooklyn Col, BA, 57; Yale Univ, MA, 59; Johns Hopkins Univ, PhD(hist sci), 69. *Mem:* Math Asn Am; Hist Sci Soc. *Res:* History of modern mathematics, particularly the development of algebra during the nineteenth and twentieth centuries. *Mailing Add:* Dept Math & Comput Sci Goucher Col Towson MD 21204-2794

KOPPELMAN, LEE EDWARD, ENVIRONMENTAL SCIENCE. *Current Pos:* PROF PLANNING & RESOURCE MGT, STATE UNIV NY, STONY BROOK, 67-, LEADING PROF & DIR, CTR REGIONAL POLICY STUDIES, 88- *Personal Data:* b New York, NY, May 19, 27; m 48; c 4. *Educ:* City Col, New York, BEE, 50; Pratt Inst Grad Sch Architecture, IASP, 64; NY Univ Grad Sch, DPA, 70. *Hon Degrees:* LD, Long Island Univ, 78. *Concurrent Pos:* Dir planning, Suffolk County Planning Comn, 60-; exec dir regional planning, Long Island Regional Planning Bd, 65-; appointee, Coastal Zone Mgt Adv Coun, Nat Oceanic & Atmospheric Admin, 73-75, Nat Shoreline Erosion Adv Panel, US Army, 74-81; adj prof, Grad Sch Environ Sci & Forestry, Syracuse Univ, 75-; consult, US Dept Housing & Urban Develop, 75-78, UN Off Ocean Econ & Technol, 81. *Mem:* Am Planning Asn; Sigma Xi; Am Inst Architect. *Res:* Integraton of coastal zone sciences and the regional planning process, including pollution studies of surface waters and the institutional management mechanisms required for coastal development. *Mailing Add:* Two Dune Ct Setauket NY 11733-1527

KOPPENAAL, THEODORE J, METALLURGY. *Current Pos:* PRES, KOPPENAAL & ASSOC, 81- *Personal Data:* b Milwaukee, Wis, Dec 19, 31; m 54; c 3. *Educ:* Univ Wis, BS, 54; Univ Ill, MS, 58; Northwestern Univ, PhD(metall), 61. *Prof Exp:* Asst metallurgist, Argonne Nat Lab, Ill, 62-66, assoc metallurgist, 66-67; suprv phys metall, Aeronutronic Div, Ford Aerospace & Commun Corp, 67-79; dir eng, Heavy Metals Div, Aerojet Ordnance Co, 79-81. *Mem:* Fel Am Soc Metals. *Res:* Technical consultant; technical marketing for diversified programs related to materials science and engineering. *Mailing Add:* 8220 Cedar Mesa Ave Las Vegas NV 89134

KOPPENHEFFER, THOMAS LYNN, BIOCHEMISTRY. *Current Pos:* from asst prof to assoc prof, 79-88, PROF BIOL, DEPT BIOL, TRINITY UNIV, 88- *Personal Data:* b Harrisburg, Pa, May 23, 42; m 67, Julie Adler; c Michael & Alex. *Educ:* Bloomsburg State Col, BS, 64; Williams Col, MA, 66; Boston Univ, PhD(biol), 70. *Prof Exp:* Asst prof biol, Boston Univ, 70-71; assoc surg, Harvard Med Sch, 72-73; asst prof biol, Williams Col, 73-79. *Concurrent Pos:* Res fel surg, Harvard Med Sch, 71-72. *Mem:* Am Asn Immunol; Am Soc Zoologists; Int Soc Develop & Comp Immunol. *Res:* Biology of vertebrate complement systems. *Mailing Add:* Dept Biol Trinity Univ 715 Stadium Dr San Antonio TX 78212-7200. *Fax:* 210-736-7229

KOPPERL, SHELDON JEROME, HISTORY OF SCIENCE. *Current Pos:* Asst prof hist sci, Grand Valley State Univ, 70-72, asst prof health sci, 72-75, assoc prof, 75-81, COORDR HIST SCI PROG, GRAND VALLEY STATE UNIV, 73-, PROF, SCH HEALTH SCI, 81- *Personal Data:* b Cleveland, Ohio, Sept 11, 43; m 67, Susan Levy; c Benjamin & Robert. *Educ:* Case Inst Technol, BS, 65; Univ Wis-Madison, PhD(chem, hist sci), 70. *Mem:* Am Chem Soc; Hist Sci Soc; Soc Hist Technol; Sigma Xi. *Res:* Historical studies in inorganic, physical and organo-metallic chemistry and medicine, chiefly since 1800; studies in the history of art and science, chiefly Renaissance and Baroque. *Mailing Add:* 1047 Ironwood Circle NW Grand Rapids MI 49544. *E-Mail:* kopperls@gvsu.edu

KOPPERMAN, RALPH DAVID, SET-THEORETIC TOPOLOGY, MATHEMATICAL LOGIC. *Current Pos:* from asst prof to assoc prof, 67-83, PROF, CITY COL NEW YORK, 84- *Personal Data:* b New York, NY, Feb 17, 42; m, Connie Hadap; c David, Leah, Amy, Gail & Susan. *Educ:* Columbia Col, AB, 62; Mass Inst Technol, PhD(math), 65. *Prof Exp:* Lectr math, Boston Univ, 63-65; asst prof, Univ RI, 65-67. *Mem:* Am Math Soc; Asn Symbolic Logic; Math Asn Am. *Res:* Generalized metric spaces and uniform spaces; general topology applied to computer graphics; spaces of ideals; asymmetric topology. *Mailing Add:* 49 Cedar St Tappan NY 10983-1948

KOPPLE, KENNETH D(AVID), PEPTIDE CHEMISTRY, NUCLEAR MAGNETIC RESONANCE. *Current Pos:* DIR PHYS & STRUCT CHEM, SMITH KLINE & FRENCH LABS, 85- *Personal Data:* b Philadelphia, Pa, Oct 21, 30; m 60. *Educ:* Mass Inst Technol, SB, 51, PhD(chem), 54. *Prof Exp:* Instr org chem, Univ Chicago, 54-56, asst prof, 56-62; res chemist, Gen Elec Co Res Lab, 62-65; from assoc prof to prof chem, Ill Inst Technol, 65-85, chmn dept, 82-85. *Concurrent Pos:* J S Guggenheim Found fel, Lab Chem Biodynamics, Univ Calif, Berkeley, 64-65; NIH res career develop award, 70-75; for res guest, SNAM Progetti Laboratori Ricerche di Base, Rome, Italy, 74. *Mem:* Am Chem Soc; fel AAAS; Am Soc Biochem & Molecular Biol; Royal Soc Chem. *Res:* Peptide chemistry, synthesis and spectroscopic determination of conformation; nuclear magnetic resonance. *Mailing Add:* Smith Kline Beecham Pharm UW2940 709 Swedeland Rd PO Box 1539 King of Prussia PA 19406-0939. *Fax:* 610-270-6608

KOPROWSKA, IRENA, PATHOLOGY, CYTOLOGY. *Current Pos:* RETIRED. *Personal Data:* b Warsaw, Poland, May 12, 17; nat US; m 38; c 2. *Educ:* Warsaw Med Sch, MD, 39. *Honors & Awards:* Woman Physician of Year, Polish Am Med Asn, 77; Papanicolaou Award, Am Soc Cytol, 85. *Prof Exp:* Intern med, Villejuif Lunatic Asylum, France, 40; asst pathologist, Rio de Janeiro City Hosps, 42-44; res asst & asst pathologist, Med Col, Cornell Univ & New York Hosp, 45-46; res asst appl immunol, Pub Health Res Inst, City of New York, 46-47; asst pathologist, New York Infirmary, 47-49; res fel & assoc anat, Med Col, Cornell Univ, 49-54; asst prof path, State Univ NY Downstate Med Ctr, 54-57; from assoc prof to prof, Hahnemann Med Col, 57-70; prof path & dir cytol serv, Health Sci Ctr, Temple Univ, 70-87. *Concurrent Pos:* Res fel, Med Col, Cornell Univ, 49-54; USPHS res grants, 54-; Runyon Mem Fund grant, 55-56; Am Cancer Soc grant, 58-61; lectr, France, Poland, India & Iran, 52-; consult, WHO, 62- *Mem:* AAAS; Am Soc Cytol; Am Asn Cancer Res; Am Soc Exp Path; Am Soc Clin Pathologists. *Res:* Studies of progressive morphologic cellular changes, especially neoplastic progression in human beings, mice and in tissue culture systems. *Mailing Add:* 334 Fairhill Rd Wynnewood PA 19096

KOPROWSKI, HILARY, BIOLOGY. *Current Pos:* dir, 57-91, inst prof, 57-93, PROF LAUREATE, WISTAR INST ANAT & BIOL, 93-; WISTAR PROF RES MED & PROF MICROBIOL, FAC ARTS & SCI, UNIV PA, 57-; PROF, DEPT MICROBIOL & IMMUNOL, THOMAS JEFFERSON UNIV, 92-, DIR, CTR NEUROVIROL, 94- *Personal Data:* b Warsaw, Poland; nat US; m 38; c 2. *Educ:* Univ Warsaw, MD, 39. *Hon Degrees:* Numerous from US & foreign univs. *Honors & Awards:* Comdr, Order of Merit, 59; Chevalier, Order of the Royal Lion, Belg; Polish Millennium Award, Alfred Jurzykowski Found, 66; Felix Wankel Tierschutz Prize, 79; Nicolaus Copernicus Medal, Polish Acad Sci, 89; John Scott Award, 90. *Prof Exp:* Res assoc, Yellow Fever Res Serv, Rockefeller Found & Ministry Educ, Rio de Janeiro, Brazil, 40-44; res assoc, Sect Viral & Rickettsial Res, Lederle Labs, Am Cyanamid Co, 44-46, asst dir, 46-57. *Concurrent Pos:* Consult, Nat Cancer Inst, NIH & USPHS, 62-70; mem, Expert Comt Rabies, WHO, Switz; co-ed, Methods in Virol, Viruses & Immunity, Current Topics in Microbiol & Immunol, 65-; Fulbright scholar, Max Planck Inst Physiol Behav, Ger, 71-72; Alexander von Humboldt Sr Scientist Award, Max Planck Inst, WGer, 74; chmn, Bd Sci Counrs, Div Cancer Etiology, Nat Cancer Inst, 87-90. *Mem:* Nat Acad Sci; NY Acad Med; NY Acad Sci (pres, 59); AAAS; Am Acad Arts & Sci; foreign mem Yugoslav Acad Arts & Sci; foreign mem Polish Acad Sci; foreign mem Russian Acad Med Sci; fel Polish Inst Arts & Sci Am; foreign mem Finnish Soc Sci & Letts. *Res:* Cell biology, virology, and immunology; cancer; vaccine against poliomyelitis, hog cholera and rabies; authored over 800 publications. *Mailing Add:* Thomas Jefferson Univ M85 Jefferson Alumni Hall 1020 Locust St Philadelphia PA 19107

KORACH, KENNETH STEVEN, STEROID HORMONE ACTION, STEROID RECEPTOR PROTEINS. *Current Pos:* staff fel, Nat Inst Environ Health Sci, 76-78, sr staff fel, 78-80, res endocrinologist, 80-84, SR RES ENDOCRINOLOGIST, NAT INST ENVIRON HEALTH SCI, 85-, CHIEF, RECEPTOR BIOL SECT, 87- *Personal Data:* b Buffalo, NY, Nov 26, 46; m 70; c 2. *Educ:* Augusta Col, Ga, BA, 69; Med Col Ga, PhD(endocrinol), 74. *Prof Exp:* Res fel endocrinol, Sch Med, Harvard Univ, 74-75, Ford res fel, 75-76. *Concurrent Pos:* Guest lectr, Dept Biochem, NC State Univ, 81-; adj prof, 90-; adj prof, lab reproductive biol, Univ NC Med Sch, 81-, adj prof, pharmacol, 89-; chmn, Radiation Safety Comt & Res Prod Subcomt, Nat Inst Environ Health Sci, 85-, Arts Graphics Comt, 87- & Res Assoc Prom Comt, 90-; transatlantic lectr, Soc Toxicol, 85; consult, Glaxo Res Inst, 90- *Mem:* Endocrine Soc; Sigma Xi. *Res:* Estrogen hormone action; investigations of estrogen receptor proteins, using a structure-activity approach; determination of intracellular sites of action; tissue responses in protein synthesis and DNA-RNA induction. *Mailing Add:* 105 Boulder Bluff Trail Chapel Hill NC 27516

KORACH, MALCOLM, ORGANIC CHEMISTRY. *Current Pos:* res chemist, org group leader & asst dir res, 49-70, dir res, 70-74, MGR RES, CHEM DIV, PPG INDUSTS, 74- *Personal Data:* b New York, NY, Apr 25, 22; m 46; c 3. *Educ:* Yale Univ, BS, 42, PhD(chem), 48. *Prof Exp:* Asst, Manhattan Proj, Columbia Univ, 43 & Oak Ridge Inst Nuclear Studies, 44-46. *Mem:* Am Chem Soc. *Res:* Heavy organic chemicals; chlorinated organics; hydrogen peroxide and its utilization. *Mailing Add:* 1745 Brookwood Dr Akron OH 44313-5058

KORAKIANITIS, THEODOSIOS, THERMODYNAMICS, POWER & PROPULSION SYSTEMS & COMPONENTS. *Current Pos:* asst prof, 88-94, ASSOC PROF MECH ENG, WASHINGTON UNIV, 94- *Personal Data:* b Athens, Greece, Jan 25, 59; US citizen. *Educ:* Newcastle Univ, UK, BSc, 81; Mass Inst Technol, SM, 82, SM(mech eng) & SM(ocean systs mgt), 87, DSc(mech eng), 87. *Honors & Awards:* Ralph R Teetor Educ Award, Soc Automotive Engrs, 89; Young Prof Award, Am Inst Aeronaut & Astronaut, 90. *Prof Exp:* Marine engr & naval architect, JJMA, 82-83; consult, NREC, 87-88. *Concurrent Pos:* Chmn, Closed Cycles Comt, Am Soc Mech Engrs, 95-96, Cycle Innovations Comt, 96-97. *Mem:* Am Soc Mech Engrs; Am Inst Aeronaut & Astronaut; Sigma Xi; Soc Automotive Engrs. *Res:* Thermal fluid sciences and design; application to power and propulsion systems design; thermodynamics, turbomachinery, piston engines and design. *Mailing Add:* Washington Univ Campus Box 1185 St Louis MO 63130. *E-Mail:* tk@zeus.wustl.edu

KORAN, LORRIN MICHAEL, OBSESSIVE-COMPULSIVE DISORDERS, AFFECTIVE DISORDERS. *Current Pos:* assoc prof, 79-84, PROF PSYCHIAT, STANFORD UNIV, 84- *Personal Data:* b Los Angeles, Calif, Apr 4, 40; m 67; c 2. *Educ:* Harvard Col, BA, 62; Harvard Med Sch, MC, 66; Am Bd Psychiat & Neurol, cert, 73. *Prof Exp:* From asst prof to assoc prof psychiat, State Univ NY, Stony Brook, 72-77. *Concurrent Pos:* Dir, med student educ psychiat, State Univ NY, Stony Brook, 73-77; dir, residency training prog, Stanford Univ, Calif, 79-81; med dir, CMU, Stanford Hosp, Stanford Calif, 80-88, dir, Obsessive Compulsive Dis Clin, Stanford Med Ctr, 88- *Mem:* Fel Am Psychiat Asn; Am Soc Clin Psychopharmacol; Am Col Psychiatrists. *Res:* Relationships between physical and mental disorders; treatment of obsessive-compulsive disorder; treatment of affective disorders. *Mailing Add:* Dept Psychiat 2363 Stanford Univ Sch Med Stanford CA 94305-5549. *Fax:* 650-725-0363

KORAN, ZOLTAN, FOREST PRODUCTS, PULP & PAPER SCIENCE & TECHNOLOGY. *Current Pos:* PROF ENG, UNIV QUE, 76- *Personal Data:* b Hungary, May 27, 34; Can citizen; m 68; c 4. *Educ:* Univ BC, BSc, 59, MF, 61; Syracuse Univ, PhD(forestry), 64. *Prof Exp:* Asst prof forestry, Univ NH, 63-64; res scientist pulp & paper, Pulp & Paper Res Inst Can, 65-68; asst prof forestry, Univ Toronto, 68-73; res scientist, Que Indust Res Ctr, 73-76. *Mem:* Forest Prod Res Soc; Int Asn Wood Anat; Can Pulp & Paper Asn; Micros Soc Can; Tech Asn Pulp & Paper Indust. *Res:* Anatomy and ultrastructure of wood, bark, fiber, pulp and paper; thermomechanical pulping; pulp and paper properties; forest products and utilization; composite boards; wood finishing and impregnation; x-ray, light and electron microscopic studies; material science engineering. *Mailing Add:* 3845 Limoges Trois-Rivieres PQ G8Y 4P9 Can

KORANT, BRUCE DAVID, VIROLOGY, ENZYMOLOGY. *Current Pos:* biochemist virol, Cent Res Dept, Exp Sta, E I Du Pont de Nemours & Co, Inc, 69-90, RES FEL, DUPONT MERCK PHARMACEUT CO, 90- *Personal Data:* b Brooklyn, NY, Aug 9, 43; m 69, Mary A; c Deborah. *Educ:* Brooklyn Col, BS, 65; Pa State Univ, MS, 67, PhD(microbiol), 69. *Concurrent Pos:* NATO fac, 78, 82 & 84. *Mem:* Am Soc Microbiol; Am Soc Virol; Soc Interferon Res. *Res:* Animal virology; bacteriophages; virus structure and replication; effects of viruses on cells; protein chemistry; proteolytic enzymes; interferon mechanism. *Mailing Add:* Res & Develop Div DuPont Merck E 336 DuPont Exp Sta Wilmington DE 19880-0336. *Fax:* 302-695-9420; *E-Mail:* korantbd@a1.lldmpc.umc.dupont.com

KORANYI, ADAM, HARMONIC ANALYSIS, LIE GROUPS & SYMMETRIC SPACES. *Current Pos:* PROF MATH, 79-85, DISTINGUISHED PROF, WASH UNIV, 85- *Personal Data:* b Szeged, Hungary, July 13, 32; US citizen; m 69, Anna Eiben. *Educ:* Univ Szeged, dipl, 54; Univ Chicago, PhD(math), 59. *Prof Exp:* Instr math, Harvard Univ, 59-60; asst prof, Univ Calif, Berkeley, 60-64; vis asst prof, Princeton Univ, 64-65; assoc prof math, Belfer Grad Sch, Yeshiva Univ, 65-68, prof, 68-79. *Mem:* Am Math Soc. *Res:* Functions of several complex variables. *Mailing Add:* Herbert H Lehman Col City Univ New York Bronx NY 10468-1589

KORC, MURRAY, ENDOCRINOLOGY. *Current Pos:* PROF & CHIEF, DIV ENDOCRINOL & METAB, UNIV CALIF, IRVINE, 89- *Personal Data:* b Ger, Apr 3, 47; m; c 3. *Educ:* Albany Med Col, MD, 74. *Prof Exp:* From asst prof to assoc prof, Dept Internal Med, Health Sci Ctr, Univ Ariz, 81-89, assoc prof internal med & biochem, 87-89. *Mem:* Am Col Physicians; AAAS; Am Soc Cell Biol; Am Diabetes Asn; Endocrine Soc; Am Fedn Clin Res. *Mailing Add:* Dept Med Div Endocrinol & Metab Univ Calif Med Sci I C240 Irvine CA 92717-0001

KORCEK, STEFAN, PHYSICAL ORGANIC CHEMISTRY, LUBRICANTS CHEMISTRY. *Current Pos:* sr res scientist, 71-76, prin res scientist assoc, 76-81, STAFF SCIENTIST LUBRICANT CHEM & PHYS ORG CHEM, RES FUELS & LUBRICANTS DEPT, FORD MOTOR CO, DEARBORN, MICH, 81- *Personal Data:* b Trnava, Czech, May 28, 34; m 65; c 2. *Educ:* Slovak Tech Univ, Bratislava, MS, 57, PhD(chem, chem eng & fuel technol), 67. *Honors & Awards:* F R McFarland Award, Soc Automotive Engrs, 81. *Prof Exp:* Assoc prof chem kinetics & reactors design, Dept Chem & Technol Petrol, Slovak Tech Univ, 57-68; fel phys org chem, Div Chem, Nat Res Coun, Ottawa, Can, 68-70. *Concurrent Pos:* Vis res off, Div Chem, Nat Res Coun, Ottawa, Can, 70-71. *Mem:* Am Chem Soc; Soc Automotive Engrs. *Res:* Kinetics and mechanisms of autooxidation and inhibited oxidation of organic substrates in liquid phase at elevated temperatures; mechanism of action of antioxidants; automotive lubricants, their chemistry and degradation in service; reactions of lubricant antioxidant additives in engines; author or coauthor of over 40 publications. *Mailing Add:* 4778 Crestview Ct Bloomfield Hills MI 48301-3565

KORCHAK, ERNEST I(AN), COATINGS & ADHESIVES TECHNOLOGY, TECHNICAL MANAGEMENT. *Current Pos:* CHMN, CHEM TECH MGT LTD, 86-; PRES, PERFORMANCE COATINGS CORP, 90- *Personal Data:* b Opava, Czech, Feb 15, 34; Australian citizen; m 59, Helen M Walker; c 3. *Educ:* Univ Melbourne, BChE, 57; Mass Inst Technol, SM, 61, ScD(chem eng), 64. *Prof Exp:* Res engr chem eng, Imp Chem Industs, Australia & NZ, 58-59; chem engr, Halcon Int, Inc, 64-67; sales exec, Sci Design Co, Inc, 67-71, vpres & gen mgr, Halcon Catalyst Industs, 71-75, pres, Halcon Res & Develop Corp, 75-80, pres, Sci Design Co, 81-86; chmn, Riverside Polymer Systs Inc, 86-90. *Concurrent Pos:* Pres, Chem Indust Asn, 84-85; chmn, Chemtech Mgt Ltd, 86- *Mem:* Am Chem Soc; Am Inst Chem Engrs. *Res:* Gas flow and turbulence, application to packed beds; process research and development of organic chemical processes, special emphasis on kinetics and separations; oxidation and carbonylation processes. *Mailing Add:* 1118 Old Gulph Rd Bryn Mawr PA 19010

KORCHAK, HELEN MARIE, PHOSPHOLIPID METABOLISM. *Current Pos:* ASSOC PROF EXP MED & DIR RES, DIV RHEUMATOLOGY, NY UNIV MED CTR, 84- *Educ:* Tufts Univ, PhD(physiol), 62. *Res:* Neutrophil activation. *Mailing Add:* Dept Pediat Children's Hosp Philadelphia Rm 1208C 34th & Civic Ctr Rd Philadelphia PA 19104-1649

KORCHEV, DMITRIY VENIAMINOVICH, mapping algorithms to parallel computer architecture, digital signal processing, for more information see previous edition

KORCHIN, LEO, ORAL & MAXILLOFACIAL SURGERY. *Current Pos:* assoc prof oral surg, Univ PR, 67-72, dir dept surg sci, 72-75, asst dean for clin instr, 79-82, assoc dean, 84-86, PROF ORAL & MAXILLOFACIAL SURG, SCH DENT, UNIV PR, SAN JUAN, 72- *Personal Data:* b Brooklyn, NY, July 1, 14; m; Norma Cruz; c Gregory & Paul. *Educ:* Cornell Univ, BS, 36; NY Univ, DDS, 41; Georgetown Univ, MS, 54; Am Bd Oral & Maxillofacial Surg, dipl; FACD; FICD. *Honors & Awards:* Novice Award, Int Asn Dent Res, 54. *Prof Exp:* Chief oral surg sect, Army Hosp, US Army, Ft Jay, NY, 48-52, instr oral surg & asst prof mil sci & tactics, Sch Dent, Georgetown Univ, 52-54, chief oral surg sect, Rodriguez Army Hosp, PR, 54-57, chief oral surg br, Dent Detachment, Ft Devens, Mass, 57-62, chief dent clin & oral surg sect, 97th Gen Hosp, Frankfurt, Ger, 62-65, chief dent serv & oral surg & dir dent intern training prog, Martin Army Hosp, Ft Benning, Ga, 65-67. *Concurrent Pos:* Fel oral path, Armed Forces Inst Path, 75-76. *Mem:* Am Soc Oral & Maxillofacial Surgeons; Am Acad Oral Path; Am Dent Asn; Int Asn Oral & Maxillofacial Surgeons. *Res:* Effects of starch sponge implanted in bone; effect of isotretinoin and triamcinolone acetonide on human skin fibroblasts in vitro. *Mailing Add:* Univ PR Sch Dent San Juan PR 00936

KORCHYNSKY, M(ICHAEL), PHYSICAL METALLURGY, MATERIALS SCIENCE. *Current Pos:* PRIN, KORCHYNSKY & ASSOCS, CONSULTS METALL, 86- *Personal Data:* b Kiev, Ukraine, Apr 11, 18; nat US; m 51, Taisija Lapin; c Michael Jr, Marina & Roksana. *Educ:* Tech Univ Lviv, Ukraine, Dipl Ing, 42. *Honors & Awards:* Am Iron & Steel Inst Medal, 65; Howe Mem lectr, Am Inst Mining, Metall & Petrol Eng, 83; W H Eiseman Award, Am Soc Metals, 84 & E C Bain Award, 86; Robert Earll McConnell Eng Achievement Award, Am Inst Mech Engrs, 92. *Prof Exp:* Asst metall, Tech Univ Lviv, 42-44; chief engr, US Army, Ger, 45-50; res metallurgist phys metall, Metals Res Labs, Union Carbide Metals Co, 51-60, tech supvr, Tech Dept, 60-61; res supvr alloy & high strength steels, Jones & Laughlin Steel Corp, 61-65, asst dir res new prod develop, Graham Res Lab, 65-70, dir prod res, 70-73; dir alloy develop, Umetco Minerals Corp, Union Carbide Corp, 73-86; consult metall, Strategic Minerals Corp, 86- *Concurrent Pos:* Sr fel, Union Carbide Corp, 79. *Mem:* Fel Am Soc Metals Int; Iron & Steel Soc-Am Inst Mining, Metall & Petrol Engrs; Soc Automotive Engrs; Acad Eng Sci Ukraine. *Res:* Physical metallurgy of steels; materials for high-temperature service; nuclear fuels; alloy design and development; technology and application of high-strength, low-alloy (microalloyed) steels; management of industrial research and product development; technological marketing. *Mailing Add:* 2770 Milford Dr Bethel Park PA 15102-1763. *Fax:* 412-787-4727

KORDA, EDWARD J(OHN), MICROSCOPY IMAGE ANALYSIS, CERAMICS. *Current Pos:* RES PROF, ATLANTA UNIV, 83- *Personal Data:* b Duluth, Minn, Nov 17, 18; m 45; c 3. *Educ:* Univ Minn, BMetE, 47; Stevens Inst Technol, MS, 51. *Prof Exp:* Lab asst chem, Duluth Jr Col, 38-39; lab asst metallog, Univ Minn, 39-41, scientist metall res, 47-48; mem res staff metall, Manhattan Proj, 44-46; proj engr metall eng, Curtiss Wright Corp, NJ, 48-49 & 50-56; prof metall eng, Drexel Inst, 56-65; dir ed & res, Del Sci Labs, Inc, 65; electron microscopist, Corning Glass Works, 65-66, sr res scientist, 66-75, res supvr, 75-79 & 81-83; vis prof, Atlanta Univ, 79-81. *Concurrent Pos:* Laboratorian, Am Steel & Wire Co, Minn, 39-41; res assoc metall, Stevens Inst Technol, 49-50, instr, 49-51; prof, Elmira Col, 66-76. *Mem:* Am Soc Testing & Mat; Am Soc Metals; Electron Micros Soc Am; Am Ceramic Soc; Sigma Xi. *Res:* Electron microscopy and optics; metallography; physical metallurgy; solid state physics, x-ray analysis; ceramography; optical microscopy; image analysis; electron diffraction. *Mailing Add:* 3913 Jericho Rd Tucker GA 30084-7412

KORDA, PETER E, ENGINEERING MECHANICS, STRUCTURAL ENGINEERING. *Current Pos:* PRES, KORDA/NEMETH ENG, 85- *Personal Data:* b Budapest, Hungary, Dec 5, 31; US citizen; m 54; c 4. *Educ:* Budapest Tech Univ, Dipl Eng, 54; Ohio State Univ, PhD(eng mech), 64. *Prof Exp:* Struct designer, Indust Bldg Design Off, Hungary, 54-56, Livesley & Henderson, Eng, 56-57 & Dominion Bridge Co, Ltd, Can, 57-60; asst proj design, Sch Archit, Ohio State Univ, 60-61, res assoc & instr eng mech, 61-63, from asst prof to prof, 64-81. *Concurrent Pos:* Consult engr, Miller & Korda, 64-67, pres, Korda Eng Co Consult Engrs, 67-85. *Mem:* Am Soc Civil Engrs; Concrete Inst Am; Int Asn Shell Struct; Nat Soc Prof Engrs; Am Soc Eng Educ. *Res:* Shallow shell theory with computer applications; dynamic stability and structural damping. *Mailing Add:* 5544 Dublin Rd Dublin OH 43017

KORDAN, HERBERT ALLEN, developmental physiology, plant morphogenetics, for more information see previous edition

KORDESCH, KARL VICTOR, ELECTROCHEMISTRY, BATTERIES & FUEL CELLS. *Current Pos:* CONSULT ELECTROCHEM, 77-; VPRES ADVAN RES, BATTERY TECHNOL INC, 88- *Personal Data:* b Vienna, Austria, Mar 18, 22; nat US; m 46; c 4. *Educ:* Univ Vienna, PhD(chem), 48. *Hon Degrees:* Dr techn hc, Tech Univ Vienna, 90. *Honors & Awards:* Nat Energy Award, Austria, 81; Vittorio De Nora-Diamond Shamrock Award, Electrochem Soc, 87; E Schroedinger Prize, Austrian Acad Sci, 90- *Prof Exp:* Asst & lectr chem, Chem Inst, Univ Vienna, 46-48, asst prof, 48-53; chem engr, Signal Corps Eng Labs, NJ, 53-55; res chemist & group leader, Develop Dept, 55-70, sr res assoc, Parma Res Lab, Union Carbide Corp, 70-74, corp res fel, Battery Prod Div, 74-77. *Concurrent Pos:* Prof, Tech Univ Graz, Austria, 77-; dir, Inst Inorg Chem Technol, 77-; secy gen, Int Electrochem Soc, 81. *Mem:* Am Chem Soc; Electrochem Soc; Austrian Chem Soc; Int Electrochem Soc (vpres, 86). *Res:* Electrochemical systems; batteries, especially with alkaline electrolytes; hydrogen-oxygen fuel cells; carbon electrodes; test and control instruments; electronic circuitry; technical management. *Mailing Add:* Tech Univ Graz Stremayrgasse 16 Graz A-8010 Austria. *Fax:* 905-881-6043

KORDOSKI, EDWARD WILLIAM, ORGANIC CHEMISTRY, SCIENCE ADMINISTRATION. *Current Pos:* sr analyst, Prog & Develop Off Indust Relations, 93-95, MGR LIBR SERVS, AM CHEM SOC, 95- *Personal Data:* b New Britain, Conn, Aug 15, 54; m 77, Donna Orischak. *Educ:* King's Col, BS, 77; Univ Md, PhD(org chem), 82; Monmouth Col, MBA, 86. *Prof Exp:* Teaching asst org chem, Univ Md, 77-79 & res asst, 79-82; process develop chemist, Dyestaffs & Chem Div, Ciba-Geigy Corp, Toms River, NJ, 82-84, sr process develop chemist, 84-87, prod chemist, Ciba-Geigy Ltd, Basel Switz, 87-88, tech proj asst, Textile Prod Div, St Gabriel, La, 88-90, chem develop res team leader, 90-91, qual assurance team leader, 91-92. *Concurrent Pos:* Bd gov, Univ Md, College Park, 95- *Mem:* Am Chem Soc; Asahs; AAAS. *Res:* Expand the existing ACS portfolio of programs, products and services for industrial chemical scientists; enhance the image and stature of chemical professionals; develop continuous small reactor technology and analytical monitoring and feedback control. *Mailing Add:* Am Chem Soc 1155 16th St NW Washington DC 20036-4800. *Fax:* 202-776-8165; *E-Mail:* e_kordoski@acs.org

KORDOVA, NONNA, RICKETTSIAL DISEASES. *Current Pos:* RETIRED. *Personal Data:* b Krasnodar, USSR; Can citizen; m 45. *Educ:* Charles Univ, Prague, MD, 45; Czech Acad Sci, PhD(med virol), 60. *Honors & Awards:* Recognition Dipl, Czech Acad Sci, 65. *Prof Exp:* Res assoc pediat, Children's Hosp, Komensky Univ, 45-54, asst prof, 54-56; res assoc rickettsioses, Inst Virol, Czech Acad Sci, 56-60, sr scientist, 60-66, chief lab, 66-68; res assoc, Univ Kans, 68-69; assoc prof, Med Col, Univ Man, 70-77, prof, 77-87. *Mem:* Can Soc Microbiol; Am Soc Microbiol; Can Pub Health Asn. *Res:* Pathogenesis of chlamydial diseases; parasite-host interactions at the cellular and subcellular level. *Mailing Add:* 501-71 Roslyn Rd Winnipeg MB R3L 0G2 Can

KORDYBAN, EUGENE S, FLUID MECHANICS. *Current Pos:* asst prof, 69-72, assoc prof civil eng, 72-81, PROF MECH ENG, UNIV DETROIT, 81- *Personal Data:* b Ukraine, May 20, 28; m 53; c 6. *Educ:* Univ Detroit, BME, 54; State Univ NY Buffalo, MS, 60, PhD(mech eng), 69. *Prof Exp:* Engr, Linde Div, Union Carbide Corp, 54-64, sr engr, 64-69. *Concurrent Pos:* NSF res grant, 70-72. *Mem:* Am Soc Mech Engrs; Am Acad Mech; AAAS. *Res:* Polyphase flow, especially slug flow, basic fluid mechanics, flow visualization techniques and flow measurement. *Mailing Add:* 4601 Carpenter St Detroit MI 48212

KORECKY, BORIVOJ, MEDICAL PHYSIOLOGY. *Current Pos:* assoc prof, 66-71, PROF PHYSIOL, UNIV OTTAWA, 71- *Personal Data:* b Prague, Czech, Sept 9, 29; c 2. *Educ:* Charles Univ, Prague, MD, 55; Czech Acad Sci, PhD, 61. *Prof Exp:* From asst prof to assoc prof path physiol, Charles Univ, Prague, 55-66. *Concurrent Pos:* Med Res Coun Can res fel, 63-64. *Mem:* Can Physiol Soc; Am Physiol Soc. *Res:* Cardiovascular and respiratory physiology. *Mailing Add:* Dept Physiol Univ Ottawa Sch Med 451 Smyth Rd Ottawa ON K1H 8M5 Can. *Fax:* 613-562-5434

KOREIN, JULIUS, NEUROLOGY. *Current Pos:* from asst prof to assoc prof, 61-72, assoc dir anal & comput methodology, Dept Radiol, 68-72, PROF NEUROL, MED CTR, NY UNIV, 72- *Personal Data:* b New York, NY, Sept 27, 28; m 57, James, Jonathan & Beth; c 3. *Educ:* NY Univ, BA, 49, MD, 53. *Honors & Awards:* Bronze Award, Diag of Brain Death, Int Film & TV Fest, NY, 83. *Prof Exp:* Intern, Maimonides Hosp, Brooklyn, 53-54; asst resident neurol, Mt Sinai Hosp, 54-55; asst & chief resident, NY Univ-Bellevue Hosp Ctr, 55-57. *Concurrent Pos:* Fel, Mt Sinai Hosp, 53-54, asst attend, 59-70, spec trainee, 60-61; spec trainee, NY Univ-Bellevue Hosp Ctr, 59-60; vis asst, Bellevue Hosp, 59-68, vis assoc, 68-72, attend, 72-, dir EEG, 61-70, chief, 70-; attend physician, Vet Admin Hosp, Manhattan, 61-73, consult, 73-87; asst attend, NY Univ Hosp, 61-72, attend, 71-; consult, Gen Elec Corp, 66-67, Children's Bur, Dept Health, Educ & Welfare, 66-71, Int Info Processing, 67-70, Nat Inst Neurol Dis & Stroke, 71-74; proj dir, Health Res Coun Grants, City of New York, 63-65 & Nat Cancer Inst, 66-70; prin investr, USV Pharmaceut Corp, 63-72, Warner-Lambert Inst, 66-67, Nat Ctr Health Serv Res & Develop, 66-70 & Hoffmann-La Roche Labs, 69-70; co-investr, Nat Inst Neurol Dis & Stroke, 65-67, proj dir & vchmn study cerebral death, 71-72; consult, sensory feedback ther, Int Ctr Disabled Res & Rehab Ctr, 72-84; assoc ed, Am Soc Cybernet Forum, 73-87; mem adv bd, Int J Neurosci, 79-; adv, President's Comn Study Ethical Problems Med, Biomed & Behav Res, Washington DC, 80-81; adv bd, Neurosci Info Ctr, Upjohn Co, 78-84; various educ video presentations, 67-84; mem, Sci & Soc Comt, NY Acad Sci, 84-86; chmn, Biomed Ethics Comt, Bellevue Hosp, 85-; career scientist award, New York City Health Res Coun, 66-72. *Mem:* AAAS; Am Neurol Asn; Am Acad Neurol; Asn Nes Nerv & Ment Dis; Am Electroencephalographic; NY Acad Sci. *Res:* Computer applications in capture, storage, retrieval and analysis of narrative medical data for the purpose of patient care and clinical research; sensory feedback therapy in neuromuscular disorders; electroencephalography and behavior, including computer analysis of the electroencephalogram, effects of drugs on the electroencephalogram and behavior, diagnosis of brain death; pathophysiology and treatment of segmental torsion dystonia; models of neurophysiological structures; ontogenesis of cerebral function in the human fetus; aquatic medicine; electro physiological probes to analyse movement of cortical and subcortical origins. *Mailing Add:* 502 Park Ave New York NY 10022. *Fax:* 212-263-8228

KOREN, EUGEN, ENDOCRINOLOGY, CELL BIOLOGY. *Current Pos:* Asst mem cell biol, 85-90, ASST MEM ENDOCRINOL RES, OKLA MED RES FOUND, 90- *Personal Data:* b Zagreb, Croatia, Oct 10, 40. *Educ:* Zagreb Univ, BA, 65, PhD(biochem), 72. *Honors & Awards:* Merrick Award, Biomed Found; Johan Blumenbach Award, Univ Gottingen. *Mem:* Am Soc Biochem & Molecular Biol; Am Soc Cell Biol; Am Chem Soc; Am Asn Endocrinol; NY Acad Sci; AAAS. *Res:* Endocrinology; cell biology. *Mailing Add:* Genentech Inc 460 Point San Bruno Blvd South San Francisco CA 94080. *Fax:* 650-225-1998

KOREN, ISRAEL, COMPUTER ENGINEERING. *Current Pos:* PROF ELEC & COMPUT ENG, UNIV MASS, AMHERST, 86- *Personal Data:* m Yuval & Yaron. *Educ:* Technion/Israel Inst Technol, BSc, 67, MSc, 70, DSc, 75. *Prof Exp:* Asst prof elec & comput eng, Univ Calif, Santa Barbara, 76-78, Univ Southern Calif, 78-79; sr lectr, Technion/Israel Inst Technol, Haifa, 79-85, head, VLSI Syst Res Ctr, 85-86. *Concurrent Pos:* Vis prof, Univ Calif, Berkeley, 82-83; consult, Tolerant Systs, 86, Digital Equip Corp, 91, Intel, 92, Advan Micro Devices, Inc, 94 & IBM, 95- *Mem:* Fel Inst Elec & Electronics Engrs; fel Japan Soc Promotion Sci; Asn Comput Mach. *Res:* Author of one book and co-author of one book. *Mailing Add:* Dept Elec & Comput Eng Univ Mass Amherst MA 01003

KORENBROT, JUAN IGAL, BIOPHYSICS. *Current Pos:* from asst prof to assoc prof, 74-85, PROF PHYSIOL, UNIV CALIF, SAN FRANCISCO, 85- *Personal Data:* b Mexico City, Mex, Nov 29, 47; m 72; c 2. *Educ:* Johns Hopkins Univ, MA, 71, PhD(biophys), 72. *Prof Exp:* Res assoc biophys, Johns Hopkins Univ, 71-72; res assoc physiol, 72-73; lectr, Univ Calif, Los Angeles, 73-74. *Concurrent Pos:* Vis scientist biochem, Nat Polytech Inst, 73. *Mem:* Soc Neurosci; Soc Gen Physiol. *Res:* Molecular mechanisms of ion transport; mechanisms of function of Rhodopsins and phototransduction; photoreceptor development. *Mailing Add:* 142 Stewart Dr Belvedere Tiburon CA 94920

KORENMAN, STANLEY G, ENDOCRINOLOGY, BIOCHEMISTRY. *Current Pos:* prof med & chmn dept, 74-89, ASSOC DEAN, SAN FERNANDO VALLEY PROG, UNIV CALIF, LOS ANGELES, 81-, ASSOC DEAN EDUC DEVELOP, SCH MED, 88-, MD, ASSOC DEAN ETHICS & MED, SCIENTIST TRAINING PROG CHIEF, DIV ENDOCRINOL, DEPT MED, CTR HEALTH SCI, 92- *Personal Data:* b New York, NY, Jan 21, 33; m 56; c 3. *Educ:* Princeton Univ, AB, 54; Columbia Univ, MD, 58. *Prof Exp:* Intern, Second Div, Bellevue Hosp & Mem Hosp, NY, 58-59; asst resident med, 50-61; clin assoc, Endocrinol Br, Nat Cancer Inst, 61-63, med officer & sr investr, 63-66; from asst prof to assoc prof med, Sch Med, Univ Calif, 66-70; prof med & biochem & chief endocrinol div, Sch Med, Univ Iowa, 70-74. *Concurrent Pos:* Collab investr, Lab Chem Biol, Inst Arthritis & Metab Dis, 64-65; clin instr, Med Ctr, George Washington Univ, 65-66; coordr regional med prog, Dept Med, Harbor Gen Hosp, 68-70, clin res ctr, 69-70; mem, Reproductive Biol Study Sect, 70-73; mem, Breast Cancer Task Force, 72; chmn dept med, San Fernando Valley Prog; chief med, Vet Admin Med Ctr, Sepulveda. *Mem:* Am Soc Clin Invest; fel Am Col Physicians; Am Fedn Clin Res; Endocrine Soc; Asn Am Physicians. *Res:* Molecular mechanisms of hormone action; clinical reproductive endocrinology and impotence. *Mailing Add:* Vet Admin Hosp Sepulveda CA 91343

KORENMAN, VICTOR, THEORETICAL CONDENSED MATTER PHYSICS. *Current Pos:* Res assoc, Univ Md, 65-67, from asst prof to assoc prof, 67-79, assoc dean, 90-91, PROF PHYSICS, UNIV MD, 79-, ASST VPRES, 91- *Personal Data:* b Brooklyn, NY, Feb 5, 37; m 68, Joan Smolin; c Edward. *Educ:* Princeton Univ, AB, 58; Harvard Univ, MA, 59, PhD(physics), 66. *Concurrent Pos:* Fel, Alfred P Sloan Found, 71. *Mem:* AAAS; fel Am Phys Soc; Fedn Am Scientists. *Res:* Theory of itinerant ferromagnetism. *Mailing Add:* Dept Physics Univ Md College Park MD 20742-4111. *E-Mail:* vk2@umail.umd.edu

KORENSTEIN, RALPH, INORGANIC CHEMISTRY, SOLID STATE CHEMISTRY. *Current Pos:* AT RES DIV, RAYTHEON CO, LEXINGTON, MASS. *Personal Data:* b Havannah, Cuba, Dec 6, 51; US citizen; m 76. *Educ:* Polytech Inst Brooklyn, BS, 73; Brown Univ, PhD(chem), 77. *Prof Exp:* Tech mem staff chem, Tex Instruments Inc, 76- *Mem:* Am Chem Soc. *Res:* Crystal growth of oxides by liquid phase epitaxy; synthesis of new inorganic compounds; thin film technology. *Mailing Add:* Res Div Raytheon Co 131 Spring St Lexington MA 02173-7801

KORETZ, JANE FAITH, IMAGE ANALYSIS, COMPUTER MODELING. *Current Pos:* from asst prof to assoc prof, Rensselaer Polytech Inst, 77-90, dir, Ctr Biophys, 91-94, head biochem & biophys prog, 92-94, PROF, DEPT BIOL, RENSSELAER POLYTECH INST, 90- *Personal Data:* b New York, NY, Aug 12, 47. *Educ:* Swarthmore Col, BA, 69; Univ Chicago, PhD(biophys), 74. *Honors & Awards:* Henry Fukui Mem Travel Award, 89. *Prof Exp:* Adj asst prof human physiol, Kean Col, NJ, 77. *Concurrent Pos:* Vis scientist, Cell Biophys Unit, Med Res Coun, London, 74-76; res affil, Dept Physiol, NJ Med Sch, 76-77; adj assoc prof, Sch Pub Health, State Univ NY, Albany, 88-; mem, Vis Study Sect, NIH, 89-93; Fulbright scholar, Univ Oxford, 91; vis prof, Open Univ Oxford, 91; hon res assoc, Open Univ Oxford Res Unit, 92- *Mem:* Biophys Soc (coun, 88-91); Optical Soc Am; Sigma Xi; Asn Women Sci; Asn Res Vision & Ophthal; Am Soc Biochem & Molecular Biol; Int Soc Eyes Res. *Res:* Characterization of native reconstituted alpha-crystallin assemblies; computer-based modelling of human and rhesus monkey visual accommodation; etiology of presbyopia. *Mailing Add:* Ctr Biophys & Dept Biol Rensselaer Polytech Inst Troy NY 12180-3590. *Fax:* 518-276-2344; *E-Mail:* koretj@rpi.edu

KOREVAAR, JACOB, MATHEMATICS. *Current Pos:* PROF, MATH INST, UNIV AMSTERDAM, 74-, DIR, 80- *Personal Data:* b Netherlands, Jan 25, 23; nat US; c 8. *Educ:* Univ Leiden, PhD(math), 49. *Hon Degrees:* Dr, Univ Gothenburg, 78. *Honors & Awards:* Reynolds Teaching Award, 58. *Prof Exp:* Asst math, Delft Univ Technol, 44-46, prof, 51-53; res assoc, Math Ctr, Univ Amsterdam, 47-49; from asst prof to prof, Univ Wis, 53-64; chmn dept, Univ Calif, San Diego, 71-73, prof math, 64-74. *Concurrent Pos:* Mem Nat Sci Found fel comt, 64-66; vis prof math, Univ Amsterdam, 74-76. *Mem:* AAAS; Am Math Soc; London Math Soc; Math Asn Am; Soc Indust & Appl Math. *Res:* Approximation; complex analysis; distributions; Fourier analysis; Tauberian theorems. *Mailing Add:* Univ Amsterdam Plantage Muidergracut 24 10181V Amsterdam Netherlands

KORF, RICHARD E, ARTIFICIAL INTELLIGENCE, HEURISTIC SEARCH. *Current Pos:* from asst prof to assoc prof, 85-95, PROF COMPUT SCI, UNIV CALIF, LOS ANGELES, 95- *Personal Data:* b Geneva, Switz, Dec 7, 56; US citizen. *Educ:* Mass Inst Technol, BS, 77; Carnegie-Mellon Univ, MS, 80, PhD(comput sci), 83. *Honors & Awards:* Presidential Young Investr Award, NSF, 86. *Prof Exp:* Asst prof comput sci, Columbia Univ, 83-85. *Concurrent Pos:* Assoc ed, J Artificial Intel Res, 93- *Mem:* Fel Am Asn Artificial Intel. *Res:* Development and analysis of heuristic search algorithms for combinatorial problems in artificial intelligence. *Mailing Add:* Comput Sci Dept Univ Calif Los Angeles CA 90095. *Fax:* 310-825-2273; *E-Mail:* korf@cs.ucla.edu

KORF, RICHARD PAUL, MYCOLOGY, TAXONOMY. *Current Pos:* Asst plant path, Cornell Univ, 47-50, from asst prof to assoc prof, 51-60, prof mycol, 69-92, prof bot, 82-92, prof & chmn theatre arts, 85-86, EMER PROF MYCOL, CORNELL UNIV, 92- *Personal Data:* b Bronxville, NY, May 28, 25; m 59, Kumiko Tachibana; c Noni, Mia, Ian F & Mario T. *Educ:* Cornell Univ, BSc, 46, PhD(mycol), 50. *Concurrent Pos:* Lectr, Glasgow Univ, 50-51; Fulbright res prof & NSF sr fel, Yokohama Nat Univ, Japan, 57-58; chmn, Nomenclature Secretariat, Int Mycol Asn, 72-77; co-ed, Mycotaxon J, 74-91; adj prof, Copenhagen Univ, 78. *Mem:* Mycol Soc Am (secy-treas, 65-68, vpres, 68-69, pres, 70-71); Brit Mycol Soc; Mycol Soc France; Mycol Soc Japan; Int Asn Plant Taxon. *Res:* Taxonomic mycology; taxonomy of discomycetes; life histories and genetics of ascomycetes; botanical nomenclature; fungi of Asia, Neotropics and Macaronesia. *Mailing Add:* Plant Path Herbarium Cornell Univ Ithaca NY 14853. *Fax:* 607-273-4357; *E-Mail:* rpk1@cornell.edu

KORFHAGE, ROBERT R, MATHEMATICS, COMPUTER SCIENCE. *Current Pos:* chmn dept, 87-89, PROF INFO SCI, UNIV PITTSBURGH, 87- *Personal Data:* b Syracuse, NY, Dec 2, 30; m 55; c 4. *Educ:* Univ Mich, BSE, 52, MS, 55, PhD(math), 62. *Prof Exp:* Engr comput res lab, United Aircraft Corp, 52-54; asst prof math, NC State Col, 60-62; from asst prof to assoc prof math & comput sci, Purdue Univ, 62-70; dir, Comput Sci/Opers Res Ctr, 70-72, actg chmn, Comput Sci & Eng, 81-83, prof comput sci, Southern Methodist Univ, 70-87. *Concurrent Pos:* Consult, Proj Comput in Eng Educ, Univ Mich, 62; Eli Lilly & Co, 64-66, Indianapolis Hosp Develop Asn, 65-66, Los Alamos Sci Lab, 65-76, Alpha Systs, Inc, 70-72, Xerox Corp, 77-78, On-Line Data, Inc, 78-84 & IBM, 82-; Fulbright prof, 73, 75. *Mem:* Sigma Xi; Asn Comput Mach; Am Soc Info Sci; Inst Elec & Electronics Engrs Comput Soc. *Res:* Finite mathematical structures; logic and algorithms; non-numeric uses of computers; information retrieval; library information systems; graph theory; visual languages. *Mailing Add:* Dept Infor Sci Univ Pittsburgh 73711S Bldg Pittsburgh PA 15260. *Fax:* 412-624-5231; *E-Mail:* korfhage@lis.pitt.edu

KORFMACHER, WALTER AVERILL, MASS SPECTROMETRY, TRACE LEVEL ANALYSIS. *Current Pos:* PRIN SCIENTIST, SCHERING-PLOUGH RES INST, 91- *Personal Data:* b St Louis, Mo, Nov 6, 51; m 74, Madeleine M Deutsch; c Mary & Joseph. *Educ:* St Louis Univ, BSCh, 73; Univ Ill, Urbana, MS, 75, PhD(anal chem), 78. *Prof Exp:* Res asst, Chem Div, Colo State Univ, Ft Collins, 76-78; chemist, Nat Ctr Toxicol Res, Food & Drug Admin, 78-83, res chemist, 83-91. *Concurrent Pos:* Adj asst prof, Dept Chem, Univ Ark, Little Rock 82-91, adj assoc prof, Dept Toxicol, 91; adj assoc prof med chem, Col Pharm, Univ Tenn, Memphis, 88-91. *Mem:* Sigma Xi; Am Chem Soc; AAAS; Am Soc Mass Spectrometry; Soc Appl Spectros; NY Acad Sci. *Res:* Analytical methods, particularly trace organic quantitative methods; development of capillary gas chromatography combined with atmospheric pressure ionization mass spectrometry, chemical ionization mass spectrometry and LC-MS; thermospray mass spectrometry, atmospheric pressure chemical ionization and tandem mass spectrometry. *Mailing Add:* Drug Metabolism K-15-3/3800 Schering Plough Res Inst 2015 Galloping Hill Rd Kenilworth NJ 07033. *Fax:* 908-298-3966

KORGEN, BENJAMIN JEFFRY, PHYSICAL OCEANOGRAPHY. *Current Pos:* OCEANOGR, US NAVAL OCEANOG OFF, 78- *Personal Data:* b Duluth, Minn, Jan 6, 31; m 59, Judith K Waggoner; c Susan K, Jeffry D & James M. *Educ:* Univ Minn, BS, 56; Univ Mich, MA, 58; Ore State Univ, PhD(phys oceanog), 69. *Prof Exp:* Asst prof phys oceanog, Univ NC Chapel

Hill, 69-74; writing & consult, 74-78. *Concurrent Pos:* Adj assoc prof, Tulane Univ, 78- *Mem:* AAAS; Am Geophys Union; Am Soc Limnol & Oceanog; Geol Soc Am; Oceangraphy Soc. *Res:* Analysis of ocean currents; non-acoustical detection of submerged objects; physical properties of sea water; underwater acoustics; tidal phenomena; analysis of ocean currents; seiches and related phenomena. *Mailing Add:* 219 Loop Dr Slidell LA 70458. Fax: 228-688-4234

KORGES, EMERSON, ELECTRICAL ENGINEERING, PHYSICS. *Current Pos:* Instr eng, Tex A&M Univ, 42-47, from asst prof to assoc prof, 47-57, prof, 57-, EMER PROF ELEC ENG, TEX A&M UNIV. *Personal Data:* b Victoria, Tex, Aug 6, 11; m 42; c 1. *Educ:* Tex Col Arts & Indust, BS, 31, MS, 42; Colo State Univ, MEE, 57. *Concurrent Pos:* Consult, Tex A&M Univ, 57- *Mem:* Am Soc Eng Educ; Inst Elec & Electronics Engrs. *Res:* Corrosion and performance of copper-to-aluminum and aluminum-to-aluminum non tension electrical connectors. *Mailing Add:* Dept Elec Eng Emer Tex A&M Univ Kingsville Campus Box 192 Kingsville TX 78363

KORIN, AMOS, MEMBRANE SCIENCE, SEPARATION TECHNOLOGY. *Current Pos:* DIR TECHNOL, W R GRACE, 87- *Personal Data:* b Rehovoth, Israel, Sept 11, 44; m 67; c 3. *Educ:* Technion Israel Inst Technol, BSc, 67; Weizmann Inst Sci, MSc, 72, PhD(polymer chem), 78. *Prof Exp:* Sr proj mgr, Israel Atomic Energy Comn, 67-73; proj engr, Weizmann Inst Sci, 73-78; dept head water distillation, Mehorot Water Co, 78-79; dir membrane develop, Gelman Sci, Inc, 79-83; independent consult, 83-85; dir technol, Stan Ohio, 85-87. *Concurrent Pos:* Lectr chem & physics, Col Eng, Tel Aviv, 73-77; consult, Amplast Co, Israel, 78-79. *Mem:* Israel Inst Chem Eng; Am Chem Soc; Filtration Soc. *Res:* Novel polymer systems; polymeric ultra filtration and microporous membranes; separation systems and their application in industrial and medical fields. *Mailing Add:* 16 Mountain View Weston CT 06883

KORIN, BASIL PETER, mathematical statistics, for more information see previous edition

KORINEK, GEORGE JIRI, PHYSICAL CHEMISTRY. *Current Pos:* RETIRED. *Personal Data:* b Jicin, Czech, July 8, 27; m 58. *Educ:* Univ BC, MSc, 54, PhD(metall), 56. *Prof Exp:* Fel, Nat Res Coun Can, 56-57; proj leader, Metals Res Lab, Union Carbide Metals Co, 57-61; group leader, Rare Metals Div, Ciba Ltd, Switz, 61-65, mgr, Rare Metals Dept, Ciba Corp, 65-70; managing dir, H C Starck Inc, 70-74, pres, 74-92. *Mem:* Am Chem Soc; Electrochem Soc; Am Soc Metals; Am Inst Mining, Metall & Petrol Eng. *Res:* Physical chemistry of extractive metallurgy; catalysis; hydrometallurgy; refractory metals; Ta capacitors. *Mailing Add:* PO Box 847 Windham NY 12496

KORITALA, SANBASIVAROA, lipid chemistry, for more information see previous edition

KORITNIK, DONALD RAYMOND, REPRODUCTIVE ENDOCRINOLOGY, ATHEROSCLEROSIS. *Current Pos:* ASSOC PROF PHARMACOL, FT WAYNE CTR MED EDUC. *Personal Data:* b Rock Springs, Wyo, Feb 28, 46; m 80; c 2. *Educ:* Univ Wyo, BS, 68, MS, 73, PhD(animal sci), 77. *Prof Exp:* Fel, Reprod Endocrinol Prog, Univ Calif, San Francisco, 77-80; asst prof comp med, Bowman Gray Sch Med, Wake Forest Univ, 80- *Mem:* Endocrine Soc; Soc Study Reprod. *Res:* Regulation of lipid and carbohydrate metabolism by reproductive hormones; binding of steroid hormones to serum binding proteins and steroid receptors during pregnancy, puberty and contraceptive steroid usage; endocrine risk factors in atherosclerosis. *Mailing Add:* 4215 River Bluff Dr Ft Wayne IN 46835

KORITZ, GARY DUANE, VETERINARY MEDICINE, PHARMACOLOGY. *Current Pos:* from asst prof to assoc prof, 75-85, PROF PHARMACOL, COL VET MED, UNIV ILL, URBANA, 85- *Personal Data:* b DeKalb, Ill, May 18, 44; m 68, Barbara Thornley; c Matthew & Laura. *Educ:* Univ Ill, Urbana, BS, 66, DVM, 68, PhD(vet pharmacol), 75. *Prof Exp:* Clinician pvt pract, Dundee Animal Hosp, 68-70. *Concurrent Pos:* NIH fel, Univ Ill, Urbana, 73-74. *Mem:* Am Vet Med Asn; Am Col Vet Toxicol; Am Acad Vet Pharmacol & Therapeut; Am Soc Vet Physiologists & Pharmacologists. *Res:* Comparative pharmacology including therapeutics, pharmacokinetics and drug disposition. *Mailing Add:* Dept Vet Biosci Univ Ill 3619 Vet Basic Sci Bldg Urbana IL 61801. Fax: 217-333-4628

KORITZ, SEYMOUR BENJAMIN, BIOCHEMISTRY. *Current Pos:* PROF BIOCHEM, MT SINAI SCH MED, 68- *Personal Data:* b Boston, Mass, Nov 25, 21; m 51; c 4. *Educ:* Univ Mass, BS, 44; Univ Wis, PhD(biochem), 51. *Prof Exp:* Res assoc, Ohio State Univ, 52-53; staff biochemist, Worcester Found Exp Biol, 53-59; from asst prof to prof biochem, Sch Med, Univ Pittsburgh, 59-68. *Concurrent Pos:* Am Cancer Soc fel, Brussels, 51-52. *Mem:* Am Soc Biol Chemists. *Res:* Mode of action of adrenocorticotropic hormone. *Mailing Add:* Mt Sinai Med Ctr One Gustave L Levy Pl Box 1020 New York NY 10029

KORKEGI, ROBERT HANI, AEROSPACE VEHICLES, SPACE SYSTEMS. *Current Pos:* VIS PROF, UNIV MD, COLLEGE PARK, 90- *Personal Data:* b Milan, Italy, Dec 3, 25; m 46, Michele Caratini; c Paulette & Danielle. *Educ:* Lehigh Univ, BS, 49; Calif Inst Technol, MS, 50, PhD(aerospace), 54. *Honors & Awards:* Pub Serv Medal, NASA, 88. *Prof Exp:* Res assoc, Eng Ctr, Univ Southern Calif, 54-57; tech dir teaching & res, von Karman Inst Fluid Dynamics, 57-64; dir res & tech admin, Hypersonic Res Lab, USAF, 64-76 & int res & develop, Adv Group Aerospace Res & Develop, NATO, 76-79; vis prof teaching & res, George Washington Univ, 79-81; dir, Aerospace Bd, Nat Res Coun, Nat Acad Sci, 81-90. *Concurrent Pos:* Mem, Adv Subcomt Fluid Mech, NASA, 67-71, US mem, Fluid Dynamics Panel, AGARD/NATO, 69-76 & bd dir, von Karman Inst Fluid Dynamics, 76-79; consult, Aerospace Res & Develop, 91; chmn, Sr Scientist & Engrs Washington Vol Org, AAAS, 94- *Mem:* Fel Am Inst Aeronaut & Astronaut. *Res:* Aerodynamics of supersonic and hypersonic flows including two-and three-dimensional shock interactions with viscous flows; supersonic and hypersonic ground test facilities; aerospace policy issues; author of 60 publications. *Mailing Add:* 4418 Springdale St NW Washington DC 20016

KORMAN, N(ATHANIEL) I(RVING), ELECTRONICS, COMPUTER SCIENCE. *Current Pos:* PRES, VENTURES RES & DEVELOP GROUP, 69- *Personal Data:* b Providence, RI, Feb 23, 16; m 41; c 2. *Educ:* Worcester Polytech Inst, BS, 37; Mass Inst Technol, MS, 38; Univ Pa, PhD(elec eng), 58. *Prof Exp:* Student engr, RCA Corp, 38-40, develop engr, 40-44, eng group leader, 44-48, eng group supvr, 48-50, adminr radar systs activities, 50-52, mgr develop eng group, 52-54, mgr systs eng group, 54, asst chief engr, 54-56, chief systs, 57-58, dir advan mil systs, 58-63, dir tech progs, 63-65, chief engr graphic systs div, 65-66, dir med electronics plans & progs, 66-69. *Mem:* Fel Inst Elec & Electronics Engrs. *Res:* Advanced development of frequency modulation transmitters; microwave and waveguide components for radar and television; development of microwave studio-to-transmitter link; fire control radar; frequency modulation techniques; waveguide techniques; systems engineering; color science; patentee in field. *Mailing Add:* 5700 Teakwood NE Albuquerque NM 87111

KORMENDY, JOHN, ASTRONOMY. *Current Pos:* AT UNIV HAWAII, 90- *Personal Data:* b Graz, Austria, June 13, 48; Can citizen; m 87, Mary. *Educ:* Univ Toronto, BSc, 70; Calif Inst Technol, PhD(astron), 76. *Honors & Awards:* Muhlmann Prize, Astron Soc Pac, 88. *Prof Exp:* Parisot fel astron, Univ Calif, Berkeley, 76-78; fel astron, Kitt Peak Nat Observ, 78-79; staff mem, Dominion Astrophys Observ, 80-89. *Concurrent Pos:* Sr vis fel, Inst Astron, Cambridge, 78 & 80; Humboldt res award, Alexander von Humboldt Found, Ger, 95. *Mem:* Am Astron Soc; Int Astron Union; Astron Soc Pac; Royal Astron Soc. *Res:* Extragalactic observational astronomy, with particular emphasis on the structure of normal and peculiar galaxies; theoretical dynamics of the structure of galaxies; astronomical image processing. *Mailing Add:* Inst Astron Univ Hawaii 2680 Woodlawn Dr Honolulu HI 96822. E-Mail: kormendy@ifa.hawaii.edu

KORN, ALFRED, STRUCTURAL & CIVIL ENGINEERING. *Current Pos:* from assoc prof to prof, 69-90, EMER PROF CIVIL ENG, SOUTHERN ILL UNIV, EDWARDSVILLE, 90- *Personal Data:* b Long Island City, NY, July 19, 30. *Educ:* Purdue Univ, BS, 52; Univ Ill, Urbana, MS, 61; Wash Univ, DSc(appl mech, struct), 67. *Prof Exp:* Designer, Bell Aircraft Corp, NY, 52-53; engr, Sverdrup & Parcel Eng Co, Mo, 55-59 & 61-63; lectr, Wash Univ, 63-66; asst prof civil eng, Univ Ky, 67-69. *Concurrent Pos:* Affil prof civil engr, Wash Univ, St Louis, 91- *Mem:* Am Soc Civil Engrs. *Res:* Structural mechanics; elastic and inelastic frame stability; plastic design; numerical and computer analysis of structures; structural optimization. *Mailing Add:* Dept Civil Eng Sch Eng Southern Ill Univ Edwardsville IL 62026

KORN, DAVID, PATHOLOGY, MOLECULAR BIOLOGY. *Personal Data:* b Providence, RI, Mar 5, 33; div; c Michael P, Stephen J & Daniel C. *Educ:* Harvard Univ, BA, 54, MD, 59. *Prof Exp:* Res assoc biochem, Nat Inst Arthritis & Metab Dis, 61-63, staff mem, 63-68, staff pathologist, NIH, 64-68; prof path & chmn dept, Sch Med, Stanford Univ, 68-84, dean, 84-95, vpres, 86-95. *Concurrent Pos:* Chmn, Nat Cancer Adv Bd, 84-91. *Mem:* Inst Med-Nat Acad Sci; Am Soc Biochem & Molecular Biol; Asn Am Med Col; Am Soc Cell Biol; AAAS; AMA; Col Am Path. *Res:* Biochemistry; nucleic acid biochemistry; regulation of gene expression; biomedical science policy; academic medicine; structure and function of medical schools. *Mailing Add:* AAMC 2450 N St NW Washington DC 20037. Fax: 202-828-1125; E-Mail: dkorn@aamc.org

KORN, EDWARD DAVID, BIOCHEMISTRY, CELL BIOLOGY. *Current Pos:* Damon Runyon fel, Lab Cellular Physiol & Metab, Nat Heart Inst, 53-54, asst scientist & sr asst scientist, Nat Heart & Lung Inst, 54-56, res chemist, Lab Cellular Physiol & Metab & Lab Biochem, Sect Cellular Physiol, 56-69, head, Lab Biochem, Sect Cellular Biochem & Ultrastruct, Nat Heart & Lung Inst, 69-74, dep sci dir, 82-88, actg sci dir, 88-89, CHIEF, LAB CELL BIOL & HEAD, SECT CELLULAR BIOCHEM & ULTRASTRUCT, NAT HEART, LUNG & BLOOD INST, 74-, SCI DIR, 89- *Personal Data:* b Philadelphia, Pa, Aug 3, 28; m 50, Muriel E Fisher; c Elizabeth G (Schoenherr) & Sarah H (Gilchrist). *Educ:* Univ Pa, AB, 49, PhD(biochem), 54. *Honors & Awards:* Super Serv Award, USPHS, 80; Mider Lectr, 85; Presidential Meritorious Exec Rank Award, 87. *Prof Exp:* Asst instr, Dept Physiol Chem, Univ Pa, 49-51, Harrison fel, 51-52, Damon Runyon fel, 52-53. *Concurrent Pos:* Vis scientist, Biochem Dept, Cambridge Univ, Eng, 58-59; fac, FAES Grad Prog, NIH, 66-76; prof, FAES Grad Prog, Johns Hopkins Univ, 66-77; vis scientist, Inst Animal Physiol, Cambridge, Eng, 69-70; assoc ed, J Biol Chem, 77-93; mem bd dirs, Found Advan Educ Sci, 77-92, treas, 80-82, vpres, 82-84, pres, 84-86; mem, Am Soc Biol Chemists to AAAS, 84-89; mem, Centennial Comt, NIH, 87, Educ Comt, 89-94, H-1 Waiver Comt, 89-91, AIDS Loan Repayment Comt, 89, Facil Planning Group, 89-91; chair, Comt Guidelines Conduct Sci Res, 90. *Mem:* Nat Acad Sci; Am Soc Biochem & Molecular Biol; Biophys Soc; Am Soc Cell Biol. *Res:* Pinocytosis and phagocytosis; cell motility; cytoplasmic actin and myosin; author of 10 books and author or co-author of over 270 publications. *Mailing Add:* Lab Cell Biol Nat Heart Lung & Blood Inst 10 Center Dr MSC 1668 Bethesda MD 20892

KORN, GRANINO A(RTHUR), COMPUTER SCIENCE, ELECTRICAL ENGINEERING. *Current Pos:* GA & TM Korn Industrial Consults, 84- *Personal Data:* b Berlin, Ger, May 7, 22; nat US; m 48; c 2. *Educ:* Brown Univ, BA, 42, PhD(physics), 48; Columbia Univ, MA, 42. *Honors & Awards:* Sr Sci Award, Soc Comput Simulation, 68; Humboldt Prize, Humboldt Found, WGer, 76. *Prof Exp:* Proj engr, Sperry Gyroscope Co, 47-48; head anal group, Airplane Div, Curtiss-Wright Corp, 48-49; staff engr, Lockheed Aircraft Co, 49-52; INDUST CONSULT, 52-; prof elec eng, Univ Ariz, 57-83. *Concurrent Pos:* Consult, Nat Acad Sci, Chile, 61; mem, NIH-Nat Adv Res Coun, 78-79. *Mem:* Int Asn Math-Simulation; fel Inst Elec & Electronics Engrs; Soc Comput Simulation. *Res:* Desire computer systems for simulation; microdare desire laboratory-automation software; mini-microcomputer system design; DESIRE simulation system; neural-network simulations. *Mailing Add:* RR1 Box 96C Chelan WA 98816

KORN, ISRAEL, DIGITAL COMMUNICATIONS. *Current Pos:* assoc prof, 78-95, VIS PROF, UNIV NSW, 95- *Personal Data:* b Zamosc, Poland, Mar 2, 34; m 61, Nurit R Better; c Yoram, Neer & Dana. *Educ:* Technion Israel Inst Technol, BSc, 62, MSc, 64, DSc, 68. *Prof Exp:* Lectr, Technion Israel Inst Technol, 68-69, sr lectr, 72-76; vis asst prof, Mich State Univ, 69-71; res assoc, NASA, 71-72; assoc prof, Univ Beer Sheva, Israel, 76-78. *Mem:* Fel Inst Elec & Electronics Engrs. *Res:* Various problems of digital communication, particularly in fading channels with application to mobile, wireless and personal communications. *Mailing Add:* Sch Elec Eng Univ NSW Sydney NSW 2052 Australia. *E-Mail:* ikorn@unsw.edu.au

KORN, JOSEPH HOWARD, RHEUMATOLOGY, CELL BIOLOGY. *Current Pos:* PROF MED & SECT CHIEF, ARTHRITIS CTR, BOSTON UNIV SCH MED, 94- *Personal Data:* b Augsburg, Ger, Jan 31, 47; US citizen; m 71; c 4. *Educ:* City Col NY, BS, 68; Columbia Univ, MD, 72. *Prof Exp:* Asst prof med & immunol, Med Univ SC, 77-78; from asst prof to prof, 78-89, Sch Med, Univ Conn, 78-94. *Concurrent Pos:* Vis prof, Weizmann Inst Sci, Israel, 85-86; assoc chief staff res & develop, Vet Admin Med Ctr, Newington, Conn, 85-94. *Mem:* Am Asn Immunologists; Am Col Rheumatology; Am Soc Clin Invest; NY Acad Sci; AAAS. *Res:* Immunobiology of connective tissue; pathogenesis of scleroderma; fibroblast biology. *Mailing Add:* Arthritis Ctr Boston Univ Sch Med 80 E Concord St Boston MA 02118-2394

KORN, ROY JOSEPH, MEDICAL ADMINISTRATION. *Current Pos:* CHIEF OF STAFF, VET ADMIN WEST SIDE HOSP, CHICAGO, 72- *Personal Data:* b Chicago, Ill, July 25, 20; m 55; c 4. *Educ:* Northwestern Univ, BS, 42, MD, 46. *Prof Exp:* Intern med, Wesley Mem Hosp, Chicago, Ill, 45-46; resident internal med, Vet Admin Hosp, Hines, Ill, 49-52; staff physician, Vet Admin Hosp, Omaha, Nebr, 52-53; from asst chief to chief med serv, West Side Vet Admin Hosp, Chicago, Ill, 53-62; adv & prof med, Chiengmai Med Sch, Thailand, 62-64; chief of staff, Vet Admin Hosp, Indianapolis, 65-72; prof med, Abraham Lincoln Sch Med, Univ IL, 72- *Concurrent Pos:* Instr, Univ Nebr, 52-53; from asst prof to assoc prof, Col Med, Univ Ill, 55-64; prof, Chicago Med Sch, 64-65; clin prof med, Sch Med, Ind Univ-Purdue Univ, Indianapolis, 65-72. *Mem:* Fel Am Col Physicians. *Res:* Liver disease. *Mailing Add:* 516 N Lincoln Hinsdale IL 60521-3447

KORNACKER, KARL, COGNITIVE SCIENCE. *Current Pos:* asst prof biophys, 68-69, ASSOC PROF, OHIO STATE UNIV, 69- *Personal Data:* b Chicago, Ill, Oct 14, 37; m 60, 79; c 2. *Educ:* Mass Inst Technol, BS, 58, PhD(neurophysiol), 62. *Prof Exp:* Res assoc biol, Mass Inst Technol, 62-68. *Mem:* AAAS; Cognitive Sci Soc. *Res:* Cognitive physiology. *Mailing Add:* Genetics Ohio State Univ 484 W 12th Ave Columbus OH 43210-1214

KORNBERG, ARTHUR, BIOCHEMISTRY. *Current Pos:* prof, 59-88, chmn dept, 59-69, EMER PROF, DEPT BIOCHEM, SCH MED, STANFORD UNIV, 88- *Personal Data:* b Brooklyn, NY, Mar 3, 18; m 43; c 3. *Educ:* City Col New York, BS, 37; Univ Rochester, MD, 41. *Hon Degrees:* Several from US & foreign univs, 60- *Honors & Awards:* Nobel Prize in Med & Physiol, 59; Paul-Lewis Award, Am Chem Soc, 51; Nat Medal Sci, Royal Soc, 79. *Prof Exp:* Intern, Strong Mem Hosp, Univ Rochester, 41-42; asst surgeon to med dir, Nat Inst Arthritis & Metab Dis, NIH, 42-53, chief enzyme & metab sect, 47-53; prof microbiol & head dept, Sch Med, Wash Univ, 53-59. *Concurrent Pos:* Mem bd gov, Weizmann Inst; sci adv, Div Schering-Plough, Inc, DNAX Res Inst Molecular & Cellular Biol, Regeneron Pharmaceut; mem bd dirs, Xoma Corp. *Mem:* Nat Acad Sci; Am Philos Soc; Am Soc Biol Chemists (pres, 65); foreign mem Royal Soc. *Res:* Enzymatic studies of DNA replication, membrane biochemistry; author of 6 publications. *Mailing Add:* Dept Biochem Beckman Ctr 400 Sch Med Stanford Univ Stanford CA 94305-5307

KORNBERG, FRED, ELECTRONICS ENGINEERING. *Current Pos:* PRES & CHIEF EXEC OFFICER, COMTECH TELECOMMUN CORP, 71-, TECHNETRONIC DATA SYSTS INC, 85- & OCTAGON COMMUN CORP, 90- *Personal Data:* b Lemberg, Poland, Jan 28, 36; US citizen; m 58; c 3. *Educ:* NY Univ, BSEE, 58, MSEE, 59. *Prof Exp:* Teacher, Col Eng, NY Univ, 58-59; staff scientist, Res Div, NY Univ, 58-59; vpres, Radio Eng Labs, Dynamics Corp Am, 59-69 & Nardcom Corp, 69-71. *Mem:* Sr mem Inst Elec & Electronics Engrs; sr mem Armed Forces Commun Eng Asn. *Mailing Add:* 17 Palatine Ct Syosset NY 11791

KORNBERG, ROGER DAVID, BIOCHEMISTRY. *Current Pos:* chmn, 84-92, PROF STRUCT BIOL, SCH MED, STANFORD UNIV, 78- *Personal Data:* b St Louis, Mo, Apr 24, 47; m 84, Yahli Deborah Lorch; c Guy Joseph, Maya Lorch & Gil Lorch. *Educ:* Harvard Univ, BA, 67; Stanford Univ, PhD(chem), 71. *Honors & Awards:* Eli Lilly Award, 80; Passano Award, 81. *Prof Exp:* Mem sci staff cell biol, Med Res Coun Lab Molecular Biol, Cambridge, Eng, 74-75; asst prof biol chem, Harvard Med Sch, 76-78. *Mem:* Nat Acad Sci. *Res:* Structure and transcription of chromosomes. *Mailing Add:* Dept Cell Biol Fairchild D123 Stanford Univ Stanford CA 94305. *Fax:* 650-723-8464; *E-Mail:* kornberg@stanford.edu

KORNBERG, SIR HANS LEO, BIOCHEMISTRY. *Current Pos:* UNIV PROF & PROF BIOL, BOSTON UNIV, 95- *Personal Data:* b Herford, Ger, Jan 14, 28; m 91, Donna Haber; c Julia M, Rachel E, Johnathan P & Simon A. *Educ:* Univ Sheffield, BSc, 49, PhD, 53; Oxford Univ, MA, 58, BSc, 61; Cambridge Univ, ScD, 75. *Hon Degrees:* ScD, Univ Cincinnati, 74; DSc, Warwick Univ, 75, Univ Sheffield, 79, Leicester Univ, 79, Bath Univ, 80, Strathclyde Univ, 85 Univ South Bank, London, 94, Univ Leeds, 95; DU, Essex Univ, 79; MD, Leipzig Univ, 84. *Honors & Awards:* Colworth Medal, Biochem Soc, 63; Otto Warburg Medal, Ger Biochem Soc, 73; Weizmann Mem Lectr, Rehovot, 75. *Prof Exp:* Commonwealth Fund fel, Yale Univ, Univ Calif, Berkeley, Pub Health Res Inst, NY, 53-55; mem sci staff, Cell Metab Res Unit, Oxford, Med Res Coun, 55-60; prof biochem, Univ Leicester, 60-75; Sir William Dunn prof biochem, Cambridge Univ, 75-95. *Concurrent Pos:* Lectr, Worcester Col, Oxford, 58-60; mem, Sci Res Coun, 67-72; chmn sci bd, 69-72; mem, UGC Biol Sci Comn, 67-76, Agr Res Coun, 81-84, Priorities Bd Res & Develop Agr, 84-90; UK rep, NATO-ASI Panel, 70-76, chmn, 74-75; managing trustee, Nuffield Found, 72-93; chmn, Royal Comn Environ Pollution, 76-81, Adv Comt Genetic Modification, 86-; hon fel, Worcester Col, Oxford, 81, Brasenose Col, Oxford, 82, Wolfson Col, Cambridge, 90; sci gov, Weizmann Inst Sci, Rehovot, Israel, 81-90, emer gov, 90-; master, Christ's Col, 82-95; pres, Biochem Soc UK, 90-95, Asn Sci Educ, 91-92, Int Union Biochem & Molecular Biol, 91-92. *Mem:* Foreign assoc Nat Acad Sci; Inst Biol (vpres, 70-72); Royal Soc Arts; Am Acad Microbiol; hon mem Am Soc Biochem & Microbiol; Am Acad Arts & Sci; Ger Soc Biol Chemists; Am Philos Soc; fel Royal Soc. *Res:* Nature and regulation of carbohydrate transport in micro-organisms. *Mailing Add:* Univ Prof Boston Univ 745 Commonwealth Ave Boston MA 02215. *Fax:* 617-353-5084; *E-Mail:* hlk@bu.edu

KORNBERG, THOMAS B, MOLECULAR & DEVELOPMENTAL BIOLOGY, GENETICS. *Current Pos:* PROF BIOCHEM & BIOPHYS, UNIV CALIF, SAN FRANCISCO, 78- *Personal Data:* b Washington, DC, Nov 10, 48. *Educ:* Columbia Col, New York, BA, 70; Columbia Univ, PhD(biochem), 73. *Prof Exp:* Res assoc biochem, Princeton Univ, 73-75; res assoc develop biol, Med Res Coun Lab Molecular Biol, Cambridge Univ, UK, 75-76; mem staff, Molecular Biol Inst, Univ Calif, Los Angeles, 76-77. *Res:* Genetic and biochemical description of the cellular events which govern determination in higher organisms. *Mailing Add:* Dept Biochem & Biophys Univ Calif Med Sch 513 Parnassus Ave San Francisco CA 94122-2722

KORNBLITH, CAROL LEE, PHYSIOLOGICAL PSYCHOLOGY, NEUROBIOLOGY. *Current Pos:* MED ED, SECT PUBLS, MAYO FOUND, 84- *Personal Data:* b Chicago, Ill, Sept 6, 45. *Educ:* Univ Mich, AB, 66, AM, 68; Calif Inst Technol, PhD(biol), 72. *Prof Exp:* Fel psychol, Princeton Univ, 72-74; asst prof, Univ NC, 74-80, interdisciplinary fel neurosci, 80-81; assoc prof psychol, Ill State Univ, 81-83; assoc prof psychol, Oberlin Col, 83-84. *Mem:* Soc Neurosci; Sigma Xi; AAAS. *Res:* Development and function of sexually dimorphic brain regions in the rat as revealed by deoxyglucose autoradiography and the development of feeding behavior and its relation to reinforcement. *Mailing Add:* 1520 NW Eighth Ave Rochester MN 55901-2536

KORNBLUM, NATHAN, organic chemistry; deceased, see previous edition for last biography

KORNBLUM, RONALD NORMAN, PATHOLOGY. *Current Pos:* MED EXAMR, VENTURA COUNTY, CALIF, 73- *Personal Data:* b Chicago, Ill, Dec 5, 33. *Educ:* Univ Calif, Los Angeles, BA, 55, MD, 59. *Prof Exp:* Resident gen path, Santa Clara County Hosp, 62-66; resident neuropath, Md Dept Ment Hyg, 66-67; fel forensic path, Md Postmortem Exam, 67-68; asst med examr, state med exam off, Md, 68-73. *Concurrent Pos:* Lectr pub health admin, Johns Hopkins Univ, 69- *Mem:* Am Acad Forensic Sci; Am Soc Clin Pathologists; Col Am Pathologists. *Res:* Forensic pathology; investigation into causes of sudden death in infancy syndrome; investigation of craniocerebral injuries and shock in relation to cerebral anoria. *Mailing Add:* 1104 N Mission Los Angeles CA 90033-1017

KORNBLUM, SAUL S, PHYSICAL PHARMACY, PHYSICAL CHEMISTRY. *Current Pos:* PRES, S S KORNBLUM ASSOCS, 85- *Personal Data:* b Far Rockaway, NY, Feb 24, 34; m 58, Sondra L Gilner; c Leslie F & Peter M. *Educ:* Brooklyn Col Pharm, BS, 55; Columbia Univ, MS, 57; Rutgers Univ, PhD(pharm, phys chem), 63. *Honors & Awards:* Lunsford Richardson Award, 63. *Prof Exp:* Instr chem, Newark Col Eng, 59-61; asst prof phys pharm, Brooklyn Col Pharm, Long Island Univ, 62-66; sr scientist, Sandoz Pharmaceut, 66-67, mgr, 67-73, assoc sect head prod develop & clin prod, Sandoz Inc, 73-85. *Concurrent Pos:* CIBA res grant, 61-62. *Mem:* Am Acad Pharmaceut Sci; NY Acad Sci; Parenteral Drug Asn. *Res:* Solid state kinetics; dissolution of poorly water-soluble drugs; sustained-release dosage forms; pharmaceutical dosage form design and evaluation; preformulation stability evaluation for new drugs; troubleshooting and reformulation. *Mailing Add:* 144 Short Hills Ave Springfield NJ 07081

KORNBLUTH, RICHARD SYD, IMMUNOLOGY. *Current Pos:* asst clin prof, 86-89, asst adj prof, 90-95, ASSOC ADJ PROF MED, DIV INFECTIOUS DIS, DEPT MED, SCH MED, UNIV CALIF, SAN DIEGO, 95- *Personal Data:* b Kansas City, Mo, Sept 14, 48; m 85; c 2. *Educ:* Harvard Col, BA, 70; NY Med Col, MD, 75; Columbia Univ, PhD(path), 83; Am Bd Internal Med, cert, 78, cert pulmonary dis, 80. *Prof Exp:* Res asst, Dept Surg, Children's Hosp, Boston, 73-74; intern & resident, Dept Med, Mt Sinai Hosp, 75-78; res fel, Cardiopulmonary Res Lab, Col Physicians & Surgeons, Columbia Univ, 78-83, instr clin med, Pulmonary Div, 81-83; res assoc, Dept Immunol, Res Inst Scripps Clin, La Jolla, Calif, 83-86. *Concurrent Pos:* Fel, Pulmonary Div, Dept Med, Col Physicians & Surgeons, Columbia Univ, 78-81, vis physician, Columbia-Presby Med Ctr, 81-83; Am Lung Asn fel, 78-80; Parker B Francis Found fel, 80-83; attend physician, Emergency Dept, Elmhurst City Hosp, Queens, NY, 81-83 & Clairemont Community Hosp, San Diego, 83-86; prin investr, USPHS, NIH, Nat Heart, Lung & Blood Inst, 89-94 & 96-, Am Found AIDS Res, 90-91 & USPHS, NIH, Nat Inst Allergy & Infectious Dis, 91-94. *Mem:* Am Thoracic Soc; Am Asn Pathologists; Am Asn Immunologists; AAAS; Soc Leukocyte Biol; Physicians Social Responsibility. *Res:* Human immunodeficiency virus; acquired immunodeficiency syndrome; macrophage immunobiology; cytokines; apoptosis; effects of human immunodeficiency virus on macrophage functions including the ability of macrophage to participate in anti-tuberculous immunity and the clearance of apoptic debris; tuberculosis; author of more than 20 technical publications; immunological regulation of macrophages in HIV infection, TB, cancer, and blood coogulation. *Mailing Add:* Dept Med-0679 Univ Calif San Diego 9500 Gilman Dr La Jolla CA 92093-0679

KORNBREKKE, RALPH ERIK, COLLOID & SURFACE SCIENCE. *Current Pos:* res chemist III, 87-90, IV, 90-91, SR RES CHEMIST, THE LUBRIZOL CORP, 92- *Personal Data:* b Brooklyn, NY, Nov 22, 51; m 74, Annette E Kingman. *Educ:* Rensselaer Polytechnic Inst, BS, 74, PhD(chem), 81. *Prof Exp:* Chemist, Petrol Action Inc, 74-75, Rensselaer Res Corp Int, 75-76; sr res chemist, The 3m Corp, 80-84; proj leader, Stand Oil Ohio, 84-87. *Concurrent Pos:* Staff mem, Nat Bur Stand, Molten Salts Data Ctr, 75-76; J Willard Gibbs res fel, Rensselaer Polytechnic Inst, 79-80; chmn, Interface Sci Chap, 3M Tech Forum, 82-84. *Mem:* Sigma Xi; Am Chem Soc; AAAS; Int Asn Colloid & Interface Sci; fel Am Inst Chemists; Soc Automotive Engrs. *Res:* Surfactant interactions at solid-liquid interfaces (effect on wetting, dispersion stability and material properties) and non-aqueous colloid properties applied to dispersions and lubrication; discovery of the stochestic nature of emulsion inversion; discovery of the complex nature of wetting near the critical point. *Mailing Add:* 8340 Tulip Lane Chagrin Falls OH 44023

KORNEGAY, ERVIN THADDEUS, ANIMAL SCIENCE. *Current Pos:* assoc prof, 67-73, PROF ANIMAL SCI, VA POLYTECH INST & STATE UNIV, 73- *Personal Data:* b Faison, NC, Mar 16, 31; m 56; c 3. *Educ:* NC State Univ, BS, 53, MS, 60; Mich State Univ, PhD(animal nutrit), 63. *Honors & Awards:* Res Award, Nutrit, Am Feed Mfg Asn, 82; Gustav Bohstedt Mineral Award, Am Soc Animal Sci, 86, Animal Mgt Award, 90. *Prof Exp:* Asst agr agent, NC State Univ, 56-59; asst, Mich State Univ, 59-63; asst res prof, Animal Nutrit, Rutgers Univ, 63-67. *Concurrent Pos:* Travel fel, Nat Feed Ingredients Asn, 83. *Mem:* Am Soc Animal Sci; NY Acad Sci; Am Inst Nutrit; Can Soc Animal Sci. *Res:* Nutrition, environment and immune response; evaluation of feedstuffs for swine; fiber and mineral utilization; sow management and nutrition; artificial rearing of baby pigs; mineral availability and interactions. *Mailing Add:* Dept Animal Sci Va Polytech Inst & State Univ Blacksburg VA 24061

KORNEL, LUDWIG, ENDOCRINOLOGY, BIOCHEMISTRY. *Current Pos:* prof med & biochem, 70-93, EMER PROF INTERNAL MED & BIOCHEM, RUSH MED COL, 93-; SR ENDOCRINOLOGIST, KUPOT HOLIN KLOLIT OUT-PATENT CLIN, JERUSALEM, ISRAEL, 96- *Personal Data:* b Jaslo, Poland, Feb 27, 23; m 52; c Eziel Edward & Amiel Maark. *Educ:* Wroclaw Univ, MD, 50; Univ Birmingham, PhD(endocrinol, steroid biochem), 58. *Honors & Awards:* Physicians Recognition Award, AMA, 69, 73, 76 & 81. *Prof Exp:* Intern med, surg, gynec & pediat, Wroclaw Univ Hosp, 49-50; from intern to resident med, Hadassah Univ Hosp, Jerusalem, 50-54; asst physician & instr, Hadassah Med Sch, Hebrew Univ, Israel, 54-55; lectr med, Univ Birmingham, 56-57; asst physician med & community health, Hadassah Univ Hosp & Community Health Ctr, Jerusalem, 57-58; from asst prof to prof med, Med Ctr, Univ Ala, 61-67, assoc prof biochem, 65-67, dir steroid sect & consult endocrinol, 63-67; dir, Steroid Unit, Rush-Presby-St Luke's Med Ctr, 67-93. *Concurrent Pos:* Res fel hemat, Hosp Broussai, Univ Paris, 51-52; Brit Coun res scholar med & steroid chem, Univ Birmingham, 55-57; res fel endocrinol & metab, Med Ctr, Univ Ala, Birmingham, 58-59; USPHS trainee, Inst Steroid Biochem, Univ Utah, 59-61; hon vis prof, Polish Acad Sci, Warsaw, 65; prof med, Col Med, Univ Ill, 67-71; sr attend physician & sr scientist, Rush-Presby-St Luke's Med Ctr, 71-; vis prof, Kanazawa Univ, Japan, 73, 82 & 88 & Inst Hypertension, Tel-Hashomer Med Ctr, Univ Tel Aviv, Israel, 90; nat corresp, Fedn Am Socs Exp Biol, 75-; mem bd dirs, Nat Acad Clin Biochem, 82-86; co-ed, Yearbook Endocrinol, 85-90. *Mem:* AAAS; Am Fedn Clin Res; Endocrine Soc; Sigma Xi; Cent Soc Clin Res; Am Asn Univ Prof; fel Am Soc Clin Pharmacol & Therapeut; Am Physiol Soc; fel Royal Soc Health; fel Nat Acad Clin Biochem. *Res:* Metabolism and mechanism of action of steroidal hormones, especially relation of corticosteroids to mechanism of arterial hypertension; mineralocorticoid receptors in arterial walls and hypertension; role of mineralocorticoids in mechanism of hypertension; control by steroids of transmembrene ionic fluxes in vascular smooth muscle; co-author of encyclopedia on human biology. *Mailing Add:* 9 Haportzim St Jerusalem 93662 Israel

KORNET, MILTON JOSEPH, PHARMACEUTICAL CHEMISTRY, ORGANIC CHEMISTRY. *Current Pos:* asst prof, 63-67, ASSOC PROF, PHARMACEUT CHEM, UNIV KY, 67- *Personal Data:* b East Chicago, Ind, Dec 31, 35; m 62, Leona; c Linda, John & Frank. *Educ:* Purdue Univ, BS, 57; Univ Ill, PhD(pharmaceut chem), 63. *Prof Exp:* Chemist, Abbott Labs, 57-59; res assoc org synthesis, Northwestern Univ, 62-63. *Mem:* Am Chem Soc. *Res:* Heterocyclic organic chemistry; medicinal chemistry; chemistry of hydrazines. *Mailing Add:* Col Pharm Univ Ky Lexington KY 40536-0082

KORNETSKY, CONAN, PSYCHOLOGY, PSYCHOPHARMACOLOGY. *Current Pos:* assoc prof, 59-62, PROF PSYCHIAT & PHARMACOL, SCH MED, BOSTON UNIV, 62- *Personal Data:* b Portland, Maine, Feb 9, 26; m 49, Marcia Smargon; c David & Lisa. *Educ:* Univ Maine, BA, 48; Univ Ky, MS, 51, PhD(psychol), 52. *Prof Exp:* Res scientist, NIMH, 52-59. *Concurrent Pos:* NIH sr res fel, Boston Univ, 59-62, NIH res scientist award, 62-70, NIMH res scientist award, 70-78, Nat Inst Drug Abuse res scientist award, 83-88; mem psychopharmacol study sect, NIH, 62-67, mem clin psychopharmacol res rev comt, NIMH, 67-71; mem comt tobacco habituation, Am Cancer Soc, 66-70; mem panel behav modification drugs for hyperkinetic children, Dept Health, Educ & Welfare, 71; mem merit rev bd neurobiol, Vet Admin, 72-76; mem psychopharmacol agents adv comt, Food & Drug Admin, 73-77; mem biomed rev comt, Nat Inst Drug Abuse, 80-84; pres, Psychopharmacol Div, Am Psychol Asn, 85-86; mem, Neurosci Rev Comt, Nat Inst Alcohol Abuse & Alcoholism, 85-89. *Mem:* Am Soc Pharmacol & Exp Therapeut; Am Psychol Asn; Am Col Neuropsychopharmacol; Int Col Neuropsychopharmacol; Psychonomic Soc; Soc Neurosci. *Res:* Neurobehavioral buses for the rewarding effects of abused substances, pain & analgesia; behavioral and neuropsychological studies of the action of antipsychotic and analgesic drugs. *Mailing Add:* Boston Univ Sch Med 80 E Concord St L602 Boston MA 02118-2394. *Fax:* 617-638-4329

KORNFEIL, FRED, PHYSICAL CHEMISTRY, ELECTROCHEMISTRY. *Current Pos:* RETIRED. *Personal Data:* b Vienna, Austria, Feb 14, 24; nat US; m 53. *Educ:* Univ Vienna, MS, 50, PhD(chem), 53. *Prof Exp:* Chemist, Power Sources Div, Electronics Technol & Devices Lab, US Army Electronics Command, Ft Monmouth, 53-59, phys scientist, Explor Res Div E, 59-71, phys scientist, Power Sources Area, 71-78. *Mem:* Am Chem Soc. *Res:* Fuel cells; battery test techniques; kinetics of electrode processes. *Mailing Add:* 112 Harwich Ct West End NC 27376-9610

KORNFELD, EDMUND CARL, MEDICINAL CHEMISTRY. *Current Pos:* RETIRED. *Personal Data:* b Philadelphia, Pa, Feb 24, 19; m 45, Virginia; c Cheryl, Marjorie & Jeanne. *Educ:* Temple Univ, AB, 40, AM, 42; Harvard Univ, MA, 44, PhD(org chem), 46. *Hon Degrees:* DSc, Temple Univ, 64. *Prof Exp:* Res chemist, Off Sci Res & Develop Contract, Harvard Univ, 45; res chemist, 46-65, res adv, Eli Lilly & Co, 65-83. *Mem:* Am Chem Soc; Am Sci Affil. *Res:* Rubber chemistry; organic structural determination; synthetic organic medicinals; organic chemicals development; medicinal chemistry of indol derivatives and ergot alkaloids. *Mailing Add:* 3550 Bay Rd S Dr Indianapolis IN 46240

KORNFELD, LOTTIE, IMMUNOBIOLOGY. *Current Pos:* RETIRED. *Personal Data:* b Vienna, Austria, Feb 8, 25; US citizen. *Educ:* Col Wooster, BA, 45; Ohio State Univ, MS, 47; Univ Chicago, PhD(microbiol), 60. *Prof Exp:* Asst bact, Ohio State Univ, 45-47; bacteriologist, Viral & Rickettsial Res Div, Lederle Labs, Am Cyanamid Co, 47-54; res asst bact, Univ Mich, 54-55; res asst bact, Dept Med, Univ Chicago, 55-60, res assoc, Dept Med & Argonne Cancer Res Hosp, 60-61; res fel microbiology, US Naval Radiol Defense Lab, 63-69 & Letterman Army Inst Res, 69-72; microbiologist, Div Biomed & Environ Res, US Atomic Energy Comn, 72-74; health scientist adminr, NIH, 74-85; Coordr, Univ-Wide AIDS Res Prog, Univ Calif, Berkeley, 85-89. *Concurrent Pos:* Lectr, Dept Microbiol, San Francisco State Col, 69-71. *Mem:* AAAS; Am Soc Microbiol; Radiation Res Soc; Reticuloendothelial Soc; Am Asn Immunologists. *Res:* Immunology; host resistance; effects of irradiation on host-parasite relationship; science administration. *Mailing Add:* 508 Tampico Dr Walnut Creek CA 94598

KORNFELD, MARIO O, NEUROPATHOLOGY. *Current Pos:* asst prof, 68-70, assoc prof path & neuropath, 70-80, PROF PATH, SCH MED, UNIV NMEX, 80- *Personal Data:* b Zagreb, Yugoslavia, July 9, 27; m 56; c 1. *Educ:* Univ Zagreb, MD, 53, ScD, 64. *Honors & Awards:* Matthew T Moore Award, Am Asn Neuropath; Weil Award, Am Asn Neuropath. *Prof Exp:* Staff pathologist, Inst Path, Gen Hosp, Zagreb, 59-64; instr neuropath, Col Physicians & Surgeons, Columbia Univ, 67-68. *Concurrent Pos:* Trainee & fel, Col Physicians & Surgeons, Columbia Univ, 64-67; staff pathologist, Bernalillo County Med Ctr, Albuquerque, 70-; attend neuropathologist, Vet Admin Hosp, 70- *Mem:* Assoc Am Asn Neuropathologists; Am Asn Pathologists; Asn Res Neuropath Ment Dis. *Res:* Histopathology of inner ear and temporal bone; ultrastructural aspects of neurolipidoses, peripheral nervous system diseases and astroglia in metabolic encephalopathies; morphometry of secretion in pituitary adenomonas. *Mailing Add:* Dept Path Univ NMex Sch Med 915 Sanford NE Albuquerque NM 87131. *Fax:* 505-277-7224

KORNFELD, ROSALIND HAUK, OLIGOSACCHARIDE STRUCTURE, GLYCOPROTEIN SYNTHESIS. *Current Pos:* from res instr to res assoc prof, 65-78, assoc prof biochem, div hemat-oncol & assoc prof, 78-81, PROF BIOCHEM, DIV HEMAT-ONCOL, DEPT MED, SCH MED & PROF, DEPT BIOL CHEM, WASH UNIV, 81-, COORDR, GRAD TRAINING PROG, 84- *Personal Data:* b Dallas, Tex, Aug 2, 35; m 59; c 3. *Educ:* George Wash Univ, BS, 57; Wash Univ, St Louis, PhD(biochem), 61. *Prof Exp:* Staff fel, Nat Inst Arthritis & Metab Dis, NIH, 63-65. *Concurrent Pos:* Mem, Comt Cancer Immunobiol, Nat Cancer Inst, NIH, 75-78, & Physiol Chem Study Sect, 80-83. *Mem:* Am Soc Hemat; Am Soc Biochem & Molecular Biol. *Res:* Biosynthesis and structural analysis of the oligosaccharides on glycoproteins and the role of mannosidases in oligosaccharide processing. *Mailing Add:* Dept Med & Biochem Box 8125 Sch Med Wash Univ 660 S Euclid St Louis MO 63110-1093

KORNFELD, STUART ARTHUR, HEMATOLOGY. *Current Pos:* from instr to asst prof med, Sch Med, Washington Univ, 66-70, from asst prof to assoc prof biochem, 68-72, dir, Div Oncol, 73-76, PROF MED, SCH MED, WASHINGTON UNIV, 72-, CO-DIR, DIV HEMAT & ONCOL, 73-, PROF BIOCHEM, 76- *Personal Data:* b St Louis, Mo, Oct 4, 36; m 59; c 3. *Educ:* Dartmouth Col, AB, 58; Washington Univ, MD, 62. *Honors & Awards:* Daneshek Prize Res, Am Soc Hemat, 81; Jubilee lectr & Harden Medallist, Biochem Soc, 89; Lewis A Connor lectr, Am Heart Asn, 90; Passano Award, 91; Kober lectr, Asn Am Physicians, 91; E Donnall Thomas lectr, 92. *Prof Exp:* Res asst, Biochem Dept, Washington Univ Sch Med, 58-62; intern ward med, Barnes Hosp, 62-63; res assoc, Nat Inst Arthritis & Metab Dis, NIH, 63-65; asst resident ward med, Barnes Hosp, 65-66. *Concurrent Pos:* Fac res assoc, Am Cancer Soc, 66-71; NIH res career develop award, 71-76; counr, Am Soc Clin Invest, 72-75 & Asn Am Physicians, 91-; mem, Cell Biol Study Sect, NIH, 74-77, Bd Sci Counselors, Nat Inst Arthritis, Diabetes & Digestive & Kidney Dis, 83-87, Sci Rev Bd, Howard Hughes Med Inst, 86- & Bd Sci Adv, Jane Coffin Childs Mem Fund Res, 87-; assoc ed, J Clin Invest, 77-81, ed, 81-82; assoc ed, J Biol Chem, 82-87; mem, Res Comt, Am Heart Asn, 85-; chmn, Prog Molecular Med Cancer Res, James S McDonnell Found, 88-, Med Genetics, Hemat & Oncol, Sect 41, Nat Acad Sci, 89- & Searle Scholars Prog, 89-93. *Mem:* Nat Acad Sci; Inst Med-Nat Acad Sci; Am Soc Clin Invest (pres, 81-82); Am Soc Hemat (pres, 91); Am Soc Biol Chemists; Asn Am Physicians (secy, 86-91); fel Am Acad Arts & Sci; Am Chem Soc; Sigma Xi; Am Fedn Clin Res; fel Am Col Physicians; fel AAAS. *Res:* Studies of the structure, biosynthesis and function of glycoproteins, especially those which are found on the surface of normal and malignant cells; targeting of newly synthesized acid hydroloses to lysosomes; author of 145 publications. *Mailing Add:* Sch Med Washington Univ St Louis MO 63110. *Fax:* 314-362-8826; *E-Mail:* skornfeld@im.wustl.edu

KORNFIELD, IRVING LESLIE, EVOLUTIONARY BIOLOGY. *Current Pos:* assoc prof zool, 77-85, PROF ZOOL, UNIV MAINE, 85- *Personal Data:* b Jacksonville, NC, July 16, 45; m 68, Victoria Jean Porter; c Molly Rebecca & Emily Caroline Porter. *Educ:* Syracuse Univ, AB, 68; State Univ NY, Stony Brook, NY, 72, PhD(ecol), 74. *Prof Exp:* Fel, Smithsonian Inst, 74-75; res collabr, Dept Genetics, Hebrew Univ, 75-76. *Concurrent Pos:* Assoc, Danforth Found, 80- *Mem:* Am Soc Ichthyologists & Herpetologists; Genetics Soc Am; Soc Study Evolution; Soc Molecular Biol & Evolution. *Res:* Evolutionary genetics of fishes; molecular systematics. *Mailing Add:* Dept Zool Univ Maine Orono ME 04469. *Fax:* 207-581-2537; *E-Mail:* irvk@maine.maine.edu

KORNFIELD, JACK I, satellite meteorology, for more information see previous edition

KORNFIELD, JULIA ANN, CHEMICAL ENGINEERING. *Current Pos:* res asst, 83-84, ASST PROF CHEM ENG, CALIF INST TECHNOL, 90- *Personal Data:* b Oakland, Calif, July 2, 62. *Educ:* Calif Inst Technol, BS, 83, MS, 84; Stanford Univ, PhD(chem eng). 88. *Prof Exp:* Res asst chem eng, Stanford Univ, 84-88, teaching asst appl math, 86 & 87; NSF/NATO fel chem eng, Max-Planck-Inst, 89. *Mem:* Am Inst Chem Engrs; Am Phys Soc; Am Chem Soc; Soc Rheology. *Res:* Chemical engineering. *Mailing Add:* Chem Eng 210-41 Calif Inst Technol Pasadena CA 91125

KORNGOLD, ROBERT, GRAFT VS HOST DISEASE, BONE MARROW TRANSPLANTATION. *Current Pos:* ASSOC PROF, MICROBIOL & IMMUNOL, JEFFERSON MED COL, 87- *Educ:* Univ Pa, PhD(immunol), 79. *Prof Exp:* Asst prof, Wistar Inst Anat & Biol, 81-87. *Mailing Add:* Dept Microbiol & Immunol Jefferson Cancer Inst 233 S Tenth St Philadelphia PA 19107-6731

KORNGUTH, STEVEN E, BIOCHEMISTRY. *Current Pos:* from asst prof to assoc prof, 63-72, PROF NEUROL & PHYSIOL CHEM, UNIV WIS-MADISON, 72- *Personal Data:* b New York, NY, Dec 1, 35; m 58; c 2. *Educ:* Columbia Univ, BA, 57; Univ Wis, MA, 59, PhD(biochem), 61. *Prof Exp:* Res scientist neurochem, NY State Psychiat Inst, 61-63. *Mem:* Am Soc Biol Chemists. *Res:* Magnetic resonance contrast agents; antigenic properties of such proteins; synaptic complexes, isolation and chemical properties; paraneoplastic disorders. *Mailing Add:* Dept Neurol & Biomolecular Chem Univ Wis Waisman Med Ctr Madison WI 53705. *Fax:* 608-265-4103

KORNHAUSER, ALAIN LUCIEN, ASTRODYNAMICS, TRANSPORTATION. *Current Pos:* assoc prof, 77-78, PROF, DEPT CIVIL ENG, PRINCETON UNIV, 78-, DIR, TRANSPORTATION PROG, 76- *Personal Data:* b Beaurepaire, France, June 12, 44; US citizen; m 65. *Educ:* Pa State Univ, BS, 65, MS, 67; Princeton Univ, MA, 69, PhD(aerospace sci), 71. *Honors & Awards:* R T Knapp & Melville Medal, Am Soc Mech Eng, 70. *Prof Exp:* Res asst cavitation, Ord Res Lab, 67; asst prof astrodyn, Univ Minn, Minneapolis, 71-77. *Concurrent Pos:* Consult, Princeton Univ 71- & Optimal Data Co, 71- *Mem:* Am Soc Mech Eng; Am Inst Aeronaut & Astronaut; Am Astronaut Soc; Sigma Xi. *Res:* Optimal space flight; cavitation; urban transportation; computer graphics; freight railroad operations and planning analysis. *Mailing Add:* 24 Montadale Circle Princeton NJ 08540

KORNHAUSER, ANDRIJA, TOXICOLOGY, BASIC MEDICAL SCIENCES. *Current Pos:* res biologist, res & mgt, Div Toxicol, 78-80, CHIEF, DERMAL & OCULAR BR, DIV TOXICOL, CFSAN, FOOD & DRUG ADMIN, 80- *Personal Data:* b Zagreb, Yugoslavia, Feb 5, 30; US citizen; m 78. *Educ:* Univ Zagreb, Yugoslavia, BSci, 54, PhD(biochem), 62. *Prof Exp:* Res assoc, Sch Med, Univ Frankfurt, Ger, 64-66; assoc prof, Rudjer Boskavic Inst, Univ Zagreb, 66-70; mem fac, Sch Med, Harvard Univ & Sch Dent Med, 70-78. *Concurrent Pos:* Lectr oral path, Sch Dermal Med, Harvard Univ, 78-; adj assoc prof dermat, Sch Med, George Washington Univ, 78- *Mem:* AAAS; Am Asn Photobiol; Soc Investigative Dermat Inc; NY Acad Sci; hon fel Skin Cancer Found. *Res:* Cutaneous toxicol; phototoxicity; carcinogenesis; photocarcinogenesis; photomedicine; molecular toxicology; pharmacology; protection against phototoxicity and carcinogenesis by dietary antioxidants; development of animal models for clinical studies. *Mailing Add:* 4517 Pine Crest Height Annandale VA 22003

KORNICKER, LOUIS SAMPSON, GEOLOGY. *Current Pos:* assoc cur, 64-67, CUR DIV CRUSTACEA, US NATURAL HIST MUS, SMITHSONIAN INST, 67- *Personal Data:* b Brooklyn, NY, May 23, 19; m 51; c 3. *Educ:* Univ Ala, BS, 41 & 42; Columbia Univ, MA, 54, PhD, 58. *Prof Exp:* Prod supvr trinitrotoluene, Tech Invest Group, Hercules Powder Co, 42-44; sr process engr & pilot plant supt, Cities Serv Ref Co, 44-47; treas & plant supt, Uncle Sam Chem Co, Inc, 47-54; asst, Columbia Univ, 54-57; asst dir, Inst Marine Sci, Univ Tex, 57-60; geologist, Off Naval Res, Chicago, 60-61; from assoc prof to prof oceanog, Tex A&M Univ, 61-64. *Concurrent Pos:* Adj prof biol, George Washington Univ, 70- *Mem:* Soc Syst Zool; Crustacean Soc. *Res:* Marine geology; micropaleontology; paleoecology; ecology; ostracodes; coral reefs; ostracoda systematics and ecology. *Mailing Add:* 10400 Lake Ridge Dr Oakton VA 22124

KORNICKER, WILLIAM ALAN, ROCK-WATER INTERACTIONS, GEOCHEMICAL MODELING. *Personal Data:* b New York, NY, July 24, 56. *Educ:* Old Dominion Univ, BS, 78, MS, 80; Tex A&M Univ, PhD(oceanog), 88. *Prof Exp:* Fel chem & environ eng, McMaster Univ, 88-91; res assoc & asst prof, Clemson Univ, 91-93. *Mem:* AAAS; Am Chem Soc; Am Geophys Union; Am Soc Limnol & Oceanog; Geochem Soc; Sigma Xi. *Res:* Thermodynamics and kinetic control of mineral formation, dissolution and solute transport in low temperature environments. *Mailing Add:* 10400 Lake Ridge Dr Oakton VA 22124-1511

KORNMAN, BRENT D, ARTIFICIAL INTELLIGENCE. *Current Pos:* ADV PROGRAMMER, IBM CORP, 82- *Personal Data:* b Dothan, Ala, Sept 20, 56; m 81; c 2. *Educ:* Univ Md, BS, 78. *Prof Exp:* Staff programmer, PAR Technol Corp, 79-82. *Mem:* Am Asn Artificial Intel. *Res:* Expert system applications; automated plan construction; knowledge representation languages; knowledge base design and development techniques; knowledge base verification. *Mailing Add:* 402 Sand Willow Ct Chesapeake VA 23320

KORNREICH, HELEN KASS, PEDIATRICS, RHEUMATOLOGY. *Current Pos:* From instr to asst prof, 63-70, ASSOC PROF PEDIAT, SCH MED, UNIV SOUTHERN CALIF, 70- *Personal Data:* b Newark, NJ, Sept 4, 31; m 65. *Educ:* Rutgers Univ, BS, 52; Hahnemann Med Col, MD, 56. *Concurrent Pos:* Arthritis & Rheumatism Found fel pediat rheumatology, Childrens Hosp, Los Angeles, Calif, 63-65. *Mem:* Am Rheumatism Asn; Am Acad Pediat. *Res:* Connective tissue diseases of childhood; medical education. *Mailing Add:* 4650 Sunset Blvd Los Angeles CA 90027-6016

KORNREICH, PHILIPP G, SOLID STATE PHYSICS, SOLID STATE MICROWAVE DEVICES. *Current Pos:* from asst prof to assoc prof, 67-78, PROF ELEC ENG, SYRACUSE UNIV, 78- *Personal Data:* b Vienna, Austria, Nov 4, 31; US citizen; m 60; c 3. *Educ:* Carnegie Inst Tech, BS, 62; Univ Pa, PhD(elec eng), 67. *Prof Exp:* Sr res engr thin film technol res, Sperry Rand Univac, 60-66; res assoc solid state physics res, Univ Pa, 66-67. *Concurrent Pos:* Consult, Gen Elec Co; consult & co-founder, DEFT Labs; vis prof, Technon Israel Inst Technol, 80-81; consult, Electronic Device Reliability Group, RADC, Rome, NY, 82-; res remote optical sensing & light frequency electronic devices optical comput, US Air Force Photonics Lab, RADC, 88- *Mem:* Am Phys Soc; Inst Elec & Electronics Engrs; Sigma Xi; AAAS; Soc Photo-Optical Instrumentation Engrs; Int Soc Optical Eng. *Res:* Phonon microwave oscillator; variable delay magnetic strip line; directional dependence of photoconductivity; direct electronic fourier transforms of images; systems with delay and memory; vibrational modes of superlattices; ultra high speed electron devices for both microwave and very high speed integrated circuits applications; three dimensional integrated circuits; light frequency devices for optical computing. *Mailing Add:* Dept Elec & Comput Eng Syracuse Univ Link Hall Syracuse NY 13244

KORNSTEIN, EDWARD, ELECTRO-OPTICS, ENGINEERING MANAGEMENT. *Current Pos:* vpres, Object Recognition Systs, Inc, 77-86, vpres & gen mgr, ORS Automation, Inc, 86-87, PRES, ORS AUTOMATION, INC, 87- *Personal Data:* b New York, NY, Sept 7, 29; m 58, Marion B Stein; c Sandra P & Martin R. *Educ:* NY Univ, BA, 51; Drexel Inst Technol, MS, 54. *Prof Exp:* Physicist optics, Radio Corp Am, 51-57 & Phys Res Lab, Boston Univ, 58; consult optics, 59-60; physicist, Radio Corp Am, 60-70; vpres, Optel Corp, 70-72; pres, Kortron Consults, 72-80. *Concurrent Pos:* Dir, Affiliated Mfrs, Inc, Orthosonics, Inc. *Mem:* Optical Soc Am; Inst Elec & Electronics Engrs; Soc Info Display. *Res:* Infrared optical and detection systems; physical optics; laser devices and systems; electro-optical displays; electronic digital timepieces; pattern recognition; machine vision systems. *Mailing Add:* 10 Channing Way RD 1 Cranbury NJ 08512. *E-Mail:* emkor@aol.com

KOROBKIN, IRVING, PHYSICS, SYSTEMS ANALYSIS. *Current Pos:* OPERS RES ANALYST MIL OPERS RES, NAVAL SURFACE WEAPON CTR, 68- *Personal Data:* b New York, NY, Oct 18, 25; m 47; c 4. *Educ:* City Col New York, BME, 45; Columbia Univ, BS, 48; Univ Md, PhD(physics), 60. *Honors & Awards:* Meritorious Civil Serv Award, Naval Ord Lab, 57. *Prof Exp:* Instr physics, City Col New York, 47-48; instr mech eng, Syracuse Univ, 48-51; res scientist & adminr fluid dynamics, US Naval Ord Lab, 51-61; sr systs analyst, IBM Corp, 61-68. *Concurrent Pos:* Consult, Missile & Space Vehicle Dept, Gen Elec Co, 56-59; assoc prof lectr, George Washington Univ, 57-66. *Mem:* Sigma Xi; assoc fel Am Inst Aeronaut & Astronaut; AAAS. *Res:* High speed fluid dynamics; reentry physics; nuclear weapons effects; military systems analyst with emphasis on strategic warfare. *Mailing Add:* 8510 Hunter Creek Trail Potomac MD 20854-2561

KOROL, BERNARD, PSYCHOPHARMACOLOGY. *Current Pos:* RES ADMIN, ENQUAY PHARMACEUT ASSOCS, 87- *Personal Data:* b Chicago, Ill, Feb 2, 29; m 52; c 3. *Educ:* Roosevelt Col, BS, 49; Univ Chicago, MS, 52; McGill Univ, PhD(pharmacol), 56. *Prof Exp:* Res pharmacologist, Smith Kline & French Labs, 56-58 & Chas Pfizer & Co, Inc, 58-61; group leader pharmacol, Geigy Res Labs, 61-64; asst prof physiol & pharmacol & chief pharmacol sect, Sch Med, Univ Mo, St Louis, 64-69; assoc prof psychiat, Sch Med, St Louis Univ & supvr psychopharmacol, St Louis Vet Admin Hosp, 69-87. *Res:* Physiology and pharmacology of mental illness. *Mailing Add:* Enquay 2840 NW Second Ave Boca Raton FL 33431

KOROLENKO, KYRILL V, UNDERWATER OBJECT DETECTION TECHNOLOGY. *Current Pos:* PRIN ENGR, CONSULT & CHIEF SCIENTIST, NAVAL UNDERSEA WARFARE CTR, 72- *Personal Data:* b Kharkov, Russia, May 12, 32; US citizen; m 58, Svetlana Vagelis-Salmsen; c George & Alexandra. *Educ:* Syracuse Univ, BEE, 59; State Univ NY, Buffalo, MS, 67. *Honors & Awards:* David Bushnell Award, Am Defense Preparedness Asn, 91. *Prof Exp:* Engr, Heavy Mil Div, Gen Elec Co, 59-65 & 66-67; feelance translr, Inst Elec & Electronics Engrs, 65-66; sr engr, Submarine Signal Div, Raytheon Co, 67-72. *Concurrent Pos:* Consult, US Naval Activ Fleet Command, Prog Off, Pentagon, 72-; chief scientist, Sharem Prog, 74-86; vis lectr, US Naval War Col, 85-90, US Anti Submarine Training Ctr, 86-91; Surface Officer Sch Command, 87-94. *Mem:* Sr mem Inst Elec & Electronics Engrs; Am Defense Preparedness Asn. *Res:* Using state of the art technology and hardware to solve underwater detection problems; anti-submarine sonar systems; granted 2 patents covering critical technology of sonar systems. *Mailing Add:* Code 309 Naval Undersea Warfare Ctr Newport RI 02841-1708. *Fax:* 401-841-7478; *E-Mail:* korolenko@1.vsdec.npt.nuwc.navy.mil

KOROLY, MARY JO, CELL BIOLOGY. *Current Pos:* ASST PROF CELL BIOL, UNIV FLA, 79- *Personal Data:* b Philadelphia, Pa, Jan 28, 43; c 1. *Educ:* Bryn Mawr Col, PhD(biochem), 69. *Prof Exp:* Asst prof cell biol, Bryn Mawr Col, 72-77, Harvard Univ, 77-79. *Mem:* AAAS; Am Soc Cell Biol; Am Women Sci; Am Soc Protozool; Am Soc Biol Chemists; Sigma Xi. *Mailing Add:* Dept Biochem & Molecular Biol Univ Fla 111 NRN Hall JHMHC Box 117035 Gainesville FL 32611-7035. *Fax:* 352-392-2344

KOROPCHAK, JOHN, ATOMIC MOLECULAR & MASS SPECTROMETRY, CHROMATOGRAPHY. *Current Pos:* from asst prof to assoc prof, 84-93, PROF CHEM, SOUTHERN ILL UNIV, 93- *Personal Data:* m 81, Diane Clark; c Shannon & Sara. *Educ:* Lafayette Col, BA, 76; Univ Ga, PhD(chem), 80. *Prof Exp:* Res chem, US Army Chem Res & Develop Ctr, 80-84. *Concurrent Pos:* Prog chmn, Fedn Anal Chem & Spectros Socs, 94. *Mem:* Am Chem Soc; Soc Appl Spectros; Am Soc Mass Spectrometry. *Res:* Development of methods of chemical analysis capable of detecting smaller quantities of various chemical species; methods for trace element analysis (e.g. heavy metals such as lead); techniques intended to be able to selectively detect single molecules. *Mailing Add:* Dept Chem & Biochem Southern Ill Univ Carbondale IL 62901-4409

KOROS, AURELIA M CARISSIMO, IMMUNOLOGY, CELL BIOLOGY. *Current Pos:* MEM FACULTY, GRAD SCH PUB HEALTH, UNIV PITTSBURGH, 81- *Personal Data:* b Boston, Mass, Aug 28, 34; m 57, Peter J; c Nina, Alicia, Sonya, Beatrice & Ariel. *Educ:* Radcliffe Col, AB, 56; Univ Pittsburgh, MS, 60, PhD(microbiol), 65. *Prof Exp:* Res asst cell physiol, Sch Med, Harvard Univ, 56-58; Am Cancer Soc Inst res grant immunol, Sch Med, Univ Pittsburgh, 65-66, from instr to asst prof microbiol, 66-73; res asst prof obstet & gynec, 73-75, res asst prof path, 75-76; res assoc, Allegheny Gen Hosp, Pittsburgh, 77-78, asst biologist, Cancer Res Unit, 78-80; mem staff, Allegheny Co Health Dept, 80-83. *Concurrent Pos:* NIH grants, 66-74, NCI grants, 80-83; Health Res & Serv Found grants, 69 & 70, Cancer Fedn, Inc, 83- & Candle Found; FIDIA fel neurosci, 88. *Mem:* AAAS; Am Soc Microbiol; Am Asn Immunologists; NY Acad Sci; Am Asn Cancer Res; Int Asn Study Lung Cancer; Clin Immunol Soc; Am Soc Hemat; Marine Biol Asn UK; Am Soc Hematol. *Res:* Elucidation of the mechanism by which antigen and antibody regulate the proliferation of antibody-producing cells; immunological relations in maternal-fetal interactions; immunoregulation in tumor models; biology of lung cancer; evolutionarily conserved antigens on lung cancer cells; sea urchin coelomocytes. *Mailing Add:* 154 Maple Heights Rd Pittsburgh PA 15232. *Fax:* 412-383-8926

KOROS, PETER J, METALLURGY, MATERIALS SCIENCE. *Current Pos:* SR RES CONSULT, LTV STEEL CORP, 84- *Personal Data:* b Berlin, Ger, July 14, 32; US citizen; m 57, Aurelia Carissimo; c 5. *Educ:* Drexel Univ, BS, 54; Mass Inst Technol, SM, 55 & ScD, 58. *Honors & Awards:* Toy Award, 62 & McKune & Herty Mem Awards, 63, Am Inst Mining, Metall & Petrol Engrs; Jalmet Award, Jones & Laughlin Steel Corp, 63; Silver Medal, Am Iron & Steel Inst, 69, Gold Medal, 77; Design & Appln Award, Int Magnesium Asn, 78. *Prof Exp:* Res engr & sr res engr, Jones & Laughlin Steel Corp, 58-63; res supvr steelmaking, 63-65, chief process metallurgist, Qual Control Div, 65-75, dir process metall res, 75-78, dir res spec projs, 78-80, mgr process develop & qual control, 80-82, sr res assoc, 82-84. *Concurrent Pos:* Chmn, Iron & Steel Div, Am Inst Mining, Metall & Petrol Engrs, 69-70, bd dirs, 74, chmn prog comt, 5th Int Iron & Steel Cong, Iron & Steel Soc, 86; mem, US Bur Mines, Generic Technol Res Ctr Pyrometall, 82- & Chmn, 84-85; adv bd, NSF Ctr Iron & Steel Res, Carnegie-Mellon Univ, 85-; mem, Steel Initative Task Force, Am Iron & Steel Inst, 85-95, chmn, Task Force on Degalvanizing Scrap, 89-91 & adv panel, Argonne Lab Prog for Electrochem Dezinc Scrap, 91-96. *Mem:* Am Iron & Steel Inst; fel Iron & Steel Soc, Am Inst Mining, Metall & Petrol Engrs; fel Am Soc Metals Int. *Res:* Process and quality control in steel production; physical chemistry of iron and steelmaking; applied research in steelmaking, steel waste recycling, direct iron/steelmaking. *Mailing Add:* LTV Steel Co Technol Ctr 6801 Brecksville Rd Independence OH 44131-5099. *Fax:* 216-642-7080

KOROS, WILLIAM JOHN, POLYMER & MEMBRANE SCIENCE, ENGINEERING. *Current Pos:* chmn dept, 93-97, PROF CHEM ENG, UNIV TEX, AUSTIN, 84- *Personal Data:* b Omaha, Nebr, Aug 31, 47; m 70. *Educ:* Univ Tex, Austin, BS, 69, MS, 75, PhD(chem eng), 77. *Prof Exp:* Engr polymer processing, E I Du Pont de Nemours & Co, 69-73; from asst prof to prof chem eng, NC State Univ, 77-84. *Concurrent Pos:* Prin investr dual mode sorption & transport in glassy polymers, NSF grant, 77-79 & 80-82; Army Res Off grant, 80-83; res award, Sigma Xi, 80; ed-in-chief, J Membrane Sci; managing ed, Membrane Quart. *Mem:* Am Inst Chem Eng; Sigma Xi; Am Chem Soc. *Res:* Sorption and transport of low molecular weight compounds such as gases, solvents, monomers and additives in the polymeric solid state; development of advanced membrane materials and structures; diffusion in polymers. *Mailing Add:* Dept Chem Eng Univ Tex Austin TX 78712-1062. *Fax:* 512-471-9643

KOROSTOFF, EDWARD, DENTAL MATERIALS. *Current Pos:* RETIRED. *Personal Data:* b Philadelphia, Pa, Feb 25, 21; m 51, Loretta Marcacci; c Lisa K (Rooney), Pamela K (Thompson) & Heather E K (Murray). *Educ:* Univ Pa, BS, 41, MS, 50, PhD(metall eng), 61. *Prof Exp:* Chem plant engr, Tenn Valley Authority, 41-43; res technologist, Leeds & Northrup Co, 44-55; metall consult, Remington Rand Univac, 55-59; grad student, Univ Pa, 59-61, sr res investr, ICR, 61-63, lectr dent mat sci, 63-65, from asst prof to assoc prof biomat, Sch Dent Med, Sch Med & Col Eng & Appl Sci, 65-75, prof restorative dent, Sch Dent Med, 75-87. *Concurrent Pos:* USPHS career develop award, Univ Pa, 66; chmn med-dent mat comt, Metall Soc, 69-71. *Mem:* Soc Biomat; Acad Dent Mat; Int Asn Dent Res; AAAS; Am Asn Univ Prof. *Res:* Stress generated electrical potentials in bone and dentin; viscoelastic properties of bone and dentin; electric stimulation of bone remodeling. *Mailing Add:* LRSM Bldg 33/Walnut Univ Pa Philadelphia PA 19104. *E-Mail:* korostof@sol1.lrsm.upenn.edu

KOROTEV, RANDALL LEE, LUNAR GEOCHEMISTRY. *Current Pos:* sr res scientist, 79-91, RES ASSOC PROF GEOCHEM, WASHINGTON UNIV, 91- *Personal Data:* b Green Bay, Wis, May 15, 49; m 74. *Educ:* Univ Wis-Madison, BS, 71, PhD(chem), 76. *Prof Exp:* Proj assoc soil sci, Univ Wis-Madison, 76-79. *Concurrent Pos:* Mem, Lunar & Planetary Sample Team, NASA, 82-85, Lunar & Planetary Geosci Rev Panel, 92-94. *Mem:* Geochem Soc; Am Geophys Union; Sigma Xi; Meteoritical Soc. *Res:* Factors affecting the distribution of elements in geologic and environmental systems; geochemistry of lunar soils and rocks; chemical analysis by neutron activation. *Mailing Add:* Dept Earth & Planetary Sci Campus Box 1169 Wash Univ St Louis MO 63130. *Fax:* 314-935-7361; *E-Mail:* rlk@levee.wustl.edu

KORPEL, ADRIANUS, OPTICS, ACOUSTICS. *Current Pos:* PROF ELEC ENG, UNIV IOWA, 77- *Personal Data:* b Rotterdam, Neth, Feb 18, 32; m 56; c 1. *Educ:* Delft Technol Univ, MSEE, 56, PhD, 69. *Honors & Awards:* Alexander von Humboldt Award, 84. *Prof Exp:* Res engr commun, Postmaster Gen Dept, Melbourne, Australia, 56-60; div chief laser appln, Zenith Radio Corp, 60-73, dir res eng physics, 73-77. *Mem:* Acoust Soc Am; fel Inst Elec & Electronics Engrs; fel Optical Soc Am; Soc Photog Instrumentation Eng; foreign assoc mem Royal Acad Belg. *Res:* Information and communication theory; microwaves; laser optics; acoustic holography and microscopy; acousto-optics; nonlinear waves; optical metrology and microscopy. *Mailing Add:* 2013 Laurence Ct NE Iowa City IA 52240

KORPER, SAMUEL, aging research, for more information see previous edition

KORPMAN, RALPH ANDREW, HEMATALOGY, MEDICAL INFORMATION SCIENCE. *Current Pos:* Intern, Med Ctr, Loma Linda Univ, 74-75, resident path, 75-78, fel hemat, 78-79, from asst prof to assoc prof hemat & path, 83-87, PROF PATH & LAB MED, LOMA LINDA UNIV, 87-, DIR LABS, 79- *Personal Data:* b New York, NY, Aug 9, 52. *Educ:* Loma Linda Univ, BA, 71, MD, 74; Claremont Grad Sch, CEM, 78. *Honors & Awards:* Sheard-Sanford Award, Am Soc Clin Pathologists, 76. *Concurrent Pos:* Dir, Med Data Corp, 76-81; consult, Technician Instruments Corp, 78-81; mem, comput adv comt, finance comt & chmn, govt rels, Am Soc Clin Path, 78-; sci adv, HBO & Co, 81-83; pres & chmn, Health Data Sci, 83- *Mem:* Fel Col Am Pathologists; fel Am Soc Clin Path; NY Acad Sci; fel Am Col Physician Execs. *Res:* Characterization of cellular membranes, especially red blood cells, laboratory quality control, applications of computers to medical care and instrument design and evaluation. *Mailing Add:* PO Box 548 Loma Linda CA 92354

KORR, IRVIN MORRIS, PHYSIOLOGY, NEUROSCIENCES. *Current Pos:* RETIRED. *Personal Data:* b Philadelphia, Pa, Aug 24, 09; m 39, 84, Janet Meneley; c David. *Educ:* Univ Pa, BA, 30, MA, 31; Princeton Univ, PhD(cellular physiol), 35. *Hon Degrees:* DSc, Kirksville Col Osteop Med, 76; DOsteop Educ, Col Osteop Med Pac, 82. *Honors & Awards:* Robert A Kistner Award, Am Asn Col Osteop Med, 83. *Prof Exp:* Asst instr physiol, Princeton Univ, 32-33; instr, Col Med, NY Univ, 36-43; sr physiologist, Signal Lab, US War Dept, Ft Monmouth, NJ, 43-44; physiol investr wound ballistics, Princeton Univ, 45; from prof & chmn, Div Physiol Sci to distinguished prof & dir, Prog Neurobiol, Kirksville Col Osteop Med, Mich State Univ, 45-75, emer prof physiol, 75-78; prof med educ, Tex Col Osteop Med, 78-90, emer prof, 90. *Concurrent Pos:* Procter fel, Princeton Univ, 35-36; investr, Aviation Res Labs, Columbia Univ, 42-43; prof biomech, Col Osteop Med, Mich State Univ, 75-78. *Mem:* AAAS; Am Physiol Soc; Soc Exp Biol & Med; Soc Neurosci; Am Soc Neurochem; Harvey Soc; emer mem Am Inst Biol Sci. *Res:* Bioluminescence; oxidation-reduction potentials; cellular metabolism; renal physiology; aviation and climatic physiology; human spinal reflexes; referred pain mechanisms; interchange between somatic and autonomic nervous systems; trophic functions of nerves. *Mailing Add:* 911 Ninth St Boulder CO 80302

KORRINGA, JAN, THEORETICAL PHYSICS, GEOPHYSICS. *Current Pos:* RETIRED. *Personal Data:* b Heemstede, Netherlands, Mar 31, 15; m 43, Johanna M Regnault; c Maarten, Wouter & Derk-Jan. *Educ:* Delft Univ Technol, DSc, 42. *Hon Degrees:* DSc, Univ Besancon, France, 63. *Prof Exp:* From asst to instr physics, Delft Univ Technol, 41-46; from lectr to sr lectr, Univ Leiden, 46-53; from assoc prof to prof physics, Ohio State Univ, 53-80; sr res assoc, Chevron Oil Field Res Co, 80-86. *Concurrent Pos:* Guggenheim fel, 63; vis prof, Univ Besancon, 63 & Univ Paris, 68; consult, Chevron Oil Field Res Co, 55-80 & Union Carbide Nuclear Co, 57-80. *Mem:* Fel Am Phys Soc; Neth Phys Soc. *Res:* Statistical physics; metals physics; theory of solids; theory of heterogeneous materials. *Mailing Add:* 620 Mystic Way Laguna Beach CA 92651

KORSCH, BARBARA M, PEDIATRICS. *Current Pos:* assoc prof, 64-69, PROF PEDIAT, SCH MED, UNIV SOUTHERN CALIF, LOS ANGELES, 69- *Personal Data:* b Jena, Ger, Mar 30, 21; US citizen; wid; c 1. *Educ:* Smith Col, BA, 41; Johns Hopkins Univ, MD, 44; Am Bd Pediat, cert, 50. *Honors & Awards:* George Armstrong Lectr, Ambulatory Pediat Asn, 73; Katherine D McCormick Distinguished Lectr, Standford Univ, 77; Kathy Newman Mem Lectr, Tulane Univ, 87; C Anderson Aldrich Award, Am Acad Pediat, 88. *Prof Exp:* Asst resident, Bellevue Hosp, 45, Mary Imogene Basset Hosp, 46, NY Hosp, 47; fel, Inst Child Develop, NY Hosp, 48-49; asst pediat, Med Col, Cornell Univ, 49-50, from instr to assoc prof, 50-61; assoc clin prof prev med, Sch Med, Univ Calif, Los Angeles, 61-64. *Concurrent Pos:* Asst outpatient pediatrician, NY Hosp, 49-50, asst attend pediatrician, 50-55, clin dir, Pediat Outpatient Dept, 50-61, assoc attend pediatrician, 55-61; pediat consult, Dept Health, NY, 49-51, Hosp Spec Surg, 55-61, Gen Pediat, Children's Hosp Los Angeles, 61-65, Med Ctr, Univ Southern Calif, 69-74; coordr, Pediat Rehab Prog, Nat Found Infantile Paralysis, 63-61; pediat dir, Observ Clin Children Los Angeles, 61-64; assoc attend pediatrician, Cedars Lebanon Hosp, 61-; dir, Introd Clin Med & Res & Training Rehab, Sch Med, Univ Southern Calif, 69-74, consult, 74-; vis prof numerous US & foreign univs, 73-89; hon staff mem, Dept Pediat, Cedars-Sinai Med Ctr, 76-; staff, Div Gen Pediat, Children's Hosp Los Angeles, 81-91; chair, Coun Am Pediat Soc, 89. *Mem:* Inst Med-Nat Acad Sci; Am Acad Pediat; Sigma Xi; Am Pediat Soc; Soc Behav Pediat (pres, 85); Soc Pediat Res. *Res:* Doctor-patient communication; health care delivery; psychosocial aspects of pediatrics including growth and development; medical education; comprehensive care of patients with chronic illness; high risk infants, transition from hospital to home; author of numerous technical publications. *Mailing Add:* Div Gen Pediat Childrens Hosp 4650 Sunset Blvd MS 76 Los Angeles CA 90027

KORSCH, DIETRICH G, astronomy, for more information see previous edition

KORSH, JAMES F, COMPUTER SCIENCE, OPERATIONS RESEARCH. *Current Pos:* assoc prof, 72-76, PROF COMPUT SCI, TEMPLE UNIV, 77-, CHMN, 75-78 & 89- *Personal Data:* b Philadelphia, Pa, June 16, 38; m 62; c 3. *Educ:* Univ Pa, BS, 60, PhD(comput sci), 66; Univ Ill, MS, 62. *Prof Exp:* Asst prof comput sci, Univ Pa, 66-71; sr res fel, Calif Inst Technol, 71-72. *Concurrent Pos:* Chmn, CIS Dept, Temple Univ, 75-78. *Mem:* Asn Comput Mach. *Res:* Quantitative methods in computer systems; analysis of algorithms; data structures. *Mailing Add:* Dept Comput & Info Sci Temple Univ Broad & Montgomery St Philadelphia PA 19122-2585

KORSLUND, MARY KATHERINE, THERAPEUTIC NUTRITION. *Current Pos:* ASSOC PROF HUMAN NUTRIT & FOOD, VA POLYTECH INST & STATE UNIV, 64- *Educ:* Univ Nebr, Lincoln, PhD(nutrit), 72. *Mailing Add:* NVa Grad Ctr Va Tech 1013 Mourning Dove Dr Blacksburg VA 24060

KORSMEYER, STANLEY JOEL, INTERNAL MEDICINE, IMMUNOLOGY. *Current Pos:* assoc prof, 86-90, PROF, DIV HEMAT-ONCOL, DEPT MED & MOLECULAR MICROBIOL, HOWARD HUGHES MED INST, SCH MED, WASH UNIV, 90-, CHIEF MOLECULAR ONCOL & PROF MED & PATH, 92-, INVESTR, 93- *Personal Data:* b Beardstown, Ill, June 8, 50. *Educ:* Univ Ill, BS, 72, MD, 76; Am Bd Internal Med, dipl, 79; Am Bd Allergy & Immunol, dipl, 81. *Honors & Awards:* Pasarow Med Res Award, 93; William C Moloney Lectr, Harvard Med Sch, 94; Albert Coons Lectr, 96; Carter Wallace Lectr, Princeton Univ, 95; BJ Kennedy Lectr, Univ Minn, 96; Ciba Drew Award, 96; E Donnall Thomas Prize, Am Soc Hemat, 96; G H A Clowes Award, Am Asn Cancer Res, 97; Reider Lectr, St John's Mercy Med Ctr, 97; Karolinska Res Lectr, 97. *Prof Exp:* Intern med, Univ Calif Hosps, San Francisco, 76-77, resident med, 77-79; clin assoc, Metab Br, Nat Cancer Inst, NIH, Bethesda, Md, 79-82, sr investr, 82-86. *Concurrent Pos:* Assoc ed, J Immunol, 84-88; Charles B Smith vis res prof, Mem Sloan Kettering Cancer Ctr, 95. *Mem:* Nat Acad Sci; Am Asn Immunologists; AAAS; Asn Am Physicians; Am Soc Hemat; Am Asn Cancer Res; Am Soc Clin Invest; Am Fedn Clin Res. *Mailing Add:* Dept Med & Path Washington Univ Sch Med 660 S Euclid Box 8022 St Louis MO 63110

KORSON, ROY, PATHOLOGY. *Current Pos:* RETIRED. *Personal Data:* b Philadelphia, Pa, Oct 24, 22; m 46, Lorraine Bagdon. *Educ:* Univ Pa, AB, 43; Jefferson Med Col, MD, 47; Am Bd Path, dipl, 56. *Prof Exp:* Asst, Col Med, Univ Vt, 50-51, asst prof path, 51-52 & 54-57, assoc prof, 57-67, actg chmn dept, 74, prof, 67-92. *Concurrent Pos:* Nat Cancer Inst res fel, Columbia Univ, 48-49 & Col Med, Univ Vt, 49-50; USPHS sr res fel, 58-63; resident, Mary Fletcher Hosp, Burlington, Vt, 51-52. *Mem:* AAAS; Am Asn Pathologists; Col Am Pathologists; Int Acad Path; Sigma Xi; Am Soc Cytol. *Res:* Cytology; histopathology; histochemistry. *Mailing Add:* Med Alumni Bldg Univ Vt Col Med Burlington VT 05405-0068

KORSRUD, GARY OLAF, ANTIBIOTIC RESIDUE ANALYSIS. *Current Pos:* RES SCIENTIST, AGR CAN, 77- *Personal Data:* b Peterborough, Ont, Mar 23, 42; m 65; c 3. *Educ:* Univ Sask, BSA, 64, MSc, 66; Univ Calif, Davis, PhD(nutrit), 70. *Prof Exp:* Res asst, Univ Sask, 64-66; teaching asst animal sci, Univ Calif, Davis, 66-67, res asst, 67-70; res scientist, Health & Welfare Can, 70-77. *Mem:* Agr Inst Can; Can Soc Animal Sci; Can Soc Nutrit Sci; Soc Toxicol Can; Am Col Vet Toxicologists. *Res:* Antibiotic residue analysis research; nutritional and biochemical aspects of veterinary toxicology; human carbohydrate nutrition research and advising; lipid nutrition; detection and assessment of chemically induced liver damage. *Mailing Add:* Health Animals Lab Agr Can 116 Vet Rd Saskatoon SK S7N 2R3 Can

KORST, DONALD RICHARDSON, internal medicine; deceased, see previous edition for last biography

KORST, HELMUT HANS, GAS DYNAMICS, PROPULSION. *Current Pos:* vis lectr gas dynamics, Univ Ill, Urbana, 48-49, from assoc prof to prof mech eng, 49-84, head dept mech & indust eng, 62-74, EMER PROF MECH ENG, UNIV ILL, URBANA, 84- *Personal Data:* b Vienna, Austria, Jan 4, 16; US citizen; m 42; c 4. *Educ:* Vienna Tech Univ, Dipl Ing, 41, Dr tech Sc, 47. *Prof Exp:* Res engr, Maschinenfabrik Augsburg-Nurnberg AG, Ger, 41-45; asst prof mech eng, Vienna Tech Univ, 45-48. *Concurrent Pos:* Vis prof, Kans State Univ, 50, Va Polytech Inst, 54 & Vienna Tech Univ, 57; design specialist, Gen Dynamics Convair, Ft Worth, 55; sr fel, NSF, 57; consult, Gen Elec Co, 59; propulsion specialist, Rocketdyne Div, N Am Aviation, 60 & 65-68; owner, H H Korst engrs consult, Urbana, 60, 70; consult, Adv Group Aeronaut Res & Develop, NATO, 64 & US Army Missile Command, 71-; res chair naval air power, Navy Postgrad Sch, Monterey, Calif, 79; Ebaugh chair prof mech eng, Univ Fla, 84. *Mem:* Fel Am Soc Mech Engrs; fel Am Inst Aeronaut & Astronaut; Am Soc Eng Educ; Sigma Xi. *Res:* Internal and external aerodynamics; jet and rocket propulsion; heat transfer. *Mailing Add:* 3 Eton Ct Champaign IL 61820-7602

KORST, JAMES JOSEPH, ORGANIC CHEMISTRY. *Current Pos:* Chemist, Chas Pfizer & Co, Inc, 59-70, supvr, 70-71, mgr qual control, 71-73, OPERS MGR, QUALITY CONTROL, PFIZER INC, 73- *Personal Data:* b Joliet, Ill, Nov 24, 31; m 60; c 3. *Educ:* Univ Ill, BS, 53; Dartmouth Col, MA, 55; Univ Wis, PhD(org chem), 59. *Mem:* Am Chem Soc. *Res:* Structures of steroid intermediates; tetracycline chemistry; quality control aspects of organic chemicals and pharmaceuticals; quality control management. *Mailing Add:* 5 Ledgewood Dr Old Lyme CT 06371

KORST, WILLIAM LAWRENCE, INORGANIC CHEMISTRY, PHYSICAL CHEMISTRY. *Current Pos:* RETIRED. *Personal Data:* b Joliet, Ill, Mar 23, 22; m 54, Mary Coutts; c David W, Lisa M, Timothy J & Pamela T. *Educ:* Univ Chicago, PhB, 46, SB, 47, SM, 49; Univ Southern Calif, PhD, 56. *Prof Exp:* Asst res chemist, Univ Calif, 56-57; asst prof chem, Polytech Inst Brooklyn, 57-58; sr res chemist, Atomics Int Div, N Am Aviation, Inc, 58-59, res specialist, 59-67; instr chem, Los Angeles City Col, 69-70; from instr to prof chem, W Los Angeles Col, 70-93. *Concurrent Pos:* Fel US AEC,, Univ Southern Calif, 52-53; Fulbright scholar, Univ Amsterdam, 54-55; vis prof, Tech Univ Vienna, 78. *Mem:* Am Chem Soc. *Res:* X-ray diffraction and crystal structures; solid-state chemistry; heavy metal hydrides; high-vacuum and high-temperature techniques; atmospheric chemistry. *Mailing Add:* 7106 Quartz Ave Canoga Park CA 91306-3636

KORSTAD, JOHN EDWARD, LIMNOLOGY, AQUACULTURE. *Current Pos:* PROF BIOL, ORAL ROBERTS UNIV, 80- *Personal Data:* b Woodland, Calif, July 4, 49; m 72, Sally Steffen; c Shauna, Sarah, Joya & Janna. *Educ:* Calif Lutheran Col, BA & BS, 72; Calif State Univ, Hayward, MS, 74; Univ Mich, Ann Arbor, MS, 79, PhD(zool), 80. *Prof Exp:* Teaching asst, Calif Lutheran Col, 70-71, Calif State Univ, Hayward, 72-74 & Univ Mich, Ann Arbor, 75-79. *Concurrent Pos:* Asst geologist, Cities Serv Oil Co, Alaska, 71; res asst, Calif State Univ, Hayward, 73; asst consult, Univ Calif, Davis, 74; asst limnologist, Great Lakes Res Div, Univ Mich, Ann Arbor, 75 & res asst, 75 & 80; vis scientist, Sintef Ctr for Aquacult, Trondheim, Norway, 87-88; col acad dir, Okla Acad Sci, 83-86; adj instr, Tulsa Community Col, 85-; vis scientist, SINTEF Ctr Aquacult, Trondheim, Norway, 87-88 & 93-94; Fulbright Scholar, Norway, 93-94. *Mem:* Am Soc Limnol & Oceanog; Great

Plains Limnologist; World Aquacult Soc; Am Asn Zool Parks & Aquariums. *Res:* Ecology; limnology, particularly phytoplankton-zooplankton interactions, nutrient regeneration, life history of zooplankton; aquaculture, particularly live feed with rotifers and Artemia; Tilapia. *Mailing Add:* Dept Biol Oral Roberts Univ Tulsa OK 74171-0001. *Fax:* 918-495-6033; *E-Mail:* jkorstad@oru.edu

KORT, MARGARET ALEXANDER, HISTOLOGY, CELL BIOLOGY. *Current Pos:* RETIRED. *Personal Data:* b Jerusalem, Jordan, Jan 16, 28; US citizen. *Educ:* Georgetown Col, BS, 58; Univ Louisville, MS, 60; Univ Northern Colo, EdD, 68. *Prof Exp:* Instr biol, Coe Col, 61-63; prof biol, Southwest Baptist Col, 67-90. *Mem:* AAAS; Nat Sci Teachers Asn. *Res:* Acid phosphatase patterns in the involuting rat uterus. *Mailing Add:* 1623 Northwood St Bolivar MO 65613

KORTANEK, KENNETH O, OPERATIONS RESEARCH, SYSTEMS ANALYSIS. *Current Pos:* PROF MATH SCI, CARNEGIE-MELLON UNIV, 69- *Personal Data:* b Chicago, Ill, Nov 13, 36; c 1. *Educ:* Northwestern Univ, BSBA, 58, MA, 59, PhD(eng sci), 64. *Prof Exp:* Asst prof appl math & indust adminr, Univ Chicago, 65-66; assoc prof opers res, Cornell Univ, 66-69. *Concurrent Pos:* Vis prof, Col Eng, Va Polytech Inst & State Univ, 79 & Univ NC, 81; pres, Kwel Corp, 81; mem, Int Symp Semi-Infinite Prog & Applns, 81. *Mem:* Opers Res Soc Am; Inst Mgt Sci; Am Math Soc; Economet Soc; Soc Indust & Appl Math. *Res:* Linear programming; duality theory in mathematical programming; applications to engineering plasticity design; equilibrium theory in economic systems; theory and applications of semi-infinite programming and design of telecommunications networks. *Mailing Add:* Dept Mgt Sci Col Bus Admin Univ Iowa Iowa City IA 52242-0001

KORTE, CLARE A, CELL DIVISION INHIBITORS, CELL MUTATIONS. *Current Pos:* PROF BIOL, ST MARYS UNIV MINN, 75-, CHAIR BIOL, 84- *Personal Data:* b Pocahontas, Ill, Jan 31, 34. *Educ:* Alverno Col, BA, 50; St Marys Col, Minn, MS, 67; Univ NDak, Grand Forks, DA, 80. *Prof Exp:* Teacher biol, Madonna High Sch, 60-65, Boylan High Sch, 65-75. *Mem:* Nat Asn Biol Teachers. *Res:* Investigations on viruses, tradescantia and chironomid larvae to determine mitotic errors after exposure to electromagnetic fields. *Mailing Add:* St Marys Univ Minn 700 Terrace Heights Winona MN 55987-1321. *Fax:* 507-457-1633; *E-Mail:* ckorte@rexmnsmcedu

KORTE, WILLIAM DAVID, ORGANIC CHEMISTRY, ORGANIC ANALYSIS. *Current Pos:* From asst prof to assoc prof, 66-75, chmn dept, 77-80, PROF CHEM, CALIF STATE UNIV, CHICO, 75- *Personal Data:* b Chicago, Ill, Oct 11, 37; m 64, Margaret Wong; c Jennifer, Christopher & Alison. *Educ:* Northwestern Univ, BA, 60; Univ Mich, MS, 62; Univ Calif, Davis, PhD(chem), 66. *Concurrent Pos:* Am Chem Soc-Petrol Res Fund res grants, 70-72; NSF grant, 83, 87; US Army res assoc, IPA, 87-89. *Mem:* AAAS; Am Chem Soc; Sigma Xi. *Res:* Stereochemistry; organometallic reaction mechanisms; organic analysis. *Mailing Add:* Dept Chem Calif State Univ Chico CA 95929-0210

KORTELING, RALPH GARRET, NUCLEAR CHEMISTRY. *Current Pos:* from asst prof to assoc prof, 65-81, PROF CHEM & CHMN, SIMON FRASER UNIV, 81- *Personal Data:* b Madanapalle, India, Jan 2, 37; US citizen; m 61; c 2. *Educ:* Hope Col, AB, 58; Univ Calif, Berkeley, PhD(chem), 63. *Prof Exp:* Fel chem, Carnegie Inst Technol, 62-63, asst prof, 63-65. *Mem:* Am Phys Soc. *Res:* High energy nuclear reactions. *Mailing Add:* Dept Chem Simon Fraser Univ Burnaby BC V5A 1S6 Can

KORTH, GARY E, METALLURGY, MATERIALS SCIENCE. *Current Pos:* MAT RES SCIENTIST, IDAHO NAT ENG LAB, 68- *Personal Data:* b Tremonton, Utah, Feb 27, 38; m 61; c 5. *Educ:* Univ Utah, BS, 63, PhD(metall), 68. *Prof Exp:* Test lab engr, Gen Dynamics-Convair, 63-64. *Mem:* Am Soc Mat Int. *Res:* Elevated temperature fatigue and creep fatigue; mechanical properties; neutron irradiation effects of metals; rapidly solidified metals technology; dynamic consolidation of rapidly solidified metal powders using explosives. *Mailing Add:* 5 S 645 W Blackfoot ID 83221

KORTH, MICHAEL STEVEN, SUPERFLUID HELIUM, MANY-BODY QUANTUM MECHANICS. *Current Pos:* Asst prof, 84-90, ASSOC PROF PHYSICS, UNIV MINN, MORRIS, 90- , CHAIR, DIV SCI & MATH, 91- *Personal Data:* b Breckenridge, Minn, Mar 18, 56; m 82, Sandra Golembeck; c Andrew M, Rebecca A & Laura J. *Educ:* Univ Minn, BA, 78; Univ Md, MS, 81, PhD(physics), 84. *Mem:* Am Phys Soc; Am Asn Physics Teachers. *Res:* Superfluid helium dynamics via an approach which builds on the idea of correlated basis functions. *Mailing Add:* Div Sci & Math Univ Minn Morris MN 56267. *E-Mail:* korthms@caa.mrs.umn.edu

KORTHUIS, RONALD JOHN, ISCHEMIA & REPERFUSION, MICROVASCULAR DYSFUNCTION. *Current Pos:* from asst prof to assoc prof, 87-94, ASST DEAN GRAD STUDIES, MED CTR, LA STATE UNIV, 92-, PROF, DEPT PHYSIOL, 94- *Personal Data:* b Grand Rapids, Mich, Feb 7, 55; m 75, Mary E Black; c 3. *Educ:* Mich State Univ, PhD(physiol), 83. *Honors & Awards:* Travel Award, World Cong Microcirculation, 84, Europ Microcirculatory Soc, 89. *Prof Exp:* Fel, Univ SAla, 83-84, instr, 84-85; asst prof, Univ Mo, 85-87. *Concurrent Pos:* Prin investr, NIH, 85-; estab investr, Nat Heart Asn, 88-93. *Mem:* Am Physiol Soc; Microcirculatory Soc; Am Gastroenterol Soc. *Res:* Reperfusion of ischemic tissues paradoxically injured tissues; production of postischemic tissue injury; role for reactive oxygen metabolites and neutrophils in the pathogenesis of ischemia/reperfusion. *Mailing Add:* Dept Physiol La State Univ Med Ctr 1501 Kings Hwy Shreveport LA 71130-3932. *Fax:* 318-675-4528

KORTRIGHT, JAMES MCDOUGALL, medical physics, radiological physics, for more information see previous edition

KORUS, ROGER ALAN, BIOREMEDIATION FOR POLLUTANT DEGRADATION, FERMENTATION TECHNOLOGY. *Current Pos:* PROF & DEPT CHAIR CHEM ENG, UNIV IDAHO, 78- *Personal Data:* b Jan 9, 43; m 71, Jean A Meyerott; c David D & Jeannine A. *Educ:* Univ Wash, BS, 65; Stanford Univ, MS, 67; Univ Waterloo, PhD(chem eng), 74. *Honors & Awards:* Cert Recognition, NASA, 80. *Prof Exp:* Instr chem, Barber-Scotia Col, 67-68; res assoc, Western Regional Res Ctr, USDA, 74-76; res specialist, Ames Res Ctr, NASA, 76-78. *Mem:* Am Inst Chem Engrs; Am Soc Microbiol; Am Soc Eng Educ. *Res:* Developed processes for the biodegradation of chlorinated and nitrated aromatic compounds that are environmental pollutants; developed a process for the production of a diesel fuel substitute from vegetable oils. *Mailing Add:* 1038 Virginia Moscow ID 83843. *Fax:* 208-885-7462; *E-Mail:* rkorus@uidaho.edu

KORWEK, ALEXANDER DONALD, MODERN & FINANCIAL MANAGEMENT TECHNIQUES, RESOURCE MANAGEMENT. *Current Pos:* PRIN, A D KORWEK CONSULTS, 75-77 & 90- *Personal Data:* b Madison, Ill, Feb 20, 32; m 75, Judith Joy; c Alexander D Jr, Brian P, Lizabeth E & Theodore (Sofranos). *Educ:* Washington Univ, St Louis, BSBA, 62; Univ Utah, Salt Lake City, MBA, 67. *Prof Exp:* Asst secy & asst treas, Hoechst (Hystron) Fibers Inc, 66-72; vpres finance, Reeves/Teletape Corp, 72-76; chief finance off & bus mgr, Queens Col, City Univ New York, 77-79; managing dir, Am Soc Civil Engrs, 79-81; secy gen mgr, chief exec officer, United Eng Trustees, Inc, 81-90. *Concurrent Pos:* Exec secy, Eng Found, 81-90; Guggenheim Medal Award bd, 81-90; exec secy, Eng Socs Libr, 81-90, John Fritz Medal Bd, 81-90, Frank F Aplan Bd Award, 89-90. *Mem:* Coun Eng & Sci Soc Execs; NY Acad Sci; Am Soc Civil Engrs. *Res:* Management and cost containment in the plant environment inclusive of all interfaces with corporate and administrative functions; role of systems in all phases of modern business. *Mailing Add:* 27 Cool Water Ct Palm Coast FL 32137-8330

KORWIN-PAWLOWSKI, MICHAEL LECH, ELECTRICAL ENGINEERING. *Current Pos:* MGR ENG, GEN INSTURMENT, IRELAND MACROOM, CO, CORK, IRELAND, 94- *Personal Data:* b Warsaw, Poland, Apr 10, 41; US citizen; m 74, Barbara Bocquet; c Wendy. *Educ:* Warsaw Tech Univ, MS, 63; Univ Waterloo, Can, PhD(elec eng), 74; Long Island Univ, MBA, 93. *Prof Exp:* Sr scientist elec eng, Inst Electron Technol, Polish Acad Sci, 63-69; res & teaching asst elec eng, Dept Elec Eng, Univ Waterloo, Can, 69-74; product line mgr rectifiers, Erie Technol Prod, Can, 74-78; vpres & chief engr, Nat Semiconductors Ltd, 78-82; dir eng, Gen Instrument Taiwan, 82-87; mgr develop eng, Power Semiconductor Div, Gen Instrument Corp, Melville, NY, 87-94. *Res:* Silicon rectifiers; transient voltage suppressors; semiconductor process technology; semiconductor devices. *Mailing Add:* Gen Instrument Corp 10 Melville Park Rd Melville NY 11747. *Fax:* 353-21-42176

KORY, MITCHELL, BIOLOGICAL SCIENCE, MEDICINE. *Current Pos:* RETIRED. *Personal Data:* b Brooklyn, NY, Jan 6, 14; m 43; c 2. *Educ:* Univ Calif, Los Angeles, AB, 42, PhD(physiol bact), 53. *Prof Exp:* Instr bact, Univ Kans, 46-51; sr res biochemist, Res Labs, Eli Lilly & Co, 53-63, mgr pub info, 63-66, mgr med educ serv, 66-83. *Mem:* Am Soc Biol Chemists; Brit Biochem Soc. *Res:* Intermediary metabolism. *Mailing Add:* 129 Willow Rd Greenfield IN 46140

KORY, ROSS CONKLIN, medicine, physiology; deceased, see previous edition for last biography

KOS, EDWARD STANLEY, MICROBIOLOGY. *Current Pos:* assoc prof, 61-69, PROF BIOL, ROCKHURST COL, 69- *Personal Data:* b Chicago, Ill, Aug 10, 28; m 52; c 2. *Educ:* Loyola Univ, Ill, BS, 50; Marquette Univ, MS, 52; Univ Ill, PhD(microbiol), 58. *Prof Exp:* Actg instr life sci, Univ Calif, Riverside, 57-58; instr microbiol, Col Med, Univ Ill, 58-60; prof biol & chmn dept, Parsons Col, 60-61. *Mem:* Am Soc Microbiol; Sigma Xi. *Res:* Nutrition and metabolism of bacteria; Melanin pigmentation in Azotobacter chrococcum. *Mailing Add:* 5926 McGee St Kansas City MO 64113-2206

KOS, JOSEPH FRANK, solid state physics, for more information see previous edition

KOSAI, KENNETH, SEMICONDUCTOR DEVICE PHYSICS, INFRARED DETECTORS. *Current Pos:* MEM TECH STAFF, SANTA BARBARA RES CTR, 81- *Personal Data:* b Spokane, Wash, July 27, 44; m 62, Carol M Fuller; c Kim M. *Educ:* Calif Inst Technol, BS, 66; Univ Southern Calif, MSEE, 68, PhD(elec eng), 73. *Prof Exp:* Mem tech staff, Philips Labs, Briarcliff Manor, NY, 73-81. *Concurrent Pos:* Vis scientist, Dept Solid State Physics, Univ Lund, Sweden, 79. *Mem:* Inst Elec & Electronics Engrs; Am Phys Soc; Sigma Xi. *Res:* Device physics of semiconductor heterojunctions and infrared detectors; semiconductor device modeling. *Mailing Add:* 234 Old Ranch Dr Goleta CA 93117. *E-Mail:* 5102@msmail3.hac.com

KOSAK, ALVIN IRA, ORGANIC CHEMISTRY. *Current Pos:* asst prof indust med, NY Univ, 52-56, from assoc prof to prof chem, 56-95, chmn dept, 62-65, head, All-Univ Dept, 65-77, actg dean fac arts & sci, 77-78, dir grad study chem, 84-87, EMER PROF CHEM, NY UNIV, 96- *Personal Data:* b New York, NY, Feb 29, 24; m 58, Judith Shankman; c Deborah (Gussoff), Andrew & David. *Educ:* City Col New York, BS, 43; Ohio State Univ, PhD(org chem), 48. *Prof Exp:* Res chemist, Socony-Vacuum Oil Co, 43-45; asst chem, Ohio State Univ, 45-46, asst instr, 48; Jewett fel, Harvard Univ, 48-49; asst prof, Univ Cincinnati, 49-52. *Concurrent Pos:* USPHS spec fel, Univ Zurich, 62. *Mem:* Fel AAAS; Am Chem Soc; fel NY Acad Sci; Sigma Xi. *Res:* Thiophene chemistry; natural products; polynuclear hydrocarbons. *Mailing Add:* Dept Chem Rm 1018 NY Univ 4 Washington Pl New York NY 10003. *E-Mail:* kosak@152.nyu.edu

KOSAK, JOHN R, INDUSTRIAL ORGANIC CHEMISTRY. *Current Pos:* sr chemist, 57-80, RES ASSOC, E I DU PONT DE NEMOURS & CO, INC, 80- *Personal Data:* b Wilmington, Del, May 18, 30; m 57; c 3. *Educ:* Univ Del, BS, 51, MS, 52; Mich State Univ, PhD(org chem), 57. *Prof Exp:* Instr org & gen chem, Ferris State Col, 55-56. *Mem:* Am Chem Soc; Catalysis Soc. *Res:* Catalysis; catalytic hydrogenation. *Mailing Add:* 103 Willowspring Rd Wilmington DE 19807-2433

KOSAKA, MICHIKO, COMPUTER SCIENCE. *Current Pos:* FAC, COMPUT SCI DEPT, MONMOUTH UNIV. *Res:* Speech and natural language understanding. *Mailing Add:* Comput Sci Dept Monmouth Univ West Long Branch NJ 07764. *Fax:* 732-571-3554; *E-Mail:* kosaka@monmouth.edu

KOSANKE, ROBERT MAX, PALEOBOTANY. *Current Pos:* GEOLOGIST, US GEOL SURV, 63- *Personal Data:* b Park Ridge, Ill, Sept 4, 17; m 41; c 2. *Educ:* Coe Col, BA, 40; Univ Cincinnati, MS, 42; Univ Ill, PhD(paleobot), 52. *Honors & Awards:* Cady Award, Geol Soc Am, 89. *Prof Exp:* Lab instr geol, Coe Col, 39-40; asst bot, Univ Cincinnati, 40-43; asst, Ill Geol Surv, 43, from asst geologist to geologist, 43-63. *Concurrent Pos:* Assoc prof bot, Univ Ill, 59-63. *Mem:* AAAS; fel Geol Soc Am; Bot Soc Am; Soc Econ Geol; Paleont Soc. *Res:* Spore studies of coal beds of Pennsylvania age; Pennsylvanian stratigraphy and paleobotany. *Mailing Add:* 12085 W Applewood Knolls Dr Lakewood CO 80215

KOSANOVICH, ROBERT JOSEPH, MATHEMATICS. *Current Pos:* PROF MATH, FERRIS STATE COL, 65-, HEAD DEPT, 75- *Personal Data:* b Monroe, Mich, Sept 27, 38; m 60; c 3. *Educ:* Eastern Mich Univ, BS, 60, MA, 62; Univ Detroit, MA, 63; Mich State Univ, PhD, 72. *Mailing Add:* 717 Novak Lane Big Rapids MI 49307

KOSARAJU, S RAO, COMPUTER THEORY. *Current Pos:* PROF, JOHN UNIV, 77- *Personal Data:* b Cadhra Pradesh, India, Feb 20, 43. *Educ:* Univ Pa, PhD(comput sci eng) 69. *Mem:* Asn Comput Mach; Soc Int Appl Math; Instr Elec & Electronics Engrs. *Mailing Add:* Dept Comput Sci John Hopkins Univ 224 New Eng Bldg Baltimore MD 21218

KOSARIC, NAIM, ENVIRONMENTAL BIOTECHNOLOGY, BIOSURFACTANTS FOR ENVIRONMENTAL & COSMETIC APPLICATIONS. *Current Pos:* RETIRED. *Personal Data:* b Sarajevo, Yugoslavia, Sept 27, 28; Can citizen; m 55, Zekija Cejvan; c Senad & Alan. *Educ:* Univ Zagreb, dipl, 55; Univ Western Ont, PhD(biochem), 69. *Prof Exp:* Process engr & lab head, Iron, Coke Oven & Steelworks, Zenica, Yugoslavia, 56-59; process mgr, Pulp & Paper Indust, Maglay, 59-61; sr process eng, petrochem, Organic Chem Indust, Zagreb, Yugoslavia, 61-65; sr res eng, Bur Res & Partic Ministry, Rabat, Morocco, 65-66; res asst, Dept Biochem, Univ Western Ont, 66-69; from asst prof to assoc prof, Univ Western Ont, 69-79, chmn, 77-80 & 84-85, prof chem & biochem eng, Fac Eng & Sci, 79-96. *Concurrent Pos:* Vis scientist, USSR Acad Sci, Moscow, 57-58 & Europ Nuclear Ctr, Mol, Belgium, 60; vis engr, Nippon Kokan Chem, Tokyo-Kawasaki, Japan, 62; consult, Indust & Govt, 70-; vis prof, Swiss Fed Inst Technol, Switz, 75-76, Inst Fermentation & Biotechnol, Tech Univ, Ger, 83, Inst Microbiol, Czech Acad Sci, Prague, 75 & 84, Inst Biochem Technol & Microbiol Tech Univ, Vienna, Austria, 84 & Fed Inst Biotechnol, Fed Repub Ger, 84; chmn chem & biochem eng, Univ Western Ont, 77-80 & 84-85; expert, CIDA consult, Agr & Food Eng, Unicamp, Compinas, Brazil, 79, 81 & 83. *Mem:* Am Inst Chem Engrs; NY Acad Sci; Am Oil Chemists Soc; AAAS; Int & Can Asn Water Pollution Res; Can Soc Chem Eng. *Res:* Development of new processes and products in biochemical and food engineering; industrial wastewater treatment; biotechnology; microbial facts and oils; biosurfactants; fuel alcohol; anaerobic digestion of industrial pollutants; microbial detoxification; microbial proteins; economics in biotechnology. *Mailing Add:* 71 Sherwood Ave London ON N6A 5B9 Can. *Fax:* 519-649-1154

KOSASKY, HAROLD JACK, GYNECOLOGY, INFERTILITY. *Current Pos:* INSTR OBSTET & GYNEC, HARVARD MED SCH, 66- *Personal Data:* b Winnipeg, Man, Oct 19, 27; m 55, Shirley A Johnston; c 3. *Educ:* Univ Man, BA, 48, MD, 53; FRCS, 60; Am Bd Obstet & Gynec, dipl, 64. *Prof Exp:* Rotating intern, Deer Lodge Vet & Grace Hosps, Winnipeg, Can, 52-53; resident gen surg, Colonel Belcher Hosp, Calgary, 53-54; resident psychiat, Warren State Hosp, Warren, Pa, 55-56; asst resident obstet & gynec, Chicago Lying-In Hosp, Univ Chicago, 56-58, sr res, 58-59; from asst prof to assoc prof, Sch Med, Univ Louisville, 61-65. *Concurrent Pos:* Exchange fel, Univ Durham, 59-60; dir, dept obstet & gynec, Cambridge Hosp, 68-70, jr assoc surgeon, Peter Bent Brigham Hosp, 66-80, obstetrician & gynecologist, Boston Hosp Women, 66-80; consult, Jordan Hosp, 69-; active staff, Brigham & Women's Hosp, 80-; pres & res chief, Saltine Res Co. *Mem:* Fel Am Col Obstetricians & Gynecologists; fel Am Col Surgeons; Royal Col Obstetricians & Gynecologists. *Res:* Endocrinology; gynecologic surgery; infertility. *Mailing Add:* 25 Boylston St Chestnut Hill MA 02167. *Fax:* 617-566-3463

KOSBAB, FREDERIC PAUL GUSTAV, PSYCHIATRY, INTERNAL MEDICINE. *Current Pos:* prof psychiat & chmn dept, 82-86, EMER PROF BIOL MED & PSYCHIAT & CHMN DEPT, SCH MED, ORAL ROBERTS UNIV, TULSA, 87- *Personal Data:* b Berlin, Ger, Mar 29, 22; US citizen; m 51. *Educ:* Univ Berlin, MD, 45; Am Bd Psychiat & Neurol, dipl, 63; Okla State Univ, MA, 89. *Prof Exp:* Intern, Army Hosps & Refugee Infirmary, Friedland, WGer, 45-46; resident internal med, Dist Hosp, Hannoversch Muenden, WGer, 46-48 & Evangel Hosp, Goettingen-Weende, WGer, 48-51; pvt pract internal med, 51-55; rotating intern, Swed Covenant Hosp, Chicago, Ill, 56-57; staff physician I, Psychiat Serv, Manteno State Hosp, Ill, 57-58; resident psychiat, Col Med, Univ Nebr, 58-59; staff physician II, Psychiat Serv, Northern State Hosp, Sedro-Woolley, Wash, 59-60; resident psychiat, Sch Med, Univ Wash, 60-61 & Northern State Hosp, Sedro-Woolley, Wash, 61-62; clin instr psychiat, Med Sch, Univ Ore, 62-64; from asst prof to prof psychiat, Med Col Va, Va Commonwealth Univ, 64-73, dir residency training in psychiat, 66-69, from actg chmn dept to assoc chmn dept, 69-73; med dir, E Plains Ment Health Ctr, 74-77; chief psychiat servs, Hampton, Va Med Ctr, 77-82. *Concurrent Pos:* Consult, WGer Vet Admin, Landau, 52-56 & Residency Training Prog, East State Hosp, Williamsburg, Va, 68-73; sr staff psychiatrist & unit med dir, Ore State Hosp, Salem, 62-63; pvt pract psychiat, 63-; mem, Med Col Va Hosps, 64-73, bd gov, City Faith Med & Res Ctr, 82-, Med Pract Coun, Conf Med & Res Ctr, 82-; attend & consult, McGuire Vet Admin Hosp, Richmond, Va, 64-73; chmn, Comt Postgrad Training in Psychiat, 67-70; mem dean's comt, Richmond Vet Admin Hosp, 69-70; prof dir NIMH grant, 69-73; prof, Dept Psychiat & Behav Sci, Eastern Va Med Sch, 77-82; chief, Dept Behav Med & Psychiat, City Faith Med & Res Ctr, Tulsa, Okla, 82-86. *Mem:* Fel Am Psychiat Asn; hon fel Arbeitsgemeinschaft F Katathymes Bilderleben, WGer; AMA. *Res:* Contribution to the problem of superfetation and superfecundation in twins; camptocormia in the female; introduction of a buddy system for hospitalized geriatric patients; symbol formation; affective imagery and its didactic uses in psychiatry; teaching and learning in medical school. *Mailing Add:* PO Box 701677 Tulsa OK 74170-1677

KOSCHIER, FRANCIS JOSEPH, TOXICOLOGY, PHARMACY. *Current Pos:* SR TOXICOL CONSULT, ARCO, 89- *Personal Data:* b New York, NY, June 16, 50. *Educ:* Bard Col, AB, 72; Univ Miss, PhD(pharmacol), 76. *Prof Exp:* Res asst prof, State Univ NY, Buffalo, 76-79; sr toxicologist, Food & Drug Res Labs, 79-80; sr toxicologist, Am Cyanamid Corp, 80-83; mgr toxicol, Ciba-Geigy Corp, 83-89. *Mem:* Soc Toxicol; Am Soc Pharmacol & Exp Therapeut; Soc Environ Toxicol & Anal Chem. *Res:* Health and environmental risk assessment of petroleum products and synthetic chemicals. *Mailing Add:* ARCO AP 4151 515 S Flower St Los Angeles CA 90071-2202

KOSCHMIEDER, ERNST LOTHAR, FLUID DYNAMICS. *Current Pos:* from asst prof to assoc prof, 68-85, PROF, UNIV TEX, AUSTIN, 86- *Personal Data:* b Danzig, Ger, May 1, 29; m 62, Kale Glaser; c 2. *Educ:* Univ Bonn, Dipl Physics, 58, Dr Rer Nat(physics), 63. *Prof Exp:* Res fel, Harvard Univ, 63-65; res assoc, Univ Chicago, 65-67. *Concurrent Pos:* Consult, Apollo XVII Convection Exp, Lockheed Space & Missiles Co, 71-74; mem, Ctr Statist Mech, Univ Tex, Austin, 72-; sr vis fel, Nat Ctr Atmospheric Res, Colo, 73-74; vis sci, Ctr Nuclear Studies, Saclay, France, 81. *Res:* Hydrodynamic stability; Benard convection; Rayleigh-Benard convection; Taylor Vorler flow; rotating annulus; planetary circulation. *Mailing Add:* E Cockrell Jr Hall 8-6 Univ Tex Austin TX 78712

KOSCO, JOHN C(ARROLL), METALLURGY, POWDER METALLURGY. *Current Pos:* DIR RES, KEYSTONE CARBON CO, 72- *Personal Data:* b Du Bois, Pa, Sept 20, 32; m 56, Mary Mullaney; c Thomas, Mary Patricia, Anne, Ellen, Maurus & Joseph. *Educ:* Univ Notre Dame, BS, 54; Princeton Univ, MSE, 56; Pa State Univ, PhD(metall), 58. *Prof Exp:* Res metallurgist, Stackpole Carbon Co, 58-66, chief engr metals, 66-67, dir metall res, 67-71. *Mem:* Am Soc Metals; Am Powder Metal Inst; Am Chem Soc. *Res:* Powder metallurgy of ferrous and non-ferrous materials, high temperature materials and electrical contacts; electrical ceramics and thermoelectric materials; coatings and metal joining. *Mailing Add:* Keystone Powder Metal Co 1933 State St St Marys PA 15857. *Fax:* 814-781-4280; *E-Mail:* jckosco@ncentral.com

KOSEL, GEORGE EUGENE, ELECTROPHOTOGRAPHY. *Current Pos:* RETIRED. *Personal Data:* b Rochester, NY, July 22, 23; m 50, Jenn Glenn; c Liza G, Leslie A & Ellen M. *Educ:* Cornell Univ, AB, 44; Univ Rochester, MS, 51. *Prof Exp:* Res assoc biochem, Atomic Energy Comn, Univ Rochester, 47-50; chief biochemist dental res, Passaic Gen Hosp, NJ, 50-54; mgr res graphic arts, Philip A Hunt Chem Corp, 54-67, mgr res, Electrostatic Div, 67-70, asst dir res, 70-75, dir basic chem res, 75-81, consult, electrophotography, 82-83; chief chemist, Am Gas & Chem Co, Ltd, 83-94. *Mem:* AAAS; Am Chem Soc. *Res:* Fluoride metabolism; solid state and physical chemistry; powders and liquid developers for electrophotography; chemicals for non-destructive testing. *Mailing Add:* 181 North Ave Park Ridge NJ 07656-1652

KOSEL, PETER BOHDAN, MICROELECTRONIC DEVICES. *Current Pos:* Assoc prof, 80-89, PROF ELEC ENG, UNIV CINCINNATI, 89- *Personal Data:* b Northeim, Ger, Aug 20, 46; Australian citizen; m 73; c 2. *Educ:* Univ Sydney, Australia, BSc, 68; Univ NSW, Australia, PhD(elec eng),

76. *Concurrent Pos:* Consult, Universal Energy Syst, Dayton, Ohio, 88- *Mem:* Inst Elec & Electronics Engrs; Sigma Xi; Electrochem Soc; Optical Soc Am; Soc Indust & Appl Math; Soc Photo-Optical Instrumentation Engrs. *Res:* High speed charge-coupled devices in gallium arsenite and fabrication technology of compound semiconductor devices; computer aided design and simulation of signal processing devices and circuits; photonic devices and optical communications; fabrication process simulation; chalcopyrite semiconductors. *Mailing Add:* Dept Elec & Comput Eng Univ Cincinnati ML30 Cincinnati OH 45221. *Fax:* 513-556-7326; *E-Mail:* kosel@kosel.ece.uc.edu

KOSERSKY, DONALD SAADIA, PHARMACOLOGY. *Current Pos:* ASSOC PROF PHARMACOL & COORDR GRAD PROG, MASS COL PHARM & ALLIED HEALTH SCI, 81- *Personal Data:* b Waterbury, Conn, Oct 16, 32; m 60. *Educ:* Univ Conn, BA, 57, MS, 68; Univ Pac, PhD, 71. *Prof Exp:* Res assoc, Sch Med, Univ NC, Chapel Hill, 71-73; asst prof, Northeastern Univ, 73-77, assoc prof pharmacol, 77-81. *Mem:* AAAS; Am Soc Pharmacol & Exp Therapeut; Neurosci Soc. *Res:* Autonomic and central nervous system pharmacology; pharmacology of addiction and drugs of abuse; classical pharmacology. *Mailing Add:* 62 Old Lancaster Rd Sudbury MA 01176

KOSH, JOSEPH WILLIAM, NEUROPHARMACOLOGY. *Current Pos:* From asst prof to assoc prof pharmacol, 71-80, AT DEPT PHARMACOL, UNIV SC, COLUMBIA. *Personal Data:* b Hempstead, Tex, Sept 30, 40. *Educ:* Univ Tex, BS, 64, MS, 67; Univ Colo, PhD(pharmacol), 71. *Mem:* AAAS; Sigma Xi. *Res:* Cardiovascular and neuropharmacology; pharmacology of gamma-aminobutyric acid intermediates and relation to convulsive threshold. *Mailing Add:* Col Pharmacol Univ SC Columbia SC 29208-0001

KOSHEL, RICHARD DONALD, NUCLEAR PHYSICS. *Current Pos:* PROF PHYSICS, 85-, ASSOC PROVOST RES & DEAN GRAD STUDIES, ILL STATE UNIV, 85- *Personal Data:* b Argo, Ill, Feb 1, 36; m 62, 80; c 2. *Educ:* Univ Ill, BS, 58, MS, 59; Univ Kans, PhD(theoret nuclear physics), 63. *Prof Exp:* From asst prof to prof physics, 63-85, assoc dean, Col Arts & Sci, Ohio Univ, 80-85. *Concurrent Pos:* Vis prof, Fla State Univ, 69-70 & Univ Md, 78-79. *Mem:* Am Phys Soc; Am Asn Physics Teachers. *Res:* Theoretical nuclear physics and numerical analysis; nuclear structure using many body techniques and nuclear reactions; non-linear system. *Mailing Add:* 305 Williamsburg Dr Starkville MS 39759

KOSHER, ROBERT ANDREW, DEVELOPMENTAL BIOLOGY. *Current Pos:* asst prof, 74-80, ASSOC PROF ANAT, SCH MED, UNIV CONN, 80- *Personal Data:* b Key West, Fla, Mar 1, 45; m 68; c 3. *Educ:* Wilkes Col, BA, 67; Temple Univ, PhD(biol), 72. *Prof Exp:* NIH fel anat, Sch Med, Univ Pa, 72-74. *Mem:* Soc Develop Biol; Am Soc Zoologists; Am Asn Anatomists. *Res:* The role of extracellular matrix components in tissue interactions and other developmental processes; the control of somite chondrogenesis by extracellular matrix components produced by the embryonic notochord and spinal cord. *Mailing Add:* Dept Anat Univ Conn Sch Med 263 Farmington Ave Farmington CT 06030-0001

KOSHI, JAMES H, DAIRY SCIENCE, ANIMAL SCIENCE. *Current Pos:* RETIRED. *Personal Data:* b Agate, Colo, June 13, 19; m 77. *Educ:* Colo Agr & Mech Col, BS, 48; Univ Minn, PhD(dairy sci), 55. *Prof Exp:* Dairy specialist & prof, Univ Hawaii, 55-74; gen mgr agr, Micronesian Develop Co, Tinian, 75-77; consult dairy prod, Hawaiian Agron Co Int, Iran, 77-78; gen mgr, 50th State Diary Farmers Coop, 79-82, consult, 83-85. *Concurrent Pos:* Consult & prof, Kasetsart Univ Thailand, 62-65. *Mem:* Am Dairy Sci Asn; Sigma Xi. *Res:* All areas of dairy cattle management and milk production. *Mailing Add:* 2333 Kapiolani Blvd Apt 2011 Honolulu HI 96826-4444

KOSHLAND, DANIEL EDWARD, JR, BIOCHEMISTRY. *Current Pos:* PROF BIOCHEM, UNIV CALIF, BERKELEY, 65- *Personal Data:* b New York, NY, Mar 30, 20; m 45. Marian Elliott; c Ellen, Phyllis, James, Gail & Douglas. *Educ:* Univ Calif, BS, 41; Univ Chicago, PhD(biochem), 49. *Hon Degrees:* PhD, Weizman Inst Sci, 84; DSc, Carnegie-Mellon Univ, 85; LLD, Simon Fraser Univ, 86, Univ Chicago, 93; LHD, Mt Sinai Univ. *Honors & Awards:* T Duckett Jones Award, Helen Hay Whitney Found, 77; Pauling Award & Edgar Fahs Smith Award, Am Chem Soc, 79; Rosentiel Award, Brandeis Univ, 84; Waterford Prize, Scripps Clin & Res Found, 84; Nat Medal Sci, 90; Merck Award, Am Soc Biochem & Molecular Biol, 91. *Prof Exp:* Anal chemist, Shell Chem Co, 41-42; asst, Manhattan Proj, Univ Chicago, 42-44; group leader, 44-46; fel, Harvard Univ, 49-51; assoc biochemist, Brookhaven Nat Lab, 51-54, biochemist, 54-56, sr biochemist, 56-65. *Concurrent Pos:* Affil, Rockefeller Univ, 58-65; mem panel, USPHS, 59-64; vis fel, All Souls Col, Oxford, 72-73; fel, Guggenheim Found, 72-73; distinguished lectr, Soc Gen Physiol, 78; ed-in-chief, Sci Mag, 85- *Mem:* Nat Acad Sci; AAAS; Am Chem Soc; Am Soc Biol Chemists (pres, 73-74); Japanese Biochem Soc; Royal Swed Acad Sci; Am Acad Arts & Sci; Am Philos Soc. *Res:* General principles of enzymology and regulatory control; understanding of memory and sensory processes; correlation of protein structure and function. *Mailing Add:* 3991 Happy Valley Rd Lafayette CA 94549-2423. *Fax:* 510-643-6386

KOSHLAND, DOUGLAS E, GENETICS. *Current Pos:* STAFF MEM GENETICS, CARNEGIE INST WASHINGTON, 88- *Personal Data:* b New York, NY, Dec 10, 53. *Educ:* Haverford Col, BA, 76; Mass Inst Technol, PhD(biol), 82. *Honors & Awards:* Helen Haynes Award; Lucy P Markell Award. *Prof Exp:* Res fel genetics, Univ Calif, San Francisco, 84-86. *Mem:* Am Chem Soc; NY Acad Sci. *Res:* Genetics. *Mailing Add:* Dept Embryol Carnegie Inst Washington 115 W University Pkwy Baltimore MD 21210-3399. *Fax:* 410-243-6311

KOSHLAND, MARIAN ELLIOTT, MOLECULAR BIOLOGY. *Current Pos:* from assoc res immunologist to res immunologist, 65-70, chmn Dept Microbiol & Immunol, 82-89, PROF IMMUNOL, DIV IMMUNOL, UNIV CALIF, BERKELEY, 70- *Personal Data:* b New Haven, Conn, Oct 25, 21; m 45; c 5. *Educ:* Vassar Univ, BA, 42; Univ Chicago, MS, 43, PhD(bact), 49. *Honors & Awards:* R E Dyer Lectr, NIH, 88; Excellence in Sci Award, Fedn Am Soc Exp Biol, 89. *Prof Exp:* Asst, Cholera Proj, Off Sci Res & Develop, Chicago, 43 & 44-45; asst, Comn Air Borne Dis, Colo, 43-44; jr chemist, Atomic Bomb Proj, Manhattan Dist, Tenn, 45-46; from assoc bacteriologist to bacteriologist, Brookhaven Nat Lab, 53-65. *Concurrent Pos:* Fel bact & immunol, Harvard Univ, 49-51; mem, Nat Sci Bd, NSF, 76-82, coun, Nat Acad Sci, 85-88, Comn Life Sci, Nat Res Coun, 89; vis prof, Cancer Ctr, Mass Inst Technol, 79 & 85-86; mem coun, Nat Inst Allergy & Infectious Dis, NIH, 91-95. *Mem:* Nat Acad Sci; Am Asn Immunologists (pres, 82-83); Am Soc Biol Chemists; Sigma Xi; Am Acad Microbiologists. *Res:* Mechanism of antibody biosynthesis; lymphokine regulation of immunoglobin gene expression; mechanisms of lymphokine signaling of B lymphocytes. *Mailing Add:* Dept Molecular & Cell Biol Univ Calif 439 LSA No 3200 Berkeley CA 94720

KOSHY, K THOMAS, PHARMACY, PHARMACEUTICAL CHEMISTRY. *Current Pos:* RETIRED. *Personal Data:* b Kerala, India, Sept 22, 24; m 50; c 2. *Educ:* Kerala Univ, India, BSc, 43; Benares Hindu Univ, BA, 48; Univ Iowa, MS, 58, PhD (pharm & pharmaceut chem), 60. *Prof Exp:* Mfg chemist, Sterling Pharmaceut, India, 48-49; jr sci asst, Inspectorate of Gen Stores Lab, 49-51; med serv rep, Parke Davis & Co, Ltd, 51-56; asst col pharm, Univ Iowa, 60-61; sr res pharmacist, Miles Labs, Inc, 61-66; sr res scientist, UpJohn Co, 66-89. *Mem:* Acad fel Am Pharmaceut Asn; Am Chem Soc. *Res:* Analytical methods development for drugs and pharmaceuticals; kinetic studies and stability testing of pharmaceuticals; residue analysis in plants and animals; metabolism in plants and animals; photolysis of pesticides and herbicides. *Mailing Add:* 5330 Glenharbor Dr Kalamazoo MI 49009

KOSHY, THOMAS, DISCRETE MATHEMATICS. *Current Pos:* from asst prof to assoc prof, 70-78, PROF & CHAIR MATH, FRAMINGHAM STATE COL, 78- *Personal Data:* b Kozhancheri, Kerala, India, Aug 21, 42; m 67, Gracy Philip; c Suresh & Sheeba. *Educ:* Kerala Univ, BSc, 62, MSc, 64; Boston Univ, PhD(math), 71. *Prof Exp:* Asst prof math, Kerala Univ, 64-67; teaching fel, Boston Univ, 67-70. *Mem:* Math Asn Am; Nat Coun Teachers Math; Fibonacci Asn. *Res:* Discrete mathematics; author of several publications. *Mailing Add:* Framingham State Col Framingham MA 01701. *Fax:* 508-626-4592; *E-Mail:* tkhosy@madmax.frc.mass.edu

KOSIBA, WALTER LOUIS, PHYSICAL CHEMISTRY. *Current Pos:* SPECIALIST, LA JOLLA RADIOCARBON & TRITIUM LAB, UNIV CALIF, SAN DIEGO, 71- *Personal Data:* b Braddock, Pa, Feb 13, 21. *Educ:* Canisius Col, BS, 43; Ohio State Univ, MSc, 49, PhD(chem), 51. *Prof Exp:* Res assoc, S A M Labs, Columbia Univ, 44-45; chemist, Phys Chem Uranium, Tenn Eastman Corp, 45-46; res chemist, Phys Chem Solids, Vitro Corp Am, 51-53; assoc physicist, Brookhaven Nat Lab, 53-58; mem res staff, Gen Atomic Div, Gen Dynamics Corp, 58-61; consult, European Atomic Energy Community, Belgium, 61-63; sr scientist, Nuclear Dept, Douglas Aircraft Co, Inc, 64-66 & Aerospace Corp, 66; asst to dir, NAm Rockwell Sci Ctr, 66-70. *Concurrent Pos:* Consult, Int Atomic Energy Agency, Austria, 61. *Mem:* AAAS; Am Chem Soc; Sigma Xi. *Res:* Materials sciences; radiation effects; solid state chemistry; radiocarbon dating. *Mailing Add:* 3920 Ingraham St Apt 118 San Diego CA 92109-5915

KOSIER, FRANK J, MATHEMATICS. *Current Pos:* assoc prof, 66-69, PROF MATH, UNIV IOWA, 69- *Personal Data:* b Lansing, Mich, July 2, 34; m 52; c 2. *Educ:* Mich State Univ, BS, 56, MS, 57, PhD(math), 60. *Prof Exp:* Instr math, Univ Calif, Berkeley, 60-61 & Univ Wis, 61-63; asst prof, Syracuse Univ, 63-64 & Univ Wis-Madison, 64-66. *Mem:* Am Math Soc; Math Asn Am. *Res:* Non-associative rings. *Mailing Add:* Dept Math Univ Iowa Iowa City IA 52240

KOSIEWICZ, STANLEY TIMOTHY, NUCLEAR WASTE MANAGEMENT, RADIOLYSIS. *Current Pos:* staff mem analytical chem, Los Alamos Nat Lab, 73-86, staff scientist, Nuclear Waste Mgr, 89-92, technol interface, Environ Restoration, 92-93, TRANSURANIC WASTE MGT, LOS ALAMOS NAT LAB, UNIV CALIF, 93- *Personal Data:* b Chicago, Ill, July 21, 44; m 89, Amy E Anderson; c 1. *Educ:* Univ Ill, BS, 67; Univ Wis, MS, 69, PhD(analytical chem), 73. *Prof Exp:* Process engr chem eng, Olin Corp, 68-69; independent consult, 86-89. *Mem:* Am Chem Soc; AAAS; Sigma Xi. *Res:* Transuranium radioactive waste degradation; nuclear waste management; trace element geochemistry and archaeology; waste management and environmental restoration technology development. *Mailing Add:* Group EM MS J534 Los Alamos Nat Lab Los Alamos NM 87545. *E-Mail:* stan@lanl.gov

KOSIKOWSKI, FRANK VINCENT, food science; deceased, see previous edition for last biography

KOSINSKI, ANTONI A, MATHEMATICS. *Current Pos:* PROF MATH, RUTGERS UNIV, 66-, DEPT CHMN, 93- *Personal Data:* b Warsaw, Poland, May 25, 30; div; c Marta. *Educ:* Univ Warsaw, PhD, 56. *Prof Exp:* Asst prof inst math, Polish Acad Sci, 56-59 & Univ Calif, Berkeley, 59-62; mem, Inst Adv Study, 62-64; assoc prof math, Univ Calif, Berkeley, 64-66. *Concurrent Pos:* Mem, INst Advan Study, 66-67, 85-86 & 96-97; vis prof, Univ Bonn, 73-74; mem, Cont Profession, Am Math Soc, 93- *Mem:* Am Math Soc. *Res:* Topology and differential topology. *Mailing Add:* Dept Math Rutgers Univ New Brunswick NJ 08903. *E-Mail:* kosinski@math.rutgers.edu

KOSINSKI, LESZEK ANTONI, GEOGRAPHY, DEMOGRAPHY. *Current Pos:* SECY-GEN, INT SOCIAL SCI COUN, PARIS, 94- *Personal Data:* b Warszawa, Poland, June 13, 29; nat Can; m 51, Maria L Bodakiewicz. *Educ:* Cent Sch Planning & Statist, MA, 51; Univ Warsaw, MA, 54; Polish Acad Sci, PhD, 58, Docent, 63. *Honors & Awards:* Medal, SAfrican Geog Soc, 87; Award for Serv to Prof Geog, Can Asn Geogrs, 94. *Prof Exp:* Jr researcher, Inst Town Planning & Archit, Poland, 50-54; sr researcher, Inst Geog, Polish Acad Sci, 54-68; prof geog, Univ Alta, Can, 69-94. *Concurrent Pos:* Vis prof, Univ Calif, Berkeley, 62, Ind Univ, 62, Univ Minn, 67, Pa State Univ, 68, Northwestern Univ, 68, Queen's Univ, Can, 68, Univ Wash, 71, Univ Liverpool, UK, 81, Univ Nat Autonoma de Mex, 81 & Univ Guadalajara, 85; chair, Comn Pop Geog, Int Geog Union, 72-80; bd mem, Int Soc Sci Coun, 86-90, Can Global Change Prog, 91- *Mem:* Int Union Sci Study Pop; Europ Asn Pop Studies; Asn Pop Geogr India; Asn Am Geogr; Pop Asn Am Avocations; fel Royal Soc Can; Can Pop Soc (pres, 84-86); Int Geog Union (secy & treas, 84-92); hon mem Russ Geog Soc; hon mem Geog Soc France; hon mem Polish Geog Soc; corresp mem Geog Soc Italy. *Res:* Human migration; human geography/demography. *Mailing Add:* ISSC Maison of UNESCO 1 rue Miollis Paris 75732 Cedex 15 France

KOSINSKI, ROBERT JOSEPH, POPULATION ECOLOGY, LIMNOLOGY. *Current Pos:* asst prof, 84-86, ASSOC PROF, BIOL PROG, CLEMSON UNIV, 86- *Personal Data:* b Montclair, NJ, Jan 8, 49; m 89, Margaret Chastain; c Robert M & Joseph D. *Educ:* Seton Hall Univ, BS, 72; Rutgers Univ, PhD(ecol), 77. *Prof Exp:* Asst prof biol, Tex A&M Univ, 77-84. *Concurrent Pos:* Grants, Environ Protection Agency, NSF & Dept Educ; software author, Worth Publ Co & Benjamin/Cummings Publ Co. *Mem:* AAAS; Ecol Soc Am; Am Soc Limnol & Oceanog; Nat Asn Biol Teachers; Nat Sci Teachers Asn. *Res:* Stream ecology; primary productivity in streams; effects of pesticides in streams; computer modeling of antigenic variation of trypanosome infections; use of computers as teaching tools. *Mailing Add:* Biol Prog Clemson Univ 330 Long Hall Clemson SC 29634-1902. *Fax:* 864-656-3839; *E-Mail:* rjksn@clemson.edu

KOSKI, RANDOLPH A, MARINE GEOLOGY. *Current Pos:* CHIEF SCIENTIST, WESTERN REGION, MINERAL RESOURCES PROG, US GEOL SUPV, 96- *Personal Data:* b Cloquet, Minn, June 22, 46. *Educ:* Univ Minn, BA, 69; Stanford Univ, MS, 74, PhD(geol), 78. *Mem:* Fel Geol Soc Am; fel Soc Econ Geologists; Am Geophys Union. *Mailing Add:* US Geol Surv MS 941 345 Middlefield Rd Menlo Park CA 94025

KOSKI, WALTER S, PHYSICAL CHEMISTRY. *Current Pos:* assoc prof phys chem, 47-55, chmn dept, 58-69, PROF CHEM, JOHNS HOPKINS UNIV, 55-, BERNARD N BAKER PROF CHEM, 74- *Personal Data:* b Philadelphia, Pa, Dec 1, 13; m 40, Helen I Tag; c Carol L, Ann L, Nancy C & Phyllis. *Educ:* Johns Hopkins Univ, PhD(phys chem), 42. *Prof Exp:* Res chemist, Hercules Powder Co, 42-43; group leader, Los Alamos Sci Lab, 44-47. *Concurrent Pos:* Physicist, Brookhaven Nat Lab, NY, 47-48; consult chem corps, US Army, 49- *Mem:* Am Chem Soc; fel Am Phys Soc. *Res:* Radioactive and stable isotopes as tracers; chemistry of boron hydrides; electron and nuclear magnetic resonance; mass spectroscopy; nuclear chemistry; ion-molecule reactions; reactive scattering of ions: mechanism of drug action. *Mailing Add:* Dept Chem Johns Hopkins Univ 3400 N Charles St Baltimore MD 21218. *Fax:* 410-516-8420; *E-Mail:* chm___zjjk@jhuvms.hcf.jhu.edu

KOSKY, PHILIP GEORGE, MATERIALS SCIENCE, HEAT TRANSFER POLYMER CHEMISTRY & ENGINEERING. *Current Pos:* mgr fuel sci unit, 80-82, STAFF CHEM ENGR, GEN ELEC RES & DEVELOP CTR, 77- *Personal Data:* b London, Eng, March 25, 39; m 64, Mary Boeker; c Deirdre A & Nicole S. *Educ:* Univ London, BSc, 61; Univ Calif, Berkeley, MS, 63, PhD(chem eng), 66. *Prof Exp:* Res asst chem eng, Univ Calif, Berkeley; sr sci officer, Harwell Nat Lab, Eng; chem engr, Res & Develop Ctr, Gen Elec; assoc prof mech eng & mech, Lehigh Univ. *Concurrent Pos:* Adj assoc prof mech eng, Union Col, Schenectady, NY; Fulbright Scholar. *Mem:* Am Chem Soc. *Res:* Chemical vapor deposition synthesis and properties of abrasive materials; kinetics of polymer reactions; transport properties and measurements; modeling chemical and physical phenomena. *Mailing Add:* Gen Elec Res & Develop Ctr PO Box 8 Schenectady NY 12301-0008. *Fax:* 518-387-6384; *E-Mail:* kosky@crd.ge.com

KOSLOW, JULIAN ANTHONY, FISHERIES OCEANOGRAPHY. *Current Pos:* sr res scientist, 90-93, PRIN RES SCIENTIST, DIV FISHERIES, COMMONWEALTH SCI & INDUST RES ORGN, 93- *Personal Data:* b Los Angeles, Calif, May 14, 47; div; c 2. *Educ:* Harvard Univ, BA, 69; Univ Wash, BA, 73; Univ Calif, San Diego, PhD(biol oceanog), 80. *Honors & Awards:* E W Fager Award, Scripps Inst Oceanog, 80; Chapman-Schaefer Award, Marine Technol Soc, 75. *Prof Exp:* Res asst biol oceanog, Scripps Inst Oceanog, Univ Calif, San Diego, 74-79; asst prof fisheries oceanog, Oceanog Dept, Dalhousie Univ, 80-88; res assoc, Dept Fisheries & Oceans, Halifax, 88-89. *Concurrent Pos:* Hon res assoc, Zool Dept, Univ West Indies, Jamaica, 86. *Res:* Deep water fisheries biology; oceanography; management; physical oceanography and plankton behavior; the regulation between stock and recruitment in fish populations; interactions with biological and climatic change and larval ecology; effect of fisheries management on fishing communities; reef fish ecology and management. *Mailing Add:* Div Marine Res Commonwealth Sci & Ind Res Orgn Marine Lab GPO Box 1538 Hobart Tas 7001 Australia. *Fax:* 61-3-62325000; *E-Mail:* tony.koslow@marine.csiro.au

KOSLOW, STEPHEN HUGH, PHARMACOLOGY, PSYCHOPHARMACOLOGY. *Current Pos:* staff fel, Lab Preclin Pharmacol, St Elizabeth's Hosp, NIMH, Washington, DC, 70-73, chief unit neurobiol & appl mass spectrometry, Lab Preclin Pharmacol, 73-75, chief, neurosci res, Biol Res Sect, Clin Res Br, 75-81, chief, Div Extramural Res, 81-85, chief, Neurosci Res Br, Div Basic Sci, 85-89, dir, Div Basic Brain & Behav Sci, 89-90, DIR, DIV NEUROSCI & BEHAV SCI, NIMH, NIH, 90- *Personal Data:* b New York, NY, Oct 14, 40; m 62, Diane Heiller; c Karin & James. *Educ:* Columbia Univ, BS, 62; Univ Chicago, PhD, 67. *Honors & Awards:* Meritorious Achievement Award, Alcohol Drug Abuse & Ment Health Admin, 79, 85 & 86, Pub Health Serv Spec Recognition Award, 92. *Prof Exp:* Fel pharmacol, Karolinska Inst, Stockholm, Sweden, 68-69. *Concurrent Pos:* Dir, Clin Res Br Collab Prog Psychol Depression, NIMH, 75-, Presidential Comn Mental Health, Special Asst Res Panel, 78; med adv bd, Tourette Syndrome Asn; chair, Fed Interagency Coord Comt on Human Brain Proj, 92; mem, White House Off Sci & Technol Deleg Orgn Econ Coop & Develop, Megascience Forum, Paris, 96- *Mem:* Am Soc Pharmacol & Exp Therapeut; Soc Neurosci; Am Col Neuropsychopharmacol; Soc Biol Psychiat; Am Soc Neurochem; Collegium Internationale Neuro-Psychopharmacologicum. *Res:* Neuropharmacology and psychopharmacology; depression and schizophrenia; neurotransmitters; metabolites and central nervous system function; neuroendocrinology; neuroscience. *Mailing Add:* NIMH Parklawn Bldg Rm 11-103 5600 Fishers Lane Rockville MD 20857. *Fax:* 3301-443-4822; *E-Mail:* nfh@wiltch

KOSLOWSKY, VERNON THEODORE, NUCLEAR PHYSICS. *Current Pos:* ASST RES OFFICER, CHALK RIVER LABS, ONT, CAN, 85- *Personal Data:* b Leamington, Ont, Can, Dec 15, 53; m 77. *Educ:* Univ Waterloo, BSc 77; Univ Toronto, MSc, 78, PhD(physics), 83. *Prof Exp:* Res fel, GSI, Darmstadt, Fed Repub Germany, 83-84. *Mem:* Can Asn Physicists. *Res:* Experimental nuclear physics; use of accelerated heavy ions as probes of the nucleus; weak interaction and the nucleus; nuclei far from stability; accelerator mass spectrometry. *Mailing Add:* Chalk River Labs Chalk River ON K0J 1J0 Can

KOSMAHL, HENRY G, ELECTRON PHYSICS. *Current Pos:* CONSULT, ELECTRON DYNAMICS DIV, HUGHES AIRCRAFT, 84- *Personal Data:* b Wartha, Ger, Dec 14, 19; US citizen; m 43; c 3. *Educ:* Dresden Tech Univ, MS, 43; Darmstadt Tech Univ, DS(electron physics), 49. *Honors & Awards:* Sci Achievement Medal, NASA, 74; Technol Adv Award, 77, CECON Centennial Award, Inst Elec & Electronics Engrs, 83. *Prof Exp:* Asst prof physics, Darmstadt Tech Univ, 49-51; res physicist, AEG-Telefunken Res Ctr, Ger, 52-56; head power amplifier, Electron Lab, US Army, 56-62; head power amplifier, Lewis Res Ctr, NASA, 62-84. *Concurrent Pos:* Consult, Aeronaut Systs & Space Div, USAF, Dayton, 62-84, Westinghouse Elec Defense Div, 82-83. *Mem:* Fel Inst Elec & Electronics Engrs. *Res:* Interaction of charged particles with waves and matter. *Mailing Add:* 12700 Lake Ave Apt 606 Cleveland OH 44107

KOSMAN, DANIEL JACOB, BIOCHEMISTRY. *Current Pos:* from asst prof to assoc prof, 70-81, PROF BIOCHEM, STATE UNIV NY BUFFALO, 81- *Personal Data:* b Chicago, Ill, Nov 29, 41; m 64; c 2. *Educ:* Oberlin Col, BA, 63; Univ Chicago, PhD(phys org chem), 68. *Prof Exp:* Res assoc biophys, Univ Hawaii, 68-69; Cornell Univ res assoc molecular biol, Dept Chem, Cambridge Univ & Med Res Coun Lab of Molecular Biol, Cambridge, Eng, 69-70. *Mem:* AAAS; Am Chem Soc. *Res:* Mechanism of enzyme action; enzyme modification; bio-inorganic chemistry; protein biosynthesis. *Mailing Add:* Dept Biochem 140 Farber Hall State Univ NY Buffalo NY 14214

KOSMAN, WARREN MELVIN, CHEMICAL PHYSICS. *Current Pos:* from asst prof to assoc prof, 77-89, PROF CHEM, VALPARAISO UNIV, 89- *Personal Data:* b Chicago, Ill, Mar 23, 46; m 70; c 1. *Educ:* Valparaiso Univ, BS, 67; Univ Chicago, MS, 69, PhD(chem physics), 74. *Prof Exp:* Instr chem, Valparaiso Univ, 69-70, instr math, 70-71; asst prof chem, Ohio State Univ, 74-77. *Mem:* Am Chem Soc. *Res:* Molecular spectroscopy and ab initio molecular orbital calculations of atoms and small molecules. *Mailing Add:* 4502 Bristol Lane Valparaiso Univ Valparaiso IN 46383-2310

KOSMATKA, JOHN BENEDICT, STRUCTURAL DYNAMICS, COMPOSITE MATERIALS. *Current Pos:* ASSOC PROF AEROSPACE STRUCT, DEPT APPL MECH, UNIV CALIF, 89- *Personal Data:* b Milwaukee, Wis, Aug 24, 56; m 88, Ellen Pecchia; c Janell & Joel. *Educ:* Univ Wis-Madison, BS, 78; Univ Mich, MS, 80; Univ Calif, Los Angeles, PhD(aerospace eng), 86. *Honors & Awards:* Aerospace Struct & Mat Award, Am Soc Mech Engrs, 91. *Prof Exp:* Engr, Aerospace Corp, El Segundo, Calif, 80-82; sr engr, TRW Corp, Redondo Beach, Calif, 82-86; asst prof mech eng, Va Polytech Inst, Blacksburg, 86-89. *Concurrent Pos:* Fac fel, Ames Res Ctr, NASA, Moffettfield, Calif, 88; Langley Res Ctr, Hampton, Va, 89 & Newport News Shipbuilding, San Diego, Calif, 90. *Mem:* Am Inst Aeronaut & Astronaut; Am Soc Mech Engrs; Am Helicopter Soc. *Res:* Structural dynamic and aeroelastic analysis of advanced composite helicopter, tilt-rotor, and turbo-propeller blades; hybrid composite materials that have reduced vibration behavior using passive and/or active techniques; author of various publications. *Mailing Add:* Dept Appl Mech & Eng Sci Univ Calif San Diego CA 92093-0085

KOSNETT, VERDA DOGULU, INTERNET-BASED EMERGING TECHNOLOGIES, INTELLIGENT SYSTEMS. *Current Pos:* CHIEF SCIENTIST, COMPUT DATA SYSTS INC, 96- *Personal Data:* b Ankara, Turkey, Jan 30, 60; US citizen; m 85, Philip Scott; c Alexander K & Nicole A. *Educ:* Gazi Univ, BS, 81; George Washington Univ, MS, 89. *Prof Exp:* Res scientist, Intellitek, 88-89; instr comput sci, Cent Tex Col, 90-91; instr bus applns & comput, Nanzan Univ, Japan, 91-92. *Concurrent Pos:* Instr artificial intel, Trident Col, 91-92. *Res:* Development of advance search algorithms; design of internet-based security systems/transactions systems. *Mailing Add:* Comput Data Systs Inc 1 Curie Ct Rockville MD 20850. *Fax:* 301-921-1004; *E-Mail:* verda.kosnett@cdsi.com, verda.kosnett@ncts.navy.mil

KOSOW, DAVID PHILLIP, ENZYMOLOGY, BLOOD COAGULATION. *Current Pos:* DIR TECH SERV, BAXTER HEALTHCARE, 91- *Personal Data:* b Jersey City, NJ, Mar 15, 36; m 58; c 2. *Educ:* Antioch Col, BS, 58; Va Polytech Inst, MS, 60, PhD(biochem & nutrit), 62. *Prof Exp:* Asst prof biochem, Va Polytech Inst, 62-63; Am Cancer Soc fel, Oak Ridge Nat Lab, 63-65; neurochemist, Philadelphia Gen Hosp, 65-66; res assoc, Inst Cancer Res, 66-70, sr res assoc, 70-73; res scientist, Am Red Cross Blood Serv, 73-77, sr res scientist, 77-81, asst dir, 81-84, coordr res & develop, 85-91. *Concurrent Pos:* Fel, Fogarty Int Ctr, Oxford, UK, 80-81; adj assoc prof, Dept Biol, Cath Univ Am, 84-87. *Mem:* Am Soc Biol Chemists; Am Chem Soc; Sigma Xi; Int Soc Thrombosis & Haemostasis. *Res:* Regulation and mechanism of plasma coagulation factors; development of blood plasma derivatives for clinical use; inactivation of viruses in plasma derivatives. *Mailing Add:* 525 N Canyon Blvd Monrovia CA 91016. *Fax:* 818-507-8635

KOSOWER, EDWARD MALCOLM, BIOPHYSICAL ORGANIC CHEMISTRY. *Current Pos:* STAFF MEM, DEPT CHEM, TEL-AVIV UNIV, ISRAEL. *Personal Data:* b Brooklyn, NY, Feb 2, 29; m 61, Nechama Sternschuss; c David A & Daria C. *Educ:* Mass Inst Technol, SB, 48; Univ Calif, Los Angeles, PhD(chem), 52. *Honors & Awards:* Weizmann Prize, 77; Kolthoff Award, 84; Lemburg Lectr, Australian Acad Sci, 91; Rothschild Prize, 96. *Prof Exp:* NIH res fel org chem, Univ Basel, 52-53 & Harvard Univ, 53-54; asst prof chem, Lehigh Univ, 54-56; from instr to asst prof, Univ Wis, 56-61; from assoc prof to prof chem, State Univ NY, Stony Brook, 61-72, adj prof, 72- *Concurrent Pos:* Alfred P Sloan fel, 60-64; NSF fel, Weizmann Inst Sci, Israel, 68-69; prof, Tel-Aviv Univ, 72-; John Simon Guggenheim fel, 77-78; vis prof, Univ Calif, San Diego, 77, Univ Calif, Berkeley, 78, Kyoto, Japan, 78, Mass Inst Technol, 83 & Bologna, Italy, 87. *Mem:* Am Chem Soc; Royal Soc Chem; Am Soc Biochem; Soc Neurosci; Israel Chem Soc; fel AAAS. *Res:* Charge-transfer spectra; pyridinium ion chemistry; solvent effects on spectra; stable free radicals; molecular medicine; neurophysiology; glutathione in chemistry, biochemistry, biology and medicine; fluorescence mechanisms; membrane mobility agents; mechanism of cell fusion; bimanes (diazabicyclo(3.3.0) octadienediones); sodium channel and acetylcholine receptor models; mechanism of fast intramolecular electron transfers; molecular basis learning and memory. *Mailing Add:* Dept Chem Tel Aviv Univ Ramat-Aviv Tel Aviv 69978 Israel. *Fax:* 972-3-6409293; *E-Mail:* kosower@chemsq6.tau.a.il

KOSOWER, NECHAMA S, CELLULAR BIOCHEMISTRY, DIFFERENTIATION & AGING. *Current Pos:* assoc prof, 72-79, chmn, Dept Human Genetics, 86-90, PROF HUMAN GENETICS, SACKLER SCH MED, TEL AVIV UNIV, 79- *Personal Data:* b Tel Aviv, Israel, Apr 27, 28; US & Israeli citizen; m 61, Edward M; c David A & Daria (Inbar). *Educ:* Univ Geneva, BS, 52; Hebrew Univ, Jerusalem, MD, 57. *Honors & Awards:* Weizmann Prize, Tel Aviv Munic, 77. *Prof Exp:* Residency, Tel-Hashomer Hosp, Israel, 57-58; resident & fel, Albert Einstein Col Med, NY, 58-60, res assoc med, 61-67, asst prof, 67-70, assoc prof, 70-72; postdoctoral fel, Univ Wis, 60-61. *Concurrent Pos:* Asst, assoc & attend physician, Bronx Munic Hosp Ctr, 67-72; Career appointment award, NIH, 68-73; genetic counr, Inst Genetics, Tel-Hashomer, Israel, 73-77; vis assoc prof med, Sch Med, Univ Calif, San Diego, 77-78; mem, Nat Bioethics Comt, Ministry Health, Israel, 80-83. *Mem:* Am Soc Clin Invest; Am Soc Hemat; Am Soc Human Genetics; Israeli Soc Cell Biol; Israeli Soc Hemat; Israeli Soc Biol Psychiat. *Res:* Cell differentiation and aging; genetics of schizophrenia; calpain-calpastatin system. *Mailing Add:* Sackler Sch Med Tel Aviv Univ Tel Aviv 69978 Israel. *Fax:* 972-6409900; *E-Mail:* nkosower@ccsg.tau.ac.il

KOSOWSKY, DAVID I, HEALTH SCIENCES, ELECTRONICS. *Current Pos:* PRES, DAMON CORP, 61-, CHMN & CHIEF EXEC OFFICER, 83- *Personal Data:* b New York, NY, Feb 27, 30; c 3. *Educ:* City Col New York, BEE, 51; Mass Inst Technol, SM, 52, ScD(network theory), 55. *Prof Exp:* Res asst & staff mem, Res Lab Electronics, Mass Inst Technol, 51-55; dir crystal div, Hermes Electronics Co, 55-60; vpres, Itek Electro-Prod Co, 60-61. *Concurrent Pos:* Trustee, New Eng Aquarium, 68- & Univ Hosp Boston, 70-; vchmn, Childrens Hosp Med Ctr, 76-83, chmn, 83. *Mem:* Inst Elec & Electronics Engrs; Sigma Xi; AAAS; NY Acad Sci. *Res:* Network theory; statistical theory of communication; crystal filters; voltage controlled crystal oscillators; spectrum analyzers; health service delivery systems; medical and electronic instrumentation. *Mailing Add:* 403D Dedham St Newton MA 02159-3300

KOSS, DONALD A, METALLURGY. *Current Pos:* PROF METALS SCI & ENG & CHMN DEPT, PA STATE UNIV, 86- *Personal Data:* b Dodge Co, Minn; m 64; c 3. *Educ:* Univ Minn, BS, 60; Yale Univ, MS, 62, PhD(metall), 65. *Prof Exp:* Res assoc, Pratt & Whitney Aircraft, 65-70; from assoc prof to prof metall eng, Mich Technol Univ, 70-85. *Concurrent Pos:* NSF fel, Los Alamos Nat Lab, 78-79. *Mem:* Am Soc Metals; Metall Soc; Mat Res Soc. *Res:* Processing, deformation, and fracture of high performance alloys. *Mailing Add:* 1374 Deerfield Dr State College PA 16803

KOSS, LEOPOLD GEORGE, PATHOLOGY, CYTOLOGY. *Current Pos:* prof, 73-92, EMER PROF PATH, ALBERT EINSTEIN COL MED, 93-; EMER CHMN, DEPT PATH, MONTE FIORE HOSP, 93- *Personal Data:* b Danzig, Poland, Oct 2, 20; nat US; m; c 3. *Educ:* Univ Bern, MD, 46. *Honors & Awards:* Wien Award, 61; Goldblatt Award, 62; Papanicolaou Award, Am Soc Cytol, 66; Stewart Award, 84; Vandenberge-Hill Award, 84. *Prof Exp:* Asst path, St Gallen, Switz, 47 & Long Island Col Med, 49; instr, Col Med, State Univ NY Downstate Med Ctr, 50-52; from assoc dir to dir cytol, Mem Hosp Cancer & Allied Dis, 52-60, from asst attend pathologist to assoc attend pathologist, 53-60, chief cytol serv & attend pathologist, 60-70; prof path, Jefferson Med Col, 70-73; chmn, Dept Path, Montefiore Hosp, 73-92. *Concurrent Pos:* From asst to assoc, Sloan-Kettering Inst, 53-60, head secy cytopath, 60-70; from asst prof to assoc prof, Sloan-Kettering Div, Med Col, Cornell Univ, 54-70; vis pathologist, James Ewing Hosp, 60-68; consult, NY State Dept Health, 62-; pathologist-in-chief, Sinai Hosp Baltimore, Inc, 70-73; mem, Ger Acad Sci, 89. *Mem:* Fel Am Soc Clin Pathologists; Am Asn Pathologists & Bacteriologists; Am Soc Cytol (pres, 62); fel Col Am Path; Int Acad Path; fel Int Acad Cytol; Soc Surg Oncol. *Res:* Cytology and pathology of cancer. *Mailing Add:* Montefiore Hosp & Med Ctr 111 E 210th St Bronx NY 10467-2490. *Fax:* 718-515-5315

KOSS, MICHAEL CAMPBELL, PHARMACOLOGY. *Current Pos:* From asst to assoc prof, 71-81, PROF PHARMACOL, COL MED, UNIV OKLA, 81- *Personal Data:* b Ann Arbor, Mich, Sept 24, 40. *Educ:* NY Univ, BA, 66; Columbia Univ, PhD(pharmacol), 71. *Mem:* Asn Res Vision & Ophthal; Soc Neurosci; Am Soc Pharmacol & Exp Therapeut; Sigma Xi. *Res:* Neuropharmacology; neurophysiology; brain stem regulatory mechanisms; autonomic nervous system. *Mailing Add:* Dept Pharmacol Univ Okla PO Box 26901 Oklahoma City OK 73190-0901

KOSS, PETER, METALLURGY. *Current Pos:* head, Dept Metall, 63-81, TECH SCI MANAGING DIR, AUSTRIAN RES CTR, 81- *Personal Data:* b Vienna, Austria, Mar 21, 32; m 56, Elsa Vedra; c Michael, Christoph & Stephan. *Educ:* Univ Vienna, PhD, 58. *Honors & Awards:* Hon Merit Silver, Austrian Govt, 69. *Prof Exp:* Res fel, Mass Inst Technol, 59. *Concurrent Pos:* Staff, Atomics Int, Calif, 59; prof, Univ Vienna, 81. *Mem:* Austrian Phys Soc; Int Plansee Soc Power Metall; Chem Phys Soc. *Mailing Add:* Osterreiches Forschungszentruti Seibersdorf GmbH 2444 Seibersdorf Vienna Kramergasse 1 A-1010 Austria

KOSS, VALERY ALEXANDER, MATHEMATICAL PHYSICS. *Current Pos:* Sr scientist, 82-88, CONSULT SCIENTIST, TECH CTR, BOC GROUP, INC, 88- *Personal Data:* b Dnepropetrovsk, USSR, Aug 4, 41; US citizen; m 67; c 1. *Educ:* Leningrad Polytech Inst, USSR, MS, 64; Phys Tech Inst, Leningrad, PhD(math physics), 72. *Res:* Modeling of various phenomena pertaining to chemistry, vacuum technologies and optics. *Mailing Add:* 1056 Carteret Rd Bridgewater NJ 08807

KOSSIAKOFF, ALEXANDER, PHYSICAL CHEMISTRY, SYSTEM ENGINEERING. *Current Pos:* physicist, Appl Physics Lab, Johns Hopkins Univ, 46-48, asst dir, 48-61, assoc dir, 61-66, dep dir, 66-69, dir, 69-80, EMER DIR & CHIEF SCIENTIST, APPL PHYSICS LAB, JOHNS HOPKINS UNIV, 80-, CHAIR, TECH MGT, SCH ENG, 80- *Personal Data:* b St Petersburg, Russia, June 26, 14; US citizen; m 39, Arabelle Davies; c Tanya A (Schmieler) & Anthony A. *Educ:* Calif Inst Technol, BS, 36; Johns Hopkins Univ, PhD(chem), 38. *Prof Exp:* Fel, Calif Inst Technol, 38-39; instr chem, Cath Univ, 39-42; tech aide, Nat Defense Res Comt, 42-43; dep dir res, Allegheny Ballistics Lab, George Washington Univ, 44-46. *Concurrent Pos:* Consult tech apl panel aeronaut, Defense Dept, 54-58; mem panel launching & handling comt guided missiles, Res & Develop Bd, 48-52; Carmrand comt, Nat Planning Asn, 62-73; mem Gov's Sci Adv Coun, 79- *Mem:* Fel Am Inst Chemists; AAAS. *Res:* Prediction and determination of molecular structure; relation between molecular structure and physical and chemical properties; mechanism of chemical reactions; mechanism of neural processes; administration of research; computer languages; computer aided instruction for handicapped children; technical management. *Mailing Add:* 120 Haviland Mill Rd Brookeville MD 20833. *E-Mail:* ak@aplexus.jhuapl.edu

KOSSLER, WILLIAM JOHN, PHYSICS. *Current Pos:* from asst prof to assoc prof, 69-78, PROF PHYSICS, COL WILLIAM & MARY, 78- *Personal Data:* b Charleston, SC, Mar 26, 37; m 61, Margaret O'Neil; c Neil, William & Paul. *Educ:* Mass Inst Technol, BS, 59; Princeton Univ, PhD(physics), 64. *Prof Exp:* Staff mem nuclear physics, Mass Inst Technol, 64-66, asst prof physics, 66-69. *Mem:* Am Phys Soc. *Res:* Experimental nuclear and solid state physics; use of miron spin rotation for the study of superconductors and magnetic systems. *Mailing Add:* Dept Physics Col William & Mary Williamsburg VA 23187

KOSSMANN, CHARLES EDWARD, medicine; deceased, see previous edition for last biography

KOSSOR, STEVEN ALBERT, CLINICAL PSYCHOLOGY, EDUCATIONAL RESTRUCTURING-REFORM. *Current Pos:* Clin psychologist, Devereuk Found, 77-92, CLIN PSYCHOLOGIST, PVT PRACT, 81- & STATE OF PA, 92- *Personal Data:* b Plainfield, NJ, Nov 29, 54; m 80, Kathleen Zampana; c Nicholas & Jaclyn. *Educ:* Montclair State Col, BA, 75; Fairleigh Dickinson Univ, MA, 77. *Mem:* Am Psychol Asn. *Res:* Exposing and stopping the illicit, inappropriate use of psychological methods in American public schools and the reform of the American education system to renew its commitment to focus on honest academic and vocational development. *Mailing Add:* W Kings Hwy Coatesville PA 19320. *Fax:* 610-383-1432

KOSSOY, AARON DAVID, ORGANIC CHEMISTRY, ANALYTICAL CHEMISTRY. *Current Pos:* sr anal chemist, 69-80, RES SCIENTIST, ELI LILLY RES LABS, 80- *Personal Data:* b New York, NY, Aug 19, 36; m 70, Joan L Pesikoff. *Educ:* City Col New York, BS, 58; Polytech Inst Brooklyn, PhD(org chem), 66. *Prof Exp:* Analytical chemist, Trubek Labs, Inc, 58-61; fel chem, Univ Calif, Berkeley, 66-69. *Mem:* Am Chem Soc; Sigma Xi. *Res:* Chemical and physical properties of organic compounds; spectroscopic characterization of organic compounds; organic structure determination; correlation of physical properties of organic compounds with biological activities. *Mailing Add:* 7627 Almaden Ct Indianapolis IN 46278. *Fax:* 317-276-5281

KOSSUTH, SUSAN, PLANT PHYSIOLOGY, GENETICS. *Current Pos:* PROJ LEADER, US FOREST SERV, 79- *Personal Data:* b Boston, Mass, Apr 28, 46. *Educ:* Colo State Univ, BS, 68, MS, 71; Yale Univ, MS, 72, MPhil, 73, PhD(tree physiol-genetics), 74. *Prof Exp:* Consult, Fla Citrus Comn, 74-76; asst prof tree physiol, Univ Ark, 76-77; asst res scientist, Univ Fla, 77-78. *Concurrent Pos:* Adj asst prof, Univ Fla, 74-76; prin investr, Weyerhaeuser Corp, Eli-Lilly Co, Ark Kraft Co, Southern Regional Educ Bd, 76; co-prin investr, Fla Citrus Comn, 77-79. *Mem:* Am Soc Plant Physiol; Sigma Xi; Soc Am Foresters; Am Forestry Asn; Plant Growth Regulator Soc Am. *Res:* Reproductive physiology and breeding and improvement of Southern pines; vegetative propagation of pines; flowering in pines; early genetic testing of pines; effects of ultraviolet light on plants. *Mailing Add:* Fruit Crops Dept 1119 HS-PP Bldg Univ Fla Gainesville FL 32611

KOSTANT, BERTRAM, GEOMETRIC QUANTIZATION. *Current Pos:* prof, 63-93, EMER PROF MATH, MASS INST TECHNOL, 93- *Personal Data:* b New York, NY, May 24, 28; m 49, 68; c 5. *Educ:* Purdue Univ, BS, 50; Univ Chicago, MS, 51, PhD(math), 54. *Hon Degrees:* DSc, Purdue Univ, 97. *Prof Exp:* NSF fel, Inst Advan Study, 53-54, mem, 54-56; from asst prof to prof math, Univ Calif, Berkeley, 56-63. *Concurrent Pos:* Higgins lectr, Princeton Univ, 55-56; mem, Miller Inst Basic Res, 58-59; Guggenheim fel, Paris, France, 59-60; prof, Oxford Univ, Tel Aviv Univ & Paris, France, 74-75, 81-82. *Mem:* Nat Acad Sci; Am Acad Arts & Sci; Am Math Soc. *Res:* Operator theory; Lie groups; representation theory; differential geometry; mathematical physics. *Mailing Add:* Dept Math Mass Inst Technol Cambridge MA 02139. *E-Mail:* kostant@math.mit.edu

KOSTELNICEK, RICHARD J, ELECTRICAL ENGINEERING. *Current Pos:* SR RES ASSOC, ESSO PROD RES CO, 69- *Personal Data:* b Chicago, Ill, May 16, 42; m 67. *Educ:* Univ Ill, Urbana, BS, 64, MS, 65, PhD(elec eng), 69. *Mem:* AAAS; Soc Explor Geophys; Inst Elec & Electronics Engrs. *Res:* Antennas; plasma physics; wave propagation in inhomogeneous media; geoscience. *Mailing Add:* 609 Bayou Crest Dr Dickinson TX 77539

KOSTENBAUDER, HARRY BARR, PHARMACY. *Current Pos:* PROF PHARM & ASSOC DEAN RES, COL PHARM, UNIV KY, 68- *Personal Data:* b Danville, Pa, Apr 9, 29. *Educ:* Phila Col Pharm, BSc, 51; Temple Univ, MSc, 53; Univ Wis, PhD(pharm), 56. *Prof Exp:* Asst pharm, Temple Univ, 51-53 & Univ Wis, 55; from asst prof to prof, Temple Univ, 56-68. *Mem:* Am Chem Soc; Am Pharmaceut Asn; NY Acad Sci; fel Acad Pharmaceut Sci (pres, 71-72); fel Am Asn Pharmaceut Scientists. *Res:* Drug binding by macromolecules; drug stability; pharmacokinetics. *Mailing Add:* 727 Cooper Dr Lexington KY 40502

KOSTER, DAVID F, PHYSICAL CHEMISTRY, SPECTROSCOPY. *Current Pos:* from asst prof to assoc prof 67-81, PROF CHEM, SOUTHERN ILL UNIV, CARBONDALE, 81- *Personal Data:* b Houston, Tex, Nov 3, 36; m 59, Dolores Ozuna; c 5. *Educ:* St Thomas Univ, BA, 59; Tex A&M Univ, MS, 63, PhD(chem), 65. *Prof Exp:* Chemist, Diamond Alkali Co, 59-60; res fel, Mellon Inst, 64-67. *Concurrent Pos:* Asst chair, Dept Chem & Biochem, Southern Ill Univ, Carbondale. *Mem:* Am Chem Soc; Sigma Xi; Nat Sci Teachers Asn. *Res:* Chemistry. *Mailing Add:* Dept Chem Southern Ill Univ Carbondale IL 62901. *E-Mail:* koster@chem.siu.edu

KOSTER, GEORGE FRED, PHYSICS. *Current Pos:* Res assoc, Mass Inst Technol, 51-52, Lincoln Lab, 52-55, from asst prof to assoc prof, 56-64, PROF PHYSICS, MASS INST TECHNOL, 64- *Personal Data:* b New York, NY, Apr 9, 27; m 51; c 3. *Educ:* Mass Inst Technol, SB, 48, PhD(physics), 51. *Concurrent Pos:* Guggenheim fel, 55-56. *Mem:* Am Phys Soc. *Res:* Theoretical physics including theory of solids and molecular theory. *Mailing Add:* Dept Physics Mass Inst Technol Cambridge MA 02139

KOSTER, JEAN NICOLAS, THERMOFLUID MECHANICS & SOLIDIFICATION OF METALLIC MELTS. *Current Pos:* res asst, 85-86, asst prof, 85-94, ASSOC PROF, UNIV COLO, 94- *Educ:* Univ Karlsruhe, Ger, Dr-Ing(fluid mech), 80. *Prof Exp:* Postdoctorate res asst, Univ Utah, 80-82; res scientist, Nuclear Res Ctr, Karlsruhe, 82-84; vis res scientist, Lewis Res Ctr, NASA, 84-85. *Res:* Visualization capabilities to study fluid mechanics and heat transfer-convective flow-in opaque metallic melts and alloys. *Mailing Add:* 872 Welsh Ct Louisville CO 80027. *Fax:* 303-492-7881

KOSTER, ROBERT ALLEN, ORGANIC CHEMISTRY. *Current Pos:* Res chemist, Dow Chem USA, 68-70, proj leader, Org Chem Prod Res, 70-80, res leader, Styrene Plastics, 80-82, RES ASSOC, DOW CHEM USA, 82- *Personal Data:* b Grand Rapids, Mich, July 12, 41; m 63, Judith Vonk; c Kimberly & Tamara. *Educ:* Hope Col, AB, 63; Univ Mich, Ann Arbor, MS, 65, PhD(chem), 68. *Mem:* Soc Plastics Engrs. *Res:* Carbonium ion chemistry; reaction mechanisms via kinetic studies; process development on fine organic chemicals; chemistry of 2.2.1 bicyclic systems; polymer process development; materials science. *Mailing Add:* 50 Wiley Lane Midland MI 48640. *E-Mail:* rakoster@dow.com

KOSTER, RUDOLF, PHARMACOLOGY. *Current Pos:* RETIRED. *Educ:* State Univ Iowa, PhD(embryol & endocrinol), 41. *Prof Exp:* Sr pharmacologist, Burroughs Wellcome Co, Research Triangle Park, NC, 53-78. *Mailing Add:* 232 Hayes Rd Chapel Hill NC 27514-5633

KOSTER, W(ILLIAM) P(FEIFFER), METALLURGICAL ENGINEERING. *Current Pos:* Staff mem, Metcut Res Assoc Inc, 53-57, vpres, 57-78, pres, 78-92, DIR METALL ENG, METCUT RES ASSOC INC, 57-, CHMN, 92- *Personal Data:* b Fords, NJ, Apr 18, 29; m 54, Marcia Kyrlach; c Kenneth, Frank, Barrett & James. *Educ:* Rutgers Univ, BS, 50; Univ Cincinnati, MS, 51, PhD(metall eng), 53. *Hon Degrees:* LHD, Cincinnati Tech Col, 70. *Honors & Awards:* Gold Medal, Soc Mfg Engrs. *Mem:* Fel Am Soc Metals; fel Soc Adv Mat & Process Eng; fel Soc Mfg Eng. *Res:* Properties of materials surfaces. *Mailing Add:* Metcut Res Inc 3980 Rosslyn Dr Cincinnati OH 45209-1196. *Fax:* 513-271-9511

KOSTER, WILLIAM HENRY, SYNTHETIC ORGANIC CHEMISTRY. *Current Pos:* vpres, Div Chem, 90-91, VPRES, CARDIOVASC DRUG DISCOVERY, BRISTOL-MYERS SQUIBB PHARM RES INST, PRINCETON, NJ, 91- *Personal Data:* b Teaneck, NJ, Apr 20, 44; m 68; c 1. *Educ:* Colby Col, BA, 66; Tufts Univ, PhD(chem), 72. *Honors & Awards:* Thomas Alva Edison Award, 92. *Prof Exp:* Fel, Squibb Inst Med Res, 71-72, res investr, 72-77, sr res investr, 77-80, group leader synthetic antibact agents & nat prods, 80-83, sect head, 83-84, dir, dept chem, Infectious & Metabolic Dis, 84-87, exec dir, 87-90. *Mem:* Am Chem Soc; Am Heart Asn; AAAS; NY Acad Sci; Fedn Am Soc Exp Biol. *Res:* Synthetic organic chemistry; bioorganic chemistry; mechanism-based design of new antibacterials/ antifungals; antiviral agents; cardiovascular agents and inhibitors of cholesterol biosynthesis; natural products isolation; structure elucidation; semi-synthetic modification; research administration. *Mailing Add:* Bristol-Myers Squibb PO Box 4000 Princeton NJ 08543-4000. *Fax:* 609-252-6964

KOSTER VAN GROOS, AUGUST FERDINAND, GEOCHEMISTRY. *Current Pos:* asst prof, 70-75, ASSOC PROF GEOL SCI, UNIV ILL, CHICAGO CIRCLE, 75- *Personal Data:* b Leeuwarden, Neth, Jan 9, 38; m 71. *Educ:* Univ Leiden, BSc, 58, MS, 62, PhD(exp petrol), 66. *Prof Exp:* Res assoc, Goddard Space Flight Ctr, NASA, 66-68; asst prof petrol, State Univ Utrecht, 68-70. *Mem:* AAAS. *Res:* Genesis of carbonatite, experimental work in synthetic systems containing carbon dioxide and water at elevated pressure and temperature; salt-silicate-water systems; studies of liquid immiscibility occurring in rocks; partitioning of minor elements in multi- phase systems; mantle metapomatsm crystal development. *Mailing Add:* Dept Geol Sci-MC 186 Univ Ill 845 W Taylor St Chicago IL 60607

KOSTIC, NENAD M, BIOINORGANIC CHEMISTRY, ORGANOMETALLIC CHEMISTRY. *Current Pos:* asst prof chem, 84-89, assoc prof chem & adj assoc prof biochem, 89-94, PROF CHEM & ADJ PROF BIOCHEM, IOWA STATE UNIV, 94- *Personal Data:* b Belgrade, Yugoslavia, Nov 18, 52; m 76, Dragana Dimitrijevic; c Dimitrije N & Bogdan N. *Educ:* Univ Belgrade, Yugoslavia, dipl, 76; Univ Wis-Madison, PhD(inorg chem), 82. *Honors & Awards:* Presidential Young Investr Award, NSF, 88. *Prof Exp:* Teaching & res asst, Univ Wis-Mad, 78-82; res fel chem, Calif Inst Technol, 82-84. *Concurrent Pos:* Sloan res fel, A P Sloan Found, 91. *Mem:* Am Chem Soc; Serbian Chem Soc. *Res:* Bioinorganic chemistry; stereochemistry; electron-transfer reactions. *Mailing Add:* Dept Chem Iowa State Univ Ames IA 50011

KOSTINER, EDWARD S, SOLID STATE CHEMISTRY. *Current Pos:* assoc prof, 72-77, head dept, 85-93, PROF CHEM, UNIV CONN, 77- *Personal Data:* b New York, NY, Feb 25, 40; m 60; c 2. *Educ:* Tufts Univ, BS, 60; Polytech Inst Brooklyn, PhD(inorg chem), 66. *Prof Exp:* Asst prof, Cornell Univ, 66-72. *Concurrent Pos:* Chair, Coun Comt Econ & Prof Affairs & mem gov bd, Coun for Chem Res, Am Chem Soc. *Mem:* Am Chem Soc; NY Acad Sci; Am Asn Crystal Growth; Mineral Soc Am; Am Crystallog Asn. *Res:* Crystal growth; crystal and structural chemistry of apatites and other halophosphates and orthophosphates; Mossbauer effect spectroscopy. *Mailing Add:* Dept Chem Univ Conn U-60 Storrs CT 06269-4060. *Fax:* 860-486-2981; *E-Mail:* chemadm3@uconnvm.uconn.edu

KOSTISHACK, DANIEL F(RANK), ELECTRICAL ENGINEERING, SOLID STATE PHYSICS. *Current Pos:* mem res staff, 67-81, GROUP LEADER, LINCOLN LAB, MASS INST TECHNOL, 81- *Personal Data:* b Pittsburgh, Pa, Mar 25, 40; m 66; c 2. *Educ:* Carnegie Inst Technol, BS, 63, MS, 65; Carnegie-Mellon Univ, PhD(elec eng), 68. *Res:* Solid-state and high frequency devices and circuits; solid-state imaging devices and electro-optical systems. *Mailing Add:* Lincoln Lab MS S3-3673 Mass Inst Technol 244 Wood St Lexington MA 02173-9108

KOSTIUK, THEODOR, SPACE PHYSICS. *Current Pos:* Nat Acad Sci resident res assoc, 73-74, space scientist, Infrared Astron Br, 74-83, head Molecular Astrophys Sect, 83-84, SPACE SCIENTIST, PLANETARY SYSTS BR, GODDARD SPACE FLIGHT CTR, NASA, 85- *Personal Data:* b Plauen, Ger, Aug 12, 44; m 70. *Educ:* City Col New York, BS, 66; Syracuse Univ, PhD(physics), 73. *Concurrent Pos:* Discipline leader, Auroral Discipline, Int Jupiter Watch. *Mem:* Am Phys Soc; Optical Soc Am; Soc Photo-Optical Instrument Engrs; AAAS; Am Astron Div Planetary Sci. *Res:* Atmosphere of planets, comets, the sun, stars and the earth's stratosphere using ultra-high resolution infrared spectroscopy; infrared heterodyne spectroscopy; discovery of the first natural laser (carbon dioxide on Mars); molecular spectroscopy; hydrocarbon chemistry on outer planets; global circulation on Mars and Venus; dynamics and planetary oscillations on Jupiter; aurorae and infrared emission on Jupiter. *Mailing Add:* Code 693 NASA Goddard Space Flight Ctr Greenbelt MD 20771

KOSTKOWSKI, HENRY JOHN, SPECTRORADIOMETRY. *Current Pos:* PROPRIETOR SPECTRORADIOMETRY CONSULT, 81- *Personal Data:* b Garwood, NJ, May 16, 26; m 47, 76; c 3. *Educ:* Johns Hopkins Univ, PhD(physics), 54. *Honors & Awards:* Gold Medal Award, US Dept Com, Edward Bennett Rosa Award. *Prof Exp:* Molecular physicist, Nat Inst Stand & Technol, 54-56, physicist high temperature, 56-58, supvry physicist, 58-65, chief radiation thermometry sect, 65-71, chief optical radiation sect, 71-81. *Concurrent Pos:* Consult, Inst Advan Study, 54, 55 & 57. *Mem:* Fel Optical Soc Am. *Res:* Spectroradiometry; optical pyrometry; spectral line intensity measurements; physical optics. *Mailing Add:* 439 Gershwin Dr Charlotte Hall MD 20622

KOSTOFF, MORRIS R, NUCLEAR PHYSICS, ACOUSTICS. *Current Pos:* RETIRED. *Personal Data:* b Jamestown, NDak, Dec 2, 33; m 55, Effie M Whitfield; c Sherrie, Terrie, Matthew, Kristine M & Mark A. *Educ:* Pac Lutheran Univ, BS, 62; Univ Tex, Austin, PhD(physics), 67. *Prof Exp:* Res asst nuclear physics, Ctr Nuclear Studies, Univ Tex, Austin, 63-66; engr-scientist, Sci & Systs Div, Tracor, Inc, 66-70, sr scientist, 70-79, prin scientist, Anal & Appl Res Div, Appl Sci Group, 79-82, dir acoust warfare prof, 82-91. *Concurrent Pos:* Sen Warren G Magnuson Scholarship, 60-61; Nat Defense Educ Act fel, 63-66; asst prof physics, Southwestern Univ, Tex, 71-74. *Mem:* Am Phys Soc. *Res:* Spin polarization measurements for elastic and inelastic proton scattering; systems analysis and simulation of signal processors for sonar systems; propagation of acoustic waves in water medium; operator interactive; realtime computer simulation of state-of-the-art sonar systems for evaluating mission effectiveness in a countermeasure environment. *Mailing Add:* 11513 Juniper Ridge Dr Austin TX 78759-3845

KOSTREVA, DAVID ROBERT, ANESTHESIOLOGY, CARDIOLOGY. *Current Pos:* SR SCIENTIST, PROCTER & GAMBLE PHARMACEUT, 93- *Personal Data:* b Milwaukee, Wis, Aug 14, 45; m 75; c 4. *Educ:* Univ Wis, Milwaukee, Ba, 72; Med Col Wis, MS, 74, PhD(physiol), 76. *Honors & Awards:* Young Cardiovasc Investr Award, 79, NIH, Res Career Develop Award, 82; Henry Pickering Bowditch lectr, 83. *Prof Exp:* Fel, Am Heart Asn, 76-77 & Nat Heart, Lung & Blood Inst, NIH, 77-78; from asst prof to assoc prof physiol & anesthesia, Med Col Wis, 81-93. *Concurrent Pos:* Chmn, Ad Hoc Study Sect, NIMH, 81. *Mem:* Am Physiol Soc; Soc Neurosci; Sigma Xi; Soc Exp Biol & Med; Int Soc Heart Res. *Res:* Neural control of circulation and respiration in adult and fetal dogs, cats and monkeys, rabbits and chickens using afferent and efferent recording techniques and brain and heart mapping studies of visceral reflexes using the carbon-fourteen-deoxyglucose technique; antiarrhythmic and cardiotonic drug development. *Mailing Add:* Procter & Gamble Pharmaceut 10200 Alliance Rd Cincinnati OH 45242. *Fax:* 513-626-6481

KOSTREVA, MICHAEL MARTIN, MATHEMATICS. *Current Pos:* assoc prof, 86-89, PROF MATH, CLEMSON UNIV, 89- *Personal Data:* b Pittsburgh, Pa, May 9, 48; m 71; c 3. *Educ:* Clarion State Col, BA, 71; Rensselaer Polytech Inst, MS, 73, PhD(math), 76. *Prof Exp:* Asst prof math, Univ Maine, Orono, 76-78; res scientist, Gen Motors Res Labs, 78-84; prin mem tech staff, GTE Labs, Inc, 84-86; mem tech staff, Alphatech, Inc, 86. *Concurrent Pos:* Consult, Gen Motors Corp, 87-, Gillette Res Inst, 90-; pres, Systematica Inc, Clemson, 89- *Mem:* Soc Indust & Appl Math; Am Math Soc; Opers Res Soc Am; Math Programming Soc. *Res:* Complementarity theory of mathematical programming, multiple objective programming, game theory, lubrication theory, scheduling, circadian rhythms. *Mailing Add:* Dept Math Sci Clemson Univ Clemson SC 29634

KOSTROUN, VACLAV O, ATOMIC PHYSICS. *Current Pos:* Res assoc & lectr, 68-70, asst prof, 70-77, ASSOC PROF APPL & ENG PHYSICS, CORNELL UNIV, 77- *Personal Data:* b Brasov, Rumania, Dec 30, 38; US citizen; m 63; c 2. *Educ:* Univ Wash, BSc, 61, MSc, 63; Univ Ore, PhD(physics), 68. *Mem:* AAAS; Am Phys Soc. *Res:* Interactions of highly charged ions with atoms at lee V energies; production of low energy, very highly charged ions; theoretical atomic physics. *Mailing Add:* Ward Reactor Lab Cornell Univ Ithaca NY 14853

KOSTRZEWA, RICHARD MICHAEL, DOPAMINE & SEROTONIN NEURAL SYSTEMS. *Current Pos:* assoc prof, 78-84, PROF PHARMACOL, E TENN STATE UNIV, 84- *Personal Data:* b Trenton, NJ, July 22, 43; m 65, Florence Palmer; c Theresa, Richard, Joseph, Maria, Krystyna, Thomas J, John P, Frank, Roseanna & Monica. *Educ:* Philadelphia Col Pharm & Sci, BS, 65, MS, 67; Univ Pa, PhD(pharmacol), 71. *Prof Exp:* Res pharmacologist, Vet Admin Hosp, New Orleans, 71-75; asst prof physiol, La State Univ Med Ctr, New Orleans, 75-78. *Concurrent Pos:* Asst prof pharmacol, Tulane Univ Med Ctr, New Orleans, 74-75; prin investr, NIH grant, 75-81, 91-95, March Dimes grant, 77-79 & Am Parkinson's Dis Asn grant, 77-78; res award, E Tenn State Univ Found, 81; res grant, Scottish Rite Schizophrenia, 89-92, John E Fogarty Int Ctr, 90 & 92; vis prof, Silesian Med Acad, Poland. *Mem:* Am Soc Pharmacol & Exp Therapeut; Neurosci Soc; Int Brain Res Orgn; Soc Toxicol; Fedn Am Socs Exp Therapeut. *Res:* Development of monoaminergic neurons; dopamine receptors and behavior; Parkinson's disease; neurotoxins; psychopharmacology; schizophrenia; tardive dyseinesia; attention deficit hyperactivity disorder. *Mailing Add:* Col Med East Tenn State Univ Johnson City TN 37614-0577. *Fax:* 423-439-5847; *E-Mail:* rmkost@juno.com

KOSTYNIAK, PAUL J, TOXICOLOGY. *Current Pos:* asst prof, 77-84, ASSOC PROF PHARMACOL, STATE UNIV NY, BUFFALO, 84-; DIR TOXICOL RES CTR, 85- *Personal Data:* b Schenectady, NY, April 8, 47; m 70; c 3. *Educ:* St John Fisher Col, BS, 70; Univ Rochester, PhD(toxicol), 75. *Prof Exp:* Fel radiation, biol & biophys, Univ Rochester, 75-77. *Concurrent Pos:* Reviewer, Toxicol & Appl Pharmacol, J Pharmacol & Exp Therapeut, J Appl Toxicol, Archives Biochem Biophys & Toxicol Letters; speaker, Gordon Conf, 87; dipl, Am Bd Toxicol. *Mem:* Soc Toxicol; Sigma Xi; Am Chem Soc; AAAS; NY Acad Sci. *Res:* Toxicology of heavy metals, antidote development and the metabolism and toxicity of organofluroic compounds; mechanisms of metal transport and disposition; role of endogenous thiols in the elimination of toxic metal pollutants; developing new in vitro models of nephrotoxicity and animal models of neurotoxicity; mechanisms of degradation of polymer films. *Mailing Add:* Pharmacol Dept State Univ NY 102 Farber Hall Buffalo NY 14214-3000

KOSTYO, JACK LAWRENCE, PHYSIOLOGY, ENDOCRINOLOGY. *Current Pos:* ASSOC DIR, MICH DIABETES RES & TRAINING CTR, 86- *Personal Data:* b Elyria, Ohio, Oct 1, 31; m 53; c 2. *Educ:* Oberlin Col, AB, 53; Cornell Univ, PhD(zool), 57. *Hon Degrees:* MD, Univ Goteborg, 78. *Honors & Awards:* Ernst Oppenheimer Mem Award, Endocrine Soc, 69. *Prof Exp:* From asst prof to prof physiol, Duke Univ, 59-68; prof physiol & chmn dept, Emory Univ, 68-79; chmn dept, 79-85, prof physiol, Med Sch, Univ Mich, 79- *Concurrent Pos:* Nat Res Coun fel, Harvard Med Sch, 57-59; Lederle med fac award, 61-64; mem endocrinol study sect, NIH, 67-71; chmn educ comt, Am Physiol Soc, 70-76, mem coun, 79-82, rep to coun Acad Socs, Asn Am Med Cols, 81-89, chmn, Coun Endocrinol & Metabolism Sect, 90-91; vis foreign scientist, Swed Med Res Coun, 72; mem physiol test comt, comprehensive part II comt, 86-, Nat Bd Mem Examnr, 74-77; mem Com Med Physiol; Int Union Physiol Sci; ed-in-chief, endocrinol, 78-82; pres, Asn Chmn Dept Physiol, 79-80; sect ed, Endocrinol, Ann Rev Physiol, 82-86; mem sci adv comt, Searle Scholars Prog, 82-85; mem admin bd, Coun Acad Socs, Am Asn Med Cols, 83-86. *Mem:* Am Physiol Soc; Endocrine Soc; Sigma Xi; Am Diabetes Asn. *Res:* Mechanism of action of pituitary growth hormone; relationship between structure and functions of growth hormone; nature of growth hormone in blood. *Mailing Add:* Dept Physiol Univ Mich Med Sch 1331 E Ann St Ann Arbor MI 48109-0580

KOSTYRKO, GEORGE JURIJ, CIVIL ENGINEERING. *Current Pos:* ASSOC PROF CIVIL ENG, SACRAMENTO STATE COL, 68-, HEAD PROG APPL MECH, 71- *Personal Data:* b Ukraine, May 9, 37; US citizen. *Educ:* City Col New York, BChE, 57; Univ Mich, Ann Arbor, MSE, 58; Sacramento State Col, MS, 63; Univ Calif, Davis, PhD(civil eng), 69. *Prof Exp:* Develop engr, Air Prod Inc, Pa, 57; Aerojet-Gen Corp, Calif, 58-61, sr res engr, 61-68. *Concurrent Pos:* NSF grant, Sacramento State Col, 71-72. *Mem:* Sigma Xi. *Res:* Detection of static and dynamic stresses in solids and structures by means of acoustic wave propagation, holography and photoelasticity. *Mailing Add:* 1721 Cathay Way Sacramento CA 95864

KOSTYU, DONNA D, IMMUNOLOGY. *Current Pos:* Res assoc, 81-86, ASST RES PROF IMMUNOL, SCH MED, DUKE UNIV, 86- *Personal Data:* b Ashtabula, Ohio, Oct 17, 47; m 70; c 2. *Educ:* Duke Univ, PhD(microbiol & immunol), 79. *Mem:* Am Asn Immunologists; Am Soc Histocompatibility & Immunogenetics. *Res:* Research focuses on the immunogenetics of the HLA supergene, the human major histocompatibility complex. *Mailing Add:* Dept Microbiol & Immunol Duke Univ Med Ctr Box 3010 Durham NC 27710-0001

KOSZALKA, THOMAS R, BIOCHEMISTRY. *Current Pos:* assoc prof radiol, 65-70, assoc prof biochem, 67-75, PROF RADIOL, JEFFERSON MED COL, 70-, PROF BIOCHEM, 75-, PROF PEDIAT, 87- *Personal Data:* b Rochester, NY, Jan 25, 27; m 54; c 3. *Educ:* Univ Rochester, BA, 50, PhD, 59. *Prof Exp:* From instr to asst prof biochem, Sch Med & Dent, Univ Rochester, 59-65. *Concurrent Pos:* Assoc dir, Eleanor Roosevelt Res Labs & dir, Harry Bock Labs, 65- *Res:* Developmental biochemistry; teratology. *Mailing Add:* 934 Irvin Rd Huntingdon Valley PA 19006

KOSZIL, LOUIS A, ELECTRO-OPTICAL COMPONENTS. *Current Pos:* sr tech aide, AT&T Bell Labs, 70-73, assoc mem tech staff, 73-80, mem tech staff, 80-88, DISTINGUISHED MEM TECH STAFF, AT&T BELL LABS, 88- *Personal Data:* b Bethlehem, Pa, Oct 7, 44; m 70, Lorraine F; c Laura Lyn & Lacene Fay. *Educ:* Moravian Col, BS, 70. *Honors & Awards:* Eng Excellence Award, Optical Soc Am, 92. *Res:* Electro-optical components; fabrication processes; fundamental semiconductor designs; applicable transmission systems; fundamental semiconductor designs; electro-optical components including fabrication processes; author of numerous articles; awarded 17 US and 5 European patents. *Mailing Add:* AT&T Bell Res Lab 600 Mountain Ave New Providence NJ 07974-2008

KOSZTARAB, MICHAEL, ENTOMOLOGY, INSECT TAXONOMY. *Current Pos:* from assoc prof to prof entom, 62-92, dir, Ctr Systs Collections, 87-91, EMER PROF ENTOM, VA POLYTECH INST & STATE UNIV, 92-; FOUNDING DIR, VA MUS NATURAL HIST, VA TECH, 90- *Personal Data:* b Bucharest, Romania, July 7, 27; US citizen; m 53, Matilda Pinter; c Eva. *Educ:* Hungarian Univ Agr Sci, HortE, 51; Ohio State Univ, PhD(entom), 62. *Hon Degrees:* Dr, Univ Haiti, Budapest, 94. *Prof Exp:* Exten asst, Hungarian State Bur Plant Protection, 47-50; asst prof hort entom, Hungarian Univ Agr Sci, 51-56; consult entomologist, Insect Control & Res Inc, Md, 57-58, asst dir res, 59-60. *Concurrent Pos:* chmn, Planning Comt, Nat Biol Surv Proj, 84-88; pres, Va Natural History Soc, 92-93; external mem, Hungarian Acad Sci, Budapest, 95. *Mem:* Nat Mem Entom Soc Am; Am Syst Collections; hon mem Hungarian Entom Soc. *Res:* Systematics and biology of scale insects (Homoptera Coccoidea) in North America and Europe; author of 165 publications including three books. *Mailing Add:* Dept Entom Va Polytech Inst & State Univ Blacksburg VA 24061-0319. *E-Mail:* idlab@vt.edu

KOT, PETER ALOYSIUS, CARDIOVASCULAR PHYSIOLOGY. *Current Pos:* Intern med, Med Ctr, Georgetown Univ, 57-58, resident, 58-60, instr physiol, 60-64, instr med, 63-64, from asst prof to assoc prof physiol, 64-76, asst prof med, 64-69, PROF PHYSIOL, MED SCH, GEORGETOWN UNIV, 76- *Personal Data:* b Stanley, Wis, Jan 13, 32; m 58; c 6. *Educ:* Marquette Univ, MS, 56, MD, 57. *Concurrent Pos:* Fel coun circulation, Am Heart Asn, 63, investr, 64-69; lectr physiol, US Naval Dent Sch, Bethesda, Md, 66-71; lectr, US Army Inst Dent Res, 68-71. *Mem:* AAAS; Am Fedn Clin Res; Am Physiol Soc; Soc Exp Biol & Med; Am Heart Asn. *Res:* Cardiovascular physiology, especially hemodynamic effects of the prostaglandins and their precursors; radiation injury. *Mailing Add:* Dept Physiol/Biophys Georgetown Univ Med Sch 3900 Reservoir Rd NW Washington DC 20007

KOT, RICHARD ANTHONY, METALLURGY, MATERIALS SCIENCE. *Current Pos:* MGR MAT TECH, RES & DEVELOP, WORTHINGTON INDUST, 89- *Personal Data:* b Syracuse, NY, May 22, 41; m 61; c 3. *Educ:* LeMoyne Col, BS, 64; Syracuse Univ, MS, 67, PhD(solid state sci), 69. *Prof Exp:* Res metallurgist, 69-74, supvr, 74-75, sect chief, 75-78, res adv, 78-80, sr res adv, 80-81, asst div head metall, Repub Steel Res Ctr, 81-86; dir res & develop, Touchstone Res Lab, 86-88. *Mem:* Am Soc Metals; Am Inst Mining, Metall & Petrol Engrs; Sigma Xi; NY Acad Sci. *Res:* Physical metallurgy; plastic deformation; recrystallization. *Mailing Add:* 4628 Bridle Path Lane Dublin OH 43017

KOTANSKY, D(ONALD) R(ICHARD), fluid mechanics, aerodynamics, for more information see previous edition

KOTB, MALAK Y, BIOCHEMISTRY, IMMUNOLOGY. *Current Pos:* asst prof, Div Infectious Dis, Dept Med, 86-90, ASST PROF, DEPT SURG & DIR SURG IMMUNOL, UNIV TENN, MEMPHIS, 90- *Personal Data:* b Cairo, Egypt, July 20, 53; m 86. *Educ:* Ain Shams Univ, Cairo, Egypt, BS, 74; Univ Tenn, Memphis, PhD(biochem), 82. *Prof Exp:* Instr, Aim Shams Univ, 74; res assoc, Duke Univ Med Ctr, 82-85. *Concurrent Pos:* Rotary Int Educ fel, 77; mem res serv, Va Med Ctr, Memphis, 86-; consult, Nat Inst Child Health & Develop. *Mem:* Am Soc Biochemists & Molecular Biologists; Sigma Xi. *Res:* Synthesis and metabolism of S-Adenosylmethonine; biochemical regulation of T lymphocyte differentiation; mechanism of pathogenesis of poststreptococcal autoimmune diseases; role of superantigenesis autoimmunity. *Mailing Add:* Dept Surg/Microbiol Univ Tenn Vet Admin Med Ctr 1030 Jefferson Ave No 151 Memphis TN 38104

KOTCH, ALEX, SCIENCE & ACADEMIC ADMINISTRATION. *Current Pos:* RETIRED. *Personal Data:* b Edwardsville, Pa, Aug 18, 26; m 52, Anne M Brinkman; c Marianne, Robert, Axel & Jennifer. *Educ:* Pa State Col, BS, 46, MS, 47; Univ Ill, PhD(org chem), 50. *Honors & Awards:* Evan Pugh Scholar, Pa State Col, 46. *Prof Exp:* Asst org chem, Pa State Col, 46-47 & Univ Ill, 47-49; Fulbright fel, Delft Tech Univ, 50-51; Little fel, Mass Inst Tech, 51-52; res chemist, Cent Res Dept, Exp Sta, E I du Pont de Nemours & Co, 52-54, Org Chem Dept, Jackson Lab, 54-59; assoc prog dir chem, NSF, 59-63, prog dir org chem, 63-65; chief biosci div, Off Saline Water, US Dept Interior, 65-66; staff assoc, Sci Develop Eval Group, Div Instnl Progs, Nat Sci Found, 66-67; prof chem & assoc chmn dept, Univ Wis-Madison, 67-77; asst dir info, educ & int progs, Solar Energy Res Inst, 77-78, spec asst to dir, 78-79, br chief, Educ & Univ Progs, 78-81, prog mgr, Univ Res & Storage Progs, 81-82; prof & dir, Off Res & Develop, Univ NDak, 82-91, emer prof chem, 91-97. *Concurrent Pos:* Consult-exam, NCent Asn Cols & Schs, 69-91, comnr-at-large, 84-88; bd dir, Assoc Western Univ, 82-91, mem exec comt bd dir, 88-91. *Mem:* Am Chem Soc. *Res:* Synthetic organic chemistry; polymers; heterocyclics; fluorescent whitening agents; dyes; science research and academic administration. *Mailing Add:* 3030 Eldridge St Golden CO 80401-1407

KOTCHOUBEY, ANDREW, COMPUTER SCIENCE, APPLIED MATHEMATICS. *Current Pos:* MGR, TRAIN SMITH COUNSEL, INC, 83- *Personal Data:* b Florence, Italy, Mar 31, 38; US citizen; m 68; c 5. *Educ:* Stevens Inst Technol, ME, 59; Columbia Univ, MA, 61, PhD(appl math), 66. *Prof Exp:* Supvr comput installation, Watson Sci Comput Lab, IBM Corp, 60-62, res assoc appl math, Watson Lab, 62-66, sr staff mem appl math & comput, 66-69; dir info systs, Interway Corp, 69-71; pres, subsidiary I/W Data Systs, Inc, 71-73; vpres, Automatech Graphics Corp, 73-83. *Concurrent Pos:* Assoc grad facs math, Columbia Univ, 67-68, adj asst prof, 68-69. *Mem:* AAAS; Asn Comput Mach; Sigma Xi; Soc Indust & Appl Math. *Res:* Calculations in atomic and molecular physics; mathematical physics; numerical analysis. *Mailing Add:* 50 E 96th St New York NY 10128

KOTCON, JAMES BERNARD, NEMATOLOGY, ENVIRONMENTAL IMPACTS OF PESTICIDES. *Current Pos:* ASST PROF PLANT PATH, WVA UNIV 85- *Personal Data:* b Neillsville, Wis, Nov 24, 54; m, Candice Elliot; c Sarah B & Rebekah J. *Educ:* Univ Wis-Stevens Points, BS, 76; Mich State Univ, MS, 79; Univ Wis-Madison, PhD(plant path), 83. *Prof Exp:* Res assoc, Cornell Univ, 83-85. *Concurrent Pos:* Chair, Nematol Comt, Am Phytopath Soc, 78-; chair, Ecol Comt, Soc Nematologists, 78-; prin investr several grants, 86-; assoc ed, J Nematol, 88-89 & 92-93. *Mem:* AAAS; Am Phytopath Soc; Ecol Soc Am; Orgn Nematologists Trop Am; Soc Nematologist; Union Concerned Scientists. *Res:* Nematode ecology, population dynamics, yield loss and control; efficacy of pesticides and environmental impacts to groundwater and nontarget organisms; biologic control, integrated pest management and sustainable agriculture. *Mailing Add:* RR 12 PO Box 400 Morgantown WV 26505. *Fax:* 304-293-2872

KOTHEIMER, WILLIAM CONRAD, ELECTRICAL ENGINEERING. *Current Pos:* dir eng, Allentown, Pa, 86-91, TECH DIR, ABB POWER T&D CO, CORAL SPRINGS, FLA, 91- *Personal Data:* b Louisville, Ky, May 26, 25; m 60, Anne Sheila Collins; c William Conrad II. *Educ:* Univ Louisville, BEE, 51. *Prof Exp:* Sr engr, Gen Elec Co, Phila, 51-65, mgr develop eng, 65-80, construct engr, 80-82, Malvern, Pa, 82-83; construct engr, Kotheimer Assocs, Lansdowne, Pa, 83-86. *Mem:* Fel Inst Elec & Electronics Engrs; Nat Soc Prof Engrs. *Res:* Author numerous articles; awarded patents in field. *Mailing Add:* 5900 NW 99th Ave Coral Springs FL 33706-2566

KOTHMANN, MERWYN MORTIMER, RANGE SCIENCE, RANGE MANAGEMENT. *Current Pos:* res asst range nutrit, 64-67, from asst prof to assoc prof range mgt, Tex Agr Exp Sta, 67-79, PROF RANGE SCI, TEX A&M UNIV, 79- *Personal Data:* b Castell, Tex, Jan 30, 40; m 62, Sara K Wells; c Cynthia, Kevin & Sara. *Educ:* Tex A&M Univ, BS, 61, PhD(range sci), 68; Utah State Univ, MS, 63. *Prof Exp:* Res asst range nutrit, Utah State Univ, 61-64. *Mem:* Soc Range Mgt; Am Soc Animal Sci; Am Forage & Grassland Coun. *Res:* Simulation of natural vegetation and livestock responses to various grazing management systems; nutrition of range livestock and botanical and chemical characteristics of diets of grazing animals. *Mailing Add:* Dept Rangeland Ecol & Mgt Tex A&M Univ College Station TX 77843-2126. *Fax:* 409-845-6430; *E-Mail:* m]kothmann@tamu.edu

KOTHNY, EVALDO LUIS, AIR POLLUTION. *Current Pos:* RETIRED. *Personal Data:* b Buenos Aires, Argentina, Oct 6, 25; US citizen; m 60, Monica Albertz; c Cecilia (Person) & Lilian (McGlothlen). *Educ:* Univ Buenos Aires, MS, 55, PhD(chem), 64. *Prof Exp:* Plant chemist, Coplan Br, US Rubber Co, Argentina, 55-56; res chemist, Buenos Aires, 56-57; asst anal instrumentation, Univ Buenos Aires, 57-60 & 61-63; asst specialist qual control, Monsanto, Argentina, 60-61; sr specialist, Gen Elec, Argentina, 61-64; res chemist, Calif Dept Health Serv, 64-91. *Concurrent Pos:* Mem, Intersoc Comt, Am Pub Health Asn, mem subcomt, No 3, 66-86, chmn, 71-74 & 76-79. *Mem:* Am Chem Soc; Asn Explor Geochem. *Res:* Industrial inorganic preparative chemistry; trace inorganic analysis; geochemistry; environmental chemistry; geochemistry of noble metals; nitrogen oxides analysis; geochemical cycle of mercury; platinum and palladium in the environment; exploration of noble metals; biogeochemistry of palladium. *Mailing Add:* 3016 Stinson Circle Walnut Creek CA 94598-3621

KOTHS, JAY SANFORD, FLORICULTURE. *Current Pos:* prof, 55-86, EMER PROF FLORICULTURE, UNIV CONN, 86- *Personal Data:* b Taylor, Mich, July 22, 26; m 47, Margaret Edwards; c Kirston, Gwen & Kim. *Educ:* Mich State Univ, BS, 48; Purdue Univ, MS, 50; Univ Mass, PhD, 67. *Honors & Awards:* Extension Award A&A Fel, Am Soc Hort Sci. *Prof Exp:* Instr floricult, Purdue Univ, 48-50; greenhouse mgr, Kemble-Smith Co, Iowa, 50-53; asst greenhouse mgr, A Washburn & Sons, Ill, 53-54; gen mgr, A Weiler Greenhouse, Wis, 54-55. *Concurrent Pos:* Consult greenhouse mgt. *Mem:* Am Soc Agron; fel Am Soc Hort Sci; Soil Sci Soc Am; Int Soc Hort Sci; Am Hort Soc. *Res:* Automation of greenhouse microclimate; greenhouse crop fertility control; biological control of soilborne diseases; pollution effects on soil nitrification. *Mailing Add:* Dept Plant Sci Univ Conn Box U-67 Storrs CT 06268

KOTHS, KIRSTON EDWARD, PROTEIN ENGINEERING, PROTEIN CHEMISTRY OF PHARMACEUTICALS. *Current Pos:* DIR BIOL THER RES, CHIRON CORP, 91- *Personal Data:* b La Fayette, Ind, Dec 24, 48; m 85, Catherine Lutes. *Educ:* Amherst Col, BA, 71; Harvard Univ, PhD(biochem & molecular biol), 79. *Prof Exp:* Scientist, Cetus Corp, 79-84, mgr protein chem, 82-84, sr scientist & dir protein chem, 84-91, sr dir res, 89-91. *Mem:* AAAS. *Res:* Characterization of rare human proteins with therapeutic potential; development of cloned human proteins for clinical use; protein engineering; lectin-binding proteins; prohormone convertase inhibition; apoptosis; protease inhibitor screens. *Mailing Add:* Chiron Corp 4560 Horton St Emeryville CA 94608. *Fax:* 510-923-4115; *E-Mail:* kirston_koths@cc.chiron.com

KOTICK, MICHAEL PAUL, RECOMBINANT DNA, MEDICINAL CHEMISTRY. *Current Pos:* res scientist, Molecular Biol Dept, Miles Labs, 69-75, sr res scientist, Chem Dept, 75-81, prin res scientist, biotechnol group, 81-88, supvr, recombinant DNA & prin staff scientist, Food Ingredients Div, 88-90, MGR, PROPRIETARY SERV, MILES PHARMACEUT DIV, MILES LABS, 90- *Personal Data:* b Buffalo, NY, Dec 28, 40; m 65; c 2. *Educ:* State Univ NY Buffalo, BS, 62, PhD(med chem), 68; Ind Univ, MS, BBA, 81. *Prof Exp:* Res asst med chem, Sch Pharm, State Univ NY Buffalo, 63-68; fel org chem, Walker Labs, Sloan-Kettering Inst Cancer Res, 68-69. *Mem:* AAAS; Am Chem Soc. *Res:* Chemistry of oligonucleotides, nucleosides, carbohydrates, narcotic drugs; medicinal chemistry; recombinant DNA technology; microbiology, molecular biology; research and resource management. *Mailing Add:* 6121 Main St Trumbull CT 06611

KOTILA, PAUL MYRON, AQUATIC ECOLOGY, ENTOMOLOGY. *Current Pos:* ASSOC PROF BIOL, FRANKLIN PIERCE COL, 88- *Personal Data:* b Hancock, Mich, Oct 14, 50. *Educ:* Mich Technol Univ, BS, 72, MS, 74; Univ Wis-Madison, PhD(entom), 78. *Prof Exp:* Asst prof biol, Allegheny Col, 78-; asst prof environ studies, St Lawrence Univ, 86-88. *Mem:* AAAS; Am Fisheries Soc; Entom Soc Am; NAm Benthological Soc; Sigma Xi. *Res:* Effects of impoundments, toxicants and other disturbances on stream insects; ecology of aquatic invertebrates. *Mailing Add:* RR 1 PO Box 262 Franklin Pierce Col College Rd MH 106 Fitzwilliam NH 03447

KOTIN, LEONARD, PHYSICAL CHEMISTRY. *Current Pos:* ASST PROF CHEM, UNIV ILL, CHICAGO CIRCLE, 61- *Personal Data:* b New York, NY, June 3, 32. *Educ:* Queens Col, BS, 54; Harvard Univ, AM, 55, PhD(chem physics), 60. *Prof Exp:* Res assoc chem, Inst Study Metals, Chicago, 59-61. *Concurrent Pos:* Res assoc, Nat Acad Sci-Nat Res Coun, 59-61; asst prof, Wash Univ, 61-65. *Mem:* AAAS; Am Chem Soc; NY Acad Sci. *Res:* Equilibrium and transport properties of synthetic and biological macromolecules; polyelectrolytes; thermodynamics and statistical mechanics of condensed phases. *Mailing Add:* Dept Chem MC 111 Univ Ill 845 W Taylor St Chicago IL 60607

KOTIN, PAUL, PATHOLOGY. *Current Pos:* CONSULT PATHOLOGIST, 81- *Personal Data:* b Chicago, Ill, Aug 13, 16; m 70, Pauline Stephan; c Joel & David. *Educ:* Univ Ill, BS, 37, MD, 40; Am Bd Path, dipl, 53. *Honors & Awards:* Sappington lectr, Am Occup Med Asn, 80, Knudsen Award, 81; Gehrmann lectr, Am Acad Occup Med, Nashville, 81. *Prof Exp:* From instr to prof path, Univ Southern Calif, 51-60, Paul Peirce prof, 60-62; chief, Carcinogenesis Studies Br, Nat Cancer Inst, 62-63, sci dir etiology, 64-66; dir, Div Environ Health Sci, Nat Inst Environ Health Sci, 66-69, dir, Inst, 69-71; prof path, vpres health sci & dean, Sch Med, Temple Univ, 71-74; sr vpres health, safety & environ, Johns-Manville Corp, 74-81. *Concurrent Pos:* Res fel path, Sch Med, Univ Southern Calif, 49-50, NSF sr fel, 59-60; med microbiologist, Los Angeles Co Gen Hosp, 50-51, attend staff pathologist, 51-62. *Mem:* Am Asn Cancer Res; Am Asn Pathologists & Bacteriologists; fel Col Am Pathologists. *Res:* Mechanisms of carcinogenesis; experimental cancer production; environmental factors in cancer; air pollution; teratogenesis. *Mailing Add:* 2304 E Sausalito Trail Tucson AZ 85737

KOTLARSKI, IGNACY ICCHAK, MATHEMATICS. *Current Pos:* PROF MATH & STATIST, OKLA STATE UNIV, 69- *Personal Data:* b Warsaw, Poland, July 29, 23; US citizen. *Educ:* Univ Warsaw, MA, 52; Wroclaw Univ, PhD(math), 61; Warsaw Tech Univ, Docent, 67. *Prof Exp:* Lectr math & statist, Planning & Statist Acad, Warsaw, 50-53; asst sampling inspection, Math Inst, Polish Acad Sci, 53-54; lectr math, Warsaw Tech Univ, 54-68; vis prof, Rome Univ, 68-69 & Univ Md, College Park, 69. *Concurrent Pos:* Mem staff sampling inspection, Polish Stand Comt, 50-53; lectr math, Army Tech Acad, Warsaw, 53-59. *Mem:* Inst Math Statist. *Res:* Characterization problems in probability; mathematical modeling. *Mailing Add:* 2723 Pioneer Trail Stillwater OK 74074

KOTLER, DONALD P, GASTROENTEROLOGY, CLINICAL IMMUNOLOGY. *Current Pos:* asst prof, 79-87, ASSOC PROF MED, COLUMBIA COL, 87- *Personal Data:* b New Brunswick, NJ, Sept 30, 47; m 73; c Dana (Helice) & Aaron. *Educ:* Rutgers Univ, BS, 69; Albert Einstein Col Med, MD, 73. *Prof Exp:* House officer internal med, Bronx Munic Hosp Ctr, 73-76; fel gastroenterol, Hosp Univ Pa, 76-78, asst prof med, Univ Pa, 78-79. *Concurrent Pos:* Assoc attend physician, St Lukes Roosevelt Hosp Ctr, 79- *Mem:* AAAS; NY Acad Sci; Am Gastroenterol Asn; Am Fedn Clin Res; Int AIDS Soc. *Res:* Currently engaged in research to define, describe and control the gastrointestinal and nutritional complications of the acquired immunodeficiency syndrome. *Mailing Add:* GI Div St Lukes Roosevelt Hosp Ctr 421 W 113 St New York NY 10025-1708. *Fax:* 212-523-3678

KOTLIAR, ABRAHAM MORRIS, PHYSICAL CHEMISTRY, POLYMER PHYSICS. *Current Pos:* ASSOC PROF, UNIV GA, 88- *Personal Data:* b Brooklyn, NY, Oct 8, 26; m 55; c 4. *Educ:* Adelphi Col, BA, 49; Polytech Inst Brooklyn, PhD(chem), 55. *Prof Exp:* Res assoc & fel chem, Duke Univ, 55-56; chemist radiation effects, US Naval Res Lab, 56-60; chemist polymer physics, Esso Res & Eng Co, 60-64; group leader, Allied Chem Corp, 64-66, sr scientist, 66-69, sr res assoc, 69-88. *Mem:* Am Chem Soc; Am Phys Soc; Soc Rheology; Sigma Xi. *Res:* Solution properties; molecular weight distributions; random processes; rheology and mechanical properties of plastics. *Mailing Add:* 112 Skyview Ct Athens GA 30606-3847

KOTLYAKOV, VLADIMIR MICHAILOVICH, GEOGRAPHY, GLACIOLOGY. *Current Pos:* Researcher, Inst Geog, USSR Acad Sci, Moscow, 54-68, head dept, 68-86, prof, 71, DIR, INST GEOG, USSR ACAD SCI, 86- *Personal Data:* b Lobnya, Russia, Nov 6, 31; m 62, Valentina Bazanova; c Michail & Andrei. *Educ:* Inst Geog, Russia, PhD(sci), 67. *Honors & Awards:* Litke Gold Medal, Russian Geog Soc, 85, Przhevalski Gold Medal, 96. *Concurrent Pos:* Ed, Data Glaciological Studies, 61-, World Atlas Snow & Ice Resources, 76- & Izvestiya Acad Nauk, 86-; pres, Int Comn Snow & Ice, 87-91; sci comt mem, Geosphere Biosphere Prog, Stockholm Int, 87-93; people's dep, USSR Supreme Court, Moscow, 89-91; academician, Russian Acad Sci, 91. *Mem:* Fel Am Geog Soc; Int Geog Union (vpres, 88-96); Int Glaciol Soc; Int Asn Hydrol Sci (vpres, 83-87); Mex Geog Soc; Ital Geog Soc; Acad Sci USSR; Georgian Acad Sci. *Res:* Contribution to the study of the earth's snow cover, glaciers and ice sheets as well as to the synthesis of socio-economic and natural resource information on Russia and the world as a whole. *Mailing Add:* Inst Geog Russ Acad Sci Staromonetny St 29 Moscow 109017 Russia. *Fax:* 7-095-959-0033; *E-Mail:* geography@glas.azc.org

KOTOVYCH, GEORGE, BIOPHYSICAL CHEMISTRY. *Current Pos:* from asst prof to assoc prof, 70-89, PROF CHEM, UNIV ALTA, 89- *Personal Data:* b Jan 3, 41; Can citizen; m 74; c 4. *Educ:* Univ Man, BSc, 63, MSc, 64, PhD(phys chem), 68. *Prof Exp:* Nat Res Coun Can fel bio-phys chem, Lawrence Radiation Lab, Univ Calif, Berkeley, 68-69. *Mem:* Chem Inst Can; Am Chem Soc. *Res:* Application of nuclear magnetic resonance techniques to the study of biological systems; structure and conformation of polypeptides, bradykinin agonists and antagonists, receptor-antagonist interactions. *Mailing Add:* Dept Chem Univ Alta Edmonton AB T6G 2G2 Can. *Fax:* 403-492-8231; *E-Mail:* george.kotovych@ualberta.ca

KOTT, EDWARD, ZOOLOGY. *Current Pos:* asst prof biol, 69-86, PROF BIOL, WATERLOO LUTHERAN UNIV, 86- *Personal Data:* b Toronto, Ont, Mar 25, 39. *Educ:* Univ Toronto, BA, 60, PhD(ecol), 65. *Prof Exp:* Lectr zool, Lakehead Col, 63-65; assoc scientist fisheries res, Bedford Inst Oceanog, 65-69. *Mem:* Am Soc Mammalogists; Soc Syst Zool. *Res:* Mammalian and fish population ecology. *Mailing Add:* Dept Biol Wilfrid Laurier Univ Waterloo ON N2L 3C5 Can

KOTTAS, HARRY, MECHANICAL ENGINEERING. *Current Pos:* PRES, K-SERV, 76- *Personal Data:* b Milligan, Nebr, Oct 24, 10; m 38; c 2. *Educ:* Univ Nebr, BSc, 32, MSc, 33. *Prof Exp:* Mech engr food processing, Roberts Dairy Co, Nebr, 33-36 & Swift & Co, 36-37; chief mech eng div, Nat Adv Comt Aeronaut, Ohio, 37-52; chief tech panels, Redstone Arsenal, Ala, 52-56; asst dir eng, AK Div, Avco Mfg Corp, Ind, 56-59; chief spec prod eng, Curtiss-Wright Corp, 59-60; chief engr, Tuthill Spring Co, Ill, 60-62; mgr eng, Int Staple & Mach Co, Pa, 62-64; mfg mgr, Am Device Mfg Co, 64-69; prof design & drafting technol, Lake Land Col, 69-76. *Res:* Product-market characteristics; mobile vehicles materials handling; industrial noise phenomena; tillage components; fluid and solid metal flow phenomena; automated packaging; engineering and industrial human factors; manufacturing optimization. *Mailing Add:* 403 S Randall St Steeleville IL 62288-2002

KOTTAS, JAMES ALAN, NEUTRAL NETWORKS & ADAPTIVE SYSTEMS, IMAGE PROCESSING & PATTERN RECOGNITION. *Current Pos:* CHIEF SCIENTIST, MIROS INC, 94- *Personal Data:* b Buffalo, NY, Feb 8, 61; m 92, Cynthia Bone; c Joel. *Educ:* Carnegie-Mellon Univ, BS, 83; Mass Inst Technol, SM, 86, PhD(elec eng), 91. *Prof Exp:* Res scientist, Symbus Technol Inc, 91-94. *Concurrent Pos:* Consult electronics, robotics & software, 88- *Mem:* Sigma Xi; Inst Elec & Electronics Engrs; Int Neural Network Soc. *Res:* Application of adaptive systems to intelligent pattern recognition; coinventor of the Trueface face recognition system and its associated family of products. *Mailing Add:* 207 Adams Ave West Newton MA 02165. *Fax:* 781-235-0720; *E-Mail:* jimk@miros.com

KOTTAYIL, SANTOSH GEORGE, DRUG MANUFACTURING DEVELOPMENT, MEDICINAL CHEMISTRY. *Current Pos:* MGR PHARMACEUT DEVELOP, UNIMED PHARMACEUT INC, 93- *Personal Data:* b Kerala, India, Apr 18, 63; US citizen; m 93, Anita George. *Educ:* Univ Poona, BSc, 83, MSc, 85; Univ Ky, PhD(org chem), 93. *Prof Exp:* Res intern, Dupont Merck, 91; sr scientist, Oramed, 92-93. *Mem:* Am Chem Soc. *Res:* Synthesis of novel and improved chemical entities for the efficient treatment of pain; chemical characterization, evaluation for pharmacological activity and study of the mechanism of action in animals and humans. *Mailing Add:* Unimed Pharmaceut Inc 2150 E Lake Cook Rd Buffalo Grove IL 60089-1862. *Fax:* 847-541-2569; *E-Mail:* kots@worldnet.att.com

KOTTCAMP, EDWARD H, JR, METALLURGY & PHYSICAL METALLURGICAL ENGINEERING. *Current Pos:* GROUP VPRES, SPS TECHNOLS, INC, 87- *Personal Data:* b York, Pa, July 12, 34; c 3. *Educ:* Lehigh Univ, BS, 56, MS, 57, PhD(metall eng & mat sci), 60. *Honors & Awards:* William Sparagan Award for Outstanding Res, 73; William Eisenman Award, Am Soc Metals, 88. *Prof Exp:* Vpres res, Bethlehem Steel Corp, 82-85, sr vpres, 85-86, exec vpres, 86-87. *Concurrent Pos:* Prof, Lehigh Univ Col Eng. *Mem:* Fel Am Soc Metals; Indust Res Inst; Am Iron & Steel Inst; Welding Res Coun. *Res:* Cold extrusion of steels; pressure vessel design; research management and innovation; high-strength steels; pressure vessels; microstructure; fracutre; metal forming; author of numerous technical articles. *Mailing Add:* 36 Latham Ct Doylestown PA 18901

KOTTER, F(RED) RALPH, ELECTRICAL MEASUREMENTS, HIGH VOLTAGE PHENOMENA. *Current Pos:* RETIRED. *Personal Data:* b Salt Lake City, Utah, Dec 8, 15; m 49, Lora Norman; c Loralee, Wade, Nola, Shauna & Virginia. *Educ:* Univ Utah, BSc, 37; George Washington Univ, AM, 40; Mass Inst Technol, ScD, 55. *Prof Exp:* Physicist, Nat Bur Stand, 37-47 & 55-81; from instr to asst prof elec eng, Mass Inst Technol, 47-54. *Concurrent Pos:* Consult, 82- *Mem:* Inst Elec & Electronics Engrs. *Res:* Precise electrical measurements; high voltage measurements. *Mailing Add:* 12921 Crisfield Rd Silver Spring MD 20906

KOTTKE, BRUCE ALLEN, EXPERIMENTAL PATHOLOGY, INTERNAL MEDICINE. *Current Pos:* Consult, Mayo Found & Clin, 62-71, from asst prof to assoc prof med, 62-76, PROF MED, MAYO GRAD SCH MED, UNIV MINN, 76- *Personal Data:* b Blue Earth, Minn, Jan 22, 29; m 79; c 2. *Educ:* Hamline Univ, BS, 51; Univ Minn, Minneapolis, MD, 54, PhD, 62. *Concurrent Pos:* Fel int med, Mayo Found, 57-61; mem coun arteriosclerosis, Am Heart Asn, mem coun atherosclerosis, mem coun thrombosis, fel coun circulation. *Mem:* Am Heart Asn; Am Fedn Clin Res; Sigma Xi. *Res:* Atherosclerosis; cholesterol metabolism; bile acid metabolism. *Mailing Add:* Mayo Clin Rochester MN 55905

KOTTKE, FREDERIC JAMES, PHYSICAL MEDICINE & REHABILITATION. *Current Pos:* Asst physiol, Univ Minn, , 41-44, from asst prof to prof, 47-86, dir div, 49-52, head dept, 52-82, EMER PROF PHYS MED & REHAB, UNIV MINN, MINNEAPOLIS, 86- *Personal Data:* b Hayfield, Minn, May 26, 17; m 39; c 3. *Educ:* Univ Minn, BS & MS, 41, PhD(physiol), 44, MD, 45; Am Bd Phys Med & Rehab, dipl, 49. *Honors & Awards:* Frank H Krusen Award, Am Acad Phys Med & Rehab, 79; Sidney Licht lectr, Univ Pa, 79 & Ohio State Univ, 81; Lewis Leavitt Mem lectr, Baylor Univ Med Sch, 82. *Concurrent Pos:* Baruch fel phys med, Univ Minn, Minneapolis, 46-47; mem, Am Bd Phys Med & Rehab, 55-70, chmn, 64-70;

consult, Minneapolis Vet Admin Hosp, 56; mem, Minn Gov Adv Comt Voc Rehab, 56-60; mem exec comt, prog chmn & vpres, Int Cong Phys Med, 60; mem med adv comt, Off Voc Rehab, 60-67; mem Med Res Study Sect, Voc Rehab Admin, 61-63; secy & mem bd dirs & mem expert med comt, Am Rehab Found, 64; mem, Minn State Bd Health, 64-67, Med Adv Comt, Social & Rehab Serv, 68-69 & Coun Cerebrovasc Dis & Coun Clin Cardiol, Am Heart Asn, 70-83. *Mem:* Fel AMA; fel Am Cong Phys Med & Rehab (vpres, 54-58, pres elect, 58-59, pres, 59-60); Am Acad Phys Med & Rehab (pres-elect, 77, pres, 78); Int Soc Rehab Disabled; hon mem Columbian Soc Phys Med & Rehab; hon mem Mex Acad Surg; hon mem Brazilian Acad Rehab Med; hon mem Venezuelan Soc Phys Med & Rehab; hon mem Neth Soc Phys Med & Rehab. *Res:* Circulation; neuromuscular diseases; poliomyelitis; rehabilitation; work of the heart. *Mailing Add:* 2741 Drew Ave S Minneapolis MN 55416

KOTTLOWSKI, FRANK EDWARD, ECONOMIC GEOLOGY, COAL GEOLOGY. *Current Pos:* econ geologist, NMex Bur Mines & Mineral Res, 51-66, asst dir & sr geologist, 66-73, dir & state geologist, 73-91, EMER DIR STATE GEOLOGIST, NMEX BUR MINES & MINERAL RES, 91- *Personal Data:* b Indianapolis, Ind, Apr 11, 21; m 45, Florence J Chrisco; c Karen S (Harvey), Janet M (Wallace) & Dianna V (Schoderbek). *Educ:* Ind Univ, AB, 47, AM, 49, PhD(econ geol), 51. *Honors & Awards:* Distinguished Serv Award, Am Asn Petrol Geologists; Public Serv Award, Am Inst Prof Geologists, 86; Caby Coal Geol Award, Geol Soc Am, 96. *Prof Exp:* Asst geologist econ geol, State Geol Surv, Ind, 46-51. *Concurrent Pos:* Asst, Ind Univ, 47-48, instr, 50; fac assoc, NMex Inst Mining & Technol, 54-73, adj prof, 74-; ed, Am Asn Petrol Geologists, 71-75; chmn, Nat Acad Sci Codes Comt, 80-81, Nat Acad Sci Comre Comt, 82-83; pres, Energy Minerals Div, Am Asn Petrol Geologists, 87-88. *Mem:* Fel AAAS; Soc Econ Geol; fel Geol Soc Am; Soc Econ Paleont & Mineral; hon mem Am Asn Petrol Geologists; Asn Am State Geologists (pres, 85-86). *Res:* Coal geology; Pennsylvanian and Permian stratigraphy; Cenozoic sediments and volcanic rocks; industrial minerals and rocks; areal mapping in Indiana, New Mexico and Montana; measuring stratigraphic sections. *Mailing Add:* 703 Sunset Dr Socorro NM 87801-4657. Fax: 505-835-6333

KOTTMAN, CLIFFORD ALFONS, MATHEMATICS. *Current Pos:* EXEC MGR, INER GRAPH CORP, 90- *Personal Data:* b San Diego, Calif, Aug 3, 42; m 66; c 3. *Educ:* Loyola Univ, Los Angeles, BS, 64; Univ Iowa, MS, 66, PhD(math), 69. *Prof Exp:* Asst prof math, La State Univ, 69-70; asst prof math, Ore State Univ, 70-75, assoc prof, 75-77; mathematician, Defense Mapping Agency, 77-90. *Concurrent Pos:* Consult in non-destructive testing. *Mem:* AAAS; Am Math Soc; Math Asn Am; Am Soc Photogram. *Res:* Functional analysis; Banach spaces; photogrammetry. *Mailing Add:* 6614 Rockland Dr Clifton VA 22024-2414. Fax: 703-266-9789

KOTTMAN, ROY MILTON, animal breeding; deceased, see previous edition for last biography

KOTTMEIER, PETER KLAUS, SURGERY. *Current Pos:* from asst prof to assoc prof, 67-70, PROF SURG, STATE UNIV NY DOWNSTATE MED CTR, 70-; DIR PEDIAT SURG SERV, UNIV HOSP, 67-; DIR PEDIAT SURG SERV, KINGS COUNTY HOSP, BROOKLYN, 62- *Personal Data:* b Munich, Ger, Feb 1, 28; m 56; c 4. *Educ:* Univ Munich, MD, 51, Ohio State Univ, MMSc, 60. *Prof Exp:* Asst instr surg, State Univ NY Downstate Med Ctr, 57-60; instr, Ohio State Univ, 60-61. *Mem:* Fel Am Acad Pediat; fel Am Col Surgeons; fel Am Pediat Surg Asn. *Res:* Pediatric surgery. *Mailing Add:* 450 Clarkson Ave Brooklyn NY 11203-2012

KOTULA, ANTHONY W, FOOD SCIENCE. *Current Pos:* PROF IN RESIDENCE, UNIV CONN, 92- *Personal Data:* b Holyoke, Mass, June 12, 29; m 57, Joan Ryzicwicz; c Kathryn & Valerie. *Educ:* Univ Mass, BS, 51, MS, 54; Univ Md, PhD(food sci), 64. *Honors & Awards:* Res Award, Poultry Sci Res Asn, 67; Signal Serv Award, Am Meat Sci Asn, 83, Distinguished Res Award; Meat Res Award, Am Soc Animal Sci, 88, Distinguished Serv Award, 92. *Prof Exp:* Proj leader, Animal Sci Inst, Agr Res Serv, USDA, 54-67, invests leader, 67-71, supvry res food technologists & chief, Meat Sci Res Lab, 71-92. *Mem:* Poultry Sci Asn; Inst Food Technologists; World Poultry Sci Asn; Am Meat Sci Asn; fel Am Soc Animal Sci; Sigma Xi. *Res:* Maintaining and improving quality of animal products; food safety. *Mailing Add:* 135 Maple Rd Storrs CT 06268. Fax: 860-429-9200

KOTVAL, PESHO SOHRAB, MEDICAL ENGINEERING, MANAGEMENT SCIENCE. *Current Pos:* res physician radiol, 83-87, ASSOC PROF RADIOL, NY MED COL, 87-, ASSOC PROF SURG, 90- *Personal Data:* b Nagpur, India, Aug 31, 42; US citizen; m 65; c 2. *Educ:* Univ Nagpur, BSc, 60; Univ Sheffield, MMet, 62, PhD(phys metall), 65; Pace Univ, MBA, 77; NY Med Col, MD, 83; Nat Bd Med Examr, dipl, 84; Am Bd Radiol, dipl, 87. *Honors & Awards:* Coatings Award, Am Soc Metals, 73. *Prof Exp:* Scientist, res assoc & mgr superally metall, Stellite Div, Union Carbide Corp, 66-70; vis scientist metall, Res Inst Advan Studies, 70-71; sr group leader metals & ceramics, Cor Res Lab, Union Carbide Corp, 71-78, res mgr mat sci, Med Prod Div, 78-80. *Concurrent Pos:* Fel, Sheffield Univ, 65-66; adj prof physics, Ind Univ, 67-68; adj prof mgt econ, Pace Univ, 77- *Mem:* Fel Am Soc Metals; Brit Inst Metallurgists; AMA; Radiol Soc NAm; Am Inst Ultrasound Med. *Res:* Superalloys for high temperature gas turbines and corrosion resistance; powder metallurgy; crystal growth; process development; low cost solar cells; medical instruments; blood flow technology. *Mailing Add:* 280 Dobbs Ferry Rd Ste 103 White Plains NY 10607-1910

KOTVIS, PETER VAN DYKE, EXTREME PRESSURE TRIBOLOGY OF METALS, LUBRICANT APPLICATIONS & THEIR THERMODYNAMICS. *Current Pos:* RES DIR, BENZ OIL, INC, 79- *Educ:* Univ Wis, BS, 69, MS, 71, PhD(surface phys chem), 91. *Prof Exp:* Instr, Univ Wis, 71-75; res chemist, Vet Admin Med Ctr, 75-79. *Res:* Application of thermodynamics, metallurgy, etc. to establish fundamental understanding of tribology, especially involving metals and lubricants. *Mailing Add:* 15725 Monterey Dr New Berlin WI 53151

KOTYK, MICHAEL, METALLURGY, CERAMICS. *Current Pos:* RETIRED. *Personal Data:* b Ford City, Pa, Mar 10, 29; m 52; c 5. *Educ:* Pa State Univ, BS, 54, MS, 56; NC State Univ, PhD(metall, ceramics), 68. *Prof Exp:* Instr metall, Pa State Univ, 54-56; sr technologist, US Steel Corp, 56-63; assoc dir metall & ceramics div, US Army Res Off, 63-68; sect supvr, Appl Res Lab, US Steel Corp, 68-73, div chief sheet prod res, 73-82, div chief, Basic Res Div, 82-84, div mgr tech serv, 84-92, technol coordr, prod technol, 84-92. *Mem:* Am Soc Metals; Am Inst Mining, Metall & Petrol Engrs; fel Am Chem Soc; Iron & Steel Inst Japan. *Res:* Formability of sheet steels; gases in metals; physical and mechanical properties of ferrous alloys; phase equilibria studies; productions sheet steel products. *Mailing Add:* 1017 Edgewood Rd New Kensington PA 15068

KOTZ, ARTHUR RUDOLPH, SOLID STATE ELECTRONICS. *Current Pos:* Jr physicist, 3M Co, 55-57, sr physicist, 57-58, supvr phys res, 58-60, proj leader, 60-61, res specialist, 66-68, sr res specialist, 68-70, mgr electronic imaging group, 70-73, CORP SCIENTIST, 3M CO, 73- *Personal Data:* b Eau Claire, Wis, Feb 21, 33; m 55; c 3. *Educ:* Univ Minn, BA, 55; Univ Wis, MS, 62, PhD(solid state physics), 66. *Mem:* Am Phys Soc; Soc Photog Sci & Eng. *Res:* Electrical transport properties of organic semiconductors; electron beam recording; gas discharge devices; photoeffects in solids, including photoconductivity, photovoltaic effect and photoemission; electrophotography; electronic imaging; electrography; reprography; electronic printing. *Mailing Add:* 5826 S Hobe Lane St Paul MN 55110

KOTZ, JOHN CARL, INORGANIC & ORGANOMETALLIC CHEMISTRY, CHEMICAL EDUCATION. *Current Pos:* prof chem, 70-87, DISTINGUISHED TEACHING PROF, DEPT CHEM, STATE UNIV NY, COL ONEONTA, 87- *Personal Data:* b Massillon, Ohio, June 27, 37; m 61; c 2. *Educ:* Wash & Lee Univ, BS, 59; Cornell Univ, PhD(inorg chem), 64. *Honors & Awards:* Catalyst Award Chem Educ, Chem Mfr Asn, 92. *Prof Exp:* NIH fel chem, Manchester Col Sci & Technol, Eng, 63-64 & Ind Univ, 64-65; asst prof, Kans State Univ, 65-70. *Concurrent Pos:* Fulbright lectr & res scholar, Portugal, 79. *Mem:* Am Chem Soc. *Res:* Synthetic organometallic chemistry; electrochemistry of organometallic compounds. *Mailing Add:* Dept Chem State Univ NY Col Oneonta NY 13820-1381. E-Mail: kotzjc@ snyoneva.cc.onconta.edu

KOTZ, SAMUEL, MATHEMATICAL STATISTICS, APPLIED PROBABILITY. *Current Pos:* PROF STATIST, UNIV MD, 79- *Personal Data:* b Harbin, China, Aug 28, 30; m 63, Rosalie Greenwald; c Tamara, Harold & Pauline. *Educ:* Hebrew Univ, Israel, MSc, 56; Cornell Univ, PhD(math statist), 60. *Hon Degrees:* DSc, Univ Athens, Greece, 95, Bowling Green State Univ, Ohio, 97. *Honors & Awards:* Wolfowitz Prize, 83. *Prof Exp:* Instr math, 56-58, lectr, Bar-Ilan Univ, Israel, 60-62; res assoc, Inst Statist, Univ NC, 62-63; sr res fel indust eng, 63-64, assoc prof, Univ Toronto, 64-67; prof math, Temple Univ, 67-79. *Concurrent Pos:* Assoc ed, J Am Statist Asn; distinguished vis prof, Bucknell Univ, 77, Guelph Univ, 86; co-ed Encycl Statist Sci; adv prof, Harbin Polytech Inst; distinguished prof, Bowling Green State Univ, 92 & 94; Univ Lulea, Sweden, 94 & 95; vis prof, Univ Copenhagen, 96. *Mem:* Am Math Soc; fel Am Statist Asn; fel Inst Math Statist; Intern Statist Inst; fel Royal Statist Soc. *Res:* Information theory; statistical distribution theory and methodology; scientific terminology; probabilistic models with special applications to business and engineering; history of statistics in 20th century; encyclopedia of statistical sciences 10 volumes. *Mailing Add:* 619 Kenbrook Dr Silver Spring MD 20962

KOTZEBUE, KENNETH LEE, ELECTRICAL ENGINEERING. *Current Pos:* RETIRED. *Personal Data:* b San Antonio, Tex, Dec 4, 33; m 54; c 3. *Educ:* Univ Tex, BS, 54; Univ Calif, Los Angeles, MS, 56; Stanford Univ, PhD(elec eng), 59. *Prof Exp:* Sr engr, Tex Instruments, Inc, 58-59; mem tech staff elec eng, Watkins-Johnson Co, 59-63, dept head solid state devices res & develop, 63-64; from assoc prof to prof elec eng, Univ Calif, Santa Barbara, 64-92. *Mem:* Inst Elec & Electronics Engrs. *Res:* Microwave solid-state device electronics. *Mailing Add:* 4737 Woodview Dr Santa Rosa CA 95405

KOUBA, DELORE LOREN, CHEMICAL ENGINEERING, ORGANIC CHEMISTRY. *Current Pos:* RETIRED. *Personal Data:* b Lincoln, Nebr, Apr 18, 19; m 71. *Educ:* Univ Nebr, BSc, 41. *Prof Exp:* Analytical chemist, Smokeless Powder Plant, Hercules, Inc, NJ, 41-42; lab supvr, 42, chief chemist, 42-43, analytical chemist, Res & Develop Res Ctr, Del, 43-46, explosives chemist, 46-50, res chemist, 50-78, sr res chemist, Res & Develop Res Ctr, Hercules, Inc, Del, 79-82. *Mem:* Am Chem Soc. *Res:* Smokeless powder testing; high explosives; semi-plant nitration; oxidation of aromatic compounds and hazardous chemicals evaluation; synthetic lubricants. *Mailing Add:* 1808 Windermere Ave Wilmington DE 19804-4025

KOUBEK, EDWARD, INORGANIC CHEMISTRY. *Current Pos:* from asst prof to assoc prof, 67-75, PROF CHEM, US NAVAL ACAD, 75- *Personal Data:* b Bayshore, NY, July 25, 37; m 63; c 2. *Educ:* State Univ NY Albany, BS, 59; Brown Univ, PhD(chem), 64. *Prof Exp:* Fel, Bell Tel Labs, NJ, 63-64. *Concurrent Pos:* Vis prof, Stanford Univ, 71, Dartmouth Col, 81 & Univ Canterbury, NZ, 91. *Mem:* Am Chem Soc. *Res:* Kinetics and mechanisms of inorganic reactions. *Mailing Add:* Dept Chem US Naval Acad Annapolis MD 21402-1398. E-Mail: koubek@artic.nadn.navy.mil

KOUCKY, FRANK LOUIS, JR, MINERALOGY, GEOCHEMISTRY. *Current Pos:* prof, 71-92, EMER PROF GEOL, COL WOOSTER, 92- *Personal Data:* b Chicago, Ill, June 24, 27; m 49, Virginia Ruhl; c Frank III, David, Walter & Jonathan. *Educ:* Univ Chicago, MS, 53, PhD(geol), 56. *Honors & Awards:* Bucher Award, 67. *Prof Exp:* Instr phys sci, Navy Pier, Univ Ill, 51-55; from instr to assoc prof, Mont Sch Mines, 55-57; asst prof & dir field camp, Univ Ill, 57-71. *Concurrent Pos:* From asst prof to assoc prof, Univ Cincinnati, 60-71; Assoc, Danforth Found, 68; res assoc, Mass Inst Technol, 78 & 83-; fel Nat Endowment Humanities, 87. *Mem:* Am Mineral Soc; Geol Soc Am; Am Schs Oriental Res; Geochem Soc; Clay Mineral Soc; Soc Econ Geologists; Sigma Xi. *Res:* X-ray crystallography; sulfide and sulfosalt minerals; geology of Wyoming and Montana; Precambrian geology; ancient technology related to mining and smelting; archaeological geology of Cyprus, Israel and Jordan. *Mailing Add:* 122 W Easton Rd Burbank OH 44214

KOUL, ASHOK KUMAR, SUPERALLOY TESTING & MICROSTRUCTURAL DESIGN, LIFE PREDICTION OF GAS TURBINE ENGINE COMPONENTS. *Current Pos:* RES OFFICER, INST AEROSPACE RES, NAT RES COUN, 80-, GROUP LEADER HIGH TEMPERATURE METALL & GAS TURBINES, 90- *Personal Data:* m, Anju Kachroo; c Abhinav & Kalhan. *Educ:* Banaras Hindu Univ, India, BSc, 73; Coun Nat Acad Awards, PhD(metall), 78. *Prof Exp:* Res investr, Sheffield Labs, Brit Steel Corp, 78-80. *Concurrent Pos:* Prof, Dept Mech Eng, Univ Ottawa, 93- *Mem:* Am Soc Metals Int. *Res:* Structure properties correlations in a wide variety of gas turbine engine materials; failure analysis and repair technologies. *Mailing Add:* Inst Aerospace Res Nat Res Coun Bldg M-13 Montreal Rd Ottawa ON K1A 0R6 Can

KOUL, HIRA LAL, MATHEMATICAL STATISTICS. *Current Pos:* asst prof statist, 68-72, assoc prof, 72-77, PROF STATIST & PROBABILITY, MICH STATE UNIV, 77- *Personal Data:* b Srinagar, India, May 27, 43. *Educ:* Univ Jammu & Kashmir, India, BA, 62, Univ Poona, MA, 64; Univ Calif, Berkeley, PhD(math statist), 67. *Prof Exp:* Asst, Univ Calif, Berkeley, 65-67. *Mem:* Fel Inst Math Statist. *Res:* Nonparametric statistics; inference on stochastic processes; reliability theory and survival analysis. *Mailing Add:* 1739 Ann St East Lansing MI 48823

KOUL, MAHARAJ KISHEN, MATERIALS SCIENCE, METALLURGY. *Current Pos:* VPRES & GEN MGR, ATLANTIC METALS CORP, PHILADELPHIA, PA. *Personal Data:* b Srinagar, India, Sept 10, 41; m; c 2. *Educ:* Univ Jammu & Kashmir, BSc, 59; Banaras Hindu Univ, BSc, 63; Mass Inst Technol, PhD(mat sci), 68. *Prof Exp:* Metall asst, Union Carbide India Pvt Ltd, 63-65; res asst mat sci, Mass Inst Technol, 65-68, fel, 68-69; res scientist, Res & Develop, Mining & Metals Div, Union Carbide Corp, 69-70, proj engr, New Prod Develop, 70-76; mgr, Steel Res & Develop, Foote Mineral Co, 76-79; exec vpres, Div Indian Metals & Ferro Alloys Ltd, Newmont Mining Co, 79-80; sr res scientist, Johnson & Johnson, 80-82. *Mem:* Am Inst Mining, Metall & Petrol Engrs; Am Soc Metals; Iron & Steel Soc. *Res:* Electron microscopic investigation of phase transformation and deformation behavior in Beta-isomorphous titanium alloys; strengthening mechanisms and their application to the development of high strength-low alloy steels; dissolution kinetics of solids in liquid metals; thermodynamics and its application to metallurgical phenomenon; boron steel developments; deoxidation, desulfurization and sulfide modification in steel; dental alloy development; mold powders for casting of steel. *Mailing Add:* 136 E Delaware Ave Pennington NJ 08534

KOUL, OMANAND, NEUROCHEMISTRY, GLYCOCONJUGATES. *Current Pos:* res assoc, Eunice Kennedy Shriver Ctr Ment Retardation, 76-82, SCIENTIST, E K SHRIVER CTR, 87- *Personal Data:* b Kashmir, India, Feb 17, 47; US citizen; m 71, Prana; c Sidharth & Pamposh. *Educ:* Banaras Hindu Univ, India, MSc, 68, PhD(zool), 74. *Prof Exp:* Lectr physiol & biochem, Banaras Hindu Univ, India, 70-74; asst prof genetics & biol, Govind Ballabh Pant Univ Agr & Technol, India, 75-76; asst biochem, McLean Hosp, 84-86. *Concurrent Pos:* Res fel, Dept Neurol, Mass Gen Hosp, 76-82, asst biochem, Dept Neurol, 86-94, asst biochemist, 94-; adj fac, Anat & Physiol, Bunker Hill Community Col; res assoc, Med Sch, Harvard Univ, 84-86 & 88-; vis prof, Claude Bernard Univ, Lyon I, France, 96. *Mem:* Am Soc Neurochem; Soc Gerantol; Soc Glycobiol. *Res:* Brain function in health and disease; enzymology of lipids; metabolism of glycolipids in animals and cell cultures; myelin biosynthesis during development; regulation of glycosylation in tissues; fetal alcohol. *Mailing Add:* 15 Ardmore Ave Burlington MA 01803-4826

KOULOURIDES, THEODORE I, DENTISTRY, ORAL BIOLOGY. *Current Pos:* RETIRED. *Personal Data:* b Preveza, Greece, Sept 11, 25; US citizen; m 56; c 3. *Educ:* Nat Univ Athens, Dent Surgeon, 50; Univ Rochester, MS, 58; Univ Ala, DMD, 60. *Prof Exp:* From asst prof to assoc prof, Med Ctr, Univ Ala, Birmingham, 60-69, prof dent, Med Ctr, 69-, emer prof; sr scientist, Inst Dent Res, 71-91. *Concurrent Pos:* Fel pedodontics, Guggenheim Dent Clin, NY, 55; fel, Eastman Dent Dispensary, Rochester, NY, 55-56; USPHS res career develop award, 63-68. *Mem:* Am Dent Asn; Am Col Dent; Sigma Xi; Int Dent Fedn; Int Asn Dent Res. *Res:* Biological mineralization, especially factors involved in dental caries and calculus formation. *Mailing Add:* 2228 Garland Dr Birmingham AL 35216

KOUNOSU, SHIGERU, HIGH ENERGY PHYSICS, THEORETICAL PHYSICS. *Current Pos:* RETIRED. *Personal Data:* b Tokyo, Japan, Aug 23, 28; m 61; c 2. *Educ:* Fukushima Univ, Japan, BEd, 51; Univ Pa, MS, 63, PhD(physics), 65. *Prof Exp:* Res assoc physics, Princeton Univ, 65-67; from asst prof to assoc prof physics, Univ Lethbridge, 67-90. *Mem:* Am Phys Soc. *Res:* Elementary particle physics. *Mailing Add:* 1054 Henderson Lake Blvd Lethbridge AB T1K 3B2 Can

KOURANY, MIGUEL, MICROBIOLOGY, PUBLIC HEALTH. *Current Pos:* Dir, Pub Health Lab, Ministry Health, 54-63, chief, Bact Dept, 63-83, dir, Gorgas Mem Lab & Tech Servs, 83-94, ASSOC INVESTR, GORGAS MEM LAB, MIN HEALTH, PANAMA, 94- *Personal Data:* b Panama City, Panama, Sept 16, 24; div; c 4. *Educ:* Iowa State Col, BS, 50; Loyola Univ, Chicago, MS, 53; Univ Mich, Ann Arbor, MPH, 54, PhD(epidemiol sci), 63. *Honors & Awards:* Romulo Roux Medal, Ministry Health, 97. *Concurrent Pos:* Consult, Pan Am Health Orgn Lab Serv var countries, 71-; supv ad honoratium, Pub Health Lab Serv, Ministry Health, 63-83; mem, Epert Adv Panel Health Lab Serv, WHO, 67-96; mem, Pan Am Health Org Sci Adv Comt to Zoonosis Ctr, Argentina, 74 - *Mem:* Am Soc Trop Med & Hyg; AAAS; Panamanian Soc Microbiol & Parasitol (pres, 68, 69 & 78); Panamanian Acad Med & Surg. *Res:* Intracellular infections; etiological agents of diarrheal disease; ecology of vibrio parahaemolyticus; zoonosis in Panama. *Mailing Add:* Gorgas Mem Lab Ministry Health Panama 1 Panama

KOURI, DONALD JACK, THEORETICAL CHEMISTRY, CHEMICAL PHYSICS. *Current Pos:* from asst prof to prof, 67-88, distinguished univ prof, 88-96, H R & L C CULLEN DISTINGUISHED UNIV PROF CHEM & PHYSICS, UNIV HOUSTON, 96- *Personal Data:* b Hobart, Okla, July 25, 38; m 65, Shirley A Stewart; c Lisa R & David M. *Educ:* Okla Baptist Univ, BA, 60; Univ Wis, MS, 62, PhD(phys chem), 65. *Honors & Awards:* US Sr Scientist Award, Alexander von Humboldt Found, 73; Spec Creativity Award, NSF, 92. *Prof Exp:* Instr chem & physics, Okla Baptist Univ, 62-63; res assoc physics & mem joint inst lab astrophys, Univ Colo, 65-66; asst prof chem, Midwestern Univ, 66-67. *Concurrent Pos:* Fel, A P Sloan Found, 72-74; Weizmann Inst fel, 73; J S Guggenheim fel, 78-79; fel Inst Advan Studies, Hebrew Univ, Jerusalem, 78-79. *Mem:* Fel Am Phys Soc; Am Chem Soc; Am Asn Physics Teachers. *Res:* Theoretical research on quantum mechanical scattering phenomena; reactive and nonreactive molecular collisions; approximations for inelastic and reactive collisions; accurate representation of multivariate functions and derivatives. *Mailing Add:* Dept Chem Univ Houston Houston TX 77204-5641. *Fax:* 713-743-2709; *E-Mail:* kouri@uh.edu

KOUSHANPOUR, ESMAIL, PHYSIOLOGY, BIOPHYSICS. *Current Pos:* Asst prof, 63-68, assoc prof anesthesia, 82-92, ASSOC PROF PHYSIOL, MED SCH, NORTHWESTERN UNIV, ILL, 68. *Personal Data:* b Teheran, Iran, June 9, 34; US citizen; m 78; c 4. *Educ:* Columbia Univ, AB, 58; Mich State Univ, MS, 61, PhD(physiol), 63. *Concurrent Pos:* Nat Heart Inst fel, 65-; vis prof, Heidelberg Univ, WGer, 83-84; sr Fulbright prof, 83-84. *Mem:* AAAS; Am Physiol Soc; NY Acad Sci; Am Heart Asn. *Res:* Mathematical and experimental analyses of the cardiovascular and renal regulators; mechanism of the baroceptor process in the carotid sinus; role of carotid sinus in renal hypertension. *Mailing Add:* Dept Physiol Northwestern Univ Med Sch Chicago IL 60611

KOUSKOLEKAS, COSTAS ALEXANDER, ENTOMOLOGY. *Current Pos:* RETIRED. *Personal Data:* b Thessaloniki, Greece, May 10, 27; m 58; c 2. *Educ:* Univ Thessaloniki, Dipl agr, 51; Univ Mo-Columbia, MS, 58; Univ Ill, Urbana, PhD(entom), 64. *Prof Exp:* Teacher agron, Am Farm Sch, Thessaloniki, 54-56; res assoc agr entom, Natural Hist Surv & Agr Exp Sta, Univ Ill, Urbana, 62-63; consult, Doxiadis Assocs Int, Athens, Greece, 64-65; sr res officer entom, Benaki Phytopath Inst, Athens, 65-67; assoc prof entom, Auburn Univ, 67-93. *Mem:* Entom Soc Am; Int Orgn Biol Control. *Res:* Biology and control of insects of ornamentals and vegetables; integrated pest management. *Mailing Add:* 529 Sundilla Ct Auburn AL 36830

KOUSKY, VERNON E, DYNAMIC METEOROLOGY, CLIMATE VARIABILITY. *Current Pos:* RES METEOROLOGIST, CLIMATE ANALYSIS CTR, 84- *Personal Data:* b Detroit, Mich, Nov 2, 43; m 73, Jamie Vavra; c Timothy, Jason & Justin. *Educ:* Pa State Univ, BS, 65, MS, 67; Univ Wash, PhD(atmospheric sci), 70. *Honors & Awards:* Silver Medal, Dept Com. *Prof Exp:* Asst prof meteorol, Univ Utah, 70-75; prof collabr, Inst Astron & Geophys, Univ Sao Paulo, 75-77; assoc researcher & researcher, Inst Space Res, Brazil, 77-83. *Mem:* Am Meteorol Soc. *Res:* Synoptic meteorology; diagnostic study of wave motions in the tropical stratosphere; severe local storms; jetstream formation; tropopause deformation; atmospheric teleconnections; tropical meteorology; climate anomalies; weather and climate forecasting. *Mailing Add:* 2272 Ingleside Ct Waldorf MD 20602

KOUTCHER, JASON ARTHUR, NMR SPECTROSCOPY, METABOLIC STUDIES OF TUMORS. *Current Pos:* ASSOC PROF RADIOL & PHYSICS, MEM SLOAN KETTERING CANCER CTR, 85-, CHIEF DIAG IMAGING PHYSICS, 89-; ASSOC PROF RADIOL & PHYSICS, SCH MED, CORNELL UNIV, 89- *Personal Data:* b Brooklyn, NY, Feb 18, 50; m 75, Sharon Raretch; c Lawrence, Stephanie & Sara. *Educ:* Mass Inst Technol, BS, 72; State Univ NY, MD, 79, PhD(biophysics), 79. *Prof Exp:* Instr med, Tufts Univ Sch Med, 83-85; asst prof med, Harvard Med Sch, 85; asst prof radiol & physics, Cornell Univ Sch Med, 86-89. *Concurrent Pos:* Prin investr, NIH & Am Chem Soc, 84-97. *Mem:* Radiation Res Soc; Soc Magnetic Resonance Med; Am Asn Cancer Res. *Res:* Measuring changes in tumor metabolism that are caused by anti-cancer treatment, particularly chemotherapy and radiation, these studies include non-invasive measurements made on cells, animal tumors, and patients using nuclear magnetic resonance spectroscopy; long range goal to enhance the effectiveness of these agents. *Mailing Add:* 9 Brewster Terr New Rochelle NY 10804. *Fax:* 212-717-3010

KOUTS, HERBERT JOHN CECIL, NUCLEAR ENERGY, NUCLEAR REACTOR SAFETY. *Current Pos:* MEM, DEFENSE NUCLEAR FACIL SAFETY BD, US GOVT, 89- *Personal Data:* b Bisbee, Ariz, Dec 18, 19; m 42, 74, Barbara Stokes; c Anne (Golden) & Catherine. *Educ:* La State Univ, BS, 41, MS, 46; Princeton Univ, PhD(physics), 52. *Honors & Awards:* E O Lawrence Award, AEC, 63 & Distinguished Serv Award, 75; Distinguished Serv Award, US Nuclear Regulatory Comn, 76; Theos Thompson Award, Am Nuclear Soc. *Prof Exp:* Assoc physicist, Brookhaven Nat Lab, 50-51, asst group leader, 51-52, group leader reactor physics, 52-58, sr scientist & assoc div head, 58-73; dir, Div Reactor Safety Res, AEC, 73-75; dir, Off Nuclear Regulatory Res, US Nuclear Regulatory Comn, 75-76; chmn, Dept Nuclear Energy, Brookhaven Nat Lab, 77-87, sr scientist, 88-89. *Concurrent Pos:* Mem, Europ-Am Comt Reactor Physics, Europ Nuclear Energy Agency, 62-68; mem, Mayor's Tech Adv Comt on Radiation, NY, 69-73; chmn, Nuclear Adv Comt, Hall of Sci, NY, 69-73; prin adv reactor safety, NY State Atomic & Space Develop Authority, 69-73; mem, Int Nuclear Safety Adv Group, chmn, 88-91. *Mem:* Nat Acad Eng; fel Am Nuclear Soc; Int Atomic Energy Agency; Int Nuclear Safety Soc Group. *Res:* Elementary particle physics; shielding and physics of nuclear reactors. *Mailing Add:* 249 S Country Rd Brookhaven NY 11719

KOUTSKY, JAMES A, chemical engineering, polymer science; deceased, see previous edition for last biography

KOUVEL, JAMES SPYROS, SOLID STATE PHYSICS, SUPERCONDUCTORS. *Current Pos:* PROF PHYSICS, UNIV ILL, CHICAGO, 69- *Personal Data:* b Jersey City, NJ, May 23, 26; m 53, Audrey Lumsden; c Diana & Alexander. *Educ:* Yale Univ, BEng, 46, PhD(phys & elec eng), 51. *Prof Exp:* Res engr, Microwave Devices, Fed Telecommun Labs, NJ, 47-48; res fel physics, Univ Leeds, 51-53; res fel solid state physics, Harvard Univ, 53-55; physicist, Res & Develop Ctr, Gen Elec Co, 55-69. *Concurrent Pos:* Guggenheim fel, 67-68; vis scientist, Atomic Energy Res Estab, Harwell, Eng, 67-68; consult, Argonne Nat Lab, 69-89, mem rev comts, Solid State Sci & Mat Sci Div, 70-72, vis scientist, 73-74; mem, Mat Res Adv Comt, NSF, 80-82, eval panels, Nat Res Coun, 81-85; vis prof, Univ Paris, Orsay, 81. *Mem:* Fel Am Phys Soc; fel AAAS. *Res:* magnetic materials; critical phenomena; phase transitions; superconductors. *Mailing Add:* Dept Physics Univ Ill 845 W Taylor St Chicago IL 60607-7059. *Fax:* 312-996-9016

KOUYOUMJIAN, ROBERT G, ELECTROMAGNETICS, ANTENNAS. *Current Pos:* From asst to assoc prof, 55-62, prof, 62-82, EMER PROF, ELEC ENG DEPT, OHIO STATE UNIV, 82. *Personal Data:* b Cleveland, Ohio, Apr 26, 23. *Educ:* Ohio State Univ, BS, 48, PhD(physics), 53. *Honors & Awards:* Centennial Medal Award, Inst Elec & Electronics Engrs, 84, Tech Achievement Award, 92. *Concurrent Pos:* Distinguished lectr, Int Elec & Electronics Engr, 73-75. *Mem:* Nat Acad Eng; fel Inst Elec & Electronics Engrs. *Res:* Application of electromagnetic theory to the analysis of antennas and scatterers; asymptotic high frequency methods and their ray optical interpretation; uniform geometrical theory of diffraction; contributed articles to professional journals. *Mailing Add:* Ohio State Univ 654 Stinson Dr Columbus OH 43214

KOUZES, RICHARD THOMAS, nuclear physics, scientific instrumentation, for more information see previous edition

KOVAC, JEFFREY DEAN, PHYSICAL CHEMISTRY. *Current Pos:* from asst prof to assoc prof, 76-91, PROF CHEM, UNIV TENN, 91- *Personal Data:* b Cleveland, Ohio, May 29, 48; m 73, Susan Davis; c Peter J & Rachel S. *Educ:* Reed Col, BA, 70; Yale Univ, MPhil, 72, PhD(chem), 74. *Prof Exp:* Res assoc chem, Mass Inst Technol, 74-76. *Concurrent Pos:* Consult, Oak Ridge Nat Lab, 84-88; assoc, Univ Tenn Knoxville Ctr Appl & Prof Ethics. *Mem:* AAAS; Am Phys Soc; Am Chem Soc. *Res:* Statistical mechanics of polymers and simple fluids; equilibrium and non equilibrium thermodynamics; rubber elasticity; structure and formation of coal; computer simulation; scientific ethics; chemical education. *Mailing Add:* Dept Chem Univ Tenn Knoxville TN 37996-1600. *Fax:* 423-974-3454; *E-Mail:* jkovac@utk.edu

KOVACH, ARISZTID G B, MEDICAL RESEARCH. *Current Pos:* assoc prof, Dept Biochem, Semmelweis Univ Med Sch, Budapest, Hungary, 49-50, from assoc prof to prof physiol, 50-91, founder & head, Exp Res Dept, 59-91, chmn, Inst Physiol, 79-91, PROF PHYSIOL & SCI ADV, INST PHYSIOL, SCH MED, SEMMELWEIS UNIV, BUDAPEST, HUNGARY, 91-; RES PROF NEUROL, CVRC, DEPT NEUROL, UNIV PA, PHILADELPHIA, 92- *Educ:* Pazmany Peter Univ, Budapest, MD, 44; Karl Ruprecht Univ, Heidelberg, MS, 42; Hungarian Acad Sci, Budapest, PhD, 52. *Prof Exp:* Asst prof & chief, Physiol Lab, Biol Res Inst, Hungarian Acad Sci, Tihany, Lake Balaton, 45-48. *Concurrent Pos:* Adj prof physiol, Dept Neurol, Univ Pa, 70-92; secy gen, Int Union Physiol Sci, 74-80, first vpres, 80-83. *Mem:* Int Union Physiol Sci. *Res:* Irreversibility of hemorrhagic shock, the role of regulatory and metabolic processes; control of heart and peripheral circulation; neuroendocrinology; cerebral blood flow and metabolism; the role of nitric oxide in cerebral blood flow metasbolism and function. *Mailing Add:* 429 Johnson Pavillion 36th & Hamilton Walk Philadelphia PA 19104-6063

KOVACH, EUGENE GEORGE, ORGANIC CHEMISTRY, SCIENCE ADMINISTRATION. *Current Pos:* mem staff, Off Technol Policy, 78-80, dir, 80-82, CONSULT, OFF ADVAN TECHNOL, US DEPT STATE, 83- *Personal Data:* b Irvington, NJ, May 18, 22; m 50; c 5. *Educ:* Wayne State Univ, BS, 43, MS, 44; Harvard Univ, MA, 48, PhD, 49. *Prof Exp:* Res tutor, Harvard, 46-49; instr, Univ Fla, 49-50, asst prof, 51-54; asst prof, Colgate Univ, 50-51; sci adv, US Naval Forces, Ger, 54-57; chem prog, NSF, 57-59; asst sci adv, Int Sci & Tech Affairs, US Dept State, 59-65, actg dir, Off Gen Sci Affairs, 65-70; dep asst secy gen for sci affairs, NATO, 70-76; with Div of Policy Res, NSF, 76-78. *Mem:* AAAS; Am Chem Soc; Ger Chem Soc; Sigma Xi. *Res:* Structure of natural products; chelate compounds; theoretical organic chemistry; science education and administration; international relations. *Mailing Add:* 4118 Aspen St Chevy Chase MD 20815

KOVACH, JACK, GEOLOGY. *Current Pos:* From asst prof to assoc prof, 68-82, PROF GEOL, MUSKINGUM COL, 83- *Personal Data:* b Rices Landing, Pa, Mar 23, 40; m 65, Frances Block; c Thomas & John. *Educ:* Waynesburg Col, BSc, 62; Ohio State Univ, MSc, 67, PhD(geol), 74. *Concurrent Pos:* Res assoc, Nat Res Coun, Nat Acad Sci, 79-80; assoc, US Geol Surv, Denver. *Mem:* Geochem Soc. *Res:* Strontium isotope geochemistry and rubidium-strontium geochronology; biogeochemistry of nonmarine mollusk shells; composition of atmospheric precipitation; silurian stratigraphy and paleontology; biogeochemistry and isotopic composition of conodonts. *Mailing Add:* Dept Geol Muskingum Col New Concord OH 43762. *Fax:* 614-825-8404

KOVACH, LADIS DANIEL, mathematics, for more information see previous edition

KOVACHICH, GYULA BERTALAN, neurochemistry, for more information see previous edition

KOVACIC, GREGOR, APPLIED NONLINEAR DYNAMIC SYSTEMS, NEAR INTEGRABLE DYNAMIC SYSTEMS. *Current Pos:* Asst prof, 91-97, ASSOC PROF MATH, RENSSELAER POLYTECH INST, 97- *Personal Data:* b Koper, Slovenia, Oct 16, 60; m 90, Miriam E Herrera. *Educ:* Univ Ljub, BSc, 85; Calif Inst Technol, PhD(appl math), 90. *Honors & Awards:* Career Award, NSF, 95. *Concurrent Pos:* Director's funded postdoctoral fel, Los Alamos Nat Lab, 89-91; res fel, A P Sloan Found, 96. *Mem:* Soc Indust & Appl Math; Am Phys Soc. *Res:* Theory of nonlinear dynamical systems for ordinary and partial differential equations and its applications to laser and non-linear fiber optics, classical mechanics and fluid mechanics. *Mailing Add:* Math Sci Dept Rensselaer Polytech Inst Troy NY 12180-3590. *Fax:* 518-276-4824; *E-Mail:* kovacq@rpi.edu

KOVACIC, JOSEPH EDWARD, organic chemistry, for more information see previous edition

KOVACIC, PETER, ORGANIC CHEMISTRY. *Current Pos:* PROF CHEM, UNIV WIS-MILWAUKEE, 68- *Personal Data:* b Wylandville, Pa, Aug 1, 21; m 46; c 6. *Educ:* Hanover Col, AB, 43, DSc, 64; Univ Ill, PhD(chem), 46. *Prof Exp:* Asst org chem, Mass Inst Technol, 46-47; instr, Columbia Univ, 47-48; res chemist, E I du Pont de Nemours & Co, 48-55; from asst prof to prof chem, Case Inst Technol, 55-68. *Mem:* Am Chem Soc. *Res:* N-Halamines; bridgehead imines; rearrangements; nitrenium ions; polymerization of aromatic nuclei; charge transfer and oxy radicals in living systems. *Mailing Add:* Dept Chem San Diego State Univ 5500 Campanile Dr San Diego CA 92182-1030

KOVACS (NAGY), HANNA, ORGANIC CHEMISTRY. *Current Pos:* RETIRED. *Personal Data:* b Szeged, Hungary, Oct 31, 19; US citizen; m 50; c 2. *Educ:* Univ Szeged, PhD(org chem), 45. *Prof Exp:* Res assoc org chem, Univ Szeged, 44-46, physiol, 46-50; res assoc org chem, Univ Budapest, 50-56; res assoc bact, Univ Basel, 57 & Detroit Inst Cancer Res, 58-59; res assoc peptide chem, St John's Univ, NY, 59-63; res chemist, Naval Appl Sci Lab, Brooklyn, 63-70; clin chemist, Mt Sinai Hosp, NY, 70-85. *Mem:* Nat Acad Clin Biochem; Am Chem Soc; NY Acad Sci; Sigma Xi; Am Asn Clin Chem. *Res:* Author or coauthor of twenty-eight publications in the field of peptide, heterocyclic, polymer, medicinal and clinical chemistry. *Mailing Add:* 639 S Grand Ave Pasadena CA 91105-3322

KOVACS, BELA A, PHARMACOLOGY, ALLERGY. *Current Pos:* SCI ADV, DEPT NAT HEALTH & WELFARE, FOOD & DRUG DIRECTORATE, 69- *Personal Data:* b Nagykoros, Hungary, Aug 28, 21; Can citizen; m 52; c Eva Maria. *Educ:* Med Univ Szeged, MD, 46; Univ London, DrPhil(pharmacol), 61. *Prof Exp:* From asst prof to assoc prof pharmacol, Med Univ Szeged, 49-56; asst prof, 61-64, assoc prof pharmacol & exp med, 64-69, assoc prof exp med, McGill Univ, 69- *Concurrent Pos:* Res fel org chem, Univ Basel, 56-57; res fel pharmacol, Nat Inst Med Res, London, 57-61; lectr, Sch Pharm, Univ London, 59-61. *Mem:* Am Soc Pharmacol & Exp Therapeut; Pharmacol Soc Can; Brit Pharmacol Soc; Am Col Clin Pharmacol & Therapeut; Can Soc Immunol. *Res:* Histamine and antihistaminics; inflammation; gastric secretion; pulmonary edema. *Mailing Add:* Dept Health & Welfare Can 300 Driveway No 9D Ottawa ON K1S 3M6 Can

KOVACS, BELA VICTOR, ACOUSTICS TESTING. *Current Pos:* VPRES, ATMOSPHERE FURN CO TECH CTR, 87- *Personal Data:* b Tiszaors, Hungary, Nov 9, 30; m 64; c 2. *Educ:* Wayne State Univ, BSME,65; Univ Conn, MSMET, 69. *Honors & Awards:* Tech Achievement Award, Ford Motor Co, 86. *Prof Exp:* Design engr, Luster Corp of Can, 58-60; res engr, Ford Sci Res Lab, 62-87. *Concurrent Pos:* Adj prof, Univ Mich & Wayne State Univ, 85; consult, Hentschel Instruments. *Mem:* Am Foundrymens Soc; Am Inst Mining & Metall Eng; Am Soc Non Destructive Testing; Am Soc Metals. *Res:* Solid state thermodynamics, crystallography acoustical properties of metals and composites cast iron metallurgy. *Mailing Add:* 1250 Club Dr Bloomfield Hills MI 48302

KOVACS, CHARLES J, EXPERIMENTAL BIOLOGY. *Current Pos:* PROF RADIATION ONCOL & DIR, DIV RADIATION THER, RADIATION ONCOL CTR, SCH MED, E CAROLINA UNIV, GREENVILLE, NC, 85- *Personal Data:* b Fairfield, Conn, Apr 7, 41. *Educ:* Siena Col, BS, 63; St John's Univ, MS, 65, PhD(microbiol & biochem), 69. *Prof Exp:* USPHS fel, Nat Cancer Inst, NIH, 69-71; res instr, Dept Med, Hahnemann Med Col, Philadelphia, Pa, 71-72; instr, Div Radiobiol & Biophys, Sch Med, Univ Va, Charlottesville, 72-75; asst prof, Dept Pediat, 75-76; assoc scientist, Cancer Res Unit, Div Radiation Oncol, Allegheny Gen Hosp, Pittsburgh, Pa, 76-79, sr scientist, Cancer Res Labs, 79-80; assoc prof, Dept Radiol, Div Radiation Oncol, Col Med, Univ SAla, Mobile, 80-81; assoc prof & dir, Radiation Oncol Labs, Dept Radiol, Sect Radiother, Bowman Gray Sch Med, Winston-Salem, NC, 81-85. *Concurrent Pos:* Res assoc, Brookhaven Nat Lab, AEC, 70-71; prin investr or co-prin investr grants, NIH, 83-86, 84-86 & 90-; consult, NIH, Vet Admin, Mariculture, Inc, NC Biotechnol Ctr. *Mem:* Sigma Xi; AAAS; Am Asn Cancer Res; Am Soc Cell Biol; Int Soc Exp Hemat; Am Soc Clin Immunol. *Mailing Add:* Dept Radiation Ther Sch Med ECarolina Univ Greenville NC 27858

KOVACS, EVE MARIA, MEDICINE. *Current Pos:* RETIRED. *Personal Data:* b Budapest, Hungary, Apr 13, 25; m 52, B A. *Educ:* Univ Szeged, MD, 52. *Prof Exp:* Lectr pharmacol, Univ Szeged, 52-54; lectr internal med, Univ Clin, 54-55, asst prof, 55-56; pharmacologist, Geigy AG, Switz, 57-58; lectr, McGill Univ, 61-64, asst prof pharmacol, 64 -; sci adv, Dept Nat Health & Welfare, Food Directorate, 70-92. *Concurrent Pos:* Cancer res fel, Dept Pharmacol, Univ London, 58-61. *Mem:* Pharmacol Soc Can; Am Soc Pharmacol & Exp Therapeut; Int Soc Biochem Pharmacol; Can Med Asn. *Res:* Cancer immunology; allergy; histamine; histamine metabolites; gastric secretion. *Mailing Add:* 300 Driveway No 9D Ottawa ON K1S 3M6 Can

KOVACS, EVE VERONIKA, COMPUTER SCIENCE. *Current Pos:* AT ARGONNE NAT LAB. *Personal Data:* b Melbourne, Australia, Nov 12, 54. *Educ:* Univ Melbourne, BSc, 76, PhD(physics), 80, dipl comput sci, 80. *Prof Exp:* Vis Scientist, Stanford Linear Accelerator Ctr, 80-81; res assoc. Rockefeller Univ, 81- *Mem:* Am Phys Soc. *Res:* Monte Carlo simulations of lattice guage theories with particular emphasis on finite size effects and the interquark potential. *Mailing Add:* Fermilab MS 318 PO Box 500 Batavia IL 60510

KOVACS, JULIUS STEPHEN, THEORETICAL PHYSICS. *Current Pos:* from asst prof to assoc prof, 56-68, PROF PHYSICS, MICH STATE UNIV, 68-, ASSOC CHMN DEPT, 77- *Personal Data:* b Trenton, NJ, Aug 20, 28; m 56; c 2. *Educ:* Lehigh Univ, BS, 50; Ind Univ, MS, 52, PhD, 55. *Prof Exp:* Asst prof physics, Univ Toledo, 54-55; res assoc, Ind Univ, 55-56. *Res:* Meson physics; elementary particles. *Mailing Add:* 1016 Beech St East Lansing MI 48823

KOVACS, KALMAN T, ENDOCRINOLOGY, ELECTRON MICROSCOPY. *Current Pos:* PATHOLOGIST, ST MICHAEL'S HOSP, TORONTO, 71-; PROF PATH, UNIV TORONTO, 80- *Personal Data:* b Szeged, Hungary, July 11, 26; Can citizen; m 62, Eva Horvath. *Educ:* Univ Szeged, Hungary, MD, 50; Univ Liverpool, PhD(path), 66; FCAP & FRCP(C), 73; FRCPath, 80, DSc 66. *Honors & Awards:* Hungarian Acad Sci Award, 68; Selye Medal; Hetenyi Medal. *Prof Exp:* Demonstr & lectr, Dept Path, Univ London, 50-54, sr lectr, Dept Med, 54-68; vis scientist exp med, Univ Montreal, 68-71; asst prof, Univ Toronto, 71-80. *Concurrent Pos:* Res fel path, Docent Univ Szeged, 60 & Crosby res fel, Univ Liverpool, 64-65. *Mem:* Int Acad Path; Am Path Soc; US Endocrine Soc; corresp mem, Romanian Acad Sci. *Res:* Morphologic study of endocrine glands, especially human pituitaries and pituitary adenomas; correlation of structural features with secretory activity. *Mailing Add:* Dept Pathol Univ Toronto St Michael's Hosp 30 Bond St Toronto ON M5B 1W8 Can. *Fax:* 416-864-5870

KOVACS, KIT M, PARENTAL INVESTMENT STRATEGISTS, MATING SYSTEMS. *Current Pos:* ASSOC PROF BIOL, UNIV WATERLOO, 87- *Personal Data:* b Iserloln, Ger, Nov 7, 56; Can citizen; m 81. *Educ:* York Univ, Toronto, HBSC, 79; Lakehead Univ, Thunder Bay, MSC, 82; Univ Guelph, PhD(zool), 86. *Prof Exp:* Post doctorate fel zool, NSERC & NATO, 86-87. *Concurrent Pos:* Res assoc, La Vie Wildlife Res Assoc Ltd, 82- *Mem:* Marine Mammal Soc; Can Zool Soc; Am Ornith Union; Animal Behav Soc. *Res:* Behavioral ecology, evolution, mating systems, parental investment, pinnipeds. *Mailing Add:* Biol Dept Univ Waterloo Waterloo ON N2L 3G1 Can

KOVACS, MIKLOS I P, ANALYTICAL CHEMISTRY. *Current Pos:* res scientist marine lipids, fisheries & oceans res, 75-79, RES SCIENTIST GEN CHEM, AGR CAN RES INST, 79- *Personal Data:* b Budapest, Hungary, Feb 1, 36; Can citizen; m 61; c 2. *Educ:* Univ Keszthely, Hungary, BS, 60; Univ Budapest, BSc, 68; Univ Guelph, MSc, 69; Univ Man, PhD(biochem), 74. *Prof Exp:* Teaching fel biochem, Univ Sask, 74-75. *Mem:* Am Asn Cereal Chemists. *Res:* Wheat quality; interaction of protein, starch and lipids. *Mailing Add:* Agr & Agri Food Can Winnipeg Res Ctr 195 DaFoe Rd Winnipeg MB R3T 2M9 Can

KOVACS, SANDOR J, JR, CARDIOLOGY. *Current Pos:* res fel, dept med, 82-85, ASST PROF CARDIOL & RADIOL, DEPT INTERNAL MED, WASHINGTON UNIV, 85- *Personal Data:* b Budapest, Hungary, Aug 17, 47; US citizen. *Educ:* Cornell Univ, BS, 69; Calif Inst Technol, MS, 72, PhD(theoret physics), 77; Univ Miami, MD, 79. *Prof Exp:* Res asst theoret physics, Calif Inst Technol, 71-77. *Concurrent Pos:* Med consult & lectr, Nat Asn Underwater Instrs, 74- *Mem:* Sigma Xi; Int Soc Gen Relativity & Gravitation; AAAS; Am Col Physicians; Am Col Cardiol; Am Bd Internal Med; Am Physiol Soc. *Res:* Noninvasive cardiological diagnostic methods including cardiac electrophysiology, arrythmia detection and analysis; biophysics. *Mailing Add:* Three Buckhammon Pl St Louis MO 63124-1730

KOVAL, CARL ANTHONY, CHEMISTRY. *Current Pos:* asst prof chem, 80-87, ASSOC PROF, UNIV COLO, 87- *Personal Data:* b York, Pa, June 28, 52; div; c 1. *Educ:* Juniata Col, BS, 74; Calif Inst Technol, PhD(chem), 79. *Prof Exp:* Fel, Purdue Univ, 78-80. *Mem:* Am Chem Soc. *Res:* Electrochemistry at semiconductor electrodes; steric inhibition of exothermic redox reactions; facilitated transport of molecules across liquid membranes. *Mailing Add:* 8897 Ute Dr Golden CO 80403-8319

KOVAL, CHARLES FRANCIS, OUTREACH PROGRAMMING. *Current Pos:* Res asst, Univ Wis-Madison, 60-65, from instr to prof, 65-95, exten entomologist, 65-80, dir, Univ Exp Farms, 80-83, dean, Wis Coop Exten Serv, 83-87, chmn dept, 88-90, EMER PROF ENTOM, UNIV WIS-MADISON, 95- *Personal Data:* b Ashland, Wis, May 10, 38; m 57, Patricia L Riley; c Michael, Daniel & Mary L. *Educ:* Northland Col, BA, 60; Univ Wis, MS, 63, PhD(entom), 66. *Concurrent Pos:* Village Forester, Shorewood Hills. *Mem:* Entom Soc Am; Inst Sci Anal; Acad Health Sci. *Res:* Insect management on turf, landscape plants and greenhouse crops with emphasis on integrated pest management strategies; urban forestry; development of extension outreach programs. *Mailing Add:* Dept Entom 237 Russell Labs Madison WI 53706. *Fax:* 608-262-3322; *E-Mail:* koval@caishp.cals.wisc.edu

KOVAL, DANIEL, MATHEMATICS. *Current Pos:* chmn dept, 71-77, PROF MATH, PAC UNION COL, 71- *Personal Data:* b Fitchburg, Mass, Nov 28, 22; m 45; c 2. *Educ:* Worcester Polytech Inst, BS, 44; Boston Univ, AM, 52, PhD(math), 65. *Prof Exp:* Physicist radiation lab, Mass Inst Technol, 44-46; asst prof appl math & physics, Atlantic Union Col, 46-60; assoc prof math, Columbia Union Col, 60-71. *Mem:* Math Asn Am. *Res:* Partial differential equations. *Mailing Add:* 1405 Crestmont Dr Angwin CA 94508

KOVAL, DON O, BIOLOGICAL ENGINEERING. *Current Pos:* PROF ELEC ENG, UNIV ALTA, EDMONTON, 80- *Personal Data:* b Pickle Crow, Ont, Mar 20, 42. *Educ:* Univ Saskatoon, Sask, BE, 65, MSc, 69, PhD, 78. *Honors & Awards:* Commemorative Medal Honor, Am Biog Inst, 91. *Prof Exp:* Subtransmission design engr distrib, Sask Power Corp, Can, 65-66; spec studies engr distrib, B C Hydro Power Authority, Can, 67-79. *Mem:* Fel Inst Elec & Electronics Engrs; Int Asn Sci & Technol Develop; Int Inst Advan Studies Systs Res & Cybernetics; fel Am Biog Inst; fel Int Biog Asn. *Mailing Add:* Dept Elec Eng Univ Alta Edmonton AB T6G 2G7 Can

KOVAL, LESLIE R(OBERT), ENGINEERING MECHANICS, STRUCTURAL ACOUSTICS. *Current Pos:* assoc prof mech eng, 71-76, PROF MECH & AEROSPACE ENG, UNIV MO, ROLLA, 76-, ASSOC CHMN MECH ENG, 85- *Personal Data:* b Rochester, NY, Jan 12, 33; m 56, Barbara Glenn; c Marshall, Deborah & Jerald. *Educ:* Univ Rochester, BS, 55; Cornell Univ, MS, 57, PhD(eng mech), 61. *Prof Exp:* McMullen fel, Cornell Univ, 55-56, instr eng mech, 58-61; mem tech staff, Ramo-Wooldridge Corp, 57-58; mem tech staff, TRW Systs Group, 61-66, staff engr, TRW Systs, Inc, Calif, 66-69; USAID vis prof, Fed Univ Rio de Janeiro, 69-70. *Concurrent Pos:* Consult, Fed Systs Div, IBM, Inc, 59 & Lockheed-Calif Co, 78-85; lectr, Univ Southern Calif, 62-69; mem tech staff, Litton Ship Systs, Calif, 71. *Mem:* Am Soc Mech Engrs; Acoust Soc Am; Am Acad Mech; Am Inst Aeronaut & Astronaut. *Res:* Vibrations and dynamic response of shell structures; liquid sloshing in rigid and flexible tanks; shimmy of aircraft landing gears; liquid behavior in low-gravity environments; acoustics; structure-borne noise propagation; smart structures. *Mailing Add:* Dept Mech & Aeronaut Eng and Eng Mech Univ Mo Rolla MO 65409-0050. *Fax:* 573-341-4607; *E-Mail:* lkoval@umr.edu

KOVAL, THOMAS MICHAEL, CELL BIOLOGY, RADIATION BIOLOGY. *Current Pos:* SR STAFF SCIENTIST, NAT COUN RADIATION PROTECTION & MEASUREMENT, 93- *Personal Data:* b Brownsville, Pa, Nov 20, 50; m 84, Amy Cvengros; c Thomas II, Matthew & Rachel. *Educ:* Pa State Univ, BS, 72; Ohio State Univ, MS, 74, PhD(zool), 76. *Prof Exp:* Nat Res Serv award fel physiol & biophys, Univ Ill, 76-77; res assoc cancer res, Allegheny Gen Hosp, 77-79; from asst prof to assoc prof radiation ther & nuclear med, Hahnemann Med Col, 79-82; assoc res prof radiol, George Wash Univ Sch Med, 82-88; assoc staff scientist, Nat Coun Radiation Protection & Measurements, 82-86, staff scientist, 87-88; sr assoc consult, Div Radiation Oncol, Mayo Clin, 88-93, prof oncol, 88-93. *Mem:* Radiation Res Soc; Am Soc Cell Biol; Tissue Cult Asn; Sigma Xi; Am Soc Photobiol; Am Asn Cancer Res; AAAS. *Res:* Stress-inducible processes in eukaryotic cells; cell and molecular biology; cell differentiation; radiation biology; mechanisms of radioresistance of cultured lepidopteran insect cells. *Mailing Add:* 4653 Cherry Valley Dr Rockville MD 20853. *Fax:* 301-907-8768

KOVALAK, WILLIAM PAUL, AQUATIC BIOLOGY. *Current Pos:* ASST PROF AQUATIC BIOL, UNIV MICH, DEARBORN, 78- *Personal Data:* b Detroit, Mich, Apr 12, 46; m 70; c 3. *Educ:* Eastern Mich Univ, BS, 67; Univ Mich, MS, 69, PhD(fisheries), 75. *Prof Exp:* Asst prof biol, Allegheny Col, 75-78. *Concurrent Pos:* Biol systs scientist, Detroit Edison, 79- *Mem:* NAm Benthological Soc. *Res:* Behavioral ecology of stream insects; ecology of Great Lakes fishes. *Mailing Add:* Dept Nat Sci Univ Mich Dearborn 4901 Evergreen Rd Dearborn MI 48128-2406

KOVALY, JOHN J, radar, missile systems, for more information see previous edition

KOVAR, FREDERICK RICHARD, NUCLEAR PHYSICS, PLASMA PHYSICS & MECHANICS. *Current Pos:* INSTR PHYSICS, DIABLO VALLEY COL, 94- *Personal Data:* b Cleveland, Ohio, Sept 20, 33; m 62, Margaret Wright; c Kathleen, Karen, Frederick Jr & Christine. *Educ:* John Carroll Univ, BS, 55; Washington Univ, St Louis, MA, 57, PhD(physics), 63. *Prof Exp:* Instr physics, St Bonaventure Univ, 59-61; sr physicist & proj mgr, Lawrence Livermore Lab, Univ Calif, 63-93. *Concurrent Pos:* Consult, Bradford Components Co, NY, 60; spec sci adv, Asst Secy Defense Atomic Energy, 84-86. *Mem:* Am Phys Soc. *Res:* Hydrodynamics, strategic analysis, and nuclear energy. *Mailing Add:* 1078 Hacienda Dr Walnut Creek CA 94598

KOVAR, JOHN ALVIS, SOIL MORPHOLOGY, SOIL FERTILITY. *Current Pos:* area dir, 67-86, REGIONAL DIR, TENN VALLEY AUTHORITY, 86- *Personal Data:* b Ennis, Tex, Nov 30, 32; div; c John D & Tera (Shivitz). *Educ:* Tex Tech Univ, BS, 56; Tex A&M Univ, MS, 63; Iowa State Univ, PhD(agron), 67. *Prof Exp:* Soil scientist, Soil Conserv Serv, USDA, 53-56 & 59-60; res asst soil anal, Tex A&M Univ, 60-62; res assoc soil surv, Iowa State Univ, 62-67. *Concurrent Pos:* Fel, Welder Wildlife Found. *Mem:* Sigma Xi; Am Soil Sci Soc; Am Soc Agron; Coun Agr Sci & Technol; Soil & Water Conserv Soc; Int Soc Soil Sci. *Res:* Soil morphology and genesis; soil fertility. *Mailing Add:* 6515 Mimms Dr Dallas TX 75252-5432

KOVATCH, GEORGE, ELECTRONICS & SYSTEMS ENGINEERING, TRANSPORTATION SYSTEMS. *Current Pos:* proj mgr, US Dept Transp, 70-76, chief, Transp Indust Anal Br, 76-81, chief, Indust Anal & Productivity Div, 81-83, CHIEF, UNIV RES & TECHNOL INNOVATION OFF, TRANSP SYSTS CTR, US DEPT TRANSP, 83-, DIR, SMALL BUS INNOVATION RES PROG, 84- *Personal Data:* b Scranton, Pa, Feb 20, 34; m 68; c 4. *Educ:* Princeton Univ, BSE, 55; Cornell Univ, MS, 60, PhD, 62. *Honors & Awards:* Bronze Medal, US Dept Transp. *Prof Exp:* Engr electronics, Gen Elec Co, 55-60; commun officer, USAF, 56-57; instr control eng, Cornell Univ, 60-62; sr eng specialist control & guid systs, Martin Co, 62-64; lab chief control & info systs, NASA, 64-67, dept dir, Off Control Theory & Appln, 67-70. *Concurrent Pos:* Mem vis sci staff, Res Inst Adv Studies, Md, 62-64; vis lectr, Drexel Inst, 63-64, Brown Univ, 68-70. *Mem:* Sr mem Inst Elec & Electronics Engrs. *Res:* Analysis and synthesis of automatic control and guidance systems utilizing modern control theory and techniques; analysis of intermodal transportation systems including new urban systems; automotive fuel economy studies; automotive industry analysis; university research and small business innovative research programs management; defense conversion small business; high technology research and development. *Mailing Add:* Three Saw Mill Pond Rd Hingham MA 02043-3457. *Fax:* 617-494-2370; *E-Mail:* kovatch@volpe1.dot.gov

KOVATS, ANDRE, mechanical engineering; deceased, see previous edition for last biography

KOVELMAN, ROBERT, VIROLOGY, TRANSCRIPTIONAL REGULATION. *Current Pos:* SCIENTIST, SIGNAL PHARMACEUT, 94- *Personal Data:* b New York, NY, Oct 30, 63. *Educ:* Columbia Univ, AB, 85; Rockefeller Univ, PhD(biochem & molecular biol), 92. *Prof Exp:* Postdoctoral fel, Scripps Res Inst, 92-94. *Mem:* AAAS. *Mailing Add:* 5555 Oberlin Dr San Diego CA 92121

KOVES, WILLIAM JOHN, STRESS THERMAL & DYNAMIC ANALYSIS OF PROCESS EQUIPMENT, COMPUTATIONAL FLUID MECHANICS FOR PROCESS EQUIPMENT. *Current Pos:* eng staff, 73-87, tech mgr, 87-92, ENG FEL, UOP, 92- *Personal Data:* b Chicago, Ill, Nov 5, 43; m 77, Evelyn G Cober; c Brian & Melissa. *Educ:* Univ Ill, BS, 66, MS, 67; Ill Inst Technol, PhD(mech eng), 93. *Prof Exp:* Engr/scientist, Douglas Aircraft, 67-71; sr engr, Aerojet Gen Corp, 71-73. *Concurrent Pos:* Chmn, Design Task Group, Am Soc Mech Engrs, 79-, Subgroup High Pressure Piping, 80-84, Comt Flaw Eval, 96-, mem, High Pressure Vessels, 80-82, Subgroup Design Anal/External Pressure, 80-, Mech Design Comt, 86-, Comt Post Construct, 96-; chmn, Comt Elevated Temperature Design, Pressure Vessel Res Coun, 91-, chmn Task Group Large Shell Intersections, 93- *Mem:* Fel Am Soc Mech Engrs. *Res:* Stress analysis of pressure vessels and piping systems, specifically high temperature design, fatigue vibration, fracture mechanics and finite element analysis; fluid mechanics, multi-phase flow and granular solids as they apply to the performance of process equipment. *Mailing Add:* 1015 Cobble Hill Ct Hoffman Estates IL 60195. *Fax:* 847-391-2253

KOVESI-DOMOKOS, SUSAN, ELEMENTARY PARTICLE PHYSICS. *Current Pos:* assoc res scientist, Johns Hopkins Univ, 69-74, asst prof theoret physics, 74-79, assoc prof physics, 79-82, PROF THEORET PHYSICS, JOHNS HOPKINS UNIV, 82- *Personal Data:* b Budapest, Hungary, Aug 16, 39; US citizen; m 67. *Educ:* Eotvos Lorand Univ, dipl physics, 63. *Prof Exp:* Res asst theoret physics, Eotvos Lorand Univ, 62-63; res assoc, Cent Res Inst Physics, Budapest, 63-68. *Concurrent Pos:* Vis sci consult, Rutherford Lab, Eng, 73; vis scientist, Europ Orgn Nuclear Res, Switz, 75-76, Univ Florence, Italy, 83 & Stanford Linear Acceleration Ctr, 84; vis sci staff mem, Deutsches Electronen-Synchrotron, Hamburg, Ger, 76. *Mem:* Ital Phys Soc; Europ Phys Soc; Am Math Soc. *Res:* Strong interactions of elementary particles at high energy; critical phenomena. *Mailing Add:* Dept Physics & Astron Johns Hopkins Univ Baltimore MD 21218-2689

KOVITZ, ARTHUR A(BRAHAM), FLUID DYNAMICS. *Current Pos:* from asst prof to assoc prof, 58-69, actg chmn dept mech eng & astronaut sci, 71-73, PROF MECH ENG, NORTHWESTERN UNIV, EVANSTON, 69- *Personal Data:* b Detroit, Mich, Aug 6, 28; m 57, Valerie Silverman; c Claudia R & Jordan A. *Educ:* Univ Mich, BSE, 50, MS, 51; Princeton Univ, PhD(aeronaut eng), 57. *Prof Exp:* Rocket res engr, Bell Aircraft Corp, NY, 51-52; res assoc, Princeton Univ, 57, asst dir proj Squid, 57-58. *Concurrent Pos:* Consult, Aeronaut Res Assocs, Princeton, 57-58, Bendix Aviation Corp, 60, Am Mach & Foundry, 62, Argonne Nat Labs, 79-80 & 81-82, Southern Conf Eng Educ, 84, Universal Energy Systs, 85, AFOSR, 86-87 & Vislaase Corp, 88-. *Res:* Heat transfer; fluid mechanics. *Mailing Add:* Dept Mech Eng Technol Inst Northwestern Univ Evanston IL 60201-2970

KOW, LEE-MING, HYPOTHALAMUS, NEUROPEPTIDES. *Current Pos:* SR RES ASSOC, ROCKEFELLER UNIV, 72- *Educ:* Calif Inst Technol, PhD(neurophysiol), 72. *Mailing Add:* Dept Neurobiol Rockefeller Univ 1230 York Ave New York NY 10021-6399

KOWAL, CHARLES THOMAS, ASTRONOMY. *Current Pos:* STAFF SCIENTIST, COMPUT SCI CORP, SPACE TELESCOPE SCI INST, 86- *Personal Data:* b Buffalo, NY, Nov 8, 40; m 68; c 1. *Educ:* Univ Southern Calif, BS, 63. *Honors & Awards:* James Craig Watson Medal, Nat Acad Sci, 79. *Prof Exp:* Res asst astron, Calif Inst Technol, 63-65 & Univ Hawaii, 65-66; res asst, Calif Inst Technol, 66-75, assoc scientist, 76-77, scientist astron, 78-81, mem prof staff, 81-85. *Mem:* Am Astron Soc; Int Astron Union. *Res:* Supernovae; planetary satellites; asteroids; comets. *Mailing Add:* 7394 Eden Brook Dr Apt 417 Columbia MD 21046. *E-Mail:* kowal@stsci.edu

KOWAL, GEORGE M, NUCLEAR ENGINEERING, MECHANICAL ENGINEERING. *Current Pos:* DEPT MGR APPL ENG ANALYSIS, GILBERT ASSOCS INC, 73- *Personal Data:* b July 6, 38; US citizen; m 63; c 4. *Educ:* Univ Detroit, BS, 61; Pa State Univ, MS, 64. *Prof Exp:* Nuclear eng radiation protection, Elec Boat Div, Gen Dynamics Corp, 64-67; nuclear proj engr gen anal, 67-73. *Concurrent Pos:* Mem indust prof adv coun, Pa State Univ, 73-77; instr, Reading Area Community Col, 76-; adj assoc prof, Drexel Univ, 76- *Mem:* Am Nuclear Soc. *Res:* Analysts associated with nuclear power generation, especially nuclear safety, shielding, heaalth physics, fuel management, licensing, regulation and emergency core cooling systems. *Mailing Add:* 1512 Colony Dr Reading PA 19610

KOWAL, JEROME, INTERNAL MEDICINE & GERIATRICS, BIOCHEMISTRY. *Current Pos:* ASSOC CHIEF STAFF, GERIATRIC EXTENDED CARE, CLEVELAND VA MED CTR, 84- *Personal Data:* b New York, NY, Mar 16, 31; m 58, Martine Janney; c Ann & Robert. *Educ:* Tufts Univ, BS, 52; Johns Hopkins Univ, MD, 56. *Prof Exp:* Steroid trainee, Worcester Found Exp Biol, 62-63; from asst prof to assoc prof med, Mt Sinai Sch Med, 65-70; assoc prof, Sch Med, Case Western Res Univ, 70-74, assoc dean vet affairs, 77-84; chief staff, Cleveland Vet Admin Med Ctr, 77-84; dir, Geriatrics Ctr Clin Assessment, Educ & Res, 84, Div Geriatric Med, Case Western Res Univ, 84. *Concurrent Pos:* Fel endocrinol, Mt Sinai Sch Med, 60-61; fel molecular biol, Albert Einstein Col Med, 63-65; chief med serv, Cleveland Vet Admin Hosp, 73-77. *Mem:* Endocrine Soc; Am Soc Clin Invest; Am Soc Biol Chemists; Am Geriat Soc; Geront Soc Am. *Res:* Mechanisms of hormone and enzyme action; biochemical regulation of adrenal cells; aging. *Mailing Add:* Dept Med Case Western Res Univ 12200 Fairhill Rd Cleveland OH 44120. *Fax:* 216-844-7254

KOWAL, NORMAN EDWARD, wastewater treatment, computer simulation, for more information see previous edition

KOWAL, ROBERT RAYMOND, SYSTEMATIC BOTANY, BIOMETRY. *Current Pos:* asst prof, 71-76, ASSOC PROF BOT, UNIV WIS-MADISON, 76- *Personal Data:* b Paterson, NJ, Apr 23, 39. *Educ:* Cornell Univ, BA, 60, PhD(plant taxon & ecol), 68. *Prof Exp:* Fel biomath, Dept Exp Statist, NC State Univ, 67-69; vis asst prof biol, Kans State Univ, 69-71. *Mem:* AAAS; Bot Soc Am; Soc Study Evolution; Am Soc Plant Taxon; Am Inst Biol Sci; Int Asn Plan Taxon. *Res:* Systematics of Senecio aureus and allied species; multivariate analysis, especially canonical analysis, as a tool in plant systematics; cytology of asteraceae tribe senecioneae. *Mailing Add:* Dept Bot 132 Birge Hall Univ Wis-Madison 430 Lincoln Dr Madison WI 53706-1381. *Fax:* 608-262-7509; *E-Mail:* rrkowal@macc.wisc.edu

KOWALAK, ALBERT DOUGLAS, PHYSICAL INORGANIC CHEMISTRY, BIOINORGANIC CHEMISTRY. *Current Pos:* asst prof, 67-71, ASSOC PROF CHEM, LOWELL TECHNOL INST, 71-, CHMN DEPT, 77- *Personal Data:* b Portsmouth, Va, Aug 14, 36; div; c 2. *Educ:* Col William & Mary, BS, 58; Va Polytech Inst, MS, 63, PhD(chem), 65. *Honors & Awards:* Fulbright lectr, Univ Repub, Montevideo, Uruguay. *Prof Exp:* Teacher chem high sch, Va, 58-59; rubber chemist, O'Sullivan Rubber Corp, 60; teacher math high sch, Va, 60-61; res asst, Air Force Off Sci Res, 63; instr inorg chem, Rose Polytech Inst, 65-67. *Mem:* Am Chem Soc. *Res:* Kinetics of the arsenicic-chromium reaction in various buffer solutions; synthesis coordination compounds. *Mailing Add:* Dept Chem Univ Lowell One University Ave Lowell MA 01854-2881

KOWALCZYK, JEANNE STUART, BIOCHEMISTRY. *Current Pos:* ASSOC PROF BIOL, UNIV SC, SPARTANBURG, 78- *Personal Data:* b Atlanta, Ga, Dec 22, 42; m 82; c 3. *Educ:* Jacksonville State Univ, BS, 65, MS, 66; Auburn Univ, PhD(zool), 72. *Prof Exp:* Teacher French, Calhoun County Bd Educ, Ala, 65-67; instr biol, Jacksonville State Univ, 67-68; teaching asst zool, Auburn Univ, 68-72, res assoc biochem, 72-73; asst prof biol & head dept, Belmont Abbey Col, 73-78. *Mem:* AAAS; Sigma Xi; Am Soc Parasitologists; Am Inst Biol Sci. *Res:* Immunological phenomena associated with trichostrongylid parasitism and ecological factors in the distrubution of pathogenic Naegleria Fowleri. *Mailing Add:* Dept Math & Sci Univ SC 800 University Way Spartanburg SC 29303-4932

KOWALCZYK, LEON S(TANISLAW), chemical engineering, for more information see previous edition

KOWALENKO, CHARLES GRANT, SOIL FERTILITY, SOIL BIOCHEMISTRY. *Current Pos:* res scientist, Soil Res Inst, 74-78, RES SCIENTIST, AGR CAN RES STA, 78- *Personal Data:* b Saskatoon, Sask, May 14, 46; m 71, Joan Grace Eddison; c Andrew Charles & Joanne Lynne. *Educ:* Univ Sask, BSA, 68, MSc, 70; Univ BC, PhD(soil sci), 74. *Prof Exp:* Soils adv, Sri Lanka-Can Dry Zone Res & Develop Proj, Kandy, 82-83. *Concurrent Pos:* Assoc ed, Can J Soil Sci, 80-82 & 88-89; ed, Can J Soil Sci, 90-93. *Mem:* Can Soc Soil Sci; Int Soc Soil Sci; Agron Soc Am; Soil Sci Soc Am; Agr Inst Can-BC Inst Agrologists. *Res:* Studies on the nutrient requirements of a wide range of crops including forages, vegetables, and fruit; while minimizing environmental pollution with primary specialization in nitrogen and sulfur but also concerned with entire range of nutrients, both macro and micro. *Mailing Add:* Pac Agri-Food Res Ctr Box 1000 Agassiz BC V0M 1A0 Can. *Fax:* 604-796-0359; *E-Mail:* kowalenkog@em.agr.ca

KOWALEWSKI, EDWARD JOSEPH, FAMILY MEDICINE. *Current Pos:* RETIRED. *Personal Data:* b Mt Carmel, Pa, Apr 21, 20; m 42; c 3. *Educ:* Gettysburg Col, BS, 42; George Washington Univ, MD, 45. *Honors & Awards:* Clarence E Shaffner Award, 71. *Prof Exp:* Pvt pract, 33-71; prof family med & chmn dept, Sch Med, Univ Md, Baltimore, 72-91. *Mem:* Am Acad Family Physicians (pres, 69-70); Soc Teachers Family Med. *Res:* Teaching of family medicine; core content of family medicine. *Mailing Add:* 1210 Buckingham Rd Arnold MD 21012

KOWALIK, JANUSZ SZCZESNY, KNOWLEDGE-BASED SYSTEMS, HIGH PERFORMANCE COMPUTING. *Current Pos:* MGR, SCI COMPUT & ANALYSIS, BOEING CO, 83-; AFFIL PROF COMPUT SCI, UNIV WASH, SEATTLE, 85- *Personal Data:* b Krzemieniec, Poland, Feb 28, 34; US citizen; m 59, Krystyna Jermakowicz; c 1. *Educ:* Gdansk Tech Univ, MSc, 57; Polish Acad Sci, Dr Techn Sc, 61. *Prof Exp:* Head comput ctr, Cent Shipbuilding Design Off, Poland, 61-64; res fel, Royal Norweg Coun Sci & Indust Res, 64-66; res fel comput sci, Inst Advan Studies, Australian Nat Univ, 66-67; sr specialist & mgr math anal, Boeing Comput Serv, Inc, 67-73; mem fac, Dept Comput Sci, Sir George Williams Univ, 73-74; dir systs & comput & prof comput sci, Wash State Univ, 74-83. *Concurrent Pos:* Consult; vis prof, Univ Calabria, Italy. *Mem:* Am Asn Artificial Intel; Asn Comput Mach; Inst Elec & Electronics Engrs. *Res:* Parallel computation; artificial intelligence; knowledge based systems; coupling numerical and symbolic computation; supercomputing. *Mailing Add:* PO Box 24346 MS 7L-49 Seattle WA 98124. *E-Mail:* kowalik@espresso.boeing.com

KOWALIK, VIRGIL C, MATHEMATICS. *Current Pos:* from asst prof to assoc prof, 65-69, chmn dept, 66-80, PROF MATH, TEX A&M UNIV, KINGSVILLE, 69- *Personal Data:* b Sinton, Tex, Feb 8, 32; m 59, Marilyn LeClerc. *Educ:* St Mary's Univ, Tex, BS, 53; Univ Tex, MA, 59, PhD(math), 66. *Prof Exp:* Instr math & physics, St Edward's Univ, 61-63. *Mem:* Am Math Soc; Am Soc Eng Educ; Math Asn Am. *Res:* Uniqueness and existence theorems for differential equations in complex space, application of functional analysis techniques to these theorems; real variables; functional analysis; generalized derivatives; metric spaces. *Mailing Add:* 839 W Avenue G Kingsville TX 78363

KOWALSKI, BRUCE RICHARD, ANALYTICAL CHEMISTRY. *Current Pos:* from asst prof to assoc prof, 75-77, PROF, UNIV WASH, 78-, DIR, CTR PROCESS ANALYTICAL CHEM, 83-, DISTINGUISHED PROF ANALYTICAL CHEM, 91- *Personal Data:* b Chicago, Ill, Mar 7, 42; m 74; c 2. *Educ:* Millikin Univ, BA, 65; Univ Wash, PhD, 69. *Honors & Awards:* Res Award, Eli Lilly Res Lab, 76; Alexander von Humboldt Award, 80; Coun Chem Res Award, 87. *Prof Exp:* Chemist, Shell Develop Co, Emerville, Calif, 69-71 & Houston, Tex, 71-72; asst prof, Colo State Univ, 72-73. *Concurrent Pos:* Chemist, Lawrence Livermore Lab, Univ Calif, 71-72 & consult, 72-; mem, Dir Res Appln, NSF. *Mem:* Pattern Recognition Soc: Am Chem Soc; AAAS; NY Acad Sci; Chemometrics Soc. *Res:* Chemometrics-the development of novel mathematical approaches for improving the measurement process; application of pattern recognition and other multivariant analysis methods to chemical data; process analytical chemistry including non invasive chemical analysis. *Mailing Add:* Chem Dept BG-10 Univ Wash Seattle WA 98195

KOWALSKI, CHARLES JOSEPH, STATISTICS, BIOMETRICS. *Current Pos:* Asst prof dent, Sch Dent, 68-74, ASSOC PROF DENT, SCH DENT, UNIV MICH, ANN ARBOR, 74-, ASST DIR STATIST RES LAB, 71-; DIR BIOMET LAB, DENT RES INST, 68- *Personal Data:* b Chicago, Ill, May 8, 38; m 62; c 3. *Educ:* Roosevelt Univ, BS, 62; Mich State Univ, MS, 65; Univ Mich, Ann Arbor, PhD(biostatist), 68. *Concurrent Pos:* Consult, Statist Res Lab, 68-71; Nat Football League, 69 & Parke, Davis & Co, 70. *Mem:* Am Statist Asn; Biomet Soc; Inst Math Statist; Int Asn Dent Res; Am Asn Phys Anthrop. *Res:* Multivariate statistical analysis, especially as applied to biomedical research; problems in growth and development; sequential and time series analysis. *Mailing Add:* 308 Arbana Dr Ann Arbor MI 48103

KOWALSKI, CONRAD JOHN, CARBANION CHEMISTRY, SYNTHETIC METHODOLOGY. *Current Pos:* asst dir, Smith Kline Beecham, 82-85, assoc dir, 85-86, dir, 86-88, GROUP DIR, SYNTHETIC CHEM, SMITH KLINE BEECHAM, 88- *Personal Data:* b Chicago, Ill, July 9, 47; m 68; c 2. *Educ:* Mass Inst Technol, SB, 68; Calif Inst Technol, MS, 71, PhD(chem), 74. *Prof Exp:* NIH fel, Columbia Univ, 74-76; asst prof chem, Univ Notre Dame, 76-82. *Concurrent Pos:* Founder & ed, Synthetic Pathways J, 81-84. *Mem:* Am Chem Soc; AAAS; Sigma Xi. *Res:* Development of new reactions and reactive intermediates for organic synthesis; devising syntheses of pharmaceutical products. *Mailing Add:* 1724 Jennings Way Paoli PA 19301-1021

KOWALSKI, DAVID FRANCIS, DNA ENZYMOLOGY, DNA STRUCTURE. *Current Pos:* RES SCIENTIST BIOCHEM, ROSWELL PARK CANCER INST, 74- *Personal Data:* b Chester, Pa, Feb 20, 47; m 81; c 2. *Educ:* LaSalle Col, BA, 68; Purdue Univ, PhD(chem), 74. *Prof Exp:* Chemist, Eastern Regional Lab, USDA, 68; asst, Purdue Univ, 69-73. *Mem:* Am Soc Biol Chemists. *Res:* Structure, reactivity and functions of supercoiled DNA; occurrence, properties and functions of DNA topoisomerses; purification and characterization of mung bean nuclease. *Mailing Add:* Dept Molecular & Cell Biol Roswell Park Cancer Inst Buffalo NY 14263-0001. *Fax:* 716-845-8169

KOWALSKI, DONALD T, MYCOLOGY. *Current Pos:* RETIRED. *Personal Data:* b Dearborn, Mich, Mar 23, 38; c 3. *Educ:* Univ Mich, BS, 60, MS, 61, PhD(bot), 64. *Prof Exp:* From asst prof to prof biol, Calif State Univ, Chico, 64-90. *Concurrent Pos:* NSF res grants, 65-75. *Mem:* Mycol Soc Am; Am Bryol & Lichenol Soc; Brit Mycol Soc; Sigma Xi. *Res:* Developmental and cytological studies in the Ascomycetes and taxonomy of Myxo mycetes; biosystematics of Myxomycetes; lichen distribution. *Mailing Add:* Box 1415 Ft Bragg CA 95437

KOWALSKI, KENNETH L, SCATTERING THEORY, STRONG-INTERACTION & NONLINEAR OPTICS PHYSICS. *Current Pos:* res assoc, Case Western Res Univ, 62-63, from asst prof to assoc prof, 63-73, exec officer, Dept Physics, 70-71, chmn dept, 71-76, PROF PHYSICS, CASE WESTERN RES UNIV, 73- *Personal Data:* b Chicago, Ill, July 24, 32; m 60, Audrey Bellin; c Claudia & Eric. *Educ:* Ill Inst Technol, BS, 54; Brown Univ, PhD(physics), 63. *Prof Exp:* Aeronaut res scientist, Nat Adv Comt Aeronaut, 54-56; res assoc physics, Brown Univ, 62. *Concurrent Pos:* Vis prof, Inst Theoret Physics, Univ Leuven, 68-69; scientist-in-residence, Argonne Nat Lab, 86-87. *Mem:* Am Phys Soc. *Res:* Properties of field theories and elementary particle interactions at high energies. *Mailing Add:* Dept Physics Case Western Res Univ Cleveland OH 44106. *Fax:* 216-368-4671; *E-Mail:* klk3@po.cwru.edu

KOWALSKI, LUDWIK, NUCLEAR PHYSICS & NUCLEAR CHEMISTRY, COMPUTER SCIENCE. *Current Pos:* assoc prof, 69-78, PROF PHYSICS, MONTCLAIR STATE COL, 78- *Personal Data:* b Warsaw, Poland, Oct 24, 31; m 67. *Educ:* Warsaw Tech Univ, ME, 55; Univ Paris, MS, 62, PhD(nuclear physics), 63; Kean Col NJ, MA, 85. *Prof Exp:* Res assoc nuclear chem, Columbia Univ, 64-69. *Concurrent Pos:* Teaching & using VAX/VMS Comput Simulations; teaching gifted children comput sci, 90- *Mem:* Am Asn Physics Teachers. *Res:* Experimental nuclear physics; high energy fission; nuclear reactions at low energies; heavy ion nuclear reactions; application of semiconductor detectors and mica track detectors for nuclear research. *Mailing Add:* Dept Physics & Earth Sci Montclair State Col Upper Montclair NJ 07043

KOWALSKI, RICHARD, MATHEMATICS. *Current Pos:* Group mgr, 75-81, SR PROJ LEADER, ARINC RES CORP, 81- *Personal Data:* b Boston, Mass, April 8, 40. *Educ:* Northeastern Univ, BS, 62; Case Inst Technol, MS, 63, PhD(math), 67. *Concurrent Pos:* Mem, Reliability Soc Admin Comt, Inst Elec & Electronics Engrs, 84-, ed, Trans on Reliability, 86-87. *Mem:* Armed Forces Commun & Electronics Asn; Math Asn Am; Sigma Xi; Inst Elec & Electronics Engrs (secy, 89-90, treas, 91-). *Res:* Software quality assurance and reliability. *Mailing Add:* ARINC Res Corp 2551 Riva Rd Annapolis MD 21401

KOWALSKI, STANLEY BENEDICT, NUCLEAR PHYSICS. *Current Pos:* Res physicist, 63-64, asst prof physics, 64-77, SR RES SCIENTIST, MASS INST TECHNOL, 64- *Personal Data:* b Wishart, Sask, Feb 23, 35; m 61; c 2. *Educ:* Univ Sask, BEng, 57, MSc, 58; Mass Inst Technol, PhD(physics), 63. *Mem:* Am Phys Soc. *Res:* Photonuclear reactions; accelerator physics. *Mailing Add:* Mass Inst Technol 26/427 Cambridge MA 02139

KOWALSKI, STEPHEN WESLEY, INORGANIC CHEMISTRY, SCIENCE EDUCATION. *Current Pos:* prof sci, 56-95, chmn, Physics-Geosci Dept, 68-72, EMER PROF, MONTCLAIR STATE UNIV, 95- *Personal Data:* b Bayonne, NJ, June 24, 31; m 55, 71; c 6. *Educ:* Fairleigh Dickinson Univ, BS, 53; NY Univ, MA, 54, PhD(sci educ), 64. *Prof Exp:* Instr, Upsala Col, 53-54 & NY Univ, 54-55; teacher high sch, NJ, 55-56. *Concurrent Pos:* Res chemist & consult, Shulton, Inc, NJ, 53-56; guest lectr, Upsala Col, 54-65 & Fairleigh Dickinson Univ, 55-64, res chemist, Hoffmann-La Roche, 56-67, consult, sr assoc, Danforth Found, 62-; coordr-supvr, Summer Sci Insts, AID, India, 66 & 67; coordr & supvr sci & math, MA in Teaching Prog, 68-69; consult, NSF & Memory Flavors, Inc. *Mem:* AAAS; Am Chem Soc; Nat Sci Teachers Asn. *Res:* Consumer testing; polyethylene permeability; synthetic flavor derivatives; chromatography; consumer science. *Mailing Add:* 23 Dwyer Rd Wayne NJ 07470

KOWALSKY, ARTHUR, BIOPHYSICAL CHEMISTRY. *Current Pos:* RETIRED. *Personal Data:* b Utica, NY, Nov 16, 23. *Educ:* Clarkson Col Technol, BS, 47; Univ Chicago, MS, 50, PhD(chem), 54. *Prof Exp:* Res assoc, Brookhaven Nat Lab, 54-56 & Univ Minn, 58-62; res assoc, Johnson Found, Univ Pa, 62-63, asst prof, 63-69; assoc scientist, Papanicolaou Cancer Res Inst, 69-71; assoc prof biophys, Albert Einstein Col Med, 71-78; prog dir biophys, NSF, 78-93. *Concurrent Pos:* Res fel physiol chem, Univ Minn, 56-58. *Mem:* Am Chem Soc; Am Soc Biol Chemists; Biophys Soc; AAAS. *Res:* Protein structure; nuclear magnetic resonance; mechanism of ion and electron transfer. *Mailing Add:* 2745 29th St NW Apt 522 Washington DC 20008-5527

KOWANKO, NICHOLAS, ORGANIC CHEMISTRY. *Current Pos:* chmn dept chem, 69-73, assoc prof, 68-77, PROF CHEM, MOORHEAD STATE UNIV, 77- *Personal Data:* b Charkov, Ukraine, June 7, 34; div; c 2. *Educ:* Univ Adelaide, BSc, 56, PhD(org chem), 61. *Prof Exp:* Teacher high sch, Australia, 57; Fulbright travel grant to US, 60; res assoc chem, Univ Calif, Berkeley, 61; fel, Univ Minn, 61-62, asst prof, 62-64; sr chemist cent res labs, Minn Mining & Mfg Co, 64-68. *Concurrent Pos:* Instr chem exten div, Univ Minn, 62-68. *Mem:* Am Chem Soc; Royal Soc Chem; Royal Australian Chem Inst. *Res:* Catalysis and desulfurization of organic compounds by metals; structure and synthesis of natural products, biosynthesis of natural products; direct fluorination studies. *Mailing Add:* Dept Chem Moorhead State Univ Moorhead MN 56560

KOWARSKI, A AVINOAM, PEDIATRICS, ENDOCRINOLOGY. *Current Pos:* PROF & DIR, DIV PEDIAT ENDOCRINOL, SCH MED, UNIV MD, 81- *Personal Data:* b Tel-Aviv, Israel, Dec 30, 27; m 50; c 2. *Educ:* Hebrew Univ, MD, 55. *Prof Exp:* Asst physician, Hadassah Univ Hosp, Israel, 55-62, chief physician, 65-67; from instr to asst prof, 67-72, assoc prof pediat, Sch Med, Johns Hopkins Univ, 72- *Concurrent Pos:* Fel pediat endocrinol, Sch Med, Johns Hopkins Univ, 62-65. *Mem:* Endocrine Soc; Am Pediat Soc; Soc Pediat Res; Am Fedn Clin Res. *Res:* Human metabolism of hormones in healthy and diseased children and adults; growth hormone; diabetes; hypoglycemia; hypertension. *Mailing Add:* Pediat Sch Med Univ Md 655 W Baltimore St Baltimore MD 21201-1559

KOWARSKI, CHANA R, PHARMACEUTICS. *Current Pos:* fel, 63-65, Temple Univ, vis prof, 67-69, assoc prof, 69-75, PROF PHARM, TEMPLE UNIV, 75- *Personal Data:* b Kaunas, Lithuania, June 1, 29; US citizen; m 50; c 2. *Educ:* Sch Pharm, Switz, BS, 53; Sch Pharm, Israel, PhD(pharm chem), 62. *Honors & Awards:* Lederle Res Award, 76. *Prof Exp:* Chief pharmacist, RAFA Labs, Israel, 53-59; teaching fel, Sch Pharm, Israel, 57-62; fel phys chem, Hebrew Univ, Jerusalem, 66-67. *Mem:* Am Pharmaceut Asn; Am Pharmaceut Soc; Sigma Xi; Am Asn Cols Pharm. *Res:* Absorption and bioavailability of drugs using the nonthrombogenic continuous withdrawal method; exemplary subjects include sulfamthiazole, sulfaethylthiadiazole, aspirin; insulin glucagon; novel delivery systems; nasal delivery, drugs and proteins (insulin, growth hormone). *Mailing Add:* Dept Pharmaceut Sci Temple Univ Sch Pharm 3307 N Broad St Philadelphia PA 19140-5101

KOWEL, STEPHEN THOMAS, ELECTRICAL ENGINEERING, OPTOELECTRONICS. *Current Pos:* PROF & CHMN, DEPT ELEC & COMPUT ENG, UNIV ALA, HUNTSVILLE, 90-, DIR, PHD PROG OPTICAL SCI & ENG, 92- *Personal Data:* b Philadelphia, Pa, Nov 20, 42; m 70, Janis L Zoltan; c Ann, Eugene & Rose. *Educ:* Univ Pa, BSEE, 64, PhD(elec eng), 68; Polytech Univ, MSEE, 66. *Honors & Awards:* Centennial Medal, Inst Elec & Electronics Engrs, 84. *Prof Exp:* Assoc elec eng, Moore Sch, Univ Pa, 68-69; from asst prof to assoc prof, Syracuse Univ, 69-79, prof elec eng, 79-84; prof, Dept Elec Eng & Comput Sci, Univ Calif, Davis, 84-90, vchmn, 86-90, dir, Organized Res Prog Polymeric Thin Film Systs, 88-90. *Concurrent Pos:* Prin investr, Syracuse Univ; grants & res contracts, NSF, US Army Night Vision & Electrooptics Lab, USAF Rome Air Develop Ctr, 71-; consult, Electronics Lab, Gen Elec Co, 76-84; vis prof, Nat Nanofabrication Facil, Cornell Univ, 82-83, Sch Elec Eng; vpres, Deft Labs, Inc, 76-84. *Mem:* Fel Sr mem Inst Elec & Electronics Engrs; Sigma Xi; AAAS; Int Soc Optical Eng; fel Optical Soc Am. *Res:* Acoustooptics and electrooptics; optical imaging with surface acoustic waves; optical and electronic applications of polymers, liquid crystals; three-dimensional displays. *Mailing Add:* Dept Elec & Comput Eng Univ Ala Huntsville Huntsville AL 35899. *Fax:* 205-890-6803; *E-Mail:* kowel@ebs330.eb.uah.edu

KOWERT, BRUCE ARTHUR, PHYSICAL CHEMISTRY. *Current Pos:* mem fac chem, 77-79, ASSOC PROF CHEM, ST LOUIS UNIV, 79- *Personal Data:* b Fredericksburg, Tex, Feb 11, 42. *Educ:* Univ Tex, Austin, BS, 64, PhD(chem), 71. *Prof Exp:* Res assoc phys chem, Phys Chem Inst, Univ Basel, 71-73 & Univ Calif, Los Angeles, 73-75; asst prof phys chem, Mich State Univ, 75-77. *Mem:* Am Chem Soc; Am Phys Soc. *Res:* Spin relaxation, molecular motion in liquids, electron transfer reactions, and the electronic structure of organic ion radicals employing electron spin resonance. *Mailing Add:* Dept Chem St Louis Univ 221 N Grand St Louis MO 63103-2006

KOWKABANY, GEORGE NORMAN, ORGANIC CHEMISTRY. *Current Pos:* RETIRED. *Personal Data:* b Jacksonville, Fla, Sept 16, 23. *Educ:* Univ Fla, BS, 47; Yale Univ, MS, 49, PhD(chem), 51. *Prof Exp:* Fel carbohydrate res, Ohio State Univ, 50-52; chemist, Nat Bur Standards, 52-53; from instr to asst prof, 53-60, assoc prof org chem, Cath Univ Am, 60-86. *Concurrent Pos:* NIH spec fel, Univ Ferrara, 63-64; vis assoc prof, Med Sch, Univ Miami, 70-71; res chemist, USDA, Beltsville, Md, 80-81. *Mem:* Fel AAAS; fel Am Inst Chemists; Am Chem Soc. *Res:* Paper chromatography; separation of amino acids and carbohydrates; structures of polysaccharides; enzymology. *Mailing Add:* 9252 San Jose Blvd No 604 Jacksonville FL 32257-5576

KOWLES, RICHARD VINCENT, GENETICS. *Current Pos:* from asst prof to prof, 72-86, PROF BIOL WITH DISTINCTION, ST MARYS UNIV MINN, 86- *Personal Data:* b Ivanhoe, Minn, May 9, 32; m 56; c 5. *Educ:* Winona State Col, BS, 54, MS, 63; St Mary's Col Minn, MS, 67; Univ Minn, St Paul, PhD(genetics), 72. *Prof Exp:* Teacher high schs, Minn, 54-68; asst prof, Univ Wis, River Falls, 71-72. *Concurrent Pos:* vis res prof, Univ Minn, 83-84. *Mem:* Genetics Soc Am; Am Genetic Asn; Soc Study Evolution; Radiation Res Asn; AAAS; Am Bot Soc. *Res:* Chromosome aberrations; molecular cytogenetics of endosperm in maize. *Mailing Add:* Dept Biol St Marys Univ Minn 700 Terrace Heights Winona MN 55987-1321. *Fax:* 507-457-1633

KOWLESSAR, O DHODANAND, MEDICINE. *Current Pos:* PROF & ASSOC CHMN, DEPT MED, THOMAS JEFFERSON UNIV, 87- *Personal Data:* b India. *Educ:* Univ Rochester, PhD(med), 55. *Prof Exp:* Resident internal med, Cornell Hosp, NY, fel; asst prof, Med Sch, Cornell Univ, dir med, 64, dir gastroneurol, 66. *Mem:* Sigma Xi; Am Soc Clin Nutrit; Inst Nutrit. *Mailing Add:* Dept Med Jefferson Med Col Thomas Jefferson Univ 1025 Walnut St Philadelphia PA 19107-5083. *Fax:* 215-955-2318

KOWOLENKO, MICHAEL D, IMMUNOTOXICOLOGY. *Current Pos:* MGR IMMUNOTOXICOL, DEPT INVESTIGATIVE TOXICOL, BRISTOL-MYERS SQUIBB PHARMACEUT RES INST, 89- *Personal Data:* b July 23, 55. *Educ:* Northeastern Univ, BS, 78, MS, 81, PhD(med lab sci), 86. *Prof Exp:* Teaching asst, Northeastern Univ, 83-85; Nat Inst Environ Health Sci fel, Albany Med Col, 87-88, asst res prof, Dept Microbiol & Immunol & Dept Med, 88-89. *Mem:* Am Asn Immunologists; Soc Toxicol. *Res:* Investigative toxicology; author of more than 20 technical publications. *Mailing Add:* Dept Inflam/Exp Med Miles Pharmaceut Div 400 Morgan Lane West Haven CT 06516-4175. *Fax:* 203-937-2526

KOZAI, YOSHIHIDE, celestial mechanics, satellite geodesy, for more information see previous edition

KOZAK, ANTAL, FOREST BIOMETRICS. *Current Pos:* from asst prof to assoc prof, 65-72, PROF FAC FORESTRY, UNIV BC, 72-, ASSOC DEAN, 78- *Personal Data:* b Tiszapuspoki, Hungary, May 22, 36; Can citizen; m 63; c 2. *Educ:* Univ BC, BSF, 59, MF, 61, PhD(biomet), 63. *Hon Degrees:* DSc, Sopron, Hungary, 89. *Prof Exp:* Res asst data processing, Univ BC, 62-63; res off statist, Can Dept Forestry, 63-65. *Concurrent Pos:* Vis lectr, Univ BC, 63-65. *Mem:* Am Statist Asn; Biomet Soc; Can Inst Forestry. *Res:* Application of statistics for forestry problems; development of estimating systems for forest inventory; taper equations; biomass equations. *Mailing Add:* Fac Forestry Univ BC 270-2357 Main Mall Vancouver BC V6T 1Z4 Can

KOZAK, GARY S, ANALYTICAL CHEMISTRY, PHYSICAL CHEMISTRY. *Current Pos:* RETIRED. *Personal Data:* b Pittsburgh, Pa, June 13, 38; m 57, 96, Carole D Palmieri; c Scott L, Gretchen L & Troy S. *Educ:* Ind Univ, BS, 60; Univ Ariz, PhD(chem), 63. *Prof Exp:* Sr assoc chemist, IBM Corp, 63-64; staff chemist, 64-66, proj chemist, 66-68, proj mgr & develop chemist, 68-69, mgr PhD recruitment progs, 69-71, mgr educ & sci rels, IBM World Trade Corp, 71-74, dir sci & contrib progs, IBM Europe, Paris, 74-78, dir spec univ prog, 78-81, prog dir tech personnel resources, 81-86, prog dir, Tech Interchange Prog, 87-93; prog dir, Health & Environ Progs, CHQ/Armonk, 93-95. *Mem:* AAAS; Am Chem Soc; World Wildlife Fund. *Res:* Kinetic studies with electrogenerated halogens; photosensitive polymers; epoxy resins and laminates. *Mailing Add:* Fox Run at Redcoat Rd West Norwalk CT 06850

KOZAK, JOHN JOSEPH, CHEMICAL PHYSICS, BIOPHYSICAL CHEMISTRY. *Current Pos:* DEAN & PROF CHEM, FRANKLIN COL ARTS & SCI, UNIV GA, 89- *Personal Data:* b Cleveland, Ohio, Sept 14, 40; m 69; c 3. *Educ:* Case Inst Technol, BS, 61; Princeton Univ, PhD(chem), 65. *Prof Exp:* NIH fel chem, Free Univ Brussels, 65-67; res assoc, Univ Chicago, 67-68; from asst prof to prof chem, Univ Notre Dame, 76-88. *Concurrent Pos:* Chmn, Prog Unified Sci, Univ Notre Dame, 70-; vis prof, Free Univ Brussels, 75, Ecole Polytechnique Federale de Lausanne, 78. *Mem:* Am Chem Soc; Sigma Xi. *Res:* Interaction of radiation and matter; investigations of liquid dissolved state; theory of phase transitions; studies on nature of irreversibility; reaction-diffusion theory. *Mailing Add:* 107 Beardshear Hall Iowa State Univ Ames IA 50011-2021

KOZAK, LESLIE P, BIOLOGY. *Current Pos:* SR STAFF SCIENTIST, THE JACKSON LAB, 70- *Personal Data:* b Dauphin, Manitoba, Oct 28, 40. *Educ:* Univ Notre Dame, PhD(biochem), 69. *Res:* Molecular genetics of mammals. *Mailing Add:* The Jackson Lab Bar Harbor ME 04609

KOZAK, MARILYN SUE, BIOCHEMISTRY OF PROTEIN SYNTHESIS. *Current Pos:* PROF BIOCHEM, JOHNSON MED SCH, 90- *Educ:* Johns Hopkins Univ, PhD(microbiol), 72. *Prof Exp:* Prof biol, Univ Pittsburgh, 85-90. *Mailing Add:* Dept Biochem Johnson Med Sch UMDNJ-RN 675 Hoes Lane Piscataway NJ 08854-5635. *Fax:* 732-235-5356

KOZAK, SAMUEL J, GEOLOGY. *Current Pos:* Asst prof, 61-70, PROF GEOL, WASHINGTON & LEE UNIV, 70- *Personal Data:* b Peabody, Mass, Apr 13, 31; m 59; c 2. *Educ:* Bates Col, BS, 54; Brown Univ, MS, 58; Univ Iowa, PhD(geol), 61. *Mem:* Geol Soc Am; Nat Asn Geol Teachers. *Res:* Structural geology; igneous and metamorphic petrology; geology of the Central Appalachians. *Mailing Add:* Dept Geol Washington & Lee Univ Lexington VA 24450-9904

KOZAK, WLODZIMIERZ M, VISUAL PHYSIOLOGY, PSYCHOPHYSICS. *Current Pos:* from assoc prof to prof, 70-95, EMER PROF PHYSIOL & BIOENG, CARNEGIE-MELLON UNIV, 95- *Personal Data:* b Warsaw, Poland, May 7, 27; m 74, Eva Tumiel; c J Ashot. *Educ:* Univ Lodz, MS, 51; Univ Sydney, PhD(visual electrophysiol), 64; Polish Acad Sci, DSc(visual electrophysiol), 66. *Honors & Awards:* Sci Award, Div Natural Sci, Polish Acad Sci, 55. *Prof Exp:* Asst prof neurophysiol, Nencki Inst Exp Biol, Univ Lodz, 46-56, assoc prof & sr scientist, Nencki Inst Exp Biol, Polish Acad Sci, Warsaw, 56-64, head, Lab Electrophysiol, 64-67 & Lab Afferent Systs, 67-68; vis assoc res prof visual physiol, State Univ NY, Buffalo, 68-70. *Concurrent Pos:* Lectr, Univ Lodz, 52-55 & Warsaw Tech Univ, 65; Rockefeller Found fel, 59-60, vis fel, Aust ralian Nat Univ, Canberra, 79; fel, Ophthalmic Res Inst Australia, Univ Sydney, 60-63; recipient habitation grant, Div Natural Sci, Po lish Acad Sci, 65-66; visitor, Brit Coun, Gt Brit, 65, Polish Acad Sci & Acad Sci, USSR, 65, Kkarolinska Inst, Sweden, 66, Sch Med, Johns Hopkins Univ, Chile, 70 & NSF, Japan, 78; Wellcome Trust fel, Inst Ophthal, Univ London, 68; United Health Found Western NY grant & Res Found grant, State Univ NY Albany, 69-70; Scaife Fund grant & Ford Found grant, Carnegie-Mellon Univ, 71-72, Health Res & Serv Found grant, 73-75, 88, NSF grant, 76-77 & Juv Diabetes Found grant, 78-80 & 85-87, Diabetes Res & Educ Found grant, 89-90; sr scientist dept med, Shadyside Hosp, Pittsburgh, 75-; NAS exchange scholar, Hungary, 84; Pfizer, Inc grant, 84; res scholar, Monash Univ, Australia, 86; Hewlett-Packard, Inc grant, 87. *Mem:* Int Brain Res Orgn; Polish Inst Arts & Sci Am. *Res:* Electrophysiology and conditioning of salivary secretion; plasticity and memory traces of spinal cord reflexes; eye optics; electrophysiology of retina and visual pathway; oscillatory components of electroretinograms and evoked potentials; electroretinograms in diabetic retinopathy; coding of brightness and color information in eye and brain; subjective color sensations; computer Fourier analysis; neurophysiology; aldose reductase inhibition in diabetes mellitus; nuclear magnetic resonance imaging of the eye; integrity of blood retinal barrier in diabetes mellitus. *Mailing Add:* Biomed Eng Prog Doherty Hall 2313 Carnegie-Mellon Univ Pittsburgh PA 15213-3890. *Fax:* 412-268-1173; *E-Mail:* wk01@andrew.cmu.edu

KOZAM, GEORGE, ANATOMY, PATHOLOGY. *Current Pos:* from asst prof to assoc prof, 58-71, PROF ANAT, COL MED & DENT NJ, 71- *Personal Data:* b Union City, NJ, Mar 28, 24; m 53. *Educ:* NY Univ, BA, 45, MS, 46, PhD(human anat), 50, DDS, 53. *Prof Exp:* Asst biol, NY Univ, 46-47, instr anat, Dent Col, 47-50, instr bact, 53-54. *Concurrent Pos:* Vis asst prof path, Dent Col, Fairleigh Dickinson Univ, 64-65. *Mem:* Am Dent Asn; fel Am Acad Oral Path; NY Acad Sci; Int Asn Dent Res. *Res:* Capillary fragility; circulation in dental pulp; respiration of rat and rabbit dental pulp; effects of local anesthetics on the respiration of dental pulp; research on trigeminal nerve; effect of eugenol on nerve transmission and oral mucous membranes. *Mailing Add:* Dept Anat Univ Med & Dent NJ Med Sch 185 S Orange Ave Newark NJ 07103-2714

KOZARICH, JOHN WARREN, BIOLOGICAL CHEMISTRY, BIOCHEMISTRY. *Current Pos:* PROF CHEM & BIOCHEM, UNIV MD, 84-; PROF, AGR BIOTECH CTR, MD BIOTECH INST, 87-; VPRES BIOCHEM, MERCK RES LABS, 93- *Personal Data:* b Jersey City, NJ, June 20, 49; m 85, Marcia Durso. *Educ:* Boston Col, BS, 71; Mass Inst Technol, PhD(biol chem), 75. *Honors & Awards:* Pfizer Award in Enzyme Chem, Am Chem Soc, 88. *Prof Exp:* NIH fel biochem, Harvard Univ, 74-77; from asst prof to prof pharmacol, Yale Univ, 77-84; vpres res & develop, Alkermes, Inc, Cambridge, Mass, 89-92. *Concurrent Pos:* Bioorg & Natural Prod Study Sect, NIH, 83-87; Am Cancer Soc Fac Res Award, 83-88; Metallobiochem Study Sect, NIH, 92- *Mem:* Am Chem Soc; Sigma Xi; Am Soc Biochem & Molecular Biol. *Res:* Design of enzyme inhibitors; mechanisms and stereochemistry of enzyme action; chemistry and biochemistry of modified nucleosides; mechanisms of drug induced DNA degradation. *Mailing Add:* PO Box 2000 R80M-101 Rahway NJ 07065-0900. *Fax:* 732-594-3695; *E-Mail:* john_kozarich@merck.com

KOZEK, WIESLAW JOSEPH, IMMUNOLOGY, ULTRASTRUCTURE. *Current Pos:* ASSOC PROF, DEPT MICROBIOL & MED ZOOL, MED SCI CAMPUS, UNIV PR, 84- *Personal Data:* b Poniatowka, Poland, Feb 6, 39; US citizen; m 71, Mireya E Guillen; c Mark R, Laura W & Robert C. *Educ:* Canisius Col, BS, 61; Tulane Univ, MS, 67, PhD(parasitol), 69. *Prof Exp:* Fel, Dept Microbiol, Univ Chicago, 69-71; Dept Immunol & Med Microbiol, Univ Fla, Gainesville, 71-72; asst res parasitologist, Calif Primate Res Ctr, Univ Calif, Davis, 73-77; scientist, Int Collabr Infectious Dis Res Prog, Tulane Univ, Calif, Colombia, 77-84. *Concurrent Pos:* Adj assoc prof, Dept Trop Med, Tulane Sch Pub Health & Trop Med, 80-84; prin investr human filariasis, Int Collabr Infectious Dis Res Prog, Cali, Colombia, 80-84. *Mem:* Am Soc Trop Med & Hyg; Am Soc Vet Parasitologists; Am Soc Parasitologists; Sigma Xi; Wildlife Dis Asn; Am Soc Trop Vet Med. *Res:* Medical helminthology; immunology, morphology, ultrastructure, animal models, and host-parasite relationship of filariae; epidemiology of human filariases in Colombia; culture of helminth cells; characterization of intracellular microorganisms of filarids; host-parasite relationships of trichinella spiralis. *Mailing Add:* Microbiol Med Univ PR PO Box 365067 San Juan PR 00936-5067. *Fax:* 787-758-4808

KOZEL, THOMAS RANDALL, MEDICAL MYCOLOGY, MEDICAL BACTERIOLOGY. *Current Pos:* from asst prof to assoc prof, 71-82, dir med admis, 72-76, PROF & CHMN MICROBIOL, UNIV NEV, RENO, 82- *Personal Data:* b Ft Dodge, Iowa, Jan 31, 46. *Educ:* Univ Iowa, BA, 67, MS, 69, PhD(microbiol), 71. *Prof Exp:* Instr microbiol, Univ Iowa, 69-70. *Concurrent Pos:* vis assoc prof, Rockefeller Univ, 80-81. *Mem:* Am Soc Microbiol; Harvey Soc; Sigma Xi. *Res:* Cellular and molecular mechanisms of infection and resistance in systemic mycoses. *Mailing Add:* Sch Med Sci Microbiol Dept Univ Nev Reno NV 89557-0901

KOZIAR, JOSEPH CLEVELAND, POLYMER CHEMISTRY, ORGANIC CHEMISTRY. *Current Pos:* sr res chemist plastics & coatings, 75-90, LEAD CHEMIST, EMULSION PROCESS GROUP, ROHM & HAAS CO, 90- *Personal Data:* b Baltimore, Md, Jan 6, 46; m 68; c David. *Educ:* Johns Hopkins Univ, BA, 68, PhD(org chem), 75. *Prof Exp:* Res chemist process develop, Diamond Shamrock Corp, 69-71. *Mem:* Am Chem Soc; AAAS. *Res:* Polymer synthesis and characterization; monomer synthesis; organic photochemistry; polymer process research. *Mailing Add:* 219 Liberty Dr Langhorne PA 19047

KOZICKI, WILLIAM, THERMODYNAMICS. *Current Pos:* from asst prof to prof, 62-96, assoc dean eng, 76-96, EMER PROF CHEM ENG, UNIV OTTAWA, 96- *Personal Data:* b Kenora, Ont, June 11, 31; m 63; c 1. *Educ:* Univ Toronto, BASc, 53, MASc, 57; Calif Inst Technol, PhD(thermodyn), 62. *Prof Exp:* Process engr, Textile Fibres Div, Du Pont Can, 53-55; res fel thermodyn, Calif Inst Technol, 61-62. *Mem:* Sigma Xi. *Res:* Transport phenomena: rheology and flow of complex systems with particular emphasis on characterization of polymer adsorption and its role in improved oil recovery, turbulent drag reduction and as filtration aid. *Mailing Add:* Dept Chem Eng Univ Ottawa Ottawa ON K1N 6N5 Can

KOZICKY, EDWARD LOUIS, WILDLIFE MANAGEMENT. *Current Pos:* DIR CONSERV DEPT, WINCHESTER-WESTERN DIV, OLIN CORP, 56- *Personal Data:* b Elberon, NJ, Feb 11, 18; m 41; c 3. *Educ:* Univ Maine, BS, 41; Pa State Col, MS, 42, PhD(zool), 48. *Prof Exp:* Chief res, State Div Fish & Game, NJ, 48; leader, Co-op Wildlife Res Unit, Iowa State Col, 48-56. *Concurrent Pos:* Dir, Wildlife Legis Fund. *Mem:* Wildlife Soc (pres, 69-70); Am Forestry Asn. *Res:* Life history, ecology and management of game birds and mammals; the development, evaluation and improvement of game animal census techniques; development and promotion of shooting preserves. *Mailing Add:* 817 Southmoor Pl Godfrey IL 62035

KOZIK, EUGENE, COMPUTER SCIENCE, OPERATIONS RESEARCH. *Current Pos:* PRES, KOZIK & ASSOCS, 70- *Personal Data:* b Duquesne, Pa, Sept 22, 24; m 56; c 2. *Educ:* Univ Pittsburgh, BS, 49, ML, 50, PhD, 60. *Prof Exp:* Engr, Gulf Oil Corp, 48-50; tech adminstr res & develop, Wright Air Develop Ctr, 53-57; mgt sci consult, Univ Pittsburgh, 59-60; mgr planning & controls, Gen Dynamics Corp, 60-61; prog mgr mgt sci, Opers Res, Inc, 61-62; dir adv studies, Burroughs Corp, 62-66; mgr info sci, Gen Elec Co, 66-70. *Concurrent Pos:* Lectr, Duquesne Univ, 60, Univ Rochester, 61 & Pa State Univ, 64-; mem, Int Comt Sci Mgt, Hist Eval Res Orgn, McLean, Va, 62-, comput comt, Am Inst Planners, 67- & urban info & measurement comt, Nat Acad Sci, 68- *Res:* Management and information science; intergrated management system; data management; computer technology. *Mailing Add:* 38 Rabbit Run Rd Malvern PA 19355

KOZIKOWSKI, ALAN PAUL, ORGANIC CHEMISTRY, NEUROCHEMISTRY. *Current Pos:* VPRES MED CHEM, TROPHIX PHARMACEUT, 94- *Personal Data:* b Menominee, Mich, Oct 27, 48; m 75; c 2. *Educ:* Univ Mich, BS, 70; Univ Calif, Berkeley, PhD(org chem), 74. *Honors & Awards:* Ciba-Geigy Award, 82. *Prof Exp:* NIH fel org chem, Harvard Univ, 74-76; asst prof, Univ Pittsburgh, 76-80, assoc prof & Camille & Henry Dreyfus teacher scholar, 80-83, Alfred P Sloan Fel Org Chem, 76-90, prof chem, 84-90; dir chem, Mayo Clin, 90-94. *Concurrent Pos:* Fel, Japan Soc for Promoting Sci, 84; prof behav neurosci, 88. *Mem:* Am Chem Soc; Chem Soc; Sigma Xi; Soc Neurosci. *Res:* Synthetic organic chemistry; synthesis of alkaloids and carbohydrates; organometallics; neuroscience. *Mailing Add:* 12 Mershon Dr Princeton NJ 08540

KOZIKOWSKI, BARBARA ANN, PHYSICAL CHEMISTRY. *Current Pos:* STAFF SCIENTIST, PROCTER & GAMBLE CO, 81- *Personal Data:* b Chicago, Ill, Jan 20, 54. *Educ:* Loyola Univ, BS, 75; Univ Ill, Chicago Circle, MS, 77, PhD(phys chem), 81. *Mem:* Am Chem Soc; Soc Biomolecular Screening. *Res:* Electronic structure of heavy transition metal complexes; developing high throughput assays for pharmaceutical drug development. *Mailing Add:* Procter & Gamble Co Health Care Res Ctr PO Box 8006 Mason OH 45040

KOZINSKI, ANDRZEI, biochemistry, for more information see previous edition

KOZIOL, BRIAN JOSEPH, CLINICAL BIOCHEMISTRY, CLINICAL NUTRITION. *Current Pos:* ASSOC PROF BIOL, UNIV BRIDGEPORT, 84- *Personal Data:* b Gardner, Mass, Aug 24, 51. *Educ:* Univ Mass, Amherst, BS, 73; Univ Calif, Los Angeles, MS, 77, PhD (exp & clin nutrit), 84. *Prof Exp:* Res asst biochem, Univ Mass, Amherst, 69-73; res asst physiol, Dept Kinesiol, 73-78, dir, Lipid Lab, Div Nutrit, Univ Calif, Sch Pub Health, Los Angeles, 78-, res assoc, Lipid Metab, Div Nutrit, Sch Pub Health & Ctr Health Enhancement, 84-, asst prof biochem & nutrit, dept med, Div Clin Nutrit, 84-, dir, Lipid-Hormone Lab, 85- *Concurrent Pos:* Adj lectr biochem, dept chem & biochem & NIH scholar, Univ Calif, Sch Pub Health, Los Angeles, 84; consult-lectr, Northrop Aircraft Div, 82-; consult, Calif Museum Sci & Ind, 83-; mem, Jonsson Comprehensive Cancer Ctr, 85- *Mem:* Am Inst Nutrit; Am Soc Clin Nutrit; Sigma Xi; AAAS; Am Coun Sci & Health. *Res:* Effect(s) of both the quantity and quality of dietary fat on the incidence of breast tumors in humans and experimental animals; possible link between dietary fat, the breast tissue hormonal milieu and breast cancer development. *Mailing Add:* 19116 Killoch Way 842 Northridge 30401 Agoura Rd Agoura Hills CA 91326

KOZIOL, DELORIS E, PATHOLOGY. *Current Pos:* Med technologist, Dept Transfusion Med, 73-83, DEPT CHIEF HOSP EPIDEMIOL SERV, CLIN CTR, NIH, 83- *Personal Data:* b Alexandria, Va, Apr 29, 49. *Educ:* Univ Del, BA, 71; Johns Hopkins Univ, MPH, 86, PhD(epidemiol), 90. *Mem:* Soc Epidemiol Res; Am Pub Health Asn; Am Soc Clin Path. *Mailing Add:* Clin Ctr-NIH Bldg 10 Rm 4A21 9000 Rockville Pike Bethesda MD 20892-1354. *Fax:* 301-496-0457; *E-Mail:* dee_koz.iol@nih.gov

KOZLIK, ROLAND A, METALLURGY. *Current Pos:* RETIRED. *Personal Data:* b Hackensack, NJ, Mar 31, 21. *Educ:* Columbia Univ, BS, 43; Univ Ky, MS, 44. *Mailing Add:* 301 Sunrise Ridge Dr Spruce Pine NC 28777-3329

KOZLOFF, EUGENE NICHOLAS, ZOOLOGY. *Current Pos:* PROF ZOOL, UNIV WASH, 66- *Personal Data:* b Teheran, Iran, Sept 26, 20; nat US; m 44, Anne Solomon; c Rae Annettte. *Educ:* Univ Calif, AB, 42, MA, 46, PhD(zool, protozool), 50. *Prof Exp:* Asst zool, Univ Calif, 44, lectr micros tech, 45; from instr to prof biol, Lewis & Clark Col, 45-66, chmn dept, 60-66. *Concurrent Pos:* Guggenheim fel, 53-54; vis prof, Inst Marine Biol, Univ Ore, 57-60, 64 & 94-95; vis prof, Friday Harbor Labs, Univ Wash, 61 & 62, resident assoc dir, 66-73; vis prof, Pac Marine Sta, 63; dir, NSF Inst Col Teachers, Univ Ore, 64. *Mem:* Marine Biol Asn UK; Western Soc Naturalists. *Res:* Cytology, morphology and taxonomy of protozoa; commensal ostracodes; acoel and rhabdocoel Turbellaria; Orthonectida Mesozoa; development of kinorhynchs. *Mailing Add:* Friday Harbor Lab Friday Harbor WA 98250

KOZLOFF, LLOYD M, VIROLOGY, MOLECULAR BIOLOGY. *Current Pos:* PROF MICROBIOL & DEAN, GRAD DIV, UNIV CALIF, SAN FRANCISCO, 81- *Personal Data:* b Chicago, Ill, Oct 15, 23; m 47; c 4. *Educ:* Univ Chicago, BS, 43, PhD(biochem), 48. *Prof Exp:* Res assoc biochem, Univ Chicago, 49-52, from asst prof to prof, 52-64; prof microbiol, Univ Colo Med Ctr, Denver, 64-80, chmn dept, 66-76, assoc dean fac affairs, 76-79. *Concurrent Pos:* Mem virol & rickettsiology study sect, NIH, 63-68; ed, J Virol, 66-74; vchmn, Virol Sect, Am Soc Microbiol, 74-75, chmn, 75-76; Found Microbiol lectr, 75-76. *Mem:* Hon fel AAAS; Am Soc Microbiol; Am Soc Biol Chemists; Am Chem Soc. *Res:* Virus structure, function and assembly; reactions during viral invasion. *Mailing Add:* 2106 Jackson No 6 San Francisco CA 94115-1551

KOZLOSKI, RICHARD PETER, HPLC ANALYSIS OF PRESTICIDES & EXPLOSIVES, GC ANALYSIS OF ENVIRONMENTAL STANDARDS. *Current Pos:* ANALYTICAL CHEMIST, ACCUSTANDARD, INC, 91- *Personal Data:* b Derby, Conn, June 25, 46; m 76, Elizabeth Zanishka; c Allen & Paul. *Educ:* Univ Conn, BA, 68; Va Polytech Inst & State Univ, PhD(chem), 77. *Prof Exp:* Scientist II, Cohn Agr Exp Sta, 79-85; sr scientist, Upjohn, Fine Chem Div, 86-90. *Mem:* Am Chem Soc. *Res:* Investigation of the chemistry of decompostions in environmental standard formulations. *Mailing Add:* 200 Vineyard Kensington CT 06483. *Fax:* 203-786-5287

KOZLOV, ALEKSEY A, EPOXY & POLYURETHANE ADHESIVES. *Current Pos:* RES & DEVELOP CHEMIST, ABATRON INC, 97- *Personal Data:* b Kiev, Ukraine, Jan 2, 57; m 91, Olga Y Zakharova; c Gleb & Sofya. *Educ:* Leningrad Technol Inst, PhD(radiation chem), 86. *Prof Exp:* Head, Radiation Chem Lab, Inst Phys Chem, Kiev, 89-97. *Res:* Epoxy and polyurethane adhesives and coatings for special applications. *Mailing Add:* 2562 18th St No 12 Kenosha WI 53140. *E-Mail:* info@abatron.com

KOZLOWSKI, ADRIENNE WICKENDEN, INORGANIC CHEMISTRY, CHEMICAL INFORMATION. *Current Pos:* from asst prof to assoc prof, 70-82, PROF CHEM, CENT CONN STATE UNIV, 82- *Personal Data:* b Hackensack, NJ, Apr 26, 41; m 68, 77, John A Jr. *Educ:* MacMurray Col, AB, 62; Univ Conn, MS, 64, PhD(chem), 68. *Prof Exp:* Res asst phys chem, Univ Conn, 68, fel biol sci, 69-70. *Concurrent Pos:* Lectr, Univ Copenhagen, 69; vis educr, Chem Abstrs Serv, 84-85. *Mem:* Am Chem Soc; Sigma Xi. *Res:* Coordination compounds; inorganic structural chemistry; information retrieval, computerized searching by inorganic structure. *Mailing Add:* Dept Chem Cent Conn State Univ 1615 Stanley St New Britain CT 06053-2439

KOZLOWSKI, BETTY ANN, NUTRITION. *Current Pos:* ASSOC PROF NUTRIT, DEPT HUMAN NUTRIT & FOOD MGT & CHIEF NUTRIT, NISONGER CTR MENTAL RETARDATION & DEVELOP DISABILITIES, OHIO STATE UNIV, 74- *Personal Data:* b Dothan, Ala, Dec 14, 43; m 78; c 1. *Educ:* Ala Col, BS, 65; Univ Tenn, Knoxville, PhD(nutrit), 70. *Prof Exp:* Res asst nutrit, Univ Tenn, Knoxville, 69-70; asst prof, Auburn Univ, 70-74. *Mem:* Sigma Xi. *Res:* Nutritional needs, and ways of meeting them in persons with developmental disabilities. *Mailing Add:* 4360 Woodhill Rd Columbus OH 43220-4380

KOZLOWSKI, DON ROBERT, AVIONICS. *Current Pos:* sect mgr advan reconnaissance systs, 65-72, sr prog engr, 72-80, CHIEF PROG ENGR ADVAN ENG, MCDONNELL AIRCRAFT CO, MCDONNELL DOUGLAS CORP, 80- *Personal Data:* b St Louis, Mo, Dec 5, 37; m 60; c 3. *Educ:* Univ St Louis, BS, 59; Washington Univ, St Louis, MS, 67. *Prof Exp:* Sr engr, McDonnell Aircraft Co, McDonnell Douglas Corp, 59-62; mgr prog develop, Electronic Specialty Co, 62-64; vpres, Aerospace Systs Corp, 64-65. *Concurrent Pos:* Dir & consult, USAF/Air Force Systs Command Offensive Air Support Mission Anal, 74-76. *Mem:* Inst Elec & Electronics Engrs; Am Soc Photogram; Am Inst Aeronaut & Astronaut; Am Defense Preparedness Asn. *Res:* Avionics, displays and data processing systems for reconnaissance and intelligence; communications and electronic warfare; aircraft systems design. *Mailing Add:* Mcdonnell Douglas PO Box 516 64-2142 St Louis MO 63136

KOZLOWSKI, GERALD P, NEUROENDOCRINOLOGY. *Current Pos:* ASSOC PROF, DEPT PHYSIOL, SOUTHWESTERN MED CTR, DALLAS, TEX, 80- *Personal Data:* b Grand Rapids, Mich, Dec 24, 42. *Educ:* Aquinas Col, BS, 64; Mich State Univ, MS, 67; Univ Ill, Urbana-Champaign, PhD(anat), 71. *Prof Exp:* Technician histopath, Mich State Univ, 64-65, asst instr anat, 65-66; res assoc, Univ Mo-Columbia, 67-68; instr, Univ Ill, Urbana-Champaign, 68-70; teaching fel, Sch Med & Dent, Univ Rochester, 71-73; asst prof anat, Col Vet Med & Biomed Sci, Colo State Univ, 73-76, assoc prof, 76-78; assoc prof neurobiol & anat, Univ Tex Health Sci Ctr, Houston, 78-80. *Concurrent Pos:* NIH grant, 74-92; ed, Histochem. *Mem:* Am Asn Anatomists; Int Soc Neuroendocrinologists; Biol Stain Comn; Soc Neurosci; Res Soc Alcoholism. *Res:* Effects at alcohol on central nervous system; vasopressin and oxytocin; scanning and high-voltage electron microscopy of the median eminence; immunocytochemistry of HIV receptor; neuroimmunology; light and election microscopic immunocytochemistry for visualization of releasing-hormines and neuropeptides of the hypothalamus. *Mailing Add:* Dept Physiol Southwestern Med Ctr Univ Tex 5323 Harry Hines Blvd Dallas TX 75235-9040

KOZLOWSKI, LESTER JOSEPH, HIGH DENSITY INFRARED FOCAL PLANE ARRAYS DESIGN, ULTRA LOW NOISE FOCAL PLANE ARRAYS DESIGN & TEST. *Current Pos:* MEM TECH STAFF, ROCKWELL INT SCI CTR, 87- *Personal Data:* b Chicago, Ill, Aug 31, 53; m 83, Dawn; c Amanda & Daniel. *Educ:* Univ Ill, Chicago, BSEE, 75, MSEE, 77. *Prof Exp:* Tech asst elec eng, Univ Ill, Chicago, 75-77; sr scientist, Hughes Aircraft Missile Systs Group, 78-87. *Mem:* Inst Elec & Electronics Engrs Electronic Devices Soc; Optical Soc Am; Soc Photo-Optical Instrumentation Engrs. *Res:* Design, development and characterization of infrared focal plane arrays for a variety of applications including military and astronomy. *Mailing Add:* Rockwell Int MS A7A 1049 Camino Dos Rios Thousand Oaks CA 91360

KOZLOWSKI, RICHARD WILLIAM HUGH, OBSERVATIONAL PLANETARY ASTRO-ATMOSPHERE & MINERALOGY REMOTE SENSE. *Current Pos:* From asst prof to assoc prof, 83-93, PROF, DEPT PHYSICS & ASTRON, SUSQUEHANNA UNIV, 93- *Personal Data:* b Ogden, Utah, Oct 10, 53; m 90. *Educ:* Susquehanna Univ, BA, 75; Univ Maine, MS, 77, PhD(physics), 82. *Concurrent Pos:* Vis scientist, Lunar & Planetary Lab, Univ Ariz, 86-; chair physics, Susquehanna Univ, 89- *Mem:* Am Geophys Union; Am Astrological Soc Div Planetary Sci; Am Asn Physics Teachers. *Res:* Observational planetary astronomy; sodium and potassium atmospheres of the planet Mercury and Earths moon-done with telescopes in Arizona; remote sensing of surface rock type Mercury, the moon, and asteroids with thermal infrared telescopes in Hawaii, Arizona and the Kuiper Airborne Observatory. *Mailing Add:* 219 W Snyder St Selinsgrove PA 17870. *Fax:* 717-372-4040; *E-Mail:* kozlow@ssa1.arc.nasa.gov

KOZLOWSKI, ROBERT H, PETROLEUM CHEMISTRY. *Current Pos:* Res chemist, Chevron Corp, 55-60, sr res chemist, 60-64, supvry res chemist, 64-66, sr res assoc, Petrol Process Res & Develop, Chevron Res Co Div, 66-76, litigation support coordr, Secy's Dept, 76-77, litigation support mgr, Secy's Dept, Stand Oil Co Calif, 78-84, litigation support mgr, 85-88, MGR, ADMIN SUPPORT, LAW DEPT, CHEVRON CORP, 88- *Personal Data:* b Duquesne, Pa, May 17, 28; div; c Michael & Nancy. *Educ:* St Mary's Col Calif, BS, 50; Northwestern Univ, PhD(chem), 55. *Concurrent Pos:* Consult, Kenwood Vineyards, 70-86; Ipatieff fel. *Mem:* Am Chem Soc; Am Soc Enol. *Res:* Petroleum processing; hydrocarbon reactions and mechanisms. *Mailing Add:* 41 Sutter St #1300 San Francisco CA 94104

KOZLOWSKI, THEODORE R, PHYSICAL INORGANIC CHEMISTRY. *Current Pos:* sr chemist, Corning Glass Works, 63-64, res chemist, 66-70, mgr, indust prod develop, 70-73, mgr, sunglass proj, France, 73-76, portfolio mgr, consumer prod, 76-82, develop mgr, elec & electronic prod, 82-84, develop mgr, tech & elec prod, 84-87, dir tech prod develop, 87-94, BUS TECHNOL DIR, CORNING-ASHAHI VIDEO, 94- *Personal Data:* b Niagara Falls, NY, Dec 21, 37; m 61, Ann Mills; c Christopher M, Karen E (Kennedy), Maureen M (Schurman), David M & Natalie A. *Educ:* Niagara Univ, BS, 59; Rensselaer Polytech Inst, PhD(phys inorg chem), 63; Harvard Univ, PMD, 72. *Concurrent Pos:* Researcher, Picatinny Arsenal, US Army, 64-66. *Mem:* AAAS; Am Chem Soc; Sigma Xi; Nat Geog Soc. *Res:* Glass-molten salt interactions; high strength glasses and glass ceramics by ion exchange from molten salts; high strength materials; product development of photochromic ophthalmic and sunglass products; consumer tableware ovenware clear glass ceramics, hybrid PC boards; low dielectric materials, strong glass ceramics, epoxy products, specialty glasses, LCD display glasses, magnetic disk substrates, dental glass ceramics, sheet, pressing and tubing processes; granted seven patents. *Mailing Add:* Corning Glass Works Sullivan Sci Park Corning NY 14831. *Fax:* 607-974-2103; *E-Mail:* kozlowski_tr@corning.com@in

KOZLOWSKI, THEODORE THOMAS, PLANT PHYSIOLOGY, FOREST BIOLOGY. *Current Pos:* VIS SCHOLAR, DEPT ENVIRON SCI, POLICY & MGT, UNIV CALIF, BERKELEY, 93- *Personal Data:* b Buffalo, NY, May 21, 17; m 54, Maude Peters. *Educ:* Syracuse Univ, BS, 39; Duke Univ, MA, 41, PhD(plant physiol), 47. *Hon Degrees:* DSc, Univ Louvain, Belg, 78, State Univ NY, 80 & Agr Univ Poznan, Poland, 92. *Honors & Awards:* Auth Award, Int Shade Tree Conf, 71; Barrington Moore Res Award Biol Sci, Soc Am Foresters, 74; George Lamb lectr, Univ Nebr, 74; Arboricult Res Award, Inst Soc Arboricult, 76; George S Long lectr, Univ Wash, 78; Merit Award, Bot Soc Am, 84; Merit Award, Int Soc Arborcult, 87; Gold Medal Forest Physiol Res, Asn Forestry Poland, 97. *Prof Exp:* From asst prof to prof bot, Univ Mass, 47-58, head dept, 50-58; prof, Univ Wis-Madison, 58-72, chmn dept, 61-64, A J Riker prof forestry, 72-87, dir biotron, 77-87;

distinguished prof, Wis Alumni Res Found, 84-87. *Concurrent Pos:* Vis prof, Univ Pa, 54; vis scientist, Soc Am Foresters, 63, 66, 68, 69 & 70; Fulbright sr res scholar & exchange lectr, Oxford Univ, 64-65; assoc ed, Am Midland Naturalist, 65-71, Can J Forest Res, 70-76; Int Shade Tree Conf res fel, 69, 70 & 71-; external PhD thesis examr, Australian Nat Univ, Univ Western Australia, Univ Ibadan, Nigeria, Sri Venkateswara Univ, India & Univ WI Found; res collabr, US Forest Serv; consult, UN Food & Agr Orgn, Nat Park Serv, Oak Ridge Nat Lab, Stanford Res Inst, NSF, Fed Forest Res Sta, Brazil & Univ BC; adj prof, Environ Studies Prog & Dept Biol Sci, Univ Calif, Santa Barbara, 87-93; trustee, Santa Barbara Bot Garden, 92-93. *Mem:* Soc Am Foresters; Am Soc Plant Physiol; Bot Soc Am; Ecol Soc Am; Am Inst Biol Sci; Sigma Xi; Scand Soc Plant Physiologists; Int Soc Arboricult; hon mem Finnish Forestry Soc; hon mem Polish Bot Soc. *Res:* Physiology of woody plants; plant water relations; physiological ecology; effects of environmental stresses on plant growth. *Mailing Add:* Dept Environ Sci Policy & Mgt Univ Calif 145 Mulford Hall Berkeley CA 94720. *Fax:* 510-643-5438

KOZMA, ADAM, RADAR SYSTEMS, ELECTROOPTICS. *Current Pos:* CONSULT ENGR, 93- *Personal Data:* b Cleveland, Ohio, Feb 2, 28; m 93, Rebecca B Chelius; c Paul (deceased) & Peter. *Educ:* Univ Mich, BSE, 52, MSE, 64; Wayne State Univ, MSEM, 61; Univ London, PhD(elec eng), 68 & dipl, Imp Col, 69. *Honors & Awards:* Ord Medal, Avionics Sect, Am Defense Preparedness Asn. *Prof Exp:* Design engr, US Broach Co, Mich, 51-56, sales engr, 56-58; asst mech & electrooptical design, Inst Sci & Technol, Univ Mich, Ann Arbor, 58-61, res assoc, 61-63, assoc res engr, 63-65, res engr & asst head, Optics Group, Radar & Optics Lab, 65-69; gen mgr, Electrooptics Ctr, Radiation Div, Harris, Inc, 69-73; sr res engr & mgr, Electromagnetics & Electronics Dept, Environ Res Inst, Mich, 73-75, mgr tech staff, 75-76, vpres & dir, Radar & Optics Div, 75-85, vpres corp develop, 85-86; vpres & dir, Defense Electronics Eng Div, Syracuse Res Corp, 86-88; head, Advan Systs Dept, Mitre Corp, 89-93. *Concurrent Pos:* Consult, Conductron Corp, 65-66, IBM Systs Develop Div, 66-67, UK Atomic Weapons Estab, 67-68 & Radiation Inc, Fla, 68-69; on leave, Imp Col, Univ London, 66-68, acad visitor & lectr, 67-68; consult phys sci directorate, USAMRDEL, MICOM, Redstone, Ala, 74-78; co-chmn & lectr, Synthetic Aperture Radar Intensive Course, Col Eng, Univ Mich, Ann Arbor, 80-, adj prof, 92- *Mem:* Fel Optical Soc Am; fel Inst Elec & Electronics Engrs; Am Defense Preparedness Asn; Sigma Xi; Soc Photog & Instrument Engrs. *Res:* Coherent optics with application to signal processing and optical correlation; holography; speckle effects in coherent systems; radar instrumentation, synthetic aperture radar systems and applications. *Mailing Add:* 2996 Appleway Dr Ann Arbor MI 48104-1808. *Fax:* 313-663-5857

KOZMETSKY, GEORGE, COMPUTER SCIENCE. *Current Pos:* prof mgt & comput sci, dean, Col Bus Admin & Grad Sch Bus, 66-82, EXEC ASSOC ECON AFFAIRS UNIV SYST, UNIV TEX, AUSTIN, 66- *Personal Data:* b Seattle, Wash, Oct 5, 17; m 43, Ronya Keosiff; c Gregory A & Nadya A (Scott). *Educ:* Univ Wash, BA, 38; Harvard Univ, MBA, 47, DCS, 57. *Honors & Awards:* Leatherbee Lectr, Harvard Univ, 67; Nat Medal of Technol, 93. *Prof Exp:* Asst prof, Carnegie-Mellon Univ, Pittsburg, 50-52; mem tech staff, Hughes Aircraft Co, Los Angeles, 54-59; vpres & asst gen mgr, Electronic Equip Div, Litton Co, 59-60; exec vpres, Teledyne Corp, Beverly Hills, 60-66. *Concurrent Pos:* Bd dirs, La Quinta Hydril, Teledyne Corp, Dell Comp Corp; vis scholar, Univ Wash, 68, Walker Ames prof, 70. *Mem:* Fel AAAS; Inst Mgt Sci (pres); Asn Advan Med Instrumentation; Brit Interplanetary Soc; Am Soc Oceanog. *Mailing Add:* PO Box 2253 Austin TX 78768-2253

KOZUB, RAYMOND LEE, NUCLEAR PHYSICS. *Current Pos:* assoc prof, 77-80, dept chmn, 86-96, PROF PHYSICS, TENN TECHNOL UNIV, 80- *Personal Data:* b Ladysmith, Wis, June 16, 40; m 65, Sandra Nye; c John & Racheall. *Educ:* Univ of Wis-River Falls, BS, 62; Mich State Univ, MS, 64, PhD(physics), 67. *Prof Exp:* Asst prof physics, Tex A&M Univ, 67-71, res scientist, Cyclotron Inst, 71-72; res assoc chem, Columbia Univ, 72-74; asst prof physics, Queen's Univ, Kingston, Ont, 74-77. *Concurrent Pos:* Prin investr sponsored res, Dept Energy, 78- *Mem:* Am Phys Soc; Sigma Xi; Am Asn Phys Teachers. *Res:* Nuclear structure studies; transfer reactions; stripping reactions to unbound final states; isobaric analog states; nuclear lifetime measurements; heavy ion reactions; neutron-rich nuclei; rare electron capture processes. *Mailing Add:* Dept Physics Tenn Technol Univ Cookeville TN 38505. *E-Mail:* rlk6642@tntech.edu

KRA, IRWIN, MATHEMATICS. *Current Pos:* from asst prof to assoc prof, 68-71, chmn dept, 75-81, PROF MATH, STATE UNIV NY, STONY BROOK, 72-, DEAN, DIV PHYS SCI & MATH, 91- *Personal Data:* b Poland, Jan 5, 37; US citizen; m 61, Eleanor Traub; c Douglas, Bryna & Gabriel. *Educ:* Polytech Inst Brooklyn, BS, 60; Columbia Univ, MA, 64, PhD(math), 66. *Prof Exp:* C L E Moore instr math, Mass Inst Technol, 66-68. *Concurrent Pos:* Guggenheim Found fel, 70-71; actg chmn, Dept Math, State Univ NY Stony Brook, 70-71, actg provost, Div Math Sci, 71-72; vis, Israel, Chile, Eng, Japan & China; adv prof, Fudan Univ, Shargai, China. *Mem:* Am Math Soc. *Res:* One complex variable, particularly moduli of Riemann surfaces and Kleinian groups. *Mailing Add:* Dept Math State Univ NY Stony Brook NY 11794-3651. *E-Mail:* irwin@mesh.sunysb.edu

KRAAKEVIK, JAMES HENRY, ATMOSPHERIC PHYSICS. *Current Pos:* chair, Physics Dept, 60-64 & 70-81, from asst prof to prof physics, 70-84, DIR, BILLY GRAHAM CTR, WHEATON COL, ILL, 84- *Personal Data:* b Chicago, Ill, Feb 18, 28; m 50, Marilyn Morrison; c Timothy, Thomas, John, Mark, Stephen & Joel. *Educ:* Wheaton Col, Ill, BS, 48; Univ Md, PhD(physics), 57. *Prof Exp:* Physicist, US Naval Res Lab, 48-54, res sect head, 54-58. *Concurrent Pos:* Consult, US Naval Res Lab, 58-73, Ill State Water Surv, 61-64 & Coronet Instr Films, 62-65; teacher, Titcombe Col, Nigeria, 64-66, prin, 66-67; educ secy, Sudan Interior Mission, 69-70, educ consult, 70-, dir, res & ministry, 81-84; educ consult, Ministry Educ, Sudan, 73-76. *Mem:* Am Asn Physics Teachers; AAAS; Am Meteorol Soc; Am Sci Affil. *Res:* Electrical properties of atmosphere and relationship with meteorology; electrical characteristics of upper atmosphere and relationship with radiation; conduction of electricity through gases; characteristics of sub-micron particles in the atmosphere. *Mailing Add:* 26 W 509 Prairie Ct Winfield IL 60190. *Fax:* 630-752-5916

KRAATZ, CHARLES PARRY, BOTULINUM TOXIX, MUSCLE POTENTIALS. *Current Pos:* CONSULT, 72- *Educ:* Univ Cincinnati, PhD(physiol), 36. *Prof Exp:* Prof pharmacol, Med Col, Jefferson Univ, 47-72. *Mailing Add:* 329 S Norwinden Dr Apt B Springfield PA 19064-3616

KRAAY, GERRIT JACOB, GENETICS. *Current Pos:* HEAD BLOOD TYPING SECT, ANIMAL DIS RES INST EAST, CAN DEPT AGR, 72-, DIR GENETIC BR, 97- *Personal Data:* b Amsterdam, Neth, Oct 14, 35; m 63; c 4. *Educ:* State Agr Univ Wageningen, BSc, 60, MSc, 63, PhD, 67. *Prof Exp:* Res scientist, Found for Blood Group Res, Wageningen, Netherlands, 63; res scientist, Dept Animal Sci, State Agr Univ Wageningen, 64-67; asst prof vet bact, Univ Guelph, 67-69, asst prof biomed sci, 69-72. *Mem:* Royal Dutch Soc Agr Sci; Int Soc Animal Bloodgroup Res; Genetics Soc Can. *Res:* Population genetics of blood groups and serum-protein polymorphisms in animals; immuno-reproduction. *Mailing Add:* Beva-Can Lab Saskatoon Res Coun 15 Innovation Blvd Saskatoon SK F7N 2X8 Can

KRABACHER, BERNARD, PHYSICAL ORGANIC CHEMISTRY. *Current Pos:* RETIRED. *Personal Data:* b Cincinnati, Ohio, Dec 25, 25. *Educ:* Univ Cincinnati, Chem Eng, 49, PhD(phys org chem), 61. *Prof Exp:* Chemist, Emery Industs, Inc, 49-57, group leader ozone res, 61-63; from assoc prof to prof chem, WVa State Col, 63-90, chmn dept, 76-82. *Mem:* Am Chem Soc; fel Am Inst Chemists. *Res:* Reactions of organic compounds with cobalt carbonyls and ozone; preparation of unusual compounds; reaction mechanisms. *Mailing Add:* 1982 Baltimore Ave Cincinnati OH 45225-1905

KRABACHER, JAY E, PHYSICAL SCIENCE. *Current Pos:* TECH ED & WRITER, SCI APPLN INT CORP, 87- *Personal Data:* b Denver, Colo, Mar 15, 49; m 73, Deborah; c Garth & Gamma-Rae. *Educ:* Colo State Univ, BS, 77. *Hon Degrees:* PhD, Inst Metamorphysical, Eng, 72. *Prof Exp:* Geophys engr, Bendix Field Eng, 78-87. *Mem:* Soc Prof Well Log Analysts. *Res:* Certification that contaminated hazardous waste properties are cleaned up in accord with the canonically conjugate variables as per Heisenberg uncertainty; proposed the Bulbyon particle in opposition to tachyons; proposed that bulbyons are absolutely fixed and motionless with respect to all frames of reference. *Mailing Add:* Sci Appln Int Corp 2597 B 3/4 Rd Grand Junction CO 81503

KRABBE, GREGERS LOUIS, MATHEMATICAL ANALYSIS. *Current Pos:* RETIRED. *Personal Data:* b Roskilde, Denmark, Jan 5, 20; nat US; m 55; c 2. *Educ:* Univ Calif, AB, 49, MS, 51, PhD, 54. *Prof Exp:* Assoc prof math, Purdue Univ, 54-60 & Yale Univ, 60-61; NATO fel, Univ Rennes, 61-62; assoc prof math Purdue Univ, 62-68, Prof, 68-88. *Mem:* Am Math Soc. *Res:* Algebraic operational calculus, as applied to lumped systems; theory of linear operators; electrical engineering, linear networks, signal and system analysis. *Mailing Add:* 779 Spruce St Berkeley CA 94707-2040

KRABBENHOFT, HERMAN OTTO, ORGANIC CHEMISTRY. *Current Pos:* Staff chemist, Gen Elec Plastics, 82-87, STAFF CHEMIST, GEN ELEC CORP RES & DEVELOP CTR, 76-81, 88- *Personal Data:* b Detroit, Mich, July 15, 45; m 76; c 2. *Educ:* Wayne State Univ, BS, 70; Univ Mich, MS, 71, PhD(chem), 74. *Concurrent Pos:* NIH grant chem, Univ Calif, Berkeley, 75-76. *Mem:* Am Chem Soc. *Res:* Structure and mechanism in organic chemistry; organic synthesis. *Mailing Add:* Gen Elec Corp/Res & Develop PO Box 8 Schenectady NY 12301-0008

KRABBENHOFT, KENNETH LOUIS, MICROBIOLOGY. *Current Pos:* RETIRED. *Personal Data:* b Page, NDak, Feb 24, 31; m 55; c 3. *Educ:* Univ Valparaiso, BA, 53; NDak State Univ, MS, 56; Ore State Univ, PhD(microbiol), 65. *Prof Exp:* Instr biol, Mankato State Col, 58-62; asst prof, NMex State Univ, 65-67; assoc prof, Mankato State Univ, 67-70, prof, 70-; mem fac, Wayne State Univ, Mich, 91. *Concurrent Pos:* NASA res grant, 65-67; NSF res grant, 69-71. *Mem:* AAAS; Am Soc Microbiol; Inst Food Technologists; Sigma Xi. *Res:* Mechanisms of radiation resistance in microorganisms. *Mailing Add:* 5050 Anthony Wayne Dr Detroit MI 48202

KRACHER, ALFRED, METEORITICS, COSMOCHEMISTRY. *Current Pos:* ASST SCIENTIST & MICROPROBE SPECIALIST, IOWA STATE UNIV, 84- *Personal Data:* b Vienna, Austria, Sept 21, 45; m 74; c 2. *Educ:* Univ Vienna, PhD(chem), 74. *Prof Exp:* Res asst chem, Univ Vienna, 72-74, res asst petrol, 74-76; staff scientist mineral & petrol, Mus Natural Hist, Vienna, 76-81; researcher earth sci, Inst Meteoritics, Univ NMex, 81-82. *Concurrent Pos:* Researcher chem, Inst Geophys, Univ Calif, Los Angeles, 77-78; counr, Meteoritical Soc, 85-86. *Mem:* Meteoritical Soc; Am Geophys Union; Geochem Soc. *Res:* Petrology and composition of meteorites and impact rocks; computer application to petrologic problems; theory of science. *Mailing Add:* 1403 Coolidge Dr Ames IA 50010. *Fax:* 515-294-6049; *E-Mail:* akracher@iastate.edu

KRACKOV, MARK HARRY, ORGANIC & FLUORINE CHEMISTRY, ORGANIC PROCESS DEVELOPMENT. *Current Pos:* CONSULT CHEM RES & DEVELOP, 95- *Personal Data:* b Brooklyn, NY, June 2, 32; m 54, Julia Kennedy; c Laureace & Michael. *Educ:* Univ Calif, Berkeley, BS, 55; Ore State Univ, PhD(org chem), 62. *Prof Exp:* Instr chem, Ore State Univ, 61-62; USPHS fel org chem, Sch Med, Yale Univ, 62-65; sr res assoc, Chem & Pigments Dept, E I Du Pont, 65-93; adj prof math, Wilmington Col, 94-95; adj prof chem, Rosemont Col & Del Co Community Col, 94-95. *Mem:* Am Chem Soc; AAAS; Sigma Xi; Catalysis Soc. *Res:* Synthesis and physical properties of heterocyclic nitrogen, sulfur and selenium compounds; chemical synthesis of polynucleotides; labelling compounds via neutron activation; photopolymerization; reverse osmosis membranes; organic chemical process development; catalysis; fluoroaromatic chemistry; anthraquinone chemistry. *Mailing Add:* 906 Brinton's Bridge Rd West Chester PA 19382

KRAELING, ROBERT RUSSELL, ANIMAL SCIENCE. *Current Pos:* res animal physiologist, Animal Physiol & Genetics Inst, Reproduction Lab, Md, 70-74, Animal Prod Lab, Russell Agr Res Ctr, Athens, 74-77, SUPVR RES PHYSIOLOGIST, ANIMAL PHYSIOL RES UNIT, RUSSELL RES CTR, AGR RES SERV, USDA, 77- *Personal Data:* b Pittsburgh, Pa, Aug 22, 42; m 62, Lois C Sunderland; c David, Williams, Michael, James & Margaret. *Educ:* Univ Md, BS, 64, MS, 67; Iowa State Univ, PhD(animal sci physiol reprod), 70. *Honors & Awards:* Animal Physiol & Endocrinol Res Award, Am Soc Animal Sci, 90. *Prof Exp:* Res asst, Swine Res Br, Animal Husb Res Div, Agr Res Serv, USDA, 64-66, agr res technician, 66-67, agr res scientist, 67; res assoc, Iowa State Univ, 67-70. *Concurrent Pos:* Adj prof, Dept Animal & Dairy Sci, Univ Ga, 74-, mem grad fac, 79-; sr scientist, SAtlantic Area, Agr Res Serv, USDA, 93. *Mem:* Am Soc Animal Sci; Soc Study Reproduction; Sigma Xi. *Res:* Determining the physiological and endocrinlogoical factors which control puberty, ovulation, corpus luteum function and the post-partum interval in swine and cattle and the effects of environment and management systems. *Mailing Add:* Richard B Russell Agr Res Ctr USDA PO Box 5677 Athens GA 30613. *Fax:* 706-546-3586

KRAEMER, DUANE CARL, REPRODUCTIVE PHYSIOLOGY, MEDICINE. *Current Pos:* assoc prof, 75-77, PROF VET PHYSIOL & PHARMACOL, COL VET MED, TEX A&M UNIV, 77- *Personal Data:* b Willow, Wis, Oct 27, 33; m 60; c 2. *Educ:* Univ Wis, BS, 55; Tex A&M Univ, MS, 60, BS, PhD(physiol of reprod) & DVM, 66. *Prof Exp:* Asst scientist, Southwest Found Res & Educ, 66-75. *Mem:* Soc Study Reproduction; Sigma Xi; Am Vet Med Asn; Am Soc Animal Sci; Am Asn Lab Animal Sci. *Res:* Reproductive gamete physiology; contraceptive development and testing. *Mailing Add:* 1101 Foster Ave College Station TX 77845

KRAEMER, HELENA CHMURA, BIOSTATISTICS. *Current Pos:* Actg asst prof, Stanford Univ, 64-69, res assoc, 69-72, from asst prof to assoc prof, 72-86, PROF BIOSTATIST, DEPT PSYCHIAT & BEHAV SCI, SCH MED, STANFORD UNIV, 86- *Personal Data:* b Derby, Conn, July 10, 37; m 62, Arthur R; c Stacey A & Karen Clowe. *Educ:* Smith Col, BA, 58; Stanford Univ, PhD(statist), 63. *Concurrent Pos:* Lectr, Div Biostatist, Dept Community & Prev Med, Stanford Univ, 71- *Mem:* Fel Am Statist Asn; Psychomet Soc. *Res:* Development of statistical methods for use in clinical and behavioral research, with particular emphasis on correlational methods. *Mailing Add:* Dept Psychiat & Behav Sci Sch Med Stanford Univ Stanford CA 94305-9991

KRAEMER, JOHN FRANCIS, ORGANIC CHEMISTRY, POLYMER CHEMISTRY. *Personal Data:* b St Louis, Mo, June 20, 41. *Educ:* St Louis Univ, BS, 63; Loyola Univ, MS, 65, PhD(org chem), 68. *Prof Exp:* Org chemist, Int Minerals & Chem Corp, 68-86. *Mem:* Am Chem Soc. *Res:* Organic synthesis; synthesis of biologically active compounds. *Mailing Add:* 6179 S State Rd 63 Terre Haute IN 47802-9133

KRAEMER, KENNETH H, DNA REPAIR, CARCINOGENESIS. *Current Pos:* res scientist, Lab Molecular Carcinogenesis, NIH, 76- *Personal Data:* b Newark, NJ, June 22, 43; m 65; c 4. *Educ:* Brown Univ, BS, 65; Tufts Univ, MD, 69, diplomat, Nat Bd Med Examiners, 70; Am Bd Internal Med, 73; Am Bd Dermat, 76. *Prof Exp:* Med intern & resident, Harlem Hosp Ctr, NY, 69-71; clin assoc dermat, Dermat Br, NIH, 71-74; resident dermat, Univ Miami Sch Med, 74-76. *Concurrent Pos:* Surgeon, US Pub Health Serv, NIH, 71-74, sr surgeon, 74-86, med dir, 86- *Mem:* Am Acad Dermat; Soc Invest Dermat; Am Soc Photobiol; Am Soc Clin Invest. *Res:* Cancer-prone human genetic disease, xerodorma pigmentosum, familial malignant melanoma or displastic nevus syndrome, atoxin telangiectasia; DNA repair; photo carcinogenesis. *Mailing Add:* Nat Cancer Inst Molecular Carcinogenesis Lab Bldg 37 Rm 3E24 Bethesda MD 20892

KRAEMER, LOUISE MARGARET, PHYSICAL CHEMISTRY, BIOCHEMISTRY. *Current Pos:* EMER PROF, UNIV ARK, 83- *Personal Data:* b New York, NY, Dec 26, 10. *Educ:* Univ Pa, AB, 43; Univ Chicago, PhD(chem), 49. *Prof Exp:* Asst engr, Brown Instrument Co, 43-45; asst chem, Univ Chicago, 45-49; res assoc med, Univ Minn, 49-51; assoc chemist, Argonne Nat Lab, 51-53; asst prof natural sci, Univ Chicago, 53-59, assoc prof phys sci, 59-64; prof chem, New Col, 64-65; prof phys sci, Univ Colo, Boulder, 66-76, emer prof, 76-83. *Concurrent Pos:* Prof, Dept Biol Sci, Univ Ark. *Mem:* AAAS; Am Chem Soc. *Res:* Enzymes in wheat germ; porphyrin chemistry; color centers in alkali halides. *Mailing Add:* Dept Biol Sci Univ Ark Sci Eng Bldg Fayetteville AR 72701

KRAEMER, LOUISE RUSSERT, MALACOLOGY. *Current Pos:* asst prof zool, 48-50, instr, 56-58 & 59-66, from asst prof to assoc prof, 66-77, PROF ZOOL, UNIV ARK, FAYETTEVILLE, 77- *Personal Data:* b Milwaukee, Wis, Dec 17, 23; m 50; c 4. *Educ:* Marquette Univ, BS, 45; Univ Mich, Ann Arbor, MS, 47, PhD(malacol), 66. *Prof Exp:* Asst zool & fisheries, Univ Mich, Ann Arbor, 46-48. *Mem:* AAAS; Am Malacol Union (pres, 81-82); Am Soc Zoologists; Sigma Xi; Animal Behav Soc. *Res:* Functional morphology; behavior of freshwater mollusks; nervous systems and reproductive systems of Lampsilis and Corbicula; macrobenthic communities in lotic systems. *Mailing Add:* Dept Zool 632 Sci-Eng Bldg Univ Ark Fayetteville AR 72701

KRAEMER, PAUL MICHAEL, CELL BIOLOGY. *Current Pos:* Group leader exp pathol, 79-81, STAFF MEM CELLULAR BIOL, LOS ALAMOS NAT LAB, 64- *Personal Data:* b Philadelphia, Pa, Mar 19, 30. *Educ:* Univ Colo, BA, 57; Tulane Univ, MPH, 59, DrPH, 61; Univ Pa, PhD(microbiol), 64. *Concurrent Pos:* Fel, Wistar Inst, 61-64; ed, J Cellular Physiol; cellular physiol study sect, NIH, 77-81, Am Cancer Soc, 87-90. *Mem:* Am Soc Biol Chemists; Am Soc Cell Biol; Am Soc Exp Path. *Res:* Mammalian cell surface complex carbohydrates; chromosome changes in cancer; tumor biology. *Mailing Add:* 191 Cascabel St Los Alamos NM 87544

KRAEMER, ROBERT WALTER, EXPERIMENTAL HIGH ENERGY PHYSICS. *Current Pos:* res assoc, 64-65, from asst prof to assoc prof, 65-74, PROF PHYSICS, CARNEGIE-MELLON UNIV, 74- *Personal Data:* b Philadelphia, Pa, Jan 27, 35; m 60, 87; c 3. *Educ:* La Salle Col, BA, 57; Johns Hopkins Univ, PhD(physics), 62. *Prof Exp:* Instr physics, Johns Hopkins Univ, 61-62, res assoc, 62-64. *Mem:* Am Phys Soc. *Res:* High energy experimental nuclear physics. *Mailing Add:* Dept Physics Carnegie-Mellon Univ Pittsburgh PA 15213

KRAEUTER, JOHN NORMAN, BIOLOGICAL OCEANOGRAPHY, MARINE ECOLOGY. *Current Pos:* ASSOC DIR, FISHERIES & AQUACULT TECH CTR, RUTGERS UNIV, 87- *Personal Data:* b Glen Gardner, NJ, Mar 26, 42; m 70, Carol Foster; c Kirtis & Kristopher. *Educ:* Fla State Univ, BA, 64; Col William & Mary, MA, 66; Univ Del, PhD(biol sci), 71. *Prof Exp:* Res fel biol sci, Marine Inst, Univ Ga, 71-73; res assoc, Skidaway Inst Oceanog, Ga, 73-74; asst marine scientist, Va Inst Marine Sci, 74-80, asst prof, 74-80, assoc prof marine sci, Univ Va & Col William & Mary, 81-82, assoc marine scientist, Va Inst Marine Sci, 81-82; Baltimore Gas & Elec, 82-87. *Mem:* Atlantic Estuarine Res Soc (pres, 77-79); Estuarine Res Fedn (treas, 82-85, secy, 87-88); Malacol Soc London; AAAS; Am Malacol Union; Am Fisheries Soc; Nat Shellfisheries Asn (pres, 93-94). *Res:* Systematics and ecology of scaphopod mollusks; zoogeography of the western Atlantic marine invertebrates; benthic infaunal ecology; aquaculture. *Mailing Add:* 722 Jonathan Hoffman Rd Cape May NJ 08204. *Fax:* 609-785-1544; *E-Mail:* kraeuter@vertigo.rutgers.edu

KRAFFT, GEOFFREY ARTHUR, ACCELERATOR PHYSICS. *Current Pos:* beam diagnostics group leader, 92-93, STAFF SCIENTIST, CONTINUOUS ELECTRON BEAM ACCELERATOR FACIL, 86-, ACCELERATOR PERFORMANCE GROUP LEADER, 93- *Personal Data:* b Enid, Okla, May 14, 58; m 94, Alicia S Hofler. *Educ:* Rutgers Univ, BA, 78; Univ Calif, Berkeley, MA, 80, PhD(physics), 86. *Mem:* Am Phys Soc. *Res:* Theory of particle accelerators; collective effects in intense particle beams; beam diagnostic devices. *Mailing Add:* TJNAF MS-89 12000 Jefferson Ave Newport News VA 23606-1909. *Fax:* 757-269-7352; *E-Mail:* krafft@jlab.org

KRAFFT, GRANT A, ALZHEIMERS DRUG DISCOVERY, BIO-ORGANIC CHEMISTRY. *Current Pos:* lab head, Abbott Diags Div, 88-91, PROG DIR, NIA ALZHEIMERS DRUG DISCOVERY, ABBOTT LABS, 91-, SR GROUP LEADER, 93- *Personal Data:* b Milwaukee, Wis, Feb 6, 54; m 84; c 2. *Educ:* Valparaiso Univ, BS, 76; Univ Ill, Urbana, PhD(org chem), 80. *Prof Exp:* NIH fel, Univ Wis, 80-82; asst prof chem, Syracuse Univ, 82-88, res assoc prof, 88-90. *Concurrent Pos:* Assoc res fel, Abbott Labs, 91- *Mem:* Soc Neurosci; Am Chem Soc; Biophys Soc; AAAS; NY Acad Sci; Sigma Xi. *Res:* Therapeutic targets to prevent neurodegeneration in Alzheimer's disease; development of organic molecular probes to elucidate biochemical and cellular pathways; development of molecular diversity strategies to enhance new lead drug discovery. *Mailing Add:* Dept Molecular Pharmacol & Biol Chem Univ Northwestern 303 E Chicago Ave Suite 215 Chicago IL 60611-3008. *Fax:* 847-937-9195; *E-Mail:* krafft.grant@igate.abbott.com

KRAFFT, JOSEPH MARTIN, PHYSICS. *Current Pos:* physicist res & develop terminal ballistics, dynamic plastic flow & fracture fatigue mech, 48-70, head, Mech Mat Br, 70-81, CONSULT, STRUCT INTEGRITY BR, NAVAL RES LAB, WASHINGTON, DC, 81- *Personal Data:* b Alexandria, Va, Jan 13, 23. *Educ:* Cath Univ Am, Washington, DC, BME, 43, PhD, 51. *Prof Exp:* Various positions teaching, eng, patent search & writing, DC, 41-49. *Concurrent Pos:* Tech ed, Trans, Am Soc Mech Engrs, J Eng Mat & Technol, 78-81. *Mem:* Fel Am Soc Metals; fel Am Soc Testing & Mat; Am Soc Mech Engrs. *Mailing Add:* 1709 Oakcrest Dr Alexandria VA 22302

KRAFFT, MARIE ELIZABETH, TOTAL SYNTHESIS OF NATURAL PRODUCTS, ORGANOMETALLIC CHEMISTRY. *Current Pos:* ASST PROF, FLA STATE UNIV, 85- *Personal Data:* b Washington, DC, Aug 15, 56; m 84. *Educ:* Va Polytech Inst & State Univ, BA, 79, MS, 80, PhD(org chem), 83. *Concurrent Pos:* NIH res fel, Columbia Univ, 83-85. *Mem:* Am Chem Soc; Sigma Xi. *Res:* Synthetic organic and organometallic chemistry; natural products synthesis; synthetic methodology. *Mailing Add:* Dept Chem Fla State Univ Tallahassee FL 32306

KRAFSUR, ELLIOT SCOVILLE, ENTOMOLOGY. *Current Pos:* from asst prof to assoc prof, 76-85, PROF ENTOM, IOWA STATE UNIV, 85- *Personal Data:* b May 15, 39; m 66, Helen J O'Meara; c Edwin P. *Educ:* Univ Md, BS, 62, MS, 64; Univ London PhD(zool), 72. *Prof Exp:* Res asst entomol, Dept Entomol, Univ Md, 62-64; ens lt entomol, USN, 64-69; fel zool, US Nat Sci Found, 70-72, Oxford Univ, 72-73; res entomologist, Animal, Plant & Health Inspection Serv, USDA, 74-76. *Concurrent Pos:* Res med entomologist, USN, 64-69; prin invstr, US Army Biol labs, 64-67 & USN Med Res Unit, Ethiopia, 67-69; consult, Commonwealth Sci & Indust Res Org, New Guinea & Australia, USDA, 86-87, Food & Agr Orgn, 91 & Int Agr Exchange Asn/USDA, 93. *Mem:* Entom Soc Am; Soc Study Evolution; fel Royal Entom Soc; Molecular Biol Evolution Soc; Int Orgn Biol Control. *Res:* Population ecology and genetics of synanthropic flies with special reference to age, breeding structure and phenology; epidemiology of arthropod borne disease; population genetics of predacious coccinellid beetles; sterile insect technique. *Mailing Add:* Dept Entom Iowa State Univ Ames IA 50011-2010. *Fax:* 515-295-5957

KRAFT, ALAN M, PSYCHIATRY. *Current Pos:* PROF PSYCHIAT & CHMN DEPT, ALBANY MED COL, 67- *Personal Data:* b Passaic, NJ, May 24, 25; m 51; c 2. *Educ:* Chicago Med Sch, MD, 51. *Prof Exp:* Staff psychiatrist, Vet Admin Hosp, Denver, Colo, 55-57; chief psychiatrist, Ment Health Ctr Am, 58-61; dir, Ft Logan Ment Health Ctr, 61-67. *Concurrent Pos:* Fel psychiat, Menninger Sch Psychiat, 52-55; consult, Vet Admin Hosp, Albany, NY, 71-; dir, Capital Dist Psychiat Ctr, Albany, 67-79. *Mem:* Am Psychiat Asn. *Res:* Treatment of chronic schizophrenia; program evaluation. *Mailing Add:* 47 New Scotland Ave Albany NY 12208-3412

KRAFT, ALLEN ABRAHAM, FOOD TECHNOLOGY. *Current Pos:* from asst prof to assoc prof, 59-72, PROF FOOD TECHNOL, IOWA STATE UNIV, 72-, PROF MICROBIOL, 81- *Personal Data:* b New York, NY, 1923; m 47; c 2. *Educ:* Cornell Univ, BS, 47, MS, 49; Iowa State Col, PhD(food technol), 53. *Prof Exp:* Asst food technol & bact, Iowa State Col, 49-53; asst poultry prod technologist, Animal & Poultry Husb Res Br, Agr Res Serv, USDA, 53-59. *Mem:* Fel AAAS; Poultry Sci Asn; Inst Food Technologists; Am Soc Microbiol; World Poultry Sci Asn. *Res:* Microbiology and technology of meat and poultry products. *Mailing Add:* 3624 Ross Rd Ames IA 50014

KRAFT, CHRISTOPHER COLUMBUS, JR, AEROSPACE ENGINEERING. *Current Pos:* PVT CONSULT, 93- *Personal Data:* b Phoebus, Va, Feb 28, 24; m 50; c 2. *Educ:* Va Polytech Inst, BS, 44. *Hon Degrees:* DEng, Ind Inst Technol, 66 & St Louis Univ, 67. *Honors & Awards:* Arthur S Flemming Award, 63; Louis W Hill Award, Am Inst Aeronaut & Astronaut, 70, Space Flight Award, 70, W Randolph Lovelace II Award, 77; Von Karman lectr, Am Inst Aeronaut & Astronaut, 77; Daniel & Florence Guggenheim Int Astronaut Award, 78; Goddard Mem Trophy, Nat Space Club, 79. *Prof Exp:* Aeronaut res engr, Langley Aeronaut Lab, Nat Adv Comt Aeronaut, Va, 45-48, space task group, NASA, 58-59, supvry aeronaut res engr, 59-61, asst chief flight opers div, 61-62, chief div, 62-63, dir flight opers, 63-69, dep dir ctr, 69-72, dir, Lyndon B Johnson Space Ctr, 72-82; aerospace consult, Rockwell Int, Houston, 82-93. *Mem:* Nat Acad Eng; fel Am Inst Aeronaut & Astronaut; fel Am Astronaut Soc. *Mailing Add:* 14919 Village Elm St Houston TX 77062

KRAFT, DAVID WERNER, THEORETICAL & EXPERIMENTAL PHYSICS, RESEARCH ADMINISTRATION. *Current Pos:* chair, Math Dept, Univ Bridgeport, 82-83, assoc dean grad studies & res, 84-86, dir, Res Corp, 85, dir, Technol Develop Unit, 85-88, prof elec eng, 85-96, PROF MATH & PHYSICS, UNIV BRIDGEPORT, 96- *Personal Data:* b Worms, Ger, Apr 21, 33; nat US; m 58; c Arthur, Mark & Jill. *Educ:* City Col New York, BS, 54; Pa State Univ, PhD(physics), 59. *Honors & Awards:* Harry Epstein Award, Am Asn Physics Teachers. *Prof Exp:* Res physicist, Pa State Univ, 59-60; sr physicist, Philips Labs Div, NAm Philips Co, Inc, 60-64 & Electronics Systs Div, Loral Corp, 64; sr res physicist, Cent Res Div, Am Cyanamid Co, 65; res scientist, Hudson Labs, Columbia, 65-68; from assoc prof to prof physics, Cooper Union, 68-76; vis prof opers res, Grad Sch Bus Admin, NY Univ, 76-77; dir, Manpower Placement Div, Am Inst Physics, 77-79; dep exec secy, Am Phys Soc, 79-82. *Concurrent Pos:* Consult, Electronic Systs Div, Loral Corp, 65; vis scientist & consult, Gen Tel & Electronics Labs, 69-70; adj prof, Statist & Oper Res, NY Univ, 69-; vis scientist, NY Univ, 72-74 & Philips Labs Div, NAm Philips Co, 75; consult, NY Tel Co, 76-77, Am Inst Physics, 77 & SL Electrostatic Technol, 88-90; found pres & dir, Conn Venture Group, 85-89; prin invstr, Conn Coop High Technol Grant, 88-90; vpres, A&D Assoc, 89-; corresp mem, UN Comn Disarmament & Arms Control, 92-; fac fel, Goddard Inst Space Studies, NASA, 92-93; chair, Physics & Astron Sect, NY Acad Sci, 92-; dir, Kardell Technol Corp, NY, 93-; vis prof physics, US Mil Acad, West Point, NY, 93-94. *Mem:* Am Phys Soc; Am Asn Physics Teachers; NY Acad Sci. *Res:* Ultrasonic absorption; scattering of elastic waves; solid state physics; nuclear fusion; astrophysics. *Mailing Add:* Div Sci & Math Univ Bridgeport Bridgeport CT 06601

KRAFT, DONALD HARRIS, INFORMATION RETRIEVAL, FUZZY SET THEORY. *Current Pos:* assoc prof, 76-82, chmn, 85-91, PROF COMPUTER SCI, LA STATE UNIV, 82- *Personal Data:* b Omaha, Nebr, Dec 21, 43; m 68, Linda G Ohlbaum; c Elizabeth & Suzanne. *Educ:* Purdue Univ, BS, 65, MS, 66, PhD(indust eng), 71. *Honors & Awards:* K S Fu Award, N Am Fuzzy Info Processing Soc, 86; Watson Davis Award, Am Soc Info Sci, 95. *Prof Exp:* Asst prof libr & info serv, Univ Md, 70-75; vis asst prof librarianship, Univ Calif, Berkeley, 75-76. *Concurrent Pos:* Adj prof libr & info sci, La State Univ, 83-; mem, NAm Fuzzy Info Processing Soc Coun, 90-92; ed, J Am Soc Info Sci; vis prof libr & info sci, Univ Calif, Los Angeles, 94. *Mem:* Asn Comput Mach; Inst Elec & Electronics Engrs Computer Soc; Asn Libr & Info Sci Educ; Am Soc Info Sci; Inst Elec & Electronics Engrs. *Res:* Use of fuzzy set theory to model generalized Boolean information retrieval mechanisms; use of operations research to model and evaluate ranked retrieval output. *Mailing Add:* Dept Computer Sci La State Univ Baton Rouge LA 70803-4020. *Fax:* 504-388-1465; *E-Mail:* kraft@bid.csc.lsu.edu

KRAFT, DONALD J, PLANT PHYSIOLOGY. *Current Pos:* asst prof, 69-72, assoc prof, 72-79, PROF, BEMIDJI STATE UNIV, 79- *Personal Data:* b Strasburg, NDak, Nov 9, 36; m 60, Beverly A Rodger; c Terrence, Brian, Karen & Margaret. *Educ:* NDak State Univ, BS, 59, PhD(plant physiol), 68. *Prof Exp:* Teacher high sch, NDak, 61-62, chmn dept sci, 62-63; asst prof biol, St Mary's Col Minn, 68-69. *Concurrent Pos:* Prin invstr grants, NIH, 68-69 & Minn State Col Bd, 69-70 & 73-74. *Mem:* AAAS; Am Soc Plant Physiologists; Sigma Xi. *Res:* Biochemistry of seed germination as a means to eliminate noxious weeds through natural components of seeds rather than through use of sprays. *Mailing Add:* Dept Biol Bemidji State Univ Bemidji MN 56601

KRAFT, EDWARD MICHAEL, AERODYNAMICS, WIND TUNNEL TECHNOLOGY. *Current Pos:* EXEC VPRES OPERS, MICRO CRAFT, 95- *Personal Data:* b Cincinnati, Ohio, Nov 13, 44; m 71; c 1. *Educ:* Univ Cincinnati, BS, 68; Univ Tenn, MS, 72, PhD(aerodyn eng), 75. *Prof Exp:* Res asst, Space Inst, Univ Tenn, 68-69; proj engr, Sverdrup/Aro, Inc, 69-72, res engr, 72-78, engr supv, 78-80; br mgr, Calspan Field Serv Inc, 81-95. *Concurrent Pos:* Asst prof, Space Inst, Univ Tenn, 77- *Mem:* Am Inst Aeronaut & Astronaut. *Res:* Wind tunnel wall interference, including subsonic, transonic and vertical/short take off and landing theories and development of the adaptive wall concept. *Mailing Add:* Micro Craft 207 Big Springs Ave Tullahoma TN 37388

KRAFT, GERALD F, ENTOMOLOGY, SCIENCE EDUCATION. *Current Pos:* Asst prof zool, 61-66, chmn dept biol, 71-74 & 77-85, ASSOC PROF BIOL, WESTERN WASH UNIV, 66- *Personal Data:* b Salinas, Calif, Feb 22, 28; m 48, 79; c 4. *Educ:* San Jose State Col, BA, 54; Wash State Univ, MS, 56; Ore State Univ, PhD(entom), 62. *Concurrent Pos:* City of Bellingham grant, 62-64; dir inst freshwater studies, Western Wash State Col, 64-68; US Dept Interior grant, 66-; res assoc, Univ Calif, Berkeley, 68-69. *Mem:* Entom Soc Am; Nat Acad Advising Asn. *Res:* General entomology; aquatic insects. *Mailing Add:* Dept Biol Western Wash Univ MS 9060 Bellingham WA 98225-5996

KRAFT, IRVIN ALAN, CHILD PSYCHIATRY, PSYCHOANALYSIS. *Current Pos:* prof, 75-91, EMER PROF MENT HEALTH, UNIV TEX SCH PUB HEALTH, HOUSTON, 91- *Personal Data:* b Huntington, WVa, Nov 20, 21; m 51, Sherry; c 4. *Educ:* NY Univ, MD, 49. *Prof Exp:* Asst prof psychiat, Baylor Col Med, 57-61, asst prof pediat, 58-61, assoc prof psychiat & pediat, 61-77, clin prof psychiat, 77- *Concurrent Pos:* Med dir, Tex Inst Family Psychiat, 64-79. *Mem:* Fel Am Psychiat Asn; fel Am Acad Psychoanal; fel Am Acad Child Psychiat; fel Am Orthopsychiat Asn. *Res:* Child psychiatry; psychoanalysis. *Mailing Add:* 2423 Gramercy Houston TX 77030. *Fax:* 713-850-1522

KRAFT, JOAN CREECH, RETINOIC ACID, DYSMORPHOGENESIS. *Current Pos:* POST GRAD RES, VET ADMIN MED CTR, 97- *Personal Data:* b Washington, DC, June 8, 43; c 3. *Educ:* Univ Pa, BS, 65; Free Univ Berlin, Ger, dipl biol, 75, Dr rer nat (biol), 77. *Prof Exp:* Lab asst molecular biol, Free Univ Berlin, 76-81, teaching asst biol, 79-83; sr res scientist, Inst Toxicol & Embyopharmacol, Berlin, 84-88; sr res fel teratology, Dept Pharmacol, Univ Wash, 90-97. *Concurrent Pos:* Postdoctoral res protein biosynthesis, Inst Biochem & Molecular Biol, Free Univ Berlin & Max Planck Inst Molecular Genetics, 78-79. *Mem:* Teratology Soc. *Res:* Teratology; pharmacokinetics, metabolism and placental transfer of the potent teratogen accutane. *Mailing Add:* Vet Admin Med Ctr 4150 Clement St Rm 111 N San Francisco CA 94121

KRAFT, JOHN CHRISTIAN, HOLOCENE GEOLOGY, ARCHAEOLOGICAL GEOLOGY. *Current Pos:* from asst prof to assoc prof, 64-69, chmn dept, 69-84, PROF GEOL, UNIV DEL, 69-, H FLETCHER BROWN PROF GEOL & MARINE STUDIES, 83- *Personal Data:* b Schwenksville, Pa, Nov 15, 29; m 92, Linda J Graves Schlick; c Christine L, John F & Amanda L Schlick. *Educ:* Pa State Univ, BS, 51; Univ Minn, MS, 52, PhD(micropaleont), 55. *Honors & Awards:* Archaeol Geol Award, Geol Soc Am, 87; John C Kraft Celebration, Coastal Sediments, Am Soc Civil Engrs & Soc Econ Paleontologists and Mineralogists, 91. *Prof Exp:* Geologist, Shell Can Ltd, 55-61, div stratigr, 61-64. *Mem:* Fel AAAS; Am Asn Petrol Geologists; fel Geol Soc Am; Soc Econ Paleont & Mineral; Am Inst Prof Geologists; Archaeol Inst Am. *Res:* Geology of coasts; Holocene sedimentary environments; Ordovician and Holocene Ostracoda; archaeological geology. *Mailing Add:* Dept Geol Univ Del Newark DE 19716. *Fax:* 302-831-4158; *E-Mail:* 00218@udel.edu

KRAFT, JOHN M, PLANT PATHOLOGY. *Current Pos:* RES PLANT PATHOLOGIST, CROP RES DIV, AGR RES SERV, USDA, 66-, RES LEADER VEG & FORAGE CROP RES, 95- *Personal Data:* b Gary, Ind, July 14, 38; m 64; c 2. *Educ:* Ariz State Univ, BSc, 60; Univ Minn, St Paul, MS, 62; Univ Calif, Riverside, PhD(plant path), 66. *Prof Exp:* Res asst plant path, Univ Minn, St Paul, 60-62 & Univ Calif, Riverside, 62-66. *Concurrent Pos:* Mem grad fac, Dept Plant Path, Wash State Univ & Dept Plant Sci, Univ Idaho. *Mem:* Am Phytopath Soc; Am Soc Agron & Soil Sci; Pisum Genetics Asn; Sigma Xi; Nat Pea Improv Asn. *Res:* Soil-borne diseases of peas and their etiology, biology of the fungi, their control and the nature and inheritance of resistance when found; control of soil-borne diseases of peas; breeding for root disease resistance in peas. *Mailing Add:* Irrigated Agr Res & Exten Ctr 24106 N Bunn Rd Prosser WA 99350-9689. *Fax:* 509-786-9277

KRAFT, KENNETH J, INVERTEBRATE ECOLOGY. *Current Pos:* asst prof, 61-64, ASSOC PROF BIOL, MICH TECHNOL UNIV, 64- *Personal Data:* b Dows, Iowa, Mar 3, 30; m 68; c 1. *Educ:* Bemidji State Col, BS, 52; Univ NDak, MS, 53; Univ Minn, PhD(entom), 58. *Prof Exp:* Instr biol, Univ Minn, 56-58; asst prof, Moorhead State Col, 58-59 & Bemidji State Col, 59-61. *Mem:* Entom Soc Am. *Res:* Ecology of aquatic insects. *Mailing Add:* Sch Forestry Mich Technol Univ 1400 Townsend Dr Houghton MI 49931-1200

KRAFT, LISBETH MARTHA, PATHOLOGY, RADIOBIOLOGY. *Current Pos:* RES SCIENTIST, AMES RES CTR, NASA, 77- *Personal Data:* b Vienna, Austria, May 16, 20; nat US. *Educ:* Cornell Univ, BS, 42, DVM, 45. *Honors & Awards:* Griffin Award, Am Asn Lab Animal Sci, 72; Charles River Prize, Am Vet Med Asn, 81. *Prof Exp:* Asst parasitol, Cornell Univ, 45-46 & nutrit, Harvard Univ, 46; bacteriologist, NY State Dept Health, 47-49; asst, Yale Univ, 49-51, from instr to asst prof, 51-55; asst prof, NY Univ, 55-57; res assoc path & vet, Sch Med, Yale Univ, 57-61; asst dir, New York City Bur Labs & assoc mem, Pub Health Res Inst, 61-65; staff scientist, Bioquest Div, Becton Dickinson Co, 65-66; res vet, Oak Ridge Assoc Univs, 66-68; owner, L M Kraft Assocs, 68-74; specialist, Space Sci Lab, Univ Calif, Berkeley, 74-75; assoc scientist dept physics, Univ San Francisco, 75-77. *Concurrent Pos:* Consult, Sloan-Kettering Inst Cancer Res, NY, 59-61. *Mem:* AAAS; Am Soc Microbiol; Am Vet Med Asn; Am Asn Lab Animal Sci; Am Col Lab Animal Med; Sigma Xi. *Res:* Central nervous system effects of cosmic ray (homogeneous differential equation) particles as applicable to manned spaceflight safety standards; investigations on health status of animals in spaceflight research; laboratory animal medicine and science. *Mailing Add:* 2101B Fallen Leaf Lane Los Altos CA 94024

KRAFT, PATRICIA LYNN, toxicology, for more information see previous edition

KRAFT, R(ALPH) WAYNE, systems theory, physical metallurgy; deceased, see previous edition for last biography

KRAFT, ROBERT PAUL, ASTROPHYSICS. *Current Pos:* actg dir, Univ Calif, Santa Cruz, 68-70, 71-73 & 80-81, prof astron & astronr, Lick Observ, 67-92, dir, Lick Observ, 81-91, dir, Univ Calif Observ, 88-91, ASTRONR/EMER PROF, UNIV CALIF, SANTA CRUZ, 93- *Personal Data:* b Seattle, Wash, June 16, 27; m 49, Rosalie Reichmuth; c Kenneth & Kevin. *Educ:* Univ Wash, BS, 47, MS, 49; Univ Calif, Berkeley, PhD(astron), 55. *Hon Degrees:* DSc, Ind Univ, 95. *Honors & Awards:* Warner Prize lectr, Am Astron Soc, 62, Henry Norris Russell Lectr, 95. *Prof Exp:* Instr math & astron, Whittier Col, 49-51; NSF fel, Mt Wilson & Palomar Observs, 55-56; asst prof astron, Ind Univ, 56-58 & Univ Chicago, 58-59; mem staff, Mt Wilson & Palomar Observs, 60-67. *Concurrent Pos:* chmn bd studies astron & astrophys, Univ Calif, Santa Cruz, 68-70 & 78-80; vis fel, Univ Colo, 70; Fairchild scholar, Cal Inst Technol, 80; Beatrice Tinsley vis prof, Univ Tex, 91-92. *Mem:* Nat Acad Sci; Am Astron Soc (pres, 74-76)); Am Acad Arts & Sci; Int Astron Union (vpres, 82-88, pres-elect, 94-); fel AAAS. *Res:* Stellar spectroscopy; galactic structure. *Mailing Add:* 830 Pinetree Lane Aptos CA 95003-3528. *Fax:* 408-426-3115; *E-Mail:* kraft@ucolick.org

KRAFT, SUMNER CHARLES, INTERNAL MEDICINE, GASTROENTEROLOGY. *Current Pos:* From instr to assoc prof, 59-73, PROF MED, SCH MED, UNIV CHICAGO, 74- *Personal Data:* b Lynn, Mass, Aug 21, 28; m 63, Patricia P Pink; c Gary, Jennifer & Steven. *Educ:* Tufts Col, BS, 48; Boston Univ, AM, 49; Univ Chicago, MD, 55; Am Bd Internal Med, dipl, 62, Am Bd Gastroenterol, dipl, 65. *Honors & Awards:* William Beaumont Award, 77. *Concurrent Pos:* USPHS spec res fel, 61-66, USPHS res career develop award, 67-71; res fel, Div Allergy, Immunol & Rheumatol, Scripps Clin & Res Found, La Jolla, Calif, 64-66; vis affil prof med, Uniformed Serv Univ Health Sci, Bethesda, 79-87. *Mem:* AAAS; Am Asn Immunologists; Am Col Physicians; Am Fedn Clin Res; Am Gastroenterol Asn; Am Soc Gastrointestinal Endoscopy; Sigma Xi. *Res:* Gastrointestinal immunolgy. *Mailing Add:* Dept Med Univ Chicago MC 4076 5841 S Maryland Ave Chicago IL 60637-1463

KRAFT, WALTER H, MARKETING, CIVIL & ENGINEERING. *Current Pos:* FROM ASST ENG TO PARTNER & SR VPRES, EDWARDS & KELCEY, INC, 62-; PARSONS BRINCKERHOFF. *Personal Data:* b Newark, NJ, Dec 31, 38; m 59; c Robin, Karen & Lynda. *Educ:* Newark Col Eng, BS, 62, MS, 65; NJ Inst Technol, DEngSc, 75. *Honors & Awards:* Robert Ridgward Award, Am Soc Civil Engrs, 62, Frank Masters Award, 82; Ivor S Wisepart Transp Eng Award & Distinguished Serv Award, Inst Transp Engrs, 86. *Concurrent Pos:* Adj prof, NJ Inst Technol & Polytech Inst, NY; chairperson, Urban Transp Div, Am Soc Civil Engrs, 77-79, Nat Transp Policy Comt, 80-82, Comt AIE03 Intermodal Transfer Facil, Nat Res Coun, Transp Res Bd, 82-85; mem, Comt A3A10 Hwy Capacity & Qual Serv, 80-85; lectr, Carnegie-Mellon Univ, St Johns Univ, Int Conf Traffic Eng & Planning, Beijing, Peoples Repub China, 87 & Sino-Am-British Urban Transp Planning Sem, Beijing, Peoples Repub China, 88. *Mem:* Fel Inst Transp Engrs (pres, 87); Am Soc Civil Engrs. *Res:* Civil engineering; traffic engineering and planning; author of numerous technical articles. *Mailing Add:* 2 Ashwood Ct Summit NJ 07901. *Fax:* 973-994-4902

KRAFT, WILLIAM GERALD, BACTERIAL PATHOGENESIS, MICROBIAL PHYSIOLOGY. *Current Pos:* sr res microbiologist, 77-82, group leader, 82-84, SECT HEAD, PROCTER & GAMBLE PHARMACEUT, 84- *Personal Data:* b Evansville, Ind, July 15, 44; m 77, Barbara A Betz. *Educ:* Purdue Univ, BS, 66; Univ Wash, MS, 72; Ind Univ, PhD(microbiol), 77. *Prof Exp:* Res eng chem, Dow Chem Co, 66-68. *Mem:* Am Soc Microbiol. *Res:* Physiology and pathogenesis of campylobacters; thermal resistance of aerobic bacilli spores and define sterilization cycles for pharmaceutical products; microbial ecology of natural and synthetic substances; develop novel antibacterials. *Mailing Add:* 8700 Mason-Montgomery Rd Mason OH 45040

KRAG, SHARON S, BIOCHEMISTRY. *Current Pos:* PROF BIOCHEM, SCH HYG & PUB HEALTH, JOHNS HOPKINS UNIV, 76-, ASSOC DEAN RES, 94- *Personal Data:* b Wharton, Tex, Aug 11, 47. *Educ:* Tex Lutheran Col, BS, 69; Johns Hopkins Univ, PhD(biochem), 74. *Prof Exp:* Fel, Cancer Res Ctr, Mass Inst Technol, 74-76. *Concurrent Pos:* Res career develop award, NIH, 80 & 85. *Mem:* Fedn Am Socs Exp Biol; Am Cell Biol Soc; AAAS. *Mailing Add:* Dept Biochem Sch Hyg & Pub Health Johns Hopkins Univ 615 N Wolfe St Baltimore MD 21205-2103

KRAH, DAVID LEE, VIROLOGY, CELL BIOLOGY. *Current Pos:* sr res virologist, Merck Sharp & Dohme Res Labs, 88-91, res fel, 91-95, SR RES FEL, MERCK RES LABS, MERCK & CO, INC, 95- *Personal Data:* b Ashland, Pa, Jan 23, 56. *Educ:* Pa State Univ, BS, 77; Hahnemann Med Col, MS, 80; Hahnemann Univ, PhD(microbiol & immunol), 82. *Prof Exp:* Fel, Rockefeller Univ, 82-85, res assoc, 85-86; sr res scientist, Schering Corp, 86-88. *Mem:* AAAS; Am Soc Microbiol; Am Soc Virol; Soc Gen Microbiol; Tissue Cult Asn. *Res:* Development and characterization of live virus vaccines; measurement of humoral immune responses following viral infection or vaccination; interactions of viruses with cell membrane receptors. *Mailing Add:* Dept Virus & Cell Biol Merck Res Labs West Point PA 19486

KRAHENBUHL, JAMES LEE, INFECTIOUS DISEASES, LEPROSY. *Current Pos:* chief, immunol res, 83-94, CHIEF, LAB RES BR, G W LONG HANSEN'S DIS CTR, CARVILLE, LA, 94- *Personal Data:* b Appleton, Wis, Oct 7, 42; m 65, Betty Poquette; c Jeffrey Lee. *Educ:* Univ Wis-Madison, BS, 64, MS, 67, PhD(med microbiol), 70. *Honors & Awards:* Distinguished Serv Award Biomed Res, USPHS, 90. *Prof Exp:* Fel, Palo Alto Med Res Found, 70-71, sr res assoc immunol & infectious dis, 72-79; chief, Leprosy Res Unit, USPHS Hosp, San Francisco, 79-83. *Concurrent Pos:* Fel med, Med Ctr, Stanford Univ, 70-71, res assoc, 72-78; USPHS res career develop award, Nat Inst Allergy & Infectious Dis, 74-79; prof vet microbiol, Sch Vet Med, La State Univ, Baton Rouge, 85- *Mem:* AAAS; Am Asn Immunologists; Soc Exp Biol & Med; Am Soc Microbiol; Int Leprosy Asn. *Res:* Mechanisms of host resistance to leprosy, tuberculosis and toxoplasmosis. *Mailing Add:* Lab Res Br La State Univ PO Box 25072 Baton Rouge LA 70894. *Fax:* 504-346-5786; *E-Mail:* krahenbuhl@vt8200.vetmed.lsu.edu

KRAHL, MAURICE EDWARD, ENDOCRINOLOGY, BIOCHEMISTRY. *Current Pos:* vis prof, 67-69, chmn & prof, 69-77, EMER PROF PHYSIOL, STANFORD UNIV, 77- *Personal Data:* b Cambridge City, Ind, Sept 17, 08; m 32, 67, Ardis Lostroh. *Educ:* Depauw Univ, AB, 29; Johns Hopkins Univ, PhD(chem), 32. *Hon Degrees:* LLD, Univ Toronto, 71. *Honors & Awards:* Banting lectr, Eng Biabetic Asn, 50. *Prof Exp:* Res chemist, Eli Lilly & Co, 33-44; instr pharmacol, Col Physiol & Surg, Columbia Univ, 44-46; asst prof to assoc prof pharmacol & biochem, Wash Univ, St Louis, 46-53; prof physiol, Univ Chicago, 53-69. *Concurrent Pos:* Vis prof physiol, Univ Rio Grande Do Sul, Brazil, 59; consult, endocrine study sect, NIH, 61-65 & pvt found, 77-; vis prof biochem, Monash Univ, Australia, 66-77; trustee, Marine Biol Lab, Woods Hole. *Mem:* Am Soc Biol Chemists; Am Soc Pharmocol & Exper Therapeut; Soc Gen Physiologists; Am Diabetes Asn. *Res:* Physical chemistry of drugs and hormones; etiology of diabetes mellitus. *Mailing Add:* 2783 W Casas Circle Tucson AZ 85741-9771

KRAHMER, ROBERT LEE, FOREST PRODUCTS. *Current Pos:* From instr to prof, 59-91, EMER PROF FOREST PROD, ORE STATE UNIV, 91- *Personal Data:* b Forest Grove, Ore, Dec 28, 32; m 57; c 2. *Educ:* Ore State Univ, BS, 58, MS, 60; State Univ NY Col Forestry, Syracuse Univ, PhD(wood prod eng), 62. *Mem:* Forest Prod Res Soc; Soc Wood Sci & Technol; Int Asn Wood Anat. *Res:* Light and electron microscope studies of fine structure of wood; variability of anatomical properties of wood. *Mailing Add:* 1040 NE Granger Ave Corvallis OR 97330

KRAHN, ROBERT CARL, ORGANIC CHEMISTRY. *Current Pos:* HEALTH CONSULT, 82-; DIR, GOLDEN PATHWAYS HEALING CTR. *Personal Data:* b Minneapolis, Minn, Dec 1, 41; m 78; c Megan Bliss & Tara Cole. *Educ:* Univ Minn, BChE, 63; Univ Wash, PhD(org chem), 68. *Prof Exp:* Res chemist, Org Chem Dept, E I Du Pont de Nemours & Co, Inc, 68-73, process chemist, 73-78, sr chemist, Chem, Dyes & Pigments Dept, Jackson Lab, 78-82. *Mem:* Am Chem Soc. *Res:* Emulsion polymerization; monomer synthesis; flurochemicals; surfactant chemistry; ethoxylation; textile finishing. *Mailing Add:* 17 Polaris Dr N Star Newark DE 19711-3056. *E-Mail:* bobkrahn@msn.com

KRAHN, THOMAS RICHARD, HORTICULTURE. *Current Pos:* Exten specialist, 67-72, head lab serv, 72-83, DIR, ALTA HORT RES CTR, 83- *Personal Data:* b Swiftcurrent, Sask, May 23, 43; m 67; c 2. *Educ:* Univ Alta, BSc, 67; Mich State Univ, MSc, 73. *Mem:* Agr Inst Can. *Res:* Post harvest physiology, mainly storage and handling practices for vegetables, potatoes, and nursey crops. *Mailing Add:* Alta Spec Crops & Hort Res Ctr SS4 Brooks AB T1R 1E6 Can

KRAHNKE, HAROLD C, PHYSIOLOGICAL CHEMISTRY, PHARMACY. *Current Pos:* RETIRED. *Personal Data:* b Beloit, Wis, Oct 12, 07; m 31; c 2. *Educ:* Univ Wis, BS, 40, MS, 41. *Prof Exp:* Pharmacist, Retail Pharm, 26-36; res asst physiol chem, Univ Wis, 40-41; res chemist, Lakeside Labs, Inc, 41-47, chief control chemist, 47-52, chief pharmaceut div, 52-62; dir pharmaceut dept, Lakeside Labs Div, Colgate-Palmolive Co, 62-73. *Mem:* Am Chem Soc; Am Pharmaceut Asn; Acad Pharmaceut Sci. *Res:* Pharmaceutical research and product development; formulation and manufacturing procedures; synthesis of organic medicinal compounds; quality control of pharmaceuticals. *Mailing Add:* 6770 N Yates Rd Milwaukee WI 53217

KRAHULA, JOSEPH L(OUIS), MECHANICS. *Current Pos:* from asst prof to assoc prof, 52-67, PROF MECH, HARTFORD GRAD CTR, RENSSELAER POLYTECH INST, 67- *Personal Data:* b Czech, July 22, 23; nat US; m 59; c 2. *Educ:* Rensselaer Polytech Inst, BME, 46, MS, 50; Univ Ill, PhD(mech), 52. *Prof Exp:* Instr mech, Rensselaer Polytech Inst, 46-50; asst, Univ Ill, 50-52. *Mem:* Assoc fel Am Inst Aeronaut & Astronaut; Int Asn Bridge & Struct Engrs. *Res:* Vibrations and elasticity. *Mailing Add:* Dept Eng & Sci Rensselaer 275 Windsor St Hartford CT 06120-2991

KRAICER, JACOB, endocrinology, neuroendocrinology, for more information see previous edition

KRAICHNAN, ROBERT HARRY, STATISTICAL MECHANICS. *Current Pos:* INDEPENDENT CONSULT, 62-; CONSULT, LOS ALAMOS NAT LAB, 82- *Personal Data:* b Philadelphia, Pa, Jan 15, 28; m 89, Judy Moore; c John L. *Educ:* Mass Inst Technol, BS, 47, PhD, 49. *Honors & Awards:* Otto Laporte Award, Am Phys Soc, 93 & Lars Onsager Prize, 97. *Prof Exp:* Mem, Inst Advan Study, 49-50; mem tech staff, Bell Tel Labs, Inc, 50-52; res assoc, Electronics Res Lab, Columbia Univ, 52-56; inst math sci, NY Univ, 56-59, sr res scientist, 59-62. *Concurrent Pos:* Consult, Naval Res Lab, 57-59 & NASA, 61-; assoc physics, Woods Hole Oceanog Inst, 60- *Mem:* Fel Am Phys Soc. *Res:* Quantum and classical statistical mechanics; random processes; turbulence, quantum field and relativity theory. *Mailing Add:* 369 Montezuma No 108 Sante Fe NM 87501

KRAIG, ELLEN, MOLECULAR IMMUNOGENETICS. *Current Pos:* ASST PROF CELL BIOL, HEALTH SCI CTR, UNIV TEX, 83- *Personal Data:* b Ft Worth, Tex, Feb 9, 53; m 78; c 1. *Educ:* Univ Denver, BS, 75; Brandeis Univ, PhD(biol), 81. *Prof Exp:* Teaching fel biol, Calif Inst Technol, 80-83. *Mem:* Am Asn Immunologists; Sigma Xi. *Res:* Use of recombinant DNA approaches to elucidate the molecular bases of immune response regulation. *Mailing Add:* Dept Cell Biol Univ Tex Health Sci Ctr 7703 Floyd Curl Dr San Antonio TX 78284-7762

KRAIHANZEL, CHARLES S, INORGANIC CHEMISTRY. *Current Pos:* From asst prof to assoc prof, 62-70, PROF CHEM, LEHIGH UNIV, 70- *Personal Data:* b New Bedford, Mass, Sept 6, 35; m 57, Pauline Tripp; c 5. *Educ:* Brown Univ, ScB, 57; Univ Wis, MS, 59, PhD(chem), 62. *Mem:* AAAS; Am Chem Soc; Sigma Xi. *Res:* Syntheses, reactions, nature of bonding and physical properties, of organosilicon, organophosphorous and transition metal compounds; molecular modeling of inorganic and organometallic compounds. *Mailing Add:* Dept Chem 6 E Packer Ave Bethlehem PA 18015. *E-Mail:* csk1@lehigh.edu

KRAIMAN, EUGENE ALFRED, POLYMER CHEMISTRY. *Current Pos:* PRES, POLYMER SYSTS CORP, 68- *Personal Data:* b Philadelphia, Pa, Apr 11, 29; m 56. *Educ:* Univ Pa, BS, 50; Univ Ill, MS, 51, PhD(chem), 53. *Prof Exp:* Res chemist, Union Carbide Plastics Co, 53-56 & Hooker Chem Co, 56-58; supvr, Plastics Div, Nopco Chem Co, 58-61; res sect head, Sun Chem Corp, 61-68. *Mem:* Am Chem Soc. *Res:* Polyurethanes; organic chemicals; elastomers; coatings; adhesives; ultraviolet radiation cured systems. *Mailing Add:* 7922 Sandpoint Blvd Orlando FL 32819

KRAINES, DAVID PAUL, TOPOLOGY. *Current Pos:* asst prof, 71-73, ASSOC PROF MATH, DUKE UNIV, 73- *Personal Data:* b Chicago, Ill, Mar 7, 41; m 64; c 2. *Educ:* Oberlin Col, AB, 61; Univ Calif, Berkeley, MA, 63, PhD(math), 65. *Prof Exp:* Instr math, Mass Inst Technol, 65-67; asst prof, Haverford Col, 67-70, actg chmn, 68-69; guest prof, Aarhus Univ, 70-71. *Mem:* Am Math Soc. *Res:* Algebraic topology. *Mailing Add:* Dept Math Duke Univ Durham NC 27706

KRAINTZ, LEON, PHYSIOLOGY, ENDOCRINOLOGY. *Current Pos:* from assoc prof to prof oral biol, 64-87, head dept, 69-81, EMER PROF ORAL BIOL & HON PROF PHYSIOL, UNIV BC, 87- *Personal Data:* b Johnstown, Pa, Oct 3, 24; m 49, Frances D Whitcomb; c Dona (Sturmanis), Franz P & Erika (Schmidt). *Educ:* Harvard Univ, AB, 50; Rice Inst, MA, 52, PhD(biol), 54. *Prof Exp:* Res asst, Sloan Kettering Inst Cancer Res, 48-50; res scientist exp med, Univ Tex, M D Anderson Hosp & Tumor Inst, 51-52, from instr to assoc prof physiol, Dent Br, 54-62; prof biol, Rice Univ, 62-64. *Concurrent Pos:* Asst, Rice Inst, 51-52; NSF fel, 52-54; vis instr, Col Med, Baylor Univ, 56-63; vis lectr, Univ St Thomas, Tex, 57-63; USPHS spec fel physiol, Howard Florey Inst Exp Physiol, Univ Melbourne, 68-69; vis prof, Dent Sci Inst, Houston, 81-82. *Mem:* Fel AAAS; Endocrine Soc; Am Physiol Soc; Can Physiol Soc; Soc Exp Biol Med; Int Asn Dent Res; Sigma Xi. *Res:* Radioisotopic techniques in biology and medicine; protein hormones; mineral metabolism; salivation. *Mailing Add:* 6478 Dunbar St Vancouver BC V6N 1X6 Can. *Fax:* 604-822-6698

KRAITCHMAN, JEROME, INSTRUMENTATION, SURFACE SCIENCE. *Current Pos:* supvr, Cent Res Facil, 76-80, ASST DIR, MAT RES LAB, CARNEGIE-MELLON UNIV, 80- *Personal Data:* b New York, NY, Mar 5, 26; m 57; c 3. *Educ:* Syracuse Univ, AB, 48; Columbia Univ, AM, 50, PhD(chem physics), 54. *Prof Exp:* Asst, Columbia Univ, 49-53; res physicist, Res Labs, Westinghouse Elec Corp, 53-66; res physicist, Glass Res Ctr, PPG Industs, Inc, 66-75. *Mem:* Am Phys Soc. *Res:* Materials science; microwave spectroscopy; molecular structure; dielectrics; semiconductors; physics and chemistry of surfaces; thin films; adhesion. *Mailing Add:* 2409 Collins Rd Pittsburgh PA 15235

KRAJCA, KENNETH EDWARD, ADHESIVES & ADHESION, COATINGS TECHNOLOGY. *Current Pos:* group leader, 84-86, develop mgr, Chem Div, 86-92, MGR TECH SERV, UNION CAMP CORP, 92- *Personal Data:* b Wichita Falls, Tex, April 1, 44; m 67, Sherry Walters; c Larur L & Shannon D. *Educ:* Midwestern State Univ, BS, 67; Univ Fla, PhD(chem), 72. *Prof Exp:* Res scientist, Union Camp Corp, 72-76; res chemist, SCM Corp, 76-80, sect head, 80-84, tech mgr, 84. *Mem:* Am Chem Soc; Adhesion Soc. *Res:* Design and develop tall oil-based products for the adhesives industry (from thermoplastic polyamides and epoxy curing agents to rosin-based tackifying resins). *Mailing Add:* 110 N Cromwell Rd Savannah GA 31410

KRAJCINOVIC, DUSAN, MICROMECHANICS, DAMAGE & FRACTURE MECHANICS. *Current Pos:* PROF MECH SOLIDS, ARIZ STATE UNIV, 89- *Personal Data:* b Zaqreb, Yugoslavia, Mar 28, 35; US citizen; m 63, Tanya Pavlic; c Ivana & Maya. *Educ:* Univ Belgrade, Yugoslavia, BSc, 58, MSc, 66; Northwestern Univ, PhD(theoret appl mech), 68. *Prof Exp:* Proj engr, Energoprojekt, Belgrade, 59-61; teaching asst mech, Univ Belgrade, 61-66; res asst, Northwestern Univ, 66-68; mem tech staff, Ingersoll Rand Res, 68-69, Argonne Nat Lab, 69-73; prof mech, Univ Ill, Chicago, 73-89. *Concurrent Pos:* Consult, Argonne Nat Lab, 73-80, Gabinete da Area de Sines, Portugal, 80-84, E Fermi Nat Lab, 83-87, Allied Signal, 92-; mem, USA Plasma Team, US Dept Energy, 76-80; vis prof, Univ de Paris VI, 87-88; mem, Inst Theoret Physics, Univ Calif, Santa Barbara, 92- *Mem:* Fel Am Soc Mech Engrs; fel Am Acad Mech. *Res:* Brittle deformation of solids with disordered microstructure; nondeterministic models of critical states in solids weakened by diffused microcracks; formulation of continuum damage theories based and inspired by micromechanics. *Mailing Add:* Mech & Aerospace Eng Ariz State Univ Tempe AZ 85287-6106. *E-Mail:* krajcino@asuvax.eas.asu.edu

KRAJEWSKI, JOHN J, SYNTHETIC ORGANIC CHEMISTRY, POLYMER CHEMISTRY. *Current Pos:* POLYMER & COATINGS CONSULT, 95- *Personal Data:* b Chicago, Ill, Mar 27, 31; m 59; c 2. *Educ:* Loyola Univ Ill, BS, 53, MS, 54; Carnegie Inst Technol, PhD(org chem), 58. *Prof Exp:* Res chemist, Swift & Co, 58-60, div head, 60-62; res chemist, Int Minerals & Chem Corp, 62-67, synthetic org specialist, 67-70; res chemist, De Soto, Inc, 70-73, tech mgr, 73-79, mgr polymer develop, 79-87, mgr, New Venture Res, 87-89; mgr new venture polymers, Allied Signal Corp, 91-94. *Concurrent Pos:* Polymer chem instructor, De Paul Univ, 90, adv res proj selection & mgt, dir, Innovative Prob Solving Serv. *Mem:* Am Chem Soc. *Res:* Organic synthesis; polymer chemistry; natural products; photopolymerization; organic photoconductors; chemical coatings; laser curing of resins. *Mailing Add:* 932 Valley Stream Dr Wheeling IL 60090-3949

KRAKAUER, HENRY, BIOMETRICS-BIOSTATISTICS. *Current Pos:* med adv, Off Med Rev, Health Care Financing Admin, 85-88, dir, Off Prog Assessment & Info, 88-91, MED ADV, HEALTH STANDARDS & QUAL BUR, HEALTH CARE FINANCING ADMIN, 91- *Personal Data:* b Jaworzno, Poland, May 31, 39; US citizen; m 74; c 2. *Educ:* Yeshiva Univ, BA, 60, BHL, 60; NY Univ, MD, 64; Yale Univ, PhD(chem), 68. *Honors & Awards:* Commendation Medal, USPHS, 81, Outstanding Serv Medal, 88, Meritorious Serv Medal, 91; Distinguished Serv Award, Dept Health & Human Serv, 89. *Prof Exp:* From asst prof to assoc prof chem, Wash State Univ, 68-79; chief, Genetics & Transplantation Biol Br, Nat Inst Allergy & Infectious Dis, 79-83. *Concurrent Pos:* Res assoc prof, Sch Med, Univ Md, 87- *Mem:* Am Soc Biochem & Molecular Biol; Am Asn Immunologists; Biophys Soc; Am Chem Soc; Biomet Soc; Sigma Xi. *Res:* Epidemiologic analysis of medical practice. *Mailing Add:* Uniformed Serv Univ Health Sci 4301 Jones Bridge Rd Bethesda MD 20814-4799. *Fax:* 301-295-3891

KRAKAUER, TERESA, BIOCHEMISTRY, CELL BIOLOGY. *Current Pos:* MICROBIOLOGIST, DEPT PATHOGENESIS & IMMUNOL DIS ASSESSMENT DIV, US ARMY MED RES INST INFECTIOUS DIS. *Personal Data:* b China; US citizen. *Educ:* Wash State Univ, BSc(chem) & BSc(biochem), 71; Iowa State Univ, PhD(biochem), 75. *Prof Exp:* Res assoc biochem, Wash State Univ, 75-78; NIH staff fel biochem, Nat Inst Arthritis, Metab & Digestive Dis, Nat Inst Dent Res, 78-80, NIH staff fel, 80- *Mem:* Am Chem Soc; Sigma Xi; Biophys Soc. *Res:* Molecular biology; cell surface proteins; molecular basis of immunogenicity; developmental biology; gene transfer. *Mailing Add:* Dis Assessment Div USAMRIID Ft Detrick Frederick MD 21702-5011

KRAKOFF, IRWIN HAROLD, medicine, for more information see previous edition

KRAKOW, BURTON, PHYSICAL CHEMISTRY, SPECTROSCOPY. *Current Pos:* PROJ MGR ADV TECHNOL, NY STATE ENERGY RES & DEVELOP AUTHORITY, 78- *Personal Data:* b Brooklyn, NY, Feg 12, 28. *Educ:* City Col New York, BS, 49; Brooklyn Col, MA, 58; Mass Inst Technol,

PhD(phys chem), 62. *Prof Exp:* Jr engr extractive metall, Metall Lab, Sylvania Elec Prod, 54-57; sr phys chemist molecular spectros, Control Instrument Div, Warner & Swasey Co, 62-69; sr prin develop engr, Honeywell Inc, 69-73; res engr, ARO Inc, 73-78. *Mem:* Am Chem Soc; Am Phys Soc; Coblentz Soc. *Res:* Infrared spectroscopy; radiant heat transfer; spectroscopic pyrometry; infrared instrumentation; solar energy conversion. *Mailing Add:* Dept Elec Eng Eng 118 4202 E Fowler Ave Tampa FL 33620-5350

KRAKOW, JOSEPH S, BIOCHEMISTRY, MOLECULAR BIOLOGY. *Current Pos:* PROF BIOL SCI, HUNTER COL, 71- *Personal Data:* b New York, NY, Dec 23, 29; m 55; c 2. *Educ:* Univ Mich, BS, 55; Yale Univ, PhD(pharmacol), 61. *Prof Exp:* USPHS fel biochem, NY Univ, 61-63; assoc res biochemist, Space Sci Lab, Univ Calif, Berkeley, 63-71, lectr, Dept Med Physics, 64-71. *Concurrent Pos:* Biochem Study Sect, NIH, 75-, chmn, 78. *Mem:* Am Chem Soc; Am Soc Biol Chem. *Res:* Nucleic acids; enzymology. *Mailing Add:* Dept Biol Hunter Col City Univ NY New York NY 10021

KRAKOWSKI, FRED, MATHEMATICS. *Current Pos:* assoc prof, Sacramento State Col, 67-70, PROF MATH, CALIF STATE UNIV, SACRAMENTO, 70- *Personal Data:* b Zuoz, Switz, July 31, 27; m 58; c 1. *Educ:* Swiss Fed Inst Technol, DSc(math), 57. *Prof Exp:* From instr to asst prof math, Univ Calif, Davis, 57-67. *Mem:* Am Math Soc. *Res:* Algebra. *Mailing Add:* 2202 Woodside Lane Sacramento CA 95825-7480

KRAL, ROBERT, PLANT TAXONOMY. *Current Pos:* from asst prof to assoc prof biol, 65-72, PROF BIOL, VANDERBILT UNIV, 72- *Personal Data:* b Highland Park, Ill, Feb 28, 26; m 57; c 1. *Educ:* NC State Col, BS, 52; Fla State Univ, PhD(bot), 59. *Prof Exp:* Asst bot, Fla State Univ, 55-58; instr, Northeast La State Col, 58-59; asst prof, Va Polytech Inst, 59-65; assoc prof, LA Tech, 62-65. *Res:* Vascular plant taxonomy; floristics of southeastern coastal plain; studies in Annonaceae, Cyperaceae and Xyridaceae; flora of Alabama and Tennessee; flora of North America. *Mailing Add:* Dept Gen Biol Vanderbilt Univ 2201 W End Ave Nashville TN 37240-0001

KRALEWSKI, JOHN EDWARD, PHARMACY, HEALTH ADMINISTRATION. *Current Pos:* asst prof, 65-69, PROF, UNIV MINN, MINNEAPOLIS, 78- *Personal Data:* b Durand, Wis, May 20, 32; m 57, Marjorie Gustafson; c Judy, Ann & Sara. *Educ:* Univ Minn, BS, 56, MHA, 62, PhD, 69. *Prof Exp:* Prof, Univ Colo, Denver, 69-78. *Mem:* Am Pub Health Asn; Asn Health Servs Res. *Res:* Health administration. *Mailing Add:* Univ Minn 420 Delaware St SE 15-205 Minneapolis MN 55455

KRALL, ALBERT RAYMOND, metabolism of pb ca & mg; deceased, see previous edition for last biography

KRALL, ALLAN M, MATHEMATICS. *Current Pos:* From asst prof to assoc prof, 63-71, PROF MATH, PA STATE UNIV, 71- *Personal Data:* b Bellefonte, Pa, Feb 25, 36; m 58; c 4. *Educ:* Pa State Univ, BS, 58; Univ Va, MA, 60, PhD(math), 63. *Concurrent Pos:* Grants, NASA, 65-69 & USAF, 77-79. *Mem:* Math Asn Am; Am Math Soc. *Res:* Differential operators. *Mailing Add:* 845 N Thomas St State College PA 16803-3659

KRALL, ELIZABETH A, NUTRITION. *Current Pos:* Res fel nutrit, 84-87, res assoc, 87-92, SCIENTIST NUTRIT, USDA, TUFTS UNIV, 92-, ASST PROF, SCH NUTRIT, 92- *Personal Data:* b Lebanon, Pa, Nov 22, 51. *Educ:* Pa State Univ, BS, 73; Univ Pittsburgh, MS, 80, PhD(enzym), 84. *Honors & Awards:* Pub Health Award, Pittsburgh Univ, 85. *Mem:* Am Inst Nutrit; Am Soc Mineral Res; Sigma Xi. *Res:* Nutrition. *Mailing Add:* USDA Health Nutrit Res Ctr on Aging Tufts Univ 711 Washington St Boston MA 02111-1524

KRALL, HARRY LEVERN, mathematics; deceased, see previous edition for last biography

KRALL, JOHN MORTON, BIOSTATISTICS, RESEARCH. *Current Pos:* DIR RES, ST LUKES HOSP, 92- *Personal Data:* b Bellefonte, Pa, July 28, 38; div; c Philip & Andrew. *Educ:* Pa State Univ, BA, 60; Univ Iowa, MS, 62, PhD(statist), 69. *Prof Exp:* Mathematician, Comput Br, NIH, 62-65; asst prof biomet, Univ Tex MD Anderson Hosp & Tumor Inst Houston, 69-70; asst prof pub health & prev med, WVa Univ, 70-73, from assoc prof to prof biostatist, 73-82; sr biostatistician, Am Col Radiol, Philadelphia, 82-92. *Mem:* Am Statist Asn. *Res:* Development of methodology for medical statistical applications; study of factors affecting survival. *Mailing Add:* St Lukes Hosp Res Inst 801 Ostrum St Bethlehem PA 18105. *Fax:* 610-954-4979

KRALL, NICHOLAS ANTHONY, PHYSICS. *Current Pos:* CO-FOUNDER, KRALL ASSOCS, 88- *Personal Data:* b Kansas City, Kans, Feb 16, 32; m 54, 85, Diane Miller; c 6. *Educ:* Univ Notre Dame, BSc, 54; Cornell Univ, PhD(theoret physics), 59. *Prof Exp:* Mem res staff solid state physics, RCA Labs, NJ, 54; mem res staff theoret physics, John Jay Hopkins Lab Pure & Appl Sci, Gen Atomic Div, Gen Dynamics Corp, 59-67, asst mgr theory, Gen Atomic Controlled Fusion Res Prog, 67; prof physics, Univ Md, College Park, 67-73; vis res prof physics, Univ Calif, San Diego, 73-74; dir lab appl plasma studies, Sci Applns Inc, 74-78, vpres, 77-78; vpres, Jaycor, San Diego, 78-87. *Concurrent Pos:* Dir joint prog plasma physics, Naval Res Lab, Univ Md, 71-73; Guggenheim Found fel, 73-74; chmn, APS/DPP, 81; chmn, Fusion Power Asn, 82-84. *Mem:* Fel Am Phys Soc; Sigma Xi; AAAS. *Res:* Controlled thermonuclear fusion; plasma physics; high energy nuclear physics; electron scattering; application of dispersion relation technique to atomic physics; magnetohydrodynamics; plasma stability theory; laser system modeling; Raman cell modeling. *Mailing Add:* Krall Assocs 1070 America Way Del Mar CA 92014. *Fax:* 619-481-7827

KRAMAN, STEVE SETH, PULMONARY MEDICINE. *Current Pos:* CHIEF OF STAFF, VET ADMIN MED CTR, LEXINGTON, KY, 86- *Personal Data:* b Chicago, Ill, Aug 30, 44; div; c 3. *Educ:* Univ PR, BS, 67, MD, 73. *Prof Exp:* Asst prof, 78-84, assoc prof med, Univ KY, 84- *Mem:* Am Col Chest Physicians; Am Thoracic Soc; Inst Elec & Electronics Engrs; Acoust Soc Am; Am Physiol Soc. *Res:* Determination of the acoustic properties of the respiratory system including lung sounds and transmitted sounds. *Mailing Add:* Vet Admin Med Ctr 2250 Leestown Rd Lexington KY 40511. *E-Mail:* sskram01@pop.uky.edu

KRAMER, AARON R, MECHANICAL ENGINEERING, INSTRUMENTATION. *Current Pos:* assoc prof eng, 63-71, PROF ENG, STATE UNIV NY, MARITIME COL, 71- *Personal Data:* b New York, NY, Apr 26, 32; m 60; c 3. *Educ:* State Univ NY Maritime Col, BME, 54; City Col New York, MME, 63. *Prof Exp:* Appl engr instr, Bailey Meter Co, 56-63. *Concurrent Pos:* Consult, Simulation Autodyn Inc, 67- & Stone & Webster Eng Corp, 73-; Inst Environ Sci res grant, 68-69; Maritime Admin, US Dept Commerce res grant, 69-73; prof eng, NY, NJ. *Mem:* Instrument Soc Am; Am Soc Mech Engrs; Am Soc Eng Educ. *Res:* Automatic control design and analysis; simulation of mechanical, chemical processes and energy management techniques with analogue, digital and hybrid computers; instrumentation and data collection systems and analysis. *Mailing Add:* Dept Engr State Univ NY Maritime Col 6 Tennyfield Ave Bronx NY 10465-4198

KRAMER, ALFRED WILLIAM, JR, morphological biology, teaching, for more information see previous edition

KRAMER, BARNETT SHELDON, MEDICAL ONCOLOGY, CANCER PREVENTION-PUBLIC HEALTH. *Current Pos:* sr investr med oncol, 86-96, DEP DIR, DIV CANCER PREV & CONTROL, NAT CANCER INST, 96- *Personal Data:* b Baltimore, Md, July 29, 48; m 72; c 1. *Educ:* Univ Md, MD, 73. *Prof Exp:* Intern, Washington Univ, 73-74, resident, 74-75; from asst prof to assoc prof med oncol, Univ Fla, 78-86; clin assoc oncol, Nat Cancer Inst, 75-78; assoc prof, 86-89, Uniformed Serv Univ Health Sci, prof, 89- *Mem:* Am Asn Cancer Res; Am Soc Clin Oncologists; Asn Clin Trials. *Res:* Infections in febrile neutropenic cancer patients; lung cancer; new drug development; cancer prevention and control. *Mailing Add:* Nat Cancer Inst Bldg 31 Rm 10A49 31 Center Dr Bethesda MD 20892-2580. *Fax:* 301-496-9931; *E-Mail:* bk76p@nih.gov

KRAMER, BERNARD, SOLID STATE PHYSICS. *Current Pos:* ADJ PROF, FAIRLEIGH DICKINSON UNIV, 86- *Personal Data:* b New York, NY, Nov 12, 22; m 46; c 2. *Educ:* City Col New York, BS, 42; NY Univ, PhD(physics), 52. *Prof Exp:* Physicist, Fed Tel & Radio Corp, 42-47; instr, Brooklyn Col, 47-49; res asst, NY Univ, 49-52, res assoc, 52-65, res scientist, 65-69; lectr, Hunter Col, City Univ New York, 53-55, from asst prof to prof physics, 55-86, chmn dept physics & astron, 60-71. *Concurrent Pos:* Vis prof, Munich Technol Univ, 59-60; vis fel, Princeton Univ, 73-74; sci collab, Brookhaven Nat Lab, 80-81; vis scholar, Univ Del, 81. *Mem:* Am Phys Soc. *Res:* Luminescence; photoconductivity; photovoltaic effects. *Mailing Add:* 115 Carnation St Bergenfield NJ 07621

KRAMER, BRADLEY ALAN, PRODUCTION PLANNING & CONTROL, ARTIFICIAL INTELLIGENCE APPLICATIONS IN MANUFACTURING. *Current Pos:* Asst prof, 85-91, assoc dir res, Ctr Res Comput Controlled Automation, 88-90, ASSOC PROF INDUST ENG, KANS STATE UNIV, 91- *Personal Data:* b Manhattan, Kans, May 30, 58; m 78; c 3. *Educ:* Kans State Univ, BS, 80, MS, 81, PhD(indust eng), 85. *Concurrent Pos:* Dow outstanding young fac award, Am Soc Eng Educ, 90. *Mem:* Soc Mfg Engrs; Am Soc Eng Educ; Inst Indust Engrs. *Res:* Manufacturing engineering; integration of the production process from product design to manufacturing to assembly with focus in production planning, scheduling and control. *Mailing Add:* Dept Indust Eng Kans State Univ 238 Manhattan KS 66506-5101

KRAMER, BRIAN DALE, PHYSICAL ORGANIC CHEMISTRY. *Current Pos:* RETIRED. *Personal Data:* b Pottsville, Pa, Nov 17, 42; m 67. *Educ:* Pa State Univ, BS, 64; Harvard Univ, PhD(chem), 68. *Prof Exp:* Res chemist, Cent Res Div, Paper Technol Group, Hercules Inc, 68-73, sr res chemist, 73-76, res supvr, New Enterprises Res Div, 76-77, res scientist, Chem Sci Div & Mat Sci Div, 77-82, proj leader paper chem, 80-87, res assoc, Mat Sci Div, 82-87, dir labs, Res Ctr, 87-89, dir technol, 89-95. *Mem:* Am Chem Soc; Tech Asn Pulp Paper Indust. *Res:* Kinetics and mechanisms of 1, 2 cycloaddition reactions; photochemical generation of reactive intermediates; Ziegler polymerization of alpha-olefins; physical and chemical characterization of organic polymers; radiation chemistry; chemical additives for paper. *Mailing Add:* 3 Boysenberry Dr Ramsey Ridge Hockessin DE 19707

KRAMER, BRUCE MICHAEL, MECHANICAL ENGINEERING. *Current Pos:* STAFF MEM, NSF, 95- *Personal Data:* b New York City, NY, July 23, 49; m, Patricia Joffee; c Katherine & Andrew. *Educ:* Mass Inst Technol, SB & SM, 72, PhD(mech eng), 79. *Honors & Awards:* Blackall Award, Am Soc Mech Eng, 82; F W Taylor Medal, Int Inst Prod Eng Res, 84; R F Bunshah Award, Int Conf Metal Coating, 86. *Prof Exp:* From asst prof to assoc prof mech eng, Mass Inst Technol, 79-85; prof mech eng, George

Washington Univ, 85-95. *Concurrent Pos:* Chmn, Zoom Telephonics, Inc, Boston, 76-89; consult, 79- *Mem:* Am Soc Mech Engrs; Am Soc Metals; Sigma Xi. *Res:* Machining automation and tool material development; tribology and wear theory. *Mailing Add:* NSF 4201 Wilson Blvd Rm 550 Arlington VA 22230. *Fax:* 703-524-6956; *E-Mail:* kramer@seas.gwu.edu

KRAMER, CAROLYN MARGARET, HIGH TECHNOLOGY CERAMICS. *Current Pos:* DIR RES & DEVELOP, CERAMCO, INC, 89- *Personal Data:* b Chicago, Ill, Mar 12, 53. *Educ:* Univ Ill, Champaign, BS, 74; Univ Calif, Berkeley, MS, 75; Univ Calif, Davis, PhD(mat sci & eng), 80. *Prof Exp:* Staff mem, Sandia Nat Lab, 73-81; postdoctoral, Nat Acad Sci, Nat Res Coun, 81-82; ceramic engr, Naval Res Lab, 82-83; mat scientist, Advan Technol Lab, Gillette, 83-84, mgr & group mgr mat res, Boston Res & Develop Lab, 84-89. *Mem:* AAAS; Soc Women Engrs; corp mem Am Ceramic Soc; Int Asn Dent Res; Am Soc Metals. *Res:* Uses of high technology ceramics. *Mailing Add:* 312 Highland Ave Moorestown NJ 08057

KRAMER, CHARLES EDWIN, POLYMER CHEMISTRY. *Current Pos:* sr res assoc, 77-81, asst dir res, 81-93, RES DIR, ALBANY INT CORP, 93- *Personal Data:* b Lancaster, Pa, Apr 1, 47; m 69, Elizabeth; c Christopher & Timothy. *Educ:* Franklin & Marshall Col, BS, 69; Northeastern Univ, MS, 71, PhD(chem), 75. *Prof Exp:* Res chemist, Celanese Corp, 74-77. *Mem:* Am Chem Soc; Sigma Xi; Tech Asn Pulp & Paper Indust. *Res:* Polymer chemistry; monomer and polymer synthesis; polymer flammability; membrane science; polymer blends; polymer structure-property relationships. *Mailing Add:* 7 Metacomet St Walpole MA 02081-2039

KRAMER, CHARLES LAWRENCE, MYCOLOGY. *Current Pos:* from asst prof to assoc prof, 58-73, PROF BOT, KANS STATE UNIV, 73- *Personal Data:* b Leavenworth, Kans, Apr 4, 28; m 51; c 2. *Educ:* Univ Kans, BA, 50, MS, 53, PhD(bot), 57. *Prof Exp:* Asst prof biol, Western Ill Univ, 57-58. *Concurrent Pos:* Grants, USPHS, 58- & NSF, 67- *Mem:* Am Mycol Soc; Int Asn Plant Taxon; Brit Mycol Soc. *Res:* Kansas fungi, especially parasitic forms; taxonomy of Taphinales; aeromycology. *Mailing Add:* Dept Biochem Kans State Univ 104 Wilard Hall Manhattan KS 66506-3702

KRAMER, DAVID BUCKLEY, mechanical engineering, computer science, for more information see previous edition

KRAMER, EARL SIDNEY, MATHEMATICS. *Current Pos:* from asst prof to assoc prof, 70-82, PROF MATH, UNIV NEBR, 82- *Personal Data:* b Chippewa Falls, Wis, Nov 13, 40. *Educ:* Wis State Univ, Eau Claire, BS, 62; Univ Mich, MS, 64 & 66, PhD(math), 69. *Prof Exp:* Temp lectr, Univ Birmingham, 69-70. *Mem:* Am Math Soc; Math Asn Am. *Res:* Existence of various combinatorial structures. *Mailing Add:* Dept Math Univ Nebr Lincoln NE 68588-0323

KRAMER, EDWARD J(OHN), MATERIALS SCIENCE. *Current Pos:* from asst prof to prof, 67-88, Samuel B Eckert prof mat sci & eng, 88-97, PROF MAT & CHEM ENG, UNIV CALIF, SANTA BARBARA, 97- *Personal Data:* b Wilmington, Del, Aug 5, 39; m 63, Gail Woodford; c Eric W & Jeanne N. *Educ:* Cornell Univ, BChE, 62; Carnegie-Mellon Univ, PhD(metal & mat sci), 67. *Hon Degrees:* Dr, Ecole Polytech Federale de Lausanne, 95. *Honors & Awards:* High Polymer Physics Prize, Am Phys Soc, 85; Swinburne Award, Inst Mat, 96. *Prof Exp:* NATO fel metall, Oxford Univ, 66-67. *Concurrent Pos:* Vis scientist, Argonne Nat Lab, 74-75; Gauss prof, Acad Wissenschaften, Gottingen, 79; vis prof, Polytech Sch Fed Lausanne, 82 & Johannes Gutenberg Univ, Mainz, 87-88. *Mem:* Nat Acad Eng; Am Chem Soc; Mat Res Soc; Soc Plastic Engrs; fel AAAS; fel Am Phys Soc. *Res:* Surfaces, interfaces, diffusion, deformation and fracture of polymeric materials. *Mailing Add:* Dept Mats Univ Calif Santa Barbara CA 93106

KRAMER, ELIZABETH, DIETETICS, BIOCHEMISTRY. *Current Pos:* CONSULT DIETITIAN, VILLA CLEMENT NSG HOME, MILWAUKEE, 85 - *Personal Data:* b Milwaukee, Wis, June 7, 18. *Educ:* Alverno Col, BSE, 43; De Paul Univ, MS, 48; St Louis Univ, PhD(chem), 54; Mt Mary Col, BS, 81. *Prof Exp:* Instr biol & math, high sch, Ill, 43-47; instr biol, Alverno Col, 47-49, assoc prof chem & chmn dept, 54-69, prof chem, 69-79; dietitian, Vet Admin Med Ctr, Milwaukee, Wis, 81-85. *Concurrent Pos:* Fel biochem, Univ Iowa, 69-70; asst archivist, Sch Sister St Francis, Milwaukee, Wis. *Mem:* Am Dietetic Asn; Sigma Xi; Soc Nutrit Educ. *Res:* Studies of drug binding, especially aspirin, salicylates and D-tubocurarine to purified proteins of human blood as well as to serum and plasma using fluorometric and gel filtration techniques. *Mailing Add:* 1425 S 26th St Milwaukee WI 53204

KRAMER, ELMER E, PATHOLOGY. *Current Pos:* assoc dir, 79-85, EMER PROF SURG PATH & OBSTET & GYNEC & HON CONSULT, NY HOSP, 85- *Personal Data:* b New Orleans, La, Sept 22, 14; m 47, Anne Gleysteen; c Antonette & Dirk. *Educ:* Tulane Univ, BS 35, MD, 38; Am Bd Obstet & Gynec, dipl, 51. *Prof Exp:* Intern, Hotel Dieu Hosp, New Orleans, La, 38-39, resident, 39-40; asst obstet & gynec, Med Col, Cornell Univ, 46-49, from instr to prof obstet & gynec, 49-70, prof surg path, 69-85, prof obstet & gynec, 70-85. *Concurrent Pos:* Intern, NY Lying-In-Hosp, 46, from asst resident to resident, 46-50, asst pathologist, 50-56, pathologist, 56-; asst attend obstetrician & gynecologist, NY Hosp, 50-53, attend pathologist, 69-; consult, Payne Whitney Psychiat Clin, 52-56, from assoc attend obstetrician & gynecologist to attend obstetrician & gynecologist, 53-57; consult, Lenox Hill Hosp, 74-79; Am Bd Qual Assurance & Utilization Rev Physicians, 78-; Am Col Utilization Rev Physicians, 78- *Mem:* AMA; fel Am Col Surgeons; Am Col Obstetricians & Gynecologists. *Res:* Obstetrical and gynecological pathology. *Mailing Add:* NY Hosp 525 E 68 St New York NY 10021

KRAMER, FRANKLIN, PROCESS & EQUIPMENT DEVELOPMENT & ENGINEERING. *Current Pos:* PRES, FREMARK CO, FOOD PROCESS CONSULTS, 88- *Personal Data:* b Brooklyn, NY, Mar 6, 23; m 51, Barbara Richter; c Nancy K (Ducharme) & Harold. *Educ:* City Col New York, BChE, 44; Polytech Inst Brooklyn, MChE, 47. *Prof Exp:* Res chem engr, Cent Res Labs, Gen Foods Corp, 44-53, tech supt, Atlantic Gelatin Div, 53-59; mgr res & develop, Walter Baker Chocolate Co, 59-62 & Cracker Jack Co Div, Borden Co, 62-65; mgr equip & process develop, Kitchens of Sarah Lee, 65-68; vpres mfg & eng, La Touraine-Bickford's Foods Inc, 68-73; vpres mfg, Seapak Div, W R Grace & Co, 73-75; prin scientist process eng, Cent Res Div, Gen Foods Corp, 75-88. *Concurrent Pos:* Sr consult, Ctr Advan Food Technol, Rutgers Univ, 88-93, vis prof & adj fac mem, 90-; chmn, Tech Achievement Awards, Gen Foods Corp; managing dir, Zuckek, Kramer Assoc Inc, 90-; eng consult. *Mem:* Sr mem Am Chem Soc; fel Am Inst Chem Engrs; Inst Food Technol. *Res:* Development of food processes from lab bench scale through commercialization; technical management and teaching. *Mailing Add:* 132 Holbrook Rd Briarcliff Manor NY 10510. *Fax:* 914-923-1609; *E-Mail:* frankbrk@aol.com

KRAMER, FRED RUSSELL, MOLECULAR BIOLOGY, BIOCHEMISTRY GENETICS & BIOTECHNOLOGY. *Current Pos:* RES PROF, DEPT MICROBIOL, NY UNIV MED SCH, 87- *Personal Data:* b New York, NY, July 7, 42; m 65; c 2. *Educ:* Univ Mich, BS, 64; Rockefeller Univ, PhD(molecular biol), 69. *Prof Exp:* Am Cancer Soc fel, Inst Cancer Res, Col Physicians & Surgeons, Columbia Univ, 69-71, res assoc molecular biol, 71-72, instr, 72-73, asst prof, human genetics & develop, 73-80, sr res assoc, 80-83, res scientist, 83-86; mem & chmn, dept molecular genetics, Pub Health Res Inst, 86- *Concurrent Pos:* Adv panalist, Nat Sci Found Biochem, 85; prin investr, NIH grant, 84-, Am Cancer Soc grant, 84-86, 89, Am Cancer Soc grant, 84-86, NSF grant, 87-90; mem Corp Bermuda Biol Asn; pres, Kramer Consult Inc. *Mem:* NY Acad Sci; Am Soc Molecular Biol & Biol Chem; Am Soc Microbiologists; Am Asn Univ Prof; Sigma Xi. *Res:* Evolution and synthesis of nucleic acids in vitro; morphology, physiology, genetics and evolution of replicatable nucleic acids; molecular beacons and binary probes for diagnostic clinical assays. *Mailing Add:* Dept Molecular Genetics Pub Health Res Inst 455 First Ave New York NY 10016-9102

KRAMER, GEORGE MORTIMER, PHYSICAL ORGANIC CHEMISTRY. *Current Pos:* chemist, Process Res Div, Esso Res & Eng Co, 57-64, Baytown Res & Develop Div, Tex, 65-66, res assoc, Cent Basic Res Lab, 66-69, res assoc, 69-78, SR RES ASSOC, CORP RES LAB, EXXON RES & ENG CO, NJ, 78- *Personal Data:* b Brooklyn, NY, May 15, 29; m 51, Vivian Kaplan; c 2. *Educ:* Queen's Col NY, BS, 51; Univ Pa, MS, 55, PhD(phys chem), 57. *Prof Exp:* Chemist, Frankford Arsenal, Pa, 51-52. *Mem:* Am Chem Soc. *Res:* Pressure-volume-temperature behavior of gases; equation of state; surface chemistry; thermochemical data; acid catalyzed alkylation and isomerization; catalysis; hydride transfer reactions; free radical reactions; carbonium ion rearrangement mechanisms and acid characterization; uranium chemistry; coal decomposition. *Mailing Add:* 36 Arden Ct Berkeley Heights NJ 07922. *E-Mail:* gmchess@aol.com

KRAMER, GERALD M, PERIODONTOLOGY, DENTISTRY. *Current Pos:* RETIRED. *Personal Data:* b Gloucester, Mass, June 11, 22; m 45; c 2. *Educ:* Tufts Univ, DMD, 44; Reisman Clin, cert, 52; Am Bd Periodont, dipl. *Prof Exp:* Instr periodont, Sch Dent Med, Univ Pa, 55-60; from asst prof to prof periodont & chmn dept, Sch Grad Dent, Boston Univ, 63-79. *Concurrent Pos:* Head, Periodont Sect, Reisman Dent Clin, Beth Israel Hosp, Boston & Boston Univ Hosp, 68- *Mem:* AAAS; Am Dent Asn; fel Am Col Dent; Am Acad Periodont; hon mem Periodont Soc SAfrica. *Res:* Clinical periodontics and oral medicine. *Mailing Add:* 470 Puritan Rd Swampscott MA 01907

KRAMER, GISELA A, REGULATION OF PROTEIN SYNTHESIS, PHOSPHORYLATION. *Current Pos:* RES SCIENTIST, UNIV TEX, AUSTIN, 74-, LECTR, 92- *Personal Data:* b Nov 29, 36; wid. *Educ:* Univ Kiel, Ger, PhD(biochem), 67; Univ Hamburg, Ger, Habilitation, 73. *Prof Exp:* Res assoc, Univ Hamburg, Ger, 69-74. *Mem:* Am Soc Biochem & Molecular Biol; Ger Soc Biol Chem. *Res:* In vitro transcription/translation of prokaryotic and eukaryotic coding sequences from plasmids to study synthesis and folding of polypeptides. *Mailing Add:* Dept Chem & Biochem Univ Tex Austin TX 78712. *Fax:* 512-471-8696

KRAMER, HENRY HERMAN, NUCLEAR MEDICINE, DIAGNOSTIC MEDICINE. *Current Pos:* CONSULT, 90- *Personal Data:* b New York, NY, Aug 19, 30; m 59, Carol; c 3. *Educ:* Columbia Univ, BA, 52, MA, 53; Univ Ind, PhD(phys chem), 60. *Prof Exp:* Res chemist nuclear methods anal, Union Carbide Corp, Nuclear Res Ctr, 60-65, group leader, Nucleonics Res & Develop, 66-73, sr group leader, Tarrytown Tech Ctr, 73-76, mgr, Sterling Forest Res Ctr, 76-78; vpres res & develop, Medi Physics Inc, 78-89. *Concurrent Pos:* Exec dir, Corar. *Mem:* Am Chem Soc; Am Nuclear Soc; Soc Nuclear Med; fel Am Col Nuclear Physicians. *Res:* Radiochemicals; radiodiagnostics; nuclear methods of analysis; biomedical significance of trace elements; nucleonics in industry and ore body exploration; diagnostic medicine. *Mailing Add:* 3911 Campolindo Dr Moraga CA 94556

KRAMER, IRVIN RAYMOND, metallurgy; deceased, see previous edition for last biography

KRAMER, J DAVID R, JR, ELECTRICAL ENGINEERING. *Current Pos:* Mem tech staff, Mitre Corp, 64-69, group leader, 69-79, assoc dept hed, 79-84, CONSULT SCIENTIST, MITRE CORP, 84- *Personal Data:* b Bayonne, NJ, Oct 29, 35; m 66; c Carolyn, Kirsten & John. *Educ:* Univ Pa,

BSEE, 57; Mass Inst Technol, MS, 58, ScD(elec eng), 64. *Concurrent Pos:* Lectr, Northeastern Univ, 65-68. *Mem:* Inst Elec & Electronics Engrs. *Res:* Systems optimization; signal design and processing; operations research. *Mailing Add:* 26 Fairbanks Rd Lexington MA 02173. *E-Mail:* dkramer@mitre.org

KRAMER, JAMES M, MOLECULAR BIOLOGY. *Current Pos:* ASSOC PROF LAB MOLECULAR BIOL, UNIV ILL, 90- *Mailing Add:* Dept CMS Biol Ward 7-334 Northwestern Univ Med Sch 303 E Chicago Ave Chicago IL 60611-3072

KRAMER, JAMES R(ICHARD), AQUATIC CHEMISTRY, METAL SPECIATION. *Current Pos:* assoc prof, 68-71, PROF GEOCHEM, MCMASTER UNIV, 72- *Personal Data:* b Marine City, Mich, Oct 27, 31; m 55, Miriam Parker; c Judith, William, Michael & Stephen. *Educ:* Mass Inst Technol, BS, 53; Univ Mich, MS, 54, PhD(geol), 58. *Prof Exp:* Asst, Res Lab, Carter Oil Co, 54; instr geol, Univ Mich, 57-58; fel, Nat Res Coun Can, Western Ont Univ, 58-59, lectr, 59-61, asst prof 61-63; res assoc, Univ Mich, 63-64; from asst prof to assoc prof, Syracuse Univ, 64-68. *Concurrent Pos:* Invited prof, Univ Que, 82. *Mem:* Am Geol Soc; Mineral Soc Am; Geochem Soc; Am Asn Petrol Geologists; Am Chem Soc. *Res:* Physical chemistry of carbonate minerals; limnological investigation of the Great Lakes; sedimentation and facies analysis of the Proterozoic sediments of Canada; aquatic chemistry of shield lakes. *Mailing Add:* Dept Geochem McMaster Univ Hamilton ON L8S 4M1 Can. *Fax:* 905-522-3141; *E-Mail:* kramer@mcmail.mcmaster.ca

KRAMER, JERRY MARTIN, CHEMICAL PHYSICS. *Current Pos:* MEM TECH STAFF, GTE LABS, 72- *Personal Data:* b Bronx, NY, Dec 16, 42; m 70; c 2. *Educ:* Univ Calif, Berkeley, BS, 65; Univ Chicago, PhD(chem), 71. *Prof Exp:* Res assoc chem, Case Western Reserve Univ, 71-72. *Mem:* Am Phys Soc; Am Chem Soc. *Res:* Arc and discharge physics optogalvanic spectroscopy laser chemistry; low energy ion-electron excitation of inorganic phosphors; photodissociation of gaseous ions; chemical kinetics. *Mailing Add:* Philips Labs 345 Scarborough Rd Briarcliff Manor KY 10510-2027

KRAMER, JOHN HOWARD, VADOSE ZONE MONITORING. *Current Pos:* SR HYDROGEOLOGIST, CONDOR EARTH TECHNOL INC, 94- *Personal Data:* b Cleveland, Ohio, Sept 10, 50; m 83, Renae Eckert; c Russell, Natalie & Stephanie. *Educ:* Amherst Col, BA, 73; Pa State Univ, MS, 76; Univ Calif, Santa Barbara, PhD(geol, geog & environ eng), 94. *Prof Exp:* Proj hydrogeologist, Metcalf & Eddy, Inc, 90-92; prin scientist, Geraghty & Mitler, Inc, 92-94. *Mem:* Am Geophys Union; Nat Groundwater Asn; Geol Soc Am; Am Soc Testing & Mat. *Res:* Innovative strategies to monitor soils above the water table; combination of network optimization and development of sensor technology to enhance environmental monitoring. *Mailing Add:* PO Box 400 Vallecito CA 95251-9999. *Fax:* 209-532-0773; *E-Mail:* kramer@geog.ucsb.edu

KRAMER, JOHN J(ACOB), PHYSICAL METALLURGY, MATERIAL SCIENCE. *Current Pos:* assoc prof elec eng, 65-69, PROF ELEC ENG, UNIV DEL, 69- *Personal Data:* b Pittsburgh, Pa, July 9, 31; m 56; c 3. *Educ:* Carnegie Inst Technol, BS, 53, MS & PhD(metall), 56. *Prof Exp:* Sr engr, magnetic mat develop sect, Westinghouse Elec Corp, 56-60, res metallurgist, res lab, 60-63, supv metallurgist, 63-64, sect mgr, 64-65, adv metallurgist, 65. *Concurrent Pos:* Phys metallurgist, ballistics res lab, Aberdeen Proving Grounds, Md, 57. *Mem:* Am Soc Metals; Am Inst Mining, Metall & Petrol Engrs; Sigma Xi. *Res:* Application of thermodynamics; surfaces; grain and crystal growth; solid state reactions; magnetic and electrical properties of solids. *Mailing Add:* 410 Arbour Dr Arbour Park Newark DE 19713-1204

KRAMER, JOHN KARL GERHARD, BIOCHEMISTRY, ORGANIC CHEMISTRY. *Current Pos:* RES SCIENTIST, CTR FOOD ANIMAL RES BR, AGR CAN, OTTAWA, 71- *Personal Data:* b Bololo, Zaire, Oct 6, 39; Can citizen; m 68, Ana-Maria Goertz; c David J. *Educ:* Univ Man, BSc, 63, MSc, 65; Univ Minn, Minneapolis, PhD(biochem), 68. *Honors & Awards:* CSP Canola Res Award, 84. *Prof Exp:* Hormel fel, Hormel Inst, Univ Minn, Austin, 68-70; Nat Res Coun Can fel, Univ Ottawa, 70-71. *Concurrent Pos:* Eastman Kodak fel, 64. *Mem:* Am Oil Chemists Soc. *Res:* Lipid chemistry, biochemistry and nutrition; pesticide metabolism in animals. *Mailing Add:* Ctr Food Animal Res Res Br Agr Can Ottawa ON K1A 0C6 Can. *Fax:* 613-943-2353

KRAMER, JOHN MICHAEL, CONTINUUM MECHANICS, RHEOLOGY. *Current Pos:* MECH ENGR, ARGONNE NAT LAB, 74- *Personal Data:* b Nov 22, 41; US citizen. *Educ:* Univ Wis, BS, 63, MS, 64, PhD(eng mech), 69. *Prof Exp:* Asst prof mech eng, Lamar Univ, 69-71, 72-74; res fel, Rheology Res Ctr, Univ Wis, 71-72. *Concurrent Pos:* Guest worker, Nat Bur Stand, US Dept Com, 73 & 74. *Res:* Engineering problems requiring an interdisciplinary approach in the general areas of continuum mechanics, materials behavior and heat transfer; behavior of materials and structures in hostile stress, temperature and irradiation environments. *Mailing Add:* Reactor Eng Div Bldg 207 Argonne Nat Lab 9700 S Cass Ave Argonne IL 60439

KRAMER, JOHN PAUL, INSECT PATHOLOGY. *Current Pos:* from assoc prof to prof, 65-90, EMER PROF INSECT PATH & MICROBIOL, CORNELL UNIV, 90- *Personal Data:* b Elgin, Ill, Mar 13, 28; div; c 2. *Educ:* Beloit Col, BS, 50; Univ Mo, MS, 52; Univ Ill, PhD(entom), 58. *Prof Exp:* Asst res prof entom, NC State Col, 58-59; asst entomologist econ entom, Ill Natural Hist Surv, 59, assoc entomologist, 59-65. *Concurrent Pos:* NIH res grant, 59-72; lectr, 8th Int Cong Microbiol, Montreal, 62; dept biol sci, Northwestern Univ, 64, 2nd Int Conf Protozool, London, 65; Dept Biol, Ithaca Col, 81, Dept Biol, State Univ NY, Cortland, 83, Col Biol Sci, Ohio State Univ, 84; consult, Environ Biol Unit, WHO, Geneva, 62-; mem trop med & parasitol study sect, NIH, 66-69; NSF vis insect pathologist, Japan, 67; NSF, fel, 67; mem, Eval Panel Life Sci, Nat Res Coun, 69-; NIH-Off Naval Res res grant microbiol, 71-74; vis biologist, Arctic Health Res Ctr, Inst Arctic Biol, Alaska, 72 & WHO res agreement, 78-; res grant, WHO, 79-82, US Dept Agr, 80-81; vis prof entom, Ohio State Univ, Columbus, 84. *Mem:* Soc Invert Path; NY Entom Soc. *Res:* Infectious diseases of insects, especially those caused by microsporidians and entomophthorans; ecology of microsporidians; epidemiology of diseases of insects. *Mailing Add:* Dept Entom 3142 Comstock Hall Cornell Univ Ithaca NY 14853

KRAMER, JOHN WILLIAM, CLINICAL PATHOLOGY. *Current Pos:* assoc prof, 72-77, PROF VET CLIN SURG & MED, COL VET MED, WASH STATE UNIV, 77- *Personal Data:* b Dearborn, Mich, Aug 17, 35; m 59; c 2. *Educ:* Mich State Univ, BSc, 58, DVM, 60, MSc, 68; Univ Calif, Davis, PhD(comp path), 72; Am Col Vet Pathologists, dipl & cert vet clin path. *Prof Exp:* Vet, NZ Dept Agr, 60-64; adv clin path, Mich State Univ, Nsukka, Nigeria, 64-66, asst instr, Univ, 66-68; trainee, Col Vet Med, Univ Calif, Davis, 68-72. *Mem:* Am Vet Med Asn; Am Soc Vet Clin Pathologists; Am Col Vet Pathologists; Am Asn Clin Chem. *Res:* Pathophysiology of diabetes mellitus. *Mailing Add:* 1415 NW Douglas Dr Pullman WA 99163

KRAMER, KARL JOSEPH, ENTOMOLOGY, BIOCHEMISTRY. *Current Pos:* RES CHEMIST BIOCHEM, USDA, 74- *Personal Data:* b Evansville, Ind, Aug 20, 42; m 66; c 2. *Educ:* Purdue Univ, BS, 64; Univ Ariz, PhD(chem), 71. *Prof Exp:* Res assoc biochem, Univ Chicago, 71-74. *Concurrent Pos:* NIH fel, 71; from asst prof to assoc prof biochem, Kans State Univ, 74-82, prof, 82- *Mem:* Am Soc Biol Chemists; Am Chem Soc; Entom Soc Am; Am Inst Biol Sci; AAAS. *Res:* Insect biochemistry; endocrinology; physiology. *Mailing Add:* US Grain Mkt Res Lab 1515 College Ave Manhattan KS 66502-2736

KRAMER, MARTIN A, HEAVY ION PHYSICS. *Current Pos:* PROF PHYSICS, CITY COL NEW YORK, 73- *Personal Data:* b Ellenville, NY, Oct 20, 41; m 63, Caroline F Hess; c Scott & Karen. *Educ:* Columbia Univ, BA, 63, MA, 64, PhD(physics), 69. *Prof Exp:* Res assoc physics, Enrico Fermi Inst, Univ Chicago, 69-71; physicist, Brookhaven Nat Lab, 71-73. *Mem:* Am Phys Soc. *Res:* Designing, building, running and analyzing experiments in high energy and heavy ion physics. *Mailing Add:* Brookhaven Lab Bldg 510A Upton NY 11973-5000

KRAMER, MILTON, PSYCHIATRY. *Current Pos:* Assoc dir res, Dept Psychiat, 72-80, PROF PSYCHIAT, SCH MED, UNIV CINCINNATI, 72-, DIR, DREAM & SLEEP LAB & SLEEP DISORDERS CTR, 80- *Personal Data:* b Chicago, Ill, Nov 11, 29; c 4. *Educ:* Univ Ill, BS, 50, BS, 52, MD, 54; Am Bd Psychiat & Neurol, dipl & cert psychiat, 61. *Concurrent Pos:* Pvt practr psychiat, Cincinnati, 60-; clinician psychiat, Outpatient Dept, Cincinnati Gen Hosp, 61- & attend staff psychiatrist, 65-; consult, Coun Drugs, AMA, 62-; dir psychiat res, Vet Admin Hosp, Cincinnati, 63- & asst chief, Dept Psychiat, 64-80; Upjohn Co grant, 70-72; mem, Therapeut Care Comt, Group Advan Psychiat, 70-; res investr, Wm S Merrell Co, 70-72 & Upjohn, 70-; proj dir sonic boom res data anal, Fed Aviation Admin, 70-72; prin investr, US Vet Admin, 75-; mem, Ohio Ment Health & Ment Retardation Adv Bd, 71-75; mem staffs, Christian R Holmes Hosp, Jewish Hosp & Good Samaritan Hosp. *Mem:* Fel Am Psychiat Asn; AMA; Asn Psychophysiol Study Sleep (mem exec comt, 71); sci assoc Am Acad Psychoanal; Am Col Psychiat; Sigma Xi. *Res:* Psychology and psychophysiology of dreaming; drugs and sleep. *Mailing Add:* 3900 Rose Hill Ave Apt 1102B Cincinnati OH 45229

KRAMER, MORTON, BIOSTATISTICS, EPIDEMIOLOGY. *Current Pos:* prof, Dept Ment Hyg, 76-84, EMER PROF, SCH HYG & PUB HEALTH, JOHNS HOPKINS UNIV, 84- *Personal Data:* b Baltimore, Md, Mar 21, 14; m 39, Pauline Weinstein; c Barry K, James L, Nancy L & Richard A. *Educ:* Johns Hopkins Univ, AB, 34, ScD, 39. *Honors & Awards:* Superior Serv Award, Dept HEW, 62, Distinguished Serv Award, 74; Rema Lapousse Award, Am Pub Health Asn, 73; WHO Health for All Medal, 87. *Prof Exp:* Asst biostatist, Sch Hyg & Pub Health, Johns Hopkins Univ, 37-38; instr prev med, Col Med, NY Univ, 38; statistician, State Dept Health, NY, 39-40; asst prof biostatist, Sch Trop Med, Univ PR & statistician, Insular Dept Health, San Juan, 40-42; econ analyst, US Dept Treas, DC, 42-43; assoc biostatist, Sch Med, Western Res Univ, 43-46; chief info & res, Off Int Health Rels, USPHS, DC, 46-49, chief, Biomet Br, NIMH, 49-75, dir, Div Biometry & Epidemiol, 75-76. *Concurrent Pos:* Consult, Am Psychiat Asn, 49-80; consult ment health unit, WHO, 59-; mem expert panel health statist, WHO, 61-84; vis scientist, Dept Pub Health Admin, London Sch Hyg & Trop Med & Soc Med Res Unit Med Res Coun, Eng, 68-69; mem, Task Panel, President's Comn Ment Health, 77-78, Adv Comn Secy Health on Health Res Studies Three Mile Island Disaster, 79-85, Selection Panel Multidisciplinary Dept Geriatrics & Gerontol, Govt Ont, Can, 87. *Mem:* Inst Med-Nat Acad Sci; fel Am Pub Health Asn; fel Am Statist Asn; fel Am Orthopsychiat Asn; Am Epidemiol Soc; Am Col Epidemiol; fel Am Psychiat Asn. *Res:* Epidemiology of mental disorders; application of biostatistical and epidemiologic methods to planning mental health and related mental health res services and evaluating their effectiveness; classification of mental disorders. *Mailing Add:* Dept Ment Hyg Johns Hopkins Univ Sch Hyg & Pub Health Baltimore MD 21205

KRAMER, NOAH HERBERT, ELECTRICAL ENGINEERING. *Current Pos:* TECH MGR, LITTON DATA COMMAND SYSTS, 80- *Personal Data:* b New York, NY, Apr 10, 24; m 54; c 3. *Educ:* Mich State Univ, BS, 47, MS, 49, PhD(elec eng), 51. *Prof Exp:* Asst, Mich State Univ, 47-49, instr, 49-51; engr, Int Bus Mach Corp, 51-57 & Stelma, Inc, 57-70; mgr transmission planning, Int Tel & Tel Corp, 73-78; pres, N H Kramer & Assocs, 78-79; mem staff, Am Satellite Corp, 79-80. *Mem:* Inst Elec & Electronics Engrs. *Res:* Communication systems and equipment; digital data transmission; digital techniques; solid state electronics; computer peripherals. *Mailing Add:* 24410 Victory Blvd No 1 Woodland Hills CA 91367

KRAMER, NORMAN CLIFFORD, INTERNAL MEDICINE, IMMUNOLOGY. *Current Pos:* from instr to prof, 60-85, EMER PROF INT MED, GEORGE WASHINGTON UNIV, 85- *Personal Data:* b New York, NY, Aug 16, 28; m 54, Patricia Elly; c M Virginia, John D, Bernard M, Peter A & Anne M. *Educ:* The Citadel, BS, 48; George Washington Univ, MS, 50, MD, 54; Am Bd Internal Med, dipl, 63. *Prof Exp:* Consult biochem, Vet Admin Hosp, Martinsburg, WVa, 50-53. *Concurrent Pos:* USPHS res fel, 59-60, USPHS res career develop award, 61-66; dir, Washington Regional Histocompatability Typing Lab; dir, Hemopheresis Serv, Med Ctr, George Washington Univ; dir, Immunogenetics & Immunohemat, Md Med Lab, Baltimore, 87-95. *Mem:* Fel Am Col Physicians; Am Soc Histocompatibility & Immunogenetics; Int Soc Forensic Heamogenetics; Am Asn Blood Banks; Am Soc Transplant Physicians. *Res:* Pathophysiology and immunology of diseases of the kidney; transplantation immunogenetics and forensic immunogenetics; nephrology. *Mailing Add:* 14505 Hollyhock Way Burtonsville MD 20866-1717

KRAMER, PAUL ALAN, PHYSICAL PHARMACY, BIOPHARMACEUTICS. *Current Pos:* PROF PHARM & ASSOC PROF LAB MED, UNIV CONN, 76-, ASST PROF PEDIAT, 86- *Personal Data:* b Hartford, Conn, July 22, 42; m 64, 87; c 2. *Educ:* Rensselaer Polytech Inst, BChE, 64; Univ Wis, MS, 66, PhD(pharm), 68. *Prof Exp:* Res biochemist, Walter Reed Army Inst Res, 68-71; asst prof phys pharm, Purdue Univ, 71-76. *Mem:* Am Asn Pharm Scientists; Controlled Release Soc; Int Asn Dent Res. *Res:* Pharmacokinetics of drugs in the elderly; drug dispositon in the neonate; drug delivery systems; dental pharmaceutics. *Mailing Add:* Dept Pharm Univ Conn Health Ctr Farmington CT 06032

KRAMER, PAUL JACKSON, plant physiology, tree physiology; deceased, see previous edition for last biography

KRAMER, PAUL ROBERT, PHYSICS, INSTRUCTIONAL TECHNOLOGY. *Current Pos:* assoc prof, State Univ NY, 70-75, chmn dept, 77-81, dean acad serv, 81-84, PROF PHYSICS, STATE UNIV NY COL TECHNOL, FARMINGDALE, 75- *Personal Data:* b Montclair, NJ, Nov 17, 35; m 64; c 2. *Educ:* Cornell Univ, BA, 57; Rutgers Univ, MS, 59, PhD(physics), 66. *Prof Exp:* Instrumentation specialist physics, State Univ NY Stony Brook, 64-66, asst prof, 66-69. *Concurrent Pos:* Dir, Comput Assisted Instr, State Univ NY, Stony Brook, 67-68, proj coordr, Instr Resources Ctr, 68-69, chmn, student comput access prog Adv Comt, State Univ, NY, 81; treas & sci mkt consult, Safety Corp Am, Huntington, NY, 84-87; mem, Fac Access, Comput Technol Adv Comt, State Univ NY, 89- *Res:* Instructional technology using computers and other media; improvement of instruction in physics and other fields; elementary school science. *Mailing Add:* State Univ NY Col Technol Farmingdale NY 11735. *Fax:* 516-673-1095; *E-Mail:* kramerpr@snyfarva.cc.farmingdale.edu

KRAMER, PHILIP, medicine; deceased, see previous edition for last biography

KRAMER, RAYMOND ARTHUR, ANALYTICAL CHEMISTRY. *Current Pos:* phys chemist, Alcoa Res Labs, 58-67, ANALYTICAL CHEMIST, ALCOA TECH CTR, ALUMINUM CO AM, 67- *Personal Data:* b Buffalo, NY, Dec 7, 29; m 55. *Educ:* Canisius Col, BS, 54; Rensselaer Polytech Inst, PhD(anal chem), 59. *Prof Exp:* Technician, Aluminum Co Am, NY, 48-54; asst, Rensselaer Polytech Inst, 54-58. *Mem:* Am Chem Soc; Soc Appl Spectros; Am Soc Testing & Mat. *Res:* Neutron activation analysis; x-ray diffraction and fluorescence; characterization of ultra-pure aluminum and gallium; emission spectroscopy; aluminum in fusion reactors. *Mailing Add:* 4377 Frederick Dr Lower Burrell PA 15068-6857

KRAMER, RAYMOND EDWARD, ELECTRICAL ENGINEERING, PHYSICS. *Current Pos:* Asst prof, Youngstown State Univ, 50-54, chmn dept, 54-78, assoc prof, 54-78, PROF ELEC ENG, YOUNGSTOWN STATE UNIV, 78- *Personal Data:* b Warren, Ohio, Feb 2, 19; m 47; c 3. *Educ:* Heidelberg Col, BSc, 43; Case Inst Technol, MSc, 50. *Concurrent Pos:* Consult elec engr, US Steel Corp, 51 & ARC Res Inc, 51-53; consult develop engr, Westinghouse Elec Corp, 54 & 55 & Ohio Bell Tel, 61. *Mem:* Inst Elec & Electronics Engrs; AAAS. *Res:* Spark machining; ferromagnetic domains and computer cores; particle physics; electrical, kinetic and quantum properties of fundamental particles; gravity waves. *Mailing Add:* Dept Elec Eng Youngstown State Univ 410 Wick Ave Youngstown OH 44555

KRAMER, RICHARD ALLEN, MOLECULAR BIOLOGY. *Current Pos:* DEPT MOLECULAR BIOL & ENZYMOL, CIBA-GEIGY PHARMACEUT, 89- *Educ:* Yale Univ, PhD(biochem), 75. *Prof Exp:* Res investr, Dept Molecular Genetics, Hoffman-Laroche, Inc, 81-89. *Res:* Yeast gene expression; recombinant DNA technology. *Mailing Add:* Pharmacol Div Ciba-Geigy Pharmaceut 556 Morris Ave Summit NJ 07901-1398

KRAMER, RICHARD MELVYN, HERBICIDES, PLANT GROWTH REGULATORS. *Current Pos:* sr res engr, Monsanto Co, 66-73, sr res group leader, 73-79, res mgr, 79-82, res mgr opers, 82-90, SR FORMULATION CONSULT, MONSANTO CO, 90- *Personal Data:* b Brooklyn, NY, Dec 20, 35; m 57, Elaine Feingold; c Roy, Eric & Ian. *Educ:* Polytech Inst Brooklyn, BChE, 57, MChE, 60, PhD(chem eng), 63; St Louis Univ, MBA, 71. *Prof Exp:* Res assoc electrodialysis, Bioferm Div, Int Minerals & Chem Co, 62-63, develop engr, 63-65, sr process engr, 65-66. *Mem:* Am Chem Soc. *Res:* Herbicide and plant growth regulator research and development; pesticide residue chemistry; pesticide formulation and environmental science. *Mailing Add:* 800 N Lindbergh Blvd Monsanto Res Ctr St Louis MO 63167

KRAMER, ROBERT, ELECTRICAL & SYSTEMS ENGINEERING. *Current Pos:* STAFF ENGR, LINCOLN LAB, MASS INST TECHNOL, 71- *Personal Data:* b Boston, Mass, Apr 25, 27; m 50; c 4. *Educ:* Mass Inst Technol, SB, 49, SM, 52, ScD(elec eng), 59. *Prof Exp:* Proj engr, Servomech Lab, Mass Inst Technol, 49-62, lectr elec eng, Univ, 59-62, staff engr, Lincoln Lab, 62-69; sr consult, Harrington, Davenport & Curtis, Inc, 69-71. *Mem:* Inst Elec & Electronics Engrs; Optical Soc Am. *Res:* Optical and data systems. *Mailing Add:* Lincoln Lab 244 Wood St MS 343 Lexington MA 02173-9185

KRAMER, ROBERT ALLEN, ENERGY, ELECTRIC TRANSMISSION & GENERATION. *Current Pos:* Nuclear fuel engr, Northern Ind Pub Serv, 73-81, mgr appl res, 81-83, dir electric eng, 83-86, dir electric opers, 86-91, DIR ELECTRIC SERVS, NORTHERN IND PUB SERV, 92- *Personal Data:* b Gary, Ind, Jan 6, 49. *Educ:* Purdue Univ, BS, 71, MS, 73, MS, 79, PhD(nuclear eng), 85. *Concurrent Pos:* Lectr physics, Purdue Univ, 75- *Mem:* Am Phys Soc; Inst Elec & Electronics Engrs; Am Nuclear Soc. *Res:* Energy and energy related fields; engineering in development and management; energy research and competitive aspects of industry. *Mailing Add:* 910 S Ridge St Crown Point IN 46307

KRAMER, SHELDON J, chemical engineering, for more information see previous edition

KRAMER, SHERMAN FRANCIS, PHARMACY, PHARMACOLOGY. *Current Pos:* RETIRED. *Personal Data:* b Elcho, Wis, Nov 15, 28; m 59; c 4. *Educ:* Univ Wis, BS, 50, PhD(pharm), 60. *Prof Exp:* Res assoc, Upjohn Co, 60-66, sect head, 66-90. *Mem:* Am Pharmaceut Asn; Acad Pharmaceut Sci. *Res:* Pharmaceutical product research and development. *Mailing Add:* 9701 Oakview St Kalamazoo MI 49002

KRAMER, STANLEY PHILLIP, medicinal chemistry, pharmacology; deceased, see previous edition for last biography

KRAMER, STANLEY ZACHARY, NEUROPHARMACOLOGY. *Current Pos:* RETIRED. *Personal Data:* b Philadelphia, Pa, Sept 10, 21; m 41; c 1. *Educ:* Univ Pa, AB, 52, PhD(physiol), 58. *Prof Exp:* Asst instr physiol, Univ Pa, 53-58; instr, Vassar Col, 58-60; instr, NY Med Col, 60-64, asst prof physiol, 64-67; from assoc prof to prof biol, Seton Hall Univ, 67-86. *Res:* Effects of drugs on brain electrical activity and behavior; neurophysiology. *Mailing Add:* 1801 J F Kennedy Blvd Philadelphia PA 19103

KRAMER, STEPHEN LEONARD, EXPERIMENTAL HIGH ENERGY PHYSICS, ACCELERATOR PHYSICS. *Current Pos:* PHYSICIST BROOKHAVEN NAT LAB, 90-, PHYSICIST VUV RING MGR, 91- *Personal Data:* b Philadelphia, Pa, July 22, 43; m, Jean K Hotchkiss; c Robyn T & Keith O. *Educ:* Drexel Inst Technol, BS, 66; Purdue Univ, MS, 67, PhD(physics), 71. *Honors & Awards:* Lark Horovitz Award; George Tautfest Award. *Prof Exp:* Res asst high energy physics, Argonne Nat Lab, 71-74, asst physicist, 74-81, physicist, 81-90. *Mem:* Am Phys Soc. *Res:* Synchrotron radiation sources; accelerator physics; radiographic imaging; applications of particle accelerators to medical research; high energy accelerator system design and application; nuclear instrumentation. *Mailing Add:* Brookhaven Nat Lab Nat Synchrotron Light Source Bldg 725C Upton NY 11973

KRAMER, STEVEN DAVID, LASER PHYSICS, NONLINEAR OPTICS. *Current Pos:* RES STAFF, INST DEFENSE ANALYSIS, 87- *Personal Data:* b Lakewood, NJ, Aug 27, 48. *Educ:* Cornell Univ, AB, 70; Harvard Univ, AM, 71, PhD(physics), 76. *Honors & Awards:* IR-100 Award, 84 & 87. *Prof Exp:* Res fel, Harvard Univ, 72-76, teaching fel, 74-75; res staff, Oak Ridge Nat Lab, 76-87. *Concurrent Pos:* Consult, 82-85. *Mem:* Am Phys Soc; Optical Soc Am; Archeol Soc Am; AAAS; Inst Elec & Electronics Engrs. *Res:* Optics; optical sensors; nonlinear optics; spectroscopy; trace analysis. *Mailing Add:* Inst Defense Analysis 1801 N Beuregard St Alexandria VA 22311

KRAMER, THEODORE TIVADAR, VETERINARY MICROBIOLOGY, IMMUNOLOGY. *Current Pos:* PROF VET MICROBIOL & PREV MED, COL VET MED, IOWA STATE UNIV, 80- *Personal Data:* b Novi-Sad, Yugoslavia, Jan 4, 28; US citizen; m 57; c 3. *Educ:* Nat Vet Sch, Alfort, France, DVM, 52; Univ Strasbourg, dipl, 53; Colo State Univ, MSc, 63, PhD(microbiol), 65; Am Col Vet Microbiol, dipl, 70. *Prof Exp:* Res off microbiol, Can Dept Agr, 57-60; jr pathologist, Colo State Univ, 60-65; asst prof microbiol, Univ Col, Nairobi, Kenya, 65-67; assoc prof vet microbiol, Western Vet Col Med, Univ Sask, 67-70; prof microbiol & head dept, Sch Vet Med, Auburn Univ, 71-80. *Mem:* Am Soc Microbiol; Am Asn Immunologists; Am Vet Med Asn. *Res:* Experimental colibacillosis in piglets; immunoglobulins of bovine colostrum; vaccine against bovine vibriosis; maternal immunity and the newborn; cell-mediated immunity to infectious diseases of animals; salmonellosis. *Mailing Add:* VMRI 1802 Elwood Dr Ames IA 50011-0001

KRAMER, TIM R, MICROBIOLOGY. *Current Pos:* RES BIOLOGIST, NIH, 79- *Personal Data:* b Garden Plain, Kans, Mar 1 ,43. *Educ:* Okla Univ, MA, PhD(med sci), 73. *Prof Exp:* Postdoctoral sr fel, Sloan Cancer Inst, NY, 73-76; mem proj, Sch Med, St Louis Univ & Fai-Land Anemia & Malnutrit Ctr, Chiang-Mai Univ, 76-78. *Mem:* Soc Exp Biol; Inst Nutrit. *Mailing Add:* Beltsville Human Nutrit Res Ctr Bldg 307 BARC-E Beltsville MD 20705-2350

KRAMER, WILLIAM GEOFFREY, PHARMACY, PHARMACOKINETICS. *Current Pos:* SR TECH ADV, QUINTILES, 96- *Personal Data:* b Pittsburgh, Pa, Sept 16, 48; m 73, Beverly Schlachman. *Educ:* Univ Pittsburgh, BS, 71; Ohio State Univ, PhD, 76. *Prof Exp:* From asst prof to assoc prof pharmaceut, Col Pharm, Univ Houston, 76-86; mgr pharmacokinetics, Schering-Plough, 86-89; assoc dir clin res, Boehringer Manheim Pharmaceut, 89-92, dir clin res, 92-96. *Concurrent Pos:* Res assoc, Inst Cardiovasc Studies, Col Pharm, Univ Houston, 77-86. *Mem:* Am Asn Pharm Scientists; Drug Info Asn; Am Asn Clin Pharmacol; Am Soc Clin Pharmacol & Therapeut. *Res:* Pharmacokinetics and pharmacodynamics as the pertain to drug development areas of specialty-cardiovascular, metabolic. *Mailing Add:* Quintiles 15825 Shady Grove Rd Suite 90 Rockville MD 20850-4008. *Fax:* 301-548-1548

KRAMER, WILLIAM J, ORGANIC CHEMISTRY, ANALYTICAL CHEMISTRY. *Current Pos:* From instr to assoc prof, 53-68, PROF CHEM, ST JOSEPH'S COL IND, 68-, CHMN DEPT, 77- *Personal Data:* b Coldwater, Ohio, Oct 13, 19. *Educ:* Univ Fribourg, Lic es Sci, 52, ScD(chem), 53. *Hon Degrees:* ScD, Univ Fribourg, 53. *Mem:* Am Chem Soc. *Res:* Reactivity of methyl groups in substituted benzene rings; history and philosophy of science. *Mailing Add:* Dept Chem St Joseph's Col Rensselaer IN 47979

KRAMER, WILLIAM S, DENTISTRY. *Current Pos:* RETIRED. *Personal Data:* b Butte, Nebr, Jan 10, 22; m 44; c 4. *Educ:* Univ Nebr, BSc, 46, DDS, 48, MSc, 54; Am Bd Pedodont, dipl. *Prof Exp:* Instr operative dent, Univ Nebr, Lincoln, 48-52, prof operative dent, 54-58, chem dept, pedodont, 58-80, prof pedodont, 80-87. *Concurrent Pos:* Dir, Dent Asst Utilization Prog; past examr, Am Bd Pedodont, exec secy, 74- *Mem:* Am Acad Pedodont (pres, 78-); Int Asn Dent Res. *Res:* Clinical studies on local anesthetic solutions; morphology of the primary dentition; physical properties of gold foil; ultrasonic sterilization; pedodontic failures. *Mailing Add:* 5124 Ventura Dr Fremont NE 68025

KRAMERICH, GEORGE L, CONTROL & ELECTRICAL ENGINEERING. *Current Pos:* from asst prof to assoc prof, 69-77, PROF ELEC ENG, CLEVELAND STATE UNIV, 77- *Personal Data:* b Aliquippa, Pa, Nov 26, 29; m 54; c 3. *Educ:* Fla State Univ, BS, 63, MS, 64; Case Western Res Univ, PhD(control eng), 70. *Prof Exp:* Teaching asst eng sci, Fla State Univ, 63-64; teaching asst elec eng, Case Western Res Univ, 64-69. *Concurrent Pos:* Consult, Gen Elec Lighting Res Lab, 70-, Chemstress Consults, 77-, Gould Instrument Div, 77- & Ohio Legis Serv Comn, 78-79. *Mem:* Sr mem Instrument Soc Am; Inst Elec & Electronics Engrs; Am Soc Eng Educ. *Res:* Economic and management decision making applied to the evaluation of advanced process control technology; computer simulation. *Mailing Add:* Dept Elec Eng Cleveland State Univ Stillwell Hall Rm 332 Cleveland OH 44115-2425

KRAMISH, ARNOLD, NUCLEAR PHYSICS, INTERNATIONAL RELATIONS. *Current Pos:* TECHNOL CONSULT, 81-; AUTHOR, 86- *Personal Data:* b Denver, Colo, June 6, 23; m 52; c 2. *Educ:* Univ Denver, BS, 45; Harvard Univ, MA, 47. *Prof Exp:* Mass spectroscopist, Oak Ridge Nat Lab, 44-45; physicist, Los Alamos Sci Labs, 45-46; staff physicist, AEC, 47-51 & physics dept, Rand Corp, Calif, 51-69; adj prof int studies, Univ Miami, 69-73; US sci liaison attache, UNESCO, 70-73; counr sci & technol, US Mission, Orgn Econ Coop & Develop, 74-76; sr scientist, Res & Develop Assocs, Arlington, 76-81. *Concurrent Pos:* Consult, Int Bank Reconstruct & Develop, 58; fel, Coun For Rels, 58-59; consult, NSF, 59-62; prof in residence, Univ Calif, Los Angeles, 65-66; Guggenheim fel, 66-67; fel, Woodrow Wilson Ctr, Smithsonian Inst, 82-83; Rockefeller scholar, Bellagio, Italy, 84; sr fel & assoc, Global Bus Access Ltd, 90- *Res:* Fission physics; applied nuclear energy; political and economic implications of nuclear energy; research and development policy and planning; space and strategic defense systems; international energy policy; technology transfer; history. *Mailing Add:* 2065 Wethersfield Ct Reston VA 22091

KRAMP, ROBERT CHARLES, RADIATION BIOLOGY, ENDOCRINOLOGY. *Current Pos:* RETIRED. *Personal Data:* b Alexandria, Va, Aug 2, 42; m 65; c 2. *Educ:* Univ Md, BS, 64; Univ Okla, MS, 69; Univ Tenn, PhD(radiation biol), 73. *Prof Exp:* Fel endocrinol, Inst Clin Biochem, 73-75; res instr, Vanderbilt Univ, 75-78; asst prof biol, Va Polytech Inst & State Univ, 78-83. *Mem:* Am Diabetes Asn; Europ Asn Study Diabetes. *Res:* Diabetes; transplantation of pancreatic islet tissue in mice; experimental and genetic diabetes in rodents. *Mailing Add:* RR 3 Floyd VA 24091

KRANBUEHL, DAVID EDWIN, PHYSICAL CHEMISTRY, POLYMER PHYSICS. *Current Pos:* PROF CHEM, COL WILLIAM & MARY, 70- *Personal Data:* b Madison, Wis, Apr 16, 43; m 66; c 2. *Educ:* DePauw Univ, BA, 65; Univ Wis, PhD(chem), 69. *Prof Exp:* Res chemist polymers, Nat Bur Standards, 69-70. *Concurrent Pos:* Nat Acad Sci fel, 69-70; consult, Nat Bur Standards, 70-, Union Carbide, Gen Elec, US Steel Corp, McDonnell Douglas Corp. *Mem:* Am Chem Soc. *Res:* Physical properties of polymers; dielectric phenomena; molecular dynamics in the liquid and glassy state; materials science engineering. *Mailing Add:* Dept Chem Col William & Mary Williamsburg VA 23185-3647

KRANC, GEORGE M(AXIMILIAN), ELECTRICAL ENGINEERING. *Current Pos:* assoc prof, 63-71, PROF SCH ENG, CITY COL NEW YORK, 71- *Personal Data:* b Lodz, Poland, Feb 1, 20; nat US; m 60, Joanna. *Educ:* St Andrews Univ, BSc, 44; Columbia Univ, MS, 53, DEng Sc(elec eng), 56. *Prof Exp:* Radio engr, Jewel Radio Co, 49-51; asst elec eng, Columbia Univ, 51-53, from instr to assoc prof, 53-62; vis prof, Polytech Inst Brooklyn, 62-63. *Concurrent Pos:* Consult, Gen Appl Sci Labs, 57 & Norden Labs, 58-59; sci ed, Scripta Technica Inc, 63-71. *Mem:* Inst Elec & Electronics Engrs; Sigma Xi. *Res:* Control systems theory, particularly sampled data systems and optimal controls. *Mailing Add:* 25 Fifth Ave New York NY 10003-4307

KRANC, STANLEY CHARLES, MECHANICAL ENGINEERING, CHEMICAL PHYSICS. *Current Pos:* from asst prof to assoc prof, 71-78, PROF ENG, UNIV SFLA, 71- *Personal Data:* b Peoria, Ill, Sept 29, 42. *Educ:* Northwestern Univ, BS, 64, PhD(mech eng), 69. *Prof Exp:* Asst prof eng sci, Fla State Univ, 67-71. *Mem:* Am Inst Aeronaut & Astronaut; Newcomen Soc; Am Soc Mech Engrs. *Res:* Gas dynamics; plasma physics; combustion; two phase flow. *Mailing Add:* Col Eng Univ SFla Tampa FL 33620

KRANE, KENNETH SAUL, EXPERIMENTAL NUCLEAR PHYSICS. *Current Pos:* from asst prof to assoc prof, 74-84, PROF & CHMN PHYSICS, ORE STATE UNIV, 84- *Personal Data:* b Philadelphia, Pa, May 15, 44; m 66; c 1. *Educ:* Univ Ariz, BS, 65; Purdue Univ, MS, 67, PhD(physics), 70. *Prof Exp:* Res assoc physics, Los Alamos Sci Lab, 70-72 & nuclear chem, Lawrence Berkeley Lab, 72-74; res assoc nuclear chem, Lawrence Berkeley Lab, 72-74. *Concurrent Pos:* Physics prog officer, NSF, 93-94. *Mem:* Fel Am Phys Soc; Am Asn Physics Teachers; Sigma Xi. *Res:* Angular distributions and correlations of gamma rays; nuclear spectroscopy; nuclear physics at ultralow temperatures; beta decay. *Mailing Add:* Dept Physics Ore State Univ Corvallis OR 97331. *E-Mail:* kranek@physics.orst.edu

KRANE, STANLEY GARSON, CELL BIOLOGY, MOLECULAR BIOLOGY. *Current Pos:* asst prof, 75-80, ASSOC PROF BIOL, FITCHBURG STATE COL, 80- *Personal Data:* b New York, NY, Feb 16, 37. *Educ:* City Col New York, BS, 57; Mich State Univ, MS, 58; Calif Inst Technol, PhD(biochem), 66. *Prof Exp:* Res fel biochem, Brandeis Univ, 66-67; asst prof biol, Univ Mass, Boston, 68-75. *Mem:* AAAS; Am Inst Biol Sci. *Res:* Mutagenesis of microorganisms. *Mailing Add:* Dept Biol Fitchburg State Col 160 Pearl St Fitchburg MA 01420-2631

KRANE, STEPHEN MARTIN, MEDICINE, BIOCHEMISTRY. *Current Pos:* PHYSICIAN, MASS GEN HOSP, 69- *Personal Data:* b New York, NY, July 15, 27; m 52; c 4. *Educ:* Columbia Col, AB, 46; Columbia Univ, MD, 51; Am Bd Internal Med, dipl. 58. *Hon Degrees:* AM, Harvard Univ, 68; MD, Univ Geneva, Switz, 89. *Honors & Awards:* Geigy Rheumatism Prize, 77; Heberden Medal, London, 80; Kleruperer Medal, 90. *Prof Exp:* Asst, Harvard Med Sch, 55-59, instr, 59-60, assoc, 60-63, from asst prof to prof, 63-87, Persis, Cyros & Marlow B Harrison Prof Med, Harvard Med Sch, 87- *Concurrent Pos:* Fel med, Harvard Med Sch, 53-55; fel, Sch Med, Wash Univ, 56; Guggenheim fel, Oxford Univ, 73-74. *Mem:* Am Soc Clin Invest; Endocrine Soc; Asn Am Physicians; Am Col Rheumatology; Am Fedn Clin Res; fel AAAS; Am Soc Biol Chemists; Am Soc Bone & Mineral Res. *Res:* Connective tissue biology and metabolism; internal medicine and rheumatology; transport mechanisms. *Mailing Add:* Mass Gen Hosp 32 Fruit St Boston MA 02114-2698

KRANER, HOBART WILSON, SEMICONDUCTOR RADIATION DETECTORS. *Current Pos:* assoc physicist, 66-71, physicist, 71-80, SR PHYSICIST, BROOKHAVEN NAT LAB, 80- *Personal Data:* b Louisville, Ky, Jan 15, 34; m 56, Carol Bostock; c Keith, Neil, Jeffrey & Jennifer. *Educ:* Mass Inst Technol, SB, 55, PhD(physics), 60. *Prof Exp:* Res assoc, Mass Inst Technol, 60-66. *Mem:* Inst Elec & Electronics Engrs. *Res:* Development of semiconductor radiation detectors for application in high energy physics and x-ray spectroscopy; position sensitive silicon detectors using integrated circuit technology and study radiation effects on such devices; applications of nuclear and x-ray spectroscopy to analytical problems in fields such as medicine and material science. *Mailing Add:* 16 S Howells Pt Rd Bellport NY 11713

KRANIAS, EVANGELIA GALANI, ION TRANSPORT, PHOSPHORYLATION REGULATION. *Current Pos:* ASSOC PROF PHOSPHORYLATION, COL MED, UNIV CINCINNATI, 78- *Educ:* Northwestern Univ, PhD(biochem), 74. *Mailing Add:* Dept Pharmacol & Cell Biophys Univ Cincinnati Med Ctr 231 Bethesda Ave Cincinnati OH 45267-0575

KRANNICH, LARRY KENT, MAIN GROUP CHEMISTRY. *Current Pos:* from asst prof to assoc prof, 69-76, actg chmn dept, 74-75, PROF & CHMN DEPT CHEM, UNIV ALA, BIRMINGHAM, 76. *Personal Data:* b Pekin, Ill, Sept 5, 42; m 74, Beverley Turner; c Emily, Louis, Laura & Rachel. *Educ:* Ill State Univ, BS, 63, MS, 65; Univ Fla, PhD(inorg chem), 68. *Prof Exp:* Asst chem, Ill State Univ, 63-65; asst, Univ Fla, 65-68, res asst, 68; asst prof, Univ Miss, 68-69. *Concurrent Pos:* Vis prof, Tech Univ Vienna, 69. *Mem:* Am Chem Soc; Sigma Xi. *Res:* Chemistry of the arsenic-nitrogen bond; reactivity of alanes and gallanes with amines, phosphines, arsines and stibines; reactivity of boranes with arsenic-nitrogen and phosphorus-nitrogen containing bases. *Mailing Add:* Dept Chem Univ Ala Birmingham AL 35294. *Fax:* 205-934-2543; *E-Mail:* krannich@uab.edu

KRANTZ, ALLEN, biochemistry, for more information see previous edition

KRANTZ, DAVID S, MEDICAL PSYCHOLOGY, BEHAVIORAL MEDICINE & CARDIOVASCULAR DISORDERS. *Current Pos:* from asst prof to assoc prof, 78-87, PROF MED PSYCHOL, UNIFORMED SERV UNIV HEALTH SCI, 87-; PROF PSYCHIAT, GEORGETOWN UNIV MED CTR, 93-, PROF CARDIOL, 96- *Personal Data:* b New York, NY, Feb 9, 49; m 82, Marsha L Dovma; c Michael & Della. *Educ:* City Col New York, BS, 71; Univ Tex, Austin, PhD(psychol), 75. *Honors & Awards:* Health Psychol Ann Award, Am Psychol Asn, 81, Early Career Sci Award, 82. *Prof Exp:* Asst prof psychol, Univ Southern Calif, 75-78. *Concurrent Pos:* Clin prof psychiat, Georgetown Univ Med Ctr, 91-93, prof psychiat, 93-; ed-in-chief, Health Psychol, 94- *Mem:* Fel Am Psychol Asn; Am Psychosomatic Soc; Soc Psychophysiol Res; fel Acad Behav Med Res (pres, 94-); fel Am Psychol Soc; fel Soc Behav Med. *Res:* Behavioral and psychophysiological factors in cardiovascular disorders; psychological stress; silent cardiac bichemia; silent cardiac ischemia; triggers of sudden cardiac death. *Mailing Add:* Dept Med Psychol Uniformed Serv Univ Health Sci 4301 Jones Bridge Rd Bethesda MD 20814-4799. *Fax:* 301-295-3034; *E-Mail:* krantz@bob.usuf2.usuhs.mil

KRANTZ, GERALD WILLIAM, ACAROLOGY, FUNCTIONAL MORPHOLOGY & BEHAVIOR. *Current Pos:* From asst prof to prof, 55-96, chmn, 91-94, EMER PROF ENTOM, ORE STATE UNIV, 94- *Personal Data:* b Pittsburgh, Pa, Mar 12, 28; m 55, Vida J Kersch; c Wayne, Georgia & Valerie. *Educ:* Univ Pittsburgh, BSc, 51; Cornell Univ, PhD, 55. *Honors & Awards:* Berlese Award, 79; Associe du Museum d'Histoire Naturelle, Paris, 84-; Gilfillan Award, 87. *Concurrent Pos:* Microzoologist, Am Quintana Roo Exped, 65, zoologist & dep leader, Exped II, 68; mem, Gov Bd, Acarology Soc Am, 71-76, chmn, 75-76; sr res scientist, Commonwealth Sci & Ind Res Organ, Pretoria, SAfrica, 79; exec comt, Int Cong Acarology, 82-; prog officer, Systematic Biol, NSF, Washington, DC, 84-85; assoc, Nat Mus Natural Hist, Paris, 84-, vis prof, 87. *Mem:* Entom Soc Am; Acarology Soc Am (pres, 95); Sigma Xi. *Res:* Systematics and behavior of Acari diversi; systematics, behavior, and functional morphology of mites (Acari), with emphasis on insect associates and marine forms. *Mailing Add:* Dept Entom Ore State Univ Corvallis OR 97331. *Fax:* 541-737-3643; *E-Mail:* krantzg@bcc.orst.edu

KRANTZ, KARL WALTER, ORGANIC CHEMISTRY, POLYMER CHEMISTRY. *Current Pos:* res chemist, 50-75, SPECIALIST SILICONE RES TECHNOL, SILICONE PROD DEPT, GEN ELEC CO, 75- *Personal Data:* b Waterbury, Conn, May 9, 18; m 42, Elizabeth Durkee; c David W & Kathryn E. *Educ:* Univ Conn, BS, 39, MS, 40; Stanford Univ, PhD(chem), 51. *Prof Exp:* Asst chem, Stanford Univ, 40-41; instr, Univ Conn, 42-43; res fel, Purdue Univ, 43-45; res chemist, E I du Pont de Nemours & Co, 45-50. *Mem:* Am Chem Soc; fel Am Inst Chemists. *Res:* Aliphatic diamines; local anesthetics; fluorocarbons; catalytic oxidation of hydrocarbons; silicones. *Mailing Add:* 1609 S Arlington Dr Seneca SC 29672

KRANTZ, KERMIT EDWARD, MEDICINE, ANATOMY. *Current Pos:* prof & chmn, Dept Gynec & Obstet, Univ Kans Med Ctr, 59-91, prof anat, 63-92, dean clin affairs, 72-74, assoc to exec vchancellor facil develop, Med Ctr, 74-83, distinguished prof, 91-94, EMER PROF ANAT, UNIV KANS MED CTR, 94- *Personal Data:* b Oak Park, Ill, June 4, 23; m 46. *Educ:* Northwestern Univ, BS, 45, BM & MS, 47, MD, 48; Am Bd Obstet & Gynec, dipl. *Hon Degrees:* DLitt, William Woods Col, 71. *Honors & Awards:* Found Award, SAtlantic Asn Obstetricians, Gynecologists, 50, Am Asn Obstetricians & Gynecologists, 50; Leslie Arey Lectr, Northwestern Univ Sch Med, 66, Thomas W McElin Lectr, 86; Distinguished Serv Award, Am Col Obstetricians & Gyecologists, 82; Edward Crown Mem Lectr, Columbus Hosp, Chicago, 83. *Prof Exp:* Asst zool, Northwestern Univ, 43; resident anat, Med Sch, 44-47; intern obstet & gynec, New York Lying-In-Hosp, Cornell Univ, 47-48; asst resident, New York Lying-In-Hosp, Cornell Univ, 47-48; from instr to asst prof, Univ Vt, 51-55; asst prof, Sch Med, Univ Ark, 55-59. *Concurrent Pos:* NY Acad Med Bowen-Brooks fel, New York Hosp, 48-50; res fel, Col Med, Univ Vt, 50-51; Markle scholar, Sch Med, Univ Kans, 57-62; asst dir, Div Maternal & Child Health & Welfare, Vt State Dept Health, 51-55, civilian Nat Consult, Surgeon Gen, US Air Force, 64-; pres, Int Family Planning Res Asn Inc, 75-76; Charles Jones Newcomb vis prof obstet & gynec, Univ Ariz Health Sci Ctr, 79; adj prof obstet & gynec, Sch Med, Univ NDak, 81. *Mem:* AAAS; Am Asn Anatomists; found fel Am Col Obstetricians & Gynecologists; Am Med Writers Asn; Soc Med Consults Armed Forces (pres, 90-91). *Res:* Human placenta; anatomy and physiology; female anatomy, urethra, bladder, vagina, uterus, tubes and ovaries; renal function in pregnancy. *Mailing Add:* Univ Kans Med Ctr 39th Rainbow Blvd Kansas City KS 66103

KRANTZ, SANFORD B, INTERNAL MEDICINE, HEMATOLOGY. *Current Pos:* CHIEF HEMAT UNIT, VET ADMIN HOSP, NASHVILLE, 70- *Personal Data:* b Chicago, Ill, Feb 6, 34; m 58, Sandra Rae Goldstein; c Michael, Marcy (Glisczinski), Alan & Sarah (Derks). *Educ:* Univ Chicago, AB & BS, 55, MD, 59. *Honors & Awards:* Joseph A Capps Prize, Inst Med Chicago, 64. *Prof Exp:* Intern med, Univ Chicago Hosps, 60-61, asst resident, 61-62, res assoc, 63-64; asst prof med, Univ Chicago Hosps & Argonne Cancer Res Hosp, 65-68; asst chief hemat serv, Clin Ctr, NIH, 68-70; assoc prof, 70-75, prof med & dir hemat, Sch Med, Vanderbilt Univ, 75- *Concurrent Pos:* USPHS fel, Univ Chicago Hosps, 62-64; NATO fel biochem, Univ Glasgow, 64-65; Leukemia Soc scholar, 65-68. *Mem:* AAAS; Am Soc Clin Invest; Am Fedn Clin Res; Am Soc Hemat; Asn Am Physicians; Int Soc Exp Hematol. *Res:* Erythropoietin; erythropoietic diseases; polycythemia vera and red cell aplasia; anemia of chronic disease. *Mailing Add:* Vet Admin Med Ctr 2-A229 1310 24th Ave S Nashville TN 37212-2637. *Fax:* 615-321-6327

KRANTZ, STEVEN GEORGE, SEVERAL COMPLEX VARIABLES. *Current Pos:* PROF MATH, WASHINGTON UNIV, ST LOUIS, 86- *Personal Data:* b San Francisco, Calif, Feb 3, 51; m 74. *Educ:* Univ Calif, Santa Cruz, BA, 71; Princeton Univ, PhD(math), 74. *Honors & Awards:* Chauvenet Prize, 92; Kemper Award, 93; Beckenbach Prize, 94. *Prof Exp:* Asst prof math, Univ Calif, Los Angeles, 74-81; assoc prof, Pa State Univ, Univ Park, 81-84, prof, 84-87. *Concurrent Pos:* NSF res fel, 75- *Mem:* Am Math Soc; Math Asn Am. *Res:* Function theory on pseudoconvex domains in complex n-space; harmonic analysis of Euclidean spaces, real function theory, differentiability of functions, and interpolation theory. *Mailing Add:* Dept Math Campus Box 1146 Washington Univ St Louis MD 63130. *E-Mail:* sk@math.wustl.edu

KRANTZ, WILLIAM BERNARD, POLYMERIC MEMBRANES, GEOMORPHOLOGY. *Current Pos:* Asst prof, 68-77, assoc prof, 77-79, PROF CHEM ENG, UNIV COLO, BOULDER, 79- *Personal Data:* b Freeport, Ill, Jan 27, 39; m 68, June Clair Gaspar; c Brigette Elise. *Educ:* St Joseph's Col, Ind, BA, 61; Univ Ill, Urbana, BS, 62; Univ Calif, Berkeley, PhD(chem eng), 68. *Honors & Awards:* Spec Achievement & Outstanding Performance Awards, NSF, 78; George Westinghouse Award, Am Soc Eng Educ, 80; John Wesley Powell Mem Lectr, AAAS, 95. *Concurrent Pos:* Consult, Dow Chem Co, Mich, 69-71; Fulbright-Hays lectr, Istanbul Tech Univ, 74-75; NSF, NATO sr fel, Univ Essex, Eng, 75; consult, Laramie Energy Technol Ctr, Dept Energy, 76-; dir, Thermodyn & Mass Transfer Prog, NSF, 77-78; mem area adv comt, US Coun Int Exchange Scholar, Int Commun Agency, 77-80; consult, US Dept Com, 79-80; Fulbright-Hayes sr res fel, Aachen Tech Univ, WGer, 81-82; Nat res lectr, Sigma Xi, 84-86; Guggenheim fel, Univ Oxford, Eng, 88-89; consult, Bend Res, 90-; vis fac researcher, Univ Twente, Neth, 95; NSF GOALI fac fel, Chevron Res & Technol Co, Calif, 96, 3M Co, Minn, 96. *Mem:* Fel AAAS; Am Inst Chem Engrs; Am Soc Eng Educ; Am Chem Soc; Sigma Xi; NAm Membrane Soc. *Res:* Polymeric membrane morphology; self-organization in geophysical processing; materials science in low-gravity; global change in polar and sub polar regions. *Mailing Add:* Dept Chem Eng Univ Colo Campus Box 424 Boulder CO 80309-0424. *Fax:* 303-492-5637; *E-Mail:* krantz@spot.colorado.edu

KRANTZBERG, GAIL, CONTAMINANT TOXICITY & BIOAVAILABILITY, ECOLOGICAL RESTORATION. *Current Pos:* ECOTOXICOLOGIST, ONT MINISTRY ENVIRON & ENERGY, 88- *Personal Data:* b Montreal, Que, Aug 19, 57; m, Douglas Markoff. *Educ:* McGill Univ, BS, 79; Univ Toronto, MS, 82, PhD(ecotoxicol), 87. *Prof Exp:* Fel, Univ Toronto, 87-88. *Concurrent Pos:* Lectr, Univ Toronto, 79-84, adj prof environ mgt & aquatic chem, 90-; consult sediment mgt, Ont Ministry Environ & Energy, 82-84, sediment specialist & remedial action plan coordr, 88-; Great Lakes Remedial Action Plan coordr, 88-94; prin investr, Environ Can, 91-; fac, Restoration ecol, York Univ, 96- *Mem:* Int Asn Great Lakes Res; Soc Environ Toxicol & Chem; NAm Benthological Soc; Nature Conservancy; Can Wildlife Fedn. *Res:* Bioavailability and toxicity of contaminants in sediment; remedial action plans to rehabilitate Great Lakes ecosystems; structural and functional indicators of aquatic ecosystem health, environmental sustainability. *Mailing Add:* Ont Ministry Environ & Energy 40 St Clair Ave W Toronto ON M4V 1M2 Can. *Fax:* 416-314-3924; *E-Mail:* krantzga@epo.gov.on.ca

KRANZ, EUGENE FRANCIS, AERONAUTICAL ENGINEERING. *Current Pos:* flight opers dir shuttle prog, 80-83, FLIGHT DIR GEMINI, APOLLO & SKYLAB MISSIONS, MANNED SPACECRAFT CTR, NASA, 64-, CHIEF FLIGHT CONTROL DIV, 69-, DIR MISSION OPERS, NASA, JOHNSON SPACE CTR, 83- *Personal Data:* b Toledo, Ohio, Aug 17, 33; c 6. *Educ:* St Louis Univ, BS. *Honors & Awards:* Lawrence Sperry Award, Am Inst Aeronaut & Astronaut, 67. *Prof Exp:* Flight test engr, McDonnell Aircraft Co, 54-55; supvr carrier flight test maintenance & checkout, Holloman AFB, NMex, 58-60. *Concurrent Pos:* Flight controller, Mercury Missions. *Mem:* Fel Am Astronaut Soc. *Mailing Add:* 1108 Shady Oak Lane Dickinson TX 77539

KRANZER, HERBERT C, APPLIED MATHEMATICS, CONSERVATION LAWS. *Current Pos:* assoc prof, 59-63, PROF MATH, ADELPHI UNIV, 63- *Personal Data:* b New York, NY, Apr 10, 32; m 58; c 3. *Educ:* NY Univ, BA, 52, PhD(math), 57. *Honors & Awards:* Putnam Awards, 51 & 52. *Prof Exp:* Asst math, NY Univ, 52-57, assoc res scientist, 57-58, instr, 58-59. *Concurrent Pos:* Consult, Los Alamos Sci Lab, 56-68; NSF sr fel, 66; vis prof, Imp Col London, 66-67; vis scholar, Columbia Univ, 76-77; consult, FONAR Corp, 83- *Mem:* Am Math Soc; Soc Indust & Appl Math; Math Asn Am; AAAS. *Res:* Magnetohydrodynamics; numerical analysis; Weiner-Hopf problems; conservation laws; magnetic resonance imaging. *Mailing Add:* Dept Math & Comput Sci Adelphi Univ Garden City NY 11530-0701

KRANZLER, ALBERT WILLIAM, MATHEMATICS. *Current Pos:* RETIRED. *Personal Data:* b Bismarck, NDak, July 11, 16; m 39; c 2. *Educ:* Univ NDak, BS, 37; Univ Minn, MS, 50. *Prof Exp:* Prin pub sch, NDak, 37-41; teacher, SDak, 41-42; instr training div, Sioux Falls Army Air Force Sch, 42-43; prin pub sch, Colo, 43-45; from assoc prof to prof math, SDak State Univ, 45-81, actg head dept, 61-68. *Mem:* Math Asn Am; Am Math Soc. *Res:* Reorganization of high school mathematics curriculum. *Mailing Add:* 808 Christine Ave No 206 Brookings SD 57006

KRAPCHO, ANDREW PAUL, ORGANIC CHEMISTRY. *Current Pos:* from asst prof to assoc prof, 60-67, PROF CHEM, UNIV VT, 67- *Personal Data:* b Alden, Pa, Mar 6, 32; m 58, M Arlene Fisher; c Karen J, Susan D & Douglas P. *Educ:* Pa State Univ, BS, 53; Harvard Univ, MA, 57, PhD(chem), 58. *Prof Exp:* Instr chem, Smith Col, 57-59; res fel, Pa State Univ, 59-60. *Concurrent Pos:* Fulbright scholar, France, 68-69. *Mem:* Am Chem Soc. *Res:* Chemistry of thiones and photochemistry of cyclic ketones; physical-organic chemistry; metal-amine reductions; solvolytic studies of spirane systems; sesquiterpene syntheses; bivalent carbon species; synthesis of antitumor agents. *Mailing Add:* Dept Chem Univ Vt Burlington VT 05405. *Fax:* 802-656-8705

KRAPF, GEORGE, ANALYTICAL CHEMISTRY. *Current Pos:* RETIRED. *Personal Data:* b Millvale, Pa, July 20, 22; m 46, Thelma Rheam. *Educ:* Univ Pittsburgh, BS, 44. *Prof Exp:* Instr chem, sec schs, WPa, 44-50; res chemist, US Steel Res Labs, 50-70, sr res chemist, 70-83. *Concurrent Pos:* Consult, 83- *Mem:* Am Chem Soc. *Res:* Polarography, thermal analysis and second phase analysis in steels; twenty publications on polargraphy and thermal analysis. *Mailing Add:* Thompson Manor 307 Russell St Pittsburgh PA 15209-1613

KRAPU, GARY LEE, WILDLIFE RESEARCH, ANIMAL ECOLOGY. *Current Pos:* RES SCIENTIST, NORTHERN PRAIRIE SCI CTR, US FISH & WILDLIFE SERV, 71- *Personal Data:* b Oakes, ND, Mar 12, 44; m 67, 85, Madeline Luke; c Jeff, Amy, Anne & Chris. *Educ:* NDak State Univ, BS, 66; Iowa State Univ, MS, 68, PhD(animal ecol), 72. *Mem:* Wildlife Soc; Am Ornithologist's Union; Wilson Soc. *Res:* Ecological aspects of waterfowl reproduction; sandhill crane biology; feeding ecology and nutrition; reproductive physiology; lipid storage; bioenergetics; marsh ecology; role of midcontinent staging areas to arctic-nesting geese, shorebirds and sandhill cranes. *Mailing Add:* Northern Prairie Sci Ctr 8711 37th St SE Jamestown ND 58402-9736. *Fax:* 701-252-4217; *E-Mail:* gary_krapu@nbs.gov

KRASAVAGE, WALTER JOSEPH, INDUSTRIAL TOXICOLOGY. *Current Pos:* SR TOXICOLOGIST INDUST TOXICOL, HEALTH SAFETY & HUMAN FACTORS LAB, EASTMAN KODAK CO, 65-, MGR REPROD & DEVELOP TOXICOL, HEALTH & ENVIRON LABS, EASTMAN KODAK CO, 65- *Personal Data:* b Luzerne, Pa, Mar 12, 33; m 55; c 4. *Educ:* King's Col, BS, 55; Univ Rochester, MS, 63. *Prof Exp:* Technician parasitol, Merck Inst Therapeut Res, 55-56; sr res assoc, Atomic Energy Proj, Dept Radiation Biol & Biophys, Sch Med & Dent, Univ Rochester, 58-65. *Concurrent Pos:* Instr biol, Rochester Inst Technol, 63-65. *Mem:* Soc Toxicol; Teratol Soc; Environ Mutagen Soc. *Res:* Subchronic and chronic toxicology of industrial chemicals, especially reproduction and embryo-fetotoxicity. *Mailing Add:* 288 Shorecliff Dr Rochester NY 14612

KRASHES, DAVID, METALLURGY. *Current Pos:* PRES, LEHIGH TESTING LABS, 72- *Personal Data:* b Brooklyn, NY, Jan 31, 25; m 56; c 1. *Educ:* Rensselaer Polytech Inst, BS, 49, MS, 52, PhD(metall), 58. *Prof Exp:* Res assoc metall, Rensselaer Polytech Inst, 53-54; mem staff, Nuclear Metals, Inc, 55-57; assoc prof, Worcester Polytech Inst, 57-65; pres, Mass Mat Res, Inc, 65- *Concurrent Pos:* Consult, Wyman-Gordon Co, 59- & Reed Rolled Thread Die Co, 60-; dir, Richard D Brew Co; pres, Conn Metall, Inc, 81- *Mem:* Fel Am Soc Metals (treas, 71-73, vpres, 80-81, pres, 81-82); Am Inst Mining, Metall & Petrol Engrs; Am Soc Testing & Mat; Am Foundry Soc. *Res:* Failure analysis of metals and mechanical products; solving industrial manufacturing problems relating to materials; fabrication; microscopy; economic studies. *Mailing Add:* Rhodes Rd Princeton MA 01541

KRASHIN, BERNARD R(OBERT), METALS. *Current Pos:* RETIRED. *Personal Data:* b Buffalo, NY, Nov 9, 18; m 46; c 2. *Educ:* Western Reserve Univ, BS, 41. *Prof Exp:* Chief chemist, Cosma Labs Co, 41-43; dir metals labs, 43-45; chief chemist & asst tech dir, 45-50; vpres, Colton Chem Co Div, Air Reduction Co, Inc, 50-56, pres, 56-62; pres, Macco Chem Co Div, Glidden Co, 62-64, vpres & gen mgr, 64-67, vpres opers, Glidden-Durkee Div, 67-70, vpres & gen Mgr, Macco Adhesives Group, SCM Corp, 71-86. *Mem:* Am Chem Soc; Am Ord Asn; Am Inst Chem. *Res:* Fungicides; vinyl resins; emulsions, wax and synthetic resin; process for fusion of bronze to steel; fungicide for ropes, nets and twine; radiological physics; synthetic resins; analytic chemistry. *Mailing Add:* 22150 Shaker Blvd Shaker Heights OH 44122

KRASKIN, KENNETH STANFORD, MICROBIOLOGY. *Current Pos:* TECH CONSULT, 88- *Personal Data:* b Kearny, NJ, Dec 28, 29; m 54, Barbara Adler; c Richard & Andrew. *Educ:* Rutgers Univ, BS, 51, MS, 53, PhD(bact), 57. *Prof Exp:* Lab instr bact, Rutgers Univ, 54-57; microbiologist, Rohm & Haas Co, 57-70; head microbiol, Personal Prod Co, Johnson & Johnson, 71-77, dir appl res, 77-88. *Mem:* Am Soc Microbiol; Sigma Xi; Soc Indust Microbiol. *Res:* Antibiotics; enzyme fermentations; sterility; disinfectants; biodegradation; vaginal microbiology and physiology. *Mailing Add:* 14 N Garden Terr Milltown NJ 08850. *Fax:* 732-297-9522

KRASNA, ALVIN ISAAC, BIOCHEMISTRY. *Current Pos:* Res worker, 54-56, from instr to assoc prof, 56-70, PROF BIOCHEM, COLUMBIA UNIV, 70- *Personal Data:* b New York, NY, June 23, 29; m 55, Elaine Cohen; c Susan, Gary & Allen. *Educ:* Yeshiva Col, BA, 50; Columbia Univ, PhD(biochem), 55. *Concurrent Pos:* Guggenheim Mem Found fel, 62-63. *Mem:* AAAS; Am Chem Soc; Harvey Soc; Am Soc Biol Chemists; Am Soc Microbiol; Am Soc Photobiol. *Res:* Bioconversion of solar energy; regulation of biosynthesis of enzymes. *Mailing Add:* Col Physicians & Surgeons Columbia Univ New York NY 10032. *Fax:* 212-305-7932

KRASNEGAR, NORMAN A, HUMAN LEARNING & BEHAVIOR. *Current Pos:* health sci adminr, Nat Inst Drug Abuse, 72-80, CHIEF, HUMAN LEARNING & BEHAV BR, NAT INST CHILD HEALTH & HUMAN DEVELOP, NIH, 80- *Personal Data:* b Boston, Mass, Nov 17, 39. *Educ:* Boston Univ, BA, 61; Columbia Univ, MA, 63; Univ Md, PhD(exp psychol), 70. *Honors & Awards:* Distinguished Serv Award, Am Psychol Asn, 81; Distinguished Serv Award, Int Soc for Develop Psychol & Biol, 95. *Prof Exp:* Exp Psychologist, Walter Rood Army Inst Res, 66-72. *Mem:* Fel Am Psychol Asn; Am Psychol Soc. *Mailing Add:* Nat Inst Child Health & Human Develop NIH Rm 4B05 9000 Rockville Pike Bethesda MD 20892. *Fax:* 301-480-7773; *E-Mail:* krasnegn@cd01.nichd.nih.gov

KRASNER, JEROME L, MANAGEMENT. *Current Pos:* DIR, INT CTR BIOMED TECHNOLOGIES, BECKER HILL COMMUNITY COL, BOSTON; VIS PROF, UNIV LOS PALMAS, SPAIN. *Personal Data:* b St Louis, Mo, Feb 25, 40; wid; c Randy, Brett, Jay, Rachael, Douglas & Peter. *Educ:* Wash Univ, BS, 61, MS, 64; Boston Univ, PhD(medsci), 69; Nichols Col, MBA, 87. *Honors & Awards:* Cert of Commendation, NASA, 69. *Prof Exp:* Chmn, Dept Biomed Eng & assoc prof health sci, physiol & biomed eng, Boston Univ, 69-74; pres, Clinco, Inc, 75-81; exec vpres, Plasmedics, Inc, 81-85; vpres re & develop, Clin Develop Corp, 83-89; dept head & prof, Dept Elec Eng Technol, Wentworth Inst Technol, 90-92. *Concurrent Pos:* Pres, Biocybernetics, Inc, 69-75; dir, Ctr Med Sci, Carnegie-Mellon Inst Res, 77-79 & Ctr Clin Eng, Wentworth Inst Technol. *Mem:* Inst Elec & Electronics Engrs; Asn Advan Med Instrumentation; Sigma Xi; NY Acad Sci; AAAS. *Res:* Design, development and international marketing of clinical instrumentation and medical devices. *Mailing Add:* 638 Main St Ashland MA 01721. *Fax:* 508-881-7085

KRASNER, JOSEPH, BIOCHEMISTRY. *Current Pos:* assoc res prof pediat, 66 79, ASSOC RES PROF OBSTET & GYNEC, STATE UNIV NY-BUFFALO, 79- *Personal Data:* b Buffalo, NY, Jan 10, 26; m 53; c 2. *Educ:* Univ Buffalo, BS, 48, EdM, 50, MA, 63, PhD(biochem), 65. *Prof Exp:* High sch teacher, 50-51; asst cancer res scientist, Roswell Park Mem Inst, 51-61; res assoc, Children's Hosp, Buffalo, NY, 65-66; cancer res scientist II, Roswell Park Mem Inst, Buffalo, 79-92. *Concurrent Pos:* Dir core labs, Children's Hosp, NY, 66-72. *Mem:* AAAS; Am Chem Soc; NY Acad Sci; Am Asn Clin Chemists; Am Soc Pharmacol & Exp Therapeut; Sigma Xi; Am Soc Biochem & Molecular Biol. *Res:* Biochemical changes during mammalian development and the effect of endogenous and exogenous compounds on development; drug-protein interactions during development and in pathological situations; physical biochemical techniques as used to study the antibody combining site. *Mailing Add:* 60 Snughaven Tonawanda NY 14150-8510

KRASNER, ROBERT IRVING, MICROBIOLOGY. *Current Pos:* From instr to assoc prof, 58-65, PROF BIOL, PROVIDENCE COL, 65- *Personal Data:* b Providence, RI, Dec 3, 29; m 64; c 2. *Educ:* Providence Col, BS, 51; Boston Univ, AM, 52, PhD(biol), 56. *Concurrent Pos:* Mem, La State Univ Sch Med Interim Training Prog Trop Med in Cent Am, 62, adv coun clin labs, RI Dept Health, 62- & US Army Biol Labs, Ft Detrick, Md, 65-66; vis prof, Sch Med, Georgetown Univ, 69-71, Haddasah Med Sch, Hewbrew Univ, Jerusalem. *Mem:* AAAS; Am Soc Microbiol; Nat Asn Biol Teachers; Nat Sci Teachers Asn. *Res:* Medical bacteriology; host-parasite relationships. *Mailing Add:* Dept Biol Providence Col River Ave & Eaton St Providence RI 02918-0001

KRASNER, SOL H, physics, for more information see previous edition

KRASNEY, JOHN ANDREW, CARDIOVASCULAR PHYSIOLOGY. *Current Pos:* assoc prof, 74-83, PROF PHYSIOL, STATE UNIV NY, BUFFALO, 83- *Personal Data:* b Long Beach, Calif, Nov 29, 40; m 64, 75; c 5. *Educ:* Elmhurst Col, BS, 62; Univ Wis-Madison, PhD(physiol), 66. *Prof Exp:* From instr to assoc prof physiol, Albany Med Col, 67-74. *Concurrent Pos:* Nat Heart Inst fel physiol, Univ Wis-Madison, 66-67; mem, Coun Cardiopulmonary Dis & Coun Circulation, Am Heart Asn; animal care & experimentation comt, Am Physiol Soc, 82-85. *Mem:* Am Physiol Soc; Can Physiol Soc; Am Heart Asn; Undersea Med Soc. *Res:* Regulation of circulation; respiration; renal function and blood volume during environmental stresses including chronic hypoxia, water immersion and exercise; neuroendocrine and mechanisms in control of fluid and electrolyte balance; cerebral circulation in chronic hypoxia; mechanisms of high-altitude cerebral edema and acute mountain sickness; ethanol on cerebral blood flow; cardiac function and arterial blood pressure. *Mailing Add:* State Univ Ny Sch Med & Biomed Sci 124 Sherman Hall Buffalo NY 14214

KRASNO, LOUIS RICHARD, MEDICINE. *Current Pos:* DIR CLIN RES, UNITED AIR LINES, 57- *Personal Data:* b Chicago, Ill, Sept 2, 14; m 40; c 1. *Educ:* Northwestern Univ, BS, 36, MS, 37, PhD(physiol), 39, MD, 44. *Prof Exp:* Asst physiol, Northwestern Univ, 36-39; instr, Chicago City Jr Col, 39-40; instr, Med Sch, Northwestern Univ, 40-47; asst prof clin sci, Univ Ill, 47-57; asst prof med, Stanford Univ, 57- *Concurrent Pos:* Practicing physician, Ill, 47-57. *Mem:* Soc Exp Biol & Med; fel Int Col Angiol; fel AMA; fel Aerospace Med Asn; fel Am Col Cardiol; Sigma Xi. *Res:* Aviation medicine; physiology; cardiovascular medicine. *Mailing Add:* 149 Flying Cloud Isle Foster City CA 94404-1301

KRASNOW, FRANCES, biochemistry, for more information see previous edition

KRASNOW, MARVIN ELLMAN, PHYSICAL CHEMISTRY, ELECTRICAL ENGINEERING. *Current Pos:* RETIRED. *Personal Data:* b Chicago, Ill, Apr 27, 24; m 49; c 5. *Educ:* Ohio State Univ, PhD(chem), 52. *Prof Exp:* Res assoc electron scattering, Ohio State Univ, 52-53; res chemist polyethylene, Visking Corp, 53-56; mgr chem, Physics & Petrol Lab, Inland Testing Labs, 56-59; dir govt res & develop, Hallicrafters Co, 59-64; coordr indust rels, Univ Ill, Urbana, 85-89, asst dean, Col Eng, 59-64; asst to dean, Col Eng, Ariz State Univ, Phoenix, 89-93. *Mem:* Inst Elec & Electronics Engrs; Am Soc Eng Educ. *Res:* Electron scattering by gases; investigation of structure of polyethylene; interaction of electromagnetic radiation with matter; evaluation of fuels and lubricants; quantum phenomena. *Mailing Add:* 2526 E Taxidea Way Phoenix AZ 85048-9077

KRASNY, HARVEY CHARLES, DRUG METABOLISM, PHARMACOKINETICS. *Current Pos:* VPRES LICENSING, CAROTECH LLC, 96- *Personal Data:* b Highpoint, NC, July 27, 45. *Educ:* Lynchburg Col, BS, 67; Univ NC, MS, 69, PhD(biochem), 76. *Prof Exp:* Sr res scientist, Wellcome Res Labs, Burroughs Wellcome Co, 69-95. *Mem:* Am Soc Clin Pharmacol & Therapeut; Am Soc Pharmacol & Exp Therapeut; Soc Toxicol; Sigma Xi; Lic Exec Soc; Asn Univ Tech Mgrs. *Res:* preclinical and clinical development of chemotherapeutic agents. *Mailing Add:* PO Box 13416 Research Triangle Park NC 27709-3416. *Fax:* 919-967-7745; *E-Mail:* hkrasny@mindspring.com

KRASS, ALLAN S(HALE), THEORETICAL PHYSICS, SCIENCE POLICY. *Current Pos:* assoc prof, 74-79, PROF PHYSICS & SCI POLICY, HAMPSHIRE COL, 81- *Personal Data:* b Milwaukee, Wis, May 16, 35. *Educ:* Cornell Univ, BS, 58; Stanford Univ, PhD(theoret physics), 63. *Prof Exp:* Res assoc physics, Univ Iowa, 62-64; lectr, Univ Calif, Santa Barbara, 64-65, asst prof, 65-72; lectr, Princeton Univ, 72-73; vis lectr, Open Univ Gr Brit, 73-74. *Concurrent Pos:* Consult, Off Technol Assessment, US Cong, 76-; NSF fac fel, 76-77; vis researcher, Stockholm Instrnl Peace Res Inst, 80-81, 83-84; sr arms analyst, Union Concerned Scientists, 85-89. *Res:* Elementary particle physics; theoretical high energy physics; science policy, especially arms control, energy and environmental. *Mailing Add:* Sch Natural Sci Hampshire Col Amherst MA 01002-3359

KRASSNER, STUART M, PARASITOLOGY, COUNSELING THERAPY. *Current Pos:* asst prof organismic biol, Univ Calif, Irvine, 65-69, assoc prof develop & cell biol, 69-73, from vchmn to chmn dept, 69-84, assoc dean grad div, 74-76, biol sci, 77-80 & grad studies & res, 84-85, actg dean grad studies & res, 85-89, JOINT PROF DEVELOP & CELL BIOL & MED MICROBIOL, UNIV CALIF, IRVINE, 73- *Personal Data:* b New York, NY, Aug 21, 35; m 86, Liza Bello; c David & Sarah. *Educ:* Brooklyn Col, BS, 57; Johns Hopkins Univ, ScD(parasitol), 61. *Prof Exp:* NIH fel, int coop med res & training prog, Johns Hopkins Univ-Sch Trop Med, Univ Calcutta, 61-62; guest investr & NIH res trainee, Rockefeller Univ, 62-65; instr invert zool, Hunter Col, 64-65. *Concurrent Pos:* Fac Am Behav Studies Inst, 96- *Mem:* AAAS; Am Soc Parasitol; Soc Protozool; Am Soc Trop Med Hyg. *Res:* Immune responses in hemoflagellate infections; control of transformation in parasitic hemoflagellates. *Mailing Add:* Dept Develop & Cell Biol Univ Calif Irvine CA 92717. *Fax:* 714-824-4709; *E-Mail:* smkrassn@uci.edu

KRASSOWSKA, WANDA, ELECTROPHYSIOLOGY, MODELS OF CARDIAC MUSCLE IN ELECTRIC FIELD. *Current Pos:* res assoc, 88-91, ASST PROF BIOMED ENG, DUKE UNIV, 91- *Personal Data:* b Warsaw, Poland, No 1, 54. *Educ:* Warsaw Tech Univ, MS, 78; Duke Univ, PhD(biomed eng), 87. *Prof Exp:* Res assoc, Inst Biocybernetics & Biomed Eng, 78-83. *Mem:* Inst Elec & Electronics Engrs; Eng Med and Bio Soc. *Res:* Electrophysiology of syncytial tissues; mechanisms of pacing and defibrillation of the heart. *Mailing Add:* Three Post Oak Rd Durham NC 27705

KRATOCHVIL, BYRON, ANALYTICAL CHEMISTRY. *Current Pos:* assoc prof, 67-71, chair, 89-96, PROF CHEM, UNIV ALTA, 71-, ASSOC PRES RES, 96- *Personal Data:* b Osmond, Nebr, Sept 15, 32; m 60, Marianne Spain; c Susan J, Daniel J, Jean M & John D. *Educ:* Iowa State Univ, BS, 57, MS, 59, PhD(anal chem), 61. *Honors & Awards:* Fisher Award, Can Soc Chem. *Prof Exp:* Instr chem, Univ Wis-Madison, 61-62, asst prof, 62-67. *Concurrent Pos:* Bd dirs, Chem Inst Can, 77-80; guest worker, Nat Bur Stand, Washington, DC, 80-81; ed bd, Can J Chem, 82-85, anal ed, 85-88, sr ed, 88-93. *Mem:* Fel AAAS; Am Chem Soc; fel Chem Inst Can. *Res:* Metal complex studies; metal ion speciation; analysis using nonaqueous solvents; clinical analysis; sampling for chemical analysis. *Mailing Add:* Dept Chem Univ Alta Edmonton AB T6G 2G2 Can. *E-Mail:* ron.kratochvil@ualberta.ca

KRATOCHVIL, CLYDE HARDING, PHYSIOLOGY, BIOCHEMISTRY. *Current Pos:* ACTG MED DIR, FAMILY HEALTH CTR, KALAMAZOO, MICH, 91- *Personal Data:* b Racine, Wis, Aug 3, 23; m 44, Janice S Meissner; c Joanne (Claney), Pamela (Tyson), Antoinette (Pax), Patricia & Simone (Vanbellinger). *Educ:* Univ Wis, Madison, BS, 50, MD, 52, PhD(physiol, biochem), 56. *Prof Exp:* Intern, USAF, William Beaumont Army Hosp, Tex, 52-53, officer-in-chg, Dept Physiol & Biophys, Sch Aviation Med, Randolph AFB, 55-59, proj officer biosci div, Europ Off, Off Aerospace Res, Brussels, Belg, 59-61, chief, Biosci Div, 61-63, comdr, 6571st Aeromed Res Lab, Holloman AFB, NMex, 63-68 & 6570th Aerospace Med Res Labs, Wright Patterson AFB, 68-70; group mgr, Med Serv, Upjohn Co, 70-74, dir clin res, Europe, 74-82, int med dir, 82-88. *Concurrent Pos:* Flight controller, Proj Mercury, 59-62; consult, Manned Spacecraft Ctr, NASA, 62-; clin prof prev med, Ohio State Univ, 69-71. *Mem:* AAAS; Am Physiol Soc; fel Aerospace Med Asn; Am Soc Clin Pharmacol & Therapeut; Int Acad Aviation & Space Med; fel Am Inst Chemists. *Res:* Aerospace medical research; immunohematology; use of primates in medical research; protein chemistry; renal physiology; central nervous system function in high stress environments; circadian rhythms. *Mailing Add:* Health Int Ltd 6403 Liteolier St PO Box 1805 Kalamazoo MI 49081-1805. *Fax:* 616-324-0771

KRATOCHVIL, JIRI, ELECTROCHEMISTRY, BIOMEDICAL SCIENCES. *Current Pos:* PRES, IE SENSORS INC, SALT LAKE CITY, UTAH, 84- *Personal Data:* b Prague, Czech, June 11, 44; m 72; c 1. *Educ:* Southampton Univ, PhD(electrochem), 72. *Prof Exp:* Fel electrochem, Univ Okla, 72-73; lectr physiol, St Thomas' Hosp Med Sch, London, 73-75; res fel, Webb-Waring Lung Inst, Denver, 75-76; sr chemist electrochem, Beckman Instruments Inc, 77-79; mgr res & develop, Critikon Inc, Salt Lake City, 79-83. *Mem:* Fel The Chem Soc; Am Chem Soc. *Res:* Ion-selective electrodes; electrochemistry of membranes; polarography; biomedical transducers; semiconductor technology; semiconductor packaging. *Mailing Add:* IE Sensors Inc 247 W 3680 South Salt Lake City UT 84115

KRATOHVIL, JOSIP, COLLOID CHEMISTRY, POLYMER PHYSICAL CHEMISTRY. *Current Pos:* res assoc, 60-64, from asst prof to assoc prof, 64-67, PROF CHEM, CLARKSON COL TECHNOL, 67-, DIR, INST COLLOID & SURFACE SCI, 81- *Personal Data:* b Morovic, Yugoslavia, Feb 26, 28; m 52; c 2. *Educ:* Univ Zagreb, BS, 52, PhD(chem), 54. *Prof Exp:* Asst chem, Med Sch, Univ Zagreb, 52-59; res fel, Nat Res Coun Can, 59-60. *Mem:* AAAS; Am Chem Soc; Fine Particle Soc; NY Acad Sci; Sigma Xi. *Res:* Coagulation and stability of colloids; light scattering; physical biochemistry; polymer chemistry; micellar systems; bile salts; polyelectrolytes and macromolecules in solutions. *Mailing Add:* Dept Chem Clarkson Univ Box 5010 Potsdam NY 13699-0001

KRATTIGER, JOHN TRUBERT, MATHEMATICS. *Current Pos:* from assoc prof to prof, 48-84, vpres student serv, 75-84, EMER PROF MATH, SOUTHEASTERN OKLA STATE UNIV, 84- *Personal Data:* b Denison, Tex, Aug 30, 16; wid; c 1. *Educ:* Austin Col, BA, 38; Southern Methodist Univ, MA, 39; Univ Okla, EdD, 58. *Prof Exp:* Asst math, Southern Methodist Univ, 39-40; teacher pub sch, Tex, 40-41; asst prof, Col Ozarks, 41-44; instr, Univ Okla, 46-48. *Mem:* Math Asn Am. *Res:* Educational guidance. *Mailing Add:* 1729 Asberry St Durant OK 74701

KRATZ, HOWARD RUSSEL, EXPERIMENTAL PHYSICS. *Current Pos:* RETIRED. *Personal Data:* b Mattoon, Wis, Nov 2, 16; m 42, Mary Katherine Bunsa; c William H & Marilyn J (Locker). *Educ:* Ripon Col, AB, 38; Univ Wis, PhD(physics), 42. *Prof Exp:* Asst physics, Univ Wis, 38-40; asst spectros, Princeton Univ, 40-42; res assoc, Metall Lab, Univ Chicago, 42-44; Los Alamos Sci Lab, 44-46, Northwestern Univ, 46, Res Lab, Gen Elec Co, 46-59, Gen Atomic Co, 59-72; sr res scientist, S-Cubed, 72-79. *Mem:* Am Phys Soc; Sigma Xi. *Res:* Ultraviolet and infrared spectroscopy; thermal conduction and transfer; plasma physics; explosion phenomena; accelerator development; nuclear weapons effects; instrumentation. *Mailing Add:* 2620 Kanuga Pines Dr Hendersonville NC 28739

KRATZEL, ROBERT JEFFREY, IMMUNOHEMATOLOGY, MICROBIOLOGY. *Current Pos:* dir tech serv, 78-81, SCI DIR BUFFALO REGION, AM RED CROSS BLOOD SERV, 81- *Personal Data:* b New York, NY, Feb 5, 49; m 75. *Educ:* Hofstra Univ, BA, 71; State Univ NY, Buffalo, MA, 73, PhD(microbiol), 77. *Prof Exp:* Trainee lab med, Erie Co Lab, E J Meyer Mem Hosp, Buffalo, 77. *Concurrent Pos:* Clin instr, Dept Microbiol, State Univ NY, Buffalo, 77-81, clin asst prof, 81-; mem bd dir, Blood Bank Asn NY State Inc. *Mem:* Am Asn Blood Banks; Am Soc Microbiol; Am Soc Histocompatibility & immunogenetics; Am Coun Transplantation. *Res:* The chemical characterization and localization of blood group antigens on blood and tissue cells; health care management. *Mailing Add:* 47 Bywater Dr Getzville NY 14068

KRATZER, D DAL, ANIMAL BREEDING, STATISTICS. *Current Pos:* BIOSTATISTICIAN, UPJOHN CO, 78- *Personal Data:* b Amazonia, Mo, Dec 16, 37; m 63; c 2. *Educ:* Univ Mo, BS, 59; Iowa State Univ, MS, 64, PhD(animal breeding), 65. *Prof Exp:* Asst animal breeding, Iowa State Univ, 59-62, res assoc animal breeding & comput sci, 62-65, asst prof animal sci & comput sci, 65-68; from asst prof to prof animal sci & statist, Univ Ky, 68-77. *Mem:* Am Soc Animal Sci; Biomet Soc. *Res:* Behavior of domestic animals. *Mailing Add:* Upjohn Co 5300 N 28th St Richland MI 49083

KRATZER, FRANK HOWARD, NUTRITION. *Current Pos:* asst prof, Col Agr & Environ Sci, 45-49, from assoc prof to prof poultry husb, 49-83, chmn dept, 76-81, EMER PROF AVIAN SCI, COL AGR & ENVIRON SCI, UNIV CALIF, DAVIS, 83- *Personal Data:* b Baldwinsville, NY, Jan 24, 18; m 46; c 3. *Educ:* Cornell Univ, BS, 40; Univ Calif, PhD(animal nutrit), 44. *Honors & Awards:* Nat Turkey Fedn Res Award, 49; Am Feed Mfrs Res Award, 60; CPC Res Award, 73. *Prof Exp:* Asst poultry husb, Univ Calif, 40-43, res assoc, 43-44; assoc prof, Colo Agr & Mech Col, 44-45. *Concurrent Pos:* NSF fel, Nat Inst Res Dairying, Reading, Eng, 59-60; guest prof, Justus Liebig Univ, Giessen, Germany, 68-69; vis prof, Univ Sydney, 75-76, Fed Univ of Rio Grande do Sol, Porto Alegre, Brasil, 82. *Mem:* Am Chem Soc; Soc Exp Biol & Med; fel Am Inst Nutrit; fel Poultry Sci Asn; Biochem Soc; fel Am Asn Adv Sci. *Res:* Nutrition of poultry amino acid requirements of chickens and turkeys; vitamin needs and function; minerals and mineral availability; growth inhibitors. *Mailing Add:* Dept Avian Sci Univ Calif Davis CA 95616. *Fax:* 530-752-5513

KRATZER, REINHOLD, POLYMER CHEMISTRY. *Current Pos:* MGR, CHEM DEPT, ULTRASYSTS INC, 70- *Personal Data:* b Kaaden, CSR, Nov 14, 28. *Educ:* Univ Munich, Dr rer nat(inorg chem), 60. *Prof Exp:* Res asst inorg chem, Univ Southern Calif, 60-62; res chemist, Naval Ord Lab, Corona, Calif, 62-64; sr scientist, MHD Res Inc, Hercules Powder Co, 64-66; spec mem adv tech staff, Marquardt Corp, 66, mgr chem res, 66-70. *Mem:* Am Chem Soc; Royal Soc Chem; Ger Chem Soc; AAAS; NY Acad Sci. *Res:* Hydrides of low atomic weight elements and their Lewis base adducts; organometallic chemistry of these elements; phosphonitriles; arc and glow discharge processes; degradation and flammability of polymers; mechanism of acid formation in coal mines; corrosion and oxidation inhibition in lubricating fluids; fluids-seals interactions; preceramic polymers and ceramics. *Mailing Add:* 17 Shooting Star Irvine CA 92714

KRATZKE, THOMAS MARTIN, STATISTICS, COMPUTER SCIENCE. *Current Pos:* ANALYST, METRON, INC, 88- *Personal Data:* b Seattle, Wash, Oct 29, 53; m 79; c 3. *Educ:* Pac Lutheran Univ, BS, 75; Wash State Univ, MA, 78; Univ Ill, Urbana-Champaign, PhD(math), 88. *Prof Exp:* Adv mem tech staff, Boeing Computer Serv, 78-80; statistician, Rockwell Hanford Opers, 80-82; teaching & res asst, Math Dept, Univ Ill, 82-88. *Mem:* Soc Indust & Appl Math; Discrete Math Activ Group. *Res:* Bayesian updating algorithm for use in anti-submarine warfare on different computers. *Mailing Add:* 2373 Old Trail Dr Reston VA 20191

KRAUEL, DAVID PAUL, TURBULENT DIFFUSION, WIND-WAVE MODELLING. *Current Pos:* asst prof, 74-79, head, Physics Dept, 81-88 ASSOC PROF PHYS OCEANOG, ROYAL ROADS MIL COL, 79-, DEAN GRAD STUDIES, 88- *Personal Data:* b Kitchener, Ont, Nov 20, 44; m 69; c 2. *Educ:* McMaster Univ, BSc, 66; Dalhousie Univ, MSc, 69; Liverpool Univ, PhD(phys oceanog), 72. *Prof Exp:* Res scientist coastal oceanog, Bedford Inst Oceanog, 66-74. *Concurrent Pos:* Consult, 79- *Mem:* Am Geophys Union; Can Meteorol & Oceanog Soc; Estuarine & Brackish-Water Sci Asn. *Res:* Modelling turbulent diffusion in coastal waters and wind-wave hindcast modelling; estuarine circulation; the effects of flux of wave energy on coastlines and coastal structures. *Mailing Add:* Royal Roads Univ 2005 Sooke Rd Victoria BC V9B 5Y2 Can

KRAUS, ALFRED ANDREW, JR, PHYSICS. *Current Pos:* RETIRED. *Personal Data:* b Richmond, Calif, May 24, 25; m 49; c 4. *Educ:* Mass Inst Technol, BS, 49; Calif Inst Technol, PhD(physics), 53. *Prof Exp:* Asst, Calif Inst Technol, 50-52; res assoc nuclear physics, Rice Univ, 53-55; from res assoc to instr physics, Univ Pac, 55-61, chmn dept, 56-61; from assoc prof to prof, NMex Highlands Univ, 61-64, chmn, Dept Physics & Math, 63-64; phys sci proj dir, Killgore Res Ctr, WTex State Univ, 64-65 & 67-68, dir, 65-67, prof physics, 64-68; owner, Canyon Res Co, 68-88. *Concurrent Pos:* Radiol physicist, San Joaquin Gen Hosp, 57-60. *Mem:* Am Phys Soc. *Res:* Nuclear physics; computers; relativistic astrophysics. *Mailing Add:* 5201 Roma Ave NE Albuquerque NM 87108

KRAUS, ALFRED PAUL, MEDICINE. *Current Pos:* from asst prof to prof, Univ Tenn, Memphis, 53-81, chief sect hemat, 64-81, dir, Ctr Res & Serv Sickle Cell Dis, 74-79, EMER PROF MED, COL MED, UNIV TENN, MEMPHIS, 81- *Personal Data:* b Vienna, Austria, June 24, 16; nat US; m 44; c 2. *Educ:* Univ Chicago, MD, 41. *Prof Exp:* Intern, Michael Reese Hosp, Ill, 41-42, asst resident & resident internal med, 42-44, resident dept hemat res, 48; chief hemat sect, Vet Admin Hosp, Ala, 49; asst chief, Kennedy Vet Admin Hosp, Tenn, 50-52. *Concurrent Pos:* Consult hematologist, Baptist Mem Hosp, 53-, Le Bonheur Children's Hosp, Methodist Hosp & St Joseph's Hosp; vis asst prof, Univ Indonesia, 55-56; investr natural hist sickle cell dis, 79- *Mem:* AAAS; Am Soc Hemat; fel AMA; fel Am Col Physicians; Am Fedn Clin Res. *Res:* Hematology; sickle cell disease; abnormal hemoglobins; hemorrhagic diseases; red cell enzymes. *Mailing Add:* 1597 Peabody Ave Memphis TN 38104

KRAUS, ARTHUR SAMUEL, EPIDEMIOLOGY. *Current Pos:* RETIRED. *Personal Data:* b New York, NY, Aug 2, 25; m 46; c 3. *Educ:* City Col New York, BS, 49; Columbia Univ, MS, 53; Univ Pittsburgh, ScD(biostatist), 58. *Prof Exp:* Biostatistician, NY State Dept Health, 50-57; chief, Div Statist, Res & Rec, Md State Dept Health, 58-62; asst dir, Off Res, New York City Dept Health, 62-65; head dept biostatist, Montefiore Hosp & Med Ctr, Bronx, NY, 65-66; prof biostatist, Dept Community Health & Epidemiol, Queen Univ Ont, 66-85, prof & coordr grad studies, 85-90. *Concurrent Pos:* Consult biostatist, Ont Dept Health, 66- *Mem:* Fel Am Pub Health Asn; Am Heart Asn; Can Pub Health Asn; Soc Epidemiol Res. *Res:* Epidemiologic and health care studies, particularly regarding the elderly and conditions which are disabling to them, such as stroke, dementia, incontinence, deafness and depression. *Mailing Add:* 163 Casterton Ave Kingston ON K7M 1R9 Can

KRAUS, ERIC BRADSHAW, ATMOSPHERE-OCEAN INTERACTION. *Current Pos:* prof, Univ Miami, 66-77, Div Atmospheric Sci, 69-77, dir, Coop Inst Marine & Atmospheric Studies, 77-81, EMER PROF METEOROL & PHYS OCEANOG, UNIV MIAMI, 81- *Personal Data:* b Liberec, Czech, Mar 22, 12; m 42, Heather Johnson; c Nigel, Sibella & Deborah. *Educ:* Charles Univ, Prague, PhD(geophysics), 46. *Hon Degrees:* ScD, Univ Liege, Belg, 92. *Honors & Awards:* Mem prize, Royal Meteorol Soc. *Prof Exp:* Sr res officer, Div Radiophysics, Commonwealth Sci & Indust Res Orgn, Australia, 46-49; authority meteorologist, Snowy Mt, Hydro-Elec Authority, 52-61; sr scientist, Woods Hole Oceanog Inst, 61-66; sr res assoc, Coop Inst Res Environ Sci, 81-89. *Concurrent Pos:* Lectr, Univ Sydney, 47-51; mem, Australian Nat Comt Geophys & Geod, 49-55; convener sub-comt oceanog, 52-55; chief, UN tech assistance mission, Nairobi, Kenya, 55-56; mem panel water resources develop, World Meteorol Orgn, 55-56; adj prof, Yale Univ, 61-63; dir, NATO Atmospheric Studies Inst, Urbino Italy 75, trustee, Univ Corp Atmospheric Res, 74-80, dir NATO Atmospheric Res Inst, Bonas, France, 81; vis prof, Paris, France, 81, Monash Univ, Melbourne, Australia, 83, Univ Liege, Belgium, 87, India Nat Inst Oceanog Soc, Indian, 88. *Mem:* Fel Am Meteorol Soc; Am Geophys Union; fel Royal Meteorol Soc; fel AAAS. *Res:* Symmetry Breaks and resulting progressive growth of Organized Diversity; author of 200 papers and several books on Atmosphere-Ocean Interaction and Climate; coberent structures in fluids. *Mailing Add:* 610 Orchard St Ashland OR 97520. *E-Mail:* 73114.701@compuserve.com

KRAUS, GEORGE ANDREW, ORGANIC CHEMISTRY. *Current Pos:* From asst prof to assoc prof, 76-86, PROF, DEPT CHEM, IOWA STATE UNIV, 86-, CHMN DEPT, 93- *Personal Data:* b Buffalo, NY, June 28, 50; m 85; c 2. *Educ:* Univ Rochester, BS, 72; Columbia Univ, PhD(chem), 76. *Concurrent Pos:* DuPont young fac grant, 76-78; 3M Young Fac grant, 81-82. *Mem:* AAAS; Am Chem Soc; fel The Chem Soc. *Res:* Active in the development of new synthetic methods and the application of these methods to the total synthesis of natural products; interests include kinetic anions, photochemistry and thermal chemistry; research on antiprotozoan diseases, suicide enzyme inhibitors and antiretroviral drugs; author of 147 publications. *Mailing Add:* Dept Chem Iowa State Univ Ames IA 50011

KRAUS, HUBERT ADOLPH, QUANTUM CHEMISTRY, THEORETICAL PHYSICS. *Current Pos:* RETIRED. *Personal Data:* b Graz, Austria, Nov 28, 07; nat US; m 29, Ersilia Z Petku; c Hubert & Zili. *Educ:* Drexel Inst, Philadelphia, Pa, BS, 28; City Col NY, MS, 34. *Prof Exp:* Consult protective coatings, Durok Bldg Mat, Inc, Hastings-on-Hudson, NY, 59-81; assoc prof chem, Burlington Community Col, 71-73. *Mem:* Am Chem Soc; AAAS; Am Inst Chemists; Int Union Pure & Appl Chem; NY Acad Sci. *Res:* Protective coating components and products; the twelve basic physical charges. *Mailing Add:* 833 Drexel Ave Cinnaminson NJ 08077

KRAUS, JAMES ELLSWORTH, HORTICULTURE. *Current Pos:* assoc horticulturist, Univ Idaho, 45-47, horticulturist, Agr Exp Sta, 48-49, prof hort & head dept, 48-49, prof plant sci, 49-72, assoc dir, 49-55, dir, Agr Exp Sta & Agr Exten Serv & dean, Col Agr, 55-72, EMER DEAN COL AGR & EMER PROF PLANT SCI, UNIV IDAHO, 72- *Personal Data:* b Rocky Ford, Colo, Nov 19, 09; m 35, Barbara J; c 1. *Educ:* Colo State Col, BS, 32; Univ Wis, MS, 34; Cornell Univ, PhD(veg crops), 40. *Hon Degrees:* Prof, Univ Ecuador, SAm, 56; DSc, Univ Idaho, 83. *Prof Exp:* Asst hort, Univ Wis, 33-34; asst veg crops, Cornell Univ, 39-40; asst physiologist, Bur Plant Indust, USDA, 36-41; assoc horticulturist, Aberdeen Br Exp Sta, Idaho, 41-44; plant breeder, Calif Packing Corp, Ill, 44-45. *Mem:* Sigma Xi. *Res:* Culture and physiology of potatoes; genetics and breeding hybrid onions; culture and physiology of freezing and canning crops; vegetable seed production. *Mailing Add:* 536 N Eisenhower St Moscow ID 83843

KRAUS, JESS F, EPIDEMIOLOGY, ENVIRONMENTAL HEALTH. *Current Pos:* from asst prof to assoc prof community health, Sch Med, Univ Calif, Davis, 69-80, prof, 80-, AT DEPT PUB HEALTH, UNIV CALIF, LOS ANGELES. *Personal Data:* b Los Angeles, Calif, Apr 4, 36; m 57; c 5. *Educ:* Sacramento State Col, BA, 59, MS, 63; Univ Calif, Berkeley, MPH, 64; Univ Minn, Minneapolis, PhD(environ epidemiol), 67. *Prof Exp:* Instr epidemiol & environ health, Univ Minn, 67-68; adj asst prof, Univ Cincinnati, 68-69. *Concurrent Pos:* Chief environ epidemiol, USPHS, 68-69, epidemiologist, Bur Environ Mgt, 69-71; fel coun epidemiol, Am Heart Asn. *Mem:* Am Pub Health Asn; Soc Epidemiol Res; Asn Teachers Prev Med. *Res:* Design and execution of community and epidemiologic research involving the interrelationship of man with his physical environment. *Mailing Add:* Dept Epidemiol Univ Calif Los Angeles 405 Hilgard Ave Los Angeles CA 90024-1301

KRAUS, JOHN DANIEL, ELECTRICAL ENGINEERING, ASTRONOMY. *Current Pos:* from assoc prof to prof elec eng, Ohio State Univ, 46-71, dir, Radio Observ, 52-80, Taine G McDougal prof elec eng & astron, 71-80, EMER PROF ELEC ENG & ASTRON, OHIO STATE UNIV, 80- *Personal Data:* b Ann Arbor, Mich, June 28, 10; m 41; c 2. *Educ:* Univ Mich, BS, 30, MS, 31, PhD(physics), 33. *Honors & Awards:* Sullivan Medal, Inst Elec & Electronics Engrs, 78, Edison Medal, 84 & 85, Heinrich Hertz Medal, 90. *Prof Exp:* Asst physics, Univ Mich, 31-32, res assoc, Dept Eng Res, 34-35, res physicist, Dept Physics, 36-37; res physicist, Physicist Res Co, 37-38; independent res & consult, Ann Arbor, 38-40; physicist, Naval Ord Lab, 40-43; res assoc, Radio Res Lab, Harvard Univ, 43-46. *Mem:* Nat Acad Eng; Am Phys Soc; Am Astron Soc; Inst Elec & Electronics Engrs. *Res:* Electromagnetic theory; antennas; radio astronomy; author of several textbooks. *Mailing Add:* 1854 Home Rd Delaware OH 43015

KRAUS, JOHN FRANKLYN, FOREST GENETICS. *Current Pos:* RETIRED. *Personal Data:* b Brooklyn, NY, Nov 12, 29; m 57, Jeanie A Bell; c John II, Brenda, Rachel, Erica & Kirstin. *Educ:* Univ Mich, BSF, 53, MF, 56; Univ Minn, PhD(forestry), 66. *Prof Exp:* Res forester, Southeastern Forest Exp Sta, US Forest Serv, 56-64, plant geneticist, 64-72, plant geneticist, Ga Forestry Ctr, 72-86. *Mem:* AAAS; Soc Am Foresters; Sigma Xi. *Res:* Breeding improved strains of southern pines. *Mailing Add:* 1211 Timberlane Dr Macon GA 31210

KRAUS, JON ERIC, FUNCTIONAL ANALYSIS, OPERATOR ALGEBRAS. *Current Pos:* Hill res instr, 77-79, from asst prof to assoc prof, 79-95, PROF MATH, STATE UNIV NY, BUFFALO, 95- *Personal Data:* b Cambridge, Mass, May 16, 51; m 77, Veronica Fabian; c Rebecca & Jeffrey. *Educ:* Univ Calif, Santa Barbara, BA, 72; Univ Calif, Berkeley, MA, 75,

PhD(math), 77. *Mem:* Am Math Soc. *Res:* Operator algebras including von Neumann, C-algebras and reflexive algebras; noncommutative dynamical systems. *Mailing Add:* Dept Math State Univ NY 106 Diefendorf Hall Buffalo NY 14214. *E-Mail:* mthjekg@csu.buffalo.edu

KRAUS, KENNETH WAYNE, ORGANIC CHEMISTRY. *Current Pos:* From asst prof to assoc prof, 60-72, chmn dept, 65-69 & 70-71, PROF CHEM, LORAS COL, 72- VPRES ACAD AFFAIRS, 87- *Personal Data:* b Waterloo, Iowa, Oct 20, 35; m 56; c 4. *Educ:* Loras Col, BS, 57; Univ Calif, Berkeley, PhD(chem), 60. *Concurrent Pos:* NSF grant, 64-66; lectr, Dept Chem, Calif State Col Long Beach, 69-70. *Mem:* Am Chem Soc. *Res:* Mechanism and use of the reaction of organocadmium reagents with acid chlorides, dipole moments, syntheses and structure proof. *Mailing Add:* Dept Chem Loras Col Dubuque IA 52001-4399

KRAUS, LORRAINE MARQUARDT, BIOCHEMISTRY. *Current Pos:* res assoc, Univ Tenn, Memphis, 57-60, from asst prof to assoc prof, 60-72, chair, Dept Biochem, 82-84, PROF BIOCHEM, CTR HEALTH SCI, UNIV TENN, MEMPHIS, 72- *Personal Data:* b Suffern, NY, Sept 6, 22; m 44; c 2. *Educ:* Mt Mary Col, BS, 43; Univ Tenn, MS, 52, PhD, 56; Memphis Col Art, BFA, 82. *Prof Exp:* Res technician, Dept Endocrinol & Metab Dis, Michael Reese Hosp, 43-44, 48; instr chem, Univ Indonesia, 55-56. *Concurrent Pos:* Mem, Blood Dis & Resources Adv Comt, Blood Div, Nat Heart, Lung & Blood Inst, 79-83. *Mem:* Int Soc Hemat; Am Chem Soc; Am Soc Hemat; Am Soc Human Genetics; Am Soc Biol Chemists; Sigma Xi. *Res:* Biosynthesis of abnormal human hemoglobins; erythropoietin; tissue culture of hemic cells; immunochemistry; chemistry of sickle cell disease; carbamoylation of amino acids and proteins in renal diseases. *Mailing Add:* Dept Biochem Univ Tenn Med Units 800 Madison Ave Memphis TN 38163-0001. *Fax:* 901-448-5513

KRAUS, OLEN, PHYSICS. *Current Pos:* chmn dept, 67-77, PROF PHYSICS, UNIV NDAK, 67-, ASSOC DEAN, COL ARTS & SCI, 77- *Personal Data:* b Berwick, Pa, Apr 7, 24; m 46; c 2. *Educ:* Pa State Univ, BS, 50; Mich State Univ, MS, 52, PhD(physics), 65. *Prof Exp:* Physicist, Nat Bur Stand, 55-62; chmn, Dept Physics, Univ SDak, 62-67. *Mem:* Am Phys Soc; Am Asn Physics Teachers. *Res:* Nuclear magnetic resonance; quantum mechanics; mathematical physics; electron resonance. *Mailing Add:* 2614 Olive St Grand Forks ND 58201

KRAUS, SAMUEL, AEROTHERMODYNAMICS, FLUID MECHANICS. *Current Pos:* RETIRED. *Personal Data:* b Irvington, NJ, Mar 15, 25; m 54, Joan D Bramson; c Barbara D, Edward O & Russell A. *Educ:* Rensselaer Polytech Inst, BAeroEng, 44, MAeroEng, 49. *Prof Exp:* Jr engr, preliminary aeronaut design, propeller div, Curtiss-Wright Corp, 46-47; aeronaut res engr, Ames Res Ctr, NASA, 49-62; res specialist, space div, 62-67, lead engr, S-II aerothermodynamics, 67-69; lead engr, 69-, mem tech staff, Shuttle Aerodynamic Loads, 69-85; prin eng specialist, gas dynamics, shuttle aerodyn, aero sci, Space Transp Systs Div, Rockwell Int Corp, 85-90. *Mem:* Assoc fel Am Inst Aeronaut & Astronaut; Sigma Xi. *Res:* Experimental and theoretical research in aerothermodynamics; planning, development and utilization of corporate experimental facilities; preflight prediction and postflight verification of aerospace vehicle environment; ignition overpressure; wake recirculation; venting of aerospace vehicles; free molecular flow forces. *Mailing Add:* 6108 Monero Dr Rancho Palos Verdes CA 90275-3319

KRAUS, SHIRLEY RUTH, CLINICAL PHARMACOLOGY. *Current Pos:* assoc prof pharmacol, Long Island Univ, prof, Brooklyn Col Pharm, 65-75, prof pharmacol & physiol, 75-82, dir, Div Pharmacotherapeut & Health Sci, 79-82, EMER PROF PHARMACOL & PHYSIOL, ARNOLD & MARIE SCHWARTZ COL PHARM & HEALTH SCI, LONG ISLAND UNIV, 82- *Personal Data:* b New York, NY, Dec 24, 19; m 46; c 2. *Educ:* Hunter Col, BA, 40; Cornell Univ, MA, 42; Univ Ill, PhD(physiol), 46. *Hon Degrees:* DSc, Arnold & Marie Schwartz Col Pharm & Health Sci, Long Island Univ, 96. *Prof Exp:* Asst, Dept Exp Biol, Am Mus Natural Hist, NY, 40-41; hematologist, Jewish Mem Hosp, 41; asst biol & chem, Adelphi Col, 42-43, instr, Sch Nursing, 43; asst, Dept Zool & Physiol, Univ Ill, 43-46; high sch teacher, 46-47; physiologist, Gastroenterol Res Lab, Mt Sinai Hosp, 47-48; biochemist, Cancer Res Found, Harlem Hosp, 48-50; lectr physiol, Col Dent, NY Univ, 50-51; pharmacologist, Cancer Res & Metab Unit, Mt Alto Hosp, Washington, DC, 51-53; instr pharmacol, Sch Med, Howard Univ, 55-56. *Concurrent Pos:* Instr, Eve Sch, Brooklyn Col, 47-48; assoc prof, Downstate Med Ctr, State Univ NY, 69-70; vis fel clin pharmacol, Med Col, Cornell Univ, 77-78; mem, Instnl Rev Bd, Clin Drug Investr Inc, 81; vis prof physiol & pharmacol, NY Col Pediat Med, 83-84. *Mem:* Soc Exp Biol & Med; Endocrine Soc; Am Physiol Soc; Am Soc Pharmacol & Exp Therapeut; Am Soc Clin Pharmacol & Therepeut; fel Am Col Clin Pharmacol. *Res:* Alloxan diabetes-anaphylaxis and granuloma pouch formation; pituitary-adrenal stress response in alloxan diabetes; anti-estrogenic action of B glycyrrhetinic acid; hyperthermia on blood platelets in male rats; corticosterone and adrenocorticotropic hormone in alloxan diabetic rats. *Mailing Add:* 13901 Coolidge Ave Jamaica NY 11435. *Fax:* 718-261-9589

KRAUS, WILLIAM LUDWIG, cardiology; deceased, see previous edition for last biography

KRAUSCHE, DOLORES SMOLENY, PHYSICS, ELECTRICAL ENGINEERING. *Current Pos:* Res asst radioastron, 65-75, fel physics, 76-77, RES PHYSICIST, UNIV FLA, 78- *Personal Data:* b Cleveland, Ohio, Jan 27, 42. *Educ:* Univ Fla, BS, 65, MS, 67, BSEE, 67, PhD(physics, astron), 75. *Concurrent Pos:* Interim engr, Electronic Commun Inc, 67; prin staff mem, Oper Res Inc, 78- *Mem:* Am Astron Soc; assoc mem Sigma Xi; assoc mem Inst Atmospheric Optics & Remote Sensing. *Res:* Electromagnetic phenomena relating to engineering problems and astronomical research. *Mailing Add:* PO Box 271 Gainesville FL 32602-0271

KRAUSE, BRIAN ROBERT, MEDICAL RESEARCH. *Current Pos:* Sr scientist athero-pharmacol, Warner Lambert/Parke-Davis, 82-85, res assoc, 85-89, sr res assoc, 89-90, ASSOC RES FEL PHARMACOL, WARNER LAMBERT/PARKE-DAVIS, 90- *Personal Data:* b Dec 2, 1949; m 76, Lisa; c Christopher, Matthew & Kara. *Educ:* Univ Ill, BS, 72; La State Univ Med Ctr, PhD, 78. *Honors & Awards:* Am Soc Pharmacol & Exp Therapeut; Am Physiol Soc; Am Heart Asn Coun Aerteriosclerosis. *Prof Exp:* Teaching asst, Univ Ill Med Ctr, 73-75, trainee pharmacol, 75-76; trainee physiol, La State Univ Med Ctr, 76-79, asst prof physiol, 81-82; res fel, NIH, 79-81. *Res:* Lipoprotein metabolism. *Mailing Add:* Warner-Lambert/Parke Davis Astherosclerosis Therapeutics 2800 Plymouth Rd Ann Arbor MI 48105-2430

KRAUSE, DANIEL, JR, CHEMICAL OCEANOGRAPHY. *Current Pos:* RES ASSOC OCEANOG, AMHERST COL, 72- *Personal Data:* b Sudbury, Mass, Feb 21, 45; m 75. *Educ:* Univ Mass, BS, 66, PhD(physics), 72. *Mem:* Sigma Xi; Am Phys Soc; Am Geophys Union. *Res:* Mass spectrometric and gasometric studies of gases dissolved in water. *Mailing Add:* 734 Bay Rd Amherst MA 01002-3544

KRAUSE, DAVID WILFRED, ANATOMY. *Current Pos:* From asst prof to assoc prof, 82-93, PROF ANAT, STATE UNIV NY, STONY BROOK, 93- *Personal Data:* b Medicine Hat, Alta, Feb 15, 50; m 78, Susan M Knispel; c Wyatt M & Tyler M. *Educ:* Univ Alta, BSc, 71, MSc, 76; Univ Mich, PhD(geol), 82. *Honors & Awards:* Anna M Jackson Award, Am Soc Mammalogists, 81. *Concurrent Pos:* Res assoc, Mus Rockies, Bozeman, Mont, 85- *Mem:* Am Soc Mammalogists; Paleont Soc; Sigma Xi; Soc Syst Zool; Soc Vert Paleont; AAAS. *Res:* Evolution of late Mesozoic and early Cenozoic vertebrates, particularly mammals, and the form and function of the mammalian dentition and postcranial skeleton. *Mailing Add:* Dept Anat Sci State Univ NY Health Sci Col Med 100 Nicholls Rd Stony Brook NY 11794-0001. *Fax:* 516-444-3947; *E-Mail:* dkrause@epo.som.sunysb.edu

KRAUSE, ELIOT, POPULATION GENETICS, BIOSTATISTICS. *Current Pos:* instr, Seton Hall Univ, 65-68, grad biol adv, 77-88, dept chmn, 88-89, ASST PROF BIOL, SETON HALL UNIV, 68- *Personal Data:* b New York, NY, June 7, 38; m 59; c 3. *Educ:* Cornell Univ, BS, 60; Purdue Univ, MS, 63, PhD(genetics), 68. *Prof Exp:* Res asst pop genetics, Purdue Univ, 60-65. *Mem:* AAAS; Genetics Soc Am; Biomet Soc; Am Genetic Asn; Sigma Xi. *Res:* Cytogenetic research with various mutagens using human lymphocytes as detected by sister chromatic exchange; selection of quantitative traits in Tribolium castaneum using genotype-environment, nutrition, interactions; study of cannibalism and competitive factors which affect population size in Tribolium; study of fragile sites in cytogenetics. *Mailing Add:* Dept Biol Seton Hall Univ South Orange NJ 07079

KRAUSE, EUGENE FRANKLIN, MATHEMATICS. *Current Pos:* From instr to assoc prof, 63-76, PROF MATH, UNIV MICH, ANN ARBOR, 76- *Personal Data:* b Kenosha, Wis, Apr 7, 37; m 59; c 2. *Educ:* Univ Wis, BS, 59, MA, 60, PhD(math), 63. *Mem:* Nat Coun Teachers Math. *Res:* Mathematics education. *Mailing Add:* Dept Math Univ Mich Main Campus Ann Arbor MI 48109

KRAUSE, HELMUT G L, LOW DENSITY AERODYNAMICS, THERMODYNAMICS. *Current Pos:* RETIRED. *Personal Data:* b Koenigsberg, Ger, Nov 10, 11, US citizen; m 55; c 1. *Educ:* Albertus Univ, Ger, PhD(astron), 38. *Honors & Awards:* Ernst Heinckel Space Flight Award, 51. *Prof Exp:* Sci res asst, Koenigsberg Univ Observ, 37-44; res scientist, Inst Ballistics, Ger Air Force Acad, 44-45 & Carl Zeiss Optical Factory, 45-47; sci res asst, Inst Theoret Physics, Univ Jena, 47 & Hamburg Univ Observ, 47-48; tech physicist, Glycerine & Aliphatic Acid Factory, 49-50; dep chief, Astronaut Res Inst, Univ Stuttgart, 51-54; sr res scientist, Res Inst Physics Jet Propulsion, 54-57; spec asst space sci, Army Ballistic Missile Agency, Ala, 57-60; sci adv studies off, Marshall Space Flight Ctr, NASA, 60-65, sci adv to dir aero-astrodyn lab, 65-74; mgr bur anal res, 75-78; aerospace scientist, Marshall Space Flight Ctr, NASA, 78-89. *Mem:* Assoc fel Am Inst Aeronaut & Astronaut; sr mem Am Astronaut Soc; Am Astron Soc; fel Brit Interplanetary Soc; Ger Soc Rocket & Space Flight. *Res:* Rocket ballistics, space mechanics and astronautical sciences; first-order perturbation theory used for Explorer I and Vanguard I; author or coauthor of 50 scientific publications. *Mailing Add:* 2718 Briarwood Dr Huntsville AL 35801

KRAUSE, HERBERT FRANCIS, ATOMIC PHYSICS, CHEMICAL PHYSICS, LASER PHYSICS. *Current Pos:* SR RES PHYSICIST, OAK RIDGE NAT LAB, 71- *Personal Data:* b Woodbury, NJ, Mar 10, 42; m 70, Carolyn Hay; c Stephen A & Diane E. *Educ:* Drexel Univ, BS, 65; Univ Pittsburgh, PhD(physics), 71. *Concurrent Pos:* Pvt computer consult. *Mem:* Am Phys Soc; Am Asn Physics Teachers; AAAS; Sigma Xi. *Res:* Atomic and molecular beam research; thermal-high energies, laser spectroscopy; molecular dynamics studies involving inner and outer shell excited species; high energy and ultra-relativistic atomic physics and particle solid interactions. *Mailing Add:* 1068 W Outer Dr Oak Ridge TN 37830. *Fax:* 423-574-1188; *E-Mail:* krause@orph01.phy.ornl.gov

KRAUSE, HORATIO HENRY, ANALYTICAL CHEMISTRY. *Current Pos:* RETIRED. *Personal Data:* b St Paul, Minn, Oct 11, 18; m 50, Marguerite Gerdes; c Gregory & Marcia. *Educ:* St Mary's Col Minn, BS, 39; Univ Minn, PhD(chem), 55. *Prof Exp:* Teacher pvt sch, 39-43; instr chem & physics, De LaSalle Mil Acad, 43-48; asst, Univ Minn, 49-54; prin chemist, Battelle Mem Inst, 55-57; proj leader chem, 57-62, sr chemist, 62-70, prin res scientist, 70-80, sr res scientist, 80-94. *Mem:* AAAS; Am Chem Soc; Am Soc Mech Eng; Nat Asn Corrosion Engrs; Sigma Xi. *Res:* High temperature chemistry, deposits and corrosion in boilers and incinerators; molten salts; solid propellants; air pollution; sulfur oxides. *Mailing Add:* 4254 Lyon Dr Columbus OH 43220

KRAUSE, IRVIN, MECHANICAL ENGINEERING. *Current Pos:* dir, Comput Integrated Mfg, 85-86 MANAGING PARTNER, CTR MFG TECHNOL, COOPERS & LYBRAND, 86-; VPRES MERITUS CONSULT SERV, 91-. *Personal Data:* b New York, NY, July 18, 32; m 53; c 3. *Educ:* City Col New York, BME, 54; Columbia Univ, MS, 55; NY Univ, EngScD(mech eng), 60. *Prof Exp:* Lectr graphics, City Col New York, 54-59; asst mech eng, NY Univ, 59-60; res scientist, Res Div, American-Standard Corp, 60-63; assoc prof mech eng & dir mat labs, Fairleigh Dickinson Univ, 63-66; chief res & develop, Diehl Div, Singer Co, 66-70, mgr eng, Indust Prod Div, 70-76; dir eng, Acushnet Co, 76-78; mgr, Mfg Technol, Arthur D Little, Inc, 78-81, tech dir, Comput Integrated Mfg, 81-85. *Concurrent Pos:* NSF fel, 59; consult, Army Res Off NC, 64-. *Mem:* AAAS; Am Soc Mech Engrs; Sigma Xi; Soc Mfg Engrs. *Res:* Visco-elastic behavior of polymeric materials; fracture in brittle materials; kinematics and mechanism synthesis; tunnel diode accelerometers; laser system metrology; electric motors and controls; automated production systems; computerization and automation as applied to the design and manufacturing activities in industry; benchmarking research and development productivity. *Mailing Add:* 1 Seaward Lane South Dartmouth MA 02748

KRAUSE, JOSEF GERALD, ORGANIC CHEMISTRY. *Current Pos:* PROF CHEM, NIAGARA UNIV, 68-. *Personal Data:* b Kearny, NJ, Mar 21, 42; m 63; c 2. *Educ:* Hobart Col, BS, 63; Northeastern Univ, PhD(org chem), 67. *Prof Exp:* NSF res fel org chem, Univ Mass, 67-68. *Concurrent Pos:* Sigma Xi res grant-in-aid, Niagara Univ, 68-69. *Mem:* Am Chem Soc. *Res:* Organic nitrogen compounds; organic synthesis; reaction mechanisms; bicyclic ring systems. *Mailing Add:* 829 92nd St Niagara Falls NY 14304

KRAUSE, LEONARD ANTHONY, BIOCHEMISTRY. *Current Pos:* mgr environ hyg serv, 63-75, DIR ENVIRON HYG & TOXICOL, OLIN CORP, 75-. *Personal Data:* b Hartford, Conn, May 13, 25; m 55, 68; c 4. *Educ:* Univ Conn, BA, 50, MS, 51; Univ Cincinnati, ScD(indust health, med), 62; Am Bd Indust Hyg, dipl. *Prof Exp:* Instr physiol & zool, Univ Conn, 49-51; biochemist-indust hygienist, Bur Labs, Conn, 51-55, sr indust hygienist, 56-59; Virginia, chief indust hyg-air pollution, Resources Res, DC, 61-62; dir environ hyg, Nat Insts Health, 62-63. *Concurrent Pos:* Instr environ sci, Middlesex Coun Col, 66-75; dir, Chem Indust Inst Toxicol. *Mem:* AAAS; Am Indust Hyg Asn; Air Pollution Control Asn; Am Pub Health Asn; Chem Indust Inst Toxicol. *Res:* Physiology of invertebrates; aspects of metal fume fever; use of vaporphase chromatography; insecticides and effects on human metabolism. *Mailing Add:* 19 Wellsweep Rd Branford CT 06405

KRAUSE, LLOYD O(SCAR), ELECTRICAL ENGINEERING. *Current Pos:* systs analyst, Space Div, 76-84, PRIN ENG SPECIALIST, SATELLITE SYSTS DIV, ROCKWELL INT CORP, 84-. *Personal Data:* b Hamburg, Wis, Oct 23, 18; m 42; c 2. *Educ:* Rose-Hulman Inst Technol, BS, 40; Syracuse Univ, MEE, 64, PhD(elec eng), 66. *Honors & Awards:* Coffin Award, Gen Elec Co, 53. *Prof Exp:* Test engr, Gen Elec Co, 40-41, prog engr, 41-43, develop engr, 43-47, proj engr, 47-52, asst sect engr, 52-53, mgr elec eng, 53-63, consult eng, 63-67; tech adv, Autonetics Div, NAm Rockwell Corp, 67-76. *Mem:* Sigma Xi; Electronic Industs Asn; Inst Elec & Electronics Engrs; Nat Soc Prof Engrs. *Res:* Radio frequency and microwave radiators; antennas; transmission lines and networks; solid state microwave; paramagnetic amplifiers; phase shifters; switches; ferrites; ferroelectrics; ground screens; electronic systems; computer reliability; correlation loops; low angle radiation; satellite sensors; navigation error analysis; adaptive arrays and noise filtering; coding and data compression; probability estimation and system simulation. *Mailing Add:* 4015 Topside Lane Corona Del Mar CA 92625

KRAUSE, LUCJAN, PHYSICS, ATOMIC & MOLECULAR COLLISIONS & SPECTROSCOPY. *Current Pos:* head dept, 59-83, prof, 63-93, EMER PROF PHYSICS, UNIV WINDSOR, 93-. *Personal Data:* b Poznan, Poland, Jan 8, 28; nat Can; m 50; c 6. *Educ:* Univ London, BSc, 51, DSc(physics), 68; Univ Toronto, MA, 53, PhD(physics), 55. *Hon Degrees:* DSc, Copernicus Univ, Torun, Poland, 83. *Prof Exp:* Assoc prof physics, Mem Univ, 55-58 & Assumption Univ, 58-63. *Concurrent Pos:* Hon res fel, Univ Col, Univ London, 70-71; adj prof eng sci, Wayne State Univ, Detroit, 72-85; fel, Churchill Col, Cambridge; res fel, Japan Soc Promotion Sci, 88. *Mem:* Fel Am Phys Soc; Can Asn Physicists; fel Brit Inst Physics; Optical Soc Am. *Res:* Laser spectroscopy of atoms and molecules; sensitized fluorescence and quenching, lifetimes of excited atomic and molecular states particularly metal excimers and exciplexes. *Mailing Add:* 890 Bartlet Dr Windsor ON N9G 1V4 Can. *Fax:* 519-973-7075; *E-Mail:* f34@server.uwindsor.ca

KRAUSE, MANFRED OTTO, ATOMIC PHYSICS, CHEMICAL PHYSICS. *Current Pos:* sr scientist, 63-95, EMER SCIENTIST ELECTRON SPECTROMETRY, OAK RIDGE NAT LAB, 95-. *Personal Data:* b Stuttgart, Ger, Mar 11, 31; m 63. *Educ:* Univ Stuttgart, dipl phys, 57; Max Planck Inst, Dr rer nat, 60. *Prof Exp:* Sr scientist mass spectrometry, William H Johnston Lab, Inc, Md, 60-63. *Concurrent Pos:* Exchange prof, Lab Curie, Paris France, 75; Alexander von Humboldt awardee, Stiftung, Ger, 75-76. *Mem:* AAAS; Sigma Xi; fel Am Phys Soc. *Res:* Transuranic chemistry; electron spectrometry; x-ray analysis; photoionization; atomic and molecular physics. *Mailing Add:* Oak Ridge Nat Lab Box 2008 4500N Oak Ridge TN 37831-6201

KRAUSE, MARGARIDA OLIVEIRA, CELL BIOLOGY, GENETICS. *Current Pos:* res assoc, 66-70, assoc prof, 70-76, PROF CELL BIOL, UNIV NB, 76-. *Personal Data:* b Lisbon, Portugal, Jan 13, 31; Can citizen; m 56, Helmut H; c Henry M, George A & Edward A. *Educ:* Univ Lisbon, BSc, 53; Univ Wis, MSc, 57, PhD(cell biol), 60. *Prof Exp:* Res assoc cell biol, Univ Wis, 60-61 & Univ Toronto, 63-66. *Concurrent Pos:* Res grants, Banting Res Found, 65 & 67, Med Res Coun Can, 65-66, Nat Res Coun Can, 67-78, Nat Cancer Inst Can, 76-79 & 84-87, Cancer Res Soc Inc, 88-90, Nat Sci & Eng Res Coun Can, 78-94 & Fed Centres Excellence Prog in Insect Biotech Network, 90-94; mem, Can Nat Comt Int Union Biol Soc, 80-83, chmn, 83-86, mem int sci & technol affairs, 81-87; mem, Nat Sci & Eng Res Coun Can grant selection comts, 80-86; exchange scientists, Int Prog, Nat Res Coun, 84-87; co-chmn, Prog Comt Int Congress Cell Biol, 88. *Mem:* Biol Coun Can; Am Soc Cell Biol; Can Soc Cell Biol (pres, 84-86); Int Cell Cycle Soc. *Res:* Role of chromosomal proteins and small nuclear RNA in gene expression; c-myc promoter utilization in transformation; baculovirus-based insecticides. *Mailing Add:* Dept Biol Univ NB Fredericton NB E3B 6E1 Can. *Fax:* 506-453-3583; *E-Mail:* mkrause@unb.ca

KRAUSE, PAUL CARL, JR, ELECTRICAL ENGINEERING. *Current Pos:* PROF ELEC ENG, PURDUE UNIV, 70-. *Personal Data:* b Reynolds, Nebr, Jan 27, 32; m 53; c 4. *Educ:* Univ Nebr, BS, 56 & 57, MS, 58; Univ Kans, PhD(elec eng), 61. *Prof Exp:* Instr elec eng, Univ Kans, 58-61; res elec eng, Allis-Chalmers Mfg Co, 61-62; asst prof elec eng, Univ Wis-Milwaukee, 62-65; assoc prof, Univ Wis-Madison, 65-70. *Concurrent Pos:* Consult, Allis-Chalmers Mfg Co, 63-66. *Mem:* Sr mem Inst Elec & Electronics Engrs; Am Soc Eng Educ. *Res:* Electric machines, power systems and control systems; hybrid computer applications in analysis of systems. *Mailing Add:* Dept Elec & Comp Eng Purdue Univ West Lafayette IN 47907

KRAUSE, PAUL FREDERICK, PHYSICAL CHEMISTRY. *Current Pos:* ASST PROF CHEM, UNIV CENT ARK, 77-. *Personal Data:* b Racine, Wis, July 30, 45; m 70; c 1. *Educ:* Dubuque Univ, BS, 67; Univ Iowa, PhD(chem), 72. *Prof Exp:* Res asst chem, Univ Iowa, 68-72; res assoc, Univ Pittsburgh, 72-73; res assoc, Miami Univ, 73-74; instr, 74, teaching fel & vis asst prof chem, 74-77. *Mem:* Sigma Xi. *Res:* Molecular spectroscopy and its use for structural considerations, particularly in the solid state. *Mailing Add:* Dept Chem Univ Cent Ark 201 Donaghey Ave Conway AR 72035-5001

KRAUSE, PETER JAMES, PEDIATRICS, PEDIATRIC INFECTIOUS DISEASES. *Current Pos:* PHYSICIAN PEDIAT INFECTIOUS DIS, CONN CHILDREN'S MED CTR, SCH MED, UNIV CONN, 79-, PROF PEDIAT, 91-. *Personal Data:* b Denver, Colo, Mar 17, 45; m 75, Carol; c Rebecca, Peter & Kathleen. *Educ:* Williams Col, BA, 67; Tufts Univ Sch Med, MD, 71. *Prof Exp:* Intern/resident pediat, New Haven Hosp, Yale Univ, 71-73; resident pediat, Med Ctr, Stanford Univ, 73-74; physician pediat, US Army, Bad Kreuznach, WGer, 74-76; res fel pediat infectious dis, Med Ctr, Univ Calif, Los Angeles, 76-79. *Concurrent Pos:* Chief pediat infectious dis, Hartford Hosp, Sch Med, Univ Conn, 79-, from asst prof to assoc prof pediat, 79-91. *Mem:* Am Soc Microbiol; fel Infectious Dis Soc Am; Am Fedn Clin Res; Sigma Xi; AAAS. *Res:* Epidemiology, pathogenesis, immunology, diagnosis and treatment of human tick-borne zoonoses including babesiosis, ehrlichiosis and lyme disease; neutrophil function including: neutrophil function in neonates, neutrophil subsets. *Mailing Add:* Dept Pediat Conn Childrens Med Ctr Hartford CT 06106. *Fax:* 860-545-9371; *E-Mail:* pkrause@ccmckids.org

KRAUSE, RALPH A(LVIN), ENGINEERING. *Current Pos:* RETIRED. *Personal Data:* b San Francisco, Calif, Nov 11, 09; m 34, 76; c 4. *Educ:* Univ Calif, BA, 32. *Prof Exp:* Biophys res, Inst Exp Biol, Univ Calif, 30-33; radio engr, Remler Co, 32-37; electronic res engr, Instrumentation Res & Develop Dept, Calif Res Corp, 37-41; electronics res, Off US Secy Navy, 41-45; sci br, Off Naval Res, 45-46; asst dir, Lab Nuclear Sci & Eng, Mass Inst Technol, 46-47; asst to pres, Raytheon Mfg Co, Mass, 47-48; dir res, Stanford Res Inst, 48-54, assoc dir, 54-64; dir dept appl sci, UNESCO, 64-68; int consult, Res Anal Corp, 68-69. *Concurrent Pos:* Sr eng consult, Brookhaven Nat Lab & Res & Develop Bd. *Mem:* AAAS; Am Soc Naval Engrs; Am Nuclear Soc; Solar Energy Soc; Inst Elec & Electronics Engrs. *Res:* Laboratory organization and research administration; electronic engineering; electrical masking of nerves; electro-encephalographic equipment design; radio speech input design; acoustic engineering; magnetostrictive pressure gauges; nuclear research administration; health physics and nuclear instrumentation; radar; loran; radio and radar counter measures. *Mailing Add:* 550 Battery St Apt 2109 San Francisco CA 94111

KRAUSE, RALPH M, MATHEMATICS. *Current Pos:* PROG DIR, NSF, 62-. *Personal Data:* b New York, NY, Nov 23, 31; m 60, Marianne Schuelein; c Peter & Steven. *Educ:* Harvard Univ, BA, 53, MA, 54, PhD(math), 59. *Prof Exp:* Asst prof math, Univ Ill, 58-60 & Ill Inst Technol, 60-62. *Mem:* Am Math Soc; Math Asn Am. *Res:* Topology. *Mailing Add:* Topology & Foundations NSF 4201 Wilson Blvd Arlington VA 22230. *E-Mail:* rkrause@nsf.gov

KRAUSE, REGINALD FREDERICK, biochemistry; deceased, see previous edition for last biography

KRAUSE, RICHARD MICHAEL, MICROBIOLOGY, IMMUNOLOGY. *Current Pos:* SR SCI ADV, FOGARTY INT CTR, NIH, BETHESDA, MD, 89- *Personal Data:* b Marietta, Ohio, Jan 4, 25. *Educ:* Marietta Col, AB, 47; Case Western Res Univ, MD, 52. *Hon Degrees:* DSc, Marietta Col, 78, Sch Med & Dent, Univ Rochester, 79, Med Col Ohio, 81, Hahnemann Med Col & Hosp, 82; LLD, Thomas Jefferson Univ, 82. *Honors & Awards:* Robert Koch Gold Medal, 84; Humboldt Award, 86. *Prof Exp:* Intern med, Barnes Hosp, 52-53, asst resident, 53-54; asst, Rockefeller Inst, 54-57, from asst prof to assoc prof, 57-62; from assoc prof to prof epidemiol, Sch Med, Wash Univ, 62-66; from assoc prof to prof microbiol & immunol & sr physician, Univ Hosp, Rockefeller Univ, 66-75, adj prof, 75-; dir, Nat Inst Allergy & Infectious Dis, 75-84, asst surgeon gen, 77-84; Woodruff prof med & dean, Sch Med, Emory Univ, 84-89. *Concurrent Pos:* Mem, Coun Rheumatic Fever & Congenital Heart Dis & mem, Coun Epidemiol, Am Heart Asn, mem, Res Comt, 63-66; mem, Comn Streptococcal & Staphylococcal Dis, Armed Forces Epidemiol Bd, 63-72; chmn, Allergy & Immunol A Study Sect, NIH, 66-70; consult & mem, Coccal Expert Comt, WHO, 67- & mem steering comt, Biomed Sci Working Group, 78-83; mem bd dirs, NY Heart Asn, 67-73; mem, Infectious Dis Adv Comt, Nat Inst Allergy & Infectious Dis, 70-74; mem bd dirs, Royal Soc Med Found, Inc, 71-77, treas, 73-75; chmn, Bd Int Health, Inst Med, Nat Acad Sci, 84-88; chmn, Middle East Res Prog, Inst Med, 89. *Mem:* Inst Med-Nat Acad Sci; Am Soc Clin Invest; Harvey Soc; Asn Am Physicians; Am Acad Allergy; Am Acad Microbiol; fel AAAS; Am Asn Immunologists; Am Epidemiol Soc; Am Col Allergists. *Res:* Pathogenesis and epidemiology of streptococcal diseases; immunochemistry; immunogenetics; antibody structure and mechanisms that generate antibody diversity; studies on streptococcal antigens; genetic control of the immune response; author or co-author of over 150 publications and 3 books. *Mailing Add:* Fogarty Int Ctr Bldg 16 Rm 202 16 Center Dr MSC6705 Bethesda MD 20892. *Fax:* 301-496-8496; *E-Mail:* harrisos@fic16.fic.nih.gov

KRAUSE, RONALD ALFRED, INORGANIC CHEMISTRY. *Current Pos:* from asst prof to prof, 67-91, EMER PROF CHEM, UNIV CONN, 91- *Personal Data:* b Boston, Mass, Oct 30, 31; m 52, 77, Kirsten Nielsen; c 2. *Educ:* Ohio State Univ, BSc, 56, PhD(chem), 59. *Prof Exp:* Res scientist, Am Cyanamid Co, Conn, 59-62. *Concurrent Pos:* Guest prof, Univ Copenhagen, Denmark, 68-69, 76, 83 & 90; consult, Arco, 78-81. *Mem:* Am Chem Soc. *Res:* Synthesis, reactions, structure, spectra and photochemistry of coordination compounds. *Mailing Add:* PO Box 59 Williamsville VT 05362-0059. *E-Mail:* rkkrause@sover.net

KRAUSE, SONJA, PHYSICAL CHEMISTRY, POLYMER CHEMISTRY. *Current Pos:* from asst prof to assoc prof, 67-78, PROF CHEM, RENSSELAER POLYTECH INST, 78- *Personal Data:* b St Gall, Switz, Aug 10, 33; nat US; m 70, Walter W Goodwin. *Educ:* Rensselaer Polytech Inst, 54; Univ Calif, PhD(phys chem), 57. *Prof Exp:* Res chemist, Rohm & Haas Co, Pa, 57-64; US Peace Corps vol, Lagos Univ, Nigeria, 64-65 & Gondar Health Col, Ethiopia, 65-66; asst prof chem, Univ Southern Calif, 66-67. *Concurrent Pos:* Mem coun, Gordon Res Conf, 81-84; sabbatical leave, Inst Charles Sadron, Strasbourg, France, 87, Nat Res Coun; mem, Polymer Sci & Technol Comt, 91-93, Naval Res Lab Polymers Panel, 93-94. *Mem:* AAAS; Am Chem Soc; fel Am Phys Soc; NY Acad Sci. *Res:* Dilute solution properties of polymers; block copolymers; polymer compatibility; transient electric birefringence; biophysical chemistry; membranes; effects of electric fields on polymer alloys; interfaces between semicrystalline polymers. *Mailing Add:* Dept Chem Rensselaer Polytech Inst Troy NY 12180-3590. *Fax:* 518-276-4887; *E-Mail:* krauss@rpi.edu

KRAUSE, STEPHEN MYRON, CARDIAC MUSCLE BIOCHEMISTRY, MYOCARDIAL ISCHEMIA. *Personal Data:* b Grand Rapids, Mich, Apr 4, 54; m 89, Jennifer Turpin; c 2. *Educ:* Mich State Univ, BS, 76; Med Col Va, MS, 78, PhD(physiol), 83. *Prof Exp:* Fel cardiol, Johns Hopkins Med Inst, 83-86; asst prof physiol, Jefferson Med Col, Thomas Jefferson Univ, 86-91. *Mem:* Am Physiol Soc; Int Soc Heart Res; Biophys Soc; Am Heart Asn. *Res:* Understanding the subcellular alterations in calcium 2 regulation in the post-ischemic heart, focus is on sarcoplasmic reticulum function as well as contractile protein function; drug development for treatments for heart failure. *Mailing Add:* Merck Sharp & Dohme Res Labs WP46-200 West Point PA 19486. *Fax:* 215-652-3811; *E-Mail:* stephen_krause@merck.com

KRAUSE, THOMAS OTTO, THEORETICAL PHYSICS, GALACTIC STRUCTURE. *Current Pos:* ASST PROF, DEPT PHYSICS, TOWSON STATE UNIV, 76- *Personal Data:* b Grand Rapids, Mich, May 5, 44; m 82, Mary L Maguire; c Peter. *Educ:* Mass Inst Technol, BS, 66; Ohio State Univ, PhD(physics), 73. *Prof Exp:* Vis asst prof, Dept Physics, Ohio State Univ, 73-76. *Mem:* Am Phys Soc; Sigma Xi. *Res:* Theoretical astrophysics. *Mailing Add:* Dept Physics Towson State Univ Towson MD 21252. *Fax:* 410-830-3511; *E-Mail:* d7pcpy6@toe.towson.edu

KRAUSE, WILLIAM JOHN, ANATOMY, HISTOLOGY. *Current Pos:* from asst prof to assoc prof, 71-83, PROF ANAT, UNIV MO, COLUMBIA, 83- *Personal Data:* b Glasgow, Mont, Mar 24, 42; m 67; c 2. *Educ:* Augustana Col, BA, 64; Univ Iowa, MS, 66; Univ Mo, Columbia, PhD(anat), 69. *Prof Exp:* Lectr anat, Monash Univ, 69-71. *Concurrent Pos:* Vis prof, Univ Western Australia, Perth, 91 & St George's Univ, Grenada, 93; Burroughs Wellcome res travel grant, Univ Southampton, UK, 92. *Mem:* Am Asn Anatomists; Anat Soc Gt Brit & Ireland. *Res:* Postnatal development of respiratory, urinary and digestive systems; biology of Brunner's glands; distribution of heat-stable enterotoxin guanylin receptors. *Mailing Add:* Dept Anat Univ Mo Columbia MO 65202. *Fax:* 573-884-4123

KRAUS-FRIEDMANN, NAOMI, PHYSIOLOGY. *Current Pos:* from asst prof to assoc prof, 74-86, PROF PHYSIOL, SCH MED, UNIV TEX, HOUSTON, 86 - *Personal Data:* b Budapest, Hungary, July 4, 33; div; c Daphna. *Educ:* Hebrew Univ, Jerusalem, MSc, 60, PhD(biochem), 65. *Prof Exp:* Res assoc, Columbia Univ, 65-66; res assoc physiol, Vanderbilt Univ, Nashville, 66-68; instr biochem, Sch Med, Univ Pa, 68-74. *Concurrent Pos:* Vis prof, Eidgenossische Tech Hochschule, Zurich, 81-82. *Mem:* Am Soc Cell Biol. *Res:* Hormonal regulation of gluconeogenesis; role of calcium and other ions in signal transduction and regulation of metabolic processes.. *Mailing Add:* Sch Med Univ Tex PO Box 20708 Houston TX 77025. *Fax:* 713-794-1349

KRAUSHAAR, JACK JOURDAN, NUCLEAR PHYSICS. *Current Pos:* from asst prof to prof, 56-88, EMER PROF PHYSICS, UNIV COLO, BOULDER, 88- *Personal Data:* b Newark, NJ, Sept 6, 23; m 51, Nancy W Curtis; c Jeffrey C, Steven L & Matthew J. *Educ:* Lafayette Col, BS, 44; Syracuse Univ, MS, 48, PhD, 52. *Prof Exp:* Asst physics, Syracuse Univ, 46-50; res assoc nuclear spectros, Brookhaven Nat Lab, 51-53; instr physics, Stanford Univ, 53-56. *Concurrent Pos:* Fulbright award, Free Univ, Amsterdam, 67-68; fac fel, Tri-Univ Meson Facil, Univ BC, Vancouver, 78-79; vis prof, Osaka Univ, 85; mem, Rocky Flats citizen Adv Bd, 93-96. *Mem:* AAAS; fel Am Phys Soc; Fedn Am Sci. *Res:* Nuclear reactions and spectroscopy; pi meson interactions and scattering; energy and environmental problems in the United States; author. *Mailing Add:* Dept Physics Univ Colo Campus PO Box 390 Boulder CO 80309-0390. *Fax:* 303-492-7486

KRAUSHAAR, WILLIAM LESTER, PHYSICS. *Current Pos:* prof, 65-80, Max Mason prof, 80-85, EMER PROF PHYSICS, UNIV WIS-MADISON, 85- *Personal Data:* b Newark, NJ, Apr 1, 20; m 80; c 3. *Educ:* Lafayette Col, BS, 42; Cornell Univ, PhD(physics), 49. *Prof Exp:* Physicist, Nat Bur Stand, 42-45; res assoc, Mass Inst Technol, 49-51, from asst prof to prof physics, 51-65. *Mem:* Nat Acad Sci; fel Am Acad Arts & Sci; fel Am Phys Soc. *Res:* High energy astrophysics; space science; cosmic rays. *Mailing Add:* Chamberlin Hall Dept Physics Univ Wis Madison WI 53706. *Fax:* 608-238-0886

KRAUSKOPF, JOHN, PSYCHOPHYSIOLOGY. *Current Pos:* DEPT PSYCHOL, NY UNIV, 88- *Personal Data:* b New York, NY, Mar 30, 28; m 52; c 3. *Educ:* Cornell Univ, AB, 49; Univ Tex, PhD, 53. *Prof Exp:* Asst psychol, Cornell Univ, 49-50; asst, Univ Tex, 50-52, res assoc, 52-53; USPHS fel, Brown Univ, 56-57, asst prof, 57-59; asst prof, Rutgers Univ, 59-62; res assoc, Univ Md, 62-64; res scientist, Inst Behav Res, 64-66; mem tech staff, Bell Labs, 66-87. *Concurrent Pos:* Vis asst prof, Bryn Mawr Col, 59-60; mem vision comt, Armed Forces-Nat Res Coun, 60- *Mem:* Optical Soc Am. *Res:* Vision; visual perception. *Mailing Add:* Ctr Neural Sci NY Univ 4 Washington Pl Rm 809 New York NY 10003

KRAUSKOPF, KONRAD BATES, GENERAL EARTH SCIENCES. *Current Pos:* actg instr phys sci, Dept Geol, Stanford Univ, 35-39, from asst prof to assoc prof geol, 39-50, prof, 50-76, EMER PROF GEOCHEM, STANFORD UNIV, 76- *Personal Data:* b Madison, Wis, Nov 30, 10; m 36, Kathryn I McCune; c Karen (Hyde), Frances (Conley), Karl & Marion (Foerster). *Educ:* Univ Wis, AB, 31; Univ Calif, PhD(chem), 34; Stanford Univ, PhD(geol), 39. *Hon Degrees:* DSc, Univ Wis-Milwaukee, 71. *Honors & Awards:* Day Medal, Geol Soc Am, 61; Goldschmidt Medal, Geochem Soc, 82; Ian Campbell Medal, Am Geol Inst, 84. *Prof Exp:* Instr chem, Univ Calif, 34-35. *Concurrent Pos:* Fulbright & Guggenheim fels, Norway, 52-53; NSF fac fel, Gt Brit, 60-61; chmn bd, Radioactive Waste Mgt, Nat Acad Sci, 81-85. *Mem:* Nat Acad Sci; fel Geol Soc Am (pres, 67); Am Geol Inst (pres, 64); Geochem Soc (pres, 70); Soc Econ Geologists; Am Philos Soc; Am Geophys Union. *Res:* Petrology of igneous and metamorphic rocks; physical chemistry of ore solutions; trace elements in sea water and in sedimentary rocks. *Mailing Add:* Dept Geol Stanford Univ Stanford CA 94305-2115. *Fax:* 650-725-2199; *E-Mail:* konrad@pangea.stanford.edu

KRAUSMAN, PAUL RICHARD, WILDLIFE ECOLOGY. *Current Pos:* asst prof wildlife ecol & asst res assoc, 78-81, ASSOC PROF WILDLIFE ECOL, UNIV ARIZ, 81- *Personal Data:* b Washington, DC, Nov 17, 46; m 66; c 2. *Educ:* Ohio State Univ, BS, 68; NMex State Univ, MS, 71; Univ Idaho, PhD(wildlife sci), 76. *Prof Exp:* Res asst environ alteration, Aeromed Res Lab, NMex, 68-71; res asst, Environ Res Lab & Radiation Lab, Brooks AFB, Tex, 71-72; asst prof wildlife ecol, Auburn Univ, 76-78. *Concurrent Pos:* Welder wildlife fel ecol, 72-76. *Mem:* Wildlife Soc; Am Soc Mammalogists; Soc Range Mgt. *Res:* Ungulate ecology. *Mailing Add:* Sch Natural Resources Univ Ariz 1600 E University Blvd Tucson AZ 85721-0001

KRAUSS, ALAN ROBERT, PHYSICS, SURFACES. *Current Pos:* asst physicist, 74-80, PHYSICIST SURFACE PHYSICS, ARGONNE NAT LAB, 80-, GROUP LEADER, 84- *Personal Data:* b Chicago, Ill, Oct 3, 43; m 65, Julie Rosado; c Susan. *Educ:* Univ Chicago, BS, 65; Purdue Univ, MS, 69, PhD(physics), 72. *Honors & Awards:* Significant Contrib Energy Technol Award, Dept Energy, 89; R&D 100 Award, 92; R A Bursha Award, Am Vacuum Soc, 94. *Prof Exp:* Res assoc surface physics, James Franck Inst, Univ Chicago, 71-74. *Concurrent Pos:* Assoc ed, Appl Physics Lett; adj prof, Univ Wis. *Mem:* Am Phys Soc; Am Vacuum Soc; Sigma Xi; Mat Res Soc. *Res:* Surface physics and chemistry; sputtering; secondary ion emission and ion-bombardment phenomena; thin film growth; diamond films; low beam surface analysis; ferroelectric thin films. *Mailing Add:* 24461 W Blvd De John Naperville IL 60564. *Fax:* 630-252-9555; *E-Mail:* alan_krauss@qmgate.anl.gov

KRAUSS, BEATRICE HILMER, PLANT PHYSIOLOGY, ETHNOBOTANY. *Current Pos:* RETIRED. *Personal Data:* b Honolulu, Hawaii, Aug 4, 03. *Educ:* Univ Hawaii, BS, 26, MS, 30. *Honors & Awards:* Award Merit, Am Asn Bot Garden & Arbor. *Prof Exp:* From asst plant physiologist to plant physiologist, Pineapple Res Inst Hawaii, 26-68; lectr ethnobot & res affil pineapple physiol, Univ Hawaii, Manoa, 68-73; res affil Hawaiian Ethnobot, Lyon Arboretum, 74-93. *Mem:* Fel AAAS; Sigma Xi; fel Asn Trop Biol. *Res:* Morphology and anatomy of pineapple plant; pineapple nutrition, especially micronutrients; Hawaiian ethnobotany. *Mailing Add:* 2437 Parker Pl Honolulu HI 96822

KRAUSS, GEORGE, PHYSICAL METALLURGY, METALLURGICAL ENGINEERING. *Current Pos:* Amax Found prof, 75-90, PROF PHYS METALL, COLO SCH MINES, 90-, DIR, ADVAN STEEL PROCESSING & PROD RES CTR, 84- *Personal Data:* b Philadelphia, Pa, May 14, 33; m 60; c 4. *Educ:* Lehigh Univ, BS, 55; Mass Inst Technol, MS, 58, ScD, 61. *Honors & Awards:* Adolf Martens Medal, 90. *Prof Exp:* Mem staff div sponsored res, Mass Inst Technol, 61-62; NSF fel, Max-Planck Inst Iron Res, 62-63; from asst prof to prof metall, Lehigh Univ, 63-75, dir electron micros lab, 69-75. *Concurrent Pos:* Ed, J Heat Treating, 78-82 & Prof Engr Pa & Co; pres, Int Fedn Heat Treatment, 88-90. *Mem:* Am Inst Mining, Metall & Petrol Engrs; fel Am Soc Metals; Electron Micros Soc Am. *Res:* Mechanical and fracture behavior of steels; microstructural characterization by light and electron microscopy; failure analysis; author of over 170 publications; principles of heat treatment of steel. *Mailing Add:* Dept Metall Eng Colo Sch Mines Golden CO 80401

KRAUSS, HERBERT HARRIS, CLINICAL PSYCHOLOGY, REHABILITATION PSYCHOLOGY. *Current Pos:* PROF PSYCHOL, HUNTER COL, CITY UNIV NY, 71-, CHAIR PSYCHOL, 93- *Personal Data:* b Philadelphia, Pa, June 13, 40; m 65, Beatrice J Osgood; c Michael C & Daniel A. *Educ:* Pa State Univ, BS, 62, MS, 63; Northwestern Univ, PhD(psychol), 66. *Prof Exp:* Asst prof psychiat & psychol, Univ Kans Med Ctr, 66-67 & Col Med, Ohio State, 67-69; assoc prof psychol, Univ Ga, 69-71. *Concurrent Pos:* Adj assoc psychologist, Payne Whitney Clin, NY Hosp, 79-; adj assoc prof psychol & psychiat, Cornell Med Sch, 79-; dir res, Int Ctr Disabled, 83- *Mem:* Int Orgn Study Group Tensions; Am Psychol Asn; NY Acad Sci; Am Coun Ger; Sigma Xi; Eastern Psychol Asn. *Res:* Psycho-social etiology and treatment of behavioral abnormalities; social construction of reality. *Mailing Add:* Six Downing Ct Irvington NY 10533-2330. *Fax:* 212-772-5620; *E-Mail:* hkrauss@shiva.hunter.suny.edu

KRAUSS, JONATHAN SETH, HEMATOLOGY, COAGULATION. *Current Pos:* from asst prof to assoc prof, 78-93, DIR, HEMAT & HEMOSTASIS LAB, MED COL GA, 78-, PROF PATH, 93-, DIR, AMBULATORY CARE LAB, 93-, DIR, FLOW CYTOMETRY LAB, 95- *Personal Data:* b Brooklyn, New York, May 25, 45; m 72, Robin Livingston; c Timothy & Rachel. *Educ:* Cornell Univ, AB, 66; Univ Fla, Gainesville, MD, 70. *Prof Exp:* Intern med, Med Col Va, 70-71; gen med officer, US Naval Reserve, 71-73; resident path, NC Mem Hosp, 73-78. *Concurrent Pos:* Fel path, Univ NC, Chapel Hill, 75-76. *Mem:* Am Col Physicians; Col Am Pathologists; Soc Hematopath; Am Soc Hematol; Asn Clin Scientists; Soc Hemophilia. *Res:* Von Willebrand factor antigen in body fluids; glycosylated hemoglobin determination hemolysis; measurement of fetal hemoglobin; granulocytic fragments in sepsis; factor VII deficiency. *Mailing Add:* 2407 McDowell St Augusta GA 30904-4635. *Fax:* 706-721-7837; *E-Mail:* jkrauss@mail.mcg.edu

KRAUSS, LAWRENCE MAXWELL, PARTICLE & ASTROPHYSICS INTERFACE. *Current Pos:* AMBROSE SWASEY PROF PHYSICS, PROF ASTRON & CHMN, PHYSICS DEPT, CASE WESTERN RES UNIV, 93- *Personal Data:* b New York, NY, May 27, 54; Can & US citizen; m 80; c 1. *Educ:* Carleton Univ, BSc, 77; Mass Inst Technol, PhD(physics), 82. *Honors & Awards:* First Prize Award, Gravity Res Found, 84. *Prof Exp:* Jr fel, Harvard Soc Fels, 82-85; asst prof, Yale Univ, 85-88, assoc prof physics & astron, 88-93. *Concurrent Pos:* Vis scientist, Smithsonian Ctr Astrophys, Harvard Univ, 85-88, Boston Univ, 85-86; assoc, Physics Dept, Harvard Univ, 87-88; pres young research annual, NSF, 86; Nat Comt Lectureships, Sigma Xi, 88; nat lectr, Sigma Xi, 91-; distinguished vis scholar, Lawrence Berkeley Lab, Dept Energy, 95; sci assoc, Europ Orgn Nuclear Res, 96-97. *Mem:* Am Phys Soc; Sigma Xi; Am Asn Physics Teachers; Am Astron Soc; NY Acad Sci; AAAS. *Res:* The interface of particle physics and astrophysics and cosmology; particle physics phenomenology; field theory; ultrasensitive detection and particle physics. *Mailing Add:* Dept Physics Case Western Res Univ 10900 Euclid Ave Cleveland OH 44106

KRAUSS, MORRIS, QUANTUM PHYSICS. *Current Pos:* STAFF SCIENTIST, CTR ADVAN RES BIOTECHNOL, 93- *Personal Data:* b New Haven, Conn, Apr 9, 32. *Educ:* City Col New York, BS, 51; Univ Utah, PhD(physics), 55. *Prof Exp:* Res scientist, Nat Inst Stand & Technol, 56-93. *Mem:* Am Phys Soc. *Mailing Add:* Ctr Advan Res Biotechnol 9600 Gudelsky Dr Rockville MD 20850

KRAUSS, ROBERT WALLFAR, BIOCHEMISTRY, ECOLOGY. *Current Pos:* CONSULT, 92- *Personal Data:* b Cleveland, Ohio Dec 27, 21; m 47; c 2. *Educ:* Oberlin Col, BA, 47; Univ Hawaii, MS, 49; Univ Md, College Park, PhD(bot), 51. *Honors & Awards:* Darbaker Award, Bot Soc Am, 56; Presidents Leadership Award, Am Inst Biol Sci, 74; Achievement Awards, NASA, 76 & 89. *Prof Exp:* Asst bot, Univ Hawaii, 47-49; asst bot, Univ Md, College Park, 49-51, res assoc plant physiol, 51-55, from asst prof to prof, 55-73, head dept bot, 64-73; dean col sci, Ore State Univ, 73-80; exec dir, Fedn Am Soc Biol, 79-90; vis sr scientist, Calif Inst Technol, JPL, 90-92. *Concurrent Pos:* Res fel, Carnegie Inst, 51-55; biologist, Coastal Studies Inst, La State Univ, 58-59; mem, Nat Res Coun, 59-60; sr res affil, Chesapeake Biol Lab, 68-73; mem bd dirs, Ed Projs Inc, 69-; consult, US Air Force Sch Aviation Med, NASA & NSF; mem corp, Marine Biol Lab, Woods Hole, Mass. *Mem:* Phycol Soc Am (pres, 64); Bot Soc Am; Am Soc Plant Physiol; Am Inst Biol Sci (secy-treas, 63-69, vpres, 72, pres, 73); Sigma Xi. *Res:* Algal physiology and biochemistry; science policy. *Mailing Add:* River-Bend Farm PO Box 291 Denton MD 21629-0291

KRAUSS, RONALD, LIPOPROTEIN METABOLISM. *Current Pos:* staff scientist, 76-84, SR SCIENTIST, LAWRENCE BERKELEY LAB, 84-, HEAD, DEPT MOLECULAR MED, 92- *Personal Data:* b New York, NY, May 12, 43; m 69, Sharon A Wald; c Daniel & Jeffrey. *Educ:* Harvard Univ, BA, 64, MD, 68. *Prof Exp:* Intern, Boston City Hosp, 68-70; clin assoc, NIH, 70-73; sr investr, 73-74; asst clin prof med, Univ Calif, San Francisco, 74-82. *Concurrent Pos:* Assoc adj prof med, Univ Calif, San Francisco, 82-; dir, Endocrine & Metab Serv, Alta Bates Hosp, 86-89; head, Molecular Med Res Prog, Donner Lab, Lawrence Berkeley Lab, 89-92; fel, Arteriosclerosis Coun, Am Heart Asn. *Mem:* Am Fed Clin Res; Am Soc Clin Invest; Am Diabetes Asn; Am Inst Nutrit. *Res:* Genetic traits affecting lipoprotein metabolism and risk for cardiovascular disease; structure and function of plasma lipoproteins. *Mailing Add:* Donner Lab Lawrence Berkeley Lab Univ Calif Berkeley CA 94720-0001. *Fax:* 510-486-5342; *E-Mail:* rmkrauss@lbl.gov

KRAUSZ, ALEXANDER STEPHEN, MATERIALS SCIENCE, MECHANICAL ENGINEERING. *Current Pos:* assoc prof mech eng, Univ Ottawa, 70-72, prof & chmn dept, 72-81, prof mech eng & dir, Eng Mgt Prog, 81-86, EMER PROF MECH ENG, UNIV OTTAWA, 90- *Personal Data:* b Budapest, Hungary, Sept 16, 24; Can citizen; m 49. *Educ:* Budapest Tech Univ, BSc, 51; Queens Univ, Ont, MSc, 59; Univ Toronto, PhD(metall), 65. *Prof Exp:* Mgr mfg, Gamma Instrument Co, Hungary, 49-52; res off plastic deformation, Nat Res Coun Can, 59-70. *Concurrent Pos:* Assoc ed, J Eng Mat & Technol; regional ed, Int J Fracture. *Mem:* Am Soc Metals; Eng Inst Can; fel Can Soc Mech Eng. *Res:* Fracture mechanics; deformation kinetics, thermally activated plastic flow and fracture and deformation processes in manufacturing; product design. *Mailing Add:* 300 Queen Elizabeth Dr No 10D Ottawa ON K1S 3M6 Can

KRAUSZ, STEPHEN, SCIENCE EDUCATION, ANIMAL PHYSIOLOGY. *Personal Data:* b Salford, Eng, Aug 4, 50; US citizen; m 72, Vicki Sigman; c Joseph, Dora, Elisheva, Nili, Raphael & Gavriella. *Educ:* City Univ New York, BSc, 71; Hebrew Univ, Jerusalem, Israel, MSc, 73, PhD(physiol), 77. *Prof Exp:* Res fel, Sch Med, Univ Calif, Los Angeles, 77-78; asst prof anat & physiol Howard Univ Med Sch, Washington, DC, 78-83; lab coordr gen sci, Hillel Acad, Denver, Colo, 83-87; adj prof human anat & physiol, metrop state col, 92-94. *Concurrent Pos:* Asst dir, Jewish Children's Adoption Network, 91- *Mem:* Sigma Xi; Am Physiol Soc. *Res:* Respiratory, cardiovascular and endocrinological responses of mammals to extremes of environment. *Mailing Add:* 1376 Utica Denver CO 80204. *Fax:* 303-893-1447

KRAUT, EDGAR A, PHYSICS. *Current Pos:* MEM TECH STAFF, SCI CTR, ROCKWELL INT CORP, 67- *Personal Data:* b Cleveland, Ohio, May 4, 34; m 80. *Educ:* Univ Calif, Los Angeles, AB, 56, MA, 57, PhD(physics), 62. *Mem:* AAAS; Am Phys Soc; Inst Elec & Electronics Engrs; Soc Indust Appl Math. *Res:* Theoretical and mathematical physics; wave propagation; physics of semiconductor surfaces and interfaces; heterojunctions; energy bands; device modeling. *Mailing Add:* Rockwell Int Sci Ctr Rm 167 1049 Camino Dos Rios Thousand Oaks CA 91360

KRAUT, JOSEPH, PROTEIN CRYSTALLOGRAPHY. *Current Pos:* from assoc prof to prof, 62-95, actg chmn dept, 72-73, RES PROF & EMER PROF CHEM, UNIV CALIF, SAN DIEGO, 95- *Personal Data:* b New York, NY, Dec 5, 26; m 53, Jean M Campbell; c Isabel, Samuel & Rachel. *Educ:* Bucknell Univ, SB, 50; Calif Inst Technol, PhD(phys chem), 54. *Honors & Awards:* Keilin Medal, Brit Biochem Soc, 80. *Prof Exp:* From instr to asst prof biochem, Univ Wash, 53-62. *Concurrent Pos:* Fel, Howard Hughes Med Inst, 55-60. *Mem:* Nat Acad Sci; Am Chem Soc; Am Crystallog Asn; Am Soc Biol Chem; AAAS. *Res:* Structure, function and evolution of biological macromolecules; x-ray diffraction crystallography. *Mailing Add:* Dept Chem & Biochem Univ Calif San Diego CA 92093-0506. *Fax:* 619-534-6128; *E-Mail:* jkraut@ucsd.edu

KRAUTER, ALLAN IRVING, MECHANICAL ENGINEERING. *Current Pos:* R&D MGR, WELCH ALLYN, 85- *Personal Data:* b Newark, NJ, Oct 15, 41; m 68; c 3. *Educ:* Stevens Inst Technol, ME, 63; Stanford Univ, MS, 64, PhD(mech eng), 68. *Prof Exp:* Asst prof mech eng, Cornell Univ, 68-74; sr consult engr & mgr, Technol Dept, Shaker Res Corp, 75-81; prog mgr, mech systs, Carrier Corp, 81-85. *Mem:* Am Soc Mech Engrs; Soc Automotive Engrs. *Res:* Vibrations and dynamics of mechanical systems; simulation of mechanical and economic system behavior. *Mailing Add:* 4312 Kasson Rd Syracuse NY 13215

KRAUTHAMER, GEORGE MICHAEL, NEUROSCIENCE. *Current Pos:* assoc prof, 69-79, PROF ANAT, ROBERT WOOD JOHNSON MED SCH, UNIV MED & DENT NJ, 79- *Personal Data:* b Ger, Sept 14, 26; nat US; div; c 6. *Educ:* City Col New York, BS, 51, MA, 52; NY Univ, PhD(psychol), 59. *Prof Exp:* Asst psychophysiol, Sch Med, NY Univ, 57-59, instr psychol, 59-60; res assoc, Univ Paris, 63-66; asst prof, Col Physicians & Surgeons, Columbia Univ, 67-69. *Concurrent Pos:* Lectr psychol, City Col NY, 59-60; res assoc, Hillside Hosp, Glen Oak, NY, 59-60; USPHS res fel, Ctr Study

Physiol of Cent Nerv Syst, Univ Paris, 60-63; asst to exec secy, Int Brain Res Orgn-UNESCO, 65-68. *Mem:* AAAS; Soc Neurosci. *Res:* Electrophysiology and neuroanatomy of brain; behavior correlates of brain function; effects of brain injury; perception and intersensory relationships; electroencephalography; drug effects. *Mailing Add:* Dept Anat Robert Wood Johnson Med Sch UMDNJ 675 Hoes Lane Piscataway NJ 08854-5635. *Fax:* 732-235-4029

KRAUTZ, FRED GERHARD, FIBER GLASS REINFORCEMENTS, FIBER GLASS COMPOSITES. *Current Pos:* res & develop dir, Certainteed Corp, 87-90, dir res & develop, 90-91, VPRES RES & DEVELOP, VETROTEX CERTAINTEED CORP, 91- *Personal Data:* b Cottbus, Ger; US citizen; m 62; c 2. *Educ:* Univ Cincinnati, ChE, 61, MS, 66. *Prof Exp:* Engr, Cincinnati Milacron, 61-63, consult, 63-65; sr engr, Owens-Corning Fiberglas Corp, 65-72, supvr reinforcements & mats, 72-78, mgr reinforcement & tires, 78-81, mgr composite prod, 81-83, tech support mgr, 83-87. *Mem:* Soc Plastics Engrs; Am Inst Chem Engrs. *Res:* Fiberglass products for all thermosetting and thermoplastic composites for Vetrotex Certainteed fiberglass reinforcements division. *Mailing Add:* Vetrotex Certainteed Corp 4515 Allendale Rd Wichita Falls TX 76310

KRAVITZ, EDWARD ARTHUR, BIOCHEMISTRY, NEUROBIOLOGY. *Current Pos:* Nat Inst Neurol Dis & Blindness res fel neurophysiol & neuropharmacol, Harvard Med Sch, 60-61, instr neurophysiol & neuropharmacol, 61-63, assoc, 63-66, from asst prof to assoc prof, 66-69, prof neurobiol, 69-86, dir prog neurosci, 82-90, GEORGE PACKER BERRY PROF NEUROBIOL, HARVARD MED SCH, 86- *Personal Data:* b New York, NY, Dec 19, 32; m 58; c 2. *Educ:* City Col New York, BS, 54; Univ Mich, PhD(biochem), 59. *Honors & Awards:* Flexner Lectr, Univ Pa, 72; Krantz Lectr, Univ Md, 75; Magnes Mem Lectr, Hebrew Univ Med Sch, Jerusalem, 81; Snider Lectr, Univ Toronto, 87; Lang Lectr, Marine Biol Lab, 83; Schmitt Lectr, Univ Pa, 91; Von Humboldt Award, 91. *Prof Exp:* Nat Heart Inst fel biochem, 59-60. *Concurrent Pos:* USPHS spec fel, 61-64, career develop award, 66-71; mem, Bd Trustees & Exec Comt, Marine Biol Lab, dir neurobiol course, 75-79; mem, Governing Coun, Inst Med, 91-93; co-founder, Neurobiol Dis Teaching Workshops, Soc Neurosci. *Mem:* Inst Med-Nat Acad Sci; Soc Neurosci; Am Acad Arts & Sci; Am Soc Biol Chemists; NY Acad Sci. *Res:* Biochemical studies on single physiologically identified nerve cells; identification of gamma-aminobutyric acid and other neurotransmitters in the lobster nervous system; amines, peptides neurohormones and behavior in lobsters. *Mailing Add:* Dept Neurobiol Harvard Med Sch 220 Longwood Ave Boston MA 02115. *Fax:* 617-734-7557; *E-Mail:* ekravitz@warren.med.harvard.edu

KRAVITZ, HENRY, PSYCHIATRY, PSYCHOANALYSIS. *Current Pos:* chmn psychiat, 67-88, EMER CHIEF, JEWISH GEN HOSP & DIR, INST COMMUNITY & FAMILY PSYCHIAT, 88- *Personal Data:* b Poland, Oct 18, 18; Can citizen; m 42, Mona Samuels; c Susan. *Educ:* McGill Univ, BA, 45, MD, CM, 49; dipl psychiat, 54; Royal Col Physicians & Surgeons Can, cert psychiat, 54; FRCP(C). *Prof Exp:* Assoc prof, McGill Univ, 67-72, prof psychiat, 72-, actg chmn, Dept Psychiat, 85- *Concurrent Pos:* Training analyst, Can Psychoanal Inst, 62-, assoc dir, 68-, dir, 80-; chmn psychiat, Jewish Gen Hosp, 67-88; chmn bd examiners, Royal Col Physicians & Surgeons, 78-82, chmn, Sect Psychiat, 82-88. *Mem:* Fel AAAS; fel Am Col Psychiat; fel Am Psychiat Asn; Can Psychoanal Soc (pres, 68-71); fel Am Col Psychoanalysts; Can Psychiat Asn. *Res:* Theoretical and practical considerations for unwed mothers; use of methadone and other substitute therapies in drug addiction; psychiatric education. *Mailing Add:* Dept Psychiat Jewish Gen Hosp Montreal PQ H3T 1E2 Can

KRAVITZ, JOSEPH HENRY, MARINE GEOTECHNIQUE, PROGRAM MANAGER. *Current Pos:* sci off, 84-86, PROG MGR, MARINE GEOL & GEOPHYS PROG, OFF NAVAL RES, 86- *Personal Data:* b Nanticoke, Pa, Aug 14, 35; m; c 2. *Educ:* Syracuse Univ, BS, 57; George Washington Univ, MS, 75, MPH, 77, PhD(geol), 83. *Prof Exp:* Res asst, Geol Dept, Yale Univ, 61-64; marine geologist, Lamont-Doherty Geol Observ, Columbia Univ, 64-65; oceanographer, US Naval Oceanog Off, 65-71, head, Geol Lab, 71-78, actg head, marine geol & geophys br, 78; sr geologist, outer continental shelf environ assessment, Nat Ocean & Atmospheric Admin, 78-80, actg dir, Marine Ecosyst Anal Div, Off Marine Pollution Assessment, 80-82, hq staff geologist, Ocean Assessment Div, 82-84, sr oceanogr, prog develop & coord staff, Off Oceanic & Atmoshperic Res, Nat Oceanic & Atmospheric Admin, 84. *Concurrent Pos:* Res assoc, Inst Artic & Alpine Res, 81-86; assoc prof lectr geol, George Wash Univ, 87- *Mem:* Fel Geol Soc Am; fel Artic Inst NAm; fel Explor Club; Soc Econ Paleontologists & Mineralogists. *Res:* High resolution seismic profiling; geotechnical analysis of sediments and its relation to depositional environments. *Mailing Add:* 11014 Old Coach Rd Potomac MD 20854

KRAVITZ, LAWRENCE C, PHYSICS, ELECTRONICS. *Current Pos:* ALLIED SIGNAL. *Personal Data:* b New York, NY, July 27, 32; m 58; c 3. *Educ:* Kans Univ, BS, 54; Air Force Inst Technol, MS, 55; Harvard Univ, PhD(physics), 63. *Prof Exp:* Physicist solid state, Corp Res & Develop Ctr, Gen Elec Co, 63-71, mgr display prog, 72-73; dir electronics, 73-78, Air Force Off Sci Res, 78-81; dir res, Bendix Advan Technol Ctr, 81- *Mem:* Inst Elec & Electronics Engrs. *Res:* Solid state science. *Mailing Add:* 7128 Wolftree Lane Rockville MD 20852

KRAWETZ, ARTHUR ALTSHULER, ANALYTICAL CHEMISTRY, PHYSICAL CHEMISTRY. *Current Pos:* Vpres, 54-74, PRES, PHOENIX CHEM LAB, INC, CHICAGO, 74- *Personal Data:* b Chicago, Ill, Oct 30, 32. *Educ:* Northwestern Univ, BS, 52; Univ Chicago, SM, 53, PhD(chem), 55. *Mem:* Am Chem Soc; Am Soc Testing & Mat; Am Inst Chem; Royal Soc Chem; Nat Fire Protection Asn. *Res:* Fuel and lubricant technology; spontaneous ignition; flammability; air and water pollution; forensic chemistry; differential thermal analysis; solution chemistry; thermodynamics; molecular spectroscopy; industrial hygiene; safety; hydraulic fluids; protective coatings; rubber and plastic. *Mailing Add:* 1010 Isabella St Evanston IL 60201. *E-Mail:* pclinc@net.com

KRAWETZ, STEPHEN ANDREW, HUMAN GENOME INITIATIVE, MEDICAL GENETICS & BIOTECHNOLOGY. *Current Pos:* asst prof res, Dept Molecular Biol & Genetics & Ctr Molecular Biol, Wayne State Univ, 89-90, asst prof, Dept Molecular Biol & Genetics, 90-92, asst prof, 92-94, ASSOC PROF DEPT OBSTETS & GYNEC, CTR MOLECULAR MED & GENETICS, WAYNE STATE UNIV, 94- *Personal Data:* b Fort Frances, Ont, Sept 17, 55; m 77, Qorraine R St John; c Rhochelle T & Alexandra R. *Educ:* Univ Toronto, BSc, 77 & PhD(biochem), 83. *Honors & Awards:* Intel Genetics Comput Appln Award, 88. *Prof Exp:* Occas teacher math, music & sci, Scarborough Bd Educ, 76-77; lab demonstr biochem, Univ Toronto, 77-81; fel, Dept Med Biochem, Univ Calgary, 83-89. *Concurrent Pos:* Brit Columbia Children's Hosp res fel, 84; Alta Heritage Found med res fel, 84-89; Biotechnol Consult, 85-; prin investr, Comput Video Expert Systs Biochem Appl, 87; cofounder & med res dir, Genetic Imaging Inc, 87-88. *Mem:* AAAS; Am Soc Human Genetics; Int Soc Matrix Biol; Soc Study Reproduction. *Res:* Control of development and differentiation of spermatogenic and elastic tissue genes; human genome initiative; computer assisted sequence analysis; molecular diagnostic probes; gene therapy targeted to the ameliozation of human disease. *Mailing Add:* 805 Canterbury Rd Grosse Pointe Woods MI 48236-1417. *Fax:* 313-577-8534; *E-Mail:* Internet Home Page: http://compbio.med.wayne.edu

KRAWIEC, STEVEN STACK, MOLECULAR BIOLOGY, MICROBIOLOGY. *Current Pos:* from asst prof to assoc prof, Lehigh Univ, 70-82, chmn, 76-78, assoc dean, Col Arts & Sci, 85-87, PROF, LEHIGH UNIV, 82- *Personal Data:* b Corvallis, Ore, Nov 4, 41; m 65, Margaret Macpherson; c Matthew & Rebecca. *Educ:* Brown Univ, AB, 63; Yale Univ, PhD(microbiol), 68. *Prof Exp:* Trainee, Univ Wis-Madison, 68-69, Nat Inst Gen Med Sci fel, 69-70. *Concurrent Pos:* Fogarty int fel, Autonomous Univ Madrid, 78-79; vis scientist, Univ Edinburgh, 92-93. *Mem:* Am Soc Microbiol; AAAS; Sigma Xi. *Res:* Characterization of chromosome organization of bacteria; acquisitive evolution; degradation of xenobiotics. *Mailing Add:* Dept Biol Sci Lehigh Univ Bethlehem PA 18015-4732. *Fax:* 610-758-4004; *E-Mail:* sk08@lehigh.edu

KRAY, LOUIS ROBERT, PETROLEUM CHEMISTRY, FUELS. *Current Pos:* RES CHEMIST ORG CHEM, CHEVRON RES CO, STAND OIL CO CALIF, RICHMOND, 67-, SR STAFF SCIENTIST. *Personal Data:* b San Bernardino, Calif, Oct 20, 38; m 87, Bettye Smallwood; c Leonard L, Roger K, Robert B, Katherine M & Ann L. *Educ:* Univ Calif, Riverside, BA, 61, PhD(org chem), 65. *Prof Exp:* Researcher, 65-67. *Mem:* Am Chem Soc; Soc Tribologists & Lubrication Engrs; Soc Mfg Engrs. *Res:* Fuel additive synthesis and development; industrial oil formulator. *Mailing Add:* 700 Bamboo Terr San Rafael CA 94903. *Fax:* 510-242-3758

KRAYBILL, EDWARD K(READY), ELECTRICAL ENGINEERING. *Current Pos:* RETIRED. *Personal Data:* b Lancaster, Pa, June 3, 17; m 39; c 1. *Educ:* Pa State Univ, BS, 39, EE, 51; Univ Mich, MSE, 48, PhD, 66. *Prof Exp:* From instr to assoc prof elec eng, Duke Univ, 39-71, asst to dean, Col Eng, 53-62, asst dean, 62-66, assoc dean, 66-71; dir, Worthington Scranton Campus, Pa State Univ, 71-78, prof eng, 71-82, emer prof, 82-84. *Mem:* Am Soc Eng Educ; Illum Eng Soc; Inst Elec & Electronics Engrs; Nat Soc Prof Engrs; Am Asn Higher Educ. *Res:* Higher education. *Mailing Add:* 500 E Marylyn Ave State College PA 16801

KRAYBILL, HENRY LAWRENCE, EXPERIMENTAL HIGH ENERGY PHYSICS. *Current Pos:* RETIRED. *Personal Data:* b Washington, DC, Apr 13, 18; m 44, Helen E Hardy; c April & Robert. *Educ:* Univ Chicago, SB, 38, PhD(physics), 49. *Prof Exp:* From instr to prof physics, Yale Univ, 48-84. *Mem:* Am Phys Soc; Am Asn Physics Teachers. *Res:* High energy particles; bubble chamber analysis of hadron interactions. *Mailing Add:* 960 Benham Hamden CT 06514

KRAYBILL, HERMAN FINK, ENVIRONMENTAL CANCER, PESTICIDE TOXICOLOGY. *Current Pos:* CONSULT BIOMED SCI, 85- *Personal Data:* b Marietta, Pa, June 27, 14; m 41, Dorothy Ramsey; c Linda J (Asper), Cynthia L & David R. *Educ:* Franklin & Marshall Col, BS, 36; Univ Md, MS, 38, PhD(biochem), 41. *Honors & Awards:* Merit Award, NIH, 81. *Prof Exp:* Instr chem, Univ Md, 36-39; res chemist, Swift & Co, 41-43; res biochemist, Moorman Mfg Co, Ill, 46 & Nat Dairy Res Labs, Md, 46-48; Bur Animal Indust, USDA, 49-53; res assoc, Nat Res Coun, DC, 48-49; supvry biochemist & chief chem div, Army Med Nutrit Lab, 53-59; sr scientist, Curtiss Wright Corp, NJ, 59-60; sr biochemist & scientist adminstr, Div Radiation Health, Nat Cancer Inst, 60-63; chief pesticides prog, USPHS, 62-66; assoc dir biol sci, Food & Drug Admin, 66-72; sci coordr, environ cancer, Nat Cancer Inst, 72-84. *Concurrent Pos:* Lectr biochem, Univ Colo, 54-58 & lectr nutrit, Univ Denver, 55-58; adj prof community health, Mt Sinai Sch Med, 68-70. *Mem:* Pan Am Med Asn; Am Chem Soc; Am Inst Nutrit; Soc Toxicol; NY Acad Sci; Sigma Xi. *Res:* Food research; fat enzymes; animal and human nutrition; dairy products; meats and fishery products; allergy; cancer; toxicology of irradiated foods; pesticides; radiological health. *Mailing Add:* 17708 Lafayette Dr Olney MD 20832

KRAYBILL, RICHARD R(EIST), CHEMICAL ENGINEERING, POLYMER PROCESSING. *Current Pos:* RETIRED. *Personal Data:* b Dover, NH, July 31, 20; m 45, Jean Gilbert; c Mary (Allen), Virginia (Patsos), Anne (Krecko) & Elizabeth. *Educ:* Purdue Univ, BChE, 42; Univ Mich, MS, 43, PhD(chem eng), 53. *Prof Exp:* Asst res engr, Calif Res Corp, 44-46; from asst prof to assoc prof chem eng, Univ Rochester, 50-67; tech assoc develop, Mfg Tech Div, Eastman Kodak Co, Rochester, 67-83. *Concurrent Pos:* Sr lectr, Univ Rochester, 78-79. *Mem:* Am Chem Soc; Am Soc Eng Educ; fel Am Inst Chem Engrs; sr mem Soc Plastics Engrs; Sigma Xi. *Res:* Fluid flow; heat transfer; extrusion. *Mailing Add:* 6415 21st Ave W C-221 Bradenton FL 34209

KRAYCHY, STEPHEN, ORGANIC CHEMISTRY, NUCLEAR MEDICINE. *Current Pos:* GROUP LEADER CHEMICAL DEVELOP, NUTRASWEET CO, UNIVERSITY PARK. *Personal Data:* b Redwater, Alta, Feb 18, 28; nat US; m 54; c 3. *Educ:* Univ Alta, BSc, 50; Univ Wis, PhD(org chem), 55. *Prof Exp:* Asst mem, Sloan-Kettering Inst Cancer Res, 54-56; sr investr chem res, G D Searle & Co, 56-71, asst dir biochem res, 71-73, asst dir drug metab-radiochem, 73-75, mgr radiopharmaceut, Searle Labs, 75-78, sr res scientist, G D Searle & Co, 78-; Searle Food Resources, Park Forest. *Mem:* Am Chem Soc. *Res:* Synthesis of steroids; steroid metabolism; microbiological transformations of steroids; drug metabolism; radiochemicals; research and development of radiopharmaceuticals; anti-infective agents; peptide synthesis. *Mailing Add:* 2301 S Millbend Dr Spring TX 77380

KRAYNAK, MATTHEW EDWARD, NUTRITION. *Current Pos:* RETIRED. *Personal Data:* b Scranton, Pa, Dec 19, 27; m 68. *Educ:* Scranton Univ, BS, 50; Univ Tenn, MS, 52, PhD(biochem), 56. *Prof Exp:* Instr chem, Univ Tenn, 53-55; asst prof biochem & vis chmn dept, Indonesia, 56-60; asst prof, Univ Tenn, 61-62; from asst prof to prof chem & nutrit, Univ Okla, 62-90. *Concurrent Pos:* Mem, Okla Nutrit Task Force. *Mem:* AAAS; Am Chem Soc; Am Dietetic Asn. *Res:* Nutritional availability of plant galactosides; biochemistry of galactosemia and lactose intolerance. *Mailing Add:* 717 Chautauqua Norman OK 73069-4605

KRBECHEK, LEROY O, ORGANIC CHEMISTRY. *Current Pos:* sr res chemist, James Ford Bell Res Ctr, Gen Mills, Inc, 69-72, sr res chemist, Gen Mills Chem Inc, 72-80, SR RES CHEMIST, HENKEL INC, 80- *Personal Data:* b Thief River Falls, Minn, May 21, 34; m 60; c 3. *Educ:* Univ NDak, BS, 57; Univ Mich, MS & PhD, 61. *Prof Exp:* Chemist, Aerospace Corp, 61-64 & Int Minerals & Chem Corp, 64-69. *Mem:* Am Chem Soc. *Res:* Organic azides and synthesis. *Mailing Add:* 1119 Humboldt St Santa Rosa CA 95404

KRC, JOHN, JR, CHEMICAL MICROSCOPY, CRYSTALLOGRAPHY. *Current Pos:* RETIRED. *Personal Data:* b Chicago, Ill, May 17, 20; m 49, Bessie Neboska; c 5. *Educ:* Univ Chicago, BS, 43. *Prof Exp:* Chemist, E J Brach & Sons, 47, Swift & Co, 48 & Armour Res Found, Ill Inst Technol, 49-61; sr res pharmacist, Warner-Lambert/Parke-Davis Pharmaceut Res Div, 61-80, res assoc, 80-82. *Concurrent Pos:* Adj prof, Sch Pharm, Univ Mich, Ann Arbor, 70-79. *Mem:* Am Chem Soc. *Res:* Chemical, x-ray and optical crystallography; chemical microscopy; phase diagrams; thermal stability; crystallization kinetics; solvation; polymorphism; recrystallization; nucleation and crystal growth; physical properties of nonhomogeneous solids. *Mailing Add:* 1514 Chipmunk Lane Oviedo FL 32765

KREAM, BARBARA ELIZABETH, BIOCHEMISTRY, ENDOCRINOLOGY. *Current Pos:* res assoc, 77-78, instr med & endocrinol, 78-79, asst prof, 79-85, ASSOC PROF, DEPT MED, DIV ENDOCRINOL & METAB, UNIV CONN HEALTH CTR, 85- *Personal Data:* b New York, NY, Mar 11, 48; m 80; c 2. *Educ:* Mt Holyoke Col, BA, 69; Yale Univ, PhD(molecular biophys, biochem), 74. *Prof Exp:* NIH fel, Dept Biochem, Univ Wis, 74-77. *Concurrent Pos:* Res grants, Am Diabetes Asn, 78-79, Juvenile Diabetes Found, 79-81, Proctor & Gamble Co, 81 & NIH, 81- *Mem:* Sigma Xi; Endocrine Soc; AAAS; Am Soc Bone & Mineral Res; Am Soc Biol Chemists. *Res:* Bone and calcium metabolism; mechanism of action of hormones; effect of insulin on collagen synthesis in bone; hormonal regulation of bone collagen synthesis. *Mailing Add:* Univ Conn Health Ctr 263 Farmington Ave Farmington CT 06030. *Fax:* 860-679-1258

KREAM, JACOB, CLINICAL CHEMISTRY, HORMONE IMMUNOASSAY. *Current Pos:* CONSULT CLIN CHEM & ENDOCRINOL/HORMONE ASSAY, 86- *Personal Data:* b New York, NY, Apr 16, 19; m 42, Rhoda Benson; c Richard, Barbara, Steven & Shelley. *Educ:* City Col NY, BS, 42; Columbia Univ, PhD(biochem), 52; Nat Registry Clin Chem, dipl; Nat Acad Clin Biochem, dipl. *Prof Exp:* Asst, Rockefeller Inst Med Res, 43; chemist, Kellex Corp, 43-44 & Pyridium Corp, 44-46; asst biochem, Columbia Univ, 46-49, William J Geis fel biol chem, 48-49; biochemist, Inst Cancer Res, 50-52 & US Vet Admin Hosp, NY, 52-53; res assoc biochem, Columbia Univ, 53-54; chief, Dept Clin Chem, Hosp Joint Dis, 54-65; dir, Core Lab, Clin Res Ctr & sr investr, Steroid Inst, Montefiore Hosp & Med Ctr, 65-82; assoc prof lab med, Albert Einstein Col Med, 78-82; dir, Biochem Labs, Inst Chronobiol, NY Hosp-Cornell Med Ctr, Cornell Univ Med Col, 82-86, assoc prof biochem psychiat, 82-86. *Concurrent Pos:* Mem bd examr, Bur Labs, NY Dept Health; lectr, Hunter Col, 51-65; lectr-consult, US Naval Hosp, St Albans, NY, 58-62; chmn, NY Sect, Am Asn Clin Chem, 59-60 & 78-79, Nat Comt, 70-75, Nat Comt Radionuclides & Radioassay, 74-76; consult clin radioimmunoassay, Union Carbide Corp, 75-79. *Mem:* AAAS; Am Chem Soc; Am Asn Clin Chem; Sigma Xi; Endocrine Soc. *Res:* Enzymology; purine and pyrimidine metabolism; purine analogs and cancer; nucleic acid chemistry; polypeptide metabolism; clinical chemistry; automated clinical methods; steroid analysis; radioimmunoassay; competitive protein binding analysis; episodic secretion of pituitary hormones and corticosteroids; radioisotopes, endocrinology of cancer, hormonal studies of mental illness. *Mailing Add:* 3 Milford Lane Glen Cove NY 11542

KREAR, HARRY ROBERT, ETHOLOGY, ECOLOGY. *Current Pos:* RETIRED. *Personal Data:* b Pittsburgh, Pa, Apr 13, 22. *Educ:* Pa State Univ, BSF, 49; Univ Wyo, MS, 53; Univ Colo, PhD(ecol, ethology), 65. *Prof Exp:* Biologist wildlife res, Mont Fish & Game Dept, 53-54; explor & res, Arctic Wildlife Range Exped, 56; instr biol, Univ Colo, 60-61; asst prof, Mankato State Col, 65-66; chmn div sci & math, US Int Univ, Colo Alpine Campus, 67-73; assoc prof biol sci, Mich Technol Univ, 73-84. *Concurrent Pos:* Vis lectr zool, NSF Insts, Univ Colo, 59-64. *Mem:* Animal Behav Soc; Ecol Soc Am; Am Soc Mammalogists. *Res:* Ecology of selected vertebrates of Ungava; reproduction of cow fur seals pribilots; Arctic wildlife range; ecology of muskrats; behavior and ecology of sea otters amchitka; ecology and ethology of pikas. *Mailing Add:* 944 Ramshorn Rd Estes Park CO 80517

KREBILL, RICHARD G, FOREST PATHOLOGY. *Current Pos:* Plant pathologist, 62-76, ASST DIR, ROCKY MOUNTAIN FOREST & RANGE EXP STA, US FOREST SERV, 79- *Personal Data:* b Upland, Calif, Mar 9, 36; m 58; c 3. *Educ:* Univ Calif, Berkeley, BS, 58; Univ Wis, PhD(plant path), 62. *Mem:* Am Phytopath Soc; Soc Am Foresters. *Res:* Tree diseases; rust fungi; shrub diseases; research administration. *Mailing Add:* 6209 Woodland Dr Ogden UT 84403

KREBS, EDWIN GERHARD, BIOCHEMISTRY. *Current Pos:* investr, Sch Med, Univ Wash, Seattle, 77-80, chmn dept, 77-84, prof pharmacol, 77-88, sr investr, Howard Hughes Med Inst, 80-90, EMER PROF, DEPT PHARMACOL & BIOCHEM, SCH MED, UNIV WASH, SEATTLE, 88-, EMER SR INVESTR, HOWARD HUGHES MED INST, 91- *Personal Data:* b Lansing, Iowa, June 6, 18; m 45; c 3. *Educ:* Univ Ill, AB, 40; Washington Univ, MD, 43. *Hon Degrees:* DSc, Univ Geneva, 79; Dr, Med Col Ohio, 93; DSc, Univ Ind, 93. *Honors & Awards:* Nobel Prize, 92; Distinguished Lectureship Award, Int Soc Endcrinol, 72; J J Berzelivs lectr, Karolinska Inst, 82; George W Thorn Award Sci Excellence, 83; Sir Frederick Hopkins Mem lectr, London, 84; Res Achievement Award, Am Heart Asn, 87; Life Sci Award, 3M, 89; Albert Lasker Basic Med Res Award, 89; Louisa Gross Horwitz Award, Columbia Univ, 89; Kawi Found Award, 96. *Prof Exp:* Intern & asst resident, Barnes Hosp, St Louis, 44-45; NIH res fel, Wash Univ, 46-48, from asst prof to prof biochem, 48-68, asst dean planning, Sch Med, 66-68; prof biochem & chmn dept, Sch Med, Univ Calif, Davis, 68-76. *Concurrent Pos:* Guggenheim fel, 59, 66; Gairdner found award, Toronto, Ont, 78 & Passano found award, Baltimore, Md, 88; mem, Educ Affairs Comt, Am Soc Biol Chemists, 65-68; mem, Biochem Test Comt, Nat Bd Med Examiners, 68-71; mem, Res Comt, Am Heart Asn, 70-74; assoc ed, J Biol Chem, 72-93. *Mem:* Nat Acad Sci; Am Acad Arts & Sci; Am Soc Biochem & Molecular Biol (pres, 85-86); Am Pharm Soc; Am Soc Pharm & Exp Theopeuts. *Res:* Enzyme chemistry; regulation of carbohydrate metabolism; mechanism of action of cyclic amp and other second messages; protein phosphorylation reactions. *Mailing Add:* Box 357280 Univ Wash Seattle WA 98195. *Fax:* 206-685-9720; *E-Mail:* egkrebs@u.washington.edu

KREBS, JAMES J(OHN), EXPERIMENTAL SOLID STATE PHYSICS. *Current Pos:* PHYSICIST MAGNETIC RESONANCE, US NAVAL RES LAB, 58- *Personal Data:* b St Louis, Mo, Feb 28, 32; m 72, Catherine Kaiser; c Christopher & Matthew. *Educ:* St Louis Univ, BS, 54, PhD(physics), 59. *Concurrent Pos:* Nat Res Coun res assoc, 58-59; vis fel, Princeton Univ, 75-76. *Mem:* Fel Am Phys Soc; Sigma Xi. *Res:* Investigation of electron-nuclear interactions by means of magnetic double resonance; resonance and optical absorption in exchange coupled systems; deep impurity resonance in III-V semiconductors; properties of ultra-thin magnetic single crystals. *Mailing Add:* Code 6340 Naval Res Lab Washington DC 20375-5000. *Fax:* 202-767-1697

KREBS, JAMES N, JET ENGINE DESIGN & DEVELOPMENT. *Current Pos:* RETIRED. *Personal Data:* b Sauk Center, Minn, Apr 20, 24. *Educ:* Northwestern Univ, BS, 45. *Honors & Awards:* Reed Aeronaut Award, Am Inst Aeronaut & Astronaut, 92. *Prof Exp:* Design develop mgr & mkt mgr, Gen Elec Co, 46-78, vpres, Mil Eng Progs, 78-82, LYNN Eng Opers, 82-84 & technol & mgt assessment, aircraft eng group, 84-85. *Mem:* Nat Acad Eng; Am Inst Aeronaut & Astronaut. *Mailing Add:* 84 Harbor Ave Marblehead MA 01945

KREBS, JULIA ELIZABETH, TEACHING, ORNITHOLOGY. *Current Pos:* PROF BIOL, FRANCIS MARION COL, 77-, DISTINGUISHED PROF, 86- *Personal Data:* b Baton Rouge, La, Mar 29, 43; m 80, Roger K Hux. *Educ:* Oberlin Col, AB, 65; Boston Col, MEd, 69; Univ Ga, MSc, 72, PhD(zool), 77. *Mem:* Ecol Soc Am; Asn Biol Lab Educ. *Res:* Nutrient cycling; effect of man on natural systems; bird populations. *Mailing Add:* Dept Biol Francis Marion Uni Florence SC 29501-0547

KREBS, MARTHA, ENERGY RESEARCH. *Current Pos:* DIR, OFF ENERGY RES, DEPT ENERGY, 93- *Educ:* Cath Univ Am, PhD(theoret physics), 66. *Prof Exp:* Staff dir, House Subcomt Energy Develop Applns, Washington, 77-83; assoc dir planning & develop, Lawrence Berkeley Lab, 83-93. *Mailing Add:* Off Energy Res Dept Energy 1000 Independence Ave SW Washington DC 20585

KREBS, ROBERT DIXON, SOIL MECHANICS, FOUNDATION ENGINEERING. *Current Pos:* RETIRED. *Personal Data:* b Gowanda, NY, Mar 12, 31; m 54; c 3. *Educ:* Rutgers Univ, BS, 52, PhD(soil sci), 56; Purdue Univ, MSE, 59. *Prof Exp:* From asst to assoc prof agron, Va Polytech Inst, 55-57; instr eng geol, Purdue Univ, 58-59; assoc prof civil eng, Va Polytech Inst & State Univ, 59-91, asst head dept, 70-91. *Concurrent Pos:* Assoc, Hwy Res Bd, Nat Acad Sci-Nat Res Coun. *Mem:* AAAS; Am Soc Civil Engrs; Am Soc Eng Educ. *Res:* Soil mechanics, physics, mineralogy and chemistry; soils and geologic engineering; soil genesis and classification; soil stabilization; soil behavior. *Mailing Add:* 101 Alleghany St Blacksburg VA 24060

KREBS, WILLIAM H, INDUSTRIAL HYGIENE, TOXICOLOGY. *Current Pos:* VPRES, INDUST HEALTH SCI INC, 93- *Personal Data:* b Detroit, Mich, Apr 6, 38; m 83, Jane Germer; c Elizabeth L & William T II. *Educ:* Univ Mich, Ann Arbor, BS, 60, MPH, 63, MS, 65, PhD, 70; Am Bd Indust Hyg, cert. *Prof Exp:* Res asst indust health, Sch Pub Health, Univ Mich, Ann Arbor, 62; indust hygienist, Lumbermens Mutual Casualty Co, Chicago, Ill, 63-64; indust hygienist, Indust Hyg Dept, Gen Motors Corp, 70-77, mgr, 77-81, dir, Toxic Mat Control Activ, 81-90, dir, Indust Hyg Activ, 90-92, asst dir, Occup Safety & Health Sect, 92-93. *Concurrent Pos:* Dir, Am Indust Hyg Asn, 76-79, vpres, 86-87, pres-elect, 87-88, pres, 88-89; pres, Mich Indust Hyg Soc, 80-81; vpres, Int Occup Hyg Asn, 90-91, pres-elect, 91-92, pres, 92-93. *Mem:* AAAS; NY Acad Sci; fel Am Indust Hyg Asn; Am Acad Indust Hyg; Brit Occup Hyg Soc; Am Pub Health Asn; hon mem Am Indust Hyg Asn; Int Commn Occup Health. *Res:* Formation of ferruginous bodies. *Mailing Add:* Indust Health Sci Inc 1014 Bishop Rd Grosse Pointe Park MI 48230. *Fax:* 313-885-3130

KREBS-SMITH, SUSAN M, NUTRITION. *Current Pos:* NUTRITIONIST, NAT CANCER INST, NIH, 91- *Personal Data:* b St Louis, Mo, June 2, 55. *Educ:* Bradley Univ, BA, 76; Univ Minn, MS, 80; Pa State Univ, PhD(nutrit), 85. *Prof Exp:* Res assoc dietary monitoring, Pa State Univ, 85-86; nutritionist, USDA, 86-91, br chief, 90-91. *Mem:* Sigma Xi; Am Dietary Asn; Am Inst Nutrit; Soc Clin Nutrit; Am Pub Health Asn. *Mailing Add:* Nat Cancer Inst Exec Plaza N Rm 313 NIH 9000 Rockville Pike Bethesda MD 20892. *Fax:* 301-496-8667

KREDICH, NICHOLAS M, INTERNAL MEDICINE, RHEUMATIC DISEASES. *Current Pos:* from asst prof to assoc prof, 68-80, PROF INTERNAL MED, MED CTR, DUKE UNIV, 80- *Personal Data:* b Chicago, Ill, Sept 23, 35; m 57; c 3. *Educ:* Duke Univ, BA, 57; Univ Mich, MA, 60, MD, 62. *Prof Exp:* Intern internal med, Duke Hosp, Durham, NC, 62-63, asst resident, 63-64; res assoc molecular biol, Nat Inst Arthritis & Metab Dis, 64-66, staff assoc, 66-68. *Concurrent Pos:* Nat Inst Arthritis & Metab Dis res grant, 68-81; investr, Howard Hughes Med Inst, 73-89. *Res:* Regulation of metabolic pathways, including feedback inhibition and repression and induction of enzymes; bacterial and human genetics; sulfur metabolism in bacteria; adenosine deaminase deficiency; immunodeficiency disease; genetics; molecular biology. *Mailing Add:* Dept Med & Biochem Duke Med Ctr Box 3100 Durham NC 27710. *Fax:* 919-684-5230

KREEGER, RUSSELL LOWELL, CELLULOSICS, PERSONAL CARE POLYMERS. *Current Pos:* SR RES SCIENTIST, SPECIALTY CHEM DIV, UNION CARBIDE CORP, 76- *Personal Data:* b Amherst, Ohio, Jan 24, 46; m 73; c 2. *Educ:* Kent State Univ, BS, 68; Ohio State Univ, Columbus, PhD(org chem), 76. *Mem:* Am Chem Soc; Sigma Xi. *Res:* Research and development; natural polymer process research; cellulosic derivatives; personal care polymers; water-soluble polymers. *Mailing Add:* Union Carbide PO Box 670 Bound Brook NJ 08822-0670

KREER, JOHN B(ELSHAW), ELECTRICAL ENGINEERING. *Current Pos:* from assoc prof to prof, 64-92, chmn, Dept Elec Eng & Systs Sci, 77-87, EMER PROF ELEC ENG, MICH STATE UNIV, 92- *Personal Data:* b Brooklyn, NY, Sept 25, 27; m 57, Vivienne Huffman; c Carolyn K (Bratzel) & Kenneth J. *Educ:* Iowa State Col, BS, 51; Univ Ill, MS, 54, PhD(elec eng), 56. *Prof Exp:* From instr to asst prof elec eng, Univ Ill, 55-59; from assoc prof to prof, Univ WVa, 59-64. *Mem:* Inst Elec & Electronics Engrs; Am Soc Eng Educ. *Mailing Add:* Dept Elec Eng Mich State Univ East Lansing MI 48824-1226. *E-Mail:* kreer@msu.edu

KREEVOY, MAURICE M, CHEMICAL KINETICS, MEMBRANE DYNAMICS. *Current Pos:* from asst prof to prof, 56-94, EMER PROF CHEM, UNIV MINN, MINNEAPOLIS, 94- *Personal Data:* b Boston, Mass, Aug 28, 28; wid; c Edith K (Pang) & William S. *Educ:* Univ Calif, Los Angeles, BS, 50; Mass Inst Technol, PhD, 54. *Prof Exp:* Res assoc chem, Pa State Univ, 53-55; NSF fel, Univ Utah, 55-56. *Concurrent Pos:* Consult, Gen Mills Inc, 59-78, Ventron Corp, 75-79, Henckel Am Inc, 78-85, Honeywell Inc, 85-86, Medtronic Inc, 88-; Sloan Found fel, 60-64; NSF sr fel, Oxford Univ, 62-63; partic, US Acad Sci exchange prog with Coun of Acad Socialist Fed Repub of Yugoslavia, 69-70. *Mem:* Am Chem Soc; Croatian Chem Soc; Sigma Xi. *Res:* Physical and theoretical organic chemistry; chemical kinetics and dynamics in solution; isotope effects; dynamics of membrane transport. *Mailing Add:* Dept Chem Univ Minn Minneapolis MN 55455. *Fax:* 612-626-7541; *E-Mail:* kreevoy@chemsun.chem.umn.edu

KREFT, ANTHONY FRANK, III, ORGANIC CHEMISTRY, MEDICINAL CHEMISTRY. *Current Pos:* Supvr, Wyeth Res Labs, 78-87, prin scientist, 88-91, SUPVR MED CHEM, WYETH-AYERST LABS, 87-, RES FEL, 91- *Personal Data:* b Detroit, Mich, May 28, 48; m 79, Margaret M Doyle; c Anthony. *Educ:* Univ Mich, BS, 70; Columbia Univ, MPh, 73, PhD(org chem), 76. *Concurrent Pos:* Fel, Stanford Univ, 76-78. *Mem:* Am Chem Soc; Inflammation Res Asn; NY Acad Sci. *Res:* Design and synthesis of drugs of medicinal interest especially in the areas of inflammation, allergy, asthma, and diseases of the central nervous system; author of 70 publications and granted 67 patents. *Mailing Add:* Wyeth-Ayerst Labs CN 8000 Princeton NJ 08540. *Fax:* 732-274-4503; *E-Mail:* kreft@war.wyeth.com

KREH, DONALD WILLARD, ORGANIC CHEMISTRY. *Current Pos:* chemist, 67-68, SR CHEMIST, TENN EASTMAN CO, 69- *Personal Data:* b Frederick, Md, Mar 17, 37; m 66; c 4. *Educ:* Univ Richmond, BS, 59, MS, 61; Va Polytech Inst, PhD(org chem), 66. *Prof Exp:* Chemist, Great Lakes Res Corp, 66-67. *Mem:* Am Chem Soc. *Res:* Reactions and synthesis of small ring sulfides, sulfoxides and sulfones; synthesis of photographic chemicals, antioxidants, stabilizers, and industrial chemical intermediates. *Mailing Add:* Eastman Chem Co PO Box 511 Kingsport TN 37622-5075

KREH, E(DWARD) J(OSEPH), JR, ENGINEERING. *Current Pos:* CONSULT ENGR, O'DONNELL & ASSOC, 82- *Personal Data:* b Pittsburgh, Pa, Feb 26, 15; m 38; c 3. *Educ:* Carnegie Inst Technol, BS, 37. *Prof Exp:* Design engr, Westinghouse Elec Corp, 37-42; plant engr, Camillus Cutlery Co, 46-51; mgr equip develop, Westinghouse Elec Corp, 51-56, mem div mgr staff, Stress Corrosion & Hydraul Fields, Bettis Plant, 56-58, div apparatus engr, 58-59, mgr, Nuclear Core Dept, 59-61, mgr, Core Mat Dept, 61-65, mgr cent labs, 65-67, mgr opers, Bettis Plant, 67-72, Prod Assurance, Westinghouse Pressurized Water Reactors Div, 72-79, consult engr, 79-82. *Mem:* Am Soc Mech Engrs; Nat Asn Corrosion Engrs; Am Inst Mgt; Am Nuclear Soc; Am Soc Chem Engrs. *Res:* Thermal, mechanical and electrical design; corrosion studies; development of fabrication processes for nuclear reactors; development and management of quality assurance systems to assure reactor safety and reliability. *Mailing Add:* 624 Trotwood Circle Pittsburgh PA 15241

KREH, RICHARD EDWARD, BIOLOGICAL SCIENCES. *Current Pos:* RES ASSOC FOREST BIOL, VA POLYTECH INST & STATE UNIV, 69- *Personal Data:* b Waterbury, Conn, Dec 22, 41; m 67; c 2. *Educ:* Univ Conn, BS, 69; Va Polytech Inst & State Univ, MS, 74. *Mem:* Soc Am Foresters. *Res:* Silviculture research on site preparation; root growth analysis of forest tree nursery growth seedlings; nitrogen dynamics of mine spoil soils for forestry reclamation; hybrid performance of selected pine crosses. *Mailing Add:* Reynolds Homestead Res Ctr PO Box 70 Critz VA 24082-0070

KREIBICH, GERT, CELL BIOLOGY. *Current Pos:* from asst prof to assoc prof, 72-82, PROF CELL BIOL, MED CTR, NY UNIV, 82- *Personal Data:* b Komotau, Czech, Nov 14, 39; Ger citizen; m 66; c 1. *Educ:* Univ Heidelberg, dipl chem, 65, Dr rer nat, 68. *Prof Exp:* Fel chem carcinogenesis, Ger Cancer Res Ctr, Heidelberg, 65-70; res assoc cell biol, Rockefeller Univ, 70-72. *Concurrent Pos:* Res fel, Ger Res Soc, 70-72; NIH res career develop award, 77-82; mem cell biol study sect, NIH, 78-82, Irma Hirschl Award, 82-86. *Mem:* Ger Soc Biol Chem; NY Acad Sci; Am Soc Cell Biol; Am Soc Biol Chemists. *Res:* Structure and function of subcellular membranes in eukaryotic cells; function of membrane bound polysomes in membrane biogenesis. *Mailing Add:* Dept Cell Biol Sch Med NY Univ 550 First Ave MSB 697 New York NY 10016-6402

KREIBICH, ROLAND, ORGANIC CHEMISTRY. *Current Pos:* RETIRED. *Personal Data:* b Glasert, Bohemia, July 30, 22; m 58. *Educ:* Univ Graz, Magister Pharmaciae, 49, PhD(chem), 51. *Prof Exp:* Res chemist, Can Westinghouse, 52-54 & Durez Plastics, Inc, 54-56; proj engr, Gen Elec, 57-58; mgr, Polymer Res Dept, Weyerhaeuser Co, 58-82. *Res:* Polymers; resins. *Mailing Add:* 4201 S 344th St Auburn WA 98001

KREIDER, DONALD LESTER, MATHEMATICAL LOGIC. *Current Pos:* from asst prof to assoc prof, 60-68, PROF MATH, DARTMOUTH COL, 68- *Personal Data:* b Lancaster, Pa, Dec 5, 31; m 52; c 3. *Educ:* Lebanon Valley Col, BS, 53; Mass Inst Technol, PhD(math), 59. *Prof Exp:* Instr, Lebanon Valley Col, 52-53; asst, Mass Inst Technol, 53-55, instr math, 55-60. *Mem:* Am Math Soc; Asn Symbolic Logic; Math Asn Am (pres); Soc Indust & Appl Math; Nat Asn Math; Asn Women Math. *Res:* Recursive functions; automata theory. *Mailing Add:* Dept Math & Comput Sci Dartmouth Col 6211 Sudikoff Hanover NH 03755-3510

KREIDER, EUNICE S, international product development, hematology & oncology, for more information see previous edition

KREIDER, HENRY ROYER, PHYSICAL CHEMISTRY, ORGANIC CHEMISTRY. *Current Pos:* CONSULT DRUG COSMETIC INDUSTS, 71- *Personal Data:* b Baltimore, Md, Dec 31, 11; m 36; c 2. *Educ:* Univ Toledo, BA, 33; Ohio State Univ, MS, 35, PhD(chem), 36. *Prof Exp:* Chemist, Am Med Asn, Chicago, 36-42 & Mead Johnson & Co, Ind, 42-45; exec asst to vpres, William S Merrell Co, 45-50, assoc dir res, 50-56; dir res, Chesebrough-Ponds, Inc, 56-59; exec vpres, Viobin Corp, 59-60; dir res, Sherman Labs, 60-68; dir prod develop, Cooper Labs, Inc, 68-71. *Mem:* AAAS; Am Chem Soc; Soc Cosmetic Chem; Am Pharmaceut Asn; Asn Res Dirs; Sigma Xi. *Res:* Development of foods, drugs & cosmetics; vitamins; proteins; fats; micronutrients. *Mailing Add:* 830 N Shore Dr NE Apt 14A St Petersburg FL 33701

KREIDER, JACK LEON, ANIMAL SCIENCE, EQUINE REPRODUCTIVE PHYSIOLOGY. *Current Pos:* PROF ANIMAL SCI & RESIDENT DIR, DEAN LEE RES STA, ALEXANDRIA, LA, 85- *Personal Data:* b Afton, Okla, Mar 12, 41; m 67; c 3. *Educ:* Okla State Univ, BS, 68; Univ Ky, MS, 70, PhD(animal sci), 71. *Prof Exp:* Asst prof animal sci, Univ Mo, Columbia, 72; from asst prof to assoc prof animal sci, La State Univ, Baton Rouge, 73-79; assoc prof animal sci, Tex A&M Univ, 79-84. *Concurrent Pos:* Mem, La Forage & Grasslands Coun, Am Forage & Grasslands Coun. *Mem:* Am Soc Animal Sci; Am Registry Prof Animal Scientists. *Res:* Reproductive physiology and endocrinology of the mare as related to improving efficiency of production of horses, particularly the perparturient period; reproductive physiology of the stallion, particularly semen physiology; administration of research in beef cattle and and service management as well as agronomy and weed control. *Mailing Add:* 214 Middleton Dr Alexandria LA 71302-9608

KREIDER, JOHN WESLEY, CANCER RESEARCH, TUMOR IMMUNOLOGY. *Current Pos:* MEM FAC PATH, HERSHEY MED CTR, 68- *Personal Data:* b Philadelphia, Pa, Mar 24, 37; m 63; c 2. *Educ:* La Salle Col, AB, 59; Univ Pa, MD, 63. *Honors & Awards:* Borden Award, AOA. *Prof Exp:* Mem fac path, Med Sch, Univ Pa, 67-68. *Concurrent Pos:* Career develop award, USPHS, 69; mem, Path B Study Sect, NIH, 79-, Am Cancer Soc Study Sect, VA Study Sect. *Mem:* Am Asn Pathologists; Am Asn Cancer Res; Am Asn Immunologists. *Res:* Host regulation of tumor growth; neoplastic cell differentiation; papillomavirus transformation. *Mailing Add:* Dept Path Pa State Univ Col Med PO Box 850 Hershey PA 17033-0850

KREIDER, KENNETH GRUBER, THIN FILMS, SENSORS. *Current Pos:* DIV CHIEF, & SR SCIENTIST, NAT BUR STAND, 75- *Personal Data:* b Lancaster, Pa, May 21, 37; m 61, Carole Compton; c Kenneth B, Cynthia L & Christopher L. *Educ:* Mass Inst Technol, SB, 59, SM, 61, ScD, 63. *Honors & Awards:* Bronze Medal, US Dept Com. *Prof Exp:* Res supvr, United Aircraft Res Labs, 65-73. *Concurrent Pos:* Chmn, Inst Elec & Electronics Engrs Tech Comt Sensor Standards; judge, Am Paper Inst Energy & Environ Awards, 78-90; adv panel, UPA Ctr Chem Elec, 85-86, Mass Inst Technol, Electronic Package, 90-92. *Mem:* Am Vacuum Soc; Am Soc Testing & Mat; Mat Res Soc; Am Soc Metals; Inst Elec & Electronics Engrs Instruments & Measurements Soc. *Res:* Thin Film Sensors; instrumentation for harsh environments; metal matrix composites; infrared thermography; sputtering of thin films; thin film electronics. *Mailing Add:* Nat Inst Stand & Technol Bldg 221 Rm A303 Gaithersburg MD 20899. *Fax:* 301-548-0206

KREIDER, LEONARD C(ALE), CHEMISTRY. *Current Pos:* RETIRED. *Personal Data:* b Sterling, Ohio, Feb 16, 10; m 33, Rachel Weaver; c Leonard E, Anna R & Sara K. *Educ:* Goshen Col, AB, 31; Ohio State Univ, MSc, 33, PhD(org chem), 36. *Prof Exp:* Preparations asst, Ohio State Univ, 31-32, asst chem, 32-36; res chemist, Rockefeller Inst, 36-37; from asst prof to prof chem, Bethel Col Kans, 37-49, chmn, Div Natural Sci, 46-49; chemist tech serv, Res Ctr, B F Goodrich Co, 49-50, pioneering res, 50-56 & org res, 56-59, sr res chemist polymerization res, 59-75. *Mem:* Am Chem Soc; Sigma Xi. *Res:* Development of catalyst for manufacture of cis-1, 4-polyisoprene and for Hydrin rubbers; oligosaccharides; alkaline degradation of carbohydrates; galacturonic acid chemistry; pigment reinforcement in rubber; alkali metal catalyzed rubbers; polyester urethane rubbers; rubber hysteresis; aluminum alkyls; metalloorganic catalyzed polymerizations. *Mailing Add:* 1320 Greencroft Dr Goshen IN 46526-5135

KREIDL, NORBERT J(OACHIM), glass science & technology; deceased, see previous edition for last biography

KREIDL, TOBIAS JOACHIM, DIGITAL IMAGE PROCESSING. *Current Pos:* ASTRONR, LOWELL OBSERV, 80- *Personal Data:* b Rochester, NY, May 6, 54. *Educ:* Univ Vienna, Austria, PhD(astron), 79. *Prof Exp:* Res assoc, Ruhr Univ, Bochum, WGer, 79-80. *Concurrent Pos:* Lectr comput sci, Northern Ariz Univ, 81. *Mem:* Am Astron Soc; Sigma Xi. *Res:* Digital image processing and image processing systems; photometry of peculiar A-type stars; computer analysis of astronomical data of various nature. *Mailing Add:* 30 Pine Del Dr Flagstaff AZ 86001

KREIDLER, ERIC RUSSELL, PHASE EQUILIBRIA, LUMINESCENCE. *Current Pos:* ASSOC PROF CERAMIC ENG, OHIO STATE UNIV, 80- *Personal Data:* b Lock Haven, Pa, July 21, 39; m 68; c 2. *Educ:* Pa State Univ, BS, 61, MS, 63, PhD(ceramic sci), 67. *Prof Exp:* Res chemist, Gen Elec Co, 66-80. *Concurrent Pos:* Consult, Gen Elec Co, 80-82; contrib ed, Communications of the Am Ceramic Soc, 81-; assoc ed, Phase Diagrams for Ceramists, 81- *Mem:* Fel Am Ceramic Soc; Electrochem Soc; Mat Res Soc. *Res:* Determination of phase diagrams; crystal chemistry and luminescence of inorganic materials; phosphors and luminescence; glass-metal composites; high temperature ceramic superconductors; electronic ceramics; ceramic processing. *Mailing Add:* 2041 College Rd Columbus OH 43210-1124

KREIER, JULIUS PETER, PROTOZOOLOGY, IMMUNOLOGY. *Current Pos:* RETIRED. *Personal Data:* b Philadelphia, Pa, Nov 30, 26; m 55; c 2. *Educ:* Univ Pa, VMD, 53; Univ Ill, MS, 59, PhD, 62. *Honors & Awards:* Fulbright Award, Inst Hyg, Montevideo, 77. *Prof Exp:* Vet, Agr Res Serv, USDA, 53-56; instr vet physiol, Univ Ill, 56-59, instr vet path & hyg, 59-61, USPHS fel, 61-62; from asst prof to assoc prof, Ohio State Univ, 62-72, prof microbiol, 72-89. *Concurrent Pos:* Vis prof, State Univ de Sao Paulo, Botucatu, Brazil, 81; lectr, China Nat Ctr Prev Med, Inst Parasitol, 85. *Mem:* Am Soc Trop Med Hygiene; Soc Protozoologists; Am Soc Parasitol; Am Asn Immunol; Am Soc Microbiol. *Res:* Host-parasite interactions, primarily the blood inhabiting protozoa; malaria parasites, babesia and trypanosomes; procaryotic protists which parasitize the blood; Anaplasmataceae and Bartonellaceae; pathogenesis of the anaemic changes associated with infection and the mechanisms by which the host controls the parasite population; immunological and biochemical events associated with disease and recovery from disease; isolation and identification of parasites and parasite parts for use as antigens. *Mailing Add:* 2047 Iuka Ave Columbus OH 43201

KREIFELDT, JOHN GENE, ENGINEERING DESIGN, ERGONOMICS & HUMAN FACTORS. *Current Pos:* From asst prof to assoc prof, 69-80, PROF ENG DESIGN & HUMAN FACTORS ENG, TUFTS UNIV, 80- *Personal Data:* b Manistee, Mich, Oct 7, 34; m 64; c 2. *Educ:* Univ Calif, Los Angeles, BS, 61; Mass Inst Tech, MS, 64; Case Western Res Univ, PhD(biomed & human factors eng), 69. *Concurrent Pos:* USPHS grants, Tufts Univ & New Eng Med Ctr, 71-81; Nat Res Coun associateship, NASA-Ames Res Ctr, 73; Dept Health, Educ & Welfare grant; NASA grants; NSF grant. *Mem:* Human Factors & Ergonomics. *Res:* Electromyographic processing and control; man-machine system design; air traffic control studies; computers in automation of radiotherapy treatment; multidimensional scaling in design; mathematical models of human operators; consumer product design; safety design. *Mailing Add:* Dept Mech Eng Tufts Univ Medford MA 02155. *E-Mail:* jkreifel@pearl.tufts.edu

KREIGHBAUM, WILLIAM EUGENE, MEDICINAL CHEMISTRY, SCIENCE COMMUNICATIONS. *Current Pos:* SR INFO ANALYST, BRISTOL MYERS SQUIBB CO, WALLINGFORD, 87- *Personal Data:* b Elkhart, Ind, June 17, 34; m 61, M Carolyn Walsh; c David & Carol. *Educ:* Wabash Col, AB, 56; Ind Univ, PhD(org chem), 60. *Prof Exp:* Bristol Labs res fel org chem, Ind Univ, 60-61; sr res scientist, 61-67, group leader, 68-69, sr investr, 70-73, prin investr, Mead Johnson Res Ctr, Mead Johnson & Co, 74-86. *Mem:* Am Chem Soc. *Res:* Synthesis and pharmacological activity of organic sulfur compounds; heterocyclic compounds containing sulfur or nitrogen; chemistry of the sympathetic nervous system. *Mailing Add:* Sci Info Dept 809 Bristol Myers Squibb Co Wallingford CT 06492-7660. *Fax:* 203-284-6006; *E-Mail:* tnbd70a@prodigy.com

KREILICK, ROBERT W, PHYSICAL CHEMISTRY. *Current Pos:* From asst prof to assoc prof, 64-71, PROF CHEM, UNIV ROCHESTER, 71- *Personal Data:* b Kalamazoo, Mich, Jan 3, 38; m 59; c 2. *Educ:* Wash Univ, AB, 59, PhD(magnetic resonance), 64. *Concurrent Pos:* Alfred P Sloan fel, 69-71; consult, NIH; founder Adaptable Lab Software, 83. *Mem:* Am Chem Soc. *Res:* Nuclear magnetic resonance and electron spin resonance; biophysical chemistry; study of biologically important metal complexes; computer software for chemistry. *Mailing Add:* Dept Chem Univ Rochester Rochester NY 14627-1001

KREILING, DARYL, MATHEMATICS. *Current Pos:* dean arts & sci, 80-87, PROF MATH, UNIV TENN, 80- *Personal Data:* b Minatare, Nebr, May 18, 36; m 56; c 3. *Educ:* Chadron State Col, BS, 61; Bowling Green State Univ, MA, 63; Univ Wyo, PhD(math), 69. *Prof Exp:* Instr math, Univ Wyo, 66-69; from asst prof to assoc prof math, Western Ill Univ, 73-80, asst dean, 74-80. *Mem:* Am Math Soc; Math Asn Am. *Res:* Associative and non-associative rings; radicals of rings and ring-like structures. *Mailing Add:* 428 Moody Ave Martin TN 38237

KREILING, WILLIAM H(ERMAN), CHEMICAL ENGINEERING. *Current Pos:* RETIRED. *Personal Data:* b Brooklyn, NY, Dec 20, 23; m 51, Joyce Wurl; c David, Daryl & Ann. *Educ:* Polytech Inst Brooklyn, BChE, 49. *Prof Exp:* Chem res engr pilot plant design, M W Kellogg Co Div, Pullman, Inc, 42-49; dept chemist paper coatings, Lowe Paper Co, 49-53, res chemist, 53-55, gen foreman coatings dept, 55-57, tech supt finishing mill, 57-58, qual control supvr, 58-59; chem engr coating develop, Keuffel & Esser Co, 59-64, mgr process eng, 64-68; sect leader, paper & coatings group, Corp Res Ctr, Int Paper Co, 68-70, sr res assoc paper develop, Corp Res & Develop Div, 70-78; sr develop engr, Specialty Papers & Packaging Div, Ludlow Corp, 78-80, sr develop engr, Laminating & Coatings Div, 80-82; res engr, Timex Corp, 82-84; sr proj mgr, Luminescent Syst Inc, 84-88. *Concurrent Pos:* Chmn, Testing Div, Tech Asn Pulp & Paper Indust, 72-74. *Mem:* Tech Asn Pulp & Paper Indust; fel Am Inst Chem; NY Acad Sci; Soc Info Display. *Res:* Protective, decorative, printing and photographic coatings and specialty papers; electroluminescent coatings & technology; patents in electrophotography and electroluminescent technology. *Mailing Add:* 53 Hadley Village Rd South Hadley MA 01075

KREIMER, HERBERT FREDERICK, JR, RING THEORY. *Current Pos:* From asst prof to assoc prof, 62-77, dept chair, 90-93, PROF MATH, FLA STATE UNIV, 77- *Personal Data:* b Cincinnati, Ohio, Feb 19, 36; m 61, Sarah J Klein; c Caroline L & Herbert F III. *Educ:* Yale Univ, BS, 58, PhD(math), 62. *Concurrent Pos:* Univ Res Coun grant, 64 & 67; vis assoc prof, Northwestern Univ, 65-66; NSF grant, 65-66 & 68-71. *Mem:* Am Math Soc; Math Asn Am; Sigma Xi. *Res:* Hopfalgebras; separable algebras; Galois theory and its generalizations for rings; Galois cohomology. *Mailing Add:* Dept Math Fla State Univ Tallahassee FL 32306-3027. *E-Mail:* kreimer@gauss.math.fsu.edu

KREIN, PHILIP T, POWER ELECTRONICS, ELECTROSTATICS. *Current Pos:* vis asst prof, 82-84, asst prof, 87-92, ASSOC PROF ELEC ENG, UNIV ILL, URBANA, 92- *Personal Data:* b Orange, Calif, Apr 22, 56. *Educ:* Lafayette Col, BS, 78, AB, 78; Univ Ill, Urbana, MS, 80, PhD(elec eng), 82. *Prof Exp:* Physicist, Tektronix, Inc, Beaverton, Ore, 84-87. *Concurrent*

Pos: Vis researcher, Sundstrand Corp, Rockford, Ill, 83; vpres, Power Electronics Soc, Inst Elec & Electronics Engrs, 97- *Mem:* Inst Elec & Electronics Engrs; Electrostatics Soc Am. *Res:* Large-signal and nonlinear control issues in power electronics; advanced switching power converters; electrohydrodynamics and other applications of electrostatics; electric machines and drive systems. *Mailing Add:* Dept Elec & Comput Eng Univ Ill 1406 W Green Urbana IL 61801. *Fax:* 217-333-1162; *E-Mail:* krein@ece.uiuc.edu

KREIPKE, MERRILL VINCENT, GEOTECHNICAL ENGINEERING, CIVIL ENGINEERING. *Current Pos:* CONSULT, 75- *Personal Data:* b Evansville, Ind, Feb 14, 16; m 37, Dorothy L Neu; c Karen J & Jane A. *Educ:* Purdue Univ, BS, 36. *Honors & Awards:* Meritorious Civilian Serv Medal, Dept Army, 66. *Prof Exp:* Resident engr, Off City Engr, Evansville, Ind, 36-39; inspector, US Army Engrs Dist, Ky, 39-41, jr engr, 41-42, asst engr, 42-44, engr, 46-51, civil engr, 51-56 & Off Chief Engrs, US Dept Army, 56-61, engr, Off Chief Res & Develop, 61-69, chief geophys sci br, US Army Res Off, 69-74, chief mil res & develop team, Chief Engrs, Dept Army, 74-75. *Concurrent Pos:* Permanent secy, quadripartite standing working group ground mobility, Armies of US, UK, Can & Australia, 59-66; proj officer for US, NATO long-term sci study land-based mobility, 66-; US nat leader, NATO long-term sci study mobility interface, 69-; exec mem & US leader, subgroup T-ground mobility, Tech Coop Prog, US, UK, Can & Australia, 69-; US nat leader, NATO long-term sci study on Arctic opers, 71- *Mem:* Fel Am Soc Civil Engrs; Soc Am Mil Engrs; Nat Soc Prof Engrs; Int Soc Soil Mech & Found Eng; Int Soc Terrain-Vehicle Systs. *Res:* Soil mechanics; terrain-vehicle interaction; quantitative terrain evaluation; design and construction of earth and rockfill dams; rapid earthwork; soil stabilization; soil surfacings. *Mailing Add:* 12191 Clipper Dr No 403 Woodbridge VA 22192. *Fax:* 703-643-9812

KREIS, RONALD W, physical chemistry, for more information see previous edition

KREIS, WILLI, CLINICAL PHARMACOLOGY, CHEMOTHERAPY. *Current Pos:* asst prof, Sloan-Kettering Inst Cancer Res, Cornell Univ, 67-72, assoc mem, 69-81, chmn biochem unit, 74-75, ASSOC PROF, SLOAN-KETTERING DIV, GRAD SCH MED SCI, CORNELL UNIV, 72- *Personal Data:* b Ebnat, Switz, Nov 3, 24; m 62; c 4. *Educ:* Univ Zurich, MD, 54; Univ Basel, PhD(org chem), 57. *Prof Exp:* Res mem biochem pharmacol, Sandoz, Ltd, Basel, Switz, 58-61; res assoc, Sloan-Kettering Inst Cancer Res, 61-64, assoc, 64-69. *Concurrent Pos:* Damon Runyon grant, 73; Nat Cancer Inst grant, 75; asst attend clin pharmacologist, Dept Med, Mem Hosp, 75-; Am Cancer Soc grants, 76, 78, 79, 80 & 81; assoc prof pharmacol & therapeut, Sloan-Kettering Div Grad Sch Med Sci, Cornell Univ, 70-80, adj staff mem, Mem Sloan-Kettering Cancer Ctr, 82-87; assoc attending res prof, North Shore Univ Hosp, Cornell Univ Med Col, 89- *Mem:* Swiss Med Soc; Swiss Chem Soc; Am Asn Cancer Res; NY Acad Sci; Am Soc Biol Chemists; Am Soc Clin Oncol. *Res:* Biochemical pharmacology of anticancer drugs; experimental and clinical pharmacology of cancer; biochemistry of nucleic acids; phase I and II evaluation of new anticancer agents, especially prostate cancer. *Mailing Add:* Dept Med N Shore Univ Hosp 300 Commun Dr Manhasset NY 11030. *Fax:* 516-562-8950

KREISER, RALPH R, INORGANIC CHEMISTRY, ANALYTICAL CHEMISTRY. *Current Pos:* PROF CHEM & CHMN DEPT, COMMUNITY COL RI, 72- *Personal Data:* b Lebanon, Pa, Oct 7, 41; m; c 2. *Educ:* Lebanon Valley Col, BSc, 63; Brown Univ, MSc, 66; Univ Conn, PhD(chem), 69. *Prof Exp:* Asst solid state chem, Philips Nature Sci Lab, Eindhoven, Holland, 69-70; inst chem, Univ Conn, 71-72. *Concurrent Pos:* Mem comn math & sci, State of RI, 84-85. *Mem:* Am Chem Soc; Sigma Xi. *Res:* Interface of science and the arts in the areas of conservation and restoration. *Mailing Add:* Dept Chem Community Col RI 400 East Ave Warwick RI 02886. *E-Mail:* rkreiser@cccri.cc.ri.us

KREISER, THOMAS H(ARRY), ANALYTICAL CHEMISTRY. *Current Pos:* SR SCIENTIST, ENVIRON TEST SYSTS, INC, 87- *Personal Data:* b Ono, Pa, Aug 12, 35; m 79; c 3. *Educ:* Lebanon Valley Col, BS, 58; Univ Nebr, MS, 60, PhD(chem), 65. *Prof Exp:* Res biochemist, Miles Labs Inc, 62-86. *Mem:* Sigma Xi. *Res:* Analytical test systems research and development. *Mailing Add:* 30182 Blue Spruce Dr Elkhart IN 46514-9723

KREISHMAN, GEORGE PAUL, BIOPHYSICAL CHEMISTRY. *Current Pos:* from asst prof to assoc prof, 75-90, PROF CHEM, UNIV CINCINNATI, 90- *Personal Data:* b Nurnberg, Ger, Jan 28, 46; US citizen; m 72, Ilze Incis; c Mara & Peter. *Educ:* Univ Wis-Milwaukee, BS, 67; Calif Inst Technol, PhD(chem), 72. *Prof Exp:* Fel chem, Int Chem Nuclear Corp, 71-72; fel biophys, Univ Pittsburgh, 72-74; vis teaching asst chem, Mich Technol Univ, 74-75. *Mem:* Am Chem Soc; Res Soc Alcoholism. *Res:* Application of nuclear magnetic resonance spectroscopy and electrochemical techniques to the study of biologically important systems. *Mailing Add:* Dept Chem Univ Cincinnati 2600 Clifton Ave Cincinnati OH 45220-2872. *Fax:* 513-556-9239

KREISLE, LEONARDT F(ERDINAND), mechanical engineering, for more information see previous edition

KREISLER, MICHAEL NORMAN, HIGH ENERGY PHYSICS. *Current Pos:* assoc prof, 72-76, grad dean res, 75-77, PROF PHYSICS, UNIV MASS, AMHERST, 76-, DIV LEADER, N DIV, 94- *Personal Data:* b Bronx, NY, Oct 30, 40; m 63, Barbara Laurence; c David, Michele & Jeffrey. *Educ:* Princeton Univ, AB, 62; Stanford Univ, MS, 63, PhD(physics), 66. *Prof Exp:* From instr to asst prof physics, Joseph Henry Labs, Princeton Univ, 66-72. *Concurrent Pos:* Sci assoc, Europ Orgn Nuclear Res, Geneva, 78-79; consult, Lawrence Livermore Labs, Los Alamos Labs. *Mem:* Am Phys Soc; Sigma Xi. *Res:* Investigation of the strong interactions of neutrons and protons, especially cross sections; study of the decays of multi-pionic resonances such as the eta meson; search for rare phenomena in weak interactions, kaon decays, beta decay of Lambda hyperon; search for tachyons; polarization in inclusive reactions; charm searches; macron accelerators; hadronic production of particles with strange, charm, and bottom quarks; new approaches to ultra high speed computation. *Mailing Add:* N Div L056 Lawrence Livermore Nat Lab Livermore CA 94550. *Fax:* 510-423-8086; *E-Mail:* kreisler1@llnl.gov

KREISMAN, NORMAN RICHARD, NEUROPHYSIOLOGY. *Current Pos:* Instr, 71-73, asst prof, 73-79, ASSOC PROF PHYSIOL, SCH MED, TULANE UNIV, 79- *Personal Data:* b Chicago, Ill, June 26, 43; m 75; c 1. *Educ:* Ariz State Univ, BA, 65; Univ Mich, MS, 68; Med Col Pa, PhD(physiol), 71. *Concurrent Pos:* Vis prof neurol, Case Western Res Univ Sch Med, 93. *Mem:* Int Soc Cerebral Blood Flow & Metab; Soc Neurosci; Am Heart Asn; Am Physiol Soc. *Res:* Electrophysiological and metabolic relationships in brain in physiological and pathophysiological states; epilepsy; hypoxia. *Mailing Add:* Dept Physiol SL-39 Sch Med Tulane Univ 1430 Tulane Ave New Orleans LA 70112-2699

KREITH, FRANK, SOLAR ENGINEERING, THERMODYNAMICS. *Current Pos:* RETIRED. *Personal Data:* b Vienna, Austria, Dec 15, 22; nat US; m 51; c 3. *Educ:* Univ Calif, BS, 45; Univ Calif, Los Angeles, MS, 49; Univ Paris, Dr Univ Paris(sci), 65. *Honors & Awards:* Worcester Award, 80; Max Jacob Award, 85; Charles Greeley Abbott Award, 88. *Prof Exp:* Res engr, Jet Propulsion Lab, Calif Inst Technol, 45-49; asst prof mech eng, Univ Calif, 51-53; assoc prof, Lehigh Univ, 53-59; chief thermal conversion, Solar Energy Res Inst, 77-84; prof mech & chem eng, 59-78, fac res assoc, Inst Behav Sci, 71-77, emer prof chem eng, Univ Colo, Boulder, 78-; pres, Kreith Eng Inc, 88-94. *Concurrent Pos:* Consult, Proj Squid, 50, Air Prod, Inc, 55-57, Metals Disintegrating Co, 57-69, Beech Aircraft Co, 59 & Nat Ctr Atmos Res, 67-69; mem staff, Nat Bur Standards, 61-63; Fulbright grants & vis lectr, France, Israel & Spain, 64-65; mem, Nat Adv Group Aeronaut Res & Develop-NATO, 64-65; fac res asst, Inst Arctic & Alpine Res, 65-71; NATO sr fel, 75; pres, Environ Consult Serv, 75-77; sr res fel, Solar Energy Res Inst, 84-87, consult engr, 87-88. *Mem:* Fel Am Soc Mech Engrs; Am Inst Chem Engrs; Inst Soc Solar Energy. *Res:* Heat transfer; boundary layer theory; solar engineering; solar energy thermal conversion; heat transfer & energy conservation; design of energy conversion & cogeneration systems; author of books on heat transfer, waste management, renewable energy conversion & solar building design; technical editor. *Mailing Add:* 1485 Sierra Dr Boulder CO 80302-7846. *Fax:* 303-863-8003

KREITH, KURT, MATHEMATICS. *Current Pos:* assoc prof, 65-69, PROF MATH, UNIV CALIF, DAVIS, 69- *Personal Data:* b Vienna, Austria, May 3, 32; US citizen; m 57. *Educ:* Univ Calif, Berkeley, AB, 53, MA, 57, PhD(math), 60. *Prof Exp:* Asst prof math, Univ Calif, Davis, 60-63; phys sci officer, US Arms Control & Disarmament Agency, 63-65. *Mem:* Am Math Soc; Math Asn Am. *Res:* Differential equations and differential operators in Hilbert space. *Mailing Add:* Dept Math Univ Calif Davis CA 95616-8633

KREITZBERG, CARL WILLIAM, METEOROLOGY. *Current Pos:* assoc prof, 70-76, PROF PHYSICS & ATMOSPHERIC SCI, DREXEL UNIV, 77- *Personal Data:* b Missoula, Mont, Mar 25, 37; m 58; c 4. *Educ:* Univ Wash, BS, 59, PhD(meteorol), 63. *Prof Exp:* Res physicist, Meteorol Lab, Air Force Cambridge Res Labs, 63-67; asst prof meteorol, Pa State Univ, 67-69. *Mem:* AAAS; Am Meteorol Soc; Sigma Xi. *Res:* Atmospheric structure, dynamics and prediction on the mesoscale, especially scale interactions due to clouds and boundary layer processes as determined from numerical simulation and field experiments. *Mailing Add:* Dept Physics Drexel Univ 3141 Chestnut St Philadelphia PA 19104-2816

KREITZER, MELVYN, OPTICAL DESIGNING. *Personal Data:* b Cape Town, SAfrica, Oct 21, 45; m 71, Sharon Meyerowitz; c Jason & David. *Educ:* Univ Cape Town, BS, 64, BS(Hons), 66; Rochester Inst Technol, MS, 68; Univ Ariz, MS & PhD, 76. *Honors & Awards:* Eng Excellence Award, Optical Soc Am, 95. *Mem:* Optical Soc Am. *Res:* Granted patents in professional field. *Mailing Add:* 8816 Tulipwood Ct Cincinnati OH 45242

KREIZINGER, JEAN DOLLOFF, GENETICS. *Current Pos:* assoc prof, 70-79, assoc dean arts & sci, 82-84, PROF BIOL, WESTERN CONN STATE UNIV, 79-, CHMN DEP BIOL & ENVIRON SCI, 94- *Personal Data:* b Presque Isle, Maine, Oct 17, 31; div; c Diane (Ross), Kary (Evans) & Tracy (Johnson). *Educ:* Univ Maine, BS, 53; Cornell Univ, MS, 56, PhD(genetics), 58; Univ Conn, MBA, 81. *Prof Exp:* Asst prof biol, Danbury State Col, 65-67; NIH res fel human genetics, M D Anderson Hosp & Tumor Inst, Univ Tex, 67-69, res assoc biol, Univ Tex, Houston, 69-70. *Concurrent Pos:* Vis prof, Cornell Univ, 81 & 86, Univ Conn, 91 & Iowa State Univ, 92. *Mem:* Sigma Xi; Bot Soc Am. *Res:* Chemical mutagenesis; plant cytogenetics. *Mailing Add:* Dept Biol & Environ Sci Western Conn State Univ 181 White St Danbury CT 06810-6845

KREJCI, ROBERT HENRY, SOLID ROCKET MOTORS, BALLISTIC MISSILES. *Current Pos:* mgr advan technol, Wasatch Div, 78-84, space motor progs, Strategic Div, 84-86, MGR SPEC PROJS, STRATEGIC DIV, THIOKOL CORP, 86- *Personal Data:* b Shenandoah, Iowa, Nov 15, 43; m 68, Carolyn R Meyer; c Christopher & Ryan. *Educ:* Iowa State Univ, BS, 67, ME, 71; Nat Defense Univ, dipl, 91. *Prof Exp:* Officer, USAF Space Div, 69-73, Ballistic Missiles Off, 75-78; res assoc, Lawrence Livermore Lab, 73-75. *Concurrent Pos:* Aeronaut engr, USAF, Wright Lab, Propulsion & Power Div, 85-96. *Mem:* Am Inst Aeronaut & Astronaut; Nat Planetary Soc; Nat Space Soc. *Res:* Develop and produce test vehicles to advance rocket motor propulsion understanding, including ignition mechanisms and motor dynamics. *Mailing Add:* 885 N 300 E Brigham City UT 84302

KREJSA, RICHARD JOSEPH, CONODONT PALEOBIOLOGY, CYCLOSTOME TOOTH DEVELOPMENT. *Current Pos:* from asst prof to assoc prof, Calif Polytech State Univ, 68-78, prof biol sci, 78-94, prof polit sci, 88-94, EMER PROF, CALIF POLYTECH STATE UNIV, 94- *Personal Data:* b Cleveland, Ohio, Apr 4, 33; m 62; c 6. *Educ:* Mich State Univ, BS, 54; Univ Calif, Los Angeles, MA, 58; Univ BC, PhD(zool), 65. *Honors & Awards:* Frederick H Stoye Award, Am Soc Ichthyologists & Herpetologists, 63. *Prof Exp:* Asst cur fishes, Scripps Inst Oceanog, Univ Calif, 58-59; instr gen zool & biol, Western Wash State Col, 64-65; vis asst prof zool, Univ Hawaii, 65-66; Nat Inst Dent Res trainee comp calcification, Col Physicians & Surgeons, Columbia Univ, 66-68. *Concurrent Pos:* NSF stipend, Summer Inst Animal Behav, Utah State Univ, 65; elected mem, San Luis Obispo Co Bd Supvrs, 73-80, chmn bd, 75, co-chmn, 76; co-chmn & bd dirs, San Luis Obispo Environ Ctr & hon life mem, 80; hon life mem, Red Wind Found, 80; vis scholar, Mus Comp Zool, Harvard Univ, Cambridge, Mass, 82-83. *Mem:* Am Soc Zoologists; Am Soc Ichthyologists & Herpetologists; Europ Soc Comp Skin Biol; AAAS; Pander Soc; Am Fisheries Soc. *Res:* Comparative morphology and embryology of vertebrate skin, teeth and scales; origin of craniata; paleobiology of conodonts; effects of gold mining and other historic natural resource exploitations on California salmonid fisheries. *Mailing Add:* Biol Sci Dept Calif Polytech State Univ San Luis Obispo CA 93407-0001

KREKELER, CARL HERMAN, ZOOLOGY, ENTOMOLOGY. *Current Pos:* prof biol, 47-87, EMER PROF BIOL, VALPARAISO UNIV, 87- *Personal Data:* b Levenworth, Kans, Jan 12, 20; m 44; c 2. *Educ:* Concordia Sem, BA, 41; Univ Chicago, PhD(zool), 55. *Prof Exp:* Instr biol, Bethany Col, 42-44. *Mem:* Ecol Soc Am; Soc Study Evolution; Soc Syst Zoologists; Nat Speleol Soc. *Res:* Speciation pattern in cave beetles; systematic entomology. *Mailing Add:* 8060 E Broadway Blvd Tucson AZ 85710

KREKORIAN, CHARLES O'NEIL, ANIMAL BEHAVIOR. *Current Pos:* from asst prof to assoc prof, 70-79, PROF ZOOL, SAN DIEGO STATE UNIV, 79- *Personal Data:* b Los Angeles, Calif, Apr 17, 41; m 67, Jane Jernegan; c Karl & Quinn. *Educ:* Calif State Col, Los Angeles, BA, 63, MA, 66; Univ Toronto, PhD(zool), 70. *Prof Exp:* Res assoc behav res, Am Inst Res, 64-66. *Mem:* AAAS; Animal Behav Soc; Herpet Soc. *Res:* Ethology of fish and reptiles with emphasis on their agonistic and gamopractic behavior. *Mailing Add:* Biol Dept San Diego State Univ San Diego CA 92182-0001

KRELL, ROBERT DONALD, IMMUNOPHARMACOLOGY. *Current Pos:* AT ICI AM INC. *Personal Data:* b Toledo, Ohio, Dec 2, 43; m 66; c 2. *Educ:* Univ Toledo, BS, 66; Ohio State Univ, PhD(pharmacol), 72. *Prof Exp:* Fel, Sch Hyg & Pub Health, Johns Hopkins Univ, 72-73; sr scientist pharmacol, SmithKline Corp, 73-81; sr mgr, pulmonary pharmacol sect, Stuart Pharmaceut, 81- *Mem:* Soc Neurosci; AAAS; Am Acad Allergy; Am Soc Pharmacol & Exp Therapeut; Am Thoracic Soc; Sigma Xi. *Res:* Biochemical, pharmacological, physiological and immunological investigation into the mechanisms of asthma, immediate-type hypersensitivity reactions and chronic obstructive pulmonary diseases. *Mailing Add:* PO Box 847 Pocono Pines PA 18350

KREMBS, G(EORGE) M(ICHAEL), COMPUTER SYSTEMS INTEGRATION. *Current Pos:* staff engr, Systs Develop Div, IBM Corp, 64-65, mgr adv graphic technol, 65-68, mgr adv display systs, 68-70, mgr, Eng Dept Adv Systs Develop, 70-77, mgr display prod technol, 77-78, mgr adv display prod, 78-79, mgr adv display technol, 79-87, TOTAL SYSTS STRATEGIST, IBM CORP, 87- *Personal Data:* b Merrill, Wis, Sept 2, 34; m 57; c 5. *Educ:* Notre Dame Univ, BS, 56; Stanford Univ, PhD, 59. *Prof Exp:* Elec engr, Ampex Corp, 57-58; group supvr solid state mat, Philco Res Labs, 59-61, sect mgr solid state mat, Ford-Philco Appl Res Labs, 61-64. *Concurrent Pos:* Guest lectr, IBM Systs Res Inst, New York, 80-82. *Mem:* Inst Elec & Electronics Engrs; Asn Comput Mach. *Res:* Computer displays; electronic scanning; graphic image processing; electro-optical systems; television engineering; broadband communications; electron tube devices; solid state device and materials technology; transistor circuit design; design and development of multi-vendor computer networks for IBM large systems used by engineers and scientists. *Mailing Add:* 123 Pleasant Ridge Dr West Hurley NY 12491. *Fax:* 914-433-8469

KREMENAK, CHARLES ROBERT, MAXILLOFACIAL GROWTH & DEVELOPMENT. *Current Pos:* instr ped dent, Univ Iowa, 59-61, asst prof orthodont, 61-69, asst prof otolaryngol & maxillofacial surg, 66-69, assoc prof, 69-72, prof otolaryngol head & neck surg, 72-84, prog dir, 69-94, prof orthodont, 72-94, EMER PROF ORTHODONT, UNIV IOWA, 94- *Personal Data:* b Newell, Iowa, Apr 17, 31; m 54, Nellie Wilson; c Sarah M H (Meyers), Erica A, Martha V & Charles V. *Educ:* Univ Iowa, DDS, 55, MS, 61. *Prof Exp:* Dent officer, USN, 55-58. *Concurrent Pos:* Prog writer & consult, Encycl Britannica Films, Inc, 61-62; Nat Inst Dent Res fel, Univ Iowa, 63-64, Nat Inst Dent Res investr cleft palate prog proj, 65-71, co-prin investr, 71-91; pres, Craniofacial Biol Group, Int Asn Dent Res, 87-88, Am Cleft Palate Asn, 87-88. *Mem:* Int Asn Dent Res; AAAS; Am Cleft Palate Asn; Am Polar Soc. *Res:* Maxillofacial growth, especially elucidation of maxillofacial growth control systems; cleft palate habilitation with emphasis on prevention of postsurgical growth aberration; role of postsurgical wound contraction in midfacial growth and development. *Mailing Add:* Univ Iowa Oakdale Hall Iowa City IA 52242-5000. *E-Mail:* kremenak@aol.com

KREMENTZ, EDWARD THOMAS, SURGICAL ONCOLOGY, CLINICAL RESEARCH. *Current Pos:* from instr to prof surg, Tulane Univ, 50-87, dir, Cancer Res Clin, 62-75, chief, sect oncol, 78, cancer teaching coordr, Am Cancer, 53-82, prof clin oncol, 77-83, EMER PROF SURG, TULANE UNIV, 88- *Personal Data:* b Newark, NJ, Apr 30, 17; m 46, Carolyn Butler; c 5. *Educ:* Wesleyan Univ, AB, 39; Univ Rochester, MD, 43; Am Bd Surg, dipl, 52. *Honors & Awards:* Lucy Wortham James Clin Cancer Res Award, Soc Surg Oncol, 85; Res Center Award, Nat Cancer Inst, Nat Inst Health, 62-67; Margaret Hay Edwards Award Medal for Cancer Educ, Am Asn Cancer Educ, 89. *Prof Exp:* Asst surg, Yale Univ, 43, 44-48, asst resident surg path, 45-46, instr surg, 48-50, Childs fel med res, 48-49. *Concurrent Pos:* Fel, New Haven Hosp, 43, 44-45, asst resident, 46-48, assoc resident, 48-49, chief resident, 49-50; sr vis surgeon, Charity Hosp, La & consult surg, various hosps, 50-; surgeon, Touro Infirmary, 57-63, sr assoc, 63-; prof clin oncol, Am Cancer Soc, 77-83. *Mem:* Am Cancer Soc; Soc Univ Surgeons; Soc Exp Biol & Med; Am Col Surgeons; Am Asn Cancer Res; Soc Surgical Oncol; Am Surg Asn; Am Soc Clin Oncol; Am Med Asn; Soc Int Surg. *Res:* Cancer chemotherapy; experimental surgery; immunotherapy; author or coauthor of 268 publications. *Mailing Add:* Tulane Sch Med Surg 1430 Tulane Ave New Orleans LA 70112

KREMER, JAMES NEVIN, BIOLOGICAL OCEANOGRAPHY, ECOLOGY. *Current Pos:* asst prof, 76-83, ASSOC PROF BIOL SCI, UNIV SOUTHERN CALIF, 83- *Personal Data:* b Montclair, NJ, July 19, 45; m 69; c 2. *Educ:* Princeton Univ, BA, 67; Univ RI, PhD(oceanog), 75. *Prof Exp:* Res asst marine ecol, Grad Sch Oceanog, Univ RI, 70-75. *Concurrent Pos:* NATO fel, 75-76. *Mem:* Am Soc Limnol & Oceanog; Estuarine Res Fedn; Am Geophys Union; Sigma Xi. *Res:* Marine plankton ecology; systems ecology and computer simulation, especially physical processes and nutrient dynamics in planktonic systems. *Mailing Add:* 17640 Virginia Ave Bellflower CA 90706

KREMER, PATRICIA MCCARTHY, zooplankton ecology, for more information see previous edition

KREMER, RUSSELL EUGENE, CRYSTAL GROWTH, SEMICONDUCTOR CHARACTERIZATION. *Current Pos:* STAFF SCIENTIST, CRYSTAL SPECIALTIES INT, 87- *Personal Data:* b Milford, Nebr, May 10, 54; m 84; c 1. *Educ:* Goshen Col, BA, 75; Purdue Univ, MS, 78, PhD(physics), 83. *Prof Exp:* From asst prof to assoc prof appl physics & elec eng, Ore Grad Ctr, 83-87. *Concurrent Pos:* Consult, United Epitaxial Technol, 85-86; adj assoc prof, Ore Grad Ctr, 87-90, Colo Univ, Colo Springs, 90. *Mem:* Am Phys Soc; Mat Res Soc; Sigma Xi; Am Asn Crystal Growth. *Res:* Growth and characterization of compound semiconductor single crystal material; development of a process to grow semi-insulating GaAs using a vertical bridgman technique. *Mailing Add:* Crystal Specialties Int 2853 Janitell Rd Colorado Springs CO 80906

KREMERS, HOWARD EARL, industrial chemistry, for more information see previous edition

KREMKAU, FREDERICK WILLIAM, MEDICAL ULTRASOUND. *Current Pos:* instr med, 72-74, res asst prof, 74-80, DIR, CTR MED ULTRASOUND, BOWMAN GRAY SCH MED, 85- *Personal Data:* b Mechanicsburg, Pa, Apr 30, 40; m 67; c 1. *Educ:* Cornell Univ, BEE, 63; Univ Rochester, MS, 69, PhD(elec eng), 72. *Prof Exp:* Teaching asst elec eng, Univ Rochester, 67-69, res asst, 69-72; assoc prof, Yale Univ, 81-85. *Mem:* Inst Elec & Electronics Engrs; Am Inst Ultrasound Med; Acoust Soc Am. *Res:* Safety of ultrasound; acoustic properties of biological material; sonographic and doppler ultrasound artifacts. *Mailing Add:* Ctr Med Ultrasound Bowman Gray Sch Med Winston-Salem NC 27157-1039

KREMP, GERHARD OTTO WILHELM, geology; deceased, see previous edition for last biography

KREMPL, ERHARD, MECHANICS OF MATERIALS. *Current Pos:* from assoc prof to prof mech, 68-93, head, Dept Mech Eng, Aeronaut Eng & Mech, 87-96, DIR, MECH MAT LAB, RENSSELAER POLYTECH INST, 75-, ROSALIND & JOHN J REDFERN JR PROF ENG, 93- *Personal Data:* b Regensburg, Ger, Mar 5, 34; wid; c 2. *Educ:* Munich Tech Univ, Dipl Ing, 56, Dr Ing(mech of mat), 62. *Honors & Awards:* Nadai Award, Am Soc Mech Engrs. *Prof Exp:* Res proj engr, Munich Tech Univ, 56-64; mech of mat engr, Gen Elec Co, NY, 64-68. *Concurrent Pos:* Fulbright fel, Austria, 85; Humboldt sr scientist, Ger, 93-94. *Mem:* Fel Am Soc Mech Engrs; Am Soc Exp Stress Anal; Am Soc Testing & Mat; Soc Eng Sci; fel Am Acad Mech. *Res:* Mechanics of deformation and fracture behavior of metals and composites; creep, fatigue, fracture; applications to power plant such as steam and gas turbines and nuclear reactors; constitutive equation theory to describe time-dependent material behavior; inelastic analysis. *Mailing Add:* Dept Mech Eng Aeronaut Eng & Mech Rensselaer Polytech Inst Troy NY 12180-3590. *E-Mail:* krempe@rpi.edu

KREMSER, THURMAN RODNEY, PHYSICS. *Current Pos:* Prof & chmn dept, 56-94, EMER PROF PHYSICS, ALBRIGHT COL, 94- *Personal Data:* b Temple, Pa, Aug 29, 32; m 88, Ruth P Bickel; c Thurman R, Melanie L, Thomas R & Thaddeus R. *Educ:* Lehigh Univ, BS, 54, MS, 56; Temple Univ, PhD(physics), 68. *Mem:* Am Asn Physics Teachers; Sigma Xi. *Mailing Add:* RR 3 Box 240 Kutztown PA 19530-9229

KREMZNER, LEON T, BIOCHEMISTRY. *Current Pos:* RETIRED. *Personal Data:* b Poland, Sept 16, 24; US citizen; m 56; c 3. *Educ:* Seton Hall Univ, BS, 49; Rutgers Univ, MS, 52, PhD(biochem), 55. *Prof Exp:* Res chemist biochem, Gen Foods Corp, 49-51; asst, Bur Biol Res, Rutgers Univ, 52-55; proj leader, Res Ctr, Gen Foods Corp, 55-58; res assoc neurochem, Col Physicians & Surgeons, Columbia Univ, 59-63; neurochemist, Bur Res, NJ Neuropsychiat Inst, 63-67; from asst prof to assoc prof neurochem, Col Physicians & Surgeons, Columbia Univ, 67-87. *Mem:* NY Acad Sci; Am Soc Biol Chemists. *Res:* Enzyme chemistry; intermediate metabolism; cholinergic system; histamine and polyamine metabolism; neurochemistry. *Mailing Add:* Canaan St Canaan NH 03741

KRENDEL, EZRA SIMON, HUMAN FACTORS ENGINEERING. *Current Pos:* dir, Mgt Sci Ctr, Univ Pa, 67-69, chmn bd adv, Ctr, 69-70, prof statist & opers res, 66-90, PROF SYSTS, SCH ENG & APPL SCI, UNIV PA, 83, EMER PROF STATIST OPERS & RES, 90- *Personal Data:* b New York, NY, Mar 5, 25; m 92, Janet Allen; c David A, Jennifer J (Hall) & Tamara Krendel-Clark. *Educ:* Brooklyn Col, BA, 45; Mass Inst Technol, ScM, 47; Harvard Univ, AM, 49. *Hon Degrees:* MA, Univ Pa, 71. *Honors & Awards:* Louis E Levy Gold Medal, Franklin Inst, 60. *Prof Exp:* From res engr to mgr engr, Psychol Lab, Labs Res & Develop, Franklin Inst, 49-63, tech dir opers res, Res Labs, 63-66. *Concurrent Pos:* Consult to indust, res, non-profit, local & fed govt orgn, 67-; NATO vis guest lectr in univs & res insts, Greece, Turkey, Eng, Italy, France & Ger, 68-71; prin scientist, Systs Technol, Inc, 87-88. *Mem:* Fel AAAS; fel Inst Elec & Electronics Engrs; fel Am Psychol Asn; fel Human Factors Soc; Ergonomics Soc; fel Am Psychol Soc. *Res:* Human control dynamics, tracking, decision making, power output and human error; command control and man-machine systems design. *Mailing Add:* 211 Cornell Ave Swarthmore PA 19081-1933. *Fax:* 610-543-9107; *E-Mail:* krendel@wharton.upenn.edu

KRENER, ARTHUR JAMES, APPLIED MATHEMATICS, SYSTEMS THEORY. *Current Pos:* Asst prof, 71-76, assoc prof, 76-80, PROF MATH, UNIV CALIF, DAVIS, 80- *Personal Data:* b Brooklyn, NY, Oct 8, 42; m; c 3. *Educ:* Col of the Holy Cross, BS, 64; Univ Calif, Berkeley, MA, 67, PhD(math), 71. *Concurrent Pos:* Res fel eng & appl physics, Harvard Univ, 74-75; Fullbright Hays fel, Univ Rome, 79; vis sr res fel, Imperial Col, London, 80-81. *Mem:* Soc Indust & Appl Math; Am Math Soc; Inst Elec & Electronics Engrs; Sigma Xi. *Res:* Nonlinear systems theory; stochastic processes. *Mailing Add:* Dept Math Univ Calif Davis CA 95616-8633

KRENITSKY, THOMAS ANTHONY, biochemistry, for more information see previous edition

KRENKEL, PETER ASHTON, WATER QUALITY MANAGEMENT, THERMAL POLLUTION. *Current Pos:* dean, Col Eng, 82-87, prof civil eng, 88-95, PROF EMER CIVIL ENG, UNIV NEV, RENO, 96- *Personal Data:* b San Francisco, Calif, Jan 3, 30; m 85, Jessica A Jones; c Joshua H, Kim H & Heather H. *Educ:* Univ Calif, Berkeley, BS, 56, MS, 58, PhD(environ eng), 60. *Honors & Awards:* Rudolf Hering Award, Am Soc Civil Engrs, 63; Serv, Integrity, Responsibility Award, Asn Gen Contractors, 84; Eminent Speaker, Inst Engr, Australia, 86. *Prof Exp:* Instr, Col Eng, Univ Calif, Berkeley, 58-60; chmn & prof, Dept Environ & Water Resources Eng, Vanderbilt Univ, 60-74; dir, Div Environ Planning, Tenn Valley Authority, 74-78; exec dir, Water Resources Ctr, Desert Res Inst, Reno, Nev, 78-82. *Concurrent Pos:* Lectr, Am Inst Chem Engrs, 68-; chmn thermal pollution, Nat Water Comn, 72-74; consult, WHO, 68-, Environ Protection Agency, 82-84, Gen Motors Corp, Monsanto Res Corp, Mead Corp, Stouffer Chem Corp, Inland container, Olin Corp, Korean Adv Inst Sci Tech, Ministry Water & Power, Repub of China, 86. *Mem:* Am Inst Chem Engrs; Am Soc Civil Engrs; Am Acad Environ Engrs; Am Water Works Asn; Int Asn Water Pollution Res; Water Environ Fedn. *Res:* Water quality management; thermal pollution; gas absorption in water; turbulent diffusion and mixing analysis; mercury in the aquatic environment; water, waste water treatment. *Mailing Add:* 3500 Cashill Blvd Reno NV 89509. *Fax:* 702-784-4466

KRENOS, JOHN ROBERT, CHEMICAL PHYSICS. *Current Pos:* asst prof, 73-78, ASSOC PROF CHEM, RUTGERS UNIV, 78- *Personal Data:* b New Britain, Conn, Sept 4, 45. *Educ:* Univ Conn, BA, 67; Yale Univ, MS, 68, PhD(chem), 72. *Prof Exp:* Fel chem, Harvard Univ, 72-73. *Mem:* Am Phys Soc; Am Chem Soc. *Res:* Energy transfer in hyperthermal collisions and collisions involving electronically excited reactants; molecular beam chemiluminescence; model calculations of chemical reactions. *Mailing Add:* Dept Chem Rutgers Univ New Brunswick NJ 08903

KRENZ, JERROLD H(ENRY), ELECTRICAL ENGINEERING. *Current Pos:* asst prof elec eng, 63-77, dir eng honors prog, 69-73, assoc prof, 77-81, PROF ELEC ENG, UNIV COLO, BOULDER, 81- *Personal Data:* b Buffalo, NY, Apr 24, 34. *Educ:* Univ Buffalo, BS, 56; Stanford Univ, MS, 58, PhD(elec eng), 64. *Prof Exp:* Engr antennas, Lockheed Missile Systs, Lockheed Aircraft Corp, 56-57; engr microwave tubes, Gen Elec Microwave Lab, 58-61. *Concurrent Pos:* Consult, Gen Elec Co, 62. *Mem:* Inst Elec & Electronics Engrs; Int Solar Energy Soc; AAAS; Sigma Xi. *Res:* Energy systems and policy; modeling; economic studies. *Mailing Add:* 10107 Gold Hill Rd Boulder CO 80302

KRENZELOK, EDWARD PAUL, TOXICOLOGY, PHARMACY. *Current Pos:* PROF PHARM & MED & DIR, PITTSBURGH POISON CTR, 83- *Personal Data:* b Ladysmith, Wis, Mar 11, 47. *Educ:* Univ Wis, BS, 71; Univ Minn, PharmD, 74. *Prof Exp:* From asst prof to assoc prof pharm, Univ Minn, 74-83. *Concurrent Pos:* Dir toxicol, Hennepin Poison Ctr, Hennepin Co Med Ctr, Minneapolis, 76-83 & mem fac toxicol, Dept Emergency Med, 78-83; Minneapolis Community Health Serv grant poison prev prog children in day care ctrs, 77-82; consult, Emergency Med Serv Div, Minn Dept Health, Minneapolis, 78 & Emergency Med Serv Div, Metrop Coun, St Paul, 78-83; chmn, Dept Prof Educ, Nat Poison Ctr Network, Pittsburgh, 78-83; adj res scientist, Hunt Inst, Carnegie-Mellon Univ. *Mem:* Am Asn Poison Ctr; Am Soc Hosp Pharm; Am Acad Clin Toxicol; Soc Acad Emergency Med; Am Bd Appl Toxicol. *Res:* Gastric decontamination of victims suffering from poisoning emergencies; drug overdosage; drug abuse; malpractice; standards of toxicologic care. *Mailing Add:* Pittsburgh Poison Ctr 3705 Fifth Ave Pittsburgh PA 15213. *Fax:* 412-692-7497; *E-Mail:* krenzee@chplink.chp.edu

KREPINSKY, JIRI J, ORGANIC CHEMISTRY, MOLECULAR GENETICS. *Current Pos:* sr res scientist, Dept Med Genetics, Univ Toronto, 76-80, assoc prof, 80-88, sr staff scientist, Ludwig Inst Cancer Res, Toronto Br, 81-88, prof med biophysics, 88-90, PROF, DEPT MED GENETICS, UNIV TORONTO, 88- *Personal Data:* b Prague, Czech, July 15, 34; Can citizen; m 88; c 2. *Educ:* Charles Univ, Prague, MSc, 57, Dr rer nat, 66; Czech Acad Sci, PhD(chem), 61. *Prof Exp:* Res asst org chem, Inst Org Chem & Biochem, Czech Acad Sci, 57-61, res assoc natural prod, 61-66 & 67-68; vis scientist, Inst Org Chem, Univ Milan, 66-67; fel synthesis natural prod, Univ NB, 68-70, lectr, 70-72; dir, Chem Res Lab of Simes, Milan, 72-75. *Concurrent Pos:* Mem bot exped, Soviet Cent Asia, 61; consult, Ont Cancer Inst, 78-81. *Mem:* Am Chem Soc; Royal Soc Chem; Chem Soc Can; NY Acad Sci. *Res:* Determination of structures of biologically important compounds, particularly glycoproteins; roles of oligosaccharides moieties of glycoproteins and glycolipids development and malignancy, in particular colon cancer; organic chemistry and mass spectrometry of carbohydrates and glycopeptides; development of protocols for population cancer screening. *Mailing Add:* Dept Molecular Med Genetics Sci Bldg Univ Toronto Toronto ON M5S 1A8 Can

KREPS, DAVID PAUL, MICROBIOLOGY, IMMUNOLOGY. *Current Pos:* ASSOC PROF BIOL, MANCHESTER COL, 67- *Personal Data:* b Pottstown, Pa, Jan 13, 43; m 65; c 2. *Educ:* Manchester Col, BS, 64; Ohio State Univ, MS, 68; Chicago Med Sch, PhD(microbiol), 76. *Prof Exp:* Teaching asst microbiol, Ohio State Univ, 65-67. *Concurrent Pos:* Res asst microbiol, Chicago Med Sch, 74-75; Res Corp res grant, 78-79; dir, NSF Int Soc Educ Planners grant, Manchester Col, 78-81. *Mem:* Sigma Xi; Am Soc Microbiol. *Res:* Immunological responses to salmonella typhimurium vaccines and cell fractions in inbred and outbred mice. *Mailing Add:* Biol Dept Manchester Col 600 E College Ave North Manchester IN 46965-1225

KREPS, JUANITA MORRIS, ECONOMICS, EDUCATION. *Current Pos:* mem fac, Duke Univ, 55-77, assoc prof, 62-68, prof econ, 68-77, asst provost, 69-72, James B Duke prof, 72-77, vpres, 73-77, EMER JAMES B DUKE PROF & EMER VPRES, DUKE UNIV, 79- *Personal Data:* b Lynch, Ky, Jan 11, 21; m 44, Clifton H Jr; c Sarah, Laura & Clifton III. *Educ:* Berea Col, AB, 42; Duke Univ, MA, 44, PhD, 48. *Hon Degrees:* Numerous hon degrees from US univs, 72-93. *Honors & Awards:* Stephen Wise Award, 78; Woman Yr Award, Ladies Home J, 78; Achievement Award, Am Asn Univ Women, 81; Dirs Choice Leadership Award, Nat Women's Econ Alliance Found, 87. *Prof Exp:* Instr econ, Denison Univ, 45-46, asst prof, 48-50; secy, US Dept Com, 77-79. *Concurrent Pos:* Bd dirs, Am Coun Ger, Res Triangle Found, Educ Testing Serv, 72-77; trustee, Berea Col, 72-78 & 80-, Duke Endowment, 79-, HumRRO, 80-83, Nat Humanities Ctr, 83-86, Coun Foreign Rels, 83-89, Univ NC, Wilmington, 93- & Kenan Inst Pvt Enterprise, Univ NC, Chapel Hill, 95-; mem, Pres Comn Nat Agenda 80's, 79, Nat Manpower Policy Task Force. *Mem:* Fel Gerontol Soc (vpres, 71-72); fel Am Acad Arts & Sci; Am Asn Univ Profs; Am Asn Univ Women; Am Econ Assn (vpres, 83-84); Indust Rels Res Asn. *Res:* Contributed to numerous publications. *Mailing Add:* Duke Univ 115 E Duke Bldg Durham NC 27708. *Fax:* 919-684-8351

KRESA, KENT, AERONAUTICS. *Current Pos:* vpres & mgr, Res & Technol Ctr, Northrop Gruman Corp, 75-76, vpres & gen mgr, Ventura Div, 76-82, vpres aircraft group, Advan Systs Div Aircraft Div, Ventura Div & Aircraft Sens Div, 82-86, sr vpres technol develop & planning, 86-87, PRES, NORTHROP GRUMAN CORP, 87-, CHIEF EXEC OFFICER & CHMN, 90- *Personal Data:* b New York, NY, Mar 24, 38. *Educ:* Mass Inst Technol, BS, 59, MS, 61, EAA, 66. *Honors & Awards:* Meritorious Civilian Serv Medal, Secy Defense, 74; Meritorious pub Serv Citation, USN, 75; Arthur D Flemming Award, US Govt, 75; Decoration Except Civilian Serv, USAF, 87; Bob Hope Distinguished Citizen Award, Nat Security Indust Asn, 96. *Prof Exp:* Sr scientist, Res & Advan Develop Div, Avco, 59-61; staff, Lincoln Lab, Mass Inst Technol, 61-68; dep dir, Strategic Technol Off, Defense Advan Res Projs Agency, 68-72, spec asst to dir, 72-73, dir tactical technol, 73-75. *Concurrent Pos:* Bd dir, Arco Corp, Chrysler Corp, John Tracy Clinic, W M Keck Found, Los Angeles World Affairs Coun; bd trustees, Calif Inst Technol; bd govs, Los Angeles Music Ctr. *Mem:* Nat Acad Eng; fel Am Inst Aeronaut & Astronaut. *Res:* Integration and manufacturing of military surveillance and combat aircraft defense electronics and systems, airspace management systems and information systems. *Mailing Add:* Northrop Grumman Corp 1840 Century Park E Los Angeles CA 90067

KRESCH, ALAN J, PHYSICAL CHEMISTRY, DATA PROCESSING. *Current Pos:* Sr res chemist, Nat Cash Register Co, Ohio, 60-73, STAFF RES ASSOC, APPLETON PAPERS INC, 73- *Personal Data:* b New York, NY, June 25, 31; m 75; c 1. *Educ:* Cornell Univ, AB, 52; Rutgers Univ,

PhD(solution kinetics), 61. *Mem:* AAAS; Am Chem Soc; Sigma Xi. *Res:* Solution kinetics of inorganic polymers; reversible photochemical reactions in solution; color technology; laboratory computer. *Mailing Add:* 39 S Meadows Dr Appleton WI 54915-2349

KRESGE, ALEXANDER JERRY, PHYSICAL ORGANIC CHEMISTRY. *Current Pos:* chmn chem group, 74-78, PROF CHEM, SCARBOROUGH COL, UNIV TORONTO, 74- *Personal Data:* b Wilkes-Barre, Pa, July 17, 26; m 50, 63, Yvonne Chiang; c Nell S, Peter B & Nicole. *Educ:* Cornell Univ, BA, 49; Univ Ill, PhD(chem), 53. *Honors & Awards:* Mardi Gras Lectr, La State Univ, 81; Mobay Lectr, Univ NH, 82-; Nelson J Leonard Lectr, Univ Ill, 86; Morley Medal, 88; Sytnex Award, 88; Richard & Doris Arnold Lectr, Univ Ill, 89; Ingold Lectr, 94. *Prof Exp:* Fulbright scholar, Univ Col, Univ London, 53-54; res assoc, Purdue Univ, 54-55 & Mass Inst Technol, 55-57; assoc chemist, Brookhaven Nat Lab, 57-60; from asst prof to prof chem, Ill Inst Technol, 60-74. *Concurrent Pos:* Guggenheim fel, 64, Killam fel, 84-86 & Yamada fel, 85; NSF sr fel, 64-65; vis lectr, Bedford Col, London, 64-65; vis prof, Oxford Univ, 65, Univ Toronto, 70-71, Univ Mich, 79, Univ Lausanne, 81, Tech Univ Denmark, 82, Univ San Paulo, 84, Fed Univ Santa Catarina, 84 & Kyoto Univ, 85; guest, Mass Inst Technol, 65; chmn, Gordon Res Conf Physics & Chem Isotopes, 68; vis scientist, Fritz Haber Inst, 81 & Univ Goteborg, 83; lectr, Frontier Chem, Wayne State Univ, 92. *Mem:* Am Chem Soc; fel Royal Soc Can; fel Chem Inst Can; Sigma Xi; AAAS; hon mem Argentinian Soc Org Chem. *Res:* Reaction mechanisms; isotope effects; acid-base catalysis; kinetics. *Mailing Add:* Dept Chem Univ Toronto Toronto ON M5S 3H6 Can. *Fax:* 416-978-7259; *E-Mail:* akresge@chem.utoronto.ca

KRESGE, EDWARD NATHAN, POLYMER CHEMISTRY. *Current Pos:* HEAD ELASTOMERS EXPLOR RES, ELASTOMERS TECHNOL DIV, EXXON CHEM CO, 75-, CHIEF POLYMER SCIENTIST, 78- *Personal Data:* b Noxen, Pa, Aug 14, 35; m 63. *Educ:* Univ Tampa, BS, 57; Univ Fla, PhD(chem), 61. *Honors & Awards:* Chmn Gordon Res Conf, Elastomers, 87. *Prof Exp:* Res chemist, 61-63, proj leader elastomers, 63-75. *Mem:* AAAS; Am Chem Soc. *Res:* Elastomer, morphology, polymer rheology and physics. *Mailing Add:* 68 Parlin Lane Watchung NJ 07060

KRESH, J YASHA, ARTIFICIAL INTERNAL ORGANS, MODELING & SIMULATION. *Current Pos:* PROF & DIR RES, DEPT CARDIOTHORACIC SURG, ALLEGHENY UNIV HEALTH SCI, 86-, PROF MED & DIR CARDIOVASC BIOPHYS & COMPUT, 86- *Personal Data:* b L'vov, Russia, July 13, 48; US citizen; m 86, Myrna Blickman. *Educ:* NJ Inst Technol, BS, 71; Rutgers Univ, MSBME, 73, PhD(biomed eng & cardiovasc physics), 77. *Prof Exp:* Res intern biomed eng, Rutgers Univ, 71-75; res intern comp-med, Mt Sinai-Rutgers Health Care Comp Lab, 75-77; res assoc, Dept Surg, Newark Beth Israel Med Ctr, 76-79; res asst prof surg, Thomas Jefferson Univ, 79-83, res mem, Ischemia Shock Res Inst, 81-86. *Concurrent Pos:* Assoc prof surg, Thomas Jefferson Univ, 83-86, assoc prof pharmacol, 84-86; adj prof bioeng, Biomed Eng & Sci Inst, Drexel Univ, 84- *Mem:* Sr mem Inst Elec & Electronics Engrs; sr mem Biomed Eng Soc; Am Heart Asn; Cardiovasc Syst Dynamics Soc; fel Am Col Cardiol; fel Acad Surg Res; Sigma Xi. *Res:* Cardiovascular system dynamics; heart assist devices; computers and cardiology; patient monitoring systems; physiological and biophysical sensors; closed-loop physiological control; numerous scientific publications. *Mailing Add:* Dept Cardiothoracic Surg Allegheny Univ Health Sci Mail Stop 110 Broad & Vine Sts Philadelphia PA 19102-1192. *E-Mail:* kresh.cvi.allegheny.edu

KRESHECK, GORDON C, PHYSICAL BIOCHEMISTRY. *Current Pos:* asst prof, 65-68, assoc prof, 68-78, DIR, CTR BIOCHEM & BIOPHYS STUDIES, NORTHERN ILL UNIV, 75-, PROF CHEM, 78- *Personal Data:* b North Tonawanda, NY, Sept 3, 33; m 61; c 3. *Educ:* Ohio State Univ, BS, 55, MS, 59, PhD(dairy technol), 61. *Prof Exp:* Res asst biochem, Nobel Med Inst, Stockholm, Sweden, 62-63; vis scientist, Procter & Gamble Co, 63; NIH res fel chem, Cornell Univ, 63-65. *Concurrent Pos:* Res assoc, Argonne Nat Lab, 66-; assoc ed, Bull Thermodynamics & Thermochem, 71-76. *Mem:* Am Chem Soc; Biophys Soc; Am Soc Biol Chemists; Sigma Xi. *Res:* Protein chemistry; solution calorimetry; lipids. *Mailing Add:* Dept Chem Northern Ill Univ De Kalb IL 60115

KRESHOVER, SEYMOUR J, PATHOLOGY. *Current Pos:* RETIRED. *Personal Data:* b New York, NY, June 22, 12; m 46; c 4. *Educ:* NY Univ, BA, 34, MD, 49; Univ Pa, DDS, 38; Yale Univ, PhD(clin med, path), 42; Am Bd Oral Med, dipl. *Hon Degrees:* DSc, State Univ NY Buffalo, 61, Univ Pa, 67, Boston Univ, 69, Univ Mich, 75; DOdont, Gothenburg Univ, 73. *Honors & Awards:* Pierre Fouchard Medal, 72; Callahan Medal, 72. *Prof Exp:* Asst instr, Sch Med Lowell, Univ Ill, 38-39; clin asst dent surg, Yale Univ, 42-43; teaching fel histoanat, NY Univ, 46-47, instr, 47; prof oral path & dir dent res, Grad & Postgrad Study, Med Col Va, 49-56; assoc dir, Nat Inst Dent Res, 46-66, dir, 66-75; vis prof oral biol, State Univ NY, Buffalo, 75-80. *Concurrent Pos:* Assoc trustee, Bd Med Educ & Res, Univ Pa, 56-66; chmn comn dent res, Int Dent Fedn, 61-67. *Mem:* Am Dent Asn; Am Pub Health Asn; Am Acad Oral Path; Int Asn Dental Res (pres, 62). *Res:* Dental histology and embryology; dental pathology; prenatal factors in congenital defects. *Mailing Add:* 838 John Anderson Dr Ormond Beach FL 32176

KRESINA, THOMAS FRANCIS, immune network interactions, somatic cell hybridization, for more information see previous edition

KRESPAN, CARL GEORGE, ORGANIC CHEMISTRY. *Current Pos:* RETIRED. *Personal Data:* b Erie, Pa, Aug 10, 26; m 49; c 3. *Educ:* Univ Rochester, BS, 48; Univ Minn, PhD(org chem), 52. *Prof Exp:* Res schemist, E I DuPont de Nemours & Co, 52-60, res supvr org chem, 60-70, res scientist, Cent Res Dept, 70-93. *Mem:* Am Chem Soc. *Res:* Organic fluorine chemistry; free radical, sulphur, cyanocarbon, macroheterocycle chemistry, and fluoropolymer. *Mailing Add:* Mozart Dr Wilmington DE 19804

KRESS, BERNARD HIRAM, ORGANIC CHEMISTRY. *Current Pos:* PRES, KRESS ASSOCS, 82- *Personal Data:* b New York, NY, Apr 18, 17; c 3. *Educ:* City Col New York, BS, 38; Columbia Univ, MA, 40, PhD(org chem), 47. *Prof Exp:* Asst biochem, Col Physicians & Surgeons, Columbia Univ, 38-40; jr biochemist neuropsychiat res unit, US Vet Admin, Long Island, 41-42; res chemist, Fed Telecommun Labs, NJ, 42-46 & Celanese Corp Am, 47-48; sr res chemist & group leader, Plaskon Div, Libbey-Owens-Ford Glass Co, 49-53; dir org res, Quaker Chem Prod Co, 53-64, mgr polymer res & develop, Quaker Chem Corp, 64-70, sr scientist, 70-82. *Mem:* Am Chem Soc; Am Asn Textile Chem & Colorists; Am Tech Asn Pulp & Paper Indust; Am Soc Lubrication Eng; fel Am Inst Chem; Sigma Xi. *Res:* High polymers; textile, metal and paper chemicals. *Mailing Add:* 4018 Kottler Dr Lafayette Hill PA 19444

KRESS, DONNIE DUANE, GENETICS, ANIMAL BREEDING. *Current Pos:* asst & assoc prof, 70-80, PROF GENETICS & ANIMAL BREEDING, MONT STATE UNIV, 80- *Personal Data:* b American Falls, Idaho, Mar 17, 42; m 70, Charlotte Grinols; c Ellen R & Benjamin D. *Educ:* Univ Idaho, BS, 64; Univ Wis, MS, 66, PhD(genetics & animal sci), 69. *Honors & Awards:* Rockefeller Prentice Mem Award, Am Soc Animal Sci, 96. *Prof Exp:* NIH fel quant genetics, Univ Minn, 69-70. *Concurrent Pos:* Guest partic, Cong Vet Med & Animal Prod, Buenos Aires, Arg, 85. *Mem:* Am Soc Animal Sci; Sigma Xi. *Res:* Quantitative genetics and animal breeding; selection, genetic by environment interaction; maternal ability of beef cattle of varying biological types and beef sire evaluation. *Mailing Add:* 1438 Ash Dr Bozeman MT 59717

KRESS, KENNETH A, BIOPHYSICS. *Current Pos:* OWNER, K-TECH CO, 84- *Personal Data:* b Pittsburgh, Pa, Apr 19, 42. *Educ:* Valparaiso Univ, BS, 64; Mont State Univ, PhD(physics), 69. *Mem:* Am Phys Soc. *Mailing Add:* K-Tech Co 6666 Van Winkle Dr Falls Church VA 22044

KRESS, LANCE WHITAKER, AIR POLLUTION. *Current Pos:* RES PLANT PATHOLOGIST, FOREST SERV, USDA, 86- *Personal Data:* b Camp Lejeune, NC, Sept 2, 45; m 69, Diane Bickel; c Nicole, Kerri & Nathan. *Educ:* Pa State Univ, BS, 68, MS, 72; Va Polytech Inst & State Univ, PhD(plant path), 78. *Prof Exp:* Jr res aide, Pa State Univ, 72-73; res assoc, Va Polytech Inst & State Univ, 75-80; asst ecologist, Argonne Nat Lab, 80-84, ecologist, 84-86. *Mem:* Sigma Xi. *Res:* Evaluating the impacts of low concentrations of air pollutants and pollutant combinations on the growth of forest tree species; investigating the effects of elevated carbon dioxide. *Mailing Add:* USDA Forest Serv PO Box 12254 Research Triangle Park NC 27709-2254

KRESS, LAWRENCE FRANCIS, BIOCHEMISTRY. *Current Pos:* Am Heart Asn adv res fel, Roswell Park Cancer Inst, 76-68, sr res scientist, 68-78, res scientist IV, 78-80, RES CANCER SCIENTIST V, ROSWELL PARK CANCER INST, 80- *Personal Data:* b Milwaukee, Wis, Oct 5, 36; div; c 4. *Educ:* Marquette Univ, BS, 59, MS, 61, PhD(physiol), 64. *Prof Exp:* NSF fel biochem, Med Sch, Dartmouth Univ, 64-66. *Mem:* Am Soc Biochem & Molecular Biol; Int Soc Toxinol. *Res:* Enzymology; proteolytic enzymes and their inhibitors; interactions between snake venom proteinases and plasma proteinase inhibitors. *Mailing Add:* 620 Youngs Rd Williamsville NY 14221

KRESS, THOMAS JOSEPH, ORGANIC CHEMISTRY. *Current Pos:* sr org chemist, 68-74, res scientist, 74-80, RES ASSOC, ELI LILLY & CO, 80- *Personal Data:* b Indianapolis, Ind, Oct 31, 40; m 65; c 4. *Educ:* Xavier Univ Ohio, BS, 62, MS, 64; Ohio Univ, PhD(org chem), 67. *Prof Exp:* Res assoc, Ohio Univ, 67-68. *Mem:* Int Soc Heterocycle Chem; Am Chem Soc; Royal Soc Chem; Sigma Xi. *Res:* The synthesis and reactions of nitrogen heterocycles. *Mailing Add:* Lilly Corp Ctr Res Chem Bldg 110 Indianapolis IN 46285

KRESS, THOMAS SYLVESTER, NUCLEAR ENGINEERING, AEROSOL SCIENCE. *Current Pos:* engr reactor safety, 59-76, prog mgr & group leader advan reactor syst, Nuclear Div, 76-80, MGR, NUCLEAR RES COUN, UNION CARBIDE CORP, 80- *Personal Data:* b Kingsport, Tenn, Dec 5, 33; m 56; c 3. *Educ:* Univ Tenn, BS, 56, MS, 65, PhD(eng sci), 71. *Prof Exp:* Engr aircraft nuclear propulsion, Pratt & Whitney Aircraft, 56-59. *Mem:* AAAS; Am Soc Mech Engrs; Am Nuclear Soc; Nat Soc Prof Engrs; Nat Mgt Asn. *Res:* Thermal sciences, heat ransfer, fluid transfer, fluid mechanics and thermodynamics; nuclear safety; aerosol science. *Mailing Add:* 102 Newridge Rd Oak Ridge TN 37830

KRESSE, JEROME THOMAS, ORGANIC CHEMISTRY. *Current Pos:* asst prof, D'Youville Col, 66-69, assoc prof chem & chmn dept chem & physics, 69-74, chmn, Div Math & Natural Sci, 74-78, PROF CHEM, D'YOUVILLE COL, 74- *Personal Data:* b Buffalo, NY, Dec 29, 31; m 62; c 5. *Educ:* Mich State Univ, BS, 58; Univ Fla, PhD(org chem), 65. *Prof Exp:* Asst prof chem, Muskingum Col, 65-66. *Mem:* AAAS; Am Asn Univ Prof; Am Chem Soc. *Res:* Studies of factors influencing the stereochemistry of the Wittig reaction; synthesis of amino acid antagonists. *Mailing Add:* 51 Harwood Rd Buffalo NY 14224-4231

KRESSEL, HENRY, ELECTROOPTICS. *Current Pos:* MANAGING DIR, WARBURG PINCUS & CO, 83- *Personal Data:* b Vienna, Austria, Jan 24, 34; US citizen; m 56, Bertha Horowitz; c Aron & Kim. *Educ:* Yeshiva Col, BA, 55; Harvard Univ, MS, 56; Univ Pa, MBA, 59, PhD(mat sci), 65. *Honors & Awards:* Achievement Award, RCA Corp, 62, 68 & 69; Centennial Medal, Inst Elec & Electronics Engrs, 84, David Sarnoff Award, 85; Distinguished Serv Award, Inst Elec & Electronics Engrs Lasers & Electro-Optics Soc. *Prof Exp:* Engr, Semiconductor Div, Radio Corp Am, 59-61, group head microwave device, 61-63, group device physics, Tech Progs Lab, 65-66, mem tech staff, RCA Labs, 67-69, group head, 69-77, lab dir, 77-79, staff vpres, 79-83. *Concurrent Pos:* Co-founder, J Lightwave Technol; consult, Dept Defense; mem, Adv Coun Eng, NSF. *Mem:* Nat Acad Eng; fel Am Phys Soc; fel Inst Elec & Electronics Engrs; Inst Elec & Electronics Engrs Laser & Electrooptics Soc. *Res:* New semiconductor devices, particularly in area of microwaves and optical devices; lasers; properties of defects in semiconductors; author of 120 technical publications; awarded 33 US patents. *Mailing Add:* E M Warburg Pincus & Co 466 Lexington Ave New York NY 10017

KRESSEL, HERBERT YEHUDE, RADIOLOGY, MAGNETIC RESONANCE IMAGING. *Current Pos:* RADIOLOGIST-IN-CHIEF, BETH ISRAEL HOSP, BOSTON, MASS, 94- *Personal Data:* b Brooklyn, NY, Nov 20, 47; c 2. *Educ:* Brandeis Univ, Waltham, Mass, BA, 68; Univ Southern Calif, MD, 72. *Honors & Awards:* Crues Kressel Award, Soc Magnetic Resonance Med, 91; Sylvia Sorkin Greenfield Award, Am Asn Physicists Med, 93. *Prof Exp:* Clin instr radiol, Univ Calif, San Francisco, 76-77; from asst prof to prof radiol, Univ Pa, Philadelphia, 77-93; prof radiol, Harvard Med Sch, 93. *Concurrent Pos:* NIH fel radiol, Univ Calif, San Francisco, 76; mem, Comn Magnetic Resonance, Am Col Radiol, 87-, chmn, Comt Magnetic Resonance Clin Appln, 87-; trustee, Soc Magnetic Resonance Med, 87, prog chair, 90; med dir, RI Magnetic Resonance Imaging Network, Providence, 88-; fel, Am Col Radiol, 91; chmn, Joint Merger Eval Comt, Soc Magnetic Resonance Med, Soc Magnetic Resonance Int, 92-93. *Mem:* Asn Univ Radiologists; Soc Gastrointestinal Radiologists; Am Col Radiol; Radiol Soc NAm; Soc Magnetic Resonance Med (pres-elect, 89-90, pres, 90-91). *Res:* Improved magnetic resonance for the abdomen and pelvis; magnetic resonance imaging of the liver. *Mailing Add:* Dept Radiol Beth Israel Hosp Sherman 358 Brookline MA 02115. Fax: 617-278-8212

KRESTA, JIRI ERIK, POLYMER CHEMISTRY, CHEMICAL ENGINEERING. *Current Pos:* RES PROF POLYMER SCI, DEPT CHEM & CHEM ENG, POLYMER INST, UNIV DETROIT, 71- *Personal Data:* b Kosice, Czech, Apr 19, 34. *Educ:* Inst Chem Technol, Prague, MChE, 57; Tech Univ Prague, MS, 64; Czech Acad Sci, PhD(polymer sci), 67. *Prof Exp:* Res assoc, Res Inst Synthetic Rubber, Zlin, Czech, 57-62; res scientist, Res Inst Macromolecular Chem, Brno, 62-69; res assoc, Dept Chem, Wayne State Univ, 69-71. *Mem:* Am Chem Soc; Soc Plastics Engrs; Czech Chem Soc; NY Acad Sci. *Res:* Reaction kinetics and catalysis of polyreactions; characterization, flammability degradation and stabilization of polymers, morphological and viscoelastic studies of polymers; research in polyurethanes; cellular materials, polyolefins; elastomers; thermostable polymers; plastics failure. *Mailing Add:* Polymer Inst Univ Detroit-Mercy 4001 W McNichols Detroit MI 48221. Fax: 313-993-1409

KRESTENSEN, ELROY R, ENTOMOLOGY. *Current Pos:* RETIRED. *Personal Data:* b New York, NY, Sept 6, 21; m 48; c 1. *Educ:* Univ Fla, BSA, 49, MS, 51; Univ Md, PhD(entom), 62. *Prof Exp:* Asst entom, Univ Fla, 49-51, interim instr, 51-52; entomologist, Fla Bd Health, 52-54; from instr to assoc prof entom, Sharpsburg Res Ctr, Univ Md, 55-84; consult, 84-86. *Mem:* Entom Soc Am. *Res:* Insect pests and control methods for fruit. *Mailing Add:* 1050 St Clair St Hagerstown MD 21742

KRETCHMER, NORMAN, nutritional science, pediatrics & diabetes; deceased, see previous edition for last biography

KRETCHMER, RICHARD ALLAN, SYNTHETIC ORGANIC CHEMISTRY. *Current Pos:* assoc gen patent atty, Patents & Licensing Dept, 76, GEN PATENT ATTY, LAW DEPT, AMOCO CORP, 76- *Personal Data:* b Tracy, Minn, Dec 12, 40; m 67, Karla M Prust; c Erich, Sarah & Jeffrey. *Educ:* Univ Minn, BChem, 62; Univ Wis, PhD(org chem), 66; Chicago-Kent Col Law, JD, 75. *Prof Exp:* USPHS fel chem, Columbia Univ, 66-68; from asst prof to assoc prof chem, Ill Inst Technol, 68-76. *Concurrent Pos:* Law firm assoc, 75-76; adj prof law, Chicago Kent Col Law, 83-84 & 87-89. *Res:* Organic chemistry; structure and synthesis; chemistry of natural products; the organic chemistry of mercury. *Mailing Add:* 270 Walker Ave Clarendon Hills IL 60514

KRETSCH, MARY JOSEPHINE, NUTRITIONAL STATUS ASSESSMENT, DIETARY ASSESSMENT. *Current Pos:* RES NUTRIT SCIENTIST, WESTERN HUMAN NUTRIT RES CTR, AGR RES SERV, USDA, 80- *Personal Data:* US citizen. *Educ:* Univ Minn, BS, 69; Univ Calif, San Francisco, RD, 70; Univ Calif, Davis, PhD(nutrit sci), 75. *Prof Exp:* Teaching asst nutrit, Univ Calif, Berkeley, 71-73, postdoctoral fel human nutrit, 75-77; nutrit scientist, Dept Defense, Letterman Army Inst Res, 77-80. *Concurrent Pos:* Dir, Human Metab Res Unit, Western Human Nutrit Res Ctr, 80-83, res leader, Ctr, 83-86. *Mem:* Am Inst Nutrit; Am Soc Clin Nutrit; Am Dietetic Asn. *Res:* Nutritional status assessment with expertise in dietary assessment and biological markers of dietary exposure; vitamin B-6; nutrition & cognitive function; human metabolic research study techniques; nutrition surveys. *Mailing Add:* USDA ARS, Western Human Nutrit Res Ctr PO Box 29997 San Francisco CA 94129-0602

KRETSCHMER, ALBERT EMIL, JR, TROPICAL AGROSTOLOGY. *Current Pos:* Soil chemist, Everglades Exp Sta, 52-55, AGRONOMIST, IFAS INDIAN RIVER RES & EDUC CTR, UNIV FLA, 55- *Personal Data:* b New York, NY, Nov 15, 25; m 49; c 3. *Educ:* Univ Fla, BA, 49; Rutgers Univ, PhD(soil chem), 52. *Concurrent Pos:* Consult soil chemist, Univ Fla-AID Prog, Costa Rica, 58-60, chief, 69-70; pvt consult trop pastures, overseas. *Mem:* Am Soc Agron; Sigma Xi. *Res:* Evaluation of tropical pasture legumes and grasses; micro and macro nutrient requirements of forages; management of grass-legume mixtures. *Mailing Add:* IFAS Indian River Res & Educ Ctr PO Box 248 Univ Fla 2199 S Rock Rd Ft Pierce FL 34945-3138

KRETSCHMER, FRANK FREDERICK, JR, RADAR SIGNAL PROCESSING. *Current Pos:* res electronics eng, 70-87, supvry electronics engr, 87-90, CONSULT, NAVAL RES LAB, 90- *Personal Data:* b Philadelphia, Pa, July 31, 30; m 58, Shirley J Bacon; c Frank F III, John, Diane, Linda & Thomas. *Educ:* Pa State Univ, BSEE, 57; Drexel Inst Tech, MSEE, 61; Johns Hopkins Univ, PhD(elec eng), 70. *Prof Exp:* Asst develop engr, Burroughs Corp, 57-58; proj engr, Bendix Radio Corp, 58-64; res assoc, Johns Hopkins Univ, 64-70. *Mem:* Fel Inst Elec & Electronics Eng; Sigma Xi. *Res:* Over 30 publications in journals, national and international conferences; co-author of one book; awarded over 20 patents. *Mailing Add:* 514 Pennyroyal Pl Venice FL 34293

KRETSINGER, ROBERT, MOLECULAR BIOLOGY, BIOPHYSICS. *Current Pos:* assoc prof, 67-75, chmn dept biol, 79-84, PROF BIOL, UNIV VA, 75- *Personal Data:* b Denver, Colo, Mar 20, 37. *Educ:* Univ Colo, AB, 58; Mass Inst Technol, PhD(biophys), 64. *Prof Exp:* Helen Hay Whitney Found fel, Med Res Coun Lab Molecular Biol, Cambridge Univ, Eng, 64-65; fel, Inst Molecular Biol, Geneva, Switz, 66-67. *Mem:* Am Crystallog Asn. *Res:* Protein structure determination by x-ray crystallography; function and evolution of calcium modulated proteins; role of calcium as cytosolic messenger. *Mailing Add:* Dept Biol Univ Va 229 Gilmer Hall Charlottesville VA 22903

KRETZ, RALPH, PETROLOGY, GEOCHEMISTRY. *Current Pos:* assoc prof, 67-71, PROF GEOL, UNIV OTTAWA, 71- *Personal Data:* Can citizen. *Educ:* Univ Chicago, PhD(geol), 58. *Prof Exp:* Geologist, Geol Surv Can, 58-61; sr lectr geol, Univ Queensland, 61-65. *Mem:* Geochem Soc; Mineral Asn Can. *Res:* Chemical composition and texture of metamorphic rocks. *Mailing Add:* Dept Geol Univ Ottawa Ottawa ON K1N 6N5 Can

KRETZMER, ERNEST R(UDOLF), ELECTRONICS, COMMUNICATION. *Current Pos:* RETIRED. *Personal Data:* b Ger, Dec 24, 24; nat US; m 54, 83, Alisa Sperling; c 2. *Educ:* Worcester Polytech Inst, BS, 45; Mass Inst Technol, SM, 46, ScD(elec eng), 49. *Prof Exp:* Mem tech staff, Mass Inst Technol, 45-49, res assoc, 49; mem tech staff, Bell Tel Labs, Inc, 49-56, supvr, 56-65, dept head, 65-70, dir, 70-83. *Mem:* Fel Inst Elec & Electronics Engrs. *Res:* Pulse modulation; phase measurement; redundancy in television; coded facsimile; transistor applications; electronic telephone system development; data communication. *Mailing Add:* 118 N Polk Dr Sarasota FL 34236

KREUTEL, RANDALL WILLIAM, JR, ANTENNAS, SATELLITE COMMUNICATIONS. *Current Pos:* TEAM LEADER, SATCOM DIV, MOTOROLA, 93- *Personal Data:* b Norwood, Mass, May 3, 34; m 75, Alice J Guillory; c John, James, Karen, Robert, Jacqueline & Michael. *Educ:* Northeastern Univ, BS, 61, MS, 64; George Washington Univ, DSc(electrophys), 78. *Prof Exp:* Res eng antennas, Sylvania Electron Syst, 57-66; mem tech staff, Communications Satellite Corp, 66-68, mgr, Antennas Dept, 68-77, sr staff scientist res & develop, 77-79, dir optical commun, 79-81, dir, div develop eng, Comsat Labs, 81- 84; dir, System Planning Corp, 84-87; dir, Sci-Atlanta, 87-89; prin engr, Electromagnetic Sci, 89-93. *Concurrent Pos:* Bd dir, SPC Antenna Corp, 86-88. *Mem:* Inst Elec & Electronics Engrs; Int Sci Radio Union; Am Inst Aeronaut & Astronaut; Sigma Xi; NY Acad Sci. *Res:* Antennas, microwave circuits, fiber optics and communications; satellite communications; electromagnetics. *Mailing Add:* Satcom Div Motorola 2501 S Price Rd Chandler AZ 85248. Fax: 602-732-2332

KREUTNER, WILLIAM, PHARMACOLOGY, BIOCHEMISTRY. *Current Pos:* sect leader, 78-88, ASSOC DIR, SCHERING CORP, 88- *Personal Data:* b Brooklyn, NY, Feb 20, 41; m 63; c 2. *Educ:* Brooklyn Col, BS, 62; Univ Minn, PhD(pharmacol), 67. *Concurrent Pos:* Adj asst prof biochem, Fairleigh Dickinson Univ, 72-79. *Mem:* Am Acad Allergy & Immunol; NY Acad Sci; Am Soc Pharmacol Exp Ther; Am Thoracic Soc; Am Col Allergy & Immunol. *Res:* Prostaglandins; leukotrienes; cyclic nucleotides; neuronal pathways and neuropeptides; antihistamines. *Mailing Add:* Schering-Plough Corp 2015 Galloping Hill Rd MS 1660 Kenilworth NJ 07033-0539. Fax: 908-298-7175

KREUTZ-DELGADO, KENNETH KEITH, ROBOTICS, MACHINE INTELLIGENCE. *Current Pos:* sci programmer, Dept Neurosci, 78-80, asst prof robotics, Dept Appl Mech & Eng Sci, 89-91, ASST PROF, DEPT ELEC & COMPUT ENG, UNIV CALIF, SAN DIEGO, 91- *Personal Data:* b Aguadilla, PR. *Educ:* Univ Calif, San Diego, BA, 76, MS, 78, PhD(systs sci), 85. *Prof Exp:* Mem tech staff, Mach Intel Systs Group, NASA Jet Propulsion Lab, Calif Inst Technol, 85-89. *Concurrent Pos:* Vis assoc mech eng, Calif Inst Technol, 89-90; NSF presidential young investr, 90; tech ed, Inst Elec & Electronics Engrs J Robotics & Automation, 91-92. *Mem:* AAAS; Inst Elec & Electronics Engrs Robotics & Automation Soc; Inst Elec & Electronics Engrs Comput Soc; Inst Elec & Electronics Engrs Systs Man & Cybernet Soc; Inst Elec & Electronics Engrs Controls Soc. *Res:* Sensor-based real-time robot planning and control; robotic manufacturing, servicing and assembly;

kinematics and dynamics of multibody systems with time-varying interconnection topologies. *Mailing Add:* Dept Chem & Elec Comput Eng 0407 Univ Calif San Diego 9500 Gilman Dr La Jolla CA 92093-0407. *Fax:* 619-534-2486; *E-Mail:* kkreutzd@ucsd.edu

KREUTZER, RICHARD D, CYTOGENETICS, BIOCHEMISTRY OF LEISHMANIA. *Current Pos:* from asst prof to assoc prof, 69-79, PROF BIOL, YOUNGSTOWN STATE UNIV, 79- *Personal Data:* b Evergreen Park, Ill, June 23, 36; m, Patricia Cain; c Kimberly & Tamara. *Educ:* Univ Ill, BS, 63, MS, 65, PhD(zool), 68. *Prof Exp:* Instr zool, Univ Ill, Urbana, 67-69. *Concurrent Pos:* Chief vector, Biol Sect, Gorgas Mem Lab, 77-79. *Mem:* Am Soc Zoologists; Am Mosquito Control Asn; Genetics Soc Am; Entom Soc Am; Am Soc Trop Med Hyg. *Res:* Genetics; invertebrates; parasitology; entomology; cytogenetics and evolution of anophelines; isozyme studies on insects and protozoan parasites. *Mailing Add:* Dept Biol Youngstown State Univ 410 Wick Ave Youngstown OH 44555-0001. *Fax:* 330-742-1483

KREUTZER, WILLIAM ALEXANDER, PLANT PATHOLOGY. *Current Pos:* prof, 62-74, EMER PROF BOT & PLANT PATH, COLO STATE UNIV, 74- *Personal Data:* b Gunnison, Colo, Apr 13, 08; m 39; c 3. *Educ:* Colo Agr Col, BS, 30, MS, 32; Iowa State Col, PhD(plant path), 39. *Prof Exp:* From instr to asst prof bot, Colo Agr Col, 31-34; asst bot & plant path, Iowa State Col, 34-36; from asst prof to prof, Colo State Col, 36-46; plant pathologist, Agr Lab, Shell Develop Co, 46-62. *Mem:* Fel AAAS; Am Phytopath Soc; Mycol Soc; NY Acad Sci. *Res:* Soil fungicides and soil microecology. *Mailing Add:* 868 Gregory Rd Ft Collins CO 80524

KREUZ, JOHN ANTHONY, ORGANIC POLYMER CHEMISTRY. *Current Pos:* Res chemist, E I Du Pont de Nemours & Co, Inc, 59-64, staff scientist, 65-77, res assoc, 77-85, sr res assoc, 85-88, res fel, 88-95, FEL, E I DUPONT DE NEMOURS & CO, INC, 95- *Personal Data:* b Buffalo, NY, Sept 18, 33; m 96, Frances Patricia; c 6. *Educ:* St Bonaventure Univ, BS, 55; Univ Notre Dame, PhD(org chem), 60. *Mem:* Am Chem Soc. *Res:* Alkaline decomposition of aliphatic disulfides; addition and condensation polymerizations; polyimides and other high temperature polymers; polymer surface chemistry, polyimide and other adhesives. *Mailing Add:* 1614 McCoy Rd Columbus OH 43220. *Fax:* 614-474-0244

KREUZER, HANS JURGEN, SURFACE SCIENCE, NON-EQUILIBRIUM STATISTICAL MECHANICS. *Current Pos:* Killam res prof, 82-90, prof physics, 90-95, KILLAM PROF, DALHOUSIE UNIV, 95-, AC FALES PROF THEORET PHYSICS, 96- *Personal Data:* b Lahnstein, Ger, Aug 9, 42; Can citizen; m 86, Kim M Thornton; c Sophia A. *Educ:* Univ Bonn, dipl, 66, Dr rer nat, 67. *Prof Exp:* Asst theoret nuclear physics, Inst Theoret Nuclear Physics, Univ Bonn, 67-69; postdoctoral fel theoret physics, Theoret Physics Inst, Univ Alta, 69-71, from asst prof to prof physics, 71-85. *Concurrent Pos:* Lady Davies prof, Technion, Haifa, Israel, 77; vis fel, Wolfson Col, Oxford, 87; fel, Max-Planck Soc, Ger, 87; external sci mem, Fritz-Haber Inst, Berlin, 88-; bd mem, Int Soc Theoret Chem Physics; Humboldt res award, 96. *Mem:* Can Asn Physicists; Chem Inst Can; Int Soc Theoret Chem Physics; fel Royal Soc Can. *Res:* Theoretical surface science; transport processes at surfaces and interfaces; kinetics of adsorption, desorption, diffusion and reactions at surfaces; physics and chemistry in high electric fields; holography. *Mailing Add:* Dept Physics Dalhousie Univ Halifax NS B3H 3J5 Can. *Fax:* 902-494-5191; *E-Mail:* kreuzer@is.dal.ca

KREUZER, LLOYD BARTON, MICROCOMPUTERS, MICROCOMPUTER OPERATING SYSTEMS. *Current Pos:* PRES, KREUZER SOFTWARE CORP, 86- *Personal Data:* b Los Angeles, Calif, Aug 26, 40. *Educ:* Swarthmore Col, BA, 62; Princeton Univ, PhD(physics), 66. *Prof Exp:* Mem tech staff physics, Bell Tel Labs, NJ, 66-73; vpres, Diax Corp, Calif, 73-74; mem tech staff, Hewlett-Packard Lab, 74-78; vpres eng, 78-81, vpres adv develop, Dynabyte Inc, 81-82; pres, Menlo Corp, 83-86,. *Mem:* Am Phys Soc; Inst Elec & Electronics Engrs. *Res:* Nonlinear optics, optical parametric effects; experimental gravitation; air pollution detection by IR laser; optoacoustic spectroscopy; microcomputers and microcomputer software. *Mailing Add:* Acuson 1220 Charleston Rd Mountain View CA 94043

KREVANS, JULIUS RICHARD, HEMATOLOGY. *Current Pos:* prof med & dean, Sch Med, Univ Calif, San Francisco, 71-82, chancellor, 82-93, consult, 93-96, MED DIR, INT MED CARE, UNIV CALIF, SAN FRANCISCO, 96- *Personal Data:* b New York, NY, May 1, 24; c 5. *Educ:* NY Univ, BS, 44, MD, 46; Am Bd Internal Med, dipl, 56. *Hon Degrees:* LLD, Rush Univ, 84. *Honors & Awards:* Abraham Flexner Award, 83; Convocation Medal, Am Col Cardiol, 84; Belkin Mem Lectr, Albert Einstein Col Med, 86. *Prof Exp:* Intern, Queens Gen Hosp, 46-47; resident path, Flushing Hosp, 47; fel hemat, Johns Hopkins Univ, 50-51, asst resident, 51-52, resident, 52-53, dir, Blood Bank, 53-62, from asst prof to prof med, Sch Med, 60-71, asst dean, 62-63, dean acad affairs, 68-71. *Concurrent Pos:* Vis hematologist, Baltimore City Hosps, 53-63, physician-in-chief, 63-; asst prof, Johns Hopkins Univ, 55-60; chmn, Asn Am Med Cols, 80-81 & Comt Humanistic Qual Internist, Am Bd Internal Med, 83; mem numerous comts, nat found, govt agencies & orgns; consult, Sch Med, Univ Wash, Univ Colo & Med Serv Found, 86. *Mem:* Inst Med-Nat Acad Sci; Am Soc Hemat; assoc Am Col Physicians; Am Fed Clin Res; Int Soc Hemat. *Mailing Add:* Med Dir Int Med Care Univ Calif San Francisco CA 94143. *Fax:* 412-502-6696

KREVSKY, SEYMOUR, RADIATION PROTECTION, TACTICAL COMMUNICATIONS SATELLITES-SYSTEMS-HF ANTENNAS & PROPAGATION. *Current Pos:* CHIEF EXEC OFFICER & PRES, NESS, INC, 92- *Personal Data:* b Elizabeth, NJ, July 2, 20; m 44, Gladys Welt; c Joan & Ell. *Educ:* Newark Col Eng, BS, 42, MS, 50. *Honors & Awards:* Professional Achievement Award, Inst Elec & Electronics Engrs; Diamond Jubilee Award, Quarter Century Wireless Asn. *Prof Exp:* Dep dir eng, US Army Commun Systs Agency, Ft Monmouth, NJ, 42-58 & 68-80; sr mem tech staff, RCA Astro Electronics, Princeton, NJ, 58-68; sr engr, PRC Inc, Eatontown, NJ, 80-84; mem tech staff, Mitre Inc, 84-85; prin engr, Analytics Inc, Tinton Falls, NJ, 85-89, & C3I Systs Inc, Eatontown, NJ, 89-90; prin staff mem, BDM Int Inc, Eatontown, NJ, 90-91. *Concurrent Pos:* Pres, Int Test & Eval Asn, Ft Monmouth, 86-; mem, Nat Defense Exec Reserve, Region II, Fed Emergency Mgt Agency, Washington, DC, 87-; dipl, Am Asn Environ Engrs. *Mem:* Fel AAAS; fel Radio Club Am; Armed Forces Commun & Electronics Asn; Inst Elec & Electronics Engrs Eng Mgt Soc (vpres, 89-91, pres, 92-93, treas, 96-97); Int Test & Eval Asn. *Res:* Engineering management; participative management in corporate, middle management and working level group management arenas; communications engineering; tactical systems engineering; wire antennas; high frequency propagation. *Mailing Add:* 69 Judith Rd Little Silver NJ 07739-1559. *Fax:* 732-842-6606

KREY, LEWIS CHARLES, NEUROENDOCRINOLOGY. *Current Pos:* ASSOC PROF, NEW YORK UNIV, 91- *Personal Data:* b New York, NY, Oct 1, 44; m 67; c 3. *Educ:* Brown Univ, AB, 66; Duke Univ, PhD(physiol), 71. *Prof Exp:* Res assoc & fel physiol, Univ Pittsburgh Sch Med, 71-73, asst prof, 73-75; from asst prof to assoc prof neuroendocrinol, Rockefeller Univ, 81-91. *Concurrent Pos:* Alfred P Sloan Found fel, 78-80, Irma T Hirschl Found fel, 80-85; assoc ed, Endocrinol, 83-88; Reproductive Endocrinol Study Sect, NIH, 85-88. *Mem:* Endocrine Soc; Sigma Xi; Int Soc Neuroendocrinol. *Res:* Role of hypothalamic and hypophyseal steroid receptors in the neuroendocrine regulation of anterior pituitary gland function; in particular, the control of gonadotropin release in several mammalian species. *Mailing Add:* Obstet & Gynec NY Univ Sch Med 550 First Ave New York NY 10016-6481

KREY, PHILIP W, RADIOCHEMISTRY, ENVIRONMENTAL SCIENCE. *Current Pos:* dir radioactivity in surface air prog, US Dept Energy, 65-67, dir stratospheric radioactivity prog, Health & Safety Lab, 67-75, environ scientist, US Energy Res & Develop Admin & US Dept Energy, 75-80, dir, Anal Chem Div, 80-88, ACTG DEP LAB DIR, ENVIRON MEASUREMENTS LAB, US DEPT ENERGY, 88- *Personal Data:* b Brooklyn, NY, June 18, 27; m 52; c 5. *Educ:* St Francis Col, BS, 48; Duquesne Univ, MS, 50. *Prof Exp:* Chemist, Nuclear Defense Lab, 50-55, chief radiochem div, 55-57; mgr radiochem div, Isotopes, Inc, 57-64. *Concurrent Pos:* Mem task group on C-14 waste disposal, Nat Coun Radiation Protection & Measurements, 75- *Mem:* AAAS; NY Acad Sci. *Res:* Behavior and transport of artificial and natural radioactivity; trace metal and gaseous pollutants in the environment, including soil, troposphere and stratosphere from both local and global sources of contamination. *Mailing Add:* 7 Bluefield Ct Hillsdale NJ 07642

KREY, PHOEBE REGINA, RHEUMATOLOGY. *Current Pos:* asst prof med & dir rheumatology, 75-77, ASSOC PROF MED, COL MED & DENT, NJ, 77- *Personal Data:* b Ambridge, Pa; m 60; c 3. *Educ:* Northeastern Univ, BS, 55; Boston Univ, MD, 60. *Prof Exp:* Intern, Newton-Wellesley Hosp, 60-61; clin fel rheumatology, Boston City Hosp & res fel, Univ Hosp, 63-69; instr med, Boston Univ Med Sch, 69-74, asst prof, 74-75. *Mem:* Am Rheumatism Asn; Reticuloendothelial Soc; Electron Micros Soc Am. *Res:* Rheumatoid arthritis, fine structure and culture of the synovial membrane; gout, systemic lupus erythematons; immune experimental arthritis in animals. *Mailing Add:* One Far View Rd Millburn NJ 07041

KREYSA, FRANK JOSEPH, ORGANIC CHEMISTRY, RESOURCE MANAGEMENT. *Current Pos:* RETIRED. *Personal Data:* b Stankov, Czech, Apr 21, 19; nat US; m 50, Aida C Maehlmann; c Francis J, Henry J, Charles G & Peter G. *Educ:* Macalester Col, BA, 40; Columbia Univ, MA, 43, PhD(org chem), 48. *Prof Exp:* Anal chemist, Rockefeller Inst, 40-41; asst chem, Col Pharm, Columbia Univ, 43-44; from instr to assoc prof chem, St John's Univ NY, 46-55; from sr res chemist to asst to vpres Europ develop, W R Grace & Co, NY & Md, 55-61; from sr prof assoc to vpres, Smithsonian Inst Sci Info Exchange, DC, 61-73; chief, Sci Serv Div, Bur Alcohol, Tobacco & Firearms, Treas Dept, Washington, DC, 73-82. *Concurrent Pos:* Tech consult, Chemo Puro Mfg Co, NY & NJ, 51-55; chmn bd trustees, Am Soc Safety Res, 66-70; comnr, Sci Manpower Comn, 69-73. *Mem:* Am Inst Chem; Am Chem Soc. *Res:* Research and development management; forensic science; instrumentation; analytical chemistry. *Mailing Add:* 1186 Willoughby Ct Frederick MD 21702

KREZANOSKI, JOSEPH Z, PHARMACEUTICAL CHEMISTRY. *Current Pos:* AT COOPER VISION INC. *Personal Data:* b Mundare, Alta, Apr 14, 27; nat US; m 49, 54; c 3. *Educ:* Univ Calif, BS, 51, MS, 53, PhD(pharmaceut chem), 56. *Honors & Awards:* Borden Award, 51; Brunswick Award, 51. *Prof Exp:* Asst pharm, Univ Calif, 51-55; asst prof, Med Col Va, 56-59; dir pharmaceut res & develop, Barnes-Hind Labs, Inc, 59-67; vpres & tech adv, Flow Pharmaceut, Inc, 67-77; dir res & develop, Cooper Labs, Inc, 77- *Mem:* AAAS; Am Pharmaceut Asn; Am Chem Soc; Asn Am Acad Dermat; Am Mgt Asn; Sigma Xi. *Res:* Physical pharmacy; mechanism of drug action at the cellular level; pharmaceutical formulation. *Mailing Add:* 810 Amber Lane Los Altos CA 94024-4617

KREZDORN, ROY R, ELECTRICAL ENGINEERING. *Current Pos:* CONSULT, 78- *Personal Data:* b Shreveport, La, Jan 30, 10; m 35; c 2. *Educ:* Texas A&M Univ, BS, 32, PhD(elec eng), 52; Texas Univ, Austin, MS, 51. *Prof Exp:* Prof elec eng, Univ Texas Austin, 41-78. *Concurrent Pos:* Mgt adv, Lower Colo River Authority, 44-75; chief elec eng engr, Fargo Eng Co, 41-51; owner, Texas Eng Assoc, 51-81; asst dir eng res, Univ Texas, 70-78. *Mem:* Fel Inst Elec & Electronics Engrs. *Res:* Various subjects concerning power distribution and transmission. *Mailing Add:* 1501 Hillmont St Austin TX 78704

KREZOSKI, JOHN R, MARINE BIOGEOCHEMISTRY. *Current Pos:* proj assoc, 82-84, asst scientist, 84-88, ASSOC SCIENTIST, CTR GREAT LAKES STUDIES, UNIV WIS-MILWAUKEE, 88- *Personal Data:* b Kalamazoo, Mich, Jan 15, 47; m 72; c 2. *Educ:* Kalamazoo Col, BA, 69; Univ Mich, MS, 76, PhD(natural resources), 81. *Prof Exp:* Res scientist, Argonne Nat Lab, 81-82. *Concurrent Pos:* Guest fac res partic, Argonne Nat Lab, 82-84; dir, Dept Environ Health & Safety, 88- *Mem:* AAAS; Am Soc Limnol & Oceanog; Int Asn Great Lakes Res; Int Asn Theoret & Appl Limnol; NAm Benthological Soc; Am Chem Soc. *Res:* Multiple radiotracer techniques to study benthic community structure, biogenic nutrient regeneration from sediments, and burial and redistribution of hazardous substances by aquatic and marine invertebrates. *Mailing Add:* Environ Health & Safety Univ Wis-Milwaukee PO Box 413 Milwaukee WI 53201. *Fax:* 414-229-6729; *E-Mail:* jrk@csd4.csd.uwm.edu

KRIBEL, ROBERT EDWARD, plasma physics, magnetohydrodynamics, for more information see previous edition

KRICHER, JOHN C, ECOLOGY. *Current Pos:* From asst prof to assoc prof, 70-80, PROF BIOL, WHEATON COL, MASS, 80- *Personal Data:* b Philadelphia, Pa, Feb 7, 44. *Educ:* Temple Univ, BA, 66; Rutgers Univ, NB, PhD(zool), 70. *Concurrent Pos:* Cottrell sci grants, Res Corp, 74 & 75; Earthwatch grants, 81-83. *Mem:* Am Inst Biol Sci; Ecol Soc Am; Am Ornith Union; Cooper Ornith Soc; Sigma Xi; Asn Field Ornith (pres, 84-87); Soc Study Evol. *Res:* Bird species diversity in relation to secondary succession; species diversity of intertidal communities; tropical bird species diversity; ecology of migrant birds in the tropics; range expansions of North American birds. *Mailing Add:* Biol Dept Wheaton Col Norton MA 02766

KRICHEVSKY, MICAH I, MICROBIOLOGY, BIOCHEMISTRY. *Current Pos:* biochemist, 61-68, chief environ mechanisms sect, 68-74, CHIEF MICROBIAL SYSTEMATICS SECT, NAT INST DENT RES, 74- *Personal Data:* b Chicago, Ill, May 4, 31; m 52; c 2. *Educ:* Univ Conn, BA, 52; Univ Ill, MS, 55, PhD(dairy sci), 58. *Prof Exp:* Asst dairy sci, Univ Ill, 53-57, 58; biochemist, Nat Inst Allergy & Infectious Dis, 58-59; biochemist, Nat Heart Inst, 59-61. *Mem:* Am Soc Microbiol; Sigma Xi. *Res:* Biochemical differentiation in slime molds; metabolic pathways in bacteria; automation and computer technology in biomedical research. *Mailing Add:* Biocomm Int 12221 Parklawn Dr Rockville MD 20852

KRICK, IRVING PARKHURST, meteorology, physics; deceased, see previous edition for last biography

KRICK, MERLYN STEWART, NUCLEAR SCIENCE. *Current Pos:* MEM STAFF NUCLEAR SAFEGUARDS, LOS ALAMOS NAT LAB, UNIV CALIF, 75- *Personal Data:* b Shillington, Pa, Jan 13, 38; m 68. *Educ:* Albright Col, BS, 59; Univ Pa, PhD(physics), 66. *Prof Exp:* Res assoc physics, Univ Rochester, 66-68; res appointee, Los Alamos Sci Lab, 68-70; from asst prof to assoc prof nuclear eng, Kans State Univ, 70-75. *Mem:* Am Phys Soc; Am Nuclear Soc; Inst Elec & Electronics Engrs. *Res:* Nuclear safeguards; nuclear instrumentation; delayed neutron physics. *Mailing Add:* Los Alamos Nat Lab MS-E540 PO Box 1663 Los Alamos NM 87545

KRIDEL, DONALD JOSEPH, CHEMICAL ENGINEERING. *Current Pos:* RETIRED. *Personal Data:* b Rochester, NY, Apr 2, 16; m 45; c 6. *Educ:* Univ Rochester, BS, 37; Mass Inst Technol, ScD, 40. *Prof Exp:* Staff engr, Eastman Kodak Co, 40-64, asst supt, 64-66, supt, 66-78. *Concurrent Pos:* Civilian employee, Corp Engrs, Manhattan Proj, 43-45. *Mem:* Am Chem Soc; Am Inst Chem Engrs. *Res:* Photographic chemicals. *Mailing Add:* PO Box 4974 Woodland Park CO 80866-4974

KRIDER, EDMUND PHILIP, ATMOSPHERIC ELECTRICITY, ATMOSPHERIC PHYSICS. *Current Pos:* asst res prof, Inst Atmospheric Physics, Univ Ariz, 71-75, from asst prof to assoc prof, 73-80, head & dir, 86, PROF, DEPT ATMOSPHERIC SCI & INST ATMOSPHERIC PHYSICS, UNIV ARIZ, 80-, HEAD & DIR, 86- *Personal Data:* b Chicago, Ill, Mar 22, 40; div; c Ruth & Reed. *Educ:* Carleton Col, BA, 62; Univ Ariz, MS, 64, PhD(physics), 69. *Honors & Awards:* Outstanding Contrib to Advan Appl Meteorol, Am Metrol Soc, 85. *Prof Exp:* Nat Acad Sci resident res assoc, Manned Spacecraft Ctr, NASA, 69-71. *Concurrent Pos:* Prin investr numerous res grants & contracts, 71-; adv, NASA, 76; mem, Lightning & Sferics Subcomn, Int Comn Atmospheric Elec, 76-; assoc ed, J Geophys Res, 77-79; co-chief ed, J Atmos Sci, 90-92; pres, Int Comn Atmospheric Elec, 92- *Mem:* Sigma Xi; fel Am Meteorol Soc; Am Geophys Union; Am Asn Physics Teachers; Inst Elec & Electronics Engrs. *Res:* Lightning and atmospheric electricity; lightning physics, protection and lightning detection and warning systems. *Mailing Add:* Inst Atmospheric Physics Univ Ariz Tucson AZ 85721. *Fax:* 520-621-6833

KRIDER, JAKE LUTHER, ANIMAL NUTRITION. *Current Pos:* prof, 63-79, EMER PROF ANIMAL SCI, PURDUE UNIV, 79- *Personal Data:* b Lewistown, Ill, Dec 12, 13; m 36. *Educ:* Univ Ill, BS, 39, MS, 41; Cornell Univ, PhD(animal husb), 42. *Honors & Awards:* Res Award, Am Feed Mfrs Asn, 49; Res Award, Am Soc Animal Prod, 49; E G Cherbonnier Nat Award, Grain & Feed Dealers Nat Asn, 66; Animal Indust Award, Am Soc Animal Sci, 78. *Prof Exp:* Asst animal husb, Univ Ill, 39-40 & Cornell Univ, 40-42; assoc, Univ Ill, 42-43, asst prof swine husb, 43-46, assoc prof, 46-47, prof animal sci, 47-50, dir feed res & nutrit, 50-51; vpres & dir feed sales, McMillen Feed Div, Cent Soya Co, Inc, 51-56, vpres & dir pub rels, 56-59, vpres personnel develop & pub rels, 59-63. *Mem:* Hon fel Am Soc Animal Sci (vpres, 67-68, pres, 68-69); Poultry Sci Asn. *Res:* Nutritive requirements of the baby pig; value of pastures; causes of reproductive failures in sows; vitamin B-12 in baby pig nutrition; dose range antibiotic protocols; choline requirement and choline-methionine responses of young pigs. *Mailing Add:* 2201 Camelback Trace 22 West Lafayette IN 47906-1886

KRIEBEL, HOWARD BURTT, FOREST GENETICS, MOLECULAR BIOLOGY CELL CULTURE. *Current Pos:* from instr to assoc prof forestry, Ohio Agr Res & Develop Ctr, 53-62, from asst prof to prof bot & plant path, Ohio State Univ, 55-69, prof forestry, Ohio Agr Res & Develop Ctr, 62-88, prof genetics, 69-88, EMER PROF, OHIO STATE UNIV, 88- *Personal Data:* b Philadelphia, Pa, July 31, 21; m 49; c 1. *Educ:* Haverford Col, BA, 46; Yale Univ, MF, 48, PhD, 56. *Honors & Awards:* Fulbright lectr, Univ Zagreb, 71-72. *Prof Exp:* Instr forestry, Univ NH, 49-52. *Concurrent Pos:* Vis scientist, Royal Col Forestry, Stockholm, 63; actg chmn, Dept Forestry, Ohio Agr Res & Develop Ctr, 66-69; Fulbright distinguished scientist, Yugoslavia, 86; coordr & mem exec bd, Div 2, Int Union Forestry Res Orgn, 91-95. *Mem:* Fel AAAS; fel Soc Am Foresters; Am Soc Plant Physiologists; hon mem Asn Genetic Socs Yugoslavia. *Res:* Heritability studies; incompatibility systems; molecular biology of embryogenesis; developmental regulation of gene expression; hybrid and ecotype testing. *Mailing Add:* 2545 Christmas Run Blvd Wooster OH 44691

KRIEBEL, MAHLON E, PHYSIOLOGY, NEUROMUSCULAR TRANSMITTER. *Current Pos:* PROF PHYSIOL, STATE UNIV NY UPSTATE MED CTR, 69- *Personal Data:* b Garfield, Wash, Nov 18, 36; m 56, 80; c 3. *Educ:* Wash State Univ, BS, 58; Univ Wash, MS, 64, PhD(zool), 67. *Prof Exp:* Fel, Albert Einstein Col Med, 67-69. *Concurrent Pos:* Mem, Marine Biol Lab, Woods Hole; vis prof, Univ Konstanz, Max-Plank-Gottingen & Univ Calif, Irvine; Alexander von Humboldt sr scientist award. *Mem:* Am Soc Cell Biologists; Soc Neurosci. *Res:* Transmitter release at the n-m junction; physiology of tunicate heart; neurophysiolgy of fish oculomotor neurons; degranulation of mast cells; squid chromatophore nerve-muscle studies. *Mailing Add:* 202 Hillsboro Pkwy Syracuse NY 13214

KRIEBEL, RICHARD MARVIN, NEUROANATOMY. *Current Pos:* assoc prof anat, 87-92, PROF ANAT, PHILADELPHIA COL OSTEOP MED, 92- *Personal Data:* b WReading, Pa, Apr 12, 47; m 66; c 5. *Educ:* Albright Col, BA, 69; Temple Univ, PhD(anat), 74. *Prof Exp:* Instr & asst prof anat, Med Col Va, Va Commonwealth Univ, 73-75; from asst prof to assoc prof anat & neurobiol, Col Med, Univ Vt, 80-87. *Mem:* Am Asn Anatomists; Soc Neurosci. *Res:* Neuroendocrine mechanisms synaptology of thalamic nuclei in mammals with specific interest in lateral geniculate; automatic control both central and peripheral cardiovascular system. *Mailing Add:* Dept Anat Philadelphia Col Osteop Med 4150 City Ave Philadelphia PA 19131-1610

KRIEBLE, JAMES G(ERHARD), CHEMICAL ENGINEERING. *Current Pos:* Res assoc chem process eng, Res Lab, Gen Elec Co, NY, 49-57, process engr, Refractory Metals Lab, 57-61, mgr powder prod eng, 61-68, MGR ENG, REFRACTORY METAL POWDER & GAS OPER, GEN ELEC CO, 68- *Personal Data:* b NJ, Oct 23, 20; m 43; c 3. *Educ:* Princeton Univ, BS, 42, PhD(chem eng), 49. *Concurrent Pos:* Fel, Textile Res Inst, 49. *Mem:* Am Chem Soc; Am Inst Chem Engrs; NY Acad Sci. *Res:* Development and economic evaluation of processes for refractory metals and gases used in lamps. *Mailing Add:* 3646 Tolland Rd Cleveland OH 44122

KRIEG, ARTHUR F, PATHOLOGY. *Current Pos:* RETIRED. *Personal Data:* b East Orange, NJ, Oct 23, 30; wid; c Arthru M, Eric A & Sandra L. *Educ:* Yale Univ, AB, 52; Tufts Univ, MD, 56. *Prof Exp:* Rotating intern, Western Reserve Univ, 56-57, resident path, 57-60, resident, New Eng Deaconess Hosp, 63-64; asst prof path, State Univ NY Upstate Med Ctr, 64-68; assoc prof path, Pa State Univ, 68-71; prof & dir clin labs, Hershey Med Ctr, 71-96. *Mem:* Fel Acad Clin Lab Physicians & Scientists; fel Am Soc Clin Pathologists; fel Col Am Pathologists. *Res:* Clinical pathology; clinical laboratory management; computer applications to medical care. *Mailing Add:* Milton S Hershey Med Ctr Pa State Univ Hershey PA 17033

KRIEG, DANIEL R, PLANT PHYSIOLOGY, BIOCHEMISTRY. *Current Pos:* From asst prof to assoc prof, 70-77, PROF PLANT PHYSIOL, TEX TECH UNIV, 77- *Personal Data:* b Taylor, Tex, May 19, 43; m 65; c 2. *Educ:* Tex A&M Univ, BS, 65, PhD(plant physiol), 70. *Concurrent Pos:* Assoc ed, Agron J. *Mem:* Am Soc Plant Physiologists; Crop Sci Soc Am; Am Soc Agron. *Res:* Sorghum and cotton, physiological responses to environmental stress; environmental effects on biochemical changes in germinating cotton seeds; drought tolerance and photosynthetic activity of sorghum; environmental effects on seed development of grain sorghum. *Mailing Add:* Plant Physiol Lab Plant & Soil Sci Dept Tex Tech Univ Lubbock TX 79409-0001

KRIEG, DAVID CHARLES, ANIMAL BEHAVIOR, VERTEBRATE ZOOLOGY. *Current Pos:* RETIRED. *Personal Data:* b Bradford, Pa, June 10, 36; m 58; c 3. *Educ:* Mansfield State Col, BS, 58; St Bonaventure Univ, MS, 61, PhD(biol), 64. *Honors & Awards:* Marcia Brady Tucker Award, Am Ornith Union, 66. *Prof Exp:* Instr biol high sch, NY, 59-62; asst prof zool, State Univ NY, Col Cortland, 62-64; grad asst, St Bonaventure Univ, 64-67; assoc prof biol, State Univ NY, Col New Paltz, 67-92. *Concurrent Pos:* Frank M Chapman grants, Am Mus Natural Hist, 66, 71, 72 & 73. *Mem:* AAAS; Am Ornith Union; Am Soc Zoologists; Animal Behav Soc; Am Soc Ichthyologists & Herpetologists. *Res:* Comparative behavior of genus Sialia; hybridization of bluebirds in great plains. *Mailing Add:* 913 State Rte 213 High Falls NY 12440

KRIEG, NOEL ROGER, MICROBIOLOGY. *Current Pos:* from asst prof to prof, 60-83, ALUMNI DISTINGUISHED PROF MICROBIOL, VA POLYTECH INST & STATE UNIV, 83- *Personal Data:* b Waterbury, Conn, Jan 11, 34. *Educ:* Univ Conn, BA, 55, MS, 57; Univ Md, PhD(microbiol), 60. *Honors & Awards:* US Fedn Culture Collections J Roger Porter Award, Am Soc Microbiol, 96. *Prof Exp:* Asst bact, Univ Conn, 55-57 & microbiol, Univ Md, 57-60. *Concurrent Pos:* Bergey's Manual Trust, 71-91 & 96-; chmn, Acad Teaching Excellence, Va Polytech Inst & State Univ, 82-83. *Mem:* Am Soc Microbiol; Soc Gen Microbiol; Am Acad Microbiol; Sigma Xi. *Res:* Bacterial systematics; microaerophily; physiology and taxonomy of microaerophilic bacteria including campylobacter, spirillum, and azospirillum. *Mailing Add:* Dept Biol Va Polytech Inst & State Univ Blacksburg VA 24061-0406. *Fax:* 540-231-9307; *E-Mail:* nrk@vt.edu

KRIEG, RICHARD EDWARD, JR, bacteriology, for more information see previous edition

KRIEG, WENDELL JORDAN, NEUROANATOMY. *Current Pos:* assoc prof neurol, Inst Neurol, 44-46, prof neurol & dir inst, Med Sch, 46-48, prof anat, 48-74, EMER PROF ANAT, MED SCH, NORTHWESTERN UNIV, CHICAGO, 74- *Personal Data:* b Lincoln, Nebr, Apr 13, 06; m 52; c 2. *Educ:* Univ Nebr, BSc, 28; NY Univ, MS, 31, PhD(anat), 35. *Prof Exp:* Instr anat, Univ Nebr, 28-29; instr, Col Dent, NY Univ, 29-32, from instr to asst prof, Col Med, 32-44. *Concurrent Pos:* Mem corp, Marine Biol Lab, Woods Hole. *Mem:* Am Neurol Asn; Am Asn Anatomists. *Res:* Originator of electroneuroprosthesis; structure and connections of cerebral cortex and diencephalon of rat, monkey and man; illustration of nervous system; design of stereotaxic machines; models, reconstructions, and illustrations of the brain. *Mailing Add:* 1236 Hinman Ave Evanston IL 60202

KRIEGE, OWEN HOBBS, APPLIED CHEMISTRY. *Current Pos:* RETIRED. *Personal Data:* b Toledo, Ohio, Nov 6, 29; m 52; c 3. *Educ:* Ohio State Univ, BSc, 51, MSc, 52, PhD(anal chem), 54. *Prof Exp:* Staff mem, Los Alamos Sci Lab, 54-60; sr chemist, Res & Develop Ctr, Westinghouse Elec Corp, 60-66; group leader anal chem, Adv Mat Res & Develop Lab, Pratt & Whitney Aircraft 66-67, group leader anal & struct chem, 67-68, res supvr, 68-70, tech supvr appl chem, 71-76, asst mgr, Mat Eng & Res Lab, 76-87. *Mem:* Am Chem Soc; Sigma Xi. *Res:* Analytical chemistry of refractory materials; phase separations in superalloys; trace analysis in complex alloys; atomic absorption; polymer chemistry; electroplating. *Mailing Add:* 370 Deer Pass Dr Sedona AZ 86351

KRIEGEL, MONROE W(ERNER), CHEMICAL ENGINEERING. *Current Pos:* prof chem eng, eng exten, Okla State Univ, 64-78, asst dir exten, 64-66, dir, 66-78, EMER PROF CHEM ENG, OKLA STATE UNIV, 78-; CONSULT CONTINUING ENG EDUC, 78- *Personal Data:* b Giddings, Tex, July 30, 12; m 42; c 1. *Educ:* Univ Tex, BS, 34, MS, 36, PhD(chem eng), 39. *Honors & Awards:* Distinguished Serv Award & Pioneer Award, Am Soc Eng Educ. *Prof Exp:* Instr chem, Univ Tex, 34-36, res assoc, bur indust chem, 37-39; assoc prof chem eng, Tex Col Arts & Indust, 39-40; sr geochemist, Carter Oil Co, 40-45, res engr & group supvr, 45-49, head prod & pipe line res, 49-58; dir tech placement & col rels, Jersey Prod Res Co, 58-64. *Concurrent Pos:* Field test engr, oil & gas div, Tex RR Comn, 39. *Mem:* Soc Petrol Engrs; Am Inst Chem Engrs; Am Soc Eng Educ. *Res:* Microgas analysis; geochemistry; corrosion in hydrogen sulphide; geochemical method of prospecting for petroleum; personnel selection; research management; hiring, training and placement of technical personnel; continuing engineering education; industry-university relations. *Mailing Add:* 2123 Countryside Dr Stillwater OK 74074

KRIEGER, ALLEN STEPHEN, SOLAR PHYSICS, X-RAY OPTICS. *Current Pos:* PRES, RADIATION SCI INC, 86- *Personal Data:* b New York, NY, Feb 23, 41; m 66, Jeanne Kann; c Sara & Ruth. *Educ:* Mass Inst Technol, BS, 62, PhD(physics), 67. *Prof Exp:* Res assoc cosmic ray physics, Ctr Space Res, Mass Inst Technol, 67-68; sr scientist, Am Sci & Eng Inc, 68-71, staff scientist, 72-73, sr staff scientist, 74-77, dir solar res, 78-79, vpres space systs, 80-83, sr vpres space sci, 84-86. *Mem:* Fel Am Phys Soc; Am Astron Soc; Am Geophys Union; Int Soc Optical Eng. *Res:* Applicaiton of x-ray optics to solar astronomy and plasma diagnostics. *Mailing Add:* Radiation Sci Bldg 200 One Kendall Sq Suite 2200 Cambridge MA 02139. *Fax:* 617-577-1209; *E-Mail:* ask@world.std.com

KRIEGER, GARY LAWRENCE, HEALTH PHYSICS, RADIATION PROTECTION PHYSICS. *Current Pos:* EMERGENCY PLANNING SCIENTIST, LONG ISLAND LIGHTING CO, 85- *Personal Data:* b New York, NY, May 2, 48; m 74; c 2. *Educ:* NY Inst Technol, BS, 71; Univ Kans, MS, 76. *Prof Exp:* Health physics supvr, Siemens Corp, 76-79; assoc scientist, Brookhaven Nat Lab, 79-82; lead sr engr, Impell Corp, 82-84; proj health physicist, KLM Eng, 84-85. *Mem:* Health Physics Soc; Am Nuclear Soc. *Res:* Dose assessment modeling technique for accidental radiological releases to the environment; impact of this exposure on man. *Mailing Add:* 22 Huyler Rd East Setauket NY 11733

KRIEGER, HENRY ALAN, PROBABILITY & MATHEMATICAL STATISTICS. *Current Pos:* from asst prof to assoc prof math, 68-83, PROF MATH, HARVEY MUDD COL, 83- *Personal Data:* b Denver, Colo, May 7, 36; m 57; c 2. *Educ:* Rensselaer Polytech Inst, BAE, 57; Brown Univ, PhD(appl math), 64. *Prof Exp:* Bateman res fel math, Calif Inst Technol, 64-65, asst prof, 65-68. *Concurrent Pos:* Vis assoc prof statist, Israel Inst Technol, 74-75; vis prof statist, Hebrew Univ Jeusalem, 81, Australian Nat Univ, 82; vis res scientist, Commonwealth Sci Res Orgn, Div Math Statist, 82. *Mem:* Am Math Soc; Math Asn Am; Soc Indust Appl Math; Sigma Xi. *Res:* Probability theory, particularly limit theorems; measure theory. *Mailing Add:* Dept Math Harvey Mudd Col 1250 Dartmouth Ave Claremont CA 91711-5990

KRIEGER, IRVIN MITCHELL, PHYSICAL CHEMISTRY. *Current Pos:* instr chem, Case Western Reserve Univ, 49-51, from asst prof to assoc prof phys chem, 51-68, prof phys chem & macromolecular sci, 68-88, dir, Ctr Adhesives, Sealants & Coatings, 82-88, EMER PROF CHEM, CASE WESTERN RESERVE UNIV, 88- *Personal Data:* b Cleveland, Ohio, May 14, 23; m 65, Theresa Melamed; c Laura. *Educ:* Case Inst Technol, BS, 44, MS, 48; Cornell Univ, PhD(phys chem), 51. *Honors & Awards:* Bingham Medal, Soc Rheol, 89. *Prof Exp:* Asst, Cornell Univ, 47-48. *Concurrent Pos:* Vis prof, Nat High Sch Chem, Mulhouse, 87-; prof invite, Ecole Nationale Superieure de Chimie de Mulhouse, 87; assoc dir res, Univ Louis Pasteur, Strasbourg. *Mem:* Am Chem Soc; Soc Rheol (pres, 77-79); Am Inst Chem Eng; Sigma Xi. *Res:* Rheology and statistical mechanics of colloids and polymers. *Mailing Add:* 3460 Green Rd Beachwood OH 44122. *Fax:* 216-932-7314

KRIEGER, JEANNE KANN, PHYSICAL ORGANIC CHEMISTRY. *Current Pos:* area supvr, 83-87, MGR RES PROD OPERS, DUPONT MED PRODS, 87- *Personal Data:* b Hartford, Conn, Apr 16, 44; m 66; c 2. *Educ:* Bryn Mawr Col, BA, 66; Mass Inst Technol, PhD(org chem), 71; Boston Col, MBA, 84. *Prof Exp:* Res assoc chem, Mass Inst Technol, 71-72, instr, 72-75, lectr, 75-78, proj leader, 78-80, asst to dir mgr, New England Nuclear, 81-83. *Mem:* Am Chem Soc; AAAS; Am Nat Standard. *Res:* Radioactive waste disposal; scintillation techniques. *Mailing Add:* 44 Webster Rd Lexington MA 02173-8235

KRIEGER, JOHN NEWTON, UROLOGY, INFECTIOUS DISEASES. *Current Pos:* from asst prof to assoc prof, 82-90, PROF UROL, UNIV WASH, 90- *Personal Data:* b Philadelphia, Pa, May 3, 48; m 72. *Educ:* Princeton Univ, AB, 70; Cornell Univ Med Col, MD, 74. *Honors & Awards:* Cornell Award Excellence Surg, 74. *Prof Exp:* Asst surgeon, gen surg, New York Hosp-Cornell Med Ctr, 74-76, urol, 76-79, surgeon, 70-80; instr urol, Univ Va, 80-82. *Concurrent Pos:* Scholar, Am Urol Asn, 80-82; attend surgeon, Univ Va Hosp, 80-82, Univ Hosp, Seattle, 82-, Harborvion Med Ctr, Seattle, 82-, Children's Orthop Hosp, 82-; consult urol, Vet Admin Hosp, Seattle, 82- *Mem:* Am Fedn Clin Res; Am Venereal Dis Asn; Am Urol Asn; Am Soc Microbiol; Infectious Dis Soc Am; Sigma Xi. *Res:* Genitourinary tract infections; bacteriuria; sexually transmitted diseases; prostatis. *Mailing Add:* Dept Urol RL-10 Univ Wash Seattle WA 98195

KRIEGER, JOSEPH BERNARD, THEORETICAL SOLID STATE PHYSICS, DENSITY FUNCTIONAL THEORY WITH APPLICATIONS TO ATOMS & MOLECULES. *Current Pos:* assoc prof, 72-74, PROF PHYSICS, BROOKLYN COL, 74- *Personal Data:* b Brooklyn, NY, July 10, 37; m 64, Rose Meyerson; c Stephen. *Educ:* Columbia Univ, AB, 59, PhD(physics), 65. *Prof Exp:* From asst prof to assoc prof physics, Polytech Inst Brooklyn, 65-72. *Concurrent Pos:* Vis assoc prof, Brooklyn Col, 71-72, chmn dept, 76-80; acad assoc, Calif Inst Technol, 79; exec officer, Doctoral Prog Physics, City Univ NY, 90-97. *Mem:* Fel Am Phys Soc; Sigma Xi. *Res:* Transport theory in solids; density functional theory; density functional theory with applications to atoms and molecules. *Mailing Add:* Dept Physics Brooklyn Col Brooklyn NY 11210. *Fax:* 718-951-4407

KRIEGER, ROGER B, MECHANICAL ENGINEERING. *Current Pos:* SR STAFF RES ENGR, ENGINE RES DEPT, GEN MOTORS RES LABS, 69- *Personal Data:* b Milwaukee, Wis, May 4, 41; m 68, 79. *Educ:* Univ Wis-Madison, BS, 64, PhD(mech eng), 68. *Prof Exp:* Res engr, Fr Inst Petrol, 68-69. *Mem:* Soc Automotive Engrs; Am Soc Mech Engrs; Combustion Inst. *Res:* Combustion; pollutant formation and destruction during combustion; combustion modelling and internal combustion engine simulation. *Mailing Add:* 636 Lakeview Ave Birmingham MI 48009

KRIEGER, STEPHAN JACQUES, THEORETICAL PHYSICS. *Current Pos:* STAFF SCIENTIST, LAWRENCE LIVERMORE NAT LAB, 80- *Personal Data:* b San Francisco, Calif, Aug 2, 37; m 58; c 4. *Educ:* Univ Calif, Berkeley, BS, 59, PhD(physics), 63. *Prof Exp:* Res physicist, Carnegie Inst Technol, 63-66; assoc prof physics, Univ Ill, Chicago Circle, 71-78, prof, 78-80. *Mem:* Am Phys Soc. *Res:* Nuclear structure; many body problem. *Mailing Add:* L-291 Lawrence Livermore Nat Lab PO Box 808 Livermore CA 94550. *Fax:* 510-422-9523; *E-Mail:* krieger@ocfkms.llnl.gov

KRIEGER-BROCKETT, BARBARA, CHEMICAL ENGINEERING, CHEMICAL PHYSICS. *Current Pos:* asst prof, 75-80, ASSOC PROF CHEM ENG, UNIV WASH, 80- *Personal Data:* b Madison, Wis, Jan 27, 47. *Educ:* Univ Wis-Madison, BS, 68; Wayne State Univ, MS, 72, PhD(chem eng), 75. *Prof Exp:* Res engr, Inst Francais du Petrole, 68-69; res technician auto emission control, Gen Motor Res Labs, 70-71; res asst, Wayne State Univ, 71-75. *Concurrent Pos:* Consult, Rocket Res Corp, 77-, Hanford Energy Develop Lab, 78- & Nat Acad Adv Bd, Environ Protection Agency, 76- *Mem:* Am Inst Chem Engrs; Am Chem Soc; AAAS; Sigma Xi. *Res:* Chemical kinetics, chemical physics and transport related to chemical reaction engineering as applied to high temperature-high energy phenomena such as combustion, pyrolysis, laser and plasma processing, air pollution and atmospheric chemistry. *Mailing Add:* 2906 Fuhrman Ave E Seattle WA 98102

KRIEGH, JAMES DOUGLAS, CIVIL ENGINEERING. *Current Pos:* RETIRED. *Personal Data:* b Dodge City, Kans, Dec 29, 28. *Educ:* Univ Colo, BS, 55, MS, 58. *Prof Exp:* Asst, Cryogenics Lab, Nat Bur Standards, Colo, 53-54; asst, Eng Exp Sta, Univ Colo, 54-55; instr civil eng, 55-58; from asst prof to prof civil eng, Univ Ariz, 58-86, prof eng mech, 81-86. *Concurrent Pos:* NSF fac fel, Univ Colo, 63-64; comt chmn, Hwy Res Bd, Nat Acad Sci-Nat Res Coun, 64-70. *Mem:* Am Soc Civil Engrs; Am Concrete Inst. *Res:* Epoxy resins for concrete construction and structural adhesives. *Mailing Add:* 40 E Calle Concordia Tucson AZ 85737

KRIEGSMAN, HELEN, MATHEMATICS. *Current Pos:* from instr to assoc prof, 47-67, PROF MATH & CHMN DEPT, PITTSBURG STATE UNIV, 67- *Personal Data:* b Pittsburg, Kans, Feb 27, 24. *Educ:* Kans State Teachers Col Pittsburg, BS, 44, MS, 47; Ohio State Univ, PhD(math educ), 64. *Prof Exp:* Teacher, High Sch, Kans, 44-47. *Mem:* Math Asn Am; Am Math Soc; Nat Coun Teachers Math. *Res:* Curriculum and methods of teaching mathematics on the secondary school and college levels. *Mailing Add:* Pittsburg State Univ Wilkinson Alumni Ctr 401 E Ford Pittsburg KS 66762-9987

KRIEGSMANN, GREGORY A, APPLIED MATHEMATICS. *Current Pos:* PROF MATH, NJ TECH INST, 90- *Personal Data:* b Chicago, Ill, Sept 20, 46; m 69; c 2. *Educ:* Marquette Univ, BS, 69; Univ Calif, Los Angeles, MS, 70, PhD(appl math), 74. *Prof Exp:* Instr math, Courant Inst, NY Univ, 74-76; mem tech staff, Hughes Aircraft Co, 76-77; asst prof math, Univ Nebr, 77-79, assoc prof, 79-80; from assoc prof to prof appl math, Northwestern Univ, 80-90. *Mem:* Soc Indust Appl Math; Am Math Soc; fel Acoust Soc Am; fel Inst Math & Appins. *Res:* Numerical and asymstotic analysis of wave propagation; bifurcation problems in the physical sciences; microwave processing of materials. *Mailing Add:* Dept Math NJ Tech Inst Technol Newark NJ 07102-9938

KRIENKE, ORA KARL, JR, ASTRONOMY. *Current Pos:* RETIRED. *Personal Data:* b Seattle, Wash, Jan 31, 31; m 60; c 2. *Educ:* Seattle Pac Col, BA, 53, MA, 55; Univ Wash, MS, 59 & 69, PhD(astron), 73. *Prof Exp:* Instr math, Seattle Pac Univ, 53-59, asst prof physics & math, 59-63, assoc prof physics, math & philos, 63-71, prof physics, math & philos, 71-97, dean, Sch Nat & Math Sci, 80-97. *Concurrent Pos:* Vis lectr, Univ Wash, 64 & 68. *Mem:* AAAS; Am Asn Physics Teachers; Am Astron Soc. *Res:* Structure of galaxies, especially irregular type II galaxies. *Mailing Add:* 9251 20th Ave NW Seattle WA 98117

KRIENS, RICHARD DUANE, ORGANIC CHEMISTRY. *Current Pos:* RETIRED. *Personal Data:* b Belmond, Iowa, Oct 16, 32; m 67, Linda J Hazel; c John, Heidi & Rebecca. *Educ:* Iowa State Teachers Col, BA, 56; Iowa State Univ, PhD(org chem), 63. *Prof Exp:* Teacher, High Sch, Iowa, 57-58; asst prof chem, Iowa Wesleyan Col, 63-65; assoc prof, Ashland Univ, 65-73, prof chem, 73- *Mem:* Am Inst Chem; Royal Soc Chem; Am Chem Soc. *Res:* Free radical organic chemistry; reaction mechanisms in organic chemistry. *Mailing Add:* Dept Chem Ashland Univ Ashland OH 44805

KRIER, CAROL ALNOTH, MATERIALS SCIENCE & ENGINEERING, PRODUCTION ENGINEERING. *Current Pos:* RETIRED. *Personal Data:* b Bismarck, NDak, July 22, 28; m 57, Carol A Wilt; c David A & Elizabeth A. *Educ:* St Martin's Col, BS, 50; Univ Pittsburgh, PhD(chem), 55. *Honors & Awards:* NASA-Apollo Achievement Award, 70; Apollo/Saturn V Roll of Honor, 71; Apollo 11 Manned Flight Awareness Award, 71. *Prof Exp:* Lab asst fuel oils, State Labs Dept, NDak, 45-46; asst instr chem, pvt sch, Wash, 48-50; asst, Univ Pittsburgh, 50-51, asst phys chem, 51-55; prin chemist, proj leader & sr scientist, Battelle Mem Inst, 55-62; metals res specialist, Boeing Co, 62-67, supvr mat stress & environ simulation, 67-70, mgr advan develop & spec studies, 70-71, eng mgr, Boeing Aerospace, 71-83, mgr mfg tech, 84-86, mgr, prod eng, Boeing Aerospace & Electronics, 87-91, mgr opers techol, Boeing Defense & Space, 91-93. *Concurrent Pos:* Consult, Defense Metals Info Ctr, 59-62; mat adv bd mem, Nat Acad Sci, 61-69, Aerospace Industs Asn, 86-89. *Mem:* Am Chem Soc; Am Soc Metals; Sigma Xi. *Res:* Thermodynamics; calorimetry; cryogenics; theory of metals and alloys; extractive metallurgy; refractory, structural and electronic materials; high temperature coatings for metals; oxidation of metals and alloys; alkali metals; platinum-group metals; high temperature corrosion; physical metallurgy; vapor deposition; manufacturing processes; automation; environmental engineering. *Mailing Add:* 4520 133 Rd Ave SE Bellevue WA 98006

KRIER, JACOB, NEUROPHYSIOLOGY. *Current Pos:* PROF GASTROINTESTINAL PHYSIOL & NEUROPHYSIOL, MICH STATE UNIV, 80- *Personal Data:* b Marlboro, Utah, Sept 5, 45. *Educ:* LaSalle Col, BS, 67; Duquesne Univ, MS, 69; Univ Pittsburgh, PhD(neuropharmacol), 77. *Prof Exp:* Res asst prof & res fel, Mayo Clin, 77-80. *Mem:* Am Physiol Soc. *Res:* Neurogenic control of gastrointestinal smooth muscle. *Mailing Add:* Dept Physiol Mich State Univ 204 Giltner Hall East Lansing MI 48824-0001. *Fax:* 517-355-5125

KRIESBERG, JEFFREY IRA, EXPERIMENTAL PATHOLOGY. *Current Pos:* from asst prof to assoc prof path, 80-89, assoc prof med, 83-89, PROF MED & PATH, HEALTH SCI CTR, UNIV TEX, SAN ANTONIO, 89-; CAREER SCIENTIST, VET ADMIN, 89- *Personal Data:* b Far Rockaway, NY, July 7, 49; c 3. *Educ:* State Univ NY, Albany, BS, 71; Univ Md, PhD(exp path), 75. *Prof Exp:* Res assoc, Dept Path, Univ Ala Med Ctr, 75-76; res fel, Dept Path, Harvard Univ, 76-77; from instr to asst prof, 77-80. *Concurrent Pos:* Lectr, var univs, socs & hosps, 78-91; asst biologist, Dept Med, Mass Gen Hosp, 79-80; consult path, Sch Med, Yale Univ, Kidney Dis Inst, NY Dept Health, 79 & Cystic Fibrosis Core Ctr, Case Western Univ, 86-91; prin investr, NIH, 81-95; mem, Spec Study Sect, NIH, 84 & 87, Spec Planning Comt, Nat Inst Arthritis & Diabetes & Digestive Kidney Dis, 85, Path A Study Sect, 85-88, Coun Kidney Cardiovasc Dis, Am Heart Asn, 86, Prog Comt, Am Soc Nephrology, 88-89; prog chmn, Tissue Cell Cult, Am Soc Nephrology, 87; Nat Kidney Found fel, 87-88 & 89-90. *Mem:* AAAS; Am Soc Nephrology; Am Asn Pathologists; Am Soc Cell Biol; Am Diabetes Asn; Tissue Cult Asn; Int Soc Nephrology; Am Heart Asn. *Res:* Author of more than 50 technical publications. *Mailing Add:* Dept Path Health Sci Ctr Univ Tex 7703 Floyd Curl Dr San Antonio TX 78284. *Fax:* 512-567-2490

KRIGBAUM, WILLIAM RICHARD, PHYSICAL CHEMISTRY. *Current Pos:* from instr to prof, 52-69, chmn dept, 76-79, JAMES B DUKE PROF CHEM, DUKE UNIV, 69- *Personal Data:* b Ill, Sept 29, 22; m 46; c 3. *Educ:* Millikin Univ, BS, 44; Univ Ill, MS, 48, PhD(chem), 49. *Hon Degrees:* DSc, Millikin Univ, 66. *Prof Exp:* Nat Res Coun fel, Cornell Univ, 49-50, res assoc & instr, 50-52. *Concurrent Pos:* Sloan res fel, 56-60; NSF sr fel, 59-60; mem adv panel chem, NSF. *Mem:* Am Chem Soc; Am Phys Soc; Am Crystallog Asn. *Res:* Wide and low angle x-ray diffraction; physical chemical studies of polymers in solution and in bulk state; physical chemistry of macromolecules. *Mailing Add:* 2504 Wilson St Durham NC 27705

KRIKORIAN, ABRAHAM D, PLANT PHYSIOLOGY, BIOCHEMISTRY. *Current Pos:* from asst prof to assoc prof biol sci, 66-81, assoc prof biochem, 81-88, PROF BIOCHEM, STATE UNIV NY, STONY BROOK, 88- *Personal Data:* b Worcester, Mass, May 5, 37. *Educ:* Mass Col Pharm, BS, 59; Cornell Univ, PhD(plant physiol), 65. *Honors & Awards:* Cosmos Achievement Award, NASA, 75 & 81; Founders' Award, Am Soc Gravitational & Space Biol, 92. *Prof Exp:* From teaching asst to teaching assoc plant physiol, Cornell Univ, 60-64, from instr to asst prof, 63-66. *Concurrent Pos:* Ed, Ann Bot, 76-82; plant sci book rev consult, Quart Rev Biol, 79-; mem comt space res, Int Coun, Sci Union, 84-; gov bd, Am Soc Gravitational & Space Biol, 85-87. *Mem:* AAAS; Am Soc Pharmacog; Int Soc Plant Morphologists; Int Asn Plant Tissue Cult; Soc Develop Biol; Tissue Cult Asn; Soc Econ Bot (vpres, 81-82, pres, 82-83); Bot Soc Am; Am Soc Plant Physiologists; Scand Soc Plant Physiol; Am Soc Gravitational & Space Biol (pres, 87-88); Int Palm Soc; Plant Growth Regulator Soc Am. *Res:* Physiological and morphological aspects of growth and development in flowering plants; morphogenesis and biochemical differentiation; nitrogen metabolism; production of secondary products and expression of biochemical potentialities by cells and tissues grown in culture; clonal stability; totipotency of higher plant cells in terms of morphogenesis and biochemical competence. *Mailing Add:* Dept Biochem & Cell Biol State Univ NY Stony Brook NY 11794-5215

KRIKORIAN, JOHN SARKIS, JR, ELECTRICAL ENGINEERING, APPLIED MATHEMATICS. *Current Pos:* VPRES, SARKIS CORP, 81- *Personal Data:* b Providence, RI, Sept 18, 41. *Educ:* Univ RI, BS, 63; Syracuse Univ, MS, 67; Univ RI, PhD(elec eng), 68. *Prof Exp:* Res specialist elec eng, Elec Boat Div, Gen Dynamics Corp, Groton, Conn, 68-73; asst prof, Univ RI, 73-80; mem tech staff, Mitre Corp, 83-84. *Concurrent Pos:* Lectr elec eng, Univ Conn, 69; adj prof, Brown Univ, 80-81. *Mem:* Sigma Xi. *Res:* Electrical engineering and related interdisciplinary activities. *Mailing Add:* Five Thayer Pl Warwick RI 02888

KRIKORIAN, OSCAR HAROLD, HIGH TEMPERATURE CHEMISTRY. *Current Pos:* RES CHEMIST, LAWRENCE LIVERMORE NAT LAB, 55- *Personal Data:* b Fresno, Calif, Nov 22, 30; m 53; c 2. *Educ:* Fresno State Col, BS, 52; Univ Calif, PhD(chem), 55. *Mem:* Am Chem Soc. *Res:* High temperature chemistry; thermodynamic properties of gaseous species that exist at high temperatures; molten metal containment studies, estimation of heat capacities and thermal expansivities of refractory materials. *Mailing Add:* 22 Rio Del Ct Danville CA 94526

KRIKOS, GEORGE ALEXANDER, PATHOLOGY. *Current Pos:* prof pathobiol, Univ Colo, 68-75, chmn dept, 68-73, assoc dean oral biol affairs, 75-76, prof 75-86, clin prof, 86-91, EMER PROF ORAL BIOL, SCH DENT UNIV COLO, 91- *Personal Data:* b Old Phaleron, Greece, Sept 17, 22; US citizen; m 49, Aspasia Manoni; c Helen, Alexandra & Alexios. *Educ:* Univ Pa, DDS, 49; Univ Rochester, PhD(path), 59. *Hon Degrees:* Dr, Univ Athens, Greece, 81. *Prof Exp:* NIH res fel path, Univ Rochester, 54-58; from asst prof to prof, Sch Dent Med, Univ Pa, 58-68, chmn path, 64-68. *Concurrent Pos:* Assoc prof oral path, Grad Sch Arts & Sci, Div Grad Educ, Sch Med, Univ Pa, 62-68; vis prof, Sch Dent, Univ Athens, Greece, 80-81. *Mem:* Am Asn Pathologists; Int Asn Dent Res; Sigma Xi. *Res:* Oral biology. *Mailing Add:* 350 Ivy St Denver CO 80220-5855

KRILL, ARTHUR MELVIN, MECHANICAL ENGINEERING, ENGINEERING GENERAL. *Current Pos:* chmn, 76-78, PRES, ARTHUR M KRILL CONSULTS, 79-; CHMN, OGDEN DEVELOP CORN, 70- *Personal Data:* b Burlington, Colo, Oct 17, 21; m 44; c 3. *Educ:* Univ Colo, BS, 43, MS, 51; Indust Col Armed Forces, Dipl, 52. *Prof Exp:* Prod engr, Pratt-Whitney Aircraft Div, United Aircraft Corp, 42, exp test engr, 43-47; from instr to assoc prof mech engr, Col Eng, Univ Denver, 47-62, coord coop plan, 48-56, head admin eng, 51-52, proj supvr, 51-56; dir opers anal unit, Denver Res Inst, 55-62, head mech div, 56-62; pres, Falcon Res & Develop, 62-70; pres, Ken R White Co, 63-76. *Concurrent Pos:* Consult, Bond Eng Co, 50-52; mem, Colo State Air Pollution Variance Bd; mgr corp planning, Stearns Roger Corp, 82-83; mem, Metrop Air Qual Coun. *Mem:* Fel AAAS; Am Soc Mech Engrs; Am Soc Eng Educ; Nat Soc Prof Engrs; Am Inst Consult Engrs. *Res:* Theoretical and applied mechanics; operations research; behavioral sciences; magnetohydrodynamics. *Mailing Add:* 450 Westwood Dr Denver CO 80206

KRIM, MATHILDE, CYTOGENETICS, VIROLOGY. *Current Pos:* CHMN BD, AM FOUND AIDS RES, 88- *Personal Data:* b Como, Italy, July 9, 26; US citizen; m 58; c 1. *Educ:* Geneva Univ, BS, 48, PhD(cytogenetics), 53. *Prof Exp:* Jr scientist & res assoc cancer res, Weizmann Inst, 53-59; res assoc virol, Div Virus Res, Med Col, Cornell Univ, 59-62; assoc, Sloan-Kettering Inst Cancer Res, 62-75, assoc & mem, 75- *Concurrent Pos:* Mem, President's Comt Ment Retardation, 66-69, Nat Endowment for Humanities, 69-73, Comt of 100 for Nat Health Ins, 69-; consult spec virus cancer prog & mem adv comt, Nat Colorectal Cancer Prog, Nat Cancer Inst, 71; trustee, Rockefeller Found, 71-; co-chmn, Nat Comt to Save our Schs of Health, 71-; mem bd trustees, Nat Biomed Res Found; mem bd dirs, Inst Soc, Ethics & Life Sci; pres, Comn Study Ethnical Probs in Med, Biomed & Behav Res, 80-; secy, Adv Comt Health Protection & Dis Prev, Dept Health, Educ & Welfare, 69-70; mem panel consult conquest of cancer, Comt Labor & Pub Welfare, US Senate, 71. *Mem:* AAAS; Am Cancer Soc; Am Asn Ment Deficiency. *Res:* Structure of chromosomes; prenatal determination of sex; aberrations in human sexual development; cell biology and mechanisms of oncogenic transformation; interferon research. *Mailing Add:* Am Found AIDS Res 733 Third Ave New York NY 10017

KRIMIGIS, STAMATIOS MIKE, SPACE PHYSICS. *Current Pos:* from sr staff scientist to supvr space physics, Johns Hopkins Univ, 68-74, head, Space Physics & Instrumentation Group, 74-81, chief scientist, 80-90, DEPT HEAD, SPACE DEPT, APPL PHYSICS LAB, JOHNS HOPKINS UNIV, 91- *Personal Data:* b Chios, Greece, Sept 10, 38; US citizen; m 90, Maria Anastasopoulou; c Michael & John. *Educ:* Univ Minn, BPhys, 61; Univ Iowa, MS, 63, PhD(physics), 65. *Honors & Awards:* Except Sci Achievement Medal, NASA, 81 & 86; Basic Sci Award, Nat Acad Astronaut, 94. *Prof Exp:* Res assoc space physics, Univ Iowa, 65-66, asst prof physics, 66-68. *Concurrent Pos:* Co-investr, Mariner IV & Injun IV, 63, Orbiting Geophys Observ-4, Explorer 33 & 35 & Injun V, 65, Mariner V Venus, 66, prin investr, Interplanetary Monitoring Platform on 7 & 8, 67; mem var NASA adv comts on space invests; prin investr, Multiple-Charged Energetic Trapped Nuclei in Radiation Belt, NSF, 71-74, Voyager Low Energy Charged Particle Exp, 72, Light Ion Release Exp, NASA, 73, Active Magnetospheric Particle Tracer Explorers, 77, Studies of Solar & Magnetospheric Particles, NSF, 77-83; assoc ed, J Geophys Res, Space Physics, 75-77; co-prin investr, Galileo Mission, Energetic Particle Detector Exp, 77 & co-investr, Ulysses Spacecraft, LAN Exp, 77; mem, Space Sci Bd, Nat Acad Sci, 83-86, chmn, Comt Solar & Space Physics, 83-86, NASA Space & Earth Sci Adv Comt, 87-90; prin investr, Imaging Neutral Particle Detector, NASA Innovative Res Prog, 85-89; mem, Space Sci Working Group, Asn Am Univs; prin investr, Cassini mission to Saturn, 90- *Mem:* AAAS; fel Am Geophys Union; fel Am Phys Soc; fel Am Inst Aeronaut & Astronautd Asn; Athens Acad Greece; Int Acad Astronaut. *Res:* Space plasma physics; solar and heliospheric physics; geomagnetically trapped radiation; planetary magnetospheres; cosmic rays; particle instrumentation; over 300 publications in journals and books. *Mailing Add:* Appl Physics Lab Johns Hopkins Univ Laurel MD 20723. *Fax:* 301-953-5969; *E-Mail:* torn-audskrimigis@jhuapl.edu

KRIMM, SAMUEL, BIOPHYSICS, POLYMER PHYSICS. *Current Pos:* Fel, Univ Mich, Ann Arbor, 50-52, from instr to assoc prof, 52-63, assoc dean res, Col Lit Sci & Arts, 72-75, chmn biophysics res div, 76-86, dir prog protein struct & design, 85-94, PROF PHYSICS, UNIV MICH, ANN ARBOR, 63- *Personal Data:* b Morristown, NJ, Oct 19, 25; m 49, Marilyn Neveloff; c David & Daniel. *Educ:* Polytech Inst Brooklyn, BS, 47; Princeton Univ, MA, 49, PhD(phys chem), 50. *Honors & Awards:* High Polymer Physics Prize, Am Phys Soc, 77; Alexander von Humboldt Prize, 83. *Concurrent Pos:* NSF sr fel, 62-63; chmn, Gordon Res Conf, 68; vis prof, Weizmann Inst, 70, Univ Mainz, 83 & Univ Paris, 91; sr fel, Univ Mich, 71-76; mem, Nat Bur Standards Polymers Div Eval Panel, Nat Acad Sci/Nat Res Coun, 73-76, chmn, 75-76; chmn biopolymers subgroup, Biophys Soc, 74-75; vchmn, Div Biol Physics, Am Phys Soc, 78, chmn, 79; mem, Mat Res Adv Comt, NSF, 81-86, chmn, 84-85, mem, Coun Mat Sci, DOE, 86 -; invited prof, French Govt, 91. *Mem:* Fel AAAS; Am Chem Soc; Biophys Soc; fel Am Phys Soc; Am Crystallog Asn. *Res:* Infrared and Raman spectroscopy; high polymers; protein structure; potential functions. *Mailing Add:* Dept Physics Univ Mich 729 Dennison Bldg Ann Arbor MI 48109. *Fax:* 313-764-3323

KRIMMEL, C PETER, MEDICINAL CHEMISTRY. *Current Pos:* RETIRED. *Personal Data:* b Erie, Pa, June 23, 17; m, Margaret Weis; c Stephen & Herbert. *Educ:* Pa State Univ, BS, 39, Northwestern Univ, MS, 41; Pa State Univ, PhD(Chem), 45. *Prof Exp:* Instr chem, Pa State Univ, 44-45; res chemist, G D Searle & Co, 46-78. *Concurrent Pos:* Vchmn, Conf Med Chem, Gordon Res Confs, 64, chmn, 65, monitor Confs, 79-88; consult, 79-; writer, 93- *Mem:* AAAS; Am Chem Soc. *Res:* Organic chemistry applied to pharmaceuticals; spasmolytics; diuretics; cardioactive drugs; anti-atherosclerotic drugs; anti-virals and antibiotics; chemistry of sugars, kojic acid, adamantane, squaric acid, polyaromatic substituted aliphatic carboxylic acids; receptors; continuing education management and design; granted 49 US patents. *Mailing Add:* 723 C Shoreline Rd Barrington IL 60010

KRIMMER, EDWARD CHARLES, PHARMACOLOGY, PSYCHOPHARMACOLOGY. *Current Pos:* Fel pharmacol, 74-76, asst prof, 76-81, ASSOC PROF PHARMACOL, UNIV PITTSBURGH, 81- *Personal Data:* b Youngstown, Ohio, Dec 31, 33; m 58; c 3. *Educ:* Univ Pittsburgh, BS, 68, PhD(pharmacol), 74. *Concurrent Pos:* Consult, ICI US, 74-75; fel, Nat Inst Drug Abuse grant, 74-76; co-investr, NIMH grant, 76-; investr, Nat Inst Drug Abuse grant, 79-83; co-investr, Nat Inst Alcohol Abuse. *Mem:* AAAS; Behav Pharmacol Soc; Am Soc Pharmacol & Exp Therapeut; Soc Stimulus Properties Drugs (secy-treas, 78-80); Soc Neurosci; Res Soc Alcoholism; Sigma Xi. *Res:* Investigate the stimulus properties of various sedatives, axiolytics, narcotics and cannabinoids and the pharmacological antagonism or enhancement of these perceived effects. *Mailing Add:* 318 Elmwood Dr Kent OH 44240-2890

KRINER, WILLIAM ARTHUR, INORGANIC CHEMISTRY. *Current Pos:* asst prof, 65-70, ASSOC PROF CHEM, ST JOSEPHS UNIV, PA, 70- *Personal Data:* b Pottsville, Pa, Feb 8, 31; m 57; c 2. *Educ:* West Chester State Col, BS, 53; Univ Pa, PhD(inorg chem), 59. *Prof Exp:* Res chemist, Rohm and Haas Co, Pa, 59-61; lectr chem, Univ Pa, 62-65. *Mem:* Am Chem Soc; Sigma Xi. *Res:* Small ring heterocyclics of Group IV preparation and reactivity; organometallic polymers; synthesis of novel organosilicon compounds; silicon hydride chemistry; boron cyanides and siloxy aluminum compounds. *Mailing Add:* Dept Chem St Josephs Univ 5600 City Ave Philadelphia PA 19131

KRING, JAMES BURTON, ENTOMOLOGY. *Current Pos:* ADJ PROF ENTOM, UNIV FLA, 82- *Personal Data:* b Monett, Mo, May 25, 21; m 47; c 5. *Educ:* Rockhurst Col, BS, 47; Kans State Col, MS, 48, PhD(entom), 52. *Honors & Awards:* L O Howard Award, 82. *Prof Exp:* Asst Instr, Kans State Col, 50; asst biol, Rockhurst Col, 50; from asst entomologist to entomologist, Conn Agr Exp Sta, 51-77; head dept, dean & dir, Col Food & Nat Resource, Agr Exp Sta & Coop Ext Serv, 79-81; prof entom, Univ Mass, 77-82. *Concurrent Pos:* Mem grad fac, Univ Conn, 59-78. *Mem:* Entom Soc Am (pres, 79); AAAS; Royal Entom Soc London; Entom Soc Can. *Res:* Ecology and systematics of Aphididae; control pests of vegetables and ornamentals; behavior of vectors of plant diseases. *Mailing Add:* Dept Math & Sci Roanne State Comm Col Patton Lane Harriman TN 37748-8915

KRINITZKY, E(LLIS) L(OUIS), ENGINEERING GEOLOGY. *Current Pos:* CHIEF GEOL RES, WATERWAYS EXP STA, ARMY CORPS ENGRS, 63- *Personal Data:* b Norfolk, Va, July 1, 24; m 52. *Educ:* Va Polytech Inst, BS, 45; Univ NC, MS, 47; La State Univ, PhD(geol), 50. *Honors & Awards:* Richard H Jahns Distinguished Lectr Eng Geol, 91. *Prof Exp:* Asst prof geol, Southwestern La Inst, 46-47; geologist, Army Corps Engrs, 48-53; sr geologist, Creole Petrol Corp, 53-61; vis prof, Univ Houston, 62-63. *Mem:* Fel Geol Soc Am; Earthquake Eng Res Inst; Am Soc Civil Engrs; Int Soc Rock Mech; Seismol Soc Am; Asn Eng Geologists. *Res:* Engineering geology; earthquake hazards; x-radiography. *Mailing Add:* 3309 Highland Dr Vicksburg MS 39180

KRINSKY, HERMAN Y, CHEMICAL ENGINEERING, THERMODYNAMICS. *Current Pos:* From instr to assoc prof, 51-66, chmn dept, 64-74, PROF CHEM ENG, PRATT INST, 66- *Personal Data:* b Hudson, NY, Aug 6, 24; m 48; c 2. *Educ:* Univ Del, BChE, 48; Columbia Univ, MS, 51. *Mem:* Am Chem Soc; Am Inst Chem Eng; Sigma Xi. *Res:* Thermodynamics of irreversible processes, particularly as applied to transport. *Mailing Add:* 327 Oakford St West Hempstead NY 11552-3220

KRINSKY, NORMAN IRVING, BIOCHEMISTRY. *Current Pos:* USPHS fel, Harvard Univ, 53-55, Nat Coun to Combat Blindness fel, 55-56, instr biol, 56-59, lectr, 59-60, from asst prof pharmacol to prof biochem, 60-70, prof biochem & pharmacol, 70-87, PROF BIOCHEM, SCH MED, TUFTS UNIV, 87- *Personal Data:* b Iron River, Mich, June 29, 28; m 60; c 2. *Educ:* Univ Southern Calif, BA, 48, MS, 50, PhD(biochem), 53. *Honors & Awards:* Lotte Arnrich lectr, Iowa State Univ, 90. *Concurrent Pos:* Vis prof, Univ Calif, Berkeley, 73; res assoc, Boston Vet Admin Med Ctr, 81-82; scientist, Human Nutrition Res Ctr Aging, Tufts Univ, 93- *Mem:* Am Chem Soc; Oxygen Soc; NY Acad Sci; Am Soc Photobiol (secy-treas, 75-81, pres, 82-83); Am Soc Biochem & Molecular Biol; Soc Free Radical Res; hon mem Vitamin Soc Japan. *Res:* Function and metabolism of carotenoids. *Mailing Add:* Dept Biochem Tufts Univ Sch Med 136 Harrison Ave Boston MA 02111-1837

KRINSKY, SAMUEL, ACCELERATOR PHYSICS. *Current Pos:* asst physicist, Brookhaven Nat Lab, 73-75, assoc physicist, 75-78, physicist, 78-85, SR PHYSICIST, BROOKHAVEN NAT LAB, 85- *Personal Data:* b Brooklyn, NY, Jan 14, 45; m 72, Faith Kuniholm; c Benjamin & Sylvia. *Educ:* Mass Inst Technol, BS, 66; Yale Univ, PhD(physics), 71. *Honors & Awards:* R&D 100 Award, 89. *Prof Exp:* Res assoc physics, Inst Theoret Physics, State Univ NY, Stony Brook, 71-73. *Mem:* Fel Am Phys Soc. *Res:* Particle beam dynamics in storage rings, undulators and wigglers as sources of synchrotron radiation; free electron lasers. *Mailing Add:* NSLS Brookhaven Nat Lab Bldg 725B Upton NY 11973

KRINSKY, WILLIAM LEWIS, MEDICAL FORENSIC ENTOMOLOGY, BIOSYSTEMATICS. *Current Pos:* from asst prof to assoc prof epidemiol, Sect Med Entom, Dept Epidemiol & Public Health, 77-87, ASSOC CLIN PROF EPIDEMIOL, SCH MED, YALE UNIV, 87- *Personal Data:* b Brooklyn, NY, Jan 10, 47; m 70; c 2. *Educ:* Yale Univ, AB, 67, MD, 74; Cornell Univ, PhD(entom), 74. *Prof Exp:* Res assoc med entom, Rocky Mountain Lab, Nat Inst Allergy & Infectious Dis, 74-77. *Concurrent Pos:* Fac affil entomol, Peabody Mus Natural Hist, Yale Univ, 80- *Mem:* Entom Soc Am; Coleopterist Soc; Am Entom Soc. *Res:* Forensic entomology; medical entomology, acarology and parasitology; Coleoptera systematics. *Mailing Add:* 5 Norway Rd New Haven CT 06473. *E-Mail:* william.krinsky@yale.edu

KRINSLEY, DANIEL B, NATURAL HAZARDS. *Current Pos:* CONSULT GEOLOGIST, 80- *Personal Data:* b New York, NY, Jun 22, 23. *Educ:* Brooklyn Col, AB, 44, Brown Univ, MSc, 49, Univ Md, PhD(geomorphol), 70. *Prof Exp:* Chief environ impact anal prog, US Geol Surv, Washington, DC, 49-80. *Mem:* fel Geol Soc Am. *Res:* Arctic-desert geomorphological research into permafrost and saline crusts in arid regions; siting of roads, airfields and large installations away from areas of natural hazards. *Mailing Add:* 2475 Virginia Ave NW Washington DC 20037

KRINSLEY, DAVID, SEDIMENTOLOGY. *Current Pos:* chmn dept, 76-82, PROF GEOL, ARIZ STATE UNIV, 76- *Personal Data:* b Chicago, Ill, Jan 9, 27; m 58; c 3. *Educ:* Univ Chicago, PhB, 48, SB & SM, 50, PhD(geol), 56. *Prof Exp:* Asst geol, Univ Ill, 54-55, instr, 55-56; micropaleontologist & geochemist oceanog & geochem, Lamont Geol Observ, Columbia Univ, 56-57; from instr to prof geol, Queens Col, NY, 57-76, chmn dept geol & geog, 62-65, assoc dean fac, 66-70, actg dean fac, 70. *Concurrent Pos:* Grants, Am Philos Soc, Petrol Res Fund, Am Chem Soc, NASA, NSF, NATO, Dept Energy; overseas fel, Churchill Col, Cambridge Univ, 70-71. *Mem:* Fel AAAS; Soc Econ Paleont & Mineral; Geol Soc Am; Sigma Xi. *Res:* Backscattered electron microscopy of fine grained sedimentary rocks. *Mailing Add:* Dept Geol Univ Ore Eugene OR 97403-1272

KRIPALANI, KISHIN J, DRUG METABOLISM, BIOPHARMACEUTICS. *Current Pos:* res group leader drug metab, 69-89, ASSOC DIR, SQUIBB INST MED RES, E R SQUIBB & SONS, INC, 89- *Personal Data:* b Karachi, W Pakistan, Oct 3, 37; m 66, Shanti Narwani; c Anjali & Renu. *Educ:* Univ Bombay, BSc Hons, 57, BSc(tech), 59; Univ Calif, PhD(pharmaceut chem), 66. *Prof Exp:* Staff scientist, Worcester Found Exp Biol, Shrewsbury, Mass, 67-68, NIH fel steroid biochem, 68-69. *Mem:* Am Chem Soc; Am Soc Pharmacol Exp Therapeut; Int Soc Study Xenobiotics; Am Asn Pharmaceut Sci. *Res:* Drug metabolism; drug-protein interactions; biotransformations, and biopharmaceutics of drugs in animal species and humans, mechanism of drug-induced drug-enzyme interactions. *Mailing Add:* Bristol Myers-Squibb PO Box 4000 Princeton NJ 08543. *Fax:* 609-252-6802; *E-Mail:* kripalani@bms.com

KRIPKE, BERNARD ROBERT, VISION, LEARNING DISABILITIES. *Current Pos:* MGR PPC ADV SYST CORP, ELECTRONIC DATA SYST, 91- *Personal Data:* b Washington, DC, Aug 25, 39; m 79; c 1. *Educ:* Harvard Col, AB, 59; Harvard Univ, AM, 60, PhD(math), 64. *Prof Exp:* Staff mem math, Mass Inst Technol, 62-63; asst prof, Univ Tex, Austin, 63-64 & Univ Calif, Berkeley, 64-69; vis lectr vision, Hadassah Hosp, Hebrew Univ, 69-70; vis fel biophys, Ohio State Univ, 70-72; res instr, Univ Utah Sch Med, 72-76, asst prof physiol, 76-82; vpres, Future Software Inc, 82-83; partner, WKCG Software Develop Corp, 83-86; sr design consult, Gen Data Syst, 88-91. *Concurrent Pos:* Consult, Utah State Budget Off, 80-81 & Utah State Div Data Processing, 81-82. *Mem:* AAAS; Soc Neurosci. *Res:* Effects of visual deprivation on cat striate cortex; hereditary learning disability; analytic functions of several complex variables; approximation in banach spaces. *Mailing Add:* 1530 N Key Blvd 706 Arlington VA 22209

KRIPKE, DANIEL FREDERICK, SLEEP DISORDERS, BIOLOGICAL RHYTHMS. *Current Pos:* from asst prof to assoc prof, 71-82, PROF, DEPT PSYCHIAT, UNIV CALIF, SAN DIEGO, 82- *Personal Data:* b Washington, DC, Oct 12, 41; c 2. *Educ:* Harvard Col, BA, 61; Col Physicians & Surgeons, Columbia Univ, MD, 65. *Prof Exp:* Intern, Bronx Munic Hosp Ctr, 65-66; resident psychiat, Albert Einstein Col Med, 68-71. *Concurrent Pos:* Attend physician, Dept Psychiat, Univ Hosp, Univ Calif, San Diego, 71- *Mem:* AAAS; Sleep Res Soc; Int Soc Chronobiol; Am Psychiat Asn. *Mailing Add:* Dept Psychiat Univ Calif San Diego 0667 La Jolla CA 92093. *E-Mail:* dkripke@ucsd.edu

KRIPKE, MARGARET LOUISE (COOK), CANCER. *Current Pos:* PROF & CHMN DEPT IMMUNOL, M D ANDERSON CANCER CTR, UNIV TEX, 83- *Personal Data:* b Concord, Calif, July 21, 43; m 75; c 1. *Educ:* Univ Calif, Berkeley, AB, 65, MA, 67, PhD(immunol), 70. *Honors & Awards:* Edna Roe Mem lectr, Int Cong Photo Biol, 80; Lila Gruber Hon Award in Cancer Res; Thomas P Infusino Lectr Cancer Causation Epidemiol, 93. *Prof Exp:* Teaching asst immunol, Univ Calif, Berkeley, 65-66; res assoc, Ohio State Univ, Columbus, 70-72; res assoc, Sch Med, Univ Louisville, 72; asst prof path, Col Med, Univ Utah, 72-75; sr prin scientist cancer, Frederick Cancer Res Ctr, 75-79, dir, Cancer Biol Prog, 79-83. *Concurrent Pos:* Chancellors distinguished lectr, Univ Calif, Berkeley, 80. *Mem:* Am Asn Cancer Res; Am Soc Photobiol; Soc Leukocyte Biol; AAAS; Soc Investigative Dermat; Am Asn Immunol. *Res:* Mechanisms of immunologic responses to tumors; relationship between the immune system and carcinogenesis; nature and significance of tumor antigens using the system of experimental ultraviolet carcinogenesis; effects of ultraviolet radiation on immunologic processes. *Mailing Add:* Dept Immunol M D Anderson Cancer Ctr Univ Tex 1515 Holcombe Blvd Box 178 Houston TX 77030

KRIPPNER, STANLEY CURTIS, CROSS-CULTURAL STUDIES, PSYCHOLOGY OF CONSCIOUSNESS. *Current Pos:* PROF PSYCHOL, SAYBROOK INST GRAD SCH, SAN FRANCISCO, 72- *Personal Data:* b Edgerton, Wis, Oct 4, 32; m 66, Lelie Harris; c Robert & Carie. *Educ:* Univ Wis-Madison, BS, 54; Northwestern Univ, MA, 57, PhD(educ psychol), 61. *Hon Degrees:* LHD, Univ Humanistic Studies, 82. *Honors & Awards:* Citation Merit, Nat Asn Creative Children & Adults, 74; Cert Recognition, US Dept Health & Human Serv, 76. *Prof Exp:* Dir, Child Study Ctr, Kent State Univ, Ohio, 61-64 & Dream Lab, Maimonides Med Ctr, Brooklyn, 64-73. *Concurrent Pos:* Lectr, Acad Pedag Sci, Moscow, 71 & Acad Scis, Beijing, China, 81; vis prof, Univ PR, Santurce, 72, Sonoma State Univ, 72-73, Univ Life Scis, Bogota, 74; Inst Psychodrama, Caracas, 75 & West Ga Col, Carrollton, Ga, 76. *Mem:* Fel Am Psychol Asn; Asn Humanistic Psychol (pres 74-75); Parapsychol Asn (pres, 83); fel Am Soc Clin Hypn; fel Soc Sci Study Sex; Am Soc Psychical Res; fel Am Psychol Soc. *Res:* Anomalous effects in dreams; indigenous healing systems; creative problem-solving in altered states of consciousness; the effects of "personal myths" on cognition and behavior; hypnotherapy and learning. *Mailing Add:* Saybrook Inst 450 Pacific Ave No 300 San Francisco CA 94133. *Fax:* 650-433-9271

KRISCH, ALAN DAVID, HIGH ENERGY PHYSICS. *Current Pos:* from asst prof to assoc prof, 64-68, PROF PHYSICS, UNIV MICH, ANN ARBOR, 68- *Personal Data:* b Philadelphia, Pa, Apr 19, 39; m 61, Jean L Peck; c Kathleen S. *Educ:* Univ Pa, BA, 60; Cornell Univ, PhD(physics), 64. *Prof Exp:* Instr physics, Cornell Univ, 64. *Concurrent Pos:* Guggenheim fel, 71; trustee, Argonne Univ Assoc, 72-73 & 80-83, chmn, Argonne ZGS Users Group, 74-76 & 78-79; vis prof, Niels Bohr Inst, Copenhagen, 75-76; chmn, Int Comt for High Energy Spin Physics Symposia, 77-94. *Mem:* AAAS; fel Am Phys Soc. *Res:* Experiments on high energy elastic and inelastic scattering of strongly interacting particles; experiments on spin dependence of strong interactions; phenomenology of strong interactions; acceleration of polarized beams. *Mailing Add:* Randall Lab Physics Univ Mich Ann Arbor MI 48109. *Fax:* 313-936-0794; *E-Mail:* krisch@umich.edu

KRISCH, JEAN PECK, GRAVITATIONAL PHYSICS. *Current Pos:* res assoc, 65-75, lectr, 76-89, ASSOC PROF PHYSICS, UNIV MICH, 89- *Personal Data:* b Washington, DC, May 23, 39; m 61, Alan D; c Kathleen S. *Educ:* Univ Md, BS, 60; Cornell Univ, MS, 62, PhD(physics), 65. *Prof Exp:* Teaching asst physics, Cornell Univ, 60-65. *Mem:* Am Asn Physics Teachers; Am Phys Soc. *Res:* Study of exact solutions and of spin fluid solutions to the field equations; general relativity. *Mailing Add:* Dept Phys Univ Mich Ann Arbor MI 48109

KRISCH, ROBERT EARLE, RADIATION BIOLOGY, BIOPHYSICS. *Current Pos:* ASSOC PROF RADIATION ONCOL, SCH MED, UNIV PA, 80- *Personal Data:* b Philadelphia, Pa, Jan 29, 37; m 70; c 1. *Educ:* Univ Pa, BA, 56, MS, 62, PhD(physics), 64; Temple Univ, MD, 60. *Prof Exp:* Instr physics, Univ Pa, 64-65; asst biophysicist, Argonne Nat Lab, 65-72, biophysicist, Div Biol & Med Res, 72-77; spec fel, Dept Radiation Ther, Harvard Med Sch, 77-80. *Mem:* Radiation Res Soc; Am Soc Ther Radiol & Oncol; AAAS. *Res:* Radiation biology; radiation damage to DNA and its modification by the chemical environment. *Mailing Add:* Dept Radiation Oncol Univ Pa Philadelphia PA 19104

KRISCIUNAS, KEVIN L, REAL-TIME DATA ACQUISITION & ANALYSIS, ASTRONOMICAL PHOTOMETRY. *Personal Data:* b Chicago, Ill, Sept 12, 53. *Educ:* Univ Ill, Urbana-Champaign, BS, 74; Univ Chicago, MA, 76. *Prof Exp:* Programmer & onboard operator, Kuiper Airborne Observ, Ames Res Ctr, NASA, 77-82; programmer & pub rels person, Joint Astron Ctr, 82-96. *Concurrent Pos:* Astron lectr, WValley Col, Saratoga, Calif, 78-82. *Mem:* Int Astron Union; Am Astron Soc; Astron Soc Pac. *Res:* Photometry of variable stars; infrared photometry and spectroscopy; astronomical site evaluation; history of astronomy. *Mailing Add:* Wash Univ Dept Astron Box 351S80 Seattle WA 98195-1580. *Fax:* 808-961-6516; *E-Mail:* kevin@jach.hawaii.edu

KRISE, GEORGE MARTIN, PHYSIOLOGY. *Current Pos:* admin officer, Dept Biol, 69-74, prof, 58-82, EMER PROF PHYSIOL, TEX A&M UNIV, 82- *Personal Data:* b San Antonio, Tex, May 12, 19; m 43; c 2. *Educ:* Univ Tex, BS, 46, MA, 48, PhD(zool), 52. *Prof Exp:* From instr to asst prof biol, St Edward's Univ, 49-51; res scientist physiol, Univ Tex, 52-58,. *Res:* Microbial physiology; effects of ionizing radiations on various species. *Mailing Add:* 2301 Hillside Dr Bryan TX 77802

KRISHAN, AWTAR, CANCER RESEARCH & CHEMOTHERAPY. *Current Pos:* PROF & CHIEF, DIV EXP THERAPEUT, DEPT RADIOL/ONCOL, UNIV MIAMI, 96- *Personal Data:* b Srinagar, India, Oct 11, 37; US citizen; m 65, Sarla; c Aruna, Ameeta & Neal. *Educ:* Panjab Univ, India, PhD(zool), 63; Univ Western Ont, PhD(anat), 65. *Honors & Awards:* Collip Medal, Univ Western Ont, 65. *Prof Exp:* Res prof cytogenetics, Univ Minn, St Paul, 65-66; cytologist, Children's Cancer Res Found, Boston, 66-71, chief cancer res, Div Exp Path & Lab Cytokinetics, 72-77; from assoc prof to prof oncol, Med Sch, Univ Miami, 77-93, sci dir, Comp Cancer Ctr, 79-93; sci dir, Mich Cancer Found, Detroit, 93-96. *Concurrent Pos:* Chief, Div Cytokinetic, Comp Career Ctr, State Fla, 77-, sci dir, 81- *Mem:* Am Asn Cancer Res; Cell Kinetics Soc Am; Electron Micros Soc (pres, 75-76). *Res:* Tumor cell kinetics; effect of cancer chemotherapy on tumor growth; use of laser flow cytometry for monitoring drug uptake. *Mailing Add:* Papanicolau Cancer Res Bldg 1556 NW Tenth Suite 100 PO Box 0169-60 R-71 Miami FL 33101. *Fax:* 305-243-5555

KRISHEN, ANOOP, TECHNICAL MANAGEMENT. *Current Pos:* sr res chemist, 63-83, SECT HEAD, RES DIV, GOODYEAR TIRE & RUBBER CO, 83- *Personal Data:* b Ludhiana, India, Aug 7, 27; wid; c 2. *Educ:* Univ Panjab, India, BSc, 48, MSc, 49; Univ Pittsburgh, PhD, 57. *Prof Exp:* Lectr chem, Govt Col, Ludhiana, India, 49-50; res asst anal chem, Nat Phys Lab, India, 50-52; sr res chemist, B F Goodrich Co Res Ctr, 57-62; chief chemist, Synthetics & Chem Ltd, India, 62-63. *Mem:* Am Chem Soc. *Res:* Pyrolysis-gas chromatography; high speed liquid chromatography; instrumental analysis; gas chromatography; laboratory robotics; laboratory information management. *Mailing Add:* Goodyear Tire & Rubber Co Res Div 142 Goodyear Blvd Akron OH 44305-0001. *Fax:* 330-796-3304; *E-Mail:* akrishen@goodyear.com

KRISHEN, KUMAR, ELECTRONICS, REMOTE SENSING. *Current Pos:* proj mgr earth resources microwave prog, Johnson Space Ctr, NASA, 76-78, mgr advan microwave prog, 78-82, mgr advan progs, Tracking & Commun Div, 82-88, asst to dir tech & advan progs mission support, 88-90, chief technologist, nio, 90-94, CHIEF TECHNOLOGIST, TECH TRANSFER & COMMERCIALIZATION, JOHNSON SPACE CTR, NASA, 95- *Personal Data:* b Srinagar, India, June 22, 39; US citizen; m 61, Vijay L Raina; c Lovely, Sweetie & Anjala. *Educ:* Univ Jammu & Kashmir, BA, 59; Univ Calcutta, BTech, 62, MTech, 63; Kans State Univ, MS, 66, PhD(electronics), 68. *Prof Exp:* Res fel, Univ Calcutta, 64-65; res asst & instr elec eng, Kans State Univ, 65-68, asst prof, 68-69; staff scientist & engr earth observ, Lockheed Electronics Co, 69-76. *Concurrent Pos:* Consult applns investr, NASA, 69-76, proj leader, Skylab Microwave Sensors Eval Team, 73-75, mem, NASA active microwave workshops, 74-77, mem agr panel earth resources, 76-77, chmn water resources panel, Microwave Remote Sensing Symp, 77; reviewer, Radio Sci, 75-; mem, Synthetic Aperture Radar Team, NASA, 76-80 & Coun Sci & Technol, 88-; lectr, Univ Houston, 77-79; prog chmn, World Cong Superconductivity, 94-; adj prof, Rice Univ, 90-96. *Mem:* Sr mem Inst Elec & Electronics Engrs; sr mem Am Inst Aeronaut & Astronaut; Radio Physics & Electronics Asn; Sigma Xi; fel Soc Design & Process Sci. *Res:* Applications of optical, infrared & microwave sensors to the field of remote sensing of earth resources and ocean/weather phenomena and human health; developing specifications for space borne systems for earth resources, ocean and weather sensing and robotic vision. *Mailing Add:* NASA Johnson Space Ctr Code HA Houston TX 77058. *Fax:* 281-244-8452; *E-Mail:* kumar.krishen@jsc.nasa.gov

KRISHNA, C R, ENGINEERING, COMBUSTION. *Current Pos:* res assoc, 74-76, MECH ENGR, BROOKHAVEN NAT LAB, 76- *Personal Data:* b Bangalore, India, May 31, 39; m 74; c 3. *Educ:* Indian Inst Sci, ME, 61; State Univ NY, Stony Brook, PhD(eng), 74. *Prof Exp:* Engr, Hindustan Aeronaut Ltd, India, 61-69. *Mem:* Combustion Inst; Am Soc Mech Engrs. *Res:* Fluidized beds; coal-slurries and liquid fuels. *Mailing Add:* 71 Osbourne Ave Mt Sinai NY 11766. *E-Mail:* krishna@bnl.gov

KRISHNA, GOPALA, GENETIC TOXICOLOGY, CYTOGENETICS & MUTAGENESIS. *Current Pos:* sr scientist, 86-91, mgr & res assoc, 91-96, SR MGR & GROUP LEADER, PARKE-DAVIS PHARMACEUT RES, WARNER-LAMBERT CO, 96- WARNER-LAMBERT CO, 91- *Personal Data:* b Kaiwara, Karnataka, India, Feb 14, 56; US citizen; m 86, Leela D Ramappa; c Kavya A. *Educ:* Univ Agr Sci, Bangalore, India, BS, 78, MS, 80; WVa Univ, PhD(genetics), 84; Eastern Mich Univ, Ypsilanti, MBA, 92; Am Bd Toxicol, cert, 91. *Prof Exp:* Teaching asst genetics, Univ Agr Sci, India, 78-80; res asst, WVa Univ, 82-84; scientist, Nat Inst Occup Safety & Health, 84-86; res assoc, Oak Ridge Nat Lab, 86. *Concurrent Pos:* Guest lectr cytogenetics, WVa Univ, 84- & genetic toxicol, Eastern Mich Univ, 87-, Hope Col, Holland Mich, 95- *Mem:* Environ Mutagen Soc; Soc Toxicol; Int Environ Mutagen Soc; Sigma Xi. *Res:* Induction of gene mutation in bacteria and chromosome damage in human cells by air particulate extract; in vivo and in vitro comparative bone marrow and spleen systems in animals for toxicology testing; antibodies to detect chromosome damage; genotoxicity of vitamin C, ethylene dibromide, dimethylnitrosamine, cyclophosphomide, mitomycin C, vinblastine, vincristine, methyl methanesulfonate, x-rays, acrylamide, chlorambucil, coaldust extract and azodyes, molecular toxicology, b53 gene expression, apoptosis; toxicological safety evaluation of a variety of pharmaceuticals; author of various publications. *Mailing Add:* Parke-Davis Pharmaceut Res Warner-Lambert Co 2800 Plymouth Rd Ann Arbor MI 48105. *Fax:* 313-996-5001; *E-Mail:* krishng@aa.wl.com

KRISHNA, J HARI, SURFACE WATER RESOURCES, CONSERVATION & MANAGEMENT. *Current Pos:* SR HYDROLOGIST, TNRCC, 93- *Personal Data:* b Madras, India, May 13, 48; m, Laxmi. *Educ:* Osmania Univ, BS, 67; Kans State Univ, MS, 71; Utah State Univ, PhD(irrig eng & hydrol), 79. *Honors & Awards:* Cert Outstanding Serv, Am Water Resources Asn, 90. *Prof Exp:* Scientist soil & water eng, Int Crops Res Inst Semi-Arid Tropics, 72-81; consult, Food & Agr Orgn, UN, 81-82; asst prof water resources, Utah State Univ, 82-84; res scientist hydrol, Tex A&M Univ, 84-88; assoc prof & dir, VI Water Resource Res Inst, Univ VI. *Concurrent Pos:* Vpres, Am Inst Hydrol, Tex Sect, 87-88; mem tech adv group, Consortium of Caribbean Univs, 89-93, bd dirs, Int Rainwater Catchment Systs Asn, 89- *Mem:* Am Water Resources Asn; Am Inst Hydrol; Am Soc Agr Engrs; Int Rainwater Catchment Systs Asn; Int Water Resources Asn; World Asn Soil & Water Conserv. *Res:* Conduct research/assessment in the areas of hydrology and water conservation; author and co-author of approximately 50 technical/scientific papers and publications. *Mailing Add:* 12405 Uttimer Lane Austin TX 78753

KRISHNA, KUMAR, ZOOLOGY, ENTOMOLOGY. *Current Pos:* from instr to assoc prof, 62-74, PROF BIOL, CITY COL NEW YORK, 74- *Personal Data:* b Dehradun, India, June 21, 30; US citizen; m 60. *Educ:* Agra Univ, BS, 50; Univ Lucknow, MS, 52; Univ Chicago, PhD(zool), 61. *Prof Exp:* Res asst, Forest Res Inst, India, 52-54; teaching asst biol, Univ Ill at Chicago Circle, 58-60; res assoc, Univ Chicago, 60-62. *Concurrent Pos:* Res assoc, Am Mus Natural Hist, 62-; NSF res grant, 62- *Mem:* Am Soc Zoologists; Soc Syst Zoologists; Int Union Study Soc Insects. *Res:* Taxonomy, ecology, zoogeography and evolution of termites; general evolutionary theory. *Mailing Add:* Dept Biol City Univ NY City Col 160 Convent Ave New York NY 10031-9101

KRISHNA, N RAMA, BIOPHYSICAL CHEMISTRY, STRUCTURAL BIOLOGY. *Current Pos:* PROF BIOCHEM & DIR NUCLEAR MAGNETIC RESONANCE CORE FACIL, CANCER CTR. *Personal Data:* b 45. *Educ:* India Inst Technol, Kampur, PhD(physics), 72. *Concurrent Pos:* Leukemia Soc of Am Scholar, 82-87. *Mem:* AAAS; Biophys Soc; Am Soc Biol Chemists. *Res:* Nuclear magnetic resonance; biomolecular conformations. *Mailing Add:* Dept Biochem Univ Ala Birmingham AL 35294

KRISHNAKUMAR, KALMANJE, INTELLIGENT CONTROL, FLIGHT SIMULATION. *Current Pos:* ASSOC PROF, UNIV ALA, 88- *Personal Data:* b Madras, India, Feb 25, 60; m 86, Sujatha; c Priya & Nithya. *Educ:* Indian Inst Technol, BTech, 82; Univ Ala, MS, 85, PhD(aerospace & elec eng), 88. *Concurrent Pos:* Prin investr, NSF & NASA, 91-; consult, Charles River Analytics, Inc, 94-; chmn, Tech Comt, Am Inst Aeronaut & Astronaut, 96-; prin scientist, Flexible Intelligence Group, Tuscaloosa, Ala. *Mem:* Am Inst Aeronaut & Astronaut; Inst Elec & Electronics Engrs. *Res:* Intelligent control applications to aerospace problems; flight dynamics and simulation. *Mailing Add:* Dept Aero Eng Univ Ala Box 870280 Tuscaloosa AL 35487-0280. *Fax:* 205-348-2094; *E-Mail:* kkumar@coe.eng.ua.edu

KRISHNAMOORTHY, GOVINDARAJALU, STRUCTURAL MECHANICS, CIVIL ENGINEERING. *Current Pos:* from asst prof to assoc prof, 68-74, PROF CIVIL ENG, SCH ENG, SAN DIEGO STATE UNIV, 74- *Personal Data:* b Tanjore, India, Jan 1, 31; m 56; c 1. *Educ:* Col Eng, Guindy, India, BSCE, 52; Ill Inst Technol, MSCE, 60, PhD(struct), 65. *Prof Exp:* Jr engr, Madras Hwy Dept, India, 52-57; from instr to asst prof civil eng, Ill Inst Technol, 61-68. *Concurrent Pos:* Consult, Ill Inst Technol Res Inst, 67-, Rohr Corp, 69-70, SAI, La Jolla & Gen Elec, Calma, 89-90. *Mem:* Am Soc Civil Engrs; Am Soc Eng Educ; Sigma Xi. *Res:* Buckling of shells; computer applications in structures; analysis and design of ocean structures; reinforced concrete masonry structures; dynamic and thermal response of mountings on main cooling pipe of nuclear reactors; computer graphics; computer aided design. *Mailing Add:* 5439 Maisel Way San Diego CA 92115. *Fax:* 619-286-3430

KRISHNAMOORTHY, MUKKAI S, COMBINATORICS. *Current Pos:* From vis asst prof to asst prof, 79-85, ASSOC PROF, RENSSELAER POLYTECH INST, 85- *Personal Data:* b Nagerkoil, India, Jan 20, 48; US citizen; m 86, Janaki Narayanaswamy; c Subrahmanya. *Educ:* Coimbatore Inst Technol, India, BE, 69; Indian Inst Technol, India, MTech, 71, PhD(comput sci), 76. *Mem:* Inst Elec & Electronics Engrs Comput Soc; Soc Photo-Optical Inst rumentation Engrs. *Res:* Develop tools to make problem solving easier. *Mailing Add:* Comput Sci Dept Rensselaer Polytech Inst 110 Eighth St Troy NY 12180. *E-Mail:* moorthy@cs.rpi.edu

KRISHNAMURTHY, LAKSHMINARAYANAN, COMBUSTION THEORY, COMPUTATIONAL FLUID DYNAMICS. *Current Pos:* res engr, 78-82, SR RES ENG FLUID MECH, UNIV DAYTON RES INST, 82- *Personal Data:* b Kumbakonam, Madras, India, Oct 23, 41; US citizen; m. *Educ:* Univ Madras, BEng, 62; Indian Inst Sci, MEng, 64; Univ Calif, San Diego, PhD(eng sci), 72. *Prof Exp:* Scientist power eng, Cent Mech Eng Res Inst, India, 65-67; res engr, Univ Calif, San Diego, 72-73; staff scientist propulsion, Duvvuri Res Assocs, Chula Vista, Calif, 73-74; res staff mem aerospace eng, Princeton Univ, 75-76; res assoc propulsion, Purdue Univ, 77-78. *Concurrent Pos:* Sr res fel, Cent Mech Eng Res Inst, Durgapur, India, 64-65; res fel, Univ Calif, San Diego, 67-68, res assist, 68-71; reviewer, Appl Mech Revs, 73-84 & Am Inst Aeronaut & Astronaut J, 82-; prin investr, Res Inst, Univ Dayton, 78-, instr, Sch Eng, 81-; mem propellants & combustion tech comt, Am Inst Aeronaut & Astronaut, 84-86. *Mem:* Am Inst Aeronaut & Astronaut; Am Soc Mech Engrs; Am Acad Mech; Combustion Inst; Sigma Xi; Soc Indust & Appl Math; Planetary Soc; Union Concerned Scientists. *Res:* Fluid mechanics and combustion; analytical and computational fluid dynamics of nonreacting and reacting gas flows. *Mailing Add:* Dept Mech & Aerospace Eng Fla Inst Technol 150 W University Blvd Melbourne FL 32907

KRISHNAMURTHY, RAMANATHAPUR GUNDACHAR, FOOD CHEMISTRY, BIOCHEMISTRY. *Current Pos:* from group leader, to sr group leader edible oil prod, 67-87, TECHNOL MGR, RES & DEVELOP DIV, KRAFT, INC, 87- *Personal Data:* b Mysore, India, May 8, 31; m 60; c 3. *Educ:* Univ Mysore, BS, 51; Rutgers Univ, MS, 64, PhD(food sci), 65. *Prof Exp:* Lab asst metall, Indian Inst Sci, India, 51-54; sci asst food technol, Cent Food Technol Res Inst, Mysore, 54-61; res asst food sci, 61-63, res fel, 63-65, asst res prof, Rutgers Univ, 65-66; res chemist, Best Foods Div, Corn Prod Co, 66-67. *Mem:* Am Chem Soc; Am Oil Chemists Soc; Inst Food Technol. *Res:* Autoxidation and thermal oxidation of fats and oils; investigation of flavors and flavor precursors in foods; chemistry and technology of oils and fats and products derived from them. *Mailing Add:* 3059 Crestwood Lane Glenview IL 60025

KRISHNAMURTHY, SUBRAHMANYA, extraction & recovery of heavy metals from contaminated soil; deceased, see previous edition for last biography

KRISHNAMURTHY, SUNDARAM, ORGANIC CHEMISTRY. *Current Pos:* MEM RES STAFF, RES LAB, EASTMAN KODAK CO, 80- *Personal Data:* b Coimbatore, Madras, India, Nov 26, 44; m 75. *Educ:* Univ Madras, BSc, 64, MSc, 66; Purdue Univ, PhD(chem), 71. *Prof Exp:* Sr res assoc chem, Purdue Univ, West Lafayette, 71-80. *Mem:* Am Chem Soc. *Res:* Synthesis and application of trialkylborohydrides in stereospecific and reguospecific organic synthesis; selective reductions; organometallics in organic synthesis. *Mailing Add:* 172 Hillrise Dr Penfield NY 14526

KRISHNAMURTI, CUDDALORE RAJAGOPAL, animal physiology, animal biochemistry, for more information see previous edition

KRISHNAMURTI, PULLABHOTLA V, VETERINARY MICROBIOLOGY. *Current Pos:* RETIRED. *Personal Data:* b Gudivada, India, Mar 1, 23; m 49; c 5. *Educ:* Univ Madras, BVSc, 49, DVP, 58; Univ Wis-Madison, MS, 61; Tex A&M Univ, PhD(vet microbiol), 67. *Prof Exp:* State vet, Andhra Vet Serv, India, 48-54; instr vet sci & exten vet, Exten Training Ctr, 55-56; asst lectr, Andhra Vet Col, 57-58; res asst, Univ Wis-Madison, 59-63; researcher poultry dis, Hy-line Poultry Farms, Iowa, 64-65; res asst vet microbiol, Tex A&M Univ, 65-66; from asst prof to assoc prof, Sch Vet Med, Tuskegee Inst, 66-69; assoc prof microbiol, Savannah State Col, 69-74, prof biol, 74-92. *Mem:* Am Vet Med Asn; Am Soc Parasitol; Poultry Sci Asn; Am Asn Avian Path. *Res:* Parasites and parasitism; plasmodium in Wisconsin chickens; cultivation of Histomonas meleagridis free of bacteria and its demonstration in tissues and cell cultures using fluorescent labeled antibody techniques; therapeutic agents in canine distemper. *Mailing Add:* 6002 Fairview Ave Savannah GA 31406

KRISHNAMURTI, RUBY EBISUZAKI, PHYSICS, FLUID MECHANICS. *Current Pos:* assoc prof oceanog, 71-75, SR RES ASSOC, GEOPHYS FLUID DYNAMICS INST, FLA STATE UNIV, 67-, PROF OCEANOG, 75- *Personal Data:* b Haney, BC, Oct 23, 34; m 60. *Educ:* Univ Western Ont, BSc, 57; Univ Chicago, MS, 60; Univ Calif, Los Angeles, PhD(physics), 67. *Prof Exp:* Res assoc fluid mech, Stanford Univ, 67. *Concurrent Pos:* Asst prof oceanog, Fla State Univ, 68-71. *Mem:* Am Phys Soc; Am Meteorol Soc; Am Geophys Union. *Res:* Geophysical fluid dynamics, particularly theoretical and experimental studies of convection and ocean circulation modelling. *Mailing Add:* Dept Oceanog Fla State Univ Tallahassee FL 32306

KRISHNAMURTI, TIRUVALAM N, METEOROLOGY, ATMOSPHERIC SCIENCE. *Current Pos:* assoc prof, 67-70, PROF METEOROL, FLA STATE UNIV, 70- *Personal Data:* b Madras, India, Jan 10, 32; nat US. *Educ:* Univ Delhi, BS, 51; Andhra Univ, India, MS, 53; Univ Chicago, PhD(meteorol), 59. *Honors & Awards:* Half-Century Award, Am Meteorol Soc, 74, Rossby Award, 85; Creativity Award, NSF, 82. *Prof Exp:* Prof meteorol, Univ Calif, Los Angeles, 60-67. *Concurrent Pos:* Mem, Global Atmospheric Res Prog working group on struct of the trop atmosphere, 69-71; mem, Adv Panel to Nat Oceanic & Atmospheric Admin on Nuclear Metal Conf, 71-73; consult synoptic subprog, GATE, Nat Acad Sci, 73-74; external examr, Univ Nairobi, Kenya, 73-76 & McGill Univ PhD students, 74-77; consult, MONEX Comt, World Meteorol Orgn, 75-76; vis lectr, Ctr Theoret Physics, Trieste, Italy, 75; mem, US Global Atmospheric Res Prog, 75-; assoc ed, J Atmospheric Sci, 75-; chmn, US MONEX Panel, Nat Acad Sci, 76-; mem, Working Group on Numerical Experimentation Global Atmospheric Res Prog, Joint Organizing Comt; mem, Comt Atmospheric Sci, Nat Acad Sci, 79- *Mem:* Fel Am Meteorol Soc; Am Geophys Union; fel Royal Meteorol Soc; Meteorol Soc Japan. *Res:* Dynamic and synoptic meteorology, including diagnostic and prognostic studies of tropical and mid-latitude systems using real input data together with analyses of tropical weather systems using satellite and aircraft information in sparse conventional data areas; global tropical mapping of the subtropical jet of winter; semilagravgian advection; multilevel non-linear balances omega equation; tropical east-west circulation; physical initialization; prediction of a life cycle of super typhoon with a global model. *Mailing Add:* 3014 Southshore Circle Fla State Univ Tallahassee FL 32312

KRISHNAN, B RAJENDRA, GENOME ANALYSIS & LARGE SCALE DNA SEQUENCING, MOLECULAR CHARACTERIZATION OF GENES. *Current Pos:* SR RES SCIENTIST, PFIZER CENT RES, 95- *Personal Data:* b Pune, Maharashtra, India, Aug 25, 61; m 91, Lalitha Ramachandran. *Educ:* Univ Madras, MS, 83, MPhil, 85, PhD(genetics), 90; Carleton Univ, PhD(molecular biol), 90. *Prof Exp:* Res fel genetics, Univ Madras, 82-85; commonwealth res scholar biol, Carleton Univ, 86-89; res assoc, Wash Univ Sch Med, 90-92; res instr med, 92-95. *Concurrent Pos:* Arthritis Found fel, Wash Univ Sch Med, 93- *Res:* Primary structure analysis of a 150 kilobae DNA region on human chromosome 6 by transposon-/polymerase chain reaction and automated flourescent DNA sequencing to characterize genes in this portion of the human genome; developed methods for rapid DNA sequencing on phage and plasmid DNA templates; molecular genetic analysis of DNA replication; bacterial transposons as tools in molecular analyses of gene function. *Mailing Add:* Pfizer Cent Res Campus Box 1221 Eastern Point Rd Groton CT 06340. *Fax:* 314-454-0486; *E-Mail:* krishnan@borcim.wustl.edu

KRISHNAN, ENGIL KOLAJ, RADIATION ONCOLOGY, TUMOR IMMUNOLOGY. *Current Pos:* teaching assoc, 71-75, instr oncol, 75-82, ASST PROF SURG & DIR RES, MED CTR, UNIV KANS, 82- *Personal Data:* b Bangalore, India, 42; US Citizen. *Educ:* Univ Mysore, BSc(physics) & (math), 64, Univ Mo, MS, 70, Cetec Univ, WI, MD, 82. *Prof Exp:* Supvr electronics, Elec Radar Develop Eng, 65-67. *Concurrent Pos:* Consult, VA Med Ctr, 82- *Mem:* Am Asn Cancer Res; Am Asn Physicians Med; Am Asn Pediat Oncol; Soc Clin Trials. *Res:* Published approximately fifty journal articles in the areas of biophysics, immunology and oncology. *Mailing Add:* Dept Surg WHE Univ Kans Med Ctr Col Health Sci Rainbow Blvd & 39th Kansas City KS 66103

KRISHNAN, GOPAL, CANCER IMMUNOLOGY, TRANSPLANTATION IMMUNOLOGY. *Current Pos:* DIR, TISSUE-TYPING LAB, OUR LADY OF LOURDES MED CTR, 84- *Personal Data:* b Kancheepuram, India, Mar 15, 35; US citizen; m 67, Prema; c Madhavan & Deepa. *Educ:* Annamala; Univ, India, MA, 55, MSc, 56; Univ Madras, PhD(chem), 65. *Prof Exp:* res assoc immunol, Univ Pa, 67-74; asst prof biochem & res instr med, Jefferson Med Col, Philadelphia, 74-76; res assoc, Pa Col Podiatric Med, 76-77; immunologist, St Vincent Med Ctr, 77-82; dir, immunol res sect, mercy cath med ctr, 82- *Concurrent Pos:* Lectr, Univ Madras Cols, India, 56-61. *Mem:* Am Asn Med Lab Immunologists; Am Soc Transplant Physicians; Am Asn Immunologists; NY Acad Sci; Am Asn Histocompatibility & Immunogenetics. *Res:* Human cancer; transplantation immunology; transplant rejections and factors affecting the allograft survival. *Mailing Add:* Delmont Labs Inc PO Box 269 Swarthmore PA 19081-0269. *Fax:* 610-543-6298

KRISHNAN, K RANGA RAMA, AFFECTIVE DISORDERS, CHRONIC PAIN. *Current Pos:* fel neurobiol, Duke Univ, 82-84, asst prof, Div Biol Psychiat, 85-90, assoc prof, 90-95, MED DIR, AFFECTIVE DISORDERS UNIT, MED CTR, DUKE UNIV, DURHAM, CC, 85-, PROF, 95- *Personal Data:* b Madras, India, April 22, 56; m 87. *Educ:* Univ Madras, MBBS, 78. *Honors & Awards:* Laughlin Award, Am Col Psychiat, 84; Rafaelsen Award, Col Int Neuro-Psychopharmacol. *Prof Exp:* Sr house officer, Dept Emergency Med, Queen Elizabeth Hosp, Univ WI, Barbados, 80-81. *Concurrent Pos:* Resident psychiat, John Umstead Prog, 81-83, chief resident, Duke Umstead Prog, 82-83. *Mem:* Int Asn Study Pain; Soc Biol Psychiat; AAAS; NY Acad Sci; Int Soc Psychoneuroendocrinol; Am Col Neropsychopharmacol. *Res:* Understanding the physiology & pathophysiology of the hypothalamo pituitary adrenal function in affective disorders; drug trials for the treatment of affective disorders; brain imaging, Magnetic Resonance Imaging and PET in affective disorders and Alzheimers disease. *Mailing Add:* Med Ctr Duke Univ PO Box 3018 Durham NC 27710

KRISHNAN, KAMALA SIVASUBRAMANIAM, OPTICAL PHYSICS, SOLID STATE SCIENCE. *Current Pos:* SR ENG, COMPUT DEVICES INT, 93- *Personal Data:* b Tiruchirappalli, India, Nov 12, 37; US citizen; m 58, Shantha Santhanam; c Kamala Harsha, Murali Swathi & Kantha Rajyashree. *Educ:* Univ Madras, MA, 57; Indian Inst Sci, Bangalore, DIISc, 60; Univ Fla, PhD(physics), 66. *Prof Exp:* Res scientist solid state physics, Res Div, Am Standard Inc, 65-68; sr res physicist, Stanford Res Inst, 68-77; mgr electro-optics, Systs Control Technol, Inc, 77-82; mgr optical signal processing, Litton Appl Technol, 82-85; sr staff engr, Lockheed Missiles & Space Co, 85-92. *Concurrent Pos:* Vis prof mat sci, San Jose State Univ, 74-84. *Mem:* Optical Soc Am; Soc Photo-Optical Instrumentation Engrs. *Res:* Optical and infrared systems; laser physics and applications; nonlinear optics; applied statistics; remote sensing; oceanography; fiber-optics. *Mailing Add:* 180 Walter Hays Dr Palo Alto CA 94303

KRISHNAN, RAMAYYA, DECISION SUPPORT SYSTEMS, CONCEPTUAL MODELING. *Current Pos:* Asst prof, 87-94, assoc prof mgt sci & info systs, 94-97, PROF MGT SCI & INFO SYSTS, CARNEGIE-MELLON UNIV, 97- *Personal Data:* b Rajkot, India, Feb 20, 60; m 87, Rema Padman; c Divya. *Educ:* Indian Inst Technol, BTech, 81; Univ Tex, Austin, MSE, 83, PhD(mgt sci & info systs), 87. *Concurrent Pos:* Assoc ed, Decision Support Systs, Opers Res Soc Am J Comput, 92- *Mem:* Asn Comput Mach; Inst Mgt Sci; Inst Elec & Electronics Engrs. *Res:* Development of relevant theory tools and techniques to facilitate decision making support through the use of reliable information systems and technology; internet, information networking and electronic commerce. *Mailing Add:* Heinz Sch Carnegie-Mellon Univ Pittsburgh PA 15213. *E-Mail:* rk2x@andrew.cmu.edu

KRISHNAN, VAIDYANADHAN, CONTROL & SYSTEMS ENGINEERING. *Current Pos:* PROF, DEPT ELEC ENG, SAN FRANCISCO STATE UNIV, 76- *Personal Data:* b Hyderabad, India, Jan 19, 43. *Educ:* Indian Inst Technol, BTech, 64, MTech, 66; Univ Calif, Berkeley, MS, 67, PhD, 72. *Prof Exp:* Design engr, Charles Bailey Co, 68-70; postdoctoral fel, Univ Calif, Berkeley, 72-74. *Mem:* Inst Elec & Electronics Engrs; Am Soc Eng Educ; Am Soc Mech Engrs; Instrument Soc Am. *Res:* Systems modeling; biological control systems. *Mailing Add:* Sch Eng San Francisco State Univ 1600 Holloway Ave San Francisco CA 94132

KRISHNAN, VENKATARAMA, ELECTRICAL & SYSTEMS ENGINEERING. *Current Pos:* PROF, DEPT ELEC ENG, UNIV MASS, LOWELL. *Personal Data:* b Madras, India, Oct 20, 29; c 2. *Educ:* Univ Madras, BSc, 48; Banares Hindu Univ, BSc, 53; Princeton Univ, MSE, 59; Univ Pa, PhD(elec eng), 63. *Prof Exp:* Instr chem, Loyola Col, Madras Univ, 48-49; sr res asst elec eng, Indian Inst Sci Bangalore, 53-56; instr, Princeton Univ, 57-58; asst prof, Villanova Univ, 58-61; assoc, Moore Sch Elec Eng, Pa, 61-64; asst prof, Polytech Inst Brooklyn, 64-66, assoc prof, 66-76. *Concurrent Pos:* Co-dir, Ctr Advan Comput & Telecommun, 93- *Mem:* Sr mem Inst Elec & Electronics Engrs. *Res:* Probabilistic and statistical modeling; tomographic studies; time series analysis; navigation and guidance. *Mailing Add:* Dept Elec Eng Univ Mass North Campus 1 University Ave Lowell MA 01854

KRISHNAPPA, GOVINDAPPA, sound intensity measurements, aeroacoustics, for more information see previous edition

KRISHNAPPAN, BOMMANNA GOUNDER, HYDRAULICS, FLUID MECHANICS. *Current Pos:* RES SCIENTIST HYDRAUL, NAT WATER RES INST, CAN CTR INLAND WATERS, ONT, 78- *Personal Data:* b Madras, India, Jan 15, 43; Can citizen; m 72; c 2. *Educ:* Madras Univ, BE, 66; Univ Calgary, MSc, 68; Queen's Univ, Ont, PhD(civil eng), 72. *Prof Exp:* Res scientist, Can Ctr Inland Waters, 72-77; flow syst engr, Ont Hydro, 77-78. *Concurrent Pos:* Asst, Nat Res Coun Can, 66-72. *Mem:* Int Asn Hydraul Res. *Res:* Sediment transport in open channel flows; dispersion of mass in open channels; mathematical models for river morphology; thermal models. *Mailing Add:* 204 Lynbrook Dr Hamilton ON L9C 2L3 Can

KRISHNAPRASAD, PERINKULAM S, SYSTEM THEORY. *Current Pos:* from asst prof to assoc prof, 80-87, PROF ELEC ENG, UNIV MD, 87- *Personal Data:* b Bombay, India, May 15, 49; m 86, Cheryl Snell. *Educ:* Indian Inst Technol, BTech, 72; Syracuse Univ, MS, 73; Harvard Univ, PhD(eng), 77. *Prof Exp:* Asst prof systs eng, Case Inst Technol, 77-80. *Mem:* Fel Inst Elec & Electronics Engrs; Am Math Soc; Am Inst Aeronaut & Astronaut; Am Acad Mech; Soc Indust Appl Math. *Res:* System theory and applications to modeling; geometric methods applied to problems in systems; control theory and nonlinear mechanics; robotics; real-time control; biologically-inspired control system architectures. *Mailing Add:* Dept Elec Eng Univ Md College Park MD 20742-0001. *E-Mail:* krishna@src.umd.edu

KRISHNASWAMY, S V, THIN FILM DEPOSITION, MICROWAVE ACOUSTICS. *Current Pos:* FEL SCIENTIST, WESTINGHOUSE RES & DEVELOP CTR, 81- *Personal Data:* b Villianallur, India, April 15, 40; US citizen; m 71; c 2. *Educ:* N Wadia Col, BSc, 59; Univ Poona, MSc, 61; Indian Inst Technol, MTech, 66; Pa State Univ, PhD(physics), 74. *Prof Exp:* Res assoc, Pa State Univ, 74-76, asst prof physics, 76-78, sr res assoc, 78-81. *Concurrent Pos:* Sr scientist, Armament Res & Develop, Kirkee, India, 62-64; res assoc, Indian Inst Technol, Bombay, 64-68; mem prog comt, Thin Film Div, Am Vacuum Soc, 88-, Ultrasonics Div, Inst Elec & Electronics Engrs, 88- *Mem:* Am Phys Soc; Am Vacuum Soc; Indian Vacuum Soc. *Res:* Preparation and characterization of thin films of wide range of materials, using ion beam deposition, magnetron sputtering and other novel techniques; microwave acoustics and magnetics; high temperature super conducting applications. *Mailing Add:* Northrop Grumman 1350 Beulah Rd Pittsburgh PA 15235-5080

KRISHTALKA, LEONARD, MAMMALIAN PALEONTOLOGY. *Current Pos:* DIR, MUS NATURAL HIST, UNIV KANS. *Personal Data:* b Montreal, Can, Jan 30, 46; m 86; c 1. *Educ:* Univ Alta, BSc, 69, MSc, 71; Tex Tech Univ, Lubbock, PhD(biol & vert paleont), 75. *Prof Exp:* Fel, Carnegie Mus Natural Hist, 75-76, res fel, 76-77, asst cur, 77-80, assoc cur, 80-87, cur & asst dir sci, 87- *Concurrent Pos:* Adj lectr, Univ Pittsburgh, 76-77, adj asst prof, 77-80, adj assoc prof, 80-; ed, Sci Publs, 86-; prog dir, Div Environ Biol, NSF, Washington, DC, 92-93. *Mem:* Soc Vert Paleont; AAAS; Paleont Soc. *Res:* Origin, evolution, relationships, paleoecology and systematics of early Tertiary and Mesozoic mammals, especially primates, artiodactyls, insectivores and multituberculates; African Neogene hominids and microfaunal paleontology. *Mailing Add:* Natural Hist Mus Dyche Hall Univ Kans Lawrence KS 66045. *Fax:* 412-622-8837; *E-Mail:* krishtalkal@clp2.clpgh.org

KRISS, MICHAEL ALLEN, PHYSICS, COMPUTER SCIENCES. *Current Pos:* CONSULT, 93- *Personal Data:* b San Diego, Calif, Dec 14, 40; m 63, Gretchen V Renzel; c Deborah J, Aaron A & Rebecc L. *Educ:* Univ Calif, Los Angeles, AB, 62, MS, 64, PhD(physics), 69. *Prof Exp:* Res assoc, Color Photog Div, Eastman Kodak, 69-79, mgr, Physics & Comput Sci Dept, Kodak, Japan, 85-88, res assoc, Physics Div, Res Lab, 79-90, mgr, External Res Prog, Electronic Imaging Res Labs, 88-90, mgr, Image Processing Lab, 90-92. *Concurrent Pos:* Lectr, Univ Col, Univ Rochester, 76- *Mem:* Soc Photog Scientists & Engrs; Sigma Xi; Soc Motion Picture & TV; NY Acad Sci. *Res:* Photographic sciences; photographic research with emphasis on the mechanisms of color reproduction and image structure photographic film systems; development of methods to measure and evaluate the color reproduction and image structure of photographic and non-photographic systems; image processing by use of computers; electronic imaging systems. *Mailing Add:* 3146 St Paul Blvd Rochester NY 14617-3433. *Fax:* 716-336-9472; *E-Mail:* mkrs@troi.cc.rochester.edu

KRISST, RAYMOND JOHN, INDUSTRIAL & MANUFACTURING ENGINEERING, OPERATIONS RESEARCH. *Current Pos:* dir eng, Appl Ctr, 85-91, CONSULT & TEACHER, UNIV HARTFORD, 91-; GUEST RES COLLABR, BROOKHAVEN NAT LAB, 96- *Personal Data:* b Lithuania, USSR, May 29, 37; m 62; c Rima, Abe & Lara. *Educ:* Univ Conn, AB, 58; Mich State Univ, PhD(physics), 65. *Prof Exp:* Res asst physics, Mich State Univ, 62-65; res fel, Harvard Univ & res affil, Mass Inst Technol, 65-70; vis scientist, German Electron-Synchrotron Inst, 70-74; prin physicist, Nuclear Power Dept, Combustion Eng Inc, 74- 85. *Concurrent Pos:* Instr, Nuclear Weapons Effects, US Army, 59 & nuclear physics, Mich State Univ, 60-63; adj fac atomic physics, Harvard Univ, 67-70; adj prof nuclear eng & numerical math, Univ Conn, 83-84, adj prof mech eng & elec eng, Univ Hartford, 85-; consult, Hartford Area Indust, 84- *Mem:* Am Mgt Asn; Am Phys Soc; Am Nuclear Soc; Am Asn Physics Teachers; Sigma Xi. *Res:* Nuclear, high-energy and accelerator physics; nuclear engineering; polarized electron beams; nuclear instrumentation. *Mailing Add:* 1018 Troutbrook Dr West Hartford CT 06119. *E-Mail:* krisrim@worldnet.att.net

KRISTA, LAVERNE MATHEW, VETERINARY ANATOMY. *Current Pos:* asst prof, 69-73, assoc prof, 73-81, PROF VET ANAT & HISTOL, AUBURN UNIV, 81- *Personal Data:* b Webster, SDak, Dec 24, 31; m 64; c 3. *Educ:* SDak State Univ, BS, 58, MS, 60; Univ Minn, PhD(poultry sci), 66, DVM, 69. *Prof Exp:* Res asst, SDak State Univ, 58-60; res asst poultry nutrit & phys, Univ Minn, 60-69. *Mem:* Sigma Xi; Am Asn Vet Anat; World Poultry Sci; Am Vet Med Asn; Sigma Xi. *Res:* Nutrition; atherosclerosis; cardiovascular physiology. *Mailing Add:* 235 Pine Hills Ave Auburn AL 36830

KRISTAL, MARK BENNETT, BIOPSYCHOLOGY, BEHAVIOR-ETHOLOGY. *Current Pos:* from asst prof to assoc prof, 73-91, PROF PSYCHOL, STATE UNIV NY, BUFFALO, 91- *Personal Data:* b New York, NY, Apr 19, 44; m 67; c 1. *Educ:* Rutgers Univ, BA, 65; Kans State Univ, MS, 70, PhD(psychol), 71. *Prof Exp:* Trainee behav genetics & neuroendocrinol, Jackson Lab, 71-73. *Concurrent Pos:* Dir, Biopsychol Prog, Psychol Dept, State Univ NY, Buffalo, 78-86, interim assoc dean, Sch Related Health Professions, 86-88, assoc dean, Fac Soc Sci, 89-90, chmn, Dept Psychol, 95-96, dean, Fac Soc Sci, 96-; NSF, NIMH, Nat Inst Drug Abuse grants. *Mem:* AAAS; Int Soc Develop Psychobiol; Soc Neurosci; Int Soc Behav Neuro Sci; Soc Behav Neuroendo. *Res:* Neural, endocrine, and genetic bases of maternal, ingestive and sexual behaviors; functions of the hypothalamus; limbic-hypothalamic function interactions; opiates and analgesia; endocrinology; pharmacology. *Mailing Add:* State Univ NY Dept Psychol Buffalo NY 14260

KRISTIAN, JEROME, PHYSICS, ASTRONOMY. *Current Pos:* MEM STAFF, MT WILSON & LAS CAMPANAS OBSERV, CARNEGIE INST WASH, 67- *Personal Data:* b Milwaukee, Wis, June 5, 34; m 55; c 1. *Educ:* Univ Chicago, MS, 56, PhD(physics), 62. *Prof Exp:* Mem staff, Argonne Nat Lab, 57-59; vis lectr physics & math, Univ Tex, 62-64; asst prof astron, Univ Wis, 64-67. *Mem:* Am Phys Soc; Am Astron Soc; Int Astron Union. *Res:* Cosmology; extra-galactic astronomy. *Mailing Add:* 813 Santa Barbara St Pasadena CA 91101

KRISTIANSEN, MAGNE, PULSED POWER TECHNOLOGY. *Current Pos:* from asst prof to prof elec eng, 66-77, P W HORN PROF ELEC ENG, TEX TECH UNIV, 77-, C B THORNTON PROF ELEC ENG, 90-; VPRES RES & DEVELOP, INTEGRATED TECH INC, 90- *Personal Data:* b Elverum, Norway, Apr 14, 32; nat US; m 57, Aud Bohn; c Sonja & Eric. *Educ:* Univ Tex, BS, 61, PhD(elec eng), 67. *Honors & Awards:* Nuclear & Plasma Sci Soc Merit Award, Inst Elec & Electronics Engrs, 91; Peter Haas Award, 87. *Prof Exp:* Res engr, Univ Tex, 63-66. *Concurrent Pos:* NSF grants, 67-86 & US Atomic Energy Comn grant, 67-72; US Army & Air Force grants, 69-; consult to various industs; vis staff mem, Los Alamos Nat Lab & Lawrence Livermore Nat Lab; contractor, Sandia Labs, Lawrence Livermore Nat Lab, Los Alamos Nat Lab, Defense Nuclear Agency, Strategic Defense Initiative Off & US Navy, 77-87, NASA, 91- & BMDO, 91-; sci adv bd, US Air Force, 81-85; assoc ed, Trans Plasma Sci, Inst Elec & Electronics Engrs, 79-89. *Mem:* AAAS; fel Inst Elec & Electronics Engrs; fel Am Phys Soc; Am Soc Eng Educ; Nat Soc Prof Eng; foreign mem Oral Br Russian Acad Sci. *Res:* Plasma dynamics, pulsed power technology and physical electronics; high power switching and radio frequency wave propagation and technology; high power microwaves; author of 330 publications, co-author of two books, editor of series of books. *Mailing Add:* Dept Elec Eng MS 3102 Tex Tech Univ Lubbock TX 79409-3102. *Fax:* 806-742-1281; *E-Mail:* nukrs@ttacs1.ttu.edu

KRISTMANSON, DANIEL D, chemical engineering, for more information see previous edition

KRISTOFFERSEN, THORVALD, FOOD SCIENCE. *Current Pos:* RETIRED. *Personal Data:* b Denmark, May 6, 19; nat US; m 48; c 1. *Educ:* Royal Vet & Agr Col, Denmark, BS, 44; Iowa State Univ, MS, 48, PhD(dairy bact), 54. *Honors & Awards:* Pfizer-Paul Lewis Award Cheese Res, 65. *Prof Exp:* Asst milk & milk prod, Govt Res Inst Denmark, 44-46; lab asst cheese, Iowa State Univ, 46-54; res assoc sanitizers, Ohio State Univ, 55-56, from asst prof to prof dairy technol, 56-84, chmn dept, 72-84. *Mem:* Fel AAAS; Am Soc Microbiol; Am Dairy Sci Asn; Inst Food Technol. *Res:* Mechanism of flavor development in cheese; enzyme system of milk, its function and purpose; butter and its physical structure; dairy sanitizers; analysis and evaluation of dairy products. *Mailing Add:* 1433 Clubview Blvd S Worthington OH 43235-1652

KRISTOL, DAVID SOL, BIOENGINEERING. *Current Pos:* from asst prof to assoc prof, 66-81, PROF CHEM, NJ INST TECHNOL, 81-, DIR, BIOMED ENG PROG, 82- *Personal Data:* b Brooklyn, NY, June 4, 38; m 75, Newman; c Rachel & Joshua. *Educ:* Brooklyn Col, BS, 58; NY Univ, PhD(chem), 69. *Prof Exp:* Res asst, Jewish Hosp Brooklyn, 58-62. *Mem:* Am Chem Soc; Sigma Xi; Inst Elec & Electronics Engrs Eng & Med & Biol Soc; NY Acad Sci. *Res:* Effect of structure upon reactivity of organic molecules; reaction of amines with chlorocarbons; modeling of the cardiovascular system; molecular modeling of the acetylcholinesterase. *Mailing Add:* Chem Div NJ Inst Technol 323 King Blvd Newark NJ 07102. *Fax:* 973-596-2316; *E-Mail:* kristol@admin.njit.edu

KRITCHEVSKY, DAVID, LIPID METABOLISM, NUTRITION. *Current Pos:* asst prof, Sch Med, Univ Pa, 57-65, prof, Sch Vet Med, 65-67, Wistar prof biochem, 67-72, chmn grad group molecular biol, 71-84, prof, 72-90, MEM, WISTAR INST, UNIV PA, 57-, EMER PROF BIOCHEM IN SURG, 90-; INST PROF, 91- *Personal Data:* b Kharkov, Russia, Jan 25, 20; nat US; m 47, Evelyn Sholtes; c Barbara, Janice & Stephen. *Educ:* Univ Chicago, BS, 39, MS, 42; Northwestern Univ, PhD(chem), 48. *Honors &*

Awards: Borden Award, Am Inst Nutrit, 74; Am Col Nutrit Award, 78; Herman Award, Am Soc Clin Nutrit, 92; Spec Recognition Award, Am Heart Asn, 93; Avenbrugger Medal, Univ Graz, Austria, 94; Supelco-Aocs Award, 96; Res Achievement Award, Am Inst Cancer Res, 96. *Prof Exp:* Jr chemist, Ninol Labs, 41-42, chemist, 42-46; asst & quiz instr, Northwestern Univ, 46-48; Am Cancer Soc fel, Swiss Fed Inst Technol, 48-50; mem staff, Radiation Lab, Univ Calif, 50-52; res chemist, Lederle Labs Div, Am Cyanamid Co, 52-57. *Concurrent Pos:* Caspar Wistar Scholar, 94- *Mem:* AAAS; Soc Exp Biol & Med; Am Soc Biol Chem; Am Chem Soc; Sigma Xi; Am Inst Nutrit. *Res:* Synthesis and metabolism of compounds labeled with isotopic carbon and hydrogen; experimental atherosclerosis; organic synthesis; steroids; biology of deuterium oxide; lipid metabolism; nutrition and cancer. *Mailing Add:* Wistar Inst 36th & Spruce Sts Philadelphia PA 19104-4268

KRITIKOS, HARALAMBOS N, ELECTRICAL ENGINEERING. *Current Pos:* from asst instr to assoc prof, 56-76, PROF ELEC ENG, MOORE SCH ELEC ENG, UNIV PA, 76- *Personal Data:* b Tripolis, Greece, Mar 8, 33; US citizen; m 64. *Educ:* Worcester Polytech Inst, BS, 54, MS, 56; Univ Pa, PhD(elec eng), 61. *Prof Exp:* Res asst elec eng, Worcester Polytech Inst, 54-56. *Concurrent Pos:* Res fel, Calif Inst Technol, 66; exec ed, Inst Elec & Electronics Engrs Trans of Geosci Electronics, 76-80. *Mem:* Inst Elec & Electronics Engrs. *Res:* Diffraction theory; antennas; propagation; microwave hazards; remote sensing; electromagnetic field theory. *Mailing Add:* Moore Sch Elec Eng Univ Pa 200 S 33rd St Philadelphia PA 19104

KRITSKY, GENE RALPH, ETHNOENTOMOLOGY, CICADA EVOLUTION & BIOGEOGRAPHY OF CICINDELIDAE. *Current Pos:* assoc prof, 83-87, CHAIRPERSON BIOL, COL MT ST JOSEPH, 85-, PROF, 87- *Personal Data:* b Minot, NDak, June 26, 53. *Educ:* Indiana Univ, AB, 74; Univ Ill, MS, 76, PhD(entom), 77. *Prof Exp:* From asst prof to assoc prof biol, Tri-State Univ, 77-83. *Concurrent Pos:* Entomologist, Tri-State Agri-Res, 79-83; adj curator, Cincinnati Mus Natural Hist, 90-; Fulbright Award, Coun Int Exchange Scholars, 81-82. *Mem:* Entom Soc Am; fel AAAS; Coleopterists Soc; Am Entom Soc. *Res:* Insect evolution; insect systematics; history of biology especially Darwin and entomology; Coleoptera; fossil insects. *Mailing Add:* Dept Biol Col Mt St Joseph Cincinnati OH 45233-1670. *Fax:* 513-244-4222; *E-mail:* cdurwin@aol.com

KRITZ, ARNOLD H, PLASMA PHYSICS. *Current Pos:* PROF, LEHIGH UNIV, 91-, CHAIR, DEPT PHYSICS, 91- *Personal Data:* b Providence, RI, Jan 6, 35; m 57, Barbara Boredach; c Ann-Sheryl, Barry & David. *Educ:* Brown Univ, ScB, 56; Yale Univ, MS, 57, PhD(physics), 61. *Prof Exp:* Res asst, Yale Univ, 57-61; sr physicist, Space Sci Lab, Gen Dynamics/Astronaut, 61-63, staff scientist, 63-65; sr staff physicist, Aeronaut Res Assocs Princeton, Inc, 65-69; from asst prof to prof, Hunter Col, 69-96, chmn, Dept Physics & Astron, 71-77. *Concurrent Pos:* Lectr, New Haven Col, 59-60 & Southern Conn State Col, 60-61; asst prof, San Diego State Col, 63-64; consult, Oak Ridge Nat Lab, 74-; sci adj, Ctr Plasma Physics Res, Ecole Polytech Lausanne, 75-76 & 82-83; vis res fel, Princeton Univ, 77-; vis scientist, Lawrence Livermore Lab, 86- *Mem:* AAAS; Am Phys Soc; Am Asn Physics Teachers; Sigma Xi. *Res:* Nonequilibrium statistical mechanics; kinetic description of plasma; microwave interactions with inhomogeneous plasma; radio frequency heating of toroidal plasmas. *Mailing Add:* Physics Dept Lehigh Univ 16 Memorial Dr E Bethlehem PA 18015. *Fax:* 215-758-5730

KRITZ, J(ACOB), electronics, electroacoustics; deceased, see previous edition for last biography

KRITZMAN, JULIUS, MEDICINE, HEMATOLOGY. *Current Pos:* STAFF INTERNAL MED, NEW ENG MED CTR HOSPS, 67- *Personal Data:* b Lawrence, Mass, Sept 15, 24; m 50, Elinor S Stone; c Julia & Marjorie. *Educ:* Harvard Univ, AB, 47; Boston Univ, MD, 51; Am Bd Internal Med, dipl, 58, dipl hemat, 74, dipl med oncol, 75, dipl advan achievement internal med, 87. *Honors & Awards:* Internist of the Year, Mass Capitol Am Col Physicians, 90. *Prof Exp:* Res fel hemat, New Eng Ctr Hosp, 53-54. *Concurrent Pos:* Physician, Med Clin, Boston Dispensary, 58-; res assoc, Arthur G Rotch Lab, 60-; attend physician, Boston Vet Admin Hosp, 60-; asst vis physician, Beth Israel Hosp, 61-67, assoc in med, 67-; instr, Harvard Med Sch, 61-70; mass lectureship, Am Col Physicians, 90. *Mem:* Am Soc Hemat; Am Col Physicians; Mass Med Soc. *Res:* Synthesis and function of antibodies, especially the use of in vitro systems for study of antibody synthesis; medical oncology. *Mailing Add:* 750 Washington St Boston MA 02111

KRITZ-SILVERSTEIN, DONNA, WOMENS HEALTH, STATISTICS. *Current Pos:* res assoc, 86-89, asst adj prof, 89-96, ASSOC ADJ PROF EPIDEMIOL, UNIV CALIF, SAN DIEGO, 96- *Personal Data:* b Brooklyn, NY, Aug 22, 57; m 86, Irvin B; c Sarah & Sharona. *Educ:* Brooklyn Col, BS, 79; NY Univ, MA, 81, PhD(social psychol), 84. *Prof Exp:* Data processing supvr, Components & Effective Fertil Regulation Study, Downstate Med Ctr, State Univ NY, 82-84, asst prof, 84-86. *Concurrent Pos:* Adj prof personality psychol, San Diego State Univ, 86-87. *Mem:* Am Psychol Asn; Western Psychol Asn; NAm Menopause Soc; Am Pub Health Asn. *Res:* Women's health, specifically the long term effects of pregnancy on the risk for diabetes and other diseases; menopause; menstrual symptoms; employment and health; osteoporosis; long term effects of hysterectomy. *Mailing Add:* Dept Family & Prev Med Univ Calif San Diego 9500 Gilman Dr 0631-C La Jolla CA 92093-0631

KRIVAK, THOMAS GERALD, INORGANIC CHEMISTRY. *Current Pos:* SR RES ASSOC, INDUST CHEM DIV, PPG INDUSTS, 69- *Personal Data:* b Johnstown, Pa, Aug 21, 40; m 63; c 3. *Educ:* Univ Pittsburgh, BS, 62, MEd, 64; Univ Notre Dame, PhD(inorg chem), 69. *Prof Exp:* Res asst chem, Radiation Labs, Mellon Inst, 62-64. *Mem:* Am Chem Soc; Sigma Xi. *Res:* Silica pigments for paint, paper, plastics and rubber applications. *Mailing Add:* Two Highview Circle Irwin PA 15642-1303

KRIVAN, HOWARD C, MICROBIOLOGY, GLYCOBIOLOGY. *Current Pos:* PRES & CHIEF SCI OFFICER, LEGERE PHARMACEUT LTD, 95- *Personal Data:* b Swickley, Pa, Aug 24, 54. *Educ:* Univ NMex, BS, 80, MS, 82; Va Polytech Inst & State Univ, PhD(microbiol), 86. *Honors & Awards:* Intramural Res Training Award, NIH, 87. *Prof Exp:* Staff fel, NIH, 87-89; dir microbiol & sr scientist, BioCarb, Inc, 89-90, vpres, 90-91; pres, MicroCarb Inc, 91, exec vpres & chief sci officer, 91-93; vpres res & develop, Lectin BioPharmaceut Inc, 94-95. *Concurrent Pos:* Consult, Lectin BioPharma Inc, 94; assoc prof microbiol, Am Univ Caribbean, 94. *Mem:* AAAS; Am Soc Microbiol. *Res:* Adhesin, receptor technology and infectious agents; botanical biopharmaceuticals to treat and prevent infectious diseases; lectins; complex carbohydrates; vaccines. *Mailing Add:* Legere Pharmaceut Ltd 3123 Research Way Suite 215 Carson City NV 89706. *Fax:* 702-841-2263; *E-Mail:* caribe824@aol.com

KRIVANEK, NEIL DOUGLAS, TOXICOLOGY. *Current Pos:* res toxicologist, 74, consult, 86, STAFF TOXICOLOGIST, HASKELL LAB TOXICOL & INDUST MED, E I DU PONT DE NEMOURS & CO, INC, 75- *Personal Data:* b Milwaukee, Wis, June 11, 44; m 69. *Educ:* Univ Wis, BS, 66; Wayne State Univ, MS, 68, PhD(physiol), 72. *Prof Exp:* Instr toxicol, Dept Occup & Environ Health, Col Med, Wayne State Univ, 72-74. *Mem:* Am Chem Soc; Am Indust Hyg Asn; Am Bd Indust Hyg Asn; Sigma Xi; Am Bd Toxicol; Soc Toxicol. *Res:* Biochemical mechanisms of industrial toxicology; methods development for measuring toxic effects. *Mailing Add:* DuPont Haskell Lab PO Box 50 Newark DE 19714

KRIVANEK, ONDREJ LADISLAV, ELECTRON MICROSCOPY, ELECTRON SPECTROSCOPY. *Current Pos:* DIR RES, GATAN, INC, 85- *Personal Data:* b Prague, Czech, Aug 1, 50; Brit citizen. *Educ:* Univ Leeds, BSc, 71; Univ Cambridge, PhD(physics), 76. *Prof Exp:* Res fel physics, Cavendish Lab, Cambridge, 75-76; res consult electron micros, Bell Lab, 76-77; asst res engr mat sci, Univ Calif, Berkeley, 77-80; asst prof solid state sci, 81-85, ADJ ASSOC PROF PHYSICS, ARIZ STATE UNIV, 85- *Mem:* Am Phys Soc; Electron Micros Soc Am; Brit Inst Physics. *Res:* High resolution and analytical electron microscopy; electron optics; electron energy loss spectroscopy; UHV electron microscopy. *Mailing Add:* Gatan Inc 6678 Owens Dr Pleasanton CA 94588. *Fax:* 510-463-0204

KRIVI, GWEN GRABOWSKI, GROWTH FACTORS, INFLAMMATION. *Current Pos:* Sr res chemist, Dept Molecular Biol, Monsanto Co, 80-82, res specialist, 82-84, res group leader I, Dept Biol Sci, 84-85, res group leader II, 85-86, sci fel, 86-89, sr fel, Dept Biol Sci, 89-96, VPRES RES & DEVELOP, MONSANTO, CO, 96- *Personal Data:* b Huntington, NY, Feb 11, 50; c 1. *Educ:* Bucknell Univ, BA, 72; Mass Inst Technol, PhD(biochem), 78; Wash Univ, MBA, 90. *Concurrent Pos:* Mem, Comt Biotechnol, Agr Res Serv, USDA, 86-; adj prof, Wash Univ, 91- *Mem:* AAAS; Am Chem Soc; Endocrine Soc. *Res:* Function relationships of growth proteins and their receptors; role of arachidonic acid metabolites in inflammation; animal cell engineering; immunoassay; cell biology; molecular genetics technologies in support of human pharmaceutical product development. *Mailing Add:* 14 Coach N Four Frontenac MO 63131-3401

KRIVIS, ALAN FREDERICK, analytical chemistry, for more information see previous edition

KRIVIT, WILLIAM, PEDIATRICS, HEMATOLOGY. *Current Pos:* PROF PEDIAT, MED SCH, UNIV MINN, MINNEAPOLIS, 51-, HEAD DEPT, 79- *Personal Data:* b Jersey City, NJ, Nov 28, 25; m 51; c 4. *Educ:* Duke Univ, 42-44; Tulane Univ, MD, 48; Am Bd Pediat, dipl, 53, dipl pediat hemat, 75. *Prof Exp:* Intern, Charity Hosp, New Orleans, 48-49; resident pediat, Col Med, Univ Utah, 49-50, chief resident, 50-51. *Mem:* Soc Pediat Res; Am Soc Hemat; Soc Exp Biol & Med; NY Acad Sci. *Mailing Add:* Health Sci Mayo Bldg Univ Minn PO Box 47 St Paul MN 55455

KRIZ, GEORGE JAMES, AGRICULTURAL ENGINEERING, SOIL SCIENCE. *Current Pos:* PROF & DIR RES, NC AGR EXP STA, 73- *Personal Data:* b Brainard, Nebr, Sept 20, 36; m 89, Rhoda M Whitacre; c Rosalie S, Richard P & Thomas G. *Educ:* Iowa State Univ, BSAE, 60, MSAE, 62; Univ Calif, Davis, PhD(eng), 65. *Prof Exp:* Teaching asst agr eng, Iowa State Univ, 60-62; asst engr, Univ Calif, Davis, 64-65, lectr groundwater hydrol, 65; from asst prof to assoc prof biol & agr eng, NC State Univ, 65-73, assoc head dept, 69-73. *Concurrent Pos:* Consult, Int Basic Econ Corp & Indian Inst Technol, 67; educ & res dir, Am Soc Agr Engrs, 83-85; bd trustees, Am Soc Agr Engrs Found; bd dirs, Agr Res Inst, 92-96. *Mem:* Fel Am Soc Agr Engrs; Coun Agr & Sci Technol; Agr Res Inst. *Res:* Animal waste management; saturated flow in porous media, especially soil water relationships. *Mailing Add:* NC State Univ Box 7643 100 Patterson Hall Raleigh NC 27695-7643. *Fax:* 919-515-7745; *E-mail:* george_kriz@ncsu.edu

KRIZ, GEORGE STANLEY, PHYSICAL ORGANIC CHEMISTRY. *Current Pos:* asst prof, Western, Wash Univ, 67-72, exec asst to dean arts & sci, 75-77, assoc prof, 77-79, PROF CHEM, WESTERN WASH UNIV, 79- *Personal Data:* b Santa Cruz, Calif, Oct 20, 39; m 89, Carolyn M; c Brian, Kenneth & Michelle. *Educ:* Univ Calif, Berkeley, BS, 61; Ind Univ, PhD(org chem), 66. *Prof Exp:* Foreign asst chem, Univ Montpellier, 65-66; vis res assoc, Ohio State Univ, 66-67. *Concurrent Pos:* Vis prof, Indiana Univ, 84-85. *Mem:* AAAS; Am Chem Soc; Royal Soc Chem. *Res:* Deuterium kinetic isotope effects; mechanisms of organic reactions; nuclear magnetic resonance spectroscopy; linear free energy relationships. *Mailing Add:* Dept Chem Western Wash Univ Bellingham WA 98255-9150. *Fax:* 360-650-2826; *E-Mail:* kriz@chem.wwu.edu

KRIZEK, DONALD THOMAS, ENVIRONMENTAL PHYSIOLOGY, STRESS PHYSIOLOGY. *Current Pos:* res plant physiologist, Phyto-Eng Lab, USDA, 66-72, res plant physiologist, Plant Stress Lab, 72-89, RES PLANT PHYSIOLOGIST, CLIMATE STRESS LAB, BELTSVILLE AGR RES CTR, AGR RES SERV, USDA, 89-; ADJ ASSOC PROF DEPT HORT, UNIV MD, 86- *Personal Data:* b Cleveland, Ohio, June 25, 35; m 62, Betty White; c Kathleen, Beth & Susan. *Educ:* Western Reserve Univ, BA, 57; Univ Chicago, MS, 58, PhD(bot), 64. *Prof Exp:* Res & develop officer, Arctic, Desert, Tropic Info Ctr, Res Studies Inst, Air Univ, 58-62; instr bot & biol, Univ Chicago, 64-66. *Concurrent Pos:* Instr, Montgomery Ctr, Univ Ala, 59-61; mem, Am Soc Hort Sci Working Group Controlled Environ, 69-, Am Soc Agr Eng Plant & Animal Physiol Adv Group, 66-; USDA rep, White House Task Force Inadvertent Modification Stratosphere, 75-78; consult, NASA, 79-, ARS rep; NCR-101 comt Growth Chamber Use, 75-; chmn Inadvertent Modification of Stratosphere subcomt, Biol & Climate Effects Res, 75-78; chmn, Environ Protection Agency Interagency Task Group, Biol (non human) Effects, 76-78; mem Plant Phys Adv Group, Am Inst Biol Sci/NASA, 79-90; chmn, Am Inst Biol Sci, Kennedy Space Ctr Biomass prod tech panel, 87-90; mem NASA Controlled Ecol Life Support Systs Discipline Working Group, 89-; chmn Comn Int de l'Eclairage Tech Comt Action Spectra in Plants, 88- *Mem:* Am Soc Plant Physiol; fel Am Soc Hort Sci; Brit Soc Exp Biol; Japanese Soc Plant Physiol; Scand Soc Plant Physiol; Am Inst Biol Sci; Am Soc Photobiol; AAAS; Int Soc Hort Sci. *Res:* Plant growth and development; senescence of vascular plants; photoperiodism and photomorphogenesis; plant growth regulators; controlled environments; environmental stress physiology; carbon dioxide enrichment; plant growth chambers; ultra-violet radiation effects; water stress; global climate change. *Mailing Add:* Climate Stress Lab USDA ARS, B-046A, BARC-W Beltsville MD 20705-2350. *Fax:* 301-504-6626; *E-Mail:* dkrizek@asrr.arsusda.gov

KRIZEK, RAYMOND JOHN, GEOTECHNICAL ENGINEERING, PROJECT MANAGEMENT. *Current Pos:* from asst prof to assoc prof, 63-70, chmn dept, 80-92, PROF CIVIL ENG, NORTHWESTERN UNIV, 70-, DIR, MASTER PROJ MGT PROG, 94- *Personal Data:* b Baltimore, Md, June 5, 32; m 64, Claudia Stricker; c Robert A & Kevin J. *Educ:* Johns Hopkins Univ, BE, 54; Univ Md, MS, 61; Northwestern Univ, PhD(geotech eng), 63. *Honors & Awards:* C A Hogentogler Award, Am Soc Testing & Mat, 70; Walter L Huber Res Prize, Am Soc Civil Engrs, 71; Palmes Academiques, French Govt, 93; Terzaghi Award, Am Soc Civil Engrs, 97. *Prof Exp:* Instr civil eng, Univ Md, 57-61; lectr soil mech, Cath Univ, 61. *Concurrent Pos:* Consult, 63-; vpres, GeoInst, Am Soc Civil Engrs. *Mem:* Am Soc Civil Engrs. *Res:* Soil-structure interaction of buried conduits; use of dredgings for landfill; relationship between soil fabric and its engineering properties; constitutive relations for soils; flow through porous media; disposal of solid waste materials; soil stabilization by grouting. *Mailing Add:* Dept Civil Eng Northwestern Univ A114 Tech Inst Evanston IL 60208-3109. *E-Mail:* rjkrizek@nwu.edu

KRIZEK, THOMAS JOSEPH, PLASTIC SURGERY, RECONSTRUCTIVE SURGERY. *Current Pos:* prof surg & chief Plastic & Reconstructive Surg, 84-87, CHMN, DEPT SURG, UNIV CHICAGO, 87- *Personal Data:* b Milwaukee, Wis, Dec 1, 32; m 59; c 3. *Educ:* Marquette Univ, BS, 54, MD, 57. *Hon Degrees:* MA, Yale Univ, 74. *Prof Exp:* Asst prof plastic surg, Johns Hopkins Univ & Univ Md, 66-68; assoc prof, Sch Med, Yale Univ, 68-73, prof plastic surg, 73-78, assoc dean grad & continuing educ, 75-77; prof surg, Col Physicians & Surgeons, Columbia Univ & Chief, Div Plastic & Reconstructive Surg, Columbia-Presby Med Ctr, 78-81; prof surg, Univ Southern Calif & chief, Div Plastic Surg, Los Angeles County, Univ Southern Calif, Med Ctr, 81-84. *Mem:* Am Asn Plastic Surgeons; Asn Hand Surg (pres, 80-81); Am Asn Surg of Trauma; Am Burn Asn; Am Col Surgeons. *Res:* Surgical infection, particularly as related to burns and other trauma; surgery and epidemiology of head and neck cancer; aging. *Mailing Add:* Dept Plastic & Reconstructive Surg Univ SFla Harbourside Med 4 Columbia Dr No 730 Tampa FL 33606

KRNJEVIC, KRESIMIR, NEUROPHYSIOLOGY, NEUROPHARMACOLOGY. *Current Pos:* Drake prof & chmn, Dept Physiol, 78-87, HEAD, DEPT ANESTHESIA RES, MCGILL UNIV, 65- *Personal Data:* b Zagreb, Yugoslavia, Sept 7, 27; m 54, Jeanne Bowyer; c Peter & Nicholas. *Educ:* Univ Edinburgh, MB, ChB, 49, BSc, 51, PhD(physiol), 53. *Honors & Awards:* Forbes lectr, 78; Gairdner Award, 84; Officer Order of Can, 87. *Prof Exp:* Beit Mem res fel, Univ Edinburgh, 51-54; res assoc & asst prof, Univ Wash, 54-56; from prin sci officer to sr prin sci officer, ARC Inst Animal Physiol, Eng, 59-65. *Concurrent Pos:* Drake prof physiol, McGill Univ, 78-; mem coun, Int Union Physiol Sci, 83-93. *Mem:* Can Physiol Soc; Int Soc Neurochem; Soc Neurosci; Royal Soc Can; Physiol Soc UK; AAAS. *Res:* Central synaptic mechanisms and disruptive effects of anoxia, hypoglycemia and anesthesia. *Mailing Add:* Dept Anesthesia Res McGill Univ McIntyre Bldg 3655 Drummond St Montreal PQ H3G 1Y6 Can. *Fax:* 514-398-4386; *E-Mail:* mc94@musica.mcgill.ca

KROC, ROBERT LOUIS, PHYSIOLOGY. *Current Pos:* RETIRED. *Personal Data:* b Chicago, Ill, June 19, 07; m 34, Alice Voelker; c Alice A (Hattemer) & Lois S. *Educ:* Oberlin Col, BA, 29, MA, 31; Univ Wis, PhD(zool, physiol), 33. *Hon Degrees:* DSc, Oberlin Col, 79. *Honors & Awards:* Addison B Scoville Award, Am Diabetes Asn, 84. *Prof Exp:* Asst, Univ Wis, 30-33; from instr to asst prof zool, Ind Univ, 33-44; biologist, Res Div, Maltine Co, 44-47, dir physiol res, Chilcott Labs Div, 47-51, Warner-Chilcott Labs Div, Warner-Hudnut, Inc, 51-58 & Warner-Lambert Res Inst, 58-69; pres, The Kroc Found, 69-85. *Concurrent Pos:* Mem bd dirs, Med Found Buffalo Res Inst, 85- & Sansum Med Res Found, Santa Barbara, 86- *Mem:* Endocrine Soc; Am Physiol Soc; Am Thyroid Asn; NY Acad Sci; AAAS. *Res:* Endocrinology, especially thyroid and reproductive physiology; prothrombin time reagent simplastin. *Mailing Add:* 4737 Sierra Madre Rd Santa Barbara CA 93110-1319

KROCHMAL, ARNOLD, economic botany; deceased, see previous edition for last biography

KROCHMAL, JEROME J(ACOB), ORGANIZATION DEVELOPMENT, ORGANIZATIONAL EFFECTIVENESS. *Current Pos:* RETIRED. *Personal Data:* b New York, NY, Dec 17, 30; m 52, Regina Maslia; c Kenneth, Frances & Linda. *Educ:* Ga Inst Technol, BCerE, 52. *Prof Exp:* Staff mem ceramics, Battelle Mem Inst, 52; staff mem ceramics & graphites, USAF Propulsion Lab, 54-57; staff mem, US Air Force Mat Lab, USAF, 57-60, sr proj officer, 60-69, sr plans analyst, 71-75, sr mgt analyst, Aeronaut Labs, 75-88. *Concurrent Pos:* Staff consult, Mat Adv Bd, Nat Acad Sci-Nat Res Coun, 60-61; Stanford-Sloan fel, 69-70. *Mem:* Orgn Develop Network; Orgn Develop Inst; Asn Psychol Type; Acad Mgt; Am Soc Training & Develop. *Res:* Organization effectiveness; instrumentation and simulations; synergistic problem solving in advanced technology; fostering creativity and innovation; high temperature materials. *Mailing Add:* PO Box 567764 Atlanta GA 31156

KROCHTA, WILLIAM G, ANALYTICAL CHEMISTRY. *Current Pos:* SR SUPVR, CHEM DIV, PPG INDUSTS, BARBERTON, 62- *Personal Data:* b Piney Fork, Ohio, Sept 24, 30; m 54; c 3. *Educ:* Mt Union Col, BS, 52; Purdue Univ, MS, 54, PhD(chem), 57. *Prof Exp:* Sr res chemist, Columbia-Southern Chem Corp, 56-59, supvr, 59-62. *Mem:* Am Chem Soc; Am Indust Hyg Asn. *Res:* Absorption spectroscopy; gas chromatography. *Mailing Add:* 237 Tanglewood Trail Wadsworth OH 44281-2354

KROCK, HANS J, ENVIRONMENTAL WATER QUALITY, OCEAN ENGINEERING. *Current Pos:* ASSOC PROF OCEAN ENG & DIR, J K K LOOK LAB, UNIV HAWAII, MANOA, 80-; PRES, OCEAN ENG & ENERGY SYST INT INC, HONOLULU, HAWAII, 88-;. *Personal Data:* b Cracow, Poland, Aug 30, 42; US citizen. *Educ:* Ariz State Univ, BS, 65, MS, 67; Univ Calif, Berkeley, PhD, 72. *Prof Exp:* Pub health engr, Dept Health, State of Ariz, 65-66; res engr tertiary treat, Los Angeles County Sanit Dists, Calif, 67-68; assoc engr hydraul, Alameda County Flood Dist, Calif, 69; res assoc, Sanit Eng Res Lab, Univ Calif, Berkeley, 70-72; sr environ engr, M&E Pac, Inc, Honolulu, Hawaii, 72-80. *Concurrent Pos:* Consult engr, 80-; prin investr, Open Cycle Ocean Thermal Energy Conversion, 82-; mem nat comt on Ocean Energy, Am Soc Civil Engrs, 87- *Mem:* Fel Am Inst Chemists; Am Soc Civil Engrs; Water Pollution Control Fedn; Marine Technol Soc; Am Soc Limnol & Oceanog; AAAS; Am Chem Soc. *Res:* Physical, chemical and biological interactions in the oceans and estuaries; gas exchange characteristics in sea water related to ocean thermal energy conversion; water quality standards. *Mailing Add:* 3786 Pakalani Pl Honolulu HI 96816-3814

KROCK, LARRY PAUL, STRESS PHYSIOLOGY, ENVIRONMENTAL PHYSIOLOGY. *Current Pos:* res physiologist environ physiol function, 85-87, res physiologist acceleration effects function, Crew Technol Div, Sch Aerospace Med, USAF, 87-94, DIR RES, HYPERBARIC MED, ARMSTRONG LAB, USAF. *Personal Data:* b Santa Monica, Calif, Oct 18, 49; m, Becky L Smith; c Melissa, Laura & Anastasia. *Educ:* San Fernando Valley State Col, BA, 72; Calif State Univ, MA, 74; Tex A&M Univ, PhD(physiol), 85. *Prof Exp:* Res asst, Dept Phys Educ, Calif State Univ, 73-74, lectr, 75-77, dir, Sports Med Facil & Undergrad Curric Sports Med, 75-82, asst prof, 79-82; res asst, Dept Physiol & Appl Physics Lab, Col Vet Med, Tex A&M Univ, 83-84, asst, Dept Health & Kinesiology, 82-85. *Concurrent Pos:* Res asst, Dept Med, Baylor Col Med, 84-85; adj prof, Univ Tex, San Antonio, 90- & Tex Lutheran Col, 91; mem, Coun Circulation, Am Heart Asn, Basic Res Rev Bd, Naval Res & Develop Command, 90 & Sci Prog Rev Comt, Aerospace Med Asn, 91; adj prof, Sch Aero Med, USAF, 90- *Mem:* Fel Aerospace Med Asn; Aerospace Physiologists Soc; AAAS; fel Am Col Sports Med; Am Heart Asn; Am Physiol Soc; Inst Elec & Electronics Engrs; Sigma Xi; NY Acad Sci. *Res:* Increase understanding about the interaction between elevated oxygen concentrations and increased ambient pressure on the structure and function of the cell; immune response maintaining homeostasis during exposure to stressful environmental conditions. *Mailing Add:* Hyperbaric Med Div Armstrong Lab Brooks AFB TX 78235-5304. *Fax:* 210-536-2946; *E-Mail:* larry.p.krock@platinum.brooks.af.mil

KROEGER, DONALD CHARLES, PHARMACOLOGY. *Current Pos:* RETIRED. *Personal Data:* b Boise, Idaho, Sept 18, 25; m 48; c 2. *Educ:* Ore State Col, BS, 47; Purdue Univ, MS, 49, PhD(pharmacol), 51. *Prof Exp:* From asst prof to assoc prof pharmacol, Univ Houston, 51-56; from asst prof to prof, Univ Tex, Dent Br, Houston, 56-88, chmn dept, 68-88. *Mem:* AAAS; Am Pharmaceut Asn; Soc Exp Biol & Med; Am Soc Pharmacol & Exp Therapeut; Int Asn Dent Res. *Res:* Neuropharmacology; electrophysiological stimulation and recording of autonomic neural centers in the brain and relationship of chemical changes in tissues to brain stimulation. *Mailing Add:* 9325 Lugary Houston TX 77074-6609

KROEGER, PETER G, fluid dynamics, heat transfer, for more information see previous edition

KROEGER, RICHARD ALAN, GAMMA-RAY OBSERVATIONS, GAMMA-RAY DETECTOR DEVELOPMENT. *Current Pos:* ASTROPHYSICIST, NAVAL RES LAB, 89- *Personal Data:* b Waterloo, Iowa, May 28, 55. *Educ:* Univ Northern Iowa, BA, 77; Univ Chicago, MS, 79, PhD(physics), 85. *Prof Exp:* Res assoc astrophys, Enrico Fermi Inst, 85; vis scientist astrophys, Univ Space Res Asn, 85-87; staff engr, Hughes Aircraft Corp, 87-89. *Mem:* Am Inst Physics; Am Astron Soc. *Res:* High energy astrophysics; gamma ray observations; measurements of cosmic rays. *Mailing Add:* 3805 Northrop Pl Bowie MD 20716

KROEKER, RICHARD MARK, ELECTRON TUNNELING. *Current Pos:* fel, 80-81, SR ENGR, GEN PROD DIV, IBM CORP, SAN JOSE, 81- *Personal Data:* b Bakersfield, Calif, Sept 7, 52; m 78; c 2. *Educ:* Washington Univ, St Louis, BA, 74; Univ Calif, Santa Barbara, PhD(physics), 79. *Prof Exp:* Fel, Physics Dept, Univ Calif, Santa Barbara, 79-80. *Mem:* Am Phys Soc. *Res:* Physical chemistry of surfaces, including monolayer spectroscopy, radiation chemistry of thin films and mechanisms of heterogeneous catalysis; tribology and wear. *Mailing Add:* 700 Spring Hill Dr Morgan Hill CA 95037

KROEMER, HERBERT, SEMICONDUCTORS. *Current Pos:* PROF ELEC ENG, UNIV CALIF, SANTA BARBARA, 76- *Personal Data:* b Weimar, Ger, Aug 25, 28; m 50; c 5. *Educ:* Univ Gottingen, dipl, 51, Dr rer nat, 52. *Hon Degrees:* Dr, Tech Univ Aachen, Ger, 84. *Honors & Awards:* J Ebers Award, Inst Elec & Electronics Engrs, 73, Jack A Morton Award, 86; Sr Res Award, Am Soc Eng Educ, 82; Heinrich Walker Medal, 82. *Prof Exp:* Res scientist, Ger Post Off Lab, 52-54 & labs, Radio Corp Am, 54-57; res group leader, Ger Philips Lab, 57-59; sr scientist, Varian Assocs, 59-66; head, New Phenomena Sect, Semiconductor Res & Develop Lab, Fairchild, 66-68; prof elec eng, Univ Colo, Boulder, 68-76. *Concurrent Pos:* Nat lectr, Inst Elec & Electronics Engrs Device Soc, 83. *Mem:* Foreign assoc Nat Acad Eng; fel Inst Elec & Electronics Engrs; fel Am Phys Soc. *Res:* Semiconductor physics and exploratory research on new device principles; physics and technology of semiconductor materials and devices; heterojunctions; molecular beam epitaxy. *Mailing Add:* Dept Elec & Comput Eng Univ Calif Santa Barbara CA 93106

KROENBERG, BERNDT, FOOD SCIENCE, NUTRITION. *Current Pos:* RETIRED. *Personal Data:* b Riga, Latvia, Oct 31, 36; m 59; c 1. *Educ:* Inst Divi Thomae, MS, 61, PhD(biochem), 63. *Prof Exp:* Instr Ger, Our Lady Cincinnati Col, 61-63; instr, Xavier Univ, Ohio, 62-63; group leader leaf chem, Brown & Williamson Tobacco Corp, 63-66; mgr emulsion develop, Celanese Coatings Co, 66-69; dir prod develop res, Ross Labs Div, Abbott Labs, Columbus, 69-76; dir licensing, 76-84; staff vpres technol & develop, Bausch & Lomb Inc, 84-96. *Mem:* AAAS; Am Chem Soc; Licencing Exec Soc. *Res:* Isolation and identification of natural products of animal and plant origin; amino acids, alkaloids, sterols; medicinal use of natural products; infant and geriatric foods; pediatric and obstetrics and gynecology drugs; diagnostic kits; enteral feeding pumps; contact lenses, ophthalmic drugs. *Mailing Add:* 16046 Autumn Oaks Circle Ballwin MO 63021

KROENERT, JOHN THEODORE, ELECTRICAL ENGINEERING, COMMUNICATIONS. *Current Pos:* RETIRED. *Personal Data:* b Arkansas City, Kans, Nov 28, 21; m 47; c 2. *Educ:* Purdue Univ, BSEE, 43. *Prof Exp:* Res engr sonar, US Navy Underwater Sound Lab, 43-51; br head servodyn group, 51-55; sr engr sonar develop, Ultrasonic Corp, 55-56; engr supvr airborne sonar, Light Mil Electronic Equip, Gen Elec Co, 56-58; sr engr, Raytheon Corp, 58-61, prin engr, Submarine Signal Div, 61-64, consult engr, 64-87. *Mem:* Sr mem Inst Elec & Electronics Engrs; fel Acoust Soc Am; assoc Sigma Xi. *Res:* Sonar signal processing; detection, classification, location and underwater telephone. *Mailing Add:* 349 New Meadow Rd Barrington RI 02806-3730

KROENING, JOHN LEO, PHYSICS. *Current Pos:* Res assoc physics, Univ Minn, Minneapolis, 62-65, asst prof, 65-68, ASSOC PROF PHYSICS, UNIV MINN, DULUTH, 68- *Personal Data:* b Princeton, Minn, Aug 18, 34; m 56; c 4. *Educ:* Univ Minn, Minneapolis, BS, 56, MS, 59, PhD(physics), 62. *Mem:* Am Geophys Union. *Res:* Atmospheric physics and electricity; small ion content; atmospheric ozone distribution; chemiluminescent detection; atmospheric aerosol-effect on ozone and small ion content; stratosphere-troposphere transport. *Mailing Add:* 1933 W Kent Rd Duluth MN 55812

KROENKE, LOREN WILLIAM, MARINE GEOLOGY. *Current Pos:* asst geophys, Hawaii Inst Geophys, Univ Hawaii, 63-66, jr geophysicist, 67-72, asst geophysicist, 72-75, assoc geophysicist marine geol & geophys, 75-86, GEOPHYSICIST, HAWAII INST GEOPHYS, UNIV HAWAII, 86- *Personal Data:* b Milwaukee, Wis, July 2, 38. *Educ:* Univ Wis-Madison, BS, 60; Univ Hawaii, MS, 68, PhD(geol), 72. *Prof Exp:* Proj asst marine geol & geophys, Geophys & Polar Res Ctr, Univ Wis, 61-63. *Concurrent Pos:* Tech adv, Comt Coord, Joint Prospecting Mineral Resources SPac Offshore Areas, Econ Comn Asia & Far East, UN, 72-73; sci adv, US-Japan Coop Prog Marine Sea-Bottom Surv Panel, 73-74; marine geologist & regional adv, UN Develop Prog, 74-76; mem, Adv Panel Ocean Margin, Joint Oceanog Inst Deep Earth Sampling-Int Prog Ocean Drilling, 74- *Mem:* Am Geophys Union; Seismol Soc Am; Geol Soc Am; AAAS; Sigma Xi. *Res:* Marine geology and geodynamics of the Pacific Ocean Basin with particular reference to the formation and deformation of oceanic crust and continental margins in the southwest Pacific. *Mailing Add:* Hawaii Inst Geophys Univ Hawaii Sch Ocean & Earth Sci & Technol Honolulu HI 96822

KROENKE, WILLIAM JOSEPH, MATERIALS SCIENCE, TECHNOLOGY TRANSFER. *Current Pos:* RES PROF, DEPT CHEM & NUCLEAR ENG, UNIV NMEX, 96- *Personal Data:* b Cleveland, Ohio, Aug 16, 34; m 61; c 2. *Educ:* Case Inst Technol, BS, 56, PhD(inorg chem), 63. *Prof Exp:* Chemist, Nat Carbon Res Lab, Union Carbide Corp, 56-61; res chemist, Res Ctr, B F Goodrich Co, 63-65, sr res chemist, 65-70, res assoc, 70-74, sr res assoc, 74-80, res & develop fel & mgr, 80-94; NSF evaluator, Ctr Micro-Eng Ceramics, 94-95. *Concurrent Pos:* Assoc dir, Ctr Micro-Eng Mat, 95- *Mem:* Am Chem Soc. *Res:* Inorganic and organometallic chemistry; goechemistry; smoke retarders; synthesis; coordination numbers; molecular and crystal structure; property-structure relationships; solid state chemistry; phase relationships; fire retardants; catalysis; polymers; high-temperature chemistry; carbon/carbon composites. *Mailing Add:* 6201 Peachtree Pl NE Albuquerque NM 87111-7205. *Fax:* 505-277-1024; *E-Mail:* yunder@unm.edu

KROES, ROGER L, SOLID STATE PHYSICS. *Current Pos:* PHYSICIST, MARSHALL SPACE FLIGHT CTR, NASA, 68- *Personal Data:* b Racine, Wis, Dec 3, 35; m 64; c 2. *Educ:* Univ Mo-Columbia, BS, 57; Univ Mo-Columbia, PhD(physics), 68. *Mem:* Am Phys Soc. *Res:* Color centers in alkaline earth oxides; optical properties of solids; crystal characterization; solution crystal growth. *Mailing Add:* 902 Coronado Ave Huntsville AL 35802. *Fax:* 205-544-2102

KROFTA, MILOS, ENGINEERING. *Current Pos:* PRIN, LENOX INST WATER TECHNOL, 51- *Personal Data:* b Ljubljana, Slovenia, July 23, 12; m 37, Maria Hybler; c Tjasa & Hanka. *Educ:* Univ Ljubljana, BS, 32; Univ Prague, MSME, 34; Univ Darmstadt, Ger, PhD(papermaking), 37. *Prof Exp:* Chemist, Paper Mill VGM, Ljubljana, Yugoslavia, 35-37, tech mgr, 37-45; prin, Krofta Eng Co, 45-51. *Concurrent Pos:* Owner & mgr, Krofta Apparatebau, Ger, 60-, Krofta UK, 60-, Krofta Switz, France, Japan, Tawian, Korea, Mex, Brazil & Arg, 70- *Res:* Flotation technology for water-waste water clarification; granted 30 patents. *Mailing Add:* 58 Yokun Ave Lenox MA 01240

KROGDAHL, WASLEY SVEN, COSMOLOGY. *Current Pos:* assoc prof math & astron, Univ Ky, 58-64, prof math & astron, 64-65, prof physics & astron, 65-86, EMER PROF, UNIV KY, 86- *Personal Data:* b Springfield, Ill, Jan 17, 19; m 42, Margaret Kiess; c Matthew, John & Marthine. *Educ:* Univ Chicago, BS, 39, PhD(astron), 42. *Prof Exp:* Jr physicist, Naval Ord Lab, 42-43; instr physics, Army Specialized Training Prog, Ripon Col, 43-44; assoc prof math & astron, Univ SC, 44-45; instr, Yerkes Observ, 45-46; asst prof astron & astrophys, Dearborn Observ, Northwestern Univ, Ill, 46-58. *Mem:* Int Astron Union. *Res:* Theoretical astrophysics; relativistic cosmology. *Mailing Add:* 3493 Castleton Way N Lexington KY 40517

KROGER, F(ERDINAND) A(NNE), PHYSICAL CHEMISTRY, THERMODYNAMICS. *Current Pos:* prof mat sci & chem, 64-85, David Packard prof elec eng, 72-85, EMER PROF MAT SCI, UNIV SOUTHERN CALIF, 85- *Personal Data:* b Amsterdam, Netherlands, Sept 11, 15; div; c 2. *Educ:* Univ Amsterdam, BSc, 34, Drs, 37, PhD(phys chem), 40. *Honors & Awards:* Chaudron Gold Medal, Fr Soc High Temperatures & Refractors. *Prof Exp:* Res worker, Philips Res Labs, Netherlands, 38-40, res group leader, 40-58; sci adv, Mullard Res Labs, Eng, 58-64. *Concurrent Pos:* Corresp, Royal Dutch Acad Sci, 78. *Res:* Solid state luminescence; compound semiconductors; imperfection chemistry. *Mailing Add:* 4604 Newport Ave San Diego CA 92107

KROGER, HANNS H, INORGANIC CHEMISTRY, ELECTROCHEMISTRY. *Current Pos:* electrochemist, NY, 62-65, ELECTROCHEMIST, BATTERY BUS SECT, EVEREADY CO, FLA, 65- *Personal Data:* b Hamburg, Ger, Sept 25, 26; US citizen; m 59; c 2. *Educ:* Univ Hamburg, Cand, 53, Dipl, 56, Dr rer nat (chem, mineral), 58. *Prof Exp:* Sci asst chem, Univ Hamburg, 56-59; chemist, Accumulatorenfabrik AG, Ger, 59-61. *Mem:* Am Chem Soc. *Res:* Battery technology; analytical chemistry. *Mailing Add:* 3841 Second Ave Gainesville FL 32607

KROGER, HARRY, SOLID STATE ELECTRONICS, EXPERIMENTAL SOLID STATE PHYSICS. *Current Pos:* AT WATSON SCH, BINGHAMPTON UNIV, 92- *Personal Data:* b Brooklyn, NY, Aug 13, 36; m 58; c 3. *Educ:* Univ Rochester, BS, 57; Cornell Univ, PhD(physics), 62. *Prof Exp:* Mem res staff, Sperry Res Ctr, 62-68, group leader microwave semiconductors, 68-69, mgr, Semiconductor Device Dept, 69-75, mgr, Advan Device Dept, 75-92. *Concurrent Pos:* MCC Echelon, Austin, 75-92. *Mem:* Inst Elec & Electronics Engrs; Am Phys Soc. *Res:* Soft x-ray spectroscopy; semiconductor memories; conduction through thin insulators; microwave semiconductor devices; Josephson devices. *Mailing Add:* 1 Elec Eng Comput Watson Sch Binghampton Univ Binghampton NY 13902

KROGER, HELMUT KARL, COMPUTATIONAL PHYSICS, LATTICE GAUZE THEORY. *Current Pos:* res assoc, 82-84, PROF RES, UNIV LAVAL, QUEBEC, 84- *Personal Data:* b Kassel, W Ger, Mar 12, 49. *Educ:* Univ Mainz, WGer, dipl, 73; Univ Bonn, PhD(physics), 77. *Prof Exp:* Res assoc, Univ Giessen, WGer, 77-79 & 80; res vis, Oak Ridge Nat Lab, 79-80; res staff, KWU Siemens Co, Erlanger, WGer, 81-82. *Concurrent Pos:* Fel Ger Acad Exchange Serv, N Atlantic Treaty Orgn, 79-80; fel Natural Sci & Eng Res Coun Can, 83- *Mem:* Am Phys Soc; Can Phys Soc; Inst Particle Physics. *Res:* Nuclear physics; qual control data; gauge theories. *Mailing Add:* Dept Physics Univ Laval Quebec PQ G1K 7P4 Can

KROGER, LARRY A, NUCLEAR PHYSICS, MEDICAL PHYSICS. *Current Pos:* HEALTH PHYSICIST, MED SYST DIV, GEN ELEC CO, 78- *Personal Data:* b Hastings, Nebr, Dec 6, 43; m 68; c 2. *Educ:* Hastings Col, BA, 66; Univ Wyo, PhD(physics), 72. *Prof Exp:* Res assoc physics & NSF-Nat Res Coun fel, Nat Reactor Testing Sta, 71-73; res assoc, Univ Pa, 73-75; sr physicist, Emergency Care Res Inst, 75-78. *Concurrent Pos:* Lectr energy. *Mem:* Am Inst Physics; AAAS; Am Asn Physicist Med; Sigma Xi; Am Phys Soc. *Res:* Medical applications of x and gamma rays and performance of radiology systems; study of radioactivity and nuclear decay schemes; radiation safety. *Mailing Add:* 2210 Woodhill Way Waukesha WI 53186

KROGER, MANFRED, FOOD SCIENCE, SCIENCE COMMUNICATIONS. *Current Pos:* Asst dairy sci, 61-63, from instr to assoc prof, 66-78, PROF FOOD SCI & SCI TECHNOL & SOC, PA STATE UNIV, UNIVERSITY PARK, 78- *Personal Data:* b Bad Oeynhausen, Ger, May 19, 33; Can & US citizen; m 62, Goldie Laris; c Hans, Erika & Stefan. *Educ:* Univ Man, BSA, 61; Pa State Univ, MS, 63, PhD(food chem), 66. *Honors & Awards:* Res Award, Int Dairy Foods Asn, 94. *Concurrent Pos:* Tech ed dairy & other food jour; consult food indust; assoc ed, J Food Sci; co-ed, Nutrit Forum; food sci communicator, Inst Food Technologists. *Mem:* Am Chem Soc; Am Dairy Sci; fel Inst Food Technologists; World Future Soc; Ger Dairy Sci Asn. *Res:* Food flavor chemistry; pesticide residue analysis; chemistry of food contaminants; food safety; food laws and regulations; instrumental analysis of fat and protein in foods; milk processing; dairy products manufacture; yogurt quality; fermented milk. *Mailing Add:* 711 McKee St State College PA 16803

KROGH, LESTER CHRISTENSEN, ORGANIC CHEMISTRY. *Current Pos:* RETIRED. *Personal Data:* b Ruskin, Nebr, Aug 22, 25; m 46; c 2. *Educ:* Univ Nebr, BS, 45, MS, 48; Univ Minn, PhD(chem), 52. *Hon Degrees:* DSc, Univ Minn, 90. *Honors & Awards:* Maurice Holland Award, Indust Res Inst, 89; E B Barnes Award, Am Chem Soc, 91. *Prof Exp:* Asst, Univ Nebr, 46-48; asst, Univ Minn, 48-51; sr chemist, Cent Res Lab, Minn Mining & Mfg Co & mgr res group, Abr Lab, 55-59, mgr res & develop group, 59-60, asst tech dir, 60-62, tech dir, 62-64, dir, Chem Res Lab, Cent Res Lab, 64-65, corp tech planning & coordr, 65-69, gen mgr, New Bus Ventures Div, 69-70, exec dir, Cent Res Labs, 70-73, vpres, Com Chem Div, 73-81, vpres, res & develop, Indust & Consumer Sector, 81-82, vpres res & develop, Minn Mining & Mfg Co, 82-88; sr vpres, res & develop, 3M, 88-90. *Concurrent Pos:* Mem bd regents, Milwaukee Sch Eng Space Appln Bd, Comt Indust Appln Microgravity Environ, Nat Res Coun, adv panel, Off Tech Assessment, Cong US, Mat & Indust Appln Panel, Strategic Defense Orgn, Dept Defense, Nat Acad Eng; mem bd dirs, Indust Res Inst Inc; trustee, Univ Nebr Found; Minn Mining & Mfr Indust Res Inst Inc; chmn, Minn High Technol Coun, 90-91. *Mem:* Nat Acad Eng; fel AAAS; Am Chem Soc; Am Inst Chem Engrs. *Res:* Preparation and reaction of polymers; fluorocarbons and the Michael reactions; coated abrasives; analysis of research projects; technology transfer; innovation in a large corporation. *Mailing Add:* 3570 Village Ct Woodbury MN 55125. *Fax:* 612-578-1763

KROGH, THOMAS EDVARD, U-PB ISOTOPIC DATING, CRUSTAL EVOLUTION. *Current Pos:* DIR GEOCHRONOLOGY LAB, GEOL DEPT, ROYAL ONT MUS, 75- *Personal Data:* b Peterborough, Ont, Jan 12, 36; m 61, Kathleen H Myers; c Erik, Kari, Sara & Jason. *Educ:* Queen's Univ, Ont, BSc, 59, MSc, 61; Mass Inst Technol, PhD(isotope geol), 64. *Hon Degrees:* DSc, Queens Univ, 91. *Honors & Awards:* Logan Medal, Geol Asn Can, 89; J Tuzo Wilson Medal, Can Geophys Union, 91; Past President's Medal, Mineral Asn Can, 96. *Prof Exp:* Fel, Dept Terrestrial Magnetism, Carnegie Inst, 64-66, mem sci staff, 66-75. *Concurrent Pos:* Fel, Carnegie Inst Dept Terrestrial Magnetism, 64-66. *Mem:* Geol Asn Can; fel Am Geophys Union; Norweg Acad Sci & Lett. *Res:* Isotope geology; use of isotopic variation in nature as natural tracers in geological processes; geochronology and genesis of rock systems; uranium-lead dating of zircon and low level lead isotopic analyses. *Mailing Add:* Dept Geol 100 Queen's Park Toronto ON M5S 2C6 Can. *Fax:* 416-586-5814

KROGMANN, DAVID WILLIAM, BIOCHEMISTRY. *Current Pos:* prof, 67-97, EMER PROF BIOCHEM, PURDUE UNIV, WEST LAFAYETTE, 97- *Personal Data:* b Washington, DC, Oct 21, 31; m 58, Loretta Kurek; c 3. *Educ:* Cath Univ Am, AB, 53; Johns Hopkins Univ, PhD(biochem), 57. *Prof Exp:* Fel biochem, Johns Hopkins Univ, 57-58; res assoc, Univ Chicago, 58-60; from asst prof to prof, Wayne State Univ, 60-67. *Mem:* Am Soc Biol Chemists; Am Soc Plant Physiol. *Res:* Biological chemistry; biochemistry of electron transport and phosphate metabolism in photosynthesis; understanding of the photosynthetic mechanism in green plants by studying the structures of individual proteins and the interaction of these proteins in the photosynthetic membrane. *Mailing Add:* Dept Biochem Purdue Univ West Lafayette IN 47907

KROGSTAD, BLANCHARD ORLANDO, INSECT ECOLOGY, INVERTEBRATE ECOLOGY. *Current Pos:* from asst prof to assoc prof, 54-63, PROF BIOL, UNIV MINN, DULUTH, 63-, HEAD DEPT, 78- *Personal Data:* b Winger, Minn, Oct 6, 21; m 46; c 3. *Educ:* Bemidji State Col, BA, 46; Univ Minn, MA, 48, PhD, 51. *Prof Exp:* Asst prof biol, St Olaf Col, 51-54. *Concurrent Pos:* Mem staff, Rockefeller Found, Chapingo, Mex, 63-64; researcher, Mexican Inst Coffee, Xalapa, 70-71. *Mem:* Ecol Soc Am; Entom Soc Am; Sigma Xi; Am Inst Biol Sci. *Res:* Ecology of insects and other invertebrates. *Mailing Add:* R 1 Winger MN 56592-9801

KROGSTAD, DONALD JOHN, MEDICINE, BIOLOGY. *Current Pos:* AT TULANE SCH PUP HEALTH & TROP MED. *Personal Data:* b New York, NY, Feb 18, 43; m 65; c 2. *Educ:* Bowdoin Col, AB, 65; Harvard Med Sch, MD, 69. *Prof Exp:* Intern, Mass Gen Hosp, Boston, 69-70, from asst resident to sr resident, 70-76, clin & res fel med, 76-78; epidemic intel serv officer, Parasitic Dis Div & Parasitic Dis Drug Serv, Ctr Dis Control, Ga, 71-73; lectr physiol & med, Med Asst Training Sch, Lilongwe, Malawi, 73-75; asst prof med & path, Sch Med, Wash Univ, 78. *Concurrent Pos:* Physician, Lilongwe Gen Hosp, 73-75; dir, Microbiol Lab, Barnes Hosp, St Louis, 78-; consult, Jewish Hosp, St Louis, 78- *Mem:* Am Soc Microbiol; Am Soc Trop Med & Hyg; Am Col Physicians; Am Asn Pathologists; Am Col Epidemiology. *Res:* Mechanisms of drug resistance; pathogenicity; epidemiology of nosocomial infection. *Mailing Add:* Tulane Sch Pub Health & Trop Med Dept Trop Med 1430 Tulane Ave New Orleans LA 70112

KROH, GLENN CLINTON, PLANT ECOLOGY. *Current Pos:* ASST PROF BIOL, TEX CHRISTIAN UNIV, 75- *Personal Data:* b Philadelphia, Pa, Dec 20, 41; m 67; c 1. *Educ:* Pa State Univ, BS, 66, MS, 70; Mich State Univ, PhD(plant ecol), 75. *Mem:* Ecol Soc Am; Am Inst Biol Sci; AAAS. *Res:* The effects of intra and interspecific competition on the strategies of annual herbs with regard to how they partition available resources into roots, shoots and reproductive tissue. *Mailing Add:* Dept Biol Tex Christian Univ 2800 S University Dr Ft Worth TX 76129-0001

KROHMER, JACK STEWART, DIAGNOSTIC & THERAPEUTIC RADIOLOGICAL PHYSICS. *Current Pos:* RETIRED. *Personal Data:* b Cleveland, Ohio, Nov 7, 21; m 46; c 3. *Educ:* Western Res Univ, BS, 43, MA, 47; Univ Tex, PhD(biophys), 61. *Honors & Awards:* William D Coolidee Award, Am Asn Physicists Med, 85, Robert J Shalek Award, 88; Marie Curie Award, Health Physics Soc, 85. *Prof Exp:* Sec assoc radiol physics, Atomic Energy Med Res Proj, Western Res Univ, 47-57; prof, Univ Tex, Southwestern Med Sch, 57-63; res prof, Roswell Park Mem Inst, 63-66; assoc, Geisinger Med Ctr, 66-72 & Radiol Assocs Erie, 72-79; prof radiol & radiation oncol, Wayne State Univ, Sch Med, 79-84; pres, J S Krohmer Radiol Physics Consult, 84-97. *Concurrent Pos:* Chief physicist, Univ Hosp Cleveland, 47-57 & Parkland Mem Hosp, Dallas, Tex, 57-63; physicist, Radiation Ctr, Ft Worth, Tex, 58-63; prof biophys, State Univ NY, Buffalo, 63-66 & physics, Bucknell Univ, Lewisburg, Pa, 66-72; pres, Erie Clin Inc, Pa, 73-76; dir, Div Radiol Physics, Wayne State Univ, 79-84; assoc mem staff, Mt Carmel Mercy Hosp & Detroit Receiving Hosp, 80-84, Harper-Grace Hosp, 82-84; bd trustees, Am Bd Radiol, 81-93; consult, US Vet Admin Hosp, Temple, Tex, 84-90; mem, Tex Radiation Adv Bd, 86-, chmn, 89-, Georgetown Tex Hosp, Georgetown, Tex Health Care Syst Bd, 87, chmn, 89- *Mem:* Am Asn Physicists Med (pres, 74-75); Am Bd Radiol; Radiol Soc NAm (vpres, 79); Am Roetgen Ray Soc; Health Physics Soc; Sigma Xi. *Res:* Biological effects of radiation; radiation imaging; uses of radioactive materials; radiation therapy and radiation protection. *Mailing Add:* 1610 Mimosa St Georgetown TX 78626

KROHN, BURTON JAY, MOLECULAR PHYSICS. *Current Pos:* STAFF MEM MOLECULAR PHYSICS, THEORET DIV, LOS ALAMOS NAT LAB, 74- *Personal Data:* b St Louis, Mo, Feb 25, 41; m 67; c 2. *Educ:* Vanderbilt Univ, BA, 64; Ohio State Univ, MS, 66, PhD(physics), 71. *Prof Exp:* Fel chem physics, Battelle Mem Inst, 71-72; res assoc infrared spectros, Fla State Univ, 73-74. *Mem:* Am Phys Soc. *Res:* Quantum-mechanical theory; modeling and computations of energies and properties of vibrating, rotating polyatomic molecules; analysis of positions of absorption lines and band- and line-intensities in high-resolution infrared spectra. *Mailing Add:* 2377 45th St No A Los Alamos NM 87544

KROHN, JOHN LESLIE, INSTRUMENTAL NEUTRON ACTIVATION ANALYSIS, NEUTRON SPECTRAL CHARACTERIZATION. *Personal Data:* b Clarksville, Ark, Dec 7, 58; m; c 2. *Educ:* Univ Ark, BS, 81, MS, 83. *Prof Exp:* Grad asst basic nuclear eng, Mech Eng Dept, Univ Ark, 81-83; eng res assoc, Nuclear Sci Ctr, Tex Eng Exp Sta, 84-86; mgr reactor opers, Tex A&M Univ, 86-88, asst dir, Nuclear Sci Ctr, 88-91. *Concurrent Pos:* Rad safety officer, AAE/BCS Traders, Inc, 86- *Mem:* Am Nuclear Soc; Am Soc Testing & Mat. *Res:* Instrumental neutron activation analysis; prompt gamma neutron activation analysis; characterization of neutron energy spectra and damage to electronic components by fast neutrons. *Mailing Add:* 10 Water Oak Lane Russellville AR 72801

KROHN, KENNETH ALBERT, NUCLEAR CHEMISTRY. *Current Pos:* assoc prof, 81-85, PROF RADIOL & RADIATION ONCOL, SCH MED, UNIV WASH, SEATTLE, 85- *Personal Data:* b Stevens Point, Wis, June 19, 45; m 68; c 1. *Educ:* Andrews Univ, BA, 66; Univ Calif, Davis, PhD(chem), 71. *Prof Exp:* Instr radiation sci, Washington Univ, 71-73; from asst prof to assoc prof radiol, Sch Med, Univ Calif, Davis, 73-81, assoc dir, Crocker Nuclear Lab, 78-80. *Concurrent Pos:* Mem comt radiopharmaceut & radioassay, Am Col Nuclear Physicians, 75-78. *Mem:* Am Chem Soc; Soc Nuclear Med; Radiation Res Soc; AAAS; Sigma Xi. *Res:* Application of isotopes to biological problems; development of new cyclotron produced radiopharmaceuticals for diagnostic procedures for cancer and heart disease; halogen and technetium chemistry and chemical effects of nuclear transformations. *Mailing Add:* Univ Wash Hosp Box 356004 Seattle WA 98195-6004

KROL, GEORGE J, PHYSICAL CHEMISTRY, ANALYTICAL CHEMISTRY. *Current Pos:* supvr, 78-84, STAFF SCIENTIST, BAYER CORP, 84- *Personal Data:* b Wilno, Poland, June 6, 36; US citizen; m 62; c 3. *Educ:* Univ Rochester, BS, 58; Rutgers Univ, PhD(phys anal chem), 68. *Prof Exp:* Res technician, Med Sch, Univ Rochester, 58-59; chemist,

Hoffmann-La Roche Inc, 60-62; res asst phys chem, Rutgers Univ, 63-67; sr res chemist, 67-75, sect head, Ayerst Labs, Inc, 75-78. *Mem:* Am Chem Soc; Am Asn Pharmaceut Scientists. *Res:* Biochemistry; radiochemistry and kinetics; analytical method development, especially chromatography; drug metabolism and pharmacokinetic analysis. *Mailing Add:* Bayer Corp 400 Morgan Lane West Haven CT 06516-4134

KROLAK, JOHN MICHAEL, CLINICAL LABORATORY MEDICINE. *Current Pos:* health scientist, 92-93, SUPVRY HEALTH SCIENTIST, CTRS DIS CONTROL & PREVENT, NAT INST OCCUP SAFETY & HEALTH, 93- *Personal Data:* b Kenmore, NY, Feb 1, 53; m 83, Janet E Koehler; c Julia E, John M Jr & Joy E. *Educ:* Va Commonwealth Univ, BS, 75, MS, 77; Okla State Univ, PhD(insect biochem), 81. *Prof Exp:* NIH res fel, Univ Tex Med Sch, 81-85; res biochemist, Armed Forces Radiobiol Res Inst, USAF, 85-89, dir clin chem, Epidemiol Res Div, 89-92, dir clin & forensic toxicol, 89-92. *Concurrent Pos:* Adj fac, Dept Pathol, Uniformed Serv, Univ Health Sci, 86-88. *Mem:* Soc Toxicol; Sigma Xi; AAAS; Entom Soc Am; Am Soc Cell Biol. *Res:* Evaluation of clinical and public health laboratory standards and practices; evaluate information contained in national databases with the objective of identifying and defining clinical and public health laboratory managerial and technical problems; evaluation of scientific data as it relates to performance and practices of clinical and public health laboratory systems; design and implementation of scientific studies to assess the quality of laboratory testing in the Nation's laboratories; develop intervention strategies for improving the quality of laboratory testing and develops technically and scientifically valid plans for evaluating the changes/improvements in clinical outcomes associated with implementing improvements in testing. *Mailing Add:* 3650 Stillwood Dr Snellville GA 30278-4493

KROLICK, KEITH A, IMMUNOLOGY. *Current Pos:* PROF MICROBIOL & IMMUNOL, UNIV TEX, 92- *Personal Data:* b Chicago, Ill, May 21, 51. *Educ:* Univ Calif, Los Angeles, PhD(microbiol). *Res:* Immunology. *Mailing Add:* Dept Microbiol Univ Tex Health Sci Ctr 7703 Floyd Curl Dr San Antonio TX 78284-7758

KROLIK, JULIAN H, THEORETICAL ASTROPHYSICS. *Current Pos:* from asst prof to assoc prof 84-91, PROF PHYSICS & ASTRON, JOHNS HOPKINS UNIV, 91- *Personal Data:* b Detroit, Mich, Apr 4, 50; m 83; c 2. *Educ:* Mass Inst Technol, SB, 71; Univ Calif, Berkeley, PhD(physics), 77. *Prof Exp:* Mem, Inst Advan Study, Mass Inst Technol, 77-79, scientist, Ctr Theoret Physics & Space Res, 79-81; res assoc, Smithsonian Ctr Astrophys, Harvard Univ, 81-84. *Concurrent Pos:* Lectr, Dept Astron, Harvard Univ, 81-84; vis prof, Col France, 84. *Mem:* Am Astron Soc. *Mailing Add:* Dept Physics & Astron Johns Hopkins Univ Baltimore MD 21218

KROLL, BERNARD HILTON, STATISTICS, SYSTEMS SCIENCE. *Current Pos:* RETIRED. *Personal Data:* b Brooklyn, NY, Sept 8, 22; m 47; c 3. *Educ:* Brooklyn Col, BA, 47. *Prof Exp:* Air transp economist, Civil Aeronaut Bd, 48-51; anal statistician, NIMH, 51-58; supvry statistician, Nat Inst Neurol Dis & Blindness, 58-67, supvry syst analyst, Nat Inst Neurol & Commun Disorders & Stroke, 67-77, assoc chief off biomet & epidemiol, 77-81. *Concurrent Pos:* Consult, NIH, 80-81. *Mem:* Fel AAAS; Asn Systs Mgt; fel Am Pub Health Asn; fel Royal Soc Health. *Res:* Design of management and administrative systems involving the use of computers; management of epidemiologic and statistical research in medical and related fields; epidemiology, manpower and information systems. *Mailing Add:* 3507 Farthing Dr Silver Spring MD 20906

KROLL, HARRY, ELECTROLESS GOLD DEPOSITION, BRIGHT TIN LEAD ELECTROPLATING. *Current Pos:* SR SCIENTIST, TECHNIC INC, 83- *Personal Data:* b Chicago, Ill, Nov 28, 14; m 45; c 3. *Educ:* Univ Ill, BS, 38, Univ Chicago, PhD(org chem), 42. *Prof Exp:* Chemist, Alrose chem co, Cranston, RI, 42-49; prin investr, Am Cancer Soc, Yale Univ, 51-58; res dir, Geigy Chem Corp, 51-58; prin investr, US Atomic Energy Comt, 58-64; res dir & vpres, Philip A Hunt Chem Corp, 64-82. *Concurrent Pos:* Adj prof, Univ RI, 74-75. *Mem:* Am Chem Soc. *Res:* Chelating afents, photo resist and metal deposition. *Mailing Add:* 615 Middle Rd East Greenwich RI 02818-2343

KROLL, JOHN ERNEST, FLUID DYNAMICS, PHYSICAL OCEANOGRAPHY. *Current Pos:* asst prof, 76-80, ASSOC PROF APPL MATH, OLD DOMINION UNIV, 81- *Personal Data:* b Los Angeles, Calif, Aug 15, 40; m 73; c 3. *Educ:* Univ Calif, Los Angeles, BS, 63, MS, 66; Yale Univ, PhD(eng & appl sci), 73. *Prof Exp:* Res fel phys oceanog, Nova Oceanog Lab, 72-75; instr, Mass Inst Technol, 75-76. *Concurrent Pos:* Sr Res Assoc, Nat Res Coun Dept Oceanog, Naval Postgrad Sch, Monterey, Calif, 85-86. *Mem:* Soc Indust & Appl Math; Am Geophys Union. *Res:* Theoretical investigation of the generation and propagation of inertial oscillations and the stability of fronts and eddies. *Mailing Add:* Dept Math Old Dominion Univ Bal 500 Hampton Blvd Norfolk VA 23529-0077

KROLL, KEITH, CARDIOVASCULAR PHYSIOLOGY. *Current Pos:* fel, Dept Physiol & Biophysics, Univ Wash, Seattle, 83-84, sr fel, 87-89, res assoc, 89-91, RES ASST PROF, CTR BIOMED ENG, DEPT PHYSIOL & BIOPHYSICS, UNIV WASH, SEATTLE, 91- *Personal Data:* b Seattle, Wash, Dec 9, 48; m 84; c 1. *Educ:* Stanford Univ, BA, 71; Univ Wash, PhD(cardiovasc physiol), 83. *Prof Exp:* Res tech, Recon Cardiovasc Res Ctr, Providence Hosp, Seattle, Wash, 72-74; res asst, Dept Physiol, Univ Leiden, Neth, 75-78. *Concurrent Pos:* Fel, NATO, 84-85, Physiol Inst I, Univ Dusseldorf, Ger, 84-87; William Lochner fel, Ger Soc Heart & Circulation Res, 85-87; prin investr, NATO, 91-92. *Mem:* Am Physiol Soc; Microcirculatory Soc; Biomed Eng Soc. *Res:* Control of myocardiol energy balance; role of adenosine and its metabolites in the heart; application of dynamic systems modeling analysis to the investigation of tissue transport, metabolic and energetic processes. *Mailing Add:* Ctr Bioeng WD-12 Univ Wash Box 357962 Seattle WA 98195-7962. *Fax:* 206-685-3300; *E-Mail:* keith@nsr.bioeng.washington.edu

KROLL, MARTIN HARRIS, CLINICAL CHEMISTRY, CLINICAL BIOCHEMISTRY. *Current Pos:* ASSOC DIR, CLIN CHEM DIV, JOHNS HOPKINS HOSP, 94-; ASSOC PROF, DEPT PATH, SCH MED, JOHNS HOPKINS UNIV, 94- *Personal Data:* b Washington, DC, June 19, 52; m 75, Ellen L Coonin; c Allison, Jonathan & Lauren. *Educ:* Univ Md, College Park, BS, 74; Univ Sch Med, MD, 78. *Honors & Awards:* Young Investr, Acad Clin Lab Physicians & Scientists, 83; Past Chmn Award, Capital Sect, Am Asn Clin Chem, 90; Roe Award, Capital Sect, Am Asn Clin Chem, 95. *Prof Exp:* Resident, path, Univ Md Hosp, 78-82; fel clin chem, NIH, 82-84, med staff, Clin Chem Serv, Clin Path Dept, 84-94. *Concurrent Pos:* Fel, NSF Summer Res, 73. *Mem:* Am Asn Clin Chem; Am Chem Soc; Acad Clin Lab Physicians & Scientists; Col Am Pathologists; Soc Math Biol. *Res:* Assessment of interferences in clinical chemistry; standardization of cholesterol determinations; biological roles of magnesium; dynamics of biological systems. *Mailing Add:* Dept Path Clin Chem Div Johns Hopkins Hosp 600 N Wolfe St Meyer B-125 Baltimore MD 21287-7065. *Fax:* 410-955-0767

KROLL, NORMAN MYLES, MATHEMATICAL PHYSICS. *Current Pos:* chmn dept, 63-65 & 83-88, prof, 62-91, EMER PROF PHYSICS, UNIV CALIF, SAN DIEGO, 91- *Personal Data:* b Tulsa, Okla, Apr 6, 22; m 45; c 4. *Educ:* Columbia Univ, AB, 42, AM, 43, PhD(physics), 48. *Prof Exp:* Asst physics, Columbia Univ, 42-44, mem sci staff, Radiation Lab, 43-62, from asst prof to prof physics, 49-62. *Concurrent Pos:* Nat Res Coun fel, Inst Advan Study, 48-50; Guggenheim fel, Rome, 55-56; Fulbright scholar, 55-56; mem staff, Jason Div, Inst Defense Anal, 60-81; NSF sr fel, Europ Orgn Nuclear Res, 65-66. *Mem:* Nat Acad Sci; fel Am Phys Soc; Am Acad Arts & Sci; Sigma Xi. *Res:* Nonlinear optics; microwave and nuclear physics; magnetron design; elementary particle theory; quantum field theory; free electron lasers; accelerator physics; plasma physics. *Mailing Add:* 9500 Gilman Dr MS 0319 La Jolla CA 92093-0319. *E-Mail:* nkroll@ucsd.edu

KROLL, ROBERT J, AEROSPACE & STRUCTURAL ENGINEERING. *Current Pos:* RETIRED. *Personal Data:* b Cincinnati, Ohio, May 1, 28; m 54, Marilyn A Wolfer; c Stephen, Kenneth, Gregory, James & Thomas. *Educ:* Univ Cincinnati, BS, 49, MS, 56; Mich State Univ, PhD(appl mech), 62. *Honors & Awards:* Weston Award, 49. *Prof Exp:* Engr reinforced concrete, Pollak Steel Co, 49-51; sr engr stress & design, Gen Elec Co, 52-57; asst prof aeronaut eng, Univ Cincinnati, actg head dept, 70-71 & 78-79, Bradley Jones prof aerospace eng, 75-82, prof aerospace eng, 57-95. *Concurrent Pos:* Consult, Gen Elec Corp, 57-, Univ Dayton Res Div, 62-63, Aeronca Mfg Corp, 64-, Rockwell Stand Corp, 64-, Cincinnati Shaper Co, 65- & Cincinnati Industs, 67-; NSF sci fac fel, 61-62; proj adv student design terms, 81-82 & 82-83. *Mem:* Assoc fel Am Inst Aeronaut & Astronaut; Soc Exp Mech; Am Soc Eng Educ; Sigma Xi. *Res:* Thermal stresses and stability; energy methods applied to lightweight structures; structural testing using strain gages and photostress; experimental wave propagation. *Mailing Add:* 2579 Beechmar Dr Cincinnati OH 45230-1204. *Fax:* 513-556-5038

KROM, MELVEN R, MATHEMATICS. *Current Pos:* Asst prof, 63-69, assoc prof, 69-76, PROF MATH, UNIV CALIF, DAVIS, 76- *Personal Data:* b Hospers, Iowa, Oct 4, 31; m 53. *Educ:* Univ Iowa, BA, 54, MS, 57; Univ Mich, PhD(math), 63. *Mem:* Asn Symbolic Logic; Math Asn Am; Am Math Soc. *Res:* Mathematical logic. *Mailing Add:* Dept Math Univ Calif Davis CA 95616-5224

KROMAN, RONALD AVRON, GENETICS. *Current Pos:* From asst prof to assoc prof, 59-69, PROF BIOL, CALIF STATE UNIV, LONG BEACH, 69- *Personal Data:* b Minneapolis, Minn, Mar 30, 27; m 62; c 3. *Educ:* Univ Minn, PhD(zool), 57. *Concurrent Pos:* Consult revision jr high & high sch math curricula, Sch Math Study Group & Calif State Dept Educ; statist consult, Arthritis Found, Mem Hosp, Long Beach, Calif; adj prof, Chapman Col, 75- *Mem:* Sigma Xi. *Res:* Soc Study Evolution; Am Genetic Asn; Genetics Soc Am; Am Inst Biol Sci; Sigma Xi. *Res:* Drosophila genetics; tumors; melanin metabolism; eye pigmentation; symbiotic associations in the Acarina. *Mailing Add:* Dept Biol Calif State Univ Long Beach CA 90840-0001

KROMANN, PAUL ROGER, PHYSICAL CHEMISTRY. *Current Pos:* ASST PROF CHEM, FT VALLEY STATE COL, 71- *Personal Data:* b Racine, Wis, Nov, 15, 29; m 60. *Educ:* Hope Col, AB, 52; Univ Calif, PhD, 57. *Prof Exp:* Chemist org synthesis, Hope Col, 52; asst chem, Univ Calif, 52-55; chemist, Plastics Fundamental Res Lab, Dow Chem USA, Mich, 57-71. *Mem:* Am Chem Soc. *Res:* Radiation chemistry; photochemistry; fluorescence lifetimes. *Mailing Add:* 348 Clairmont Dr Warner Robins GA 31088-5364

KROMANN, RODNEY P, ANIMAL NUTRITION, BIOENERGETICS. *Current Pos:* OWNER, KROMANN NUTRIT, 96- *Personal Data:* b Stockton, Calif, Sept 3, 31; m 79; c 4. *Educ:* Calif State Polytech Univ, BS, 58; Univ Calif, Davis, MS, 60, PhD(nutrit), 66. *Prof Exp:* Asst prof nutrit, NMex State Univ, 63-68; nutritionist, Shell Develop Co, 68-70; asst prof nutrit, Wash State Univ, 71-73, assoc prof, 73-78; pres, Nutrit Int, 78-93; dir feed formulations, Hubbard Milling Co, 93-; dir nutrit & res, Yoder Inc, 95-96; dir nutrit tech serv, DuCoa, 96. *Concurrent Pos:* Nutrit consult, 65-68. *Mem:* AAAS; Am Soc Animal Sci; Am Inst Nutrit; Am Dairy Sci Asn. *Res:*

Animal bioenergetics and nutrient and energy metabolism; mathematical modeling of protein and fat synthesis and of heat loss for the determination of maintenance by a radiometer. *Mailing Add:* 34195 CSAH 30 Grove City MN 56243

KROMBEIN, KARL VON VORSE, ENTOMOLOGY. *Current Pos:* chmn dept entom, Smithsonian Inst, 65-71, sr entomologist, 71-80, sr scientist, 80-93, EMER SCIENTIST, SMITHSONIAN INST, 93- *Personal Data:* b Buffalo, NY, May 26, 12; m 42, Dorothy Buckingham; c Kristin, Kyra & Karlissa. *Educ:* Cornell Univ, BS, 34, AM, 35, PhD(entom), 60; Univ Peradeniya, Sri Lanka, PhD(zool), 80. *Prof Exp:* Asst, NY State Exp Sta, 36-38; entomologist, Niagara Sprayer & Chem Co, NY, 39-40; assoc entomologist, Bur Entom & Plant Quarantine, USDA, 41-42, entomologist & invests leader, 46-65. *Concurrent Pos:* Civilian consult, Surgeon Gen, US Air Force, 72-79, emer consult, 79- *Mem:* Fel AAAS; corresp mem Am Entom Soc; hon mem Egyptian Entom Soc; fel Entom Soc Am. *Res:* Systematics, bionomics, ecology and behavior of Hymenoptera Aculeata (solitary wasps and bees). *Mailing Add:* Dept Entom NHB Stop 165 Smithsonian Inst Washington DC 20560

KROMER, LAWRENCE FREDERICK, NEUROBIOLOGY, NEURAL REGENERATION. *Current Pos:* AT GEORGETOWN UNIV, 85- *Personal Data:* b Sandusky, Ohio, Sept 1, 50. *Educ:* Univ Chicago, BA, 72, PhD(anat), 77. *Prof Exp:* Fel, Dept Histol, Univ Lung, Sweden, 77-79; asst res neuroscientist, Univ Calif, San Diego, 79-81; asst prof, Dept Anat & Neurobiol, Univ Vt, 81- *Concurrent Pos:* Prin investr, pvt found res grants, NIH, 79-; fel, A P Sloan Found, 80-86. *Mem:* Soc Neurosci; Int Soc Develop Neurosci; Am Asn Anatomists; AAAS. *Res:* Development and regeneration in the mammalian central nervous system by utilizing and intracephalic implantation technique which allows the transplantation of embryonic and neonatal neural tissue into the brain of neonatal and adult rodents. *Mailing Add:* Dept Anat & Cell Biol Georgetown Univ Med Dent Bldg 3900 Reservoir Rd NW Washington DC 20007-2187

KROMHOUT, ROBERT ANDREW, CHEMICAL PHYSICS. *Current Pos:* from asst prof to prof, 56-92, head dept, 60-62, EMER PROF PHYSICS, FLA STATE UNIV, 92- *Personal Data:* b Elgin, Ill, Oct 23, 23; m 50, Ora Morlier; c 3. *Educ:* Kans State Univ, BS, 47; Univ Ill, Urbana-Champaign, MS, 48, PhD(physics), 52. *Prof Exp:* Asst prof physics, Univ Ill, 52-56. *Mem:* Am Phys Soc; Am Asn Physics Teachers; Sigma Xi. *Res:* Phase transitions; statistical mechanics; intermolecular forces; Van der Waal's interactions, phase transitions, statistical mechanisms. *Mailing Add:* Dept Physics Fla State Univ Tallahassee FL 32306-3016

KROMM, DAVID ELWYN, WATER MANAGEMENT IN NORTH AMERICAN HIGH PLAINS. *Current Pos:* PROF GEOG, KANS STATE UNIV, 67- *Personal Data:* b Grosse Pointe, Mich, Sept 1, 38; m 60, Roberta Retzel; c David, Randall & Christopher. *Educ:* Eastern Mich Univ, BS, 60; Mich State Univ, MA, 64, PhD(geog), 67. *Concurrent Pos:* Happold vis prof, Univ Nebr, 83; vis prof, Lethbridge Univ, 90. *Mem:* Nat Coun Geog Educ; Asn Am Geogrs; Am Water Resources Asn; Am Asn Advan Slavic Studies. *Res:* Examine response to ogaliala aquifer depletion. *Mailing Add:* Geog Dept Kans State Univ 201 Dickens Hall Manhattan KS 66506-0801. *Fax:* 785-532-7310; *E-Mail:* Bitnet: krommgeo@ksuvm

KROMMINGA, ALBION JEROME, THEORETICAL PHYSICS. *Current Pos:* assoc prof, 65-69, PROF PHYSICS, CALVIN COL, 69- *Personal Data:* b Mille Lacs Co, Minn, June 20, 33; div; c 2. *Educ:* St Cloud State Col, BS, 55; Univ Minn, PhD(physics), 61. *Prof Exp:* Asst prof physics, Iowa State Univ, 61-63 & Idaho State Univ, 63-65. *Mem:* Am Phys Soc; Sigma Xi; Am Sci Affil. *Res:* Theory of electromagnetic, atomic, and nuclear reactions. *Mailing Add:* Dept Physics Calvin Col 3201 Burton St SE Grand Rapids MI 49546-4388

KRON, GERALD EDWARD, ASTRONOMY. *Current Pos:* RETIRED. *Personal Data:* b Milwaukee, Wis, Apr 6, 13; m 46; c 5. *Educ:* Univ Wis, BS, 33, MS, 34; Univ Calif, PhD(astrophys), 38. *Prof Exp:* Jr astronr, Lick Observ, Univ Calif, 38-42, asst astronr, 42-47, assoc astronr, 47-52, astronr, 52-65; dir, US Naval Observ, Flagstaff Sta, 65-73; sr res fel, Australian Nat Univ, 74-76. *Concurrent Pos:* Res assoc, Mass Inst Technol, 40-41 & Calif Inst Technol, 42-45; physicist, US Naval Ord Test Sta, Calif, 45; astron res, Pinecrest Observ, Flagstaff, Ariz, 76-85; Pinecrest Observ, Hawaii, 85- *Mem:* AAAS; Am Astron Soc; Int Astron Union; Royal Astron Soc. *Res:* Electronic camera research and development; investigation of integrated properties of globular clusters; distribution of interstellar reddening. *Mailing Add:* 2929 Poni Moi Rd Honolulu HI 96815

KRON, RICHARD G, ASTRONOMY. *Current Pos:* PROF, DEPT ASTRON & ASTROPHYS UNIV CHICAGO; DIR, YERKES OBSERV. *Res:* Astrophysics; astronomy. *Mailing Add:* 415 Grand View Ave Williams Bay WI 53191

KRONAUER, RICHARD ERNEST, MECHANICAL ENGINEERING, BIOMEDICAL PHYSICS. *Current Pos:* From instr to assoc prof, 51-64, PROF MECH ENG, HARVARD UNIV, 64- *Personal Data:* b Paterson, NJ, Aug 5, 25; m 48, Joanne Edwards; c 3. *Educ:* Stevens Inst Technol, MechEng, 47; Harvard Univ, SM, 48, PhD, 51. *Concurrent Pos:* Consult, Pratt & Whitney Aircraft Div, United Aircraft Corp, 51-58, Flow Corp, 53-67, Baldwin-Lima-Hamilton Corp, 56-61, Arthur D Little Co, 60-67 & Campbell-Kronauer Assoc, 80-95, Brigham & Women's Hosp, 91-; NSF fel, 64 & 71; NIH int fel, 78. *Mem:* Am Soc Mech Engrs; AAAS; Sleep Res Soc; Sigma Xi. *Res:* Fluid dynamics and turbulence; nonlinear oscillations; visual system information processing; human circadian oscillators. *Mailing Add:* 14 Chauncy St Unit 7 Cambridge MA 02138. *Fax:* 781-995-9837; *E-Mail:* kronauer@deas.harvard.edu

KRONBERG, PHILIPP PAUL, RADIO ASTRONOMY, ASTROPHYSICS. *Current Pos:* from asst prof to assoc prof, 68-78, PROF PHYS SCI & ASTRON, UNIV TORONTO, 78-, KILLAM RES FEL & PROF, 93- *Personal Data:* b Toronto, Ont, Sept 16, 39; m 63; c 3. *Educ:* Queen's Univ Kingston, BSc, 61, MSc, 63; Univ Manchester, PhD(physics), 67. *Hon Degrees:* DSc, Univ Manchester, 95. *Honors & Awards:* Humboldt Res Prize, 90. *Prof Exp:* Lectr physics, Univ Manchester & Jodrell Bank, 66-68. *Concurrent Pos:* Mem, Assoc Comt Astron, Nat Res Coun Can, 71-74, ed, 74; mem grant selection comt, Univ Astron & Space Res Can, 74-78; Alexander von Humboldt sr res fel, Max-Planck-Inst fur Radioastronomie, Ger, 75-77 & 90-91; sr von Humboldt fel, 75-77; mem, Univ Toronto Res Bd, 78-82; mem & chmn, VLA Adv Comt, 78-82; vis comt, US Nat Radio Astron Observ, 82; chmn, Nat Res Coun Millimetre Telescope Steering Comt, 83-84; Guggenheim fel, 85; chmn, Assoc Univ Inc; Killam fel, 93. *Mem:* Am Astron Soc; Int Astron Union; Can Astron Soc; Sigma Xi; Can Inst Int Affairs; Atlantic Coun Can. *Res:* Measurement and analysis of magnetic fields in space; structure of our galaxy; extragalactic astrophysics; radioastronomy; high-energy processes in space. *Mailing Add:* Dept Astron Univ Toronto 60 St George St Toronto ON CAN

KRONBERGER, KARLHEINZ, POLYMER CHEMISTRY, ORGANIC CHEMISTRY. *Current Pos:* sr res chemist, 68-78, sect mgr, 78-90, RES DEPT MGR, RES DIV, ROHM & HAAS CO, 90- *Personal Data:* b Vienna, Austria, Jan 24, 40. *Educ:* Vienna Tech Univ, Dipl Ing, 64; Univ Nebr, PhD(org chem), 67. *Prof Exp:* Res assoc, Mass Inst Technol, 67-68. *Mem:* Am Chem Soc. *Res:* Coatings and polymer research; aqueous polymers; acrylics. *Mailing Add:* Rohm & Haas Res Labs Spring House PA 19477

KRONE, LESTER H(ERMAN), JR, MANAGEMENT SCIENCE. *Current Pos:* MGR PROD PLANNING & MKT, MCDONNELL-DOUGLAS AUTOMATION CO, 73- *Personal Data:* b St Louis, Mo, Oct 8, 31; m 53; c 3. *Educ:* Wash Univ, BS, 52, DSc(chem eng), 55; Univ Ill, MS, 53. *Prof Exp:* Group leader process develop dept, Uranium Div, Mallinckrodt Chem Works, 55-56; appl sci rep, Int Bus Mach Corp, 56-57, mgr appl sci, Mo, 57-58; mgr oper anal, Monsanto Co, 58-68; independent consult, 68-73. *Concurrent Pos:* Lectr, Wash Univ; assoc prof, Southern Ill Univ. *Mem:* Asn Comput Mach; Am Inst Chem Engrs; Opers Res Soc Am; Inst Mgt Sci. *Res:* Applied mathematics; computer techniques; operations research; mathematical programming, statistics and simulation. *Mailing Add:* 749 Chatelet Woods Dr St Louis MO 63135

KRONE, RALPH WERNER, NUCLEAR PHYSICS. *Current Pos:* RETIRED. *Personal Data:* b Berlin, Ger, May 18, 19; US citizen; m 42; c 3. *Educ:* Antioch Col, BS, 42; Univ Ill, MS, 43; Johns Hopkins Univ, PhD, 49. *Prof Exp:* From asst prof to assoc prof, Univ Kans, 48-61, actg chmn dept, 65-66, prof physics, 61-82, prof physics & astron, 82. *Mem:* Fel Am Phys Soc. *Res:* Nuclear structure; spectroscopy of light and medium light nuclei. *Mailing Add:* Box 21 Washington NH 03280

KRONE, RAY B, HYDRAULIC & SANITARY ENGINEERING, TIDAL HYDRAULICS & SEDIMENT TRANSPORT. *Current Pos:* from assoc prof to prof, Univ Calif, Davis, 64-88, chmn, Dept Civil Eng, 68-72, assoc dean res, Col Eng, 72-88, EMER PROF CIVIL ENG, UNIV CALIF, DAVIS, 88- *Personal Data:* b Long Beach, Calif, June 7, 22; m 46, C Jane Baldrige; c C Ann & Ray B. *Educ:* Univ Calif, BS, 50, MS, 58, PhD(sanit eng), 62. *Honors & Awards:* H A Einstein Award, Am Soc Civil Engrs, Moffitt-Nichol Award. *Prof Exp:* From asst to assoc res engr, Univ Calif, Berkeley, 50-64, lectr, 62-64. *Concurrent Pos:* Consult, US Army Corps Engrs, 60-, Calif Atty Gen, 69- & engr firms. *Mem:* Nat Acad Eng; Am Geophys Union; fel AAAS; Am Soc Civil Engrs; Estuarine Res Fedn. *Res:* Soil science; sediment transport in estuaries, particle transport in surface and ground waters; properties of water; soil water relations. *Mailing Add:* Dept Civil & Environ Eng Univ Calif Davis CA 95616

KRONEBERGER, GERALD F, COMBUSTION & EMISSIONS, ENERGY EFFICIENCY. *Current Pos:* PRES, AAA/CSI, 84- *Personal Data:* b Chicago, Ill, Sept 7, 29; m 57, Kathryn B Stanton; c Diane, Cris & Kevin. *Educ:* Ill Tech, BS, 51; Pepperdine Univ, MBA, 79. *Prof Exp:* Sci & Prof Personnel Prog, USA/CC, 51-53; regional mgr, GATX, 53-64; tech dir, BSP/ ENVIRTECH/LURGI, 64-84. *Concurrent Pos:* Nat bd dirs & nat chmn, Environ Div, Am Inst Chem Eng, 74-76, ed, Nat Symposia Ser, 76; expert witness servs, AAA/CSI, 85- *Mem:* Fel Am Inst Chem Eng; Am Acad Environ Engrs; Water & Environ Fedn. *Res:* Extensive publications in thermal and combustion processes as well as environmental and reclamation processes; energy recovery and storage system; forensic expert services; awarded US & foreign patents. *Mailing Add:* 61 Montego Novato CA 94949. *Fax:* 415-883-6846

KRONENBERG, RICHARD SAMUEL, MEDICINE, PHYSIOLOGY. *Current Pos:* prof & chmn, Dept Med, 84-95, EXEC ASSOC DIR, CLIN AFFAIRS, UNIV TEX HEALTH CTR, 95- *Personal Data:* b Chicago, Ill, Aug 7, 38; m 63; c 3. *Educ:* Northwestern Univ, BA, 60, MD, 63. *Prof Exp:* USPHS res fel, Cardiovasc Res Inst, Med Ctr, Univ Calif, San Francisco, 68-70; asst prof, Pulmonary Div, Univ Minn Hosp, 70-74, assoc prof, 74-78, prof med & head, 78-84. *Concurrent Pos:* Consult, Vet Admin Hosp,

Minneapolis, 71-84. *Mem:* AAAS; Am Physiol Soc; fel Am Col Physicians; Am Fedn Clin Res; Am Thoracic Soc. *Res:* Repiratory physiology; pulmonary disease. *Mailing Add:* Dept Clin Affairs Univ Tex Health Ctr PO Box 2003 Tyler TX 75710-2003

KRONENBERG, STANLEY, NUCLEAR RADIATION PHYSICS. *Current Pos:* RES PHYSICIST, US ARMY COMMUN COMMAND, FT MONMOUTH, NJ, 53- *Personal Data:* b Krosno, Poland, May 3, 27; US citizen; m 53, Eva Kroupa; c Eric & Olga. *Educ:* Univ Vienna, PhD(physics), 52. *Concurrent Pos:* Consult, Fed Emergency Mgt Agency & Dept Energy; RSG Rep, NATO. *Mem:* Am Phys Soc. *Res:* Nuclear radiation detection; radiology; radiation imaging. *Mailing Add:* 42 Stouts Rd Skillman NJ 08558. Fax: 732-427-2667

KRONENTHAL, RICHARD LEONARD, POLYMER CHEMISTRY, SURGICAL DEVICES. *Current Pos:* PRES, KRONENTHAL ASSOCS, INC, 89- *Personal Data:* b New York, NY, Oct 6, 28; m 49; c 2. *Educ:* Brooklyn Col, BS, 51; Polytech Inst New York, PhD(chem), 55. *Prof Exp:* Sr proj chemist org chem, Colgate Palmolive Co, 54-57; mgr dept org & polymer chem, Ethicon, Inc, Johnson & Johnson, 57-68, assoc dir res, 68-72, dir res, 72-84, dir res & develop, 84-89. *Concurrent Pos:* Instr, Polytech Inst New York, 58-64. *Mem:* AAAS; Am Chem Soc; Am Soc Artificial Internal Organs; Am Inst Chem; Royal Soc Chem; Sigma Xi. *Res:* Chemistry of proteins; surgical devices; biomaterials; biodegradable polymers. *Mailing Add:* Kronenthal Assoc Inc 301 Rte 17 N Suite 800 Rutherford NJ 07070

KRONENWETT, FREDERICK RUDOLPH, BACTERIOLOGY. *Current Pos:* DIR, AM BIOL CONTROL LABS, 57- *Personal Data:* b Newark, NJ, July 29, 23; m 50; c 5. *Educ:* Upsala Col, BSc, 48; Rutgers Univ, MS, 50, PhD(dairy bact), 54. *Prof Exp:* Dir qual control, Hohneker Dairy Co, 54-57; fel, Rutgers Univ, 58; from instr to prof biol sci, Fairleigh Dickinson Univ, 58-89. *Concurrent Pos:* Lectr, Upsala Col, 58-59; chmn Adv Panel Biol Indicators, US Pharmacopeia, mem, Steril Comt, US Pharmacopeia XVIII; consult, Bergen Pines Hosp, 59; dir bioanal lab, NJ Bd Med Examr, 59; expert adv, Int Atomic Energy Agency, Vienna, 72; specialist microbiol, Am Soc Clin Pathologists, 65; fel, Upsala Col, 72- *Mem:* Am Soc Microbiol; Am Pub Health Asn; Inst Food Technologists; NY Acad Sci; Sigma Xi. *Res:* Identification of thermophilic bacteria; thermal death time studies on Brucella abortus; food poisoning; general microbiology; sterilization and disinfection; irradiation microbiology and dosimetry; medical device development; water microbiology. *Mailing Add:* PO Box 505 Tenafly NJ 07670

KRONER, KLAUS E(RLENDUR), INDUSTRIAL ENGINEERING, ENGINEERING GRAPHICS. *Current Pos:* RETIRED. *Personal Data:* b Gottingen, Ger, July 19, 26; nat US; m 59; c 2. *Educ:* Col Wooster, BA, 49; NY Univ, BEE, 57; Am Int Col, MBA, 62. *Honors & Awards:* Distinguished Serv Award, Graphics Div, Am Soc Eng Educ, 85. *Prof Exp:* Instr eng drawing, NY Univ, 50 & 51-55; instr eng graphics, Univ Maine, 55-57; from asst prof to assoc prof basic eng, Univ Mass Amherst, 57-69, assoc prof indust eng & opers res, 69-88, asst head, 81-86, emer prof indust eng & opers res, 87. *Concurrent Pos:* Res scientist, indust develop div, Ga Inst Technol, 71. *Mem:* Am Soc Eng Educ. *Res:* Computer graphics; engineering economy; plant location and layout; industrial development. *Mailing Add:* 30 Plumtree Rd Sunderland MA 01375

KRONFELD, DAVID SCHULTZ, NUTRITION, VETERINARY PHYSIOLOGY. *Current Pos:* from asst prof to assoc prof pharmacol, 60-67, chief sect nutrit, 81-88, PROF NUTRIT, SCH VET MED, UNIV PA, 67-, POULTRY MELLON PROF AGR & VET MED, 88- *Personal Data:* b Auckland, NZ, Nov 5, 28; m 57; c 2. *Educ:* Univ Queensland, BVSc, 52, BSc, 54, MVSc, 57, DSc(biochem), 72; Univ Calif, Davis, PhD(physiol), 59; Am Col Vet Internal Med, dipl, 73. *Hon Degrees:* MA, Univ Pa, 71. *Prof Exp:* Demonstr physiol, Univ Queensland, 53-54, lectr vet physiol, 54-57; lectr vet med, Univ Calif, Davis, 58-59, asst prof physiol, 59-60. *Mem:* Am Dairy Sci Asn; Am Physiol Soc; Am Vet Med Asn; Am Inst Nutrit. *Res:* Nutrition and high performance of exercise, growth, pregnancy and lactation; metabolic disorders, ketosis, hypercholesterolemia, hypoglycemia, hypocalcemia, hypomagnesemia; tracer methodology, kinetic analysis, regulatory models; preventive medicine, health economics. *Mailing Add:* Dept Animal & Poultry Sci Poly Tech & State Univ Blacksburg VA 24061-0306

KRONGELB, SOL, PHYSICS. *Current Pos:* CONSULT, 93- *Personal Data:* b Jersey City, NJ, Aug 15, 32; m 53, Gladys Steinfeld; c Harold, Philip & Lisa. *Educ:* NY Univ, BS, 53; Mass Inst Technol, MS, 55, PhD, 58. *Prof Exp:* Asst physics, Res Lab Electronics, Mass Inst Technol, 54-58; assoc, Int Bus Mach Corp, 58-60, mem res staff, 60-93, mgr device fabrication & magnetics, 86-93. *Mem:* Am Vacuum Soc; Inst Elec & Electronics Engrs; Electrochem Soc. *Res:* Microwave spectroscopy; paramagnetic resonance; parametric devices; semiconductor technology; thin film adhesion; deposition and properties of magnetic and glass thin films; device fabrication technology. *Mailing Add:* Greenlawn Rd Katonah NY 10536

KRONICK, PAUL LEONARD, SOLID-STATE PROPERTIES OF COLLAGEN, BIOMECHANICS OF SKIN. *Current Pos:* LEAD SCIENTIST, AGR RES & ECONS SERV, USDA, 82- *Personal Data:* b North Adams, Mass, Oct 19, 31; m, Jane Collier; c Rani, Oren & Ivar. *Educ:* Williams Col, AB, 53; Yale Univ, PhD(chem), 57. *Prof Exp:* Res chemist, E I Dupont de Nemours, Inc, 58-60; prin scientist, Franklin Inst, 60-82. *Concurrent Pos:* Fulbright res scholar, Norweg Radium Hosp, 68-69; fel, NIH, 71-73; vis lectr, Robert Wood Johnson Found, Univ Pa, 71-73, assoc med, Med Sch, 74-79; prin investr, NIH, 71-81, Clamer Fund, 77-79, Benners Fund, 78-79; EMBO fel, Norsk Hydro Inst Cancer Res, 78; consult, FMC Corp, 80-82, Armstrong Cork, Inc, 82, AAAS, 86-88; assoc ed, J Am Leather Chemists Asn, 92- *Mem:* Am Chem Soc; AAAS; Sigma Xi; NY Acad Sci; Am Leather Chemists Asn. *Res:* Connective tissue biophysics and collagen-platelet interactions; applies basic biophysics to making useful products from animal connective tissue; magnetophoretic cell separation. *Mailing Add:* 721 Millbrook Lane Haverford PA 19041. *E-Mail:* pkronick@arserrc.gov

KRONK, HUDSON V, MATHEMATICS. *Current Pos:* asst prof, 64-68, ASSOC PROF MATH, STATE UNIV NY, BINGHAMTON, 68- *Personal Data:* b Port Jervis, NY, Oct 6, 38; m 59; c 3. *Educ:* Rensselaer Polytech Inst, BS, 59; Mich State Univ, MS, 60, PhD(math), 64. *Prof Exp:* Lectr math, Kalamazoo Col, 63. *Mem:* Am Math Soc; Math Asn Am. *Res:* Graph theory. *Mailing Add:* Dept Math State Univ NY PO Box 6000 Binghamton NY 13902-6000

KRONMAL, RICHARD AARON, BIOSTATISTICS. *Current Pos:* From instr to assoc prof, 64-75, chmn biomath group, 73-85, PROF BIOSTATIST, SCH PUB HEALTH, UNIV WASH, 75- *Personal Data:* b Los Angeles, Calif, May 3, 39; m 60; c 3. *Educ:* Univ Calif, Los Angeles, AB, 61, PhD(biostatist), 64. *Concurrent Pos:* Career develop award, 68-73; mem, Renal Cardiovasc Ad Comt, Food & Drug Admin; mem, Epidemiol Study Sect, NIH. *Mem:* Fel Am Statist Asn; Soc Study Human Biol; AAAS; Biomet Soc. *Res:* Mathematical statistics; statistical computing; public health and epidemiology. *Mailing Add:* Dept Biostatist SC 32 Univ Wash 2900 Seventh Ave NE Seattle WA 98195-0001

KRONMAN, JOSEPH HENRY, anatomy, dentistry, for more information see previous edition

KRONMAN, MARTIN JESSE, PHYSICAL CHEMISTRY. *Current Pos:* PROF BIOCHEM, STATE UNIV NY UPSTATE MED CTR, 68- *Personal Data:* b New York, NY, Sept 30, 27; m 65; c 3. *Educ:* Rutgers Univ, BS, 50; Temple Univ, PhD, 55. *Honors & Awards:* Chem of Milk Award, Am Chem Soc, 68. *Prof Exp:* Nat Heart Inst fel, Purdue Univ, 55-56; phys chemist, Eastern Regional Res Lab, USDA, 56-61; head biochem lab, US Army Natick Labs, 61-68. *Mem:* AAAS; Am Chem Soc; Am Soc Biol Chemists. *Res:* Physico-chemical properties of proteins and nucleic acids; theory and technique of light scattering; optical rotation dispersion, absorption and emission spectra as applied to biological macromolecules; protein denaturation in enzyme action. *Mailing Add:* 100 Dewitt Rd Syracuse NY 13214-2005

KRONSTAD, WARREN ERVIND, GENETICS, AGRONOMY. *Current Pos:* from instr to assoc prof genetics & agron, 59-72, distinguished prof plant genetics, 89, PROF PLANT BREEDING & AGRON CROP SCI, ORE STATE UNIV, 72-, DIR GENETICS INST. *Personal Data:* b Bellingham, Wash, Mar 3, 32; m 52; c 4. *Educ:* Wash State Univ, BS, 57, MS, 59; Ore State Univ, PhD(crop sci, genetics), 63. *Honors & Awards:* Alexander von Humboldt Award, 81; Presidential End Hunger Award; Crop Sci Award, Crop Sci Soc Am, 83. *Prof Exp:* Sr exp aide genetics, Wash State Univ, 59. *Concurrent Pos:* Consult, US AID, Turkey, 67-, Washington, DC, 69, Ecuador, Korea, & Peoples Repub China; Nixon & Fergusson distinguished prof. *Mem:* Fel Am Soc Agron; fel Crop Sci Soc Am; Sigma Xi; fel AAAS. *Res:* Cereal improvement; environment-genotype interaction; use of biometrical models to partition genetic variation; disease resistance; influence of chelating agents on genetic recombination; aluminum tolerance in plants. *Mailing Add:* Dept Crop Sci & Soil Sci Ore State Univ 231 Crop Sci Bldg Corvallis OR 97331-7307

KRONSTEIN, KARL MARTIN, ALGEBRA. *Current Pos:* from instr to asst prof, 58-69, ASSOC PROF MATH, UNIV NOTRE DAME, 69- *Personal Data:* b Heidelberg, Ger, Feb 9, 28; US citizen; m 60; c 3. *Educ:* Georgetown Univ, BS, 51; Harvard Univ, AM, 52, PhD(math), 64. *Prof Exp:* Instr math, Reed Col, 57-58. *Concurrent Pos:* NATO res fel, Univ Frankfurt, 64-65. *Mem:* Am Math Soc; Math Asn Am; Sigma Xi. *Res:* Finite group theory, particularly Schur index. *Mailing Add:* 1328 E Wayne St South Bend IN 46615

KRONTIRIS-LITOWITZ, JOHANNA KAYE, INVERTEBRATE NEUROBIOLOGY, CENTRAL REGULATION OF CARDIOVASCULAR FUNCTION. *Current Pos:* ASST PROF, YOUNGSTOWN STATE UNIV, 88- *Personal Data:* b Wheeling, WVa, June 7, 52; m 77, Harvey Litowitz; c 3. *Educ:* Case Western Res Univ, BS, 74, MS, 77; Cleveland State Univ, PhD(regulatory biol), 83. *Prof Exp:* Postdoctoral fel, Baylor Col Med, 83-85 & Univ Tex Med Ctr, Houston, 85-87. *Mem:* Sigma Xi; Soc Neurosci; Asn Women Sci; Women Neurosci; Am Physiol Soc. *Res:* Regulation of cardiovascular function and stress-evoked humoral responses in molluses especially Aplysia Californica. *Mailing Add:* Dept Biol Sci Youngstown State Univ 410 Wick Ave Youngstown OH 44555. *Fax:* 330-742-1483

KRONZON, ITZHAK, ECHOCARDIOGRAPHY, DOPPLER. *Current Pos:* Assoc prof, 78-83, PROF CLIN MED, NY UNIV, 83- *Personal Data:* b Haifa, Israel, Sept 14, 39; US citizen; m 60; c 3. *Educ:* Hebrew Univ, MD, 64; Am Col Physicians, dipl, 79 & 81. *Concurrent Pos:* Vis prof, Tel Aviv Univ, 87-, Hebrew Univ, Jerusalem, 89- *Mem:* AMA; Am Heart Asn; Am Soc Echocardiography; fel Am Col Physicians; fel Am Col Cardiol; fel Am Col Chest Physicians. *Res:* Clinical applications of computorized technologies in the non-invasive diagnosis and evaluation of heart diseases; hemodynamics; angiography; cardiac imaging; non-invasive cardiology. *Mailing Add:* 550 First Ave New York NY 10016-6402

KROODSMA, DONALD EUGENE, ANIMAL COMMUNICAION, BEHAVIORAL ECOLOGY. *Current Pos:* assoc prof, 80-87, PROF ZOOL, UNIV MASS, AMHERST, 87- *Personal Data:* b Zeeland, Mich, July 7, 46; m 68; c 3. *Educ:* Hope Col, BA, 68; Ore State Univ, PhD(zool), 72. *Prof Exp:* Fel, animal behav, Rockefeller Univ, 72-74, asst prof, 74-80. *Concurrent Pos:* Mem adv panel, psychobiol, NSF, 80, 85-88 & prin investr, grants, 76- *Mem:* Fel Am Ornithologists Union; fel Animal Behav Soc; Cooper Ornith Soc. *Res:* Diversity of vocal behaviors among birds; development, evolution, and functions of these diverse vocal communication systems. *Mailing Add:* Dept Biol Univ Mass Amherst MA 01003-0027

KROODSMA, ROGER LEE, WILDLIFE ECOLOGY, ORNITHOLOGY. *Current Pos:* mgr environ impacts prog, 77-79, MEM RES STAFF, ENVIRON SCI DIV, OAK RIDGE NAT LAB, 74- *Personal Data:* b Zeeland, Mich, Jan 23, 44; div; c 3. *Educ:* Hope Col, BA, 66; ND State Univ, MS, 68, PhD(zool), 70. *Prof Exp:* Asst prof biol, Union Univ, Jackson, Tenn, 70-73; res assoc ecol, Univ Ga, Athens, 73-74. *Mem:* Wildlife Soc; Am Ornithologists Union. *Res:* Community ecology of birds in man-affected habitats, such as transmission line rights-of-way and pine plantations; edge effect. *Mailing Add:* 113 N Seneca Rd Oak Ridge TN 37830

KROOK, LENNART PER, VETERINARY PATHOLOGY. *Current Pos:* assoc prof, 59-65, PROF VET PATH, NY STATE COL VET MED, CORNELL UNIV, 65-, ASSOC DEAN POSTDOCTORAL EDUC, 81- *Personal Data:* b Eksh-rad, Sweden, Aug 28, 24; m 58; c 2. *Educ:* Royal Vet Col Sweden, DVM, 53, PhD(vet path), 57. *Prof Exp:* From asst prof to assoc prof vet path, Royal Vet Col Sweden, 51-57; assoc prof, Res Inst Nat Defense, Sundbyberg, 58; assoc prof, Sch Vet Med, Kans State Univ, 58-59. *Mem:* Am Inst Nutrit; Int Acad Path; Sigma Xi. *Res:* Nutritional pathology. *Mailing Add:* Dept Path NY State Col Vet Med Cornell Univ Ithaca NY 14853-0001

KROON, JAMES LEE, SCIENCE EDUCATION. *Current Pos:* assoc prof, 69-79, PROF CHEM, BETHEL COL, 79- *Personal Data:* b Grand Rapids, Mich, Apr 24, 26; m 52; c 3. *Educ:* Calvin Col, AB, 48; Purdue Univ, MS, 51, PhD(chem), 54. *Prof Exp:* Asst, Purdue Univ, 48-51; chemist, Dow Chem Co, 53-58, proj leader, 58-69. *Mem:* Am Chem Soc; Sigma Xi; Am Sci Affiliation. *Res:* Polarography; electrochemistry; aerosols. *Mailing Add:* 56211 Harman Dr Mishawaka IN 46544

KROON, PAULUS ARIE, PHYSICAL BIOCHEMISTRY. *Current Pos:* ASSOC PROF BIOCHEM, UNIV QUEENSLAND, 89-, DIR, CTR PROTEIN STRUCT, FUNCTION & ENG, 95- *Personal Data:* b Rotterdam, Neth, June 1, 45; US citizen; m 68, Ferguson; c Lisa, Natasha & Joanna. *Educ:* Univ Auckland, BS, 67, MS, 68; Calif Inst Technol, PhD(chem), 75. *Prof Exp:* Res assoc, Life Sci Dept, Univ Pittsburgh, 75-77; sr res fel, Merck Res Lab, 77-89. *Concurrent Pos:* Res scientist, Biosci Div, Jet Propulsion Lab, 70-73. *Mem:* Australian Soc Biochem & Molecular Biol; Am Soc Biochem & Molecular Biol; Am Heart Asn. *Res:* Structure and function of lipoproteins and their receptors, protein engineering. *Mailing Add:* Dept Biochem Univ Queensland St Lucia Qld 4072 Australia. *Fax:* 617-3365-4699; *E-Mail:* pkroon@biosci.uq.edu.au

KROONTJE, WYBE, AGRONOMY. *Current Pos:* assoc prof, 56-74, PROF AGRON, VA POLYTECH INST & STATE UNIV, 74- *Personal Data:* b Rotterdam, Neth, Aug 2, 22; nat US; m 48; c 1. *Educ:* Cornell Univ, BS, 51; Univ Nebr, MS, 53, PhD(soils), 56. *Prof Exp:* Asst, Univ Nebr, 51-56. *Concurrent Pos:* Prof & chmn dept soil sci, Ataturk Univ, Turkey, 63-65. *Mem:* Am Soc Agron; Soil Sci Soc Am; Int Soil Sci Soc; Turkish Soil Sci Soc. *Res:* Soil fertility and management of tobacco, soybeans and field crops; transformation and uptake of nitrogen; development of agronomic and higher education. *Mailing Add:* 5 Dogwood Circle Blacksburg VA 24060

KROP, STEPHEN, PHARMACOLOGY, TOXICOLOGY. *Current Pos:* CONSULT, 79- *Personal Data:* b New York, NY, Sept 24, 11; m 34, Mary Lulick; c Elaine S, Marianne E, Paul N & Thomas M. *Educ:* George Washington Univ, BS, 39; Georgetown Univ, MS, 40; Cornell Univ, PhD(pharmacol), 42. *Prof Exp:* Asst pharmacol, Med Col, Cornell Univ, 39-42, instr, 42-44; from instr to asst prof, Sch Med, Yale Univ, 44-46; chief pharmacol sect, Med Div, Army Chem Ctr, Md, 46-48, dep chief physiol div, Chem Corps Med Labs, 52-57; assoc mem, Squibb Inst Med Res, 48-49; dir pharmacol div, Warner Inst Therapeut Res, Div Warner-Hudnut, Inc, 49-51; res assoc & asst dir chem-biol coord ctr, Nat Res Coun, 51-52; chief pharmacol dept & pres, Ethicon Res Found Div, Johnson & Johnson Co, NJ, 57-63; chief drug pharmacol br, US Food & Drug Admin, 63-79. *Concurrent Pos:* Prof lectr, Med Sch, Georgetown Univ, 51-58 & 63-67; spec lectr, Med Sch, Univ Md, 52-57. *Mem:* Soc Toxicol; Am Soc Pharmacol & Exp Therapeut; Soc Exp Biol & Med; Am Physiol Soc; Harvey Soc; Sigma Xi. *Res:* Pharmacology of central nervous system; circulation; nerve-muscle; smooth muscle; local anesthetics; respiration; toxicology; chemical warfare agents. *Mailing Add:* 7908 Birnam Wood Dr McLean VA 22102-2744

KROPF, ALLEN, BIOPHYSICAL CHEMISTRY. *Current Pos:* from instr to assoc prof, 58-68, PROF NAT SCI, 85- *Personal Data:* b Queens, NY, Oct 3, 29; m 50, Rita Berliner; c Noel, Julie & Aaron. *Educ:* Queens Col, NY, BS, 51; Univ Utah, PhD(chem), 54. *Hon Degrees:* MA, Amherst Col, 69. *Prof Exp:* Chemist, Appl Physics Lab, Johns Hopkins Univ, 54-56; Am Cancer Soc res fel chem vision, Harvard Univ, 56-58. *Concurrent Pos:* NSF sci fac fel, Univ Calif, Berkeley, 62-63; NIH spec res fel, Weizmann Inst Sci, 68-69; mem Visual Sci Sect, NIH, 73-77; vis prof biophys, Kyoto Univ, 75-76; vis prof phys chem, Hebrew Univ, 76; assoc chmn, Gordon Conf Visual Transduction, 78, 80; vis scholar biol, Harvard Univ, 82-83; vis scientist, Membrane Sci, Weizmann Inst Sci, 86-87, Hebrew Univ, 91. *Res:* Photochemistry of visual pigments; preparation and properties of visual pigments; chemistry of olfaction. *Mailing Add:* Dept Chem Amherst Col Amherst MA 01002. *Fax:* 413-542-2735; *E-Mail:* akropf@amherst

KROPF, DONALD HARRIS, MEAT SCIENCE, ANIMAL HUSBANDRY. *Current Pos:* assoc prof, 62-72, PROF ANIMAL SCI & MEAT RES SCI, KANS STATE UNIV, 72- *Personal Data:* b Watertown, Wis, Mar 8, 31; m 62, Gwendolyn Slover; c Gregory, Bradley & Martha. *Educ:* Univ Wis, BS, 52, PhD(animal husb), 57; Univ Fla, MS, 53. *Prof Exp:* Res asst meat sci, Univ Fla, 52-53 & Univ Wis, 53-56; asst prof animal husb, Clemson Col, 58-62. *Mem:* Fel AAAS; Am Soc Animal Sci; Am Meat Sci Asn; Inst Food Technologists; Int Asn Milk, Food, Environ Sanit. *Res:* Meat color; effect of freezing system and rate packaging, display temperature and lighting on color; muscle histochemistry; carcass and live animal evaluation; processing and quality control. *Mailing Add:* Dept Animal Sci & Indust Kans State Univ Call Hall Manhattan KS 66506

KROPP, JAMES EDWARD, ORGANIC CHEMISTRY. *Current Pos:* SR RES SPECIALIST, MINN MINING & MFG CO, 67- *Personal Data:* b Chicago, Ill, July 25, 39; m 61; c 4. *Educ:* Wabash Col, BA, 61; Univ Colo, PhD(org chem), 65. *Prof Exp:* Res chemist, Film Dept, E I du Pont de Nemours, Inc, 65-67. *Mem:* Am Chem Soc. *Res:* Organic synthesis, mechanisms, stereochemistry; polymer synthesis, mechanisms, morphology, solvent effects; rheology; adhesion; new product development, marketing and production. *Mailing Add:* 675 Eldridge Ave St Paul MN 55117

KROPP, JOHN LEO, PHYSICAL CHEMISTRY, SPECTROSCOPY. *Personal Data:* b Salem, Ore, June 26, 34; m 59, Joann Laure; c David, Michael, Daniel & Rachel. *Educ:* Univ Santa Clara, BS, 56; Univ Notre Dame, PhD(phys chem), 61. *Prof Exp:* Res assoc radiation lab, Univ Notre Dame, 61-62; mem tech staff, TRW Space & Technol Group, 62-80, sr proj engr, 80-84, proj mgr, 84-92. *Mem:* AAAS; Sigma Xi; Am Inst Aeronaut & Astronaut. *Res:* Photochemistry of large organic molecules, especially fluorescence and phosphorescence of aromatic hydrocarbons; microgravity research experiment development; development of instrument systems especially space-oriented instruments; cost modelling of space communication and sensor systems. *Mailing Add:* 315 Via San Sebastian Redondo Beach CA 90277-6659

KROPP, PAUL JOSEPH, ORGANIC CHEMISTRY. *Current Pos:* chmn, Curric Appl Sci, 84-91, PROF CHEM, UNIV NC, CHAPEL HILL, 70- *Personal Data:* b Springfield, Ohio, June 29, 35; m 63, Patricia M Morrissey; c David E & Sonia M. *Educ:* Univ Notre Dame, BS, 57; Univ Wis, PhD(org chem), 62. *Prof Exp:* Res chemist, Procter & Gamble Co, 61-70. *Concurrent Pos:* Alfred P Sloan Found res fel, 72; vis prof, Univ Calif, Los Angeles, 77-78, Univ Bordeaux, 82 & Duke Univ, 89-90. *Mem:* Am Chem Soc. *Res:* Photochemistry; surface-mediated reactions; organic synthesis. *Mailing Add:* Dept Chem Univ NC Chapel Hill NC 27599-3290. *E-Mail:* kropp@unc.edu

KROPP, WILLIAM RUDOLPH, JR, COSMIC RAY PHYSICS, ELEMENTARY PARTICLE PHYSICS. *Current Pos:* asst res physicist, Univ Calif, 66-67, asst res physics, 67-73, assoc res physicist 73-80, RES PHYSICIST, UNIV CALIF, IRVINE, 80- *Personal Data:* b Chicago, Ill, Nov 10, 36; div; c Marianne & Kathryn. *Educ:* DePaul Univ, BS, 58; Case Inst Technol, PhD(physics), 64. *Honors & Awards:* Rossi Prize, Am Astrophys Soc, 89. *Prof Exp:* Res assoc, Case Inst Technol, 64-66. *Mem:* Am Phys Soc. *Res:* Low background detection systems; neutrino interactions; cosmic rays. *Mailing Add:* Dept Physics Univ Calif Irvine CA 92697-4575. *E-Mail:* wkropp@vci.edu

KROPSCHOT, RICHARD H, CRYOGENICS, SOLID STATE PHYSICS. *Current Pos:* assoc dir energy sci, Lawrence Berkeley Lab, 85-90, LIAISON OFFICER, OFF PRES, UNIV CALIF, 90- *Personal Data:* b Kalamazoo, Mich, May 25, 27; m 50, Claire Mills; c Susan & Anne. *Educ:* Mich State Univ, BS, 48, MS, 50, PhD(physics), 59. *Honors & Awards:* Exceptional Serv Award, US Dept Com. *Prof Exp:* Res engr low temp res, NAm Aviation Co, 50-51; physicist, Nat Bur Stand, Boulder, Colo, 51-79; dir, Off Basic Energy Sci, US Dept Energy, 79-85. *Concurrent Pos:* Guest prof, ETH, Zurich, 64-65; adj prof, Univ Colo, Boulder, 69-79. *Mem:* Fel Am Phys Soc. *Res:* Solid state research at low temperatures; cryogenic engineering; properties of liquid helium; superconductivity and superconducting magnets. *Mailing Add:* 929 Calle Arco Santa Fe NM 87501. *Fax:* 505-667-0365; *E-Mail:* kropschot@lanl.gov

KROSCHEWSKY, JULIUS RICHARD, BOTANY, PHYTOCHEMISTRY. *Current Pos:* ASST DIR, EDWARD'S AQUIFER RES & DATA CTR, SOUTHWESTERN UNIV, 88- *Personal Data:* b Taylor, Tex, Dec 14, 24; m 46; c 3. *Educ:* Univ Tex, BA, 47, MA, 49, PhD(bot), 67. *Prof Exp:* Instr biol, Lee Col, Tex, 49-52, Odessa Col, 54-59 & high sch, Calif, 60-61; asst prof, St Edward's Univ, 61-67; prof biol, Bloomsburg State Col, 67-87. *Mem:* AAAS; Phytochem Soc NAm. *Res:* Determination of structures and taxonomic significances of flavonoid compounds of plants; plant tissue culture studies. *Mailing Add:* 2935 Philo St San Marcos TX 78666

KROSS, ROBERT DAVID, POLYMER CHEMISTRY, ANALYTICAL CHEMISTRY. *Current Pos:* PRES, KROSS-LINK LABS, 81- *Personal Data:* b Brooklyn, NY, Apr 25, 31; m 52; c 2. *Educ:* Brooklyn Col, BS, 52; Iowa State Col, PhD(phys chem), 56. *Prof Exp:* Anal group leader, Rayonier Inc,

57-59; chief chemist, Food & Drug Res Labs, 59-66; res dir, Foster D Snell, 66-69; dir, Kross Ref Lab, 69-80; vpres & dir res, Hydro Optics Inc, 73-80; vpres, Mkt-Tech Indust Ltd, 81-83. *Concurrent Pos:* Vpres & dir res, Alcide Corp, 84-91. *Res:* Consulting and analysis in nutrition, pharmaceuticals, cosmetics, plastics and polymers; life sciences; biochemistry; infrared spectroscopy; physical analytical chemistry; federal regulations pertaining to chemically-oriented products; environmental sciences; microbiocidal systems for pharmaceutical, food and environmental applications. *Mailing Add:* 2506 Florin Ct Bellmore NY 11710

KROTHE, NOEL C, GEOLOGY. *Current Pos:* asst prof, 76-81, ASSOC PROF GEOL, IND UNIV, 81- *Personal Data:* b Shickshinny, Pa, May 22, 38. *Educ:* Bloomsburg State Univ, BS, 61; Ind Univ, MAT, 69; Penn State Univ, MS, 73, PhD(geol), 76. *Prof Exp:* Teacher, sci, Tarrytown, NY & Baltimore, Md, 61-68. *Mem:* Fel Geol Soc Am; Int Asn Hydrologists. *Res:* Chemical aspects of hydrology; isotopes in ground water. *Mailing Add:* Dept Geol Ind Univ Bloomington IN 47405

KROTKOV, ROBERT VLADIMIR, ATOMIC PHYSICS. *Current Pos:* assoc prof, 66-73, PROF PHYSICS, UNIV MASS, AMHERST, 73- *Personal Data:* b Toronto, Ont, July 17, 29; m 58; c 4. *Educ:* Queen's Univ, Ont, BA, 51, MA, 52; Princeton Univ, PhD, 58. *Prof Exp:* Instr physics, Palmer Lab, Princeton Univ, 56-58, res asst, 58-60; from instr to asst prof, Yale Univ, 60-66. *Mem:* Am Phys Soc; Sigma Xi. *Res:* Relativity and gravitation. *Mailing Add:* Dept Physics Univ Mass Hasbrouck Lab Amherst MA 01003

KROTO, HAROLD WALTER, CHEMISTRY. *Current Pos:* lectr, Univ Sussex, Eng, 68-77, reader, 77-85, prof chem, 85-91, ROYAL SOC RES PROF, UNIV SUSSEX, ENG, 91- *Personal Data:* b Oct 7, 39; m 63, Margaret H Hunter; c 2. *Honors & Awards:* Nobel Prize in Chem, 96; Tilden Lectr, 81-82; Int New Mat Prize, Am Phys Soc, 92; Italgas Prize Innovation Chem, 92; Longstaff Medal, Royal Soc Chem, 93. *Prof Exp:* Postdoctoral fel, Nat Registry Clin Chem, 64-66; res scientist, Bell Tel Labs, NJ, 66-67. *Res:* Contributed many articles to professional journals. *Mailing Add:* Sch Chem & Molecular Sci Falmer Univ Sussex Brighton Sussex BN1 9QJ England

KROTOSK, DANUTA MARIA, research administration, for more information see previous edition

KROUSE, HOWARD ROY, PHYSICS, CHEMISTRY. *Current Pos:* prof physics & chmn dept, 71-97, EMER PROF, UNIV CALGARY, 97- *Personal Data:* b Norfolk Co, Ont, Jan 8, 35; m 58; c 2. *Educ:* McMaster Univ, BSc, 56, PhD(physics), 60. *Prof Exp:* From asst prof to prof physics, Univ Alta, 60-71, asst chmn dept 70-71. *Concurrent Pos:* NATO fel & res assoc, Univ Calif, San Diego, 66-67; exchange scientist, USSR, 69; vis scientist, Japan, 71; res grants, Nat Res Coun Can, Defence Res Bd Can & Geol Surv Can. *Mem:* AAAS; Am Geophys Union; Am Phys Soc; Geochem Soc; Can Asn Physicists; Sigma Xi. *Res:* Isotope fractionation studies in physical, geological, chemical, biological and environmental processes; mass spectrometry. *Mailing Add:* Dept Physics Univ Calgary 2500 Universityy Dr Calgary AB T2N 1N4 Can

KROUSKOP, THOMAS ALAN, BIOENGINEERING, BIOMATERIALS. *Current Pos:* assoc prof, 78-87, PROF, BAYLOR COL MED, 87- *Personal Data:* b Washington, DC, July 11, 45; m 68, Arlene A Swatsworth; c Peter E, Barbara J & Mark A. *Educ:* Carnegie Inst Technol, BS, 67; Carnegie-Mellon Univ, MS, 69, PhD(civil eng, biotechnol), 71. *Honors & Awards:* BCM Res Achievement Award, 87; Koziak Award, 93. *Prof Exp:* Design engr, Gen Analytics Inc, 68; from asst to assoc prof bioeng, Tex A&M Univ, 71-78. *Concurrent Pos:* Adj prof, Tex Woman's Univ, 87-, Rice Univ, 90- & Univ Tex Dent Sch, 95- *Mem:* Am Soc Testing & Mat; Rehab Eng Soc NAm. *Res:* Design of prosthetic appliances; materials for use as medical implants; effects of mechanical stress on soft tissue metabolism; development of assistive devices for the physically handicapped. *Mailing Add:* 11915 Meadowtrail Lane 1333 Moursund Ave Stafford TX 77477. *E-Mail:* krouskop@bcm.tmc.edu

KROW, GRANT REESE, ORGANIC CHEMISTRY. *Current Pos:* from asst prof to assoc prof, 69-80, PROF CHEM, TEMPLE UNIV, 80- *Personal Data:* b Reading, Pa, June 30, 41; m 70; c 2. *Educ:* Albright Col, BS, 63; Princeton Univ, MFA, 64, PhD(chem), 67; Temple Univ, JD, 78. *Honors & Awards:* Golden Key, Nat Honor Soc. *Prof Exp:* Res assoc chem, Ohio State Univ, 67-69. *Concurrent Pos:* Sci & legal consult, 78- *Mem:* Am Chem Soc; Sigma Xi. *Res:* Stereochemistry; chemistry of heterocycles; synthetic methods applied to natural products. *Mailing Add:* Dept Chem Temple Univ Philadelphia PA 19122. *Fax:* 215-204-1532

KROWN, SUSAN E, MEDICAL ONCOLOGY, AIDS RESEARCH. *Current Pos:* fel med oncol & clin immunol, Mem Sloan Kettering Cancer Ctr, 74-77, res assoc immunbiol, Sloan Kettering Inst Cancer Res, 77-84, assoc prof, 83-94, assoc mem med, 84-94, MEM MED, MEM SLOAN KETTERING CANCER CTR, CORNELL UNIV, 94-, PROF MED, 94- *Personal Data:* b Bronx, NY, Sept 8, 46; div; c Catherine Pitt. *Educ:* Barnard Col, AB, 67; State Univ NY Downstate Med Ctr, MD, 71. *Honors & Awards:* Milstein Award, 95. *Prof Exp:* Intern internal med, Mt Sinai Hosp, NY, 71-72, resident, 72-74. *Concurrent Pos:* Clin asst & asst attend physician med, Mem Hosp, 77-82, assoc attend, 82-; mem, Oncol Drugs Adv Comt, US Food & Drug Admin, 86-90, consult, 90-96; vchair, Oncol Comt, AIDS Clin Trials Group, Nat Inst Allergy & Infectious Dis, NIH, 87-89, chair, 90-92; adv bd, Cancer Treat Reports, 84-87; bd dirs, Soc Biol Ther, 86-89; mem ed bd, J Interferon Res, J AIDS; mem, Int Soc Interferon Res; chair, AIDS Task Force, Mem Sloan Kettering Cancer Ctr, 89-; mem, AIDS Clin Drug Discovery Comt, NIH, 90-92. *Mem:* Am Asn Cancer Res; Am Soc Clin Oncol; AAAS; Soc Biol Ther; Int Soc Interferon Res. *Res:* Clinical investigations of biological agents and antivirals in the treatment of cancer and AIDS; mechanisms of action of biological response modifiers; identification of immunological prognostic parameters in cancer and AIDS. *Mailing Add:* Mem Hosp 1275 York Ave New York NY 10021. *E-Mail:* krowns@mskcc.org

KRSTENANSKY, JOHN LEONARD, MEDICINAL CHEMISTRY, PEPTIDE CHEMISTRY. *Current Pos:* RES SECT LEADER, SYNTEX, 91- *Personal Data:* b Chicago, Ill, Sept 8, 55. *Educ:* Loyola Univ, Chicago, AB & BS, 77; Univ Ill, Chicago, PhD(med chem), 83. *Prof Exp:* Res assoc, Univ Ariz, 83-85; sr res biochemist, Marion Merrell Dow, 85-91. *Concurrent Pos:* Lectr med chem peptides, Univ Calif, Berkeley Extension, 94. *Mem:* Am Chem Soc; Sigma Xi; Am Peptide Soc; Europ Peptide Soc; NY Acad Sci; Philos Sci Asn. *Res:* Design of peptides and peptide mimetics for therapeutic applications. *Mailing Add:* 3455 Rambow Dr Palo Alto CA 94306. *Fax:* 650-354-2442

KRUBINER, ALAN MARTIN, organic chemistry, for more information see previous edition

KRUCKEBERG, ARTHUR RICE, BOTANY. *Current Pos:* from instr to assoc prof, Univ Wash, 51-63, chmn dept 71-77, prof, 64-88, EMER PROF BOT, UNIV WASH, 88- *Personal Data:* b Los Angeles, Calif, Mar 21, 20; m 42, 53; c 5. *Educ:* Occidental Col, AB, 41; Univ Calif, Berkeley, PhD(bot), 51. *Prof Exp:* Asst biol, Occidental Col, 39-41; field asst, Carnegie Inst, 41; asst biol, Stanford Univ, 41-42; asst bot, Univ Calif, Berkeley, 46-51. *Concurrent Pos:* Instr, Occidental Col, 46. *Mem:* Am Soc Plant Taxon. *Res:* Experimental plant taxonomy; edaphic ecology of serpentine soils. *Mailing Add:* 20312 15th NW Shoreline WA 98195

KRUCZYNSKI, WILLIAM LEONARD, RESOURCE MANAGEMENT. *Current Pos:* PROG SCIENTIST, WATER QUAL PROTECTION PROG, FLA KEYS NAT MARINE SANCTUARY, 95- *Personal Data:* b Buffalo, NY, July 18, 43; m 66, Mary C Cantwell; c Gregory C & Amy M. *Educ:* Canisius Col, BS, 65; Univ NC, Chapel Hill, PhD(marine biol), 71. *Honors & Awards:* Bronze Medal, US Environ Protection Agency. *Prof Exp:* Asst prof biol, Hartwick Col, 70-74; asst prof res, Fla A&M Univ, 74-79; life scientist, US Environ Protection Agency, 79-85, chief, Wetlands Protection Sect, Region IV, 85-87, wetlands specialist, Gulfbreeze, Fla, 87-95. *Concurrent Pos:* Consult, Environ Anal, Inc, 72-75, Conservation Consult, Inc, 77 & Tex A&M Univ & Tex Instruments, Inc, 78-79; vis prof, Col Ctr Finger Lakes, 73; res assoc, Fla State Univ, 74-77; vpres, Environ Systs Serv, Inc, 74-76. *Mem:* Am Soc Zoologists; AAAS; Ecol Soc Am; Estuarine Res Fedn. *Res:* Ecology of a crab symbiotic with mollusk hosts; systematics of marine isopod crustaceans; ecology of saline marshes; wetland restoration. *Mailing Add:* 3681 Monteigne Dr Pensacola FL 32504. *Fax:* 305-743-3304; *E-Mail:* kruczynski.bill@epmail.epa.gov

KRUEGEL, ALICE VIRGINIA, ORGANIC CHEMISTRY, FORENSIC SCIENCE. *Current Pos:* Res chemist, Spec Testing & Res Lab, Drug Enforcement Admin, 70-78, supvry chemist forensic drug chem, Western Field Lab, 78-88, prog mgr, Off Forensic Sci, 88-92, LAB DIR, NORTHEAST LAB, DRUG ENFORCEMENT ADMIN, 92- *Personal Data:* b Louisville, Ky, May 29, 39; m 65, David; c Scott & Ann. *Educ:* Spalding Col, Louisville, BA, 61; Univ Ky, PhD(org chem), 72. *Mem:* Am Chem Soc; Am Acad Forensic Sci; Am Soc Crime Lab Dir. *Res:* Forensic drug analysis; identification of impurities in illicitly manufactured drugs. *Mailing Add:* 300 Rector Pl No 3E New York NY 10280

KRUEGER, ANNE O, INTERNATIONAL ECONOMICS & DEVELOPMENT. *Current Pos:* HERALD L & CAROLYN L RITCH PROF HUMANITIES & SCI, STANFORD UNIV, 93-, SR FEL, HOOVER INST, 93- *Personal Data:* b Endicott, NY, 34. *Educ:* Oberlin Col, BA, 53; Univ Wis, MS, 56, PhD(econ), 58. *Hon Degrees:* Dr, Hacettepe Univ, 90, Monash Univ, 96; LHD, Georgetown Univ, 93. *Honors & Awards:* Robertson Prize, Nat Acad Sci, 84; Frank E Seidman Distinguished Award, 93. *Prof Exp:* Instr econ, Univ Wis, 58-59; from asst prof to prof, Univ Minn, 59-82; vpres econ & res, World Bank, 82-86; arts & sci prof econ, Duke Univ, 87-93. *Concurrent Pos:* Vis prof, Mass Inst Technol, 73-74, Northwestern Univ, 76, Australian Nat Univ, 77, Univ Aarhus, 79, Univ Paris, 80, Monash Univ, Australia, 81, Univ Md, 83, Univ Warsaw, 93, Delhi Sch Econs, 95 & Kiel Inst World Econs, 96; mem, Panel Technol & Employment, Nat Acad Sci, 85-87; res assoc, Nat Bur Econ Res, 86-; trustee, Oberlin Col, 87-95; mem, Task Force Struct Rev Biol, Behav & Social Sci Directorate, NSF, 90-91, chair, Task Force Int Econ Res Related to Global Warming, 91-92; sr res fel, Inst Policy Reform, 90-92. *Mem:* Nat Acad Sci; Am Econ Asn (vpres, 77-78, pres-elect, 95, pres, 96-); fel Am Acad Arts & Sci; Royal Econ Soc; fel Economet Soc; Int Econ Asn (vpres, 94-). *Res:* Analysis of trade and exchange rate regemes and global systems with special reference to international economic organizations and developing countries. *Mailing Add:* Dept Econ Stanford Univ Stanford CA 94305-6072. *Fax:* 650-725-5702; *E-Mail:* akrueger@leland.stanford.edu

KRUEGER, ARLIN JAMES, STRATOSPHERIC OZONE, REMOTE SENSING. *Current Pos:* AEROSPACE TECHNOLOGIST & ASTROPHYSICIST, GODDARD SPACE FLIGHT CTR, NASA, GREENBELT, MD, 69- *Personal Data:* b Lamberton, Minn, Oct 22, 33; m

78, Susan Peacock; c Sandra, Timothy & Terry. *Educ:* Univ Minn, BA, 55; Colo State Univ, PhD(atmospheric sci), 84. *Honors & Awards:* Except Achievement Award, Goddard Space Flight Ctr, 86. *Prof Exp:* Physicist, Naval Weapons Ctr, China Lake, Calif, 59-69. *Concurrent Pos:* Prin investr, ROCOZ rocket ozonesonde, 60-84; sr scientist, Nimbus 7 Total Ozone Mapping Spectrometer, TOMS, 73-93; instrument scientist, Meteor 3/TOMS, 88-; prin investr, ADEOS/TOMS, 88-; instr scientist, Earth Probe/TOMS, 89- *Mem:* Am Geophys Union; Am Meteorol Soc; Sigma Xi; AAAS. *Res:* Atmospheric chemistry; development of satellite and rocket instruments to measure ozone and sulfur dioxide; analysis of ozone variability and volcanic clouds; modelling of stratospheric chemistry; Mars atmosphere; remote sensing. *Mailing Add:* Goddard Space Flight Ctr NASA Code 916 Greenbelt MD 20771. *Fax:* 301-286-1754; *E-Mail:* krueger@chapman.gsfc.nasa.gov

KRUEGER, CHARLES ROBERT, forage crop management, forage crop utilization, for more information see previous edition

KRUEGER, DAVID ALLEN, THEORETICAL PHYSICS. *Current Pos:* from asst prof to assoc prof, 69-80, PROF PHYSICS, COLO STATE UNIV, 80- *Personal Data:* b Sidney, Mont, Aug 21, 39; m 61; c 4. *Educ:* Mont State Univ, BS, 61; Univ Wash, PhD(physics), 67. *Prof Exp:* Wis Alumni Res Found res assoc physics, Univ Wis, Madison, 67-69. *Concurrent Pos:* Vis prof, Watson Res Lab, Int Bus Mach Corp, Yorktown Heights, NY, 75 & Dept Energy, Energy Technol Ctr, Bartlesville, Okla, 80; mem tech staff, Sandia Lab, Albuquerque, 78-79; vis scientist, Marathon Oil Co Res Ctr, Littleton, Colo, 85-86. *Mem:* AAAS; Am Phys Soc; Am Asn Phys Teachers; Soc Petrol Engrs. *Res:* Theoretical many-body problem; dynamics of second order phase transitions; particle size effects on phase transitions; fluids (stability of flow in porous media); thermal physics. *Mailing Add:* Dept Physics Colo State Univ Ft Collins CO 80523. *Fax:* 970-491-7947

KRUEGER, EUGENE REX, MATHEMATICS, COMPUTER SCIENCES. *Current Pos:* PRES, KROEGER & ASSOCS, 89- *Personal Data:* b Grand Island, Nebr, Mar 30, 35; m 57; c 3. *Educ:* Rensselaer Polytech Inst, BS, 57, MS, 60, PhD(appl math), 62. *Prof Exp:* Physicist, Res Ctr, Int Bus Mach Corp, 57-58; vis fel, Math Res Ctr, Univ Wis, 62-63; asst prof math, Univ Colo, Boulder, 63-68, dir, Comput Ctr, 67-74, from asst prof to prof math & comput sci, 68-74; vchancellor educ syst, Ore State Syst Higher Educ, 74-82; prof comput sci, Ore State Univ, 74-82; gen mgr, Control Data Corp, 82-85, vpres, 85-89; exec dir, William C Norry Inst, 89-95, vpres, 95-96. *Mem:* Am Soc Eng Educ. *Res:* Fluid mechanics with emphasis on hydrodynamic stability; mathematical methods of physics; numerical analysis; interactive computer graphics. *Mailing Add:* 3205 NW Kidd Pl Bend OR 97701

KRUEGER, GEORGE CORWIN, OPTICS. *Current Pos:* From instr to assoc prof, 50-62, PROF PHYSICS, UNIV MAINE, ORONO, 62- *Personal Data:* b Seattle, Wash, Nov 29, 22. *Educ:* Reed Col, AB, 45; Brown Univ, PhD(physics), 51. *Concurrent Pos:* Air Force Weapons Lab, NMex, 65-66. *Mem:* Am Phys Soc; Optical Soc Am. *Res:* Atmospheric turbulence and heat transfer; physical optics; electromagnetic theory. *Mailing Add:* Dept Physics Bennett Hall Univ Maine Orono ME 04473

KRUEGER, GERHARD R F, ANATOMIC PATHOLOGY, LABORATORY IMMUNOLOGY. *Current Pos:* PROF PATH, DEPT PATH LAB MED, UNIV TEX, HOUSTON, 91- *Personal Data:* b Berlin, Ger, Nov 21, 36; m 60; c 3. *Educ:* Intern med rotating, Hosps Free Univ, 62-64. *Prof Exp:* resident path, City Hosp Spandau, Berlin, 64-65; res pathologist, Nat Cancer Inst, NIH, 65-67, pathologist, Lab Path, 68-72; resident path, Dept Path, Free Univ, Berlin, 67-68; asst prof path, Dept Path, Univ Cologne, Ger, 72-74, prof path & head immunopath, 74-91. *Concurrent Pos:* Chmn, Int Inst Immunopath, Inc, Cologne-Washington, 89-; vis prof, Dept Path Lab Med, Univ Tex, Houston, 90-91. *Mem:* Am Asn Pathologists; Am Soc Microbiol; Hematopath Soc; Int Asn Res Leukemia Asn Dis. *Res:* Relationships between reactivated herpesvirus infections to immune deficiency, autoimmunity and lymphoproliferative disorders; influence of virus infection on cell membrane function. *Mailing Add:* Dept Path Univ Cologne Joseph-Stelzmann-Str 9 50931 Cologne Germany 50924

KRUEGER, JACK N, ELECTRICAL & AGRICULTURAL ENGINEERING. *Current Pos:* RETIRED. *Personal Data:* b St Paul, Minn, Aug 29, 22; m 58; c 2. *Educ:* Univ Minn, BEE, 44, MS, 49. *Prof Exp:* Instr elec eng, Univ Minn, 44-49; res prof agr eng, Univ Ky, 49-51; consult engr, 51-55; assoc prof elec eng, Va Polytech Inst, 55-56; head, Electromech Develop Dept, Pillsbury Mills, Inc, 56-58; assoc prof elec eng, SDak State Univ, 58-59; from assoc prof to prof elec eng, Univ NDak, 69-88. *Mem:* Inst Elec & Electronics Engrs. *Res:* Electrical power and machinery; electrical instrumentation; biomedical and industrial electronics; environmental conditioning of production, processing and storage areas for agricultural products; forensic engineering; solar and wind energy systems. *Mailing Add:* Rte 1 Box 104B East Grand Forks MN 56721

KRUEGER, JAMES ELWOOD, ORGANIC CHEMISTRY. *Current Pos:* VPRES, QUAL ASSURANCE, IND MGT, 90- *Personal Data:* b Marinette, Wis, Apr 2, 26; m 53; c 3. *Educ:* Univ Wis, BS, 49; Mass Inst Technol, PhD(org chem), 54. *Prof Exp:* Res fel chem, Harvard Med Sch, 53-55; chemist, Dow Chem Co, 55-61; chemist, Lederle Labs Div, Am Cyanamid Co, 61-79, qual auditor, qual mgt, 79-90. *Concurrent Pos:* Cert qual auditor, Am Soc Qual Control. *Mem:* AAAS; Am Chem Soc; Sigma Xi; Acad Pharmaceut Sci; Am Soc Qual Control. *Res:* Pharmaceutical science; research quality assurance; laboratory quality assurance. *Mailing Add:* Six Lucille Blvd New City NY 10956-4421

KRUEGER, JAMES HARRY, INORGANIC CHEMISTRY. *Current Pos:* From asst prof to assoc prof, 61-76, PROF CHEM, ORE STATE UNIV, 76- *Personal Data:* b Milwaukee, Wis, May 18, 36; m 59; c 3. *Educ:* Univ Wis-Madison, BS, 58; Univ Calif, Berkeley, PhD(chem), 61. *Mem:* Am Chem Soc. *Res:* Kinetics and mechanisms of inorganic reactions; synthesis and characterization of transition metal complexes containing thiolate amino acid ligands. *Mailing Add:* Dept Chem Ore State Univ Gilbert Hall 153 Corvallis OR 97331-4003

KRUEGER, JAMES MARTIN, NEUROBIOLOGY. *Current Pos:* assoc prof, 85-87, PROF NEUROBIOL, UNIV TENN, 87- *Personal Data:* b New York, NY, Sept 8, 44. *Educ:* Univ Wis, BS, 66; Univ Pa, PhD(physiol), 74. *Prof Exp:* Res fel, Harvard Med Sch, 74-81; from asst prof to assoc prof neurobiol, Chicago Med Sch, 81-85. *Mem:* Am Sleep Res Soc; Am Physiol Soc; Europ Sleep Res Soc. *Res:* Biochemistry of sleep regulation. *Mailing Add:* Dept Physiol & Biophys Univ Tenn 894 Union Ave Memphis TN 38163-0001. *Fax:* 901-448-7126

KRUEGER, KARL E, BIOCHEMISTRY, DRUG RECEPTORS. *Current Pos:* Asst prof, 86-92, ASSOC PROF MED & NEUROBIOL, GEORGETOWN UNIV MED SCH, 92- *Personal Data:* b Poughkeepsie, NY, Sept 28, 54. *Educ:* Marist Col, BA, 76; Vanderbilt Univ, PhD(biochem), 81. *Mem:* Am Soc Biochem & Molecular Biol; Soc Neurosci. *Mailing Add:* Dept Cell Biol Georgetown Univ Sch Med Washington DC 20057-0001. *Fax:* 202-687-1823

KRUEGER, PAUL A, organic chemistry; deceased, see previous edition for last biography

KRUEGER, PAUL CARLTON, INORGANIC CHEMISTRY, PHYSICAL CHEMISTRY. *Current Pos:* Res chemist, Air Reduction Co, 63-65, sr res chemist, Cent Res Labs, 65-78, supvr, Indust Health Serv & Safety, 78-80, mgr environ affairs, 80-84, mat selection & performance, 84-87, MGR ENVIRON AFFAIRS, AIRCO, INC, 87- *Personal Data:* b Louisville, Ky, June 1, 36; m 65; c 2. *Educ:* Marquette Univ, BS, 58; Case Inst Technol, PhD(chem), 63. *Mem:* Am Chem Soc. *Res:* Chelate, silicon and slag chemistry; coordination compounds; inorganic and high temperature polymers; ferroalloy production; cutting of metals; corrosion of stainless steel alloys; development of stainless steel alloys; industrial hygiene sampling and interpretation; failure analysis of equipment and compressed gas cylinders. *Mailing Add:* BOC Group Inc Group Tech Ctr 100 Mountain Ave Murray Hill NJ 07974-2069

KRUEGER, PETER GEORGE, AVIONICS & NAVIGATION. *Current Pos:* SR TECH ADV, DEFENSE MAPPING AGENCY HQ, FAIRFAX, VA, 93- *Personal Data:* b Lodz, Poland, May 20, 40; US citizen; div; c 3. *Educ:* Loma Linda Univ, La Sierra Campus, BA, 62; Univ Calif, Riverside, MA, 66, PhD(physics), 70. *Prof Exp:* Physicist, Naval Weapons Ctr, 62-80; Naval Air Systs Command, Wash, DC, 80-86; staff scientist, secy defense, Wash, DC, 86-93. *Mem:* Am Phys Soc; Inst Navig; US Naval Inst. *Res:* Defense mapping; agency research, development and production programs. *Mailing Add:* 11109 Timberhead Ct Reston VA 20191

KRUEGER, PETER J, CONFORMATIONS OF ORGANIC MOLECULES, INFRARED & RAMAN SPECTROSCOPY. *Current Pos:* head dept, Univ Calgary, 66-70, prof chem, 66-91, vdean fac arts & sci, 70-72, mem bd govs, 70-73, acad vpres & provost, 76-90, EMER PROF CHEM, UNIV CALGARY, 91-, ACAD-IN-RESIDENCE, INT CTR, 91- *Personal Data:* b Altona, Man, Nov 11, 34; m 59, Dorothy Lashley; c Kathryn, Vivian & Jonathan. *Educ:* Univ Man, BSc, 55, MSc, 56; Oxford Univ, DPhil(infrared spectros), 58. *Honors & Awards:* Coblentz Award Spectros, Coblentz Soc, 67; Gerhard Herzberg Award, Spetros Soc Can, 73. *Prof Exp:* Fel, Org Spectrochem Sect, Div Pure Chem, Nat Res Coun Can, Ont, 58-59; from asst prof to assoc prof chem, Univ Alta, 59-66. *Concurrent Pos:* Vis scientist, Nat Res Coun Can, Ottawa, 66-67; Nat coordr, Can Univ Stud Exchange-Consortium, 92-93. *Mem:* Fel Chem Inst Can; Spectros Soc Can; fel Royal Soc Chem; Coblentz Soc. *Res:* University governance and administration; organic spectrochemistry; infrared and Raman spectra of organic compounds; normal coordinate analysis of vibrational spectra; molecular structure determination; internationalization of university programs. *Mailing Add:* Dept Chem Univ Calgary 2500 University Dr NW Calgary AB T2N 1N4 Can. *Fax:* 403-282-0683; *E-Mail:* pkrueger@ucdasvm1.admin.ucalgary.ca

KRUEGER, ROBERT A, ORGANIC CHEMISTRY. *Current Pos:* GEN MGR, ICI RESINS US, 85- *Personal Data:* b Oak Park, Ill, Dec 29, 35; m 59; c 3. *Educ:* Knox Col, AB, 57; Kans State Univ, PhD(org chem), 65. *Prof Exp:* Chemist, Visking Div, Union Carbide Corp, 57-58 & 60; res chemist, 65-69, sect leader, 69-72, tech adminr, 72-73, facility mgr, 73-75, vpres res & develop eng, 77-78, vpres additives & specialty polymers & develop function, 77-79, sr vpres elastomers, latex & specialty chem, 79-80, sr vpres & gen mgr, Polyvinyl Chloride Div, 80-81, sr vpres staff support serv, B F Goodrich Chem Co, 81-85. *Concurrent Pos:* Consult, mgmt, res & develop. *Mem:* Am Chem Soc; Indust Res Inst. *Res:* Synthesis and reactions of carbenes; olefin synthesis; antioxidants; polyvinyl chloride stabilization; organometallic chemistry. *Mailing Add:* 160 Carlton Lane North Andover MA 01845-5617

KRUEGER, ROBERT CARL, BIOCHEMISTRY. *Current Pos:* asst prof, 50-56, ASSOC PROF BIOL CHEM, COL MED, UNIV CINCINNATI, 56- *Personal Data:* b Philadelphia, Pa, Oct 11, 20; m 47; c 2. *Educ:* Univ Pa, BS, 42; Columbia Univ, PhD(biochem), 48. *Prof Exp:* Res assoc immunochem, Col Physicians & Surgeons, Columbia Univ, 47-50. *Concurrent Pos:* Res assoc, Brookhaven Nat Lab, 59-60; vis scientist, Univ Brussels, 66-67; NIH spec fel, 66-67. *Mem:* Am Soc Biol Chemists. *Res:* RNA synthesis; deoxribonucleoprotein structure and function. *Mailing Add:* Dept Biol Chem Univ Cincinnati Col Med 231 Bethesda Ave Cincinnati OH 45267-0001

KRUEGER, ROBERT GEORGE, IMMUNOLOGY, VIROLOGY. *Current Pos:* CONSULT, 89- *Personal Data:* b Duluth, Minn, Apr 22, 38; m 60; c 2. *Educ:* Col St Thomas, BS, 60; Univ Detroit, MS, 62; Univ Chicago, PhD(microbiol), 66. *Prof Exp:* Asst prof immunol, New York Med Col, 66-67; asst prof microbiol, Univ Wash, 67-71; assoc prof, Mayo Grad Sch Med, Univ Minn & Mayo Med Sch, 71-75; dir, Lab Molecular Oncol, Christ Hosp Inst Med Res, Cincinnati, 75-81; dir, Div Tumor Biol, 78-81; prof exp med & assoc prof microbiol, Col Med, Univ Cincinnati, 75-81; regional med assoc, Smith Kline & Fr Labs, 81-85. *Concurrent Pos:* USPHS grants, 67-81; Am Cancer Soc grant, 69-71; consult microbiol & immunol, Mayo Clin, 71-75. *Mem:* AAAS; Am Asn Immunologists; Soc Exp Biol & Med; Am Soc Microbiol; Am Diabetes Asn. *Res:* Genetic regulation of immunoglobulin synthesis; mechanisms of neoplastic transformation by oncogenic viruses; protein synthesis in differentiated mammalian cells; structure of oncogenic viruses. *Mailing Add:* 9620 Timbermill Ct Cincinnati OH 45231

KRUEGER, ROBERT HAROLD, PHYSICAL CHEMISTRY. *Current Pos:* SCIENTIST, BIRL LAB, NORTHWESTERN UNIV 90- *Personal Data:* b Sioux City, Iowa, Jan 25, 26; m 56; c 3. *Educ:* Morningside Col, BS, 50; Northwestern Univ, MS, 55; Loyola Univ, PhD(chem), 67. *Prof Exp:* Chemist, Cent Com Co, 51-54 & Diversey Corp, Ill, 54-56; res chemist, Roy C Ingersoll Res Ctr, Borg-Warner Corp, 56-62, sr res chemist, 62-70, group leader 70-78, mgr phys chem, 78-89. *Mem:* Am Chem Soc; Nat Asn Corrosion Engrs; Steel Struct Paint Coun; Am Soc Testing & Mat. *Res:* Development of materials for bearings and seals; cement additives; new fluids for refrigeration; corrosion, friction and wear of materials; development of corrosion and scale inhibitors; plasma treatment of metals; protective coatings; sensors. *Mailing Add:* 11514 Michigan Dr Spring Grove IL 60081-8129

KRUEGER, ROBERT JOHN, PHARMACOGNOSY, PHARMACEUTICAL CHEMISTRY. *Current Pos:* from asst prof to assox prof, 75-86, PROF PHARMACOG, FERRIS STATE UNIV, 86- *Personal Data:* b Milwaukee, Wis, Apr 15, 48; m 71; c 2. *Educ:* Univ Conn, BS, 71; Univ Iowa, PhD(pharm), 75. *Concurrent Pos:* NDEA fel, 71-74; Eli Lilly & Co fel, 74-75, PMA; vis scientist, Abbott, 83; chmn, Am Chem Soc Western MI Region, 85; pres, Sigma Xi, Grand Valley St Univ, 86-87. *Mem:* AAAS; Am Soc Pharmacog; Am Chem Soc; Phytochem Soc NAm; Am Asn Col Pharm; Sigma Xi. *Res:* Plant tissue culture; isolation and identification of natural products; xenobiotic metabolism by plant cell cultures; fungal ellicitor stimulation of plant cell culture. *Mailing Add:* 701 Magnolia Big Rapids MI 49307

KRUEGER, ROBERT WILLIAM, PHYSICS. *Current Pos:* PRES, PROF SERV INT, 73- *Personal Data:* b Philadelphia, Pa, Nov 16, 16; m 41, Marjorie E Jones; c Arlene R (Pappan) & Diane L (Lane). *Educ:* Univ Calif, Los Angeles, AB, 37, MA, 38, PhD(physics), 42. *Prof Exp:* Res physicist, Douglas Aircraft Co, 42-46; asst chief, Missiles Div, Rand Corp, 47-53; pres, Planning Res Corp, 54-73. *Concurrent Pos:* Pres-founder, Prof Serv Coun, 71-74, dir, 71- *Mem:* Am Phys Soc; Opers Res Soc Am. *Res:* Operations research; systems engineering; aerodynamics; propulsion; quantum mechanics; spectroscopy. *Mailing Add:* 1016 Moraga Dr Los Angeles CA 90049

KRUEGER, ROGER WARREN, AGRICULTURE, BIOTECHNOLOGY. *Current Pos:* MGR TECHNOL, GLOBAL PROD STEWARDSHIP MONSANTO-LIFE SCI, 96- *Personal Data:* b Manhassett, NY, Nov 8, 53; m 76, Ann S Schaumburg; c Van, Mara & Hanna. *Educ:* Univ NH, BS, 76; Univ RI, MS, 79; Univ Mo-Columbia, PhD(biol), 83. *Prof Exp:* Res assoc biochem, Univ Mo, 83-85; sr res scientist, Dekalb Plant Genetics, DeKalb-Pfizer, 85-91; res scientist genetics, Biol Dept, Yale Univ, 91; sr biologist, Am Cyanamid, 91-93, sr prod develop mgr, 94, mgr biotechnol, 95-96. *Concurrent Pos:* Invited lectr biol, Conn Col, 86-91; mem biotech educ comt, Future Farmers Am, Biotech Indust Orgn; Maize Genetics Soc, 93- *Mem:* Am Soc Plant Physiologists; Int Soc Plant Molecular Biol; Future Farmers Am; Biotech Indust Orgn; Maize Genetics Soc. *Res:* Molecular genetics to plant development; using transposable elements to gain a better understanding of genes controlling development; commercial application to modern agriculture. *Mailing Add:* 800 N Lindbergh Blvd St Louis MO 63167. *Fax:* 314-694-1139; *E-Mail:* rwkrue@ccmail.monsanto.com

KRUEGER, ROLAND FREDERICK, WELLBORE MECHANICS, OIL RECOVERY. *Current Pos:* PRIN, KGK PETROL CONSULTS, 86- *Personal Data:* b Fond du Lac, Wis, Oct 18, 18; m 43; c 3. *Educ:* Ripon Col, BA, 39; Univ Ill, MA, 41. *Honors & Awards:* Distinguished Serv Award, Soc Petrol Engrs, 82; Citation Serv, Am Petrol Inst, 83. *Prof Exp:* Lab instr, Univ Ill, 39-41; physicist, Tenn Eastman Corp, 41-42; Holston Ord Works, 42; physicist, radiation lab, Univ Calif, 43; tech supvr, Manhattan Proj, Oak Ridge Nat Labs, 43-44, asst dept support, 44-46; physicist & res engr, Douglas Aircraft Co, Calif, 46-48; physicist & res engr, Union Oil Co, 48-51, sect leader, Prod Res Dept, 51-55, sr sect leader, 55-62, supvr, 62-81, mgr, 81-85, staff consult to pres sci & technol div, 85-86. *Concurrent Pos:* Distinguished lectr, Soc Petrol Engrs, 75-76, sr tech ed, J Petrol Technol, 79-82 & mem bd dirs, 83-86. *Mem:* Soc Petrol Engrs; Am Petrol Inst; AAAS; Asn Advan Eng. *Res:* Isotope separation; mass spectroscopy; combustion; spectrophotometry; thermodynamics; flow of fluids in porous media; production mechanics; formation damage in oil and gas wells; oil recovery processes; well stimulation. *Mailing Add:* 561 Peralta Hills Dr Anaheim CA 92807

KRUEGER, WILLIAM ARTHUR, AGRONOMY. *Current Pos:* Asst prof agron, 68-74, ASSOC PROF PLANT & SOIL SCI, UNIV TENN, KNOXVILLE, 74- *Personal Data:* b Milford, Iowa, Mar 24, 41. *Educ:* Univ Minn, BS, 63; Univ Ill, PhD(agron), 68. *Mem:* Plant Growth Regulator Soc; Weed Sci Soc Am. *Res:* The effects that herbicides exert on the physiology of plants, particularly mode of action and basis of selectivity. *Mailing Add:* Canton Hollow Rd Knoxville TN 37922

KRUEGER, WILLIAM CLEMENT, RANGE SCIENCE. *Current Pos:* asst prof, 71-75, leader rangeland resources prog, 75-80, HEAD, DEPT RANGELAND RESOURCES, ORE STATE UNIV, 81- *Personal Data:* b Medford, Ore, Aug 19, 42; m 65; c 2. *Educ:* St Mary's Col, Calif, BS, 64; Humboldt State Col, MS, 67; Utah State Univ, PhD(range sci), 70. *Prof Exp:* Res technician range sci, Intermountain Forest & Range Exp Sta, 67-70; asst prof, Humboldt State Col, 70-71. *Concurrent Pos:* Head, Dept Range Sci, Colo State Univ, 80-81. *Mem:* Soc Range Mgt. *Res:* Range restoration; interaction of livestock grazing, wildlife and timber production through integration of management systems. *Mailing Add:* Rangeland Resources Dept Ore State Univ Strand Agr Hall Corvallis OR 97331

KRUEGER, WILLIAM E, ORGANIC CHEMISTRY. *Current Pos:* from asst prof to assoc prof, 66-85, PROF CHEM, STATE UNIV NY COL PLATTSBURGH, 85- *Personal Data:* b St Louis, Mo, June 26, 40. *Educ:* Univ Notre Dame, BS, 62; Univ NH, PhD(org chem), 67. *Prof Exp:* Res fel org chem, Univ Ill, Chicago Circle, 66. *Mem:* Am Chem Soc. *Res:* Partially reduced pyridines; nitrenes; phosphorus additions. *Mailing Add:* Colligan Point Rd Plattsburgh NY 12901-2698

KRUEGER, WILLIE FREDERICK, POULTRY HUSBANDRY, GENETICS. *Current Pos:* from asst prof to assoc prof, 53-59, PROF POULTRY SCI, TEX A&M UNIV, 59-, HEAD DEPT, 72- *Personal Data:* b Riesel, Tex, Oct 12, 21; m 46; c 2. *Educ:* Tex A&M Univ, BS, 43, MS, 49; Univ Mo, PhD(genetics, animal breeding), 52. *Prof Exp:* Teacher & prin pub sch, Tex, 41-42; flock supvr, Tex Poultry Improv Asn, 42-43; instr poultry husb, Miss State Univ, 46-47; asst, Agr & Mech Col Tex, 47-49; asst, Univ Mo, 49-50, from instr to asst prof, 50-53. *Mem:* Poultry Sci Asn; Am Genetic Asn; Sigma Xi. *Res:* Application of the principles of population genetics to poultry; embryology; embryology and incubation of chicken and turkey eggs; environmental factors influencing chickens and turkeys. *Mailing Add:* Dept Poultry Sci Tex A&M Univ College Station TX 77843-2472

KRUER, WILLIAM LEO, PLASMA PHYSICS. *Current Pos:* GROUP LEADER LASER PLASMA THEORY & SIMULATION, LAWRENCE LIVERMORE LAB, 72- *Personal Data:* b Louisville, Ky, Apr 20, 42; m 65; c 3. *Educ:* Univ Louisville, BS, 64, MS, 65; Princeton Univ, MA, 67, PhD(astron), 69. *Prof Exp:* Res assoc, Plasma Physics Lab, Princeton Univ, 69-70, mem res staff, 70-72. *Concurrent Pos:* Lectr, Univ Calif, Davis/Livermore, 76-; affil mem Ctr Plas Physics & Fusion Eng, Univ Calif, Los Angeles, 76- *Mem:* Fel Am Phys Soc. *Res:* Plasma theory; computer simulation of plasmas; nonlinear plasma waves; plasma heating; laser fusion. *Mailing Add:* 4055 Suffolk Way Pleasanton CA 94566

KRUESI, WILLIAM R, protective equipment, for more information see previous edition

KRUG, EDWARD CHARLES, ENVIRONMENTAL GEOCHEMISTRY. *Current Pos:* ENVIRON CONSULT, 90- *Personal Data:* b New Brunswick, NJ, Aug 24, 47; m 88, Nancy C Wegner. *Educ:* Rutgers Univ, BSc, 75, MSc, 78, PhD(environ geochem), 81. *Prof Exp:* asst soil scientist, Conn Agr Exp Sta, 80-85; assoc prof scientist, Ill State Water Surv, 85-90. *Mem:* Soil Sci Soc Am; Am Geophys Union; AAAS; Int Soc Soil Sci. *Res:* Reactions, weathering, and biogeochemical cycling of elements and materials in soil, water, and lake sediment; environmental policy making. *Mailing Add:* 521 Deborah Ave Winona MN 55987-2103

KRUG, JOHN CHRISTIAN, MYCOLOGY, LICHENOLOGY. *Current Pos:* res assoc mycol, 75-77, asst cur, 81-82, LECTR, UNIV TORONTO, 77-, CUR, 82- *Personal Data:* b Toronto, Can, July 11, 38; m 74, Beatrix Guyer; c Isobel Maja & Bruce Robert. *Educ:* Univ Toronto, BSc, 63, MA, 64, PhD(mycol), 70. *Prof Exp:* Fel mycol, Inst Bot, Swiss Fed Inst Technol, 70-72; fel, Univ Waterloo, 73; res assoc & fel, Univ Toronto, 73-74; cur asst cryptogamic bot, Royal Ont Mus, 74-75. *Concurrent Pos:* Collabr, Excerpta Botanica Sectio A: Taxonomica et Chorologica, 75-; res fel, Royal Ontario Mus, 78-; link scientist, Int Mycol Inst, 97- *Mem:* Mycol Soc Japan; Brit Mycol Soc; Mycol Soc Am; Am Bryolog & Lichenolog Soc; Brit Lichen Soc; Int Asn Lichenology; Asn for Taxon Study Flora of Trop Africa. *Res:* Systematic and phytogeographical studies of Coprophilous Ascomycetes; Ascomycetes of over-wintering twigs; phytogeographical studies of Canadian arctic lichens; systematic studies of Ascomycetes from tropical soils; molecular systematics of Ascomycetes. *Mailing Add:* Dept Bot Univ Toronto 25 Willcocks St Toronto ON M5S 3B2 Can. *Fax:* 416-978-6573; *E-Mail:* jkrug@botony.utoronto.ca

KRUG, MAURICE F, MECHANICAL ENGINEERING. *Current Pos:* FOUNDER, CHMN & CHIEF EXEC OFFICER, KRUG INT CORP, 59- *Personal Data:* b 1929. *Educ:* Univ Dayton, Ohio, BS, 55. *Prof Exp:* Researcher, Univ Dayton, Ohio, 55-60. *Mailing Add:* Krug Int Corp 6 N Main St Suite 1900 Dayton OH 45402-1900

KRUG, ROBERT M, MEDICAL RESEARCH. *Current Pos:* PROF CHMN, DEPT MOLECULAR BIOL & BIOCHEM, RUTGERS UNIV, 90-; DIR JOINT GRAD PROG BIOCHEM, UNIV MED & DENT, ROBERT WOOD JOHNSON MED SCH, 90- *Personal Data:* b Newark, NJ, Aug 27, 39. *Educ:* Harvard Univ, AB; Rockefeller Univ, PhD. *Honors & Awards:* Karl Meyer Lecturer, Univ Calif, San Francisco Med Ctr, 86. *Prof Exp:* From asst prof to assoc prof molecular biol, Cornell Univ Grad Sch Med, 69-79, prof, 80-90. *Concurrent Pos:* Res assoc, Mem Sloan-Kettering Cancer Ctr, NY, 65-68, asst mem, 68-71, assoc mem, 72-79, chmn, Molecular Biol Prog, 83-86, head, Lab Viral & Cellular Gene Expression, 78-90, mem, 79-90. *Mem:* Am Soc Microbiol; Am Soc Virology; Am Soc Biochem & Molecular Biol. *Res:* Molecular biology and biochemistry. *Mailing Add:* Dept Molecular Biol & Biochem Rm 305 Ctr Adv Biotechnol & Med 679 Hoes Lane Piscataway NJ 08855-1179. *Fax:* 732-235-4880

KRUG, SAMUEL EDWARD, PSYCHOLOGICAL & EDUCATIONAL MEASUREMENT, PERSONALITY ASSESSMENT. *Current Pos:* PRES, METRITECH INC, 82-; PRES, INDUST PSYCHOL INT, LTD, 89- *Personal Data:* b Chicago, Ill, Nov 15, 43; m 68, Marion E Besch; c Mark, Michael, David & Timothy. *Educ:* Col Holy Cross, AB, 65; Univ Ill Urbana-Champaign, MA, 68, PhD(psychol), 71. *Prof Exp:* Managing dir, Inst Personality & Ability Testing, 71-82. *Concurrent Pos:* Adj prof, Univ Ill, Urbana-Champaign, 87- *Mem:* Fel Am Psychol Asn; fel Soc Personality Assessment; Nat Coun Measurement Educ; Am Educ Res Asn. *Res:* Applied psychological and educational measurement, including test development and computer-based interpretation of test results. *Mailing Add:* MetriTech Inc 4106 Fieldstone Champaign IL 61820. *Fax:* 217-398-5798

KRUGER, ALBERT AARON, SOLID STATE CHEMISTRY, MATERIALS SCIENCE. *Personal Data:* b Brooklyn, NY, Oct 3, 52; c Evelyne & Nathaniel R. *Educ:* Brooklyn Col, BS, 74; Syracuse Univ, MS, 78. *Prof Exp:* Sr tech assoc, Bell Tel Labs, 75-78; team leader & sr chemist, 3M Cent Res Labs, 78-82; supvr & confirmed res scientist, St Gobain Res, 82-87; adj, Dept Physics, Brooklyn Col, 87-88; sr res scientist, Batelle-Pac NW Labs, 88-90; prin scientist, Westinghouse Hanford, 91-97. *Concurrent Pos:* Site eval team mem, NSF, 93-; consult, Ore Grad Inst, 94- *Mem:* Fel Am Inst Chemists; Sigma Xi; Am Chem Soc; Mat Res Soc; Am Ceramic Soc; Int Union Pure & Appl Chem. *Res:* Materials science and in particular the preparation and synthesis of solids with novel electrical properties; surface treatments and correlating their effects on bulk physical properties of materials. *Mailing Add:* 2175 Clearview Ave Richland WA 99352-1809. *E-Mail:* albertk1@aol.com

KRUGER, CHARLES HERMAN, JR, PHYSICAL GAS DYNAMICS, PARTIALLY IONIZED PLASMAS. *Current Pos:* from asst prof to assoc prof, Standord Univ, 62-70, chmn, 82-88, sr assoc dean, 88-92, PROF MECH ENG, STANFORD UNIV, 70-, VICE PROVOST & DEAN RES & GRAD POLICY, 93- *Personal Data:* b Oklahoma City, Okla, Oct 4, 34; m 77; c 4. *Educ:* Mass Inst Technol, SB, 56, PhD(mech eng), 60; Univ London, dipl, Imp Col, 57. *Honors & Awards:* Fluid & Plasmadynamics Award & Medal, Am Inst Aeronaut & Astronaut, 79. *Prof Exp:* From instr to asst prof mech eng, Mass Inst Technol, 59-60; res scientist, Res Labs, Lockheed Missiles & Space Co, Calif, 60-62. *Concurrent Pos:* Sr fel, Nat Sci Found, 68-69; vis prof, Harvard Univ, 68-69 & Princeton Univ, 78-79; mem hearing bd, Bay Area Air Pollution Control Dist, 70-83; chmn, Steering Comt, Eng Aspects of Magnetohydrodyn, 78-81; vis scientist, Norwegian Inst Technol, 79; mem, Environ Studies Bd, Nat Acad Sci, 80-83, adv coun, MAE Dept, Princeton Univ, 81-91. *Mem:* Am Phys Soc; Am Soc Mech Engrs; Am Inst Aeronaut & Astronaut; Combustion Inst. *Res:* Physical gas dynamics; partially ionized plasmas; plasma chemistry; plasma diagnostics; diamond synthesis. *Mailing Add:* Bldg 10 Stanford Univ Stanford CA 94305

KRUGER, FRED W, MECHANICAL ENGINEERING. *Current Pos:* Instr mech eng, Valparaiso Univ, 47-55, chmn dept, 55-65, dean col eng, 65-72, vpres, 74-87, EMER PROF, VALPARAISO UNIV, 87- *Personal Data:* b Chicago, Ill, Dec 17, 21; m 47, Esther Foelber; c 3. *Educ:* Univ Purdue, BS, 43, BS, 47; Univ Notre Dame, MS, 54. *Concurrent Pos:* Consult, McDonnell Aircraft Co, Caterpillar Tractor Co, Argonne Nat Lab, Northern Ill Gas Co & Ind State Bd Registr Prof Eng; mem city coun, City of Valparaiso, 72-96 & City Planning Comn, 76-85. *Mem:* Am Soc Mech Engrs; Am Soc Eng Educ. *Res:* Heat power systems. *Mailing Add:* Gellerson Eng Bldg Valparaiso Univ Valparaiso IN 46383

KRUGER, FREDRICK CHRISTIAN, ECONOMIC GEOLOGY. *Current Pos:* CONSULT, 77-; EMER PROF, STANFORD UNIV, 77- *Personal Data:* b St Paul, Minn, Apr 1, 12; m 36, Helene Anderson; c Kurn F & Jan C (Anderson). *Educ:* Univ Minn, BS, 35, MS, 36; Harvard Univ, PhD, 41. *Honors & Awards:* Hardinge Award, Am Inst Mining, Metall & Petrol Eng, 72. *Prof Exp:* Asst, Univ Minn, 35-36; instr geol, Dartmouth Col, 36-38; asst, Harvard Univ, 38-41; from asst geologist to asst chief geologist, Cerro de Pasco Copper Corp, 41-49; lectr geol, Northwestern Univ, 49; from assoc prof to prof, Univ Tenn, 49-52; asst chief geologist, Reynolds Metals Co, 52-57; chief geologist to vpres mining & explor div, Int Minerals & Chem Corp, 57-66; head dept, 66-74, prof mineral eng, 66-78, Donald Steel chair econ geol, 71-78, assoc dean, Stanford Univ, 72-78. *Concurrent Pos:* Asst, Radcliffe Col, 38-41; Krumb lectr, Am Inst Mining, Metall & Petrol Eng, 68; lectr geol, Univ Texas, 78. *Mem:* Fel Am Geol Soc; Soc Econ Geol; Am Inst Mining, Metall & Petrol Eng; Can Inst Mining & Metall; Peruvian Geol Soc. *Res:* Mining geology; administration. *Mailing Add:* 145 Wildwood Way Woodside CA 94062

KRUGER, JAMES EDWARD, ENZYMOLOGY, CEREAL CHEMISTRY. *Current Pos:* RES SCIENTIST CHEM CEREAL, GRAIN RES LAB, 66-, WHEAT ENZYME & ASIAN END PROD RES, 89- *Personal Data:* b Winnipeg, Man, Oct 14, 38; m 60; c 1. *Educ:* Univ Man, BSc, 60, MSc, 63; Univ Sask, PhD(phys org), 65. *Mem:* Am Asn Cereal Chemists; Chem Inst Can; Am Asn Plant Physiologists. *Res:* Wheat systems such as amylase, proteases, polyphenol, and oxidoases; high performance liquid chromatography of sugars and proteins; automation of analytical techniques in cereal chemistry; pre-harvest sprouting problems. *Mailing Add:* 303 Main St Rm 1404 Winnipeg MB R3C 3G8 Can

KRUGER, JEROME, CORROSION SCIENCE & ENGINEERING. *Current Pos:* chmn mat sci & eng, 86-88, PROF, JOHNS HOPKINS UNIV, 84- *Personal Data:* b Atlanta, Ga, Feb 7, 27; m 55, Mollee Coppel; c Lennard & Joseph. *Educ:* Ga Inst Technol, BS, 48, MS, 50; Univ Va, PhD, 53. *Honors & Awards:* Silver Medal, Com Dept, 62, Gold Medal, 72; W R Whitney Award, Nat Asn Corrosion Engrs, 76; U R Evans Award, Brit Inst Corrosion, 91. *Prof Exp:* Du Pont fel, Univ Va, 51-52; mem staff, Naval Res Lab, Washington, 52-55; mem staff, Nat Bur Stand, Com Dept, Washington, 55-83, sect chief, Corrosion & Electrodeposition, 66-80. *Concurrent Pos:* Consult, Argonne Nat Lab, Lockheed, Baltimore Gas & Elec, Teletech, Thompson, Dalton & DeRose & Mueller Brass; div ed, J Electrochem Soc, 66-83; chmn, Int Corrosion Coun, 87-90. *Mem:* Fel & hon mem Electrochem Soc (treas, 82-86); fel Nat Asn Corrosion Engrs; AAAS; Am Inst Conserv; Fedn Mat Soc (pres, 77); Sigma Xi. *Res:* Material science & engineering; corrosion science and engineering, electrochemistry, electrodeposition, passivity, breakdown of passivity and localized corrosion, x-ray absorption spectroscopy, economics of corrosion; underground, marine and atmospheric corrosion, conservation (artistic and historical objects) science. *Mailing Add:* Dept Mat Sci & Eng Johns Hopkins Univ Baltimore MD 21218. *Fax:* 410-516-5293; *E-Mail:* jk2727@aol.com

KRUGER, LAWRENCE, NEUROANATOMY, NEUROPHYSIOLOGY. *Current Pos:* USPHS sr res fel anat, 59-60, from asst prof to assoc prof, 60-66, PROF ANAT, UNIV CALIF, LOS ANGELES, 66- *Personal Data:* b New Brunswick, NJ, Aug 15, 29; m 61, Virginia Findlay; c Erika & Paula. *Educ:* Wagner Col, BS, 49; Yale Univ, PhD(physiol), 54. *Prof Exp:* Asst physiol, Yale Univ, 50-53, asst neurophysiol, Inst Living, Conn, 53-54; USPHS fel physiol, Johns Hopkins Univ, 55-58; Nat Res Coun fel, Col France, 58; Nat Res Coun fel anat, Oxford Univ, 58-59. *Concurrent Pos:* Lederle med fac award, 61-64; mem, Int Brain Res Orgn, UNESCO; Wellcome vis prof, 81. *Mem:* AAAS; Am Asn Anatomists; Am Physiol Soc; Soc Neurosci. *Res:* Cutaneous receptors and their central nervous system representation; organization of the visual system in vertebrates with particular reference to the midbrain; thalamo-cortical relations; electron microscopy of neural degeneration; pain. *Mailing Add:* Dept Neurobiol 73-235 Health Sci Ctr Univ Calif Los Angeles CA 90024. *Fax:* 310-825-2224; *E-Mail:* lkruger@neurobio.medsch.ucla.edu

KRUGER, OWEN L, CERAMICS, METALLURGY. *Current Pos:* SR ENGR & COST ANALYST, EXXON NUCLEAR CO, INC, 77- *Personal Data:* b Oak Park, Ill, Dec 1, 32; m 54; c 4. *Prof Exp:* Metall engr, Ill Inst Technol, 54; metallurgist, Continental Foundry & Mach Co, 54-55; assoc metallurgist, Argonne Nat Lab, 57-69; assoc chief, Plutonium Technol & Mat, Thermodyn Div, Columbus Div, Battelle Mem Inst, 69-77. *Mem:* Fel Am Ceramic Soc; Am Nuclear Soc. *Res:* Light water reactor fuel fabrication; plutonium ceramics and metallurgy; fast reactor fuel development. *Mailing Add:* 2360 Harris Ave Richland WA 99352

KRUGER, PAUL, NUCLEAR CIVIL ENGINEERING. *Current Pos:* PROF NUCLEAR CIVIL ENG, STANFORD UNIV, 62- *Personal Data:* b Jersey City, NJ, June 7, 25; m 72, Claudia Mathis; c Sharon, Kenneth & Louis. *Educ:* Mass Inst Technol, BS, 50; Univ Chicago, MS, 52, PhD(nuclear chem), 54. *Prof Exp:* Asst instr nuclear & phys chem, Univ Chicago, 50-53; res physicist, Res Labs Div, Gen Motors Corp, 53-54; vpres & head, Dept Phys Sci, Nuclear Sci & Eng Corp, Pa, 54-60; mgr nuclear proj, Hazelton-Nuclear Sci Corp, 60-62. *Mem:* Fel Am Nuclear Soc; Am Soc Civil Engrs; Am Chem Soc. *Res:* Nuclear methods in civil engineering and environmental sciences; environmental radioactivity; energy and environment; geothermal engineering. *Mailing Add:* Dept Civil Eng Stanford Univ Stanford CA 94305. *Fax:* 650-725-8662; *E-Mail:* kruger@cive.stanford.edu

KRUGER, RICHARD PAUL, ELECTRICAL ENGINEERING. *Current Pos:* CHIEF SCIENTIST, SAIC, 93- *Personal Data:* b Chicago, Ill, July 27, 44; m 69; c 2. *Educ:* Purdue Univ, BS, 67; Univ Mo, MS, 68, PhD(elec eng), 71; Univ NMex, MBA, 79. *Prof Exp:* Asst prof elec eng & radiol, Univ Southern Calif, 71-75; asst vpres, Sci Int Applns Inc, 82-89; staff mem elec eng, Los Alamos Nat Lab, Univ Calif, 75-82, group leader, 89-93. *Concurrent Pos:* Consult, Rockwell Corp, 73, Aerospace Corp, 75 & Univ Southern Calif, 76-77. *Mem:* Sr mem Inst Elec & Electronics Engrs; Sigma Xi. *Res:* Computer image processing applied to biomedical and industrial images; industrial automation; pattern recognition; computed tomography. *Mailing Add:* SAIC 1710 Goodridge Dr PO Box 1303 McLean VA 22102

KRUGH, THOMAS RICHARD, BIOPHYSICAL CHEMISTRY. *Current Pos:* from asst prof to assoc prof, 70-78, PROF CHEM, UNIV ROCHESTER, 78- *Personal Data:* b Pittsburgh, Pa, May 3, 43; m 70, Rosemary F Donohue; c Bradley. *Educ:* Univ Pittsburgh, BS, 65; Pa State Univ, PhD(phys chem), 69. *Prof Exp:* NIH fel, Stanford Univ, 69-70. *Mem:* AAAS; Biophys Soc; Am Chem Soc; Am Asn Cancer Res. *Res:* Biophysical chemistry; drug-nucleic acid complexes; carcinogen-nucleic acid complexes; structures of nucleic acids; nuclear magnetic resonance. *Mailing Add:* Dept Chem Univ Rochester Rochester NY 14627-0216. *Fax:* 716-473-6889; *E-Mail:* krugh@chem.rochester.edu

KRUGLAK, HAYM, PHYSICS, SCIENCE EDUCATION. *Current Pos:* from assoc prof to prof, 54-77, EMER PROF PHYSICS, WESTERN MICH UNIV, 78- *Personal Data:* b Ukraine, Mar 24, 09; m 41, Mary L Stewart; c Joyce & David. *Educ:* Univ Wis, BA, 34, MA, 36; Univ Minn, PhD, 51. *Prof Exp:* Instr pub sch, Wis, 36-38 & Milwaukee Voc Jr Col, 38-42, supvr radio training, 42-44; vis asst prof physics, Princeton Univ, 44-46; instr, Univ Minn, 46-51, asst prof physics, astron & gen studies, 51-54. *Concurrent Pos:* Vis scholar, Univ Ariz, 82-89. *Mem:* Am Asn Physics Teachers; Am Asn Univ Professors; fel AAAS. *Res:* Performance tests in laboratory instruction; design of laboratory and demonstration apparatus; physics, mathematics and astronomy education. *Mailing Add:* Dept Physics Western Mich Univ Kalamazoo MI 49008-5151

KRUGMAN, SAUL, medicine; deceased, see previous edition for last biography

KRUGMAN, STANLEY LIEBERT, FOREST GENETICS, FOREST PHYSIOLOGY. *Current Pos:* FOREST CONSULT, 95- *Personal Data:* b St Louis, Mo, June 8, 32; m 58, Judith R Alfend; c Jeffrey J & Mark B. *Educ:* Univ Mo, BS, 54; Univ Calif, MS, 56, PhD(plant physiol), 61. *Honors & Awards:* William Schlich Memorial Medal, Soc Am Foresters, 90; Forestry Gold Medals, Czech Repub & Repub Poland. *Prof Exp:* Res specialist, Univ Mo, 53-55; teaching asst, Univ Calif, 56-58, res asst forestry, 58-60, res specialist, 60-62; plant physiologist forest genetics, Pac Southwest Forest Range & Exp Sta, US Forest Serv, 62-66, proj leader genetics res proj, Inst Forest Genetics, 66-71, chief br genetic & related res, 71-74, rrin res forest geneticist, 74-81, dir, Forest Mgt Res, 81-95. *Concurrent Pos:* Res assoc, Agr Exp Sta, Univ Calif, 62-71; biotechnol comt, USDA, 74-87, Nat Genetics Resources Bd, 78-86; sr forest consult, World Bank, 90-97. *Mem:* Fel Soc Am Foresters; Soc Plant Physiol; fel AAAS; Int Union Forestry Res Orgn. *Res:* Pigments, hormones and reproductive physiology as related to trees; forest and tree improvement/diversity; international research, including forest restoration, ecology and genetic resource conservation; forest biology/ diversity. *Mailing Add:* 6515 Dryden Dr McLean VA 22101. *Fax:* 202-205-1551

KRUH, DANIEL, RESEARCH & DEVELOPMENT, EXTERNAL TECHNOLOGY TRANSFER. *Current Pos:* sr res assoc, 87-88, Block Drug Co, Inc, mgr new technol, 88-89 & 92-93, mgr, licensing & acquisitions, 88-92, SR RES ASSOC NEW TECHNOL, BLOCK DRUG CO, INC, 93- *Personal Data:* b Brooklyn, NY, May 22, 34; m 61, Sheila R Reinhard; c Andrew & Ira (deceased). *Educ:* WVa Wesleyan Col, BS, 55; Rensselaer Polytech Inst, PhD(org chem), 63. *Honors & Awards:* Inventors Award, Gen Elec. *Prof Exp:* Res chemist, Hercules Powder Co, 63-66; specialist-adv develop composites bus oper, Insulating Mat Dept, Gen Elec Co, 66-70, mgr wire enamel develop, 70-72; res assoc, Johnson & Johnson Dental Prods Co, 72-75, sr res scientist, 75-76, supvr polymer tech serv, 76-83; sr chemist, Electro-Science Labs Inc, 83-84; proj mgr, Int Hydron Corp, 84-87. *Concurrent Pos:* Elected mem bd dirs, Soc Plastics Eng, Med Plastics Div, 87-90. *Mem:* Am Chem Soc; Soc Plastics Eng; Am Inst Chem; Controlled Release Soc; Int Asn Dental Res; Licensing Execs Soc; Soc Cosmetic Chemists; Am Asn Pharmaceut Scientists; Am Asn Textile Chemists & Colorists; Am Oil Chemists Soc. *Res:* Antiradiation drugs; phthalocyanine pigments; polyimides; chemical and light cured dental materials; high performance polymers in coatings and composites; silicone gas permeable and tinted soft contact lenses; conductive polymer thick films; consumer products (over-the-counter drugs, dental, household); granted 5 patents. *Mailing Add:* 8 Braddock St East Brunswick NJ 08816. *Fax:* 201-434-0842

KRUH, ROBERT FRANK, PHYSICAL CHEMISTRY. *Current Pos:* PROF CHEM & DEAN GRAD SCH, KANS STATE UNIV, 67- *Personal Data:* b St Louis, Mo, June 15, 25; m 48; c 3. *Educ:* Washington Univ, AB, 48, PhD(chem), 51. *Prof Exp:* Asst prof chem, DePauw Univ, 51-52; from asst prof to prof chem & dean col arts & sci, Univ Ark, 52-67. *Concurrent Pos:* Vis prof, Wash Univ, 60-61; mem coun res policy and grad educ, Nat Asn State Univs & Land Grant Cols, 68-72; mem policy comt, Coun Grad Schs, US, 69-73, chmn, Bd Dirs, 78-79; mem bd trustees, Argonne Univ Asn, 70-77; pres, Kans State Univ Res Found, 70-; mem, Grad Record Exam Bd, 77-, chmn, 80-81. *Mem:* Sigma Xi; AAAS; Am Chem Soc; fel Am Inst Chemists; Am Phys Soc. *Res:* Crystallography; x-ray diffraction; structure of liquids. *Mailing Add:* 2155 Blue Hills Rd Manhattan KS 66502-4561

KRUISBEEK, ADA M, DEVELOPMENTAL BIOLOGY. *Current Pos:* Vis scientist, 79-82, cancer expert, 82-86, SR INVESTR, NIH, 86- *Personal Data:* b Rotterdam, Netherlands, Oct 2, 38. *Educ:* Leiden Univ, BS, 73, PhD(immunol), 78. *Mem:* Am Asn Immunologists; Brit Soc Immunologists; Europ Soc Geront. *Mailing Add:* Netherlands Kanker Inst Res Bldg H7 Plesmanlaan 121 Amsterdam 1066CX Netherlands. *Fax:* 31-20-512-2057

KRUKAR, RICHARD HAROLD, DISTRIBUTED INTELLIGENT CONTROL, OPTICAL METROLOGY. *Current Pos:* CONTROL SYSTS ENGR, LAM RES, 96- *Personal Data:* b Aurora, Colo, May 24, 62. *Educ:* Univ NMex, BUS, 84, MSEE, 87, PhD(elec eng), 93. *Prof Exp:* Pres, Desert Sage, 92-94; mem tech staff, Lucent Bell Labs, 94-96. *Res:* Distributed controls, pattern recognition and statistical analysis; designing and building instrumentation and writing software. *Mailing Add:* 39120 Argonaut Way No 132 Fremont CA 94538

KRUKOWSKI, MARILYN, CELL BIOLOGY, DEVELOPMENTAL BIOLOGY. *Current Pos:* from res asst prof to asst prof, 69-75, assoc prof, 75-87, PROF BIOL, WASH UNIV, 87- *Personal Data:* b New York, NY, May 3, 32; m 55, Lucian; c Samantha. *Educ:* Brooklyn Col, BA, 54; NY Univ, MA, 62, PhD(biol), 65. *Prof Exp:* Res asst endocrinol exp cardiovasc dis, NY Med Col, Flower & Fifth Ave Hosps, 56-62, res assoc, 62-66, asst prof pharmacol & coinvestr endocrinol and exp cardiovasc dis, 66-69, instr pharmacol, 64-66. *Mem:* AAAS; Am Soc Cell Biol; Am Soc Bone & Mineral Res; Sigma Xi; Orthop Res Soc. *Res:* Bone development; origin, induction and cytodifferentiation of bone-resorbing cells; factors and materials that stimulate bone formation. *Mailing Add:* Dept Biol Washington Univ Box 1229 St Louis MO 63130-4899. *Fax:* 314-935-4432

KRULICH, LADISLAV, NEURO-ENDOCRINOLOGY. *Current Pos:* from asst prof to assoc prof, 70-79, PROF PHYSIOL, UNIV TEX SOUTHWESTERN MED SCH, 79- *Personal Data:* b Cesky Broad, Czech, Oct 22, 25; m 51, Ludmila Rakusanova; c Eva & Jan. *Educ:* Univ Charles, Prague, MD, 51, PhD(physiol), 58. *Prof Exp:* From asst prof to assoc prof physiol, Univ Charles, Prague, 51-70. *Mem:* Endocrine Soc; Am Physiol Soc; Soc Exp Biol & Med; AAAS; Int Soc Neuroendocrinol. *Res:* Neuro-endocrinology; discovery of receptors for glucose in the brain (1961); discovery of the hypochalmic growth hormone-inhibiting hormone (somatostatin) 1968; studies on the role of multiple adrenergic and opioid receptors in the regulation of the secretion of pituitary hormones. *Mailing Add:* Dept Physiol Univ Tex Southwestern Med Ctr 5323 Harry Hines Blvd Dallas TX 75235-7200

KRULL, IRA STANLEY, ANALYTICAL CHEMISTRY. *Current Pos:* sr scientist & fac fel, Barnett Inst, 79-92, ASSOC PROF CHEM, DEPT CHEM, NORTHEASTERN UNIV, 84- *Personal Data:* b New York, NY, Oct 21, 40; m 73, Erica Meghid; c Marc A. *Educ:* City Col New York, BS, 62; NY Univ, MS, 66, PhD(org chem), 68. *Honors & Awards:* Innovative Res Award Anal Chem, Barnett Inst, 83; Bioanal Sci Recognition Outstanding Achievement Award, 88; Recognition Award, Am Asn Pharmaceut Scientists, 88. *Prof Exp:* Weizmann fel chem, Weizmann Inst Sci, 70-73; asst scientist, Boyce Thompson Inst Plant Res, 73-76; sr scientist chem, Thermo Electron Corp, 77-79. *Concurrent Pos:* Union Carbide fel, 68-70; Boston Dist Sci Adv, Food & Drug Admin, 80-, sci adv, res assoc prog, 83-87, ad hoc res review comt, 85-91; NIH Small Bus Innovation Res Study Sect, 83, 84, 86 & 88, Spec Study Sect & site visit, Univ Wash, 83; proposal reviewer, NSF, 83-, Am Chem Soc Petrol res fund, 85-; vis sabbatical prof, Anal Res Dept, Ciba-Geigy Corp, Switz, 90; vis scholar, Bioanal Systs Inc & Purdue Univ, Ind, 91. *Mem:* Am Chem Soc; NY Acad Sci; Soc Electroanal Chem; Sigma Xi; AAAS. *Res:* Analytical biotechnology; analytical biochemistry; trace organic analytical chemistry; analytical method development; instrumentation research and development; drug analysis; bioanalytical chemistry; author of numerous publications. *Mailing Add:* Northeastern Univ Dept Chem 360 Huntington Ave Boston MA 02115. *Fax:* 617-373-8795

KRULL, JOHN NORMAN, ECOLOGY, WILDLIFE BIOLOGY. *Current Pos:* assoc prof, 71-75, PROF WILDLIFE BIOL & CONSERV, CENT MICH UNIV, 75- *Personal Data:* b Albany, NY, July 31, 39; m 63; c 2. *Educ:* State Univ NY Col Forestry, Syracuse Univ, BS, 61, MS, 63, PhD(wetland ecol), 67. *Prof Exp:* Asst prof Southern Ill Univ, 67-71. *Mem:* Soc Am Foresters; Conserv Educ Asn; Soil & Water Conserv Soc; Wildlife Soc. *Res:* Wetland ecology, especially green-tree reservoir ecology, waterfowl use and production from various wetland habitats, and aquatic plant-invertebrate associations; wildlife management investigations; conservation. *Mailing Add:* Dept Biol Cent Mich Univ 100 W Preston Rd Mt Pleasant MI 48859-0001

KRULL, ULRICH JORG, BIOSENSORS, CHEMICALLY MODIFIED SURFACES. *Current Pos:* Asst prof anal chem, Univ Toronto, 85-90, asst chair chem, 90-92, assoc prof anal chem, 90-95, ASSOC DEAN SCI & VPRIN RES, UNIV TORONTO, ERINDALE CAMPUS, 94-, PROF ANAL CHEM, 95- *Personal Data:* b Berlin, Ger, Oct 28, 56; Can citizen; m 80, Carol B Walters; c Jeffrey M & Justin U. *Educ:* Univ Toronto, BSc, 79, MSc, 80, PhD(anal chem), 83. *Honors & Awards:* McBryde Medal, Can Soc Chem, 94. *Concurrent Pos:* Prin investr, Chem Sensors Group, Univ Toronto, 85-, res fac, Inst Environ Studies, 89-, res assoc, Ctr Plant Biotechnol, 92-95; chair, Anal Chem Div, Chem Inst Can, 92-94; sec vpres, Royal Can Inst, 93-94, counr, 94-; counr, Can Int Inst, 95- *Mem:* Fel Chem Inst Can; Royal Can Inst; Royal Astron Soc Can; Can Int Inst. *Res:* Investigation of organized organic monolayers for biosensor development, this has involved the study of lipid membranes as electrochemical and flourescent transducers of selective binding interactions of proteins; development of analytical techniques such as photopyroelectric spectroscopy and immobilization of amphiphile/enzyme assemblies and single stranded DNA for preparation of fibre-optic biosensors. *Mailing Add:* Dept Chem Erindale Col Univ Toronto Mississauga ON L5L 1C6 Can. *Fax:* 905-828-5425; *E-Mail:* ukrull@credit.erin.utoronto.ca

KRULWICH, TERRY ANN, BIOCHEMISTRY & BIOENERGETICS, MICROBIAL PHYSIOLOGY. *Current Pos:* from asst prof to assoc prof, 70-81, PROF BIOCHEM & DEAN GRAD SCH, MT SINAI SCH MED, 81- *Personal Data:* b New York, NY, Apr 7, 43; m 73; c 3. *Educ:* Goucher Col, BA, 64; Univ Wis-Madison, MS, 66, PhD(bact), 68. *Hon Degrees:* DSc, Goucher Col, 87. *Prof Exp:* NIH trainee bact, Univ Wis, 68; postdoctoral fel molecular biol, Albert Einstein Col Med, 68-70. *Concurrent Pos:* NSF predoctoral fel, 64-68, NSF postdoctoral fel, 68-70; NIH, Res Career Develop Award, 75-80; NIH, mem Cellular Molecular Basic Dis Comt, 78-82, mem, Microbiol Physiol Genetics Study Sect, 83-87. *Mem:* AAAS; Am Soc Microbiol; Am Chem Soc; Am Soc Biol Chemists; NY Acad Sci; Biophys Soc; Sigma Xi. *Res:* Microbial bioenergetics; alkalophilic and acidophilic bacteria; protonophore resistance. *Mailing Add:* Dept Biochem Mt Sinai Sch Med Box 1020 One Gustave L Levy Pl New York NY 10029-6504

KRUM, ALVIN A, PHYSIOLOGY. *Current Pos:* from asst prof to assoc prof, 61-73, PROF PHYSIOL, MED CTR, UNIV ARK, LITTLE ROCK, 73- *Personal Data:* b Fresno, Calif, May 14, 28; m 54; c 2. *Educ:* Univ Calif, AB, 50, PhD(physiol), 57. *Prof Exp:* Res physiologist, Univ Calif, 57-61. *Concurrent Pos:* Fel, Steroid Training Prog, Univ Utah, 58-59; Lederle Med Fac Award, 64-67. *Mem:* AAAS; Am Physiol Soc; Endocrine Soc; Soc Exp Biol & Med; Sigma Xi. *Res:* Endocrinology; steroid biosynthesis; metabolism. *Mailing Add:* 1829 Whispering Oaks Poplar Bluff MO 63901-2069

KRUM, JACK KERN, FOOD TECHNOLOGY. *Current Pos:* PRES, TECHNIQUES, INC, 80- *Personal Data:* b Kansas City, Mo, Mar 17, 22; m 46, Miriam Siebert; c Meredith, Mark, Eric & Andrew. *Educ:* Hope Col, AB, 44; Mich State Univ, MS, 48; Univ Mass, PhD(food tech), 49. *Honors & Awards:* Fel, Inst Food Technol, 83. *Prof Exp:* Assoc prof food technol, Univ Tenn, 49-50; food technologist in charge prod control labs, Oscar Mayer & Co, 50-52; res chemist, Nat Biscuit Co, 52-56; asst tech dir, Sterwin Chem Inc, 56-61, tech dir, 61-69; asst res dir, R T French Co, 69-70, dir res & develop, 71-72, vpres & dir res & develop, 72-73; tech dir, ITT Paniplus Co, 73-79. *Concurrent Pos:* Mem food additive comt, Flavoring Extract Mfrs Asn US, 61-72, chmn, 67-71; mem indust comt, Food Protection Comn, Nat Acad Sci, 64-66; White House Conf Food Nutrit & Health, 69 & tech comt, Grocery Mfrs Am, 70-73. *Mem:* Am Asn Cereal Chem; Inst Food Technol. *Res:* Food additives; new product development; fermentation; nutrition; food processing; dry mixes; food additives; dehydration; food flavors; stabilizers, emulsifiers and enrichment; research administration. *Mailing Add:* Techniques Inc 16705 W 327th St Paola KS 66071

KRUMBEIN, AARON DAVIS, REACTOR PHYSICS, PLASMA PHYSICS. *Current Pos:* RETIRED. *Personal Data:* b New York, NY, Apr 6, 21; m 50, Hilda Beim; c Esther, David & Deborah. *Educ:* Brooklyn Col, AB, 41; NY Univ, PhD(physics), 51. *Prof Exp:* Lab asst physics, Bartol Res Found, 41-42; asst, NY Univ, 42-46, asst, Cosmic Ray Proj, 46-47, consult physicist, Upper Atmosphere Res, Res Div, 47-49; asst prof, Univ Md, 50-56; adv scientist, Develop Div, United Nuclear Corp, 56-71; sr scientist, Soreg nuclear Res Ctr, Yavne, Israel, 71-86, consult, 86-96. *Concurrent Pos:* Sr scientist solid state physics, US Naval Ord Lab, 55; vis asst prof, Yeshiva Univ, 61-70; vis sr res assoc, Plasma Physics Group, Univ Md, 78-79, vis prof, Plasma Lab, 85-86. *Mem:* Israel Phys Soc (treas, 75-78); Am Nuclear Soc; Israel Nuclear Soc; Am Phys Soc; Sigma Xi. *Res:* Gaseous electronics; nuclear detectors; nuclear reactor and reactor shielding physics; intermetallic semiconductors; Geiger-Muller counters; radiation transport; space physics; laser produced plasma; thermonuclear reactors. *Mailing Add:* 134/17 Netter St Jerusalem 97763 Israel

KRUMBEIN, SIMEON JOSEPH, ELECTROCHEMISTRY, SURFACE PHYSICS. *Current Pos:* sr eng scientist, Res Div, 77-91, SR MEM TECH STAFF, TECHNOL DIV, AMP, INC, 91- *Personal Data:* b Brooklyn, NY; m 57; c 3. *Educ:* Brooklyn Col, BS, 56; NY Univ, PhD(phys chem), 61. *Honors & Awards:* Lowenheim Mem Award, Am Soc Testing & Mat, 92. *Prof Exp:* Chemist, TRG, Inc, 56-57; phys chemist, Fuel Cell Lab, Gen Elec Co, 61-64; sr scientist, Res Div, Burndy Corp, 64-69; asst prof, Stern Col, Yeshiva Univ, 69-75, assoc prof chem, 75-79. *Concurrent Pos:* Consult, US Army Electronic Components Lab, 70; co-adj asst prof chem, Univ Coll, Rutgers Univ, 72-74; consult, Res Div, AMP, Inc, 73-76. *Mem:* Am Chem Soc; Electrochem Soc; Am Soc Testing & Mat; Sigma Xi; Int Inst Connector & Interconnection Technol. *Res:* Experimental methods in fuel cell research; electrical contact phenomena; metallic corrosion; experimental electrode kinetics; contact materials; environmental testing; electromigration; plating porosity. *Mailing Add:* 3106 Labyrinth Rd Baltimore MD 21208. *Fax:* 717-986-5218

KRUMDIECK, CARLOS L, BIOCHEMISTRY, NUTRITION. *Current Pos:* asst prof biochem & med, Univ Ala, Birmingham, 67-70, assoc prof biochem, 70-81, assoc dir nutrit prog, 76-85, PROF BIOCHEM, UNIV ALA, BIRMINGHAM, 77-, ASSOC PROF PEDIAT, 76- *Personal Data:* b Lima, Peru, Nov 11, 32;; c 2. *Educ:* San Marcos Univ, Lima, BMed & MD, 58; Tulane Univ La, PhD(biochem), 64. *Honors & Awards:* Bordeu Award in Nutrit, 85. *Prof Exp:* Resident med, Hosp 2nd of May, Lima, Peru, 58-59; biochemist, Hektoen Inst Med Res, Chicago, Ill, 59-60; Rockefeller Found fel biochem, Tulane Univ La, 60-62 & 64, USPHS fel, 62-63; prof biochem, Univ Cayetano Heredia, Peru, 65-70. *Mem:* Am Soc Biol Chemists; Sigma Xi; Am Inst Nutrit; Am Soc Clin Nutrit; NY Acad Sci; AAAS; Physicians Social Responsibility. *Res:* Biochemistry of folic acid polyglutamates; biochemical assessment of nutrient status; pathogenesis of atherosclerosis; nutrition and cancer. *Mailing Add:* Dept Nutrit Sci Univ Med Ala 1675 University Blvd Rm 304 Birmingham AL 35294-3360

KRUMHANSL, JAMES ARTHUR, CONDENSED MATTER PHYSICS, BIOPHYSICS. *Current Pos:* dir lab atomic & solid state physics, 60-64, Horace White prof physics, 81-90, PROF PHYSICS, CORNELL UNIV, 59-, EMER HORACE WHITE PROF PHYSICS, 90- *Personal Data:* b Cleveland, Ohio, Aug 2, 19; m 45, 83, Marilyn Dahl; c James L, Carol L & Peter A. *Educ:* Univ Dayton, BS, 39; Case Inst Technol, MS, 40; Cornell Univ, PhD(physics), 43. *Hon Degrees:* DSc, Case Western Res, 80. *Honors & Awards:* Fulbright lectr, 76; lectr, Yamada Found Japan, 82 & 89. *Prof Exp:* Instr physics, Cornell Univ, 43-44; physicist, Stromberg-Carlson Co, 44-46; from asst prof to assoc prof physics & appl math, Brown Univ, 46-48; from asst prof to assoc prof physics, Cornell Univ, 48-55; from asst dir res to assoc dir res, Nat Carbon Co, 55-58. *Concurrent Pos:* Consult to var industs, 64-; mem adv comts, AEC, Dept Defense & Nat Acad Sci, 56-; ed, J Appl Physics, 57-60; Guggenheim fel, 59-60; assoc ed, Solid State Commun, 63- & Rev Mod Physics, 68-73; NSF sr fel, Oxford Univ, 66-67; mem gov bd, Am Inst Physics, 73-; ed, Phys Rev Lett, 74-; asst dir, math phys sci & eng, NSF, 77-79; adj prof physics, Univ Pa, 80-82; fel, Los Alamos Nat Lab; dir, Allied Corp, 80-87; vis fel, All Souls, Oxford, 77, 82-83, Gonville & Caius, Cambridge, 83, Yamada Found Japan, 82 & 89; lectr, Yamada Found Japan, 89 & 89; adj prof, Univ Mass, Amherst, 90- *Mem:* Fel Am Phys Soc (pres, 89); fel AAAS; Sigma Xi. *Res:* Condensed matter physics; materials science; biomolecular physics; applied mathematics; research administration; nonlinear phenomena in physics, materials and biology. *Mailing Add:* 515 Station Rd Amherst MA 01002. *E-Mail:* jimk@msc.cornell.edu

KRUMM, CHARLES FERDINAND, ELECTRICAL ENGINEERING. *Current Pos:* mem tech staff, Hughes Res Lab, 76-77, sect head, 77-78, from asst dept mgr to dept mgr, 78-86, mgr, Micoelectronics Lab, 86-89, prog mgr, 89-96, gas prod line mgr, 96, MICROELECTRONICS DIV MGR, HUGHES RADAR SYSTS, 96- *Personal Data:* b Macomb, Ill, Aug 3, 41; m 67, Patricia Kosanke; c Jennifer & Frederick. *Educ:* Univ Mich, BSE, 63, MSE, 65, PhD(elec eng), 70. *Prof Exp:* Res asst, Electron Physics Lab, Univ Mich, 65-69; sr res scientist, Res Div, Raytheon Co, 69-76. *Concurrent Pos:* Mem, Adv Group Electron Devices, Dept Defense. *Mem:* Fel Inst Elec & Electronics Engrs. *Res:* Design, fabrication and testing of Gallium Arsenide & Silicon integrated circuits including ion implantation; electron beam and optical lithography; high resolution dry processing and molecular beam epitaxy. *Mailing Add:* Hughes Aircraft Co Microelectronics Div PO Box H Newport Beach CA 92658-2027. *Fax:* 714-759-7353; *E-Mail:* ckrumm@ccmail.hac.com

KRUMMEL, DEBRA A, NUTRITION, CELLULAR VASCULAR DISEASE PREVENTION. *Current Pos:* CONSULT NUTRIT, 94- *Personal Data:* b Akron, Ohio, July 31, 57. *Educ:* Kent State Univ, BS, 78; Case Western Res Univ, MS, 80; Pa State Univ, PhD(nutrit), 86. *Honors & Awards:* Huddelson Award, Am Dietetic Asn, 93. *Prof Exp:* Asst prof nutrit, Kent State Univ, 86-88; nutritionist, Catherine McCauley Health Ctr, Ann Arbor, 88-89; res fel internal med, Sinai Hosp, Detroit, 89-90; res scientist, Hershey Foods Corp, 90-94. *Concurrent Pos:* Asst prof nutrit, Oakland Community Col, 86-88. *Mem:* Am Inst Nutrit; Soc Nutrit Educ; Am Dietetic Asn; Sports & Cardiovasc Nutrit Group. *Res:* Nutrition; cellular vascular disease prevention. *Mailing Add:* Community Med WVa Univ PO Box 9005 Morgantown WV 26506-9005. *Fax:* 304-293-8624

KRUMMEL, WILLIAM MARION, BIOMEDICAL ENGINEERING, ELECTRICAL ENGINEERING. *Current Pos:* RETIRED. *Personal Data:* b New York, NY, Aug 15, 28; m 62; c 3. *Educ:* City Col NY, BEE, 49; Columbia Univ, MS, 63; NY Univ, PhD(biomed eng), 67. *Prof Exp:* Engr, Control Div, Gen Elec Co, 49-54, systs engr, 56-62; asst prof elec eng, Univ Conn, 67-69 & NY Univ, 69-71, adj assoc prof, 71-73; assoc prof math, Bronx Community Col, City Univ NY, 71-73; assoc dean, Westchester Community Col, 73-80; pres, Norwalk State Tech Col, 80-86 & Bridgeport Eng Inst, 86-95. *Concurrent Pos:* Chair, New Eng Sect, Soc Mfg Engrs. *Mem:* AAAS; Inst Elec & Electronics Engrs; NY Acad Sci; Sigma Xi; Am Soc Eng Educ. *Res:* Application of mathematical and engineering techniques to experimental and theoretical biomedical problems; application of electrical engineering techniques to industrial process control. *Mailing Add:* Little Fox Lane Norwalk CT 06850

KRUMMENACHER, DANIEL, GEOLOGY, CHEMISTRY. *Current Pos:* RETIRED. *Personal Data:* b Geneva, Switz, Mar 14, 25; m 51. *Educ:* Univ Geneva, dipl chem eng, 52, PhD(geol), 59. *Prof Exp:* Res scientist, Univ Geneva, 59-62, assoc prof geochem, 62-68; from asst prof to prof geol, San Diego State Univ, 68-88. *Concurrent Pos:* Researcher mass spectros, Univ Calif, Berkeley, 60-61, res assoc, 67-68. *Mem:* Geol Soc Am. *Res:* Isotope geology; geochronometry. *Mailing Add:* Box 168 Rancho Sante Fe CA 92067

KRUMREI, W(ILLIAM) C(LARENCE), PROCESS DEVELOPMENT, PRODUCT DEVELOPMENT. *Current Pos:* RETIRED. *Personal Data:* b Cleveland, Ohio, Mar 31, 24; m 52, Betty Dotzauer; c Thomas & James. *Educ:* Case Inst Technol, BS, 50; Mass Inst Technol, MS, 51. *Prof Exp:* Develop engr, Process Develop Dept, Procter & Gamble Co, 51-54, tech brand mgr, Soap Prod Res Dept, 54-55, sect head, 55-58, assoc dir, Foods Div, Prod Develop Dept, 58-62, assoc dir, Household Soap Prod Develop Div, 62-63, dir prod develop, Household Soap Div, 63-70, dir tech govt rels, 70-72, sr dir, Corp Res & Develop Dept, 72-82. *Concurrent Pos:* Mem adv comt, NIH, 77-78. *Mem:* AAAS; Am Mgt Asn; Sigma Xi; NY Acad Sci; Am Indust Health Counc. *Res:* Oil, food and detergent chemistry and processing. *Mailing Add:* 6 N Calibogue Cay Rd Hilton Head Island SC 29928

KRUPA, SAGAR, PHYTOPATHOLOGY, AIR POLLUTION. *Current Pos:* res fel soil sci, Dept Microbiol, Univ Minn, St Paul, 72-73, res fel plant path, 73-74, from asst prof to assoc prof, 74-85, ENVIRON PATHOLOGIST, UNIV MINN, ST PAUL, 74-, PROF PLANT PATH & PLANT PHYSIOL, DEPT PLANT PATH, 85- *Personal Data:* b Madras, India, Oct 11, 40; US citizen; m 67. *Educ:* Andhra Univ, BSc, 59; Univ Wis, MS, 68; Univ Uppsala, PhD(plant physiol), 71. *Prof Exp:* Swed Nat Sci Res Coun res fel physiol bot, Inst Physiol Bot, Univ Uppsala, 72. *Concurrent Pos:* Docent, Inst Physiol Bot, Univ Uppsala, 73- *Mem:* Am Phytopath Soc; Air Pollution Control Asn; AAAS; fel Air & Waste Mgt Asn. *Res:* Atmospheric chemistry and effects of air pollution on vegetation. *Mailing Add:* Dept Plant Path Univ Minn St Paul MN 55108

KRUPKA, LAWRENCE RONALD, PLANT PATHOLOGY. *Current Pos:* from asst prof to assoc prof, 65-68, PROF NATURAL SCI, MICH STATE UNIV, 68-, CHMN, DEPT GREAT ISSUES & INTERDEPT COURSES, 73- *Personal Data:* b New York, NY, Mar 7, 33; m 58. *Educ:* Cornell Univ,

BS, 54; Univ Del, MS, 56; La State Univ, PhD, 59. *Prof Exp:* Asst plant path, Univ Del, 54-56 & La State Univ, 56-58; asst pathologist, Univ Nebr, 59-60; biologist, Rohm and Haas Chem Co, Pa, 61-63; asst prof biol, Philadelphia Col Pharm, 63-65. *Concurrent Pos:* USPHS fel, 59-60; co-dir, sci, technol & human values, NSF. *Mem:* Mycol Soc Am; Am Phytopath Soc; Soc Indust Microbiol; Sigma Xi. *Res:* Host-parasite relationships of plant pathogens, especially rusts; respiration studies; enzyme and organic acid metabolism; drug toxicity; effects of science and technology upon society. *Mailing Add:* Dept Natural Sci Mich State Univ 100 N Kedzie Hall East Lansing MI 48824-1031

KRUPKA, MILTON CLIFFORD, HIGH TEMPERATURE & HIGH PRESSURE PHYSICAL CHEMISTRY, SYSTEMS ENGINEERING MATERIALS. *Current Pos:* RETIRED. *Personal Data:* b New York, NY, Jan 1, 24; m 54, Emilia T Clara; c Denise, John & Nilda. *Educ:* City Univ New York, BA, 44; Univ NMex, MS, 58, PhD(phys chem), 62. *Prof Exp:* Jr chemist, SAM Labs, Columbia Univ, 44-45; asst chemist, Los Alamos Nat Lab, Univ Calif, 45-46, lab supvr explosives, 46-50, proj engr weapons develop, 50-59, mat scientist high temp chem, 59-71, staff mem & asst mgr high temp chem, 71-75, mem staff & prin investr, technol & environ assessment, New Energy Technol & Conversion Systs, 76-78, syst analyst & prin investr, 78-89. *Concurrent Pos:* Consult, 89-91. *Mem:* Fel Am Inst Chemists; Am Chem Soc; Sigma Xi; Sci Res Soc. *Res:* Elucidation of high temperature thermodynamics and properties of various refractory materials; ultrahigh pressure and temperature research; preparation of new materials and new superconductors; corrosion research in natural silicate melts; technology assessment; systems analysis for advanced energy systems; physics. *Mailing Add:* 6401 Turnberry Lane NE Albuquerque NM 87111-5860

KRUPKA, RICHARD M(ORLEY), BIOCHEMISTRY. *Current Pos:* RES SCIENTIST, CAN DEPT AGR, 60- *Personal Data:* b Winnipeg, Man, Jan 17, 32; m 58; c 2. *Educ:* Univ Sask, BA, 53, MA, 55; McGill Univ, PhD(plant biochem), 57. *Prof Exp:* Fel enzyme kinetics, Univ Ottawa, 58-60. *Mem:* Can Fedn Biol Socs; Fedn Am Soc Exp Biol. *Res:* Transport kinetics; enzyme kinetics. *Mailing Add:* Res Ctr Can Agr London Res Ctr 1391 Sanford St London ON N5V 4T3 Can

KRUPKE, WILLIAM F, SOLID STATE PHYSICS. *Current Pos:* MEM STAFF, LAWRENCE LIVERMORE NAT LAB, 74- *Personal Data:* b Springfield, Mass, Jan 30, 37; m 61. *Educ:* Rensselaer Polytech Inst, BS, 58; Univ Calif, Los Angeles, MA, 60, PhD(spectros), 66. *Prof Exp:* Mem tech staff laser res, Minneapolis Regulator Co, 61-62; mem tech staff solid state res, Aerospace Corp, 62-66; staff physicist, Hughes Aircraft Co, Culver City, 66-74. *Mem:* Am Phys Soc. *Res:* Spectroscopic research on solid and gaseous systems as related to the dynamics of lasers; electronic structure of rare earth elements in solids; transition intensities and energy transfer processes. *Mailing Add:* Lawrence Livermore Lab L-488 UCL PO Box 5508 Livermore CA 94551

KRUPP, DAVID ALAN, BIOCHEMISTRY OF CORAL MUCUS, CALORIMETRY OF TISSUES. *Current Pos:* INSTR BIOL & MARINE SCI, WINDWARD COMMUNITY COL, 84-, FAC COORDR, MARINE OPTION PROG, 84- *Personal Data:* b Blue Island, Ill, Feb 6, 53; m 86; c 2. *Educ:* Univ Calif, Los Angeles, BA, 76; Univ Hawaii, PhD(zool), 82. *Concurrent Pos:* Prin investr, Summer Prog Enhancement Basic Educ Oceanog, 85-90; co-prin investr, Marine Option Prog Sea Grant Projs, 85-91; sci fac coordr, Math-Sci Dept, Windward Community Col, 85-89, dept chairperson, 89-91; vis researcher, Marine Lab, Univ Guam, 89; lectr, summer advan res & training prog, Hawaii Inst Marine Biol, 91- *Mem:* AAAS; Am Soc Zoologists. *Res:* Aspects of the biology of reef corals: reproduction, production of mucus and its properties, diffusion barriers and carbon limitation, pollution effects on coral reefs; biochemistry of sea cucumber body walls. *Mailing Add:* Sci Univ Hawaii Windward Community Col 45-720 Keaahala Rd Kaneohe HI 96744-3528

KRUPP, EDWIN CHARLES, ASTRONOMY. *Current Pos:* Cur, 72-74, actg dir, 74-76, DIR ASTRON, GRIFFITH OBSERV, CITY LOS ANGELES, 76- *Personal Data:* b Chicago, Ill, Nov 18, 44; m 68, Robin Rector; c Ethan H. *Educ:* Pomona Col, BA, 66; Univ Calif, Los Angeles, MA, 68, PhD(astron), 72. *Hon Degrees:* LHD, WCoast Univ, 96. *Honors & Awards:* Klumpke-Roberts Award for Contrib to Pub Understanding of Astron, Astron Soc of the Pac, 89. *Concurrent Pos:* Inst, El Camino Col, 69-74 & Univ Southern Calif, 74-75; consult, Los Angeles County Supt Sch, Community Col Consortium, 74-82; lectr & course coord, Univ Calif Exten, 75- *Mem:* Am Astron Soc; Sigma Xi; fel Explorer's Club; Int Astron Union; Astron Soc Pac. *Res:* Archaeoastronomy; ethnoastronomy; public astronomy education; childrens books on science. *Mailing Add:* Griffith Observ 2800 E Observatory Rd Los Angeles CA 90027. *Fax:* 213-663-4323; *E-Mail:* ekrupp@earthlink.net

KRUPP, IRIS M, PARASITOLOGY, ALLERGY. *Current Pos:* RETIRED. *Personal Data:* b New Orleans, La, May 1, 28; m 78, Robert E Post. *Educ:* La State Univ, BS; Tulane Univ, MS, 55, PhD(parasitol), 58, MD, 71. *Prof Exp:* Res asst, Med Sch, Tulane Univ, 49-53; instr vet parasitol, Mich State Col, 53-54; asst, Med Sch, Tulane Univ, 54-58, from instr to asst prof trop med & pub health, 59-66, assoc prof trop med & pub health, 66-81, clin assoc prof med, 71-76. *Concurrent Pos:* Observer res technol, London Sch Hyg & Trop Med, 59-60; consult, USPHS grant, 60-65; intern, USPHS Hosp, 71-72; res fel, Vet Admin Hosp, New Orleans, 72-73; mem adv bd parasitic dis & consult to surgeon gen, Dept Army, 73-75; resident dermat, Charity Hosp, New Orleans, 73-76; pvt pract dermat, 76- *Mem:* Am Soc Dermat Surg; Int Soc Dermat Surg; Am Acad Dermat. *Res:* Immunology of parasitic infections; schizophrenia; dermatology. *Mailing Add:* 4357 Folse Dr Metairie LA 70002

KRUPP, MARCUS ABRAHAM, MEDICINE, METABOLISM. *Current Pos:* dir, Palo Alto Med Clin Lab, 50-80, dir, 50-86, EMER DIR, PALO ALTO MED RES FOUND, 86- *Personal Data:* b El Paso, Tex, Feb 12, 13; m 41, 58, Donna Goodheart; c Michael, David (deceased), Peter & Sara. *Educ:* Stanford Univ, AB, 34, MD, 39; Am Bd Int Med, dipl, 47. *Honors & Awards:* Albion Walter Hewlett, 87. *Prof Exp:* Dir clin path, Vet Admin Hosp, San Francisco, 46-50. *Concurrent Pos:* Asst clin prof, Sch Med, Stanford Univ, 46-56, assoc clin prof, 56-65, clin prof, 65- *Mem:* Am Col Physicians; Am Fedn Clin Res; AAAS. *Res:* Renal physiology; water and electrolyte metabolism; author of several medical textbooks. *Mailing Add:* 860 Bryant St Palo Alto CA 94301

KRUPP, PATRICIA POWERS, GROSS ANATOMY, EXPERIMENTAL MORPHOLOGY. *Current Pos:* ASSOC PROF ANAT, COL MED, UNIV VT, 78- *Personal Data:* b New York, NY. *Educ:* Beaver Col, BA, 64; Hahnemann Med Col, PhD(anat), 70. *Prof Exp:* Asst instr nursing anat & physiol, Pa State Univ, Ogontz Campus, 63-66; sr instr gross anat, Hahnemann Med Col, 70-71, asst prof, 71-78. *Mem:* Am Asn Anatomists; AAAS; NY Acad Sci; Am Fedn Clin Res; Am Women Sci. *Res:* Experimental modification of thyroid gland structure and function; effects of diet, drugs, spontaneous hypertension and chronic stimulation. *Mailing Add:* Dept Anat & Neurobiol Col Med Univ Vt Given Bldg Burlington VT 05401

KRUSBERG, LORIN RONALD, PLANT PATHOLOGY. *Current Pos:* From asst prof to assoc prof, 60-70, PROF PLANT PATH, UNIV MD, COLLEGE PARK, 70- *Personal Data:* b July 18, 32; m; c 3. *Educ:* Univ Del, BS, 54; NC State Univ, MS, 56, PhD(plant path), 59. *Concurrent Pos:* Fel, NSF, Rothamsted Exp Sta, Eng, 59-60. *Mem:* Am Phytopath Soc; fel Soc Nematol; Sigma Xi. *Res:* Biology and control of nematodes parasitic on corn, soybeans and vegetables. *Mailing Add:* Dept Bot Univ Md College Park MD 20742-0001

KRUSCHWITZ, WALTER HILLIS, PHYSICS. *Current Pos:* RETIRED. *Personal Data:* b Edgerton, Ohio, July 20, 20; m 47, Virginia Stone; c Nancy & Sharon. *Educ:* Taylor Univ, AB, 42; Vanderbilt Univ, MA, 48; Univ Mich, PhD(higher ed), 61. *Prof Exp:* Assoc prof physics, Cumberland Univ, 48-50; asst prof physics & math, Union Univ, Tenn, 51-60, prof & head physics dept, 61-63; prof physics, Mobile Col, 63-67; assoc prof physics & educ, Univ SFla, 67-69, assoc prof phys sci & physics, 69-72, assoc prof physics, 73- *Mem:* Am Asn Physics Teachers. *Res:* Measurement of the velocity of a gas immediately before combustion; undergraduate college physics research and its sponsorship; science education. *Mailing Add:* 3307 Korina Lane Tampa FL 33618

KRUSE, ARTHUR HERMAN, MATHEMATICS. *Current Pos:* RES PROF MATH SCI, NMEX STATE UNIV, 60- *Personal Data:* b Easton, Kans, Feb 5, 28; m 54; c 2. *Educ:* Univ Kans, BA, 49, MA, 51; Univ Chicago, PhD(math), 56. *Prof Exp:* Res assoc math, Univ Kans, 54-60, from instr to asst prof, 54-60. *Mem:* Am Math Soc; Math Asn Am. *Res:* Topology; axiomatic set theory; analysis. *Mailing Add:* Dept Math NMex State Univ Las Cruces NM 88003-0105

KRUSE, CARL WILLIAM, coal desulfurization, coal analyses, for more information see previous edition

KRUSE, CONRAD EDWARD, BACTERIOLOGY. *Current Pos:* PROF ENVIRON ENG, TEMPLE UNIV, 90- *Personal Data:* b Philadelphia, Pa, Sept 14, 23; m 49; c 2. *Educ:* Philadelphia Col Pharm, BSc, 49, DSc(bact), 53; Univ Wis, MSc, 51. *Prof Exp:* Instr bact, Philadelphia Col Pharm, 51-56; res assoc, can div, Crown Cork & Seal Co, Pa, 56-57 & Col Dept, Lea & Febiger, 57-60; asst prof biol sci, Drexel Inst, 60-67; assoc prof biol, Ursinus Col, 67-89. *Concurrent Pos:* Dept supvr bact, Childrens Hosp, Philadelphia, 53-56; instr, Misericordia Hosp, Philadelphia, 55-56. *Mem:* AAAS; Am Soc Microbiol; Am Pharmaceut Asn; Inst Food Technologists. *Res:* Industrial and medical microbiology; biochemistry; food technology; development of pharmaceutical and food products; development of biochemical fuel cell. *Mailing Add:* Dept Environ Eng CECSA Temple Univ 1701 N Broad St Philadelphia PA 19122-2504

KRUSE, FERDINAND HOBERT, physical chemistry, for more information see previous edition

KRUSE, JAMES ALEXANDER, CRITICAL CARE MEDICINE, CLINICAL RESEARCH. *Current Pos:* instr internal med, 84-86, asst prof med, 86-91, ASSOC PROF MED, SCH MED, WAYNE STATE UNIV, 91- *Personal Data:* b Cleveland, Ohio, Aug 28, 52. *Educ:* Ohio State Univ, BA, 75, MD, 79. *Prof Exp:* Intern med, Akron City Hosp, Northeastern Ohio Univ, Col Med, 79-80, resident, 80-81, chief med resident; fel critical care med, Mt Carmel Mercy Hosp, Detroit, 82-84. *Concurrent Pos:* Dir, Respiratory Care Unit, Detroit Receiving Hosp, 85-93; vis prof, Univ Ill & Univ Mich, 87-93; consult, Food & Drug Admin Working Group, 88-93; specialist site vis, Accreditation Coun Grad Med Educ, 89-90; guest ed, Critical Care Clins, WB Saunders Co, Philadelphia, 91-92. *Mem:* Fel Am Col Critical Care Med. *Res:* Clinical studies of investigational drugs and medical devices (eg, intravascular catheters) and clinical and laboratory studies involving sepsis, oxygen transport, lactate metabolism, lactic acidosis, acid-base and electrolyte disorders. *Mailing Add:* DRH 5S-10 4201 St Antoine Blvd Detroit MI 48201

KRUSE, KIPP COLBY, BEHAVIORAL ECOLOGY. *Current Pos:* from asst prof to assoc prof, 79-87, PROF ZOOL, EASTERN ILL UNIV, 87- *Personal Data:* b Norfolk, Nebr, Nov 21, 49; m 75, Linda L Erwin; c Colby E & Hilary P. *Educ:* Wayne State Col, BSE, 71; Univ SDak, MA, 73; Univ Nebr, PhD(Ecol), 78. *Prof Exp:* Instr biol, Univ Nebr, 78-79. *Mem:* Sigma Xi; Soc Study Amphibians & Reptiles; Herpetologists League; Animal Behav Soc; Wildlife Soc. *Res:* Aspects of sexual selection in frogs, toads and waterbugs. *Mailing Add:* Dept Zool Eastern Ill Univ Charleston IL 61920. *Fax:* 217-521-2122; *E-Mail:* cfkck@eiu.edu

KRUSE, LAWRENCE IVAN, pharmaceutical chemistry, for more information see previous edition

KRUSE, OLAN ERNEST, PHYSICS. *Current Pos:* prof & chmn dept, 56-87, PROF PHYSICS, TEX A&I UNIV, 87- *Personal Data:* b Coupland, Tex, Sept 6, 21; m 42, Lucille Thomas; c 2. *Educ:* Tex Col Arts & Indust, BS, 42; Univ Tex, MA, 49, PhD, 51. *Prof Exp:* Jr radio engr, Signal Corps Labs, Camp Evans, NJ, 42-43; from asst prof to prof physics & chmn dept, Stephen F Austin State Col, 51-56. *Concurrent Pos:* Instr, Naval Officers Pre-Radar Sch, Harvard Univ, 43-44 & Bowdoin Col, 44-45; ensign, Lt JG & Lt US Naval Res, 43-46. *Mem:* Am Asn Physics Teachers. *Res:* Electronic circuitry; mechanics; electricity and magnetism; multiple scattering of charged particles by thin foils. *Mailing Add:* Dept Physics Tex A&I Univ Santa Gertrudis Kingsville TX 78363

KRUSE, PAUL WALTERS, JR, SOLID STATE PHYSICS, ELECTROOPTICS. *Current Pos:* CHIEF SCIENTIST, INFRARED SOLUTIONS, INC, 94- *Personal Data:* b Hibbing, Minn, Nov 24, 27; m 54; c 9. *Educ:* Univ Notre Dame, BS, 51, MS, 52, PhD(physics), 54. *Honors & Awards:* Recipient, H W Sweatt Award, Honeywell, Inc, 66; Alan Gordon Mem Award, Int Soc Optical Eng, 81. *Prof Exp:* Physicist, Farnsworth Electronics Co, 54-56; sr res scientist, Res Ctr, Minn-Honeywell Regulator Co, 56-59, prin res scientist, 59-60, staff scientist, 60-69, sr staff scientist, 70-77, prin staff scientist, 78-80, prin res fel, Corp Technol Ctr, 80-83, chief res fel, Sensor & Syst Develop Ctr, Honeywell, Inc, 83-93; consult infrared technol, 93-94. *Concurrent Pos:* Mem, US Army Sci Adv Panel, 65-77, ground warfare panel, President's Sci Adv Comt, 70-72, comt mat for electromagnetic radiation detection devices, Nat Acad Sci, 71-73 & Army Countermine Adv Comt, 71-74; mem planning comt, Third Int Photoconductivity Conf, 69-71; chmn, US Army ERADCOM Technol Panel, 75-76; mem, US Army Near-Millimeter Wave Technol Base Develop Study, 76-77; mem, Army Sci Bd, 78-82, 85-90; Mem comt phys sci, adv bd military personnel supplies, Nat Res Coun, Nat Acad Sci, 69-71, NATO rev panel Pres's Sci Adv Comt & Vietnam Panel, 71-72 & US/USSR Tech Balance Assessment Study, US Naval Res Adv Comt, 79-80; mem, Comt Biol & Chem Sensor Technol, Nat Res Coun, Nat Acad Sci, 83-84; mem, Sci & Technol Operating Comt, Am Electronics Asn, 90- *Mem:* Fel Am Phys Soc; assoc fel Am Inst Aeronaut & Astronaut; fel Optical Soc Am; sr mem Inst Elec & Electronics Engrs. *Res:* Electrooptical physics; nonlinear optics; infrared detectors; crystal growth; solid state devices; lasers; photoeffects in high temperature superconductors. *Mailing Add:* 6828 Oaklawn Ave Edina MN 55435. *Fax:* 612-551-0038; *E-Mail:* isi@visi.com

KRUSE, ROBERT LEROY, DATA STRUCTURES, ALGORITHM ANALYSIS. *Current Pos:* chmn dept, 76-79, PROF MATH & COMPUT SCI, ST MARY'S UNIV, HALIFAX, 79- *Personal Data:* b Jacksonville, Fla, Jan 7, 41. *Educ:* Pomona Col, BA, 62; Calif Inst Technol, MS, 62, PhD(math), 64. *Prof Exp:* Staff mem, Sandia Lab, 64-70; assoc prof math, Emory Univ, 73-76. *Concurrent Pos:* Fulbright-Hays grant & vis reader, Univ Canterbury, NZ, 70-72; vis prof, Univ Alberta, 82; Erskine fel, Univ Canterbury, New Zealand, 90. *Mem:* Am Math Soc; Asn Comput Mach. *Res:* Data structures; applications of computers in abstract algebra; finite rings. *Mailing Add:* Dept Math & Comput Sci St Mary's Univ Halifax NS B3H 3C3 Can. *E-Mail:* kruse@stmarys.ca

KRUSE, ROBERT LOUIS, CHEMICAL ENGINEERING, POLYMER CHEMISTRY & ENGINEERING. *Current Pos:* chem engr, Monsanto Co, 67-70, res group leaser, 70-78, sci fel 78-85, sr sci fel, 85-96, CONSULT, MONSANTO CO, 96- *Personal Data:* b Fairmont, Minn, Aug 23, 38; c Donna & Brian. *Educ:* Univ Minn, Minneapolis, BS, 60; Univ Ill, Urbana, MS, 62; Columbia Univ, EngSciD(chem eng), 67. *Prof Exp:* Chem engr, Esso Res & Eng Co, NJ, 61-64. *Concurrent Pos:* Lectr polymer processing, Univ Mass, 67-68; lectr math, Western New Eng Col, 68-89; lectr polymer characterization, St Joseph Col, Conn, 70-71. *Mem:* Am Chem Soc; Soc Petrol Engrs. *Res:* Polymerization kinetics; rheology and surface properties of polymers; molecular characterization; continuum properties; composites; structure/property relationships. *Mailing Add:* 444 Michael Sears Rd Belchertown MA 01007. *Fax:* 413-283-3544; *E-Mail:* r.l.kruse@juno.com

KRUSE, ULRICH ERNST, PHYSICS. *Current Pos:* from asst prof to prof physics, 59-, EMER PROF PHYSICS, UNIV ILL, URBANA. *Personal Data:* b Berlin, Ger, May 22, 29; nat US. *Educ:* Harvard Univ, PhD(physics), 54. *Prof Exp:* From instr to asst prof physics, Univ Chicago, 54-59. *Mem:* Fel Am Phys Soc. *Res:* Experimental nuclear physics. *Mailing Add:* 2210 Combs St Urbana IL 61801

KRUSE, WALTER M, INORGANIC CHEMISTRY, PHYSICAL CHEMISTRY. *Current Pos:* CONSULT, 90- *Personal Data:* b Heide, Ger, Oct 6, 28; m 60, Edith Blackbird; c Elke & Lakota. *Educ:* Univ Cologne, PhD, 58. *Prof Exp:* Fel, Univ Chicago, 58-60; asst kinetics, Max Planck Inst Phys Chem, 60-64; res chemist, Hercules Res Ctr, Del, 64-71; Atlas Chem Industs, Inc, 71-74, ICI United States, Inc, 74-79, sr res chemist, ICI Americas, Inc, 79-90. *Concurrent Pos:* Res info scientist, 88-91. *Mem:* Am Chem Soc; Sigma Xi. *Res:* Preparative inorganic chemistry; complex chemistry; oxidation of olefins; hydrogenation of carbohydrates; homogeneous catalysis. *Mailing Add:* One Woodbury Ct Wilmington DE 19805

KRUSEN, EDWARD MONTGOMERY, MEDICINE. *Current Pos:* RETIRED. *Personal Data:* b Philadelphia, Pa, Feb 7, 20; m 48, 75, Ruth Trescott; c Richard & Nancy. *Educ:* Univ Pa, BA, 41, MD, 44; Univ Minn, MS, 50. *Honors & Awards:* Tex Award Planning Voc Rehab, 68; Distinguished Clinician, Am Acad Phys Med & Rehab, 85. *Prof Exp:* Med dir phys ther sch, Baylor Univ Med Ctr, 51-71, prof phys ther, Univ, 58-71, chief Dept Phys Med & Rehab, 50-85. *Concurrent Pos:* From asst prof to assoc prof phys med & rehab, Univ Tex Health Sci Ctr, 51-61, chmn dept, 51-55, clin prof phys med & rehab, 61-; area consult, Vet Admin, 54-; chmn med adv bd, United Cerebral Palsy, Tex, 55-73; consult, Elizabeth Kenney Found, 55-57 & Am Rehab Found, 57-; chmn, Coun Med Dirs Phys Ther Schs, 60; mem, Am Bd Phys Med & Rehab, 65-77, Gov Coun Develop Disabilities, 71 & Residency Review Comt, 76-82. *Mem:* AMA; Am Rheumatism Asn; Am Cong Rehab Med; Am Acad Phys Med & Rehab; Sigma Xi. *Res:* Cervical syndrome; backache; hemiplegia; exercise; rehabilitation of the elderly; electromyography. *Mailing Add:* 3500 Colgate Dallas TX 75225

KRUSHENSKY, RICHARD D, GEOLOGY, VOLCANOLOGY. *Current Pos:* geologist, Br Spec Projs, US Geol Surv, 61-64 & Br Int Geol, 64-70, geologist, Br Eastern Environ Geol & dep chief, Off Environ Geol, 74-79, actg chief, Off Environ Geol, 79-80, geologist, Br Eastern Environ Geol, 80-83, DEP CHIEF LATIN AM, ASSOC CHIEF & CHIEF EUROPE, OFF INT GEOL, US GEOL SURV, 83- *Personal Data:* b Ferndale, Mich, June 3, 32; m 60, Arvene L Pell; c Kari L. *Educ:* Wayne State Univ, BS, 55, MS, 57; Ohio State Univ, PhD(geol), 60. *Prof Exp:* Geologist, Orinoco Mining Co Div, US Steel Corp, 60-62. *Res:* Mineral exploration and training of local personnel in Turkey; study of Irazu Volcano, Costa Rica and other active and inactive volcanoes in Central America; volcanic petrology and petrography; volcanology; mineral exploration; regional geology of volcanogenic and intrusive rocks in Puerto Rico. *Mailing Add:* 8106 Timber Valley Ct Dunn Loring VA 22027. *Fax:* 703-648-4227; *E-Mail:* rkrushen@usgs.gov

KRUSIC, PAUL JOSEPH, ELECTRON SPIN RESONANCE, FREE RADICAL CHEMISTRY. *Current Pos:* RES CHEMIST, CENT RES DEPT, E I DU PONT DE NEMOURS & CO, INC, 66- *Personal Data:* b Trieste, Italy, Nov 28, 34; m 56; c Paul Jr, Sonja & Mara. *Educ:* Wesleyan Univ, BA, 59; Univ Calif, Berkeley, PhD(chem), 65. *Honors & Awards:* Delaware Sec Award, Am Chem Soc, 74. *Prof Exp:* Chemist, Cent Res Lab, Gen Elec Co, NY, 59-61. *Concurrent Pos:* Vis scholar, Centre d'Etudes Nucleaires de Grenoble, France, 81-82; vis prof, Ecole Normale Superieure, Paris, 87. *Mem:* Am Chem Soc. *Res:* Microwave spectroscopy; electron spin resonance spectroscopy; free radical chemistry; organometallic reaction mechanisms; homogeneous catalysis; organometallic photochemistry; autoxidation of hydrocarbons; radical chemistry of fullerenes; gas-phase nuclear magnetic resonance; fluorine chemistry. *Mailing Add:* Cent Res Dept E I du Pont de Nemours & Co Inc Wilmington DE 19880-0328. *E-Mail:* krusic@esvax.dnet.dupont.com

KRUSKAL, BENJAMIN A, PHAGOCYTOSIS, MYCOBACTERIAL INFECTIONS. *Current Pos:* ASST MED, INFECTIOUS DIS, CHILDREN'S HOSP, 93-; ASST PEDIATRICIAN, MASS GEN HOSP, 96- *Personal Data:* b Ann Arbor, Mich, May 15, 59; m 84, Maureen O'Brien; c Meira, Shoshana & Adina. *Educ:* Univ Pa, BA, 81; NY Univ, MS, 84, MD, 88, PhD(pharmacol), 88. *Concurrent Pos:* Fel, Cancer Res Inst, 91-94; Charles Janeway fel child health res, Children's Hosp, 94. *Mem:* Am Soc Cell Biol; AAAS; Infectious Dis Soc Am; Pediat Infectious Dis Soc; Am Acad Pediat; Am Soc Microbiol. *Res:* Cell biology of phagocytosis; phagosome-lysosome fusion and its inhibition by microbial pathogens; the macrophage mannose receptor. *Mailing Add:* 300 Longwood Ave Boston MA 02115. *Fax:* 617-355-6575; *E-Mail:* kruskal@a1.tch.harvard.edu

KRUSKAL, JOSEPH BERNARD, COMBINATORICS, STATISTICS. *Current Pos:* RETIRED. *Personal Data:* b New York, NY, Jan 29, 28; m 53, Rachel Solomon; c Joyce & Benjamin. *Educ:* Univ Chicago, PhB & BS, 48, MS, 49; Princeton Univ, PhD, 54. *Prof Exp:* Instr math, Princeton Univ, 55; res instr, Univ Wis, 56-58; asst prof, Univ Mich, 58-59; mem tech staff, Bell Labs, 59-93. *Concurrent Pos:* Vis prof, Yale Univ, 66-67, Columbia Univ, 76, Rutgers Univ, 77; assoc ed jour, Soc Indust & Appl Math, 67-70. *Mem:* Am Math Soc; Classification Soc NAm (pres, 74-77); fel AAAS; fel Am Statist Asn; Psychometric Soc (pres, 74-75). *Res:* Statistics, psychometrics and statistical linguistics. *Mailing Add:* 42 Oakland Rd Maplewood NJ 07040. *E-Mail:* kruskal@research.bell-labs.com

KRUSKAL, MARTIN DAVID, MATHEMATICAL PHYSICS, APPLIED MATHEMATICS. *Current Pos:* DAVID AILBERT PROF MATH, RUTGERS UNIV, NEW BRUNSWICK, 89- *Personal Data:* b New York, NY, Sept 28, 25; m 50; c 3. *Educ:* Univ Chicago, BS, 45; NY Univ, MS, 48, PhD(math), 52. *Honors & Awards:* Fulbright lectr, Grenoble, France, 59 & 78; Gibbs lectr, Am Math Soc, 79; Dannie-Helmman Prize Math Physics, 83; Potts Gold Medal, Franklin Inst, 86; Appl Math & Numerical Anal, Nat Acad Sci, 89; Nat Med Sci, 93. *Prof Exp:* Asst & instr math, NY Univ, 46-51; res scientist, Plasma Physics Lab, Princeton Univ, 51-59, sr res assoc & lectr astron, 59-61, prof astrophys sci, 61-89, dir, Prog Appl Math, 68-86, prof, 79-, emer prof math, 79-89. *Concurrent Pos:* Consult, Los Alamos Sci Lab, 53-59,

Radiation Lab, Univ Calif, 54-57, Oak Ridge Nat Lab, 55-58, 63-, Radio Corp Am, 60-62 & IBM Corp, 63-; assoc head, Theoret Div, Plasma Physics, Lab, Princeton Univ, 56-64; NSF sr fel, Max Planck Inst Physics & Astrophysics, Ger, 59-60; vis prof, Weizman Inst Sci, Israel, 73-74; fel, Japanese Soc Prom Sci, Nagoya Univ, 79-80; mem bd dir, Soc Indust & Appl Math, 85-; co dir, Inst Termenoild Physics, Santa Barbara, 85. *Mem:* Nat Acad Sci; Am Math Soc; Math Asn Am; Am Phys Soc; Soc Indust & Appl Math; Am Acad Arts & Sci. *Res:* Plasma physics; general mathematics; asymptotic phenomena; logic; magnetohydrodynamics; controlled fusion; relativity; minimal surfaces. *Mailing Add:* Dept Math Hill Centre Rutgers Univ Busch Campus New Brunswick NJ 08903. *E-Mail:* kruskal@math.rutgers.edu

KRUSKAL, WILLIAM HENRY, STATISTICS. *Current Pos:* from instr to prof, Univ Chicago, 50-73, chmn dept, 66-73, Ernest Dewitt Burton distinguished serv prof statist & col, 73- 89, dean, Div Social Sci, 74-84, EMER ERNEST DEWITT BURTON DISTINGUISHED SERV PROF STATIST & COL, UNIV CHICAGO, 90- *Personal Data:* b New York, NY, Oct 10, 19; m 42; c 3. *Educ:* Harvard Univ, SB, 40, MS, 41; Columbia Univ, PhD(math statist), 55. *Honors & Awards:* Ronald A Fisher Mem lectr, Comt Pres Statist Socs, 78; Samuel S Wilks Mem Medal, 78. *Prof Exp:* Mathematician, US Naval Proving Ground, 41-46; vpres, Kruskal & Kruskal, Inc, 46-48; lectr math, Columbia Univ, 49-50. *Concurrent Pos:* Vis asst prof, Univ Calif, Berkeley, 55-56; ed, Annals Math Statist, Inst Math Statist, 58-61; chmn math sci panel & mem cent planning comt, Behav & Soc Sci Surv Comt, 66-70; mem adv comt, Encycl Britannica, 66-76, adv comt probs census enumeration, Nat Res Coun, 69-71 & President's Comn Fed Statist, 70-71; fel, Ctr Advan Study in Behav Sci, 70-71; NSF sr fel, 70-71; trustee, Nat Opinion Res Ctr, 70-; dir, Social Sci Res Coun, 75-78; chmn comt Nat Statist, Nat Acad Sci-Nat Res Coun, 71-78; mem adv coun, NSF, 77-; mem adv comt, Fed Statist Syst Reorgn, 78-80; John Simon Guggenheim Mem Found fel, 79-80, mem educ adv board, 80-88. *Mem:* Fel AAAS; fel Inst Math Statist (pres, 70-71); fel Am Statist Asn (vpres, 72-74, pres, 82); Int Statist Inst; Math Asn Am; fel Am Acad Arts & Sci; hon fel Royal Statist Soc. *Res:* Theoretical statistics, especially nonparametric analysis and analysis of variance; public policy aspects of statistics. *Mailing Add:* Dept Statist Univ Chicago Chicago IL 60637

KRUTAK, JAMES JOHN, SR, CHEMISTRY OF FUNCTIONAL DYES, DESIGN OF NEAR-ULTRAVIOLET NEAR INFRARED & VISIBLE DYES. *Current Pos:* res chemist, Tenn Eastman Co, Eastman Kodak Co, 67-69, sr res chemist, 69-75, res assoc, 75-93, SR RES ASSOC, TENN EASTMAN CO, EASTMAN KODAK CO, 94- *Personal Data:* b Atlanta, Ga, Apr 5, 42; m 80, Elsa Thur de Koos; c James, Kim, Kari, Juan, Jon, David & Khristopher. *Educ:* La State Univ, BS, 64; Univ NC, PhD(org chem), 68. *Concurrent Pos:* Coordr, Photog Chem Res Lab, Eastman Kodak, 73-83, asst to chem res dir, 84-85, lab head, Colorants Res Lab, 86-91; mem sci adv comt, Cosmetic, Toiletry & Fragrance Asn; functional dye consult, 91- *Mem:* Am Chem Soc; Int Soc Heterocyclic Chem; Am Asn Textile Chemists & Colorists; Tech Asn Pulp & Paper Indust; Soc Plastics Engrs; Soc Cosmetic Chemists. *Res:* Synthesis of natural products; development of novel indole synthesis; study of mechanisms of indole forming reactions using stable and radioactive isotope tracer methodology; cycloaddition reactions; chemical uses of lasers; photographic dye and developer synthesis and related technology; functional dye design and synthesis for plastics, fibers, inks, coatings, personal and household care products, safe coloration and UV-screen systems for cosmetics, medical products, construction products, security and automation systems; synthetic paper compositions and advanced materials of construction from recyclable polymers; automation of plastics recycling near infrared dye design; granted over 40 patents. *Mailing Add:* Res Labs Eastman Chem Co PO Box 1972 Kingsport TN 37662-5150. *Fax:* 423-229-4558

KRUTAK, PAUL RUSSELL, PETROLEUM GEOLOGY, OSTRACODE ECOLOGY & SYSTEMATICS. *Current Pos:* CHMN GEOSCI, FT HAYS STATE UNIV, 92- *Personal Data:* b Pueblo, Colo, Oct 6, 34; m 55, Jerri Nichols; c Paul R Jr, Helen E, Krag F, Kurt M & Lars F. *Educ:* La State Univ, BS, 56, MS, 60, PhD(struct geol), 63. *Honors & Awards:* Silver Medal, Geol Inst, Univ Mex, 80. *Prof Exp:* Geologist, Stanolin Oil & Gas Co, Wyo, 56-58; asst geol, La State Univ, 58-63, res asst, 60-63, res dir, Basin Res Inst, 88-91; asst prof geol, Ball State Univ, 63-65; assoc prof, Eastern NMex Univ, 65-70; prof geol, Univ Nebr, Lincoln, 70-82; sr geologist, Arco Explor Co, Lafayette, La, 82-85; consult geologist, Terra-Mar Geoserv Int, 86-88. *Concurrent Pos:* Micropaleontologist, Shell Oil Co, 60; Geol Soc Am Grand, 65-66; field geologist, Idaho Bur Mines, 67 & 68; Sigma Xi grant, 67; consult, Sunrise Explor Co, Phoenix, Ariz, 68; vis prof geol, Univ Mex, 79 & La State Univ, 79; Fulbright Res Award, Nuevo Leon, Mex, 80-81; asesor, Inst Geol, Univ Mex, 80; vchmn, Global Sedimentary Geol Prog, 88; co-convenor, Geol Soc Am, 90; lectr, Korea Ocean Res Develop Inst, 97; mem, Cushman Found Foraminiferal Res. *Mem:* Am Asn Petrol Geologists; fel Geol Soc Am. *Res:* Regional structure and stratigraphy; mesozoic-cenozoic micropaleontology; petrography; seismic stratigraphy; copper porphry exploration. *Mailing Add:* Dept Geosci Ft Hays State Univ 600 Park St Hays KS 67601-4099. *Fax:* 785-628-4096; *E-Mail:* gspk@fhsuvm.fhsu.edu

KRUTCHEN, CHARLES M(ARION), CHEMICAL ENGINEERING. *Current Pos:* RETIRED. *Personal Data:* b Gadsen, Ala, Sept 7, 34; m 59, Mary A Metaxas; c Carolyn P, Anne E, James C & Melissa M. *Educ:* Vanderbilt Univ, BE, 56; Cornell Univ, PhD(chem eng), 64. *Prof Exp:* Chem engr, Res Ctr, Hercules Powder Co, 56-58, res engr, Fiber Dept, 62-64; sr res engr, Res Div, W R Grace & Co, 64-66; staff chem engr, Gen Elec Res & Develop Ctr, 66-76; eng assoc, Res & Develop Lab, Mobil Chem, Edison, NJ, 76-77, res supvr, Plastics Div, 77-90, sr res assoc, 90-92, sr res assoc, Macedon, NY, 92-95. *Mem:* Am Inst Chem Engrs; Am Chem Soc; AAAS; Soc Plastics Engrs. *Res:* Chemical process studies; polymer fiber, film and foam technology; polymer processing; morphology-physical property relationships in polymers; polymer recycling; granted 27 patents. *Mailing Add:* 30514 Laurel Ct Daphne AL 36527. *Fax:* 315-986-5213

KRUTCHKOFF, DAVID JAMES, ORAL PATHOLOGY, DENTISTRY. *Current Pos:* PROF ORAL DIAGNOSIS-PATH, UNIV CONN, 73- *Personal Data:* b Eureka, Calif, June 7, 38; m 66, Sumiko Takao; c Tamara, Todd & Laurel. *Educ:* Univ Calif, Berkeley, AB, 60; Wash Univ, DDS, 64; Univ Mich, MS, 70. *Prof Exp:* Res asst path, Wash Univ, 67-68; Nat Inst Dent Res fel & instr oral path, Univ Mich, 68-70; asst prof oral path, Univ Louisville, 70-73. *Concurrent Pos:* Vis prof, Tohoku Univ, Sendai, Japan, 87. *Mem:* Int Asn Dent Res; Am Acad Oral Path; Eastern Soc Teachers Oral Path. *Res:* Dental caries; clinical studies; dental enamel; infrared internal reflection spectroscopy; oral cancer; lichenoid dysplasia; forensic consultation. *Mailing Add:* Dept Oral Path Univ Conn Health Ctr MC 0925 263 Farmington Ave Farmington CT 06030. *Fax:* 860-679-4334

KRUTCHKOFF, RICHARD GERALD, APPLIED STATISTICS. *Current Pos:* from asst prof to prof, 64-96, EMER PROF STATIST, VA POLYTECH INST & STATE UNIV, 96- *Personal Data:* b Brooklyn, NY, Dec 23, 33; m 87, Debra Jarrett; c Barbara, Robyn & Daniel. *Educ:* Columbia Univ, AB, 56, MA, 58, PhD(math statist), 64. *Prof Exp:* Instr physics, Wilkes Col, 58-60; lectr, Queens Col, NY, 60-64. *Concurrent Pos:* Ed, J Statist Comput & Simulation, 72- *Mem:* AAAS; fel Am Statist Asn. *Res:* Statistical inference; empirical Bayes decision theory; water pollution statistics; simulation; chaos. *Mailing Add:* Dept Statist Va Polytech Inst & State Univ Blacksburg VA 24061

KRUTTER, HARRY, PHYSICS. *Current Pos:* CONSULT, DIGITAL SYST GROUP, 86- *Personal Data:* b Boston, Mass, Mar 17, 11; m 35; c 1. *Educ:* Mass Inst Technol, 32, SM, 33, PhD(physics), 35. *Honors & Awards:* Distinguished Civilian Serv Award, USN, 56; Distinguished Civilian Serv Award, US Dept Defense, 57. *Prof Exp:* Teaching fel physics, Mass Inst Technol, 33-35; instr, Purdue Univ, 35-36; asst prof petrol eng, Pa State Col, 36-42; res assoc & staff mem, Mass Inst Technol, 42-45; chief scientist, Field Sta, Naval Res Lab, 46-49, tech dir, Aero Electronics & Elec Lab, 49-56, chief scientist, 56-67, tech dir, 67-73, consult, Naval Air Develop Ctr, 73-85. *Concurrent Pos:* Lectr, Wharton Sch, Univ Pa, 73-79. *Mem:* Am Phys Soc; fel Inst Elec & Electronics Engrs; assoc fel Am Inst Aeronaut & Astronaut. *Res:* X-ray crystal structure; theory of metals; flow of gases through porous media; antennas; radar; electronics. *Mailing Add:* 310 S Easton Rd Glenside PA 19038

KRUTZ, RONALD L, COMPUTER ENGINEERING. *Current Pos:* fac mem, Dept Elec Eng, 75-78, ASSOC DIR, CARNEGIE-MELLON RES INST, PITTSBURGH, 78-, DIR & FOUNDER, COMPUT ENG CTR, 78- *Personal Data:* b McKeesport, Pa, Aug 27, 38; m 61, Hilda M Napolitano; c Sheri R & Lisa M. *Educ:* Univ Pittsburgh, BSEE, 60, MSEE, 67, PhD(elec eng), 72. *Prof Exp:* Proj engr, Gulf Res & Develop Co, 64-74; mgr, Comput Sci Dept, Res & Develop Ctr, Singer Corp, 74-75. *Mem:* Sr mem Inst Elec & Electronics Engrs. *Res:* Microprocessors and logic design; developed video tape course on microprocessors and software; contributed articles to professional journals; distributed computing; awarded seven patents for computer and digital systems. *Mailing Add:* Carnegie-Mellon Res Ctr 700 Technology Dr Pittsburgh PA 15213

KRUTZSCH, HENRY C, PROTEIN BIOCHEMISTRY. *Current Pos:* sr staff fel, Lab Chem, Nat Heart, Lung & Blood Inst, NIH, 73-77, Lab Immunogenetics, Nat Inst Allergy & Infectious Dis, 77-79, expert, 79-82, Lab Exp Carcinogenesis, Nat Cancer Inst, 82-86, spec expert, Diabetes Br, Nat Inst Diabetes & Digestive & Kidney Dis, 86-87, cancer expert, lab path, 87-92, CHEMIST LAB PATH, NAT CANCER INST, NIH, 92- *Personal Data:* b Fairbanks, Alaska, Feb 7, 42; m 74, Christine Bekiesz. *Educ:* Univ Calif, Riverside, BA, 64; Univ Iowa, PhD(org chem), 68. *Prof Exp:* Res chemist, Pioneering Res Div, Exp Sta, E I du Pont de Nemours & Co, 68-73. *Mem:* AAAS; Am Soc Biochem & Molecular Biol; Protein Soc; Am Chem Soc; Sigma Xi. *Res:* Protein biochemistry. *Mailing Add:* Path Lab NIH Bldg 10 Rm 2A33 Bethesda MD 20892

KRUTZSCH, PHILIP HENRY, ANATOMY, ZOOLOGY. *Current Pos:* head dept, 64-73, prof, 64-89, EMER PROF ANAT, COL MED, UNIV ARIZ, 90- *Personal Data:* b St Louis, Mo, July 12, 19; m 40, Dorothy Edens; c Eric W & Lynda C. *Educ:* San Diego State Col, BA, 43; Univ Calif, MA, 48; Univ Kans, PhD(zool,anat), 53. *Prof Exp:* Asst, Univ Calif, 47-48; asst instr, Univ Kans, 48-52, asst, 49; instr anat, Sch Med, Univ Pittsburgh, 53-54; asst prof, Univ Tex Health Sci Ctr, Dallas, 55-56; assoc prof, Sch Med, Univ Pittsburgh, 57-64. *Mem:* Am Soc Mammal; Am Asn Anatomists; Am Soc Zoologists; Soc Study Reproduction. *Res:* Physiology of reproduction; studies of brown adipose tissue, prolonged sperm longevity and male reproduction. *Mailing Add:* Dept Cell Biol & Anat Univ Ariz Col Med 1501 N Campbell Tucson AZ 85724. *Fax:* 520-626-2097

KRUUS, JAAN, ELECTRICAL ENGINEERING, INSTRUMENTATION. *Current Pos:* vpres, 81-89, PRES, COMM INSTRUMENTS & METHODS OBSERVATION, WORLD METEOROL ORGN, 89- *Personal Data:* b Kuimetsa, Estonia, July 23, 36; Can citizen; m 62, Reet Luhaki; c Erik, Karin, Kaia & Robert. *Educ:* Univ Toronto, BASc, 59; Univ Ill, MS, 61, PhD(elec eng), 63. *Prof Exp:* Engr, Spruce Falls Power & Paper Co, Ont, 59-60; asst prof elec eng, Queen's Univ, Ont, 63-65; assoc prof, Univ Ottawa, 65-69; head, Instrumentation Sect, Hydrol Sci Div, Inland Waters Br, Environ Can, 69-74, coordr remote sensing, Off Sci Adv, 74-78, planning analyst, Atmospheric Environ Serv, 78-80, dir, Data Acquisition Serv Br, 80-91. *Mem:* Inst Elec & Electronics Engrs; Sigma Xi. *Res:* Application of artificial intelligence for meteorological measurements. *Mailing Add:* 15 Michigan Dr Willowdale ON M2M 3H9 Can

KRUUS, PEETER, PHYSICAL CHEMISTRY. *Current Pos:* From asst prof to assoc prof, 65-77, PROF CHEM, CARLETON UNIV, 77- *Personal Data:* b Tallinn, Estonia, July 8, 39; Can citizen; m 63; c 4. *Educ:* Univ Toronto, BSc, 61, PhD(phys chem), 65; Tech Univ Denmark, Lic Techn, 63. *Concurrent Pos:* Sci adv, Sci Coun Can, 69-70; res scientist, Cominco Ltd, 79-80; adv, Int Orgn Consumers Unions, 87-88. *Mem:* Chem Inst Can. *Res:* Structure and dynamics in liquids and solutions; cavitation-induced chemical reactions; supercritical extraction. *Mailing Add:* Dept Chem Carleton Univ Colonel By Dr Ottawa ON K1S 5B6 Can

KRUUV, JACK, CRYOBIOLOGY, RADIOBIOLOGY. *Current Pos:* RETIRED. *Personal Data:* b Tartu, Estonia, June 1, 38; Can citizen; m 60, Joan Lederman; c Cindy, Wendy & Sean. *Educ:* Univ Waterloo, BASc, 62, MSc, 63; Univ Western Ont, PhD(biophys), 66. *Prof Exp:* Ont Cancer Found fel & lectr, Victoria Hosp, 66; fel, Argonne Nat Lab, 66-67; from asst prof to assoc prof physics, Univ Waterloo, 67-77, prof physics & biol, 77-96. *Concurrent Pos:* Vis prof biophysics, Pa State Univ, 74-75; vis prof, Univ Calif, 93. *Mem:* Radiation Res Soc; Cryobiol Soc. *Res:* Cancer research; radiation biophysics; research with synchronized tissue culture cells; effects of low oxygen atmospheres on cells; radiotherapy of cancer cells; repair of radiation and freeze-thaw damage; cryobiology; multi-cellular tissue culture systems; hypothermia; hyperthermia; mechanisms of freeze-thaw damage. *Mailing Add:* Dept Physics Univ Waterloo Waterloo ON N2L 3G1 Can. *Fax:* 519-746-8115

KRYDER, MARK HOWARD, MAGNETIC RECORDING, MAGNETO-OPTIC RECORDING. *Current Pos:* assoc prof, 78-80, dir, Magnetics Technol Ctr, 82-90, PROF ELEC & COMP ENG, CARNEGIE-MELLON UNIV, 80-, DIR, DATA STORAGE SYSTS CTR, 90- *Personal Data:* b Portland, Ore, Oct 7, 43; m 65, Sandra L Curtis; c Christa M & Matthew C. *Educ:* Stanford Univ, BS, 65; Calif Inst Technol, MS, 66, PhD(elec eng, physics), 70. *Honors & Awards:* Magnetics Soc Achievement Award, Inst Elec & Electronics Engrs. *Prof Exp:* NSF res fel, Calif Inst Technol, 69-71; scientist solid state physics, Univ Regensburg, 71-73; res staff mem, IBM Res Ctr, 73-75, mgr explor bubble devices, 75-78. *Concurrent Pos:* Consult, IBM, Gen Elec, Nat Semiconductor Corp, Motorola, & Alcoa; distinguished lectr, Inst Elec & Electronics Engrs, 85. *Mem:* Nat Acad Eng; fel Inst Elec & Electronics Engrs; Am Phys Soc. *Res:* Applied magnetics; magneto-optical, and magnetic recording devices including materials, fabrication, device design and use in systems. *Mailing Add:* Dept Elec & Comput Eng Carnegie-Mellon Univ Pittsburgh PA 15213

KRYGER, ROY GEORGE, PHYSICAL ORGANIC CHEMISTRY. *Current Pos:* PROF CHEM, LOMA LINDA UNIV, RIVERSIDE, CALIF, 84- *Personal Data:* b Brooklyn, NJ, June 7, 36; m 58; c 2. *Educ:* Atlantic Union Col, AB, 57; Stevens Inst Technol, MS, 66; Boston Univ, PhD(org chem), 73. *Prof Exp:* Chemist qual control, Lederle Lab Div, Am Cyanamid Co, 57-58; chemist food analyst, US Army Med Res & Nutrit Lab, 59-60; anal methods develop & antibiotic res & develop chemist, Lederle Lab Div, Am Cyanamid Co, 60-66; prof chem, Atlantic Union Col, 81-84, chmn dept, 66-84. *Mem:* AAAS; Nat Sci Teachers Asn. *Res:* Relative and absolute reactivities of free radicals and relation of structure of free radicals to their reactivity. *Mailing Add:* 20265 Silktassel Rd Riverside CA 92508-3025

KRYNITSKY, JOHN ALEXANDER, PETROLEUM FUELS, CHEMISTRY. *Current Pos:* CONSULT, FUELS & PETROL PROD, 81- *Personal Data:* b Far Rockaway Beach, NY, June 15, 18; m 49; c 1. *Educ:* Univ Md, BS, 39; Univ NC, PhD(org chem), 43. *Prof Exp:* Asst chem, Univ NC, 39-43; chemist, Naval Res Lab, DC, 43-44 & 45-64; staff asst, Off Dir Defense Res & Eng, 64-67; dir tech opers, Defense Fuel Supply Ctr, 67-81. *Mem:* Am Chem Soc; Am Soc Testing & Mat. *Res:* Fuels; lubricants; petroleum products; organic materials; synthetic organic chemistry; detection and identification of organic substances; preparations and properties of some highly chlorinated hydrocarbons; hydrazine; aircraft and rocket fuels. *Mailing Add:* 4904 Cumberland Ave Chevy Chase MD 20815-5454

KRYSAN, JAMES LOUIS, INSECT PHYSIOLOGY. *Current Pos:* res leader, res entomologist, Yakima Res Lab, Agr Res Serv, 84-92, USDA, AT USDA, BELTSVILLE, MD, 92- *Personal Data:* b Calmar, Iowa, Mar 12, 34; m 60; c 3. *Educ:* Iowa State Teachers Col, BA, 61; Univ Ill, MS, 64, PhD(entom), 65. *Prof Exp:* Asst prof biol, St Mary's Col, Minn, 65-68; entomologist, Northern Grain Insects Res Lab, Sci & Educ Admin-Agr Res, USDA, 68-84. *Mem:* Entom Soc Am; AAAS; Am Soc Nat; Coleopterists Soc. *Res:* Management of insect pests of pear; biosystematics of Diabrotica; seasonality of insects. *Mailing Add:* 5802 Nicholson Lane Rockville MD 20852

KRYSTEK, STANLEY R, JR, COMPUTATIONAL BIOCHEMISTRY, PROTEIN & PEPTIDE MODELING. *Current Pos:* Res fel, 89-90, res investr I, 90-92, RES INVESTR II, BRISTOL-MEYERS SQUIBB, 92- *Personal Data:* b Ft Belvoir, Va, May 6, 61. *Educ:* State Univ NY, Albany, BS, 83; Albany Med Col, MS, 85, PhD(biochem), 89. *Mem:* Biophys Soc; Protein Soc; Am Peptide Soc; AAAS; Am Chem Soc. *Res:* Computational biochemistry; protein and peptide modeling. *Mailing Add:* Bristol-Myers Squibb Res Inst PO Box 4000 Princeton NJ 08543-4000. *Fax:* 609-252-6030

KRYTER, KARL DAVID, PSYCHOPHYSIOLOGY, PSYCHOACOUSTICS. *Current Pos:* LECTR & ADJ PROF, SAN DIEGO STATE UNIV, 91- *Personal Data:* b Indianapolis, Ind, Oct 13, 14; m 46; c 3. *Educ:* Butler Univ, AB, 39; Univ Rochester, PhD(psychol), 43. *Honors & Awards:* Distinguished Award Sci, Am Speech & Hearing Asn; Franklin V Taylor Award in Eng Psychol. *Prof Exp:* Fel psycho-acoust, Harvard Univ, 42-46; asst prof psychol, Univ Wash, St Louis, 46-48; dir human factors oper res lab, USAF, 48-52 & oper appln lab, Cambridge Res Ctr, 52-57; head psychoacoust dept, Bolt Beranek & Newman, Inc, 57-65; dir, Sensory Res Ctr, Stanford Res Inst, 65-85; staff scientist, SRI Int, 85-91. *Concurrent Pos:* Pres, Acousis Co; mem comt hearing, bioacoust & biomech, Nat Acad Sci-Nat Res Coun, 57-, chmn exec coun, 61-64; mem adv panel psychol & soc sci, Off Asst Secy Defense, 58-63; Int Orgn Standard & Int Electrotechnol Comn, 62-; adv, President's Comt Sci & Technol. *Mem:* Fel AAAS; Soc Eng Psychol (pres, 66); Am Psychol Asn; Acoust Soc Am (pres, 71); Human Factors Soc. *Res:* Audition; psychoacoustics; speech communication; electrophysiology. *Mailing Add:* 1515 San Antonio Creek Rd Santa Barbara CA 93111

KRYWOLAP, GEORGE NICHOLAS, MICROBIAL ECOLOGY. *Current Pos:* From asst prof microbiol to assoc prof, Schs Pharm & Dent, 64-77, PROF MICROBIOL, UNIV MD, 77- *Personal Data:* b Ukraine, May 4, 36; US citizen; m 57, Olha Nikitich; c George W. *Educ:* Drexel Univ, BS, 60; Pa State Univ, MS, 62, PhD(microbiol), 64. *Concurrent Pos:* Vis prof, Col Dent, Univ Fla, 88-89. *Mem:* AAAS; Am Soc Microbiol; Int Asn Dent Res; Brit Soc Gen Microbiol. *Res:* Antibiotics; production of antibiotics by mycorrhizal fungi; microbial ecology of the oral cavity; microbiology of the periodontum. *Mailing Add:* 221 Edridge Way Baltimore MD 21228. *Fax:* 410-706-0193

KRZANOWSKI, JOSEPH JOHN, JR, PHARMACOLOGY, PHYSIOLOGY. *Current Pos:* from asst prof to assoc prof, 71-83, PROF PHARMACOL, COL MED, UNIV SFLA, 83-, VCHMN DEPT, 81-, ASSOC DEAN RES & GRAD AFFAIRS, 91- *Personal Data:* b Hartford, Conn, Feb 4, 40; m 63, Patricia Teper; c Karen M & Jenifer A. *Educ:* Univ Conn, BS, 62; Univ Tenn, MS, 65, PhD(pharmacol, physiol), 68; Barry Col, MA, 87. *Prof Exp:* Fel pharmacol, Med Sch, Wash Univ, 68-71. *Concurrent Pos:* NIH pulmonary young investr award, 74-76; co-chmn, Am Acad Allergy & Immunol Role & Care Animals Res, 88-93. *Mem:* Am Soc Pharmacol & Exp Therapeut; NY Acad Sci; AAAS; Am Acad Allergy & Immunol; Am Col Clin Pharmacol. *Res:* Autonomic pharmacology; smooth muscle pharmacology; pulmonary and cardiac cyclic nucleotides; prostaglandins; pulmonary and immunopharmacol; Red Tide Toxin. *Mailing Add:* Dept Pharmacol & Therapeut Col Med Univ SFla Tampa FL 33612. *Fax:* 813-974-3081; *E-Mail:* jkrzanow@com1.med.usf.edu

KRZEMINSKI, STEPHEN F, PHYSICAL CHEMISTRY, ANALYTICAL CHEMISTRY. *Current Pos:* Sr res chemist, Bristol Res Labs, 69-75, proj leader, Res Div, 75-77, mgr, Govt Regulatory Rels, 77-80, CORP MGR, GOVT RELS & PROD STAND, AGR CHEM-NORTH AM, ROHM AND HAAS CO, 80- *Personal Data:* b Philadelphia, Pa, Dec 26, 43; m 66; c 3. *Educ:* La Salle Col, BA, 65; Univ Pittsburgh, PhD(phys chem), 69. *Mem:* Am Chem Soc. *Res:* Transition metal chemistry; coordination compounds; Mossbauer spectroscopy; pesticide residues; metabolism and environmental fate of pesticides; drug delivery systems; pharmacokinetics. *Mailing Add:* 9 Rymill Terr Cherry Hill NJ 08003

KRZYCH, URSZULA, IMMUNOLOGY. *Current Pos:* PROF IMMUNOL, CATH UNIV, 82-, RES SCIENTIST, 86- *Personal Data:* b Lancut, Poland, July 23, 49. *Educ:* Rutgers Univ, BA, 72, PhD(physiol), 77. *Prof Exp:* Fel immunol, Univ Calif, Los Angeles, 77-82. *Concurrent Pos:* Vis prof for women, NSF, 86. *Mem:* Am Asn Immunologists. *Res:* Immunology. *Mailing Add:* Dept Immunol Walter Reed Army Inst Res 16th & Dahlia Sts NW Washington DC 20307-5100

KRZYZANOWSKI, PAUL, COMPILER DESIGN. *Current Pos:* Mem tech staff, UNIX Systs Lab, 85-89, MEM TECH STAFF, COMPUT SYSTS RES, AT&T BELL LABS, 89- *Personal Data:* b New York, NY, Feb 7, 64. *Educ:* NY Univ, BS, 85; Cooper Union, BE, 85; Columbia Univ, MS, 87. *Mem:* Inst Elec & Electronics Engrs. *Mailing Add:* 180 Marion Ave Fanwood NJ 07023

KSHIRSAGAR, ANANT MADHAV, STATISTICS. *Current Pos:* PROF BIOSTATIST, UNIV MICH, 77- *Personal Data:* b Satara, India, Aug 16, 31; m 57; c 2. *Educ:* Univ Bombay, MSc, 51; Univ Manchester, PhD(statist), 61. *Hon Degrees:* DSc, Univ Manchester, 76. *Prof Exp:* Lectr statist, Univ Bombay, 51-63; sr sci officer, Defence Sci Lab, India, 63-68; assoc prof statist, Southern Methodist Univ, 68-71; prof statist, Tex A&M Univ, 71-77. *Mem:* Fel Am Statist Asn; fel Inst Math Statist; Int Inst Statist. *Res:* Design of experiments; multivariant and discriminant analysis; renewal theory, especially Markovian renewal theory. *Mailing Add:* 112 S Morehead Ct Ann Arbor MI 48103

KSIENSKI, A(HARON), ELECTRICAL ENGINEERING. *Current Pos:* prof elec eng & tech dir commun systs, Electrosci Lab, 67-87, EMER PROF ELEC ENG, OHIO STATE UNIV, 87- *Personal Data:* b Warsaw, Poland, June 23, 24; nat US; m 54; c 2. *Educ:* Univ Southern Calif, MS, 52, PhD(elec eng), 58. *Honors & Awards:* Lord Brabazon Award, Inst Radio & Electronic Engrs, London, 67 & 76. *Prof Exp:* Consult engr, W L Schott Co, Calif, 52-53; staff engr, Wiancko Eng Co, 53-57; staff engr, Antenna Res Dept, Hughes Aircraft Co, 58-60, sr staff engr, 60, head res staff, 60-67. *Concurrent Pos:* Lectr, Univ Southern Calif, 54-57; assoc ed, Antennas, Inst Elec & Electronics Engrs, 70-72. *Mem:* Fel Inst Elec & Electronics Engrs; Int Union Radio Sci. *Res:* Antennas and antenna systems; information theory; data processing; radar detection and identification; target identification; signal processing arrays communication. *Mailing Add:* Dept Elec Eng Ohio State Univ 1320 Kinnear Rd Columbus OH 43212

KSIR, CHARLES JOSEPH, PSYCHOPHARMACOLOGY. *Current Pos:* asst prof, 72-76, assoc prof, 76-80, PROF PSYCHOL, UNIV WYO, 80-*Personal Data:* b Albuquerque, NMex, May 19, 45; m 67; c 1. *Educ:* Univ Tex, Austin, BA, 67; Ind Univ, Bloomington, PhD(psychol), 71. *Prof Exp:* Fel neurobiol, Worcester Found Exp Biol, 71-72. *Concurrent Pos:* Vis scientist, Salk Inst Biol Study, 81, Univ Cambridge, Eng, 83. *Mem:* Behav Pharmacol Soc; Psychonomic Soc; AAAS; Sigma Xi; Soc Neurosci; Am Psychol Asn. *Res:* Behavioral pharmacology; neuropharmacology. *Mailing Add:* Dept Psychol Box 3415 Univ Wyo Laramie WY 82071-3415. *Fax:* 307-766-2926; *E-Mail:* cksir@uwyo.edu

KSYCKI, MARY JOECILE, RADIATION CHEMISTRY. *Current Pos:* RETIRED. *Personal Data:* b Du Bois, Ill, May 26, 13. *Educ:* St Louis Univ, BSc, 36, MS, 40, PhD(chem), 42. *Hon Degrees:* MI, St Mary's Col, 85. *Honors & Awards:* Sci Prof of the Year Award, Nat Sci Teachers Asn, 60. *Prof Exp:* Instr chem, Le Clerc Col, 42-43; prof & head dept, 43-49; prof, Webster Col, 49-50; head dept sci pvt sch, Ill, 50-54; prof & head dept, Notre Dame Col, Mo, 54-77; prof chem & chmn sci, St Mary's Col, Orchard Lake, Mich, 77-91. *Concurrent Pos:* Assoc radiation proj, Univ Notre Dame, 58; fel, Univ Okla, 61 & 63, Univ Ill, 62 & Kans State Univ, 64; NIH res award, 61-64; NSF res grant, 63-65; Japan Soc Promotion Sci res grant, Kyoto Univ, 71-72. *Mem:* Am Chem Soc; Nat Sci Teachers Asn. *Res:* Electrodeposition of molybdenum; alloxan diabetes; electrodeposition potentials of copper, nickel and cobalt; radiation chemistry; effects of drugs on iodine metabolism; protective power of nucleotides against gamma ray inactivation of ribonuclease. *Mailing Add:* 320 E Ripa Ave St Louis MO 63125-2835

KU, ALBERT B, ENGINEERING MECHANICS, APPLIED MATHEMATICS. *Current Pos:* from asst prof to assoc prof, 64-76, chmn dept civil eng, 82-85, PROF ENG MECH, UNIV DETROIT, MERCY, 76-*Personal Data:* b Changsha, China, June 15, 33; m 65, Jane Wu; c Natalie & Elizabeth. *Educ:* Univ Taiwan, BSCE, 56; Va Polytech Inst, MSCE, 61; Ohio State Univ, PhD(soil mech), 65. *Prof Exp:* Jr engr, Mil Construct Comt, 58-59; engr, Kai-Nan Eng Corp, 59-60. *Concurrent Pos:* Consult, Chrysler Corp, 66-, Burrough's Corp, 70- & Gen Motors, 72- *Mem:* Am Acad Mech. *Res:* Rheological properties of bituminous concrete; linear viscoelasticity; nonlinear mechanics; static and dynamic stability; finite element analysis; artificial intelligence; computer software. *Mailing Add:* Col Eng & Sci Univ Detroit Mercy Detroit MI 48221

KU, AUDREY YEH, organic chemistry, polymer chemistry, for more information see previous edition

KU, BERNARD SIU-MAN, NEXT GENERATION SWITCHING TECHNOLOGIES, ADVANCED SOFTWARE ENGINEERING RESEARCH & DEVELOPMENT. *Current Pos:* MEM TECH STAFF TELECOMMUN RES & DEVELOP ENG, ADV SWITCHING LAB, NEC AM, INC, IRVING, TEX, 89- *Personal Data:* b Hong Kong. *Educ:* Univ Hong Kong, BS, 81; Univ Tex, MBA, 83; Univ NTex, MS, 85; Southern Methodist Univ, PhD(telecommun), 91. *Prof Exp:* Chairperson, Computer Sci Dept, Univ Mary Hardin-Baylor, Belton, Tex, 85-88; computer mgr, Southern Methodist Univ, Dallas, Tex, 88-89. *Concurrent Pos:* Teaching fel & res assistantship, Southern Methodist Univ, Dallas, Tex, 88; vis prof computer sci, Richland Col, 89. *Mem:* Int Commun Asn; Inst Elec & Electronics Engrs; Asn Comput Mach. *Res:* Advanced software technology for telecommunication switching software development, e.g. software reuse, case tools and integrated software engineering environment; telecommunication industry trends and technology assessment. *Mailing Add:* 3608 Legendary Lane 1525 Walnut Hill Lane Plano TX 75023

KU, DAVID NELSON, BIOFLUID DYNAMICS, VASCULAR SURGERY. *Current Pos:* from asst prof to assoc prof, 86-95, PROF BIOENG, GA INST TECHNOL, 95-; ASSOC PROF & DIR VASCULAR LAB, EMORY UNIV, 86- *Personal Data:* b St Louis, Mo, Mar 15, 56; m 80; c 3. *Educ:* Harvard Univ, BA, 78; Ga Inst Technol, MS, 82, PhD(aerospace eng & biofluid dynamics), 83; Emory Univ, MD, 84. *Honors & Awards:* NSF Presidential Young Investrs Award, 87; Y C Fung Young Investr Award, Am Soc Mech Engrs, 89, Gustus A Larson Mem Award, 96. *Prof Exp:* Surg resident, Univ Chicago, 84-85; dir, Vascular Lab, Hyde Park Community Hosp, 85-86. *Concurrent Pos:* Fulbright Gastprofessor, Munich, Ger, 85; fel cardiovascular path, Univ Chicago, 85-86; mem, Coun Arteriosclerosis, Am Heart Asn. *Mem:* Am Soc Mech Engrs; Am Heart Asn; AMA; Am Col Angiol; Am Phys Soc. *Res:* Biofluid dynamics research on the development, diagnosis, and treatment of arterial disease; mechanisms of atherogenesis and the thrombosis of athersclerotic arteries; magnetic resonance imaging. *Mailing Add:* Sch Mech Eng Ga Inst Technol Atlanta GA 30332-0405

KU, EDMOND CHIU-CHOON, LIPID METABOLISM. *Current Pos:* RETIRED. *Personal Data:* b Canton, China, Aug 11, 32; US citizen; m 59; c 2. *Educ:* Taiwan Prov Col, BS, 56; Va Polytech Inst, PhD(biochem), 62. *Prof Exp:* Res scientist biochem, Parke, Davis & Co, 63-67; NIH spec res fel, Cornell Univ, 67-69; sr staff scientist, Ciba-Geigy Corp, 70-79, mgr, 80-85, sr res fel, 85-97. *Mem:* Am Chem Soc; Sigma Xi; NY Acad Sci; Inflammable Res Asn. *Res:* Enzyme kinetics and its application to the study of drug action at molecular level; regulatory mechanism involved in the biosynthesis and degradation of prostaglandins at subcellular level; cholesterol and triglyceride biosynthesis regulation. *Mailing Add:* 8 Albert Dr Upper Saddle River NJ 07458

KU, HAN SAN, PLANT PHYSIOLOGY, BIOCHEMISTRY. *Current Pos:* SR RES ASSOC BIOCHEM, T R EVANS RES CTR, 74-; VPRES, RICERCA INC, 90- *Personal Data:* b Hsin-Chu, Taiwan, Nov 20, 35; m 65, Lily S; c 2. *Educ:* Nat Taiwan Univ, BS, 58; Osaka Univ, MS, 63; Univ Calif, Davis, PhD(plant physiol), 68. *Honors & Awards:* Japanese Food Sci Soc Award, 66; Campbell Award, Am Inst Biol Sci, 69. *Prof Exp:* Lectr agr, Taipei Agr Prof Sch, 57-58; asst plant physiol, Nat Taiwan Univ, 60-61; res asst, Univ Calif, Davis, 64-68, NIH fel ethylene biosynthesis, 68; NSF fel ethylene physiol, Purdue Univ, 68-70; res biologist, Allied Chem Res Lab, 70-71, biologist & res leader plant sci, 72-73; plant biochemist, Mich State Univ, 73-74. *Concurrent Pos:* Mgr, Biol Eval SDS Biotech & Agr Chem Biol Evaluation; vpres, Ricenca, Inc & ISK Interprise. *Mem:* AAAS; Am Soc Plant Physiologists; Am Soc Agron; Japanese Biochem Soc; Soil Sci Soc Am; Am Chem Soc; Japanese Silver Chem Soc. *Res:* Ethylene biogenesis and action in plant tissue; plant growth regulator; photorespiration; nitrogen fixation; crop production pesticide; pesticide metabolism; animal, plant metabolism; Environ Fate EPA; allochemical mode of pesticide. *Mailing Add:* 8060 Conestoga Trail Mentor OH 44060

KU, HARRY HSIEN HSIANG, MATHEMATICAL STATISTICS, ENGINEERING. *Current Pos:* RETIRED. *Personal Data:* b Peking, China, Mar 3, 18; US citizen; m 42, 81, Helen Hamstra; c Richard. *Educ:* Purdue Univ, BS, 40, MSE, 41; George Washington Univ, MS, 60, PhD, 68. *Prof Exp:* Civil engr, M W Kellogg Co, 42-43; math statistician, Ctr Appl Math, Nat Eng Lab, Nat Bur Stand, 59-79, chief statist eng div, 78-85. *Concurrent Pos:* Consult, Ctr Measurement Stand, Hsinchu, Taiwan; vis scientist, Cent Bur Nuclear Measurements, Geel, Belgium. *Mem:* AAAS; fel Am Statist Asn; Int Statist Inst. *Res:* Statistical analysis of measurement data in engineering and physical sciences; propagation of error, precision and accuracy; application of information theory in analysis of multi-dimensional contingency tables and Markov chains. *Mailing Add:* 9608 Glencrest Lane Kensington MD 20895

KU, HSU-TUNG, TOPOLOGY. *Current Pos:* asst prof, 68-73, assoc prof, 73-79, PROF MATH, UNIV MASS, AMHERST, 79- *Personal Data:* b Formosa, Oct 24, 33; m 64. *Educ:* Taiwan Prov Norm Univ, BSc, 61; Tulane Univ, MSc, 64, PhD(math), 67. *Prof Exp:* Mem math, Inst Adv Study, 67-68. *Concurrent Pos:* Vis mem math, Inst Adv Study, 77. *Mem:* Am Math Soc. *Res:* Transformation groups; algebraic topology. *Mailing Add:* Dept Math Univ Mass Amherst MA 01003-4515

KU, JENTUNG, THERMODYNAMICS & FLUID MECHANICS, COMPUTER MODELING & SIMULATION. *Current Pos:* SR ENGR, NASA GODDARD SPACE FLIGHT CTR, 91- *Personal Data:* b Hsinchu, Taiwan, Mar, 1950. *Educ:* Nat Tsing Hua Univ, BS, 72; Purdue Univ, MS, 76, PhD (mech eng), 80. *Prof Exp:* Mem tech staff, Advan Technol Ctr, Bendix Corp, 80-83; sect head & prog mgr, OAO Corp, 83-91. *Mem:* Am Soc Mech Engrs; Am Inst Aeronaut & Astronaut; Am Nuclear Soc. *Res:* Two-phase heat transport and thermal control systems; capillary pumped loops for spacecraft thermal management. *Mailing Add:* NASA Goddard Space Flight Ctr Code 724-2 Greenbelt MD 20771

KU, MEI-CHIN HSIAO, TOPOLOGY, GEOMETRY. *Current Pos:* from asst prof to assoc prof, 70-82, PROF MATH, UNIV MASS, AMHERST, 82- *Personal Data:* b Formosa, Nov 1, 37; m 64, Hsu-Tung; c 2. *Educ:* Taiwan Norm Univ, BSc, 61; Syracuse Univ, MS, 64; Tulane Univ, La, PhD(math), 67. *Prof Exp:* Mathematician, Inst Advan Study, 67-68. *Concurrent Pos:* Vis mem, Inst Advan Study, 77 & 84. *Mem:* Math Asn Am. *Res:* Transformation groups; geometry; PDE. *Mailing Add:* Dept Math & Statist Univ Mass Amherst MA 01003. *Fax:* 413-545-1801; *E-Mail:* meiku@math.umass.edu

KU, PAO KWEN, ANIMAL NUTRITION. *Current Pos:* RES SPECIALIST, DEPT ANIMAL SCI, MICH STATE UNIV, 73- *Personal Data:* b Anhing, China, Dec 18, 33. *Educ:* Mich State Univ, PhD(animal nutrit), 70. *Res:* Animal nutrition. *Mailing Add:* Dept Animal Sci Animal Nutrit Lab Mich State Univ East Lansing MI 48824-0001

KU, PEH SUN, ENVIRONMENTAL PHYSICS. *Current Pos:* RETIRED. *Personal Data:* b Shangtung, China, Aug 23, 22; US citizen; m 57, Hui Chen Sun; c John & George. *Educ:* Nat Cent Univ, BS, 47; Univ Rochester, MS, 55; Yale Univ, DEng(chem eng), 60. *Prof Exp:* Chem engr, Chinese Petrol Corp, Taiwan, 47-54; res asst, Carnegie Inst Technol, 54-55; res engr, Boeing Co, 60-65; theoret physicist, Reentry Systs Div, Gen Elec Co, 65-69, staff scientist, 69-70; chem engr air pollution control, Consol Edison Co, NY, 70-73, sr engr, 73-78, sr environ engr, Environ Affairs, 78-92. *Mem:* AAAS; Am Chem Soc; Am Phys Soc; Am Geophys Union. *Res:* Acoustics; high temperature thermodynamics and transport properties of matter; physical properties of matter under high pressures; chemical kinetics; control and dispersion of air pollutants in the atmosphere and their removal from industrial processes; water pollution and hazardous wastes; novel methods of energy conversion. *Mailing Add:* 244 Old State Rd Berwyn PA 19312

KU, ROBERT TIEN-HUNG, FIBER OPTICS, LASER COMPONENT PACKAGING & LASER APPLICATIONS. *Current Pos:* mem tech staff, Laser Develop Dept, 81-88, supvr, Lightwave Device Packaging Dept, 88-94, DEPT HEAD, SUBMARINE DEVICE PACKAGING ENG & MFG, AT&T BELL LABS, 95- *Personal Data:* b Shanghai, China, Jan 19, 47; US citizen; m 71; c 2. *Educ:* Univ Ill, Urbana, BS, 67, MS, 68, PhD(elec eng), 73. *Prof Exp:* Res asst, Gaseous Electronics Lab, Univ Ill, 67-73; mem tech staff, Optics Div, Lincoln Lab, Mass Inst Technol, 73-81. *Concurrent Pos:* Fel, NSF. *Mem:* Am Phys Soc; Inst Elec & Electronics Engrs; Optical Soc Am; Sigma Xi. *Res:* Laser and optical components for fiber communication systems; laser spectroscopy studies of pollutant gases; laser diagnostics of plasma and chemically excited media; laser radars; high power lasers. *Mailing Add:* PO Box 13396 Reading PA 19612. *Fax:* 610-939-7648; *E-Mail:* rku@lucent.com

KU, TEH-LUNG, GEOCHEMISTRY, OCEANOLOGY. *Current Pos:* assoc prof, 69-75, PROF GEOL SCI, UNIV SOUTHERN CALIF, 75- *Personal Data:* b Shanghai, China, Aug 30, 37; m 70, Theresa Shen; c Pamela, Christina & Joanna. *Educ:* Nat Taiwan Univ, BS, 59; Columbia Univ, PhD(geochem), 66. *Prof Exp:* Post-doctoral, Lamont Geol Observ, Columbia Univ, 66-67; asst scientist, Woods Hole Oceanog Inst, 67-69. *Concurrent Pos:* Guggenheim fel, 83-; Fulbright Sr Scholar, 83-; vis prof, Hartwell Lab, UK, 83- & Nat Taiwan Univ, 91-; Fulbright prof, Ctr Weak Radioactivity, Nat Ctr Sci Res, 84-; fel, Japan Soc Prom Sci, 91- *Mem:* AAAS; fel Am Geophys Union; Geol Soc Am; Geochem Soc. *Res:* Isotope geochemistry; chemical oceanography; geochronology; Pleistocene geology; climatology; hydrogeochemistry. *Mailing Add:* Dept Earth Sci Univ Southern Calif Los Angeles CA 90089-0002

KU, TIMOTHY TAO, FORESTRY. *Current Pos:* from asst prof to assoc prof, 59-63, PROF FORESTRY, UNIV ARK, MONTICELLO, 63- *Personal Data:* b Chaochow, China, Mar 26, 26; m 50, Victoria Feng; c 2. *Educ:* Nanking Univ, BS, 48; Mich State Univ, MF, 50, PhD(forest ecol, silvicult), 54. *Prof Exp:* Forester, T S Coile, Inc, Forest Land Consults, 56-58. *Concurrent Pos:* Vis prof forestry, Nat Taiwan Univ, Taipei, 83; fel, Soc Am Foresters, 85. *Mem:* Soc Am Foresters; Soil Sci Soc Am. *Res:* Silviculture; forest soils and ecology; biomass production and nutrient cycling in forest stands, site evaluation and classification, and applied silviculture. *Mailing Add:* 236 Mason Hill Rd Monticello AR 71655

KU, VICTORIA FENG, ORGANIC CHEMISTRY. *Current Pos:* asst prof, 69-75, ASSOC PROF CHEM, UNIV ARK, MONTICELLO, 76- *Personal Data:* b Peking, China, Mar 14, 30; US citizen; m 50; c 2. *Educ:* Barat Col, BS, 50; Univ Ark, MS, 64, PhD(chem), 76. *Prof Exp:* Chemist, Mich State Health Dept Lab, 52-56 & Hercules Powder Co, 57-59. *Mem:* Am Chem Soc. *Mailing Add:* 236 Mason Hill Monticello AR 71655

KU, Y(U) H(SIU), ELECTRICAL ENGINEERING, SYSTEMS ENGINEERING. *Current Pos:* vis prof, 52-54, prof, 54-71, EMER PROF ELEC & SYSTS ENG, UNIV PA, 72- *Personal Data:* b Wusih, China, Dec 24, 02; m 29; c 7. *Educ:* Mass Inst Technol, SB, 25, SM, 26, ScD, 28. *Hon Degrees:* MA & LLD, Univ Pa, 72. *Honors & Awards:* Gold Medal, Ministry Educ, 60; Lamme Medal, Inst Elec & Electronic Engrs, 72; Gold Medal, Chinese Inst Elec Engrs, 72; Pro Mundi Beneficio Medal, Brazilian Acad Humanities, 75. *Prof Exp:* Prof elec eng & head dept, Chekiang Univ, 29-30; dean eng, Cent Univ, China, 31-32; pres, 44-45, prof elec eng, 47-49; dean eng, Tsing Hua Univ, 32-37; vminister, Ministry Ed, 38-44; educ comnr, Shanghai Munic Govt, 45-47; pres, Chengchi Univ, 47-49. *Concurrent Pos:* Dir, Aeronaut Res Inst, China, 34-37 & Electronics Res Inst, 35-37; head, Chinese Educ Mission to India, 43; chief Chinese deleg, Int Tech Cong, Paris, 46; mem gen assembly, Int Union Theoret & Appl Mech, 46-92; vis prof elec eng, Mass inst Technol, 50-52; consult, Gen Elec Co, NY, 51-55, Univac, 52-53, Radio Corp Am, 59-60; hon prof, Shanghai Jiao-Tong Univ, 79-, Xian, Southwestern, Northern Jiao-Tong Univ, 85-, Northeast Univ of Sci & Eng & Northwest Telecommunication Univ, 86-, Southeast Univ, Nanjing, 88-; hon adv, Huazhong Univ of Sci & Eng, 87- *Mem:* Am Soc Eng Educ; fel Inst Elec & Electronics Engrs; Brit Inst Elec Engrs; Chinese Inst Eng (vpres, 45-46); Chinese Inst Elec Engr (pres, 40-41). *Res:* Analysis and control of linear and nonlinear systems; electric energy conversion; transient circuit analysis. *Mailing Add:* 1420 Locust St No 22G Univ Pa Philadelphia PA 19102-4213

KU, YI-YIN, PROCESS RESEARCH ON SYNTHESIS OF PHARMACEUTICAL DRUG CANDIDATES. *Current Pos:* res scientist, 89-92, SR RES SCIENTIST, ABBOTT LABS, 92- *Personal Data:* b Xian, China, May 15, 59; m 85, Yao-En Li; c Kory K Li & Katherine H Li. *Educ:* Northwestern Univ, China, BS, 82; Univ Ill, Chicago, MS, 85, PhD(org chem), 88. *Prof Exp:* Res assoc, Univ Ill, Chicago, 88-89. *Mem:* Am Chem Soc. *Res:* Discovery of new and efficient synthetic methods for the pharmaceutical drug candidates; process research and development of commercial chemical processes for synthesis of pharmaceutical bulk drugs. *Mailing Add:* 493 Satinwood Terr Buffalo Grove IL 60089. *Fax:* 847-938-5932

KUAN, SHIA SHIONG, DEVELOPMENT OF BIOSENSORS. *Current Pos:* DIR, NATURAL TOXINS RES CTR, FOOD & DRUG ADMIN, 80- *Personal Data:* b Canton, China, Oct 18, 33; US citizen; m 73; c 1. *Educ:* Nat Chung Hsing Univ, BS, 53; WVa Univ, MS, 65, PhD(biochem), 68. *Prof Exp:* Dir, Nanchow Sugar Factory, 58-63; res asst, WVa Univ, 63-68; res fel, La State Univ, New Orleans, 68-70; sr res assoc, Univ New Orleans, 71-80. *Concurrent Pos:* Consult, Taiwan Sugar Res Inst, 68- & W China Univ Med Sci, 85-; adj prof chem, Univ New Orleans, 81- *Mem:* Am Chem Soc; Sigma Xi; NY Acad Sci; AAAS; Asn Anal Chemists; Inst Food Technologists. *Res:* Induction, isolation, purification and immobilization of enzymes and the application of immobilized enzymes to agricultural, chemical and clinical analyses; the isolation of naturally occuring toxins and the development of fast, simple and inexpensive procedures for the determination of these toxins. *Mailing Add:* 3020 Transcontinental Dr Metairie LA 70006

KUAN, TUNG-SHENG, ELECTRON MICROSCOPY, ELECTRONIC MATERIALS. *Current Pos:* PROF PHYSICS, STATE UNIV NY, ALBANY, 95- *Personal Data:* b Taiwan, Dec 13, 47; US citizen; m 77; c 2. *Educ:* Nat Taiwan Univ, BS, 70; Cornell Univ, MS, 73, PhD(mat sci), 77. *Prof Exp:* Res staff mem, IBM Thomas J Watson Res Ctr, 77-95. *Concurrent Pos:* Mem, Metal Soc, Am Inst Mech Engrs. *Mem:* Am Phys Soc; Mat Res Soc; Am Inst Mech Engrs; Electron Micros Soc Am. *Res:* Structural, mechanical and electrical properties of electronic materials; electron microscopy of thin film materials and interfaces. *Mailing Add:* Dept Physics State Univ NY 1400 Washington Ave Albany NY 12222

KUANG, YUNAN, EXPERIMENTAL PHYSICS. *Current Pos:* res assoc, 88-93, ASST PROF, COL WILLIAM & MARY, 93- *Personal Data:* b Wuhan, China, Mar 7, 62; m 91, Feng Liao; c Guang Y & Amy M. *Educ:* Wuhan Univ, BS, 82; Yale Univ, PhD(physics), 88. *Res:* Studied the fundamental principles of physics using muonium; observed for the first time the formation of muonium negative ion in vacuum; experimental test of muon number conservation in rare kaon decay and muon decay. *Mailing Add:* Physics Dept Col William & Mary Williamsburg VA 23187-8795. *E-Mail:* kuang@wmheg.physics.wm.edu

KUBAS, GREGORY JOSEPH, TRANSITION-METAL & SMALL MOLECULE CHEMISTRY. *Current Pos:* mem staff chem, 72-88, LAB FEL, LOS ALAMOS NAT LAB, 88- *Personal Data:* b Cleveland, Ohio, Mar 12, 45; m 73; c 2. *Educ:* Case Inst Technol, BS, 66; Northwestern Univ, PhD(inorg chem), 70. *Honors & Awards:* Am Chem Soc Award in Inorg Chem, Am Chem Soc, 93. *Prof Exp:* Fel chem, Princeton Univ, 71-72. *Mem:* Am Chem Soc. *Res:* Coordination chemistry of dihydrogen and sulfur dioxide, structure and reactivity of transition metal SO_2 complexes; synthesis, characterization and structure of organometallic small molecule complexes of molybdenum and tungsten. *Mailing Add:* 29 Camino Cielo Santa Fe NM 87501

KUBENA, KAREN SIDELL, NUTRITION IN PREGNANCY, DIETARY ASSESSMENT. *Current Pos:* lectr nutrit, Tex A&M Univ, 79-82, dir dietetic internship, 82-90, asst prof, 82-88, ASSOC PROF NUTRIT, TEX A&M UNIV, 88- *Personal Data:* b Madison, Wis, Oct 1, 45; m 68, Leon F; c Lance & Angela. *Educ:* Univ Wis-Madison, BS, 67; Miss State Univ, MS, 76; Tex A & M Univ, PhD(nutrit), 82. *Honors & Awards:* Outstanding Serv Award, Am Dietetic Asn, 89 & 90. *Prof Exp:* Therapeut dietitian, Vet Admin Ctr, Temple, Tex, 68-69; consult dietitian, nursing homes & hosps, Miss, 70-74; prog coordr & instr, Dietary Asst Course, Blinn Col, Brenham, Tex, 76-77; dir, Dietary Dept, Grimes Mem Hosp, Navasoto, Tex, 77-79. *Concurrent Pos:* Prog dir, undergrad prog dietetics, Tex A&M Univ, 82-, prin investr, 82-, sect leader, Human Nutrit Sect, 84- *Mem:* Am Dietetic Asn; Am Inst Nutrit; Am Soc Clin Nutrit; Inst Food Technologists. *Res:* Magnesium adequacy during reproduction in rats and humans with regard to immune function and mineral metabolism; lipid metabolism; nutrition and social support through life cycle. *Mailing Add:* Dept Animal Sci Human Nutrit Sect Tex A&M Univ College Station TX 77843-2471

KUBENA, LEON FRANKLIN, NUTRITION, TOXICOLOGY. *Current Pos:* Res nutritionist, South Cent Poultry Res Lab, Animal Sci Div, 70-75, RES ANIMAL SCIENTIST BIOCHEM & NUTRIT, FOOD ANIMAL PROTECTION RES LAB, AGR RES SERV, USDA, COLLEGE STATION, TEX, 76- *Personal Data:* b Caldwell, Tex, July 6, 40; m 68; c 2. *Educ:* Tex A&M Univ, BS, 65, PhD(poultry sci), 70. *Concurrent Pos:* Mem fac, Tex A&M Univ, 80- *Mem:* Poultry Sci Asn; Asn Off Anal Chemists; AAAS; World Poultry Sci Asn; US Animal Health Assoc; Coun Agr Sci & Technol. *Res:* Interrelationships of environment and nutrition; toxicology of environmental toxicants in poultry with special emphasis on interaction of these toxicants. *Mailing Add:* 2010 Langford St College Station TX 77840

KUBERSKY, EDWARD SIDNEY, LIMNOLOGY, ECOLOGY. *Current Pos:* CHMN & ASSOC PROF BIOL, FELICIAN COL, 93- *Personal Data:* b Brooklyn, NY, Feb 25, 47. *Educ:* Brooklyn Col, CUNY, BS, 67; Ind Univ, MA, 68, PhD(zool), 73. *Prof Exp:* from instr to assoc prof biol, Upsala Col, 72-89, chmn dept, 79-84; chmn & assoc prof biol, St Francis Col, 89-93. *Concurrent Pos:* Proj dir, NSF grant, 72-74 & 76-77; Danforth assoc, 80-86; consult-Lake Restoration & Mgt. *Mem:* Int Asn Theoret & Appl Limnol; Freshwater Biol Asn; Am Soc Limnol & Oceanog; NAm Lake Mgt Soc. *Res:* Ecology and taxonomy of cladocera; lake restoration. *Mailing Add:* Dept Biol Felician Col 262 S Main St Lodi NJ 07644

KUBES, GEORGE JIRI, PULP CHEMISTRY. *Current Pos:* res scientist pulping, 72-77, head Chem Pulping & Bleaching Sect, 77-85, SR SCIENTIST, PULP & PAPER RES INST CAN, 85-; AUXILIARY PROF, CHEM ENG DEPT, MCGILL UNIV, 85- *Personal Data:* b Prague, Czech, Feb 14, 34; Can citizen; m 59; c 2. *Educ:* Tech Univ, Prague, MSc, 58; Tech Univ, Bratislava, PhD(pulp chem). *Prof Exp:* Supvr res group, NBohemian Pulp & Paper Mill, Czech, 58-62, mgr res pulping, papermaking & pollution, 62-67; head pulping group, Pulp & Paper Res Inst Czech, 68; sr res chemist, CIP Res Ltd, Can, 69-72. *Concurrent Pos:* Indust consult, Chem Eng Designing Inst, Czech, 58-68; lectr, Chem Eng Fac, Tech Univ, 62-67. *Mem:* Can Pulp & Paper Asn; Tech Asn Pulp & Paper Indust; Chem Inst Can. *Res:* Pulping with an effort to develop a sulphur-free pulping and chlorine-free bleaching process; consultant services to pulp and paper manufacturing industry all over the world; improvements in existing processes, pulping of tropical wood species and annual plants; viscosity of pulp; reaction kinetics in cellulose degradation during alkaline deliquification which resulted in the development of G-factor; differential thermal analysis of black liquor quality; reaction engineering studies and chemical kinetics, also fundamental studies in fluidized bed technology. *Mailing Add:* Chem Eng Dept McGill Univ 3420 University St Pulp & Paper Res Inst Montreal PQ H3A 2A7 Can

KUBIAK, CLIFFORD P, ORGANOMETALLIC PHOTOCHEMISTRY & CHARGE TRANSFER, ORGANOMETALLIC POLYMER CHEMISTRY. *Current Pos:* from asst prof to assoc prof, 82-90, PROF CHEM, PURDUE UNIV, 90- *Personal Data:* b Stamford Conn, July 16, 53; m, Pam. *Educ:* Brown Univ, BS, 75; Univ Rochester, PhD, 80. *Prof Exp:* fel, Mass Inst Technol, 80-81. *Concurrent Pos:* fel, Alfred P Sloan Found, 87-91; counr, Div Inorg Chem, Am Chem Soc, 90-92; consult, Elf Ato Chem NAm, 92- *Mem:* Am Chem Soc; Inter-Am Photochem Soc; Sigma Xi. *Res:* organometallic photochemistry and charge transfer; organometallic polymer chemistry. *Mailing Add:* Purdue Univ Dept Chem 1393 Brown Bldg West Lafayette IN 47907-1393. *Fax:* 765-494-0239; *E-Mail:* cliff@cv3chem.purdue.edu

KUBICA, GEORGE P, MEDICAL BACTERIOLOGY, BIOSAFETY. *Current Pos:* CONSULT, TUBERCULOSIS BACT & DIRECTIONAL AIR FLOW DYNAMICS, 89- *Personal Data:* b Little Falls, NY, June 18, 29; m 53, Beverly G Smith; c Scott P & Kimberly A (Jones). *Educ:* Cornell Univ, BA, 51; Univ Mich, MA, 52; Univ Wis, PhD(med bact), 55. *Honors & Awards:* Commendation Medal, Surg Gen, USPHS, 68, Meritorious Serv Medal, 88. *Prof Exp:* Actg chief, Tuberc Unit, Commun Dis Ctr, USPHS, 55-62, chief, 62-69; mem & head mycobact sect, Trudeau Inst, Inc, 69-74; microbiologist consult, Mycobact Ctr Dis Control, 74-86, chief, 87-89. *Concurrent Pos:* Instr, Sch Med, Emory Univ, 59-69; assoc prof, Univ NC, 64-69; chmn, Assembly on Microbiol & Immunol, Am Thoracic Soc, 73-74; secy, Comt on Bacteriol, Int Union Against Tuberc, 76-82; adv/lectr, Int Tuberc Course, Japan, 84-90; chmn, Mycobact Div, 85-86. *Mem:* Am Thoracic Soc; Am Soc Microbiol; Int Union Against Tuberc; fel Am Acad Microbiol; Am Biol Safety Asn. *Res:* Tuberculosis. *Mailing Add:* 2383 Welton Pl Atlanta GA 30338

KUBICEK, JOHN D, MATHEMATICS. *Current Pos:* PROF MATH, SOUTHWEST MO STATE UNIV, 81-, ACTG DIR, MATH CTR, 88- *Personal Data:* b Owatonna, Minn, Feb 1, 43. *Educ:* St Johns Univ, BA, 65, MS, 67; Univ Mo, PhD(math), 75. *Mem:* Am Math Soc. *Res:* Developmental education in colleges. *Mailing Add:* Dept Math Southwest Mo State Univ Springfield MO 65804

KUBIK, PETER W, ACCELERATOR MASS SPECTROMETRY. *Current Pos:* SR RES ASSOC, PAUL SCHERRER INST, 91- *Personal Data:* b Penzberg, Ger, Dec 31, 49; m 92, Sabine G Teichmann. *Educ:* Tech Univ Munich, Ger, MSc, 78, PhD(physics), 83. *Prof Exp:* Res fel, Inst Nuclear Physics, Tech Univ Munich, Ger, 78-83; res assoc, Univ Rochester, 83-87, sr res assoc, Nuclear Struct Res Lab, 87-91. *Mem:* Am Phys Soc; Ger Phys Soc. *Res:* Measurements of long-lived radioisotopes in natural samples like meteorites, glacial ice, ground water, ocean sediments, surface rocks, etc, using accelerator mass spectrometry. *Mailing Add:* Paul Scherrer Inst Particle Physics c/o ETH Hohggerberg Zurich CH-8093 Switzerland. *Fax:* 41-1-633-1067; *E-Mail:* kubik@particle.phys.ethz.ch

KUBIK, PHILIP ROMAN, SQUID MAGNETOMETRY, THIN FILM SUPERCONDUCTIVE ELECTRONICS. *Current Pos:* SR PHYSICIST, CTF SYSTS, INC, 84- *Personal Data:* b London, UK, Jan 4, 53. *Educ:* Univ BC, BS, 74, MS, 77, PhD(physics), 84. *Mem:* Am Phys Soc; Can Asn Physicists. *Res:* Used nuclear magnetic resonance at temperatures from 0.3K-20K to discover orientational ordering phase transitions of hydrogen and D2 on graphite; established a thin film deposition and lithography facility for fabrication of niobium squids; participated in the development of commercial systems for squid magnetometry, especially magnetoencephalography. *Mailing Add:* CTF Systs Inc 15-1750 McLean Ave Port Coquitlam BC V3C 1M9 Can. *Fax:* 604-941-8561; *E-Mail:* pkubik@ctf.bc.ca

KUBIK, ROBERT N, COMPUTER SCIENCE, CONTROL SYSTEMS. *Personal Data:* b Honolulu, Hawaii, Nov 17, 31; m 55; c 4. *Educ:* Univ Calif, Berkeley, AB, 54. *Prof Exp:* Programmer, Atomic Energy Div, Babcock & Wilcox Co, 57-61, sr programmer, 61-62, prog supvr, 62-63, chief comput serv, 63-66; acct rep, IBM Corp, 67; prin engr, Nuclear Power Generating Dept, Babcock & Wilcox Co, 68-69, chief instrument develop, Res & Develop Div, 69-71, mgr process control, Lynchburg Res Ctr, 71-72, mgr indust systs, 72-76, mgr advan control & exp physics lab, Lynchburg Res Ctr, 76-79. *Mem:* Inst Elec & Electronics Engrs; Am Soc Nondestructive Testing; Am Nuclear Soc. *Res:* methodology; nondestructive examination. *Mailing Add:* PO Box 503 Point Reyes Station CA 94956

KUBIN, ROSA, BIOCHEMISTRY, VETERINARY PATHOLOGY. *Current Pos:* RETIRED. *Personal Data:* b St Poelten, Austria, Dec 15, 06; nat US; m 31. *Educ:* St Poeltner Obergym, Austria, BS, 25; Univ Vienna, MS, 29, PhD(org chem), 31. *Prof Exp:* Asst, Austrian Chem Works, 31-35 & Syngala, Inc, Austria, 35-38; AMA fel, Med Sch, Univ Ore, 38, Lilly fel, 39-40, asst 40-41; asst prof biochem & clin path, Med Sch, Middlesex Univ, 41-47; asst prof chem, Univ Mass, 47-49; assoc prof biochem, New Eng Col Pharm, 50-51; consult vet pathologist, 51-90. *Concurrent Pos:* Lectr, Wellesley Col, 55-57 & Concord Acad, 57-61; teacher advan chem & molecular biol, Waltham High Sch, 61-73. *Mem:* Fel AAAS; Am Chem Soc; NY Acad Sci. *Res:* Medical biochemistry; bleaching of textiles; hormone extraction; laboratory methods applied in veterinary clinical pathology; diseases in veterinary medicine. *Mailing Add:* 865 Central Ave N Hill B301 Needham MA 02192-1338

KUBIS, JOSEPH J(OHN), NONLINEAR MECHANICS, COMPUTATIONAL FLUID DYNAMICS. *Current Pos:* SR RES ENGR, FORD MOTOR CO, 85- *Personal Data:* b New York, NY, Apr 15, 38; m 68, 84, Kathleen M Doody; c Joseph H & Anne M. *Educ:* Mass Inst Technol, SB, 59; Princeton Univ, AM, 61, PhD(physics), 64. *Hon Degrees:* MA, Cambridge Univ, 67. *Prof Exp:* Asst prof physics, Tex A&M Univ, 64-67; sr res physicist, Cavendish Lab & fel, Clare Hall, Cambridge Univ, 67-69; asst prof physics, Mich State Univ, 69-71; mem tech staff, Theory & Comput Div, KMS Fusion, Inc, 72-82; prog specialist, Software Serv Corp, 83-85. *Concurrent Pos:* Consult, Brookhaven Nat Lab, 67 & Los Alamos Sci Lab, 68 & 71. *Mem:* Am Phys Soc; Asn Comput Mach; Inst Elec & Electronics Engrs Computer Soc; Sigma Xi; Soc Indust & Appl Math. *Res:* Nonlinear crash mechanics; finite element methods; computational fluid dynamics; optical ray tracing; numerical analysis; scientific computing; software engineering. *Mailing Add:* 3489 Oak Dr Ypsilanti MI 48197-3747

KUBISEN, STEVEN JOSEPH, JR, PHYSICAL ORGANIC CHEMISTRY, ORGANIC CHEMISTRY. *Current Pos:* DIR DEVELOP MKTS & PARTNERSHIPS, ALCOA. *Personal Data:* b Iowa City, Iowa, June 21, 52; m 77. *Educ:* Cornell Univ, AB, 74; Harvard Univ, MA, 75, PhD(org chem), 78. *Prof Exp:* Res chemist, Union Carbide Corp, 78-81, proj scientist, 81-84, group leader, 84-86; polymer lab dir, Akeo Coatings Am, 86-87; technol mgr, Electromat Dept, Gen Elec, 87-91. *Concurrent Pos:* Vpres, Werner-Gershan Assoc, 94- *Mem:* Am Chem Soc; Sigma Xi; Inst Paper Chem. *Res:* Phosphate ester hydrolysis; process chemistry; epoxidation chemistry; natural oils chemistry; acrylic, urethane technology; radiation cure; epoxy resins. *Mailing Add:* Alcoa 100 Technical Dr Bldg D Alcoa Center PA 15069

KUBISKE, MARK E, FOREST TREE PHYSIOLOGICAL ECOLOGY, STRESS PHYSIOLOGY. *Current Pos:* RES ASSOC, DEPT FORESTRY, MICH STATE UNIV, 93- *Personal Data:* b East Lansing, Mich, Sept 30, 58; m 82, Alice Nevel. *Educ:* Univ Wis-Stevens Point, BS, 88; Pa State, MS, 90, PhD(forestry), 93. *Mem:* Am Soc Foresters; Ecol Soc Am. *Res:* Responses of eastern deciduous tree species to climatic drought; response of above and below ground processes to elevated atmospheric carbon dioxide from a forest ecology perspective. *Mailing Add:* 326 Pilgrim Rd Houghton MI 49931. *Fax:* 517-336-1143; *E-Mail:* 21338mek@msu.edu

KUBITZ, WILLIAM JOHN, HARDWARE SYSTEMS, COMPUTER SCIENCE. *Current Pos:* teaching asst elec eng, 64-65, res asst comput sci, 65-68, res asst prof, 68-69, from asst prof to assoc prof, 70-85, PROF COMPUT SCI & ASSOC HEAD DEPT, UNIV ILL, 85- *Personal Data:* b Freeport, Ill, Dec 27, 38; m 60, Carol A Hay; c Emily & James. *Educ:* Univ Ill, Urbana-Champaign, BS, 61, MS, 62, PhD(elec eng), 68. *Prof Exp:* Develop engr, Gen Elec, 62-64. *Mem:* Inst Elec & Electronics Engrs; AAAS; Sigma Xi; Asn Comput Mach. *Res:* Automated chip and module layout of digital circuits based on automatic generation from a topological data structure with size, shape and timing constraints; object oriented graphics for a networked workstation environment with application to user interfaces, design systems and visualization; computeer graphics. *Mailing Add:* Dept Comput Sci 3270 DCL Univ Ill 1304 W Springfield Ave Urbana IL 61801. *E-Mail:* kubitz@cs.uiuc.edu

KUBLER, DONALD GENE, ORGANIC CHEMISTRY. *Current Pos:* from assoc prof to chmn dept, 61-85, chmn dept, 67-72, EMER PROF, FURMAN UNIV, 85- *Personal Data:* b Easton, Md, Apr 4, 23; m 47; c Matthew, Robbie, John & William. *Educ:* Univ SC, BS, 47; Univ Md, PhD(chem), 52. *Prof Exp:* Instr chem, Univ SC, 47-48; chemist, Develop Dept, Union Carbon Chem Co, WVa, 52-58; asst prof chem, Univ SC, 58-59 & Hampden-Sydney Col, 59-61. *Concurrent Pos:* NSF fac fel sci, Clemson Univ, 75; vis prof, Univ Sterling, 82, Grinnell Col, 86-87 & King Col, 88-89. *Mem:* Am Chem Soc; Sigma Xi. *Res:* Structure and mechanism for acetal and carbohydrate hydrolysis; forensic chemistry. *Mailing Add:* 136 Conder Dr Marietta SC 29661-9786

KUBLER, HANS, FOREST PRODUCTS. *Current Pos:* PROF WOOD SCI, UNIV WIS-MADISON, 67- *Personal Data:* b Ger, Sept 11, 22; m 60, 84. *Educ:* Univ Hamburg, dipl wood tech, 50, Dr rer nat(wood sci), 57. *Prof Exp:* Res asst wood tech, Nat Res Ctr Wood Prod, Ger, 50-54, proj leader wood sci, 59-66. *Concurrent Pos:* Proj leader, Ger Res Asn, 57-58; Fulbright fel, US Forest Prod Lab, Madison, Wis, 58-59; exchange scientist, Acad Wood Tech, Leningrad, USSR, 62; int ed, Forest Prod Res Soc, 67-74. *Mem:* Forest Prod Res Soc; Soc Wood Sci & Technol. *Res:* Wood at low temperatures; growth stresses in trees; drying of wood; cracks in stems of trees; self heating of wood and other organic materials; wood as building material; ignition and fire performance of wood; spiral grain in trees. *Mailing Add:* 4913 Waukesha St Madison WI 53705

KUBLER-ROSS, ELISABETH, MEDICINE, PSYCHIATRY. *Current Pos:* PRES & CHMN BD, SHANTI NILAYA GROWTH & HEALTH CTR, 77- *Personal Data:* b Zurich, Switz, July 8, 26; nat US; c Kenneth L & Barbara L. *Educ:* Univ Zurich, MD, 57; Univ Notre Dame, LLD, 74; Hamline Univ, LLD, 75; DPedagogy, Keuka Col, NY, 76. *Hon Degrees:* DSc, Albany Med Col, 74, Smith Col, 75; Molloy Col, 76, Regis Col, 77, Farleigh Dickinson Univ, 79; hon degree, Med Col Pa, 75, Anna Maria col, 78; LittD, St Mary's Col, Notre Dame, Ind, 75, Hood col, 76, Rosary Col, River Forest, Ill, 76; LHD, Amherst Col, 75, Loyola Univ, 75, Bard Col, NY, 77, Union Col, NY, 78, D'Youville Col, 79; Univ Miami, 76. *Honors & Awards:* Teilhard Prize, Tielhard Found, 81; Golden Plate Award, Am Acad Achievement, 80. *Prof Exp:* Rotating intern, Community Hosp, Glen Cove, NY, 58-59; resident, Montefiore Hosp, NY, 61-62; fel psychiat, Psychopathic Hosp, Univ Colo Med Sch, 62-63, instr psychiat, Colo Gen Hosp, 62-65; asst prof psychiat, Billings Hosp, Univ Chicago, 65-70; med dir, Family Serv & Ment Health Ctr,

S Cook County, Chicago Heights, 70-73; pres, Ross Med Assocs, 73-77. Concurrent Pos: Res fel, Manhattan State Hosp, 59-62; mem staff, LaRabida Children's Hosp & Res Ctr, 65-70, chief consult & res liaison sect, 69-70. Mem: AAAS; Am Holistic Med Asn; Am Med Women's Asn; Am Psychiat Asn; Am Psychosomatic Soc; Asn Cancer Victims & Friends; Soc Psychophysiol Res. Mailing Add: c/o Celestial Arts Publ PO Box 7123 Berkeley CA 94707

KUBO, RALPH TERUO, MOLECULAR IMMUNOLOGY, IMMUNOCHEMISTRY. Current Pos: PRIN SCIENTIST, CYTEL CORP, 91- Personal Data: b Hilo, Hawaii, Mar 28, 42; m 67, June K Kaneshire; c Todd J Y & Kelly Ann M. Educ: Univ Calif, Los Angeles, BA, 65; Univ Hawaii, MS, 67, PhD(microbiol), 70. Prof Exp: Asst prof microbiol, Univ Hawaii, Honolulu, 70-71; sr fel, Nat Jewish Ctr Immunol Respiratory Med, 71-73, mem immunol, 73-89; from assoc prof to prof, Dept Microbiol, Med Sch, Univ Colo, 80-91; sr fac mem, Nat Jewish Ctr Immunol, 89-91. Concurrent Pos: Asst prof, Med Sch, Univ Colo, 75-80; assoc ed, J Immunol & Develop Comp Immunol, 78-82; Japan Soc for the Prom of Sci Fels, Univ Tokyo, 87; mem study sect, NIH, 89-93. Mem: Am Soc Microbiol; Sigma Xi; Am Asn Immunologists; NY Acad Sci; Am Soc Cell Biol. Res: Characterization of modified synthetic peptides by analytical methods to support manufacter of such products for vaccine development; monocloral antibody reactivity with peptide-mitc liquads. Mailing Add: Cytel Corp 3525 Johns Hopkins Ct San Diego CA 92121-1121. Fax: 619-552-8801; E-Mail: ralph_kubo@cytelcorp.com

KUBOTA, MITSURU, INORGANIC CHEMISTRY. Current Pos: From instr to assoc prof, 59-71, PROF CHEM, HARVEY MUDD COL, 71- Personal Data: b Eleele, Hawaii, Sept 25, 32; m 56, Jane Taketa; c Lynne K & Keith N. Educ: Univ Hawaii, BA, 54; Univ Ill, MS, 58, PhD, 60. Honors & Awards: Award Res Undergrad Inst, Am Chem Soc, 92. Concurrent Pos: NSF fel, Univ NC, Chapel Hill, 66-67; Fulbright-Hays advan res fel, Univ Sussex, Eng, 73-74; NIH spec fel, Calif Inst Technol, 74-75; consult, Chevron Res, 81-82; NSF develop award, Univ Calif, Berkeley, 81-82; vis prof, Univ Venice, 88 & Cambridge Univ, 89. Mem: Fel AAAS; Am Chem Soc; Royal Soc Chem; Sigma Xi. Res: Organometallic chemistry; homogeneous catalysis; inorganic synthesis. Mailing Add: Dept Chem Harvey Mudd Col Claremont CA 91711

KUBOTA, TOSHI, AERONAUTICS. Current Pos: Asst, Calif Inst Technol, 52-57, res fel, 57-59, from asst prof to assoc prof, 59-71, PROF AERONAUT, CALIF INST TECHNOL, 71- Personal Data: b Westmoreland, Calif, Feb 25, 26; m 52; c 3. Educ: Univ Tokyo, BEng, 47; Calif Inst Technol, MS, 52, PhD(aeronaut), 57. Concurrent Pos: Consult, AER, Inc, 57-59, Calif Div, Lockheed Aircraft Corp, 59-61, NESCO, 61-62, NAm Aviation, 62-69, TRW Systs Group, 68- & Aerospace, 69- Mem: Am Inst Aeronaut & Astronaut; Phys Soc Japan; Sigma Xi. Res: Hypersonic aerodynamics and heat transfer. Mailing Add: 140 Lowell Ave Sierra Madre CA 91024

KUBU, EDWARD THOMAS, PHYSICAL CHEMISTRY, POLYMER PHYSICS. Current Pos: PVT CONSULT, 86- Personal Data: b New York, NY, Nov 19, 26; m 51. Educ: NY Univ, BA, 49; Princeton Univ, MA, 51, PhD(chem), 52. Prof Exp: Sect leader, Textile Physics Sect, Res Ctr, B F Goodrich Co, 52-59; supvr characterization res, Cent Res Lab, Allied Corp, 59-61, asst dir lab res, 61-62, dir lab res, 62-63, dir res & develop, Fibers Div, asst to pres, 68-70, tech dir, Fibers Div, 70-73, dir tech opers, 73-77, mgr Govt & Indust Liaison, 77-86. Concurrent Pos: Bd trustees exec comt, Textile Res Inst, 71-78; mem adv bd, Textile Res Inst Regulatory Tech Info Ctr. Mem: Am Chem Soc; Sigma Xi. Res: Physical, chemical and mechanical properties of high polymers; manufacture and use of synthetic fibers; impact of government regulations on synthetic fiber, plastics and chemical manufacture and use. Mailing Add: 4720 Southmoor Rd Richmond VA 23234-3748

KUC, JOSEPH, PLANT BIOCHEMISTRY, PLANT PHYSIOLOGY. Current Pos: prof, 74-95, EMER PROF, UNIV KY, 95-, CONSULT PLANT PATH. Personal Data: b New York, NY, Nov 24, 29; m 91, Karola Maywald; c Paul, Rebecca & Miriam. Educ: Purdue Univ, BS, 51, MS, 53, PhD(biochem), 55. Honors & Awards: Campbell Award, Am Phytopath Soc, Sturgill Award; Medal, Int Plant Protection. Prof Exp: Asst biochem, Purdue Univ, 51-54, from asst prof to prof, 55-74. Concurrent Pos: Fulbright fel, 60 & 66; fel, Brazilian Coffee Inst, 69 & 71; Alexander von Humboldt Found res prize; sr sci awards, 80-90; hon prof Univ Repub, Montevideo, Uzuaquay, Shandone Agr, Univ China. Mem: Am Chem Soc; fel Am Phytopath Soc; Am Soc Plant Physiol; Phytochem Soc; fel Am Inst Chemists; Am Soc Biochem & Molecular Biol. Res: Biochemistry of disease resistance in plants; synthesis of natural products; plant immunization; plant microbe interactions. Mailing Add: 700 Front St Residence 1202 San Diego CA 92101. Fax: 619-237-1224

KUCERA, CLARE H, oilwell chemicals, organic & inorganic chemistry; deceased, see previous edition for last biography

KUCERA, LOUIS STEPHEN, VIROLOGY, AIDS. Current Pos: from asst prof to assoc prof, 70-80, PROF MICROBIOL, BOWMAN GRAY SCH MED, WAKE FOREST UNIV, 80- Personal Data: b New Prague, Minn, June 23, 35; m 59, JoAnn; c Gregory, Gary, Stephen & Scott. Educ: St John's Univ, Minn, BA, 57; Creighton Univ, MS, 59; Univ Mo, PhD(microbiol), 64. Honors & Awards: Microbiol Distinguished Serv Award, Am Soc Microbiol. Prof Exp: Res bacteriologist, Radioisotope Serv, Vet Admin Hosp, Omaha, Nebr, 60; res asst virol, Sect Microbiol, Mayo Clin, 64-65, res assoc, 65-66, res assoc, Virol Lab, St Jude Res Hosp, Memphis, Tenn, 66-68, staff mem, 68-70. Concurrent Pos: Reviewer, Human Cell Biol Prog, NSF; cancer res, proceedings, Nat Acad Sci; site visit reviewer, NC Biotechnol Ctr; prin investr & vis scientist, German Cancer Res Ctr, Heidelberg, 86; asst prof, Dept Microbiol, Univ Tenn Med Units, Memphis, 68-70; NIH grant; NC biotechnol grant. Mem: Int AIDS Soc; Am Soc Microbiol; fel Am Acad Microbiol; Sigma Xi; Am Soc Virol; Int Soc Antiviral Res; Am Asn Cancer Res. Res: Herpes simplex virus DNA sequences; prostaglandin synthesis and tumorigenesis; consequences of herpes simplex virus-alveolar macrophage interactions; tumor promoters; chemical carcinogens and herpes viruses; human immunodeficiency virus and herpes virus interactions; ether lipids and chemotherapy of HIV infections. Mailing Add: Dept Microbiol & Immunol Bowman Gray Sch Med Winston-Salem NC 27157-1064. Fax: 910-716-9928; E-Mail: lkucera@bgsm.edu

KUCERA, THOMAS J, ORGANIC CHEMISTRY. Current Pos: CONSULT, 82- Personal Data: b Oak Park, Ill, Feb 22, 25; m 64; c 3. Educ: Loyola Univ, Ill, BS, 45; Ill Inst Technol, MS, 52; Purdue Univ, PhD, 53. Prof Exp: Res chemist, Miner Labs, Mid-West Div, Arthur D Little, Inc, 45-50; Fulbright scholar, Univ Auckland, 53-54; res fel, Purdue Univ, 54-55; asst to pres, Mid-West Labs, 55-56; mgr chem res, Charles Bruning Co, Inc, 56-61; consult, 61-64; vpres res & eng, Apeco Corp, 64-81. Concurrent Pos: Fulbright scholar, New Zealand. Mem: AAAS; Am Chem Soc; The Chem Soc; Soc Photog Sci & Eng. Res: Photoreproduction; organic photoreactions; inorganic photoconductors; electrostatics; organic mechanisms. Mailing Add: 9310 Hamlin Ave Evanston IL 60203-1302

KUCESKI, VINCENT PAUL, ORGANIC CHEMISTRY. Current Pos: sr chemist, C P Hall Co Ill, 52-59, dir res, 59-71, vpres res, 71-74, VPRES RES & DEVELOP, C P HALL CO ILL, 74- Personal Data: b Superior, Wis, Apr 1, 20; m 44; c 2. Educ: Univ Wis, BS, 42, MS, 48, PhD(chem), 50. Prof Exp: Res chemist, Southern Cotton Oil Co, 50-52. Mem: Am Chem Soc; Am Inst Chemists; Am Oil Chemists Soc. Res: Oxidations of organic compounds; oils and fats; analytical organic chemistry. Mailing Add: 293 W Elmwood Chicago Heights IL 60411-1068

KUCHAR, NORMAN RUSSELL, MATERIALS PROCESSING, MANUFACTURING TECHNOLOGY. Current Pos: Fluid dynamicist fluid physics, Space Sci Lab, Gen Elec Co, 67-69, group leader biofluid mech, Environ Sci Lab, 69-72, mech engr, 72-80, mgr process physics prog, 80-82, mgr, Process Technol Br, 83-90, mfg, Process Physics Lab, 90-93, MGR MFG TECH LAB, GEN ELEC CO, 93- Personal Data: b Cleveland, Ohio, June 22, 39; m 67; c 2. Educ: Case Inst Technol, BS, 61, MS, 65; Case Western Res Univ, PhD(eng), 67. Mem: Am Soc Mech Engrs; Am Soc Mat; Sigma Xi. Res: Intelligent processing of materials; process modeling; computer-aided engineering; process sensors; laser and quality technology. Mailing Add: 60 Fredericks Rd Scotia NY 12302

KUCHAREK, THOMAS ALBERT, PLANT PATHOLOGY. Current Pos: asst prof & asst exten plant pathologist, 70-74, assoc prof, 75-80, PROF PLANT PATH & EXTEN PLANT PATHOLOGIST, UNIV FLA, 80- Personal Data: b Cleveland, Ohio, Nov 16, 39; m 63; c 2. Educ: Kent State Univ, BS, 62; Univ Minn, MS, 65, PhD(plant path), 69. Prof Exp: Asst plant path, Univ Minn, 62-65; instr, Okla State Univ, 65-68 & Univ Minn, 69. Mem: Am Phytopath Soc; Sigma Xi. Res: Diagnosis and control of diseases on field crops and vegetables. Mailing Add: Dept Plant Path Univ Fla PO Box 110680 Gainesville FL 32611-2002

KUCHEL, OTTO GEORGE, NEPHROLOGY. Current Pos: CONSULT, 96- Personal Data: b Spis Stara Ves, Czech, June 22, 24; Can citizen; m 53, Gabriel Szalaf; c George, Erica & Marie. Educ: Charles Univ, Prague, MD, 50, PhD(endocrinol), 56, ScD(nephrology), 65. Honors & Awards: Res Award, Asn French Speaking Physicians Can, 72. Prof Exp: Instr int med, Safarik Univ, Kosice, 56; asst prof, III Dept Med, Charles Univ, Prague, 57-65; instr, Vanderbilt Univ, 66; prof, III Dept Med, Charles Univ, Prague, 67-68; prof nephrology, Clin Res Inst, Univ Montreal, 68-96, dir, Lab Sympathetic Nerv Syst, Inst, 75-96. Concurrent Pos: Mem serv nephrology, Hotel-Dieu Hosp & Univ Montreal, 68; mem, Hypertension Task Force, NIH, 75-79; mem, Coun High Blood Pressure Res, Cleveland. Mem: Endocrine Soc; Royal Soc Med; Am Col Physicians; Royal Col Physicians & Surgeons Can. Res: Clinical nephrology and endocrinology related to research of mechanisms of hypertension, particularly the role of the sympathetic nervous system, adrenals and the kidney. Mailing Add: Clin Res Inst Montreal 110 Pine Ave W Montreal PQ H2W 1R7 Can. Fax: 514-987-5675

KUCHERLAPATI, RAJU SURYANARAYANA, HUMAN GENETICS. Current Pos: CHMN & PROF GENETICS, ALBERT EINSTEIN COL MED, 89-, SAUL & LOLA KRAMER PROF, 89- Personal Data: b Kakinada, India, Jan 18, 43; m; c 1. Educ: Andhra Univ, India, BSc, 60, MSc, 62; Univ Ill, Urbana, PhD(genetics), 72. Prof Exp: Res fel human genetics, Yale Univ, 72-75; asst prof, Princeton Univ, 75-82; prof genetics, Univ Ill, 82-88. Concurrent Pos: Damon Runyon Cancer Fund res fel, Yale Univ, 73-74; NIH fel, 74-75; mem, Mammalian Genetics Study Sect, NIH, 85-89. Mem: AAAS; Genetics Soc Am; Am Soc Microbiol. Res: Human gene mapping; study of regulation of gene action in human cells; gene transfer, gene therapy; homologous recombination. Mailing Add: Dept Molecular Genetics Albert Einstein Col Med 1300 Morris Park Ave Bronx NY 10461. Fax: 718-823-6550; E-Mail: kucherla@aecom.yu.edu

KUCHINSKAS, EDWARD JOSEPH, BIOCHEMISTRY. *Current Pos:* from asst prof to assoc prof, 56-67, from asst dean to assoc dean sch grad studies, 67-73, PROF BIOCHEM, STATE UNIV NY DOWNSTATE MED CTR, 67- *Personal Data:* b Maspeth, NY, Feb 11, 27; Wid; c 1. *Educ:* Queen's Col, NY, BS, 49; Cornell Univ, PhD, 54. *Prof Exp:* Instr biochem, Med Col, Cornell Univ, 54-56. *Mem:* AAAS; Am Chem Soc; Soc Exp Biol Med; Harvey Soc; Am Soc Biol Chemists; NY Acad Sci. *Res:* Metabolic effects of cysteine analogues, especially vitamin requirements and enzyme activation; catalase; semisynthetic penicillins; S-methyl group oxidations; peroxidative mechanisms; metabolism of penicillamine. *Mailing Add:* 118-11 84 Ave Apt 604 Kew Gardens NY 11415-2935

KUCHLER, ROBERT JOSEPH, MICROBIOLOGY. *Current Pos:* from asst prof to prof bact, 62-75, dir coord grad prog microbiol, 78-81, PROF MICROBIOL, RUTGERS UNIV, 75- *Personal Data:* b Pittsburgh, Pa, Mar 28, 28; m 58; c 3. *Educ:* Univ Pittsburgh, BS, 50, MS, 52; Univ Mich, PhD, 58. *Prof Exp:* Asst bact, WVa Univ, 52-54 & Univ Mich, 54-58; bacteriologist & head dept, William Singer Res Lab, Allegheny Gen Hosp, 58-62. *Mem:* Am Soc Microbiol; Tissue Cult Asn; Am Soc Cell Biol; Sigma Xi. *Res:* Development of metazoan cell populations in tissue culture with emphasis on their permeability to small molecular species and on the organization of macromolecules within these cells; viral nucleic acids. *Mailing Add:* 11 Dogwood Ct East Brunswick NJ 08816

KUCHNIR, FRANCA TABLIABUE, MEDICAL PHYSICS, RADIOLOGICAL SCIENCE. *Current Pos:* trainee, Univ Chicago, 71-73, asst prof, 73-74, dir, Sect Med Physics, 80-84, ASSOC PROF MED PHYSICS, UNIV CHICAGO, 74- *Personal Data:* b Russe, Bulgaria, July 18, 35; US citizen; m 60; Moyses; c Louis & Deborah. *Educ:* Univ San Paulo, BS, 58; Univ Ill, MS, 62, PhD(physics), 65. *Prof Exp:* Res asst physics, Univ Ill, 60-65; fel, Argonne Nat Lab, 66-68; asst prof, Univ Ill, 69-70; asst physicist, Argonne Nat Lab, 70-71. *Concurrent Pos:* Prog dir, Nat Res Serv Awards, Nat Cancer Inst, 79-88. *Mem:* Am Asn Physicists Med; Radiol Soc NAm; Am Col Radiol; Am Soc Ther Radiol Oncol. *Res:* Radiation physics and dosimetry specifically related to radiation therapy and diagnosis. *Mailing Add:* Dept Radiation Oncol Univ Chicago 5758 S Maryland Ave MC9006 Chicago IL 60637. *Fax:* 773-702-0610; *E-Mail:* franca@rover.uchicago.edu

KUCHNIR, MOYSES, LOW TEMPERATURE PHYSICS, SUPERCONDUCTIVITY APPLICATIONS. *Current Pos:* PHYSICIST & APPL SCIENTIST, FERMI NAT ACCELERATOR LAB, 74- *Personal Data:* b Sao Paulo, Brazil, May 18, 36; US citizen; m 60; c 2. *Educ:* Univ Asn Paulo, BS, 57; Univ Ill, Urbana, MS, 62, PhD(physics), 66. *Prof Exp:* Mem staff solid state physics, Argonne Nat Lab, 66-68, asst physicist, 68-73; proj assoc cryogenics, Univ Wis-Madison, 73; prof physics, Univ Estadual Campinas, Brazil, 74. *Mem:* AAAS; Am Phys Soc; Inst Elec & Electronics Engrs; Mat Res Soc. *Res:* Properties of quantum fluids; magnetic properties of superconductors; cryogenic and superconducting equipment and techniques; superconducting magnets for accelerators; properties of materials at low temperatures. *Mailing Add:* 934 Parkside Elmhurst IL 60126

KUCK, DAVID JEROME, COMPUTER SCIENCE, COMPUTER ENGINEERING. *Current Pos:* from asst to prof, 65-93, dir, Ctr Comput Res & Develop, 84-93, EMER PROF COMPUT SCI, UNIV ILL, URBANA-CHAMPAIGN, 93-; CHMN, KUCK & ASSOCS INC. *Personal Data:* b Muskegon, Mich, Oct 3, 37; m 77, Sharon McCure; c Julianne & Jonathen. *Educ:* Univ Mich, Ann Arbor, BS, 59; Northwestern Univ, MS, 60, PhD(eng), 63. *Honors & Awards:* Emanuel R Piore Award, Inst Elec & Electronics Engrs, 87, Eckert Mauchiy Award. *Prof Exp:* Ford fel & asst prof elec eng, Mass Inst Technol, 63-65. *Concurrent Pos:* NSF res grant, 70-; consult, Burroughs Corp, 72- & Los Alamos Nat Lab, 78-; assoc ed, Inst Elec & Electronics Engrs Trans Comput, 73-75, Asn Comput Mach Database Systs, 77-, Int J Comput & Info Sci, 77-, J Asn Comput Mach, 80- & J Digital Systs, 80-; pres, Kuck & Assoc Inc; mem tech adv bd, Sequent Comput Systs, Portland, Ore, 85-, Sci Comput Systs, San Diego, Calif, 85-, Dana Group, Sunnyvale, Calif, 86-; mem, Comput Sci & Technol Bd, Nat Res Coun, Washington, DC, 86-; bd dirs, Supercomput Systs Inc, 88- *Mem:* Nat Acad Eng; fel Inst Elec & Electronics Engrs; fel AAAS; fel Asn Comput Match. *Res:* Parallel, pipeline and multiprocessor computation methods; interconnection networks; memory hierarchies; compilation of ordinary programs for such machines. *Mailing Add:* Kuck & Assocs Inc 1906 Fox Dr Champaign IL 61820

KUCK, JAMES CHESTER, AGRICULTURAL BIOCHEMISTRY, ORGANIC CHEMISTRY. *Current Pos:* RES CHEMIST, SOUTHERN REGIONAL RES CTR, SCI & EDUC ADMIN, AGR RES, USDA, NEW ORLEANS, 53- *Personal Data:* b New Orleans, La, Dec 24, 12; m 69. *Educ:* La State Univ, Baton Rouge, BS, 38. *Prof Exp:* Prof math & sci, Rugby Mil Acad, New Orleans, 41-42; asst chemist, La State Bd Health, 42; sr res chemist, Celotex Corp, Marrero, La, 42-49. *Mem:* Am Oil Chemists Soc; Sigma Xi. *Res:* Chemical and physical properties of oil-bearing seed, especially cottonseed, peanuts, soybean, sunflower, rape and properties relating to improvements in present industrial processing and development of higher quality and utility of these products. *Mailing Add:* 1373 Madrid St New Orleans LA 70122

KUCK, JOHN FREDERICK READ, JR, BIOCHEMISTRY. *Current Pos:* from asst prof to prof ophthal, 63-88, asst prof biochem, 63-88, EMER PROF OPHTHAL, SCH MED MED, EMORY UNIV, 88-, EMER PROF, EYE RES LAB, 93- *Personal Data:* b Savannah, Ga, Jan 27, 18; m 49; c 5. *Educ:* Va Polytech Inst, BS, 39, MS, 40; Univ NC, PhD(biochem), 51. *Prof Exp:* Chemist, Nat Adv Comn Aeronaut, 40-46; prof chem, St Procopius Col, 50-51; res assoc surg, Col Med, Wayne State Univ, 51-56; res assoc, Kresge Eye Inst, 57-63. *Concurrent Pos:* Adj prof, Sch Chem, Ga Inst Technol, 87-88, vis prof, 88-93. *Mem:* AAAS; Am Chem Soc; Asn Res Vision & Ophthal; Sigma Xi. *Res:* Lens metabolism; diabetic and radiation cataracts; anti-cataractogenic drugs; Raman spectroscopy of lens. *Mailing Add:* Eye Res Lab Emory Univ Atlanta GA 30322-4750. *Fax:* 404-778-4143

KUCK, JULIUS ANSON, ORGANIC CHEMISTRY, HIGH PRESSURE LIQUID CHROMATOGRAPHY. *Current Pos:* res assoc, Dept Chem, 77-90, ADJ PROF CHEM RES, BANNOW SCI CTR, FAIRFIELD UNIV, 90- *Personal Data:* b Willimantic, Conn, Jan 6, 07; m 32, 55; c John H Jr & Peter H. *Educ:* Hamilton Col, AB, 28; Cornell Univ, PhD(org chem), 32. *Prof Exp:* Asst chem, Cornell Univ, 28-32; fel, City Col New York, 34-35, tutor, 35-36, from instr to assoc prof, 37-64; vis prof & actg chmn dept, Inter-Am Univ, PR, 65-66; from asst prof to assoc prof chem, Stamford Br, Univ Conn, 66-77. *Concurrent Pos:* Consult org microanal, Am Cyanamid Co, 43-64. *Mem:* Am Chem Soc; AAAS; Am Microchem Soc; Sigma Xi. *Res:* Synthetic organic chemistry; aliphatic boric acids; cardiac lactones; microanalysis; analytical methods and development; saxitoxin in paralytic shellfish poison; HPLC for natural product analysis; determination of alpha-tocopherol, retinol, and betacarotene in human serum; development and operation of the quartz crystal, high frequency nanogram ultramicro balance; piezoelectric effect upon a 10 megahertz oscillator by imposing an appropriate mass and noting the frequency change produced. *Mailing Add:* 57 Mimosa Dr Cos Cob CT 06807. *Fax:* 203-254-4034

KUCZENSKI, RONALD THOMAS, PSYCHOPHARMACOLOGY. *Current Pos:* ASST PROF PHARMACOL, VANDERBILT UNIV, 74-, ASST PROF BIOCHEM, 80- *Personal Data:* b Detroit, Mich, July 27, 44. *Educ:* Univ San Diego, BS, 66; Mich State Univ, PhD(biochem), 70. *Prof Exp:* Res psychobiologist psychiat, Univ Calif, San Diego, 70-73, asst prof, 73-74. *Res:* Regulation of biochemical events of central nervous system synaptic transmission and relationship to effects of pharmacological manipulations on behavioral parameters. *Mailing Add:* Dept Psych Univ Calif San Diego La Jolla CA 92093-0603

KUCZKOWSKI, JOSEPH EDWARD, ALGEBRA, MATHEMATICS EDUCATION. *Current Pos:* from assoc prof to prof math, 71-87, asst dean, 84-87, ASSOC DEAN, SCH SCI, IND UNIV, PURDUE, 87- *Personal Data:* b Buffalo, NY, Nov 18, 39; m 65, Elizabeth Bayley; c Edward, Ann, James & Laura. *Educ:* Canisius Col, BS, 61; Purdue Univ, MS, 63, PhD(math), 68. *Prof Exp:* From instr to asst prof math, Purdue Univ, 66-71. *Mem:* Math Asn Am; Nat Coun Teachers Math. *Res:* Subsemigroups of groups, with emphasis on nilpotent groups; semigroups satisfying certain non-tautological laws. *Mailing Add:* Dept Math Sci Ind Univ-Purdue Univ 402 N Blackford St Indianapolis IN 46202. *Fax:* 317-274-0628; *E-Mail:* jkuczkow@indyvax.iupui.edu

KUCZKOWSKI, ROBERT LOUIS, PHYSICAL INORGANIC CHEMISTRY. *Current Pos:* from asst prof to assoc prof, 66-74, PROF CHEM, UNIV MICH, ANN ARBOR, 74-, CHAIR DEPT, 91- *Personal Data:* b Buffalo, NY, Aug 2, 38; m 62; c 3. *Educ:* Canisius Col, BS, 60; Harvard Univ, MA, 62, PhD(chem), 64. *Prof Exp:* Nat Acad Sci res fel chem, Nat Bur Stand, 64-66. *Mem:* Am Chem Soc; Am Phys Soc; AAAS. *Res:* Microwave spectroscopy of inorganic compounds; weakly bound complexes; vun der waals molecules. *Mailing Add:* Dept Chem Univ Mich Ann Arbor MI 48109-1055

KUCZMARSKI, EDWARD R, CELL BIOLOGY. *Current Pos:* ASSOC PROF PHYSIOL, CHICAGO MED SCH, 89- *Personal Data:* b Cleveland, Ohio, Sept 4, 49. *Educ:* Hiram Col, BS, 71; Yale Univ, PhD(cell biol), 77. *Prof Exp:* Postdoctoral, Stanford Univ, 77-82; asst prof cell biol, Northwestern Univ Med Sch, 82-89. *Mem:* AAAS; Am Soc Cell Biol; Am Physiol Soc; Am Soc Biochem & Molecular Biol. *Res:* Mechanism and regulation of cell motility; cytoskeleton and signal transduction. *Mailing Add:* Dept Physiol Chicago Med Sch 3333 Green Bay Rd Suite 3274 North Chicago IL 60064-3095

KUDENOV, JERRY DAVID, INVERTEBRATE ZOOLOGY, PHYLOGENETIC SYSTEMATICS OF POLYCHAETOUS ANNELIDS. *Current Pos:* from asst prof to assoc prof, 80-87, chair, Dept Biol Sci, 86-90, PROF, DEPT BIOL SCI, UNIV ALASKA, ANCHORAGE, 87- *Personal Data:* b Lynwood, Calif, Dec 19, 46; m 69, Kathryn A Brown; c Peter A & Michael W. *Educ:* Univ Calif, San Diego, BA, 68; Univ of the Pac, MSc, 70; Univ Ariz, PhD(zool), 74. *Prof Exp:* Res scientist zool & pollution biol, Marine Pollution Studies Group, Fisheries & Wildlife Div, Australia, 74-79; vis prof, Dept Biol Sci & cur polychaeta, Allan Hancock Found, Univ Southern Calif, 79-80. *Concurrent Pos:* Mem, Biol Soc Wash. *Mem:* Am Soc Zoologists; Sigma Xi; AAAS; Int Asn Polychaetology. *Res:* Functional morphology of feeding, biometrics and phylogenetic systematics of polychaaetous annelids, especially of the order amphimomida. *Mailing Add:* Dept Biol Univ Alaska Anchorage Col 3211 Providence Dr Anchorage AK 99508-4614. *Fax:* 907-786-4607; *E-Mail:* afjdk@acad2.alaska.edu

KUDER, JAMES EDGAR, ORGANIC CHEMISTRY. *Current Pos:* RES ASSOC, CELANESE RES CO, 77- *Personal Data:* b Madang, New Guinea, Dec 28, 39; US citizen; m 62; c 2. *Educ:* Capital Univ, BS, 62; Ohio Univ, PhD(org chem), 68. *Prof Exp:* Chemist water anal, US Geol Surv, Ohio, 62-63; res fel, Rensselaer Polytech Inst, 68-69; scientist, Res Labs, Xerox Corp, 69-77. *Mem:* Am Chem Soc; The Chem Soc; Sigma Xi; Soc Photo-Optical Instrumentation Engrs. *Res:* Electronic structure and properties of organic dyes; photochemical rearrangements; quantum chemistry; reactions and spectroscopic studies of heterocyclic compounds; organic electrochemistry; optical recording materials. *Mailing Add:* 91 Willoughby Rd Fanwood NJ 07023-1244

KUDER, ROBERT CLARENCE, PLASTICS CHEMISTRY. *Current Pos:* RETIRED. *Personal Data:* b North Baltimore, Ohio, Dec 31, 18; m 42, Agnes Ewert; c 7. *Educ:* Ohio State Univ, AB, 39; Northwestern Univ, PhD(org chem), 42. *Prof Exp:* Jr chemist, Ethyl Gasoline Corp, 39; res chemist, Stand Oil Co, Ind, 42-46; asst prof chem, Univ Dayton, 46-48; sr res chemist, Barrett Div, Allied Chem Corp, 48-52, asst supvr res, 52-57, supvr polymer res, 57; tech dir, Bemis Bros Bag Co, 57-58; dir res & develop, Mol-Rez Div, Am Petrochem Corp, 58-63; res assoc, Gen Mills, Inc, 63-68; tech dir resins, Whittaker Corp, 68-77, tech dir, Minneapolis Coatings & Chem Div, 77-80; res chemist, Precision Cosmet Co, 80-83. *Concurrent Pos:* Consult, 84- *Mem:* Am Chem Soc. *Res:* Polyesters; polyurethanes. *Mailing Add:* 222 W Eagle Lake Dr Maple Grove MN 55369-6149

KUDMAN, IRWIN, metallurgy, physics, for more information see previous edition

KUDO, AKIRA, ENVIRONMENTAL SCIENCES, WATER CHEMISTRY. *Current Pos:* SR RES OFFICER, INST ENVIRON CHEM, 90- *Personal Data:* b Japan, Apr 6, 39; m 74, Yumiko; c Hiroki & Satoshi. *Educ:* Kyoto Univ, Japan, BSc, 63, MSc, 65; Univ Tex, Austin, PhD(environ health eng), 69; Kyoto Univ, Japan, DEng, 79. *Prof Exp:* Sr res officer biol, Nat Res Coun Can, 71-90. *Concurrent Pos:* Vis prof, Univ Ottawa, Can, 75-; vis scientist, Japan, 76, 85, 88 & 90 & France, 81, 83, 85 & 90; assoc ed, J Environ Conserv Eng, 80- *Mem:* Int Asn Water Pollution Res; Am Soc Civil Eng; Am Water Pollution Control Fedn. *Res:* Distribution, transport, transformation, and transfer of heavy metal pollutants, including radioactive materials (plutonium etc), in the aquatic systems such as rivers, lakes, and estuaries; anaerobic treatment of wastewater; Arctic ice core studies. *Mailing Add:* Inst Environ Chem Rm 236/M-12 Nat Res Coun Montreal Rd Ottawa ON K1A 0R6 Can

KUDO, ALBERT MASAKIYO, PETROLOGY, VOLCANOLOGY. *Current Pos:* from asst prof to assoc prof, 66-85, PROF GEOL, UNIV NMEX, 85- *Personal Data:* b New Westminster, BC, May 30, 37; m 62; c 2. *Educ:* Univ Toronto, BS, 60; McMaster Univ, MS, 62; Univ Calif, San Diego, PhD(earth sci), 67. *Prof Exp:* Lab instr geol, McMaster Univ, 60-62; res asst geochem, Univ Calif, San Diego, 62-66. *Concurrent Pos:* Petrologist-geochemist, Leg 65, Deep Sea Drilling Proj, 79; fel, Japan Soc Prom Sci, Tohuku Univ, Japan, 82; consult, Morrison-Knudsen Engrs, 88. *Mem:* Am Geophys Union; Geochem Soc; Geol Soc Am; fel Mineral Soc Am. *Res:* Igneous petrology; geochemistry. *Mailing Add:* 4116 Coe Dr NE Albuquerque NM 87110

KUDO, SHINICHI, MOLECULAR GENETICS. *Current Pos:* Res fel, 87-90, RES ASSOC MOLECULAR GENETICS, LA JOLLA CANCER RES FOUND, 90- *Personal Data:* b Yubaryri, Japan, Aug 29, 56. *Educ:* Asahikawa Med Col, Japan, MD, 82; Sapporo Med Sch, PhD(virol), 86. *Mem:* Am Soc Biochem & Molecular Biol; Am Soc Cell Biol. *Res:* Molecular genetics. *Mailing Add:* Dept Virol Hokaido Inst Pub Health Kita-19 Nishi-12 Kita-Ku Sapporo 060 Japan. *Fax:* 81 11 7369476

KUDYNSKA, JADWIGA, solid state physics, spectroscopy & spectrometry, for more information see previous edition

KUDZIN, STANLEY FRANCIS, ORGANIC CHEMISTRY. *Current Pos:* assoc prof, 62-70, PROF CHEM, STATE UNIV NY COL NEW PALTZ, 70- *Personal Data:* b Jersey City, NJ, Mar 1, 26; m 50; c 3. *Educ:* Fordham Univ, BS, 47, MS, 49, PhD(chem), 51. *Prof Exp:* Res & tech serv chemist, E I du Pont de Nemours & Co, 51-56; tech supvr, Ciba Co, Inc, 56-60; assoc prof org chem, Clemson Col, 60-61; ed, Acad Press, Inc, 61-62. *Concurrent Pos:* Consult, Acad Press, Inc. *Mem:* AAAS; Am Chem Soc. *Res:* Chemical education and literature. *Mailing Add:* 35 Ferris Lane Poughkeepsie NY 12601-5111

KUEBLER, JOHN RALPH, JR, INDUSTRIAL CHEMISTRY. *Current Pos:* RETIRED. *Personal Data:* b Indianapolis, Ind, Oct 22, 24; m 57; c 2. *Educ:* Univ Wis, BS, 48; Univ Ill, MS, 49, PhD, 51. *Prof Exp:* Inorg res chemist, Mallinckrodt Chem Works, 51-85, qual control mgr, Calsicat Div, 70-81. *Mem:* Am Chem Soc; Am Soc Qual Control. *Res:* Inorganic stereochemistry; inorganic analytical methods development. *Mailing Add:* 3922 Sterrettania Rd Erie PA 16506-4266

KUEBLER, WILLIAM FRANK, JR, chemistry; deceased, see previous edition for last biography

KUECKER, JOHN FRANK, PHYSICAL CHEMISTRY. *Current Pos:* from asst prof to assoc prof, 65-71, head dept, 69-72, PROF CHEM, KEARNEY STATE COL, 71- *Personal Data:* b Webster, SDak, Mar 21, 32; m 58; c 4. *Educ:* Northern State Col, BS, 54; SDak Sch Mines & Technol, BS, 58; Univ Nebr, MS, 63, PhD(chem), 65. *Prof Exp:* Teacher high sch, SDak 54-55 & 56-57; asst prof chem, Doane Col, 63-65. *Mem:* AAAS; Am Chem Soc; Nat Sci Teachers Asn. *Res:* Viscosity of aqueous salt solutions; ultracentrifugation of inorganic polymer solutions. *Mailing Add:* 3101 11th Ave Kearney NE 68847

KUEHL, GUENTER HINRICH, CATALYSTS, ZEOLITES. *Current Pos:* CONSULT, 93-; ADJ PROF, CHEM ENG DEPT, UNIV PA, 94- *Personal Data:* b Geesthacht, Ger, Jan 2, 28; m 57, Christel Kuehl; c Gerald, Gunda & Marianne. *Educ:* Brunswick Tech Univ, dipl, 55, Dr rer nat(chem), 57. *Prof Exp:* USPHS fel, Ind Univ, 57-59; res chemist, Kali-Chemie AG, Ger, 60-61; sr res chemist, Cent Res Div, Socony Mobil Oil Co, 62-69; sr res chemist, Process Res & Develop Serv Div, Mobil Res & Develop Corp, 69-75, assoc 75-83, res assoc, Paulsboro Res Lab, Catalyst Res & Develop Sect, 83-91, sr res assoc, Chem Catalyst Div, 91-93. *Concurrent Pos:* Counr, Am Chem Soc, 84-92; mem, Synthesis Comn, Int Zeolite Asn. *Mem:* Soc Ger Chem; Am Chem Soc; Int Zeolite Asn; Catalysis Soc. *Res:* Crystallization, modification, characterization, and chemistry of zeolites; catalyst research and development for application in petroleum and petrochemical industry; preparation and investigation of hydrogenphosphato-carbonato-apatites; phosphato complexes; preparation and properties of organo-metallic acetylene compounds. *Mailing Add:* 1956 Cardinal Lake Dr Cherry Hill NJ 08003-2904. *Fax:* 215-573-2093; *E-Mail:* kuehl@eniac.seas.upenn.edu

KUEHL, HANS H(ENRY), ELECTRICAL ENGINEERING. *Current Pos:* res scientist plasmas, Eng Ctr, 59-60, from asst prof to assoc prof, 60-72, PROF ELEC ENG, UNIV SOUTHERN CALIF, 72-, CHMN, ELEC ENG & ELECTROPHYSICS, 87- *Personal Data:* b Detroit, Mich, Mar 16, 33; m 65, Anna Meidinger; c Susan & Michael. *Educ:* Princeton Univ, BSEE, 55; Calif Inst Technol, MS, 56, PhD(elec eng), 59. *Prof Exp:* Mem tech staff, Hughes Aircraft Co, 58-59. *Concurrent Pos:* Res fel, Calif Inst Technol, 59-60, vis assoc, 76. *Mem:* Am Phys Soc; fel Inst Elec & Electronics Engrs; Int Sci Radio Union. *Res:* Plasma physics; electromagnetic theory; antennas. *Mailing Add:* Dept Elec Eng PHE 604 Univ Southern Calif Los Angeles CA 90089-0271. *Fax:* 213-740-8677

KUEHL, LEROY ROBERT, BIOCHEMISTRY. *Current Pos:* from instr to assoc prof, 65-80, PROF BIOCHEM, UNIV UTAH, 80- *Personal Data:* b Ketchikan, Alaska, Aug 15, 31; m 59; c 3. *Educ:* Iowa State Univ, BS, 53; Ore State Univ, MS, 55; Univ Calif, Berkeley, PhD(comp biochem), 61. *Prof Exp:* NIH fel, Max Planck Inst Biol, Tubingen, Ger, 62-65. *Mem:* Fedn Am Soc Exp Biol; Am Chem Soc; AAAS. *Res:* Biochemistry of the cell nucleus; chromosomal proteins. *Mailing Add:* Dept Biochem Sch Med Univ Utah 50 N Medical Dr Salt Lake City UT 84132-0001

KUEHLER, JACK D, ELECTRON OPTICS. *Current Pos:* INDEPENDENT CONSULT. *Personal Data:* b Grand Island, NB, Aug 29, 32; m, Carmen. *Educ:* Santa Clara Univ, BS & MS. *Hon Degrees:* DSc, Clarkson Univ, Univ Santa Clara, 89. *Prof Exp:* Assoc engr, San Jose Res Lab, IBM Corp, 58-67, dir, Raleigh Commun Lab, NC, 67-70, dir, San Jose & Menlo Park Develop Labs, 70-72, vpres, Gen Prod Div, 72-74, vpres develop, 74-77, pres, Syst Prod Div, 78-80, IBM vpres & pres, Gen Technol Div, 80-81, sr vpres, 82, IBM vchmn bd, 88-89, pres & mem exec comt, 89-93. *Concurrent Pos:* Asst group exec systs develop, Data Processing Prod Group, 77-78, info systs & tech group exec, 81, mem corp mgmt bd & US mfg, 85, mem bd dir, 86, exec vpres, 87; mem bd dir, Olin Corp & Nat Asn Mfrs. *Mem:* Nat Acad Eng; fel Inst Elec & Electronics Engrs; fel Am Acad Arts & Sci. *Mailing Add:* PO Box 11130 Telluride CO 81435

KUEHN, GLENN DEAN, BIOCHEMISTRY, MOLECULAR BIOLOGY. *Current Pos:* from asst prof to assoc prof, 70-75, PROF CHEM, NMEX STATE UNIV, 80- *Personal Data:* b Terry, Mont, Apr 13, 42; m 65, Donna F; c Tara L. *Educ:* Concordia Col, BA, 64; Wash State Univ, PhD(biochem), 68. *Prof Exp:* NIH fel, Univ Calif, Los Angeles, 68-70. *Concurrent Pos:* Am Cancer Soc res support award, 71-76 & 81-83; NSF res support award, 73-79; NIH res support award, 74-77, 80-83, 80-85, 85-89, 90-95 & 96, USDA res support award, 86-91 & 92-97, USGS res support, 87-92; dir, Minorities Biomed Res Support Group, 75-97; Roche Found Fel, Univ Berne, Switz, 79; dir, Bridges to Am Indians in Community Colg, 92-97. *Mem:* AAAS; Am Chem Soc; Fedn Am Soc Exp Biol; Am Soc Microbiol; Soc Adv Chicanos & Nat Am Sci. *Res:* Biosynthesis and regulatory functions of polyamines; carbon dioxide fixation in autotrophs; regulatory enzymology; biochemical mechanisms of drought and heat tolerance in plants. *Mailing Add:* Grad Prog Molecular Biol Box 3MLS NMex State Univ Las Cruces NM 88003-0001. *Fax:* 505-646-6448; *E-Mail:* gkuehn@nmsu.edu

KUEHN, JEROME H, FISH BIOLOGY, FISHERIES ADMINISTRATION. *Current Pos:* RETIRED. *Personal Data:* b Minneapolis, Minn, July 20, 20; m 45; c 3. *Educ:* Univ Minn, BS, 42, MS, 49. *Prof Exp:* Aquatic biologist aide, State Natural Resources Dept, Minn, 46, aquatic biologist, 47-52, asst wildlife projs coordr, 52-56, supvr, Survs & Inventories Unit, 56-66, natural resource planning dir, 66-79, chief fisheries, 79-82. *Mem:* Am Fisheries Soc. *Res:* Techniques of fisheries survey procedures; development of fisheries management investigations; fish toxicants; natural resource planning; environmental impact review; water resources planning. *Mailing Add:* 3198 Manitou Dr St Paul MN 55110

KUEHN, LORNE ALLAN, biophysics, for more information see previous edition

KUEHNE, DONALD LEROY, CHEMICAL ENGINEERING. *Current Pos:* SR RES ENGR & SR DEVELOP ENGR, CHEVRON RES & TECHNOL, RICHMOND, CALIF, 88- *Personal Data:* b Oak Park, Ill, Jan 24, 52. *Educ:* Cornell Univ, BS, 73; Calif Inst Technol, MS, 75, PhD(chem eng), 79. *Prof Exp:* Res engr, Chevron Oil Field Res Co, Chevron Corp, 78-88. *Mem:* Am Inst Chem Engrs; Soc Petrol Engrs. *Res:* Development and reservoir applications of enhanced oil recovery chemicals; technology for improving sweep efficiency in oil production. *Mailing Add:* Chevron Res & Technol 100 Chevron Way Bldg 10 Rm 2214 Richmond CA 94806

KUEHNE, MARTIN ERIC, ORGANIC CHEMISTRY. *Current Pos:* from asst prof to assoc prof & Sloan fel, 61-68, chmn dept, 76-78, PROF CHEM, UNIV VT, 68- *Personal Data:* b Floral Park, NY, May 29, 31; m 53; c 1. *Educ:* Columbia Univ, AB, 52, PhD(chem), 56; Harvard Univ, MA, 53. *Prof Exp:* Sr chemist, Chem Res Dept, Ciba Pharmaceut Prod, Inc, 55-61. *Mem:* Am Chem Soc. *Res:* Synthetic and degrative problems in natural products; general organic chemistry; medicinal chemistry. *Mailing Add:* 169 S Cove Rd Burlington VT 05401

KUEHNER, CALVIN CHARLES, MEDICAL MICROBIOLOGY, PUBLIC HEALTH. *Current Pos:* RETIRED. *Personal Data:* b Put-in-Bay, Ohio, Dec 12, 22; m 47, Bonnie Murphy; c Charles, Carol & Mary. *Educ:* Ohio State Univ, BS, 49, MS, 50, PhD(mycol), 53. *Prof Exp:* Zymologist, Fermentation Div, Northern Regional Res Lab, Peoria, Ill, 51-54; asst prof microbiol, Univ Detroit, 54-58; assoc prof biol, Univ Windsor, 58-67; prof & chmn dept, St Dominic Col, 67-69; prof microbiol, Moraine Valley Community Col, 69-75; dir, Basic Sci Div, Nat Col Chiropractic, 75-89, prof microbiol & pub health, 75-93. *Concurrent Pos:* Consult microbiol, Palos Med Labs, Palos Heights, Ill, 74-76; assoc ed, J Manipulative & Physiol Therapeut, 78- *Mem:* Am Inst Biol Sci; Am Pub Health Asn. *Res:* Teaching of general and medical micrbiology; community health problems. *Mailing Add:* 995 W River Pt Circle Murray VT 84123

KUEHNER, JOHN ALAN, NUCLEAR PHYSICS. *Current Pos:* PROF PHYSICS, MCMASTER UNIV, 66- *Personal Data:* b Lennoxville, Que, Oct 8, 31; div; c 3. *Educ:* Bishop's Univ, BSc, 51; Queen's Univ, Ont, MA, 54; Univ Liverpool, PhD(physics), 56. *Prof Exp:* Res officer, Chalk River Nuclear Labs, 56-66. *Mem:* Am Phys Soc; Can Asn Physicists; Royal Soc Can. *Res:* Nuclear structure studies using reactions induced with accelerated ion beams. *Mailing Add:* Dept Physics McMaster Univ Hamilton ON L8S 4K1 Can

KUEHNERT, CHARLES CARROLL, PLANT MORPHOGENESIS. *Current Pos:* from asst prof to assoc prof bot, 64-71, ASSOC PROF BIOL, SYRACUSE UNIV, 71- *Personal Data:* b Springdale, Ark, Nov 21, 30; m 68. *Educ:* Mankato State Col, BA, 53; Purdue Univ, MS, 55, PhD(bot), 59. *Prof Exp:* Asst bot, Purdue Univ, 53-58, res asst, 59; Nat Res Coun Can fel & res assoc biol, Univ Sask, 60-62; res assoc, Brookhaven Nat Lab, 62-64. *Concurrent Pos:* Res collabr, Brookhaven Nat Lab, 64-67; vis prof, 65-66, asst botanist, 70-71; adv except undergrad, NSF undergrad res partic prog, Syracuse Univ, 66-67 & adv except sec sch students, NSF Pre-Col Studies Ctr, 68 & 71; sci consult, L W Singer Publ Co, 67; organizing co-chmn, Int Conf Dynamics Meristem Cell Pop, Univ Rochester, 71. *Mem:* Bot Soc Am. *Res:* Dynamics of meristem cell populations; cell biology; cell population kinetics; developmental and experimental morphology. *Mailing Add:* 168 Edgehill Rd Syracuse NY 13244

KUEKER, DAVID WILLIAM, LOGIC. *Current Pos:* asst prof, 73-76, assoc prof math, 76-84, PROF MATH, UNIV MD, COLLEGE PARK, 84- *Personal Data:* b Denver, Colo, Dec 14, 43; div. *Educ:* Univ Calif, Los Angeles, BA, 64, MA, 66, PhD(math), 67. *Prof Exp:* Actg asst prof math, Univ Calif, Los Angeles, 67-68; Hildebrandt res instr, Univ Mich, Ann Arbor, 68-70, asst prof, 70-73. *Mem:* Am Math Soc; Asn Symbolic Logic. *Res:* Mathematical logic, especially model theory for finitary, infinitary and other non-classical languages. *Mailing Add:* Dept Math Univ Md College Park MD 20742-0001

KUEMMEL, DONALD FRANCIS, ANALYTICAL CHEMISTRY. *Current Pos:* RETIRED. *Personal Data:* b Milwaukee, Wis, Dec 27, 27; m 49, Juanita Beaudoin; c Victoria, Jerome & Katherine. *Educ:* Marquette Univ, BS, 50, MS, 52; Purdue Univ, PhD(anal chem), 56. *Prof Exp:* Chemist, Allis-Chalmers Mfg Co, Wis, 51-53; res chemist, Procter & Gamble Co, 55-88. *Mem:* Am Chem Soc; Am Oil Chem Soc. *Res:* Chromatography; separations. *Mailing Add:* 3367 Nandale Dr Cincinnati OH 45239-4013

KUEMMERLE, NANCY BENTON STEVENS, molecular genetics, dna repair mechanisms, for more information see previous edition

KUENHOLD, KENNETH ALAN, GENERAL PHYSICS, ENGINEERING PHYSICS. *Current Pos:* Asst prof, 73-76, ASSOC PROF PHYSICS, UNIV TULSA, 76-, CHMN ENG PHYSICS, 77- *Personal Data:* b Cleveland, Ohio. *Educ:* Cornell Univ, BEP, 64; Ohio State Univ, PhD(physics), 73. *Concurrent Pos:* Adj res partic, Oak Ridge Assoc Univs, 73-78. *Mem:* Am Phys Soc; Am Asn Physics Teachers; Sigma Xi. *Res:* Two-phase oil and gas instrumentation and measurement. *Mailing Add:* Dept Physics Univ Tulsa 600 S College Tulsa OK 74104-3189

KUENZEL, WAYNE JOHN, POULTRY PHYSIOLOGY, ORNITHOLOGY. *Current Pos:* asst prof poultry sci, 74-78, assoc prof physiol, 78-84, PROF PHYSIOL, UNIV MD, COLLEGE PARK, 84- *Personal Data:* b Philadelphia, Pa, Jan 22, 42; c 2. *Educ:* Bucknell Univ, BS, 64, MS, 66; Univ Ga, PhD(zool), 69. *Prof Exp:* NIH fel neurophysiol, Cornell Univ, 71-73, res assoc, 73-74. *Concurrent Pos:* Sabbatical leave, Scotland, 81; Fulbright-Hays sr res fel award, Gt Brit. *Mem:* AAAS; World's Poultry Sci Asn; Poultry Sci Asn; Am Ornithologists Union; Am Soc Zoologists; Soc Neurosci. *Res:* Avian physiology; regulation of food and water intake; neuroanatomy; neurobiology; neural control of precocious puberty; neurosciences. *Mailing Add:* 6829 Pineway Hyattsville MD 20792-1160

KUENZI, NORBERT JAMES, MATHEMATICS. *Current Pos:* asst prof, 64-66 & 69-70, assoc prof, 70-80, PROF MATH, UNIV WIS-OSHKOSH, 80-, CHAIRPERSON DEPT, 76- *Personal Data:* b Beaver Dam, Wis, Aug 5, 35; m 60; c 5. *Educ:* Wis State Univ-Eau Claire, BS, 59; Univ Ill, Urbana, MA, 63; Univ Iowa, PhD(statist), 69. *Prof Exp:* Teacher high sch, Wis, 59-62. *Mem:* Inst Math Statist; Am Statist Asn; Math Asn Am. *Res:* Probability theory; mathematical statistics. *Mailing Add:* 414 E New York Ave Oshkosh WI 54901

KUENZLER, EDWARD JULIAN, WETLAND ECOLOGY, ENVIRONMENTAL NUTRIENT CYCLING. *Current Pos:* assoc prof environ sci & eng, Univ NC, Chapel Hill, 65-70, prof marine sci, 68-93, prof bot, 69-75, prof environ sci & eng, 70-93, EMER PROF, UNIV NC, CHAPEL HILL, 93- *Personal Data:* b West Palm Beach, Fla, Nov 11, 29; m 65, Jutta G Koslowski; c Doreen F & Dirk E. *Educ:* Univ Fla, BS, 51; Univ Ga, MS, 53, PhD(ecol), 59. *Prof Exp:* From res asst to res assoc marine biol, Woods Hole Oceanog Inst, 59-64, assoc scientist, 64-65. *Concurrent Pos:* Prog dir biol oceanog, NSF, Washington, DC, 71-72; prog area dir, Environ Chem & Biol, 80-83, Aquatic & Atmospheric Sci, 90-93; dep chmn, Environ Sci Eng, 84-87; chmn, marine sci curric, Univ NC, 68-73, prof ecol, 71-93. *Mem:* Estuarine Res Fedn; Ecol Soc Am; Am Soc Limnol & Oceanog; Soc Wetland Scientists. *Res:* Ornithology; spider ecology; energy and nutrient flows through marine animals; nutrition of marine, estuarine, and freshwater phytoplankton; ecology of estuaries; aquatic and wetland ecology; wastewater renovation by forested wetlands. *Mailing Add:* 6015 Old Greensboro Rd Chapel Hill NC 27516. *E-Mail:* ekuenzler@aol.com

KUEPER, THEODORE VINCENT, EXPERIMENTAL STATISTICS. *Current Pos:* PRES, WIS DATA LAB, LTD, 89- *Personal Data:* b Dubuque, Iowa, Aug 13, 41; m 63; c 3. *Educ:* Iowa State Univ, BS, 63. *Prof Exp:* Scientist biochem, Beatrice Foods Co, 63, statistician exp statist, 63-67, head statist, 67-70, res mgr sci serv, 70-74, res mgr new prod develop, 74-78, dir formulated foods res, 78-81, dir res & develop qual assurance grocery foods, 81-83, dir res & develop qual assurance cheese, 83-84, vpres qual assurance cheese, 84-87; consult & high sch chem teacher, 87-89. *Res:* New food products, both consumer and industrial; statistical analysis, experimental design and computer applications in regard to food research and development; prediction of food sensitivities for patients of health practitioners. *Mailing Add:* 415 Cymric Ct Wales WI 53183

KUESEL, THOMAS ROBERT, BRIDGES, TUNNELS. *Current Pos:* Mem staff, Parsons, Brinckerhoff, Quade & Douglas, NY, 47-63, proj mgr, San Francisco, 67-68, partner & sr vpres, 68-83, dir, 68-90, chmn bd, 83-91, EMER CHMN BD, PARSONS, BRINCKERHOFF, QUADE & DOUGLAS, NY, 91-; CONSULT ENGR, 91- *Personal Data:* b Richmond Hill, NY, July 30, 26; m 59, Lucia Elodia Fisher; c Robert & William. *Educ:* Yale Univ, BEng, 46, MEng, 47. *Honors & Awards:* Ernest E Howard Award, Am Soc Civil Eng, 88. *Concurrent Pos:* Asst mgr eng, Parsons Brinckerhoff-Tudor-Bechtel, San Francisco, 63-67; vchmn, OECD Tunneling Conf, Washington, DC, 70; mem, US Nat Comt Tunneling Technol, 72-74; chmn, Geotech Bd, Nat Res Coun, 87- *Mem:* Nat Acad Eng; fel Am Soc Civil Eng; Int Asn Bridge, Struct Eng; Brit Tunneling Soc; Sigma Xi. *Res:* Structural engineering; designer of 120 bridges and 135 tunnels world wide. *Mailing Add:* 5 Wood Lane Charlottesville VA 22901

KUETHER, CARL ALBERT, biochemistry; deceased, see previous edition for last biography

KUETTNER, KLAUS E, BIOCHEMISTRY. *Current Pos:* assoc biochemist, Dept Biochem, Rush Col Health, 66-79, asst prof, 71-72, assoc prof, Dept Orthop Surg & Biochem, Rush Col Health Sci & Rush Med Col, 72-77, PROF, DEPT BIOCHEM & ORTHOP SURG, RUSH MED COL, RUSH PRESBY-ST LUKE'S CTR, 77-, SR BIOCHEMIST, DEPT ORTHOP SURG, 79-, CHMN, DEPT BIOCHEM, 80-, CO-DIR, RUSH ARTHRITIS & ORTHOP INST, 91-, ASSOC DEAN BASIC SCI & RES, 94- *Personal Data:* b Bunzlau, Ger, June 25, 33; m 90, Erzsebet Stock. *Educ:* Univ Freiburg, MS, 58; Univ Berne, PhD(pharmaceut chem), 61. *Honors & Awards:* Kappa Delta Award, Am Acad Orthop Surgeons & Orthop Res Soc, 78; Carol Nachman, Mainz, Fed Repub Ger, 87; Pauwels Mem Medal, Ger Soc Orthop & Traumatology, 88. *Prof Exp:* Res assoc biochem, Ciba Pharmaceut Co, Switz, 61-62; fel, Div Biol & Med Res, Argonne Nat Lab, 62-64; from instr to asst prof biol chem, Univ Ill Col Med, 64-65. *Concurrent Pos:* Res assoc, Dept Osthop Surg, Presby St Luke's Hosp, 64-71; prof, Cook Co Grad Sch Med, 77-82; organizer & chmn, Int Workshop Conf Articular Cartilage Biochem, Wiesbaden, Fed Repub fo Ger, 87 & 91; co-chmn, Bat Sheva Seminar, Nof Ginosor, Israel, 89; consult ed, Europ J Exp Musculoskeletal Res, 90-; head, Collab Ctr Field Osteoarthritis/Rheumatol, WHO, 91- *Mem:* Soc Complex Carbohydrates; Orthop Res Soc; Int Asn Dent Res; Am Soc Biol Chemists; Am Soc Cell Biol; Am Chem Soc; Am Soc Biol Chemist; Am Rheumatism Asn; Am Soc Bone & Mineral Res; Am Asn Advan Sci; Soc Biol Chem; NY Acad Sci; Sigma Xi. *Res:* Biochemistry of connective tissue; biochemical changes during cartilage calcification; bone formation and development of diseases especially osteoarthritis; cartilage calcification. *Mailing Add:* Dept Biochem Rush Presby St Luke Med Ctr 1653 W Congress Pkwy Chicago IL 60612. *Fax:* 312-942-3053

KUFF, EDWARD LOUIS, MOLECULAR BIOLOGY, RETROVIRUSES. *Current Pos:* EMER PROF, NAT CANCER INST, 96- *Personal Data:* b Baltimore, Md, June 1, 24; m 47, Suzanne Seff; c Karen. *Educ:* Johns Hopkins Univ, AB, 43, MD, 47; Washington Univ, PhD(cytol), 52. *Prof Exp:* Intern med, Barnes Hosp, Washington Univ, 47-48; instr anat, Sch Med, 48-52; med officer, Nat Cancer Inst, 52-96, head, Bio Synthesis Sect, 68-96, actg chief,

KUFFEL, EDMUND, HIGH VOLTAGE ENGINEERING. *Current Pos:* prof elec engr, Univ Man, Winnipeg, 68-70, head, 78-79, dean eng, 79-89, PROF ELEC ENG & DEAN EMER, UNIV MAN, WINNIPEG, 89- *Personal Data:* b Poland, Oct 28, 24; m 52, Alicja; c Anna, John, Richard & Peter. *Educ:* Univ Col, Dublin, BSc, 53, MSc, 54, PhD, 59; Univ Manchester, Eng, DSc, 67. *Prof Exp:* Res engr, Met Vickers Elec Co, 54-60; mem fac & elec engr, Univ Manchester Inst Sci & Technol, 60-68; head elec eng, Univ Windsor, Ont, 70-78. *Concurrent Pos:* Consult prof, Xi'an Jiaotong Univ, China, 86-; bd dirs, Manchester Hydro Elec Bd, Indust Appln Microelectronic Ctr. *Mem:* Fel Inst Elec & Electronics Engrs; Can Acad Eng. *Res:* Author or co-author of over 150 published technical papers on high voltage engineering. *Mailing Add:* 2661 Knowles Ave Winnipeg MB R2G 2K7 Can

KUFFLER, DAMIEN PAUL, NERVE REGENERATION, SYNAPTIC PHYSIOLOGY. *Current Pos:* ASSOC PROF, INST NEUROBIOL, UNIV PR, 90- *Personal Data:* b Chicago, Ill, Jan 13, 47. *Educ:* Univ Mass, Amherst, BS, 69; Univ Calif, Los Angeles, PhD(neurobiol), 74. *Prof Exp:* Asst prof, Univ Basel, Switz, 83-90. *Res:* Examination of factors promoting and directing axon regeneration. *Mailing Add:* Inst Neurobiol Univ PR Blvd Del Valle 201 San Juan PR 00901. *Fax:* 787-725-3804; *E-Mail:* d_kuffler@rcmad.upr.clu.edu

KUFTINEC, MLADEN M, ORTHODONTICS, NUTRITION. *Current Pos:* PROF & CHMN, ORTHOD, NY UNIV, 90- *Personal Data:* b Zagreb, Yugoslavia, Apr 18, 43; US citizen; div; c 1. *Educ:* Univ Sarajevo, Yugoslavia, DStom, 65; Harvard Sch Dent Med, cert orthod, 68, DMD, 72. *Hon Degrees:* ScD, Mass Inst Technol, 71. *Prof Exp:* Instr nutrit & health, Cambridge Ctr Adult Educ, 71; res assoc & instr, Mass Inst Technol, 71-72; staff assoc orthod, Forsyth Dent Ctr, Boston, 72; assoc prof, Va Commonwealth Univ, 72-76; prof & chmn orthod, Univ Louisville, Sch Dent, 76-87, chmn growth & spec care, 87-90. *Concurrent Pos:* Consult, Cranio Facial Anamalies Team, Louisville, 76- & Nat Bd Dent Examr, 77-80; reviewer, J Dent Educ, 76-81, J Dent Res, 77-80 & J Am Orthod, 79- *Mem:* Am Asn Orthod; Am Dent Asn; Int Asn Dent Res; Nutrit Today Soc. *Mailing Add:* One Washington Sq Village Apt O-10 New York NY 10012

KUGEL, HENRY W, NUCLEAR FUSION RESEARCH. *Current Pos:* PRIN RES PHYSICIST, PRINCETON PLASMA PHYSICS LAB, 78- *Personal Data:* b 1940; US citizen. *Educ:* Canisius Col, BS, 62; Univ Notre Dame, PhD(physics), 67. *Prof Exp:* Res assoc nuclear physics, Univ Notre Dame, 67; res assoc, Univ Wis, 68-70; res fel nuclear & atomic physics, Rutgers Univ & Bell Lab, 70-72; asst prof atomic physics, Rutgers Univ, 72-78. *Mem:* Am Phys Soc; AAAS; Sigma Xi. *Res:* Neutral beam operations; tokamak operation; neutral beam diagnostics; radiological studies; plasma surface interactions. *Mailing Add:* Princeton Plasma Physics Lab PO Box 451 Princeton NJ 08543. *E-Mail:* hkugel@pppl.gov

KUGEL, ROBERT BENJAMIN, DEVEOPMENTAL PEDIATRICS, ACADEMIC ADMINISTRATION. *Current Pos:* RETIRED. *Personal Data:* b Chicago, Ill, May 2, 23; m 50, Dorothy Bowdle; c Rebecca, Gretchen & Jennie. *Educ:* Univ Mich, AB, 45, MD, 46. *Hon Degrees:* Brown Univ, MS, 64. *Honors & Awards:* Mildred Thomson Award, 73. *Prof Exp:* Intern, Univ Hosp, Univ Mich, 47, resident pediat, 48-50; Commonwealth Fund fel, Child Study Ctr, Yale Univ, 50-52; instr, Univ, 52-53; res assoc, Sch Hyg & Pub Health & asst prof pediat, Johns Hopkins Univ, 55-56; assoc prof, Col Med, Univ Iowa & dir, Child Develop Clin, Univ Hosp, 56-63; from prof med sci to prof child health, Brown Univ, 63-66; found prof pediat, 66-69, chmn dept pediat, 66-69; prof pediat & dean Col Med, Univ Nebr, Omaha, 69-74; prof pediat & vpres health sci, Univ NMex Health Sci Ctr, 74-76; exec vchancellor, Univ Kans Med Ctr, 76-77; vpres, Community Health Plan, Georgetown Univ, Washington, DC, 77-80; med dir, Cardinal Cooke Hearth Care Ctr, New York, 81-89. *Concurrent Pos:* Dir, Sch Health, Baltimore Health Dept, Md, 55-56; mem, President's Comn on Ment Retardation, 66-70; consult, State Hosp & Sch, Woodward, Iowa; Ment Retardation Br, Div Hosp & Med Facilities, USPHS, Health Res Facilities Br, NIH & US Children's Bur; chief admin officer, Bernalillo Co Med Ctr, Albuquerque, NMex, 74-76. *Mem:* Soc Res Child Develop; fel Am Asn Ment Retardation; fel Am Acad Pediat; Am Pediat Soc; Am Col Physicians; AMA. *Res:* Child development; medical ecology; mental retardation. *Mailing Add:* 6016 Claiborne Dr McLean VA 22101-2401

KUGELMAN, IRWIN JAY, ENVIRONMENTAL ENGINEERING. *Current Pos:* dir, Ctr Marine & Environ Syst, 81-88, CHMN, CIVIL ENG DEPT, LEHIGH UNIV, 85- *Personal Data:* b Brooklyn, NY, Feb 15, 37; m 58; c 4. *Educ:* Cooper Union, BCE, 58; Mass Inst Technol, SM, 60, ScD(civil eng),63. *Honors & Awards:* Bronze Medal, US Environ Protection Agency, 81. *Prof Exp:* Asst prof civil eng, NY Univ, 62-65; res scientist process res, Am-Standard Corp, 65-70; res sanit engr, Phys & Chem Res Sect, Advan Waste Treatment Prog, 70-74, chief pilot & field eval, Munic Environ Res Lab, US Environ Protection Agency, 74-81. *Concurrent Pos:* Sci Adv Comt, Univ Ill, 80-82 & 86-90 & Notre Dame, 80-82; Peer Review Panel, US Environ Protection Agency, 80-; Water Pollution Mgt Comt, Am Soc Civil Engrs, 85; NJ Govnrs Sci Adv Comt, 85-; consult, Nat Acad Sci, Potomic Estuary Study, 87-88; vice chair, Water Pollution Control Fedn Res Comt, 88-; dept chair coun, Am Soc Civil Engrs, 90- *Mem:* Sigma Xi; Am Soc Civil Engrs; Am Waterworks Asn; Water Pollution Control Fedn; Air Pollution Control Asn; Int Asn Water Pollution Res; Am Chem Soc. *Res:* Treatment of water and wastes; hazardous waste management. *Mailing Add:* 524 Kevin Dr Bethlehem PA 18017

KUGLER, GEORGE CHARLES, analytical chemistry, for more information see previous edition

KUGLER, LAWRENCE DEAN, GENERAL MATHEMATICS. *Current Pos:* PROF MATH, UNIV MICH, FLINT, 66- *Personal Data:* b Orange, Calif, Feb 18, 41; m 62; c 2. *Educ:* Calif Inst Technol, BS, 62; Univ Calif, Los Angeles, MA, 65, PhD(math), 66. *Concurrent Pos:* NSF grants, 67-71. *Mem:* Am Math Soc; Math Asn Am. *Res:* Application of nonstandard analysis to the theory of almost periodic functions; division algebra. *Mailing Add:* Dept Math Univ Mich Flint MI 48502-2186

KUH, ERNEST SHIU-JEN, ELECTRICAL ENGINEERING. *Current Pos:* assoc prof, Univ Calif, Berkeley, 56-62, Miller res prof, 65-66, chmn, Dept Elec Eng & Comput Sci, 68-72, dean, Col Eng, PROF ELEC ENG, UNIV CALIF, BERKELEY, 62-, WILLIAM S FLOYD PROF ENG, 90- *Personal Data:* b Peking, China, Oct 2, 28; nat US; m 57, Bettine Chow; c Anthony & Theodore. *Educ:* Univ Mich, BS, 49; Mass Inst Technol, SM, 50; Stanford Univ, PhD, 52. *Honors & Awards:* Guillemin-Cauer Award, Inst Elec & Electronics Engrs, 73; Alexander von Humboldt Award, 77; Educ Medal, Inst Elec & Electronics Engrs, 81, Centennial Medal, 83; Lamme Award, Am Soc Eng Educ, 81; Circuits & Systs Soc Award, 88; C & C Prize, Found C & C Promotion, Japan, 96. *Prof Exp:* Mem tech staff, Bell Tel Labs, NJ, 52-56. *Concurrent Pos:* Consult, Res Lab, IBM Corp, 57-62; NSF sr fel, 62-63; mem adv panel elec sci, NSF, 76-77, vis comt, Gen Motors Inst, Sci Adv Bd, Mills Col & Peer Rev Panel, Nat Bur Stand; mem adv panel eng NSF, 79-; hon prof, Shanghai Jiao Tong Univ, 79, Tsinghua Univ, 85 & Tianiin Univ, 85; Brit Sci & Eng fel, 81; mem vis comt, Elec Eng & Comput Sci Dept, Mass Inst Technol; adv coun, Elec Eng Dept, Princeton Univ; bd counr, Sch Eng, USC. *Mem:* Nat Acad Eng; fel Inst Elec & Electronics Engrs; Acad Sinica; fel AAAS. *Res:* Network system theory and computer-aided design in microelectronics; electric circuit theory; computer-aided design of integrated circuits. *Mailing Add:* Dept Elec Eng & Comput Sci Univ Calif Berkeley CA 94720

KUHAJEK, EUGENE JAMES, CRYSTALLIZATION, ION EXCHANGE. *Current Pos:* Res chemist, Morton Thiokol, 62-78, MGR RES & DEVELOP, MORTON SALT DIV, MORTON INT, 78- *Personal Data:* b Chicago, Ill, Mar 4, 34; m 70, Margaret Callaghan; c Dan & Jeanne. *Educ:* Loyola Univ, Chicago, BS, 55; Univ Minn, PhD(inorg chem), 62. *Mem:* Am Chem Soc; Am Soc Animal Sci; Am Water Works Asn; Int Desalination Asn. *Res:* Product development, product and process improvements relate to sodium chloride and potassium chloride. *Mailing Add:* 973 Amberwood Dr Crystal Lake IL 60014. *Fax:* 815-337-5390

KUHAR, MICHAEL JOSEPH, NEUROPHARMACOLOGY, NEUROSCIENCE. *Current Pos:* from asst prof to assoc prof 72-81, PROF NEUROSCI, PHARMACOL & PSYCHIAT, SCH MED, JOHNS HOPKINS UNIV, 81-; CHIEF NEUROSCI BR, NAT INST DRUG ABUSE ADDN RES CTR, 85- *Personal Data:* b Scranton, Pa, Mar 10, 44; m 69; c 2. *Educ:* Univ Scranton, BS, 65; Johns Hopkins Univ, PhD(biophys, pharmacol), 70. *Honors & Awards:* Daniel H Efron Award, 81; Mathilde Solowey Award, 85; Otto Krayer Award, 92. *Prof Exp:* Fel psychiat, Sch Med, Yale Univ, 70-72. *Mem:* AAAS; Soc Neurosci; Int Brain Res Orgn; Am Soc Pharmacol & Exp Therapeut; Am Col Neuropsychopharmacol. *Res:* Interaction of drugs with central nervous system neurotransmitters. *Mailing Add:* Yerkes Regional Primate Ctr Emory Univ 954 Gatewood Rd NE Atlanta GA 30329

KUHI, LEONARD VELLO, ASTROPHYSICS. *Current Pos:* sr vpres acad affairs & provost, 88-91, PROF ASTRON, UNIV MINN, 91- *Personal Data:* b Hamilton, Ont, Oct 22, 36; nat US; m 89, Mary E Ostern; c Alison & Christopher. *Educ:* Univ Toronto, BASc, 58; Univ Calif, Berkeley, PhD(astron), 63. *Prof Exp:* Carnegie fel astron, Mt Wilson & Palomar Observs, 63-65; from asst prof to assoc prof astron Univ Calif, Berkeley, 65-74, chmn dept, 75-76 dean phys sci, 76-82, prof astron, 74-89, dean, Col Lett & Sci, 82-89. *Concurrent Pos:* Vis prof, Joint Inst Lab Astrophys, Boulder, 69, Inst d'Astrophysique, Paris, 72-73 & Univ Heidelberg, Landessternwarte, 78; foreign prof, Col de France, Paris, 72-73; Alexander von Humboldt US sr scientist, 80-81. *Mem:* Fel AAAS; Astron Soc Pac (pres, 78-80); Int Astron Union; Am Astron Soc; Sigma Xi. *Res:* Pre-main sequence stellar evolution; extended stellar atmospheres and mass flow problems. *Mailing Add:* Astron Dept Univ Minn 116 Church St SE Minneapolis MN 55455-0110

KUHL, DAVID EDMUND, NUCLEAR MEDICINE. *Current Pos:* PROF INTERNAL MED & RADIOL, MED SCH, UNIV MICH, 86-, CHIEF, DIV NUCLEAR MED, 86- *Personal Data:* b St Louis, Mo, Oct 27, 29; m 54, Eleanor Kasales; c David Stephen. *Educ:* Temple Univ, AB, 51; Univ Pa, MD, 55. *Hon Degrees:* LHD, Loyola Univ, Chicago, 93. *Honors & Awards:* Nuclear Med Pioneer Citation, Soc Nuclear Med, 76; numerous hon lect awards, 77-; Ernst Jung Prize Med, Ernst Jung Found, Ger, 81; William C Menninger Mem Award, Am Col Physicians, 89; Javits Neurosci Investr Award, NIH, 89; Benedict Cassen Prize Res, Soc Nuclear Med, 96; Outstanding Researcher Award, Radiol Soc NAm, 96. *Prof Exp:* Asst instr radiol, Sch Med, Univ Pa, 58-61, from instr to prof, 61-76, chief, Nuclear Med

Div, Univ Pa Hosp, 63-76, prof eng, Moore Sch Elec Eng, 74-76, vchmn, Dept Radiol, Hosp, 75-76; chief, Div Nuclear Med, Dept Radiol Sci, Sch Med, Univ Calif, Los Angeles, 76-84, assoc dir, Lab Biomed & Environ Sci & chief, Lab Nuclear Med, 76-84, prof radiol sci, 76-86, vchmn dept, 77-86. *Concurrent Pos:* Mem, Adv Comt, med uses isotopes, US Atomic Energy Comn, Nat Res Coun, 67-79, Comt Radiol, Nat Acad Sci, 67-71 & Radiation Study Sect, NIH, 68-73; chmn, Diag Radiol Comt, Nat Cancer Inst, NIH, 73-77; fel, Coun Circulation, Am Heart Asn, 78; bd trustees, James T Case Radiol Found, 82-86; consult, Outstanding Investr Prog, Nat Cancer Inst, 84-; dir, Positron Emission Tomography Ctr, Univ Mich, 86- *Mem:* Inst Med-Nat Acad Sci; fel Am Col Radiol; Soc Nuclear Med; Am Neurol Asn; fel Am Col Nuclear Physicians; Asn Am Physicians. *Res:* Measuring altered cerebral neurochemistry using radiotracers and emission tomography in early degenerative brain disease. *Mailing Add:* Univ Mich Med Ctr Ann Arbor MI 48109-0028. *Fax:* 313-936-8182; *E-Mail:* dkuhl@umich.edu

KUHL, FRANK PETER, JR, ELECTRICAL ENGINEERING. *Current Pos:* PROJ LEADER, US ARMY ARMAMENT RES & DEVELOP COMMAND, 78- *Personal Data:* b New York, NY, Oct 28, 35; m 64, C Maxine Barrett; c Ellen, Francie (DeBeer), Peter, Margaret & Raymond. *Educ:* Columbia Univ, BSEE, 57, MSEE, 58; Yale Univ, MEng, 61, DEng, 63. *Honors & Awards:* Region I Award, Inst Elec & Electronics Engrs. *Prof Exp:* Engr, Sperry Gyroscope Co, NY, 62-63; sr engr, Missile Systs Div, Digital Systs Dept, Raytheon Co, 63-65; asst prof elec eng, Union Col, NY, 65-67 & US Naval Acad, 68-73; eng specialist, Singer-Kearfott, 74-76; sr engr, Avionics Div, ITT, 76-78. *Concurrent Pos:* Adj prof, Fla Inst Technol, 82-84. *Mem:* Sr mem Inst Elec & Electronics Engrs. *Res:* Pattern recognition using computers, specifically handprinted letters and numbers; polarized radar backscatter of solid objects in free space; video images of airplanes; lead-angle prediciton of maneuvering targets. *Mailing Add:* 64 E Shawnee Trail Wharton NJ 07885

KUHL, PATRICIA K, SPEECH & HEARING SCIENCE. *Current Pos:* from asst prof to assoc prof, 77-82, PROF, UNIV WASH, 82- *Personal Data:* b Nov 5, 46; m, Andrew N Meltzoff; c Katherine. *Educ:* St Cloud State Univ, BA, 67; Univ Minn, MA, 71, PhD(psychol, speech), 73. *Prof Exp:* Postdoctoral fel, Cent Inst Deaf, 73-76. *Concurrent Pos:* Adj prof psychol, Univ Wash, 85-, otolaryngol, 87-, Virgina Merrill Bloedel scholar, 92-94, Neurosci Prog, 94-; assoc ed, J Acoust Soc Am 88-92, Neurosci, 89-; neurosci fel, G Edelmans Neurosci Res Group, 94-; bd dirs, Am Inst Physics, 94-96, Wash Technol Ctr, 94-; bd trustees, Neuroscis Res Found Inc, 94- *Mem:* Fel Acoust Soc Am (vpres, 97-); fel Am Phychol Soc; fel AAAS. *Mailing Add:* Univ Wash Eagelson Hall 204 PO Box 354875 Seattle WA 98195

KUHLERS, DARYL LYNN, ANIMAL BREEDING. *Current Pos:* assoc prof, 78-84, PROF ANIMAL & DAIRY SCI, AUBURN UNIV, 84- *Personal Data:* b Mason City, Iowa, Nov 12, 45; m 76; c 3. *Educ:* Iowa State Univ, BS, 67; Univ Wis, MS, 70, PhD(animal sci & genetics), 73. *Prof Exp:* Asst prof animal sci, Iowa State Univ, 74-78. *Concurrent Pos:* Res assoc, Univ Wis, 73-74; consult, US Feed Grains Coun, 77, Am Soybean Asn, 82, 85 & 87 Thailand, 86. *Mem:* Am Soc Animal Sci; Coun Agr Tech. *Res:* Swine breeding; genetics; selection and swine production. *Mailing Add:* Animal Sci Auburn Univ Auburn AL 36849-3501

KUHLMAN, ELMER GEORGE, PLANT PATHOLOGY. *Current Pos:* Plant pathologist, Southeastern Forest & Range Exp Sta, US Forest Serv, 61-68, prin plant pathologist, 68-71, supvry plant pathologist, 71-73, prin plant pathologist, proj leader, Forestry Sci Lab, Southeastern Forest & Range Exp Sta, 90-94, EMER SCIENTIST, US FOREST SERV, 94- *Personal Data:* b Beaver Dam, Wis, Dec 15, 34; m 61, Linda Seburn; c Jennifer, Sara & Kathleen. *Educ:* Univ Wis, BS, 56; Ore State Univ, PhD(plant path), 61. *Concurrent Pos:* Adj prof plant path, NC State Univ, 75-83; assoc ed, Plant Dis, 78-81 & 93-96; adj prof plant path, Univ Ga, 84-; assoc ed, Phytopath, 83-85; assoc ed, Southern J Appl Forestry, 87-90. *Mem:* Mycol Soc Am; Am Phytopath Soc; Soc Am Foresters. *Res:* Ecological studies of soil organisms; epidemiology of pitch canker disease; effect of environment and mycoparasites on sporulation by Cronartium fusiforme; hyperparasites and hypovirulence; taxonomy of Gibberella fujikuroi and Mortierella; resistance to fusiform rust and variation in virulence. *Mailing Add:* Forestry Sci Lab 320 Green St Athens GA 30602. *Fax:* 706-546-2454

KUHLMAN, JOHN MICHAEL, EXPERIMENTAL FLUID MECHANICS & AERODYNAMICS. *Current Pos:* assoc prof, 85-87, PROF MECH & AEROSPACE ENG, WVA UNIV, MORGANTOWN, 87- *Personal Data:* b Akron, Ohio, June 1, 48; m 70, Patricia Barrett; c Jennifer, Benjamin, Melissa & Emily. *Educ:* Case Western Reserve Univ, BS, 70, MS, 73, PhD(eng), 75. *Prof Exp:* From asst prof to assoc prof mech eng, Dept Mech Eng & Mech, Old Dom Univ, 74-85. *Concurrent Pos:* NSF grant, 78-80 & 84-85, prin investr, Langley Res Ctr, NASA grants; prin investr, Naval Surface Weapons Ctr, 75-77, 78-83, & 85- 93, co-prin investr, 81-84; prin investr, Air Force Wright Aeronaut Lab, 89-91; prin investr, Off Sci Res, USAF, 95-97; co-prin investr, Army Res Off, 96-99. *Mem:* Am Soc Mech Engrs; Am Soc Eng Educ; assoc fel Am Inst Aeronaut & Astronaut; Sigma Xi. *Res:* Experimental and theoretical fluid mechanics and aerodynamics; laser velocimetry. *Mailing Add:* Mech & Aerospace Eng Dept WVa Univ Eng Sci Bldg Morgantown WV 26506-6106. *Fax:* 304-293-6689

KUHLMANN, GEORGE EDWARD, ORGANIC CHEMISTRY, PHYSICAL CHEMISTRY. *Current Pos:* Proj chemist, Amoco Chem Corp, 68-71, res chemist, 71-78, staff res chemist, 78-83, SR RES CHEMIST, AMOCO CHEM CORP, 83-, ASSOC RES SCIENTIST, 92- *Personal Data:* b Bronxville, NY, Apr 7, 42. *Educ:* City Col New York, BS, 64; Syracuse Univ, MS, 65, PhD(org chem), 68. *Mem:* AAAS; Am Chem Soc. *Res:* Sulfur chemistry; aromatic acids; hydrocarbon oxidation. *Mailing Add:* Amoco Chem Corp E-1 PO Box 3011 Naperville IL 60566-7011

KUHLMANN, KARL FREDERICK, BIOPHYSICAL CHEMISTRY, ANALYTICAL DATA SYSTEMS. *Current Pos:* SR DEVELOP ENGR, NELSON ANALYSTS INC, 81- *Personal Data:* b Ogden, Utah, Feb 3, 37; m 77; c 2. *Educ:* Johns Hopkins Univ, BA, 59; Univ Utah, PhD(chem), 63. *Prof Exp:* Res fel chem, Harvard Univ, 62-64 & Int Bus Mach fel, Comput Ctr, 63-64; Alumni Res Found fel, Univ Wis, 64-65; asst prof, Dartmouth Col, 65-71; assoc prof, Stanford Univ, 71-73; phys chemist, Life Sci Div, Stanford Res Inst, 73-81. *Mem:* Am Phys Soc. *Res:* Magnetic resonance; structure and relaxation in liquids; drug design; binding of drugs to macromolecules. *Mailing Add:* 1115 Hermosa Way Menlo Park CA 94025

KUHLMANN-WILSDORF, DORIS, TRIBOLOGY, SLIDING ELECTRICAL CONTACTS. *Current Pos:* prof eng physics, 63-66, UNIV PROF APPL SCI, PHYSICS & MAT SCI, UNIV VA, CHARLOTTESVILLE, 66- *Personal Data:* b Bremen, Ger, Feb 15, 22; US citizen; m 50, Heinz G; c Gabriele & Michael. *Educ:* Gottingen Univ, BS, 44, MS, 46, PhD(mat sci), 47. *Hon Degrees:* DSc, Univ Witwatersrand, Johannesburg, SAfrica, 54. *Honors & Awards:* Medal for Excellence in Res, Am Soc Eng Educ, 65 & 66; Heyn Medal, Ger Soc Mat Sci, 88; Achievement Award, Soc Women Engrs, 89; Ragnar Helm Sci Achievement Award, Inst Elec & Electronics Engrs, 91. *Prof Exp:* Fel mat sci, Univ Gottingen, Ger, 47-48; fel physics, Bristol Univ, Eng, 49-50; lectr, Univ Witwatersrand, SAfrica, 50-56; from assoc prof to prof metall, Univ Pa, Philadelphia, 57-63. *Concurrent Pos:* Vis prof physics, Pretoria Univ, SAfrica, 82-83. *Mem:* Nat Acad Eng; fel Am Soc Metals; fel Am Phys Soc; Am Inst Mech Engrs; Am Asn Univ Professors; Soc Women Engrs. *Res:* Publications in the areas of crystal defect theory; theory of workhardening and plastic deformation of metals, triboloby, electrical sliding contacts. *Mailing Add:* 304 Dept Physics Univ Va Charlottesville VA 22901. *Fax:* 804-924-4576

KUHLTHAU, A(LDEN) R(OBERT), TRANSPORTATION, SYSTEMS ENGINEERING. *Current Pos:* RETIRED. *Personal Data:* b New Brunswick, NJ, Apr 29, 21; m 43, Gay Harris; c Peyton, Richard & Linda. *Educ:* Wake Forest Col, BS, 42; Univ Va, MS, 44, PhD(physics), 48. *Prof Exp:* Asst physics, Wake Forest Col, 41-42 & Off Sci Res & Develop & Naval Bur Ord Contracts, 42-48; asst prof, Univ NH, 48-51; asst dir, Ord Res Lab, Univ Va, 51-54, dir, Res Lab Eng Sci, 54-67, assoc dean, Sch Eng & Appl Sci, 59-67, prof aerospace eng, 59-77, assoc provost for res, 67-71, pres, Univ Space Res Asn, 69-75, prof transp, Dept Civil Eng, 77-86. *Res:* Rarefied gas dynamics; human factors in transportation; air transportation systems. *Mailing Add:* 1817 Meadowbrook Heights Rd Charlottesville VA 22901

KUHN, CEDRIC W, PLANT PATHOLOGY. *Current Pos:* from asst plant pathologist to assoc plant pathologist, Univ Ga, 60-65, head, Dept Plant Path, 66-68, from assoc prof to prof, 68-90, EMER PROF PLANT PATH, UNIV, GA, 90- *Personal Data:* b Milroy, Ind, Dec 23, 30; m 56, Barbara J Buhler; c Mark A & Kathy J. *Educ:* Purdue Univ, BS, 56, MS, 58, PhD(plant path), 60. *Honors & Awards:* Outstanding Plant Pathologist, Am Phytopath Soc. *Prof Exp:* Grad asst, Purdue Univ, 56-60. *Mem:* Fel Am Phytopath Soc; Am Soc Virol. *Res:* Plant virus research. *Mailing Add:* 1231 Creekshore Dr Athens GA 30606

KUHN, CHARLES, III, PULMONARY PATHOLOGY. *Current Pos:* PROF PATH, SCH MED, BROWN UNIV, 87- *Personal Data:* b Cambridge, Mass, May 18, 33; m 59, Nobuko Obayashi; c 3. *Educ:* Harvard Univ, AB, 55; Wash Univ, MD, 59. *Prof Exp:* Intern path, Barnes Hosp, St Louis, Mo, 59-60, from asst resident to resident, 60-62; Am Cancer Soc fel, Wash Univ, 62-63, from instr to prof path, Sch Med, 65-87. *Concurrent Pos:* Vis prof biochem, Univ Manchester, UK, 80-81. *Mem:* Am Soc Cell Biologists; Am Thoracic Soc; Int Acad Path; Am Soc Investigative Path; Histochem Soc. *Res:* Pulmonary ultrastructure; pulmonary connective tissue; experimental emphysema and fibrosis; natriuretic peptides in pulmonary vascular disease. *Mailing Add:* Dept Path Mem Hosp 111 Brewster St Pawtucket RI 02860. *Fax:* 401-729-2990

KUHN, DAISY ANGELIKA, BACTERIOLOGY. *Current Pos:* from instr to assoc prof microbiol, 59-71, PROF BIOL, CALIF STATE UNIV, NORTHRIDGE, 71- *Personal Data:* b Heidelberg, Germany, Aug 3, 30. *Educ:* Univ Pa, AB, 52; Univ Calif, PhD(microbiol), 60. *Prof Exp:* Asst bact, Univ Calif, 57-59. *Mem:* AAAS; Am Soc Microbiol; Brit Soc Gen Microbiol; Can Soc Microbiologists. *Res:* Systematics of bacteria; microbial ecology. *Mailing Add:* Dept Biol Calif State Univ Northridge CA 91330-8303

KUHN, DAVID TRUMAN, GENETICS. *Current Pos:* asst prof, 70-72, assoc prof, 72-79, PROF BIOL, UNIV CENT FLA, 79- *Personal Data:* b Tucson, Ariz, Apr 4, 40; m 68, Judy; c Christopher & Carrie. *Educ:* Colo State Col, BA, 63; Univ Utah, MS, 65; Ariz State Univ, PhD(zool), 68. *Prof Exp:* Asst prof biol, Creighton Univ, 68-70. *Concurrent Pos:* Sabbatical, Univ Geneva, Switz, 78; Sabbatical, Ariz State Univ, Tempe, 84. *Mem:* AAAS; Genetics Soc Am; Sigma Xi; Am Genetic Asn. *Res:* Developmental and molecular genetics of Drosophila. *Mailing Add:* Dept Biol Sci Univ Cent Fla Orlando FL 32816. *Fax:* 407-823-5769; *E-Mail:* fdkuhn@ucf1vm.cc.ucf.edu

KUHN, HANS HEINRICH, POLYMER CHEMISTRY. *Current Pos:* group leader textile chem, Milliken Res Co, 60-61, sect leader, 61-65, mgr polymer res, 65-79, sr scientist, 79-96, RES FEL, MILLIKEN RES CO, 96- *Personal Data:* b Uzwil, Switz, Jan 12, 24; m 54, Edith L Peyer; c Johann H & Barbara E. *Educ:* Swiss Fed Inst Technol, ChemEng, 49. *Hon Degrees:* DSc, Swiss Fed Inst Technol, 54. *Prof Exp:* Res chemist, Dewey & Almy Div, W R Grace & Co, 57-60. *Concurrent Pos:* Asst to Prof H Hopff, Swiss Fed Inst Technol, 53-57; hon consul Switz for SC & NC, 70-95. *Mem:* Am Chem Soc; New

Swiss Chem Soc. *Res:* Chemistry of epoxy steroids, aliphatic and aromatic epoxides; polymer chemistry, specifically oriented toward textile applications including electroactive polymers. *Mailing Add:* 176 W Park Dr Spartanburg SC 29306

KUHN, HAROLD WILLIAM, MATHEMATICS. *Current Pos:* assoc prof, 59-63, PROF MATH & ECON, PRINCETON UNIV, 63- *Personal Data:* b Santa Monica, Calif, July 29, 25; m 49, Estelle Henkin; c Clifford, Nicholas & Jonathan. *Educ:* Calif Inst Technol, BS, 47; Princeton Univ, MA, 48, PhD(math), 50. *Honors & Awards:* John von Neumann Theory Prize, Opers Res Soc Am. *Prof Exp:* Fine instr math, Princeton Univ, 49-50; Fulbright res scholar, dept sci, Univ Paris, 50-51; lectr, Princeton Univ, 51-52; from asst prof to assoc prof, Bryn Mawr Col, 52-59. *Concurrent Pos:* Exec secy, div math, Nat Acad Sci-Nat Res Coun, 57-58 & 59-61; NSF fel & vis mem, London Sch Econ, 58-59 & 71-72; sr consult, Mathematica, Inc, 61-83; mem adv comt, Army Res Off, 62-65 & div math, Nat Res Coun, 63-65 & 69-71; NSF fel, Univ Rome, 65-66; Guggenheim fel, 82-83. *Mem:* Am Math Soc; Soc Indust & Appl Math (pres, 53-54); fel Economet Soc; Math Asn Am; Math Prog Soc; fel Am Acad Arts & Scientists. *Res:* Mathematical economics; mathematical programming; combinatorial problems. *Mailing Add:* Fine Hall Washington Rd Princeton NJ 08544-0001

KUHN, HOWARD A, MANUFACTURING ENGINEERING, METALLURGICAL ENGINEERING. *Current Pos:* tech vpres, Metalworking Technol Inc, 89-92, VPRES & CHIEF TECH OFFICER, CONCURRENT TECHNOL CORP, 92-; ADJ PROF METALL ENG & MECH ENG, UNIV PITTSBURGH, 89- *Personal Data:* b Pittsburgh, Pa, Dec 6, 40; m 62, Beverly Burke; c Amy, Jeffrey, David & Stephen. *Educ:* Carnegie-Mellon Univ, BS, 62, MS, 63, PhD(mech eng), 66. *Honors & Awards:* Zay Jeffries Award, Am Soc Metals, 87. *Prof Exp:* Instr mech eng, Carnegie-Mellon Univ, 65-66; from asst prof to assoc prof metall eng, Drexel Univ, 66-74; from assoc prof to prof mat eng & mech eng, Univ Pittsburgh, 75-89. *Concurrent Pos:* Consult engr, 66-88; tech dir, Deformation Control Technol, Inc, 80-87. *Mem:* Fel Am Soc Metals; Am Soc Mech Engrs; Am Powder Metall Inst; Soc Mfg Engrs. *Res:* Powder metallurgy; metal flow analysis; process design; mechanical and metallurgical analysis of net-shape forming processes (powder consolidation, precision forging); fracture during forming, expert systems for metalworking processes. *Mailing Add:* 128 McCaffrey Lane Johnstown PA 15905. *Fax:* 814-269-2795; *E-Mail:* kuhn@ctc.com

KUHN, JANICE OSETH, TOXICOLOGY. *Current Pos:* toxicologist, 88-90, SR TOXICOLOGIST, STILLMEADOW INC, 90- *Personal Data:* b Canacao, Philippines, June 29, 40; US citizen;; m; c 3. *Educ:* Univ RI, BS, 62, PhD(biochem), 70. *Prof Exp:* Asst prof biol sci, Va Polytech Inst & State Univ, 69-72; res assoc biochem, Univ SFla, 72-73, from asst prof to assoc prof chem, 73-83; res asst prof, Dept Med, Baylor Col Med, 83-88. *Mem:* Am Chem Soc; AAAS; NY Acad Sci; Sigma Xi; Soc Toxicol. *Res:* Role of intracellular calcium in cell injury and metabolic regulation; mechanisms of chemical injury. *Mailing Add:* 2118 S Fountain Valley Dr Missouri City TX 77459-1899

KUHN, KLAUS, CELL MATRIX. *Current Pos:* sci mem, Max-Planck Inst Proteinchem, 66-72, dir, connective tissue dept, 73-95, exec dir, Max-Planck Inst Biochem, 77-80, chmn, Biol Med Sect, 87-90, MEM SCI COUN, MAX PLANCK INST BIOCHEM, 66- *Personal Data:* b Breslau, May 1, 27; Ger citizen; m 56, Barbara Bleimund; c Thomas, Sabine & Gabriele. *Educ:* Univ Munich, dipl, 50 & 52; Max Planck Inst EiweiB-u Lederforschung, PhD(biochem), 55. *Hon Degrees:* Dr, Univ Ouler, Finland, 94. *Prof Exp:* Fel Deutsche Forschungsgemeinschaft Inst Technol, Darmstadt, 56-58, asst prof, 58-60; assoc prof, Univ Heidelberg, 60-66; dir, Dept Connective Tissue Res & exec dir, Max Planck Inst Biochem, 77-80; Fogarty scholar, Fogarty Intern Ctr, NIH, Bethesda, 81-82. *Concurrent Pos:* Mem sci adv bd, Inst Arteriosclerosis Res, Munster, 81-91, Int Inst Cellular & Molecular Path, Brussels, 84-91, Inst Environ Res, Neuherberg nr Munich, 91-93; co-chmn, Gordon Res Conf Struct Macromolecules, Collagen, 91. *Mem:* Hon mem Am Soc Biol Chemists; Europ Molecular Biol Orgn. *Res:* Structure and function of extracellular matrix constituents; cell matrix interaction; molecular biology of collagen genes and other extracellular matrix constituents. *Mailing Add:* Max-Planck Inst Biochem 82152 Martinsried nr Munich Germany. *Fax:* 49-89-8578-2422

KUHN, LESLIE A, CARDIOLOGY. *Current Pos:* Assoc prof med, 66-75, assoc attend cardiologist, Hosp, 66-75, CLIN PROF MED, MT SINAI SCH MED, 75-, ATTEND CARDIOLOGIST, MT SINAI HOSP, NY, 75-, DIR, CORONARY CARE UNIT, 70- *Personal Data:* b South Falls, NY, May 10, 24; m 50; c 2. *Educ:* State Univ NY Downstate Med Ctr, MD, 48. *Concurrent Pos:* Prin investr, Nat Heart Inst res grant, 60; fel coun clin cardiol, Am Heart Asn, 65-; consult cardiologist, US Vet Admin Hosp, Bronx, 69-; sr asst ed, J Am Col Cardiol; Consult, Coronary Care Unit, Mt Sinai Hosp, New York, 81- *Mem:* Fel Am Col Cardiol; fel Am Col Physicians; Am Fedn Clin Res; Am Soc Artificial Internal Organs; Am Col Chest Physicians. *Res:* Hemodynamic and cardiac metabolic effects of pharmacological agents and methods of mechanical circulatory support in experimental and clinical acute myocardial infarction with shock. *Mailing Add:* Cardiol Div Mt Sinai Sch Med 1050 Fifth Ave New York NY 10028-0110

KUHN, MARTIN CLIFFORD, METALLURGY. *Current Pos:* PRES, DIR & CHIEF EXEC OFFICER, KEN CON INC, 87-; DIR, PRES & CHIEF EXEC OFFICER, WESTERN STATES ENG, 92- *Personal Data:* b Tucson, Ariz, Apr 4, 40; m 63, Priscilla Seymour; c Katherine E R (Salah), Fletcher T & Clifford S. *Educ:* Colo Sch Mines, Met Eng, 63, MS, 67, PhD(metall), 68. *Prof Exp:* Sr res engr, Anaconda Co, 68-72, supvr mineral processing, 72-74, mgr process technol, 74-75; proj mgr, Hazen Res, 75-76; mgr, Tech Develop Ctr, Mineral Sci Div, UOP Inc, 76-79; vpres & gen mgr, Minerals Separation Corp, 79-87. *Concurrent Pos:* Vpres new ventures, Mountain States Mineral Enterprises Inc; dir, Mountain States Mineral Enterprises, 84-90; dir, Netwest Develop Corp, 85- *Mem:* Am Inst Mining Metall & Petrol Engrs; Soc Mining Engrs; Mining & Metallurgical Soc Am; Am Mining Congress; Mining Found SW. *Res:* Mineral processing; froth flotation; hydrometallurgy; extractive metallurgy; heavy media and ultrasonics. *Mailing Add:* 5760 W Placita Del Risco Tucson AZ 85745. *Fax:* 520-889-2733

KUHN, MATTHEW, MICROELECTRONICS, TELECOMMUNICATIONS & COMPUTING. *Current Pos:* PRES, ECONTECH CONSULT SERVS, 94- *Personal Data:* b Sacalaz, Rumania, Mar 19, 36; Can citizen; c 2. *Educ:* Queen's Univ, Ont, BSc, 62; Univ Waterloo, MASc, 63, PhD(elec eng), 67. *Hon Degrees:* DEng, Univ Waterloo, Ont, Can, 85. *Prof Exp:* Advan Res Proj Agency fel, Div Eng, Brown Univ, 67-68; mem staff, device res & develop, Bell Tell Labs Inc, 68-70, supvr electroluminescence device develop, 70-73, res mgr, Elec Mat & Process Dept, Bell Northern, 73-76, mgr, Advan Technol Lab, 76-79, dir, Tech Dept, 79-84, asst vpres resource develop univ rel, 84-89; pres, Microelectronics Ctr NC, 89-93. *Concurrent Pos:* Pres, Electron Devices Soc, Inst Elec & Electronics Engr, 80-81; mem, Queen's Univ Adv Coun on Eng, 80-86; mem, Nat Sci & Eng Res Coun Can, (Commun & Comput), 81-84; bd vis, Duke Fac Eng. *Mem:* Fel Inst Elec & Electronics Engrs; AAAS. *Res:* Solid state device physics; electroluminescence; semiconductor-insulator interface physics; solid state display development; silicon integrated circuit research; optoelectronics, fiber optics and telecommunications systems applications; management and administration of advanced technology research laboratory & telecommunications systems research programs; special experience in collaborative university-industry- government consortium research and development administration. *Mailing Add:* Two Whisper Lane Chapel Hill NC 27514. *Fax:* 919-544-8970; *E-Mail:* kuhn@mcnc.org

KUHN, NICHOLAS J, MATHEMATICS. *Current Pos:* ASSOC PROF, DEPT MATH, UNIV VA, 86- *Personal Data:* b Feb 15, 55. *Educ:* Princeton Univ, AB, 76; Univ Chicago, MS, 77, PhD(math), 80. *Prof Exp:* Actg asst prof, Dept Math, Univ Wash, Seattle, 80-82; vis fel, Dept Math, 82-83, asst prof, Princeton Univ, 83-86. *Concurrent Pos:* Fel, Am Math Asn, 82-83; vis scholar, Northwestern Univ, Evanston, IL, 83; Sloan Found Fel, 85-87; vis fel, Cambridge Univ, Cambridge, Eng, 86-87. *Mem:* Am Math Soc; Math Asn Am. *Mailing Add:* Dept Math Univ Va Charlottesville VA 22903-3145

KUHN, PETER MOUAT, METEOROLOGY, ATMOSPHERIC PHYSICS. *Current Pos:* SR RES SCIENTIST, NSI TECHNOL SERVS, INC, AMES RES CTR, NASA, CALIF, 80-; SR CONSULT, COLLINS DIVS, ROCKWELL INT CORP, 90- *Personal Data:* b Janesville, Wis, Feb 2, 20; m 53, Beth Earson; c Lori. *Educ:* Univ Wis, BS, 51, MS, 52, PhD(atmospheric physics), 62. *Honors & Awards:* Group Spec Achievement Award, NASA. *Prof Exp:* Res meteorologist, US Weather Bur, Washington, DC, 52-54; res assoc meteorol, Univ Wis, 54-56; res meteorologist, US Weather Bur, Univ Wis, 56-67; proj leader, Radiation Group, Atmospheric Phys & Chem Lab, Nat Oceanic & Atmospheric Admin Res Labs, 67-70, chief Thermal Modification Br, 70-80. *Concurrent Pos:* Staff meteorologist, WKOW-TV, 54-56; consult, atmospheric remote sensing, Stoughton, Wis, 88- *Mem:* AAAS; fel Explorers Club; fel Optical Soc Am; Sigma Xi; Am Meteorol Soc; Am Inst Aeronaut & Astronaut. *Res:* Experimental meteorology, especially infrared radiation measurements surface through 30 kilometers, remote sensing of clear air turbulence and volcanic ash. *Mailing Add:* 1780 Skyline Dr Stoughton WI 53589. *Fax:* 608-873-3473

KUHN, RAYMOND EUGENE, IMMUNOBIOLOGY, PARASITOLOGY. *Current Pos:* Assoc prof, 68-80, PROF BIOL, WAKE FOREST UNIV, 80- *Personal Data:* b Biloxi, Miss, Sept 6, 42; m 64. *Educ:* Carson-Newman Col, BS, 65; Univ Tenn, PhD(zool), 68. *Mem:* Am Soc Parasitologists; Am Asn Immunol; Am Soc Trop Med & Hyg. *Res:* Immunology of parasitic diseases. *Mailing Add:* Dept Biol Wake Forest Univ PO Box 7325 Winston-Salem NC 27109-7325

KUHN, THOMAS S, history of physics, conceptual change; deceased, see previous edition for last biography

KUHN, WILLIAM FREDERICK, ANALYTICAL CHEMISTRY, SPECTROCHEMISTRY. *Current Pos:* RETIRED. *Personal Data:* b Kittanning, Pa, Apr 1, 30; m 53, Norma Truhlik; c Jeffrey, Timothy, Diane & Gregory. *Educ:* St Vincent Col, BS, 57; Univ Richmond, MS, 62. *Honors & Awards:* William J Poehlman Award, Soc Appl Spectros, 75; St Vincent Gold Medal in chem. *Prof Exp:* Chemist, Philip Morris Inc, 57-59, res chemist, 59-62, group leader tech info, 62-64, sr scientist mass spectros, 64-69, facil leader Instrument Sect, 69-72, proj leader smoke condensation, 72-74, mgr biochem res, 74-81, mgr anal res, 81-84, dir appl res, dir res & develop support, 87-91, asst to vpres res & develop, Philip Morris USA, 91-93. *Mem:* Soc Appl Spectros; AAAS; Am Chem Soc; Am Soc Mass Spectrometry; Sigma Xi. *Res:* Spectroscopic methods; chromatographic techniques; computer applications; technical information; environmental pollution; tobacco and smoke composition; ionization phenomena; entomology. *Mailing Add:* 2140 Galloway Terr Midlothian VA 23113-6447

KUHN, WILLIAM LLOYD, pharmacology, for more information see previous edition

KUHN, WILLIAM R, PALAEOCLIMATE, CLIMATE DYNAMICS. *Current Pos:* asst prof, Univ Mich, 67-71, assoc prof atmosphere & ocean sci, 72-77, dept chmn, 80-90, PROF ATMOSPHERIC OCEANIC SCI, UNIV MICH, ANN ARBOR, 77- *Personal Data:* b Columbus, Ohio, May 7, 38; m 57; c 3. *Educ:* Capital Univ, BS, 61; Univ Colo, PhD(astro-geophys), 66. *Prof Exp:* Fel astro-geophys, Univ Colo, 66-67. *Mem:* Am Geophys Union; Am Astron Soc; AAAS. *Res:* Radiation and photochemical studies applicable to planetary atmospheres and the prebiotic earth atmosphere; climatology; radiative transfer. *Mailing Add:* Dept Atmospheric Sci Univ Mich N Campus Ann Arbor MI 48109-2143

KUHNEN, SYBIL MARIE, BOTANY. *Current Pos:* CONSULT, 55- *Personal Data:* b Haledon, NJ, Sept 12, 17. *Educ:* Montclair State Col, BA, 41; Columbia Univ, MA, 46; NY Univ, PhD(sci educ), 60. *Prof Exp:* Pub sch teacher, NJ, 41-43; asst bot, Columbia Univ, 43-46; from instr to assoc prof bact & bot, Montclair State Col, 46-66, chmn dept, 69-76, prof biol, 66-87. *Mem:* AAAS; Bot Soc Am; Nat Sci Teachers Asn. *Res:* Plant ecology. *Mailing Add:* 5 Charles Ct Clifton NJ 07013

KUHNERT, BETTY R, OBSTETRICAL ANESTHESIA. *Current Pos:* SR DIR CLIN RES & DEVELOP, WYETH-AYERS RES, 84- *Personal Data:* b New York, NY Dec 16, 44. *Educ:* Kent State Univ, PhD(biol), 72. *Prof Exp:* Asst prof, Case Western Res Univ, 75-84, assoc prof reproductive biol, 84- *Mem:* Fedn Am Socs Exp Biol; Am Soc Pharmacol & Exp Therapeut; Perinatal Res Soc; Sigma Xi; Soc Obstet Anesthesia & Perinatology; Am Soc Clin Pharm & Therapeut. *Mailing Add:* Clin Commun Wyeth-Ayerst Res PO Box 8299 Philadelphia PA 19101

KUHNLEIN, HARRIET V, ECOLOGY, STUDY OF DIETS. *Current Pos:* PROF NUTRIT, SCH DIETETICS & HUMAN NUTRIT & DIR, CTR INDIGENOUS PEOPLES NUTRIT & ENVIRON, MACDONALD CAMPUS, MCGILL UNIV, 85- *Personal Data:* b Sadsburyville, Pa, Aug 14, 39; m; c 3. *Educ:* Pa State Univ, BS, 61; Ore State Univ, MS, 69; Univ Calif, Berkeley, PhD(nutrit), 76. *Prof Exp:* Res fel, Int Ctr Med Res & Training, Calif, Colombia & Tulane Univ, 67; res asst, Inst Molecular Biol, Univ Ore, 69-72; NIH trainee nutrit sci, Univ Calif, Berkeley, 73-76; assoc prof nutrit, Sch Family & Nutrit Sci, Univ BC, 76-85. *Concurrent Pos:* Can rep, Comt Nutrit Anthrop, Int Union Nutrit Sci, 83-; mem adv bd, Herb Res Found, 83-; mem, Nutrit Working Group, Int Strategic Issues for Health Prom, Med Serv Health & Welfare Can, 84; consult, PCB contamination inuit diet, Health & Welfare Can, 86; ed, Ecol Food & Nutrit, 89- *Mem:* Am Dietetic Asn; Can Dietetic Asn; Soc Ethnobiol; Can Soc Nutrit Sci; Am Inst Nutrit; Can Soc Circumpolar Health. *Res:* Cultural and ecological determinants of diets and human nutritional status; nutrient levels in foods of indigenous people; Nuxalk of British Columbia, Canadian and other indigenous people. *Mailing Add:* Ctr Indigenous Peoples Nutrit & Environ Macdonald Campus McGill Univ Ste Anne de Bellevue PQ H9X 3V9 Can. *Fax:* 514-398-1020; *E-Mail:* kuhnlein@agradm.lan.mcgill.ca

KUHNLEY, LYLE CARLTON, MICROBIOLOGY. *Current Pos:* RETIRED. *Personal Data:* b Buffalo, Minn, Dec 23, 25; m 53; c 4. *Educ:* Univ Minn, BA, 49; Univ Tex, MA, 55, PhD(bact), 61. *Prof Exp:* Bacteriologist, Ariz State Dept Health, 49-50 & 53-55; from assoc to emer prof biol, Tex Tech Univ, 59-88. *Mem:* AAAS; Am Soc Microbiol. *Res:* Inducible enzyme formation; rumen microbiology; ecology of coliphage; geomicrobiological prospecting; resistance mechanisms. *Mailing Add:* Box 409 Monroe OR 97456-0409

KUHNS, ELLEN SWOMLEY, PHYSICS, RESEARCH ADMINISTRATION. *Current Pos:* RETIRED. *Personal Data:* b Chester, Pa, Feb 6, 19; m 74 Charles C; c James L Stewart. *Educ:* Coe Col, BA, 41; Johns Hopkins Univ, PhD(physics), 46. *Prof Exp:* Instr astron, Teachers Col, Johns Hopkins Univ, 41-45; instr physics, Conn Col, 45-46; asst prof, NJ Col for Women, Rutgers Univ, 46-51; physicist, Naval Electronics Lab Ctr, 51-66, head, Optical Physics Div, 66-68, res mgr, 68-70, planning office, 70-74, tech prog mgt off, 74-77; dep independent res & independent exp develop dir, Naval Ocean Systs Ctr, 77-82. *Mem:* Fel Am Phys Soc. *Res:* Ultrasonics; underwater acoustics. *Mailing Add:* 875 Albion St San Diego CA 92106-2933

KUHNS, JOHN FARRELL, WATER CHEMISTRY, ICHTHYOLOGY. *Current Pos:* CO-OWNER, THE WRITTEN WORD, 79- *Personal Data:* b Albuquerque, NMex, Mar 2, 47; m 67; c 1. *Educ:* Univ Mo, Kansas City, BS, 69. *Prof Exp:* Co-owner, Fish Ltd, 67-69, Piscean Fantasy, 69; partner & pres, Mid-Continent Fish Ltd, 70; vpres & pres, Montserrat Educ & Sci Co, 70-73; res dir, Gen Drug & Chem Corp, 74-82; PRES, CORP SECY & RES DIR, AQUASCI RES GROUP INC, 82- *Concurrent Pos:* Founder, chmn bd & pres, Friends of the Aquarium, Inc, 77-; ed, J Aquaricult & Aquatic Sci, 79-, ed & compiler, Codex Fishery Chem, 84- & Drum & Croaker, 89-; consult, Tex A&M Col Sta, Aqua Med Prog, 82-83; asst syst oper, Aquaria-Fish Forum, 84-; reviewer, AAAS Books & Films; mgr, Aquatic Data Ctr, 89-; pres, EECHO Systs, 89- *Mem:* AAAS; Am Chem Soc; Am Soc Ichthyologist & Herpetologist; Am Fisheries Soc; World Aquaculture Soc; Am Cichlid Asn; Int Asn Aquatic Animal Med. *Res:* Development of products for aquaculture, aquariculture and sport fisheries designed to control water quality in closed systems. *Mailing Add:* 1100 Gentry North Kansas City MO 64116-4112

KUHNS, WILLIAM JOSEPH, CHEMISTRY. *Current Pos:* VIS INVESTR, HOSP SICK CHILDREN, TORONTO, 84- *Personal Data:* b Allentown, Pa, Sept 2, 18; m 61; c 7. *Educ:* Muhlenberg Col, BS, 40; Lehigh Univ, MS, 42; Johns Hopkins Univ, MD, 48. *Prof Exp:* Chemist, Lederle Labs Div, Am Cyanamid Corp, 42-44; intern med, Salt Lake County Gen Hosp, 49-50; fel microbiol, Col Med, NY Univ, 50-51; vis investr & asst physician, Hosp, Rockefeller Inst, 51-54; assoc prof path, Sch Med, Univ Pittsburgh, 54-59; assoc prof path, Sch Med, NY Univ, 60-77; dir transfusion serv, NC Mem Hosp, 77-81, prof, 77-81, Res Prof Path, Univ NC, 81- *Concurrent Pos:* Biochem res, Lister Inst, Univ London, 74-75; fel biochem, Res Inst, Hosp Sick Children, Toronto, 84-86; summer res, Marine Biol Lab, Woods Hole, MA, 88-90. *Mem:* Am Soc Clin Invest; Soc Exp Biol & Med; Am Asn Immunologists; Am Asn Pathologists; fel AAAS; fel Am Acad Microbiol; Am Soc Cell Biol; Soc Develop Biol; Am Soc Hematol. *Res:* Glycosyltransferases of O-linked glycans, sulfotransferases; blood groups and their precursors on cultured cells; blood groups on cells on culture; blood groups in infrahuman species; blood groups and antibodies in transplantation and cancer. *Mailing Add:* Biochem Res Hosp Sick Children 555 University Ave Toronto ON M5G 1X8 Can

KUHR, RONALD JOHN, ENTOMOLOGY, INSECT TOXICOLOGY. *Current Pos:* prof & head, Dept Entom, 80-86, assoc dean & dir res, Col Agr Life Sci, 87-91, PROF, DEPT ENTOM & TOXICOL, NC STATE UNIV, 92- *Personal Data:* b Appleton, Wis, Dec 29, 39; m 61; c 3. *Educ:* Univ Wis, BS, 63; Univ Calif, Berkeley, PhD(agr chem), 66. *Prof Exp:* NIH fel, Pest Infestation Lab, Slough, Eng, 66-68; from asst prof to assoc prof insect toxicol, NY State Agr Exp Sta, 73-77; prof entom, assoc dir res & assoc dir, Agr Exp Sta, Cornell Univ, 77-80. *Mem:* Am Chem Soc; Entom Soc Am. *Res:* Metabolism of carbamate insecticide chemicals in plants and insects; environmental degradation of pesticides. *Mailing Add:* NC State Univ Box 7613 Raleigh NC 27695-7613. *E-Mail:* ron_kuhr@ncsu.edu

KUIDA, HIROSHI, INTERNAL MEDICINE, PHYSIOLOGY. *Current Pos:* chief resident med, Univ Utah, 57-58, instr, 58-61, asst res prof, 61-64, assoc prof, 64-69, assoc prof physiol, 65-69, PROF MED & PHYSIOL, COL MED, UNIV UTAH, 69-, CHIEF, DIV CARDIOL, 80- *Personal Data:* b Ogden, Utah, Oct 23, 25; m 51; c 4. *Educ:* Univ Utah, BS, 49, MD, 51. *Prof Exp:* Intern med, Salt Lake County Gen Hosp & Univ Utah, 51-52, asst resident, 52-53; fel cardiol, Harvard Med Sch & Peter Bent Brigham Hosp, 53-54, res fel, 54-56; res fel physiol, Univ Minn, 56-57. *Concurrent Pos:* USPHS fel, 53-55, res career develop award, Am Heart Asn res fel, 55-57. *Mem:* Am Physiol Soc; Am Fedn Clin Res. *Res:* Pulmonary vascular hemodynamics; hemodynamics of endotoxin shock; pathophysiology of pulmonary hypertensive heart disease in cattle. *Mailing Add:* 2651 S 9040 W Magna UT 84044

KUIJT, JOB, PLANT ANATOMY, PLANT MORPHOLOGY. *Current Pos:* assoc prof, 68-70, PROF BIOL, UNIV LETHBRIDGE, 70- *Personal Data:* b Velsen, Holland, May 25, 30; nat Can; div; c Steven, Ian, David, Tony & Nicola. *Educ:* Univ BC, BA, 54; Univ Calif, MA, 55, PhD(anat), 58. *Prof Exp:* From instr to asst prof biol & bot, Univ BC, 59-68. *Concurrent Pos:* Adj prof, Univ Victoria, 89- *Mem:* Bot Soc Am. *Res:* Structure and taxonomy of parasitic angiosperms; systematics of mistletoes. *Mailing Add:* Dept Biol Univ Victoria Victoria BC V8W 3N5 Can. *Fax:* 250-721-7120

KUIKEN, KENNETH (ALFRED), BIOCHEMISTRY. *Current Pos:* RETIRED. *Personal Data:* b Chicago, Ill, Oct 14, 18; m 44; c 2. *Educ:* Geneva Col, BS, 39; Univ Pittsburgh, PhD(biochem), 43. *Prof Exp:* Assoc nutritionist & assoc prof biochem & nutrit, Exp Sta, Agr & Mech Col Tex, 43-50; mem staff, Cellulose & Specialties Tech Div, Procter & Gamble Co, 50-74, sr res chemist, Buckeye Cellulose Corp, 74-83. *Mem:* AAAS; Tech Asn Pulp & Paper Indust; Am Chem Soc; Soc Exp Biol & Med; fel Am Oil Chemists' Soc; Sigma Xi. *Res:* Microbiological methods of amino acid analysis; cottonseed processing; nutritional requirements of laboratory and farm animals; manufacture and application of wood and cotton cellulose; analytical methods for cellulose. *Mailing Add:* 4796 Gwynne Rd Memphis TN 38117-3210

KUIPER, LOGAN KEITH, GROUNDWATER HYDROLOGY, FLUIDS. *Current Pos:* HYDROLOGIST, US GEOL SURV, 79- *Personal Data:* b Oskaloosa, Iowa, Sept 12, 40; m 72; c 3. *Educ:* Univ Iowa, BA, 62, MS, 65, PhD(physics), 69; Calif Inst Technol, MS, 63. *Prof Exp:* Asst prof physics, SDak Sch Mines, 70; res geologist, Iowa Geol Surv, 72-78. *Mem:* Am Geophys Union; Soc Indust & Appl Math. *Res:* Groundwater hydrology and particularly the mathematical modelling; applied mathematics. *Mailing Add:* Los Alamos Nat Lab PO Box 1663 MS D446 Los Alamos NM 87545

KUIPER, THOMAS BERNARDUS HENRICUS, RADIOASTRONOMY. *Current Pos:* Sr scientist, 75-77, MEM TECH STAFF ASTRON, JET PROPULSION LAB, CALIF INST TECHNOL, 77- *Personal Data:* b Amersfoort, Neth, July 14, 45; Can citizen; m 70. *Educ:* Loyola Col, Montreal, BSc, 66; Univ Md, PhD(astron), 73. *Concurrent Pos:* Resident res assoc, US Nat Res Coun & Jet Propulsion Lab, 73-75. *Mem:* Am Astron Soc; Can Astron Soc; Int Astron Union; AAAS; Int Union Radio Sci. *Res:* Spectroscopy observations with emphasis on instrumentation and techniques; very large baseline interferometer; solar physics; radio search for extraterrestrial intelligence and evolution of civilization in space. *Mailing Add:* Jet Propulsion Lab 169-506 Calif Inst Technol 4800 Oak Grove Dr Pasadena CA 91109

KUIPER-GOODMAN, TINE, TOXICOLOGY RISK ASSESSMENT, ELECTRON MICROSCOPY. *Current Pos:* RES SCIENTIST CELL TOXICOL & TOXICOLOGIST, HEALTH PROTECTION BR, BUR CHEM SAFETY, HEALTH & WELFARE, CAN, 66- *Personal Data:* b Leeuwarden, Netherlands, Sept 11, 37; div; c Margaret. *Educ:* McMaster Univ, BSc, 61, MSc, 63; Nat Res Coun Can & Ont fels & PhD(histol, embryol), Univ Ottawa, 67. *Mem:* Can Soc Cell Biol; Micros Soc Can; Soc Toxicol Can; Am Soc Toxicol. *Res:* Effect of exogenous substances that may be present in food on cell organelles of animal tissues; risk assessment of mycotoxins and natural toxicants present in food; development of quantitative morphological methods. *Mailing Add:* Health Can Bur Chem Safety Toxicol Eval Sect 2204 D1 Tunneys Pasture ON K1A 0L2 Can. *Fax:* 613-957-1688; *E-Mail:* tinc__kuiper@inet.hwc.cal

KUIPERS, BENJAMIN JACK, INTELLIGENT SYSTEMS. *Current Pos:* assoc prof, Dept Comput Sci, 85-92, BRUTON CENTENNIAL PROF COMPUT SCI, UNIV TEX, AUSTIN, 92- *Personal Data:* b Grand Rapids, Mich, Apr 7, 49; m 75, Laura Lein; c Anna, Rebecca & David. *Educ:* Swarthmore Col, BA, 70; Mass Inst Technol, PhD(math), 77. *Prof Exp:* Systs Programmer, Psychol Dept, Harvard Univ, 70-72; res assoc, Div Study Res Educ, Mass Inst Technol, 77-78; asst prof comput sci, Dept Math, Tufts Univ, 78-84; res assoc, lab computer sci, Mass Inst Technol, 84-85. *Concurrent Pos:* Vis scientist, Lab Computer Sci, Mass Inst Technol, 80-84; asst prof med, Tufts Univ, 83-85; Univ Tex Health Sci Ctr, San Antonio, 88-90; consult, MCC, 85-87, USCG, 86-87, CISE, 86-88, Peat Marwick Found, 89-90. *Mem:* AAAS; Inst Elec & Electronics Engrs; Asn Comput Mach; Cognitive Sci Soc; fel Am Asn Artificial Intel; Comput Prof Soc Responsibility; fel Soc Values Higher Educ. *Res:* Artificial intelligence; qualitative simulation and modeling of physical systems; artificial intelligence in medicine; knowledge representation; spatial learning, exploration and problem solving; robotics and intelligent control. *Mailing Add:* Comput Sci Dept Univ Tex Austin TX 78712. *Fax:* 512-471-8885; *E-Mail:* kuipers@cs.utexas.edu

KUIPERS, JACK, MATHEMATICS. *Current Pos:* PROF MATH, CALVIN COL, 67- *Personal Data:* b Grand Rapids, Mich, Mar 27, 21; m 48; c 5. *Educ:* Calvin Col, AB, 43; Univ Mich, BSEE, 43, MSE, 59, Info & ContE, 66. *Prof Exp:* Asst to dir res, Elec Sorting Mach Co, 46-50; proj engr, Lear, Inc, 50-53; chief engr, R C Allen Bus Mach, Inc, 53-54; sr proj engr, Lear, Inc, 54-59; sr physicist, Cleveland Pneumatic Industs, 59-62; lectr aerospace eng, Inst Sci & Technol, Univ Mich, 62-65, assoc res engr, Univ, 65-67. *Concurrent Pos:* Consult, Precision Prod Dept, Nortronics Div, Northrop Corp, 67-, Precision Prod Dept & Avionics Div, Lear Jet Industs, 67-, Polhemus Navigation Sci, Inc & Advan Technol Systs, Div Austin Co, Cleveland, Ohio, 75- *Mem:* Inst Elec & Electronics Engrs; Math Asn Am; Sigma Xi. *Res:* Automatic control; analog-digital computer simulation; special purpose computer design; navigation and guidance control and instrumentation; coordinate converters for gyroscope inertial reference systems; mathematical models and optimization. *Mailing Add:* 3805 Baker Park Dr SE Grand Rapids MI 49508

KUITERT, LOUIS CORNELIUS, ENTOMOLOGY. *Current Pos:* RETIRED. *Personal Data:* b Spring Lake, Mich, Aug 20, 12; m 46; c 3. *Educ:* Kalamazoo Col, BA, 39; Univ Kans, MA, 40, PhD(entom), 47. *Prof Exp:* Asst entomologist, State Entom Comn, Kans, 40-41; high sch instr, 41-42; asst instr biol, Univ Kans, 46-47; asst prof entom, Kans State Col, 47-48; asst entomologist, Agr Exp Sta, Univ Fla, 48-52, assoc entomologist, 52-55, entomologist, 55-61, head dept, 61-66, prof entom, 66-76. *Mem:* Entom Soc Am. *Res:* Control of insect and arachnid pests of woody ornamentals, pastures, tobacco; taxonomy of western hemisphere water scorpions; biology and control of tobacco insects. *Mailing Add:* 2325 NW 38th Dr Gainesville FL 32605

KUIVANIEMI, S HELENA, GENETICS INTRACRANIAL & AORTIC ANEURYSMS, DNA LINKAGE ANALYSIS. *Current Pos:* ASSOC PROF, WAYNE STATE UNIV, 95- *Personal Data:* b Karsamaki, Finland, Oct 7, 59; m 87, Gerardus Cornelus Tromp. *Educ:* Univ Oulu, Finland, MD, 84, PhD(med biochem), 85, Docent, 93. *Prof Exp:* Teaching asst med biochem, Univ Oulu, Finland, 81-87; fel, Rutgers Med Sch, 85-86; fel, Thomas Jefferson Univ, 86, instr, 86-90, res asst prof biochem, 90-95. *Concurrent Pos:* Vis scientist, MeiKai Univ, Japan, 92, Univ Oulu, Finland, 93. *Mem:* AAAS; Am Soc Human Genetics; NY Acad Sci; Am Genetic Asn. *Res:* Genetic basis of connective tissue disorders including familial aortic aneurysms, intracranial aneurysms, the Blau syndrome and Dupuytrens contracture. *Mailing Add:* Ctr Molecular Med & Genetics Wayne State Univ Scott Hall Rm 3106 540 E Canfield Ave Detroit MI 48201. *Fax:* 215-955-5393; *E-Mail:* kuivanie@sanger.bcm.tju.edu

KUIVILA, HENRY GABRIEL, ORGANIC CHEMISTRY. *Current Pos:* chmn dept, 64-69, 82-85, prof, 64-88, EMER PROF CHEM, STATE UNIV NY, ALBANY, 88- *Personal Data:* b Fairport Harbor, Ohio, Sept 17, 17; m 43; c 3. *Educ:* Ohio State Univ, BSc, 42, MA, 44; Harvard Univ, PhD(chem), 48. *Prof Exp:* Jr chemist, Manhattan Proj, Monsanto Chem Co, Ohio, 44-46; from asst prof to prof chem, Univ NH, 48-64. *Concurrent Pos:* NSF sr fel & Guggenheim fel, 59; vis prof, Japan Soc Prom Sci, 73. *Mem:* Fel AAAS; Am Chem Soc; Royal Soc Chem. *Res:* Organic reaction mcchanisms; organometallic chemistry. *Mailing Add:* Dept Chem State Univ NY Albany NY 12222

KUJATH, MAREK RYSZARD, DYNAMICS OF MACHINES, MACHINE DESIGN. *Current Pos:* ASSOC PROF MECH ENG, TECH UNIV NS, 82- *Personal Data:* b Poznan, Poland, Apr 25, 50; Can citizen. *Educ:* Warsaw Tech Univ, MASc, 74; Polish Acad Sci, PhD(mech eng), 80. *Prof Exp:* Proj mgr, Cent Inst Indust Safety, Poland, 78-81; postdoctoral mech eng, Norweg Inst Technol, 81-82. *Concurrent Pos:* Vis prof, Can Space Agency, 90-91. *Mem:* Am Soc Mech Engrs. *Res:* Machine dynamics; machine design; time varying systems; robotics, rotors and vibration; signal processing; space structures; space mechanics. *Mailing Add:* Dept Mech Eng Dalhousie Univ PO Box 1000 Halifax NS B3J 2X4 Can

KUKAL, GERALD COURTNEY, LOG ANALYSIS, PETROLEUM GEOLOGY. *Current Pos:* SR GEOLOGIST & FORMATION EVALUATION SPECIALIST, CER CORP, 77- *Personal Data:* b St Louis, Mo, Oct 1, 43; m 63; c 4. *Educ:* Southwest Mo Univ, BS, 67; Purdue Univ, MS, 73. *Prof Exp:* Teacher geol, Riverview Gardens Sch Dist, 67-70; teaching asst & instr geol, Purdue Univ, 70-73; field engr, Dresser Atlas, 73-77. *Mem:* Soc Prof Well Log Analysts; Am Asn Petrol Geologists. *Res:* Development of log interpretation systems for low-permeability gas reservoirs. *Mailing Add:* 5010 Reno Ct Las Vegas NV 89119

KUKES, SIMON G, catalysis in petroleum, for more information see previous edition

KUKI, ATSUO, QUANTUM BIOPHYSICS, MULTI-COMPONENT ELECTRON TRANSFER SYSTEMS. *Current Pos:* ASST PROF CHEM, CORNELL UNIV, 86- *Personal Data:* b Chicago, Ill; m; c 1. *Educ:* Yale Univ, BS, 78; Stanford Univ, PhD(phys chem), 85. *Prof Exp:* NIH-NRSA postdoctoral fel, Univ Ill, 85-86. *Concurrent Pos:* NSF presidential young investr, 89; Camille & Henry Dreyfus Found teacher-scholar, 89. *Mem:* Am Phys Soc; Am Chem Soc; Biophys Soc. *Res:* Chemical physics of electron transfer reactions; electronically active peptides of de novo design; quantum theory of electronic interactions; biophysics. *Mailing Add:* Alanex Corp 3550 General Atomics Ct San Diego CA 92121-1194

KUKIN, IRA, ENVIRONMENTAL CHEMISTRY. *Current Pos:* PRES & FOUNDER, APOLLO CHEM CORP, 63- *Personal Data:* b New York, NY, Apr 4, 24; m 54; c 3. *Educ:* City Col New York, BS; Harvard Univ, MA, 50, PhD(inorg chem), 51. *Hon Degrees:* Yeshiva Univ, 86. *Prof Exp:* Instr chem, Sampson Col, 46-48; group leader, Gulf Res & Develop Co, 51-57; res dir & scientist, res Sonneborn Chem & Ref Corp, Div Witco Corp, 57-63. *Concurrent Pos:* Chmn, Apollo Technol Int. *Mem:* Am Chem Soc. *Res:* Energy conservation; pollution control; consultant with government agencies on air pollution. *Mailing Add:* 45 Edgemont Rd West Orange NJ 07052-2037

KUKKONEN, CARL ALLAN, RESEARCH & DEVELOP MANAGEMENT, SPACE MICROELECTRONICS. *Current Pos:* DIR, CTR SPACE MICROELECTRONICS TECHNOL & MGR SUPERCOMPUT, JET PROPULSION LAB, CALIF INST TECHNOL, 84- *Personal Data:* b Duluth, Minn, Jan 25, 45; m 68; c 2. *Educ:* Univ Calif, Davis, BS, 68; Cornell Univ, MS, 71, PhD(physics), 75. *Prof Exp:* Res assoc physics, Purdue Univ, 75-77; res staff, Ford Motor Co, 77-84. *Mem:* Am Phys Soc. *Res:* Theory of electrons in metals; direct injection diesel engines; design and development of small high speed direct injection diesel engines for passenger cars; technological assessment of hydrogen as an alternative automotive fuel; concurrent computing; neural networks; solid state devices; photonics; custom microcircuits; supercomputing and computer sciences; solid state and theoretical physics; electrical engineering. *Mailing Add:* JPL-180-604 Cal Tech Pasadena CA 91109. *Fax:* 818-593-5629

KUKLA, MICHAEL JOSEPH, PHARMACEUTICAL CHEMISTRY. *Current Pos:* SR SCIENTIST, MCNEIL PHARMACEUT, 78- *Personal Data:* b Frankfort, Ger, Sept 23, 47; US citizen; m 69; c 3. *Educ:* Kalamazoo Col, BA, 69; Ohio State Univ, PhD(org chem), 74. *Prof Exp:* res investr chem, G D Searle & Co, 74-78. *Mem:* Am Chem Soc. *Res:* Synthesis of heterocyclic ring systems which may alter functions in the central nervous system. *Mailing Add:* 1551 Oak Hollow Dr Maple Glen PA 19002-2834

KUKOLICH, STEPHEN GEORGE, PHYSICAL CHEMISTRY, STRUCTURAL CHEMISTRY. *Current Pos:* assoc prof, 74-79, PROF CHEM, UNIV ARIZ, 79- *Personal Data:* b Appleton, Wis, Feb 3, 40; m 74, Penelope E Graves; c Stephen A, Keith G & Kari G. *Educ:* Mass Inst Technol, BS, 62, DSc(physics), 66. *Prof Exp:* Instr physics, Mass Inst Technol, 66-68; asst prof chem, Univ Ill, 68-69 & Mass Inst Technol, 69-74. *Concurrent Pos:* NSF res grants, 70-79 & 83-86, Am Chem Soc, 77-81, 83-86, 89-91 & 92-94, Res Corp, 88-90. *Mem:* Am Phys Soc; Sigma Xi; Am Chem Soc. *Res:* Structures of weakly bound complexes, high resolution microwave spectroscopy; microwave measurements of structures of transition metal complexes; quadrupole coupling measurements; electron paramagnetic resonance spectroscopy of biological molecules; molecular relaxation studies. *Mailing Add:* Dept Chem Univ Ariz 1600 E University Blvd Tucson AZ 85721-0001. *Fax:* 520-621-8407; *E-Mail:* kukolich@cgf.chem.arizona.edu

KUKSIS, ARNIS, BIOCHEMISTRY. *Current Pos:* from asst prof to assoc prof, Banting & Best Dept Med Res, 65-74, PROF, DEPT BIOCHEM & BANTING & BEST DEPT MED RES, C H BEST INST, UNIV TORONTO, 74- *Personal Data:* b Valka, Latvia, Dec 3, 27; nat Can; m 53, Inese Jekabsons; c Anda, Davis, Lauris & Inga. *Educ:* Iowa State Col, BS, 51, MS, 53; Queen's Univ, Ont, PhD(biochem), 56. *Prof Exp:* Res fel org chem, Royal Mil Col, Ont, 56-58,; res assoc biochem, Queen's Univ, Ont, 58-59, asst prof, 60-65. *Concurrent Pos:* Career investr, Med Res Coun Can, 60- & dir, Regional Gas Chromatography/Mass Spectrometry Lab, 72-; fel coun arteriosclerosis, Am Heart Asn; vis prof, Japanese Soc Prom Sci, 81 & Ensbana, Dijon, France, 92. *Mem:* Am Oil Chem Soc; Can Biochem Soc; Am Soc Biol Chemists; Am Inst Nutrit; fel Royal Soc Can; Can Soc Biochem & Molecular Biol; Am Soc Biochem & Molecular Biol. *Res:* Composition of food fats; mechanics of lipid digestion and absorption; metabolism of triglycerides and phospholipids, sterols and bile acids; chromatographic separations and mass spectrometry of lipids. *Mailing Add:* Banting & Best Dept Med Res C H Best Inst Univ Toronto Toronto ON M5G 1L6 Can. *Fax:* 416-978-8528; *E-Mail:* arnis.kuksis@utoronto.ca

KULA, ERIC BERTIL, PHYSICAL METALLURGY. *Current Pos:* RETIRED. *Personal Data:* b New York, NY, July 4, 29; m 51; c 2. *Educ:* Mass Inst Technol, BS, 48, MS, 52, ScD(metall), 54. *Prof Exp:* Metallurgist, Downarvet's Steelworks, Sweden, 48-49; asst, Royal Inst Technol, Sweden, 49-50; asst, Mass Inst Technol, 50-54; supvry metallurgist, US Army Mat Technol Lab, Watertown, Mass, 56-93, br chief, 73-93, div dir, 88-93. *Mem:* Am Soc Metals; Am Inst Mining, Metall & Petrol Engrs. *Res:* Mechanical behavior of metals; high strength steels; failure analysis. *Mailing Add:* 23 Mason St Lexington MA 02173

KULACKI, FRANCIS ALFRED, MECHANICAL ENGINEERING, HEAT TRANSFER. *Current Pos:* dean, Inst Technol, 93-95, PROF MECH ENG, UNIV MINN, 93- *Personal Data:* b Baltimore, Md, May 21, 42; m, Jane H Davidson; c Sarah A (Huff) & Nancy B. *Educ:* Ill Inst Technol, BSME, 63, MSGE, 66; Univ Minn, PhD(mech eng), 71. *Prof Exp:* From asst prof to assoc prof mech eng, Ohio State Univ, 71-80; prof & chmn, Dept Mech & Aerospace Eng, Univ Del, Newark, 80-85; dean, Col Eng, Colo State Univ, 86-93. *Concurrent Pos:* Consult to indust, govt labs & litigation. *Mem:* Sigma Xi; fel Am Soc Mech Engrs; Am Soc Eng Educ; fel AAAS. *Res:* Heat and mass transfer; convective heat transfer; hydrodynamic stability; electrofluid mechanics; nuclear waste disposal; technology-based education; engineering education. *Mailing Add:* Dept Mech Eng Univ Minn Inst Technol Minneapolis MN 55455. *Fax:* 612-624-1398

KULAK, GEOFFREY LUTHER, CIVIL ENGINEERING. *Current Pos:* PROF CIVIL ENG, UNIV ALTA, 70- *Personal Data:* b Edmonton, Alta, Nov 26, 36; m 58; c 2. *Educ:* Univ Alta, BSc, 58; Univ Ill, Urbana, MS, 61; Lehigh Univ, PhD(civil eng), 67. *Honors & Awards:* Moiseff Award, Am Soc Civil Engrs, 85. *Prof Exp:* Design engr, Bridge Br, Prov of Alta Dept Hwy, 58-60; instr civil eng, Univ Alta, 61-62; asst prof, NS Tech Col, 62-64; res asst, Lehigh Univ, 64-67; assoc prof, NS Tech Col, 67-70. *Concurrent Pos:* Mem, Res Coun Struct Conn, 67-; invited prof, Swiss Fed Inst Technol, 84. *Mem:* Am Soc Civil Engrs; Can Standards Asn; Can Soc Civil Eng. *Res:* Strength and behavior of steel structures; strength of high-strength bolts and welds; behavior of welded and bolted connections; fatigue strength of steel structures. *Mailing Add:* Dept Civil Eng Univ Alta Edmonton AB T6G 2M7 Can

KULAKOWSKI, ELLIOTT C, SCIENCE ADMINISTRATION. *Current Pos:* ASSOC PROF BIOCHEM, SCH MED, TEMPLE UNIV, 89-, ASSOC VPROVOST HEALTH SCI RES DEVELOP, 89- *Personal Data:* b Feb 18, 51; c 3. *Educ:* Fairfield Univ, BS, 72; Long Island Univ, MS, 75; Lehigh Univ, PhD(biochem), 80. *Prof Exp:* Med technologist, Cent Gen Hosp, Plainview, NY, 73; res & teaching asst, Mich State Univ, 74; clin chemist, Upjohn Co, 74-77; res assoc & instr chem, Lehigh Univ, 77-80; staff fel, Hypertension Endocrine Br, NIH, 80-83, prog officer biochem, Cardiac Functions Br, 83-84, sci prog adminr res grants, Cardiac Dis Br, Div Heart & Vascular Dis, Nat Heart Lung & Blood Inst, 84-88, sci prog adminr Ischemic Heart Dis, Specialized Ctr Res, 85-86, sr sci adv, Nat Heart, Lung & Blood Inst, 86-89. *Mem:* Am Soc Pharmacol & Therapeut; Am Heart Asn; Nat Coun Univ Res Admin; Soc Res Admin. *Res:* Cardiovascular pharmacology and metabolism; clinical biochemistry. *Mailing Add:* Sch Med Temple Univ 406 Univ Serv Bldg Philadelphia PA 19122

KULANDER, BYRON RODNEY, ROCK FRACTURES, FORELAND FOLD BELTS. *Current Pos:* PROF GEOL, DEPT GEOL SCI, WRIGHT STATE UNIV, 79-, CHMN GEOL, 89- *Personal Data:* b Huntington, WVa, Aug 27, 37; m 68; c 1. *Educ:* Kent State Univ, BS, 62; WVa Univ, MS, 64, PhD(geol), 68. *Prof Exp:* From asst prof to assoc prof geol, Dept Geol, Alfred Univ, 66-79. *Concurrent Pos:* Coop res geologist, WVa Geol Surv, 69-; consult, Dept Energy, 76-78, Mound Labs, 81-82, Terra Tek, 83-85, BDM Corp, 85-88, Amoco Corp, 86-89, Oryx Energy Co, 89-90; vis prof, Dept Geol, WVa, Univ, 78. *Mem:* Am Asn Petrol Geologists; fel Geol Soc Am. *Res:* Rock fractures-fractured reservoirs, including application of fractography to fractured core and outcrop rocks; structural geology of foreland fold belts; application of geophysics to detached sedimentary rocks and basement structures. *Mailing Add:* Dept Geol Sci Wright State Univ 3640 Colonel Glenn Dayton OH 45435-0002

KULANDER, KENNETH CHARLES, MOLECULAR COLLISIONS, MULTIPHOTON PROCESSES. *Current Pos:* staff scientist, Laser Prog, Lawrence Livermore Nat Lab, 78-82, chemist, Chem Dept, 82-85, physicist, Physics Dept, 85-86, GROUP LEADER, THEORET ATOMIC & MOLECULAR PHYSICS GROUP, LAWRENCE LIVERMORE NAT LAB, 86- *Personal Data:* b St Paul, Minn, Nov 26, 43; m 69, Monica Romanovski. *Educ:* Cornell Col, BS(math), 65; Univ Minn, PhD(phys chem), 72. *Prof Exp:* Fel, Chem Dept, Univ Minn, 72-75; sr res assoc, Daresbury Lab, Sci Res Coun, Warrington, Eng, 75-78. *Concurrent Pos:* Vis scientist, Max Planck Inst Quantum Optics, Garching, Ger, 82-83; vis fel, Univ Colo, 93-94; chmn, Few Body Sci Topical Group, Am Phys Soc, 96-97; mem, Tech Coun, Optical Soc Am, 97- *Mem:* Fel Am Phys Soc; Optical Soc Am. *Res:* Atomic and molecular collision theory; multiphoton processes; laser interactions with atoms and molecules; development of computational methods for quantum dynamics. *Mailing Add:* Lawrence Livermore Nat Lab PO Box 808 Livermore CA 94551. *Fax:* 510-422-9180; *E-Mail:* kulander@lnl.gov

KULAWIEC, ROBERT JOSEPH, HOMOGENEOUS CATALYSIS, ORGANOMETALLIC CHEMISTRY. *Current Pos:* ASST PROF CHEM, GEORGETOWN UNIV, 92- *Personal Data:* b St Louis, Mo, Aug 1, 62; m 87, Suzanne T Michel. *Educ:* Univ Calif, Berkeley, BS, 84; Yale Univ, MS, 86, PhD(chem), 89. *Prof Exp:* NIH res fel, Dept Chem, Stanford Univ, 89-92. *Concurrent Pos:* Dreyfus new fac award, Camille & Henry Dreyfus Found, 92. *Mem:* Am Chem Soc; Sigma Xi. *Res:* Synthetic organic and organometallic chemistry; application of transition metal complexes in selective synthesis. *Mailing Add:* Dept Chem Georgetown Univ Washington DC 20057-1227. *Fax:* 202-687-6209; *E-Mail:* kulawiecr@guvax.acc.georgetown.edu

KULCINSKI, GERALD LA VERN, NUCLEAR ENGINEERING, MATERIALS. *Current Pos:* PROF NUCLEAR ENG, UNIV WIS, 72-, DIR FUSION TECHNOL INST, 74- *Personal Data:* b LaCrosse, Wis, Oct 27, 39; m 61, Janet N Berg; c 3. *Educ:* Univ Wis, BS, 61, MS, 62, PhD(nuclear eng), 65. *Honors & Awards:* Curtis McGraw Res Award, Am Soc Eng Educ, 78; Outstanding Achievement Award, Am Nuclear Soc, 80; Leadership Award, Fusion Power Assocs, 92; NASA Pul Serv Medal, Nat Acad Eng, 93. *Prof Exp:* Asst scientist nuclear rockets, Los Alamos Sci Lab, 63; sr res scientist & group leader radiation damage reactor mats, Battelle Northwest Lab, 65-72; adj prof nuclear eng, Ctr Grad Study, Richland, 68-71. *Concurrent Pos:* Assoc ed, Nuclear Engr & Design, 83-; Grainger chair nuclear engrs, 84-; vis scientist, Karlsruhe Nuclear Res Ctr, Ger, 77, Bechtel, San Francisco, 89 & 95. *Mem:* Nat Acad Eng; Fel Am Nuclear Soc; Am Inst Aeronaut & Astronaut. *Res:* Fission reactors; fusion reactor design; materials; radiation damage; environmental effects; nuclear power. *Mailing Add:* Nuclear Eng/ 443 Engr Res Univ Wis 1500 Eng Dr Madison WI 53706. *Fax:* 608-263-4499; *E-Mail:* kulcinski@engr.wisc.edu

KULCZYCKI, ANTHONY, JR, IMMUNOCHEMISTRY, ALLERGY. *Current Pos:* from instr to asst prof med, 76-82, asst prof microbiol & immunol, 80-85, ASSOC PROF MED, DEPT MED, DIV ALLERGY & IMMUNOL, SCH MED, WASHINGTON UNIV, 82-, ASSOC PROF MICROBIOL & IMMUNOL, 85- *Personal Data:* b Easton, Pa, Dec 17, 44; m 69, Judy; c Alexander & Amy-Elizabeth. *Educ:* Princeton Univ, AB, 66; Harvard Univ, MD, 70. *Honors & Awards:* J D Lane Award, USPHS, 74. *Prof Exp:* Intern med, Buffalo Gen Hosp, & E J Meyer Hosp, 70-71; med resident, State Univ NY, Buffalo, 71-72; res assoc, Nat Inst Arthritis, Metab & Digestive Dis, NIH, Bethesda, 72-74; NIH res fel, Sch Med, Washington Univ, 74-76. *Concurrent Pos:* Assoc investr, Howard Hughes Med Inst, Wash Univ, 77-84; asst physician, Dept Med, Barnes Hosp, St Louis, 77- *Mem:* Am Asn Immunologists; fel Am Acad Allergy & Immunol; Am Soc Clin Invest; Collegium Internationale Allergologicum. *Res:* Chronic hives; infantile colic; allergic reactions to aspartame (NutraSweet). *Mailing Add:* Dept Int Med Wash Univ Sch Med 660 S Euclid Ave St Louis MO 63110. *Fax:* 314-362-0640; *E-Mail:* akulczyc@imgate.waste.edu

KULCZYCKI, LUCAS LUKE, PEDIATRICS. *Current Pos:* DIR, CYSTIC FIBROSIS CTR, GEORGETOWN UNIV HOSP, 77- *Personal Data:* b Jurjampol, Poland, Aug 19, 11; US citizen; c 2. *Educ:* Univ Lwow, BSc, 34, DVM, 36; Univ Edinburgh, MB BCh, 44, MD, 46; Univ London, dipl pub health, 48; Royal Col Physicians & Surgeons Can, cert pediat, 58. *Honors & Awards:* Physician's Recognition Award, AMA, 69, 81 & 84. *Prof Exp:* Resident physician med & surg, Raigmore Hosp, Dept Health, Scotland, 46-47; asst physician, London Exec Coun, Eng, 47-50; med dir pub health, Local Health Unit, Dept Health, Winnipeg, Can, 51-53; residential training pediat, Children's Hosp Med Ctr, Boston, Mass, 53-55, asst physician, 55-62; dir, Cystic Fibrosis Ctr, Children's Hosp Nat Med Ctr, 62-77; prof clin pediat, 73-78, prof Pediat, Med Sch, Georgetown Univ, 78- *Concurrent Pos:* Res fel, Children's Hosp Med Ctr, Boston, 55-61; instr, Harvard Med Sch, 56-62; clin dir, Wrentham State Sch, 57-58; consult pediatrician, Dept Health Maine & Maine Med Ctr, Portland, 58-68; clin assoc prof pediat, Georgetown Univ, 62-67, assoc prof, 67-72; consult pediatrician & co-worker, Children's Hosp, Boston, Mass, 62-68; guest worker, NIH, 62-68; consult pediatrician, Children's Convalescent Hosp, Washington, DC, 63-75. *Mem:* Fel Am Acad Pediat; fel Am Col Chest Physicians; AMA; fel NY Acad Sci; hon mem Polish Pediat Soc; fel Royal Soc Health; Lung & Thoracic Soc; Brit Med Asn; Can Med Asn; fel Am Pub Health Asn; fel Am Lung Asn. *Res:* Cystic fibrosis in caucasians and negroes; cyctic fibrosis, tuberculosis and allergy; upper respiratory tract in cystic fibrosis; hearing and cystic fibrosis; bronchoscopy and bronchial lavage in cystic fibrosis; impact of cystic fibrosis on the patient and his parents; patient home care; mucus retention and over-inflation as a basic pulmonary complication in cystic fibrosis; use and abuse of antibiotics in management of cystic fibrosis. *Mailing Add:* Childrens Hosp Nat Med Ctr Washington DC 20009

KULEVSKY, NORMAN, PHYSICAL CHEMISTRY. *Current Pos:* From asst prof to assoc prof, 62-74, PROF CHEM, UNIV NDAK, 74- *Personal Data:* b New York, NY, July 28, 35; m 61; c 3. *Educ:* Brooklyn Col, BS, 56; Univ Mich, MS, 58, PhD, 63. *Mem:* Am Chem Soc. *Res:* Molecular and charge transfer complexes; hydrogen bonding studies. *Mailing Add:* 1720 Cottonwood St Grand Forks ND 58201

KULFINSKI, FRANK BENJAMIN, ECOLOGY, ENVIRONMENTAL STUDIES. *Current Pos:* assoc prof, 69-77, PROF BIOL SCI & COORDR ENVIRON STUDIES MS PROG, SOUTHERN ILL UNIV, EDWARDSVILLE, 77- *Personal Data:* b New Brunswick, NJ, May 30, 30; m 56; c 3. *Educ:* Rutgers Univ, BS, 52; Univ Mass, MS, 54; Iowa State Col, PhD(ecol), 57. *Prof Exp:* Instr bot, Iowa State Col, 56-57; asst prof biol sci, Western Ill Univ, 57-60; assoc prof biol, Ill Wesleyan Univ, 60-69. *Concurrent Pos:* Vis assoc prof zool, Southern Ill Univ, Carbondale, 68; instr, Civil Serv Comn Workshop Environ Impact Statements, 73-77; consult biol portions environ impact statements, eng firms, 71-81. *Res:* Cytology; phycology; pathology; ecology. *Mailing Add:* 34 Wiltshire Ct Edwardsville IL 62025

KULGEIN, NORMAN GERALD, ENGINEERING, APPLIED PHYSICS. *Current Pos:* Res scientist, Aerospace Sci Lab, 60-67; staff scientist & mgr aerophys group, 67-91, CONSULT SCIENTIST, LOCKHEED PALO ALTO RES LABS, 91- *Personal Data:* b Bridgeport, Conn, Mar 6, 34; m 60; c 2. *Educ:* Mass Inst Technol, BS, 55, MS, 56; Harvard Univ, PhD(eng, appl physics), 60. *Concurrent Pos:* Lectr, Univ Santa Clara, 63-; Stanford Univ, 69-70. *Mem:* Am Inst Aeronaut & Astronaut; Combustion Inst. *Res:* High temperature viscous flows; radiation gas dynamics; hydrodynamics; reentry vehicle hardening technology; infrared systems analysis. *Mailing Add:* 711 Gailen Ave Palo Alto CA 94303

KULHAWY, FRED HOWARD, GEOTECHNICAL ENGINEERING. *Current Pos:* assoc prof, 76-81, PROF CIVIL ENG, CORNELL UNIV, 81- *Personal Data:* b Topeka, Kans, Sept 8, 43; m 66, Gloria Ianna. *Educ:* NJ Inst Technol, BSCE, 64, MSCE, 66; Univ Calif, Berkeley, PhD(civil eng), 69. *Honors & Awards:* Edmund Friedman Young Eng Award, Am Soc Civil Eng, 74; Walter L Huber Res Prize, Am Soc Civil Eng, 82; Cross-Can lectr, Can Geotech Soc, 88; Ardaman Lectr, Univ Fla, 95; Casagrande Lectr, Boston Soc Civil Engrs, 96. *Prof Exp:* Asst inst civil eng, Newark Col Eng, 64-66; soils engr, Storch Engrs, 66; res asst & jr res specialist, Univ Calif, Berkeley, 66-69; assoc, Raamot Assoc PC, 69-71; from asst prof to assoc prof, Syracuse Univ, 69-76. *Concurrent Pos:* Numerous consults to govt agencies, indust firms, eng & archit consults & attys, 69-; vis prof, Univ Cambridge, Univ Sydney, Univ Hawaii, 85-86; Fulbright Scholar, 85; vis prof, Univ Hong Kong, Univ Queensland, 93; Maunsell fel, Univ Hong Kong, 93. *Mem:* Fel Am Soc Civil Eng; fel Geol Soc Am; Int Soc Rock Mech; Int Soc Soil Mech & Found Eng; Int Asn Eng Geol; Int Asn of Found Drilling Contractors. *Res:* Numerical methods applications in geotechnical engineering; soil and rock stress-strain-strength behavior; model and full-scale behavior of geotechnical structures; foundation engineering. *Mailing Add:* Sch Civil & Environ Eng Cornell Univ Hollister Hall Ithaca NY 14853-3501. *Fax:* 607-255-9004; *E-Mail:* fhk1@cornell.edu

KULIER, CHARLES PETER, SYNTHETIC ORGANIC CHEMISTRY, PHARMACEUTICAL CHEMISTRY. *Current Pos:* from assoc res chemist to res chemist, Warner-Lambert Co, 63-70, sr res chemist, 70-72, sr scientist, 72-75, res assoc, 76-89, info serv, 90-92, SR INFO SCIENTIST, PARKE DAVIS DIV, WARNER-LAMBERT CO, 93- *Personal Data:* b Chicago, Ill, Aug 11, 35; m 59, Beatrice Marquis; c David & Nancy. *Educ:* Ill Wesleyan Univ, BS, 57; Univ Kans, PhD(org chem), 62. *Honors & Awards:* F Spencer Mortimer, Chem Award. *Prof Exp:* Asst chem, Ill Wesleyan Univ, 56-57 & Univ Kans, 57-61; res assoc & fel org chem, Johns Hopkins Univ, 62-63. *Mem:* Am Chem Soc. *Res:* Organic synthesis of heterocyclic compounds and natural products; use of newer reaction methods for preparation of organic compounds of potential medicinal use; process research; information science and systems. *Mailing Add:* 1181 Oak Hampton Rd Holland MI 49424-2663. *Fax:* 616-392-8916; *E-Mail:* kulierc@aa.wl.com

KULIK, MARTIN MICHAEL, PLANT PATHOLOGY. *Current Pos:* RETIRED. *Personal Data:* b Brooklyn, NY, Apr 20, 32; m 62; c 3. *Educ:* Cornell Univ, BS, 54; La State Univ, MS, 56, PhD(plant path), 59. *Prof Exp:* Plant pathologist, Seed Br, USDA, 61-63, res platn pathologist, Seed Qual Lab, 63-72, Seed Res Lab, 72-85, Germplasm Qual & Enhancement Lab, 86-90, plant pathologist, soybean & alfalfa res lab, Agr Res Serv, 90-96. *Mem:* Am Soc Agron; Am Phytopath Soc; Mycol Soc Am. *Res:* Diseases of seeds and forages. *Mailing Add:* 5100 Moorland Lane Bethesda MD 20814. *Fax:* 301-504-5463; *E-Mail:* mkulik@asrr.arsusda.gov

KULIKOWSKI, CASIMIR A, ARTIFICIAL INTELLIGENCE, BIOMEDICAL COMPUTING. *Current Pos:* RETIRED. *Personal Data:* b Hertford, Eng, May 4, 44; m, Christine Wilk; c Michael E & Victoria A. *Educ:* Yale Univ, BE, 65, MS, 66; Univ Hawaii, PhD(elec eng), 70. *Prof Exp:* From asst prof to prof, Comput Sci Dept, Rutgers Univ, 70-90, chmn 84-90, dir lab, 85-96. *Mem:* Inst Med-Nat Acad Sci; fel Am Acad Med Informatics; AAAS; Am Asn Artificial Intel; fel Inst Elec & Electronics Engrs. *Res:* Knowledge-based systems; biomedical imaging; pattern recognition and machine learning; medical decision analysis; interpretation of DNA and protein structures; multimedia systems modeling and simulation. *Mailing Add:* Dept Comp Sci Rutgers Univ New Brunswick NJ 08903. *Fax:* 732-932-0537; *E-Mail:* kulikowsi@cs.rutgers.edu

KULKA, JOHANNES PETER, PATHOLOGY, PSYCHIATRY. *Current Pos:* RETIRED. *Personal Data:* b Vienna, Austria, Feb 7, 21; nat US. *Educ:* Cornell Univ, AB, 41; Johns Hopkins Univ, MD, 44; Am Bd Path, dipl. *Prof Exp:* Intern path, Strong Mem Hosp, NY, 44-45; asst res, Mass Gen Hosp, Boston, 45-47; instr anat, Harvard Med Sch, 47-49, instr path, 49-52, assoc, 52-58, clin assoc, 58-61, from asst clin prof to assoc clin prof, 61-70; resident psychiat, McLean Hosp, 70-73; child psychiat trainee, South Shore Ment Health Ctr, Quincy, Mass, 73-74; gen physician health serv & clin instr med, Tufts Univ, 75-79. *Concurrent Pos:* Pathologist, Lovett Mem, 47-52; assoc path, Peter Bent Brigham Hosp, 55-58, asst med, 58-61, assoc staff, 61-70; pathologist, Robert B Brigham Hosp, Boston, 55-58, clin & res assoc, 58-61, pathologist, 61-70; clin fel psychiat, Harvard Med Sch, 70-73 & McLean Hosp, 73-74; mem courtesy staff, Lawrence Mem Hosp, Medford, Mass, 75-79. *Res:* Pathology of rheumatic diseases, cold injury and microcirculatory disorder; psychosomatic disorders. *Mailing Add:* PO Box 316 Lincoln MA 01773-9701

KULKARNI, ANAND K, ELECTRONIC MATERIALS, ELECTRONIC DEVICES. *Current Pos:* vis asst prof electronics, 78-80, asst prof, 80-85, ASSOC PROF ELECTRONICS, MICH TECHNOL UNIV, 85- *Personal Data:* b Gokak, Karnatak, India, Oct 18, 46; m 71; c 1. *Educ:* Karnatak Univ, Dharwad, India, BS, 67, MS, 70; Iowa State Univ, Ames, MS, 75; Univ Nebr-Lincoln, PhD(eng), 79. *Honors & Awards:* Ralph R Teetor Educ Award, Soc Automotive Engrs, Inc, 86. *Prof Exp:* Asst engr, Pvt Electronics Co, 71; jr sci asst, govt orgn, 71-72; res & teaching asst physics, Iowa State Univ, 73-75; res asst elec eng, Univ Nebr-Lincoln, 76-78. *Concurrent Pos:* Prin investr, NSF, 83-86; co-investr, Int Bus Mach, 85-86, Ramtron Corp, 87-88, NSF, 89-92; proj dir, Mich State, 90-91, dir grad prog, 91-92, Elec Eng Dept, 91-93. *Mem:* Inst Elec & Electronics Engrs; Am Vacuum Soc; Int Soc Hybrid Microelectronics. *Res:* Ohmic contacts and schottky contacts to gallium arsenide; ferroelectric thin film memory devices; solder joints and metal/ceramic contacts; diamond thin films and thin film sensors. *Mailing Add:* 105 W Houghton Ave Houghton MI 49931

KULKARNI, ANANT SADASHIV, CLINICAL PHARMACOLOGY, IMMUNOLOGY. *Current Pos:* PRES, AM CTR CLIN RES, 85- *Personal Data:* b Kolhapur, India, July 31, 34; m 60; c 2. *Educ:* Podar Med Col, GFAM (MD), 58; Univ Minn, PhD(pharmacol), 66. *Prof Exp:* Intern med, Sisters Hosp, Buffalo, NY, 59-60; surg resident, St Anthony's Hosp St Louis, 60-61; res asst pharmacol, Univ Wis, 61-62; res asst pharmacol, Univ Minn, 62-65; sr scientist, Mead Johnson Res Ctr, 65-67; res pharmacologist, Dow Human Health Res Lab, 67-71, clin monitor, Med Dept, Dow Chem Co, 71-73; sect head neuropsychiat & assoc dir clin res, Abbott Lab, 73-75; assoc dir, G D Searle & Co, 75-77, dir clin res, gen med & neuropsychiat, 78-85. *Concurrent Pos:* Vis lectr, Med Ctr, Ind Univ, Indianapolis, 68-71, clin asst prof, 71-73. *Mem:* Acad Psychosom Med; Am Soc Pharmacol & Exp Therapeut; Sigma Xi; Am Psychol Asn; Am Pharmaceut Asn. *Res:* CNS pharmacology; clinical psychopharmacology; animal behavior; rheumatology; drug behavior interactions. *Mailing Add:* 608 Carter St Libertyville IL 60048

KULKARNI, ASHOK BALKRISHNA, GENE KNOCKOUT MOUSE TECHNOLOGY, MOLECULAR ENDOCRINOLOGY. *Current Pos:* SR STAFF FEL, NIH, 87- *Personal Data:* b Satara, India, Nov 5, 47; US citizen; m 75, Chhaya A Chandorkar; c Monica, Deepti & Vandance. *Educ:* MS Univ, Baroda, India, PhD(biochem), 80. *Prof Exp:* Sci officer, Haffkine Inst, Bombay, 76-82; res scientist, Columbia Univ, NY, 82-87. *Mem:* Fedn Am Socs Exp Biol; NY Acad Sci. *Res:* Molecular biology. *Mailing Add:* NIH Bldg 30 MS 132 9000 Rockville Pike Bethesda MD 20892. *Fax:* 301-496-9480

KULKARNI, BIDY, MATERNAL & CHILD HEALTH, ABNORMAL PREGNANCY. *Current Pos:* assoc prof obstet & gynec, 80-93, CONSULT RES & EDUC SERVS, CHICAGO MED SCH, 92- *Personal Data:* b Maharashtra, India, Apr 18, 30; m 57; c 2. *Educ:* Univ Poona, India, MS, 56, PhD, 62. *Honors & Awards:* Outstanding New Citizen of Year, 73. *Prof Exp:* Jr sci asst biochem & steroid chem, Nat Chem Lab, Poona, India, 52-56, sr sci asst steroid chem, 56-61; fel steroid biochem, Clark Univ, 61-64; fel org chem, Nat Res Coun Can, 64-66; sr sci officer biochem, Nat Chem Lab, Poona, 66-67; sect chief, Dept Endocrinol, Div Clin Sci, Southwest Found Res & Educ, 67-70; asst prof obstet & gynec, Pritzker Sch Med, Univ Chicago, 70-73; assoc prof obstet & gynec & dir reproductive endocrinol, Stritch Sch Med, Loyola Univ Chicago, 73-79; dir, reproductive endocrinol, Cook County Hosp, Chicago, 79-83. *Concurrent Pos:* Dir labs, Sect Gynecic Endocrinol, Michael Reese Hosp & Med Ctr, 70-73; dir perinatal ctr labs, Forster G McGaw Hosp, Maywood, 73-77; consult, Gottlieb Mem Hosp, 77-81; sci officer, Cook County Hosp, 79- *Mem:* AAAS; Endocrine Soc; Soc Study Reproduction; Asn Clin Scientist; Nat Acad Clin Biochem; Chicago Gynec Soc; Am Fertil Soc; Int Fertil Soc; Am Soc Reproductive Med. *Res:* Natural and contraceptive steroid hormone metabolism in man and nonhuman primates; methods in hormone assays involving competitive protein binding and radioimmunoassays; clinical endocrinology fetoplacental function population control research; steroid biochemistry; abnormal pregnancy; contraception; clinical chemistry. *Mailing Add:* Nine S 155 Nantucket Darien IL 60561. *Fax:* 630-963-4692

KULKARNI, PADMAKAR VENKATRAO, NUCLEAR CHEMISTRY, RADIOPHARMACEUTICALS. *Current Pos:* asst prof, 76-84, ASSOC PROF, SOUTHWESTERN MED SCH, UNIV TEX, 84- *Personal Data:* b Inamhongal, India, Nov 1, 42; m 68, Suma; c Brinda, Vishwas & Moha. *Educ:* Janata Col, BS, 63; Rensselaer Polytech Inst, MS, 72, PhD(chem), 73. *Prof Exp:* Sci officer trainee radiochem, Bhabha Atomic Res Ctr, Bombay, 63-64, sci officer, 64-68; radiopharmaceut specialist, Cambridge Nuclear Radiopharm Corp, Mass, 72-73; isotope chemist, Abbott Diag Div, Abbot, Ill, 73-76. *Concurrent Pos:* Radiopharmaceut scientist, Parkland Mem Hosp, Dallas, Tex, 76- *Mem:* Am Chem Soc; Soc Nuclear Med; AAAS; Soc Magnetic Resonance Med. *Res:* Development of radioisotope labeled compounds as radiopharmaceuticals for diagnostic purposes; development of radioimmunoassay systesm; diagnostic nuclear cardiology; radioisotope tracer techniques in health sciences; contrast agents for magnetic resonance imaging. *Mailing Add:* Radiol Imaging Ctr 5323 Harry Hines Blvd Dallas TX 75235-9058. *Fax:* 214-648-4538; *E-Mail:* pkulka@mednet.swmed.edu

KULKARNI, PRASAD SHRIKRISHNA, PHARMACOLOGY, OPHTHALMOLOGY. *Current Pos:* assoc prof, 87-93, PROF, DEPT OPHTHAL, UNIV LOUISVILLE, 93- *Personal Data:* b Karad, India, May 22, 43; US citizen. *Educ:* Downstate Med Sch, State Univ NY, New York, MS, 71, PhD, 74. *Prof Exp:* Fel, Washington Univ, St Louis, Mo, 74-76; teaching fel, dept ophthal, Columbia Univ, 76-78, res assoc, 78-80, asst prof, 80-87. *Mem:* Am Soc Pharmacol & Exp Therapeut; Int Soc Eye Res; Asn Res Vision & Ophthal; Brit Pharmacol Soc; Inflam Res Asn. *Res:* Role of prostaglandins, leukotrienes and other arachidonic acid metabolites in ocular inflammation; mechanism of steroidal and nonsteroidal anti-inflammatory agents in ocular inflammation; retinal microcirculation physiology and pathology. *Mailing Add:* Ky Lions Eye Res Inst Univ Louisville Louisville KY 40202. *E-Mail:* pskulkol@wlkyvm.louisville.ed

KULKARNI, SHRINIVAS R, RADIO ASTRONOMY. *Current Pos:* PROF, DEPT RADIO ASTRON CALIF INST TECHNOL. *Honors & Awards:* Alan T Waterman Award, NSF, 92. *Mailing Add:* Dept Radio Astron Calif Inst Technol Pasadena CA 91125

KULKARNI, SUDHIR RAJARAM, CHRONIC FORMULATIONS, THICK FILM CONDUCTORS. *Current Pos:* mem tech staff, AVX Corp, 87-90, sr mem, 90-94, mgr, Assembly & Pkg Lab, 94-96, DIR, PROD DEVELOP GROUP, AVX CORP, 96- *Personal Data:* b Bombay, India, Nov 11, 51; US citizen; m 80, Vandana; c Tyaj & Ruta. *Educ:* MS Univ, Baroda,India, BE, 74; Indian Inst Technol, Kanpur, MTech, 76; Ore Grad Ctr, PhD(mat sci), 85. *Prof Exp:* Sr res engr, Asia Brown Boveri, 76-80; res scientist, Ceramated Inc, 86-88, sr res scientist, 88-89. *Mem:* Am Ceramic Soc. *Res:* Electronic ceramics; developing formulations for various applications; developed thick film conductors for various applications. *Mailing Add:* AVX Corp PO Box 867 17th Ave S Myrtle Beach SC 29575

KULKARNI, VITTHAL SHRINIWAS, LIPID BIOPHYSICAL CHEMISTRY, TRANSMISSION ELECTRON MICROSCOPY. *Current Pos:* ASSOC RES SCIENTIST, YALE UNIV, 97- *Personal Data:* b Hangandi, India, July 7, 57; m 85, Anuvadha Kavathekar; c Girindra, Prajacta & Chaitrali. *Educ:* Shivaji Univ, India, BSc, 77, MSc, 79; Univ Pune, India, PhD(chem), 84. *Prof Exp:* Res asst prof, Univ Provence, France, 84-85; res assoc, Jeol Ltd, Tokyo, 88-90, Vanderbilt Univ, 90-92 & Univ Minn, 92-97. *Mem:* Am Chem Soc; Am Oil Chemists Soc; Micros Soc Am. *Res:* Exploring microstructural self-assemblies of lipids and sufactants; exploring their formations and applications in biotechnology; physical chemistry of biliary lipids. *Mailing Add:* Brady Mem Lab B130 Dept Path Sch Med Yale Univ New Haven CT 06520-8023. *Fax:* 203-737-1064; *E-Mail:* vitthal.kularni@yale.edu

KULKARNY, VIJAY ANAND, FLUID DYNAMICS, APPLIED PHYSICS. *Current Pos:* MEM TECH STAFF, ENG SCI LAB, TRW DEFENSE & SPACE SYSTS GROUP, 78- *Personal Data:* b Karwar, India, May 3, 47. *Educ:* Indian Inst Technol, Bombay, BTech, 69; Calif Inst Technol, MS, 70, PhD(aeronaut), 75. *Prof Exp:* From res fel to sr res fel aeronaut, Calif Inst Technol, 75-78. *Concurrent Pos:* Instr aeronaut, Calif Inst Technol, 76-77; consult, TRW Defense & Space Systs Group, 78. *Mem:* Am Phys Soc; Sigma Xi. *Res:* Gas dynamics; acoustics; shock waves and associated linear and nonlinear wave phenomena in multidimensions and inhomogeneous media; dynamics of vortex interactions and vorticity dominated flows; flow and acoustics of high energy pulsed gas lasers. *Mailing Add:* 30427 Via Rivera Rancho Palos Verdes CA 90274-4449

KULKE, BERNHARD, electron beams, diagnostics, for more information see previous edition

KULKOSKY, PAUL JOSEPH, PHYSIOLOGICAL PSYCHOLOGY. *Current Pos:* from asst prof to assoc prof, 82-89, chair, Dept Psychol, 88-91, PROF PSYCHOL, UNIV SOUTHERN COLO, 89- *Personal Data:* b Newark, NJ, Mar 3, 49; m 78, Tanya M Weightman. *Educ:* Columbia Col, BA, 71, MA, 72; Univ Wash, PhD(psychol), 75. *Prof Exp:* Staff fel, Nat Inst Alcohol Abuse & Alcoholism, 76-80; from res assoc to instr, Cornell Univ Med Col, 80-82. *Concurrent Pos:* Affil prof psychol, Am Univ, 77-80; bd dir, Pueblo Zool Soc, 85-88, bd adv, 88-91; prin investr, NIH grant, 84-; Consortium Aquariums, Univs & Zoos, 89-; from vchair to chair, Psychol Sci Sect, Southwestern & Rocky Mountain Div, AAAS, 90-92, coun, Undergrad Psychol Progs, 90-, exec comt, 91-94; regional liaison, Rocky Mountain Area, 90-91. *Mem:* Psychonomic Soc; Soc Neurosci; Int Soc Biomed Res Alcoholism; Sigma Xi; NY Acad Sci; Soc Ingestive Behav; Am Psychol Soc; AAAS (pres elect, 94-95, pres, 95-96, past pres, 96-); Int Brain Res Orgn. *Res:* Regulatory behaviors in mammals, including the learned and physiological controls of ingestive behaviors. *Mailing Add:* Dept Psychol Univ Southern Colo Pueblo CO 81001. *Fax:* 719-549-2705; *E-Mail:* kulkosky@meteor.uscolo.edu

KULL, FREDERICK CHARLES, SR, RESEARCH ADMINISTRATION. *Current Pos:* GLAXO WELLCOME CO, RES TRIANGLE PARK, NC, 95- *Personal Data:* b Newark, NJ, Apr 10, 19; m 43, Marguerite McCauley; c 5. *Educ:* Villanova Univ, BS, 41; Ind Univ, MA, 49; Univ Mich, PhD(bact), 52; Am Bd Med Microbiol, dipl. *Prof Exp:* Chemist, Sherwin-Williams Co, NJ, 41-43; asst bact, Ind Univ, 47-49; from asst to instr, Univ Mich, 49-51; sr bacteriologist, Ciba-Geigy Pharmaceut Co, 52-58, dir virol, 58-59, dir bact, 59-61, dir sci info ctr, 61-68; adminr, 68-77, dir admin, res, develop & med, Burroughs Wellcome Co, 77-85; consult, 85-95. *Concurrent Pos:* Instr, Rutgers Univ, 55-58; adj prof, Sch Pharm, Univ NC, 72-92; consult, Nat Serv Exec Corp, 85-90, Glaxo Inc, 86-90; vpres, Exec Serv Corp Carolinas, 90- *Mem:* Am Acad Microbiol; Am Soc Microbiol; Sigma Xi; Drug Info Asn. *Res:* Medical information; documentation; biological sciences; virology; enzymology. *Mailing Add:* 3804 St Marks Rd Durham NC 27707-5013

KULL, FREDRICK J, ENZYMOLOGY. *Current Pos:* from asst to assoc prof biol sci, State Univ NY, 69-91, dir biochem, 75-84, acad coordr off campus col, 85-89 & 91, EMER PROF BIOL SCI, STATE UNIV NY, BINGHAMTON, 91- *Personal Data:* b Mar 9, 35; m, Barbara E Crute; c F Jon & Carrie L. *Educ:* Kent State Univ, BS, 60; Ohio State Univ, MS, 62, Brandeis Univ, PhD(biochem), 67. *Prof Exp:* Fel, Oak Ridge Nat Lab, Oak Ridge, 67-69. *Concurrent Pos:* Vis prof chem. *Mem:* Am Chem Soc Biol Chem Div; AAAS; Sigma Xi; Fedn Am Soc Exp Biol; Am Soc Biochem & Molecular Biol. *Mailing Add:* Dartmouth Col 260 Poverty Lane Lebanon NH 03766-1432

KULL, LORENZ ANTHONY, NUCLEAR PHYSICS. *Personal Data:* b Chicago, Ill, Dec 25, 37; m 85; c 2. *Educ:* Ill Inst Technol, BSc, 63; Mich State Univ, PhD(physics), 67. *Prof Exp:* Physicist, Gulf Gen Atomic, Inc, 67-69; physicist, Sci Applns Int Corp, 69-75, vpres & mgr appl sci & technol group, 75-79, exec vpres, 79-88, pres & chief oper officer, 88-96. *Concurrent Pos:* Mem, Air Force Studies Bd, 84-90. *Mem:* Am Phys Soc; Am Nuclear Soc; Inst Elec & Electronics Engrs. *Res:* Development of nuclear materials assay instrumentation; experimental studies of direct particle transfer reactions with light nuclei; experimental studies of photoneutron cross-sections, threshold photoneutrons and photo fission; modeling and analysis of nuclear fuel cycle systems; design of military electronics, components and systems. *Mailing Add:* 2018 Demayo Rd Del Mar CA 92014

KULLBACK, JOSEPH HENRY, MATHEMATICAL STATISTICS. *Current Pos:* CHIEF STAFF SCIENTIST, GRUMMAN DATA SYSTS INC, 81- *Personal Data:* b Washington, DC, July 16, 33; m 60; c 3. *Educ:* George Washington Univ, BA, 55; Stanford Univ, MS, 57, PhD(math statist), 60. *Prof Exp:* Mathematician, Stanford Res Inst, 60-67; math statistician, US Naval Res Lab, 67-81. *Concurrent Pos:* Prof lectr, George Washington Univ, 77- *Mem:* Armed Forces Commun Electronics Asn. *Res:* Operations research; simulation techniques. *Mailing Add:* Grumman Data Systs 5201 Leesburg Pike Suite 701 Falls Church VA 22041

KULLBACK, SOLOMON, MATHEMATICAL STATISTICS, APPLIED STATISTICS. *Current Pos:* Prof, 38-75, EMER PROF STATIST, GEORGE WASHINGTON UNIV, 75- *Personal Data:* b Brooklyn, NY, Apr 3, 07; m 30, 74; c 2. *Educ:* City Col New York, BS, 27; Columbia Univ, MA, 29; George Washington Univ, PhD(math), 34. *Mem:* Inst Math Statist; Am Statist Asn; Royal Statist Soc. *Res:* Information theory; analysis of count or categorical data. *Mailing Add:* Dept Statist George Washington Univ Washington DC 20052-0001

KULLBERG, RUSSELL GORDON, BOTANY. *Current Pos:* From assoc prof to prof, 65-89, EMER PROF BIOL, SOUTHEAST MO STATE UNIV, 89- *Personal Data:* b Flint, Mich, Aug 4, 22; m 45, Mary Whitney; c Kristine & Gayle. *Educ:* Univ Mich, BS, 49, MS, 50; Mich State Univ, PhD(bot), 66. *Mem:* Phycol Soc Am; Ecol Soc Am. *Res:* Phycology; ecology of hot spring algae. *Mailing Add:* 1824 Westridge Cape Girardeau MO 63701

KULLEN, MARK K, OPTICS, PHYSICS. *Current Pos:* ENG SCIENTIST, GEN DYNAMICS, 89- *Educ:* Wayne State Univ, BS, 84, MS, 87. *Mem:* Am Phys Soc. *Mailing Add:* 36719 Bobrich Livonia MI 48152

KULLER, ROBERT G, MATHEMATICS. *Current Pos:* ASSOC PROF MATH, NORTHERN ILL UNIV, 68- *Personal Data:* b Baltimore, Md, Nov 29, 26; m 59; c 5. *Educ:* Swarthmore Col, AB, 48; Univ Mich, MS, 49, PhD(math), 55. *Prof Exp:* Instr math, Dartmouth Col, 53-55; from instr to asst prof, Wayne State Univ, 55-59; asst prof, Dartmouth Col, 59-60, 61-62 & Univ Colo, 62-65; assoc prof, Wayne State Univ, 65-68. *Concurrent Pos:* Vis lectr, Nat Taiwan Univ, 60-61. *Mem:* Am Math Soc; Math Asn Am; Soc Indust & Appl Math. *Res:* Functional analysis; computers in undergraduate mathematics curriculum. *Mailing Add:* 528 S Third St Apt 5 Dekalb IL 60115-2854

KULLGREN, THOMAS EDWARD, MECHANICAL ENGINEERING. *Current Pos:* DEAN & PROF MECH ENG, SAGINAW VALLEY STATE UNIV, 84- *Personal Data:* b Grand Rapids, Mich, Apr 10, 41; m 89, Elizabeth A Kornacki; c Kristin, Erin, Jeffrey & Ian. *Educ:* USAF Acad, BS, 64; Stanford Univ, MS, 72; Colo State Univ, PhD(mech eng), 76. *Prof Exp:* From asst prof to assoc prof eng mech, USAF Acad, 76-82, prof & actg head, 82-84. *Concurrent Pos:* Vis scientist, Air Force Mats Lab, 77, prin investr, Wind Energy Res Proj, 77-84; dir, Ctr Appl Technol Res, Saginaw Valley State Univ, 85 & Bus & Indust Develop Inst, 88-90. *Mem:* Am Soc Mech Engrs; Am Soc Engr Educ; Soc Mfg Engrs. *Res:* Numerical solution of three-dimensional problems in fracture mechanics; international wind energy resource assessments and feasibility studies; technology transfer and economic development. *Mailing Add:* PO Box 444 Midland MI 48640. *Fax:* 517-790-2717

KULLMAN, DAVID ELMER, MATHEMATICS EDUCATION, HISTORY OF MATHEMATICS. *Current Pos:* from asst prof to assoc prof, 69-81, PROF MATH, MIAMI UNIV, 81-, DEPT CHAIR, 93- *Personal Data:* b Kenosha, Wis, May 27, 40; m 65, Karen Holzhauser; c Bradley & Kristen. *Educ:* Northwestern Univ, BA, 62; Cornell Univ, MA, 63; Univ Kans, PhD(math), 69. *Prof Exp:* High sch teacher, Ill, 63-65. *Mem:* Nat Coun Teachers Math; Sigma Xi; Math Asn Am; Can Soc Hist & Philos Math; Am Math Soc. *Res:* History of mathematics; problem solving and applications in school mathematics. *Mailing Add:* Dept Math & Statist Miami Univ Oxford OH 45056. *E-Mail:* dekullman@miavx1.muohio.edu

KULLNIG, RUDOLPH K, PHYSICAL ORGANIC CHEMISTRY. *Current Pos:* ADJ PROF, RENSSELAER POLYTECH INST, TROY, NY, 83-, SR FEL, 90- *Personal Data:* b Kirchberg, Lower Austria, Oct 2, 18; US citizen; m 54, Charlotte Voisard. *Educ:* Univ Ottawa, Can, PhD(chem), 58. *Prof Exp:* Chemist, Bell-Craig Ltd, Ont, 52-55; asst res chemist, Sterling Res Group, 58-64, res chemist & group leader, 64-68, sect head, 68-90. *Mem:* Am Chem Soc; Am Crystallog Asn. *Res:* Nuclear magnetic resonance spectroscopy; indoles and other heterocyclic compounds; single cryst x-ray diffraction. *Mailing Add:* 284 Kingman Rd Nassau NY 12123-9743. *E-Mail:* kullnr@rpi.edu

KULM, LAVERNE DUANE, GEOLOGICAL OCEANOGRAPHY. *Current Pos:* From asst prof to assoc prof, 64-74, PROF OCEANOG, ORE STATE UNIV, 74- *Personal Data:* b Mobridge, SDak, Feb 17, 36; m 62. *Educ:* Monmouth Col, BA, 59; Ore State Univ, PhD(oceanog), 65. *Concurrent Pos:* Fel, Marathon Oil Co, 71. *Mem:* AAAS; Soc Econ Paleontologists & Mineralogists; fel Geol Soc Am; Am Geophys Union. *Res:* Continental margin structure, tectonics, sedimentation; deep-sea sedimentation. *Mailing Add:* Col Oceanog Ore State Univ Corvallis OR 97331-5503

KULMAN, HERBERT MARVIN, ENTOMOLOGY. *Current Pos:* RETIRED. *Personal Data:* b Sayre, Pa, June 12, 29; div; c 2. *Educ:* Pa State Univ, BS, 52; Duke Univ, MF, 55; Univ Minn, PhD, 60. *Prof Exp:* Entomologist, Southeastern Forest Exp Sta, USDA, 56-57; asst prof entom, WVa Univ, 59-62; from asst to assoc prof forest entom, Va Polytech Inst, 62-69; assoc prof entom, Univ Minn, St Paul, 69-72, prof, 72-89. *Concurrent Pos:* Latin Inst Forestry, Merida Vez, 70; NSF res group, Korea & Taiwan. *Mem:* Entom Soc Am. *Res:* Forest entomology, especially biological control and damage evaluation. *Mailing Add:* 1037 Spruce St W San Diego CA 92103

KULP, BERNARD ANDREW, PHYSICS. *Current Pos:* CHIEF SCIENTIST & DIR LABS, AIR FORCE SYSTS COMMAND, 75- *Personal Data:* b Columbus, Ohio, Aug 3, 23; m 52; c 9. *Educ:* Univ Minn, BEE, 46; Ohio State Univ, MS, 47, PhD(physics), 55. *Prof Exp:* Asst, Ohio State Univ, 46-47; res metallurgist, Carnegie-Ill Steel Corp, 47-48; res engr, Battelle Mem Inst, 48-55; physicist, Linde Co, 55-58; physicist, Aerospace Res Lab, Wright-Patterson AFB, 58-69; chief scientist, Air Force Armament Lab, Eglin AFB, 69-75. *Mem:* Fel AAAS; Am Phys Soc; Am Defense Preparedness Asn. *Res:* Solid state physics; radiation damage; electrooptics; ordnance engineering. *Mailing Add:* 13418 Queens Lane Ft Washington MD 20744

KULPA, CHARLES FRANK, JR, APPLIED MICROBIOLOGY IN ENVIRONMENTAL AREAS, GENE EXCHANGE IN MIXED CULTURES. *Current Pos:* from asst prof to assoc prof, 72-79, PROF MICROBIOL, UNIV NOTRE DAME, 91-, ASSOC DEAN, COL SCI, 93- *Personal Data:* b Jackson, Mich, Jan 1, 44; m 84, Loretta M Blanford; c David, Andrew, Marlo & Edward. *Educ:* Univ Mich, BS, 66, MS, 68, PhD(microbiol), 70. *Prof Exp:* Staff fel, NIH, 70-72. *Concurrent Pos:* Vis scientist, Kyoto Univ, 81; consult, Amoco Chem, 81-93, Construct Technol Lab, 89-, Newmont Metall Serv, 90-93, Energy Biosysts, 91-; prin investr, Argonne Nat Lab, 89-94, res assoc, 90-, Chevron, 92-, Amoco Oil, 94- *Mem:* Am Soc Microbiol; Am Acad Microbiol; AAAS; Soc Indust Microbiol. *Res:* Use of bacteria for waste remediation and biodesulfurization of petroleum distillates; investigation of genetic exchange within mixed cultures for the maintenance of biodegradative genes. *Mailing Add:* Dept Biol Sci Univ Notre Dame Notre Dame IN 46556-0369. *E-Mail:* charles.f.kulpa.1@nd.edu

KULSRUD, RUSSELL MARION, PLASMA PHYSICS. *Current Pos:* PROF ASTROPHYS SCI, PRINCETON UNIV, 67- *Personal Data:* b Lindsborg, Kans, Apr 10, 28; m 55; c 3. *Educ:* Univ Md, BA, 49; Univ Chicago, MS, 52, PhD(physics), 54. *Hon Degrees:* MS, Yale Univ, 66. *Prof Exp:* Mem staff physics, Proj Matterhorn, Princeton Univ, 54-59, sr res assoc, 59-64, head theoret sect, Plasma Physics Lab, 64-66; prof appl sci & astron, Yale Univ, 66-67. *Concurrent Pos:* Consult, Oak Ridge Nat Lab, 55, RCA Corp, 60 & Gen Atomic Div, Gen Dynamics Corp, 60. *Mem:* Fel Am Phys Soc; Int Astron Union; Am Astron Soc. *Res:* Plasma physics with application to controlled fusion reactor research; astrophysics. *Mailing Add:* Peyton Hall Princeton Univ Princeton NJ 08544

KULWICH, ROMAN, BIOCHEMISTRY. *Current Pos:* CONSULT, 78- *Personal Data:* b New York, NY, Oct 18, 25; m 48; c 3. *Educ:* Univ Fla, BS, 49, PhD(animal nutrit), 51. *Prof Exp:* Animal nutritionist & animal husbandman, Animal Husb Res Div, Agr Res Serv, USDA, 51-57; biochemist & supvry chemist, Mkt Qual Res Div, Agr Mkt Serv, Plant Indust Sta, Beltsville, 57-62; grants assoc, Div Res Grants, NIH, 62-63; scientist adminr, Nat Inst Child Health & Human Develop, 63-64; endocrinol prog dir extramural prog, Nat Inst Arthritis & Metab Diseases, 64-69; health scientist adminr, Nat Ctr Health Serv Res & Develop, 69-71; asst for rev & eval, 71-73, from asst to assoc dir extramural progs, Nat Inst Allergy & Infectious Dis, 73-78. *Res:* Nutritional and biochemical research on trace mineral and sulfur metabolism in laboratory and farm animals involving the use of radioactive tracers; body composition research involving 4-pi low level gamma ray measurements; biomedical science administration. *Mailing Add:* 9504 SE 107th Pl Belleview FL 34420

KULWICKI, ANAHID, NURSING, MEDICINE. *Current Pos:* ASSOC PROF, SCH NURSING, OAKLAND UNIV, ROCHESTER, MICH. *Concurrent Pos:* Fulbright grantee cardiovasc risk, Univ Jordon, Amman, Jordon, 96. *Res:* Cardiovascular risk assessment and risk reduction. *Mailing Add:* Sch Nursing Oakland Univ Rochester MI 48309-4401

KULWICKI, BERNARD MICHAEL, CHEMICAL ENGINEERING, MATERIALS SCIENCE. *Current Pos:* proj engr semiconductor mat res, Tex Instruments Inc, 64-69, sect leader, 69-70, br mgr active mat develop, Mat & Elec Prod Group, Mat & Controls Div, 71-79, SR MEM TECH STAFF, ADVAN DEVELOP, TEX INSTRUMENTS INC, 80- *Personal Data:* b Detroit, Mich, July 3, 35. *Educ:* Univ Detroit, BChE, 58; Univ Mich, MSE, 60, PhD(chem eng), 63. *Prof Exp:* Res fel, Inst Solid State Physics, Czech Acad Sci, 63-64. *Concurrent Pos:* Assoc ed, J Am Ceramic Soc, 90- *Mem:* AAAS; Am Ceramic Soc; Electrochem Soc; Am Chem Soc; Mat Res Soc; Soc Advan Mat & Process Eng. *Res:* Phase equilibria; thermodynamic and electrical properties of semiconducting materials; ferroelectric materials; thermistors; ceramic varistors. *Mailing Add:* 19 Poppasquash Rd North Attleboro MA 02760

KUMAGAI, LINDY FUMIO, MEDICINE. *Current Pos:* assoc prof, 69-71, PROF INTERNAL MED, SCH MED, UNIV CALIF, DAVIS, 71-, HEAD ENDOCRINE SECT, 69- *Personal Data:* b Rock Springs, Wyo, Aug 5, 27; m 52; c 3. *Educ:* Univ Utah, BA, 49, MS, 50, MD, 54. *Prof Exp:* Asst anat, Sch Med, Univ Utah, 49-54; med intern, Mass Mem Hosp, 54-55; USPHS res fel, Thorndyke Mem Lab, Boston City Hosp, Harvard Med Sch, 55-57; asst resident med, Univ Hosp, Utah, 57-58, from instr to assoc prof, Col Med, 58-69, asst dean, 68-69. *Concurrent Pos:* Clin investr, Vet Admin Hosp, Salt Lake City, Utah, 58-61; chief radioisotope serv, 61-69; assoc ed, Endocrinology, 73-77; mem, Endocrine Study Sect, Dept Health & Human Sci, NIH, 80-; mem, Calif Bd Med Quality Assurance, 80- *Mem:* Endocrine Soc. *Res:* Metabolism of adrenocortical and thyroidal hormones. *Mailing Add:* Dept Med-Endocrinol Univ Calif Davis Med Ctr 2315 Stockton Blvd Sacramento CA 95817-2201

KUMAI, MOTOI, CLOUD PHYSICS, EARTH SCIENCES. *Current Pos:* RES PHYSICIST, SCI & TECHNOL CORP, 90- *Personal Data:* b Nagano, Japan, Mar 22, 20; m 48, Yamanouchi Mutsuko; c Keiko I & Etsuko (Azar). *Educ:* Sci Univ Tokyo, BS, 41; Hokkaido Univ, PhD(physics), 57. *Prof Exp:* Res assoc physics, Hokkaido Univ, 42-55, lectr, 55-58; res assoc cloud physics, Univ Chicago, 58-61; res physicist atmospheric sci, US Army Cold Regions Res & Eng Lab, 61-90. *Mem:* Am Meteorol Soc; Sigma Xi; Japanese Soc Snow & Ice; Meteorol Soc Japan; Clay Minerals Soc. *Res:* Physics of atmosphere, research on snow crystal nuclei, and ice fog nuclei; electron diffraction of ice and aerosols, and attenuation of infrared radiation; scanning electron microscopy and acid snow and rain. *Mailing Add:* 21 Marlyn Dr Burnt Hills NY 12027-9737

KUMAMOTO, JUNJI, PHYSICAL ORGANIC CHEMISTRY. *Current Pos:* LECTR & CHEMIST, UNIV CALIF, RIVERSIDE, 66- *Personal Data:* b Sacramento, Calif, May 9, 24; m 50; c 4. *Educ:* Univ Calif, Los Angeles, BS, 50; Univ Chicago, PhD(phys org chem), 53. *Prof Exp:* NSF grant, Harvard Univ, 53-55; chemist, Shell Develop Co, 55-60 & res lab, IBM Corp, 60-66. *Mem:* Am Chem Soc; NY Acad Sci; AAAS; Sigma Xi. *Res:* Reaction mechanisms of phosphate ester hydrolysis; free radical-metal ion reactions; relationship between structure and spectra; thermodynamic basis for temperature breaks in arrhenius plots. *Mailing Add:* Dept Bot & Plant Sci Univ Calif Riverside CA 92521-0001

KUMAR, AJIT, CELL BIOLOGY, MOLECULAR GENETICS. *Current Pos:* ASSOC PROF BIOCHEM, SCH MED, GEORGE WASHINGTON UNIV, 79- *Personal Data:* b Bihar, India, Mar 2, 40; m 71; c 1. *Educ:* Bihar Univ, India, BSc, 58, MSc, 60; Univ Chicago, PhD(biol), 68. *Prof Exp:* Fel biochem, Albert Einstein Col Med, 68-71; res assoc, Harvard Med Sch, 71-75, asst prof microbiol & molecular genetics, 77; tutor biochem & molecular biol, Harvard Univ, 77-79. *Concurrent Pos:* Vis fel microbiol, Uppsala Univ, Sweden, 71; vis scientist biochem, Cambridge Univ, 77; assoc prof genetics, George Washington Univ, 80-; guest res scientist, Lab Biochem, Nat Cancer Inst, NIH, 80- *Mem:* Am Soc Cell Biol; Am Soc Biol Chemists. *Res:* RNA protein complexes and their role in eukaryotic gene expression. *Mailing Add:* Dept Biochem Sch Med George Washington Univ 2300 Eye St NW Washington DC 20037. *Fax:* 202-994-8974

KUMAR, ALOK, COMPUTER AIDED DESIGN. *Current Pos:* ASST PROF MECH ENG, UNIV DEL, NEWARK, 81- *Personal Data:* b Meerut, India, Sept 22, 51; m 80. *Educ:* Indian Inst Technol, Kanpur, India, BTech, 72, MTech, 76; Univ Houston, PhD(mech eng), 80. *Prof Exp:* Asst prof mech eng, Univ Wis-Platteville, 79-81. *Concurrent Pos:* Res & teaching asst, Indian Inst Technol, Kanpur, India, 73-76; res & teaching fel, Univ Houston, 76-79. *Mem:* Am Soc Mech Engrs; Soc Mfg Engrs; Am Soc Eng Educ. *Res:* Computer-aided design; kinematics; robotics and mechanical manipulator characterization; design and control; mathematical modeling of manufacturing processes; biomechanics. *Mailing Add:* WVa Univ PO Box 4260 Morgantown WV 26506

KUMAR, ASHOK, MATERIALS SCIENCE & ENGINEERING, ENVIRONMENTAL SCIENCE. *Current Pos:* BR CHIEF, CONSTRUCT ENG RES LAB, US ARMY CORPS ENGRS, 73-, SR SCIENTIST, 93- *Personal Data:* m 62, Rosetta Campbell; c Derek & Dana. *Educ:* Bihar Univ, India, BS, 58, Univ Calif, Berkeley, MS, 62, PhD(eng), 66. *Honors & Awards:* IR-100 Award, 84. *Prof Exp:* Teaching fel, Univ Calif, Berkeley, 66-68; res engr, Gen Motors Corp, 66-68; unit head, Martin Marietta Corp, 68-73. *Concurrent Pos:* Adj prof, Univ Ill, 85-; mem, pub affairs comt, Nat Assoc Corrosion Engrs, 86-89; ed comt, J Thermal Spray, 95- *Mem:* Fel Am Soc Metals; Am Ceramic Soc; Nat Asn Corrosion Engrs; Am Soc Testing & Mat. *Res:* Materials science and engineering as applied to corrosion and coatings used in infrastructure; new technologies to remove lead based paint using thermal spray vitrification process from steel structures; ceramic coated anodes for corrosion protection. *Mailing Add:* 2313 Blackthorn Dr PO Box 9005 Champaign IL 61821

KUMAR, BALASUBRAMANIAN SHIVA, HIGH ENERGY PHYSICS. *Current Pos:* PROF, DEPT PHYSICS, YALE UNIV, 86- *Personal Data:* b India. *Educ:* India Univ, BS, 77, MS, 79; Yale Univ, MS, 80, PhD(physics), 86. *Mem:* Am Phys Soc. *Res:* High energy physics. *Mailing Add:* WNSL Yale Univ 272 Whitney Ave New Haven CT 06520

KUMAR, CIDAMBI KRISHNA, ASTROPHYSICS, ATOMIC PHYSICS. *Current Pos:* from asst prof to assoc prof, 72-84, PROF PHYSICS & ASTRON, HOWARD UNIV, 84- *Personal Data:* b Madras, India, Sept 24, 37; m 68; c 2. *Educ:* Andhra Univ, India, BSc, 57; Univ Wis, MS, 65; Univ

Mich, PhD(astron), 69. *Prof Exp:* Jr sci officer nuclear physics, AEC, India, 58-63; Carnegie fel atomic physics & astrophys, Carnegie Inst Washington Dept Terrestrial Magnetism, 70-72. *Concurrent Pos:* Res assoc, Carnegie Inst Washington Dept Terrestrial Magnetism, 73- *Mem:* Am Astron Soc; Sigma Xi. *Res:* Spectrophotometry of galaxies and comets; beam-foil spectroscopy; radio astronomy. *Mailing Add:* Dept Physics & Astron Howard Univ 2355 Sixth St Rm 105 Washington DC 20059-0001

KUMAR, DEVENDRA, laser spectroscopy, optogalvanic & photoacoustic spectroscopy, for more information see previous edition

KUMAR, GANESH N, POLYMER SCIENCE, CHEMICAL ENGINEERING. *Current Pos:* STAFF MEM, JOHNSON & JOHNSON MED KK, TOKYO, JAPAN. *Personal Data:* b Madras, India, Oct 4, 48; m 75, Prema; c Bharat & Ramya. *Educ:* Univ Madras, BTech, 70; Clarkson Col Technol, MS, 72; Case Western Reserve Univ, PhD(polymer sci), 75; MBA, 88. *Honors & Awards:* Gold Medal, Univ Madras, 70; Johnson Medal, Johnson & Johnson, 92. *Prof Exp:* Assoc scientist, Xerox Corp, 74-78; sr res scientist, Johnson & Johnson Dent Prod Co, 78-80, mgr polymer res, 80-81,; dir polymer sci, Vistakon Inc, Jacksonville, Fla, 83-85, dir polymer sci & qual assurance, 85-87, vpres res & develop, 87- *Concurrent Pos:* Res assistantship, Clarkson Univ, 70-71; res fel, CWRU, 71-74. *Mem:* Am Chem Soc; Am Phys Soc; NAm Thermal Analysis Soc; Sigma Xi; AAAS. *Res:* Polymer structure property relationships; polymer mechanical and rheological properties; polymer blends and composites. *Mailing Add:* Johnson & Johnson Med KK 3-2 Toyo 6-Chome Kotoku Tokyo 135 Japan

KUMAR, K S P, ELECTRICAL ENGINEERING. *Current Pos:* PROF ELEC ENG, UNIV MINN, 64- *Personal Data:* US citizen. *Educ:* Purdue Univ, MS, 61, PhD(elec eng), 64. *Mem:* Inst Elec & Electronics Engrs; Am Soc Eng Educ. *Res:* Adaptive control of processes; stochastic filtering algorithms; robotic control. *Mailing Add:* 1155 W Sandhurst Dr Roseville MN 55113. *E-Mail:* kumar@ee.umn.edu

KUMAR, K SHARVAN, high temperature structural materials & intermetallics, aerospace lightweight alloy development, for more information see previous edition

KUMAR, KAPLESH, INERTIAL INSTRUMENTS. *Current Pos:* Staff scientist, Charles Stark Draper Lab, Inc, 75-80, chief, Mat Develop Sect, 80-88, chief, Mat Sci & Technol Sect, 88-91, PRIN MEM TECH STAFF, CHARLES STARK DRAPER LAB, INC, 91- *Personal Data:* b Lucknow, India, Nov 9, 47; m 74, Savinder Kaur; c Priyadarshini & Ruchira. *Educ:* Indian Inst Technol, Kanpur, BTech, 69, Stevens Inst Technol, MS, 71; Mass Inst Technol, ScD, 75. *Honors & Awards:* Invention Disclosure Award, NASA. *Concurrent Pos:* Vis lectr, Am Soc Metals Int, 89; mem, Mat Tech Comt, Am Inst Aeronaut & Astronaut, 91-; mem, Int Mat Rev Comt, Am Soc Metals Int, 92- *Mem:* Am Soc Metals Int; Am Inst Aeronaut & Astronaut. *Res:* Samarium-transition-metal permanent magnets; metal matrix composites; ion implantation; chemical vapor deposition; dimensional stability; flex lead corrosion; printed circuit board adhesion degradation; manganese-zinc ferrites; rotating electrical contacts; high Tc superconductors; interial instruments. *Mailing Add:* 25 Redwing Rd Wellesley MA 02181

KUMAR, MADHURENDU B, HYDROLOGY & WATER RESOURCES. *Current Pos:* GEOLOGIST SUPVR, OIL & GAS DIV, OFF CONSERV, LA DEPT NATURAL RESOURCES, 82- *Personal Data:* b Khagaria, India, Jan 4, 42; m; c 2. *Educ:* Indian Sch Mines, Ranchi Univ, BS, 61, MS, 62; La State Univ, PhD(geol), 72. *Honors & Awards:* Sir Henry Hayden Medal, Mining, Metal & Geol Inst India, 78; Presidential Cert Merit Prof Dedication & Leadership, Am Inst Prof Geol, 93. *Prof Exp:* Instr, Indian Sch Mines, Minerol & Petrol, 62-63; sci officer, Atomic Mines & Minerals Div, Dept Atomic Energy, Govt India, 63; sr exec oil geologist, Oil India, Ltd, 63-69; instr geol & geography, City Univ New York, Hunter Col, 74-77; res assoc geol, Inst Environ Studies, 75, sr investr geohydrol, 78-82, sr res assoc, La State Univ, 78-82. *Concurrent Pos:* Consult, 72-; vis prof, La State Univ, 77-78, Southern Univ, 78-90, Univ Southwest La, 79. *Mem:* Am Asn Petrol Geologists; Am Inst Prof Geologists; fel Geol Soc Am. *Res:* Subsurface of petroleum geology; salt domes; mine hydrology; petroleum resource conservation. *Mailing Add:* 5802 Highland Rd Baton Rouge LA 70808

KUMAR, MAHESH C, VETERINARY MICROBIOLOGY, PUBLIC HEALTH. *Current Pos:* DIR VET SERV, E B OLSON FARMS, ATWATER, MINN, 89- *Personal Data:* b Montgomery, WPakistan, Sept 21, 35; m 85, Shashi Luther; c Sanjai, Ashwin, Sheen & Salil. *Educ:* Univ Bihar, BVSc & AH, 58; Univ Minn, Minneapolis, MS, 64, PhD(vet microbiol), 67. *Prof Exp:* Vet asst surg, Animal Husb Dept, Bihar, India, 58-61; res fel, Univ Minn, St Paul, 67, res assoc vet microbiol, 67-76; dir vet servs, Mile High Turkey Hatchery, Longmont, Colo, 76-84; dir, Mill Farms Co, Paynesville, Minn, 84-85; dir, Koronis Mills, 86-89. *Mem:* Am Vet Med Asn; Am Asn Avian Path; Poultry Sci Asn; Am Soc Microbiol. *Res:* Poultry diseases; mycoplasma and salmonella infections in turkeys; elimination of salmonella from turkeys and their environment; prevention and treatment of diseases in turkeys. *Mailing Add:* E B Olson Farms Div Jennie-O Foods Box 439 Atwater MN 56209. *Fax:* 320-974-8499

KUMAR, NIRJAN, molecular biology, for more information see previous edition

KUMAR, PANGANAMALA RAMANA, STOCHASTIC SYSTEMS, MANUFACTURING SYSTEMS. *Current Pos:* assoc prof, 85-87, PROF ELEC & COMPUT ENG, UNIV ILL, URBANA-CHAMPAIGN, 87- *Personal Data:* b Nagpur, India, Apr 21, 52; m 82, Jayashree Sundaram; c Ashwin & Shilpa. *Educ:* Indian Inst Technl, BTech, 73; Wash Univ, MS, 75, DSc, 77. *Honors & Awards:* Donald P Eckman Award, Am Automotive Control Coun, 85. *Prof Exp:* From asst prof to assoc prof math, Univ Md, Baltimore Co, 77-84. *Mem:* Fel Inst Elec & Electronics Engrs. *Res:* Systems theory and its applications; adaptive control; stochastic systems; manufacturing systems; optimization; game theory; neural networks; communication networks. *Mailing Add:* Univ Ill CSL 1308 W Main St Urbana IL 61801. *Fax:* 217-244-1653; *E-Mail:* prkumar@decision.csl.uiu.edu

KUMAR, PRADEEP, NONLINEAR PHENOMENA, SUPERCONDUCTIVITY. *Current Pos:* from asst prof to assoc prof, 79-93, PROF PHYSICS, UNIV FLA, 93-; PROG DIR MAT THEORY, DIV MAT RES, NSF, 95- *Personal Data:* b Allahabad, India, Jan 1, 49; m 87, Diana Tonnessen; c Casey A & Vijay A. *Educ:* Univ Lucknow, India, BSc, 66; Indian Inst Technol, Kanpur, MSc, 68; Univ Calif, San Diego, PhD(physics), 73. *Prof Exp:* Res assoc physics, Univ Wis-Milwaukee, 73-75; res assoc, Univ Southern Calif, 75-77, asst prof, 77-78. *Concurrent Pos:* Nordita prof, Helsinki Univ Technol, Finland, 78-79; guest prof, Nordita, Copenhagen, Denmark, 78-79; vis scientist, Helsinki Univ Technol, 84, CEA, France, 89. *Mem:* Am Phys Soc. *Res:* Theoretical ultra low temperature physics; nonlinear phenomena; solitons; magnetism; superconductivity. *Mailing Add:* Phys Dept Univ Fla Gainesville FL 32611. *E-Mail:* pkumar@nsf.gov

KUMAR, RAVINDER, COMMUTATIVE ALGEBRA, INSTRUCTIONAL TECHNOLOGIES. *Current Pos:* asst prof, 90-95, ASSOC PROF MATH, ALCORN STATE UNIV, 95- *Personal Data:* b Gujranwala, Jan 31, 45; Indian citizen; m, Kanchan B Manaktala; c Preeti. *Educ:* Delhi Univ, India, BA, 64, MA, 66, PhD(math), 72. *Prof Exp:* From asst prof to assoc prof math, Ramjas Col, Delhi Univ, India, 66-90. *Concurrent Pos:* Mombusho postdoctoral fel, Kyoto Univ, Japan, 79-82, vis res guest scholar math, 88; consult, Clark Atlanta Univ, 91-; coordr, Title III grant, Alcorn State Univ, 92-94, prin investr, 96-97; prin investr, Teacher Enhancement Projs, Miss Insts Higher Learning, 93, 95-97; co-prin investr, USDA, 93-96; coordr, Coop Consortium Clark Atlanta Univ, 94-96; ed, Teaching Math Technol, Alcorn State Univ, 96- *Mem:* Am Math Soc; Math Asn Am; Nat Coun Teachers Math. *Res:* Commutative rings in multiplicative ideal theory; local rings; instructional technologies in mathematics. *Mailing Add:* 120 Linda Dr Vicksburg MS 39180. *Fax:* 601-877-6256; *E-Mail:* rkumar@academic.alcorn.edu

KUMAR, ROMESH, ENERGY SYSTEMS DESIGN & ANALYSIS, FUEL CELL SYSTEMS. *Current Pos:* Appointee, 72-74, asst chem engr, 74-76, CHEM ENGR, ARGONNE NAT LAB, 76- *Personal Data:* b Rajpura, India, Oct 18, 44; m 76, Kumkum Khanna; c Rahul & Ritu. *Educ:* Panjab Univ, BSc, 65; Univ Calif, Berkeley, MS, 68, PhD(chem eng), 72. *Honors & Awards:* R&D-100 Awards. *Concurrent Pos:* US Deleg, Int Energy Agency's Polymer Electrolyte Fuel Cell Annex VIII. *Mem:* Am Inst Chem Engrs; Am Soc Mech Engrs. *Res:* Fuel cell and systems for transportation; fuel processing of hydrocarbon and alcohol fuels for use in fuel cell systems; granted six patents. *Mailing Add:* Chem Eng Div Argonne Nat Lab Argonne IL 60439-4837. *Fax:* 630-252-4176; *E-Mail:* kumar@cmt.anl.gov

KUMAR, S, SOLID STATE PHYSICS. *Current Pos:* RES PHYSICIST, QUANTUM MAGNETICS INC, 90- *Personal Data:* b Ernakulam, India, July 31, 59. *Educ:* Indian Inst Technol, MS, 80; Pa State Univ, PhD(physics), 86. *Prof Exp:* Grad asst, Pa State Univ, 80-86; postdoctoral researcher, Ohio State Univ, 86-89; asst prof, Northeast Mo State Univ, 89-90. *Mem:* Am Phys Soc. *Res:* Liquid helium and the design and construction of cryogenic apparatus; design, construction and testing of SQUID-based magnetometers. *Mailing Add:* 7740 Kenamar Ct San Diego CA 92121-2425

KUMAR, S ANAND, BIOCHEMISTRY. *Current Pos:* RES SCIENTIST CLIN SCI, WADSWORTH CTR LABS & RES, NY STATE DEPT HEALTH, 78- *Personal Data:* b Bangalore, India, Mar 12, 36; m 63. *Educ:* Univ Mysore, BSc, 54; Univ Poona, MSc, 57; Indian Inst Sci, PhD(biochem), 63. *Prof Exp:* Fel biochem, Sch Med, Tufts Univ, Boston, Mass, 63-65; res assoc biochem, Scripps Clin & Res Found, La Jolla, Calif, 65-66; lectr biochem, Indian Inst Sci, Bangalore, 66-71; guest scientist biochem, Roche Inst Molecular Biol, Nutley, NJ, 71-72; vis asst prof biol, Hunter Col, City Univ NY, 72-77. *Concurrent Pos:* Adj prof, State Univ NY, 80-; mem gov bd, Astra Res & Develop Ctr, Bangalore, India, 84-, consult, Fine Chem Div, Astra-IDL, Ltd, 85- *Mem:* Sigma Xi; Am Soc Biol Chemists; NY Acad Sci. *Res:* Structure and mode action of enzymes; genetic transcriptions; bacterial RNA polymerase and its site-specific inhibitors; steroid hormone receptors-DNA interactions; steroid hormone controlled gene expression. *Mailing Add:* Astra Res Ctr PO Box 359 Malleswaram Bangalore 560003 India

KUMAR, SHIV SHARAN, ASTRONOMY. *Current Pos:* asst prof, 65-68, ASSOC PROF ASTRON, UNIV VA, 68- *Personal Data:* b Bannu, India, Mar 15, 39; m 64; c 3. *Educ:* Univ Mich, PhD(astron), 62. *Prof Exp:* Asst astron, Univ Observ, Univ Mich, 57-60; astrophysicist, Smithsonian Astrophys Observ, 60-61; res assoc, Goddard Inst Space Studies, 62-63; staff mem, Phys Res Lab, India, 63-65. *Mem:* Fel AAAS; Int Astron Union; Am Astron Soc; fel Royal Astron Soc. *Res:* Stellar atmospheres; stellar structure and evolution; origin of the solar system; celestial mechanics. *Mailing Add:* Dept Math-Astron Rm 314 Univ Va PO Box 3818 Univ Sta Charlottesville VA 22903

KUMAR, SHRAWAN, BIOMECHANICS, ERGONOMICS. *Current Pos:* from asst prof to assoc prof, 77-82, PROF PHYS THER, UNIV ALTA, 82-, PROF NEUROSCI, 92- *Personal Data:* b Allahabad, India, July 1, 39; m 65, Rita Srivastava; c Rajesh & Sheela. *Educ:* Univ Allahabad, BSc, 59, MSc, 62; Univ Surrey, PhD(physiol), 71. *Hon Degrees:* DSc, Univ Surrey, 94. *Honors & Awards:* Sir Frederic Bartlett Medal. *Prof Exp:* Lectr zool, Univ Allahabad, 62-66; fel eng, Univ Dublin, 71-73; pool officer orthop, All-India Inst Med Sci, 73-74; res assoc rehab med, Univ Toronto, 74-77. *Mem:* Am Soc Biomech; Orthop Res Soc; Human Factors Soc; Human Factors Soc Can; Ergonomics Soc; Int Soc Study Lumbar Spine. *Res:* Work physiology; occupational biomechanics; tissue biomechanics. *Mailing Add:* Dept Phys Ther Univ Alta Edmonton AB T6G 2G4 Can

KUMAR, SHRAWAN, MOLECULAR GENETICS. *Current Pos:* ASST PROF, BOYS TOWN NAT RES HOSP, 93-; ASST PROF ANTHROP, UNIV NEBR, OMAHA, 93-; ASST PROF GENETICS, CREIGHTON UNIV, MED CTR, 93- *Personal Data:* b Calcutta, India, Feb 28, 53; m 92, Lina Kumar. *Educ:* Calcutta Univ, BS, 72; Ranchi Univ, MS, 76, PhD(serogenetics), 84. *Prof Exp:* Res fel, Bur Police Res & Develop, 77-82; sr fel, Anthrop Surg, India, 82-88; res assoc, Univ Nebr, Med Ctr, 88-89; res assoc, Boys Town Nat Res Hosp, 89-92. *Mem:* India Soc Human Genetics; Indian Anthrop Soc; SAsian Anthropologists; Am Soc Human Genetics; Asn Res Otolerjyngol; AAAS. *Res:* Localization of human genetic diseases to its specific location in the human genome; clone and characterize the disease gene. *Mailing Add:* 2184 N 124th Ave Circle Omaha NE 68164. *Fax:* 402-498-6331

KUMAR, SHRAWAN, GEOMETRIC TECHNIQUE IN REPRESENTATION THEORY. *Current Pos:* PROF MATH, UNIV NC, 91- *Personal Data:* b Ghazipur, U.P., India, June 12, 53; m 78, Shyama Agrawal; c Neeraj & Niketa. *Educ:* Gorakhpu Univ, BSc, 73; Bombay Univ, MSc, 75, PhD(math), 86. *Prof Exp:* Post-doctoral fel, Math Sci Res Inst, 83-84; CLE Moore instr, Mass Inst Technol, 84-85; mem, Inst Advan Study, Princeton, NJ, 88-89; reader, Tata Inst Fund Res, India, 89-92. *Concurrent Pos:* Mem, Tata Inst Fund Res, India, 75-89; prin investr, NSF, 92-95, 96-99; vis prof, Max Planck Inst Math, 93, Ecole Norm Sub, Paris, 94, RIMS, Kyoto Univ, Kyoto, 96. *Mem:* Am Math Soc. *Res:* Topology and geometry of finite and infinite dimensional flag varieties and also use them in some problems of representation theory of finite dimensional semi-simple groups as well as Kac-Moody groups. *Mailing Add:* Dept Math Univ NC Chapel Hill NC 27599-3250

KUMAR, SOMA, BIOCHEMISTRY. *Current Pos:* from asst prof to assoc prof, 58-72, PROF CHEM, GEORGETOWN UNIV, 72- *Personal Data:* b Lucknow, India, May 16, 24; m 55; c 3. *Educ:* Univ Lucknow, BSc, 44, MSc, 45; Univ Md, PhD, 53. *Prof Exp:* Res assoc, Univ Md, 53-54; lectr biochem, Univ Lucknow, 54-56; asst prof, All-India Inst Med Sci, New Delhi, 56-58. *Mem:* AAAS; Am Chem Soc; Am Soc Biol Chemists; Sigma Xi. *Res:* Biosynthesis of fatty acids; phospholipase A2. *Mailing Add:* Dept Chem Georgetown Univ 37th & O St NW Washington DC 20057-0001

KUMAR, SUDHIR, RAILROAD ENGINEERING. *Current Pos:* chmn, 71-78, PROF MECH & AEROSPACE ENG, ILL INST TECHNOL, 71-, DIR, RR ENG LAB, 78-, DIR, ACAD RR ENG & TRANSP MGR, 91- *Personal Data:* b Saharanpur, India, Oct 31, 33; m 60, Jyotsna Kapil; c Nisha, Raj & Anita. *Educ:* Agra Univ, BSc, 50, MSc, 52; Indian Inst Sci, Bangalore, AIISc, 55; Pa State Univ, PhD(eng mech), 58. *Honors & Awards:* Octave Chanute Medal, Western Soc Engrs, 86. *Prof Exp:* Demonstr physics, Bareilly Col, Agra Univ, 50-51; res asst eng mech, Pa State Univ, 55-57, res assoc, 57-58, asst prof, 58-59; asst solid mech br, Eng Sci Div, Off Ord Res, US Army, 58-59, chief, 59-62, assoc dir, Eng Sci Div, US Army Res Off-Durham, 62-71. *Concurrent Pos:* Vis lectr, Duke Univ, 58-62, vis assoc prof, 62-71 & NC State Univ, 68-71; vis lectr, Acad Railway Sci, People's Repub China, 83-84; mem, Fac Adv Comn, Ill Bd Higher Educ, 85-87. *Mem:* Am Inst Aeronaut & Astronaut; Indian Soc Theoret & Appl Mech; Assoc Railway Engrs Am; Am Acad Mech; Am Soc Mech Engrs. *Res:* Wheel and rail interaction; railroad engineering; materials; helicopters; performance and efficiency of trains depends very much on optimizing the wheel-rail contact conditions separately for the powered and the nonpowered units, this still has not been accomplished, understanding wheel rail interaction is the key to it. *Mailing Add:* Dept Mech & Aerospace Eng Ill Inst Technol 3300 S Fed St Chicago IL 60616-3732. *Fax:* 312-567-7230

KUMAR, SUDHIR, BIOCHEMISTRY, NEUROCHEMISTRY. *Current Pos:* from asst prof to assoc prof, 76-86, PROF BIOCHEM & NEUROL SCI, MED SCH, RUSH UNIV, 86-, DIR & PROF, CLIN REGION LAB, HAZEL CREST, ILL, 88-; PROF BIOL, TRITON COL, ILL, 93- *Personal Data:* b Anjhi, India, Sept 16, 42; m 68, Nilima Jain; c Avanti & Anjali. *Educ:* Univ Rajasthan, India, BS, 59, MS, 61; Univ Lucknow, India, PhD(biochem), 66. *Prof Exp:* Res assoc pharmacol, Baylor Col Med, 67-68; sr res scientist, NY State Res Inst Neurochem, Columbia Univ, 68-69; chief biochemist pediat, Methodist Hosp, Brooklyn, 69-73; res biochemist hematol, Vet Admin Hosp, Brooklyn, 73-75; dir perinatal res & lab, Christ Hosp, Oak Lawn, Ill, 75-81, dir pediat res, 78-81. *Concurrent Pos:* Int Brain Res Org res fel award, UNESCO & Govt France, 71; Dreyfus Med Found fel, 71 & 73; consult scientist med res, Vet Admin Hosp, Hines, Ill, 76-79; dir & pres, Clin Diagnostics, Hazel Crest, Oak Forest, Ill, 82-88; consult, Govt India & UNESCO Prog, 87, 89 & 91. *Mem:* Fel NY Acad Sci; Am Soc Biol Chemists; Am Inst Nutrit; Am Soc Neurochem; Am Soc Exp Biol & Med; Am Soc Clin Nutrit; Soc Pediat Res; Am Soc Microbiol; Int Soc Neurochem; fel Nat Acad Clin Biochemists; fel Am Inst Chemists. *Res:* Study of vitamin B12 metabolism; effect of malnutrition on brain development and its correlation to mental retardation; changes in levels of nucleic acids and enzymes of purine catabolism; changes in amino acid levels; developing brain and metabolic disorders in newborn; perinatal medicine and development of screening tests for metabolic disorders in newborn; development of serum-free culture media and its use in growing neural and amniotic fluid cells; development of rapid tests for use in clinical laboratory; alzheimer's disease; effects of drugs in controlling syndromes associated with HIV (AIDS etc). *Mailing Add:* 18901 Springfield Flossmoor IL 60422. *Fax:* 708-799-8713

KUMAR, SURIENDER, ORGANIC CHEMISTRY, BIOCHEMISTRY. *Current Pos:* asst prof biochem, 71-75, assoc prof, 75-81, PROF BIOCHEM, COL MED & DENT NJ, 81- *Personal Data:* b Panjab, India, Dec 5, 38; m 65; c 4. *Educ:* Univ Delhi, BSc, 58, MSc, 60; Boston Univ, PhD(org chem), 67. *Prof Exp:* Lectr chem, Deshbandhu Col, Delhi, 60-62; fel, Cornell Univ, 66-68; fel, Univ Wis-Madison, 68; res chemist, Vet Admin Hosp, 68-70. *Mem:* AAAS; Am Chem Soc; fel Am Inst Chemists; NY Acad Sci; Am Soc Biol Chemists; Am Asn Cancer Res. *Res:* Cancer research; proteolytic enzymes; all transformation. *Mailing Add:* Dept Biochem Univ Md-NJ Med Sch Newark NJ 07103

KUMAR, VIJAY, LABORATORY MEDICINE, IMMUNOLOGY. *Current Pos:* ASSOC RES PROF, STATE UNIV NY, BUFFALO, 87-; PRES, IMMCO DIAG, 87- *Personal Data:* b Punjab, India, Apr 15, 45; m 73. *Educ:* Panjab Univ, BS, 66, MS, 68; State Univ NY, Buffalo, PhD(biochem), 73; Am Bd Med Microbiol, dipl; Am Bd Med Lab Immunol, dipl. *Prof Exp:* Teaching asst biochem, State Univ NY, Buffalo, 69-73; fel, E J Meyer Mem Hosp, 73-74, fel immunol, Erie County Lab, E J Meyer Mem Hosp, 74-76; asst prof, Dept Microbiol, If Testing Serv Buffalo, 76-87, asst dir. *Concurrent Pos:* From clin instr to clin asst prof, Dept Microbiol, State Univ NY, Buffalo, 74-76. *Mem:* Am Soc Microbiol; Soc Investigative Dermat; Am Asn Clin Chem. *Res:* Isolation of proteins, enzymes, autoimmunity, and immunochemistry; Sluten Sensince entoromail. *Mailing Add:* 60 Pine View State Univ NY Amherst NY 14228

KUMAR, VINAY, CANCER, IMMUNOLOGY. *Current Pos:* assoc prof, 82-83, Charles T Ashworth prof, 86-94, PROF PATH, SOUTHWESTERN MED CTR, UNIV TEX, 83-, VERNIE A STEMBRIDGE, CHAIR PATH, 94- *Personal Data:* b Montgomery, India, Dec 24, 44; m 72, Raminder; c Rohit & Ambika. *Educ:* Poona Univ, BSc, 62; Punjab Univ, MBBS, 67; All India Inst Med Sci, MD(path), 72. *Prof Exp:* Tutor path, All India Inst Med Sci, 69-72; from instr to asst prof, Boston Univ, 72-78, assoc prof path & microbiol, Sch Med, 78-82. *Concurrent Pos:* Med Found Inc fel, Boston, 74-76; prin investr, Nat Cancer Inst, 77-; Am Cancer Soc res scholar award, 78; mem, Immunobiol Study Sect, NIH, 84-87. *Mem:* Am Asn Immunol; Sci Res Soc NAm; Am Soc Invest Path (vpres, 97-98). *Res:* Tumor immunology; virus induced cancer; bonemarrow transplantation; natural killer cells; hematopoiesis; coauthor of two publications. *Mailing Add:* Dept Path Southwestern Med Sch Univ Tex 5323 Harry Hines Blvd Dallas TX 75235-9072. *Fax:* 214-648-4033; *E-Mail:* kumerol@utsw.swmed.edu

KUMAR, VIPIN, PARALLEL COMPUTING, ARTIFICIAL INTELLIGENCE. *Current Pos:* ASSOC PROF, DEPT COMPUT SCI, UNIV MINN, 89- *Personal Data:* b Muzaffarnagar, Uttar Prad, Oct 21, 56; m 82; c 2. *Educ:* Univ Roorkee, Uttar Prad, India, BE, 77; Philips Int Inst, Eindhoven, Neth, ME, 79; Univ Md, College Park, PhD(computer sci), 82. *Prof Exp:* Asst prof, Dept Comput Sci, Univ Tex, Austin, 83-89. *Mem:* Inst Elec & Electronics Engrs; Asn Comput Mach; Am Asn Artificial Intel. *Res:* Algorithms for solving various scientific and artificial intelligence problems on massively parallel computers. *Mailing Add:* Dept Comput Sci Univ Minn 4-192 Elec Eng/Comput Sci Bldg 200 Union St SE Minneapolis MN 55455

KUMARAN, A KRISHNA, DEVELOPMENTAL BIOLOGY, MOLECULAR ENDOCRINOLOGY OF INSECTS. *Current Pos:* assoc prof, 69-73, PROF BIOL, MARQUETTE UNIV, 73-, WEHR PROF, 93- *Personal Data:* b Govada, India, July 17, 32; US citizen; m 56, Jyoti Thummala; c Nanda K Alapati. *Educ:* Univ Madras, BSc, 50, MSc, 55, PhD(zool), 59. *Prof Exp:* Demonstr zool, Sri Venkateswara Univ, India, 55-57, lectr, 57-62; NIH trainee, Western Res Univ, 62-65; reader, Osmania Univ, India, 65-68; sr res assoc biol, Case Western Res Univ, 68-69. *Concurrent Pos:* NSF res grants, 70-; NIH res grant, 75-; vis scientist, Czech Acad Sci, 78; vis scientist biol, Harvard Univ, 83; USDA res grant, 86-; vis lectr, Univ Guam, 88; vis scientist, Chinese Acad Sci, 89. *Mem:* Fel AAAS; Entom Soc Am; Am Soc Cell Biol; Am Soc Zoologists; Int Soc Develop Biol; Am Soc Develop Biol. *Res:* Molecular entomology; role of hormones in control of insect development; hormonal control of specific gene expression during post embryonic development in insects. *Mailing Add:* Dept Biol Marquette Univ Milwaukee WI 53233. *E-Mail:* kumaran@vms.csd.mu.edu

KUMARAN, MAVINKAL KIZHAKKEVEETTIL, INSULATION, TRANSPORT PROPERTIES. *Current Pos:* res assoc, 81-84, res officer, 84-89, SR RES OFFICER, NAT RES COUN, CAN, 90- *Personal Data:* b Cannonore, Kerala, India, June 1, 46; Can citizen; m 71, Dakshayani P Ramath; c Jyothi & Ranjith. *Educ:* Univ Kerala, India, BS, 65, MS, 67; Univ London, PhD (chem thermodynamics), 76. *Prof Exp:* Lectr phys chem, Sree Narayana Col, Ind, 67-80; res fel thermodynamics, Massey Univ, NZ, 80-81. *Concurrent Pos:* Res fel, Calcut Univ, India, 72-73; commonwealth scholar, Univ London, 73-76; fel, Japan Soc Prom Sci, 92. *Res:* Experimental and theoretical investigations on properties of liquids and liquid mixtures, especially in the critical region; experimental and theoretical investigation on heat and moisture transport properties of building materials. *Mailing Add:* Inst Res Construct Nat Res Coun Can Ottawa ON K1A 0R6 Can. *Fax:* 613-954-3733; *E-Mail:* Bitnet: kumaran@irc.lan.nrc.ca

KUMARI, DURGA, ORGANIC CHEMISTRY, ANALYTICAL CHEMISTRY. *Current Pos:* RESEARCHER CHEM, MAT DIV, FED HWY ADMIN, 87- *Personal Data:* b New Delhi, India, Apr 27, 51. *Educ:* Meerut Univ, India, BS, 72, MS, 74; Delhi Univ, India, PhD(chem), 80. *Prof Exp:* Scientist chem, Indian Inst Technol, 79-81; res assoc chem, Univ Minn, Bemidji State Univ, Fla A&M Univ & Okla State Univ, 81-87. *Concurrent Pos:* Fulbright scholar, Fulbright Off, Wash, DC, 77-78; postdoctoral fel chem, Okla State Univ, Fla A&M Univ, Bemidji State Univ, Univ Minn, 81-87. *Mem:* Am Chem Soc; Am Soc Mass Spectrometry; AAAS; Indian Women Sci Asn. *Res:* Isolation, identification and synthesis of novel compounds using organic chemistry; material science chemistry; author of various publications. *Mailing Add:* 4006 Birchwood Ct North Brunswick NJ 08902

KUMAROO, KUZIYILETHU KRISHNAN, BIOCHEMISTRY. *Current Pos:* RES BIOCHEMIST, DEPT HYPERBARIC MED, NAVAL MED RES INST, BETHESDA, MD, 79- *Personal Data:* b Kerala, India, Apr 6, 31; m 67, Vatsala; c Vnod & Manoj. *Educ:* Kerala Univ, India, BSc, 55; Univ NC, PhD(biochem), 69. *Prof Exp:* Chemist, Capsulation Serv, India, 55-56; clin chemist, Grant Med Col, Bombay, 56-57; petrol chemist, Kuwait Oil Co, Arabia, 57-63; res asst biochem, Univ NC, Chapel Hill, 63-68; NIH trainee, Univ Mich Med Ctr, 68-71; asst prof biochem, Univ NC, Chapel Hill, 71-79. *Mem:* Sigma Xi; Am Soc Biochem & Molecular Biol; Oxygen Soc; Nat Asn Retarded Citizens; Undersea Soc Int; Planetary Soc Int. *Res:* Biochemistry of circulating blood factors and cells that regulate pulmonary, cardiovascular and central nervous system functions in normal and pathological conditions; cerebral ischemia and thrombosis; biochemistry of decompression sickness; regulatory role of proteases; basic chromosomal proteins in differentiating cells; biochemistry of oxygen/hydrogen gases in diving; complements in decompression sickness. *Mailing Add:* 2614 Urbana Dr Wheaton MD 20906. *Fax:* 301-949-5330

KUMBAR, MAHADEVAPPA M, PHYSICAL CHEMISTRY, BIOPHYSICS. *Current Pos:* CHIEF, INFO MGT SYSTS, PILGRIM PSYCHOL CTR, b Tallur, India, Nov 15, 39; m 2. *Educ:* Karnatak Univ, India, BSc, 61, MSc, 63; Adelphi Univ, PhD(phys chem), 69. *Prof Exp:* Lectr, Parle Col, India, 63-65; res assoc biophys, 69-71, adj asst prof, 71-79, ADJ ASSOC PROF BIOPHYS, ADELPHI UNIV, 79- *Concurrent Pos:* Adj fac, Nassau Community Col, 71- *Mem:* Am Chem Soc. *Res:* Statistical mechanics of macromolecules; dynamic and mechanical properties, conformational changes and conformational studies. *Mailing Add:* 2 Essex Rd Plainview NY 11803-2704

KUMBARACI-JONES, NURAN MELEK, TEACHING, BIOLOGICAL CHEMISTRY. *Current Pos:* asst prof, 79-84, ASSOC PROF CHEM, STEVENS INST TECHNOL, 84- *Personal Data:* b Istanbul, Turkey, Apr 3, 44; m 81, Francis T; c Anne & Marian. *Educ:* Robert Col, Istanbul, Turkey, BS, 66; Columbia Univ, MS, 73, MA, 75, MPhil, 76, PhD(physiol), 77. *Prof Exp:* Chemist res & develop, Eczacibasi Pharmaceut Co, 66-71; NIH fel, dept physiol, Col Physicians & Surgeons, Columbia Univ, 77-79. *Mem:* Am Physiol Soc; Soc Neurosci; NY Acad Sci; Sigma Xi. *Res:* Thrombogenesis on artificial surfaces; biochemistry and biophysics of skeletal muscle contraction; electrophysiological properties of excitable membranes and synaptic transmission; immune mechanisms activating the complement system and inflammatory processes. *Mailing Add:* Dept Chem & Chem Eng Stevens Inst Technol Hoboken NJ 07030. *Fax:* 201-216-8240

KUMINS, CHARLES ARTHUR, SURFACE CHEMISTRY. *Current Pos:* CONSULT, 82- *Personal Data:* b New York, NY, Jan 13, 15; m 40; c 3. *Educ:* City Col New York, BS, 36; Polytech Inst Brooklyn, MS, 41. *Honors & Awards:* Roon Awards, Fed Socs Coatings Technol, 65 & 76; Matticello lectr, 79; Sci Achievement Award, Fed Soc Coatings Technol. *Prof Exp:* Jr chemist, Titanium Div, Nat Lead Co, NJ, 37-41; res chemist & group leader, Wyandotte Chem Co, Mich, 41-42; sr res chemist, Res Labs, Interchem Corp, 42-50, head dept inorg & phys chem, 50-54, dir dept, 54-59, dir textile chem, 59-63, asst dir, 63-67; dir res lab, Charles Bruning Co, 67-71; dir res & develop, Graphics Develop Lab, Addressograph-Multigraph Co, 71-73; dir res & develop, Tremco Corp, 73-80; vpres sci & technol, Sherwin Williams Co, 80-81. *Concurrent Pos:* Secy & trustee, Paint Res Inst, 75- *Mem:* AAAS; Am Chem Soc; fel Am Inst Chemists. *Res:* Rheology and particle size; colloids and surface chemistry; high temperature reactions; inorganic pigments; metallo-organics; iron compounds; alumina silicates; physical chemistry of polymers; transport phenomena in polymers; photochemistry; imaging systems; electrophotography; sealants and adhesives. *Mailing Add:* 6589 Locust Grove Rd Easton MD 21601-9251

KUMKUMIAN, CHARLES SIMON, MEDICINAL CHEMISTRY. *Current Pos:* CONSULT, 97- *Personal Data:* b Meriden, Conn, June 17, 20; m 61; c 4. *Educ:* Temple Univ, BS, 44, MS, 51; Univ Md, PhD(med chem), 62. *Prof Exp:* Instr, Temple Univ, 47-51; instr chem, Univ Md, 57-60; asst ed, Chem Abstr Serv, 62-63; chemist, Bur Med, US Food & Drug Admin, 64-68, supvry chemist, Bur Drugs, 68-72, asst dir chem, Off Drug Res & Rev, 72-95; dir regulatory affairs, Otsuka Am Pharmaceut Inc, 95-97. *Mem:* Am Chem Soc. *Res:* Synthesis and biological activity of steroids; structure activity relationships; analytical chemistry. *Mailing Add:* 5919 Holland Rd Rockville MD 20851

KUMLER, PHILIP L, ORGANIC & POLYMER CHEMISTRY, THERMAL ANALYSIS. *Current Pos:* assoc prof, 76-80, PROF CHEM, STATE UNIV NY, FREDONIA, 80- *Personal Data:* b Columbus, Ohio, May 23, 41; div; c 1. *Educ:* Miami Univ, BA, 62; Univ Rochester, PhD(chem), 67. *Prof Exp:* Jr chemist indust res, Procter & Gamble Co, 62, summer staff, Indust Soap & Chem Prod, 63 & 64; fac asst chem, Wabash Col, 64; NATO fel, Univ Copenhagen, 67-68; fel & res assoc, Univ Chicago, 68-69, NIH fel, 69-70, fel & res assoc, 70; from asst prof to assoc prof chem, Saginaw Valley State Col, 70-76. *Concurrent Pos:* Vis res assoc macromolecular sci, Case Western Res Univ, 81; vis prof, Mich Molecular Inst, 87, 88, 89 & 90; adj fac, State Univ NY, Buffalo, 89- *Mem:* AAAS; Am Chem Soc; Sigma Xi; NY Acad Sci; NAm Thermal Anal Soc. *Res:* Polymer chemistry and physics; surface analysis of polymers; thermal analysis. *Mailing Add:* Dept Chem State Univ NY Fredonia NY 14063. *Fax:* 716-673-3347; *E-Mail:* kumler@fredonia.edu

KUMLI, KARL F, ORGANIC CHEMISTRY. *Current Pos:* from asst prof to assoc prof, 64-71, PROF CHEM, CALIF STATE UNIV, CHICO, 71-, CHMN DEPT, 75- *Personal Data:* b Denver, Colo, Oct 9, 27; m 53; c 2. *Educ:* Kans State Teachers Col, AB, 55; Univ Kans, PhD(chem), 59. *Prof Exp:* Res chemist, Celanese Chem Corp, 59-61; res scientist, Weyerhaeuser Co, 61-64. *Mem:* Am Chem Soc. *Res:* Stereochemistry and mechanisms of reactions of the phosphorus atom; synthesis and characterization of polyoxymethylene, phenol-formaldehyde, epoxy. *Mailing Add:* 1340 Manchester Rd Chico CA 95929

KUMMER, JOSEPH T, SOLID STATE CHEMISTRY. *Current Pos:* RETIRED. *Personal Data:* b Baltimore, Md, Oct 21, 19; m 47, Ruth Lambrix; c Frederic J, Marian E, David T & Joseph T. *Educ:* Johns Hopkins Univ, BE, 41, PhD(chem eng), 45. *Honors & Awards:* Mobay Award & Thomas Midgley Award, Am Chem Soc, 81. *Prof Exp:* Fel catalysis, Mellon Inst, 45-51; assoc scientist, Dow Chem Co, 51-60; sr staff scientist, Sci Lab, Ford Motor Co, 60-84. *Mem:* Nat Acad Eng; Am Chem Soc. *Res:* Catalysis; electrochemistry; plant process design; heat engines. *Mailing Add:* 3904 Golfside Ypsilanti MI 48197

KUMMER, MARTIN, MATHEMATICAL PHYSICS, APPLIED MATHEMATICS. *Current Pos:* from asst prof to assoc prof, 66-75, PROF MATH, UNIV TOLEDO, 75- *Personal Data:* b Glarus, Switz, June 11, 36; m 67, Regula Josi; c Lukas. *Educ:* Swiss Fed Inst Technol, predipl math, 57, dipl math (physics), 59, PhD(math physics), 62. *Prof Exp:* Asst theoret physics, Swiss Fed Inst Technol, 60-64; NSF res assoc, Univ Mich, 64-66. *Concurrent Pos:* Sabbatical leave, Courant Inst, NY Univ, 78; res grant, Swiss Fed Inst Technol, 81, Naval Res Lab, Summer, 87 & 88; vis prof, Univ NMex, 93. *Mem:* Am Phys Soc; Math Asn Am; Int Asn Math Physicists; Am Math Soc. *Res:* Study of linear and nonlinear Hamiltonian systems; in particular, perturbations of integrable systems with applications to celestial and quantum mechanics. *Mailing Add:* 3411 Queenswood Blvd Toledo OH 43606. *Fax:* 419-530-4720; *E-Mail:* mkummer@uoft02.utoledo.edu

KUMMER, W(OLFGANG) H(ELMUT), ELECTRICAL ENGINEERING. *Current Pos:* head res sect, Antenna Dept, 59-66, sr scientist, Antenna Dept, 66-76, CHIEF SCIENTIST, RADAR MICROWAVE LAB, HUGHES AIRCRAFT CO, CULVER CITY, 76- *Personal Data:* b Stuttgart, Ger, Oct 10, 25; nat US; m 56; c 4. *Educ:* Univ Calif, BS, 46, MS, 47, PhD(elec eng), 54. *Prof Exp:* Asst elec eng, Univ Calif, 46-50, lectr, 50-53; mem tech staff, Bell Tel Labs, 53-59. *Concurrent Pos:* Mem comns B & F, Int Sci Radio Union. *Mem:* Fel Inst Elec & Electronics Engrs (pres, Antennas & Propagation Soc, 74). *Res:* Electromagnetic theory; signal processing and electronically scanned antennas and tropospheric propagation beyond the horizon; microwave field; slot radiators in wave-guides. *Mailing Add:* 1310 Sunset Ave Santa Monica CA 90405

KUMMEROW, FRED AUGUST, FOOD SCIENCE. *Current Pos:* assoc prof food chem, 50-59, PROF FOOD CHEM, UNIV ILL, URBANA, 59- *Personal Data:* b Berlin, Ger, Oct 4, 14; nat US; m 42; c 3. *Educ:* Univ Wis, BS, 39, MS, 41, PhD(biochem), 43. *Prof Exp:* Assoc nutritionist, Clemson Col, 43-45; assoc prof chem, Kans State Col, 45-50. *Concurrent Pos:* Mem, Assocs Food & Container Inst, Chicago; mem comn arteriosclerosis, Am Heart Asn. *Mem:* AAAS; Am Chem Soc; Sigma Xi; Fedn Am Socs Exp Biol; Am Soc Microbiol. *Res:* Nutrition; biochemistry; fat and oil chemistry. *Mailing Add:* 205 Burnsides Res Lab Univ Ill Rm 205 1208 W Pennsylvania St Urbana IL 61801-4727. *Fax:* 217-833-3585

KUMMLER, RALPH H, CHEMICAL ENGINEERING, ENVIRONMENTAL ENGINEERING. *Current Pos:* assoc prof, 70-74, CHMN & PROF CHEM ENG, WAYNE STATE UNIV, 74- *Personal Data:* b Jersey City, NJ, Nov 1, 40; m 62; c 3. *Educ:* Rensselaer Polytech Inst, BS, 62; Johns Hopkins Univ, PhD(chem eng), 66. *Prof Exp:* Res chemist, Gen Elec Space Sci Lab, 65-70. *Concurrent Pos:* Consult, Gen Elec Space Sci Lab, 70-74, Phys Dynamics Inc, 70-78, Urban Sci Appl, 77-, KMS Fusion, 77, Urban Consult Inc, 87- & Limnotech, 87-88; mem sci adv bd, Environ Protection Agency, 76-78. *Mem:* Am Inst Chem Engrs; Am Chem Soc; Air & Waste Mgt Asn; Am Inst Chem. *Res:* Chemical kinetics; environmental chemistry and transport including computer simulation of natural and polluted air and aquatic environments; chemiluminescence and hydrocarbon reactivity; hazardous waste management. *Mailing Add:* Dept Chem Eng Wayne State Univ 1100 Eng Bldg Detroit MI 48202-1053

KUMOSINSKI, THOMAS FRANCIS, PHYSICAL CHEMISTRY. *Current Pos:* PHYS CHEMIST BIOCHEM, EASTERN REGIONAL LAB, USDA, 61- *Personal Data:* b Philadelphia, Pa, Apr 19, 41. *Educ:* Drexel Univ, BSc, 64, PhD(phys chem), 73. *Mem:* Am Chem Soc; Sigma Xi. *Res:* Physical chemistry of biological macromolecules; theoretical and experimental quantum chemistry; small angle x-ray and light scattering; general spectroscopy of small molecular weight biological systems, porphyrins, flavins, etc. *Mailing Add:* 4752 Melrose St Philadelphia PA 19137-1111

KUMP, LEE ROBERT, SEDIMENTARY GEOCHEMISTRY, ATMOSPHERIC & OCEANIC EVOLUTION. *Current Pos:* asst prof, 86-91, ASSOC PROF GEOSCI, PA STATE UNIV, 91- *Personal Data:* b Minneapolis, Minn, Apr 3, 59; m 84, Michelle McClung; c Katherine & Sean. *Educ:* Univ Chicago, AB, 81; Univ SFla, PhD(marine sci), 86. *Prof Exp:* Geologist, US Geol Surv, 81-82; res asst, Univ SFla, 81-86. *Concurrent Pos:* Secy gen working group, Int Asn Geochem & Cosmochem. *Mem:* Geol Soc Am; Am Geophys Union; Geochem Soc; Clay Minerals Soc; Am Chem Soc. *Res:* Charges in oceanic and atmospheric composition, and climate, through earth history; numerical models of biogeochemical cycles; clay diagenesis; marine chemistry of trace metals; chemical weathering. *Mailing Add:* Dept Geosci Pa State 210 Deike Bldg University Park PA 16802. *Fax:* 814-865-3191; *E-Mail:* kump@geosc.psu.edu

KUMPEL, PAUL GREMMINGER, TOPOLOGY. *Current Pos:* from asst prof to assoc prof math, 64-84, dir teacher prep, Div Math Sci, 71-74, PROF MATH, STATE UNIV NY, STONY BROOK, 84- *Personal Data:* b Riverside, NJ, Sept 3, 35; div; c 2. *Educ:* Trenton State Col, BS, 56; Brown Univ, PhD(math), 64. *Prof Exp:* Instr math, Lafayette Col, 56-59; asst, Brown Univ, 59-63, instr, 63-64. *Concurrent Pos:* Sci Res Coun sr vis fel, Univ Hull, 71, dir undergrad prog math, 76-82; vis scholar, 78 & assoc chair, Wesleyan Univ, 87. *Mem:* Math Asn Am. *Res:* Topology of H-spaces. *Mailing Add:* Dept Math State Univ NY Stony Brook NY 11794-3651

KUMTA, PRASHANT NAGESH, ELECTRONIC PACKAGING, ELECTROCHEMICAL SYSTEMS. *Current Pos:* ASSOC PROF, CARNEGIE-MELLON UNIV, 90- *Personal Data:* b Madras, India, Aug 17, 60. *Educ:* Indian Inst Technol, BTech, 84; Univ Ariz, MS, 87, PhD(mat sci & eng), 90. *Concurrent Pos:* Summer Fac fel, USAF, 93; res initiation award, NSF, 93. *Mem:* Am Ceramic Soc; Mat Res Soc; Mat Soc; Electrochem Soc. *Res:* Chemical processing and structure property correlation of electronic and optical ceramics, glasses and composites. *Mailing Add:* 4 Bayard Rd No 62 Pittsburgh PA 15213. *Fax:* 412-268-7596; *E-Mail:* kumta@cmu.edu

KUN, ERNEST, BIOCHEMISTRY, PHARMACOLOGY. *Current Pos:* PROF BIOCHEM, ROMBERG CTR ENVIRON STUDIES, 90-; HEAD SCIENTIST, OCTAMER INC, 90- *Personal Data:* b Sopron, Hungary, Oct 22, 19; nat US. *Educ:* Eotvos Lorand Univ, Budapest, MD, 43. *Prof Exp:* Asst physiol, Eotvos Lorand Univ, 39-43, asst prof pharmacol, 44-46; asst, Univ Chicago, 46-47, res assoc, 47-49; asst prof med & pharmacol & lectr biochem, Tulane Univ, 49-53; fel, Inst Enzyme Res, Univ Wis, 53-56; lectr pharmacol, Med Ctr, Univ Calif, San Francisco, 56-60, from assoc prof to prof exp pharmacol, biochem & biophys & exp therapeut, 60-90. *Concurrent Pos:* Estab investr, Am Heart Asn, 56-61. *Mem:* AAAS; Am Chem Soc; Am Soc Pharmacol & Exp Therapeut; Soc Exp Biol & Med; Am Soc Biol Chemists. *Res:* Enzymology of dehydrogenases; enzymes of sulfur metabolism; metabolic regulation studies by F-containing substrate homologs; bioenergetics; molecular mechanisms of growth regulation in eukaryotic cells at the chromatin level (poly adenosine diphosphate R). *Mailing Add:* Ct Environ Studies San Francisco State Univ PO Box 855 Tiburon CA 94920-0855

KUN, KENNETH ALLAN, TECHNICAL PLANNING & IMPLEMENTATION, SHORT & LONG TERM PLANNING & IMPLEMENTATION. *Current Pos:* CONSULT, 92- *Personal Data:* b Brooklyn, NY, July 14, 30; m 55, Carolyn Cohen; c Michael E & Deborah S. *Educ:* Brooklyn Col, BS, 52; Polytech Inst Brooklyn, MS, 55; Yale Univ, MS, 59, PhD(chem), 61. *Prof Exp:* Chemist, US Elec Mfg Co, 52-53, Warner-Chilcott Res Labs, 53-55 & Am Cyanamid Co, 55-57; asst redox polymers, Yale Univ, 57-60; sr res chemist, Rohm & Haas Co, 60-66, Far East regional mgr indust chem, Foreign Opers Div, Tokyo, 66-72, sales/mkt coordr, Latin Am Opers, Int Div, 72-76, mem staff corp hq, 76-78; dir mkt, Specialty Chem Div, Church & Dwight Co Inc, 78-79; dir specialty chem res, Calgon Corp, Div Merck & Co Inc, 79-81; chief tech officer & vpres, Polychrome Corp, Div Dainippon Ink & Chem, 81-83; pres & chief exec officer, Syracuse Res Corp, 83-92. *Concurrent Pos:* Bd dirs, Am Asn Lab Accreditation; grad asst, NIH; mem Am Chamber Com Japan, Chmn, Lic, Patents & Trade Comt; chmn, Syracuse sect, Am Chem Soc; mem bd dirs, Cent NY Technol Develop Orgn; chmn, Econ Develop Comn, Dewitt, NY. *Mem:* AAAS; Am Chem Soc; Sigma Xi; fel Am Inst Chemists; Am Soc Testing & Mat; NY Acad Sci; Soc Chem Indust Eng; Am Mgt Asn. *Res:* Synthesis of monomers and polymers; application of polymers for surface coatings, fibers, redox polymers and ion-exchange resins; structures of porous solids; pharmaceuticals; batteries and dry cells; environmental chemistry; acid deposition; purification systems; technical business management and strategic business planning. *Mailing Add:* 1754 Morgan Lane Collegeville PA 19426. *Fax:* 610-409-9997; *E-Mail:* kenakan@aol.com

KUN, ZOLTAN KOKAI, CRYSTAL GROWTHS OF SOLID STATE MATERIALS. *Current Pos:* CONSULT, CARNEGIE MELLON RES INST, 96- *Personal Data:* b Satoraljaujhely, Hungary, Feb 28, 32; US citizen; m 63, Joan L Kies; c John, Daniel & Zoe. *Educ:* Univ Miskolc, Hungary, Dipl Ing, 54. *Prof Exp:* Metallurgist I, Zenith Radio Corp, 60-77; sr engr, Westinghouse Res & Develop Ctr, 78-82, fel engr, 82-85, adv engr, 85-90, consult scientist, Sci & Technol Ctr, 90-91, consult scientist, Westinghouse Info & Security Systs Div, 91-95. *Mem:* Soc Info Display; Soc Imaging Sci & Technol. *Res:* Electro-optical materials; light emitting diodes in wide bandgap II-VI compounds; high field electroluminescence in thin films; discovery of high output edge emission from thin film electroluminescent devices leading to a light array replacing lasers in electrophotographic printers. *Mailing Add:* 2604 Saybrook Dr Pittsburgh PA 15235

KUNA, SAMUEL, PHARMACOLOGY. *Current Pos:* prof & dir Toxicol Prog, Grad Sch, 80-84, EMER PROF, RUTGERS UNIV, 84- *Personal Data:* b Velke Levare, Czech, May 7, 12; nat US; m 36; c 2. *Educ:* NY Univ, BA, 43, PhD(biol), 56; Temple Univ, MA, 49. *Prof Exp:* Mem, Merck Inst Therapeut Res, 34-43, res asst to dir, 43-50, res assoc & head pharmacol res unit, 50-57; head pharmacol dept, Bristol-Myers Prod Div, Bristol-Myers Co, 57-62, asst dir res & develop, 63-67; dir pharmacol & toxicol, Calgon Consumer Prod Co Div, Merck & Co, 67-74, dir biol res, 74-80. *Concurrent Pos:* Head biol control dept, Merck Inst Therapeut Res, 47-50, 53-56; instr, Temple Univ, 47-50. *Mem:* Am Soc Pharmacol & Exp Therapeut; Soc Toxicol; NY Acad Sci. *Res:* Action of chemical agents on interchange of tissue fluids; analgesics; physiology of the stomach; psychopharmacology; product development. *Mailing Add:* Dept Internal Med Plum Div Univ Tex Med Br Galveston TX 77555-0561. *Fax:* 409-772-9539

KUNAPULI, SATYA P, CARDIOVASCULAR BIOLOGY, MOLECULAR CARDIOLOGY. *Current Pos:* ASST PROF PHYSIOL, THROMBOSIS RES CTR, TEMPLE UNIV, 90- *Personal Data:* b Kakinada, India, Aug 12, 54. *Educ:* Andhra Univ, India, BSc, 75, MSc, 77; Indian Inst Sci, PhD(enzymol), 84. *Prof Exp:* Fel molecular biol, Univ Tex Med Br, Galveston, 84-85, instr physiol, 86-88; scientist, Astra Res Ctr, Bangalore India, 88-90. *Mem:* Am Soc Biochem & Molecular Biol; Am Soc Cell Biol. *Res:* Cardiovascular biology; molecular cardiology. *Mailing Add:* Thrombosis Res Ctr Temple Univ 3400 N Broad Philadelphia PA 19140-5104. *Fax:* 215-707-4003

KUNASZ, IHOR ANDREW, ECONOMIC GEOLOGY. *Current Pos:* Staff geologist, Foote Mineral Co, 70-72, chief geologist, 72-88, gen mgr, Cyprus Minera Chile, 88-90, mgr bus develop, Cyprus Minerals Co, 90-93, DIR PROJ DEVELOP, CYPRUS FOOTE MINERAL CO, 93- *Personal Data:* b Montlucon, France, Sept 24, 39; US citizen; m 65, Zenovia Tarczanyn; c Markian & Marta. *Educ:* Case Western Res Univ, BA, 63; Pa State Univ, MS, 68, PhD(geol), 70. *Concurrent Pos:* Chmn, Indust Minerals Div, Soc Mining Eng, Am Inst Mining Eng, 87, bd mem, 89-; consult, 90- *Mem:* Soc Mining Eng, Am Inst Mining Eng; Geol Soc Am; Geochem Soc; Shevchenko Sci Soc. *Res:* Economic and exploration geology associated with industrial minerals, especially saline deposits and lithium deposits of the world, precious metals and non-ferrous metals development; project development in the CIS. *Mailing Add:* 973 Maykut Ave Collegeville PA 19426. *Fax:* 215-889-0246

KUNAU, ROBERT, JR, EXPERIMENTAL BIOLOGY. *Current Pos:* PVT PRACT NEPHROLOGY, 89- *Mailing Add:* Dallas Nephrology 7777 Forest Lane Suite B-245 Dallas TX 75230-2509

KUNC, JOSEPH ANTHONY, NON-EQUILIBRIUM PHENOMENA IN HIGH-TEMPERATURE GASES, MOLECULAR INTERACTIONS. *Current Pos:* res assoc prof, Dept Aerospace Eng & Dept Physics, 80-85, assoc prof, 85-89, PROF, DEPT AEROSPACE ENG & DEPT PHYSICS, UNIV SOUTHERN CALIF, LOS ANGELES, 90- *Personal Data:* b Baranowicze, Poland, Nov 1, 43; US citizen; m 79, Mary Smolska; c Robert. *Educ:* Warsaw Tech Univ, MS, 70, PhD(plasma sci), 74. *Prof Exp:* Assoc prof, Warsaw Tech Univ, 74-78. *Concurrent Pos:* Vis scholar, Atomic & Plasma Radiation Div, Nat Bur Stand, 79, Dept High-Temp Plasma, Nat Inst Nuclear Studies, Warsaw, Poland, 91, Inst Theoret Atomic & Molecular Physics, Harvard Univ, Cambridge, 91; res affil, Jet Propulsion Lab, Calif Inst Technol, Pasadena, 82-83; prin investr numerous grants, 83-; consult, Nat Tech Systs, Los Angeles, 84-86, Phys Optics Corp, 88- & B P Wolfsdorf & Assocs, 91; mem, Comt Arcs & Flames, Nat Res Coun 85-86; Harvard/Smithsonian fel, 91; mem, Thermophys Comt, Am Inst Aeronaut & Astronaut; chmn, Thermophysics Publ Comt, Am Inst Aeronaut & Astronaut, 95-97. *Mem:* Fel Am Phys Soc; assoc fel Am Inst Aeronaut & Astronaut; sr mem Inst Elec & Electronics Engrs. *Res:* General nonlinear collisional-radiative models of non-equilibrium in partially-ionized plasmas; atomic and molecular interactions with transfer of electronic, rotational and vibrational energy; kinetic processes in supersonic and hypersonic flows, thyratrons, high-power light sources. *Mailing Add:* 2017 Summerland Rancho Palos Verdes CA 90275. *E-Mail:* kunc@spock.usc.edu

KUNCE, HENRY WARREN, COMPUTER SIMULATION, HUMAN-SOCIAL RELATIONS. *Current Pos:* CHIEF SCI OFFICER, SOCIOCYBERNETICS INC, 95- *Personal Data:* b St Louis, Mo, Apr 18, 25; m 48, Avon Estes; c Catherine, Nancy, Christopher, Cynthia & James. *Educ:* Washington Univ, BA, 46; McCormick Theol Sem, Chicago, BD & MDiv, 49; Univ Miami, MSIE, 71, PhD(statist), 79. *Prof Exp:* Clergyman, Ohio & Mo, 49-61; planner-analyst parish develop, Bd Missions, United Presby Church, Mo & Fla, 61-70; systs analyst, Clin Campesina, Homestead, Fla, 70-71; res scientist sociocybernet, Univ Miami, 71-72; chief mgr syst eng, Mgt Info Systs & Opers Res, Metro Dade Co Govt, Fla, 72-95. *Concurrent Pos:* Adj math fac, Univ Miami, Coral Gables, Fla, 80-; pres, Sociocybernet, Inc, South Miami, Fla. *Mem:* Opers Res Soc Am; Am Inst Indust Engrs; Inst Mgt Sci; Soc Comput Simulation; AAAS; Sigma Xi. *Res:* Sociocybernetics, the application of cybernetics to the dynamics of human interaction and social structures, using systems analysis and computer simulation of stochastic and deterministic mathematical models, a discrete system, finite state automata, and a continuous model analyzed by phase space analysis; applications made in management; counseling education; personnel problems. *Mailing Add:* 5025 SW 74th Terr Miami FL 33143. *E-Mail:* kunce@ibm.net

KUNDEL, HAROLD LOUIS, RADIOLOGY. *Current Pos:* WILSON PROF RES RADIOL, UNIV PA, 80- *Personal Data:* b New York, NY, Aug 15, 33; m 58, Alice M Pape; c 3. *Educ:* Columbia Univ, AB, 55, MD, 59; Temple Univ, MS, 63. *Hon Degrees:* MA, Univ Pa, 80. *Honors & Awards:* Mem

Award, Asn Univ Radiologists, 63, Stauffer Award, 82. *Prof Exp:* Intern med, Mary Imogene Bassett Hosp, Cooperstown, NY, 59-60; resident radiol, Temple Univ Hosp, 60-63; resident radiobiol, Sch Aerospace Med, 63-64; James Picker Found advan acad fel physiol, Sch Med, Temple Univ, 64-66, attend radiologist, Univ Hosp, 66-80, prof radiol, 68-80. *Concurrent Pos:* Attend radiologist, Hosp Univ Pa, 80- *Mem:* AAAS; Am Col Radiol; Asn Univ Radiologists. *Res:* Image information processing and analysis; visual perception; diagnostic decision making. *Mailing Add:* Dept Radiol Hosp Univ Pa Philadelphia PA 19104

KUNDELL, FREDRICK AUSTIN, POLYMERIZATION OF VEGETABLE OIL. *Current Pos:* assoc dean col, 72-76, chair, Dept Chem, 80-96, PROF CHEM, SALISBURY STATE UNIV, 70- *Personal Data:* b Pulaski, NY, Oct 20, 40; m, Karen Gabrys; c 3. *Educ:* Univ Md, PhD(phys chem), 66. *Prof Exp:* Sci specialist, US House Reps, 78. *Mem:* Am Chem Soc. *Res:* Develop polymerization processes for corn and soybean oil. *Mailing Add:* 21506 Wetipquin Rd Tyaskin MD 21865. *Fax:* 410-548-3318; *E-Mail:* fakundell@ssu.edu

KUNDERT, ESAYAS G, ALGEBRA. *Current Pos:* prof, 62-82, EMER PROF MATH, UNIV MASS, AMHERST, 82- *Personal Data:* b Ruti, Switz, May 7, 18; US citizen; m 54; c Berta (Garafalo), Antony & Diana (Blackburn). *Educ:* Swiss Fed Inst Technol, dipl, 45, Dr Math, 50. *Prof Exp:* Asst prof math, Univ Tenn, 50-51; from asst prof to prof, La State Univ, 51-62. *Concurrent Pos:* US Army grant, 52-53. *Res:* Algebraic geometry and algebraic topology; elementary number theory. *Mailing Add:* 19 Van Meter Dr Amherst MA 01002

KUNDIG, WERNER, BIOLOGY. *Current Pos:* EMER PROF BIOL, HOOD COL, FREDERICK, MD, 88- *Personal Data:* b 1931. *Mailing Add:* PO Box 247 Eastsound WA 98245-0241

KUNDSIN, RUTH BLUMFELD, MEDICAL MICROBIOLOGY. *Current Pos:* res assoc, 61-76, ASSOC PROF MICROBIOL & MOLECULAR GENETICS, HARVARD SCH MED, 76-; PRES, KUNDSIN LAB INC, 81- *Personal Data:* b New York, NY, July 30, 16; m 35, Edwin; c Andrea K (Dupree) & Dennis E. *Educ:* Hunter Col, BA, 36; Boston Univ, MA, 49; Harvard Univ, ScD(microbiol), 58. *Hon Degrees:* ScD, Univ Mass, 75. *Prof Exp:* Res bacteriologist, Sch Pub Health, Harvard Univ, 36-37 & Sch Med, Univ Pa, 37-38; res bacteriologist, Peter Bent Brigham Hosp, 51-58, asst surg, 58-64, mem assoc staff, 64-70; epidemiologist, Brigham & Women's Hosp, Boston, Mass, 70- *Mem:* AAAS; Am Soc Microbiol; fel NY Acad Sci; Int Org Mycoplasmology; Am Acad Microbiol. *Res:* Dynamics of disinfection as applied to environmental bacteriology; sanitary bacteriology; maintenance of standards for a hygienic environment; epidemiology of staphylococcal disease; skin disinfection; mycoplasmas and reproductive failure in humans; chlamydia infections. *Mailing Add:* Brigham & Women's Hosp 75 Francis St Boston MA 02115. *E-Mail:* rbkundsin@bics.bwh.harvard.edu

KUNDT, JOHN FRED, DENDROLOGY, FORESTRY EDUCATION. *Current Pos:* RETIRED. *Personal Data:* b Denver, Colo, Dec 21, 26; m 48; c 2. *Educ:* WVa Univ, BS, 52; NC State Univ, PhD(forestry), 72. *Prof Exp:* Mgt chief, Forest Mgt Serv, Div Forestry, Va, 52-57; forest supvr prod, Union Camp Paper Corp, 57-64; fel dendrol, NC State Univ, 64-69; asst prof bot, genetics & plant taxon, State Univ NY, 69-73; assoc prof & exten forestry specialist, Univ Md, 74-88. *Mem:* Soc Am Foresters. *Res:* Effects of adding composted sewage sludge to newly planted Pinus Taeda and Pinus Virginiana; developing pine hybrids between Pinus Taeda and Pinus Rigida by selecting superior parental phenotypes, and producing experimental seed orchard; developing a Pinus Virginiana seed orchard to produce seed for Christmas tree production; development of Paulownia tomentosa in plantations, initial establishment and cold hardiness development. *Mailing Add:* 103 Fox Run Laurel DE 19956

KUNDU, MUKUL RANJAN, RADIOPHYSICS, ELECTRONICS. *Current Pos:* actg dir astron, 78-79, dir astron, 80-85, PROF PHYSICS & ASTRON, UNIV MD, COLLEGE PARK, 68- *Personal Data:* b Calcutta, India, Feb 10, 30; m 58, Ranu Paul; c Krishna, Rina & Sanjit. *Educ:* Univ Calcutta, BSc, 49, MSc, 51; Univ, Paris, DSc, 57. *Honors & Awards:* Sr US Scientist Award, Alexander von Humboldt Found, 78. *Prof Exp:* Asst, Coun Sci & Indust Res, Univ Calcutta, 52-54, vis SK Mitra distinguished prof, 93; French Govt scholar radio astron, Ecole Normale Superieure & Meudon Observ, 54-56; asst, Nat Ctr Sci Res, Ministry Educ, France & Meudon Observ, 56-58; jr res fel, Nat Phys Lab, India, 58-59; res assoc solar radio astron, Observ, Univ Mich, 59-62; assoc prof astron, Cornell Univ, 62-65 & Tata Inst Fundamental Res, Bombay, 65-68. *Concurrent Pos:* Sr res assoc, Nat Acad Sci-Nat Res Coun, 67, 74-75 & 86-87; vis prof, Nat Astron Observ, Japan, 93 & Inst Space Astronaut Studies, Japan, 94. *Mem:* Int Astron Union; sr mem Inst Elec & Electronics Engrs; Am Astron Soc; Int Radio Sci Union; fel Royal Astron Soc; fel Am Phys Soc; Am Geophys Union. *Res:* Solar, stellar and galactic radio astronomy. *Mailing Add:* Astron Dept Space Sci Bldg Univ Md College Park MD 20742. *Fax:* 301-314-9067; *E-Mail:* kundu@antso.umd.edu

KUNDU, SAMAR K, EXPERIMENTAL BIOLOGY. *Current Pos:* SR SCIENTIST, DIAG DEPT, ABBOTT LABS, 83- *Mailing Add:* Dept 9D3 Bldg R1B/5 Abbott Labs North Chicago IL 60064. *Fax:* 847-937-1219

KUNELIUS, HEIKKI TAPANI, PLANT SCIENCE, FORAGE MANAGEMENT. *Current Pos:* head, Forage-Beef Sect, 85-91, asst dir, 91-93, RES SCIENTIST PLANT SCI, RES BR, AGR CAN, 70- *Personal Data:* b Konginkangas, Finland, Mar 21, 40; Can citizen; m 71; c 2. *Educ:* Univ Helsinki, BSA & MSc, 66; Univ Man, PhD(plant sci), 70. *Prof Exp:* Res asst plant path, Agr Res Ctr, 66. *Concurrent Pos:* Fel plant sci, Univ Man, 70; study leave, NZ-Australia, 79-80; mem, Expert Comt, Forage Breeding, Can, 79- *Mem:* Fel Can Soc Agron; Am Soc Agron; Agr Inst Can; Finnish Asn Agr Grad; Swed Seed Asn. *Res:* Physiology and management of forage grasses and legumes; pasture management; minimum tillage for pasture renovation. *Mailing Add:* Agr Can Res Sta PO Box 1210 Charlottetown PE C1A 7M8 Can. *Fax:* 902-566-6821

KUNESH, CHARLES JOSEPH, FINE PARTICLE TECHNOLOGY, PAPER SCIENCE. *Current Pos:* DIR RES, MINERALS TECHNOL, INC, 92- *Personal Data:* b Greensburg, Pa, Oct 18, 48; m 74; c 2. *Educ:* Carnegie-Mellon Univ, BS, 70; Univ Pittsburgh, PhD(phys chem), 73. *Prof Exp:* Res chemist, Pfizer Inc, 73-77, sr res chemist, 77-80, sr res scientist, 80-82, res mgr, 82-88, dir res, 88-92. *Mem:* Am Chem Soc; Tech Asn Pulp & Paper Indust; Mat Res Soc. *Res:* Synthesis and crystal engineering of fine particle inorganic materials, especially precipitated calcium carbonate; application of inorganic fine particles in filled and-or coated paper and in polymer composites. *Mailing Add:* 3305 Altonah Rd Bethlehem PA 18017-1846. *Fax:* 610-861-3412; *E-Mail:* ckunesh@aol.com

KUNESH, JERRY PAUL, CLINICAL PHARMACOLOGY, MEDICINE. *Current Pos:* Instr vet med & surg, 61-62, NIH fel physiol, 64-65, asst prof physiol & pharmacol, 65-70, assoc prof pharmacol & med, 70-75, PROF VET MED & SURG, IOWA STATE UNIV, 75- *Personal Data:* b Kewaunee, Wis, Jan 19, 38; m 61; c 3. *Educ:* Iowa State Univ, DVM, 61, MS, 66, PhD(physiol), 69. *Mem:* Am Asn Swine Practitioners; Am Asn Bovine Practitioners; Am Vet Med Asn. *Res:* Porcine hemorrhagic syndromes and clinical evaluation of antimicrobial agents as well as their mechanisms of action. *Mailing Add:* 2034 Jensen Ave Ames IA 50010

KUNG, CHING, GENETICS, NEUROBIOLOGY. *Current Pos:* assoc prof, 74-77, Hilldale prof, 90, PROF MOLECULAR BIOL & GENETICS, UNIV WIS-MADISON, 77- *Personal Data:* b Kwang Tung, China, Apr 28, 39; US citizen; m; c 3. *Educ:* Chung Chi Col, Chinese Univ Hong Kong, dipl, 63; Univ Pa, PhD(biol), 68. *Prof Exp:* Fel genetics, Ind Univ, Bloomington, 68-70; fel electrophysiol, Univ Calif, Los Angeles, 70-71; from asst prof to assoc prof molecular biol, Univ Calif, Santa Barbara, 71-74. *Mem:* AAAS; Genetic Soc Am; Am Soc Cell Biol. *Res:* Genetic dissection of sensory transductions in microbes; ion channels of paramecium, yeast, and e coli. *Mailing Add:* 305 Molecular Biol Univ Wis 1525 Linden Dr Madison WI 53706-1596

KUNG, ERNEST CHEN-TSUN, METEOROLOGY. *Current Pos:* assoc prof, 67-70, PROF ATMOSPHERIC SCI, UNIV MO, COLUMBIA, 70-, DEPT CHMN SOIL & ATMOSPHERIC SCIS, 93- *Personal Data:* b Ping-tung, Taiwan, China, Jan 1, 31; m 59, Susan Hwang; c Felicia, Denise & David. *Educ:* Nat Univ Taiwan, BS, 53; Univ Ariz, MS, 59; Univ Wis, PhD(meteorol), 63. *Honors & Awards:* Res Award, Sigma Xi, 83. *Prof Exp:* Specialist agron, Taiwan Prov Govt, 54-58; proj assoc meteorol, Univ Wis, 63; res meteorologist, Geophys Fluid Dynamics Lab, Environ Sci Serv Admin, 63-67. *Concurrent Pos:* NSF grants, 67-69, 70-75, 76-88; pres grad fac senate, Univ Mo-Columbia, 77-78; Nat Oceanic & Atmospheric Admin grant, 83-88; Nat Ctr Atmospheric Sci, 92-94; US Dept Interior, 94-99. *Mem:* Fel Am Meteorol Soc; fel Royal Meteorol Soc; Meteorol Soc Japan; Sigma Xi. *Res:* Atmospheric general circulation; long-range forecasting; dynamic climatology. *Mailing Add:* Atmospheric Sci Prog Univ Mo Columbia MO 65211. *Fax:* 573-884-5333

KUNG, HAROLD HING CHUEN, CATALYSIS, KINETICS. *Current Pos:* from asst prof to assoc prof, 76-84, chmn, 86-92, PROF CHEM ENG, NORTHWESTERN UNIV, 84-, DIR, CTR CATALYSIS & SURFACE SCI, 93- *Personal Data:* b Hong Kong, Oct 12, 49; m 71. *Educ:* Univ Wis-Madison, BS, 71; Northwestern Univ, MS, 72, PhD(chem), 74. *Honors & Awards:* P H Emmett Award, Catalysis Soc, 91; Henske Lectr, Yale Univ, 86. *Prof Exp:* Res chemist, E I du Pont de Nemours & Co, Inc, 74-76. *Concurrent Pos:* Fel, Japanese Soc Promoton Sci, 94. *Mem:* Am Chem Soc; Am Inst Chem Engrs; Catalysis Soc. *Res:* Surface chemistry and physics; catalysis; chemical reaction engineering. *Mailing Add:* Dept Chem Eng Northwestern Univ Evanston IL 60208. *Fax:* 847-467-1018; *E-Mail:* hkung@nwu.edu

KUNG, HSIANG-FU, BIOCHEMICAL PHYSIOLOGY. *Current Pos:* CHIEF, LAB BIOCHEM PHYSIOL, NAT CANCER INST, DCT, BIOL RESPONSE MODIFIERS PROG, NIH, 86- *Personal Data:* b Chungking, China, Sept 4, 42; US citizen; m; c 2. *Educ:* Nat Chung-hsing Univ, BS, 63; Vanderbilt Univ, PhD, 66. *Prof Exp:* Fel, Lab Biochem, Sect Enzymes, NIH, 69-70; sci asst, Max-Planck Inst Biol, 70-71; res fel, Dept Biochem, Roche Inst Molecular Biol, 71-73, asst mem, 73-80, res fel, 81-82, res leader, Dept Molecular Genetics, Res Div, Hoffman-La Roche Inc, 80-81, sr res fel, 82-86. *Concurrent Pos:* Vis asst prof, Dept Biochem, Col Med & Dent NJ, 71-73 & 73-76; adj prof, Dept Zool & Physiol, Rutgers State Univ, 76-78. *Mem:* Fedn Am Socs Exp Biol; AAAS. *Res:* Biochemical physiology. *Mailing Add:* Nat Cancer Inst Lab Biochem Physiol Frederick Cancer Res Facil Bldg 567 Rm 152 Frederick MD 21702-1201. *Fax:* 301-846-6863

KUNG, HSIANG-TSUNG, COMPUTER ARCHITECTURE & NETWORKS, PARALLEL COMPUTATION. *Current Pos:* GORDON MCKAY PROF ELEC ENG & COMPUT SCI, HARVARD UNIV, 92- *Personal Data:* b Shanghai, China, Nov 9, 45; m 70, Ling-Ling Chang; c 2. *Educ:* Nat Tsing Hua Univ, BS, 68; Univ NMex, MA, 70; Carnegie Mellon Univ, PhD(math), 74. *Prof Exp:* Res assoc, Carnegie Mellon Univ, 73-74, from asst prof to prof comput sci, 74-92. *Concurrent Pos:* Archit consult, ESL, Inc, 82; Guggenheim fel, 83-84. *Mem:* Nat Acad Eng; Inst Elec & Electronics Engrs; Asn Comput Mach. *Res:* Computer algorithms; computational complexity; parallel computation; multiprocessors; very large scale integration; numerical analysis; computer architectures; supercomputers; computer and telecommunications networks. *Mailing Add:* Div Eng & Appl Sci Harvard Univ 29 Oxford St Pierce Hall 110 Cambridge MA 02138

KUNG, PATRICK C, EXPERIMENTAL BIOLOGY. *Current Pos:* VCHMN BD & CHIEF SCI OFFICER, T CELL SCI INC, 89- *Mailing Add:* T Cell Sci Inc 119 Fourth Ave Needham MA 02194-2725

KUNG, SHAIN-DOW, MOLECULAR BIOLOGY. *Current Pos:* RETIRED. *Personal Data:* b Lini, China, Mar 14, 35; US citizen; m 64; c 3. *Educ:* Chung Hsing Univ, Taiwan, BSc, 58; Univ Guelph, MSc, 65; Univ Toronto, PhD(bot), 68. *Honors & Awards:* Philip Morris Award, 79. *Prof Exp:* Instr bot, Chung Hsing Univ, Taiwan, 58-62; res assoc biochem, Univ Toronto, 68-71 & biol, Univ Calif, Los Angeles, 71-74; from asst prof to assoc prof, 74-82, actg chmn, 82-84, prof biol, 82-86, assoc dean, Univ Md, Baltimore County, 85-87; actg dir, Ctr Agr Biotechnol, Univ Md, College Park, 86-93, dir, 88-93. *Concurrent Pos:* Fulbright Award, 83. *Mem:* AAAS; Am Soc Plant Physiologists. *Res:* Biochemistry and genetics of chloroplast protein; properties, function and evolution of chloroplast DNA; molecular biology of genetic tumors. *Mailing Add:* 14713 Harvest Lane Silver Spring MD 20905

KUNG, SILAS, MAGNETIC SENSING TECHNOLOGY FOR INDUSTRIAL & BIOMEDICAL IMAGING APPLICATIONS, INTEGRATION OF WIRELESS NETWORKS WITH FIBER OPTIC NETWORKS. *Current Pos:* CHIEF SCIENTIST, ITRON INC, 95- *Personal Data:* b Hong Kong, Nov 11, 48. *Educ:* Lanchow Univ, BSc, 67, MSc, 68; Columbia State Univ, PhD(appl physics & elec eng), 97. *Hon Degrees:* PhD, Dalian Inst Geront, 88. *Prof Exp:* Opers mgr, Carter Semiconductor Inc, 70-71; asst pres, Bowmar Instrument Corp, 72-76; supt, Fairchild Corp, 66-68, sr eng mgr, 76-82; pres, AIMS Inc, 82-84; group mgr, Unisys Corp, 85-88, sr prin consult, 88-89; prog mgr, Compaq Comput Corp, 89-90; dir photonic device res, develop & mfg, PCO Corp, 90-91; chief consult, SPI Inc, 92-94. *Concurrent Pos:* Mem, Pvt Indust Coun, City Sunnyvale, Calif, 84-85; emer prof physics, Dalian Inst Geront, 88; potential staff, Superconductive Super Collider Lab, Tex, 91; vis scientist, Biomed Imaging Resource Lab, Mayo Clin, 95-96. *Mem:* Inst Elec & Electronics Engrs. *Res:* Indium phosphide/silicon, giant magnetresistive/indium phosphide/silicon and high temperature superconductor/silicon materials systems and processing technologies to build low cost intelligent fiber optic links and low cost intelligent wireless to fiber optic links; superconductive quantum interference device based biomag physiological imaging system for non-invasive diagnostics for heart, brain and other organs preventive health care. *Mailing Add:* 712 First St N Waterville MN 56096-1042. *Fax:* 507-362-8090

KUNG, TED TESHIH, ALLERGY, INFLAMMATION. *Current Pos:* assoc scientist, Schering Corp, 71-75, sr res scientist, 79-89, PRIN RES SCIENTIST, SCHERING-PLOUGH RES INST, 90- *Personal Data:* b Beijing, China, Jan 17, 36; US citizen; m, Christina Y Peng; c Victor H & Cary W. *Educ:* Nat Taiwan Univ, BS, 57; Fairleigh Dickinson Univ, MS, 68; NY Univ, PhD(biol), 78. *Prof Exp:* Instr genetics, Nat Taiwan Univ, 62-64; asst scientist, NY Univ Med Ctr, 68-71. *Concurrent Pos:* Lectr human anat & physiol, Bloomfield Col, 84-90; adj assoc prof endocrinol, Fairleigh Dickenson Univ, 89-90; adj prof human anat & physiol, Kean Col, NJ, 90- *Mem:* Soc Invest Dermat; Inflammation Res Asn; NY Acad Sci; Soc Leukocyte Biol; Am Thoracic Soc. *Res:* Pulmonary inflammation in allergic mice or other rodents; effects of various cytokines on the pathogenesis of eosinophilia; involvement of mast cells in the development of eosinophilia in allergic mice. *Mailing Add:* Schering Plough Res Inst Kenilworth NJ 07033-0539

KUNHARDT, ERICH ENRIQUE, ELECTROKINETICS, COMPUTATIONAL PHYSICS & TRANSPORT PHENOMENA. *Current Pos:* GEORGE MEADE BOND PROF PHYSICS & ENG PHYSICS, STEVENS INST TECHNOL, 96- *Personal Data:* b Montecristy, Dominican Rep, May 31, 49; m 76, Christine Koza. *Educ:* NY Univ, BS, 69, MS, 72; Polytechnic Univ, PhD(electrophys), 76. *Hon Degrees:* ME, Stevens Inst Technol, 96. *Honors & Awards:* Halliburton Found Award, 83. *Prof Exp:* From asst prof to prof elec eng & physics, Tex Tech Univ, 76-85; prof electrophysics, Polytech Univ, 85-92, dir, Weber Res Inst, 86-96. *Concurrent Pos:* Consult, Los Alamos Nat Lab, 79-87, GTE Labs, 82-85 & Lawrence Livermore Labs, 88-91; adv bd, Transport Theory & Statist J, 82- *Mem:* Am Phys Soc; Sigma Xi; Inst Elec & Electronics Engrs. *Res:* Experimental, theoretical and computational investigations of the non-equilibrium behavior of quantum and classical electron assemblies in matter under the influence of place-time varying electric and magnetic fields. *Mailing Add:* Physics Dept Stevens Inst Technol Hoboken NJ 07030. *Fax:* 201-216-5638; *E-Mail:* ekunhard@stevens-tech.edu

KUNIN, ARTHUR SAUL, MEDICINE, PHYSIOLOGICAL CHEMISTRY. *Current Pos:* from instr to assoc prof, 57-82, PROF, COL MED, UNIV VT, 82- *Personal Data:* b Brooklyn, NY, Aug 11, 25; m 59; c 4. *Educ:* Columbia Univ, BA, 48; Univ Vt, MD, 52. *Prof Exp:* Intern med, Peter Bent Brigham Hosp, Boston, Mass, 52-54, jr asst resident, 53-54, sr asst resident, 56-57; NIH fel, Med Sch, Boston Univ, 54-56. *Concurrent Pos:* Lederle Med fac award, Col Med, Univ Vt, 65-68; NIH spec fel, Mass Gen Hosp & Harvard Med Sch, 62-64; Am Col Physicians Willard Thompson traveling scholar, Univ Col Hosp Med Sch, London, 64; vis prof, Inst Chem Med, Univ Bern, 70-71; fel Dept Physiol, Harvard Med Sch, 78-79. *Mem:* Am Col Physicians; Am Fedn Clin Res. *Res:* Renal physiology; mitochondrial metabolism; nutrition in renal disease; nephrology; diseases of metabolism; metabolic bone diseases and the intermediary metabolism of epiphyseal cartilage. *Mailing Add:* 7 Windmill Bay Rd Shelburne VT 05482

KUNIN, CALVIN MURRY, INTERNAL MEDICINE, INFECTIOUS DISEASE. *Current Pos:* prof & chmn dept, 79-84, POMERENE PROF MED, COL MED, OHIO STATE UNIV, 83- *Personal Data:* b Burlington, Vt, May 3, 29; m 76, Ilene Jacobson; c 3. *Educ:* Columbia Univ, AB, 49; Cornell Univ, MD, 53. *Prof Exp:* Intern med, New York Hosp, 53-54; sr asst surg, USPHS, 54-56; asst resident, Peter Bent Brigham Hosp, Boston, 56-57; res fel, Harvard Med Sch, 57-59; from asst prof to assoc prof med & prev med, Sch Med, Univ Va, 59-70; prof med & assoc chmn dept, Univ Wis-Madison, 70-79; chief med, Vet Admin Hosp, 70-70. *Mem:* Am Fedn Clin Res; Am Asn Immunologists; Am Assoc Physicians; Am Soc Clin Invest; Soc Exp Biol & Med; fel Infectious Dis Soc Am (past pres). *Res:* Epidemiology; antibiotic therapy; urinary tract infections. *Mailing Add:* Dept Med Ohio State Univ 410 W Tenth Ave Columbus OH 43210

KUNIN, ROBERT, PHYSICAL CHEMISTRY. *Current Pos:* CONSULT, 76- *Personal Data:* b West New York, NJ, July 16, 18; m 42; c 2. *Educ:* Rutgers Univ, BS, 39, PhD(colloidal chem), 42. *Honors & Awards:* Franklin Inst Gold Medal, 66. *Prof Exp:* Assoc chemist, Tenn Valley Authority, 42-44; sr chemist, Manhattan Proj, Columbia Univ, 44-45; Gulf fel, Mellon Inst, 45-46; lab head chg res & develop ion exchange resins, 46-59, res assoc, 59-70, sr staff assoc, Rohm & Haas Co, 70-76. *Concurrent Pos:* Lectr, Univ Pa & Am Univ. *Mem:* AAAS; Am Chem Soc; Am Inst Chem Engrs; Electrochem Soc; Israel Chem Soc; Sigma Xi. *Res:* Desalination; adsorption; liquid extraction; theory and application of ion exchange; inorganic chemistry of phosphates, uranium fluorides; analytical chemistry of inorganic constituents; ion exchange in silicates; electrochemistry of membrane processes; catalysis; water treatment and purification. *Mailing Add:* 860 Lower Ferry Rd No 2J Trenton NJ 08628

KUNISHI, HARRY MIKIO, SOIL CHEMISTRY. *Current Pos:* RETIRED. *Personal Data:* b Honolulu, Hawaii, Aug 30, 32; m 59. *Educ:* Univ Hawaii, BS, 55, MS, 56; Univ Wash, BS, 58; Univ Wis, PhD(soils), 63. *Prof Exp:* Soil scientist, Agr Res Serv, USDA, 62-90. *Mem:* Int Soc Soil Sci; Am Soc Agron; Am Chem Soc; Sigma Xi. *Res:* Chemistry and mineralogy of potassium in soils; adsorption and movement of radionuclides in soils; phosphate reactions in field and streams; rates of phosphate supplied to plants by acid soils of southeastern United States; phosphorus management under no-tillage; model of phosphorus transport from agricultural fields; soil-water-plant-phosphorus reactions in fresh water and brackish water systems. *Mailing Add:* 2288 W Valley Westminster MD 21158

KUNISI, VENKATASUBBAN S, ORGANIC CHEMISTRY. *Current Pos:* from asst prof to assoc prof, 81-89, PROF CHEM, UNIV NFLA, 89-, CHAIR, 94- *Personal Data:* b Kottayam, India; m 74, Saraswathi; c Sharmila & Satish. *Educ:* Univ Madras, India, BSc, MSc; Univ Kans, PhD(chem), 75. *Prof Exp:* Fel, Emory Univ, 74-76; lectr, Tex A&M Univ, 76-79; assoc pharmacol, Univ Fla, 79-80. *Mem:* Am Chem Soc. *Res:* Bio-organic mechanisms; chemical and enzyme catalysis; organic reaction mechanisms; solution kinetics; istope effects; nuclear magnetic resonance studies of drugs using shift reagents. *Mailing Add:* Dept Natural Sci Bldg 3 Rm 2203 Univ NFla Jacksonville FL 32216

KUNKEE, RALPH EDWARD, MICROBIOLOGY, ENOLOGY. *Current Pos:* asst res biochemist, 60-63, prof enol, 63-91, EMER PROF ENOL, UNIV CALIF, DAVIS, 91- *Personal Data:* b San Fernando, Calif, July 30, 27. *Educ:* Univ Calif, AB, 50, PhD(biochem), 55. *Prof Exp:* Asst biochemist, Univ Calif, 50-53; res biochemist, E I du Pont de Nemours & Co, 55-60. *Concurrent Pos:* Fulbright fel, Ger, 70-71; France fel, Montpellier, 77-78; consult, UN Food & Agr Orgn, Bangalore, India, 96. *Mem:* Fel AAAS; Am Soc Microbiol; Am Soc Enol (secy-treas, 81-83). *Res:* Intermediary metabolism and control; fermentation; microbiology. *Mailing Add:* Dept Viticult & Enol Wickson Hall Univ Calif Davis CA 95616. *Fax:* 530-752-0382; *E-Mail:* rekunkee@ucdavis.edu

KUNKEL, BARBARA NICOLE, PLANT DISEASE RESISTANCE, BACTERIAL PATHOGENICITY. *Current Pos:* ASST PROF BIOL, WASHINGTON UNIV, 94- *Personal Data:* b Berkeley, Calif, Dec 26, 62. *Educ:* Univ Calif, Davis, BS, 84; Harvard Univ, PhD(molecular genetics), 90. *Prof Exp:* Postdoctoral fel, Univ Calif, Berkeley, 90-94. *Concurrent Pos:* Life sci res fel, 90-93; Am Chem Soc postdoctoral fel, 93-94; Searle scholar, 96-; Packard fel, 96- *Mailing Add:* 1 Brookings Dr St Louis MO 63130. *E-Mail:* kunkel@biodec.wnstl.edu

KUNKEL, HARRIOTT ORREN, NUTRITION, PHILOSOPHY OF AGRICULTURAL SCIENCE. *Current Pos:* from asst prof to assoc prof animal sci & biochem, Tex A&M Univ, 51-57, assoc dir, Tex Agr Exp Sta, 62-68, dean, Col Agr & actg dir, Tex Agr Exp Sta, 68-72, dean agr, 72-88, PROF ANIMAL SCI BIOCHEM & BIOPHYS, TEX A&M UNIV, 57-, EMER DEAN AGR & LIFE SCI, 91- *Personal Data:* b Olney, Tex, July 3, 22; m 60, Beverly Davies; c 2. *Educ:* Tex A&M Univ, BS, 43, MS, 48; Cornell Univ,

PhD(biochem), 50. *Prof Exp:* Instr biochem, Univ Wis, 50-51. *Mem:* Am Chem Soc; Am Soc Animal Sci; Am Soc Biochem & Molecular Biol; Am Inst Nutrit; Soc Exp Biol & Med. *Res:* Science administration; philosophy of agricultural science; theory of higher education in agriculture and life sciences. *Mailing Add:* Dept Animal Sci Tex A&M Univ 100 Kleberg Ctr College Station TX 77843-2471. *Fax:* 409-845-6433

KUNKEL, JOSEPH GEORGE, DEVELOPMENTAL BIOLOGY, INSECT PHYSIOLOGY. *Current Pos:* from asst prof to assoc prof, 70-85, PROF ZOOL, UNIV MASS, AMHERST, 85- *Personal Data:* b Oceanside, NY, Aug 17, 42; m 64, Gerda I Balding; c David & Peter. *Educ:* Columbia Col, AB, 64; Case Western Res Univ, PhD(biol), 68. *Prof Exp:* Trainee biomet, Case Western Res Univ, 68; NIH trainee develop biol, Yale Univ, 68-70. *Concurrent Pos:* Instr biol, Yale Univ, 69-70; prin investr, NIH, Cockroach Develop, NSF, Role Oligosaccharides in Vitellogenesis, USDA, Gypsy Moth pop biol, Storage Proteins as indices of nutritive quality; vis scholar, Dept Biochem, Univ Calif, Berkeley, 77-78; adj prof molecular & cellular biol prog, Univ Mass, 84-, entom, 85-; vis scientist, Marine Biol Lab, Woods Hole, MA, 93-94. *Mem:* AAAS; Am Soc Zoologists; Classification Soc. *Res:* Insect physiology and development; chemistry and function of vitellogenin; evolution; biometry; effect of oligosaccharides on proteins; role of ions in early development of oocytes; pattern formation. *Mailing Add:* Dept Biol Univ Mass Amherst Amherst MA 01003-0002. *E-Mail:* joe@bio.umass.edu

KUNKEL, LOUIS M, MEDICINE. *Current Pos:* res fel pediat, 80-82, from instr to assoc prof, 82-90, PROF PEDIAT & GENETICS, HARVARD MED SCH, 90-, CHIEF, DIV GENETICS, CHILDREN'S HOSP, BOSTON, 89- *Personal Data:* b New York, NY, Oct 13, 49. *Educ:* Gettysburg Col, BA, 71; Johns Hopkins Univ, PhD, 78. *Honors & Awards:* Duchenne-Erb-Preis, Ger Muscular Dystrophy Asn, 86; George Cotzias Mem Lectr, Am Acad Neurol, 88; Royal Soc Wellcome Found Prize, Eng, 88; Warren Alpert Found Prize, 88; Passano Found Young Scientist Award, 89; Nat Med Res Award, Nat Health Coun, 89; Pruzansky Lectr, March of Dimes Birth Defects Found, 89; Gairdner Found Int Award, 89; E Mead Johnson Award, 91; Silvio O Conte Decade of the Brain Award, 91. *Prof Exp:* Fel, Univ Calif, San Francisco, 78-80; res fel med, Children's Hosp Med Ctr, Boston, 80. *Concurrent Pos:* George Meany postdoctoral fel, Muscular Dystrophy Asn, 80-82; lectr neurobiol, Harvard Med Sch, 83-89, tutor human genetics, 87-89; assoc investr, Howard Hughes Med Inst, 87-90, investr, 90- *Mem:* Nat Acad Sci; Muscular Dystrophy Asn (vpres, 87-89). *Res:* Linkage of human genetic diseases with DNA markers; molecular genetics of Duchenne muscular dystrophy; differential gene expression during development; structural organization of mammalian DNA. *Mailing Add:* Children's Hosp 300 Longwood Ave Boston MA 02115

KUNKEL, STEVEN L, IMMUNOLOGY, REGULATION OF CYTOKINE GENE EXPRESSION. *Current Pos:* instr, 80-82, from asst prof to assoc prof, 82-91, PROF PATH & IMMUNOL, UNIV MICH, 91- *Educ:* NDak State Univ, BS, 73, MS, 74; Univ Kans, PhD(biochem & microbiol), 78. *Honors & Awards:* Establ Investr, Am Heart Asn, 85. *Prof Exp:* Fel, inflammation & immunol, Univ Conn, 78-80. *Mem:* Am Soc Invest Path; Am Asn Immunol; Shock Soc; Am Thoracic Soc. *Res:* Immunology; regulation of cytokine gene expression. *Mailing Add:* Dept Path Univ Mich Med Sch Box 0602 1301 Catherine Rd Ann Arbor MI 48109-0602. *Fax:* 313-764-2397

KUNKEL, THOMAS A, DEVELOPMENTAL BIOLOGY. *Current Pos:* sr staff fel, 82-86, RES GENETICIST, LAB MOLECULAR GENETICS, NAT INST ENVIRON HEALTH SERV, NIH, 86- *Personal Data:* b Cincinnati, Ohio, Aug 8, 49. *Educ:* Thomas More Col, BA, 71; Univ Cincinnati, MS, 73, PhD(develop biol), 77. *Prof Exp:* Res assoc, Inst Cancer Res, Philadelphia, 77-78; fel, NIH, 78-81, Univ Wash, 78-82. *Concurrent Pos:* Adj prof, Dept Microbiol & Immunol, Univ NC, Chapel Hill, 82-, Genetics, Univ Food Genetics, Duke Univ, 86- *Mem:* Am Soc Biochem & Molecular Biol; Am Asn Cancer Res. *Res:* Developmental biology. *Mailing Add:* Lab Genetics NIEHS NIH PO Box 12233 Research Triangle Park NC 27709-2233. *Fax:* 919-541-7613

KUNKEL, WILLIAM ECKART, astronomy, for more information see previous edition

KUNKEL, WULF BERNARD, PLASMA PHYSICS. *Current Pos:* Asst res engr aerodyn, Univ Calif, Berkeley, 51-54, lectr, 53-67, assoc res eng, 54-55, physicist, Lawrence Berkeley Lab, 56-70, prof physics, 67-91, group leader Magnetic Fushion Energy Res Proj, Lawrence Berkeley Lab, 70-91, EMER PROF PHYSICS, UNIV CALIF, BERKELEY, 91- *Personal Data:* b Eichenau, Ger, Feb 6, 23; nat US; m 47; c 2. *Educ:* Univ Calif, BA, 48, PhD(physics), 51. *Honors & Awards:* Alexander von Humboldt award, 80. *Concurrent Pos:* Guggenheim fel, 55-56 & 72-73; consult, Aerospace Corp, 61-71; ed, Plasma Physics, 70-80. *Mem:* Fel Am Phys Soc; Sigma Xi. *Res:* Physics of ionized gases; magnetohydrodynamics; controlled-fusion research. *Mailing Add:* 4-230 Lawrence Berkeley Lab Univ Calif Berkeley CA 94720

KUNKLE, DONALD EDWARD, PHYSICS, MATHEMATICS. *Current Pos:* TECH CONSULT, ANALYTE CORP, 91- *Personal Data:* b New Kensington, Pa, Mar 9, 28; m 50; c 3. *Educ:* Lafayette Col, BS, 50. *Prof Exp:* Res physicist spectros, 50-55, group leader nondestructive testing, 55-62, process control, Alcoa Res Lab, 62-70; staff physicist process technol, Kaiser Aluminum & Chem Corp, 70-80, mgr prod anal & test syst, qual control, 80-86; nuclear engr, Dept Navy, 87-90. *Mem:* Am Soc Non-destructive Testing; Anal Chem Appl Spectros; Am Soc Testing & Mat. *Res:* Applied emission spectroscopy; eddy current testing; new principles of radiation thickness gauging for non-ferrous rolling mills; closed loop process control systems; quality control in metals industry; nuclear instrumentation for submarine program. *Mailing Add:* 1419 Village Ctr Dr Medford OR 97504-4501. *E-Mail:* hrfj25a@prodigy.com

KUNKLE, GEORGE ROBERT, ENVIRONMENTAL GEOLOGY, HYDROLOGY. *Current Pos:* PRES & PRIN HYDROGEOLOGIST, G R KUNKLE & ASSOC, INC, 86- *Personal Data:* b Elyria, Ohio, Mar 27, 34; m 58; c 4. *Educ:* Iowa State Univ, BS, 56; Univ Mich, MS, 58, PhD(geol), 61. *Prof Exp:* Geologist, Res Coun Alta, Can, 60-62 & US Geol Surv, 62-66; asst prof geol, Univ Toledo, 66-71; pres & environ consult, Earthview, Inc, 71-77; sr scientist, Jones & Henry Eng, LTD, 77-80; assoc & mgr, Neyer, Tiseo & Hindo, Ltd, 80-86. *Mem:* Nat Water Well Asn; Am Inst Prof Geologists. *Res:* Groundwater resources and environmental geology; influence of land use and natural processes on the quality and quantity of ground and surface waters. *Mailing Add:* 319 Bay Run Newport NC 28570

KUNO, H JOHN, MICROWAVE & SOLID STATE ELECTRONICS. *Current Pos:* FOUNDER, QUINSTAR TECH INC, 93- *Educ:* Univ Calif, Los Angeles, BSEE, 61, MSEE, 63, PhD, 66. *Prof Exp:* Res engr, Elec Div, NCR, 61-66; mem tech staff, David Sarnoff Res Ctr, RCA, 66-69; mem tech staff & asst div mgr, Hughes Aircraft Co, 69-93. *Mem:* Fel Inst Elec & Electronics Engrs. *Res:* Contributed over 100 articles on microwave and solid state electronics to professional journals. *Mailing Add:* 28009 Seashell Way Rancho Palos Verdes CA 90275-3816

KUNOS, GEORGE, MOLECULAR PHARMACOLOGY, RECEPTOR RESEARCH. *Current Pos:* PROF & CHMN, DEPT PHARMACOL & TOXICOL, MED COL VA, RICHMOND, 92- *Personal Data:* b Budapest, Hungary, May 14, 42; US citizen; m 67, Ildiko Vermes; c Anne-Marie & Doreen. *Educ:* Budapest Med Sch, MD, 66; McGill Univ, Montreal, PhD(pharmacol), 73. *Prof Exp:* Asst prof pharmacol, McGill Univ, Montreal, 74-79, from assoc prof to prof pharmacol & med, 79-88; lab chief physiol & pharmacol, Nat Inst Alcohol Abuse & Alcoholism, Bethesda, Md, 87-92. *Concurrent Pos:* Fel, Coun High Blood Pressure Res, Am Heart Asn. *Mem:* Am Soc Pharmacol & Exp Therapeut; Am Soc Biochem & Moleuclar Biol; Int Soc Hypertension; Soc Exp Biol & Med; Hungarian Acad Sci. *Res:* Pharmacology, molecular biology and physiological regulation of drug and hormone receptors; neural mechanisms of blood pressure regulation; author of over 100 publications and four books. *Mailing Add:* 6606 Marywood Rd Bethesda MD 20817. *Fax:* 804-371-7519; *E-Mail:* gkunos@gems.vcu.edu

KUNOV, HANS, PHYSIOLOGICAL ACOUSTICS, ACOUSTICAL COMMUNICATION PROCESSES. *Current Pos:* from asst prof to assoc prof, 67-82, PROF BIOMED ENG, ELEC & COMPUT ENG & OTOLARYNGOL, UNIV TORONTO, 82-, DIR, INST BIOMED ENG, 89- *Personal Data:* b Copenhagen, Denmark, Mar 14, 38; Can citizen; m 64, 77, D Clare Lamb; c Mads J & Niels P. *Educ:* Tech Univ Denmark, MASc, 63, PhD(elec eng), 66. *Prof Exp:* Fel biomed eng, Tech Univ Denmark, 66-67. *Concurrent Pos:* Pres, Div 934533 Ont Inc, Artel Eng, 75-; dir, Elec Eng Consociates, 90-92; mem, Grant Selection Comt Elec Eng, Natural Sci & Eng Res Coun Can, 90-; assoc ed, Inst Elec & Electronics Engrs Trans Biomed Eng, 91-; dir res & co-foundr, Paul Madsen Med Devices Ltd, 92- *Mem:* Inst Elec & Electronics Engrs; Acoust Soc Am; AAAS; Can Med & Biol Eng Soc; Sigma Xi; Instrument Soc Am. *Res:* Acoustics and hearing; acousto-mechanical models of the head; hearing assistive devices; signal processing by the ear; signal processing for amelioration of hearing deficit; advanced audiometric instrumentation. *Mailing Add:* 4 Princeton Rd Etobicoke ON M8X 2E2 Can. *Fax:* 416-978-4317; *E-Mail:* hkunov@vm.utcc.utoronto.ca

KUNSELMAN, A(RTHUR) RAYMOND, NUCLEAR PHYSICS, PARTICLE PHYSICS. *Current Pos:* FAC MEM PHYSICS, UNIV WYO, 69- *Personal Data:* b Witchita Falls, Tex, Feb 22, 42; m 92, Donna. *Educ:* Univ Calif, Berkeley, BA, 64, MA, 65, PhD(physics), 69. *Prof Exp:* Physicist, Lawrence Berkeley Lab, 69. *Concurrent Pos:* Consult, Rutherford Lab, Eng, 75. *Mem:* Am Asn Physics Teachers; Sigma Xi. *Res:* Muonic and hadronic atoms; leptonic conservations; muonic hydrogen isotopes. *Mailing Add:* Dept Physics Univ Wyo Box 3905 Laramie WY 82071. *E-Mail:* rk@uwyo.edu

KUNSTADTER, JOHN W, NON-PROFIT ADMINISTRATION. *Current Pos:* SELF EMPLOYED, 69- *Personal Data:* b Chicago, Ill, Oct 20, 27; m 49; c 4. *Educ:* Mass Inst Technol, BS, 49. *Mem:* Am Phys Soc. *Mailing Add:* 1035 Fifth Ave Apt 15C New York NY 10028

KUNTZ, GARLAND PARKE PAUL, CORROSION, COMPUTER ASSISTED INSTRUCTION. *Current Pos:* ASSOC PROF PHYSICS & CHEM, CONCORDIA COL, EDMONTON, 75-, HEAD CHEM DEPT, 96- *Personal Data:* b Ft Worth, Tex. *Educ:* Fla State Univ, BS, 66; Case Western Res Univ, MS, 69, PhD(chem), 72. *Prof Exp:* Fel, Dept Chem, Case Western Res Univ, 72-73; res assoc, Univ Alta, 73-75. *Mem:* Nat Asn Corrosion Engrs. *Res:* Computer assisted instruction. *Mailing Add:* Dept Sci Concordia Col 7128 Ada Blvd Edmonton AB T5B 4E4 Can. *Fax:* 403-474-1933

KUNTZ, IRVING, POLYMER CHEMISTRY, ORGANIC CHEMISTRY. *Current Pos:* from sr chemist to sect head, Esso Res & Eng Co, 55-63, res assoc, 63-68, SR RES ASSOC, EXXON CHEM CO, 68- *Personal Data:* b New York, NY, Feb 16, 25; m 47, 77; c 2. *Educ:* City Col New York, BS, 48; Polytech Inst Brooklyn, MS, 50, PhD(chem), 55. *Prof Exp:* Res chemist, Sprague Elec Co, Mass, 50-53. *Res:* Organic reaction mechanisms; polymer chemistry; ionic polymerizations; kinetics. *Mailing Add:* 725 Haven Pl Linden NJ 07036-5820

KUNTZ, IRWIN DOUGLAS, JR, PHYSICAL CHEMISTRY. *Current Pos:* assoc prof, 71-76, PROF CHEM, UNIV CALIF, SAN FRANCISCO, 77- *Personal Data:* b Nashville, Tenn, Aug 31, 39; m 61; c 3. *Educ:* Princeton Univ, AB, 61; Univ Calif, Berkeley, PhD(chem), 65. *Prof Exp:* Asst prof chem, Princeton Univ, 65-71. *Mem:* Fel AAAS; Sigma Xi; Am Chem Soc. *Res:* Physical chemistry of liquid state; hydration of macromolecules; spectroscopic studies of biological materials and fast reactions in biological systems; design of ligands. *Mailing Add:* Dept Pharmaceut Chem Univ Calif 513 Parnassus Ave Box 0446 San Francisco CA 94143-0446

KUNTZ, MEL ANTON, PETROLOGY, VOLCANOLOGY. *Current Pos:* RES GEOLOGIST, US GEOL SURV, 74- *Personal Data:* b Minneapolis, Minn, July 4, 39; m 67, 93, Carmela S Realmonte; c David, Brian, Stacy, Robert & Jeffrey. *Educ:* Carleton Col, BA, 61; Northwestern Univ, MS, 64; Stanford Univ, PhD(geol), 68. *Prof Exp:* Asst prof geol, Amherst Col, 68-74. *Mem:* Mineral Soc Am; Geol Soc Am. *Res:* Petrogenesis of epizonal and catazonal plutons; application of experimental studies to natural igneous and metamorphic rocks; petrogenesis of basalts; basalts of Snake River Plain, Idaho; geology of intermountain western United States; geology of the Idaho batholith; geology of Lake Mead area, Nevada and Arizona. *Mailing Add:* US Geol Surv Mail Stop 913 Box 25046 Denver Fed Ctr Denver CO 80225. *Fax:* 303-236-0214

KUNTZ, RICHARD A, MATHEMATICS. *Current Pos:* from asst prof to assoc prof, Monmouth Col, NJ, 68-76, chmn dept, 74-76, dean grad sch, 76-80, vpres admin, 80-87, PROF MATH, MONMOUTH COL, NJ, 76-, VPRES & DEAN, SCH INFO SCI, 87- *Personal Data:* b Lakewood, NJ, Sept 7, 39; m 60; c 2. *Educ:* Monmouth Col, BS, 64; Univ Md, MA, 67, PhD(math), 69. *Prof Exp:* Teaching asst math, Univ Md, 64-68. *Mem:* Am Math Soc; Math Asn Am. *Res:* Abstract algebra; ideal theory in commutative rings. *Mailing Add:* Monmouth Univ West Long Branch NJ 07764

KUNTZ, ROBERT ELROY, PARASITOLOGY, HELMINTHOLOGY. *Current Pos:* CONSULT, 85- *Personal Data:* b Lawton, Okla, Feb 23, 16; m 38; c 3. *Educ:* Univ Okla, BA, 39, MS, 40; Univ Mich, PhD(zool), 47; Am Bd Med Microbiol, dipl. *Prof Exp:* Asst zool, Univ Okla, 38-40; teaching fel, Univ Mich, 40-43; mem staff, Naval Med Sch, Bethesda, Md, 43, head epidemic teams, SPac, 43-45, res parasitologist, Naval Med Res Inst, 45-48, head parasitol dept, Naval Med Res Unit 3, Cairo, 48-53, instr, Naval Med Sch, 53-57, head parasitol dept, Naval Med Res Unit 2, Taipei, 57-62, res parasitologist & head tech serv dept, Naval Med Res Inst, 62-64; head parasitol dept, Southwest Found Res & Educ, 64-84. *Concurrent Pos:* Exam parasitol, Fac Med, Ain Shams Univ, Cairo, 50-52; res Univ Md & adj prof, microbiol, Univ Tex Med Sch, San Antonio; consult, Parasitic Div, WHO. *Mem:* Am Soc Trop Med & Hyg; Am Soc Parasitologists; Am Micros Soc; Int Primatol Soc; SW Asn Parasitol. *Res:* Biology of schistosomes and other helminths; survey-type investigations on parasites of man and lower vertebrates; epidemiology of helminth diseases and zoogeography of parasites of vertebrates, especially the parasites of primates. *Mailing Add:* 14794 Cadillac Dr San Antonio TX 78248

KUNTZ, ROBERT ROY, PHYSICAL CHEMISTRY. *Current Pos:* From asst prof to assoc prof, 62-71, chmn dept, 78-79, assoc chair, 79-81, PROF CHEM, UNIV MO, COLUMBIA, 71- *Personal Data:* b Barry, Ill, Apr 10, 37; m 59; c 2. *Educ:* Culver-Stockton Col, BA, 59; Carnegie Inst Technol, MS, 62, PhD(chem), 63. *Prof Exp:* Assoc prog dir, NSF, 73-74. *Mem:* Am Soc Photobiol; Sigma Xi; Am Chem Soc; Am Phys Soc; Inter Am Photochem Soc. *Res:* Photolysis and radiolysis of organic compounds, free radical kinetics, radiation protection; flash photolysis; photobiology; photocatalysis. *Mailing Add:* Dept Chem Univ Mo Columbia MO 65211-0001

KUNTZMAN, RONALD GROVER, BIOCHEMISTRY, PHARMACOLOGY. *Current Pos:* VPRES RES & DEVELOP, HOFFMANN-LA ROCHE INC, NUTLEY, NJ, 84- *Personal Data:* b New York, NY, Sept 17, 33; m 55; c 2. *Educ:* Brooklyn Col, BS, 55; George Washington Univ, MS, 57, PhD(biochem), 62. *Honors & Awards:* John Jacob Abel Award, Am Soc Pharmacol & Exp Therapeut, 69. *Prof Exp:* Chemist, Nat Inst Health; sr biochemist, Wellcome Res Labs, Burroughs & Co, 62-70, dep head biochem pharmacol dept, 67-70; assoc dir dept biochem & drug metab, Hoffmann-La Roche, Inc, 70-72, assoc dir biol res, 72-73, asst vpres & dir therapeuts res, 73-81; vpres & dir Pharmaceut Res & Develop, Hoffmann-La Roche Inc, 80-84. *Concurrent Pos:* Res & develop steering comt, chmn subcomt on Adv Comt Systs, Comn Drugs for Rare Dis, Pharmaceut Mfrs Asn, 85-; chmn Drug Metab Div, Am Soc Pharmacol & Exp Therapeut; res adv coun, Nat Orgn Rare Dis; mem Adv Bd, Univ Pa Natural Sci Asn; mem Adv Bd, Univ Ariz Col Pharm Nat Adv Bd; mem, Am Soc Pharmacol & Exp Therapeut Coun; corp mem, Muscular Dystrophy Asn. *Mem:* Am Soc Pharmacol & Exp Therapeut (secy-treas, 81-83); Am Soc Biol Chemists; Sigma Xi; Am Col Neuropsychopharmacol; Soc Toxicol; AAAS. *Res:* Biochemical effects and metabolism of drugs and steroid hormones, induced enzyme syntheses; syntheses metabolism and storage of biogenic amines; preclinical development of new drugs; pharmacokinetics and efficacy studies on new therapeutics. *Mailing Add:* 12 Augustine Ave Ardsley NY 10502-2203. *Fax:* 973-235-7605

KUNZ, ALBERT BARRY, CHEMICAL PHYSICS, SOLID STATE SCIENCE. *Current Pos:* res asst prof, 69-71, from asst prof to assoc prof, 71-76, PROF PHYSICS, UNIV ILL, URBANA, 76- *Personal Data:* b Philadelphia, Pa, Oct 2, 40; m 64; c 1. *Educ:* Muhlenberg Col, BS, 62; Lehigh Univ, MS, 64, PhD(physics), 66. *Prof Exp:* Res assoc physics, Lehigh Univ, 66-69. *Concurrent Pos:* Consult, US Air Force Aerospace Res Lab, 71 & E I du Pont de Nemours & Co, Inc, 73-79; adj prof physics, Mich Technol Univ, 81- *Mem:* Am Phys Soc; Sigma Xi. *Res:* Solid state, atomic and molecular theory; band theory of solids, solid state spectroscopy; spectra of ions, atoms and molecules; theory of ground state properties of polyatomic systems; theory of catalysis is being developed. *Mailing Add:* Dept Elec & Eng Mich Tech Univ Houghton MI 49931

KUNZ, ALBERT L, PHYSIOLOGY. *Current Pos:* from instr to assoc prof, 62-76, prof, 76-, EMER PROF PHYSIOL, OHIO STATE UNIV. *Personal Data:* b Bloomington, Ind, Oct 3, 33; m 57; c 5. *Educ:* Ind Univ, AB, 56, MD, 59; Ohio State Univ, MS, 65. *Honors & Awards:* Perkin's Award, Am Physiol Soc, 74. *Concurrent Pos:* Nat Heart Inst fel, 63-65; Alexander Von Humboldt fel, 74-75. *Mem:* Am Physiol Soc; Am Heart Asn; Am Asn Univ Professors. *Res:* Respiratory control; anomalous viscosity of blood. *Mailing Add:* 110 Glenmont Ave Columbus OH 43214

KUNZ, BERNARD ALEXANDER, dna repair, mutagenesis, for more information see previous edition

KUNZ, HAROLD RUSSELL, THERMODYNAMICS, HEAT TRANSFER. *Current Pos:* adj prof, Dept Chem Eng, 92-94, PROF IN RESIDENCE, UNIV CONN, 94-; FUEL CELL CONSULT, 92- *Personal Data:* b Troy, NY, Oct 3, 31; wid; c Daryl L (Gottier) & Roderick R. *Educ:* Rensselaer Polytech Inst, BME, 53, MS, 58, PhD(heat transfer), 66. *Prof Exp:* Jr anal engr heat transfer & fluid mech res, Pratt & Whitney Aircraft Div, United Technologies Corp, 53-54, anal engr, 54-57, sr anal engr, 57-60, asst proj engr heat transfer res, 60-63, proj engr heat transfer & fuel cell res, 63-68, sr proj engr, 68-74, sr proj engr, Power Systs Div, 75, sr proj engr fuel cell res, Power Systs Div, 75-85; sr proj engr fuel cell res, Int Fuel Cells, 85-92. *Concurrent Pos:* Adj asst prof mech eng, Hartford Grad Ctr, 66-70, adj assoc prof, 70-94. *Mem:* Electrochem Soc; Am Soc Mech Engrs. *Res:* Electrochemistry; thermodynamics; electrocatalysis; single-phase and two-phase fluid mechanics and heat transfer. *Mailing Add:* 26 Valley View Lane Vernon CT 06066. *Fax:* 860-486-2959

KUNZ, HEINZ W, PATHOLOGY, IMMUNOGENETICS. *Current Pos:* from res asst prof to assoc prof, Univ Pittsburgh, 76-90, asst dir, Div Exp Path, 87-90, assoc dir, 87-88, dir grad prog, 88-91, PROF PATH, UNIV PITTSBURGH, 90- *Personal Data:* b Zurich, Switz, Feb 8, 33; US citizen; m, Nancy I. *Educ:* Univ Pittsburgh, PhD(immunogenetics), 78. *Prof Exp:* Res asst, Dept Path, Harvard Med Sch, Boston, 62-65, sr res asst, 65-69, tech assoc, 69-70, assoc, 70-71; clin asst staff, Presby-Univ Hosp, 71-84. *Concurrent Pos:* Assoc staff, Presby-Univ Hosp, 84-; mem, Pittsburgh Cancer Inst, 86-; consult, Nat Res Coun, 90- *Mem:* AAAS; Am Chem Soc; Genetics Soc Am; Transplantation Soc; Am Asn Pathologists; Am Asn Immunologists; Int Soc Immunol & Reprod; Am Soc Immunol & Reprod; Am Asn Cancer Res. *Res:* Experimental pathology; reproduction immunology; immunogenitics. *Mailing Add:* Dept Path Sch Med Univ Pittsburgh Terrace & DeSoto St Pittsburgh PA 15261-0001. *Fax:* 412-648-1916; *E-Mail:* hwk@med.pitt.edu

KUNZ, KAISER SCHOEN, PHYSICS. *Current Pos:* res prof physics & elec eng, 60-76, RES PROF PHYSICS, NMEX STATE UNIV, 76- *Personal Data:* b New Middletown, Ind, Oct 16, 15; m 44; c 3. *Educ:* Univ Ind, AB, 36; Univ Cincinnati, AM, 37, PhD(theoret physics), 39. *Prof Exp:* Instr math, Univ Cincinnati, 39-42; instr electronics, Cruft Lab, Harvard Univ, 42-45, res assoc, 45-46, res fel, 46-47, lectr appl math, comput lab, 47-49; assoc prof elec eng, Case Inst Technol, 49-51; from res physicist to head interpretation res dept, Schlumberger Well Surv Corp, 51-60. *Mem:* Fel AAAS; Am Phys Soc; Inst Elec & Electronics Engrs; Am Math Soc; Am Asn Physics Teachers; Sigma Xi. *Res:* Propagation of electromagnetic waves in dynamic media; quantum electronics and lasers; electrodynamics; field theory; numerical analysis. *Mailing Add:* 2047 Crescent Dr Las Cruces NM 88005

KUNZ, PETER DALE, THEORETICAL NUCLEAR PHYSICS. *Current Pos:* RETIRED. *Personal Data:* b Hubbard, Ore, July 20, 28. *Educ:* Ore State Col, BS, 50, MS, 53; Univ Wash, PhD, 59. *Prof Exp:* Instr, Univ Wash, 60; res assoc, Univ Calif, Los Angeles, 60-61; asst prof, Univ BC, 61-62; from asst prof to prof, Univ Colo, 62-92. *Mem:* Fel Am Phys Soc. *Res:* Research nuclear structure; nuclear reaction theory and nuclear reaction codes. *Mailing Add:* Nuclear Physics Labs Univ Colo PO Box 446 Boulder CO 80309

KUNZ, SIDNEY EDMUND, ENTOMOLOGY, ECOLOGY. *Current Pos:* res entomologist, Agr Res Serv, USDA, Kerrville, 67-69, res entomologist, Col Sta, 69-77, res leader & res entomologist, sci & educ, 77-86, LAB DIR, AGR RES SERV, USDA, KERRVILLE, 86- *Personal Data:* b Fredericksburg, Tex, Dec 24, 35; m 62; c 3. *Educ:* Tex A&M Univ, BS, 58, MS, 62; Okla State Univ, PhD(entom), 67. *Prof Exp:* Surv entomologist, Okla State Univ, 61-64, exten entomologist, 64-67. *Concurrent Pos:* Entom consult, Food & Agr Orgn UN Develop Prog, Mauritius, 73-74 & USAID, Tanzania, IAEA, Somalia, 82. *Mem:* Entom Soc Am; Am Registry Prof Entomologists; Sigma Xi. *Res:* Biology, ecology and area integrated pest management control of biting flies of cattle, horn flies and stable flies. *Mailing Add:* HC 5 Aqua Vista Estates Kerrville TX 78028

KUNZ, THOMAS HENRY, ANIMAL PHYSIOLOGY, BEHAVIOR-ETHOLOGY. *Current Pos:* from asst prof to assoc prof, Boston Univ, 71-84, dir grad studies, 78-81, assoc chmn, 81-85, chmn, 85-90, DIR GRAD PROGS, ECOL & BEHAV EVOLUTION, BOSTON UNIV, 83-, PROF BIOL, 84-, DIR, CTR ECOL & CONSERV BIOL, 96- *Personal Data:* b Kansas City, Mo, June 11, 38; m 62, Margaret Brown; c Pamela L & David

T. *Educ:* Cent Mo State Univ, BS, 61, MS, 62; Drake Univ, MA, 68; Univ Kans, PhD(ecol), 71. *Honors & Awards:* Gerritt S Miller Award, 84. *Prof Exp:* Instr biol, Shawnee Mission Schs, 62-67; res fel, Kans Nat Hist Surv, 67-70; teaching fel, Univ Kans, 70-71. *Concurrent Pos:* Prin investr, NSF, 73-, Nat Geog Soc, 84-85 & 96-97; assoc ed, Am Midland Naturalist, 78-80; res assoc, Carnegie Mus Natural Hist, 78-; Orgn Am States grant, 84-85; res assoc, Smithsonian Inst, 94- *Mem:* Fel AAAS; Am Soc Mammalogists; Ecol Soc Am; Am Soc Naturalists; Soc Study Evolution. *Res:* Behavioral and physiological ecology of bats, with emphasis on social behavior, energetics, reproductive biology and feeding ecology of temperate and tropical species. *Mailing Add:* Dept Biol Boston Univ Boston MA 02215. *Fax:* 617-353-6340; *E-Mail:* kunz@bu__bio.bu.edu

KUNZE, A(DOLF) W(ILHELM) GERHARD, GEOPHYSICS. *Current Pos:* from asst prof to assoc prof, 74-85, PROF GEOL, UNIV AKRON, 85- *Personal Data:* b Philadelphia, Pa, Aug 23, 36; m 67, 92, Diana Maira Duch; c Peter & Karl. *Educ:* Pa State Univ, BS, 63, PhD(geophys), 73. *Prof Exp:* Nat Res Coun res assoc lunar geophys, Johnson Space Ctr, NASA, Houston, 73-74. *Concurrent Pos:* Vis prof, Inst Geophys, Kiel, Fed Repub Ger, 82, 90, 94; Fulbright sr prof teaching/res award, 90. *Mem:* Am Geophys Union; Soc Explor Geophysicists; Asn Eng Geologists. *Res:* Engineering geophysics: shallow subsurface investigations using gravity/magnetic, electrical resistivity and seismic refraction methods; seismotectonic studies and focal mechanism determinations. *Mailing Add:* 2471 Brice Rd Akron OH 44313. *Fax:* 330-972-7611; *E-Mail:* akunze@uakron.edu

KUNZE, DIANA LEE, MEDICAL PHYSIOLOGY. *Current Pos:* asst prof cardiovasc physiol, 73-78, ASSOC PROF PHYSIOL & BIOPHYS, UNIV TEX MED BR GALVESTON, 78- *Personal Data:* b Winthrop, Mass, Dec 19, 39. *Educ:* Stetson Univ, BS, 61; Emory Univ, MS, 66; Univ Utah, PhD(physiol), 70. *Prof Exp:* Researcher neurophysiol, Nat Ctr Sci Res, France, 71-72; res assoc cardiovasc physiol, Univ Utah, 72-73. *Res:* Studies of control mechanisms of cardiac rhythm by neural input and by local factors. *Mailing Add:* 9831 Hillsdale Rd Brecksville OH 44141

KUNZE, ERIC, OCEANOGRAPHY. *Current Pos:* Res asst, 79-85, res asst prof, 87-93, ASSOC PROF, SCH OCEANOG, UNIV WASH, SEATTLE, 93- *Personal Data:* b Nelson, BC, June 13, 56. *Educ:* Univ BC, Vancouver, BSc, 79; Univ Wash, MS, 82, PhD(oceanog), 85. *Honors & Awards:* Father James B Macelwane Young Investr Medal, Am Geophys Union, 92; Sverdrup lectr, 92. *Concurrent Pos:* Fel, Woods Hole Oceanog Inst, 83, res assoc, 85-86, res scientist, 86-87; asst ed, J Marine Res, 87- *Mem:* Fel Am Geophys Union; Am Meteorol Soc; Nat Conserv; Can Meteorol & Oceanog Soc. *Res:* Interactions of meso- to microscale oceanic phenomena including fronts, eddies, internal waves, turbulence, double diffusion, bottom topography and surface forcing and their effects, through mixing and water-mass modification on larger scales; demonstration that internal waves are sensitive to rotation in the ocean. *Mailing Add:* Oceanog Univ Wash Box 357940 Seattle WA 98195-7940

KUNZE, GEORGE WILLIAM, SOIL MINERALOGY. *Current Pos:* RETIRED. *Personal Data:* b Warda, Tex, Sept 16, 22; m 48; c 2. *Educ:* Tex A&M Univ, BS, 47, MS, 50; Pa State Univ, PhD(soil mineral), 52. *Prof Exp:* From asst prof to assoc prof, Tex A&M Univ, T52-60, from assoc dean to dean grad col, 67-84, prof soils & crop sci, 60-84. *Concurrent Pos:* Consult ed, Soil Sci, 58-; grad prog consult, Bangladesh Agr Univ, 70 & Grad Sch Agr Sci, Castelar, Arg, 72; vpres, Conf Southern Grad Schs, 79-80, pres, 80-81. *Mem:* Fel AAAS; fel Am Soc Agron; Soil Sci Soc Am; Clay Minerals Soc; fel Mineral Soc Am. *Res:* Soil chemistry. *Mailing Add:* 5100 S US Hwy 77 LaGrange TX 78945

KUNZE, JAY FREDERICK, PHYSICS, MEDICAL PHYSICS. *Current Pos:* DEAN, COL ENG, IDAHO STATE UNIV, 95- *Personal Data:* b Pittsburgh, Pa, Feb 24, 33; m 56; c 3. *Educ:* Carnegie Inst Technol, BS, 54, MS, 55, PhD(nuclear physics), 59. *Prof Exp:* Proj physicist & asst, Carnegie Inst Technol, 54-58; physicist, Idaho Test Sta, Gen Elec Co, 58-65, mgr nuclear technol, 65-69; mgr oper & anal, Aerojet Nuclear Corp, 69-70, mgr reactor technol, LPT, 70-74; mgr geothermal & adv technol, EG&G Idaho, Inc, 74-78; vpres & gen mgr, Energy Serv Inc, 78-83; chmn nuclear eng, Univ Mo, 83-95. *Concurrent Pos:* Site leader, Air Force solar eclipse expeds, 54-55; affil prof, Univ Idaho, 59-; assoc prof, Univ Utah, 69- *Mem:* Am Nuclear Soc; Nat Soc Prof Engrs. *Res:* Geothermal energy; experimental reactor physics and reactor analysis; energy engineering and conservation; astronomy. *Mailing Add:* Col Eng Idaho State Box 8060 Pocatello ID 83209

KUNZE, OTTO ROBERT, ENGINEERING, AGRICULTURE. *Current Pos:* assoc prof to prof, 57-90, EMER PROF ELEC POWER & PROCESSING, TEX A&M UNIV, 90- *Personal Data:* b Warda, Tex, May 27, 25; m 51, Alice R Eifert; c Glenn, Allen, Charles & Karen. *Educ:* Tex A&M Univ, BS, 50; Iowa State Univ, MS, 51; Mich State Univ, PhD(agr eng), 64. *Prof Exp:* Agr & indust engr, Cent Power & Light Co, 51-56; assoc prof elec power & processing, Tex A&M Univ, 57-61 & 64-69, prof, 69-90. *Concurrent Pos:* Consult post-harvest rice processing, India, 75 & 85; mem, Tex Air Control Bd, 78-90; lectr & consult, Taiway, 85, 87 & 94, China, 93, Thailand, 95. *Mem:* Fel Am Soc Agr Engrs; Am Asn Cereal Chemists; AAAS; Nat Soc Prof Engrs; Sigma Xi. *Res:* Electric power and processing in agriculture; physical properties of agricultural products; hygroscopicity of rice and its effects on the grain; moisture absorption in low-moisture rough rice and rapid moisture removal in grains. *Mailing Add:* 1002 Milner Dr College Station TX 77840-2215

KUNZE, RAY A, MATHEMATICS. *Current Pos:* chmn dept, 69-74, PROF MATH, UNIV CALIF, IRVINE, 69- *Personal Data:* b Des Moines, Iowa, Mar 7, 28; m 51; c 5. *Educ:* Univ Chicago, BS, 50, MS, 51, PhD(math), 57. *Prof Exp:* Asst prof math, Brandeis Univ, 60-62; from assoc prof to prof, Wash Univ, 63-69. *Concurrent Pos:* Consult, Inst Defense Anal, 54-, Prentice Hall & McGraw Hill, 61- *Mem:* Am Math Soc. *Res:* Harmonic analysis; representations of Lie Groups. *Mailing Add:* Univ Ga Athens GA 30602-3024

KUNZE, RAYMOND J, soil physics, for more information see previous edition

KUNZLE, HANS PETER, MATHEMATICAL PHYSICS, RELATIVITY. *Current Pos:* from asst prof to assoc prof, 70-80, PROF MATH, UNIV ALTA, 80- *Personal Data:* b Kreuzlingen, Switz, Sept 1, 40; m 68, Nicole Maruani; c Frederick, Caroline, Cyril & Elisabeth. *Educ:* ETH, dipl, 64; Univ London, PhD(relativity), 67. *Prof Exp:* Res asst, Kings Col, Univ London, 67-68; lectr & asst res mathematician, Univ Calif, Berkeley, 68-70. *Concurrent Pos:* Vis scientist, Centre Phys Theor Nat Inst Sci Res, Marseille, France, 75-76, Max Planck Inst Astrophy, Garching, 82-83, Albert-Einstein-Inst, Potsdam, Ger, 96, Inst Theoret Physics, Univ of Zurich, 96. *Mem:* Am Math Soc; Am Phys Soc; Can Math Soc. *Res:* Mathematical problems in general relativity; applications of differential geometry to physics, especially relativistic mechanics and field theories; solutions to Einstein-Yang-Mills field equations. *Mailing Add:* Dept Math Sci Univ Alta Edmonton AB T6G 2G1 Can. *Fax:* 403-492-6826; *E-Mail:* hp.kunzle@ualberta.ca

KUNZLER, JOHN EUGENE, SOLID STATE DEVICES, SUPERCONDUCTIVITY. *Current Pos:* RETIRED. *Personal Data:* b Willard, Utah, Apr 25, 23; m 50, Lois McDonald; c Carol (Blaine), Marilyn (Barker), Bonnie & Kim (Tomeo). *Educ:* Univ Utah, BS, 45; Univ Calif, PhD(phys chem), 50. *Honors & Awards:* John Price Wetherill Award, Franklin Inst, 64; Int Prize New Mat, Am Phys Soc, 79; Kamerlingh Onnes Medal, Neth Asn Refrig, 79. *Prof Exp:* Asst, Purdue Univ, 45-46; from asst to res assoc, Univ Calif, 46-52; mem tech staff, AT&T Bell Labs, 52-61, head, Metal Physics Res Dept, 61-69, dir, Electronic Mat & Device Lab, 69-79, dir, Electronic Mat, Processes & Devices Lab, 79-85, dir, Future Device Studies Ctr, 85-86. *Mem:* Nat Acad Eng; Am Chem Soc; fel Am Phys Soc. *Res:* Electrical, thermal and magnonic properties of solids at low temperatures; Fermi surface; galvanomagnetic and magnetothermal effects; high purity metals; high-field superconductivity; superconducting magnets; low temperature heat capacity and related thermal effects. *Mailing Add:* Rte 2 PO Box 130 Port Murray NJ 07865

KUO, ALBERT YI-SHUONG, PHYSICAL OCEANOGRAPHY, HYDRODYNAMICS. *Current Pos:* assoc marine scientist, 70-78, sr marine scientist & head, Hydraulics Sect, 78-81, PROF, COL WILLIAM & MARY, 81- *Personal Data:* b Tayuan, Taiwan, Nov 4, 39; m 65; c 2. *Educ:* Nat Taiwan Univ, BS, 62; Univ Iowa, MS, 65; Johns Hopkins Univ, PhD(fluid mech), 70. *Prof Exp:* Jr instr fluid mech, Johns Hopkins Univ, 67-69, res assoc, 70; dir, Va Inst Marine Sci, 91-92, dept chair, 93-95. *Concurrent Pos:* From asst prof to assoc prof, Univ Va & Col William & Mary, 70-80; vis prof, Nat Taiwan Univ, 77-78. *Mem:* Am Soc Civil Engrs; Estuarine Res Fedn; Int Asn Hydraul Res. *Res:* Turbulence, diffusion, dispersion; estuarine mathematical model; estuarine hydrodynamics; sediment transport; coastal circulation. *Mailing Add:* Dept Phys Sci Va Inst Marine Sci Gloucester Point VA 23062. *Fax:* 804-642-7195

KUO, BENJAMIN CHUNG-I, ELECTRICAL ENGINEERING. *Current Pos:* asst, 54-57, from asst prof to assoc prof, 58-66, PROF ELEC ENG, UNIV ILL, URBANA, 66- *Personal Data:* b China, Oct 5, 30; m 54; c 1. *Educ:* Univ NH, BS, 54; Univ Ill, MS, 56, PhD(elec eng), 58. *Prof Exp:* Plant engr, Laible Mfg Co, 53-54. *Mem:* Inst Elec & Electronics Engrs. *Res:* Feedback control systems; sampled-data systems. *Mailing Add:* 3206 Valley Brook Dr Champaign IL 61821

KUO, CHAN-HWA, ORGANIC CHEMISTRY. *Current Pos:* Res chemist, 58-74, SR RES CHEMIST, MERCK & CO, INC, 74- *Personal Data:* b Shanghai, China, Oct 7, 31; US citizen; m 57; c 3. *Educ:* Hartwick Col, BS, 57; Rensselaer Polytech Inst, MS, 58; Polytech Inst Brooklyn, PhD(org chem), 75. *Mem:* Sigma Xi. *Res:* Synthesis of griseofulvin, fluoro- and polychlorogriseofulvin, estrone, prostaglandin E1; synthesis and conformational analysis of pantetheine analogs; synthesis and relative configurational studies of the chiral lactone derived from thermozymocidin (myriocin). *Mailing Add:* 105 E Nassau Ave South Plainfield NJ 07080-5219

KUO, CHAO-YING, CELLULAR TRANSPLANTATION. *Current Pos:* from instr to asst prof, Dept Med, Microbiol & Immunol, Univ Tenn, 80-84, res assoc, Dent Res Ctr, 88 & Dept Pediat, 89-90, ASST PROF, DEPT PEDIAT, CTR HEALTH SCI, UNIV TENN, 91- *Personal Data:* b Taiwan, Apr 27, 40; m 67, Grace Lo; c Alice A & Bobby F. *Educ:* Nat Taiwan Normal Univ, BS, 64; Ind State Univ, MA, 70; Univ Iowa, PhD(microbiol), 74. *Prof Exp:* Teaching asst, Lab Invert, Zool & Human Physiol, Taiwan Normal Univ, 65-67, Gen Bot, Human Anat & Physiol, Ind State Univ, 68-70; asst immunol, Univ Iowa, 70-73, asst res scientist, Div Allergy & Immunol, Dept Med, 74-77, instr, 80-81. *Concurrent Pos:* Res assoc, Lady Davis Inst Med Res, Jewish Gen Hosp, Montreal, 73-74; assoc mem, Barbara Kopp Geriat Res Ctr, Auburn, NY, 77-80; grants, Leukemia Res Found, Inc, 78-79, Nat Cancer Inst, NIH, 79-83, Am Cancer Soc, 81-82 & LeBonheur Diabetes Res Fund, 91-92; res microbiologist, Res Serv, Vet Admin Med Ctr, Memphis, Tenn, 81-84; pvt enterprise, 84-88; vis assoc prof, Dept Pediat, Nat Taiwan Univ,

93; vis res assoc prof, Nat Sci Coun, Repub China, 93. *Mem:* Am Asn Immunologists; Asn Am-Chinese Professionals. *Res:* Allergy & tumor immunology; monoclonal antibody production; islet transplantation and islet gland equivalent development; aging and cancer; author of numerous scientific publications. *Mailing Add:* Dept Pediat Col Med Univ Tenn WPT 301 50 N Dunlap Memphis TN 38103. *Fax:* 901-572-5036

KUO, CHARLES C Y, MATERIALS & PROCESSES, MICROELECTRONICS. *Current Pos:* TECH DIR RES & DEVELOP MAT, CTS CORP, ELKHART, IND, 77- *Personal Data:* b Hubei, China; m 49, Deborah; c Sze-Ping, Sze-Wen-Seot & Stanley. *Educ:* Col Ord Eng, China, BS, 45; Lehigh Univ, Bethlehem, Pa, MS, 57, PhD(chem), 61. *Honors & Awards:* John Wagnon Tech Achievement Award, Int Soc Hybrid Microelectronics, 87. *Prof Exp:* Asst prof chem eng, Col Ord Eng, Taiwan, China, 49-55; res fel chem eng, Lehigh Univ, Bethlehem, Pa, 55-61; mem staff, res & develop mat, Bell Tel Labs, AT&T, Pa, 61-67; eng specialist, res & develop mat, Res & Develop Lab, GTE, NY, 67-71; dept head, res & develop mat, Engelhard Industs, NJ, 71-77. *Concurrent Pos:* Mem prog comt, Int Conf Electronic Components & Mat, 89-; spec ed, Soc Functional Mat, 90- *Mem:* Am Chem Soc; Am Ceramic Soc; Am Soc Metals; Int Soc Microelectronics; Soc Functional Mat. *Res:* Materials and processes of hybrid microelectronics; thick and thin films; resistors; conductors; dielectrics; reliability; interconnection; packaging; author of more than 80 publications; granted 34 patents. *Mailing Add:* CTS Corp 905 West Blvd N Elkhart IN 46514

KUO, CHENG-YIH, polymer science, for more information see previous edition

KUO, CHIANG-HAI, CHEMICAL, ENVIRONMENTAL & PETROLEUM ENGINEERING. *Current Pos:* assoc prof, 70-77, PROF CHEM ENG, MISS STATE UNIV, 77- *Personal Data:* b Tainan, Taiwan, Feb 10, 36; m 59; c 2. *Educ:* Nat Taiwan Univ, BS, 57; Univ Houston, MS, 61, PhD(chem eng), 64. *Honors & Awards:* Award, Am Inst Chem Engrs, 64; Bronze Medal Award, US Environ Protection Agency, 75. *Prof Exp:* Teaching asst, Nat Taiwan Univ, 57-59; engr, Shell Develop Co, 62-64, res engr, 64-70. *Concurrent Pos:* Hearin-Hess distinguished prof, Miss State Univ, 90-93. *Mem:* Am Inst Chem Engrs; Am Inst Mining Metall & Petrol Engrs. *Res:* Mass transfer and chemical reactions; reaction kinetics; flow through porous media; heat transfer; petroleum recovery processes; air and water pollution control. *Mailing Add:* Dept Chem Eng Miss State Univ Mississippi State MS 39762. *Fax:* 601-325-2482; *E-Mail:* kuo@che.msstate.edu

KUO, CHING-CHIANG, STRUCTURAL DYNAMICS, SYSTEM INTEGRATION. *Current Pos:* MGR STRUCT DYNAMICS, BOEING NAM, 96- *Personal Data:* m, Ju-pi Chen; c Roger W & Lillian W. *Educ:* Cheng Kung Univ, BS, 65; Univ Iowa, MS, 68; Mass Inst Technol, PhD(aeronaut & astronaut), 72. *Prof Exp:* Mem tech staff, Rockwell Int, 73-87, supvr vehicle & syst dynamics, 87-91, mgr struct dynamics, 91-95 & 96; spec adv, Mayor Taipei Rapid Transit Systs, Taipei Munic Govt, 95-96. *Concurrent Pos:* Blue Ribbon Comn Rapid Transit Systs, Taipei Munic Govt, 95. *Mem:* Assoc fel Am Inst Aeronaut & Astronaut; Sigma Xi. *Res:* Nonlinear panel flutter when subject to forcing function; past flutter of the panel with various forcing amplitudes and frequencies; unsteady aerodynamics on lifting body using bath sources and doublets. *Mailing Add:* 16938 Mt Hanna Circle Fountain Valley CA 92708. *Fax:* 562-922-1214; *E-Mail:* ching.kuo@boeing.com

KUO, CHO-CHOU, MEDICAL MICROBIOLOGY. *Current Pos:* Fel, Univ Wash, 67-71, asst prof, 71-76, assoc prof, 76-80, PROF PATHOBIOL, UNIV WASH, 80- *Personal Data:* b Taiwan, Sept 12, 34; m 64; c 1. *Educ:* Nat Taiwan Univ, MD, 60; Univ Wash, PhD(prev med), 70. *Mem:* Am Pub Health Asn; Am Col Prev Med; Am Soc Microbiol; Am Asn Immunologists; Am Sexually Transmitted Dis Asn. *Res:* Microbiology and immunology of the Chlamydia Trachomatis organisms which cause eye and genital infection and chlamydia pneumonic which causes respiratory infection; development of diagnostic methods and prevention of the disease. *Mailing Add:* Dept Path & Biol Univ Wash Seattle WA 98195. *E-Mail:* cckuo@u.washington.edu

KUO, CHUNG-MING, CELLULOSE, PULP & PAPER SCIENCES. *Current Pos:* Res chemist, 68-71, sr res chemist, 71-81, RES ASSOC, EASTMAN CHEM CO, 81- *Personal Data:* b Chang-Hwa, Taiwan, China, Aug 6, 35; US citizen; m 66, Freda Lai; c Michael & Susan. *Educ:* Chung-Shing Univ, Taiwan, BS, 58; Syracuse Univ, MS, 64, PhD(org chem), 69. *Mem:* Am Chem Soc. *Res:* Chemistry and new and improved methods for the preparation of cellulose and its derivatives; modification of cellulose and cellulose derivatives for fibers, films and plastics end uses; new products based on cellulose and the related carbohydrate materials. *Mailing Add:* 2625 Brighton Ct Kingsport TN 37660. *Fax:* 423-229-4558

KUO, ERIC YUNG-HUEI, ONCOLOGY, VETERINARY MEDICINE. *Current Pos:* vet med officer, 76-80, RES STAFF, USDA, 80- *Personal Data:* b Chiayi, Taiwan, Aug 8, 34; US citizen; m 68; c 2. *Educ:* Nat Taiwan Univ, BS, 60; Univ Ill, Urbana, MS, 66, PhD(vet med sci), 70. *Prof Exp:* Asst vet parasitol, Dept Vet Med, Nat Taiwan Univ, 61-63; res asst vet physiol, Col Vet Med, Univ Ill, Urbana, 63-69; res assoc endocrinol, Dept Physiol, Sch Med, Boston Univ, 69-71; sr investr vet endocrinol, Mason Res Inst, 71-74, prin investr oncol, 75-76. *Concurrent Pos:* Vet, Southeast Vet Hosp, Taiwan, 61-63; lectr, Grad Div, Anna Maria Col, Mass, 76- *Mem:* AAAS; Endocrine Soc; Am Vet Med Asn. China. *Res:* The roles of infection, infection hormonal imbalance, radiation and immunosuppression in mammary oncogenesis; the responses of hosts and tumors to surgery, radiation and chemotherapy. *Mailing Add:* 2455 Sedgefield Dr Chapel Hill NC 27514

KUO, FRANKLIN F(A-KUN), ELECTRICAL ENGINEERING. *Current Pos:* EXEC DIR, SRI INT, MENLO PARK, CALIF, 82- *Personal Data:* b China, Apr 22, 34; m 58; c 2. *Educ:* Univ Ill, BS, 55, MS, 56, PhD(elec eng), 58. *Prof Exp:* Asst prof elec eng, Polytech Inst Brooklyn, 58-60; mem tech staff, Bell Tel Labs, Inc, 60-66; prof elec eng, Univ Hawaii, 66-82. *Concurrent Pos:* Mem Cosine comt, Nat Acad Eng, 65-72; liaison scientist, US Off Naval Res, London, 71-72; consult ed, Prentice-Hall, Inc; dir info systs, Off Secy Defense, 76-77; coun mem, Asn Comput Mach. *Mem:* Fel Inst Elec & Electronics Engrs; Asn Comput Mach. *Res:* Digital computers; information transmission; computer networks; data communications. *Mailing Add:* 824 La Mesa Dr Portola Valley CA 94028

KUO, HARNG-SHEN, CHEMISTRY, BIOCHEMISTRY. *Current Pos:* anal res chemist, 71-72, radiation safety officer, 72-75, SR STAFF SCIENTIST, CUTTER LABS, 75- *Personal Data:* b Hangchow, China, June 9, 35; m 67; c 3. *Educ:* Cheng Kung Univ Taiwan, BS, 59; La State Univ, New Orleans, MS, 66; Pa State Univ, PhD(chem), 70. *Prof Exp:* Analyst cement, Taiwan Chi Hsin Co, 61; engr, Taiwan Fertilizer Co, 61-64; chemist & fel, Lawrence Berkeley Lab, 70-71. *Mem:* Am Chem Soc. *Mailing Add:* 1012 Leland Dr Lafayette CA 94549

KUO, HSIAO-LAN, DYNAMIC METEOROLOGY, FLUID DYNAMICS. *Current Pos:* PROF METEOROL, UNIV CHICAGO, 62- *Personal Data:* b Mancheng, China, Jan 7, 15; m 49; c 3. *Educ:* Tsing Hua Univ, BS, 37; Univ Chicago, PhD(meteorol), 48. *Prof Exp:* From res assoc meteorol to res meteorologist, Mass Inst Technol, 49-57; vis assoc prof meteorol, Univ Chicago, 57-58; supvr res meteorol & hurricane res proj, Mass Inst Technol, 58-62. *Res:* Dynamics of planetary atmospheres and atmospheric vortices; general circulation; atmospheric radiation; high atmosphere; climate change. *Mailing Add:* 55 S Kimbark Ave Chicago IL 60637

KUO, HUI-HSIUNG, STOCHASTIC DIFFERENTIAL EQUATIONS, BROWNIAN FUNCTIONALS. *Current Pos:* assoc prof, 77-82, PROF RES & TEACHING, LA STATE UNIV, 82- *Personal Data:* b Ta-chia, Taichung, Taiwan, Oct 21, 41; US citizen; m 69, Fukuko Tanaka; c Isaac J & Henry G. *Educ:* Taiwan Univ, BA, 65; Cornell Univ, MA, 68, PhD(math), 70. *Prof Exp:* Vis mem res, Courant Inst, NY Univ, 70-71,; asst prof, res & teaching, Univ Va, 71-75; vis asst prof res & teaching, State Univ NY, Buffalo, 75-76; assoc prof res & teaching, Wayne State Univ, 76-77. *Concurrent Pos:* Mem, Comt Summer Inst, Am Math Soc, 83-86; Ctr STochastic Processes, Univ NC, 84; vis prof, Nagoya Univ, 84, Univ Bielefeld, 86 & 88, Kyushu Univ, 91 & Meijo Univ, 96; prin investr, ARO Res Grant, 94-97; prin investr, ARO Res Grant, 94-97. *Mem:* Am Math Soc; Math Soc Japan; Korean Math Soc. *Res:* Stochastic differential equations, infinite dimensional stochastic analysis, probability and harmonic analysis on infinite dimensional spaces, white noise distribution theory. *Mailing Add:* Dept Math La State Univ Baton Rouge LA 70803. *Fax:* 504-388-4276; *E-Mail:* mmkuo@lsuvax.sncc.lsu.edu

KUO, JOHN TSUNG-FEN, GEOPHYSICS. *Current Pos:* res scientist, Lamont Geol Observ, Columbia Univ, 60-64, from assoc prof to prof mining (geophysics), 64-82, Vinton prof mining (geophysics), 83-85, Ewing & Wurzel prof geophys, 85-, EMER PROF GEOPHYS, COLUMBIA UNIV. *Personal Data:* b Hangchow, China, Apr 1, 22; m 57; c 2. *Educ:* Univ Redlands, BS, 52; Calif Inst Technol, MS, 54; Stanford Univ, PhD(geophys), 58. *Hon Degrees:* ScD, Univ Redlands, 78. *Prof Exp:* From instr to asst prof geol & geophys, San Jose State Col, 56-60. *Concurrent Pos:* Res assoc, Stanford Univ, 58-60; NSF sr fel, Cambridge Univ, 70-71; consult; vis prof, Univ Tex, Austin, 77, Cornell Univ, 78, Technische Universitat Clausthal, WGer, 87; distinguished US sr scientist, Alexander von Humboldt Award, 86-87. *Mem:* Seismol Soc Am; Am Geophys Union; Soc Explor Geophys; fel Geol Soc Am; fel Royal Astron Soc. *Res:* Acoustic, elastical, EM wave scattering and diffractions; geophysical exploration; solid earth and ocean dynamics. *Mailing Add:* Dept Geophys Columbia Univ-2960 New York NY 10027-6902

KUO, JYH-FA, BIOCHEMISTRY, PHARMACOLOGY. *Current Pos:* assoc prof, 72-76, prof biochem, 85-92, PROF PHARMACOL, SCH MED, EMORY UNIV, 76- *Personal Data:* b Kaoshiung, Taiwan, May 19, 33; m 65, Alexandra Loh; c Calvin & Frances. *Educ:* Nat Taiwan Univ, BS, 57; SDak State Univ, MS, 61; Univ Ill, Urbana, PhD(biochem), 64. *Hon Degrees:* MD, Linkoping Univ, Sweden, 80. *Prof Exp:* Res biochemist, Lederle Labs, Am Cyanamid Co, 64-68; from asst prof to assoc prof pharmacol, Sch Med, Yale Univ, 68-72. *Concurrent Pos:* Vis prof, Swedish Med Res Found, Linkoping Univ, Sweden, 70, Peking Univ, China, 83 & Max-Planck Inst Biophys Chem, Ger, 89; Res Career Develop Award, NIH, 71-75; Merit Award, NIH, 86-96; vis lectr, Nat Sci Coun, Taiwan, 93. *Mem:* AAAS; Am Soc Biochem & Molecular Biol; Am Soc Pharmacol & Exp Therapeut. *Res:* Protein kinase C and protein phosphorylation/dephosohorylation systems in signal transduction, cancer, and cardiac function and pathophysiology. *Mailing Add:* Dept Pharmacol Emory Univ Sch Med Atlanta GA 30322. *Fax:* 404-727-0365

KUO, KENNETH K, AERONAUTICAL & ASTRONAUTICAL ENGINEERING. *Current Pos:* DISTINGUISHED ALUMNI PROF MECH ENG, PA STATE UNIV. *Honors & Awards:* Propellants & Combustion Award, Am Inst Aeronaut & Astronaut, 95. *Mailing Add:* Dept Mech Eng Pa State Univ University Park PA 16802

KUO, LAWRENCE C, MOLECULAR ENZYMOLOGY, STRUCTURAL BIOLOGY. *Current Pos:* SR DIR, BIOL CHEM, DEPT INTIVIRAL RES, MERCK & CO. *Personal Data:* b Hong Kong, Feb 8, 51; US citizen; m, Michelle Sparks; c Iain Garrihan & Anna Sophie. *Educ:* Cornell Univ, BS, 74; Univ Chicago, PhD(biophys), 81. *Honors & Awards:* Harold Lamport Award, Biophys Soc. *Prof Exp:* Res fel chem, Harvard Univ, 81-85. *Concurrent Pos:* Res fel, Jane Coffin Childs Fund Med Res, 81-84; Pew scholar; NIH res career develop award; asst prof, Boston Univ, 85- *Mem:* Am Chem Soc; AAAS; Am Soc Biochem & Molecular Biol. *Res:* Biologically related organic and inorganic chemistry; use of chemical methods and approaches to the solution of enzyme actions; the roles of metal ions in metalloenzymes; protein isomerization; anti-HIV therapy; virol proteins. *Mailing Add:* Merck & Co PO Box 4 West Point PA 19486

KUO, LIH, HEMODYNAMICS & CIRCULATORY PHYSIOLOGY, CORONARY MICROCIRCULATION. *Current Pos:* res assoc, 86-89, asst res scientist, 90-91, ASST PROF HEALTH SCI CTR, TEX A&M UNIV, 92- *Personal Data:* b Taipei, Taiwan, Aug 28, 57; m 89, Athena CL-Wu; c Enoch & Esther (Ning. *Educ:* Tung-Hai Univ, BS, 79; Nat Taiwan Univ, MS, 83; Med Col Va, PhD(physiol), 87. *Honors & Awards:* Grega-Zacharkow Young Investr Award, Microcirculatory Soc, 80. *Prof Exp:* Res asst, Nat Defence Med Ctr, 79-81. *Concurrent Pos:* World Cong Microcirculation Travel award, Microcirculation Soc, 81; grad fac, Tex A&M Univ, 90-; mem, Cent Res Rev Comt, Am Heart Asn Tex, 92-; mem, Exp Cardiovasc Sci Study Sect, NIH, 94- *Mem:* Fel Am Physiol Soc; Microcirculatory Soc; fel Am Heart Asn. *Res:* Pathophysiological study of coronary microcirculation; investigating the mechanisms of local regulation of microvascular tone; studying the signal transduction in endothelial cells; studying the interaction of endothelium and vascular smooth muscle in the regulation of vascular resistance. *Mailing Add:* Dept Med Physiol Tex A&M Univ College Station TX 77843-1114

KUO, MINGSHANG, SPECTROSCOPY, CHROMATOGRAPHY. *Current Pos:* SCIENTIST ANALYTICAL CHEMIST NATURAL PROD, PHARMACIA & UPJOHN CO, 79-, SR RES SCIENTIST, 89-, PROJ LEADER CHEM & BIOL SCREENING, UPJOHN LABS, 92- *Personal Data:* b Kaohsiung, Taiwan, Oct, 11, 49; m 74, Hwa M Lin; c Alexander & Michelle. *Educ:* Nat Tsing-Hua Univ, Taiwan, BS, 71; Mich State Univ, PhD(chem), 79. *Mem:* Am Chem Soc. *Res:* Isolation and identification of fermentation products; natural products chemistry; pharmacokinetics drug metabolism research. *Mailing Add:* Upjohn Co 7700 Portage Rd Kalamazoo MI 49001. *Fax:* 616-833-2225

KUO, PAO-KUANG, THEORETICAL PHYSICS. *Current Pos:* asst prof, 69-71, ASSOC PROF PHYSICS, WAYNE STATE UNIV, 71- *Personal Data:* b Hopei, China, Feb 23, 35; m 61; c 2. *Educ:* Nat Taiwan Univ, BSc, 57; Univ Minn, PhD(physics), 64. *Prof Exp:* Instr physics, Cornell Univ, 64-66; from res assoc to instr, Mass Inst Technol, 66-68; vis lectr, Johns Hopkins Univ, 68-69. *Mem:* Am Phys Soc. *Res:* Quantum electrodynamics; theory of elementary particles and coherence phenomena. *Mailing Add:* Dept Physics & Astron Rm 235 Bldg 666 W Hancock Wayne State Univ 5950 Case Ave Detroit MI 48202

KUO, PETER TE, CARDIOLOGY, INTERNAL MEDICINE. *Current Pos:* clin prof med, 87-88, PROF MED, BAYLOR COL MED, 88-; DIR HYPERLIPIDEMIA PROG, HOUSTON VET ADMIN MED CTR, 87- *Personal Data:* b Fukien, China, Mar 21, 16; m 49; c 2. *Educ:* St John's Univ, China, MD, 39; Univ Pa, MMSc, 49, DSc(med), 50. *Honors & Awards:* Sci Award, Am Chinese Asn, 77, 88, 92 & 93. *Prof Exp:* From asst to asst prof med, Med Sch, St John's Univ, China, 40-46; from instr to prof, Sch Med, Univ Pa, 50-73; sr staff mem, Robineete Found Cardiovasc Res, Hosp Univ Pa, 52-73; prof med & dir, Cardiovascular Div, Robert Wood Johnson Med Sch, Univ Med & Dent NJ, 73-82, John G Detwiler prof cardiol, 82-87. *Concurrent Pos:* Consult cardiol & probs lipid metab; estab investr, Am Heart Asn, 55-60, Arteriosclerosis Coun, 58; USPHS career develop award, 61-66; consult, Med & Cardiol Med Ctr, Muhlenberg Hosp, St Peter's Med Ctr, 73-87; hon prof, 2nd Med Col, Shanghai, China, 81; dir, Atherosclerosis Res, Univ Med & Dent, Robert Wood Johnson Med Sch, 82-87; fel, Arteriosclerosis Coun, Am Heart Asn. *Mem:* Fel Gerontol Soc; fel Am Col Physicians; fel Am Col Cardiol; Am Soc Clin Nutrit; Am Nutrit Inst; fel AAAS; Am Fedn Clin Res; Am Med Asn; Asn Univ Cardiologists; fel Am Col Chest Physicians. *Res:* Blood and tissue lipids and their relationship to the problem of arteriosclerosis; circulatory hemodynamics; promote detection, prevention and treatment of dyslipidemias and coronary heart disease; role of lipoprotein (a), oxidized low-density lipoprotein on atherosclerosis and very low blood cholesterol of less than 160 mg/dL on male all-cause mortality. *Mailing Add:* 4215 Milton Houston TX 77005. *Fax:* 713-794-7492

KUO, SCOT CHARLES, CELL BIOPHYSICS. *Current Pos:* ASST PROF, DEPT BIOMED ENG, JOHNS HOPKINS UNIV, 93- *Personal Data:* b July 4, 61; m 92. *Educ:* Harvard Univ, BA, 82; Univ Calif, Berkeley, DPhil, 88. *Prof Exp:* Tech, Dept Chem, Harvard Univ, 81, res, Dept Biochem, 79-82; mem res proj, Dept Biochem, Univ Calif, Berkeley, 82-88; res fel, Dept Cell Biol, Duke Univ, 88-93. *Concurrent Pos:* Fel, Jane Coffin Childs Mem Fund Med Res, 89-92. *Mem:* Am Soc Cell Biol; Biophys Soc. *Res:* Biophysics of microtubule-dependent motility; cellular cytoskeletal mechanics; optical tools for biophysics. *Mailing Add:* Dept Biomed Eng Johns Hopkins Univ Sch Med 720 Rutland Ave Baltimore MD 21205. *E-Mail:* skuo@bme.jhu.edu

KUO, SHAN SUN, APPLIED MATHEMATICS, COMPUTER SCIENCE. *Current Pos:* prof math, Univ NH, 64-77, prof comput sci, 77-96, dir, Comput Ctr, 64-96, EMER PROF, UNIV NH, 96- *Personal Data:* b Nanking, China, Nov 22, 22; m 58; c 1. *Educ:* Nat Chung Cheng Univ, China, BEng, 44; Ohio State Univ, MSc, 48; Harvard Univ, MEng, 54; Yale Univ, DEng, 58. *Prof Exp:* Instr, Nat Chung Cheng Univ, China, 44-46; lectr, Formosa Inst Technol, 46-47; struct engr, Ohio State Univ, 48-52; engr, Carew Steel Prod Corp, 52-53; engr, Fay Spofford & Thorndike, 54-55; from asst prof to assoc prof civil eng, Tufts Univ, 58-64, dir, Comput Ctr, 61-64. *Mem:* Am Math Soc; Asn Comput Mach; Am Soc Civil Engrs; Am Soc Mech Engrs; Am Soc Eng Educ. *Res:* Numerical analysis; computer applications. *Mailing Add:* Dept Comput Sci Univ NH Kingsbury Durham NH 03824

KUO, SHIOU, SOIL CHEMISTRY, PHYSICAL CHEMISTRY. *Current Pos:* ASST SOIL SCIENTIST, WESTERN WASH RES & EXTEN CTR, WASH STATE UNIV, 78- *Personal Data:* b Ping-Tung, Taiwan, Oct 8, 43; m 69; c 3. *Educ:* Chung-Hsing Univ, Taiwan, BS, 66; Utah State Univ, 70; Univ Maine, PhD(soil chem), 73. *Prof Exp:* Res assoc soils, Iowa State Univ, 74-75; res assoc agron, Univ Calif, Davis, 75-78. *Mem:* Am Soc Agron; Soil Sci Soc Am; Chinese Agr Asn; Sigma Xi. *Res:* Nitrogen transformations in soils and their relation to the nitrogen uptake by plant; cations and anions reactions with soil colloidal particles and the plant growth. *Mailing Add:* 2505 Manorwood Dr SE Puyallup WA 98374

KUO, THOMAS TZU SZU, THEORETICAL PHYSICS. *Current Pos:* assoc prof, 68-72, PROF PHYSICS, STATE UNIV NY, STONY BROOK, 72- *Personal Data:* b Peiping, China, July 31, 32; m 62; c 2. *Educ:* Naval Col Eng, Taiwan, BS, 54; Tsing Hua Univ, Taiwan, MS, 59; Univ Pittsburgh, PhD(physics), 64. *Honors & Awards:* Humboldt Award Sr Am Scientists, 77. *Prof Exp:* From instr to asst prof physics, Princeton Univ, 64-68; vis scientist, Argonne Nat Lab, 68 & 69. *Concurrent Pos:* Nordita guest prof physics, Univ Oslo, 74-75, 78 & 83; vis prof, Julich Nuclear Res Ctr, WGer, 79; hon prof, Inst High Energy Physics, China, Jilin Univ & Fudan Univ, 81. *Mem:* Fel Am Phys Soc. *Res:* Theoretical nuclear physics; nuclear structure and the free nucleon nucleon interaction; nuclear matter phase transitions; finite temperature; many body problems. *Mailing Add:* Dept Physics State Univ NY Stony Brook NY 11794

KUO, TZEE-KE, HIGH ENERGY PHYSICS. *Current Pos:* asst prof, 65-68, assoc prof, 68-77, PROF PHYSICS, PURDUE UNIV, WEST LAFAYETTE, 77- *Personal Data:* b Peking, China, Apr 13, 37; m 61. *Educ:* Nat Taiwan Univ, BS, 57; Univ Chicago, MS, 60; Cornell Univ, PhD(physics), 63. *Prof Exp:* Res assoc physics, Brookhaven Nat Lab, 63-65. *Mem:* Am Phys Soc. *Res:* Elementary particle physics. *Mailing Add:* Dept Physics Purdue Univ West Lafayette IN 47907

KUO, WAY, RELIABILITY ENGINEERING, APPLIED STATISTICS. *Current Pos:* PROF & HEAD, INDUST ENG DEPT, TEX A&M UNIV, 93- *Personal Data:* b Taipei, Taiwan, Jan 5, 51; m 77, Suzanne Lee; c Tiffany & Wendy. *Educ:* Nat Tsing-Hua, Taiwan, BS, 72; Kans State Univ, MS, 77, 78, PhD(eng), 80. *Prof Exp:* Tech staff mem, Bell Labs, 80-83; from asst prof to prof, Iowa State Univ, 84-88, prof & chair, indust mfg syst eng, 89-93. *Concurrent Pos:* Vis sci, Oak Ridge Nat Lab, 81; sr res assoc, Nat Res Coun, 86; sr Fulbright Scholar, 91-92. *Mem:* Fel Inst Elec & Electronics Eng; Am Soc Qual Control; Inst Indust Engrs. *Res:* Modeling, evaluation and estimating quality and reliability of modern systems, with emphasis on optional system design. *Mailing Add:* Ind Eng Dept Tex A&M Univ College Station TX 77843-3131

KUO, YEN-LONG, ELECTRICAL ENGINEERING. *Current Pos:* MEM TECH STAFF ELEC ENG, BELL TEL LABS INC, 70- *Personal Data:* b Taipei, Taiwan, Nov 18, 36; m 66; c 1. *Educ:* Taipei Inst Technol, Taiwan, Dipl elec eng, 57; Okla State Univ, MS, 61; Univ Calif, Berkeley, PhD(elec eng), 66. *Prof Exp:* Actg asst prof elec eng, Univ Calif, Berkeley, 66; asst prof, Purdue Univ, 66-70. *Mem:* Inst Elec & Electronics Engrs. *Res:* Computer-aided circuit analysis and synthesis; nonlinear distortion analysis; system theory. *Mailing Add:* 11 Brentwood Circle North Andover MA 01810

KUO, YING L, TELECOMMUNICATION FIELD DESIGN, COMPUTER QUALITY CONTROL PLANNING. *Current Pos:* ENG STAFF, RES & DEVELOP DEPT, FOUNTAIN TECH INC, 89-, DIR, ENG RES & DEVELOP DEPT. *Personal Data:* b Taipei, Taiwan, Aug 19, 58. *Educ:* Van-Nam Inst Technol, BS, 81; Calif Century Univ, BS, 88, MS, 89; Century Univ NMex, PhD(comput eng), 91. *Prof Exp:* Chief engr, Res & Develop Dept, Microtel Inc, 82-84; supvr, Res & Develop Dept, All Best Inc, 84-86; mgr, Res & Develop Dept, Telemate Tech, Inc, 86-88. *Res:* Microcomputer and microprocessor; hardware design and software design. *Mailing Add:* Fountain Tech Inc 50 Randolph Rd Somerset NJ 08873

KUO, YUE, PLASMA PROCESSING TECHNOLOGY, THIN FILM TRANSISTORS. *Current Pos:* RESEARCHER, IBM TJ WATSON RES CTR, 87- *Personal Data:* b Taipei, Taiwan, Jan 2, 53; US citizen; m, Kiyomi Murai. *Educ:* Nat Taiwan Univ, BS, 74; Columbia Univ, MS, 78, PhD(chem eng), 79. *Prof Exp:* Res asst, Columbia Univ, 76-79; pilot lab mgr, Mobay Chem Co, 80-82; prin process engr, Semiconductor Div, Data Gen Co, 84-87. *Concurrent Pos:* Vis res engr, Univ Calif, Berkeley, 82-84; instr semiconductor processing, Northeastern Univ, 85-86. *Mem:* Sr mem Inst Elec & Electronics Engrs; Electrochem Soc; Mat Res Soc. *Res:* Transistors; liquid crystal displays; published over 100 articles. *Mailing Add:* 143 Deer Run Chappaqua NY 10514. *E-Mail:* ykuo@watson.ibm.com

KUPCHELLA, CHARLES E, CANCER BIOLOGY, ENVIRONMENTAL EDUCATION. *Current Pos:* PROVOST, SE MO STATE UNIV, 93- *Personal Data:* b Nanty Glo, Pa, July 7, 42; m 63, Adele Kiel; c Richard, Michele & Jason. *Educ:* Ind Univ Pa, BSEd, 64; St Bonaventure, PhD(physiol), 68. *Prof Exp:* From asst prof to assoc prof, Bellarmine Col, 68-73; assoc dir, Cancer Res Ctr & assoc prof oncol, Sch Med, Univ Louisville, 73-79; chmn biol, Murray State Univ, 79-85; dean, Ogden Col Sci Technol & Health, Western Ky Univ, 85-93. *Concurrent Pos:* NIH/NCI Sci Rev & Eval Comt, 93-; mem, Inst Res Grants Sci Adv Comt, Am Cancer Soc, 93-96; consult environ progs var insts. *Mem:* AAAS; Sigma Xi; Am Asn Cancer Educ (treas, 94-). *Res:* Biology of cancer; biology of the glycosaminoglycans-involvement in metastasis and wound repair; diseases of the skin; environmental science. *Mailing Add:* SE Mo State Univ One Univ Plaza Cape Girardeau MO 63701

KUPCHIK, EUGENE JOHN, ORGANOMETALLIC CHEMISTRY, CHEMICAL GRAPH THEORY. *Current Pos:* from asst prof to assoc prof, 60-68, PROF ORG CHEM, ST JOHN'S UNIV, NY, 68- *Personal Data:* b Wallington, NJ, Aug 26, 29; m 65, Barbara Smith. *Educ:* Rutgers Univ, BS, 51, PhD(org chem), 59. *Prof Exp:* First lt chemist, Wright-Patterson AFB, USAF, 51-52; res chemist, Union Carbide Plastics Co, 54-55; Alfred P Sloan res fel, 56; teaching fel, Du Pont, 57; instr chem, Rutgers Univ, 58-60. *Mem:* Am Chem Soc. *Res:* Organometallic chemistry; organotin compounds; biological properties of organometallic compounds; chemical graph theory; quantitative structure: activity relationships in chemistry, biology and pharmacy. *Mailing Add:* Dept Chem St John's Univ Jamaica NY 11439

KUPCHIK, HERBERT Z, CANCER. *Current Pos:* from asst prof to assoc prof, 76-91, PROF MICROBIOL, PATH & LAB MED, SCH MED, BOSTON UNIV, 91- *Personal Data:* b Brooklyn, NY, Dec 6, 40; m 64; c 2. *Educ:* Bethany Col, BS, 62; Wayne State Univ, MS, 65, PhD(biochem), 67. *Prof Exp:* Asst chem, Wayne State Univ, 62-63, res asst biochem, 64-67; assoc med, Harvard Med Sch, 69-71, assoc biol chem, 71-72, prin res assoc biochem, 72-78. *Concurrent Pos:* Instr biochem & org chem, Marygrove Col, 64-65; NIH fel enzym, Cancer Res Inst, New Eng Deaconess Hosp, Boston, 67-69; res fel enzym, Harvard Med Sch, 68-69; clin assoc, Thorndike Mem Lab, 69-73; res assoc, Mallory Gastroenterol Lab, Boston City Hosp, 69-74, sr res assoc, 74-80; res assoc, Sch Med, Boston Univ, 71-76, mem staff, Hubert H Humphrey Cancer Res Ctr, 80-; mem spec sci staff, Boston City Hosp & Mallory Inst Path, 78- *Mem:* Am Asn Pathologists; Am Soc Microbiol; Am Asn Cancer Res; Am Fedn Clin Res; NY Acad Sci. *Res:* Properties of invasive human tumors; in-vitro screening and evaluation of immunotherapeutic agents; development of monoclonal antibodies to human tumors; in-vitro transformation of human colonic adenomas to carcinomas. *Mailing Add:* Dept Microbiol Boston Univ Sch Med 80 E Concord St Boston MA 02118-2394

KUPEL, RICHARD E, ORGANIC CHEMISTRY, INORGANIC CHEMISTRY. *Current Pos:* CONSULT, SKC INC, 80- *Personal Data:* b Peoria, Ill, Nov 8, 20; m 46; c 1. *Educ:* Monmouth Col, Ill, BS, 48. *Prof Exp:* Chemist, Gen Elec Co, Wash, 48-50, supvr mass spectrometry lab, 50-52, chemist, Ohio, 52-54, unit leader instrumental anal lab, 54-61; asst chief lab phys & chem anal br, Nat Inst Occup Safety & Health, USPHS, 61-73, hazard eval coordr, 73-80. *Concurrent Pos:* Chmn subcomt seven, Intersoc Comt Manual Methods Ambient Air Sampling & Anal. *Mem:* Am Chem Soc; Am Conf Govt Indust Hyg; Am Indust Hyg Asn; Soc Appl Spectros (pres elect, 65). *Res:* Quantitative analytical methods for analysis of trace elements in biological tissues and environmental samples using emission spectrographic, mass spectrometric, x-ray diffraction, gas chromatographic and spectrophotometric procedures and instrumentation; charcoal tube for sampling organic vapors; K-2 spot test of asbestos. *Mailing Add:* 3935 Freeman Ave Hamilton OH 45015-1919

KUPERMAN, ALBERT SANFORD, PHARMACOLOGY, EDUCATIONAL ADMINISTRATION. *Current Pos:* ASSOC DEAN EDUC AFFAIRS, ALBERT EINSTEIN COL MED, 75-, ASSOC PROF MOLECULAR PHARMACOL, 89- *Personal Data:* b New York, NY, Aug 1, 31; m 56, Barbara Noah; c Laura & Meredith. *Educ:* NY Univ, AB, 52; Cornell Univ, PhD(pharmacol), 57. *Prof Exp:* Res fel pharmacol, Med Col, Cornell Univ, 57-58, instr, 58-59; asst prof, Col Med, NY Univ, 59-61; asst prof, Med Col, Cornell Univ, 61-65; assoc prof, Hunter Col, 65-68, prof biol sci, 68; Rockefeller Found vis prof & actg chmn dept pharmacol, Fac Med Sci, Mahidol Univ, Thailand, 68-75. *Concurrent Pos:* USPHS fel, 57-59. *Mem:* Am Soc Pharmacol & Exp Therapeut; fel Am Col Clin Pharmacol. *Res:* General pharmacology; physiology and pharmacology of excitable cells. *Mailing Add:* Off Educ Albert Einstein Col Med 1300 Morris Park Ave Bronx NY 10461. *Fax:* 718-430-8255; *E-Mail:* kuperman@aecom.yu.edu

KUPERS, RUDOLF CARL, IMMUNOLOGY. *Current Pos:* SR SCIENTIST, SCI APPLNS INT CORP, 93- *Personal Data:* b Los Angeles, Calif, Jan 21, 45. *Educ:* Calif State Univ, Northridge, BS, 69, MS, 76; Johns Hopkins Univ, PhD(microbiol), 78. *Prof Exp:* Res fel mech cell mediated cytotoxicity, Max Planck Inst, 80-83; asst prof chem, Johns Hopkins Univ, 83-93. *Mem:* Am Asn Immunologists. *Res:* Autoimmune diseases. *Mailing Add:* Sci Applns Int Corp 5340 Spectrum Dr Suite N Frederick MD 21703

KUPFER, CARL, OPHTHALMOLOGY. *Current Pos:* DIR, NAT EYE INST, 70- *Personal Data:* b New York, NY, Feb 9, 28. *Educ:* Yale Univ, AB, 48; Johns Hopkins Univ, MD, 52. *Hon Degrees:* DSc, Univ Pa, 82. *Honors & Awards:* Pisart Vision Award. *Prof Exp:* Intern & asst resident, Wilmer Eye Inst, Johns Hopkins Hosp, 52-53, lab asst biostatist, Med Sch, Johns Hopkins Univ, 53-54 & 57-58; from instr to asst prof ophthal, Harvard Med Sch, 60-66; prof & chmn dept, Sch Med & res affil, Primate Ctr, Univ Wash, 66-70. *Concurrent Pos:* Res fel ophthal, Wilmer Eye Inst, 57-58; res fel, Harvard Med Sch, 58-60; prog dir ophthal training grant, Mass Eye & Ear Infirmary, 62-66; mem, Vision Res Training Comt, NIH, 63-64 & Neurol Prog Proj B, 67-69; mem, Adv Comt Basic & Clinical Res, Nat Soc Prev Blindness, 69-; clin assoc prof, Howard Univ, 70-; mem, Sci Adv Panel, Res to Prevent Blindness, Inc, 71-75; mem, Sci Adv Comt, Fight for Sight, 71-; chmn, Proj & Priorities Comt, Int Agency Prevention Blindness, 75-; mem, Bd Dirs, Helen Keller Int Inc, 75- *Mem:* Inst Med-Nat Acad Sci; Am Physiol Soc; Asn Res Vision & Ophthal; Am Acad Ophthal; Am Ophthal Soc; Pan Am Ophthal Soc. *Res:* Intraocular pressure and neurophysiology; glaucoma; neuroophthalmology. *Mailing Add:* Nat Eye Inst 31 Center Dr MSC 2510 Bethesda MD 20892-2510. *Fax:* 301-496-9970; *E-Mail:* cak@b31.nei.nih.gov

KUPFER, DAVID, BIOCHEMICAL PHARMACOLOGY, DRUG METABOLISM. *Current Pos:* SR SCIENTIST, WORCESTER FOUND EXP BIOL, 71- *Personal Data:* b Warsaw, Poland, Nov 27, 28; US citizen; m 61; c 3. *Educ:* Univ Calif, Los Angeles, BA, 52, PhD(biochem), 58. *Prof Exp:* Scientist, Worcester Found Exp Biol, 58-60; intermediate scientist & fel, Weizmann Inst Sci, 61-62; res scientist, Lederle Labs, Am Cyanamid Co, 62-71. *Mem:* Am Chem Soc; Am Soc Biol Chemists; Soc Pharmacol & Exp Therapeut. *Res:* Drug-drug interactions; prostaglandin metabolism; hepatic monoxygenases; hormonal activity of environmental pollutants. *Mailing Add:* Worcester Found Exp Biol 222 Maple Ave Shrewsbury MA 01545-2737

KUPFER, DAVID J, PSYCHIATRY. *Current Pos:* PROF & CHMN, DEPT PSYCHIAT, UNIV PITTSBURGH; dir res, Western Psychiat Inst & Clin. *Mem:* Inst Med-Nat Acad Sci. *Mailing Add:* Western Psychiat Inst & Clin 3811 O'Hara St Pittsburgh PA 15213

KUPFER, DONALD HARRY, STRUCTURAL & SALT DOME GEOLOGY. *Current Pos:* from asst prof to assoc prof, 55-66, prof, 66-80, EMER PROF GEOL, LA STATE UNIV, BATON ROUGE, 81- *Personal Data:* b Los Angeles, Calif, Oct 4, 18; m 52, Romaine Littlefield; c Madeline (Van Epps) & John C. *Educ:* Calif Inst Technol, BS, 40; Univ Calif, Los Angeles, AM, 42; Yale Univ, MS, 51, PhD(geol), 51. *Honors & Awards:* A I Levorsen Award, 75. *Prof Exp:* Geologist, Gladding McBean & Co, 41-42 & US Geol Surv, 42-55. *Concurrent Pos:* Indust mineral consult, 58-; NSF sr fel, NZ, 62-63; Cent Treaty Orgn minerals mapping consult, Turkey, 66 & Pakistan, 67; fel, Salt Domes, Spain & Ger, 69, Can, Mexico, Israel, 79; pres, Geol Res Indust Minerals Corp, 77-92. *Mem:* Fel AAAS; Am Asn Petrol Geologists. *Res:* Earthquakes; faults; salt domes; nonmetal mining; tectonics; areal geology; Gulf Coast geology; salt mine safety; energy resources; history of geology. *Mailing Add:* 210 West Circle Dr Canon City CO 81212

KUPFER, JOHN CARLTON, SYSTEMS PERFORMANCE ANALYSIS. *Current Pos:* mem tech staff, Rockewell Int, 85-96, MEM TECH STAFF, BOEING NAM, 96- *Personal Data:* b Los Angeles, Calif, Feb, 12, 55; m 87, Joan M Todd. *Educ:* Rice Univ, BA, 77; Univ Ariz, MS, 81 & PhD(physics), 85. *Mem:* Am Phys Soc; Mat Res Soc. *Res:* Systems analysis; development and operation of system performance models for requirements definition; design tradestudies, error tree flowdown and impact of baseline changes. *Mailing Add:* PO Box 577 Atwood CA 92811

KUPFER, SHERMAN, INTERNAL MEDICINE, PHYSIOLOGY. *Current Pos:* assoc prof med, Mt Sinai Sch Med, 66-72, from assoc dean to sr assoc dean, 68-80, dep dean, 80-85, assoc prof physiol, 68-93, PROF MED, MT SINAI SCH MED, 72-, PROF PHYSIOL, 94- *Personal Data:* b Jersey City, NJ, Apr 28, 26; m 51, Adele Glassman; c Marcia A, Joel M & Kenneth C. *Educ:* Cornell Univ, MD, 48. *Prof Exp:* Res fel physiol, Sch Med, Western Reserve Univ, 49-50; res fel, Med Col, Cornell Univ, 50-51, from instr to asst prof physiol, 55-66. *Concurrent Pos:* Asst to dir med res, Mt Sinai Hosp, 56-58, res assoc, 58-60, asst attend physician, 60-65, dir clin res ctr, 63-86, assoc attend physician, 65-72, attend physician, 72- *Mem:* Am Physiol Soc; Am Fedn Clin Res; Am Soc Artificial Internal Organs; Am Heart Asn; Harvey Soc; Am Soc Nephrology. *Res:* Renal and cardiovascular physiology; quantitative measurement of organ blood flow and function-noninvasively; granted one US patent. *Mailing Add:* Dept Med Mt Sinai Sch Med Box 1100 One E 100th St New York NY 10029-6574

KUPFERBERG, HARVEY J, PHARMACOLOGY. *Current Pos:* PHARMACOLOGIST, EPILEPSY BR, NEUROL DIS PROG, NAT INST NEUROL & COMM DIS & STROKE, 71- *Personal Data:* b New York, NY, Jan 4, 33; m 62; c 2. *Educ:* Univ Calif, Los Angeles, BS, 55; Univ Southern Calif, PharmD, 59; Univ Calif, San Francisco, PhD(pharmacol), 62. *Prof Exp:* USPHS fel pharmacol, Univ Calif, San Francisco, 60-62 & 62-63; staff fel, Nat Heart Inst, 63-65; from instr to asst prof, Univ Minn, Minneapolis, 65-71. *Concurrent Pos:* USPHS res grant, 66-69. *Mem:* AAAS; Am Pharmaceut Asn; Acad Pharmaceut Sci; Am Soc Pharmacol & Exp Therapeut; Soc Toxicol. *Res:* Pharmacodynamics; metabolism of drugs; mechanism of action of anticonvulsant drugs. *Mailing Add:* Epilepsy Br Nat Inst Neurol & Comm Dis & Stroke NIH Fed Bldg Rm 512 Bethesda MD 20892-0001

KUPFERBERG, LENN C, MATERIALS ANALYSIS. *Current Pos:* sr res scientist, 84-87, SR DEVELOP SCIENTIST & MGR, MAT ANALYSIS LAB, ELECTRONIC SYSTS LAB, RAYTHEON, 87- *Personal Data:* b Flushing, NY, July 27, 51; m 76, Karen F Fink; c David & Beth. *Educ:* Trinity Col, Conn, BS, 73; Univ Rochester, NY, MA, 75, PhD(physics), 79. *Prof Exp:* Assoc fel physics, Mass Inst Technol, 78-80; asst prof physics, Worcester Polytech Inst, 80-84. *Concurrent Pos:* Vis scientist physics, Mass Inst Technol, 80-84. *Mem:* Am Phys Soc; AAAS; Inst Elec & Electronics Engrs;

Sigma Xi; Mat Res Soc; Micros Soc Am. *Res:* Materials anaylsis; characterization of IR-optical materials. *Mailing Add:* Raytheon Electronic Systs Lab 131 Spring St Lexington MA 02173. *Fax:* 781-860-3194; *E-Mail:* lenn_c_kupferberg@raytheon.com

KUPFERMAN, ALLAN, PHARMACOLOGY, OPHTHALMOLOGY. *Current Pos:* Asst prof pharmacol, 69-78, ASSOC PROF PHARMACOL & OPHTHAL, SCH MED, BOSTON UNIV, 78- *Personal Data:* b New York, NY, Aug 5, 35; m 59; c 2. *Educ:* Univ Bridgeport, BA, 59; Clark Univ, AM, 61; Univ Vt, PhD(pharmacol), 66. *Res:* Pharmacokinetics of topically applied steroids in the eye. *Mailing Add:* 28 Moose Hill St Sharon MA 02067

KUPFERMAN, STUART L, METROLOGY, PHYSICAL OCEANOGRAPHY. *Current Pos:* SR MEM TECH STAFF, SANDIA NAT LABS, 80- *Personal Data:* b New York, NY, June 30, 37; m 66, Virginia Sullivan; c Jocelyn S & Kimberly J. *Educ:* Polytech Inst Brooklyn, BS, 59; Harvard Univ, AM, 64, PhD(physics), 67. *Prof Exp:* Res assoc phys oceanog, Univ RI, 68-70; asst prof phys oceanog, Univ Del, 70-78; vis investr, Woods Hole Oceanog Inst, 78-80. *Concurrent Pos:* Grantee, Univ Del Res Found, 71-72 & NSF, 71-78. *Mem:* AAAS; Am Phys Soc. *Res:* Automation of high accuracy calibration and measurement systems. *Mailing Add:* Dept 1542 Sandia Nat Lab PO Box 5800 Albuquerque NM 87185-0665

KUPFERMANN, IRVING, NEUROPSYCHOLOGY. *Current Pos:* assoc prof med psychol, 74-79, PROF PHYSIOL & PSYCHIAT, COL PHYSICIANS & SURGEONS, COLUMBIA UNIV, 79-; ASSOC RES SCIENTIST, NY STATE PSYCHIAT INST, 73- *Personal Data:* b New York, NY, Jan 26, 38; m 65; c 2. *Educ:* Univ Fla, BS, 59; Univ Chicago, PhD(biopsychol), 64. *Honors & Awards:* Richard Temple Award, Univ Chicago, 65; Res Scientist Develop Award, NIMH, 69, Merit Award, 90. *Prof Exp:* Res fel, Harvard Med Sch, 65-66; from instr to assoc prof, NY Univ Med Sch, 66-74. *Concurrent Pos:* Mem, NIMH Neuropsychol Study Sect, 75-; assoc ed, J Neurosci, Neurosci Letts & Brain Behav Sci. *Mem:* Soc Neurosci. *Res:* Invertebrate behavior and learning; neural mechanisms of learning and motivation; Aplysia; feeding behavior in Aplysia. *Mailing Add:* Columbia Univ 722 W 168th St New York NY 10032

KUPIECKI, FLOYD PETER, BIOCHEMISTRY. *Current Pos:* RES SCIENTIST, UPJOHN CO, 60- *Personal Data:* b Bronson, Mich, May 1, 26; m 50, Rose Johnson; c Erik & Stephanie. *Educ:* Western Mich Univ, BS, 50; Univ Notre Dame, PhD(chem), 53. *Prof Exp:* Res chemist, Michael Chem Corp, 53-55; res assoc org chem & biochem, Univ Pa, 55-56; from res assoc to instr biochem, Univ Mich, 56-59; Fulbright fel, Biochem Inst, Helsinki, Finland, 59-60. *Mem:* Am Soc Biochem & Molecular Biol; Am Chem Soc; Sigma Xi. *Res:* Diabetes research; lipid metabolism and adipose tissue enzymes; metabolism in islets of diabetic animals. *Mailing Add:* 5409 Circlewood Dr Kalamazoo MI 49001-5546

KUPIEC-WEGLINSKI, JERZY W, TRANSPLANTATION IMMUNOBIOLOGY, CELLULAR IMMUNOLOGY. *Current Pos:* res fel, Harvard Med Sch, 79-81, instr, 82-84, asst prof, 85-87, ASSOC PROF SURG, HARVARD MED SCH, 87- *Personal Data:* b Warsaw, Poland, July 11, 51; US citizen; m 92, Krystyna Czerpak. *Educ:* Warsaw Med Acad, MA, 75; Polish Acad Sci, PhD(immunol), 79. *Prof Exp:* Asst surg res, Polish Acad Sci, 76-79; res fel med, Brigham Women's Hosp, 80-83; fel, Oxford Univ, 86. *Concurrent Pos:* Prin investr, Am Heart Found, 87-89, NIH grant, 88-; consult pharmaceut, Smith Kline Beecham, Bayer Inst; vis prof, over 30 univs & hosps, USA, Europe & SAm; mem, Sci Studies Comt, Am Soc Transplant Physicians, 93- *Mem:* Fel Transplant Soc; fel Am Soc Transplant Physicians; fel Am Asn Immunologists; fel Am Fedn Clin Res; fel Europ Soc Surg Res. *Res:* Dissection of the host immune response after organ transplantation; efficiency and therapeutic applicability of various modalities which may prove beneficial as immunosuppressive drugs in allograft recipients; testing intricate cellular, humoral and cytokine events in transplanted hosts. *Mailing Add:* Surg Res Lab Harvard Med Sch 260 Longwood Ave Boston MA 02115-6092. *Fax:* 617-432-4353

KUPKE, DONALD WALTER, BIOCHEMISTRY. *Current Pos:* from asst prof to prof, 57-92, chmn dept, 64-66, EMER PROF BIOCHEM, SCH MED, UNIV VA, 92- *Personal Data:* b Omaha, Nebr, Mar 16, 22; m 49, Carol Fulton; c 5. *Educ:* Valparaiso Univ, AB, 47; Stanford Univ, MS, 49, PhD(chem), 52. *Prof Exp:* Nat Res Coun fel med sci, Carlsberg Lab, Denmark, 52-53 & Uppsala Univ, Sweden, 53-54; USPHS fel, Carlsberg Lab & Stanford Univ, 55; mem staff, Carnegie Inst, Stanford Univ, 55-56. *Concurrent Pos:* Vis prof, Otago Univ, NZ, 84. *Mem:* AAAS; Am Soc Biol Chemists; Am Chem Soc; Biophys Soc; Protein Soc. *Res:* Protein biophysical chemistry; magnetic balancing methods; density, viscosity and osmotic pressure; volume change on metal-ion coordination to biological molecules; hydration changes of DNA. *Mailing Add:* Dept Biochem Univ Va Sch Med Charlottesville VA 22901. *Fax:* 804-924-5069; *E-Mail:* dwk@uva.pcmail.virginia.edu

KUPPENHEIMER, JOHN D, JR, OPTICS, NON-IMAGING OPTICS. *Current Pos:* asst mgr, Diffraction Ltd, Div, Sanders Assocs, 72-73, dir, Optical Metrology Lab, 73-79, sr prin physicist, 79-84, ENG FEL LOCKHEED SANDERS, 84-; PROF PHYSICS, TUFTS UNIV, 84- *Personal Data:* b Orange, NJ, Sept 15, 41; div. *Educ:* Lafayette Col, BS, 63; Boston Univ, MA, 65; Worcester Polytech Inst, PhD(physics), 89. *Honors & Awards:* Tech Achievement Award, Sanders Assoc, 84; Chmn's Award, Sanders Asn, 86; Robert E Gross Award, Lockheed Corp, 87. *Prof Exp:* Fel physics, Worcester Polytech Inst, 69-70, asst prof, 70-71; scientist, Diffraction Ltd, Inc, 71-72. *Concurrent Pos:* Adj prof physics, Univ Lowell, 75-87. *Mem:* Optical Soc Am; Sigma Xi. *Res:* Quantum optics; photon count statistics; lasers; optical constants of semiconductors; atmospheric optics; optical guidance; optical counter measures; development of IR lasers; development of IR countermeasures; applications of non-imaging optics to laser pumping; IR countermeasures and illumination. *Mailing Add:* 100 Brookfield Rd Tewksbury MA 01876-2123

KUPPERMAN, HERBERT SPENCER, endocrinology; deceased, see previous edition for last biography

KUPPERMAN, MORTON, MATHEMATICAL STATISTICS. *Current Pos:* RETIRED. *Personal Data:* b New York, NY, Mar 19, 18; m 46, Anita. *Educ:* City Col New York, BS, 38; George Washington Univ, MA, 50, PhD(math statist), 57. *Prof Exp:* Statistician, Gen Staff, US War Dept, 40-41 & Europ Cent Inland Transp Orgn, France, 46; statistician, Med Statist Div, Off Army Surgeon Gen, 47-55; mathematician, Nat Security Agency, 55-73; sr lectr math statist, Univ Leicester, Eng, 73-78. *Concurrent Pos:* Prof lectr, George Washington Univ, 57-73. *Mem:* Inst Math Statist; Royal Statist Soc; Math Asn Am; Am Statist Asn; Sigma Xi. *Res:* Distribution theory; application of information theory to multivariate analysis and statistical inference; counterexamples in probability and statistics. *Mailing Add:* 5904 Mt Eagle Dr Apt 214 Alexandria VA 22303-2535

KUPPERMAN, ROBERT HARRIS, APPLIED MATHEMATICS, OPERATIONS RESEARCH. *Current Pos:* exec dir, Sci Technol, 79-85, SR ADVISOR, CTR STRATEGIC & INT STUDIES, GEORGETOWN UNIV, 83-, SCI ADVISOR, 93- *Personal Data:* b New York, NY, May 12, 35; m 67, Helen Slotnick; c 1. *Educ:* NY Univ, BA, 56, PhD(appl math), 62. *Honors & Awards:* Outstanding Serv Awards, Exec Off President, 68-71; Order of Paul Revere Patriot, 70; Presidential Citations, 71-73,. *Prof Exp:* Instr math, NY Univ, Pratt Inst & Hunter Col, 56-60; sr engr, Jet Propulsion Lab, Calif Inst Technol, 60-62; exec adv opers res, Douglas Aircraft Co, Inc, 62-64; mem sr staff, Inst Defense Anal, 64-67; asst dir, Natural Resource Anal Ctr, Exec Off of Pres, 67-70, dep asst dir, President's Off Emergency Preparedness, 70-71, asst dir, 71-73; chief scientist, US Arms Control & Disarmament Agency, 73-79. *Concurrent Pos:* Prin engr, Repub Aviation Corp, 59-60; consult, US Civil Serv Comn, 65 & US Army Security Agency, Army Intel & Army Electronic Warfare Bd, 66; lectr, Univ Md, 65, vis prof govt & polit, 74-76; expert consult, Exec Off President, 67-68; dep exec dir, President's Property Rev Bd, 70-73; mem, Army Sci Bd, 79-, Coun Foreign Relations, 84-; pres, Kuppeman Assocs, Inc, 79-; sr lab fel, Los Alamos Nat Lab, 80- *Mem:* Fel NY Acad Sci; fel Opers Res Soc; Soc Indust & Appl Math; Int Inst Strategic Studies; Mil Opers Res Soc. *Res:* Strategic analysis and arms race stability; conversational computer systems and crisis management; conventional arms transfers; terrorism. *Mailing Add:* 2832 Ellicott St NW Washington DC 20008

KUPPERMANN, ARON, CHEMICAL PHYSICS. *Current Pos:* PROF CHEM PHYSICS, CALIF INST TECHNOL, 63- *Personal Data:* b Sao Paulo, Brazil, May 6, 26; nat US; m 51, Roza Davidson; c Baruch, Miriam, Nathan & Sharon. *Educ:* Univ Sao Paulo, Brazil, ChemE, 48, CE, 53; Univ Notre Dame, PhD(phys chem), 55. *Honors & Awards:* Venable lectr, Univ NC, 67; Werner lectr, Univ Kans, 68; Reilly Lectr, Univ Notre Dame, 65. *Prof Exp:* Asst prof phys chem, Cath Univ Sao Paulo, 49-50 & chem, Inst Aeronaut Technol, 50-51; head anodizing sect, Ajax Indust & Trade Co, 52; res assoc phys chem, Radiation Proj, Univ Notre Dame, 53-55; from instr to assoc prof, Univ Ill, 55-63. *Concurrent Pos:* Resident res assoc, Argonne Nat Lab, 57; res assoc, Inst Atomic Energy, Sao Paulo, 59-60; NSF fel, 68-69; Guggenheim fel, 76-77; consult, Jet Propulsion Lab, 65-69, TRW Systs Group, 70-77, World Bank, 83-; chmn joint chem study group, Nat Acad Sci-Nat Res Coun, Brazil, 73-76. *Mem:* Fel Am Inst Chem; fel Am Phys Soc; Am Chem Soc; AAAS. *Res:* Experimental and theoretical chemical dynamics; collisions in crossed molecular beams; laser spectroscopy and photochemistry; radiation chemistry; low energy electron impact phenomena, experiment and theory; variable angle photoelectron spectroscopy. *Mailing Add:* Dept Chem 127-72 Calif Inst Technol Pasadena CA 91125

KUPPERS, JAMES RICHARD, PHYSICAL CHEMISTRY. *Current Pos:* RETIRED. *Personal Data:* b Newland, Ind, Aug 4, 20; m 44, Faith Farnham; c James F, Theresa (Lanning), Kathryn & Mary (Stewart). *Educ:* Univ Fla, BS, 43, PhD(chem), 57; La State Univ, MS, 47. *Prof Exp:* Food technologist, United Fruit Co, 47-49, assoc biochemist, 49-54; res chemist textile fibers dept, E I Du Pont de Nemours & Co, 57-60; assoc prof chem, Pfeiffer Col, 60-64; from assoc prof to prof chem, Univ NC, Charlotte, 65-86. *Mem:* Am Chem Soc. *Res:* Solution thermodynamics. *Mailing Add:* Dept Chem Univ NC Charlotte NC 28223-0001

KUPRIYANOV, VALERY V, BIOENERGETICS, ION TRANSPORT. *Current Pos:* vis res scientist, 92-94, assoc res officer, 94-96, SR RES OFFICER, INST BIODIAG, NAT RES COUN CAN, 96- *Personal Data:* b Zhukorka, USSR, Jan 28, 47; m 79, Smirnova Elena; c Nina & Mikhail. *Educ:* Lomonosov Moscow State Univ, BSc, 70, PhD(chem), 75; USSR Cardiol Res Ctr, Moscow, DSc, 87. *Prof Exp:* Jr res scientist, Lomonosov Moscow State Univ, 72-76; jr res scientist, USSR Cardiol Res Ctr, Moscow, 76-81, sr res scientist, 81-88, prin investr, 88-92. *Concurrent Pos:* Adj prof, Dept Biochem, Univ Man, 97- *Mem:* Int Soc Heart Res; Int Soc Magnetic Resonance Med; Am Heart Asn; NY Acad Sci. *Res:* Studies of relationship between energetics and ion fluxes in normal and abnormal cardiac muscle, using nuclear magnetic resonance; development of new methods for drug testing and non-invasive diagnostics. *Mailing Add:* Inst Biodiag 435 Ellice Ave Winnipeg MB R3B 1Y6 Can. *Fax:* 204-984-6978; *E-Mail:* kupriyanov@ibd.nrc.ca

KUPSCH, WALTER OSCAR, GEOLOGY. *Current Pos:* Prof, Univ Sask, 50-86, dir, Inst North Studies, 65-72, dir, Churchill River Study, 73-76, EMER PROF, UNIV SASK, 86- *Personal Data:* b Amsterdam, Neth, Mar 2, 19; nat Can; m 45, Emmy H de Long; c Helen E, Yvonne T & Richard C. *Educ:* Univ Amsterdam, BSc, 43; Univ Mich, MS, 48, PhD(geol), 50. *Hon Degrees:* LLD, Univ Sask, 97. *Concurrent Pos:* Prin geologist, Geol Surv, Sask, 50-56, consult, 56-; ed, Musk-Ox; mem, Sci Coun Can, 76-82; mem, NWT Sci Adv Bd, 76-82, petrol adv, 80-83, North Dev Adv Coun, 85-88. *Mem:* Fel Arctic Inst NAm; fel Geol Asn Can; fel Geol Soc Am; Am Asn Petrol Geol; fel Royal Can Geog Soc; fel Royal Soc Can. *Res:* Stratigraphy; geomorphology; glacial geology. *Mailing Add:* Dept Geol Sci Univ Sask Saskatoon SK S7N 0W0 Can. *Fax:* 306-966-8593

KUPSTAS, EDWARD EUGENE, ORGANIC CHEMISTRY. *Current Pos:* RETIRED. *Personal Data:* b Eynon, Pa, Aug 1, 21; m 57; c 5. *Educ:* Fordham Col, BS, 51, MS, 53, PhD(chem), 58. *Prof Exp:* Res chemist, Textile Fibers Dept, E I du Pont de Nemours & Co, Inc, 55-88. *Mem:* Am Chem Soc. *Res:* Structure and synthesis of ichtiamin; dyes; polymers; polyesters. *Mailing Add:* 1614 Hardee Rd Kinston NC 28501-2018

KURACHI, KOTOKU, HUMAN GENETICS, MOLECULAR BIOLOGY. *Current Pos:* assoc prof, 86-90, PROF, DEPT HUMAN GENETICS & CELLULAR & MOLECULAR BIOL PROG, UNIV MICH, 90- *Personal Data:* b Amagi City, Japan, Nov 16, 41; c 2. *Educ:* Kyushu Univ, Japan, BS, 65, MS, 67, PhD, 70. *Honors & Awards:* Res Career Develop Award, NIH; Int Prize, French Asn Hemophiliacs-World Fedn Hemophilia. *Prof Exp:* Res assoc, Dept Biochem, Kyushu Univ, Japan, 70; sr fel, Dept Biochem, Univ Wash, Seattle, 70-72 & 74-75, Dept Biol Struct, 72-74, from sr res assoc to res assoc prof biochem, 75-86. *Concurrent Pos:* Vis lectr, Ctr Biochem & Biophys Sci & Med, Harvard Med Sch, 83-86; travel award, Am Soc Biochem & Molecular Biol, 88; mem, Res Peer Rev Comt, Am Heart Asn, Mich, 89-; consult. *Mem:* Am Chem Soc; Am Soc Biol Chem & Molecular Biol; AAAS; Am Soc Human Genetics; Am Soc Hemat. *Res:* Human genetics; author of numerous scientific publications; blood coagulation; protease; gene therapy. *Mailing Add:* Dept Human Genetics Med Sch Univ Mich 3712 Med Sci II Bldg Ann Arbor MI 48109-0618. *Fax:* 313-747-3158; *E-Mail:* kotoku.kurachi@med.umich.edu

KURAJIAN, GEORGE MASROB, MECHANICAL DESIGN, SOLID MECHANICS. *Current Pos:* RETIRED. *Personal Data:* b Highland Park, Mich, Oct 28, 26; m 55; c 3. *Educ:* Univ Detroit, BME, 48, ME, 63; Univ Mich, MSE, 53. *Prof Exp:* From instr to asst prof eng mech, Univ Detroit, 48-64; from asst prof to prof mech eng & eng mech, Univ Mich, Dearborn, 72-92, chmn, Dept Mech Eng, 75-92. *Concurrent Pos:* Consult, indust & govt agencies, 54- *Mem:* Am Soc Eng Educ; fel Am Soc Mech Engrs; Soc Exp Stress Anal; Indust Math Soc; Int Asn Vehicle Design; Int Asn Struct Mech Reactor Technol. *Res:* Design and stress analysis of structural shells; space frames; amphibious vehicles; chemical machinery; automotive components; automotive dynamometers and test cells; physical testing laboratory projects; mechanical design; finite element; solid mechanics; theories of failure; fatigue. *Mailing Add:* 1754 Cass Lake Rd Keego Harbor MI 48320

KURAMITSU, HOWARD KIKUO, BIOCHEMISTRY. *Current Pos:* PROF ORAL BIOL, STATE UNIV NY, BUFFALO, 93- *Personal Data:* b Los Angeles, Calif, Oct 18, 36; m 70, Kim Chua; c Tracy Kristine. *Educ:* Univ Calif, Los Angeles, BS, 57, PhD(biol chem), 62. *Prof Exp:* Jr res biochemist, Sch Med, Univ Calif, Los Angeles, 61-62; res fel bact, Harvard Med Sch, 62-63; res assoc microbiol, Sch Med, Univ Southern Calif, 63-67; from asst prof to assoc prof, Med Sch, Northwestern Univ, 67-79, prof microbiol, 79-89; prof pediat dent, Univ Tex Health & Sci Ctr, San Antonio, 89-93. *Concurrent Pos:* NIH Oral Biol & Med Study Sect, 84-89. *Mem:* AAAS; Am Soc Biol Chemists; Am Soc Microbiol; Int Asn Dent Res. *Res:* Regulation of carbohydrate metabolism in oral microorganisms; isolation and characterization of genes involved in pathogenic proper ties of oral microorganisms. *Mailing Add:* Dept Oral Biol State Univ NY 3435 Main St Buffalo NY 14214-3092. *Fax:* 716-829-3942; *E-Mail:* kuramits@acsu.buffalo.edu

KURATA, MAMORU, SEMICONDUCTOR DEVICE MODELING. *Current Pos:* engr, Illum Div, Toshiba Corp, 61-64, researcher, Res & Develop Ctr, 67-82, sr researcher, 82-86, CHIEF RES SCIENTIST, RES & DEVELOP CTR, TOSHIBA CORP, 86- *Personal Data:* b Nagoya, Japan, Apr 27, 36. *Educ:* Yokohama Nat Univ, Bachelor, 61; Univ Tokyo, Dr(elec eng), 73. *Prof Exp:* Guest researcher semiconductors, Tech Univ Aachen, Ger, 64- 66. *Mem:* Fel Inst Elec & Electronics Engrs. *Res:* Semiconductor device modeling with its application to high power devices; gate turn-off thyristors; high speed devices such as heterojunction bipolar transistors; author of several books. *Mailing Add:* Toshiba Res Corp 1 Koukai Toshiba-Cho Saiwai-Ku Kawasaki Kanagawa 210 Japan

KURATH, DIETER, THEORETICAL NUCLEAR PHYSICS. *Current Pos:* assoc physicist, 51-60, SR PHYSICIST, ARGONNE NAT LAB, 60- *Personal Data:* b Evanston, Ill, Oct 17, 21; m 45; c 4. *Educ:* Brown Univ, AB, 42; Univ Chicago, PhD(physics), 51. *Prof Exp:* Asst, Univ Chicago, 47-51. *Concurrent Pos:* Guggenheim fel, 57-58; vis prof, Univ Wash, 61-62 & State Univ NY Stony Brook, 69-70; sr vis fel, Nuclear Physics Lab, Oxford Univ, 73-74, Univ Melbourne, 88. *Mem:* Am Phys Soc. *Res:* Shell model of nuclear structure. *Mailing Add:* Argonne Nat Lab Argonne IL 60439. *Fax:* 630-252-3903; *E-Mail:* b03477@anlos

KURATH, PAUL, ORGANIC CHEMISTRY. *Current Pos:* RETIRED. *Personal Data:* b St Gallen, Switz, June 18, 24; nat US; div; c 5. *Educ:* Swiss Fed Inst Technol, dipl, 48, DSc, 51. *Prof Exp:* Res assoc & fel pharmaceut chem, Univ Kans, 51-53 & org chem, Univ Rochester, 54-58; res chemist, Res Div, Abbott Labs, 58-88. *Mem:* Am Chem Soc; The Chem Soc; Swiss Chem Soc; Sigma Xi. *Res:* Organic synthesis; natural products; steroids; antibiotics; peptides. *Mailing Add:* 5247 Rockpointe Ct Gurnee IL 60031-1804

KURATH, SHELDON FRANK, POLYMER CHEMISTRY, RHEOLOGY. *Current Pos:* assoc prof phys chem, 65-69, prof chem, 69-93, EMER PROF CHEM, UNIV WIS, OSHKOSH, 93- *Personal Data:* b Moscow, Idaho, Mar 29, 28; m 54; c 3. *Educ:* Univ Wis, BS, 50, MS, 51, PhD(chem), 54. *Prof Exp:* Res aide, Inst Paper Chem, Lawrence Univ, 53-65. *Mem:* Am Chem Soc; Soc Rheol; Am Inst Chem Eng; Tech Asn Pulp & Paper Indust. *Res:* Non-Newtonian flow of polymers and pigment suspensions; polymer viscoelasticity; colloid chemistry. *Mailing Add:* 2413 S Greenview Appleton WI 54915-4832

KURCHACOVA, ELVA S, ORGANIC CHEMISTRY. *Current Pos:* RETIRED. *Personal Data:* b Oriente, Cuba, Aug 5, 21; m 44; c 2. *Educ:* Univ Havana, DSc(physics, chem), 45. *Prof Exp:* Dir res, Linner Labs, Cuba, 45-61; assoc res chemist, Miles Labs, Inc, 61-78; sr assoc res scientist, 78-89. *Concurrent Pos:* Pres & dir, Yelene Prod, 53-61. *Mem:* AAAS; Am Chem Soc; NY Acad Sci. *Res:* Pharmaceuticals; organic synthesis; development of medicinal drugs. *Mailing Add:* 3355 Jaywood Terr No J 112 Boca Raton FL 33431-6579

KURCZEWSKI, FRANK E, ENTOMOLOGY. *Current Pos:* from asst prof to prof entom, 66-77, PROF ENVIRON & FOREST BIOL, COL ENVIRON SCI & FORESTRY, STATE UNIV NY, 77- *Personal Data:* b Erie, Pa, May 24, 36; m 59; c 4. *Educ:* Allegheny Col, BS, 58; Cornell Univ, MS, 62, PhD(insect taxon), 64. *Prof Exp:* Res assoc entom, Univ Kans, 64-66, vis asst prof, 66. *Concurrent Pos:* NSF fel, 64-65; NIH fel, 65-66. *Res:* Comparative behavior and systematics of digger wasps; insect behavior. *Mailing Add:* Dept Environ Sci State Univ NY Col Environ Sci 320 Bray Hall Syracuse NY 13210-2723

KURCZYNSKI, THADDEUS WALTER, CLINICAL GENETICS, CHILD NEUROLOGY. *Current Pos:* PROF, DEPT PEDIAT & PATH & DIR, GENETICS CTR NORTHWEST OHIO, MED COL OHIO, 81- *Personal Data:* b Hamtramck, Mich, Oct 31, 40; m 92, Margaret Nadeau Gray; c Peter L & Karen L. *Educ:* Univ Mich, BS, 62, MS, 63; Case Western Reserve Univ, PhD(human genetics), 69, MD, 70; Am Bd Psychiat & Neurol, with spec competence in child neurol; Am Bd Med Genetics, cert clin genetics & clin biochem genetics. *Prof Exp:* From intern to resident neurol, Univ Mich Hosps, 70-73; resident pediat, Children's Hosp Mich, 73-74; fel pediat neurol, Albert Einstein Col Med, 74-76; asst prof, Dept Pediat, Div Pediat Neurol, Dept Med, Div Neurol & Human Genetics & Genetics Ctr, Case Western Reserve Univ, 76-81. *Mem:* Am Soc Human Genetics; Am Acad Neurol; Child Neurol Soc; Am Med Asn; Am Col Med Genetics. *Res:* Clinical genetics; metabolic disorders of the nervous system. *Mailing Add:* Dept Pediat Med Col Ohio PO Box 10008 Toledo OH 43699-0008

KUREY, THOMAS JOHN, NUCLEAR PHYSICS, REACTOR PHYSICS. *Current Pos:* AT MED SYST, GEN ELEC CO, MILWAUKEE. *Personal Data:* b Boston, Mass, Feb 21, 37. *Educ:* Boston Col, BS, 58; Pa State Univ, MS, 61, PhD(physics), 63. *Prof Exp:* Physicist, Knolls Atomic Power Lab, Gen Elec Co, 64-80. *Mem:* Am Phys Soc; Am Nuclear Soc. *Res:* Beta and gamma spectroscopy; applications of solid state nuclear detectors; electron spin resonance study of decay of unstable free radicals in gamma irradiated solids; reactor physics analytical methods; critical experiments. *Mailing Add:* 2130 La Rochelle Ct Brookfield WI 53045

KURFESS, JAMES DANIEL, ASTROPHYSICS. *Current Pos:* ASTROPHYSICIST, E O HULBURT CTR SPACE RES, US NAVAL RES LAB, 69- *Personal Data:* b Perrysburg, Ohio, Nov 8, 40; div; c 2. *Educ:* Case Inst Technol, BS, 62, MS, 63, PhD(physics), 67. *Prof Exp:* Res assoc space sci, Rice Univ, 67-69. *Concurrent Pos:* Mem data base group study uses sci balloons, Nat Acad Sci, 75; mem, Sci Adv Panel Long Duration Balloon Develop Prog; prin investr, Oriented Scintillation Spectros Exp, Gamma Ray Observ, NASA; mem, Comt Space Astron & Astrophys, Nat Acad Sci, 83-87; secy-treas, Div Astrophysics, Am Phys Soc, 80-84, vchairperson, 90, chairperson, 91. *Mem:* Am Phys Soc; Am Astron Soc; Int Astron Union. *Res:* Hard x-ray and gamma-ray observations of solar and extra-solar sources using balloons and satellite instrumentation; development of long duration balloon-borne capabilities. *Mailing Add:* Naval Res Lab Code 7650 4555 Overlook Ave SW Washington DC 20375-5352

KURFESS, THOMAS ROLAND, PRECISION ENGINEERING, QUALITY ASSURANCE. *Current Pos:* ASSOC PROF MECH ENG, CARNEGIE MELLON UNIV, 89- *Personal Data:* m 88, Adriana D Praddaude. *Educ:* Mass Inst Technol, SB, 86, SM, 87 & 88, PhD(mech eng), 89. *Honors & Awards:* Young Investr Award, NSF, 92; George Tallman Ladd Award, Carnegie Inst Technol, 92. *Prof Exp:* Draper fel, C S Draper Lab, 85-89. *Concurrent Pos:* Expert, Lawrence Livermore Nat Lab, 92- *Mem:* Am Soc Mech Engrs; Soc Mfg Engrs; Inst Elec & Electronics Engrs; Am Soc Eng Educ; Nat Soc Prof Engrs. *Res:* Research and development in system dynamics and control with applications to CAD/CAM/CAE systems. *Mailing Add:* Ga Tech Sch Med Eng Atlanta GA 30332

KURIAKOSE, AREEKATTUTHAZHAYIL, MATERIAL SCIENCE, CERAMICS PROCESSING & CHARACTERIZATION. *Current Pos:* RES SCIENTIST, NATURAL RESOURCES CAN, GOVT CAN, 81- *Personal Data:* b Palai, India, Aug 20, 33; Can citizen; m 60, Alice Joseph; c Neena, Binny & Joseph. *Educ:* Univ Madras, India, BSc, 53, MA, 55, PhD(chem), 61. *Prof Exp:* Lectr chem, St Thomas Col, Palai, India, 55-56; res engr, Norton Res Corp Can Ltd, 66-69, sr res engr, 69-75, supvr mat res, 75-81. *Concurrent Pos:* Ed-in-chief, J Can Ceramic Soc, 87-89. *Mem:* Can Ceramic Soc; Am Ceramic Soc; Sigma Xi. *Res:* High temperature chemistry; abrasive materials; ceramics microstructure and properties; solid electrolytes and energy storage and generating systems; hydrogen fuel cells and sensors; toughened ceramics; silicon carbide. *Mailing Add:* Natural Resources Can 555 Booth St Ottawa ON K1A 0G1 Can. *E-Mail:* akuriaks@nrcan.gc.ca

KURIGER, WILLIAM LOUIS, ELECTRICAL ENGINEERING. *Current Pos:* From asst prof, to assoc prof, 66-80, PROF ELEC, ENG, UNIV OKLA, 80- *Personal Data:* b Waterloo, Iowa, Aug 7, 33; m 56; c 7. *Educ:* Univ Iowa, BSEE, 58; Iowa State Univ, ME, 63, PhD(elec eng), 66. *Prof Exp:* Engr, Collins Radio Co, 58-64. *Mem:* Inst Elec & Electronics Engrs; Optical Soc Am; Sigma Xi. *Res:* Laser applications; electronics. *Mailing Add:* Dept Elec Eng & Comput Sci Univ Okla Norman OK 73019

KURIHARA, NORMAN HIROMU, ORGANIC CHEMISTRY. *Current Pos:* RES SPECIALIST, AGR ORG DEPT, DOW CHEM CO, 66- *Personal Data:* b Oxnard, Calif, Mar 23, 38; m 65. *Educ:* Univ Calif, Santa Barbara, BA, 61; Univ Calif, Davis, PhD(org chem), 65. *Prof Exp:* Res fel, Univ Calif, 65-66. *Mem:* Am Chem Soc; Sigma Xi. *Res:* Agricultural and pesticide chemistry. *Mailing Add:* 503 Rock Oak Rd Walnut Creek CA 94598

KURIHARA, YOSHIO, METEOROLOGY. *Current Pos:* res meteorologist, Environ Sci Serv Admin, 67-70, RES METEOROLOGIST, GEOPHYS FLUID DYNAMICS LAB, NAT OCEANIC & ATMOSPHERIC ADMIN, 70- *Personal Data:* b Korea, Oct 24, 30; Japan citizen; m 60, Michiko Ishihara; c Junko & Takao. *Educ:* Univ Tokyo, BA, 53, PhD(geophys), 62. *Honors & Awards:* Meteorol Soc Japan Award, 75; B Miller Award, Am Meteorol Soc, 84, J Charney Award, 96; Gold Medal Award, US Dept Com, 93; Fujiwara Award, Meterol Soc Japan, 94. *Prof Exp:* Tech officer, Japan Meteorol Agency, 53-59; res officer, Meteorol Res Inst, 59-63; res meteorologist, Geophys Fluid Dynamics Lab, US Weather Bur, 63-65; res officer, Meteorol Res Inst, 65-67. *Concurrent Pos:* Vis lectr, Princeton Univ, 71-86, lectr & prof, 91- *Mem:* Fel Am Meteorol Soc; Am Geophys Union; Meteorol Soc Japan. *Res:* Construction of statistical-dynamical model of the atmosphere; simulation of the hurricane; prediction of tropical cyclones. *Mailing Add:* Geophys Fluid Dynamics Lab Princeton Univ PO Box 308 Princeton NJ 08542

KURIS, ARMAND MICHAEL, PARASITOLOGY, MARINE ECOLOGY. *Current Pos:* ASSOC PROF BIOL SCI, UNIV CALIF, SANTA BARBARA, 75- *Personal Data:* b New York, NY, May 16, 42. *Educ:* Tulane Univ, BS, 63; Univ Calif, Berkeley, MA, 66, PhD(zool), 71. *Prof Exp:* Asst prof zool, Univ Fla, 73-74; asst prof zool & marine sci, Univ NC, Chapel Hill, 74-75. *Concurrent Pos:* NIH fel, G W Hooper Found, Univ Calif, San Francisco, 71-72; NIH fel, Dept Zool, Univ Mich, Ann Arbor, 72-73; actg asst prof, Bodega Marine Lab, Univ Calif, Bodega Bay, 73, 74 & 75; prin investr, Marine Sci Inst, Univ Calif, Santa Barbara, 78- *Mem:* Am Soc Ichthyol & Herpetol; AAAS; Ecol Soc Am; Soc Protozool; Am Soc Parasitol; Crustacean Soc. *Res:* Parasite ecology; biological control; crustacean biology; molting physiology; nemertean biology; competition; parasitic castration; shrimp taxonomy; limb regeneration; population biology; prawn aquaculture. *Mailing Add:* Dept Biol Sci Univ Calif Santa Barbara 552 University Ave Santa Barbara CA 93106-0002

KURITZKES, ALEXANDER MARK, ORGANIC CHEMISTRY. *Current Pos:* RETIRED. *Personal Data:* b Leipzig, Ger, May 3, 24; nat US; wid; c Linda A & Michael S. *Educ:* Univ Calif, BA, 48; Univ Basel, PhD(chem), 59. *Prof Exp:* Res chemist, R J Strasenburgh Co, NY, 49-52 & Mattin Labs, Mearl Corp, 59-92. *Mem:* Sigma Xi. *Res:* Isolation and determination of structures of natural products; organic analytical chemistry; spectroscopy. *Mailing Add:* 6 Murray Hill Sq No 203 New Providence NJ 07974-1528

KURIYAMA, KINYA, DRUG RECEPTOR, GAMA-AMINOBUTYRIC ACID. *Current Pos:* from instr to asst prof, 58-63, PROF PHARMACOL & CHMN DEPT, KYOTO PREFECTURAL UNIV MED, 71-, DIR, GRAD SCH, 79- *Personal Data:* b Kyoto, Japan, July 11, 32; m 59, Chieko; c Takuya & Nagato. *Educ:* Kyoto Prefectural Univ Med, MD, 57, PhD(pharmacol), 63. *Honors & Awards:* Sci Award, Japanese Med Asn, 82. *Prof Exp:* Res assoc pharmacol, Johns Hopkins Univ Sch Med, 63-64; sr res scientist, City Hope Nat Med Ctr, 64-67; assoc prof pharmacol, Sch Med, Loma Linda Univ, 67-69; prof neurochem, Sch Med, State Univ NY, 70-71. *Concurrent Pos:* Mem coun, Japanese Pharmacol Soc, 74-, Japanese Soc Neuropsychopharmacol, 87-90 & Asian WPac Pharmacol Soc, 88-; ed, Neurochem Int, 82-; assoc ed, Alcohol & Alcoholism, 85-; pres, Japanese Pharmacol Soc, 93-, 15th Cong Int Soc Neurochem, 93. *Mem:* Int Soc Neurochem; Int Soc Biomed Res Alcoholism (pres, 95-); Am Soc Pharmacol & Exp Therapeut; Japanese Med Soc Alcohol & Drug Studies (pres, 87). *Res:* Neurochemical and pharmacological studies on amino acid neurotransmitters, drug receptors, drug dependence and signal transductions in exitable cells. *Mailing Add:* 69-1 Iwagakakiuchi-cho Kamigamo Kita-Ku Kyoto 603 Japan. *Fax:* 81-075-251-5314

KURIYAMA, MASAO, X-RAY PHYSICS, MATERIALS SCIENCE. *Current Pos:* CONSULT, 90- *Personal Data:* b Tokyo, Japan, Oct 29, 31; m 58; c 1. *Educ:* Tokyo Metrop Univ, BS, 53; Univ Tokyo, MS, 55, DSc(physics), 58. *Honors & Awards:* Silver Medal, US Dept Com, 74, IR-100, 79. *Prof Exp:* Res assoc, Tokyo Metrop Univ, 58-59; res assoc x-ray physics, Inst Solid State Physics, 59-62; sr scientist, Westinghouse Elec Corp, 62-66; assoc prof physics, Univ Tokyo, 66-67; physicist, Inst Mat Sci & Eng, Nat Bur Standards, 67-80, supvry physicist, 80-90. *Concurrent Pos:* Vis prof, Nat Lab High Energy Physics, Japan, 86. *Mem:* Am Crystallog Asn; Am Phys Soc; Phys Soc Japan. *Res:* Magnetism; x-ray dynamical diffraction; crystal perfection; crystal growth; x-ray inelastic scattering; synchrotron radiation topography; x-ray microscopy; x-ray nondestructive evaluation; x-ray tomographic imaging. *Mailing Add:* 20337 Bickleton Pl Gaithersburg MD 20879

KURKJIAN, CHARLES R(OBERT), CERAMICS. *Current Pos:* SCIENTIST, BELL COMMUN RES, 94- *Personal Data:* b Wanamassa, NJ, Dec 7, 29; m 55; c 3. *Educ:* Rutgers Univ, BS, 52; Mass Inst Technol, ScD(ceramics), 55. *Prof Exp:* Res assoc glass, Mass Inst Technol, 55-57; fel, Univ Sheffield, Eng, 57-59; mem tech staff inorg chem, Bell Tel Labs, 59-94. *Mem:* Nat Acad Eng; fel Brit Soc Glass Technol; fel Am Ceramic Engrs; Acad Ceramics. *Res:* Glass; ceramics; general high temperature inorganic chemistry. *Mailing Add:* 82 Harrison Brook Dr Basking Ridge NJ 07920

KURKOV, VICTOR PETER, ORGANIC CHEMISTRY, CATALYSTS. *Personal Data:* b Zrenjanin, Yugoslavia, Mar 29, 36; US citizen; m 57, Sara Semeredi; c Paul & Theodore. *Educ:* NY Univ, BChE, 63; Columbia Univ, MA, 65, PhD(org chem), 67. *Prof Exp:* Res asst biochem, Col Med, NY Univ, 58-63; res chemist, Chevron Res Co, 67-74, sr res chemist, Chem Res Dept, 74-83, sr res assoc, 83-91, staff scientist, 91-96. *Mem:* Am Chem Soc. *Res:* Free radical reactions; oxidation; homogeneous catalysis; new petrochemical processes; polymer chemistry; reactive extrusion. *Mailing Add:* 66 Dunfires Terr Centerville CA 94901

KURLAND, ALBERT A, PSYCHIATRY. *Current Pos:* RES PROF PSYCHIAT, SCH MED, UNIV MD, 79- *Personal Data:* b Wilkesbarre, Pa, June 29, 14; m 41; c 2. *Educ:* Univ Md, BS, 36, MD, 40. *Prof Exp:* Staff psychiatrist, Spring Grove State Hosp, State of Md, 49-53, dir med res, 53-60, dir res, Dept Ment Hyg, 60-69, dir, Md Psychiat Res Ctr, 69-77. *Mem:* AMA; Am Psychiat Asn. *Res:* Chlorpromazine in the treatment of schizophrenia; clinical reaction and tolerance to lysergic acid diethylamine tartrate in chronic schizophrenia; the drug placebo and its psychodynamic and conditional reflex action; comparative effectiveness of eight phenothiazines; author of over 185 publications in clinical Psychopharmacology. *Mailing Add:* Taylor Manor Hosp 6317 Park Heights NE Baltimore MD 21215-2937

KURLAND, JEFFREY ARNOLD, SOCIOBIOLOGY, PRIMATOLOGY. *Current Pos:* asst prof, 75-84, ASSOC PROF ANTHROP, PA STATE UNIV, UNIV PARK, 84- *Personal Data:* b New York, NY, Nov 19, 43; m 67; c 2. *Educ:* Cornell Univ, BA, 67; Harvard Univ, PhD(anthrop), 76. *Prof Exp:* Res assoc primatol, Primate Res Inst, Kyoto Univ, 72-73; instr anthrop, Harvard Univ, 74-75. *Mem:* AAAS; Animal Behav Soc; Int Primatol Soc; Soc Study Evolution; Am Asn Phys Anthropologists; Sigma Xi. *Res:* Primate sociobiology and behavioral ecology; crab-eating, rhesus, Japanese and barbary macaques; human sociobiology. *Mailing Add:* Dept Anthrop Pa State Univ 409 Carpenter Bldg University Park PA 16802-3404

KURLAND, JONATHAN JOSHUA, PHYSICAL ORGANIC CHEMISTRY. *Current Pos:* chemist, 68-75, proj scientist, 75-84, RES SCIENTIST, UNION CARBIDE CHEM & PLASTICS CO INC, 84- *Personal Data:* b Boston, Mass, Jan 11, 39; m 64, Dorothy Baker; c Brenda & Zelig. *Educ:* Univ Pa, BA, 60; Harvard Univ, MA, 67, PhD(chem), 68. *Prof Exp:* Res assoc chem, Columbia Univ, 67-68. *Mem:* Am Chem Soc; Am Soc Testing Mat; Am Inst Chem Engrs. *Res:* Oxidation and free-radical chemistry; process research and development; process safety technology. *Mailing Add:* 1617 Kirklee Rd Charleston WV 25314-2426

KURLAND, LEONARD T, MEDICINE, EPIDEMIOLOGY. *Current Pos:* RETIRED. *Personal Data:* b Baltimore, Md, Dec 24, 21; m 42, Miriam Feinstein; c Geoffrey, Steven, Robert, Keith & Ellen (Hussey). *Educ:* Johns Hopkins Univ, BA, 42, DrPH, 51; Univ Md, MD, 45; Harvard Univ, MPH, 48. *Honors & Awards:* Golden Sci Hope Chest Award, Nat Mult Sclerosis Soc, 66; Charcot Award, Int Fedn Mult Sclerosis Soc, 83; Maurice C Pincoffs lectr in Med, Univ Md Sch Med, 90; Peripheral Neuropathy Asn Award, Introducing/Applying Epidemiol Methods, 92; James D Bruce Mem Award, Pre Med, Am Col Physicians, 96. *Prof Exp:* Intern, Univ Md Hosp, 45-46; asst resident, Glenn Dale Tuberc Sanatorium, 46; asst dir, Div Tuberc Control & Sanatoria, State Mass, 46-47; epidemiologist, NIMH, 48-54; chief, Epidemiol Br, Nat Inst Neurol Dis & Blindness, NIH, 55-64, consult, Collab & Field Prog, 65-86; fel neurol, Mayo Clin, 52-53, res assoc biometry & med statist, 53-55, prof epidemiol, Mayo Grad Sch Med, 64-94, consult & chmn, Dept Med Statist, Epidemiol & Pop Genetics, Mayo Clin & Mayo Found, 64-86, sr consult, Dept Health Sci Res, Sect Clin Epidemiol, 87-94. *Concurrent Pos:* Res assoc, Dept Epidemiol, Johns Hopkins Univ, 50-51, assoc epidemiol, Sch Hyg & Pub Health, 74-81; adj fac mem, San Diego State Univ, 85; fel neuropath, Armed Forces Inst Path, 55-56; vis lectr, Dept Neurol, Med Col SC, 56; prof lectr neurol, Georgetown Univ, 57; clin asst prof neurol, Howard Univ, 59-62, prof, 62-64; med dir, USPHS, 64; mem res comt, Mayo Clinn, 66-70, consult comt, 72-74, clin coord comt, 73-75, subcomt cancer prog eval, 73-74; assoc ed, Am J Epidemiol, 72-; contrib ed, Am J Indust Med, 80-89; adj fac mem, San Diego State Univ, 85; consult-ed, J Clin Epidemiol, 81- *Mem:* Am Soc Human Genetics; fel AMA; fel Am Pub

Health Asn; Am Neurol Asn; Am Epidemiol Soc (vpres, 72, pres, 74); Am Acad Neurol; Int Epidemiol Asn; Am Asn Hist Med; Soc Epidemiol Res; Asn Teachers Prev Med; Am Col Prev Med; fel Soc Adv Med Systs; Int Soc Pharmacoepidemiol; Int Fedn Med Systs Soc; World Fedn Neurol; Am Col Physicians. *Res:* Human ecology; medical record systems; geographic pathology; human genetics as applied to neurology; epidemiology of chronic disease; author of three books and 493 technical papers. *Mailing Add:* 1165 Plummer Circle Rochester MN 55902. *Fax:* 507-284-5036

KURLAND, ROBERT JOHN, NUCLEAR MAGNETIC RESONANCE. *Current Pos:* SR RESEARCHER, DEPT SPEC IMAGING-RADIOL, GEISINGER MED CTR, 85- *Personal Data:* b Denver, Colo, Apr 2, 30; m 64; c 5. *Educ:* Calif Inst Technol, BS, 51; Harvard Univ, MA, 53, PhD(chem physics), 55. *Prof Exp:* Res assoc, Nat Bur Standards-Nat Res Coun, 56-58; from instr to assoc prof chem, Carnegie Mellon Univ, 58-68; assoc prof chem, State Univ NY Buffalo, 68-85. *Mem:* Am Asn Phys Med; Soc Magnetic Resonance Imaging. *Res:* Magnetic imaging and spectroscopy. *Mailing Add:* RR 4 Danville PA 17821

KURLAND, SUSAN L, AVIATION LAW. *Current Pos:* chief asst corp coun, 87-88, DEP CORP COUN, DEPT LAW, CITY CHICAGO, 88-; GEN COUN, CHICAGO-GARY REGIONAL AIRPORT AUTHORITY, 95-; ASSOC ADMINR AIRPORTS, FED AVIATION ADMIN. *Educ:* Brandeis Univ, BA, 73; Boston Univ, JD, 76. *Prof Exp:* Asst city solicitor, Law Dept, City Newton, Mass, 76-82; attorney, Ancal, Glink, Diamond, Murphy & Cope, PC, Chicago, 82-87. *Concurrent Pos:* Chmn, Infrastructure Comt, US Dept Transp. *Res:* National airport planning, including safety standards, design and engineering. *Mailing Add:* 2555 Pennsylvania Ave NW Apt 1011 Washington DC 20037-1651

KURMES, ERNEST A, FORESTRY. *Current Pos:* assoc prof, 67-80, PROF FORESTRY, NORTHERN ARIZ UNIV, 80- *Personal Data:* b Brooklyn, NY, Jan 19, 31; m 91, Patricia A Hall; c 2. *Educ:* Lehigh Univ, BA, 53; Yale Univ, MS, 57, MF, 58, PhD(forest ecol), 61. *Prof Exp:* Asst prof forestry, Southern Ill Univ, Carbondale, 61-67. *Mem:* Fel AAAS; Soc Am Foresters; Ecol Soc Am; Sigma Xi. *Res:* Forest ecology; regeneration of forest tree species. *Mailing Add:* Forestry Northern Ariz Univ Box 4098 N Flagstaff AZ 86011-0001. *Fax:* 520-523-1080

KURNICK, ALLEN ABRAHAM, chemistry, nutrition; deceased, see previous edition for last biography

KURNICK, JOHN EDMUND, HEMATOLOGY, ONCOLOGY. *Current Pos:* ASSOC CLIN PROF MED (HEMAT/ONCOL), UNIV CALIF, IRVINE, 79- *Personal Data:* b New York, NY, Feb 9, 42; m 69, Luann Fogliani; c David S & Katherine R. *Educ:* Harvard Univ, BA, 62; Univ Chicago, MD, 66. *Prof Exp:* Intern, Univ Wash Hosps, 66-67; resident med, Stanford Univ Hosps, 67-68; fel hemat, 68-70, asst prof med, Univ Colo Med Ctr & chief, Hemat Serv, Denver Vet Admin Hosp, 73-78. *Mem:* Am Col Physicians; Am Fedn Clin Res; Am Soc Clin Oncol; Am Soc Hemat; Int Soc Exp Hemat. *Res:* Hematopoietic cellular differentiation and control of granulopoiesis; erythropoiesis in anemias of chronic diseases and uremia; chemotherapy of malignant disorders. *Mailing Add:* 11411 Brookshie Suite 103 Downey CA 90241. *Fax:* 562-862-4034

KURNICK, NATHANIEL BERTRAND, BIOCHEMISTRY, MEDICINE. *Current Pos:* assoc prof med in residence & assoc internist, 65-68, chmn div hemat, 66-71, CLIN PROF MED, UNIV CALIF, IRVINE, 68- *Personal Data:* b Brooklyn, NY, Nov 8, 17; m 89, Sally A Kreger; c John E, Katherine J (deceased) & James T. *Educ:* Harvard Univ, BA, 36, MD, 40; Am Bd Internal Med, dipl, 51, cert oncol, 73, cert hemat, 74. *Prof Exp:* Workman fel med & biochem, Mass Gen Hosp, Harvard Univ, 40-41; intern, Mt Sinai Hosp, NY, 41-42, resident med, 46-47; Nat Res Coun & Am Cancer Soc res fel biochem & cytochem, Rockefeller Inst, 47-48 & Karolinska Nobel Inst, Stockholm, 48-49; asst prof med & dir lab cell res, Med Sch, Tulane Univ, 49-54; assoc clin prof med, Univ Calif, Los Angeles, 54-65, assoc internist, 59-65. *Concurrent Pos:* Vis physician, Charity Hosp, New Orleans, La, 49-54 & Touro Infirmary, 52-54; consult, Charity Hosp, Pineville, La, 49-54; mem staff, Vet Admin Hosp, Long Beach, Calif, 54-59, consult, 59-; vis physician, Harbor Gen Hosp, Torrance Calif, 54-59, consult, 59-66; vis physician, Los Angeles County Hosp, 65-68; chmn dept med, Long Beach Community Hosp, 66-67; staff mem var hosps; dir oncol-hemat lab, Long Beach Community Hosp, 81- *Mem:* Histochem Soc; Am Soc Hemat; Soc Exp Biol & Med; Int Soc Hemat; Int Soc Exp Hemat. *Res:* Nucleic acids; chemistry and metabolism; nucleolytic enzymes; cytochemistry; hematology; in vitro chemosensitivity research (oncology); radiation biology; Sigma Xi. *Mailing Add:* 1760 Termino Ave G20 Long Beach CA 90804. *Fax:* 562-498-4435; *E-Mail:* nbkurnick@pol.net

KURNIT, DAVID MARTIN, GENETICS, MOLECULAR BIOLOGY. *Current Pos:* INVESTR, HOWARD HUGHES MED INST, 86-; PROF PEDIAT & HUMAN GENETICS, MED SCH, UNIV MICH, 86- *Personal Data:* b Brooklyn, NY, Dec 24, 47; m 93, Kristine Tewksbury; c Heather (Spicer), Katherine & Jennifer. *Educ:* Brooklyn Col, BA, 68; Albert Einstein Col Med, PhD(cell biol), 74, MD, 75. *Prof Exp:* From asst prof to assoc prof pediat, Harvard Med Sch, 79-86. *Concurrent Pos:* Nat Res Serv award, NIH, 77-79, clin investr award, Nat Inst Child Health & Human Develop, 82-85, res career develop award, 85-90. *Mem:* Am Soc Human Genetics; Soc Pediat Res; Cytogenetics & Cell Genetics; Am Soc Biochem & Molecular Biol; Sigma Xi. *Res:* Molecular analysis of cardiogenesis and Down syndrome; sequence copy changes in cancer. *Mailing Add:* Univ Mich 3520 MSRB I Ann Arbor MI 48109-0650. *Fax:* 313-936-9353; *E-Mail:* david.kurnit@med.umich.edu

KURNOW, ERNEST, STATISTICS. *Current Pos:* From instr to prof econ, Schs Bus, NY Univ, 48-62, chmn quant anal area, 62-76, chmn doctoral prog, Grad Sch Bus Admin, 76-85, prof statist, 62-86, EMER PROF STATIST, SCHS BUS, NY UNIV, 86- *Personal Data:* b New York, NY, Oct 21, 12; m 38, Joyce Litzky; c Ruth (Jarrett), Susan (Weistrop) & Alice (Morin). *Educ:* City Col New York, BS, 32, MS, 33; NY Univ, PhD(econ), 51. *Concurrent Pos:* Lincoln Found grant, 58-61; study dir, Tri-State Transp Comt, 64-66, Finance Mass Transit, 71-72 & Gov Spec Comn, 71-72; Fulbright grant, Athens, Greece, 66-67; consult, Tri-State Regional Planning Comn, 73-75 & New York Temp Comn City Finances, 75-76; dir, Careers Bus Prog, 78-86. *Mem:* Fel Am Statist Asn; Int Statist Inst; Inst Mgt Sci; Am Econ Asn; Am Inst Decision Sci. *Res:* Applications of statistics in fields of transportation and state and local government; design of sampling studies. *Mailing Add:* 3 Washington Sq Village New York NY 10012

KURODA, PAUL KAZUO, CHEMISTRY. *Current Pos:* from asst prof to prof, 52-81, DISTINGUISHED PROF CHEM, UNIV ARK, FAYETTEVILLE, 81- *Personal Data:* b Fukuoka, Japan, Apr 1, 17; nat US; m 53; c 3. *Educ:* Univ Tokyo, BS, 39, ScD(inorg chem), 44. *Honors & Awards:* Nuclear Appln Award, Am Chem Soc, 78. *Prof Exp:* Asst prof chem, Univ Tokyo, 44-49; fel, Univ Minn, 49-52. *Concurrent Pos:* Assoc chemist, Argonne Nat Lab, 57-58. *Mem:* AAAS; Am Phys Soc; Geochem Soc; Am Chem Soc; Am Geophys Union; Sigma Xi. *Res:* Natural radioactivity; nuclear and radiochemistry; cosmochemistry; geochemistry; spontaneous fission; low-level counting; radioactive fallout. *Mailing Add:* 4191 Del Rosa Ct Las Vegas NV 89121-5011

KUROHARA, SAMUEL S, RADIOBIOLOGY, RADIOTHERAPY. *Current Pos:* ASSOC RADIOTHERAPIST, WHITTIER ONCOL MED CLIN, 75- *Personal Data:* b Hilo, Hawaii, Apr 21, 31; m 56; c 3. *Educ:* Wash Univ, BA, 53, MD, 57; Univ Rochester, PhD(radiobiol), 64. *Prof Exp:* Intern gen med, Jewish Hosp, St Louis, 57-58; res radiol, Strong Mem Hosp, 58-61, asst radiotherapist, 61-64; radiotherapist, US Naval Hosp, San Diego, 64-66; assoc dir radiation & assoc chief cancer res, Roswell Park Mem Inst, NY, 66-68; asst dir radiother, Med Ctr, 68-74, prof radiol, 68-74, CLIN PROF RADIOL, SCH MED, UNIV SOUTHERN CALIF, 75- *Concurrent Pos:* Instr radiol, Sch Med, Univ Rochester, 61-64; clin consult, Roswell Park Mem Inst, NY, 68-; specialist physician, Los Angeles County Univ Southern Calif Med Ctr, 68-; consult, Tech Serv Corp, 60-71; Good Samaritan Hosp, Los Angeles, 69-72, Whittier Oncol Med Clin, 71- & Alpha Omega Serv, 73- *Mem:* Radiol Soc NAm; AMA; Am Soc Therapeut Radiol; Radiation Res Soc; Sigma Xi. *Res:* Computer applications in the study of medical and biological data; computer application to automated system in radiotherapy; effects of ionizing radiation on normal tissues; mechanisms of tumor control with radiation. *Mailing Add:* 825 Oak Knoll Circle Pasadena CA 91106

KUROKAWA, KANEYUKI, MICROWAVES, OPTICAL COMMUNICATIONS. *Current Pos:* dep dir, Fujitsu Labs, 75-79, dir, 79-85, managing dir, 85-92, vpres, 92-94, FUJITSU FEL, FUJITSU LABS, 94- *Personal Data:* b Tokyo, Japan, Aug 14, 28; m 57, Yasuko Nomura; c Michiko & Hiroko. *Educ:* Univ Tokyo, Bachelor Eng, 51, Dr Eng, 58. *Honors & Awards:* Pioneer Award, Inst Elec & Electronics Engr, 96; Distinguished Contrib Award, Inst Electronic Info & Commun Engrs, 96. *Prof Exp:* Asst prof, Univ Tokyo, 57-63; mem tech staff, Bell Labs, 63-64; supvr, 64-75. *Concurrent Pos:* Vis prof, Inst Indust Sci, Univ Tokyo, 86-89. *Mem:* Fel Inst Elec & Electronics Engrs; Asn Comput Mach; Inst Electronics, Info & Commun Engrs Japan. *Res:* Microwave circuit theory; parametric amplifier; balanced transistor amplifier; solid state oscillators theory; solid state switches; analysis of head crash of hard discs; technical management; optical fiber communication. *Mailing Add:* Fujitsu Labs Ltd 4-1-1 Kamiodanaka Nakaharaku Kawasaki 211 Japan

KUROKAWA, KIYOSHI, MEDICINE. *Current Pos:* DEAN & PROF MED, SCH MED, TOKAI UNIV, 96- *Personal Data:* b, Tokyo, Japan, Sept 11, 36. *Educ:* Univ Tokyo, MD, 62, DMS, 67; Am Bd Internal Med, cert. *Prof Exp:* Clin training internal med & nephrol, Dept Med, Univ Tokyo, 62-69; res assoc, Dept Med, Univ Pa, 69-71; sr res fel, Cedars Sinai Med Ctr, 71-73; sr res fel, Univ Calif, Los Angeles, 71-73, from asst prof to prof med, Dept Med, 77-84; asst prof med, Dept Med, Univ Southern Calif, 74-77; assoc prof, Dept Med, Univ Tokyo, 83-89, prof & chmn, 89-96. *Concurrent Pos:* Chmn bd, Japanese Soc Internal Med, 90-93. *Mem:* Foreign assoc Inst Med Nat Acad Sci; Japanese Soc Internal Med (pres, 95-96); Int Soc Nephrol (pres-elect, 95-97); Japanese Soc Nephrology (pres, 93-94); Am Soc Clin Invest; Asn Am Physicians. *Mailing Add:* Sch Med Tokai Univ 143 Shimokasuya Isehara Kanagawa 259 11 Japan

KUROKI, GARY W, AGRICULTURAL BIOTECHNOLOGY, PROTEIN BIOCHEMISTRY. *Current Pos:* RES SCIENTIST, DNA PLANT TECHNOL CORP, 90- *Personal Data:* b Jan 16, 56. *Educ:* Ft Lewis Col, BS, 79; Univ Iowa, MS, 82, PhD(bot), 85. *Prof Exp:* Res fel, Dept Bot, Univ Iowa, 80-85; scholar, Dept Biochem & Biophys, Univ Calif, Davis, 86-88, Dept Bot & Plant Sci, Riverside, 88-90. *Mem:* Am Soc Biochem & Molecular Biol; Am Soc Plant Physiologists; Phytochem Soc NAm. *Res:* Purification and characterization of plant proteins; analysis of metabolic pathways and metabolite pools associated with primary and secondary plant metabolism; analysis of the kinetic characteristics of chorismate mutase 1 purified from Solanum tuberosum tubers; author of numerous scientific publications. *Mailing Add:* Core Lab Appl Biosyst 850 Lincoln Center Dr Foster City CA 94404. *Fax:* 650-638-5981

KUROSAKA, MITSURU, MECHANICAL ENGINEERING, AERONAUTICAL & ASTRONAUTICAL ENGINEERING. *Current Pos:* from assoc prof to prof mech & aerospace eng, Univ Tenn Space Inst, 77-87, PROF AERONAUT & ASTRONAUT, UNIV WASH, 87- *Personal Data:* b Shenyang, China, Mar 26, 35; US citizen; m 63; c 3. *Educ:* Univ Tokyo, BS, 59, MS, 61; Calif Inst Technol, PhD(mech eng), 68. *Honors & Awards:* Gen H H (Hap) Arnold Award, Am Inst Aeronaut & Astronaut, 83. *Prof Exp:* Design engr, Hitachi Ltd, 61-63; grad res & teaching asst, Calif Inst Technol, 63-67; eng specialist, AiResearch Mfg Co, 67-69; fluid mech engr, Gen Elec Res & Develop Ctr, 69-77. *Concurrent Pos:* Consult, Gen Elec Co, ARO, Inc, AiResearch Mfg Co, Calspan & Pratt & Whitney Can; vis prof, Mass Inst Technol, 84-85. *Mem:* Assoc fel Am Inst Aeronaut & Astronaut; fel Am Soc Mech Engrs; Sigma Xi. *Res:* Aerothermodynamics of gas turbines; aeroacoustics; unsteady flow, aeroelasticity; thermodynamics and heat transfer; fluid dynamics. *Mailing Add:* Dept Aeronaut & Astronaut Univ Wash Seattle WA 98195. *Fax:* 206-543-0217; *E-Mail:* kurosaka@aa.washington.edu

KUROSE, GEORGE, CHEMICAL ENGINEERING. *Current Pos:* Chem engr, Am Cyanamid Co, 50-55, res chem engr, 55-62, sr res chem engr, 62-77, GROUP LEADER, AM CYANAMID CO, 77- *Personal Data:* b Eatonville, Wash, June 13, 24; m 56; c 3. *Educ:* Columbia Univ, BS, 49, MS, 50. *Mem:* Am Chem Soc; Am Inst Chem Eng. *Res:* Process development; process design; process and economic evaluation; synthetic fiber process development. *Mailing Add:* Ten Wayfaring Rd Norwalk CT 06851

KUROSKI DE BOLD, MERCEDES LINA, IMMUNOCYTOCHEMISTRY. *Current Pos:* ASST PROF PATH & SCIENTIST, HEART INST, UNIV OTTAWA, 86- *Personal Data:* b Cordoba, Argentina, Sept 23, 42; Can citizen; m 68; c 5. *Educ:* Nat Univ, Cordoba, Argentina, BSc, 68; Queen's Univ, Can, MSc, 72, PhD(path), 74. *Prof Exp:* Res fel path, Queen's Univ, Kingston, 68-74; instr, 72-74, res assoc, 77-85, asst prof, 85-86. *Concurrent Pos:* Bd dirs, Child Life & Play Ottawa Liaison; bd dirs, Can-Arg Inst; tutor, GI Block, Second Yr Fac Med, Univ Ottawa, 92- vchair, Animal Care Comt, 95-, actg chair, 96- *Mem:* Soc Exp Biol & Med; Int Soc Heart Res; Can Cardiovasc Soc. *Res:* Correlation between the structure and function of mammalian and non-mammalian cells; sequence cardionatrins; functional morphology of mammalian atrial cardiocytes. *Mailing Add:* Ottawa Civic Hosp Univ Ottawa Heart Inst 1053 Carling Ave Ottawa ON K1Y 4E9 Can

KUROSKY, ALEXANDER, PROTEIN STRUCTURE, PROHORMONE PROCESSING. *Current Pos:* from asst prof to assoc prof, 75-82, PROF HUMAN BIOL CHEM & GENETICS, MED BR, UNIV TEX, GALVESTON, 82- *Personal Data:* b Windsor, Ont, Can, Sept 12, 38; US citizen; m 63, Anna Kinik; c Lisa K, Tanya K & Stepanie A. *Educ:* Univ BC, BSc, 65; Univ Toronto, MSc, 69, PhD, 72. *Honors & Awards:* John G Sinclair Award, Sigma Xi, 88. *Prof Exp:* Res technician, Dept Agr, Harrow, Ont & Vancouver, BC, Can, 59-64; res & develop chemist, Can Breweries, Ltd, Toronto, 65-67. *Concurrent Pos:* NIH & NSF res grants, Burkitt Found, 76- *Mem:* Am Soc Biochem & Molecular Biol; Am Chem Soc; Can Biochem Soc; AAAS; Sigma Xi; Am Inst Chem. *Res:* Biochemistry; structure, function and genetics. *Mailing Add:* Dept Human Biol Chem & Genetics Univ Tex Med Br Galveston TX 77555. *Fax:* 409-747-4753; *E-Mail:* akurosky@mspoi.med.utmb.edu

KUROWSKI, GARY JOHN, NUMERICAL ANALYSIS. *Current Pos:* from asst prof to assoc prof math, 63-72, dir comput ctr, 69-71, PROF MATH, UNIV CALIF, DAVIS, 72- *Personal Data:* b Fargo, NDak, Mar 22, 31; m 63; c 3. *Educ:* Univ Minn, BS, 53, MS, 54; Carnegie Inst Technol, PhD(math), 59. *Prof Exp:* Res assoc math, Off Ord Res, Duke Univ, 59-63. *Mem:* Am Math Soc; Asn Comput Mach; Soc Indust & Appl Math. *Res:* Applied mathematics, especially discrete and semi-discrete analogues of the classic fields of analysis and their application to numerical analysis. *Mailing Add:* 1009 Vassar Dr Davis CA 95616

KUROYANAGI, NORIYOSHI, DIGITAL TELECOMMUNICATIONS SYSTEMS, HIGH SPEED DIGITAL TRANSMISSIONS. *Current Pos:* PROF TELECOMMUN, TOKYO ENG UNIV, 86- *Personal Data:* b Tokyo, Japan, Feb 7, 30; m 59, Emiyo; c Noriko, Chiyoko & Yuri. *Educ:* Tokyo Inst Technol, Bachelor, 54, DrEng(comput), 62. *Honors & Awards:* Maejima Award, Asn Post & Telecommun, 79; Sci & Technol Minister Award, Japanese Govt, 80; Donald W McLellan Meritorious SErv Award, Inst Elec & Electronics Engrs, Commun Soc, 87. *Prof Exp:* Mem tech staff, Nippon Tel & Tel Pub Corp, 54-64, staff engr, Elec Commun Labs, 64-71, dept head, 71-74, sr staff engr, 74-77, dep dir, 78-81, dir, 81-86. *Concurrent Pos:* Head, Info Networks Dept, Tokyo Eng Univ. *Mem:* Inst Elec & Electronics Engrs Commun Soc; Inst Elec Inf & Commun Engrs; fel Inst Elec & Electronics Engrs. *Res:* High speed computer-arithmetic circuits; high speed digital transmission systems; synchronization techniques; enhanced digital communication networks; local area networks; spread spectrum communication systems; development of PCM-400 Mb/s coaxial transmission systems. *Mailing Add:* Tokyo Eng Univ 1404-1 Katakura Hachiohji Tokyo 192 Japan

KURSHAN, JEROME, MATHEMATICS. *Current Pos:* RETIRED. *Personal Data:* b Brooklyn, NY, Mar 10, 19; m 46, Phyllis Sterman; c Neil & Rachel. *Educ:* Columbia Univ, AB, 39; Cornell Univ, PhD(physics), 43. *Prof Exp:* Asst physics, Columbia Univ, 39 & Cornell Univ, 39-43; res physicist, RCA Labs, 43-55, mgr employ & training 55-59, mgr, Res Serv Lab, 59-66, mgr mkt, 66-73, mgr admin serv, 73-83, mgr admin proj, 83-87. *Concurrent Pos:* Instr, Rutgers Univ, 44. *Mem:* Inst Elec & Electronics Engrs. *Res:* Ion sources; gated amplifiers; frequency modulated magnetrons; automatic frequency control oscillators; transistors; semiconductors physics; materials analysis; computer applications; research management; research administration. *Mailing Add:* 73 Random Rd Princeton NJ 08540. *E-Mail:* pandj@aol.com

KURSS, HERBERT, MATHEMATICS. *Current Pos:* assoc prof, 62-69, prof, 69-90, EMER PROF MATH, ADELPHI UNIV, 90- *Personal Data:* b Brooklyn, NY, Mar 30, 24; m 63, Rachel Gani. *Educ:* Cooper Union, BEE, 43; Polytech Inst Brooklyn, MEE, 52; NY Univ, PhD, 57. *Prof Exp:* Tech writer radar, Techlit Consult, Inc, 47; instr elec eng, US Merchant Marine Acad, 47-48; res assoc appl math, Microwave Res Inst, Polytech Inst Brooklyn, 48-54; res asst math, NY Univ, 54-57; res assoc appl math, Microwave Res Inst, Polytech Inst Brooklyn, 57-59, res asst prof, 59-62. *Mem:* Am Math Soc; Math Asn Am; Sigma Xi; Soc Indust & Appl Math; Inst Elec & Electronics Engrs. *Res:* Problems associated with ordinary differential equations and with electromagnetic theory. *Mailing Add:* Dept Math Adelphi Univ Garden City NY 11530

KURSTEDT, HAROLD ALBERT, JR, NUCLEAR ENGINEERING. *Current Pos:* ASSOC PROF MECH & NUCLEAR ENG, VA POLYTECH INST & STATE UNIV, 76- *Personal Data:* b Columbus, Ohio, Sept 15, 39; m 61; c 3. *Educ:* Va Mil Inst, BS, 61; Univ Ill, Urbana, MS, 63, PhD(nuclear eng), 68. *Prof Exp:* Instr mech eng, Va Mil Inst, 61-62; res & develop coordr, Ballistic Res Labs, Aberdeen Proving Ground, Md, 66-68; asst prof nuclear eng, Col Eng, Ohio State Univ, 68-70; prog mgr, Fed Systs Div, Indust Nucleonics Corp, 70-76. *Mem:* Am Soc Civil Eng; Am Soc Eng Educ; Am Nuclear Soc; Sigma Xi. *Res:* Nuclear reactor kinetics and heat transfer, particularly experimental and analytical techniques in pulsed thermal and fast reactors; nuclear instrumentation and control; nondestructive inspection. *Mailing Add:* Dept Indust & Systs Eng Va Tech 212 Hancock Hall Blacksburg VA 24061-0118

KURSUNOGLU, BEHRAM N, THEORETICAL PHYSICS. *Current Pos:* PROF PHYSICS, UNIV MIAMI, 58-, DIR, CTR THEORET STUDIES, 65- *Personal Data:* b Bayburt, Turkey, Mar 14, 22; m 52; c 3. *Educ:* Univ Edinburgh, BSc, 49; Cambridge Univ, PhD, 52. *Hon Degrees:* DSc, Fla Inst Technol, 82. *Honors & Awards:* Presidential Sci Prize, 72; Sci Award, Asn of Turkish Am Scientists of USA, 88. *Prof Exp:* Res assoc, Cornell Univ, 52-54; vis prof physics, Miami Univ, 54-55; sr fel, Yale Univ, 55; dean fac nuclear sci & technol, Mid E Tech Univ, Ankara, Turkey, 56-58. *Concurrent Pos:* Adv, Turkish Gen Staff Atomic Matters, 56-58; mem, Turkish Atomic Energy Comn, 56-58; Turkish mem sci comt, NATO, 58; consult, Brit Atomic Energy Res Estab, 61 & Max Planck Inst Physics & Astrophys, 61; consult, Oak Ridge Nat Lab, 62-64, chmn, Ann High Energy Physics Conf, Fla, 64-83; chmn, Ann Int Sci Forum, Energy, 77-; pres & chmn bd, Global Foundation Inc, 78- *Mem:* Fel Am Phys Soc; Am Asn Physics Teachers; Turkish Am Sci Asn. *Res:* Theoretical high energy, relativity and plasma physics; arms control; energy. *Mailing Add:* Global Found Inc PO Box 249055 Coral Gables FL 33124

KURT, CARL EDWARD, CIVIL ENGINEERING, STRUCTURAL ENGINEERING. *Current Pos:* PROF, DEPT CIVIL ENG, UNIV KANS, 82- *Personal Data:* b Muskogee, Okla, June 3, 43; m 69, Judith Berryman; c David. *Educ:* Okla State Univ, BS, 65, MS, 66, PhD(civil eng), 69. *Prof Exp:* Instr civil eng, Okla State Univ, 69; sr engr strength, McDonnell Douglas Astronaut Corp, 69-74; from asst prof to assoc prof, Dept Civil Eng, Auburn Univ, 74-82. *Concurrent Pos:* Pres, EnGraph; prin investr, numerous proj. *Mem:* Am Soc Civil Engrs; Am Soc Testing & Mat; Am Inst Steel Construct. *Res:* Geographical information systems; behavior of structural materials and structural steel design; structural analysis and stability; engineering properties of thermoplastic water well casings; computer aided design. *Mailing Add:* Dept Civil Eng Univ Kans Lawrence KS 66045. *Fax:* 785-864-3787

KURTA, ALLEN, BATS, ENDANGERED SPECIES. *Current Pos:* asst prof, 88-91, ASSOC PROF BIOL, EASTERN MICH UNIV, 91- *Personal Data:* b Detroit, Mich, Sept 6, 52; m 80; c 1. *Educ:* Mich State Univ, BS, 75, MS, 80; Boston Univ, PhD(biol), 86. *Prof Exp:* Asst prof biol, Nazareth Col, 85-86; res assoc, Boston Univ, 86-88. *Concurrent Pos:* Consult, 80- *Mem:* Am Soc Mammalogists; Am Soc Naturalists; Am Soc Zoologists. *Res:* Physiology, ecology and natural history of bats and other mammals. *Mailing Add:* Dept Biol Eastern Mich Univ Ypsilanti MI 48197. *Fax:* 313-487-9235; *E-Mail:* bio_kurta@emunix.emich.edu

KURTENBACH, AELRED J(OSEPH), ELECTRICAL ENGINEERING. *Current Pos:* PRES, DAKTRONICS, INC, BROOKINGS, SDAK, 69- *Personal Data:* b Dimock, SDak, Jan 3, 34; m 60; c 5. *Educ:* SDak Sch Mines & Technol, BS, 61; Univ Nebr, MS, 62; Purdue Univ, PhD(elec eng), 68. *Prof Exp:* Instr elec eng, SDak State Univ, 62-65, asst prof, 65-69, assoc prof, 69-72. *Concurrent Pos:* Instr elec eng, Purdue Univ, 65-66. *Mem:* Inst Elec & Electronics Engrs. *Res:* Biomedical telemetry; pulse-code modulation telemetry. *Mailing Add:* Daktronics Inc PO Box 5128 Brookings SD 57006

KURTH, CARL FERDINAND, RESEARCH ADMINISTRATION. *Current Pos:* RETIRED. *Personal Data:* b Zwickau, Ger, May 11, 28; m 51, Ursula L Pfeifer; c Mattias C & Cornelia L. *Educ:* Grad engr, Polytechnikum, Mittweida, Ger, 51. *Honors & Awards:* Nachrichtentechnische Gesellschaft Award, Ger Commun Soc, 64; Darlington Prize, Circuits & Systs Soc, Inst Elec & Electronics Engrs, 77; Centennial Medal, Int Elec & Electronics Engrs, 84. *Prof Exp:* Head dept, Ferhmeldewerk, Leipzig, 51-60, Stand Elektrik Lorenz, Stuttgart, 60-64; instr, Lehigh Univ, 65; supvr, Bell Labs,

65-89, elec engr res, 89-93. *Concurrent Pos:* Assoc ed, Trans, Circuits & Systs J, 77-79; touring lectr, China, Inst Elec & Electronics Engrs, 79; group leader, MITRE Corp, 90-93. *Mem:* Fel Inst Elec & Electronics Engrs; Inst Elec & Electronics Engrs Circuits & Systs Soc (pres, 80). *Res:* Contributed over 30 technical papers and articles to professional journals; holder of 17 patents. *Mailing Add:* 1566 SE Hatfield Ct Port St Lucie FL 34952-4290

KURTH, JANICE H, HUMAN GENETICS, EVOLUTIONARY GENETICS. *Current Pos:* STAFF SCIENTIST, ST JOSEPHS HOSP & MED CTR, 93- *Personal Data:* b Dec 26, 63; m 87, Matthias C; c Carol M & Susan A. *Educ:* Austin Col, BA, 85; Stanford Univ, PhD(genetics), 91; Univ Ariz, MD, 95. *Honors & Awards:* Frances Kallman Award, Stanford Univ, 91. *Prof Exp:* Res assoc, Tex Tech Univ, 91-93. *Concurrent Pos:* Physician, Ariz Physicians, 96- *Mem:* AAAS; AMA; Am Soc Human Genetics; Am Col Med Genetics. *Res:* Defining genetic predisposition to Parkinson's disease through population genetic analysis; linkage projects also in progress to localize genes for cavernous malformations, Navajo neuropathy and others. *Mailing Add:* St Josephs Hosp & Med Ctr 350 W Thomas Rd Phoenix AZ 85013-4496. *Fax:* 602-406-7172; *E-Mail:* jkurth@mha.chw.edu

KURTTI, TIMOTHY JOHN, INSECT PATHOLOGY, INSECT PHYSIOLOGY. *Current Pos:* asst prof entom, 86-89, ASSOC PROF ENTOM, UNIV MINN, 89- *Personal Data:* b Minneapolis, Minn, Mar 8, 42; m 85. *Educ:* Univ Minn, BA, 65, PhD(entom), 74. *Prof Exp:* From jr scientist to asst scientist insect microbiol, 66-69, res asst, 69-70, res fel, 70-73, res assoc insect microbiol, Dept Entom, Fisheries & Wildlife, Univ Minn, St Paul, 73-77; scientist, Int Lab for Res on Animal Dis, Nairobi, Kenya, 77-80; asst res prof microbiol, Waksman Inst Microbiol, Rutgers Univ, 80-85. *Mem:* Soc Invert Path; Entom Soc Am; Sigma Xi; Am Soc Parasitol; Soc Protozool. *Res:* Insect microbiology; bovine and tick tissue culture; development physiology of insects; insect nutrition; biological calorimetry; theileriosis; intracellular parasitism; microbial control; Lyme disease. *Mailing Add:* Dept Entomol Univ Minn St Paul MN 55108

KURTZ, A PETER, PESTICIDE CHEMISTRY, STRUCTURE-ACTIVITY RELATIONSHIPS. *Current Pos:* res chemist, Tech Ctr, Rhone-Poulenc Agr Co, 71-78, group leader pesticide chem, 78-85, sr group leader pesticide chem, 85- 88, MGR SCI INFO MGMT & SYSTS, TECH CTR, RHONE-POULENC AGR CO, 89- *Personal Data:* b Staten Island, NY, June 12, 42; m 64, Marie Ueberwasser; c Christine & Catherine. *Educ:* Fordham Univ, BS, 63; Columbia Univ, MA, 64, PhD(org chem), 68. *Prof Exp:* Res chemist, Letterman Army Inst Res, 69-71. *Mem:* Am Chem Soc. *Res:* Development of quantitative structure; activity relationships and application to the design of selectively toxic pesticide chemicals; computerized chemical/biological information storage and analysis systems. *Mailing Add:* Tech Ctr Rhone-Poulenc Agr Co PO Box 12014 Research Triangle Park NC 27709. *E-Mail:* peter.kurtz@rtp.fwexc.rp.fr

KURTZ, ANTHONY DAVID, PHYSICAL METALLURGY. *Current Pos:* dir res & develop, 59-66, PRES, KULITE SEMICONDUCTOR PROD, 66- *Personal Data:* b New York, NY, May 3, 29; m 55, 85, Nora Morcos; c Jennifer (Unger), John & Sandria. *Educ:* Mass Inst Technol, SB, 51, SM, 52, ScD(phys metall), 55. *Honors & Awards:* Si Fluor Technol Award, Instrument Soc Am, 78. *Prof Exp:* Res asst, Mass Inst Technol, 51-54, staff mem, Lincoln Lab, 54-55; sr engr, Transistor Prod, Inc Div, Clevelite Corp, 56; supvr appl res, Semiconductor Div, Minneapolis-Honeywell Regulator Co, 56-59. *Mem:* Am Soc Metals; Am Phys Soc; Inst Elec & Electronics Engrs; Sigma Xi. *Res:* Solid state physics and tranducer design; semiconductor devices and materials; diffusion in solids; imperfections in metals and semiconductors; experimental mechanics; stress analysis. *Mailing Add:* Kulite Semiconductor Prod One Willow Tree Rd Hackensack NJ 07605

KURTZ, CLARK N, OPTICS. *Current Pos:* Design engr electronics, Eastman Kodak Co, 59-62, sr res physicist, 66-72, res assoc optics, 72-79, lab head res labs, 79-84, dir Optical Rec Prod, Photo Div, 84-85, Adv Dev Mgr Mass Mem, 85-88, sr tech asst to dir res, 88-89, DIR INFO & COMPUTER TECH DIV, RES, EASTMAN KODAK CO, 89- *Personal Data:* b Stillwater, Minn, Nov 24, 37; m 65; c 2. *Educ:* SDak Sch Mines & Technol, BS, 59; Univ Ill, MS, 63; Univ Rochester, PhD(elec eng), 67. *Honors & Awards:* Charles Ives Award, Soc Photog Scientists & Engrs, 72. *Concurrent Pos:* Adv bd, Nat Ctr Supercomputing, Univ Ill, Cornell Theory Ctr. *Mem:* Optical Soc Am; Am Inst Physics. *Res:* Physics of forming images on paper in copying; theory of light propagation in waveguides; design of optical screens and diffusers; optical disk; light waves. *Mailing Add:* 4355 W Lake Rd Canandaigua NY 14424

KURTZ, DAVID ALLAN, PESTICIDE CHEMISTRY, CHEMOMETRICS. *Current Pos:* CONSULT, 95- *Personal Data:* b Evanston, Ill, Jan 31, 32. *Educ:* Knox Col, AB, 54; Pa State Univ, MS, 58, PhD(org chem), 60. *Prof Exp:* Instr gen chem, Pa State Univ, 59-60; sr chemist, HRB-Singer, Inc, 60-62; res assoc appl chem, Mat Res Lab, Pa State Univ, 62-66, asst prof pessticides anal, 67-71, anal chemist, Pesticides Res Lab, 71-93, sr res assoc & environ chemist, Environ Resource Res Inst, 93-95. *Concurrent Pos:* Co-leader, Coop Regional Proj NE-115, Pa Agr Exp Sta, 78-83. *Mem:* Am Chem Soc; Chemometrics Soc; Soc Environ Toxicol & Chem; Asn Off Anal Chemists; Int Union Pure & Appl Chem; Int Asn Great Lakes Res. *Res:* Methods of analysis for pesticides and herbicides; chemometric methods (statistical calibration methods in trace residue analysis for pesticides and environmental compounds); pesticide analysis in marine and marine atmosphere environments; long range transport of pesticides; groundwater kinetics of pesticide movement. *Mailing Add:* 118 E South Hills Ave State College PA 16801. *Fax:* 814-237-5562; *E-Mail:* dave_kurtz@agcs.cas.psu.edu

KURTZ, DAVID WILLIAMS, PHOTOCHEMISTRY, EDUCATION. *Current Pos:* from asst prof to assoc prof, 73-83, PROF ORG CHEM, OHIO NORTHERN UNIV, 84-, CHMN CHEM, 95- *Personal Data:* b Altoona, Pa, July 27, 42; m 72, Saddie King; c Stella A, Kimberly C & Eleanor J. *Educ:* Houghton Col, NY, BS, 64; Syracuse Univ, PhD(chem), 71. *Prof Exp:* Res assoc photochem, Univ Wis, 71-73. *Concurrent Pos:* Petrol Res Found fel, Iowa State Univ, 83. *Mem:* Am Chem Soc; Sigma Xi. *Res:* Torsional processes in photochemical transformations and other syntheitic applications in organic chemistry. *Mailing Add:* Dept Chem Ohio Northern Univ Ada OH 45810. *E-Mail:* dkurtz@onv.edu

KURTZ, EDWIN BERNARD, JR, SCIENCE EDUCATION. *Current Pos:* prof life sci & chmn dept, 72-89, EMER PROF, UNIV TEX PERMIAN BASIN, 89- *Personal Data:* b Wichita, Kans, Aug 11, 26; m 52, Lois Leecing; c Kathryn & Jane. *Educ:* Univ Ariz, BS, 48, MS, 49; Calif Inst Technol, PhD, 52. *Prof Exp:* Instr bot, Univ Ariz, 47, from asst prof to prof, 51-68, actg head dept, 54-55; prof biol & head dept, Kans State Teachers Col, 68-72. *Concurrent Pos:* Asst dir educ, AAAS, Washington, DC, 65-67. *Mem:* AAAS; Am Inst Biol Sci; Nat Sci Teachers Asn. *Res:* Science education. *Mailing Add:* 1620 N Kutch Dr Flagstaff AZ 86001

KURTZ, GEORGE WILBUR, ANALYTICAL CHEMISTRY. *Current Pos:* RETIRED. *Personal Data:* b Harrisburg, Pa, Dec 8, 28; m 53; c 3. *Educ:* Pa State Univ, BS, 50, MS, 52, PhD(dairy sci), 54. *Prof Exp:* Res chemist, Swift & Co, 54; head, Flavor & Phys Chem Lab, Armed Forces Qm Food & Container Inst, Chicago, 56-62; chemist, Dalare Assocs, 62-69; mgr qual control, R P Scherer, Monroe, NC, 69-79, plant mgr, 79-89, consult, Clearwater, 89-94. *Mem:* Am Chem Soc; Inst Food Technol. *Res:* Analytical chemistry; food technology. *Mailing Add:* 3029 Brookfield Lane Clearwater FL 34621

KURTZ, HAROLD JOHN, VETERINARY PATHOLOGY. *Current Pos:* Instr vet surg, 60-61 & vet med, 61-62, fel vet path, 62-66, from asst prof to assoc prof, 66-74, PROF VET PATH, COL VET MED, UNIV MINN, ST PAUL, 74- *Personal Data:* b Brookings, SDak, Feb 18, 31; m 53; c 3. *Educ:* SDak State Univ, BS & MS, 54; Univ Minn, DVM, 58, PhD(vet path), 66. *Mem:* Am Vet Med Asn; Am Col Vet Path; Int Cad Path. *Res:* Dissecting aortic rupture in turkeys; neuropathology and pathology of animal diseases; comparative pathology; edema disease of swine. *Mailing Add:* 236-E Vet Diag Lab Univ Minn Col Vet Med St Paul MN 55108

KURTZ, LAWRENCE ALFRED, NUMERICAL ANALYSIS. *Current Pos:* PROF MATH, UNIV MONTEVALLO, 78- *Personal Data:* b Providence, RI, Dec 29, 40; m, Jane Lanyon. *Educ:* Univ RI, BS, 62; Univ Conn, MS, 65; Univ Tenn, Knoxville, PhD(math), 69. *Prof Exp:* Engr, Eastman Kodak Co, 62-63; teaching asst math, Univ Conn, 63-65; teaching asst, Univ Tenn, Knoxville, 65, instr, 70; statist comput analyst, 71, asst prof, Hollins Col, 70-77. *Mem:* Am Math Soc; Soc Indust & Appl Math. *Res:* Computational fluid dynamics; numerical analysis of partial differential equations; mathematics education. *Mailing Add:* Dept Math & Phys Montevallo AL 35115

KURTZ, LESTER TOUBY, AGRONOMY. *Current Pos:* RETIRED. *Personal Data:* b Howard Co, Ind, Nov 7, 14; m 40; c 2. *Educ:* Purdue Univ, BS, 38; Univ Ill, PhD(agron), 43. *Prof Exp:* Asst soil chemist, Dept Agron, Univ Ill, Urbana, 38-43, assoc, 43-44, instr US army spec training prog, 43-45, from asst prof to assoc prof, 44-50, prof soil fertil & fertilizers, Exp Sta, 50-82. *Concurrent Pos:* Guggenheim fel, soils lab, Agr Res Serv, USDA, 53-54; Fulbright fel, Waite Inst, SAustralia, 61-62 & soil & fertilizer br, Tenn Valley Authority, Ala, 68-69; Lady Davis fel, Soils & Fertilizer Div, Israel Inst Tech, Haifa, Israel. *Mem:* AAAS; fel Am Soc Agron; Am Chem Soc; Soil Sci Soc Am. *Res:* Soil chemistry and fertility; analytical chemistry; phosphate fixation in Illinois soils; fate of fertilizer nitrogen in soils as indicated by nitrogen 15; role of fertilizer in water pollution. *Mailing Add:* 607 E Washington St Urbana IL 61801

KURTZ, MARGOT, MEDICAL EDUCATION. *Current Pos:* coordr, Mich State Univ, 76-77, co-dir preceptor prog, 77-, co-dir jr partnership progs, 80-, asst prof, 85-87, assoc prof, 87-, PROF, DEPT FAMILY MED, MICH STATE UNIV. *Personal Data:* b WGer, Aug 30, 41; m 65; c 1. *Educ:* Mich State Univ, BA, 72, MA, 73, PhD, 76. *Prof Exp:* Fac behav sci, Lansing Community Col, 74-76. *Res:* Educational and psychological aspects of clinical training; behavioral aspects of physician-patient relationship; processes in medical interviewing; psychological aspects of student personal development and relationship patterns while in medical school. *Mailing Add:* Dept Family & Community Med Mich State Univ East Lansing MI 48824

KURTZ, MARK EDWARD, WEED SCIENCE, CROP ROTATION & FIBER RESEARCH. *Current Pos:* ASSOC PLANT PHYSIOLOGIST, RES DEPT, DELTA BR, MISS AGR & FORESTRY EXP STA, STONEVILLE, MS, 80- *Personal Data:* b Trenton, Mo, Nov 8, 46; m 52, 71; c 2. *Educ:* Mo Valley Col, BS, 69; Miss State Univ, MS, 77, PhD(weed sci), 80. *Concurrent Pos:* Adj assoc prof, Dept Plant Path & Weed Sci, Miss State Univ, 81- *Mem:* Weed Sci Soc Am; Int Kenaf Asn. *Res:* Soybean and rice cotton weed control, utilizing existing techniques and improvising new ideas to solve unanswered problems as they arise in varied cropping systems; evaluating herbicides in a soybean-rice rotation; herbicide tolerance in Kenaf (Hibiscus Cannabinus). *Mailing Add:* 304 S Deer Dr E Leland MS 38756

KURTZ, MICHAEL E, MEDICINE, RESEARCH ADMINISTRATION. *Current Pos:* res assoc, Surg & Transplant Servs, 89-90, MGR & ASSOC DIR, SURG RES INST, ST LOUIS UNIV, 90- *Personal Data:* b St Louis, Mo, Mar 30, 52; m 83, Karen Rodefeld; c Brian, Alison & Brendan. *Educ:* Univ Mo, St Louis, BA, 76, MS,80. *Prof Exp:* Sr res tech, Cancer Biolsect, Washinton Univ, St Louis, 76-81; res biologist, John Cochran Vet Admin Hosp, St Louis, 81-85, mgr, Histocompatibility Lab, 85-89. *Concurrent Pos:* Consult, HLA Servs, 86-, instr res methodology, 90-, mem lab adv comt, 92 & 93. *Mem:* Soc Res Adminr; Asn Acad Surg Admin; Am Soc Histocompatibility & Immunogenetics; Am Asn Lab Animal Sci; Nat Coun Univ Res Adminr. *Res:* Medical & health sciences. *Mailing Add:* 5833 Morning Field Pl St Louis MO 63128. *Fax:* 314-268-5181; *E-Mail:* kurtzme@wpogate.slu.edu

KURTZ, MYRA BERMAN, MICROBIOLOGY, GENETICS. *Current Pos:* sr res fel, 88-89, dir, 89-96, SR DIR, MERCK RES LABS, RAHWAY, NJ, 96- *Personal Data:* b New York, NY, July 20, 45; m 70, Stuart J; c Rachel L. *Educ:* Goucher Col, AB, 66; Harvard Univ, PhD(microbiol), 71. *Prof Exp:* Res assoc, State Univ NY, Albany, 71-72; assoc prof microbiol, Fed Univ Sao Carlos, Brazil, 72-74; res assoc, Rutgers Univ, 75-76, asst res prof, Waksman Microbiol, 76-82; sr res scientist, Squibb Inst, Princeton, NJ, 82-87. *Concurrent Pos:* Ed, Fungal Genetics & Biol. *Mem:* Am Soc Microbiol; AAAS; Sigma Xi. *Res:* Molecular genetics of the dimorphic human pathogenic fungus; Candida albicans; systemic fungal disease; fungal cell wall synthesis. *Mailing Add:* 16 Redwood Rd Martinsville NJ 08836. *Fax:* 732-594-1399; *E-Mail:* myra__kurtz@merck.com

KURTZ, PETER, JR, CERAMIC ENGINEERING, THERMODYNAMICS. *Current Pos:* RETIRED. *Personal Data:* b Chicago, Ill, May 12, 27; m 50. *Educ:* Univ Mo, Rolla, BS, 52, MS, 53; Univ Calif, Los Angeles, PhD(eng), 64. *Prof Exp:* Grad res engr, Univ Calif, Los Angeles, 53-55, jr res engr, 55-57, asst res engr, 57-58, assoc eng, 56-62, actg asst prof, 63-64, asst prof, 64-68; prof eng, Biola Col, 68-80, chmn, Div Sci, 71-80, prof physics, 80-92. *Mem:* Am Asn Physics Teachers; Sigma Xi. *Res:* Mechanical properties of ceramic materials; thermodynamic properties of multicomponent polyphase systems. *Mailing Add:* 115 Copa De Oro Dr Brea CA 92621

KURTZ, RICHARD LEIGH, SURFACE SCIENCE, SYNCHROTRON RADIATION. *Current Pos:* ASSOC PROF PHYSICS, LA STATE UNIV, 90- *Personal Data:* b Dubuque, Iowa, Oct 19, 56; m 87, Helene Davne; c 1. *Educ:* Brandeis Univ, BA, 78; Yale Univ, MS, 79, PhD(appl physics), 83. *Honors & Awards:* Harding Bliss Prize, 83. *Prof Exp:* Nat Res Coun assoc, Nat Bur Stand, 83-85; res physicist, Nat Inst Stand & Technol, 85-91. *Mem:* Am Phys Soc; Am Vacuum Soc; Sigma Xi; AAAS; Mat Res Soc. *Res:* Synchrotron radiation applications in surface science; photoelectron spectroscopy; surface electronic structure; molecular adsorption; stimulated desorption; transition-metal oxides; high temperature superconductors; high Tc thin films. *Mailing Add:* Dept Physics & Astron La State Univ 202 Nicholson Hall Baton Rouge LA 70803-4001. *Fax:* 504-388-5855; *E-Mail:* phkurt@lsuvm.sncc.lsu.edu

KURTZ, RICHARD ROBERT, SYNTHETIC ORGANIC CHEMISTRY. *Current Pos:* researcher, Upjohn Co, 73-80, res head, 80-83, res mgr, 83-84, ASSOC DIR, UPJOHN CO, 84- *Personal Data:* b Moose Jaw, Sask, Mar 20, 45; m 70; c 2. *Educ:* Univ Calgary, BSc, 67; Mass Inst Technol, PhD(org chem), 71. *Prof Exp:* Assoc org chem, John C Sheehan Inst Res, 71-73. *Mem:* Am Chem Soc; AAAS; NY Acad Sci. *Res:* Pharmaceutical research and development; synthesis of heterocycles. *Mailing Add:* Chem Process Res & Develop Upjohn Co Unit 1510-91-1 Kalamazoo MI 49001-3298

KURTZ, STANLEY MORTON, PATHOLOGY. *Current Pos:* PROF PATH, SOUTHWESTERN MED CTR, DALLAS & STAFF PATHOLOGIST, DALLAS VET ADMIN HOSP, 85- *Personal Data:* b Philadelphia, Pa, May 11, 26; m 57; c 2. *Educ:* George Washington Univ, BS, 49, MS, 50, PhD(anat), 53; Univ Ala, MD, 58. *Prof Exp:* Instr anat, Bowman Gray Sch Med, Wake Forest Col, 52-54; instr anat, Med Sch, Univ Ala, 54-58; sr res fel path, Univ Pittsburgh, 58-61; assoc prof, Med Ctr, Duke Univ, 61-65; dir dept toxicol, Res Labs, Parke Davis & Co, 65-76; prof path, Med Univ SC, Charleston & staff pathologist, Charleston Vet Admin Hosp, 76-85. *Concurrent Pos:* Consult, Vet Admin Hosps, 61-65, Nat Acad Sci-Nat Res Coun, 72- & Nat Inst Drug Abuse, 74- *Mem:* AAAS; Am Soc Path & Bact; Am Soc Exp Path; Soc Toxicol. *Res:* Cytology; electron microscopy; development, structure and pathology of mammalian renal glomerulus. *Mailing Add:* Dept Anat & Cell Biol Tex Col Osteo Med 3500 Camp Bowie Blvd Fort Worth TX 76107-2699

KURTZ, STEVEN ROSS, ELECTRONIC MATERIALS, PHOTODETECTOR DEVELOPMENT. *Current Pos:* SR MEM TECH STAFF, SANDIA NAT LAB, 80- *Personal Data:* b Washington, DC, Oct 3, 53; m 78. *Educ:* Bucknell Univ, BS, 75; Univ Ill, Urbana-Champaign, MS, 77, PhD(physics), 80. *Mem:* Am Phys Soc. *Res:* Electronic materials, semiconductors and insulators; photoconductivity and transport in layered semiconductors and disordered materials; optical and electron paramagnetic resonance spectroscopies; photodetector development, novel infrared materials and photodetectors; diode lasers; infrared optoelectronics. *Mailing Add:* Div 0603 Sandia Nat Lab PO Box 5800 Albuquerque NM 87185

KURTZ, STEWART K, ELECTROOPTICS. *Current Pos:* vchair & elec adminr, Mat Res Inst, Murata prof mat res, 89-93, PROF ELEC ENG, PA STATE UNIV, 87- *Personal Data:* b Bryn Mawr, Pa, June 9, 31; m 51, Dora Grandinetti; c Philip, David, Timothy & John. *Educ:* Ohio State Univ, BSc, 56, MSc, 57, PhD(physics), 60. *Prof Exp:* Staff scientist, Bell Tel Labs, Inc, 60-69; group dir explor res, Philips Labs Div, NAm Philips Corp, 69-78; vpres eng, vpres technol & sr scientist, Bristol Myers, Clairol Appliance Div, 78-87. *Mem:* Am Phys Soc; sr mem Inst Elec & Electronics Engrs; NY Acad Sci; Mat Res Soc; Am Ceramic Soc. *Res:* Grain growth in polyrystaline materials; microstructural simulation; ferroelectrics, primarily optical and electrooptical properties; nonlinear optical materials; powder survey methods; second harmonic coefficients; Raman scattering; statistical topology; phase transitions; crystal chemistry. *Mailing Add:* Mat Res Inst Pa State Univ 188 MRI Bldg University Park PA 16802-1013. *Fax:* 814-863-1465; *E-Mail:* skkl@psu.edu

KURTZ, THOMAS EUGENE, MATH STATISTICS, COMPUTER SYSTEMS. *Current Pos:* VCHMN, TRUE PASIC INC, 83- *Personal Data:* b Oak Park, Ill, Feb 22, 28; m 53, 74; c 3. *Educ:* Knox Col, BA, 50; Princeton Univ, PhD(math), 56. *Hon Degrees:* DSc, Knox Col, 85. *Honors & Awards:* Pioneer Award, Am Fed Info Processing Socs, 74. *Prof Exp:* From instr to assoc prof math, 56-66, dir, Comput Ctr, 59-75, dir, Off Acad Comput, 75-78, vchmn, Prog Comput Info Sci, 80-88, PROF MATH, DARTMOUTH COL, 66- *Concurrent Pos:* Consult, Vet Admin, White River Junction, Vt; mem Pierce panel, Presidents Sci Adv Coun Comput in Higher Educ, 65-67; chmn coun, EDUCOM, 73-74; chmn bd, NERComP Inc, 74- *Mem:* Am Statist Asn; Asn Comput Mach; Inst Elec & Electronics Engrs. *Res:* Computer languages; computer systems and their applications; computer use in education; statistics applications. *Mailing Add:* 3 Lakeview Hanover NH 03755-3407

KURTZ, THOMAS GORDON, STOCHASTIC PROCESSES. *Current Pos:* Vis lectr math, Univ Wis-Madison, 67-69, from asst prof to assoc prof, 69-75, dept chair, 85-88, PROF MATH, UNIV WIS-MADISON, 75-, DIR, CTR MATH SCI, 90- *Personal Data:* b Kansas City, Mo, July 14, 41; m 63, Carolyn Neville; c 2. *Educ:* Univ Mo, Columbia, BA, 63; Stanford Univ, MS, 65, PhD(math), 67. *Mem:* Math Asn Am; Soc Indust & Appl Math; Am Math Soc; fel Inst Math Statist; Opers Res Soc Am; Int Statist Inst. *Res:* Probability theory and stochastic processes; Markov processes; approximation for stochastic process; filtering; stochastic control; stochastic analysis, applications to gentics and networks. *Mailing Add:* Dept Math Univ Wis-Madison Madison WI 53706-1388

KURTZ, VINCENT E, STRATIGRAPHY, ENVIRONMENTAL GEOLOGY. *Current Pos:* CONSULT GEOL, 91- *Personal Data:* b Duluth, Minn, Apr 12, 26; m 53; c 5. *Educ:* Univ Minn, BA, 46, MS, 49; Univ Okla, PhD(geol), 60. *Prof Exp:* Geologist, Aurora Gasoline Co, Colo, 52-55, dist geologist, Kans, 56-58; consult geologist, Mich, 60-65; from asst prof to assoc prof earth sci, Southwest Mo State Col, 65-74, prof geol, 74-91. *Mem:* Am Inst Prof Geologists. *Res:* Late Cambrian and early Ordovician stratigraphy; paleontology and paleoecology of trilobites, inarticulate brachiopods and conodonts. *Mailing Add:* 1643 S St Charles Ave Springfield MO 65804

KURTZ, WILLIAM BOYCE, FOREST RESOURCE ECONOMICS, SOCIAL FORESTRY. *Current Pos:* assoc prof, 75-80, PROF FORESTRY, UNIV MO-COLUMBIA, 80- *Personal Data:* b Austin, Tex, July 15, 41; m 65; c 2. *Educ:* NMex State Univ, BS, 63, MS, 66; Univ Ariz, PhD(natural resource econ), 71. *Prof Exp:* Range conservationist, Soil Conserv Serv, USDA, 63-64; res assoc watershed mgt, Univ Ariz, 68-69; proj economist, Daniel Mann Johnson & Mendenhall, 69; sr economist, Voorhies, Trindle & Nelson, Orange County, 69-70; asst prof natural resources mgt, Calif Polytech State Univ, 70-75. *Concurrent Pos:* Walnut Coun Res Award, 84. *Mem:* Sigma Xi; Am Agri Econ Asn; Soil Conserv Soc Am; Soc Am Foresters. *Res:* Social forestry; agroforestry economics; non-industrial forest owner decision making. *Mailing Add:* Forest Dept Univ Mo Agr Bldg Rm 1 30 Columbia MO 65211-0001. *E-Mail:* snrkurtz@mizzou1.missouri.edu

KURTZE, DOUGLAS ALAN, PATTERN FORMATION, STATISTICAL PHYSICS. *Current Pos:* PROF PHYSICS, NDAK STATE UNIV, 90- *Personal Data:* b Mt Vernon, NY, Oct 15, 54; m 92, Elena Knickman; c Jocelyn B & Benedict Z. *Educ:* Lehigh Univ, BA & BS, 74; Cornell Univ, MS, 78, PhD(physics), 80. *Prof Exp:* Res physicist, Carnegie-Mellon Univ, 79-82; asst prof physics, Clarkson Univ, 82-90. *Concurrent Pos:* Resident vis, AT&T Bell Lab, 83-84; res physicist, Inst Theoret Physics, 87. *Mem:* Am Phys Soc; Soc Indust & Appl Math; Am Asn Crystal Growth; Am Asn Physics Teachers. *Res:* Instabilities and pattern formation in solidifying and crystallizing systems; analytical and numerical methods for moving boundary problems; zeros of partition functions. *Mailing Add:* Dept Physics NDak State Univ Fargo ND 58105-5566. *Fax:* 701-237-7088; *E-Mail:* kurtze@plains.nodak.edu

KURTZIG, SANDRA L, MATHEMATICS, AERONAUTICAL ENGINEERING. *Current Pos:* FOUNDER, ASK GROUP INC, 72-, EMER CHMN, 93- *Personal Data:* b Chicago, Ill, Oct 21, 46; c Andrew Paul & Kenneth Alan. *Educ:* Univ Calif, Los Angeles, BS, 68; Stanford Univ, MS, 68. *Prof Exp:* Mkt rep, Gen Elec Co, 69-72; chmn bd, chief exec officer & pres, ASK Comput Systs, 72-85, chmn bd, 86-89, chmn, pres & chief exec officer, 89-93. *Mailing Add:* 2420 Sand Hill Rd Suite 201 Menlo Park CA 94025-6942

KURTZKE, JOHN F, SR, NEUROLOGY, EPIDEMIOLOGY. *Current Pos:* clin assoc prof, Sch Med, Georgetown Univ, 63-65, assoc prof, 65-68, prof neurol, community & family med, 68-95, vchmn, Dept Neurol, 76-95, DISTINGUISHED PROF NEUROL, UNIFORMED SERV UNIV HEALTH SCI, SCH MED, GEORGETOWN UNIV, 92- *Personal Data:* b Brooklyn, NY, Sept 14, 26; m 50, Margaret Nevin; c John F Jr, Catherine

(Brown), Elizabeth (Siebert), Joan (Brennan), Robert N, James S & Christine (Hughes). *Educ:* St John's Univ, NY, BS, 48; Cornell Univ, MD, 52; Am Bd Psychiat & Neurol, dipl neurol, 58, cert, 90. *Honors & Awards:* Zimmerman Lectr, Stanford Univ, 80; Hope Chest Award, Nat Mult Sclerosis Soc, 82; Gold Vicennial Medal, Georgetown Univ, 82; Tarbox Lectr, Tex Tech Univ Health Sci, 89; Geigy Lectr in Mult Sclerosis, Univ Western Ont, 89; US Legion of Merit, 86; John Jay Dystel Prize for Mult Sclerosis Res, Nat Mult Sclerosis Soc & Am Acad Neurol, 97. *Prof Exp:* Intern, Kings County Hosp, 52-53; resident, Vet Admin Hosp, Bronx, 53-56; instr neurol, Jefferson Med Col, 58-61, asst neurologist, Hosp & Clin, 58-63, assoc clin neurol, Col, 61-63, asst prof, 63. *Concurrent Pos:* Rear adm, Med Corps, USNR, 44-86; chief neurol serv, Vet Admin Hosp, Coatesville, Pa, 56-63, assoc chief staff res, 57-62; examr, Am Bd Psychiat & Neurol, 61-; consult neurol, Nat Naval Med Ctr, Bethesda, 66-; chief Neurol Serv, Vet Affairs Med Ctr, Washington, DC, 63-95; Neurol Epidermial Sect, 95-; mem exec comt coop study of adrenocorticotropic hormone in mult sclerosis, Nat Inst Neurol Dis & Blindness, 64-71; Vet Admin rep, Neurol Study Sect, Div Res Grant, 64-72; mem, World Fedn Neurol, comn geog neurol, epidemiol & statist, 64-76, comn Mult Sclerosis, 67-, comn neuroepidemiol, 77-, mem med adv bd, Nat Multiple Sclerosis Soc, 66-; consult to Surgeon Gen, Dept Navy, 70-; mem int med adv bd, Int Fedn Mult Sclerosis Soc, 72-; consult ad hoc comt spinal cord injury, Nat Inst Neurol Dis & Stroke, 73-76; mem epilepsy adv comt, NIH, 74-77; mem, task force on neurol serv, Joint Comn Neurol, 71-75 & work group on epidemiol, Nat Mult Sclerosis Soc, 73; chmn work group on epidemiol, biostatist & pop genetics, Comn for Control of Huntington's Dis, 76-77; liaison officer, USN Med Sch, 79-86; established investr, Nat Mult Sclerosis Soc, 87; mem working group on design clin studies, Nat Mult Sclerosis Soc, 76-84; mem, Comt Nat Needs for Neurol, Am Acad Neurol, 79-85; mem, Manpower Comt, Soc Med Consult Armed Forces, 84-; mem, Inst Res Bd, Nat Inst Neurol Dis & Stroke, 89-, Neurol Panel, Inst Med, 90 & Stroke Coun, Am Heart Asn, 92-; residency, Rev Comt Neurol, 83-88, vchmn, 85-86, chmn, 87-88. *Mem:* Fel Am Col Epidemiol; Am Neurol Asn; fel Am Col Physicians; fel Am Acad Neurol; Am Epidemiol Soc; fel Am Col Prev Med; hon mem Danish Neurol Soc; hon foreign mem French Neurol Soc; hon corresp mem, Ger Soc Neurol. *Res:* Neuroepidemiology; author of over 400 publications. *Mailing Add:* 7509 Salem Rd Falls Church VA 22043. *Fax:* 703-560-6490

KURTZMAN, CLETUS PAUL, YEAST TAXONOMY, MOLECULAR SYSTEMATICS OF YEASTS & OTHER FUNGI. *Current Pos:* Microbiologist, Northern Regional Res Ctr, USDA, 67-70, Cur Yeast Col, 70-81, res leader, Agr Res Serv Cult Col, 81-85, RES LEADER, MICROBIOL PROPERTIES RES, NAT CTR AGR UTILIZATION RES, USDA, 85- *Personal Data:* b Mansfield, Ohio, July 19, 38; m 62, Mary A Dombrink; c Mary, Mark & Michael. *Educ:* Ohio Univ, BS, 60; Purdue Univ, MS, 62; WVa Univ, PhD(mycol/microbiol), 67. *Honors & Awards:* J Roger Porter Award, US Fedn Cult Col, Am Soc Microbiol, 90. *Concurrent Pos:* US res, Int Comn Yeasts, 80-, Int Mycol Asn, 83-; adj prof mycol, Ill State Univ, 81- *Mem:* Int Comn Yeasts; fel Am Acad Microbiol; Am Soc Microbiol; Int Mycol Asn (secy, 90-); US Fedn Cult Collections (vpres, 77-78, pres, 78-80); World Fedn Cult Collections. *Res:* Molecular systematics of yeasts and yeastlike fungi with emphasis on correlation of molecular divergence with organismal evolution. *Mailing Add:* 5326 N Robinhood Dr Peoria IL 61614. *Fax:* 309-681-6686

KURTZMAN, RALPH HAROLD, JR, BIOCHEMISTRY, MYCOLOGY. *Current Pos:* ED, INT J MUSHROOM SCI, 95-; CONSULT, 97- *Personal Data:* b Minneapolis, Minn, Feb 21, 33; m 55, N Virginia Leusslser; c Steven & Sue K (Anderson). *Educ:* Univ Minn, BS, 55; Univ Wis, MS, 58, PhD(plant path biochem), 59. *Prof Exp:* Asst prof plant path, Univ RI, 59-62; asst prof biol, Univ Minn, 62-65; biochemist, Western Regional Res Lab, USDA, 65-97. *Concurrent Pos:* NASA contract res with A H Brown & A O Dahl, Univ Minn, 63; lectr, Pakistan & Thailand, 74, Pakistan & India, 78 & Univ Helsinki, 80; guest scientist, VTT Tech Res Ctr Finland, 80; consult mushroom growing, 81. *Mem:* Mushroom Growers Asn Gt Brit; Mycol Soc Am; Am Mushroom Inst; World Soc Mushroom Biol & Mushroom Sci; Mycol Soc Japan. *Res:* Physiology of plant diseases, particularly Dutch elm disease; alkaloid metabolism of fungi; fungal decomposition of cellulose and lignin; mushroom production from wastes; bureaucratic vasilation; mushroom physiology; ethanol fermentation. *Mailing Add:* Western Regional Res Lab USDA 800 Buchanan St Albany CA 94710. *Fax:* 510-526-2492; *E-Mail:* rhktzl@worldnet.att.net

KURUCZ, ROBERT LOUIS, ASTROPHYSICS. *Current Pos:* PHYSICIST, SMITHSONIAN ASTROPHYS OBSERV, 74- *Personal Data:* b Columbus, Miss, Sept 7, 44. *Educ:* Harvard Col, AB, 66, PhD(astron), 73. *Prof Exp:* Res fel, Harvard Col Observ, 73-74. *Mem:* Am Astron Soc; Int Astron Union. *Res:* Stellar atmospheres; solar physics; radiative transfer; atomic and molecular physics. *Mailing Add:* Smithsonian Astrophys Observ 60 Garden St Cambridge MA 02138. *E-Mail:* kurucz@cfa.harvard.edu

KURUGANTY, SASTRY P, POWER SYSTEM RELIABILITY EVALUATION FOR PLANNING BULK POWER SYSTEM SECURITY ASSESSMENT. *Current Pos:* DEPT ENERGY SAMUEL MASSIE CHAIR EXCELLENCE, UNIV TURABO, 95- *Personal Data:* b Masulipatam, India, Jan 12, 41; Can citizen; m 62, Lakshmi Bhagaratula; c Sailaja, Padmaja & Saroja. *Educ:* Andhra Univ, BSc, 59, ME, 67; Birla Inst, BE, 64; Univ NB, MScE, 74; Univ Sask, PhD(power syst reliability), 79. *Prof Exp:* Asst prof elec eng, J N Technol Univ, India, 66-71; from res asst to res assoc elec eng, Univ NB, 71-75; from res asst to res assoc, Univ Sask, 75-80; reliability specialist, Man Hydro, 80-89; prof & chmn, Dept Elec Eng, Univ NDak, 89-95. *Concurrent Pos:* Consult, Man HVDC Res Ctr, 86- *Mem:* Sr mem Inst Elec & Electronics Engrs; Nat Soc Prof Engrs; Am Soc Eng Educ. *Res:* Power system planning using probabilistic methods; generation planning, transmission, planning and distribution planning; development of methodology for reliability and risk evaluation of power systems; rotating machine dynamics. *Mailing Add:* Dept Elec Eng Univ Turabo PO Box 3030 Univ Sta Gurabo PR 00778-3030

KURUP, PRADEEP UNNIKRISHNAN, GEOTECHNICAL ENGINEERING, GEOENVIRONMENTAL ENGINEERING. *Current Pos:* ASST PROF, UNIV MASS, LOWELL, 97- *Personal Data:* b North Parur, Kerala, India, May 5, 63; m 94, Meenakshi. *Educ:* Univ Kerala, India, BTech, 85; Indian Inst Technol, Madras MTech, 87; La State Univ, PhD(civil eng), 93. *Prof Exp:* Postdoctoral researcher, La State Univ, 93-94; res assoc IV, La Transp Res Ctr, 94-96, res assoc V, 96-97. *Concurrent Pos:* Prin investr, NSF, 96-, Nat Res Coun, 96-97; affil mem, Grad Fac, La State Univ, 96-; mem, Transp Res Bd, 97- *Mem:* Am Soc Civil Engrs; Am Soc Testing & Mat; Int Asn Comput Methods & Advan Geomech. *Res:* Site characterization by in situ methods; advanced laboratory calibration chamber studies of piezocone penetrometers; development of novel test devices for highway applications; geoenvironmental screening tool; underground space. *Mailing Add:* Dept Civil Eng Univ Mass 1 University Ave Lowell MA 01854. *Fax:* 504-767-9108; *E-Mail:* pkurup@ltrc.lsu.edu

KURUP, VISWANATH PARAMESWAR, MEDICAL MYCOLOGY, IMMUNOLOGY. *Current Pos:* from asst prof to assoc prof, 73-86, PROF MED, MED COL WIS, 86-; MICROBIOLOGIST MED MYCOL, VET ADMIN MED CTR, 73- *Personal Data:* b Thattayil, India, Jan 20, 36; US citizen; m 62, Indira; c Mini, Manoj & Vinod. *Educ:* Univ Poona, BS, 57, MS, 59; Univ Delhi, PhD(med mycol), 67. *Prof Exp:* Fel med mycol, Ohio State Univ, 68-70; microbiologist, St Anthony Hosp, Columbus, Ohio, 70-73. *Concurrent Pos:* Vis prof, PR, 81-; Fulbright fel, Finland, 84; consult, UN Develop Prog, 90. *Mem:* Fel Am Soc Microbiol; Am Asn Immunologists; Int Soc Human & Animal Mycol; fel Am Acad Allergy & Clin Immunol; Med Mycol Soc Am; fel Am Acad Microbiol. *Res:* Isolation and purification of antigens and allergens associated with HP from pathogenic fungi; characterization of the antigens and development of immunological tests for the early diagnosis of hypersensitivity lung disease and immune regulation in HP. *Mailing Add:* Vet Admin Res Serv 151 5000 W National Ave Milwaukee WI 53295-1000

KURYLA, WILLIAM C, ORGANIC CHEMISTRY. *Current Pos:* res & develop chemist, Chem Div, Union Carbide Corp, 60-69, res scientist, Tech Ctr, 69-71, group leader, 71-73, mgr recruiting & univ rels, 73-77, technol mgr, Occup Health, Res & Develop Dept, Tech Ctr, 77-80, sr group leader, indust hyg & environ anal, 78-80, corp mgr appl toxicology serv, 80-84, corp mgr into resources & technol, 84-85, dir prod safety CIPS group, 85-86, corp mgr prod & distrib risk, 86-87, ASST DIR PROD SAFETY, UNION CARBIDE CORP, 80- *Personal Data:* b Cuyahoga Falls, Ohio, Sept 3, 34; m 57; c 2. *Educ:* Kent State Univ, BSc, 56; Univ Minn, MSc, 58, PhD(org chem), 60. *Prof Exp:* Microanalyst, Univ Minn, 56-59. *Concurrent Pos:* Adj prof, WVa State Col. *Mem:* Am Chem Soc; Am Inst Chem; Am Ind Hyg Asn; Sigma Xi; NY Acad Sci; Am Col Toxicol. *Res:* Polyurethane chemistry and technology; ketene acetals and indole chemistry; radiochemical studies with polymers; textile and fiber chemicals; flame retardants; health effects of chemicals. *Mailing Add:* 4 Peaceful Dr New Fairfield CT 06812-3215

KURYLO, MICHAEL JOHN, III, ATMOSPHERIC KINETICS, PHOTOCHEMISTRY. *Current Pos:* Nat Res Coun res assoc, 69-71, RES CHEMIST, NAT INST STAND & TECHNOL, 71- *Personal Data:* b Meriden, Conn, July 20, 45; m 66, Mary E Tomko; c Michelle M, Michael J IV, Melinda S & Meredith L. *Educ:* Boston Col, BS, 66; Cath Univ Am, PhD(phys chem), 69. *Honors & Awards:* Bronze Medal, US Dept Com, 83, Silver Medal, 91. *Concurrent Pos:* Mem, Panel Lab Measurement & Data Eval, NASA, 78-; sci asst to dir, Nat Measurement Lab, Nat Bur Stand, 79-80; sci prog mgr, NASA, 87- *Mem:* Am Chem Soc; Am Phys Soc. *Res:* Rates and mechanisms of gas phase reactions of importance to atmospheric chemistry and combustion processes; temperature and pressure effects in free radical reactions; role of anthropogenic emissions on stratospheric ozone. *Mailing Add:* Chem Sci & Technol Lab Nat Inst Stand & Technol Gaithersburg MD 20899. *E-Mail:* mkurylo@nist.gov, mkurylo@hq.nasa.gov

KURYLO-BOROWSKA, ZOFIA, BIOPHYSICS OF THE ORIGIN OF LIFE. *Current Pos:* Asst prof, 67-72, ASSOC PROF, ROCKEFELLER UNIV, 72- *Personal Data:* b Lublin, Poland, May 13, 29; US citizen. *Educ:* Polytech Univ, Poland, MSci, 50, PhD(biochem), 58. *Mem:* Am Chem Soc; Am Polish Inst Art & Sci. *Res:* Biosynthesis of biological active peptides; origin of life. *Mailing Add:* 1230 York Ave Rockefeller Univ New York NY 10021

KURZ, DAVID W, POLYMER COMPOSITES, SOLID POLYMER ELECTROLYTES. *Current Pos:* RES STAFF SCIENTIST, GOULD ELECTRONICS, INC, 89- *Personal Data:* m 84, Soo Chang; c Shelby S. *Educ:* Univ Ill, Champaign, BS, 79; Case Western Res Univ, MS, 85; Univ Southern Miss, PhD(polymer sci), 89. *Prof Exp:* Polymer scientist, Esmark, Inc, 80-81 & Lawter, Inc, 81-82. *Mem:* Am Chem Soc; Soc Plastics Engrs; AAAS. *Res:* Polymer electrolytes; water soluble polymers; synthetic polymers; composites; initiators. *Mailing Add:* 7886 Skyline View Concord OH 44060

KURZ, JAMES ECKHARDT, PHYSICAL CHEMISTRY, POLYMER CHEMISTRY. *Current Pos:* prin tech specialist, 86-93, GROUP MGR, MCDONNELL-DOUGLAS CORP, 93- *Personal Data:* b Louisville, Ky, Oct 8, 34; m 63; c 2. *Educ:* Centre Col, AB, 56; Duke Univ, MA, 58,

PhD(phys chem), 61. *Prof Exp:* Sr res chemist, Monsanto Co, 61-66, sr res specialist, 66-75, sr group leader, 75-82, mgr res, 82-84, mgr res & develop, 84-85. *Mem:* Am Chem Soc; Soc Advan Mat & Process Eng. *Res:* Characterization of polymers by dilute solution methods; column fractionation of polymers and gel permeation chromatography; physical, mechanical and thermal characterization of polymers and polymer structure; membrane structure and use in industrial processes; structure, property and applications of polymers; structural composites; processing science of aerospace materials. *Mailing Add:* 14317 Aitken Hill Chesterfield MO 63017. *Fax:* 314-777-1171; *E-Mail:* jkurz@mdc.com

KURZ, JOSEPH LOUIS, PHYSICAL ORGANIC CHEMISTRY. *Current Pos:* from asst prof to assoc prof, 64-73, PROF CHEM, WASH UNIV, 73- *Personal Data:* b St Louis, Mo, Dec 13, 33. *Educ:* Wash Univ, AB, 55, PhD(chem), 58. *Prof Exp:* Res fel, Harvard Univ, 58-60; res chemist, Cent Basic Res Lab, Esso Res & Eng Co, 60-64. *Concurrent Pos:* Vis prof, Wash Univ, 63-64. *Mem:* Am Chem Soc; AAAS. *Res:* Mechanisms, kinetics and thermodynamics of reactions in solution; mechanisms of homogeneous catalysis; transition state structure; kinetic and equilibrium isotope effects. *Mailing Add:* 3640 Yellow Dog Rd Lonedell MO 63130-4899

KURZ, KENNETH D, THROMBOSIS. *Current Pos:* sr scientist, 79-87, RES SCIENTIST, ELI LILLY & CO, 87- *Personal Data:* b Palmer, Nebr, Oct 14, 48. *Educ:* Univ Nebr, BS, 72; Univ Ill, PhD(physiol), 76. *Prof Exp:* Res fel hypertension, Univ Mo, Columbia, 77-79. *Concurrent Pos:* Mem, Thrombosis Coun, Am Heart Asn. *Mem:* Am Physiol Soc; Am Heart Asn. *Res:* Thrombosis. *Mailing Add:* Dept Cardiovasc Pharmacol Eli Lilly & Co Lilly Corp Ctr Indianapolis IN 46285. *Fax:* 317-277-0892

KURZ, MICHAEL E, ORGANIC CHEMISTRY. *Current Pos:* from asst prof to assoc prof, 68-76, actg chmn dept, 74-75, PROF CHEM, ILL STATE UNIV, 76-, CHMN DEPT, 87- *Personal Data:* b Detroit, Mich, Mar 5, 41; m 64; c 4. *Educ:* St Mary's Col, BA, 63; Case Western Reserve Univ, PhD(chem), 67. *Prof Exp:* Instr & res assoc chem, Columbia Univ, 67-68. *Concurrent Pos:* Petrol res fund res grant, 69-72 & 85-87, NSF grant, 85, 89; Sabbatical Res, La State Univ, 76-77, Univ Ill, 88. *Mem:* Am Chem Soc; Int Assoc Arson Investr. *Res:* Free radical aromatic substitution utilizing oxidative and photolytic methods of radical generation; oxidative aromatic substitutions; trace residue analysis; fire debris. *Mailing Add:* Dept Chem Ill State Univ Normal IL 61761-4160. *Fax:* 309-438-5538

KURZ, RICHARD J, space research, instrumentation, for more information see previous edition

KURZ, RICHARD KARL, PHOTOGRAPHIC CHEMISTRY. *Current Pos:* RETIRED. *Personal Data:* b New York, NY, Feb 4, 36; m 60, Catharine Morphy; c Ann, Carolyn, Patricia, Mark & Karl. *Educ:* St John Fisher Col, NY, BS, 57; Univ Ill, Urbana-Champaign, PhD(org chem), 61. *Prof Exp:* Res chemist, Res Labs, Eastman Kodak Co, 61-69, res assoc, 69-74, lab head photog chem, 74-81, sr lab head, 81-85, prod develop mgr, Graphics Imaging Syst Div, 85-89, sr tech staff, 89-92. *Res:* Design and development of advanced photographic materials for use in radiography, graphic arts, micrographics and instrumentation recording applications; environmental conformance technology. *Mailing Add:* 40 True Hickory Dr Rochester NY 14615

KURZ, WOLFGANG GEBHARD WALTER, MICROBIOLOGY, PLANT PHYSIOLOGY. *Current Pos:* assoc res officer microbiol & fermentation technol, Nat Res Coun Can, 67-73, sr res officer Microbiol & Fermentation Technol, Prairie Regional Lab, 73-87, head, Biotechnol Sect, 81-86, head plant prod technol, 83-86, INT PROJ COORDR, PLANT BIOTECHNOL INST, NAT RES COUN CAN, 85-, HEAD BIOTECHNOL DEVELOP DEPT, 89- *Personal Data:* b Innsbruck, Austria, June 9, 33; m 63, Monica Birgit Sjostedt; c Kristina (Malin), Barbara (Asa) & Ulrika (Ebba). *Educ:* Univ Vienna, PhD(microbiol, biochem), 58. *Honors & Awards:* Can Soc Microbiologists Award, 79. *Prof Exp:* Res asst microbiol & biochem, Royal Inst Technol, Sweden, 55-63; fel, Prairie Regional Lab, Nat Res Coun Can, 63-65; res scientist, Tech Res Coun Sweden, 65-67. *Concurrent Pos:* Adj prof, Dept Appl Microbiol, Univ Sask, Saskatoon, Can. *Mem:* Fel Chem Inst Can; Can Soc Microbiologists; Int Asn Plant Tissue Cult. *Res:* Biological dinitrogen fixation; continuous cultivation of microbes and plant cells; fermentation biology; enzymology; microbial physiology; process development; apparatus design; biosynthesis of secondary metabolites by microbes and plant cells. *Mailing Add:* Plant Biotechnol Inst Nat Res Coun Can 310 Gymnasium Pl Saskatoon SK S7N 0W9 Can. *Fax:* 306-975-4839; *E-Mail:* wkurz@pbi.nrc.ca

KURZE, THEODORE, neurosurgery, for more information see previous edition

KURZROCK, RAZELLE, LEUKEMIA, MEDICINE. *Current Pos:* ASSOC PROF MED ONCOL & HEMAT, M D ANDERSON CANCER CTR, UNIV TEX, 89- *Personal Data:* b Toronto, Ont, Sept 29, 54; m 85. *Educ:* Univ Toronto, BS, 73, MD, 78. *Mem:* AMA; AAAS; Am Soc Hemat; Am Soc Clin Oncol; Am Asn Cancer Res. *Res:* Elucidation of the molecular genetic mechanisms responsible for leukemia and the treatment of this disorder. *Mailing Add:* 805 Anderson St Houston TX 77401-2806

KURZWEG, FRANK TURNER, SURGERY. *Current Pos:* RETIRED. *Personal Data:* b Plaquemine, La, Aug 7, 17; m 56; c 2. *Educ:* Harvard Univ, SB, 38; Harvard Med Sch, MD, 42; Univ Minn, MS, 47. *Prof Exp:* Instr surg, Med Sch, Tulane Univ, 49-56; from assoc prof to prof, Med Sch, Univ Miami, 56-68; prof, Surg Div, Sch Med, La State Univ, Shreveport, 68-80, head dept & div, 68-76. *Mem:* Am Col Surgeons. *Res:* General, thoracic and vascular surgery. *Mailing Add:* 58 Star Lake Rd Pensacola FL 32507-3475

KURZWEG, ULRICH H(ERMANN), FLUID MECHANICS, APPLIED MATHEMATICS. *Current Pos:* assoc prof, 68-76, PROF ENG SCI, UNIV FLA, 76- *Personal Data:* b Jena, Ger, Sept 16, 36; US citizen; m 63, Sophia Speth; c Tina. *Educ:* Univ Md, BS, 58; Princeton Univ, MA, 59, PhD(physics), 61. *Prof Exp:* Fulbright res grant appl math, Univ Freiburg, 61-62; res scientist physics, United Technol Res Labs, Conn, 62-64, sr theoret physicist, 64-68. *Concurrent Pos:* Adj asst & assoc prof, Hartford Grad Ctr, Rensselaer Polytech Inst, 63-68. *Mem:* AAAS; Am Phys Soc; Sigma Xi; NY Acad Sci. *Res:* Hydrodynamic and hydromagnetic stability of rotating flows; thermal instability of electrically conducting fluids; two-phase magnetohydrodynamic flows; numerical solutions of partial differential equations; optics of solar concentrators; heat exchange and gas separation by high frequency oscillations; fluid mechanics of time-periodic compressisble flow; micro-fluid mechanics. *Mailing Add:* Dept Aerospace Eng Mech & Eng Sci Univ Fla Gainesville FL 32611. *Fax:* 352-392-7303; *E-Mail:* uhk@koala.aero.ufl.edu

KUSALIK, PETER GERARD, COMPUTER SIMULATION, LIQUID STATE THEORY. *Current Pos:* ASST PROF, DEPT CHEM, DALHOUSIE UNIV, 89- *Personal Data:* b Taber, Alta, Can, July 17, 59; m 84; c 2. *Educ:* Univ Lethbridge, BSc, 81; Univ BC, MSc, 84, PhD(chem), 87. *Prof Exp:* Vis fel, Res Sch Chem, Australian Nat Univ, 87-89, 93. *Concurrent Pos:* NSERC postdoctoral fel, Australian Nat Univ, 87-89, postdoctoral fel, Res Sch Chem, 89; NSERC univ res fel, Dept Chem, Dalhousie Univ, 89- *Mem:* Chem Inst Can. *Res:* Computer simulation and theoretical studies of polar solvents and electrolyte solutions; non-equilibrium molecular dynamics techniques; applied field simulations; dynamics of polar liquids and solutions; solvation. *Mailing Add:* Dept Chem Dalhousie Univ Halifax NS B3H 4J3 Can. *Fax:* 902-494-1310; *E-Mail:* kusalik@ac.dal.ca

KUSANO, KIYOSHI, NEUROPHYSIOLOGY. *Current Pos:* assoc prof, 70-73, PROF BIOL, ILL INST TECHNOL, 73- *Personal Data:* b Nagasaki, Japan, Feb 1, 33; m 61. *Educ:* Kumamoto Univ, BSc, 56; Kyushu Univ, DSc, 60. *Prof Exp:* Instr physiol, Med Sch, Kumamoto Univ, 56-59 & Tokyo Med & Dent Univ, 59-60; jr res zoologist, Univ Calif, Los Angeles, 60-61; res assoc neurol, Columbia Univ, 61-63; asst prof physiol, Tokyo Med & Dent Univ, 63-65; from asst prof to assoc prof physiol, Med Sch, Ind Univ, 65-70. *Concurrent Pos:* Corp mem, Marine Biol Lab, 67; USPHS res grant, Med Sch, Ind Univ, 67-69, NSF grant, 68-70; USPHS res grant, Ill Inst Technol, 71-; mem, Physiol Study Sect, NIH, 79- *Mem:* Am Physiol Soc; Soc Gen Physiol; Soc Neurosci; Biophys Soc. *Res:* Synaptology; comparative neurophysiology. *Mailing Add:* NIH Bldg 36 Rm 4D-20 Bethesda MD 20892

KUSCHNER, MARVIN, PATHOLOGY. *Current Pos:* prof path, Health Sci Ctr, 70-87, dean sch med, 72-87, DISTINGUISHED SERV PROF PATH, STATE UNIV NY, STONY BROOK, 87- *Personal Data:* b New York, NY, Aug 13, 19; m 48; c 3. *Educ:* NY Univ, AB, 39, MD, 43. *Prof Exp:* Asst path, Col Med, NY Univ, 47-49; from instr to assoc prof, Col Physicians & Surgeons, Columbia Univ, 49-55; prof, Col Med, NY Univ, 55-70, dir path, Univ Hosp, 68-70. *Concurrent Pos:* Asst pathologist, Bellevue Hosp, 49-54, actg dir path, 54-55, dir, 55-70; res prof path & environ med, NY Univ, Col Med, 70-; trustee, Assoc Univs, Inc, 80; chmn, Environ Health Sci Rev Comt, Nat Inst Environ Health Sci, NIH, 81-86; mem, Environ Health Comt, Sci Adv Bd, US Environ Protection Agency, 83-85. *Mem:* Am Asn Path & Bact; Am Soc Exp Pathologists; Am Soc Clin Pathologists; Am Asn Cancer Res; Int Acad Path. *Res:* Pathology of cardiopulmonary diseases; causes of lung cancer. *Mailing Add:* 64 E Gate Dr Huntington NY 11743

KUSERK, FRANK THOMAS, MICROBIAL ECOLOGY, ENVIRONMENTAL MICROBIOLOGY. *Current Pos:* From asst prof to assoc prof, 77-92, dir, Acad Comput, 88-94, PROF BIOL, MORAVIAN CO, BETHLEHEM, PA, 92- *Personal Data:* b Philadelphia, Pa, Mar 26, 51; m 75, Evelyn Hundley; c Claire & Laura. *Educ:* Univ Notre Dame, BS, 73; Univ Del, Newark, PhD(biol), 78. *Concurrent Pos:* Res fel, Marine Biol Lab, Woods Hole, Mass, 79; res assoc, Acad Natural Sci Philadelphia, 81-82; consult ecol, ITT Res Inst, Chicago, Ill, 84-90; dean asst info technol, Moravian Co, Bethlehem, 96- *Mem:* Am Inst Biol Sci; Ecol Soc Am; Sigma Xi; Nat Cent Sci Educ; Nat Asn Biol Teachers; Nat Sci Teachers Asn. *Res:* Microbial ecology; population dynamics and community structure of a group of soil amoebae, the dictyostelid cellular slime molds; uptake and utilization of dissolved organic carbon by streamed micro-organisms. *Mailing Add:* Dept Biol Moravian Col Bethlehem PA 18018. *Fax:* 610-861-3979; *E-Mail:* kuserk@moravian.edu

KUSHICK, JOSEPH N, THEORETICAL BIOPHYSICAL CHEMISTRY. *Current Pos:* from asst prof to assoc prof, 76-88, chmn, dept chem, 92-95, PROF CHEM, AMHERST COL, 88- *Personal Data:* b New York, NY, July 18, 48; m 70, Marilyn Massler; c Rafael & Maia Shoshana. *Educ:* Columbia Col, AB, 69; Columbia Univ, PhD(chem phys), 75. *Hon Degrees:* AM, Amherst Col, 88. *Honors & Awards:* L P Hammett Award, Columbia Univ, 73. *Prof Exp:* Res assoc chem, Univ Chicago, 74-76. *Concurrent Pos:* Fel NSF, 76-78; vis scholar, Harvard Univ, 79-80; Camille & Henry Dreyfus teacher scholar grant, 80; adj assoc prof physiol & biophys, Mt Sinai Sch Med, NY, 86-88, adj prof, 88- *Mem:* Am Chem Soc. *Res:* Computer simulation of biological molecules; statistical mechanics. *Mailing Add:* Dept Chem Amherst Col Amherst MA 01002. *E-Mail:* jnkushick@amherst.edu

KUSHIDA, TOSHIMOTO, SOLID STATE PHYSICS. *Current Pos:* RES PROF, WAYNE STATE UNIV, 87- *Personal Data:* b Tokyo, Japan, Feb 13, 20; m 46, Mieko Kanemori; c Hiroko, Makiko & Yayoi. *Educ:* Hiroshima Univ, BSc, 44, ScD(physics), 56; Harvard Univ, MSc, 56. *Prof Exp:* Asst physics, Hiroshima Univ, 44-48, from instr to prof, 48-61; res scientist, Sci Lab, Ford Motor Co, 61-87. *Concurrent Pos:* Res fel, Harvard Univ, 56-58. *Mem:* Fel Am Phys Soc; Inst Elec & Electronics Engrs; Sigma Xi. *Res:* Nuclear magnetic resonance; high pressure physics; the puli susceptibility of alkali metals as a function of pressure; phase transitions in high temperature superconductors. *Mailing Add:* 22836 Nona Dearborn MI 48124

KUSHINSKY, STANLEY, BIOANALYTICS, DRUG METABOLISM. *Current Pos:* RETIRED. *Personal Data:* b Brooklyn, NY, Sept 20, 30; div. *Educ:* City Col New York, BS, 51; Columbia Univ, MA, 52; Univ Boston, PhD(chem), 55; Nat Registry Clin Chem, dipl, 68. *Prof Exp:* Res asst, Worcester Found Exp Biol, 52-55; steroid chemist, Dept Surg, Sch Med, Univ Southern Calif, 55-57, res assoc, 57-58, adj asst prof surg & biochem, 58-62, asst prof, 62-64, asst prof biochem, 64-65; from assoc res biochemist to res biochemist, Dept Obstet & Gynec, Sch Med, Univ Calif, Los Angeles, 65-70; dir biochem res, Rees-Stealy Clin Res Found, 70-79; prin scientist, Syntex Res, 79-81, dept head, Anal & Metab chem, 81-86, sr scientist, 82-84, asst dir, Inst Pharmacol & Metab, 84, dir bioanal chem & metab, 84-86, dir bioanal & metab res, 86-93. *Concurrent Pos:* USPHS res career develop award, 65-70; adj prof chem, San Diego State Univ, 73-76. *Mem:* Fel AAAS; Am Chem Soc; Am Asn Clin Chem; Nat Acad Clin Biochem; Endocrine Soc; Am Asn Pharmaceut Scientists. *Res:* Synthesis, isolation and metabolism of steroid hormones; enzyme kinetics; betaglucuronidase; gas chromatographic and radioimmunologic determination of steroids in blood and tissues; high performance liquid chromatography; drug metabolism; bioavailability; pharmacokinetics. *Mailing Add:* 2449 Geranium St San Diego CA 92109-2338

KUSHLAN, JAMES A, ORNITHOLOGY, WETLAND ECOLOGY. *Current Pos:* chair, 88-94, PROF ECOL, UNIV MISS, 88-; DIR, PATUXENT WILDLIFE RES CTR, 94- *Personal Data:* b Cleveland, Ohio, Oct 11, 47; m, Paula Frohring; c 2. *Educ:* Univ Miami, BS, 69, MS, 72, PhD(biol), 74. *Hon Degrees:* DSc, Thiel Col, 96. *Prof Exp:* Maytag fel, Univ Miami, 69-72; biol technician, Nat Park Serv, 73-75; Supvry res biologist, US Dept Interior, 75-84; from assoc prof to prof biol, E Tex State Univ, 84-88. *Concurrent Pos:* Res fel, Univ Miami, 72-74; hydrol technician, US Geol Surv, 72-73; mem, Fed Fla Panther Recovery Team, 75-82, Fed Am Crocodile Recovery Team, 75-83, Fed Cape Sable Sparrow Recovery Team, 79-83; vis scientist, Darwin Res Sta, 78; res assoc, Inst Trop Zool, Cent Univ Venezuela, 79-83; adj assoc prof biol, Univ Miami, 80-86; lectr, Nordic Inst Ecol, 80; mem, Crocodile Specialist Group, 81-, N Am Prairie Conf Comt, 86, Nat Riparian Coun, 86-87, Asn Miss Biol Chairs, 88-, Sci & Math Task Force, Miss Pub Educ Forum, 93; assoc ed, Wetlands, 93-95; coun mem, Am Ornithologists Union, 94- *Mem:* Fel Am Ornithologists Union; Soc Wetland Scientists; Colonial Waterbird Soc (pres-elect, 93-, pres, 96-98); Ecol Soc Am. *Res:* Wetland ecology, especially the adaptation and accommodation of animal populations to fluctuating water conditions using waterbirds and fishes; population and community ecology, especially the influence of environmental fluctuations on population and community dynamics. *Mailing Add:* Patuxent Wildlife Res Ctr 12100 Beech Front Dr Laurel MD 20708. *Fax:* 301-497-5505; *E-Mail:* james_kushlan@nbs.gov

KUSHMERICK, MARTIN JOSEPH, RADIOLOGY, BIOPHYSICS. *Current Pos:* asst prof, 70-76, ASSOC PROF PHYSIOL, HARVARD MED SCH, 76-, ASSOC PROF BIOL, HARVARD UNIV, 78- *Personal Data:* b Pa, May 21, 37; m 62; c 4. *Educ:* Univ Scranton, BS, 58; Univ Pa, MD, 63, PhD(molecular biol), 66. *Prof Exp:* Asst prof biochem, Univ Pa, 66-67; staff assoc, Lab Phys Biol, Nat Inst Arthritis & Metab Dis, NIH, 67-69; hon res assoc & Brit-Am exchange fel, Am Heart Asn, Univ Col, Univ London, 69-70. *Concurrent Pos:* NIH Res Career Develop Awards, 76-81. *Mem:* Am Physiol Soc; AAAS; Biochem Soc Eng; Biophys Soc; Soc Gen Physiologists; Am Soc Biol Chem; Soc Mag Res Med. *Res:* Muscle physiology; energetics, metabolism and their control; mechanism and control of contraction; nuclear magnetic resonance. *Mailing Add:* Dept Radiol Imaging Res Lab SB-05 Univ Wash Seattle WA 98195-0001

KUSHNARYOV, VLADIMIR MICHAEL, ELECTRON MICROSCOPY. *Current Pos:* from asst prof to assoc prof med microbiol, 78-80, DIR, ELECTRON MICROS INSTNL FAC, MED COL WIS, 80-, PROF MICROBIOL, 89- *Personal Data:* b Odessa, USSR, Jan 2, 31; m 54; c 1. *Educ:* 1st Moscow Med Inst, MD, 54; Acad Med Sci, USSR, PhD(microbiol), 61, DSc, 69. *Prof Exp:* Chief & lab prof, Moscow Inst Vaccines & Serim, 75-77. *Concurrent Pos:* Lectr, Moscow Postgrad Med Sch, 60-77. *Mem:* AAAS; Am Soc Microbiol; NY Acad Sci; Int Soc Interferon Res; Electron Micros Soc Am. *Res:* Interaction of biologically active ligands-diphteria toxin, staphyloccocal toxic shock syndrome toxin, interferons with mammalian cells; analysis of internalization of ligands by cells, employing quantitative immunocytochemistry, electron microscopy and biochemical techniques. *Mailing Add:* Dept Microbiol Med Col Wis 8701 Watertown Plank Milwaukee WI 53226-3548

KUSHNER, ARTHUR S, ORGANIC CHEMISTRY, BIOLOGICAL INSECT CONTROLS. *Current Pos:* vpres marketing & sales, 84-88, DIR OPERS, BIOSYS INC, 88- *Personal Data:* b New York, NY, May 9, 40; m 64; c 2. *Educ:* Univ Evansville, BA, 62; Pa State Univ, PhD(org chem), 66; Cleveland State Univ, MBA, 78. *Prof Exp:* Fel chem, Univ Chicago, 66-68; asst prof, Cleveland State Univ, 68-74; supvr film chem sect, Photohorizons Div, Horizons Res, Inc, Cleveland, 74-75, mgr tech support serv, 75-76; group leader cooling water prod, Mogul Div, Dexter Corp, Chagrin Falls, 76-78, prod mgr, 78-79, sales mgr, 79-80; prod develop mgr, Woodhill Permatex Div, Loctite Corp, Cleveland, 80-81; mkt mgr, Chromatix, 81-84. *Concurrent Pos:* Dir, Kushner Electroplating Sch, 78- *Mem:* Am Soc Metals; Am Electroplaters & Surface Finishers Soc; Am Chem Soc; Sigma Xi. *Res:* Synthesis and reactions of bridged polycyclic systems; corrosion inhibition; treatment of cooling water; preparation of new corrosion inhibition materials; photochemistry of free-radical film systems; corrosion inhibition; metal finishing and electroplating; development of biological insect controls. *Mailing Add:* 732 Glencoe Ct Sunnyvale CA 94087-3412

KUSHNER, DONN JEAN, MICROBIAL BIOCHEMISTRY, MICROBIAL PHYSIOLOGY. *Current Pos:* prof, 89-92, EMER PROF MICROBIOL & BOT, UNIV TORONTO, 92-; EMER PROF BIOL, UNIV OTTAWA, 89- *Personal Data:* b Lake Charles, La, Mar 29, 27; m 49, Eva Dubska; c Daniel, Roland & Paul. *Educ:* Harvard Univ, SB, 48; McGill Univ, MSc, 50, PhD(biochem), 52. *Honors & Awards:* Can Soc Microbiologists Award, 92. *Prof Exp:* Asst, Res Inst, Mont Gen Hosp, 52-53; Nat Found Infantile Paralysis fel, 53-54; res officer bact physiol & genetics, Forest Insect Lab, 54-61; assoc res officer, Nat Res Coun Can, 61-65. *Concurrent Pos:* Nat Inst Med Res, London, Eng, 58-59, Inst Pasteur, Paris, 72, MacDonald Col, 80, Cornell Univ, 81- & Inst Jacques Monod, Paris, 86-87; from assoc prof to prof biol, Univ Ottawa, 65-89; co-ed, Can J Microbiol, 80-84, Archives of Microbiol, 86-94; vis prof microbiol & environ studies, Univ Toronto, 88-89. *Mem:* Am Soc Biol Chem & Molecular Biol; Am Soc Microbiol; Can Soc Microbiol (pres, 80-81). *Res:* Physiology of halophilic and psychrophilic bacteria; action of microorganisms in natural environments on polymers and heavy metals; bacterial drug resistance. *Mailing Add:* Dept Bot Univ Toronto Toronto ON M5S 3B2 Can. *Fax:* 416-978-5878; *E-Mail:* kushner@botany.utoronto.ca

KUSHNER, HAROLD J(OSEPH), STOCHASTIC SYSTEMS, OPERATIONS RESEARCH. *Current Pos:* chmn, Div Appl Math, 88-92, PROF APPL MATH & ENG, BROWN UNIV, 64- *Personal Data:* b New York, NY, July 29, 33; m 60, Linda Rosen. *Educ:* City Col New York, BSc, 55; Univ Wis, MSc, 56, PhD(elec eng), 58. *Honors & Awards:* Control Theory Field Award, Inst Elec & Electronics Engrs; Lewis Levy Medal, Franklin Inst. *Prof Exp:* Staff mem, Lincoln Lab, Mass Inst Technol, 58-63 & Res Inst Advan Studies, Martin-Marietta Corp, Md, 63-64. *Concurrent Pos:* Dir, Lefscelcz Ctr Dynamical Syst, 87- *Mem:* Inst Math Statist; Soc Indust & Appl Math; Opers Res Soc Am; Inst Elec & Electronics Engrs. *Res:* Theoretical study of automatic control and communication systems, especially when random phenomenon are of some significance; applied probability; stochastic systems theory. *Mailing Add:* Dept Appl Math Brown Univ Providence RI 02912

KUSHNER, HARVEY, MATHEMATICAL BIOMEDICAL STATISTICS. *Current Pos:* PROF MATH & BIOSTATIST & CHMN, DEPT BIOMET, HAHNEMANN UNIV, 78- *Personal Data:* b Philadelphia, Pa, Nov 2, 50; m 73; c 4. *Educ:* Temple Univ, AB, 72, MA, 74, PhD(math), 78. *Concurrent Pos:* Adj assoc prof, Dept Math, Temple Univ, 79- & Grad Sch, Med Col Pa, 80-81 & 85-86; treas, Biomed Comput Res Inst. *Mem:* Am Math Soc; Am Statist Asn. *Res:* Time series analysis; categorical data analysis. *Mailing Add:* 9743 Redd Rambler Rd Philadelphia PA 19115

KUSHNER, HARVEY D(AVID), OPERATIONS RESEARCH. *Current Pos:* pres, ORI Inc, 69-83, chmn & chief exec officer, 83-85, CHMN & CHIEF EXEC OFFICER, THE ORI GROUP, INC, 85- *Personal Data:* b New York, NY, Dec 28, 30; m 51; c 3. *Educ:* Johns Hopkins Univ, BE, 51. *Prof Exp:* Engr, Mach Evals Group, Bur Ships, US Navy Dept, 51 & Performance & Sci Sect, 52-53; mem tech staff, Cent Res Lab, Melpar, Inc Div, Westinghouse Air Brake Co, 53-54 & Flight Simulator Dept, 54-55; res engr, Reliance Group Inc, 55-57, group leader, 57-59, prog dir, 59-61, vpres & dir, Eastern Div, 61-62, vpres & dir, Phys Systs Div, 63-64, dir, Govt & Indust Systs Div, 64-68, exec vpres, 62-69, vpres, 71-77; pres, Disclosure, Inc, 72-77. *Concurrent Pos:* Consult, Appl Physics Lab, Johns Hopkins Univ, 57-58 & Nat Acad Sci Comt Undersea Warfare, 63-64. *Mem:* Opers Res Soc Am; Inst Mgt Sci; Am Inst Aeronaut & Astronaut; sr mem Inst Elec & Electronics Engrs; Am Soc Mech Engrs; fel NY Acad Sci. *Res:* Systems analysis; operations research. *Mailing Add:* 9743 Redd Rambler Rd Philadelphia PA 19115

KUSHNER, IRVING, RHEUMATOLOGY, MEDICINE. *Current Pos:* PROF MED, SCH MED, CASE WESTERN RES UNIV, 74- *Personal Data:* b New York, NY, Jan 16, 29; m 55; c Ellen, Philip & David. *Educ:* Columbia Univ, BA, 50; Wash Univ, MD, 54. *Prof Exp:* Intern med, New Haven Hosp, 54-55; asst resident, 2 & 4 med serv, Boston City Hosp, 57-58; demonstr med, Case Western Res Univ, 58-59, instr, 60-61, sr instr, 61-64, from asst prof to assoc prof, 64-73; prof, WVa Univ, 73-74. *Concurrent Pos:* USPHS res fel, 58-59; Helen Hay Whitney Found res fel, 59-62; foreign fel, Inst Sci Res Cancer, France, 62-63; sr int fel, Fogarty Ctr, NIH, 76; med dir, Metro Health Ctr Rehab, 85-91. *Mem:* Am Col Physicians; Am Rheumatism Asn; Soc Exp Biol & Med; NY Acad Sci; Am Asn Immunol. *Res:* Acute phase reaction; C-reactive protein; mechanisms which regulate the acute phase response to inflammatory stimuli with particular emphasis on induction of c-reaction protein by cytokines. *Mailing Add:* Dept Med Metro Health Med Ctr Cleveland OH 44109. *Fax:* 216-778-8376

KUSHNER, LAWRENCE MAURICE, MATERIALS SCIENCE, TOXIC & HAZARDOUS SUBSTANCE REGULATION. *Current Pos:* RETIRED. *Personal Data:* b New York, NY, Sept 20, 24; m 72, Shirley Brown; c Robb & Leslie. *Educ:* Queens Col, BS, 45; Princeton Univ, AM, 47, PhD, 49. *Honors & Awards:* Students Medal, Am Inst Chemists, 45; Gold Medal, Dept

Com, 68; Meritorious Serv Award, Am Nat Students Inst, 73. *Prof Exp:* Teaching asst, Princeton Univ, 47-48; staff mem, Nat Bur Stand, 48-56, chief, Metal Physics sect, 56-61 & Metall Div, 61-66, dep dir, Inst Appl Tech, 66-68, dir, Inst Appl Technol, 68-69, dep dir, Bur, 69-73, actg dir, 72-73; comnr, Consumer Prod Safety Comn, 73-77; coordr policy develop, Nat Bur Stand, 77-80; sr staff scientist, Mitre Corp, 80-85, consult scientist, 85-89. *Concurrent Pos:* Lectr chem, Am Univ, 52-60; mem ad hoc int group metal physics, Org Econ Coop & Develop, 61; fel, Sci & Technol Fel Prog, Dept Com, 64-65; mem, Md Gov Sci Adv Coun, 72-75; adj prof eng & pub policy, Carnegie-Mellon Univ, 81-92. *Mem:* Fel AAAS; hon mem Am Soc Testing & Mat; Am Chem Soc; Am Phys Soc; Sigma Xi (pres, 76). *Res:* Physical chemistry of surface active agents; relationship between physical properties of materials and their molecular and crystal structures. *Mailing Add:* 20506 Beaver Ridge Rd Gaithersburg MD 20879-4326

KUSHNER, MARK JAY, COMPUTER SIMULATION, COMPUTER AIDED DESIGN. *Current Pos:* PROF ELEC & COMPUT ENG, UNIV ILL, URBANA, 86- *Personal Data:* b Los Angeles, Calif, Dec 21, 52. *Educ:* Univ Calif Los Angeles, BA & BS, 76; Calif Inst Technol, MS, 77, PhD(appl physics), 79. *Honors & Awards:* Techn Excellence Award, Semiconductor Res Corp, 95. *Prof Exp:* Postdoctoral, Calif Inst Technol, 79-80; physicist, Sandia Nat Labs, 80-81, Lawrence Livermore Nat Labs, 81-83; dir electron, atomic & molecular physics, Spectra Technol, 83-86. *Concurrent Pos:* Assoc ed, Trans Plasma Sci, 89-, Plasma Sources Sci & Technol, 94- *Mem:* Fel Inst Elec & Electronics Engrs; fel Am Phys Soc; fel Optical Soc Am; Am Vacuum Soc; Mat Res Soc; Am Soc Eng Educ. *Res:* Low temperature plasmas for materials fabrication, lighting sources, plasma chemistry and lasers. *Mailing Add:* Univ Ill 1406 W Green St Urbana IL 61801-2918. *Fax:* 217-244-7097; *E-Mail:* mjk@uiuc.edu

KUSHNER, SAMUEL, PHARMACEUTICAL CHEMISTRY. *Current Pos:* RETIRED. *Personal Data:* b Auburn, NY, Apr 25, 15; m 37; c 4. *Educ:* Univ Mich, BS, 39, MS, 40, PhD(chem), 42. *Prof Exp:* Res chemist, Am Cyanamid Co, 42-44, group leader, 44-55, unit leader, 55-56, head dept med chem of infectious dis, 56-71, head chem of infectious res dis sect, Lederle Labs, Am Cyanamid Co, 71-81. *Mem:* AAAS; Am Chem Soc; NY Acad Sci. *Res:* Structure of penicillin; chemotherapy related to tropical diseases; tuberculosis and virus; structure and synthesis of antibiotics; antineoplastics. *Mailing Add:* 138 Highview Ave Nanuet NY 10954-3315

KUSHNER, SIDNEY RALPH, MOLECULAR GENETICS, ENZYMOLOGY. *Current Pos:* assoc prof, 80-82, head dept, 87-95, PROF GENETICS, UNIV GA, 82- *Personal Data:* b New York, NY, Dec 14, 43; m, Deena Dash; c Aaron & Ze'eva. *Educ:* Oberlin Col, BA, 65; Brandeis Univ, PhD(biochem), 70. *Prof Exp:* NIH fel molecular biol, Univ Calif, Berkeley, 70-71; NIH fel, Med Sch, Stanford Univ, 71-73, from asst prof to assoc prof biochem, 73-80. *Concurrent Pos:* NIH res career develop award, 75; assoc ed, Gene, 80-; Microbiol Genetics Study Sect, NIH, 81-85; bd dirs, Am Type Cult Collection, 88-93. *Mem:* Am Soc Microbiol; fel AAAS; Am Soc Biol Chemists; Genetics Soc Am. *Res:* Analysis of messenger RNA degradation; genetic control and enzymology of recombination and DNA repair; functional expression of eukaryotic DNA in prokaryotes. *Mailing Add:* Dept Genetics Univ Ga Athens GA 30602. *E-Mail:* skushner@uga.cc.uga.edu

KUSHNICK, THEODORE, PEDIATRICS, MEDICAL GENETICS. *Current Pos:* PROF PEDIAT & DIR MED GENETICS, SCH MED, ECAROLINA UNIV, 79- *Personal Data:* b Brooklyn, NY, Mar 29, 25; m 49; c 3. *Educ:* Ohio State Univ, BS, 44, MS, 47; Harvard Med Sch, MD, 51. *Prof Exp:* Intern med, Boston City Hosp, 51-52; resident pediat, Boston Children's Med Ctr, 52-53, 54-55; clin res asst, Boston Children's Cancer Res Found, 55-56; pvt pract, NJ, 56-59; clin instr pediat, Col Med & Dent NJ, Newark, 58-59, from asst prof to prof, 59-79, dir, div human genetics, 61-79. *Concurrent Pos:* Jr physician, Wrentham State Sch, Mass, 53; resident psychiat, Boston State Hosp, 53-54; clin instr, Harvard Med Sch, 55-56; genetic consult, Nat Found March of Dimes Spec Birth Defects Treatment Ctr, Babies Hosp, Newark; Mead-Johnson res grant, 60-62; NIH res grant, 61-63; Nat Found-March of Dimes Med Serv Prog Grants, 74-75 & 76-77; Sci Adv Comm, Nat Tay-Sachs & Allied Dis Asn, 74- *Mem:* AAAS; Am Asn Ment Deficiency; fel Am Acad Pediat; Am Soc Human Genetics; NY Acad Sci. *Res:* Clinical pediatrics; clinical genetics mental retardation; cytogenetics; immunology. *Mailing Add:* Dept Pediat Sch Med ECarolina Univ Greenville NC 27834

KUSHWAHA, RAMPRATAP S, LIPID METABOLISM. *Current Pos:* SCIENTIST, SOUTHWEST FOUND BIOMED RES, 82- *Personal Data:* b India, July 11, 43. *Educ:* Wash State Univ, PhD(nutrit), 73. *Concurrent Pos:* Adj prof, Dept Path, Univ Tex Health Sci Ctr, 82- *Mem:* Am Heart Asn; Am Inst Nutrit; Med & Health Sci; Biol Sci. *Res:* Metabolic and molecular basis of genetic dyslipoproteinemias in pedigreed baboons; metabolic and molecular mechanisms by which dietary factors such as cholestrol and sex steroid hormones modulate lipoprotein metabolism in normal and dyslipoproteinemic subjects. *Mailing Add:* Dept Physiol & Med Southwest Found Biomed Res PO Box 28147 San Antonio TX 78284-0147. *Fax:* 210-670-3323

KUSIAK, ANDREW, ENGINEERING DESIGN, MANUFACTURING & ARTIFICIAL INTELLIGENCE CONCURRENT ENGINEERING. *Current Pos:* chair, 88-95, PROF INDUST ENG, UNIV IOWA, 88- *Personal Data:* b Kozia Wola, Poland, June 14, 49; Can citizen; m 74; c 3. *Educ:* Warsaw Tech Univ, BS, 72, MS, 74; Polish Acad Sci, PhD(oper res), 79. *Prof Exp:* Proj mgr, Dept Automation, Inst Mgt & Org, 79-81; asst prof indust eng, Tech Univ, Nova Scotia, 82-85; assoc prof, indust eng, Univ Man, Can, 85-88. *Concurrent Pos:* Ed, Artificial Intel in Indust, 86-, Appl Artificial Intel, 88-; res award, Univ Man, 86; chmn, Int Conf Adv Prod, 87, Int Conf Artificial Intel, 90; vis prof, Inst Adv Studies, Vienna, Austria, 91; hon prof, Huazong Univ Sci & Technol, China. *Mem:* Sr mem Soc Mfg Engrs; Oper Res Soc Am; sr mem Am Asn Artificial Intel; Inst Indust Engrs; Int Fedn Automation & Control; Int Fedn Info Processing. *Res:* Knowledge-based systems for design of products and manufacturing systems; group technology; design of facilities; process planning; concurrent engineering; design automation; design methodologies. *Mailing Add:* Dept Indust Eng Univ Iowa Iowa City IA 52242

KUSIC, GEORGE LARRY, JR, CONTROL ENGINEERING, COMPUTER SCIENCE. *Current Pos:* asst prof, 67-77, ASSOC PROF ELEC ENG & GRAD PROG COORDR, UNIV PITTSBURGH, 77- *Personal Data:* b Aliquippa, Pa, Aug 26, 35; m 69; c 1. *Educ:* Carnegie Inst Technol, BSEE, 57, MSEE, 66, PhDEE, 68. *Prof Exp:* Res engr, Sikorsky Aircraft Co, 57-59; elec develop engr, TRW Corp, 59-63. *Concurrent Pos:* NASA-Am Soc Eng Educ fac res fel, 69; sr Fulbright-Hays lect grant, Univ Belgrade, 70-71; consult, NSF-Agency Int Develop India Prog, 68, IBM Data Processing Div, 68 & Westinghouse Res Lab, 69-70. *Mailing Add:* 5470 Fair Oaks St Pittsburgh PA 15217

KUSIK, CHARLES LEMBIT, WASTE MINIMIZATION, RECYCLING. *Current Pos:* MNR metals & energy mgt, 64-88, dir technol & prod develop, 89-96, PRIN, ARTHUR D LITTLE INC, 96- *Personal Data:* b New York, NY, Apr 24, 34. *Educ:* Mass Inst Technol, BS, 56; NY Univ, DSc(chem eng), 61. *Prof Exp:* Scientist opers res, Mass Inst Tchnol, 61-62; scientist gas dynamics, Avco Corp, 63-64. *Mem:* Am Inst Chem Engrs; Am Chem Soc; Am Inst Mining, Metall & Petrol Engrs. *Res:* Energy assessments; recycling; process development; economics; commercial feasibility studies; pollution prevention. *Mailing Add:* Arthur D Little Inc 20 Acorn Park Cambridge MA 02140

KUSKA, HENRY (ANTON), PHYSICAL CHEMISTRY. *Current Pos:* RETIRED. *Personal Data:* b Chicago, Ill, July 28, 37; m 64; c 3. *Educ:* Cornell Col, BA, 59; Mich State Univ, PhD(phys chem), 65. *Prof Exp:* Res assoc & res fel phys chem, Mich State Univ, 64-65; assoc prof phys chem, Univ Akron, 65-94. *Mem:* Am Chem Soc. *Res:* Spectroscopy; nuclear magnetic resonance; electron spin resonance; electron-nuclear double resonance; infrared, visible ultraviolet. *Mailing Add:* 7352 Ashburton Circle NW Canton OH 44720

KUSKO, ALEXANDER, ELECTRICAL ENGINEERING. *Current Pos:* div dir, 88-94, CORP VPRES, FAILURE ANALYSIS ASSOC, 94- *Personal Data:* b New York, NY, Apr 4, 21; m 41; c 2. *Educ:* Purdue Univ, BS, 42; Mass Inst Technol, SM, 44, ScD, 51. *Prof Exp:* Asst, Mass Inst Technol, 42-44, from instr to assoc prof, 46-58, lectr, 58-88. *Concurrent Pos:* Pres, Alexander Kusko Inc, 56-88. *Mem:* Inst Elec & Electronics Engrs. *Res:* Energy conversion and control. *Mailing Add:* Failure Analysis Assoc 3 Cambridge Ctr Cambridge MA 02142

KUSLAN, LOUIS ISAAC, HISTORY OF SCIENCE. *Current Pos:* RETIRED. *Personal Data:* b New Haven, Conn, Feb 14, 22; m 47; c 2. *Educ:* Univ Conn, BS, 43; Yale Univ, MA, 49, PhD(sci educ), 54. *Prof Exp:* Instr high schs, Conn, 43-46; asst chem, Univ Conn, 46-47, instr, Waterbur Br, 47-49; from instr to asst prof sci, Southern Conn State Univ, 50-56, assoc chem, 56-60, prof chem & chmn dept sci, 60-66, dean arts & sci, 66-78, prof chem, 78-88. *Concurrent Pos:* Fel chem, Yale Univ, 58-59, hist sci, 62-63. *Mem:* Am Chem Soc; Hist Sci Soc. *Res:* History of analytical and American chemistry; elementary science education; nineteenth century American chemistry. *Mailing Add:* 653 Gaylord Mountain Rd Hamden CT 06518

KUSMIK, WILLIAM F, ANALYTICAL CHEMISTRY. *Current Pos:* mgr cell biol & immunol, 87-91, mgr qual control creative biomolecules, 91-93, MGR ASSAY DEVELOP, 93- *Personal Data:* b Hartford, Conn, June 7, 42; m 92, Elaine Stamstevis; c William Aldo & Alexa Rae. *Educ:* Col Holy Cross, Mass, BA, 65; Cent Conn State Univ, MA, 76; Univ Conn, PhD(cell physiol), 82. *Prof Exp:* Res fel steroid receptor biochem, Res Inst, Temple Univ, 82-85; res scientist, Univ Conn Med Sch, 85-86, Univ Miami Med Sch, 86-87. *Mem:* AAAS; Wound Healing Soc; Am Soc Cell Biol; Tissue Cult Asn; Parenteral Drug Asn; Regulatory Affiars Prof Soc. *Res:* Development of biological immunological and analytical assays for the testing of recombinant protein pharmaceuticals. *Mailing Add:* Dept Bioassay Creative Biomolecules 35 South St Hopkinton MA 01748. *Fax:* 508-435-0454

KUSPIRA, J, CYTOGENETICS. *Current Pos:* RETIRED. *Personal Data:* b Yorkton, Sask, Nov 20, 28; m 58; c 4. *Educ:* Univ Sask, BSc, 51, MSc, 52; Univ Alta, PhD(genetics), 55. *Prof Exp:* Asst cytogeneticist, Univ Alta, 55-57, assoc res prof cytogenetics, 58- 62, assoc prof, 62-70, prof genetics, 70-90, assoc dean sci, 72-90. *Mem:* Am Genetic Asn; Genetics Soc Can. *Res:* Cytogenetic analysis of tetraploid and hexaploid wheats. *Mailing Add:* 12416 47th Ave Edmonton AB T6H 0B4 Can

KUSSE, BRUCE RAYMOND, PLASMA PHYSICS. *Current Pos:* res assoc, Lab Plasma Studies, 70-71, asst prof, 71-76, ASSOC PROF PLASMA PHYSICS, CORNELL UNIV, 76- *Personal Data:* b Rochester, NY, Aug 10, 38. *Educ:* Mass Inst Technol, SB, 60, SM, 64, PhD(elec eng), 69. *Prof Exp:* Sr scientist, Eastern Sci & Technol Div, EG&G, 69-70; res assoc plasma physics, Res Lab Electronics, Mass Inst Technol, 70. *Mem:* Sigma Xi; Am Phys Soc. *Res:* Plasma physics-experimental studies of intense, relativistic beam-plasma interactions, particularly in toroidalgeometry. *Mailing Add:* 144 N Sunset Dr Ithaca NY 14850

KUSSMAUL, KEITH, DESIGN & ANALYSIS OF EXPERIMENTS, STATISTICAL PROCESS CONTROL. *Current Pos:* STATIST CONSULT, 93- *Personal Data:* b Sterling, Ill, Apr 9, 39; m 65, Carol Cowan; c Clifton, Kimberly, Katherine & Craig. *Educ:* Univ Mich, BS, 60, MS, 61; NC State Univ, PhD(statist), 66. *Prof Exp:* Mathematician, Int Bus Mach Corp, 61-62; statistician, Westinghouse Elec Corp, 66-93. *Concurrent Pos:* Lectr indust eng, Univ Pittsburgh, 67-70, vis lect prog, Soc Indust Appl Math, 77-83. *Mem:* Am Statist Asn; Biomet Soc; Am Soc Qual Control. *Res:* Design and analysis of industrial experiments; statistical methods; general linear hypothesis; general statistical consulting. *Mailing Add:* 9 Oakmore Dr Round Rock TX 78664-9612. *E-Mail:* oakmoore@.aol.com

KUSSY, FRANK WERNER, ELECTRICAL DISTRIBUTION & CONTROL. *Current Pos:* CONSULT, 80- *Personal Data:* b Dresden, Ger, Oct 13, 10; m, Adelaide Maria; c Edward & Henrietta. *Educ:* Tech Univ Munich, MS, 34; Tech Univ Vienna, Dr Technische Wissenschaften, 36. *Prof Exp:* Pres, Rheastab-Habege GmbH, Dresden; proj engr, Square D Co, 54-56, asst chief engr, 56-58, chief engr, 58-59; res engr & engr mgr, ITE, 59-68, adv develop engr, 68-75, dir prod develop, 75-80. *Concurrent Pos:* Vol, Int Exec Serv Corp, Egypt, Zimbabwe, 87, 90 & 91. *Mem:* Fel Inst Elec & Electronics Engrs. *Res:* Patents in field of electrical distribution and control; combination starters; author of several books. *Mailing Add:* 21394 Magnolia Ct Farmington Hills MI 21133

KUST, ROGER NAYLAND, INORGANIC CHEMISTRY, PHYSICAL CHEMISTRY. *Current Pos:* MGR METALS RECOVERY, TETRA TECHNOL, INC, 87- *Personal Data:* b Berwyn, Ill, Apr 20, 35; m 57; c 2. *Educ:* Purdue Univ, BS, 57; Iowa State Univ, PhD(fused salts), 63. *Prof Exp:* Asst prof inorg chem, Tex A&M Univ, 64-65 & Univ Utah, 65-71; sr inorg chemist, Ledgemont Lab, Kennecott Copper Corp, 71-77, group leader chem, 77-78, sect head chem, 78-79; sr staff engr, Exxon Minerals Co, 79-80, sect head, 80-81, mgr, Minerals Processing Res Div, 81-87. *Mem:* AAAS; Am Chem Soc; Electrochem Soc; Am Acad Arts & Sci; Am Inst Chemists; Metall Soc. *Res:* Acid-base reactions in fused salts; electrochemical investigations in nonaqueous media with emphasis on fused salts; chemistry of metallurgical processes. *Mailing Add:* 8408 Crescent Wood Lane Spring TX 77379

KUSTIN, KENNETH, INORGANIC CHEMISTRY, PHYSICAL CHEMISTRY. *Current Pos:* from asst prof to prof, 61-97, chmn dept, 74-77, EMER PROF CHEM, BRANDEIS UNIV, 97- *Personal Data:* b Bronx, NY, Jan 6, 34; m 56, Myrna M Jacobson; c Brenda, Michael & Franklin. *Educ:* Queens Col, NY, BSc, 55; Univ Minn, Minneapolis, PhD(inorg chem), 59. *Prof Exp:* USPHS fel, Max Planck Inst Phys Chem, 59-61. *Concurrent Pos:* Vis prof, Dept Pharmacol, Harvard Med Sch, 77-78; Fulbright lectr, 78; counr, Am Chem Soc, 83-85; prog dir, NSF, 85-86; adj res sci, Res Develop & Eng Ctr, US Army Natick, 91. *Mem:* Am Chem Soc; Western Soc Naturalists; AAAS; Inst Food Technologists. *Res:* Inorganic biochemistry; oscillating reactions; fast reactions. *Mailing Add:* 5210 Fiore Terr Apt 111 San Diego CA 92122. *E-Mail:* kmkustin@ix.netcom.com

KUSTOM, ROBERT L, ION ACCELERATION & FOCUSING, POWER ELECTRONIC NETWORKS. *Current Pos:* Elec engr particle detect develop, Accelerator Res Facil Div, Argonne Nat Lab, 58-69, elec engr radio frequency separators & microwave discharge chambers, 69-71, group leader zero gradient synchrotron oper, 71-73, assoc div dir, Plasma Support Syst, Tokamaks & Accelerator Exp Area, 73-78, mgr accelerator syst intense pulsed neutron source, 78-79, div dir accelerator res & develop, 79-81, assoc proj dir electron accelerator, 81-83, sr elec engr, Seven Giga Electronvolt Storage Ring-Advan Photon Source Proj, 83-88, interim dir, Advan Photon Source Accelerator Syst Div, 89-90, SR ELEC ENGR, ADVAN PHOTON SOURCE, GROUP LEADER, RF GROUP, ARGONNE NAT LAB, 90- *Personal Data:* b Chicago, Ill, July 11, 34; c 3. *Educ:* Ill Inst Technol, BSEE, 56, MSEE, 58; Univ Wis-Madison, PhD(elec eng), 69. *Concurrent Pos:* Vis scientist, Rutherford High Energy Lab, Didcot, UK, 70-71; Tokamak Fusion Test Reactor eng rev comt, Princeton Plasma Physics Lab, 75-77; vis prof, Elec & Comput Eng Dept, Univ Wis-Madison, 78-79 & 80-81, consult, Superconductive Energy Storage Group, 81, adj prof, Elec & Comput Eng Dept, 83- *Mem:* Inst Elec & Electronics Engrs; Sigma Xi. *Res:* Development of ion acceleration, focussing, and detection techniques, and the electrodynamic interactions between ions and electromagnetic fields; theoretical and experimental development of superconductive energy storage and transfer techniques using power electronic circuits and electronic circuits and electrodynamic devices; radio frequency systems and accelerating cavities. *Mailing Add:* Argonne Nat Lab 9700 S Cass Ave Argonne IL 60439

KUSTU, SYDNEY GOVONS, BACTERIOLOGY, GENETICS. *Current Pos:* from asst prof to assoc prof bact, Davis, 74-87, PROF PLANT & MICROBIOL, UNIV CALIF, BERKELEY, 87-, PROF MOLECULAR CELL BIOL, 87- *Personal Data:* b Baltimore, Md, Mar 18, 43. *Educ:* Harvard Univ, BA, 63; Univ Calif, Davis, PhD(biochem), 70. *Mem:* Nat Acad Sci; Am Soc Microbiol; Am Soc Biol Chemists; Sigma Xi; AAAS. *Res:* Regulation of bacterial nitrogen metabolism. *Mailing Add:* Plant & Microbiol Univ Calif 111 Koshland Ave Berkeley CA 94720-3102. *Fax:* 510-642-4995; *E-Mail:* kustu@mendel.berkeley.edu

KUSUDA, TAMAMI, MECHANICAL ENGINEERING. *Current Pos:* CONSULT, JAPAN TECHNOL PROG, US DEPT COM, 87- *Personal Data:* b Seattle, Wash, June 24, 25; m 55, Selma Kornreich; c Leo, Kay & Yuri. *Educ:* Univ Tokyo, BS, 47; Univ Wash, Seattle, MS, 52; Univ Minn, PhD(mech eng), 55. *Honors & Awards:* Wolverline Award, Am Soc Heating, Refrig & Air-Conditioning Engrs, 57, Crosby-Field Award, William Holladay Distinguished Fel Award, 87; Gold Medal, US Dept Com, 80. *Prof Exp:* Staff engr, Worthington Corp, 55-62; mech engr, Nat Bur Stand, 62-70, asst chief, Environ Eng Sect, 70-74, chief, Thermal Eng Sect, 74-78, chief, Thermal Anal Prog, 78-83, chief, Bldg Physics Div, 83-86. *Concurrent Pos:* Prof lectr, George Wash Univ, 87- *Mem:* Am Soc Mech Engrs; fel Am Soc Heating, Refrig & Air-Conditioning Engrs; hon mem Automated Procedure Eng Consult; AAAS. *Res:* Heat transfer and thermodynamics related to environmental science, such as air conditioning, heating, ventilating, refrigeration, ground heat exchange and psychrometrics; energy conservation; indoor air quality. *Mailing Add:* 5000 Battery Lane Apt 506 Bethesda MD 20814. *Fax:* 301-913-5760; *E-Mail:* kusuda@cais.com

KUSWA, GLENN WESLEY, EXPERIMENTAL PHYSICS, TECHNOLOGY TRANSFER. *Current Pos:* mgr future options planning, Sandia Labs, 84-85, mgr, Technol Transfer Dept, 86-88, supr plasma diag, 88-90 & 91-92, mgr environ health & safety, 91-92, MGR, LAB ASSESSMENTS, SANDIA LABS, 95- *Personal Data:* b Milwaukee, Wis, Dec 11, 40; wid; c Kevin & Erika. *Educ:* Univ Wis-Madison, BS, 62, MS, 64, PhD(physics), 70. *Prof Exp:* Physicist, Sandia Labs, 70-74; physicist, Laser & Isotope Separation Technol Off, US Energy Res & Develop Admin, 74-76; mgr, Particle Beam Fusion Res Dept, Sandia Labs, 76-81; tech adv asst secy defense progs, US Dept Energy, 82-83. *Concurrent Pos:* Bd pres, Maxwell Mus Anthropol Found. *Mem:* Am Phys Soc; AAAS; Sigma Xi; Planetary Soc. *Res:* Plasma guns; measurement of distribution functions; holographic interferometry; production of dense plasmas; electrical break-down in vacuum; interaction of electron and ion beams with matter; inertially driven fusion technology using lasers, ions, electron beams; large scale research management; defense science technology transfer and licensing; assessment of value of technology. *Mailing Add:* 1115 San Rafael Ave NE Albuquerque NM 87122-1130. *E-Mail:* gwkuswa@sandia.gov

KUSY, ROBERT PETER, DENTAL RESEARCH, MEDICAL RESEARCH. *Current Pos:* res assoc, Med Sch, Univ NC, 72-74, asst prof oral biol, 74-79, assoc prof orthod & Dent Res Ctr, Dent Sch, 79-89, assoc prof biomed eng, Med Sch, 85-89, adj prof appl sci curric, Sch Med, 90-96, PROF DEPT ORTHOD, DENT RES CTR & BIOMED ENG, UNIV NC, 89-, PROF CURRIC APPLN & MAT SCIS, 96- *Personal Data:* b Worcester, Mass, Oct 19, 47; m 69, Gisela Bauer; c Kimberly & Kevin. *Educ:* Worcester Polytech Inst, BS, 69; Drexel Univ, MS, 71, PhD(mat eng), 73. *Prof Exp:* Res asst mats, Dept Metall Eng, Drexel Univ, 69-72. *Concurrent Pos:* Co-investr, Duke-NC Eng Res Ctr, 88-; mem, Inst Nutrit, 90-. *Mem:* Am Soc Metals; Am Chem Soc; Soc Plastics Engr; NAm Thermal Anal Soc; Int Asn Dent Res; Int Metallog Soc; Microbeam Anal Soc; Soc Biomat. *Res:* Properties of dental and medical materials; fractography and fracture work energy of polymers; fabrication of high strength/high modulus fibers; laser scattering experiments; thermal analysis and radiation properties of polymers; biosensors; ion implantation of dental and medical materials; specialize in orthodontic materials. *Mailing Add:* 113 Cynthia Dr Chapel Hill NC 27514. *Fax:* 919-966-3683; *E-Mail:* rkusy@bme.unc.edu

KUSZAK, JEROME R, PATHOLOGY. *Current Pos:* DIR ELECTRON MICROS, DEPT PATH, RUSH-PRESBY, ST LUKE'S MED CTR, 83- *Personal Data:* b May 26, 51. *Educ:* Wayne State Univ, BS, 72, MS, 76, PhD(anat), 80. *Honors & Awards:* Alcon Res Inst Award, 90. *Prof Exp:* Instr anat, cell biol & path, Rush Med Col, 80-83, asst prof path, Conjoint Appointment Anat, 83-87. *Concurrent Pos:* New investr award, Nat Eye Inst, NIH, 83-86; assoc prof path, Conjoint Appointment Anat, Rush Med Col, 87-, assoc prof ophthal, 90- *Mem:* Inst Soc Eye Res; Asn Res Vision & Ophthal; Am Soc Cell Biol. *Res:* Pathology. *Mailing Add:* Dept Path Rush-Presby St Luke Med Ctr 1653 W Congress Pkwy Chicago IL 60612-3833. *Fax:* 312-942-4228

KUTAL, CHARLES RONALD, PHOTOCHEMISTRY, PHOTOSENSITIVE MATERIALS. *Current Pos:* from instr to assoc prof, 73-85, head, 91-96, PROF CHEM, UNIV GA, 85- *Personal Data:* b Chicago, Ill, Aug 9, 44; m 73, Judy Gombos. *Educ:* Knox Col, Ill, AB, 65; Univ Ill, Urbana-Champaign, MS, 68, PhD(chem), 70. *Honors & Awards:* Res Award, Sigma Xi, 79. *Prof Exp:* Res assoc chem, Univ Southern Calif, 70-72. *Concurrent Pos:* Res fel, Nat Res Coun-Nat Acad Sci, 72-73; vis scientist, IBM Res Labs, 86. *Mem:* Am Chem Soc; AAAS; Sigma Xi; Int Soc Optical Eng. *Res:* Photochemical and photophysical investigations of transition metal and organometallic complexes, photocatalysis, photolithography. *Mailing Add:* Dept Chem Univ Ga Athens GA 30602. *Fax:* 706-542-9454; *E-Mail:* ckutal@sunchem.chem.uga.edu

KUTAS, MARTA, PSYCHOLOGY, PSYCHOPHYSIOLOGY. *Current Pos:* res neuroscientist, 78-80, asst res neuroscientist, 80-84, ASSOC RES NEUROSCIENTIST, UNIV CALIF, SAN DIEGO, 85- *Personal Data:* b Hungary, Sept 2, 49; US citizen. *Educ:* Oberlin Col, BA, 71; Univ Ill, Urbana-Champaign, MA, 74, PhD(biol psychol), 77. *Honors & Awards:* Early Career Contribution Psychol Award, Am Psychiat Asn. *Prof Exp:* Vis res assoc, Dept Psychol, Univ Ill, 77-78. *Mem:* Soc Psychophyisol Res; Int Neuropsychol Soc; Women in Neurosci. *Res:* Brain function, including recording and interpreting pattern of brain waves (event related potentials) from the scalp as humans try to comprehend the oral, written or pictorial world. *Mailing Add:* 3493 Voyager Circle San Diego CA 92130

KUTCHAI, HOWARD C, PHYSIOLOGY, BIOCHEMISTRY. *Current Pos:* from asst prof to assoc prof, 72-81, PROF PHYSIOL, SCH MED, UNIV VA, 81- *Personal Data:* b Detroit, Mich, Feb 21, 42; m 93, Elizabeth Probasco; c Joshua J. *Educ:* Univ Mich, BS, 63; Univ Calif, San Francisco, PhD(physiol), 67. *Prof Exp:* NIH trainee, Univ Mich; fel, Univ Olso , 69-70 & Johns Hopkins Univ, 70-72. *Concurrent Pos:* Assoc ed, Biophys J, 88-93. *Mem:* AAAS; Am

Physiol Soc; Biophys Soc; Soc Gen Physiol. *Res:* Function of the calcium-ATP ase of sarcoplasmic reticulum, diffusion boundary layers; oxygen transport in red blood cells; influence of membrane lipids on transport processes; biophysics. *Mailing Add:* Dept Physiol Univ Va Box 449 Charlottesville VA 22908-0449. *Fax:* 804-982-1616; *E-Mail:* hck4p@virginia.edu

KUTCHER, STANLEY PAUL, ADOLESCENT AFFECTIVE DISORDERS, PSYCHOPHARMACOLOGY. *Current Pos:* PROF & HEAD PSYCHIAT SERV, CHIEF SERV. *Personal Data:* b Toronto, Can, Dec 16, 51; c 3. *Educ:* McMaster Univ, BA, 74, MA, 75, MD, 79; FRCPS, 83. *Honors & Awards:* R O Jones Award; Renger Award. *Prof Exp:* Assoc prof psychiat & phys rehab med, Univ Toronto, 86-91, asst prof, Sch Grad Studies, 87-88; head, Div Adolescent Psychiat, Sunnybrook Med Ctr, 86-91, dir adolescent psychiat serv. *Concurrent Pos:* Vis clin scientist psychiat, Med Res Coun Gt Brit, 83-84; sci prog chair, Can Acad Child Psychiat. *Mem:* Am Psychiat Asn; Can Phys Asn; Can Col Neuropharmacol; Am Col Neuropsychopharmacol; Am Acad Child Adolescent Psychiat. *Res:* Psychopharmacology of adolescent affective disorders; neuroendovirology. *Mailing Add:* Dept Psychiat Dalhousie Univ QE2 Health Sci Ctr 5909 Jubilee Rd Lane Bldg Halifax NS B3H 2E2 Can

KUTIK, LEON, ORGANIC CHEMISTRY, TECHNICAL MANAGEMENT. *Current Pos:* MGR, COM APPLN LAB, W R GRACE & CO, DAVISON DIV TECH CTR, 83- *Personal Data:* b New York, NY, Mar 6, 27; m 63; c 3. *Educ:* City Col New York, BS, 49; Univ Chicago, MBA, 73. *Honors & Awards:* Roy H Kienle Award, 65. *Prof Exp:* Chemist, Clover Leaf Paint & Varnish Corp, 51-55; chemist, Cent Res Labs, Interchem Corp, 55-57, sr chemist, 57-59, group leader, 59, asst dept dir appl res finishes & adhesives, 59-63, prog mgr, 63-67, mgr graphic arts, 67-68; tech dir chem coatings, De Soto Inc, 68-70, mgr resin develop, Chem Coatings Div, 70-73, mgr indust res, 73-77, tech mgr construct coatings, 77-80; mgr mfg & tech serv, Sherwin Williams Corp, 80-83. *Mem:* Am Chem Soc; Soc Paint Technol; Nat Asn Corrosion Engrs. *Res:* Organic coatings for metal, paper, fiberboard, plywood, wood and plastics; adhesives for packaging and structural applications; methods of application for industrial coatings; powder coatings; matting agents; corrosion inhibiting pigments. *Mailing Add:* 704 St Paul Ave Reisterstown MD 21136

KUTILEK, MICHAEL JOSEPH, WILDLIFE ECOLOGY. *Current Pos:* asst prof, 75-80, ASSOC PROF BIOL, SAN JOSE STATE UNIV, 80- *Personal Data:* b Baltimore, Md, July 1, 43; m 68; c 1. *Educ:* San Diego State Univ, BS, 66, MS, 68; Mich State Univ, PhD(fisheries & wildlife), 75. *Prof Exp:* Res technician biol, Calif Dept Fish & Game, 65; wildlife biologist, Kenya Nat Parks, US Peace Corps, 69-71. *Mem:* Wildlife Soc. *Res:* Foraging strategies of herbivorous large mammals of Africa particularly, grazing and browsing ungulates; ecological and evolutionary aspects of plant-herbivore interactions. *Mailing Add:* Dept Biol Sci San Jose State Univ One Washington Sq San Jose CA 95192-0001

KUTKUHN, JOSEPH HENRY, ECOLOGY, FISHERIES. *Current Pos:* RETIRED. *Personal Data:* b Weehawken, NJ, Mar 28, 27; m 53, Farner; c Michael, Constance, Jacquelyn, Holly & Kenneth. *Educ:* Colo State Univ, BS, 53; Iowa State Univ, MS, 54, PhD(fishery mgt), 56. *Prof Exp:* Fishery biologist, Dept Fish & Game, Calif, 56-58; asst lab dir, US Fish & Wildlife Serv, Dept Interior, Tex, 58-65, NC, 65-69, Mich, 72-75, lab dir Mich, 76-82, assoc dir, Fishery Resources, Washington, DC, 83-87. *Concurrent Pos:* Consult, UN Develop Prog, Food & Agr Orgn, Fishery Res & Develop Proj, Lima, Peru, 70-72; consult, 87. *Mem:* Am Fisheries Soc; Am Inst Fishery Res Biol; Sigma Xi; Int Asn Great Lakes Res; Int Acad Sci. *Res:* Dynamics of exploited fish and shellfish resources. *Mailing Add:* 476 Wesman Dr Grayling MI 49738

KUTLER, BENTON, DENTISTRY. *Current Pos:* RETIRED. *Personal Data:* b Council Bluffs, Iowa, May 21, 20; m 44, Harriet Lorkis; c Laura, Robert, David, Howard & Bruce. *Educ:* State Univ Iowa, BA, 42; Creighton Univ, DDS, 45. *Prof Exp:* Instr prev med, Col Med, Univ Nebr Med Ctr, 45-65, clin asst prof oral surg & gen dent, 65-94, clin asst prof community dent & preceptor, Col Dent, 79-94; assoc clin prof restorative dent, Creighton Univ Sch Dent, 91-94. *Concurrent Pos:* Preceptor trainer, Creighton Univ Sch Dent, 71-78, vis lectr, 72-80. *Mem:* Sigma Xi; fel AAAS; fel Int Col Dentists; fel Am Col Dentists; fel Acad Gen Dent; Am Dent Asn; Am Soc Dent Children; Int Asn Dent Res; Am Asn Endodontists; Am Acad Implant Dent; Int Cong Oral Implantologists. *Res:* Fluoride applications for adult caries; caries research methods. *Mailing Add:* 9909 Essex Dr Omaha NE 68114

KUTNER, ABRAHAM, ORGANIC POLYMER CHEMISTRY, PHOTOCHEMISTRY. *Current Pos:* RETIRED. *Personal Data:* b Lynn, Mass, Mar 28, 19; m 47, Dorothy Gitnick; c Richard M, Robert S & Janet L. *Educ:* Ohio State Univ, PhD(org chem), 50. *Prof Exp:* Res chemist, Schering Corp, 46-47; res chemist, Hercules, Inc, 50-73, sr res chemist, 73-80, res scientist, 80-85. *Concurrent Pos:* Vol teaching prog sci. *Mem:* Am Chem Soc. *Res:* Organic synthesis; polymers; polymer additives; stabilization; polymer reactions; photochemistry applications. *Mailing Add:* 12971 Bucklard Ct West Palm Beach FL 33414-6229

KUTNER, LEON JAY, MEDICAL MICROBIOLOGY. *Current Pos:* RETIRED. *Personal Data:* b Camden, NJ, Mar 25, 28; c 2. *Educ:* Temple Univ, AB, 49; Pa State Univ, MS, 50, PhD(bact), 53; Univ Pittsburgh, MD, 63. *Prof Exp:* Asst, Pa State Univ, 49-53; res assoc virol, Sloan-Kettering Inst Cancer Res, 56-59; intern, Second Med Div, Bellevue Hosp, New York, 63-64; asst prof microbiol in surg, Med Col, Cornell Univ, 64-73; asst prof path in residence, 73-77, assoc clin prof path, Univ Calif, San Diego, 77-; chief microbiol lab, Lab Serv, Vet Admin Hosp, San Diego, 73-92. *Concurrent Pos:* Assoc scientist, Hosp Spec Surg, NY, 64-73. *Mem:* Am Soc Microbiol; NY Acad Sci. *Res:* Resistance to infectious disease. *Mailing Add:* 6833 Via Estradad La Jolla CA 92037

KUTNER, MICHAEL HENRY, LINEAR MODELS, VARIANCE COMPONENTS. *Current Pos:* from asst prof to assoc prof, 71-80, PROF BIOSTATIST, EMORY UNIV, 81-, ASSOC DEAN ACAD AFFAIRS, 90- *Personal Data:* b Hartford, Conn, Sept 24, 37; m 66; c 2. *Educ:* Cent Conn State Col, BS, 60; Va Polytech Inst, MS, 62; Tex A&M Univ, PhD(statist), 71. *Honors & Awards:* H O Hartley Award, Former Students Tex A&M Univ, 84. *Prof Exp:* Asst prof math & statist, Col William & Mary, 62-67; asst prof statist, Tex A&M Univ, 70-71. *Concurrent Pos:* Lectr, NASA, Langley AFB, 63-67, Ctr Dis Control, 80-; bd mem, Am Statist Asn, 81-83, pres, Atlantic Chap, 84-86, vchair publ comt, 88-90; regional adv bd, Biomet Soc, 81-83; assoc ed, Am Statistician, 86-88; dir biostatistics, Emory Univ, 87-; prog chair, Summer Res Conf, 89; consult, Norwich Eaton Pharmaceut, 89-91. *Mem:* Inst Math Statist; fel Am Statist Asn; Biomet Soc. *Res:* Repeated measures on analysis of variance; coauthor of two textbooks. *Mailing Add:* 11 Downing Lane Decatur GA 30033

KUTNEY, JAMES PETER, ORGANIC CHEMISTRY, BIOTECHNOLOGY. *Current Pos:* from instr to assoc prof, 59-66, PROF CHEM, UNIV BC, 66- *Personal Data:* b Lamont, Alta, May 2, 32; m 53; c 3. *Educ:* Univ Alta, BSc, 54; Univ Wis, MSc, 56; Wayne State Univ, PhD(org chem), 58. *Honors & Awards:* Merck, Sharp & Dohme Award, Chem Inst Can, 68. *Prof Exp:* Res fel org chem, Syntex Res Labs, Mex, 58-59. *Concurrent Pos:* NATO scholar, Bonn, WGer, 65; consult, MacMillan Bloedel, 68-78; vis prof, Japan Soc Prom Sci, 75; bd dir, Canadian Patents & Develop Ltd, 76-81; mem, Sci Coun BC, 78-81; mem, adv panel Biotechnol, NSERC, 82-84. *Mem:* Am Chem Soc; The Chem Soc; fel Chem Inst Can; Swiss Chem Soc. *Res:* Chemistry, biosynthesis and biodegradation of natural products and related biologically active compounds, particularly synthesis, isolation and structure elucidation of alkaloids, steroids and terpenes; biotechnology, plant cell cultures; microbial transformations; pharmaceutical drug development. *Mailing Add:* Dept Chem Univ BC 2036 Main Mall Vancouver BC V6T 1Z1 Can. *Fax:* 604-822-2710

KUTSCHA, NORMAN PAUL, FOREST PRODUCTS. *Current Pos:* SR SCIENTIST, WEYERHAEUSER CO, 77- *Personal Data:* b Irvington, NJ, Sept 24, 37; m 62; c 2. *Educ:* State Univ NY Col Forestry, Syracuse Univ, BS, 59, PhD(wood prod eng), 67; Univ Wis-Madison, MS, 61. *Prof Exp:* Forest prod technologist, US Forest Prod Lab, 59-62; asst prof wood prod eng, State Univ NY Col Forestry, Syracuse Univ, 67-68; from asst prof to assoc prof wood technol, Sch Forest Resources, Univ Maine, Orono, 68-77. *Concurrent Pos:* Partic, McIntire-Stennis Res Proj, Maine Agr Exp Sta, USDA, 69- *Mem:* Soc Wood Sci & Technol; Electron Micros Soc Am; Int Asn Wood Anat; Forest Prod Res Soc; Sigma Xi. *Res:* Light and electron microscopic studies of wood as a developing tissue in the growing tree and as a raw material for various products. *Mailing Add:* 4235 S 324 Pl Auburn WA 98001

KUTSHER, GEORGE SAMUEL, ANALYTICAL CHEMISTRY. *Current Pos:* RETIRED. *Personal Data:* b Reading, Pa, July 16, 21; wid; c 5. *Educ:* Albright Col, BS, 47; Lehigh Univ, MS, 49. *Prof Exp:* Head res anal dept, Nitrogen Div, Allied Chem & Dye Corp, 49-58, supvr opers eng, Allied Chem Corp, 58-60, supvry res chemist, 60-69, sr engr, Gas Purification Dept, 69-81, sr process engr, Selexol Dept, 81-82; mgr eng serv, Norton Co, 82-83, Tech consult Selexol, 83-87. *Mem:* Am Chem Soc. *Res:* Gas purification; selexol gas purification process. *Mailing Add:* 113 Gangplank Rd Moneta VA 24121

KUTSKY, ROMAN JOSEPH, BIOLOGY, CHEMISTRY. *Current Pos:* CONSULT NUTRIT & TOXICOL. *Personal Data:* b Allentown, Pa, May 13, 22; div; c 3. *Educ:* Princeton Univ, AB, 44; Univ Calif, MA, 49, PhD(zool), 53. *Prof Exp:* Asst physics, Princeton Univ, 44-46; asst zool, Univ Calif, 46-49, asst specialist plant path, 49-51, res fel biochem, Donner Lab, 53-57; res biochemist, Vet Admin Hosp, 57-67; assoc prof biol, Tex Woman's Univ, 67-73; prof life sci, Bishop Col, 73-77; chemist, Army Med Ctr, El Paso, 77-78; supvr & staff chemist, Bonneville Power Admin, 78-86. *Concurrent Pos:* Consult, Microchem Specialties Co, 59; NASA res grant, 73-76. *Mem:* AAAS; Am Chem Soc; Tissue Cult Asn; NY Acad Sci. *Res:* Biochemical extractions of biologically active materials; cellular biochemistry and physiology; physical biochemistry; tissue culture growth and form; vitamins and hormones; continuous flow preparative electrophoresis; effects of antioxidants; hormones and vitamins in tissue culture; aging; nutrition. *Mailing Add:* 5719 NE Hazel Dell Dr No D Vancouver WA 98663-1273

KUTTAB, SIMON HANNA, MEDICINAL CHEMISTRY. *Current Pos:* ASSOC PROF CHEM, BIR-ZEIT UNIV, WEST BANK, ISRAEL, 81- *Personal Data:* b Jerusalem, Palestine, Apr 17, 46; US citizen; m 78, Eileen Rizek; c Rania, Johnny & Rani. *Educ:* Am Univ Beirut, Lebanon, BSc, 68; Univ Kans, PhD(med chem), 74. *Prof Exp:* Asst res pharmacologist med chem, Univ Calif, Davis, 74-75 & Univ Calif, San Francisco, 75-76; asst prof, Northeastern Univ, 76-81. *Concurrent Pos:* Dep dir, Ctr Environ & Occup Health Sci, Birqeik Univ, West Bank, Via Israel. *Mem:* Am Chem Soc; AAAS; Sigma Xi; Acad Am Pharmaceut Asn. *Res:* Design and synthesis of compounds of biological interest; breakdown of xenobiotics and specific absorption rate correlations using such advanced analytical techniques as gas chromatography, high performance liquid chromatography and gas chromatography-mass spectrometry. *Mailing Add:* Dept Chem Bir-Zeit Univ Box 14 Bir-Zeit West Bank Israel. *Fax:* 972-2-9982166; *E-Mail:* skuttab@ceohs.birzeit.edu

KUTTEH, WILLIAM HANNA, REPRODUCTIVE ENDOCRINOLOGY & IMMUNOLOGY. *Current Pos:* instr fel reproduction endocrinol, 89-91, ASST PROF OBSTET & GYNEC & DIR REPRODUCTIVE IMMUNOL, SOUTHWESTERN MED CTR, UNIV TEX, 91- *Personal Data:* b Statesville, NC, Mar 18, 54; m 88; c 1. *Educ:* Wake Forest Univ, BA, 75; Univ Ala, Birmingham, PhD(immunol), 81; Bowman Gray Sch Med, MD, 85. *Honors & Awards:* Res Award, Sigma Xi, 80 & 84; Distinguished Res Award, Am Fertil Soc. *Prof Exp:* Res asst immunol, Duke Univ Med Ctr, 75-78; predoctoral fel microbiol, Univ Ala, Birmingham, 78-81, res instr obstet & gynec, 85-89; postdoctoral fel biochem, Bowman Gray Sch Med, 81-85. *Concurrent Pos:* Chief resident obstet & gynec, Univ Ala, Birmingham, 89, consult, dept microbiol, 89-; NIH fel, 89-91. *Mem:* Am Asn Immunologists; Am Fertil Soc; Am Col Obstet & Gynec; Soc Mucosal Immunol; NY Acad Sci; Am Asn Gynec Laparoscopists; Soc Gynec Invest; Endocrine Soc. *Res:* Secretory immune system of the female reproductive tract; immune response to human ovarian cancer; recurrent pregnancy loss; antisperm antibody mediated in fertility. *Mailing Add:* Dept Obstet & Gynec Univ Tenn 956 Court Ave Rm D324 Memphis TN 38163-2116. *Fax:* 901-448-8782

KUTTER, ELIZABETH MARTIN, MOLECULAR BIOLOGY, GENOMIC DATABASES. *Current Pos:* MEM FAC BIOPHYS, EVERGREEN STATE COL, 72- *Personal Data:* b Chicago, Ill, Aug 11, 39; c Bernard & Eric. *Educ:* Univ Wash, BS, 62; Univ Rochester, PhD(biophys), 68. *Prof Exp:* Res assoc biol, Univ Va, 69-72. *Concurrent Pos:* Res grants, NIH, 73-76, NSF, 70-72 & 76-, mem, NIH Dir Adv Comt on Recombinant DNA, 75-79; mem, NSF Adv Comt Ethics & Values in Sci & Technol, 78-80; vis scientist, Dept Biochem, Univ Calif, San Francisco, 78-79; teacher ethics & molecular biol, AAAS, Chataqua, 77-80; mem bd dir, John Bastyr Col, 79-92; Nat Acad Sci exchange mem USSR, 90. *Mem:* Biochem Soc; AAAS; Am Soc Microbiol; Genetics Soc; Protein Soc. *Res:* Biochemical developments during bacteriophage T4 infection of Escherichia coli, especially regulation of transcription and events governing the transition from host to phage metabolism; integrated genomic data bases. *Mailing Add:* Dept Sci Technol & Health Lab 1 2023 Evergreen State Col Olympia WA 98505. *Fax:* 360-866-6754; *E-Mail:* kutterb@elwha.evergreen.edu

KUTTLER, JAMES ROBERT, DIFFERENTIAL EQUATIONS, EIGENVALUES. *Current Pos:* MATHEMATICIAN, APPLIED PHYSICS LAB, JOHNS HOPKINS UNIV, 63- *Personal Data:* b Burlington, Iowa, Aug 8, 41; m 63, Evelyn Ridgley; c John, Robert & Laura. *Educ:* Rice Univ, BA, 62, Univ Md, MA, 64, PhD(math), 67. *Concurrent Pos:* Lectr, math, Johns Hopkins Univ, GWC Whiting Sch Eng, Continuing Prof Progs, 81- *Res:* Differential equations, electromagnetics, eigenvalues. *Mailing Add:* Appl Physics Lab Johns Hopkins Univ Laurel MD 20723-6099

KUTUZOVA, GALINA DMITRIEVNA, BIOLUMINESCENCE, ENZYMOLOGY. *Current Pos:* SR SCIENTIST RES & DEVELOP, PROMEGA CORP, 92- *Personal Data:* b Moscow, USSR, Mar 27, 55; m 79, Audrey A Kutuzov; c Andrey A. *Educ:* Moscow State Univ, BS, 75, MS, 76, PhD(enzym), 81. *Prof Exp:* Scientist, Chem Enzym Dept, Moscow State Univ, Russia, 76-83, sr scientist, 83-86, group leader, 86-89; res scientist, Biochem & Biophys Dept, Tex A&M Univ, 90-92. *Mem:* Am Soc Biochem & Molecular Biol; Int Soc Bioluminescence & Chemiluminescence; AAAS; Protein Soc. *Res:* Biochemistry of beetle luciferases, its kinetics, stability and mechanism of action; genetic engineering of beetle luciferases and its mutants; purification and applications; adenosin triphosphate-assays technology development. *Mailing Add:* Promega Corp 2800 Woods Hollow Rd Madison WI 53719. *Fax:* 608-277-2601

KUTZ, FREDERICK WINFIELD, ECOLOGY, MEDICAL ENTOMOLOGY. *Current Pos:* ECOLOGIST, US ENVIRON PROTECTION AGENCY, 72- *Personal Data:* b Wilmington, Del, Sept 29, 39; m 63, Arlene Clarke; c Mark D & Heather L. *Educ:* Univ Del, BS, 62, MS, 64; Purdue Univ, PhD(entom), 72. *Honors & Awards:* Cert of Recognition, Nat Marine Fisheries Serv. *Prof Exp:* Res fel & assoc entom, Univ Del, 62-64; entomologist, Med Serv Corps Officer, US Army, 64-66; res asst & instr, Purdue Univ, 66-69; entomologist & parasitologist, Insect Control & Res Inc, 69-72. *Concurrent Pos:* Mem sci adv panel, Onchocerciasis Control Prog, WHO, 74-80, monitoring panel, Fed Working Group Pest Mgr, 75-77 & subcomt, Comt Environ Carcinogens, Nat Cancer Inst, 76-; adj prof, Univ Miami Sch Med, 80- *Mem:* Entom Soc Am; Am Soc Trop Med & Hyg; Am Mosquito Control Asn; Sigma Xi. *Res:* Arthropod-insect pest management, particularly of medical significance and chemical and biological monitoring in humans and environmental components; environmental processes and effects of chemicals and other stressors. *Mailing Add:* 4967 Moonfall Way Columbia MD 21044. *Fax:* 410-573-2771; *E-Mail:* kutz.rick@epamail.epa.gov

KUTZKO, PHILIP C, NUMBER THEORY. *Current Pos:* asst prof, 74-77, assoc prof, 77-80, PROF MATH, UNIV IOWA, 80- *Personal Data:* b Brooklyn, NY, Nov 24, 46; m 67; c 1. *Educ:* City Col New York, BA, 67; Univ Wis, MA, 68, PhD(math), 72. *Prof Exp:* Instr math, Univ Wis, Green Bay, 68-69, instr, Rock County Ctr, 69-72; instr, Princeton Univ, 72-74. *Mem:* Am Math Soc. *Res:* Representation theory of p-adic linear groups and applications to non-abelian classfield theory. *Mailing Add:* 1610 Muscatine Ave Iowa City IA 52240

KUTZLER, FRANK WILLIAM, PHYSICS. *Current Pos:* PROF, DEPT PHYSICS, TENN TECHNOL UNIV, 85- *Personal Data:* b Pueblo, Colo, Aug 8, 52. *Educ:* Univ Southern Colo, BS, 74; Stanford Univ, PhD(physics), 81. *Prof Exp:* Res scientist, Naval Res Lab, 84-85. *Mem:* Am Phys Soc. *Mailing Add:* PO Box 5055 Cookeville TN 38505

KUTZMAN, RAYMOND STANLEY, TOXICOLOGY. *Current Pos:* chem mgr, Nat Toxicol Prog, Nat Inst Environ Health Sci, 85- *Personal Data:* b St Cloud, Minn, April 16, 49. *Educ:* St Cloud State Col, BA, 71; Univ Notre Dame, MS, 74; NC State Univ, PhD(zool), 77. *Prof Exp:* Res assoc, Chem Dept, 77-79, from asst scientist to assoc scientist, Med Dept, Brookhaven Nat Lab, 79-85. *Concurrent Pos:* Dir, Toxic Hazard Res Unit, Armstrong Aerospace Res Lab, USAF. *Mem:* AAAS; Soc Toxicol; Int Soc Study Xenobiotics; Soc Risk Anal; Am Soc Pharmacol & Exp Therapeut. *Res:* Biodistribution of xenobiotic agents after inhalation exposure; risk assessment; genetic disposition as an underlying factor in biochemical and physiological aspects of toxicity. *Mailing Add:* Mitretek Syst 13526 George Rd Suite 200 San Antonio TX 78230

KUTZSCHER, EDGAR WALTER, PHYSICS. *Current Pos:* CONSULT PHYSICIST, 72- *Personal Data:* b Leipzig, Ger, Mar 21, 06; nat US; m 45; c 2. *Educ:* Univ Berlin, PhD(physics), 33, Dr phil habil(appl physics), 36. *Hon Degrees:* DrEng, Hannover Univ, 63. *Honors & Awards:* Todt Prize, 44. *Prof Exp:* Asst physics, Univ Berlin, 30-33 & Inst Technol, Berlin, 33; physicist, Dept Defense, Ger, 34-37; dir res, Electroacoust Co, Kiel, Ger, 37-45 & univ exten, Flensburg, Ger, 46-47; physicist infrared, USN, 47-51 & solid state physics, Santa Barbara Res Ctr, Calif, 51-53; head dept radiation sensors & technol, Lockheed Aircraft Corp, 54-72. *Concurrent Pos:* Asst prof, Inst Technol, Berlin, 37-45. *Mem:* Optical Soc Am. *Res:* Infrared physics and detectors. *Mailing Add:* 15450 Briarwood Dr Sherman Oaks CA 91403

KUUS-REICHEL, KRISTINE, IMMUNOLOGY. *Current Pos:* RES SCIENTIST, HYBRITECH INC, 86-, MGR CELL & MOLECULAR BIOL, 93- *Personal Data:* b New York, NY, Aug 8, 53. *Educ:* State Univ NY, Buffalo, BS, 75; Med Col Va, PhD(immunol), 83. *Prof Exp:* Res fel B cell activation, Scripps Inst, 83-86. *Concurrent Pos:* Adj prof immunol, Calif State Univ, San Marcos, 92- *Mem:* Am Asn Immunologists; NY Acad Sci; AAAS; Asn Women Sci. *Res:* Immunology. *Mailing Add:* Hybritech Inc PO Box 269006 San Diego CA 92196-9006. *Fax:* 619-457-5308

KUWABARA, JAMES S, ECOLOGY. *Current Pos:* HYDROLOGIST & PROJ CHIEF, NAT RES PROG, GEOL SURV, US DEPT INTERIOR, 80- *Personal Data:* b Honolulu, Hawaii, Apr 26, 53. *Educ:* Univ Hawaii, Manoa, BS, 75; Calif Inst Technol, MS, 76, PhD(environ eng sci), 80. *Prof Exp:* Comput operator trainee, Castle & Cooke Inc, 71. *Concurrent Pos:* Res assoc, Nat Res Coun, 80-81; mem, Task Group on Biol & Microbiol, Water Resources Div, US Geol Surv, 86-89, Environ Chem Task Group, 88-92. *Mem:* Am Soc Civil Engrs; fel Am Inst Chemists; Am Soc Agr Engrs; Am Geophys Union; Phycological Soc Am; Inst Elec & Electronics Engrs; Am Inst Biol Sci. *Res:* Contributed numerous articles to professional publications. *Mailing Add:* US Dept Interior US Geol Surv 345 Middlefield Rd Menlo Park CA 94025

KUWAHARA, STEVEN SADAO, biochemistry hemostasis, analytical biochemistry, for more information see previous edition

KUWANA, THEODORE, ANALYTICAL CHEMISTRY, ELECTROCHEMISTRY. *Current Pos:* AT CTR BIOANALYTICAL RES, KANS UNIV, LAWRENCE. *Personal Data:* b Idaho Falls, Idaho, Aug 3, 31. *Educ:* Antioch Col, BS, 54; Cornell Univ, MS, 56; Univ Kans, PhD(anal chem), 59. *Prof Exp:* Res chemist, Aerojet-Gen Corp Div, Gen Tire & Rubber Co, 59; fel, Calif Inst Technol, 59-60; asst prof anal chem, Univ Calif, Riverside, 60-66; from assoc prof to prof, Case Western Reserve Univ, 66-71; PROF CHEM, OHIO STATE UNIV, 71- *Concurrent Pos:* Chmn, Gordon Res Conf Anal Chem, 64. *Mem:* AAAS; Am Chem Soc; Royal Soc Chem. *Res:* Organic electrode processes; photoelectrochemistry and electroluminescence. *Mailing Add:* Dept Chem Univ Kans 6084 Malott Hall Lawrence KS 66045

KUYATT, CHRIS E(RNIE EARL), UNCERTAINTY IN MEASUREMENT, ELECTRON OPTICS. *Current Pos:* COORDR, RADIATION MEASUREMENT SERVS, NAT INST STAND & TECHNOL, 91-, ACTG EXEC DIR, VIS COMT, 94- *Personal Data:* b Grand Island, Nebr, Nov 30, 30; m 49, Patricia Peirce; c Chris S, Brian, Alan & B Neal. *Educ:* Univ Nebr, BS, 52, MS, 53, PhD(physics), 60. *Honors & Awards:* US Dept Com Silver Medal, 64. *Prof Exp:* Res asst, dept physics, 53-59, res assoc & instr atomic physics, Univ Nebr, 59-60; physicist, Nat Bur Standards, 60-69, actg chief electron physics sect, 69-70, chief electron & optical physics sect, 70-73, chief surface & electron physics sect, 73-78, chief, Radiation Physics Div, 78-79, dir, Ctr Radiation Res, 79-91. *Concurrent Pos:* Interagency Radiation Res Comt, 80-84; com sci & technol fel, NSF, 83-84; mem, Nat Inst Standards & Technol Liaison with Nat Coun Radiation Projections & Measurement, 80-, chmn, Ionizing Radiation Safety Comt, 79-; mem, Interagency Steering Comt Acad Res Facil, 84. *Mem:* Fel Am Phys Soc; AAAS; Sigma Xi. *Res:* Electron scattering; polarized electrons; electron monochromators; electron energy analyzers; electron optics; evaluation and expression of uncertainty in measurement. *Mailing Add:* Rm A817 Bldg 101 Nat Inst Stand & Technol Gaithersburg MD 20899. *E-Mail:* akuyatt@nnt.gov

KUYPER, LEE FREDERICK, ORGANIC CHEMISTRY, MEDICINAL CHEMISTRY. *Current Pos:* SR SCIENTIST, BURROUGHS WELLCOME CO, 77- *Personal Data:* b Mitchell, SDak, Feb 28, 49; c 1. *Educ:* Ouachita Univ, BS, 71; Univ Ark, PhD(org chem), 77. *Prof Exp:* Res assoc, Univ NC, 76-77. *Mem:* Am Chem Soc. *Res:* Molecular modeling; drug design and synthesis. *Mailing Add:* Glaxo 5 Moore Dr Research Triangle Park NC 27709-4498

KUZEL, NORBERT R, ANALYTICAL CHEMISTRY, INSTRUMENTATION. *Current Pos:* RETIRED. *Personal Data:* b Angus, Minn, May 23, 23; m 49. *Educ:* NDak State Univ, BS, 48, MS, 49. *Prof Exp:* Anal chemist, Eli Lilly & Co, 49-59, dept head anal develop, 59-63, sr anal chemist, 63-67, res scientist, 68-73, res assoc, 73-84. *Mem:* Am Chem Soc; Instrument Soc Am. *Res:* Development of analytical methods; residue analysis; laboratory and process automation and computerization. *Mailing Add:* 4611 Berkshire Lane Indianapolis IN 46226-3137

KUZMA, JAN WALDEMAR, BIOSTATISTICS. *Current Pos:* chmn dept biostatist, 67-73, PROF BIOSTATIST & CHMN DEPT BIOSTATIST & EPIDEMIOL, SCH PUB HEALTH, LOMA LINDA UNIV, 73- *Personal Data:* b Warsaw, Poland, Apr 24, 36; US citizen; m 63; c 3. *Educ:* Andrews Univ, BA, 59; Columbia Univ, MS, 61; Univ Mich, PhD(biostatist), 63. *Prof Exp:* Lectr biostatist & dir clin trials unit, Univ Calif, Los Angeles, 63-67. *Concurrent Pos:* Consult biostatistician, Loma Linda Univ, 64-67. *Mem:* Am Statist Soc; Biomet Soc; Am Pub Health Asn; AAAS. *Res:* Lifestyle and longevity; health care costs; general statistical methodology. *Mailing Add:* 1280 E San Bernardino Ave Redlands CA 92374

KUZMA, JOSEPH FRANCIS, PATHOLOGY. *Current Pos:* prof path, 74-80, CLIN PROF PATH, MED COL WIS, 80- *Personal Data:* b Austria, Mar 14, 15; US citizen; m 41; c 7. *Educ:* Univ Ill, BS, 37, MD, 40; Marquette Univ, MS, 42. *Prof Exp:* From instr to prof, Marquette Univ, 46-74, dir dept, 53-69. *Concurrent Pos:* Dir lab, Milwaukee Hosp, 43-47 & Milwaukee Co Hosp, 47-54 & 64-69. *Mem:* Am Soc Clin Path; fel AMA; Am Asn Path & Bact; Am Col Physicians; Col Am Path; Sigma Xi. *Res:* Mammary tumors and diseases; sulfonamide reactions; experimental arthritis; kidney diseases; radioactive strontium; bone cancer. *Mailing Add:* 1115 Honey Creek Pkwy Wauwatosa WI 53213

KUZMAK, JOSEPH MILTON, PHYSICAL CHEMISTRY, PAPER COATINGS. *Current Pos:* RETIRED. *Personal Data:* b Man, Can, Mar 7, 22; m 42, Lillian E Ulinder; c James J, Sylvia D & Paula J (Smith). *Educ:* Univ Man, BSc, 49, MSc, 50; McGill Univ, PhD(phys chem), 53. *Prof Exp:* Res officer, Nat Res Coun Can, 53-57; res chemist, Am Viscose Corp, 74-67; sr res chemist, St Regis Paper Co, 67-84; sr scientist, Champion Int Corp, 84-86. *Mem:* Am Chem Soc; Tech Asn Pulp & Paper Indust. *Res:* Mechanism of moisture movement in porous materials; chemical modification of regenerated cellulose; chemical modification of pulp and paper; paper coatings and coating process. *Mailing Add:* 2203 Apple Rd Fogelsville PA 18051

KUZMANOVIC, B(OGDAN) O(GNJAN), CIVIL ENGINEERING STRUCTURES. *Current Pos:* SR STRUCT ENGR, VPRES & ASSOC, BEISWENGER, HOCH & ASSOCS, MIAMI BEACH, FLA, 81- *Personal Data:* b Belgrade, Yugoslavia, July 16, 14; m 50, Galina Movcanquk; c Natasha. *Educ:* Univ Belgrade, Dipl Eng, 37; Serbian Acad Sci, Dr Tech Sc, 56. *Prof Exp:* Asst designer bridges, Ministry Transp, Belgrade, 38-41, sr designer, 45-53; from asst prof to assoc prof struct, Univ Sarajevo, 53-58; Brit Coun & Gilchrist Ed Trust res fel, Sheffield Sci Sch, Yale, 58-59; prof, Univ Khartoum, 59-60, dean fac eng & head dept civil eng, 60-63, prof & head dept, 63-65; prof struct, Univ Kans, 65-81. *Concurrent Pos:* Off Civil Defense res grant, 67. *Mem:* Fel Am Soc Civil Engrs; sr mem Int Asn Bridge & Struct Engrs. *Res:* Theory of elasticity and plasticity; plastic analysis and design of steel and concrete structures; metal fatigue. *Mailing Add:* 1528 Wiley St Hollywood FL 33020. *Fax:* 305-948-6290

KUZNESOF, PAUL MARTIN, REGULATORY FOOD CHEMISTRY, FOOD ADDITIVE SAFETY EVALUATION. *Current Pos:* regulatory chemist, US Food & Drug Admin, 84-87, sect head, Food & Color Additives Rev Sect, 87-92, chief, Chem Rev Br, 92-96, ACTG DEP DIR, DIV PROD MANUFACTURE & USE, OFF PRE-MKT APPROVAL, CTR FOOD SAFETY & APPL NUTRIT, US FOOD & DRUG ADMIN, 96- *Personal Data:* b Bronx, NY, Aug 13, 41; div; c Adam. *Educ:* Brown Univ, ScB, 63; Northwestern Univ, PhD, 67. *Prof Exp:* Fel inorg mat res div, Lawrence Radiation Lab, Univ Calif, 67-69; asst prof chem, San Francisco State Col, 69-70; prof chem, Univ Campinas, Brazil, 70-75; vis lectr, Univ Mich, Ann Arbor, 75-76; vis assoc prof, Trinity Col, Hartford, Conn, 76-78; mem staff, Chem Div, Naval Res Lab, 78-79; assoc prof, Agnes Scott Col, Decatur, Ga, 79-83. *Concurrent Pos:* Grant, FAPESP Res Found, Sao Paulo, 71; grants, Res Corp, 77 & NSF, 81; vis scholar, Northwestern Univ, 82; invited expert, Comt Food Additives, Joint Expert Comt Food Additives, WHO/Food & Agr Orgn, 89, 93-97; chair, Working Group Specifications, UN Codex Comt Food Additives & Contaminants, 96 & 97. *Mem:* Am Chem Soc; Sigma Xi; AAAS; Inst Food Technologists. *Res:* Synthesis and electronic properties of boron-nitrogen compounds; hydrides of the lighter main group elements; electron donor-acceptor interactions; electroactive polymers. *Mailing Add:* Off Pre-Mkt Approval HFS-247 Ctr Food Safety & Appl Nutrit Food & Drug Admin 200 C St SW Washington DC 20204. *Fax:* 202-418-3030; *E-Mail:* pmk@fdacf.ssw.dhhs.gov

KVAAS, T(HORVALD) ARTHUR, PHYSICS, ENGINEERING. *Current Pos:* CONSULT ACOUST, 80- *Personal Data:* b Des Moines, Iowa, Jan 8, 19; m 42, Rosemary Saal; c Robert & Ronald. *Educ:* Univ Calif, Los Angeles, BA, 40, MA, 42. *Prof Exp:* Phys sci res engr, Res Lab, Douglas Aircraft Co, 42-46, phys scientist proj Rand, 46-48; proj engr, Rand Corp, 48-52; sect chief missiles adv design, Douglas Aircraft Co, 52-57; mgr, Synthesis Sect, Tech Mil Planning Oper, Gen Elec Co, 57-60, prof staff, 60-62, tech anal & appln oper, 62-63, mgr tech environ studies, tempo, Ctr Advan Studies, 63-70, pres, ADCON Corp, 70-74; vpres & opers mgr, Moseley Assocs, 74-76, consult, 77; opers mgr, Cetec Broadcast Corp, 78-80. *Concurrent Pos:* Mem comt, Am Stand Asn Comt Acoust Terminology, 46-48; Am Rocket Soc rep, Cong Int Astronaut Fedn, Amsterdam, 58. *Mem:* Assoc fel Am Inst Aeronaut & Astronaut; Acoust Soc Am. *Res:* Technological and environmental forecasting and planning with particular emphasis on future technologies, technical resources and their application to future human needs; corporate long range strategic business planning. *Mailing Add:* 933 Roble Lane Santa Barbara CA 93103

KVALNES, KALLA L, BIOCHEMISTRY. *Current Pos:* STAFF SCIENTIST, PROCTER & GAMBLE, 92- *Personal Data:* b Sept 15, 60; m; c 2. *Educ:* Univ Cincinnati, BS, 82; Hahnemann Univ PhD(biochem), 87. *Prof Exp:* Fel, Dept Biochem, Albert Einstein Col Med, 87-90, Univ NC, 90-92. *Concurrent Pos:* NIH grants, 88-91 & 89-90. *Mem:* Am Chem Soc; AAAS; Am Soc Biochem & Molecular Biol. *Res:* Protein, native and mutant, purification; chemical modification of proteins. *Mailing Add:* Procter & Gamble Co 11511 Reed Hartman Hwy Cincinnati OH 45241. *Fax:* 513-626-4399

KVALSETH, TARALD ODDVAR, STATISTICS, MATHEMATICAL MODELING. *Current Pos:* assoc prof mech eng, 79-82, head indust eng, 83-92, PROF MECH ENG, UNIV MINN, 82- *Personal Data:* b Brunkeberg, Norway, Nov 7, 38; m 64, Amy; c Erik, Lisbet & Andrew. *Educ:* Univ Durham, Eng, BSc, 63; Univ Calif, Berkeley, MS, 66, PhD(indust eng), 71. *Prof Exp:* Assoc prof indust eng, Ga Inst Technol, 71-74; sr lectr, Norweg Inst Technol, 74-79. *Concurrent Pos:* Co-prin investr, Nat Inst Occup Safety & Health, 87-91. *Mem:* Int Ergonomics Asn (vpres, 82-85); AAAS; Sigma Xi; Human Factors & Ergonomics Soc; Ergonomics Soc; Am Inst Indust Engrs. *Res:* Human factors engineering with emphasis on human performance measures, quantitative models, statistical methods, industrial ergonomics and safety. *Mailing Add:* 108 Turnpike Rd Golden Valley MN 55416. *Fax:* 612-624-1398

KVAM, DONALD CLARENCE, PHARMACOLOGY. *Current Pos:* RETIRED. *Personal Data:* b Escanaba, Mich, Oct 20, 32; m 54, Suzanne Irving; c Donald, Mark & Amy. *Educ:* Ferris State Col, BS, 54; Univ Wis, PhD(pharmacol), 60. *Prof Exp:* Sr pharmacologist, Mead Johnson & Co, 60-63, group leader pharmacol, 63-64; supvr biol res, 3M Pharmaceut, 64-67, mgr biol res, 67-71, mgr pharmacol, 71-78, mgr clin pharmacol, 78-82, assoc dir, 82-93. *Concurrent Pos:* Lectr, Col Med Sci, Univ Minn. *Mem:* AAAS; Am Soc Pharmacol & Exp Therapeut; Am Soc Clin Pharmacol & Therapeut; Soc Exp Biol Med. *Res:* Clinical pharmacology, phase 1 and pharmacokinetics studies. *Mailing Add:* 4 North Oaks Rd St Paul MN 55127-6431

KVEGLIS, ALBERT ANDREW, POLYMER CHEMISTRY, ORGANIC CHEMISTRY. *Current Pos:* MGR, INK VEHICLES, SUNCHEMICAL CORP, 82- *Personal Data:* b Brooklyn, NY, Feb 10, 34; m 61; c 3. *Educ:* Queens Col, NY, BS, 56; Stevens Inst Technol, MS, 65. *Prof Exp:* Sr res chemist polymers, Plastics Div, Allied Chem Corp, 56-71; res chemist polymers, Trimflex Div, Teleflex Corp, 71; methods develop, Biomed Sci, Inc, 71-72; group leader, Polymers & Vehicles, Inmont Corp, 72-82. *Mem:* Am Chem Soc. *Res:* Polymer synthesis and characterization, development of resins and vehicles for inks and coatings, synthesis of flame retardant monomers and additives for plastics, modification of polymers. *Mailing Add:* 6 Buckingham Circle Pine Brook NJ 07058-9712

KVENVOLDEN, KEITH ARTHUR, ORGANIC GEOCHEMISTRY. *Current Pos:* geologist, 75-92, SR SCIENTIST, US GEOL SURV, 92- *Personal Data:* b Cheyenne, Wyo, July 16, 30; m 59, Mary Ann Lawrence; c Joan A & Jon W. *Educ:* Colo Sch Mines, GpE, 52; Stanford Univ, MS, 58, PhD(geol), 61. *Honors & Awards:* Meritorious Serv Award, US Dept Interior, 85, Distinguished Serv Award, 96; Treibs Medal & Award, Org Geochem Div, Geochem Soc, 95. *Prof Exp:* Jr geologist, Socony Mobil Oil Co, Venezuela, 52-54, sr res technologist petrol geochem, Mobil Field Res Lab, Tex, 61-66; res scientist, Ames Res Ctr, NASA, Calif, 66-71, chief, Chem Evol Br, 71-74, chief, Planetary Biol Div, 74-75. *Concurrent Pos:* Consult assoc prof geol, Stanford Univ, 67-73, consult prof, 73-; chmn, Jodies Adv Panel Org Geochem, 74-80; mem, US Nat Comt Geochem, 80-83, chmn, 84-86; chmn, Gordon Res Conf Org Geochem, 84; mem, US Sci Adv Comt, Ocean Drilling Prog, 85-86. *Mem:* Am Asn Petrol Geol; fel Geol Soc Am; fel Geochem Soc; fel Am Geophys Union; fel AAAS; fel Explorers Club. *Res:* Organic geochemistry of modern and ancient sediments; petroleum geochemistry; environmental geochemistry; organic chemistry of meteorites; origin and evolution of life; geochemistry of amino acids; geochemistry of hydrocarbon gases and gas hydrates. *Mailing Add:* 2433 Emerson St Palo Alto CA 94301. *E-Mail:* kk@octopus.wr.usgs.gov

KVIETYS, PETER R, CARDIOVASCULAR PHYSIOLOGY. *Current Pos:* assoc prof, 86-91, PROF MED PHYSIOL & CARDIOVASC PHYSIOL, LA STATE UNIV MED CTR, 91- *Personal Data:* b Strasbourg, France, Jan 12, 48. *Educ:* Western Mich Univ, BS, 72, MS, 75; Mich State Univ, PhD(physiol), 79. *Prof Exp:* Fel cardiovasc physiol, Univ SAla, 79-80, from asst prof to assoc prof med & cardiovasc physiol, 81-86. *Mem:* Am Gastroenterol Asn; fel Am Physiol Soc; Am Heart Asn; AAAS; Tissue Cult Asn. *Res:* Cardiovascular physiology. *Mailing Add:* Victoria Hosp 375 South St Rm C206 London ON N6A 4G5 Can. *Fax:* 519-432-7367

KVIST, TAGE NIELSEN, DEVELOPMENTAL ANOMALIES, TERATOLOGY. *Current Pos:* from asst prof to assoc prof, 76-87, ASST DEAN BASIC SCI, PHILADELPHIA COL OSTEOP MED, 86-, PROF & CHMN ANAT, 87- *Personal Data:* b Copenhagen, Denmark, Jan 17, 42; US citizen; m 65; c 3. *Educ:* Univ BC, BS, 66, MS, 69; Univ Pa, Philadelphia,

PhD(biol), 73. *Honors & Awards:* Lindback Found Award, Christian R & Mary F Lindback Found, 85. *Prof Exp:* Teaching asst develop, Univ BC, Vancouver, 66-67; teaching fel biol, Univ Pa, Philadelphia, 69-72, res assoc develop, 73-76; lectr comp embryol, Rosemont Col, Pa, 72; chief neurosurg res, congenital anoms, Joseph Stokes Jr Res Inst, 73-76. *Concurrent Pos:* Sci res adv, Pa Gov Conf Handicapped Individuals, 76; consult, NIH Sci Rev Group, 79-; rev bd human res, Philadelphia Col Obstet Med, 81-; guest lectr, Sch Nursing, Univ Pa, 82-87; mem, Nat Comt Res Neurol Commun Dis, Spina Bifida Asn Am, 85-; reviewer, March of Dimes Birth Defects Found Grant; mem, Inst Self Study Task Force & Exec Fac, Philadelphia Col Obsteop Med, 85-; chmn animal care & utilization, Philadelphia Col Osteop Med, 86-, curric, 86-, comput asst instr, 86-, Strategic Planning Task Force, 87, dir, Sch Allied Health, 86-, rep, Health Sci Libraries Consortium, 87- *Mem:* Soc Develop Biol; Teratol Soc; Am Asn Anatomists; Spina Bifida Asn Am; Am Asn Clin Anatomists; Sigma Xi; Humanity Gifts Registry Pa Anatomists. *Res:* Birth defects involving the central nervous system; Spina Bifida Cystica; Anencephalus; Hydrocephalus; connective tissue macromolecule formation in developing embryos and in rheumatoid arthritis. *Mailing Add:* Dept Anat Philadelphia Col Osteop Med 4170 City Ave Philadelphia PA 19131

KWAAN, HAU CHEONG, INTERNAL MEDICINE, HEMATOLOGY & ONCOLOGY. *Current Pos:* assoc prof, 66-72, PROF MED, MED SCH, NORTHWESTERN UNIV CHICAGO, 72- *Personal Data:* b Hong Kong, Sept 30, 31; US citizen; m 58; c 2. *Educ:* Univ Hong Kong, MB & BS, 52, MD, 58; FRCP(E), 67; Am Bd Internal Med, cert internal med, 69, cert hemat, 74, cert med oncol, 79. *Prof Exp:* House physician, Univ Hong Kong Med Unit, Queen Mary Hosp, 52-53; sr clin asst med, Univ Hong Kong, 53-55, asst lectr, 56-59, lectr, 59-61; sr investr physiol, James F Mitchell Found, DC, 62-65. *Concurrent Pos:* China Med Bd NY fel pharmacol, 58-59; vis res fel, Col Physicians & Surgeons, Columbia Univ, 58-59; clin asst prof, Sch Med, Georgetown Univ, 64-65; mem coun thrombosis, Am Heart Asn, 64-; chief hemat-oncol sect, Vet Admin Lakeside Med Ctr, Chicago, 67-; attend physician, Northwestern Mem Hosp, Chicago, 69-; sr Fulbright travel scholar, 74. *Mem:* Fel Am Col Physicians; AMA; Am Physiol Soc; Am Soc Hemat; Am Fedn Clin Res; Int Soc Thrombosis Hemostasis. *Res:* Blood coagulation; fibrinolysis; thrombosis. *Mailing Add:* Dept Med 333 E Huron St Vet Admin Med Ctr Northwestern Univ Med Sch Chicago IL 60611-3004. *Fax:* 312-908-5057

KWAK, JAN C T, POLYMER SCIENCE, COLLOID SCIENCE. *Current Pos:* from asst prof to assoc prof, 70-83, PROF CHEM, DALHOUSIE UNIV, 83-, CHAIR, DEPT CHEM, 86- *Personal Data:* b Schagen, Neth, May 6, 42; m 65; c 3. *Educ:* Univ Amsterdam, MSc, 64, PhD, 67. *Prof Exp:* Res assoc molten salts, Neth Orgn Advan Pure Res, 64-68; res chemist, Sea Water Conversion Lab, Univ Calif, Berkeley, 68-70. *Mem:* Am Chem Soc; Chem Inst Can. *Res:* Polymer solutions; surfactants; surfactant nuclear magnetic resonance; biophysical chemistry; flocculation studies; coal beneficiation; colloid chemistry. *Mailing Add:* Dept Chem Dalhousie Univ Halifax NS B3H 4J3 Can

KWAK, NOWHAN, HIGH ENERGY PHYSICS. *Current Pos:* from asst prof to assoc prof, 65-78, PROF PHYSICS & ASTRON, UNIV KANS, 78- *Personal Data:* b Seoul, Korea, Sept 16, 28; US citizen; m 58; c 2. *Educ:* Seoul Nat Univ, BS, 52; Emory Univ, MS, 56; Univ Rochester, MA, 59; Tufts Univ, PhD(physics), 62. *Prof Exp:* Res assoc high energy physics, Tufts Univ, 62-65. *Concurrent Pos:* Sr fel, Austrian Acad Sci, 73-74; vis scientist, Cern, 74-76, Deutsches Elektronen-Synchrotron, WGer, 80-81. *Mem:* Am Phys Soc. *Res:* Experimental high energy physics. *Mailing Add:* Dept Phys Univ Kans Lawrence KS 66045. *Fax:* 785-864-5262; *E-Mail:* kwak@kuhub.cc.ukans.edu

KWAK, YUN SIK, EXPERIMENTAL BIOLOGY. *Current Pos:* PROF & CHMN, DEPT CLIN PATH, SCH MED, AJOU UNIV, SUWON, KOREA, 94- *Personal Data:* b Taegu, Korea, Aug 21, 37; m 66, Pil Nam Kim; c Kyu, Sue & Ken. *Educ:* Kyungpook Nat Univ, MD, 61; Union Univ, Albany, PhD(molecular biol & path), 72; Am Bd Path, cert analysis & clin, 78, cert chempath, 80. *Prof Exp:* Teaching fel, Dept Biochem, Sch Med, Kyungpook Univ, 64-66, from instr to asst prof, 66-69; from res instr to asst prof, Dept Path, Albany Med Col, 69-78; assoc prof, Dept Path, Sch Med, Wright & State Univ, 79-81. *Concurrent Pos:* Chief resident, Dept Path, Albany Med Ctr Hosp, 73-74; staff pathologist-in-chg clin chem, Vet Admin Hosp, Albany, NY, 75-77, mem numerous comts, 77-, chief clin path sect, Lab Serv, Cleveland, 77-79, chief lab serv, Dayton, 79-81, Cleveland, 81-, spec asst to med ctr dir, I/C Med Info Mgt Sect, Vet Admin Med Ctr, 89-93; asst prof, Dept Path, Sch Med, Case Western Res Univ, 77-95. *Mem:* Am Asn Clin Chem; fel Am Soc Clin Pathologists; Am Asn Pathologists; NY Acad Sci; fel Nat Acad Clin Biochem; fel Col Am Pathologists; AMA. *Res:* Biochemical aspects of atherogenesis; effective utilization of laboratory information in clinical medicine and laboratory management; author of numerous scientific publications. *Mailing Add:* 1908 Halls Carriage Westlake OH 44145-2033. *Fax:* 82-331-219-5778; *E-Mail:* yskwak@madang.ajou.ac.kr

KWAN, JOHN YING-KUEN, ASTROPHYSICS. *Current Pos:* assoc prof, 81-87, PROF ASTROPHYS, UNIV MASS, 87- *Personal Data:* b Hong Kong, Apr 5, 47; m 73; c 2. *Educ:* Utah State Univ, BS, 69; Calif Inst Technol, PhD(physics), 72. *Prof Exp:* Res fel astrophys, Calif Inst Technol, 73 & Inst Advan Study, 73-74; asst prof astrophys, State Univ NY Stony Brook, 75-76; mem tech staff, Bell Labs, 76-80. *Mem:* Am Astron Soc; Inst Elec & Electronics Engrs. *Res:* Theoretical studies of astrophysical masers, interstellar molecular clouds, quasars, young stellar objects. *Mailing Add:* Dept Physics & Astron Univ Mass Amherst MA 01003-0134

KWAN, KING CHIU, DRUG METABOLISM, PHARMACOKINETICS. *Current Pos:* res assoc, Merck Res Labs, 64-66, unit head, 66-69, pharmacokinetic specialist, 69-70, sr res fel, 70-76, sr invest, 76-79, sr dir biopharmaceut, 79-81, exec dir drug metab, 81-92, VPRES DRUG METAB, MERCK RES LABS, 92- *Personal Data:* b Hong Kong, Jan 14, 36. *Educ:* Univ Mich, BS, 56, MS, 58, PhD(pharmaceut chem), 62. *Prof Exp:* Res chemist, R P Scherer Corp, 62-63; lectr pharm, Univ Mich, 63-64. *Concurrent Pos:* Mem, Pharmacol Study Sect, NIH, 80-83. *Mem:* Am Pharmaceut Asn; Am Asn Pharmaceut Scientists; Am Soc Pharmacol & Exp Therapeuts; Int Soc Study Xenobiotics; Sigma Xi; Controlled Release Soc. *Res:* Pharmaceutical research and development; drug metabolism; pharmacokinetics; biopharmaceutics. *Mailing Add:* Merck Res Labs West Point PA 19486. *E-Mail:* kc_kwan@merck.com

KWAN, PAUL WING-LING, CANCER, CELL BIOLOGY. *Current Pos:* res assoc, 75-85, RES ASSOC PROF, DEPT PATH, SCH MED, TUFTS UNIV, 85- *Personal Data:* b Hong Kong, Nov 7, 42; US citizen. *Educ:* Univ Md, BS, 66; Clark Univ, MA, 71, PhD(biol), 75. *Prof Exp:* Teaching asst biol, Clark Univ, 67-73. *Concurrent Pos:* Supvr, spec procedures lab, Path Dept, New Eng Med Ctr. *Mem:* Nat Soc Histotechnol; Soc Appl Immunohistochem. *Res:* Application of immunohistochemistry to the study of tumor biology and clinical diagnosis; pathogenesis of benign prostatic hyperplasia and prostate cancer in animal models. *Mailing Add:* Dept Path Tufts Univ Sch Med 136 Harrison Ave Boston MA 02111. *E-Mail:* paul.kwan@es.nemc.org

KWANG, JIMMY, MOLECULAR VIROLOGY, GENE EXPRESSIONS. *Current Pos:* RES MICROBIOLOGIST, US MEAT ANIMAL RES CTR, 89- *Personal Data:* b China, Aug 24, 49; US citizen; m 77, Chiao-herng; c Kay & Joyce. *Educ:* Taiwan Pingtang Inst Agr, DVM, 73; Univ RI, MS, 81; Univ Calif, Davis, PhD(molecular virol), 87. *Prof Exp:* Lectr vet path & histol, Taiwan Pingtang Inst Agr, 75-79; dir res & develop, Schuyler Swine Serv, 81-84; NIH fel, Sch Med, Univ Calif, San Diego, 87-88; sr scientist, Viogene, 88-89. *Mem:* Am Soc Microbiol; US Animal Health Asn; Am Asn Vet Lab Diagnosticians. *Res:* Pathogenic mechanism of animal viral diseases; characterize each disease at the molecular level and develop a specific, sensitive, rapid, and economic diagnostic procedure for each; develop effective disease control measures for each. *Mailing Add:* USDA-Agr Res Serv US-Meat Animal Res Ctr Clay Center NE 68933

KWAN-GETT, CLIFFORD STANLEY, SURGERY. *Current Pos:* asst res prof, 68-70, ASSOC RES PROF SURG, UNIV UTAH, 70- *Personal Data:* b Emmaville, NSW, Oct 14, 34; m 61; c 2. *Educ:* Univ Sydney, BSc, 54, BE, 56, MD, 63. *Prof Exp:* Engr, Australian Postmaster Gen Dept, 60-61; resident med off, Lanceston Gen Hosp, Tasmania, 64-66. *Concurrent Pos:* Fel med, Cleveland Clin Found, 66-67; consult, Aerojet Gen Corp, Calif, 66-68; cardiol, thoracic & vascular surgeon. *Mem:* Am Soc Artificial Internal Organs; Biomed Eng Soc; AMA. *Res:* Developing total replacement artificial hearts to replace the irreparable human heart; use of artificial heart assist devices; development and use of artificial kidneys, especially for home use by patients. *Mailing Add:* Western Cardiovasc Assoc 1055 E 3900 S Salt Lake City UT 84112

KWARTLER, CHARLES EDWARD, SYNTHETIC ORGANIC CHEMISTRY. *Current Pos:* PRES, KWARTLER ASSOCS, 87- *Personal Data:* b Stanislau, Austria, Oct 5, 11; US citizen; m 41, Ruth Allenbach; c Alice, Jeanne & David. *Educ:* NY Univ, BS, 32, PhD(org chem), 36. *Honors & Awards:* Cert Merit, US Defense Dept. *Prof Exp:* Microchem technician, NY Univ, 34-36, asst instr, 36-38; res chemist, Winthrop Chem Co, 39-43, dir pilot lab, 43-45, head process develop lab, Winthrop-Stearns, Inc, 45-51, chief chemist, Winthrop Prod, Inc, 51-55; dir res & develop, Gamma Chem Co, 51-55, vpres, 55-56, exec vpres, 57-66; consult, Ashland Chem Co, 76-78 & Southland Corp, 78-87. *Concurrent Pos:* Mgr process develop, Ashland Chem Co, 69-71, asst to pres & tech coordr, 71-76; chmn bd trustees, Warren Co Community Col Comn, 81- & Warren Co Community Col Found, 84-; mem bd dir, Hackettstown Community Hosp, 86- *Mem:* Chemists' Club; Sigma Xi; Nat Hon Soc Scientists; Nat Hon Soc Chemists; emer mem Am Chem Soc. *Res:* Anesthetics; antimalarials; antiseptics; analgesics; antispasmodics; sulfanilamides; quaternary ammonium compounds; arsenicals; radiopaques; diuretics; synthetic sex hormones; organic antimony compounds; synthetic detergents; 8-hydroxyquinoline; synthetic herbicides and pecticides. *Mailing Add:* 139 E 63rd St Apt 2D New York NY 10021

KWASNY, STAN C, COMPUTER SCIENCE. *Current Pos:* ASSOC PROF COMPUT SCI, WASHINGTON UNIV, ST LOUIS. *Res:* Language processing with neural networks; recursive auto-associative memory; language identification; neurocomputation. *Mailing Add:* Dept Comput Sci Washington Univ St Louis MO 63130

KWATNY, EUGENE MICHAEL, BIOMEDICAL ENGINEERING. *Current Pos:* PRIN INVESTR VISUAL SYSTS & DIR COMPUT & INFO SCI, KRUSEN CTR RES & ENG & ASST PROF REHAB MED, SCH MED, TEMPLE UNIV, 71- *Personal Data:* b Philadelphia, Pa, Oct 25, 43; m 66; c 2. *Educ:* Drexel Univ, BS, 66, MS, 68, PhD(biomed eng), 71. *Prof Exp:* Biomed engr, Aerospace Crew Equipment Dept, US Naval Air Develop Ctr, 66-71. *Concurrent Pos:* Adj asst prof visual sci & biomed eng, Pa Col Optom, 74- *Mem:* Inst Elec & Electronics Engrs. *Res:* Sensory aids for rehabilitation; bioelectric signal processing; computers in medicine and biology. *Mailing Add:* Comput Sci Dept 38-24 Temple Univ Broad & Montgomery St Philadelphia PA 19122

KWATRA, SUBHASH CHANDER, DIGITAL SATELLITE COMMUNICATIONS. *Current Pos:* from asst prof to prof, 77-86, PROF ENG, UNIV TOLEDO, 86- *Personal Data:* b India, Nov 12, 41; m 66; c 2. *Educ:* Birla Inst Technol, BE, 62, MS, 70; Univ SFla, PhD(elec eng), 75. *Prof Exp:* Lectr eng, Birla Inst Technol & Sci, 65-70. *Concurrent Pos:* Prin investr, Lewis Res Ctr, NASA, 79- *Mem:* Inst Elec & Electronics Engrs. *Res:* Digital signal processing; satellite communications. *Mailing Add:* Col Eng Dept Elec Eng Univ Toledo 2801 W Bancroft Toledo OH 43606

KWEI, GLORIA Y, NUTRITIONAL BIOCHEMISTRY. *Current Pos:* RES FEL, MERCK & CO, 91- *Personal Data:* b Taipei, Taiwan, Mar 17, 6. *Educ:* Univ Calif, Berkeley, BS, 82, PhD(nutrit sci),87. *Prof Exp:* Res assoc nutrit & cancer, Rutgers Univ, 87-91. *Mem:* Am Asn Pharmaceut Sci; Am Inst Nutrit; AAAS; Int Soc Study Xenobiotics. *Res:* Nutritional biochemistry; drug metabolism. *Mailing Add:* Merck Res Labs RY80-A9 Rahway NJ 07090

KWEI, TI-KANG, POLYMER CHEMISTRY, PHYSICAL CHEMISTRY. *Current Pos:* PROF, POLYTECH UNIV, 84- *Personal Data:* b Shanghai, China, Mar 19, 29; US citizen; m 54, K P Shen; c Joseph, Carol & Richard. *Educ:* Chiao Tung Univ, BS, 49; Univ Toronto, MASc, 54; Polytech Inst Brooklyn, PhD(chem), 58. *Honors & Awards:* Achievement Award, Chinese Inst Eng, USA; Res Award, Sigma Xi; Achievement Award, Chinese Mat Soc; Life Achievement Award, North Jersey Sect, Am Chem Soc. *Prof Exp:* Polymer chemist, Stand Oil Co, Ind, 58-59; polymer chemist, Interchem Corp, 59-61, sr chemist, 61-63, group leader polymer chem, 63-65; mem tech staff, Bell Labs, 65-81; vpres, Indust Technol Res Inst, Taiwan, 81-84. *Mem:* Am Chem Soc. *Res:* Thermodynamics of polymer mixtures; viscoelasticity and surface chemistry of polymers; transport phenomena in polymers. *Mailing Add:* Polytech Univ 6 Metrotech Ctr Brooklyn NY 11201-2990. Fax: 718-260-3125

KWENTUS, GERALD K(ENNETH), CHEMICAL ENGINEERING. *Current Pos:* TECH DIR, OCCIDENTAL CHEM CORP, 93- *Personal Data:* b St Louis, Mo, Jan 10, 37; m 72, Carolyn Harnagel; c Susanne & Karen. *Educ:* Wash Univ, BS, 60; Mass Inst Technol, PhD(chem eng), 67. *Prof Exp:* Sr res engr, Org Div, Monsanto Co, 66-70, res specialist, 70-75, sr res specialist, 75-80, sr res group leader, 80-82, mgr res & develop, Monsanto Chem Intermediates Co, 82-93. *Mem:* Am Inst Chem Engrs. *Res:* Preparative chromatography; fractional distillation; chemical kinetics; heat transfer. *Mailing Add:* 25 Vassar Dr Amherst NY 14068

KWIATEK, JACK, INDUSTRIAL ORGANIC CHEMISTRY, POLYMER CHEMISTRY. *Current Pos:* RETIRED. *Personal Data:* b Kansas City, Mo, Feb 9, 24; m 48, Lottie West; c Sandra (Simenhoz), Kim D & Sharon (Gadoth). *Educ:* Univ Ill, BS, 44; Cornell Univ, PhD(chem), 50. *Honors & Awards:* Chemist of the Year, Cincinnati Sect, Am Chem Soc, 74. *Prof Exp:* Org res chemist, M W Kellogg Co, 50-54; res assoc, Gen Elec Co, 54-58; sr res assoc, Nat Distillers & Chem Corp, 58-88; res scientist, USI Div, Quantum Chem Corp, 88-92. *Concurrent Pos:* Adj asst prof, Eve Col, Univ Cincinnati, 61-65; sr fel, Weizmann Inst Sci, 68-70. *Mem:* Am Chem Soc; Catalysis Soc. *Res:* Homogeneous and heterogeneous catalysis; hydrogenation; syngas reactions; oxidation; carbonylation; coordination compounds; organometallics; free radical reactions; organophosphorus compounds; conductive polymers; biodegradable polymers. *Mailing Add:* 3135 N Farmcrest Dr Cincinnati OH 45213

KWIECINSKI, GARY GEORGE, REPRODUCTION & IMMUNOLOGY OF CHIROPTERA VITAMIN D REPRODUCTION FERTILITY & NUTRITIONAL PHYSIOLOGY OF MAMMALS. *Current Pos:* ASSOC PROF BIOL, UNIV SCRANTON, 88- *Personal Data:* b Suffern, NY, Aug 15, 52. *Educ:* Cornell Univ, BS, 75, PhD(zool), 84; Rutgers Univ, MS, 76. *Prof Exp:* Teaching asst physiol, Rutgers Univ, 75-76; teaching asst zool, Cornell Univ, 77-83; res assoc & instr vet cell biol, Tufts Univ, 83-85; res assoc biochem, Univ Wis, 86-88. *Concurrent Pos:* Instr vet anat, Cornell Univ, 79-83; prin investr, NIH Nat Inst Child Health & Human Develop, 92- *Mem:* Am Soc Mammalogists; Soc Study Reproduction; Endocrinol-Endocrine Soc. *Res:* Investigate nutritional and physiological adaptation in mammals; endocrinological aspects of the reproductive, thyroidal and immunological perturbations of seasonal cycling that accentuate general principles. *Mailing Add:* Dept Biol Univ Scranton Scranton PA 18510-4625. Fax: 717-941-6369; E-Mail: ggk301@uofs.edu

KWIRAM, ALVIN L, PHYSICAL CHEMISTRY, CHEMICAL PHYSICS. *Current Pos:* assoc prof, Univ Wash, 70-75, chmn dept, 77-87, from vprovost to sr vprovost, 87-90, PROF CHEM, UNIV WASH, 75-, VPROVOST RES, 90- *Personal Data:* b Man, Can, Apr 28, 37; m 64, Verla R Michel; c Andrew B & Sidney M. *Educ:* Walla Walla Col, BS(chem) & BA(physics), 58; Calif Inst Technol, PhD(chem), 63. *Hon Degrees:* PhD, Andrew Univ, 95. *Honors & Awards:* Eastman-Kodak Sci Award, 62; Univ-Indust Rel Award, Coun Chem Res, 86. *Prof Exp:* Instr & res assoc chem, Calif Inst Technol, 62-63; res assoc physics, Stanford Univ, 63-64; instr chem, Harvard Univ, 64-67, lectr, 67-70. *Concurrent Pos:* Woodrow-Wilson fel, 58; Alfred P Sloan fel, 68-70; mem, Exec Comt & secy-treas, Div Phys Chem, Am Chem Soc, 76-86, counr, 86-, founding comt & bd dirs, Coun Chem Res, 80-84, chmn, 82-83, mem, Comt Sci, 88; chair-elect, Chem Div, AAAS, 91-, mem, Sci Prog Comt, 94- *Mem:* Am Chem Soc; fel Am Phys Soc; Sigma Xi; fel AAAS. *Res:* Magnetic resonance in solids and molecular crystals; electron-nuclear double resonance; optical detection of magnetic resonance; structure and dynamics in ground and excited states of molecules. *Mailing Add:* Off Res 312 Gerberding Hall Univ Wash Seattle WA 98195-1237

KWITEROVICH, PETER O, JR, LIPOPROTEIN METABOLISM. *Current Pos:* from asst prof to assoc prof, 72-84, PROF PEDIAT & MED, JOHNS HOPKINS UNIV MED SCH, 84- *Personal Data:* b Danville, Pa, June 24, 40; m 65; c 3. *Educ:* Holy Cross Col, AB, 62; Dartmouth Med Sch, BMS, 64; Johns Hopkins Univ, MD, 66. *Honors & Awards:* Blakeslee Award, Am Heart Asn. *Prof Exp:* Intern pediat, Childrens Hosp Med Ctr, 66-67, staff assoc lipoprotein res, Molecular Dis Br, NIH 67-70; resident pediat, Johns Hopkins Hosp, 70-72. *Concurrent Pos:* Prin investr lipid res clin, Johns Hopkins Univ, 71-, chief lipid res, Athereosclerosis Unit, 76; chmn, Dietary Intervention study in children, 87; mem nutrit study sect, NIH, 87- *Mem:* Soc Pediat Res; Am Soc Clin Invest. *Mailing Add:* Dept Pediat Johns Hopkins Univ Med Sch 720 Rutland Ave Baltimore MD 21205-2109

KWITOWSKI, PAUL THOMAS, INORGANIC CHEMISTRY. *Current Pos:* assoc prof, 69-80, PROF CHEM, NIAGARA COMMUNITY COL, 80-, CHMN, DEPT PHYS SCI, 71- *Personal Data:* b Buffalo, NY, Nov 14, 39; m 63; c 4. *Educ:* Canisius Col, BS, 61; Univ Wis, PhD(inorg chem), 67. *Prof Exp:* Res chemist, Airco-Speer Res Labs, NY, 66-69. *Mem:* Am Chem Soc. *Res:* Gas chromatography; catalysis of organic reactions; halocarbon and organometallic chemistry; spectroscopy; chemistry of refractive compounds; chemical vapor deposition. *Mailing Add:* 211 Walton Dr Buffalo NY 14226

KWITTER, KAREN BETH, GASEOUS NEBULAE, EVOLUTION OF LOW-MASS STARS. *Current Pos:* Asst prof, 79-86, ASSOC PROF ASTRON, WILLIAMS COL, 86-, CHMN, ASTRON DEPT, 88- *Personal Data:* b Brooklyn, NY, Mar 20, 51; m 79, Steven P Souza; c Randall & Aaron. *Educ:* Wellesley Col, BA, 72; Univ Calif, Los Angeles, MA, 74, PhD(astron), 79. *Concurrent Pos:* Harlow Shapley vis lectr, Am Astron Soc, 81-; vis asst prof astron, Univ Ill, 83-84. *Mem:* Am Astron Soc; Sigma Xi; Int Astron Union; AAAS; Astron Soc Pac. *Res:* Gaseous nebulae, their chemical compositions and physical conditions, including nebulae around Wolf-Rayet stars and planetary nebulae; stellar evolution from planetary nebulae nucleus to sub dwarf to white dwarf. *Mailing Add:* Dept Astron Williams Col 33 Lab Campus Dr Williamstown MA 01267-2693

KWO, JUEINAI, CONDENSED MATTER PHYSICS. *Current Pos:* RES SCIENTIST, AT&T BELL LABS, 81- *Personal Data:* b Taipei, Taiwan, Oct 1, 53. *Educ:* Nat Taiwan Univ, BS, 75; Stanford Univ, MS, 77, PhD(appl physics), 81. *Mem:* Am Phys Soc. *Mailing Add:* AT&T Bell Labs 1D-232 Murray Hill NJ 07974

KWOCK, LESTER, BIOCHEMISTRY, RADIATION BIOCHEMISTRY. *Current Pos:* instr radiation biol, 73-76, ASST PROF, SCH MED, TUFTS UNIV, 76-; FAC, DEPT RADIOL, UNIV NC, CHAPEL HILL. *Personal Data:* b San Francisco, Calif, June 21, 42; m 68; c 1. *Educ:* San Jose State Univ, BS, 65; San Diego State Univ, MS, 68; Univ Calif, Santa Barbara, PhD(chem), 73. *Concurrent Pos:* NIH fel, Sch Med, Tufts Univ & Tufts-New England Med Ctr, 74-76; Nat Cancer Inst grant, Tufts-New England Med Ctr, 76- *Mem:* Am Chem Soc; Radiation Res Soc; Sigma Xi; AAAS. *Res:* Membrane transport; effects of ionizing radiation on biological systems; radioprotectors and radiosensitizers for normal and neoplastic cells. *Mailing Add:* Dept Radiol Sch Med Univ NC Chapel Hill NC 27599-7510

KWOK, CLYDE CHI KAI, MECHANICAL ENGINEERING. *Current Pos:* RETIRED. *Personal Data:* b Shanghai, China, May 26, 37; m 62; c 1. *Educ:* McGill Univ, BEng, 61, MEng, 62, PhD, 67. *Prof Exp:* Res asst mech eng, McGill Univ, 61-64; prin scientist, Aviation Elec Ltd, 64-69; assoc prof mech eng, Sir George Williams Campus, Concordia Univ, 69-77, prof eng, 77-96. *Mem:* Am Soc Mech Engrs; Am Inst Aeronaut & Astronaut. *Res:* Research and development of basic fluidic devices particularly the design and analysis of vortex type devices; fluid control elements and systems. *Mailing Add:* Dept Mech Eng 2600 Pierre DuPuy Ave Apt 232 Montreal PQ H3Z 3R6 Can

KWOK, HOI S, DISPLAY TECHNOLOGIES, MATERIALS. *Current Pos:* PROF ENG, HONG KONG UNIV SCI & TECHNOL, 92- *Personal Data:* b Hong Kong, China, Mar 1, 51; US citizen; m 78, Ying Hung Tung; c 3. *Educ:* Northwestern Univ, BS, 73; Harvard Univ, MS, 75, PhD(physics), 78. *Honors & Awards:* Presidential Young Investr Award, 84. *Prof Exp:* Res fel chem, Lawrence Berkeley Lab, Univ Calif, 78-80; from asst prof to prof eng, State Univ NY, Buffalo, 80-92. *Concurrent Pos:* Prin investr grants, NSF, US Dept Energy, 81-92; sci adv, Photochem Res Assocs, 82-89 & Excel Technologies, 87-92. *Mem:* Am Phys Soc; sr mem Inst Elec & Electronics Engrs; Am Chem Soc; fel Optical Soc Am. *Res:* Laser spectroscopy of semiconductors and superconductors; display technologies. *Mailing Add:* Dept Elec Eng Hong Kong Univ Sci & Technol Clearwater Bay Kowloon Hong Kong People's Republic of China

KWOK, MUNSON ARTHUR, ATOMIC & MOLECULAR PHYSICS, FLUIDS. *Current Pos:* mem tech staff, Aerospace Corp, 68-76, staff scientist, 76-77, res scientist, 77-84, mgr, 84-87, DEPT DIR, AEROSPACE CORP, 87- *Personal Data:* b San Francisco, Calif, Apr 28, 41; m 77, Suellen Cheng. *Educ:* Stanford Univ, BS, 62, MS, 63, PhD(aeronaut & astronaut), 67. *Prof Exp:* NSF fel, Stanford Univ, 67-68. *Concurrent Pos:* Chair, Plasmadynamics & Lasers Tech Comt, Am Inst Aeronaut & Astronaut. *Mem:* Am Phys Soc; Soc Photo-Optical Instrumentation Engrs; sr mem Am Inst Aeronaut & Astronaut; Am Soc Mech Engrs; Optical Soc Am. *Res:* Fluid mechanics; thermophysics; gas lasers; chemical lasers; kinetic theory; plasmas; high temperature gasdynamics; propulsion; microelectromechanics. *Mailing Add:* Aerospace Corp PO Box 92957 MS M5/753 Los Angeles CA 90009-2957. Fax: 310-336-7680; E-mail: mumson__kwok@qmailz.aero.org

KWOK, SUN, ASTRONOMY. *Current Pos:* from asst prof to assoc prof, 83-88, PROF ASTRON, UNIV CALGARY, 88- *Personal Data:* b Hong Kong, Sept 15, 49; Can citizen; m 73, Emily Yu; c Roberta & Kelly. *Educ:* McMaster Univ, BSc, 70; Univ Minn, Minneapolis, MS, 72, PhD(physics), 74. *Prof Exp:* Fel astron, Dept Physics, Univ BC, 74-76; asst prof, Dept Physics, Univ Minn, Duluth, 76-77; res assoc, Ctr Res Exp Space Sci, York Univ, 77-78; res assoc astron, Herzberg Inst Astrophys, 78-83. *Concurrent Pos:* Proj specialist, Int Adv Panel, World Bank, 84; vis fel, Joint Inst Lab Astrophys, Univ Colo, 89-90. *Mem:* Am Astron Soc; Can Astron Soc; Int Astron Union; Astron Soc Pac. *Res:* Stellar mass loss; the late stages of stellar evolution; planetary nebulae; infrared astronomy. *Mailing Add:* 139 Edgeland Rd NW Calgary AB T3A 2Y3 Can. *Fax:* 403-289-3331; *E-Mail:* kwok@iras.ucalgary.ca

KWOK, THOMAS YU-KIU, ELECTRONICS MATERIALS, VLSI TECHNOLOGY. *Current Pos:* RES STAFF MEM, IBM RES DIV, THOMAS J WATSON RES CTR, 82- *Personal Data:* b Hong Kong; c 2. *Educ:* Mass Inst Technol, BS, 76, MS, 78, PhD(mat sci), 82. *Mem:* Am Phys Soc; Inst Elec & Electronics Engrs; Mat Res Soc. *Res:* Grain boundary structure and diffusion; microstructure of metallic thin films and submicron metal lines; electromigration, mechanical properties and reliability of multilevel interconnection; very-large-scale integration metallization; molecular dynamics and computer simulations. *Mailing Add:* 735 Beech St Westwood NJ 07675

KWOK, WO KONG, ORGANIC CHEMISTRY, POLYMER CHEMISTRY. *Current Pos:* res chemist, Exp Sta, E I Du Pont De Nemours & Co, 66-76, sr res chemist, Kinston, 76-84, res assoc, 84-90, sr res assoc, 91-95, SR RES CHEMIST, CHESTNUT RUN, E I DU PONT DE NEMOURS & CO, INC, 81-, RES ASSOC, 95- *Personal Data:* b Hong Kong, Jan 13, 36; m 63. *Educ:* Nat Taiwan Univ, BS, 58; ETenn State Univ, MS, 63; Ill Inst Technol, PhD(phys & org chem), 67. *Honors & Awards:* DuPont Mkt Excellence Award, 96. *Prof Exp:* Chemist, SChina Bleaching & Dyeing Factory, 58-61. *Concurrent Pos:* Ill Inst Technol Res Inst fel, 65-67. *Mem:* Am Chem Soc. *Res:* Elimination reaction kinetics and mechanism; polymer degradation mechanism; nonwoven technology. *Mailing Add:* 11 McCormick Dr W Riding Hockessin DE 19707

KWOLEK, STEPHANIE LOUISE, POLYMER CHEMISTRY & PROCESSING. *Current Pos:* RETIRED. *Personal Data:* b New Kensington, Pa, July 31, 23. *Educ:* Carnegie Inst Technol, BS, 46. *Hon Degrees:* DSc, Worcester Polytech Inst, 81. *Honors & Awards:* Publ Award, Am Chem Soc, 59, Creative Invention Award, 80; Howard N Potts Medal, Franklin Inst, 76; Mat Achievement Citation, Am Soc Metals, 78; Chem Pioneer Award, Am Inst Chemists, 80; Eng/Technol Award, Soc Plastics Engrs, 85; Harold DeWitt Smith Mem Award, Am Soc Testing & Mat, 88; George Lubin Mem Award, Soc Advan Mat & Process Engrs, 91; Jack Kilby Award, Kilby Awards Found, 94; Am Innovator Award, Patent & Trademark Off, 95; Nat Medal Technol, 96; Perkin Medal, Soc Chem Indust, 97. *Prof Exp:* Chemist, Fibers Dept, Pioneering Res Lab, Exp Sta, E I Du Pont de Nemours & Co, Inc, 46-59, from res chemist to sr res chemist, 59-74, res assoc, 74-86. *Concurrent Pos:* Consult. *Mem:* Am Chem Soc; Sigma Xi; Am Inst Chem. *Res:* Condensation polymers; high temperature polymers; low temperature interfacial and solution polymerizations; high tenacity and high modulus fibers and films; liquid crystalline polymers, solutions and melts. *Mailing Add:* 312 Spalding Rd Wilmington DE 19803-2422

KWON, BYOUNG SE, IMMUNE RESPONSES & DISEASE STATES. *Current Pos:* assoc prof, 88-93, SCIENTIST, WALTHER ONCOL CTR, IND UNIV SCH MED, PROF, DEPT MICROBIOL & IMMUNOL, 93- *Personal Data:* b Seoul, Korea, Dec 17, 47; US citizen; m 71, Myung H Hahn; c David H, Ed E & Pat M. *Educ:* Seoul Nat Univ, DDS, 72; Med Col Ga, Augusta, PhD(microbiol), 81. *Prof Exp:* Assoc scientist, Dept Human Genetics Yale Univ Sch Med, 83-84, Guthrie Res Inst, 84-88. *Concurrent Pos:* Swebilius cancer res award, Yale Univ, 83-84; Nat res serv award, NIH 82-83, young investr res award, 85-88; feasibility grant prog award, Am Diabetes Asn Inc, 85-87. *Mem:* Am Soc Microbiol; Sigma Xi; AAAS; Am Diabetes Asn; Am Asn Immunologists; Nat Orgn Albinism & Hypopigmentation; Int Soc Exp Hemat. *Res:* Immune cell functions in normal immune responses and disease states; molecular genetic studies on human pigmentation and its disorders. *Mailing Add:* Ind Univ Sch Med 635 Barnhill Dr MS 255 Indianapolis IN 46202-5120

KWON, JOON TAEK, PROCESS CHEMISTRY-CATALYSIS, APPLIED INSTRUMENTAL ANALYSIS. *Current Pos:* sr res chemist, Lummus Crest Inc, 70-78, PRIN RES CHEMIST, ABB LUMMUS CREST INC, 78- *Personal Data:* b Kimpo, Kyunngi Do, Korea, Mar 10, 35; US citizen; m 64, Moon J You; c Howard A & Daphne E. *Educ:* Univ Ill, BS, 57; Cornell Univ, MS, 59, PhD(chem), 62. *Prof Exp:* Res asst chem, Cornell Univ, 57-62; res fel chem, Univ BC, 62-64; instr II, 64-65; res chemist, Chemcell Ltd, 65-67; sr res chemist, Celanese Res Co, 67-70. *Concurrent Pos:* Grantee, Univ BC, 64-65, Nat Res Coun Can, 66 & 67. *Mem:* Am Chem Soc; fel Am Inst Chemists; Soc Chem Indust; Korean Chem Soc; Royal Soc Chem. *Res:* Developing novel production of bulk chemicals and catalytic processes; lummus propylene oxide process and the Lummus-unocal ethylbenzene/cumene processes. *Mailing Add:* 142 Derby Dr Freehold NJ 07728-2767. *Fax:* 973-893-2745

KWON, TAI HYUNG, SOLID STATE PHYSICS. *Current Pos:* from asst prof to assoc prof, 69-90, PROF PHYSICS, UNIV MONTEVALLO, 90- *Personal Data:* b Yechon, Korea, Sept 15, 32; m 69, Young-Ju Choi; c Wade J. *Educ:* Univ Ga, BS, 63, MS, 65, PhD(physics), 67. *Prof Exp:* Res fel, Ga Inst Technol, 67-69. *Concurrent Pos:* Frederick Gardner Cottrell Res Corp grant, 71- *Mem:* Am Phys Soc; Am Asn Physics Teachers. *Res:* Statistical physics; spin dynamics; neutron scattering; Heisenberg system; magnetism; lattice dynamics, anharmonicity; thermoelastic properties of ionic crystals. *Mailing Add:* Dept Physics Univ Montevallo Montevallo AL 35115. *Fax:* 205-665-9495

KWON-CHUNG, KYUNG JOO, MEDICAL MYCOLOGY. *Current Pos:* res microbiologist, 68-94, HEAD, MOLECULAR MICROBIOL SECT, LCI, NAT INST ALLERGY & INFECTIOUS DIS, NIH, 95- *Personal Data:* b Seoul, Korea, Oct 5, 33; m 57; c 3. *Educ:* Ewha Womans Univ, Korea, BS, 56, MS, 58; Univ Wis, MS, 63, PhD(bact), 65. *Honors & Awards:* Director's Award, NIH, 77; Award, Int Soc Human & Animal Mycol, 82; Rhoda Benham Award, Med Mycol Soc Am, 96; Dir Award, NIH, 96. *Prof Exp:* Instr microbiol, Ewha Womans Univ, 59-61; res asst bact, Univ Wis, 61-65. *Concurrent Pos:* Fel, Univ Wis, 65; vis fel med mycol, NIH, 66-68; consult, Armed Forces Inst Path, Washington, DC, 76-86. *Mem:* Mycol Soc Am; Am Soc Microbiol; Med Mycol Soc Am; Int Soc Human & Animal Mycol. *Res:* Morphology, genetics, molecular biology and pathogenicity of fungi. *Mailing Add:* Rm 11C304 Bldg 10 NIH Bethesda MD 20892

KWONG, JOSEPH N(ENG) S(HUN), CHEMICAL ENGINEERING. *Current Pos:* RETIRED. *Personal Data:* b Chung Won, China, Oct 28, 16; nat US; m 42; c 3. *Educ:* Stanford Univ, BA, 37; Univ Mich, MS, 39; Univ Minn, PhD(chem eng), 42. *Prof Exp:* Chem engr, Minn Mining & Mfg Co, 42-44; chemist, Shell Develop Co, Calif, 44-47, chemist & res engr, 47-51; sr chemist, Minn Mining & Mfg Co, 51-60, res specialist, 60-80. *Mem:* Am Chem Soc; Am Inst Chem Engrs. *Res:* Process and resin development, design and evaluation; thermodynamics; polyethylene terephthalate polymer and film technology. *Mailing Add:* 1399 N Hamline Ave St Paul MN 55108-2407

KWONG, MAN KAM, MATHEMATICS. *Current Pos:* resident scientist, 82-83, spec term appointment, 85-87, SCIENTIST, ARGONNE NAT LAB, 87- *Personal Data:* b Canton, China, Feb 2, 47; m 70; c 2. *Educ:* Univ Hong Kong, BSc, 68; Univ Chicago, MSc, 70, PhD(math), 73. *Prof Exp:* Lectr math, Hong Kong Baptist Col, 73-75, Hong Kong Polytech, 75-77; from asst prof to prof math, Northern Ill Univ, 77-89. *Mem:* Sigma Xi; Am Math Soc; Soc Indust & Appl Math. *Res:* Ordinary differential equations; functional analysis; inequalities; image processing; scientific computation. *Mailing Add:* 1727 Beloit Dr Naperville IL 60565. *Fax:* 630-752-5986; *E-Mail:* kwong@mcs.anl.gov

KWONG, YUI-HOI HARRIS, GRAPH THEORY, INTEGER SEQUENCES. *Current Pos:* Asst prof, 87-92, ASSOC PROF MATH & COMPUT SCI, STATE UNIV NY, COL FREDONIA, 92- *Personal Data:* b Hong Kong, Oct 10, 57; m 85. *Educ:* Univ Mich, BS, 80, MS, 81; Univ Pa, PhD(math), 87. *Mem:* Am Math Soc; Math Asn Am; Sigma Xi. *Res:* Graph labeling; extremal graph theory; divisibility; congruences of integer sequences; combinatorial proof. *Mailing Add:* Dept Math & Comput Sci State Univ NY Col Fredonia Fredonia NY 14063

KWUN, KYUNG WHAN, mathematics, for more information see previous edition

KYAME, JOSEPH JOHN, MATHEMATICAL PHYSICS. *Current Pos:* Asst & instr, 44-45, asst prof, 48-58, ASSOC PROF PHYSICS, TULANE UNIV, 58- *Personal Data:* b New Orleans, La, Mar 12, 24; wid; c 1. *Educ:* Tulane Univ, BS, 44, MS, 45; Mass Inst Technol, PhD(physics), 48. *Mem:* Am Phys Soc; Sigma Xi. *Res:* Electromagnetic theory; piezoelectricity; thermodynamics. *Mailing Add:* 32 Warbler St New Orleans LA 70124

KYANKA, GEORGE HARRY, MECHANICAL ENGINEERING, WOOD SCIENCE. *Current Pos:* from asst prof to assoc prof, 68-80, PROF WOOD ENG, COL ENVIRON SCI & FORESTRY, STATE UNIV NY, 80-, CHMN DEPT, 85- *Personal Data:* b Syracuse, NY, July 17, 41; m 66; c 2. *Educ:* Syracuse Univ, BS, 62, MS, 66, PhD(mech eng), 75. *Prof Exp:* Res engr gas turbines, Caterpillar Tractor Co, 62-64; res asst aero eng, Syracuse Univ, 64-66; asst prof mech tech, Onondaga Col, 67-68. *Concurrent Pos:* NSF res fel, Syracuse Univ, 67; proj dir, NSF, 70-73, 76- & Weyerhaeuser Corp, 78-; adj prof, Onondaga Col Archit, 70-; consult engr, 70-; dir, Educ Opportunity Prog in Forestry, 73-76. *Mem:* Am Soc Mech Engrs; Am Soc Testing & Mat; Soc Exp Stress Analysis; Forest Prod Res Soc; Am Acad Mech; Soc Exp Mech. *Res:* Mechanical properties of wood and wood products; testing and design of wood products; professional responsibility and products liability in product design; wood in architecture and art. *Mailing Add:* Col Environ Sci & Forestry State Univ NY 320 Bray Hall Syracuse NY 13210-2778

KYBA, EVAN PETER, ORGANIC CHEMISTRY, SYNTHETIC MEDICINAL CHEMISTRY. *Current Pos:* dir, 88-90, SR DIR MED CHEM, ALCON LAB, INC, 90- *Personal Data:* b Canora, Sask, June 27, 40; m 62; c 1. *Educ:* Univ Sask, BA, 62; Univ Ala, PhD(org chem), 71. *Prof Exp:* Teacher chem, Regina Col Inst, Sask, 62-65; Nat Res Coun Can fel, Univ Calif, Los Angeles, 71-72; from asst prof to assoc prof, 72-85, prof chem, Univ Tex, Austin, 85-87. *Mem:* Am Chem Soc; The Chem Soc. *Res:* Reactive intermediates; organophosphorus chemistry; stereochemistry; synthesis of unusual small heterocycles and multiheteromacrocycles; homogeneous catalysis; organometallic chemistry; medicinal chemistry. *Mailing Add:* Alcon Labs Inc 6201 S Freeway R2-33 Ft Worth TX 76134-2001

KYBETT, BRIAN DAVID, PHYSICAL CHEMISTRY. *Current Pos:* from asst prof to assoc prof, 65-81, PROF CHEM & DIR, ENERGY RES UNIT, UNIV REGINA, 81- *Personal Data:* b Oxford, Eng, May 10, 38; m 63, Gaynor M Davies; c Gareth S. *Educ:* Univ Wales, BSc, 60, PhD(chem), 63. *Prof Exp:* Res assoc chem, Rice Univ, 63-65. *Mem:* Chem Inst Can; Royal Soc Chem; Am Chem Soc; Solar Energy Soc Can Inc; Int Solar Energy Soc. *Res:* Lattice energies; thermochemistry; reactivity of coal; surfactants; renewable energy; environmental chemistry. *Mailing Add:* Energy Res Unit Univ Regina Regina SK S4S 0A2 Can

KYBURG, HENRY, UNCERTAIN INFERENCE INDUCTIVE LOGIC. *Current Pos:* PROF PHILOS, UNIV ROCHESTER, 63-, PROF COMPUT SCI, 86- *Personal Data:* b New York, NY, Oct 9, 28; m 60; c 8. *Educ:* Yale Univ, BA, 48; Columbia Univ, MA, 52, PhD(philos), 55. *Prof Exp:* Asst prof math, Wesleyan Univ, 58-61; res assoc, Rockefeller Univ, 61-62. *Mem:* Fel AAAS; Am Philos Asn; Am Math Soc; Am Asn Artificial Intel; Asn Comput Mach. *Res:* Uncertain inference; inductive logic; representation of uncertainty; decision under uncertainty. *Mailing Add:* 1018 Eyer Rd Lyons NY 14489

KYCIA, THADDEUS F, HIGH ENERGY PHYSICS. *Current Pos:* Res asst high energy physics, 59-61, from asst physicist to assoc physicist, 61-66, physicist, 66-72, SR PHYSICIST, BROOKHAVEN NAT LAB, 72- *Personal Data:* b Montreal, Que, Aug 10, 33; m 57; c 1. *Educ:* McGill Univ, BS, 54, MS, 55; Univ Calif, Berkeley, PhD(high energy physics), 59. *Mem:* Fel Am Phys Soc. *Res:* Development of Cerenkov detectors; measurement of total cross sections; search for resonances; measurement of magnetic moment of hyperons; study of rare K meson decay. *Mailing Add:* Brookhaven Nat Lab Upton NY 11973

KYDD, DAVID MITCHELL, MEDICINE, METABOLISM. *Current Pos:* from assoc prof to prof, 52-69, EMER PROF MED, STATE UNIV NY DOWNSTATE MED CTR, 70- *Personal Data:* b Jersey City, NJ, May 17, 03; m 29; c 1. *Educ:* Princeton Univ, BS, 24; Harvard Univ, MD, 28. *Prof Exp:* Sterling res fel, Yale Univ, 29, Sax res fel, 29-30, from instr to asst prof med, Sch Med, 30-34; asst prof, Albany Med Col, 36-47; assoc prof, Sch Med, Yale Univ, 47-52. *Concurrent Pos:* Assoc, Bassett Hosp, NY, 34-47. *Mem:* Am Soc Clin Invest; Harvey Soc; Soc Exp Biol & Med; Am Inst Nutrit. *Res:* Electrolyte disturbances; thyroid diseases. *Mailing Add:* 48 Grove St Cooperstown NY 13326-1427

KYDD, PAUL HARRIMAN, PHYSICAL CHEMISTRY, CHEMICAL ENGINEERING. *Current Pos:* PRES, PARTNERSHIPS LTD INC, 83- *Personal Data:* b New Haven, Conn, Nov 25, 30; m 56, Priscilla Clisham; c David M & Andrew H. *Educ:* Princeton Univ, AB, 52; Harvard Univ, MA, 53, PhD(phys chem), 56. *Prof Exp:* Fel phys chem, Harvard Univ, 56-57; phys chemist, Gen Elec Res Lab, 57-66; lectr, Harvard Univ, 59-60; mgr chem processes, Gen Elec Res & Develop Ctr, 66-75; vpres technol, Hydrocarbon Res, Inc, 75-83. *Mem:* Am Chem Soc. *Res:* Coal liquifaction, gasification; petroleum production and refining; gas turbines, power generation; renewable resources, chemical intermediates; microcomputer applications; technology assessment; technology information management; contract research management. *Mailing Add:* PO Box 6042 Lawrenceville NJ 08648

KYDES, ANDY STEVE, NUMERICAL ANALYSIS, ENERGY SYSTEMS ANALYSIS. *Current Pos:* ENERGY SYST ANALYST, DEPT ENERGY & ENVIRON, BROOKHAVEN NAT LAB, 76- *Personal Data:* b Spilia, Greece, Jan 21, 45; US citizen; c 2. *Educ:* Harvard Univ, AB, 68; State Univ NY, Stony Brook, MS, 73, PhD(numerical analysis), 74. *Prof Exp:* Instr math & physics, Milton Acad, Mass, 68-71; asst prof math, State Univ NY, Stony Brook, 74-76. *Mem:* Oper Res Soc Am; Inst Mgt Sci. *Res:* Energy systems analysis; multi-criteria analysis; optimization. *Mailing Add:* 78 Stuart Ave Norwalk CT 06850

KYDONIEFS, ANASTASIOS D, applied mathematics, continuum mechanics, for more information see previous edition

KYHL, ROBERT LOUIS, ELECTRICAL ENGINEERING. *Current Pos:* from assoc prof to prof, 56-83, EMER PROF ELEC ENG, MASS INST TECHNOL, 83- *Personal Data:* b Omaha, Nebr, July 27, 17; m 43; c 1. *Educ:* Univ Chicago, SB, 37; Mass Inst Technol, PhD(physics), 47. *Honors & Awards:* Baker Award, Inst Radio Eng, 58. *Prof Exp:* Asst physics, Univ Chicago, 40-41; res associate radiation lab, Mass Inst Technol, 41-45, insulation lab, 45-47 & electronics res lab, 47-48; res assoc, Hansen Lab, Stanford Univ, 48-54 & res lab, Gen Elec Co, 54-56. *Mem:* Am Phys Soc; Inst Elec & Electronics Engrs. *Res:* Microwave spectroscopy and power tubes; electron accelerators; solid state masers. *Mailing Add:* Dept Elec Eng Mass Inst Technol 77 Massachusetts Ave Cambridge MA 02139

KYHOS, DONALD WILLIAM, PLANT TAXONOMY, PLANT CYTOGENETICS. *Current Pos:* from asst prof to assoc prof, 65-74, PROF BOT, UNIV CALIF, DAVIS, 74- *Personal Data:* b Los Angeles, Calif, Apr 10, 29; m 61; c 3. *Educ:* Whittier Col, AB, 51, MS, 56; Univ Calif, Los Angeles, PhD(bot), 64. *Prof Exp:* NIH fel biol, Stanford Univ, 64-65. *Concurrent Pos:* Australian Res Grant Comt fel, 72. *Mem:* Am Soc Plant Taxon; Bot Soc Am; Soc Study Evolution; Sigma Xi. *Res:* Plant systematics and evolutionary cytogenetics. *Mailing Add:* 909 Fordham Dr Davis CA 95616

KYLE, BENJAMIN G(AYLE), CHEMICAL ENGINEERING. *Current Pos:* From asst prof to assoc prof, 58-64, PROF CHEM ENG, KANS STATE UNIV, 64- *Personal Data:* b Atlanta, Ga, Dec 4, 27; m 52; c 4. *Educ:* Ga Inst Technol, BChE, 50; Univ Fla, MSE, 55, PhD(chem eng), 58. *Mem:* Am Chem Soc; Am Inst Chem Engrs. *Res:* Thermodynamics; mass transfer. *Mailing Add:* Dept Chem Eng Kans State Univ Manhattan KS 66506-5102

KYLE, HERBERT LEE, EARTH RADIATION BUDGET, SOLAR PHYSICS. *Current Pos:* SPACE PHYSICIST, GODDARD SPACE FLIGHT CTR, NASA, 59- *Personal Data:* b Monmouth, Ill, June 28, 30; m 60; c 1. *Educ:* Univ Ariz, BS, 54; Univ NC, MS, 59, PhD(atomic physics), 64. *Mem:* Am Phys Soc; Am Geophys Union. *Res:* Remote sensing of the earth's radiation budget; remote sensing for the cloud properties and cloud cover; atmospheric radiative transfer theory and numerical analysis; measurement of the solar constant and it's variations; application of computers to scientific problems; creation of satellite climate data sets with emphasis on long-term sensor calibration and numerical analysis. *Mailing Add:* 21 A Ridge Rd Greenbelt MD 20770

KYLE, MARTIN LAWRENCE, CHEMICAL ENGINEERING. *Current Pos:* chem engr, 60-78, ASST LAB DIR, ARGONNE NAT LAB, 78- *Personal Data:* b Akron, Ohio, Jan 2, 35; m 57, Evelyn Sveda; c 3. *Educ:* Univ Notre Dame, BS, 56; Purdue Univ, MS, 61; Univ Chicago, MBA, 71. *Prof Exp:* Chem engr, E I DuPont de Nemours & Co, 56-57. *Mem:* Am Chem Soc. *Res:* Battery development; solar energy; coal technology. *Mailing Add:* 1105 Delles Rd Wheaton IL 60187

KYLE, PHILIP R, VOLCANOLOGY. *Current Pos:* PROF GEOCHEM, NMEX INST MINING TECHNOL, 81- *Personal Data:* b Wellington, NZ, Dec 3, 47. *Educ:* Victoria Univ, PhD(geol), 76. *Mem:* Fel Geol Soc Am. *Mailing Add:* 1304 Vista Dr Socorro NM 87801

KYLE, ROBERT ARTHUR, HEMATOLOGY, GAMMOPATHIES. *Current Pos:* from asst prof to assoc prof, 66-75, CONSULT MED, MAYO MED SCH, 61-, PROF MED & LAB MED, 75- *Personal Data:* b Bottineau, NDak, March 17, 28; m 54, Charlene Showalter; c John, Mary, Barbara & Jean. *Educ:* Univ NDak, BS, 48; Northwestern Univ Med Sch, MD, 52; Univ Minn, MS, 58. *Honors & Awards:* Waldenstrom's Award Res Multiple Myeloma, Int Workshop Myeloma, Torino, Italy, 91. *Prof Exp:* Clin asst hemat, Tufts Univ Sch Med, 60-61; postdoctoral fel hemat, Nat Cancer Inst, 60-61. *Concurrent Pos:* William H Donner prof med & Lab Med, Mayo Med Sch, 81-87; prin invest, Acute Leukemia Group B, 71-72; chmn, myeloma comn, Eastern Coopr Oncol Group, 84-; consult, PDQ Info Bank, Nat Cancer Inst, 84- *Mem:* NY Acad Sci; Am Assoc Cancer Res; Am Soc Hemat; fel Am Col Physicians; Am Soc Clin Oncol; Cent Soc Clin Res. *Res:* Monoclonal gammopathies; includes multiple myeloma, amyloidosis, macroglobulinemia, and related plasma cell proliferative process. *Mailing Add:* 200 First St SW Rochester MN 55905. *Fax:* 507-266-4088

KYLE, THOMAS GAIL, INFRARED STUDIES, METEOROLOGICAL TRACERS. *Current Pos:* RETIRED. *Personal Data:* b Crawford, Okla, Sept 12, 36; m 58; c 2. *Educ:* Univ Okla, BS, 60, MS, 62; Univ Denver, PhD(physics), 65. *Prof Exp:* Res officer, Commonwealth Sci & Indust Res Orgn, Australia, 65-66; res physicist, Univ Denver, 66-71; scientist, Nat Ctr Atmospheric Res, 71-76; staff mem, Los Alamos Nat Lab, 76-92. *Concurrent Pos:* Vis prof, Clemson Univ, 81-82, Denver Univ, 82-83, Okla State Univ, 83-84. *Mem:* Optical Soc Am; Sigma Xi. *Res:* Computational physics; theoretical and experimental studies of infrared spectra; laser studies; studies of the composition and radiative properties of the atmosphere; weather modification; artificial intelligence; atmospheric modeling; image processing. *Mailing Add:* 2413 Regal Rd Plano TX 75075 England

KYLSTRA, JOHANNES ARNOLD, MEDICINE, PHYSIOLOGY. *Current Pos:* RETIRED. *Personal Data:* b Manado, Neth EIndies, Nov 30, 25; m 56; c 2. *Educ:* Univ Leiden, MD, 58. *Honors & Awards:* Lockheed Award, Marine Technol Soc, 70. *Prof Exp:* prof pulmonary & allergy, Duke Univ, 72-89. *Mem:* AAAS; Am Physiol Soc; Undersea Med Soc (pres, 73-74). *Res:* Liquid breathing and lung lavage. *Mailing Add:* Dept Med Duke Univ 4415 Malvern Rd Durham NC 27707-5645

KYNCL, J JAROSLAV, HYPERTENSION, ADRENERGIC RECEPTORS. *Current Pos:* E VOLWILER RES FEL, ABBOTT LABS RES & DEVELOP, 72- *Personal Data:* b Prague, Czech, Aug 16, 36; US citizen; m 61; c 2. *Educ:* Masaryk Univ, Czech, MS, 59; Komensky Univ, Czech, PhD(pharmacol), 63; Czech Acad Sci, Prague, ScC, 67. *Honors & Awards:* Pfizer Lectr, Clin Res Inst Montreal, 80. *Prof Exp:* Sr res scientist, Res Inst Pharm & Biochem, Prague, Czech, 63-68; A V Humboldt fel cardiovasc res, Univ Heidelberg, Ger, 68-72; res fel, Cleveland Clin Res Div, 70-72. *Concurrent Pos:* Mem, Coun High Blood Pressure, Am Heart Asn. *Mem:* Fel Am Heart Asn; Am Endocrine Soc; Am Soc Pharmacol & Exp Therapeut; Am Soc Hypertension; Int Soc Hypertension. *Res:* Pathophysiology of cardiovascular and endocrine disorders; novel concepts and specific agents useful in therapy; author of numerous scientific publications and patents; codiscoverer of Terazosin (Hytrin). *Mailing Add:* Dept 41K Bldg R13 1401 Sheridan Rd Lake Forest IL 60064

KYRALA, GEORGE AMINE, OPTICS, LASER FUSION & INTERACTIONS. *Current Pos:* MEM STAFF, PHYSICS DIV, LOS ALAMOS NAT LAB, 79-; VIS FAC, UNIV NMEX, LOS ALAMOS, 86- *Personal Data:* b Bhamdoun, Lebanon, Apr 20, 46; US citizen; m 73, Trish

Mylet; c Michaelene & Kamaal. *Educ:* Am Univ Beirut, BS, 67; Yale Univ, MPh, 69, PhD(physics), 74. *Prof Exp:* Fel physics, Joint Inst Lab Astrophys, Univ Colo, 74-76; res assoc optics & physics, Optical Sci Ctr & Dept Physics, Univ Ariz, 76-78, res fel lasers & spectros, Dept Physics, 78-79. *Concurrent Pos:* Lectr, Dept Physics, Univ Colo, 75; vis fac & consult, Al-Hazen Res Ctr, Baghdad, 75. *Mem:* Am Phys Soc; Arab Phys Soc; Int Optical Eng Soc; Optical Soc Am; fel Int Soc Photo-Optical Instrumentation Engrs. *Res:* Charge transfer in atomic collision; electron scattering from excited atoms; laser construction and use in ultra high resolution spectroscopy; laser fusion experiments and optics; plasma xray spectroscopy; ultrafast diagnostics; x-ray imaging. *Mailing Add:* MS E-526 Los Alamos Nat Lab Los Alamos NM 87545. *Fax:* 505-665-4409; *E-Mail:* kyrala@lanl.gov

KYRIAKIS, JOHN M, MEDICINE. *Current Pos:* INSTR MED, HARVARD MED SCH, 90- *Prof Exp:* RES FEL, MASS GEN HOSP, 87- *Mailing Add:* Diabetes Res Lab Mass Gen Hosp MGH E Bldg 149 13th St Charlestown MA 02129-0001. *Fax:* 617-726-5649

KYRIAKOPOULOS, NICHOLAS, SYSTEMS THEORY & CONTROLS, DIGITAL SIGNAL PROCESSING. *Current Pos:* instr elec eng, George Washington Univ, 64-66, from asst prof to assoc prof elec eng & comput sci, 66-79, PROF ENG, GEORGE WASHINGTON UNIV, 80- *Personal Data:* b Atalanti, Greece, Nov 14, 37; m 67, Irene Ioannidou; c Anastasia & Aris. *Educ:* George Washington Univ, BEE, 60, MS, 63, DSc, 68. *Honors & Awards:* Sigma Xi. *Prof Exp:* Electronic engr, Harry Diamond Labs, Dept Army, 60-62; aerospace engr, Goddard Space Flight Ctr, NASA, 62-64. *Concurrent Pos:* NASA-Am Soc Eng Educ fac fel, Goddard Space Flight Ctr, NASA, 67-68; consult, Nat Biomed Res Found, 66-67; Howard Res Corp, 67 & RCA Serv Co, 67-; summer fac fel, 74-76; vis prof, Nat Tech Univ, Athens, 72-73; NIK Assocs, 77-; sr scientist, US Arms Control & Disarmament Agency, 79-; consult, Int Atomic Energy Agency, 82- *Mem:* Inst Elec & Electronics Engrs. *Res:* Computer-aided analysis and design; performance evaluation of space communication systems; digital signal processing; monitoring and data collection systems; process automation and control; applications of technology to arms control; sensors and security systems. *Mailing Add:* Dept Elec Eng & Comput Sci George Washington Univ 2121 Eye St NW Washington DC 20052. *Fax:* 202-994-0227; *E-Mail:* kyriak@seas.gwu.edu

KYRIAZIS, ANDREAS P, PATHOLOGY. *Current Pos:* PROF PATH, UNIV MED & DENT NJ, 82- *Personal Data:* b Aigion, Greece, Jan 19, 32; m 65; c 1. *Educ:* Nat Univ Athens, MD, 57; Univ Thessaloniki, DrSc(path), 62; Jefferson Med Col, PhD(path), 68. *Prof Exp:* Resident path, Univ Thessaloniki, 60-64; attend pathologist, Piraeus Gen Hosp, Greece, 64; resident path, Jersey City Med Ctr, 65; res assoc, Univ Chicago, 68-70, asst prof path, 70-75; assoc prof path, Univ Cincinnati, 78-82. *Concurrent Pos:* Vis scientist, Argonne Cancer Res Hosp, Univ Chicago, 68-; vis prof, dept gen & tumor immunol, Hebrew Univ Hadassah Med Sch, Jerusalem, Isreal. *Mem:* Reticuloendothelial Soc; Am Asn Pathologists; NY Acad Sci; Int Acad Path; Am Asn Cancer Res; AAAS; Tissue Cult Asn. *Res:* Tissue culture; tumor biology; experimental tumor chemotherapy. *Mailing Add:* 106 Denham Ct Richmond VA 23229

KYSER, DAVID SHELDON, experimental solid state physics, for more information see previous edition

KYTE, JACK ERNST, BIOCHEMISTRY. *Current Pos:* Damon Runyon Fund fel biochem, 72-74, ASST PROF BIOCHEM, UNIV CALIF, SAN DIEGO, 74- *Personal Data:* b Pasadena, Calif, May 21, 47. *Educ:* Carleton Col, BA, 67; Harvard Univ, PhD(biochem), 72. *Res:* Molecular structure of proteins which catalyze the transport of matter across biological membranes. *Mailing Add:* Dept Chem 0506 Univ Calif at San Diego La Jolla CA 92093

KYTHE, PREM KISHORE, WAVE STRUCTURE, GEOMETRIC & COEFFICIENT PROBLEMS. *Current Pos:* from vis assoc to assoc prof, 67-74, PROF MATH, UNIV NEW ORLEANS, LA, 74- *Personal Data:* b India, Jan 29, 30; US citizen; m 55; c 2. *Educ:* Agra Univ, BSc, 50, MSc, 55; Aligarh Muslim Univ, PhD(math), 61. *Prof Exp:* Lectr math, Aligarh Muslim Univ, India, 58-60; from lectr to asst prof, Indian Inst Technol, Bombay, India, 60-67. *Concurrent Pos:* Invited speaker, NATO, Advan Inst Automotive Transl Lang, Italy, 62; fel, UNESCO, 63; consult, Inst Human Learning, Univ Calif, Berkeley, 64; vis prof, Math Dept, Imp Col, London, 73 & Comput Sci Dept, Univ Ill, Urbana-Champaign, 86. *Res:* Univalent functions; boundary-value problems in continuum mechanics; laplace transforms; wave theory; wave structure in unsteady free convection flows in a rotating medium; geometric and coefficient problems in some subclasses of univalent functions; fundamental solutions. *Mailing Add:* Dept Math Univ New Orleans-Lake Front New Orleans LA 70148. *Fax:* 504-280-5516; *E-Mail:* pkkma@uno.edu

KYUNG, JAI HO, ORGANIC CHEMISTRY. *Current Pos:* Res chemist, 74-76, SR RES CHEMIST, ASHLAND CHEM CO, 76- *Personal Data:* b Seoul, Korea, Dec 26, 47; m 73. *Educ:* Seoul Nat Univ, BS, 69; Brown Univ, PhD(org chem), 75. *Mem:* Am Chem Soc. *Res:* Synthesis of organic ligands for recovery of metals for mining industry and commercial development of solvent extraction of hydrometallurgy; homogeneous and heterogeneous catalysis of petrochemicals and industrial intermediate chemicals. *Mailing Add:* 3525 Trillium Lane Appleton WI 54915

L

LA, SUNG YUN, PHYSICS. *Current Pos:* assoc prof, 68-78, PROF PHYSICS & EARTH SCI, WILLIAM PATERSON COL NJ, 78- *Personal Data:* b Seoul, Korea, Sept 24, 36. *Educ:* WVa Wesleyan Col, BS, 59; Univ Conn, MS, 62, PhD(physics), 64. *Prof Exp:* Res assoc appl physics, Mat Res Lab, Pa State Univ, 65-68. *Mem:* Am Phys Soc. *Res:* Theoretical studies of ionic crystals; defects investigated by electron spin resonance technique, cohesive energy and compressibility. *Mailing Add:* Dept Chem & Physics Rm Sci 434 William Paterson Col NJ 300 Pompton Rd Wayne NJ 07470-2103

LAAKSO, JOHN WILLIAM, BIOCHEMISTRY. *Current Pos:* RETIRED. *Personal Data:* b Minn, Jan 28, 15; m 41; c 4. *Educ:* Winona State Col, BS, 38; Mont State Col, MS, 49; Univ Minn, PhD(biochem), 56. *Prof Exp:* Teacher high schs, Minn, 38-42; instr math, Mont State Col, 46-47; from instr to assoc prof, St Cloud State Univ, 48-63, chmn dept, 66-73, prof chem, 63-80. *Mem:* Am Chem Soc; Sigma Xi. *Res:* Synthesis and biological assay of orotic acid analogs. *Mailing Add:* 3496 160th St South Haven MN 55382

LAALE, HANS W, EXPERIMENTAL EMBRYOLOGY, TERATOLOGY. *Current Pos:* RETIRED. *Personal Data:* b Copenhagen, Denmark, Apr 20, 35; Can citizen. *Educ:* Bob Jones Univ, BSc, 59; Univ Western Ont, MSc, 61; Univ Toronto, PhD(zool), 66. *Prof Exp:* Asst lectr biol, Hong Kong Baptist Col, 61-63; lectr, Chinese Univ Hong Kong, 66-67; from asst prof to prof zool, Univ Man, 67-96. *Concurrent Pos:* Vis prof, Tunghai Univ, Taiwan, 73- & Univ BC, 80- *Mem:* Can Soc Zoologists; Sigma Xi. *Res:* Teleost embryology and teratology; in vitro fish embryo culture: differentiation and organogenesis. *Mailing Add:* Dept Zool Univ Man Winnipeg MB R3T 2N2 Can

LAALI, KENNETH KHOSROW, STRUCTURAL & MECHANISTIC CHEMISTRY, ORGANIC & ORGANOMETALLIC CHEMISTRY. *Current Pos:* from asst prof to assoc prof, 85-96, PROF CHEM, KENT STATE UNIV, 96- *Personal Data:* b Tehran, Iran, July 5, 51; US citizen. *Educ:* Univ Tehran, BS, 73; Univ Manchester, PhD(org chem), 77. *Prof Exp:* Res fel, Sci Res Coun, King's Col, Univ London, 77-79; Nat Ctr Sci res fel, Univ Strasbourg, 79-80; instr, Univ Amsterdam, 80-81; res assoc, Swiss Fed Inst Technol, 81-82; res scientist, Hydrocarbon Res Inst, Univ Southern Calif, 82-85. *Mem:* Am Chem Soc; Royal Soc Chem; Am Soc Mass Spectros. *Res:* Physical organic, organometalic, fluorine and hydrocarbon chemistry; reactive intermediates; superacid chemistry; Friedel-crafts, multinuclear nuclear magnetic resonance and modern mass spectrometry. *Mailing Add:* Dept Chem Kent State Univ Kent OH 44242. *Fax:* 330-672-3816; *E-Mail:* laali@kentvm.kent.edu

LAANE, JAAN, PHYSICAL CHEMISTRY, SPECTROSCOPY. *Current Pos:* from asst prof to assoc prof, 68-76, PROF CHEM, TEX A&M UNIV, 76-, ASSOC DEAN, COL SCI, 94- *Personal Data:* b Paide, Estonia, June 20, 42; US citizen; m 66, Tiiu Virkhaus; c Christina & Lisa. *Educ:* Univ Ill, Urbana, BS, 64; Mass Inst Technol, PhD(chem), 67. *Honors & Awards:* Kendall Award, 64; Kodak Award, 67; Alexander von Humboldt US Sr Scientist Award, 79. *Prof Exp:* Asst prof chem, Tufts Univ, 67-68; chmn, Div Phys & Nuclear Chem 77-87 & 93-94; sr policy adv, Koriyama, Japan, 90-94. *Concurrent Pos:* Vis scientist, Los Alamos Sci Lab, NMex, 64 & 67-68; vis prof, Univ Bayreuth, WGer, 79-80, 81, 83; dir, Inst Pac Asia, 87-90; ed, J Molecular Struct, 94- *Mem:* Am Chem Soc; fel Am Phys Soc; Soc Appl Spectros; Coblentz Soc (treas, 85-); fel Am Inst Chem; AAAS. *Res:* Far-infrared spectroscopy of small ring compounds; potential energy functions; organometallic syntheses; infrared and Raman spectroscopy; nitrogen-oxygen chemistry. *Mailing Add:* Dept Chem Tex A&M Univ College Station TX 77843. *Fax:* 409-845-3154; *E-Mail:* laane@chemvx.tamu.edu

LAASPERE, THOMAS, RADIOPHYSICS. *Current Pos:* from asst prof to prof, 61-89, EMER PROF ENG, THAYER SCH ENG, DARTMOUTH COL, 89- *Personal Data:* b Estonia, Mar 17, 27; US citizen; m 55, Suzanne Champagne; c Hans, Liisa & Jaan. *Educ:* Univ Vt, BS, 56; Cornell Univ, MS, 58, PhD(commun eng), 60. *Prof Exp:* Res assoc radiophys, Cornell Univ, 60-61. *Concurrent Pos:* Mem comn IV, US Nat Comt, Int Sci Radio Union, 64- *Mem:* Inst Elec & Electronics Engrs. *Res:* Scattering of radio waves in the troposphere and ionosphere; whistlers and other audio-frequency electromagnetic waves; space research; electric rates, load management. *Mailing Add:* Dartmouth Col Thayer Sch Hanover NH 03755

LAATSCH, RICHARD G, MATHEMATICAL ANALYSIS. *Current Pos:* from asst prof to assoc prof, 62-70, PROF MATH & ASSOC CHMN DEPT, MIAMI UNIV, 70- *Personal Data:* b Fairmont, Minn, July 14, 31; m 66; c 5. *Educ:* Cent Mo State Col, BS, 53; Univ Mo, MA, 57; Okla State Univ, PhD(math), 62. *Prof Exp:* Instr math, Univ Tulsa, 57-60; asst prof, Okla State Univ, 62. *Mem:* Math Asn Am. *Res:* Subadditive functions; topological vector spaces and cones of functions. *Mailing Add:* Dept Math Miami Univ 123 Bachelor Hall Oxford OH 45056

LABANA, SANTOKH SINGH, ORGANIC CHEMISTRY, POLYMER SCIENCE. *Current Pos:* prin scientist assoc, 67-70, staff scientist, 70-72, MGR POLYMER SCI DEPT, FORD MOTOR CO, 72- *Personal Data:* b Maritanda, India, Nov 15, 36; m 64. *Educ:* Univ Panjab, India, BSc, 57, MSc, 59; Cornell Univ, PhD(org chem), 63. *Prof Exp:* Lectr chem, G H G Col,

Sadhar, India, 58-60; res chemist, Univ Calif, Berkeley, 63-64; scientist, Xerox Corp, 64-67. *Concurrent Pos:* Chmn coatings & films, Gordon Res Conf, 80 & Org Coatings & Plastics Chem Div, Am Chem Soc, 81; mem adv bd, J Coatings & Technol. *Mem:* Am Chem Soc. *Res:* Synthetic organic chemistry; polymer syntheses; mechanism of organic reactions; physical and thermal properties of polymers with special reference to network polymers; radiation induced polymerizations, coating and composites. *Mailing Add:* Box 2037 Dearborn MI 48123-2037

LABANAUSKAS, CHARLES K, PLANT PHYSIOLOGY. *Current Pos:* From asst horticulturist to horticulturist, Citrus Res Ctr, 55-88, prof hort sci, 68-88, EMER PROF HORT SCI, COL NATURAL & AGR SCI, UNIV CALIF, RIVERSIDE, 88- *Personal Data:* b Upyna, Lithuania, Jan 3, 23; nat US. *Educ:* Hohenheim Agr Univ, dipl, 47; Univ Ill, MS, 53, PhD, 54. *Concurrent Pos:* Lectr, Univ Calif, Riverside, 65-68. *Mem:* Am Soc Hort Sci. *Res:* Mineral metabolism in plants. *Mailing Add:* 3682 15th St Riverside CA 92501

LABANICK, GEORGE MICHAEL, ZOOLOGY, HERPETOLOGY. *Current Pos:* from asst prof to assoc prof, 79-89, PROF BIOL, UNIV SC, SPARTANBURG, 89-, DIV CHAIR, 90- *Personal Data:* b Passaic, NJ, Sept 27, 50; m 79; c 2. *Educ:* Col William & Mary, BS, 72; Ind State Univ, MA, 74; Southern Ill Univ, PhD(zool), 78. *Prof Exp:* Asst prof biol, Emory & Henry Col, 78-79. *Mem:* Sigma Xi; Am Soc Ichthyologists & Herpetologists; Herpetologists' League; Soc Study Amphibians & Reptiles; Soc Study Evolution. *Res:* Mimicry and other defense mechanisms; salamander ecology and systematics. *Mailing Add:* Div Natural Sci & Eng Univ SC Spartanburg 800 University Way Spartanburg SC 29303-4932

LABAR, MARTIN, POPULATION BIOLOGY, BIOETHICS. *Current Pos:* Assoc prof, 64-66, PROF SCI, SOUTHERN WESLEYAN UNIV, 66-, CHMN DIV SCI, 64- *Personal Data:* b Radisson, Wis, May 15, 38. *Educ:* Wis State Univ, Superior, BA, 58; Univ Wis, MS, 63, PhD(genetics, zool), 65. *Mem:* Am Sci Affiliation; Ecol Soc Am; Soc Study Evolution. *Res:* Use of computer simulation in teaching population biology; bioethics. *Mailing Add:* Div Sci Southern Wesleyan Univ PO Box 1020 Central SC 29630-1020

LABARBERA, ANDREW RICHARD, REPRODUCTIVE BIOLOGY, MOLECULAR ENDOCRINOLOGY. *Current Pos:* assoc prof, Dept Obstet & Gynec, 88-95, ASSOC PROF, DEPT MOLECULAR & CELLULAR PHYSIOL, COL MED, UNIV CINCINNATI, 88-, PROF OBSTET & GYNEC, 95- *Personal Data:* b Teaneck, NJ, Oct 6, 48. *Educ:* Iona Col, BS, 70; Columbia Univ, MA & MPhil, 74, PhD(physiol), 75. *Prof Exp:* Staff assoc, Int Inst Study Human Reproduction, Columbia Univ, 75-77; res fel, Dept Cell Biol, Mayo Grad Sch Med, 77-80; from asst prof to assoc prof, Dept Physiol, Northwestern Univ Med Sch, 80-88, from asst prof to assoc prof, Dept Obstet & Gynec, 85-88. *Concurrent Pos:* Dir, Hormone Assay Lab, Ctr Endocrinol Metab Nutrit, Northwestern Univ Med Sch, 80-85; grantee, NIH, 82-86 & 94-, USDA, 86-92; dir, Invitro Fertil Lab, Northwestern Mem Hosp, 85-88; vchmn admin & res, Dept Obstet & Gynec, Col Med, Univ Cincinnati, 88-93; dir, Andrology Lab, Univ Cincinnati Hosp, 88-; consult, NIH, 90- *Mem:* AAAS; Am Physiol Soc; Am Fertil Soc; Endocrine Soc; Soc Exp Biol Med; Soc Study Reproduction. *Res:* Mechanisms of signal transduction in the gonads; molecular and cellular regulation of gonadotropin receptors. *Mailing Add:* Dept OB/GYN Univ Cinn Col Med PO Box 670526 Cincinnati OH 45267-0526. *Fax:* 513-558-6138; *E-Mail:* andrew.labarbera@uc.edu

LABARGE, ROBERT GORDON, CHEMISTRY. *Current Pos:* INDEPENDANT CONSULT, 93- *Personal Data:* b Buffalo, NY, July 11, 40. *Educ:* Univ Rochester, BS, 62; Carnegie-Mellon Univ, PhD(chem), 66; Cent Mich Univ, MBA, 78. *Prof Exp:* Res chemist, Consumer Prod Dept, Dow Chem Co, 66-73, dir acad educ, 73-75, res specialist, Designed Prod Dept, 75-78, mgr, New Prod Develop, 78-83, mgr, Opportunities Identification, 83-93. *Concurrent Pos:* Adj prof chem, Cent Mich Univ, 74, econ & mgt, Delta Col, 78-82; adj prof, Northwood Inst, 82. *Mem:* Am Chem Soc; Inst Food Technologists; Am Oil Chemists Soc; Sigma Xi. *Res:* New product exploration and development. *Mailing Add:* 709 Sterling Dr Midland MI 48640-2764

LABARRE, ANTHONY E, JR, MATHEMATICS. *Current Pos:* RETIRED. *Personal Data:* b New Orleans, La, July 18, 22; m 43, 77; c 2. *Educ:* Tulane Univ, BE, 43, MS, 47; Univ Okla, PhD(math), 57. *Prof Exp:* Instr math, Tulane Univ, 46-48; asst prof, Univ Idaho, 48-50; instr, Univ Okla, 50-54 & Univ Wyo, 54-56; from asst prof to assoc prof, Univ Idaho, 56-61; chmn dept, Calif State Univ, Fresno, 61-66, prof math, 61-90. *Mem:* Math Asn Am; Am Math Asn Two Year Col. *Res:* Functional analysis, differential geometry. *Mailing Add:* 2809 Mckelvy Ave Clovis CA 93612

LABARTHE, DARWIN RAYMOND, EPIDEMIOLOGY. *Current Pos:* PROF EPIDEMIOL, SCH PUB HEALTH, UNIV TEX, 77- *Personal Data:* b Berkeley, Calif, Aug 5, 39. *Educ:* Princeton Univ, AB, 61; Columbia Univ, MD, 65; Univ Calif, Berkeley, MPH, 67, PhD(epidemiol), 75. *Prof Exp:* Epidemiologist, Com Corps, Heart Dis & Stroke Control Prog, San Francisco, 67-69; dep chief & sr epidemiologist, Epidemiol Field & Training Sta, USPHS Heart Dis & Stroke Control Prog, San Francisco, 69-70; from assoc res epidemiologist to assoc prof epidemiol, Sch Pub Health, Univ Tex Health Sci Ctr, Houston, 70-73; consult epidemiol, dept med statist & epidemiol, Mayo Clin & Mayo Found, 74-77. *Concurrent Pos:* Dep dir, Coord Ctr, Hypertension Detection & Followup Prog, Nat Heart & Lung Inst, 71-73; consult, Task Force Automated Blood Pressure Devices, Nat Heart & Lung Inst, 73-74; consult, coord ctr, Hypertension Detection & Followup Prog, Nat Heart & Lung Inst, 74-; co-investr & co-dir, Study Incidence & Natural Hist Genital Tract Anomalies & Cancer in Offspring exposed in Utero to synthetic Estrogens, Nat Cancer Inst, 74-; chmn & dir, US Seminar in Cardiovasc Epidemiol, Am Heart Asn, 75-; dir design & analysis, Baylor Col Med, 77-; dep dir, Beta-Blocker Heart Attack Trial Coord Ctr. *Mem:* Fel Am Heart Asn; fel Am Col Prev Med; Soc Epidemiol Res (pres, 72-73); Am Pub Health Asn; Int Soc Cardiol. *Res:* Epidemiology and prevention, especially of cardiovascular and other chronic conditions; drugs; intra-individual variability of blood pressure and other personal characteristics. *Mailing Add:* Univ Tex HSC-EPID PO Box 20186 Astrodome Sta Houston TX 77225

LABATE, SAMUEL, ACOUSTICS. *Current Pos:* RETIRED. *Personal Data:* b Easton, Pa, Dec 19, 18; m 49; c 2. *Educ:* Lafayette Col, AB, 40; Mass Inst Technol, MS, 48. *Prof Exp:* Asst instr math, Univ Pa, 40-41; engr, E I du Pont de Nemours & Co, 41-42; consult engr, Bolt & Beranek, 48-49, consult engr, 49-53, exec vpres, 53-69, pres, 69-76, dir, Bolt Beranek & Newman, Inc, 53-83, chmn bd, 76-83. *Mem:* Fel Acoust Soc Am; Acad Appl Sci. *Res:* Engineering; applied architectural and physical acoustics. *Mailing Add:* 424 Scraggy Neck Rd Cataumet MA 02534

LABAVITCH, JOHN MARCUS, PLANT PHYSIOLOGY, BIOCHEMISTRY. *Current Pos:* asst pomologist, 76-80, ASSOC POMOLOGIST, UNIV CALIF, DAVIS, 80-, LECTR POMOL, 76- *Personal Data:* b Covington, Ky, Oct 15, 43. *Educ:* Wabash Col, AB, 65; Stanford Univ, PhD(plant physiol), 73. *Prof Exp:* Instr biol, Wabash Col, 65-67; NIH fel biochem, Univ Colo, 72-76. *Mem:* Am Soc Plant Physiologists; AAAS. *Res:* Cell wall metabolism of fruit. *Mailing Add:* Dept Bot Univ Calif Davis Davis CA 95616-5200

L'ABBE, MARY ROBERTA, TRACE ELEMENT & MINERALS NUTRITION, NUTRITION & HEALTH. *Current Pos:* chemist, 76-89, RES SCIENTIST, NUTRIT RES, HEALTH CAN, 89-, HEAD, MICRO NUTRIENTS SECT, 91- *Personal Data:* b Ottawa, Ont, Mar 4, 52. *Educ:* Carleton Univ, BSc, 75; McGill Univ, MSc, 83, PhD(nutrit), 88. *Concurrent Pos:* Lectr, Mem Univ, 92, Am Oil Chemists, 92 & 97, Univ Laval, 93, Univ Man, 94, Can Inst Food Sci, 94, USDA, 95 & Univ Alta, 95; adj prof, Dept Food & Nutrit, Univ Man, 95- *Mem:* Can Fedn Biol Socs; Can Soc Nutrit Sci (treas, 89-92); Am Nutrit Sci; Oxygen Soc; Int Soc Free Radical Res. *Res:* Trace element nutrition; vitamins and minerals; review of Canandian food fortification policy. *Mailing Add:* 2203C Health Can Ottawa ON K1A 0L2 Can. *Fax:* 613-941-6182; *E-Mail:* mlabbe@hpb.hwc.ca

LABBE, ROBERT FERDINAND, CLINICAL CHEMISTRY, NUTRITION. *Current Pos:* res asst prof pediat & lectr biochem, Univ Wash, 57-60, res assoc prof pediat, 60-68, prof pediat, 68-74, PROF LAB MED, MED SCH, UNIV WASH, 74-, HEAD, CLIN CHEM DIV, 80- *Personal Data:* b Portland, Ore, Nov 12, 22; m 55; c 3. *Educ:* Univ Portland, BS, 47; Ore State Col, MS, 49, PhD(biochem), 51. *Honors & Awards:* Ames Award, Am Asn Clin Chemists. *Prof Exp:* AEC fel med sci, Col Physicians & Surgeons, Columbia Univ, 51-53; res instr, Med Sch, Univ Ore, 53-55, res asst prof, 55-57. *Concurrent Pos:* Vis asst prof, Inst Enzyme Res, Univ Wis, 56-57; vis researcher, Commonwealth Sci & Indust Res Orgn, Australia, 65; NIH spec fel, 65 & career develop award, 66-70. *Mem:* Fel AAAS; Am Chem Soc; Am Soc Biol Chemists; Acad Clin Lab Physicians & Scientists; Am Asn Clin Chemists; Am Soc Clin Nutrit. *Res:* Heme biosynthesis; iron metabolism; related metabolic diseases; clinical nutrition, ascorbic acid metabolism, low power lasers. *Mailing Add:* Dept Lab Med Harborview Med Ctr Box 359743 Seattle WA 98104-2499. *Fax:* 206-223-3930

LABBE, RONALD GILBERT, MICROBIOLOGY. *Current Pos:* from asst prof to assoc prof, 76-87, PROF FOOD MICROBIOL, DEPT FOOD SCI, UNIV MASS, AMHERST, CHENOWETH LAB, 88- *Personal Data:* b Berlin, NH, July 16, 46; m 78; c 2. *Educ:* Univ NH, BA, 68; Univ Wis, MS, 70, PhD(bact), 76. *Prof Exp:* Res assoc microbiol, Food Res Inst, Univ Wis, 76. *Concurrent Pos:* Adj prof, Sch Pub Health, Univ Mass. *Mem:* Sigma Xi; Int Asn Milk, Food & Environ Sanitarians; Am Soc Microbiol; Inst Food Technologists; fel Am Acad Microbiol. *Res:* Clostridium perfringens food poisoning; germination and sporulation of bacterial spores; microbial food safety. *Mailing Add:* Dept Food Sci Univ Mass Amherst Chenoweth Lab Amherst MA 01003-0002

LABELLA, FRANK SEBASTIAN, BIOCHEMICAL & CELLULAR PHARMACOLOGY. *Current Pos:* lectr pharmacol, 58-60, from asst prof to assoc prof, 60-67, PROF PHARMACOL & THERAPEUT, FAC MED, UNIV MAN, 67- *Personal Data:* b Middletown, Conn, Sept 23, 31; m 52; c 3. *Educ:* Wesleyan Univ, BA, 52, MA, 54; Emory Univ, PhD(basic health sci), 57. *Honors & Awards:* John J Abel Award, Am Soc Pharmacol & Exp Therapeut, 67; E W R Steacie Prize in Natural Sci, Pharmacol Soc Can, 69, Upjohn Award, 82. *Prof Exp:* Asst biol, Wesleyan Univ, 52-54; asst physiol, Emory Univ, 54-55, asst histol, 55-57, instr physiol, 57-58. *Concurrent Pos:* Am Heart Asn fel, Emory Univ, 57-58; Can Rheumatism & Arthritis Soc res fel, Univ Man, 58-61; estab investr, Am Heart Asn, 61-66, mem coun arteriosclerosis; career investr, Med Res Coun Can, 66-; mem, Man Environ Res Comt & Int Narcotics Res Conf. *Mem:* Can Biochem Soc; Endocrine Soc; AAAS; Can Asn Geront; Am Soc Pharmacol & Exp Therapeut; Pharmacol Soc Can. *Res:* Cellular pharmacology and biochemistry; neurochemistry; aging; endocrine pharmacology; neuroendocrinology. *Mailing Add:* Dept Pharmacol & Therapeut Fac Med Univ Man 770 Bannatyne Ave Winnipeg MB R3E 0W3 Can

LABELLE, EDWARD FRANCIS, EXPERIMENTAL BIOLOGY. *Current Pos:* RES SCIENTIST, GRAD HOSP, BOCKUS RES INST, PHILADELPHIA, PA, 87- *Personal Data:* b Worcester, Mass, Aug 11, 48; m; c 2. *Educ:* Col Holy Cross, AB & MS, 70; Univ Mich, Ann Arbor, PhD(biochem), 74. *Prof Exp:* Grad teaching asst, Dept Biol Chem, Univ Mich, 70-74; postdoctoral fel, Sect Biochem, Cornell Univ, 74-76; asst prof chem, Western Ill Univ, 76-78; from asst prof to assoc prof, Div Biochem, Med Br, Univ Tex, Galveston, 78-87. *Concurrent Pos:* Prin investr, Western Ill Univ, NIH, Am Diabetes Asn, Muscular Dystrophy Asn & Am Heart Asn, 77-89; mem, Cancer Ctr Rev Comt, Med Br, Univ Tex, 78-86, Biochem Grad Student Adv Comt, 81-87 & Biohazards Comt, 83-84; co-investr, NIH, 82-91 & NSF, 84-85; adj assoc prof, Dept Physiol, Univ Pa, Philadelphia, 88- *Mem:* Am Chem Soc; AAAS; Am Soc Biol Chemists; Soc Gen Physiologists. *Mailing Add:* Bockus Res Inst Grad Hosp 415 S 19th St Philadelphia PA 19146-1464. *Fax:* 215-893-4178

LABEN, ROBERT COCHRANE, GENETICS, ANIMAL HUSBANDRY. *Current Pos:* instr animal husb & jr animal husbandman, Univ Calif, Davis, 50-52, asst prof & asst animal husbandman, 52-58, assoc prof & assoc animal husbandman, 58-64, prof, animal husbandman & dir comput ctr, 64-69, dept vchmn, 78-82, prof animal sci & geneticist, exp sta, 69-86, EMER PROF ANIMAL SCI, EXP STA, UNIV CALIF, DAVIS, 86- *Personal Data:* b Darien Center, NY, Nov 16, 20; m 46; c 4. *Educ:* Cornell Univ, BS, 42; Okla Agr & Mech Col, MS, 46; Univ Mo, PhD(animal breeding), 50. *Prof Exp:* Asst animal husb, Okla Agr & Mech Col, 46-47; asst dairy husb, Univ Mo, 47-49, asst instr, 49-50. *Mem:* Am Soc Animal Sci; Biomet Soc; Am Dairy Sci Asn; Am Genetic Asn; Sigma Xi. *Res:* Breeding and genetics of farm livestock. *Mailing Add:* 502 Oak Ave Davis CA 95616

LABER, LARRY JACKSON, PLANT PHYSIOLOGY. *Current Pos:* PVT PRACT OUTPATIENT PSYCHOLOGIST, 86- *Personal Data:* b Lincoln, Vt, July 9, 37; m 63. *Educ:* Univ Vt, BS, 59, MS, 61; Univ Chicago, PhD(bot), 67. *Prof Exp:* Asst prof, Pa State Univ, 65-66; NSF trainee, Univ Ga, 67-69; NIH trainee, Brandeis Univ, 69-70; asst prof bot, Univ Maine, Orono, 70-76, assoc prof, 77-83. *Mem:* AAAS; Am Soc Plant Physiol; Japanese Soc Plant Physiol. *Res:* Choroplast development; photophosphorylation; carbon dioxide fixation. *Mailing Add:* 17 Sunset Dr Orono ME 04473

LABERGE, GENE L, GEOLOGY. *Current Pos:* from asst prof to assoc prof, 65-74, PROF GEOL, UNIV WIS-OSHKOSH, 74- *Personal Data:* b Ladysmith, Wis, Mar 15, 32; m 62; c 2. *Educ:* Univ Wis, BS, 58, MS, 59, PhD(geol), 63. *Prof Exp:* Sponsored res officer, Commonwealth Sci & Indust Res Orgn, Melbourne, Australia, 63-64; Nat Res Coun Can fel, Geol Surv Can, 64-65. *Concurrent Pos:* Mem staff, Wis Geol & Natural Hist Surv, 72- *Mem:* AAAS; Geol Soc Am; Soc Econ Geologists. *Res:* Origin of Precambrian iron formations; Precambrian geology and mineral deposits of Wisconsin. *Mailing Add:* Dept Geol Univ Wis 800 Algoma Blvd Oshkosh WI 54901-3551

LABERGE, WALLACE E, ENTOMOLOGY. *Current Pos:* assoc taxonomist, 65-67, TAXONOMIST, ILL NATURAL HIST SURV, 67-; PROF ENTOM, UNIV ILL, URBANA, 70- *Personal Data:* b Grafton, NDak, Feb 7, 27; m 58; c 3. *Educ:* Univ NDak, BSc, 49, MS, 51; Univ Kans, PhD(entom), 55. *Prof Exp:* Asst cur, Snow Entom Mus & instr entom, Univ Kans, 54-55, asst prof, 55-56; asst prof zool, Iowa State Univ, 56-59; assoc prof entom, Univ Nebr, 59-65. *Mem:* Entom Soc Am; Soc Study Evolution; Soc Syst Zool; Am Entom Soc; Sigma Xi. *Res:* Systematics of Hymenoptera, Apoidea and Braconidae. *Mailing Add:* 2012 S Race St Urbana IL 61801

LABERGE, WALTER B, ASTROPHYSICS. *Current Pos:* CONSULT. *Personal Data:* b Chicago, Ill, Mar 29, 24; m 82; c 5. *Educ:* Univ Notre Dame, BS in Naval Sci, 44, BS, 47, PhD(physics), 50. *Prof Exp:* Vpres, Defense Div, Philco-Ford, 57-70; tech dir, Naval Weapons Ctr, China Lake, Calif, 70-73; asst secy Air Force, Res & develop, 73-75; asst secy gen, NATO, Brussels, 75-76; under secy Army, 76-79; prin dep to Dr William Perry, under Secy Defense, 79-81; exec asst to pres, Lockheed Corp, 81-82, vpres planning & technol, 82-84, vpres & gen mgr, Res & Develop Div, 84-86, vpres corp develop, 86-88; chair acquisition mgt policy, Defense Systs Mgt Col, Ft Belvoir, Va, 89- *Concurrent Pos:* Mem, Bd Army Sci & Technol, Nat Acad Eng, 82-88, Army Sci Bd, 83-89; vis scholar, Stanford Univ, 89- *Mem:* Nat Acad Eng. *Res:* One of the principal inventors of the Sidewinder air to air missile. *Mailing Add:* 8104 Shardonay Cove Austin TX 78750

LABES, MORTIMER MILTON, CHEMICAL PHYSICS. *Current Pos:* PROF CHEM, TEMPLE UNIV, 70- *Personal Data:* b Newton, Mass, Sept 9, 29; m 53, 72, Dina Shachar; c 6. *Educ:* Harvard Univ, AB, 50; Mass Inst Technol, PhD, 54. *Prof Exp:* Asst, Mass Inst Technol, 51-54, res chemist, Sprague Elec Co, 54-57; sr res chemist, Franklin Inst, 57-59, sr staff chemist, 59-60, lab mgr, 60-61, tech dir chem div, 61-66; prof chem, Drexel Inst, 66-70. *Mem:* Am Chem Soc; Am Phys Soc; Sigma Xi. *Res:* Chemistry and physics of organic solid state; molecular complexes; liquid crystals; electronic properties of polymers; synthesis and properties of carbon fibers and carbon composites; preparation and properties of fullerenes. *Mailing Add:* Dept Chem Temple Univ Philadelphia PA 19122. *Fax:* 215-204-1532; *E-Mail:* labes@materials.temple.edu

LABIANCA, DOMINICK A, ORGANIC CHEMISTRY, POLYMER CHEMISTRY. *Current Pos:* asst prof to assoc prof, New Sch Lib Arts, 72-80, assoc prof, 80-83; PROF, DEPT CHEM, BROOKLYN COL, CITY UNIV NY, 83- *Personal Data:* b Brooklyn, NY, Feb 4, 43; m 73, Carol A Rudow; c Dominick K. *Educ:* Polytech Inst Brooklyn, BS, 65; Univ Mich, PhD(chem), 69. *Prof Exp:* NSF fel org photochem, Calif Inst Technol, 69-70; res chemist, Res & Develop, Bound Brook Tech Ctr, Union Carbide Corp, 70-72. *Concurrent Pos:* Consult, expert witness in driving while intoxicated & related cases, 85- *Mem:* NY Acad Sci; Sigma Xi; Am Chem Soc; Nat Sci Teachers Asn; AAAS. *Res:* Chemical education; chemistry/humanities integration, curriculum development; chemistry of breath-alcohol testing; science education. *Mailing Add:* 189 Ribbon St Franklin Square NY 11010. *Fax:* 718-951-4607

LABIANCA, FRANK MICHAEL, UNDERWATER ACOUSTICS, ACOUSTIC SIGNAL PROCESSING. *Current Pos:* mem tech staff, 67-85, tech supvr, 85-92, TECH MGR, AT&T BELL LABS, 93- *Personal Data:* b Brooklyn, NY, Aug 17, 39; m 70, Ann Piscitelli; c Carla & Elena. *Educ:* Polytech Inst Brooklyn, BEE, 61, MS, 63, PhD(elec eng), 67. *Prof Exp:* Instr elec eng, Polytech Inst Brooklyn, 61-67. *Concurrent Pos:* Prin investr, Off Naval Res & other govt agencies. *Mem:* Inst Elec & Electronics Engrs; Sigma Xi. *Res:* Propagation in surface ducts and underwater channel, scattering of sound from the ocean surface, radiation from cavitating propellers and the origins of ambient noise; adaptive array processing for underwater acoustic detection of signals in noise; speech recognition; digital filter design; LMS techniques in algorithm design with application to active control of sound and vibration. *Mailing Add:* 2 Slope Dr Cedar Knolls NJ 07927-1516. *Fax:* 973-386-6616; *E-Mail:* hogpb!fmlab@hogpa.ho.att.com

LABINGER, JAY ALAN, INORGANIC CHEMISTRY, ORGANOMETALLIC CHEMISTRY. *Current Pos:* MEM PROF STAFF & ADMINR, BECKMAN INST, CALIF INST TECHNOL, 86- *Personal Data:* b Los Angeles, Calif, July 6, 47; m 70; c 1. *Educ:* Harvey Mudd Col, BS, 68; Harvard Univ, PhD(chem), 72. *Prof Exp:* Res assoc chem, Princeton Univ, 73-74, instr, 74-75; asst prof chem, Univ Notre Dame, 75-81; sr res chemist, Occidental Res Corp, 81-83; res adv, Arco, 83-86. *Concurrent Pos:* Assoc ed, Chem Revs, 79-81; ed, J Molecular Catalysis, 94- *Mem:* Am Chem Soc; Soc Lit & Sci; AAAS. *Res:* Synthetic and mechanistic organo-transition metal chemistry; activation of small molecules by transition metal complexes; homogeneous and heterogeneous catalysis; alkane activation. *Mailing Add:* Calif Inst Technol 139-74 Pasadena CA 91125. *Fax:* 626-449-4159; *E-Mail:* jal@cco.caltech.edu

LABISKY, RONALD FRANK, WILDLIFE BIOLOGY, FISHERIES SCIENCE. *Current Pos:* actg dir & asst dir, Univ Fla, 76-78, prof & wildlife coordr, Sch Forest Resources & Conserv, 78-84, chair, 84-87, PROF, DEPT WILDLIFE ECOL & CONSERV, UNIV FLA, 84- *Personal Data:* b Aberdeen, SDak, Jan 16, 34; div; c Dawn A & Holly H. *Educ:* SDak State Univ, BS, 55; Univ Wis, MS, 56, PhD(wildlife ecol-zool), 68. *Honors & Awards:* Grad Fac Adv Award, Am Fisheries Soc, 78; Spec Recognition Serv Award, Wildlife Soc, 88; Spec Recognition Serv Award, Nat Asn State Univ & Land-Grant Cols, 95. *Prof Exp:* Field asst game bird res, Ill State Natural Hist Surv, 56-57, from asst proj leader to proj leader, 57-59, from asst wildlife specialist to assoc wildlife specialist, 59-72, wildlife specialist, 72-76. *Concurrent Pos:* Chmn, Nat Fish & Wildlife Resources Res Coun, 78-; chmn, Fish & Wildlife Resources Sect, Nat Asn State Univ & Land Grant Col, 84-95; assoc ed, J Wildlife Mgt, 83-86, adv bd, Critical Rev in Natural Resources Mgt, 87-88. *Mem:* Am Fisheries Soc; Wildlife Soc; Am Ornith Union; Wilson Ornith Soc; Am Soc Mammal. *Res:* Ecology and physiology of gallinaceous game birds, doves and waterfowl; population ecology, social biology and spatial distribution of pheasants and white-tailed deer; ecological, ethological, physiological and nutritive factors influencing distribution and abundance of terrestrial and aquatic wildlife; biology and management of spiny lobsters and deep-water reef fishes; ecology and management of nongame and endangered wildlife, particularly red-cockaded woodpeckers; wildlife conservation. *Mailing Add:* Dept Wildlife Ecol & Conserv Univ Fla Gainesville FL 32611-0430. *E-Mail:* rfla@gnv.ifas.ufl.edu

LABODA, HENRY M, EXPERIMENTAL BIOLOGY, LIPIDS. *Current Pos:* SR SCIENTIST, SCHERING-PLOUGH HEALTHCARE PROD, MEMPHIS, TENN, 88- *Personal Data:* b Kingston, Pa, Dec 9, 50; m, Beverly A Lyman; c Alex & Elizabeth. *Educ:* Wilkes Col, BS, 72; Temple Univ, MS, 76; Hahnemann Univ, PhD(biol chem), 81. *Prof Exp:* Med technologist, Robert Packer Mem Hosp, Sayre, Pa, 72-74; biochemist, EM Sci, Gibbstown, NJ, 81-82; clin chemist, Cooper Hosp, Camden, NJ, 82-83; NIH postdoctoral trainee, Dept Physiol & Biochem, Med Col Pa, Philadelphia, 83-86; fel, Biophys Inst, Boston Univ Med Ctr, 86-88. *Concurrent Pos:* Mem, Prog Comt, Am Chem Soc, 90-92. *Mem:* Am Soc Biochem & Molecular Biol; Am Chem Soc. *Res:* Analytical and preparative chromatographic methods; enzyme assay development; peroutaneous penetration-topical drug delivery; spectrophotometric methods; enzyme-linked immunosorbent assay; surface chemistry techniques including lipid monolayers, force-area isotherms and enzymatic hydrolysis; analytical method development. *Mailing Add:* 8540 Nottingwood Dr Cincinnati OH 45255. *Fax:* 901-320-5526

LA BONTE, ANTON EDWARD, MACHINE INTELLIGENCE, TECHNOLOGY TRANSFER. *Current Pos:* RETIRED. *Personal Data:* b Minneapolis, Minn, May 6, 35; m 59, Ana M Pelak. *Educ:* Univ Minn, Minneapolis, BS, 57, MSEE, 60, PhD(elec eng), 66. *Prof Exp:* Instr elec eng, Univ Minn, Minneapolis, 59-62, res fel micromagnetics, 62-63, instr elec eng, 63-65; sr scientist, Control Data Corp, 66-69, mgr systs analysis, 69-75, sr tech consult, corp res & eng, 75-89; consult, 89. *Mem:* Inst Elec & Electronics Engrs; Cognitive Sci Soc; Am Asn Artificial Intel. *Res:* Machine intelligence with emphasis on knowledge-based information and decision systems; technology transfer strategies and techniques. *Mailing Add:* 4729 30th Ave S Minneapolis MN 55406

LABORDE, ALICE L, BIOCHEMISTRY, CELL BIOLOGY. *Current Pos:* Sr res scientist, Infectious Dis Res, 79-86, SR RES SCIENTIST, CHEM & BIOL SCREENING, UPJOHN CO, 86- *Personal Data:* b Jan 8, 47. *Educ:* La Col, BS, 70; Univ Southwestern La, MS, 72; Univ Tex, Austin, PhD(microbiol), 79. *Mem:* Am Soc Microbiol; Soc Indust Microbiol; Am Soc Biochem & Molecular Biol. *Res:* Development of screening assays and systems to detect novel therapeutic agents from natural products and/or chemical libraries; development of robotic systems to automate screens to ensure that a high volume of samples can be rapidly and successfully processed. *Mailing Add:* Chem & Biol Screening Upjohn Co 301 Henrietta St Kalamazoo MI 49007-4940. *Fax:* 616-385-5225

LABOSKY, PETER, JR, WOOD CHEMISTRY, PULP & PAPER. *Current Pos:* assoc pulp & paper, 79-85, PROF WOOD CHEM, PA STATE UNIV, 85- *Personal Data:* b Manville, NJ, Jan 9, 37; m 67, Maryann Federovich; c Kevin & MaryJo. *Educ:* Rutgers Univ, BS, 63; Va Polytech Inst, MS, 67, PhD(wood technol), 70. *Prof Exp:* Res engr, Westvaco Corp, 70-74; assoc exten, Clemson Univ, 74-79. *Mem:* Tech Asn Pulp & Paper Indust; Forest Prod Soc; Soc Wood Sci & Technol. *Res:* Relationship of fiber properties to paper properties; biopulping; kraft pulping of hardwoods; bark chemistry; author of many publications; wood composites. *Mailing Add:* 309 FRL Pa State Univ University Park PA 16802. *Fax:* 814-865-7193

LABOUNTY, JAMES FRANCIS, SR, LIMNOLOGY, LAKE MANAGEMENT. *Current Pos:* Fish & wildlife biologist, US Bur Reclamation, Boulder City, Nev, 69-72, environ specialist, Phoenix, Ariz, 72-74, res biologist, Eng & Res Ctr, Denver, 74-80, tech specialist, 80-84, HEAD, ENVIRON SCI SECT, ENG & RES CTR, US BUR RECLAMATION, DENVER, 84- *Personal Data:* b Minneapolis, Minn, Dec 14, 42; m 69; c 2. *Educ:* Univ Nev, Las Vegas, BS & BA, 67, MS, 68; Ariz State Univ, Tempe, PhD(zool), 74. *Concurrent Pos:* Prin investr, US Bur Reclamation, Denver, 74-84; lectr, Univ Colo, Denver, 77-78; bd dir, NAm Lake Mgt Soc. *Mem:* NAm Lake Mgt Soc; Am Fisheries Soc; Southwestern Asn Naturalists; Desert Fishes Coun; Am Soc Ichthyologists & Herpetologists. *Res:* Performing applied investigations on the ecology of lakes, reservoir and streams and in particular the nature of eutrophication research program for the US Bureau of Reclamation. *Mailing Add:* 13222 W LaSalle Circle Lakewood CO 80228-4932

LABOV, JAY BRIAN, PRE-COLLEGE & UNDER GRADUATE SCIENCE EDUCATION. *Current Pos:* asst prof, 79-84, ASSOC PROF BIOL, COLBY COL, 84- *Personal Data:* b Philadelphia, Pa, Sept 19, 50; m 75, Jeriestra; c Adam & Rachel. *Educ:* Univ Miami, Fla, BS, 72; Univ RI, MS, 74, PhD(biol sci), 79. *Prof Exp:* Instr biol, Wash & Lee Univ, 78-79. *Concurrent Pos:* Vis investr, Jackson Lab, 81; vis scientist, Monell Chem Senses Ctr, 85-86; fel, W K Kellogg Found Nat Fel Prog, 88-91; study dir, Comt Undergrad Educ, Nat Res Coun, 93- *Mem:* Animal Behav Soc; AAAS; Am Soc Zoologists; Am Soc Mammalogists; Nat Sci Teachers Asn; Sigma Xi. *Res:* Behavioral and physiological aspects of mammalian reproduction; pre-college and undergraduate science education. *Mailing Add:* Dept Biol Colby Col 5720 Mayflower Hill Waterville ME 04901-9989. *Fax:* 202-334-2154; *E-Mail:* jlabov@nas.edu

LABOWS, JOHN NORBERT, JR, ORGANIC CHEMISTRY. *Current Pos:* res assoc, Colgate Palmolive Co, 85-87, sr res assoc, 87-90, assoc res fel, 90-96, ASSOC DIR, COLGATE PALMOLIVE CO, 96- *Personal Data:* b Wilkes-Barre, Pa, June 27, 41; m 64, Mary L Parente; c Steven, Christopher, Gregory & Jennifer. *Educ:* Lafayette Col, BS, 63; Cornell Univ, PhD(org chem), 67. *Prof Exp:* Asst prof org chem, Wilkes Col, 67-70, assoc prof, 70-78; asst mem, Monell Chem Senses Ctr, 78-80, assoc mem, 80-85. *Concurrent Pos:* Nat Cancer Inst fel, Fels Res Inst, Temple Univ, 70-71. *Mem:* Am Chem Soc; Sigma Xi; Asn Chemoreception Sci; Soc Cosmetic Chemists. *Res:* Gas chromatography mass spectrometry analysis; physical chemistry of flavors and fragrances; chemical communication; odor/fragrance analysis. *Mailing Add:* Colgate-Palmolive Res Ctr 909 River Rd Piscataway NJ 08855-1343. *E-Mail:* john__labows@colpal.com

LABRECQUE, DOUGLAS R, EXPERIMENTAL BIOLOGY. *Current Pos:* CHIEF GI, IOWA CITY VET ADMIN HOSP, 82- *Prof Exp:* Dir liver serv, 79, PROF INTERNAL MED, UNIV IOWA, 87- *Mailing Add:* Dept Internal Med Univ Iowa Hosps & Clins 4553-G JCP 200 Hawkins Dr Iowa City IA 52242. *Fax:* 319-353-6399

LABREE, THEODORE ROBERT, BACTERIOLOGY, FOOD TECHNOLOGY. *Current Pos:* TECH DIR, CORP RES & DEVELOP QUAL ASSURANCE, ERLY JUICE INC, 89- *Personal Data:* b Lafayette, Ind, June 25, 31; m 51; c 2. *Educ:* Purdue Univ, BS, 58, MS, 60. *Prof Exp:* Res asst food technol, Purdue Univ, 58-59; assoc bacteriologist, Mead Johnson & Co, 59-62, scientist bact, 62-65, mgr med admin, 65-73; tech dir regulatory affairs, Riviana Foods, Inc, 73-86; coordr & mgr qual assurance, Trbesweet Co Inc, 86-89. *Mem:* Am Soc Microbiol; Inst Food Technologists. *Res:* Active oxygen method; spore destruction of food spoilage organisms; new methods development; microbiology; government regulations, processing, packaging, labeling; good manufacturing practices regulations; low acid; sanitation; food plant; warehouse evaluation; pesticides; fumigation. *Mailing Add:* 9839 Canoga Lane Houston TX 77080

LABRIE, DAVID ANDRE, MICROBIOLOGY, BIOCHEMICAL GENETICS. *Current Pos:* from asst prof to assoc prof, 70-81, dept head, 86-90, PROF BIOL, WTEX STATE UNIV, 81- *Personal Data:* b Baltimore, Md, Mar 23, 37; m 62; c Walter & Gwynne. *Educ:* Bethany Col, WVa, AB, 61; NMex Highlands Univ, MS, 65; NC State Univ, PhD(microbiol), 68. *Prof Exp:* NIH fel, Univ Tex, Austin, 68-70. *Mem:* AAAS; Sigma Xi; Nat Asn Biol Teachers. *Res:* Microbiology genetics of antibiotic resistance and ultraviolet light. *Mailing Add:* Dept Life Earth & Environ Sci WTex A&M Univ Canyon TX 79016

LABRIE, FERNAND, ENDOCRINOLOGY, HORMONE-SENSITIVE CANCER. *Current Pos:* From asst prof to assoc prof physiol, 66-73, HEAD, LAB MOLECULAR ENDOCRINOL, HOSP CTR, LAVAL UNIV, 69-, PROF PHYSIOL, 73-, DIR RES CTR, CTR HOSP UNIV LAVAL, 82-, HEAD, DEPT PHYSIOL, 90- *Personal Data:* b June 28, 37; Can citizen; m 63; c 4. *Educ:* Laval Univ, BA, 57, MD, 62, PhD(endocrinol), 67; FRCP(C), 73. *Hon Degrees:* DSc, Univ Caen, France, 96. *Honors & Awards:* Order of Can, 82; Nat Order of Que, 91. *Concurrent Pos:* Med Res Coun Can fels, Laval Univ, 63-66, Univ Cambridge, 66-67, Univ Sussex, 67-68 & centennial fel, Lab Molecular Biol, Univ Cambridge, 68-69; Med Res Coun Can scholar, Laval Univ, 69-, assoc, 73-; dir molecular endocrinol, Med Res Coun Group, 73-, emer scientist, 96-; pres, Can Soc Clin Invest, 82, Can Soc Endocrinol Metab, 84. *Mem:* Am Soc Biol Chemists; Am Physiol Soc; Endocrine Soc; Can Physiol Soc; Can Biochem Soc; Am Soc Androl. *Res:* Molecular biology and regulation of formation and action of androgens and estrogens with speical application in prostate and breast cancer. *Mailing Add:* Ctr Hosp Univ Laval 2705 Blvd Laurier Rm T-367 Ste Foy PQ G1V 4G2 Can. *Fax:* 418-654-2735; *E-Mail:* fernand.labrie@crchul.ulaval.ca

LABUDA, DAMIAN, BIOCHEMISTRY OF NUCLEIC ACIDS, MOLECULAR HUMAN & MAMMALIAN GENETICS. *Current Pos:* from res assoc, 82-84, from asst prof to assoc prof, 84-94, PROF GENOMICS, DEPT PEDIAT, UNIV MONTREAL, 94- *Personal Data:* b Poznan, Poland, Sept 25, 49; Can citizen; m 74, Malgorzata Kranz; c Marcin, Zuzanna & Aleksander. *Educ:* Adam Mickiewicz Univ-Poznan, Poland, MS, 71, PhD(biochem), 76. *Prof Exp:* Asst adj biochem, Inst Biol, Adam Mickiewicz Univ, 71-82. *Concurrent Pos:* Fel, Inst Plant Physiol, Hungarian Acad Sci, Szeged, 71-72; fel, Max-Planck Inst Biophys Chem, Gottingen, 78-82. *Mem:* Genetic Soc Am; Can Genetic Soc; Soc Molecular Biol & Evolution; Am Soc Human Genetics; Int Soc Molecular Evolution; Human Genome Orgn. *Res:* Structure and evolutionary history of the human genome; origins of human genomic diversity and the mechanism of mutations involved; medical applications of molecular genetics in diagnosis and mapping of hereditary disorders; after mechanism of mutations involved evolution of human populations, mammalian and primate evolution, genome mapping. *Mailing Add:* Res Ctr Ste Justine Hospital Pediat Dept Univ Montreal 3175 Ch Cote Ste Catherine Montreal PQ H3T 1C5 Can. *Fax:* 514-345-4801; *E-Mail:* labuda@ere.umontreal.ca

LABUDA, MITCHELL JOSEPH, PROCESS ENGINEERING, THIN FILMS ENGINEERING. *Current Pos:* PROCESS ENGR, CRYSTAL TECHNOL INC, 96- *Personal Data:* b Highland Park, Ill, Oct 16, 67; m, Ava V Ackerman. *Educ:* Univ Ill, BS, 90; Univ Wis-Madison, PhD(chem), 96. *Mem:* Am Chem Soc. *Res:* Crystal technology; cleaning and thin film deposition processes. *Mailing Add:* 1040 E Meadow Circle Palo Alto CA 94303-4230

LABUDDE, ROBERT ARTHUR, LASER ANNEALING, DIGITAL CODING. *Current Pos:* PRES, LEAST COST FORMULATIONS, LTD, 79- *Personal Data:* b Flint, Mich, May 28, 47; m 69; c 2. *Educ:* Univ Mich, Ann Arbor, BS, 69; Univ Wis-Madison, PhD(chem), 73. *Prof Exp:* Res asst chem, Univ Wis, 68-73, lectr comput sci, 73, asst scientist, math res ctr, 73-74; instr appl math, Mass Inst Technol, 74-75; asst prof math & comput sci, Old Dom Univ, Norfolk, Va, 76-79; exec vpres, Labudde Eng Corp, 83-86. *Concurrent Pos:* Consult, Gen Systs Div, IBM, 75-78, Res Ctr, Allied Tech Corp, 77-78, Digital Design Labs, 79, Burroughs Corp, 80-82 & Optical Coating Labs, Inc, 82-83; secy, ERB Leasing Co, Inc, 83-86; mem bd dirs, Tech Express Inc, 90. *Mem:* Am Soc Indust & Appl Math; Asn Comput Mach; Am Soc Testing & Mat; Am Soc Qual Control; Inst Indust Engrs; Inst Food Technologists; Sigma Xi. *Res:* Theoretical modeling of laser-based optical disk memory systems, including thermal, optical and thin-film properties; noise sources and kinetics of environmental degradaation; digital coding and communication. *Mailing Add:* 824 Timberlake Dr Virginia Beach VA 23464-3239

LABUDDE, SAMUEL FREEMAN, ENVIRONMENTAL ACTIVIST. *Current Pos:* STAFF BIOLOGIST, MARINE MAMMAL FUND, 87- *Personal Data:* b Madison, Wis, July 3, 56. *Educ:* Ind Univ, BA, 86. *Honors & Awards:* Goldman Award, NAm Goldman Found, 91. *Concurrent Pos:* Fisheries biologist, Nat Marine Fisheries Serv, 87; staff biologist, Earth Island Inst, 87-94; field biologist, Earthtrust, Honolulu, 89-90; field investr, Friends of Animals, 90; EC marine policy consult, Humane Soc US, 90-93. *Res:* East Pacific dolphin slaughter by tuna industry; Asian driftnet fleets; illegal trade in tigers and other endangered species. *Mailing Add:* Endangered Species Proj E-205 Ft Mason Ctr San Francisco CA 94123

LABUTE, JOHN PAUL, MATHEMATICS. *Current Pos:* asst prof, 67-70, ASSOC PROF MATH, MCGILL UNIV, 70- *Personal Data:* b Tecumseh, Ont, Feb 26, 38; m 61; c 3. *Educ:* Univ Windsor, BSc, 60; Harvard Univ, MA, 61, PhD(math), 65. *Prof Exp:* Nat Res Coun Can res fel, Col France, 65-67. *Mem:* Can Math Cong; Am Math Soc. *Res:* Algebra and number theory. *Mailing Add:* Dept Math McGill Univ 805 Sherbrooke St W West Montreal PQ H3A 2K6 Can. *Fax:* 514-398-3899; *E-Mail:* labute@math.mcgill.ca

LABUZA, THEODORE PETER, FOOD SCIENCE, PHYSICAL CHEMISTRY. *Current Pos:* assoc prof, 71-72, PROF FOOD TECHNOL, UNIV MINN, ST PAUL, 72-, ASSOC DEAN GRAD SCH. *Personal Data:* b Perth Amboy, NJ, Nov 10, 40; m 85; c 2. *Educ:* Mass Inst Technol, SB, 62, PhD(food sci), 65. *Honors & Awards:* Samuel Cate Precott Res Award, Inst Food Technologists, 72, Cruess Award, 73, Babcock Hart Award, 88; Howard Lectr, Univ Ill, 87. *Prof Exp:* From instr to assoc prof food eng, Mass Inst Technol, 65-71. *Concurrent Pos:* Food processing consult. *Mem:* Fel Inst Food Technologists (pres, 88-89); Am Inst Chem Eng; Am Chem Soc; Am Asn Cereal Chemists; Asn Food & Drug Officials; Sigma Xi. *Res:* Physical chemical factors involved in water in foods; reaction kinetics and prediction of food storage life; stability of intermediate moisture foods; nutrient degradation in processing; kinetics of microbial growth and death; plant tissue culture; edible films. *Mailing Add:* Dept Food Sci & Nutrit Univ Minn St Paul MN 55108. *Fax:* 612-483-3302; *E-Mail:* tplabuza@epx.cls.umn.edu

LACASCE, ELROY OSBORNE, JR, ACOUSTICS. *Current Pos:* from instr to prof, 54-93, chmn dept, 77-88, EMER PROF PHYSICS, BOWDOIN COL, 93- *Personal Data:* b Fryeburg, Maine, Jan 17, 23. *Educ:* Bowdoin Col, AB, 43; Harvard Univ, AM, 51; Brown Univ, PhD(physics), 55. *Prof Exp:* Instr physics, Bowdoin Col, 43 & 47-49, instr math, 51; physicist, Naval Res Lab, 44; foreign serv officer, US Dept State, 45-46; teacher, high sch, 46-47. *Concurrent Pos:* Res assoc, Yale Univ, 60-61; NSF fac fel, 60-61; vis investr, Woods Hole Oceanog Inst, 68-69, guest investr, 75-76 & 82-83. *Mem:* Emer mem Acoust Soc Am. *Res:* Ultrasonics and underwater sound. *Mailing Add:* Dept Physics & Astron Bowdoin Col Brunswick ME 04011-2546

LACEFIELD, GARRY DALE, FORAGE PRODUCTION & MANAGEMENT. *Current Pos:* from asst exten prof to assoc exten prof, 74-82, EXTEN FORAGE SPECIALIST, 74- & EXTEN PROF, UNIV KY, 82- *Personal Data:* b McHenry, Ky, Aug 22, 45; m 67; c 2. *Educ:* Western Ky Univ, BS, 70, MS, 71; Univ Mo, PhD(agron & physiol), 74. *Honors & Awards:* Exten Specialist of the Year, 83. *Prof Exp:* Lab instr & instr plant sci, Western Ky Univ, 69-71; teaching asst, Univ Mo, 71-74. *Mem:* Am Soc Agron; Am Forage & Grassland Coun. *Res:* Development and implementation of improved practices in forage establishment, production and utilization. *Mailing Add:* 304 Holly Lane Princeton KY 42445

LACELLE, PAUL (LOUIS), HEMATOLOGY, PHYSIOLOGY. *Current Pos:* from sr instr to prof, 67-74, chmn dept, 77, PROF BIOPHYS, SCH MED, UNIV ROCHESTER, 74-, SR ASSOC DEAN ACAD AFFAIRS & RES. *Personal Data:* b Syracuse, NY, July 4, 29; m 53; c 4. *Educ:* Houghton Col, BA, 51; Univ Rochester, MD, 59. *Honors & Awards:* Sr Humboldt Award. *Prof Exp:* Intern & resident, Strong Mem Hosp, Univ Rochester, 59-62; fel biophys, Atomic Energy Comn, 62-65; NIH Spec fel, Univ Saarland, 65-66. *Concurrent Pos:* Buswell fel, Sch Med, Univ Rochester, 66-67; NIH res grant, 70- *Mem:* Biophys Soc; Am Phys Soc; Am Soc Hemat; Am Fedn Clin Res; Biorheology, Europ Microcirculation. *Res:* Biophysical properties of blood cells; microcirculation. *Mailing Add:* Box 706 601 Elmwood Ave Rochester NY 14642-8408. *Fax:* 716-256-1131; *E-Mail:* pllace@biophysics.rochester.edu

LACERDA, ALEX HUGO, LOW TEMPERATURE PHYSICS, HIGH MAGNETIC FIELD PHYSICS. *Current Pos:* HEAD LOW TEMP PHYSICS, NAT HIGH MAGNETIC FIELD LAB, LOS ALAMOS NAT LAB, 93- *Personal Data:* b Pernambuco, Brazil, Jan 2, 62; m 86, Andrea Labouriau; c Hugo. *Educ:* UFPE, Brazil, BS, 85; Univ J Fourier, France, MS, 87, PhD(physics), 90. *Prof Exp:* Asst scientist, Fla State Univ, 93-96. *Concurrent Pos:* Japanese Soc Prom Sci fel & vis asst prof, 96; NSF grantee, 96. *Mem:* Am Phys Soc; Brazilian Phys Soc. *Res:* Magnetic and transport properties of novel materials at extreme conditions of very high magnetic fields and low temperature. *Mailing Add:* NHMFL Los Alamos Nat Lab MS E536 Los Alamos NM 87455. *Fax:* 505-665-4311; *E-Mail:* lacerda@lanl.gov

LACEWELL, RONALD DALE, RESOURCE ECONOMICS, PRODUCTION ECONOMICS. *Current Pos:* from asst prof to assoc prof, 70-78, PROF AGR ECON, TEX A&M UNIV, 78- *Personal Data:* b Plainview, Tex, Apr 15, 40; m 62; c 3. *Educ:* Tex Tech Univ, BS, 63, MS, 65; Okla State Univ, PhD(agr econ), 70. *Prof Exp:* Statistician, Bur Census, US Dept Com, 63-64; instr agr econ, Tex Tech Univ, 65-66; economist, Econ Res Serv, US Dept Agr, 67-70. *Concurrent Pos:* Consult, Govt, Legal & Corp. *Mem:* Am Agr Econ Asn. *Res:* Economics of water resources emphasizing agriculture; alternative energy sources and impacts of energy price adjustments; economics and environmental impacts of integrated pest management systems used for crop production. *Mailing Add:* 3337 Golden Trail College Station TX 77845

LACEY, BEATRICE CATES, PSYCHOPHYSIOLOGY. *Current Pos:* mem staff, Fel Res Inst, Wright State Univ, 53-82, sr investr, 66-72, sr scientist, 72-82, fel prof, 77-82, actg sci dir, 79-82, clin prof psychiat, 82-89, EMER FELS PROF, WRIGHT STATE UNIV, 89- *Personal Data:* b New York, NY, July 22, 19; m 38, John I; c Robert A & Carolyn E. *Educ:* Cornell Univ, AB, 40; Antioch Col, MA, 58. *Honors & Awards:* Distinguished Sci Contrib Award, Am Psychol Asn, 76; Psychol Sci Gold Medal Award, Am Psychol Found, 85. *Prof Exp:* From instr to prof psychol, Antioch Col, 56-77, adj prof, 77-82. *Concurrent Pos:* Co-prin investr, USPHS grant, 60-82; assoc ed, Psychophysiol, 71-77. *Mem:* Fel Soc Exp Psychologists; fel Acad Behav Med Res; Soc Psychophysiol Res (pres, 78-79); Soc Neurosci. *Res:* Psychophysiology of the autonomic nervous system. *Mailing Add:* 1425 Meadow Lane Yellow Springs OH 45387-1221

LACEY, ELIZABETH PATTERSON, PLANT ECOLOGY. *Current Pos:* ASST PROF BOT, UNIV NC, GREENSBORO, 78- *Personal Data:* b Cleveland, Ohio. *Educ:* Univ Colo, BA, 69; Univ Mich, MS, 74, PhD(bot), 78. *Mem:* Bot Soc Am; Brit Ecol Soc; Ecol Soc Am; Soc Study Evolution; Sigma Xi. *Res:* Plant population biology; evolution of life history patterns. *Mailing Add:* Dept Biol Univ NC Greensboro NC 27412-0001

LACEY, HOWARD ELTON, MATHEMATICS. *Current Pos:* dept head math, 80-91, ASSOC DEAN, COL SCI, UNIV TEX A&M, 91- *Personal Data:* b Leaky, Tex, Feb 9, 37; m 58; c 4. *Educ:* Abilene Christian Col, BA, 59, MA, 61; NMex State Univ, PhD(math), 63. *Prof Exp:* Asst prof math, Abilene Christian Col, 63-64 & Univ Tex, Austin, 64-67; res assoc, NASA Manned Spacecraft Ctr, 67-68; from assoc prof to prof math, Univ Tex, Austin, 68-80, mem grad fac, 68-80, vchmn dept, 75-77. *Concurrent Pos:* Res assoc, Inst Math, Polish Acad Sci, Warsaw, 72-73. *Mem:* Am Math Soc; Math Asn Am. *Res:* Functional analysis; classical Banach spaces. *Mailing Add:* Tex A&M Univ 4058 Deerfield College Station TX 77845-7847. *Fax:* 409-845-6028

LACEY, JOHN I, PSYCHOPHYSIOLOGY, NEUROPHYSIOLOGY. *Current Pos:* fels prof & chmn dept, 77-82, FELS EMER PROF PSYCHIAT, SCH MED, WRIGHT STATE UNIV, 82- *Personal Data:* b Chicago, Ill, Apr 11, 15; m 38, Beatrice Cates; c Robert A & Carolyn E. *Educ:* Cornell Univ, BA, 37, PhD(psychol), 41. *Honors & Awards:* Distinguished Contrib Award, Soc Psychophysiol Res, 70; Distinguished Sci Contrib Award, Am Psychol Asn, 76; Sci Gold Medal Award, Am Psychol Found, 85. *Prof Exp:* Instr psychol, Queens Col, NY, 41-42; res assoc, Antioch Col, 46-73, from assoc prof to prof psychophysiol & chmn dept, 48-77; sr scientist, Fels Res Inst, 73-77. *Concurrent Pos:* William James fel, Am Psychol Soc, 89; lectr, Ohio State Univ, 50 & sch med, Univ Louisville, 55; fel, Commonwealth Fund, 57-59; mem, Ment Health, Behav Sci & Exp Psychol Study Sects, USPHS, 56-60, Res Career Develop Comt, 64-65; mem, Adv Panel Life Sci Facil, NSF, 60-61; mem coun, Am Psychol Asn, 64-68, 70-73, & 78-79, pres, Div 6, 69-70, bd dirs, 71-77; mem, Clin Prog-Proj Rev Comt, NIMH, 66-71, chmn, 70-71; mem bd sci counr, Nat Inst Aging, 77-80; prof, Antioch Col, 78-82; chmn, Sect J, AAAS, 85-86. *Mem:* Nat Acad Sci; fel Soc Exp Psychologists; Soc Neurosci; fel Acad Behav Med; fel Am Psychol Asn; Int Brain Res Orgn. *Res:* Psychophysiology of the autonomic nervous system and psychosomatic medicine; brain physiology and behavior. *Mailing Add:* 1425 Meadow Lane Yellow Springs OH 45387

LACEY, RICHARD FREDERICK, MAGNETISM. *Current Pos:* physicist, 67-69, STAFF SCIENTIST, HEWLETT-PACKARD LABS, 69-. *Personal Data:* b Vallejo, Calif, May 29, 31; m 71, Ruth Murtagh. *Educ:* Mass Inst Technol, SB, 52, PhD(physics), 59. *Prof Exp:* Sr engr, Sylvania Lighting Prod Co, 59-62; sr scientist, Am Sci & Eng Co, 62-63; sr physicist, Varian Assocs, 63-67. *Mem:* Inst Elec & Electronics Engrs; Am Phys Soc. *Res:* Atomic structure; radio-frequency spectroscopy; physical and quantum electronics. *Mailing Add:* Hewlett-Packard Labs PO Box 10350 Palo Alto CA 94303-0867. *E-Mail:* lacey@hpl.hp.com

LACH, JOSEPH T, PHYSICS. *Current Pos:* chmn, Fermi Lab Physics Dept, 74-75, MEM STAFF, FERMI NAT ACCELERATOR LAB, 69-; RES AFILIARE, ILL STATE GEOL SURV, 87- *Personal Data:* b Chicago, Ill, May 12, 34; m 65. *Educ:* Univ Chicago, AB, 53, MS, 56; Univ Calif, Berkeley, PhD(physics), 63. *Prof Exp:* Res assoc physics, Yale Univ, 63-65, asst prof, 66-69. *Concurrent Pos:* Joint res prog, Leningrad Nuclear Physics Inst (USSR). *Mem:* Am Phys Soc. *Res:* Elementary particle physics; physics electronic data processing. *Mailing Add:* 28 W 364 Indian Knoll Trail West Chicago IL 60185

LACHAINE, ANDRE RAYMOND JOSEPH, OPTICS. *Current Pos:* from asst prof to assoc prof, 76-90, PROF PHYSICS, ROYAL MIL COL CAN, 90- *Personal Data:* b Ottawa, Ont, Sept 22, 45; m 68; c 3. *Educ:* Univ Ottawa, BSc Hons, 67, MSc, 70, PhD(physics), 76. *Prof Exp:* Instr physics, Univ NB, 76. *Concurrent Pos:* Investr contract, 77- *Res:* Photoacoustics and photothermal physics. *Mailing Add:* Dept Physics Royal Mil Col Kingston ON K7K 5L0 Can

LACHANCE, DENIS, FOREST PATHOLOGY, RESEARCH MANAGEMENT. *Current Pos:* res scientist forest path, Laurentian Forestry Ctr, 66-79, HEAD, FOREST INSECT & DIS SURV SECT, CAN FORESTRY SERV, 79-, RES PROJ LEADER, ENVIRON STRESS ON FORESTS, 89- *Personal Data:* b Quebec, Que, Feb 2, 39; m 64, Ruth Gagnon; c Simon, Vincent & Renee. *Educ:* Laval Univ, BSc, 62; Univ Wis-Madison, PhD(phytopath), 66. *Mem:* Can Phytopath Soc (secy-treas, 71-73); Can Inst Forestry; Int Soc Plant Path. *Res:* Hardwood cankers and conifer root rot; hardwood decline diseases (sugar maple) and impact of environmental stress on forest health. *Mailing Add:* 3374 Beauchamps Ste-Foy PQ G1X 2C6 Can. *Fax:* 418-648-5849

LA CHANCE, LEO EMERY, GENETICS. *Current Pos:* CONSULT, 92- *Personal Data:* b Brunswick, Maine, Mar, 1, 31; m 55; c 3. *Educ:* Univ Maine, AB, 53; NC State Col, MS, 55, PhD(genetics), 58. *Prof Exp:* Res assoc biol, Brookhaven Nat Lab, 58-60; insect geneticist, USDA, 60-63, proj leader, Insect Genetics & Radiation Biol Sect, Metab & Radiation Res Lab, Entom Res Div, Agr Res Serv, 63-69; sci officer & head, Insect Eradication & Pest Control Sect, Joint Food & Agr Orgn-Int Atomic Energy Agency, Austria, 69-71; proj leader, Insect Genetics & Radiation Biol Sect, Agr Res Serv, USDA, 71-77, dir, 77-82, supvr insect geneticist & nat tech adv, Metab & Radiation Res Lab, 82-86; dep dir, Joint Food & Agr Org Inst Atomic Energy

Agency, Austria, 86-92. *Concurrent Pos:* Ed, Analysis Entomol Soc Am J, 92- *Mem:* AAAS; Genetics Soc Am; Entom Soc Am. *Res:* Insect genetics and radiation biology; population genetics of screwworms, mechanism of hybrid sterility in Heliothis species; insect cytology and cytogenetic effects of radiation; factors influencing chromosome aberrations and dominant lethal mutations induced by radiation and chemicals; insect reproduction. *Mailing Add:* PO Box 5771 Fargo ND 58105

LACHANCE, MARC-ANDRE, SYSTEMATICS OF YEASTS, EVOLUTION OF YEASTS. *Current Pos:* from asst prof to assoc prof, 79-94, PROF PLANT SCI, UNIV WESTERN ONT, 94- *Personal Data:* m 80, Jane M Bowles. *Educ:* Univ Montreal, BA, 69, BSc, 72; McGill Univ, MSc, 73; Univ Calif, Davis, PhD(microbiol), 77. *Prof Exp:* Fel, Pasteur Inst, 77-78. *Concurrent Pos:* Hon lectr microbiol, Univ Western Ont, 78-; consult, var insts, 79-; mem, Int Comn Yeasts, 88-; assoc ed, Can J Microbiol, 93- *Mem:* Can Soc Microbiologists; Am Soc Microbiol. *Res:* Evolutionary systematics and ecology of yeasts; natural fermentations; speciation in yeasts; yeast predation. *Mailing Add:* Dept Plant Sci Univ Western Ont London ON N6A 5B7 Can. *Fax:* 519-661-3935; *E-Mail:* lachance@julian.uwo.ca

LACHANCE, MURDOCK HENRY, electro optics, for more information see previous edition

LACHANCE, PAUL ALBERT, NUTRITION, FOOD SCIENCE. *Current Pos:* assoc prof food sci, 67-72, dir, Sch Feeding Effectiveness Res Proj, 69-72, PROF NUTRIT & FOOD SCI, RUTGERS UNIV, 72-, DIR, GRAD PROG FOOD SCI, 87- *Personal Data:* b St Johnsbury, Vt, June 5, 33; m 55; c 4. *Educ:* St Michael's Col, Vt, BSc, 55; Univ Ottawa, PhD(biol, nutrit), 60. *Hon Degrees:* DSc, St Michael's Col, 82. *Honors & Awards:* Gemini Prog Achievement Award, NASA, 66. *Prof Exp:* Res biologist, Aerospace Med Res Lab, Wright-Patterson AFB, Ohio, 60-63; coord flight food & nutrit, NASA Manned Spacecraft Ctr, 63-67. *Concurrent Pos:* Lectr, Univ Dayton, 63; chair, Univ Senate & Fac Rep Bd Gov, Rutgers Univ, 90-, actg chair, Dept Food Sci, 90- *Mem:* Fel Inst Food Technologists; Am Soc Clin Nutrit; Am Pub Health Asn; NY Acad Sci; Am Dietetic Asn; fel Am Col Nutrit. *Res:* Aerospace food and nutrition; nutritional toxicology; nutritional aspects of food processing; micronutrient nutrification. *Mailing Add:* Dept Food Sci Rutgers Univ Box 231 New Brunswick NJ 08903-0231. *Fax:* 732-932-6776

LACHAPELLE, RENE CHARLES, MEDICAL MICROBIOLOGY. *Current Pos:* dir, Sch Allied Health, 77 & 82, CHAIRPERSON, DEPT MED TECHNOL, UNIV VT, 74- *Personal Data:* b Joliette, Que, Jan 28, 30; US citizen; m 59; c 3. *Educ:* Seminaire de Joliette, BA, 50; Univ Montreal, BSc, 53; Syracuse Univ, MS, 57, PhD(microbiol), 62. *Prof Exp:* Lab admin dir clin path, Syracuse Mem Hosp, 62-66; assoc prof biol, Univ Dayton, 66-74. *Mem:* Sigma Xi; AAAS; Am Soc Med Tech; Am Soc Microbiol; Can Soc Microbiol. *Res:* Morphogenesis and serological properties of Candida albicans; monomine oxidase and serotonin in germfree animals; skin bacteria in long-term space flights; educational aspects of medical technology; coagglutination of streptococcal groups. *Mailing Add:* Dept Med Technol 302 Rowell Bldg Univ Vt Burlington VT 05401

LACHENBRUCH, ARTHUR HEROLD, HEAT & DEFORMATION IN THE EARTHS CRUST. *Current Pos:* geophysicist, 51-, EMER GEOPHYSICIST, US GEOL SURV. *Personal Data:* b New Rochelle, NY, Dec 7, 25; m 50, Edith Bennett; c Roger, Charles & Barbara. *Educ:* Johns Hopkins Univ, BA, 50; Harvard Univ, MA, 54, PhD(geophys), 58. *Honors & Awards:* Kirk Bryan Award, Geol Soc Am, 63; Distinguished Serv Award, Dept Interior, 78; Walter H Bucher Medal, Am Geophys Union, 89. *Concurrent Pos:* Vis prof, Dartmouth Col, 63. *Mem:* Nat Acad Sci; fel AAAS; fel Am Geophys Union; fel Royal Astron Asn; fel Arctic Inst NAm; fel Geol Soc Am. *Res:* Solid earth geophysics; terrestrial heat flow; tectonophysics; permafrost. *Mailing Add:* Br Tectonophysics US Geol Surv 345 Middlefield Rd Menlo Park CA 94025

LACHENBRUCH, PETER ANTHONY, BIOSTATISTICS. *Current Pos:* STAFF, FOOD & DRUG ADMIN. *Personal Data:* b Los Angeles, Calif, Feb 5, 37; m 62. *Educ:* Univ Calif, Los Angeles, BA, 58, PhD(biostatist), 65; Lehigh Univ, MS, 61. *Honors & Awards:* Mortimer Spiegelman Gold Medal Award, Am Pub Health Asn, 71; fel, Am Statist Asn, 79. *Prof Exp:* Asst math, Lehigh Univ, 58-59; programmer, Douglas Aircraft Co, 59-60; sr opers res analyst, Syst Develop Corp, 60-61; res scientist, Am Res Inst, 61-62; USPHS fel biostatist, Univ Calif, Los Angeles, 62-65; from asst prof to prof biostatist, 65-76; Univ NC, Chapel Hill, 75-76; prof prev med, Univ Iowa, 76; Sch Pub Health, Univ Calif, Los Angeles. *Mem:* AAAS; fel Am Statist Asn; Biomet Soc; Am Pub Health Asn; Royal Statist Soc; Sigma Xi. *Res:* Discriminant analysis; statistical epidemiology; computer analysis of data; survival analysis. *Mailing Add:* Ctr Biol Eval & Res Food & Drug Admin 1401 Rockville Pike HFM 215 Rockville MD 20852-1448

LACHER, ROBERT CHRISTOPHER, TOPOLOGY, APPLIED MATHEMATICS. *Current Pos:* from asst prof to assoc prof, 68-75, PROF MATH, FLA STATE UNIV, 75- *Personal Data:* b Atlanta, Ga, Oct 14, 40. *Educ:* Univ Ga, BS, 62, MA, 64, PhD(math), 66. *Prof Exp:* Asst prof math, Univ Calif, Los Angeles, 66-67; vis mem math, Inst Advan Study, 67-68. *Concurrent Pos:* Alfred P Sloan fel, 70-72; mem, Inst Advan Study, 72; NSF res grants, 72- *Mem:* AAAS; Sigma Xi; Am Math Soc. *Res:* Geometric topology; cell-like mappings and generalized manifolds; embedding problems; catastrophe theory. *Mailing Add:* Dept Comput Sci Fla State Univ Tallahassee FL 32306

LACHER, THOMAS EDWARD, JR, TROPICAL ECOLOGY, CONSERVATION BIOLOGY. *Current Pos:* PROF, DEPT WILDLIFE & FISHERIES SCI, TEX A&M UNIV, 96- *Personal Data:* b Pittsburgh, Pa, Aug 9, 49; m 78, Susana Teixeira; c Iara L & Lais M. *Educ:* Univ Pittsburgh, BS, 72, PhD(biol sci), 80. *Prof Exp:* Teaching asst biol, Univ Pittsburgh, 72-79; asst prof zool, Univ Brazil, 79-81; from asst prof to assoc prof environ studies, Western Wash Univ, 81-89; dir trop ecol & prof, Dept Aquacult, Fisheries & Wildlife & Dept Environ Toxicol, Clemson Univ, 89-96. *Concurrent Pos:* Vis prof, Univ Fed Minas Gerais, 86; consult, World Wildlife Fund, 86, Empresa Brazil Pesquisa Agropecvaria, 88 & Kellogg Found, 91; mem, Species Survival Comm IUCN, 89-, Working Group Comt Nat Inst Environ, 90- *Mem:* AAAS; Am Soc Mammalogists; Ecol Soc Am; Asn Trop Biol; Am Asn Naturalists; Soc Conserv Biol. *Res:* Research on the ecology and conservation of tropical ecosystems; ecological research emphasizes the structure and function of communities of mammals; conservation focusses on sustainable development and restoration of degraded areas. *Mailing Add:* Dept Wildlife & Fisheries Sci 210 Nagle Hall Tex A&M Univ College Station TX 77843-2258. *Fax:* 409-845-4096; *E-Mail:* tlacher@tamu.edu

LACHICA, R VICTOR, CONTROL & MONITORING OF FOOD-BORNE PATHOGENS, MICROBIAL SPOILAGE OF FOODS. *Current Pos:* RES MICROBIOLOGIST, NATICK RES, DEVELOP & ENG CTR, US ARMY, 84- *Personal Data:* b Cebu, Philippines, Feb 24, 43; US citizen; m 74, Lois J Holmes. *Educ:* Wartburg Col, BS, 63, Iowa State Univ, PhD(bact), 67. *Prof Exp:* Res assoc, Univ Wis-Madison, 67-69; asst res microbiologist, Univ Calif-Davis, 69-74; chief, Microbiol Br, WHO, Guatemala, 74-80; adj prof food microbiol, Univ Ariz, Tucson, 81-83; vis microbiologist, USDA Eastern Res Ctr, Philadelphia, 83-84. *Mem:* Am Soc Microbiol; Inst Food Technologists; AAAS; Sigma Xi. *Res:* Accelerated detection and identification of bacterial pathogens and indicator organisms in foods including staphyloccocus aureus, Yersinia enterocolitica and Listeria monocytogenes; control of growth of these pathogens in foods. *Mailing Add:* 241 Indian Camp Lane Lincoln MA 01773. *Fax:* 508-651-5274

LACHIN, JOHN MARION, III, CLINICAL TRIALS. *Current Pos:* from asst res prof to res prof statist, George Washington Univ, 73-84, asst dir, Biostatist Ctr, 80-85, co-dir, 85-88, PROF STATIST, GEORGE WASHINGTON UNIV, 84-, DIR, BIOSTATIST CTR, 88- *Personal Data:* b New Orleans, La, July 4, 42; m 66, Teresa Bohan; c Ellen, Mark & Andrea. *Educ:* Tulane Univ, BS, 65; Univ Pittsburgh, ScD(biostatist), 72. *Prof Exp:* Epidemiologist & dir, Div Prog Info & Eval, Va, 72-73. *Concurrent Pos:* Adj asst prof biometry, Va Commonwealth Univ, 72-73; mem, Serv Res & Epidemiol Studies Rev Comt, NIMH, 77-80, Gastrointestinal Drugs Adv Comt, Food & Drug Admin, 78-82, Data Monitoring Comt, NIH Nat Coop Dialysis Study, 79-81, Opers Comt, Vet Admin Coop Study on Hypertension, 81-86; dir, Biostatist Coord Ctr, Nat Coop Gallstone Study, 78-83, Lupus Nephritis Collab Study, 81-86 & Diabetes Control & Complications Trial, 82-; mem policy adv bd, Hypertension Prevention Trial, NIH, 82-86, chmn treatment effects monitoring & adv comt, Glaucoma Laser Trial, 83- *Mem:* Biomet Soc; fel Am Statist Asn; Soc Epidemiol Res; Soc Clin Trials; Inst Math Stat; Int Soc Clin Biostatist; fel Royal Statist Soc; Int Stat Inst. *Res:* Design, coordination and analysis of medical clinical trials; statistical methodology for design and analysis of clinical trials; medical research in diabetes, renal disease, gallstone disease. *Mailing Add:* Biostatist Ctr George Washington Univ 6110 Executive Blvd Suite 750 Rockville MD 20852. *Fax:* 301-881-3742; *E-Mail:* Bitnet: biostat@gwuvm

LACHMAN, IRWIN MORRIS, CERAMICS ENGINEERING. *Current Pos:* RETIRED. *Personal Data:* b New York, NY, Aug 2, 30; m 59; c 2. *Educ:* Rutgers Univ, BSc, 52; Ohio State Univ, MSc, 53, PhD(ceramic eng), 55. *Prof Exp:* Sr scientist ceramics, Thermo Mat, Inc, 57-58; staff mem, Sandia Corp, 58-60; res assoc ceramics, Corning Glass Works, 60-95. *Mem:* AAAS; fel Am Ceramic Soc; Brit Ceramic Soc; Soc Automotive Engrs. *Res:* Mechanical and thermal properties of ceramics. *Mailing Add:* 19 E Fifth St Corning NY 14830

LACHMAN, LAWRENCE B, CELLULAR BIOLOGY. *Current Pos:* assoc prof, 83-88, PROF, DEPT CELL BIOL, M D ANDERSON CANCER CTR, UNIV TEX, HOUSTON, 88- *Personal Data:* b Denver, Colo, Nov 13, 47. *Educ:* Univ Colo, BA, 69; Boston Univ, PhD(biochem), 73. *Prof Exp:* Res assoc pharmacol, Sch Med, Yale Univ, 73-76; res assoc, Dept Microbiol & Immunol, Div Immunol, Duke Univ Med Ctr, 76-78, med res assoc, 78-79, med res asst prof, 79-82; sr staff scientist, Immunex Corp, Seattle, Wash, 82-83. *Concurrent Pos:* Mem, Duke Comprehensive Cancer Ctr, 81; ed-in-chief, Lymphokine Res, 82-; mem, Biol Response Modifiers Prog, Decision Network Comt, 82-83; NIH grants, 84-87, 86-89, 88-89 & 87-92; mem, AIDS & Related Res Rev Group, NIH-Dept Health & Human Serv, 90- *Mem:* Am Asn Immunol. *Res:* Lymphokines and cytokines; interleukin-1; author or co-author of numerous publications; recipient of one patent. *Mailing Add:* Dept Cell Biol Univ Tex M D Anderson Cancer Ctr 1515 Holcombe Blvd Houston TX 77030. *Fax:* 713-797-9764

LACHMAN, LEON, PHARMACY, QUALITY CONTROL & QUALITY ASSURANCE. *Current Pos:* PRES LACHMAN CONS SERVS INC, WESTBURY, NY, 81- *Personal Data:* b Bronx, NY, Jan 29, 29; m 51, Joan G Kantor; c Larry & Julie. *Educ:* Columbia Univ, BSc, 51, MSc, 53; Univ Wis, PhD, 56. *Hon Degrees:* Dr, Columbia Univ, 76. *Honors & Awards:* Indust Pharmaceut Technol Award, Acad Pharmaceut Sci, 70. *Prof Exp:* Asst dir pharm, Res & Develop Div, Ciba Pharmaceut Co, NJ, 56-68, dir, 68-69; vpres develop & control, Du Pont Pharmaceut, 69-79; sr vpres sci & technol, United Lab Inc, 79-81. *Concurrent Pos:* Vis scientist, Am Asn Cols Pharm; mem bd trustees, Col Pharm, Columbia Univ, 74-78; vis prof, Rutgers Univ Col Pharm, 83- *Mem:* Fel Acad Pharmaceut Sci; hon mem Parenteral Drug Asn (pres, 81-83); Am Chem Soc; Am Asn Pharmaceut Scientists; Acad Pharmaceut Sci (pres). *Res:* Process and equipment design; research and development of pharmaceutical dosage forms; analytical research; quality control practices; medical research; regulatory affairs; Food and Drug Administration regulatory submissions and compliance. *Mailing Add:* Lachman Cons Serv Inc 1600 Stewart Ave Suite 604 Westbury NY 11590-6611. *Fax:* 516-683-1887

LACHS, GERARD, ELECTRONICS. *Current Pos:* PROF ELEC ENG, UNIV SFLA, 84- *Personal Data:* b Essen, Ger, Aug 2, 34; US citizen; m 57, Sandra Jacobson; c Gregory & Melanie. *Educ:* NY Univ, BS, 56; Univ Rochester, MS, 61; Syracuse Univ, PhD(elec eng), 64. *Prof Exp:* Asst engr, Sperry Gyroscope Co, 57-58; sr res staff mem commun, Gen Dynamics/Electronics, 58-61; instr elec eng, Syracuse Univ, 61-64; from asst prof to prof elec eng, Pa State Univ, 64-84. *Mem:* Inst Elec & Electronics Engrs; Acoust Soc Am. *Res:* Coherent fiber optic communication systems; digital communication systems; coding of orthogonal wave shapes; audition and psycho-acoustics; bioengineering. *Mailing Add:* Dept Elec Eng Univ SFla Tampa FL 33620. *E-Mail:* lachs@ssunburn.ec.usf.edu

LACK, LEON, BIOCHEMISTRY. *Current Pos:* from asst prof to assoc prof, 65-71, PROF PHARMACOL, MED CTR, DUKE UNIV, 71- *Personal Data:* b New York, NY, Jan 7, 22; m 48; c 5. *Educ:* Brooklyn Col, AB, 43; Mich State Univ, MS, 48; Columbia Univ, PhD(biochem), 53. *Prof Exp:* Fel, Duke Univ, 53-55; from instr to asst prof pharmacol, Sch Med, Johns Hopkins Univ, 55-64. *Mem:* Am Soc Biol Chemists; Am Soc Pharmacol & Exp Therapeutics. *Res:* Metabolism of aromatic substances; intestinal active transport; pharamacology of androgen related disorders. *Mailing Add:* Lab Molecular Pharmacol Box 3185 Duke Univ Med Ctr Durham NC 27706

LACKEY, CAROLYN JEAN, COMMUNITY NUTRITION. *Current Pos:* EXTEN PROF, FOOD & NUTRIT, NC AGR EXTEN SERV, NC STATE UNIV, 83- *Personal Data:* b Shelby, NC, Nov 24, 48. *Educ:* Univ NC, Greensboro, BSHE, 71; Univ Tenn, Knoxville, MS, 73, PhD(food sci), 74. *Prof Exp:* Asst prof foods & nutrit, Purdue Univ, 74-76; from asst prof to assoc prof community nutrit, Mich State Univ, 76-83. *Concurrent Pos:* Proj dir, Nutrit Educ Grant, Mich Dept Educ, 78. *Mem:* Soc Nutrit Educ; Inst Food Technologists. *Res:* Investigation of determinants of food behavior and food behavior modification; development, implementation and evaluation of food and nutrition education materials. *Mailing Add:* 1608 Wedgeland Dr Raleigh NC 27615

LACKEY, HOMER BAIRD, APPLIED CHEMISTRY. *Current Pos:* res chemist, Cent Rest Dept, Crown Zellerbach Corp, 8-55, supvr prod res, Chem Prod Div, 55-68, mgr prod res, 68-80, MGR REGULATORY AFFAIRS, CHEM PROD DIV, CROWN ZELLERBACH CORP, 80- *Personal Data:* b Freewater, Ore, Nov 23, 20; m 42; c 3. *Educ:* Ore State Univ, BS, 47, MS, 48. *Prof Exp:* Asst, Ore State Univ, 47-48. *Concurrent Pos:* Consult, chem concrete, 82- *Mem:* Am Chem Soc; Am Soc Testing & Mat; Am Concrete Inst. *Res:* Forest byproduct utilization. *Mailing Add:* 804 NW 19th Ave Camas WA 98607

LACKEY, JAMES ALDEN, MAMMALOGY. *Current Pos:* PROF ZOOL, STATE UNIV NY, OSWEG O, 73- *Personal Data:* b Glens Falls, NY, Nov 25, 38; div; c Jesse S & Christopher J. *Educ:* Cornell Univ, BS, 61; Calif State Univ, San Diego, MA, 67; Univ Mich, PhD(zool), 73. *Mem:* Am Soc Mammalogists; Sigma Xi; AAAS. *Res:* Reproduction, growth, development and population ecology of mammals; biochemical genetics. *Mailing Add:* Biol Dept State Univ NY Oswego NY 13126

LACKEY, LAURENCE, geomorphology, engineering geology, for more information see previous edition

LACKEY, ROBERT T, FISHERIES & WILDLIFE MANAGEMENT. *Current Pos:* PROF FISHERIES, ORE STATE UNIV, 82-, DEP LAB DIR, 89-, ASSOC DIR, CTR ANALYSIS ENVIRON CHANGE, 91-, PROF POLIT SCI, 95- *Personal Data:* b Kamloops, BC, May 18, 44; m 67, Lana J Apparius; c Christopher R & Karen M. *Educ:* Humboldt State Univ, BS, 67; Univ Maine, Orono, MS, 68; Colo State Univ, PhD(fisheries & wildlife), 71. *Prof Exp:* Asst prof, Va Polytech Inst & State Univ, 71-74; sect leader, Fisheries Sci, 71-72 & 75-77, assoc prof fisheries, 74-79; group leader, Nat Water Res Analysis Group, 79-81; sr ecologist, Environ Res Lab, Corvallis, 81-85, assoc br chief, 85-87, br chief, 87-89. *Concurrent Pos:* Res grants, Off Econ Opportunity & Celanese Corp, Off Water Res, 72-77, US Nat Marine Fisheries Serv, 72-78, US Dept Agr, 73-78 & US Forest Serv, 75-78; consult, US Fish & Wildlife Serv, 74-76, Brandermill Corp, 74-75 & US Army Corps Engrs, 75-76; fish & wildlife adminr, US Fish & Wildlife Serv, 76-77; vis prof, George Mason Univ, 76-77, Univ Mich, 78. *Mem:* Inst Fishery Res Biologists; Am Fisheries Soc; Ecol Soc Am; fel Am Inst Fishery Res Biologists. *Res:* Effects of man's activities on aquatic and terrestrial resources; fisheries management, including structure and management of aquatic renewable natural resources; systems analysis; environmental assessment; ecological risk assessments; ecosystem management; ecological risk assessment. *Mailing Add:* Environ Protection Agency 200 SW 35th St Corvallis OR 97333. *Fax:* 541-754-4614; *E-Mail:* lackey.robert@epamail.epa.gov

LACKEY, WALTER JACKSON, CERAMIC & METALLURGICAL ENGINEERING. *Current Pos:* PRIN RES SCIENTIST, GA INST TECHNOL, 86- *Personal Data:* b Shelby, NC, Feb 6, 40; m 61, Betty Peek; c 2. *Educ:* NC State Univ, BS(metall eng) & BS(ceramic eng), 61, MS, 63, PhD(ceramic eng), 70. *Prof Exp:* Res scientist, Battelle-Northwest Lab, 63-65; mat engr, Douglas Aircraft Corp, 65-66; res asst electronic ceramics, NC State Univ, 66-69; group leader, Metals & Ceramics Div, Oak Ridge Nat Lab, 69-84. *Mem:* Fel Am Ceramic Soc; Am Soc Metals. *Res:* Fabrication, characterization and testing of nuclear fuels and waste forms; mechanisms and measurement of electrical conduction in ceramic insulators; ceramic coatings and composites; ceramic superconductors. *Mailing Add:* 3129 Wendwood Dr Marietta GA 30062

LACKNER, HENRIETTE, HEMATOLOGY. *Current Pos:* res assoc, Sch Med, NY Univ, 63-65, instr med, 65-67, from asst prof clin med to asst prof med, 67-75, ASSOC PROF CLIN MED, SCH MED, NY UNIV, 75- *Personal Data:* b Vienna, Austria, Feb 27, 22; US citizen; m 49; c 3. *Educ:* Univ Leeds, MB & ChB, 45, MD, 48. *Hon Degrees:* FRCP, Univ Leeds, 96. *Prof Exp:* Jr lectr med, Univ Cape Town, 55-62. *Concurrent Pos:* Res asst, Groote Schuur Hosp, Cape Town, SAfrica, 55-62, asst physician, Arthritis Clin, 55-56, physician-in-chg & asst physician med outpatient clin, 56-62; res scientist, Am Nat Red Cross, 63-; clin asst vis physician, Bellevue Hosp, NY, 65-75, assoc vis physician, 75-; asst, Univ Hosp, 66-75, assoc med, 75- *Mem:* Soc Study Blood; Am Soc Hemat. *Res:* Blood coagulation disorders and pathological fibrinolysis. *Mailing Add:* Dept Med NY Univ Med Ctr New York NY 10016-6451

LACKNER, JAMES ROBERT, AEROSPACE MEDICINE. *Current Pos:* From asst prof to assoc prof, 70-79, chmn dept psychol, 75-83, provost & dean fac, 86-89, RIKLIS PROF PHYSIOL, DEPT PSYCHOL, 79-, DIR ASHTON GRAYBELL SPATIAL ORIENTATION LAB, 82- *Personal Data:* b Virginia, Minn, Nov 11, 40; m 70, Ann Martin Graybiel. *Educ:* Mass Inst Technol, BSc, 66, PhD, 70. *Honors & Awards:* Arnold B Tuttle Award, Aerospace Med Asn. *Concurrent Pos:* Res assoc dept psychol & clin res ctr, MIT, Cambridge, 70-80; fabricant comt life sci exp for a space sta, 82; space sci bd, Sensory Motor Panel, Nat Acad Sci, 84-86; mem, Comt Hearing, Bioacoust & Biomech, Nat Res Coun, 85-89, Comn Vision, 87-92, Comn Space, Biol & Med, 91- *Mem:* Am Soc Gravitational & Space Biol; Aerospace Med Asn; Soc Neurosci; Psychonomics Soc; Int Brain Res Orgn; hon mem Barany Soc; hon mem Int Acad Astronaut. *Res:* Human sensory-motor and spatial orientation. *Mailing Add:* Dept Psychol Brandeis Univ 415 South St Waltham MA 02154-2700

LACKO, ANDRAS GYORGY, BIOCHEMISTRY, MICROBIOLOGY. *Current Pos:* assoc prof, 75-83, PROF BIOCHEM, DEPT BIOCHEM & MOLECULAR BIOL, UNIV NTEX HEALTH SCI CTR, FT WORTH, 83- *Personal Data:* b Budapest, Hungary, Nov 10, 36; Can citizen; m 64; c 4. *Educ:* Univ BC, BSA, 61, MSc, 63; Univ Wash, PhD(biochem), 68. *Prof Exp:* Res asst biochem, Univ Wash, 63-68; asst mem, Albert Einstein Med Ctr, 69-71; mem staff, Med Sch, Temple Univ, 71-72, asst prof med, 72-75. *Concurrent Pos:* NIH fel, Albert Einstein Col Med, 68-69. *Mem:* Am Soc Biochem & Molecular Biol; Am Heart Asn. *Res:* Structure and function of enzymes and lipoproteins. *Mailing Add:* Dept Biochem & Molecular Biol Univ NTex Health Sci Ctr 3500 Camp Bowie Blvd Ft Worth TX 76107-2690. *Fax:* 817-735-2133; *E-Mail:* tc07@unt.edu

LACKS, SANFORD, GENETICS, MOLECULAR BIOLOGY. *Current Pos:* from asst geneticist to geneticist, 61-82, SR GENETICIST, BROOKHAVEN NAT LAB, 82- *Personal Data:* b New York, NY, Jan 28, 34; m 59, Elaine Norris; c Jennifer, Daniel & Julia. *Educ:* Union Univ, NY, BS, 55; Rockefeller Univ, PhD, 60. *Prof Exp:* Instr biol, Harvard Univ, 60-61. *Mem:* Am Soc Microbiol; Am Soc Biol Chem; Genetics Soc Am. *Res:* Bacterial transformation; DNA repair; DNA methylation; restriction enzymes; folate biosynthesis. *Mailing Add:* Biol Dept Brookhaven Nat Lab Upton NY 11973-5000. *Fax:* 516-344-3407; *E-Mail:* lacks@sun2.bnl.gov

LACKSONEN, JAMES W(ALTER), CHEMICAL ENGINEERING. *Current Pos:* from asst prof to prof, 67-92, asst dean, Col Eng, 71-92, EMER PROF CHEM ENG, UNIV TOLEDO, 92- *Personal Data:* b Ashtabula, Ohio, Oct 17, 36; m 57; c 2. *Educ:* Ohio State Univ, BChE & MSc, 59, PhD(chem eng), 64. *Prof Exp:* Res engr, Battelle Mem Inst, 60-65; proj engr, Pittsburgh Plate Glass Co, 65-66; sr develop engr chem-plastics div, Gen Tire & Rubber Co, Ohio, 66-67. *Mem:* AAAS; Am Inst Chem Engrs; Am Chem Soc; Electrochem Soc. *Res:* Kinetics and surface chemistry processes; fuel cells; transport of gases in microporous media; reactor design; reinforced plastics; foam; mass transfer. *Mailing Add:* 4758 S Crestridge Rd Toledo OH 43623

LA CLAIRE, JOHN WILLARD, II, PLANT CELL BIOLOGY, PHYCOLOGY. *Current Pos:* Asst prof, 79-85, ASSOC PROF, DEPT BOT, UNIV TEX, 85- *Personal Data:* b Utica, NY, July 1, 51; m 94, Julie M Palmer. *Educ:* Cornell Univ, BS, 73; Univ SFla, MA, 75; Univ Calif, Berkeley, PhD(bot), 79. *Concurrent Pos:* Prin investr, Cell Biol Sect, NSF, 81-; prin investr plant growth develop, USDA, 87-; vis assoc prof, Dept Cell Biol, Stanford Univ, 89; prin investr marine biotechnol, ONR, 95- *Mem:* AAAS; Am Soc Cell Biol; Bot Soc Am; Brit Phycol Soc; Int Phycol Soc; Phycol Soc Am. *Res:* Cell biology and molecular biology of algae; cell motility phenomena; cellular wound healing, mitosis, cytokinesis and cytoplasmic streaming; cytoskeleton of plant cells. *Mailing Add:* Dept Bot Univ Tex Austin TX 78713-7640. *E-Mail:* laclaire@utxvms.cc.utexas.edu

LACOSS, RICHARD THADDEE, SIGNAL PROCESSING, COMPUTERIZED SENSOR DATA INTERPRETATION. *Current Pos:* Mem staff, 65-69, GROUP LEADER, LINCOLN LAB, MASS INST TECHNOL, 69- *Personal Data:* b Gardner, Mass, Aug 19, 37; m 84, Cynthia

Okoham; c Zelda & Remi. *Educ:* Columbia Univ, AB, 59, BS, 60; Univ Calif, Berkeley, MS, 62, PhD(elec eng, info & control theory), 65. *Mem:* Inst Elec & Electronics Engrs; Sigma Xi; Asn Comput Mach. *Res:* Signal processing; object recognition; radar signal analysis; neural networks; image processing; model-based algorithms; intelligent systems; atmospheric acoustics; distributed algorithms; system engineering. *Mailing Add:* No 8 Chauncy Lane Cambridge MA 02138

LACOSTE, RENE JOHN, ANALYTICAL CHEMISTRY, PESTICIDE CHEMISTRY. *Current Pos:* RETIRED. *Personal Data:* b New York, NY, Feb 19, 27. *Educ:* Rensselaer Polytech Inst, BS, 50; Univ Chicago, MS, 53. *Prof Exp:* Chemist, Am Dent Asn, 50-53; chemist, Rohm & Haas Co, 53-68; sr chemist, 68-69, int registr agr & sanit chem, 69-75, regional regulatory mgr, 75-80, foreign regulatory mgr agr chem, 80-90. *Concurrent Pos:* Agr indust rep UN, Codex Comt Pesticide Residues, 70-90. *Mem:* Fel AAAS; Am Chem Soc; Am Inst Chem; NY Acad Sci; Sigma Xi. *Res:* Physical and chemical methods of analysis; electrochemical analysis; separations of organic mixtures; developed methods for analysis of chemicals in products of industrial production; national and international industry and government groups concerned with drafting and adopting regulations regarding production and use of agricultural pesticide chemicals. *Mailing Add:* 5353 Arlington Expressway Apt 11-B Jacksonville FL 32211-5588

LACOUNT, ROBERT BRUCE, ORGANIC CHEMISTRY. *Current Pos:* from asst prof chem to prof & chmn dept, Waynesburg Col, 65-71, prof & chmn dept chem & physics, 71-91, PROF CHEM, WAYNESBURG COL, 91- *Personal Data:* b Martinsburg, WVa, Sept 16, 35; m 64, Virginia Walchak; c Victoria & Robert. *Educ:* Shepherd Col, BS, 57; Univ Pittsburgh, MLitt, 62, PhD(org chem), 65. *Prof Exp:* Res assoc fundamental org chem, Mellon Inst, 58-65. *Concurrent Pos:* Res grant, Petrol Res Fund, 65-67; res chemist, US Bur Mines, 70-75 & Energy Res & Develop Admin, 75-77 & Dept Energy, 77-89; tech dir, ViRoLac Ind, 89- *Mem:* Am Chem Soc. *Res:* Synthetic organic chemistry; organic sulfur chemistry; production of low-sulfur fuels from coal; instrumental methods. *Mailing Add:* Waynesburg Col Waynesburg PA 15370

LACOURSE, WILLIAM CARL, GLASS SCIENCE & ENGINEERING. *Current Pos:* PROF GLASS SCI, COL CERAMICS, ALFRED UNIV, 70-; VPRES, SAXON GLASS TECHNOL, 96- *Personal Data:* b Schenectady, NY, June 19, 43; m 66, Patricia Clark; c Brian C & Elisa (Rogers). *Educ:* State Univ NY, Stony Brook, BS, 66, MS, 67; Rensselaer Polytech Inst, PhD(mat eng), 70. *Prof Exp:* Nat Res Coun postdoctoral fel, Naval Res Lab, 70. *Concurrent Pos:* Vis scientist, St Gobair Res, Paris, 87 & Univ Modera, Italy, 95; dir, Ctr Glass Res, Alfred Univ, 96-97. *Mem:* Fel Am Ceramic Soc; Soc Glass Technol. *Res:* Authored over 70 publications in general area of glass science, with special emphasis on chemical and mechanical properties development of special compositions for new or improved properties. *Mailing Add:* Alfred Univ Alfred NY 14802. *Fax:* 607-871-2392; *E-Mail:* flacourse@bigvax.alfred.edu

LACOUTURE, PETER GEORGE, PHARMACOLOGY, PHYSIOLOGY. *Current Pos:* assoc dir, 92-94, DIR, PURDUE FREDERICK, 94- *Personal Data:* b Worcester, Mass, Oct 26, 51; m 78, Sheila A Foy; c Alyssa, Bryan & Timothy. *Educ:* Col Holy Cross, AB, 73; Mass Col Pharm & Allied Health Sci, MS, 81, PhD(pharmacol & physiol), 86. *Prof Exp:* Sr res asst physiol, Harvard Sch Pub Health, 80-85; res affil toxicol, Div Clin Pharmacol & Toxicol, Children's Hosp, Boston, 85-87; res fel path, Harvard Med Sch & develop officer, Clin Labs, Children's Hosp Boston, Mass, 87; sr clin scientist, Wyeth-Ayerst Res, 88-90, asst dir, 90-92. *Concurrent Pos:* Consult, Mass Poison Control Syst, 77-87 & Drug Epidemiol Unit, Boston Univ Med Ctr, 80-87; instr pediat, Harvard Med Sch, 88; asst med, Dept Med, Children's Hosp Boston, 88-89; examr, Am Bd Appl Toxicol, 89. *Mem:* Am Acad Clin Toxicol; Am Soc Pharmacol & Exp Therapeut; Am Soc Clin Pharmacol & Therapeut; Am Thoracic Soc; Am Col Allergy & Immunol; Am Pain Soc. *Res:* Rheumatology, anti-inflammatory drugs; immunology, anti-allergy and pulmonary drugs; general toxicology; pharmacoepidemiology; regulatory affairs; author of over 100 technical publications. *Mailing Add:* 16 Ashford Lane Newton CT 06470-1774. *Fax:* 203-831-9659

LACROIX, GUY, MARINE ECOLOGY. *Current Pos:* RETIRED. *Personal Data:* b Que, Apr 10, 30; m 60; c 2. *Educ:* Laval Univ, BA, 52, LPh, 53,DSc, 68; Univ Montreal, BSc, 57, MSc, 59. *Prof Exp:* Zooplanktonologist, Grande Riviere Marine Biol Sta, Que, 58-68; from asst prof to prof biol oceanog, Dept Biol, Laval Univ, 68-97, dir, Grad Studies Biol, 83-85, assoc dir, Sch Grad Studies, 85-97. *Concurrent Pos:* Exec secy, Interuniv Group Oceanog Res, Que, 70-77; mem bd, Laval Univ, 74-77 & Sci Comt Oceanic Res, Can Nat Comt, 74-78; ed, Can Naturalist, 79-86. *Mem:* Marine Biol Asn UK; Am Soc Limnol & Oceanog; Plankton Soc Japan. *Res:* Zooplankton; invertebrate zoology; primary production; marine invertebrates. *Mailing Add:* 1155 Ave Turnbull Apt 403 Quebec PQ G1R 5G3 Can

LACROIX, NORBERT HECTOR JOSEPH, MATHEMATICS, BIOLOGICAL SCIENCES. *Current Pos:* from asst prof to assoc prof, 66-77, chmn dept, 70-77, PROF MATH, LAVAL UNIV, 77- *Personal Data:* b Sarsfield, Ont, Can, Oct, 26, 40; m 65, Ghislaine Levesque; c Eric, Hugo & Carl (deceased). *Educ:* Univ Ottawa, BSc, 62; Univ Notre Dame, PhD(math), 66. *Prof Exp:* Instr math, Univ Notre Dame, 62-66. *Mem:* Can Math Soc; Asn Canadienne-Francaise Advan Sci; Can Appl Math Soc; Can Soc Theoret Biol; Am Math Soc. *Res:* Organisational principles in developmental and structural biology; mathematical models. *Mailing Add:* Dept Math Laval Univ Quebec PQ G1K 7P4 Can. *Fax:* 418-656-2817; *E-Mail:* nlacroix@mat.ulaval.ca

LACY, ANN MATTHEWS, GENE STRUCTURE & FUNCTION-FUNGI, GENERAL MOLECULAR & HUMAN GENETICS. *Current Pos:* instr genetics, Goucher Col, 59-61, from asst prof to assoc prof, 61-73, chmn, Dept Biol Sci, 69-72, 86-87 & 89, chmn, Fac Natural Sci & Math, 88-91, PROF BIOL SCI GENETICS, GOUCHER COL, 73-, ELIZABETH CONNOLLY TODD PROF, 94- *Personal Data:* b Boston, Mass, May 29, 32. *Educ:* Wellesley Col, BA, 53; Yale Univ, MS, 56, PhD(microbiol), 59. *Prof Exp:* Res asst, Dept Genetics, Carnegie Inst, Washington, Cold Spring Harbor, 53-54. *Concurrent Pos:* Prin investr, genetics tryptophan synthase in neurospora crassa, NSF res grants, Goucher Col, 60-60; sr res fel, Bot Dept, Univ Glasgow, Scotland, 68-69. *Mem:* AAAS; Genetics Soc Am; Am Asn Univ Profs; Am Inst Biol Sci; Sigma Xi. *Res:* Gene-enzyme relationships and gene regulation in Neurospora crassa (gene organization, cross-pathway regulation), especially in the tryptophan biosynthetic pathway. *Mailing Add:* Dept Biol Sci Goucher Col 1021 Dulaney Valley Rd Towson MD 21204. *Fax:* 410-337-6408

LACY, GEORGE HOLCOMBE, PHYTOPATHOLOGY, BACTERIAL GENETICS. *Current Pos:* from asst prof to assoc prof, 80-88, PROF PLANT PATH, VA POLYTECH INST & STATE UNIV, 88- *Personal Data:* b Washington, DC, Nov 13, 43; m 64; c 2. *Educ:* Calif State Univ, Long Beach, BS, 66, MS, 71; Univ Calif, Riverside, PhD(phytopath), 75. *Prof Exp:* Lab technician qual control, Am Chem & Plastics Co, Stauffer Chem Co, Calif, 64-65; biol sci instr, US Peace Corps, Corozal Town, Belize, 66-68; scientist II soil microbiol, Jet Propulsion Lab, Calif Inst Technol, 69-71; res assoc plant path, Univ Wis-Madison, 75-77; asst plant pathologist, Conn Agr Exp Sta, 77-80. *Concurrent Pos:* NIH grant, 75-76, NSF grant, Univ Wis-Madison, 76-77, 87-, USDA grants, 83-89, Environ Protection Agency, NSF grants, 87-91. *Mem:* Am Phytopath Soc; Am Microbiol Soc. *Res:* Molecular basis for plant pathogenesis and biological control of plant disease and biological control of plant disease and ecological impact of release of genetically engineered microorganisms into the environment. *Mailing Add:* 2009 Broken Oak Dr Blacksburg VA 24060

LACY, LEWIS L, MICROGRAVITY SCIENCES, MATERIAL ANALYSIS & PHYSICS FOR PETROLEUM PRODUCTION. *Current Pos:* RES SCIENTIST, BJ SERV, 93- *Personal Data:* b Bluefield, WVa, Mar 25, 41; m 64; c 2. *Educ:* Va Polytech Inst & State Univ, BS, 63, MS, 65; Univ Tenn, Knoxville, PhD(physics), 71. *Honors & Awards:* Marshall Space Flight Ctr Dirs Commendation Award, NASA, 71 & NASA Manned Flight Awareness Award, 74; NASA Group Achievement Award, Johnson Space Flight Ctr, 76; NASA New Technol Award, 80, 84. *Prof Exp:* Res assoc solid state physics, Los Alamos Sci Lab, 64; exp physicist, Nuclear & Plasma Physics Div, Space Sci Lab, Marshall Space Flight Ctr, NASA, 65-68, mat & appl physics scientist, Space Sci Lab, 68-77, br chief, Solid State & Solidification Br, 77-81, sr res specialist, 81-84; sr res staff, Exxon Prod Res Co, 84-93. *Concurrent Pos:* mem, Comt Advance Hydraul Fracturing, Soc Petrol Engrs, 86-88. *Mem:* Am Phys Soc; Soc Petrol Engrs. *Res:* Gleeble welding simulation experiments and fracture toughness of offshore platform steels; hydraulic fracture geometry and orientation, triaxial borehole seismic, tiltmeter arrays and fracture mapping; solidification and crystal growth, containerless supercooling and low-gravity solidification, low temperature and superconducting materials. *Mailing Add:* 6 Postvine Ct Woodlands TX 77381

LACY, MELVYN LEROY, PLANT PATHOLOGY, EPIDEMIOLOGY. *Current Pos:* RETIRED. *Personal Data:* b Henry, Nebr, Oct 24, 31; m 54, Shirley Chenoweth; c Matthew & Miles. *Educ:* Univ Wyo, BS, 59, MS, 61; Ore State Univ, PhD(plant path), 64. *Honors & Awards:* Distinguished Serv Award, Am Phytopath Soc. *Prof Exp:* From asst prof to prof plant path, Mich State Univ, 65-96. *Mem:* Am Phytopath Soc; Can Phytopath Soc; Am Potato Asn. *Res:* Soil-borne fungus diseases, epidemiology and control; pesticides for disease control; epidemiology, disease forecasting and disease management. *Mailing Add:* Dept Bot & Plant Path Mich State Univ East Lansing MI 48823. *E-Mail:* lacyml@aol.com

LACY, PAUL ESTON, PATHOLOGY. *Current Pos:* from instr to assoc prof, Washington Univ, 56-61, asst dean, 59-61, Mallinckrodt prof path & chmn dept, 61-85, Robert L Kroc prof, 85-95, EMER PROF PATH, WASHINGTON UNIV MED SCH, 95- *Personal Data:* b Trinway, Ohio, Feb 7, 24; m 45, Ellen Talbot; c Paul E Jr & Steven Talbot. *Educ:* Ohio State Univ, BA, 45, MSc & MD, 48; Univ Minn, PhD(path), 55. *Hon Degrees:* Dr, Uppsala Univ, Sweden, 77. *Honors & Awards:* Banting Mem Lectr, Brit Diabetic Asn, 63, Banting Award, 70; Elliot Proctor Joslin Mem Lectr, 66; Richard M Jaffe Lectr, 69; Rollin Rurner Woodyatt Mem Lectr, 70; Sci Award, Juv Diabetes Found, 73, David Rumbough Mem Award Sci Achievement, 77 & 92; 3M Life Sci Award, Fedn Am Socs Exp Biol, 81; Rous-Whipple Award, Am Asn Pathologists, Inc, 84; Maude Abbolt Lectr, Int Acad Path, 86; H P Smith Mem Award Lectr, Am Soc Clin Pathologists, 86; Gold Headed Cane, Am Soc Path, 95. *Prof Exp:* Asst instr anat, Ohio State Univ, 44-48; intern, White Cross Hosp, Columbus, Ohio, 48-49; Nat Cancer Inst fel, Med Sch, Washington Univ, 55-56. *Concurrent Pos:* Mem path B study sect, NIH, 61-66, chmn, 66-67; mem adv comt res personnel, Am Cancer Soc, 66-70; mem basic sci adv comt, Nat Cystic Fibrosis Res Found, 67-69; assoc ed, Diabetes, 73-; mem nat comn diabetes, NIH, 74-75 & mem nat adv environ health sci coun, 74-77; mem bd dirs, Am Diabetes Asn 75-79; pres, Asn Path Chmn, Inc, 81 & Am Asn Pathologists, Inc, 83; mem, Nat Diabetes Adv Bd, NIH, 85, 86; path, Barnes & Allied Hosps & St Louis Hosp, 85-95. *Mem:* Inst Med-Nat Acad Sci; Am Soc Exp Path; Am Diabetes Asn; Int Diabetes Fedn; fel AAAS; fel Am Acad Arts & Sci; Cell Transplant Soc. *Res:* Endocrine pathology; experimental diabetes; published numerous articles in various journals. *Mailing Add:* Dept Path Med Sch Washington Univ St Louis MO 63110

LACY, W(ILLARD) C(ARLETON), GEOLOGICAL ENGINEERING. *Current Pos:* found chair geol, 72-81, emer prof geol, 81-93, EMER CONSULT, JAMES COOK UNIV, NQUEENSLAND, 83- *Personal Data:* b Waterville, Ohio, July 17, 16; m 40, Jo Wipior; c 6. *Educ:* DePauw Univ, AB, 38; Univ Ill, MS, 40; Harvard Univ, PhD(geol), 50. *Honors & Awards:* Fulbright Lectr, Univ Queensland, 67; Henry Krumb Lectr, 85; Ben Dickerson Award, 91; Medal of Honor, Mining Hall of Fame, 93. *Prof Exp:* Geologist, Titanium Alloy Mfg Co, 42-43; petrologist, Cerro de Pasco Corp, 46-50, from asst chief to chief geologist, 50-55; prof geol, Univ Ariz, 55-64, prof mining & geol eng & head dept, 64-71. *Concurrent Pos:* Vis lectr, Harvard Univ, 53; prin, Lacy & Assocs, Consults. *Mem:* Fel Geol Soc Am; Soc Econ Geol; Am Inst Mining, Metall & Petrol Engrs; Int Soc Rock Mech; hon fel Australasian Inst Mining & Metall; Asn Eng Geologists. *Res:* Mining geology; localization of ore deposits; ground stabilization. *Mailing Add:* 8700 N LaCholla Blvd Tucson AZ 85742

LACY, W(ILLIAM) J(OHN), CHEMICAL ENGINEERING. *Current Pos:* PRES, LACY & CO, ENVIRON & INDUST CONSULTS, 83- *Personal Data:* b Meriden, Conn, May 26, 28; m 50; c William P, Gregory D & Debra (Gwen). *Educ:* Univ Conn, BS, 50, New York Univ, 51, Orins, 57, PhD. *Hon Degrees:* DSc, Paul Sabatier Univ, France, 83. *Honors & Awards:* Leonard Gloub Chem Award; Gold Medal, Am Water Works Asn, 60; Bronze Medal, Environ Protection Agency, 83; Paul Sabatier Univ Medal, France, 83; US Distinguished Serv Medal, 84; Govern Thailand Environ Medal, 84; Lublin Polytech Univ Medal, 88; Madam Curie Medal, Poland, 89; Washington Acad Sci Medal, 92; Polish Acad Sci Medal, 92; High Inst Pub Health Medal, Egypt, 93. *Prof Exp:* Asst chemist & res assoc, NY Univ, 50-51; chemist & sr proj engr, Eng Res & Develop Labs, Va, 51-58; chief test sta, Oak Ridge Nat Lab, Tenn, 58-59; chief radiochemist, Off Civil Defense & Mobilization, 59-62, asst dir, Post Attack Res Div, Off Civil Defense, Washington, DC, 62-67; chief indust pollution control res & develop, Fed Water Pollution Control Admin, Environ Protection Agency, 67-71, dir, Appl Sci & Technol Div, 71-74, prin eng sci adv, 74-79, dir water, waste & hazardous mat res, 79-83. *Concurrent Pos:* Partic sanit eng conf, Atomic Energy Comn, 52, 54 & 56, chmn adv comt spec weapons, 56-58; mem, Nat Adv Bd Water Decontamination, 54-56; lectr, numerous US univs; dep dir, US deleg, USSR, 75, 76 & 78; head, US Deleg UN Environ Prog, Paris, 75 & 78; co-chmn, Third Int Conf, Sorrento, Italy, 76; deleg, Tokyo Conf, 77; rep, Environ Protection Agency, World Cong Berlin, 77; sci dir, US Deleg, India, 78, Egypt, 79 & Italy, 81; co-chair III, IV, V & VI, X, Int Conf Chem, Protect Environ, Poland, 81 & 89, France, 83, Belgium, 85, Italy, 87 & Hong Kong, 90; chmn (ad hoc) EPA Hazardous Waste Res Lab Comt in Waste Minimization; vpres, Int & Exec Comt Chem Protection Environ; consult pollution prev, US Dept Energy, waste minimization, USAID & environ activ Cent Europ, Dept Com. *Mem:* Am Soc Testing & Mat; Am Chem Soc; Sigma Xi; fel Am Inst Chem Engrs; Am Acad Environ Engrs; life mem Int Ozone Asn. *Res:* Industrial waste water treatment; pollution prevention waste minimization; reactor waste disposal problems; hazardous waste monitoring and disposal; author of 201 publications and granted 4 patents. *Mailing Add:* 9114 Cherry Tree Dr Alexandria VA 22309-2905. *Fax:* 703-780-2184

LAD, PRAMOD MADHUSUDAN, RECEPTOR PHARMACOLOGY, MEMBRANE BIOPHYSICS & BIOCHEMISTRY. *Current Pos:* DIR RES, KAISER REGIONAL RES LAB, KAISER FOUND INST, LOS ANGELES, 81- *Personal Data:* b Bombay, India, Dec 25, 48; nat US; m 78; c 1. *Educ:* London Univ, BSc, 70; Cornell Univ, PhD(chem), 74. *Concurrent Pos:* Vis assoc res fac, Calif Inst Technol, Pasadena, 81-; adj assoc prof toxicol, Univ Southern Calif, 86- *Mem:* Am Soc Pharmacol & Exp Therapeut; Biophys Soc; Endocrine Soc; AAAS; Am Chem Soc; Reticuloendothelial Soc. *Res:* Major pathways of receptor mediated signaling in cells of the immune response; cells involved in inflammatory reactions such as neutrophils, lymphocytes, and mast cells; platelet-leukocyte interactions and their role in thrombus formation. *Mailing Add:* Kaiser Hosp 1515 W Vermont Ave Los Angeles CA 90027-5337

LAD, ROBERT AUGUSTIN, CHEMISTRY. *Current Pos:* RETIRED. *Personal Data:* b Chicago, Ill, May 8, 19; m 44, Delores Terwoord; c 9. *Educ:* Univ Chicago, SB, 39, SM, 41, PhD(inorg chem), 46. *Prof Exp:* Asst, Nat Defense Res Comt, Univ Chicago, 42-46; aeronaut res scientist, Nat Adv Comt Aeronaut, Lewis Res Ctr, NASA, 46-59, chief, Mat Sci Br, 59-78. *Concurrent Pos:* Mem solid state sci panel, Nat Acad Sci-Nat Res Coun, 63-78. *Mem:* AAAS; Am Phys Soc; fel Am Inst Chem. *Res:* Physics and chemistry of surfaces; radiation chemistry; materials science. *Mailing Add:* 3114 W 159th St Cleveland OH 44111

LADA, ARNOLD, biochemistry, organic chemistry; deceased, see previous edition for last biography

LADA, CHARLES JOSEPH, ASTRONOMY. *Current Pos:* SR ASTROPHYSICIST, SMITHSONIAN ASTROPHYS OBSERV, 90- *Personal Data:* b Webster, Mass, Mar 18, 49; m 84; c 2. *Educ:* Boston Univ, BA, 71; Harvard Univ, AM, 72, PhD(astron), 75. *Prof Exp:* Fel, Ctr Astrophys, Harvard Col Observ & Smithsonian Astrophys Observ, 75-77; res fel, Harvard Univ, 77-78; Bart Bok fel astron, Steward Observ, Univ Ariz, 78-80, from asst prof to assoc prof, 80-90. *Concurrent Pos:* Alfred P Sloan Found fel, 81-84; vis assoc prof, Univ Calif, Berkeley, 88-89. *Mem:* Am Astron Soc; Int Astron Union. *Res:* Formation of stars; interstellar gas dynamics; structure and evolution of interstellar molecular clouds; structure and evolution of our galaxy. *Mailing Add:* 694 Webster St Needham MA 02192

LADA, ELIZABETH A, astronomy, for more information see previous edition

LADANYI, BRANKA MARIA, THEORETICAL CHEMISTRY, PHYSICAL CHEMISTRY. *Current Pos:* from asst prof to assoc prof, 79-87, PROF CHEM, COL STATE UNIV, 87- *Personal Data:* b Zagreb, Croatia, Sept 7, 47; Can citizen; m 74, Marshall Fixman. *Educ:* McGill Univ, BSc, 69; Yale Univ, MPhil, 71, PhD(chem), 73. *Honors & Awards:* Alfred P Sloan fel, 82-85. *Prof Exp:* Vis asst prof chem, Univ Ill, Urbana, 74; res assoc chem, Yale Univ, 74-79. *Concurrent Pos:* Camille & Henry Dreyfus Teacher-Scholar, 83-87; vis fel, Joint Inst Lab Astrophys, 93-94; assoc ed, J Chem Physics, 94- *Mem:* Am Chem Soc; Am Phys Soc; AAAS; Am Women Sci. *Res:* Statistical mechanics of fluids; structure of molecular liquids; propagation and scattering of light in fluids; solvation in liquids and clusters, dielectric properties of fluids; solvent effects on chemical reactions. *Mailing Add:* Dept Chem Colo State Univ Ft Collins CO 80523. *Fax:* 970-491-1801; *E-Mail:* bl@bibm.mfbl.colostate.edu

LADANYI, BRANKO, GEOTECHNICAL ENGINEERING. *Current Pos:* prof civil eng, 67-94, prof geotech eng, Dept Civil Eng, 77-82, EMER PROF CIVIL ENG, ECOLE POLYTECH, UNIV MONTREAL, 94- *Personal Data:* b Zagreb, Yugoslavia, Dec 14, 22; Can citizen; m 46, Nevenka Zilic; c Branka, Thomas & Marc. *Educ:* Univ Zagreb, BEng, 47; Univ Louvain, PhD(civil eng), 59. *Honors & Awards:* R F Legget Geotech Award, 81; E E De Beer Geotech Award, 87; Elbert F Rice Mem Award, Am Soc Civil Engrs, 91; Roger J E Brown Mem Award, Can Geotech Soc, 93; Horst Leipholz Medal, Can Soc Civil Eng, 96; Northern Sci Award, Govt Can, 96. *Prof Exp:* Design engr found & hydraul struct, Dept Transport, Zagreb, 47-52; asst prof soil mech & found eng, Univ Zagreb, 52-58; res engr soil mech, Belg Geotech Inst, Ghent, 58-62; from assoc prof to prof geotech eng, Laval Univ, Que, 62-67. *Concurrent Pos:* Dir, Northern Eng Centre, 72- *Mem:* Fel Eng Inst Can; Can Inst Mining & Metall; fel Am Soc Civil Engrs; fel Can Soc Civil Engrs; fel Royal Soc Can; Tunnelling Asn Can (pres, 82-84); Can Rock Mech Asn (pres, 84-87); fel Can Acad Eng. *Res:* Soil and rock mechanics; permafrost engineering; mechanics of permafrost and ice; problems of foundation engineering, tunnelling and Arctic offshore construction. *Mailing Add:* Dept Civil Eng Ecole Polytech Box 6079 Centre-Ville Sta Montreal PQ H3C 3A7 Can

LADAS, GERASIMOS, DIFFERENTIAL EQUATIONS. *Current Pos:* from asst prof to assoc prof, 69-75, chmn dept, 72-78, PROF MATH, UNIV RI, 75- *Personal Data:* b Lixuri, Greece, Apr 25, 37; US citizen; m 65; c 2. *Educ:* Nat Univ Athens, BS, 61; NY Univ, MS, 66, PhD(math), 68. *Prof Exp:* Fel, NY Univ, 64-68; asst prof math, Fairfield Univ, 68-69. *Mem:* Am Math Soc. *Res:* Ordinary, functional and abstract differential equations. *Mailing Add:* Math Dept Univ RI Kingston RI 02881-0816. *Fax:* 401-792-4617

LADD, CHARLES CUSHING, III, CIVIL ENGINEERING, GEOTECHNICAL ENGINEERING. *Current Pos:* From instr to assoc prof, 57-70, PROF CIVIL ENVIRON ENG, MASS INST TECHNOL, 70- *Personal Data:* b Brooklyn, NY, Nov 23, 32; m 54, Carol L Ballou; c Melissa, Charles, Ruth & Matthew. *Educ:* Bowdoin Col, AB, 55; Mass Inst Technol, SB, 55, SM, 57, ScD(soil eng), 61. *Honors & Awards:* Croes Medal, 73; Norman Medal, 76; Terzaghi Lectr, 86; Hogentogler Award, 90; Middlebrook Award, Am Soc Chem Engrs, 96. *Concurrent Pos:* Vis consult, Haley & Aldrich, Inc, 67-68; vis sr scientist, Norweg Geotech Inst, 83. *Mem:* Nat Acad Eng; Am Soc Civil Engrs; Am Soc Testing & Mat; Am Soc Eng Educ; Nat Soc Prof Engrs; hon mem Am Soc Chem Engrs; Can Geotech Soc; Brit Geotech Soc. *Res:* Engineering properties of soils, soft ground and offshore construction as applied to civil engineering projects. *Mailing Add:* 7 Thornton Lane Concord MA 01742-4107. *Fax:* 617-253-6044

LADD, CONRAD MERVYN, POWER PLANT PROJECT MANAGEMENT, NUCLEAR & ENVIRONMENTAL ENGINEERING. *Current Pos:* CHMN & CHIEF EXEC OFFICER, SR MGT CONSULT, INC, 85- *Personal Data:* b Lakewood, Ohio, Dec 16, 26; m 47, Bonnie L Hinrichs; c Craig, Sue A, Patricia & Deborah. *Educ:* Univ Mich, BSME, 49. *Honors & Awards:* Dedicated Serv Award, Am Soc Mech Engrs, 87. *Prof Exp:* Student engr, Duquesne Light Co, 49-51; intermediate engr, Westinghouse Atomic Power Div, 51-52; sr engr, Atomic Power Develop Asn/Commonwealth Asn, 52-59; prod mgr, Brush Beryllium Corp, 59-63; mkt mgr, Atomics Int, Div Rockwell Int, 63-74; asst mgr mkt, Stone & Webster Engrs, 74-76; mgr bus develop & proj exec, Stearns Roger, Inc, 76-85. *Concurrent Pos:* Mem exec comt, Power Div, Am Soc Mech Engrs, 78-83, chmn, 81-82, chmn, Task Force Clean Coal Technol, 85-86, co-chmn, Task Force Acid Rain, 85-86, chmn energy comt, 87-90. *Mem:* Fel Am Soc Mech Engrs. *Res:* Engineering, development and testing of basic nuclear equipment and systems and nuclear fuel fabrication and processing; two infield patents. *Mailing Add:* Sr Mgt Consults Inc 1780 S Bellaire Suite 809 Denver CO 80222

LADD, JOHN HERBERT, PHYSICAL CHEMISTRY, PHYSICS. *Current Pos:* RETIRED. *Personal Data:* b Kewanee, Ill, Sept 6, 18; m 39; c 3. *Educ:* Univ Ill, BS, 40, MS, 42, PhD(phys chem), 47. *Prof Exp:* Asst phys chem, Univ Ill, 40-42; sr chemist, Eastman Kodak Co, 47-48; develop engr, 48, sr develop engr, 48-53, tech assoc, 53-57, sr develop proj engr, 57-69, sr staff mem, Kodak Res Labs, 69-81. *Concurrent Pos:* Instr, Univ Rochester, 49-51. *Mem:* Am Phys Soc. *Res:* Electron emission from metals; color photographic printers; color films in television; television test charts and standards; analog computers; digital equipment instrumentation, optical testing; digital hardware; photosensors; laser applications. *Mailing Add:* 7 Barnswallow Dr Pittsford NY 14534

LADD, KAYE VICTORIA, INORGANIC CHEMISTRY, PHYSICAL CHEMISTRY. *Current Pos:* MEM FAC CHEM, EVERGREEN STATE COL, 75- *Personal Data:* b Seattle, Wash, Aug 26, 41. *Educ:* Reed Col, BA, 63; Brandeis Univ, MA, 65, PhD(inorg chem), 74. *Prof Exp:* Staff scientist chem biol, Tyco Labs Inc, 65-68; assoc prof chem, Suffolk Univ, 68-75. *Concurrent Pos:* Consult, New Eng Aquarium, 70-75 & Corff & Shapiro, 77. *Mem:* Am Chem Soc; AAAS; Sci Inst Publ Info. *Res:* Environmental inorganic research, especially the transport of trace metals in metabolic process within and between organisms. *Mailing Add:* 1704 24th Ave NW Olympia WA 98502

LADD, SHELDON LANE, GENETICS, AGRONOMY. *Current Pos:* assoc prof, 76-80, PROF AGRON, COLO STATE UNIV, 80- *Personal Data:* b Merced, Calif, Sept 21, 41; m 62; c 2. *Educ:* Calif State Univ, Fresno, BS, 63; Univ Calif, Davis, PhD(genetics), 66. *Prof Exp:* Captain asst chief forensic toxicol, Sch Aerospace Med, USAF, 66-71; plant breeder sugarcane genetics, Dept Genetics & Path, Hawaiian Sugar Planters' Asn, 71-76. *Concurrent Pos:* Dir, Asn Off Seed Certifying Agencies, exec dir, Colo Seed Growers Asn & head seed cert, State Colo, 76- *Mem:* Crop Sci Soc Am; Am Soc Agron. *Res:* Plant breeding of agronomic species; cell and tissue culture of agronomic and revegetation species; seed quality and vigor. *Mailing Add:* Dept Crop Sci Ore State Univ 3017 Agron Life Sci Corvallis OR 97331-7306

LADD, THYRIL LEONE, JR, ENTOMOLOGY. *Current Pos:* RETIRED. *Personal Data:* b Albany, NY, Oct 10, 31; m 56; c 3. *Educ:* State Univ NY, Albany, AB, 56, MA, 58; Cornell Univ, PhD(entom), 63. *Prof Exp:* Res entomologist, Agr Res Sta, USDA, 62-69, res leader, Hort Insects Res Lab, 69-92. *Concurrent Pos:* Adj prof entom, Ohio State Univ, 71- *Mem:* AAAS; Entom Soc Am; Am Entom Soc; Sigma Xi; Coun Agr Sci & Technol. *Res:* Effects of radiation and chemicals on insect reproduction; integrated insect control; insect responses to attractants and repellents; effects of insect feeding on plant yields; improved procedures for applications of insecticides. *Mailing Add:* 2660 Winchester Woods Suite F Wooster OH 44691

LADDA, ROGER LOUIS, PEDIATRICS, CLINICAL GENETICS. *Current Pos:* from asst prof to assoc prof, 74-83, PROF PEDIAT, COL MED, PA STATE UNIV, 83-, CHIEF, DIV GENETICS, 74- *Personal Data:* b Highland, Ill, Oct 28, 36; m 57; c 5. *Educ:* Wesleyan Univ, BA, 58; Sch Med, Univ Chicago, MD, 63. *Prof Exp:* Res & clin fel, Children's Serv & Genetics Unit, Mass Gen Hosp, Sch Med, Harvard Univ, 72-74. *Concurrent Pos:* App mem, sci adv bd, Geront Res Ctr, Nat Inst Aging, 82-84. *Mem:* Am Pediat Soc; Soc Pediat Res; AAAS; Sigma Xi. *Res:* Growth regulating factors and cell division. *Mailing Add:* Dept Pediat Div Genetics Milton S Hershey Med Ctr PO Box 850 Hershey PA 17033

LADDE, GANGARAM SHIVLINGAPPA, DIFFERENTIAL EQUATIONS, APPLIED SYSTEMS ANALYSIS. *Current Pos:* PROF MATH, UNIV TEX, ARLINGTON, 80- *Personal Data:* b Jalkot, India, Mar 9, 40; US citizen; m 65; c 3. *Educ:* Marathwada Univ, BSc, 63, MSc, 65; Univ RI, PhD(math), 72. *Prof Exp:* Teaching asst, Univ RI, 67-71, instr, 71-73; from asst prof to assoc prof, State Univ NY, Potsdam, 73-80. *Concurrent Pos:* Fel, Univ Santa Clara, Calif, 74, res assoc, 81 & 87; grant-in-aid, Res Found, State Univ NY, Albany, 78-79; vis prof math, Univ Rome, Italy, 78 & Univ Tex, Arlington, 79-80; ed, Stochastic Analysis & Appln. *Mem:* Am Math Soc; Indian Math Soc; Sigma Xi; Soc Indust & Appl Math; Inst Elec & Electronics Engrs; NY Acad Sci. *Res:* Biomathematics; competitive analysis; differential games; deterministic analysis; mathematical modeling in biological, medical, physical, and social sciences; nonlinear boundary value problems; oscillation theory; stability theory; stochastic andlysis; systems analysis; filtering and control theory. *Mailing Add:* PO Box 19408 Arlington TX 76019-0001

LADDU, ATUL R, EXPERIMENTAL BIOLOGY. *Current Pos:* PRIN, CARDIOVASC, 90- *Personal Data:* b Aug 23, 40; US citizen. *Educ:* MB & BS, 62, MD, 67. *Prof Exp:* Instr pharmacol, Maulana Azad Med Col, New Delhi, 63-68; postdoctoral fel, Dept Pharmacol, Med Col Wis, 68-71, from 1st instr to asst prof, 71-73; group leader, Cardiovasc Div, Lederle Labs, Div Am Cyanamid Co, 73-75; sr clin invest assoc, Ciba-Geigy Corp, 75-76; asst med dir, Ives Labs, Inc, Div Am Home Prod Inc, 76, assoc med dir, 76-78, proj leader, 78-82; dir clin res, DuPont Critical Care, 82-88; dir clin res, Cardiovasc & Neurosci, Abbott Labs, 88-90. *Concurrent Pos:* Assoc ed, J Clin Pharmacol, Int J Clin Pharmacol. *Mem:* Fel Am Col Cardiol; fel Am Soc Clin Pharmacol & Therapeut; fel Am Col Clin Pharmacol; Am Soc Hypertension; Am Fedn Clin Res; NY Acad Sci; Am Soc Pharmacol & Exp Therapeut; Soc Exp Biol & Med; Sigma Xi; Int Study Group Res Cardiac Metab. *Res:* Conducting clinical trials with cardiovascular products and neuropharmacological agents; author or co-author of several publications. *Mailing Add:* 1216 N Claridge Way Carmel IN 46032

LADE, ROBERT WALTER, SOLID STATE ELECTRONICS. *Current Pos:* CONSULT, 91- *Personal Data:* b Fond du Lac, Wis, Apr 3, 35; m 56, Nancy Carey; c Kipton, Carey, Scot & Andrew. *Educ:* Marquette Univ, BEE, 58, MS, 61; Carnegie Inst Technol, PhD(elec eng), 62. *Prof Exp:* Instr, Marquette Univ, 59-61 & Carnegie Inst Technol, 61-62; assoc prof, NC State Univ, 63-67; prof elec eng & chmn dept, Marquette Univ, 67-77; mem staff, RWL Eng, 77-84; res mgr, Eaton Corp, 84-91. *Concurrent Pos:* Engr, AC Spark Plug, Wis, 59-60. *Mem:* Inst Elec & Electronics Engrs. *Res:* Electrical properties of free and passivated semiconductor surfaces under the influence of high energy radiation fields; computer-aided circuit design and power semiconductor device design. *Mailing Add:* 637 NE 15th Ct Cape Coral FL 33909. *E-Mail:* rwlade@cyberstreet.com

LADEFOGED, PETER NIELSEN, LINGUISTICS, PHONETICS. *Current Pos:* from asst prof to prof, 62-91, EMER PROF PHONETICS, UNIV CALIF, LOS ANGELES, 91-, RES LING, 91- *Personal Data:* b Sutton, Eng, Sept 17, 25; m 53, Jennifer Macdonald; c Lise, Thegn & Katie. *Educ:* Univ Edinburgh, MA, 51, PhD, 59. *Hon Degrees:* DLitt, Univ Edinburgh, 93. *Honors & Awards:* Silver Speech Commun Medal, Acoust Soc Am, 94. *Prof Exp:* Lectr, Univ Edinburgh, 53-61; lectr, Univ Ibadan, Nigeria, 59-60; res fel, WAfrican Lang Surv, Nigeria, 61-62. *Concurrent Pos:* Team leader, EAfrican Surv Lang Use & Lang Teaching, Uganda, 68- *Mem:* Fel Acoust Soc Am; fel Am Speech & Hearing Asn; fel Am Acad Arts & Sci; fel Am Speech Lang & Hearing Asn; Ling Soc Am (pres, 78); Int Phonetic Asn (pres, 86-91). *Res:* Author of several publications. *Mailing Add:* 10777 Massachusetts Ave Los Angeles CA 90024

LA DELFE, PETER CARL, PHYSICS, OPTICS. *Current Pos:* staff mem optical films, Los Alamos Nat Lab, 78-79, sect leader, Coating Sect, 79-82, staff mem, 82-85, proj leader, Phoenix Beam Transp, 85-88, mgr, Aurora Optics, 88-90, STAFF MEM, OPTICAL SENSORS & RADIOMETRIC INSTRUMENTS, LOS ALAMOS NAT LAB, 90- *Personal Data:* b Woburn, Mass, Feb 19, 43; m 78, Carol Thompson. *Educ:* Clarkson Col Technol, BS, 68, MS, 71. *Prof Exp:* Sr physicist optical films, Spectrum Systs Div, Barnes Eng Co, 71-74; consult pvt pract, 74-77. *Mem:* Am Vacuum Soc; Optical Soc Am; Int Soc Optical Eng. *Res:* Design and development of optical interference filters including research in the materials science of producing optical films; instrument design and system analysis for optical sensing systems. *Mailing Add:* 600 Los Pueblos Los Alamos NM 87544. *Fax:* 505-667-3815; *E-Mail:* pladelfe@sst.lanl.gov

LADENHEIM, HARRY, REACTOR ENGINEERING, PROCESS ENGINEERING. *Current Pos:* RETIRED. *Personal Data:* b Vienna, Austria, Oct 17, 32; US citizen; m 55; c 2. *Educ:* City Col New York, BS, 54; Polytech Inst Brooklyn, PhD(org polymer chem), 58. *Prof Exp:* Fel chem, Ill Inst Technol, 58-59; res chemist, Esso Res & Eng Co, 59-63; res chemist, Houdry Process & Chem Co, 63-70, sr res chemist, 70-76, sr develop engr, 76-79, prin res engr, Air Prods & Chem Inc, Marcus Hook, Pa, 79-81, process engr, 82-87, sr process engr, Air Prods & Chem Inc, Paulsboro, NJ, 82-94; consult, 87-96; PC trainer, Data Processing Trainers, Inc, 96-97. *Mem:* Am Chem Soc. *Res:* Mechanisms in physical organic chemistry; exploratory and process study in petroleum technology; use of polymers as enzyme models; catalysis; catalytic chemistry. *Mailing Add:* 459 Levering Mill Rd Bala Cynwyd PA 19004-2726

LADENSON, JACK HERMAN, CLINICAL CHEMISTRY. *Current Pos:* from asst prof to assoc prof, 72-84, HEAD, CLIN CHEM & COMPUT, SCH MED WASH UNIV, 80-, PROF PATH & CLIN CHEM MED, WASH UNIV SCH MED, 84-, OREE M CARROLL & LILLIAN B LADENSON CHAIR CLIN CHEM, 93-; DIR CLIN CHEM, BARNES HOSP, 80- *Personal Data:* b Philadelphia, Pa, Apr 8, 42; m 68, Ruth Carroll; c Michele S & Jeffrey L. *Educ:* Pa State Univ, BS, 64; Univ Md, PhD(analytical chem), 71. *Honors & Awards:* Outstanding Contrib Educ Award, Am Asn Clin Chem, 89; Cert Hon, Am Asn Clin Chem, 90; Distinguished Scientist Award, Clin Ligand Assay Soc, 94. *Prof Exp:* NSF fel, 66-70; fel clin chem, Hartford Hosp, 70-72. *Concurrent Pos:* Asst dir clin chem, Barnes Hosp, 72-76, co-dir, 76-79; dir, Am Bd Clin Chem, 79-85; mem, Bd Dirs, Am Asn Clin Chem, 81-83 & 85-87; mem, Bd Trustees, Van Slyke Soc, 93- *Mem:* Am Asn Clin Chem (pres, 86); Acad Clin Lab Physicians & Scientists. *Res:* Development of monoclonal antibodies and assays for cardiac proteins and detection of myocardial infarction. *Mailing Add:* Div Lab Med Sch Med Wash Univ Sch Med 660 S Euclid Ave Box 8118 St Louis MO 63110-1093. *Fax:* 314-362-1461

LADERMAN, A(RNOLD) J(OSEPH), FLUID MECHANICS, HEAT TRANSFER. *Current Pos:* supvr, Exp Fluid Mech Sect, 66-71, prin scientist, Fluid Mech Dept, 65-79, PRIN SCIENTIST, MECH ENG DEPT, AERONUTRONIC DIV, FORD AEROSPACE CORP, 79- *Personal Data:* b Pittsburgh, Pa, Apr 27, 30; m 59; c 2. *Educ:* Univ Calif, Berkeley, BS, 51, MS, 57, PhD(mech eng), 60. *Prof Exp:* Res engr mech eng, Mech Equip Unit, Boeing Co, 51-55; assoc res engr, Propulsion Dynamics Lab, Univ Calif, Berkeley, 57-65. *Concurrent Pos:* Lectr, Univ Calif, Berkeley, 60-61, 64; consult, Repub Aviation Co, NY, 62, Jet Propulsion Lab, Calif, 63-64 & Sandia Corp, 63-65. *Mem:* Am Inst Aeronaut & Astronaut; Combustion Inst; Sigma Xi. *Res:* Non steady gas dynamics of reactive media; shock and detonation wave phenomena; two phase flow; high power lasers; transition and turbulence in compressible boundary layers. *Mailing Add:* 2745 Temple Hills Dr Laguna Beach CA 92651

LADERMAN, JULIAN DAVID, MATHEMATICS, COMPUTER SCIENCE. *Current Pos:* From instr to asst prof math, 73-83, ASSOC PROF MATH & COMPUT SCI, LEHMAN COL, 84- *Personal Data:* b New York, NY, Oct 15, 48. *Educ:* NY Univ, BA, 70, MS, 72, PhD(comput sci), 76. *Concurrent Pos:* Consult, Systs Revisited, 78- *Mem:* Am Math Soc; Math Asn Am; Asn Comput Mach. *Res:* Computational complexity; mathematical programming; statistics; game theory; probability; operations research; programming languages; numerical analysis. *Mailing Add:* 2600 Netherland Ave Apt 824 Bronx NY 10463-4816

LADINSKY, HERBERT, pharmacology, biochemistry, for more information see previous edition

LADINSKY, JUDITH L, ENDOCRINOLOGY, PUBLIC & INTERNATIONAL HEALTH. *Current Pos:* proj assoc, Dept Gynec-Obstet, 61-68, from instr to asst prof prev med, 68-74, ASSOC PROF PREV MED, SCH MED, UNIV WIS-MADISON, 75-, DIR, OFF INT HEALTH, 85- *Personal Data:* b Los Angeles, Calif, June 16, 38; m 61, Jack; c Morissa & Mark. *Educ:* Univ Mich, BS, 61; Univ Wis-Madison, MS, 64, PhD(reproductive physiol), 68. *Prof Exp:* Med technologist, Clin Labs, St Mary's Hosp, Mich, 55-56; res asst, Dept Neuropath, Univ Mich, 56-58, Dept Anat, 58-60 & Dept Surg, 60-61. *Concurrent Pos:* Consult, Ministries Health, Southeast Asia; chair, US Comt Sci Coop with Vietnam & Laos. *Mem:* Am Soc Cell Biol; NY Acad Sci; Tissue Cult Asn; Am Pub Health Asn; Asn Teachers Prev Med; Nat Coun Int Health; Nat Asn Pub Health Policy (secy, 84-86); Sigma Xi. *Res:* Cell kinetics of normal and neoplastic tissues; automated methods of cancer detection; endocrinology of tumors; community medicine; neonatology; health care delivery; international health. *Mailing Add:* Dept Prev Med 1760 Med Sci Ctr Med Sch Univ Wis 1300 Univ Ave Madison WI 53706

LADISCH, MICHAEL R, BIOCHEMICAL ENGINEERING. *Current Pos:* Res eng biochem, 77-78, from asst prof to assoc prof, 78-81, PROF FOOD, AGR & CHEM ENG, PURDUE UNIV, 85-, GROUP LEADER RES & PROCESS ENG, LAB RENEWABLE RESOURCES, 78- *Personal Data:* b Upper Darby, Pa, Jan 15, 50; m 75; c 2. *Educ:* Drexel Univ, BS, 73; Purdue Univ, MS, 74, PhD(chem eng), 77. *Honors & Awards:* Peterson Award, Am Chem Soc, 77; US Presidential Young Investr Award, 84; James M Van Laren Serv Award, Am Chem Soc, 90. *Mem:* Am Chem Soc; Am Inst Chem Engrs; Am Soc Agr Engrs; fel Am Inst Med & Biol Eng. *Res:* Cellulose conversion; bioseparations; enzyme and chemical kinetics; liquid chromatography. *Mailing Add:* Lab Renewable Resources Eng Potter Ctr Purdue Univ West Lafayette IN 47906

LADISCH, STEPHAN, TUMORGENICITY, GLYCOBIOLOGY. *Current Pos:* from asst prof to assoc prof, 78-86, SR MEM, HUMAN IMMUNOBIOL GROUP, UNIV CALIF, LOS ANGELES, 78-, PROF PEDIAT, DIV HEMAT-ONCOL, SCH MED, 86-; DIR, CTR CANCER & TRANSPLANTATION BIOL, CHILDREN'S RES INST; PROF PEDIAT & BIOCHEM/MOLECULAR BIOL, GEORGE WASHINGTON UNIV, SCH MED. *Personal Data:* b Garmisch-Partenkirchen, WGer, July 18, 47; US citizen; m 74, Brigitte Bidault; c Gwenola & Virginie. *Educ:* Univ Pa, Philadelphia, BS, 69, MD, 73; Am Bd Pediat, cert hemat-oncol, 78. *Prof Exp:* Intern & resident pediat, Children's Hosp Med Ctr, Boston, Mass, 73-75; clin assoc, Pediat Oncol Br, Nat Cancer Inst, Bethesda, Md, 75-77, investr, 77-78. *Concurrent Pos:* NSF res grants, 68-69 & 72; NIH res grants, 80-84 & 83-, Career Develop Award, 82-87; Nat Found-March Dimes res grant, 80-84; vis scientist, Lausanne Br, Ludwig Inst for Cancer Res, Epalinges, Switz, 81-82, Inst Pasteur, Paris, 86-87; scholar, Leukemia Soc Am, 82-87. *Mem:* Am Soc Hemat; AAAS; Soc Pediat Res; Am Asn Immunologists; Am Fedn Clin Res. *Res:* Modulation of the immune response by gangliosides, membrane glycolipids shed by tumor cells and role of this process in tumorgenicity. *Mailing Add:* 111 Michigan Ave NW Ctr Cancer Transplantation Biol Children Nat Med Ctr Washington DC 20010. *Fax:* 202-884-3929

LADISH, JOSEPH STANLEY, ATOMIC & MOLECULAR PHYSICS. *Current Pos:* RES STAFF, LOS ALAMOS NAT LAB, 74- *Personal Data:* b Worcester, Mass, Aug 9, 43; m 64; c 2. *Educ:* Mass Inst Tech, BS, 65; Yale Univ, MS, 66, MPhil, 67 & PhD(physics), 74. *Concurrent Pos:* Adj fac, Univ NMex, Los Alamos, 83- *Mem:* Am Phys Soc. *Res:* Production of polarized electrons; carbon dioxide laser fusion research; detection by Cerenkav radiation; optical transition radiation. *Mailing Add:* 327 Rover Blvd Los Alamos NM 87544

LADKANY, SAMAAN GEORGE, FINITE ELEMENT ANALYSIS, EXPERIMENTAL MECHANICS. *Current Pos:* assoc prof & prin investr, 84-88, PROF & DIR, NUCLEAR WASTE STORAGE PROG, UNIV NEV, 88- *Personal Data:* b Damascus, May 16, 41; US citizen; m 82; c 2. *Educ:* Am Univ Beirut, BS, 63; Univ Wis-Madison, BS, 65, MS, 67, MS, 75, PhD(civil eng), 75. *Prof Exp:* Adj asst prof & scientist, Eng Res Sta, Univ Wis-Madison, 75-79; asst prof, Johns Hopkins Univ, 79-84. *Concurrent Pos:* Co-prin investr, Univ Nev, Las Vegas/Am Soc Heating, Refrig & Air Conditioning Engrs Prop Fans, 84-86, Univ Nev Las Vegas/Army Res Off Robotics, 85-91; expert witness/consult, Clark Co Attorneys, 85-; dir, High Level Nuclear Waste Prog, Univ Nev, Las Vegas/Dept Energy, 91-96; mem, Tubular Struct Comt, Struct Stability Res Coun, 93-, Double Curved Shells Comt, 93-; mem, Steel Bridges Comt, Am Soc Civil Engrs, 95- *Mem:* Struct Stability Res Coun; Am Soc Civil Engrs; Am Concrete Inst; Am Soc Eng Educ. *Mailing Add:* Dept Civil Eng Univ Nev Las Vegas NV 89154-4015. *Fax:* 702-895-3936; *E-Mail:* samaan@ce.unlv.edu

LADMAN, AARON J(ULIUS), ANATOMY. *Current Pos:* dean, Sch Allied Health, 81-86, prof anat, 81-96, ADJ PROF NEUROBIOL & ANAT, ALLEGHENY UNIV HEALTH SCI, MCP HAHNEMANN SCH MED, HAHNEMANN UNIV, PHILADELPHIA, 96- *Personal Data:* b Jamaica, NY, July 3, 25; m 48, 82, Patricia A Bergbauer; c Susan (Brown), Thomas J & Peter. *Educ:* NY Univ, AB, 47; Ind Univ, PhD(anat), 52. *Prof Exp:* Res fel anat, Harvard Med Sch, 52-55, assoc anat, 55-61; assoc prof, Med Units, Univ Tenn, 61-64; prof anat & chmn dept, Univ NMex, 64-81. *Concurrent Pos:* USPHS career develop award, 62-64; mem res career award comt, Nat Inst Gen Med Sci, 67-71; ed, Anat Record, 68- *Mem:* Am Soc Cell Biol; Coun Biol Ed; Histochem Soc; Am Asn Anatomists (2nd vpres, 80-81 & 1st vpres, 81-82); fel AAAS. *Res:* Cytochemistry; electron microscopy; endocrinology; experimental cytology; retina lung; tumor biology; scientific writing. *Mailing Add:* Dept Neurobiol & Anat Allegheny Univ Health Sci MCP Hahnemann Sch Med Ctr City Campus Broad & Vine Philadelphia PA 19102-1192. *E-Mail:* ladmana@allegheny.edu

LADNER, DAVID WILLIAM, QUANTITATIVE STRUCTURE-ACTIVITY RELATIONSHIPS. *Current Pos:* res chemist herbicide synthesis, Agr Res Div, Am Cyanamid, 77-80, sr res chemist herbicide synthesis, 80-83, group leader, 83-93, sr group leader herbicide synthesis, 93-96, RES MGR CHEM DISCOVERY, AGR RES DIV, AM CYANAMID, 96- *Personal Data:* b Meadville, Pa, June 22, 47; m 73, Cathy Tillman; c Rebecca & Deborah. *Educ:* Pa State Univ, BS, 69; Univ Ga, PhD(org chem), 74. *Prof Exp:* Res assoc org systhesis, Dept Chem, Univ Wash, 74-75; res fel org synthesis, Syntex, SA, Mex, DF, 75-76; sr scientist, N L Industs, 76-77. *Mem:* Am Chem Soc. *Res:* Design and synthesis of herbicides and plant regulants, particularly those affecting enzymes in amino acid biosynthetic pathways; quantitative structure-activity relationships, techniques to model activity, translocation and uptake of pesticides; high throughput synthesis. *Mailing Add:* PO Box 400 Princeton NJ 08543-0400. *E-Mail:* ladnerd@pt.cyanamid.com

LADNER, RICHARD E, COMPUTER SCIENCE. *Current Pos:* From actg asst prof to assoc prof, 71-81, PROF COMPUT SCI, UNIV WASH, 81- *Personal Data:* b Berkeley, Calif, Aug 22, 43; c 2. *Educ:* St Marys Col, Calif, BS, 65; Univ Calif, Berkeley, PhD(math), 71. *Concurrent Pos:* Vis appts, Univ Toronto, 77, Yale Univ, 78, Gallaudet Univ, 85, Math Sci Res Inst, 86 & Victoria Univ Wellington, NZ, 93; ed, J Comput, Soc Indust & Appl Math, 80-83; Guggenheim fel, 85-86; prog comt mem, Comput Profs Social Responsibility, 88 & 92; assoc ed, J Comput & Syst Sci, 89-; Fulbright travel grant, NZ, 92-93. *Mem:* Fel Asn Comput Mach; Inst Elec & Electronics Engrs Comput Soc; Am Math Soc; Asn Symbolic Logic. *Res:* Design and analysis of algorithms; parallel and distributed computation theory; computational complexity; computer networks; lossy data compression. *Mailing Add:* Dept Comput Sci & Eng Univ Wash Box 352350 Seattle WA 98195

LADNER, SIDNEY JULES, PHYSICAL CHEMISTRY. *Current Pos:* asst prof, 67-69, ASSOC PROF CHEM, HOUSTON BAPTIST UNIV, 69- *Personal Data:* b Houston, Tex, Mar 12, 36; m 59; c 2. *Educ:* Univ Houston, BS, 59, PhD(phys chem), 65. *Prof Exp:* Fel chem, Univ NMex, 65-66; chemist, Shell Develop Co, Tex, 66-67. *Mem:* Am Chem Soc. *Res:* Molecular spectroscopy; decay processes and the decay kinetics of molecules in excited electronic energy states; chemical education. *Mailing Add:* Dept Chem Houston Baptist Univ 7502 Fondren Rd Houston TX 77074-3204

LADO, FRED, THEORY OF LIQUIDS. *Current Pos:* from asst prof to assoc prof, 68-85, PROF PHYSICS, NC STATE UNIV, 85- *Personal Data:* b La Coruna, Spain, June 5, 38; US citizen; m 60; c 3. *Educ:* Univ Fla, BS, 60, PhD(physics), 64. *Prof Exp:* Fel physics, Univ Fla, 64-65; staff mem, Los Alamos Sci Lab, 65-68. *Concurrent Pos:* Fulbright sr lectr, Spain, 71-72; guest scientist, Int Ctr Theoret Physics, Trieste, Italy, 87, Inst Rocasolano, CSIC, Madrid, Spain, 97. *Mem:* Am Phys Soc; Span Physics Soc. *Res:* Statistical mechanics; equilibrium and non-equilibrium theory of liquids; many-body problem. *Mailing Add:* Dept Physics NC State Univ Raleigh NC 27695-8202. *Fax:* 919-515-6538; *E-Mail:* fred_lado@ncsu.edu

LA DU, BERT NICHOLS, JR, BIOCHEMICAL PHARMACOLOGY. *Current Pos:* chmn dept, 74-80, prof, 74-88, EMER PROF PHARMACOL, UNIV MICH MED SCH, ANN ARBOR, 88-, DIR RES, DEPT ANESTHESIOL, 91- *Personal Data:* b Lansing, Mich, Nov 13, 20; m 47; c 4. *Educ:* Mich State Col, BS, 43; Univ Mich, MD, 45; Univ Calif, PhD(biochem), 52. *Prof Exp:* Intern, Rochester Gen Hosp, NY, 45-46; asst biochem, Mich State Col, 46-47 & Univ Calif, 47-50; from sr asst surgeon to med dir, NIH, 50-63; prof pharmacol & chmn dept, Med Sch, NY Univ, 63-74. *Concurrent Pos:* Res assoc, Goldwater Mem Hosp Res Serv, NY Univ, 50-54, instr, Bellevue Med Ctr, 51-54. *Mem:* Am Soc Biol Chemists; Am Chem Soc; Am Soc Pharmacol & Exp Therapeut (pres, 78-79); Am Soc Human Genetics; NY Acad Sci (pres, 70). *Res:* Drug metabolism; metabolism of tyrosine; inborn errors of metabolism; pharmacogenetics. *Mailing Add:* Dept Pharmacol 1301 MSRB III Univ Mich Med Sch Ann Arbor MI 48109-0632. *Fax:* 313-764-9332

LADUKE, JOHN CARL, SYSTEMATIC BIOLOGY, BIOLOGICAL SCIENCES. *Current Pos:* Asst prof, 80-85, ASSOC PROF BIOL, UNIV NDAK, 85- *Personal Data:* b Jackson, Mich, Nov 21, 50; m 73; c 1. *Educ:* Tex Tech Univ, BS, 73, MS, 75; Ohio State Univ, PhD(bot), 80. *Honors & Awards:* Ralph E Alston Award, Bot Soc Am, 79. *Mem:* Int Asn Plant Taxon; Am Soc Plant Taxonomists; Bot Soc Am; Soc Syst Zool; Sigma Xi. *Res:* Plant systematics; chemosystematics; Sphaeralcea (Malvacae) including gathering morphological, cytological, flavonoid chemical data, molecula. *Mailing Add:* Dept Biol Univ NDak PO Box 9019 Grand Forks ND 58202-9019. *E-Mail:* laduke@vm1.nodak.edu

LADWIG, HAROLD ALLEN, NEUROLOGY. *Current Pos:* FAC, EEG LAB, WILSON MEM HOSP, NC, 83- *Personal Data:* b Manilla, Iowa, May 11, 22; m 46; c Stephen & Rosemary. *Educ:* Univ Iowa, MD, 47, BA, 52; Am Bd Psychiat & Neurol, dipl. *Prof Exp:* Clin instr neurol, Univ Minn, 50-53; from instr to asst prof neurol & psychiat, Sch Med, Creighton Univ, 54-56, assoc prof, 66-83; Dept Neurol, Univ Nebr Med Ctr, 66-83. *Concurrent Pos:* Dir, EEG Lab, Creighton Mem St Joseph's Hosp, 54-70, asst dir rehab ctr, 54-58, assoc dir, 58-64; attend physician, Vet Admin Hosp, 54-59, consult physician, 59-63; mem med staff, Nebr Children's Ther Ctr, 56-64; dir, EEG Lab, Children's Mem Hosp, 63-70 & Archbishop Bergan Mercy Hosp, 64-83. *Mem:* Am EEG Soc; AMA; Am Col Physicians; Am Cong Rehab Med; Am Acad Neurol. *Res:* Diagnostic neurology and rehabilitation of neurological patients; care of the aged; electroencephalography. *Mailing Add:* PO Box 3049 Wilson NC 27895-3049

LAEMLE, LOIS K, DEVELOPMENTAL NEUROBIOLOGY, VISUAL SYSTEMS. *Current Pos:* asst prof, 72-77, ASSOC PROF NEUROANAT & HISTOL, UNIV MED & DENT NJ, 77- *Personal Data:* b New York, NY, May 26, 41. *Educ:* City Univ New York, BS, 62; Columbia Univ, PhD(anat), 68. *Prof Exp:* Fel anat, Albert Einstein Col Med, 68; res fel neurosci, Rose F Kennedy Ctr Ment Retardation, 69-72. *Concurrent Pos:* Prin investr, NIH res grant, 73-81 & 82-86; vis prof, Dept Ophthal, NY Med Sch, 83; assoc ed, Am J Anat, 89- *Mem:* Am Asn Anatomists; Soc Neurosci; Sigma Xi; NY Acad Sci; Cajal Club. *Res:* Morphology and development of the central nervous system; fiber connections, neuronal maturation, and neurotransmitters in the visual system; mechanisms of arcadian timekeeping. *Mailing Add:* Dept Anat Univ Med & Dent NJ Med Sch 100 Berben St Newark NJ 07103

LAEMMLE, JOSEPH THOMAS, ORGANIC CHEMISTRY, METAL WORKING LUBRICANTS. *Current Pos:* sr scientist, Alcoa Labs, 77-80, staff scientist, 80-81, tech supvr, 81, sr tech supvr, 81-86, DIV MGR, SURFACE TECH DIV, ALCOA LABS, 86- *Personal Data:* b Louisville, Ky, Feb 7, 41; m 65, Patricia A Tincher; c Scott, Adam & Lillian. *Educ:* Bellarmine Col, BA, 64; Ga Inst Technol, MS, 68, PhD(org chem), 71; Ga State Univ, MBA, 76. *Honors & Awards:* NASA Trainee, 69. *Prof Exp:* From asst res chemist to asst, Ga Inst Technol, 67-73; asst prof chem, Kennesaw Col, 73-77. *Mem:* Am Chem Soc; Soc Tribologist & Lubrication Engrs; Sigma Xi. *Res:* Determination of the structure of organometallic compounds; lubricant testing and development; descriptions of organometallic reaction mechanisms and sterechemistry of additions with Ketones; metal working lubricants including formation, handling, reclamation and disposal. *Mailing Add:* Surface Tech Div Alcoa Tech Ctr Alcoa Lab 100 Technical Dr Alcoa Ctr PA 15069-0001. *Fax:* 412-337-2809

LAEMMLEN, FRANKLIN, PLANT PATHOLOGY, ENTOMOLOGY. *Current Pos:* farm adv, Imp Co Coop Exten, 80-92, FARM ADV, SANTA BARBARA & SAN LUIS OBISPO COUNTIES, UNIV CALIF, 92- *Personal Data:* b Reedley, Calif, Mar 8, 38; m 61, Anne; c Teresa & Louise. *Educ:* Univ Calif, Davis, BS, 60, PhD(plant path), 70; Purdue Univ, West Lafayette, MS, 67. *Prof Exp:* Res asst plant path, Univ Calif, Davis, 66-70; asst prof, Univ Hawaii, 70-72; from asst prof to assoc prof plant path, Mich State Univ, 76-80. *Concurrent Pos:* Assoc ed, Plant Dis Reporter, 74-77; vis colleague, Dept Plant Path, Univ Calif, Berkeley, 78-79. *Mem:* Sigma Xi; Am Phytopath Soc. *Res:* Extension plant pathology; ornamental plant diseases; plant disease diagnostic laboratory; field and vegetable crop diseases. *Mailing Add:* 1053 Camelot Dr Santa Maria CA 93455. *Fax:* 805-934-6240

LAERM, JOSHUA, FUNCTIONAL MORPHOLOGY. *Current Pos:* Asst prof, 76-81, ASSOC PROF ZOOL, UNIV GA, 81-, DIR, MUS NATURAL HIST, 78- *Personal Data:* b Waynesboro, Pa, Sept 27, 42; m 81. *Educ:* Pa State Univ, BA, 65; Univ Ill, MS, 72, PhD(zool), 76. *Mem:* AAAS; Soc Vert Paleont; Am Soc Mammalogists; Soc Study of Evolution; Am Soc Zoologists. *Res:* Evolution and functional morphology of vertebral column in fossil fishes; mammalian systematics; vertebrate natural history. *Mailing Add:* Dept Zool Univ Ga 1180 E Broad St Athens GA 30601-3040

LAESSIG, RONALD HAROLD, CLINICAL CHEMISTRY, PUBLIC HEALTH. *Current Pos:* assoc prof, 71-76, PROF PREV MED & PATH, MED CTR, UNIV WIS-MADISON, 76-; DIR, STATE LAB HYG, 79- *Personal Data:* b Marshfield, Wis, Apr 4, 40; m 66, Joan M Spreda; c 1. *Educ:* Wis State Univ-Stevens Point, BS, 62; Univ Wis-Madison, PhD(analytical chem), 65. *Honors & Awards:* DIFCO Award, Am Pub Health Asn, 74; Outstanding Contrib through Serv to Profession of Clin Chem Award, Am Asn Clin Chem, 90, Natelson Award for Advan Clin Chem, 90. *Prof Exp:* Fel, Princeton Univ, 65-66 & Ctr Dis Control, Atlanta, 66; asst dir, State Lab Hyg, 70-79, chief chem, 66-79. *Concurrent Pos:* Mem, Inst Bd Anal Chem, 71-; chmn diag prod comt, Food & Drug Admin, 72-74; pres, Nat Comt Clin Lab Stand, 80-82; mem bd, Am Asn Clin Chem, 85-88. *Mem:* Am Asn Clin Chem; Am Chem Soc; Am Pub Health Asn. *Res:* Automation; newborn screening; computerization of laboratory operation; public health laboratory applications of test procedures. *Mailing Add:* Dept Pathol Med Sch Univ Wis 1300 University Ave Madison WI 53706-1585. *Fax:* 608-262-3257

LAETSCH, THEODORE WILLIS, MATHEMATICAL ANALYSIS. *Current Pos:* ASSOC PROF MATH, UNIV ARIZ, 71-, HEAD, MATH DEPT, 78- *Personal Data:* b St Louis, Mo, Jan 7, 40; m 61. *Educ:* Washington Univ, St Louis, BS, 61; Mass Inst Technol, SM, 62; Calif Inst Technol, PhD(appl math), 68. *Prof Exp:* Asst prof physics, Col Idaho, 62-65; asst prof math, Ill State Univ, 68-70. *Concurrent Pos:* Nat Acad Sci-Nat Res Coun resident res associateship, Wright-Patterson AFB, Ohio, 70-71. *Mem:* Am Math Soc; Soc Indust & Appl Math. *Res:* Functional analysis in partially ordered spaces; boundary value problems for ordinary and partial differential equations. *Mailing Add:* Dept Math Univ Ariz PO Box 210089 Tucson AZ 85721-0089

LAETSCH, WATSON MCMILLAN, BOTANY. *Current Pos:* from asst prof to assoc prof bot, Univ Calif, Berkeley, 63-71, assoc dir, Lawrence Hall Sci, 69-72, dir, Univ Bot Garden, 69-73, dir, Lawrence Hall Sci, 72-80, PROF BOT, UNIV CALIF, BERKELEY, 71-, VCHANCELLOR UNDERGRAD AFFAIRS, 80- *Personal Data:* b Bellingham, Wash, Jan 19, 33; m 58; c 2. *Educ:* Wabash Col, AB, 55; Stanford Univ, PhD(biol), 61. *Hon Degrees:* DSc, Wabash Col, 85. *Prof Exp:* Fulbright fel, Univ Delhi, India, 56-57; asst prof biol, State Univ NY, Stony Brook, 61-63. *Concurrent Pos:* Fulbright fel, Univ Delhi, India, 56-57; NSF sr fel, Univ Col, London, 68-69; pres, Asn Sci-Tech Ctrs, 77-78; mem, Indo-US Subcomn Educ & Cult, 83- *Mem:* AAAS; Bot Soc Am; Am Soc Plant Physiol; Soc Exp Biol & Med. *Res:* Plant development; structure and function of the photosynthetic apparatus; science education. *Mailing Add:* 1554 LeRoy Ave Berkeley CA 94708-1942

LAEVASTU, TAIVO, OCEANOGRAPHY, METEOROLOGY. *Current Pos:* RETIRED. *Personal Data:* b Vihula, Estonia, Feb 26, 23; m 49, Irene Merikanto; c Kristina, Pia & Steve. *Educ:* Gothenburg & Lund, Fil Kand, 51; Univ Wash, Seattle, MS, 54; Univ Helsinki, PhD(oceanog), 61. *Honors & Awards:* Mil Oceanog Award, 69. *Prof Exp:* Fisheries officer, Swed Migratory Fish Comt, 51-53; res assoc oceanog, Univ Wash, Seattle, 54-55; fisheries oceanogr, Food & Agr Orgn, UN, 55-62; assoc prof, Univ Hawaii, 62-64; res oceanogr, US Fleet Numerical Weather Facil, 64-71, chief, Oceanog Div, Environ Prediction Res Facil, Naval Postgrad Sch, 71-76; ecosyst modeling expert, Nat Oceanic & Atmospheric Admin, Nat Marine Fisheries Serv, 76-94. *Concurrent Pos:* UNESCO lectr, Bombay, India, 59; mem, Panel Disposal Radioactive Waste Into Sea & Fresh Water, Int Atomic Energy Agency, 59-62; mem, Working Group Fisheries Prob Comn Maritime Meteorol, World Meteorol Orgn, 60-62; NSF & USN res grantee, 62-64; mem, World Meteor Orgn/UNESCO Panel Oceanic Water Balance, 72-84 & Sea Use Coun, Sci-Tech Bd, 71-76; proj dir, ICSC World Lab, Lausanne, 92-93. *Mem:* Japan Soc Fish Oceanog; Am Inst Fishery Res Biol. *Res:* Fisheries hydrography and oceanography; marine chemistry; sea-air interactions; oceanographic forecasting; numerical modeling in oceanography and meteorology; marine ecosystem modeling. *Mailing Add:* 10333 40th Ave NE Seattle WA 98125. *Fax:* 206-525-9154

LA FEHR, THOMAS ROBERT, GEOPHYSICS. *Current Pos:* PRES, LCT, 89- *Personal Data:* b Los Angeles, Calif, Feb 6, 34; m 57; c 5. *Educ:* Univ Calif, Berkeley, AB, 58; Colo Sch Mines, MSc, 62; Stanford Univ, PhD(geophys), 64. *Prof Exp:* Geophysicist, US Geol Surv, 62-64; geophysicist, Geophys Assocs, Int, 64-66; vpres tech develop, GAI-GMX Inc, 66-67; dir tech develop, GAI-GMX Div, EG&G Inc, 67-69; assoc prof, Colo Sch Mines, 69-75, adj prof geophys, 75-89; pres, Edcon, 75-89. *Concurrent Pos:* Lectr, Stanford Univ, 64; consult, GAI-GMS Div, EG&G, Inc, 69-70 & Explor Data Consult, 70-89. *Mem:* Hon mem Soc Explor Geophys; Am Asn Petrol Geol; Am Geophys Union. *Res:* Gravity and magnetic exploration; potential field theory; integrated seismic, gravity, well log data; borehole gravity. *Mailing Add:* 9566 Briar Forest Dr Houston TX 77063

LAFERRIERE, ARTHUR L, ORGANIC CHEMISTRY, INORGANIC CHEMISTRY. *Current Pos:* PROF CHEM, RI COL, 62- *Personal Data:* b Willimantic, Conn, Dec 3, 33; m 55; c 3. *Educ:* Brown Univ, BS, 55; Rutgers Univ, MS, 58; Univ RI, PhD(chem), 60. *Prof Exp:* Res chemist, Minerals & Chem Corp, 56-58 & Am Cyanamid Co, 60-62. *Mem:* Am Chem Soc. *Res:* Inorganic solution chemistry; organic redox mechanisms. *Mailing Add:* Dept Chem RI Col 600 Mt Pleasant Ave Providence RI 02908

LAFEVER, HOWARD N, PLANT BREEDING, GENETICS. *Current Pos:* from asst prof to prof genetics & plant breeding, 65-77, PROF AGRON, OHIO AGR RES & DEVELOP CTR, 77- *Personal Data:* b Hagerstown, Ind, May 13, 38; m 58; c 2. *Educ:* Purdue Univ, BS, 59, MS, 61, PhD(plant breeding & genetics), 63. *Honors & Awards:* Crops & Soils Award, Am Soc Agron, 77. *Prof Exp:* Instr bot, Wis State Univ, LaCrosse, 63; asst prof genetics, Purdue Univ, 63; res geneticist, Boll Weevil Res Lab, USDA, 63-65. *Mem:* Am Soc Agron; Crop Sci Soc Am. *Res:* Breeding new wheat varieties for distribution and production in midwest; genetic studies of wheat. *Mailing Add:* 500 Danberry Dr Wooster OH 44691

LAFEVERS, JAMES RONALD, MANAGEMENT OF RESEARCH & DEVELOPMENT, MANAGEMENT OF MULTIDISCIPLINARY RESEARCH IN ENERGY DEVELOPMENT. *Current Pos:* consult energy & environ res, Argonne Nat Lab, 73-74, asst scientist & prog mgr, 74-79, environ scientist & prog mgr, 79-82, dir sci & technol rev, Univ Chicago Argonne Nat Lab, 83-91, actg assoc vpres res & lab, 91-92, EXEC DIR & DEP VPRES ARGONNE NAT LAB, UNIV CHICAGO, 92- *Personal Data:* b Oakland, Calif, Nov 16, 44; m 65, Judy Isbell; c Sandra, Terri & Jamie. *Educ:* Univ Cent Ark, BS, 68; Univ Southern Miss, MS, 70; Ind State Univ, PhD(econ geog), 74. *Prof Exp:* Instr phys sci, Columbia Acad, 69-70; instr phys geog & resource mgt, Univ Southern Miss, 70-71. *Concurrent Pos:* Consult resource mgt, Southern Miss Develop Comn, 68-69; res assoc, Crane Ctr Econ Develop, 70-71, River Basin Res Ctr, 71-72; consult energy & environ sci, Los Alamos Tech Assocs, 81-82; lectr sci & environ policy, Northwestern Univ, 82-84; mem, Cong Sci & Technol Adv Comt, 91-94. *Mem:* AAAS; Asn Am Geographers; Am Nuclear Soc; Am Phys Soc; Am Mgt Asn; Inst Environ Sci. *Res:* Energy resource and facility development and related economic and environmental impacts, including the effects of legislation and policy decisions on both the energy industry and the environment; application of both basic and applied research methods. *Mailing Add:* Univ Chicago Argonne Nat Lab Bldg 201 Argonne IL 60439. *Fax:* 630-252-5329; *E-Mail:* lafevers@201hrmail.hr.anl.gov

LAFFERTY, JAMES FRANCIS, BIOMEDICAL ENGINEERING, MECHANICAL ENGINEERING. *Current Pos:* asst prof nuclear eng, Werner-Gren Res Lab, Univ Ky, 57-62, assoc prof mech eng, 62-73, actg lab dir, 67-73, prof mech eng & lab dir, 73-85, prof & dir, Biomed Eng Ctr, 85-90, EMER PROF & DIR BIOMED ENG CTR, UNIV KY, 90-; BIOMED ENG CONSULT, 90- *Personal Data:* b Pampa, Tex, Dec 23, 27; m 56; c 3. *Educ:* Univ Ky, BS, 55; Univ Southern Calif, MS, 57; Univ Mich, MS, 66, PhD(nuclear eng), 67. *Prof Exp:* Asst, Wenner-Gren Res Lab, Univ Ky, 54-55; mem tech staff, Hughes Aircraft Co, 55-57. *Concurrent Pos:* NSF fac fels, Univ Mich, 61-62 & 65-66. *Mem:* Orthop Res Soc; Am Soc Mech Eng; Soc Automotive Eng. *Res:* Biomechanics of the skeletal and cardiovascular systems; response of biosystems to impact, vibration, acceleration. *Mailing Add:* 693 Andover Village Pl Lexington KY 40509

LAFFERTY, JAMES M(ARTIN), PHYSICAL ELECTRONICS, POWER ELECTRONICS. *Current Pos:* CONSULT, 81- *Personal Data:* b Battle Creek, Mich, Apr 27, 16; m 42; c 4. *Educ:* Univ Mich, BSE, 39, MS, 40, PhD(elec eng), 46. *Honors & Awards:* Naval Ord Develop Award, 46; Lamme Medalist, Inst Elec & Electronics Engrs, 79. *Prof Exp:* Mem staff, Eastman Kodak Co, NY, 39; radio proximity fuse res, Carnegie Inst Wash, 41; res assoc, Gen Elec Co, 42-56, mgr, Plasma & Vacuum Physics Br, 56-68, mgr, Gen Physics Lab, 68-72, mgr, Physics & Elec Eng Lab, 72-74, mgr, Physics & Electronic Eng Lab, 74-75, mgr, Electronic Power Conditioning & Control Lab, 75-78, mgr, Power Electronics Lab, Res & Develop Ctr, 78-81. *Concurrent Pos:* Group leader, People to People Citizen Embassador Prog, 84-88. *Mem:* Nat Acad Eng; fel AAAS; fel Am Phys Soc; fel Inst Elec & Electronics Engrs; hon mem Am Vacuum Soc; Int Union Vacuum Sci Tech Applns (pres, 81-83). *Res:* Electrometer and microwave tubes; electron guns; lanthanum boride cathodes; color television picture tubes; gas discharge tubes; hot-cathode magnetron ionization gauge; triggered vacuum gap; vacuum switch; electric vehicles. *Mailing Add:* 1202 Hedgewood Lane Schenectady NY 12309

LAFFERTY, KEVIN D, MATHEMATICAL MODELLING, PARASITE ECOLOGY. *Current Pos:* ADJ PROF, UNIV CALIF, LOS ANGELES, 93- *Personal Data:* b Glendale, Calif, Sept 8, 63; m 92, Cristina Sandoral. *Educ:* Univ Calif, Santa Barbara, BA, 85, MA, 88, PhD(ecol), 91. *Prof Exp:* Lectr parasitol, Univ Calif, Santa Barbara, 90-92, res biologist, 93; fel, Nat Marine Sanctuary, 92-93. *Mem:* Western Soc Naturalists. *Res:* Effects that parasites have on the ecology and evolution of their hosts; degradation of the marine environment. *Mailing Add:* 1933 Lombardy Dr La Canada Flintridge CA 91011

LAFFERTY, WALTER J, PHYSICAL CHEMISTRY. *Current Pos:* CHEMIST, NAT INST STAND & TECHNOL, 62- *Personal Data:* b Wilmington, Del, Feb 10, 34; m 58; c Anne, Maura, Clare, Ellen, Paula & Brenda. *Educ:* Univ Del, BS, 56; Mass Inst Technol, PhD(phys chem), 61. *Honors & Awards:* Silver Medal, Dept Com. *Prof Exp:* Res assoc, Johns Hopkins Univ, 61-62. *Concurrent Pos:* Leverhulme vis fel, Univ Reading, England, 70-71; vis prof, Univ Paris (VI), 87, 91 & 93. *Mem:* Coblentz Soc; Am Phys Soc. *Res:* Infrared and microwave spectroscopy. *Mailing Add:* Optical Technol Div Bldg 221 Rm B250 Nat Inst Stand & Technol Gaithersburg MD 20899. *E-Mail:* wjl@tiber.nist.gov

LAFFIN, ROBERT JAMES, MICROBIOLOGY. *Current Pos:* asst prof, 64-67, assoc prof, 67-76, PROF MICROBIOL, ALBANY MED COL, 76- *Personal Data:* b New Haven, Conn, Apr 16, 27; m 74, Judith Mayba; c 4. *Educ:* Yale Univ, BS, 49, PhD(microbiol), 55; Am Bd Med Lab Immunol, dipl. *Prof Exp:* Instr microbiol, Womans Col, Univ NC, 53-55; from instr to assoc prof, Creighton Univ, 55-62; instr obstet & gynec, med sch, Tufts Univ, 62-64. *Concurrent Pos:* Immunologist, St Margaret's Hosp, 62-64. *Mem:* Emer mem Am Asn Immunologist. *Res:* Microbiology. *Mailing Add:* Dept Microbiol Albany Med Col Union Univ 47 New Scotland Ave Albany NY 12208-3479. *Fax:* 518-262-5748; *E-Mail:* riaffin@ccgateway.amc.edu

LAFFLER, THOMAS G, GENETICS. *Personal Data:* b Detroit, Mich, May 10, 46; m 68; c 3. *Educ:* Mass Inst Technol, BS, 68; Univ Wash, PhD(genetics), 74. *Prof Exp:* Fel oncol, McArdle Lab Cancer Res, 74-78, res assoc, 78-80; res asst prof microbiol, Med & Dent Schs, Northwestern Univ, 80-89. *Mem:* Genetics Soc Am; Sigma Xi. *Res:* Study of molecular basis of cell cycle control using Physarum polycephalum as a lower enkorycote model; cell cycle mutants and the regulation of tubulin biosynthesis and DNA replication. *Mailing Add:* 1964 Pinehurst Ct Libertyville IL 60048

LAFFOON, JOHN, ELECTRON MICROSCOPY. *Current Pos:* ULTRA MICROTOMY DENT RES, 79- *Personal Data:* b Albia, Iowa, June 20, 55. *Educ:* Univ Iowa, BS, 79. *Prof Exp:* Electron microscopy, Dent Col, Univ Iowa, 79-88. *Res:* Electron microsepy in dental research for the past nine years; tem and sem and micro probe, soft and hard tissue. *Mailing Add:* Electron Probe Microanalysis Facil Dows Inst Dent Res Univ Iowa Col Dent N441 Dent Sci Bldg Iowa City IA 52242

LAFLAMME, GASTON, EPIDEMIOLOGY, MYCOLOGY. *Current Pos:* RES SCIENTIST, CAN FORESTRY SERV, STE-FOY, QUE, 80- *Personal Data:* b St Prosper, Beauce, Que, July 15, 45; m 80; c 1. *Educ:* Laval Univ, Que, BScApp, 68, MSc, 71; Swiss Fed Inst Technol, Zurich, DScApp(forest path & mycol), 75. *Prof Exp:* Res scientist forest path, Can Forestry Serv, Nfld, 75-78; forest pathologist, Dept Land & Forest, Que, 78-80. *Mem:* Can Phytopath Soc; Poplar Coun Can; Can Forestry Inst. *Res:* Decay of living trees; taxonomy of fungi; scleroderris canker and other tree diseases; endophytic fungi. *Mailing Add:* PO Box 3800 Ste Foy PQ G1V 4C7 Can

LA FLEUR, JAMES KEMBLE, MECHANICAL ENGINEERING. *Current Pos:* RETIRED. *Personal Data:* b Los Angeles, Calif, Apr 23, 30; m 64; c 3. *Educ:* Calif Inst Technol, BSME, 52, Pepperdine, MBA, 80. *Prof Exp:* Engr, AiResearch Mfg Co, 52-56; pres, Kemsco Inc, 56-57, Dynamic Res Inc, 57-60 & LaFleur Corp, 60-65, chmn bd, 65-66; pres, Indust Cryogenics Inc, 66-75; chmn, pres & chief exec officer, GTI Corp, 75-90. *Mem:* Am Soc Mech Engrs; Cryogenic Soc Am; Int Solar Energy Soc; Int Asn Hydrogen Energy; Am Wind Energy Asn. *Res:* Applying knowledge gained in the development of normal turbo-machinery to the field of low temperature to develop new low temperature processes. *Mailing Add:* PO Box 2327 North Hollywood CA 91602

LAFLEUR, KERMIT STILLMAN, TEXTILE CHEMISTRY, SOIL SCIENCE. *Current Pos:* RETIRED. *Personal Data:* b Waterville, Maine, Feb 14, 15; m 39; c 1. *Educ:* Colby Col, BA, 37; Clemson Univ, MS, 64, PhD, 66. *Prof Exp:* Asst chemist, Wyandotte Worsted Co, Maine, 37-40, chief chemist, 40-46; chief chemist, Deering Milliken Maine Mills, 47-52; res chemist, Excelsior Mills, 52-56, tech supt, 56-58; group leader wool res, Deering Milliken Res Corp, 59-62, consult chemist, 62-66, sr scientist, 66-67; assoc prof soil chem, Clemson Univ, 67-75, prof, 75-80. *Mem:* AAAS; Am Soc Agron; Soil Sci Soc Am. *Res:* Wool chemistry; soil chemistry. *Mailing Add:* 206 Hunter Ave Clemson SC 29631

LAFLEUR, LOUIS DWYNN, acoustics, ultrasonics, for more information see previous edition

LAFLEUR, MICHEL, BIOPHYSICAL CHEMISTRY, SPECTROSCOPY OF BIOMOLECULES. *Current Pos:* asst prof, 90-95, ASSOC PROF PHYS CHEM, UNIV MONTREAL, 95- *Personal Data:* b Montreal, Que, Mar 14, 60. *Educ:* Univ Sherbrooke, BSc, 82; Univ Laval, PhD(chem), 87. *Prof Exp:* Postdoctoral fel, Dept Biochem, Univ BC, 87-90. *Mem:* Can Asn Advan Sci; Spectros Soc Can; Can Soc Chem; Fedn Am Soc Exp Biol; Biophys Soc. *Res:* Establish the physico-chemical laws dictating the behavior of biomolecules by characterizing the structure and dynamics by spectroscopic methods. *Mailing Add:* Dept Chem Univ Montreal Montreal PQ H3C 3J7 Can. *Fax:* 514-343-7586; *E-Mail:* lafleur@ere.umontreal.ca

LAFLEUR, ROBERT GEORGE, HYDROLOGY & WATER RESOURCES. *Current Pos:* Instr geol, 52-55, from asst prof to assoc prof, 55-82, PROF, GLACIAL GEOL & WATER RESOURCES, RENSSELAER POLYTECH INST, 82- *Personal Data:* b Albany, NY, Mar 31, 29; m 50; c 3. *Educ:* Univ Rochester, AB, 50; Rensselaer Polytech Inst, MS, 53, PhD, 61. *Concurrent Pos:* Consult, NY State Educ Dept & US Geol Surv. *Mem:* Fel Geol Soc Am; Nat Asn Geol Teachers; Am Geophys Union; Arctic Inst NAm; Soc Econ Paleontologists & Mineralogists; Sigma Xi; Am Inst Prof Geologist; Am Inst Hydrol. *Res:* Glacial geology; hydrogeology. *Mailing Add:* Taberton Rd Sand Lake NY 12153

LAFON, GUY MICHEL, GEOCHEMISTRY, PHYSICAL CHEMISTRY. *Current Pos:* sr res geologist, RES ASSOC, EXXON PROD RES CO, 79- *Personal Data:* b Bordeaux, France, June 5, 43. *Educ:* Paris Sch Mines, Civil Ing Mines, 64; Univ Alta, MSc, 65; Northwestern Univ, Ill, PhD(geol), 69. *Prof Exp:* Res Found fel, State Univ NY Binghamton, 69-70, asst prof geol, 70-72; asst prof geol, Johns Hopkins Univ, 72-79. *Mem:* Sigma Xi; AAAS; Geochem Soc; Soc Econ Paleont & Mineral; Geol Soc Am; Am Chem Soc. *Res:* Geochemistry of natural water systems; thermodynamic properties of brines and minerals; equilibrium models; experimental study of mineral-fluid reactions, hydrothermal simulation of geological processes. *Mailing Add:* PO Box 2189 Houston TX 77252-2189

LAFON, STEPHEN WOODROW, ANTIMICROBIAL THERAPY. *Current Pos:* Res asst, Dept Exp Ther, Burroughs Wellcome Co, 77-78, res scientist I, 78-81, res scientist II, 81-86, prog coordr, Dept Proj Coord, 86-87, clin res assoc III, Dept Infectious Dis, 87-89, CLIN RES SCIENTIST I, DEPT INFECTIOUS DIS, BURROUGHS WELLCOME CO, 89- *Personal Data:* b Owasso, Mich, Aug 3, 53; m 74; c 2. *Educ:* Olivet Nazarene Col, BA, 75; WVa Univ, MSc, 78. *Mem:* Assoc mem Am Soc Biol Chemists. *Res:* Metabolism and pharmacokinetics of numerous potential therapeutic agents; purine metabolism and nucleic acid synthesis in mammalian cells and protozoa; DNA damage assays and repair research; early HIV diseases and opportunist infections; author of numerous publications. *Mailing Add:* Dept Infectious Dis & Immunol Burroughs Wellcome Co 3030 Cornwallis Rd Research Triangle Park NC 27709-2700

LAFOND, ANDRE, FORESTRY. *Current Pos:* RETIRED. *Personal Data:* b Montreal, Que, July 1, 20; m 46; c 3. *Educ:* Jean-de-Brebeuf Col, BA, 42; Laval Univ, BA, 45, BASc, 46; Univ Wis, PhD, 51. *Prof Exp:* Forester, Que Forest Serv, 46-51; prof forest ecol & physiol, Laval Univ, 51-85, dean fac forestry, 71-85, pres, Res Found, 75. *Concurrent Pos:* Consult, Que Northshore Paper Co, World Bank & Can Int Develop Agency. *Mem:* Can Soc Soil Sci; Can Soc Plant Physiol; Fr-Can Asn Advan Sci; Can Inst Forestry; Int Soc Soil Sci. *Res:* Forest ecology, particularly soil vegetation relationships; forest physiology, particularly mineral nutrition of trees and fertilization; forest management, particularly site classification. *Mailing Add:* 2071 Marie-Victorin St Nicolas PQ G7A 4H4 Can

LA FOND, EUGENE CECIL, OCEANOGRAPHY, PHYSICAL OCEANOGRAPHY. *Current Pos:* secy gen, 70-87, PRES, COMN OCEANOG COOP WITH DEVELOP COUNTRIES, INT ASN PHYS SCI OCEAN, 83- *Personal Data:* b Bridgeport, Wash, Dec 4, 09; m 35, Katherine W Gehring; c William G & Robert E. *Educ:* San Diego State Col, AB, 32; Andhra Univ, India, DSc, 56. *Honors & Awards:* Ocean Sci Award, Am Geophys Union, 82; 100 Years of Int Geophys Medal, Soviet Acad Sci, 83; Distinguished Serv Award, Int Asn Phys Sci Ocean, 87. *Prof Exp:* Asst, Scripps Inst, Univ Calif, 33-40, oceanogr, 40-47; prof oceanog, Andhra Univ, India, 52-53 & 55-56; specialist oceanog, US State Dept, 56-57; sr scientist, Atomic Submarine US Ship Skate, North Pole, 58; marine biologist, Scirpps Inst & Int Coop Admin, 60-61; chief scientist, US Prog Biol, Int Indian Ocean Exped, Woods Hole Oceanog Inst, 62-63; dep dir off oceanog & dep secy, Int Oceanog Comn, UNESCO, Paris, France, 63-64; supvry res oceanogr, Navy Electronics Lab, Naval Undersea Res & Develop Ctr, 64-68, sr scientist & consult oceanog, 68-73. *Mem:* Marine Technol Soc; Soc Limnol & Oceanog (vpres, 54-55); Am Geophys Union; Int Asn Phys Sci Ocean (secy-gen,

70-87); Maratime Res Soc. *Res:* Physical oceanography; dynamics of internal waves, ocean water structures, water motion and near shore phenomena (waves, tide, circulation, beach erosion); studies carried out in Bay Bengal, South China Sea, Arctic Ocean, and North Pacific Ocean. *Mailing Add:* 4505 Santa Cruz Ave Box 7325 San Diego CA 92107

LAFONTAINE, JEAN-GABRIEL, CELL BIOLOGY, ELECTRON MICROSCOPY. *Current Pos:* asst prof path, Med Sch, 60-64, assoc prof biol, 64-68, PROF BIOL, SCI FAC, LAVAL UNIV, 68- *Personal Data:* b Sherbrooke, Que, Aug 4, 28; m 52; c 3. *Educ:* Laval Univ, Lic es Sci, 50; Univ Wis, MS, 52, PhD(zool), 54. *Honors & Awards:* Que Asn Advan Sci Prize, 82. *Prof Exp:* Res asst cytol, Sloan Kettering Inst, 54-56, Rockefeller Inst, 56-58 & Montreal Cancer Inst, 58-60. *Concurrent Pos:* Damon Runyon fel, 54-56. *Mem:* Am Soc Cell Biol; Can Soc Cell Biol; Royal Soc Can, 84; NY Acad Sci, 85. *Res:* Cytochemistry and ultrastructure of the cell nucleus. *Mailing Add:* Dept Biol Laval Univ Quebec PQ G1K 7P4 Can

LAFONTAINE, THOMAS E, AIR & WATER POLLUTION CONTROL, THERMAL PROCESS DESIGN. *Current Pos:* PRES/OWNER, TELTECH CO, 88-; VPRES & TECH DIR, INTERCON PAC INC, 90- *Personal Data:* b Clarksburg, Mass, Jan 2, 52; m 81, Catherine Hackett; c Christina & Colima. *Prof Exp:* Pres, T&C Res, 78-80; tech dir, Cameron-Yakima Inc, 81-87; vpres, ATESA USA, Inc, 87-88. *Concurrent Pos:* Consult, Ralston Brokers Int, 88-, Pac Aqua-Tech, Ltd, 90- *Mem:* Int Carbon Soc; Nat Pollution Control Fedn; Nat Air Pollution Control Asn; Am Water Works Asn. *Res:* Chemically treated activated carbons for special applications; manufacture of special purpose activated carbons; conversion of organic waste from landfills into activated carbon; process development for the disposal of waste tires. *Mailing Add:* PO Box 2784 Yakima WA 98907. *Fax:* 509-965-5963

LAFORNARA, JOSEPH PHILIP, CHEMISTRY, ENVIRONMENTAL SCIENCES. *Current Pos:* res chemist, Nat Environ Res Ctr, 71-75, Oil & Hazardous Mat Spills Br, Indust Environ Res Lab, 75-78, phys scientist, Environ Response Team, 78-87, CHIEF ENVIRON RESPONSE TEAM, US ENVIRON PROTECTION AGENCY, 87- *Personal Data:* b Buffalo, NY, Dec 5, 42; wid; c 2. *Educ:* Canisius Col, BS, 64; Univ Fla, PhD(inorg chem), 70. *Prof Exp:* Res chemist, Edison Water Qual Lab, Fed Water Qual Admin, Dept Interior, 70-71. *Concurrent Pos:* Tech adv, Hazardous Mat Adv Comt, Nat Res Coun-Nat Acad Sci, 71-; mem, Task Force for Nitrosamine Control & Task Force for Kepone Control, US Environ Protection Agency, 75-; chmn, Hazardous Mat Div, Am Soc Testing & Mat Comt, No F-20, Spill Control Syst, 78- *Mem:* Am Soc Testing & Mat; Am Chem Soc; Water Pollution Control Fedn. *Res:* Application of chemical technology to control of spills of hazardous materials; chemical analysis of inorganic and organic water and air pollutants; ultimate disposal of chemical wastes. *Mailing Add:* 894 Joan Ct North Brunswick NJ 08902-3223

LAFOUNTAIN, JAMES ROBERT, JR, CELL BIOLOGY. *Current Pos:* from asst prof to assoc prof, 72-86, PROF BIOL SCI, STATE UNIV NY, BUFFALO, 86- *Personal Data:* b Richmond, Va, Jan 8, 44; m 70; c 2. *Educ:* Princeton Univ, AB, 66; State Univ NY, Albany, PhD(biol sci), 70. *Prof Exp:* Fel, Eidgenossische Technische Hochschule, Switz, 71-72. *Mem:* Am Soc Cell Biol. *Res:* Physiology of cell division and cell motility. *Mailing Add:* Dept Biol Sci State Univ NY 657 Cooke Hall Buffalo NY 14260-1300. *Fax:* 716-645-2975

LAFOUNTAIN, LESTER JAMES, JR, GEOLOGY. *Current Pos:* CONSULT, BRYANA STIRRAT & ASSOC, 92- *Personal Data:* b Marinette, Wis, Sept 27, 42; m 64; c 1. *Educ:* Univ Wis, BS & MS, 64; Univ Colo, PhD(geol), 73. *Prof Exp:* Field geologist, US Steel Corp, 64; party chief geol, 65; geologist, Texaco Inc, 66; res assoc rock mech, Dept Geol, Univ NC, 71-74; asst proj geologist, D'Appolonia Geophys Corp, 75-76, proj geologist, 76-77, chief geologist int oper, 78-79, gen mgr corp, 80-84; vpres, Technos, 84-85; asst prog mgr, Battelle Off Nuclear Waste Isolation, 85-88; vpres, Converse Environ Consults Calif, 88-90; consult, Emot, 90-92. *Mem:* Geol Soc Am; Am Geophys Union; AAAS; Sigma Xi; Am Soc Civil Engrs; Nat Water Well Asn; Soc Explor Geophysicists. *Res:* The mechanisms and physical aspects of rock dilation, stick slip and earthquake precursors; the tectonics of the mid-continent and its relationship to seismicity. *Mailing Add:* 61 Hidden Valley Rd Monrovia CA 91016

LAFRAMBOISE, JAMES GERALD, PLASMA PHYSICS. *Current Pos:* asst prof physics, 67-71, assoc prof, 71-77, PROF PHYSICS & ASTRON, YORK UNIV, 77- *Personal Data:* b Windsor, Ont, July 26, 38; m 62; c 2. *Educ:* Univ Windsor, BSc, 57; Univ Toronto, BASc, 59, MA, 60, PhD(aerospace studies), 66. *Prof Exp:* Asst prof math, Univ Windsor, 65-67. *Concurrent Pos:* Mem prog team, WISP Shuttle Exp; assoc ed, J Geophys Res, Space Physics, 83-85. *Mem:* Can Asn Physicists; Am Geophys Union; Planetary Soc. *Res:* High-voltage electrical charging of spacecraft; electrode devices for plasma diagnostics; high-voltage antennas in space plasmas; spacecraft-plasma interactions. *Mailing Add:* Dept Physics & Astron York Univ 4700 Keele St Downsview ON M3J 1P6 Can

LAFRAMBOISE, MARC ALEXANDER, MATHEMATICS. *Current Pos:* RETIRED. *Personal Data:* b Windsor, Ont, May 18, 15; m 49; c 2. *Educ:* Univ Ottawa, BA, 42; Univ Mich, MA, 46, MSc, 49. *Prof Exp:* Prin & teacher pub & separate schs, Ont, 34-42; asst prof math, Assumption Col, 42-50; from asst prof to assoc prof math, Univ Detroit, 53-76, adj prof, 76-80. *Concurrent Pos:* Dean eve div, Assumption Col, 46-49. *Res:* Mathematics education. *Mailing Add:* 1477 Dufferin Pl Windsor ON N8X 3K3 Can

LAFRANCHI, EDWARD ALVIN, ELECTRICAL ENGINEERING. *Current Pos:* RETIRED. *Personal Data:* b Petaluma, Calif, July 23, 28; m 54; c 3. *Educ:* Univ Santa Clara, BS, 50. *Prof Exp:* Opers engr, Lawrence Livermore Lab, 53-56, design engr, 56-58, group leader, 58-66, div leader, 66-73, dept head, Dept Electronics Eng, 73-86, dep assoc dir eng, 86-91. *Mem:* Inst Elec & Electronics Engrs. *Res:* Computer science and engineering; engineering management. *Mailing Add:* 359 Polk Way Livermore CA 94550

LAFRENZ, DAVID E, MICROBIOLOGY. *Current Pos:* assoc res scientist, Dept Internal Med, 87-88, adj asst prof, 87-88, ASST PROF & ASSOC DIR, CELL & IMMUNOBIOL CORE FACIL & DIR FLOW CYTOMETRY FACIL, DEPT MICROBIOL, SCH MED, UNIV MO, COLUMBIA, 88-; RES MICROBIOLOGIST, H S TRUMAN MEM VET ADMIN HOSP, COLUMBIA, 88- *Personal Data:* b Waterloo, Iowa, Aug 13, 47; m; c 2. *Educ:* Ariz State Univ, BS, 71; Univ Iowa, PhD, 78. *Prof Exp:* Postdoctoral fel, Howard Hughes Med Inst, Stanford Univ Sch Med, 78-81, postdoctoral res affil, 81-83; res health sci specialist, Vet Admin Med Ctr, Iowa City, 83-88, dir, Animal Care Facil, 83-88. *Concurrent Pos:* Mem, Res & Develop Comt, Vet Admin Med Ctr, Iowa City, Iowa, 87-88. *Mem:* Am Asn Immunologists; AAAS; Am Soc Microbiol; Soc Anal Cytol. *Res:* Cellular immunology; immunologic memory; molecular immunology; molecular biology. *Mailing Add:* Dept Res H S Truman Mem Hosp 800 Hospital Dr Columbia MO 65201-5275. *Fax:* 573-443-2511 Ext 6453

LAFUSE, HARRY G, ELECTRICAL ENGINEERING. *Current Pos:* RETIRED. *Personal Data:* b Liberty, Ind, Jan 22, 30; m 54, Karen A Brehm; c Carrie (Robinson). *Educ:* Purdue Univ, BSEE, 57; Univ Ill, MSEE, 58, PhD, 62. *Prof Exp:* Instr elec eng, Univ Ill, 61-62; asst prof elec eng, Univ Notre Dame, 62-65, assoc prof, 65-81; elec engr, Phillips Eng Co, 81-83; staff engr, Bendix Guid Systs Div, 83-95. *Concurrent Pos:* Consult, Bendix Corp, 62-69 & McCarthy & Assocs, 70-83. *Mem:* Sigma Xi; Nat Soc Prof Engrs. *Res:* Electromagnetic field theory; network analysis and synthesis; high frequency transmission systems; microwave theory; guidance electronics systems. *Mailing Add:* 7531 Somerset Bay Indianapolis IN 46240

LAFUZE, JOAN ESTERLINE, PEDIATRICS. *Current Pos:* RES ASSOC PEDIAT HEMAT-ONCOL, SCH MED, IND UNIV, 85-; ASST PROF BIOL, IND UNIV E, 87- *Personal Data:* b Indianapolis, Ind. *Educ:* Ind Univ, AB, 59; Ball State Univ, MS, 75, Ind Univ, PhD(physiol), 81. *Prof Exp:* Lab tech & asst supvr, Gen Lab, Methodist Hosp, 59-60; student technologist, Sch Med Technol, St Vincent Hosp, 60-61; med technologist, Richmond Med Lab, 63-65; teaching supvr, In-Serv Lab, Educ Prog, Reid Mem Hosp, 65-68; educ coordr, Ind Voc Tech Col, 68-71; res & teaching asst, Dept Physiol & Biophys, Sch Med, Ind Univ, 75-81; res technologist pediat hemat-oncol, James Whitcomb Riley Hosp Children, Ind, 81-85. *Concurrent Pos:* Asst prof, Dept Physiol & Biophys, Sch Med, Ind Univ, 84-87. *Mem:* Am Soc Clin Pathologists; Am Physiol Soc; Tissue Cult Asn; AAAS. *Res:* Construction of a Molt-3 cDNA library; construction and characterization of a subtracted T-cell ALL cDNA library; construction of a subtracted T-cell ALL probe; sequencing; effect of neutrophil activation on respiration, blood pressure and absolute granulocyte count of rabbits and cats; use of antioxidants to attenuate the in vivo and in vitro effects of chemotactic agents; adherence of neutrophils to culture vascular endothelium; transendothelial migration of activated neutrophils. *Mailing Add:* Dept Pediat Ind Univ Sch Med Riley Hosp Children 702 Barnhill Dr Rm 2720 Indianapolis IN 46202-5225. *Fax:* 317-274-4471

LAGACE, LISETTE, MOLECULAR BIOLOGY & PROTEIN, BIOCHEMISTRY & CELL BIOLOGY. *Current Pos:* SR SCIENTIST, BIOMEGA INC, 89- *Personal Data:* b Oct 13, 51; c 2. *Educ:* Univ Que, BS, 75; Laval Univ, PhD(physiol), 79. *Prof Exp:* Instr cell biol, Baylor Col Med, 82-84; asst prof, Laval Univ, 84-89. *Mem:* Am Soc Cell Biol; Antiviral Res Soc. *Res:* Molecular biology; protein biochemistry; cloning expression and purifictaion of recombinant proteins; study of the role or veral protein in the virus cycle. *Mailing Add:* Dept Biochem Biomega Inc 2100 Cunard Laval PQ H7S 2G5 Can

LAGACE, PAUL ALFRED, MATERIALS & STRUCTURES ENGINEERING, COMPOSITE MATERIALS. *Current Pos:* From asst prof to assoc prof, Mass Inst Technol, 82-93, exec officer, Dept Aeronaut & Astronaut, 90-91, actg head, 91-93, PROF AERONAUT & ASTRONAUT, MASS INST TECHNOL, 93- *Personal Data:* b Lewiston, Maine, July 25, 57; m 83, Robin Pare. *Educ:* Mass Inst Technol, SB, 78, SM, 79, PhD(aeronaut & astronaut), 82. *Honors & Awards:* Von Karman Lectr, Israeli Aerospace Sci Orgn, 93; Coombes Lectr, Australian Aeronaut & Astronaut Soc, 97. *Concurrent Pos:* Pres, Int Comt Composite Mat, 93- *Mem:* Assoc fel Am Inst Aeronaut & Astronaut; Am Soc Composites; Am Soc Testing & Mat; Soc Advan Mat & Process Engrs. *Res:* Composite materials and structures, their fracture, durability, damage tolerance and applications. *Mailing Add:* Mass Inst Technol 77 Massachusetts Ave Rm 33-303 Cambridge MA 02139

LAGAKOS, STEPHEN WILLIAM, BIOSTATISTICS. *Current Pos:* assoc prof, Harvard Sch Pub Health, 80-85, PROF, HARVARD SCH PUB HEALTH, 86- *Personal Data:* b Philadelphia, Pa, June 18, 46; m 68; c 2. *Educ:* Carnegie-Mellon Univ, BS, 68; George Washington Univ, MPhil & PhD(math & statist), 72; Harvard Univ, AM, 86. *Honors & Awards:* Spiegelman Gold Medal, 86. *Prof Exp:* Math statistician, Naval Ord Sta, 68-70; statistician biostatist, Statist Lab, State Univ NY Buffalo, 72-80, asst prof statist sci, 73-80. *Concurrent Pos:* Coord statistician, Working Party Ther Lung Cancer, 72-; protocol statistician, Eastern Coop Oncol Group, 72- *Mem:* Biomet Soc; Royal Statist Soc; Inst Math Statist; Int Asn Study Lung Cancer; Am Statist Asn. *Res:* The planning, design and analysis of clinical trials with particular emphasis on survival-type data. *Mailing Add:* Dept Biostatist Harvard Sch Pub Health 677 Huntington Ave Boston MA 02115-6023

LAGALLY, MAX GUNTER, MATERIALS SCIENCE, SURFACE PHYSICS. *Current Pos:* instr physics & res assoc surface physics, 70-71, from asst prof to assoc prof 71-77, PROF MAT SCI & ENG, UNIV WIS-MADISON, 77-, DIR THIN-FILM DEPOSITION & APPLS CTR, 85- *Personal Data:* b Darmstadt, Ger, May 23, 42; US citizen; m 69; c 3. *Educ:* Pa State Univ, BS, 63; Univ Wis, MS, 65, PhD(physics), 68. *Prof Exp:* Vis fel physics, Fritz Haber Inst, Max Planck Soc, 68-69. *Concurrent Pos:* Sloan Found fel, 73-77; vis scientist surface physics, Sandia Nat Lab, 74; H I Romnes fel, 76-80; John Bascom prof surface sci & technol, Univ Wis-Madison, 86-; Gordon Godfrey vis prof physics, Univ NSW, Sydney, Australia, 87; Humboldt sr res fel, Julich, Ger, 92. *Mem:* Fel Am Phys Soc; Mat Res Soc; Am Vacuum Soc; Am Chem Soc; Am Soc Metals Int; fel Australian Inst Physics. *Res:* Crystallographic and electronic properties of surfaces, thin films, and interfaces; surface disorder; multilayer thin films for x-ray optics; diffraction; scanning tunneling microscopy. *Mailing Add:* Dept Mat Sci & Eng Univ Wis 1509 University Ave Madison WI 53706

LAGANIS, EVAN DEAN, INFRARED SYNTHESIS, ORGANOSILICONE CHEMISTRY. *Current Pos:* res chemist organofluorine, organosilicon & polyacetylene chem, Cent Res & Develop Dept, 81-84, RES CHEMIST, OPTICAL DISK MEDIA, PHOTOSYSTS & ELECTRONIC PROD DEPT, E I DU PONT DE NEMOURS & CO, INC, 85-, ACCOUNT MGR, 92-, SE REGIONAL MGR, DUPONT SAFETY & ENVIRON MGT & SERV, 93- *Personal Data:* b Detroit, Mich, June 6, 53; m 77; c 2. *Educ:* State Univ NY, Geneseo, BA, 75; Dartmouth Col, PhD(org chem), 80. *Prof Exp:* Fel organometallic & cyclophane chem, Univ Ore, 79-81. *Mem:* Am Chem Soc. *Res:* Preparation of infrared dyes for use as the active layer in Optical Disk Media; organosilicon reagents for organic synthesis. *Mailing Add:* 9703 Chatham Oaks Trail Charlotte NC 28210-7812

LAGARIAS, JEFFREY CLARK, MATHEMATICS. *Current Pos:* MEM TECH STAFF, BELL TELEPHONE LABS, 74- *Personal Data:* b Pittsburgh, Pa, Nov 16, 49. *Educ:* Mass Inst Technol, SB & SM, 72, PhD(math), 74. *Honors & Awards:* Lester Ford Award, Math Asn Am, 87. *Concurrent Pos:* Vis asst prof, Univ Md, 78-79; vis assoc prof comput sci, Rutgers Univ, 84. *Mem:* Am Math Soc; Math Asn Am; Soc Indust & Appl Math; Inst Elec & Electronics Engrs; Asn Comput Mach; Math Prog Soc. *Res:* Computational complexity theory; cryptography; number theory; discrete mathematics, dynamical systems. *Mailing Add:* AT&T Labs Res Rm 2C-373 688 Mountain Ave Murray Hill NJ 07974. *Fax:* 908-582-2379; *E-Mail:* jcl@research.att.com

LAGARIAS, JOHN S(AMUEL), PHYSICS, ELECTRONICS. *Current Pos:* PRES LAGARIAS ASSOCS, INC, 84- *Personal Data:* b Rochester, NY, July 4, 21; m 47, Virginia J Clark; c Jeffrey C, Peter C & J Clark. *Educ:* Rensselaer Polytech Inst, BS, 48. *Prof Exp:* Engr, Res Dept, Westinghouse Elec Corp, 48-51; physicist, Koppers Co, Inc, Pa, 51-53, mgr, Precipitation Br, 53-55, mgr, Metal Prod Res, 56-61, mgr, Physics & Phys Chem Lab, 61-63; mgr, Res & Develop, Am Instrument Co, 63-65; vpres, Resources Res, Inc, Va, 65-66, exec vpres, 66-67, pres, 67-71; dir environ qual, Kaiser Engrs Inc, 71-84. *Concurrent Pos:* Conf chmn, 2nd Int Clean Air Cong, 70, 1st Int Conf Electro Precipitation, 81; mem, Calif Air Resources Bd, 85- *Mem:* Fel, hon mem Air Pollution Control Asn (pres, 68-69); Am Phys Soc; sr mem Inst Elec & Electronics Engrs; Am Acad Environ Engrs; fel Int Soc Electrostatic Precipitation. *Res:* Industrial gas cleaning equipment including electrostatic precipitators, bag filters, and scrubbers; environmental controls. *Mailing Add:* Lagarias Assocs 5954 Autumnwood Dr No 5C Walnut Creek CA 94595

LAGE, GARY LEE, PHARMACOLOGY, TOXICOLOGY. *Current Pos:* PRIN, ENVIRON CORP. *Personal Data:* b Hinsdale, Ill, Nov 11, 41; m 64; c 2. *Educ:* Drake Univ, BS, 63; Univ Iowa, MS, 65, PhD(pharmacol), 67; Am Bd Toxicol, dipl, 80. *Prof Exp:* From asst prof to assoc prof pharmacol, Sch Pharm, Univ Kans, 67-73; assoc prof pharm, Univ Wis-Madison, 73-78; prof toxicol & dir toxicol progs, Philadelphia Col Pharm & Sci, 78-84, chmn dept pharmacol & toxicol, formerly. *Concurrent Pos:* USPHS res career develop award, 75-80. *Mem:* Soc Toxicol (treas, 85-87); Am Pharmaceut Asn; AAAS; Am Soc Pharmacol & Exp Therapeut; Am Asn Col Pharm. *Res:* Study of drug distribution and metabolism in relation to drug toxicity, distribution and/or metabolism, especially cardiac glycosides; hepatotocity mechanisms. *Mailing Add:* 52 River Dr Titusville NJ 08560

LAGE, JANICE M, PATHOLOGY. *Current Pos:* instr, 84-87, ASST PROF, HARVARD MED SCH, 87-; PATHOLOGIST, BRIGHAM & WOMEN'S HOSP, 87- *Personal Data:* b Exeter, Calif, July 5, 51. *Educ:* Calif State Univ, Fresno, BS, 73; Wash Univ, Mo, MD, 80; Am Bd Path, cert, 85. *Prof Exp:* Instr path, Sch Med, Stanford Univ, 80; instr path, Sch Med, Wash Univ, 81, instr obstet/gynec, 82, asst path, 83. *Concurrent Pos:* Resident path, Wash Univ, 81-82, obstet & gynec, 82-83, fel, Dept Path, 83-84; assoc pathologist, Brigham & Women's Hosp, Boston, Mass, 84-87; NIH grant, 90. *Mem:* US Acad Path; Can Acad Path; Am Asn Pathologists; Int Soc Gynec Pathologists; Soc Pediat Pathologists. *Res:* Gestational trophoblastic diseases; perinatal and obstetric pathology, with emphasis on congenital malformations; application of flow cytometry to surgical pathology of obstetric and gynecologic tumors. *Mailing Add:* Dept Path Georgetown Univ 3900 Reservoir Rd NW Washington DC 20007. *Fax:* 617-732-7513

LAGERGREN, CARL ROBERT, PHYSICS. *Current Pos:* mgr mass spectrometry, 65-68, RES ASSOC, RADIOL SCI DEPT, PAC NORTHWEST LABS, BATTELLE MEM INST, 68- *Personal Data:* b St Paul, Minn, Nov 21, 22; m 47; c 3. *Educ:* State Col, Wash, BS, 44, MS, 49; Univ Minn, PhD(physics), 55. *Prof Exp:* Sr physicist, Hanford Atomic Prod Oper, Gen Elec Co, 55-65. *Mem:* Am Phys Soc; Sigma Xi. *Res:* Mass spectrometry; electron impact phenomena; isotopic abundances; surface ionization; ion optics. *Mailing Add:* 2110 Howell Ave Richland WA 99352-2012

LAGERSTEDT, HARRY BERT, PLANT PHYSIOLOGY, HORTICULTURE. *Current Pos:* RETIRED. *Personal Data:* b Glen Ridge, NJ, Aug 2, 25; m 52; c 5. *Educ:* Ore State Univ, BS, 54, MS, 57; Tex A&M Univ, PhD(plant physiol), 65. *Prof Exp:* From instr to asst prof hort, Ore State Univ, 57-67, assoc prof, 67-; res horticulturist, Agr Res Serv, 67-; Northwest Germplasm Repository. *Mem:* Am Soc Plant Physiol; Am Soc Hort Sci; Sigma Xi. *Res:* Plant growth regulators; nut crops. *Mailing Add:* 34151 NE Electric Rd Corvallis OR 97333

LAGHARI, JAVAID RASOOLBUX, ELECTRICAL ENGINEERING. *Current Pos:* from asst prof to assoc prof, 80-92, PROF ELEC ENG, STATE UNIV NY, BUFFALO, 92-, DIR GRAD STUDIES, 93- *Personal Data:* b Hyderabad, Pakistan, June 25, 50; nat US; m 82, Shahida; c Zaid. *Educ:* Sind Univ, Pakistan, BE, 71; Middle East Tech Univ, Turkey, MS, 75; State Univ NY, Buffalo, PhD(elec eng), 80. *Prof Exp:* Asst eng, Indust Grindery, Pakistan, 71-72; asst exec engr, Airports Develop Agency, Pakistan, 75-76. *Concurrent Pos:* Prin investr, Air Force Off Sci Res, 83-90, Off Naval Res, 86-87; chmn, Radiation Soc Comt, Inst Elec & Electronics Engrs, 86-, mem, Comt Man & Radiation; mem, Tech Prog Comt, Int Symp Elec Insulation, 88-90, chmn, 92; mem, Tech Prog Comt, Int High Voltage Symp, 89; mem, ADCOM, Inst Elec & Electronics Engrs, 91- *Mem:* Inst Elec & Electronics Engrs. *Res:* High voltage and pulsed power; electrical insulation and dielectrics, as applicable to space power technology, including energy storage and transport devices; high speed diagnostics; Super vision and guidance under graduate and engineering studies. *Mailing Add:* 173 Shetland Dr Buffalo NY 14221. *Fax:* 716-645-5964; *E-Mail:* laghari@acsu.buffalo.edu

LAGNESE, JOHN EDWARD, MATHEMATICS. *Current Pos:* from asst prof to assoc prof, 64-72, PROF MATH & CHMN DEPT, GEORGETOWN UNIV, 72- *Personal Data:* b Pittsburgh, Pa, Mar 7, 37; m 60; c 3. *Educ:* Univ Dayton, BS, 59; Univ Md, College Park, MA, 61, PhD(math), 63. *Prof Exp:* Nat Acad Sci-Nat Res Coun fel, Nat Bur Stand, 63-64. *Concurrent Pos:* Consult, AID, 70. *Mem:* Am Math Soc; Math Asn Am. *Res:* Partial differential equations; operator theory. *Mailing Add:* Dept Math Georgetown Univ 37th & O Sts Washington DC 20057

LAGO, JAMES, PROCESS RESEARCH & DEVELOPMENT, FERMENTATION & ISOLATION. *Current Pos:* CONSULT, 86- *Personal Data:* b New York, NY, Nov 7, 21; m 68, Barbara Drake. *Educ:* Polytech Inst Brooklyn, BChE, 44; Mass Inst Technol, MS, 47. *Honors & Awards:* Merck Dir Award. *Prof Exp:* Asst, Manhattan Proj, 44-46; jr engr, Merck & Co Inc, Rahway, 47-51, group leader chem eng, 51-57, sect mgr, 57-64, mgr, 64-69, dir chem eng res & develop, 69-79, vpres process res & develop, 79-85. *Mem:* Nat Acad Eng; Am Chem Soc; Am Inst Chem Engrs; AAAS. *Res:* Development of processes for the preparation of medicinals; design and startup of manufacturing facilities for the processes developed. *Mailing Add:* 2399 Alamo Pintado Rd Solvang CA 93463. *Fax:* 509-493-3498

LAGO, PAUL KEITH, ENTOMOLOGY. *Current Pos:* PROF BIOL, UNIV MISS, 76- *Personal Data:* b Worthington, Minn, June 24, 47; m 69; c 1. *Educ:* Bemidji State Col, BA, 69, MA, 71; NDak State Univ, PhD(entom), 77. *Mem:* Coleopterists Soc; Entom Soc Am; Am Entom Soc; NAm Benthological Soc; Sigma Xi. *Res:* Insect taxonomy, principally coleoptera and aquatic insects; insect ecology. *Mailing Add:* Dept Biol Univ Miss Gen Delivery University MS 38677-9999

LAGOWSKI, JEANNE MUND, BIOCHEMICAL & MOLECULAR GENETICS. *Current Pos:* assoc res scientist biochem genetics, 59-63, res scientist, 63-73, lectr zool, 73-74, asst dean, Div Gen & Comp Studies, 72-78, assoc prof zool, 74-81, asst dean, 78-81, ASSOC DEAN, COL NATURAL SCI & PROF ZOOL, UNIV TEX, AUSTIN, 81- *Personal Data:* b St Louis, Mo, Nov 17, 29; m 54. *Educ:* Bradley Univ, BS, 51, MS, 52; Univ Mich, PhD(org chem), 57. *Prof Exp:* Instr analytical chem, Bradley Univ, 51-52; res chemist, Mich State Univ, 56-57; res fel phys org chem, Cambridge Univ, 57-59. *Concurrent Pos:* Res career develop award, NIH, 64-69; assoc, Danforth Found, 77- *Mem:* Am Chem Soc; Int Soc Heterocyclic Chemists. *Res:* Chemistry of nitrogen heterocycles; biochemical genetics. *Mailing Add:* Dept Zool Univ Tex Austin TX 78712

LAGOWSKI, JOSEPH JOHN, INORGANIC CHEMISTRY. *Current Pos:* From asst prof to assoc prof, 59-67, PROF CHEM, UNIV TEX, AUSTIN, 67- *Personal Data:* b Chicago, Ill, June 8, 30; m 54. *Educ:* Univ Ill, BS, 52; Univ Mich, MS, 54; Mich State Univ, PhD(inorg chem), 57; Cambridge Univ, PhD(inorg chem), 59. *Honors & Awards:* Piper Prof Award, Nat Chem Mfg Asn, 81; Chem Educ Award, Am Chem Soc, 89. *Mem:* Am Chem Soc; The Chem Soc. *Res:* Liquid ammonia solutions; organometallic compounds, borazines and derivatives; electrochemistry; development of computer-based teaching methods; non-aqueous solution chemistry; metal atom reactions. *Mailing Add:* Dept Chem Univ Tex Austin TX 78712-1104

LAGRAFF, JOHN ERWIN, AERODYNAMICS, GAS TURBINE HEAT TRANSFER. *Current Pos:* PROF FLUIDS-AERODYN, DEPT MECH & AERODYN ENG, 70-, DIR, AEROSPACE ENG PROG, SYRACUSE UNIV, 86-, DIR, CTR HYPERSONICS, 93- *Personal Data:* b Schenectady, NY, July 24, 40; m 62, Susan McAllister; c John R & Thomas. *Educ:* Mass Inst Technol, BS, 62; Oxford Univ, DPhil(eng sci), 70. *Honors & Awards:* Ralph Teetor Award, Soc Automotive Engrs, 72; Nat Fac Adv Award, Am Inst Aeronaut & Astronaut, 90. *Prof Exp:* Assoc scientist, Res & Advan Develop Div, Avco Corp, 62-66. *Concurrent Pos:* Vis prof, Oxford Univ, 83. *Mem:* Assoc fel Am Inst Aeronaut & Astronaut; Am Soc Mech Engrs; Am Asn Univ Prof; Am Asn Eng Educ. *Res:* Unsteady aerodynamics; heat transfer associated with gas turbines; boundary layer transition-hypersonics. *Mailing Add:* Syracuse Univ Col Eng 151 Link Hall Syracuse NY 13244

LAGRANGE, WILLIAM SOMERS, FOOD MICROBIOLOGY, FOOD SAFETY. *Current Pos:* EXTEN FOOD TECHNOLOGIST, IOWA STATE UNIV, 62- *Personal Data:* b Ames, Iowa, Apr 23, 31; m 54; c 3. *Educ:* Iowa State Univ, BS, 53, PhD(dairy bact), 59. *Prof Exp:* Exten technologist dairy mfg, Univ Ky, 59-62. *Mem:* Int Asn Milk, Food & Environ Sanit; fel Inst Food Technologists; Am Soc Microbiol; Am Dairy Sci Asn. *Res:* Dairy manufacturing quality control; dairy and foods microbiology; foods processing and control. *Mailing Add:* Dept Food Technol Iowa State Univ Ames IA 50011-2010. *Fax:* 515-294-8181

LAGRASSA, SUSAN, MATHEMATICS EDUCATION, COMMUTATIVE SEMIRINGS. *Current Pos:* ASST PROF MATH & MASTERS EDUC, DIR MATH, TRUMAN STATE UNIV, 95- *Personal Data:* b Kansas City, Mo, Mar 29, 65; m 95, Kevin Easley. *Educ:* NE Mo State Univ, BSE, 87, MA, 89; Univ Iowa, PhD(math), 95. *Prof Exp:* Instr math, NE Mo State Univ, 89-91. *Concurrent Pos:* Resident coordr, Connie Belin Nat Ctr Gifted Educ, 92-94; trainer, Mid Sch Math Mentoring Inst, 95-97; proj dir, A Goals 2000 Math Proj, Dept Educ, 96- *Mem:* Am Math Soc; Math Asn Am; Nat Coun Teachers Math. *Res:* Master of Arts Education program in mathematics; ideals in and polynomials over commutative semirings. *Mailing Add:* Div Math & Comput Sci Truman State Univ Kirksville MO 63501. *E-Mail:* lagrassa@truman.edu

LAGREGA, MICHAEL DENNY, hazardous waste management; deceased, see previous edition for last biography

LAGRONE, ALFRED HALL, RESEARCH ENGINEER. *Current Pos:* res engr, 46-54, from assoc prof to prof, 46-60, EMER PROF, UNIV TEX, AUSTIN, 92-, DIR ANTENNAS PROPAGATION LAB, 66- *Personal Data:* b DeBerry, Tex, Sept 25, 12; m 55, Dixie Louise Ballard; c Carrie Sue, Howard, Tracy & Kimberly. *Educ:* Univ Tex, BS, 38, MS, 48 PhD, 54. *Honors & Awards:* Scott Helt Mem Award, Inst Radio Engrs, 60. *Prof Exp:* Distrib engr, San Antonio Pub Serv Co, 38-42. *Concurrent Pos:* Consult, ABC, Collins Radio Co, Honeywell Inc & Tex Nuclear Co; chmn, US Comn Union Radio-Sci Int, 75- *Mem:* Fel Inst Elec & Electronics Engrs; Sigma Xi. *Res:* Antennas and propagation. *Mailing Add:* 3925 Sierra Dr Austin TX 78731-3911

LAGU, AVINASH L, ANALYTICAL CHEMISTRY OF RDNA DERIVED PROTEINS, CAPILLARY ELECTROPHORESIS. *Current Pos:* sr analytical chemist, Eli Lilly & Co, 79-87, RES SCIENTIST, LILLY RES LABS, 88- *Personal Data:* b Belgaum, India, Feb 14, 41. *Educ:* Bombay Univ, India, BSc, 61; Univ Cincinnati, MS, 72, PhD(analytical chem), 74. *Prof Exp:* Sr analytical chemist, Norwich Pharmacol, Proctor & Gamble, 74-76; scientist, Ortho Pharmaceut Corp, Johnson & Johnson, 76-79. *Mem:* Am Chem Soc; Sigma Xi. *Res:* Developing methods for the analysis of recombinant DNA derived proteins and peptides; biotechnology related problems; application of capillary electrophoresis and high-performance liquid chromatography to the analysis of DNA fragments and proteins. *Mailing Add:* Lilly Corp Ctr Eli Lilly & Co Indianapolis IN 46285. *Fax:* 317-276-5499

LAGUNOFF, DAVID, PATHOLOGY. *Current Pos:* chmn path, 79-96, PROF PATH, ST LOUIS UNIV, 79- *Personal Data:* b New York, NY, Mar 14, 32; m 58, Susan Powers; c Rachel, Liza & Michael. *Educ:* Univ Chicago, MD, 57. *Prof Exp:* Asst microbiol, Univ Miami, 51-53; intern, San Francisco Hosp, Calif, 57-58; from instr to prof path, Univ Wash, 60-79. *Concurrent Pos:* Nat Heart Inst fel path, Univ Wash, 58-59, USPHS trainee, 59-60; Nat Heart Inst spec fel physiol, Carlsberg Lab, Denmark, 62-64; Nat Cancer Inst spec fel path, Sir William Dunn Sch Exp Path, Oxford Univ, 69-70. *Mem:* Am Soc Invest Path; Am Soc Cell Biol; Am Asn Immunol. *Res:* Mast cell structure and function; cell secretion; inflammation; endothelial motility, angiogenesis. *Mailing Add:* Dept Path Sch Med St Louis Univ 1402 S Grand Blvd St Louis MO 63104-1079

LAGUNOWICH, LAURA ANDREWS, anatomy, for more information see previous edition

LAGUROS, JOAKIM GEORGE, SOIL MECHANICS, HIGHWAY ENGINEERING. *Current Pos:* assoc prof, 63-69, prof soils & hwys, 69-80, PROF CIVIL ENG & ENVIRON SCI, UNIV OKLA, 80- *Personal Data:* b Istanbul, Turkey, Feb 4, 24; US citizen; m 57; c 1. *Educ:* Robert Col, Istanbul, BS, 46; Iowa State Univ, MS, 55, PhD(soil mech), 62. *Prof Exp:* Asst engr, Naval Shipyard, Turkey, 48-51; instr civil eng, Robert Col, 51-54, asst prof, 56-59; res asst soils, Exp Sta, Iowa State Univ, 54-56, 59-62; asst prof soil mech, Univ Ohio, 62-63. *Concurrent Pos:* Consult, Neth Harbor Works Co, Turkey, 52, Robert Col, 58 & McFadzen, Everly & Assocs, 61; mem, Physicochem Phenomena Soils Comt, Hwy Res Bd, Nat Acad Sci-Nat Res Coun, 64-67. *Mem:* Am Soc Civil Engrs; Am Soc Eng Educ; Clay Minerals Soc. *Res:* Behavior of soils under load application; improvement of soil properties by admixtures; quality control of materials. *Mailing Add:* Dept Civil Eng & Environ Univ Okla Main Campus 900 Asp Ave Norman OK 73019-4050

LAHA, RADHA GOVINDA, ANALYTICAL MATHEMATICS, PURE MATHEMATICS. *Current Pos:* PROF MATH, BOWLING GREEN STATE UNIV, 72- *Personal Data:* b Calcutta, India, Oct 1, 30; US citizen. *Educ:* Univ Calcutta, BSc, 49, MSc, 51, PhD(math), 57. *Prof Exp:* Mem staff math, Res & Training Sch, Indian Statist Inst, Calcutta, 52-57, lectr, 57; Smith-Mundt-Fulbright fel, Cath Univ Am, 57-58, res asst prof, 58-60; reader, Div Theoret Res & Training, Indian Statist Inst, 60-61; vis res fel, Inst Statist, Univ Paris & Swiss Fed Inst Technol, 61-62; from asst prof to prof, Cath Univ Am, 62-72. *Concurrent Pos:* Vis res fel, Mass Inst Technol, 68-69 & Inst Advan Study, Canberra, Australia, 80; vis mem, Inst Advan Study, Princeton, 74. *Mem:* Fel Inst Math Statist; Int Statist Inst; Am Math Soc. *Res:* Analytical and abstract probability; harmonic analysis and representation theory of groups; application of probability and analysis to number theory. *Mailing Add:* Dept Math Bowling Green State Univ Bowling Green OH 43403-0001

LAHAIE, IVAN JOSEPH, ELECTROMAGNETIC SCATTERING & IMAGING, RADAR CROSS-SECTION ANALYSIS & MEASUREMENT TECHNOLOGY. *Current Pos:* res engr, 80-91, SR SCIENTIST, ENVIRON RES INST MICH, 91- *Personal Data:* b Bay City, Mich, May 21, 54; m 93, Kathy R Hill; c Katelyn L (Hill) & Alexandra R. *Educ:* Mich State Univ, BS, 76; Univ Mich, MS, 77, PhD(elec eng), 81. *Honors & Awards:* Radar Systs Panel Award, Inst Elec & Electronics Engrs Aerospace & Electronic Systs Soc, 91. *Prof Exp:* Res asst, Radiation Lab, Univ Mich, 76-80. *Concurrent Pos:* Assoc ed, Inst Elec & Electronics Engrs Antennas & Propagation, 86- *Mem:* Inst Elec & Electronics Engrs; Sigma Xi; Optical Soc Am. *Res:* Application of electromagnetic scattering, inverse scattering, and signal processing techniques to the analysis of radar cross-section measurements and synthetic aperture radar. *Mailing Add:* Environ Res Inst Mich PO Box 134001 Ann Arbor MI 48113-4001. *Fax:* 313-994-0944; *E-Mail:* lahaie@erim.org

LAHAM, QUENTIN NADIME, HISTOLOGY, EMBRYOLOGY. *Current Pos:* RETIRED. *Personal Data:* b Oshkosh, Wis, Feb 18, 27; m 50; c 3. *Educ:* Ripon Col, BA, 49; Marquette Univ, MS, 51; Univ Ottawa, PhD, 59. *Prof Exp:* Lectr gen biol, Univ Ottawa, 51-54, from asst prof to assoc prof, 54-58, prof histol & embryol, 68-76, chmn biol, 81, prof biol, 77-81. *Concurrent Pos:* Nuffield fel, 60-61. *Mem:* Teratology Soc; Soc Develop Biol; Can Soc Zoologists; Can Soc Cell Biol. *Res:* Ontogeny of enzyme systems during embryogenesis; influence of heavy metals on developing embryos. *Mailing Add:* 2101 Salmon Falls Rd El Dorado Hills CA 95762

LAHAM, SOUHEIL, INHALATION TOXICOLOGY, CANCER. *Current Pos:* SCI CONSULT. *Personal Data:* b Port-au-Prince, Haiti, Apr 17, 26; m 55, Marie Grintchenko; c Nadia & Beatrice. *Honors & Awards:* William P Yant Award in Toxicol & Indust Hyg. *Prof Exp:* Res assoc, Univ Paris, 54-56; guest scientist, Can Dept Health & Welfare, 56-58, head, Biochem Sect, Environ Health Directorate, 58-62, chief, Environ Toxicol Prog, Occup Health Div, 62-71, sr res scientist & consult, 62-79, head, Inhalation Toxicol Unit, Environ Health Directorate, 79-81, head, Occup Toxicol Res Sect. *Concurrent Pos:* Guest scientist, Nat Res Coun Can, 56-58; vis prof, Univ Ottawa, 71-, Univ Que, 73-, Ohio State Univ, Columbus, 74-, Carleton Univ, 77- & Univ Calif, Berkeley, 81- *Mem:* Am Indust Hyg Asn; Toxicol Soc Can; Europ Soc Toxicol; Soc Toxicol; AAAS; Europ Asn Cancer Res. *Res:* Inhalation toxicity and metabolism of toxic and carcinogenic substances; environmental and occupational cancer; chemical carcinogenesis; neurotoxicology; peripheral neuropathy induced by industrial chemicals; inhalation toxicity of indoor air pollutants. *Mailing Add:* 249 Latchford Rd Ottawa ON K1Z 5W3 Can. *Fax:* 613-728-8301

LAHAMER, AMER S, HYPERFINE INTERACTIONS USING MOSSBAUER SPECTROSCOPY, ENDOHEDRAL METALLOFULLERENES CHARACTERIZATION BY TIME-OF-FLIGHT MASS SPECTROMETERY. *Current Pos:* Instr, Berea Col, 89-90, asst prof, 90-96, actg chmn dept, 95-96, ASSOC PROF PHYSICS, BEREA COL, 96- *Personal Data:* b Ganzour, Libya, July 24, 56. *Educ:* Univ Iowa, BSEE, 80, MSEE, 81, MS, 84; Vanderbilt Univ, PhD(solid state physics), 90. *Concurrent Pos:* Hon res asst, Univ Tenn, 97- *Mem:* Am Phys Soc; Am Asn Univ Profs. *Res:* Hyperfine interactions by Mossbauer spectroscopy; production analysis and characterization of endohedral metallofullerenes. *Mailing Add:* CPO 1109 Berea Col Berea KY 40404. *Fax:* 606-9876-4506; *E-Mail:* amer_lahamer@berea.edu, nqz@ornl.gov

LAHEY, M EUGENE, PEDIATRICS. *Current Pos:* head dept, 58-74, prof, 58-83, EMER PROF PEDIAT, UNIV UTAH, 83- *Personal Data:* b Ft Worth, Tex, Dec 28, 17; m 42; c 6. *Educ:* Univ Tex, BA, 39; St Louis Univ, MD, 43. *Prof Exp:* Nat Res Coun fel med sci, Univ Utah, 49-51, asst prof pediat, 51-52; from asst prof to assoc prof, Univ Cincinnati, 52-58. *Concurrent Pos:* Mem med adv bd, Leukemia Soc, 58- & hemat training grant comt, Nat Inst Arthritis & Metab Dis, 59-63; mem, Scope Panel, US Pharmacopeia, 60-; mem residency rev comt, AMA, 61-65, pres, 65-; res dir, Children's Hosp, East Bay, 64-65; vis prof, Children's Hosp, Honolulu. *Mem:* Am Soc Hemat; Am Pediat Soc; Soc Pediat Res. *Res:* Pediatric hematology. *Mailing Add:* 50 N Medical Dr Salt Lake City UT 84132-1001

LAHEY, RICHARD THOMAS, JR, HEAT TRANSFER, FLUID MECHANICS. *Current Pos:* chmn, Dept Nuclear Eng, Rensselaer Polytech Inst, 75-87, prof nuclear eng & eng physics, 87-89, prof, Dept Chem Eng, 87-89, dir, Ctr Multiphase Res, 91-94, EDWARD E HOOD JR PROF ENG, RENSSELAER POLYTECH INST, 89-, DEAN ENG, 94- *Personal Data:* b St Petersburg, Fla, Feb 20, 39; m 61; c 3. *Educ:* US Merchant Marine Acad, BS, 61; Rensselaer Polytech Inst, MS, 64; Columbia Univ, ME, 66; Stanford Univ, PhD(mech eng), 71. *Honors & Awards:* Glen Murphy Award, Am Soc Eng Educ, 85; Tech Achievement Award, Am Nuclear Soc, 85, Arthur Holly Compton Award, 89, Glenn T Seaborg Medal, 92; E O Lawrence Mem Award, US Dept Energy, 88. *Prof Exp:* Engr, Knolls Atomic Power Lab, 61-64; res assoc, Columbia Univ, 64-66; mgr core & safety develop, Nuclear Energy Div, Gen Elec, 66-75. *Concurrent Pos:* Mem, Sci Adv Comt, EG&G Idaho Inc, 76-; mem, Advan Code Rev Group & LOFT Rev Group, US

Nuclear Regulatory Comn, 76-; pres, R T Lahey, Inc, 81-83; comnr, Eng Manpower Comn, 81-; Fulbright fel, Magdalen Col, Oxford Univ, 83-84; ed, J Nuclear Eng & Design, 83-; adj prof, Univ Pisa, Italy & Claude Bernard Univ, France, 87; Alexander von Humbolt sr scientist fel, 94-95. *Mem:* Nat Acad Eng; fel Am Nuclear Soc; Sigma Xi; NY Acad Sci; Am Soc Eng Educ; fel Am Soc Mech Engrs; Am Inst Chem Engrs. *Res:* Two-phase flow and boiling heat transfer technology; nuclear reactor thermal-hydraulics and safety. *Mailing Add:* Sch Eng Rensselaer Polytech Inst 110 Eighth St Troy NY 12181. *E-Mail:* laheyr@rpi.edu

LAHIRI, SUKHAMAY, PHYSIOLOGY. *Current Pos:* assoc prof environ physiol, 69-73, ASSOC PROF PHYSIOL, UNIV PA, 73- *Personal Data:* b Calcutta, India, Apr 1, 33; m 65. *Educ:* Univ Calcutta, BSc, 51, MSc, 53, DPhil(physiol), 56; Oxford Univ, DPhil(physiol), 59. *Honors & Awards:* Premchand-Roychand Gold Medal, Univ Calcutta, 62. *Prof Exp:* Govt of WBengal scholar, Oxford Univ, 56-59; asst prof physics, Presidency Col, Univ Calcutta, 59-65, hon lectr, Univ, 60-65; vis fel & asst prof, State Univ NY Downstate Med Ctr, 65-67; sr res assoc, Cardiovasc Inst, Michael Reese Hosp & Med Ctr, Chicago, Ill, 67-69. *Mem:* NY Acad Sci; Am Physiol Soc. *Res:* High altitude physiology; regulation and adaptation; gas exchange; chemoreceptors. *Mailing Add:* Dept Physiol G4 Univ Pa Med Sch 36th & Spruce Sts Philadelphia PA 19104

LAHIRI, SYAMAL KUMAR, MATERIALS SCIENCE, ADVANCED CERAMICS. *Current Pos:* CENT GLASS RES INST, CALCUTTA, INDIA. *Personal Data:* b Rangoon, Burma, Jan 1, 40; m 70; c 3. *Educ:* Univ Calcutta, BE, 61; Univ Notre Dame, MS, 64; Northwestern Univ, PhD(mat sci), 69. *Honors & Awards:* Outstanding Invention Award, IBM Corp, 76. *Prof Exp:* Sr sci asst, Defence Metall Res Lab, Govt of India, 61-62; res staff mem, T J Watson Res Ctr, IBM Corp, 68-84; Nat Phys Lab & Cent Electronics Inst, New Delhi, India, 84-86; T J Watson Res Ctr, IBM Corp, 87. *Concurrent Pos:* Vis scientist, Nat Phys Lab & Indian Inst Technol, New Delhi, India, 78-79; adj prof, IIT, Uharagpur, India, 88-89. *Mem:* Am Phys Soc; Inst Elec & Electronics Engrs; fel Inst Engrs India. *Res:* Thin film properties; fabrication of thin film devices; physical metallurgy; Josephson tunneling devices; microelectronic packaging; mechanical properties of materials; electronic ceramics. *Mailing Add:* Sch Appl Sci Nanyang Tech Univ Nanyang Ave Singapore 639798 Singapore

LAHITA, ROBERT GEORGE, IMMUNOLOGY, RHEUMATOLOGY. *Current Pos:* ASSOC PROF, COLUMBIA, 91- *Personal Data:* b Elizabeth, NJ, Dec 30, 45; m 71, Terry Barr; c Jason & Eric. *Educ:* St Peter's Col, BS, 67; Thomas Jefferson Univ, MD, 73, PhD(microbiol), 73. *Honors & Awards:* Fedelitas Award, Lupus Found, 96; Knowles Lectr, 97. *Prof Exp:* From asst prof to assoc prof immunol, Rockefeller Univ, 80-87; assoc prof med & pharmacol, Cornell Med Col, 80-90. *Concurrent Pos:* Lectr, Mt Sinai Med Ctr, 81-; consult, Medcom, 81-; mem exec bd, NY Arthritis Found, 82-, NY Serv Life Eval Found, Serv Life Eval Found Am, 83-; physician, Rockefeller Hosp, 83-; attend physician, Hosp Joint Dis, NY; clin scholar, Rockefeller Univ; attend phys, Hosp Spec Surg, NY; chief rheumatist, St Luke's Roosevelt Hosp, NY; chmn bd, Lupus Found Am; bd gov, NY Arthritis Found. *Mem:* Am Rheumatism Asn; Am Soc Microbiol; NY Acad Sci; Harvey Soc; AAAS; Clin Immunol Soc. *Res:* Effect of sex steroids on immune response; disease systemic lupus erythematosus. *Mailing Add:* Columbia Univ 432 W 58th St New York NY 10019. *Fax:* 201-447-6437; *E-Mail:* rlahita@mem.po.com

LAHOTI, GOVERDHAN DAS, MATERIALS SCIENCE ENGINEERING. *Current Pos:* RES SCIENTIST, TIMKEN RES, CANTON, OHIO, 82- *Personal Data:* b Jaipur, India, May 4, 48; m 75; c 3. *Educ:* Univ Burdwan, BEng, 69, Univ Calif, Berkeley, MS, 70, PhD(mech eng), 73. *Honors & Awards:* Gold Medal, Univ Burdwan, 70. *Prof Exp:* Teaching asst mech eng, Univ Calif, Berkeley, 70-72, res asst, 72-73; res scientist, Batelle Mem Inst, Columbus, Ohio, 74-81. *Concurrent Pos:* Consult mech engr, 73-74. *Mem:* Soc Mfg Engrs; Am Soc Metals; Am Soc Mech Engrs. *Res:* Development and optimization of metalworking processes, such as forging, rolling, and extrusion; computer aided modeling of metalworking techniques. *Mailing Add:* 4105 Glenmoor Rd NW Canton OH 44718

LAHR, CHARLES DWIGHT, MATHEMATICAL ANALYSIS. *Current Pos:* from asst prof to assoc prof math, Dartmouth Col, 75-84, assoc dean fac sci & dean grad studies, 81-84, prof math & comput sci & dean fac, 84-89, PROF MATH & COMPUT SCI, DARTMOUTH COL, 84- *Personal Data:* b Philadelphia, Pa, Feb 6, 45; m 69, 86; c 4. *Educ:* Temple Univ, BA, 66; Syracuse Univ, MA, 68, PhD(math), 71. *Prof Exp:* Mathematician, Bell Labs, 71-73; vis asst prof math, Savannah State Col, 73-74 & Amherst Col, 74-75. *Mem:* Am Math Soc; Sigma Xi; Math Asn Am; AAAS. *Res:* Banach algebras, particularly convolution algebras in harmonic analysis; use of computers in secondary school teaching. *Mailing Add:* Dept Math & Comput Sci Dartmouth Col Hanover NH 03755-1890. *Fax:* 603-646-1312; *E-Mail:* lahr@dartmouth.edu

LAHR, GILBERT M, METALLURGICAL ENGINEERING, FAILURE ANALYSIS OF ENGINE COMPONENTS. *Current Pos:* RETIRED. *Personal Data:* b Detroit, Mich, Sept 18, 22; wid; c Patricia A (Boone), David G & Janis E (Visser). *Educ:* Gen Motors Inst, BSIndustE, 46. *Prof Exp:* Metallurgist, Detroit Diesel Eng Div, Gen Motors, 47-62, asst chief metallurgist, 62-77, chief metallurgist in charge mat eng, Mat Qual Control, Failure Analysis & Metall Processing Diesel Engines, 77-85. *Mem:* Fel Am Soc Metals; Am Soc Non Destructive Testing. *Res:* High strength cold-worked steel; development of materials and processes for manufacturing of cylinder liners; holder of two patents. *Mailing Add:* 45152 Byrne Ct Northville MI 48167

LAHR, JOHN CLARK, EARTHQUAKE LOCATION, EDUCATION OUTREACH. *Current Pos:* GEOPHYSICIST SEISMOL, US GEOL SURV, 71- *Personal Data:* b Indianapolis, Ind, Nov 11, 44; m 66, 78, Janice Henderson; c Taya, Nils & Elizabeth. *Educ:* Rensselaer Polytech Inst, BS, 66; Columbia Univ, MS, 71, PhD(seismol), 75. *Concurrent Pos:* Affil prof geol, Univ Alaska, Fairbanks, 93- *Mem:* Seismol Soc Am; Am Geophys Union; Nat Sci Teachers Asn. *Res:* Seismicity and tectonics of Alaska, especially as related to hazards assessment. *Mailing Add:* PO Box 83245 Fairbanks AK 99708. *Fax:* 907-474-5618; *E-Mail:* lahr@usgs.gov

LAHTI, LESLIE ERWIN, CHEMICAL ENGINEERING. *Current Pos:* RETIRED. *Personal Data:* b Floodwood, Minn, July 27, 32; m 56, Alma Kelley; c David, Mark & Paul. *Educ:* Tri State Col, BS, 54; Mich State Univ, MS, 58; Carnegie Inst Technol, PhD(chem eng), 64. *Honors & Awards:* Shreve Prize, 67. *Prof Exp:* Glass technologist, Corning Glass Works, 55-57; develop engr, Ren Plastics, 57; assoc prof, Tri State Col, 58-60; asst prof chem eng, Purdue Univ, 63-67; from assoc prof to prof & chmn dept, Univ Toledo, 67-80, dean eng, 80-89, emer prof chem eng, 90-95. *Concurrent Pos:* Consult, Am Oil, Great Lakes Chem, 67-69, Inland Chem Co, 70-, Stubbs, Overbeck, 79-81. *Mem:* Am Inst Chem Engrs; Am Chem Soc; Am Soc Eng Educ; Nat Soc Prof Engrs. *Res:* Fundamentals of nucleation and crystallization from solutions; polymerization processes. *Mailing Add:* 4813 Dressage Lane Sylvania OH 43560

LAI, CHII-MING, METABOLISM. *Current Pos:* sr res assoc, Du Pont Pharmaceut, 89-90, SR RES ASSOC, STINE-HASKELL RES CTR, DU PONT MERCK PHARMACEUT CO, 91- *Personal Data:* b Taiwan, Repub China, May 25, 35; c 2. *Educ:* Kaohsiung Med Col, BS, 65; Univ Ga, MS, 71; State Univ NY, Buffalo, PhD(pharmaceut), 77. *Prof Exp:* Pharmacist, Develop Dept, Taiwan Tanabe Pharmaceut Co, 66-69; teaching asst pharm, Sch Pharm, Univ Ga, 69-71; res asst pharmaceut, Sch Pharm, State Univ NY, Buffalo, 71-77; res investr, Am Critical Care, McGaw Park, Ill, 77-78, sr res investr, 78-81, res fel, 81-86; res fel, Du Pont Critical Care, Newark, Del, 86-89. *Mem:* Am Pharmaceut Asn; Am Asn Pharmaceut Scientists; Am Soc Pharmacol & Exp Therapeut; NY Acad Sci. *Res:* Biopharmaceutics, pharmacokinetics, drug metabolism and detoxication; animal screening and screening techniques; linear and nonlinear model fitting and stimulation; statistical methods; bioanalytical methods development; isotope tracer techniques; control theory and biological feedback mechanisms; physical pharmacy and bio-organic chemistry. *Mailing Add:* 36 Autumnwood Dr Newark DE 19711-2447. *Fax:* 302-451-0054

LAI, CHING-SAN, CELL BIOPHYSICS, MEMBRANE BIOPHYSICS. *Current Pos:* res assoc, Med Col Wis, 79-80, asst prof biophys, 81-84, assoc prof, 85-90, PROF, MED COL WIS, 91- *Personal Data:* b Taiwan, Nov 27, 46; m 71, Shan-Lan Liu; c Jennifer Y & Shawn S. *Educ:* Nat Taiwan Norm Univ, BS, 70; Univ Hawaii, PhD(biophys), 78. *Prof Exp:* Fel biophys, Univ Hawaii, 78. *Concurrent Pos:* NIH grantee, 82- *Mem:* Biophys Soc; AAAS; Int Electron Paramagnetic Resonance Soc. *Res:* Molecular dynamics of cell adhesive glycoproteins; development and applications of electron spin resonance spectroscopy to biomedical systems. *Mailing Add:* Dept Radiol Med Col Wis 8701 Watertown Plank Milwaukee WI 53226-3548

LAI, CHINTU (VINCENT C), COMPUTATIONAL HYDRAULICS, HYDROMECHANICS. *Current Pos:* Res hydraul engr, Washington, DC, 61-63, Ore, 63-65 & Arlington, Va, 65-73, RES HYDROLOGIST, WATER RESOURCES DIV, US GEOL SURV, RESTON, 73- *Personal Data:* b Changhua, Formosa, Aug 5, 30; m 63; c 2. *Educ:* Taiwan Univ, BS, 54; Univ Iowa, MS, 57; Univ Mich, PhD(civil eng), 62. *Mem:* Am Soc Civil Engrs; Asn Comput Mach; Int Asn Hydraul Res; Am Geophys Union; Sigma Xi. *Res:* Computational hydraulics-surface water problems; transient flows in closed and open conduits; numerical modelling and computer simulation of unsteady flows in rivers, estuaries, embayments, closed conduits and other areas in hydromechanics and hydrologic process. *Mailing Add:* 6814 Glenmont St Falls Church VA 22042-4105

LAI, CHUN-YEN, ENZYMOLOGY, BACTERIAL TOXIN. *Current Pos:* RETIRED. *Educ:* Univ Ill, PhD(biochem), 61. *Prof Exp:* Res investr, Roche Res Ctr, 73-; adj prof biochem, Med Col, Cornell Univ, 79-; res chief, Hoffman-La Roche, Inc. *Mailing Add:* 4404 Sunflower Dr Rockville MD 20853

LAI, DAVID CHIN, ELECTRICAL ENGINEERING. *Current Pos:* SR STAFF MEM, GA TECH RES INST, 96- *Personal Data:* b Beijing, China, Nov 11, 31; US citizen; m 63; c 2. *Educ:* Nat Taiwan Univ, BSEE, 54; Johns Hopkins Univ, DEng, 60. *Prof Exp:* Asst prof eng, Brown Univ, 60-62; assoc prof elec eng, Northeastern Univ, 62-65; from assoc prof to prof elec eng, Univ Vt, 65-85; sr staff mem, Martin Marietta Orlando Aerospace, 85-95; prin res engr, Gleason Res Assocs, 95-96. *Concurrent Pos:* Vis prof elec eng, Stanford Univ, 71-75. *Mem:* Inst Elec & Electronics Engrs. *Res:* Signal processing; radar signals; pattern recognition; automatic target recognition; multi-sensor fusion; granted 2 US patents. *Mailing Add:* 175 Spring Chase Circle Altamonte Springs FL 32714

LAI, DAVID YING-LUN, STRUCTURAL-ACTIVITY RELATIONSHIPS, RISK ASSESSMENT. *Current Pos:* TOXICOLOGIST, US ENVIRON PROTECTION AGENCY, 87- *Personal Data:* b Canton, China, Aug 1, 47; US citizen; m 84; c 2. *Educ:* Chinese Univ, Hong Kong, BSc, 70; Med Col, Ga, PhD(biochem), 77. *Prof Exp:* Instr biol & biochem, Dept Biol, Chinese Univ, Hong Kong, 70-72; instr, Dept Med, Med Ctr, Tulane Univ, 77-79; sr toxicologist consult, Sci Applns Int Corp, 79-87. *Mem:* Soc Toxicol; Am Col

Toxicol; Am Asn Cancer Res; Am Soc Pharmacol & Exp Therapeut; Soc Risk Analysis; Europ Asn Cancer Res. *Res:* Development and evaluation of hazard and risk assessment of toxic substances. *Mailing Add:* OTS/HERD/OB TS-796 US EPA 401 M St SW Washington DC 20460-0001

LAI, ELAINE Y, CELL BIOLOGY. *Current Pos:* SR RES ASSOC BIOL, BRANDEIS UNIV, 82- *Personal Data:* b British Hong Kong, Nov 11, 49; m 81. *Educ:* Iowa State Univ, BS, 73; Brandeis Univ, PhD(biol), 78. *Honors & Awards:* Estherlee Runoto Gilbert Merit Award, 77. *Concurrent Pos:* Vis lectr cell-free translation, Univ NC, Chapel Hill, 79; organizer EMBO course, Max Planck Inst, WGer, 86; Max-Planck fel, Munich, 86. *Mem:* Am Soc Cell Biol. *Res:* Regulation of eukaryotic gene expression during cell differentiation; emphasis on dissection of the coordinate expression of flagellar calmodulin and tubulin genes in the amebo-flagellate, Naegleria gruberi. *Mailing Add:* Dept Biol Brandeis Univ 415 South St Waltham MA 02254-9110. *Fax:* 781-736-3107

LAI, FENG CHYUAN, HEAT TRANSFER, ENERGY CONVERSION. *Current Pos:* ASST PROF MECH ENG, UNIV OKLA, 92- *Personal Data:* b Taipei, Taiwan, Aug 6, 56; US citizen; m 86, Hongshing Cheng; c Cathy B & Anthony C. *Educ:* Nat Tsing Hua Univ, Taiwan, BS, 78; Univ Del, MS, 85, PhD(mech eng), 88. *Prof Exp:* Asst engr, Energy Res Lab, Taiwan, 80-82; res assoc, Colo State Univ, 86-92. *Concurrent Pos:* Co-prin investr, Dept Energy, 94-96 & NASA, 96; prin investr, Okla Ctr Advan Sci & Technol, 95-97. *Mem:* Am Soc Mech Engrs; Am Soc Heating Refrig & Air-Conditioning Engrs; Am Soc Eng Educ; Am Inst Aeronaut & Astronaut. *Res:* Heat and mass transfer in porous media, heat transfer enhancement using electrical field; manufacturing of composite materials and indoor air quality. *Mailing Add:* 1600 Pembroke Dr Norman OK 73072. *Fax:* 405-325-1088; *E-Mail:* lai@leo. ecn.ou.edu

LAI, FONG M, CARDIOVASCULAR PHARMACOLOGY. *Current Pos:* GROUP LEADER & PRIN PHARMACOLOGIST, LEDERLE LABS, AM CYANAMID CO, 76- *Personal Data:* b Taiwan, Aug 17, 42; m 69; c 2. *Educ:* Taipei Med Col, BS, 66; Taiwan Univ, MS, 69; Med Col Va, PhD(pharmacol), 74. *Prof Exp:* Res fel, Roche Inst Molecular Biol, 74-76. *Mem:* Am Soc Pharmacol & Exp Therapeut. *Res:* Mechanisms of the hypertension and the cerebral vasculative pharmacology. *Mailing Add:* Wyeth-Averst Res CN8000 Princeton NJ 08543. *Fax:* 732-274-4004

LAI, JAI-LUE, ACOUSTICS, STRUCTURAL DYNAMICS. *Current Pos:* MGR, PRATT & WHITNEY, 92- *Personal Data:* b Taipei, Taiwan, Dec 9, 40; US citizen; m 68; c 2. *Educ:* Nat Taiwan Univ, BS, 62; Polytech Inst Brooklyn, MSE, 66; Princeton Univ, PhD(mech eng), 69. *Prof Exp:* Engr satellite struct, RCA Corp, 67; assoc res & develop fel, B F Goodrich Co, 68-89; dir, Gencorp Automotive, 87-91. *Mem:* Am Inst Aeronaut & Astronaut; Am Soc Mech Engrs; Soc Advan Mat Process Eng; Soc Petrol Engrs; Soc Automotive Engrs. *Res:* Application of new material composite structure as new products or components. *Mailing Add:* 106 Barrington Way Glastonbury CT 06033-4343

LAI, JUEY HONG, CHEMICAL ENGINEERING, POLYMER CHEMISTRY. *Current Pos:* PRES, LAI LABS INC, 89- *Personal Data:* b Taipei, Taiwan, Dec 4, 36; US citizen; m 68, Li Huey Chung; c Eric Yo-Ping & Bruce Yo-Sheng. *Educ:* Nat Taiwan Univ, BS, 59; Univ Wash, MS, 63, PhD(phys chem), 69. *Honors & Awards:* H W Sweatt Award, Honeywell Inc, 80. *Prof Exp:* Res specialist polymer, Univ Minn, 69-73; from prin res scientist to sr prin res scientist polymer mat, Honeywell Technol Ctr, 73-83, staff scientist polymer mat, chem sensors, 83-89. *Concurrent Pos:* Lectr, State Univ NY, New Paltz, 83; Small Bus Innovation res award, Dept Health & Human Serv, 90, 93, 94 & 96. *Mem:* Am Chem Soc; Sigma Xi; fel Am Inst Chemists; Am Asn Dent Res. *Res:* Polymer materials for electronics; electron resists for electron beam microfabrication, membrane technology for gas removal, solid state chemistry and chemical sensors; dental restorative materials; maxillofacial prosthetic materials. *Mailing Add:* 14617 White Oak Dr Burnsville MN 55337-4152. *E-Mail:* jlai124@aol.com

LAI, KAI SUN, ENGINEERING. *Current Pos:* ENGR, UNITED TECHNOL, 86- *Personal Data:* b Hong Kong, China; US citizen. *Educ:* Pa State Univ, BSc, 59. *Prof Exp:* Engr, Aerojet Gen Corp, 59-62; sr analyst, Atlantic Res Corp, 62-68; mgr, Teledyne McCormick Selph, 68-80, sr scientist, 80-82, eng specialist, 82-86. *Res:* Combustion process and thermochemical analysis of solid fuels and additives, including boranes; propulsion for aerospace applications and use of explosives and pyrotechnics for safety applications. *Mailing Add:* 855 W Eighth St Gilroy CA 95020

LAI, KUO-YANN, PHYSICAL CHEMISTRY, SURFACE & COLLOID SCIENCE. *Current Pos:* Res chemist, Colgate-Palmolive Co, 77-80, sr res chemist, 80-83, res assoc, 83, sect head, 83-86, sr sect head chem res, 86-87, mgr oral prod develop, 87-93, assoc dir, household surface care prod develop, 93-95, ASSOC DIR, GLOBAL MAT SOURCING, COLGATE-PALMOLIVE CO, 96- *Personal Data:* b Miao-Li, Taiwan, Sept 13, 46; m 72, Jane M Yang; c Melody, Amy & Peter. *Educ:* Cheng Kung Univ, Taiwan, BS, 69; Univ Tex, El Paso, MS, 74; Clarkson Col Technol, PhD(chem), 77. *Honors & Awards:* Pres Award for Tech Excellence, Colgate-Palmolive, 85; Asian Am Corp Achieve Award, Org Chinese Am, 92. *Concurrent Pos:* Robert A Welch fel, 72-74; NSF fel, 74-77. *Mem:* Am Chem Soc; Am Oil Chemists Soc. *Res:* Adhesional wetting; scavenging of aerosols; surfactants and detergents; oral hygiene prods. *Mailing Add:* Colgate-Palmolive Co 330 Park Ave New York NY 10022. *E-Mail:* huo__ yann__lai@colpal.com

LAI, MICHAEL MING-CHIAO, VIROLOGY, VIRAL HEPATITIS. *Current Pos:* from asst prof to assoc prof microbiol, 73-83, PROF MICROBIOL & NEUROL, SCH MED, UNIV SOUTHERN CALIF, 83-; INVESTR, HOWARD HUGHES MED INSTR, 90- *Personal Data:* b Tainan, Taiwan, Sept 8, 42; m 71, Cathy Wung; c Cindy & Jennifer. *Educ:* Nat Taiwan Univ Col Med, MD, 68; Univ Calif, Berkeley, PhD(molecular biol), 73. *Prof Exp:* Med officer, Chinese Marine Corps, 68-69; molecular biologist, Univ Calif, Berkeley, 73. *Concurrent Pos:* Prin investr grants, Nat Cancer Inst & Am Cancer Soc, 73-85, NIH, 75-, NSF, 79-87 & Nat Mult Sclerosis Soc, 82-. *Mem:* Am Soc Microbiol; Am Soc Virol; Fedn Am Soc Exp Biol; AAAS; RNA Cos; Soc Chinese Bioscientists Am (pres, 91-92). *Res:* Molecular biology of hepatitis viruses and coronaviruses; mechanism of viral pathogenesis and viral replication. *Mailing Add:* Dept Microbiol Sch Med Univ Southern Calif 2011 Zonal Ave Los Angeles CA 90033. *Fax:* 213-342-9555; *E-Mail:* michlai@hsc.usc.edu

LAI, MING, DESIGN & ENGINEERING SOLID-STATE LASER SYSTEMS, LASER PHYSICS. *Current Pos:* laser scientist, 92-94, SR LASER SCIENTIST, NOVATEC LASER SYSTEMS INC, 94-, DIR, RES & DEVELOP DIV, 95- *Personal Data:* b Guangdong, China, May 9, 57; m 85, Meijuan Yuan. *Educ:* Univ Zhongshan, China, BSc, 82; Univ Toronto, Can, MSc, 86; Univ NMex, PhD(optical sci), 90. *Prof Exp:* Res assoc, Univ NMex, 90-92. *Mem:* Optical Soc Am; Am Phys Soc. *Res:* Solid-state lasers and medical laser systems for eye surgery; laser physics and technology, particularly on ultra short laser pulse generation, amplification and application. *Mailing Add:* 2705 Avenida De Anita No 31 Carlsbad CA 92008. *E-Mail:* mlai003@aol.com

LAI, MING-CHIA DANIEL, ENGINE COMBUSTION & SPRAY PROCESSES, COMBUSTION LASER DIAGNOSTICS & COMPUTATIONAL FLUID DYNAMICS. *Current Pos:* from asst prof to assoc prof, 87-96, CHARLES DEVLIEG PROF MECH ENG, WAYNE STATE UNIV, 96- *Personal Data:* b Taipei, Taiwan, July 28, 57; US citizen; m 85; c 4. *Educ:* Nat Taiwan Univ, BS, 79; Pa State Univ, MS & PhD(mech eng), 85. *Prof Exp:* Postdoctoral res fel, Univ Mich, 85-86; postdoctoral assoc, Mass Inst Technol, 86-87. *Concurrent Pos:* Tech assoc, Internal Combustion Div, Am Soc Mech Engrs, 87-, mem, Combustion & Fuel Comt, Int Gas Turbine Inst, 96-; consult, CFD Res Corp, 90, Inst Gas Technols, 93, Gen Motor Corp, 94-96, Honda NAm Res & Develop & Ford Motor Co, 97; vis prof mech eng, Univ Hiroshima, Japan, 94. *Mem:* Am Soc Mech Engrs; Soc Automotive Engrs; Am Inst Aeronaut & Astronaut; Combustion Inst; Inst Liquid Atomization & Spray Syst. *Res:* Applying and developing laser diagnostics and computational fluid dynamics techniques to automotive and aeronautic propulsion and manufacturing systems; spray and mixture formation process; combustion; emission and control strategies in internal combustion engine and gas turbine engines. *Mailing Add:* 5443 Berwyck Dr Troy MI 48202. *Fax:* 313-577-8789

LAI, PATRICK KINGLUN, IMMUNOVIROLOGY, IMMUNOPATHOLOGY. *Current Pos:* asst mem, 87-90, MEM VIROL, TAMPA BAY RES INST, 90- *Personal Data:* b Hong Kong, Oct 10, 44; Australian citizen; m, Priscilla T Liu; c Lee J & Chay A. *Educ:* Univ Western Australia, PhD(microbiol), 78. *Prof Exp:* Res fel biol, Univ Ottawa, Can, 78-79 & immunol, Univ Col London, UK, 79-82; sr res officer immunol, Royal Postgrad Med Sch, UK, 82-84; from instr to asst prof immunol, Univ Nebr Med Ctr, 84-87. *Concurrent Pos:* Vis scholar, Int Agency Res Cancer, France, 75; WHO fel, Rush-Presby St Luke Med Ctr, Chicago, 76-77; res fel, Imp Cancer Res Funds, UK, 79-82; Europ Molecular Biol Orgn fel, Univ Zurich, 81; vis prof, Alta Heritage Found, Univ Alta, 82; assoc prof, Salem Teikyo Univ, Salem, WVa, 93- *Mem:* Am Asn Immunologists; AAAS; NY Acad Sci. *Res:* Interaction between viruses and cellular components that give diseases; how cellular factors, including immunomodulators, regulate virus replication and pathogenesis. *Mailing Add:* Tampa Bay Res Inst 10900 Roosevelt Blvd St Petersburg FL 33716-2308

LAI, POR-HSIUNG, PROTEIN. *Current Pos:* FOUNDER, PROTEIN INST INC, 90- *Mailing Add:* Protein Inst Inc PO Box 550 Broomall PA 19008-0550

LAI, RALPH WEI-MEEN, SURFACE CHEMISTRY, MINERAL SCIENCE & ENGINEERING. *Current Pos:* SCIENTIST, US DEPT ENERGY, 85- *Personal Data:* b Tou-Lu, Taiwan, Dec 17, 36; US citizen; m 66; c 2. *Educ:* Cheng Kung Univ, Taiwan, BS, 59; SDak Sch Mines & Technol, MS, 64; Univ Calif, Berkeley, PhD(mat sci & eng), 70. *Prof Exp:* Res scientist mat res, Cyprus Mines Corp, 69-72; mineral processing scientist process develop, Anglo-Am Clays Corp, 73-74; sr proj engr metall eng, Kennecott Develop Ctr, Kennecott Copper Corp, 74-85. *Concurrent Pos:* Pres, Western Prospect Co, 78-, Toshi Co, 86- *Mem:* Am Inst Mining, Metall & Petrol Engrs; Japan Inst Mining & Metall; Clay Minerals Soc; Am Chem Soc. *Res:* Surface chemistry of oxide minerals; coal preparation and utilization. *Mailing Add:* Dept Energy Pittsburgh Energy Tech PO Box 10940 Pittsburgh PA 15236-0940. *Fax:* 412-892-4760

LAI, SAN-CHENG, chemical engineering, for more information see previous edition

LAI, SHU TIM, SPACECRAFT INTERACTIONS, SPACE PHYSICS. *Current Pos:* RES PHYSICIST, USAF GEOPHYS LAB, 81- *Personal Data:* b Hong Kong, May 23, 38; US citizen; m 72. *Educ:* Brandeis Univ, MA, 67, PhD(physics), 71. *Prof Exp:* Mem res staff, Lincoln Lab, Mass Inst Technol, 78-79; sr mem res staff, Boston Col, 79-80. *Mem:* Am Geophys Union; Am

Phys Soc; Am Asn Physics Teachers; Inst Elec & Electronics Engrs; Am Inst Aeronaut & Astronaut. *Res:* Space plasma physics, spacecraft charging; electron, ion and neutral beams emitted from spacecrafts; atmospheric physics; spacecraft interactions with space environment; digital signal processing. *Mailing Add:* 38 Hilltop Dr Burlington MA 01803. *Fax:* 781-377-5571

LAI, TZE LEUNG, MATHEMATICS, STATISTICS. *Current Pos:* PROF STATIST, STANFORD UNIV, 87- *Personal Data:* b Hong Kong, June 28, 45; m 75; c 2. *Educ:* Univ Hong Kong, BA, 67; Columbia Univ, MA, 70, PhD(statist), 71. *Honors & Awards:* Comt of Presidents Statist Soc Award, 83. *Prof Exp:* From asst prof to prof statist, Columbia Univ, 71-87. *Concurrent Pos:* Vis assoc prof math, Univ Ill, Urbana-Champaign, 75-76; vis prof statist, Stanford Univ, 78-79; John Simon Guggenheim fel, 83-84; vis prof, Math Sci Res Inst, Berkeley, 83. *Mem:* Fel Am Statist Asn; fel Inst Math Statist; Sigma Xi; AAAS; NY Acad Sci; Int Statist Inst; Biometric Soc; Drug Info Asn. *Res:* Sequential methods in statistics; statistical quality control and clinical trials; time series analysis; limit theorems in probability; renewal theory and random walks; martingales and potential theory; system identification and control; cardiorespiratory physiology; medical informatics. *Mailing Add:* Dept Statist Stanford Univ Stanford CA 94305

LAI, W(EI) MICHAEL, MECHANICAL ENGINEERING. *Current Pos:* PROF MECH ENG & ORTHOP BIOENG, COLUMBIA UNIV, 87- *Personal Data:* b Amoy, China, Nov 29, 31; US citizen; m 63; c 2. *Educ:* Nat Taiwan Univ, BS, 53; Univ Mich, Ann Arbor, MS, 59, PhD(eng mech), 62. *Honors & Awards:* Melville Medalist, Am Soc Mech Engrs. *Prof Exp:* From asst prof to prof mech, Rensselaer Polytech Inst, 61-89. *Mem:* Am Math Soc; fel Am Soc Mech Engrs; Am Soc Biomech; AAAS; Ortho Res Soc. *Res:* Hydrodynamic stability; continuum mechanics; biomechanics. *Mailing Add:* 215 W 95th St Apt 9H New York NY 10025-6340

LAI, YIH-LOONG, PHYSIOLOGY. *Current Pos:* res assoc prof, 84-92, RES PROF PULMONARY PHYSIOL, DEPT PHARMACOL, UNIV KY, 92- *Educ:* Taiwan Normal Univ, BS, 63; Kans State Univ, PhD(physiol), 72. *Prof Exp:* NIH fel, Mayo Clin, 72-74, asst mem, 76-81, assoc mem, 81-84. *Mem:* Am Physiol Soc; Am Heart Asn. *Res:* Physiology. *Mailing Add:* Dept Physiol Nat Taiwan Univ Med Col 1 Jen-Ai Rd First Sec Taipei Taiwan

LAI, YING-SAN, VALVE DESIGN & DEVELOPMENT, VALVE APPLICATIONS. *Current Pos:* VPRES ENG, TELEDYNE FLUID SYSTS, 93- *Personal Data:* b Taiwan, China, Sept 9, 37; US citizen; m 66, Nancy Tom; c Nolan, Ormond & Lynna. *Educ:* Nat Taiwan Univ, BS, 60; Univ Iowa, MS, 63; Northwestern Univ, PhD(mech eng), 73. *Prof Exp:* Design engr, CBI Industs, 63-69, stress analyst, 72-73; chief engr, Valve Div, Dresser Industs, 73-83, eng dir, Dresser Dewrance Ltd, UK, 83-84; dir eng, Valve Div, Dresser Industs, 84-92. *Mem:* Am Soc Mech Engrs; Am Petrol Inst. *Res:* Pressure relief valves and line valves for industrial applications. *Mailing Add:* 4878 Dublin Dr North Royalton OH 44133

LAI, YUAN-ZONG, WOOD CHEMISTRY. *Current Pos:* FAC, EMPIRE STATE PAPER RES INST, STATE UNIV NY, SYRACUSE. *Personal Data:* b Taiwan, Repub of China, Mar 11, 41; m 68; c 2. *Educ:* Nat Taiwan Univ, BS, 63; Univ Wash, MS, 66 & 67, PhD(wood chem), 68. *Prof Exp:* From res asst to res assoc wood chem, Col Forest Resources, Univ Wash, 64-70; sr res assoc wood chem, Univ Mont, 70-75; asst prof wood chem, dept forestry, Mich Technol Univ, 75-77, assoc prof forestry, 77- *Mem:* Tech Asn Pulp & Paper Indust; Am Chem Soc; Sigma Xi. *Res:* Lignin, cellulose and extractive chemistry; thermal properties of wood components. *Mailing Add:* Col Environ Sci & Forestry State Univ NY Syracuse NY 13210

LAI, YU-CHIN, POLYMER CHEMISTRY. *Current Pos:* sr polymer chemist, 86-90, sr scientist, 90-92, PRIN SCIENTIST, BAUSCH & LOMB, 92- *Personal Data:* b Feb 2, 49; m 79, Pi-Ching Chen; c Leslie & Sophia. *Educ:* Nat Tsing Hua Univ, Taiwan, BS, 71; Carnegie-Mellon Univ, MS, 75; Univ Fla, PhD(chem), 80. *Prof Exp:* Res assoc, Univ Mass, 80-81; res chemist polymer chem, Corp Res & Develop, Allied corp, 81-86. *Concurrent Pos:* Mem, Tech Prog Comt Polymeric Mat Sci & Eng, Am Chem Soc. *Mem:* Am Chem Soc. *Res:* Synthesis of organic compounds: monomers and polymers; kinetics and mechanism of polymerization; structure-properties relationships in polymers. *Mailing Add:* Contact Lens Div Res & Develop Bausch & Lomb Inc 1400 N Goodman St Rochester NY 14692-0450. *Fax:* 716-338-5304

LAIA, JOSEPH R, STRATEGY, TECHNOLOGY LEVERAGING & IMPLEMENTATION. *Current Pos:* Staff mem, Los Alamos Nat Lab, 87-88, sect leader, 88-90, group leader, 90-94, co-dir, Advan Mat Lab, 93-94, DIR, ENERGY TECHNOL PROG, LOS ALAMOS NAT LAB, 94- *Personal Data:* b 1958; m 80, Jill Jensen; c 2. *Educ:* State Univ NY, Stony Brook, BS, 80, MS, 83, PhD(mat sci & eng), 86. *Res:* Vapor phase processing of material, reactivity of solids, strategy in technology development, research and development portfolio management and leveraging into core business lines. *Mailing Add:* Los Alamos Nat Lab MS D453 Los Alamos NM 87545. *Fax:* 505-665-2964; *E-Mail:* jlaia@lanl.gov

LAIBINIS, PAUL EDWARD, CHEMICAL ENGINEERING. *Current Pos:* asst prof, Cambridge, 93-94, Texaco-Mangelsdorf, asst prof, 94-96, DOHERTY ASST PROF, MASS INST TECHNOL, 96- *Personal Data:* b Wilkes-Barre, Pa, Dec 8, 63. *Educ:* Mass Inst Technol, BS, 85; Harvard Univ, MA, 87, PhD(chem), 91. *Honors & Awards:* Victor K LaMer Award, Am Chem Soc, 94; Presidential Early Career Award for Scientists & Engrs, 96. *Prof Exp:* Teaching/res asst, Harvard Univ, Cambridge, 85-91; postdoctoral fel, Calif Inst Technol, Pasadena, 91-93. *Concurrent Pos:* Beckman Fedn young investr, 95-; Off Naval Res young investr, 96- *Mem:* AAAS; Am Inst Chem Engrs; Am Chem Soc; Mat Res Soc. *Res:* Contributed over 40 science publications on self-assembling strategies for surface modification controlling interfacial properties and sensor design; one patent in area of thin films and nanotechnology. *Mailing Add:* Dept Chem Eng Mass Inst Technol Cambridge MA 02139. *E-Mail:* pel@mit.edu

LAIBLE, JON MORSE, ALGEBRA. *Current Pos:* from asst prof to assoc prof, 64-79, dean, Col Lib Arts & Sci, 81-93, PROF MATH, EASTERN ILL UNIV, 79- *Personal Data:* b Bloomington, Ill, July 25, 37; m 59, Jo A Ivens; c Kathy J, Kenneth R, Jackie A & Michael H. *Educ:* Univ Ill, Urbana, BS, 59, PhD(math), 67; Univ Minn, Minneapolis, MA, 61. *Prof Exp:* Asst prof math, Western Ill Univ, 61-64. *Mem:* Math Asn Am; Sigma Xi. *Mailing Add:* Dean Col Sci Eastern Ill Univ 531 Deer Run Trail Charleston IL 61920

LAIBLE, ROY C, POLYMER PHYSICS, CHEMISTRY. *Current Pos:* CONSULT, TEL-TECH, 88- *Personal Data:* b Boston, Mass, June 16, 24. *Educ:* Northeastern Univ, BS, 45; Boston Univ, MA, 48; Mass Inst Technol, PhD, 70. *Prof Exp:* Res assoc polymerization, Univ RI, 50-52; org chemist, Cent Intel Agency, 52-53; org chemist, US Army Natick Labs, 53-58, phys sci admnr, 58-63, physics scientist, 63-70, chief, Textile Res Sect, 70-76, chief, Polymers & Org Mat Br, 76-87; properties plastics & elastomers consult, 87-94. *Concurrent Pos:* Secy of Army res & study fel viscoelastic properties polymers, Sweden & Scotland, 62-63. *Res:* Allyl polymerization; viscoelastic properties of fibrous and non-fibrous polymers; ballistic properties of polymers; chemical and mechanical properties of polymers especially elastomers; author of one book. *Mailing Add:* 101 Overbrook Dr Wellesley MA 02181

LAIBOWITZ, ROBERT (BENJAMIN), APPLIED PHYSICS. *Current Pos:* RES STAFF MEM, IBM RES CTR, 66- *Personal Data:* b Yonkers, NY, Mar 24, 37; m 58; c 3. *Educ:* Columbia Col, BA, 59; Columbia Univ, BS, 60, MS, 63; Columbia Univ, PhD(appl physics), 67. *Mem:* Am Phys Soc; fel Am Vacuum Soc. *Res:* Electrical and optical properties of materials; superconductivity. *Mailing Add:* IBM T J Watson Res Ctr PO Box 218 Yorktown Heights NY 10598

LAIBSON, PETER R, OPHTHALMOLOGY. *Current Pos:* PROF OPHTHAL, SCH MED, THOMAS JEFFERSON UNIV, 73- *Personal Data:* b New York, NY, Dec 11, 33; m 63; c 1. *Educ:* Univ Vt, BA, 55; State Univ NY Downstate Med Ctr, MD, 59; Am Bd Ophthal, dipl, 65. *Prof Exp:* NIH fel corneal dis, Retina Found & Mass Eye & Ear Infirmary, 64-65; ASSOC PROF OPHTHAL, SCH MED, TEMPLE UNIV, 66- *Concurrent Pos:* Attend surgeon & dir cornea serv, Wills Eye Hosp; consult lectr, US Naval Hosp, Philadelphia, 68-; mem ophthal staff, Lankenau Hosp, Philadelphia. *Mem:* Asn Res Ophthal; Am Acad Ophthal & Otolaryngol; AMA; Am Ophthal Soc. *Res:* Corneal diseases and surgery of the cornea, particularly viral external diseases, herpes simplex and adenoviruses. *Mailing Add:* Ninth & Walnut Philadelphia PA 19107

LAIDLAW, HARRY HYDE, JR, APICULTURE, HONEY BEE GENETICS & BREEDING. *Current Pos:* asst prof entom & asst apiculturist, Univ Calif, Davis, 47-53, assoc prof entom & assoc apiculturist, 53-59, prof entom & apiculturist, 59-74, prof genetics, 71-74, assoc dean col agr, 60-64, chmn fac & staff, Col Agr, 65-66, EMER PROF ENTOM, EXP STA, UNIV CALIF, DAVIS, 74- *Personal Data:* b Houston, Tex, Apr 12, 07; m 46, Ruth G Collins; c Barbara S (Murphy). *Educ:* La State Univ, BS, 33, MS, 34; Univ Wis, PhD(entom, genetics), 39. *Honors & Awards:* C W Woodworth Award, Entom Soc Am, 81; Gold Merit Award, Int Fedn Beekeepers Asn, 86; Alan Clemson Mem Found Int Serv Bee Breeding Award, Australia, 89. *Prof Exp:* From minor sci helper to agent, USDA, 29-34 & 35-39; asst zool & entom, La State Univ, 33-34, asst exp sta, 34-35; prof biol sci, Oakland City Col, 39-41; apiarist, State Dept Agr & Indust, Ala, 41-42; entomologist hqs, 1st Army, NY, 46-47. *Concurrent Pos:* Wis Alumni Res Found asst, Univ Wis, 37-39; Rockefeller Found grant, Brazil, 54-55, Sudan, 67; NIH grant, Univ Calif, Davis, 63-66, NSF grant, 66-73; coordr, Univ Calif Egypt agr develop prog, AID, 79-83. *Mem:* Fel AAAS; Soc Integrative & Comp Biol; fel Entom Soc Am; Am Soc Nat. *Res:* Genetics, breeding and anatomy of the honeybee; queen rearing; artificial insemination of queen bees. *Mailing Add:* 761 Sycamore Lane Davis CA 95616-3432. *Fax:* 530-752-1537; *E-Mail:* hhlaidlaw@ucdavis.edu

LAIDLAW, JOHN COLEMAN, ENDOCRINOLOGY. *Current Pos:* VPRES, RES & EDUC, ONT CANCER TREATMENT & RES FOUND, 86-; PROF MED, UNIV TORONTO, 86- *Personal Data:* b Toronto, Ont, Feb 28, 21; m 57, Ann Elliot; c Kate & Meg. *Educ:* Univ Toronto, BA, 42, MD, 44, MA, 47; Univ London, PhD(biochem), 50; FRCP(C), 55; FRSC, 75; FRCP, 81. *Prof Exp:* Jr intern, Toronto Gen Hosp, 44; demonstr biochem, Univ Toronto, 46-47; lectr biochem, Univ London, 47-50; sr intern med, Toronto Gen Hosp, 50-51; res fel, Harvard Med Sch, 51-53, instr, 53-54; assoc, 54-56, from asst prof to prof med, Univ Toronto, 56-75, dir inst med sci, 67-75; prof med & chmn dept, McMaster Univ, 75-81, dean, fac health sci, 81-85; sci adv to pres, Med Res Coun, Ottawa, 85-86. *Concurrent Pos:* Asst, Peter Bent Brigham Hosp, Boston, 51-53, jr assoc, 53-54; physician, Toronto Gen Hosp, 54-59, sr physician, 59-75; exec dir med affairs, Can Cancer Soc, 86-92. *Mem:* Endocrine Soc; Am Soc Clin Invest; Can Soc Clin Invest (pres, 62); Can Soc Endocrinol & Metab (pres, 75). *Mailing Add:* Dept Res & Educ Ont Cancer Treat & Res Found 620 University Ave Toronto ON M5G 2L7 Can. *Fax:* 416-971-6888

LAIDLAW, WILLIAM GEORGE, THEORETICAL CHEMISTRY. *Current Pos:* from asst prof to prof chem, 65-93, FAC PROF CHEM, UNIV CALGARY, 93- *Personal Data:* b Wingham, Ont, Mar 13, 36; m 61, Lucia N Mundon; c David K & Michael K. *Educ:* Univ Western Ont, BSc, 59; Calif Inst Technol, MSc, 61; Univ Alta, PhD(theoret chem), 63. *Prof Exp:* NATO fel, Math Inst, Univ Oxford, 64-65. *Concurrent Pos:* Adj prof physics, Univ Hawaii. *Mem:* Chem Inst Can; Can Asn Physics. *Res:* Hydrodynamics; flow of fluids in porous media; fluid systems near instabilities. *Mailing Add:* Dept Chem Univ Calgary Calgary AB T2N 1N4 Can

LAIDLER, KEITH JAMES, PHYSICAL CHEMISTRY, CHEMICAL KINETICS & HISTORY OF CHEMISTRY. *Current Pos:* chmn dept, Univ Ottawa, 61-66, vdean fac pure & appl sci, 62-66, prof, 55-81, EMER PROF CHEM, UNIV OTTAWA, 81- *Personal Data:* b Liverpool, Eng, Jan 3, 16; m 43, Mary Auchincloss; c Margaret (deceased), Audrey (deceased) & James. *Educ:* Oxford Univ, BA, 37, MA, 55, DSc, 56; Princeton Univ, PhD(phys chem), 40. *Hon Degrees:* LLD, Simon Fraser Univ, 97. *Honors & Awards:* Medal, Chem Inst Can, 71; Queen's Jubilee Medal, 77; Centenary Medal, Royal Soc Can, 82, Henry Marshall Tory Medal, 87; Dexter Award Excellence, Am Chem Soc, 96. *Prof Exp:* Res chemist, Nat Res Coun Can, 40-42; sci officer, Can Armaments Res & Develop Estab, 42-44, chief sci officer & supt phys & math wing, 44-46; from asst prof to assoc prof chem, Cath Univ Am, 46-55. *Concurrent Pos:* Commonwealth vis prof, Sussex Univ, 66-67. *Mem:* Royal Soc Can; fel Royal Soc Can; fel Chem Inst Can. *Res:* Chemical kinetics of gas reactions; surface, solution and enzyme reactions; photochemistry; history of physical chemistry. *Mailing Add:* Dept Chem Univ Ottawa Ottawa ON K1N 6N5 Can. *Fax:* 613-562-5170

LAI-FOOK, JOAN ELSA I-LING, zoology, for more information see previous edition

LAI-FOOK, STEPHEN J, BIOMEDICAL ENGINEERING. *Current Pos:* PROF BIOMED ENG, WENNER GREN RES LAB, UNIV KY, 87-, PROF PHYSIOL & BIOPHYS, 91- *Personal Data:* b Trinidad & Tobago, Aug 28, 40; US citizen; m 74, Michele Lund; c Kristin & Thomas. *Educ:* Loughborough Univ, Eng, BTech, 64; Southhampton Univ, Eng, MScEng, 66; Univ Wash, Seattle, PhD(mech eng), 72. *Prof Exp:* Res engr, Boeing Co, 66-69; fel, Dept Aerospace Eng & Mech, Univ Minn, 73-74; instr biophys, Mayo Med Sch, 75-78, assoc prof physiol & med, 78-81, assoc prof physiol & biophys, 81; assoc mem, Cardiovasc Res Inst, 84-87. *Concurrent Pos:* NIH young investr award, 76, res career develop award, 80; assoc consult thoracic dis, Mayo Clin, 77-80, consult, 80-81; adj asst prof physiol & med, Univ Calif, San Francisco, 81, instr orgn physiol, Pulmonary Physiol Lab, 82-85, lectr, Sch Pediat, 83, 84 & 86, adj assoc prof physiol, 84-87; mem, Respiratory & Appl Study Sect, NIH, 90-94; assoc ed, J Appl Physiol, 93- *Mem:* Am Physiol Soc; Am Soc Mech Engrs; Biomed Eng Soc; Microcirculation Soc; Am Thoracic Soc; Am Heart Asn; Am Acad Mech. *Res:* Pulmonary mechanics; mechanical properties of the lung; mechanics of lung interstitium and the pleural space in relation to liquid and solute exchange; mathematical modeling of physiological systems. *Mailing Add:* Dept Biomed Eng Univ Ky Wenner Gren Res Lab Lexington KY 40506-0001. *Fax:* 606-257-1836; *E-Mail:* bme006@ukcc.uky.edu

LAIHING, KENNETH, NONLINEAR OPTICS, LASER SPECTROSCOPY. *Current Pos:* From asst prof to assoc prof, 88-95, PROF & CHMN, DEPT CHEM, OAKWOOD COL, 96- *Personal Data:* b Trinidad, WI; US citizen; m 80, Esther Adolph; c Steven K. *Educ:* Col Staten Island, BS, 72; Long Island Univ, MS, 81; Univ Ga, PhD(chem), 88. *Honors & Awards:* Martin Reynolds Smith Mem Prize, Am Chem Soc, 87. *Concurrent Pos:* Res fel, US Army, 89 & 90, Am Chem Soc, 91; fel, NSF, 91 & 92, prin investr, 92- *Mem:* Am Chem Soc; Optical Soc Am; Am Phys Soc; Int Union Pure & Appl Chem. *Res:* Preparation and characterization of novel inorganic and organometallic compounds for nonlinear applications; new techniques for identification and sequencing of biological molecules using matrix assisted time-of-flight mass spectrometry. *Mailing Add:* Dept Chem Oakwood Col Huntsville AL 35896. *Fax:* 205-726-7111; *E-Mail:* laihing@oakwood.edu

LAIKEN, NORA DAWN, MEDICAL PHYSIOLOGY, MEDICAL EDUCATION. *Current Pos:* USPHS fel & res assoc phys biochem, Univ Calif, San Diego, 71-72, sci curric adv physics, biol & chem, Adaptive Learning Prog, 72-73, lectr med, 74-76, asst prof, 76-80, asst adj prof med, 80-83, DIR TUTORIAL PROG, UNIV CALIF, SAN DIEGO, 73-, LECTR MED, 83-, ASST DEAN CURRIC & STUDENT AFFAIRS, 83- *Personal Data:* b Chicago, Ill, June 28, 46; m 67, Stuart L; c 2. *Educ:* Univ Chicago, BS, 67; Rockefeller Univ, PhD(life sci), 70. *Prof Exp:* USPHS fel & res assoc phys biochem, Inst Molecular Biol, Univ Ore, 70-71. *Concurrent Pos:* Mem test adv, Asn Am Med Col, 74-78; mem, Undergrad Teaching Proj Comt, Am Gastroenterol Asn, 85-91. *Res:* Development of innovative instructional materials and methods in the basic medical sciences, particularly in medical physiology and pharmacology; applications of computers to biomedical problems. *Mailing Add:* 9500 Gilman Dr 0606 Univ Calif San Diego La Jolla CA 92093-0606. *Fax:* 619-534-8556; *E-Mail:* nlaiken@ucsd.edu

LAINE, RICHARD MASON, ORGANOMETALLIC CHEMISTRY. *Current Pos:* ASSOC PROF, DEPT MAT SCI & ENG/DEPT CHEM, UNIV MICH, 90- *Personal Data:* b San Fernando, Calif, Oct 31, 47. *Educ:* Calif State Univ, Northridge, BS, 69; Univ Southern Calif, PhD(chem), 73. *Prof Exp:* Fel chem, Univ Del, 73-74, Dept Chem & Dept Chem & Nuclear Eng, Univ Calif, Santa Barbara, 74-76, Stanford Res Inst, 76-77; phys inorg chemist, SRI Int, 77-87; fac, Dept Mat Sci & Eng, Univ Wash, Seattle, 87-90. *Concurrent Pos:* Prin investr, NSF Chem Eng Grant, 78-79; proj leader, NIH Grant, 78-81. *Mem:* Am Chem Soc; Catalysis Soc; Sigma Xi. *Res:* Homogeneous catalysis of the water-gas shift reaction and the catalysis of related reactions wherein water serves as a source of hydrogen. *Mailing Add:* Dept Mat Sci & Eng Univ Mich H H Dow Bldg 2300 Hayward Ann Arbor MI 48109-2136

LAINE, ROGER ALLAN, BIOCHEMISTRY. *Current Pos:* CHIEF SCIENTIST, GLYCOMED, INC, 88-, PROF, DEPT BIOCHEM & CHEM. *Personal Data:* b Cloquet, Minn, Jan 28, 41; c 2. *Educ:* Univ Minn, Minneapolis, BA, 64; Rice Univ, Houston, PhD(biochem), 70. *Prof Exp:* Fel biochem, Mich State Univ, East Lansing, 70-72; fel pathobiol, Univ Wash, 72-74; from asst prof to assoc prof biochem, Col Med, Univ Ky, 75-88; chmn, Dept Biochem, La State Univ, Baton Rouge, 88-90. *Mem:* Am Chem Soc; Soc Complex Carbohydrates; Am Soc Mass Spectrometry; Am Soc Biol Chemists. *Res:* Biochemistry of cell membrane components; gas-liquid-chromatography and mass spectrometry in carbohydrate analysis. *Mailing Add:* Dept Biochem La State Univ Baton Rouge LA 70803-0001

LAING, JOHN E, ENTOMOLOGY, ECOLOGY. *Current Pos:* RETIRED. *Personal Data:* b Ottawa, Ont, Oct 17, 39; m 64; c 2. *Educ:* Carleton Univ, BSc, 63, MSc, 64; Univ Calif, Berkeley, PhD(entom), 68. *Prof Exp:* Asst res entomologist & lectr, Div Biol Control, Univ Calif, Berkeley, 68-73; from asst prof to assoc prof environ biol, Univ Guelph, 73-96. *Mem:* Entom Soc Can (secy, 78-81); Entom Soc Am; Ecol Soc Am; Int Asn Ecol; Int Orgn Biol Control; Sigma Xi. *Res:* Ecology of tetranychid mites; populations dynamics of arthropods; ecology and control of orchard pests; biological control of insect pests and weeds. *Mailing Add:* Dept Biol & Environ Univ Guelph Guelph ON N1G 2W1 Can

LAING, PATRICK GOWANS, ORTHOPEDIC SURGERY. *Current Pos:* assoc prof orthop surg, 56-63, CLIN PROF ORTHOP SURG, UNIV PITTSBURGH, 63-; ORTHOP SURGEON, AIKEN MED, 56- *Personal Data:* b Barnes, Eng, Nov 8, 23; US citizen; m 56; c 4. *Educ:* Univ Southampton, MB & BS, 40; FRCS, 48; FRCS(C), 54, Am Bd Orthop Surg, dipl, 60. *Prof Exp:* House surgeon, Kings Col Hosp, London, Eng, 45-46; registr orthop surg, Royal Hampshire Co Hosp, Winchester, 46-47, gen & orthop surg, Queen Mary's Hosp, Sidcup, 48, orthop surg, Lewisham Hosp, London, 48-50 & Pembury Hosp, Kent, 50-52; sr registr, Bradford Hosp, Yorkshire, 52-54; chief resident surg, Vet Hosp, St John, NB, 54-55; chief serv, Vet Admin Hosp, 56-92. *Concurrent Pos:* Fel cerebral palsy, Univ Pittsburgh, 55-56. *Mem:* Orthop Res Soc; Am Orthop Asn; Am Soc Testing & Mat; NY Acad Sci; Brit Orthop Asn. *Res:* Blood supply and the dynamics of circulation in bones and joints; metallurgy and engineering in orthopedics; radioisotopes in clinical orthopedics. *Mailing Add:* 532 S Aiken Ave Pittsburgh PA 15232

LAING, RONALD ALBERT, BIOPHYSICS. *Current Pos:* ASSOC PROF OPHTHAL, MED SCH, BOSTON UNIV, 70- *Personal Data:* b Seattle, Wash, Dec 9, 33. *Educ:* Reed Col, BA, 56; Rice Univ, MA, 58, PhD(low temperature physics), 60. *Prof Exp:* Asst prof physics, Tulane Univ, 60-68; sr scientist, Space Sci Inc, 68-70; vis scientist, Univ Tokyo, 69-70. *Concurrent Pos:* NSF sci fac fel, Harvard Univ, 65-66; NIH fel, Mass Inst Technol, 66-67; vis lectr, Univ Mass, Boston, 67-68; consult, Space Sci Inc, 67-68. *Mem:* Biophys Soc; Asn Res in Vision & Ophthalmol; Optical Soc Am; AAAS; Sigma Xi. *Res:* Ophthalmic biophysics; bioengineering. *Mailing Add:* 1024 Massachusetts Ave Lexington MA 02173-3829

LAIPIS, PHILIP JAMES, MOLECULAR BIOLOGY, GENETICS. *Current Pos:* from asst prof to assoc prof, 74-86, PROF BIOCHEM, UNIV FLA, 86- *Personal Data:* b Charleston, SC, Apr 20, 44; m 70; c 2. *Educ:* Calif Inst Technol, BS, 66; Stanford Univ, PhD(genetics), 72. *Prof Exp:* Nat Cancer Inst fel, Princeton Univ, 72-74. *Concurrent Pos:* Vis scholar biochem, Harvard Univ, 81-82; vis affil, Whitehead Inst, Mass Inst Technol, 87-88. *Mem:* AAAS; Am Soc Microbiol; Sigma Xi; Am Soc Biol Chem; Am Soc Cell Biol. *Res:* Gene organization and variation in mammalian mitochondrial DNA; mechanisms of maternal inheritance, mitochondrial amplification and embryonic distribution of mitochondria on mammals; gene organization and variation in mammalian carbonic anhydrase genes; site directed mutation of human carbonic anhydrase isozymes and expression in bacterial systems. *Mailing Add:* Univ Fla PO Box 100245 HSC Gainesville FL 32610-0245

LAIR, ALAN VAN, PARABOLIC & ELLIPTIC PARTIAL DIFFERENTIAL EQUATIONS. *Current Pos:* from asst prof to assoc prof 82-91, PROF MATH, AIR FORCE INST TECHNOL, 91-, DEPT HEAD, 93- *Personal Data:* b Anna, Tex, May 2, 48; m 78, Vickie Jucht. *Educ:* Univ NTex, BA, 70; Tex Tech Univ, MS, 72, PhD(math), 76. *Prof Exp:* From asst prof to assoc prof math, Univ SDak, 76-82. *Concurrent Pos:* Reviewer, Math Rev, 80- *Mem:* Am Math Soc; Soc Indust & Appl Math. *Res:* Existence and properites of solutions to partial differential equations. *Mailing Add:* 116 Holmes Dr Fairborn OH 45324. *E-Mail:* alair@afit.af.mil

LAIRD, CAMPBELL, PHYSICAL METALLURGY. *Current Pos:* prof metall, 68-80, PROF MAT SCI & ENG, UNIV PA, 80- *Personal Data:* b Ardrishaig, Scotland, June 17, 36; m 64, Beckwith; c Katherine F, Andrew K & Lucy M. *Educ:* Cambridge Univ, BA, 59, MA, 63, PhD(metall), 63. *Prof Exp:* Res fel metall, Christ's Col, Cambridge Univ, 61-65; prin scientist, Sci Lab, Ford Motor Co, 63-68. *Concurrent Pos:* Battelle vis prof, Ohio State Univ, 68-; hon prof, Academia Sinica; vis prof physics, Univ Vienna. *Mem:* Am Inst Mining, Metall & Petrol Engrs; Am Soc Testing & Mat; Electron Micros Soc Am; Royal Inst Gt Brit; Brit Inst Metals; fel Am Soc Metals. *Res:* Fracture of materials, especially by fatigue; super-conductivity; diffusional phase transformations; electron microscopy; cyclic stress-strain response of materials; environmental effects on fractive; properties of composite materials; 270 publications. *Mailing Add:* 951 Weadley Rd Radnor PA 19087

LAIRD, CHARLES DAVID, CELL BIOLOGY, HUMAN GENETICS. *Current Pos:* assoc prof zool & adj assoc prof genetics, 71-75, PROF ZOOL & ADJ PROF GENETICS, UNIV WASH, 75-, RES AFFIL, CHILD DEVELOP & MENT RETARDATION CTR, 89- *Personal Data:* b Portland, Ore, May 12, 39; m 61; c 4. *Educ:* Univ Ore, BA, 61; Stanford Univ, PhD(genetics), 66. *Honors & Awards:* Wassenberg Mem Lectr, San Diego State Univ, 90. *Prof Exp:* NIH fel genetics, Univ Wash, 67-68; asst prof zool, Univ Tex, Austin, 68-71. *Concurrent Pos:* Distinguished vis lectr, Univ Tex, Austin, 77; vis scholar, Cambridge Univ, 78-79; mem, Fred Hutchinson Cancer Res Ctr, 90- *Mem:* AAAS; Am Soc Human Genetics; Genetic Soc Am. *Res:* Encoding the three dimensional structure of chromosomes; mechanisms of transcription control; chromosome structure and function; human genetics. *Mailing Add:* Dept Zool Univ Wash Box 351800 Seattle WA 98195

LAIRD, CHRISTOPHER ELI, NUCLEAR PHYSICS. *Current Pos:* From asst prof to assoc prof, 67-75, PROF PHYSICS, EASTERN KY UNIV, 75- *Personal Data:* b Anniston, Ala, Nov 29, 42; m 66, Mary Weaver; c 2. *Educ:* Univ Ala, BS, 63, MS, 66, PhD(physics), 70. *Concurrent Pos:* Fac res mem, Vanderbilt Univ, 69 & Argonne Nat Lab, 77-78; vis res prof, Univ Ky, 79-81 & 86, Marshall Space Flight Ctr, 82, 83, 96. *Mem:* Am Phys Soc; Sigma Xi; Sci Res Soc; Sigma Xi; Am Nuclear Soc. *Res:* Theoretical and experimental nuclear physics with primary emphasis in beta decay; atomic effects during beta decay; proton induced nuclear reactions; experimental measurement of proton-induced reaction cross-sections analysis of this data using various nuclear models. *Mailing Add:* Dept Physics & Astron Eastern Ky Univ 351 Moore Hall Richmond KY 40475. *Fax:* 606-622-1020; *E-Mail:* phylaird@acs.eku.edu

LAIRD, CLEVE WATROUS, PHYSIOLOGY, GENETICS. *Current Pos:* PRES & CONSULT, DRIAL CONSULT, 86- *Personal Data:* b Montclair, NJ, Mar 29, 38; m 65, Elizabeth Cortelyou; c Kevin W & Brian C. *Educ:* Gettysburg Col, BA, 61; Univ Nebr, MS, 63; Rutgers Univ, PhD(endocrinol & reproductive physiol), 67. *Honors & Awards:* Can Heart Prize, 76. *Prof Exp:* Biol sect head, Hycel Inc, 69-72, res assoc, Biores Inc, 72-74, sr scientist, Block Eng, 74-77, sr scientist & group leader, Union Carbide, med prod, 77-80, dir, Lab Serv Clin, Chem & Physiol, Remote Imaging Syst, 81-86. *Concurrent Pos:* Cyto chem consult, Coulter Electronics; postdoctoral fel, NIH, 67-69; staff, NATO mammalian genetics course, 68, adj assoc prof, Baylor Col Med, 69-72, adj asst prof, Boston Univ, 72-77, instr, Harvard Med Sch, 74-80. *Mem:* Am Physiol Asn; Am Heart Asn; Am Asn Clin Chem; Am Soc Vet Clin Pathologists; Soc Reproductive Physiol; Sigma Xi. *Res:* Clinical chemistry; impact of genetics and disease on the physiology and biochemistry of animals and humans. *Mailing Add:* Drial Consults Inc 3216 Sheri Dr Simi Valley CA 93063-1085. *Fax:* 805-522-1526; *E-Mail:* diabetes@ix.netcom.com

LAIRD, DON M, CLINICAL CHEMISTRY. *Current Pos:* tech specialist, 92-94, PROJ MGR, ABBOTT LABS, 94- *Personal Data:* b Johnstown, NY, Sept 27, 53. *Educ:* Campbell Univ, BS, 77; Wake Forest Univ, PhD(energy metab), 83. *Prof Exp:* NIH res fel, Johns Hopkins Univ Med Sch, Baltimore, 83-87; sr res scientist, Monsanto Co, 87-92. *Mem:* Am Asn Clin Chem. *Res:* Clinical chemistry. *Mailing Add:* Dept 9FB Abbott Labs Bldg AP8 One Abbott Park Rd North Chicago IL 60064

LAIRD, DONALD T(HOMAS), COMPUTER SCIENCE. *Current Pos:* res assoc, Ord Res Lab, Pa State Univ, 49-55, asst prof elec eng, 55-58, eng res, 58-61, dir, Comput Ctr, 58-88, assoc prof, 61-64, ASSOC PROF COMPUT SCI, PA STATE UNIV, 64-, EMER DIR, COMPUT CTR. *Personal Data:* b Sykesville, Pa, Dec 12, 26; m 48; c 4. *Educ:* Pa State Univ, BS, 46, PhD(physics), 55; Cornell Univ, MS, 51. *Prof Exp:* Asst physics, Cornell Univ, 46-49. *Concurrent Pos:* Prog dir comput sci, NSF, 63-64. *Res:* Computer programming systems including supervisors and language processors. *Mailing Add:* PO Box 223 State College PA 16804-0223

LAIRD, HUGH EDWARD, II, neuropharmacology, cellular pharmacology, for more information see previous edition

LAIRD, WILSON MORROW, geology, geomorphology & petroleum geology; deceased, see previous edition for last biography

LAITIN, HOWARD, SYSTEMS ANALYSIS & DESIGN. *Current Pos:* CONSULT, 95- *Personal Data:* b Brooklyn, NY, Nov 18, 31; m 61; c 3. *Educ:* Brooklyn Col, BA, 52; Harvard Univ, MA, 53, PhD(statist, pub health & econ), 56. *Prof Exp:* Med economist, Hosp Coun Greater NY, 54-56; dir, Michael Saphier & Assoc, 56; proj dir, Army Med Serv, 57-59; sr economist, Rand Corp, 59-62; mgr proj anal, Hughes Aircraft Co, 62-82, chief scientist, 82-95. *Concurrent Pos:* Clin assoc prof pub health, Univ Calif, Los Angeles, 59-73; adj prof, Sch Eng, Univ Southern Calif, 66-90; adv to var orgn & govt agencies. *Res:* Technical analysis; military affairs; public health; solid and hazardous waste management; air pollution; transportation; safety; economic studies. *Mailing Add:* 4916 White Ct Torrance CA 90503

LAITY, DAVID SANFORD, CHEMICAL ENGINEERING. *Current Pos:* RETIRED. *Personal Data:* b mt Kisco, NY, Nov 20, 26; m 50, Mary J Work; c David Jr & Robert. *Educ:* Haverford Col, BA, 49; Mass Inst Technol, MS, 50; NY Univ, ScD(chem eng), 56. *Prof Exp:* Plant process engr & supvr, Eng Serv Div, E I DuPont de Nemours & Co, 50-59; supv res engr, Process Design Div, Chevron Res Co, 59-66, staff econ analyst, Comptrollers Analysis Div, 67-69, asst proj mgr, Belg Refinery, 69-71, staff planner, Chevron Oil Europe, 71-73, mgr, Process Design Div, Chevron Corp, 73-86, vpres, Process Res Dept, 86-92. *Concurrent Pos:* Chmn, Adv Coun, Sch Chem Eng, Cornell Univ, 81-91 & Worcester Polytech Inst, 85-87. *Mem:* Am Inst Chem Eng; Sigma Xi. *Res:* Process engineering and research management in chemical and petroleum industries. *Mailing Add:* 96 Silverwood Dr Lafayette CA 94549

LAITY, JOHN LAWRENCE, INDUSTRIAL CHEMISTRY, PETROLEUM CHEMISTRY. *Current Pos:* CHEMIST & SUPVR, SHELL OIL CO, 68- *Personal Data:* b Helena, Mont, Feb 23, 42; m 64; c 2. *Educ:* Stanford Univ, BS, 64; Univ Wash, PhD(chem), 68. *Mem:* Am Chem Soc. *Res:* Photochemical smog; automotive and engine research; combustion; gasoline and oil additives; compositions of fuels and solvents; exhaust emissions; catalysts; atmospheric reactions; air and water pollution; polymer chemistry. *Mailing Add:* 14207 Withersdale Houston TX 77077

LAJTAI, EMERY ZOLTAN, GEOLOGY. *Current Pos:* vis lectr eng geol, Univ NB, 65-67, asst prof, 67-70, assoc prof eng geol & rock mech, 70-77, PROF GEOL, UNIV NB, 77- *Personal Data:* b Hungary, Oct 28, 34; Can citizen; m 59. *Educ:* Univ Toronto, BASc, 50, MASc, 61, PhD(Pleistocene geol), 66. *Prof Exp:* Soils engr, Subway Construct Br, Toronto Transit Comn, 61-63; eng geologist, H G Acres & Co Ltd, Ont, 63-65. *Concurrent Pos:* Nat Res Coun Can res grants, 66-68, 71-74 & 74-77; Govt Can, Geol Surv grants, 67-68 & 71-72. *Mem:* Can Geotech Soc; Can Rock Mech Group. *Res:* Brittle fracture of rocks under compressive loading with application in structural and engineering geology. *Mailing Add:* Dept Civil & Geol Eng Univ Man Winnipeg MB R3T 2N2 Can

LAJTHA, ABEL, BIOCHEMISTRY. *Current Pos:* prin res scientist, 62-66, DIR, NY STATE RES INST NEUROCHEM, 66-; PROF EXP PSYCHIAT, SCH MED, NY UNIV, 71- *Personal Data:* b Budapest, Hungary, Sept 22, 22; nat US; m 53; c 2. *Educ:* Eotvos Lorand Univ, Budapest, PhD(chem), 45. *Hon Degrees:* Dr, Univ Padua, Italy. *Prof Exp:* Asst prof biochem, Eotvos Lorand Univ, 45-47; asst prof, Inst Muscle Res, Mass, 49-50; sr res scientist, NY State Psychiat Inst, 50-57, assoc res scientist, 57-62. *Concurrent Pos:* Fel, Zool Sta, Italy, 47-48; res fel, Royal Inst Gt Brit, 48-49; asst prof, Col Physicians & Surgeons, Columbia Univ, 56-69; pres, Am Soc Neurochem & Int Soc Neurochem. *Mem:* Int Brain Res Orgn; Am Soc Biol Chemists; Am Acad Neurol; Am Col Neuropsychopharmacol; Int Soc Neurochem; Am Chem Soc. *Res:* Neurochemistry; amino acid and protein metabolism of the brain and the brain barrier system. *Mailing Add:* Ctr Neurochem NS Kline Inst Orangeburg NY 10962

LAJTHA, KATE, biogeochemistry, environmental physiology, for more information see previous edition

LAKATOS, ANDRAS IMRE, THIN FILM DEVICES, LIQUID CRYSTAL DISPLAYS. *Current Pos:* Scientist photoelec properties displays, 66-78, MGR THIN FILM DEVICE AREA, WEBSTER RES CTR, XEROX, INC, 78- *Personal Data:* b Budapest, Hungary, Aug 23, 37; US citizen; m 72; c 1. *Educ:* Alfred Univ, BS, 62, MS, 63; Cornell Univ, PhD(appl physics), 67. *Mem:* Sr mem Inst Elec & Electronics Engrs; fel Soc Info Display; Am Phys Soc; Soc Photog Sci & Eng. *Res:* Development of thin film transistors for the addressing of one and two dimensional marking or display arrays. *Mailing Add:* Xerox Corp MS 0147-59B 800 Phillips Rd Webster NY 14580. *Fax:* 716-422-8548

LAKATTA, EDWARD G, CARDIOLOGY, MUSCLE PHYSIOLOGY. *Current Pos:* DIR, GERONT RES CTR, NAT INST AGING, NIH, 76- *Personal Data:* b Scranton, Pa, May 10, 44; m, Loretta Cantwell; c 3. *Educ:* Georgetown Univ, MD, 70. *Concurrent Pos:* Prof med, Johns Hopkins Sch Med, Baltimore, Md; prof physiol, Univ Md Sch Med, Baltimore, Md. *Mem:* Am Physiol Soc; Am Heart Asn; Am Soc Clin Invest; Biophys Soc; Internation Soc Heart Res; Physiol Soc. *Res:* Conceptualize, study and characterize the basic mechanisms that control myocardial and vascular structure and function; describe the influence of age and age-related chronic pathologic conditions in man and animal models; the latter involve isolated cardiac muscle myocytes and subcellular organelles. *Mailing Add:* Geront Res Ctr Nat Inst Aging NIH 4940 Eastern Ave Baltimore MD 21224-2700. *Fax:* 410-558-8150; *E-Mail:* hal%vax.dnet@dxi.nih.gov

LAKE, BRUCE M, OCEAN REMOTE SENSING. *Current Pos:* Technol staff, Fluid Mechs Dept, 69-81, mgr, Ocean Technol Dept, 81-96, MGR COMPUT PHYSICS BUS, TRW SPACE & TECHNOL GROUP, 96- *Personal Data:* b Nov 22, 41. *Educ:* Princeton Univ, BSE, 63; Calif Inst Technol, MS, 64, PhD(aeronaut), 69. *Concurrent Pos:* Mem, Naval Studies Bd Boundary Layer Dynamics Panel, 92-95. *Mem:* Nat Acad Eng; Am Phys Soc; Sigma Xi. *Res:* Surface-wave hydrodynamics and non-acoustic anti-submarine warfare; nonlinear hydrodynamics and ocean remote sensing; wave stability, dynamics and radar scattering; author or coauthor of over 35 articles. *Mailing Add:* Dept Ocean Technol/Sensors Lasers & Res Ctr TRW Space & Technol Div One Space Park R1/1008B Redondo Beach CA 90278. *Fax:* 310-814-2359; *E-Mail:* blake@amelia.sp.trw.com

LAKE, CHARLES RAYMOND, PSYCHOPHARMACOLOGY. *Current Pos:* PROF PHARMACOL & PROF PSYCHIAT, UNIFORMED SERV UNIV HEALTH SCI, 79- *Personal Data:* b Nashville, Tenn, July 6, 43; m 67; c 2. *Educ:* Tulane Univ, BS, 65, MS, 66; Duke Univ, PhD(physiol & pharmacol), 71, MD, 72. *Prof Exp:* Resident psychiat, Duke Univ Med Ctr, 72-74; res assoc, 74-75, clin assoc, Lab Clin Sci, 75-77, attend physician, Sect

Exp Therapeut, NIMH, 78-80. *Concurrent Pos:* Psychiat consult, Nat Naval Med Ctr, Bethesda, Md, 80- *Mem:* Am Soc Pharmacol & Exp Therapeut; Soc Biol Psychiat; Am Soc Neurochem; Am Col Neuropsychopharmacol; Int Soc Hypertension. *Res:* Biogenic amine metabolism as related to neuropsychiatric disease and bloodpressure regulation; endorphins and neuropsychiatric disorders; endogenous opioid and catecholamine interrelationships. *Mailing Add:* Univ Health Sci 4301 Jones Bridge Rd Bethesda MD 20814-4799

LAKE, DAVID ALLEN, PHYSICAL THERAPY, HEALTH PROFESSIONS EDUCATION. *Current Pos:* PROF & DEPT HEAD PHYS THER, ARMSTRONG ATLANTIC STATE UNIV, 94- *Personal Data:* b Ypsilanti, Mich, Feb 10, 51. *Educ:* Univ Calif, Irvine, BS, 72; Ind State Univ, MS, 75; Tex Tech Sch Med, PhD(physiol-neurosci), 78. *Prof Exp:* Res assoc, Univ Mich, 72-73; actg asst prof zool, NC State Univ, 78-80; asst prof biol, Kean Col, NJ, 80-85; asst prof phys ther, Northeastern Univ, 85-88, assoc prof & dept head, 88-94. *Concurrent Pos:* Vis prof, St George Sch Med, 81-82. *Mem:* Am Physiol Soc; Am Phys Ther Asn; Sigma Xi; Fedn Am Socs Exp Biol; Am Col Sports Med. *Res:* Innovative teaching methodologies including cooperative learning, problem-based learning and other active learning metholdologies; volunteer programs for the elderly and teaching methods in geriatrics. *Mailing Add:* Dept Phys Ther Armstrong Atlantic State Univ 11935 Abercorn St Savannah GA 31419. *Fax:* 912-921-5838; *E-Mail:* david__lake@mailgate.armstrong.edu

LAKE, GEORGE RUSSELL, DYNAMICS OF GALAXIES, COSMOLOGY. *Current Pos:* PROF, UNIV WASH, 86- *Personal Data:* b Washington, DC, June 12, 53; c Astrid & Caitlin. *Educ:* Haverford Col, BA, 75; Princeton Univ, MA, 77, PhD(physics), 80. *Honors & Awards:* Dudley Prize. *Prof Exp:* Fel, Univ Calif, Berkeley, 79-80 & Churchill Col, Cambridge, 80-81; mem tech staff, Bell Labs, 81-86. *Concurrent Pos:* Proj scientist, NASA. *Res:* Dynamics of galaxies, galaxy formation and cosmology; low mass stars; search for extraterrestrial intelligence. *Mailing Add:* Dept Astron Univ Wash FM 20 Seattle WA 98195. *Fax:* 206-685-0403; *E-Mail:* lake@astro.washington.edu

LAKE, JAMES ALBERT, MOLECULAR & CELL BIOLOGY. *Current Pos:* PROF MOLECULAR BIOL, UNIV CALIF, LOS ANGELES, 76- *Personal Data:* b Nebr; m 67; c 2. *Educ:* Univ Colo, BA, 63; Univ Wis, Madison, PhD(physics), 67. *Honors & Awards:* Irma T Hirschl Found Award, 74; Burton Award, Electron Micros Soc Am, 75. *Prof Exp:* Fel physics, Univ Wis, 67; NIH fel molecular biol, Mass Inst Technol, 67-68 & Children's Cancer Res Found, Mass, 68-70; res fel, Harvard Univ, 69-70; asst prof cell biol, Rockefeller Univ, 70-72; from asst prof to assoc prof cell biol, Med Sch, NY Univ, 72-76. *Concurrent Pos:* Fel, Churchill Col, Cambridge, UK, 83. *Mem:* Fel AAAS; Biophys Soc; Electron Micros Soc Am; Cell Biol Soc; Am Soc X-ray Crystallog. *Res:* Molecular evolution and molecular structure of biological molecules; ribosome function and structure; protein synthesis. *Mailing Add:* Molecular Biol Inst Univ Calif 405 Hilgard Ave Los Angeles CA 90024

LAKE, LARRY WAYNE, PETROLEUM ENGINEERING. *Current Pos:* W A TEX MONCRIEF CENTENNIAL CHAIR & PROF PETROL ENG, UNIV TEX, AUSTIN, 78- *Personal Data:* b Del Norte, Colo, Jan 31, 46; m 75, Carole S Holmes; c Lelie S & Jeffrey W. *Educ:* Ariz State Univ, BS, 67; Rice Univ, PhD, 73. *Honors & Awards:* Reservoir Engr Award, Soc Petrol Engrs. *Prof Exp:* Prog engr, Motorola Co, Phoenix, 68-70; sr res eng, Shell Develop Co, Houston, 73-78. *Concurrent Pos:* Consult enhanced oil recovery. *Mem:* Nat Acad Eng; Soc Mining Engrs; Soc Petrol Engrs; Am Inst Chem Engrs. *Res:* Petroleum engineering; enhanced oil recovery. *Mailing Add:* Dept Petrol & Geosysts Eng Univ Tex Mail Code C0300 Austin TX 78712

LAKE, LORRAINE FRANCES, ANATOMY, REHABILITATION MEDICINE. *Current Pos:* Instr phys ther, Washington Univ, 49-54, instr anat & phys ther, 54-58, assoc dir phys ther curric & chg clin training, 58-63, dir phys ther, 59-60, asst dir, 60-67, assoc dir, Irene Walter Johnson Inst Rehab, 67-79, asst prof, 68-80, EMER ASST PROF PHYS THER, WASHINGTON UNIV, 80- *Personal Data:* b St Louis, Mo, Feb 12, 18. *Educ:* Washington Univ, BS, 50, MA, 54, PhD(anat), 62. *Honors & Awards:* Woodcock Mem Lectr, Univ Calif, 59. *Concurrent Pos:* Consult, Surgeon Gen, USAF, 65-67 & Birth Defects Treat Ctr, Nat Found, 65-69. *Mem:* Sigma Xi. *Res:* Normal and abnormal neuromuscular function; electromyocardiographic investigations of normal human movement; human teratology. *Mailing Add:* 900 S Hanley Rd Apt 14B Clayton MO 63105-2669

LAKE, ROBERT D, POLYMER CHEMISTRY, UNSATURATED POLYESTER & VINYLESTER RESINS. *Current Pos:* RETIRED. *Personal Data:* b Lansing, Mich, Sept 7, 30; m 64, Angeline M Fricioni; c Carolyn A & Jeffrey R. *Educ:* Mich State Univ, BS, 52; Ind Univ, PhD(org chem), 56. *Prof Exp:* Am Petrol Inst fel, Northwestern Univ, 56-57; fel chem res, Mellon Inst, 57-60; scientist, Koppers Co, Inc, 60-66, group mgr explor res, 66-72, sr scientist, Res Dept, 72-77, proj tech coordr, 77-80; develop group mgr, Reichold Chem, 80-89, mgr, flame retardant resins, 89-90; consult, 90-96. *Res:* Synthesis and properties of vinyl and condensation polymers; preparation and properties of unsaturated polyester resins; smoke and flammability behavior of polymers; development of thermoset polyester molding compounds; flame retardant and corrosion resistant polyester and vinylester resins. *Mailing Add:* 215 Thornwood Ct Coraopolis PA 15108

LAKEIN, RICHARD BRUCE, SUPERCOMPUTING, PARALLEL COMPUTING. *Current Pos:* mathematician, 75-82, COMPUT SYSTS ANALYST, NAT SECURITY AGENCY, 82- *Personal Data:* b Baltimore, Md, Mar 5, 41; m 64; c 2. *Educ:* Yale Univ, BA, 62; Univ Md, MA, 64, PhD(math), 67. *Prof Exp:* Lectr math, Univ Md, 67-68; asst prof math, State Univ NY, Buffalo, 68-74. *Mem:* Am Math Soc; Asn Comput Mach. *Res:* Parallel computing; number theory. *Mailing Add:* 8711 Bunnell Dr Potomac MD 20854-3606

LAKES, RODERIC STEPHEN, LASERS & OPTICS, MECHANICAL ENGINEERING. *Current Pos:* from asst prof to assoc prof, 78-86, PROF BIOMED ENG, UNIV IOWA, 86- *Personal Data:* b New York, NY, Aug 10, 48; m 71. *Educ:* Rensselaer Polytech Inst, BS, 69, PhD(physics, biophys), 75. *Honors & Awards:* Burlington Northern Found Award, 87. *Prof Exp:* Res assoc appl sci, Yale Univ, 75-77; asst prof physics, Tuskegee Inst, 77-78; vis asst prof biomed eng, Rensselaer Polytech Inst, 78. *Concurrent Pos:* Fel NIH fel, Yale Univ, 75-77; prin investr, Proj Bone Biomech, NIH, 79-82; vis prof, Dept Mat, Queen Mary Col, Univ London, 84; prin investr, Study Viscoelastic Elastomers, 86-88; vis prof, Univ Wis-Madison, 90. *Mem:* Am Phys Soc; Soc Photo Optical Instrumentation Engrs; Sigma Xi; fel Am Soc Mech Engrs; fel AAAS; Soc Rheology. *Res:* Novel structured materials; bone biomechanics and bioelectricity; properties of piezoelectric solids and composite materials; applied optics; holographic interferometry; granted four patents. *Mailing Add:* Biomed Eng Dept 238 IATL Univ Iowa Iowa City IA 52242

LAKEY, WILLIAM HALL, GENITO-URINARY SURGERY. *Current Pos:* RETIRED. *Personal Data:* b Medicine Hat, Alta, Nov 12, 27; m 57; c 4. *Educ:* Univ Alta, BSc, 49, MD, 53; FRCPS(C), 60. *Honors & Awards:* Surg Res Medal, Royal Col Physicians & Surgeons Can, 56. *Prof Exp:* Prof surg, Fac Med, Univ Alta, 60-97, dir, Div Urol, Univ Hosp, Edmonton, 71-97. *Mem:* Fel Am Col Surg; Am Urol Asn; Can Urol Asn; Can Acad Genito-Urinary Surg; Am Asn Genito-Urinary Surg. *Res:* Renal transplantation; renal hypertension and use of diagnostic tests; kidney preservation. *Mailing Add:* Dept Surg-Urol Univ Alta Fac Med Edmonton AB T6G 2B7 Can

LAKHTAKIA, AKHLESH, T-MATRIX WAVE SCATTERING, ELECTRODYNAMICS OF CHIRAL MEDIA. *Current Pos:* Scholar, 83-84, asst prof, 84-91, ASSOC PROF, PA STATE UNIV, 91- *Personal Data:* b Lucknow, India, July 1, 57; m 82, Mercedes Scabbiolo; c Natalya S. *Educ:* Banaras Hindu Univ, India, BTech, 79; Univ Utah, MS, 81 & PhD(elec eng), 83. *Prof Exp:* Res asst, Univ Utah, 79-83. *Concurrent Pos:* Ed-in-chief, Speculations in Sci & Technol, 90-; traveling lectr, Int Comn Optics, 92; int lectr, Optical Soc Am, 92; Scottish Amicable lectr, Univ Glasgow, 95. *Mem:* Inst Elec & Electronics Engrs; fel Optical Soc Am; fel Int Soc Optical Eng; fel Inst Physics. *Res:* Author and co-author of over 375 papers and conference publications on wave-material interaction, electromagnetics, chiral media, fractals, chaos, bioelectromagnetics; materials science; fractals; chaos; author/editor of seven research books. *Mailing Add:* 227 Hammond Bldg University Park PA 16802. *Fax:* 814-863-7967; *E-Mail:* axl4@psu.edu

LAKIN, JAMES D, ALLERGIES, CLINICAL IMMUNOLOGY. *Current Pos:* CHMN DEPT ALLERGY & IMMUNOL, OXBORO CLIN, 90-, LAB DIR, 93- *Personal Data:* b Harvey, Ill, Oct 4, 45; m 72, Sally A Stuteville; c Margaret K & Matthew A. *Educ:* Northwestern Univ, BSc, 68, PhD, 68, MD, 69. *Prof Exp:* Instr, Dept Microbiol, Northwestern Univ Med Sch, 66-68, Passavant Hosp Sch Nursing, 66-68 & Wesley Mem Hosp Sch Nursing, 66-68; intern, Dept Internal Med, Univ Mich Med Ctr, 70, resident, 71-72, fel, Allergy Sect, 73; lt commander, Med Corps, Naval Med Res Inst, USNR, 74-76, staff investr & lab dir, Allergy Res Lab, Nat Naval Med Ctr, 74, dir allergy-res training, 74-76; asst prof, Georgetown Univ Med Ctr, 75-76; pvt pract, Okla Allergy Clin, 75-89; from clin asst prof to clin prof internal med & pediat, Univ Okla Health Sci Ctr, Oklahoma City, 76-89, chmn, dept allergy, 89. *Concurrent Pos:* Dep dir, Clin Immunol Fiv, Naval Med Res Inst, Nat Naval Med Ctr, 74-75; dir, Adolescent Allergy Clin, Children's Mem Hosp, 76-, Frontiers of Sci, 79-81, Okla Allergy Clin, 80-, Okla Med Res Found, 82-; mem, Res Comt, Presby Hosp, Oklahoma City, 77; mem, Comt Allergy & Clin Immunol, Am Col Chest Physicians, 77; diving med officer, Nat Oceanic & Atmospheric Admin, 88-; staff mem, Baptist Med Ctr, St Anthony Hosp, Children's Mem Hosp, Univ Hosp, Presby Hosp, Mercy Mem Hosp & Deaconess Hosp, Oklahoma City, Okla; spec consult, Vet Admin Hosp, Oklahoma City, Okla. *Mem:* Am Asn Immunologists; fel Am Col Physicians; fel Am Col Chest Physicians; AMA; Am Soc Internal Med; Fedn Am Socs Exp Biol; fel Am Acad Allergy & Immunol; Undersea Med Soc. *Res:* Classification of hypersensitivity reactions; immune response and hypersensitivity reactions. *Mailing Add:* Oxboro Clin 600 W 98th St Bloomington MN 55420-4700. *Fax:* 612-885-6022

LAKKARAJU, H S, SURFACE SCIENCE, NONLINEAR OPTICS. *Current Pos:* PROF PHYSICS, SAN JOSE STATE UNIV, 81- *Personal Data:* b Bapatla, India, Sept 20, 46; m 69; c 2. *Educ:* Andhra Univ, India, BSc, 65, MSc, 67; Fairleigh Dickinson Univ, MS, 73; State Univ NY, Buffalo, PhD(physics), 79. *Prof Exp:* Sr sci asst, Radiosci Div, Nat Phys Lab, 70-71. *Concurrent Pos:* Vis asst prof, Tex A&M Univ, 79-81. *Mem:* Am Phys Soc; Optical Soc Am; Int Soc Optical Eng. *Res:* Laser spectroscopy and nonlinear optics, and the applications of these in the surface science; condensed matter physics and biophysics. *Mailing Add:* Physics Dept San Jose State Univ San Jose CA 95192

LAKOSKI, JOAN MARIE, NEUROPHARMACOLOGY, NEUROENDOCRINOLOGY. *Current Pos:* ASSOC PROF PHARMACOL, PA STATE UNIV COL MED, 93- *Personal Data:* b Poughkeepsie, NY, Mar 28, 53; m 78; c 2. *Educ:* Mount Holyoke Col, AB,

75; Univ Iowa, PhD(pharmacol), 81. *Prof Exp:* Biologist, NIH, 75-77; fel neuropharmacol, Yale Univ Sch Med, 81-84; asst prof pharmacol, Univ Tex Med Br, Galveston, 84-92, asst prof human biol chem & genetics, 92-93; adj mem, Marine Biomed Inst, 88-93. *Concurrent Pos:* Mem, Initial Rev Group Pharmacol Spec Rev Comt, Nat Inst Drug Abuse, 87; res career develop award, Nat Inst Aging, 89-94; mem, Teaching & Eval Mat Subcomt, Am Soc Pharmacol & Exp Therapeut, 89-91; assoc ed, Molecular & Cellular Neurosci, 89-; mem, Coord Ctr Aging Adv Comt, Univ Tex Med Br, 90-93; chmn, Comt Res, Univ Tex Med Br, 90-91; chair, Preprof Subcomt on Educ, Am Soc Pharmacol & Exp Therapeut, 91-93; co-chmn, Symp Serotonin & Drugs of Abuse, 92; mem, Young Scientists Bd, Inst Develop Neurosci & Aging 92- *Mem:* Soc Neurosci; Endocrine Soc; Sigma Xi; Serotonin Club; AAAS; Int Soc Develop Neurosci; Int Sco Neuroendocrinol; Am Soc Pharmacol & Exp Ther. *Res:* Neuropharmacologic basis of age-related changes in central nervous system function that mediate reproductive aging; role of sertonin neuronal systems in drug-induced effects of cocaine, steroids, histamine and aging. *Mailing Add:* Dept Pharmacol Milton S Hershey Med Ctr PO Box 850 Hershey PA 17033-0850. *Fax:* 717-531-5013; *E-Mail:* jlakoski@anes.hmc.psu.edu

LAKOWICZ, JOSEPH RAYMOND, BIOPHYSICS, BIOCHEMISTRY. *Current Pos:* assoc prof, 80-84, PROF BIOCHEM, SCH MED, UNIV MD, 84- *Personal Data:* b Philadelphia, Pa, Mar 15, 48; c 2. *Educ:* La Salle Col, BA, 70; Univ Ill, Urbana, MS, 72, PhD(biochem), 73. *Prof Exp:* NATO fel biochem, Oxford Univ, 73-74; asst prof biochem, Univ Minn, 75-80. *Concurrent Pos:* Estab investr, Am Heart Asn, 77. *Mem:* AAAS; Am Chem Soc; Biophys Soc; Am Soc Photobiol; Sigma Xi; Am Soc Biol Chemists; Optical Soc Am; Am Phys Soc; Protein Soc. *Res:* Fluorescence spectroscopy; membrane transport of chlorinated hydrocarbons and carcinogens; rapid relaxation phenomena in biopolymers; frequency-domain fluorometry; energy transfer; molecular dynamics; time-domain fluorometry. *Mailing Add:* Dept Biol Chem Univ Md Sch Med 108 N Greene St Baltimore MD 21201-1503

LAKRITZ, JULIAN, ORGANIC CHEMISTRY. *Current Pos:* tech dir, 75-90, VPRES SALES & MKT, ANSCOTT-SIGNAL CHEM CO, 75- *Personal Data:* b Antwerp, Belg, Feb 13, 30; US citizen; c 2. *Educ:* NY Univ, BA, 52; Univ Mich, MS, 54, PhD(org chem), 60. *Prof Exp:* Res chemist, Esso Res & Eng Co, 58-68; dir res & develop, Am Permac Inc, Garden City, NY, 68-75. *Mem:* Am Chem Soc; Am Asn Textile Chem & Colorists. *Res:* Chemistry and technology for solvent processing of textiles. *Mailing Add:* 2 Livingston Ave Edison NJ 08820-2324

LAKS, DAVID BEJNESH, defect calculations in solids, for more information see previous edition

LAKS, PETER EDWARD, WOOD PRESERVATION. *Current Pos:* SR RES SCI, MICH TECHNOL UNIV, 85- *Personal Data:* b Brisbane, Australia, Jul 15, 53; Can Citizen; m 73; c 3. *Educ:* Simon Fraser Univ, BSc, 76, MSc, 79; Univ BC, PhD(wood sci), 84. *Concurrent Pos:* Adj prof, 85- *Mem:* Am Chem Soc; Am Soc Pharmacog. *Mailing Add:* Sch Forestry Mich Technol Univ 1400 Townsend Dr Houghton MI 49931-1200

LAKSHMAN, M RAJ, LIPIDS, ALCOHOLISM. *Current Pos:* assoc res prof, 83-90, RES PROF, GEORGE WASHINGTON UNIV, 90- ; CHIEF LIPID RES, DEPT VET AFFAIRS MED CTR, WASHINGTON, DC, 80- *Personal Data:* b Calcutta, India, Aug 3, 38; US citizen; m 66, Malathi; c Vijay & Madhu. *Educ:* Poona Univ, BS, 58, MS, 59; Inst Sci, PhD(biochem), 66. *Honors & Awards:* Wash Heart Ball Award, 90. *Prof Exp:* Nat Res Coun fel, Dept Nat Health & Welfare, Can, 66-67; sr res adv, Rockefeller Found, Bangkok, 67-71; proj assoc, Vet Admin Med Ctr, Wis, 71-74; vis scientist, NIMH, 74-78; res chemist, Nat Inst Alcohol Abuse & Alcoholism, 78-80. *Concurrent Pos:* Res prof, Am Univ, 76; mem, Exp Adv Group Nutrit, Food & Drug Admin, 83. *Mem:* Am Soc Biol Chem; Res Soc Alcoholism; Am Inst Nutrit; Int Soc Biochem Res Alcoholism. *Res:* Lipid and lipoprotein regulation, alcoholic hyperlipidemia, hormonal control, regulation of alcohol dehydrogenase, mechanism of absorption, action of tetrachloro-dibenzo p-dioxin, cholesterol deposition and removal, obesity. *Mailing Add:* Lipid Res Lab 151T Dept Vet Affairs Med Ctr 50 Irving St Washington DC 20422

LAKSHMANAN, P R, ORGANIC POLYMER CHEMISTRY. *Current Pos:* TECH DIR, BAYCHEM INT, INC, 83- *Personal Data:* b Jamshedpur, Bihar, India, Apr 28, 39. *Educ:* Univ Calcutta, BS, 58; Univ Bombay, BS, 61; NDak State Univ, MS, 65, PhD(polymers & coating), 66. *Prof Exp:* Sect suprv, 66-80, dir new prods res & develop, 80-85, res chemist plastics & sr res chemist coatings & adhesives, Gulf Oil Chem Co, 66- *Mem:* Am Chem Soc; Oil & Color Chemists Asn; Soc Plastic Engrs; Am Inst Chemists. *Res:* Relationship between structure and performance of adhesives and coatings; mechanism of adhesion, polymer blends and alloys. *Mailing Add:* Baychem Int Inc Suite 400 5625 FM 1960 W Houston TX 77069-4211

LAKSHMANAN, VAIKUNTAM IYER, METALLURGICAL CHEMISTRY, HYDROMETALLURGY. *Current Pos:* MGR MINERAL RESOURCES, ORTECH INT, 81-, PROG DIR, ENVIRON & MAT PROCESSING. *Personal Data:* b Pazhaya Kayal, Madras, India, July 10, 40; m 68. *Educ:* Univ Bombay, BSc, 61, MSc, 63, PhD(chem), 68. *Honors & Awards:* Bosworth Smith Inst Award, Brit Inst Mining & Metall, 74; Sherritt Hydrometall Award; Standelman Award for Tech Excellence; Flavelle Award for Technol Develop & Transfer. *Prof Exp:* Chief chemist, H&R Johnson India (PVT) Ltd, 68-69; res fel minerals eng, Univ Birmingham, 69-72, lectr, 72-75; fel metall chem sect, Canmet, Dept Energy, Mines & Resources, Ottawa, 75-76; assoc scientist extractive metall sect, Noranda Res Ctr, Montreal, 76-77; res chemist, Eldorado Nuclear Ltd, 77-81. *Concurrent Pos:* Adj prof, Dept Metall & Mat Sci, Univ Toronto, assoc, Dept Chem Eng. *Mem:* Metall Soc; Royal Inst Chem; Brit Inst Mining & Metall; Soc Chem Indust; Can Inst Mining & Metall; Am Soc Mining Eng. *Res:* Solution chemistry; solution treatment precipitation; solvent extraction; ion exchange; treatment of effluents; radiotracer studies; precious and rad metals recovery; technology development and transfer in the areas of hydrometallurgy, environmental and materials processing. *Mailing Add:* Ortech Int 2395 Speakman Dr Mississauga ON L5K 1B3 Can. *Fax:* 905-823-1446

LAKSHMIKANTHAM, VANGIPURAM, MATHEMATICS. *Current Pos:* prof math & chmn dept, 73-86, Ashbel Smith prof, 86, DIR, DIV INTERDISCIPLINARY SCI, 83-, PROF APPL MATH, UNIV TEX, ARLINGTON, 89- *Personal Data:* b Hyderabad, India, Aug 8, 26; m 42, Sarojamma; c Sreekantham, Neerada & Niropama. *Educ:* Osmania Univ, India, PhD(math), 59. *Honors & Awards:* Distinguished Res Award, 81. *Prof Exp:* Res assoc math, Univ Calif, Los Angeles, 60-61; assoc prof, Univ Alta, 63-64; prof & chmn dept, Marathwada Univ, India, 64-66; prof & chmn dept, Univ RI, 66-73. *Concurrent Pos:* Ed, Nonlinear Analysis, Nonlinear World & Stochastic Analysis & Appl; assoc ed, J Math Anal & Applns, Applicable Analysis, Appl Math & Comput, J Math & Phys Sci, J Differential Equations & Dynamic Systs, J Nonlinear Differential Equations; vis mem, Math Res Ctr, Univ Wis-Madison, 61-62, Res Inst Advan Study, 62-63. *Mem:* Am Math Soc; Indian Math Soc; Indian Nat Acad Sci; Soc Indust & Appl Math; Int Nat Fedn Nonlinear Analysts. *Res:* Differential inequalities; theory and applications, including stability theory by Liapunov's second method; nonlinear analysis. *Mailing Add:* Dept Appl Math Fla Inst Technol 150 W University Blvd Melbourne FL 32901. *Fax:* 407-984-8461

LAKSHMINARAYAN, S, RESPIRATORY DISEASES. *Current Pos:* assoc prof, 75-82, PROF MED, SCH MED, UNIV WASH, 82-, MED DIR RESPIRATORY THER UNIT & PULMONARY FUNCTION LAB & CHIEF PULMONARY CRITICAL CARE MED SECT, VET ADMIN MED CTR, SEATTLE, WASH, 75- *Personal Data:* b Madras, India, July 2, 43; US citizen. *Educ:* India Inst Med Sci, New Delhi, MBBS, 64; Royal Col Physicians, London, MRCP, 69, FRCP, 83. *Prof Exp:* Fel, Pulmonary Div, Westminster Hosp, London, 69-70; Brompton Hosp, 70-71 & Univ Colo Med Ctr, 71-72; from instr to asst prof med, Pulmonary Div, Univ Colo Med Ctr, 72-75. *Concurrent Pos:* Vis prof, St Johns Med Col, Bangalore, India, 85-86, Royal Postgrad Med Sch & Hammersmith Hosp, London, 86; chmn, Intensive Care Comt, Vet Admin Med Ctr, Seattle, 88- *Mem:* Am Col Chest Physicians; Am Thoracic Soc; Am Fedn Clin Res; Am Heart Asn; Am Physiol Soc; NY Acad Sci. *Res:* Pulmonary medicine; respiratory therapy. *Mailing Add:* Pulmonary & Critical Care Med Seattle Vet Admin Med Ctr Pulmonary 111B 1660 S Columbian Way Seattle WA 98108

LAKSHMINARAYANA, B, AEROSPACE & MECHANICAL ENGINEERING. *Current Pos:* from asst prof to assoc prof, Pa State Univ, 63-74, dir computational fluid dynamic studies, 80-86, distinguished alumni prof, 85-86, EVAN PUGH PROF AEROSPACE ENG, PA STATE UNIV, 86-, DIR, CTR GAS TURBINES & POWER, 94- *Personal Data:* b Shimoga, India, Feb 15, 35; m 65, Saroja; c Anita & Arvind. *Educ:* Univ Mysore, BE, 58; Univ Liverpool, PhD(mech eng), 63, DEng, 82. *Honors & Awards:* Henry R Worthington Prize, 77; Outstanding Res Award, 77, 82; Premier Res Award, 83; Pandrey Lit Award & Air Breathing Propulsions Award, Am Inst Aeronaut & Astronaut; Freeman Scholar Award & Fluids Eng Award, Am Soc Mech Engrs, 90; Arch T Colwell Merit Award, Soc Automotive Engrs. *Prof Exp:* Asst engr, Kolar Gold Fields, India, 58-60. *Concurrent Pos:* Consult, Pratt & Whitney Aircraft, 72-, Garret Turbine Engine, 80-, Teledyne CAE, 83-, Ruffalo Fone Co, 84; vis assoc prof aeronaut & astronaut, Mass Inst Technol, 72; vis prof, Nat Ctr Sci Res, Ecole de Centrale Delyon, France, 87. *Mem:* Sigma Xi; Am Soc Eng Educ; AAAS; fel Am Soc Mech Engrs; fel Am Inst Aeronaut & Astronaut. *Res:* Three dimensional inviscid and viscid flow through rotor; rotor wake flow; rotor end wall flows; unsteady flow; transonic flow and acoustics of turbomachinery; aircraft and space propulsion; fluid mechanics; computational fluid dynamics; turbomachinery three dimensional flow field measurement and computation; automotive torque converter flow field. *Mailing Add:* Dept Aerospace Eng Pa State Univ 153 Hammond Bldgs University Park PA 16802

LAKSHMINARAYANA, J S S, PHYCOLOGY, WATER POLLUTION. *Current Pos:* RETIRED. *Personal Data:* b Penumantra, India, Sept 22, 31; m 60; c 2. *Educ:* Andhra Univ, India, BSc, 52; Banaras Hindu Univ, MSc, 54, PhD(bot), 60. *Prof Exp:* Lectr bot, Banaras Hindu Univ, 55; scientist & head biol, Nat Environ Eng Res Inst, India, 59-70; assoc prof to prof, Dept Biol, Univ Moncton, 70-97. *Concurrent Pos:* Fr Govt fel, ASTEF, Paris, 65-66; lectr, Visvesvaraya Regional Col Eng, India, 66-69; fel, Mem Univ Nfld, 70. *Mem:* Fel Linnean Soc UK; fel Marine Biol Asn, India. *Res:* Algology, limnology and oceanography in relation to pollution; coastal zone management; primary productivity in relation to fishery development. *Mailing Add:* 271 Argyle St Moncton NB E1C 3V5 Can

LAKSHMINARAYANAN, KRISHNAIYER, BIOCHEMISTRY, INDUSTRIAL MICROBIOLOGY. *Current Pos:* PRES, BIO-TECH INC, BENSENVILLE, ILL, 75- *Personal Data:* b Bikshandarkoil, India, July 5, 24; m 60, Kamakshi; c Gayathri & Venkatesh. *Educ:* Univ Madras, BSc, 45, MSc, 50, PhD(biochem), 55. *Prof Exp:* Jr chemist, King Inst Prev Med, India, 45-47, biochemist, Stanley Hosp, Madras, 50-51; asst prof microbiol, Birla Col, Pilani, 52; Imp Chem Industs fel, Nat Inst Sci India, 55-56; Nat Res Coun Can fel, Univ Man, 56-58; Sci & Indust Res, Govt India, 59-60; plant biochemist, Cent Bot Lab, Allahabad, 60-61; res scientist indust microbiol, John Labatt Ltd, 61-62, sr res scientist, 62-63, proj leader, 63-67, sr indust enzymologist, Dawe's Fermentation Prod, Inc, 67-69, dir fermentation develop, 69-71, res & develop, 71; mgr process develop, Searle Biochem, Div G D Searle & Co, 71-75. *Concurrent Pos:* Hon lectr, Univ Western Ont, 64-67. *Mem:* Fel Chem Inst Can; fel Royal Inst Chemists. *Res:* Microbial enzymology; plant biochemistry; toxicology; immunology; chromatography; microtechniques; industrial fermentations; enzyme production; immobilization; enzymes for clinical diagnostics and food applications. *Mailing Add:* 1310 N Belmont Ave Arlington Heights IL 60004

LAKSHMIVARAHAN, SIVARAMAKRISHNAN, COMPUTER SCIENCE. *Current Pos:* assoc prof, Sch Elec Eng & Comput Sci, Univ Okla, 78-84, Hallibuurton distinguished lectr, Col Eng, 84-86, prof, 84-92, assoc distinguished lectr, 86-87, George Lynn Cross res prof, 95, PROF, SCH COMPUT SCI, UNIV OKLA, 92- *Personal Data:* b Karaikurichi, India, June 12, 44; m 73, Shantha Sitaram Varahan; c Subha & Bharathram. *Educ:* Univ Madras, India, BSc, 64; Indian Inst Sci, Bangalore, BE, 67, ME, 69, PhD(algorithms), 73. *Prof Exp:* Res asst, Indian Inst Sci, Bangalore, 69-73, proj asst, Sch Automation, 73, lectr & asst prof, Dept Comput Sci, Madras, 73-75; vis asst prof, Div Appl Math, Brown Univ, Providence, 75-76; asst prof, Dept Eng & Appl Sci, Yale Univ, New Haven, 76-78. *Concurrent Pos:* Vis prof, Univ Bonn, 80 & 82, Univ Laval, Can, 82, Amoco Prod Res Ctr, Tulsa, 83, Nat Inst Stand & Technol, 85, Tech Inst Higher Studies, Mex, 88, 90 & 93, Nat Tsing-Huo Univ, Taiwan, 92, Indian Inst Sch, 93; consult, Amoco Res Ctr, Nat Inst Stand & Technol. *Mem:* Fel Inst Elec & Electronics Engrs; fell Asn Comput Mach. *Res:* Author and editor of numerous books; contributed various articles to science journals. *Mailing Add:* Sch Comput Sci Univ Okla Norman OK 73019. *Fax:* 405-325-4044; *E-Mail:* varahan@mailhost.ecn.uoknor.edu

LAKSO, ALAN NEIL, POMOLOGY, PLANT PHYSIOLOGY. *Current Pos:* Asst prof pomol, 73-80, assoc prof hort, Sci Dept, 80-86, PROF, NY STATE AGR EXP STA, CORNELL UNIV, 86- *Personal Data:* b Auburn, Calif, Jan 3, 48. *Educ:* Univ Calif, Davis, BS, 70, PhD(plant physiol), 73. *Honors & Awards:* Gourley Award, Am Soc Hort Sci, 80. *Mem:* Int Soc Hort Sci; Am Soc Hort Sci; Am Soc Enol & Viticult; Sigma Xi. *Res:* Environmental physiology and the physiological bases of yield and quality of apples and grapes. *Mailing Add:* Dept Hort Sci NY State Agr Exp Sta Geneva NY 14456

LAL, DEVENDRA, NUCLEAR PHYSICS, GEOCHEMISTRY & GEOPHYSICS. *Current Pos:* dir, 72-87, sr prof, 83-89, FEL, PHYS RES LAB, AHMEDABAD, INDIA, 89-; PROF NUCLEAR GEOPHYS, SCRIPPS INST OCEANOG, UNIV CALIF, SAN DIEGO, 67- *Personal Data:* b Banaras, India, Feb 14, 29; m 55. *Educ:* Banaras Hindu Univ, BSc, 47, MSc, 49; Univ Bombay, PhD(physics), 58. *Hon Degrees:* DSc, Banaras Hindu Univ, Varanasi, 81. *Honors & Awards:* Krishnan Medal, Indian Geophys Union, 65; S S Bhatnagar Award, 67; Krishnan Medal Lectr, Indian Nat Sci Acad, 81; Jawaharlal Nehru Award for Phys Sci; Raman Birth Centenary Award, 96. *Prof Exp:* From res fel to sr prof, Tata Inst Fundamental Res, Bombay, India, 49-72. *Concurrent Pos:* Mem sci adv comt to Cabinet, Govt India, 81-82; mem sci comt Indo-US joint comn sci & technol; founding fel, Third World Acad Sci, Trieste, Italy. *Mem:* Foreign assoc Nat Acad Sci; fel Indian Acad Sci; fel Indian Nat Sci Acad; assoc mem Royal Astron Soc; fel Royal Soc. *Res:* Cosmic rays; astrophysics; meteoritics; oceanography; meteorology; hydrology; geophysics; glaciology and geomorphology. *Mailing Add:* GRD 0220 Scripps Inst Oceanog La Jolla CA 92093-0220

LAL, HARBANS, PHARMACOLOGY. *Current Pos:* PROF & CHMN DEPT PHARMACOL, TEX COL OSTEOP MED, UNIV NTEX, 80-, PROF BIOL SCI, 80- *Educ:* Univ Kans, MS, 58; Univ Chicago, PhD(pharmacol), 62. *Prof Exp:* Res fel, Univ Chicago, 58-61; res pharmacologist, IIT Res Inst, 61-65; res assoc neurol & psychiat, Med Sch Northwestern Univ, 62-65; assoc prof pharmacol & toxicol, Univ Kans, 65-67; res & develop scientist, Janssen Pharmaceut, 73-74; from assoc prof to prof pharmacol & toxicol, Univ RI, 67-80, prof psychol, 70-80; res assoc, RI Inst Ment Health, 69-78, clin psychopharmacologist, 78-80; dir psychopharmacol, Inst Behav Med, 77-79. *Concurrent Pos:* Adj prof chem & behav, Tex Christian Univ, 80-; teaching asst & lectr, Univ Chicago; co-instr, Chicago Med Sch, Chicago Col Osteop Med, Univ Kans, Univ RI, Brown Univ Med Sch, Tex Col Osteop Med & Univ NTex; nat grant rev panels ad hoc appts, NSF, Nat Inst Drug Abuse Study Sect, Harry Frank Guggenheim Found, Human Embryol & Develop Study Sect; consult, Boehinger Pharmaceut Co, Burroughs Welcome Pharmaceut Co, Hoechst-Roussel Pharmaceut Co, Upjohn Pharmaceut Co, Ciba-Geigy Pharmaceut Co, McNeill Pharmaceut Co, Ortho Pharmaceut Co & Sterling-Winthrop Pharmaceut Co; grants, var corp & orgn. *Mem:* Am Col Neuropsychopharmacol; Asn Med Sch Pharmacol; Am Soc Pharmacol & Exp Therapeut; Soc Neurosci; Soc Toxicol; Behav Pharmacol Soc; fel Am Col Clin Pharmacol; Soc Biol Psychiat; Am Psychol Asn; Fedn Am Socs Exp Biol. *Res:* Pharmacology; toxicology; psychopharmacology. *Mailing Add:* Dept Pharmacol Tex Col Osteop Med 3500 Camp Bowie Ft Worth TX 76017-2699

LAL, JOGINDER, POLYMER CHEMISTRY. *Current Pos:* CONSULT, LAL ASSOCS, 87- *Personal Data:* b Amritsar, India, July 2, 23; nat US; m 51, Ardyce Lundenburg; c Anjana L Pettigrew & Rajinder K Lal. *Educ:* Punjab Univ, India, BSc Hons, 44, MSc, 46; Polytech Inst Brooklyn, MS, 49, PhD, 51. *Honors & Awards:* Gold Medal, Hindu Col Amritsar, 41; Akron Summit Polymer Conf Award, 76; IR-100 Award, 79; First Serv Award, Polymer Div, Am Chem Soc, 83; Melvin Mooney Distinguished Technol Award, Rubber Div, Am Chem Soc, 89, Mosher Award, 97. *Prof Exp:* Prof chem, Jain Col, Ambala, India, 45-47 & Hindu Col Amritsar, 51-52; head polymer res, H D Justi & Son, Inc, Pa, 52-56; res scientist, Goodyear Tire & Rubber Co, 56-67, sect head, 67-75, mgr polymer res, 75-82, sr res & develop assoc, 83-85; adj prof, Inst Biomen Eng, Univ Akron, 87- *Concurrent Pos:* Mem adv bd, J Polymer Sci, 67-90, mem adv comt, Chem Technol Prog, Univ Akron, 76-88; counr & mem several nat comts, Am Chem Soc; prog chmn, Akron Polymer Lect Group 60-61, chmn, 61-62; cong sci counr, 74-86; chmn awards comt, Polymer Div, Am Chem Soc, 79-82, alt counr, Rubber Div, 85-87; vchmn, Gordon Res Conf Elastomers, 82, chmn, 83; co-ed & assoc ed of three books on polymer chem; organized chaired Nobel Laureate Paul J Flory Mem Colloquim, Rubber Div Am Chem Soc, 91; frequent lectr, nat & int meetings & indust, univ & govt res labs; expert analyst, Chemtracts-Macromolecular Chem, 91-94; mem, Clin Permanent Artificial Heart Prog Replacement Humans & Artificial Spinal Disc Prog Acromed, Cleveland; consult, Cleveland. *Mem:* Am Chem Soc. *Res:* Block copolymers; coatings; relationship between structure and properties of polymers; vulcanization; monomer synthesis; inventor Hexsyn rubber; reinforcement; author of over 100 US patents and journal publications. *Mailing Add:* Lal Assocs 855 Shullo Dr Akron OH 44313-5852

LAL, MANOHAR, ENGINEERING SYSTEM MODELS, MATHEMATICAL PHYSICS. *Current Pos:* sr res scientist math physics, Amoco Tulsa Tech Ctr, 78-80, sr staff scientist, 80-82, res assoc 82-86, spec res assoc, 86-92, SR RES ASSOC, AMOCO TULSA TECH CTR, 92- *Personal Data:* b Lakki Marwat, India, Apr 11, 34; m 63, Urmila Rani Mehndiratta; c Gaurav, Gunjan & Garima-Lal. *Educ:* Allahabad Univ India, BSc, 55; Indian Inst Sci, DIISc, 58; Univ Ill, Urbana, MS, 61, PhD(elec eng), 63. *Prof Exp:* Lectr electronics & commun, Univ Roorkee, India, 58-60, from asst prof to prof, 63-74; prof elec eng, Wichita State Univ, 74-78. *Concurrent Pos:* Khosla res award, Univ Roorkee, India, 71; vis res prof, Coord Sci Lab, Univ Ill & Elec Eng & Comput Sci Dept, Univ Santa Clara, 75; adj prof, Univ Tulsa, 81. *Mem:* Inst Elec & Electronics Engrs; Soc Petrol Engrs. *Res:* Electricial systems and circuits; Engineering systems modeling and control, fluid mechanics, drilling and production research in petroleum, fluid flow and wave propagtion in earth models, digital signal processing, solids control, rock mechanics and wellbore stability. *Mailing Add:* Amoco Prod Co Res Ctr PO Box 3385 Tulsa OK 74102

LAL, MOHAN, MATHEMATICS. *Current Pos:* from asst prof to assoc prof math, 64-75, PROF MATH, MEM UNIV NFLD, 75- *Personal Data:* b Dharmkot, Punjab, May 8, 32; Can citizen; m 64. *Educ:* D M Col, Punjab, India, BA, 52; Aligarh Muslim Univ, MSc, 55; Univ BC, PhD(nuclear physics), 62. *Prof Exp:* Lectr physics, D A V Col, Punjab, India, 55-57; res asst, Univ BC, 57-61; res assoc, Univ Alta, 62-63; asst prof math & physics, Mt Allison Univ, 63-64. *Concurrent Pos:* Comput specialist, Fed & Prov Land Inventory Studies, Dept Mines & Natural Resources, Can, 67. *Mem:* Can Math Cong. *Res:* Numerical analysis; applied mathematics and elementary number theory. *Mailing Add:* Dept Math & Statist Mem Univ Nfld Elizabeth Ave St John's NF A1C 5S7 Can

LAL, RATTAN, SOIL PHYSICS, TROPICAL SOILS. *Current Pos:* assoc prof, 87-89, PROF SOIL PHYSICS, OHIO STATE UNIV, COLUMBUS, OHIO, 89- *Personal Data:* b Karyal, Punjab, Sept 5, 44; m 71, Sukhvarsha Sharma; c Priva, Pratibha, Abhishek & Vivek. *Educ:* Punjab Agr Univ, Ludhiana, India, BSc, 63; Indian Agr Res Inst, New Delhi, MSc, 65; Ohio State Univ, PhD(soil physics), 68. *Honors & Awards:* Int Soil Sci Award, Soil Sci Soc Am, 88; Distinguished Scientist Award, Asn Sci Indian Origin, 90. *Prof Exp:* Sr res fel soil physics, Univ Sydney, Australia, 68-69; soil physicist, Int Inst Trop Agr, Ibadan, Nigeria, 70-87. *Concurrent Pos:* Vpres, Int Comt Continental Erosion, IAHS, UK, 82-87 & World Asn Soil & Water Conserv, Ankeny, Iowa, 83-87, pres, 88-91; chmn, Working Group ISSS, Soil Erosion Res Methods, 83-88; bd mem, Int Soil Tillage Res Orgn, Holland, 84-88, pres, 88-91; coordr, Upland Prod Systs, Int Inst Trop Agr, Ibadan, Nigeria, 84-87; bd mem, Orgn Trop Studies, 89-93; soil sci appl res award, 92. *Mem:* World Asn Soil & Water Conserv (pres, 88-91); Int Soil Tillage Res Orgn (pres, 88-91); fel Soil Sci Soc Am; fel Am Soc Agron; Int Soc Soil Sci; Soil & Water Conserv Soc. *Res:* Management of soil and water resources with particular relevance to the tropics and sub-tropics; processes of soil degradation under intensive management including accelerated erosion, compaction, anaerobiosis, transport of sediment-related pollutants, emission of radiatively active gases from soils and deterioration of soil structure; soil conservation; soils and greenhouse effect. *Mailing Add:* 3080 Wareham Rd Columbus OH 43221

LAL, RAVINDRA BEHARI, MATERIALS SCIENCE-CRYSTAL GROWTH. *Current Pos:* assoc prof, 75-79, PROF PHYSICS, ALA A&M UNIV, 79- *Personal Data:* b Agra, India, Oct 5, 35; m 62, Usha; c Amit K. *Educ:* Agra Univ, BSc, 55, MSc, 58, PhD(physics), 63. *Honors & Awards:* New Technol Invention Award, 81, 83. *Prof Exp:* Lectr physics, REI Col, Agra Univ, 58-59 & Delhi Polytech, 63-64; Nat Acad Sci-Nat Res Coun resident res assoc, Marshall Space Flight Ctr, NASA, 64-67; asst prof, Indian Inst Technol, Delhi, 68-70; sr res assoc, Univ Ala, Huntsville, 71-73; asst prof physics, Paine Col, 73-75. *Concurrent Pos:* Prin investr space shuttle experiment, First Int Microgravity Lab, NASA, 92. *Mem:* Am Phys Soc; Sigma Xi; Am Asn Crystal Growth. *Res:* Solid state physics; crystal growth and characterization of materials; magnetic and electrical properties of II-VI and III-V compounds; infra-red detector materials; manufacturing in space; selected by NASA as an investigator for an experiment on International Microgravity Lab (1ML-1) for 1992; growth of nonlinear optical materials for second harmonic generation. *Mailing Add:* Dept Physics Ala A&M Univ PO Box 71 Normal AL 35762. *Fax:* 205-851-5622; *E-Mail:* lal@caos.aamu.edu

LAL, SAMARTHJI, NEUROPSYCHIATRY. *Current Pos:* from asst prof to assoc prof, 73-83, PROF PSYCHIAT, MCGILL UNIV, 83-; DIR CLIN & BASIC RES PSYCHIAT, MONTREAL GEN HOSP, 75- *Personal Data:* b London, Eng, Mar 23, 38; Can citizen; m 74, Maureen Kiely; c Sikander.

Educ: Univ London, MB, BS, 62; McGill Univ, dipl psychiat, 67; FRCP(C), 70; Am Bd Psychiat & Neurol, 78. *Honors & Awards:* Heinz Lehmann Award, 86. *Prof Exp:* Med Res Coun Can res fel psychiat, 67-71; chief consult serv, Montreal Gen Hosp, 71-75, assoc psychiatrist, 74-78. *Concurrent Pos:* Consult psychiatrist, Queen Mary Vet Hosp, 71-78; staff psychiatrist, Montreal Gen Hosp, 71-, consult, Psychiat Consultation Serv, 75-; staff psychiatrist, Douglas Hosp, 76-, bd dirs, Res Ctr, 80-; sr psychiatrist, Montreal Gen Hosp, 78-; examr, Royal Col Phys Surg, Can, 81-82; actg dir, McGill Ctr Res Schizophrenia, 92- *Mem:* Can Soc Clin Invest; Can Psychiat Asn; fel Am Psychiat Asn; fel Can Col Neuropsychopharmacol; Soc Biol Psychiat; Int Soc Psychoneuroendrinol. *Res:* Monoaminergic mechanisms in anterior pituitary secretion and in neurological and psychiatric disorders. *Mailing Add:* Dept Psychiat Montreal Gen Hosp 1650 Cedar Ave Montreal PQ H3G 1A4 Can. *Fax:* 514-934-8237

LALA, JAYNARAYAN HOTCHAND, COMPUTER ENGINEERING. *Current Pos:* Tech staff, Charles Stark Draper Lab, Inc, Cambridge, 76-83, chief systs archit sect, NASA Dept, 83-85, div leader, Fault Tolerant Systs Div, 85-91, leader, Advan Comput Archit Group, 91-93, PRIN MEM TECH STAFF, CHARLES STARK DRAPER LAB INC, 93- *Personal Data:* b Hyderabad, Pakistan, Jan 12, 1951; m 77, Michele Simone Breton. *Educ:* Indian Inst Technol, SB, 71; Mass Inst Technol, SM, 73, ScD, 76. *Concurrent Pos:* Adv, USN Combat Syst Archit Adv Panel, 85-86; mem, Battle Mgt Panel, Strategic Defense Initiative, 92. *Mem:* Fel Am Inst Aeronaut & Astronaut; Indian Inst Technol Soc New Eng (vpres, 95-); Int Fedn Info Processing; fel Inst Elec & Electronics Engrs. *Res:* Fault tolerant computer designs; contributed articles to professional journals. *Mailing Add:* 12 Bowdoin Rd Wellesley MA 02181-2509

LALA, PEEYUSH KANTI, CANCER, IMMUNOLOGY. *Current Pos:* prof & chair anat, 83-93, PROF ONCOL, UNIV WESTERN ONT, 89-, PROF ANAT CELL BIOL, 93- *Personal Data:* b Chittagong, Brit India, Nov 1, 34; m 62, 92, Shipra; c Probal & Prason. *Educ:* Univ Calcutta, MB, BS, 57, PhD(med biophys), 62. *Prof Exp:* Demonstr path, Calcutta Med Col, 59-60; demonstr path & hemat, NRS Med Col, 61-62; res assoc biol & med res, Argonne Nat Lab, 63-64; res scientist, Radiobiol Lab, Univ Calif, San Francisco, 64-66; res assoc biol & health physics, Chalk River Nuclear Labs, Atomic Energy Can Ltd, 67-68; from asst prof to prof anat, McGill Univ, 68-83. *Concurrent Pos:* Fulbright travel scholar, 62; res dir, Med Res Coun Can grant, 68- & Nat Cancer Inst Can grant, 69-; USPHS grant, 75-; vis prof, Walter & Eliza Hall Inst Med Res, Melbourne Univ, 77-78; counr, Int Soc Reprod Immunol, 86; vpres, Can Asn Anat, 89-90, pres, 91-93; JCB grant award, Can Asn Anat, 90. *Mem:* Am Asn Immunol; Am Asn Cancer Res; Int Soc Exp Hemat; Int Soc Reprod Immunol; Am Asn Anat; Am Soc Reprod Immunol (vpres, 85); Soc Leuko Biol. *Res:* Studies of cell population kinetics during normal hematopoiesis, leukemias and cancer; host-tumor cell interactions in vivo; biology of tumor-host and fetomaternal relationship; author of more than 150 research publications and 14 book chapters on hematology, immunology, cancer and reproduction; discoverer of a new mode of cancer therapy applied to human trial; biology of the placenta, invasion and metastasis. *Mailing Add:* Dept Anat Cell Biol Univ Western Ont London ON N6A 5C1 Can. *Fax:* 519-661-3936; *E-Mail:* pklala@julian.uwo.ca

LALANCETTE, JEAN-MARC, INORGANIC CHEMISTRY, ENVIRONMENTAL CHEMISTRY. *Current Pos:* PRES & CONSULT CHEMIST ENVIRON & HIGH TEMPERATURE CHEM, INOTEL INC, 85- *Personal Data:* b Drummondville, Que, Apr 21, 34; m 58; c 3. *Educ:* Univ Montreal, BSc, 57, MSc, 58, PhD(chem), 61. *Honors & Awards:* Manning Award, 85; Award, Can-Fr Asn Advan Sci, 85. *Prof Exp:* From asst prof to prof chem, Univ Sherbrooke, 60-80; vpres res & develop, Net Asbestos Soc, 80-85. *Mem:* Chem Inst Can. *Res:* Organometallic chemistry; chemistry of graphite intercalates, both catalytic and synthetic properties; photochemical reactions; use of natural materials for protection of environment; peat moss. *Mailing Add:* Inotel Inc 470 Irene-Coutre St Sherbrooke PQ J1L 1J4 Can. *Fax:* 819-346-8248

LALANCETTE, ROGER A, ANALYTICAL CHEMISTRY, STRUCTURAL CHEMISTRY. *Current Pos:* asst prof analytical chem, 69-76, assoc prof, 76-87, PROF CHEM, RUTGERS UNIV, NEWARK, 87- *Personal Data:* b Springfield, Mass, July 30, 39; m 67, 78; c Christopher & Brian. *Educ:* Am Int Col, BA, 61; Fordham Univ, PhD(analytical chem), 67. *Prof Exp:* Res fel, Brookhaven Nat Lab, 66-67; res chemist photopolymerization, Photo Prod Dept, E I du Pont de Nemours & Co, Inc, NJ, 67-69. *Concurrent Pos:* Vis scientist, Univ Calif, San Francisco, 80-81. *Mem:* Am Chem Asn; Am Mat Soc; Am Crystallog Asn. *Res:* Preparation and structural studies; x-ray powder and single crystal analysis; GC/MS of pesticides in soil and water. *Mailing Add:* Dept Chem Rutgers Univ Newark Campus 73 Warren St Newark NJ 07102-1814. *Fax:* 210-648-1264; *E-Mail:* lalancette@hades.rutgers.edu

LALAS, DEMETRIUS P, DYNAMIC METEOROLOGY, ENVIRONMENTAL FLUID DYNAMICS. *Current Pos:* adv, Ministry Energy & Indust & Ministry Environ & pres, 93-94, DIR, NAT OBSERV ATHENS & PRES GOV BD, GREEK WIND ENERGY ASN, 94- *Personal Data:* b Athens, Greece, Sept 28, 42; m 67; c 2. *Educ:* Hamilton Col, AB, 62; Cornell Univ, MAeroE, 65, PhD(aerospace), 68. *Prof Exp:* Asst prof, Dept Eng Mech & Dept Mech Eng, Wayne State Univ, 68-73, assoc prof, 73-79, prof, Dept Mech Eng, 79-90. *Concurrent Pos:* Vis fel, Coop Inst Res Environ Eng, Univ Colo, 73-74, consult, 74-75; assoc prof, Dept Meteorol, Univ Athens, Greece, 76-77, prof & chmn dept & dir, Meteorol Inst, 79-83; pres, Ctr Renewable Energy Sources, Athens, Greece, 88-91; managing dir, Lomda Tech, Ltd, 89-94. *Mem:* Am Meteorol Soc; Am Geophys Union; Greek Meteorol Soc; Am Soc Mech Eng. *Res:* Dynamics of micro and mesoscale wave dynamics, their excitation, stability and properties; solar and wind energy; air pollution modelling; environmental fluid mechanics; lubrication theory. *Mailing Add:* Papanastasiou 27 Neo Psychiko Athens 15451 Greece. *Fax:* 30-1-3421019

LALCHANDANI, ATAM PRAKASH, OPERATIONS RESEARCH, PLANNING. *Current Pos:* CONSULT, 92- *Personal Data:* b India, Oct 20, 43; US citizen; div; c 1. *Educ:* Indian Inst Technol, Bombay, BTech, 63; Cornell Univ, MS, 66, PhD(oper res), 67. *Prof Exp:* Sr oper res analyst, Procter & Gamble, 67-69; dir appl syst, Optimum Systs Inc, Santa Clara, Calif, 69-73; dir indust serv, Control Analysis Corp, 73-77; dir planning & analysis, Nat Semiconductor Corp, 77-81; treas, Nat Adv Systs, 81-83, vpres finance & admin, 83-92. *Concurrent Pos:* Vis lectr, Grad Sch Bus, Univ Santa Clara, 69-77, Univ Cincinnati, 69 & Xavier Univ, Ohio, 69. *Mem:* Opers Res Soc Am; Inst Mgt Sci; Financial Exec Inst. *Res:* Finance. *Mailing Add:* 262 Angela Dr Los Altos CA 94022

LALEHZARIAN, HAMO, HUMAN FACTORS-ERGONOMICS, STATISTICAL DESIGN & PROCESS CONTROL. *Current Pos:* PROF INDUST ENG, CALIF STATE UNIV, FRESNO, 87- *Personal Data:* b Isfahan, Iran, Dec 22, 52; US citizen; m 91, Carine Simonian; c Serjeic. *Educ:* Univ Tex, Arlington, BSIE, 80, MSIE, 81, PhD(indust eng), 87. *Prof Exp:* Financial analyst, Merchantil Nat Bank, 81-84. *Concurrent Pos:* Consult, Iranian Steel Complex, 89, Gottschalks Dept Stores, 90; assoc prof, Am Univ Armenia, 93. *Mem:* Inst Indust Engrs; Human Factors Soc; Soc Mfg Engrs. *Res:* Effects of mental work load on the p300 component of evoked brain potentials and various levels of automation. *Mailing Add:* 1386 E Portland Ave Fresno CA 93720. *Fax:* 209-278-6759; *E-Mail:* hamo_lalehzarian@csu.fresno.edu

LALEZARI, PARVIZ, MEDICINE, PHYSIOLOGY. *Current Pos:* from asst prof to assoc prof, 67-79, PROF MED, ALBERT EINSTEIN COL MED, 79-, PROF PATH, 89-; PRES, CHIEF EXEC OFFICER & MED DIR, BERGEN COMMUNITY REGIONAL BLOOD CTR, 94- *Personal Data:* b Hamadan, Iran, Aug 17, 31; m 58, Cecilia Schnitzer; c Jacob Paul & Renee. *Educ:* Univ Teheran, MD, 54. *Concurrent Pos:* City NY Res Counc res grant, 60-64; dir immunohemat & blood bank, Montefiore Hosp & Med Ctr, 60-96; NIH res grant, 65-; Am Cancer Soc res grant, 89-94. *Mem:* Am Soc Hemat; Am Soc Clin Invest; Am Asn Immunol; Am Asn Blood Banks. *Res:* Leukocyte immunology; red cell immunology autoimmune diseases, hematopoietic progenitor cells, blood substitutes. *Mailing Add:* Bergen Community Regional Blood Ctr 970 Linwood Ave W Paramus NJ 07652. *Fax:* 201-670-6174

LALIBERTE, GARLAND E, AGRICULTURAL ENGINEERING. *Current Pos:* assoc prof, Univ Man, 67-69, prof & head dept, 69-86, prof agr eng, 86-96, EMER DEAN, UNIV MAN, 96- *Personal Data:* b Walkerburn, Man, Dec 28, 36; m 59; c 2. *Educ:* Univ Sask, BEng, 56, MSc, 61; Colo State Univ, PhD(agr eng), 66. *Honors & Awards:* Maple Leaf Award, Can Soc Agr Eng, 81; Agr Eng of Year Award, Am Soc Agr Eng, 90. *Prof Exp:* Engr, Can Dept Agr, 56-61, res scientist, 61-67. *Concurrent Pos:* Agr Inst Can fel, 83; Can Soc Agr Eng fel, 84. *Mem:* Am Soc Agr Engrs; Can Soc Agr Eng (pres, 78-79); Sigma Xi; fel Agr Inst Can. *Res:* Drainage engineering; irrigation engineering; soil and water conservation. *Mailing Add:* Dept Biosysts Eng Univ Man Winnipeg MB R3T 2N2 Can

LALIBERTE, LAURENT HECTOR, ELECTROCHEMISTRY, CORROSION. *Current Pos:* sr res assoc, Int Paper, Pineville Mill, 78-79, group mgr, 79-87, mgr tech serv, 87-90, MGR PROCESS CONTROL TECH, INT PAPER, PINEVILLE MILL, 90- *Personal Data:* b Ottawa, Ont, Can, Nov 7, 43; m 66; c 2. *Educ:* Univ Ottawa, BSc, 66, PhD(chem), 69. *Honors & Awards:* Weldon Medal, Can Pulp & Paper Asn. *Prof Exp:* Fel chem, Univ Ottawa, 69-71; scientist corrosion, Pulp & Paper Res Inst Can, 71-78. *Mem:* Nat Asn Corrosion Engrs; Tech Asn Pulp & Paper Indust. *Res:* Corrosion of materials used in pulp and paper industry process equipment; chemical engineering; process control. *Mailing Add:* Int Paper 1285 Tri Ridge Blvd Loveland OH 45140

LALICH, JOSEPH JOHN, PATHOLOGY. *Current Pos:* from instr to assoc prof, 46-56, PROF PATH, MED SCH, UNIV WIS-MADISON, 56- *Personal Data:* b Slunj, Yugoslavia, Nov 23, 09; nat US; m 41. *Educ:* Univ Wis, BS, 33, MS, 36, MD, 37. *Prof Exp:* Fel exp med, Univ Kans, 38-42. *Mem:* AAAS; fel Soc Exp Biol & Med. *Res:* Hemorrhagic and traumatic shock; hemostasis; coagulation; hemoglobinuric nephrosis; experimental lathyrism; myocardial necrosis after allylamine ingestion; monocrotaline induced cor pulmonale. *Mailing Add:* 6306 Mound Dr Middleton WI 53562

LALL, ABNER BISHAMBER, VISUAL PHYSIOLOGY, SENSORY SYSTEMS. *Current Pos:* assoc prof, 88-93, PROF BIOL, HOWARD UNIV, 94- *Personal Data:* b Bareilly, UP, India, Jan 28, 33; m 68, Jean Hinson; c Sarojini. *Educ:* Univ Delhi, BSc, 54; Boston Univ, STB, 59; Syracuse Univ, MS, 62; Univ Md, PhD(zool), 71. *Prof Exp:* Investr, Eye Res Found Bethesda, 69-72; asst prof neurophysiol & comp physiol, City Col NY, 72-74; fel neurophysiol, Johns Hopkins Univ Sch Med, 74-75; sr assoc, Howard Univ Col Med, 76-79; asst prof, Skidmore Col, 77-78, Univ Miami, 82-83; assoc res scientist, Dept Biol, McCollum Pratt Inst, 79-82 & 83-85, res scientist, Dept Biophys, Johns Hopkins Univ, 85-88. *Concurrent Pos:* Grass Found fel neurophysiol, Marine Biol Lab, Woods Hole, Mass, 70. *Mem:* Asn Res Vision & Opthal; Am Soc Zoologists; AAAS; Soc Neurosci. *Res:* Neural mechanisms of instinctive visual behavior among arthropods, amphibians and fishes. *Mailing Add:* Thomas C Jenkins Dept Biophys Johns Hopkins Univ 414 Northway Baltimore MD 21218-1115

LALL, B KENT, CIVIL ENGINEERING, TRANSPORTATION ENGINEERING. *Current Pos:* assoc prof, 77-84, PROF CIVIL ENG, PORTLAND STATE UNIV, 84- *Personal Data:* b Sargodha, India, Feb 4, 39; US citizen; m 70, Margaret V Boult; c Niren N. *Educ:* Panjab Univ, India, BSc, 61; Univ Roorkee, ME, 64; Univ Birmingham, PhD(transp), 69. *Prof Exp:* Teaching fel hwy, Univ Roorkee, 61-64; asst prof & lectr civil eng, Indian Inst Technol, Delhi, 64-75; assoc prof, Univ Man, 75-77. *Concurrent Pos:* Mem, Pub Transp Comt, Urban Transp Div, Am Soc Civil Engrs, 79-, chmn, 88-90, Geometric Design Hwys Comt, 80-, Urban Transp Div, secy, Exec Comt, 90-92, chair, 94-95 & chair, Transp Cong, 95; vis prof, Univ Adelaide, SAustralia, 85; consult, Nat Rds Bd, Ministry Works, NZ, 86; mem, Unsig Intersect Comt, Transp Res Bd, 90- *Mem:* Fel Am Soc Civil Engrs; Sigma Xi; Inst Transp Engrs; High Speed Ground Transp Asn Am. *Res:* Urban transportation; traffic management and video imaging technologies, ITS, transportation planning and systems; pavement design; highway and traffic engineering; highway materials and construction; highway capacity and geometric design. *Mailing Add:* Dept Civil Eng Portland State Univ Box 751 Portland OR 97207-0751

LALL, PRITHVI C, NUCLEAR PHYSICS, ACOUSTICS. *Current Pos:* ASSOC COMNR, DEPT NAVY, NAVAL UNDERWATER SYST CTR, 71- *Personal Data:* b Panjab, India, Sept 20, 31. *Educ:* Panjab Univ, MS, 54; Oregon State Univ, PhD(physics), 62; George Washington Univ, JD, 69. *Prof Exp:* Asst prof, Howard Univ, 62-71. *Mem:* Am Phys Soc; Sigma Xi. *Mailing Add:* Off Patent Coun Naval Underwater Syst Ctr Bldg 112T Newport RI 02841

LALL, SANTOSH PRAKASH, NUTRITIONAL BIOCHEMISTRY. *Current Pos:* res scientist fish nutrit, 74-93, HEAD, AQUACULT SECT, HALIFAX LAB, 94- *Personal Data:* b Motihari, India, Sept 8, 44; Can citizen; m 74, Barbara Smith; c Carolyn & Julie. *Educ:* Allahabad Univ, BSc, 64; Univ Guelph, MSc, 68, PhD(nutrit), 73. *Prof Exp:* Res asst animal nutrit, Allahabad Agr Inst, 64-65. *Concurrent Pos:* Res asst, Nutrit Dept, Univ Guelph, 68, fel, 73. *Mem:* Can Soc Nutrit Sci; Aquacult Asn Can; NY Acad Sci; World Aquacult Soc. *Res:* Nutrient requirements of salmonid and marine fishes in fresh water and sea water. *Mailing Add:* Inst Marine Biosci Nat Res Coun 1411 Oxford St Halifax NS B3H 3Z1 Can. *Fax:* 902-426-9413; *E-Mail:* santosh.lall@nrc.ca

LALLEY, EDWARD T, PATHOLOGY, IMMUNOLOGY. *Current Pos:* Instr, 71-78, from asst prof to assoc prof, 78-91, PROF PATH, UNIV PA, 91- *Personal Data:* b Pittsburgh, Pa, Mar 30, 43. *Educ:* Univ Pa, BS, 65, PhD(path), 78; Univ Pittsburgh, DMD, 68. *Concurrent Pos:* Residency path, Univ Pa, 71-73. *Mem:* Am Cancer Soc. *Res:* Pathology; immunology. *Mailing Add:* Univ Pa 4001 Spruce St Philadelphia PA 19104-6003

LALLEY, PETER AUSTIN, HUMAN GENETICS, BIOCHEMICAL GENETICS. *Current Pos:* DIR, CTR BACCALAURATE & GRAD STUDIES, NAT TECH INST DEAF, 93- *Personal Data:* b Lackawanna, NY, Feb 19, 40; m 67; c 3. *Educ:* Siena Col, BS, 61; Cath Univ Am, MS, 69; State Univ NY, Buffalo, PhD(human genetics), 74. *Prof Exp:* Fel human genetics, Roswell Park Mem Inst, 74-75; mem staff biochem genetics, Vet Admin Oncol Br, Nat Cancer Inst, 75-77; sr investr biochem genetics, Biol Div, Oak Ridge Nat Lab, 77; contract genetic basis of mutagenesis & carcinogenesis, Dept of Energy, 78-85; fac, Inst Med Res, Bennington, Vt, 85-88; fac, Ctr Molecular Biol, Wayne State Univ, 88-93. *Concurrent Pos:* Mem, Int Comt Human Gene Mapping, 75-92. *Mem:* AAAS; Am Soc Human Genetics; Genetics Soc Am. *Res:* Comparative genetics; gene mapping; somatic cell hybrids; genetics of carcinogenesis; mutagenesis; genetics of inherited diseases. *Mailing Add:* Rochester Inst Tech Hugh Dow L Carey Bldg 96 Lomb Memorial Dr Rochester NY 14623-5604

LALLEY, PETER MICHAEL, NEUROPHYSIOLOGY, NEUROPHARMACOLOGY. *Current Pos:* asst prof, 76-80, ASSOC PROF PHYSIOL, SCH MED, UNIV WIS-MADISON, 80- *Personal Data:* b Scranton, Pa, Jan 21, 40; m 63; c 4. *Educ:* Philadelphia Col Pharm & Sci, BSc, 63, MSc, 65, PhD(pharmacol), 70. *Prof Exp:* Fel neuropharmacol, Sch Med, Univ Pittsburgh, 70-73, lectr neurosci pharmacol, 72-73, asst prof, 73-74; asst prof pharmacol, Col Med, Univ Fla, 74-76. *Concurrent Pos:* Consult, US Pharmacopoeia & Dispensing Info; vis prof physiol, Univ Heidelberg, Fed Repub Ger, 85, 86, 87, Univ Gottingen, Fed Repub Ger, 88. *Mem:* Soc Neurosci; Sigma Xi; Am Physiol Soc; AAAS; Am Pharmaceut Asn; Am Heart Asn. *Res:* Identifying the neurotransmitters in the brainstem and spinal cord which control respiration and blood pressure, and determining the conditions under which they are operative. *Mailing Add:* Dept Physiol Univ Wis Med Ctr 1300 Univ Ave Madison WI 53706-1509

LALLEY, THOMAS L, BEHAVIORAL SCIENCE. *Current Pos:* RETIRED. *Personal Data:* b Baltimore, Md, Jan 22, 28. *Educ:* Loyola Col, BA, 47; Georgetown Univ, MA, 50. *Prof Exp:* Dep chief, Antisocial & Violent Behav Br, NIMH, 76-87, chief, Serv Res Br, 87-96. *Mailing Add:* 3713 Yuma St NW Washington DC 20016-2211

LALLI, CAROL MARIE, MARINE BIOLOGY. *Current Pos:* RES ASSOC, UNIV BC, 80- *Personal Data:* b Toledo, Ohio, Dec 5, 38. *Educ:* Bowling Green State Univ, BS & BEd, 60, MA, 62; Univ Wash, PhD(zool), 67. *Prof Exp:* Lectr zool, McGill Univ, 68-69, from asst prof to assoc prof marine sci, 69-79. *Mem:* Marine Biol Asn. *Res:* Ecological studies of planktonic and benthonic gastropod molluscs. *Mailing Add:* Zool Dept Univ BC Vancouver BC V6T 1Z4 Can

LALLY, PHILIP M(ARSHALL), ELECTRICAL ENGINEERING. *Current Pos:* RETIRED. *Personal Data:* b New York, NY, Sept 30, 25; m 47, Mary A Evans; c Philip J, Stephen A & James W. *Educ:* Mass Inst Technol, SB, 48, SM, 49. *Prof Exp:* Asst elec eng, Mass Inst Technol, 48-49; engr, Electron Tube Dept, Sperry Gyroscope Co, 49-54, sr engr, 54-55, eng sect head, 55-57, eng supvr res & develop, Electronic Tube Div, Sperry-Rand Corp, 57-59, eng dept head, 59-60, asst prod eng supt, 60, prod eng mgr, 60-64, mgr res & advan devices, 64-68; mgr eng, Low Power Prod Line, Teledyne Electronics Technol, 68-85, adv develop mgr, 85-90, mgr elec eng, 90-93, mgr design eng, Vacuum Electronics Bus Unit, 93-95. *Concurrent Pos:* Lectr, Adelphi Col, 55-56 & Univ Fla, 58-59. *Mem:* Inst Elec & Electronics Engrs. *Res:* Microwave vacuum tubes, especially traveling wave tubes and klystrons. *Mailing Add:* 738 Desoto Dr Palo Alto CA 94303

LALLY, VINCENT EDWARD, METEOROLOGY, ELECTRONICS. *Current Pos:* prog head, 61-90, comt on space res, 65-75, EMER SR SCIENTIST, NAT CTR ATMOSPHERIC RES, 90- *Personal Data:* b Brookline, Mass, Oct 13, 22; m 53; c 3. *Educ:* Univ Chicago, BS, 44; Mass Inst Technol, BS, 48, MS, 49. *Honors & Awards:* Cleveland Abbe Award, Am Met Soc, 90. *Prof Exp:* Engr, Bendix-Friez, Md, 49-51; chief meteorol instrument sect, Air Force Cambridge Res Labs, 51-58; res mgr, Tele-Dynamics Div, Am Bosch Arma Corp, 58-61. *Mem:* AAAS; fel Am Meteorol Soc; Sigma Xi. *Res:* Meteorological instruments and measurement systems. *Mailing Add:* 4475 Laguna Pl Boulder CO 80303

LALONDE, ROBERT THOMAS, TOXICOLOGY. *Current Pos:* from asst prof to assoc prof, 59-68, PROF CHEM, STATE UNIV NY, 68- *Personal Data:* b Bemidji, Minn, May 7, 31; m 57, Suzanne Denniston; c Robert J, Judith M, Mary C, Jane F, Suzanne, Jerome V & Thomas A. *Educ:* St John's Univ, Minn, BA, 53; Univ Colo, PhD, 57. *Prof Exp:* Sr res engr chem, Jet Propulsion Lab, Calif Inst Technol, 57-58; res assoc, Univ Ill, 58-59. *Concurrent Pos:* NIH fel, 65-66, Fed Rep Ger Exchange, 80. *Mem:* Am Chem Soc; Am Soc Pharmacol; Environ Mutagen Soc; Sigma Xi. *Res:* Chemistry of natural products; chemistry of alkaloids, terpenoids, steroids and fatty acid derivatives; origin, synthesis, structure-activity relations and modes of inactivation of halogen containing mutagens; geogenesis of organo-sulfur compounds. *Mailing Add:* Dept Chem State Univ NY Col Environ Sci & Forestry Syracuse NY 13210-2786. *Fax:* 315-470-6856; *E-Mail:* lalonde@suvm.syr.edu

LALOR, WILLIAM FRANCIS, COTTON PRODUCTION & PROCESSING, TROPICAL FOOD CROPS. *Current Pos:* dir, Agr Res, 73-90, VPRES, AGR, COTTON INC, 91- *Personal Data:* b Dublin, Ireland, Sept 30, 35; US citizen; m 61; c 4. *Educ:* Univ Col, Dublin, B Agr Sc, 58; Mich State Univ, MS, 62; Iowa State Univ, PhD(agr eng), 68. *Prof Exp:* Lectr agr, Univ Col, Dublin, 62-65; prof agr eng, Auburn Univ, 68-71; scientist agr eng, Int Inst Trop Agr, 71-73. *Concurrent Pos:* Prof engr, dept consumer-affairs, Calif. *Mem:* Am Soc Agr Engrs. *Res:* Development of production and processing systems for cotton and cottonseed. *Mailing Add:* 904 Plateau Lane Raleigh NC 27615. *Fax:* 919-881-9874

LALWANI, NARENDRA DHANRAJ, DRUG DEVELOPMENT, INVESTIGATIVE & MECHANISTIC TOXICOLOGY. *Current Pos:* sr scientist, 90-91, res assoc, 91-93, SR MGR, DEPT PATH & EXP TOXICOL, PARKE-DAVIS PHARMACEUT RES, 93- *Personal Data:* b Gujarat, India, Sept 25, 52; US citizen; m 85, Leena Hingorani; c Nalin & Neeraj. *Educ:* Gujarat Univ, BS, 73; Univ Bombay, MS, 76, PhD(biophys), 79. *Prof Exp:* Fel, Northwestern Univ Med Sch, 79-81, res assoc, 81-83, asst prof & res scientist, 84-87; asst prof, Med Col Va, Va Commonwealth Univ, 87-90. *Concurrent Pos:* Res student, Cancer Res Inst, Bombay, India, 74-76, jr res fel, 76-79; prin investr, Nat Cancer Inst, 84-87; Am Cancer Soc, 87-88; Va Commonwealth Univ, 89. *Mem:* Am Soc Cell Biol; Am Asn Cancer Res; Soc Toxicol; Am Soc Microbiol; AAAS. *Res:* Signal transduction in cell proliferation and differentiation; cellular and molecular aspects of apoptosis; mechanisms of chemical toxicity in liver and pancreas; xenobiotic effects on peroxisomes; receptor mediated gene expression. *Mailing Add:* 9143 Silver Pine Dr South Lyon MI 48178

LAM, CHAN F, IMAGE PROCESSING, CONFORMAL DOSE PLANNING FOR STEREOTACTIC RADIOSURGERY. *Current Pos:* dir, Opers & Chief Prog, Med Univ SC, 71-72, from asst prof to assoc prof biomed eng, 70-80, dir, Time Share & Hybrid Comput Syst, 75-80, dir, Biomed Comput Ctr, 80-85, PROF BIOMED, MED UNIV SC, 80-, DIR, BIOMED IMAGE & SIGNAL PROCESSING LAB, 87-, PROF RADIOL, 91- *Personal Data:* b Kwantung, China, Oct 23, 43; m 67; c 2. *Educ:* Calif Polytech State Univ, BS, 65; Clemson Univ, MS, 67, PhD(elec & comp eng), 70. *Prof Exp:* Res asst, Grad Inst Technol, Univ Ark, 65-66; res asst comp analysis, Clemson Univ, 66-70. *Concurrent Pos:* Spec Study Sect, NIH, 79, Biomed Res Technol Rev Comt, 86-90; vis res prof, Dept Elec Eng, Cheng Kung Univ, Tainan, Taiwan, 85. *Mem:* Sigma Xi; Inst Elec & Electronics Engrs; Pattern Recognition Soc; Soc Math Biol. *Res:* Modeling of enzyme kinetic reaction mechanisms; biomedical signal and image processing; optimal dose planning for stereotactic radiosurgery; pattern recognition. *Mailing Add:* Dept Biomet Med Univ SC 171 Ashley Ave Charleston SC 29425. *Fax:* 803-792-0539; *E-Mail:* lam@tigger.musc.edu

LAM, CHEUNG-WEI, ELECTROMAGNETIC INTERFERENCE, SIGNAL INTEGRITY. *Current Pos:* TECH STAFF, QUAD DESIGN TECHNOL, 93- *Personal Data:* b Hong Kong, Mar 5, 65; m 93, Hoi-Man Hui; c Isaac S. *Educ:* Chinese Univ Hong Kong, BS, 87; Mass Inst Technol, MS, 89, PhD(elec eng), 93. *Honors & Awards:* Inst Elec & Electronics Engrs Prize, 87. *Concurrent Pos:* Researcher, Schlumberger-Doll Res, 90. *Mem:*

Inst Elec & Electronics Engrs; Sigma Xi. *Res:* Design of efficient electromagnetic interference simulator; development of nonlinear models for superconducting transmission lines; high-speed electronic interconnection and packaging; acoustic logging in borehole structures. *Mailing Add:* 1395 La Culebra Circle Camarillo CA 93012. *Fax:* 805-988-8259; *E-Mail:* lam@qdt.com

LAM, DANIEL J, PHYSICAL METALLURGY & CHEMISTRY. *Current Pos:* RETIRED. *Personal Data:* b Hong Kong, Dec 30, 30; m 59; c 3. *Educ:* Rensselaer Polytech Inst, BMetE, 56, MMetE, 58, PhD(phys metall), 60. *Prof Exp:* Res assoc metall, Rensselaer Polytech Inst, 56-58, instr, 58-60; asst metallurgist, Argonne Nat Lab, 60-66, assoc metallurgist, 66-72, metallurgist, 72-74, sr scientist, 74-96, group leader, 78-96. *Mem:* AAAS; Am Phys Soc; Am Inst Mining, Metall & Petrol Engrs. *Res:* Electronic structure and related physical and chemical properties of actinide metals, alloys and compounds; electronic structure and related physical properties of multicomponent oxides. *Mailing Add:* 10318 SW 49th Lane Gainesville FL 32608-7161

LAM, FUK LUEN, CHEMISTRY. *Current Pos:* MGR QUAL ASSURANCE, PARKE-DAVIS, WARMER-LAMBERT CO, 80- *Personal Data:* b Hong Kong, Nov 7, 37; US citizen; m 68, Irene Chan; c David & Eugene. *Educ:* Univ SC, PhD(org chem), 66. *Prof Exp:* Fel chem, Mass Inst Technol, 66-67; Brandeis Univ, 68-69; res assoc chem oncogenesis, Sloan-Kettering Inst, 70-75, assoc, 75-79. *Mem:* Am Chem Soc. *Res:* Organic and analytical chemistry. *Mailing Add:* 92 Westminster Rd Chatham NJ 07928. *Fax:* 973-631-7722

LAM, GABRIEL KIT YING, RADIATION BIOPHYSICS, CANCER RADIOTHERAPY. *Current Pos:* Staff biophysicist, BC Cancer Res Ctr, 76-84, BIOPHYSICIST, BC CANCER AGENCY, 84- *Personal Data:* b Hong Kong, Jan 1, 47; m 74, Virginia Kwan; c Sylvia, Grace & Yvonne. *Educ:* Univ Hong Kong, BSc, 70; Univ Western Ont, MSc, 71; Univ Toronto, PhD(biophys), 74. *Concurrent Pos:* Med Res Coun fel, Univ BC, 74-76, hon asst prof, 81- *Mem:* Radiation Res Soc; Am Asn Physicists Med. *Res:* Biophysical studies in the use of particle radiation for cancer radiotherapy; theoretical studies of radiation action. *Mailing Add:* Batho Biomed Facil TRIUMF Univ BC 4004 Wesbrook Mall Vancouver BC V6T 2A3 Can. *Fax:* 604-822-5997; *E-Mail:* gkylam@triumfcl.ca

LAM, GILBERT NIM-CAR, PHARMACOKINETICS, DRUG METABOLISM. *Current Pos:* ASSOC DIR, DUPONT MERCK PHARMACEUT CO, 91- *Personal Data:* b Shanghai, China, Nov 10, 51. *Educ:* State Univ NY, Buffalo, BS, 76; Univ Ill, PhD(pharm), 81. *Prof Exp:* Res biochemist, E I DuPont de Nemours & Co, Inc, 81-91. *Mem:* Am Asn Pharmaceut Scientists; Int Soc Study Xenobiotics. *Res:* Pharmacokinetics; biopharmaceutics; drug metabolism and analytical methodology of pharmaceuticals. *Mailing Add:* 25015 Stonegate Laguna Niguel CA 92677

LAM, HARRY CHI-SING, THEORETICAL HIGH ENERGY PHYSICS. *Current Pos:* from asst prof to assoc prof, 65-75, chmn dept, 76-80, PROF PHYSICS, MCGILL UNIV, 75- *Personal Data:* b Hong Kong, Nov 10, 36. *Educ:* McGill Univ, BSc, 58; Mass Inst Technol, PhD(physics), 63. *Prof Exp:* Res assoc physics, Univ Md, 63-65. *Concurrent Pos:* Asst ed, Can J Physics, 73- *Mem:* Am Phys Soc; Can Asn Physicists. *Res:* Quantum field theory; particle theory. *Mailing Add:* Rutherford Physics Bldg McGill Univ 3600 University St Montreal PQ H3A 2T8 Can

LAM, JOHN LING-YEE, CLASSICAL & QUANTUM ELECTRODYNAMICS. *Current Pos:* PRIN ENGR, BOEING DEFENSE & SPACE GROUP, 88- *Personal Data:* b Hong Kong, May 28, 40; US citizen. *Educ:* Rice Univ, BA, 62; Calif Inst Technol, PhD(physics), 67. *Prof Exp:* Res fel, Calif Inst Technol, 66-68, Univ Miami, 68-69, Nat Res Coun Can, 69-71 & Max Planck Inst Physics & Astrophys, Munich, 71-73; sr res physicist, Dikewood Corp, 74-81; sr tech specialist, Northrop Corp, 81-88. *Mem:* Am Phys Soc. *Res:* Interaction between radiation and matter in both the classical and quantum regimes, and in both the microscopoic and macroscopic aspects. *Mailing Add:* 4821 Kent-Des Moines Rd Apt 303 Kent WA 98032

LAM, KAI SHUE, PHYSICS, CHEMICAL PHYSICS. *Current Pos:* Fel & instr chem physics, 76-80, SR RES ASSOC CHEM PHYSICS, DEPT CHEM, UNIV ROCHESTER, 80- *Personal Data:* b Hong Kong, Feb 22, 49. *Educ:* Univ Calif, Berkeley, AB, 70; Mass Inst Technol, PhD(physics), 76. *Mem:* Am Phys Soc; Sigma Xi. *Res:* Atomic and molecular collision physics; atom-surface collisions; interaction of collision systems with laser radiation; spectral line broadening. *Mailing Add:* Physics Dept Calif State Polytech Univ Pomona CA 91768. *Fax:* 909-869-4396

LAM, KIN LEUNG, COMPUTATIONAL FLUID MECHANICS, NUCLEAR REACTOR SAFETY. *Current Pos:* STAFF MEM, LOS ALAMOS NAT LAB, 89- *Personal Data:* c 1. *Educ:* Univ Calif, Berkeley, BS, 81; Univ Calif, Santa Barbara, PhD(chem eng), 89. *Mem:* Am Inst Chem Engrs; Soc Indust & Appl Math; Am Soc Mech Engrs; Am Phys Soc; Am Inst Aeronaut & Astronaut. *Res:* Computational fluid dynamics with applications in nuclear and chemical plant safety problems involving turbulence, multiphase flow and heat transfer phenomena. *Mailing Add:* 554 Brighton Loop Los Alamos NM 87544

LAM, KUI CHUEN, MATHEMATICAL PROGRAMMING & ACCURACY ANALYSIS, ASTRONAUTICAL GUIDANCE. *Current Pos:* TECH STAFF ASTRONAUT GUID, C S DRAPER LABS, INC, 80- *Personal Data:* b Hong Kong, Sept 22, 43; m 74; c 1. *Educ:* Univ Hong Kong, BSc gen hons, 67, BSc spec hons, 68; Univ Ore, MS, 71; PhD(physics), 74. *Prof Exp:* Res assoc physics, Univ Ga, 74-75; asst prof physics, Pahlaui Univ, Shiraz, Iran, 75-76; lab supvr foreign lang, Western Carolina Univ, 76; res specialist atmospheric physics, Cloud Physics Dept, Univ Mo, Rolla, 76-79; res assoc radio astron, Mass Inst Technol, 79-80. *Mem:* Am Phys Soc. *Res:* Numerical analysis; mathematical physics; control and decision astronautical guidance; particle theory. *Mailing Add:* Mass Inst Technol BR PO Box 172 Cambridge MA 02139

LAM, KWOK-WAI, BIOCHEMISTRY. *Current Pos:* PROF OPHTHAL, UNIV TEX, HEALTH SCI CTR. *Personal Data:* b Kowloon, Hong Kong, Sept 21, 35; m 61; c 2. *Educ:* ETex Baptist Col, BS, 57; Univ Pittsburgh, PhD(biochem), 63. *Prof Exp:* Nat Inst Child Health & Human Develop fel enzymol & geront, 63-65, assoc, 65-66; assoc enzymol, Retina Found, Boston, 66-73; res assoc prof biochem, 73-81, res prof ophthal, Albany Med Col, 81. *Concurrent Pos:* NIH career develop award, 67; asst prof biochem, Boston Univ, Sch Med, 70-73. *Mem:* Nat Acad Clin Biochem; Am Chem Soc; Asn Res Vision & Ophthal; Fedn Am Socs Exp Biol; Nat Registry Clin Chem. *Res:* Mechanism of oxidative phosphorylation; clinical enzymology. *Mailing Add:* Dept Surg Ophthal Univ Tex Health Sci Ctr 7703 Floyd Curl Dr San Antonio TX 78284-6200

LAM, LEO KONGSUI, INERTIAL GUIDANCE INSTRUMENTS. *Current Pos:* mem tech staff, 81-88, SR MEM TECH STAFF, GUIDANCE & CONTROL SYSTS DIV, LITTON INDUSTS INC, 88- *Personal Data:* b Hong Kong, Sept 12, 46; US citizen; m 83, Florence Tsai; c Stephen & Jonathan. *Educ:* Univ Hong Kong, BSc, 69; Columbia Univ, MA, 70, PhD(physics), 75. *Prof Exp:* Res assoc physics, Joint Inst Lab Astrophys, Univ Col, 75-77; res asst prof physics, Univ Mo, Rolla, 77-79; mem fac, Univ Southern Calif, 79-81. *Concurrent Pos:* Guest worker physics, Boulder Labs, Nat Bur Stands, 75-77. *Mem:* Optical Soc Am. *Res:* Fiber optics gyroscopes; erbium doped fiber amplifiers. *Mailing Add:* Litton Guid & Control 5500 Canoga Ave Mail Sta 7 Woodland Hills CA 91367. *Fax:* 818-715-4351; *E-Mail:* lam@littongcs.com

LAM, NGHI QUOC, METAL PHYSICS & RADIATION EFFECTS. *Current Pos:* Fel metal physics, Argonne Nat Lab, 71-74, asst scientist, 74-77, scientist, 77-88, SR SCIENTIST, ARGONNE NAT LAB, 88- *Personal Data:* b Vietnam, Oct 4, 45; US citizen; m 69, Hien T Nguyen; c Albert, Alice & Tina. *Educ:* Laval Univ, BS, 68; McMaster Univ, PhD(mat sci), 71. *Honors & Awards:* Mat Sci Res Award, Dept Energy, 84. *Concurrent Pos:* Adj prof, Div Med Physics & Bioeng, Chicago Med Sch, 76-81 & 86-88; vis scientist, Ctr Nuclear Studies, Saclay, France, 76-81 & 86-88. *Mem:* Am Phys Soc; Mat Res Soc; Bohmische Physikalische Gesellschaft. *Res:* Radiation effects; atomic defects; diffusion; segregation; phase transformation; sputtering; ion implantation; electron microscopy; computer modeling and simulations. *Mailing Add:* Mat Sci Div Argonne Nat Lab Argonne IL 60439. *E-Mail:* nghi___lam@qmgate.anl.gov

LAM, SAU-HAI, APPLIED MATHEMATICS & MECHANICAL ENGINEERING. *Current Pos:* asst, Princeton Univ, 56-58, res assoc, 58-59, from asst prof to assoc prof aeronaut eng, 60-67, chmn, Eng Physics Prog, 72-81, assoc dean eng, 80-81, co-chmn, prog appl & computational math, 83-86, chmn, dept mech & aerospace eng, 83-89, PROF AERONAUT ENG, PRINCETON UNIV, 67-, EDWIN WILSEY '04 CHAIRED PROF, 73- *Personal Data:* b Macao, Dec 18, 30; m 59, Patsy Chu; c Nelson, Karen & Philip. *Educ:* Rensselaer Polytech Inst, BAeroEng, 54; Princeton Univ, PhD(aeronaut eng), 58. *Prof Exp:* Res asst, Cornell Univ, 59-60. *Concurrent Pos:* Sr NSF fel, 66-67; assoc ed, Physics of Fluids, 83- *Mem:* Fel Am Inst Aeronaut & Astronaut; Am Phys Soc; Am Soc Mech Engrs. *Res:* Theoretical gas dynamics; chemical kinetics; ionized gas flows; non-linear dynamics and control. *Mailing Add:* Dept Mech & Aerospace Eng Princeton Univ D302C Eng Quadrangle Princeton NJ 08544. *E-Mail:* lam@princeton.edu

LAM, SHEUNG TSING, APPLIED NUCLEAR PHYSICS, INFORMATION TECHNOLOGY. *Current Pos:* staff physicist & safety officer, Nuclear Res Ctr, 72-86, AMS proj coordr, 87-91, TECHNOL TRANSFER & INFO, UNIV ALTA, 91- *Personal Data:* b Hong Kong, Dec 11, 34; Can citizen. *Educ:* Univ Hong Kong, BSc, 59; Univ Ottawa, MSc, 62; Univ Alta, PhD(physics), 67. *Prof Exp:* Demonstr physics, Univ Hong Kong, 59-60; Can Nat Coun fel & res assoc nuclear physics, Univ Toronto, 67-70; asst prof, Univ Va, 70-72. *Concurrent Pos:* Attached staff mem, Chalk River Nuclear Labs, Atomic Energy Can Ltd, 67-70; Frederick Gardner Cottrell Res Corp grant, 71-72. *Mem:* Am Phys Soc. *Res:* Nuclear structure studies using electrostatic accelerators and fast neutron induced fission studies; neutron-neucleus scattering and analysis using optical potentials; study of 3-body interacton using n-D breakup reaction; trace element analysis using proton-induced X-ray emission; trace isotope analysis using accelerator mass spectrometry; use of internet for communication of data. *Mailing Add:* Centre Subatomic Res Univ Alta Edmonton AB T6G 2N5 Can. *E-Mail:* lam@phys.unlberton.ca

LAM, SIMON SHIN-SING, COMPUTER SCIENCE. *Current Pos:* from asst prof to assoc prof, 77-83, David S Bruton Centennial prof, 85-88, PROF COMPUT SCI, UNIV TEX, AUSTIN, 83-, CHMN DEPT, 92- *Personal Data:* b Macoa, July 31, 47; m 71, Amy Leung; c Eric. *Educ:* Wash State Univ, BSEE, 69; Univ Calif, Los Angeles, MS, 70, PhD, 74. *Honors & Awards:* Leonard G Abraham Prize, Inst Elec & Electronics Engrs. *Prof Exp:* Res engr,

ARPA Network Measurement Ctr, Univ Calif, Los Angeles, 71-74; res staff mem, IBM Watson Res Ctr, Yorktown Heights, NY, 74-77. *Concurrent Pos:* Chancellor's teaching fel, Univ Calif, Los Angeles, 69-73; NSF grant, 78- *Mem:* Fel Inst Elec & Electronics Engrs; Comput Mach. *Res:* Computer science; contributed articles to professional journals. *Mailing Add:* Dept Comput Sci Univ Tex Austin TX 78712

LAM, STANLEY K, SEPARATION SCIENCE, CLINICAL CHEMISTRY. *Current Pos:* ASSOC PROF LAB MED, ALBERT EINSTEIN COL MED, 78- *Personal Data:* b Hong Kong; US citizen. *Educ:* Calif State Univ, BA, 74; State Univ NY, Buffalo, PhD(chem), 80. *Mem:* Am Chem Soc; Am Asn Clin Chem. *Res:* Chromatographic methods for the monitoring of therapeutic agents and development of chromatographic techniques. *Mailing Add:* 2240 VanCortlandt Circle Yorktown Heights NY 10598

LAM, TENNY N(ICOLAS), TRANSPORTATION ENGINEERING, OPERATIONS RESEARCH. *Current Pos:* RETIRED. *Personal Data:* b Hong Kong, Nov 28, 40; m 66; c 1. *Educ:* Univ Calif, Berkeley, BS, 63, MEng, 64, DEng(transp sci), 67. *Prof Exp:* Asst prof civil eng, Univ Mo, Columbia, 66-68; sr res engr, Dept Theoret Physics, Gen Motors Res Labs, 68-74; from assoc prof to prof civil eng, Univ Calif, Davis, 74-86; reader, Univ Hong Kong, 87-89, prof, 91-94, dean eng, 92-94. *Concurrent Pos:* Assoc ed, Transp Sci, 74-77 & 80-86. *Mem:* Opers Res Soc Am; Am Soc Civil Engrs. *Res:* Traffic flow theory; transportation systems planning and analysis. *Mailing Add:* 3100 Shelter Cove Univ Calif Davis CA 95616

LAM, TSIT-YUEN, ALGEBRA. *Current Pos:* lectr, Univ Calif, 68-69, from asst prof to assoc prof, 69-76, vchmn dept, 75 & 80-81, Miller prof, 78-79, PROF MATH, UNIV CALIF, BERKELEY, 76- *Personal Data:* b Hong Kong, Feb 6, 42; m 70, Chee-King; c Juwen, Fumei, Juleen & Tsai-Yu. *Educ:* Hong Kong Univ, BA, 63; Columbia Univ, PhD(math), 67. *Honors & Awards:* Steele Prize, Am Math Soc, 83. *Prof Exp:* Fel math, Univ Ill, Urbana, 67; instr, Univ Chicago, 67-68. *Concurrent Pos:* Alfred P Sloan Found fel, 72-74; Guggenheim fel, 81-82. *Mem:* Am Math Soc; Math Asn Am. *Res:* Finite groups and group representation theory; quadratic forms; ring theory. *Mailing Add:* Dept Math Univ Calif Berkeley CA 94720-0001

LAM, VINH-TE, PHYSICAL CHEMISTRY. *Current Pos:* PROF CHEM, COL BOIS-DE-BOULOGNE, 72- *Personal Data:* b Saigon, SVietnam, Dec 12, 39; Can citizen; m 80. *Educ:* Univ Montreal, BSc, 62, PhD(phys chem), 67. *Prof Exp:* Prof org chem, Col St Laurent, 66-67; fel, Nat Res Coun Can, 67-69; lectr phys chem & Nat Res Coun Can grant, Univ Sherbrooke, 69-72. *Mem:* Am Chem Soc; Chem Inst Can. *Res:* Thermodynamics; thermochemistry; static and dynamic microcalorimetry; critical phenomena; surface and polymer chemistry; molecular interactions; structure of liquids and solutions. *Mailing Add:* 6728 Chateaubriand Montreal PQ H2S 2N8 Can. *E-Mail:* vinhteel@collegebdeb.qc.ca

LAM, YIU-KUEN TONY, ORGANIC CHEMISTRY. *Current Pos:* sr res chemist, 79-83, RES FEL, MERCK & CO, INC, 84- *Personal Data:* b Hong Kong, June 5, 47; US citizen; m 77; c 3. *Educ:* Chinese Univ, Hong Kong, BSc, 71; Univ NB, PhD(org chem), 74. *Prof Exp:* Res assoc, Univ Tex, Austin, 75-77; asst prof, Univ Alta, 77-79. *Mem:* AAAS; Am Chem Soc; Am Soc Pharmacog. *Res:* Discovery and chemistry of novel biologically interesting principles from microbial, herbal and animal sources. *Mailing Add:* 25 Hamilton Lane N Plainsboro NJ 08536-1130

LAMAN, JERRY THOMAS, EXTRACTION OF MINERALS USING WATER, RESTORATION OF GROUNDWATER. *Current Pos:* proj mgr, 83-84, VPRES, IN-SITU, INC, LARAMIE, WYO, 84-; PRES & BD DIR, SOLUTION MINING CORP, LARAMIE, 89- *Personal Data:* b Muskogee, Okla, Mar 1, 47; m 72, Lenora; c Troy T & Brian D. *Educ:* Colo Sch Mines, dipl, 69. *Prof Exp:* Refinery engr, ARCO, Torrance, Calif, 69-71; asst mine supt, Cliffs Copper Corp, 72-77, chief metallurgist, Cleveland Cliffs Iron Co, 77-83. *Mem:* Am Inst Mining Metall & Petrol Eng; Groundwater Protection Coun. *Res:* Mining; metallurgy. *Mailing Add:* Solution Mining Corp PO Box 1109 Laramie WY 82073. *Fax:* 307-721-7592; *E-Mail:* jlaman@in-situ.com

LAMANNA, JOSEPH CHARLES, NEUROPHYSIOLOGY, OPTICAL INSTRUMENTATION. *Current Pos:* assoc prof, 81-90, PROF, DEPT NEUROL, CASE WESTERN RES UNIV, 90-, ACTG CHMN, DEPT ANAT, 93- *Personal Data:* b Bronxville, NY, July 12, 49; m 71; c 3. *Educ:* Georgetown Univ, BS, 71; Duke Univ, PhD(physiol), 75. *Honors & Awards:* Young Investr Award, NIH, 77. *Prof Exp:* NIH fel & res assoc physiol, Duke Univ Med Ctr, 75-77; from asst prof to assoc prof, Dept Neurol & Physiol-Biophys, Med Sch, Univ Miami, 77-81. *Concurrent Pos:* Postdoctoral fel, NIH, 75-77; vis investr neurosurg Loma Linda Med Univ, Calif, 75, Semmelweiss Med Sch, Budapest, Hungary, 80; Res Career Develop Award, NIH, 78-81; Brain, Lung & Develop Res Study Comt, Am Heart Asn, 86-89; Merit Rev Bd, Vets Admin, 87-90. *Mem:* Am Physiol Soc; Optical Soc Am; Int Soc Oxygen Transp Tissues; Soc Neurosci; Biomed Eng Soc; Microcirculatory Soc. *Res:* Determining the role of oxygen and oxidative energy metabolism in the function of the central nervous system in mammals, utilizing optical monitoring techniques. *Mailing Add:* Dept Neurol Case Western Res Univ Sch Med 10900 Euclid Ave Cleveland OH 44106-4938. *Fax:* 216-368-1144; *E-Mail:* jcl4@po.cwru.edu

LA MANTIA, CHARLES R, CHEMICAL ENGINEERING. *Current Pos:* PRES, ARTHUR D LITTLE, INC, CAMBRIDGE, 86- *Personal Data:* b New York, NY, June 12, 39; m 61; c 2. *Educ:* Columbia Univ, BA, 60, BS, 61, MS, 63, ScD(chem eng), 65. *Prof Exp:* Res & develop proj off, Defense Atomic Support Agency, 65-67; vpres chem & metall eng, Arthur D Little Inc, Cambridge, 67-81; pres, Koch Process Systs Inc, Westborough, Mass, 81-86. *Concurrent Pos:* Mem staff, Charles F Bonilla & Assocs, 65. *Mem:* Am Inst Chem Engrs. *Res:* Chemical process design, analysis and development; air pollution control; energy technology; cryogenic technology. *Mailing Add:* 3 Goodwin Rd Lexington MA 02173

LA MAR, GERD NEUSTADTER, STRUCTURAL CHEMISTRY. *Current Pos:* from asst prof to assoc prof, 71-74, PROF CHEM, UNIV CALIF, DAVIS, 74- *Personal Data:* b Brasov, Romania, Dec 21, 37; US citizen; m 64; c 2. *Educ:* Lehigh Univ, BS, 60; Princeton Univ, PhD(chem), 64. *Prof Exp:* NSF fel, 64-66; NATO fel, 66-67; res chemist, Shell Develop Co, 67-70. *Concurrent Pos:* Fel, Alfred P Sloan Found, 72, John Simon Guggenheim Mem Found, 75. *Mem:* Am Chem Soc. *Res:* The use of magnetic resonance spectroscopy as a tool for elucidating structure-function relationships in metallo-enzymes and their model complexes. *Mailing Add:* Dept Chem Univ Calif-Davis Davis CA 95616-5224

LAMARCA, MICHAEL JAMES, DEVELOPMENTAL BIOLOGY. *Current Pos:* RETIRED. *Personal Data:* b Jamestown, NY, June 4, 31; m 54; c 3. *Educ:* State Univ NY Albany, AB, 53; Cornell Univ, PhD(zool), 61. *Prof Exp:* Instr zool, Rutgers Univ, 61-63, asst prof, 63-65; from asst prof to assoc prof biol, Lawrence Univ, 65-76, chmn dept, 70-74, prof, 76- *Concurrent Pos:* NSF res grant, 63-65; resident dir, Assoc Cols Midwest Argonne Semester Prog, Argonne Nat Lab, 68-69; NSF sci fac fel biol sci, Purdue Univ, 71-72; vis biol chem, Harvard Med Sch, 77-78. *Res:* RNA and protein synthesis in echinoderm, amphibian, and mammalian development. *Mailing Add:* 2109 Beacon St SW Rochester MN 55902

LAMARCHE, FRANCOIS, SURFACE ACTIVITY OF PROTEINS, PROTEIN STRUCTURE. *Current Pos:* RES SCIENTIST PROTEIN STRUCT, FOOD RES DEVELOP CTR, AGR CAN, 88- *Personal Data:* b Montreal, Que, Jan 2, 60; m 86; c 2. *Educ:* Univ Que Trois-Rivieres, BSc, 82, PhD(biophys), 88. *Mem:* Biophys Soc; Protein Soc. *Res:* Study of the behavior of proteins at air-water and oil-water interface; importance of structural factors of protein on their surface properties. *Mailing Add:* Food Res & Develop Ctr Agr 3600 Casavant Blvd W St-Hyacinthe PQ J2S 8E3 Can

LAMARCHE, J L GILLES, PHYSICS. *Current Pos:* From asst prof to prof, 57-92, ADJ PROF PHYSICS, UNIV OTTAWA, 92- *Personal Data:* b Montreal, Que, May 31, 27. *Educ:* Univ Montreal, BSc, 50; Univ BC, MA, 53, PhD(physics), 57. *Mem:* Am Phys Soc; Can-Fr Asn Advan Sci; Can Asn Physicists. *Res:* Low temperature physics; semimagnetic semiconductor magnetism; nuclear magnetism. *Mailing Add:* Dept Physics Univ Ottawa Ottawa ON K1N 6N5 Can. *Fax:* 613-562-5190; *E-Mail:* lamarche@physics.uottawa.ca

LAMARCHE, PAUL H, GENETICS, PEDIATRICS. *Current Pos:* chief pediat & genetics, 74-85, MED DIR, EASTERN MAINE MED CTR, 85-; PROF GENETICS, UNIV MAINE, 74- *Personal Data:* b Boston, Mass, Sept 5, 29; m 52; c 5. *Educ:* Boston Col, BS, 56; Boston Univ, MD, 60; Mass Inst Technol, ScM, 74. *Hon Degrees:* MA, Brown Univ. *Prof Exp:* Res assoc path & dir genetics lab, RI Hosp, 63-75, med dir, Birth Defects Ctr, 65-75, med dir child develop ctr, 66-75, assoc physician-in-chief pediat, 69-75. *Concurrent Pos:* Asst pediatrician, Providence Lying-In Hosp, 63-74, consult, 66-74; prin investr Nat Cancer Inst grant, 64-69; prof pediat, Sch Med, Tufts Univ, 81; consult, Child Study Ctr, Brown Univ, 67-74. *Mem:* AAAS; Genetics Soc Am; Tissue Cult Asn. *Res:* Genetics and cytogenetics of teratogenesis and oncogenesis; electron microscopy of fine structure of somatic cellular phenotypes normal and abnormal in the human. *Mailing Add:* 489 State St Bangor ME 04401-6616

LAMARCHE, PAUL HENRY, JR, PLASMA-MATERIALS INTERACTIONS, ULTRA-HIGH VACUUM SCIENCE. *Current Pos:* Head, Vacuum Systs Group, 84-93, DEP HEAD, TRITIUM SYST DIV, PRINCETON UNIV, 93- *Personal Data:* b Norwood, Mass, Apr 21, 53. *Educ:* Boston Col, BS, 75; Yale Univ, MS, 76, PhD(physics), 81. *Prof Exp:* Res physicist, Exxon Prod Res Co, 81-82; res assoc, Univ Chicago, 82-84. *Concurrent Pos:* Consult, 84-; chmn, Plasma Sci & Technol Div, Am Vacuum Soc, 89. *Mem:* AAAS; Am Phys Soc; Am Vacuum Soc. *Res:* The interaction of energetic plasma ions with solids as embodied in fusion research devices; interfacial processes at vacuum-wall boundary; consulting work on vacuum vessel and system design. *Mailing Add:* 52 Brophy Dr Trenton NJ 08638. *E-Mail:* lamarche@pppl.gov

LAMASTRO, ROBERT ANTHONY, GLASS TECHNOLOGY. *Current Pos:* Glass technologist, Wheaton Indusls, 82-84, mgr glass res & develop, 84-89. *Personal Data:* b New York, NY, Sept 11, 56; m 81; c 1. *Educ:* Rutgers Univ, BA & BS, 79, MS, 81, PhD(ceramic eng), 82. *Concurrent Pos:* Adj prof, Cumberland Co Col, 89- *Mem:* Am Ceramic Soc; Soc Glass Technol; Parenteral Drug Asn; Am Chem Soc; AAAS. *Res:* Development of specialty glass formulations for the pharmaceutical and cosmetic packaging industries. *Mailing Add:* Lawson, Mardon Wheaton Indusls 1101 Wheaton Ave Millville NJ 08332-2003

LAMATTINA, JOHN LAWRENCE, HETEROCYCLIC CHEMISTRY, MEDICINAL CHEMISTRY. *Current Pos:* RES SCIENTIST MED CHEM, PFIZER INC, 77-, DIR MED CHEM, 87- *Personal Data:* b Brooklyn, NY, Jan 22, 50; m 71; c 3. *Educ:* Boston Col, BS, 71; Univ NH, PhD(chem), 75. *Concurrent Pos:* NIH fel, Princeton Univ, 75-77. *Mem:* Am Chem Soc. *Res:* Design and synthesis of compounds which possess intriguing biological properties. *Mailing Add:* Pfizer Inc Pfizer Cent Res Div Eastern Point Rd Groton CT 06340

LAMAZE, GEORGE PAUL, NEUTRON DEPTH PROFILING, EXPERIMENTAL NUCLEAR PHYSICS. *Current Pos:* PHYSICIST, INORG ANALYSIS RES DIV, NAT INST STAND & TECHNOL, 89- *Personal Data:* b Algiers, Algeria, Jan 15, 45; US citizen; m 65, Catherine Frantz; c Theresa & Melissa. *Educ:* Fla State Univ, BA, 65; Duke Univ, PhD(physics), 72. *Honors & Awards:* Award Merit, Am Soc Testing & Mat. *Prof Exp:* Physicist neutron stand, Nat Bur Stand, 72-89. *Concurrent Pos:* Sci asst to Rep George Brown, Calif, 78-79; secy comt on Nuclear Technol & Applns, Am Soc Testing & Mat, 90-92, vchair, Subcomt Nuclear Radiation Metrol & chmn, Comt Nuclear Technol Applns, 94- *Mem:* Am Phys Soc; fel Am Soc Testing & Mat. *Res:* Measurement of neutron depth profiling; radioactivity measurements; cold neutron fluence rates. *Mailing Add:* Nat Inst Stand & Technol Bldg 235 Gaithersburg MD 20899. *Fax:* 301-208-9279; *E-Mail:* lamaze@enh.nist.gov

LAMB, DAVID E(RNEST), chemical engineering, computer science, for more information see previous edition

LAMB, DENNIS, CLOUD PHYSICS. *Current Pos:* ASSOC PROF METEROL DEPT, PA STATE UNIV, UNIVERSITY PARK, 86- *Personal Data:* b Chicago, Ill, Feb 3, 41; m 81; c 1. *Educ:* Kalamazoo Col, BA, 63; Univ Wash, PhD(atmospheric sci), 70. *Prof Exp:* Gen physicist data assessment, Naval Weapons Ctr, China Lake, Calif, 63-65; NATO res assoc meteorol, Univ Frankfurt, 71-72; from asst to res prof, Atmospheric Sci Ctr, Desert Res Inst, Univ Nev, Reno, 72-86. *Mem:* Am Meteorol Soc; Sigma Xi; Am Geophys Union. *Res:* Nucleation and growth of solids from the liquid and vapor phases; formation of cloud nuclei; cloud physics/weather modification; atmospheric chemistry. *Mailing Add:* Meteorol Dept Penn State Univ 503 Walker Bldg University Park PA 16802. *E-Mail:* lno@ems.psu.edu

LAMB, DONALD JOSEPH, PHARMACY. *Current Pos:* RETIRED. *Personal Data:* b Pittsburgh, Pa, Oct 29, 31; m 56; c 2. *Educ:* Ohio State Univ, BSc, 54, MSc, 55, PhD(pharm), 60. *Prof Exp:* Res assoc pharmaceut res & develop, Upjohn Co, 60-65, res head, 65-70, res mgr pharmaceut res, 70-83, dir proj support, 83-88, dir proj mgt, 88- *Mem:* Am Pharmaceut Asn; Am Acad Pharmaceut Sci; Am Chem Soc; Sigma Xi. *Res:* Design and evaluation of drug dosage forms, including design and evaluation of drugs to fit specific dosage forms. *Mailing Add:* 5128 Allardowne St Portage MI 49002

LAMB, DONALD QUINCY, JR, ASTROPHYSICS. *Current Pos:* dept chmn, 88-91, PROF ASTRON & ASTROPHYS, UNIV CHICAGO, 85- *Personal Data:* b Manhattan, Kans, June 30, 45; m 78, Linda Gilkerson; c Michael. *Educ:* Rice Univ, BA, 67; Univ Liverpool, MSc, 69; Univ Rochester, PhD(physics), 74. *Prof Exp:* Res asst prof physics, Univ Ill, 73-75, from asst prof to prof, 75-80; physicist, Smithsonian Ctr Astrophys, Harvard Univ, 80-85. *Concurrent Pos:* Marshall scholar, 67-69; Guggenheim fel, 78-79; vis scientist, Smithsonian Ctr Astrophys, Harvard Univ, 79-80; lectr astron, Harvard Univ, 80-85; trustee, Aspen Ctr Physics, 81-87, sect, 85-86, adv bd, 87-; vis prof physics, Inst Theoret Physics, Univ Calif, Santa Barbara, 87. *Mem:* Fel Am Phys Soc; Am Astron Soc; fel Royal Astron Soc; Brit Inst Physics; Europ Phys Soc. *Res:* Evolution and structure of white dwarfs and neutron stars; physics of compact x-ray and gamma-ray sources, supernovae; properties of matter at high densities. *Mailing Add:* Dept Astron & Astrophys Univ Chicago 5640 S Ellis Ave Chicago IL 60637. *Fax:* 773-702-8212; *E-Mail:* lamb@oddjob.uchicago.edu

LAMB, DONALD R(OY), CIVIL ENGINEERING. *Current Pos:* from supply instr to assoc prof, 51-70, PROF CIVIL ENG & HEAD DEPT, UNIV WYO, 70- *Personal Data:* b Yuma, Colo, May 6, 23; m 43; c 3. *Educ:* Hastings Col, BA, 47; Univ Wyo, BS, 51, MS, 53, CE, 58; Purdue Univ, PhD, 62. *Prof Exp:* Supt high schs, Nebr, 46-47, coach, 47-49. *Mem:* Am Soc Eng Educ; Am Soc Civil Engrs; Nat Soc Prof Engrs; Sigma Xi. *Res:* Use of radioisotopes in the study of portland cement, asphalt concrete and solids; portland cement concrete and associated aggregates; transportation; recreational engineering; engineering geology. *Mailing Add:* 1354 Indian Hills Dr Laramie WY 82070

LAMB, FREDERICK KEITHLEY, ASTROPHYSICS. *Current Pos:* Instr & res assoc, 70-72, from asst prof to assoc prof, 72-78, PROF PHYSICS, UNIV ILL, URBANA, 78- *Personal Data:* b Manhattan, Kans, June 30, 45; m 71; c 2. *Educ:* Calif Inst Technol, BS, 67; Oxford Univ, DPhil(theoret physics), 70. *Concurrent Pos:* Fel physics, Magdalen Col, Oxford Univ, 70-72; assoc, Ctr Advan Study, Univ Ill, Urbana, 73-74; res fel, Alfred P Sloan Found, 74-78; vis fel, Inst Astron, Cambridge, UK, 75-76; fel commorer, Churchill Col, Cambridge, UK, 75-76; vis assoc, Caltech, 77-78; fel, John Simon Guggenheim Found, 85-86; vis scholar, Stanford Univ Ctr Space Sci & Astrophys; sci fel, Ctr Int Security & Arms Control, Stanford Uni, 85-86. *Mem:* Fel Am Phys Soc; Am Astron Soc; fel Royal Astron Soc; Int Astron Union. *Res:* White dwarfs, neutron stars, and black holes; plasma theory and applications to pulsars and cosmic X-ray sources; the interaction of radiation with matter; arms control and international security. *Mailing Add:* Dept Physics Univ Ill 1110 W Green St Urbana IL 61801

LAMB, GEORGE ALEXANDER, pediatrics, infectious diseases, for more information see previous edition

LAMB, GEORGE LAWRENCE, JR, PHYSICS. *Current Pos:* FAC MEM & PROF MATH & PROF OPTICAL SCI, UNIV ARIZ, 74- *Personal Data:* b Norwood, Mass, Apr 28, 31; m 59; c 4. *Educ:* Boston Col, BS, 53, MS, 54; Mass Inst Technol, PhD(physics), 58. *Prof Exp:* Staff mem, Los Alamos Sci Lab, 58-63; physicist, United Aircraft Res Labs, Conn, 63-74. *Mem:* Am Phys Soc; Sigma Xi; Acoust Soc Am. *Res:* Nonlinear waves and solitons; acoustic wave propagation. *Mailing Add:* 2942 Ave Del Conquistador RR 2 Univ Ariz Tucson AZ 85749-9304

LAMB, GEORGE MARION, MICROPALEONTOLOGY, STRATIGRAPHY. *Current Pos:* prof geol, 64-89, asst to pres, 89-, EMER PROF GEOL, UNIV SALA. *Personal Data:* b Little Rock, Ark, Dec 23, 28; m 53; c 2. *Educ:* Emory Univ, BA, 50, MS, 54; Univ Colo, Boulder, PhD(geol), 64. *Prof Exp:* Geologist, Stand Oil Calif, Inc, 55-61. *Mem:* Am Asn Petrol Geol; Geol Soc Am; Am Inst Prof Geologists. *Res:* Ecology and paleoecology of Foraminifera; biostratigraphic relationships; groundwater and environmental geology; beach erosion and development. *Mailing Add:* Rte 2 Box 48 Stevenville TX 76401

LAMB, H RICHARD, PSYCHIATRY. *Current Pos:* assoc prof, 76-80, PROF PSYCHIAT, SCH MED, UNIV SOUTHERN CALIF, 80- *Personal Data:* b Philadelphia, Pa, Sept 18, 29; m 69, Doris Koehn; c Jonathan, Carolyn & Thomas. *Educ:* Univ Pa, BA, 50; Yale Univ, MD, 54. *Honors & Awards:* Presidential Commendation, Am Psychiat Asn, 85. *Prof Exp:* Chief rehab serv, San Mateo Co Ment Health Serv, 68-76. *Concurrent Pos:* Consult, NIMH, 75-; ed-in-chief, New Directions Ment Health Serv J, 78-; mem comt rehab, Am Psychiat Asn, 78-84, Comt Chronically Ment Ill, 86-, chmn, Comt Coord Hosp & Community Psychiat Serv, 83-; mem, Group Advan Psychiat. *Mem:* Fel Am Psychiat Asn; fel Am Col Psychiatrists; Group Advan Psychiat. *Res:* Social and community psychiatry and community mental health with a major focus on the long-term severely disabled psychiatric patient in the community. *Mailing Add:* Dept Psychiat Sch Med Univ Southern Calif 1934 Hosp Pl Los Angeles CA 90033. *Fax:* 213-226-4268

LAMB, J(AMIE) PARKER, JR, MECHANICAL & AEROSPACE ENGINEERING. *Current Pos:* from asst prof to prof mech eng, Univ Tex, Austin, 63-81, chmn dept, 70-76, assoc dean, Col Eng, 76-81, chmn aerospace eng, 81-88, ERNEST COCKRELL JR MEM PROF, UNIV TEX, AUSTIN, 81- *Personal Data:* b Boligee, Ala, Sept 21, 33; m 55, Nancy C Flaherty; c David & Stephen P. *Educ:* Auburn Univ, BS, 54; Univ Ill, MS, 58, PhD(mech eng), 61. *Honors & Awards:* Founders Award, Am Soc Mech Engrs, 75; Centennial Award, Am Soc Mech Engrs, 80; Joe J King Prof Eng Award, 84. *Prof Exp:* Proj engr, Flight Control Lab, Wright Air Develop Ctr, Ohio, 55-57; asst prof mech eng, NC State Univ, Raleigh, 61-63. *Concurrent Pos:* Consult, ARO, Inc, Tenn, 63-65, Tracor, Inc, Tex, 65-67, NASA, Ala, 69-70, Vought Aerospace Corp, Tex, 69-70 & Mobil Oil Corp, Tex, 77-78; assoc tech ed, J Fluids Eng, 76-79; gen chmn, Tenth US Nat Cong, Appl Mech, 86; dir eng prog, Univ Tex, Pan-Am, 93-94. *Mem:* Fel Am Soc Mech Engrs; assoc fel Am Inst Aeronaut & Astronaut; Am Soc Eng Educ; Nat Soc Prof Engrs. *Res:* Heat transfer and fluid mechanics in separated flow regions; compressible turbulent boundary layers; heat, mass and momentum transfers in free turbulent jets; energy conversion processes for low temperature sources. *Mailing Add:* Dept Mech Eng Univ Tex Austin TX 78712

LAMB, JAMES C(HRISTIAN), III, SCIENCE EDUCATION, RESEARCH ADMINISTRATION. *Current Pos:* CONSULT, 91- *Personal Data:* b Warsaw, Va, Aug 20, 24. *Educ:* Va Mil Inst, BS, 47; Mass Inst Technol, SM, 48, SE, 52, ScD(sanit eng). 53. *Prof Exp:* Instr civil eng, Va Mil Inst, 48-50; asst sanit eng, Mass Inst Technol, 51-53, res assoc, 53-55; sanit engr, Am Cyanamid Co, 55-59; from assoc prof to prof, Univ NC, Chapel Hill, 59-87. *Concurrent Pos:* Consult engr, 48-50, 52-55, 59-; lectr, Washington & Lee Univ, 49-50 & Exten Div, State Dept Educ, Mass, 51-52; adj prof, Newark Col Eng, 56-59; judge, US Nuclear Regulatory Comn, 74- *Mem:* Am Soc Civil Engrs; Am Water Works Asn; Water Pollution Control Fedn. *Res:* Industrial wastes; sewage treatment; water supply; saline water conversion; corrosion; stream pollution; refuse disposal; steam pollution, regulatory controls and standards; civil engineering. *Mailing Add:* 2401 Old Ivy Rd Charlottesville VA 22903

LAMB, JAMES L, MICROPALEONTOLOGY. *Current Pos:* CONSULT, 81- *Personal Data:* b Los Angeles, Calif, Jan 17, 25; m 45; c 2. *Educ:* Univ Southern Calif, BS, 53. *Prof Exp:* Paleontologist, Richfield Oil Corp, 53-57 & Creole Petrol Corp, 57-64; paleontologist, Exxon Prod Res Co, 64-81. *Mem:* Soc Econ Paleont & Mineral; Am Asn Petrol Geologists; Venezuelan Asn Geol, Mining & Petrol. *Res:* Historical geology and paleontology; geologic distribution of planktonic foraminifera; tertiary microfossils; Pleistocene epoch. *Mailing Add:* 1358 Lawnridge St Medford OR 97504-6246

LAMB, JOHN DAVID, MACROCYCLIC HOST-GUEST CHEMISTRY, SEPARATIONS CHEMISTRY. *Current Pos:* dir res admin, 85-90, exec dir res & creative work, 90-92, PROF CHEM, BRIGHAM YOUNG UNIV, 91- *Personal Data:* b Brockville, Can, Oct 10, 49; m 76, Betty Villella; c Michael, Jeremy, Joshua, Zachary, Matthew & Jacob. *Educ:* Brigham Young Univ, BS, 71, PhD (inorg phys chem), 78. *Prof Exp:* Prog mgr separations & analysis, US Dept Energy, 82-84. *Concurrent Pos:* Prin investr, US Dept Energy, 84-, Idaho Natural Energy Lab & Dionex Corp, 86-; vis prof, Univ Catania, Italy, 89, Univ Parma, Italy, 90 & 91, Sichuan Univ, China, 91, Univ Pavia, Italy, 95; co-ed-in-chief, J Inclusion Phenomena, 92- *Mem:* Am Chem Soc. *Res:* Macrocyclic ligands in making chemical separations by ion chromatography liquid membranes, solvent extraction and capillary electrophoresis; multimedia computer materials for chemistry instruction. *Mailing Add:* Dept Chem & Biochem Brigham Young Univ Provo UT 84602. *Fax:* 801-378-5474; *E-Mail:* john_lamb@byu.edu

LAMB, MARY ROSE, GENETIC & MOLECULAR BIOLOGY OF PHOTOTAXIS IN CHLAMYDOMONAS, ORGANELLE GENETICS. *Current Pos:* asst prof, 84-90, ASSOC PROF, DEPT BIOL, UNIV PUGET SOUND, 90- *Personal Data:* b Glen Falls, NY, Aug 8, 52. *Educ:* Reed Col, BA, 74; State Univ NY, Albany, MLS, 75; Ind Univ, PhD(zool), 84. *Prof Exp:* Asst prof biol, Bryn Mawr Col, 83-84. *Mem:* Genetics Soc Am; Am Soc Microbiol; Sigma Xi. *Res:* Genetics and molecular biology of phototaxis in chlamydomonas reinhardil; identified four genes that affect the assembly of the eyespot and are characterizing those genes. *Mailing Add:* Dept Biol Univ Puget Sound 1500 N Warner St Tacoma WA 98416-0001. *Fax:* 253-756-3500; *E-Mail:* mrlamb@ups.edu

LAMB, MINA MARIE WOLF, NUTRITION, FOOD PREPARATION. *Current Pos:* from lab asst to prof, Tex Tech Univ, 40-69, Margaret W Weeks distinguished prof, 69-75, head, Dept Food & Nutrit, 55-69, lectr & adv foreign students, 60-71, EMER PROF FOOD & NUTRIT, TEX TECH UNIV, 75- *Personal Data:* b Sagerton, Tex, Aug 14, 10; m 41; c 1. *Educ:* Tex Tech Col, BA, 32, MS, 37; Columbia Univ, PhD(nutrit, chem), 42. *Honors & Awards:* Piper Award, 65; Medallion Award, Am Dietetic Assoc, 86; Serv Award, 87. *Prof Exp:* Teacher, elem & high sch, 33-35; teacher & res worker food & nutrit, 35-37. *Mem:* AAAS; Am Dietetic Asn; Am Home Econ Asn; Am Men Sci. *Res:* Basal metabolism of college girls and children of various ages older than two years; needs of children and adults; dietary studies of children, college girls and families; animal feeding work with albino rats determining growth and reproduction responses to various diets and foods. *Mailing Add:* 6002 W 34th St Lubbock TX 79407-3102

LAMB, NEVEN P, biological anthropology; deceased, see previous edition for last biography

LAMB, PETER JAMES, METEOROLOGY. *Current Pos:* PROF & DIR, UNIV OKLA, NORMAN, 91- *Personal Data:* b Nelson, NZ, June 21, 47; m 70, Barbara H Harrison; c Karen D & Brett T. *Educ:* Univ Canterbury, Christ Church, NZ, BA, 69, MA(Hons), 71; Univ Wis, PhD, 76. *Honors & Awards:* Margary Lectr, 91. *Prof Exp:* Res asst, Univ Wis-Madison, 71-76, res assoc, 76; lectr, Univ Adelaide, Australia, 76-79; sr scientist, Ill State Water Surv, Champaign, 79-91, sect head, 84-90. *Concurrent Pos:* Vis res assoc, Univ Miami, Fla, 78-79; adj prof, Univ Ill, Urbana, 83-94; consult, Dept State, Dept Energy, Agency Int Develop, Nat Oceanic & Atmospheric Admin, NSF, World Meteorol Orgn, Kingdom of Morocco, Univ Wis, Univ Adelaide, Univs Space Res Asn & Environ Protection Agency, 83-; numerous res grants from US & Fed Agencies. *Mem:* Fel Am Meteorol Soc; Royal Meteorol Soc; Am Asn State Climatologists; Sigma Xi. *Res:* Research on heat transport by the Atlantic Ocean; role of the ocean in causing droughts in Sahelian Africa; investigations of precipitation variability in North America and North Africa. *Mailing Add:* Univ Okla CIMMS-Sarkeys Energy Ctr 100 E Boyd Rm 1110 Norman OK 73019. *Fax:* 405-325-7614; *E-Mail:* plamb@ou.edu

LAMB, RICHARD C, GAMMA RAY ASTRONOMY, ELEMENTARY PARTICLE PHYSICS. *Current Pos:* assoc prof, 67-72, PROF PHYSICS, IOWA STATE UNIV, 72- *Personal Data:* b Lexington, Ky, Sept 8, 33; m 59, Jane Oldham; c Cheryl, Richard, David & Wayne. *Educ:* Mass Inst Technol, BS, 55; Univ Ky, PhD(physics), 63. *Prof Exp:* Asst scientist, Argonne Nat Lab, 63-67. *Concurrent Pos:* Vis scientist, NASA-Goddard Space Flight Ctr, 75-76; prin investr prog observational gamma-ray astron, 80-; sr assoc, Jet Propulsion Lab, Nat Res Coun, 82-83. *Mem:* Fel Am Phys Soc; Am Astron Soc; Int Astron Union. *Res:* Very high energy gamma ray astronomy using the atmospheric Cerenkov technique; identification of gamma ray sources. *Mailing Add:* Dept Physics & Astron Iowa State Univ Ames IA 50011. *Fax:* 515-294-6027; *E-Mail:* rcl@iastate.edu

LAMB, ROBERT ANDREW, VIROLOGY, MOLECULAR BIOLOGY. *Current Pos:* JOHN EVANS PROF MOLECULAR & CELLULAR BIOL, NORTHWESTERN UNIV, 83-, INVESTR, HOWARD HUGHES MED INST, 91- *Personal Data:* b London, Eng, Sept 26, 50; US citizen; m 89, Reay G Paterson; c Alexander. *Educ:* Univ Birmingham, BSc, 71; Univ Cambridge, PhD(virol), 74. *Hon Degrees:* ScD, Univ Cambridge, 91. *Honors & Awards:* Phoebe Weinstein Award for Negative Strand Virus Res, 80; Wallace P Rowe Award for Excellence in Virol Res, 90. *Prof Exp:* Res assoc, Rockefeller Univ, 74-77, from asst prof to assoc prof virol, 77-82. *Concurrent Pos:* Fulbright-Hays travel award, 74-77; Irma T Hirschl career scientist award, 79-83; assoc ed, Virol, 80-93, ed, J Virol, 87-93; estab investr, Am Heart Asn, 82-87; ed-in-chief, Virol, 94- *Mem:* Am Soc Cell Biol; Am Soc Microbiol; Am Soc Biochem & Molecular Biol; Soc Gen Microbiol; Am Soc Virol; AAAS. *Res:* Virology; replication of influenza virus and paramyxoviruses; cell biology of integral membrane proteins. *Mailing Add:* Howard Hughes Med Inst & Dept Biochem Molecular & Cell Biol Northwestern Univ 2153 N Campus Dr Evanston IL 60208-3500. *Fax:* 847-491-2467; *E-Mail:* ralamb@nwu.edu

LAMB, ROBERT CARDON, DAIRY SCIENCE. *Current Pos:* HEAD ANIMAL DAIRY & VET SCI, UTAH STATE UNIV, 90- *Personal Data:* b Logan, Utah, Jan 8, 33; m 53; c 5. *Educ:* Utah State Univ, BS, 56; Mich State Univ, MS, 59, PhD(dairy cattle breeding), 62. *Prof Exp:* Instr dairy sci, Mich State Univ, 58-60; asst prof, Utah State Univ, 61-64; res dairy husbandman, Agr Res Serv, USDA, 64-72, res leader, 72-90. *Mem:* Am Dairy Sci Asn. *Res:* Use of incomplete records in dairy cattle selection; genetics by nutrition interactions; inheritance of abnormalities in livestock; feed utilization efficiency in dairy cattle; dairy herd management; exercise for dairy cows; integrated reproduction management; stress in dairy cattle; dairy cattle housing; use of BST in dairy cattle. *Mailing Add:* Animal Sci Utah State Univ Logan UT 84322-0001

LAMB, ROBERT CHARLES, ORGANIC CHEMISTRY. *Current Pos:* chmn dept, 66-77, PROF CHEM, ECAROLINA UNIV, 66- *Personal Data:* b Union Co, SC, Sept 28, 28; m 50; c 2. *Educ:* Presby Col, SC, BS, 48; Univ Ga, MS, 55; Univ SC, PhD(chem), 58. *Prof Exp:* Instr chem, Presby Col, SC, 50-51; asst prof, Univ Ga, 58-66; assoc prof & chmn dept, Augusta Col, 66. *Mem:* Am Chem Soc; Sigma Xi. *Res:* Organic peroxides; free radicals in solution; chemical kinetics. *Mailing Add:* 2011 Sherwood Dr Greenville NC 27858-5320

LAMB, ROBERT CONSAY, POMOLOGY, GENETICS. *Current Pos:* from asst prof to prof, 48-88, EMER PROF POMOL, NY STATE COL AGR & LIFE SCI, 88- *Personal Data:* b Saskatoon, Sask, May 11, 19; nat US; m 49; c 3. *Educ:* Univ Sask, BSA, 41; Univ Minn, MS, 47, PhD(hort), 54. *Prof Exp:* Asst hort, Univ Minn, 46-48. *Concurrent Pos:* Orgn Europ Econ Coop sr vis fel sci, John Innes Inst, Eng, 62; mem plant explor team, Int Bd Plant Genetic Resources, Nepal, 84- *Mem:* Am Soc Hort Sci; Int Soc Hort Sci; Can Soc Hort Sci; Am Pomol Soc (pres, 80-82). *Res:* Breeding disease resistant apple varieties; introduced Liberty and Freedom apples which are resistant to apple scab, mildew, cedar apple rust and fire blight. *Mailing Add:* 12 Cornwall Rd Geneva NY 14456

LAMB, ROBERT EDWARD, ANALYTICAL CHEMISTRY. *Current Pos:* from asst prof to assoc prof, 78-88, PROF CHEM, OHIO NORTHERN UNIV, 88- *Personal Data:* b Sharon, Pa, July 12, 45; m 73; c 2. *Educ:* St Louis Univ, AB, 69, BS, 70; Univ Ill, MS, 74, PhD(analytical chem), 75. *Prof Exp:* Lectr analytical chem, Sch Chem Sci, Univ Ill, 75; asst prof chem, Southern Methodist Univ, 75-78. *Mem:* Am Chem Soc. *Res:* Pulse polarography and stripping analysis; liquid chromatography; analysis of trace metal complexes; environmental applications of analytical techniques. *Mailing Add:* Dept Chem Ohio Northern Univ 525 S Main St Ada OH 45810-1555

LAMB, SANDRA INA, ORGANIC CHEMISTRY, ENVIRONMENTAL CHEMISTRY. *Current Pos:* LECTR CHEM, UNIV CALIF, SANTA BARBARA, 93- *Personal Data:* b New York, NY, Apr 20, 31; m 50; c 4. *Educ:* Univ Calif, Los Angeles, BS, 54, PhD(phys org chem), 59. *Prof Exp:* Instr chem, Santa Monica City Col, 59; asst prof, San Fernando Valley State Col, 60-61; instr, Exten Div, Univ Calif, 61-69; from asst prof to assoc prof chem, 69-76, Mt St Mary's Col, Calif, 71-76, chmn, Dept Phys Sci & Math, 69-75; lectr chem, Univ Calif, Los Angeles, 76-93. *Concurrent Pos:* Asst res pharmacologist, Med Sch, Univ Calif, 66-, lectr, 70. *Mem:* AAAS; Am Chem Soc; Sigma Xi. *Res:* Analytical applications of gas chromatography in chemistry and medicine with special interest in analysis of acetylcholine and various cholinergic agents; mechanism of action of muscarinic agents; analytical applications of gas chromatography and ion chromatography air pollution; synthesis of small ring compounds. *Mailing Add:* PO Box 1541 Port Hueneme CA 93044

LAMB, WALTER ROBERT, PHYSICS, GRAVITATION RESEARCH. *Current Pos:* PRES, ENERGY SYSTS & SOLAR INC, 90- *Personal Data:* b Weiser, Idaho, Sept 26, 22; m 46, Jean M MacArthur; c Gayna D (Bang). *Educ:* Univ Calif, AB, 48. *Prof Exp:* Physicist, US Naval Radiol Defense Lab, 48-59; solid state physicist, Res & Develop Dept, Raytheon Semiconductor Co, 59-63, Fairchild Semiconductor, 63-64 & Union Carbide Corp, 64-65, eng mgr, 78-85; mgr advan processing, Stewart-Warner Microcircuits, 65-68; physicist, Fairchild Semiconductor Corp, 68-71; physicist, Raytheon Co, 71-77; eng mgr, Acrian, 85-89; consult, Elec Power Res Inst, 89-90. *Mem:* AAAS; Am Phys Soc. *Res:* Solid state, nuclear radiation, optical, luminescent, thermodynamic and gravitational phenomena; insolation. *Mailing Add:* 148 Jacinto Way Sunnyvale CA 94086. *E-Mail:* 71700.1261@compuserve.com

LAMB, WILLIAM BOLITHO, CHEMICAL ENGINEERING. *Current Pos:* Res engr, E I Du Pont de Nemours & Co, Inc, 65-68, res supvr, 68-69, group mgr, 69-75, tech supt, Film Dept, 75-78, planning mgr, 79-80, prod mgr, Polymer Prod Dept, 80-86, regional mgr, La, 86-89, western sales mgr, 89-90, mgr film products, 90-93, prod & develop mgr, 93-96, SR TECH CONSULT, E I DU PONT DE NEMOURS & CO, INC, 96- *Personal Data:* b Chicago, Ill, May 6, 37; m 95, Eileen; c William, Karen & Daniel. *Educ:* Princeton Univ, BSE, 58; Univ Del, MChE, 63, PhD(chem eng), 65. *Mem:* Am Inst Chem Eng. *Res:* Mass transfer in gas-liquid systems; polymer rheology; extrusion and processing of polymers for packaging film applications; fluoropolymers. *Mailing Add:* 4 Sorrel Dr Surrey Park Wilmington DE 19803

LAMB, WILLIS EUGENE, JR, QUANTUM MECHANICS, ATOMIC PHYSICS. *Current Pos:* PROF PHYSICS & OPTICAL SCI, UNIV ARIZ, 74-, PROF, ARIZ RES LABS, 82- *Personal Data:* b Los Angeles, Calif, July 12, 13; m 39. *Educ:* Univ Calif, Berkeley, BS, 34, PhD, 38; Univ Pa, DSc, 53; Oxford Univ, MA, 56. *Hon Degrees:* MA, Yale Univ, 61; LHD, Yeshiva Univ, 65; DSc, Gustavus Adolphus Col, 75, Columbia Univ, 90. *Honors & Awards:* Nobel Prize in Physics, 55; Rumford Medal, Am Acad Arts & Sci, 53; Loeb Lectr, Harvard Univ, 53-54; Award, Res Corp, 55; Fulbright Lectr, Univ Grenoble, 64; Gordon Shrum Lectr, Simon Fraser Univ, 72; Einstein Medal, Soc Optical & Quantum Electronics, 92. *Prof Exp:* Asst physics, Univ Calif, 34-35 & 36-37; instr, Columbia Univ, 38-43, assoc, 43-45, from asst prof to prof physics, 45-52; prof, Stanford Univ, 51-56; fel, New Col & Wykeham prof, Oxford Univ, 56-62; Henry Ford II prof, Yale Univ, 62-72, Josiah Willard Gibbs prof, 72-74. *Concurrent Pos:* Mem staff, Radiation Lab, Columbia Univ, 43-52; Guggenheim fel, 60-61; consult, Philips Labs, Inc, NASA, Bell Tel Labs & Perkin-Elmer Corp; vis prof, Japan Soc Promo Sci, Res Inst Fundamental Res, Kyoto Univ & Tata Inst Fundamental Res, Bombay, 60, Columbia Univ, 61; sr fel, Alexander von Humboldt Found, 92-94; Vikrom Sarab-hai prof, Physics Res Lab, 97. *Mem:* Nat Acad Sci; fel

Am Phys Soc; hon mem NY Acad Sci; hon fel Brit Inst Physics; hon fel Royal Soc Edinburgh; hon fel Inst Physics; fel Optical Soc Am; hon fel Phys Soc. *Res:* Theoretical physics; atomic and nuclear structure; microwave spectroscopy; fine structure of hydrogen and helium; magnetron oscillators, statistical mechanics; masers and lasers; quantum theory of measurement. *Mailing Add:* Optical Sci Ctr Univ Ariz Tucson AZ 85721

LAMBA, RAM SARUP, INORGANIC CHEMISTRY, ORGANIC CHEMISTRY. *Current Pos:* instr chem, Inter Am Univ PR, 69-70, asst prof & chmn dept, 70-71, chmn dept natural sci, 73-77, assoc prof chem, math & physics, 73-83, dean acad affairs, 77-82, prof, 83-87, DISTINGUISHED PROF CHEM, INTER AM UNIV PR, 87- *Personal Data:* b Calcutta, India, Dec 29, 41; US citizen; m 69; c 2. *Educ:* Delhi Univ, India, BSc, 62, MSc, 64; ETex State Univ, DEd(inorg chem, educ), 73. *Prof Exp:* Res asst, Indian Inst Petrol, Dehradun, India, 64-65; chemist & supt dyeing & finishing, Beaunit Corp of NC, Humacao, PR, 68-69. *Mem:* Royal Inst Chem; Am Chem Soc; The Chem Soc; fel Inst Educ Leadership. *Res:* To develop innovative methods in the teaching of college chemistry and to integrate with biological sciences; synthesis and study of chromium (III), complexes; construction of low cost equipment in chemistry. *Mailing Add:* Inter-Am Univ PR, Dept Chem PO Box 1943 San Juan PR 00900-1293

LAMBA, SURENDAR SINGH, PHARMACY, PHARMACOGNOSY. *Current Pos:* From assoc prof to prof pharmacog, 66-88, SECT LEADER & PROF MED CHEM/NATURAL PROD, FLA A&M UNIV, 88- *Personal Data:* b India, Mar 3, 34; m 67, Betty NeSmith; c Sunjai. *Educ:* Agra Univ, BSc, 54; Univ Rajasthan, BPharm, 57; Panjab Univ, India, MPharm, 60; Univ Nebr, MS, 63; Univ Colo, PhD(pharmacog), 66. *Honors & Awards:* Lederle Fac Award, 75. *Concurrent Pos:* Vis prof, Univ Panama, 77-78 & Univ Benin, Nigeria, 81-82. *Mem:* Am Pharmaceut Asn; Acad Pharmaceut Sci; NY Acad Sci; Am Soc Pharmacog; Sigma Xi; Am Asn Col Pharm. *Res:* Evaluation of potential antisickling agents from natural and synthetic sources; phytochemistry. *Mailing Add:* Col Pharm Fla A&M Univ Tallahassee FL 32307

LAMBDIN, PARIS LEE, ENTOMOLOGY. *Current Pos:* PROF ENTOM, DEPT ENTOM & PLANT PATH, UNIV TENN, 74- *Personal Data:* b St Charles, Va, Oct 13, 41; m 64, Linda Price; c Miranda L & Michael L. *Educ:* Lincoln Mem Univ, BA, 64; Va Polytech Inst & State Univ, MS, 72, PhD(entom), 74. *Honors & Awards:* Sigma Xi Res Award, 73; Inst Res Award, 90. *Prof Exp:* Teacher biol, Bassett High Sch, 64-66. *Concurrent Pos:* Pres, Tenn Entom Soc, 95-96. *Mem:* Entom Soc Am. *Res:* Systematics of species in the superfamily Coccoidea; biological control of ornamental and forest insect pests. *Mailing Add:* Dept Entom & Plant Path Univ Tenn Knoxville TN 37901-1071. *Fax:* 423-974-4744; *E-Mail:* plambdin@utk.edu

LAMBE, JOHN JOSEPH, SOLID STATE PHYSICS. *Current Pos:* CONSULT, 86- *Personal Data:* b Cork, Ireland, Dec 1, 26; US citizen; m 50; c 2. *Educ:* Univ Mich, BSE, 48, MS, 50; Univ Md, PhD(physics), 54. *Prof Exp:* Eng physics, Airborne Instruments Lab, 48-51; physicist solid state physics, Naval Res Lab, 51-56; physicist microwave res, Univ Mich, 56-59; staff scientist solid state physics, Ford Motor Co, 59-79; consult, Jet Propulsion Lab, Pasadena, Calif, 79-86. *Mem:* Fel Am Phys Soc. *Res:* Solid state physics; magnetic resonance; luminescence; super conductivity; electron tunneling. *Mailing Add:* 205 224th Ave SE Redmond WA 98053

LAMBE, ROBERT CARL, plant pathology, for more information see previous edition

LAMBE, T(HOMAS) WILLIAM, GEOTECHNICAL ENGINEERING. *Current Pos:* from instr to asst prof soil mech, Mass Inst Technol, 45-52, assoc prof & dir, Soil Stabilization Lab, 52-59, prof geotech eng & head, Geotech Div, 59-69, Edmund K Turner prof, 69-81, EMER EDMUND K TURNER PROF CIVIL ENG, MASS INST TECHNOL, 81- *Personal Data:* b Raleigh, NC, Nov 28, 20; m 47. *Educ:* NC State Univ, BS, 42; Mass Inst Technol, SM, 44, ScD(soil mech), 48. *Honors & Awards:* Collingswood Prize, Am Soc Civil Engrs, 52, Arthur M Wellington Prize, 61 & 84, Norman Medal, 64, Terzaghi Lectr, 70 & Karl Terzaghi Award, 75; Desmond Fitzgerald Medal, Brit Soc Civil Engrs, 54 & 56; Rankine Lectr, Brit Inst Civil Engrs, 73; R P Davis Lectr, Univ WVa, 73; Terzaghi Mem Lectr, Istanbul, Turkey, 73; Moh Lectr, Taipei, Taiwan, 80, Indonesia & Singapore, 81; Ardaman Lectr, Univ Fla, 85; Shaw Lectr, NC State Univ, 85. *Prof Exp:* Struct detailer, Am Bridge Co, Pa, 42; field engr, Olsen Consult Engrs, Edenton, NC, 42; instr civil eng, Univ NH, 42-43; field engr airbase construct, US Navy, Brunswick, Maine, 43; struct & found engr, Univ Calif, San Francisco, 44; soil engr, Dames & Moore, San Francisco, 44-45. *Concurrent Pos:* Consult geotech eng, 45- *Mem:* Nat Acad Eng; hon mem Am Soc Civil Engrs; fel Brit Inst Civil Engrs; hon mem Venezuelan Soc Soil Mech & Found Eng; hon mem Southeast Asian Soc Geotech Eng. *Res:* Soil testing, stabilization and mineralogy; soil engineering; earth and rock dams. *Mailing Add:* 35250 Clay Gully Rd Myakka City FL 34251

LAMBE, THOMAS ANTHONY, OPERATIONS RESEARCH, ENGINEERING SCIENCE. *Current Pos:* ASSOC PROF, SCH PUB ADMIN, UNIV VICTORIA, 74- *Personal Data:* b Victoria, BC, Dec 27, 30; m 64. *Educ:* Univ BC, BASc, 52; Stanford Univ, MSc, 58, PhD(eng sci), 68. *Prof Exp:* Engr, Can Westinghouse, 52-54; res engr, BC Res Coun, 54-57, proj leader opers res, 58-65; assoc prof indust eng, Univ Toronto, 68-74. *Mem:* Can Oper Res Soc; Opers Res Soc Am. *Res:* Economic analysis of engineering systems, particularly the transportation and natural resource industries; decision theory and individual choice behavior. *Mailing Add:* Dept Pub Admin Univ Victoria Box 1700 HSD Bldg Rm 7326 Victoria BC V8W 2Y2 Can

LAMBECK, KURT, GEOPHYSICS. *Current Pos:* dir, 84-92, PROF GEOPHYS, RES SCH EARTH SCI, AUSTRALIAN NAT UNIV, 77- *Personal Data:* b Utrecht, Neth, Sept 20, 41; m 67, Bridget M Nicholls; c Alexis & Fiona. *Educ:* Univ NSW, BS, 63; Oxford Univ, PhD, 68, DSci, 76. *Hon Degrees:* DEng, Nat Tech Univ, Greece, 94. *Honors & Awards:* Macelwane Medal, Am Geophys Union, 76, Charles A Whitten Medal, 93; Sir Harold Jeffreys Lectr, Royal Astron Soc, 89; Alfred Wegener Medal, 97. *Prof Exp:* Geodesist, Smithsonian Astrophys Observ, 67-70; dir sci, Group Res Geodesie Spatiale, Observ Paris, 70-73; prof geophysics, Dept Earth Sci, Univ Paris, 73-77. *Concurrent Pos:* Assoc, Harvard Col Observ, 67-70; chmn, Bilateral Sci & Tech Progs, Dept Indust, Tech & Com; chmn, Comt Int Union Geodesy & Geophys Study Earth's Deep Interior. *Mem:* Fel Am Geophys Union; Australian Acad Sci; foreign mem Norweg Acad Sci & Lett; foreign mem Royal Neth Acad Art & Sci. *Mailing Add:* Res Sch Earth Sci Australian Nat Univ Canberra ACT 0200 Australia. *Fax:* 61-2-62495443

LAMBEK, JOACHIM, MATHEMATICS. *Current Pos:* Assoc prof, 54-63, PROF MATH, MCGILL UNIV, 63- *Personal Data:* b Leipzig, Ger, Dec 5, 22; nat Can; m 48; c 3. *Educ:* McGill Univ, BSc, 46, MSc, 47, PhD, 51. *Concurrent Pos:* Mem, Inst Advan Study, 59-60. *Mem:* Am Math Soc; Math Asn Am; Can Math Cong; Sigma Xi. *Res:* Algebra. *Mailing Add:* Dept Math Burnside Hall McGill Univ 805 Sherbrooke St W Montreal PQ H3A 2K6 Can. *Fax:* 514-398-3899

LAMBERG, STANLEY LAWRENCE, HEMATOLOGY, HISTOLOGY. *Current Pos:* from asst prof to assoc prof, 70-75, PROF MED LAB TECHNOL, STATE UNIV NY COL TECHNOL, FARMINGDALE, 75- *Personal Data:* b Brooklyn, NY, Oct 2, 33; m 63, Charlotte F Rothchild; c Steven K & Eric M. *Educ:* Brooklyn Col, BS, 55; Oberlin Col, MA, 57; Tufts Univ, MS, 62; NY Univ, PhD(biol), 68. *Honors & Awards:* Founder's Day Award, NY Univ, 69. *Prof Exp:* Teaching asst biol, Oberlin Col, 55-57; chief technician biochem, Sch Med, Cornell Univ, 57-58; res fel, Sch Med, Tufts Univ, 58-61; Nat Inst Dent Res fel, Col Dent, NY Univ, 61-66; lectr biol, City Col New York, 66-67; asst prof biol, Conolly Col, Long Island Univ, 67-70. *Concurrent Pos:* Asst res scientist, Guggenheim Inst Dent Res, NY Univ, 68-69; adj asst prof, Conolly Col, Long Island Univ, 70-73, adj assoc prof, 73-75, adj prof, 75-78; adj instr, 81-86, adj asst prof, 86-87, adj assoc prof, Suffolk Co Comt Col, 87- *Mem:* AAAS; NY Acad Sci; Sigma Xi; Nat Soc Histotechnol. *Res:* Mitochondrial phosphorylation reactions during embryonic development; effect of ultraviolet irradiation and various inhibitors and uncoupling reagents on mitochondrial phosphorylation reactions. *Mailing Add:* 3 Park Pl Hauppauge NY 11788-2106

LAMBERG-KARLOVSKY, CLIFFORD CHARLES, ANTHROPOLOGY, ARCHAEOLOGY. *Current Pos:* from asst prof to prof anthrop, 65-90, STEPHEN PHILLIPS PROF ARCHAEOL, HARVARD UNIV, 91-; CUR NEAR EASTERN ARCHAEOL, PEABODY MUS ARCHAEOL & ETHNOL, 69-; DIR, AM SCH PREHISTORIC RES, 92- *Personal Data:* b Praque, Czech, Oct 2, 37; m 59, Martha L Veale; c Karl E Othmar & Christopher W. *Educ:* Dartmouth Col, AB, 59; Univ Pa, MA, 64, PhD, 65. *Hon Degrees:* MA, Harvard Univ, 70. *Honors & Awards:* Reckitt Lectr, Brit Acad, 73. *Prof Exp:* Asst prof sociol & anthrop, Franklin & Marshall Col, 64-65. *Concurrent Pos:* Dir archaeol surv, Syria, 65, excavation projs, Tepe Yahya, Iran, 67-75, Saudia Arabia, 77-80, USSR, 90-91, Anau, Turkmenistan; NSF grant, 66-75, Nat Endowment Arts grant, 77-, Nat Endowment Humanities grant, 77-; trustee, Am Inst Iranian Studies, 68-, Am Sch Oriental Res, 69-71, Am Inst Yemeni Studies, 76-77; assoc, Columbia Univ, 69-; dir, Peabody Mus Archaeol & Ethnol, 77-90; Can lectr, Beersheva Univ, 93. *Mem:* Fel Soc Antiquaries Gt Brit & Ireland; Am Anthrop Asn; AAAS; NY Acad Sci; Soc Am Archaeol; Archeol Inst Am; Am Acad Arts & Sci. *Res:* Ancient civilization; archaeological surveys and excavations in Iran, Saudi Arabia, Syria and Central Asia. *Mailing Add:* 22 Stevens Rd Melrose MA 02176-2114

LAMBERSON, HAROLD VINCENT, JR, MEDICINE. *Current Pos:* ASSOC PROF PATH, STATE UNIV NY, HSC SYRACUSE, 85- *Personal Data:* b Albany, NY, July 29, 45. *Educ:* Union Col, Schenectady, NY, BS, 67, MS, 69; Albany Med Col, MD & PhD, 75. *Prof Exp:* asst prof path, asst dir clin path & dir, Diag Virol Lab & Microbiol Sect, Upstate Med Ctr, State Univ NY, 78-82, actg dir, Clin Immunol Sect, 80-81; DIR, AM RED CROSS BLOOD SERV, 82- *Mem:* Am Soc Clin Pathologists; Am Soc Microbiol. *Res:* Rapid laboratory diagnosis of infectious diseases; transfusion related viral infections; effects of blood donation on donor immune function. *Mailing Add:* American Red Cross Blood Serv 636 S Warren St Syracuse NY 13202-3304

LAMBERSON, LEONARD ROY, INDUSTRIAL & MANUFACTURING ENGINEERING. *Current Pos:* DEAN ENG, WESTERN MICH UNIV, KALAMAZOO, 89- *Personal Data:* b Stanwood, Mich, Nov 18, 37; m 75; c 3. *Educ:* Gen Motors Inst, BME, 61; NC State Univ, MS, 63; Tex A&M Univ, PhD(indust eng), 67. *Honors & Awards:* Craig Award, Am Soc Qual Control, 78. *Prof Exp:* Prod foreman, Chevrolet Div, Gen Motors Corp, 61-64; from asst prof to prof indust eng, Gen Motors Inst, 64-70, chmn dept, 69-70; asst prof, Tex A&M Univ, 65-68; assoc prof, Wayne State Univ, 70-79, prof indust eng, 79-89, chmn dept, 82-89. *Concurrent Pos:* Reliability Engr, US Army Tank Auto Command, 77-78. *Mem:* Inst Indust Engrs; Am Soc Qual Control; Am Soc Eng Educ. *Res:* Development of techniques and procedures to improve the reliability of commercial products. *Mailing Add:* Dean Eng Western Mich Univ Kalamazoo MI 49008-3804

LAMBERSON, ROLAND H, ECOLOGICAL MODELLING, CONSERVATION BIOLOGY. *Current Pos:* PROF MATH, HUMBOLDT STATE UNIV, 80- *Personal Data:* m 90, Michele Olsen; c Robyn (Verkamp) & Laurie (O'Keeffe). *Educ:* Hastings Col, BA, 63; Univ Wyo, MS, 65; Univ Northern Colo, DA, 74. *Prof Exp:* Chmn, Physics Dept, Minot State Col, 65-67; asst prof math, Hastings Col, 67-74; chmn, Math Dept, Des Moines Area Community Col, 74-80. *Concurrent Pos:* Vis prof math, Univ BC, 79-80, 87, Univ Perugia, Italy, 82, Univ Natal, SAfrica, 93. *Mem:* Resource Modeling Asn (pres, 85-86, exec secy, 89-); Math Asn Am; Soc Conserv Biol; Soc Math Biol. *Res:* Development of mathematical models for viability analysis or management of threatened or endangered species particularly the northern spotted owl and other forest dwelling species. *Mailing Add:* Math Dept Humboldt State Univ Arcata CA 95521. *Fax:* 707-826-3140; *E-Mail:* Lambersonr@axe.humboldt.edu

LAMBERT, ALAN L, MATHEMATICS. *Current Pos:* PROF MATH, UNIV NC, CHARLOTTE, 83- *Personal Data:* b New York, NY, Nov 28, 43. *Educ:* Univ Miami, BS, 66, MS, 67; Univ Mich, PhD, 70. *Mem:* Am Math Soc; Irish Math Soc. *Res:* Properties of composition operators. *Mailing Add:* Math Dept Univ NC Charlotte NC 28223-0001

LAMBERT, BRIAN KERRY, INDUSTRIAL ENGINEERING. *Current Pos:* Asst prof, 67-71, ASSOC PROF INDUST ENG, TEX TECH UNIV, 71- *Personal Data:* b Spokane, Wash, Nov 21, 41; m 63; c 2. *Educ:* Tex Tech Col, BS, 64, MS, 66, PhD(indust eng), 67. *Mem:* Soc Mfg Engrs; Inst Indust Engrs; Am Soc Eng Educ. *Res:* Manufacturing research and development, specifically machining operations research and systems analysis, specifically reliability. *Mailing Add:* Dept Indust Eng MSC 4230 NMex State Univ PO Box 30001 Las Cruces NM 88003

LAMBERT, CHARLES CALVIN, DEVELOPMENTAL BIOLOGY, REPRODUCTIVE BIOLOGY. *Current Pos:* from asst prof to assoc prof, 70-79, PROF ZOOL, CALIF STATE UNIV, FULLERTON, 79- *Personal Data:* b Rockford, Ill, Apr 10, 35; m 65; c 2. *Educ:* San Diego State Univ, BA, 64, MS, 66; Univ Wash, PhD(zool), 70. *Prof Exp:* NIH traineeship, Univ Wash, 70. *Concurrent Pos:* Vis investr, Friday Harbor Labs, 74-, Hopkins Marine Sta, 78, Bermuda Biol Sta, 80, Shimoda Marine Res Ctr, 82 & Kewalo Marine Lab, 85; vis prof, Friday Harbor Labs, 81 & Shimoda Marine Res Ctr (UNESCO/ICRO course), 82. *Mem:* Am Soc Zoologists; Soc Develop Biol; AAAS; Am Soc Cell Biol; Int Soc Develop Biol; Int Cell Res Orgn. *Res:* Development and physiology of marine invertebrates. *Mailing Add:* Dept Biol Calif State Univ-Fullerton Fullerton CA 92634

LAMBERT, DAVID L, ASTRONOMY. *Current Pos:* Prof, 69, ISABEL MCCUTCHEON HARTE CENT PROF ASTRON, UNIV TEX, 74- *Educ:* Univ Col Oxford, BS; Balliol Col, PhD. *Honors & Awards:* Dannie Heineman Prize, Am Astron Soc, 87. *Concurrent Pos:* Res fel, Calif Inst Technol, Pasadena & Mt Wilson Palomar Observ; Guggenheim fel & vis Erskine fel, Univ Canterbury, NZ, 85. *Mem:* Fel Royal Astron Soc; Am Astron Soc; Int Astron Union. *Res:* Astronomy. *Mailing Add:* Dept Astron Univ Tex Austin TX 78712-1083

LAMBERT, DIANE, MATHEMATICAL STATISTICS. *Current Pos:* RES SUPVR & DISTINGUISHED MEM TECH STAFF, BELL LABS, LUCENT TECHNOL, 96- *Personal Data:* US citizen. *Educ:* Univ Rochester, PhD(statist), 79. *Prof Exp:* From asst prof to assoc prof statist, Carnegie-Mellon Univ, 80-86. *Concurrent Pos:* Adv panel mem, Statist Income Div, US Internal Revenue Serv, 80-88; vis assoc prof statist, Univ Chicago, 84-86; assoc ed, J Am Statist Asn, 84-90, ed, 95-97; bd mem, Bd Math Sci, Nat Res Coun, 90-93; bd dir, Am Statist Asn, 96-97. *Mem:* Fel Inst Math Statist (exec secy, 90-93); fel Am Statist Asn; Int Statist Inst. *Res:* Developing, analyzing and applying innovative statistical models for nonstandard applications such as the risk of disclosure in publicly released databases and the probability of detecting low levels of environmental contaminants. *Mailing Add:* AT&T Bell Labs Rm 2C-256 600 Mountain Ave Murray Hill NJ 07974-2070. *E-Mail:* dl@bell-labs.com

LAMBERT, EDWARD HOWARD, MEDICAL PHYSIOLOGY, NEUROMUSCULAR DISORDERS. *Current Pos:* PROF NEUROL, UNIV MINN MED SCH, 85- *Personal Data:* b Minneapolis, Minn, Aug 30, 15; m 40, 75. *Educ:* Univ Ill, BS, 36, MS, 38, MD, 39, PhD(physiol), 44. *Honors & Awards:* Presidential Cert Merit, 47; Tuttle Award, Aerospace Med Asn, 52. *Prof Exp:* Instr med technol, Herzl Jr Col, 41-42; assoc med, Off Sci Res & Develop, Col Med, Univ Ill, 42-43; res asst, 43-45, from instr to prof physiol, 45-58, prof physiol, Mayo Grad Sch Med, Univ Minn, 58-73, prof physiol & neurol, Mayo Med Sch, 73-85. *Concurrent Pos:* Consult, Mayo Clin, 45-85; mem pub adv groups, NIH; prin investr, NIH grant, 81- *Mem:* Am Acad Neurol; Soc Neurosci; Am Physiol Soc; Aerospace Med Asn; Am Asn Electromyography & Electrodiag (pres, 58); hon mem Am Neurol Asn. *Res:* Neurophysiology; neuromuscular disorders in man; electromyography; neuromuscular transmission. *Mailing Add:* Dept Physiol & Neurol Mayo Med Sch Mayo Clin Guggenheim 8 Rochester MN 55905-0001

LAMBERT, FRANCIS LINCOLN, PHYSIOLOGY. *Current Pos:* asst prof biol, 55-61, assoc prof physiol & biophys, 61-80, prof & chmn biol sci, 80-84, PROF PHYSIOL & BIOPHYS, UNION COL, NY, 85- *Personal Data:* b Staunton, Va, Oct 8, 23; m 67; c 2. *Educ:* George Washington Univ, BS, 49, MS, 51; Harvard Univ, PhD(biol), 58. *Prof Exp:* Instr zool, George Washington Univ, 49-52. *Concurrent Pos:* Jacques Loeb assoc marine biol, Rockefeller Inst, 60-61; educ consult, US Agency Int Develop, India, 65-68. *Mem:* AAAS; Am Soc Zool; Sigma Xi. *Res:* Invertebrate physiology; cellular neurophysiology. *Mailing Add:* 720 Riverside Ave Scotia NY 12302-1436

LAMBERT, FRANK LEWIS, ORGANIC CHEMISTRY. *Current Pos:* from asst prof to prof, 48-80, EMER PROF CHEM, OCCIDENTAL COL, 81-; SCI CONSULT, GETTY CONSERV INST, 82- *Personal Data:* b Minneapolis, Minn, July 10, 18; m 43, Bernice Webster. *Educ:* Harvard Univ, BA, 39; Univ Chicago, PhD(org chem), 42. *Prof Exp:* Res & develop chemist, Edwal Labs, Ill, 42-43, develop chemist, 43-44, head develop dept, 46-47; instr chem, Univ Calif, Los Angeles, 47-48. *Concurrent Pos:* NSF fac fel, 57-58, 70-71. *Mem:* Am Chem Soc. *Res:* Polarography of organic halogen compounds; halogenation of organic compounds. *Mailing Add:* 2834 Lewis Dr La Verne CA 91750-4308

LAMBERT, GEORGE, VETERINARY MICROBIOLOGY. *Current Pos:* RETIRED. *Personal Data:* b Etobicoke, Ont, Oct 8, 23; US citizen; m 48; c 3. *Educ:* Univ Guelph, DVM, 47; Iowa State Univ, MS, 66. *Prof Exp:* Instr vet path, Ont Vet Col, Univ Guelph, 47-48; asst prof, WVa Univ, 48-50; coop agt, Univ Wis & USDA, 50-53; asst state vet epidemiol, Va Dept Agr, 53-57; res vet bact, Nat Animal Dis Lab, 57-65, res virol, 65-67; asst dir biol dept, Diamond Labs, Inc, 67-70; chief virol res lab, Nat Animal Dis Ctr, 70-75, asst dir, 75-80, assoc dir, 80-85 res leader immunol res, 85-89. *Mem:* Am Vet Med Asn; US Animal Health Asn; Conf Res Workers Animal Dis. *Res:* Administration of animal disease research. *Mailing Add:* 1375 231st Rd Boone IA 50036

LAMBERT, GLENN FREDERICK, BIOCHEMISTRY. *Current Pos:* RETIRED. *Personal Data:* b Columbus, Ohio, Nov 21, 18; m 45, Mary L Greager; c Sharon & Susan. *Educ:* DePauw Univ, AB, 40, Univ Ill, PhD(biochem), 44. *Prof Exp:* Spec res asst, Univ Ill, 45-46; res chemist, Abbott Labs, 46-60, sr res pharmacologist, 61-73, sr res chemist, 73-89. *Concurrent Pos:* Mem, Coun Arteriosclerosis & Coun Thrombosis, Am Heart Asn. *Mem:* Am Chem Soc; Sigma Xi. *Res:* Biochemistry and nutrition of amino acids; fat emulsions for intravenous therapy; atherosclerosis; thrombolytic drugs; high pressure liquid chromatography separation and analysis of peptides. *Mailing Add:* 318 Judge Ave Waukegan IL 60085

LAMBERT, HELEN HAYNES, ENDOCRINOLOGY. *Current Pos:* asst prof, 70-75, ASSOC PROF BIOL, NORTHEASTERN UNIV, 75- *Personal Data:* b Baton Rouge, La, July 25, 39; div; c 2. *Educ:* Wellesley Col, BA, 61; Univ NH, MS, 63, PhD(zool), 69. *Prof Exp:* Instr zool, Univ NH, 67-68; asst prof biol, Simmons Col, 69-70. *Concurrent Pos:* Mem, Sex Info & Educ Coun US. *Mem:* AAAS; Sigma Xi; Am Inst Biol Sci; Am Soc Zool. *Res:* Environmental factors affecting reproduction and sexual behavior; sex determination and development of sex differences. *Mailing Add:* Dept Biol Northeastern Univ 360 Huntington Ave Boston MA 02115-5096

LAMBERT, HOWARD W, TOPOLOGY. *Current Pos:* PROF MATH, WESTERN NMEX UNIV, 80- *Personal Data:* b Oakland, Calif, Aug 2, 37; m 57; c 3. *Educ:* Univ Calif, Berkeley, BA, 60; Iowa State Univ, MS, 61; Univ Utah, PhD(math), 66. *Prof Exp:* From asst prof to prof math, Univ Iowa, 66-80. *Mem:* Am Math Soc; Math Asn Am; Am Asn Univ Professors; Soc Indust & Appl Math. *Res:* Upper semi-continuous decompositions of topological spaces, 3-manifolds. *Mailing Add:* 203 Mariquita Rd Corrales NM 87048

LAMBERT, JACK LEEPER, ANALYTICAL CHEMISTRY, INORGANIC CHEMISTRY. *Current Pos:* from instr to prof, 50-88, EMER PROF CHEM, KANS STATE UNIV, 88- *Personal Data:* b Pittsburg, Kans, Mar 2, 18; wid; c John, Paul, Patricia & Michael. *Educ:* Kans State Teachers Col, Pittsburg, BA & MS, 47; Okla State Univ, PhD(chem), 50. *Prof Exp:* Instr chem, Kans State Teachers Col, Pittsburg, 47-48; asst, Okla State Univ, 48-50. *Concurrent Pos:* Assoc prog dir, NSF, Washington, DC, 65-66. *Mem:* Am Chem Soc; Sigma Xi; fel AAAS. *Res:* Methods research in analytical chemistry; reagents for trace analysis in air and water; insoluble, demand-type disinfectants for water. *Mailing Add:* 800 Ratone St Manhattan KS 66502. *Fax:* 785-532-6666

LAMBERT, JAMES LEBEAU, organic chemistry, analytical chemistry, for more information see previous edition

LAMBERT, JAMES MORRISON, NUCLEAR PHYSICS. *Current Pos:* from asst prof to assoc prof, 64-74, PROF PHYSICS, GEORGETOWN UNIV, 74- *Personal Data:* b Chicago, Ill, Feb 18, 28; m 53; c 3. *Educ:* Johns Hopkins Univ, BA, 55, PhD(physics), 61. *Prof Exp:* Instr physics, Johns Hopkins Univ, 60-61; asst prof, Univ Mich, 61-63. *Concurrent Pos:* Res consult, Naval Res Lab, 66- *Mem:* Am Phys Soc; AAAS; Sigma Xi. *Res:* Experimental medium energy nuclear physics; nuclear reaction studies using particle accelerators; experimental surface physics. *Mailing Add:* Dept Physics Georgetown Univ Washington DC 20007

LAMBERT, JEAN WILLIAM, AGRONOMY. *Current Pos:* from asst prof to prof, 46-82, EMER PROF AGRON & PLANT GENETICS, UNIV MINN, ST PAUL, 82- *Personal Data:* b Ewing, Nebr, June 10, 14; m 43; c 2. *Educ:* Univ Nebr, BS, 40; Ohio State Univ, MS, 42, PhD(agron), 45. *Honors & Awards:* Agron Achievement Award, Am Soc Agron, 83. *Prof Exp:* Instr agron, Ohio State Univ, 43-45. *Concurrent Pos:* Consult, Am Soybean Asn, 63, Food & Agr Orgn, Hungary, 75, US Info Agency, Romania, 76, Agr Corp Am, USSR, 79 & Food & Agr Orgn, Poland, 80; res consult, Chilean Agr Prog, Rockefeller Found, 64; partic, Vis Scientist Prog, Am Soc Agron; tech ed, Agron J, 71-73. *Mem:* Hon life mem Am Soybean Asn; fel Crop Sci Soc Am; Sigma Xi. *Res:* Bromegrass cultural research; varietal improvement in barley and soybeans; barley and soybean genetics. *Mailing Add:* 2171 Carter Ave St Paul MN 55108

LAMBERT, JERRY ROY, AGRICULTURAL ENGINEERING, AGRICULTURAL INFORMATION SYSTEMS. *Current Pos:* from asst prof to assoc prof, 64-72, PROF AGR ENG, CLEMSON UNIV, 72-; COMPUT COORDR, 85- *Personal Data:* b Benton, Ill, Sept 16, 36; div; c 3. *Educ:* Univ Fla, BAgrE, 58, MS, 62; NC State Col, PhD(agr eng), 64. *Prof Exp:* Design eng trainee, Soil Conserv Serv, USDA, 58-60. *Mem:* Am Soc Eng Educ; Am Soc Agr Engrs. *Res:* Water relations of plants; evapotranspiration; water movement in soils; simulation of agricultural systems; microcomputer applications to agriculture information delivery systems. *Mailing Add:* PO Box 1332 Clemson SC 29633

LAMBERT, JOHN B(OYD), METALLURGY & PHYSICAL METALLURGICAL ENGINEERING, MATERIALS SCIENCE ENGINEERING. *Current Pos:* CONSULT, 92- *Personal Data:* b Billings, Mont, July 5, 29; wid; c William, Thomas, Stephanie, Patricia, Catherine & Karen. *Educ:* Princeton Univ, BS, 51; Univ Wis, PhD(chem eng), 56. *Honors & Awards:* Co-Recipient, Charles Hatchett Award, Inst Metals, 86. *Prof Exp:* Res engr, Indust & Biochem Dept, E I du Pont de Nemours & Co, 56-63, sr res engr, Pigments Dept, Del, 63-68; mkt mgr, Fansteel Inc, 69-71, plant mgr, Metals Div, 71-72, mgr mfg eng, V R Wesson Div, 73-80, corp tech dir & vpres, 80-87, mkt mgr, Metals Div, 87-88, gen mgr, 88-90, corp tech dir, 91-92. *Concurrent Pos:* Instr, Am Chem Soc. *Mem:* Am Chem Soc; Am Inst Chem Engrs; Electrochem Soc; Am Soc Metals; Sigma Xi; Soc Mfg Engrs. *Res:* Inorganic colloid chemistry; physical and powder metallurgy; surface chemistry, drying, machining and metal cutting; ceramic cutting tools; technical management; refractory metals, including tantalum, niobium, and hard metals. *Mailing Add:* 617 E Greenbriar Lane Lake Forest IL 60045-3214. *Fax:* 847-295-1376; *E-Mail:* drjbl@aol.com

LAMBERT, JOSEPH B, ORGANIC CHEMISTRY. *Current Pos:* From asst prof to prof, Northwestern Univ, 65-91, dir, Integrated Sci Prog, 82-85, chmn dept, 86-89, CLARE HAMILTON HALL PROF CHEM, NORTHWESTERN UNIV, 91- *Personal Data:* b Ft Sheridan, Ill, July 4, 40; m 67, Mary W Pulliam; c Laura K, Alice P & Joseph C. *Educ:* Yale Univ, BS, 62; Calif Inst Technol, PhD(org chem), 65. *Honors & Awards:* Eastman Kodak Award, 65; Nat Fresenius Award, 76; Norris Award for Teaching Chem, Am Chem Soc, 87; Fryxell Award in Sci Archaeol, Soc Am Archaeol, 89; Nat Catalysis Award, Chem Mfrs Asn, 93. *Concurrent Pos:* Alfred P Sloan Found fel, 68-70; Guggenheim fel, 73; vis assoc, Brit Mus Res Lab, 73; vis scholar, Polish Acad Sci, 81 & Chinese Acad Sci, 88; Nat Acad Sci exchange fel, 85; ed-in-chief, J Phys Org Chem, 86-; USAF Off Sci Res fel, 90; chmn, Div Hist Chem, Am Chem Soc, 96-; distinguished lectr, Sigma Xi, 97-98. *Mem:* Fel AAAS; Sigma Xi; Am Chem Soc; fel Brit Interplanetary Soc; Soc Archeol Sci (pres int off, 86-87); fel Japan Soc Prom Sci. *Res:* Nuclear magnetic resonance spectroscopy, organic reaction mechanisms, organosilicon and organotin chemistry, applications of analytical chemistry to archaeology. *Mailing Add:* Dept Chem Northwestern Univ 2145 Sheridan Rd Evanston IL 60208-3113

LAMBERT, JOSEPH MICHAEL, APPROXIMATION THEORY, NUMERICAL METHODS. *Current Pos:* from asst prof to assoc prof math, Pa State Univ, 70-81, asst dean, Col Sci, 79-82, actg head, 80-82, ASSOC PROF & DEPT HEAD COMPUT SCI, PA STATE UNIV, 82- *Personal Data:* b Philadelphia, Pa, Nov 19, 42; m 73; c 3. *Educ:* Drexel Univ, BS, 65; Cornell Univ, MA, 67; Purdue Univ, PhD(math), 70. *Concurrent Pos:* Vis assoc prof math, Univ Tenn, Knoxville, 77-78; vis assoc prof comput sci, Cornell Univ, Ithaca, 86-87. *Mem:* Am Math Soc; Asn Comput Mach; Inst Elec & Electronics Engrs. *Res:* Functional analysis; approximation theory; numerical analysis; operations research; software metrics. *Mailing Add:* Dept Comput Sci & Eng Pa State Univ 310 Pond Lab University Park PA 16802-0001

LAMBERT, JOSEPH PARKER, DENTISTRY. *Current Pos:* RETIRED. *Personal Data:* b Bronte, Tex, Oct 6, 21; m 45; c 5. *Educ:* Baylor Univ, DDS, 52. *Prof Exp:* Instr, Col Dent, Baylor Univ, 52-56, prof prosthetics & chmn dept, 56-94. *Mem:* Am Dent Asn. *Mailing Add:* 3707 Gaston Suite 602 Dallas TX 75246

LAMBERT, LAURIE E, IMMUNOLOGY. *Current Pos:* SR ASSOC SCIENTIST, MARION MERRELL DOW, 93- *Personal Data:* b Springfield, Mass. *Educ:* Univ Wis, PhD(immunol), 87. *Res:* Immunology. *Mailing Add:* Dept Immunol Marion Merrell Dow 2110 E Galbraith Rd Cincinnati OH 45215-6300

LAMBERT, MARY PULLIAM, BIOCHEMISTRY, NEUROBIOLOGY. *Current Pos:* NIH res fel, 82-83, RES ASSOC, NORTHWESTERN UNIV, 83- *Personal Data:* b Birmingham, Ala, Apr 27, 44; m 67, Joseph B; c Laura, Alice & Joseph. *Educ:* Birmingham-Southern Col, BS, 66; Northwestern Univ, PhD(biochem), 71. *Prof Exp:* Instr biochem, Northwestern Univ, Ill, 70-72, fel reproductive biol, 81-82. *Mem:* Sigma Xi; Soc Neurosci. *Res:* Neurotransmitter receptors; receptor biochemistry; receptor development; mechanism of receptor function; Alzheimer's disease. *Mailing Add:* Dept Neurobiol & Physiol Northwestern Univ Evanston IL 60208. *Fax:* 847-491-5210

LAMBERT, MAURICE C, PHYSICAL CHEMISTRY. *Current Pos:* RETIRED. *Personal Data:* b Roosevelt, Utah, Apr 14, 18; m 42; c 5. *Educ:* Brigham Young Univ, BS, 39, MA, 41. *Prof Exp:* Assoc chemist, Indust Lab, Mare Island Naval Shipyard, 41-46; chemist, Hanford Atomic Prod Oper, 48-64; sr chemist, Gen Elec Co, 64; sr res scientist, Battelle Northwest Labs, 65-70; sr res scientist, Westinghouse Hanford Co, 70-82. *Mem:* Am Chem Soc; Soc Appl Spectros. *Res:* X-ray spectrometry, absorptiometry and diffraction; atomic absorption and flame emission spectrometry; separations of trace elements; gas-solid reactions; properties of inorganic oxides; fused salt studies; surface analysis by electron spectroscopy; automation of analytical techniques. *Mailing Add:* 2021 Stevens Dr No C1 Richland WA 99352

LAMBERT, MURIEL WIKSWO, DNA REPAIR, CHROMATIN STRUCTURE IN DNA REPAIR. *Current Pos:* assoc, 76-78, from asst prof to assoc prof, 78-91, PROF PATH, UNIV MED & DENT, NJ MED SCH, 91-, PROF MED, DIV DERMAT, 93- *Personal Data:* b Teaneck, NJ. *Educ:* Sweet Briar Col, AB, 66; Northwestern Univ, PhD(biol sci), 70. *Prof Exp:* NSF fel, Northwestern Univ, 66-70; NIH fel, Harvard Univ, Sch Dent med, 70-72, res fel, Sch Med, Yale Univ, 72-76. *Concurrent Pos:* Prin investr, NIH, 86-; mem, NIH Study Sect, Nat Inst Arthritis & Musculoskeletal & Skin Dis Res Core Ctr Grants, 92- *Mem:* Am Asn Cancer Res; Environ Mutagen Soc; Soc Invest Dermat; Am Soc Photobiol; Fedn Am Soc Exp Biol; Am Acad Dermat. *Res:* DNR repair of specific types of damage with emphasis on mammalian systems; the role of chromatin structure and protein DNA interaction on the repair process is being investigated; defects in these repair processes in certain genetic diseases such as xeroderma pigmentosum and Fanconi anemia. *Mailing Add:* Dept Path Med Sch Univ Med & Dent NJ 185 S Orange Ave Newark NJ 07103. *Fax:* 973-982-7293

LAMBERT, PAUL WAYNE, GEOMORPHOLOGY, PHOTOGRAPHY. *Current Pos:* ADJ PROF GEOG, SOUTHERN METHODIST UNIV, 97- *Personal Data:* b Ft Worth, Tex, Oct 27, 37; m 59, Janice M O'Neil; c Dean P. *Educ:* Tex Tech Univ, BA, 59; Univ NMex, MS, 61, PhD(geol), 68. *Prof Exp:* Geologist, Texaco Inc, NMex, 61-62; asst prof geol, Cent Mo State Col, 65-68; assoc prof, WTex State Univ, 68-70; geologist, Dept Prehist, Nat Inst Anthrop & Hist, Mex, 72-73; geologist, US Geol Surv, 73-81; assoc prof geol, WTex A&M Univ, 81-96. *Concurrent Pos:* Res grants, Geol Soc Am & Sigma Xi, 68-69 & NSF, 69-70; adj cur geol, Panhandle-Plains Hist Mus, WTex A&M Univ, Canyon, 94- *Mem:* Geol Soc Am; Soc Am Archaeol; Asn Am Geographers; Royal Geog Soc; Explorers Club. *Res:* Photographic documentation of physical and cultural geographic features in western United States and Mexico. *Mailing Add:* 9191 Garland Rd No 531 Dallas TX 75218. *Fax:* 806-656-2928

LAMBERT, REGINALD MAX, BACTERIOLOGY, IMMUNOLOGY. *Current Pos:* assoc dir, Blood Group Res Unit, 55-64 & 67-76, ASSOC PROF MICROBIOL, SCH MED, STATE UNIV NY, BUFFALO, 67- *Personal Data:* b Delta, Ohio, Feb 25, 26; m 52; c 3. *Educ:* Butler Univ, BA, 50; Univ Buffalo, MA, 52, PhD(bact, immunol), 55. *Prof Exp:* Asst bact & immunol, Sch Med, State Univ NY Buffalo, 51-55, instr, 55-57, assoc, 57-59, asst prof, 59-64; asst prof path, Col Med, Univ Fla, 64-67. *Concurrent Pos:* Consult, E J Meyer Mem Hosp, Buffalo, 58, 60-63 & 67- & Buffalo Gen Hosp, 63-64; dir blood bank, Shands Teaching Hosp, Univ Fla, 64-67; dir, Buffalo Regional Red Cross Bldg Prog, 73- *Mem:* AAAS; Am Soc Microbiol; Int Soc Blood Transfusion; Int Soc Hemat; Sigma Xi. *Res:* Blood groups; immunohematology; transfusion genetics. *Mailing Add:* 233 Shermin Hall State Univ NY, 3435 Main St Buffalo NY 14214

LAMBERT, RICHARD BOWLES, JR, PHYSICAL OCEANOGRAPHY. *Current Pos:* assoc prog dir, 84-91, PROG DIR PHYS OCEANOG, NSF, 91- *Personal Data:* b Clinton, Mass, Apr 20, 39; m 64, Sherrill Smith; c Lisa B. *Educ:* Lehigh Univ, AB, 61; Brown Univ, ScM, 64, PhD(physics), 66. *Prof Exp:* Fulbright fel aerodyn, Munich Tech, 66-67; from asst prof to assoc prof oceanog, Univ RI, 67-75; prog dir phys oceanog, NSF, 75-77; res oceanogr, Sci Appln Inc, 77-84, mgr, Ocean Physics Div, 79-81, asst vpres, 80-82, sr res oceanogr, 82-84, assoc prog dir oceanog, 84-90. *Mem:* Am Geophys Union; Oceanog Soc. *Res:* Hydrodynamic stability; oceanic turbulence; diffusion energy transfer; air-sea interaction; program management. *Mailing Add:* 11312 Gainsborough Rd Potomac MD 20854. *E-Mail:* rlambert@nsf.gov

LAMBERT, ROBERT F, ELECTRICAL ENGINEERING, ACOUSTICS. *Current Pos:* Asst elec eng, Univ Minn, Minneapolis, 48-49, from instr to assoc prof, 49-59, assoc dean, Inst Technol, 67-68, PROF ELEC ENG, UNIV MINN, MINNEAPOLIS, 59- *Personal Data:* b Warroad, Minn, Mar 14, 24; m 51; c 3. *Educ:* Univ Minn, BEE, 48, MS, 49, PhD, 53. *Honors & Awards:* John Johnson Mem Educ Award, Inst Noise Control Engrs, 84. *Concurrent Pos:* Vis asst prof, Mass Inst Technol, 53-55; vis scientist, III Phys Inst, Univ Goettingen, Ger, 64 & NASA Langley Res Ctr, Hampton, Va, 79; acoust consult. *Mem:* Am Soc Eng Educ; fel Acoust Soc Am; fel Inst Elec & Electronics Engrs; Sigma Xi; Inst Noise Control Engrs. *Res:* Signal analysis including random processes and noise; acoustics including flow ducts, wave filters, porous materials, wave propagation, noise control; communication technology including ink jet printing, ultrasonic scanning, speech and electro-acoustics; random processes. *Mailing Add:* Dept Elec Eng Inst Technol Univ Minn 200 Union St SE Minneapolis MN 55455

LAMBERT, ROBERT HENRY, ATOMIC PHYSICS. *Current Pos:* from asst prof to assoc prof, 61-68, PROF PHYSICS, UNIV NH, 68- *Personal Data:* b Bayshore, NY, Nov 3, 30; div; c 2. *Educ:* St Lawrence Univ, BS, 52; Harvard Univ, MS, 54, PhD(physics), 63. *Prof Exp:* Instr physics, Univ NH, 55-57; asst, Harvard Univ, 57-60. *Concurrent Pos:* Cent Univ res grants, Univ NH, 62-63, 65-66; NSF grant, 65-71. *Mem:* Am Phys Soc. *Res:* Measurement of hyperfine structure using optical pumping. *Mailing Add:* Dept Physics De Meritt Hall Univ NH Durham NH 03824. *Fax:* 603-862-2998

LAMBERT, ROBERT JOHN, PLANT GENETICS. *Current Pos:* from res asst to res assoc, 58-64, from instr to assoc prof, 64-76, PROF PLANT BREEDING & GENETICS, UNIV ILL, URBANA, 76- *Personal Data:* b Faribault, Minn, Mar 14, 27. *Educ:* Univ Minn, BS, 52, MS, 58; Univ Ill, PhD(plant breeding, genetics), 63. *Prof Exp:* Res asst plant breeding & genetics, Univ Minn, 56-58. *Concurrent Pos:* Supvr world collection of maize mutants, Maize Genetics Coop. *Mem:* AAAS; Crop Sci Soc Am; Genetics Soc Am; Am Asn Cereal Chemists. *Res:* Investigations of plant geometry of maize and breeding in high yield environment; selection and development of modified protein maize strains. *Mailing Add:* Dept Crop Sci Univ Ill 1102 S Goodwin Urbana IL 61801

LAMBERT, ROGER GAYLE, PLANT PHYSIOLOGY. *Current Pos:* RETIRED. *Personal Data:* b Minneapolis, Minn, Jan 22, 30; m 56; c 3. *Educ:* Univ Minn, BS, 53, MS, 57, PhD(plant physiol), 61. *Prof Exp:* Instr plant physiol, Univ Minn, 57-61; from asst prof to prof, Univ Louisville, 61-93, from actg head to head, Dept Biol, 63-66. *Concurrent Pos:* Fel bot & plant path, Potato Virus Lab, Colo State Univ, 70-71. *Mem:* Am Soc Plant Physiol; Sigma Xi. *Res:* Plant competition and trophic structure of ecosystems. *Mailing Add:* RR 3 Box 305 Georgetown IN 47122

LAMBERT, ROGERS FRANKLIN, ORGANIC CHEMISTRY. *Current Pos:* PROF CHEM, RADFORD COL, 65- *Personal Data:* b Kamas, Utah, July 12, 29; m 51; c 4. *Educ:* Brigham Young Univ, BS, 53; Purdue Univ, PhD(org chem), 58. *Prof Exp:* Chemist, US Bur Mines, 53; res chemist, Ethyl Corp, 58-61; res supvr, Thiokol Chem Corp, 61-65. *Mem:* Am Chem Soc. *Res:* Polymers; chemical reductions; transition metal carbonyls; reactions of heterocyclics. *Mailing Add:* 1902 Eighth St Radford VA 24142

LAMBERT, ROYCE LEONE, SOILS, AGRONOMY. *Current Pos:* ASSOC PROF SOILS, CALIF POLYTECH STATE UNIV, SAN LUIS OBISPO, 69- *Personal Data:* b Coatesville, Ind, Nov 3, 33; m 53; c 3. *Educ:* Purdue Univ, Lafayette, BS, 64, MS, 66, PhD(soil physics), 70. *Concurrent Pos:* Soil conservationist, Nat Park Serv, 71. *Mem:* Am Soc Agron; Soil Sci Soc Am; Soil Conserv Soc Am. *Res:* Soil management. *Mailing Add:* Dept Soil Sci Calif Polytech State Univ San Luis Obispo CA 93407-0001

LAMBERT, WALTER PAUL, civil engineering, for more information see previous edition

LAMBERT, WILLIAM M, JR, MATHEMATICS. *Current Pos:* RETIRED. *Personal Data:* b Wausau, Wis, Apr 6, 36. *Educ:* Univ Wis, BA, 58; Univ Calif, Los Angeles, MA, 59, PhD(math), 65. *Prof Exp:* Teaching asst math, Univ Wis, 57-58; teaching asst, Univ Calif, Los Angeles, 59-60, res asst, 60-63; from asst prof to assoc prof, Loyola Univ, Calif, 63-69; assoc prof, Univ Detroit, 69-74; prof, Dept Math, Univ Costa Rica, 74-85. *Mem:* Math Asn Am; Asn Symbolic Logic. *Res:* Effective processes of general algebraic structures; metamathematics of algebra. *Mailing Add:* Apdo 111-2070 Sabanilla 2070 Montes de Oca Costa Rica

LAMBERTI, GARY ANTHONY, STREAM ECOLOGY, PLANT-HERBIVORE INTERACTIONS. *Current Pos:* ASSOC PROF BIOL, UNIV NOTRE DAME, 89- *Personal Data:* b Oakland, Calif, Oct 5, 53; m 90, Donna Packer. *Educ:* Univ Calif, Davis, BS, 75; Univ Calif, Berkeley, PhD(aquatic biol), 83. *Prof Exp:* Assoc, Ore State Univ, 84-86, res asst prof, 86-89. *Concurrent Pos:* Consult, Clear Lake Algae Res Unit, 76-77; prin investr, NSF, 90-93, US Environ Protection Agency, 92-; assoc ed, J NAm Benthological Soc, 91-94. *Mem:* Ecol Soc Am; NAm Benthological Soc; Am Inst Biol Sci; AAAS. *Res:* Ecology of streams and rivers; benthic communities the importance of algal-herbivore interactions; the retention and processing of nutrients and organic matter; the impacts of exotic species, especially zebra mussels. *Mailing Add:* Univ Notre Dame Dept Biol Sci 105 Galvin Life Sci Notre Dame IN 46556

LAMBERTI, JOSEPH W, PSYCHIATRY. *Current Pos:* asst prof, 63-69, ASSOC PROF PSYCHIAT, MED CTR, UNIV MO, COLUMBIA, 69- *Personal Data:* b Toronto, Ont, Dec 20, 29; m 55; c 6. *Educ:* Univ Ottawa, MD, 54; Royal Col Physicians & Surgeons Can, cert psychiat, 61. *Prof Exp:* Asst psychiatrist, Winnipeg Psychiat Inst, 60-61, sr psychiatrist, 61-63. *Concurrent Pos:* Dir consult serv & lectr, Med Ctr, Univ Mo, 63-67, consult, Peace Corps, 64- & Univ Press, 65- *Mem:* Am Psychiat Asn; corresp mem Can Psychiat Asn; Sigma Xi. *Res:* Treatment of common sexual disorders; study of antisocial behavior; study of affective disorders. *Mailing Add:* Dept Psychiat Univ Mo Columbia Med Sch One Hospital Dr Columbia MO 65201-5276

LAMBERTS, AUSTIN E, MARINE ZOOLOGY, NEUROSURGERY. *Current Pos:* INDEPENDENT RES, REEF ECOL, 73- *Personal Data:* b East Saugatuck, Mich, Nov 30, 14; div; c Catherine (LeGalley), Barbara (Law), Marcia & Conrad P. *Educ:* Calvin Col, AB, 36; Univ Mich, Ann Arbor, MD, 41, MS, 50; Am Bd Neurosurg, dipl, 52; Univ Hawaii, PhD(marine zool), 73. *Prof Exp:* Resident & instr neurosurg, Univ Mich, 45-50; pvt pract neurosurg, St Mary's Hosp, Grand Rapids, 50-68; teaching asst marine zool, Univ Hawaii, 69-73. *Concurrent Pos:* Consult neurosurg, St Mary's Hosp, Grand Rapids, 50-76; vol physician displaced dependents camp site 8, Africa, Asia, Caribbean & SAm; res grant, Nat Geog Soc, 74 & 78, Nat Sci Asn, 78. *Mem:* Fel Explorers Club; Am Asn Neurosurgeons; Cong Neurosurgeons; Am Med Asn. *Res:* Study of natural life cycles of reef corals and unexplained coral kills; coral growth using the dye alizarin; effects of pesticides on coral growth; collecting and identification of modern Pacific reef corals; cataloging. *Mailing Add:* 1520 Leffingwell NE Grand Rapids MI 49505

LAMBERTS, BURTON LEE, BIOCHEMISTRY. *Current Pos:* RETIRED. *Personal Data:* b Fremont, Mich, Oct 24, 19; m 60, B Elaine Rutherford; c Susan & James. *Educ:* Calvin Col, BS, 49; Mich State Univ, PhD(chem), 58. *Prof Exp:* Chemist, Northern Regional Res Lab, Ill, 51-54; asst chem, Mich State Univ, 55-58, instr, 58-60; chief biochemist, Dent Res Facil, Naval Dent Res Inst, 60-88. *Mem:* Am Chem Soc; Int Asn Dent Res. *Res:* Dental caries; salivary gland secretions; relationship of oral microbial products to periodontal disease. *Mailing Add:* 1320 Minard Lane Libertyville IL 60048

LAMBERTS, ROBERT L, PHOTOGRAPHIC OPTICS, PHYSICAL OPTICS. *Current Pos:* RETIRED. *Personal Data:* b Fremont, Mich, Sept 8, 26; m 51; Margaret Van Mouwerik; c Ruth (DuMont), Margaret (Bendroth), Nancy (Black), William J, Robert J & Peter J. *Educ:* Calvin Col, AB, 49; Univ Mich, MS, 51; Univ Rochester, PhD(optics), 69. *Prof Exp:* Res assoc, 51-80, sr res assoc, Kodak Res Labs, Eastman Kodak Co, 80-83; teaching, Roberts-Wesleyan Col, 83-84; teaching, Daystar Univ Col, Nairobi, Kenya, 84-85, Nazareth Col, Rochester, 86-89. *Concurrent Pos:* Partner, Sine Patterns, Penfield, NY. *Mem:* Fel Optical Soc Am. *Res:* Image structure of optical systems and photographic materials; physical optics. *Mailing Add:* 236 Henderson Dr Penfield NY 14526. *Fax:* 716-248-8323

LAMBERTSEN, CHRISTIAN JAMES, PHARMACOLOGY. *Current Pos:* from instr to assoc prof pharmacol, Univ Pa, 46-52, prof pharmacol & exp therapeut, 53-85, dir, Inst Environ Med, 68-85, EMER DISTINGUISHED PROF ENVIRON MED, MED CTR, UNIV PA, 85-, DIR, ENVIRON BIOMED RES DATA CTR, 85- *Personal Data:* b Westfield, NJ, May 15, 17; wid; c Christian, David, Richard & Bailey. *Educ:* Rutgers Univ, BS, 39; Univ Pa, MD, 43. *Hon Degrees:* DSc, Northwestern Univ, 77. *Honors & Awards:* Ocean Sci & Eng Award, Marine Technol Soc, 72; Environ Sci Award, NY Acad Sci, 74 & Aerospace Med Asn, 79; Boerema Award, Undersea & Hyperbaric Med Soc, 92. *Prof Exp:* Intern, Hosp Univ Pa, 43. *Concurrent Pos:* Markle scholar, 48-53; assoc med, Univ Hosp, Univ Pa, 48-77; mem, Panel Shipboard & Submarine Med, Off Secy Defense Res Develop Bd, 50-53; vis res assoc prof, Univ Col, London, 51-52; mem, Comt Undersea Warfare & Comt Naval Med Res, Nat Res Coun, 53-72 & panel underwater swimmers, 53-56; mem, Pharmacol Comt, Nat Bd Med Examrs, 54-55, basic sci secy bd, 54-; consult, US Army Chem Ctr, 55-59; consult & lectr, Off Surgeon Gen, USN, 57-60; consult neuropharmacol, Del State Hosp, 57-61; consult, Sci Adv Bd, USAF, 59-61, mem adv panel med sci, Off Secy Defense; chmn, Man in Space Comt, Space Sci Bd, Nat Acad Sci, 60-62, consult, 62-80; mem, US Oceanogr Adv Bd, 70-; chmn, Comt Manned Undersea Activ, Off Secy Navy; mem, Comt Undersea Physiol & Med, Nat Res Coun, 72- & Comt Hyperbaric Oxygenation; med adv, SubSea Int, Inc, US & Brit, 83-; mem, Radiation & Environ Health Working Group, NASA, 89-91, Life Sci Div, Environ Biomed Sci Working Group, 91- *Mem:* Nat Acad Eng; fel Am Soc Clin Pharmacol & Therapeut; Am Physiol Soc (pres, 54-55); Am Soc Clin Invest; Am Soc Pharmacol & Exp Therapeut; Am Col Clin Pharmacol & Chemother; Asn Am Med Cols; Europ Undersea Biomed Soc; Int Acad Astronaut; Int Astronaut Fedn; Sigma Xi. *Res:* Respiratory physiology and pharmacology; aerospace and diving medicine; breathing apparatus for underwater swimmers; granted 10 US patents. *Mailing Add:* Inst Environ Med Med Ctr Univ Pa 1 John Morgan Bldg 3620 Hamilton Walk Philadelphia PA 19104-6068

LAMBERTSEN, ELEANOR C, HEALTH SERVICES DELIVERY. *Current Pos:* RETIRED. *Prof Exp:* consult nursing & health serv, 88- *Mem:* Inst Med-Nat Acad Sci. *Mailing Add:* 510 E 77th St New York NY 10021

LAMBERTSEN, RICHARD H, pathobiology, pathophysiology, for more information see previous edition

LAMBERTSON, GLEN ROYAL, ACCELERATOR SCIENCE, PARTICLE DYNAMICS. *Current Pos:* CONSULT, 91- *Personal Data:* b Paonia, Colo, Jan 14, 26; m 50, Jean Smith; c Tali, Roy & Dean. *Educ:* Univ Colo, BS, 48; Univ Calif, Berkeley, MA, 51. *Prof Exp:* Res physicist, Lawrence Radiation Lab, Berkeley, 51-54 & 55-63 & Brookhaven Nat Lab, 54-55; res physicist, Lawrence Berkeley Lab, 64-71; staff sr scientist, 71-91, group leader, 73-91. *Concurrent Pos:* Vis scientist, Europ Orgn Nuclear Res, Geneva, 63-64. *Mem:* Fel Am Phys Soc; AAAS. *Res:* Analysis, design specification, and development of particle accelerator components; items that interact electromagnetically with the beam. *Mailing Add:* 6401 Castle Dr Oakland CA 94611

LAMBETH, DAVID N, MAGNETISM. *Current Pos:* SR RES PHYSICIST, EASTMAN KODAK CO, 73- *Personal Data:* b Carthage, Mo, Mar 18, 47; m 69; c 1. *Educ:* Univ Mo-Columbia, BS, 69; Mass Inst Technol, PhD(physics), 73. *Mem:* Inst Elec & Electronics Engrs; Magnetics Soc; Am Phys Soc. *Res:* Magnetism and magneto-optics of thin film materials. *Mailing Add:* ECE Dept Carnegie Mellon Univ Pittsburgh PA 15213. *Fax:* 412-268-6978

LAMBETH, DAVID ODUS, BIOCHEMISTRY. *Current Pos:* from asst prof to assoc prof, 77-84, PROF BIOCHEM, SCH MED, UNIV NDAK, 84- *Personal Data:* b Carthage, Mo, June 16, 41; m 62, Sharon Oldham; c Gregory S & Judith C. *Educ:* Univ Mo, Columbia, BSEd, 62; Purdue Univ, MS, 67; Univ Wis-Madison, PhD(biochem), 71. *Prof Exp:* Instr chem, Columbia Pub Schs, 62-67; NIH fel biochem, Univ Mich, 71-73; asst prof chem, Univ SFla, 73-77. *Mem:* Sigma Xi; Am Chem Soc; Am Soc Biochem & Molecular Biol. *Res:* Enzymology; role of GTP in metabolism; mitochondrial bioenergetics. *Mailing Add:* Dept Biochem Univ NDak 501 N Columbia Rd Grand Forks ND 58202-9037

LAMBETH, J DAVID, BIOCHEMISTRY. *Current Pos:* from asst prof to assoc prof, 80-91, PROF, DEPT BIOCHEM, EMORY UNIV SCH MED, 91-, CHMN, 94- *Personal Data:* b El Paso, Tex, Aug 26, 50; m, Victoria Stevens; c Jonathan D, Benjamin H & Dylan R. *Educ:* Southern Methodist Univ, BA, 72; Duke Univ, PhD(biochem), 76, MD, 77. *Prof Exp:* NIH fel, Dept Biochem, Duke Univ, 77-80. *Concurrent Pos:* Prin investr, NIH, 80- *Mem:* Am Soc Biochem & Molecular Biol; AAAS; Endocrine Soc. *Res:* Enzymology, regulation and signal transductions relating to oxidative systems; neutrophil superoxide generation and its receptor-coupled regulation, including phospholipase D; cholesterol metabolism and trafficking in the adrenal cortex. *Mailing Add:* Dept Biochem Emory Univ Atlanta GA 30322

LAMBETH, VICTOR NEAL, VEGETABLE CROPS, TOMATO BREEDING. *Current Pos:* Asst instr, 39-42, from asst prof to prof, 59-90, EMER PROF HORT, UNIV MO, COLUMBIA, 90- *Personal Data:* b Sarcoxie, Mo, July 5, 20; m 46; c 2. *Educ:* Univ Mo, BS, 42, MA, 48, PhD(hort), 50. *Concurrent Pos:* NSF vis prof, Thailand, 81, res, 82-84; consult, Liberia, 87. *Mem:* AAAS; Am Soc Plant Physiol; fel Am Soc Hort Sci; Int Soc Hort Sci. *Res:* Soil fertility and plant nutrition; raw product quality; tomato breeding; water relationships; post harvest physiology; international agriculture. *Mailing Add:* 1327 Lambeth Dr Columbia MO 65202

LAMBIRD, PERRY ALBERT, PATHOLOGY. *Current Pos:* CLIN PROF PATH & ORTHOP SURG, MED ARTS LAB, 70-; CHMN PATHLOR, 95- *Personal Data:* b Reno, Nev, Feb 7, 39; m 60, Mona Salyer; c Allison (Watson), Jennifer S, Elizabeth G & Susannah J. *Educ:* Stanford Univ, BA, 58; Johns Hopkins Univ, MD, 62; Oklahoma City Univ, MBA, 73. *Honors & Awards:* Outstanding Pathologist Award, Am Path Found, 84; Distinguished Practr, Nat Academies Pract, 90. *Prof Exp:* Fel internal med, Johns Hopkins Univ, 62-63, fel path, 65-69; consult, Health Serv Admin, USPHS, 63-65; pathologist, Med Arts Lab, 69-96. *Concurrent Pos:* Consult pathologist, Off Med Examr, 69-80; adj asst prof, Oklahoma City Univ, 73-82; proj pathologist, Am Cancer Soc-Nat Cancer Inst BCDP, 74-81; proprietor, Lambird Mgt Consult Serv, 74-; consult, Okla Breast Cancer Control Network, 75-80; reviewer, Southern Med J, J AMA & Diag Cytopath, 75-; mem bd dirs, Am Path Found, 78-84, pres, 83-84; regent, Uniformed Serv, Univ Health Sci, 83-88; mem, Task Force Entitlement & Human Asst, US House Rep, 83-89; CCE award, Am Soc Clin Path, 83-91; bd govs, Col Am Pathologists, 84-93; pres, Independent Path Inst, Inc, 84-; deleg, AMA, 80-, mem, Coun Med Serv, 85- *Mem:* Am Med Asn; Am Path Found (pres, 82-83); Arthur Purdy Stout Soc Surg Pathologists; fel Col Am Pathologists; Am Soc Cytol; fel Am Soc Clin Pathologists. *Res:* Breast cancer pathology and control; health care financing and administration; medical systems management. *Mailing Add:* Pathlor PO Box 60609 Oklahoma City OK 73146-0609. *Fax:* 405-278-2722

LAMBOOY, JOHN PETER, BIOCHEMISTRY. *Current Pos:* assoc dean, Grad Sch, Baltimore Campuses, Univ Md, 69-71, prof biol chem, Sch Med, 69-74, dean grad studies & res, 71-74, prof & chmn dept, 74-85, EMER PROF BIOCHEM, SCH DENT, UNIV MD, BALTIMORE, 85- *Personal Data:* b Kalamazoo, Mich, Dec 6, 14; m 42, Irene T Slattery; c John P, Peter K, Philip J & Kathleen A. *Educ:* Kalamazoo Col, AB, 37, MS, 38; Univ Ill, MA, 39; Univ Rochester, PhD(physiol chem), 42. *Honors & Awards:* Sci Achievement Award, Sigma Xi Md Sect, 74; Md Chemist Award, Am Chem Soc, 85. *Prof Exp:* From instr to assoc prof physiol, Univ Rochester, 46-63; prof chem pharmacol & sect head biochem pharmacol, Eppley Inst Cancer Res, Col Med, Univ Nebr, 63-68, prof biochem, 64-69. *Mem:* Am Chem Soc; Sigma Xi; Am Soc Biochem & Molecular Biol. *Res:* Synthesis and biological acitivity of vitamin analogs, amino acid analogs, anesthetics, sympathomimetic amines, bacteriostatic agents, carcinolytic agents and carcinogenic agents. *Mailing Add:* 904 Huntsman Rd Baltimore MD 21286

LAMBORN, BJORN N A, PLASMA PHYSICS. *Current Pos:* from asst prof to assoc prof, 65-75, chmn dept, 70-73 & 79-91, PROF PHYSICS, FLA ATLANTIC UNIV, 75-, ASSOC DEAN, COL SCI, 95- *Personal Data:* b Stockholm, Sweden, Apr 2, 37. *Educ:* Univ Calif, Berkeley, AB, 58, MA, 60; Univ Fla, PhD(physics, math), 62. *Prof Exp:* Instr physics, Univ Miami, 63; res physicist, Inst Plasmaphysik, GmbH, Munich, Ger, 63-65. *Concurrent Pos:* Bd trustees, Thiouracil. *Mem:* Sigma Xi; Am Phys Soc. *Res:* Theoretical plasma physics; wave interaction in relativistic plasmas; nonadiabatic particle motion; diffusion; nonlinear wave coupling; space plasmas. *Mailing Add:* Col Sci Fla Atlantic Univ Boca Raton FL 33431. *Fax:* 561-367-2662; *E-Mail:* lamborn@hcc.fau.edu

LAMBRAKIS, KONSTANTINE CHRISTOS, AEROSPACE ENGINEERING. *Current Pos:* asst prof thermodynamics, Univ New Haven, 66-69, assoc prof gas dynamics, 69-72, chmn mech eng dept, 74-76, PROF ENG & GAS DYNAMICS, UNIV NEW HAVEN, 72-, DEAN ENG, 76- *Personal Data:* b Piraeus, Greece, Jan 30, 36; US citizen. *Educ:* Univ Bridgeport, BSEE, 62, MSME, 65; Rensselaer Polytech Inst, PhD(aerospace eng), 71. *Prof Exp:* Develop elec engr, Skinner Pridision Industs, 61-64; sr mech eng, MB Electronics, 64-66. *Concurrent Pos:* Consult, United Nuclear Corp, 84-85, Times Fiber Commun Inc, 86-87, Textron Inc, 80-87. *Mem:* Am Soc Mech Eng; AAAS; Am Soc Elec Eng; Am Soc Aeronaut Eng. *Res:* Compressible fluid flow and thermal sciences; new computational techniques for solving non-linear partial differential equations occurring in thermal-fluid sciences and field theory. *Mailing Add:* Dept Mech Eng Univ New Haven 300 Orange Ave West Haven CT 06516-1916

LAMBRECHT, RICHARD MERLE, radiopharmaceutical chemistry, nuclear medicine, for more information see previous edition

LAMBREMONT, EDWARD NELSON, ENTOMOLOGY, NUCLEAR SCIENCE. *Current Pos:* assoc prof nuclear sci, 66-74, PROF NUCLEAR SCI & DIR NUCLEAR SCI CTR, LA STATE UNIV, BATON ROUGE, 74- *Personal Data:* b New Orleans, La, July 29, 28; m 81, 90; c 4. *Educ:* Tulane Univ, BS, 49, MS, 51; Ohio State Univ, PhD(entom), 58. *Prof Exp:* Asst zool, Tulane Univ, 48-51; asst entom, Ohio State Univ, 54-56; entomologist, Insect Physiol, Entom Res Div, Agr Res Serv, USDA, La, 58-66. *Concurrent Pos:* Vis scientist, Oak Ridge Assoc Univs, Med & Health Sci Div, 77-, bd dirs, 79-84; consult nuclear sci & technol, pub info & radiation safety, energy issues; southeast regional dir, bd dir, Sigma Xi, 83-90; vis scientist, Int Atomic Energy Agency, Vienna, 88- *Mem:* AAAS; Entom Soc Am; Sigma Xi; Nuclear Soc. *Res:* Physiology and biochemistry of insects, especially lipid metabolism, synthesis and utilization of fatty acids, phospholipids and glycerolipids and lipid enzyme systems; radiotracer and nuclear science methodology as applied to biological problems; insect radiation biology and physiology of tumorous tissues. *Mailing Add:* Nuclear Sci Ctr La State Univ Baton Rouge LA 70803-5820

LAMBROPOULOS, PETER POULOS, THEORETICAL PHYSICS. *Personal Data:* b Tripolis, Greece, Oct 5, 35; US citizen. *Educ:* Athens Tech Univ, dipl, 58; Univ Mich, MSE, 62, MS, 63, PhD(nuclear sci), 65. *Prof Exp:* Engr, Orgn Telecommun, Greece, 59-60; sr physicist, Bendix Res Lab, Mich, 65-67; asst physicist, Argonne Nat Lab, Ill, 67-72; vis fel, Joint Inst Lab Astrophys, 72-73; from asst to assoc prof, Tex A&M Univ, 73-75; assoc prof physics, Univ Southern Calif, 75-79, prof, 79-94, co-chmn dept, 81-83. *Mem:* AAAS; Am Phys Soc; Fedn Am Scientists. *Res:* Atomic physics; interaction of radiation with matter; quantum optics; strong electromagnetic fields. *Mailing Add:* Max Planck Inst fui Quantenoptik Postfach 1513 Hans Kopfermann Strasse 85748 Garching Germany

LAMBROS, JOHN, COMPOSITE MATERIALS, FRACTURE MECHANICS. *Current Pos:* ASST PROF MECH ENG, UNIV DEL, 95- *Personal Data:* b Athens, Greece, Apr 10, 67. *Educ:* Imp Col, London, BEng, 88; Calif Inst Technol, MS, 89, PhD(aeronaut), 94. *Prof Exp:* Res fel aeronaut, Calif Inst Technol, 94-95. *Mem:* Am Soc Mech Engrs; Soc Exp Mech; Am Acad Mech. *Res:* Dynamic fracture mechanics; advanced materials; optical techniques; high speed photography and thermography; dynamic friction. *Mailing Add:* 126 Spencer Lab Univ Del Newark DE 19716. *E-Mail:* lambros@me.udel.edu

LAMBSON, ROGER O, ANATOMY. *Current Pos:* vchancellor, health policy & prog develop, 84-88, PROF ANAT, UNIV KANS, 84-, VCHANCELLOR ADMIN, 89- *Personal Data:* b Provo, Utah, Feb 5, 39; c 3. *Educ:* Univ Mont, BA, 61; Tulane Univ, PhD(anat), 65. *Prof Exp:* From instr to prof anat, Col Med, Univ Ky, 65-84, assoc dean student affairs & dir admis, 71-75, assoc dean acad affairs, 75-76, assoc dean basic sci, 76-84. *Mem:* Asn Am Med Col; Am Asn Anatomists; Am Asn Med Clins. *Mailing Add:* VChancellor Admin Univ Kansas Med Ctr Kansas City KS 66160-7100

LAMBUTH, ALAN LETCHER, ADHESIVE TECHNOLOGY, WOOD UTILIZATION. *Current Pos:* asst mgr mfg tech serv, Boise Cascade Corp, 69-70, mgr prod develop, 71-76, mgr res & develop, 77-81, MGR PROD & PROCESS DEVELOP, TIMBER & WOOD PROD DIV, BOISE CASCADE CORP, 82- *Personal Data:* b Seattle, Wash, Jan 5, 23; m 44; c 4. *Educ:* Univ Wash, BS, 47. *Honors & Awards:* Monsanto Award, 69; Borden Award, Forest Prod Res Soc, 84. *Prof Exp:* Res chemist, Western Div, Monsanto Co, 47-57, res group leader, Plastics Div, 58-68. *Concurrent Pos:* Reviewer of publ & res proposals, NSF, Forest Prod Res Soc & USDA forest prod labs & exp stas, 75-; mem, US-Can Binational Comt Plywood, 85 & Adv Comt USDA Southern Forest Exp Sta; chmn, Prod/Stand Comt, Am Plywood Asn, Treated Wood Prod Comt, Nat Forest Prod Asn; chmn, PS-1 Standing Comt Plywood, US Dept Com & Adv Bd, Univ Calif Forest Prod Lab. *Mem:* Forest Prod Res Soc (pres, 82-83); Am Chem Soc; Am Inst Timber Construct; Am Soc Testing & Mat; Int Union Forestry Res Orgn; Nat Forest Prod Asn; Am Plywood Asn; Western Wood Prod Asn. *Res:* Adhesive technology and innovation; wood resource utilization; wood product development; chemical utilization of biomass; wood engineering. *Mailing Add:* 7240 Cascade Dr Boise ID 83704

LAMDEN, MERTON PHILIP, BIOCHEMISTRY. *Current Pos:* from asst prof to prof, 47-85, EMER PROF BIOCHEM, COL MED, UNIV VT, 85- *Personal Data:* b Boston, Mass, Sept 7, 19; m 42, Bernice I Levenson; c Carol B (Sacks) & Deborah J (Lamden). *Educ:* Univ Mass, BS, 41; Mass Inst Technol, PhD(food technol), 47. *Prof Exp:* Asst, Mass Inst Technol, 41-42, mem res staff, Food Technol Labs, 43-44. *Concurrent Pos:* Commonwealth Fund fel & NSF-Orgn Europ Econ Coop sr vis fel, Univ Col, Univ London, 61-62; vis res biochem, Dept Food Sci & Technol, Univ Calif, Davis, 75. *Mem:* AAAS; Am Chem Soc; Am Inst Nutrit; Brit Biochem Soc. *Res:* Vitamin content and retention in foods; nutritional status of humans; biochemical studies on ascorbic and oxalic acids; role of ascorbic acid in metabolism. *Mailing Add:* 17 Wildwood Dr Burlington VT 05401

LAMDIN, EZRA, CLINICAL TRIALS, HYPERTENSION. *Current Pos:* CONSULT PHARMACEUT INDUST, 88- *Personal Data:* b Cleveland, Ohio, Nov 25, 23; m 69, Lois Symons; c Geoffrey P, Peter B & Andrew A. *Educ:* Harvard Univ, AB, 47, MD, 51; Am Bd Internal Med, dipl, 58. *Prof Exp:* Intern med, Harvard Med Serv, Boston City Hosp, 51-52, asst resident, 52-53; USPHS fel, Sch Med, Yale Univ, 53-55; asst, Sch Med, Boston Univ, 55-56, instr, 56-58; clin instr, Sch Med, Tufts Univ, 58-60; res fel biochem, Brandeis Univ, 61-62; asst prof med & physiol, Col Med, Univ Cincinnati, 62-67; assoc prof med, Sch Med, Univ Pittsburgh, 67-69; asst med dir, Am Heart Asn, 69-73, dir div sci affairs, 73-75; asst med dir, Ayerst Labs, 75-77, assoc med dir, 77-79; dir, med affairs, ICI Americas, Inc, 79-88. *Concurrent Pos:* Teaching fel med, Harvard Med Sch, 52-53; resident, Vet Admin Hosp, Boston, 55-56, staff physician, 56-60, clin investr, 58-60; clin & res fel med, Mass Gen Hosp, Boston, 58-59; res collabr, Med Res Dept, Brookhaven Nat Lab, 63-69; chief med serv, Vet Admin Hosp, Pittsburgh, 67-69; adj assoc prof physiol, Mt Sinai Sch Med, 69-79. *Mem:* AAAS; emer mem Am Fedn Clin Res; Am Heart Asn; emer mem Am Soc Clin Pharmacol & Therapeut; Sigma Xi; fel Royal Soc Med. *Res:* Renal physiology and disease; biochemical aspects of membrane phenomena and active transport; intermediary metabolism; diabetes and obesity; mechanism of hormone action; clinical pharmacology; mechanism and treatment of hypertension. *Mailing Add:* 9 Pinefields Lane Brunswick ME 04011-9337

LAME, EDWIN LEVER, INTERNAL MEDICINE. *Current Pos:* RETIRED. *Personal Data:* b Evanston, Ill, Feb 23, 04; m 40; c 2. *Educ:* Mass Inst Technol, BS, 26; Univ Pa, MD, 33; Am Bd Internal Med, dipl, 45; Am Bd Radiol, dipl, 45. *Prof Exp:* Asst med, Sch Med, Univ Pa, 36-42, asst radiol, 42-47; dir radiol, Presby Hosp, 47-66; chief radiol, Vet Admin Hosp, Coatesville, 66-77. *Concurrent Pos:* Fel internal med & chest dis, physician & asst to dir, Dept Res Respiratory Dis, Germantown Hosp, 36-42; asst physician, Pa Hosp, 37-43; asst pediatrist & chief chest clin, Children's Hosp, 38-45; fel radiol, Hosp Univ Pa, 42-45; chief radiol, Jeanes Hosp, 45-48, consult, 48-60; assoc prof clin radiol, Sch Med & asst prof radiol, Grad Sch Med, Univ Pa, 57-66. *Mem:* Radiol Soc NAm; Am Roentgen Ray Soc; AMA; fel Am Col Physicians; fel Am Col Radiol. *Res:* Pulmonary radiologic interpretation; pelvic and vertebral osteomyelitis arising from the urinary tract; cholecystitis; clinical and radiologic criteria; gastrointestinal barium; protection and dose reduction in diagnostic radiology; radiologic signs of preclinical heart failure. *Mailing Add:* 1400 Waverly Rd Villa 48 Gladwyne PA 19035-1254

LAMEIRO, GERARD FRANCIS, KNOWLEDGE TECHNOLOGY, COMPLEX MODELS. *Current Pos:* DIR, LAMEIRO RES INST, 91-, SR RES FEL, 92-; MKT DEVELOPER, HEWLETT PACKARD, 96- *Personal Data:* b Paterson, NJ, Oct 3, 49. *Educ:* Colo State Univ, BS, 71, MS, 73, PhD(mech eng), 77. *Honors & Awards:* Nat Distinguished Serv Award, Asn Energy Engrs, 81. *Prof Exp:* Fel, Solar Energy Appln Lab, Colo Energy Res Inst, Colo State Univ, 74-77, NSF fel solar energy, 77, sr scientist, Solar Energy Res Inst, 77-78, asst prof mgt sci & info systs, 78-83; pres, Successful Automated Off Systs, Inc, 82-84; prod mgr, Hewlett-Packard Co, 84-88; columnist, HP Chronicle, 88-91; independent mgt strategist, Comput Corp, 88-91. *Concurrent Pos:* Mem, Nat Bd Dirs, Asn Energy Engrs, 80-81. *Mem:* Asn Energy Engrs (pres-elect, 79, pres, 80). *Res:* Knowledge technology and knowledge revolution and its impact on corporation; economy and society; national economic growth; complex models. *Mailing Add:* PO Box 9580 Ft Collins CO 80525-0500

LAMELAS, FRANCISCO JAVIER, synchrotron x-ray scattering, molecular beam epitaxy growth & surface science, for more information see previous edition

LAMENSDORF, DAVID, ELECTRICAL ENGINEERING. *Current Pos:* GROUP LEADER, MITRE CORP, 85- *Personal Data:* b NY, Nov 22, 37; m, Joyce Milunsky. *Educ:* Cornell Univ, BEE, 60; Harvard Univ, SM, 61, PhD(appl physics), 67. *Prof Exp:* Mem tech staff, Sperry Res Ctr, 67-83, sr res sect head, Sperry Defense Electronics, 83-85. *Concurrent Pos:* Res assoc, Univ Col London, 72-73. *Mem:* AAAS; sr mem Inst Elec & Electronics Engrs; Sigma Xi. *Res:* Electromagnetic theory; transient analysis of antennas; microwave antennas, networks and electronics; adaptive arrays and radar. *Mailing Add:* Mitre Corp MS M114 Burlington Rd Bedford MA 01730

LA MERS, THOMAS HERBERT, ELECTRO CHEMICAL SENSORS, BIOSENSORS. *Current Pos:* prod res & develop, 69-89, DESIGN CONSULT, MECH DEVICES, YELLOW SPRINGS INSTRUMENT CO INC, 89- *Personal Data:* b New York, NY, Apr 23, 45; m 69. *Educ:* Antioch Col, BSES, 68. *Prof Exp:* Machine designer, Vernay Labs, 68-69; aircraft designer, SRL Corp, 69. *Concurrent Pos:* Consult, Ventura Labeling Co, 84-85. *Mem:* AAAS. *Res:* Integrating science and technology to accomplish new objectives in engineering design; gas sensors; thermometry; ceramic sensors. *Mailing Add:* 777 Dayton St Yellow Springs OH 45387. *Fax:* 937-767-9187

LAMEY, HOWARD ARTHUR, EXTENSION TEACHING, ROW CROP DISEASES. *Current Pos:* EXTEN PLANT PATHOLOGIST & PROF, EXTEN SERV, NDAK STATE UNIV, 77- *Personal Data:* b Bloomington, Ind, Dec 20, 29; m 56, Cynthia Hueniuk; c Timothy, Thaddeus, Linda, Suzan & Laura. *Educ:* Ohio Wesleyan Univ, BA, 51; Univ Wis-Madison, PhD(plant path), 54. *Prof Exp:* Res asst, Dept Plant Path, Univ Wis, 51-54, proj assoc, 54-55, 57-58; asst plant pathologist, US Army, Md, 56-57; plant pathologist, USDA, Camaguey, Cuba, 58-60; sr res plant pathologist, Baton Rouge, La, 60-69; plant pathologist, Int Inst Trop Agr, Ibadan, Nigeria, 69-71, coordr plant protection prog & chmn, Res Comt, 70-71; proj mgr, Food & Agr Orgn, Suweon, Korea, 71-75, consult, Cent Am & Mex, 76. *Concurrent Pos:* Rice virologist, Food & Agr Orgn, UN, Bangkok, Thailand, 66-67; proj mgr, 67-68, consult, 70. *Mem:* Fel AAAS; Am Phytopath Soc; Am Soc Sugar Beet Technologists. *Res:* Diseases of sugarbeets, sunflower, dry edible beans, soybeans, and canola; fungicides, foliar and seed treatment, epidemiology. *Mailing Add:* Dept Plant Path NDak State Univ Box 5012 Fargo ND 58105. *Fax:* 701-231-7851; *E-Mail:* alamey@ndsuext.nodak.edu

LAMEY, STEVEN CHARLES, ANALYTICAL CHEMISTRY, ORGANIC CHEMISTRY. *Current Pos:* RES CHEMIST ENERGY RES, MORGANTOWN ENERGY TECHNOL CTR, 75- *Personal Data:* b Lock Haven, Pa, Mar 5, 44; m 70, Charlotte I Orndorf. *Educ:* Lock Haven State Col, BA, 68; WVa Univ, MS, 73, PhD(analytical chem), 75. *Prof Exp:* Res chemist org synthesis, Am Aniline Corp, 68-70. *Mem:* Am Chem Soc; AAAS; Coblentz Soc; Sigma Xi. *Res:* Characterization of coal tars; electrochemistry; instrument development for coal characterization; environmental analysis; characterization of coal combustion products; mild gasification of coal-waste management-environmental chemistry; on-line instrumentation for trace element analysis; coal technology. *Mailing Add:* Morgantown Energy Technol Ctr Collins Ferry Rd Morgantown WV 26505

LAMIE, EDWARD LOUIS, COMPUTER SCIENCE. *Current Pos:* PROF DEPT COMPUT SCI, CALIF STATE UNIV, STANISLAUS, 82-, DIR INST RES, 93- *Personal Data:* b Kingsley, Mich, Aug 27, 41; m 60, Frances M Jeffries; c David, Jennifer, William, Kate, Andrew, Marla & Melissa. *Educ:* San Diego State Univ, AB, 69; Univ Southern Calif, MS, 71; Mich State Univ, PhD(comput sci), 74. *Prof Exp:* Mem tech staff, Rockwell Int, 69-71; assoc prof comput sci, Cent Mich Univ, 71-82, prof & chmn dept, 82- *Mem:* Asn Comput Mach; Inst Elec & Electronics Engrs. *Res:* Database systems; discrete simulation; artificial intelligence. *Mailing Add:* 1713 Farmington Lane Modesto CA 95355. *E-Mail:* lamie@altair.csustan.edu

LAMKEY, KENDALL RAYE, QUANTITATIVE GENETICS, APPLIED STATISTICS. *Current Pos:* RES GENETICIST PLANTS, USDA, AGR RES SERV, 84- *Personal Data:* b Springfield, Ill, Nov 22, 58; m 81, Becky M Zarf; c Collin, Nickolas & Jacob. *Educ:* Univ Ill, BS, 80, MS, 82; Iowa State Univ, PhD(plant breeding), 85. *Concurrent Pos:* Asst prof & collabr, Iowa State Univ, 85-90, assoc prof & collabr, 90-; assoc ed, Crop Sci Soc Am, 91. *Mem:* Am Soc Agron; Crop Sci Soc Am; Biometrics Soc; Genetics Soc Am. *Res:* Application of quantitative genetics and selection theory to more effectively and efficiently improve and broaden the genetics base of corn. *Mailing Add:* Dept Agron Iowa State Univ Ames IA 50011. *Fax:* 515-294-9359; *E-Mail:* krlamkey@iastate.edu

LAMM, FOSTER PHILIP, POLYMER CHEMISTRY. *Current Pos:* RES SCIENTIST, UNITED TECHNOLOGIES RES CTR, 79- *Personal Data:* b Whittier, Calif, April 18, 50; m 77; c 2. *Educ:* Univ Calif, San Diego, BA, 72; Wesleyan Univ, PhD(chem), 79. *Mem:* Am Chem Soc; Soc Mfg Engrs. *Res:* Chemistry and processing of high performance adhesives; new materials and processing techniques for electrical insulating; organic materials failure analysis. *Mailing Add:* 56 Clinton Dr South Windsor CT 06074-3012

LAMM, MICHAEL EMANUEL, IMMUNOLOGY, PATHOLOGY. *Current Pos:* JOSEPH R KAHN PROF & CHMN PATH, CASE WESTERN RES UNIV, 81- *Personal Data:* b Brooklyn, NY, May 19, 34; m 61, Ruth Kumin; c Jocelyn & Margaret. *Educ:* Univ Rochester, MD, 59; Western Res Univ, MS, 62; Am Bd Path, dipl, 65. *Prof Exp:* From intern to resident path, Univ Hosps, Cleveland, Ohio, 59-62; res assoc, NIH, 62-64; from asst prof to prof path, Sch Med, NY Univ, 64-81. *Mem:* US & Can Acad Path; Am Soc Invest Path; Clin Immunol Soc; Am Asn Immunol; Soc Mucosal Immunol. *Res:* Mucosal immunity; immunopathology. *Mailing Add:* Inst Path Case Western Res Univ 2085 Adelbert Rd Cleveland OH 44106. *Fax:* 216-368-0494; *E-Mail:* mel.6@po.cwru.edu

LAMM, WARREN DENNIS, BEEF CATTLE MANAGEMENT, COOPERATIVE EXTENSION ADMINISTRATION. *Current Pos:* exten beef specialist, Dept Animal Sci, 81-86, ASST DIR, AGR & NATURAL RESOURCES, COOP EXT, COLO STATE UNIV, 86- *Personal Data:* b West Reading, Pa, Jan 27, 47; m 71, Jean A Murphy; c Kevan & Dana. *Educ:* Del Valley Col Sci & Agr, BS, 69; Iowa State Univ, MS, 72; Univ Nebr, PhD(ruminant nutrit), 76. *Prof Exp:* Exten agt, Exten Serv, Colo State Univ, 72-73; asst prof beef cattle nutrit & eval, Va Polytech Inst & State Univ, 76-81. *Concurrent Pos:* Kellogg fel, 88. *Mem:* Am Soc Animal Sci; Coun Agr Sci & Technol. *Res:* Beef nutrition and management; energetic efficiency; protein utilization; use of underutilized feedstuffs and animal waste refeeding. *Mailing Add:* Colo State Univ 01 Admin Ft Collins CO 80523. *Fax:* 970-491-6208; *E-Mail:* dlamm@vines.colostate.edu

LAMMERS, WIM, physiology, for more information see previous edition

LAMMERTSMA, KOOP, CHEMISTRY. *Current Pos:* from asst prof to assoc prof, 83-92, PROF, UNIV ALA, 92- *Personal Data:* b Makkum, Frysland, Neth, Aug 29, 49. *Educ:* Univ Groningen, Neth, MS, 75; Univ Amsterdam, PhD, 79. *Prof Exp:* Fel, Univ Col London, Eng, 80, Univ Erlangen, Nurnberg, Ger, 80-81; res fel, Univ Southern Calif, Los Angeles, 81-83. *Mem:* Am Chem Soc. *Res:* Author of numerous publications; chemistry. *Mailing Add:* Dept Chem Vrije Univ Amsterdam Netherlands

LAMMIE, JAMES L, TRANSIT. *Current Pos:* proj dir, Parsons Brinckeroff Inc, 75-82, pres & chief operating officer, 82-90, pres & chief exec officer, 90-96, DIR, PARSONS BRINCKEROFF INC, 96- *Personal Data:* b Homestead, Pa, Sept 19, 31. *Educ:* US Mil Acad, BS, 53; Purdue Univ, MS, 57; George Washington Univ, MS, 69; US Army Command & Gen Staff Col, MMAS, 75. *Honors & Awards:* Civil Eng of Yr Award, Am Soc Civil Engrs, 91, Parcel/Sverdrup Civil Eng Mat Award, 91. *Prof Exp:* US Army Colonel, 53-74, dist engr, 72-74; dir syst develop, Harding Larson Assoc, 74-75. *Concurrent Pos:* Asst prof mil eng, Colo Sch Mines; mem, Indust Policy Adv, US Trade Rep, 96. *Mem:* Nat Acad Eng; fel & hon mem Am Soc Civil Engrs; fel Soc Am Mil Engrs; Am Pub Transit Asn. *Mailing Add:* Parsons Brinckerhoff Inc One Penn Plaza New York NY 10119

LAMMIE, PATRICK J, PARASITOLOGY. *Current Pos:* RES BIOLOGIST, CTR DIS CONTROL, 89- *Mailing Add:* Parasitol Ctr Dis Control & Prev 4770 Buford Hwy NE Atlanta GA 30341-3724

LAMMI-KEEFE, CAROL J, NUTRITION. *Current Pos:* ASST PROF NUTRIT SCI, UNIV CONN. *Personal Data:* b Acushnet, Mass, June 11, 47. *Educ:* Univ Minn, PhD(nutrit), 80. *Mailing Add:* Dept Nutrit Sci Univ Conn Storrs CT 06269-4017

LAMOLA, ANGELO ANTHONY, photobiology, photochemistry, for more information see previous edition

LAMON, EDDIE WILLIAM, cancer, immunology; deceased, see previous edition for last biography

LAMONDE, ANDRE M, PHARMACY. *Current Pos:* MGR PHARMACEUT TECHNOL, GLEXO-WELLCOME, 89- *Personal Data:* b St Lambert, Que, Oct 5, 36; m 66. *Educ:* Univ Montreal, BPharm, 61; Purdue Univ, MSc, 63, PhD(indust pharm), 65. *Prof Exp:* Asst prof pharm, Univ Montreal, 65-68; regulatory affairs coordr, Med Div, Syntex Ltd, 68-70, qual control mgr, 70-72, qual control dir, 72-79; qual control dir, Schering Can, 79-89. *Res:* Basic pharmaceutics and pharmaceutical analysis. *Mailing Add:* 1875 Georgeville Rd Magog PQ J1X 3W4 Can

LAMONDIA, JAMES A, NEMATOLOGY, SOIL MICROBIOLOGY. *Current Pos:* asst scientist res, 86-89, ASSOC SCIENTIST RES, DEPT PLANT PATH, CONN AGR EXP STA, 89- *Personal Data:* b Springfield, Mass, Dec 3, 57; m 79, Bonnie Dyer; c Jeffrey & Patrick. *Educ:* Fitchburg State Col, 79; Cornell Univ, MS, 82, PhD(plant path), 84. *Prof Exp:* Res assoc plant path, Cornell Univ, 84-86. *Concurrent Pos:* Assoc ed, J Nematol, 88-91. *Mem:* Am Phytopath Soc; Soc Nematologists. *Res:* Ecology and integrated management of soilborne plant pathogens, especially plant parasitic nematodes and fungi involved in complex diseases. *Mailing Add:* Dept Plant Path & Ecol Valley Lab Conn Agr Exp Sta PO Box 248 Windsor CT 06095. *Fax:* 860-688-9479; *E-Mail:* lamondia@caes.state.ct.us

LAMONT, GARY BYRON, CONTROL ENGINEERING, COMPUTER ENGINEERING. *Current Pos:* from asst prof to assoc prof, 70-80, PROF ELEC ENG, AIR FORCE INST TECHNOL, 80- *Personal Data:* b St Paul, Minn, Feb 14, 39; m 66, Delores Leininger; c Jon, Heather & Michael. *Educ:* Univ Minn, BPhysics, 61, MSEE, 67, PhD(control sci), 70. *Prof Exp:* Develop engr, Honeywell Inc, 61-65, systs analyst, 65-67. *Mem:* Inst Elec & Electronics Engrs; Am Soc Eng Educ; Asn Comput Mach; Soc Indust & Appl Math. *Res:* Control estimation theory; applications of small computers; computer structures; intelligent systems; operating systems; parallel distributed computing; evolutionary computation. *Mailing Add:* Air Force Inst Technol Wright-Patterson AFB AFT/ENG Dayton OH 45433

LAMONT, JOHN THOMAS, MEDICINE, GASTROENTEROLOGY. *Current Pos:* assoc prof & chief, 80-85, PROF GASTROENTEROL, UNIV HOSP, BOSTON UNIV, 85- *Personal Data:* b Lockport, NY, Oct 2, 38; m 64; c 3. *Educ:* Canisius Col, BS, 60; Univ Rochester, MD, 65. *Prof Exp:* Fel, Mass Gen Hosp, 71-73; instr, Harvard Med Sch, 73-75, asst prof med, 75-80. *Concurrent Pos:* Consult gastroenterologist, Peter Bent Brigham Hosp, Boston Hosp Women & WRoxbury Vet Admin Hosp, 75-80 & Univ, Boston City Hosp, 80-; NIH career investr award, 75; res grants, Am Cancer Soc & Nat Found for Ileitis Colitis, 77-78. *Mem:* Am Soc Clin Res; Am Gastroenterol Asn; Am Soc Study Liver Dis. *Res:* Structure and function of colonic glycoproteins; biochemistry of intestinal tract in health and disease; colon cancer; gallstones, ulcer; bacterial toxins. *Mailing Add:* 720 Harrison Ave Boston MA 02118

LAMONT, JOHN W(ILLIAM), ELECTRICAL ENGINEERING, COMPUTER SCIENCE. *Current Pos:* FAC, IOWA STATE UNIV, 87- *Personal Data:* b Cape Girardeau, Mo, Mar 7, 42; m 68; c 2. *Educ:* Univ Mo-Rolla, BSEE, 64; Univ Mo-Columbia, MSEE, 66, PhD, 70. *Prof Exp:* Instr elec eng, Univ Mo-Columbia, 66-70; asst prof, Univ Southern Calif, 70-73; asst prof, dept elec eng, Univ Tex, Austin, 73-77; proj mgr, Elec Power Res Inst, 77-87. *Mem:* Nat Soc Prof Engrs; Inst Elec & Electronics Engrs; Sigma Xi. *Res:* Application of computers to power systems. *Mailing Add:* 1005 Idaho Ave Ames IA 50010-3018

LAMONT, PATRICK, INTELLIGENT SYSTEMS, COMPUTER ALGEBRA NUMBER THEORY. *Current Pos:* asst prof quant info sci, 79-83, assoc prof, 83-91, PROF COMPUT SCI, WESTERN ILL UNIV, 91- *Personal Data:* b Dublin, Ireland, Aug 29, 36. *Educ:* Glasgow Univ, BSc, 58, PhD(math), 62. *Prof Exp:* Asst lectr math, Royal Col Sci & Technol, Scotland, 61-62; Dept Sci & Indust Res traveling fel, State Univ Utrecht & Univs Gottingen & Munich, 62-64; lectr pure math, Univ Birmingham, 64-70; assoc prof math, St Mary's Col, Ind, 70-74; chmn, Deep Springs Col, California, 74-76; asst prof math, Monmouth Col, Ill, 76-79. *Concurrent Pos:* Asst prof, Univ Notre Dame, 66-68; assoc prof math & comput sci, St Johns Univ, 88-89. *Mem:* Am Math Soc; London Math Soc; Asn Comput Mach. *Res:* Arithmetic theory of nonassociative algebras and intelligent software systems; cryptology; general computer sciences. *Mailing Add:* 141 Chandler Blvd Macomb IL 61455-1414. *Fax:* 309-298-2302; *E-Mail:* mfpjl@uxa.ecn.bgu.edu

LAMONT, SUSAN JOY, IMMUNOGENETICS, DISEASE RESISTANCE. *Current Pos:* from asst prof to assoc prof, 83-91, PROF ANIMAL SCI, IOWA STATE UNIV, 91- *Personal Data:* b Hammond, Ind, Dec 26, 53; m 74, Gregory D; c 1. *Educ:* Trinity Christian Col, BA, 75; Univ Ill Med Ctr, PhD(anat), 80. *Prof Exp:* Postdoctoral fel, Univ Mass, 80-83. *Concurrent Pos:* Vis scientist, Spelderholt, Neth, 90. *Mem:* Conf Res Workers Animal Dis; Am Asn Immunologists; Poultry Sci Asn; World Poultry Sci Asn; Int Soc Animal Genetics. *Res:* Structure and function of the chicken major histocompatibility complex; genetic resistance to disease in poultry; biomedical disease models in avian species. *Mailing Add:* Dept Animal Sci Iowa State Univ 201 Kildee Hall Ames IA 50011

LA MONTAGNE, JOHN RING, MICROBIOLOGY. *Current Pos:* influenza prog officer, Nat Inst Allergy & Infectious Dis, NIH, 76-84, viral vaccines prog officer, 83-86, dir, AIDS Prog, 86-87, actg dir, Microbiol & Infectious Dis Prog, 87-88, DIR, DIV MICROBIOL & INFECTIOUS DIS, NAT INST ALLERGY & INFECTIOUS DIS, NIH, BETHESDA, 88- *Personal Data:* b Mexico City, Mex, Jan 1, 43; US citizen; m 68. *Educ:* Univ Tex, BA, 65, MA, 67; Tulane Univ, PhD(microbiol), 71. *Prof Exp:* Teaching asst, Dept Microbiol, Univ Tex, 65-67; fel, Dept Microbiol & Immunol, Tulane Univ, Sch Med, 67-70, teaching asst, 70-71; res assoc, Dept Microbiol, Univ Pittsburgh, Sch Med, 71-74, instr, 74-76. *Concurrent Pos:* Mem, Task Force Reye's Syndrome, Pub Health Serv, 81- *Mem:* Am Soc Microbiol; AAAS; Am Soc Virol; Infectious Dis Soc Am; Am Soc Trop Med & Hyg. *Res:* Microbiology. *Mailing Add:* Div Microbiol & Infectious Dis Nat Inst Allergy & Infectious Dis Solar Bldg Rm 3A18 60033 Executive Blvd Bethesda MD 20892

LAMOREAUX, PHILIP ELMER, GEOLOGY, HYDROLOGY. *Current Pos:* RETIRED. *Personal Data:* b Chardon, Ohio, May 12, 20; m 43, Ura Mae Munro; c Philip E Jr, James W & Karen L. *Educ:* Denison Univ, BA, 43, DSc; Univ Ala, MA, 49. *Honors & Awards:* Ian Campbell Medal, Am Geol Inst, 90, William B Heroy Award, 95; Commander's Medal, US Corps Eng, 90. *Prof Exp:* Jr geologist, US Geol Surv, 43-45, asst geologist, 45-47, dist geologist, 47-48, div hydrologist, 58-59, chief, Groundwater Br, 59-61; state geologist & oil & gas suprv, Geol Surv Ala, 61-77; lectr geol, Univ Ala, Tuscaloosa, 48-59, from assoc prof to prof, 61-78, dir, Environ Inst Waste Mgt Studies, 67-78; pres, PE Lamoreauz & Assocs, Inc, 76-87, chmn bd, 87-90, sr biologist, 90- *Concurrent Pos:* Consult, Egypt, 53, 59, 61, 63-64, 65, 70 & 80, Thailand, 54, 61 & 76, Philippines, 61, Surinam, 63, Mauritania, Africa, Senegal & Colombia, 64; chmn bd trustees, Geol Soc Am; vice chmn, Interstate Oil Compact Comn, 63; chmn, Comt Publ, Am Geol Inst, 68-70, pres, 71-72; ed-in-chief, J Environ Geol, 82-; mem, Med Tech Reference Group, Oak Ridge Nat Lab, 84-88; mem bd trustee, Denison Univ, 87. *Mem:* Nat Acad Sci; Nat Acad Eng; Geol Soc Am; Am Astn Petrol Geologists; Int Asn Hydrogeologists (vpres, 73-77, pres, 77-80); Am Inst Prof Geologists; Soc Econ Geol; Am Inst Hydrol; Am Soc Testing & Mat; Am Geophys Union; Am Inst Mech Engrs; Int Union Geol & Geophys. *Res:* Groundwater geology; fluoride in groundwater; stratigraphy of Gulf Coastal Plain; hydrogeology of Karst areas. *Mailing Add:* P E LaMoreaux & Assocs Inc 2610 University Blvd Tuscaloosa AL 35401-1566

LAMORTE, MICHAEL FRANCIS, SOLID STATE ELECTRONICS, ELECTRICAL ENGINEERING. *Current Pos:* SR ENGR SOLID STATE, RES TRIANGLE INST, 76- *Personal Data:* b Altoona, Pa, Feb 20, 26; m 57; c 3. *Educ:* Va Polytech Inst & State Univ, BS, 50; Polytech Inst New York, MEE, 51. *Honors & Awards:* Eng Achievement Award, RCA Corp, 60. *Prof Exp:* Mgr solid state, RCA Corp, 59-67; pres solid state, Laser Diode Labs, 67-69; pres comput, Mathatronics Corp, 70-71; gen mgr med, Diamondhead Corp, 71-72; pres electronics, Princeton Synergestek Prod, 72-76. *Concurrent Pos:* Fel engr, Westinghouse Elec Corp, 55-59; solid state physicist, Fort Monmouth, 52-55. *Mem:* Inst Elec & Electronics Engrs; Am Inst Physics; AAAS. *Res:* Semiconductor device physics; properties of materials; device design; device and material technology; special research interest in application of III-IV materials to electrooptical, microwave and logic devices. *Mailing Add:* 222 Timberly Dr Durham NC 27707

LAMOTTE, CAROLE CHOATE, IMMUNOCYTOCHEMISTRY, ELECTRON MICROSCOPY. *Current Pos:* res assoc neurosurg, 77-78, asst prof neuroanat & neurosurg, 78-83, ASSOC PROF NEUROSURG, SCH MED, YALE UNIV, 83- *Personal Data:* b Washington, DC, May 15, 47; m 70; c 2. *Educ:* Univ Okla, BS, 67; Georgetown Univ, MS, 69; Johns Hopkins Univ, PhD(physiol), 72. *Honors & Awards:* Jacob Javitz Neurosci Investr Award, 88-95. *Prof Exp:* NIH fel anat, Sch Med, Johns Hopkins Univ, 72-74, instr anat, 74-75, asst prof anat, 75-77. *Concurrent Pos:* Prin investr, NIH Grant, 78-95; regular mem, NIH Neurol Sci & Study Sect, 85-88. *Mem:* Am Asn Anatomists; Soc Neurosci; Am Pain Soc. *Res:* Anatomy and physiology of pain and temperature sensation; sprouting and reorganization in injured spinal cord. *Mailing Add:* Res Lab Yale Univ Sch Med 333 Cedar St New Haven CT 06510

LAMOTTE, CLIFFORD ELTON, PLANT PHYSIOLOGY. *Current Pos:* assoc prof bot & plant path, 66-80, PROF BOT, IOWA STATE UNIV, 80- *Personal Data:* b Alpine, Tex, June 24, 30; m 74; c 2. *Educ:* Tex A&M Univ, BS, 53; Univ Wis, PhD(bot), 60. *Prof Exp:* Res assoc biol, Princeton Univ, 60-61; from instr to asst prof, Boston Univ, 61-66. *Concurrent Pos:* Fac leave Univ Col Wales, UK, 74-75. *Mem:* Bot Soc Am; AAAS; Am Soc Plant Physiol. *Res:* Hormonal regulation of development and orientation in plants; plant morphogenesis using tissue culture methods; growth and development in plants. *Mailing Add:* Dept Bot Iowa State Univ Ames IA 50011-2010

LAMOTTE, LOUIS COSSITT, JR, MICROBIOLOGY, EPIDEMIOLOGY. *Current Pos:* RETIRED. *Personal Data:* b Clinton, SC, Jan 21, 28; m 48, Lila J Magruder; c Barbara, Robert, Nancy, Diane & Cynthia. *Educ:* Duke Univ, AB, 48; Univ NC, MSPH, 51; Johns Hopkins Univ, ScD(virol, entom), 58. *Honors & Awards:* Pub Health Serv Super Serv Award, 1981. *Prof Exp:* Bacteriologist, State Bd Health, NC, 48-51; virologist, Chem Corps, US Dept Army, 51-58; chief, Virus Invest Unit, Dis Ecol Sect, Tech Br, Nat Commun Dis Ctr, 58-65, asst chief, Dis Ecol Sect, 65-66, chief community studies, Pesticides Prog, 66-69, dept chief, 69-70, chief, Microbiol Br, 70-72, dir, Licensure & Proficiency Testing Div, 72-82, dir, Div Tech Eval & Assistance, Ctr Dis Control, 82-86. *Concurrent Pos:* Mem grad fac, Colo State Univ, 59-66; adj prof, Ga State Univ, 71- *Mem:* AAAS; Sigma Xi; Am Soc Trop Med & Hyg; Am Pub Health Asn; Am Soc Microbiol. *Res:* Epidemiology of arthropod-borne viruses; virology, bacteriology, parasitology and epidemiology of infectious diseases. *Mailing Add:* 4820 Leeds Ct Atlanta GA 30338. *Fax:* 770-394-7977; *E-Mail:* llamotte@aol.com

LAMOTTE, ROBERT HILL, NEUROSCIENCES. *Current Pos:* ASSOC PROF ANESTHESIOL & PHYSIOL, MED SCH, YALE UNIV, 77- *Personal Data:* b Washington, DC, Nov 4, 40; m 70. *Educ:* Trinity Col, BS, 63; Kans State Univ, PhD(psychol), 68. *Prof Exp:* instr, 70-73, asst prof neurophysiol, Sch Med & asst prof psychol, Johns Hopkins Univ, 73-77. *Concurrent Pos:* Fel neurophysiol, Johns Hopkins Univ, 73-77. *Mem:* Soc Neurosci; AAAS. *Res:* Neurophysiology and psychophysics of somesthesis. *Mailing Add:* Dept Anesthesiol Yale Univ Sch Med 333 Cedar St New Haven CT 06510-3219

LAMOUREUX, CHARLES HARRINGTON, BOTANY. *Current Pos:* from asst prof to assoc prof, 59-71, assoc dean acad affairs, 85-91, PROF BOT, COLS ARTS & SCI, UNIV HAWAII, MANOA, 71-, DIR, H L LYON ARBORETUM, 92- *Personal Data:* b West Greenwich, RI, Sept 14, 33; m 54, Florence Kettelle; c Mark & Anne. *Educ:* Univ RI, BS, 53; Univ Hawaii, MS, 55; Univ Calif, Davis, PhD(bot), 61. *Prof Exp:* Asst bot, Univ Hawaii, 53-55; jr plant pathologist, Calif State Dept Agr, 55; asst bot, Univ Calif, Davis, 55-59. *Concurrent Pos:* Res assoc, Bernice P Bishop Mus, 62-; guest scientist, Nat Biol Inst Indonesia, 72-73, 79-80. *Mem:* Sigma Xi; Bot Soc Am; Int Asn Plant Taxon; Int Asn Wood Anat. *Res:* Plant morphology; island biology; pteridology; conservation biology. *Mailing Add:* Dept Bot Univ Hawaii Manoa Honolulu HI 96822-2270. *Fax:* 808-988-4231

LAMOUREUX, GERALD LEE, BIOCHEMISTRY. *Current Pos:* RES CHEMIST, METAB & RADIATION RES LAB, AGR RES SERV, USDA, 66- *Personal Data:* b Bottineau, NDak, Apr 13, 39; m 69. *Educ:* Minot State Col, BS, 61; NDak State Univ, PhD(chem), 66. *Concurrent Pos:* Adj prof, NDak State Univ, 74- *Mem:* Am Chem Soc; Sigma Xi; Weed Sci Soc; Int Union Pure & Appl Chem. *Res:* Elucidation of metabolic pathways utilized by plants and animals in the metabolism of herbicides, insecticides and other exenobiotics; glutathione-S-transferase mediated reactions; herbicide mode of action. *Mailing Add:* 2449 Lilac Lane Fargo ND 58102-2123

LAMOYI, EDMUNDO, IMMUNOCHEMISTRY, IMMUNOPARASITOLOGY. *Current Pos:* SR INVESTR, BIOMED RES INST, NAT UNIV MEX, 86- *Personal Data:* b Oaxaca, Mex, May 6, 52; m 90, Judith Dominguez; c Carla & Renata. *Educ:* Nat Univ Mex, BS, 75; Brandeis Univ, PhD(biol), 81. *Prof Exp:* Postdoctoral res assoc, Brandeis Univ, 81-83; vis assoc, Nat Inst Allergy & Infectious Dis, NIH, 83-86. *Concurrent Pos:* Nat researcher, Nat Syst Res, Pub Educ Secretariat, Mex, 86; lectr, Sci & Humanities Col, Nat Univ Mex, 87- *Mem:* Am Asn Immunologists. *Res:* Studies of the human immune response to the parasite entamoeba histolytica; analysis of parasite antigens with monoclonal antibodies. *Mailing Add:* Dept Immunol Inst Invest Biomed UNAM APDO 70-228 Mexico City DF 04510 Mexico. *Fax:* 525-550-00-48

LAMP, BENSON J, MARKETING & DEVELOPMENT, AGRICULTURAL ENGINEERING. *Current Pos:* prof, 49-61 & 87-91, EMER PROF AGR ENG, OHIO STATE UNIV, COLUMBUS, 91-; PRES, B J COMPANIES, 91- *Personal Data:* b Cardington, Ohio, Oct, 7, 25; m 48, Martha J Motz; c Elaine, Marlene, Linda & David. *Educ:* Ohio State Univ, BS(agr) & BS(agr eng), 49, MS, 52; Mich State Univ, PhD(agr eng), 60. *Honors & Awards:* Gold Medal, Am Soc Agr Engrs. *Prof Exp:* Prod mgr, Massey Ferguson Ltd, Toronto, 61-66; prod planning mgr, Ford Tractor Opers Div, Ford Motor Co, Troy, Mich, 66-71, mkt mgr, 71-76, bus planning mgr, 78-87, vpres mkt & develop, Ford Aerospace Div, Dearborn, 76-78. *Mem:* Fel Am Soc Agr Engrs (pres, 85-86). *Res:* Agricultural engineering, harvesting and management. *Mailing Add:* BJM Co Inc 6128 Inverurie Dr E Dublin OH 43017

LAMP, HERBERT F, PLANT ECOLOGY, PRAIRIE ECOLOGY. *Current Pos:* prof biol, Northeastern Ill Univ, 64-66, prof biol sci & chmn dept, 66-83, assoc dean, Arts & Sci, 83-84, EMER PROF BIOL SCI, NORTHEASTERN ILL UNIV, 85- *Personal Data:* b Davenport, Iowa, Aug 6, 19; wid; c Barbara, Majorie, Herbert Jr, Laurie, Jonathan & Kathryn. *Educ:* Chicago Teacher Col, BEd, 41; Univ Chicago, SM, 47, PhD(bot), 51. *Prof Exp:* Instr bot, Fla State Univ, 47-50; teacher biol, Ill Teachers Col Chicago-S, 50-59, from assoc prof to prof, 59-64, chmn dept natural sci, 56-64. *Concurrent Pos:* Res assoc, Univ Chicago, 52-56; vol Herbarium, Morton Arboretum, 85- *Mem:* Bot Soc Am; Ecol Soc Am; Sigma Xi. *Res:* Physiological ecology of range grasses; bromus inermis leyss; prairie ecology; commmunity ecology. *Mailing Add:* 180 Linden Ave Elmhurst IL 60126

LAMP, WILLIAM OWEN, POPULATION ECOLOGY, BIOLOGICAL CONTROL. *Current Pos:* ASST PROF ENTOM, UNIV MD, 85- *Personal Data:* b Omaha, Nebr, June 19, 51; m 73; c 2. *Educ:* Ohio State Univ, MS, 76; Univ Nebr, BS, 72, PhD(entom), 80. *Prof Exp:* Res assoc, Ill Natural Hist Surv, 80-85. *Mem:* Entom Soc Am; Weed Sci Soc Am. *Res:* Ecological interactions in agroecosystems, especially mutiple pest interactions, and their economic and environmental impact for corp protection. *Mailing Add:* Dept Entom Univ Md College Park MD 20742-0001

LAMPE, FREDERICK WALTER, PHYSICAL CHEMISTRY. *Current Pos:* from assoc prof to prof, 60-91, head dept, 83-88, EMER PROF CHEM, PA STATE UNIV, 92- *Personal Data:* b Chicago, Ill, Jan 5, 27; m 49, Eleanor F Coffin; c Joan, Kathy, Erik, Beth & Kristina. *Educ:* Mich State Col, BS, 50; Columbia Univ, AM, 51, PhD(chem), 53. *Honors & Awards:* US Sr Scientist Award, Alexander von Humboldt Found, 73-74 & 84. *Prof Exp:* Res chemist, Humble Oil & Refining Co, 53-56, sr res chemist, 56-60, res specialist, 60. *Concurrent Pos:* Consult, Socony Mobil Oil Co, 61-69, Sci Res Instruments Corp, 67-77 & W H Johnston Labs, Inc, 60-67; NSF sr fel & guest prof, Univ Freiburg, 66-67. *Mem:* AAAS; Am Chem Soc; fel Am Phys Soc; Royal Soc Chem. *Res:* Photochemistry; radiation chemistry; reactions of free radicals and of gaseous ions; mass spectrometry. *Mailing Add:* 542 Ridge Ave State College PA 16803. *E-Mail:* fwl@email.PSU.edu

LAMPE, MARTIN, PLASMA PHYSICS, CHARGED PARTICLE BEAMS. *Current Pos:* res physicist, 69-75, supvr res physicist, 75-95, SR SCIENTIST, NAVAL RES LAB, 95- *Personal Data:* b Brooklyn, NY, Apr 29, 42; m 64, Barbara Grappo; c William T & Rebecca I. *Educ:* Harvard Univ, AB, 62; Univ Calif, Berkeley, MA, 63, PhD(physics), 67. *Honors & Awards:* E O Hulburt Award, Naval Res Lab, 85. *Prof Exp:* Res assoc, NY Univ, 67-69. *Mem:* Fel Am Phys Soc; Inst Elec & Electronics Engrs; Sigma Xi. *Res:* Theory of plasma instabilities; non-linear theory and propagation of relativistic electron beams; modeling of plasma processing and low-temperature discharges. *Mailing Add:* Naval Res Lab Code 6709 4555 Overlook Ave SW Washington DC 20375-5346. *Fax:* 202-767-0631; *E-Mail:* lampe@ppd.nrl.navy.mil

LAMPEN, J OLIVER, MICROBIOLOGY, MOLECULAR BIOLOGY. *Current Pos:* RETIRED. *Personal Data:* b Holland, Mich, Feb 26, 18; m 44, Miriam Walsh; c David, Peter & Richard. *Educ:* Hope Col, AB, 39; Univ Wis, MS, 41, PhD(biochem), 43. *Hon Degrees:* LHD, Hope Col, 74. *Honors & Awards:* Lilly Award, 52. *Prof Exp:* Biochemist, Am Cyanamid Co, 43-46; res assoc, Med Sch, Wash Univ, 46-47, instr biochem, 47-48, asst prof biol chem, 48-49; assoc prof microbiol, Sch Med, Western Res Univ, 49-53; dir, Div Biochem Res, Squibb Inst Med Res, Olin Mathieson Chem Corp, 53-58; dir, Waksman Inst, Rutgers Univ, 58-80, prof, 80-88, emer prof microbiol, 88-90. *Mem:* AAAS; Am Soc Microbiol; Am Soc Biol Chemists; Am Acad Microbiol; Brit Biochem Soc; Soc Gen Microbiol. *Res:* Secretion of enzymes by microorganisms; site of exoenzyme formation, mechanism of secretion, control of synthesis; antibiotics and cell membrane. *Mailing Add:* 8 Brookfall Rd Edison NJ 08817

LAMPERT, CARL MATTHEW, ALTERNATIVE ENERGY ENGINEERING, OPTICAL SWITCHING TECHNOLOGY. *Current Pos:* OWNER & SCI CONSULT, STAR SCI, 96- *Personal Data:* b Portland, Ore, Feb 20, 52. *Educ:* Univ Calif, Berkeley, BS(electronic eng) & BS(mat sci), 74, MS, 77, PhD(mat sci), 79. *Prof Exp:* Electronics technician, Contra Costa Col, San Pablo, 70-72, comput programmer, US Forestry Serv, 72-74; res asst, Lawrence Berkeley Lab, Calif, 74-79, prin investr & staff scientist, 79-96. *Concurrent Pos:* Conf chmn, Int Optical Eng Soc, 82-, proj leader, Int Energy Agency, Paris, France, 84-96; ed-in-chief, Solar Energy Mat J, 82-; lectr, Inst Theoret Physics, Trieste, Italy, 85-; consult, Lyon & Lyon, Los Angeles, 85, UN Develop Prog, NY, 85-, Innotech, Trumbull, Conn, 86-, Optical Coating Labs Inc, Santa Rosa, 88-, Elf Atochem, France, 90-, Monsanto, St Louis, 96-, Rohm & Haas, 96- *Mem:* Fel Int Optical Eng Soc; Inst Elec & Electronics Engrs; Am Vacuum Soc; Int Solar Energy Soc; Sigma Xi. *Res:* Development of new optical materials and coatings for glass and plastic products, application to buildings, automotive and aerospace glazing; engineering and materials for energy conversion components; large scale optical switching and display products; author of over 100 papers, 1 book, 2 patents, lectured in 16 countries. *Mailing Add:* Star Sci 2384 Stanford Pl Santa Clara CA 95051-1530. *Fax:* 408-261-0171; *E-Mail:* carl@starscience.com

LAMPERT, SEYMOUR, SOLAR ENERGY & ALTERNATE ENERGY APPLICATIONS. *Current Pos:* prof eng, 75-93, EMER PROF ENG, UNIV SOUTHERN CALIF, 93- *Personal Data:* b Brooklyn, NY, Mar 5, 20; m 48, Axelrod; c Rachel B, David A & Martin D. *Educ:* Ga Inst Technol, BS, 43; Calif Inst Technol, MS, 47, AE, 48, PhD(aeronaut eng & math), 54. *Prof Exp:* Instr math, Ga Sch Technol, 43-44; res scientist, Ames Lab, Nat Adv Comt Aeronaut, 44-51; res engr, Jet Propulsion Lab, Calif Inst Technol, 51-54; asst prof eng, Univ Southern Calif, 54-55; chief engr, Odin Assocs, 55-56; mgr appl mech, Ford Aeronotronic, 56-62; dir advan syts, NAm Aviation Space & Info Systs, 62-67; vpres, Syst Assoc Inc, 67-71. *Concurrent Pos:* Consult, Jet Propulsion Lab, Calif Inst Technol, 67-68; sci adv, Dept Defense, 68-69; ed-in-chief, J Solar Sci, 81-82; vpres, Davato Corp, 85- *Mem:* Sigma Xi; Sci Res Soc Am. *Res:* Structures for spacecraft; spacecraft design; methodology for developing area transportation; fluid mechanics; wing theory; solar energy. *Mailing Add:* PO Box 4719 Irvine CA 92716-4719. *E-Mail:* sylamp@aol.com

LAMPERTI, ALBERT A, RADIATION BIOLOGY. *Current Pos:* ASSOC PROF, DEPT ANAT, TEMPLE UNIV, SCH MED, 80- *Personal Data:* b Bronx, NY, Oct 24, 47; m 72; c 2. *Educ:* Manhattan Col, BS, 69; Univ Cincinnati, PhD(anat), 73. *Prof Exp:* Asst prof anat, Univ Cincinnati, Col Med, 73-80. *Mem:* Am Asn Anatomists; Radiation Res Soc. *Res:* Reproductive neuroendocrinology; radiation biology. *Mailing Add:* Dept Anat Temple Univ Sch Med 3400 N Broad St Philadelphia PA 19140-5196

LAMPERTI, JOHN WILLIAMS, STOCHASTIC PROCESSES. *Current Pos:* assoc prof, 63-68, PROF MATH, DARTMOUTH COL, 68- *Personal Data:* b Montclair, NJ, Dec 20, 32; m 57, Claudia J McKay; c Matthew D, Steven J, Aaron M & A Noelle. *Educ:* Haverford Col, BS, 53; Calif Inst Technol, PhD(math), 57. *Prof Exp:* From instr to asst prof math, Stanford Univ, 57-61; vis asst prof, Dartmouth Col, 61-62; res assoc, Rockefeller Inst, 62-63. *Concurrent Pos:* Sci exchange visitor, USSR, 70; vis prof, Aarhus Univ, 72-73, Nat Atonomous Univ Nicaragua, 90; consult, Am Friends Serv Comt, 80, 85 & 91. *Mem:* Fedn Am Scientists; fel Inst Math Statist; Union Concerned Scientists. *Res:* Probability theory, particularly properties of stochastic processes. *Mailing Add:* Dept Math Dartmouth Col Hanover NH 03755. *Fax:* 603-646-1312; *E-Mail:* j.lamperti@dartmouth.edu

LAMPI, RAUNO ANDREW, FOOD SCIENCE & TECHNOLOGY & SERVICE SYSTEMS, CHEMICAL ENGINEERING. *Current Pos:* CONSULT, 90- *Personal Data:* b Gardner, Mass, Aug 12, 29; m 51, Betty M Noponen; c Steven, Martin, Karin & Eric. *Educ:* Univ Mass, BS, 51, MS, 55, PhD(food technol), 57. *Honors & Awards:* Rohland Isker Award, Res & Develop Assocs, 69; Indust Achievement Award, Inst Food Technol, 78; Rietter-Davis Award, Inst Food Technol Packaging Div, 95. *Prof Exp:* Res instr food technol, Univ Mass, 53-57; tech dir, New Eng Appl Prod Co, 59-62; mgr, Food Technol Sect, Cent Eng Labs, FMC Corp, 62-66; packaging technologist, Container Div, Natick Labs, US Army, 66-67, res phys scientist, Packaging Div, 67-69, chief, Systs Develop Br, Packaging Div, 69-76, chief, Food Equip Div, 76-88, chief, Adv Equip Br, Technol Acquisition Div, Natick Res Develop & Eng Ctr, 88-89. *Concurrent Pos:* Asst mgr indust instrumentation, Food Div, Foxboro Co, 57-59. *Mem:* Fel Inst Food Technol. *Res:* Continuous applesauce and juice processes; stability of freeze dried foods; thermal processing of foods in flexible packages and flat metal containers; development of food service systems; design concepts for NASA Space Station Feeding System. *Mailing Add:* 20 Wheeler Rd Westborough MA 01581. *Fax:* 508-366-8069

LAMPKY, JAMES ROBERT, MICROBIOLOGY. *Current Pos:* from asst prof to prof, 66-92, EMER PROF BACT, CENT MICH UNIV, 92- *Personal Data:* b Battle Creek, Mich, June 19, 27; m 71, Shirley Ann Kellett. *Educ:* Eastern Mich Univ, BS, 59; Univ Mo, MA, 61, PhD(microbiol), 66. *Prof Exp:* From instr to asst prof bact, Wis State Univ, 63-66. *Concurrent Pos:* Adv, SC Poison Control Ctr; lectr, Brookgreen Gardens. *Mem:* Am Soc Microbiol; Soc Indust Microbiologists; Mycol Soc Am. *Res:* Cellulolytic fruiting myxobacteria of the genus Polyangium with emphasis on morphology and ultrastructure. *Mailing Add:* 101 Inverness Ct Myrtle Beach SC 19575

LAMPMAN, GARY MARSHALL, ORGANIC CHEMISTRY. *Current Pos:* From asst prof to assoc prof, 64-73, PROF CHEM, WESTERN WASH UNIV, 73- *Personal Data:* b South Gate, Calif, Oct 8, 37; m 71, Marian Shulze; c Elizabeth & Karl. *Educ:* Univ Calif, Los Angeles, BS, 59; Univ Wash, PhD(chem), 64. *Concurrent Pos:* Res fel, Univ Col London, 78, 81 & 86. *Mem:* Am Chem Soc; Sigma Xi. *Res:* Synthetic organic chemistry; organometallic chemistry; chemical education. *Mailing Add:* Dept Chem Western Wash Univ Bellingham WA 98225-9150. *E-Mail:* lampman@chem.wwu.edu

LAMPORT, DEREK THOMAS ANTHONY, BIOCHEMISTRY. *Current Pos:* from asst prof to assoc prof, 64-74, PROF BIOCHEM, DOE PLANT RES LAB, MICH STATE UNIV, 74- *Personal Data:* b Brighton, Eng, Dec 1, 33; m 63; c 5. *Educ:* Univ Cambridge, BA, 58, PhD(biochem), 63. *Prof Exp:* Staff scientist, Res Inst Advan Studies, Martin Marietta Corp, Md, 61-64. *Mem:* Am Chem Soc. *Res:* Plant cell wall proteins; role of hydroxyproline-rich glycoproteins, notably extensin, in plant growth. *Mailing Add:* PO Box 423 Potterville MI 48876

LAMPORT, LESLIE B, CONCURRENT & DISTRIBUTED COMPUTING. *Current Pos:* SR CONSULT ENGR, DIGITAL EQUIP CORP, 85- *Personal Data:* b New York, NY, Feb 7, 41. *Educ:* Mass Inst Technol, BS, 60; Brandeis Univ, MA, 63, PhD(math), 72. *Prof Exp:* Prof math, Marlboro Col, 65-69, Mass Comput Assocs, 70-77 & SRI Int, 77-85. *Mem:* Nat Acad Eng. *Mailing Add:* Digital Equip Corp 130 Lytton Ave Palo Alto CA 94301. *Fax:* 650-853-2104

LAMPPA, GAYLE K, GENETICS, BIOLOGY. *Current Pos:* ASST PROF, DEPT MOLECULAR GENETICS & CELL BIOL, UNIV CHICAGO, 85- *Educ:* Reed Col, BA, 73; Univ Wash, PhD(bot), 80. *Prof Exp:* Postdoctoral fel, Lab Plant Molecular Biol, Rockefeller Univ, 81-84. *Concurrent Pos:* Damon Runyon-Walter Winchell Res Fund postdoctoral fel, 82-84, NIH postdoctoral fel, 82-85; Zeisler fac award, 85; Andrew Mellon fel, 85; ad hoc reviewer, Dept Energy & NSF; chmn, Univ Biosafety Comt, Univ Chicago, 86-87, mem, Ctr Photochem & Photobiol & Comt Genetics; mem study sect, Prog Plant Growth & Develop, Competitive Res Grants Off, USDA, 88, 89 & 90. *Mem:* Sigma Xi; Am Soc Plant Physiol; Int Soc Plant Molecular Biol; Am Soc Cell Biol. *Mailing Add:* Dept Molecular Genetics & Cell Biol Univ Chicago 920 E 58th St Chicago IL 60637-1432

LAMPSON, BUTLER WRIGHT, COMPUTER SCIENCE. *Current Pos:* ARCHITECT, MICROSOFT, 95- *Personal Data:* b Washington, DC, Dec 23, 43; m 67, Lois Alterman; c Michael & David. *Educ:* Harvard Univ, AB, 64; Univ Calif, Berkeley, PhD(comput sci), 67. *Hon Degrees:* DSc, Swiss Fed Inst Technol, Zurich, 86. *Honors & Awards:* Software Systs Award, Asn Comput Mach, 85, Turing Award, 92. *Prof Exp:* From asst prof to assoc prof comput sci, Univ Calif, Berkeley, 67-71; res fel, Xerox Palo Alto Res Ctr, 71-80, sr res fel, 80-84; sr corp consult engr, Digital Equip Corp, Cambridge, Mass, 85-94. *Concurrent Pos:* Dir syst develop, Berkeley Comput Corp, 69-71. *Mem:* Nat Acad Eng; fel Asn Comput Mach; Am Acad Arts & Sci. *Res:* Programming languages and operating systems. *Mailing Add:* Microsoft 180 Lakeview Ave Cambridge MA 02138. *Fax:* 617-547-9580; *E-Mail:* blampson@microsoft.com

LAMPSON, FRANCIS KEITH, METALLURGICAL ENGINEERING, MATERIALS ENGINEERING. *Current Pos:* DIR MAT ENGRS, MARQUARDT CO, DIV CCI CORP, 65- *Personal Data:* b Minneapolis, Minn, Aug 7, 24; m 45, Margaret E Snyder; c Michael K, Jan C, Andrea L & Kevin D. *Educ:* Univ Ill, BS, 49. *Prof Exp:* Jr metallurgist, NEPA Div, Fairchild Eng & Air Corp, 49-51; exp metallurgist, Allison Div, Gen Motors Corp, 51-54; group leader, Mat & Processing, Marquardt Co, Van Nuys, Calif, 54-57; Pacific Coast area tech rep, Allegheny-Ludlum Steel Corp, Los Angeles, 57-65. *Concurrent Pos:* Pres, F K Lampson Assocs, 74- *Mem:* Am Soc Metals; Soc Aerospace Mat Process Engrs; Am Soc Testing Mats; Am Inst Mining Engrs. *Res:* Propulsion technology materials; ferrous and super alloy materials; refractory materials and related disilicide coatings; biomedical materials. *Mailing Add:* 10000 Aldea Ave N Northridge CA 91325

LAMPSON, GEORGE PETER, BIOCHEMISTRY. *Current Pos:* RETIRED. *Personal Data:* b Colman, SDak, June 12, 19; m 48; c 3. *Educ:* SDak State Univ, BS, 42; Univ Wis, MS, 50. *Prof Exp:* Res assoc biochem, Ortho Pharmaceut Corp, 50-59; sr res biochemist, Dept Virus & Cell Biol, Merck Inst Therapeut Res, 59-85. *Mem:* NY Acad Sci; Am Chem Soc; Am Soc Biol Chemists. *Res:* Purification and characterization of chicken embryo interferon as a low molecular protein; synthetic and natural double-stranded RNA as inducers of inderferon and host resistance; virus chemistry. *Mailing Add:* 2012 Keystone Dr Hatfield PA 19440

LAMPSON, LOIS ALTERMAN, IMMUNE RESPONSES. *Current Pos:* ASST PROF ANAT, SCH MED, UNIV PA, 79- *Educ:* Univ Calif, Berkeley, PhD(immunol), 76. *Res:* Role of major histocompatibility complex in neural tissue; immune response to neural tumor. *Mailing Add:* Dept Neurol Harvard Med Sch Brigham & Women's Hosp LMRC 116 Boston MA 02115

LAMPTON, MICHAEL LOGAN, X-RAY ASTRONOMY. *Current Pos:* ASST RES PHYSICIST, SPACE SCI LAB, UNIV CALIF, BERKELEY, 67- *Personal Data:* b Williamsport, Pa, Mar 1, 41. *Educ:* Calif Inst Technol, BS, 62; Univ Calif, Berkeley, PhD(physics), 67. *Concurrent Pos:* NSF fel, Univ Calif, Berkeley, 68-69. *Mem:* Am Geophys Union; Am Astron Soc. *Res:* Ultraviolet astronomy. *Mailing Add:* 10821 Sterling Ave Berkeley CA 94703

LAMSTER, HAL B, GENERAL COMPUTER SCIENCE, OPERATIONS RESEARCH. *Current Pos:* EXEC VPRES, TELMAR GROUP INC, 71- *Personal Data:* b New York, NY, July 12, 41; m 67; c 1. *Educ:* NY Univ, BS, 63, MS, 70. *Prof Exp:* Consult, Gen Analysis, 68-69; pres, Time Sharing Sci Inc, 70-71. *Concurrent Pos:* Chair comt, Asn Comput Mach, 86- *Mem:* Inst Elec & Electronics Engrs; Asn Comput Mach. *Res:* Microcomputing application; data communications; man-machine interactions. *Mailing Add:* 148 Madison Ave New York NY 10016

LAMSTER, IRA BARRY, DENTISTRY, BIOCHEMISTRY. *Current Pos:* ASSOC PROF DENT & DIR PERIODONT, COLUMBIA UNIV, 88- *Personal Data:* b New York, NY, Mar 6, 50; m 71; c 2. *Educ:* Queens Col, NY, BA, 71; Univ Chicago, SM, 72; State Univ NY, Stony Brook, DDS, 77; Harvard Univ, MMSc, 80; Am Bd Oral Med, cert, 84. *Prof Exp:* Res fel, Lab Surg Res, Med Sch, Harvard Univ & teaching fel periodontol, Sch Dent Med, 77-80; from asst prof to assoc prof periodont & oral med, Fairleigh Univ, 80-88. *Concurrent Pos:* Prin investr, res contracts & grants, Lever Res Inc, Warner-Lambert Co, Johnson & Johnson & Block Drug Co, 80-, NIH dent student res training award, Nat Inst Dent Res, 82 & NIH grants, 82-86 & 85-; Salisbury fel. *Mem:* Sigma Xi; Am Dent Asn; Am Acad Periodontol; AAAS; Am Acad Oral Med. *Res:* Host response in human periodontal disease; diagnostic techniques for periodontal disease; application of a biochemical profile of gingival crevicular fluid. *Mailing Add:* Columbia Univ Sch Dent & Oral Surg 630 W 168 St New York NY 10032

LAMUNYON, CRAIG WILLIS, ANIMAL BEHAVIOR, ENTOMOLOGY. *Current Pos:* RES ASSOC, DEPT MOLECULAR & CELLULAR BIOL, UNIV ARIZ, TUCSON, 93- *Personal Data:* b Fullerton, Calif, Feb 2, 60; m 83, Cynthia A Munson; c Diana N & Kyle C. *Educ:* Calif State Univ, Fullerton, BA, 84; Cornell Univ, PhD(chem ecol), 92. *Prof Exp:* Res assoc, Cornell Univ, Ithaca, NY, 92-93. *Mem:* AAAS; Entom Soc Am; Animal Behav Soc; Sigma Xi. *Res:* Behavioral ecology of mating; sperm competition and nuptial investments in invertebrates; ecology of insect defense mechanisms. *Mailing Add:* Univ Ariz Sect Molecular & Cell Biol Tucson AZ 85721-0001. *Fax:* 520-621-3709; *E-Mail:* ward_lab@tikal.biosci.arizona.edu

LAMUTH, HENRY LEWIS, APPLIED PHYSICS, ELECTRICAL ENGINEERING. *Current Pos:* ALPHACOMM INC, COMPUT SYSTS, 87- *Personal Data:* b Painesville, Ohio, Apr 15, 42; m 69; c 2. *Educ:* Ohio State Univ, BS, 66, PhD(physics), 70. *Prof Exp:* Assoc res physicist optics, Willow Run Labs, Inst Sci & Technol, Univ Mich, 70-72; mem tech staff electro-optics, Orlando Div, Martin Marietta Aerospace, 72-74; mgr, Sensors, Electronics & Controls Group, Columbus Labs, Battelle Mem Inst, 74-; Sperry Corp, 87. *Mem:* AAAS; Am Phys Soc; Sigma Xi; Inst Elec & Electronics Engrs. *Res:* Electro-optics, infrared, radar sensors and sensing; missile systems; atmospheric transmission; fiber and integrated optics; communication systems and techniques with optical radiation; electronic control systems; analog-digital electronic systems. *Mailing Add:* 2041 Wyandotte Rd Columbus OH 43212

LAMY, PETER PAUL, geriatrics & gerontology, clinical pharmacology; deceased, see previous edition for last biography

LAN, CHUAN-TAU EDWARD, ENGINEERING MECHANICS, CIVIL ENGINEERING. *Current Pos:* from asst prof to assoc prof, 68-78, prof, 78-92, BELLOWS DISTINGUISHED PROF AEROSPACE ENG, UNIV KANS, 92- *Personal Data:* b Taiwan, China, Apr 21, 35; US citizen; m 61, Sumy Chen; c Susan, Justin & Austin. *Educ:* Nat Taiwan Univ, BS, 58; Univ Minn, MS, 63; NY Univ, PhD(aeronaut), 68. *Honors & Awards:* Cert of Recognition, NASA Langley Res Ctr, 78, 80, 82 & 86. *Prof Exp:* Asst civil engr hydraul, Bd Water Supply, NY, 63-65; assoc res scientist aeronaut, Aerospace Labs, NY Univ, 68. *Concurrent Pos:* Prin investr, NASA Langley Res Ctr, 73-; reviewer, J Aircraft & Am Inst Aeronaut & Astronaut, 75-; consult, Aeronaut Res Lab, Taiwan, 77- & Vigyan Res Assoc, Inc, 86- *Mem:* Am Inst Aeronaut & Astronaut. *Res:* Steady and unsteady aerodynamics; flight dynamics. *Mailing Add:* Dept Aerospace Eng Univ Kans Lawrence KS 66045. *Fax:* 785-864-3597; *E-Mail:* vortex@kuhub.cc.ukans.edu

LAN, MING-JYE, POLYMER SYNTHESIS, POLYMER COMPOSITE. *Current Pos:* RES CHEMIST, BAXTER INC, 92- *Personal Data:* b Kaohsiung, Taiwan, Repub China, Nov 3, 53; m 80; c 1. *Educ:* Nat Tsing-Hua Univ, Taiwan, BS, 76; Univ Mich, MS, 81, PhD(chem & macromolecular sci & eng), 85. *Prof Exp:* Teaching asst org chem, Univ Mich, 79-84; res chemist, Allied-Signal Inc, 85-87, sr res chemist, 87-92. *Mem:* Am Chem Soc; Soc Advan Mat & Process Eng. *Res:* Bipolar membranes for water splitting; synthesis and characterization of biopolymers as anti-viral agents; synthesis of monomers and polymers; thermoset polymers for composites. *Mailing Add:* 303 Southgate Dr Vernon Hills IL 60061

LAN, SHIH-JUNG, DRUG METABOLISM. *Current Pos:* res investr drug metab, 69-73, sr res investr, 73-74, RES GROUP LEADER, SQUIBB INST MED RES, 75- *Personal Data:* b Kwangtung, China, Sept 15, 38; m 67; c 2. *Educ:* Univ Tunghai, BS, 60; Okla State Univ, MS, 64; Univ Minn, PhD(biochem), 68. *Prof Exp:* Fel physiol chem, Univ Wis, 67-69. *Mem:* Am Chem Soc; Am Soc Pharmacol & Exp Therapeut. *Res:* Microsomal drug metabolism enzyme systems; mechanism of drug action. *Mailing Add:* Bristol-Myers Squibb Co PO Box 4000 Princeton NJ 08543-4000

LANA, EDWARD PETER, HORTICULTURE. *Current Pos:* prof & chmn dept, 56-81, EMER PROF HORT, NDAK STATE UNIV, 81- *Personal Data:* b Duluth, Minn, Oct 17, 14; m 42; c 3. *Educ:* Univ Minn, BS, 42, MS, 43, PhD, 48. *Prof Exp:* Canning crops res, Fairmont Canning Co, Minn, 43-47; asst prof hort, Iowa State Univ, 47-56. *Mem:* Am Soc Hort Sci; Sigma Xi. *Res:* Crop breeding; cultural studies. *Mailing Add:* 11103 Avenue N 401 W Fargo ND 58102-4648

LANAM, RICHARD DELBERT, JR, METALLURGY OF PLATINUM GROUP METALS. *Current Pos:* metall section head, 79-82, tech oper mgr, 82-88, TECH/ENG MGR, ENGELHARD CORP, 88- *Personal Data:* b Denver, Col, May 31, 43; m 65, Anna Coyle; c Richard III, Amy, Catherine. *Educ:* Northwestern Univ, BS, 66; Drexel Univ, MS, 69, PhD(mat eng), 72. *Prof Exp:* Eng Specialist, Olin Corp, 70-74; sr metall eng, Pfizer Inc, 74-79. *Mem:* Am Soc Metals; Am Inst Metall Eng. *Res:* General refining and use of platinum group metals; sputter-coated ruthenium for electrical contact applications; author of ten publications and holder of nine US patents. *Mailing Add:* 655 Fourth Ave Westfield NJ 07090

LANCASTER, BRICK, HEALTH EDUCATION ADMINSTRATION. *Current Pos:* ASSOC DIR HEALTH EDUC PRACT & POLICY, DIV ADULT & COMMUNITY HEALTH, NAT CTR CHRONIC DIS PREV & HEALTH PROM, CTR DIS CONTROL & PREV, 88- *Honors & Awards:* Sarah Mazelis Award, Am Pub Health Asn, 93; Health Prom & Educ Advocacy Award, Asn State & Territorial Dirs Health Prom & Pub Health Educ, 96. *Prof Exp:* Chief, Off Health Prom & Educ, Ariz Dept Health Serv. *Concurrent Pos:* Mem, HIV Comt, Asn State & Territorial Health Off. *Mem:* Asn State & Territorial Dirs Pub Health Educ (pres); Soc Pub Health Educ (vpres & secy). *Mailing Add:* Ctr Dis Control & Prev 4770 Buford Hwy NE Atlanta GA 30341

LANCASTER, CLEO, ANIMAL PHYSIOLOGY. *Current Pos:* SR RES BIOLOGIST, UPJOHN CO, 71- *Personal Data:* b Rocky Mount, NC, Dec 10, 48. *Educ:* Elizabeth City State Univ, NC, BS, 71; Western Mich Univ, MS, 79. *Prof Exp:* Res asst, Brookhaven Nat Lab, 71. *Mem:* AAAS; NY Acad Sci. *Res:* Experimental gastroenterology; development of experimental models of ulcers, gastric lesions, pancreatitis and surgical methods to study gastric secretion; helped develop the cytoprotection concept, antisecretory property of prostaglandins and the antipancreatitis effect of opioid agonists. *Mailing Add:* Safety Pharmacol Upjohn Co Kalamazoo MI 49001

LANCASTER, GEORGE MAURICE, DIFFERENTIAL GEOMETRY. *Current Pos:* RETIRED. *Personal Data:* b Penrith, Eng, July 18, 34; m 64, Georgia Reid; c John & Sarah. *Educ:* Univ Liverpool, BSc, 56; Univ Sask, PhD(math), 67. *Prof Exp:* Res analyst, Weapons Res Div, A V Roe & Co Ltd, Woodford, Eng, 56-58; opers res analyst, Northern Elec Co Ltd, Montreal, 58-60; lectr math, Royal Roads Mil Col, 60-64; asst prof, Univ Sask, 67-70; assoc prof, Royal Rds Mil Col, 70-80, head dept, 78-87, prof math, 80-95, dean sci & eng, 87-95. *Concurrent Pos:* Nat Res Coun Can grants, Univ Sask, 68-70; spec lectr, Univ Victoria, 71. *Mem:* Am Math Soc; Tensor Soc. *Res:* Differential geometry; imbedding of Riemannian manifolds. *Mailing Add:* 1229 St Patrick St Victoria BC V8S 4Y3 Can

LANCASTER, JACK R, JR, BIOENERGETICS, ELECTRON TRANSFER. *Current Pos:* PROF PHYSIOL, LA STATE UNIV, NEW ORLEANS, 94- *Personal Data:* b Memphis, Tenn, Aug 27, 48; c 2, Judith Roberts; c Tonya & Madeline. *Educ:* Univ Tenn, Martin, BS, 70, PhD(biochem), 74. *Prof Exp:* Res assoc biochem, Cornell Univ, 74-76 & Duke Univ, 76-80; from asst prof to assoc prof biochem, Utah State Univ, 80-92; assoc prof, Univ Pittsburgh, 92-95. *Concurrent Pos:* NSF trainee, 70-73; estab investr, Am Heart Asn, 83-88; mem, Coun Basic Sci, Am Heart Asn; nat lectr, Sigma Xi, 94- *Mem:* Am Chem Soc; Am Soc Biol Chemists; Biophys Soc; Sigma Xi; Am Heart Asn. *Res:* Basic biochemical mechanisms of biological actions of nitric oxide and immune cytotoxicity; bioenergetics; electron transfer. *Mailing Add:* Depts Physiol & Med La State Univ Med Ctr 1901 Perdido St New Orleans LA 70112. *E-Mail:* ilanca@lsumc.edu

LANCASTER, JAMES D, AGRONOMY. *Current Pos:* RETIRED. *Personal Data:* b Randolph, Miss, June 11, 19; m 42; c 3. *Educ:* Miss State Col, BS, 47, MS, 48; Univ Wis, PhD, 54. *Prof Exp:* Asst agronomist, Exp Sta & asst prof agron, 51-57, agronomist, Exp Sta & prof agron, Miss State Univ, 57-85. *Mem:* Am Soc Agron; Soil Sci Soc Am; AAAS. *Res:* Soil fertility and testing; fertilizer evaluation; crop fertilization. *Mailing Add:* 1250 Oktoc Rd Starkville MS 39759

LANCASTER, JESSIE LEONARD, JR, ENTOMOLOGY. *Current Pos:* from asst prof to assoc prof, 51-60, PROF ENTOM, UNIV ARK, FAYETTEVILLE, 60- *Personal Data:* b Horatio, Ark, Jan 26, 23; m 46; c 4. *Educ:* Univ Ark, BSA, 47; Cornell Univ, PhD(econ entom), 51. *Prof Exp:* Asst, Cornell Univ, 47-51. *Concurrent Pos:* NIH spec res fel, Rocky Mountain Lab, 63-64. *Mem:* Entom Soc Am. *Res:* Medical veterinary entomology and mosquito control. *Mailing Add:* 3076 N Lancaster Lane Fayetteville AR 72703

LANCASTER, JOHN, MICROBIAL GENETICS. *Current Pos:* from asst prof to assoc prof, 68-83, assoc dean, 84-88, PROF MICROBIOL, UNIV OKLA, 83- *Personal Data:* b Bolton, Miss, Aug 30, 37; m 64. *Educ:* Miss State Univ, BS, 59, MS, 61; Univ Tex, PhD(microbiol), 64. *Prof Exp:* NIH trainee, Univ Tex, 63-64. *Concurrent Pos:* NIH grant, 66; dir scholar-leadership enrichment prog, Univ Okla, 87-, dir lab animal resources, 88- *Mem:* AAAS; Am Soc Microbiol; Hist Sci Soc; Am Asn Lab Animal Sci. *Res:* Mechanism of conjugation in Escherichia coli; animal behavior in relations to animal rights; biological perspectives on environmental ethics. *Mailing Add:* Univ Okla Main Campus 770 Van Fleet Oval Norman OK 73019-6130

LANCASTER, MALCOLM, CARDIOLOGY, GERIATRICS. *Current Pos:* PROF CLIN MED, DEPT FAMILY PRACT, UNIV TEX HEALTH SCI CTR, SAN ANTONIO, 85- *Personal Data:* b Amarillo, Tex, July 28, 31; m 59, Patricia Pramik; c Pamela (Lancaster-Elzinga), Kimberly (Russell), Lisa & Timothy. *Educ:* Univ Tex Southwestern Med Sch, MD, 56; Univ Colo, Denver, MS, 60. *Honors & Awards:* Casimir Funk Award, Asn Mil Surgeons US, 71; USAF Res & Develop Award, 71; John Jeffries Award, Am Inst Aeronaut & Astronaut, 74; Arnold D Tuttle Award, Aerospace Med Asn, 75. *Prof Exp:* Chief med serv, 48th Tactical Hosp, Royal Air Force, Lakenheath, Eng, 60-63; chief, Cardiopulmonary Serv & chmn, Dept Med, USAF Hosp, Wright-Patterson AFB, 65-66; chief, Internal Med Br, Sch Aerospace Med, Brooks AFB, Tex, 66-73, chief, Clin Sci Div, 72-78; chief med serv & clin dir, San Antonio State Chest Hosp, 78-81; pres, Systemics, Inc, San Antonio, TX, 81- *Mem:* Fel Aerospace Med Asn; fel Am Col Cardiol; fel Am Col Physicians; Am Geriat Soc; fel Am Col Prev Med. *Res:* Medical aspects of aerospace operations; cardiovascular disease epidemiology; computers and electrocardiography; computer aided design; geriatrics aerospace medicine. *Mailing Add:* 101 Hibiscus San Antonio TX 78213

LANCE, EUGENE MITCHELL, surgery; deceased, see previous edition for last biography

LANCE, GEORGE M(ILWARD), MECHANICAL & ELECTRICAL ENGINEERING. *Current Pos:* from asst prof to prof, Univ Iowa, 61-70, assoc dean undergrad progs & student affairs, 74-79, chmn eng prog, 74-85, prof mech eng, 70-91, EMER PROF MECH ENG, UNIV IOWA, 91- *Personal Data:* b Youngstown, Ohio, Dec 4, 28; m 64, Phyllis Sprague; c Kathryn, Deborah, John, Rebecca & George. *Educ:* Case Inst Technol, BS, 52, MS, 54. *Prof Exp:* Instr eng, Case Inst Technol, 52-54; res engr, TRW, Inc, 54-56; lectr mech eng, Univ Wash, St Louis, 56-60; sr systs engr, Moog Servocontrols, Inc, 60-61. *Mem:* Am Soc Mech Engrs. *Res:* Theory of automatic control; hydraulic servosystems; system design. *Mailing Add:* 609 S Summit Univ Iowa Iowa City IA 52240

LANCE, R(ICHARD) H, MECHANICS. *Current Pos:* from asst prof to assoc prof theoret & appl mech, 62-81, assoc dean eng, 74-86, PROF THEORET & APPL MECH, CORNELL UNIV, 81- *Personal Data:* b Geneva, Ill, Nov 29, 31; m 53; c 3. *Educ:* Univ Ill, Urbana, BSME, 54; Ill Inst Technol, MSME, 57; Brown Univ, PhD(solid mech), 62. *Prof Exp:* Test engr, Minneapolis Honeywell Regulator Co, 54; mech engr, Ingersoll Milling Mach Co, Ill, 57-58; res assoc, Brown Univ, 62. *Concurrent Pos:* Lectr, Int Bus Mach Corp, NY, 66; sr scientist, Hughes Aircraft Co, 80-81, 86-87. *Mem:* Am Soc Mech Engrs; AAAS; Am Acad Mech. *Res:* Mechanical behavior of solids; engineering structural mechanics; plasticity; numerical methods in engineering. *Mailing Add:* Cornell Univ 322 Thurston Hall Ithaca NY 14853-1503

LANCE, VALENTINE A, REPRODUCTIVE PHYSIOLOGY, COMPARATIVE ENDOCRINOLOGY. *Current Pos:* ASST PROF PHYSIOL, LA STATE UNIV, 78-; ENDOCRINOLOGIST, SAN DIEGO ZOO, 87- *Personal Data:* b London, Eng, Feb 14, 40; wid; c 2. *Educ:* Long Island Univ, BS, 66; Col William & Mary, MA, 68; Univ Hong Kong, PhD(zool), 74. *Prof Exp:* Demonstr zool, Univ Hong Kong, 68-74; res assoc endocrinol, Boston Univ, 74-78. *Concurrent Pos:* Reviewer, Gen & Comp Endocrinol, J Exp Zool, Peptides, Herpetologica J Wildlife Dis; grant rev, NSF; asst prof, Sch Med, Tulane Univ, 82-87. *Mem:* Endocrine Soc; Soc Study Reproduction; Am Soc Zoologists; Soc Study Amphibians & Reptiles; Herpetologists League; Sigma Xi; AAAS. *Res:* Evolution of the endocrine system; evolution of pituitary control of gonadal steroidogenesis; role of hypothalamic hormones and related reptiles in non-mammalian vertebrates; hormonal control of seasonal reproduction; physiology and endocrinology of non-mammalian vertebrates; endocrinology of pregnancy, pancreatic hormones and peptides in non-mammalian and mammalian vertebrates. *Mailing Add:* Res Dept San Diego Zoo PO Box 551 San Diego CA 92112

LANCET, MICHAEL SAVAGE, PHYSICAL CHEMISTRY, CHEMICAL ENGINEERING. *Current Pos:* RES SCIENTIST COAL CONVERSION RES, CONSOL COAL CO, 74- *Personal Data:* b Detroit, Mich, Dec 11, 44; m 69; c 1. *Educ:* Rose Hulman Inst Technol, BS, 66; Univ Chicago, MS, 71, PhD(nuclear chem), 72. *Prof Exp:* Res assoc nuclear cosmo chem, Carnegie-Mellon Univ, 72-74. *Concurrent Pos:* Fel, Carnegie-Mellon Univ, 72-74. *Mem:* AAAS; Am Chem Soc; Sigma Xi. *Res:* Conversion of coal to substitute natural gas and synthetic liquids; utilization of all other forms of energy. *Mailing Add:* Chem Res Div Consolidation Coal Co Library PA 15129

LANCHANTIN, GERARD FRANCIS, BIOCHEMISTRY. *Current Pos:* RETIRED. *Personal Data:* b Detroit, Mich, Mar 27, 29; m 55; c 5. *Educ:* Seton Hall Univ, BS, 50; Univ Wyo, MS, 51; Univ Southern Calif, PhD(biochem), 54. *Honors & Awards:* Chaney Award Clin Chem, 81. *Prof Exp:* Res assoc, Sch Med, Univ Southern Calif, 54-55, from asst prof to assoc prof biochem, 57-69; dir biochem, St Joseph Med Ctr, 74-85. *Concurrent Pos:* Consult, Los Angeles Co Gen Hosp, 57-; adj prof biochem, Sch Med, Univ Southern Calif, 69- *Mem:* Fel AAAS; Am Asn Clin Chem; Am Chem Soc; Am Soc Hemat; Am Soc Biol Chemists. *Res:* Clinical biochemistry; blood coagulation. *Mailing Add:* 65 S La Senda South Laguna CA 92677-3346

LANCIANI, CARMINE ANDREW, ECOLOGY. *Current Pos:* Interim asst prof zool, Univ Fla, 68-70, asst prof zool & biol sci, 70-73, assoc prof zool, 73-80, PROF ZOOL, UNIV FLA, 80- *Personal Data:* b Leominster, Mass, May 16, 41; m 64; c 2. *Educ:* Cornell Univ, BS, 63, PhD, 68. *Mem:* Ecol Soc Am; Entom Soc Am; Am Soc Limnol & Oceanog; Soc Study Evolution. *Res:* Population ecology of aquatic organisms, particularly life cycles, growth, reproduction and competition of parasitic water mites; effect of parasitism on host ecology. *Mailing Add:* Dept Zool Univ Fla 416 Bar Bldg Gainesville FL 32611

LANCMAN, HENRY, NUCLEAR SPECTROSCOPY, PHOTONUCLEAR REACTIONS. *Current Pos:* instr, 68-70, from asst prof to assoc prof, 70-78, PROF PHYSICS, CITY UNIV NY, BROOKLYN COL, 78- *Personal Data:* b Warsaw, Poland, Mar 19, 32; US citizen; m 63, Ina Serf; c Steven & Anna. *Educ:* Moscow Univ, MS, 58; Inst Nuclear Res, Polish Acad Sci, PhD(physics), 66. *Prof Exp:* Asst res physics, Inst Nuclear Res, Warsaw, Poland, 58-61, sr asst res, 61-65, head, Lab Gamma Ray Spectroscopy, 65-66; res assoc, Columbia Univ, 67-68. *Concurrent Pos:* Consult, Am Inst Physics, 68-71; vis prof physics, Rijks Univ, Utrecht, Holland, 74-75; res grants, PSC-BHE, 76-88, NSF, 77-78 & US Dept Energy, 79-85. *Mem:* Am Phys Soc; Sigma Xi. *Res:* Higher order effects in beta decay; lifetimes of nuclear states; nuclear resonance flourescence and absorbtion of gamma rays; photofission. *Mailing Add:* Dept Physics Brooklyn Col Bedford Ave & Ave H Brooklyn NY 11210

LAND, CECIL E(LVIN), ELECTRONICS ENGINEERING, SOLID STATE PHYSICS. *Current Pos:* staff mem, 56-83, DISTINGUISHED MEM TECH STAFF, SANDIA NAT LABS, 83- *Personal Data:* b Lebanon, Mo, Jan 8, 26; m 47; c 2. *Educ:* Okla State Univ, BS, 49. *Hon Degrees:* DSc, Okla Christian Col, 78. *Honors & Awards:* Nat Soc Prof Engrs Award, 73; Frances Rice Darne Mem Award, Soc Info Display, 76; Recognition Award, Inst Elec & Electronics Engrs UFFC-S, 86, Achievement Award, 90. *Prof Exp:* Prof engr, Electronics Div, Westinghouse Elec Corp, Md, 49-56. *Concurrent Pos:* Chmn, Inst Elec & Electronics Engrs UFFC-S Ferroelectrics Comt, 78- *Mem:* Fel Soc Info Display; fel Inst Elec & Electronics Engrs; Am Phys Soc; fel Am Ceramics Soc; Optical Soc Am. *Res:* Ferroelectric ceramic electrooptic and piezoelectric materials and devices; ferroelectric thin films and devices. *Mailing Add:* 2118 Gretta St NE Albuquerque NM 87112

LAND, CHARLES EVEN, STATISTICS, EPIDEMIOLOGY. *Current Pos:* expert math statistician, Biometry Br, 75-77, health statistician, Environ Epidemiol Br, 77-84, HEALTH STATISTICIAN, RADIATION EPIDEMIOL BR, NAT CANCER INST, NIH, 84- *Personal Data:* b San Francisco, Calif, July 13, 37; m 60, Vera F Thyne; c David & Graham. *Educ:* Univ Ore, BA, 59; Univ Chicago, MA, 64, PhD(statist), 68. *Honors & Awards:* Outstanding Serv Medal, USPHS, 91. *Prof Exp:* Res assoc statist, Atomic Bomb Casualty Comn, Nat Acad Sci, 66-68; asst prof, Ore State Univ, 68-73; res assoc statist, Atomic Bomb Casualty Comn & Radiation Effects Res Found, 73-75. *Concurrent Pos:* Mem, Nat Coun Radiation Protections Measurements; mem comt 1 on risk assessment, Int Comn Radiol Protection. *Mem:* Radiation Res Soc; fel Am Col Epidemiol; fel Am Statist Asn; Biomet Soc; AAAS; Am Epidemiol Soc. *Res:* Risk analysis; inference problems associated with transformations of data; radiation carcinogenesis in human populations; epidemiology; biometry. *Mailing Add:* Radiation Epidemiol Br Nat Cancer Inst Exec Plaza N Rm 408 Bethesda MD 20892. *Fax:* 301-402-0207; *E-Mail:* Bitnet: cyl@nihcu

LAND, DAVID J(OHN), ATOMIC & MOLECULAR PHYSICS, MATERIALS ANALYSIS. *Current Pos:* Nat Acad Sci res assoc, 66-68, RES PHYSICIST, NAVAL SURFACE WEAPONS CTR, 68- *Personal Data:* b Boston, Mass, Feb 15, 39. *Educ:* Boston Col, BS, 59; Brown Univ, PhD(physics), 66. *Prof Exp:* Res asst physics, Brown Univ, 59-66. *Mem:* Am Phys Soc; Optical Soc Am. *Res:* Atomic collision physics; modelling and simulation of atomic collision processes. *Mailing Add:* Code 682 Carderock Div Naval Surface Warfare Ctr 841 MacArthur Blvd West Bethesda MD 20817-5700. *Fax:* 301-227-4733; *E-Mail:* landd@oasys.dt.navy.mil

LAND, GEOFFREY ALLISON, histocompatibility & immunogenetics, medical microbiology, for more information see previous edition

LAND, LYNTON S, GEOLOGY, GEOCHEMISTRY. *Current Pos:* asst prof, 67-77, PROF GEOL, UNIV TEX, AUSTIN, 77- *Personal Data:* b Baltimore, Md, Dec 30, 40. *Educ:* Johns Hopkins Univ, AB, 62, MA, 63; Lehigh Univ, PhD(geol), 66. *Prof Exp:* Res fel geol, Calif Inst Technol, 66-67. *Mem:* Soc Econ Paleontologists & Mineralogists; Int Asn Sedimentol. *Res:* Sedimentology; carbonate sedimentation; diagenesis; sedimentary geochemistry; stable isotope geochemistry. *Mailing Add:* Dept Geol Sci Univ Tex Austin TX 78712-1026

LAND, MING HUEY, CAD APPLICATIONS. *Current Pos:* chair technol, 83-89, DEAN FINE & APPL ARTS, APPALACHIAN STATE UNIV, 89- *Personal Data:* b Hsinchu, Taiwan, July 10, 40; US citizen; m 70; c 2. *Educ:* Taiwan Normal Univ, BS, 63; Northern Ill Univ, MS, 68; Utah State Univ, EdD, 70. *Honors & Awards:* Spec Recognition Award, Int Technol Educ Asn, 90. *Prof Exp:* Asst prof technol, Eastern Ill Univ, 70-71; prof indust educ, Miami Univ, 71-83. *Concurrent Pos:* Fulbright lectr, Chungnam Nat Univ Korea, 80-81; vis prof, Northeast Univ Technol, China, 86. *Mem:* Am Soc Eng Educ; Am Voc Asn; Int Technol Educ Asn; Nat Asn Indust Technol. *Res:* Theories of engineering graphics; descriptive geometry; applications in computer graphics. *Mailing Add:* 320 University Circle Boone NC 28607

LAND, PETER L, SOLID STATE PHYSICS, CERAMICS. *Current Pos:* Res scientist, Metall & Ceramics Lab, Aerospace Res Labs, 64-75, RES SCIENTIST, HARDENED MAT BR, WRIGHT LABS, WRIGHT-PATTERSON AFB, OHIO, 75- *Personal Data:* b Leasburg, Mo, Nov 20, 29; m 66, Kathleen J Wysong; c Stephanie M, Jennifer S & Debora D. *Educ:* Univ Mo, BS, 58, MS, 60, PhD(physics), 64. *Mem:* Sigma Xi. *Res:* New or improved nonlinear optical materials; optical properties of solids and liquids; laser effects on materials; optical filton theory. *Mailing Add:* 502 Land Dr Dayton OH 45440-3701. *Fax:* 937-255-3377; *E-Mail:* landpl@milgate.ml.wpafb.af.mil

LAND, ROBERT H, NUCLEAR PHYSICS, SCIENTIFIC & ENGINEERING COMPUTER APPLICATIONS. *Current Pos:* RETIRED. *Personal Data:* b Portland, Maine, Sept 17, 24. *Educ:* Univ Maine, BS, 49; Mass Inst Technol, PhD(nuclear physics), 57. *Prof Exp:* Asst physicist, Argonne Nat Lab, 56-60, assoc physicist, 60-85, physicist, 85-91. *Mem:* Am Phys Soc; Asn Comput Mach; Sigma Xi. *Res:* Photoproduction of charged pi-mesons from deuterium; reactor neutron diffusion theory; molecular physics and solid state physics calculations using digital computers. *Mailing Add:* 5528 S Everett Ave Chicago IL 60637

LAND, WILLIAM EVERETT, PHYSICAL CHEMISTRY. *Current Pos:* dep head high explosives sect, Bur Ord, 42-51, head high explosives res & develop, 51-60, div engr, Mines & Explosives Div, Bur Naval Weapons, 60-65, asst dir, Mine Warfare Proj Off, 65-66, div engr, Mine Warfare Div, Naval Ord Systs Command, 66-68, CONSULT NAVAL ORD SYSTS COMMAND, BUR NAVAL WEAPONS, NAVY DEPT, 68- *Personal Data:* b Baltimore, Md, Aug 23, 08; m 42. *Educ:* Johns Hopkins Univ, BS, 28, PhD(phys chem), 33. *Prof Exp:* Chemist, Devoe & Raynolds Co, 28-29; instr chem, Emory Univ, 33-37; asst dir res, Glidden Co, 37-42. *Concurrent Pos:* Mem ammunition & high explosives panel, Res & Develop Bd, 48-51, chmn, 51-53; US leader explosives panel, Tripartite Tech Coop Prog, 61-65. *Mem:* Am Chem Soc. *Res:* Adsorption; catalysis; titanium pigments; microscopy; chemical engineering; ordnance engineering. *Mailing Add:* 9200 Beech Hill Dr Bethesda MD 20817

LANDA, EDWARD ROBERT, ENVIRONMENTAL RADIOACTIVITY. *Current Pos:* RES HYDROLOGIST, US GEOL SURV, 78- *Personal Data:* b New York, NY, Oct 29, 48; m 92, Judith Johnson. *Educ:* City Col NY, BS, 70; Univ Minn, MS, 72, MPH, 74, PhD(soil sci), 75. *Prof Exp:* Res asst, Dept Soil Sci, Univ Minn, 70-75; res assoc, Depts Agr Chem & Soil Sci, Ore State Univ, 75-78. *Concurrent Pos:* Vis fac, St Mary's Col, Md, 91. *Mem:* Soil Sci Soc Am; Health Physics Soc; Int Asn Hydrogeologists. *Res:* Study fate, transformations, and transport of radionuclides in aquatic and terrestrial environments; uranium mill tailings. *Mailing Add:* US Geol Surv 430 National Ctr Reston VA 20192. *Fax:* 703-648-5484; *E-Mail:* erlanda@usgs.gov

LANDAHL, HERBERT DANIEL, MATHEMATICAL BIOLOGY. *Current Pos:* prof, 68-80, EMER PROF BIOPHYS & BIOMATH, UNIV CALIF, SAN FRANCISCO, 80- *Personal Data:* b Fancheng, China, Apr 23, 13; US citizen; m 40, Evelyn Blomberg; c Carl D, Carol A (Kubai) & Linda C (Shidner). *Educ:* St Olaf Col, AB, 34; Univ Chicago, SM, 36, PhD(math biophys), 41. *Honors & Awards:* Career Achievement Award, Soc Toxicol, 87. *Prof Exp:* Asst, Psychomet Lab, Univ Chicago, 37-38, asst math biophys, Dept Physiol, 39-42, res assoc, 42-45, asst prof, 45-48, from assoc prof to prof math biol, 48-58, prof biophys, 64-68, secy comt math biol, 48-64, actg chmn, 64-67. *Concurrent Pos:* Res career award, NIH, 62-68; chief ed, Bull Math Biol, 73-81. *Mem:* Biomet Soc; Biophys Soc; Soc Math Biol (vpres, 72-82, pres, 82-); Biomed Eng Soc. *Res:* Mathematical biophysics of cell division, nerve excitation and central nervous system; removal of aerosols and vapors by the human respiratory tract; biological effects of radiation; population interaction; biological periodicities; insulin production and release mechanisms. *Mailing Add:* 472 Lansdale Ave San Francisco CA 94127

LANDAHL, MARTEN T, FLUID DYNAMICS. *Current Pos:* Res eng aeroelastic lab, 54-56, assoc prof, 60-63, PROF AERONAUT & ASTRONAUT, MASS INST TECHNOL, 63- *Personal Data:* b Sweden, Aug 6, 27. *Educ:* Royal Inst Technol, Sweden. *Honors & Awards:* Wallmarks Prize, Swedish Acad Sci, 68; Guggenheim Award, 90. *Concurrent Pos:* Res scientist, Aeronaut Res Inst Sweden, 56-60; prof mech, Royal Inst Technol, Sweden, 67-88. *Mem:* AAAS; fel Am Inst Aeronaut & Astronaut; fel Am Phys Soc. *Res:* Theoretical and applied mechanics, wave mechanics, aeroelasticity; fluid mechanics, hydrodynamic stability, turbulence, geophysical fluid dynamics, acoustics, rotating flows, vortex flows, ship sydrodynamics, computational fluid dynamics. *Mailing Add:* Dept Aeronaut & Astronaut Mass Inst Technol Cambridge MA 02139

LANDAU, BARBARA RUTH, PHYSIOLOGY. *Current Pos:* RETIRED. *Personal Data:* b Pierre, SDak, Apr 28, 23. *Educ:* Univ Wis, BS, 45, MS, 49, PhD, 56. *Prof Exp:* Instr phys educ, Rockford Col, 45-47; instr physiol, Mt Holyoke Col, 49-51; instr, St Louis Univ, 56-59; from instr to asst prof, Univ Wis, 59-62; asst prof zool, Univ Idaho, 62-64; from asst prof to assoc prof physiol, Univ Wash, 64-82, emer prof, Biophys & Biol Struct, 83-85. *Res:* Neural aspects of temperature regulation, hibernation, cell activity at reduced temperature; author of textbooks of anatomy and physiology. *Mailing Add:* 4109 224th Lane SE Apt 307 Issaquah WA 98029

LANDAU, BERNARD ROBERT, MEDICINE, BIOCHEMISTRY. *Current Pos:* prof pharmacol, 70-78, PROF MED, CASE WESTERN RES UNIV, 69-, PROF BIOCHEM, 79- *Personal Data:* b Newark, NJ, June 24, 26; m 56; c 3. *Educ:* Mass Inst Technol, SB, 47; Harvard Univ, MA, 49, PhD(chem), 50; Harvard Med Sch, MD, 54. *Prof Exp:* Med house officer, 54-55, sr res physician, Peter Bent Brigham Hosp, Boston, Mass, 58-59; asst prof biochem & from asst prof to assoc prof med, Case Western Res Univ, 59-67; dir dept biochem, Merck Inst Therapeut Res, 67-69. *Concurrent Pos:* Clin assoc, Nat Cancer Inst, 55-57; USPHS res fel biochem, Harvard Med Sch, 57-58, tutor, 57-59; estab investr, Am Heart Asn, 59-64. *Mem:* Endocrine Soc; Soc Biol Chem; Am Physiol Soc; Asn Am Physicians; Am Diabetes Asn. *Res:* Carbohydrate metabolism; endocrinology; diabetes mellitus. *Mailing Add:* Dept Med Case Western Res Iniv Hosps 10900 Euclid Ave Cleveland OH 44106-4951

LANDAU, BURTON JOSEPH, MICROBIOLOGY, VIROLOGY. *Current Pos:* sr instr, 67-69, asst prof, 69-74, ASSOC PROF MICROBIOL, 74-, ASST DEAN CURRIC, SCH MED, HAHNEMANN UNIV, 87- *Personal Data:* b Boston, Mass, May 6, 33; m 57; c 2. *Educ:* Boston Univ, AB, 54; Univ NH, MS, 57; Univ Mich, PhD(microbiol), 67. *Honors & Awards:* Lindback Award. *Prof Exp:* Sr res virologist, Merck Inst Therapeut Res, Merck, Inc, 64-65; res assoc microbiol, Univ Mich, 65-67. *Mem:* Am Soc Microbiol; Soc Gen Microbiol; Tissue Cult Asn; Am Soc Virol. *Res:* Use of differentiating cell cultures to grow viruses with restricted host ranges; virus-host cell interactions leading to virus induced transformation; coxsackievirus virus infections. *Mailing Add:* Dept Microbiol & Immunol Hahnemann Univ Sch Med Broad & Vine Sts Philadelphia PA 19102-1178

LANDAU, DAVID PAUL, MAGNETISM, STATISTICAL MECHANICS. *Current Pos:* from asst prof to prof, 69-84, RES PROF PHYSICS, UNIV GA, 84- *Personal Data:* b St Louis, Mo, June 22, 41; m 66, Heidi; c 2. *Educ:* Princeton Univ, BA, 63; Yale Univ, MS, 65, PhD(physics), 67. *Honors & Awards:* Jesse Beams Medal, 87. *Prof Exp:* Asst res physics, Nat Ctr Sci Res, Grenoble, France, 67-68; lectr eng & appl sci, Yale Univ, 68-69. *Concurrent Pos:* Guest scientist, KFA Jlich, WGer, 74; Alexander von Humboldt fel, Univ Saarland, 75; Sr US scientist Humboldt fel, Univ Mainz, 88. *Mem:* Fel Am Phys Soc; Sigma Xi. *Res:* Critical phenomena associated with phase transitions; properties of magnetic solids, computer-simulation methods, phase transitions in binary alloys and adsorbed monolayers. *Mailing Add:* Ctr Simulational Physics Univ Ga Athens GA 30601. *Fax:* 706-542-2492; *E-Mail:* dlandau@uga.cc.uga.edu

LANDAU, EMANUEL, EPIDEMIOLOGY, BIOSTATISTICS. *Current Pos:* PROJ DIR & STAFF EPIDEMIOLOGIST, AM PUB HEALTH ASN, 75- *Personal Data:* b New York, NY, Nov 28, 19; m 48, Davetta Goldberg; c Elizabeth L (Rabin). *Educ:* City Col New York, BA, 39; Am Univ, PhD(econ), 66. *Honors & Awards:* Super Serv Award, HEW, 63. *Prof Exp:* Bus economist, Econ Date Analysis Br, Off Price Admin, 41-42 & 46-47; chief, Family Statist Sect, Bur Census, 48-56; mem staff, Calif State Dept Pub Health, 57-59; chief, Biomet Sect, Div Air Pollution, USPHS, 59-62; head, Lab & Clin Trials Sect, Nat Cancer Inst, 62-64; statist adv, Nat Air Pollution Control Admin, 65-69; epidemiologist, Adminr Res & Develop, Environ Health Serv, 69-71; epidemiologist, Adminr Res & Monitoring, Environ Protection Agency, 71; chief, Epidemiol Studies Br, Bur Radiol Health, Food & Drug Admin, USPHS, 71-75. *Concurrent Pos:* Mem, Career Serv Bd Math & Statist, Dept Health, Educ & Welfare, 65-69; mem, Comt Long-term Training Outside Serv, USPHS, 66-68; adv air qual criteria, WHO, Switz, 67; mem, comt study lung cancer among uranium miners, USPHS, 67; adv air qual criteria, Karolinska Inst, Sweden, 68; Nat Air Control Admin tech liaison rep, Adv Comt Toxicol, Nat Acad Sci, 68-69; adv, Dept Transp, 72-74; assoc ed, J Air Pollution Control Asn, 72 & J Clin Data & Analysis, 74-; consult, Bur Radiol Health, Food & Drug Admin, 75-83; chmn, Comt Statist & Environ, Am Statist Asn, 84-85. *Mem:* Fel Am Pub Health Asn; fel Royal Soc Health; Air & Waste Mgt Asn; Am Statist Asn; Soc Occup & Environ Health. *Res:* Problems of environmental health; public health statistics; chronic disease epidemiology. *Mailing Add:* Am Pub Health Asn 1015 15th St NW Washington DC 20005. *Fax:* 202-789-5661

LANDAU, JOSEPH VICTOR, molecular biology, for more information see previous edition

LANDAU, JOSEPH WHITE, MEDICINE, DERMATOLOGY. *Current Pos:* asst res dermatologist, Univ Calif, Los Angeles, 64, from asst prof to assoc prof med & dermat, 64-74, attend physician, Student Health Serv, 65-86, ASSOC CLIN PROF MED DERMAT, MED CTR, UNIV CALIF, LOS ANGELES, 74- *Personal Data:* b Buffalo, NY, May 23, 30; m 85; c 5. *Educ:* Cornell Univ, BA, 51, MD, 55; Am Bd Pediat, dipl, 62; Am Bd Dermat, dipl, 65, cert dermatopath, 75. *Prof Exp:* Intern, Gen Hosp, Buffalo, 55-56; resident pediat, Children's Hosp, Buffalo, 56, Children's Hosp, Boston, Mass, 59-60 & Med Ctr, Univ Calif, Los Angeles, 60-61. *Concurrent Pos:* USPHS fel hemat, Children's Hosp, Los Angeles, 61-62 & fel mycol, Med Ctr, Univ Calif, Los Angeles, 62-63; attend physician, Wadsworth Vet Admin Hosp, 66- *Mem:* Am Acad Dermat; Soc Invest Dermat. *Res:* Host-parasite relationships in mycology; genodermatoses. *Mailing Add:* 2428 Santa Monica Blvd Santa Monica CA 90404

LANDAU, MATTHEW PAUL, AQUACULTURE, CRUSTACEAN PHYSIOLOGY. *Current Pos:* asst prof, 88-90, ASSOC PROF MARINE SCI, RICHARD STOCKTON COL, 90- *Personal Data:* b New York, NY, Dec 16, 49; m 85, Brenda J Tylka; c Rose & Isaac. *Educ:* St John's Univ, BS, 72; Long Island Univ, MS, 76; Fla Inst Technol, PhD(oceanog), 83. *Prof Exp:* Res fel biol, NY Ocean Sci Lab, 74-75; technician biochem, USDA, Gainesville, Fla, 75-78 & biol, Univ WFla, 78-79; postdoctoral aquacult, Harbor Br Oceanog Inst, 83-84 & biol, Univ Conn, 85-88; res scientist aquacult, Oceanic Inst, 84-85. *Mem:* World Aquacult Soc; Am Soc Zoologists; Crustacean Soc; Am Fisheries Soc. *Res:* General aquaculture systems, especially as they relate to crustaceans; reproductive endocrinology of crustaceans, in particular concerning the mandibular organ. *Mailing Add:* Dept Math & Sci Richard Stockton Col Pomona NJ 08240-9999. *Fax:* 609-748-5515

LANDAU, RALPH, CHEMICAL ENGINEERING. *Current Pos:* OWNER, LISTOWEL INC, 82- *Personal Data:* b Philadelphia, Pa, May 19, 16; m 40; c 1. *Educ:* Univ Pa, BS, 37; Mass Inst Technol, ScD(chem eng), 41. *Hon Degrees:* ScD, Polytech Univ, Clarkson Col, Ohio State Univ & Univ Pa. *Honors & Awards:* Petrochem & Petrol Div Award, Am Inst Chem Engrs, 73; Chem Indust Medal, Soc Chem Indust, 73; Winthrop-Sears Medal, Chem Indust Asn, 77; Award, Newcomen Soc NAm, 78; Award, Asn Consult Chemists & Chem Engrs, 78; Perkin Medal, 81. *Prof Exp:* Asst chem eng, Mass Inst Technol, 38-41; process develop engr, M W Kellogg Co, 41-43 & 46; head, Chem Dept, Kellex Corp, 43-45; exec vpres, Sci Design Co, Inc, 46-63; pres, Halcon Int, Inc, 63-75, chmn, 75-81, chmn, Halcon SD Group, Inc, 81-82. *Concurrent Pos:* Dir, Aluminum Co Am, 77-; adj prof mgt, tech & soc, Univ Pa, 77-; consult prof econ, Stanford Univ, 82- *Mem:* Nat Acad Eng (vpres, 81-); fel Am Inst Chem Engrs; fel NY Acad Sci; Am Chem Soc; Dirs Indust Res. *Res:* Commercial and technical research, development and manufacture in chemical process industries; international operations of chemical industry; economics of technology and public policy implications. *Mailing Add:* Listowel Inc 2 Park Ave New York NY 10016-5601

LANDAU, RICHARD LOUIS, ENDOCRINOLOGY. *Current Pos:* From asst prof to prof, 48-88, EMER PROF MED, UNIV CHICAGO, 88- *Personal Data:* b St Louis, Mo, Aug 8, 16; m 43; c 3. *Educ:* Wash Univ, BS & MD, 40. *Concurrent Pos:* Ed, Perspectives in Biol & Med, 73- *Mem:* Am Soc Clin Invest; Endocrine Soc; AMA; Sigma Xi. *Res:* Hormonal regulation of growth processes; reproductive endocrinology; metabolic influence of progesterone; effect of steroid hormones on electrolyte metabolism. *Mailing Add:* 950 E 59th St Chicago IL 60637-2602

LANDAU, WILLIAM, MICROBIOLOGY. *Current Pos:* RETIRED. *Personal Data:* b Jersey City, NJ, July 3, 27; m 63; c 2. *Educ:* Univ Conn, BA, 49; Yale Univ, MS, 51; Univ Pa, PhD(pub health, prev med), 58. *Prof Exp:* Res assoc biochem, Roswell Park Mem Inst, 58-61; assoc dir microbiol dept, Presby-St Lukes Hosp, 61-74, assoc scientist, 74-93; from asst prof to assoc prof bact, Rush Med Ctr, 62-93. *Mem:* Am Soc Microbiol; NY Acad Sci. *Res:* Clinical bacteriology. *Mailing Add:* 8345 Kenton Ave Skokie IL 60076

LANDAU, WILLIAM M, NEUROLOGY, NEUROPHYSIOLOGY. *Current Pos:* From instr to assoc prof, 52-63, PROF NEUROL, SCH MED, WASH UNIV, 63-, HEAD DEPT, 70-, CO-HEAD, DEPT NEUROL & NEUROSURG, 75- *Personal Data:* b St Louis, Mo, Oct 10, 24; m 47; c 4. *Educ:* Washington Univ, MD, 47. *Concurrent Pos:* Sr asst surgeon & neurophysiologist, NIMH & Nat Inst Neurol Dis & Blindness, 52-54; vis prof,

Univ Munich, 63; pres, Am Bd Psychiat & Neurol, 75; chmn, Nat Comt Res Neurol & Commun Dis, 80- *Mem:* Am Physiol Soc; Am EEG Soc; Am Neurol Asn (pres, 77); Asn Univ Profs Neurol (pres, 78); Am Acad Neurol. *Res:* Sensory and motor systems. *Mailing Add:* Dept Neurol Wash Univ Sch Med 660 S Euclid Ave St Louis MO 63110

LANDAUER, MICHAEL ROBERT, NEUROTOXICOLOGY. *Current Pos:* RES TOXICOLOGIST, ARMED FORCES RADIOBIOL RES INST, 84- *Personal Data:* b New York, NY, Sept 24, 46. *Educ:* Rutgers Univ, BS, 68; Univ Ill, Urbana, MS, 70, PhD(biopsychol), 75. *Prof Exp:* Res assoc psychol, Beaver Col, 74-76; vis asst prof biol, Barnard Col, Columbia Univ, 76-79; fel toxicol & pharmacol, Med Col, Va Commonwealth Univ, 79-82, res assoc pharmacol, Med Col Va, 82-84. *Concurrent Pos:* Lectr, Philadelphia Zoo, 76; grant, NIMH, 79; vis res scientist, US Army Chem Res & Develop Ctr, 82-84; grant recipient, Vet Admin & Dept Defense, 91-96. *Mem:* Radiation Res Soc; Animal Behav Soc; Am Soc Zoologists; Europ Soc Radiation Biol; Am Col Toxicologists; Asn Govt Toxicologists (pres, 97-98); Behav Toxicol Soc; Int Neurotoxicol Soc. *Res:* Behavioral effects of ionizing radiation and chemical radiation protectors; neurotoxicology; psychopharmacology. *Mailing Add:* Dept Radiation Pathophysiol & Toxicol Bldg 42 Armed Forces Radiobiol Res Inst 8901 Wisconsin Ave Bethesda MD 20889

LANDAUER, ROLF WILLIAM, SOLID STATE PHYSICS, COMPUTER TECHNOLOGY. *Current Pos:* physicist, IBM Corp, 52-61, dir phys sci, 61-66, asst dir res, 66-69, IBM FEL, THOMAS J WATSON RES CTR, IBM CORP, 69- *Personal Data:* b Stuttgart, Ger, Feb 4, 27; nat US; m 50; c 3. *Educ:* Harvard Univ, SB, 45, AM, 47, PhD(physics), 50. *Hon Degrees:* DSc, Technion, Israel, 91. *Honors & Awards:* Scott Lectr, Cambridge Univ, UK, 91; Stuart Ballantine Medal, Franklin Buckley Inst, 92; Oliver E Buckley Prize, Am Phys Soc, 95. *Prof Exp:* Physicist, Lewis Lab, Nat Adv Comt Aeronaut, 50-52. *Mem:* Nat Acad Sci; Nat Acad Eng; fel Inst Elec & Electronics Engrs; fel Am Phys Soc; fel AAAS; Am Acad Arts & Sci; Europ Acad Arts & Sci. *Mailing Add:* Thomas J Watson Res Ctr IBM Corp PO Box 218 Yorktown Heights NY 10598. *E-Mail:* landaue@watson.ibm.com

LANDAW, STEPHEN ARTHUR, INTERNAL MEDICINE, HEMATOLOGY. *Current Pos:* assoc prof med & radiol, 73-78, PROF MED, STATE UNIV NY HEALTH SCI CTR, 78- *Personal Data:* b Paterson, NJ, June 20, 36; c Jared & Nicole. *Educ:* Univ Wis-Madison, BS, 57; George Washington Univ, MD, 59; Univ Calif, Berkeley, PhD(med physics), 69; Am Bd Internal Med, dipl, 72, cert hemat, 72, cert med oncol, 75; Am Bd Nuclear Med, dipl, 72. *Honors & Awards:* Kosmos Achievement Award, NASA, 75 & 77. *Prof Exp:* Intern, Mt Sinai Hosp, NY, 59-60, asst resident internal med, 60-61; Nat Heart Inst fel med physics, Donner Lab, Univ Calif, Berkeley, 63-70, asst physician, 70-73, lectr med physics, Univ, 70-72. *Concurrent Pos:* Attend staff physician, Alameda Co Hosp, Oakland, Calif, 69-73, chief isotope lab, 71-73; Nat Heart & Lung Inst career develop award, 70-73; assoc chief staff res, Vet Admin Hosp, Syracuse, NY, 73-95; mem attend staff med, Vet Admin Hosp, 73-, Univ Hosp & Crouse-Irving Mem Hosp, 73-95; NIH fel med & hemat, Med Col Va, 62-63. *Mem:* Fel Am Col Physicians; Am Soc Hemat; Am Fedn Clin Res; Soc Exp Biol & Med; Soc Pediat Res. *Res:* Bilirubin kinetics; quantitative red blood cell kinetics; polycythemic disorders; carbon monoxide kinetics. *Mailing Add:* Med Serv (III) Vet Admin Med Ctr 800 Irvine Ave Syracuse NY 13210. *Fax:* 315-477-4570; *E-Mail:* landaw.stephen@syracuse.va.gov

LANDAY, ALAN LEE, MICROBIOLOGY. *Current Pos:* asst prof immunol/microbiol, 83-88, asst prof path, 85-88, DIR CLIN IMMUNOL LAB & FLOW CYTOMETRY LAB, OFF CONSOL SERV, RUSH-PRESBY-ST LUKE'S MED CTR, CHICAGO, 83-, ASSOC PROF IMMUNOL/MICROBIOL, PATH & MED, 88- *Personal Data:* b Pittsburgh, Pa, Feb 13, 55. *Educ:* Pa State Univ, BS, 76; Univ Pittsburgh, PhD, 81. *Prof Exp:* Postdoctoral, Cellular Immunobiol Unit, Univ Ala Sch Med, Birmingham, 81-83. *Concurrent Pos:* Grants, Leukemia Res Found, 85-86, Rush Univ, 85-86, Rush Med Ctr, 85-86, Am Cancer Soc, 85-86, NIH, 86-89 & 87-92, Loyd Frye Found, 88-91, Coulter Immunol, 90-91, AMAC Corp, 91-92; mem, Stand Subcomt Flow Cytometry, Immunol Res Comt, Flow Cytometry Adv Comt, NIH; chmn, Nat Comt Clin Lab & Qual Control & Stand Comt, Soc Analytical Cytol; adv, Freedon Proj, Col Am Pathologists Diag & NASA Space Sta. *Mem:* AAAS; NY Acad Sci; Int Soc Analytical Cytol; Am Soc Histocompatability & Immunogenetics; Am Soc Clin Path; Am Fedn Clin Res; Am Asn Immunologists; Clin Immunol Soc; Am Soc Hemat; Am Asn Pathologists. *Res:* Effects of Vitamin C on growth characteristics of cultured cells; effects of radiation, chemotherapy & immunotherapy on a transplan; biology; pathology; numerous technical publications. *Mailing Add:* Dept Immunol Microbiol & Path Rush-Presby-St Luke's Med Ctr 1653 W Congress Pkwy Chicago IL 60612-3833

LANDBORG, RICHARD JOHN, CHEMISTRY, SCIENCE EDUCATION. *Current Pos:* asst prof, 59-63, chmn dept, 65-67, ASSOC PROF CHEM, AUGUSTANA COL, SDAK, 63- *Personal Data:* b Manchester, Iowa, May 13, 33; m 55; c 4. *Educ:* Luther Col, Iowa, BA, 55; Univ Iowa, MS, 57, PhD(chem), 59. *Prof Exp:* Part-time instr chem, Cornell Col, 57-58. *Concurrent Pos:* Fulbright exchange prof, Univ Santa Maria Antigua, Panama, 67. *Mem:* AAAS; Am Chem Soc; Sigma Xi. *Res:* Chemistry of diazomethane particularly the addition cyclization reactions with activated olefinic systems. *Mailing Add:* 1109 W 37th St Sioux Falls SD 57105-0678

LANDE, ALEXANDER, THEORETICAL NUCLEAR PHYSICS. *Current Pos:* assoc prof, 72-80, PROF PHYSICS, INST THEORET PHYSICS, STATE UNIV GRONINGEN, 80- *Personal Data:* b Hilversum, Neth, Jan 5, 36; US citizen. *Educ:* Cornell Univ, BA, 57; Mass Inst Technol, PhD(theoret physics), 64. *Prof Exp:* Instr, Palmer Phys Lab, Princeton Univ, 63-66; NSF fel, Niels Bohr Inst, 66-68, asst prof, 68-70; vis assoc prof, Nordic Inst Theoret Atomic Physics, 70-72. *Concurrent Pos:* Chmn, Inst Theoret Physics, 76-83. *Mem:* Am Phys Soc; Europ Phys Soc; Neth Phys Soc. *Res:* Theoretical nuclear structure. *Mailing Add:* Inst Theoret Physics Groningen Univ Nijenborgh 4 Groningen 9747 AG Netherlands. *Fax:* 31 50 3634947; *E-Mail:* lande@th.rug.ne

LANDE, KENNETH, ASTROPHYSICS, ELEMENTARY PARTICLE PHYSICS. *Current Pos:* from instr to assoc prof, 59-74, PROF PHYSICS, UNIV PA, 74- *Personal Data:* b Vienna, Austria, June 5, 32; nat US; c 3. *Educ:* Columbia Univ, AB, 53, AM, 55, PhD(physics), 58. *Prof Exp:* Asst physics, Columbia Univ, 54-57. *Concurrent Pos:* Actg chmn, Astron & Astrophys, 84-; assoc ed astrophys, Phys Rev Letters, 87. *Mem:* Am Phys Soc; Sigma Xi; Am Astron Soc. *Res:* Neutrino physics; cosmic rays. *Mailing Add:* Dept Physics Univ Pa Philadelphia PA 19104

LANDE, RUSSELL SCOTT, POPULATION GENETICS, EVOLUTION. *Current Pos:* PROF BIOL, UNIV ORE, 89- *Personal Data:* b Jackson, Miss, Aug 10, 51. *Educ:* Univ Calif, Irvine, BS, 72; Harvard Univ, PhD(biol), 76. *Honors & Awards:* MacArthur Fel, John D & Catherine T MacArthur Found, 97. *Prof Exp:* Asst prof biophys & theoret biol, Univ Chicago, 78-89. *Mem:* Fel genetics, Univ Wis-Madison, 76-78. *Res:* Population genetics and evolution, especially of quantitative characters and chromosomal rearrangements. *Mailing Add:* Dept Biol Univ Ore Eugene OR 97403

LANDE, SAUL, BIOCHEMISTRY, ORGANIC CHEMISTRY. *Current Pos:* STAFF, ST JOSEPHS HOSP, 85- *Personal Data:* b Philadelphia, Pa, Aug 7, 30; m 54; c 4. *Educ:* Ursinus Col, BS, 48; Univ Pittsburgh, PhD(biochem), 60. *Prof Exp:* Sr res chemist, Squibb Res Inst, 61-63; assoc prof biochem in med, Sch Med, Yale Univ, 63-76, assoc clin prof dermat, 77-89. *Mem:* Am Chem Soc. *Res:* Chemistry of biologically active peptides. *Mailing Add:* 35 Point Beach Dr Milford CT 06902

LANDE, SHELDON SIDNEY, ENVIRONMENTAL CHEMISTRY, RISK ASSESSMENT. *Current Pos:* ENVIRON SPECIALIST, 3M CO, 79- *Personal Data:* b Chicago, Ill, July 16, 41; m 64; c 2. *Educ:* Ill Inst Technol, BS, 62; Mich State Univ, PhD(chem), 66. *Prof Exp:* Mult fel petrol, Mellon Inst, 68-70; res chemist, Gulf Res & Develop Co, 70-71; res assoc water chem, Grad Sch Pub Health, Univ Pittsburgh, 71-72; pub health adminr, Allegheny Co Health Dept, Pa, 72-75; res assoc, Syracuse Univ Res Corp, 75-79. *Mem:* Air & Waste Mgt Asn; Am Chem Soc; Soc Exposure Analysis; Soc Risk Analysis. *Res:* Fate of organic substances in soil and water; analysis of organic chemicals in the environment; health risk analysis. *Mailing Add:* Bldg 21 2W 05 3M Co 3M Ctr St Paul MN 55102-1403

LANDECKER, PETER BRUCE, SPACECRAFT INSTRUMENTATION. *Current Pos:* LAB SCIENTIST, SPACE & COMMUN GROUP, HUGHES AIRCRAFT CO, 82- *Personal Data:* b New York, NY, Oct 1, 42. *Educ:* Columbia Univ, BA, 63; Cornell Univ, PhD(exp physics), 68. *Honors & Awards:* Hughes Aircraft Co Inventor Awards, 83, 88, 89, 90, 91, 92 & 93. *Prof Exp:* Instr physics, Cornell Univ, 67-68; asst res physicist, Univ Calif, Irvine, 68-70; res assoc, Columbia Univ, 70-74; mem tech staff, Aerospace Corp, 74-82. *Concurrent Pos:* Instr, El Camino Col, 77 & 86-88; consult, Columbia Univ, 74-75, Aerospace Corp, 82-83, Sumware Corp, 86; prin investr, Solar X-ray satellite Payload, 74-82. *Mem:* Int Astron Union; Am Phys Soc. *Res:* Instruments on remote sensing spacecraft; x-ray astronomy; cosmic ray physics; solar physics; spacecraft and photography; star sensing attitude determination; granted two patents; author of 73 publications. *Mailing Add:* 1736 Nelson Ave Manhattan Beach CA 90266. *E-Mail:* 0068574@ccmail.emis.hac.com

LANDEFELD, THOMAS DALE, REPRODUCTIVE ENDOCRINOLOGY, BIOCHEMISTRY. *Current Pos:* from res assoc to sr res assoc, Univ Mich, Ann Arbor, 76-78, asst res scientist, Dept Path, 78-82, asst prof, 82-87, ASSOC PROF, DEPT PHARMACOL, UNIV MICH, ANN ARBOR, 87- *Personal Data:* b Columbus, Ohio, Mar 24, 47; div; c 2. *Educ:* Marietta Col, AB, 69; Univ Wis-Madison, BS & PhD(reproductive endocrinol), 73. *Prof Exp:* Fel endocrinol div, Med Col, Cornell Univ, 73-74; fel obstet & gynec dept, Sch Med, Wash Univ, 74-76. *Concurrent Pos:* Prin investr, NIH res grant, Univ Mich, 78-90, co-investr, 79-90 & 83-90, asst dean res & grad studies, 89-93; fel, Comt Dent Coop. *Mem:* Endocrine Soc; Soc Study Reproduction; Sigma Xi; NY Acad Sci; Am Soc Biochem & Molecular Biol; Soc Sci Study Sex. *Res:* Pituitary gonadotropins; isolation, purification, and biochemical characterization; mechanisms and control of biosynthesis; mRNA purification and translation; gene expression and regulation; recombinant DNA and cloning. *Mailing Add:* Dept Pharmacol Univ Mich Med Sch 2220B MSRB III Ann Arbor MI 48109-0632. *Fax:* 313-763-4450; *E-Mail:* thomas.landefeld@med.umich.edu

LANDEL, ROBERT FRANKLIN, PHYSICAL CHEMISTRY, RHEOLOGY. *Current Pos:* RETIRED. *Personal Data:* b Pendleton, NY, Oct 10, 25; m 53, Aurora S Mamauag; c Carlisle P, Grace P, Hans F, Robert F Jr, Kevin L & Matthew N. *Educ:* Univ Buffalo, BA, 50, MA, 51; Univ Wis, PhD(phys chem), 54. *Honors & Awards:* Except Sci Achievement Award, NASA, 76, Except Serv Award, 88; Humboldt Prize, Ger, 90. *Prof Exp:* Res assoc, Univ Wis, 54-55; sr res engr, Jet Propulsion Lab, Calif Inst Technol, 55-59, chief, Solid Propellant Chem Sect, 59-61, chief, Polymer Res Sect, 61-75, mgr, Propulsion & Mat Res Sect, 75-76, chief, Energy & Mat Res Sect, 76-79 & 80-82, div technologist, Control & Energy Conversion Div, 79-80, sr res scientist, 81-92, mgr, Mat Res & Biotechnol Sect, 82-83, dept mgr, Appl

Mech Technol Sect, 83-85. *Concurrent Pos:* Sr res fel, Calif Inst Technol, 65-69; sr Fulbright fel, Italy, 71-72; sr fel, Ctr Res Macromolecules, France, 72; res affil, Rancho Los Amigos Hosp, Downey, Calif, 76-; consult, Sandia Corp, 83; vis prof, Swiss Fed Tech Inst, Lausanne, Switz & Univ Philippines, Manila, 93-94 & 97. *Mem:* Am Phys Soc; Am Chem Soc; Soc Rheology (pres, 85-87). *Res:* Mechanical properties and failure of high polymers; polymer solutions and slurries. *Mailing Add:* 300 Tahimik Trail Santa Cruz CA 95065. *E-Mail:* landel@cruzio.com

LANDER, ARTHUR DOUGLAS, COGNITIVE SCIENCE. *Current Pos:* Edward J Poitras asst prof human biol & exp med, 88-91, ASST PROF, DEPT BRAIN & COGNITIVE SCI & DEPT BIOL, MASS INST TECHNOL, 87- *Personal Data:* b Brooklyn, NY, Sept 12, 58. *Educ:* Yale Univ, BS, 79; Univ Calif, San Francisco, PhD(neurosci), 85. *Prof Exp:* Assoc, Howard Hughes Med Inst, Ctr Neurobiol & Behav, Col Physicians & Surgeons, Columbia Univ, 85-87. *Concurrent Pos:* David & Lucile Packard fel sci & eng, 88-93. *Mem:* Soc Neurosci; Soc Develop Biol; NY Acad Sci; Am Soc Cell Biol. *Res:* Molecular mechanisms of axon outgrowth and guidance; cellular responses to extracellular matrix; biologic functions of proteoglycans. *Mailing Add:* Develop & Cell Biol Univ Calif Irvine CA 92717-2300

LANDER, ERIC STEVEN, GENETICS. *Current Pos:* vis scientist, 84-89, assoc prof, 89-93, PROF, DEPT BIOL, MASS INST TECHNOL, 93-; MEM, WHITEHEAD INST BIOMED RES, 89-, DIR, WHITEHEAD/MASS INST CTR GENOME RES, 89-; GENETICIST MED, MASS GEN HOSP, 93- *Personal Data:* b Brooklyn, NY, Feb 3, 57. *Educ:* Princeton Univ, AB, 78; Oxford Univ, DPhil(math), 81. *Honors & Awards:* Christian A Herter Distinguished Lectr, NY Univ, 93; Gladstone Distinguished Lectr, Gladstone Inst, 94; Herbert Boyer Lect Genetics, Univ Calif, San Francisco, 95; Herman Beerman Lectr, Soc Investigative Dermat, 95; Rhoads Mem Award Excellence Cancer Res, Am Asn Cancer Res, 95; Kroc Distinguished Lectr, Univ Wash, 96. *Prof Exp:* Asst prof, Grad Sch Bus, Harvard Univ, 81-86, assoc prof, 87-90. *Concurrent Pos:* Fel, Whitehead Inst Biomed Res, 86-89; MacArthur prize fel res human genetics & med, 87-92; mem, Comt Math & Molecular Biol, Nat Acad Sci, 89-90, DNA Technol Forensic Sci, 90-93; Ralph R Braund distinguished vis prof, Univ Tenn, 94; US Pres Comn Nat Medal Sci, 95-97; mem, Develop Diagnostics Working Group, Nat Cancer Inst, 96-97; mem, Genetics Working Group, NIMH, 97- *Mem:* Nat Acad Sci; Human Genome Orgn; Genetics Soc Am; Am Soc Human Genetics; Math Asn Am; fel AAAS; Am Acad Forensic Sci; Am Asn Cancer Res. *Res:* Human, mouse and rat genetics; study of traits with complex inheritance; construction of genetic, physical and sequence maps of human, mouse and rat genomes; development and application of tools for function genomics. *Mailing Add:* Whitehead Inst/Ctr Genome Res Mass Inst Technol 1 Kendall Sq Bldg 300 Cambridge MA 02139-1561. *Fax:* 617-252-1933

LANDER, JAMES FRENCH, GEOPHYSICS, TSUNAMIS. *Current Pos:* RES ASST, UNIV COLO, 88- *Personal Data:* b Bristol, Va, Aug 24, 31; m 60, Corinne Earle; c Jamie S, James Jr & Vivian G. *Educ:* Pa State Univ, BS, 58; Am Univ, MS, 62, MA, 68. *Honors & Awards:* Nakashizuka Award, Tsunami Soc, 88. *Prof Exp:* Geophysicist, US Coast & Geol Surv, Nat Oceanic & Atmospheric Admin, 58-62, chief seismol invests sect, 62-63, chief seismol invests br, Environ Res Labs, 63-73, chief, Nat Earthquake Info Ctr, 66-73; dep dir, Nat Geophys & Solar-Terrestrial Data Ctr, Nat Oceanic & Atmospheric Admin, 73-88. *Concurrent Pos:* Staff, Exec Off of Pres, Off Emergency Preparedness, 70-71; dir, World Data Ctr-A Solid Earth Geophys, 73-83; mem, Tsunami Comn, Int Union Geod & Geophys, 91, secy, 96. *Mem:* AAAS; Seismol Soc Am; Am Geophys Union; Sigma Xi; Tsunami Soc; Int Soc Prevent & Miticaton Natural Hazards. *Res:* US tsunamis; earthquake intensity; tsunami warning; diaster studies; natural hazard risks; digital data bases. *Mailing Add:* Univ Colo CIRES Campus Box 449 Boulder CO 80309. *E-Mail:* jfl@ngdc.noaa.gov

LANDER, PHILIP HOWARD, DIAGNOSTIC RADIOLOGY, SPINAL IMAGING & DIAGNOSIS. *Current Pos:* SR RADIOLOGIST, SIR MORTIMER B DAVIS GEN HOSP, 72-; ASSOC PROF, MCGILL UNIV, 87- *Personal Data:* b Montreal, Que, Sept 17, 41; m 67, Freema; c 3. *Educ:* McGill Univ, Can, BSc, 64, MD, 66. *Mem:* Radiol Soc NAm; Am Roentgen Ray Soc; Int Skeletal Soc; Soc Int Spine injection; Can Asn Radiologists. *Res:* Correlation of Paget's disease, bone with radiographic pathology, histopathology and clinical findings involving the weight bearing joints and the spine; diagnostic imaging of painful intervertebral segments of the cervical and lumbar spine; correlation to provocative and analgesic clinical tests; investigation of electrocoagulation of dorsal ramii of painful vertebral segments. *Mailing Add:* Jewish Gen Hosp 3755 Cote St Catherine Rd Montreal PQ H3T 1E2 Can. *E-Mail:* plander@objectpeople.on.ca

LANDER, RICHARD LEON, PHYSICS. *Current Pos:* assoc prof physics, 66-70, assoc dean res, Grad Div, 70-73, PROF PHYSICS, UNIV CALIF, DAVIS, 70- *Personal Data:* b Oakland, Calif, Apr 23, 28; Div; c 3. *Educ:* Univ Calif, Berkeley, BA, 50, PhD(physics), 58; Ohio State Univ, MA, 51. *Prof Exp:* Staff physicist, Lawrence Radiation Lab, Univ Calif, 58-60; res specialist nuclear physics, Boeing Co, 60-61; assoc res physicist, Univ Calif, San Diego, 61-66. *Concurrent Pos:* Vis scientist, Europ Orgn Nuclear Res, Switz, 66-67. *Mem:* AAAS; Am Phys Soc. *Res:* Experimental elementary particle physics. *Mailing Add:* Dept Physics Univ Calif Davis CA 95616

LANDERL, HAROLD PAUL, ORGANIC CHEMISTRY. *Current Pos:* RETIRED. *Personal Data:* b Pittsburgh, Pa, Apr 26, 22; m 44; c 3. *Educ:* Carnegie Inst Technol, BS, 43, MS, 47, DSc(chem), 48. *Prof Exp:* Asst, Nat Defense Res Comt, Calif Inst Technol, 44-46; res chemist, Jackson Lab, E I Du Pont de Nemours & Co, Inc, 48-54, supvr res & develop, Tech Lab, 54-60, head textile dye appln div, 60-70, asst dir dyes & chem tech lab, 70-72, tech mgr dyes & chem, Belg, 72-76, tech mgr dyes, Chem, Dyes & Pigments Dept, 76-80, staff consult, Employee Rels Dept, 80-82. *Mem:* Am Chem Soc; Am Asn Textile Chemists & Colorists. *Res:* Application of dyes to fibers. *Mailing Add:* 1503 Fresno Rd Wilmington DE 19803-5123

LANDERS, EARL JAMES, INVERTEBRATE ZOOLOGY. *Current Pos:* assoc prof zool, 60-70, PROF ZOOL, ARIZ STATE UNIV, 70- *Personal Data:* b Greybull, Wyo, Dec 17, 21; m 51; c 2. *Educ:* Univ Wyo, AB, 50, MS, 52; NY Univ, PhD(zool), 58. *Prof Exp:* Instr zool, Univ Wyo, 55-56; from asst prof to assoc prof biol sci, Tex Western Col, 56-60, actg chmn dept, 59-60. *Mem:* AAAS; Am Soc Parasitol. *Res:* Parasitic protozoa life cycles; transmembrane electrolyte transport. *Mailing Add:* 3034 S Country Club Way Tempe AZ 85282

LANDERS, JAMES WALTER, PATHOLOGY. *Current Pos:* Assoc prof, 62-80, CLIN PROF PATH, SCH MED, WAYNE STATE UNIV, 80- *Personal Data:* b Norfolk, Nebr, Oct 19, 27; m 52; c 3. *Educ:* Univ Nebr, MD, 53. *Concurrent Pos:* Assoc pathologist, William Beaumont Hosp, Royal Oak, Mich, 64-68 & St John Hosp, Detroit, 68- *Mem:* Am Soc Clin Path; Col Am Path; Int Acad Path; Sigma Xi. *Res:* Neuropathology. *Mailing Add:* 1507 Sunningdale Grosse Pointe MI 48236

LANDERS, JOHN HERBERT, JR, ANIMAL NUTRITION. *Current Pos:* from asst prof to prof & exten animal scientist, 50-77, EMER PROF, ORE STATE UNIV, 77- *Personal Data:* b Stockton, Mo, Jan 24, 21; m 43, Mary Hanna; c Steven, Patricia & David. *Educ:* Univ Mo, BS, 42, MS, 50; Kans State Univ, PhD(animal nutrit), 66. *Prof Exp:* Co agent agr, Univ Mo, 45-49, instr animal sci, 49-50. *Prof Exp:* Am Romney Sheep Breeders Asn (secy, 61-); Am Soc Animal Sci. *Res:* Counseling and advising livestock growers in more efficient production of meat and fiber. *Mailing Add:* 29515 NE Weslinn Dr Corvallis OR 97333

LANDERS, ROGER Q, JR, PLANT ECOLOGY, RANGE MANAGEMENT. *Current Pos:* EXTEN RANGE SPECIALIST, TEX A&M UNIV SYST, 79-, EMER EXTEN SPECIALIST, 94- *Personal Data:* b Menard, Tex, July 23, 32; m 54, Helen Benson; c Roger III & Amy (Ness). *Educ:* Tex A&M Univ, BS, 54, MS, 55; Univ Calif, Berkeley, PhD(bot), 62. *Prof Exp:* From asst prof to assoc prof plant ecol, Iowa State Univ, 62-71, prof, 71-79. *Mem:* Ecol Soc Am; Soc Range Mgt; Sigma Xi. *Res:* Grasslands; management of grazing land by chemical, mechanical and biological methods; prescribed burning to control undesirable brush and cactus and enhance productivity of desirable forage species for livestock and wildlife. *Mailing Add:* Res & Exten Ctr Tex A&M Univ Syst 7887 N Hwy 87 San Angelo TX 76901

LANDES, HUGH S(TEVENSON), physics, electrical engineering, for more information see previous edition

LANDES, JOHN D, FRACTURE MECHANICS. *Current Pos:* prof eng sci & mech, 87-95, PROF MECH & AEROSPACE & ENG SCI, UNIV TENN, 95- *Personal Data:* b Sellersville, Pa, June 28, 42; m 64, Anne Ruth; c Jennifer, Kristina, Rebecca & David. *Educ:* Lehigh Univ, BS, 64, MS, 65, PhD(mech), 70. *Honors & Awards:* Irwin Medal, Am Soc Testing & Mat, 80, Award of Merit, 89; Fracture Mech Medal, 95. *Prof Exp:* Res assoc, Pratt & Whitney Aircraft, 65-66; grad asst mech, Lehigh Univ, 66-70; sr engr, Westinghouse Elec Co, 70-76, fel engr, 76-78, adv engr, 78-85; mgr, Am Welding Inst, 85-87. *Mem:* Am Soc Testing & Mat; Am Welding Soc; Soc Eng Sci. *Res:* Research in fracture and fatigue, fracture of ductile materials; metals and polymers including testing standards and methods of applications. *Mailing Add:* 310 Perkins Hall Univ Tenn Knoxville TN 37996-2030. *Fax:* 423-974-7663

LANDESBERG, JOSEPH MARVIN, ORGANIC CHEMISTRY. *Current Pos:* asst prof, Univ, 66-70, assoc prof, 70-75, PROF CHEM, GRAD SCH ARTS & SCI, ADELPHI UNIV, 75- *Personal Data:* b New York, NY, Apr 21, 39; m 64; c 2. *Educ:* Rutgers Univ, BS, 60; Harvard Univ, MA, 62, PhD(chem), 65. *Prof Exp:* NIH res fel, Columbia Univ, 64-66. *Mem:* AAAS; Am Chem Soc; Royal Soc Chem; Am Asn Univ Prof. *Res:* Heterocyclic chemistry; synthetic applications of organometallic compounds; synthesis of strained, small-membered rings. *Mailing Add:* Dept Chem Adelphi Univ Garden City NY 11530. *Fax:* 516-877-4191

LANDESMAN, BARBARA TEHAN, WAVE PROPAGATION & DIFFRACTION, IMAGE PROCESSING. *Current Pos:* dir res & develop, 93-96, SR SCIENTIST, APPL TECHNOL ASSOCS, 93- *Personal Data:* b Louisville, Ky, Feb 23, 55. *Educ:* Univ Louisville, BS, 76; Stanford Univ, MS, 77; Univ Ariz, MS, 84, PhD(optical scis), 88. *Prof Exp:* Subsyst engr, Ford Aerospace & Communs, 77-79; sr engr electro optics, Itek Corp, 79-80; sr mem optical staff, Talandic Res Corp, 87-89; res scientist, Lockheed Missiles & Space, 89-93. *Concurrent Pos:* Asst prof, Elec Eng Linear Systs, San Jose Univ, 79-80. *Mem:* Inst Elec & Electronics Engrs; Optical Soc Am; Soc Photo Optical Instrumentation Engrs. *Res:* Gaussian beam propagation diffraction and interaction with ice crystal clouds; laser resonator design and semiconductor laser; actively illuminated satellite targets imaged by ground based telescopes. *Mailing Add:* 13333 Arch Ct NE Albuquerque NM 87112

LANDESMAN, EDWARD MILTON, MATHEMATICS. *Current Pos:* asst prof, 69-71, assoc prof, 71-80, PROF MATH, CROWN COL, UNIV CALIF, SANTA CRUZ, 80- *Personal Data:* b Brooklyn, NY, Mar 19, 38. *Educ:* Univ Calif, Los Angeles, BA, 60, MA, 61, PhD(math), 65. *Prof Exp:* Asst prof in residence math, Univ Calif, Los Angeles, 65-66; asst prof, Univ Calif, Santa Cruz, 66-68; asst prof, Univ Calif, Los Angeles, 68-69. *Concurrent Pos:* Air Force Off Sci Res grant, Univ Calif, Santa Cruz, 70-71. *Mem:* AAAS; Am Math Soc; Math Asn Am. *Res:* Partial differential equations; combinatorial theory; calculus. *Mailing Add:* Acad Systs Math 444 Castro St Suite 1200 Mountain View CA 94041

LANDESMAN, HERBERT, INORGANIC CHEMISTRY. *Current Pos:* PROF CHEM, LOS ANGELES SOUTHWEST COL, 69- *Personal Data:* b Newark, NJ, Apr 22, 27; m 53; c 2. *Educ:* Harvard Univ, BS, 48; Purdue Univ, PhD(chem), 51. *Prof Exp:* Res chemist, Naval Ord Test Sta, 51-52, Olin Mathieson Chem Corp, 52-59 & Nat Eng Sci Co, 59-66; chem consult, West Precipitation Group, Joy Mfg Co, 66-68; vpres, Environ Resources, Inc, 68-69. *Mem:* Air Pollution Control Asn; Am Chem Soc. *Res:* Organosilicon chemistry; chemistry of boron hydrides; fire extinguishants; fluorocarbons; hazards analysis; air and water pollution. *Mailing Add:* Dept Life & Phys Sci Los Angeles Southwest Col 1600 W Imperial Hwy Los Angeles CA 90047-4810

LANDESMAN, RICHARD, DEVELOPMENTAL BIOLOGY. *Current Pos:* ASSOC PROF ZOOL, UNIV VT, 69- *Personal Data:* b Brooklyn, NY, Jan 30, 40. *Educ:* NY Univ, BA, 61, MS, 63; Univ BC, PhD(zool), 66. *Prof Exp:* NIH fel biol, Mass Inst Technol, 66-69. *Concurrent Pos:* NIH & Nat Inst Dent Res, 84-85. *Mem:* Soc Develop Biol. *Res:* Cellular and molecular basis of limb regeneration; fracture healing in the newt; differentiation and morphogenesis of the regenerating newt limb-role of hormones and secondary growth factors in regeneration; osteoinductive potential of demineralized bone matrix and bone proteins. *Mailing Add:* Dept Zool Univ Vt Marsh Life Scis Burlington VT 05405-0001

LANDGRAF, RONALD WILLIAM, FATIGUE, FRACTURE. *Current Pos:* vis prof, 88-90, PROF, ENG SCI & MECH, VA POLYTECHNIC INST & STATE UNIV, 90- *Personal Data:* b Freeport, Ill, Mar 7, 39; m 62, Nancy J Griffith; c 2. *Educ:* Carnegie Inst Technol, BS, 61; Univ Ill, Urbana, MS, 66, PhD(theoret & appl mech), 69. *Prof Exp:* Mat engr, Micro Switch Div, Honeywell, Inc, 61-65; res assoc theoret & appl mech, Univ Ill, Urbana, 66-68; res scientist, Sci Res Staff, Ford Motor Co, 68-77, mem eng & res staff, 77-79, staff scientist, eng & res staff, 79-88. *Concurrent Pos:* Assoc ed, Fatigue Eng, Mat & Struct, 79-; vis prof, Univ Ill, Urbana-Champaign, 85. *Mem:* Am Soc Metals; Am Inst Mining, Metall & Petrol Engrs; fel Am Soc Testing & Mat; Soc Automotive Engrs; Am Soc Eng Educ. *Res:* Cyclic deformation and fracture behavior of metals and alloys; influence of metallurgical structure on fatigue crack initiation and propagation; development of fatigue design procedures. *Mailing Add:* 1501 Nelson Blacksburg VA 24060. *Fax:* 540-231-4574; *E-Mail:* mc@landgraf.esm.vt.edu

LANDGRAF, WILLIAM CHARLES, pharmaceutical chemistry, software systems, for more information see previous edition

LANDGREBE, ALBERT R, CHEMISTRY. *Current Pos:* BR CHIEF CHEM STORAGE, ENERGY RES & DEVELOP ADMIN, 75- *Personal Data:* b New Rochelle, NY, Mar 4, 33; m 58; c 2. *Educ:* Fordham Univ, BS, 57; Univ Md, PhD(chem), 64. *Prof Exp:* Inorg chemist, USDA, 60-63; radiochemist, Nat Bur Standards, Md, 63-68; chemist & chmn comt sci & tech symposia, AEC, 68-75. *Mem:* AAAS; Soc Nuclear Med; Sigma Xi; Am Chem Soc. *Res:* Use of radioisotopes in analytical and inorganic chemistry; radio chromatographic methods; substoichiometric radioisotopic dilution analysis; removal of radioisotopes from milk; activation analysis; trace and micro analysis. *Mailing Add:* 3201 Dunnington Rd Beltsville MD 20705-1014

LANDGREBE, DAVID ALLEN, ELECTRICAL ENGINEERING, SIGNAL PROCESSING & REMOTE SENSING. *Current Pos:* From asst prof to assoc prof, Purdue Univ, 62-70, dir, Lab Applications Remote Sensing, 69-81, assoc dean eng & dir, Eng Exp Sta, 81-84, actg head elec & comput eng, 95-96, PROF ELEC ENG, PURDUE UNIV, 70- *Personal Data:* b Huntingburg, Ind, Apr 12, 34; m 59, Ann Swank; c James D, Carole & Mary. *Educ:* Purdue Univ, BSEE, 56, MSEE, 58, PhD(elec eng), 62. *Honors & Awards:* Except Sci Achievement Medal, NASA, 73; Geosci & Remote Sensing Soc Except Serv Award, Inst Elec & Electronics Engrs, Edinburgh, Scotland, 88; William T Pecora Award, NASA & US Dept Interior, 91; Scientific Achievement Award, Inst Elec & Electronics Engrs Geosci & Remote Sensing Soc, 92. *Concurrent Pos:* Consult, Earlham Col, 63 & Douglas Aircraft Co, 64-70; mem tech staff, Bell Tel Labs, Murray Hill, NJ, 56; electronics engr, Interstate Electronics Corp, Anaheim, Calif, 58-59; res scientist, Douglas Aircraft Co, Newport Beach, Calif, 62. *Mem:* Fel Inst Elec & Electronics Engrs; Am Soc Eng Educ; fel Amer Soc Photogram & Remote Sensing. *Res:* Representation and analysis of signals; data processing. *Mailing Add:* Prof Elec & Comput Eng Purdue Univ West Lafayette IN 47907-1285. *Fax:* 765-494-3358; *E-Mail:* landgreb@ecn.purdue.edu

LANDGREBE, JOHN A, REACTION MECHANISMS, REACTIVE INTERMEDIATES. *Current Pos:* From asst prof to assoc prof, Univ Kans, 62-71, assoc chmn, 67-70, chmn, 70-80, PROF CHEM, UNIV KANS, 71- *Personal Data:* b San Francisco, Calif, May 6, 37; m 61, Carolyn Thomson; c Carolyn J & John F. *Educ:* Univ Calif, Berkeley, BS, 59; Univ Ill, Urbana, PhD(org chem), 62. *Mem:* Am Chem Soc. *Res:* Organic reaction mechanisms; small ring compounds; carbene intermediates; reactions of carbonyl ylides. *Mailing Add:* Dept Chem Univ Kans Lawrence KS 66045-1500. *Fax:* 785-864-5396; *E-Mail:* landgreb@kuhub.cc.ukans.edu

LANDGREN, CRAIG RANDALL, PLANT TISSUE CULTURE, PLANT DEVELOPMENT. *Current Pos:* asst prof biol, Middlebury Col, 77-96, chmn dept, 82-88 & 92-96, dir, Northern Studies, 84-87, chmn, Nat Sci Div, 85-88, dir, SCIENS Prog, 87-90 & 92, dir, Freshman Writing Prog, 90-91, Col Writing Prog, 92-93, dean instrnl resources, 95-96, DIR, ACAD FACIL PLANNING & PROF, MIDDLEBURY COL, 96- *Personal Data:* b St Paul, Minn, Dec 20, 47; m 83, Susan C Gatwood; c Gari A R & Cynthia E. *Educ:* Albion Col, BA, 69; Harvard Univ, MA, 70, PhD(biol), 74. *Prof Exp:* Asst prof, George Mason Univ, 74-77; vis asst prof, Univ Ore, 76-77. *Concurrent Pos:* Res grant, George Mason Found, 75-76; res assoc, Univ Ore, 78-81; vis scientist, US-USSR Nat Acad Sci Exchange Prog, 80. *Mem:* Sigma Xi. *Res:* Studies in the culture and differentiation of isolated plant cells and plant cell protoplasts; genetic engineering through organelle transplantation and cell fusion; plant stress physiology; over wintering of plants; ethics in science. *Mailing Add:* Acad Facil Planning Middlebury Col Middlebury VT 05753. *Fax:* 802-388-0739; *E-Mail:* landgren_randy@msmail.middlebury.edu

LANDGREN, GEORGE LAWRENCE, ELECTRICAL ENGINEERING. *Current Pos:* RETIRED. *Personal Data:* b Duluth, Minn, July 22, 19; m 43, Anna J Sinamark; c Karen J, Nancy E, Larry A & David G. *Educ:* Univ Minn, BEE, 41; Northwestern Univ, MS, 55. *Prof Exp:* Elec engr, Commonwealth Edison Co, Chicago, 41-85. *Mem:* Fel Inst Elec & Electronics Engrs. *Mailing Add:* 2450 Iroquois Rd Wilmette IL 60091-1368

LANDGREN, JOHN JEFFREY, MATHEMATICS, FUNCTIONAL ANALYSIS. *Current Pos:* SR RES SCIENTIST, GA INST TECHNOL, 80- *Personal Data:* b St Paul, Minn, Nov 16, 47; m 77; c 3. *Educ:* Univ Minn, BS, 69, MS, 71, PhD(math), 76. *Prof Exp:* Vis asst prof math, Ga Inst Technol, 76-78; asst prof math, Univ Tenn, 78-80. *Mem:* Sigma Xi; Soc Indust & Appl Math. *Res:* Electronic warfare; simulation of radar/jamming systems; applied mathematics; radar countermeasures and radar signal processing; adaptive antenna arrays. *Mailing Add:* Countermeasures Develop Lab Ga Technol Res Inst Ga Inst Tech Atlanta GA 30332-0840

LANDICK, ROBERT, REGULATION OF TRANSCRIPTIONAL ELONGATION, STRUCTURE-FUNCTION OF RNA POLYMERASE. *Current Pos:* FAC, DEPT BACT, UNIV WIS. *Personal Data:* b Salem, Mass, Dec 9, 51. *Educ:* Univ Mich, BS, 75, PhD(biol chem), 83. *Honors & Awards:* Pres Young Investr Award, NSF, 89. *Prof Exp:* NIH fel, Stanford Univ, 83-86; asst prof biol, Wash Univ, 87-91, assoc prof, 91- *Concurrent Pos:* Searle Scholar Award, Chicago Community Trust, 87-90; presidential young investr, 89-93; vis scholar, Stanford Univ, 92-93. *Mem:* Am Chem Soc; Am Soc Microbiol; AAAS; Am Soc Biochem & Molecular Biol. *Res:* Studies of the mechanisms that control RNA synthesis by RNA polymerase after initiation; genetic and biochemical dissection of RNA polymerase structure and function during RNA chain elongation. *Mailing Add:* Dept Bact Univ Wis 1550 Linden Dr Madison WI 53706-1567. *Fax:* 314-935-4432; *E-Mail:* landick@wustlb.wustl.edu

LANDING, BENJAMIN HARRISON, PEDIATRIC PATHOLOGY, GENETICS. *Current Pos:* prof, 61-90, EMER PROF PATH & PEDIAT, UNIV SOUTHERN CALIF, 90-; RES PATHOLOGIST, CHILDREN'S HOSP, LOS ANGELES, 88- *Personal Data:* b Buffalo, NY, Sept 11, 20; m, Dorothy Hallas; c 4. *Educ:* Harvard Univ, AB, 42; Harvard Med Sch, MD, 45. *Honors & Awards:* Farber Mem Lectr, Soc Pediat Path, 84. *Prof Exp:* Intern, Children's Hosp, Boston, 45-46; res pathologist, Children's Med Ctr, Boston, 48-50, asst pathologist, 50-52, assoc pathologist, 52-53; from asst to instr & assoc path, Harvard Med Sch, 48-53; from asst prof to assoc prof path & pediat, Col Med, Univ Cincinnati, 53-61; pathologist-in-chief & dir labs, Children's Hosp, Los Angeles, 61-88, Winzer prof path, 76-88. *Concurrent Pos:* Res pathologist, Free Hosp for Women & Boston Lying-In-Hosp, 49; dir pathologist, Children's Hosp & Res Found, Cincinnati, 53-61. *Mem:* Histochem Soc; Endocrine Soc; Am Asn Path (asst secy, 53-57); Int Acad Path; Soc Pediat Path (pres, 72-73). *Res:* Histochemistry of metabolic diseases; pediatric pathology; morphometry of malformation syndromes; enteric nervous system involvement in neurologic diseases; neurosciences. *Mailing Add:* Children's Hosp 4650 Sunset Blvd Los Angeles CA 90027

LANDING, ED, BIOSTRATIGRAPHY & SYSTEMATICS OF EARLY-MIDDLE CAMBRAIN SHELLED ORGANISMS, DEPOSITIONAL ENVIRONMENTS OF CONTINENTAL SLOPE & PLATFORMAL SHALE BASINS. *Current Pos:* STATE PALEONTOLOGIST, NY STATE GEOL SURV, 86- *Personal Data:* b Milwaukee, Wis, Aug 10, 49. *Educ:* Univ Wis, BSc, 72; Univ Mich, MSc, 75, PhD(paleont), 78. *Prof Exp:* Fel, Univ Walterloo Can, 78, Univ Toronto, 80; res assoc, Nat Res Coun US, 79. *Concurrent Pos:* Adj asst prof, State Univ NY, Albany, 83- *Mem:* Paleont Soc; Soc Econ Paleontologists & Mineralogists. *Res:* Reconstructing the evolutionary relationships, habitats, paleogeography and biostratigraphic utility of the earliest skeletalized metazoans. *Mailing Add:* 46 Pinewood Ave Albany NY 12208. *Fax:* 518-473-8496

LANDIS, ABRAHAM L, CHEMISTRY. *Current Pos:* RETIRED. *Personal Data:* b New York, NY, May 25, 28; m 57, Eileen Pomper; c Daniel & Lawrence. *Educ:* City Col New York, BS, 51; Univ Kans, PhD(chem), 55. *Prof Exp:* Aeronaut res scientist, Nat Adv Comt Aeronaut, 55-56; sr res chemist, Atomics Int Div, NAm Rockwell, Inc, 56-61; sr staff chemist, Hughes Aircraft Co, El Segundo, Calif, 61-80, sr scientist, 80-86; sr staff scientist, Lockheed Aeronaut Syst Co, 86-91 & Lockheed Missile Res & Develop Co, 91-94. *Concurrent Pos:* Polymers consult. *Mem:* Am Chem Soc; Sigma Xi; Am Inst Chem; Am Ceramic Soc; Soc Advan Mat & Process Eng. *Res:* High temperature polymers; polymer chemistry; vacuum technology; organic synthesis; organometallic polymers; aerospace materials. *Mailing Add:* 1457 Bellevue Ave No 9 Burlingame CA 94010. *E-Mail:* allandis@aol.com

LANDIS, ARTHUR MELVIN, HETEROPOLY COMPLEXES, SEPARATIONS SCIENCE. *Current Pos:* asst prof, 87-91, ASSOC PROF CHEM, EMPORIA STATE UNIV, EMPORIA, KS, 91- *Personal Data:* b Lancaster, Pa, Jan 21, 44; m 68; c 2. *Educ:* Elizabethtown Col, BS, 66; Ohio Univ, MS, 70; Georgetown Univ, PhD(chem), 77. *Prof Exp:* Head teaching fel chem, Georgetown Univ, Washington, DC, 70-75, vis prof, 73-75; vis prof chem, Dickinson Col, Carlisle, Pa, 75-77; sr res chemist, UOP, Inc, Signal-Allied Co, Des Plaines, Ill, 77-82; asst prof chem, Col Our Lady of The Elms, Chicopee, Mass, 83-87. *Concurrent Pos:* Vis prof chem, Georgetown Univ, 83; lectr chem, Western New Eng Col, 84-; consult, Springfiled Wire, 86-89; mem, Gordon Res Conf, 80-82. *Mem:* Am Chem Soc; Sigma Xi. *Res:* Heteropolies and polyoxometallates; preparation and properties of organo-heteropoly polymers; configurations and conformations of species; separation theory of solutes via interaction with inorganic solids, for example, preparative liquid chromatography. *Mailing Add:* 1008 Burns St Emporia KS 66801-6314

LANDIS, DENNIS MICHAEL DOYLE, NEUROLOGY, NEUROSCIENCE. *Current Pos:* assoc prof neurol, develop genetics & anat, Case Western Res Univ, 85-88, assoc prof neurol & Ctr Neurosci, 88-90, PROF NEUROL & NEUROSCI, SCH MED, CASE WESTERN RES UNIV, 90-, ACTG CHMN, DEPT NEUROL; NEUROLOGIST, UNIV HOSPS CLEVELAND, 85-, DIR, DEPT NEUROL, 85- *Personal Data:* b Boston, Mass, Aug 12, 45; m 70, E Story Cleland; c Michael C. *Educ:* Harvard Col, AB, 67; Harvard Med Sch, MD, 71; Am Bd Internal Med, dipl, 75; Am Bd Psychiat & Neurol, dipl, 79. *Prof Exp:* From instr to asst prof neurol, Harvard Med Sch, 78-83, asst prof neurol-neurosci, 83-85. *Concurrent Pos:* Instr neurobiol, Marine Biol Labs, Woods Hole, Mass, 77-; teacher investr award, Nat Inst Neurol & Communicative Dis & Stroke, 78, Javits Neurosci investr award, 89; asst neurol, Mass Gen Hosp, 78-79, attend physician, Neurol Serv & Neurol Consult Serv & dir, Muscular Dystrophy Asn Clin, 78-85, asst neurologist, 79-85; assoc neuropathologist, Eunice Kennedy Shriver Ctr Ment Retardation, Waltham, Mass, 78-85; lectr, Mass Gen Hosp, Marine Biol Lab & Case Western Res Univ, 78-; attend physician, Neurol Serv, Vet Admin Hosp, Cleveland, 85- & Neurol & Consult Serv, Univ Hosps Cleveland, 85-; dir, Lab Neurocytol, 85- *Mem:* Soc Neurosci; Am Acad Neurol; Am Soc Cell Biol; Am Neurol Asn; Soc Exp Neuropath. *Res:* Structure and function at synaptic junctions in the central nervous system; membrane and cytoplasmic structure in astrocytes; astrocyte function during development, in the adult, and in the response to injury. *Mailing Add:* Dept Neurol & Neurosci Sch Med E-604 Case Western Res Univ 2119 Abington Rd Cleveland OH 44106-2333. *Fax:* 216-368-3951; *E-Mail:* ddl@po.cwru.edu

LANDIS, E K, CHEMICAL ENGINEERING. *Current Pos:* RETIRED. *Personal Data:* b Pulaski, Va, June 17, 30; m 65; c 1. *Educ:* Va Polytech Inst, BS, 54; Univ Va, MChE, 55; Carnegie Inst Technol, PhD(chem eng), 59. *Prof Exp:* From asst prof to prof chem eng, Univ Ala, Tuscaloosa, 59-88. *Concurrent Pos:* Consult, US Army Missile Command, 61- & US Bur Mines, 62-; Ford Found prof, Carnegie Inst Technol, 64. *Mem:* Am Inst Chem Engrs; Am Soc Eng Educ. *Res:* Combustion instability; thermodynamics of solution; mass transfer in fixed beds; mass and energy transfer across living cell walls. *Mailing Add:* 3309 Royal Scots Way Ft Smith AR 72908-9327

LANDIS, EDWARD EVERETT, psychiatry; deceased, see previous edition for last biography

LANDIS, FRED, MECHANICAL ENGINEERING. *Current Pos:* dean, Col Eng & Appl Sci, 74-83, prof, 84-94, EMER PROF MECH ENG, UNIV WIS, MILWAUKEE, 94- *Personal Data:* b Munich, Ger, Mar 21, 23; nat US; wid, Billie Schiff; c John D, Deborah E & Mark E. *Educ:* McGill Univ, BEng, 45; Mass Inst Technol, SM, 49, ScD, Mass Inst Technol, 50. *Honors & Awards:* Centennial Medallion, Am Soc Mech Engrs, 80. *Prof Exp:* Design engr, Can Vickers, Ltd, 45-47; asst, Mass Inst Technol, 48-50; asst prof mech eng, Stanford Univ, 50-52; thermodyn res engr, Northrop Aircraft, Inc, 52-53; from asst prof to prof mech eng, NY Univ, 61-73, chmn dept, 63-73; prof & dean intercampus progs, Polytech Univ,NY, 73-74. *Concurrent Pos:* Mem, NY State Comn on Primary & Secondary Educ, 71; staff consult, Pratt & Whitney Aircraft, 57-88; bd gov, Am Soc Mech Engrs, 89-91. *Mem:* Hon mem Am Soc Mech Engrs (vpres, 85-89, 92-95); assoc fel Am Inst Aeronaut & Astronaut; fel Am Soc Eng Educ. *Res:* Thermodynamics; fluid mechanics; heat transfer; manpower economics; engineering education. *Mailing Add:* Col Eng & Appl Sci Univ Wis PO Box 784 Milwaukee WI 53201. *Fax:* 414-229-6958

LANDIS, JOHN W, NUCLEAR POWER SAFETY. *Current Pos:* RETIRED. *Personal Data:* b Kutztown, Pa, Oct 10, 17; m 41, Muriel T Souders; c Maureen & Marcia (Dent). *Educ:* Lafayette Col, BS, 39. *Hon Degrees:* DSc, Lafayette Col. 60. *Honors & Awards:* George Washington Kidd Award, 72. *Prof Exp:* Res Engr, Eastman Kodak Co, Rochester, NY, 39-43; officer, US Navy, 43-46, consult, Bur Ord, 46-50; head sci & eng test develop, Educ Testing Serv, 48-50; proj & reactor engr, AEC, 50-53; dir customer rel, Atomic Energy Div, Babcock & Wilcox Co, 53-55, mgr opers, Lynchburg, Va, 55-62 & Atomic Energy Div, 62-65, gen mgr opers, Wash, 65-68; group vpres, Gulf Gen Atomic Co, 68-70, pres, 70-75; sr vpres & dir, Stone & Webster Eng Co, 75-93, sr exec consult, 93-95. *Concurrent Pos:* Chmn, Adv Comt Isotopes Radiation Develop & four other adv comts, US AEC, 57-70; vchmn mgt comt, Nat Environ Studies Prof, 74-; mem, Fusion Adv Panel, US House Rep, 79-; dir, Cent Fidelity Banks, 79-; charter mem, Magnetic Fusion Adv Comn, US Dept Energy, 82-84, vchmn, Energy Res Adv Bd, 84-; chmn, Comt Protection Environ, US Energy Asn & Energy Res Adv Bd; NAm regional coordr, World Energy Coun; mem, Nat Energy Outlook Comt & Secy Energy Adv Bd, Dept Energy. *Mem:* Nat Acad Eng; fel Am Nuclear Soc (pres, 71-72); fel Am Soc Mech Engrs; Am Nat Stand Inst (pres, 74-77); Am Soc Macro-Eng (pres, 85-); Fusion Power Assocs; Sigma Xi. *Res:* Color sensitometry; guided missiles; radiation detection; advanced nuclear reactors; environmental protection; alternative energy systems; published numerous articles in various journals. *Mailing Add:* Stone & Webster Eng Corp 245 Summer St Boston MA 02210

LANDIS, PHILLIP SHERWOOD, ORGANIC CHEMISTRY, AGRICULTURE & FOOD CHEMISTRY. *Current Pos:* RETIRED. *Personal Data:* b York, Pa, July 29, 22; m 44; c 2. *Educ:* Franklin & Marshall Col, BS, 43; Univ Ky, MS, 47; Northwestern Univ, PhD(chem), 58. *Honors & Awards:* Outstanding Sci Award, Am Chem Soc, 86. *Prof Exp:* Chemist, Cities Serv Refining Corp, 43-45; res chemist, Mobil Oil Corp, 47-63, res assoc, 63-66, sr res assoc, 66-69, mgr prod res group, Mobil Res & Develop Corp, 69-83; adj prof, Glassboro State Col 81-94. *Concurrent Pos:* Consult, Mobil Res & Develop, 83-85, Int Lubricants Inc, 86- *Mem:* Am Chem Soc; Sigma Xi. *Res:* Mechanisms and kinetics of organic reactions; pyrolysis of organic compounds; organo-sulfur compounds; petrochemicals; radical reactions; chemistry of jojoba oil; chemistry of plant oils. *Mailing Add:* 5753 Independence Circle Alexandria VA 22312-2629. *Fax:* 703-658-3956

LANDIS, STORY CLELAND, NEUROBIOLOGY. *Current Pos:* ASSOC PROF, DEPT PHARMACOL, CASE WESTERN RES UNIV,- *Personal Data:* b New York, NY, May 14, 45; m 69. *Educ:* Wellesley Col, BA, 67; Harvard Univ, MA, 70, PhD(biol), 73. *Prof Exp:* NIH fel neuropath, 73-75, RES FEL NEUROBIOL, HARVARD MED SCH, 75-, INSTR, 80- *Mem:* Am Asn Anatomists; Soc Neurosci; Am Soc Cell Biol. *Res:* Developmental neurobiology; cell biology. *Mailing Add:* Dept Pharmacol NINDS NIH Bldg 36 Rm 5A05 Bethesda MD 20892

LANDIS, VINCENT J, INORGANIC CHEMISTRY. *Current Pos:* From instr to assoc prof, 54-65, PROF CHEM, SAN DIEGO STATE UNIV, 65- *Personal Data:* b Minneapolis, Minn, Oct 27, 28; m 50; c 6. *Educ:* Wash State Univ, BS, 50; Univ Minn, PhD(inorg chem), 57. *Concurrent Pos:* Richland fac fel, Univ Wash, 64-65. *Mem:* Am Chem Soc. *Res:* Metal coordination compounds; radiochemistry. *Mailing Add:* Dept Chem San Diego State Univ San Diego CA 92182-0001

LANDIS, WAYNE G, AQUATIC TOXICOLOGY, METABOLISM OF XENOBIOTICS. *Current Pos:* RES BIOLOGIST, TOXICOL DIV, CHEM RES & DEVELOP CTR, 82- *Personal Data:* b Washington, DC, Jan 20, 52. *Educ:* Wake Forest Univ, BA, 74; Ind Univ, MA, 78, PhD(zool), 79. *Prof Exp:* Assoc instr biol, Dept Biol, Ind Univ, 74-79; environ & health scientist, environ & health studies group, Franklin Res Ctr, 79-82. *Mem:* Genetics Soc Am; Soc Protozoologists; Am Soc Testing & Mat; Soc Study Evolution; AAAS; Sigma Xi; Soc Environ Toxicol & Chem. *Res:* Toxicity, fate and impact on community structure of environmental toxicants on aquatic systems; characterization of the DFPases in Tetrahymena thermophila; ecology and evolution of paramecium; structure-activity derivations for toxicologic endpoints; holds two US patents. *Mailing Add:* 4158 Ridgewood Ave Bellingham WA 98226-2560. *Fax:* 360-650-7284; *E-Mail:* landis@henson.cc.wwu.edu

LANDIS, WILLIAM JOEL, STRUCTURAL BIOLOGY, BIOMINERALIZATION. *Current Pos:* assoc, Orthop Surg, Harvard Med Sch, 72-74, res assoc, anat, 74-81, asst prof, 81-84, ASSOC PROF ORTHOP SURG, CELLULAR BIOL & ANAT, HARVARD MED SCH, 84-; SR RES ASSOC, CHILDREN'S HOSP, BOSTON, 80- *Personal Data:* b Clarksville, Tenn, Mar 1, 43. *Educ:* Univ Mass, BS, 65; Mass Inst Technol, MS, 67, PhD(biophys), 72. *Honors & Awards:* C E Hall Award, Electron Micros Soc Am, 91. *Prof Exp:* Res asst Orthop Surg, Children's Hosp, Boston, 72-75, res assoc, 75-80. *Concurrent Pos:* Prin investr, NIH, 80-83 & 92-, Whitaker Health Sci Found, 81-83, William F Milton Fund, 84-86, NASA, 88-; sr res scholar, Fulbright Found, 88-89; sci consult, var co & corp, 75- *Mem:* Orthop Res Soc; Microbeam Analysis Soc; Int Asn Dent Res; Electron Microscope Soc Am; Am Soc Gravitational & Space Biol; Fulbright Asn. *Res:* Characterizing the effects of force (mechanical, electromagnetic and gravitational) on the structure of the skeleton and mineralized tissues. *Mailing Add:* Enders Bldg Rm 284 Children's Hosp Boston MA 02115. *Fax:* 617-730-5454; *E-Mail:* landis_w@a1.tch.harvard.edu

LANDISS, DANIEL JAY, ANALOG ELECTRONICS, COMPUTERS IN EDUCATION. *Current Pos:* PROF TECHNOL, ST LOUIS COMMUNITY COL, 74- *Personal Data:* b Alton, Ill, June 11, 43. *Educ:* Wash Univ, St Louis, BS, 64, MS, 66. *Prof Exp:* Res engr, Mallinckrodt Inst Radiol, 66-67; dir, Eng Tech Serv, Wash Univ, 67-69 & Biomed Eng Lab, Lewis-Howe Co, 69-72; chief engr, Artronix, Inc, 72-73. *Concurrent Pos:* Pres & owner, Quest Instruments Ltd, 80-; assoc, Senne, Kelsey & Assocs, 85-; vis prof, Czech Tech Univ, Prague, 88-89. *Res:* Biomedical ultrasound diagnostics. *Mailing Add:* 5053 Westminster Pl St Louis MO 63108

LANDMAN, ALFRED, ATOMIC PHYSICS. *Current Pos:* GEN ENGR, TRANSP SYSTS CTR, US DEPT TRANSP, 70- *Personal Data:* b Vienna, Austria, June 29, 33; US citizen; m 67; c 2. *Educ:* Univ Pa, AB, 54; Columbia Univ, PhD(physics), 63. *Prof Exp:* Lectr physics, Brooklyn Col, 59-62; res assoc, Columbia Univ, 63; res assoc chem physics, Inst Study Metals, Univ Chicago, 63-64; res engr physics, Gen Tel & Electronics Labs, 65-66, adv res engr, 66-67; physicist, NASA Electronics Res Ctr, 67-70. *Mem:* Am Phys Soc. *Res:* Spectroscopy; optical pumping; gas laser molecular stark effect; synthetic fuels. *Mailing Add:* 29 Tyler Rd Lexington MA 02173

LANDMAN, DONALD ALAN, THEORETICAL & COMPUTATIONAL PLASMA, ATOMIC PHYSICS. *Current Pos:* RES PHYSICIST, MISSION RES CORP, 85- *Personal Data:* b New York, NY, Apr 23, 38; m 70; c 2. *Educ:* Columbia Univ, AB, 59, MA, 61, PhD(physics), 65. *Prof Exp:* Asst prof physics, NY Univ, Bronx, 65-69; res scientist, Cornell Aeronaut Lab, Buffalo, 70 & Advan Res Instrument Systs Inc, 71; from assoc astron to astron, Inst Astron, Univ Haw, 72-85. *Mem:* NY Acad Sci; Am Phys Soc; Int Astron Union. *Res:* Theoretical and computational plasma and atomic physics applied to atmospheric problems; research in solar physics. *Mailing Add:* Mission Res Corp 735 State St PO Drawer 719 Santa Barbara CA 93102. *Fax:* 805-962-8530

LANDMAN, OTTO ERNEST, MICROBIAL GENETICS. *Current Pos:* RETIRED. *Personal Data:* b Mannheim, Ger, Feb 15, 25; nat US; m 48, Ruth Hallo; c Wendy, Jessica & Jonathan. *Educ:* Queens Col, BS, 47; Yale Univ, MS, 48, PhD(microbiol), 51. *Prof Exp:* USPHS fel, Calif Inst Technol, 51-52; res assoc bact, Univ Ill, 53-56; chief, Microbial Genetics Br, US Army Biol Labs, Ft Detrick, 56-61, sr investr, 61-63; assoc prof biol, Georgetown Univ, 63-66, prof, 66-90. *Concurrent Pos:* NIH spec fel, Ctr Molecular Genetics, Nat Ctr Sci Res, Gif-Sur-Yvette, France, 68-69; vis investr, Nat Inst Med Res, Mill Hill, London, 75-76. *Mem:* AAAS; Am Soc Microbiol; Genetics Soc Am. *Res:* Protoplasts and L forms of bacteria; cell division; wall biosynthesis and transformation in bacteria; phage infection of protoplasts; gene expression in dicaryotic bacterial system; inheritance of acquired characteristics; molecular-genetic mechanism of aging. *Mailing Add:* Dept Biol Georgetown Univ Washington DC 20057. *Fax:* 301-365-6558

LANDMAN, UZI, MICROMECHANICS, CHEMICAL PHYSICS. *Current Pos:* from assoc prof to prof, 75-88, assoc dean res, Col Sci & Lib Studies, 88-89, REGENTS PROF, SCH PHYSICS, GA INST TECHNOL, 88-; NORDITA PROF, CHALMERS UNIV TECHNOL, INST THEORET PHYSICS, GOTEBORG, SWEDEN, 84- *Personal Data:* b Tel-Aviv, Israel, May 22, 44. *Educ:* Hebrew Univ, Israel, BSc, 66; Weizman Inst Sci, Israel, MSc, 67; Israel Inst Technol, DSc(theoret chem), 69. *Prof Exp:* Asst prof chem, Israel Inst Technol, 69-70; vis asst prof chem, Univ Calif, Santa Barbara, 70-71; res asst prof physics, Univ Ill, Urbana, 71-72; scientist, Webster Xerox Res Lab, 72-75; sr fel, Inst Fundamental Studies, Dept Physics & Astron, Univ Rochester, 75-77. *Concurrent Pos:* Ed, J Computational Mat Sci, 91-; dir, Ctr Computational Mat Sci, 92- *Mem:* Fel Am Phys Soc; Am Vacuum Soc. *Res:* Formulation and application of a multiple scattering theory of inelastic electron diffraction from metal surfaces leading to the earliest precision determination of surface plasmon dispersion relation for aluminum; statistical physics; chemical physics; computational physics. *Mailing Add:* Sch Physics Ga Inst Technol Atlanta GA 30332

LANDMESSER, LYNN THERESE, PHYSIOLOGY, NEUROBIOLOGY. *Current Pos:* prof, Physiol Sect, Biol Sci Group, 83-85, PROF, DEPT PHYSIOL & NEUROBIOL, UNIV CONN, STORRS, 85- *Personal Data:* b Santa Ana, Calif, Nov 30, 43. *Educ:* Univ Calif, Los Angeles, BA, 65, PhD(neurophysiol), 69. *Honors & Awards:* Yntema Mem Lectr, State Univ NY, Syracuse, 81; Twelfth Ann Trotter Lectr, Dept Anat & Neurobiol, Washington Univ, 87. *Prof Exp:* NIH fel, Physiol Dept, Col Med, Univ Utah, 69-71, Dept Regulatory Biol, Univ Conn, 71-72; from asst prof to prof biol, Dept Biol, Yale Univ, 72-83. *Concurrent Pos:* NIH grant, 72-85, NSF grant, 88-91; assoc ed, Develop Biol, 77-81, J Neurosci, 81-85; mem, Sci Adv Comt, Nat Spinal Cord Injury Found, 79-87; mem, NIH Study Sect Neurol B, 82-85, Social Issues Comt, Soc Neurosci, 82-85; Grass Found vis scientist, Anat Dept, Emory Univ, Ga, 84; Jacob Javits investr award, 85-92; Arturo Rosenblueth distinguished prof, Ctr Advan Studies, Mexico City, 87; dir, NIH Postdoctoral Training Grant Neurosci, 88-; Wiersma vis prof neurosci, Calif Inst Technol, 89; mem sci adv bd, Nat Inst Child Health & Develop, NIH, 89- *Mem:* Soc Neurosci; Am Physiol Soc; Soc Develop Biol (pres, 88-89); fel AAAS. *Res:* Neurophysiology. *Mailing Add:* Dept Neurosci Case Western Res Univ 10900 Euclid Ave Cleveland OH 44106-4975

LANDO, BARBARA ANN, ALGEBRA. *Current Pos:* STATE DIR, ELDERHOSTEL, 90- *Personal Data:* b Elizabeth, NJ, Dec 7, 40; m 65. *Educ:* Georgian Court Col, BA, 62; Rutgers Univ, New Brunswick, MS, 64, PhD(math), 69. *Prof Exp:* Instr math, Douglass Col, Rutgers Univ, NB, 69; from asst prof to prof, Univ Alaska, Fairbanks, 79-90. *Mem:* Am Math Soc; Math Asn Am; Inst Elec & Electronics Engrs; Asn Comput Mach. *Res:* Differential algebra; formal language theory. *Mailing Add:* 1881 Yankovich Rd Fairbanks AK 99709

LANDO, JEROME B, POLYMER SCIENCE. *Current Pos:* asst prof polymer sci & eng, Case Western Res Univ, 65-68, assoc prof, 68-74, chmn dept, 78-85, PROF MACROMOLECULAR SCI, CASE WESTERN RES UNIV, 74-; TECH DIR, EDISON POLYMER INOVATION CORP, 85- *Personal Data:* b Brooklyn, NY, May 23, 32; m 62; c 3. *Educ:* Cornell Univ, BA, 53; Polytech Inst Brooklyn, PhD(chem), 63. *Honors & Awards:* Int Res Award, Soc Plastics Engrs, 94. *Prof Exp:* Fel, Polytech Inst Brooklyn, 63; res chemist, Camille Dreyfus Lab, Res Triangle Inst, 63-65. *Concurrent Pos:* Humboldt Found Sr Am Scientist Award, 74; vis prof, Univ Mainz, 74 & Weismann Inst, Israel, 87; mem adv bd, J Molecular Electronics, Mat Lett & Polymers Advan Technol; dir, Polymer Microdevices Lab, 87- *Mem:* Am Chem Soc; Am Crystallog Asn; Am Phys Soc; Sigma Xi; Soc Plastics Engrs. *Res:* Polymer physical chemistry; solid state reactions, especially polymerization reactions and polymer crystal structure; synthesis of stereoregular polymers, pyroelectric and piezoelectric polymers; electronic and optical properties of polymers and thin film. *Mailing Add:* Dept Macromolecular Sci Case Western Res Univ Cleveland OH 44106

LANDOLFI, NICHOLAS F, MOLECULAR IMMUNOLOGY. *Current Pos:* STAFF SCIENTIST, PROTEIN DESIGN LABS, 88- *Personal Data:* b Ashtabula, Ohio, Sept 2, 55; m 88. *Educ:* Ohio State Univ, BS, 77; Miami Univ, MS, 80; Univ Tex, PhD(immunol), 84. *Prof Exp:* Res fel, Univ Tex Southwestern Med Sch, 85-88 & Leukemia Soc Am, 87-88. *Mem:* Am Asn Immunologists; AAAS; Sigma Xi. *Res:* Structure and function analysis of molecules involved in immune response; differential control of genes in the cells of the immune system. *Mailing Add:* Protein Design Labs 2375 Garcia Ave Mountain View CA 94043-1170

LANDOLL, LEO MICHAEL, POLYMER CHEMISTRY. *Current Pos:* DIR TECHNOL, APPL EXTRUSION TECHNOL, 94- *Personal Data:* b Cleveland, Ohio, Oct 11, 50; m 71, Mary Bissler; c 2. *Educ:* Kent State Univ, BA, 70; Univ Del, MBA, 82; Univ Akron, PhD(polymer sci), 75. *Prof Exp:* Res chemist, Hercules Inc, 74-79, sr res chemist polymer synthesis, 79-82, res scientist, 82-87, proj leader, 87-94. *Mem:* Am Chem Soc; Tech Asn Pulp & Paper Indust; Soc Plastics Engrs. *Res:* Polymer synthesis and processing related to thermoplastic and thermoset systems, fibers, films, property correlations; synthesis and structure property relations of natural and synthetic water soluble polymers; steric stabilization of particles in suspension. *Mailing Add:* 1 Ice Pond Trail Hockessin Hunt Hockessin DE 19707-9412. *Fax:* 302-378-4482

LANDOLPH, JOSEPH RICHARD, JR, BIOCHEMISTRY, CHEMICAL & GENETIC TOXICOLOGY. *Current Pos:* postdoctoral res fel chem carcinogenesis, Comprehensive Career Ctr, Univ Southern Calif, 77-80, asst prof path, 80-82, asst prof, microbiol & path, 82-87, ASSOC PROF MOLECULAR MICROBIOL & IMMUNOL, PATH & MOLECULAR PHARMACOL & TOXICOL WITH TENURE, NORRIS COMPREHENSIVE CANCER CTR, SCH MED, UNIV SOUTHERN CALIF, 87- *Personal Data:* b Upper Darby, Pa, Nov 9, 48; m 80, Alice L Kaufman; c Joseph R III & Louis S. *Educ:* Drexel Univ, BS, 71; Univ Calif, Berkeley, PhD(chem), 76. *Prof Exp:* Qual control chemist, Rohn Haas Co, Philadelphia, Pa, 68; chem technician, Smith Kline & Fr Co, Philadelphia, Pa, 69; res asst chem, Dept Chem, Univ Calif, Berkeley, 71-76. *Concurrent Pos:* Postdoctoral fel, Am Cancer Soc, 77-79; prin investr, Nat Cancer Inst, Nat Inst Environ Health Sci & Environ Protection Agency grants, 83-; consult, Am Petrol Inst, 85-87; consult, Ozone Criteria Doc, Environ Protection Agency, Calif; Howard Hughes fels, Nat Res Coun, 88; Traveler's lectr, Soc Toxicol, 90; Path Study Sect, NIH, 97. *Mem:* Am Soc Biochem & Molecular Biol; Am Asn Cancer Res; Sigma Xi; Environ Mutagen Soc; Am Soc Cell Biol; Soc Toxicologists. *Res:* Mechanisms of chemical carcinogenesis studied in cultured mammalian cells; molecular biology of oncogene activation and tumor suppressor gene in activation caused by organic chemical carcinogens and carcinogenic metal salts; human carcinogenesis mechanisms; molecule oncology. *Mailing Add:* Norris Comprehensive Cancer Ctr Rm 517 MS 73 Univ Southern Calif Sch Med 1441 Eastlake Ave Los Angeles CA 90033-0800. *Fax:* 213-764-0105

LANDOLT, ARLO UDELL, ASTRONOMY. *Current Pos:* from asst prof to assoc prof, 62-68, dir observ, 70-88, PROF PHYSICS & ASTRON, LA STATE UNIV, BATON ROUGE, 68- *Personal Data:* b Highland, Ill, Sept 29, 35; m 66, Eunice J Casper; c Lynda, Barbara, Vicky, Debra & Jennifer. *Educ:* Miami Univ, BA, 55; Ind Univ, MA, 60, PhD(astron), 63. *Honors & Awards:* George van Biesbroeck Prize, 95. *Prof Exp:* Scientist aurora & airglow, US Int Geophys Year Comt, 56-58. *Concurrent Pos:* Mem first wintering-over party, Int Geophys Year Amundson-Scott S Pole Sta, Antarctica, 57; Grad Res Coun res grants, La State Univ, Baton Rouge, 64-76; res grants, 64, 66, 69, 71, 73, 75 & 92-97 & Res Corp, 64 & NASA, 65, 92; secy, sect D Astron, AAAS, 70-78, US Nat Comt, Int Astron Union, 80-89 & 95-; prog dir, NSF, Washington, DC, 75-76; Air Force Off Sci Res, grants, 77-87; guest investr, Dyer Observ, Vanderbilt Univ, Goethe Link Observ, Ind Univ, Kitt Peak Nat Observ, Cerro Tololo Inter-Am Observ & Las Campanas Observ, La Serena, Chile; actg chmn, dept physics & astron, La State Univ, Baton Rouge, 72 & 73, pres fac senate, 79-80; Space Telescope Sci Inst grant, 85-90. *Mem:* Fel AAAS; Int Astron Union; Am Astron Soc (secy, 80-89 & 95-); Royal Astron Soc Eng; Sigma Xi; Explorer's Club. *Res:* Photometric investigations of star clusters, variable stars, and eclipsing binaries; standard astronomical photometric systems; galactic structure. *Mailing Add:* Dept Physics & Astron La State Univ Baton Rouge LA 70803-4001. *Fax:* 504-388-5855; *E-Mail:* landolt@rouge.phys.lsu.edu

LANDOLT, JACK PETER, SPATIAL DISORIENTATION, BIODYNAMICS. *Current Pos:* defense scientist vestibular physiol, Defense & Civil Inst Environ Med, 68-75, group head motion sickness biodynamics, 75-76, sect head disorientation biodynamics, 76-80, sect head biophys, 80-86, sect head, aerospace physiol, 86-89 , HEAD, PLANS & POLICY, DEFENSE & CIVIL INST ENVIRON MED, 89- *Personal Data:* b Zurich, Switz, Mar 17, 34; Can citizen; m 64, C Gwendolyn Delmas; c Lydia M, Phillip L, Monica A, Christian L & Mark D. *Educ:* Univ Ottawa, BASc, 59, MSc, 62; Iowa State Univ Sci & Technol, PhD(elec eng), 68. *Honors & Awards:* A Jaan Saber Mem Award, Can Aeronaut & Space Inst, 92; Sidney P Leverett, Jr, Environ Sci Award, Aerospace Med Asn, 94; NTW Award Excellence, Transp Asn Can, 95. *Prof Exp:* Defense scientist oper res, Can Army Oper Res Estab, 61-65. *Concurrent Pos:* Mem, Can Adv Comt, Int Stand Org, 77-89, Aerospace Med Panel, Adv Group, Aerospace Res & Develop, NATO, 78- *Mem:* Soc Neurosci; Barany Soc. *Res:* Neurobiology of peripheral vestibular apparatus; space adaptation syndrome and circular vection; vestibular-visual interactions; motion cues in simulation sickness; impact protection of the human; author or coauthor of over 100 publications; high altitude and high acceleration physiology. *Mailing Add:* Defense & Civil Inst Environ Med 1133 Sheppard Ave W North York ON M3M 3B9 Can

LANDOLT, MARSHA LAMERLE, FISH PATHOLOGY, TOXICOLOGY. *Current Pos:* From asst prof to assoc prof, Univ Wash, 75-86, asst dir, 80-83, assoc dean, 83-91, PROF FISHERIES, SCH FISHERIES, UNIV WASH, 86-, DIR, 91- *Personal Data:* b Houston, Tex, Jan 19, 48. *Educ:* Baylor Univ, BS, 69; Univ Okla, MS, 70; George Washington Univ, PhD(path), 76. *Concurrent Pos:* Histopathologist, Eastern Fish Dis Lab, US Dept Interior, Leetown, WVa, 70-74; path clerk, Dept Animal Health, Nat Zool Park, Smithsonian Inst, Washington, DC, 74-75. *Res:* Development of in vitro and in vivo test systems for use in genotoxic research; fish pathology; development of vaccines for prevention of fish disease. *Mailing Add:* Sch Fisheries WH-10 Univ Wash 3900 7th Ave NE Seattle WA 98195-0001

LANDOLT, PAUL ALBERT, PHYSIOLOGY. *Current Pos:* from instr to prof 53-77, EMER PROF PHYSIOL, UNIV NEBR, LINCOLN, 77- *Personal Data:* b Shubert, Nebr, July 10, 12; wid; c Sharon (Harvey). *Educ:* Nebr State Teachers Col, Peru, BA, 33; Univ Nebr, MS, 51, PhD(zool, physiol), 60. *Prof Exp:* Teacher, High Schs, Nebr, 36-42; field dir mil welfare, Am Red Cross, Mariannas Islands, 42-46; instr biol sci, Scottsbluff Jr Col, Nebr, 46-53. *Concurrent Pos:* Instr, Southeast Community Col, Lincoln, 77-88. *Mem:* AAAS; Am Soc Cell Biol. *Res:* Vertebrate physiology; tissue culture; problems related to effects of air pollutants on lung tissue. *Mailing Add:* 1540 N Cotner Blvd No 110 Lincoln NE 68505

LANDOLT, PETER JOHN, INSECT COMMUNICATION, CHEMICAL ECOLOGY. *Current Pos:* Res assoc, Fresno, 79-81, res entomologist, Miami, 81-84, RES ENTOMOLOGIST, USDA AGR RES SERV, GAINESVILLE, 84- *Personal Data:* b Cincinnati, Ohio, June 13, 52. *Educ:* Northern Mich Univ, BS, 74; Wash State Univ, MS, 76, PhD(entom), 78. *Res:* Study of chemically mediated behavior important to host, food, and mate-finding strategies of insects, with emphasis on cabbage looper moths and tephritid fruit flies. *Mailing Add:* PO Box 14565 Gainesville FL 32604

LANDOLT, ROBERT GEORGE, ORGANIC CHEMISTRY. *Current Pos:* chmn, Chem Dept, 81-85, 82-86 & 90-93, PROF, TEX WESLEYAN UNIV, 81- *Personal Data:* b Houston, Tex, Apr 4, 39; m 62; c 3. *Educ:* Austin Col, BA, 61; Univ Tex, PhD(org chem), 65. *Prof Exp:* Res assoc org chem, Univ Ill, 65-67; from asst prof to assoc prof org chem, Muskingum Col, 67-80, chmn dept, 71-74; sr scientist, Radian Corp, 80-81. *Concurrent Pos:* Resident consult, Columbus Labs, Battelle Mem Inst, 74-75; consult & contractor, US Navy, 82-84; Cong fel, Am Chem Soc, 86-87; dir, Res Div, Tex Higher Educ Coord Bd, 91. *Mem:* AAAS; Am Asn Univ Prof; Am Chem Soc; Sigma Xi. *Res:* Abnormal claisen rearrangement and reactions in aprotic polar solvents; nitroso aromatic compounds; oxidation of coal and coal model compounds; computer assisted information retrieval; origin of organic pollutants in water; hypochlorite reactions with organics. *Mailing Add:* Dept Chem Tex Wesleyan Univ Ft Worth TX 76105. *Fax:* 817-531-4425

LANDOLT, ROBERT RAYMOND, HEALTH PHYSICS. *Current Pos:* from instr to assoc prof, 64-81, PROF HEALTH SCI, PURDUE UNIV, WEST LAFAYETTE, IND, 81- *Personal Data:* b Sherman, Tex, May 11, 37; m 70, Alice; c Sarah, Doris & George. *Educ:* Austin Col, BA, 59; Univ Kans, MS, 61; Purdue Univ, PhD(bionucleonics), 68. *Prof Exp:* Reactor health physicist, Phillips Petrol Co, Idaho, 61-64. *Mem:* Health Physics Soc. *Res:* Radioactive aerosol production during reactor decommissioning; low-level radioactive waste management. *Mailing Add:* Sch Health Sci Purdue Univ West Lafayette IN 47906. *Fax:* 765-496-1377; *E-Mail:* landoltr@purccvm.bitnet

LANDON, ERWIN JACOB, BIOCHEMISTRY. *Current Pos:* asst prof, 59-67, ASSOC PROF PHARMACOL, SCH MED, VANDERBILT UNIV, 67- *Personal Data:* b Cleveland, Ohio, Jan 22, 25; m 65. *Educ:* Univ Chicago, BS, 45, MD, 48; Univ Calif, PhD(biochem), 53. *Prof Exp:* Intern, Harper Hosp, Detroit, Mich, 48-49. *Concurrent Pos:* Sr res fel pharmacol, Sch Med, Yale Univ, 57-59. *Mem:* Am Chem Soc; Am Soc Pharmacol & Exp Therapeut; Sigma Xi. *Res:* Biochemistry of renal transport; cell calcium regulation. *Mailing Add:* Dept Pharmacol Vanderbilt Univ Nashville TN 37232-0001

LANDON, JOHN CAMPBELL, VIROLOGY, CANCER. *Current Pos:* PRES, BIOQUAL INC, 82- *Personal Data:* b Hornell, NY, Jan 3, 37; m 58; c 4. *Educ:* Alfred Univ, AB, 59; George Washington Univ, MS, 62, PhD(biol), 67. *Prof Exp:* Biologist, Nat Cancer Inst, 60-65; head virol, Litton Bionetics, Inc, 65-68; chief dept virol & cell biol, 68-71, dir spec prog develop, 71-72, dir sci, Frederick Cancer Res Ctr, 72-75; pres, Mason Res Inst, 75-82, Sema Inc, 85-91. *Concurrent Pos:* Pres & chief exec officer, Diagnow Corp, 86- *Mem:* AAAS; Am Soc Cell Biol; NY Acad Sci; Am Soc Microbiol. *Res:* Viral oncology; tissue culture; general human and simian virology; cell biology; environmental biology. *Mailing Add:* 8213 Raymond Lane Potomac MD 20854-3728

LANDON, ROBERT E, geology; deceased, see previous edition for last biography

LANDON, SHAYNE J, ORGANOSILICON & ORGANOMETALLIC CHEMISTRY. *Current Pos:* sr chemist, Spec Chems Div, Union Carbide Corp, 85-90, proj scientist, 90-94, RES SCIENTIST, OSI SPECIALTIES GROUP, WITCO CORP, 94- *Personal Data:* b Alexandria Bay, NY, July 21, 54; m 79, Martha J Poole; c Thomas P. *Educ:* State Univ NY, Plattsburgh, BA, 76, MA, 79; Univ Del, PhD, 84. *Prof Exp:* Res assoc, Pa State Univ, 84-85. *Mem:* Am Chem Soc; Sigma Xi; NY Acad Sci. *Res:* Organosilicon chemistry; silicone surfactants; urethanes; spectroscopy; reaction mechanisms and kinetics; silicon modified polymer. *Mailing Add:* OSI Specialties Group Witco Corp 777 Old Saw Mill River Rd Tarrytown NY 10591. *Fax:* 914-784-4922

LANDON, SUSAN MELINDA, PETROLEUM GEOLOGY. *Current Pos:* INDEPENDENT GEOLOGIST, DENVER, 90- *Personal Data:* b Mattoon, Ill, July, 2, 50; m 93, Richard D Dietz. *Educ:* Knox Col, BA, 72; State Univ NY, MA, 75. *Honors & Awards:* Martin Van Couvering Award, Am Inst Prof Geologists, 91. *Prof Exp:* Petrol geologist, Amoco Prod Co, Denver, 74-87, mgr, Explor Training, Amoco, Houston, 87-89. *Concurrent Pos:* Instr petrol geol & explor, Bur Land Mgt, US Forest Serv, Nat Park Serv Indust, 78-; mem & chmn, Colo Geol Surv Adv Comt, Denver, 91-93; mem bd, Earth Sci & Resources, Nat Res Coun, 92-; ed, Interior Rift Basins, 93. *Mem:* Am Asn Petrol Geologists (treas); Am Inst Prof Geologists. *Res:* Frontier explorations for hydrocarbons in US and in midcontinent rift system. *Mailing Add:* Thomasson Partner Assocs 1100 Stout St Suite 1400 Denver CO 80202. *Fax:* 303-436-1935

LANDOR, JOHN HENRY, SURGERY. *Current Pos:* CHIEF, DEPT SURG, RARITAN VALLEY HOSP, GREEN BROOK, 73- *Personal Data:* b Canton, Ohio, Sept 30, 27; m 53; c 6. *Educ:* Univ Chicago, PhB, 48, MD, 53. *Prof Exp:* Instr surg, Sch Med, Univ Chicago, 58; from instr to prof, Sch Med, Univ Mo-Columbia, 59-69; prof, Col Med, Univ Fla, 69-72; prof & chief gen surg, Col Med & Dent NJ, Rutgers Med Sch, 72- *Concurrent Pos:* Commonwealth Found fel, Royal Postgrad Med Sch, London, 66-67. *Mem:* Am Col Surgeons; Soc Univ Surgeons; Am Gastroenterol Asn; Soc Surg Alimentary Tract; Int Soc Surgeons. *Res:* Physiology of the stomach. *Mailing Add:* Health Sci Ctr Dept Surg State Univ NY 450 Clarkson Ave PO Box 40 Brooklyn NY 11203

LANDOWNE, DAVID, PHYSIOLOGY, BIOPHYSICS. *Current Pos:* asst prof physiol, 72-75, ASSOC PROF PHYSIOL, SCH MED, UNIV MIAMI, 75- *Personal Data:* b Chicago, Ill, Dec 26, 42; m 66; c 2. *Educ:* Mass Inst Technol, BS, 63; Harvard Univ, PhD(physiol), 68. *Prof Exp:* Res assoc pharmacol, Sch Med, Yale Univ, 68-72. *Concurrent Pos:* Grass Found fel, 70; NSF fel, Univ London, 70-71. *Mem:* Biophys Soc; Soc Gen Physiol. *Res:* Excitable membranes; ion movements and optical measurements of the movement of excitable molecules. *Mailing Add:* Dept Physiol & Biophys Univ Miami Sch Med R-430 PO Box 016430 Miami FL 33101-6430

LANDOWNE, MILTON, INTERNAL MEDICINE, CIRCULATORY PHYSIOLOGY. *Current Pos:* RETIRED. *Personal Data:* b New York, NY, Nov 19, 12; m 41, Eleanor Judson; c David, Stephen, Joseph, Martha & Ruth. *Educ:* City Col New York, BS, 32; Harvard Univ, MD, 36. *Prof Exp:* Intern, Mt Sinai Hosp, New York, 36-39; Libman fel, Michael Reese Hosp, Chicago, 39-41; instr, Univ Chicago, 41-46, asst prof med, 46-48; chief cardiovasc res unit, Vet Admin Hosp, 48-49; assoc chief geront sect, Nat Heart Inst, 49-57; med dir, Levindale Hebrew Home & Infirmary, Baltimore, Md, 57-65; dir med lab, US Army Res Inst Environ Med, 65-76, med adv, 76-85. *Concurrent Pos:* Asst prof, Johns Hopkins Univ, 55-65; head div cardiol & chronic dis, Sinai Hosp, Baltimore, 58-65; asst clin prof, Harvard Univ, 65-74. *Mem:* AAAS; Am Soc Clin Invest; Am Physiol Soc; Soc Exp Biol & Med; Am Heart Asn. *Res:* Disorders of the circulation; biology aging; clinical medicine; physiology of blood and circulation; metabolic and renal diseases; environmental medicine. *Mailing Add:* 67 Woodchester Dr Weston MA 02193

LANDRETH, GARY E, SIGNAL TRANSDUCTORS. *Current Pos:* asst prof neurosci, 86-89, ASSOC PROF NEUROSCI, CASE WESTERN RES UNIV, 89- *Personal Data:* b Van Nuys, Calif, Apr 26, 50. *Educ:* Univ Kans, BA, 72; Univ Mich, PhD(neurobiol), 77. *Prof Exp:* Fel neurobiol, Stanford Univ, 77-80; asst prof, Med Col Univ SC, 80-86. *Mem:* Am Soc Biol Chemists; Soc Neurosci. *Res:* Signal transductors. *Mailing Add:* Alzheimer Res Lab E504 Case Western Res Univ Sch Med Cleveland OH 44106-4928

LANDRETH, KENNETH S, ANATOMY. *Current Pos:* assoc prof microbiol, 85-91, PROF MICRO BIOL & IMMUNOL, SCH MED, WVA UNIV, 91- *Personal Data:* b Galax, Va, Aug 22, 47; m 76; c 2. *Educ:* Univ Wash, Seattle, PhD(biol struct), 80. *Prof Exp:* Sr res scientist, Okla Med Res Found, 82-85. *Concurrent Pos:* Res fel, Sloan-Kettering Cancer Ctr; mem, Mary Babb Randolph Cancer Ctr, WVa, 90- *Mem:* Am Asn Immunologists. *Res:* Regulation of B lymphocyte production in the bone marrow; lemopoiesis. *Mailing Add:* Microbiol WVa Univ Sch Med Morgantown WV 26506-0002

LANDRETH, RONALD RAY, WASTE REUSE, SULFUR OXIDE. *Current Pos:* res engr, Inland Steel, 75-79, group leader environ res, 79-85, proj mgr sorbent injection, 84-86, sr environ consult eng, 85-86, scientist res, 86-88, new ventures, 88-90, prog mgr new ventures, 90-92, MGR OPERS & TECHNOL, ADVAN GRAPHITE TECHNOL, INLAND STEEL, 92- *Personal Data:* b Mattoon, Ill, June 15, 49; m 71, Laura J Hagerman; c L Paige, Matthew C & Brittany J. *Educ:* Northwestern Univ, BA, 71; Pa State Univ, PhD(environ chem), 75. *Prof Exp:* Res fel chem, Pa State Univ, 72-75. *Mem:* Air & Waste Mgt Asn; Am Chem Soc. *Res:* Environmental sciences, primarily air and solids; airwork included air monitoring, source identification and development of innovative desulfurization controls (patented); solid waste work included recycling and reuse technology development. *Mailing Add:* 249 Meadow Ridge Rd Valparaiso IN 46383. *Fax:* 219-942-4574

LANDRIGAN, PHILIP J, ENVIRONMENTAL EPIDEMIOLOGY, OCCUPATIONAL MEDICINE. *Current Pos:* PROF ENVIRON MED, MT SINAI SCH MED, 85-, CHMN COMMUNITY MED & DIR, DIV ENVIRON MED, 90- *Personal Data:* b Boston, Mass, June 14, 42; m 76; c 3. *Educ:* Harvard Med Sch, MD, 67; Univ London MSc, 77. *Prof Exp:* Chief, Environ Hazards Activ, Ctr Dis Control, 70-73; dir surveillance hazard & eval, Occup epidemiol, Nat Inst Occup Safety & Health, 79-85. *Concurrent*

Pos: Vchair, Bd Environ Sci & Technol, Nat Acad Sci, 81-86; chair, Comt Environ Hazard, Am Acad Pediat, 83-87. Mem: Inst Med-Nat Acad Sci; Am Epidemiol Soc; Royal Soc Med; Am Acad Pediat; Am Pub Health Asn; Am Occup Med Asn; NY Acad Sci. Res: Occupational and environmental epidemiology; Lema poisoning; occupational respiratory diseases; reproductive dysfunction and neurotoxicology. Mailing Add: Dept Commun Med Mt Sinai Sch Med PO Box 1057 New York NY 10029

LANDROCK, ARTHUR HAROLD, PLASTICS, ADHESIVES MATERIALS ENGINEERING. Current Pos: CONSULT MAT SCI, 93-. Personal Data: b New York, NY, May 19, 19; m 42, Rose-Marie McDonald; c Virginia A (deceased), Nancy, Mary-Jane, Joan, Rebecca & Roberta. Educ: Queens Col, BS, 41; Boston Univ, AM, 50. Honors & Awards: Ed Excellence Award, Am Soc Testing & Mat, 77, D-20 Award Excellence, 88, Outstanding Achievement Award, 89, Comt Terminology Mem Award, 90. Prof Exp: Chemist packaging res, Paper Containers Div, Continental Can Co, 45-47; res asst & tech asst food packaging, Mass Inst Technol, 47-53; sr food packaging scientist, Film Div, Olin Mathieson Chem Corp, 53-55, sr res chemist, Viscose Res, Gen Res Orgn, 55-56; prod stand mgr, M&M'S Candies, Div Food Mfrs, 56-60; mat engr, Dept Defense Plastics Tech Eval Ctr, Armament Res, Develop & Eng Ctr, US Army, 61-93. Concurrent Pos: US deleg & mem tech adv group plastics, Int Orgn Stand, 77-; mem, Comt Terminology, Am Soc Testing & Mat, 83-89, ed reviewer, Stand in Plastics & Adhesives; liaison rep, Comt Combustion Toxicity, Nat Mat Adv Bd, 84-; mem ed bd, J Plastics & Elastomers, 78-, J Testing & Eval, 88- Mem: Fel Am Soc Testing & Mat; Int Orgn Stand; Soc Advan Mat & Process Eng; Sigma Xi; Soc Plastics Engrs; Am Soc Mat Int. Res: Plastics and adhesives; flammability of plastics and adhesive bonding; plastic foams, terminology; standardization. Mailing Add: 285 E Shore Trail Sparta NJ 07871

LANDRUM, BILLY FRANK, ORGANIC CHEMISTRY, POLYMER CHEMISTRY. Current Pos: RETIRED. Personal Data: b Atlanta, Ga, June 7, 20; m 48, Marjorie Rakestraw; c Douglas F, Charles T & Barbara E (Bozarth). Educ: Emory Univ, AB, 47, MS, 49, PhD(chem), 50. Prof Exp: Res chemist polymer chem, M W Kellogg Co, 50-53, res supvr pilot plant, 53-57; head polymer sect, Minn Mining & Mfg Co, 57-62; mgr advan projs, FMC Corp, NJ, 62-66; staff scientist, Whittaker Corp, 66-67; staff scientist, Com Develop Dept, Ciba-Geigy Corp, 67-74, mgr, Mkt Develop, Plastics & Additives Div, 74-78, tech serv mgr, comput mat dept, 81-85. Mem: Am Chem Soc; Sigma Xi; Soc Advan Mat & Processing Eng. Res: Organo-metallic reactions; polymers; fluorocarbons; urethanes; coal and coke; activated carbon; composite materials. Mailing Add: 761 Isabella Way Fairfield CA 94533

LANDRUM, LESLIE ROGER, SYSTEMATICS, PHYTOGEOGRAPHY. Current Pos: RES SCIENTIST & HERBARIUM CUR, DEPT BOT, ARIZ STATE UNIV, TEMPE, 86- Personal Data: b St Louis, Mo, Dec 1, 46; m 73, Sonia Suanes. Educ: NY State Col Forestry, BS, 69; Univ Mich, MS, 75, PhD(bot), 80. Prof Exp: Peace Corp vol, Sch Forestry, Univ Chile, Santiago, 69-73; teaching asst, Div Biol Sci, Univ Mich, Ann Arbor, 73-80; B A Krukoff res assoc, NY Bot Garden, Bronx, 80-83; Tilton fel, Calif Acad Sci, San Francisco, 83-86; vis lectr, San Francisco State Univ, 85 & Univ Calif, Berkeley, 86. Concurrent Pos: Grants, numerous insts & schs, 77-90; comn mem, Orgn Flora Neotropica, 86-; co-ed, Vascular Plants Ariz Proj, 87- & J Ariz-Nev Acad Sci, 91-94; Fulbright fel, Paraguay & Brazil, 95. Mem: Am Soc Plant Taxonomists; Int Asn Plant Taxon; Soc Econ Bot. Res: Systematics of American Myrtaceae; flora and phytogeography of temperate South America, especially Chile; analysis of phylogenetic patterns; phytogeography of Southern South America; flora of Arizona; numerical phylogenetic analysis; author of numerous publications. Mailing Add: Dept Bot Ariz State Univ Tempe AZ 85287-1601. Fax: 602-965-6899; E-Mail: iclrl@asuvm.inre.asu.edu

LANDRUM, PETER FRANKLIN, AQUATIC TOXICOLOGY SPECIALIZING IN BIOACCUMULATION PROCESSES. Current Pos: res chemist, 81-94, supvry chemist, 94-, ACTG DIR, US DEPT COM GREAT LAKES ENVIRON RES LAB, 96- Personal Data: m 72, Fawn M Atkinson. Educ: Calif State Col, San Bernardino, BA, 74; Univ Calif, Davis, PhD(pharmacol & toxicol), 79. Prof Exp: Res assoc, Savannah River Ecol Lab, 79-81; lectr toxicol, Eastern Mich Univ, 84-91. Concurrent Pos: Assoc ed, Critical Reviews Environ Sci & Technol, 92-, J Great Lakes Res, 92-; fel, Coop Inst Limnol & Ecosyst Res, 92-; adj assoc prof, Dept Environ Toxicol, Clemson Univ, 92-, Sch Pub Health, Univ Mich, 93- Ohio State Univ Dept Entom, 94- Mem: Soc Environ Toxicol & Chem; Am Chem Soc; Am Soc Testing & Mat; Int Asn Great Lakes Res. Res: Exposure and effects of organic contaminants to aquatic organisms with a special emphasis on the processes and environmental factors affecting the bioavailabilty of sediment-associated contaminants of benthos. Mailing Add: Nat Oceanic & Atmospheric Admin Great Lakes Environ Res Lab 2205 Commonwealth Blvd Ann Arbor MI 48105-1593. Fax: 313-741-2055; E-Mail: landrum@glerl.noaa.gov

LANDRUM, RALPH AVERY, JR, GEOPHYSICS. Current Pos: RETIRED. Personal Data: b Memphis, Tenn, Oct 2, 26; m 49; c 3. Educ: Rice Inst, BS, 49; Univ Tulsa, MS, 64. Prof Exp: Asst seismic observer, Amerada Petrol Corp, 49-51; res seismic observer, Stanolind Oil & Gas Co, 51-56; res engr, Pan Am Petrol Corp, 56-63, staff res engr, 63-67, staff res scientist, 67-71; res assoc, Res Ctr, Amoco Prod Co, 71-74; sr res geophysicist, Western Geophys Co Am, 74-93. Mem: Am Soc Explor Geophys; Inst Elec & Electronics Engrs; Europ Asn Explor Geophys. Res: Exploration geophysics; design of seismic instrumentation; mathematics of seismic data processing. Mailing Add: 1707 Valley Vista Dr Houston TX 77077

LANDRY, FERNAND, EXERCISE PHYSIOLOGY, HISTORY & PHILOSOPHY OF OLYMPIC MOVEMENT. Current Pos: dept head phys activ sci, 68-76, head, Phys Activ Sci Lab, 81-84, PROF PHYS ACTIV & SPORTS SCI, UNIV LAVAL, 84- Personal Data: b Levis, PQ, Can, Jan 13, 30; m 55, Monique Dumont; c Marc, Josee, Isabelle, Dominique, & Marie-France. Educ: Univ Ottawa, BSc, 54; Univ Ill, Urbana, MS, 55, PhD(phys educ exercise physiol), 68. Hon Degrees: Dr, Univ Ottawa, Can, 90, Univ Moneton, Can, 94. Honors & Awards: Medal, Que Govt, 74, Int Olympic Acad, 81. Prof Exp: From teacher-researcher phys educ to dept head, Univ Ottawa, 55-68. Mem: Can Asn Sport Sci (pres, 71-72); Int Coun Sport Sci & Phys Educ (vpres, 72-); emer fel Am Col Cardiol; fel Am Acad Phys Educ; fel Am Col Sports Med. Res: Short-term and chronic effects of physical activity and sports; use of physical activity in the prevention of and/or rehabilitation from generative diseases; causes of variations in suseptibility sensitivity to training stimuli; effects of training in patients with prosthetic aortic valves; exercise hypertension; history and philosophy of Olympic Movement and Olympic Games. Mailing Add: Dept Phys Activ Sci Laval Univ Quebec PQ G1K 7P4 Can. Fax: 418-656-3020; E-Mail: flandry@edp.ulaval.ca

LANDRY, MICHAEL RAYMOND, MARINE ZOOPLANKTON, PROTOZOAN ECOLOGY. Current Pos: assoc prof, Dept Oceanog, Univ Hawaii, 87-89, assoc chmn, 89-92, chmn, 93-96, PROF OCEANOG, DEPT OCEANOG, UNIV HAWAII, 89- Personal Data: b Berlin, NH, Apr 16, 48; m 72, Christine Benedetti; c Steve M & Scott R. Educ: Univ Calif, Santa Barbara, BA, 70; Univ Wash, PhD(oceanog), 76, MBA, 86. Honors & Awards: Spec Creativity Award, NSF, 90. Prof Exp: Res biologist, Scripps Inst Oceanog, Univ Calif, San Diego, 76-78; res asst prof, Univ Wash, 78-83, res assoc prof biol oceanog, Sch Oceanog, 83-87. Concurrent Pos: Coordr, NW Regional Oceanog Prog, US Dept Energy, 82-85; intern, Global Commun Systs working group on numerical modeling, 95-; joint Global Ocean Flux Study Prog Steering Comt, 95- Mem: Am Soc Limnol & Oceanog; Western Soc Naturalists; Soc Protozoologists; Intern Soc Copepodiologists; fel AAAS. Res: Feeding behavior and population dynamics of marine zooplankton; marine microbial ecology; marine ecosystem research and modeling; carbon and nitrogen cycling. Mailing Add: Dept Oceanog Univ Hawaii-Manoa Honolulu HI 96822. Fax: 808-956-9516; E-Mail: landry@soest.hawaii.edu

LANDRY, RICHARD GEORGES, APPLIED STATISTICS. Current Pos: Asst prof, 69-73, assoc prof, 70-80, PROF MEASUREMENT & STATIST, CTR TEACHING & LEARNING, UNIV NDAK, 80- Personal Data: b Manchester, NH, Nov 7, 42; m 66; c 3. Educ: Oblate Col, BA, 64; Boston Col, MEd, 67, PhD(res & statist), 70. Concurrent Pos: Eval auditor, numerous ESEA Title III Projs, 70-; eval consult, Grand Rapids Sch Dist, Minn, 73-; res coordr, Nat Inst Educ Proj, Univ NDak, 73- Mem: Am Asn Univ Prof; Am Educ Res Asn; Am Statist Asn; Nat Coun Measurement Educ. Res: Applied educational statistics; educational measurement and evaluation in affective domain; foreign language learning and creativity. Mailing Add: Educ Found & Res Univ NDak Box 7189 Grand Forks ND 58202

LANDRY, STUART OMER, JR, ZOOLOGY. Current Pos: actg dean grad sch, 66-68, PROF BIOL, STATE UNIV NY BINGHAMTON, 63- Personal Data: b New Orleans, La, Sept 30, 24; m 50; c 2. Educ: Harvard Univ, BS, 49; Univ Calif, PhD(zool), 54. Prof Exp: Curatorial asst, Mus Vert Zool, Calif, 50-52; asst zool, Univ Calif, 52-53, assoc, 53-54; from instr to assoc prof anat, Univ Mo, 54-59; assoc prof biol & chmn dept, La State Univ, 59-63. Mem: AAAS; Soc Syst Zool; Am Soc Mammal; Am Asn Anat; Am Soc Zoologists. Res: Comparative anatomy and classification of mammals; functional anatomy of mammals. Mailing Add: Dept Biol Sci State Univ NY Binghamton NY 13902-6000

LANDS, WILLIAM EDWARD MITCHELL, BIOCHEMISTRY. Current Pos: DIR, DIV BASIC RES, NAT INST ALCOHOL ABUSE & ALCOHOLISM, 90- Personal Data: b Chillicothe, Mo, July 22, 30; c 4. Educ: Univ Mich, Ann Arbor, BS, 51; Univ Ill, PhD(biol chem), 54. Honors & Awards: Gold Medal Bond Award, Am Oil Chemists Soc, 65; Glycerine Res Award, 69; Verhagen Lectr, 79-81; Pfizer Biomed Res Award, 85. Prof Exp: NSF fel, Calif Inst Technol, 54-55; from instr to prof biochem, Univ Mich, Ann Arbor, 55-80; head biochem, Univ Ill Med Ctr, 80-85, prof, 85-90. Concurrent Pos: Chmn subcomt biochem nomenclature, Nat Acad Sci, 62-64; Danforth Assoc, 66-; ed, Can J Biochem, 72-78; ed, Biochem & Biophys Acta, J Lipid Res, 78- Mem: AAAS; Am Chem Soc; Am Soc Biochem & Molecular Biol; Am Oil Chemists Soc; Sigma Xi; Am Inst Nutrit. Res: Metabolism of glycerides and long-chain aliphatic acids and aldehydes; formation of membranes and regulation of membrane function; prostaglandin biochemistry and control of its biosynthesis. Mailing Add: Nat Inst Abuse & Alcoholism NIH Willco Bldg 6000 Exec Blvd MSC 7003 Rockville MD 20892-7003. Fax: 301-443-6077, 594-0673

LANDSBAUM, ELLIS M(ERLE), CHEMICAL ENGINEERING. Current Pos: sect mgr, 61-84, STAFF ENGR, PROPULSION DEPT, AEROSPACE CORP, 84- Personal Data: b Chicago, Ill, Feb 28, 25; m 52; c 2. Educ: Ill Inst Technol, BSc, 49; Northwestern Univ, MSc, 53, PhD(chem eng), 55; Univ Calif, Los Angeles, cert nuclear tech, 67, cert bus mgt, 72. Prof Exp: Jr engr, Socony Oil Co, 49-51; res group supvr, Jet Propulsion Lab, Calif Inst Technol, 55-61. Mem: Am Inst Aeronaut & Astronaut; Combustion Inst. Res: Solid propellant rockets; combustion; nozzles; system analysis. Mailing Add: 518 N Alta Dr Beverly Hills CA 90210

LANDSBERG, ARNE, CHEMICAL ENGINEERING. *Current Pos:* RETIRED. *Personal Data:* b Des Moines, Iowa, June 10, 33; c Karin & Eric. *Educ:* Univ Colo, BS, 55; Ore State Univ, PhD(chem eng), 64. *Prof Exp:* Chem engr, US Bur Mines, 61-64; peace corps vol for prof, Chem Eng Prog, Costa Rica, 64-66; chem res engr, US Bur Mines, Albany, 66-91. *Mem:* Sigma Xi; Am Chem Soc. *Res:* Chemical kinetics of gas-solid reactions; vapor-solid equilibrium. *Mailing Add:* 1415 NW Greenwood Pl Corvallis OR 97330-1827

LANDSBERG, JOHANNA D (JOAN), ANALYTICAL CHEMISTRY, RESEARCH ADMINISTRATION. *Current Pos:* res chemist, 79-89, PROF LEADER, PAC NORTHWEST RES STA, SILVICULT LAB, FOREST SERV, USDA, BEND, ORE, 89- *Personal Data:* b Medford, Ore, July 15, 40. *Educ:* Ore State Univ, BS, 62, MS, 64. *Prof Exp:* Res asst, dept food sci & technol, Ore State Univ, 76-77; res chemist, Bend Res, Inc, 77-78. *Concurrent Pos:* Prin investr, US-Spain Res Proj, 86-89. *Mem:* Am Chem Soc; Sigma Xi; AAAS; Soc Am Foresters. *Res:* Effects of prescribed fire on soil, forest floor and foliar nutrients in Central Oregon ponderosa pine and mixed conifer lands. *Mailing Add:* 986 Highline Dr East Wenatchee WA 98802-5610

LANDSBERG, LEWIS, METABOLISM. *Current Pos:* IRVING S CUTTER PROF & CHMN, DEPT MED, MED SCH, NORTHWESTERN UNIV, 90-, DIR, CTR ENDOCRINOL, METAB & NUTRIT, 90- *Personal Data:* b New York, NY, Nov 23, 38. *Educ:* Williams Col, AB, 60; Yale Univ, MD, 64. *Prof Exp:* From instr to asst prof med, Sch Med, Yale Univ, 69-72; from asst prof to prof med, Harvard Med Sch, 72-90. *Concurrent Pos:* Assoc physician, Yale-New Haven Hosp, 69-71; Beth Israel Hosp, 74-79; attend physician, West Haven Vet Admin Hosp, 70-72, Yale-New Haven Hosp, 71-72; assisting physician, Boston City Hosp, 72-73, assoc vis physician, 73-74; physician, Beth Israel Hosp, 79-88, sr physician, 88-90; physician-in-chief, Dept Med, Northwestern Mem Hosp, 90- *Mem:* Am Fedn Clin Res; Endocrine Soc; NY Acad Sci; Am Heart Asn; Am Soc Pharmacol & Exp Therapeut; fel Am Col Physicians; AAAS; Am Physiol Soc; Am Soc Clin Invest; Asn Am Physicians. *Res:* Catecholamines and the sympathoadrenal system; nutrition and the sympathetic nervous system; obesity and hypertension; numerous publications. *Mailing Add:* Chmn-Dept Med Northwestern Univ Med Sch 250 E Superior St Wesley Rm 296 Chicago IL 60611-2950

LANDSBERGER, FRANK ROBBERT, PHYSICAL BIOCHEMISTRY, VIROLOGY. *Current Pos:* DIR OFF SCI & TECH DEVELOP, MT SINAI MED CTR, 91- *Personal Data:* b Amsterdam, Neth, Aug 10, 43; US citizen; div; c 1. *Educ:* Cornell Univ, BA, 64; Brown Univ, PhD(physics), 70. *Prof Exp:* Res asst physics, Brown Univ, 64-69; res fel biochem, Div Endocrinol, Sloan-Kettering Inst Cancer Res, 69-71; asst prof chem, Ind Univ, Bloomington, 71-74; from asst prof to assoc prof, Rockefeller Univ, 74-87, Andrew M Mellon found fel, 80-87, adj assoc prof, 87-91. *Mem:* AAAS; Biophys Soc; fel NY Acad Sci; Am Soc Microbiol; Am Chem Soc; Sigma Xi. *Res:* Use of physical biochemical studies of the structure and function of biological and model membranes with emphasis on enveloped viruses and parasites and their interaction with cell surfaces. *Mailing Add:* Off Sci & Tech Develop Mt Sinai Med Ctr 1 Gustav Levy Pl New York NY 10029-6574

LANDSBURG, ALEXANDER CHARLES, COMMERCIAL SHIP DESIGN & OPERATIONS, SHIP MANEUVERABILITY. *Current Pos:* Trainee, Maritime Admin, 66-67, naval archit, Off Ship Construct, 67-74, mgr, ship design develop, 74-76, chief, Environ Activ, Off Shipbldg Costs, 74-76, mgr, comput-aided ship design, 76-78, comput-aided cost analysis, Off Shipbldg Costs, 78-85, liaison, Off Advan Ship Opers, 85-87, naval archit, Off Ship Construct, 87-88, prog mgr, ship performance & safety, Off Technol Assessment, 88-95, PROG MGT SYSTS SAFETY & HUMAN FACTORS, OFF MARITIME LAB TRAINING & SAFETY, MARITIME ADMIN, 95- *Personal Data:* b Saginaw, Mich, Dec 23, 42; m 67, S Lorin Nichols; c Lori A, Alexander G, Jessica L & Eliot N. *Educ:* Univ Mich, BS, 66, MS, 69; Harvard Bus Sch, PMD, 79. *Mem:* Soc Naval Architects & Marine Engrs; Am Soc Naval Engrs; Human Factors Soc. *Res:* Innovative ship design and operations; computer-aided ship design and operations; ship maneuverability; information and training for shipboard personnel; ship design and operations for military sealift; cost analysis; human factors research. *Mailing Add:* 307 Williamsburg Dr Silver Spring MD 20901. *Fax:* 202-493-2288; *E-Mail:* alex.landsburg@marad.dot.gov

LANDSEA, CHRISTOPHER W, METEOROLOGY. *Current Pos:* PROF, DEPT ATMOSPHERIC SCI, COLO STATE UNIV. *Honors & Awards:* Banner I Miller Award, Am Meteorol Asn, 94. *Mailing Add:* Dept Atmospheric Sci Colo State Univ Ft Collins CO 80523

LANDSHOFF, ROLF, MATHEMATICAL PHYSICS. *Current Pos:* RETIRED. *Personal Data:* b Berlin, Ger, Nov 30, 11; nat US; m 41; c 4. *Educ:* Berlin Tech Inst, DrIng, 36; Univ Minn, PhD(theoret physics), 38. *Prof Exp:* Asst physics, Univ Minn, 36-40; prof, Col St Thomas, 40-44; scientist, Los Alamos Sci Lab, 44-56; sr mem, Lockheed Palo Alto Res Lab, 56-76; consult, 77-90. *Concurrent Pos:* Vis lectr, Weizmann Inst, 63-64. *Mem:* Fel Am Phys Soc. *Res:* Atomic physics; hydrodynamics; statistical mechanics. *Mailing Add:* 525 E Crescent Dr Palo Alto CA 94301

LANDSKROENER, PETER, PROCESS ENGINEERING FOR PAPER INDUSTRY, PAPER FILM & FOIL. *Current Pos:* CONSULT, 82- *Personal Data:* b Woodbury, NJ, Dec 3, 28. *Educ:* Univ Del, BS, 50, MS, 51; Cath Univ Am, PhD(phys chem), 54. *Prof Exp:* Vpres res & develop com develop, Annin Indust, 66-69; gen mgr, Columbia Magnetics, 69-76; pres coating, laminating & printing, John Dusenbery Co, 76-82. *Mem:* Am Chem Soc; Am Inst Chemists; Sigma Xi. *Mailing Add:* SW Develop Corp 418 Poppasquash Rd Bristol RI 02809

LANDSMAN, DAVID, MOLECULAR BIOLOGY, GENETICS. *Current Pos:* VIS SCIENTIST, NAT CTR BIOTECHNOL INFO, NAVAL ORDINANCE LAB & NIH. *Personal Data:* b Cape Town, SAfrica, Oct 5,53; m 82, Dawn; c Marc & Kevin. *Educ:* Univ Cape Town, S Africa, BSc, 76, PhD(biochem), 84. *Prof Exp:* Vis fel, Nat Cancer Inst, NIH, 84-87, vis assoc, Lab Molecular Carcinogenesis, NIH, 87-89. *Mem:* Am Soc Biochem & Molecular Biol. *Res:* Structure and function of interphase chromatin and nuclei; molecular and cellular interactions controlling the regulation of gene expression. *Mailing Add:* Comput Biol Br Nat Ctr Biotechnol Info Nat Libr Med Bldg 38A Rm 8N807 Bethesda MD 20892. *E-Mail:* landsman@ncbi.nlm.nih.gov

LANDSMAN, DOUGLAS ANDERSON, PHYSICAL CHEMISTRY. *Current Pos:* sr proj engr, Int Fuel Cells, 72-91, CONSULT, 91- *Personal Data:* b Dundee, Scotland, May 31, 29; div; c 4. *Educ:* Univ St Andrews, BSc, 49, Hons, 50, PhD(thermodyn), 57. *Prof Exp:* Sr sci officer, Chem Div, Atomic Weapon Res Estab, UK Atomic Energy Authority, Eng, 53-57; Nat Res Coun Can fel, 57-58; Harwell sr fel, Chem Div, Atomic Energy Res Estab, UK Atomic Energy Authority, Eng, 58-60, prin sci officer, 60-65; res supvr, Mat Eng Res Lab, Pratt & Whitney Aircraft Div, Middletown, 65-72. *Mem:* Fel Royal Soc Chem; Am Chem Soc. *Res:* Thermodynamics of ionization in aqueous solutions; chemistry of the hydrogen isotopes; isotope separation; gas chromatography; chemonuclear reactors; energy conversion; fuel cells. *Mailing Add:* 100 Wells St Apt 1001 Hartford CT 06103-2934

LANDSTREET, JOHN DARLINGTON, STELLAR MAGNETISM, STELLAR ATMOSPHERES. *Current Pos:* from asst prof to assoc prof, 70-76, chmn dept, 92-96, PROF ASTRON, UNIV WESTERN ONT, 76-, CHMN DEPT, 92- *Personal Data:* b Philadelphia, Pa, Mar 13, 40; m 86, Barbara G Keenan; c David & Sarah. *Educ:* Reed Col, BA, 62; Columbia Univ, MA, 63, PhD(physics), 66. *Prof Exp:* Instr physics, Mt Holyoke Col, 65-66, asst prof, 66-67; res assoc astron, Columbia Univ, 67-70, asst prof, 70. *Concurrent Pos:* Mem, Grant Selection Comt Space & Astron, Natural Sci & Eng Res Coun Can, 80-83, chmn, 82-83; mem, Sci Adv Comt, Can Ctr Space Sci, 81-83; mem, Sci Adv Coun, Can-France-Hawaii Telescope Corp, 80-83, vchmn, 81, chmn, 82-83; vis scientist, Inst Theoret Astrophys, Univ Heidelberg, 84-85; mem, Coun Admin, Astron Observ, Mont Megantic, 85-90; distinguished res prof, Univ Western Ont, 87-88; mem bd dirs, Telescope Corp, Can, France, Hawaii, 91-, secy, 92-93, vchmn, 94-95, chmn, 96-97; vis scientist, Observatoire Midi-Pyrenees, Toulouse, France, 91-92; mem bd dirs, Can Astron Soc. *Mem:* Am Astron Soc; Can Astron Soc (vpres, 94-96, pres, 96-98); Royal Astron Soc; Int Astron Union. *Res:* Observation of circular and linear polarization in stars and extra-galactic objects, especially white dwarfs; observation and interpretation of stellar magnetism and of stellar spectra. *Mailing Add:* Dept Physics & Astron Univ Western Ont London ON N6A 3K7 Can. *Fax:* 519-661-2033; *E-Mail:* jlandstr@phobos.astro.uwo.ca

LANDSTROM, D(ONALD) KARL, NATURAL GAS TECHNOLOGY, HVAC. *Current Pos:* prin res scientist solar mat analysis, 65-80, proj mgr energy & thermal technol, 80-90, DEP DIR, GAS APPLIANCE TECHNOL CTR, COLUMBUS LABS, BATTELLE MEM INST, 91- *Personal Data:* b Portland, Ore, Oct 12, 37. *Educ:* Mass Inst Technol, BS, 59. *Prof Exp:* Supvr electron micros, Goodyear Atomic Corp, 59-63; res engr mat environ, NAm Aviation, 63-65. *Mem:* AAAS; Int Solar Energy Soc; Am Soc Heating Refrig & Air Conditioning Engrs. *Res:* Solar energy; environmental impact analysis; thermal analysis; materials research; physical and chemical analysis; electron microscopy; electron probe analysis; nuclear waste; energy and environmental systems; agricultural controlled environment system; heat pumps and alternative energy systems; gas fired heat pumps; heating, ventilating and air conditioning systems; gas appliance technology; granted 4 patents. *Mailing Add:* 903 Neil Ave Columbus OH 43215. *Fax:* 614-424-3534

LANDUCCI, LAWRENCE L, ORGANIC CHEMISTRY, NUCLEAR MAGNETIC RESONANCE. *Current Pos:* RES CHEMIST & NUCLEAR MAGNETIC RESONANCE SPECTROSCOPIST, US FOREST PROD LAB, 67- *Personal Data:* b St Paul, Minn, May 20, 39; m 69; c 3. *Educ:* Univ Minn, BS, 62, PhD(org chem), 67. *Concurrent Pos:* Organizer, First Int Workshop Nuclear Magnetic Resonance & Wood Sci, Vancouver, BC, 85. *Mem:* Am Chem Soc. *Res:* Lignin and lignin model compound chemistry; methods of lignin degradation; mechanism of anthraquinone pulping; nuclear magnetic resonance characterization of lignin and reaction products; application of state-of-the-art nuclear magnetic resonance methods to characterization of wood components. *Mailing Add:* 3198 Shady Oak Lane Verona WI 53593-9734

LANDWEBER, LAWRENCE H, COMPUTER SCIENCE. *Current Pos:* From asst prof to assoc prof, 67-77, PROF COMPUT SCI & CHMN DEPT, UNIV WIS-MADISON, 77- *Personal Data:* b New York, NY, Nov 29, 42; m 66. *Educ:* Brooklyn Col, BS, 63; Purdue Univ, MS & PhD(comput sci), 66. *Mem:* Am Math Soc; Asn Comput Mach; Sigma Xi. *Res:* Theoretical computer science; computer networks; computer conferencing and mail. *Mailing Add:* Dept Comput Sci Univ Wis 1210 W Dayton St Madison WI 53706

LANDWEBER, LOUIS, SHIP HYDRODYNAMICS, INTEGRAL EQUATIONS. *Current Pos:* EMER PROF FLUID MECH, INST HYDRAUL RES, UNIV IOWA, 54- *Personal Data:* b New York, NY, Jan 8, 12; m 35; c Peter S & Victor A. *Educ:* City Col New York, BS, 32; George Washington Univ, MA, 35; Univ Md, PhD(physics), 51. *Honors & Awards:* Davidson Medal, Soc Naval Architects & Marine Engrs, 78; David Taylor

Lectr, David Taylor Naval Ship Res & Develop Ctr, 78; Weinblum Mem Lectr, German Inst Ship Construct & Soc Naval Architects & Marine Engrs, 81. *Prof Exp:* Physicist & head, Hydrodyn Div, David W Taylor Naval Ship Res & Develop Ctr, 32-54. *Concurrent Pos:* Prin investr, Off Naval Res, 54- & Mobil Oil Co, 85-; vis prof, Univ Mich, 61-62, Colo State Univ, 66, Technion, Israel, 72, Hokkaido Univ, 79. *Mem:* Nat Acad Eng; Soc Naval Architects & Marine Engrs; fel Am Acad Mech; corresp mem Maritime & Aeronaut Tech Asn; Sigma Xi. *Res:* Analytical, numerical and experimental research about the flow of one or more bodies or ships moving through a fluid, their added masses and the forces and moments acting upon them; ship hydrodynamics, gravity waves, boundary layers and integral equations; author, co-author or editor of approximately 150 technical papers, reports, monographs and books. *Mailing Add:* Inst Hydraul Res Univ Iowa Iowa City IA 52242

LANDWEBER, PETER STEVEN, MATHEMATICS. *Current Pos:* assoc prof, 70-74, PROF MATH, RUTGERS UNIV, NEW BRUNSWICK, 74- *Personal Data:* b Washington, DC, Aug 17, 40; m 64; c 2. *Educ:* Univ Iowa, BA, 60; Harvard Univ, MA, 61, PhD(math), 65. *Prof Exp:* Asst prof math, Univ Va, 65-68; asst prof, Yale Univ, 68-70. *Concurrent Pos:* Mem sch math, Inst Advan Study, 67-68 & 86-87; NATO fel, Univ Cambridge, 74-75; NSF grad fel commemorative lectr, 89; chmn, Russian Translations Comt, Am Math Soc, 89-92. *Mem:* Am Math Soc; Math Asn Am. *Res:* Cobordism theory of differential manifolds. *Mailing Add:* 10 Wallingford Dr Princeton NJ 08540. *E-Mail:* landwebe@math.rutgers.edu

LANDWEHR, JAMES M, STATISTICAL APPLICATIONS & COLLABORATIONS, RESEARCH ON APPLIED STATISTICS METHODOLOGIES. *Current Pos:* TECH STAFF & SUPVR, AT&T BELL LABS, MURRAY HILL, 73- *Personal Data:* b Philadelphia, Penn, Jan 12, 45; m 67; c 3. *Educ:* Yale Univ, BA, 66; Univ Chicago, PhD(statist), 72. *Prof Exp:* Lectr & asst prof statist, Univ Mich, Ann Arbor, 70-73. *Concurrent Pos:* Panel mem, Nat Acad Sci, Nat Res Coun, 84-88; co-prin investr, Quant Lit Proj, Am Statist Asn, Nat Coun Teachers Math, 84-87. *Mem:* Fel AAAS; fel Am Statist Asn; Inst Math Statist; Math Asn Am; Classification Soc. *Res:* Statistical experimentation and data analysis in manufacturing; categorical data analysis and logistic regression; graphical methods; precollege statistics education; software metrics; statistical applications. *Mailing Add:* 6 Clearview Dr Summit NJ 07901

LANDY, ARTHUR, BIOCHEMICAL GENETICS, GENE REGULATION. *Current Pos:* asst prof, 68-74, assoc prof, 75-77, PROF MED SCI, BROWN UNIV, 78- *Personal Data:* b Philadelphia, Pa, Mar 17, 39; m 65; c 2. *Educ:* Amherst Col, BA, 61; Univ Ill, PhD(microbiol & biochem), 65. *Prof Exp:* Res fel biochem genetics, Med Res Coun Lab Molecular Biol, Cambridge, Eng, 66-68. *Concurrent Pos:* NATO fel, 66-67; fel, Am Cancer Soc, 68 , fac res assoc, 75-81, mem adv bd, 78-; assoc ed, Cell, 79-; mem recombinant DNA adv comt, NIH, 81-; chmn nucleic acids, Gordon Res Conf, 83; mem, Microbiol Genetics Study Sect, NIH, 87- *Mem:* Am Soc Microbiol; Am Soc Biol Chemists. *Res:* Gene structure and regulation in prokaryotes and eukaryotes; organization of eukaryote genes; mechanisms of site-specific recombination. *Mailing Add:* Div Biol & Med Brown Univ Box G Providence RI 02912-0001

LANDZBERG, ABRAHAM H(AROLD), SEMICONDUCTOR PROCESS ENGINEERING. *Current Pos:* CONSULT, SEMICONDUCTOR & ELECTRONIC PACKAGING DEVELOP & MFG, 93- *Personal Data:* b New York, NY, Sept 10, 29; m 55, Joan E Magliacano; c Judith E, Carol A & Steven J. *Educ:* NY Univ, BSME, 51; Princeton Univ, MSE, 53. *Prof Exp:* Develop engr, Gen Elec Co, 52-59; dept mgr appl mech, Res Div, IBM, 59-65, dept mgr integrated circuits, Components Div, 65-70, advan mfg mgr, 71-76, sr eng mgr, Semiconductor Develop Eng, 76-85, sr eng mgr, Packaging Develop Eng, 85-93. *Mem:* Inst Elec & Electronics Engrs. *Res:* Physics of failure of integrated circuits; mechanical properties of materials; applied mechanics, application to electronic computer components; turbines; electrical machinery; manufacturing systems and processes for integrated circuits; electronic component packaging development; microelectronics reliability. *Mailing Add:* 685 Fieldstone Ct Yorktown Heights NY 10598

LANE, ALFRED GLEN, ANIMAL NUTRITION. *Current Pos:* RETIRED. *Personal Data:* b Stoutland, Mo, Aug 21, 32; m 57; c 2. *Educ:* Univ Mo, BS, 59, MS, 60, PhD(animal nutrit), 65. *Prof Exp:* Instr voc agr, Parkersburg Community Sch, Iowa, 60-63; asst dairy husb, Univ Mo, Columbia, 63-65, asst prof, 65-70, mgr diary res, Allied Mills, Inc, 70-77; pvt consult, 77-82; dairy specialist, Tex A&M Univ, 82-94. *Mem:* Am Dairy Sci Asn; Am Soc Animal Sci. *Res:* Ruminant nutrition; physiology. *Mailing Add:* PO Box 58 Stephenville TX 76401

LANE, BENJAMIN CLAY, PHARMACOLOGY. *Current Pos:* res pharmacologist, 85-88, sr res investr, 88-89, SR RES SCIENTIST, IMMUNOSCI PROG, ABBOTT LABS, ILL, 89- *Personal Data:* b Raleigh, NC, Feb 8, 52. *Educ:* Wash State Univ, BS, 74, MS, 76, PhD(bact), 80. *Prof Exp:* Res scholar, Div Clin Immunol & Rheumatic Dis, Med Ctr, Univ Southern Calif, 79-81; res assoc, Div Rheumatic Dis, Med Ctr, Duke Univ, 81-85. *Concurrent Pos:* Lab instr, Dept Bact & Pub Health, Wash State Univ, 75-78; NIH fel, Med Ctr, Duke Univ, 81-82 & Arthritis Found res fel, 83-84. *Mailing Add:* Abbott Labs 100 Abbott Park Rd Info Nat Libr Med NIH Bldg 38A Rm 8N807 Abbott Park IL 20894-0001

LANE, BENNIE RAY, MATHEMATICS. *Current Pos:* chmn dept, 66-78, PROF MATH, EASTERN KY UNIV, 66- *Personal Data:* b Deming, NMex, July 2, 35; m 56; c 4. *Educ:* Colo State Col, BA, 56, MA, 57; George Peabody Col, PhD(math), 62. *Prof Exp:* Asst prof math, Univ Chattanooga, 59-61; instr appl math, Vanderbilt Univ, 61-62; asst prof math, Colo State Col, 62-63; from asst prof to assoc prof, George Peabody Col, 63-66. *Mem:* Am Math Asn. *Res:* Mathematics education; teaching mathematics by television; abstract algebra; programmed instruction. *Mailing Add:* 126 Westwood Dr Richmond KY 40475

LANE, BERNARD PAUL, PATHOLOGY. *Current Pos:* assoc prof, 71-76, PROF PATH, HEALTH SCI CTR, STATE UNIV NY STONY BROOK, 76- *Personal Data:* b Brooklyn, NY, June 27, 38; m 62, Dorthy Spiegel; c Erika, Andrew & Matthew. *Educ:* Brown Univ, AB, 59; NY Univ, MD, 63; State Univ NY, MA, 92. *Prof Exp:* NIH trainee exp path, Sch Med, NY Univ, 65-66, from asst prof to assoc prof path, 66-71. *Concurrent Pos:* Attend pathologist, Bellevue & NY Univ Hosps, 69-71, Vet Admin Hosp, Northport, NY, 71- & Stony Brook Univ Hosp, 79-; vis scientist, Armed Forces Inst Path, 71; chief cell injury labs, Armed Forces Inst Path. *Mem:* Am Soc Cell Biol; Int Acad Path; Am Asn Path; Am Soc Clin Path; Am Asn Cancer Res. *Res:* Experimental pathology; electron microscopy; cellular injury. *Mailing Add:* Dept Path State Univ NY Health Sci Ctr Stony Brook NY 11790

LANE, BYRON GEORGE, BIOCHEMISTRY. *Current Pos:* PROF BIOCHEM, UNIV TORONTO, 68- *Personal Data:* b Toronto, Ont, May 16, 33; m 61. *Educ:* Univ Toronto, BA, 56, PhD(biochem), 59. *Honors & Awards:* Ayerst Award, Can Biochem Soc, 71. *Prof Exp:* Jr res asst biochem, Med Ctr, Univ Calif, San Francisco, 59-60; res assoc, Rockefeller Inst, 60-61; asst prof, Univ Alta, 61-63, assoc prof, 64-68. *Mem:* Am Soc Biol Chemists. *Res:* Biochemical investigations of germin, the marker protein for onset of growth in germinating wheat embryos. *Mailing Add:* Dept Biochem Univ Toronto One Kings College Circle Toronto ON M5S 1A8 Can

LANE, CARL LEATON, FOREST SOILS. *Current Pos:* RETIRED. *Personal Data:* b Raleigh, NC, Feb 11, 28; m 52; c 1. *Educ:* NC State Univ, BS, 52, MS, 61; Purdue Univ, PhD(forest soil microbiol), 68. *Prof Exp:* Forest mgr, State Hosp Butner, NC, 52-59; from asst prof to assoc prof forestry, Clemson Univ, 60-90, coordr, Res & Grad Progs, Dept Forestry, 85-90. *Mem:* Soc Am Foresters. *Res:* Forest soils microbiology; forest soil tree disease relationships; nitrogen fixation; effluent utilization. *Mailing Add:* 150 Folgers St Clemson SC 29631

LANE, CHARLES A, ORGANIC CHEMISTRY. *Current Pos:* asst prof, 64-73, ASSOC PROF ORG CHEM, UNIV TENN, KNOXVILLE, 73- *Personal Data:* b Wichita, Kans, Nov 18, 32. *Educ:* Univ Okla, BS, 54; Yale Univ, MS, 59; Univ Calif, PhD(chem), 63. *Prof Exp:* Org chemist, Lederle Labs, Am Cyanamid Co, 56-58; asst prof org chem, Univ Nigeria, 61-63; asst prof, Univ Calif, 63-64. *Res:* Theoretical chemistry. *Mailing Add:* Dept Chem Univ Tenn Knoxville TN 37996-1600. *E-Mail:* clane@ibm.net

LANE, DENNIS DEL, AIR POLLUTION MONITORING & CONTROL, AEROSOL SCIENCE. *Current Pos:* From asst prof to prof, 76-93, N T VEATCH DISTINGUISHED PROF ENVIRON ENG, UNIV KANS, 93- *Personal Data:* b Peoria, Ill, Feb 16, 50; m 69, Kristine L Bell; c Thomas D, Jeffrey T, T Matthew & Theresa B. *Educ:* Univ Ill, Urbana, BS, 72, MS, 73, PhD(environ eng), 76. *Honors & Awards:* Award Res Excellence, US Environ Protection Agency, 91, Bronze Medal Res Achievements, 93. *Concurrent Pos:* Consult, Midwest Res Inst, 77-91, State Kans Atty Gen, 77- & US Environ Protection Agency, 85-; prin investr, US Environ Protection Agency, 81-; mem bd sci counrs, Agency Toxic Substances & Dis Registry, 88-94; mem, Subcomt Great Lakes Appl Health, USPHS, 92-93. *Mem:* Air & Waste Mgt Asn; Am Soc Civil Engrs; Am Soc Aerosol Res; AAAS; Asn Environ Eng Profs. *Res:* Aerosol science (physics and chemistry of particles moving in the air); air quality monitoring; air pollution control; water-related areas in environmental engineering and science. *Mailing Add:* Dept Civil Eng Univ Kans Lawrence KS 66045. *Fax:* 785-864-5379; *E-Mail:* lane@kuhub.cc.ukans.edu

LANE, DONALD WILSON, PETROLEUM GEOLOGY. *Current Pos:* GEOLOGIST, OHM REMEDIATION SERV, 92- *Personal Data:* b Fayetteville, Tenn, June 23, 34; m 60, Joanne Eaker; c 3. *Educ:* Dartmouth Col, BA, 56; Univ Ill, MS, 58; Rice Univ, PhD(geol), 61. *Prof Exp:* Geologist, Tenneco Oil Co, 61-70; regional geologist, Royal Resources Corp, 70; staff geologist, Geol Surv Wyo, 70-73; mgr exp geol & Rocky Mountain area, Mich & Wis Pipeline Co, 73-76; consult geologist, 76-84; sr geologist, Britoil Ventures, 85-86; consult geologist, ERM-Southwest, 87-88, geologist, 88-91; geologist, Jones & Neuse, 91-92. *Mem:* Am Asn Petrol Geol. *Res:* Lower Paleozoic stratigraphy and hydrocarbon potential of the northeastern United States; Wyoming stratigraphy and stratigraphic resources; Lower Cretaceous stratigraphy of northwestern Colorado; eocene and cretaceous stratigraphy of Texas Gulf Coast; Pennsylvanian stratigraphy of North Texas. *Mailing Add:* 12214 Mossycup Dr Houston TX 77024

LANE, EDWIN DAVID, FISH CULTURE, FISH ECOLOGY. *Current Pos:* COORDR, FISHERIES & AGR DEPT, MALASPINA COL, NANAIMO, BC, 79- *Personal Data:* b Vancouver, BC, May 9, 34; m 58; c 2. *Educ:* Univ BC, BSC, 59, MSC, 62; Univ Tex, PhD(zool), 66. *Prof Exp:* Staff mem, Fisheries Invest Off, NZ Marine Dept, 62-63; res scientist, Res Br, Ont Dept Land & Forest, 66-68; assoc prof zool, Calif State Univ, Long Beach, 68-74, res grant, 68-69 & 71-74; head coop res, Can Wildlife Serv, Can Dept Environ, 74-79. *Concurrent Pos:* Fisheries expert, Food & Agr Orgn, 67- *Mem:* Can Soc Zoologists; NZ Limnol Soc; Am Fish Soc. *Res:* Salmonid culture especially feeding; ecology of fishes, especially in streams, estuaries and coastal bay systems; environmental impact of development, especially in the North. *Mailing Add:* Fisheries & Agr Dept Malaspina Col 900 Fifth St Nanaimo BC V9R 5S5 Can

LANE, ERIC TRENT, MICROCOMPUTER ANIMATION GRAPHICS. *Current Pos:* assoc prof, 67-77, PROF PHYSICS, UNIV TENN, CHATTANOOGA, 77- *Personal Data:* b Baton Rouge, La, Aug 30, 38; m, Chantana Varnarkomola; c Carmen & Vivian. *Educ:* La State Univ, BS, 60; Rice Univ, MA, 63, PhD(physics), 67. *Honors & Awards:* Proj Seriphim Grand Prize Software, 87. *Prof Exp:* Vis lectr physics, La State Univ, New Orleans, 63-65. *Concurrent Pos:* NSF grant, microcomput course develop; coordr exhibs, Challenger Learning Ctr. *Mem:* Am Phys Soc; Am Asn Physics Teachers; Sigma Xi. *Res:* Microcomputer animation graphics for science and physics education; research applied to improvement of teaching and human relationships. *Mailing Add:* Dept Physics Univ Tenn Chattanooga TN 37403-2598. *Fax:* 423-755-4279; *E-Mail:* ericlane@utcvm.utc.edu

LANE, ERNEST PAUL, TOPOLOGY. *Current Pos:* assoc prof, 70-75, PROF MATH, APPALACHIAN STATE UNIV, 75- *Personal Data:* b Greene Co, Tenn, Nov 14, 33; m 61; c 2. *Educ:* Berea Col, BA, 55; Univ Tenn, MA, 57; Purdue Univ, PhD(math), 65. *Prof Exp:* Programmer, Army Ballistic Missile Agency, Ala, 57-58; instr math, Berea Col, 58-60; asst prof, Va Polytech Inst, 65-70. *Mem:* Math Asn Am; Am Math Soc. *Res:* Abstract spaces; metrization; real-valued functions on abstract spaces. *Mailing Add:* Dept Math Appalachian State Univ Boone NC 28608-0001

LANE, FORREST EUGENE, PLANT PHYSIOLOGY, PLANT BIOCHEMISTRY. *Current Pos:* RETIRED. *Personal Data:* b Enola, Ark, June 24, 34; m 54, Leota M Farmer; c Sharon R, Laura K, Linda M, Dwight H & Ellen S. *Educ:* Univ Ark, BA, 56, MEd, 59, MS, 63; Univ Okla, PhD(plant physiol), 65. *Prof Exp:* Teacher, Hall High Sch, Ark, 57-58; instr biol, Univ Ark, 58-63; asst prof biol, Kans State Col Pittsburg, 65-67; from asst prof to assoc prof, Dept Bot & Bact, Univ Ark, Fayetteville, 67-96. *Concurrent Pos:* NSF fel, 63-65. *Mem:* Sigma Xi; Am Soc Plant Physiol; Scand Soc Plant Physiol; Bot Soc Am; Phytochem Soc NAm. *Res:* Dormancy in plant structures such as seeds, fruits, tubers and buds; relationship between dormancy and plant phenolics; enzymes associated with hormone control and plant growth; anthocyanin pigments. *Mailing Add:* 5450 Huntsville Rd Univ Ark Fayetteville AR 72701

LANE, GARY (THOMAS), ANIMAL NUTRITION, BIOCHEMISTRY. *Current Pos:* DIR, TECH SERV, BERKMANN MILLS, 86- *Personal Data:* b Center, Ky, Nov 8, 41; m 63; c 3. *Educ:* Berea Col, BS, 63; Purdue Univ, West Lafayette, MS, 65, PhD(animal nutrit), 68. *Prof Exp:* Res asst animal nutrit, Purdue Univ, West Lafayette, 63-67; from asst prof to assoc prof animal nutrit, Tex A&M Univ, 67-77; assoc exten prof dairy, Univ Ky, 77-86. *Mem:* Am Dairy Sci Asn; Am Soc Animal Sci. *Res:* Ration additives for ruminants; ration and its relation to milk composition and yield; mechanisms of milk synthesis; chemical preservation of high-moisture grain. *Mailing Add:* 1124 Secretariat Dr E Danville KY 40422

LANE, GEORGE ASHEL, APPLIED CHEMISTRY, THERMODYNAMICS & MATERIAL PROPERTIES. *Current Pos:* RES ASSOC, OMNITECH INT, 92- *Personal Data:* b Norman, Okla, May 9, 30; m 52, Patricia Graves. *Educ:* Grinnell Col, AB, 52; Northwestern Univ, PhD(phys chem), 55. *Honors & Awards:* IR-100 Award, 80. *Prof Exp:* Asst chem, Grinnell Col, 51-52; asst, Northwestern Univ, 52-55; spec projs chemist, Dow Chem USA, 55-56, staff asst, 56-58, chemist, 58-63, proj leader, 63-66, sr res chemist, 66-69, res specialist, 69-73, sr res specialist, 73-80, res assoc, 80-92. *Mem:* Am Chem Soc; Sigma Xi. *Res:* Solar energy; energy storage; oxygen isotope effects; trout ecology; auto crash protection; rocket propellant testing and evaluation; pyrotechnics; ceramics. *Mailing Add:* 3802 Wintergreen Dr Midland MI 48640

LANE, GEORGE H, PHYSICS. *Current Pos:* head dept, Norwich Univ, 62-79, from asst prof to prof, 66-92, dir grad studies, 68-75, 79-80, EMER PROF PHYSICS, NORWICH UNIV, 92- *Personal Data:* b Milford, NH, Feb 19, 24; m 48; c 2. *Educ:* Amherst Col, BA, 47; Yale Univ, MS, 49; Univ Conn, PhD(physics), 61. *Prof Exp:* Asst instr physics, Univ Conn, Hartford Br, 49-51; from instr to asst prof, Franklin & Marshall Col, 54-60. *Mem:* AAAS; Am Asn Physics Teachers; Sigma Xi; Astron Soc Pac. *Res:* Atomic collisions; mass spectrometry. *Mailing Add:* 4118 Wake Robin Dr Shelburne VT 05482-7576

LANE, H CLIFFORD, EXPERIMENTAL BIOLOGY. *Current Pos:* clin assoc, Lab Immunoregulation, 79-82, sr investr, 82-89, DEP CLIN DIR, NAT INST ALLERGY & INFECTIOUS DIS, NIH, BETHESDA, MD, 85-, CHIEF, CLIN & MOLECULAR RETROVIROL SECT, LAB IMMUNOREGULATION, 89-, CLIN DIR, INST, 91- *Personal Data:* b Detroit, Mich, June 15, 50. *Educ:* Univ Mich, BS, 72, MD, 76; Am Bd Internal Med, cert, 79; Am Bd Infectious Dis, cert, 84; Am Bd Allergy & Immunol, cert, 86. *Prof Exp:* Intern internal med, Univ Hosp, Ann Arbor, Mich, 76-77, resident, 77-79. *Concurrent Pos:* Prof lectr med, George Washington Univ, 93- *Mem:* Am Fedn Clin Res; Am Asn Immunologists; Am Col Physicians; fel Infectious Dis Soc Am; Am Soc Clin Invest; Am Asn Physicians. *Res:* Mechanisms of activation, proliferation and differentiation of human lymphoid cells in the normal immune response; clinical, pathophysiologic, immunologic, molecular biologic, virologic and therapeutic aspects of disease states including the vasculitic syndromes, Sjogren's syndrome, and AIDS. *Mailing Add:* Nat Inst Allergy & Infectious Dis-NIH 9000 Rockville Pike Bldg 10 Rm 115231 Bethesda MD 20892-1894. *Fax:* 302-402-0070

LANE, HAROLD RICHARD, PALEONTOLOGY, STRATIGRAPHY. *Current Pos:* Sr res scientist, Res Ctr, 68-89, MGR WORLDWIDE PALEONT, AMOCO PROD CO, HOUSTON, 89- *Personal Data:* b Danville, Ill, Mar 7, 42; m 68; c 2. *Educ:* Univ Ill, Urbana, BS, 64; Univ Iowa, MS, 66, PhD(geol), 69. *Mem:* Brit Palaeont Asn; Int Palaeont Asn; Soc Econ Paleont & Mineral. *Res:* Evolution, biostratigraphy and systematic paleontology of microfossils, conodonts, especially in Devonian through Middle Pennsylvanian strata of North America. *Mailing Add:* 6542 Auden St Houston TX 77005

LANE, HELEN W, BIOMEDICINE. *Current Pos:* DIR NUTRIT BIOCHEM, JOHNSON SPACE CTR, HOUSTON, 89-, DIR CLIN LABS, 91- *Educ:* Univ Calif, Berkeley, BS, 68; Univ Wis-Madison, MS, 71; Univ Fla, PhD(animal nutrit), 78. *Prof Exp:* Asst gastroenterol, Dept Internal Med, Univ Wis-Madison, 70-72; instr, Dept Food Sci, Univ Fla, 72-74, asst gastroenterol, Dept Internal Med, 74-75, grad teaching asst, Prog Clin & Commun Dietetics, 75-77; asst prof, Prog Nutrit & Dietetics, Univ Tex Health Sci Ctr, Houston, 77-82, assoc prof, Prog Nutrit & Dietetics & Grad Sch Biomed Sci, 82-84; prof, Dept Nutrit & Foods, Auburn Univ, 84-89. *Concurrent Pos:* Adj appt, Dept Chem, Houston Baptist Univ, 78-84, adj prof, Dept Prev Med, Univ Tex Med Br, Galveston, 89-; grant reviewer, USDA, 81, 83-85, 87 & 89, Nat Cancer Inst, NIH, 86, Am Inst Cancer Res Study Sect, 86-91 & Am Dietetic Asn, 89. *Mem:* Am Asn Cancer Res; Am Dietetic Asn; Am Home Econ Asn; Am Inst Nutrit; Am Soc Clin Nutrit; Inst Food Technologists; Sigma Xi. *Res:* Nutritional sciences; preventive medicine; dietetics. *Mailing Add:* Biomed Opers & Res SD4 NASA Johnson Space Ctr Houston TX 77058

LANE, JAMES DALE, VERTEBRATE ZOOLOGY. *Current Pos:* asst prof biol, 65-70, PROF ZOOL, MCNEESE STATE UNIV, 70- *Personal Data:* b Las Cruces, NMex, Aug 28, 37; m 58; c Christopher. *Educ:* NMex State Univ, BS, 59, MS, 62; Univ Ariz, PhD(zool), 65. *Prof Exp:* Asst biol, NMex State Univ, 59-62; asst zool, Univ Ariz, 62-65, asst geochronology, 65. *Mem:* AAAS; Soc Syst Zool; Am Soc Mammal; Soc Vert Paleont; Am Inst Biol Sci. *Res:* Ecology and systematics of various mammalians taxons, especially rodents. *Mailing Add:* Dept Biol McNeese State Univ PO Box 92000 Lake Charles LA 70605-4511

LANE, JOHN D, pharmacology; deceased, see previous edition for last biography

LANE, JOSEPH M, ORTHOPAEDIC SURGERY. *Current Pos:* dir, Res Div, 90-93, CHIEF, MBD UNIT SPEC SURG, NEW YORK, 76-, ASSOC DIR TRAUMA SERV, 96-, DIR ORTHOP LAB APPL CLIN RES & TISSUE ENG. *Personal Data:* b New York, NY, Oct 27, 39; m 63, Barbara Greenhouse; c Debra & Jennifer. *Educ:* Columbia Univ, AB, 57; Harvard, Univ, MD, 65. *Prof Exp:* Surg intern, Hosp Univ Pa, Philadelphia, 65-66, resident gen surg, 66-67, resident, 69-72, chief resident, 72-73, chief MBD Sect, 73-76; res assoc, NIH, Nat Inst Dent Res, Bethesda, Md, 67-69; res fel, Philadelphia Gen Hosp, 69-70. *Concurrent Pos:* Assoc dir, MutliPurpose Arthritis Ctr, New York, 88-; consult & collabr, Collagen Corp, Warsaw, Ind, Genetics Inst, Andover, Mass, EBI, Fairfield, NJ; chmn orthop, Univ Calif, Los Angeles, 93-96. *Mem:* Fel Am Acad Orthop Surgeons; AMA; Am Soc Bone & Mineral Res; Musculoskeletal Tumor Soc (pres, 82-83); Orthop Res Soc (pres, 84-85). *Res:* Orthopaedic surgery; oncology; characterize connective tissue injury and repair; bone regeneration with growth factors (BMP). *Mailing Add:* Hosp Spec Surg 535 E 70th St New York NY 10021-4898. *Fax:* 212-772-1061; *E-Mail:* lanej@hss.edu

LANE, JOSEPH ROBERT, PHYSICAL METALLURGY, METALLURGICAL ENGINEERING. *Current Pos:* RETIRED. *Personal Data:* b Chicago, Ill, Mar 3, 17; m 49, Wyvona Alexander. *Educ:* Univ Ill, BS, 43; Mass Inst Technol, ScD(metall), 50. *Prof Exp:* Metallurgist, Univ Chicago, Metall Lab, 43-45; res asst, Mass Inst Technol, 45-50; br head, Naval Res Lab, 50-55; sr staff metallurgist, Nat Mat Adv Bd, Nat Acad Sci, 55-89. *Mem:* Fel Am Soc Metals Int. *Res:* Superalloys, refractory metals and various aerospace structural materials. *Mailing Add:* 7211 Rebecca Dr Alexandria VA 22307

LANE, KEITH ALDRICH, ANALYTICAL CHEMISTRY. *Current Pos:* RETIRED. *Personal Data:* b Gridley, Kans, Nov 11, 21; m 45, Frances Jenkins; c Keith A Jr & Bruce K. *Educ:* Oglethorpe Univ, AB, 42, MA, 43. *Prof Exp:* Chemist, Mutual Chem Co Am, 43-51, group leader analytical res, 51-58; chemist, Solvay Process Div, Allied Chem Corp, 58-64, group leader analytical res, 64-70, environ chemist, Indust Chems Div, 70-83. *Mem:* Am Chem Soc. *Res:* All phases of chromium chemistry; organic and inorganic analytical method development; environmental studies and pollution control. *Mailing Add:* 122 Royal Rd Liverpool NY 13088

LANE, LAWRENCE JUBIN, ELECTRICAL ENGINEERING. *Current Pos:* RETIRED. *Personal Data:* b Morganton, NC, Feb 19, 27; m 47, 75, Helen E Sollazzo; c Priscilla (Purks) & Richard. *Educ:* NC State Col, BEE, 50; Univ Va, MSEE, 50. *Prof Exp:* Engr, Gen Elec, Schenectady, 50-54, class supvr, Philadelphia, 54-55, develop engr, Waynesboro, 55-63, sr develop engr, 63-78, sr systs design engr, 78-83, consult engr, 83-95. *Mem:* Fel Inst Elec & Electronics Engrs. *Res:* Patentee in field. *Mailing Add:* 1601 Chatham Rd Waynesboro VA 22980-3203

LANE, LEONARD JAMES, HYDROLOGY. *Current Pos:* HYDROLOGIST, AGR RES SERV, USDA, 84- *Personal Data:* b Tucson, Ariz, Apr 25, 45; m 64; c 2. *Educ:* Univ Ariz, BS, 70, MS, 72; Colo State Univ, PhD(civil eng), 75. *Honors & Awards:* Super Serv Award, USDA, 81; Arthur S Flemming Award, 83. *Prof Exp:* Hydrologist, Agr Res Serv, USDA, 70-81; staff mem, Univ Calif, 81-84. *Concurrent Pos:* Fac affil civil eng, Colo State Univ, 73-74; adj assoc prof renewable natural resouces, Univ Ariz, 82- *Mem:* Am Geophys Union; Am Soc Civil Engrs; Am Water Resources Asn; Brit Geomorphol Res Group; Am Soc Agr Engrs; Sigma Xi. *Res:* Hydrology of semiarid regions; runoff and sediment simulation models incorporating geomorphic features, land use and management; improved erosion prediction technology; climatic fluctuations and change. *Mailing Add:* US Dept Agr Agr Res Serv 2000 E Allen Rd Tucson AZ 85719

LANE, LESLIE CARL, PLANT VIROLOGY. *Current Pos:* fel virol, 73-75, asst prof, 75-81, ASSOC PROF PLANT PATH, UNIV NEBR-LINCOLN, 81- *Personal Data:* b Stamford, Conn, Apr 5, 42; m 66, 77; c 2. *Educ:* Univ Wis, BS, 65, PhD(biochem), 71. *Prof Exp:* Fel virol, John Innes Inst, Norwich, Eng, 71-73. *Mem:* Am Phytopath Soc; Electrophoresis Soc; Am Soc Virol. *Res:* Structure and replication of plant viruses; virus directed protein and nucleic acid synthesis; virus-host interactions; gel electrophoretic separations; fluorescence detection methods. *Mailing Add:* 5801 Enterprise Dr Apt B8 Lincoln NE 68521-1010

LANE, LEWIS BEHR, HAND SURGERY, CLINICAL & BASIC SCIENCE RESEARCH IN ORTHOPAEDICS & HAND SURGERY. *Current Pos:* CHIEF HAND SURG, DEPT ORTHOP, LONG ISLAND JEWISH MED CTR, 97- *Personal Data:* b NY, Dec 16, 48. *Educ:* Columbia Col, BA, 70, MD, 74; Am Bd Orthop Surg, cert, 81 & 89, cert surg hand, 89. *Honors & Awards:* Philip D Wilson Prize; Lewis Clark Wagner Prize. *Prof Exp:* Intern surg, NY Hosp, 74-75; fel orthop res, Hosp Spec Surg, 75-76, resident orthop surg, 75-76, vis scientist, 80-89; fel hand surg, St Lukes-Roosevelt Hosp, 79-80; clin assoc prof orthop surg, Cornell Univ Med Col, 92-97. *Concurrent Pos:* Attend orthop surgeon, Hosp Spec Surg, 89-; assoc ed, Am J Hand Surg, 91-; asst attend, Long Island Jewish Med Ctr. *Mem:* Am Soc Surg Hand; fel Am Acad Orthop Surgeons; fel Am Col Surgeons; Orthop Res Soc. *Res:* Hand surgery, both clinical and basic science; tenosynovitis; infection; arthritis. *Mailing Add:* 800 Community Dr Manhasset NY 11030. *Fax:* 516-365-1634

LANE, LOIS KAY, PROTEIN CHEMISTRY. *Current Pos:* ASSOC PROF, DEPT PHARMACOL & CELL BIOPHYS, COL MED, UNIV CINCINNATI, 77- *Educ:* Dartmouth Col, PhD(biol), 73. *Mailing Add:* Dept Pharmacol Univ Cincinnati Col Med PO Box 670575 Cincinnati OH 45267-0575

LANE, MALCOLM DANIEL, BIOCHEMISTRY, MOLECULAR BIOLOGY. *Current Pos:* prof physiol chem, 70-78, DELAMAR PROF BIOL CHEM & CHMN DEPT, MED SCH, JOHNS HOPKINS UNIV, 78- *Personal Data:* b Chicago, Ill, Aug 10, 30; m 51, Patricia L Sonquist; c Claudia J & Malcolm D Jr. *Educ:* Iowa State Univ, BS, 51, MS, 53; Univ Ill, PhD, 56. *Honors & Awards:* Mead Johnson Award, Am Inst Nutrit, 66; William C Rose Award, 81. *Prof Exp:* Res asst, Iowa State Univ, 51-53; from assoc prof biochem & nutrit to prof, Va Polytech Inst, 56-64; from assoc prof biochem to prof, Sch Med, NY Univ, 64-70. *Concurrent Pos:* Sr fel, Max Planck Inst Cell Chem, 62-63; mem, Biochem Study Sect, NIH, 70-74, Bd Sci Coun, Nat Heart, Lung & Blood Inst, 86-92. *Mem:* Nat Acad Sci; Am Chem Soc; Am Soc Biochem & Molecular Biol (pres, 91); Am Inst Nutrit; AAAS; Am Soc Cell Biol; Harvey Soc; fel Am Acad Arts & Sci. *Res:* Transcriptional control of gene expression during differentiation; differentiation of preadipocytes into adipocytes; insulin action; glucose transport; diabetes. *Mailing Add:* Dept Biol Chem Johns Hopkins Univ Sch Med 725 N Wolfe St Baltimore MD 21205. *Fax:* 410-955-0903; *E-Mail:* dan.lane@quail.bs.jhu.edu

LANE, MEREDITH ANNE, SYSTEMATICS, EVOLUTION. *Current Pos:* DIR, MCGREGOR HERBARIUM & ASSOC PROF BOT, UNIV KANS, 89- *Personal Data:* b Mesa, Ariz, Aug 4, 51; div. *Educ:* Ariz State Univ, BS, 74, MS, 76; Univ Tex, PhD(bot), 80. *Honors & Awards:* Cooley Award, Am Soc Plant Taxonomists, 82. *Prof Exp:* assoc prof bot, Dept EPO Biol, Univ Colo, Boulder, 80-89. *Concurrent Pos:* Vis asst prof, Dept Bot, Univ Tex, 82; chmn, Systs Sect, Bot Soc Am, 84-86; actg cur, Rocky Mountain Herbarium, Univ Wyo, 85-86; prog dir, Am Soc Plant Taxonomists, 85-89; consult ed, plant taxon, Encyc Sci & Eng, McGraw-Hill, 86-93; adj asst prof bot, Dept Bot, Univ Wyo, Laramie, 86-89; mem coun, Int Orgn Plant Biosyts, 90-92. *Mem:* Int Asn Plant Taxon; Am Soc Plant Taxonomists (secy, 85-87); Bot Soc Am; Int Orgn Plant Biosysts. *Res:* Angiosperm systematics, specifically of southwestern North American and Mexican Compositae (Astereae), using cytotaxonomic, ecogeographic, scanning electron microscopic, biogeographic and cladistic techniques; pollination biology of Compositae, especially micromorphological pollinator cues; forensic botany. *Mailing Add:* NSF 4201 Wilson Blvd Suite 635 Arlington VA 22230. *E-Mail:* mlane@kuhub.cc.ukans.edu

LANE, MONTAGUE, CLINICAL PHARMACOLOGY, CLINICAL ONCOLOGY. *Current Pos:* from asst prof to assoc prof, 60-67, PROF PHARMACOL & MED, BAYLOR COL MED, 67-, HEAD, DIV CLIN ONCOL, 69- *Personal Data:* b New York, NY, Aug 28, 29; div; c Laura D & Adam R. *Educ:* NY Univ, BA, 47; Chicago Med Sch, MB, 52, MD, 53; Georgetown Univ, MS 57. *Prof Exp:* Res assoc radiobiol, Cancer Res Lab, City New York, 47-48; res assoc oncol, Chicago Med Sch, 50-52; intern med, Jewish Hosp Brooklyn, NY, 52-53, asst res, 53-54; clin assoc pharmacol, Nat Cancer Inst, 54-56; asst resident med, USPHS, Rochester, 56-57; investr clin pharmacol, Nat Cancer Inst, 57-60. *Concurrent Pos:* Instr, Sch Med, George Washington Univ, 57-60; consult, Vet Admin Hosp, 63-; mem pharmacol & therapeut study sec, Nat Cancer Inst, 66-69, consult chemother study sect, 69-72, mem nat new agents & spec Krebiozen rev comts, 72-73, mem cancer clin invests rev comt, 73-79, mem subcomt med oncol, Am Bd Internal Med, 73-80; consult, Food & Drug Admin, 86- *Mem:* Am Soc Hemat; Am Soc Pharmacol & Exp Therapeut; Soc Exp Biol & Med; Am Asn Cancer Res; Am Soc Clin Pharmacol & Therapeut (pres, 71-72); Sigma Xi; Am Soc Clin Oncol. *Res:* Cancer chemotherapy alkylating agents; antimetabolites; riboflavin deficiency; drug screening; ferro-kinetics; biological response modifiers. *Mailing Add:* 6560 Fannin Suite 1510 Houston TX 77030

LANE, NANCY JANE, CELL BIOLOGY, NEUROBIOLOGY. *Current Pos:* sr prin sci officer & head electron micros, Agr Res Coun Res Unit Insect Neurophysiol & Pharmacol, Dept Zool, 68-90, WELLCOME FEL, CAMBRIDGE UNIV, 91- *Personal Data:* b Halifax, NS; m 69, R N Perham; c Temple D & Quentin S. *Educ:* Dalhousie Univ, BSc, 58, MSc, 60; Oxford Univ, DPhil(cytol), 63; Cambridge Univ, PhD, 68. *Hon Degrees:* ScD, Cambridge Univ, 81; LLD, Dalhousie Univ, 85; Dsc, Salford Univ, 94. *Prof Exp:* Res asst prof path, Albert Einstein Col Med, 64-65; res staff biologist, Yale Univ, 65-68. *Concurrent Pos:* Res fel, Girton Col, Cambridge Univ, 68-70, off fel & lectr cell biol, 70-, grad tutor, 75-; chair, govt working party women sci & eng, 93; non-exec dir, Smith & Nephew & Peptide Therapeut. *Mem:* Am Soc Cell Biol; Brit Soc Cell Biol (secy, 82-90); Soc Exp Biol; fel Royal Micros Soc; fel Zool Soc; fel Royal Soc Arts. *Res:* Freeze-fracture and tracer analysis of invertebrate central nervous systems; accessibility of nervous systems to tracer molecules; structure and biochemistry of tight junctions in endothelial cells; alzheimer's disease. *Mailing Add:* Dept Zool Downing St Cambridge CB2 3EJ England. *Fax:* 44-223-336676

LANE, NEAL F, ATOMIC PHYSICS. *Current Pos:* DIR, NSF, 93- *Personal Data:* b Oklahoma City, Okla, Aug 22, 38; m 60, Joni S Williams; c Christy (Saydjari) & John P. *Educ:* Univ Okla, BSc, 60, MS, 62, PhD(physics), 64. *Hon Degrees:* DSc, Univ Ala, 94, Mich State Univ, 95, Ohio State Univ, 96; DHL, Univ Okla, 95, Marymount Univ, 95. *Honors & Awards:* Distinguished Karcher Lectr, Univ Okla, 83. *Prof Exp:* NSF res fel physics, Queen's Univ, Belfast, 64-65; vis fel, Joint Inst Lab Astrophys, Univ Colo, 65-66; from asst prof to assoc prof physics, Rice Univ, Houston, Tex, 66-72, prof physics & space physics & astron, 72-84, chmn, Dept Physics, 77-82, provost, 86-93; chancellor, Univ Colo, Colo Springs, 84-85. *Concurrent Pos:* Alfred P Sloan res fel, 67-73; vis fel, Joint Inst Lab Astrophys, Univ Colo, 75-76; dir, Physics Div, NSF, 79-80; distinguished vis scientist, Univ Ky, 80; non-resident fel, Joint Inst Lab Astrophys, Univ Colo, 84-93. *Mem:* Fel Am Phys Soc; fel AAAS; Am Asn Phys Teachers; Sigma Xi; fel Am Acad Arts & Sci; Am Inst Phys. *Res:* Theoretical studies of collision processes involving electrons, atoms and molecules. *Mailing Add:* 3826 Whitman Rd Annandale VA 22003-2200

LANE, NORMAN GARY, PALEONTOLOGY. *Current Pos:* prof paleont, 73-94, chmn dept, 84-87, EMER PROF PALEONT, IND UNIV, BLOOMINGTON, 94- *Personal Data:* b French Lick, Ind, Feb 19, 30; m 58; c 3. *Educ:* Oberlin Col, AB, 52; Univ Kans, MS, 54, PhD(geol), 58. *Prof Exp:* From asst prof to prof geol, Univ Calif, Los Angeles, 58-73. *Concurrent Pos:* Fulbright scholar, Univ Tasmania, 55-56; Fulbright prof, Trinity Col, Dublin, 71-72; res assoc paleont, Smithsonian Inst, 71- *Mem:* Paleont Soc (pres, 88); Soc Econ Paleontologists & Mineralogists; Soc Vert Paleont; Paleont Asn. *Res:* Functional morphology and community relations of fossil crinoids. *Mailing Add:* Dept Geol Ind Univ Bloomington IN 47405

LANE, ORRIS JOHN, JR, ROAD PAVEMENT. *Current Pos:* dist mat engr, 73-83, Portland cement concrete engr, 83-87, TESTING ENGR, IOWA DEPT TRANSP, 87- *Personal Data:* b Sigourney, Iowa, Apr 21, 32. *Educ:* Iowa State Univ, BS, 57. *Prof Exp:* Asst dist mat engr, Iowa Hwy Comn, 57-62, spec invest eng, 62-63, Portland cement concrete engr, 63-73. *Concurrent Pos:* Mem, C-13 Tech Comn Concrete Pipe, Am Soc Testing & Mat, 67-73 & 83-, Stand Comt Direct Design Buried Concrete Pipe, Am Soc Civil Engrs, 90- *Mem:* Nat Soc Prof Engrs. *Res:* A principle in development of the Iowa System for concrete bridge floor repair and rehabilitation; a principle in development of the Iowa Fast Track system for concrete pavement which permits early return of the new pavement to service. *Mailing Add:* 1111 Garfield Ames IA 50014

LANE, PETER, ORNITHOLOGY. *Honors & Awards:* Commemorative Medal, Confederation Can, 93. *Res:* Author of two books. *Mailing Add:* 210 Chemin de l'Eperon CP 1654 Lac Beauport PQ G0A 2C0 Can

LANE, RAYMOND OSCAR, NUCLEAR PHYSICS. *Current Pos:* prof physics, 66-74, DISTINGUISHED PROF PHYSICS, OHIO UNIV, 74- *Personal Data:* b Asbury Park, NJ, Sept 25, 24; m 49; c 3. *Educ:* Iowa State Univ, PhD(physics), 53. *Prof Exp:* Res asst, Inst Atomic Res, Iowa State Col, 49-53; assoc physicist, Argonne Nat Lab, 53-66. *Mem:* Am Phys Soc. *Res:* Penetration of electrons in matter; beta ray spectroscopy; neutron scattering; neutron polarization; nuclear structure. *Mailing Add:* 10 Canterbury Dr Athens OH 45701

LANE, RICHARD DURELLE, MONOCLONAL ANTIBODY TECHNOLOGY, ENZYMOLOGY. *Current Pos:* NIH res technician, Med Col Ohio, 75-76, instr, 80-83, asst prof, 84-87, ASSOC PROF, DEPT ANAT, MED COL OHIO, 87- *Personal Data:* b Detroit, Mich, May 14, 53; m 75; c 3. *Educ:* Bowling Green State Univ, BS, 75; Med Col Va, PhD(anat), 80. *Mem:* Soc Neurosci; AAAS; Am Asn Immunologists. *Res:* Investigating the reorganization of the somatosensory system in response to peripheral nerve injury. *Mailing Add:* Dept Anat Med Col Ohio CS No 10008 Toledo OH 43699. *Fax:* 419-381-3008; *E-Mail:* lane@gemini.mco.edu

LANE, RICHARD L, CERAMICS, ELECTRONIC MATERIALS. *Current Pos:* PROF MICROELECTRONIC ENG, ROCHESTER INST TECHNOL, NY, 87- *Personal Data:* b Franklinville, NY, Mar 11, 35; m 58; c 4. *Educ:* State Univ NY, Alfred, BS, 57, PhD(ceramic sci), 62. *Honors & Awards:* Tech Innovation Awards, NASA. *Prof Exp:* Res scientist, Appl Res Lab, Xerox Corp, 62-65, Fundamental Res Lab, 65-68; proj leader, Hamco Mach & Electronics Corp, 68-70, mgr res & develop, 70-74, dir eng, Hamco Div, 74-78; dir, Technol Ctr, Kayex Corp, 78-87. *Mem:* Am Ceramic Soc; Am Inst Ceramic Engrs; Electrochem Soc. *Res:* Physics of glass, electrical and optical properties; chemistry of glass, surface properties and reactions, high temperature reactions and crystal-glass interactions; chemical and physical properties of crystalline ceramic materials; semiconductor materials processing; plasma etching. *Mailing Add:* 1350 Penfield Ctr Rd Penfield NY 14526. *Fax:* 716-475-5041; *E-Mail:* rllemc@ritvax.isc.rit.edu

LANE, RICHARD NEIL, MATHEMATICS, ELECTRICAL ENGINEERING. *Current Pos:* CONSULT, 75-; PRES, LANE WESTLY INC. *Personal Data:* b Richmond, Va, Sept 1, 44. *Educ:* Calif Inst Technol, BS, 65, PhD(math), 68. *Prof Exp:* Mem prof staff math, Gen Elec Co, 68-69; sr scientist, Systs Applns, Inc, 69-70, dir commun studies, 70-75. *Mem:* Am Math Soc; Inst Elec & Electronics Engrs. *Res:* Systems analysis and modeling of cost and performance of communications systems, especially mobile radio and common carrier systems. *Mailing Add:* Lane Westly Inc 330 Primrose Ave Suite 404 Hillsborough CA 94010

LANE, ROBERT HAROLD, bioinorganic chemistry, inorganic chemistry, for more information see previous edition

LANE, ROBERT KENNETH, ENVIRONMENTAL SCIENCE, RESOURCE MANAGEMENT. *Current Pos:* PRES, WESTERN ENVIRON PERSPECTIVES LTD, 92- *Personal Data:* b Brandon, Man, Can, Feb 7, 37; m 61; c 1. *Educ:* Brandon Col, BSc, 57; Ore State Univ, MS, 62, PhD(oceanog), 65. *Honors & Awards:* Centennial Medal, Govt Can, 67, Merit Award, 77. *Prof Exp:* Forecaster, Meteorol Serv Can, 57-58; oceanogr, Fisheries Res Bd Can, 59-61; instr oceanog, Ore State Univ, 63-66; res scientist, Environ Can, 66-75, sci adv, 75-79, dir, Environ Protection Serv, 82-92; dir water proj, Can West Found, 79-81. *Concurrent Pos:* Chmn, Int Joint Comn Upper Great Lakes Water Qual Bd, 72-75 & Poplar River Bd, 78-80; prin investr, Landsat & Skylab, NASA. *Mem:* Am Soc Limnol & Oceanog; Am Geophys Union; Royal Meteorol Soc; Int Asn Gt Lakes Res (pres, 74-75); Am Meteorol Soc; Sigma Xi. *Res:* Physical oceanography and limnology, especially heat and radiation exchange; remote sensing; meteorology. *Mailing Add:* 12 Gilchrist Pl St Albert AB T8N 2M3 Can

LANE, ROBERT SIDNEY, MEDICAL ENTOMOLOGY, MICROBIOLOGY. *Current Pos:* assoc specialist, 80-84, ASSOC PROF, DEPT ENTOM SCI, UNIV CALIF, BERKELEY, 84- *Personal Data:* b Worcester, Mass, Mar 7, 44; m 68; c 2. *Educ:* Univ Calif, Berkeley, BA, 66, PhD(entom), 74; San Francisco State Col, MA, 69. *Prof Exp:* Asst pub health biologist, Vector Biol & Control Sect, State Dept Health, Calif, 74-77, assoc pub health biologist, 77-79. *Concurrent Pos:* Lectr, Biol Dept, San Francisco State Univ, 79-80; fel, Calif Acad Sci. *Mem:* Entom Soc Am; Wildlife Dis Asn; Am Soc Trop Med & Hyg; Soc Vector Ecologists; Sigma Xi. *Res:* Biosystematics of Tabanidae (Diptera); ecology and epidemiology of tick-borne disease, particularly Lyme disease and other spirochetoses. *Mailing Add:* Dept Entom Sci Univ Calif 201 Wellman Hall Berkeley CA 94720-3112

LANE, ROGER LEE, ZOOLOGY, EMBRYOLOGY. *Current Pos:* asst prof, 75-80, ASSOC PROF BIOL, KENT STATE UNIV, 80- *Personal Data:* b Mt Carmel, Ill, July 4, 45; m 68; c Paulette Hruban; c Leigh S, Brooke C & Taylor C. *Educ:* Univ Nebr, BS, 68, MS, 71, PhD(zool), 74. *Prof Exp:* Vis lectr zool, John F Kennedy Col, 73-75. *Mem:* Crustacean Soc; Am Malacol Union; Am Micros Soc; Nat Asn Biol Teachers. *Res:* Histology and histochemistry of terrestrial isopod crustaceans and terrestrial pulmonate gastropods. *Mailing Add:* Kent State Univ Ashtabula OH 44004. *Fax:* 440-964-4269; *E-Mail:* lane@ashtabula.kent.edu

LANE, STEPHEN MARK, PHYSICS. *Current Pos:* PHYSICIST, LASER FUSION, LAWRENCE LIVERMORE LAB, 78- *Personal Data:* b Scott Air Force Base, Ill, Nov 22, 48. *Educ:* San Jose State Univ, BA, 71; Univ Calif, Davis, MS, 73, PhD(appl sci), 79. *Mem:* Am Phys Soc. *Res:* Atomic and nuclear spectroscopy as applied to laser fusion research. *Mailing Add:* L-447 Lawrence Livermore Nat Lab UCL PO Box 5508 Livermore CA 94550

LANE, WALLACE, preventive medicine, cultural anthropology; deceased, see previous edition for last biography

LANE, WILLIAM JAMES, ANALYTICAL CHEMISTRY. *Current Pos:* res coordr analytical chem, Universal Oil Prod Co, 69-74, group leader analytical chem res & develop, 74-78, lab supvr, spectroscopy & analytical res, 78-81, LAB SUPVR, ANALYTICAL RES & SCHEDULING, UOP, INC, 81- *Personal Data:* b Zanesville, Ohio, Dec 5, 25; m 50; c 3. *Educ:* Denison Univ, BA, 47; Miami Univ, MS, 53; Iowa State Univ, PhD(chem), 57. *Prof Exp:* Asst chemist, AEC, Mound Lab, Monsanto Chem Co, 48-51; res asst analytical chem, Ames Lab, Iowa State Univ, 52-57; analytical chemist, Columbia-Southern Chem Corp, Pittsburgh Plate Glass Co, 57-60, analytical group supvr, 60-64, res analytical chemist, Chem Div, 64-69. *Mem:* Am Chem Soc. *Res:* General wet chemical analysis; polarography; chromatography; spectrophotometry. *Mailing Add:* 444 W Norman Ct Des Plaines IL 60016-2443

LANE, WILLIAM W, ELECTRONICS ENGINEERING. *Current Pos:* PRES, W LANE & ASSOC INC, NEW YORK, 92- *Personal Data:* b Roanoke, Va, Feb 25, 34; m 78, Ronnie D; c Jonathan D, Drew H & Craig M. *Educ:* Brooklyn Col, BA, 56; Cornell Univ, MBA, 58. *Prof Exp:* Vpres, Major Electronics Corp, 59-70, chmn & dir, 70; vpres & dir, Int Transistor Corp, Burbank, 71-73; vchmn & dir, Int Chia Hsin, Taipai, Taiwan, 73-76; chmn & dir, Emerson, Hong Kong, 76; chmn, chief exec officer & dir, Emerson Radio Corp, North Bergen, NJ, 74-91. *Concurrent Pos:* Pres, Majorette Enterprises, 61-; chmn, Maj Exco Imports Inc, 77-85, Emerson Comput Corp, 89-91, H H Scott, Inc Cardiac Resuscitator Corp, Emerson Investment Corp, Major Realty Corp, Emteck Technol Ltd; mem bus adv bd, US Senate. *Mailing Add:* 760 Park Ave New York NY 10021-4152

LANEWALA, MOHAMMED A, CHEMICAL ENGINEERING, SOFTWARE SYSTEMS. *Current Pos:* OWNER, RES SYSTS, 92- *Personal Data:* b Dohad, India; Sept 16, 31; US citizen; m 68, Emma J France; c Rani J & Shirin A. *Educ:* Univ Calcutta, BSc, 56, MSc, 59; Univ Toronto, MASc, 61; NY Univ, PhD(chem eng), 67. *Prof Exp:* Develop engr, Molecular Sieve Dept, Linde Div, Union Carbide Corp, 64-69, proj leader, Eastview, 69-77, comput tech coordr, 77-84, consult, 84-88; consult, UOP, 88-92. *Concurrent Pos:* Adj instr, Bishop State Community Col, 87- & Univ SAla, 96- *Mem:* Am Soc Testing & Mat. *Res:* Catalysis; adsorption; petroleum processes; computer technology; laboratory automation. *Mailing Add:* 5909 Ole Mill Rd Mobile AL 36609

LANFORD, OSCAR E, III, MATHEMATICAL PHYSICS, ANALYSIS & FUNCTIONAL ANALYSIS. *Current Pos:* PROF MATH, SWISS FED INST TECHNOL, ZURICH, 87- *Personal Data:* b New York, NY, Jan 6, 40; m 61, Regina Krigman; c Lizabeth M. *Educ:* Wesleyan Univ, BA, 60; Princeton Univ, MA, 62, PhD(physics), 66. *Hon Degrees:* ScD, Wesleyan Univ, 90. *Honors & Awards:* Award in Appl Math & Numerical Analysis, Nat Acad Sci, 86. *Prof Exp:* Instr math, Princeton Univ, 65-66; from asst prof to prof math, Univ Calif, Berkeley, 66-87. *Concurrent Pos:* Vis prof physics, Inst des Haute Estudes Sci, Bures-sur-Yvette, France, 67-68; prof physics, 82-87; Alfred Sloan Found res fel, 69-71; mem, Inst Advan Studies, 70; exchange prof, Univ Aix Marseille, 71. *Mem:* Am Math Soc. *Res:* Mathematical physics, especially statistical mechanics and dynamical systems theory. *Mailing Add:* D-Math ETH - Zentrum Zurich 8092 Switzerland. *E-Mail:* lanford@math.ethz.ch

LANFORD, ROBERT ELDON, IMMUNOLOGY, VIROLOGY. *Current Pos:* asst scientist, 84-85, assoc scientist, 86-89, SCIENTIST, DEPT VIROL & IMMUNOL, SOUTHWEST FOUND BIOMED RES, SAN ANTONIO, TEX, 90- *Personal Data:* b Ft Worth, Tex, Apr 18, 51; m 72, Deborah Hanna; c Shane & Jeremiah. *Educ:* Univ Tex, BS, 74; Baylor Col Med, PhD(virol), 79. *Prof Exp:* Asst prof, Dept Virol & Epidemiol, Baylor Col Med, Houston, Tex, 82-84. *Concurrent Pos:* From adj prof to adj assoc prof, 84-91, adj prof, Dept Microbiol, Univ Tex Health Sci Ctr, San Antonio, 91- *Mem:* Am Soc Microbiol; Am Soc Virol; Am Soc Cell Biol. *Res:* Hepatitis B virus; hepatitis C virus; lipoprotein (a). *Mailing Add:* Dept Virol & Immunol Southwest Found Biomed Res 7620 NW Loop 410 San Antonio TX 78228-0147

LANFORD, WILLIAM ARMISTEAD, ION BEAM ANALYSIS OF MATERIALS, THIN FILM PHYSICS. *Current Pos:* assoc prof, 79-83, dir, Accelerator Lab, 88-94, PROF PHYSICS, STATE UNIV NY, ALBANY, 83-, CHAIR PHYSICS DEPT, 90-92. *Personal Data:* b Albany, NY, Nov 15, 44; m 66, Cynthia Smith; c Catherine, William & Anne. *Educ:* Univ Rochester, BS, 66, PhD(physics), 72. *Prof Exp:* Res assoc, Mich State Univ, 71-72, asst prof, 72-73; from asst prof to assoc prof physics, Yale Univ, 73-79. *Concurrent Pos:* Consult, Exxon, 79-93, Sotheby's, 79, IBM, 80-, Nat Semiconductor, 84 & Bell Labs, 85-92; assoc ed, Appl Nuclear Sci, 79-92, ed, Radiation Effects, 83-89; fel, Alfred P Sloan Found, 79-83; mem, Int Adv Comt, Ion Beam Analysis Conf, 81-; vchmn, NY State Sect, Am Phys Soc, 85-87, chmn, 87-89, coun rep, 89-91; chmn, Physics Dept, State Univ NY, Albany, 90-92; vis prof, Univ Uppsala, Sweden, 94-96; guest researcher, Royal Swedish Acad Sci, 94-96. *Mem:* Am Ceramic Soc; Am Phys Soc; Mat Res Soc; Hist Metall Soc; Bohmtsche Phys Soc; Sigma Xi; AAAS. *Res:* Use of neuron beams in the study of materials including nuclear reaction analysis of hydrogen in materials; reaction of glass with water; microelectronic materials; archaeological materials. *Mailing Add:* Dept Physics State Univ NY Albany NY 12222. *Fax:* 518-442-4486; *E-Mail:* lanford@thor.albany.edu

LANG, ANTON, developmental plant biology; deceased, see previous edition for last biography

LANG, BRUCE Z, PARASITOLOGY, IMMUNOLOGY. *Current Pos:* from asst prof to assoc prof, 67-74, chmn dept, 78-80, PROF BIOL, EASTERN WASH UNIV, 74- *Personal Data:* b St Joseph, Mo, May 31, 37; m 59; c 2. *Educ:* Chico State Col, BS, 60; Univ NC, Chapel Hill, MSPH, 61, PhD(parasitol), 66. *Prof Exp:* Vis asst prof zool, Univ Okla, 66-67. *Concurrent Pos:* NIH fel zool, Univ Okla, 66-67; NSF grants, 69-72; affil fac mem, Univ Idaho, 75-; USDA grants, 77-83; mem grad fac, Wash State Univ, 77- *Mem:* AAAS; Am Soc Parasitol; Am Soc Zoologists; Am Soc Trop Med & Hyg; Am Inst Biol Sci. *Res:* Host-parasite relationships; ecology of parasitism; ecology of fresh-water gastropod molluscs. *Mailing Add:* Dept Biol Eastern Wash Univ M/S 72 Cheney WA 99004-2496

LANG, C MAX, LABORATORY ANIMAL MEDICINE. *Current Pos:* CHMN, DEPT COMP MED, COL MED, MILTON S HERSHEY MED CTR, PA STATE UNIV, 66- *Personal Data:* b Paris, Ill, Dec 29, 37; m 65, Sylvia Smith; c Karen E, John A & Susan C L (Swiegert). *Educ:* Univ Ill, BS,

59, DVM, 61. *Honors & Awards:* Res Award, Am Asn Lab Animal Sci, 79 & 80; Charles River Prize, 87. *Concurrent Pos:* George T Harrel prof. *Mem:* Am Col Lab Animal Med (secy-treas, 81-90, pres-elect, 90-91, pres, 91-92). *Res:* Environmental factors that can influence interpretation of research data. *Mailing Add:* Milton S Hershey Med Ctr Pa State Univ PO Box 850 Hershey PA 17033

LANG, CALVIN ALLEN, GERONTOLOGY, NUTRITION. *Current Pos:* from asst prof to assoc prof, 59-72, dir biomed aging res prog, 71-74, PROF BIOCHEM, SCH MED, UNIV LOUISVILLE, 72-, DIR, LOUISVILLE LONGITUDINAL LONGEVITY PROG, 83- *Personal Data:* b Portland, Ore, June 13, 25; m 49; c 4. *Educ:* Princeton Univ, AB, 47; Johns Hopkins Univ, ScD(biochem), 54. *Honors & Awards:* Tanner Lectr, Inst Food Tech, 73. *Prof Exp:* Res collabr, Brookhaven Nat Labs, 49-51; asst scientist insect biochem, Conn Agr Exp Sta, 54-56; res assoc, Sch Hyg & Pub Health, Johns Hopkins Univ, 56-59. *Concurrent Pos:* Fel, Sch Hyg & Pub Health & McCollum-Pratt Inst, Johns Hopkins Univ, 56-59; NIH fel, 57-59 & res career develop award, 67-72; Nat Sigma Xi lectureship, 90. *Mem:* Am Soc Biol Chem; Am Inst Clin Nutrit; Soc Exp Biol & Med; fel Geront Soc (vpres, 71); Sigma Xi. *Res:* Biochemistry of growth and aging; insect and nutritional biochemistry; glutathione detoxification and aging. *Mailing Add:* Dept Biochem MDR 412 Univ Louisville Sch Med Louisville KY 40292-0001

LANG, CHARLES H, INSULIN RESISTANCE, TRACER METHODOLOGY. *Current Pos:* PROF SURG, UNIV HOSP, STATE UNIV NY STONY BROOK. *Personal Data:* b Pittsburgh, Pa, July 7, 54; m 81; c 3. *Educ:* Westminster Col, BS, 76; Hahnemann Med Col, MS, 79, PhD(physiol), 81. *Prof Exp:* Fel metab, La State Univ Med Ctr, 81-84, res asst prof metab & shock, 84-86, from asst prof to assoc prof metab & shock, 86- *Mem:* Shock Soc; Am Physiol Soc; Am Diabetes Asn; Internal Endotoxin Soc; Res Soc Alcoholism; Surg Infection Soc. *Res:* The role of glucose counterregulatory hormones in mediating insulin action in various pathophysiological conditions, including sepsis, diabetes, chronic alcoholism and burn; the influence of various cytokines on carbohydrate homeostasis and their putative role in endotoxemia and sepsis. *Mailing Add:* Dept Surg State Univ NY Stony Brook NY 11794-8191

LANG, CONRAD MARVIN, PHYSICAL CHEMISTRY. *Current Pos:* from instr to assoc prof, 64-78, PROF CHEM, UNIV WIS-STEVENS POINT, 78- *Personal Data:* b Chicago, Ill, July 1, 39; m 61; c 3. *Educ:* Elmhurst Col, BS, 61; Univ Wis-Madison, MS, 64; Univ Wyo, PhD(chem), 70. *Prof Exp:* Teaching asst chem, Univ Wis-Madison, 61-63, res assoc, 63-64. *Concurrent Pos:* Consult, Crowns, Merklin, Midthun & Hill, Attorneys at Law, 70-; NSF res grant, Univ Wis-Stevens Point, 71-73; W B King vis prof, Iowa State Univ, 76-77; bd dirs, Am Chem Soc, 89- *Mem:* Am Chem Soc. *Res:* Application of electron spin resonance to molecular structure and macromolecular aspects of binary fluid mixtures; semiempirical quantum chemical calculations on systems of biological interest; physiochemical aspects of vision; chemical philately; chemical demonstrations; history of science. *Mailing Add:* Dept Chem Univ Wis Stevens Point WI 54481

LANG, DAVID (VERN), SEMICONDUCTORS, PHYSICS. *Current Pos:* mem tech staff, Bell Labs, 72-81, head, Semiconductor Electronics Res Dept, 81-87, LUCENT TECHNOL, 87-, ADJ MAT PHYSICS DIR, 96- *Personal Data:* b Willmar, Minn, July 11, 43; m 68; c 3. *Educ:* Concordia Col, Moorhead, Minn, BA, 65; Univ Wis-Madison, PhD(physics), 69. *Honors & Awards:* Morris E Leeds Award, Inst Elec & Electronics Engrs, 88. *Prof Exp:* Res assoc physics, Univ Ill, Urbana, 69-70, res asst prof, 70-72. *Mem:* Fel Am Phys Soc; sr mem Inst Elec & Electronics Engrs. *Res:* Capacitance spectroscopy (DLTS); defects in III-V semiconductors; recombination enhanced solid state defect reactions; radiation damage in semiconductors; gap states in amorphous semiconductors. *Mailing Add:* Bell Labs 600 Mountain Ave Murray Hill NJ 07974

LANG, DIMITRIJ ADOLF, BIOPHYSICS, MOLECULAR BIOLOGY. *Current Pos:* RETIRED. *Personal Data:* b Berlin, Ger, Aug 30, 26; m 59; c 2. *Educ:* Univ Frankfurt, MS, 53, PhD(biophys), 59. *Prof Exp:* Res asst biophys, Max Planck Inst Biophys, 53-58 & Hyg Inst, Univ Frankfurt, 58-65; from asst prof to prof biol, Univ Tex, Dallas, 65-91. *Concurrent Pos:* NIH res career develop awards, 67-71 & 72-76. *Mem:* Electron Micros Soc Am; Biophys Soc. *Res:* Electronics; physics of ionizing radiations; high-output x-ray machines; standard dosimetry of x-rays; electron microscopy of bacteria, viruses and nucleic acids; physical chemistry of nucleic acids. *Mailing Add:* 802 St Lukes Dr Richardson TX 75080

LANG, ENID ASHER, PSYCHIATRY. *Current Pos:* FAC MEM PSYCHIAT, MT SINAI SCH MED, NY, 81-, CLIN ASSOC PROF PSYCHIAT. *Personal Data:* b Los Angeles, Calif, Aug 28, 44; m, Norton D; c Eugene & Aaron. *Educ:* Radcliffe Col, AB, 66; Univ Southern Calif, MD, 70; Columbia Univ, MS, 74. *Hon Degrees:* MPN, Columbia Univ, 74. *Prof Exp:* Med intern, Beth Israel Hosp, NY, 71-72; resident psychiat, Columbia Psychiat Inst, 72-74; res fel, Columbia Univ Health Serv, 74-75; fac mem, Sch Med, NY Univ, 75-80. *Concurrent Pos:* Dir, Group Psychiat & Training Psychiat Residents, Bellevue Hosp, Sch Med, NY Univ, 75-, dir, Socialization Prog Psychiat Outpatients, 75-; process groups psychiat residents training, Mt Sinai Med Ctr, Dept Psychiat, Psychoanal & Lit, teaching course fac. *Mem:* Am Psychiat Asn; NY Acad Sci; Am Women's Med Asn. *Res:* A longitudinal comparative study of treatment-outcome of discharged psychiatric outpatients who receive group therapy with medication versus individual therapy with medication only. *Mailing Add:* 10 Innes Rd Scarsdale NY 10583

LANG, ERICH KARL, RADIOLOGY, INTERVENTIONAL RADIOLOGY. *Current Pos:* chmn dept, 67-76, PROF RADIOL & UROL, SCH MED, LA STATE UNIV, NEW ORLEANS, 76-; PROF RADIOL, SCH MED, TULANE UNIV, 76- *Personal Data:* b Vienna, Austria, Dec 7, 29; US citizen; m 56, Nicole J Miller; c Erich C & Cortney A. *Educ:* Columbia Univ, MS, 51; Univ Vienna, MD, 53. *Prof Exp:* Assoc radiol, Johns Hopkins Hosp & Univ, 56-59, assoc radiologist, 59-61; radiologist, Methodist Hosp, Indianapolis, Ind, 61-67; prof radiol & chmn dept, Sch Med, La State Univ, Shreveport, 67-76. *Concurrent Pos:* Prof radiol, Univ Med & Dent NJ, 95- *Mem:* AMA; Radiol Soc NAm; Soc Nuclear Med; Am Col Radiol; Am Col Chest Physicians. *Res:* Diagnostic, vascular roentgenographic examinations; diagnostic roentgenographic evaluation of tumors and tumor diagnosis. *Mailing Add:* La State Univ Med Ctr Dept Radiol 1542 Tulane Ave New Orleans LA 70110. *Fax:* 504-568-8955

LANG, FRANK ALEXANDER, SYSTEMATIC BOTANY. *Current Pos:* from asst prof to assoc prof, 66-77, chmn dept, 76-80, PROF BIOL, SOUTHERN ORE STATE COL, 77-, CHMN DEPT, 90- *Personal Data:* b Olympia, Wash, May 14, 37; m 59, Suzanne DeArmond; c Thomas & Amy. *Educ:* Ore State Univ, BS, 59; Univ Wash, MS, 61; Univ BC, PhD(bot), 65. *Prof Exp:* Asst prof biol, Whitman Col, 65-66. *Concurrent Pos:* Vis scholar, Harvard Univ, Herbaria, 81-82. *Mem:* Am Soc Plant Taxon; Int Asn Plant Taxon; Am Fern Soc; Bot Soc Am. *Res:* Biosystematics and cytotaxonomy of vascular plants; flora of the Siskiyou Mountains. *Mailing Add:* Dept Biol Southern Ore State Col 1250 Siskiyou Blvd Ashland OR 94520-5001. *Fax:* 541-552-6415; *E-Mail:* flang@sosc2.sosc.osshe.edu

LANG, FRANK THEODORE, PHYSICAL CHEMISTRY. *Current Pos:* assoc prof phys chem, 67-80, chmn, Dept Chem, 70-73 & 89-93, PROF CHEM, FAIRLEIGH DICKINSON UNIV, FLORHAM-MADISON, 80- *Personal Data:* b New York, NY, Jan 25, 38; m 63; c 3. *Educ:* St Francis Col, NY, BS, 59; Rensselaer Polytech Inst, PhD(phys chem), 64. *Prof Exp:* Res assoc photochem, Univ Sheffield, 64-65; res assoc-instr energy transfer, Univ NC, Chapel Hill, 65-67. *Mem:* Am Chem Soc. *Res:* Charge transfer complexes; flash photolysis; low temperature photochemistry; energy transfer processes; luminescence studies; oscillating reactions. *Mailing Add:* Dept Chem Fairleigh Dickinson Univ Madison NJ 07940. *E-Mail:* lang@alpha.fdu.edu

LANG, GEORGE E, JR, TOPOLOGY. *Current Pos:* ASSOC PROF MATH & COMPUT SCI, FAIRFIELD UNIV, 70- *Personal Data:* b Chicago, Ill, June 29, 42; m 68; c 2. *Educ:* Loyola Univ Chicago, BS, 64; Univ Dayton, MS, 66; Purdue Univ, PhD(math), 70. *Prof Exp:* Teaching asst, Univ Dayton, 64-66 & Purdue Univ, 67-69. *Mem:* Am Math Soc; Math Asn Am; Am Asn Univ Profs; Asn Comput Mach. *Res:* Homotopy theory; subgroups of homotopy groups; direct limits of CW complexes with an eye to group theoretic applications. *Mailing Add:* Dept Math & Comput Sci Fairfield Univ Fairfield CT 06430-7524

LANG, GERALD EDWARD, PLANT ECOLOGY. *Current Pos:* from asst prof to assoc prof, 76-84, PROF BIOL & ASST DEAN, WVA UNIV, 84- *Personal Data:* b Chicago, Ill, Mar 1, 45; m 73; c 1. *Educ:* Western Ill Univ, BS, 67; Univ Wyo, MS, 69; Rutgers Univ, PhD(bot), 73. *Prof Exp:* Res instr terrestrial ecol, Dartmouth Col, 73-76. *Concurrent Pos:* NSF res grants, 74-76, 76-79, 77, 79-82, 83-85 & 84; Army Corps Engrs res contract, 79-82, Environ Protection Agency res contract, 82-85; NASA res grant, 85-88. *Mem:* AAAS; Brit Ecol Soc; Ecol Soc Am. *Res:* Vegetation patterns and biogeochemical processes in high-elevation wetland ecosystems in the Appalachian Mountains; decomposition rates for leaf and wood litter; concomitant elemental mineralization patterns in forest ecosystems. *Mailing Add:* Dean Arts & Sci WVa Univ 1600 University Ave Morgantown WV 26506-0001

LANG, GERHARD HERBERT, MEDICAL MICROBIOLOGY, VETERINARY MEDICINE. *Current Pos:* RETIRED. *Personal Data:* b Neunkirchen, WGer, Jan 6, 27; Can citizen; m 59; c 2. *Educ:* Univ Lyons, France, DVM, 55; Pasteur Inst, Paris, cert bact, 55; Univ Toronto, MVSc, 62. *Prof Exp:* Assoc vet, Beauxsenne, France, 55-57; from asst prof to assoc prof vet virol, Ont Vet Col, Univ Guelph, 61-92. *Concurrent Pos:* Animal health expert virol, Food & Agr Orgn, Rome, 71-73. *Mem:* Am Asn Avian Pathologists; World Vet Poultry Asn; Can Soc Microbiologists; Am Soc Microbiologists; Can Vet Med Asn. *Res:* Animal and human virus infections, their diagnosis and control; medical and veterinary microbiology. *Mailing Add:* 87 Hearn Ave Guelph ON N1H 5Y6 Can

LANG, GERHARD PAUL, INORGANIC CHEMISTRY. *Current Pos:* RETIRED. *Personal Data:* b Omaha, Nebr, Feb 20, 17; m 44, Elsie Reese; c Miriam, Allen, Karen & Elizabeth. *Educ:* Valparaiso Univ, BA, 43; Wash Univ, MA, 55. *Prof Exp:* Chemist, Visking Corp, 44-45; chemist, Uranium Div, Mallinckrodt Chem Works, 46-64; res chemist, Emerson Elec Mfg Co, 64-66; sr engr, McDonnell Douglas Corp, 66-82. *Mem:* Am Chem Soc; Sigma Xi. *Res:* Uranium chemistry; liquid-liquid extraction; radiochemistry; aerospace chemistry. *Mailing Add:* 7430 Hiawatha Ave Richmond Heights MO 63117

LANG, HARRY GEORGE, PHYSICS. *Current Pos:* Asst prof, Rochester Inst Technol, Nat Tech Inst Deaf, 70-80, prof physics, 80-84, coordr, Off Fac Develop, 84-90, PROF, DEPT EDUC RES & DEVELOP, ROCHESTER INST TECHNOL, NAT TECH INST DEAF, 90- *Personal Data:* b Pittsburgh, Pa, June 2, 47; m 73, Bonnie Meath. *Educ:* Bethany Col, WVa, BS, 69; Rochester Inst Technol, MS, 74; Univ Rochester, EdD, 79.

Concurrent Pos: Consult, Proj Handicapped Sci, AAAS, 78-, Res Better Sch, Inc & Am Printing House for Blind; vis prof, Univ Rochester, 81-; ed, Testing Phys Handicapped Students in Sci; vis lectr, Univ Leeds, Eng, 88. *Mem:* Nat Sci Teachers Asn; AAAS; Am Educ Res Asn; Nat Asn Res Sci Teaching; Asn Educ Teachers Sci. *Res:* Test measurement theory; criterion referenced measurement; science curriculum research for handicapped students; digital computer analysis and synthesis of speech; historical contributions of deaf persons to science; research on effective teaching. *Mailing Add:* Nat Tech Inst for the Deaf 52 Lomb Mem Dr Rochester NY 14623. *E-Mail:* hgl9008@rit.edu

LANG, HELGA M (SR THERESE), biochemistry, nutrition; deceased, see previous edition for last biography

LANG, IVAN MARSHALL, SWALLOWING, VOMITING. *Current Pos:* From asst prof to assoc prof surg, 83-92, ADJ ASSOC PROF MED, MED COL WIS, 96- *Personal Data:* b Wilkes-Barre, Pa, Oct 26, 47; m 73, div; c 2. *Educ:* Univ Pittsburgh, BS, 69; Temple Univ, MS, 75, PhD(physiol & biophys), 80; Univ Wis, DVM, 96. *Mem:* Am Physiol Soc; Am Gastroenterol Asn; Soc Neurosci; Am Motility Soc; Am Vet Med Asn. *Res:* Physiology of swallowing with special interest in bolus transport from pharynx to stomach and in the mechanisms of airway protection; physiology of vomiting and belching; peripheral and central neurol control of these phenomena. *Mailing Add:* Dysphagia Res Lab Med Col Wis 8701 Watertown Plank Rd Milwaukee WI 53226. *E-Mail:* imlang@post.its.amcw.edu

LANG, JAMES FREDERICK, DRUG METABOLISM. *Current Pos:* RETIRED. *Personal Data:* b Dayton, Ohio, Mar 19, 31; m 58; c 2. *Educ:* Univ Cincinnati, BS, 58, MS, 70. *Prof Exp:* Res asst toxicol & drug metab, Christ Hosp Inst Med Res, Subsid Elizabeth Gamble Deaconess Home Asn, 58-63; from res asst biochem to biochemist, Merrell Dow Pharmaceut, Inc, 63-72; sect head drug metab, 72-82, sr res biochemist, Merrell Dow Res Inst, 82-85, group leader, drug metab clin res support, 85-90. *Res:* Isolation and identification of drug metabolites, pharmacokinetics; development and application of analytical methods for trace analysis of drug residues in biological media. *Mailing Add:* 2894 Pineridge Ave Cincinnati OH 45208-2818

LANG, JOHN CALVIN, JR, PHYSICAL CHEMISTRY. *Current Pos:* ASST TECH DIR, ALCON LABS, 86- *Personal Data:* b Montclair, NJ, May 6, 42; m 66, Elizabeth H; c Phebe D. *Educ:* Wesleyan Univ, BA, 64; Cornell Univ, MS, 68, PhD(chem), 72. *Prof Exp:* Fels, Cornell Univ, 72 & 73-75, Univ Reading, Eng, 72-73; res scientist phys chem, Procter & Gamble Co, 75-84; res assoc, Arco Oil & Gas Co, 84-86. *Concurrent Pos:* Adv, Ctr Surface Sci & Eng, Univ Fla; adj assoc prof chem, Univ Tex, Arlington, 86- *Mem:* Am Phys Soc; Sigma Xi; Am Chem Soc; Controlled Release Soc. *Res:* Phase equilibria; phase transitions; critical phenomena; thermodyamics of aqueous solutions; magnetic resonance; light scattering; surfactant, polymer and colloid physical chemistry; drug delivery, especially ophthalmologic; drug assessment. *Mailing Add:* 2106 Riverforest Dr Arlington TX 76017-1637

LANG, JOSEPH EDWARD, THEORETICAL PHYSICS. *Current Pos:* asst prof physics, 71-80, ASSOC PROF PHYSICS, THOMAS MORE COL, 80- *Personal Data:* b Covington, Ky, Aug 10, 42. *Educ:* Thomas More Col, AB, 64; Univ Ill, MS, 65, PhD(physics), 70. *Prof Exp:* NSF fel, Lawrence Radiation Lab, Univ Calif, Berkeley, 70-71. *Concurrent Pos:* Vis scientist, Air Force Mat Lab, Wright-Patterson AFB, 78-79. *Mem:* Am Phys Soc; Am Asn Physics Teachers, Sigma Xi. *Res:* Elementary particle physics; magnetic anisotropy; computers in education. *Mailing Add:* Wright Bros Br PO Box 301 Dayton OH 45409-0301

LANG, KENNETH LYLE, FRESHWATER ECOLOGY. *Current Pos:* Assoc prof biol, 70-77, ASSOC PROF ZOOL, HUMBOLDT STATE UNIV, 77- *Personal Data:* b Cuba City, Wis, Apr 12, 36; m 61; c 1. *Educ:* Iowa State Col, BS, 59; Univ Iowa, MS, 66, PhD(zool), 70. *Mem:* Am Soc Zool; Am Soc Limnol & Oceanog. *Res:* Freshwater zooplankton populations; dispersion patterns and species diversity of benthic and planktonic Cladoceran assemblages. *Mailing Add:* Dept Biol Humboldt State Univ 1 Harps St Arcata CA 95521-8299

LANG, LAWRENCE GEORGE, SOLID STATE PHYSICS. *Current Pos:* prof, 73-96, EMER PROF PHYSICS, PA STATE UNIV, 97- *Personal Data:* b Pittsburgh, Pa, Mar 25, 31; m 53; c 2. *Educ:* Carnegie Inst Technol, BS, 52, MS, 53, PhD(physics), 57. *Prof Exp:* Res physicist, Carnegie Inst Technol, 56-57 & 58-60, asst prof to assoc prof physics, 60-66; eng specialist, Philco Corp, 57-58; res physicist, Atomic Energy Res Estab, Eng, 63-65 & 66-73. *Concurrent Pos:* Nat Acad Sci-Nat Res Coun fel, 63-64. *Mem:* Am Phys Soc. *Res:* Angular correlation of radiation from positron annihilation in solids; Mossbauer effect in compounds; paramagnetic and diamagnetic salts; biological macromolecules. *Mailing Add:* Dept Physics Pa State Univ 104 Davey Lab University Park PA 16802-6300

LANG, MARTIN, ENVIRONMENTAL ENGINEERING. *Current Pos:* PVT CONSULT ENGR, 89- *Mem:* Nat Acad Eng. *Mailing Add:* 11 A Pine Dr N Roslyn NY 11576

LANG, MARTIN T, COMPUTER IN MATHEMATICS EDUCATION. *Current Pos:* from asst prof to assoc prof, 69-78, PROF MATH, CALIF POLYTECH STATE UNIV, 78- *Personal Data:* b Yokohama, Japan, May 7, 36; US citizen; m 65, Barbara Parks; c Rebecca, Ruth & Jonathan. *Educ:* NCent Col, BA, 59; Univ Kans, MA, 63; Univ Tex-Austin, PhD(math educ), 73. *Prof Exp:* From lectr to asst prof math, San Diego State Univ, 64-69. *Concurrent Pos:* Nat Woodrow Wilson fel, 59; Nat Defense Educ Award, 59; Asst instr math, Univ Kans, 63-65. *Mem:* Math Asn Am; Nat Coun Teachers Math; Am Asn Univ Profs; Nat Educ Asn. *Res:* Use of computers in math education at the college level; computer augmented instruction. *Mailing Add:* 1444 Tanglewood Ct San Luis Obispo CA 93401. *Fax:* 805-756-6537; *E-Mail:* mlang@calpoly.edu

LANG, NEIL CHARLES, CHEMICAL PHYSICS. *Current Pos:* CHEMIST, LASER PROG, LAWRENCE LIVERMORE LAB, 76- *Personal Data:* b Montreal, Que, Jan 24, 48; US citizen. *Educ:* McGill Univ, BSc, 68; Mass Inst Technol, PhD(phys chem), 74. *Concurrent Pos:* Fel, Nat Res Coun Can, 74-76. *Mem:* Am Phys Soc; Sigma Xi. *Res:* Chemical physics, reaction dynamics and energy transfer processes in gas phase collisions; applications in laser technology and isotope enrichment. *Mailing Add:* 670 Vernon St No 404 Oakland CA 94610

LANG, NORMA JEAN, phycology, for more information see previous edition

LANG, NORMA M, NURSING & PUBLIC POLICY. *Current Pos:* DEAN & PROF, SCH NURSING, UNIV PA, 92- *Personal Data:* b Wausau, Wis, Dec 27, 39; c 2. *Educ:* Alverno Col, BSN, 61; Marquette Univ, MSN, 63, PhD(educ admin), 74. *Prof Exp:* Staff nurse & asst instr, St Joseph's Hosp, 61-62; instr & coodr med-surg nursing, St Mary's Sch Nursing, 64-65; instr & asst prof, 65-69, Sch Nursing, Univ Wis, Milwaukee, from asst prof to prof, 68-92, proj dir res develop grant, 77-79, dean, 80-92. *Concurrent Pos:* Nursing coodr, Wis Regional Med Prog, 68-73; res assoc, Sch Nursing, Univ Wis, Milwaukee, 77, ctr scientist , Urban Res Ctr, 77-79; Medicus Corp, 86. *Mem:* Inst Med-Nat Acad Sci; fel Am Acad Nursing; Am Nurses' Asn; Am Heart Asn; Am Asn Univ Profs; Am Pub Health Asn. *Res:* Nursing; nursing and policy; education administration; numerous articles and publications. *Mailing Add:* Sch Nursing Univ Pa 420 Guardian Dr Philadelphia PA 19104. *Fax:* 215-573-2114; *E-Mail:* nlang@pobox.upenn.edu

LANG, NORTON DAVID, PHYSICS. *Current Pos:* STAFF MEM, IBM CORP, 69- *Personal Data:* b Chicago, Ill, July 5, 40; m 69, Enid Asher; c Eugenie & Aaron. *Educ:* Harvard Univ, AB, 62, AM, 65, PhD(physics), 68. *Honors & Awards:* Davisson-Germer Prize, Am Phys Soc, 77. *Prof Exp:* Asst res physicist, Univ Calif, San Diego, 67-69. *Concurrent Pos:* Assoc ed, Phys Rev Lett, 80-83; chmn of the fel comt, Div Condensed Matter Physics, Am Phys Soc, 85-87, chmn, Davisson-Germer Prize Comt, 90; mgr, Elec Struct Theory Group, 84-93. *Mem:* Fel NY Acad Sci; fel Am Phys Soc. *Res:* Condensed matter physics; surface science; atomic-scale electronics. *Mailing Add:* IBM Res Ctr Yorktown Heights NY 10598. *E-Mail:* lang@watson.ibm.com

LANG, PETER MICHAEL, chemical & nuclear engineering, for more information see previous edition

LANG, PHILIP CHARLES, ORGANIC CHEMISTRY. *Current Pos:* SR RES CHEMIST & DIR CHEM, CIBA-GEIGY CORP, 80- *Personal Data:* b Jamestown, NY, Nov 16, 34; m 55; c 3. *Educ:* Allegheny Col, BS, 57; Ohio Univ, MS, 59; Rensselaer Polytech Inst, PhD(org chem), 66. *Prof Exp:* Res chemist, Diamond Alkali Co, 59-62; assoc res chemist, Sterling Winthrop Res Inst, 62-67; res chemist, GAF Corp, 67-73 & Toms River Chem Corp, 73-80. *Mem:* Am Chem Soc. *Res:* Synthetic medicinal chemistry; heterocyclic and acteylene compounds; aromatics and synthetic dyes. *Mailing Add:* 216 Edgemere Dr RD 5 Toms River NJ 08755

LANG, RAYMOND W, MICROBIOLOGY. *Current Pos:* assoc prof, 68-72, PROF MED MICROBIOL, COL MED, OHIO STATE UNIV, 72- *Personal Data:* b Syracuse, NY, Aug 1, 30; m 53; c 5. *Educ:* LeMoyne Col, NY, BS, 52; Mich State Univ, MS, 57, PhD(microbiol), 59. *Prof Exp:* Asst prof microbiol, St John's Univ, NY, 59-62; fel bact & immunol, Sch Med, State Univ NY Buffalo, 62-63, from instr to asst prof bact & immunol, 63-68. *Concurrent Pos:* Consult urol res sect, Millard Fillmore Hosp, 64-66; consult training prog, Nat Inst Dent Res, 72-75; consult, Ohio Dept Health, 83- *Mem:* AAAS; Am Soc Microbiol; Am Asn Immunol. *Res:* Immunochemistry of tissue antigens; autoimmunity. *Mailing Add:* Dept Med Microbiol Ohio State Univ Col Med 370 W Ninth Ave Columbus OH 43210-1238

LANG, ROBERT PHILLIP, PHYSICAL CHEMISTRY. *Current Pos:* From instr to assoc prof 62-74, chmn dept, 71-88, PROF CHEM, QUINCY COL, 74- *Personal Data:* b Chicago, Ill, June 15, 32. *Educ:* Univ Ill, BS, 55; Univ Chicago, MS, 60, PhD(phys chem), 62. *Concurrent Pos:* NSF res grant, 65-68 & 70-72. *Mem:* AAAS; Am Chem Soc; Am Asn Physics Teachers. *Res:* Thermodynamic and electronic spectral characteristics of molecular complexes of iodine; amino acid sequences in enzymes. *Mailing Add:* Dept Chem Quincy Univ Quincy IL 62301-2200

LANG, ROGER H, COMMUNICATION THEORY. *Current Pos:* PROF ENG APPL SCI, GEORGE WASHINGTON UNIV, 70-, CHMN DEPT, 84- *Personal Data:* b New York, NY, July 8, 40. *Educ:* Polytech Inst Brooklyn, BSEE, 62, MSEE, 64, PhD(electrophys), 68. *Concurrent Pos:* Fel Nat Res Consult. *Mem:* Fel Inst Elec & Electronics Engrs. *Mailing Add:* Dept Elec Eng & Comput Sci George Washington Univ 801 22nd St NW Washington DC 20052

LANG, ROY, PHYSICS. *Current Pos:* researcher, Ctr Res Labs, 73-91, gen mgr, Fundamental Res Labs, 91-97, RES FEL, RES & DEVELOP GROUP, NEC CORP, JAPAN, 97- *Personal Data:* b Tokyo, Japan, Apr 5, 42; m 72, Junko; c Eugene & Mariko. *Educ:* Univ Tokyo, BS, 66; Mass Inst Technol, PhD(physics), 71. *Honors & Awards:* Sakurai Mem Award, Optoelectronics Indust & Technol Asn, 92. *Prof Exp:* Res assoc, Inst Lab Astrophys, Univ Colo & Nat Bur Stand, 71-73. *Mem:* Fel Inst Elec & Electronics Engrs; Japan Appl Physics Soc; Japan Phys Soc. *Res:* Contribution to development of optoelectronic devices, especially of semiconductor lasers; granted 16 Japanese patents in field. *Mailing Add:* Res & Develop Group NEC 4-1-1 Miyazaki Miyamae-ku Kawasaki 216 Japan. *Fax:* 81-44-856-2130; *E-Mail:* lang@rdq.cl.nec.co.jp

LANG, SERGE, NUMBER THEORY, ALGEBRAIC GEOMETRY. *Current Pos:* PROF MATH, YALE UNIV, 72- *Personal Data:* b Paris, France, May 19, 27. *Educ:* Calif Tech Univ, BS, 46; Princeton Univ, PhD(math), 51. *Honors & Awards:* Cole Prize, Am Math Soc, 59; Alexander von Humboldt Award, 84. *Prof Exp:* Instr math, Princeton Univ, 51-52 & Univ Chicago, 53-55; fel, Inst Advan Studies, 52-53; from asst prof to prof, Columbia Univ, 55-71. *Concurrent Pos:* Vis scholar, Inst Advan Study, 52-53; Fulbright fel, 56-57. *Mem:* Nat Acad Sci; Am Math Soc. *Mailing Add:* Dept Math Yale Univ 10 Hillhouse Ave New Haven CT 06520

LANG, STANLEY ALBERT, JR, ORGANIC CHEMISTRY. *Current Pos:* res chemist, Lederle Labs, Am Cyanamid Inc, 74, group leader, Info Dis Ther Sect, 74-77, group leader, 77-80, HEAD, CHEM DEPT, INFECTIOUS DIS THER SECT, MED RES DIV, AM CYANAMID INC, 80- *Personal Data:* b Cleveland, Ohio, Mar 30, 44. *Educ:* John Carroll Univ, BS, 66; Brown Univ, PhD(org chem), 70. *Prof Exp:* Res fel, Ohio State Univ, 70, Nat Cancer Inst fel, 71. *Mem:* Am Chem Soc. *Res:* Synthetic organic chemistry; medicinal drugs; antibiotics, anticancer agents; immunoregulants. *Mailing Add:* 7 Colony Dr Blauvelt NY 10913-1319

LANG, THOMAS G(LENN), MECHANICAL ENGINEERING. *Current Pos:* HYDRODYNAMICS CONSULT. *Personal Data:* b San Jose, Calif, July 28, 28; m 62; c 2. *Educ:* Calif Inst Technol, BS, 48 & 50; Univ Southern Calif, MS, 53; Pa State Univ, PhD(aerospace eng), 68. *Prof Exp:* Operator, Southern Calif Coop Wind Tunnel, 48-49; stress analyst, NAm Aviation, Inc, 50-51; designer, US Naval Ord Test Sta, 51-52, hydrodynamicist, 52-58, head oceanic res group, 58-61, head hydrodyn res group, 61-66; US Naval Ord Test Sta scholar, Pa State Univ, 66-68; tech consult, Ocean Technol Dept, Naval Undersea Warfare Ctr, 68; head advan design, Systs Analysis Group, Naval Undersea Ctr & Naval Ocean Systs Ctr, 68-70, head, Advan Concepts Group, 70-73, head, Advan Concepts Div, 73-78. *Concurrent Pos:* Consult, 78-79; pres, Semi-Submerged Ship Co, 79- *Mem:* Am Inst Aeronaut & Astronaut; Marine Technol Soc; Soc Naval Architects & Marine Engrs. *Res:* Hydrodynamics, especially stability and control, propulsion, boundary layer control, vented hydrofoils, sea animal hydrodynamics, polymer additives for drag reduction; semisubmerged ship design. *Mailing Add:* 417 Loma Larga Dr Solana Beach CA 92075

LANG, VALERIE ILONA, ATMOSPHERIC SCIENCES, SPECTROSCOPY & PHYSICAL CHEMISTRY. *Current Pos:* mem tech staff, 88-92, PROJ ENGR GOVT & ENVIRON PROGS, AEROSPACE CORP, 93- *Personal Data:* b New Market, Ont, Mar 24, 59. *Educ:* McGill Univ, BSc, 79; Univ Miami, MS, 82; Dartmouth Col, PhD(phys chem), 86. *Prof Exp:* Resident res assoc, Nat Res Coun, Jet Propulsion Lab, NASA, 86-88; cong sci fel, Am Geophys Union, 92-93. *Mem:* Am Geophys Union; AAAS; Am Chem Soc. *Res:* Chemical kinetics; atmospheric spectroscopy; space launch chemistry. *Mailing Add:* Aerospace Corp PO Box 92957 M5/742 Los Angeles CA 90009. *Fax:* 310-336-6435; *E-Mail:* valerie_lang@qmail2.aero.org

LANG, WILLIAM HARRY, PETROLEUM CHEMISTRY, FUEL SCIENCE. *Current Pos:* RETIRED. *Personal Data:* b Etna, Pa, Mar 29, 18; m 46, K Eileen Hewitt; c William H Jr & June E (Koch). *Educ:* Grove City Col, BS, 40. *Prof Exp:* Sr res chemist, Cent Res Div, Mobil Res & Develop Corp, 40-81. *Mem:* Am Chem Soc; Catalysis Soc. *Res:* Development of new and alternate fuels and energy sources to use as a petroleum substitute; co-inventor of methanol to gasoline and methanol to olefins processes. *Mailing Add:* 307 Water St Exeter NH 03833

LANG, WILLIAM WARNER, ACOUSTICAL & NOISE CONTROL ENGINEERING. *Current Pos:* PRES, INT INST NOISE CONTROL ENG, 92- *Personal Data:* b Boston, Mass, Aug 9, 26; m 54, Asta L Ingard; c Robert. *Educ:* Iowa State Univ, BS, 46, PhD(physics), 58; Mass Inst Technol, SM, 49. *Honors & Awards:* Achievement Award, Inst Elec & Electronics Engrs Group Audio & Electroacoust, 72, Centennial Medal, 84; Silver Medal, Acoust Soc Am, 84; Pro Silentio Medal, Hungarian Optical Acoust & Film Tech Soc, 89. *Prof Exp:* Acoust engr, Bolt, Beranek & Newman, Inc, 49-51; instr physics, US Naval Post-Grad Sch, 51-55; spec engr, E I du Pont de Nemours & Co, Inc, 55-57; adv physicist, IBM Corp, 58-64, sr physicist & mgr, Acoust Lab, 64-75, prog mgr acoust technol, 75-90, sr tech staff mem, 91-92. *Concurrent Pos:* Mem eval panel, Mech Div, Nat Bur Stand, 74-75, chmn, 75-76; adj prof physics, Vassar Col, 79- *Mem:* Nat Acad Eng; Inst Noise Control Eng (pres, 78, 88); Acoust Soc Am; fel Inst Elec & Electronics Engrs; fel Audio Eng Soc; fel Inst Acoust. *Res:* Acoustics; effects and control of noise; theory and design of acoustical materials; determinations of sound power levels of noise sources. *Mailing Add:* 29 Hornbeck Ridge Poughkeepsie NY 12603-4205. *Fax:* 914-473-9325

LANGACKER, PAUL GEORGE, THEORETICAL PHYSICS, ELEMENTARY PARTICLE PHYSICS. *Current Pos:* from res assoc to prof, 74-93, WILLIAM SMITH PROF PHYSICS, UNIV PA, 93-, CHAIR, DEPT PHYSICS & ASTRON, 96- *Personal Data:* b Evanston, Ill, July 14, 46; m 83, Irmgard Sieker. *Educ:* Mass Inst Technol, BS, 68; Univ Calif, Berkeley, MA, 69, PhD(physics), 72. *Hon Degrees:* MS, Univ Pa, 81. *Prof Exp:* Res assoc, Rockefeller Univ, 72-74. *Concurrent Pos:* Alexander von Humboldt award, 87-88. *Mem:* Fel Am Phys Soc; fel AAAS. *Res:* Theoretical elementary particle physics especially the experimental consequences of fundamental theories. *Mailing Add:* Dept Physics Univ Pa Philadelphia PA 19104-6396

LANGAGER, BRUCE ALLEN, POLYMER CHEMISTRY. *Current Pos:* Sr res chemist, 68-74, res specialist, 74-78, TECH SUPVR, 3M CO, 78- *Personal Data:* b Willmar, Minn, Jan 17, 42; m 64; c 2. *Educ:* Augsburg Col, BA, 64; Univ Minn, Minneapolis, PhD(org chem), 68. *Mem:* Sigma Xi. *Res:* Life sciences; surface chemistry. *Mailing Add:* 3104 13th Terr NW St Paul MN 55112

LANGAN, THOMAS AUGUSTINE, BIOCHEMISTRY. *Current Pos:* assoc prof, 71-83, PROF PHARMACOL, MED SCH, UNIV COLO, DENVER, 83- *Personal Data:* b Providence, RI, July 25, 30; m 60; c 2. *Educ:* Fordham Univ, BS, 52; Johns Hopkins Univ, PhD(biochem), 59. *Prof Exp:* Mem res staff, Med Nobel Inst, Stockholm, Sweden, 59-60; guest investr biochem, Rockefeller Inst, 60-61; mem res staff, Wenner-Gren Inst, Stockholm, Sweden, 61-62; res assoc biochem, Rockefeller Inst, 62-65; staff scientist, C F Kettering Res Lab, 65-67, investr, 67-70, sr investr, 70-71. *Concurrent Pos:* NSF fel, 59-62; from asst prof to assoc prof, Antioch Col, 67-71. *Mem:* Am Soc Biol Chemists; Am Soc Cell Biol; Am Soc Pharmacol & Exp Therapeut. *Res:* Metabolism and function of histones and nuclear phosphoproteins; control of histone phosphorylation by cyclic adenosine monophosphate and cell growth; regulation of nucleic acid synthesis in eukaryotes; effects of histone phosphorylation on chromotin structure; role of cdc2 protein kinase substrates in control of cell cycle progression. *Mailing Add:* Dept Pharmacol Univ Colo Med Ctr 4200 E Ninth Ave Denver CO 80262

LANGAN, WILLIAM BERNARD, PHYSIOLOGY. *Current Pos:* assoc prof biol, 63-80, ASST TO DIR RES, VILLANOVA UNIV, 81- *Personal Data:* b Wayne Co, Pa, Oct 31, 13; m 57; c 2. *Educ:* Univ Scranton, BS, 36; Columbia Univ, MA, 37 & 44; Fordham Univ, PhD(zool), 42. *Prof Exp:* Asst sci, Teachers Col, Columbia Univ, 36-37; asst biol, Fordham Univ, 40-42; instr physiol, NY Med Col, 42-47, assoc, 47-50, asst prof biol, 50-60, asst prof pharmacol, 58-60; sect head physiol, Food & Drug Res Labs, Inc, 60-61; NIH spec fel, State Univ NY Downstate Med Ctr, 61-62, asst prof, 62-63. *Concurrent Pos:* Lectr, Hunter Col, 60-62; consult, Food & Drug Res Labs, Inc, 61-63; training prog partic, Int Lab Genetics & Biophys, Italy, 65; vis prof, Dept Pharmacol, Thomas Jefferson Med Col, Philadelphia, 80- *Mem:* Fel AAAS; Harvey Soc; Endocrine Soc; Am Soc Zool; NY Acad Sci; Sigma Xi. *Res:* Steroids and cardiac electrophysiology; steroids and ovulation in sub-mammalian species; mechanism of hormone action at the cellular level. *Mailing Add:* 5 Langan Ave Hawley PA 18428-1523

LANGDALE, GEORGE WILFRED, MANAGEMENT OF CROP RESIDUES, CONSERVATION TILLAGE. *Current Pos:* RETIRED. *Personal Data:* b Walterboro, SC, Sept 14, 30; m 55, Eugenia Boatwright. *Educ:* Clemson Univ, BS, 57, MS, 61; Univ Ga, PhD(soil sci), 69. *Honors & Awards:* H H Bennett Award, Soil & Water Conserv Soc, 92. *Prof Exp:* Res soil scientist, Agr Res Serv, USDA, 57-96. *Mem:* Fel Am Soc Agron; fel Soil Sci Soc Am; Int Soil Sci Soc; fel Soil & Water Conserv Soc; World Asn Soil & Water Conserv. *Res:* Soil and soil sciences; agronomy; hydrology and water resources; management of crop residues with conservation tillage to control soil erosion and enhance environmental quality. *Mailing Add:* 125 Orchard Knob Lane Athens GA 30605

LANGDELL, ROBERT DANA, PATHOLOGY. *Current Pos:* fel path, 49-51, from instr to assoc prof, 51-64, PROF PATH, SCH MED, UNIV NC, CHAPEL HILL, 67- *Personal Data:* b Pomona, Calif, Mar 14, 24; m 48, Alice Pritt; c Robert D Jr & Sara E (Hendrick). *Educ:* George Washington Univ, MD, 48. *Honors & Awards:* Landsteiner Mem Award, Am Asn Blood Banks, 95. *Prof Exp:* Intern, Henry Ford Hosp, Detroit, Mich, 48-49. *Concurrent Pos:* USPHS sr res fel, 56-62 & career develop award, 62-67; mem, Hemat Study Sect, USPHS, 67-70; ed-in-chief, Transfusion, 72-82; pres, Am Asn Blood Banks, 72-73; mem, Panel Rev Blood & Blood Derivatives, Food & Drug Admin, 75-80; mem bd gov, Col Am Path, 75-80; assoc ed, Arch Path & Lab Med, 81- *Mem:* AMA; Am Soc Clin Path; Col Am Path; Am Asn Blood Banks. *Res:* Hematologic pathology; physiology of blood coagulation; hemorrhagic disorders. *Mailing Add:* 707 William Circle Chapel Hill NC 27516

LANGDON, ALLAN BRUCE, PLASMA THEORY, COMPUTATIONAL PHYSICS. *Current Pos:* staff physicist, 70-91, ASSOC DIV LEADER, PHYSICS DEPT, LAWRENCE LIVERMORE LAB, 91- *Personal Data:* b Edmonton, Alta, Dec 14, 41; m 66; c 3. *Educ:* Univ Man, BSc, 63; Princeton Univ, PhD(astrophys), 69. *Prof Exp:* Actg asst prof elec eng, Univ Calif, Berkeley, 67-69. *Concurrent Pos:* Lectr elec eng, Univ Calif, Berkeley, 69-73 & 81-82; affil mem, Ctr Plasma Physics & Fusion Eng, Univ Calif, Los Angeles, 77-78. *Mem:* Fel Am Phys Soc; Sigma Xi; Can Asn Physicists; Asn Comput Mach. *Res:* Plasma theory; computational physics; computer simulation of plasmas; numerical analysis. *Mailing Add:* L-472 Lawrence Livermore Lab Box 808 Livermore CA 94550

LANGDON, EDWARD ALLEN, MEDICINE, RADIOLOGY. *Current Pos:* RETIRED. *Personal Data:* b Los Angeles, Calif, Feb 9, 22. *Educ:* Western Res Univ, BS, 42; Univ Mich, MD, 45. *Prof Exp:* From asst prof to assoc prof, Sch Med, Univ Calif, Los Angeles, 59-70, prof radiol & chief, Radiother Div & asst dean student affairs, 70-78, prof & vchmn, Dept Radiol Oncol & asst dean student affairs, 70- *Mem:* AMA; Am Col Radiol; Radiol Soc NAm; Soc Nuclear Med; Asn Univ Radiol. *Res:* Radiation therapy. *Mailing Add:* 200 UCLA Med Plaza Suite B265 Los Angeles CA 90024

LANGDON, GLEN GEORGE, JR, COMPUTER ENGINEERING & COMPUTER SCIENCE, DATA COMPRESSION IMAGE CODING. *Current Pos:* PROF COMPUT ENG, UNIV CALIF, SANTA CRUZ, 87- *Personal Data:* b Morristown, NJ, June 30, 36; m 63, Marian Jacobsen; c Karen. *Educ:* Wash State Univ, BSEE, 57; Univ Pittsburgh, MSEE, 63; Syracuse Univ, PhD(elec eng), 68. *Prof Exp:* Engr, Westinghouse Elec Corp, 60-63; engr, IBM Corp, 63-73, res staff comput sci, 74-87. *Concurrent Pos:* Lectr, Syracuse Univ, NY, 68-69, Univ Santa Clara, 75-78, 80 & Stanford Univ, 84-85; vis prof, Univ Sao Paulo, Brazil, 71-72; mem gov bd, Comput Soc, Inst Elec & Electronics Engrs, 84-85. *Mem:* Fel Inst Elec & Electronics Engrs; Asn Comput Mach. *Res:* Data compression and arithmetic coding; image compression and processing; computer logic design. *Mailing Add:* 220 Horizon Way Aptos CA 95003-2739

LANGDON, HERBERT LINCOLN, GROSS ANATOMY, DEVELOPMENTAL ANATOMY. *Current Pos:* asst prof, 72-78, ASSOC PROF ANAT, SCH DENT MED, UNIV PITTSBURGH, 78- *Personal Data:* b Malone, NY, July 7, 35; m 72. *Educ:* St Lawrence Univ, BS, 57; Univ Mo, MA, 63; Univ Miami, PhD(biol struct), 72. *Prof Exp:* Asst prof biol, Miami-Dade Community Col, 65-68. *Concurrent Pos:* Res consortium, Cleft Palate Ctr, Univ Pittsburgh, 76. *Mem:* Am Cleft Palate Asn; Sigma Xi; Am Asn Anatomists. *Res:* Normal and abnormal morphology and development of human tongue and velopharyngeal mechanism; craniofacial development and growth; neuroanatomy. *Mailing Add:* Univ Pittsburgh 620 Salk Hall Pittsburgh PA 15261

LANGDON, KENNETH R, PLANT TAXONOMY, ENDANGERED SPECIES. *Current Pos:* RETIRED. *Personal Data:* b Cache, Okla, Aug 20, 28; m 61; c 3. *Educ:* Okla State Univ, BS, 58, MS, 60; Univ Fla, PhD(plant path, nematol, bot), 63. *Prof Exp:* Nematologist & botanist, Div Plant Indust, Fla Dept Agr & Consumer Serv, 63-91. *Mem:* Soc Europ Nematologist; Int Asn Plant Taxon; Am Soc Plant Taxonomists. *Res:* Plant systematics. *Mailing Add:* 2216 NW 49th Terr Gainesville FL 32605

LANGDON, ROBERT GODWIN, BIOCHEMISTRY. *Current Pos:* RETIRED. *Personal Data:* b Dallas, Tex, Jan 18, 23; m 45; c 4. *Educ:* Univ Chicago, MD, 45, PhD(biochem), 53. *Prof Exp:* From instr to prof physiol chem, Sch Med, Johns Hopkins Univ, 53-67; prof biochem & chmn dept, Col Med, Univ Fla, 67-69; chmn dept, Univ Va, 77-82, prof biochem, 69-82. *Concurrent Pos:* USPHS fel, Univ Chicago, 51-53; Lederle award, 54-57. *Mem:* Am Soc Biol Chemists; Am Chem Soc. *Res:* Membrane biochemistry; glucose transport; mechanism of hormone action. *Mailing Add:* Buck Creek Farm PO Box 464 Nemo TX 76070

LANGDON, TERENCE GEORGE, MECHANICAL PROPERTIES, CREEP & SUPERPLASTICITY. *Current Pos:* assoc prof, 71-76, PROF, UNIV SOUTHERN CALIF, 76- *Personal Data:* b Trowbridge, Eng, Jan 24, 39; m 68, Mady M Rodriguez. *Educ:* Univ Bristol, Eng, BSc, 61, DSc, 80; Univ London, PhD(phys metall), 65. *Prof Exp:* Res metallurgist, Univ Calif, Berkeley, 65-67; vis scientist, US Steel Corp, 67-68; res fel, Cavendish Lab, Univ Cambridge, 68-69; res assoc, Univ BC, 69-71. *Concurrent Pos:* Vis prof, Univ Melbourne, 77-78; vis scientist, Riso Nat Lab, Denmark, 84; prof, Univ NSW, 84; Japan Soc Prom Sci sr del, Kyushu Univ, 91; hon academician, Acad Sci Bashkortostan Repub, 93. *Mem:* Fel Inst Physics; fel Inst Metallurgists; fel Am Ceramic Soc; fel Am Soc Metals Int; Minerals, Metals & Mat Soc; Mat Res Soc. *Res:* Mechanical properties at high temperatures of crystalline materials including metals, ceramics, composites and rocks; emphasis on deformation mechanisms in creep and superplasticity, especially the role of grain boundaries. *Mailing Add:* Depts Mat Sci & Mech Eng Univ Southern Calif Los Angeles CA 90089-1453. *Fax:* 213-740-7797; *E-Mail:* langdon@usc.edu

LANGDON, WILLIAM KEITH, ORGANIC CHEMISTRY. *Current Pos:* RETIRED. *Personal Data:* b Hubbardston, Mich, May 8, 16; m 40; c 4. *Educ:* Mich State Univ, BS, 38, MS, 40. *Prof Exp:* Res chemist, Chrysler Corp, 39-43; res chemist, Wyandotte Chem Corp, 43-69, res supvr org chem, BASF Wyandotte Corp, 69-81. *Mem:* Am Chem Soc; Sigma Xi. *Res:* New organic chemical synthesis including heterocyclic nitrogen compounds, surfactants, acetals, epoxides and plastic intermediates. *Mailing Add:* 8091 O'Donnell Grosse Ile MI 48138-1142

LANGDON, WILLIAM MONDENG, chemical engineering; deceased, see previous edition for last biography

LANGE, BARRY CLIFFORD, PROCESS RESEARCH, FORMULATION CHEMISTRY. *Current Pos:* Process chemist, 80-84, agr chem discovery chemist, 84-87, RES MGR, ROHM & HAAS CO, 87- *Personal Data:* b Philadelphia, Pa, June 14, 52; m 74, Linda Leedom; c Julianna & Jillian. *Educ:* Stevens Inst Technol, BS, 74; Pa State Univ, PhD(chem), 79. *Concurrent Pos:* Res assoc, Mass Inst Technol, 80. *Mem:* Am Chem Soc. *Res:* Research management, design of biologically active compounds, chemical process research, kinetics and mechanisms of organic reactions; synthesis of penicillin and cephalosporin analogs and other antibiotics; physical organic chemistry including enolate alkylation; polymer chemistry; agricultural and food chemistry; biochemistry. *Mailing Add:* 1031 Barley Way Lansdale PA 19446-3200

LANGE, BRUCE AINSWORTH, CHEMISTRY OF SURFACES, CEMENT CHEMISTRY. *Current Pos:* group leader, Pinawa, Man, Atomic Energy Can, 83-86, br mgr anal chem, 86-91, br mgr, Chalk River Lab, 91-96, DIR, WASTE MGT & DECOMMISSIONING OPERS, ATOMIC ENERGY CAN, 97- *Personal Data:* b Springfield, Mass, Aug 3, 48; m 77; c 2. *Educ:* Lowell Technol Inst, BS, 70; Univ NH, PhD(chem), 74. *Prof Exp:* Fel chem, Northwestern Univ, 74-75, Univ Cincinnati, 75-76; res chemist, Nat Inst Occup Safety & Health, Cincinnati, Ohio, 76-79; group leader chem, W R Grace & Co, Cambridge, Mass, 79-83. *Mem:* Am Ceramic Soc. *Res:* X-ray crystallography; inorganic synthesis; radiopharmaceuticals; development of analytical methods for hazardous materials; surface chemistry; cement chemistry; comminution of minerals; process design; computer modelling; analytical chemistry. *Mailing Add:* Chalk River Labs Chalk River ON K0J 1J0 Can

LANGE, CARINA BEATRIZ, MARINE PHYTOPLANKTON, DIATOMS. *Current Pos:* SRA, Scripps Inst Oceanog, 86-89, asst specialist, 90-91, assoc specialist, 91-95, ASSOC RESEARCHER, SCRIPPS INST OCEANOG, 96- *Personal Data:* b Buenos Aires, Arg, July 27, 55; c Alexander Pillard. *Educ:* Univ Buenos Aires, Licenciada, 80, PhD(marine biol), 88. *Concurrent Pos:* Vis scientist, Univ Oslo, 91 & Univ Breinen, 91-93 & 96; lectr, Univ Concepcion, Chile, 92-93 & Cath Univ, Puerto Rico, 95. *Mem:* Am Soc Limnol & Oceanog; Am Geophys Union; Int Soc Diatom Res; Oceanog Soc. *Res:* Annual and interannual variations of marine phytoplankton fluxes to the sea floor; paleoproductivity; morphological studies on marine diatoms; toxic diatoms. *Mailing Add:* 9500 Gilman Dr La Jolla CA 92093-0215. *Fax:* 619-534-0784; *E-Mail:* clange@ucsd.edu

LANGE, CHARLES FORD, BIOCHEMISTRY, IMMUNOLOGY. *Current Pos:* assoc prof microbiol, 70-75, prof, 75-95, EMER PROF MICROBIOL, 96- *Personal Data:* b Chicago, Ill, Feb 16, 29; m 53; c 3. *Educ:* Roosevelt Univ, BS, 51, MS, 53; Univ Ill, PhD(biochem), 59; Am Bd Med Lab Immunol, dipl, 81. *Prof Exp:* Res assoc biochem, Univ Ill, 60-61; res assoc, Hektoen Inst Med Res, Cook Co Hosp, 61-63, head phys chem, 63-69. *Concurrent Pos:* Consult immunologist, Hines Vet Admin Hosp, 75-95. *Mem:* Am Chem Soc; Am Soc Biochem & Molecular Biol; Transplantation Soc; Am Soc Microbiol; Am Asn Immunol; AAAS. *Res:* Urinary glycoproteins; immunochemistry of streptococcal related glomerulonephritis; streptococcal M-proteins; transplantation antigens; immunology of aging; autoimmune diseases; monoclonal antitissue antibodies. *Mailing Add:* Dept Microbiol Stritch Sch Med Loyola Univ Maywood IL 60153. *E-Mail:* clange@luc.edu

LANGE, CHARLES GENE, applied mathematics; deceased, see previous edition for last biography

LANGE, CHRISTOPHER STEPHEN, RADIATION BIOPHYSICS, GENOME STRUCTURE. *Current Pos:* PROF RADIATION ONCOL & DIR RADIATION RES, COL MED, STATE UNIV NY, HEALTH SCI CTR BROOKLYN, 80-, PROF PHYSIOL & BIOPHYS, SCH GRAD STUDIES, 92- *Personal Data:* b Chicago, Ill, Feb 11, 40; m 64, 73, Eleanor E Gitlin; c Tamara A & Theodore O. *Educ:* Mass Inst Technol, Cambridge, BS, 61; Oxford Univ, Eng, DPhil, 68. *Prof Exp:* Med Res Coun res asst radiobiol, Churchill Hosp, Headington, Oxford, 61-62; NHS res officer radiobiol, Christie Hosp & Holt Radium Inst, Manchester, Eng, 62-68, NHS sr res officer, 68-69; asst prof radiol, radiobiol, biophys, Sch Med & Dent, Univ Rochester, 69-80. *Concurrent Pos:* Prin investr, Grants USDOE, NSF, NCI, NIGMS, Mathers Found, etc, 72-; vis radiobiologist, Am Inst Biol Sci, 73-79; vis prof chem, Univ Calif, San Diego, 75-76; presidential distinguished lectr, Univ Hirosaki, Japan, 79; guest scientist, Brookhaven Nat Lab, 83-; mem, Tumor Biol Comt & tumor repository utilization comt, Radiation Ther Oncol Group, Nat Proj, NIH/NCI, 88- & 93-; scholar adv comt, Kosciuszko Found, 89-; res career develop award, USDHEW/NCI, 72-77; NIH/Div Res Grants, SBIR Special Study Sect-2, 93. *Mem:* Radiation Res Soc; Biophys Soc; NY Acad Sci; Sigma Xi; AAAS. *Res:* Molecular and cellular bases of cellular and organisimal radiation effects and aging; DNA damage and repair; DNA structure in mammalian chromosomes; viscoelastometry and other hydrodynamic behavior of DNA; differentiation control (polarity) in tissues; assays for improved cancer therapy. *Mailing Add:* State Univ NY Health Sci Ctr 450 Clarkson Ave PO Box 1212 Brooklyn NY 11203. *E-Mail:* lange_c@hscbklyn.edu

LANGE, EUGENE ALBERT, STRUCTURAL INTEGRITY TECHNOLOGY, FRACTURE MECHANICS. *Current Pos:* RETIRED. *Personal Data:* b Stevens Pt, Wis, Oct 22, 23; m 51. *Educ:* Univ Wis, BS, 45, MS, 51. *Honors & Awards:* Res Pub Award, Naval Res Lab, 68. *Prof Exp:* Res metal, Univ Wis, 51-53; res engr, Gray Iron Res Inst, 53-56; surv res metal, Naval Res Lab, 56-80; consult, Eugene A Lange, 80-90. *Concurrent Pos:* Lectr, Union Col, Schenectady, NY, 70-88. *Mem:* Am Soc Metals. *Res:* Casting technology; non-magnetic steels; fracture mechanics; dynamic fracture toughness. *Mailing Add:* 9503 Veirs Dr No 3 Rockville MD 20850

LANGE, GAIL LAURA, ALGEBRA. *Current Pos:* CONSULT, 80- *Personal Data:* b Chicago, Ill, June 28, 46. *Educ:* Univ Wis, BS, 69, PhD(math), 75. *Prof Exp:* Instr math, Univ Maine, Farmington, 72-75, asst prof, 75-80. *Mem:* Am Math Soc; Math Asn Am. *Res:* Investigation of which finite p-groups can be the Frattini subgroup of finite p-groups. *Mailing Add:* Shaw Hill Rd Rd 1 PO Box 1203 Farmington ME 04938

LANGE, GORDON DAVID, NEUROPHYSIOLOGY, BIOLOGICAL OCEANOGRAPHY. *Current Pos:* NEUROPHYSIOLOGIST, NAT INST NEUROL & COMMUN DIS & STROKE, NIH, 84- *Personal Data:* b Douglas, Ariz, Jan 15, 36; c 3. *Educ:* Calif Inst Technol, BS, 58; Rockefeller Univ, PhD(biophys), 65. *Prof Exp:* Res assoc biophys, Rockefeller Univ, 65-66; asst res neuroscientist, Univ Calif, San Diego, 66-68, asst prof, 68-74, assoc prof neurosci, 74-84. *Mem:* Soc Neurosci; NY Acad Sci; Sigma Xi. *Res:* Neurophysiology of sensory systems; studies of the dynamics of interactions among nerve cells; mathematical and computer models of interactions of organisms. *Mailing Add:* Nat Inst Neurol Dis & Stroke Div Intramural Res Bldg 36 Rm 2A03 Bethesda MD 20892

LANGE, GORDON LLOYD, TERPENOID SYNTHESIS, PHOTOCHEMICAL CYCLOADDITIONS. *Current Pos:* from asst prof to assoc prof chem, 67-84, PROF CHEM & BIOCHEM, UNIV GUELPH, 85- *Personal Data:* b Edmonton, Alta, Mar 1, 37; m 64; Gail Stephen; c Stephen & Margot. *Educ:* Univ Alta, BSc, 59; Univ Calif, Berkeley, PhD(org chem), 63. *Honors & Awards:* Union Carbide Award for Chem Educ, 86. *Prof Exp:* Res chemist, Procter & Gamble Co, 62-65; lectr org chem, Univ Western Ont, 65-67. *Concurrent Pos:* Fel, 3M, 91. *Mem:* Am Chem Soc; fel Chem Inst Can. *Res:* Synthesis of natural products and compounds with potential biological activity; organic photochemistry; structural elucidation of natural products; free radical fragmentation reactions. *Mailing Add:* Dept Chem & Biochem Univ Guelph Guelph ON N1G 2W1 Can. Fax: 519-766-1499; E-Mail: lange@chembio.uoguelph.ca

LANGE, IAN M, GEOLOGY, GEOCHEMISTRY. *Current Pos:* assoc prof, 73-77, PROF GEOL, UNIV MONT, 77-, CHMN DEPT. *Personal Data:* b New York, NY, Nov 11, 40. *Educ:* Dartmouth Col, BA, 62, MA, 64; Univ Wash, PhD(geol), 68. *Prof Exp:* Asst prof geol, Fresno State Col, 68-73. *Mem:* Geochem Soc; Geol Soc Am. *Res:* Isotope geology, economic geology. *Mailing Add:* Dept Geol Univ Mont Missoula MT 59802-0001

LANGE, JAMES NEIL, JR, PHYSICS. *Current Pos:* VPRES, INTERCOMP INC, STILLWATER, 85- *Personal Data:* b Bridgeport, Conn, May 4, 38; m 58; c 2. *Educ:* Pa State Univ, PhD(physics), 64. *Prof Exp:* From asst prof to assoc prof, 65-71, prof physics, Okla State Univ, 71-, Regents Prof Physics, 81- *Concurrent Pos:* Vis prof, Univ Nottingham, 76, Nat Univ Mex, 78; sr vis fel, Gt Brit, 76. *Mem:* Am Phys Soc; Am Geophys Union. *Res:* Acoustics; geophysics. *Mailing Add:* 6920 Redlands Rd Stillwater OK 74075

LANGE, KENNETH L, GENETICS & MEDICAL IMAGING, COMPUTATIONAL PROBABILITY & STATISTICS. *Current Pos:* PROF BIOSTAT & PHARMACIA & UPJOHN FOUND RES PROF BIOSTAT & PROF MATH, UNIV MICH, 94- *Personal Data:* b Angola, Ind, June 16, 46; m 70; c 2. *Educ:* Mich State Univ, BS, 67; Mass Inst Technol, MS, 68, PhD(math), 71. *Honors & Awards:* George W Snedecor Award, 93. *Prof Exp:* Asst prof math, Univ NH, 71-72; NIH postdoctoral fel biomath, Univ Calif, Los Angeles, 72-74, from asst prof to assoc prof, 74-83, prof, 83-94, dept chair, 85-94. *Concurrent Pos:* NIH res career develop award, Univ Calif, Los Angeles, 79-84; vis prof statist, Mass Inst Technol, 83-84 & Harvard Univ, 90-91; mem, Joint Comt Math Life Sci, Am Math Soc & Soc Indust & Appl Math, 84-89. *Mem:* Soc Indust & Appl Math; Am Soc Human Genetics; Am Statist Asn. *Res:* Biomathematical modeling in genetics, medical imaging, demography, and physiology; applied stochastic processes and computational statistics. *Mailing Add:* Dept Biomath Univ Mich Sch Pub Health II 1420 Washington Heights Ann Arbor MI 48109-2029

LANGE, KLAUS ROBERT, PHYSICAL CHEMISTRY, SURFACE CHEMISTRY. *Current Pos:* CONSULT, 90- *Personal Data:* b Berlin, Germany, Jan 15, 30; US citizen; m 51, Sulvia Pollack; c Stephen M & Karen J. *Educ:* Univ Pa, AB, 52; Univ Del, MS, 54, PhD(phys chem), 56. *Prof Exp:* Res chemist, Atlantic Refining Co, 55-59; sr res chemist, Philadelphia Quartz Co, 59-67, res assoc, 67-69; lab mgr, Betz Lab Inc, 69-74; res dir, Quaker Chem Corp, 75-86, sr tech adv, 86-90. *Concurrent Pos:* Mem bd dir, Chem Data Systs, 70-75. *Mem:* Am Chem Soc; Tech Asn Pulp & Paper Inst. *Res:* Physical adsorption; heterogeneous catalysis; surface chemistry of silica and related solids; silicate solutions, fundamental properties; colloidal suspensions; detergency; pollution control; polymer applications; lignin and paper chemistry; defoamers. *Mailing Add:* 805 Lombard St Philadelphia PA 19147-1316

LANGE, LEO JEROME, MATHEMATICS. *Current Pos:* from asst prof to assoc prof, 60-83, dept chmn, 88-91, PROF MATH, UNIV MO, COLUMBIA, 83-,. *Personal Data:* b New Rockford, NDak, Aug 29, 28; m 55; c 4. *Educ:* Regis Col, Colo, BS, 52; Univ Colo, MA, 56, PhD(math), 60. *Prof Exp:* Instr math, Univ Colo, 52-56, asst, 58-60; mathematician, Boulder Labs, Nat Bur Stand, 56-60. *Mem:* Math Asn Am; Am Math Soc. *Res:* Continued fractions; complex analysis; approximations & expansions. *Mailing Add:* Univ Mo Columbia MO 65211-0001

LANGE, LESTER HENRY, MATHEMATICS. *Current Pos:* SPEC ASST TO DEAN, MOSS LANDING MARINE LAB, CALIF, 88- *Personal Data:* b Concordia, Mo, Jan 2, 24; m 47, 62; c 5. *Educ:* Valparaiso Univ, AB, 48; Stanford Univ, MS, 50; Univ Notre Dame, PhD, 60. *Honors & Awards:* L R Ford Sr Award, Math Asn Am, 72. *Prof Exp:* Instr math, Valparaiso Univ, 50-53, asst prof, 54-56; instr, Univ Notre Dame, 56-57 & 59-60; from asst prof to prof, San Jose State Univ, 60-70, actg head dept, 61-62, chmn dept, 62-70, dean sch sci, 70-88, emer dean & emer prof math, San Jose State Univ, 88- *Mem:* AAAS; Math Asn Am; London Math Soc; Nat Coun Teachers Math. *Res:* Complex variable; topology. *Mailing Add:* Moss Landing Marine Lab PO Box 450 Moss Landing CA 95039-0450

LANGE, ROBERT CARL, MAGNETIC RESONANCE IMAGING, RADIOLOGICAL PHYSICS. *Current Pos:* asst prof, 69-76, ASSOC PROF RADIOL PHYSICS, SCH MED, YALE UNIV, 76- *Personal Data:* b Stoneham, Mass, Aug 26, 35; m 59, 82; c 2. *Educ:* Northeastern Univ, BS, 57; Mass Inst Technol, PhD(chem), 62. *Prof Exp:* Group leader physics, Monsanto Res Corp, 62-69. *Concurrent Pos:* Consult, R J Schulz Assocs, 73-; tech dir magnetic resonance imaging, Yale New Haven Hosp, 69- *Mem:* AAAS; Am Chem Soc; Am Phys Soc; Soc Nuclear Med; Sigma Xi. *Res:* Magnetic resonance imaging; computer applications to medicine. *Mailing Add:* Dept Radiol MR Sect Sch Med Yale Univ 333 Cedar St PO Box 208042 New Haven CT 06520-8042

LANGE, ROBERT DALE, HEMATOLOGY. *Current Pos:* dir, Univ Tenn, Knoxville, 77-81, prof, 78-85, chmn dept, 78-81, RES PROF, MEM RES CTR, UNIV TENN, KNOXVILLE, 65-, EMER PROF & CHMN, DEPT MED BIOL, 85- *Personal Data:* b Redwood Falls, Minn, Jan 24, 20; m 44; c 2. *Educ:* Macalester Col, AB, 41; Wash Univ, MD, 44. *Prof Exp:* Dir, St Louis Regional Blood Ctr, 48-51; instr med, Washington Univ, 51-53; instr clin med, Univ Minn, 53-54; asst prof med, Washington Univ, 56-61; chief physician, Vet Admin Hosp, 61-62; assoc prof med, Med Col, Univ Ga, 62-65. *Concurrent Pos:* Consult, Milledgeville State Hosp & Vet Admin Hosp, Augusta, Ga; hematologist, Atomic Bomb Casualty Comn, 51-53. *Mem:* Am Soc Hemat; Am Fedn Clin Res; fel Am Col Physicians; fel Int Soc Hemat. *Res:* Internal medicine. *Mailing Add:* Univ Tenn Mem Res Ctr 1924 Alcoa Hwy Knoxville TN 37920

LANGE, ROBERT ECHLIN, JR, WILDLIFE DISEASES, WILDLIFE DISEASE PREVENTION. *Current Pos:* dept asst regional dir Fed Aid, 88-94, CHIEF FED AID, FISH & WILDLIFE, 94- *Personal Data:* b Janesville, Wis; m 70. *Educ:* Colo State Univ, BS, 68, 70, MS, 73, DVM, 74. *Prof Exp:* Wildlife vet wildlife dis, NMex Dept Game & Fish, 74-80; adj prof, NMex State Univ, 78-80; field diagnostician, Nat Wildlife Health Lab, 80-88. *Concurrent Pos:* Wildlife dis consult, Colo Wild Animal Dis Ctr, 72-74; adj prof, Biol Dept, NMex Highlands Univ, 75-77. *Mem:* Wild Animal Dis Asn; Am Vet Med Asn; Wildlife Soc; Am Asn Wildlife Vet (secy treas, 81-). *Res:* Investigation into the game management implications of wildlife diseases in elk, Rocky Mountain bighorn sheep and other mammals; wildlife disease management in migratory waterfowl; mammals and wildlife disease prevention. *Mailing Add:* Fish & Wildlife Serv Div Fed Aid 4401 N Fairfax Dr Rm 140 Arlington VA 22203

LANGE, WILLIAM JAMES, SURFACE PHYSICS. *Current Pos:* RETIRED. *Personal Data:* b Sandusky, Ohio, Jan 20, 30; m 51; c 4. *Educ:* Oberlin Col, AB, 51; Mass Inst Technol, PhD(physics), 56. *Prof Exp:* Asst phys electronics, Mass Inst Technol, 51-56; physicist, Res Labs, Westinghouse Elec Corp, 56-64, mgr vacuum physics, 64-88. *Mem:* Am Phys Soc; Am Vacuum Soc. *Res:* Ultrahigh vacuum; interaction of gases with surfaces. *Mailing Add:* 3917 Hickory Hill Rd Murrysville PA 15668

LANGE, WINTHROP EVERETT, PHARMACY. *Current Pos:* dir labs, 68-74, VPRES, INT DIR TECH SERV, PURDUE FREDERICK CO, 74- *Personal Data:* b Appleton, Wis, Sept 22, 25; m 48; c 2. *Educ:* Univ Wis, BS, 52, MS, 53, PhD(pharm, chem), 55. *Prof Exp:* Asst pharm, Univ Wis, 52-54; asst prof, SDak State Col, 55-58; from asst prof to assoc prof, 58-66, prof & chmn dept, Mass Col Pharm, 66-68. *Concurrent Pos:* Adj prof, A&M Schwartz Col Pharm & Health Sci, 78-82. *Mem:* Am Chem Soc; Am Pharmaceut Asn; Soc Cosmetic Chem; Acad Pharmaceut Sci; Int Fedn Socs Cosmetic Chem (pres, 76-77). *Res:* Synthesis of metal chelates as pro-drugs; pharmaceutical analysis. *Mailing Add:* 124 Woodside Dr Greenwich CT 06830-6732

LANGE, YVONNE, MEMBRANE BIOGENESIS, CHOLESTEROL MOVEMENT IN CELLS. *Current Pos:* assoc prof, 81-86, PROF BIOCHEM & PATH, RUSH MED COL, 84- *Personal Data:* b Durban, SAfrica, Apr 5, 41; m 82. *Educ:* London Univ, BSc, 62; Oxford Univ, DPhil(theoret physics), 66. *Prof Exp:* Instr biophys, Harvard Med Sch, 70-72, lectr, 73-75; res fel, Sch Med, Boston Univ, 75-76, from asst prof to assoc prof, 76-81. *Mem:* Am Soc Biol Chemists; Am Soc Cell Biol. *Res:* Intracellular movement of newly synthesized cholesterol in cultured cells with the objective of elucidating mechanisms by which eukaryotic cells regulate their membrane cholesterol content. *Mailing Add:* Dept Biochem Rush Univ 1653 W Congress Pkwy Chicago IL 60612. Fax: 312-942-4228

LANGEBARTEL, RAY GARTNER, MATHEMATICS, ASTRONOMY. *Current Pos:* Asst math, 46-48, from instr to assoc prof, 48-70, PROF MATH, UNIV ILL, URBANA, 70- *Personal Data:* b Quincy, Ill, Apr 27, 21; m 45; c 4. *Educ:* Univ Ill, AB, 42, AM, 43, PhD(math), 48. *Concurrent Pos:* Vis res assoc, Stockholm Observ, 50-51. *Res:* Function theory; stellar dynamics. *Mailing Add:* 1107 S Lynn Champaign IL 61820-6330

LANGEL, ROBERT ALLAN, GEOPHYSICS. *Current Pos:* physicist, Commun Br, 62-63, Fields & Plasmas Br, 63-74, GEOPHYSICIST GEOMAGNETISM, GEOPHYS BR, GODDARD SPACE FLIGHT CTR, NASA, 74- *Personal Data:* b Pittsburgh, Pa, May 25, 37; m 59, Carolyn M Wills; c 3. *Educ:* Wheaton Col, AB, 59; Univ Md, College Park, MS, 71, PhD(physics), 73. *Honors & Awards:* Except Performance Award, NASA, 81, Except Sci Achievement Medal, 82. *Prof Exp:* Physicist, Optics Br, US Naval Res Lab, 59-62. *Concurrent Pos:* Proj scientist for Magsat Spacecraft; ed, Earth & Planet Int, 76, Geophys Res Lect, 82, J Geophys Res, 85; vis scholar, Bullard Labs, Cambridge Univ, 83-84, Purdue Univ, 92-93; chmn, Working Group Mainfield & Secd Vacation, Int Asn Geomagnetism &

Aeronomy, 87-91; assoc ed, J Geophys Res, 91- *Mem:* Fel Am Geophys Union; Int Asn Geomagnetism & Aeronomy. *Res:* Utilization of surface and near-earth satellite magnetic field measurements to study lithospheric magnetic anomalies, upper mantle conductivity and core-mantle processes; derivation of geomagnetic field models. *Mailing Add:* 14910 Laurel Oaks Lane Laurel MD 20707. *Fax:* 301-286-1616; *E-Mail:* langel@geomag.gsfc.nasa.gov

LANGELAND, KAARE, DENTAL MATERIALS, EXPERIMENTAL PATHOLOGY. *Current Pos:* prof, Dept Gen Dent, Sch Dent Med, 69-70, prof & chmn, Dept Endodontics, 70-87, EMER PROF, DEPT RESTORATIVE DENT & ENDODONTOLOGY, SCH DENT MED, UNIV CONN HEALTH CTR, FARMINGTON, 87-; ADJ PROF, DEPT ENDODONTICS, SCH GRAD DENT, BOSTON UNIV, 92- *Personal Data:* b Saltdal, Norway, Nov 3, 16. *Educ:* Vet Col Norway, grad, 38; Norweg State Dent Sch, DDS, 42; Univ Oslo, PhD, 57. *Honors & Awards:* Badge of Honor in Silver & Prize, Norweg Dent Asn, 59. *Prof Exp:* Asst, Dent Diag Dept, Gaustad Hosp, 42-52; res assoc, Norweg Inst Dent Res, 52-63; assoc prof oral histol & chmn dept, univ & proj dir, Minn Mining & Mfg, State Univ NY Buffalo, 63, prof oral biol, 64-69. *Concurrent Pos:* USPHS grants, Res Found, State Univ NY Buffalo, 63; 3M grant, 63-69; USPHS grants, 63-68, 69-70 & 77-79; Serco grant, 66-67; Univ Conn Res Found grants, 70-73 & 76-77; Off Naval Res Contract, 71-77; teacher, Norweg State Dent Sch, 48-49; ed, Scand Dent J, 57-63; vis lectr, Boston Univ; vchmn comn dent res, Int Dent Fedn, chmn working group biol testing dent mat; mem, Coun Stand Dent Mats & Devices, Am Mat Stand Inst; Norweg state rep, Inter-Nordic Comt Planning Nordic Bur Stand Dept Mat, 61-62; mem, Working Group Dent Terminology, Int Orgn Stand, 65. *Mem:* Norweg Dent Asn; hon mem Dent Asn SAfrica; hon mem Dent Asn South Rhodesia; hon mem SAfrican Prosthodont Soc; corresp mem Finnish Dent Soc. *Res:* Experimental pathology regarding biomaterials; evaluation of the biologic properties of methods; devices, and materials used in dentistry before they are released for general use; author of numerous books, chapters, articles and abstracts. *Mailing Add:* 340 Westmont West Hartford CT 06117

LANGENAU, EDWARD E, JR, WILDLIFE BIOLOGY, PSYCHOLOGY. *Current Pos:* Wildlife res biologist, 74-85, BIG GAME SUPVR, STATE MICH, 86- *Personal Data:* b Brooklyn, NY, Oct 28, 46; m 69, Diana G; c Erik & David. *Educ:* Rensselaer Polytech Inst, BS, 68; Mich State Univ, MS, 73, PhD(wildlife mgt), 76; MPA, 81. *Mem:* Soc Am Foresters; Wildlife Soc. *Res:* Public behavior; white-tailed deer behavior; forest recreation; attitude toward clearcutting; hunter behavior; natural resource policy analysis; public administration. *Mailing Add:* PO Box 1067 Indian River MI 49749-1067

LANGENBERG, DONALD NEWTON, SOLID STATE PHYSICS. *Current Pos:* CHANCELLOR, UNIV MD SYST, 90- *Personal Data:* b Devils Lake, NDak, Mar 17, 32; m 53, Patricia Warrington; c Karen, Julia, John & Amy. *Educ:* Iowa State Univ, BS, 53; Univ Calif, Los Angeles, MS, 55, Berkeley, PhD(physics), 59. *Hon Degrees:* MA, Univ Pa, 71, DSc, 85. *Honors & Awards:* John Price Wetherill Medal, Franklin Inst, 75. *Prof Exp:* Actg instr physics, Univ Calif, Berkeley, 58-59; NSF fel, 59-60; from asst prof to assoc prof physics, Univ Pa, 60-67, prof physics, 67-, dir lab res struct matter, 72-74, vprovost grad studies & res, 74-79, prof elec eng & sci, 76-; chancellor, Univ Ill, Chicago, 83-90. *Concurrent Pos:* Sloan Found fel, 62-64; Guggenheim Found fel, 66-67; assoc prof, Advan Normal Sch, Univ Paris, 66-67; distinguished vis scientist, Mich State Univ, 69; mem, Nat Acad Sci-Nat Acad Eng-Nat Res Coun Panel Adv to Cryogenics Div, Nat Bur Stand, 69-70, chmn, 70-75; mem, Comn I, Int Union Radio Sci, 69-; vis prof, Calif Inst Technol, 71; guest researcher, Cent Inst Low Temperature Study, Bayer Acad Sci & Tech Univ Munich, 74; mem, Adv Comt Res, NSF, 74-77, Coun Govt Relations & chmn, Adv Coun, 77-80, dep dir, NSF, 80-82; trustee, Assoc Univs, Inc, 75-80; mem, Nat Comn Res, 78-80; mem, bd trustees, Univ Pa, 90-; chmn & bd dir, Nat Asn State Univ & Land-Grant Col, 91- *Mem:* Fel AAAS (pres, 90); fel Am Phys Soc (pres, 93). *Res:* Cyclotron resonance and Fermi surface studies in metals and semiconductors; tunneling and Josephson effects in superconductors; precision measurement and fundamental physical constants; low temperature physics; nonequilibrium phenomena in superconductors. *Mailing Add:* 3112 Old Court Rd Baltimore MD 21208. *E-Mail:* dnl@umsa.umd.edu

LANGENBERG, PATRICIA WARRINGTON, BIOSTATISTICS, CLINICAL TRIALS & WOMENS HEALTH. *Current Pos:* ASSOC PROF BIOSTATIST, UNIV MD, BALTIMORE, 90-, VCHAIR, DEPT EPIDEMIOL & PREV MED, 96- *Personal Data:* b Des Moines, Iowa, Sept 10, 31; m 53, Donald N; c Karen K, Julia A, John N & Amy P. *Educ:* Iowa State Univ, BS, 53; Temple Univ MA, 75, PhD(math), 78. *Prof Exp:* From instr to asst prof math, LaSalle Col, 75-80; asst prof statist, Temple Univ, 80-83; assoc prof biomet, Sch Pub Health, Univ Ill, 83-90. *Concurrent Pos:* Co-chair, Women's Health Group, Univ Md, Baltimore; mem, Rehab Merit Rev, Dept Veterans Affairs. *Mem:* Am Statist Asn; Biomet Soc; Caucus Women Statist. *Res:* Clinical trials; biostatistics; mathematical statistics; women's health. *Mailing Add:* Dept Epidemiol & Prev Med Univ Md Baltimore 660 W Redwood St Baltimore MD 21201. *Fax:* 410-706-8013; *E-Mail:* plangenb@umabnet.ab.umd.edu

LANGENBERG, WILLEM G, PLANT PATHOLOGY, PLANT VIROLOGY. *Current Pos:* RES PLANT PATHOLOGIST, AGR RES SERV, USDA, 67- *Personal Data:* b Djombang, Indonesia, Apr 16, 28; US citizen; m 55; c 3. *Educ:* Calif State Col Long Beach, BS, 63; Univ Calif, Berkeley, PhD(plant path), 67. *Prof Exp:* Assoc prof plant path, 67-80, prof, life sci dept, Univ Nebr-Lincoln, 80- *Mem:* Am Phytopath Soc. *Res:* Study of plant-virus-vector relationships with labeled antibodies or viruses; light and electron microscopy radioautography. *Mailing Add:* RR Martell Martell NE 68404

LANGENHEIM, JEAN HARMON, PLANT BIOCHEMICAL ECOLOGY & EVOLUTION. *Current Pos:* from asst prof to assoc prof, 66-73, chmn, Biol Dept, 74-76, PROF BIOL, UNIV CALIF, SANTA CRUZ, 73- *Personal Data:* b Homer, La, Sept 5, 25; div. *Educ:* Univ Tulsa, BS, 46; Univ Minn, MS, 49, PhD(bot, geol), 53. *Prof Exp:* Investr, Nat Geol Serv, Colombia, 53; res assoc, Univ Calif, Berkeley, 54-59; teaching assoc, Univ Ill, 59-62; Asn Univ Women fel, Harvard Univ, 62-63; res assoc, Bot Mus, 63-66. *Concurrent Pos:* Mem teaching staff & bd trustees, Rocky Mountain Biol Lab, 54-65; lectr, Mills Col, 55-56; from instr to asst prof, San Francisco Col Women, 56-59; scholar, Radcliffe Inst Independent Study, 63-64; mem exec comt, Org Trop Studies, 72-77, acad vpres, 75-77; vis prof biol, Harvard Univ, 74; mem, NSF comn floral inventory Amazon, 75-87; mem, ecol adv comm, Environ Protection Agency, 77-81; mem, US Nat Comt, Int Union Biol Sci, 89-94. *Mem:* Int Soc Chem Ecol (pres, 86-87); Bot Soc Am; Ecol Soc Am (vpres, 80-81, pres, 86-87); fel AAAS; Asn Trop Biol (pres, 85); Soc Econ Biol (pres, 93-94). *Res:* Paleoecological studies of amber; evolutionary and physio-ecological studies of tropical resin-producing and other terpene-producing plants; concepts of ecology; plants and human affairs. *Mailing Add:* Dept Biol Univ Calif Santa Cruz CA 95064. *Fax:* 408-459-3139; *E-Mail:* lang@biology.ucsc.edu

LANGENHEIM, RALPH LOUIS, JR, PALEONTOLOGY, STRATIGRAPHY. *Current Pos:* from asst prof to prof geol, 59-92, cur paleont, Mus Natural Hist, 83-92, EMER PROF GEOL, UNIV ILL, URBANA, 92-, EMER CUR PALEONT, MUS NATURAL HIST, 92- *Personal Data:* b Cincinnati, Ohio, May 26, 22; m 46, 62, 70, 94, Casey D; c Victoria & Ralph L. *Educ:* Univ Tulsa, BS, 43; Univ Colo, MS, 47; Univ Minn, PhD(geol), 51. *Prof Exp:* Asst prof geol, Coe Col, 50-52; asst prof paleont, Univ Calif, 52-59. *Concurrent Pos:* Foreign expert, Inst Geol Nac, Colombia, 53; adv, Geol Surv Can, 57 & Cent Geol Surv, Repub China, 81; foreign assoc, Geol Surv Iran, 73; partner, Lanman Assocs, Consult Geologists, 74-; consult curric & prog, Fac Geol & Mining, Polytech Univ Albania, 92. *Mem:* Geol Soc Am; Paleont Soc (secy, 62-70); Am Asn Petrol Geol; Soc Econ Paleont & Mineral; Geol Soc London. *Res:* Invertebrate paleontology and stratigraphy; Paleozoic of western and central North America; Tertiary of southern Mexico; Permian and Carboniferous of Iran; petroleum and energy geology; approximately 125 publications. *Mailing Add:* Univ Ill Dept Geol 245 NHB 1301 W Green St Urbana IL 61801

LANGER, ARTHUR M, MINERALOGY, ENVIRONMENTAL SCIENCES. *Current Pos:* res assoc environ sci, 65-66, asst prof mineral, 66-68, ASSOC PROF MINERAL MT SINAI SCH MED, 68-, ASSOC PROF POLYPEPTIDE, MEMBRANE RES, 85; DIR, ENVIRON SCI LAB, INST APPL SCI, BROOKLYN COL, CITY UNIV NEW YORK, 85- *Personal Data:* b New York, NY, Feb 18, 36; m 62, 67; c 4. *Educ:* Hunter Col, BA, 56; Columbia Univ, MA, 62, PhD(mineral), 65. *Prof Exp:* Res assoc mineral, Columbia, 62-65. *Concurrent Pos:* Adj assoc prof, Queens Col, NY, 68-70; consult, NIH, Bethesda Md, 74, Int Agencies Res Cancer, Lyon WHO, 74, Inst Pub Health, Norway, 77, Ministry Mines, Johannesburg, SAfrica, 77, Int Metalworkers Fedn, Geneva, 80, Ctr Dis Control, Atlanta, 84, Nat Acad Sci, 84, Consumer Prod Safety Comn, Washington, DC, 86. *Mem:* AAAS; Geol Soc Am; Electron Probe Analysis Soc Am; Geochem Soc; Mineral Soc Am. *Res:* Metamorphic and igneous petrology; clay mineralogy; secondary mineralization; instrumentation; microparticulate identification, analysis and interaction in the human environment. *Mailing Add:* 6 Rochambeau Dr Hartsdale NY 10530

LANGER, DIETRICH WILHELM, SOLID STATE PHYSICS. *Current Pos:* PROF ELEC ENG, UNIV PITTSBURGH, 87- *Personal Data:* b Berlin, Ger, Aug 13, 30; US citizen; m 61; c 4. *Educ:* Tech Univ Berlin, MS, 57, PhD(physics), 60. *Honors & Awards:* Alexander von Humboldt Award, 72. *Prof Exp:* From res physicist to sr res physicist, Aerospace Res Labs, Wright-Patterson Air Force Base, 57-65, group leader, electronic properties, Semiconductors Group, 65-87. *Concurrent Pos:* Eve lectr, Univ Dayton, 59-60; grant, Ecole Normale Superieure, Paris, 64-65; adv, Max Planck Inst Solid State Study, 72-73; fel Indust Col Armed Forces, 75-76. *Mem:* Fel Am Phys Soc; sr mem Inst Elec & Electronics Engrs. *Res:* Optical, electronic and electrooptical properties of semiconductors and devices; materials research; research and development administration. *Mailing Add:* Elec Eng Dept Univ Pittsburgh 348 Benedum Hall Pittsburgh PA 15261

LANGER, GEORGE EDWARD, OBSERVATIONAL STELLAR EVOLUTION, CHEMICAL EVOLUTION OF THE MILKY WAY. *Current Pos:* from asst prof to assoc prof, 69-85, PROF PHYSICS, COLO COL, 85- *Personal Data:* m 63, Josephine Moroney; c Mary A, Sara, & James. *Educ:* Univ Notre Dame, BS & BA, 59; Cornell Univ, MS, 63; Univ Colo, PhD(astrophys), 69. *Prof Exp:* Woodrow Wilson Found teaching intern, Tuskegee Univ, 63-65. *Concurrent Pos:* Vis astronr, Lick Observ & Univ Calif Observ, 71-96. *Mem:* Am Astron Soc; Int Astron Union; Royal Astron Soc; AAAS. *Res:* Physics; atomic abundances in old stellar populations, nucleosynthesis and mixing in small mass stars, stellar mass loss, cold interstellar clouds, and the early chemical evolution of the galaxy. *Mailing Add:* 1928 N Prospect St Colorado Springs CO 80903. *E-Mail:* elanger@cc.colorado.edu

LANGER, GLENN A, MEDICINE. *Current Pos:* assoc prof, Univ Calif, Los Angeles, 66-69, assoc dir, Cardiovasc Res Lab, 66-87, vchmn, Dept Physiol, 67-87, PROF MED & PHYSIOL, MED CTR, UNIV CALIF, LOS ANGELES, 69-, CASTERA PROF CARDIOL, 78-, DIR, CARDIOVASC RES LAB & ASSOC DEAN RES, 87- *Personal Data:* b Nyack, NY, May 5, 28; m 54; c 1. *Educ:* Colgate Univ, BA, 50; Columbia Univ, MD, 54. *Prof Exp:* Intern, Mass Gen Hosp, 54-55; asst res, Columbia-Presby Med Ctr, 57-58; sr resident, Mass Gen Hosp, 59-60; clin instr, Los Angeles Co Cardiovasc Res

Lab & Med Ctr, Univ Calif, Los Angeles, 60-62; asst prof med, Columbia Univ, 63-66. *Concurrent Pos:* Chmn exec comt, Basic Sci Coun & bd dirs, Am Heart Asn, 76-78; Griffith vis prof cardiol, 79; Macy fac scholar, 79-80. *Mem:* Am Heart Asn; Am Physiol Soc; Am Soc Clin Invest; Am Asn Physicians; Soc Gen Physiologists. *Res:* Myocardial physiology and metabolism. *Mailing Add:* Dept Med & Physiol Univ Calif Sch Med 675 Circle Dr S Rm 3645 Los Angeles CA 90095-1760

LANGER, HORST G, INORGANIC CHEMISTRY. *Current Pos:* res chemist, 58-64, sr res chemist, 64-68, ASSOC SCIENTIST, DOW CHEM USA, 68- *Personal Data:* b Breslau, Ger, Dec 29, 27; US citizen; m 55; c 2. *Educ:* Brunswick Tech Univ, Dipl, 54, Dr rer nat(chem), 56. *Prof Exp:* Asst inorg analytical chem, Brunswick Tech Univ, 51-56; res assoc inorg chem, Ind Univ, 56-58. *Mem:* Am Chem Soc; Am Soc Mass Spectrometry; Int Confedn Thermal Analysis; fel NAm Thermal Analytical Soc; Ger Chem Soc. *Res:* Analytical, dental and organometallic chemistry; mass spectrometry; thermal analysis; fire retardants; catalysts. *Mailing Add:* 28 Joyce Rd Wayland MA 01778-4516

LANGER, JAMES STEPHEN, STATISTICAL MECHANICS. *Current Pos:* dir, Inst Theoret Physics, 89-95, PROF PHYSICS, UNIV CALIF, SANTA BARBARA, 82- *Personal Data:* b Pittsburgh, Pa, Sept 21, 34; m 58, Elinor G Aaron; c Ruth, Stephen & David. *Educ:* Carnegie Inst Technol, BS, 55; Univ Birmingham, PhD, 58. *Honors & Awards:* Oliver Buckley Prize, Am Phys Soc, 97. *Prof Exp:* Instr physics, Carnegie-Mellon Univ, 58-64, from asst prof to prof, 64-82, assoc dean, Mellon Inst Sci, 71-74. *Concurrent Pos:* Vis assoc prof, Cornell Univ, 66-67; Guggenheim fel, Harvard Univ, 74-75. *Mem:* Nat Acad Sci; fel Am Phys Soc; Am Acad Arts & Sci; fel AAAS. *Res:* Theoretical solid state physics; kinetics of phase transformations. *Mailing Add:* Physics Dept Broida Hall Univ Calif Santa Barbara CA 93106. *Fax:* 805-893-2902; *E-Mail:* langer@physics.ucsb.edu

LANGER, LAWRENCE MARVIN, NUCLEAR PHYSICS. *Current Pos:* from instr to prof, Ind Univ, Bloomington, 38-59, actg chmn dept, 61-62 & 65-66, chmn, 66-73, EMER PROF PHYSICS, IND UNIV, BLOOMINGTON, 79- *Personal Data:* b New York, NY, Dec 22, 13; m 36. *Educ:* NY Univ, BS, 34, MS, 35, PhD(physics), 38. *Hon Degrees:* DSc, Ind Univ, 88. *Honors & Awards:* Samuel F B Morse Medal. *Prof Exp:* Asst physics, NY Univ, 34-38. *Concurrent Pos:* Res assoc, Radiation Lab, Mass Inst Technol, 41-42; alt group leader, Los Alamos Atomic Bomb Proj, 43-45; sci consult, US War Dept, 45; expert consult, AEC, 48-74, US Energy Res & Develop Admin, 74-; consult & observer, Greenhouse Atomic Bomb Tests, Marshall Islands, 51; adv consult, Nat Res Coun, 57-60; dir, Off Naval Res & NSF res nuclear spectros, 63-; adv consult, Nuclear Data Proj, Nat Acad Sci-Nat Res Coun. *Mem:* AAAS; fel Am Phys Soc. *Res:* Nuclear physics; artificial and natural radioactivity; beta ray spectra; neutron scattering; D-D reaction; beta and gamma coincidence measurements; Cockroft-Walton accelerator; Geiger Counter; cyclotron; counting equipment; microwave radar; underwater sound; ballistics; nuclear spectroscopy and nuclear weapons; double beta decay; mass of the neutrino; shapes of the allowed and forbidden beta spectra. *Mailing Add:* 1342 Southdowns Dr Bloomington IN 47401

LANGER, R M, OPTICS, BIOPHYSICS. *Current Pos:* RETIRED. *Personal Data:* b New York, NY, Dec 1, 99. *Educ:* Calif Inst Technol, PhD(physics), 26. *Prof Exp:* Sr physicist, Tech Opers, 50-52; mgr, Bege Co, 52-70. *Mem:* Am Phys Soc; AAAS. *Mailing Add:* 46 Park St Arlington MA 02174

LANGER, ROBERT MARTIN, CHEMICAL ENGINEERING. *Current Pos:* RETIRED. *Personal Data:* b Boston, Mass, May 29, 25. *Educ:* Yale Univ, BS, 45, DEng, 52; Mass Inst Technol, SM, 48. *Prof Exp:* dep mgr dir, Badger BV, The Hague, Neth, 70-74, mgr dir, 74-78; sr vpres, Badger Am Inc, Cambridge, 81-83; sales mgr, Badger Co Inc, Cambridge, Mass, 68-70, vpres proj admin, 78-80, vpres & treas, 83-87. *Mem:* Am Inst Chem Engrs. *Mailing Add:* 280 Commonwealth Ave Boston MA 02116-2422

LANGER, ROBERT SAMUEL, BIOENGINEERING, BIOMEDICAL SCIENCE. *Current Pos:* From asst prof to assoc prof, Dept Nutrit & Food Sci, 78-85, prof, Dept Appl Biol Sci, 85-88, GERMESHAUSEN PROF, DEPT CHEM ENG, MASS INST TECHNOL, 88-; RES ASSOC SURG, BOSTON CHILDREN'S HOSP, 74- *Personal Data:* b Aug 29, 48; US citizen; m 88, Laura Feigenbaum; c Michael & Susan. *Educ:* Cornell Univ, BS, 70; Mass Inst Technol, ScD, 74. *Hon Degrees:* Dr, Eidgenossische Tech Sch, Zurich, 96. *Honors & Awards:* Walter F Enz Lectr, Univ Kans, 89; Founders Award, Controlled Release Soc, 89, Outstanding Pharmaceut Paper Award, 90 & 92; Creative Polymer Chem Award, Am Chem Soc, 89, Perlman Mem Award Lectr, 92, Phillips Award, 92; Clemson Award, Soc Biomat, 90; Prof Prog Award, Am Inst Chem Engrs, 90, Charles M A Stine Award, 91, William Walker Award, 96; Sandoz-Dorsey lectr, Ohio State Univ, 91; Ashton-Cary Lectr, Ga Inst Technol, 91; Sidney Riegelman Lectr, Univ Calif, San Francisco, 91; Organon Teknika Award, Europ Soc Artificial Organs, 91; Louis W Busse Lectr, Univ Wis, 91; Miles Distinguished Lectr, Univ Pittsburgh, 92; Kelly Distinguished Lectr, Purdue Univ, 92; Priestley Lectr, Pa State Univ, 93; Kurt Wohl Mem Lectr, Univ Del, 93; Distinguished Pharmaceut Scientist Award, Am Asn Pharmaceut Scientists, 93, Ebert Prize, Am Pharmaceut Asn, 95 & 96. *Concurrent Pos:* Vis asst prof nutrit & food sci, Mass Inst Technol, 77-78; consult, numerous co; ed, Biomat, 83-; pres, Controlled Release Soc, 91-92; chair, Am Inst Med & Biol Eng Col Fels, 95-96. *Mem:* Nat Acad Sci; Inst Med - Nat Acad Sci; Biomed Engr Soc; Controlled Release Soc; Am Soc Artificial Internal Organs; Am Chem Soc; fel Soc Biomat; fel Am Inst Med & Biol Eng; Am Inst Chem Engrs; Am Acad Arts & Sci; Sigma Xi. *Res:* Polymer drug delivery systems; tumor neovascularization; application of enzymes in medicine; biomaterials; tissue engineering. *Mailing Add:* Dept Chem Eng Mass Inst Technol 77 Massachusetts Ave Cambridge MA 02139. *Fax:* 617-258-8827

LANGER, SIDNEY, INORGANIC CHEMISTRY. *Current Pos:* RETIRED. *Personal Data:* b New York, NY, Dec 15, 25; m 51; c Gail. *Educ:* NY Univ, AB, 49; Ill Inst Technol, PhD(chem), 55. *Prof Exp:* Chemist, Oak Ridge Nat Lab, 54-60; mem res staff, Gen Atomic Div, Gen Dynamics Corp, 60-69, group leader, Nuclear Fuels Group, Res & Develop Div, Gulf Gen Atomic, 69-71, mgr gas cooled fast breeder reactor fuels, 77-81, mem sr res staff, 69-83; prin prog specialist, TMI-2 Accident Eval Prog, EG&G Idaho, Inc; sr scientist, Sci Appl Int, 89-93. *Concurrent Pos:* Group leader fuels & mat develop, gas-cooled fast reactor project, Gen Atomic Co, 71- *Mem:* AAAS; Sigma Xi; Am Chem Soc; fel Am Nuclear Soc. *Res:* Nuclear reactor chemistry; physical chemistry and thermodynamics of high temperature systems; phase equilibria; fission product behavior in fuels; fission product release; fuel processing and reprocessing; nuclear reactor safety. *Mailing Add:* PO Box 22062 San Diego CA 92192. *E-Mail:* philane@aol.com

LANGERMAN, NEAL RICHARD, CHEMICAL & ENVIRONMENTAL SAFETY. *Current Pos:* asst prof, 75-83, ASSOC PROF CHEM, UTAH STATE UNIV, 83-; PRES, CHEM SAFETY ASN, SAN DIEGO, CALIF, 83. *Personal Data:* b Philadelphia, Pa, Mar 11, 43. *Educ:* Franklin & Marshall Col, AB, 65; Northwestern Univ, PhD(chem), 69. *Prof Exp:* NIH fel chem, Yale Univ, 69-70; asst prof biochem, Sch Med, Tufts Univ, 70-75. *Mem:* Am Soc Biol Chemists; Biophys Soc; Calorimetry Soc; Undersea Med Soc; Am Chem Soc. *Res:* Thermodynamic studies of protein reactions, especially flavin-flavoprotein interactions; microcalorimetry; fluorescence spectroscopy; analytical ultracentrifugation; chemical safety; management of hazardous waste; chemical resource recovery. *Mailing Add:* Chem Safety Asn 9163 Chesapeake Dr San Diego CA 92123-1002. *Fax:* 619-565-6267; *E-Mail:* chemsaf@ix.netcom.com

LANGFELDER, LEONARD JAY, GEOTECHNICAL & COASTAL ENGINEERING. *Current Pos:* CONSULT ENGR, 88- *Personal Data:* b Lynbrook, NY, Feb 5, 33; m 55; c 3. *Educ:* Univ Fla, BSCE, 59, MSE, 60; Univ Ill, PhD(civil eng), 64. *Prof Exp:* Res assoc coastal eng, Univ Fla, 60-62; vis lectr civil eng, Univ Ill, 64; from asst prof to prof civil eng, NC State Univ, 69-78, prof marine sci & eng & head dept, 78-80, dir, Ctr Marine, Earth, Atmospheric Sci, 69-78, prof & head, Dept Marine, Earth & Sci, 80- 82, 83-85; asst secy, Nat Resources, NC, 82-83; vpres & mgr dir, Harbor Br, Oceanog Inst, Inc, 86-88. *Concurrent Pos:* Mem soils, geol & found cmt, Hwy Res Bd, Nat Acad Sci-Nat Res Coun, 65- *Mem:* Am Soc Civil Engrs. *Res:* Soil properties, principally shear strength and compaction properties of cohesive soils; improved foundation engineering principles; coastal processes. *Mailing Add:* 129 S Plantation Circle Pointe Vedra Beach FL 32082

LANGFITT, THOMAS WILLIAM, NEUROSURGERY. *Current Pos:* SR FEL, MGT DEPT, WHARTON SCH, UNIV PA, 97- *Personal Data:* b Clarksburg, WVa, Apr 20, 27; m 53; c 3. *Educ:* Princeton Univ, AB, 49; Johns Hopkins Univ, MD, 53. *Prof Exp:* Intern gen surg, Johns Hopkins Univ Hosp, 53-54; asst resident gen surg, Johns Hopkins Univ Hosp, 54-55, from asst resident to chief resident neurosurg, 57-61; assoc, Univ Pa, 61-63, from asst prof to assoc prof, 63-68, Charles Frazier prof neurosurg, Med Sch, 68-87, head dept, Univ Hosp, 68-87, vpres health affairs, 74-87; pres & chief exec officer, Glen Meade Trust Co, 87-97. *Concurrent Pos:* Res fel, Johns Hopkins Univ Hosp, 57-60; contractor, US Army Chem Corp, 57-; head, Sect Neurosurg, Pa Hosp, 61-68; bd dir, NY Life Ins Co. *Mem:* Inst Med-Nat Acad Sci; Am Philos Soc (secy). *Res:* Pathophysiology and metabolism in acute brain injuries. *Mailing Add:* 260 Beech Hill Rd Wynnewood PA 19096

LANGFORD, COOPER HAROLD, III, PHYSICAL INORGANIC CHEMISTRY. *Current Pos:* VPRES RES, UNIV CALGARY, 92- *Personal Data:* b Ann Arbor, Mich, Oct 14, 34; m 59, Martha Whitney; c Robert, Cooper & Holly. *Educ:* Harvard Univ, AB, 56; Northwestern Univ, PhD(chem), 59. *Prof Exp:* NSF fel, Univ Col, London, 59-60; instr chem, Amherst Col, 60-61, from asst prof to assoc prof, 61-67; from assoc prof to prof, Carleton Univ, 67-80; prof chem & chmn dept, Nat Sci & Eng Res Coun Can, Concordia Univ, 80-87, assoc vrector res, 87-90, dir phys & math sci, 90-92. *Concurrent Pos:* Vis asst prof, Columbia Univ, 64; Alfred P Sloan Found fel, 68-70; consult, Inland Waters Directorate, Can, 73; consult, Nat Health & Welfare Can, 77; mem, Chem Grants Comt, Nat Res Coun Can, 75-78, chmn, 77-78; chem chmn, Coun Can Univ, 81-83; mem, strategic grants comt, open sect, Nat Sci Eng Res Coun Can, 85- *Mem:* Fel AAAS; Am Chem Soc; Royal Soc Chem; fel Chem Inst Can; fel Royal Soc Can. *Res:* Applications to energy problems; inorganic photochemistry; kinetics in analysis; solution physical chemistry. *Mailing Add:* Univ Calgary 2500 University Dr NW Calgary AB T2N 1N4 Can. *Fax:* 403-289-8926

LANGFORD, DAVID, MECHANICAL ENGINEERING, NUCLEAR ENGINEERING. *Current Pos:* RETIRED. *Personal Data:* b New York, NY, May 6, 34; m 90, Stephney A Foster; c Laura J, Meryl D, Jennie (Hubbard) & Joshua B. *Educ:* NY Univ, BS, 56, MS, 57; Ill Inst Technol, MS, 59; Rensselaer Polytech Inst, DEngSc, 65. *Prof Exp:* From asst physicist to assoc physicist, IIT Res Inst, 57-59; from sr analytical engr to asst proj engr, Pratt & Whitney Aircraft, United Aircraft Corp, 59-66; from asst prof to assoc prof mech eng, Drexel Univ, 66-72; regional radiation noise rep, US Environ Protection Agency, 72-82; engr, US Nuclear Reg Comn, 82-91. *Mem:* AAAS; Am Phys Soc; Am Nuclear Soc; Am Soc Mech Engrs; NY Acad Sci. *Res:* Psychology and education of engineers; nuclear engineering; magnetohydrodynamics; superconductivity; conduction heat transfer; fluid flow; environmental science/Nuclear Environmental Protection Agency. *Mailing Add:* 1201 Seminole Blvd Apt 94 Largo FL 33770

LANGFORD, DEAN TED, LIGHTING & PRECISION. *Current Pos:* PRES, OSRAM SYLVANIA INC, 93- *Personal Data:* b June 19, 39; m, Nancy Hirsch; c Douglas T & John P. *Educ:* Univ Ill, BS, 62. *Hon Degrees:* LHD, Salem State Col, 90. *Prof Exp:* Regional sales mgr, IBM, 80-81; corp dir mgt develop, Armonk, 81-82; group dir commun, Ryebrook, NY, 82-83; vpres mkt, GTE Commun Systs, 83-84; pres, GTE Elec Prod, 84-93. *Mem:* Nat Elec Mfg Asn; Phys Sci Inc. *Mailing Add:* Osram Sylvania Inc 100 Endicott St Danvers MA 01923-3623

LANGFORD, ERIC SIDDON, MATHEMATICS. *Current Pos:* PROF MATH, CALIF STATE UNIV, CHICO, 82- *Personal Data:* b New York, NY, May 23, 38; m 59; c 1. *Educ:* Mass Inst Technol, SB, 59; Rutgers Univ, MS, 60, PhD(math), 63. *Honors & Awards:* L R Ford Award, Math Asn Am, 71. *Prof Exp:* Res specialist, Autonetics Div, NAm Rockwell, 63-64; asst prof math, Naval Postgrad Sch, 64-69; assoc prof math, Univ Maine, Orono, 69-77, prof, 77-82. *Concurrent Pos:* Vis assoc, Daniel H Wagner, Assocs, 66; collab ed, Am Math Monthly, 69-71, assoc ed, 71-75; vis assoc prof math, Calif Inst Technol, 72-73; vis scholar, Univ Calif, Berkeley, 76; vis distinguished prof math, Calif Polytech State Univ, San Luis Obispo, 77-78. *Res:* Geometrical aspects of Banach spaces; Riesz spaces. *Mailing Add:* Dept Math & Statist Calif State Univ Chico CA 95929-0525

LANGFORD, FLORENCE, NUTRITION. *Current Pos:* from asst prof to assoc prof, 42-61, actg dean, 70-72, PROF FOOD & NUTRIT, TEX WOMAN'S UNIV, 62- *Personal Data:* b Celina, Tex, Sept 20, 12. *Educ:* Tex Woman's Univ, BS, 32, MA, 38; Iowa State Univ, PhD(nutrit), 60. *Prof Exp:* High sch teacher, Tex, 32-34; teacher home econ, Kilgore Jr Col, 35-37; instr nutrit & home mgt, Univ Tenn, 38-41. *Mem:* Am Chem Soc; Am Dietetic Asn; Am Home Econ Asn; Am Pub Health Asn; Int Fedn Home Econ; Sigma Xi. *Res:* Food and nutrition; human nutrition; energy metabolism. *Mailing Add:* PO Box 425767 Denton TX 76204

LANGFORD, FRED F, ECONOMIC GEOLOGY. *Current Pos:* assoc prof, 62-71, PROF GEOL SCI, UNIV SASK, 71- *Personal Data:* b Toronto, Ont, Dec 19, 29; m 53; c 3. *Educ:* Univ Toronto, BA, 53; Queen's Univ, Ont, MA, 55; Princeton Univ, PhD(geol), 60. *Prof Exp:* Geologist, Imp Oil Co, 53-54; geologist, Ont Dept Mines, 54-57; assoc prof geol, Univ Kans, 58-62. *Mem:* Mineral Asn Can; Geol Asn Can. *Res:* Economic geology; potash geology; uranium deposits. *Mailing Add:* Dept Geol Sci Univ Sask Saskatoon SK S7N 0W0 Can

LANGFORD, GEORGE, PHYSICAL & MECHANICAL METALLURGY. *Current Pos:* ASSOC PROF MAT ENG, DREXEL UNIV, 75- *Personal Data:* b Chicago, Ill, Dec 26, 36; m 68; c 2. *Educ:* Mass Inst Technol, SB, 59, ScD(metall), 66. *Prof Exp:* Instr metall, Mass Inst Technol, 60-62; scientist, Edgar C Bain Lab Fundamental Res, US Steel Corp, Pa, 66-71; res specialist, Monsanto, Chemstrand Res Ctr, Inc, Durham, 72-75. *Mem:* AAAS; Am Soc Metals; Am Inst Mining, Metall & Petrol Engrs. *Res:* Optical and electron metallography of heavily deformed metals and theory of their strain hardening; wire drawing; steel casting by diffusion solidification and liquid infiltration. *Mailing Add:* 32 Bodine Rd Berwyn PA 19312-1237

LANGFORD, GEORGE MALCOLM, CELL BIOLOGY, MICROTUBULES. *Current Pos:* PROF, DARTMOUTH COL, 93- *Personal Data:* b Halif, NC, Aug 26, 44; m 68, Sylvia Tyler; c Joy, Grant & George III. *Educ:* Fayetteville State Univ, BS, 66; Ill Inst Technol, MS, 69, PhD(cell biol), 71. *Hon Degrees:* MA, Dartmouth Col, 94. *Prof Exp:* Fel biophys cytol, Univ Pa, 71-73; asst prof cell biol, Univ Mass, 73-76, Col Med, Howard Univ, 77-79; from assoc prof to prof cell biol, Sch Med, Univ NC, Chapel Hill, 79-91. *Concurrent Pos:* NIH fel, 71-73; Macy fel, Marine Biol Lab, 76 & 77, Steps fel, 78; consult, NIH, 81-; Marine Biol Lab, 82-; NSF Adv Comt Cell Molecular Biol, 84-; trustee, Marine Biol Lab, 84-; cell biol prog dir, NSF, 88-89; prof, Dartmouth Col, 91-, Ernest Everett Just Prof Natural Sci, Dept Biol Sci, Fac Arts & Sci, 91- *Mem:* AAAS; Am Soc Cell Biol; Sigma Xi; NY Acad Sci. *Res:* Vesicle transport on axoplasmic microtubules and the structure and function of microtubules; wave propagation in the microtubular axostyle; properties of axonal and dendritic microtubules; axonal transport. *Mailing Add:* Dartmouth Col Dept Biol Sci 6044 Gilman Labs Hanover NH 03755-3576

LANGFORD, PAUL BROOKS, PHYSICAL ORGANIC CHEMISTRY. *Current Pos:* from asst prof to assoc prof, 62-70, PROF CHEM, DAVID LIPSCOMB COL, 70-, CHMN DEPT, 80- *Personal Data:* b Lockesburg, Ark, Aug 11, 30; m 59; c 1. *Educ:* Okla State Univ, BS, 52, MS, 54; Ga Inst Technol, PhD(chem), 62. *Prof Exp:* Instr chem, Ga Inst Technol, 56-62. *Mem:* Am Chem Soc. *Res:* Rates and mechanisms of reactions of organic halogen compounds; charge transfer complex compounds. *Mailing Add:* Dept Chem David Lipscomb Univ Granny White Pike Nashville TN 37204-3951

LANGFORD, ROBERT BRUCE, ORGANIC CHEMISTRY, CHEMICAL EDUCATION. *Current Pos:* from instr to prof, 64-86, chmn dept, 68-74, EMER PROF CHEM, E LOS ANGELES COL, 86-; ADJ PROF CHEM, L A PIERCE COL, 92- *Personal Data:* b San Francisco, Calif, Mar 7, 19; m 57, Wilma R Ostrander. *Educ:* Univ Calif, Los Angeles, BS, 48; Univ Southern Calif, MS, 63, PhD, 72. *Prof Exp:* Chemist petrol analysis, Southern Pac Co, 49-54; res chemist pesticides, Stauffer Chem Co, 54-58; lab mgr org synthesis, Cyclo Chem Corp, 58-61; teacher chem, Los Angeles City Schs, 61-64. *Mem:* Am Chem Soc; Sigma Xi. *Res:* Organic synthesis; sulfur compounds; photochemistry. *Mailing Add:* 644 Haverkamp Dr Glendale CA 91206

LANGFORD, ROLAND EVERETT, TOXICOLOGY. *Current Pos:* CONSULT HAZARDOUS MAT & INDUST HYG, 85-; LT COLONEL MED SERV CORP, US ARMY, 92- *Personal Data:* b Owensboro, Ky, Apr 11, 45; m 67, Son Hee Shin; c John E & Lee S. *Educ:* Ga Southern Univ, BS, 67; Univ Ga, MS, 71, PhD(phys chem), 74; Univ NC, PhD(health physics), 94. *Prof Exp:* Chemist & instr, Environ Sci Educ Agency, 71-72; instr chem & math, Bainbridge Col, 73-74; res assoc, Chem Dept, Univ Ga, 74; asst prof chem & geol, Ga Mil Col, 75-77, head, Sci Dept, 76-77; asst prof chem, Ga Southern Col, 77-78; chief, Clin Chem Lab Sci Div, US Army Acad Health Sci, 78-79; sanit engr & environ sci officer, US Army Environ Hyg Agency, 79-81; comdr environ sanitation team, Fifth Prevent Med Unit, 81-83. *Concurrent Pos:* adj fac, Univ MD Korea, 81-83, Purdue Univ, 95. *Mem:* Am Chem Soc; fel Am Inst Chemists; Asn Mil Surgeons US; Nat Environ Health Asn; Am Acad Sanitarians; Royal Asiatic Soc; Health Physics Soc. *Res:* Toxicology of mlitary releant chemicals and exposures especially weapon system combustion products. *Mailing Add:* US Army Med Res Detachment MCMR-UWW 2800Q St Bldg 824 Wright-Patterson AFB OH 45433-7947. *E-Mail:* langfordr@falcon.al.mil

LANGFORD, RUSSELL HAL, HYDROLOGY, ENVIRONMENTAL CHEMISTRY. *Current Pos:* RETIRED. *Personal Data:* b North Platte, Nebr, Nov 14, 25; m 46, Mary Imogene Ellenbecker; c Stephen R, David G, Amy L & Russell J. *Educ:* Univ Nebr, BSc, 49. *Prof Exp:* Hydrologist, US Geol Surv, 49-66, asst chief, Off Water Data Coord, 66-68, chief, Off Water Data Coord, 68-80, assoc chief hydrologist, 80-85. *Concurrent Pos:* Mem, Int Souris-Red River Eng Bd, Int Joint Comn US & Can; alt chmn, US Nat Comt Sci Hydrol; US mem comn hydrol, World Meteorol Org, Intergovt Coun, Int Hydrolog Prog, UNESCO. *Mem:* Am Chem Soc; Am Water Works Asn; Am Geophys Union; Water Pollution Control Fedn; AAAS. *Res:* Water chemistry; geochemistry; hydrology of the Missouri River basin, Colorado River basin, great basin. *Mailing Add:* 8380 Greensboro Dr Apt 926 McLean VA 22102

LANGFORD, WILLIAM FINLAY, DIFFERENTIAL EQUATIONS, BIFURCATION THEORY. *Current Pos:* assoc prof, 82-87, chair, Dept Math & Statist, 90-96, PROF MATH, UNIV GUELPH, CAN, 88- *Personal Data:* b Thunder Bay, Ont, Sept 11, 43; m 92, Anne Ellis; c Cathena, Anne, Allison & Robert. *Educ:* Queens Univ, Can, BSc, 66; Calif Inst Technol, PhD(appl math), 71. *Prof Exp:* From asst prof to assoc prof math, McGill Univ, 70-82. *Concurrent Pos:* Res visitor, Univ Nice, France, 79-80; adj prof appl math, Univ Waterloo, 83-; vis prof math, Univ Houston, 85-87; mem bd dirs, Can Math Soc, 85-89; vis prof, Tianjin Univ China, 87; res visitor, Inst Math & Appl, Minn, 89; Univ Guelph Forster fel, 89; Can-UK Bilateral Exchange fel, 89; prog organizer, Fields Inst Res Math Sci, 92-93, dep dir, 96-97; BC Mattews Alumni fel, 96. *Mem:* Am Math Soc; Soc Indust & Appl Math; Can Math Soc; Can Appl Math Soc. *Res:* Theory of bifurcation for nonlinear differential equations; effects of symmetry; numerical algorithms for bifurcation problems and applications in science and engineering. *Mailing Add:* Dept Math & Statist Univ Guelph Guelph ON N1G 2W1 Can. *Fax:* 519-837-0221; *E-Mail:* wlangfor@uoguelph.ca

LANGHAM, ROBERT FRED, PATHOLOGY. *Current Pos:* RETIRED. *Personal Data:* b Grand Ledge, Mich, Jan 31, 12; m 37; c 5. *Educ:* Calvin Col, AB, 35; Mich State Univ, MS, 37, DVM, 42, PhD, 50. *Prof Exp:* From instr to prof vet path, 38-88, actg chmn, Dept Path, Col Vet Med, 73-75, emer prof vet path, Mich State Univ, 88-. *Mem:* Am Vet Med Asn; Am Col Vet Path; Conf Res Workers Animal Dis; Int Acad Path. *Res:* Leptospirosis; neoplasms and joint disease in animals; co-author and author. *Mailing Add:* 330 Shoesmith Haslett MI 48840

LANGHANS, ROBERT W, FLORICULTURE. *Current Pos:* From asst prof to assoc prof, 56-68, PROF FLORICULT, CORNELL UNIV, 68- *Personal Data:* b Flushing, NY, Dec 29, 29; m 52; c 3. *Educ:* Rutgers Univ, BS, 52; Cornell Univ, MS, 54, PhD(floricult), 56. *Honors & Awards:* Blauvelt Award, 55; Kenneth Post Award, Am Soc Hort Sci, 65. *Mem:* Am Soc Hort Sci; Am Soc Plant Physiol; Int Soc Hort Sci. *Res:* Effects of photoperiod and temperature on growth and flowering. *Mailing Add:* Dept Floriculture Cornell Univ Col Agr 15-D Plant Sci Bldg Ithaca NY 14853

LANGHEINRICH, ARMIN P(AUL), CHEMISTRY, FUEL ENGINEERING. *Current Pos:* Asst chemist, Utah Cooper Div, 59, jr scientist, Res Ctr, Western Mining Div, 59-62, from asst scientist to scientist, 62-71, sr scientist, Res Dept, Metal Mining Div, 71-79, MGR, TECH & ADMIN SERV, KENNECOTT MINERALS CO, 79- *Personal Data:* b Planitz, Ger, Sept 1, 26; US citizen; m 49; c 3. *Educ:* Univ Utah, BS, 58, MA, 62. *Concurrent Pos:* Spec instr chem, Salt Lake Ctr Continuing Educ, Brigham Young Univ, 63-77. *Mem:* Am Chem Soc; Am Soc Testing & Mat (secy, 77-82). *Res:* Application of x-ray fluorescence techniques to laboratory and on-stream analyses; energy dispersion x-ray analysis with conventional and radioisotope excitation; optical emission spectroscopy applied to geochemical samples and to refined copper; development of high purity copper standards; environmental analysis. *Mailing Add:* 230 M St Salt Lake City UT 84103-3544

LANGHOFF, CHARLES ANDERSON, CHEMICAL PHYSICS. *Current Pos:* DOW CHEM, 81- *Personal Data:* b New Orleans, La, June 27, 47; m 73; c 3. *Educ:* Tulane Univ, BS, 69; Calif Inst Technol, PhD(chem), 74. *Prof Exp:* Fel chem, IBM Res Lab, San Jose, 73-75; asst prof chem, Ill Inst Technol, 75-81. *Concurrent Pos:* Res Corp grant, 77-78. *Mem:* Am Chem Soc; Am Phys Soc. *Res:* Picosecond spectroscopy; dynamic of liquids; theory of radiationless transitions; nonlinear optics. *Mailing Add:* Dow Chem Co 1776 Bldg Midland MI 48674

LANGHOFF, PETER WOLFGANG, COMPUTATIONS, APPLIED SCIENCE. *Current Pos:* from asst prof to assoc prof, 69-77, PROF CHEM, IND UNIV, BLOOMINGTON, 77- *Personal Data:* b New York, NY, Jan 19, 37; m 62, Judith D Perrotta; c Lisa, Kristen (Grunnan) & Allison. *Educ:* Univ Hofstra, BS, 58; State Univ NY, Buffalo, PhD(physics), 65. *Prof Exp:* Physicist, Cornell Aeronaut Labs, Inc, Cornell Univ, 62-65; fel, Harvard Univ, 67-69. *Concurrent Pos:* Vis fel, Joint Inst Lab Astrophys, 75-76, Nat Res Coun fel, 78-79; vis prof, Univ Colo, Boulder, 76 & Univ Paris, Orsay, 81,; prof chem & fac assoc, Supercomput Res Inst, Fla State Univ, 85-86; vpres res, SRT, Inc, 86-88. *Mem:* Am Phys Soc; Am Chem Soc. *Res:* Atomic and molecular physics; interaction of radiation and matter; atomic and molecular structure; molecular photoionization; supercomputer computations; advanced solar energy technology; hydrogen production; x-ray photophysics and chemistry. *Mailing Add:* Dept Chem Ind Univ Bloomington IN 47405. *Fax:* 812-855-8300; *E-Mail:* langhoff@othello.ucs.indiana.edu

LANGILLE, ALAN RALPH, CROP PHYSIOLOGY. *Current Pos:* From asst prof to assoc prof agron, 73-79, PROF AGRON & BOT, UNIV MAINE, ORONO, 79- *Personal Data:* b Amherst, NS, Apr 2, 38; m 67; c 1. *Educ:* McGill Univ, BS, 60; Univ Vt, MS, 62; Pa State Univ, PhD(agron), 67. *Concurrent Pos:* Vis prof, dept plant path, Kan State Univ, 79-80. *Mem:* Am Soc Agron; Am Soc Hort Sci; Potato Asn Am. *Res:* Hormonal control of tuber initiation and subsequent growth in the potato; growth regulator physiology; salt tolerance in conifers; protoplast regeneration. *Mailing Add:* Dept Plant Sci Univ Maine Deering Hall Orono ME 04469-0001

LANGILLE, BRIAN LOWELL, CARDIOVASCULAR CELL BIOLOGY. *Current Pos:* assoc prof path, 85-94, ASSOC PROF PATH, OBSTET & GYNEC, UNIV TORONTO, 94- *Personal Data:* b Victoria, BC, July 26, 47; m 93, Susan Lee Adamson; c Ellen Rebecca. *Educ:* Univ BC, BSc, 69, MSc, 70, PhD(zool), 75. *Prof Exp:* Asst prof biophys, Univ Western Ont, 77-79, asst prof physiol, 79-85. *Concurrent Pos:* Sr res fel, Heart & Stroke Found, Ont, 78-79, career investr, 89-; mem, Coun Basce Sci, Am Heart Asn; counr, Biophys Soc Can, 91- *Mem:* Am Asn Pathologists; AAAS; Biophys Soc Can; Can Atherosclerosis Soc; Am Heart Asn. *Mailing Add:* Toronto Hosp 200 Elizabeth St CCRW 1-836 Toronto ON M5G 2C4 Can

LANGLAND, OLAF ELMER, RADIOLOGY, DENTISTRY. *Current Pos:* PROF & HEAD, DIV ORAL & MAXILLOFACIAL DENT RADIOL, DENT DIAG SCI, SCH DENT, HEALTH SCI CTR, UNIV TEX, SAN ANTONIO, 75-, PROF, DEPT RADIOL, SCH MED, 75- *Personal Data:* b Madrid, Iowa, May 30, 25; wid; c 4. *Educ:* Univ Iowa, DDS, 51, MS, 61; Am Bd Oral & Maxillo-Facial Radiol, dipl, 81; Am Bd Oral Med, dipl, 84. *Honors & Awards:* Merit Award, Coun Int Rels, Am Dent Asn, 75. *Prof Exp:* From instr to assoc prof oral diag & radiol, Col Dent, Univ Iowa, 59-69, head dept, 64-69; prof oral diag-med-radiol & head dept, Sch Dent, La State Univ, New Orleans, 69-75. *Concurrent Pos:* USPHS grant, Col Dent, Univ Iowa, 64-66; consult, Wilford Hall USAF Hosp, Lackland, Tex, 68-77; mem subcomt proposed dent x-ray mach, Am Nat Stand Inst, 68-74; staff dentist, Charity Hosp, New Orleans, 69-75; vis prof, Univ Fed Alagoas, Maceio, Brazil, 73; chmn, oral diag/med sect, Am Asn Dent Schs, 73 & dent radiol sect, 84; mem Nat Bd Test Const Comt Oral Path & Dent Radiol, Am Dent Asn, 79-83. *Mem:* Fel Am Col Dent; Am Acad Dent Radiol (pres, 84); Orgn Teachers Oral Diag (pres, 73); Am Asn Dent Schs; Int Asn Oral & Maxillo-Facial Radiol. *Res:* Panoramic radiography; educational research in dentistry; clinical research in oral manifestations of systemic disease; application of modern intensifying screens in diagnostic radiology. *Mailing Add:* Radiol Univ Tex Health Sci Ctr San Antonio 7703 Floyd Cur Dr San Antonio TX 78229-3992

LANGLANDS, ROBERT P, MATHEMATICS. *Current Pos:* PROF MATH, INST ADVAN STUDY, 72- *Personal Data:* b New Westminster, BC, Oct 6, 36; m 56, Charlotte L Cheverie; c William, Robert, Sarah & Thomasin. *Educ:* Univ BC, BA, 57, MA, 58; Yale Univ, PhD(math), 60. *Hon Degrees:* DSc, Univ BC, McMaster Univ, City Univ New York Grad Ctr, 85, Univ Waterloo, 88, Universite de Paris VII, 89 & McGill Univ, 92, Toronto, 93. *Honors & Awards:* Wilbur Cross Medal, Yale Univ, 75; Cole Prize, Am Math Soc, 82; Common Wealth Award, 84; Nat Acad Sci Award in Math, 88; Wolf Prize, 96. *Prof Exp:* Instr math, Princeton Univ, 60-61, lectr, 61-62, from asst prof to assoc prof, 62-67; prof math, Yale Univ, 67-72. *Concurrent Pos:* Mem, Inst Advan Study, 62-63; Miller fel, Univ Calif, Berkeley, 64-65; Sloan fel, 64-66; res prof, Ctr Math, 94- *Mem:* Nat Acad Sci; Royal Soc London; Am Math Soc; Can Math Soc; AAAS; Sigma Xi; Royal Soc Can. *Res:* Group representations; automorphic forms. *Mailing Add:* Inst Advan Study Princeton NJ 08540. *E-Mail:* rpl@math.ias.edu

LANGLEBEN, MANUEL PHILLIP, GLACIOLOGY, MICROMETEOROLOGY. *Current Pos:* Res atmospheric physics, McGill Univ, 53-57, lectr, 57-59, from asst prof to assoc prof, 59-69, dir, McGill Ctr Northern Studies & Res, 77-80, prof, 69-89, asst chmn, 84-89, EMER PROF PHYSICS, MCGILL UNIV, 89- *Personal Data:* b Poland, Apr 9, 24; nat Can; m 48; c 3. *Educ:* McGill Univ, BSc, 49, MSc, 50, PhD(physics), 53. *Mem:* Royal Meteorol Soc; Glaciol Soc; Am Geophys Union; Sigma Xi; fel Royal Soc Can. *Res:* Physics of ice; sea ice; ice drift. *Mailing Add:* Rutherford Physics Bldg 3600 University St Montreal PQ H3A 2T8 Can. *Fax:* 514-398-8434; *E-Mail:* plangl@physics.lan.mcgill.ca

LANGLEY, ALBERT E, PHARMACOLOGY, TOXICOLOGY. *Current Pos:* from asst prof to prof, Dept Pharmacol & Toxicol, Wright State Univ, 77-90, vchair dept, 80-82, chair dept, 82-85, ASSOC DEAN ACAD AFFAIRS, SCH MED, WRIGHT STATE UNIV, DAYTON, OHIO, 90- *Personal Data:* b July 2, 43. *Educ:* Waynesburg Col, BS, 67; Ohio State Univ, Columbus, PhD(pharmacol), 74. *Prof Exp:* Postdoctoral fel, Dept Pharmacol, Med Ctr, Univ Colo, Denver, 74-76; scientist, Cardiovasc Sect, Warner-Lambert Res Inst, Morris Plains, NJ & Ann Arbor, Mich, 76-77. *Concurrent Pos:* Course dir med pharmacol, Wright State Univ, 78-83, mem, Lab Animal Utilization Comt, 82-87 & chmn, Radiation Safety Comt, 84-; res grants, var insts & asns, 79-; invited lectr, var asns, univs & insts, 82-; consult, Eurand Am, Inc, 84- *Mem:* Am Soc Pharmacol & Exp Therapeut; Asn Med Sch Pharmacol; Soc Toxicol. *Res:* Autonomic and ocular drugs; antihypertensives, antilipidemics, and antiarrythmics; diuretics; cardiotonics; histamine and antihistamines; vasoactive peptides; drugs used to treat migraine; alcohols; antianginals; respiratory drugs; thrombolytics. *Mailing Add:* Dept Pharmacol & Toxicol Wright State Univ Sch Med Dayton OH 45435

LANGLEY, G R, INTERNAL MEDICINE, HEMATOLOGY. *Current Pos:* lectr internal med, Dalhousie Univ, 63-64, from asst prof to assoc prof med, 64-68, head dept, 74-82, PROF MED, DALHOUSIE UNIV, 68- *Personal Data:* b Sydney, NS, Oct 6, 31; m 57, Jean M Ballentyne; c Joanne, Mark R & Richard. *Educ:* Mt Allison Univ, BA, 52; Dalhousie Univ, MD, 57; FRCP(C), 61, FACP, 65. *Hon Degrees:* FRCP(E), 83. *Honors & Awards:* Queens Jubilee Medal, 77; Medal, Nat Can Inst, 85. *Prof Exp:* Asst resident internal med, Victoria Gen Hosp & Toronto Gen Hosp, 57-60; J Arthur Haatz fel hemat, Univ Melbourne, 60-61; Med Res Coun Can fel, Sch Med & Dent, Univ Rochester, 61-62 & Dalhousie Univ, 63. *Concurrent Pos:* John & Mary R Markle scholar med, 63-68; head Dept Med, Camp Hill Hosp, 69-74; head Dept Med, 74-82, sr physician, Victoria Gen Hosp, 82-; Wightman vis prof, Royal Col Physicians & Surgeons, 90. *Mem:* Fel Am Col Physicians; Can Soc Clin Invest; Can Soc Bioethics; Am Soc Hemat; Royal Col Physicians & Surgeons Can; Am Soc Clin Oncol. *Res:* Hematological oncology; quantitative analysis of bioethical issues. *Mailing Add:* Dept Med Q E II Health Sci Ctr Victoria Gen Hosp Site 1278 Tower Rd Halifax NS B3H 2Y9 Can. *Fax:* 902-428-4436; *E-Mail:* langley@ac.dal.ca

LANGLEY, KENNETH HALL, LASER LIGHT SCATTERING. *Current Pos:* from asst prof to assoc prof, 63-81, PROF PHYSICS, UNIV MASS, AMHERST, 81. *Personal Data:* b Ft Collins, Colo, Sept 1, 35; m 59; c 2. *Educ:* Mass Inst Technol, SB, 58; Univ Calif, Berkeley, PhD(physics), 66. *Prof Exp:* Actg asst prof & res assoc physics, Univ Calif, Berkeley, 66. *Concurrent Pos:* Cofounder, Langley-Ford Instruments. *Mem:* Am Phys Soc; AAAS. *Res:* Experimental dynamic light scattering from polymers and biological macromolecules; dynamic nuclear orientation; light scattering from critical point fluids; biological systems. *Mailing Add:* Dept Physics & Astron Univ Mass Amherst MA 01003. *E-Mail:* langley@phast.umass.edu

LANGLEY, MAURICE N(ATHAN), AGRICULTURAL ENGINEERING. *Current Pos:* SR CONSULT, 88- *Personal Data:* b Dorchester, Nebr, July 6, 13; m 39, Ruby E Frederiksen; c Susan I (Thomas), Gilbert W & Richard J. *Educ:* Colo Agr & Mech Col, BS, 39. *Honors & Awards:* Meritorious Serv Award, US Bur Reclamation, 56 & 69; Outstanding Serv Award, USBR, 47; Meritorious Serv Award, USBR, 56 & 69; Int Water for Peace Conf Commendation, 67; Distinguished Serv Award, Dept of Interior, 68; Outstanding Serv & Leadership Award, US Comt on Irrig & Drainage, 84; Distinguished Serv Award, Nat Water Resources Asn, 89. *Prof Exp:* Soil surveyor, Agr Exp Sta, Colo State Col, 39-40; jr soil surveyor, Soil Conserv Serv, USDA, Tex, 40-42, asst soil technologist & chief land classification div, 46-48, land use specialist & head land use & settlement div, 49-56, agr engr & chief opers div, 56-59, hydraul engr, Land & Water Br, 59-60, chief, Irrig Br, 60-62, asst chief div irrig & land use, 62-64, chief water & land, 64-73; vpres, Bookman-Edmonston Eng, Inc, 73-88. *Concurrent Pos:* Pres, US Comt Irrig, Drainage & Flood Control, 70, 71 & 72; US nat chmn, US Comt Irrig & Drainage, 70-72 & Int Comn Irrig & Drainage, vpres, 74, 75 & 76; bd dirs, Am Water Found, 84-88. *Mem:* Am Soc Agr Engrs; Soil Sci Soc Am; Am Soc Agron; Int Comn Irrig & Drainage (pres, 73-75); Am Water Found; Int Eng Comt Am Consult Engrs Coun; Nat Water Resources Asn; Am Registry Cert Prof Agronomist & Soil Scientist. *Res:* Water holding capacity of soils for land classification purposes. *Mailing Add:* 6825 Algonquin Ave Bethesda MD 20817-4813

LANGLEY, NEAL ROGER, POLYMER CHEMISTRY. *Current Pos:* chemist, 68-80, ASSOC RES SCIENTIST, DOW CORNING CORP, 80- *Personal Data:* b Sumas, Wash, July 27, 39. *Educ:* Univ Wash, BS, 61; Univ Wis, PhD(chem), 68. *Prof Exp:* Sr res scientist, Pac Northwest Lab, Battelle Mem Inst, 67-68. *Mem:* Am Chem Soc. *Res:* Structure and viscoelastic properties of cross-linked polymers; structure and thermo-mechanical properties of ceramic fibers. *Mailing Add:* Dow Corning Corp Mail No 500 Midland MI 48686-0995

LANGLEY, ROBERT ARCHIE, VACUUM TECHNOLOGY, MATERIAL SCIENCE. *Current Pos:* RETIRED. *Personal Data:* b Athens, Ga, Oct 21, 37; div; c 3. *Educ:* Ga Inst Technol, BS, 59, MS, 60, PhD(physics), 63. *Prof Exp:* Asst physics, Ga Inst Technol, 59-63; physicist, Air Force Cambridge Res Labs, 63-65 & Oak Ridge Nat Lab, 66-68; staff mem, Sandia Corp, 68-78; prog coordr, Oak Ridge Nat Lab, 78-80 & Int Atomic Energy Agency, 80-81; staff scientist, Oak Ridge Nat Lab, 81-96. *Mem:* Am Phys Soc; Am Nuclear Soc; Am Vacuum Soc; Health Physics Soc. *Res:* Plasma-wall interactions in controlled fusion devices; ion implantation; hydrogen and helium migration in metals; surface physics; ion backscattering; nuclear microanalysis. *Mailing Add:* 374 Marney Cove Rd Kingston TN 37763

LANGLEY, ROBERT CHARLES, ORGANIC CHEMISTRY. *Current Pos:* res dir, Hanovia Div, 54-62, SECT HEAD, RES & DEVELOP DIV, ENGELHARD INDUSTS, INC, 62- *Personal Data:* b NJ, Apr 11, 25; m 54; c 1. *Educ:* St Peters Col, BS, 49. *Prof Exp:* Chemist, E I du Pont de Nemours & Co, 50-54. *Mem:* Am Chem Soc; Am Ceramic Soc. *Res:* Organic compounds of metals; thin films; gas purification. *Mailing Add:* 214 Old Forge Rd Millington NJ 07946

LANGLEY WOOD, ROBERTSON HARRIS, ENVIRONMENTAL PHYSIOLOGY. *Current Pos:* RETIRED. *Personal Data:* b Lynchburg, Va, Aug 22, 24; m 51; c 5. *Educ:* Col William & Mary, BS, 49; Columbia Univ, AM, 50; Cornell Univ, PhD(biol), 65. *Prof Exp:* Instr sociol, Winthrop Col, 50-51; pvt bus, 52-56; researcher, Bur Com Fisheries, US Fish & Wildlife Serv, 56-57; res asst biol, Woods Hole Oceanog Inst, 57-58, Inst Fish Res, Univ NC, 59 & Lerner Lab, Am Mus Natural Hist, 59-60; assoc marine scientist & head dept, Va Inst Marine Sci, 61-67; sr marine scientist & head dept environ physiol, 67-69; prof zool & chmn dept, Univ NH, 69-72; prof environ studies & dir prog, Sweet Briar Col, 72-82. *Concurrent Pos:* From asst prof to assoc prof, Col William & Mary, 61-69; asst prof, Univ Va, 63-69. *Mem:* AAAS; Am Soc Limnol & Oceanog; Am Soc Zoologists; Animal Behav Soc; Estuarine Res Soc. *Res:* Physiological and behavioral effects upon marine organisms of changes in sensory and biochemical characteristics of environment. *Mailing Add:* 104 Monacan Pl Madison Heights VA 24572-3411. *Fax:* 804-384-6380

LANGLOIS, BRUCE EDWARD, FOOD MICROBIOLOGY. *Current Pos:* from asst prof to assoc prof dairy sci, 64-74, PROF ANIMAL SCI, UNIV KY, 74- *Personal Data:* b Berlin, NH, Sept 16, 37; m 60; c 2. *Educ:* Univ NH, BS, 59; Purdue Univ, PhD(dairy microbiol), 62. *Prof Exp:* Asst prof dairy, Purdue Univ, 62-64. *Mem:* Am Soc Microbiol; Inst Food Technologists; Int Asn Milk, Food & Environ Sanit; Sigma Xi. *Res:* Staphyloccocal mastitis; transferable drug resistance in farm animals; microflora of dairy and meat products. *Mailing Add:* Dept Animal Sci Univ Ky 500 S Limestone St Lexington KY 40506-0001

LANGLOIS, GORDON ELLERBY, PHYSICAL CHEMISTRY. *Current Pos:* Sr res chemist, Calif Res Corp, Chevron Res Co, 43-69, sr res chemist, 69-73, mgr, Synthetic Fuels Div, 73-78. *Personal Data:* b Burley, Idaho, Aug 30, 18; m 44; c 3. *Educ:* Northwestern Univ, BS, 42; Univ Calif, PhD(phys chem), 52. *Mem:* Am Chem Soc. *Res:* Catalytic reactions of hydrocarbons, as polymerization, alkylation and isomerization; synthetic fuels technology. *Mailing Add:* 15 Doral Dr Moraga CA 94556-1042

LANGLYKKE, ASGER FUNDER, MICROBIOLOGY. *Current Pos:* RETIRED. *Personal Data:* b Pleasant Prairie, Wis, July 17, 09; m 39; c 4. *Educ:* Univ Wis, BS, 31, MS, 34, PhD(biochem), 36. *Hon Degrees:* ScD, Trinity Col, 65. *Honors & Awards:* Barnett Cohen Award, Am Soc Microbiol, 78; James M Van Lanean Award, Am Chem Soc, 83. *Prof Exp:* Foreman, Procter & Gamble Co, Ill, 31-32; asst, Univ Wis, 32-36, Dow fel, 36-37; res chemist, Hiram Walker & Sons, Inc, 37-40; supt butyl alcohol plant, Cent Lafayette, PR, 40-43; div head, Northern Regional Res Lab, USDA, Ill, 43 & 45-47; chief pilot plant div & chief tech officer, Chem Warfare Serv, Md & Ind, 43-45; dir, Microbiol Develop, E R Squibb & Sons, 47-49, dir res & develop labs, 49-64, vpres, 64-68; exec dir, Am Acad Microbiol & Am Soc Microbiol, 68-74; proj mgr, Frederick Cancer Res Ctr, 77-79. *Concurrent Pos:* Consult, Res & Develop Bd, US Army, 45-53 & Chem Corp, 53-66; off dir, Defense Res & Eng, 60-63; mem, Comt Agr Sci, USDA, 64-68; Adv Bd Res & Grad Educ, Rutgers Univ & Sci Adv Comt, Rutgers Inst Microbiol, 64-68; vpres, Appl Chem Div Comt, Int Union Pure & Appl Chem, 77-81; adj prof, Rutgers Univ, 68-74; exec staff scientist, Genex Corp, 79-85. *Mem:* Fel AAAS; fel NY Acad Sci; emer mem Biochem Soc UK; Am Inst Chem Engrs; Am Soc Microbiol. *Res:* Fermentation processes for antibiotics steroids, industrial and pharmaceutical chemicals; biochemical engineering. *Mailing Add:* 240 Dill Ave Frederick MD 21701

LANGMAN, CRAIG BRADFORD, METABOLIC BONE DISEASE, KIDNEY STONE DISEASE. *Current Pos:* assoc prof, 87-93, PROF PEDIAT, NORTHWESTERN UNIV, 93- *Personal Data:* b Philadelphia, Pa, Feb 15, 53. *Educ:* Temple Univ, BS, 73; Hahnemann Univ, MD, 77. *Prof Exp:* Asst prof pediat, Univ Chicago, 81-85. *Concurrent Pos:* Assoc chair pediat, Northwestern Univ, 89-92. *Mem:* Am Soc Pediat Nephrology; Nat Kidney Found; Int Soc Kidney & Urinary Tract; Am Soc Bone & Mineral Res; Soc Pediat Res. *Res:* Clinical expression and basic mechanisms of metabolic bone and stone disease in children, including the expression of forerunners of adult diseases such as osteoporosis; bone cell biology; cytokine regulation. *Mailing Add:* Nephrology Div Children's Mem Hosp 2300 Children's Plaza Chicago IL 60614

LANGMUIR, CHARLES H, GEOCHEMISTRY. *Current Pos:* ARTHUR STORKE PROF GEOL, DEPT EARTH & ENVIRON SCI, LAMONT-DOHERTY EARTH OBSERV, COLUMBIA UNIV. *Personal Data:* b Ont, Nov 24, 50. *Educ:* Harvard Univ, BA, 73; State Univ NY, Stony Brook, PhD(geol), 80. *Honors & Awards:* Bowen Award, Am Geophys Union, 96. *Concurrent Pos:* Arthur Sloane res fel, 84. *Mem:* Fel Am Geophys Union. *Mailing Add:* Lamont-Doherty Earth Observ Columbia Univ Rte 9N Palisades NY 10964. *Fax:* 914-365-8155; *E-Mail:* langmuir@ldeo.columbia.edu

LANGMUIR, DAVID BULKELEY, PHYSICS. *Current Pos:* RES CONSULT, 73- *Personal Data:* b Los Angeles, Calif, Dec 14, 08; m 42, Marianna Lawrence; c Diana (Rosenthal), Jean (Blinn) & Charles H. *Educ:* Yale Univ, BS, 31; Mass Inst Technol, ScD(physics), 35. *Prof Exp:* Res physicist, Radio Corp Am Mfg Co, NJ, 35-41; liaison officer, Off Sci Res & Develop, Washington, DC & London, 41-45; secy, Guided Missiles Comt, Joint Chiefs of Staff, Washington, DC, 45-46; dir planning div, Res & Develop Bd, 46-48; exec officer, Prog Coun, AEC, 48-50; USAEC liaison officer, Atomic Energy Can, Ltd, Chalk River, 50-54; mem tech staff, Ramo-Wooldridge Corp, 54-56, dir res lab, Ramo-Wooldridge Div, Thompson Ramo Wooldridge Corp, 56-60 & TRW Space Technol Labs, 60-65, dir, Phys Res Ctr, TRW Systs, Calif, 65-70, dir res planning, 70-73. *Concurrent Pos:* Prof lectr, George Washington Univ, 48-50; mem sci adv group, Off Aerospace Res, US Air Force, 63-70, chmn, 69-70; chmn, Joint Workshop Indust Innovation, Nat Acad Sci, Taiwan, 75. *Mem:* Fel Am Phys Soc; fel Inst Elec & Electronics Engrs; Am Inst Aeronaut & Astronaut; Sigma Xi. *Res:* Thermionics; television light valves; high frequency tubes; diffusion in metals; ionic propulsion. *Mailing Add:* 350 21st St Santa Monica CA 90402

LANGMUIR, DONALD, GEOCHEMISTRY. *Current Pos:* PROF GEOCHEM, DEPT CHEM & GEOCHEM, COLO SCH MINES, 78- *Personal Data:* b Nashua, NH, Apr 5, 34; c 2. *Educ:* Harvard Univ, AB, 56, MA, 61, PhD(geol sci), 65. *Prof Exp:* Geochemist, Water Resources Div, US Geol Surv, 64-66; lectr water resources, Rutgers Univ, 66-67; from asst prof to prof geochem, Pa State Univ, University Park, 67-78. *Concurrent Pos:* Adj prof geochem, Desert Res Inst, Univ Nev, Reno, 74-75; assoc ed, Geochim Cosmochim Acta, 75-80; pres, Hydrochem Systs Corp, 79-; vis prof inorg chem, Univ Sidney, Australia, 80; dir, Earth Search, Inc, 81-85; mem, President's Nuclear Waste Tech Rev Bd, 89; pres, Colo Mountain Club, 90. *Mem:* Fel AAAS; Am Chem Soc; Am Geophys Union; fel Mineral Soc Am; Geochem Soc; Sigma Xi; Soc Environ Geochem & Health. *Res:* Geochemistry of subsurface waters; thermodynamic properties of minerals and dissolved species in water; adsorption of dissolved inorganic species on geological materials; geochemistry of exploration for ore deposits, of solution mining, and of groundwater pollution and restoration. *Mailing Add:* 129 S Eldridge Way Golden CO 80401

LANGMUIR, MARGARET ELIZABETH LANG, PHYSICAL CHEMISTRY, PHOTOCHEMISTRY. *Personal Data:* b Chicago, Ill, Nov 11, 35; m 62, D Bruce; c Lisa D (Maypother) & Jonathan B. *Educ:* Culver-Stockton Col, BA, 56; Purdue Univ, PhD(chem), 63. *Prof Exp:* Instr analytical & inorg chem, Wellesley Col, 60-63; phys chemist, Pioneering Res Div, US Army Natrick Labs, 63-69; consult, 69-74; res assoc, Northeastern Univ, 76-78; sr scientist, EIC Corp, 78-81 & Giner Inc, 81-83; sr scientist, Covalent Assoc, Inc, 84. *Mem:* AAAS; Am Chem Soc; Electrochem Soc; Sigma Xi. *Res:* Organic photochemistry; acidity functions; flash photolysis; fast reaction mechanisms; excited state proton transfer; fluorescence, phosphorescence and charge transfer spectra; electrochemistry; implantable electrodes; isomerization; semiconductor electrochemistry; photoelectrochemical cells; solar cells; polymer modified electrodes, ion selective electrodes, ion selective fluorophores; electrochemistry. *Mailing Add:* Covalent Assoc Inc 10 State St Woburn MA 01801-6820. *Fax:* 978-443-7878

LANGNER, GERALD CONRAD, PHYSICS. *Current Pos:* MEM STAFF NONDESTRUCTIVE TESTING, LOS ALAMOS NAT LAB, 74- *Personal Data:* b Austin, Minn, Feb 13, 44; m 73; c 1. *Educ:* St John's Univ, BA, 66; NDak State Univ, MA, 68. *Prof Exp:* Physicist control syst eng, US Navy, 68-69; scientist II physics, Albuquerque Div, EG&G Inc, 69-73. *Mem:* Am Soc Nondestructive Testing; Am Phys Soc. *Mailing Add:* 90 Mimbres Dr Los Alamos NM 87544

LANGNER, RONALD O, BIOCHEMICAL PHARMACOLOGY. *Current Pos:* ASSOC PROF PHARMACOL, UNIV CONN, 69- *Personal Data:* b Chicago, Ill, May 10, 40; m 63; c 2. *Educ:* Blackburn Col, BA, 62; Univ RI, MS, 66, PhD(pharmacol), 69. *Mem:* Am Biol Chem. *Res:* Metabolism of collagen and its relationship to experimental atherosclerosis. *Mailing Add:* Dept Sci Univ Conn Sch Pharmacol U-92 Storrs CT 06269-2092

LANGONE, JOHN JOSEPH, BIO-ORGANIC CHEMISTRY. *Current Pos:* STAFF FEL IMMUNOCHEM, NAT CANCER INST, 75- *Personal Data:* b Cambridge, Mass, Aug 20, 44; m 73; c 2. *Educ:* Boston Col, BS, 66; Boston Univ, PhD(org chem), 72. *Prof Exp:* Fel org chem, Boston Univ, 71-72; sr res assoc biochem, Brandeis Univ, 72-75. *Mem:* Am Chem Soc; Am Soc Biol Chemists. *Res:* Immunopharmacology and immunochemistry of biologically active compounds; cancer immunochemistry. *Mailing Add:* Molecular Biol Br FDA OST HFZ-113 12709 Twinbrook Pkwy Rockville MD 20852-1719

LANGRANA, NOSHIR A, COMPUTER AIDED DESIGN, BIOMECHANICS. *Current Pos:* From asst prof to assoc prof, 76-87, PROF MECH DESIGN, COL ENG, RUTGERS UNIV, 87- *Personal Data:* b Bombay, India, Oct 1, 46; US citizen; m 72, Dinaz; c 2. *Educ:* Univ Bombay, India, BE, 68; Cornell Univ, MS, 71, PhD(mech eng), 75. *Honors & Awards:* Ralph R Teetor Award, Soc Automotive Engrs, 77. *Concurrent Pos:* Adj prof surg, NJ Med Sch, 95- *Mem:* Am Soc Mech Engrs; Orthop Res Soc; NAm Spine; Sigma Xi; fel Am Soc Mech Engrs. *Res:* Computer-aided design technology in the investigation of musculoskeletal problems; designing and developing layered manufacturing, virtual reality and devices for medical use. *Mailing Add:* Mech Engr Rutgers Univ Busch Campus PO Box 909 Piscataway NJ 08855. *Fax:* 732-445-3124

LANGRETH, DAVID CHAPMAN, THEORETICAL CONDENSED MATTER PHYSICS, THEORETICAL SURFACE PHYSICS. *Current Pos:* from asst prof to prof, 67-80, assoc chmn dept & dir grad progs, 70-73, PROF II PHYSICS, RUTGERS UNIV, NEW BRUNSWICK, 80- *Personal Data:* b Greenwich, Conn, May 22, 37; m 66, Ellen Connolly; c Robert & Katrina. *Educ:* Yale Univ, BS, 59; Univ Ill, MS, 61, PhD(physics), 64. *Prof Exp:* Res assoc physics, Univ Chicago, 64-65 & Cornell Univ, 65-67. *Concurrent Pos:* Rutgers Res Coun fel, Univ Calif, San Diego, 73-74; guest prof, Nordita, Copenhagen, 75-76; prin investr, NSF grants, 69-; coordr surface prog, Inst Theoret Physics, Santa Barbara, 83; mem, Davisson-Germer Prize Comt, 84-, chmn, 88; vis prof, Chalmers Univ, Göteborg, Sweden, 88 & 93. *Mem:* AAAS; Am Phys Soc. *Res:* Theoretical solid state physics, specializing in the many body problem; theoretical surface physics. *Mailing Add:* Dept Physics & Astron Rutgers Univ PO Box 849 Piscataway NJ 08855-0849. *Fax:* 732-445-4400; *E-Mail:* langreth@physics.rutgers.edu

LANGRIDGE, ROBERT, MOLECULAR BIOLOGY. *Current Pos:* prof biochem & biophys, Sch Med, Univ Calif, 77-94, prof, Dept Pharmaceut Chem, 77-94, dir, Comput Graphics Lab, 77-94, EMER PROF BIOCHEM & BIOPHYS, UNIV CALIF, 94- *Personal Data:* b Essex, Eng, Oct 26, 33; m 60; c 2. *Educ:* Univ London, BSc, 54, PhD(crystallog), 57. *Prof Exp:* Res fel biophys, Yale Univ, 57-59; res assoc biophys, Mass Inst Technol, 59-61 & Children's Hosp, Med Ctr, Boston Univ, 61-66; res assoc, Harvard Univ, 63-64, lectr, 64-66; prof biophys & info sci, Univ Chicago, 66-68; prof biochem, Princeton Univ, 68-76. *Concurrent Pos:* Vis prof biochem biophys, Ore State Univ, 94- *Mem:* Inst Med-Nat Acad Sci; Biophys Soc; Am Crystallog Asn; Am Chem Soc; AAAS. *Res:* X-ray diffraction and physical-chemical studies of the structures of biological macromolecules, particularly nucleic acids, nucleoproteins, viruses and ribosomes; applications of high speed digital computers. *Mailing Add:* Dept Pharmaceut Chem Univ Calif San Francisco CA 94143-0446

LANGRIDGE, WILLIAM HENRY RUSSELL, VIROLOGY, DEVELOPMENTAL BIOLOGY. *Current Pos:* PROF, DEPT PLANT SCI, UNIV ALTA, 87- *Personal Data:* b New York, NY, Jan 30, 38; m 60; c 2. *Educ:* Univ Ill, Urbana, BS, 62, MS, 64; Univ Mass, PhD(biochem), 74. *Prof Exp:* NIH fel virol, Boyce Thompson Inst, Ithaca, NY, 74-87. *Mem:* AAAS; Soc Invert Path; Am Soc Microbiol; Sigma Xi. *Res:* Metabolism of baculoviruses and vertebrate and insect poxviruses; the mechanism of infection and the structure of the virus genome and virus protein; plant molecular biology. *Mailing Add:* 11856 Westminster Ct Loma Linda CA 11856

LANGSAM, MICHAEL, POLYMER CHEMISTRY. *Current Pos:* sr res chemist, 67-75, MGR POLYMER PROCESS DEVELOP, AIR PROD & CHEM, INC, 75- *Personal Data:* b Brooklyn, NY, Nov 4, 38; m 62; c 3. *Educ:* Rensselaer Polytech Inst, BS, 59; Polytech Inst Brooklyn, PhD(polymer sci), 64. *Prof Exp:* Res chemist polymer, B F Goodrich Lab, Brecksville, Ohio, 64-67. *Mem:* Sigma Xi; Am Chem Soc. *Res:* Polymer synthesis, rheology, polymer kinetics, and particle morphology. *Mailing Add:* 1114 N 26th St Allentown PA 18104

LANGSDORF, ALEXANDER, JR, nuclear physics; deceased, see previous edition for last biography

LANGSDORF, WILLIAM PHILIP, PHYSICAL ORGANIC CHEMISTRY. *Current Pos:* RETIRED. *Personal Data:* b Cambridge, Ohio, Apr 6, 19; m 41, Mary A McCleary; c Philip. *Educ:* Ohio State Univ, BSc, 41; Mass Inst Technol, PhD(chem), 47. *Prof Exp:* Res chemist, Indust & Biochem Dept, E I Du Pont de Nemours & Co, Inc, 49-62, res assoc, 62-79. *Mem:* Sigma Xi. *Res:* Organic reactions; mechanism of organic reactions; kinetics. *Mailing Add:* 2149 Culver Dr Wilmington DE 19810-1309

LANGSETH, MARCUS G, GEOPHYSICS, OCEANOGRAPHY. *Current Pos:* SR RES ASSOC GEOPHYS, LAMONT-DOHERTY GEOL OBSERV, COLUMBIA UNIV, 58- *Personal Data:* b Lebanon, Tenn, Nov 24, 32; m 63. *Educ:* Waynesburg Col, BS, 54; Columbia Univ, PhD(geol), 64. *Concurrent Pos:* Adj prof, Columbia Univ. *Mem:* AAAS; Am Geophys Union; Geol Soc Am; Sigma Xi. *Res:* Terrestrial heat flow; lunar heat flow; oceanographic instrumentation; submarine geology. *Mailing Add:* Lamont-Doherty Geol Observ Palisades NY 10964-8000

LANGSETH, ROLLIN EDWARD, ELECTRICAL ENGINEERING, MATHEMATICS. *Current Pos:* DIST MGR, AM TEL & TEL CO, 81- *Personal Data:* b St Paul, Minn, Apr 13, 40; m 66; c 2. *Educ:* Univ Minn, Minneapolis, BS, 62, MSEE, 65, PhD(elec eng), 68. *Prof Exp:* Mem tech staff, Bell Tel Labs, 68-80. *Mem:* Inst Elec & Electronics Engrs. *Res:* Communication in multipath propagation media; diversity systems; effects of noise and interference; data networks; satellite systems. *Mailing Add:* AT&T Bell Labs Crawfords Corner Rd Rm 3M 526 Holmdel NJ 07733

LANGSJOEN, ARNE NELS, ORGANIC CHEMISTRY. *Current Pos:* RETIRED. *Personal Data:* b Dalton, Minn, Apr 6, 19; m 43, Carol L Gaustad; c Karen (Zins), Peter L & Thor V (deceased). *Educ:* Gustavus Adolphus Col, BA, 42; Univ Iowa, MS, 43, PhD, 49. *Prof Exp:* From asst prof to assoc prof, Gustavus Adolphus Col, 48-56, chmn dept, 56-66, prof chem, 56-86. *Concurrent Pos:* NSF res fel, Uppsala & Royal Inst Technol, Sweden, 58-59; vis prof chem, Tunghai Univ, Taichung, Taiwan, 69-70, Univ Alaska, Fairbanks, 82-83. *Mem:* Am Chem Soc; Sigma Xi. *Res:* Biological chemistry. *Mailing Add:* 410 N Fourth St St Peter MN 56082

LANGSJOEN, PER HARALD, MEDICINE, CARDIOLOGY. *Current Pos:* CLIN PROF, COL MED, TEX A&M UNIV, 75- *Personal Data:* b Fergus Falls, Minn, Aug 9, 21; m 45; c 5. *Educ:* Gustavus Adolphus Col, AB, 43; Univ Minn, Minneapolis, MD, 50, MD, 51. *Prof Exp:* Intern & residency internal med, Letterman Army Hosp, San Francisco, Calif, 50-54; staff physician, Coco Solo Hosp, Cristobal, CZ, 54-56; resident cardiol, Fitzsimmons Army Hosp, Denver, Colo, 56-58; chief cardiovasc serv, Wm Beaumont Gen Hosp, El Paso, Tex, 58-60; chief cardiovasc serv, Scott & White Clin, 60-75. *Concurrent Pos:* Fel coun clin cardiol, Am Heart Asn, 65-; consult, US Army Hosp, Ft Hood, Tex, 61-75 & Vet Admin Hosp, Temple, 61-75. *Mem:* Fel Am Col Physicians; fel Am Col Cardiol. *Res:* Rheologic aspects of the circulatory system in health and in disease states. *Mailing Add:* Salr Hosp Clin 22736 Bullard TX 75757-8202

LANGSLEY, DONALD GENE, PSYCHIATRY, PSYCHOANALYSIS. *Current Pos:* PROF PSYCHIAT, NORTHWESTERN UNIV MED SCH, 82- *Personal Data:* b Topeka, Kans, Oct 5, 25; m 55, Pauline Royal; c Karen, Dorrie & Susan. *Educ:* State Univ NY Albany, AB, 49; Univ Rochester, MD, 53. *Honors & Awards:* Hofheimer Award, Am Psychiat Asn, 71, Admin Psychiat Award, 93. *Prof Exp:* Intern, USPHS Hosp, San Francisco, 53-54; resident psychiat, Langley Porter Clin, Sch Med, Univ Calif, San Francisco, 54-59, NIMH career teacher award psychiat, 59-61; from asst to assoc prof psychiat, Sch Med, Univ Colo, 61-68; prof psychiat & chmn dept, Sch Med, Univ Calif, Davis, 68-76 & Univ Cincinnati, 76-81; prof psychiat & chmn dept, Sch Med, Univ Cincinnati, 76-81. *Concurrent Pos:* Dir inpatient serv, Colo Psychiat Hosp, Denver, 61-68; dir ment health serv, Sacramento Med Ctr, Univ Calif, Davis, 68-73; mem psychiat training comt, NIMH, 71-75, mem psychiat test comt, Nat Bd Med Examr, 72-76; chief staff, Sacramento Med Ctr, 74-75; chmn dept defense select comt psychiat care eval, NIMH, 75-78; dir, Am Bd Psychiat & Neurol, 75-80; exec vpres, Am Bd Med Specialties, 81-91. *Mem:* Am Psychiat Asn (vpres, 77-79, pres, 80-81); Am Psychoanalysis Asn; AMA. *Res:* Family crisis therapy; evaluation of therapy, medical education and psychiatric education. *Mailing Add:* 9445 Monticello Ave Evanston IL 60203. *Fax:* 847-679-7605; *E-Mail:* langsley@nwu.edu

LANGSTON, CHARLES ADAM, SEISMOLOGY. *Current Pos:* from asst prof to assoc prof, 77-86, PROF GEOPHYS, PA STATE UNIV, 86- *Personal Data:* b 1949. *Educ:* Case Western Res Univ, BS, 72; Calif Inst Technol, MS, 74, PhD(geophys), 76. *Prof Exp:* Res geophys, Calif Inst Technol, 72-74, Louis D Beaumont fel, 74-75, res asst, 75-76, res fel, 76-77. *Concurrent Pos:* Assoc ed, J Geophys Res, 80-82; dir, Seismic Observ, Pa State Univ, 85-; bd dirs, Seismol Soc Am, 88-91; mem, Comt Seismol, Nat Res Coun, 90- *Mem:* Am Geophys Union; Seismol Soc Am (pres, 90-91); Geol Soc Am. *Res:* Theoretical and observation seismology; wave propagation in elastic media; seismic source parameter estimation; crustal and upper mantle structure. *Mailing Add:* Dept Geosci Pa State Univ 440 Deike Bldg University Park PA 16802

LANGSTON, CLARENCE WALTER, MICROBIOLOGY. *Current Pos:* PRES, LANGSTON LABS, INC, KANS & PR, 71- *Personal Data:* b Gainesville, Tex, July 4, 24; m 48; c 2. *Educ:* Southern Methodist Univ, BS, 49; NTex State Univ, MA, 51; Univ Wis, PhD(bact), 55. *Prof Exp:* Bacteriologist, Kraft Foods Co, 50-51; asst, Univ Wis, 51-54; bacteriologist, Dairy Cattle Res Br, Agr Res Serv, USDA, 54-62; chief virus & rickettsial div, Directorate Biol Opers, Pine Bluff Arsenal, US Army, Ark, 62-66; head bact sect, Midwest Res Inst, 66-71. *Mem:* Am Acad Microbiol; Am Soc Microbiol; Soc Indust Microbiol. *Res:* Dairy and food bacteriology; microbiology and chemistry of fermentations; physiology of bacteria; taxonomy and nomenclature of bacteria; research development and production of viruses and rickettsiae. *Mailing Add:* 12432 Linden Leawood KS 66209-2606

LANGSTON, DAVE THOMAS, ENTOMOLOGY. *Current Pos:* res assoc, 70-74, ASSOC PROF ENTOM, UNIV ARIZ, 80-, EXTEN SPECIALIST ENTOM, 74- *Personal Data:* b Chickasha, Okla, Apr 19, 45; m 65; c 4. *Educ:* Southwestern Okla State Univ, BS, 67; Okla State Univ, MS, 70; Univ Ariz, PhD(entom), 74. *Prof Exp:* Res asst, Okla State Univ, 67-70. *Mem:* Entom Soc Am. *Res:* Insect management as it influences production agriculture, specifically those insects which are economically important in the Southwestern United States. *Mailing Add:* 5902 S College Ave Tempe AZ 85283

LANGSTON, GLEN IRVIN, RADIO ASTRONOMY. *Current Pos:* SCIENTIST, NAT RADIO ASTRON OBSERV, 89- *Personal Data:* b Marion, Ohio, Nov 22, 56; m 87; c 1. *Educ:* Mass Inst Technol, BS, 81, PhD(physics), 87. *Prof Exp:* Scientist, Max Planck Inst, 87-88 & Naval Res Lab, 88-89. *Res:* Gravitational lensing. *Mailing Add:* 1604 Marticello Ave Apt G Charlottesville VA 22902

LANGSTON, HIRAM THOMAS, THORACIC SURGERY. *Current Pos:* prof surg, 52-78, clin prof, 78-80, EMER PROF, COL MED, UNIV ILL, 80- *Personal Data:* b Rio de Janeiro, Brazil, Jan 12, 12; US citizen; m 41; c 3. *Educ:* Univ Louisville, AB, 30, MD, 34; Univ Mich, MS, 41; Am Bd Surg, dipl, 42; Am Bd Thoracic Surg, dipl, 48. *Prof Exp:* Intern, Garfield Mem Hosp, Washington, DC, 34-35, resident path, 35-37; from asst resident to resident surg, Univ Mich Hosp, 37-39, resident thoracic surg, 39-40, instr, Univ, 40-41; assoc surg, Med Sch, Northwestern Univ, Ill, 41-42, asst prof, 46-48; assoc prof, Col Med, Wayne State Univ, 48-52. *Concurrent Pos:* Chief surgeon, Chicago State Tuberc Sanitarium, State Dept Pub Health, 52-71; mem staff, Grant & St Joseph's Hosps, 52- *Mem:* Am Thoracic Soc; Am Asn Thoracic Surg (secy, 56-61, vpres, 68-69, pres, 69-70); fel Am Col Surg; Soc Thoracic Surgeons; Am Surg Asn. *Res:* Surgery for diseases of the chest; tuberculosis and cancer of the lung. *Mailing Add:* 39 N Mason Ave Chicago IL 60644

LANGSTON, JAMES HORACE, ORGANIC CHEMISTRY. *Current Pos:* RETIRED. *Personal Data:* b Garrison, Tex, Oct 8, 17; m 84, Edith Gates. *Educ:* Stephen F Austin State Col, BA, 37; Univ NC, MA, 39, PhD(org chem), 41. *Prof Exp:* Asst chem, Univ NC, 37-40; res chemist, Columbia Chem Div, Pittsburgh Plate Glass Co, 41-46; from assoc prof to prof textile chem & dyeing, Clemson Col, 46-58; prof chem, Samford Univ, 58-84, head dept, 58-78, chmn, Div Natural Sci & Math, 68-72. *Concurrent Pos:* Fulbright lectr, Cent Univ & Nat Polytech Sch, Ecuador, 59-60, Fulbright lectr & res consult, Nat Univ Honduras, 67-68. *Mem:* Am Chem Soc; fel Am Inst Chemists. *Res:* Drugs; polymers; plastics; plasticizers; catalysis; fibers; textile finishing materials; sulfone formation. *Mailing Add:* 542 Hillyer High Rd Anniston AL 36207-6246

LANGSTON, JIMMY BYRD, physiology, pharmacology; deceased, see previous edition for last biography

LANGSTON, WANN, JR, VERTEBRATE PALEONTOLOGY. *Current Pos:* VPRES LAB, BALCONES RES CTR, AUSTIN. *Personal Data:* b Oklahoma City, Okla, July 10, 21; m 46; c 2. *Educ:* Univ Okla, BS, 43, MS, 47; Univ Calif, PhD(paleont), 51. *Prof Exp:* Instr geol, Tex Tech Col, 46-48; preparator, Mus Paleont, Univ Calif, 49-54, lectr, 51-52; vert paleontologist, Nat Mus Can, 54-62; res scientist, Tex Mem Mus, 62-, dir, Vertebrate Paleont Lab, 69-; prof dept geol sci, Univ Tex, Austin, 75-, Yaeger prof, 83-. *Concurrent Pos:* Res assoc, Cleveland Mus Natural Hist, 74- *Mem:* Geol Soc Am; Soc Vert Paleont (vpres, 73-74, pres, 74-75); Am Soc Icthyol & Herpet; Am Asn Petrol Geologists; Sigma Xi. *Res:* Fossil amphibians and reptiles; stucture and relationships of extinct crocodylia and large pterosaurs; cretaceous non-mammalian tetrapods in Texas. *Mailing Add:* Univ Tex Balcones Res Ctr Vertebrate Paleont Austin TX 78712

LANGSTROTH, GEORGE FORBES OTTY, PHYSICS. *Current Pos:* Res assoc physics, Dalhousie Univ, 62-63, from asst prof to assoc prof, 67-69, asst dean grad studies, 67-68, actg dean, 68-69, dean, 69-72, PROF PHYSICS, DALHOUSIE UNIV, 69- *Personal Data:* b Montreal, Que, July 13, 36; m 60; c 2. *Educ:* Univ Alta, BSc, 57; Dalhousie Univ, MSc, 59; Univ London, PhD(physics), 62. *Concurrent Pos:* Mem, Defence Res Bd Can, 71-77. *Mem:* Can Asn Physicists. *Res:* Microwave breakdown in gases; ions in afterglows; positron annihilation; optical properties of metals. *Mailing Add:* Dept Physics Dalhousie Univ Halifax NS B3H 4H6 Can

LANGVARDT, PATRICK WILLIAM, MASS SPECTROMETRY, CHROMATOGRAPHY. *Current Pos:* RES LEADER ANALYTICAL CHEM, DOW CHEM CO, 74- *Personal Data:* b Dodge City, Kans, Mar 20, 50. *Educ:* Kans State Teachers Col, BS, 72; Purdue Univ, MS, 74. *Mem:* Am Soc Mass Spectrometry; Sigma Xi; Am Chem Soc. *Res:* Analytical chemistry in support of toxicology studies; metabolite identification; analytical toxicology; trace determinations in biological matrices; automated sample preparation and analysis. *Mailing Add:* Dow Corning Co Health & Environ Sci C03101 Midland MI 48686-0994

LANGWAY, CHESTER CHARLES, JR, GEOLOGY. *Current Pos:* PROF GEOL SCI & CHMN DEPT, STATE UNIV NY BUFFALO, 77- *Personal Data:* b Worcester, Mass, Aug 15, 29; m 59; c 4. *Educ:* Boston Univ, AB, 55, MA, 56; Univ Mich, PhD(geol, glaciol), 65. *Prof Exp:* Res geologist, US Army Snow, Ice & Permafrost Res Estab, 56-59; res assoc properties of snow & ice, Res Inst, Univ Mich, 59-61; res glaciologist, US Army Cold Regions Res & Eng Lab, 61-65, chief snow & ice br, 66-77. *Concurrent Pos:* Mem panel glaciol, Comt Polar Res, Nat Acad Sci, 69-75, secy, Int Comt Ice Core Studies; chmn dept geol sci, State Univ NY Buffalo, 75- *Mem:* AAAS; fel Geol Soc Am; Am Geophys Union; Am Polar Soc; fel Arctic Inst NAm; Sigma Xi. *Res:* Basic and applied research related to the properties of snow and ice, including field and laboratory techniques of analyzing shallow and deep ice cores for stratigraphy and age dating; isotopic and ionic constituents, terrestrial and extraterrestrial inclusions. *Mailing Add:* 25 Wendys Way Harwich MA 02645

LANGWEILER, MARC, PATHOLOGY. *Current Pos:* INSTR, DARTMOUTH MED SCH & TECH SPECIALIST, MARY HITCHCOCK MEM HOSP, DEPT PATH, DARTMOUTH-HITCHCOCK MED CTR, 88- *Personal Data:* b Astoria, NY, Jan 27, 52. *Educ:* Cornell Univ, BS, 72, DVM, 75, MS, 80, PhD, 83. *Prof Exp:* Vet clinician, Flushing Vet Hosp, NY, 75-76, Henry Bergh Mem Hosp, New York, 76-77; grad res asst, NY State Col Vet Med, Cornell Univ, Ithaca, 77-79, grad vet asst, 79-82; postdoctoral res fel, NIH, Dept Microbiol/Immunol, Duke Univ Med Ctr, 82-84, clin immunol fel, 83-84; res assoc, Dept Path, State Univ NY Med Ctr, 84-85; res tech, Dept Radiation Biol/Oncol, Sch Med, ECarolina Univ, 86-88. *Mem:* Am Asn Immunologists; Am Asn Vet Immunologists; Am Vet Med Asn; Am Asn Med Lab Immunologists; Int Soc Analytical Cytol. *Res:* Microbiology; immunology; veterinary medicine. *Mailing Add:* Dept Path Dartmouth-Hitchcock Med Ctr One Medical Ctr Dr Lebanon NH 03756

LANGWIG, JOHN EDWARD, FOREST PRODUCTS, WOOD SCIENCE. *Current Pos:* from asst prof to prof, Okla State Univ, 71-86, chmn, dept forestry, 75-81, exten prof, 81-86, EMER PROF WOOD SCI, OKLA STATE UNIV, 86- *Personal Data:* b Albany, NY, Mar 5, 24; m 46, Margaret Kirk; c Nancy A (Davis). *Educ:* Univ Mich, Ann Arbor, BS, 48; State Univ NY Col Forestry, Syracuse Univ, MS, 68, PhD(wood sci), 71. *Prof Exp:* Instr wood prod eng, State Univ NY Col Forestry, Syracuse Univ, 69-70. *Mem:* Soc Wood Sci & Technol; Forest Prod Res Soc; Soc Am Foresters; Sigma Xi; Tech Asn Pulp & Paper Indust. *Res:* Neutron activation analysis of trace elements in wood and effects on physical properties; physical properties of wood-polymer composites. *Mailing Add:* Dept Forestry Okla State Univ Stillwater OK 74078-0491

LANGWORTHY, HAROLD FREDERICK, MATHEMATICS, OPTICS. *Current Pos:* res assoc, Res Labs, Eastman Kodak Co, Rochester, 67-79, lab head, 79-81, asst dir, 81-83, dir, Physics Div, Kodak Res Labs, 83-86, dir, Res Labs, CISG, 86-89, dir res, IISG, 89-90, gen mgr thermal printing, 90-91, assoc dir, MR&E, 91-92, DIR MFG RES & ENG, EASTMAK KODAK CO, ROCHESTER, 92- *Personal Data:* b White Plains, NY, Aug 1, 40; m 65; c Katherine, Kristen & Thomas. *Educ:* Rensselaer Polytech Inst, BS, 62; Univ Minn, PhD(math), 70. *Mem:* Optical Soc Am; AAAS. *Res:* Mathematical optics; rheology. *Mailing Add:* 732 Hightower Way Webster NY 14580. *E-Mail:* hal@kodak.com

LANGWORTHY, JAMES BRIAN, NUCLEAR PHYSICS, MATHEMATICAL PHYSICS. *Current Pos:* Physicist math physics, Radiation Div, 59-69, res physicist particle transp, Theory Br, Nuclear Physics Div, 69-76, RES PHYSICIST RADIATION DAMAGE, RADIATION EFFECTS BR, CONDENSED MATTER & RADIATION SCI DIV, NAVAL RES LAB, 76- *Personal Data:* b Billings, Mont, Feb 18, 34; m 65, Alva Lawhorne; c Alan & Shelby. *Educ:* Univ Colo, BS, 56; Univ Md, MS, 66. *Concurrent Pos:* Pres, Youth Resources Ctr, Inc, 71-87. *Mem:* Am Phys Soc; AAAS; Sigma Xi. *Res:* Radiation damage, hardening and shielding; energetic particle transport by Monte Carlo computer codes; microdosimetry in single event upset of memory cells; chord distributions; radiation hardening of satellite electronics. *Mailing Add:* Code 6613 Naval Res Lab Washington DC 20375-5345. *E-Mail:* Langworthy@radef.nrl.navy.mil

LANGWORTHY, THOMAS ALLAN, MICROBIAL PHYSIOLOGY. *Current Pos:* Res assoc, Univ SDak, 71-72, from asst prof to assoc prof, 72-82, prof microbiol, 82-91, prof & interim chair microbiol, 91-95, PROF MICROBIOL, UNIV SDAK, 95- *Personal Data:* b Oak Park, Ill, Aug 7, 43; m 88, Jane Moser; c 2. *Educ:* Grinnell Col, AB, 65; Univ Kans, PhD(microbiol), 71. *Honors & Awards:* Alexander von Humboldt US Sr Scientist Prize, 84; Burlington Northern Found Award, 87. *Mem:* Am Soc Microbiol; AAAS; Am Acad Microbiol; Int Orgn Mycoplasmology. *Res:* Structure and function of the membranes and cell surfaces of bacteria from extreme environments, mycoplasmas, archaebacteria and cellular evolution. *Mailing Add:* Dept Microbiol Sch Med Univ SDak Vermillion SD 57069-2390. *Fax:* 605-677-5658; *E-Mail:* tlangwor@usd.edu

LANGWORTHY, WILLIAM CLAYTON, ORGANIC CHEMISTRY, ENVIRONMENTAL CHEMISTRY. *Current Pos:* VPRES ACAD AFFAIRS, FT LEWIS COL, DURANGO, CO, 83- *Personal Data:* b Watertown, NY, Sept 3, 36; m 58, Margaret Amos; c Kenneth & Geneva. *Educ:* Tufts Univ, BSChem, 58; Univ Calif, Berkeley, PhD(org chem), 62. *Prof Exp:* NIH fel chem, Mass Inst Technol, 61-62; asst prof, Alaska Methodist Univ, 62-65; from asst prof to prof, Calif State Col, Fullerton, 65-73; prof chem & head dept, 73-76, dean sch sci & math, Calif Polytech State Univ, San Luis Obispo, 76-83. *Concurrent Pos:* Assoc dean, Sch Lett, Arts & Sci, Calif State Col, Fullerton, 70-73, dir environ studies prog, 70-72. *Mem:* AAAS; Am Chem Soc; Sigma Xi. *Res:* Physical organic chemistry; organic reactions in liquid ammonia; environmental chemistry, especially analysis and effects of trace pollutants. *Mailing Add:* Ft Lewis Col 1000 Rim Dr Durango CO 81301

LANHAM, RICHARD HENRY, JR, EDUCATIONAL ADMINISTRATION. *Current Pos:* PROF PODIATRIC MED, VPRES & DEAN ACAD AFFAIRS, CALIF COL PODIATRIC MED, 85- *Personal Data:* b Shelbyville, Ill; m 59; c 2. *Educ:* Ohio Col Podiatric Med, DPM, 58; Univ Louisville, MEd, 80. *Prof Exp:* Pvt pract, Clarksville, Ind, 59-85. *Concurrent Pos:* Clin investr, Sutter Biomed, 79-85 & Dow Corning Corp, 79-82; adj clinician, Ohio Col Podiatric Med, 81- *Mem:* Am Podiatric Med Asn (pres, 85-86); Am Col Foot Surgeons; Am Col Foot Orthopedists (pres, 70-71); Am Pub Health Asn; Am Bd Podiatric Orthop; Am Bd Podiatric Surg. *Res:* Clinical investigation of three designs for foot implants; author of articles on foot surgery, drug use surveys and case reports. *Mailing Add:* 6257 Meadowstone Dr Santa Rosa CA 95409

LANHAM, URLESS NORTON, ENTOMOLOGY. *Current Pos:* vis cur entom, Univ Colo Mus, Boulder, 61-62, assoc cur, 62-73, cur entom & prof natural hist, 73-90, EMER CUR ENTOM, UNIV COLO MUS, BOULDER, 90- *Personal Data:* b Grainfield, Kans, Oct 17, 18; m 45; c Robert, Margaret & Carl. *Educ:* Univ Colo, BA, 40; Univ Calif, Berkeley, PhD(entom), 48. *Prof Exp:* Asst zool, Univ Calif, Los Angeles, 40-41, biol, Scripps Inst, 41-42, entom, 47-48; from instr to asst prof zool, Univ Mich, 48-56, res asst & consult, NSF Proj Insect Ecol, 56-61. *Concurrent Pos:* Consult, Biol Sci Curric Study, Univ Colo, Boulder, 63-66, lectr, Inst Develop Biol, 66-67, asst prof biophys, 68-71; adv ed, Columbia Univ Press, 64-72; assoc prof, Div Natural Sci, Monteith Col, Wayne State Univ, 59-61; consult, Smithsonian Inst, 67. *Mem:* Kans Entom Soc; Sigma Xi. *Res:* Faunistics and systematics of Apoidea, especially of the genus Andrena. *Mailing Add:* Univ Colo Mus Boulder CO 80309

LANIER, LEWIS L, EXPERIMENTAL BIOLOGY. *Current Pos:* SR SCI STAFF, DEPT IMMUNOL, DNAX RES INST MOLECULAR & CELLULAR BIOL, INC, 91- *Personal Data:* b Memphis, Tenn, July 1, 53. *Educ:* Va Polytech Inst & State Univ, BS, 75; Univ NC, PhD(microbiol & immunol), 78. *Prof Exp:* Fel, Dept Path, Damon Runyon-Walter Winchell Cancer Fund, Sch Med, Univ NMex, 79-81, res asst prof, 81; sr res scientist, Becton Dickinson Monoclonal Ctr, 81-88, assoc res dir, 88-90. *Concurrent Pos:* Transmitting ed, Int Immunol, 88-; mem, Int Health Reviewers Rev, NIH, 89-93; assoc ed, J Immunol, 86-; res assoc, Cancer Res Inst, Sch Med, Univ Calif, San Francisco, 89- *Mem:* Am Asn Immunologists; Soc Anal Cytol; Clin Immunol Soc; Sigma Xi. *Res:* Experimental biology. *Mailing Add:* Dept Human Immunol DNAX Res Inst 901 California Ave Palo Alto CA 94304-1104

LANIER, ROBERT GEORGE, NUCLEAR PHYSICS. *Current Pos:* fel, 69-71, STAFF MEM, NUCLEAR CHEM DIV, LAWRENCE LIVERMORE NAT LAB, UNIV CALIF, 71- *Personal Data:* b Chicago, Ill, Oct 27, 40; div; c 2. *Educ:* Lewis Col, BS, 62; Fla State Univ, PhD(nuclear chem), 68. *Prof Exp:* US AEC fel, Chem Div, Oak Ridge Nat Lab, 67-69. *Mem:* AAAS; Am Phys Soc. *Res:* Experimental low energy nuclear structure studies; charged-particle reaction spectroscopy, cross section measurements and in-beam gamma ray spectroscopy. *Mailing Add:* Nuclear Chem Div L 232 Univ Calif Lawrence Livermore Nat Lab PO Box 808 Livermore CA 94550

LANING, J HALCOMBE, MANUFACTURING AUTOMATION. *Current Pos:* RETIRED. *Personal Data:* b Kansas City, Mo, Feb 14, 20; m 43, Betty Kolb; c Christine, James, Susan & Linda. *Educ:* Mass Inst Technol, BA, 40, PhD(appl math), 47. *Prof Exp:* Sr staff mem, Instrumentation Lab, Mass Inst Technol, 45-73; head, mfg & comput dept, C S Draper Lab, Inc, 73-82, sr fel automation, 82-85, head, Automation Technol Dept, 85-89. *Mem:* Nat Acad Eng; Asn Comput Mach; Am Math Soc; Am Inst Aeronaut & Astronaut; Soc Indust & Appl Math; Inst Elec & Electronics Engrs. *Mailing Add:* 130 Temple St West Newton MA 02165

LANING, STEPHEN HENRY, ANALYTICAL CHEMISTRY. *Current Pos:* RETIRED. *Personal Data:* b Albany, NY, Oct 18, 18; m 46, Marjorie A Metzner; c Barbara A & Malcolm H. *Educ:* Union Col, NY, BS, 41; Rutgers Univ, PhD(phys chem), 47. *Prof Exp:* Asst, Rutgers Univ, 41-44, instr, 45-46; res chemist, Chem Div, Pittsburg Plate Glass Co, 47-61, supvr res & tech serv, 61-67, supvr res & tech serv, 67-86. *Mem:* Am Chem Soc; AAAS; Soc Appl Spectros. *Res:* Development of methods for x-ray analysis of glass, silica and titania pigments, minerals, cements and other types of materials; developed x-ray methods for determining quartz in airborne dusts. *Mailing Add:* 1219 Greenvale Ave Akron OH 44313-6745

LANKFORD, EDWARD B, MUSCLE MECHANICS, CARDIAC MECHANICS. *Current Pos:* fel,90-94,instr, 94-95, ASST PROF, CARDIOVASC SECT, HOSP UNIV PA, 95- *Personal Data:* b Salisbury, Md, Jan 31, 58. *Educ:* Va Polytech Inst & State Univ, BS, 80; Univ Md, MD, 84; Johns Hopkins Univ, PhD(biomed eng), 91. *Prof Exp:* Resident, Hershey Med Ctr, 88-90. *Mem:* Am Col Physicians. *Res:* Mechanics of muscle in human diseased states; cardiac mechanics in hypertrophic cardiomyopathy and dilated cardiomyopathy. *Mailing Add:* 809A Stellar-Chance Bldg 422 Curie Blvd Philadelphia PA 19104-6100. *E-Mail:* lankford@mail.med.upenn.edu

LANKFORD, J(OHN) L(EWELLYN), PROPULSION, HYPERBALLISTICS. *Current Pos:* RETIRED. *Personal Data:* b Hampton, Va, Sept 13, 20; m 45; c 2. *Educ:* Va Polytech Inst, BS, 42. *Prof Exp:* Aeronaut res scientist, Nat Adv Comt Aeronaut, 45-53; res engr, Cent Res Lab, Melpar, 53-54; head, dept gas dynamics, Exp Inc, 54-58; aeronaut res engr, Naval Ord Lab, 58-62; chief adv studies lunar logistics flight systs, NASA, 62-64; actg chief, Missile Dynamics Div, Naval Ord Lab, 64-65, prin investr & mgr rain erosion & hypersonic reentry mat, Naval Surface Weapons Ctr, White Oak, Md, 65-70, consult & prog mgr, US Navy, 70-75. *Concurrent Pos:* Consult, Bur Weapons, US Navy, 64-75; consult, energy & heat transfer, 76-; assoc staff & consult energy prog, Univ Md, 79-80; lectr, Montgomery Col, 78-79. *Mem:* Assoc fel Am Inst Aeronaut & Astronaut; AAAS. *Res:* Supersonics; hypersonics; propulsion aerodynamics; inlets; aeroballistics. *Mailing Add:* 1717 Marymont Rd Silver Spring MD 20906

LANKFORD, WILLIAM FLEET, NUCLEAR & SOLID STATE PHYSICS. *Current Pos:* from asst prof to assoc prof, 69-78, PROF PHYSICS, GEORGE MASON UNIV, 78- *Personal Data:* b Charlottesville, Va, Jan 9, 38. *Educ:* Univ Va, BA, 60; Univ SC, MS, 64, PhD(physics), 69. *Prof Exp:* Instr physics, Univ NC, Greensboro, 62-63; fel, Col William & Mary, 69. *Mem:* Am Inst Physics; Am Phys Soc. *Res:* Experimental solid state research. *Mailing Add:* 10718 Scott Dr Fairfax VA 22030

LANKS, KARL WILLIAM, PATHOLOGY, MOLECULAR BIOLOGY. *Current Pos:* from asst prof to assoc prof, 74-88, PROF PATH, STATE UNIV NY DOWNSTATE MED CTR, 88- *Personal Data:* b Philadelphia, Pa, Nov 1, 42. *Educ:* Pa State Univ, BS, 63; Temple Univ, MD, 67; Columbia Univ, PhD(path), 71. *Prof Exp:* Intern, Columbia-Presby Hosp, 67-68; instr path, Columbia Univ, 71-72. *Concurrent Pos:* NIH res fel, Dept Chem, Harvard Univ, 71-72. *Mem:* Am Soc Biol Chemists; Am Soc Exp Path; Am Soc Cell Biol. *Res:* Structure and metabolism of messenger ribonucleic acids; mechanism of cell attachment; regulation of protein and RNA messenger synthesis in cultured cells; structure and function of heat shock proteins. *Mailing Add:* Dept Path Staten Island Univ Hosp 475 Seaview Ave Staten Island NY 10305

LANMAN, ROBERT CHARLES, BIOCHEMICAL PHARMACOLOGY, TOXICOLOGY. *Current Pos:* vpres, 84-91, EXEC VPRES, KANSAS CITY ANALYTICAL SERV, 91-; PROF PHARMACOL & MED, UNIV MO, KANSAS CITY, 81- *Personal Data:* b Bemidji, Minn, Oct 2, 30; m 57, Dorothy; c Michael, Dianne, Douglas & Krista. *Educ:* Univ Minn, BS, 56, PhD(pharmacol), 67. *Prof Exp:* Teaching asst, Col Pharm, Univ Minn, 58-59; pharmacologist, Sect Biochem Drug Action, Lab Chem Pharmacol, Nat Heart Inst, 62-66; assoc prof pharmacol & med, Univ Mo, Kansas City, 66-81, chmn, Div Pharmacol, 87-92. *Concurrent Pos:* Consult, Marion Merrell Dow, Inc. *Mem:* Am Asn Cols Pharm; Am Soc Pharmacol & Exp Therapeut; Fedn Am Socs Exp Biol; Am Asn Pharmaceut Scientists; Am Pharmaceut Asn. *Res:* Passage of drugs across body membranes; mechanism and kinetics of drug absorption, distribution, metabolism and excretion; analysis of drugs in biological fluids and tissues. *Mailing Add:* Kansas City Analytical Serv Inc 12700 Johnson Dr Shawnee KS 66216. *Fax:* 913-268-3240

LANN, JOSEPH SIDNEY, ORGANIC CHEMISTRY. *Current Pos:* RETIRED. *Personal Data:* b Washington, DC, Sept 16, 17; m 45; c 3. *Educ:* Univ Md, BS, 37, PhD(org chem), 41. *Prof Exp:* res chemist, Jackson Lab, E I du Pont de Nemours & Co, Inc, 46-54, dir, Freon Prod Lab, 54-64, asst mgr new prod & mkt develop, Freon Prod Div, 64-65, asst dist mgr, 65-68, mgr develop prod, Freon Prod Div, 68-80. *Mem:* Am Chem Soc. *Res:* Surface active agents and neoprene; organic compounds; fluorinated hydrocarbons. *Mailing Add:* 608 Haverhill Rd Sharpley Wilmington DE 19803-2437

LANNER, RONALD MARTIN, FOREST GENETICS, TREE PHYSIOLOGY. *Current Pos:* prof, 67-95, EMER PROF FOREST GENETICS & DENDROL, UTAH STATE UNIV, 96- *Personal Data:* b Brooklyn, NY, Nov 12, 30; m 57, Harriette Flanigan; c Deborah & David. *Educ:* Syracuse Univ, BS, 52, MF, 58; Univ Minn, Minneapolis, PhD(forestry), 68. *Prof Exp:* Res forester, Pac Southwest Forest & Range Exp Sta, US Forest Serv, 58-64. *Concurrent Pos:* Consult, Forestry Proj, Food & Agr Orgn, UN, Taiwan, 69; res fel, Univ Fla, 73-74; vis prof, Univ Wash, 82-83; ed,Western J Appl Forestry, 84-96. *Mem:* Soc Am Foresters. *Res:* Morphogenesis and growth of woody plants; evolution and ecology of pines with bird-dispersed seeds; author of books about trees. *Mailing Add:* Dept Forest Res Utah State Univ Logan UT 84322. *Fax:* 435-750-4040

LANNERS, H NORBERT, ELECTRON MICROSCOPY. *Current Pos:* ASST PROF, ROCKEFELLER UNIV, 80- *Personal Data:* b Volkmarsen, Ger, June 23, 43; m 73. *Educ:* Univ Tubingen, Ger, Dr rer nat, 73. *Prof Exp:* Fel, Rockefeller Univ, 73-76; res assoc, Cornell Univ Med Col, 76-80. *Concurrent Pos:* Vis scientist, Agr Exp Sta, Univ Puerto Rico, 76; adj res assoc, Rockefeller Univ, 76-79. *Mem:* Soc Protozoologists; Electron Microsc Soc Am. *Res:* Cultivation of human malaria parasites. *Mailing Add:* 4552 N Palm Ave Fresno CA 93704

LANNERT, KENT PHILIP, INDUSTRIAL ORGANIC CHEMISTRY. *Current Pos:* Res chemist, Monsanto Co, 69-72, res specialist, 72-76, sr res specialist, 76-82, group leader, 82-83, sr group leader, 83-86, MGR TECHNOL, MONSANTO CO, 86- *Personal Data:* b Belleville, Ill, Nov 29, 44; m 70; c 2. *Educ:* Southern Ill Univ, Carbondale, BA, 66; Vanderbilt Univ, PhD(chem), 69. *Mem:* Am Chem Soc. *Res:* Organic synthesis; chelation; synthesis of chelants and other detergent related chemicals; phosphates processing. *Mailing Add:* Monsanto 800 N Lindbergh Blvd St Louis MO 63166

LANNI, FREDERICK, BIOLOGY. *Current Pos:* SR RES SCIENTIST, BIOL DEPT, CARNEGIE-MELLON UNIV, 90- *Mailing Add:* Carnegie-Mellon Univ 4400 Fifth Ave Box 32 Pittsburgh PA 15213-2683

LANNIN, JEFFREY S, MATERIALS SCIENCE ENGINEERING. *Current Pos:* asst prof, 76-81, assoc prof, 81-86, PROF PHYSICS, PA STATE UNIV, 86- *Personal Data:* b New York, NY, Aug 21, 40; m 71; c Joshua. *Educ:* Purdue Univ, BS, 62; Univ Ill, Urbana, MS, 64; Stanford Univ, PhD(solid state physics), 71. *Prof Exp:* Physicist thin films, Fairchild Semiconductor Res Lab, 66-67 & semiconductor physics, Lockheed Palo Alto Res Labs, 67-68; staff physicist raman scattering, Max Planck Inst Solid State Res, 71-74; vis scientist optical properties, Argonne Nat Lab, 74-75; vis asst prof mat sci, Univ Del, 75-76. *Concurrent Pos:* Consult, Lockheed Palo Alto Res Lab, 68-71. *Mem:* Am Phys Soc; Am Vacuum Soc. *Res:* Raman and neutron scattering in ordered and disordered solids and liquids; amorphous materials; thin film physics; cluster vibrational and electronic properties; fullerene materials. *Mailing Add:* 634 W Fairmount Ave State College PA 16801. *Fax:* 814-865-3604; *E-Mail:* jsl@phys.psu.edu

LANNING, DAVID D(AYTON), NUCLEAR ENGINEERING. *Current Pos:* PROF NUCLEAR ENG, MASS INST TECHNOL, 69- *Personal Data:* b Baker, Ore, Mar 30, 28; m 50; c 3. *Educ:* Univ Ore, BA, 51; Mass Inst Technol, PhD(nuclear eng), 63. *Prof Exp:* Physicist, Hanford Atomic Prod Oper, Gen Elec Co, 51-57; res assoc & reactor supt, Mass Inst Technol, 57-62, from asst prof to assoc prof nuclear eng, 62-65, asst dir res reactor, 62-65; unit mgr reactor physics, Battelle-Northwest, 65-66, sect mgr, 66-69. *Concurrent Pos:* Consult, Stone & Webster Eng Corp, 77-78, Boston Edison Co; mem, Monticello Nuclear Power Reactor Safety Audit Comt, Nat Res Coun, NSF. *Mem:* Am Nuclear Soc. *Res:* Nuclear engineering education; design, safety, control and operation of nuclear reactor systems. *Mailing Add:* Dept Nuclear Eng Mass Inst Technol 77 Massachusetts Ave Cambridge MA 02139-4307

LANNING, FRANCIS CHOWING, CHEMISTRY. *Current Pos:* from instr to prof, 42-78, EMER PROF CHEM, KANS STATE UNIV, 78- *Personal Data:* b Denver, Colo, Jan 5, 08; m 34; c 2. *Educ:* Univ Denver, BS, 30, MS, 31; Univ Minn, PhD(phys chem), 36. *Prof Exp:* Asst, Univ Denver, 30-31; analytical chemist, Minn State Hwy Dept, 36-42. *Mem:* Am Chem Soc; Sigma Xi; Am Soc Hort Sci. *Res:* Organosilicon compounds; silicon and other minerals in plants; chemical composition of limestones. *Mailing Add:* Dept Chem Kans State Univ Manhattan KS 66504

LANNING, WILLIAM CLARENCE, PHYSICAL CHEMISTRY. *Current Pos:* RETIRED. *Personal Data:* b Boicourt, Kans, Dec 9, 13; wid; c Patricia L, John G & Marianne. *Educ:* Sterling Col, AB, 34; Univ Kans, AM, 36, PhD(chem), 38. *Prof Exp:* Asst instr chem, Univ Kans, 35-38; res chemist & sect mgr, Naval Res Lab, 38-45; res chemist, Phillips Petrol Co, 46-73, sect mgr, 57-73; res chemist, Bartlesville Energy Res Ctr, ERDA, 74-80. *Mem:* Am Chem Soc; Sigma Xi. *Res:* Non-aqueous solutions; inorganic preparations; catalytic hydrocarbon and petroleum processes; fundamentals of crude oil production; refining of synthetic crude oils. *Mailing Add:* 1530 Pecan Pl Bartlesville OK 74003

L'ANNUNZIATA, MICHAEL FRANK, ANALYSIS OF RADIONUCLIDES, INTERNATIONAL CONSULTING. *Current Pos:* managing dir, Cornado, Calif, 91-94, MANAGING DIR, WORLDTECH INT TECH SERV, OCEANSIDE, CALIF, 95- *Personal Data:* b Springfield, Mass, Oct 14, 43; m 73, Maria Del Carmen Salazar; c Michael, Helen & Frank E. *Educ:* St Edward's Univ, BS, 65; Univ Ariz, MS, 67, PhD(agr chem &

soils), 70. *Hon Degrees:* Hon Teaching Dipl, Cent Univ Ecuador, 78. *Prof Exp:* Res chemist herbicides, Amchem Prods, Inc, 71-72; res assoc, Univ Ariz, 72-73; prof & res investr, Univ Chapingo, Mex, 73-75; res investr, Nat Inst Nuclear Energy, Mex, 75-77; assoc officer, Int Atomic Energy Agency, Vienna, 77-80, second officer, 80-83, first officer, 83-86, sr officer, head fel & training sect, 86-91. *Concurrent Pos:* Consult health veg, Caborca, Mex, 72; consult, Govt Nicaragua, 78, Costa Rica, 78 & 80, Guatemala, 79, Columbia, 79, Arg, 80, Panama, 80, Spain, 80, Uruguay, 80, US Dept State, 85 & 89, USSR State Comm on Utilization Atomic Energy, 80 & 85, Fed Rep Ger, 87, France, 87 & 88, Poland, 88 & 90, People's Repub China, 88, Thailand, 88, Vietnam, 88, Czech, 89, Sweden, 89 & 90, Ger Dem Repub, 89, Mex, 89, Hungary, 90, Israel, 90, Belg, 90 & Italy, 90, Romania 91, Repub Korea, 91; consult & lectr, Atomic Sch Trop Agr, Cardenas, Mex, 73 & Atomic Energy Comn, Quito, Ecuador, 78, Nat Atomic Energy Agency, Baton, Jakarta, Indonesia, 91-94, Ministry Energy Resources, Beijing, China, 92, Nuclear Energy Comn, Santiago, Chile, 92, Int Atomic Energy Agency, Vienna, Austria, 93, Nat Coun Sci Res, Lusaka, Zambia, 94, Forest Res Inst Nigeria, Ibadan, 94-95, Egypt Atomic Energy Authority, Cairo, Egypt, 95-96, Ministry Educ, Jakarta, Indonesia, 95, Sudan Atomic Energy Com, Khartoum, Sudan, 95, Ethiopian Sci & Technol Com, Addis Ababa, Ethiopia, 96, Nat Radiation Com, Arusha, Tanzania, 96 & Packard Instrument Co, Meriden Conn, 95-97; vis lectr, Timiryazev Agr Acad, Moscow, Inst Nuclear Appln Vet Sci, Turkey & Univ Guanajuato, Mex, 81; mem bd gov, Uppsala Univ, Int Sci Progs, Uppsala, Sweden, 88-91; hon prof, Zhejiang Agr Univ, Hangzhou, Peoples Repub China, 92. *Mem:* Sigma Xi; AAAS. *Res:* Detection and measurement of radio nuclides; analysis of radioactivity; use of radioisotopes in fertilizer use efficiency studies; use of isotopes in the elucidation of biochemical pathways and mechanisms. *Mailing Add:* 4317 Cassanna Way No 1608 Oceanside CA 92057-7621. *Fax:* 760-439-0689; *E-Mail:* lannunzi@sprynet.com

LANNUTTI, JOSEPH EDWARD, EXPERIMENTAL HIGH ENERGY PHYSICS, MARINE AQUACULTURE. *Current Pos:* from asst prof to assoc prof, 57-64, PROF PHYSICS, FLA STATE UNIV, 64- *Personal Data:* b Cedar Hollow, Pa, May 4, 26; m 54, Margaret Judge; c Dominique, John & Kathryn. *Educ:* Pa State Univ, BS, 50; Univ Pa, MS, 53; Univ Calif, PhD(physics), 57. *Prof Exp:* Admin asst, Pa RR, 43-47; asst, Univ Pa, 51-52; physicist, NAm Aviation Inc, 52-53; asst, Univ Calif, 54-57. *Concurrent Pos:* Physicist, Lawrence Radiation Lab, Univ Calif, 59-60; mem, bd dir, Univs Res Assoc, Southeastern Univs Res Assoc & Oak Ridge Assoc Univs; assoc vpres acad affairs & assoc vpres res, Fla State Univ. *Mem:* Am Phys Soc. *Res:* Physics of elementary particles; research administration. *Mailing Add:* Dept Physics Fla State Univ Tallahassee FL 32306-3016. *Fax:* 850-644-3612; *E-Mail:* lanuttir@res.fsu.edu

LANOU, ROBERT EUGENE, JR, EXPERIMENTAL PHYSICS. *Current Pos:* mem fac, 59-66, chmn dept, 85-92, PROF PHYSICS, BROWN UNIV, 66- *Personal Data:* b Burlington, Vt, Feb 13, 28; m 60, Cornelia Wheeler; c Katharine B, Gregory P, Elizabeth M & Steven M. *Educ:* Worcester Polytech Univ, BS, 52; Yale Univ, PhD(physics), 57. *Prof Exp:* Physicist, Lawrence Radiation Lab, Univ Calif, 57-59. *Concurrent Pos:* Chmn, High Energy Discussion Group, Brookhaven Nat Lab, 81-83; consult, Brookhaven Nat Lab & US Dept Energy; mem, High Energy Physics Adv Panel Comt, Future High Energy Comput, Solar Neutrino Res; mem, exec comt, Div Particles & Fields, Am Phys Soc. *Mem:* Fel AAAS; fel Am Phys Soc. *Res:* Elementary particle physics; particle astrophysics. *Mailing Add:* Dept Physics Brown Univ Providence RI 02912

LANOUE, ALCIDE MOODIE, HEALTH CARE ADMINISTRATION. *Current Pos:* COMDT, ACAD HEALTH SCI, US ARMY, FT SAM HOUSTON, 86-; SURGEON GEN, DEPT ARMY GENERAL'S OFF, COMDR, ARMY MED COMMAND, FT SAM HOUSTON, 94- *Personal Data:* b Tonawanda, NY, Nov 2, 34; m 86, Beth Gortner; c Claire L, Alcide J, George E & Michelle. *Educ:* Harvard Univ, BA, 56; Yale Univ, MD, 60; Am Bd Orthop Surg, dipl. *Prof Exp:* Intern, Brooke Army Med Ctr, Tex, 60-61, res orthop surg, 63-66; mem staff, 2nd Surg Hosp, Repub Vietnam, 66-67, 24th Evacuation Hosp, Repub Vietnam, 67, Valley Forge Gen Hosp, Pa, 67-70, 71-73, Command & Gen Staff Col, Kans, 70-71, Walter Reed Army Med Ctr, Washington, DC, 73-77, Hanau Clin, Ger, 77-80, US Army MEDDAC, Ft Benning, Ga, 82-84; comdr, US Army MEDDAC, Ft Stewart, Ga, 80-82; cmndg gen, Dwight David Eisenhower Army Med Ctr, Ft Gordon, Ga, 84-86; Maj Gen, US Army Med Corps, 88. *Mem:* Fel Am Chem Soc; Am Acad Orthop Surg. *Res:* Orthopedic surgery; contributed many chapters to books and articles to professional journals. *Mailing Add:* Surgeon Gen Off 5109 Leesburg Pike No 6 Falls Church VA 22041-3208

LA NOUE, KATHRYN F, BIOCHEMISTRY, CELL PHYSIOLOGY. *Current Pos:* assoc prof, 74-81, PROF PHYSIOL, MILTON S HERSHEY MED CTR, PA STATE UNIV, 81- *Personal Data:* b Camden, NJ, Dec 21, 34; m 76; c 4. *Educ:* Bryn Mawr Col, AB, 56; Yale Univ, PhD(biochem), 60. *Prof Exp:* Res chemist, US Army Surg Res Unit, 61-67; NIH fel, Johnson Res Found, Sch Med, Univ Pa, 68-70, res assoc, 70, asst prof, 71-74. *Concurrent Pos:* Dr W D Stroud estab investr, Am Heart Asn, 71-76. *Mem:* AAAS; Am Chem Soc; Am Soc Biol Sci; Biophys Soc; Am Physiol Soc. *Res:* Control of mitochondrial metabolism; membrane transport mechanisms; mechanism of transmembrane signalling. *Mailing Add:* Dept Cell & Molecular Biol Milton S Hershey Med Ctr Pa State Univ Hershey PA 17033

LANOUX, SIGRED BOYD, INORGANIC CHEMISTRY. *Current Pos:* from asst prof to assoc prof chem, 74-81, PROF CHEM, UNIV SOUTHWESTERN LA, 66-74, head, Dept Chem, 72-86, dean sci, 86-92, PROF CHEM, UNIV SOUTHWESTERN LA, 74- *Personal Data:* b New Orleans, La, Nov 1, 31; m 54, Emily Broussard; c Yvonne & Jeannine. *Educ:* Southwestern La Univ, BS, 57; Tulane Univ, PhD(inorg chem), 62. *Prof Exp:* Res assoc, Univ Ill, Urbana, 61-62; res chemist, Textile Fibers Dept, E I du Pont de Nemours & Co, Inc, 62-66. *Mem:* Am Chem Soc; Sigma Xi. *Res:* Phosphazene chemistry. *Mailing Add:* 104 Ridgewood Lafayette LA 70506-3222. *Fax:* 318-482-5676; *E-Mail:* lanoux@usl.edu

LANPHERE, MARVIN ALDER, GEOLOGY, GEOCHEMISTRY. *Current Pos:* geologist, 63-67, dep asst chief geologist, Washington, DC, 67-69, RES GEOLOGIST, US GEOL SURV, CALIF, 69- *Personal Data:* b Spokane, Wash, Sept 29, 33; m 61, Joyce E Brown; c Christine, Darcy & Andrew. *Educ:* Mont Sch Mines, BS, 55; Calif Inst Technol, MS, 56, PhD(geol), 62. *Honors & Awards:* Meritorious Serv Award, Interior Dept. *Prof Exp:* Postdoctoral fel, Calif Inst Technol, 62-63. *Concurrent Pos:* Secy, Volcanol, Geochem & Petrol Sect, Am Geophys Union, 70-72; vis prof, Stanford Univ, 72; vis fel, Australian Nat Univ, 75-76. *Mem:* Fel Geol Soc Am; Am Geophys Union. *Res:* Geochronology, application of techniques of radioactive age determination of rocks and minerals to geological problems; isotope tracer studies of geological processes. *Mailing Add:* US Geol Surv 1036 Oakland Ave Menlo Park CA 94025. *Fax:* 650-329-4664; *E-Mail:* alder@mojave.wr.usgs.gov

LANPHIER, EDWARD HOWELL, DIVING MEDICINE, ENVIRONMENTAL PHYSIOLOGY. *Current Pos:* sr scientist prev med, 76-92, asst dir, 78-93, EMER SCIENTIST, UNIV WIS-MADISON, 93- *Personal Data:* b Madison, Wis, May 29, 22; m 78, Karron Baird. *Educ:* Univ Wis, BS, 46; Univ Ill, MS & MD, 49; MDiv, Nashotah House, 76. *Honors & Awards:* Behnke Award, Undersea & Hyperbaric Med Soc, 77. *Prof Exp:* Am Col Physicians res fel physiol, Grad Sch Med, Univ Pa, 50-51; asst med officer & physiologist, Exp Diving Unit, USN, 52-58, diving med officer, Eniwetok Proving Ground, 58, med officer, Underwater Demolition Team, Norfolk, Va, 58-59; from asst prof to assoc prof physiol, Sch Med, State Univ NY, Buffalo, 59-73. *Mem:* Am Physiol Soc; Undersea & Hyperbaric Med Soc; Am Acad Underwater Scis. *Res:* Respiratory physiology; submarine and diving medicine; physiological problems of immersion and exposure to increased pressure; hyperbaric medicine. *Mailing Add:* Dept Prev Med 504 Walnut St Madison WI 53705. *E-Mail:* lanphier@facstaff.wisc.edu

LANPHIER, ROBERT C, III, ENGINEERING. *Current Pos:* PRES, AGMED INC. *Personal Data:* b Nov 13, 32; wid; c 4. *Educ:* Dale Univ, REEE, 56, RSIA, 57. *Prof Exp:* Pres, Dickey Sch Corp. *Mem:* Nat Acad Eng. *Mailing Add:* AGMED Inc 713 W Prospect Springfield IL 62704. *Fax:* 217-744-0630

LANSBURY, PETER THOMAS, ORGANIC CHEMISTRY. *Current Pos:* from asst prof to assoc prof chem, 59-65, PROF CHEM, STATE UNIV NY BUFFALO, 65- *Personal Data:* b Vienna, Austria, Feb 24, 33; US citizen; m 57; c 3. *Educ:* Pa State Univ, BS, 53; Northwestern Univ, PhD(chem), 56. *Prof Exp:* Res scientist chem, E I du Pont de Nemours & Co, Inc, 56-58; lectr org chem, Univ Del, 58-59. *Concurrent Pos:* Prin investr, NSF res grants, 60-; vis prof chem, Univ Ill, Urbana, 63-64; fel, Alfred P Sloan Found, 63-67; consult, Hooker Chem Corp, 65-74; res award, Ciba-Geigy Corp, 73-74. *Mem:* Am Chem Soc; Sigma Xi. *Mailing Add:* 26 Morning Star Ct Buffalo NY 14221

LANSDELL, HERBERT CHARLES, NEUROPSYCHOLOGY, ANIMAL RESEARCH ETHICS. *Current Pos:* res supvr, 58-70, HEALTH SCI ADMINR, NAT INST NEUROL DIS & STROKE, 70- *Personal Data:* b Montreal, Que, Dec 22, 22; US citizen; div; c Grant & Bret. *Educ:* Sir George Williams Eve Col, BSc, 44; McGill Univ, PhD(psychol), 50. *Prof Exp:* Asst prof psychol, McGill Univ, 49-50; defense res sci officer, Defense Res Med Labs, 50-54; asst prof psychol, Univ Buffalo, 54-58. *Mem:* Fel Am Psychol Asn; fel AAAS; Soc Neurosci; Psychomet Soc; Int Brain Res Orgn. *Res:* Statistical analysis of psychological test results obtained from neurological patients to investigate brain function, especially hemispheric and sex differences; test construction. *Mailing Add:* Dis & Stroke Fed Bldg Rm 916 NIH Bethesda MD 20892-9170. *Fax:* 301-402-1501; *E-Mail:* hcl@nihcu

LANSDOWN, A(LLEN) M(AURICE), civil, structural & transportation engineering, for more information see previous edition

LANSFORD, EDWIN MYERS, JR, BIOCHEMISTRY, MICROBIOLOGY. *Current Pos:* RETIRED. *Personal Data:* b Houston, Tex, June 26, 23; m 50, 81, Ingrid Gimm; c Elayne, Daniel & Ralph. *Educ:* Univ Calif, Los Angeles, BA, 46; Rice Univ, BA, 48; Univ Tex, MA, 51, PhD(biochem), 51. *Prof Exp:* Fel, Univ Ill, 51-52; res scientist, Clayton Found Biochem Inst, Univ Tex, 53-67; prof biochem, Southwestern Univ, Georgetown, Tex, 67-93. *Mem:* Am Chem Soc; Sigma Xi; NY Acad Sci. *Res:* Microbial intermediary metabolism; amino acid activating enzymes; metabolic effects of alcohol; single carbon unit metabolism and its control. *Mailing Add:* 1202 Peachtree St Georgetown TX 78626

LANSING, ALLAN M, CARDIOVASCULAR SURGERY, ORGAN TRANSPLANTATION. *Current Pos:* DIR CARDIOVASC SURG, AUDUBON HEART INST, 93- *Personal Data:* b St Catherines, Ont, Sept 12, 29; m 51; c 3. *Educ:* Univ Western Ont, MD, 53, PhD(physiol), 57; FRCS(C), 59. *Hon Degrees:* LHD, Bellarmine Col, Louisville, Ky, 85; DSc, Transylvania Univ, Lexington, Ky, 85. *Honors & Awards:* Hon G Ferguson Trophy, Western Ont Fac Med, 53. *Prof Exp:* Nat Res Coun Can scholar, Univ Western Ont, 55-57; asst prof surg & physiol, Fac Med, Univ Western Ont, 61-63; assoc prof, Sch Med, Univ Louisville, 63-69, chief, Sect

Cardiovasc Surg, 69-74, prof surg, 69-80, prog surg thoracic & cardiovasc, 80-84; dir cardiovasc surg, Humana Heart Inst Int, Louisville, Ky, 83-93. *Concurrent Pos:* Markle scholar med sci, 61-; bd mem, Nat Kidney Found, Louisville, Western Ky, Bellarmine Col, Louisville, Ky & Transylvania Univ, Lexington, Ky, 85- *Mem:* Fel Am Col Surg; fel Am Col Cardiol; Soc Univ Surg; Royal Col Surg Can; Warren H Cole Soc. *Res:* Cardiovascular physiology and shock; pulmonary atelectasis; renal transplantation; open heart surgery; 055912110research in heart replacement, including transplantation and the mechanical heart and the major fields at present; promotion and improvement of college education. *Mailing Add:* 3200 Boxhill Lane Louisville KY 40222

LANSINGER, JOHN MARCUS, GEOPHYSICS, IONOSPHERIC PHYSICS. *Current Pos:* PVT CONSULT, QUITEK, 80- *Personal Data:* b July 20, 32; US citizen; m 53; c 2. *Educ:* Lewis & Clark Col, BS, 54; Univ Alaska, MS, 56. *Prof Exp:* Instr geophys, Univ Alaska, 56-57; sr engr, Philco Corp, 57-59; staff assoc, Boeing Sci Res Labs, Northwest Environ Technol Labs, Inc, 59-69, vpres, 69-76; staff mem, Phys Dynamics Inc, 76-79. *Mem:* Am Geophys Union; Inst Elec & Electronics Engrs; Air Pollution Control Asn; Am Phys Soc. *Res:* Environmental sciences; ionospheric research; atmospheric propagation at optical wavelengths. *Mailing Add:* 9301 26th Pl NW Seattle WA 98117

LANSKA, DOUGLAS JOHN, ADULT & GERIATRIC NEUROLOGY, NEUROEPIDEMIOLOGY & DEMENTIA. *Current Pos:* asst prof neurol, 89-92, ASSOC PROF NEUROL, PREV MED & ENVIRON HEALTH, UNIV KY, 89-; STAFF NEUROLOGIST, VET AFFAIRS MED CTR, 89- *Personal Data:* b Milwaukee, Wis, Aug 6, 59; m 82, Mary Jo Brook; c Joseph & John. *Educ:* Univ Wis, BS, 80; Med Col Wis, MS, 84, MD, 84; Univ Ky, MSPH, 96. *Honors & Awards:* Career Investr Develop Award, Nat Inst Neurol Dis & Stroke, 91; McHenry Award, Am Acad Neurol, 97. *Prof Exp:* Consult comput programmer, CSI Corp, 82-84; resident physician, Univ Hosps Cleveland, 84-88, instr neurol, 88-89. *Concurrent Pos:* Nat res serv award, Nat Inst Aging, 84; assoc, Sanders Brown Ctr Aging, 89-; assoc med staff, Div Maternal & Child Health, Commonwealth Ky, 89-; consult, Ky Med Rev Bd, 89-, Commonwealth Ky Ctr Excellence in Stroke, 91, Internal Med Ctr Advan Res & Educ, 91-; adv panel mem, Am Med Asn, 91-; staff neurologist, Vet Affairs Med Ctr, Lexington, 91-; mem, Agency Health Care Policy & Res Clin Pract Guidelines, 92-94, Am Bd Psychiat & Neurol Test Comt, 92- & Dept Vet Affairs Comt, 93-94; fac res award, Col Med, Univ Ky, 93. *Mem:* Am Acad Neurol; World Fedn Neurol; Am Heart Asn Stroke Coun; Am Col Physician Execs; Am Neurol Asn; Asn Univ Profs Neurol. *Res:* Epidemiologic studies of neurologic diseases especially investigations of factors producing temporal trends and large scale patterns of morbidity and mortality; stroke, dementia, Alzheimer's disease, Parkinson's disease, amyotrophic lateral sclerosis and Huntington's disease. *Mailing Add:* Dept Neurol Univ Ky Ky Clin L-412 Lexington KY 40536-0284. *Fax:* 606-323-5943; *E-Mail:* djlansva@ukcc.uky.edu

LANSKI, CHARLES PHILIP, MATHEMATICS, NONCOMMUTATIVE RING THEORY. *Current Pos:* From asst prof to assoc prof, 69-81, PROF MATH, UNIV SOUTHERN CALIF, 82- *Personal Data:* b Chicago, Ill, Oct 19, 43. *Educ:* Univ Chicago, SB, 65, SM, 66, PhD(math), 69. *Concurrent Pos:* NSF grant, 71-78. *Mem:* Am Math Soc; Math Asn Am. *Res:* Noncommutative ring theory; rings with involution; derivations and identities of prime rings. *Mailing Add:* Univ Southern Calif Los Angeles CA 90089-1113

LANSON, HERMAN JAY, ORGANIC CHEMISTRY. *Current Pos:* TECH CONSULT, 85- *Personal Data:* b Utica, NY, Feb 22, 13; m 35; c 3. *Educ:* Syracuse Univ, BS, 34, MS, 36; Polytech Inst New York, PhD(org chem), 45. *Honors & Awards:* St Louis Gateway Award. *Prof Exp:* Org res chemist, Nuodex Prod Co, Inc, NJ, 36-40; res chemist, H D Roosen Co, NY, 40-43; chief chemist, Crown Oil Co Prod Corp, 43-45; supvr, Vehicle Res & Prod, Grand Rapids Varnish Corp, 45-50; supvr, resin & plasticizer develop, Chem Mat Dept, Gen Elec Co, 50-57; vpres & tech dir, US Vehicle & Chem Co, 57-61; vpres & res dir, Lanson Chem Corp, 61-70, pres & res dir, Washburn Lanson Corp, 70-75; pres & res dir, Lanchem Corp, 75-84. *Concurrent Pos:* Lectr, Washington Univ, Roosevelt Univ, Chicago, Univ Houston, Univ Mo & St Louis Univ. *Mem:* Am Oil Chem Soc; Soc Plastics Engrs; fel Am Inst Chemists; Am Chem Soc. *Res:* Synthetic resins; drying oils; protective coatings; electrical insulation materials; development of water-soluble polymers, synthetic latexes, synthetic resins for electrical insulation and coatings. *Mailing Add:* 564 Sarah Lane St Louis MO 63141

LANTER, ROBERT JACKSON, PHYSICS, NUCLEAR WEAPON ENGINEERING. *Current Pos:* Alt group leader physics, 46-48, STAFF MEM PHYSICS & ENG, LOS ALAMOS NAT LAB, UNIV CALIF, 49- *Personal Data:* b Middletown, Ohio, Nov 9, 14; m 47; c 2. *Educ:* Univ Utah, BA, 42; Univ NMex, MS, 57. *Mem:* Am Phys Soc; AAAS. *Res:* Neutron production and detection; developed 1-meter diameter liquid scintillation counter for detection of bursts of fewer than 100 neutrons; helped develop D-T pulsed neutron sources; silver counter for detecting and counting deutron-deutron reaction and deutrium-tritium reaction neutrons. *Mailing Add:* 2438 Club Rd Los Alamos NM 87544

LANTERMAN, ELMA, ANALYTICAL CHEMISTRY. *Current Pos:* RETIRED. *Personal Data:* b Elkhart, Ill, Jan 25, 17. *Educ:* Univ Ill, BS, 40; Ind Univ, MA, 48, PhD(analytical chem), 51. *Prof Exp:* Chem technician, Mayo Clin, 41-42; chemist, Devoe & Raynolds Co, 42-43 & Metal & Thermit Corp, 43-46; asst, Univ Ind, 46-51; asst prof physics, NC State Col, 51-53; supvr, Metal Groups, Indianapolis Naval Ord Plant, 53-55; sr res chemist, Am Can Co, 55-59; sr res chemist, Borg-Warner Corp, 59-61, scientist, 61-63, mgr analytical chem, 63-74, staff scientist, Res Ctr, 74-82. *Concurrent Pos:* Comnr, Environ Comn, Des Plaines, Ill, 74-79. *Mem:* Am Chem Soc; Electron Micros Soc Am; Am Crystallog Asn; Soc Appl Spectros (treas, 70-74); Sigma Xi. *Res:* X-ray diffraction and spectroscopy; electron microscopy; technology forecasting. *Mailing Add:* 1124 E Vilas Marshfield WI 54449-1640

LANTERMAN, WILLIAM STANLEY, III, PLANT PATHOLOGY. *Current Pos:* Head, Plant Quarantine Sect, 85-87, DIR CTR PLANT HEALTH, AGR CAN RES & QUARANTINE STA, SIDNEY, BC, 87-, DIR, PLANT PROTECTION DIV, 94- *Personal Data:* b Portsmouth, Va, Sept 8, 47; m 75, Denise M MacDonald; c Samuel MacDonald & Ian Kennedy. *Educ:* Univ Maine, BS, 80; Cornell Univ, MPS, 82, PhD, 85. *Concurrent Pos:* Dir & exec mem coop adv bd, Univ Victoria, BC, 88-; chmn, Comt Cert Stand, NAm Plant Protection Orgn, Ottawa, Ont, 89- *Res:* Plant pathology and regulatory aspects of the international movement of plant germ plasm. *Mailing Add:* Agr Can Ctr Plant Health 8801 E Saanich Rd Sidney BC V8L 1H3 Can. *Fax:* 250-363-6661; *E-Mail:* lantermanw@em.agr.ca

LANTERO, ORESTE JOHN, JR, BIOCHEMISTRY, ORGANIC CHEMISTRY. *Current Pos:* RES SCIENTIST BIOCHEM, SOLVAY INC, 73- *Personal Data:* b Chicago, Ill, Aug 26, 42; m 67; c 2. *Educ:* Purdue Univ, BS, 64; NDak State Univ, PhD(biochem), 71. *Prof Exp:* Res fel, Merrell Nat Lab, 71-73. *Mem:* AAAS. *Res:* Isolation and characterization of enzymes; preparation and characterization of immobilized enzymes. *Mailing Add:* 59731 Ridgewood Dr Goshen IN 46526

LANTOS, P(ETER) R(ICHARD), CHEMICAL ENGINEERING. *Current Pos:* PRES, TARGET GROUP, INC, 80- *Personal Data:* b Budapest, Hungary, July 18, 24; nat US; m 47; c 4. *Educ:* Cornell Univ, BChE, 45, PhD(chem eng), 50. *Prof Exp:* Develop chemist, Gen Elec Co, 46-47; res engr, E I du Pont de Nemours & Co, Inc, 50-55, res supvr, 55-60; mgr appln & prod develop, Celanese Plastics Co, 61-63, mgr res & develop, 64-69; dir develop, Sun Chem Corp, 69-70, vpres res & develop, 70-75; gen mgr, Plastics Div, Rhodia Inc, 75; dir res & develop, Arco Polymers, Inc, 76-77, vpres, 78-79. *Concurrent Pos:* Chmn, Chem Mkts & Econ, Div Am Chem Soc; chmn, Res Mgt Group, Philadelphia. *Mem:* Asn Consult Chemists & Chem Engrs; Am Chem Soc; Am Inst Chem Engrs; Plastic Inst Am; Soc Plastics Engrs. *Res:* Polymers; plastics; fibers. *Mailing Add:* 1000 Harston Lane Glenside PA 19038

LANTZ, THOMAS LEE, POWER HYDRAULICS, LUBRICATION OF INDUSTRIAL MACHINERY. *Current Pos:* MTCE engr, 59-67, PLANT HYDRAUL & LUBRICATION ENGR, WHEELING-PITTSBURGH STEEL, 67- *Personal Data:* b Clarksburg, WVa, July 12, 36; m 61; c 2. *Educ:* WVa Univ, BS, 59; Univ Pittsburgh, MA, 67. *Concurrent Pos:* Dir, Am Soc Lubrication Engrs, 74-84; comt mem, Asn Iron & Steel Engrs, 75-; instr tech math & physics, Belmont Tech Community Col, 77-87; instr hydraul, drafting, eng, WVa Northern Community Col, 87- *Mem:* Fel Am Soc Lubrication Engrs (vpres, 74-84). *Res:* Power hydraulics; lubrication of industrial machinery; several technical articles. *Mailing Add:* 124 E Cardinal Ave Wheeling WV 26003

LANYI, JANOS K, BIOCHEMISTRY. *Current Pos:* PROF PHYSIOL & BIOPHYS, UNIV CALIF, IRVINE, 80-, DEPT CHAIR, 95- *Personal Data:* b Budapest, Hungary, June 5, 37; US citizen; m 88; c Brigitte Schobert. *Educ:* Stanford Univ, BS, 59; Harvard Univ, MA, 61, PhD(biochem), 63. *Honors & Awards:* Except Sci Achievement Medal, NASA, 77; H Julian Allen Award, 78; Alexander von Humbolt Prize, 79. *Prof Exp:* NIH fel genetics, Sch Med, Stanford Univ, 63-65; Nat Acad Sci-Nat Res Coun res assoc biochem, 65-66; res scientist, Planetary Biol Div, Ames Res Ctr, NASA, 66-80. *Mem:* Biophys Soc; Am Soc Biol Chem; Hungarian Acad Sci. *Res:* Structure and function of enzymes and membranes in halophilic microorganisms; bacteriorhodopsin, halorhodopsin; energetics and mechanism of proton and chloride transport. *Mailing Add:* Dept Physiol & Biophys Univ Calif Irvine CA 92717. *Fax:* 714-824-8540; *E-Mail:* jlanyi@orion.oac.uci.edu

LANYON, HUBERT PETER DAVID, SOLID STATE PHYSICS. *Current Pos:* assoc prof, 67-77, PROF ELEC ENG, WORCESTER POLYTECH INST, 77- *Personal Data:* b Halesowen, Eng, June 25, 36; m 79; c 5. *Educ:* Cambridge Univ, BA, 58, MA, 62; Leicester Univ, PhD(physics), 61. *Prof Exp:* Res demonstr physics, Leicester Univ, 58-61; res assoc elec eng, Univ Ill, Urbana, 61-63; mem tech staff, RCA Labs, 63-66; assoc prof elec eng, Carnegie Inst Technol, 66-67. *Mem:* Inst Elec & Electronics Engrs; Sigma Xi. *Res:* Physics of solid state devices; device modelling; integrated circuits; solar cell physics; instrumentation. *Mailing Add:* Elec Eng & Comput Dept Worcester Polytech Inst 100 Institute Rd Worcester MA 01609-2247

LANYON, SCOTT MERRIL, ORNITHOLOGY, BIOCHEMICAL SYSTEMATICS. *Current Pos:* From asst cur to assoc cur, 85-92, chair, Dept Zool, 90-93, PRITZKER CUR SYSTEMATIC BIOL, FIELD MUS NATURAL HIST, 93- *Personal Data:* b Tucson, Ariz, July 17, 56; m 81, Vicki Umbach; c Ashley & Cassandra. *Educ:* State Univ NY Col Geneseo, BA, 77; Ind Univ, MA, 80; La State Univ, PhD(evolutionary biol), 85. *Concurrent Pos:* Lectr, Univ Chicago, 85-; prin investr, NSF Grant, 86-89, 87-90 & 91-96; adj prof, Ill State Univ, 88-, Univ Ill, Chicago, 93-; counr, Wilson Ornith Soc, 90-91, Am Ornith Union, 93- *Mem:* Fel Am Ornithologists Union; Wilson Ornithol Soc; Cooper Ornithol Soc; Soc Syst Zoologists; Soc Study Evolution. *Res:* Using DNA sequence data to construct and test hypotheses of evolutionary relationships for birds; studies of the evolution of behavior, morphology and ecology. *Mailing Add:* 6665 Sherman Lake Rd Hugo MN 55038. *E-Mail:* lanyon@fmnh785.fmnh.org

LANYON, WESLEY EDWIN, ornithology, for more information see previous edition

LANZA, GIOVANNI, PHYSICS. *Current Pos:* assoc prof, 58-60, PROF PHYSICS, NORTHEASTERN UNIV, 60- *Personal Data:* b Trieste, Italy, Aug 5, 26; m 50; c 4. *Educ:* Univ Trieste, PhD, 50. *Prof Exp:* Asst prof quantum theory, Univ Trieste, 50-52; prof, Univ Cagliari, Univ Sardinia & Univ Padua, 52-54; vis physicist nuclear physics, Mass Inst Technol, 54-55; res fel, Harvard Univ, 55-58. *Concurrent Pos:* Fulbright & Smith Mundt scholars, 54; consult, Lab Electronics, Inc, 58- & Saunders Assocs, 63- *Mem:* Ital Phys Soc; Sigma Xi. *Res:* Magnetohydrodynamics; plasma physics; energy conversion techniques; nuclear physics; physics of upper atmosphere. *Mailing Add:* PO Box 1083 Campton NH 03223

LANZA, GUY ROBERT, AQUATIC ECOLOGY. *Current Pos:* PROF ENVIRON HEALTH, ETENN STATE UNIV, 89- *Personal Data:* b Englewood, NJ, Jan 27, 39; m 68; c 2. *Educ:* Fairleigh Dickinson Univ, BS, 61; Univ Ky, MS, 69; Va Polytech Inst & State Univ, PhD(zool), 72. *Prof Exp:* Res biologist, Merck Inst Therapeut Res, 63-69; aquatic ecologist, Smithsonian Inst, 71-73 & NY Univ, 73-75; aquatic ecologist, Univ Tex, Dallas, 75-89, assoc prof environ sci, 75-90. *Concurrent Pos:* Consult ecologist, Int Ctr Med Res & Training, Malaysia, 72-73; asst dir, Aquatic ecol prog, NY Univ Med Ctr, 73-75; subcomt partic, Nat Comn Water Qual, 75. *Mem:* AAAS; Water Pollution Control Fedn. *Res:* Structure and function of aquatic ecosystems; pollution ecology and the environmental physiology and energetics of aquatic organisms. *Mailing Add:* Dept Environ Health E Tenn State Univ PO Box 10001 Johnson City TN 37614-0002

LANZA, RICHARD CHARLES, PHYSICS. *Current Pos:* Res assoc physics, Mass Inst Technol, 66-68, asst prof, 68-74, mem res staff, 74-83, PRIN SCIENTIST, MASS INST TECHNOL, 83- *Personal Data:* b New York, NY, Apr 28, 39; m 63; c 1. *Educ:* Princeton Univ, AB, 59; Univ Pa, MS, 61, PhD(physics), 66. *Concurrent Pos:* Assoc radiol, Harvard Med Sch & Peter Bent Brigham Hosp, 74-; res fel, Mass Gen Hosp, 75-76. *Mem:* AAAS; Inst Elec & Electronics Engrs; Am Phys Soc. *Res:* Experimental particle physics, nuclear and electronic instrumentation, medical instrumentation, especially in radiology and nuclear medicine; imaging for nondestructive testing and evaluation. *Mailing Add:* Dept Nuclear Eng Rm NW13-219 Mass Inst Technol Cambridge MA 02139. *Fax:* 617-253-2343; *E-Mail:* lanza@mit.edu

LANZA-JACOBY, SUSAN, NUTRITION, INFECTION. *Current Pos:* PROF, THOMAS JEFFERSON UNIV, 79- *Personal Data:* m 78; c 1. *Educ:* Hunter Col, BS, 65; Columbia Univ, MS, 68; Rutgers Col, PhD(nutrit biochem), 79. *Concurrent Pos:* Lectr, Hunter Col, 68-72; instr, Philadelphia Gen Hosp Sch Nursing, 72-77. *Mem:* Am Inst Nutrit; Am Dietetic Asn; Shock Soc; Am Soc Parenteral Nutrit. *Res:* Lipid metabolism in infection, tumor growth, and parenteral feeding; lipids and lipoproteins. *Mailing Add:* Dept Surg Thomas Jefferson Univ 1025 Walnut St Philadelphia PA 19107-5001. *Fax:* 215-923-1420

LANZANO, BERNADINE CLARE, COMPUTER SCIENCE, MATHEMATICS. *Current Pos:* SR STAFF ENGR COMPUT SCI, TRW SYSTS GROUP, 57- *Personal Data:* b Stanberry, Mo, Oct 29, 33; m 57. *Educ:* Benedictine Col, BS, 55. *Prof Exp:* Mathematician, Lockheed Corp, 56-57. *Mem:* Math Asn Am; Soc Indust & Appl Math. *Res:* Design and development of computer software in the areas of trajectory analysis, optimization, targeting, and in the fields of information processing of financial and scientific data; management of database management systems applications software development, installation, and operational support. *Mailing Add:* 1630 Eagle Nest Circle Winter Springs FL 32706

LANZANO, PAOLO, APPLIED MATHEMATICS, SPACE PHYSICS. *Current Pos:* head math res ctr, 72-76, SR RES SCIENTIST, NAVAL RES LAB, 76- *Personal Data:* b Cairo, Egypt, Nov 29, 23; nat US; m 57. *Educ:* Univ Rome, BS, 43, PhD(math), 47. *Prof Exp:* Asst prof math, Univ Rome, 46-49 & St Louis Univ, 50-56; design specialist, Douglas Aircraft Co, Calif, 56-58; mem tech staff, Space Tech Labs, Calif, 58-60; res scientist, Nortronics Div, Northrop Corp, 60-61; prin scientist, Space & Info Systs Div, NAm Aviation, 61-71; assoc prof math, Nicholls State Univ, 71-72. *Concurrent Pos:* Fel, Inst Advan Studies, Univ Rome, 46-48. *Mem:* Am Math Soc; Am Geophys Union Soc; Soc Indust & Appl Math; assoc fel Am Inst Aeronaut & Astronaut. *Res:* Celestial mechanics; theory of relativity; Riemannian geometry; space physics; geodesy; geophysics. *Mailing Add:* 1630 Eagle Nest Circle Winter Springs FL 32708

LANZEROTTI, LOUIS JOHN, GEOPHYSICS, SPACE PHYSICS. *Current Pos:* Fel, 65-67, mem, 67-82, DISTINGUISHED MEM TECH STAFF, BELL LABS LUCENT TECHNOLOGIES, 82- *Personal Data:* b Carlinville, Ill, Apr 16, 38; m 65; c 2. *Educ:* Univ Ill, BS, 60; Harvard Univ, AM, 63, PhD(physics), 65. *Honors & Awards:* Lisle Abbott Rose Eng Award, 60; NASA Distinguished Pub Serv Medal, 88; Antarctica Geog Feature named in honor, Mt Lanzerotti; 24th Harry G Armstrong Lectr, Aerospace Med Asn, 89; Dean John R Benton Lectr, Col Eng, Univ Fla, 94. *Concurrent Pos:* Assoc ed, J Geophys Res, 71-75; mem, Space Sci Adv Comt, NASA, 75-79, Space & Earth Sci Adv Comt, 84-88, Adv Coun, 84-; adj prof, Univ Fla, 78-; mem, Space Sci Bd, Nat Acad Sci, 79-83 & 88-, Polar Res Bd, 82-90; regents lectr, Univ Calif, Los Angeles, 87. *Mem:* Nat Acad Eng; fel Am Phys Soc; fel Am Geophys Union; sr mem Inst Elec & Electronics Engrs; Soc Terrestial Magnetism & Elec Japan; assoc fel Am Inst Aeronaut & Astronaut; fel AAAS; Int Acad Astronaut; Am Astron Soc; Europ Geophys Soc. *Res:* Particles and fields in planetary magnetospheres; solar cosmic ray composition and propagation; ionosphere-magnetosphere coupling; planetary magnetospheres; geomagnetic depth sounding; impacts of space effects on technologies. *Mailing Add:* Bell Labs Lucent Technologies Rm 1E-439 600 Mountain Ave Murray Hill NJ 07974

LANZEROTTI, MARY YVONNE DEWOLF, PHYSICAL CHEMISTRY. *Current Pos:* RES PHYS SCIENTIST, E&W DIV, US ARMY ARDEC, 65- *Personal Data:* b Phoenix, Ariz, Nov 7, 38; m 65, Louis J; c Mary & Louis. *Educ:* Univ Calif, Berkeley, BS, 60; Harvard Univ, PhD(phys chem), 65. *Honors & Awards:* Res & Develop Achievement Award, Dept Army Res, 95. *Prof Exp:* Chemist, US Naval Ord Test Sta, 60; asst, Harvard Univ, 60-64; res chemist, Mithras Inc, Mass, 64-65. *Mem:* AAAS; Am Chem Soc; Am Phys Soc; Am Soc Mech Engrs; Am Defense Preparedness Asn; Mat Res Soc. *Res:* Mechanical behavior of materials under high acceleration; power spectral analysis of fracture surface topography; crystal growth of energetic materials during high acceleration using an ultracentrifuge. *Mailing Add:* E&W Div Bldg 3022 US Army ARDEC Picatinny Arsenal NJ 07806-5000

LANZKOWSKY, PHILIP, PEDIATRICS, HEMATOLOGY. *Current Pos:* PROF PEDIAT, STATE UNIV NY STONY BROOK, 70- *Personal Data:* b Cape Town, SAfrica, Mar 17, 32; m 55; c 5. *Educ:* Univ Cape Town, MB ChB, 54, MD, 59; Royal Col Physicians & Surgeons, dipl child health, 60; Am Bd Pediat, dipl, 66, cert pediat hematol-oncol, 75; FRCP(E), 73. *Hon Degrees:* DSc, St Johns Univ NY, 95. *Honors & Awards:* Joseph Arenow Prize, 59. *Prof Exp:* From intern to sr intern, Groote Schuur Hosp, Univ Cape Town, 55-56; gen pract, 56-57; from registr to sr registr, Red Cross War Mem Children's Hosp, 57-60, consult pediatrician & pediat hematologist, 63-65; asst prof pediat, NY Hosp-Cornell Med Ctr, 65-67, assoc prof, 67-70. *Concurrent Pos:* Dr C L Herman res grants, 58 & 64; Cecil John Adams mem traveling fel & Hill-Pattison-Struthers bursary, 60; Benger Labs traveling grant, 61; registr pediat unit, St Mary's Hosp Med Sch, Univ London, 61; clin & res fel pediat hemat, Duke Univ, 61-62; res fel, Col Med, Univ Utah, 62-63; lectr, Univ Cape Town, 63-65; dir pediat hemat, New York Hosp-Cornell Med Ctr, 65-70; pediatrician-in-chief, chmn pediat & chief pediat hemat, Long Island Jewish-Hillside Med Ctr, 70-; pediatrician-in-chief, Queens Hosp Ctr, 70-; mem pediat adv comt NY City Dept Health, 70-73. *Mem:* Am Soc Hemat; Am Acad Pediat; Am Soc Clin Oncol; Am Asn Cancer Res; Am Pediat Soc. *Res:* Nutritional anemias in children, especially iron, folate and protein deficiency; pediatric oncology. *Mailing Add:* L I Jewish Med Ctr New Hyde Park NY 11040

LANZKRON, ROLF W, ASTROPHYSICS, AERONAUTICAL & ASTRONAUTICAL ENGINEERING. *Current Pos:* PRES, R W L ASSOCS, 95- *Personal Data:* b Hamburg, Ger, Dec 9, 29; nat US; m 61, Virginia Yarri; c Paul, Sophie & Lisa. *Educ:* Milwaukee Sch Eng, BS, 54; Univ Wis, MS, 55, PhD, 56. *Honors & Awards:* Outstanding Achievement Award, NASA, 64. *Prof Exp:* Asst, Univ Wis, 55-56; asst res & develop, Univac Div, Sperry Rand Corp, 56-57; design engr, Martin Co, 57-62; chief flight projs, Div, Apollo, NASA, 62-68; prog mgr, Fed Aviation Admin Display Systs, Raytheon Co, 68-73; prog mgr Air Force AN-TPN/19 Prog, 73-78, opers mgr graphic oper, 78-81, graphic systs mgr, 81-83, dep dir, Air Traffic Control, 83-92, dir, Air Traffic Control, 93-95. *Mem:* Am Inst Aeronaut & Astronaut; Sigma Xi; Math Asn Am; Inst Elec & Electronics Engrs. *Res:* Several papers on control system; several papers on automatic checkout of space craft; paper on display technology; research in air traffic control; vessel traffic control. *Mailing Add:* 2 Mallard Way Gloucester MA 01930

LANZL, LAWRENCE HERMAN, PHYSICS, MEDICAL PHYSICS. *Current Pos:* sr physicist, Univ Chicago, 51-55, from asst prof to assoc prof, Dept Radiol, Sch Med, 55-68, prof med physics, div biol sci, 68-80, EMER PROF, DIV BIOL SCI, PRITZKER SCH MED & FRANKLIN MCLEAN MEM RES INST, UNIV CHICAGO, 80-; PROF MED PHYSICS & EMER CHMN DEPT MED PHYSICS, COL HEALTH SCI, RUSH UNIV, RUSH PRESBY ST LUKES MED CTR, CHICAGO, 80- , EMER PROF, DEPT RADIATION ONCOL, RUSH MED COL, 91- *Personal Data:* b Chicago, Ill, Apr 8, 21; m 47, Elisabeth Farber; c Eric L & Barbara. *Educ:* Northwestern Univ, BS, 43; Univ Ill, MS, 47, PhD(physics), 51; Am Bd Health Physics, dipl, 60, 85 & 93, Am Bd Radiol, dipl, 67, Am Bd Med Physics, dipl, 90. *Honors & Awards:* Coolidge Award, Am Asn Physicists Med, 78; Landauer Award, 89; Farrington Daniels Award, 84; Inst named in honor of Lawrence H Lanzl, Inst Med Physics, Seattle, Wash; Failla Mem Lect, NY, 96. *Prof Exp:* Asst, Dearborn Observ, Ill, 41-42, Northwestern Univ, 42-43, Univ Chicago, 44, asst, Univ Ill, 46-50; jr scientist, Los Alamos Sci Lab, 44-45; assoc physicist, Argonne Nat Lab, 51. *Concurrent Pos:* Fac, Argonne Cancer Res Hosp, 51-; first officer, Int Atomic Energy Comn, Vienna, Austria, 67-68; bd mem, Am Int Sch, Vienna, 67-68; mem, Nat Coun Radiation Protection, 67 & US Nat Comt Med Physics, 70-; chmn, Radiation Protection Adv Coun, State of Ill, 71-; mem tech adv panel, Los Alamos Meson Physics Facil, Los Alamos, NMex & steering comt, radiol physics ctr, Univ Tex M D Anderson Hosp & Tumor Inst; consult, Int Atomic Energy Agency, Vienna, Hines Vet Admin Hosp, Ill, NIH & WHO, Geneva; consult radiation dosimetry prob, India, 73, Turkey, 75, Saudia Arabia, 75, Iran, 76, Israel, 77, Ghana, 78, Thailand, 79 & Nigeria, 81; chmn, Comn Accreditation Educ Progs Med Ph, 82-88; consult, Pan Am Health Org, Wash, DC, 93. *Mem:* AAAS; Asn Med Physicists India; Brit Hosp Physicists' Asn; fel Am Asn Physicists Med (pres, 67-68); Radiol Soc NAm; fel Health Physics Soc; Sigma Xi; fel Am Col Radiol; Int Orgn Med Physics (pres, 85-88); Int Union Phys & Eng Sci Med (pres, 88-91); hon mem Chinese Soc Med Physics. *Res:* Accelerators; radiation as applied to medicine; radiation physics; high energy x-rays and electrons; isotopes in medicine; nuclear reactors; health physics; radiation dosimetry. *Mailing Add:* 5750 S Kenwood Ave Chicago IL 60637-1744. *Fax:* 312-942-2339

LANZONI, VINCENT, PHARMACOLOGY, CLINICAL MEDICINE. *Current Pos:* dean & prof med, NJ Med Sch, 75-87, DEAN & PROF MED, GRAD SCH BIOMED SCIS, UNIV MED & DENT NJ, 87- *Personal Data:* b Kingston, Mass, Feb 23, 28; m 60, Phoebe Krey; c Susan, Karen & Margaret. *Educ:* Tufts Univ, PhD(pharmacol), 53; Boston Univ, MD, 60. *Prof Exp:* Instr pharmacol, Sch Med, Tufts Univ, 53-54; from intern to resident, Boston City Hosp, 60-63; asst prof pharmacol & instr med, Sch Med, Boston Univ, 63- 66, assoc prof pharmacol & med, 66-73, assoc dean sch med, 69-75, prof pharmacol, 73-75. *Concurrent Pos:* Res fel, NIH, 53-54; fel med, Boston City Hosp, 63-65. *Mem:* Sigma Xi. *Res:* Cardiovascular pharmacology. *Mailing Add:* 1 Fairview Rd Millburn NJ 07041

LAO, BINNEG YANBING, ELECTRONICS ENGINEERING, APPLIED PHYSICS. *Current Pos:* VPRES, SIERRA MONOLITHICS, INC, 88- *Personal Data:* b Szechwan, China, Feb 25, 45; US citizen; m 70, Jennifer Dai; c Catherine & Richard. *Educ:* Univ Calif, Los Angeles, BS, 67; Princeton Univ, MA, 69, PhD(physics), 71. *Prof Exp:* NSF fel solid state physics, Ctr Theoret Physics, Univ Md, 71-73; sr res physicist instrumentation, Eastern Div Res Labs, Dow Chem Co, 73-76; prin physicist appl physics, Bendix Res Labs, Bendix Corp, 76-80; mgr, Microelectronics Magnavox Res Oper, Magnavox Adv Prod & Syst Co, 80-86; consult, 86-88. *Mem:* Am Phys Soc; Sigma Xi; Inst Elec & Electronics Engrs. *Res:* Radio frequency and microwave system development; superconducting sensors and electronics; wireless systems; nonlinear and excitonic effects in semiconductors; sensors and solid state devices. *Mailing Add:* 29722 Grandpoint Lane Rancho Palos Verdes CA 90275. *Fax:* 310-318-8635; *E-Mail:* blao@ix.netcom.com

LAO, CHANG SHENG, MEDICAL DEVICE & CLINICAL TRIALS REVIEW, IN-VITRO DIAGNOSTIC TESTS ANALYSIS. *Current Pos:* math statistician, Ctr Drugs Eval & Res, Food & Drug Admin, 74-80 & Ctr Radiol Health Devices, 80-86, supvry math statistician, Ctr Drugs Eval & Res, 86-87, MATH STATISTICIAN, CTR RADIOL HEALTH DEVICES, FOOD & DRUG ADMIN, 87- *Personal Data:* b Shanghai City, China, Dec 10, 35; US citizen; m 66, Ching C Wang; c Allen, Lawrence & Cathy. *Educ:* Nat Taiwan Univ, BA, 60; Univ Mass, MS, 66; Yale Univ, PhD(biostatist), 73. *Prof Exp:* Statistician, E I du Pont de Nemours & Co Inc, 66-68; med res scientist, Pa Dept Health, 73-74; epidemiologist, US Environ Protection Agency, 80. *Concurrent Pos:* Statist reviewer, Asn Off Analytical Chemists, 77-91; lectr med statist, Howard Univ Sch Med, 83. *Mem:* Am Statist Asn; Biomet Soc; Asn Off Analytical Chemists. *Res:* Statistical reviews of medical devices clinical trials; analyze the statistical and epidemiological data related to public health; design and analyze laboratory data on heart valve study; ethylene oxide study; in-vitro diagnostic tests. *Mailing Add:* 15429 Narcissus Way Rockville MD 20853. *Fax:* 301-443-8559; *E-Mail:* csl@fdadr.cdrh.fda.gov

LAO, LANG LI, NUCLEAR FUSION. *Current Pos:* PRIN SCIENTIST, GEN ATOMICS, 82- *Personal Data:* b Hai Duong, Vietnam, Jan 28, 54; m 79, Ngan Hua; c Bert J & Brian J. *Educ:* Calif Inst Technol, BS & MS, 76; Univ Wis-Madison, MS, 77 PhD, 79. *Honors & Awards:* Award for Excellence in Plasma Physics, Am Phys Soc, 94. *Prof Exp:* Staff scientist, Oak Ridge Nat Lab, Tenn, 79-81; Tactical Recon Wing, Redondo Beach, Calif, 81-82. *Mem:* Fel Am Phys Soc. *Res:* Equilibrium analysis of magnetic fusion; plasma physics experiments; developed a widely used computer code; published numerous articles. *Mailing Add:* Gen Atomics 3550 Gen Atomics Ct San Diego CA 92121-1122

LAO, YAN-JEONG, CHEMICAL ENGINEERING, ENVIRONMENTAL HEALTH. *Current Pos:* from asst prof to assoc prof, 73-81, chmn dept, 85-97, PROF ENVIRON HEALTH, ECAROLINA UNIV, 81- *Personal Data:* b Nanking, China, Feb 5, 36; US citizen; m 65; c 2. *Educ:* Nat Taiwan Univ, BS, 58; Univ Mich, MS, 62; PhD(chem eng), 69. *Prof Exp:* Res engr chem eng, E I du Pont de Nemours & Co, Inc, 69-71; sr engr, Monsanto Co, 72-73. *Mem:* Nat Environ Health Asn; Am Indust Hyg Asn; Sigma Xi. *Res:* Monitoring and analyzing environmental pollutants, the study of their effects and health related problems. *Mailing Add:* Dept Environ Health ECarolina Univ Greenville NC 27858

LAPALME, DONALD WILLIAM, PHOTOGRAPHIC ENGINEERING, PHYSICAL CHEMISTRY. *Current Pos:* Sr res chemist photo eng, Photo Div, Gaf Bldg Mats Corp, 67-72, sr prod engr, 72-74, prod mgr reprographics, 74-76, tech dir process eng, Res & Develop, 76-78, plant mgr prod, Photo Div, 78-81, VPRES OPERS, GAF BLDG MATS CORP, 81- *Personal Data:* b Woonsocket, RI, July 27, 37; m 61; c 4. *Educ:* St John's Univ NY, BS, 59, MS, 61, PhD(chem), 68. *Mem:* Soc Photog Scientists & Engrs (pres, 73-74); Am Chem Soc. *Res:* Photographic science. *Mailing Add:* 3002 Tudor Dr Wayne NJ 07444

LAPERRIERE, JACQUELINE DOYLE, AQUATIC FISHERIES. *Current Pos:* Water resource technician, Univ Alaska, Fairbanks, 71-72, res biologist, 72-73, aquatic biologist, 73-74, instr water resources, 74-79, asst prof, Inst Water Resources, 79-85, asst prof fisheries, 80-85, ASSOC PROF FISHERIES & WATER RESOURCES, COL NATURAL SCI & INST WATER RESOURCES, UNIV ALASKA, FAIRBANKS, 85-, ASST LEADER, ALASKA COOP FISHERY RES UNIT, 80- *Personal Data:* b Northampton, Mass, Dec 31, 42; div; c 2. *Educ:* Univ Mass, BS, 64; Iowa State Univ, MS, 71, PhD(water resources), 81. *Concurrent Pos:* Andrew W Mellon Found travel grant, 80. *Mem:* Am Fisheries Soc; Am Soc Limnol & Oceanog; Int Asn Limnol; NAm Benthol Soc; NAm Lake Mgt Soc; Sigma Xi. *Res:* Stream ecology, primary and secondary production, water quality and effects of development; limnology of subarctic lakes, thermal regime, chemical cycling and production; toxicity testing of Alaskan fishes. *Mailing Add:* PO Box 81547 Fairbanks AK 99708-1547

LAPETINA, EDUARDO G, PLATELET AGGREGATION, PHOSPHOLIPIDS. *Current Pos:* PROF MED, CASE WESTERN RES UNIV, 76- *Educ:* Univ Buenos Aires, Argentina, PhD(biochem), 67. *Prof Exp:* Group leader molecular biol, Wellcome Res Labs, Burroughs Wellcome Co, 76- *Res:* Thrombosis. *Mailing Add:* Molecular Cardiovasc Res Ctr Dept Med Case Western Res Univ 10900 Euclid Ave Cleveland OH 44106-4958

LAPEYRE, GERALD J, SOLID STATE PHYSICS, SURFACE PHYSICS. *Current Pos:* From asst prof to assoc prof physics, 62-74, PROF PHYSICS, MONT STATE UNIV, 74- *Personal Data:* b Riverton, Wyo, Jan 3, 34; m 60; c 3. *Educ:* Univ Notre Dame, BS, 56; Univ Mo, MA, 58, PhD(physics), 62. *Mem:* Fel Am Phys Soc; Am Asn Physics Teachers; Am Vacuum Soc. *Res:* Solid state physics surface science with emphasis on synchrotron photoemission and electronic structure. *Mailing Add:* Dept Physics Mont State Univ AJM Johnson Hall Bozeman MT 59717

LAPEYRE, JEAN-NUMA, MOLECULAR PATHOLOGY. *Current Pos:* proj investr, Exp Path Sect, M D Anderson Cancer Ctr, Univ Tex, 77-78, res assoc, 78-79, from instr to asst prof & asst biochemist, 79-85, ASSOC BIOCHEMIST & ASSOC PROF BIOCHEM, EXP PATH SECT, M D ANDERSON CANCER CTR, UNIV TEX, 85- *Personal Data:* b Los Angeles, Calif, Oct 17, 45. *Educ:* Univ Calif, Los Angeles, BS, 67, MS, 69; Univ Southern Calif, PhD(molecular biol), 75. *Prof Exp:* Lectr cell biol & dent biochem, Univ Southern Calif, 73-75; Fogarty Int fel, Swiss NSF, Univ Geneva, 75-77. *Concurrent Pos:* Lectr chem embryol, Molecular Biol Grad Sch, Univ Geneva, 76; vis exchange scientist, Nat Ctr Sci Res, Inst Molecular Biophys, Orleans, France, 82; mem NIH Study Sect, Clin Sci IV, 85-89, NSF Rev Bd, 90-; consult, DNA Sci, Inc, Houston & Cytol Technol, Inc. *Mem:* Am Soc Biochem & Molecular Biol; AAAS; Biophys Soc; Am Asn Cancer Res. *Res:* DNA chemical synthetic methods and DNA sequencing; DNA structure and conformation; author of numerous scientific publications. *Mailing Add:* Dept Gene Therapeut Tampa Bay Res Inst 10900 Roosevelt Blvd St Petersburg FL 33716

LAPHAM, LOWELL WINSHIP, NEUROPATHOLOGY. *Current Pos:* assoc prof path, 64-69, prof, 69-92, EMER PROF NEUROPATH, MED CTR, UNIV ROCHESTER, 92- *Personal Data:* b New Hampton, Iowa, Mar 20, 22; div; c Joan, Steven, Judith & Jennifer. *Educ:* Oberlin Col, BA, 43; Harvard Med Sch, MD, 48. *Prof Exp:* Sr instr path, Case Western Res Univ, 55-57, from asst prof to assoc prof, 57-64. *Concurrent Pos:* Nat Mult Sclerosis Soc fel cytochem, Case Western Res Univ, 56-58; consult neuropath, Univ Rochester Affil Hosps. *Mem:* Am Asn Neuropath; Sigma Xi. *Res:* Studies of developmental diseases of nervous system; brain tumors; nature and function of glia; effects of environmental substances on nervous system. *Mailing Add:* 121 Kendal Dr Oberlin OH 44074

LAPICKI, GREGORY, INNER SHELL IONIZATION. *Current Pos:* assoc prof, 81-87, PROF PHYSICS, E CAROLINA UNIV, 88- *Personal Data:* b Warsaw, Poland; US citizen. *Educ:* Warsaw Univ, MS, 67; NY Univ, PhD(physics), 75. *Prof Exp:* Post doc physics, NY Univ, 75-76, res scientist, 77-78; vis asst prof physics, Tex A&M Univ, 79-80; asst prof physics, Northwestern State Univ La, 80-81. *Concurrent Pos:* Prin investr, Nat Bur Stand, 82-84; partic, Oak Ridge Nat Lab, 81-87; panel reviewer, Off Naval Technol Postdoc Fel, 87; Fulbright Award, Arg, 91-92. *Mem:* Am Phys Soc; Sigma Xi. *Res:* Penetration of charged particles in matter; development of theories of inner-shell direct ionization and electron capture; study of asymmetric and symmetric ion-atom collisions; published over 80 refereed articles. *Mailing Add:* Dept Physics E Carolina Univ Greenville NC 27858. *Fax:* 919-757-6314; *E-Mail:* phgreg@ecuvm.cis.ecu.edu

LAPIDES, JACK, urology; deceased, see previous edition for last biography

LAPIDUS, ARNOLD, MATHEMATICS. *Current Pos:* ENTREPRENEUR, ADVAN MATH, 87- *Personal Data:* b Brooklyn, NY, Nov 6, 33; m 52. *Educ:* Brooklyn Col, BS, 56; NY Univ, MS, 60, PhD(math), 67. *Prof Exp:* Asst math, Courant Inst, NY Univ, 58-60, asst res scientist, AEC comput facil, 61-65, assoc res scientist, 61-68; math analyst, Comput Applns Inc-NASA, 68-69, sci prog mgr, 69-71; asst math prof, Fairleigh Dickinson Univ, 71-76, assoc prof quant analysis, 77-83, prof & chmn, Dept Comput & Decision Syst, 83-85; sr engr, Singer Electronic Syst Corp, 86-87. *Mem:* Soc Indust & Appl Math; Math Asn Am; Am Math Soc; AAAS. *Res:* Partial and ordinary differential equations, Monte Carlo methods; scientific programming; artificial intelligence; tedious algebra by computer; fluid dynamics by computer; shock calculations; numerical methods and analysis; linear programming; kalman filters; analysis of biological graphics. *Mailing Add:* 160 Rockwood Pl Englewood NJ 07631

LAPIDUS, HERBERT, PHARMACY, PHARMACOLOGY. *Current Pos:* tech dir, 70-77, VPRES RES & DEVELOP, COMBE INC, 77- *Personal Data:* b New York, NY, Aug 10, 31; m 52, Iris Felber; c Lani R & William S. *Educ:* Columbia Univ, BS, 53, MS, 55; Rutgers Univ, PhD(pharm), 67. *Prof Exp:* Proj leader, Julius Schmid Co, 57-60; proj leader pharm, Bristol-Myers Co, 60-63, group leader, 63-67, dept head, 67-70. *Mem:* Am Chem Soc; Sigma Xi; Soc Cosmetic Chemists; NY Acad Sci; Am Soc Clin Pharmacol & Therapeut; Am Asn Pharmaceut Scientists. *Res:* Development of pharmaceutical dosage forms, especially sustained release medication, biopharmaceutics and percutaneous absorption; development of new technology, such as hair dyes, skin and dental products, and veterinary products; granted 16 patents in the chemical and drug fields. *Mailing Add:* Combe Inc 1101 Westchester Ave White Plains NY 10604

LA PIDUS, JULES BENJAMIN, MEDICINAL CHEMISTRY. *Current Pos:* From asst prof to prof, Ohio State Univ, 58-67, assoc dean res, Grad Sch, 72-74, vprovost res & dean, 74-84, PROF MED CHEM, OHIO STATE UNIV, 67-; PRES, COUN GRAD SCHS, US, 84- *Personal Data:* b Chicago, Ill, May 1, 31; m 54, 70, Anne M LuPidus; c Steven, Amy, Mark & Marilyn. *Educ:* Univ Ill, BS, 54; Univ Wis, MS, 57, PhD(pharmaceut chem), 58. *Concurrent Pos:* Consult, Pharmacol & Toxicol Training Grants Comt, Nat Inst Gen Med Sci, NIH, 65-67, Prog Comt, 71-75; Pres Coun Grad Sch US, 84- *Mem:* Am Chem Soc; fel AAAS. *Res:* Structure-action relationships; autonomic pharmacology. *Mailing Add:* Coun Grad Schs One Dupont Circle NW Suite 430 Washington DC 20036-1173

LAPIDUS, MICHEL LAURENT, FUNCTIONAL ANALYSIS, MATHEMATICAL PHYSICS. *Current Pos:* PROF MATH, UNIV CALIF, RIVERSIDE, 90- *Personal Data:* b Casablanca, Morocco, July 4, 56; m 80, Odile Ioos; c Julie A & Michael A. *Educ:* Univ Pierre & Marie Curie, Paris VI, MS, 77, DEA, 78, Dr(math), 80, Doctoral d'Etatès Sci Math, 86. *Honors & Awards:* Michael Award Res Sci, Univ Ga, Athens, 89-90. *Prof Exp:* Res assoc, math, Rectorat de Paris, Inst Pure Math, Univ Paris VI, 78-80; Georges Lurcy fel math, Univ Calif, Berkeley, 79-80; asst prof math, Univ Southern Calif, Los Angeles, 80-85; vis asst prof, Univ Iowa, Iowa City, 85-86; assoc prof math, Univ Ga, Athens, 86-90. *Concurrent Pos:* Award, Fac Res & Innovation Fund, Univ Southern Calif, 84; mem, Math Sci Res Inst, Berkeley, 84-85; vis prof, Yale Univ, 90-91; creative res medal, Univ Ga, Athens, 89-90; vis prof, Inst Higher Sci Studies, Paris, 95-96. *Mem:* Math Asn Am; Fr Math Soc; AAAS; Int Asn Math Physicists; Soc Indust & Appl Math; Am Math Soc; Am Phys Soc. *Res:* Mathematical research in analysis, partial differential equations, and in mathematical physics; study of the Trotter-Lie formula and modification of the Feynman integral; Feynman path integrals in quantum mechanics; Feynman's operational calculus for noncommuting operators; eigenvalues and eigenfunctions of elliptic boundary value problems with indefinite weights; spectral and fractal geometry; vibrations of fractal drums; connections with number theory, particularly the theory of the Riemann Zeta-function. *Mailing Add:* Dept Math Univ Calif Sproul Hall Riverside CA 92521

LAPIDUS, MILTON, BIOCHEMISTRY. *Current Pos:* SR BIOCHEMIST, WYETH LABS, INC, 59- *Personal Data:* b New York, NY, May 8, 22; m 58; c 2. *Educ:* Univ Wis, BS, 48, MS, 53, PhD(biochem), 56. *Prof Exp:* Res chemist, Abbott Labs, 48-51; sr fel, Eastern Regional Res Lab, USDA, 56-59. *Mem:* AAAS; Am Chem Soc. *Res:* Isolation of vitamin B12b; microbiological transformation of steroids; chromatographic purification of viruses; prostaglandin biosynthesis and isolation; synthesis of penicillins and sweeteners; synthesis of peptides, complement inhibitors. *Mailing Add:* 412 Yorkshire Way Rosemont PA 19010-1119

LAPIERRE, YVON DENIS, PSYCHOPHARMACOLOGY. *Current Pos:* Lectr, 70-73, from asst prof to assoc prof, 73-81, PROF PSYCHIAT & PHARMACOL, UNIV OTTAWA, 81-, CHMN, PSYCHIAT DEPT, 86- *Personal Data:* b Bonnyville, Alta, Oct 19, 36; m 60, Nicole Beauregard; c Michel, Denis & Stephan. *Educ:* Ottawa Univ, BA, 57, MD, 61; Univ Montreal, MSc, 70; FRCP(C), 72. *Honors & Awards:* Tait-MacKenzie Medal, Ottawa Acad Med, 80; Medal of Hon, Can Col Neuropschopharmacol, 88. *Concurrent Pos:* Sci dir psychiat, Pierre Janet Hosp, Que, 70-76; dir psychopharmacol, Ottawa Gen Hosp, 76-79; chmn, Expert Standing Comt Psychotrop Drugs, 82; dir res & psychiat, Royal Ottawa Hosp, 79-86; dir outpatient clin, 80-85, psychiatrist in chief, 86- *Mem:* Can Col Neuropsychopharmacol; fel Royal Col Physicians & Surgeons Can; Soc Biol Psychiat; Col Int Neuropsychopharmacol; fel Am Psychiat Asn; fel Am Col Psychiat. *Res:* Drugs used in the treatment of psychiatric disorders plus biochemical clinical and electrophysiological research in the underlying biological factors contributing to mental illness. *Mailing Add:* Royal Ottawa Hosp 1145 Carling Ave Ottawa ON K1Z 7K4 Can

LAPIETRA, JOSEPH RICHARD, PHYSICAL CHEMISTRY, THERMODYNAMICS. *Current Pos:* from asst prof to assoc prof, 64-77, acad dean, 69-75, PROF CHEM, MARIST COL, 77- *Personal Data:* b New York, NY, July 20, 32. *Educ:* Marist Col, BA, 54; Cath Univ Am, PhD(chem), 61. *Prof Exp:* Teacher high sch, NY, 54-56; instr chem, Cath Univ Am, 60-61. *Mem:* Am Chem Soc. *Res:* Chemistry of transition metal complexes; thermochemistry; history of science; electrochemistry. *Mailing Add:* 12 Wilmot Terr Poughkeepsie NY 12603

LAPIN, A I E, ELECTRICAL ENGINEERING. *Current Pos:* PRIN SCIENTIST ENGR, HUGHES MISSILE SYSTS CO, 92- *Personal Data:* b Montreal, Que, May 13, 38; m 64, Ruth Heath; c Kathleen, Heather & Amy. *Educ:* McGill Univ, BEng, 60; Univ Sheffield, PhD(elec eng), 63. *Prof Exp:* Mem tech staff, Bell Tel Labs Inc, 63-70; eng staff specialist, Gen Dynamics Corp, 70-92. *Mem:* Inst Elec & Electronics Engrs. *Res:* Microwave diode and transistor circuitry; microwave systems for tactical missiles. *Mailing Add:* 1302 Albright Ave Upland CA 91786. *Fax:* 909-868-4716

LAPIN, ABRAHAM, CHEMICAL ENGINEERING, MATHEMATICS. *Current Pos:* RETIRED. *Personal Data:* b Cairo, Egypt, Sept 30, 23; US citizen; wid; c Jonathan & Josh. *Educ:* Univ Mich, BScE(chem eng) & BScE(math), 49; Polytech Inst Brooklyn, MSc, 55; Lehigh Univ, PhD(chem eng), 63. *Prof Exp:* Asst port engr, Am Israeli Shipping Co, Inc, 49-51; sales mgr, Dapor Trading Co, Inc, 51-52; mat engr, US Corps Eng, 53; chem engr, Mineral Beneficiation Lab, Columbia Univ, 54; chem engr, Air Prod & Chem, Inc, 55-57, proj engr, 57-59, group leader, 59-63, sect mgr cryogenic eng res & develop, 63-75. *Concurrent Pos:* Lectr, Pa State Univ, 61 & Lehigh Univ, 64. *Mem:* Am Chem Soc; Am Inst Chem Engrs; fel Am Inst Chemists; Am Soc Heating, Refrig & Air-Conditioning Eng; Am Soc Testing & Mat. *Res:* Cryogenic engineering; low temperature separation; distillation; heat transfer; insulation; fluid flow. *Mailing Add:* The Pavillion 845 Palmer Ave Mamaroneck NY 10543

LAPIN, DAVID MARVIN, BIOLOGY. *Current Pos:* PROF BIOL SCI & CHMN BIOL DEPT, TOURO COL, 85- *Personal Data:* b New York, Apr 12, 39; m 67; c 2. *Educ:* NY Univ, BA, 60, MS, 63, PhD(biol). *Prof Exp:* From instr to prof biol sci, Fairleigh Dickinson Univ, 66-85, chmn dept, 76-85. *Concurrent Pos:* Grants in aid, Fairleigh Dickinson Univ, 68-72. *Mem:* AAAS; Am Soc Hemat. *Res:* Kinetics of hematopoiesis; humoral regulation of hematopoiesis. *Mailing Add:* 1124 E 81st St Brooklyn NY 11236-4741

LAPIN, EVELYN P, NEUROCHEMISTRY, ENZYMOLOGY. *Personal Data:* b Montreal, Que, Aug 29, 33; c 3. *Educ:* McGill Univ, BSc, 54, PhD(biochem), 57. *Prof Exp:* Am Cancer Soc fel, Dept Path, Albert Einstein Col Med, 57-59; instr math & chem, Herzliah Acad, 62-65; lectr biochem, McGill Univ, 65-66; NIH fel, Mt Sinai Sch Med, 70-73, instr neurochem, 74-81, res asst prof, 81-88. *Concurrent Pos:* Lectr, Queen's Col, NY, 73-; vis asst prof, Stern Col Women, Yeshiva Univ, NY; vis assoc prof, Columbia Univ. *Mem:* Brit Biochem Soc; Am Soc Neurochem; Can Fedn Univ Women; Int Soc Neurochem; NY Acad Sci. *Res:* Subcellular compartmentalization of respiratory activity and energy metabolism; protein and lipid chemistry of nervous system, localization, separation and identification and function; biochemical mechanisms of hydrocarbon neurotoxins in central and distal axonopathy; brain catecholamines, dopamine, sub P, CCK in selected areas in animal Parkinsonian model. *Mailing Add:* 142-05 Roosevelt Apt 325 Flushing NY 11354

LAPIN, GREGORY D, BRAIN TUMORS. *Current Pos:* ASST PROF BIOMED ENG & NEUROL, NORTHWESTERN UNIV, 88- *Personal Data:* b Chicago, Ill, July 28, 56. *Educ:* Northwestern Univ, BS, 78, MS, 79, PhD(elec eng), 87. *Mem:* Inst Elec & Electronics Engrs; Biomed Eng Soc; Am Chem Soc. *Mailing Add:* 1206 Sommerset Ave Deerfield IL 60015

LAPITAN, NORA L, PLANT GENOME ORGANIZATION & EVOLUTION, GENOME MAPPING. *Current Pos:* ASST PROF GENETICS, COLO STATE UNIV, 89- *Personal Data:* b Manila, Philippines, Aug 23, 56; m 81, Romel. *Educ:* Univ Philippines, BS, 78; Kans State Univ, MS, 83, PhD(genetics), 86. *Prof Exp:* Assoc, Cornell Univ, 86-89. *Concurrent Pos:* Consult, UN Develop Prog, 88; prin investr, Agr Exp Sta, Colo State Univ, 89-, USDA, 90- *Mem:* Am Soc Agron; Sigma Xi. *Res:* Use of molecular techniques to genetically improve crop plants; use of DNA markers to locate and isolate genes for important traits, such as resistance to diseases and insects; molecular organization of plant genomes. *Mailing Add:* Dept Soil Sci Colo State Univ Ft Collins CO 80523-0001

LAPKIN, MILTON, POLYMER CHEMISTRY. *Current Pos:* DIR RES, ICI RESINS, USA, 86- *Personal Data:* b New York, NY, July 29, 29; m 64; c 3. *Educ:* Polytech Inst New York, BS, 51, PhD(org chem), 55. *Prof Exp:* Group leader, Olin Corp, 55-59, sect leader, 59-60, dir res, 69-73; dir res, Beatrice Foods, Polyvinyl Chem Indust, 73-86. *Mem:* Am Chem Soc; AAAS; Am Inst Chem; Fedn Soc Coating Technol. *Res:* Free radical polymerization; polyvinyl chloride; acrylic and methacyclic polymers; epoxies; propylene oxide; ethylene oxide; polyutheranes; suspension polymerization; emulsion polymerization. *Mailing Add:* 194 Greenwood Ave Beverly Farms MA 01915

LAPLANCHE, LAURINE A, PHYSICAL CHEMISTRY, PHARMACEUTICAL CHEMISTRY. *Current Pos:* from asst prof to assoc prof, 65-91, PROF CHEM, NORTHERN ILL UNIV, 91- *Personal Data:* b New York, NY, July 4, 38; m. *Educ:* Univ Md, BS, 59; Mich State Univ, PhD(chem), 63. *Prof Exp:* Asst prof physics, WVa State Col, 64-65. *Concurrent Pos:* Vis prof pharmaceut chem, Univ Calif, San Francisco, 84-85. *Mem:* Am Chem Soc; Sigma Xi. *Res:* Nuclear magnetic resonance; two dimensional nuclear magnetic resonance; energy barriers to internal rotation; molecular structure of biological molecules; proton exchange; hydrogen bonding; lanthanide shift reagents and conformational analysis. *Mailing Add:* 5265 Redman Rd Las Cruces MN 88011-7558

LAPLAZA, MIGUEL LUIS, MATHEMATICS. *Current Pos:* assoc prof, 67-76, PROF MATH, UNIV PR, MAYAGUEZ, 76- *Personal Data:* b Zaragoza, Spain, Mar 20, 38; m 69; c 4. *Educ:* Univ Barcelona, MD, 60; Univ Madrid, PhD(math), 65. *Prof Exp:* Instr math, Univ Barcelona, 60-61; from asst prof to assoc prof, Univ Madrid, 60-66. *Mem:* Am Math Soc; Math Asn Am. *Res:* Category theory. *Mailing Add:* Dept Math Univ PR Mayaguez Col Cont St Mayaguez PR 00680-9998

LAPOINTE, JACQUES, PROTEIN BIOSYNTHESIS, MOLECULAR GENETICS. *Current Pos:* Adj prof, 73-77, assoc prof, 77-81, PROF BIOCHEM, UNIV LAVAL, 81- *Personal Data:* b Montreal, Que, Nov 22, 42; m 67; c 1. *Educ:* Univ Montreal, BSc, 64, MSc, 66; Yale Univ, PhD(molecular biophys), 72. *Concurrent Pos:* Vis assoc prof molecular biophys & biochem, Yale Univ, 80-81. *Mem:* Am Soc Microbiol; Am Soc Biochem & Molecular Biol; Can Biochem Soc. *Res:* Regulation of the expression of genes encoding aminoacyl-t RNA synthetases in gram-negative and gram-positive bacteria; structure-function studies of bacterial aminoacyl-t RNA synthetases. *Mailing Add:* Dept Biochem Laval Univ Fac Sci et Genie Quebec City PQ G1K 7P4 Can

LA POINTE, JOSEPH L, zoology, for more information see previous edition

LAPOINTE, LEONARD LYELL, SPEECH PATHOLOGY. *Current Pos:* chmn, 84-92, PROF, DEPT SPEECH & HEARING SCI, ARIZ STATE UNIV, TEMPE, 92- *Personal Data:* b Iron Mountain, Mich, June 28, 39; m 63, Corinne Abraham; c Chris & Adrienne. *Educ:* Mich State Univ, BA, 61; Univ Colo, MA, 66, PhD(speech path), 69. *Honors & Awards:* Award, Sci Exhib, XV World Cong Logopedics & Phoniatrics, 71. *Prof Exp:* Dir speech path commun dis, Bd Educ, Menasha, Wis, 61-64; speech pathologist, Gen Rose Mem Hosp, 66; asst prof phonetics, Univ Colo, Denver, 68-69; coordr & instr audiol & speech path, Vet Admin Med Ctr, Gainesville, 69-84, res investr speech sci, 71-84. *Concurrent Pos:* Fel neurogenic commun dis, Vet Admin Hosp, Denver, 68-69; adj prof commun dis, Univ Fla, 69-, mem res fac neuroling, Ctr Neurol-Behav Ling Res, 74-; consult, Vet Admin Med Ctr, Phoenix & Vet Admin Outpatient Clin, Los Angeles. *Mem:* Acad Aphasia; fel Am Speech-Lang-Hearing Asn; Int Asn Logopedics & Phoniatrics; Int Neuropsychol Soc; Nat Aphasia Asn. *Res:* Development of measurement strategies of human oral sensation-perception; oral physiology and neurolinguistics; diagnosis and treatment strategies in aphasia and related neurogenic communication impairments; developing reading tests for aphasia; memory attention disorders in left and right hemisphere damage; cognitive-linguistic interactions. *Mailing Add:* Dept Speech & Hearing Sci Ariz State Univ Tempe AZ 85287-0001. *Fax:* 602-965-8516; *E-Mail:* lapointe@asu.edu

LAPONSKY, ALFRED BAER, PHYSICAL ELECTRONICS. *Current Pos:* RETIRED. *Personal Data:* b Cleveland, Ohio, Nov 24, 21; m 57, Ellen Anglesey; c Mark & Laura. *Educ:* Lehigh Univ, BS, 43, MS, 47, PhD(physics), 51. *Prof Exp:* Instr physics, Lehigh Univ, 47-51; physicist electron physics, Res Lab, Gen Elec Co, 51-63; assoc prof elec eng, Univ Minn, Minneapolis, 63-66; fel engr, Indust & Govt Tube Div, Westinghouse Elec Corp, 66-83. *Mem:* Sigma Xi. *Res:* Electron physics; electro-optics; image sensing and display techniques. *Mailing Add:* 176 Greenridge Dr Horseheads NY 14845

LAPORTE, DAVID COLEMAN, REGULATION OF GENE EXPRESSION, PROTEIN PHOSPHORYLATION CASCADES. *Current Pos:* asst prof, PROF BIOCHEM, UNIV MINN, 83- *Personal Data:* b Bryn Mawr, Pa, July 31, 51; m 75, Donna Stowell; c David W & Joan M. *Educ:* Univ Wis, BSc, 76; Univ Ill, PhD(biochem), 80. *Prof Exp:* Fel, Univ Calif, Berkeley, 80-83. *Mem:* Am Soc Biochem & Molecular Biol; Genetics Soc Am; Am Soc Microbiol. *Res:* Regulation of cellular functions; regulation of glycogen metabolism in yeast and of the glyoxylate bybass in E coli, these systems employ protein phosphorylation and control of transcription as regulatory strategies. *Mailing Add:* Dept Biochem 4-225 Millard Hall Univ Minn Med Sch 435 Delaware St SE Minneapolis MN 55455-0347. *Fax:* 612-625-2163; *E-Mail:* david_1@microbe.med.umn.edu

LAPORTE, LEO FREDRIC, GEOLOGY. *Current Pos:* PROF EARTH SCI, UNIV CALIF, SANTA CRUZ, 71- *Personal Data:* b Englewood, NJ, July 30, 33; m 56, 85, Margaret Liniecki; c Leo G, Eva R & Noel A. *Educ:* Columbia Univ, AB, 56, PhD(geol), 60. *Prof Exp:* From instr to prof geol, Brown Univ, 59-71. *Concurrent Pos:* Co ed, Palaios, 86-89; secy, US Nat Off, Hist Geol, Nat Res Coun, 91-93, chair, 94-96; provost, Crown Col, 93-98, assoc vchancellor, Undergrad Educ, 94-98. *Mem:* Soc Vert Paleont; Geol Soc Am; Soc Sedimentary Geol (pres, 95-96); Hist Sci Soc; Hist Earth Sci Soc (pres, 94); AAAS. *Res:* Paleoecology and environmental stratigraphy; history and evolution of life; history of paleontology. *Mailing Add:* Earth Sci Univ Calif Santa Cruz CA 95064. *Fax:* 408-459-2098

LAPORTE, RONALD E, EPIDEMIOLOGY. *Current Pos:* EPIDEMIOLOGIST, DEPT EPIDEMIOL, UNIV PITTSBURGH, 78- *Personal Data:* b Buffalo, NY, May 29, 49; m 71. *Educ:* Univ Buffalo, BA, 71; Univ Pittsburgh, MS, 73, PhD(psychol), 76. *Concurrent Pos:* Fel epidemiol, Univ Pittsburgh, 76- *Mem:* AAAS; Soc Epidemiol Res; Am Psychol Asn. *Res:* Chronic disease epidemiology; investigating possible protective factors of coronary heart disease and diabetes epidemeology. *Mailing Add:* 717 Duncan Ave Pittsburgh PA 15237

LAPOSA, JOSEPH DAVID, PHYSICAL CHEMISTRY. *Current Pos:* from asst prof to assoc prof, 67-86, PROF CHEM, MCMASTER UNIV, 86- *Personal Data:* b St Louis, Mo, July 21, 38; m 68, Karen Frantzen; c Rebecca, Jessica & Judith. *Educ:* St Louis Univ, BS, 60; Univ Chicago, MS, 62; Loyola Univ, Ill, PhD(chem), 65. *Prof Exp:* NIH fel chem, Cornell Univ, 65-67. *Res:* Molecular luminescence. *Mailing Add:* Dept Chem McMaster Univ 1280 Main St W Hamilton ON L8S 4M1 Can

LAPOSATA, MICHAEL, EXPERIMENTAL BIOLOGY. *Current Pos:* ASSOC PROF PATH, HARVARD MED SCH, 89- *Personal Data:* b Johnstown, Pa, Apr 22, 52. *Educ:* Bucknell Univ, BS, 74; Johns Hopkins Univ, MD, 81, PhD(cellular & molecular biol), 82; Am Bd Path, dipl, 89. *Prof Exp:* Postdoctoral res fel, Div Hemat-Oncol, Dept Med, Sch Med Wash Univ, St Louis, Mo, 81-82, resident, Div Lab Med, Depts Path & Med, 83-84, chief resident, 84-85; asst dir, Hemostasis Lab, Hosp Univ Pa, 85-86, co-dir, 85-89; asst prof path & lab med, Med Sch Univ Pa, 85-89; dir clin labs & chief, div clin labs, Mass Gen Hosp, 89- *Concurrent Pos:* Sheryl N Hirsch Award, Lupus Found, 87-88; assoc physician Lab Med, Dept Med & assoc pathologist, Dept Path, Mass Gen Hosp, 89-; mem, Coun Thrombosis, Am Heart Asn. *Mem:* Am Asn Clin Res; Am Asn Pathologists; Acad Clin Lab Physicians & Scientists; Am Heart Asn; NY Acad Sci; Am Soc Clin Pathologists. *Res:* Cellular and molecular biology; pathology; hematology, coagulation and blood transfusion. *Mailing Add:* Dir Clin Labs Gray 239 Mass Gen Hosp 32 Fruit St Boston MA 02114-2696

LAPOSTOLLE, PIERRE MARCEL, DYNAMICS OF PARTICLES IN ELECTROMAGNETIC FIELDS, SPACE CHARGE PHENOMENA. *Current Pos:* CONSULT, 85- *Personal Data:* b Vanves, France, May 29, 22; m 47, Descolas; c Bertrand, Xavier, Emmanuel, Anne & Benedicte. *Educ:* Paris Univ, PhD(traveling wave tube theory), 47. *Prof Exp:* Engr, Nat Ctr Telecommun, Paris, 45-54, sci dir, 72-78; physicist, Europ Orgn Nuclear Res, Geneva, 54-71; sci adv, Ganil Caen, France, 78-85. *Concurrent Pos:* Consult, Europ Orgn Nuclear Res & Los Alamos Nat Lab, 85- *Mem:* Fel Inst Elec & Electronics Engrs; Soc France Physique. *Res:* Theory of the interaction between an electromagnetic wave and a beam of particles; amplification in a traveling wave tube; acceleration of particles in a linear accelerator. *Mailing Add:* 3 Rue Victor Daix Neuilly Sur Seine 92200 France

LAPOTA, DAVID, BIOLOGICAL OCEANOGRAPHY, ENVIRONMENTAL TOXICOLOGY. *Current Pos:* biologist, 79-80, biol lab technician, 80-82, SR SCIENTIST (DP-III), NAVAL COMMAND, CONTROL & OCEAN SURVEILLANCE CTR, 82- *Personal Data:* b June 1, 49; m 75, Jeannette Harward. *Educ:* San Diego State Univ, BS, 73, MA, 82; Univ Calif, Santa Barbara, PhD, 97. *Prof Exp:* Data analyst, San Diego State Univ Found, 74-79. *Concurrent Pos:* Comt Biol Effects, Am Soc Testing & Mats. *Mem:* Am Geophys Union; Oceanog Soc; fel Explorer's Club; AAAS. *Res:* Bioluminescence projects involved with at sea expeditions; biological tests for environmental risk assessment; author of approximately 30 publications and granted 4 patents. *Mailing Add:* Naval Command Control & Surveillance Ctr Res Develop Test Eval Div D362 53475 Strothe Rd San Diego CA 92152-6310. *Fax:* 619-553-6305; *E-Mail:* lapota@nosc.mil

LAPP, H(ERBERT) M(ELBOURNE), AGRICULTURAL ENGINEERING. *Current Pos:* RETIRED. *Personal Data:* b Alameda, Sask, Feb 2, 22; m 50; c 3. *Educ:* Univ Sask, BE, 49; Univ Minn, MS, 62. *Prof Exp:* Water develop, Prairie Farm Rehab Admin, Dom Govt Can, 49-51; exten engr, Man Dept Agr, 51-53; from asst prof to prof, Univ Man, 53-89, head dept, 58-67, emer prof agr eng, 89- *Concurrent Pos:* Colombo plan adv, Khon Kaen Univ, Thailand, 65-67; local prog head develop grad studies in agr eng for Latin Am region, Nat Agrarian Univ, Peru, 67-70; consult, Can Int Develop Agency, Nigeria, 73 & 76, F F Sloney Co, Consult Engrs, Vancouver, Honduras, 74, Int Bank Reconstruct & Develop, Philippines, 76, Pakistan, 77, Brazil Agr Res Dept, 81, US Agency for Int Develop, Peru, 82, Can Int Develop Agency, 82, Int Develop Res Ctr, India, 83 & Lavalin-Crippen Int, Honduras, 83. *Mem:* Fel Can Soc Agr Eng (pres, 75-76); Am Soc Agr Engrs; Agr Inst Can. *Res:* Farm structure; soil and water. *Mailing Add:* 592 Borebank St Winnipeg MB R3N 1E9 Can

LAPP, M(ARSHALL), LASER GAS DIAGNOSTICS, LIGHT SCATTERING. *Current Pos:* SANDIA NAT LAB. *Personal Data:* b Buffalo, NY, Aug 20, 32; m 58, 80; c 2. *Educ:* Cornell Univ, BEngPhys, 55; Calif Inst Technol, PhD(eng sci), 60. *Prof Exp:* Physicist, Corp Res & Develop, Gen Elec Co, 60-80, actg mgr, Combustion Inst, 81- *Concurrent Pos:* Sci Res Coun sr vis fel, Sch Physics, Univ Newcastle, 68-69. *Mem:* AAAS; fel Am Phys Soc; fel Optical Soc Am; Am Inst Aeronaut & Astronaut; fel Brit Inst Physics. *Res:* Optical diagnostics of flames; laser Raman spectroscopy; radiative properties of metal vapors and gases; optical diagnostics of gases and surfaces; atomic and molecular physics; physics of fluids. *Mailing Add:* PO Box 3500 Walnut Creek CA 94598-0500

LAPP, MARTIN STANLEY, CONIFER BIOTECHNOLOGY. *Current Pos:* RETIRED. *Personal Data:* b Toronto, Ont. *Educ:* York Univ, BSc, 69, MSc, 72; Univ Alta, PhD(plant path), 77. *Prof Exp:* Res assoc, Nat Res Coun Can, 77-80, res officer numerical taxon, 80-96. *Mem:* Can Phytopath Soc. *Res:* Micropropagation of conifers; genetic engineering. *Mailing Add:* 763 Wilkinson Way Saskatoon SK S7N 3L8 Can

LAPP, N LEROY, MEDICINE, PULMONARY DISEASES. *Current Pos:* From instr to prof, WVa Univ, 66-96, asst dean, 75-77, chmn, Dept Med, Pulmonary Dis Sect, 78-88, EMER PROF, SCH MED, WVA UNIV, MORGANTOWN, 96- *Personal Data:* b May 16, 32; m 56, Catherine Alger; c Thomas & Anne. *Educ:* Eastern Mennonite Col, BS, 56; Temple Univ, MD, 61. *Mem:* Fel Am Col Physicians; fel Am Col Chest Physicians; Cent Soc Clin Res; Am Thorac Soc; Am Physiol Soc; Brit Thorac Soc. *Res:* Studies on subjects occupationally exposed to a variety of inorganic mineral dusts; investigating mechanisms of lung fibrosis and the cytokines which are involved in this process. *Mailing Add:* Dept Med Health Sci Ctr Univ WVa PO Box 9166 Morgantown WV 26506

LAPP, NEIL ARDEN, PLANT PATHOLOGY, NEMATOLOGY. *Current Pos:* FIELD DEVELOP FEL, MERCK & CO, 81- *Personal Data:* b Bloomington, Ill, Dec 7, 42; m 67; c 2. *Educ:* Goshen Col, BA, 64; WVa Univ, MS, 67; NC State Univ, PhD(plant path), 70. *Prof Exp:* Plant pathologist, Plant Protection Div, NC Dept Agr, 71-81. *Concurrent Pos:* Adj asst prof plant path, NC State Univ, 71-77, adj assoc prof, 77- *Mem:* Am Phytopath Soc; Soc Nematologists. *Res:* Plant disease and nematode survey and detection; chemical control. *Mailing Add:* 7208 Madiera Ct Raleigh NC 27615

LAPP, P(HILIP) A(LEXANDER), REMOTE SENSING. *Current Pos:* PRES, PHILIP A LAPP LTD, 69- *Personal Data:* b Toronto, Ont, May 12, 28; m 52; c 3. *Educ:* Univ Toronto, BASc, 50; Mass Inst Technol, SM, 51, ScD(instrumentation), 54. *Prof Exp:* Instr aeronaut eng, Mass Inst Technol, 52-53, res assoc, 53-54; systs eng, De Havilland Aircraft Can Ltd, 54-56, proj engr, Guided Missile Div, 55-60, chief engr, Spec Prod & Appl Res Div, 60-65, dir tech opers, 65-68; sr vpres, Spar Aerospace Prod Ltd, 68-69.

Concurrent Pos: Chmn working group sensors, Can Ctr Remote Sensing, 70-76; mem, Can Accreditation Bd, 71-75; mem, Bd Govs, York Univ, 80-; fel, Ryerson Polytech Inst, 85. *Mem:* Am Inst Aeronaut & Astronaut; Inst Elec & Electronics Engrs; Can Res Mgt Asn. *Res:* Dynamics of vehicles; guidance and control of missiles and aircraft; military and industrial instrumentation and automatic control; educational planning and research on public policy; remote sensing applied to resource management and environmental monitoring. *Mailing Add:* 128 Elgin St Thornhill ON L3T 1W6 Can

LAPP, THOMAS WILLIAM, ENVIRONMENTAL CHEMISTRY, RISK ASSESSMENT. *Current Pos:* assoc chemist, 74-77, sr chemist, 77-87, PRIN ENVIRON SCIENTIST, MIDWEST RES INST, 87- *Personal Data:* b Joliet, Ill, Oct 6, 37; m 61. *Educ:* Coe Col, BA, 59; Kans State Univ, MS, 61, PhD(inorg chem), 63. *Prof Exp:* Fel radiation chem, NAm Aviation Sci Ctr, 63-64; asst prof nuclear chem, Univ WVa, 64-66; assoc chemist, Midwest Res Inst, Mo, 66-69; mem staff, Univ Mo, Kansas City, 70-74. *Res:* Production and utilization of industrial chemicals suspected of possessing toxic properties; environmental transport and fate; risk assessment; hazardous waste incineration studies. *Mailing Add:* 102 Glen Alpine Circle Cary NC 27513

LAPP, WAYNE STANLEY, TRANSPLANTATION BIOLOGY. *Current Pos:* from asst prof to assoc prof, 68-82, PROF PHYSIOL IMMUNOL, DEPT PHYSIOL, MCGILL UNIV, 82-, PROF, CTR CLIN IMMUNOBIOL & TRANSPLANT. *Personal Data:* b Stevensville, Ont, Can, Nov 11, 36; m 64; c 4. *Educ:* Univ Toronto, BSA, 62, MSA, 64; McGill Univ, Montreal, PhD(transplantation physiol), 67. *Prof Exp:* Fel transplantation immunol, Karolinska Inst, Stockholm, 67-68. *Concurrent Pos:* Guest prof immunol, Ger Cancer Rec Ctr, Heidelberg, 77-78; assoc mem, Dept Med, McGill Univ, Montreal, 80-; counr, Can Soc Immunol. *Mem:* Can Physiol Soc; Can Soc Immunol; Am Asn Immunol; Transplantation Soc; NY Acad Sci. *Res:* Graft-versus-host induced immunosuppression of T and B lymphocyte functions; effect of the GVH reaction on T and B cell ontogency and thymus function. *Mailing Add:* Dept Physiol Ctr Clin Immunobiol & Transplant McGill Univ McIntyre Med Sci Bldg 3655 Drummond St Montreal PQ H3G 1Y6 Can

LAPPAS, LEWIS CHRISTOPHER, PHARMACEUTICAL CHEMISTRY. *Current Pos:* CONSULT, 84- *Personal Data:* b Lynn, Mass, May 14, 21; m 49, Arlene Rockwood; c John, Robert & Janet. *Educ:* Mass Col Pharm, BS, 43, MS, 48; Purdue Univ, PhD(pharmaceut chem), 51. *Prof Exp:* Res scientist, Eli Lilly & Co, 51-84. *Mem:* Am Chem Soc; Am Pharmaceut Asn. *Res:* Drug encapsulation processes; basic gelatin research as applied to capsular forms; study of filmogens as drug release mechanisms; stabilization of drugs and drug forms; pharmaceutical aspects of drug absorption; investigation of new antimicrobials in drug and cosmetic formulations. *Mailing Add:* 12240 Brompton Rd Carmel IN 46033

LAPPE, RODNEY WILSON, CARDIOVASCULAR. *Current Pos:* DIR CARDIOVASC RES, CIBA-GEIGY PHARMACEUT DIV, 90- *Personal Data:* b Breese, Ill, Sept 12, 54; c 2. *Educ:* Blackburn Col, BA, 76; Ind Univ, PhD(pharmacol), 80. *Prof Exp:* Postdoctoral pharmacol, Univ Iowa, 80-82; res scientist, Hypertension Sect, Wyeth Labs, Inc, 82-85, mgr, 85-87, mgr, Vascular Dis Sect, Wyeth-Ayerst Res, 87-88; res fel, Hypertension Sect, Rorer Cent Res, 88-90. *Concurrent Pos:* Res fel, Iowa Cardiovasc Ctr Inst, 82; chmn, Cardiovasc Subcomt, 87 & 88; mem, Animal Use Comt, Wyeth-Ayerst Res, 88. *Mem:* Am Soc Hypertension; Am Soc Pharmacol & Exp Therapeut; Inter-Am Soc Chemother; Coun High Blood Pressure. *Res:* Cardiovascular system. *Mailing Add:* Cardiovasc Res Ciba-Geigy 556 Morris Ave Summit NJ 07901-1398

LAPPIN, GERALD R, CHEMISTRY. *Current Pos:* RETIRED. *Personal Data:* b Caro, Mich, Apr 14, 19; m 45; c 2. *Educ:* Alma Col, BS, 41; Northwestern Univ, PhD(org chem), 46. *Prof Exp:* Asst, Northwestern Univ, 41-43, interim instr chem, 44, asst, 44-46; asst prof, Antioch Col, 46-49 & Univ Ariz, 49-51; sr res chemist, Tenn Eastman Co Div, Eastman Kodak Co, 51-69, res assoc, 69-83. *Concurrent Pos:* Consult, Vernay Labs, Ohio, 46-49. *Mem:* Am Chem Soc. *Res:* Additives for foods; plastics and petroleum products; chemistry of polyesters; technology forecasting as applied to research and development planning. *Mailing Add:* 4047 Skyland Dr Kingsport TN 37664

LAPPLE, CHARLES E, CHEMICAL ENGINEERING, FLUID & PARTICLE MECHANICS. *Current Pos:* CONSULT, 79- *Personal Data:* b New York, NY, Feb 11, 16; m 41; c 2. *Educ:* Columbia Univ, BS, 36, ChE, 37. *Honors & Awards:* Colburn Award, Am Inst Chem Engrs, 46. *Prof Exp:* Chem engr, E I du Pont de Nemours & Co, 37-45, process engr, 45-46, chem engr, 46-48, res proj eng, 48-50; assoc prof chem eng, Ohio State Univ, 50-55; sr scientist, SRI Int, 55-79. *Concurrent Pos:* Lectr, Columbia Univ, 41-48 & Univ Del, 48-50; indust consult, 50-; consult, Atomic Energy Comn, 50-58, USPHS, 61-66 & US Dept Interior, 66- *Mem:* Am Chem Soc; Am Inst Chem Engrs. *Res:* Fluid mechanics; heat transfer; dust and mist collection; particle dynamics; aerosols; atmospheric pollution abatement; fine particle technology. *Mailing Add:* 260 Calle Linda Fallbrook CA 92028-9425

LAPPORTE, SEYMOUR JEROME, ORGANIC & PETROLEUM CHEMISTRY, MATERIALS CHEMISTRY. *Current Pos:* prog officer, 87-90, PROG DIR, NSF, 91- *Personal Data:* b Chicago, Ill, Mar 26, 30; m 64, Anne Frankel; c Daniel & Michael. *Educ:* Univ Chicago, MS, 53; Univ Calif, Los Angeles, PhD(chem), 57. *Prof Exp:* Asst, Univ Calif, Los Angeles, 53-56; sr res assoc, Chevron Res Co, 56-74, mgr, Pioneering Div, 74-86, sr res scientist, 80-86. *Concurrent Pos:* Teacher, Exten, Univ Calif, 60-; vis scholar, Stanford Univ, 68-69. *Mem:* Am Chem Soc; Royal Soc Chem; Mat Res Soc. *Res:* Organic reaction mechanisms; organometallics; oxidation; transition metal chemistry; homogenous catalysis; ultraviolet stabilization; polymers; solid state chemistry; materials chemistry. *Mailing Add:* NSF 4201 Wilson Blvd Rm 1059 Arlington VA 22230. *Fax:* 510-376-8333; *E-Mail:* slapporte@note.nsf.gov

LAPRADE, MARY HODGE, ZOOLOGY. *Current Pos:* instr zool, 58-60 & 64-65, dir, Clark Sci Ctr, 73-90, LECTR BIOL SCI, SMITH COL, 65- *Personal Data:* b Oakland, Calif, Feb 6, 29; m 58; c 2. *Educ:* Wilson Col, AB, 51; Radcliffe Col, AM, 52, PhD(biol), 58. *Prof Exp:* Instr biol, Simmons Col, 52-55. *Concurrent Pos:* Instr, NSF In Serv Inst High Sch Biol Teachers, 65-66. *Mem:* Sigma Xi. *Res:* Growth and regeneration, particularly in crustaceans; fine structure of endocrine organs in crustaceans. *Mailing Add:* Dept Biol Sci Smith Col Northampton MA 01063-0048

LAPSLEY, ALWYN COWLES, PHYSICS. *Current Pos:* RETIRED. *Personal Data:* b Albemarle Co, Va, Mar 12, 20. *Educ:* Univ Va, BEE, 41, MS, 44, PhD(physics), 47. *Prof Exp:* Instr physics, Univ Va, 41-43, asst, Manhattan Proj & Navy Fire Control, 43-46; sr physicist, Photo Prod Dept, E I du Pont de Nemours & Co, 47-51, res engr, Atomic Energy Div, 51-60; lectr nuclear eng, Reactor Facil, Sch Eng & Appl Sci, Univ Va, 60-77, sr scientist, 60-85, res assoc prof, 77-85. *Mem:* Am Phys Soc; Am Nuclear Soc. *Res:* Mechanics; physical optics; Kerr effect with high frequency fields; nuclear physics; ion chambers; reactor kinetics; isotope separation. *Mailing Add:* 1609 Inglewood Dr Charlottesville VA 22901-2651

LAPUCK, JACK LESTER, FOOD CHEMISTRY, BACTERIOLOGY. *Current Pos:* OWNER & MGR, LAPUCK LABS, 66- *Personal Data:* b Jamaica Plain, Mass, Aug 28, 24; m 48, Ruth G; c Robert, Susan & Debra. *Educ:* Northeastern Univ, BS, 46; Univ Mass, MS, 49; Calvin Coolidge Col, DSc, 60. *Prof Exp:* Food sanitarian, Montgomery Co Health Dept, Md, 50-51; food chemist, Food & Drug Res Labs, NY, 51; chemist, Waltham Labs, Inc, 51-55, lab dir & vpres, 55-66. *Concurrent Pos:* Instr, Univ Exten, Mass Dept Educ, 55-; past pres, Analytical Group NE Sect. *Mem:* Am Chem Soc; Am Soc Microbiol; Inst Food Technologists; Nat Environ Health Asn. *Res:* Food technology; microbiology; analytical chemistry; environmental analyses. *Mailing Add:* 8 Lovett Rd Box 311 Newtown MA 02159

LAQUATRA, IDAMARIE, NUTRITION. *Current Pos:* nutritionist, Heinz USA, 84-89, MGR NUTRIT SERV, WEIGHT WATCHERS DIV, HEINZ USA, PITTSBURGH, PA, 90- *Educ:* Pa State Univ, BS, 75, MS, 79, PhD(appl nutrit), 83. *Prof Exp:* Clin dietitian, Custom Mgt Corp, 76-77; instr & consult, Pa State Univ, University Park, 78-82; pvt nutrit consult, State Col, Pa, 80-82; consult, Clin Nutrit Staff, Vet Admin Med Ctr, Bronx, NY, 83-84. *Concurrent Pos:* Grad asst, Pa State Univ, 77-81, lab asst, 78 & 79; postdoctoral fel, Prev Cardiol Prog, Univ Med & Dent NJ, 82-84; adj fac, Home Econ Dept, Montclair State Col, NJ, 83-84; mem, Col Bd Adv, Col Home Econ, Ohio State Univ, 86-89, adv group, Plan V Dietetics Prog, Pa State Univ, 88- & Coun Res, Am Dietetic Asn, 89- *Mailing Add:* Sci Affairs & Training 1538 Ingomar Heights Rd 921 Pa Ave 9th Floor Pittsburgh PA 15237

LAQUER, HENRY L, CRYOGENICS, SUPERCONDUCTIVITY. *Current Pos:* PRIN, CRYOPOWER ASSOCS, 84- *Personal Data:* b Frankfurt-am-Main, Ger, Nov 28, 19; nat US; m 47, Justine Harwood; c Frederic C, Emily K, Lydia J & H Turner. *Educ:* Temple Univ, AB, 43; Princeton Univ, MA, 45, PhD(phys chem), 47. *Prof Exp:* Res chemist, Ladox Labs, Pa, 46; mem staff, Los Alamos Sci Lab, Univ Calif, 47-77, consult, 77-83. *Concurrent Pos:* Adj prof, Los Alamos Residence Ctr, Univ NMex, 70-73. *Mem:* Am Phys Soc. *Res:* High magnetic fields; applied superconductivity; dielectric studies; elastic properties of metals; cryogenics; high temperature superconductivity materials and applications. *Mailing Add:* Rte 5 Box 445 Espanola NM 87532-8906. *E-Mail:* laquerhl@roadrunner.com

LARABELL, CAROLYN A, DEVELOPMENTAL BIOLOGY. *Current Pos:* scholar, Dept Biochem & Biophys & Dept Zool, Davis, 88-90, MGR, WEST COAST FACIL INTERMEDIATE VOLTAGE ELECTRON MICROS, LAWRENCE BERKELEY LAB, UNIV CALIF, BERKELEY. *Personal Data:* b Detroit, Mich, Dec 16, 47. *Educ:* Mich State Univ, BA, 70; Ariz State Univ, BS, 81, PhD(zool), 88. *Prof Exp:* Supvr, Dept Neurophysiol, Good Samaritan Hosp, Phoenix, 71-75; teaching asst, Dept Zool, Ariz State Univ, 83, res assoc, 83-88. *Concurrent Pos:* NIH reprod biol training grant, Univ Calif, Davis, 89. *Mem:* Am Soc Cell Biol; Soc Develop Biol; AAAS; Micros Soc Am. *Res:* Egg cytoskeleton and its modification during fertilization and development; signal transduction at fertilization. *Mailing Add:* 160A Donner Lab Lawrence Berkeley Lab Univ Calif Berkeley CA 94720-0001. *Fax:* 510-486-6488; *E-Mail:* larabell@lbl.gov

LARA-BRAUD, CAROLYN WEATHERSBEE, BIOCHEMISTRY. *Current Pos:* asst res scientist biochem 73-75, asst prof, 75-80, ASSOC PROF HOME ECON, UNIV IOWA, 80- *Personal Data:* b Waco, Tex, Jan 4, 40; m 70. *Educ:* Univ Tex, Austin, BA, 62, PhD(chem), 69. *Prof Exp:* Res assoc biochem, Clayton Found Biochem Inst & lectr home econ, Nutrit Div, Univ Tex, Austin, 71-73. *Mem:* AAAS; Am Chem Soc; Sigma Xi, Inst Food Technol; Am Home Econ Asn. *Res:* Intermediary metabolism; regulation of inducible enzyme systems. *Mailing Add:* 810 W Benton 313-B Iowa City IA 52246-5924

LARACH, SIMON, PHYSICAL INORGANIC CHEMISTRY, SOLID STATE CHEMISTRY. *Current Pos:* PRES, DEVTECH INC, 87- *Personal Data:* b Brooklyn, NY, Apr 21, 22; m 48; c 2. *Educ:* City Col New York, BS, 43; Princeton Univ, MA, 51, PhD(chem), 54. *Prof Exp:* Res chemist, Third Res Div, Goldwater Hosp, Col Med, NY Univ, 43 & 46; res chemist luminescence & solid state, David Sarnoff Res Ctr, Radio Corp Am, 46-59, head photoelectronic, magnetic & dielec res, 59-61, assoc lab dir, 61-67, overseas fel, 69, fel, 67-87. *Concurrent Pos:* Vis fel, Princeton Univ, 67-68; liaison lectr, Indust Res Inst-Am Chem Soc, 68; vis prof, Hebrew Univ, Jerusalem, 69-70, adj prof, 71-73; UN consult, UNESCO Div Tech Educ & Res, 71; prin lectr, NATO Adv Study Inst, Norway, 72; vis prof, Swiss Fed Inst Technol, 72 & Princeton Univ, 73; div ed electronics, J Electrochem Soc; res prof radiol, Hahnemann Med Col & Hosp, 74-; adj prof radiol, Col Physicians & Surgeons, Columbia Univ, 78-86; invited lectr, People's Repub China, 87, Taiwan, 87, Kyoto, 91 & Helsinki, 92; consult, 88- *Mem:* Am Chem Soc; fel Am Phys Soc; fel Am Inst Chem; Electrochem Soc. *Res:* Synthesis and properties of electronically-active solids; medical ultrasound. *Mailing Add:* 1 Windsor Rd Great Neck NY 11021-3920

LARAGH, JOHN HENRY, PHYSIOLOGY, MEDICINE. *Current Pos:* HILDA ALTSCHUL MASTER PROF MED, MED COL, CORNELL UNIV, 75-, DIR CARDIOVASC CTR, NY HOSP-CORNELL MED CTR, 75- *Personal Data:* b Yonkers, NY, Nov 18, 24; m 74; c 3. *Educ:* Cornell Univ, MD, 48. *Honors & Awards:* Stouffer Prize Med Res, 69. *Prof Exp:* Intern med, Presby Hosp, New York, 48-49, asst resident, 49-50, asst, 50-55, instr, 55-57, assoc, 57-59, from asst prof to prof clin med, Col Physicians & Surgeons, Columbia Univ, 67-75. *Concurrent Pos:* Nat Heart Inst trainee, 50-51; asst physician, Presby Hosp, NY, 50-54, from asst attend physician to assoc attend physician, 54-69, attend physician, 69-75, vchmn in chg med affairs, Bd Trustees, 74; NY Heart Asn res fel, 51-52; mem med adv bd, Coun High Blood Pressure Res, Am Heart Asn, 61, chmn, 68-72; consult cardiovasc study sect, USPHS, 64-68 & heart prog proj A, 67-72; dir, Hypertension Ctr & Nephrol Div, Columbia-Presby Med Ctr, 71-75; mem policy adv bd, Hypertension Detection & Follow-Up Prog, Nat Heart & Lung Inst, 71-, mem bd sci coun, 74-; mem adv bd, Am Soc Contemp Med & Surg, 74. *Mem:* Am Soc Clin Invest; fel Am Col Physicians; Am Soc Nephrol; assoc Harvey Soc; Asn Am Physicians. *Res:* Cardiovascular and renal diseases; endocrinology. *Mailing Add:* NY Hosp 525 E 68th St Starr H New York NY 10021-4873

LARAMORE, GEORGE ERNEST, PHYSICS, MEDICINE. *Current Pos:* from asst prof to assoc prof, 78-85, PROF, DEPT RADIATION ONCOL, UNIV WASH, 85-, VCHMN, DEPT RADIATION ONCOL, 95- *Personal Data:* b Ottawa, Ill, Nov 5, 43; m 87, Sheley D Pemberton; c Parker & Patricia. *Educ:* Purdue Univ, BS, 65; Univ Ill, Urbana, MS, 66, PhD(physics), 69; Univ Miami, MD, 76. *Prof Exp:* NSF fel, Univ Ill, Urbana, 69-70, res assoc physics, 70-71; res physicist, Sandia Labs, 71-75. *Mem:* Am Phys Soc; Am Vacuum Soc; AMA; Am Radiation Soc; Am Soc Therapeut Radiol & Oncol; Am Soc Radiation Oncol. *Res:* Theory of low-energy electron diffraction; fast neutron radiotherapy for human malignancies; interaction of fast electrons with solids; boron neutron capture therapy; radiation oncology. *Mailing Add:* Dept Radiation Oncol Med Ctr Univ Wash 1959 NE Pacific St MS Box 356043 Seattle WA 98195-6043. *Fax:* 206-548-6218; *E-Mail:* george@radonc.washington.edu

LARBALESTIER, DAVID C, SUPERCONDUCTIVITY. *Current Pos:* from asst prof to prof, 76-81, L V SHUBNIKOV PROF MAT SCI & PHYSICS & DIR, APPL SUPERCONDUCTIVITY CTR, UNIV WIS, 91-, GRAINGER PROF SUPERCONDUCTIVITY, 96- *Personal Data:* b Somerset, UK, May 22, 43; US citizen; m 67; c Nikolai, Laura & Lucy. *Educ:* Imp Col, BS, 65; Univ London, PhD(metall), 70. *Honors & Awards:* IR-100 Award, Indust Res, 79; Particle Accelerator Technol Award, Inst Elec & Electronics Engrs, 91. *Prof Exp:* Scientist, Batelle Res Lab, Switz, 70-72; sr sci officer, Rutherford Lab, UK, 73-76. *Concurrent Pos:* Vis scientist, Brookhaven Nat Lab, 78; vis prof, Univ Rennes, France, 92; chair, Univ Wis, 89- *Mem:* Fel Am Phys Soc; Mat Res Soc. *Res:* Critical current density of high field superconducting materials; developed conductors at the state of the art made from both low and high temperature superconductors. *Mailing Add:* 1500 Engineering Dr Madison WI 53706. *Fax:* 608-263-1087; *E-Mail:* larbales@engr.wisc.edu

L'ARCHEVEQUE, REAL VIATEUR, nuclear engineering & electronics, research & development, for more information see previous edition

LARCOM, LYNDON LYLE, BIOPHYSICS, PHOTOBIOLOGY. *Current Pos:* CONSULT, 72- *Personal Data:* b Olean, NY, Apr 11, 40. *Educ:* Carnegie-Mellon Univ, BS, 62; Univ Pittsburgh, MS, 65, PhD(biophysics), 68. *Prof Exp:* NIH fel chem, Univ Pittsburgh, 68-70, res assoc, 70-72. *Mem:* Biophys Soc; Am Soc Photobiol; Am Soc Microbiol; Am Chem Soc; Sigma Xi. *Res:* Mechanisms of DNA damage and repair; the biophysical properties of nucleic acids; molecular quantum mechanics; DNA-protein interactions; virus structure; mechanisms of carcinogenesis. *Mailing Add:* Dept Physics Clemson Univ Clemson SC 29634-0001

LARD, EDWIN WEBSTER, ANALYTICAL CHEMISTRY. *Current Pos:* RETIRED. *Personal Data:* b Ala, July 17, 21; m 45; c 4. *Educ:* Ark State Col, BS, 49; Memphis State Univ, MA, 61. *Prof Exp:* Chemist, Ethyl Corp, 49-52 & Chemstrand Corp, 52-54; sr chemist, Nitrogen Prod Div, W R Grace & Co, Tenn, 54-62, res supvr, Res Div, Clarksville, Md, 62-74; chem engr, Naval Sea Systs Command, Washington, DC, 74-84. *Mem:* Am Chem Soc. *Res:* Trace gas analysis with infrared; separation and determination of argo, oxygen and nitrogen by chromatography; trace analysis of acetylene, methane, carbon monoxide and carbon dioxide; synthesis of aryl dimethyl sulfonium chloride compounds; chemical warfare agents; unsaturates in auto emissions; water energy conservation on naval ships; issued 23 patents and author of 17 publications. *Mailing Add:* 12703 Beaverdale Lane Bowie MD 20715

LARDNER, JAMES F, COMPUTER DESIGN, SCIENCE ADMINISTRATION. *Current Pos:* DIR, POTASH CORP, SASK, 89-; DIR, SEARS MFG CO, 95- *Personal Data:* b Davenport, Iowa, May 24, 24. *Educ:* Cornell Univ, BME, 45. *Prof Exp:* Eng & mfg mgr, Deere & Co, 46-56, mgr, Overseas Mfg Group, 56-62, managing dir, John Deer Iberica SA, 62-67, asst gen mgr, Des Moines Works, 67-68, Harvester Works, 68-69, mgr, Corp Plant & Prod Eng Dept, 69-70, corp dir mfg eng, 70-80, vpres mfg develop, 80-82, vpres, Govt Prod & Component Sales, 82-85, vpres, Component Group, 85-90; dir, Am Stand, 84-90. *Concurrent Pos:* Mem, Comt Comput-Aided Mfg, Nat Res Coun, 80-81, Panel Comput Design & Mfg, 83, Comt Indust/Acad Coop in Mfg, 84- 85, Mfg Studies Bd, 84-, Comn Eng & Tech Systs, 84-86, Cross-Disciplinary Eng Res Comt, 85-87, Comt Labor Mkt Adjustments, 87, Comt Defense Mfg Strategy, Panel Pvt Contractors, 90-, chmn, Mfg Studies Bd, 90-; dir, Comput Aided Mfg Int Inc, 81-84; mem, Panel Eng Res Ctrs, Nat Acad Eng, 84, Foundations Mfg Comt, 89-; mem, Panel Mfg Eng, Bd Assessment Nat Inst Stand & Technol, 86-91. *Mem:* Nat Acad Eng; fel Soc Mgr Eng; fel Soc Mfg Engrs. *Mailing Add:* 2752 Nichols Lane Davenport IA 52803

LARDNER, ROBIN WILLMOTT, APPLIED MATHEMATICS, COMPUTATIONAL MECHANICS & OCEANOGRAPHY. *Current Pos:* assoc prof, Simon Fraser Univ, 67-70, prof, 70-95, chmn dept, 71-73, EMER PROF MATH, SIMON FRASER UNIV, 95- *Personal Data:* b Leicester, Eng, Feb 9, 38; m 58, 79, Niki Papalou; c 4. *Educ:* Cambridge Univ, BA, 59, PhD(appl math), 63, ScD, 86. *Prof Exp:* Res assoc physics, Columbia Univ, 61-63; NATO fel appl math & theoret physics, Peterhouse Col, Cambridge Univ, 63-65; lectr math & physics, Univ EAnglia, 65-67. *Concurrent Pos:* Prof appl math, Univ Petrol & Minerals, Dhahran, Saudi Arabia, 82-87; sr res scientist, KFUPM Res Inst, Dhahran, Saudi Arabia, 91-93 & 95-97. *Res:* Numerical solution of partial differential equations; numerical tidal modelling and modelling of other oceanographic flows; pollutant transport modelling; inverse problems in oceanography, data assimilation; nonlinear vibrations and waves in solids and fluids. *Mailing Add:* Dept Math Simon Fraser Univ Burnaby BC V5A 1S6 Can. *E-Mail:* rwl@cs.sfu.ca

LARDNER, THOMAS JOSEPH, ENGINEERING MECHANICS. *Current Pos:* PROF CIVIL ENG, UNIV MASS, 78- *Personal Data:* b New York, NY, July 19, 38; m 64, Anne Jeanne; c Joseph, Theresa & Deborah. *Educ:* Polytech Inst Brooklyn, BAeroE, 58, MS, 59, PhD(appl mech), 61. *Prof Exp:* Res assoc appl mech, Polytech Inst Brooklyn, 59-61; res engr, Jet Propulsion Lab, Calif Inst Technol, 62-63; instr math, Mass Inst Technol, 63-67, asst prof appl math, 67-70, assoc prof mech eng, 70-73; prof theoret & appl mech, Univ Ill, Urbana, 73-78. *Concurrent Pos:* Fulbright lectr, Univ Nepal, 65-66; consult, Polytech Inst Brooklyn & Jet Propulsion Lab, Calif Inst Technol. *Mem:* Fel Am Soc Mech Engrs; Soc Indust & Appl Math. *Res:* Applied mathematics and mechanics; applied solid mechanics. *Mailing Add:* 175 Amity St Amherst MA 01002. *E-Mail:* lardner@ecs.umass.edu

LARDY, HENRY ARNOLD, CELL BIOLOGY, ENDOCRINOLOGY. *Current Pos:* from asst prof to prof biol sci, Univ Wis-Madison, 45-50, Vilas prof, 66-88, chmn, Res Dept, Enzyme Inst, 50-88, EMER PROF BIOL SCI, UNIV WIS-MADISON, 88- *Personal Data:* b Roslyn, SDak, Aug 19, 17; m 43, Annrita Dresselhuys; c Nicholas, Diana, Jeffrey & Michael. *Educ:* SDak State Univ, BS, 39; Univ Wis, MS, 41, PhD(biochem), 43. *Hon Degrees:* DSc, SDak State Univ, 78. *Honors & Awards:* Neuberg Medal, 56; Lewis Award, Am Chem Soc, 49; Wolf Found Award Agr, 81; Nat Award Agr Excellence, Agr Mkt Asn, 82; Carl Hartman Award, Soc Study Reproduction, 84; Amory Prize, Am Acad Arts & Sci, 84; William Rose Award Biochem, Am Soc Biol Chemists, 88. *Prof Exp:* Fel, Nat Res Coun, Banting Inst, Univ Toronto, 44-45. *Mem:* Nat Acad Sci; Am Philos Soc; Am Chem Soc; Am Soc Biol Chem (pres, 64); Am Acad Arts & Sci; Soc Study Reproduction; hon mem Japanese Biochem Soc. *Res:* Enzymes; intermediary metabolism; hormones; sperm storage for artificial insemination; induction of thermogenic enzymes by thyroid hormone and by specific steriods. *Mailing Add:* Enzyme Inst Univ Wis-Madison 1710 University Ave Madison WI 53705. *Fax:* 608-265-2904; *E-Mail:* Lardy@enzyme.wisc.edu

LARDY, LAWRENCE JAMES, NUMERICAL ANALYSIS. *Current Pos:* from asst prof to assoc prof, 64-74, dept chmn, 82-88, PROF MATH, SYRACUSE UNIV, 74- *Personal Data:* b Sentinel Butte, NDak, Aug 23, 34; m 56; c 2. *Educ:* NDak State Col, Dickinson, BS, 57; Univ NDak, MS, 59; Univ Minn, PhD(math), 64. *Prof Exp:* Instr math, Univ NDak, 59-60 & Univ Minn, 62-64. *Concurrent Pos:* Res fel, Yale Univ, 67-68; vis assoc prof, Univ Md, 73-74. *Mem:* Soc Indust & Appl Math; Math Asn Am; Am Math Soc; Sigma Xi. *Res:* Functional analysis. *Mailing Add:* 4838 Westfield Dr Manlius NY 13104-2122

LARDY, MATHIAS M, NUCLEAR & ANALYTICAL CHEMISTRY, HEALTH PHYSICS. *Current Pos:* TECH DIR, QUANTERRA ENVIRON SERV, 94- *Personal Data:* b Sentinel Butte, NDak, May 24, 32; m 58, Deanna Brown; c Steven, Renee, Cheryl & Robert. *Educ:* Dickinson State Univ, BS, 54; Ore State Univ, MS, 58; Univ Mont, MS, 62. *Prof Exp:* Instr, Culbertson High Sch, 54-57, Anaconda Sr High Sch, 58-60; chemist radioanal, Gen Elec, 62-64; chemist radioanal, US Testing Co, 65-66, supvr radiochem anal, 66-67, mgr, 67-74, asst vpres, 74-90; tech dir, IT Corp, 90-94. *Concurrent Pos:* Lab dir radiobioassay & radiochem, Clin Lab Improvement Act, 68 & 70. *Mem:* Am Chem Soc; Health Physics Soc; Am Soc Testing & Mat. *Res:* Analysis of environmental and biological samples for radionuclides from tritium to curium; standards for quality assurance of radiochemical laboratories. *Mailing Add:* 1967 Pine St Richland WA 99352. *Fax:* 509-375-5590

LAREW, H(IRAM) GORDON, CIVIL ENGINEERING, SOIL MECHANICS. *Current Pos:* from assoc prof to prof, 56-92, EMER PROF CIVIL ENG, UNIV VA, 92- *Personal Data:* b Independence, WVa, June 5, 22; m 46, Mary Jo Thompson; c Jane Jo, Hiram G III & Elizabeth T. *Educ:* Univ WVa, BS, 44; Purdue Univ, MS, 51, PhD, 60. *Prof Exp:* Jr engr, NY Cent Syst, 46; instr civil eng, Purdue Univ, 47-56. *Concurrent Pos:* Consult, 54- *Mem:* Fel Am Soc Civil Engrs; Am Soc Eng Educ. *Res:* Utilization of solid wastes; the effects of repeated loads upon soils; soil strength; earth dams; blast damage. *Mailing Add:* 2500 Hillwood Pl Charlottesville VA 22901

LARGE, ALFRED MCKEE, SURGERY. *Current Pos:* RETIRED. *Personal Data:* b Listowel, Ont, Mar 7, 12; nat US; m 43; c 1. *Educ:* Univ Toronto, BA, 33, MD, 36. *Prof Exp:* Instr surg, Sch Med, Washington Univ, 43-44; from asst prof to assoc prof clin surg, Col Med, Wayne State Univ, 46-80. *Concurrent Pos:* Attend surgeon, St John Hosp, Ben Secours Hosp & Cottage Hosp; pvt pract. *Mem:* AMA. *Res:* Clinical surgery. *Mailing Add:* 131 Park Shores Circle Apt 9E Apt 208 E Vero Beach FL 32963-3847

LARGE, RICHARD L, SOIL SCIENCE, AGRONOMY. *Current Pos:* VPRES, A&L AGR LABS, INC, 71- *Personal Data:* b Rochester, Ind, June 9, 40; m 62; c 3. *Educ:* Purdue Univ, BSc, 62; Okla State Univ, MSc, 66; Ohio State Univ, PhD(soil sci), 69. *Prof Exp:* Agronomist, US Testing Co, Inc, 69-71. *Mem:* Soil Sci Soc; Am Soc Agron; Coun Agr Sci & Technol. *Res:* Soil fertility; crop nutrition; land application of sludge. *Mailing Add:* 411 N Third St Memphis TN 38105

LARGENT, DAVID LEE, MYCOLOGY. *Current Pos:* asst prof bot, 68-74, assoc prof, 74-77, PROF BOT, HUMBOLDT STATE COL, 77- *Personal Data:* b San Francisco, Calif, Oct 30, 37; m 70. *Educ:* San Francisco State Col, BA, 60, MA, 63; Univ Wash, PhD(bot), 68. *Prof Exp:* Instr bot, Foothills Jr Col, 63; instr bot & biol, Phoenix Jr Col, 63-64. *Mem:* Am Soc Plant Taxon; Mycol Soc Am; Am Bryol & Lichenological Soc; Sigma Xi. *Res:* Taxonomy and ecology of the Rhodophylloid fungi on the Pacific coastal states of America; cryptogamic botany. *Mailing Add:* 141 Carter Lane Eureka CA 95503-9549

LARGENT, MAX DALE, dentistry, for more information see previous edition

LARGIS, ELWOOD EUGENE, BROWN ADIPOSE TISSUE METABOLISM, HYPOGLYCEMIC DRUGS. *Current Pos:* RES PHARMACOLOGIST, DEPT METAB DIS, LEDERLE LABS, 73- *Educ:* Univ NDak, PhD(biochem), 70. *Mailing Add:* Prin Sci Wyeth-Ayerst Res CN 8000 Rm 1806 Princeton NJ 08543-8000

LARGMAN, COREY, BIOCHEMISTRY. *Current Pos:* asst adj prof, 78-82, assoc res prof, 84-89, RES PROF INTERNAL MED & BIOL CHEM, SCH MED, UNIV CALIF, DAVIS, 90-; ASSOC CAREER SCIENTIST, VET ADMIN, 85- *Personal Data:* c 2. *Educ:* Reed Col, BA, 66; Mass Inst Technol, PhD(org chem), 70. *Prof Exp:* Fel biochem, Univ Calif, Berkeley, 71-74. *Concurrent Pos:* Asst dir, Enzym Res Lab, Martinez Vet Med Ctr, Calif, 74-82, actg assoc chief staff res, 89, dir, Core Biochem Lab, 82-; vis scientist, Dept Biochem, Univ Calif, San Francisco, 83-84; res prog specialist basic sci, Vet Admin, Washington, DC, 87-90, merit rev bd, 90-; Dept Nutrit Res Training Ctr, Univ Calif, Davis, 90- *Mem:* Am Soc Biol Chemists; AAAS. *Res:* Expression of homeotic genes during differentiation; structure and function of proteolytic enzymes; role of homeobox genes in hematopoiesis; elastase structure and function. *Mailing Add:* Dept 151 H Vet Admin Med Ctr 4150 Clement St Dept ISI H Rm 12 San Francisco CA 94121-1598

LARGMAN, THEODORE, ORGANIC CHEMISTRY. *Current Pos:* RETIRED. *Personal Data:* b Philadelphia, Pa, Nov 16, 23; wid; c 4. *Educ:* Temple Univ, AB, 48; Ind Univ, PhD(org chem), 52. *Prof Exp:* Sr res chemist, Nitrogen Div, Allied Signal Corp, 62-66, scientist, Cent Res Labs, 66-68, res group leader, Corp Chem Res Lab, 51-81, res assoc, 81-88, sr res assoc, 88-92. *Concurrent Pos:* Consult, Triad Enterprises, 90- & Teltech, 96- *Res:* Organic synthesis; fine chemicals; agricultural pesticides; flame retardant chemicals and polymers; uranium extraction; polymer adhesion; bioresorbable polymers; fiber research; granted 35 US patents. *Mailing Add:* Seven Upper Field Rd Morristown NJ 07960

LARI, ROBERT JOSEPH, PHYSICS. *Current Pos:* RETIRED. *Personal Data:* b Aurora, Ill, 31; m 56; c 4. *Educ:* St Procopius Col, BS, 53; Univ Notre Dame, MS, 55. *Prof Exp:* Instr physics, St Procopius Col, 57-61; physicist, Argonne Nat Lab, 61-88; vpres, Vector Fields Inc, 88-93. *Mem:* Am Asn Physics Teachers; Asn Comput Mach. *Res:* Particle accelerator magnet design, other electromagnetic devices design. *Mailing Add:* 800 W Marywood Ave Aurora IL 60504

LARIMER, FRANK WILLIAM, PROTEIN ENGINEERING, MOLECULAR GENETICS. *Current Pos:* Res scientist, Chem Mutagenesis Prog, Biol Div, 76-84, SR RES SCIENTIST, PROTEIN ENG PROG, BIOL DIV, OAK RIDGE NAT LAB, 84- *Personal Data:* b Mt Pleasant, Mich, Feb 26, 48; m 72, Constance A Zendel. *Educ:* Albion Col, BA, 71; Fla State Univ, MS, 73, PhD(genetics), 75. *Concurrent Pos:* Adj prof, Oak Ridge Grad Sch Biomed Sci, Univ Tenn, 77-; adj prof, biotech concentration, Bio Consortium, 85-, Cell, Molecular & Develop Biol Prog, Univ Tenn, Knoxville, 89- *Mem:* Am Soc Microbiol; Am Soc Biochem & Molecular Biol; Genetics Soc Am; Int Soc Plant Molecular Biol; Protein Soc. *Res:* Protein engineering: enzyme structure/function analysis, modeling of binding sites and catalytic complexes, subunit interactions and assembly; molecular genetics of mutagenesis and DNA repair. *Mailing Add:* Biol Div Oak Ridge Nat Lab PO Box 2009 Oak Ridge TN 37831-8077. *Fax:* 423-574-0793; *E-Mail:* larimer@bioux1.bio.ornl.gov

LARIMER, JAMES LYNN, NEUROBIOLOGY. *Current Pos:* From asst prof to assoc prof, 59-68, actg chmn dept, 73-74, PROF ZOOL, UNIV TEX, AUSTIN, 68- *Personal Data:* b Washington Co, Tenn, Jan 7, 32; div; c 2. *Educ:* ETenn State Univ, BS, 53; Univ Va, MA, 54; Duke Univ, PhD, 59. *Honors & Awards:* Javits Neurosci Res Award, 88-95. *Concurrent Pos:* Guggenheim fel, 67-68; mem physiol study sect, NIH, 72-86; mem marine sci panel, NSF, 86. *Mem:* Soc Neurosci; Am Physiol Soc; Sigma Xi; fel AAAS. *Res:* Comparative physiology; behavior and neurophysiology of invertebrates. *Mailing Add:* Dept Zool Univ Tex Austin TX 78712-1104

LARIMER, JOHN WILLIAM, GEOCHEMISTRY. *Current Pos:* from asst prof to assoc prof, 74-77, PROF GEOL, ARIZ STATE UNIV, 77- *Personal Data:* b Pittsburgh, Pa, Sept 4, 39; m 65; c 2. *Educ:* Lehigh Univ, BA, 62, MS, 63, PhD(geol), 66. *Honors & Awards:* Nininger Award, 66. *Prof Exp:* NASA-AEC res assoc geochem, Enrico Fermi Inst, Univ Chicago, 66-69. *Concurrent Pos:* Prin invesr, Lunar & Planetary Sci Prog, NASA, 72-; NATO fel, Max Planck Inst, 75-76; vis prof, Calif Inst Technol, 79. *Mem:* AAAS; Geochem Soc; Am Geophys Union; Meteoritical Soc; Sigma Xi. *Res:* Cosmochemistry; mineralogy and composition of meteorites. *Mailing Add:* 440 E Alameda Dr Tempe AZ 85282

LARIMORE, RICHARD WELDON, FISH BIOLOGY. *Current Pos:* Asst aquatic biol, Univ Ill, Urbana, 46-54, assoc, 54-58, prof zool, 70-76, prof environ eng, 69-88, EMER PROF, UNIV ILL, URBANA, 89- *Personal Data:* b Rogers, Ark, Feb 10, 23; m 47; c 3. *Educ:* Univ Ark, BS, 46; Univ Ill, MS, 47; Univ Mich, PhD(zool), 50. *Honors & Awards:* Fisheries Pub Award, Wildlife Soc, 57; Am Fisheries Soc Award, 60. *Concurrent Pos:* Aquatic biologist, Ill State Natural Hist Surv, 58-89; fishery expert, Food & Agr Orgn, 63-64 & 72-73; sr lectr, Fulbright Comn, 80, 83, 90. *Mem:* Am Soc Ichthyol & Herpet; Am Fisheries Soc; Am Inst Fishery Res Biol. *Res:* Ecology of stream and reservoir fishes; dynamics of cooling lakes; utilization of tropical aquatic resources. *Mailing Add:* 277 Nat Res Bldg Univ Ill Pennsylvania Ave Champaign IL 61820

LARIS, PHILIP CHARLES, PHYSIOLOGY. *Current Pos:* assoc prof, 66-75, PROF BIOL, UNIV CALIF, SANTA BARBARA, 75- *Personal Data:* b Perth Amboy, NJ, Sept 5, 31; m 56; c 4. *Educ:* Rutgers Univ, BS, 52; Princeton Univ, MA, 54, PhD(physiol), 56. *Prof Exp:* Instr biol, Univ Calif, 56-58, from asst prof to assoc prof, 58-65; assoc prof, Franklin & Marshall Col, 65-66. *Mem:* Am Physiol Soc; Soc Gen Physiol. *Res:* Cell permeability membrane potentials; amino acid and ion transport. *Mailing Add:* 132 W Alamar Ave Santa Barbara CA 93105

LARIVEE, JACQUES, CONSERVATION. *Mailing Add:* 194 Ouellet Rimouski PQ G5L 4R5 Can

LARK, CYNTHIA ANN, MICROBIOLOGY. *Current Pos:* assoc res prof biochem, 70-72, ASSOC PROF BIOL, UNIV UTAH, 72- *Personal Data:* b Shawnee, Okla, Dec 31, 28; m 51; c 4. *Educ:* Mt Holyoke Col, BA, 50; St Louis Univ, PhD, 62. *Prof Exp:* Lab technician, Carnegie Inst, 50-51 & Sloan-Kettering Inst Cancer Res, 51-53; res asst, Univ Geneva, 55-56 & St Louis Univ, 59-62; NIH fel, Washington Univ, 62-63; asst prof microbiol, Kans State Univ, 63-70. *Res:* Microbial genetics; molecular biol; DNA reproducing bacteria. *Mailing Add:* 3605 Mill Circle Univ Utah 201 S Biol Bldg Salt Lake City UT 84112-1196

LARK, KARL GORDON, MOLECULAR BIOLOGY, GENETICS. *Current Pos:* chmn dept, 70-77, PROF BIOL, UNIV UTAH, 77- *Personal Data:* b Lafayette, Ind, Dec 13, 30; m 51; c 4. *Educ:* Univ Chicago, PhB, 49; NY Univ, PhD(microbiol), 53. *Prof Exp:* Am Cancer Soc res fel, Statenserum Inst, Denmark, 53-55; Nat Found res fel, Biophys Lab, Univ Geneva, 55-56; instr microbiol, Sch Med, St Louis Univ, 56-57, sr instr, 57-58, from asst prof to assoc prof, 58-63; prof, Kans State Univ, 63-70. *Concurrent Pos:* Nat Inst Gen Med Sci career develop award, 63-70; mem, Genetics Panel, NSF, 66-69; consult, Eli Lilly & Co, 68-74; mem, Genetics Study Sect, NIH, 71-75; ad hoc mem, Nat Inst Gen Med Sci Coun, 78-79, mem, 79- *Mem:* Biophys Soc; Am Soc Cell Biol; Am Soc Biol Chem; Am Soc Microbiol. *Res:* Cell growth and division; DNA replication and segregation in bacteria and eucaryotes; plant genetics and tissue culture. *Mailing Add:* Dept Biol Univ Utah 201 Biol Bldg Salt Lake City UT 84112

LARK, NEIL LAVERN, NUCLEAR PHYSICS. *Current Pos:* from asst prof to prof natural sci, Raymond Col, 62-75, PROF PHYSICS, UNIV PAC, 75- *Personal Data:* b Baker, Ore, Sept 10, 34; m 58; c 2. *Educ:* Chico State Col, AB, 55; Cornell Univ, PhD(phys chem), 60. *Honors & Awards:* Sigma Xi. *Prof Exp:* Res asst, Los Alamos Sci Lab, 55-56; res asst, Brookhaven Nat Lab, 57, jr res assoc, 58-59, res assoc, 60-61; NATO fel, Inst Nuclear Res, Amsterdam, Neth, 61-62, res assoc, 62. *Concurrent Pos:* Res asst, Univ NMex, 54; consult & res collabr, Los Alamos Sci Lab, 69; Ford Found fel & Fulbright grantee, Niels Bohr Inst, Copenhagen, Denmark, 67-68; NSF lectr, Tex A&M Univ, 70; res collabr, Brookhaven Nat Lab, 71-72, vis physicist, 75; vis fel, Australian Nat Univ, 76; vis astronr, Univ Hawaii, 86, 87. *Mem:* Am Phys Soc; Am Asn Physics Teachers; Am Astron Soc; Am Asn Univ Prof. *Res:* Nuclear spectroscopy; teaching of physics and astronomy. *Mailing Add:* Dept Physics Univ Pac Stockton CA 95211

LARKE, R(OBERT) P(ETER) BRYCE, VIROLOGY, INFECTIOUS DISEASES. *Current Pos:* dir, 88-90, MED DIR, PROV AIDS PROG, ALTA HEALTH, 90-; PROF PEDIAT, UNIV ALTA, 76-, PROF MED MICROBIOL & INFECTIOUS DIS, 86- *Personal Data:* b Blairmore, Alta, Nov 14, 36; m 60, Shirle Mae Mills; c Krista, Bryce Jr & Donald. *Educ:* Queen's Univ, Ont, MD & CM, 60; Univ Toronto, DCISc, 66. *Honors & Awards:* Parkin Prize, Royal Col Physicians, Edinburgh, 66. *Prof Exp:* Intern, St Michael's Hosp, Toronto, Ont, 60-61; resident pediat, Hosp for Sick Children, Toronto, Ont, 61-62, res fel virol, Res Inst, 62-66; instr prev med, Sch Med, Case Western Res Univ, 66-68, sr instr, 68; asst prof pediat, McMaster Univ, 69-72, asst prof path, 71-72, assoc prof pediat & path, 72-75; assoc prof pediat, Univ Alta, 75-76, clin virologist, Prov Lab Pub Health, 75-85, hon prof Med, Div Infectious Dis, 77-86; assoc med dir, Can Red Cross Blood Transfusion Serv, Edmonton, Alta, 85-88. *Concurrent Pos:* Fel Microbiol, Sch Hyg, Univ Toronto, 63-66; Med Res Coun Can res fel, 64-66; dir virol lab, St Joseph's Hosp, Hamilton, Ont, 71-75; vis scientist, Viral Oncol Unit, Pasteur Inst, Paris, France, 86-87; dep med dir, Can Red Cross Blood Transfusion Serv, 88- *Mem:* Am Soc Microbiol; Am Soc Virol; Am Pediat Soc; Infectious Dis Soc Am; Can Pediat Soc; Can Soc Clin Invest. *Res:* Clinical virology and infectious diseases of children and adults; mechanisms of host resistance to viral infections; interaction between viruses and blood platelets; epidemiology of viral infections; immunization against hepatitis B. *Mailing Add:* Dept Pediat Univ Alta Edmonton AB T6G 2R7 Can. *Fax:* 403-439-2683

LARKIN, DAVID, ELECTROCHEMISTRY. *Current Pos:* asst prof, 73-80, ASSOC PROF CHEM, TOWSON STATE UNIV, 80- *Personal Data:* b London, Eng, Oct 6, 41. *Educ:* Loughborough Univ Technol, BTech, 65, PhD(electrochem), 68; Royal Inst Chem, ARIC, 70. *Prof Exp:* Asst prof chem, Fla Technol Univ, 72-73. *Mem:* Am Chem Soc; Royal Soc Chem; Sigma Xi. *Res:* Study of electro kinetics at solid metal electrodes. *Mailing Add:* Dept Chem Towson State Univ Towson MD 21204

LARKIN, EDWARD CHARLES, HEMATOLOGY. *Current Pos:* from assoc prof to prof med, 75-83, PROF MED & PATH, UNIV CALIF, DAVIS, 83- *Personal Data:* b Waltham, Mass, Aug 7, 37; m 65; c 2. *Educ:* Harvard Col, AB, 59; Yale Univ Sch Med, MD, 63. *Prof Exp:* Asst prof med, Univ Tex Med Br, 70-74, assoc prof, 74-75; chief hemat oncol, Marinez Va Hosp, 75-84. *Mem:* Am Soc Hemat; Int Soc Hemat; Am Col Physicians; Western Soc Clin Res. *Mailing Add:* Vet Admin Univ Calif Med Hosp 150 Muir Rd Martinez CA 94553

LARKIN, EDWARD P, FOOD MICROBIOLOGY, VIROLOGY. *Current Pos:* RETIRED. *Personal Data:* b Watertown, Mass, Sept 27, 20; m 49, Clara M Cronin; c 3. *Educ:* Mass State Col, BS, 46; Univ Mass, MS, 48, PhD(bact), 54. *Hon Degrees:* Hon BS, Mass State Col, 43. *Prof Exp:* Instr bact, Univ Mass, 48-54, asst prof, 54-61; dir, Med Sch Study, CIC, Purdue Univ, 60-61; adminr & assoc mem virol, Inst Med Res, NJ, 61-68; chief biophys lab, New Bolton Ctr, Sch Vet Med, Univ Pa, 68-70; chief virol br, Ctr Food Safety & Appl Nutrit, Food & Drug Admin, 70-87. *Concurrent Pos:* Vis assoc, Univ Pa, 61-65; Leukemia Soc scholar, 65-70. *Mem:* Am Soc Microbiol; Sigma Xi; Int Asn Comp Res on Leukemia & Related Dis (secy, 69-71). *Res:* Food virology; physical characterization of viruses; kinetic studies of physical and chemical inactivation of viruses. *Mailing Add:* 400 Stanton Ave Terrace Park OH 45174-1244

LARKIN, JOHN MICHAEL, ORGANIC CHEMISTRY. *Current Pos:* SR RES SUPVR, HUNTSMAN CHEM CORP, 93- *Personal Data:* b York, Nebr, Aug 11, 37; m 65, Sheila Kern; c Ellen, Paul & Michael. *Educ:* Univ Nebr, Lincoln, BS, 59; Univ Colo, Boulder, MS, 63, PhD(org chem), 65. *Prof Exp:* Chemist, Qual Water Br, US Geol Surv, Nebr, 59-60; from chemist to sr chemist, Texaco Inc, Beacon, 65-70, res chemist, 70-74, sr res chemist, 74-76; sr proj chemist, Jefferson Chem Co, Austin, Tex, 76-87; supvr res sect, Texaco Chem Co, Austin, TX, 87-93. *Mem:* Am Chem Soc. *Res:* Organic synthesis; structure elucidation; reaction mechanisms; organic nitrogen compounds; free radical rearrangements; steroidal heterocycles; air pollution; lubricant additive synthesis; chemicals from synthesis gas; heterogeneous catalysis. *Mailing Add:* Texaco Chem Corp PO Box 15730 Austin TX 78761-5730. *E-Mail:* larkijm@texaco.com

LARKIN, JOHN MONTAGUE, MICROBIAL PHYSIOLOGY, MICROBIAL ECOLOGY. *Current Pos:* from asst prof to assoc prof, 67-81, PROF MICROBIOL, LA STATE UNIV, BATON ROUGE, 81-, ASSOC DEAN GRAD SCH, 94- *Personal Data:* b Philadelphia, Pa, Apr 7, 36; div; c Laura & Jennifer. *Educ:* Ariz State Univ, BS, 61, MS, 63; Wash State Univ, PhD(microbiol), 67. *Prof Exp:* Asst microbiol, Ariz State Univ, 61-63 & Wash State Univ, 63-67. *Mem:* AAAS; Am Soc Microbiol. *Res:* Bacterial taxonomy; biology of gliding bacteria; filamentous sulfur bacteria; microbiology of cold, hydrocarbon marine seeps. *Mailing Add:* Grad Sch La State Univ Baton Rouge LA 70803. *Fax:* 504-388-1370; *E-Mail:* gradassd@lsuvm.sngg.lsu.edu

LARKIN, JOHN W, NUTRITION. *Current Pos:* CHIEF, FOOD PROCESS HAZARD ANALYSIS BR, CTR FOOD SAFETY & APPL NUTRIT, 91- *Personal Data:* b Ossining, NY, Aug 2, 54. *Educ:* Ohio State Univ, BS, 78, MA, 80; Mich State Univ, PhD(food sci), 84. *Mailing Add:* Ctr Food Safety & Appl Nutrit 6502 S Archer Rd Summit-Argo IL 60501

LARKIN, K(ENNETH) T(RENT), ELECTRICAL ENGINEERING. *Current Pos:* PALO ALTO MGT GROUP. *Personal Data:* b Fowler, Colo, Nov 11, 20; m 46; c 2. *Educ:* Southern Methodist Univ, BS, 43. *Prof Exp:* Jr engr, Lone Star Gas Co, 39-42; instr radio eng, Southern Methodist Univ, 42-43; scientist, US Naval Res Lab, DC, 43-45; mgr receiver & indicators br, Waltham Labs, Raytheon Mfg Co, 46-55, dept mgr radar & radar develop, Santa Barbara Labs, 55-56; mgr telecommun dept, Lockheed Missiles & Space Co, 56-57, mgr electronics div, 57-58, assoc dir electronics res & develop, 58-62, assoc dir eng electronics, 62-63, asst dir eng, Res & Develop Div, 63, dir, 63-65, dir info systs, 65-71; pres, Technicon Med Info Systs Corp, 71- *Mem:* Sr mem Inst Elec & Electronics Engrs. *Res:* Computer systems, especially as applied to health care. *Mailing Add:* 215 Golden Hills Dr Portola Valley CA 94028

LARKIN, LAWRENCE A(LBERT), FINITE ELEMENT ANALYSIS, ELASTO-PLASTIC FLOW. *Current Pos:* res scientist, 70-74, CONSULT ENGR, DATA SYSTS DIV, A O SMITH CORP, 74- *Personal Data:* b Kansas City, Mo, Jan 5, 37; m 60. *Educ:* Univ Kans, BA, 59, MS, 60, PhD(civil eng), 64. *Prof Exp:* Asst prof civil eng, State Univ NY Buffalo, 64-69. *Mem:* Am Soc Civil Engrs. *Res:* Development of finite element computer codes; finite element computation of elasto-plastic response of vehicle structures during crash conditions. *Mailing Add:* 7728 W Coventry Dr Franklin WI 53132

LARKIN, LYNN HAYDOCK, ANATOMY, REPRODUCTIVE BIOLOGY. *Current Pos:* from asst prof to assoc prof, 68-79, PROF ANAT, COL MED, UNIV FLA, 79- *Personal Data:* b Highland Co, Ohio, Jan 29, 34; div; c 2. *Educ:* Otterbein Col, BS, 56; Univ Colo, PhD(anat), 67. *Prof Exp:* Instr anat, Sch Med, Univ Colo, 66-67, res assoc molecular, cellular & develop biol, 67-68. *Mem:* Sigma Xi; Am Asn Anatomists; Soc Study Reproduction; Am Asn Clin Anatomists. *Res:* Role of relaxin in pregnancy and parturition. *Mailing Add:* Univ Fla Col Med PO Box 100235 JHMHC Gainesville FL 32610

LARKIN, PETER ANTHONY, fisheries; deceased, see previous edition for last biography

LARKIN, ROBERT HAYDEN, ANALYTICAL CHEMISTRY. *Current Pos:* res chemist, Rohm & Haas Co, 73-79, sect mgr analytical res, 79-84, sect mgr environ sci, 84-86, DIR REGULATORY AFFAIRS, ROHM & HAAS CO, 86- *Personal Data:* b New York, NY, Mar 26, 46; m 67; c 4. *Educ:* Providence Col, BS, 68; Univ Mass, PhD(phys chem), 72. *Prof Exp:* Res assoc chem, Mass Inst Technol, 72-73. *Mem:* Am Chem Soc; Nat Agr Chem Asn. *Res:* Determination of the environmental fate and metabolism of agricultural pesticides. *Mailing Add:* 207 Hemlock Circle North Wales PA 19454-2663

LARKIN, RONALD PAUL, WILDLIFE ECOLOGY IN DISTURBED ENVIRONMENTS, CHARACTERIZATION OF ANIMALS MOVEMENTS. *Current Pos:* ASSOC PROF SCIENTIST & WILDLIFE ECOLOGIST, ILL NATURAL HIST SURV. 80-; DEPT AFFIL, DEPT ECOL, ETHOLOGY & EVOLUTION, UNIV ILL, 81-, ADJ ASSOC PROF, DEPT NATURAL RESOURCES & ENVIRON SCI. *Personal Data:* b St Louis, Mo, July 27, 45. *Educ:* Univ Mo, Columbia, AB, 67; Rockefeller Univ, PhD, 73. *Prof Exp:* Res assoc, Rockefeller Univ, 73-75, asst prof, 75-80. *Concurrent Pos:* Prin investr, USAF, US Fish & Wildlife Serv, USN, NSF, US Army & State Ill, 78-; consult & lectr, Bird Hazard Team, USAF, 85-; mem & lectr, Bird Strike Comt Europe, Copenhagen, Madrid, 86 & 88; consult & lectr, Soc Protection Nature, Israel, 89; attendee & lectr, Next Generation Weather Radar Oper Support Facil, USAF, Fed Aviation Admin & Nat Weather Serv, 93. *Mem:* Am Ornithologists' Union; Animal Behav Soc; Am Soc Naturalists; Nat Ctr Sci Educ; Am Meteorol Soc; Sigma Xi. *Res:* Interdisciplinary approaches; computer applications in ecology, especially spatial statistics and automated systems for locating and recognizing animals; bird flight, migration, orientation, dispersal, radar ornithology, bird hazards to aircraft, and birds' use of atmospheric structure; bioacoustics. *Mailing Add:* Ill Natural Hist Surv 607 E Peabody Dr Champaign IL 61820. *E-Mail:* r_larkin@uiuc.edu

LARKIN, WILLIAM (JOSEPH), NUCLEAR ENGINEERING, ENGINEERING MANAGEMENT. *Current Pos:* ENG MGT CONSULT, 88- *Personal Data:* b Morristown, NJ, Aug 18, 18; m 49, Margaret Power; c Lawrence. *Educ:* Mass Inst Technol, BS & MS, 49; Univ Tenn, MS, 56. *Prof Exp:* Design draftsman, Ford Instrument Co, NY, 42; mech engr, Los Alamos Sci Lab, 44-46; asst dir eng sch, Mass Inst Technol, 49-50; engr, US AEC, Dept Energy, 50-55, chief, Reactor Projs Br, 55-66, actg dir, Reactor Div, 66-69, dir, Off Nuclear & Criticality Safety, 69-70, dir off safety, 70-73, chief, Uranium Enrichment Expansion Proj Br, Res Develop Admin, Res Develop Admin, 73-76, dir, Planning, Analysis, Control & Reports Div, 77-78; consult engr, 78-88. *Res:* Uranium enrichment plant engineering; construction project planning and management control; operational safety. *Mailing Add:* 112 Blue Ridge Ct Oak Ridge TN 37830

LARKIN, WILLIAM ALBERT, FLAME RETARDANTS, GLASS COATINGS. *Current Pos:* CONSULT, TECHNOL, 92- *Personal Data:* b Boston, Mass, Dec 17, 26; m 53, Winifred Swierczek; c 7. *Educ:* Boston Col, BS, 49. *Honors & Awards:* Lifetime Innovation Award, Soc Nat Elf Aquitane, Paris, France, 93. *Prof Exp:* Dist mgr, McKesson & Robbins Inc, 53-57; dist mgr, Atochem NAm, 57-61, mgr tech serv, 61-68, mgr prod develop, 68-73, tech dir, 73-80, plant gen mgr, 80-81, dir technol, 82-92. *Concurrent Pos:* Consult polymer additives & functional glass coatings. *Mem:* Soc Plastics Engrs; Licensing Exec Soc; Am Chem Soc. *Res:* Polymer stabilizers; flame retardants; modifiers; glass coatings for strengthening and electroconductivity; organometallic, organotin chemistry and applications; holder of 35 US patents. *Mailing Add:* 38 Sylvania Ave Avon By The Sea NJ 07717. *Fax:* 732-774-2422; *E-Mail:* 1quest4@aol.com

LARKINS, BRIAN ALLEN, PLANT PHYSIOLOGY, PLANT BIOCHEMISTRY. *Current Pos:* Res assoc biochem genetics, 75-76, from asst prof to assoc prof, 76-83, PROF GENETICS, PURDUE UNIV, 84- *Personal Data:* b Bellville, Kans, Aug 12, 46; m 69; c 2. *Educ:* Univ Nebr, BSEd, 69, PhD(bot), 74. *Honors & Awards:* Charles Albert Schull Award, Am Soc Plant Physiologists, 83. *Concurrent Pos:* Porterfield prof plant sci, Univ Ariz; Hovde distinguished prof, Purdue Univ, 86. *Mem:* Nat Acad Sci; AAAS; Sigma Xi; Am Soc Biochem & Molecular Biol; Soc Develop Biol; Am Soc Plant Physiologists. *Res:* Protein and nucleic acid biosynthesis; seed storage protein metabolism; regulation of gene activity during seed formation. *Mailing Add:* Dept Plant Sci Univ Ariz Tucson AZ 85721. *Fax:* 520-621-3692; *E-Mail:* larkins@ag.arizona.edu

LARKINS, THOMAS HASSELL, JR, INORGANIC CHEMISTRY. *Current Pos:* Sr res chemist, Tenn Eastman Co, 63-80, RES ASSOC, EASTMAN CHEM DIV, EASTMAN KODAK CO, 80- *Personal Data:* b Dickson, Tenn, Mar 1, 39; m 60; c 3. *Educ:* Austin Peay State Col, BS, 60; Vanderbilt Univ, MA, 62, PhD(chem), 63. *Mem:* Am Chem Soc. *Res:* Coordination chemistry; catalysis; coal gasification; chemicals from coal. *Mailing Add:* 4408 Beechcliff Dr Kingsport TN 37664

LARKY, ARTHUR I(RVING), ELECTRICAL ENGINEERING, COMPUTER ENGINEERING. *Current Pos:* From res asst prof to prof elec eng, Lehigh Univ, 56-95, prof comput eng, 64-95, EMER PROF ELEC & COMPUT ENG, LEHIGH UNIV, 95- *Personal Data:* b Bound Brook, NJ, Feb 27, 31; m 81, Joan Ullman; c Susan, David, Steven, Wayne, Barbara & Melissa. *Educ:* Lehigh Univ, BS, 52; Princeton Univ, MS, 53; Stanford Univ, PhD(elec eng), 57. *Concurrent Pos:* Consult, 62-; academician, Int Higher Educ Acad Sci, Moscow, Russia, 95- *Mem:* Inst Elec & Electronics Engrs. *Res:* Computer design; automated testing. *Mailing Add:* Lehigh Univ 215 Packard Bldg 19 Bethlehem PA 18015. *Fax:* 610-974-6468; *E-Mail:* ail0@lehigh.edu

LARMIE, WALTER ESMOND, FLORICULTURE. *Current Pos:* RETIRED. *Personal Data:* b Smithfield, RI, Sept 6, 20; m 43, Una Mullen; c Walter C, Wayne C & Wendy C (Butler). *Educ:* Univ RI, BS, 49, MS, 54. *Prof Exp:* From asst prof to prof hort, Univ RI, 49-83, chmn, Dept Plant & Soil Sci, 72-83. *Res:* Storage of flowers and plants; weed control; growth regulators; propagation and culture of poinsettias; floral design. *Mailing Add:* 65 Blackbird Rd West Kingston RI 02892

LARMORE, LAWRENCE LOUIS, MATHEMATICS. *Current Pos:* assoc prof, 70-77, PROF MATH, CALIF STATE COL, DOMINGUEZ HILLS, 77- *Personal Data:* b Washington, DC, Nov 23, 41; m 64; c 2. *Educ:* Tulane Univ, BS, 61; Northwestern Univ, PhD(math), 65. *Prof Exp:* Asst prof math, Univ Ill, Chicago Circle, 65-68 & Occidental Col, 68-70. *Mem:* Am Math Soc. *Res:* Algebraic topology; obstruction theory; classification of liftings, embeddings and immersions; twisted extraordinary cohomology. *Mailing Add:* Dept Math Univ Calif 900 University Ave Riverside CA 92521-0001

LARNER, ANDREW CHARLES, MOLECULAR BIOLOGY. *Current Pos:* SR RES SCIENTIST, DEPT CYTOKINE BIOL, FOOD & DRUG ADMIN, 88- *Personal Data:* b St Louis, Mo, Apr 1, 53. *Educ:* Haverford Col, BA, 75; Univ Va, PhD(pharmacol), 81, MD, 82. *Prof Exp:* Res fel infeforons, Rockefeller Univ, 82-85; residency path, Nat Cancer Inst, 85-88. *Mem:* Am Soc Exp Pathologists; Int Soc Interferon Res. *Res:* Molecular biology. *Mailing Add:* Dept Cytokine Biol Food & Drug Admin Bldg 29A Rm 2D20 Bethesda MD 20892-1029

LARNER, JOSEPH, BIOCHEMISTRY, PHARMACOLOGY. *Current Pos:* prof pharmacol & chmn dept, Sch Med, 69-90, ALUMNI PROF PHARMACOL, UNIV VA, 74- *Personal Data:* b Brest-Litovsk, Poland, Jan 9, 21; nat US; m 47; c 3. *Educ:* Univ Mich, BS, 42; Columbia Univ, MD, 45; Univ Ill, MS, 49; Wash Univ, PhD(biochem), 51. *Hon Degrees:* Dr, Univ Barcelona, 83. *Honors & Awards:* David Rumbaugh Award, Juv Diabetes Found, 80; Sandoz Lectr, Can Soc Endocrinol & Metab, 81; Banting Lectr Can Diabetes Asn, Univ Toronto, 81; E W Sutherland Mem Lectr, Univ Miami, 81; Paul K Smith Mem Lectr, George Washington Univ, 82; Diaz Christobal Award, Int Diabetes Fedn, 82; Claude P Brown Mem Lectr, Am Asn Clin Pathologists, 83; William Creacy Estab Lectr, Temple Univ Med Sch, 83; John Lynch Lectr, Univ Notre Dame, 84; Res Award, Japan Soc Starch Res, 85; Res Award, Asn Am Med Col, 87; Banting Medal, Am Diabetes Asn, 87; Lifetime Sci Achievement Award, Commonwealth Va, 92. *Prof Exp:* Instr biochem, Wash Univ, 51-53; asst prof, Noyes Chem Lab, Univ Ill, 53-57; from assoc prof to prof pharmacol, Sch Med, Western Res Univ, 57-64; Hill prof metab enzym, Col Med Sci, Univ Minn, Minneapolis, 64-69. *Concurrent Pos:* Travel award, Int Cong Biochem, 55; mem, Metab Study Sect, NIH, 62-66, mem, Training Comt, Nat Inst Arthritis & Metab Dis, 66; Commonwealth Fund fel, Lab Molecular Biol, Cambridge Univ, 63-64; NIH res career award, 63-64; mem, Subcomt Enzymes, Nat Res Coun-Nat Acad Sci, 64-; mem rev bd, Am Cancer Soc, 70-74; dir, Univ Diabetes Res & Training Ctr, 74-91. *Mem:* Inst Med-Nat Acad Sci; Am Soc Biol Chemists; fel Royal Col Med; Am Soc Pharmacol & Exp Therapeut; hon mem Japan Biochem Soc; Am Chem Soc; hon mem Can Soc Endocrinol & Metab; NY Acad Sci; Sigma Xi; Am Diabetes Asn; Am Inst Chemists; fel AAAS. *Res:* Enzymatic aspects of intermediary carbohydrate metabolism, genetic and hormonal control. *Mailing Add:* Dept Pharmacol Univ Va Sch Med Charlottesville VA 22903. *Fax:* 804-924-1992; *E-Mail:* jlgd@virginia.edu

LARNER, KENNETH LEE, EXPLORATION GEOPHYSICS. *Current Pos:* GREEN CHAIR PROF GEOPHYS, COLO SCH MINES, GOLDEN, COLO, 88- *Personal Data:* b Chicago, Ill, Nov 1, 38; m 76; c 2. *Educ:* Colo Sch Mines, GpE, 60; Mass Inst Technol, PhD(geophys), 70. *Prof Exp:* Res scientist image enhancement, EG&G, Inc, 67-69; sr res geophysicist, Western Geophys Co, 70-74, mgr res & develop explor geophys, 75-80, vpres & develop, 80-88. *Concurrent Pos:* Lectr geophys, Univ Houston, 73-74. *Mem:* Soc Explor Geophysicists; Seismol Soc Am; Europ Asn Explor Geophysicists; Sigma Xi. *Res:* Seismic signal enhancement and wave propagation; estimation of geophysical parameters from seismic measurements. *Mailing Add:* 8132 Citation Trail Evergreen CO 80439-6408

LARNEY, VIOLET HACHMEISTER, MATHEMATICS. *Current Pos:* RETIRED. *Personal Data:* b Chicago, Ill, May 19, 20; m 50. *Educ:* Ill State Univ, BEd, 41; Univ Ill, AM, 42; Univ Wis, PhD(math), 50. *Prof Exp:* Teacher high sch, Ill, 42-44; asst math, Univ Wis, 44-48, instr, Exten Div, 48-50; asst prof, Kans State Univ, 50-52; from assoc prof to prof math, State Univ NY, Albany, 52-82, emer prof, 82. *Mem:* Math Asn Am; Am Math Soc. *Res:* Abstract algebra. *Mailing Add:* 573 Leisure World Mesa AZ 85206-3129

LARNTZ, KINLEY, APPLIED STATISTICS, MATHEMATICAL STATISTICS. *Current Pos:* PROF APPL STATIST, UNIV MINN, ST PAUL, 71- *Personal Data:* b Coshocton, Ohio, Oct 2, 45; m 65; c 3. *Educ:* Dartmouth Col, AB, 67; Univ Chicago, PhD(statist), 71. *Mem:* Am Statist Asn; Royal Statist Soc; Biomet Soc; Inst Math Statist; Sigma Xi; AAAS. *Res:* Analysis of qualitative data; comparison of small sample distributions for chi-square goodness-of-fit statistics; data analysis applied statistical methods. *Mailing Add:* Dept Appl Statist 352 COB Univ Minn 1994 Buford Ave St Paul MN 55108

LAROCCA, ANTHONY JOSEPH, PHYSICS, ELECTRICAL ENGINEERING. *Current Pos:* RES PHYSICIST, ENVIRON RES INST MICH, 73- *Personal Data:* b New Orleans, La, May 15, 23; m 54, Anne-Marie Blain; c 6. *Educ:* Tulane Univ, BS in EE, 49; Univ Mich, MS, 52. *Prof Exp:* Res asst physics, Tulane Univ, 49-51; res asst, Inst Sci & Technol, Univ Mich, Ann Arbor, 56-58, res assoc, 58-60, from assoc res physicist to res physicist, 60-73. *Concurrent Pos:* Adj prof, Univ Mich, 73- *Mem:* AAAS; Optical Soc Am. *Res:* Infrared and optical technology; radiation phenomena; propagation and attenuation; techniques of measurement of radiation; design and use of electrooptical devices; standards of radiation; study of techniques of remote sensing of environment. *Mailing Add:* 2600 Englave Ann Arbor MI 48103

LA ROCCA, JOSEPH PAUL, MEDICINAL CHEMISTRY. *Current Pos:* RES & DEVELOP, BECTON-DICKINSON LABWARE, 88- *Personal Data:* b La Junta, Colo, July 5, 20; m 47; c 4. *Educ:* Univ Colo, BS, 42; Univ NC, MS, 44; Univ Md, PhD(pharmaceut chem), 48. *Prof Exp:* Res chemist, Naval Res Lab, 47-49; from assoc prof to prof pharm, Univ Ga, 49-88, head, dept med chem, 70-88. *Mem:* Am Chem Soc; Am Pharmaceut Asn. *Res:* Synthetic sedative-hypnotics; anticonvulsant compounds; chemotherapy of cancer. *Mailing Add:* 115 Fortson Circle Athens GA 30606-4129

LA ROCCA, PAUL JOSEPH, CELL PHYSIOLOGY. *Current Pos:* mgr biol res, 84-86, MGR BIOL SCI & TECHNOL, BECTON DICKINSON LABWARE, 86- *Personal Data:* b Newburgh, NY, Jan 30, 54; c 2. *Educ:* George Washington Univ, BS, 77; Univ Ill, Chicago, PhD(cell & develop biol), 82. *Prof Exp:* Sr fel physiol, Div Cell Growth & Regulation, Dana-Farber Cancer Inst & Dept Physiol & Biophys, Harvard Med Sch, 82-84. *Concurrent Pos:* Nat res serv award, NIH, 82-83, fel, 83-85. *Mem:* Sigma Xi; Tissue Cult Asn; Am Soc Cell Biol; NY Acad Sci; Am Chem Soc. *Res:* Product development and testing; manufacturing technologies; new technologies that impact cell culture. *Mailing Add:* Dept Res & Develop Becton Dickinson Labware 1 Becton Dr Franklin Lakes NJ 07417-1886

LAROCHE, ANDRE, IDENTIFICATION OF DNA MARKERS & GENES FOR DISEASE RESISTANCE, FREEZING TOLERANCE IN HIGHER PLANTS. *Current Pos:* RES SCIENTIST, AGR CAN RES CTR, LETHBRIDGE, ALTA, 89- *Personal Data:* b Que, Can, May 31, 56; m 80, Mireille Cloutier; c Guillaume, Philippe, Francois J & Antoine. *Educ:* Univ Sherbrooke, Que, BSc, 79, MSc, 83; Univ Western Ont, PhD(plant sci), 87. *Prof Exp:* Vis fel, Agr Can Plant Res Ctr, Ottawa, Ont, 87-89. *Concurrent Pos:* Adj prof, Dept Biol Sci, Univ Lethbridge, Alta, 92- *Mem:* Am Soc Plant Physiologists; Can Soc Plant Physiologists; Int Soc Plant Molecular Biol; Can-Fr Asn Advan Sci. *Res:* Identification of markers linked to different disease resistance genes in cereals; identification of DNA sequences involved in the vernalization process of wheat; identification of DNA fragments unique to specific plant pathogens. *Mailing Add:* Agr Can Res Sta PO Box 3000 Main Lethbridge AB T1J 4B1 Can. *Fax:* 403-382-3156

LA ROCHE, GILLES, ENDOCRINOLOGY, WATER POLLUTION TOXICOLOGY. *Current Pos:* PRES, VIT-VITAILLE-VIRON INC, 79- *Personal Data:* b Bienville, Que, July 11, 22. *Educ:* Univ Montreal, BS, 47; McGill Univ, MS, 51; Univ Wash, PhD(biochem), 56. *Prof Exp:* Researcher, Univ Calif, Berkeley, 56-58, res biochemist & dir metab unit, 58-66; prof toxicol & endocrinol, Sch Oceanog, RI Univ, 66-72; prof toxicol, McGill Univ Inst Oceanog, 72-81. *Concurrent Pos:* Sci advr, Int Joint Comn Great Lakes, 80-85. *Mem:* AAAS; Am Physiol Soc; Endocrine Soc; Asn Clin Scientists. *Res:* Endocrinology; water pollution toxicology. *Mailing Add:* Vit-Vitaille-Viron Inc 1455 Sherbrooke St W PH-3 Montreal PQ H3G 1L2 Can

LAROCHELLE, JACQUES, ANIMAL PHYSIOLOGY. *Current Pos:* from asst prof to assoc prof, 77-92, PROF PHYSIOL, LAVAL UNIV, 92- *Personal Data:* b Que, Can, Sept 4, 46; m 72; c 2. *Educ:* Laval Univ, BA, 66, BSc, 71, DSc, 76. *Prof Exp:* Lectr physiol, Laval Univ, 74-75; Que Ministry Educ fel & vis scholar zool, Duke Univ, 76. *Mem:* Can Soc Zoologists. *Res:* Temperature regulation and locomotion in birds and mammals. *Mailing Add:* Dept Biol Laval Univ Quebec PQ G1K 7P4 Can. *Fax:* 418-656-2043; *E-Mail:* jacques.larochelle@bio.ulaval.ca

LA ROCHELLE, JOHN HART, PHYSICAL CHEMISTRY. *Current Pos:* RETIRED. *Personal Data:* b Longmeadow, Mass, Aug 17, 24; m 48; c 4. *Educ:* Univ Mass, BS, 48; Northeastern Univ, MS, 50; Univ Mich, PhD(chem), 55. *Prof Exp:* Res chemist, Shell Chem Co, 55-60, sr res chemist, 60-68, res supvr, 68-72, res supvr, Shell Develop Co, 72-74, staff chemist, Geismar Plant, 74-83. *Mem:* AAAS; Am Inst Chemists; Sigma Xi. *Res:* Dielectric polarization of gases. *Mailing Add:* 2757 Woodland Ridge Baton Rouge LA 70816

LAROCK, BRUCE E, CIVIL ENGINEERING, HYDRODYNAMICS. *Current Pos:* From asst prof to assoc prof, 66-79, PROF CIVIL ENG, UNIV CALIF, DAVIS, 79- *Personal Data:* b Berkeley, Calif, Dec 24, 40; m 68, Susan E Gardner; c Lynne M & Jean E. *Educ:* Stanford Univ, BS, 62, MS, 63, PhD(civil eng), 66. *Concurrent Pos:* Sr US scientist award, Alexander von Humboldt-Stiftung, 86-87. *Mem:* Am Soc Civil Engrs. *Res:* Hydraulics and fluid mechanics; finite element methods. *Mailing Add:* Dept Civil & Environ Eng Univ Calif Davis CA 95616. *Fax:* 530-752-7872; *E-Mail:* belarock@ucdavis.edu

LAROCK, PAUL ANTHONY, ENVIRONMENTAL SCIENCES, GEOMICROBIOLOGY. *Current Pos:* PROF, DEPT OCEANOG & COASTAL SCI, LA STATE UNIV, 92- *Personal Data:* b New York, NY, Nov 18, 37. *Educ:* Rensselaer Polytech Inst, BCE, 60, MS, 64, PhD(environ eng), 68. *Honors & Awards:* Nat Tech Achievement Award, NAm Lakes Mgt Soc, 87. *Prof Exp:* From asst prof to prof, Fla State Univ, 68-92. *Concurrent Pos:* Assoc prof, Univ Hawaii, 75-76. *Mem:* Am Soc Microbiol; Am Geophys Union; Am Soc Limnol & Oceanog. *Res:* Environmental microbiology and biogeochemical cycling of minerals and toxic materials; Marine microbiology, bacterial cycling of minerals, stormwater effects on receiving bodies and microbiol ecology. *Mailing Add:* Dept Oceanog & Coastal Sci La State Univ Baton Rouge LA 70803. *Fax:* 504-388-6307; *E-Mail:* oclaro@unix1.sncc.lsu.edu

LAROCK, RICHARD CRAIG, ORGANIC CHEMISTRY. *Current Pos:* From instr to assoc prof, 72-85, PROF CHEM, IOWA STATE UNIV, 85- *Personal Data:* b Berkeley, Calif, Nov 16, 44. *Educ:* Univ Calif, Davis, BS, 67; Purdue Univ, PhD(chem), 72. *Concurrent Pos:* Du Pont Young fac scholar, 75-76; A P Sloan fel, 77-79. *Mem:* Am Chem Soc; Sigma Xi. *Res:* Synthesis of biologically active compounds; new synthetic methods; organometallic and heterocyclic chemistry; polymer chemistry. *Mailing Add:* Dept Chem 2751 Gilman Hall Iowa State Univ Ames IA 50011-0061. *Fax:* 515-294-0105; *E-Mail:* larock@iastate.edu

LAROS, GERALD SNYDER, II, orthopedic surgery; deceased, see previous edition for last biography

LAROSSA, ROBERT ALAN, AGRICULTURE PRODUCTION. *Current Pos:* prin investr, Cent Res & Develop Dept, 80-90, SR RES BIOLOGIST, AGR PRODS DEPT, E I DU PONT DE NEMOURS & CO, INC, 90- *Personal Data:* b New York, NY, Jan 29, 51; c 2. *Educ:* Johns Hopkins Univ, BA, 73; Yale Univ, MPhil, 76, PhD(molecular biophys & biochem), 77. *Prof Exp:* Postdoctoral fel, Dept Molecular Biophys & Biochem, Yale Univ, 77; postdoctoral fel, Dept Biochem, Stanford Univ, 77-80, res assoc, 80. *Concurrent Pos:* Teaching asst, Yale Univ, 73-74; Am Chem Soc postdoctoral fel, 77-79, NSF postdoctoral fel, 79-80; invited lectr, numerous insts & univs, 79-; lectr molecular genetics, DuPont Continuing Educ Prog, 81; adj asst prof, Sch Life & Health Sci, Univ Del, 83-86; spec reviewer, Microbial Genetics & Physiol Study Sect II, NIH, 89. *Mem:* Am Soc Microbiol; Genetics Soc Am; Am Soc Biochem & Molecular Biol. *Mailing Add:* Cent Res Dept E I du Pont de Nemours & Co 672 Kadar Dr West Chester PA 19382-8124. *Fax:* 302-695-9183

LAROW, EDWARD J, AQUATIC ECOLOGY, INVERTEBRATE ZOOLOGY. *Current Pos:* From asst prof to assoc prof, 68-74, chmn dept, 71-80, PROF BIOL, SIENA COL, NY, 74- *Personal Data:* b Albany, NY, Dec 22, 37; m 63, Nancy L Jarvis; c Mary A, Edward Jr, John & Catherine. *Educ:* Siena Col, BS, 60; Kans State Univ, MS, 65; Rutgers Univ, PhD(zool), 68. *Concurrent Pos:* Nat Res Coun Int Biol Prog grant, 70-74; vis lectr, State Univ NY Albany, 70-75 & Col Environ Sci & Forestry, 76-85. *Mem:* Ecol Soc Am; Am Soc Limnol & Oceanog; Int Soc Limnol. *Res:* Biological rhythms and their role in the vertical migration of zooplankton; secondary production of zooplankton; effect of acid precipitation on zooplankton populations. *Mailing Add:* Dept Biol Siena Col 515 Loudonville Rd Loudonville NY 12211-1459

LARRABEE, ALLAN ROGER, BIOCHEMISTRY. *Current Pos:* SYSTS PROGRAMMER, BOEING COMPUT SERV, BELLEVUE, 86- *Personal Data:* b Flushing, NY, Feb 24, 35; m 60; c 3. *Educ:* Bucknell Univ, BS, 57; Mass Inst Technol, PhD, 62; Ore Inst Sci & Technol, MS, 86. *Prof Exp:* Staff fel biosynthesis of fatty acids, NIH, 64-66; asst prof chem, Univ Ore, 66-72; from assoc prof to prof chem, Memphis State Univ, 72-83. *Concurrent Pos:* NIH res grant, 67-70; NSF res grant, 70-75; consult 81- 86. *Mem:* Am Soc Biol Chemists. *Res:* Role of vitamin B-12, folic acid and pantothenate as coenzymes; biosynthesis of fatty acids; multienzyme complexes; protein turnover; parallel computers. *Mailing Add:* Boeing Info & Support Syst PO Box 3707 Seattle WA 98124-2207

LARRABEE, MARTIN GLOVER, NEUROCHEMISTRY, NEUROPHYSIOLOGY. *Current Pos:* assoc prof, 49-63, PROF BIOPHYS, JOHNS HOPKINS UNIV, 63- *Personal Data:* b Boston, Mass, Jan 25, 10; m 32, 44; c 2. *Educ:* Harvard Univ, AB, 32; Univ Pa, PhD(biophys), 37. *Hon Degrees:* MD, Univ Lausanne, 74. *Prof Exp:* Asst, Univ Pa, 34-35, fel med physics, 37-40; asst prof physiol, Med Col, Cornell Univ, 40-41; fel, Johnson Found, Univ Pa, 41-42, assoc, 42-43, from asst prof to assoc prof biophys, 43-48. *Mem:* Nat Acad Sci; Am Physiol Soc; Am Soc Neurochem; Int Soc Neurochem; Soc Neurosci (treas, 72-75). *Res:* Metabolism in relation to physiological function and embryological development in sympathetic ganglia. *Mailing Add:* Dept Biophys Johns Hopkins Univ Baltimore MD 21218

LARRABEE, R(OBERT) D(EAN), OPTICAL METROLOGY, SEM METROLOGY. *Current Pos:* physicist, 76-81, group leader, 81-93, GUEST RESEARCHER, NAT INST STAND & TECHNOL, 94- *Personal Data:* b Flushing, NY, Nov 29, 31; m 53, Ramona Rogers; c David A & Susan (Albohn). *Educ:* Bucknell Univ, BS & MS, 53; Mass Inst Technol, SM, 55, ScD, 57; Rider Col, MBA, 76. *Prof Exp:* Res engr, David Sarnoff Res Ctr, RCA Corp, 57-71, sr engr, Advan Technol Lab, 72-76. *Concurrent Pos:* Mem adj fac, Univ Md, 81-82. *Mem:* AAAS; sr mem Inst Elec & Electronics Engrs; Am Phys Soc; Sigma Xi. *Res:* Semiconductor materials and devices; solid-state plasma physics; semiconductor microwave oscillators and amplifiers; infrared physics and detectors; characterization of semiconductor materials; optical and scanning electron microscope submicrometer metrology; granted 9 patents. *Mailing Add:* 18801 Woodway Dr Derwood MD 20855

LARRICK, JAMES WILLIAM, HUMAN MONOCLONAL ANTIBODIES, CANCER THERAPEUTICS. *Current Pos:* FOUNDER, PANORAMA RES, 88- *Personal Data:* b Englewood Colo, Jan 4, 50; m 95, Zi Hua; c 14. *Educ:* Colo Col, BA, 72; Duke Univ, PhD(immunol), 79, MD, 80. *Prof Exp:* Intern, Stanford Med Ctr, Palo Alto, 81; scientist & proj leader, Cetus Immune Res Labs, 82-84, sr scientist, 85, dir, Genelabs Inc, 85-88, dir explor res, 90. *Concurrent Pos:* Thomas J Watson fel. *Mem:* Am Asn Immunologists; Am Fedn Clin Res; AAAS. *Res:* Discovery and characterization of novel biopharmaceuticals for therapy and diagnosis of diseases; human monoclonal antibodies, cytokines. *Mailing Add:* Palo Alto Inst Molecular Med 2462 Wyandotte Mountain View CA 94043. *Fax:* 650-694-7717; *E-Mail:* jwlarrick@aol.com

LARROWE, BOYD T, ELECTRONIC ENGINEERING. *Current Pos:* RETIRED. *Personal Data:* b Merriam, Kans, May 6, 23; m 59, Kathryn Tittiger; c Ann (Baca), John, Martha (Henry) & David. *Educ:* Univ Kans, BS, 50; Univ Ill, MS, 51. *Prof Exp:* Mem staff digital comput design, Univ Ill, 50-51; res assoc, Univ Mich, 52-57; sr engr, Strand Eng Co, 57-62; chief engr, Comput Displays, Burroughs Corp Labs, Mich, 62-64; res engr, Inst Sci Technol, Univ Mich, 64-73 & Environ Res Inst Mich, 73-89. *Mem:* Inst Elec & Electronics Engrs. *Res:* Digital computer design; automatic radar image interpretation; display techniques; real time electronic processor design for synthetic aperture radar. *Mailing Add:* 403 Seneca St Tecumseh MI 49286-1022

LARROWE, VERNON L, ELECTRICAL ENGINEERING. *Current Pos:* res engr, 73-83, sr res engr, 83-86, EMER MEM TECH STAFF, ENVIRON RES INST MICH, 89- *Personal Data:* b Galax, Va, Feb 21, 21; m 66, Florence Glinicki; c Victoria. *Educ:* Univ Kans, BS, 50; Univ Ill, MS, 51; Univ Mich, PhD(elec eng), 64. *Prof Exp:* Asst elec eng, Univ Ill, 50-51; res assoc, Inst Sci & Technol, Univ Mich, Ann Arbor, 51-53, assoc res engr, 53-57, head analog comput lab, 53-65, res engr, 57-65; res engr, Infrared & Optics Lab, Willow Run Labs, 65-73. *Mem:* Inst Elec & Electronics Engrs; Soc Comput Simulation; Soc Photo-Optical & Instrumentation Engrs; NY Acad Sci. *Res:* Application of electronic analog computers; data processing; information theory; remote sensing; automatic pattern recognition; high density digital recording; servo controls. *Mailing Add:* Environ Res Inst Mich Box 134001 Ann Arbor MI 48113-4001. *E-Mail:* vernon2616@aol.com

LARRY, JOHN ROBERT, PHYSICAL CHEMISTRY. *Current Pos:* Res chemist, E I du Pont de Nemours & Co, Inc, 66-74, sr res chemist, 74-76, res supvr, 77-84, RES MGR, ELECTRONICS DEPT, RES & DEVELOP DIV, E I DU PONT DE NEMOURS & CO, INC, WILMINGTON, DEL, 84- *Personal Data:* b Mt Clare, WVa, Nov 13, 39; m 63; c 3. *Educ:* WVa Univ, BS, 61; Ohio State Univ, PhD(chem), 66. *Honors & Awards:* Tech Achievement Award, Int Soc Hybrid Microelectronics, 82. *Mem:* Am Chem Soc; Int Soc Hybrid Microelectronics. *Res:* Charge transfer and molecular complexes; ultracentrifugation; emulsion polymerization; colloid chemistry; rheology; solid state conductors; solid state resistors; multilayer capacitors. *Mailing Add:* DuPont Co Exp Sta PO Box 80334 Rm 210 Wilmington DE 19880-0334

LARSEN, ARNOLD LEWIS, botany, agronomy, for more information see previous edition

LARSEN, AUBREY ARNOLD, MEDICINAL CHEMISTRY. *Current Pos:* RETIRED. *Personal Data:* b Rockford, Ill, Sept 27, 19; m 43; c 5. *Educ:* Antioch Col, BS, 43; Mich State Col, MS, 44; Cornell Univ, PhD(org chem), 46. *Prof Exp:* Mem staff, Sterling-Winthrop Res Inst, 46-60; asst dir org chem, Mead Johnson & Co, Ind, 60-63, dir chem res, 63-67, vpres phys sci, 67-70; vpres & sci dir, Bristol-Myers Int, 70-75; vpres res & develop, Mead Johnson & Co, 75-82. *Mem:* AAAS; NY Acad Sci; Am Chem Soc; Sigma Xi. *Res:* Pharmaceutical and nutritional research and development. *Mailing Add:* 2920 Cypress Ct Evansville IN 47711-6725

LARSEN, AUSTIN ELLIS, VETERINARY MEDICINE, MICROBIOLOGY. *Current Pos:* RETIRED. *Personal Data:* b Provo, Utah, Nov 1, 23; m 45; c 4. *Educ:* Wash State Univ, BS, 48, DVM, 49; Univ Utah, MS, 56, PhD(microbiol), 69. *Prof Exp:* Vet pvt pract, Utah, 49-68; clin instr microbiol, Col Med, Univ Utah, 61-68, asst prof, 68-80, dir, Vivarium, 68-87, assoc prof cellular, viral & molecular virol, 80-87. *Concurrent Pos:* Vet & dir, Res Lab, Fur Breeders Agr Coop Lab, 52-68, consult vet, 68-; consult, Schering Corp, 63-; non-med med asst res, Vet Admin, 69-; mem, Adv Comt Fur Farmers Res Inst; mem, Health Task Force Utah. *Mem:* Am Soc Microbiol; Am Soc Exp Path; Am Soc Lab Animal Pract; Sigma Xi. *Res:* Slow virus research. *Mailing Add:* 1825 S 230 E Salt Lake City UT 84108

LARSEN, BARBARA SELIGER, MASS SPECTROMETRY. *Current Pos:* RES SCIENTIST, CENT RES, DUPONT CO, 84- *Personal Data:* b Englewood, NJ, Oct 22, 56; m 80; c 2. *Educ:* Santa Clara Univ, BS, 78; Univ Del, PhD(phys chem), 83. *Prof Exp:* Res assoc, Int Diagnostics Tech, 78-79; NSF postdoctoral fel, Johns Hopkins Univ, 83-84. *Mem:* Am Soc Mass Spectrometry; Am Chem Soc; Int Protein Soc. *Res:* Mass spectrometry as applied to the area of life sciences including sequence of proteins, identification of metabolites; new ionization techniques to expand the application of mass spectrometry. *Mailing Add:* Dupont Co PO Box 80228 Wilmington DE 19898

LARSEN, CHARLES MCLOUD, MATHEMATICS EDUCATION. *Current Pos:* From instr to prof, 54-88, EMER PROF MATH, SAN JOSE STATE UNIV, 88- *Personal Data:* b Staten Island, NY, Dec 6, 24; m 48; c 4. *Educ:* Cornell Univ, AB, 45, AM, 50; Stanford Univ, PhD(educ), 60. *Concurrent Pos:* Vis prof, Beijing Agr Univ, China, 85 & 86-87. *Mem:* Math Asn Am; Nat Coun Teachers Math. *Res:* History of mathematics; mathematics education. *Mailing Add:* 1675 Ellis Hollow Rd Ithaca NY 14850

LARSEN, CHARLES ROBERT, SYSTEMS ENGINEERING, MANAGEMENT. *Current Pos:* AEROSPACE ENGR, FED AVIATION ADMIN, US DEPT TRANSP, 94- *Personal Data:* b Independence, Mo, Aug 7, 44; div; c Peter Charles & Caryn Elizabeth. *Educ:* Univ Calif, Berkeley, BS, 66. *Prof Exp:* Lead thermal systs engr, Aerojet-Gen Corp, 67-70; sr proj engr, Bendix Aerospace, 70-72; payloads & mech systs mgr, Ford Aerospace & Commun Corp, 72-83; sr advan prog mgr, Aerospace Div, Gen Elec, 83-91; tech staff specialist, Fairchild Space & Defense Corp, 91-94; consult & aerospace engr, Aerospace Consult Group, Inc, 94. *Mem:* Assoc fel Am Inst Aeronaut & Astronaut. *Res:* Aerospace safety of launch vehicles, with emphasis on the X-33 and X-34 programs leading to the development of the commercial reusable vehicle. *Mailing Add:* 30 Steeple Ct Germantown MD 20874. *Fax:* 202-366-9945; *E-Mail:* chuck.larsen@faa.dot.gov

LARSEN, CURTIS E, QUATERNARY GEOLOGY, COASTAL GEOMORPHOLOGY. *Current Pos:* Res geologist, 80-95, ASSOC EASTERN REGIONAL GEOLOGIST, GEOL DIV, US GEOL SURV, 95- *Personal Data:* b Elmhurst, Ill, Oct 8, 39. *Educ:* Univ Ill, BS, 64; Western Wash Univ, MA, 71; Univ Chicago, PhD(anthrop), 80. *Mem:* Am Quaternary Asn. *Mailing Add:* US Geol Surv 953 Nat Ctr Reston VA 20194. *Fax:* 703-648-6684; *E-Mail:* clarsen@usgs.gov

LARSEN, DAVID M, THEORETICAL PHYSICS. *Current Pos:* PROF, UNIV MASS, LOWELL, 87- *Personal Data:* b Hawthorne, NJ, Mar 8, 36; m 58; c 3. *Educ:* Mass Inst Technol, SB, 57, PhD(physics), 62. *Prof Exp:* Nat Res Coun-Nat Bur Stand fel physics, Nat Bur Stand, Washington, DC, 62-64; staff physicist, Lincoln Lab, Mass Inst Technol, 64-76, staff physicist, Francis Bitter Nat Magnet Lab, 76-87. *Mem:* Fel Am Phys Soc. *Res:* Impurities in semiconductors; polaron theory. *Mailing Add:* 6 Fessenden Way Lexington MA 02173

LARSEN, DAVID W, PHYSICAL CHEMISTRY. *Current Pos:* asst prof, 64-66, assoc prof chem, 66-80, PROF, UNIV MO-ST LOUIS, 80- *Personal Data:* b Chicago, Ill, Feb 21, 36; m 63. *Educ:* Dana Col, BA, 58; Northwestern Univ, PhD(phys chem), 63. *Prof Exp:* Res assoc nuclear magnetic resonance spectros, Washington Univ, 63-64. *Mem:* Am Chem Soc. *Res:* Nuclear magnetic resonance spectroscopy; exchange reactions of Lewis acids and bases in non-aqueous media; ionic interactions in aqueous media. *Mailing Add:* Dept Chem Univ Mo-St Louis St Louis MO 63121

LARSEN, DON HYRUM, industrial microbial, medical microbiology; deceased, see previous edition for last biography

LARSEN, EDWARD WILLIAM, APPLIED MATHEMATICS. *Current Pos:* MEM STAFF MATH, LOS ALAMOS NAT LAB, 77- *Personal Data:* b Flushing, NY, Nov 12, 44; m 74. *Educ:* Rensselaer Polytech Inst, BS, 66, PhD(math), 71. *Prof Exp:* Asst prof math, NY Univ, 71-76; assoc prof, Univ Del, 76-77. *Concurrent Pos:* Ed, Transport Theory & Statist Physics, 75- & J Appl Math, 76- *Mem:* Soc Indust & Appl Math; Am Nuclear Soc. *Res:* Asymptotic expansions; spectral theory; numerical analysis; transport theory. *Mailing Add:* Dept Nuclear Eng Univ Mich Ann Arbor MI 48109

LARSEN, EDWIN MERRITT, ZIRCONIUM, LITHIUM & TRITIUM CHEMISTRY. *Current Pos:* RETIRED. *Personal Data:* b Milwaukee, Wis, July 12, 15; m 46, Kathryn M Behm; c Robert, Lynn & Richard. *Educ:* Univ Wis-Madison, BS, 37; Ohio State Univ, PhD(chem), 42. *Prof Exp:* Chemist, Rohm & Haas, Pa, 37-38; asst chem, Ohio State Univ, 38-42; instr, Univ Wis, 42-43; group leader, Manhattan Dist Proj, Monsanto Chem Co, Ohio, 43-46; from asst prof to assoc prof, Univ Wis-Madison, 46-58, prof chem, 58-86, assoc chmn dept, 77-86. *Concurrent Pos:* Vis prof, Univ Fla, 58; Fulbright lectr, Inst Inorg Chem, Vienna Tech Inst, 66-67; Wis Fusion Tech Inst, 77- *Mem:* Fel AAAS; Am Chem Soc; Am Nuclear Soc; Sigma Xi. *Res:* Chemistry of the transitional elements; reduced states; chemistry of nuclear fusion; synthesis in liquid aluminum halides. *Mailing Add:* Dept Chem Univ Wis Madison WI 53705

LARSEN, ELLEN WYNNE, DEVELOPMENTAL GENETICS. *Current Pos:* asst prof, 74-79, ASSOC PROF GENETICS, DEPT ZOOL, UNIV TORONTO, 79- *Personal Data:* b Paterson, NJ, Apr 28, 42; US & Can citizen; c 1. *Educ:* Univ Mich, BSc, 63, MSc, 67, PhD(zool), 69. *Prof Exp:* Fel cytogenetics, York Univ, 69-70; fel genetics, Simon Fraser Univ, 70-74. *Mem:* AAAS; Genetics Soc Am; Genetics Soc Can. *Res:* Genes and morphogenesis in fruit fly; imaginal discs evolutionary development biology. *Mailing Add:* Dept Zool 25 Harvard St Univ Toronto Toronto ON M5S 1A1 Can

LARSEN, ERIC RUSSELL, ORGANIC CHEMISTRY. *Current Pos:* RETIRED. *Personal Data:* b Port Angeles, Wash, July 7, 28; m 51; c Eric, Karen, Elisabeth & Kathryn. *Educ:* Univ Wash, BS, 50; Univ Colo, PhD(org chem), 54. *Prof Exp:* Res chemist, Chem Eng Lab, Dow Chem Co, 56-59, proj leader, 59-62, sr res chemist, 62-64, group leader, Halogens Res Lab, 64-68, assoc res scientist, 68-74, res scientist, Halogens Res Lab, 74-86, consult, 86-96. *Concurrent Pos:* Consult assoc, Omni-Tech Int, Teltech, Inc. *Mem:* AAAS; Am Chem Soc; Sigma Xi. *Res:* Primary research in bromine and fluorine chemistry; flammability of organic compounds, including polymers and in the mechanism of flame suppression; fire research, especially flame retardancy in plastics; inert gas narcosis. *Mailing Add:* 314 W Meadowbrook Dr Midland MI 48640

LARSEN, FENTON E, HORTICULTURE, POMOLOGY. *Current Pos:* From asst horticulturist to assoc horticulturist, 59-73, PROF & HORTICULTURIST, WASH STATE UNIV, 73- *Personal Data:* b Preston, Idaho, Mar 22, 34; m 54, ReNae Buxton; c Steven, Kent, JulieAnn & Michael. *Educ:* Utah State Univ, BS, 56; Mich State Univ, PhD(hort), 59. *Concurrent Pos:* Consult, Columbia, 75, Venezuela, 77, Costa Rica, 79, 87, 88, Indonesia, 82, Ecuador, 85 & Jordan, 88; vis prof, Univ Jordan, Amman, 79. *Mem:* Am Soc Hort Sci; Am Pomol Soc; Int Plant Propagators Soc; Sigma Xi. *Res:* Pomology; propagation; rootstocks, growth regulators; leaf abscission and branching of nursery stock. *Mailing Add:* Dept Hort Wash State Univ Pullman WA 99164-6414. *Fax:* 509-335-8690; *E-Mail:* flarsen@wsu.edu

LARSEN, FREDERICK DUANE, GEOMORPHOLOGY. *Current Pos:* From instr to asst prof geol, 57-89, PROF, NORWICH UNIV, 80- *Personal Data:* b St Johnsbury, Vt, Mar 20, 30; m 52; c 4. *Educ:* Middlebury Col, BA, 52; Boston Univ, MA, 60; Univ Mass, PhD(geol), 72. *Concurrent Pos:* US Geol Surv, 68-82, VT & NH Geol Surv, 83- *Mem:* Geol Soc Am; Soc Sedimentary Geol; Nat Asn Geol Teachers. *Res:* Glacial geology if the Connecticut Valley of Mass, Vermont and New Hampshire; glacial geology of central Vermont. *Mailing Add:* Dept Earth Sci Norwich Univ 65 S Main St Northfield VT 05663-1004

LARSEN, HAROLD CECIL, AERODYNAMICS, ASTRODYNAMICS. *Current Pos:* from asst prof to assoc prof aerodyn, 46-56, PROF AERODYN & HEAD DEPT, USAF INST TECHNOL, 56- *Personal Data:* b Granite, Utah, June 15, 18; m 56, A Caroline Kelly; c John H, Robert G & Kistin L. *Educ:* Univ Utah, BSc, 41; Calif Inst Technol, MSc, 46, AE, 55. *Prof Exp:* Prod engr, Lockheed Aircraft Corp, Calif, 41. *Concurrent Pos:* Dir, Aerospace Design Ctr & Windtunnel Res & Testing, AFIT. *Mem:* Am Inst Aeronaut & Astronaut; Sigma Xi. *Res:* Wind energy conversion; vortex theory of the cyclogiro and application to vertical axis wind turbine; Giro mill and Madaras rotor design of sky-diver wind tunnel; energy conversion of ocean and tidal currents. *Mailing Add:* 2829 Rugby Rd Dayton OH 45406-2004

LARSEN, HARRY STITES, FORESTRY. *Current Pos:* RETIRED. *Personal Data:* b Pittsburgh, Pa, Aug 12, 27; m 56; c 3. *Educ:* Rutgers Univ, BS, 50; Mich State Univ, MS, 53; Duke Univ, PhD, 63. *Prof Exp:* Forester, Southern Timber Mgt Serv, 53-56; asst prof, Auburn Univ, 59-71, assoc prof silvicult, Dept Forestry, 71-80, assoc prof forestry, 89-92. *Mem:* Ecol Soc Am; Soc Am Foresters. *Res:* Tree physiology; nursery seedling quality. *Mailing Add:* 316 Buena Vista Dr Lillian AL 36549

LARSEN, HOWARD JAMES, DAIRY NUTRITION. *Current Pos:* from asst prof to prof, 55-88, EMER PROF DAIRY SCI, MARSHFIELD EXP STA, UNIV WIS, 88- *Personal Data:* b Duluth, Minn, Jan 21, 25; m 46; c 2. *Educ:* Univ Wis, BS, 50; Iowa State Col, MS, 52, PhD(dairy husb), 53. *Prof Exp:* Assoc & instr dairy husb, Iowa State Col, 54-55. *Concurrent Pos:* Consult, US Feed Grains Coun, 81. *Mem:* Fel AAAS; Coun Agr Sci & Technol; Am Soc Animal Sci; Am Dairy Sci Asn; Sigma Xi. *Res:* Forage utilization by dairy cattle; forage and concentrate preservation and utilization by dairy cattle; environmental studies with ruminants. *Mailing Add:* 1020 Many Penny Ave Bayfield WI 54814

LARSEN, HOWLAND AIKENS, CHEMICAL ENGINEERING. *Current Pos:* res engr, E I du Pont de Nemours & Co, Inc, 57-64, sr res engr, 64-66, res supvr, 67-68, sr supvr, Fluorocarbons Div, 69-80, RES ASSOC, PLASTICS PROD DEPT, E I DU PONT DE NEMOURS & CO, INC, 80- *Personal Data:* b Seattle, Wash, June 29, 28; m 62; c 6. *Educ:* Mass Inst Technol, SB, 50; Univ Ill, MS, 51, PhD(chem eng), 57. *Prof Exp:* Jr engr, Shell Develop Co, 51-53. *Mem:* Am Chem Soc. *Res:* Thermoplastics; irreversible chemical effects of high pressure and shear. *Mailing Add:* 1360 Market St Parkersburg WV 26101

LARSEN, JAMES BOUTON, COMBUSTION TOXICOLOGY, NATURAL TOXINS. *Current Pos:* from asst prof to assoc prof, 73-93, PROF BIOL, UNIV SOUTHERN MISS, 93- *Personal Data:* b Detroit, Mich, July 28, 41; m 64, Anne Struhsaker; c Nathan & Susan. *Educ:* Kalamazoo Col, BA, 63; Univ Miami, MS, 66, PhD(marine biol), 68. *Prof Exp:* Fel biochem, Colo State Univ, 67-68; asst prof biol, Hamline Univ, 68-73. *Concurrent Pos:* Investr, Marine Biol Lab, Woods Hole, 82; res prof, Sch Pharm, Univ Conn, 87. *Mem:* AAAS; Sigma Xi; Am Soc Zoologists; Int Soc Toxinology. *Res:* Physiological effects of carbon monoxide; combustion toxicology of polymers; physiology, toxicology and pharmacology of natural toxins. *Mailing Add:* Dept Biol Sci Univ Southern Miss Box 9236 Hattiesburg MS 39406-9236. *E-Mail:* jlarsen@ocean.st.usm.edu

LARSEN, JAMES VICTOR, CHEMICAL & MATERIALS ENGINEERING. *Current Pos:* PRES, WESTECH ENG, 84- *Personal Data:* b Salt Lake City, Utah, June 16, 42; m 66. *Educ:* Univ Utah, BS, 67; Univ Md, College Park, MS, 69, PhD(chem eng), 71. *Prof Exp:* Chem engr, US Naval Ord Lab, 67-71; sales mgr, Eimco Div, Envirotech Corp, 71-73, gen mgr, Eimcomet Plastics, 73-76, gen mgr, opers, Eimco PMD, 76-77, pres, Molded Prod Div, 77-, pres, Eng Dept, 77-84. *Mem:* Am Inst Chem Engrs; Am Inst Mining Engrs. *Res:* Nonmetallic materials; carbon fiber composites; plastics. *Mailing Add:* 2906 Kennedy Dr Salt Lake City UT 84108

LARSEN, JOHN HERBERT, JR, VERTEBRATE ZOOLOGY. *Current Pos:* from asst prof to assoc prof, 65-75, chmn dept, 78-84, PROF ZOOL, WASH STATE UNIV, 75-, DIR, ELECTRON MICROS CTR, 83- *Personal Data:* b Tacoma, Wash, July 20, 29; m 51. *Educ:* Univ Wash, BA, 55, MS, 58, PhD(zool), 63. *Prof Exp:* Instr embryol, Univ Wash, 60; instr biol, Univ Puget Sound, 60-61; cur & instr zool, Univ Wash, 61-62, NIH res fel, 63-64, USPHS sr fel electron micros, 64-65. *Mem:* Am Inst Biol Sci; Am Soc Zoologists; Sigma Xi; Soc Syst Zool; Am Soc Ichthyologists & Herpetologists. *Res:* Evolution and functional morphology of feeding systems in amphibians; implications of neoteny to urodele evolution; mechanisms of ovulation in lower vertebrates. *Mailing Add:* Electron Micros Ctr Wash State Univ Pullman WA 99164-4210

LARSEN, JOHN W, ORGANIC CHEMISTRY, PHYSICAL CHEMISTRY. *Current Pos:* DEPT CHEM, LEHIGH UNIV. *Personal Data:* b Hartford, Conn, Oct 30, 40; c 3. *Educ:* Tufts Univ, BS, 62; Purdue Univ, PhD(chem), 67. *Honors & Awards:* Storch Award, Am Chem Soc. *Prof Exp:* Res fel chem, Univ Pittsburgh, 66-68; from asst prof to assoc prof chem, Univ Tenn, Knoxville, 68-78, prof, 78-; chem div, Oak Ridge Nat Lab, 76- *Mem:* AAAS; Am Chem Soc; Sigma Xi. *Res:* Coal chemistry; thermodynamics of organic intermediates; chemistry in strong acid solutions and molten salts; environmentally benign organic synthesis. *Mailing Add:* Dept Chem Lehigh Univ 6 E Packer Ave Bethlehem PA 18015. *Fax:* 610-758-3461; *E-Mail:* jwl0@lehigh.edu

LARSEN, KENNETH MARTIN, APPLIED MATHEMATICS. *Current Pos:* from asst prof to prof, 60-89, EMER PROF MATH, BRIGHAM YOUNG UNIV, 89- *Personal Data:* b Ogden, Utah, June 26, 27; m 55, Merlee Smith; c 9. *Educ:* Univ Utah, BA, 50; Brigham Young Univ, MA, 56; Univ Calif, Los Angeles, PhD(math), 64. *Prof Exp:* Teaching asst math, Brigham Young Univ, 54-55 & Univ Calif, Los Angeles, 56-60. *Mem:* Sigma Xi; Soc Indust & Appl Math. *Res:* Numerical analysis; ordinary and partial differential equations; plasma confinement and stability. *Mailing Add:* 2270 N 300 E Brigham Young Univ Provo UT 84604-5860

LARSEN, LAWRENCE HAROLD, PSYCHIATRY. *Current Pos:* res asst prof, 67-71, RES ASSOC PROF PSYCHIAT, UNIV WASH, 71- *Personal Data:* b Staten Island, NY, July 22, 39; m 69; c 1. *Educ:* Stevens Inst Technol, BS, 61; Johns Hopkins Univ, PhD(hydrodyn), 65. *Prof Exp:* NSF fel meteorol, Univ Oslo, 65-66; vis res asst prof, Johns Hopkins Univ, 66-67. *Concurrent Pos:* Prog dir phys & chem oceanog, NSF, 72-73. *Mem:* Am Meteorol Soc; Am Geophys Union. *Res:* Physical oceanography; wave motion; estuaries; sediment dynamics; electroencephalogram; Alzheimer's diagnostics; computers. *Mailing Add:* Dept Psychiat Behav Sci RP-10 Univ Wash Seattle WA 98195

LARSEN, LELAND MALVERN, ALGEBRA. *Current Pos:* assoc prof, 48-67, head dept, 67-80, PROF MATH, KEARNEY STATE COL, 67- *Personal Data:* b Blair, Nebr, Aug 20, 15; m 40; c 3. *Educ:* Dana Col, BA, 41; Univ Nebr, MA, 48, PhD, 67. *Prof Exp:* Pub sch teacher, Nebr, 36-41, supt schs, 41-43; instr, Univ Nebr, 43-44. *Mem:* Math Asn Am; Nat Coun Teachers Math. *Res:* Theory of fields; various algorithms. *Mailing Add:* 4311 Sunset Trail Kearney NE 68847

LARSEN, LLOYD DON, FOOD MICROBIOLOGY, EARLY DETECTION OF MICROBES. *Current Pos:* MICROBIOLOGIST, DUGWAY, UTAH, 84- *Personal Data:* b Terre Haute, Ind, Sept 13, 44; m 69; c Michael, David, Peter, Joanna, Nathan, James, Gregory & Kathryn. *Educ:* Brigham Young Univ, BS, 69, MS, 74; Univ Minn, PhD(food microbiol), 79. *Prof Exp:* Sr scientist, Carnation Res Lab, 79-84. *Mem:* Am Soc Microbiol; Inst Food Technol. *Res:* Plasmids in industrial microorganisms including group N streptococci; improving fermentations via biotechnology; development of substitute dairy products; microbial detection kits. *Mailing Add:* 115 E 2075 S Orem UT 84058-8174. *Fax:* 435-833-5716

LARSEN, LYNN ALVIN, NUTRITION. *Current Pos:* chemist, GRAS Rev Br, Div Food & Color Additives, Ctr Food Safety & Appl Nutrit, Food & Drug Admin, 77-78, consumer safety officer, 78-81, assoc dir prog develop, Div Nutrit, 81-90, sci policy analyst, 90-91, dir, exec opers staff, 91-92, SPEC ASST, ADV COMTS, POLICY, PLANNING & STRATEGIC INITIATIVES, CTR FOOD SAFETY & APPL NUTRIT, FOOD & DRUG ADMIN, 92- *Personal Data:* b Grand Forks, NDak, Aug 2, 43; m 66, Bette J Tandberg; c Rachel A & Kirk D. *Educ:* Univ NDak, BS, 65; Univ Wash, PhD(inorg chem), 71. *Prof Exp:* Res assoc, Div Nephrology, Dept Med, Univ Wash, 71-77. *Concurrent Pos:* Wash State Heart Asn fel, Div Nephrology, Dept Med, Univ Wash, 72-74; instr, Prog Educ Gifted, Prince William Co, Va, 79-83. *Mem:* Am Chem Soc; AAAS; Inst Food Technologists. *Mailing Add:* Off Policy Planning & Strategic Initiatives Ctr Food Safety & Appl Nutrit Food & Drug Admin HFS-5 200 C St SW Washington DC 20204. *Fax:* 202-205-4970; *E-Mail:* llarsen@bangate.fda.gov

LARSEN, MARLIN LEE, CLINICAL CHEMISTRY. *Current Pos:* CONSULT, 79-; PRES, HARVARD LAB & XRAY INC, ROSEBURG, ORE, 81- *Personal Data:* b Grand Island, Nebr, Nov 22, 42; m 64; c 3. *Educ:* Kearney State Col, BS, 64; Wash State Univ, PhD(chem), 68. *Prof Exp:* Dir res & develop, ICN Med Labs, Inc, 68-79. *Mem:* Am Asn Clin Chemists; Am Asn Bioanalysts; Am Chem Soc. *Res:* Automation and methodology research of medical laboratory procedures. *Mailing Add:* 160 Rivershore Dr Roseburg OR 97470

LARSEN, MAX DEAN, ALGEBRA. *Current Pos:* From asst prof to assoc prof, 66-73, dean, Col Arts & Sci, 74-82, PROF MATH, UNIV NEBR-LINCOLN, 73- *Personal Data:* b Pratt, Kans, Jan 23, 41; m 62. *Educ:* Kans State Teachers Col, BA, 61; Univ Kans, MA, 63, PhD(math), 66. *Concurrent Pos:* NSF res grant, 68-70. *Mem:* Am Math Soc; Math Asn Am; Nat Coun Teachers Math; Sigma Xi. *Res:* Extension of integral domain concepts to general commutative rings, particularly valuation theory; module theory over commutative rings. *Mailing Add:* 641 Haverford Circle Lincoln NE 68510-2313

LARSEN, MICHAEL JOHN, MYCOLOGY, FOREST PATHOLOGY. *Current Pos:* RES SCIENTIST, US FOREST SERV, USDA, 70- *Personal Data:* b London, Eng, Apr 27, 38; m 70; c 2. *Educ:* Syracuse Univ, BSc, 60; State Univ NY, MSc, 63, PhD(mycol path), 67. *Prof Exp:* Res scientist, Can Forestry Serv, 66-70. *Concurrent Pos:* Adj assoc prof, Univ Wis-Madison, 71- & Mich Technol Univ, 78- *Mem:* Mycol Soc Am; Am Phytopath Soc; Int Asn Plant Taxon & Nomeclature; Int Mycol Soc. *Res:* Speciation, taxonomy, physiology of North American wood inhabiting fungi and their ecological roles in forest ecosystems. *Mailing Add:* USDA Forest Serv 1221 S Main St Moscow ID 83843-4211

LARSEN, MIGUEL FOLKMAR, MESOSCALE & RADAR METEOROLOGY. *Current Pos:* ASST PROF PHYSICS, CLEMSON UNIV, 84- *Personal Data:* b Caracas, Venezuela, June 2, 53; US citizen; m 78. *Educ:* Univ Rochester, BS, 71; Cornell Univ, MS, 77, PhD(meteorol), 79. *Prof Exp:* Res assoc ionospheric physics, Cornell Univ, 79-84. *Concurrent Pos:* Mem, sci adv comt, Arecibo Observ, 85-87; prin investr, Air Force Off Sci Res grant, 85-88 & NASA grant, 86-88. *Mem:* Am Geophys Union; Am Meteorol Soc. *Res:* Mesoscale meteorological research using radar wind profilers; studies of neutral and ion interactions in the auroral zone thermosphere using sounding rockets and radars. *Mailing Add:* 102 Blue Ridge Dr Clemson SC 29631-1713

LARSEN, PAUL M, BOTANY. *Current Pos:* ASST PROF BIOL, ANNE ARUNDEL COMMUNITY COL, 94- *Prof Exp:* Res assoc bot, Univ Md, 87-94. *Mailing Add:* Dept Biol Anne Arundel Community Col Arnold MD 21012

LARSEN, PETER FOSTER, BIOLOGICAL OCEANOGRAPHY. *Current Pos:* res scientist, 76-77, SR RES SCIENTIST, BIGELOW LAB OCEAN SCI, 77-; PRIN INVESTR, KENNEBEC AREA RES ENDOWMENT, 91- *Personal Data:* b Mt Kisco, NY. *Educ:* Univ Conn, BA, 67, MS, 69; Col William & Mary, PhD(marine sci), 74. *Prof Exp:* Lectr chem, Norwalk Community Col, 68-70; res asst marine biol, Va Inst Marine Sci, 70-72, asst marine scientist ecol, 72-73; state oceanogr, Maine Dept Marine Resources, 73-76. *Concurrent Pos:* Pres, Coastal Sci, 73-; consult, Res Inst Gulf Maine, 73- & Bigelow Lab Ocean Sci, 75-76; gov bd, Estuarine Res Fedn, 80-84 & secy, 81-83; adj prof life sci, Univ New Eng, 96- *Mem:* New Eng Estuarine Res Soc (secy-treas, 80-82, pres, 82-84, past pres, 84-86); Estuarine & Coastal Sci Asn; Estuarine Res Fedn. *Res:* The documentation of benthic community structure and function in the estuarine and marine environments of the Gulf of Maine region; environmental quality of the Kennebec River estuary and its influences on the coastal ocean. *Mailing Add:* Bigelow Lab Ocean Sci West Boothbay Harbor ME 04575. *Fax:* 207-633-9641; *E-Mail:* plarsen@bigelow.org

LARSEN, PHILIP O, PLANT PATHOLOGY, TURFGRASS PATHOLOGY. *Current Pos:* PROF & DEPT HEAD, DEPT PLANT PATH, UNIV MINN, 85-, ASSOC DEAN RES & ASST DIR ARCHAEOL EXP STAT. *Personal Data:* b Audubon Co, Iowa, Dec 1, 40; m 61; c 3. *Educ:* Iowa State Univ, BS, 63; Univ Ariz, MS, 67, PhD(plant path), 69. *Prof Exp:* From asst prof to prof plant path, Ohio State Univ, 69-85. *Mem:* Am Phytopath Soc. *Res:* Diseases of turf grasses. *Mailing Add:* 277 Coffey Univ Minn 1420 Eckles Ave St Paul MN 55108. *Fax:* 612-625-9728

LARSEN, RALPH IRVING, ENVIRONMENTAL ENGINEERING, MATHEMATICAL MODELING OF AIR POLLUTANT CONCENTRATIONS & EFFECTS. *Current Pos:* environ res engr, Environ Opers Br, Meteorol & Assessment Div, Atmospheric Sci Res Lab, 71-88, ENVIRON RES ENGR, HUMAN EXPOSURE PROCESSES BR, ATMOSPHERIC RES DIV, NAT ENVIRON RES LAB, US ENVIRON PROTECTION AGENCY, 88- *Personal Data:* b Corvallis, Ore, Nov 26, 28; m 50, 91, Anne Harmon King; c Karen (Cleeton), Eric, Kristine (Burns), Jan, Vikki K (Ball), Terri K (Readling) & Cindi K (King). *Educ:* Ore State Univ, BS, 50; Harvard Univ, MS, 55, PhD(air pollution, indust hyg), 57. *Honors & Awards:* Commendation Medal, USPHS, 79. *Prof Exp:* Sanit engr, Div Water Pollution Control, USPHS, 50-54; chief tech serv, State & Community Serv Sect, Nat Air Pollution Control Admin, 57-61; chief, Biomet Sect, Field Studies Br, 63-65, asst chief br, 65-67, res engr, Off Criteria & Stand, 67-71. *Concurrent Pos:* Lectr adj fac, Inst Air Pollution Training, Environ Protection Agency, 69- *Mem:* Air & Waste Mgt Asn; Sigma Xi; AAAS. *Res:* Studies on the concentration, effects and control of air pollution; mathematical modeling; computer analyses. *Mailing Add:* 4012 Colby Dr Raleigh NC 27609-6045

LARSEN, ROBERT PAUL, HORTICULTURE, UNIVERSITY ADMINISTRATION. *Current Pos:* RETIRED. *Personal Data:* b Vineyard, Utah, Dec 1, 26; m 48, Lorna Anderson; c Nanette (Dunford), Peggy (Rinehart), Mark & Cynthia (Bennett). *Educ:* Utah State Univ, BS, 50; Kans State Univ, MS, 51; Mich State Univ, PhD(hort), 55. *Prof Exp:* From asst prof to prof hort, Mich State Univ, 55-68; prof hort & supt, Tree Fruit Res Ctr, Wash State Univ, 68-82; vpres univ exten, Utah State Univ, 82-92. *Mem:* Fel Am Soc Hort Sci (pres, 75-76); Int Soc Hort Sci; fel AAAS. *Res:* Physiology, nutrition and management of tree fruit crops. *Mailing Add:* 1175 N Cedar Heights Dr Logan UT 84341

LARSEN, RONALD JOHN, MATHEMATICAL ANALYSIS. *Current Pos:* adj assoc prof, Clarkson Col Technol, 77-78. *Personal Data:* b Chicago, Ill, Jan 1, 37; m 62; c 1. *Educ:* Mich State Univ, BS, 57, MS, 59; Stanford Univ, PhD(math), 64. *Prof Exp:* Instr math, Yale Univ, 63-65; asst prof, Cowell Col, Univ Calif, Santa Cruz, 65-70; assoc prof math, Wesleyan Univ, 70-75; vis assoc prof, State Univ NY, Binghamton, 75-76 & Albany, 76-77. *Concurrent Pos:* Fulbright-Hays advan res grant, Univ Oslo, 68-69, vis asst, 73-74; Fulbright-Hays travel award, Norway, 73-74. *Mem:* Am Math Soc; Math Asn Am; Norweg Math Soc. *Mailing Add:* 174 County Rte 35 Canton NY 13617

LARSEN, RUSSELL D, CHEMICAL PHYSICS, STATISTICS. *Current Pos:* DEPT CHEM, TEX TECH UNIV, LUBBOCK, 83- *Personal Data:* b Muskegon, Mich, June 6, 36; m 58; c 2. *Educ:* Kalamazoo Col, BA, 57; Kent State Univ, PhD(chem), 64. *Prof Exp:* Teaching asst chem, Univ Cincinnati, 58-60; asst instr, Kent State Univ, 64; res assoc, Princeton Univ, 64-65; Robert A Welch fel, Rice Univ, 65-66; asst prof, Ill Inst Technol, 66-72; asst prof chem, Tex A&M Univ, 72-76; actg assoc prof, dept chem, Univ Nev, Reno, 76-77; assoc prof, dept chem, Univ Mich, 77-83. *Mem:* Am Chem Soc; Am Phys Soc; Am Statist Asn; Sigma Xi; AAAS. *Res:* Chemical and biomedical signal processing; spectral analysis; Walsh functions; spline representations; zero-based signal representations; chemical education, chaos. *Mailing Add:* Tex Dept Health T801 1100 W 49th St Austin TX 78756

LARSEN, SIGURD YVES, THEORETICAL PHYSICS. *Current Pos:* assoc prof, 68-75, PROF PHYSICS & CHMN DEPT, TEMPLE UNIV, 75- *Personal Data:* b Brussels, Belg, Aug 14, 33; US citizen. *Educ:* Columbia Univ, AB, 54, MA, 56, PhD(physics), 62. *Prof Exp:* Asst physics, Columbia Univ, 54-57 & 60-62; consult, Nat Bur Stand, 62; Nat Acad Sci-Nat Res Coun assoc, 62-63, physicist, Washington, DC, 63-68. *Concurrent Pos:* Consult, Los Alamos Sci Lab, 64, Lawrence Radiation Lab, 67-72 & Nat Bur Stand, 68-71; mem panel quantum fluids, Int Union Pure & Appl Chem, 66-; vis prof, Mex Inst Petrol, 71-72 & Nat Univ Mex, 72. *Mem:* Am Phys Soc; Ital Phys Soc; Sigma Xi. *Res:* Statistical physics; quantum theory; numerical analysis. *Mailing Add:* Dept Physics Temple Univ Philadelphia PA 19122. *Fax:* 215-787-5652

LARSEN, STEVEN H, CHLAMYDIA TRACHOMATIS, HETEROLOGOUS GENE EXPRESSION. *Current Pos:* asst prof, 79-95, ASSOC PROF MICROBIOL, IND UNIV SCH MED, 95- *Personal Data:* b Bringham City, Utah, Aug 28, 44; m 68, Mary Kimber; c Jill, Bert, Hans, Jacob & Kimberly. *Educ:* Utah State Univ, BA, 68, MS, 70; Univ Wis, PhD(biochem), 74. *Prof Exp:* Teaching asst chem & physics, Utah State Univ, 66-70; trainee biochem, Univ Wis, 70-74, fel genetics, 74-75; fel microbiol, Johns Hopkins Univ Sch Med, 75-79, instr, 77. *Concurrent Pos:* Consult, Human Amylase Cloning Group, Dept Genetics, Ind Univ, 80-86; Eli Lilly Young Scientist Res Awards, 83-85; vis prof, Tokushimo Univ, 91. *Mem:* Am Soc Microbiol; AAAS. *Res:* Development of eukaryotic cloning vectors; chlamydia trachomatics genetics. *Mailing Add:* Dept Microbiol & Immunol Ind Univ Sch Med 635 Barnhill Dr Indianapolis IN 46202. *Fax:* 317-274-4090; *E-Mail:* slarsen@iupui.edu

LARSEN, TED LEROY, PHYSICS, SEMICONDUCTORS. *Current Pos:* DIR RES & DEVELOP, ENG OPTOELECTRONICS DIV, GEN INSTRUMENT CORP, 79- *Personal Data:* b Jerome, Idaho, Mar 18, 35; m 57; c 2. *Educ:* Univ Calif, Berkeley, BS, 61, MS, 62; Stanford Univ, PhD(mat sci), 70. *Prof Exp:* Mem tech staff, Hewlett-Packard Co, 62-65, res & develop group leader, 68-71, res & develop sect mgr semiconductors, 71-79. *Mem:* Electrochem Soc; Inst Elec & Electronics Engrs. *Res:* III-V compound materials and devices for optoelectronic and microwave applications, including single crystal and epitaxial growth, crystalline defects, impurity diffusion and minority carrier recombination processes; III-IV and silicon device and product development including led lamps and displays and optocouplers. *Mailing Add:* 1109 Hamilton Ave Palo Alto CA 94301

LARSEN, WILLIAM L(AWRENCE), CORROSION, FAILURE ANALYSIS. *Current Pos:* CONSULT PROF METALL ENGR, 62- *Personal Data:* b Crookston, Minn, July 16, 26; m 54, Gracie Richey; c Eric & Thomas. *Educ:* Marquette Univ, BME, 48; Ohio State Univ, MS, 50, PhD(metall eng), 56. *Prof Exp:* Res assoc metall eng, Ohio State Univ, 51-56; res metallurgist, E I du Pont de Nemours & Co, Inc, 56-58; asst prof mech eng & chem, Iowa State Univ, 58-62, from assoc metallurgist to metallurgist, Ames Lab, 58-69, from assoc prof to prof metall, 69-93. *Concurrent Pos:* Consult mat design, mat failure & educ progs for superior students; prof engr, Iowa. *Mem:* Am Soc Metals Int; Nat Col Hons Coun; Nat Asn Corrosion Engrs Int; Am Soc Eng Educ; Am Soc Testing & Mat; Nat Soc Prof Engrs. *Res:* Metallurgical engineering design and failure analysis; expert witness-product liability; consultant to industry and legal profession. *Mailing Add:* 335 N Franklin Ave Ames IA 50014-3424

LARSEN-BASSE, JORN, MATERIALS SCIENCE, CORROSION. *Current Pos:* PROG DIR, SURFACE ENG & TRIBOLOGY, NSF, 88- *Personal Data:* b Maribo, Denmark, Oct 14, 34; US citizen; m 59, Maka Simpson; c Kai E. *Educ:* Tech Univ Denmark, MS, 58, PhD(metall), 61. *Prof Exp:* Actg asst prof metall, Tech Univ Denmark, 59-61; researcher, Soderfors Bruk, Sweden, 61-62; res assoc mat sci, Stanford Univ, 63; asst prof, San Jose State Col, 63-64; from asst prof to prof mech eng, Univ Hawaii, 64-86, chmn dept, 76-80 & 82-85; prof mech eng, Ga Inst Technol, 86-91. *Concurrent Pos:* Ford Found resident indust, 68-69; hon vis prof, Univ NSW, 71 & Commonwealth Sci & Indust Res Orgn, Melbourne, 72; prog dir, NSF, 88-91; vis scientist, Nat Inst Sci & Technol, 88- *Mem:* Am Inst Mining, Metall & Petrol Engrs; Nat Asn Corrosion Engrs; Am Soc Mech Engrs; Sigma Xi; Soc Tribologists & Lubrication Engrs; fel Am Soc Metals. *Res:* Abrasion resistance of metals; corrosion in marine and volcanic environments; ocean thermal energy conversion; microstructure-property relations; surface engineering. *Mailing Add:* Tribology Prog 4201 Wilson Blvd Rm 545 Arlington VA 22230. *Fax:* 703-306-0291; *E-Mail:* jlarsenb@nsf.gov

LARSH, HOWARD WILLIAM, MEDICAL MYCOLOGY. *Current Pos:* assoc prof bact, med, mycol & plant path, Univ Okla, 45-48, chmn, Dept Plant Sci, 45-62 & Dept Microbiol & Bot, 66-76, PROF PLANT SCI, UNIV OKLA, 48-, RES PROF, 62- *Personal Data:* b East St Louis, Ill, May 29, 14; m 38; c 1. *Educ:* McKendree Col, BA, 36; Univ Ill, MS, 38, PhD, 41. *Prof Exp:* Asst bot, Univ Ill, 38-41; instr, Dept Bot & Bact, Univ Okla, 41-42; plant pathologist, Bur Plant Indust, Soils & Agr Eng, USDA, 43-45. *Concurrent Pos:* Spec consult, McKnight State Tuberc Hosp & Nat Commun Dis Ctr, USPHS, 50-; med mycologist consult & co-dir lab, Mo State Chest Hosp, Mt Vernon, 55-, dir labs, 77; consult, Manned Spacecraft Ctr, NASA; res reviewer, Immunol & Infectious Dis Comt, Vet Admin Hosp, Oklahoma City, 72; cert bioanal lab dir, Am Bd Bioanal, 74-; ed rev bd, J Clin Microbiol, 74-; ed-in-chief, Sabouraudia, 75-79; consult med mycol. *Mem:* Fel AAAS; fel Am Pub Health Asn; fel Am Acad Microbiol; Bot Soc Am; Mycol Soc Am; Sigma Xi. *Res:* Medical mycosis; systemic mycoses; histoplasmosis; cryptococcosis. *Mailing Add:* 611 Broad Lane Norman OK 73069

LARSON, ALLAN, SYSTEMATIC BIOLOGY. *Current Pos:* asst prof, 86-92, ASSOC PROF, DEPT BIOL, WASHINGTON UNIV, 92- *Personal Data:* b Silver Spring, Md, Nov 7, 53. *Educ:* Univ Md, College Park, BS, 75, MS, 77; Univ Calif, Berkeley, PhD(genetics), 82. *Prof Exp:* Res assoc, Dept Biochem, Univ Calif, Berkeley, 83-86. *Concurrent Pos:* Assoc ed, Evolution, 92-96, Syst Biol, 92- *Mem:* Am Soc Naturalists; Genetics Soc Am; Herpetologist's League; Soc Study Evolution; Soc Molecular Biol & Evolution; Soc Syst Biologists. *Res:* Molecular population genetics and systematics, especially of amphibians and lizards; laboratory activities include amplification and sequencing of mitochondrial and nuclear DNA, and use of DNA sequence variation to study phylogenetic relationships among species and the genetic structures of populations. *Mailing Add:* PO Box 2904 St Louis MO 63130-0304. *Fax:* 314-935-4432; *E-Mail:* larson@wustlb.wustl.edu

LARSON, ALLAN BENNETT, INDUSTRIAL PHARMACY, COSMETIC CHEMISTRY. *Current Pos:* dir, process res & develop, Ayerst Labs, 84-87, DIR PROCESS RES & DEVELOP, WYETH-AYERST RES, AM HOME PROD, 87- *Personal Data:* b Chicago, Ill, Feb 9, 43; m 71, Virginia L House; c Michael A & Jacie L. *Educ:* Drake Univ, BS, 66; Univ Wis, MS, 69; Purdue Univ, PhD(phys & indust pharm), 72. *Prof Exp:* Sr res pharmacist, Dorsey Labs Div, Sandoz-Wander Inc, 72-76; sr pharmaceut scientist, Richardson-Merrell, Inc, 76-77, group leader, Vick Divs Res & Develop, 77-80, mgr tech serv, Vicks Personal Care Div, 80-84. *Mem:* Am Pharmaceut Asn; Acad Pharmaceut Sci; Soc Cosmetic Chemists; Am Asn Pharmaceut Scientists; Drug Info Asn. *Res:* Pharmaceutical and skin care product development and stability, preformulation, uniformity of mixing, scale-up technology, process improvements, process validation, process optimization; technology transfer. *Mailing Add:* 5 Bouchard Dr Peru NY 12972-9714

LARSON, ANDREW HESSLER, EXTRACTIVE CHEMICAL METALLURGY. *Current Pos:* METALL CONSULT, 88- *Personal Data:* b Peru, Ill, Sept 14, 31; m 55, Margo Miller; c Eric H, Karl A & Kurt G. *Educ:* Mo Sch Mines, BS, 53, MS, 54; Univ Mo, PhD(metall), 59. *Prof Exp:* From asst prof to assoc prof metall eng, Mo Sch Mines, 59-63; from assoc prof to prof, Colo Sch Mines, 63-68; sr res metallurgist, Bunker Hill Co, 68-69; mgr res & develop, 69-78; dir prod develop & eng, Metals Div, Gould Inc, 78-84; dir metals eng, GNB Inc, 84-88. *Concurrent Pos:* Ford Found Prog prod specialist, Tex Div, Dow Chem Co, 66-67. *Mem:* Am Inst Mining, Metall & Petrol Engrs; Sigma Xi. *Res:* High temperature thermodynamic and kinetic studies of metallurgical systems involving the extraction and refining of metals. *Mailing Add:* 4116 Strawberry Lane Eagan MN 55123-1421

LARSON, ARVID GUNNAR, SIGNAL PROCESSING, COMPUTER ARCHITECTURE. *Current Pos:* CHMN, NICOLE LARSON ASSOC, 91-, CHIEF SCIENTIST, WALCOFF ASSOC, 93- *Personal Data:* b Chicago, Ill, July 26, 37; m 89, Nicole Sours; c Gregory M. *Educ:* Ill Inst Tech, BS, 59; Stanford Univ, MS, 66, PhD(elec eng), 73. *Honors & Awards:* Centennial Medal, Inst Elec & Electronics Engrs. *Prof Exp:* Res engr, Stanford Res Inst, 64-74; mgr, Appl Res Group, Planning Res Corp, 74-78; proj mgr, Syst Planning Corp, 78-80; div mgr, Advan Res & Appln Corp, 80-85; vpres, Analytical Disciplines Inc, 85-86; prin, Booz, Allen & Hamilton Inc, 86-89; sr vpres, Syntek Eng & Comput Systs, 89-90; res prof, George Mason Univ, 91-92. *Concurrent Pos:* Bd dir, Res Inst Info Sci & Eng; chmn, Res & Develop Policy Task Force, Am Asn Eng Socs; chmn, US Activ Bd, Govt fel comt; vpres-prof activ, Inst Elec & Electronics Engrs. *Mem:* Sigma Xi; fel Inst Elec & Electronics Engrs. *Res:* Computer systems and network architecture, high speed signal processing; software engineering; systems science. *Mailing Add:* 6921 Espey Lane McLean VA 22101-5455. *Fax:* 703-893-9008; *E-Mail:* a.larson@ieee.com

LARSON, BENNETT CHARLES, X-RAY DIFFRACTION, CRYSTAL DEFECTS. *Current Pos:* Physicist, 69-79, group leader, 80-90, SECT HEAD, SOLID STATE DIV, OAK RIDGE NAT LAB, 90- *Personal Data:* b Buffalo, NDak, Oct 9, 41; m 69, Pat Taliaferro; c Chris & Andrea. *Educ:* Concordia Col, BA, 63; Univ NDak, MS, 65; Univ Mo, PhD(physics), 70. *Honors & Awards:* Bertram E Warren Diffraction Physics Award, Am Crystallog Asn, 85. *Mem:* Am Phys Soc; Am Crystallog Asn; Mat Res Soc. *Res:* X-ray diffraction study of intrinsic and induced defects in crystalline solids using diffuse scattering; x-ray diffraction study of pulsed-laser annealing; x-ray diffraction using synchrotron radiation; inelastic scattering. *Mailing Add:* Bldg 3025 PO Box 2008 Oak Ridge Nat Lab Oak Ridge TN 37831. *E-Mail:* bcl@ornl.gov

LARSON, BRUCE LINDER, BIOCHEMISTRY, NUTRITION. *Current Pos:* RETIRED. *Personal Data:* b Minneapolis, Minn, June 24, 27; m 54, Marjorie Hersleth; c Eric, David & Brian. *Educ:* Univ Minn, BS, 48, PhD(biochem), 51. *Honors & Awards:* Gold Medal, Am Chem Soc, 66; Fulbright lectr, Arg, 65. *Prof Exp:* Asst, Univ Minn, 48-51; from instr to prof biol chem, Univ Ill, Urbana, 51-90, head, Dept Dairy Sci, 79-81, mem nutrit sci fac, 72-90, emer prof biol chem & nutri sci, 90- *Concurrent Pos:* Prin investr, NSF, 59-74, 79-82, NIH, 72-75, Nat Dairy Coun, 76-79; mem, Milk Proteins Comn, Am Dairy Sci Asn, 55-86, Milk Synthesis Comn, 69. *Mem:* Fel AAAS; Am Chem Soc; Am Soc Biochem & Molecular Biol; Am Dairy Sci Asn. *Res:* Lactation and mammary gland metabolism in the formation of mammary secretions; cellular ejection of products and biological significance of colostrum and milk; pathways of radioactive contaminants into milk and other foods. *Mailing Add:* Dept Animal Sci 312 Animal Sci Lab Univ Ill 1207 W Gregory Dr Urbana IL 61801

LARSON, CHARLES CONRAD, FORESTRY ADMINISTRATION. *Current Pos:* forest economist & res assoc forestry, State Univ NY, 50-58, from assoc prof to prof world forestry, 59-83, dir int forestry, 64-79, dean, Sch Environ & Resource Mgt, 71-79, EMER PROF FORESTRY, COL ENVIRON SCI & FORESTRY, STATE UNIV NY, 83- *Personal Data:* b Pettibone, NDak, Nov 17, 14; m 58; c 2. *Educ:* Univ Minn, BS, 40; Univ Vt, MS, 43; Inst Pub Admin, NY, cert, 50; State Univ NY Col Forestry, Syracuse Univ, PhD(forestry admin), 52. *Prof Exp:* Summer res asst, Lake States Forest Exp Sta, 40-41; asst forest supvr, Crossett Lumber Co, Ark, 44; res & stat exten forester, Univ Vt, 44-47; res assoc, Inst Pub Admin, NY, 48-49. *Concurrent Pos:* Ford Found overseas res fel, 54-; consult, Syracuse Univ Res Inst, 57-59; vis prof & proj leader, AID-State Univ NY Res Found Assistance Contract, Col Forestry, Univ Philippines, 59-62; mem bd dirs, Orgn Trop Studies, 71-; chmn educ comn, Int Union Socs Foresters, 71-79. *Mem:* Soc Am Foresters; Int Soc Trop Foresters (pres, 79-81). *Res:* Forestry administration, policy and economics; tropical vegetation; world forestry development with emphasis on the tropics; range management. *Mailing Add:* 200 Ridgecrest Rd Syracuse NY 13214

LARSON, CHARLES FRED, MECHANICAL ENGINEERING, RESEARCH & TECHNOLOGY MANAGEMENT. *Current Pos:* EXEC DIR, INDUST RES INST, INC, 75- *Personal Data:* b Gary, Ind, Nov 27, 36; m 59, Joan Grupe; c Gregory P & Laura A. *Educ:* Purdue Univ, BS, 58; Fairleigh Dickinson Univ, Rutherford, MBA, 73. *Prof Exp:* Proj engr, Combustion Eng, Inc, 58-60; asst dir, Welding Res Coun, 60-75. *Concurrent Pos:* Secy, Indust Res Inst Res Corp, 75- *Mem:* Fel AAAS; Am Soc Mech Engrs; Soc Res Adminr; Nat Soc Prof Engrs. *Res:* Pressure vessels; fatigue of welded structures; fracture toughness of metals; non-destructive examination; heavy-section steels; research management; research and technical management. *Mailing Add:* 1550 M St NW Washington DC 20005. *Fax:* 202-776-0756

LARSON, CLARENCE EDWARD, PHYSICAL CHEMISTRY. *Current Pos:* RETIRED. *Personal Data:* b Cloquet, Minn, Sept 20, 09; m 34, 57; c 3. *Educ:* Univ Minn, BS, 32; Univ Calif, PhD(chem), 36. *Honors & Awards:* Soc Advan Mgt Award, 65. *Prof Exp:* Instr chem, Univ Calif, 32-36; res assoc, Mt Zion Res Found, Calif, 36-37; assoc prof, Col Pac, 37-39, prof & head dept, 39-40; chief, Analytical Sect, Radiation Lab, Univ Calif, 40-43; head tech staff, Electromagnetic Plant, Carbide & Carbon Chem Co Div, Union Carbide Corp, 43-46, dir res & develop, 46-49, supt, 49-50, dir, Oak Ridge Nat Lab, 50-55, vpres chg res, Nat Carbon Co Div, 55-59, assoc mgr res admin, 59-61, vpres, Union Carbide Nuclear Co Div, 61-64, pres, Nuclear Div, Union Carbide Nuclear Co, 64-69; comnr, Energy Res & Develop Admin, Washington, DC, 69-74. *Concurrent Pos:* Am Nuclear Soc fel, 62; mem bd dirs, Oak Ridge Inst Nuclear Studies, 63-65; energy consult, Systs Control, Inc, 64-74; comnr, US AEC, 69-74, energy consult, 74-83; deleg, UN Conf Peaceful Uses of Atomic Energy. *Mem:* Nat Acad Eng; AAAS; Am Chem Soc; fel Am Inst Chemists; fel Am Nuclear Soc; Pioneers Sci & Technol Hist Asn (pres, 83-). *Res:* Inorganic chemistry of biological systems; separation methods for isotopes; radiochemistry; analytical methods; uranium chemistry; colloids; chemical separation methods. *Mailing Add:* 6514 Bradley Blvd Bethesda MD 20817

LARSON, CURTIS L(UVERNE), AGRICULTURAL & CIVIL ENGINEERING. *Current Pos:* From instr to assoc prof, 48-65, PROF AGR ENG, INST AGR, UNIV MINN, ST PAUL, 65- *Personal Data:* b Cottonwood, Minn, Oct 10, 20; m 44; c 3. *Educ:* Univ Minn, BAgrE, 43, MS, 49; Stanford Univ, PhD(civil eng), 65. *Concurrent Pos:* Water mgt consult, Colombia, 72-73; Nicaragua, 75; Chile, 76 & Panama, 78. *Mem:* Am Soc Agr Engrs; Am Geophys Union; Am Water Resources Asn; Soil Conserv Soc Am. *Res:* Surface water hydrology; watershed modeling; erosion control; water resources. *Mailing Add:* 2232 Ferris Lane St Paul MN 55113

LARSON, D WAYNE, PHYSICAL CHEMISTRY. *Current Pos:* asst prof, 68-71, ASSOC PROF CHEM, UNIV REGINA, 71- *Personal Data:* b Prince Albert, Sask, Dec 2, 38; m 62, Kathleen Uvery; c Gregor, Brian, Steven & Graham. *Educ:* Univ Sask, BA, 61, MA, 62; Univ Toronto, PhD(inorg chem), 65. *Prof Exp:* Mem res staff, Can Forces Inst Aviation Med, 65-68. *Concurrent Pos:* Asst to dean, Fac Grad Studies & Res, Univ Regina, 73-79. *Mem:* Chem Inst Can; Can Nuclear Soc. *Res:* Science education, attitudes toward science; technology assessment, ethics, public policy; social issues, perceptions of risk, energy resources; uranium development in Saskatchewan. *Mailing Add:* Dept Chem Univ Regina Regina SK S4S 0A2 Can

LARSON, DANIEL JOHN, LASER SPECTROSCOPY, NEGATIVE IONS. *Current Pos:* from assoc prof to prof, Univ Va, 78-96, assoc dean, Fac Arts & Sci, 89-91, chair dept, 91-97, MAXINE S & JESSE W BEAMS PROF PHYSICS, UNIV VA, 96- *Personal Data:* b Minneapolis, Minn, Nov 8, 44; m 94, Tanya Furman. *Educ:* St Olaf Col, Northfield, Minn, BA, 66; Harvard Univ, Cambridge, Mass, MA, 67, PhD(physics), 71. *Prof Exp:* From asst prof to assoc prof physics, Harvard Univ, 70-78. *Concurrent Pos:* Vis scientist, Nat Bur Stand, 85-86 & Lab Aime Cotton, Orsay, France, 91; vis prof, Chalmers Univ, Gothenburg, Swed, 86. *Mem:* Am Phys Soc; Optical Soc Am. *Res:* High resolution optical and microwave spectroscopy of atoms and ions, especially negative ions, using tunable lasers and atom and ion storage and beam techniques; atomic structure and interactions in strong fields. *Mailing Add:* Dept Physics Univ Va McCormick Rd Charlottesville VA 22901. *Fax:* 804-924-4576; *E-Mail:* djl@virginia.edu

LARSON, DAVID MICHAEL, VASCULAR CELL BIOLOGY, INTERCELLULAR COMMUNICATION & GAP JUNCTION. *Current Pos:* asst prof, 84-95, ASSOC PROF PATH LAB MED, BOSTON UNIV SCH MED, 95- *Personal Data:* b St Paul, Minn, Jan 12, 51; m, Susan L Carlson. *Educ:* Univ Minn, BS, 72, PhD(zool), 80. *Prof Exp:* Fel cytoskeletal & vascular smooth muscle cell differentiation, Brigham & Women's Hosp, 80-83. *Concurrent Pos:* Fel, Mallory Inst Path, 83-84; prin investr, 84-; special sci staff, Boston City Hosp, 84-96, Boston Med Ctr, 96- *Mem:* Am Soc Cell Biol; AAAS; Microcirculatory Soc; NY Acad Sci; Am Heart Asn; NAm Vascular Biol Orgn. *Mailing Add:* Mallory Inst Path Boston Univ Sch Med 784 Massachusetts Ave Boston MA 02118. *Fax:* 617-534-5315; *E-Mail:* davlar@bu.edu

LARSON, DENNIS LUVERNE, SOLAR ENERGY ENGINEERING, SYSTEMS ENGINEERING APPLICATIONS. *Current Pos:* asst prof agr eng, 73-79, ASSOC PROF AGR & BIOSYSTS ENG, UNIV ARIZ, TUCSON, 79- *Personal Data:* b Mason City, Iowa, Feb 3, 40; m; c Scott, Kristine, Steven & Kathryn. *Educ:* Iowa State Univ, BS, 63; Univ Ill, MS, 64; Purdue Univ, PhD(agr eng), 71. *Prof Exp:* Lt, Signal Corps, US Army, Ger, 64-66; proj design engr, John Deere Planter Works, 66-68; asst prof, Univ Nebr, Nat Univ, Medellin, Colombia & Nat Res Ctr, Bogota, Colombia, 71-73; exten agr engr, Mich State Univ, 73. *Concurrent Pos:* Vis prof agr eng, Univ Melbourne, 83-84; Unicamp, Campinas, Brazil, 94. *Mem:* Am Soc Agr Engrs; Am Solar Energy Soc; Am Soc Eng Educ. *Res:* Evaluation of renewable energy application and energy use management; systems engineering analysis of agriculture resource management issues; evaluation of electro-migration for control of chemical movement in soils. *Mailing Add:* Univ Ariz 403 Shantz Bldg Tucson AZ 85721. *Fax:* 520-621-3963; *E-Mail:* larson@ccit.arizona.edu

LARSON, DONALD ALFRED, BOTANY. *Current Pos:* assoc vpres health sci, 73-81, PROF BIOL HEALTH SCI, STATE UNIV NY, BUFFALO, 73- *Personal Data:* b Chicago, Ill, Sept 15, 30; m 53; c 3. *Educ:* Wheaton Col, Ill, BS, 53; Univ Ill, MS, 55, PhD(bot), 59. *Prof Exp:* Assoc prof bot, Univ Tex, Austin, 59-69, prof & dir health prof, 69-73. *Mem:* Bot Soc Am; Am Soc Cell Biologists. *Res:* Electron microscopy; cytology; palynology; taxonomic uses; paleobotany. *Mailing Add:* Dept Biol Sci Cooke Hall State Univ NY Buffalo Buffalo NY 14260-0001

LARSON, DONALD CLAYTON, SOLID STATE PHYSICS. *Current Pos:* assoc prof, 67-83, PROF PHYSICS, DREXEL UNIV, 83- *Personal Data:* b Wadena, Minn, Jan 29, 34; m 60; c Tor & Erika. *Educ:* Univ Wash, BS, 56; Harvard Univ, SM, 57, PhD(appl physics), 62. *Prof Exp:* Asst prof physics, Univ Va, 62-67. *Mem:* Am Phys Soc; Int Solar Energy Soc; Am Soc Testing & Mat. *Res:* Electrical properties of metallic, organic and amorphous semiconducting films; biomechanics; solar energy; insulation studies; integrated optics. *Mailing Add:* Dept Physics Drexel Univ Philadelphia PA 19104. *Fax:* 215-895-5934; *E-Mail:* larsond@coasmail.drexel.edu

LARSON, DONALD W, AGRICULTURAL ECONOMICS. *Current Pos:* from asst prof to assoc prof, 70-82, PROF AGR ECON, OHIO STATE UNIV, 82- *Personal Data:* b Avoca, Minn, Aug 7, 40; m 62; c 3. *Educ:* SDak State Univ, BS, 62; Mich State Univ, MS, 64, PhD(agr econ), 68. *Prof Exp:* Asst prof agr econ, Mich State Univ, 68-70. *Concurrent Pos:* Mkt consult, 73, Loan consult, US AID, 74, 85, 86-93; consult, mkt & price policy, World Bank, 78, 80, 82, 84, 86, 87, 92, 93. *Mem:* Am Agr Econ Asn; Int Asn Agr Economists; Brazilian Agr Econ Asn. *Res:* Grain marketing and transportation systems, marketing and market policy in developing countries; rural financial markets in developing countries. *Mailing Add:* Ohio State Univ Dept Agr Econ Columbus OH 43210

LARSON, EDWARD WILLIAM, JR, STRUCTURAL ENGINEERING. *Current Pos:* RETIRED. *Personal Data:* b New Haven, Conn, Apr 17, 23; m 52; c 2. *Educ:* Ind Technol Col, BSCE, 43; Northwestern Univ, MS, 48, PhD(civil eng), 53. *Prof Exp:* Jr engr, Bur Ships, US Dept Navy, 43-44, physicist, David Taylor Model Basin, 44-46; res assoc struct, Northwestern Univ, 49-52, instr struct eng, 52-53; engr, Hughes Tool Co, Calif, 53-55; res engr, Lockheed Aircraft Corp, 55-57; supv stress analysis, Rocketdyne Div, Rockwell Int, 57-62, group leader dynamic sci, 62-63, sect chief & mgr turbomach, 63-69, mgr tech specialties, 69-75, assoc chief engr, 75-79, dir, design technol, 79-86. *Concurrent Pos:* Lectr, Univ Calif, Los Angeles, 53-64, Calif State Univ, 86-92. *Mem:* Soc Exp Stress Analysis; Am Inst Aeronaut & Astronaut; Sigma Xi; Am Soc Eng Educ. *Res:* Failure investigation of engine components under actual operating conditions and structural behavior of liquid rocket engines to transient, steady state and flow-induced vibrations. *Mailing Add:* 18621 Ringling St Tarzana CA 91356

LARSON, EDWIN E, GEOPHYSICS, GEOLOGY. *Current Pos:* from asst prof to assoc prof, 66-75, PROF GEOL SCI, UNIV COLO, BOULDER, 75- *Personal Data:* b Los Angeles, Calif, Jan 5, 31. *Educ:* Univ Calif, Los Angeles, BA, 54, MA, 58; Univ Colo, PhD(geol), 65. *Prof Exp:* Explor geologist, Humble Oil & Refining Co, 57-60; NSF fel, 65-66. *Mem:* AAAS; Geol Soc Am; Am Geophys Union; Sigma Xi. *Res:* Investigation of rock magnetic properties; paleomagnetism and its application to the solution of geological problems; lunar magnetism. *Mailing Add:* Dept Geol Univ Colo Campus Box 250 Boulder CO 80309-0250

LARSON, ELAINE LUCILLE, NURSING. *Current Pos:* PROF & DIR, SCH NURSING, GEORGETOWN UNIV, 91-, DEAN, 92- *Personal Data:* b Apr 27, 43. *Educ:* Univ Wash, Seattle, BS, 65, MS, 69, PhD(epidemiol), 81. *Prof Exp:* Staff nurse, Univ Wash Hosp, Seattle, 65-66, clin specialist, cardiovasc nursing, 66-67, hosp epidemiologist, 67-70, nurse coordr, staff develop, 76-77, nursing res coordr, 77-81, assoc dir nursing, 81-83; clin nurse, Robert Wood Johnson Sch Nursing, Univ Pa, 83-85; M Adelaide Nutting chair clin nursing, Sch Nursing, Johns Hopkins Univ, 85-91, prof & dir, Ctr Nursing Res, 90-91. *Concurrent Pos:* Instr, cardiopulmonary resuscitation, Regional Med Prog & Wash State Red Cross, 66-67; asst prog dir, Sch Nursing, Univ Wash, 69-70, clin asst prof, Dept Physiol Nursing, 78-81; consult, St Elizabeth's Hosp, 71, Health Sci Learning Resource Ctr, Univ Wash, 78, Wash State Dept Social & Health Serv & Ctrs Dis Control, 80, Philadelphia Naval Hosp, 84, Purdue Frederick Co, Norwalk, 85, Keck Found & Columbia Univ, NY, 86; recipient, Biomed Res Support Grant, Robert Wood Johnson Found clin nurse fel, Ctr Dis Control grant; nurse practr coronary care, Kaiser-Permanente Sunnyside Med Ctr, Portland, 75-76; mem, Cert Bd Infection Control, 83-86, Res Comt, Asn Practr Infection, 86-88, Task Force Severity Illness Adjusters, Soc Hosp Epidemiologists Am, 87-88, Comt Study Resources Clin Invest, Inst Med, 88, Gov Coun & Priorities & Planning Comt, Am Acad Nursing, 88-89, Gov Coun Prog Planning Comt, 90-92 & Planning Panel Health Effects Stress & Emotions, 91; ed, Riv Mag, 83-87, Annals Int Med, 88, Sour Am Med Asn, 83- *Mem:* Inst Med-Nat Acad Sci; Am Nurses Asn; Am Pub Health Asn; Asn Practrs Infection Control; Soc Hosp Epidemiol Am; Soc Res Nursing Educ Forum; Am Soc Microbiol; fel Am Acad Nursing; Sigma Xi. *Res:* Author of over 99 articles, journals and books. *Mailing Add:* Sch Nursing Georgetown Univ 3700 Reservoir Rd NW Washington DC 20007

LARSON, ERIC GEORGE, PHOTOCHEMISTRY. *Current Pos:* Sr chemist, Corp Res Lab, 3M Co, 84-86, Indust Abrasives Div, 86-88, res specialist, 88-91, SR RES SPECIALIST, ABRASIVES SYSTS DIV, 3M CO, 91- *Personal Data:* b Chicago, Ill, Apr 25, 57; m 85; c 1. *Educ:* Purdue Univ, BS, 80; Northwestern Univ, MS, 81, PhD(org chem), 85. *Mem:* Am Chem Soc. *Res:* High performance polymers; structural adhesives; rapid cure resins; radiation curable resins; photochemistry; new polymer synthesis. *Mailing Add:* 251-1A-03 3M Ctr St Paul MN 55144-1000

LARSON, ERIC HEATH, POLYELECTROLYTE CHEMISTRY, POLYMERIZATION REACTION ENGINEERING. *Current Pos:* group leader, 90-94, PRIN SCIENTIST, RHONE POULENC SPECIALTY CHEMS, 94- *Personal Data:* b Medford, Mass, Apr 8, 50; m 75, Maria V Contreras; c Richard & Peter. *Educ:* Tufts Univ, BS, 73; Yale Univ, MS, 74; Syracuse Univ, PhD(chem eng), 78. *Prof Exp:* Res engr III, Allied Signal Corp, 78-81; sr res engr, 81-84, res assoc, 84-90. *Mem:* Tech Asn Pulp & Paper Indust; Am Chem Soc. *Res:* Investigate polyelectrolyte synthesis, structure-property relationships, applications in various water treatment related industries; inverse emulsion synthesis and reactor engineering, including advanced control strategies. *Mailing Add:* 132 Derby Dr Freehold NJ 08512. *Fax:* 732-294-0659; *E-Mail:* eric.larson@f620.h2605.z1.ieee.org

LARSON, EVERETT GERALD, SOLID STATE PHYSICS, MOLECULAR PHYSICS. *Current Pos:* assoc prof, 69-75, PROF PHYSICS, BRIGHAM YOUNG UNIV, 75- *Personal Data:* b Logan, Utah, Nov 12, 35; m 63; c 4. *Educ:* Mass Inst Technol, SB, 57, SM, 59, PhD(electron correlation), 64. *Prof Exp:* Asst, Mass Inst Technol & mem staff, Lincoln Labs, 57-64; asst prof physics, Brigham Young Univ, 64-68; vis asst prof chem, Univ Ga, 68-69. *Mem:* Am Phys Soc. *Res:* Atomic molecular and solid state theory; correlation effects; cooperative phenomena; theory of irreversible processes. *Mailing Add:* Dept Physics & Astron Brigham Young Univ 263 FB Provo UT 84602-1022

LARSON, FRANK CLARK, MEDICINE. *Current Pos:* Instr, Univ Wis-Madison, 50-51, asst clin prof, 51-56, from asst prof to assoc prof, 56-63, PROF MED & PATH, UNIV WIS-MADISON, 63-, DIR CLIN LABS, HOSP, 58- *Personal Data:* b Columbus, Nebr, Jan 17, 20; m 48; c 3. *Educ:* Nebr State Teachers Col, AB, 41; Univ Nebr, MD, 44; Am Bd Internal Med, dipl. *Concurrent Pos:* Asst chief med & tuberc serv, Vet Admin Hosp, Madison, 51-56, chief invest med serv, 52-56. *Mem:* Endocrine Soc; Am Col Physicians; Cent Soc Clin Res; Sigma Xi. *Res:* Thyroid metabolism. *Mailing Add:* Salr Hosp Clin 600 Highland Ave Madison WI 53792-0001

LARSON, FREDERIC ROGER, FOREST MANAGEMENT, SYSTEMS ANALYSIS. *Current Pos:* Forester, Kaibab & Nez Perce Nat Forests, 65-67, res forester, Rocky Mountain Exp Sta, 67-78, RES FORESTER, PAC NORTHWEST EXP STA, US FOREST SERV, 79- *Personal Data:* b Los Angeles, Calif, Mar 26, 42; m 74, Angela DiSandro; c 1. *Educ:* Northern Ariz Univ, BSF, 66, MS, 68; Colo State Univ, PhD(forestry), 75. *Concurrent Pos:* Prof, Northern Ariz Univ Forestry Sch, 71-72, adj prof, 75-78. *Mem:* Soc Am Foresters; Am Soc Photogram; Soc Range Mgt; Wildlife Soc; Sigma Xi. *Res:* Quantifying and simulating growth and management of southwestern coniferous forests; computer simulation models ecosystems; forest multi-resource inventories. *Mailing Add:* 3301 C St Suite 200 Anchorage AK 99503-3954. *Fax:* 907-271-2898

LARSON, G(USTAV) OLOF, ORGANIC CHEMISTRY. *Current Pos:* assoc prof, 66-71, PROF CHEM, FERRIS STATE UNIV, 71- *Personal Data:* b Cedar City, Utah, Dec 24, 26; m 55; c 4. *Educ:* Univ Utah, BS, 48, MA, 51; Wash State Univ, PhD, 59. *Prof Exp:* Asst prof chem, Utah State Univ, 57-62; assoc prof & head dept, Westminster Col, Utah, 62-65; NSF fac fel, Univ Colo, 65-66. *Mem:* AAAS; Am Chem Soc. *Res:* Organic reaction mechanisms; stereochemistry; teaching aids, including patents on paper steromodels and pK-pH calculator. *Mailing Add:* 285 Shoshane Ave Rexburg ID 83440

LARSON, GARY EUGENE, BOTANY, BIOPHYSICS. *Current Pos:* asst prof, Bethany Col WVa, 64-66, assoc prof, 66-81, chmn dept, 68-81, PROF BOT, BETHANY COL, WVA, 81- *Personal Data:* b Jersey Shore, Pa, Aug 10, 36; m 60; c 2. *Educ:* State Univ NY Albany, BS, 58, MS, 60; Rutgers Univ, PhD(bot), 64. *Prof Exp:* Asst bot, Rutgers Univ, 61-62, instr biol, Douglass Col, 62-64. *Concurrent Pos:* WVa Heart Asn grant, 67-68; teacher & dir, Col Educ Prog, WVa Penitentiary, 68-78; Peace Corps sci curric adv, Gambian Govt, 70-71; dir, Nat Defense Educ Act Title I Proj, 72-73; exec dir, Brooke-Hancock Comprehensive Health Planning Asn, 74-75; vis Fulbright Lectr, Dept Biol, Univ Ile, Nigeria, 77-78; AAAS rep to West African Sci Asn meeting, Lome, Togo, 79. *Mem:* Fel AAAS; Sigma Xi; Am Inst Biol Sci; Audubon Soc. *Res:* Bioelectric potentials surrounding the roots of plants; computer aided instruction; audio-tutorial education. *Mailing Add:* Dept Biol Bethany Col Bethany WV 26032

LARSON, GEORGE H(ERBERT), AGRICULTURAL ENGINEERING. *Current Pos:* assoc prof agr eng, Kans State Univ, 46-50, head dept, 50-56, prof agr eng, 50-84, EMER PROF AGR ENG, KANS STATE UNIV, 84- *Personal Data:* b Lindsborg, Kans, Jan 28, 15; m 41, Susan Spearie; c Laurence G. *Educ:* Kans State Univ, BS, 39, MS, 40; Mich State Univ, PhD, 55. *Prof Exp:* Asst, Kans State Univ, 39-40; asst instr agr eng, Univ Wis, 40-42; instr, Panhandle Agr & Mech Col, 42; jr instr, US Dept Navy, 42-43. *Concurrent Pos:* Prof & proj leader agr eng, Nebr Mission, USAID, Bogota, Colombia, 70-72; prof agr eng & head dept agron with Kans State Univ Proj, USAID, Ahmadu Bello Univ, Nigeria, 72-74; consult with Kans State Univ Proj, USAID, Central Luzon State Univ, Philippines, 78-80. *Mem:* Am Soc Agr Engrs; Nat Soc Prof Engrs. *Res:* Utilizing liquefied petroleum gas for weed control by flaming; power and machinery, utilizing liquefied petroleum gas in tractors; operating costs of field machinery; agricultural mechanization in developing countries. *Mailing Add:* 419 Oakdale Dr Manhattan KS 66502

LARSON, GERALD LOUIS, ORGANIC CHEMISTRY, SYNTHETIC INORGANIC & ORGANOMETALLIC CHEMISTRY. *Current Pos:* HEAD, SILICON APPL, HULS AM, 90-, LAB DIR CHEM TECHNOL, 93- *Personal Data:* b Tacoma, Wash, Jan 14, 42; m 66, Marilyn K Rudenick; c Michael E & Jeris K. *Educ:* Pac Lutheran Univ, BSc, 64; Univ Calif, Davis, PhD(chem), 68. *Honors & Awards:* Igarravides Award, Am Chem Soc, 87. *Prof Exp:* Fel chem, Wash State Univ, 68-69, Mass Inst Technol, 69-70; from asst prof to prof chem, Univ PR, Rio Piedras, 70-86; mgr res prods, Huls Am Petrarch Systs, 86-88, mgr res chem, 88-90. *Concurrent Pos:* Chmn, PR Sect, Am Chem Soc, 76; vis prof, Polytech Inst Mex, 82, Bari Univ, Italy, 83,

Wurzburg Univ, 86 & La State Univ, 84-85. *Mem:* Am Chem Soc; Sigma Xi. *Res:* Organosilicon chemistry with an emphasis on the synthetic applications of organosilanes; new routes to organosilicon compounds, new applications of organosilicones in industry. *Mailing Add:* Huls Am Inc 2 Turner Pl Piscataway NJ 08854. Fax: 732-981-5033

LARSON, HAROLD JOSEPH, MATHEMATICAL STATISTICS. *Current Pos:* prof opers analysis, 62-80, PROF OPERS RES & STATIST, NAVAL POSTGRAD SCH, 80- *Personal Data:* b Eagle Grove, Iowa, Nov 16, 34; m 62; c 4. *Educ:* Iowa State Univ, BS, 56, MS, 57, PhD(math, statist), 60. *Prof Exp:* Instr statist, Iowa State Univ, 59-60; math statistician, Stanford Res Inst, 60-62. *Concurrent Pos:* Consult, Autonetics Div, NAm Aviation, Inc, 63-64, Data Dynamics, Inc, 65-67 & Field Res Corp, 65-69; Fulbright prof, Univ Sao Paulo, 70-71. *Mem:* Am Statist Asn. *Res:* Probability theory; general statistical methods. *Mailing Add:* Dept Opers Res Naval Postgrad Sch Monterey CA 93943-5000

LARSON, HAROLD OLAF, ORGANIC CHEMISTRY. *Current Pos:* RETIRED. *Personal Data:* b Port Wing, Wis, May 27, 21. *Educ:* Univ Wis, BS, 43; Purdue Univ, MS, 47; Harvard Univ, PhD, 50. *Prof Exp:* Navigator, Pan Am Airways, 44-45; chemist, Hercules Powder Co, 50-54; res fel chem, Harvard Univ, 54-55; asst prof, Univ WVa, 55-57; res fel, Purdue Univ, 57-58; from asst prof to prof chem, Univ Hawaii, 58-90. *Mem:* Am Chem Soc. *Mailing Add:* Dept Chem Univ Hawaii Honolulu HI 96822

LARSON, HAROLD PHILLIP, ASTRONOMY. *Current Pos:* from asst prof to assoc prof astron, 71-76, RES PROF, LUNAR & PLANETARY LAB, UNIV ARIZ, 83- *Personal Data:* b Hartford, Conn, July 13, 38; m 60; c 2. *Educ:* Bates Col, BS, 60; Purdue Univ, MS, 63, PhD(physics), 67. *Prof Exp:* Res assoc physics, Purdue Univ, 67-68; fel, Aime-Cotton Lab, Nat Ctr Sci Res, France, 68-69. *Mem:* Am Astron Soc. *Res:* Infrared astronomy of planetary atmospheres and surfaces. *Mailing Add:* 2373 Miraval Segundo Tucson AZ 85718

LARSON, HARRY THOMAS, LARGE SCALE COMMAND & CONTROL SYSTEM ENGINEERING, DISPLAY ENGINEERING. *Current Pos:* PRES, LARBRIDGE ENTERPRISES, 70- *Personal Data:* b Berkeley, Calif, Oct 16, 21; div; c Kristin E (Beltz), Margit M (Mills) & Megan M (Hoyt). *Educ:* Univ Calif, Berkeley, BS, 47; Univ Calif, Los Angeles, MS, 54. *Honors & Awards:* Centennial Medal, Inst Elec & Electronics Engrs, 84. *Prof Exp:* Comput engr, Nat Bur Stand Inst Numerical Analysis, 49-51; syst engr, Hughes Aircraft Co, 51-54; mgr, Bus Appl Dept, Ramo Woolbridge Corp, 54-56; prog engr, Aeronutronic Div, Philco-Ford Corp, 56-68; asst dir, software & info systs div, TRW Systs, 68-69; dir planning, CalComp, 69-74; sr scientist, Hughes Aircraft, 78-87. *Concurrent Pos:* Chmn, Nat Prof Group Electronic Comput, Inst Radio Engrs, 53-54, guest ed, 60-61; lectr, comput design, Univ Southern Calif Grad Sch, 54-55; mem, bd gov, Am Fed Info Processing Soc, 56-59; chmn, tech prog, Joint Comput Conf, 67; mem, Army Sci Bd, 88-92; chmn, Soc Implications Computs, 56-70. *Mem:* Fel Inst Elec & Electronics Engrs; Soc Info Displays. *Res:* Computer system design; architecture of large scale computerized systems; social implications of science and technology; public understanding of technology and science. *Mailing Add:* 236 Calle Aragon Apt A Laguna Hills CA 92653-3492

LARSON, INGEMAR W, ZOOLOGY, PARASITOLOGY. *Current Pos:* CONSULT, 83- *Personal Data:* b Clarissa, Minn, Dec 4, 28; m 62. *Educ:* Concordia Col, Moorhead, Minn, AB, 51; Kans State Univ, MS, 57, PhD(parasitol), 64. *Prof Exp:* Instr biol, Concordia Col, 51-52; asst zool, Kans State Univ, 55-57, from instr to asst zool, 57-63; asst parasitol, Biol Sta, Univ Mich, 57; res assoc, Ore State Univ, 63-66; from asst prof to prof biol, Augustana Col, Ill, 63-83, chmn dept biol, 77-83. *Mem:* Am Soc Parasitologists; Am Micros Soc; Sigma Xi. *Res:* Parasitic protozoa; floodplain insects. *Mailing Add:* 2128 31st St Rock Island IL 61201

LARSON, JAMES D, BEAM TRANSPORT ANALYSIS, ACCELERATOR TECHNOLOGY. *Current Pos:* RETIRED. *Personal Data:* b Kansas City, Mo, Feb 16, 35. *Educ:* Mass Inst Technol, BS, 57; Calif Inst Technol, MS, 59, PhD(physics), 65. *Mem:* Am Phys Soc. *Mailing Add:* 10011 E 35th St Terr Independence MO 64052

LARSON, JAY MICHAEL, ENGINE VALVE TRAIN DESIGN, MATERIALS & METALLURGY. *Current Pos:* chief engr mats & basic proc, Eaton Corp, 76-85, mat & serv, 85-91, mgr eng, 91-96, TECH DIR, EATON CORP, 96- *Personal Data:* m 66, Karen Ann Frantzen; c Kristin, Jeffrey, Gregory & Danielle. *Educ:* Univ Wash, BS, 65, MS, 68, PhC, 69, PhD(metall), 70; Western Mich Univ, MBA, 90. *Prof Exp:* Res metallurgist, Int Nickel, 70-76. *Concurrent Pos:* Prof, Kellogg Community Col, 78; chmn, Iron & Steel Tech Comt, Soc Automotive Engrs, 95-97; mem, Oaklawn Hosp Develop Bd, 96- *Mem:* Fel Soc Automotive Engrs; fel Am Soc Metals Int; Am Inst Mech Engrs; Sigma Xi. *Res:* Patentee in field; electron microscopy; superconductors; alloy development; valve train design; standards on valve train materials; order-disorder phenomenon; ultralite engine valves; new product development process. *Mailing Add:* 337 N Kalamazoo Marshall MI 49068

LARSON, JAY REINHOLD, MECHANICAL & NUCLEAR ENGINEERING. *Current Pos:* RETIRED. *Personal Data:* b Urbana, Ill, Dec 6, 32; m 58; c 4. *Educ:* Univ Ill, Urbana, BS, 55; Univ Wash, MS, 60; Purdue Univ, PhD(mech eng), 64. *Prof Exp:* Engr, Gen Elec Co, 60-61; assoc scientist, Aerojet Nuclear Co, 64-77; scientist & eng supvr, EG&G Idaho Inc, 77-94. *Concurrent Pos:* Affil prof, Univ Idaho. *Mem:* Am Soc Mech Engrs; Nat Soc Prof Engrs. *Res:* Heat transfer; nuclear reactor safety research. *Mailing Add:* 1033 E 25 St Idaho Falls ID 83404. Fax: 208-524-3595

LARSON, JERRY KING, CLINICAL PHARMACOLOGY. *Current Pos:* asst to dir clin res, 70-76, MGR CLIN SCI SERV, PFIZER CENT RES, PFIZER INC, 76- *Personal Data:* b Willmar, Minn, May 15, 41; m 64; c 2. *Educ:* Macalester Col, BA, 63; Mass Inst Technol, PhD(org chem), 67. *Prof Exp:* Res chemist, Chas Pfizer & Co, Inc, 67-70. *Mem:* Am Chem Soc. *Res:* Clinical trials with new potential drug candidates, particularly the administration and monitoring of such trials. *Mailing Add:* Pfizer Cent Res Eastern Point Rd Groton CT 06340-5196

LARSON, JOHN GRANT, CATALYSIS, SURFACE SCIENCE. *Current Pos:* head, Phys Chem Dept, 73-85, HEAD, PHYSICS DEPT, GEN MOTORS RES LABS, 85- *Personal Data:* b Galesburg, Ill, Aug 17, 33; m 59; c 2. *Educ:* Bradley Univ, BS, 55; Univ Ill, Urbana, PhD(phys chem), 62. *Prof Exp:* Proj officer, Mat Lab, Wright Field, USAF, 55-57; fel, Mellon Inst, 61-64; group leader, Gulf Res & Develop Co, 64-66, supvr, Chem Physics Sect, 66-69, dir, 70-73. *Mem:* Catalysis Soc; Am Chem Soc; Sigma Xi; Am Phys Soc. *Res:* Catalysis, both oxide and supported metals especially for emission control; combustion chemistry; surface chemistry; magnetic materials; metal physics; layered materials. *Mailing Add:* Physics Dept Gen Motors NAO Res & Develop Ctr 30500 Mound Rd Warren MI 48090

LARSON, JOSEPH STANLEY, WETLAND ECOLOGY & POLICY. *Current Pos:* adj asst prof wildlife biol & asst unit leader, Mass Coop Wildlife Res Unit, Univ Mass, Amherst, 67-69, assoc prof, 69-77, chmn dept, 80-83, PROF, DEPT FORESTRY & WILDLIFEMMGT, UNIV MASS, AMHERST, 77-, DIR, ENVIRON INST, 83- *Personal Data:* b Stoneham, Mass, June 23, 33; m 58, Wendy Nichols; c Marion Elizabeth & Sandra Frances. *Educ:* Univ Mass, BS, 56, MS, 58; Va Polytech Inst, PhD(zool), 66. *Honors & Awards:* Conserv Award for Except Pub Serv in the Cause of Conserv, Chevron, 90. *Prof Exp:* Exec secy, Wildlife Conserv Inc, Mass, 58-59; state ornithologist & asst to dir, Mass Div Fisheries & Game, 59-60; head, Conserv Educ Div, Natural Resources Inst, Univ Md, 60-62, res asst prof wildlife, 65-67. *Concurrent Pos:* Consult wetland ecol to var pub, pvt & int agencies & foreign govts; exec chmn, Nat Wetlands Tech Coun, 77-; deleg, Ramsar Conv Wetlands Int Importance, 87, 90 & 93; chmn, US Nat Ramsar Comt, 89-96; adv wetlands & mem ecol comn ecosyst mgt, Int Union Conserv Nature & Natural Resources, Switz. *Mem:* AAAS; Wildlife Soc; Ecol Soc Am; Am Soc Mammal; Soc Wetland Scientists. *Res:* Wetland ecology and management specializing in techniques for assessing functions of wetlands and wetland policy; beaver behavior. *Mailing Add:* 27 Arnold Rd Pelham MA 01002-9757. E-Mail: larson@tei.umass.edu

LARSON, KENNETH ALLEN, IMMUNOLOGY, VETERINARY MEDICINE. *Current Pos:* PRES, ELARS BIORES LABS INC, 76- *Personal Data:* b Havre, Mont, July 6, 35; m 61; c 4. *Educ:* Wash State Univ, DVM, 61, MS, 65, PhD(immunol), 66. *Prof Exp:* Vet pvt pract, Mont, 61-63; asst prof vet med, Colo State Univ, 66-69, assoc prof vet med & microbiol, 69-76. *Mem:* AAAS; Am Soc Microbiol; Am Vet Med Asn. *Res:* Immunology of tumors in animals. *Mailing Add:* 1305 Teakwood Dr Ft Collins CO 80525

LARSON, KENNETH BLAINE, biophysics, biomathematics, for more information see previous edition

LARSON, KENNETH CURTIS, PAPER CHEMISTRY, WOOD CHEMISTRY. *Current Pos:* Sci specialist res & develop, Scott Paper Co, Philadelphia, Pa, 67-74, sci assoc, 74-77, proj head, 77-80, Mgr Res & Develop, 80-81, DIR, WORLDWIDE CONSUMER TOWEL PROD DEVELOP, SCOTT PAPER CO, PHILADELPHIA, 81- *Personal Data:* b Madison, Wis, July 7, 40; m 64, Barbara; c Christopher & James. *Educ:* Calif Inst Technol, BS, 62; Lawrence Univ, MS, 64, PhD(wood chem), 67. *Honors & Awards:* E J Albert Award, Tech Asn Pulp & Paper Indust. *Mem:* Tech Asn Pulp & Paper Indust. *Res:* Colloid and surface chemistry of wood pulp fibers; product and process development. *Mailing Add:* Kimberly Clark 2300 Winchester Rd PO Box 2007 Neenah WI 54957-2007

LARSON, LARRY LEE, REPRODUCTIVE PHYSIOLOGY. *Current Pos:* asst prof, 72-77, ASSOC PROF REPRODUCTIVE PHYSIOL, UNIV NEBR, LINCOLN, 77- *Personal Data:* b Horton, Kans, Nov 18, 39; m 63; c 2. *Educ:* Kans State Univ, BS, 62, MS, 65, PhD(animal breeding), 68. *Prof Exp:* NIH fel, Cornell Univ, 68-70, asst prof reproductive physiol, 70-72. *Mem:* Soc Study Reproduction; Brit Soc Study Fertil; Am Soc Animal Sci; Am Dairy Sci Asn. *Res:* Estrus control and determination; conception failures; management factors to improve reproductive performance. *Mailing Add:* Dept Animal Sci Univ Nebr E Campus C203 Animal Sci Lincoln NE 68583-0001

LARSON, LAURENCE ARTHUR, PLANT PHYSIOLOGY, BIOLOGY EDUCATION. *Current Pos:* from asst prof to assoc prof, 63-75, PROF BOT, OHIO UNIV, 75- *Personal Data:* b Cleveland, Ohio, Mar 17, 30; m 56; c 2. *Educ:* Ohio Univ, BS, 56; Univ Tenn, MS, 59; Purdue Univ, PhD(amino acid metab), 63. *Prof Exp:* Phys oceanogr, US Navy Hydrographic Off, 56-57; instr bot, Univ Tenn, 59. *Mem:* Am Inst Biol Sci; Asn Am Biol Teachers; Inst Relig Age Sci. *Res:* Germination physiology. *Mailing Add:* Dept Biol Sci Ohio Univ Athens OH 45701-2979

LARSON, LAWRENCE T, ECONOMIC GEOLOGY, MINERALOGY. *Current Pos:* prof geol & chmn dept, 75-90, PROF ECON GEOL, MACKAY SCH MINES, UNIV NEV, RENO, 90- *Personal Data:* b Waukegan, Ill, Dec 3, 30; m 57; c 3. *Educ:* Univ Ill, BS, 57; Univ Wis, MS, 59, PhD(geol), 62. *Prof Exp:* From asst prof to prof geol, Univ Tenn, Knoxville, 61-75. *Concurrent Pos:* Consult, Oak Ridge Nat Lab, 63-69 & mining firms, 68-, UN Develop Prog, WHO & US Dept Energy; partner, Appl Explor Concepts, 72-79; Fulbright lectr, Turkey, 85-86, UN Develop Prog, 90. *Mem:* Geol Soc Am; Am Inst Mining, Metall & Petrol Engrs; Soc Econ Geologists. *Res:* Manganese mineralogy and ore deposits; ore microscopy; uranium mineralization in Great Basin; geologic thermometry; ceramic and high alumina clay deposits; applied geochemistry and gold exploration; ore deposit geology of Turkey. *Mailing Add:* Dept Geol Sci Univ Nev Reno NV 89557-0001

LARSON, LEE EDWARD, PHYSICS. *Current Pos:* from asst prof to assoc prof, 66-78, PROF PHYSICS, DENISON UNIV, 78- *Personal Data:* b Bristol, Conn, Dec 2, 37; m 63; c 2. *Educ:* Univ NH, PhD(ionospheric physics), 67. *Honors & Awards:* Distinguished Serv Citation, Am Asn Physics Teachers. *Prof Exp:* Instr physics, Allegheny Col, 61-63. *Mem:* Am Asn Physics Teachers; Am Geophys Union. *Res:* High resolution molecular spectroscopy. *Mailing Add:* Dept Physics Denison Univ Granville OH 43023. *E-Mail:* larson@cc.denison.edu

LARSON, LESTER LEROY, VETERINARY MEDICINE, DISEASES OF REPRODUCTION. *Current Pos:* RETIRED. *Personal Data:* b Amherst Junction, Wis, Feb 12, 23; m 51, Norma L Kirkpatrick; c Susan L, Paul L & Charlene A. *Educ:* Univ Minn, BS, 50, DVM & MS, 53, PhD(vet med), 57; Am Col Theriogenologists, dipl, 70. *Honors & Awards:* M S D Agvet Dairy Prev Med Award, Am Asn Bovine Practitioners, 85. *Prof Exp:* Vet, 53-54; from instr to asst prof vet med, Univ Minn, 54-58; assoc vet, Am Breeders Serv, 58-73, vet & head vet dept, 74-85. *Concurrent Pos:* Chmn comt exam, Am Col Theriogenologists, 73; guest lectr genital path in the bull, Univ Venezuela, 78; pvt vet pract, 85- *Mem:* Am Vet Med Asn; US Animal Health Asn; Am Asn Bovine Practitioners; Am Col Theriogenologists. *Res:* Neuroanatomical and neurophysiological aspects of reproductive process-male; surgical technique for anesthesia of penis-bull; control of venereal diseases of cattle through artificial insemination; actuarial studies of bull under conditions of an artificial insemination center. *Mailing Add:* 2039 Cty T Amherst Junction WI 55407-9216

LARSON, LESTER MIKKEL, chemistry; deceased, see previous edition for last biography

LARSON, M(ILTON) B(YRD), MECHANICAL ENGINEERING. *Current Pos:* PROF MECH ENG, ORE STATE UNIV, 69- *Personal Data:* b Portland, Ore, July 3, 27; m 50; c 4. *Educ:* Ore State Univ, BS, 50, MS, 55; Yale Univ, MEng, 51; Stanford Univ, PhD(mech eng), 61. *Prof Exp:* From instr to assoc prof mech eng, Ore State Univ, 52-64; dean eng, Univ NDak, 64-68. *Concurrent Pos:* Ford Found resident, Washington Works, E I Du Pont de Nemours & Co, Inc, 68-69. *Mem:* Am Soc Mech Engrs; Am Soc Eng Educ. *Res:* Heat transfer. *Mailing Add:* Dept Mech Eng Ore State Univ 204 Rogers Hall Corvallis OR 97331-6001

LARSON, MAURICE A(LLEN), CHEMICAL ENGINEERING. *Current Pos:* from asst prof to prof, 58-77, chmn dept, 78-83, DISTINGUISHED PROF CHEM ENG, IOWA STATE UNIV, 77- *Personal Data:* b Iowa, July 19, 27; m 53, Ruth Gugeler; c Richard (deceased), Janet & John. *Educ:* Iowa State Univ, BS, 51, PhD(chem eng), 58. *Honors & Awards:* Wester Fund Award, Am Soc Engr Educ, 70. *Prof Exp:* Chem engr res & develop, Dow Corning Corp, 51-52, chem engr mfg, 53-54. *Concurrent Pos:* NSF sci fac fel, Stanford Univ, 65-66; Shell vis prof, Univ Col, Univ London, 71-72; vis prof, Univ Queensland, 81 & Inst Sci & Technol, Univ Manchester, 84-85. *Mem:* Am Chem Soc; Am Soc Eng Educ; fel Am Inst Chem Engrs. *Res:* Process dynamics and control; crystallization; analysis of particulate system. *Mailing Add:* Dept Chem Eng Iowa State Univ Ames IA 50011. *Fax:* 515-294-2689; *E-Mail:* malarson@iastate.edu

LARSON, MERLYN MILFRED, FOREST PHYSIOLOGY, TROPICAL FORESTRY. *Current Pos:* assoc prof silvicult, 66-70, PROF FORESTRY, OHIO AGR RES & DEVELOP CTR, 70-; PROF NATURAL RESOURCES, OHIO STATE UNIV, 70- *Personal Data:* b Story City, Iowa, Sept 11, 28; m 54; c 6. *Educ:* Colo State Univ, BS, 54; Univ Wash, MF, 58, PhD, 62. *Prof Exp:* Jr forester, US Forest Serv, 55, res forester, Rocky Mountain Forest & Range Exp Sta, 55-64, forest physiologist, 64-66. *Concurrent Pos:* Asst, Univ Wash, 58-59; consult, Cath Univ, Dominican Repub, 83, G B Plant Univ Agr Technol, India, 88; vis prof, Trop Agr Res & Training Ctr, Costa Rica, 84. *Mem:* Soc Am Foresters; Int Soc Trop Foresters. *Res:* Forest regeneration; tree physiology; forest nurseries. *Mailing Add:* Sch Nat Resources Ohio State Univ 2021 Coffey Rd Columbus OH 43210-1044

LARSON, NANCY MARIE, NEUTRON PHYSICS, DATA ANALYSIS & EVALUATION. *Current Pos:* SR RES STAFF, COMPUT ENG & PHYSICS DIV, OAK RIDGE NAT LAB, LOCKHEED MARTIN, 72- *Personal Data:* b Dickinson, ND, Sept 30, 46; m 68, Duane C; c Linnea M. *Educ:* Mich State Univ, BS, 67, MS, 69, PhD(theoret physics), 72. *Mem:* Am Phys Soc. *Res:* Generalized least square (Bayes method); Reich-Moore R-matrix theory; analysis of neutron scattering data; data reduction and uncertainty propagation. *Mailing Add:* Oak Ridge Nat Lab Bldg 6011 MS 6370 PO Box 2008 Oak Ridge TN 37831-6370. *Fax:* 423-574-3527; *E-Mail:* nml@ornl.gov

LARSON, OMER R, ENTOMOLOGY. *Current Pos:* from asst prof to assoc prof, Univ NDak, 64-76, actg chmn dept, 66-67, assoc dean arts & sci, 69-70 & 75-76, chmn dept, 78-80, PROF BIOL, UNIV NDAK, 76- *Personal Data:* b Roseau, Minn, Dec 1, 31; m 60, Patricia A Saumur; c Kristin, Katherine, Elizabeth & Margaret. *Educ:* Univ NDak, BA, 54; Univ Minn, MS, 60, PhD(fish parasites), 63. *Prof Exp:* Instr biol, Minot State Col, 63-64. *Concurrent Pos:* Vis prof, Dept Biol, USAF Acad, 90-91. *Mem:* Am Soc Parasitologists; Wildlife Dis Asn; Sigma Xi; Soc Vector Ecologists; Am Entom Soc. *Res:* Helminth life cycles; parasites and diseases of fish; biogeography and cold tolerance of fleas. *Mailing Add:* Biol Dept Univ NDak Box 8238 Grand Forks ND 58202

LARSON, PHILIP RODNEY, FOREST PHYSIOLOGY, PLANT ANATOMY. *Current Pos:* RETIRED. *Personal Data:* b North Branch, Minn, Nov 26, 23; m 48; c 2. *Educ:* Univ Minn, BS, 49, MS, 52; Yale Univ, PhD(forestry), 57. *Honors & Awards:* Distinguished Serv Award, USDA, 75; Barrington Moore Biol Res Award, Soc Am Foresters, 75; New York Bot Garden Award, Bot Soc Am, 77. *Prof Exp:* Res forester, US Forest Serv, Fla, 52-54, plant physiologist, Lake States Forest Exp Sta, 56-62, leader physiol wood formation, Pioneering Res Unit, NCent Forest Exp Sta, 62. *Mem:* Am Soc Plant Physiologists; Soc Am Foresters; fel Int Acad Wood Sci; Bot Soc Am; Int Asn Wood Anatomists. *Res:* Wood formation; vascular anatomy; physiology of growth and development. *Mailing Add:* 3012 S Rifle Rd Rhinelander WI 54501

LARSON, REGINALD EINAR, air mass tracers, nuclear spectroscopy, for more information see previous edition

LARSON, RICHARD ALLEN, ENVIRONMENTAL ORGANIC CHEMISTRY. *Current Pos:* PROF, INST ENVIRON STUDIES, UNIV ILL, URBANA, 79- *Personal Data:* b Minot, NDak, July 9, 41; m 63; c 2. *Educ:* Univ Minn, Minneapolis, BA, 63; Univ Ill, Urbana, PhD(org chem), 68. *Prof Exp:* USPHS fels, Univ Liverpool, 68-69 & Cambridge Univ, 69-70; res assoc bot, Univ Tex, Austin, 70-72; asst cur, Stroud Water Res Ctr, Acad Natural Sci Philadelphia, 72-79. *Concurrent Pos:* Spec lectr, Univ Pa, 73-74; Nat Res Coun sr res assoc, Environ Protection Agency, Athens, Ga, 85-86. *Mem:* Phytochem Soc NAm; Am Chem Soc; Am Soc Photobiol; Sigma Xi. *Res:* Natural products; phytochemistry; aquatic organic chemistry; photobiology. *Mailing Add:* 1101 W Peabody Dr Urbana IL 61801

LARSON, RICHARD BONDO, STAR FORMATION, GALACTIC EVOLUTION. *Current Pos:* From asst prof to assoc prof, Yale Univ, 68-75, dir undergrad studies, 71-81, chmn dept, 81-87, PROF ASTRON, YALE UNIV, 75- *Personal Data:* b Toronto, Ont, Jan 15, 41; Can citizen. *Educ:* Univ Toronto, BSc, 62, MA, 63; Calif Inst Technol, PhD(astron), 68. *Concurrent Pos:* Tinsley vis prof, Univ Tex, 90. *Mem:* Int Astron Union; Am Astron Soc; Royal Astron Soc Can; Royal Astron Soc; Sigma Xi; Astron Soc Pac. *Res:* Theoretical studies of star formation and early stellar evolution; stellar dynamics, formation and evolution of galaxies. *Mailing Add:* Dept Astron Yale Univ Box 208101 New Haven CT 06520-8101. *Fax:* 203-432-5048; *E-Mail:* larson@astro.yale.edu

LARSON, RICHARD CHARLES, QUEUEING THEORY, LOGISTICS. *Current Pos:* Asst prof elec eng, Mass Inst Technol, 69-71, asst prof urban studies & planning & elec eng, 71-72, assoc prof urban studies & planning, elec eng & comput sci, 72-79, co-dir, Opers Res Ctr, 77-86 & 91-95, prof elec eng & urban studies & planning, 79-88, PROF ELEC ENG, MASS INST TECHNOL, 88-, DIR, CTR ADVAN EDUC SERV, 95- *Personal Data:* b Apr 10, 43; m 79, M Elizabeth Murray; c Erik, Evan & Ingrid. *Educ:* Mass Inst Technol, SB, 65, SM, 67, PhD(elec eng), 69. *Honors & Awards:* Lanchester Prize, Opers Res Soc Am, 72; Cecil T Holmes Math Lectr, Bowdoin Col, 91. *Concurrent Pos:* Mem, Sci & Technol Task Force, President's Comn Law Enforcement & Admin Justice, Inst Defense Analysis, 66; prin investr, NSF, 73-76, 84-87, 87-90, 88-91 & 92-95, US Dept Justice, 77-79, 80-82, 83-85, 84-85 & 85-87, Mass Inst Technol Ctr Transp Studies/ US Dept Transp, 91-93; founder & pres, Pub Systs Eval, Inc, 74-85; vis assoc prof opers res, Dept Indust Eng & Opers Res, Univ Calif, Berkeley, 76; chmn, Enforth Corp, 80-90; Queues-Enforth Develop, Inc, 90-; consult, Nat Inst Justice, 80-93; Union Carbide Corp, 83-85, Harvard Univ, 85-89, First Boston Corp, 87-88, Kuwait Found Advan Sci, 89, Coca-Cola Corp, 91-92, United Artists & Johnson Controls, 93; vis prof opers res, Tech Univ Denmark, 81; Wharton Sch distinguished lectr, Univ Pa, 91. *Mem:* Nat Acad Eng; Opers Res Soc Am (pres, 93-94); Inst Mgt Sci; Sigma Xi; AAAS; Inst Elec & Electronics Engrs; Prod & Opers Mgt Soc. *Res:* Operations research, especially decisions involving the allocation of resources; complex operational systems involving queueing type congestion, logistics distribution, scheduling of personnel, location of facilities, assisted command and control and statistical inference from transactional data; using advanced technologies for distance learning; operations research applied to private and public systems; transportation and logistics; psychology of queueing, queueing theory; criminal justice and municipal public safety. *Mailing Add:* Mass Inst Technol Bldg 9-215 77 Massachusetts Ave Cambridge MA 02139. *Fax:* 617-252-1566

LARSON, RICHARD GUSTAVUS, COMPUTER MATHEMATICS, HOPF ALGEBRAS. *Current Pos:* from asst prof to assoc prof, 67-77, PROF MATH, UNIV ILL, CHICAGO, 77- *Personal Data:* b Pittsburgh, Pa, May 16, 40; m 94, Roberta L Raymond; c 3. *Educ:* Univ Pa, AB, 61; Univ Chicago, MS, 62, PhD(math), 65. *Honors & Awards:* Fulbright lectr, Philippines, 78. *Prof Exp:* Instr math, Mass Inst Technol, 65-67. *Mem:* Am Math Soc; Asn Comput Mach; Math Asn Am; Soc Indust & Appl Math. *Res:* Algebraic and arithmetic structure of Hopf algebras; symbolic algorithms; computational problems of algebra; theoretical computer science; applications of hopf algebras to control theory. *Mailing Add:* Dept Math Univ Ill MC 249 851 S Morgan St Chicago IL 60607. *E-Mail:* rgl@uic.edu

LARSON, RICHARD I, CHEMICAL ENGINEERING. *Current Pos:* Engr, 63-66, proj engr, Knolls Atomic Power Lab, Schenectady, 68-77, PRIN ENGR, NUCLEAR FUEL DEPT, GEN ELEC CO, 75- *Personal Data:* b Chicago, Ill, Dec 29, 37; m 61; c 3. *Educ:* Northwestern Univ, BSChE, 60; Cornell Univ, MChE, 63; Rensselaer Polytech Inst, PhD(chem eng), 69. *Prof Exp:* Consult, Atomic Energy Comn, 66-68. *Mem:* Am Inst Chem Engrs; Am Chem Soc; Am Nuclear Soc. *Res:* Nuclear fuel processing, turbulent flow-heat and mass transfer; colloidal and surface chemistry; numerical solution; ordinary and partial differential equations; system analysis; fluidization production equipment. *Mailing Add:* 2009 Spanish Wells Dr Wilmington NC 28405-4283

LARSON, ROBERT ELOF, PHARMACOLOGY, TOXICOLOGY. *Current Pos:* from asst prof to assoc prof, 65-76, chmn dept, 70-76, PROF PHARMACOL & TOXICOL, SCH PHARM, ORE STATE UNIV, 76- *Personal Data:* b Spokane, Wash, Oct 9, 32; m 57; c 3. *Educ:* Wash State Univ, BS, & BPharm, 57, MS, 62; Univ Iowa, PhD(pharmacol), 64. *Prof Exp:* Pharmacist, Manito Pharm, Wash, 57-59; staff fel toxicol, Nat Cancer Inst, 64-65. *Mem:* Soc Toxicol; Am Soc Pharmacol & Exp Therapeut; Soc Exp Biol Med; Sigma Xi. *Res:* Hepatotoxicity and nephrotoxicity of halogenated hydrocarbons; toxicity of nitrosoureas. *Mailing Add:* 680 Floral Pl Hood River OR 97031-1168

LARSON, ROGER, MARINE GEOPHYSICS, TECTONICS. *Current Pos:* PROF MARINE GEOPHYS, UNIV RI, 80- *Personal Data:* b Stratford, Iowa, Jan 12, 43. *Educ:* Iowa State Univ, BS, 65; Univ Calif, San Diego, PhD(oceanog), 70. *Prof Exp:* Sr res assoc, Lamont-Doherty Geol Observ, Columbia Univ, 76-80. *Mem:* Fel Geol Soc Am; Geophys Union. *Mailing Add:* Dept Oceanog Univ RI 15 S Ferry Rd Narragansett RI 02882-1197

LARSON, ROLAND EDWIN, MATHEMATICS. *Current Pos:* From asst prof to assoc prof, 70-83, PROF MATH, BEHREND COL, PA STATE UNIV, 83- *Personal Data:* b Ft Lewis, Wash, Oct 31, 41; m 60; c 2. *Educ:* Lewis & Clark Col, BS, 66; Univ Colo, Boulder, MA, 68, PhD(math), 70. *Concurrent Pos:* Mem. Nat Coun Teachers Math. *Mem:* Am Math Soc; Math Asn Am; Nat Coun Teachers Math; Am Math Asn Two Year Col. *Res:* Author of numerous publications. *Mailing Add:* Behrend Col Pa State Univ Erie PA 16563-1500

LARSON, ROY AXEL, HORTICULTURE. *Current Pos:* Assoc prof, 61-69, PROF HORT, NC STATE UNIV, 69- *Personal Data:* b Cloquet, Minn, Feb 5, 31; m 53; c 4. *Educ:* Univ Minn, BS, 53, MS, 57; Cornell Univ, PhD(floricult), 61. *Mem:* Am Soc Hort Sci. *Res:* Floriculture, particularly investigations on effects of environment and regulators on flowering and plant growth. *Mailing Add:* Dept Hort NC State Univ PO Box 7609 Raleigh NC 27695-0001

LARSON, RUBY ILA, CYTOGENETICS. *Current Pos:* RETIRED. *Personal Data:* b Hatfield, Sask, Can, May 30, 14. *Educ:* Univ Sask, BS, 42 & 43, MA, 45; Univ Mo, PhD(genetics), 52. *Prof Exp:* Cytogeneticist, Cereal Div, Dom Exp Sta, Sask, 45-48; cytogeneticist, Sci Serv Lab, Can Dept Agr, 48-59, cytogeneticist, Res Sta, 59-79. *Res:* Wheat cytogenetics. *Mailing Add:* 20 Third St S Unit 410 Lethbridge AB T1J 4P1 Can

LARSON, RUSSELL EDWARD, AGRICULTURAL EDUCATION, ACADEMIC ADMINISTRATION. *Current Pos:* asst prof veg gardening, Pa State Univ, 44-45, assoc prof plant breeding, 45-47, head, Dept Hort, 52-61, dir agr & home econ exten, 61-63, dean & dir, Col Agr, 63-74, provost, 72-77, prof, 47-77, EMER PROVOST, EMER DEAN & EMER PROF HORT, PA STATE UNIV, UNIVERSITY PARK, 77-; CONSULT AGR, 77- *Personal Data:* b Minneapolis, Minn, Jan 2, 17; m 39, Margaret A Johnson; c 3. *Educ:* Univ Minn, BS, 39, MS, 40, PhD(genetics, plant breeding), 42. *Hon Degrees:* DSc, Del Valley Col Sci & Agr, 66. *Honors & Awards:* Vaughan Award, Am Soc Hort Sci, 48. *Prof Exp:* Asst hort, Univ Minn, 39-41. *Concurrent Pos:* Sci aide, Mex Agr Prog, Rockefeller Found, 60; chmn comn educ agr & natural resources, Nat Acad Sci-Nat Res Coun, 66-; adv sci affairs, Am Cocoa Res Inst, 77-88. *Mem:* AAAS; Am Soc Hort Sci; Genetics Soc Am; Am Genetics Asn. *Res:* Administration of agricultural research development and education. *Mailing Add:* 608 Elmwood St State College PA 16801-7053

LARSON, RUSSELL L, BIOCHEMISTRY. *Current Pos:* RES CHEMIST, USDA, UNIV MO, COLUMBIA, 65- *Personal Data:* b Bridgewater, SDak, Dec 9, 28; wid; c 1. *Educ:* SDak State Univ, BS, 57, MS, 59; Univ Ill, PhD(biochem), 62. *Prof Exp:* Fel microbiol, Ore State Univ, 62-64. *Mem:* Am Chem Soc; Phytochem Soc NAm; Am Soc Plant Physiol. *Res:* Biochemistry of disease resistance in plants; alteration in metabolic processes in maize as a result of alteration in the genetic systems in maize. *Mailing Add:* 438 Airwood Ave Springfield MO 65802

LARSON, SANFORD J, NEUROANATOMY, NEUROSURGERY. *Current Pos:* assoc prof, 63-68, PROF NEUROSURG, MED COL WIS, 68-, CHMN DEPT, 63- *Personal Data:* b Chicago, Ill, Apr 9, 29; m 57; c 3. *Educ:* Wheaton Col, Ill, BA, 50; Northwestern Univ, MD, 54, PhD(anat), 62. *Prof Exp:* Resident neurosurg, Northwestern Univ, 55-57 & 59-61; USPHS res fel, 61-62; dir neurosurg educ, Cook Co Hosp, Chicago, 62-63. *Concurrent Pos:* Chief neurosurg, Vet Admin Hosp, Wis, 91, Milwaukee Co Gen Hosp & Froedtert Mem Lutheran Hosp; consult, Columbia & Milwaukee Children's Hosps, Wis & Shriners Hosps Crippled Children, Chicago, Ill. *Mem:* Soc Univ Surg; Am Asn Neurol Surg; Am Col Surg; Soc Neurol Surgeons. *Res:* Neurophysiology; neurological surgery. *Mailing Add:* Dept Neurosurg Med Col Wis 9200 W Wisconsin Ave Milwaukee WI 53226

LARSON, STEVEN MARK, NUCLEAR MEDICINE, CANCER MEDICINE. *Current Pos:* CHIEF NUCLEAR MED SERV, DEPT RADIOL, MEM SLOAN KETTERING CANCER CTR, 88-, DIR LAURENT & ALBERTA GERSCHELL PET CTR, 88- *Personal Data:* m 64, Elaine L Williamson; c Nathan P & Justine J. *Educ:* Univ Wash, MD, 68. *Prof Exp:* Chief nuclear med, NIH, 83-88. *Concurrent Pos:* Captain, USPHS, 83-88; prof radiol, Med Col, Cornell Univ, 88- *Mem:* Inst Clin Pet (pres, 94-95); Soc Nuclear Med. *Res:* Development and application of radiolasers for diagnosis and therapy in oncology. *Mailing Add:* Mem Sloan Kettering Cancer Ctr 1275 York Ave New York NY 10021

LARSON, THOMAS D, TRANSPORTATION MANAGEMENT. *Current Pos:* PVT CONSULT TRANSP, 92- *Personal Data:* b Sept 28, 28; c 3. *Educ:* Pa State Univ, BS, 52, MS, 59, PhD(civil eng), 62. *Honors & Awards:* Secy's Gold Medal Award for Outstanding Achievement, Secy Transp, 90. *Prof Exp:* Prof, Col Bus Admin & Col Eng, Pa State Univ, 62-89; adminr, Fed Hwy Admin, 89-92. *Concurrent Pos:* Secy transp, Commonwealth Pa, 79-87; chair, Nat Gov's Task Force on New Fed Transp Legis. *Mem:* Nat Acad Eng; fel Nat Soc Civil Engrs; fel Nat Acad Pub Admin. *Mailing Add:* PO Box 324 Lamont PA 16851

LARSON, THOMAS E, PHYSICAL CHEMISTRY, ORGANIC CHEMISTRY. *Current Pos:* RETIRED. *Personal Data:* b Waupaca, Wis, Apr 13, 26; m 49; c 3. *Educ:* Lewis & Clark Col, BA, 50; Johns Hopkins Univ, MA, 51, PhD(phys chem), 56. *Honors & Awards:* Award of Excellence, Dept Energy, Fogbank, 84, Terrazzo, 85. *Prof Exp:* Jr instr chem, Johns Hopkins Univ, 50-53, res asst, Inst Coop Res, 53-56; staff mem, Los Alamos Nat Lab, 56-75, alt group leader WX-2, 75-84, group leader explosive technol, 84-91. *Concurrent Pos:* Assoc, Los Alamos Nat Lab, 91- *Mem:* Am Chem Soc. *Res:* Kinetics of exchange reactions in boron hydrides; sensitivity of explosives to various stimuli; radioactive materials. *Mailing Add:* 2711 Walnut St Los Alamos NM 87544. *Fax:* 505-667-3407

LARSON, VAUGHN LEROY, veterinary medicine, for more information see previous edition

LARSON, VERNON C, AGRICULTURE, ACADEMIC ADMINISTRATION. *Current Pos:* dir int agr progs, 72-87, asst provost & dir int prog, 87-91, EMER PROF, KANS STATE UNIV, 91- *Personal Data:* b Stambough, Mich, Apr 8, 23; m 46; c 3. *Educ:* Mich State Univ, BS, 47, MS, 50, EdD(educ admin), 54. *Prof Exp:* From asst prof to assoc prof dairy & asst to dean, Mich State Univ, 47-59; prof agr & asst dean, Am Univ, Beirut, 59-62; prof dairy agr & dir int agr prog, Kans State Univ, 62-65; prof agr sci & dean agr, Ahmadu Bello Univ, Nigeria & chief party, AID & Kans State Univ Team in Nigeria, 66-68; dir int agr progs, Kans State Univ, 68-70; chief party, AID & Kans State Univ Team in India, 70-72. *Concurrent Pos:* AID consult, Jordan, 60, Cyprus & Sudan, 61, Kenya, 68, Colombia, 69, Sierre Leon, 75, Philippines, 77, Paraguay, 78 & Peru, 78, Morocco, 85, Nepal, 85, Botswana, 87, Brazil 89. *Mem:* AAAS; Int Asn Agr Students; Nat Asn State Univs & Land-Grant Cols. *Res:* Agricultural administration. *Mailing Add:* 1951 Bluestem Terr Manhattan KS 66502

LARSON, VINCENT H(ENNIX), MECHANICAL ENGINEERING. *Current Pos:* prof mech eng, 72-85, chmn dept, 72-78, EMER PROF MECH ENG, CLEVELAND STATE UNIV, 85- *Personal Data:* b Clinton, Minn, Feb 23, 17; m 55, Shirley Slettum. *Educ:* Univ Minn, BS, 51, ME, 64, PhD(mech eng), 65. *Prof Exp:* Proj engr, Research, Inc, Minn, 54-58, chief analytical engr, 58-63; assoc prof mech eng & astronaut sci, Northwestern Univ, 65-72. *Mem:* Am Inst Aeronaut & Astronaut; Am Soc Mech Engrs. *Res:* Control system theory and practice; systems engineering; conception; analysis, evaluation, synthesis and optimization of mechanical and electromechanical systems; analysis of robotic mechanisms. *Mailing Add:* 1823 Colfax Ave S Minneapolis MN 55403

LARSON, VIVIAN M, VIROLOGY. *Current Pos:* RETIRED. *Personal Data:* b Erie, NDak, Oct 3, 31. *Educ:* NDak State Col, BS, 53; Univ Mich, MPH, 58, PhD(virol), 63. *Prof Exp:* Bacteriologist, Detroit Dept Health Labs, Mich, 53-59; from res fel to sr res fel virol, Merck Sharp & Dohme Res Labs, 63-71, dir, NIH Virus Lab, 71-80, dir, 80-90. *Mem:* Am Soc Microbiol; Am Acad Microbiol; AAAS. *Res:* Cell biology; immunology; viral; vaccines. *Mailing Add:* 362 Park Dr Harleysville PA 19438

LARSON, WILBUR JOHN, ANALYTICAL CHEMISTRY. *Current Pos:* RETIRED. *Personal Data:* b Rockford, Ill, Nov 19, 21; m 45, Betty J Swanson; c Kurt E, Gail D (Akins) & Neil F. *Educ:* Augustana Col, Ill, BA, 46; Univ Wis, MS, 48, PhD, 51. *Prof Exp:* Chemist, Mallinckrodt Chem Works, 51-57, head, Analytical Develop Lab, 57-63, asst dir qual control, 64-72; res assoc, Mallinckrodt Inc, 72-84, qual control mgr, 84-86. *Mem:* Am Chem Soc; Sigma Xi. *Res:* Trace analysis; quality control; electronic grade chemicals; reagent chemicals. *Mailing Add:* 1364 Stein Ave Ferguson MO 63135-1709

LARSON, WILBUR S, INORGANIC CHEMISTRY, ANALYTICAL CHEMISTRY. *Current Pos:* assoc prof, 63-76, PROF CHEM, UNIV WIS, OSHKOSH, 76- *Personal Data:* b Downing, Wis, Jan 28, 23; m 53; c 1. *Educ:* Wis State Univ, River Falls, BS, 45; Univ Wyo, MS, 58, PhD(inorg chem), 64. *Prof Exp:* Teacher high schs, Wis, 44-55; asst gen chem, Univ Wyo, 55-63. *Mem:* Am Chem Soc; Sigma Xi. *Res:* Colorimetric sulfide, sulfite and thiosulfate analysis; stability of antimony addition compounds; equilibrium exchange mechanisms of metallic sulfides; mechanism studies of antimony pentachloride. *Mailing Add:* 1538 Kentucky St Oshkosh WI 54901

LARSON, WILLIAM EARL, SOIL SCIENCE. *Current Pos:* prof, 67-89, EMER PROF SOIL SCI, UNIV MINN, ST PAUL, 89- *Personal Data:* b Creston, Nebr, Aug 7, 21; m 47; c 4. *Educ:* Univ Nebr, BS, 44, MS, 46; Iowa State Univ, PhD, 49. *Hon Degrees:* DSc, Univ Nebr, 82. *Honors & Awards:* Soil Sci Award, Am Soc Agron; Bennett Award, Soil Conserv Soc, 85; Black Award, 87. *Prof Exp:* Asst prof agron, Iowa State Univ, 49-50; soil scientist, USDA, Mont State Col, 51-54; from assoc prof to prof soils, Iowa State Univ, 54-67. *Concurrent Pos:* Soil scientist, USDA, Iowa State Univ, 54-67; vis prof, Univ Ill, 60 & Univ Minn, 63; Fulbright scholar, Australia, 65-66. *Mem:* Fel AAAS; fel Am Soc Agron; fel Soil Sci Soc Am; Int Soc Soil Sci; fel Soil Conserv Soc Am. *Res:* Soil structure and mechanics; water infiltration; nutrient interrelations in plants; crop response to soil moisture levels and soil temperature; tillage requirements of crops; utilization of sewage wastes on land. *Mailing Add:* 3334 Richmond Ave St Paul MN 55126

LARTER, EDWARD NATHAN, GENETICS, PLANT BREEDING. *Current Pos:* Rosner res chair prof plant sci & dir tritical res prog, 69-89, EMER PROF PLANT SCI, UNIV MAN, 89- *Personal Data:* b Can, Feb 13, 23; m 45; c 3. *Educ:* Univ Alta, BSc, 51, MSc, 52; State Col Wash, PhD(genetics, plant breeding), 54. *Prof Exp:* Assoc prof genetics & plant breeding, Univ Sask, 54-69. *Mem:* Genetics Soc Can; Can Soc Agron; Agr Inst Can. *Res:* Plant breeding and cytogenetics of barley, triticale and related species. *Mailing Add:* 92 Tunis Bay Winnipeg MB R3T 2X1 Can

LARTER, RAIMA, NONLINEAR DYNAMICS. *Current Pos:* vis asst prof, Ind Univ-Purdue Univ, Indianapolis, 81-83, asst prof, 83-87, assoc prof, 88-91, PROF CHEM, IND UNIV-PURDUE UNIV, INDIANAPOLIS, 92-, ASSOC DEAN GEN EDUC, 96- *Personal Data:* b Kingsville, Tex, May 1, 55; m 77, Kenneth B Lipkowitz; c Nathan & Benjamin. *Educ:* Mont State Univ, BS, 76; Ind Univ, Bloomington, PhD(phys chem), 80. *Prof Exp:* Res assoc chem, Princeton Univ, 80-81. *Concurrent Pos:* Prin investr, Petrol Res Fund, Am Chem Soc & NSF, 87- *Mem:* Am Chem Soc; Am Phys Soc; Asn Women Sci (secy, 86-88). *Res:* Chemical oscillations, chaos, self-organization phenomena and biochemical and biophysical applications. *Mailing Add:* Chem Dept Ind Univ-Purdue Univ 402 N Blackford St Indianapolis IN 46202. *Fax:* 317-274-4701; *E-Mail:* larter@chem.iupui.edu

LARTIGUE, DONALD JOSEPH, BIOCHEMISTRY, ENZYMOLOGY. *Current Pos:* RETIRED. *Personal Data:* b Baton Rouge, La, Sept 7, 34; m 62; c 2. *Educ:* La State Univ, BS, 57, MS, 59, PhD(biochem), 65. *Prof Exp:* Analyst, US Food & Drug Admin, 59-60; marine biologist, Marine Lab, Univ Miami, 60; biochemist, USPHS Hosp, Carville, La, 60-62, R J Reynolds Tobacco Co, NC, 65-70; asst biochem, La State Univ, 62-63, assoc, 63-65; sr clin biochemist, J T Baker Chem Co, 70-71; sr res biochemist, Corning Glass Works, 71-74; clin chemist, Ochsner Clin, 74-76, Southern Baptist Hosp, 76-87; assoc prof med technol, La State Univ Med Ctr, 87-89, asst prof path, 90-95; clin chemist, Vet Admin Med Ctr, New Orleans, 90-95. *Concurrent Pos:* Vis prof, Wake Forest Univ, 68. *Mem:* Am Asn Clin Chemists. *Res:* Clinical chemistry; industrial enzymology; immobilized enzymes. *Mailing Add:* 135 Belle Grove Circle Vidalia LA 71373

LARUE, JAMES ARTHUR, MATHEMATICS. *Current Pos:* RETIRED. *Personal Data:* b Rivesville, WVa, Apr 24, 29; m 47; c 2. *Educ:* WVa Univ, AB, 48, MS, 49; Univ Pittsburgh, PhD(math), 61. *Prof Exp:* Asst prof math, Morris Harvey Col, 49-54; from asst prof to prof math, Fairmont State Col, 54-88, chmn dept, 65-88. *Res:* Mathematical analysis; divergent series. *Mailing Add:* 1114 S Park Dr Fairmont WV 26554

LA RUE, JERROLD A, METEOROLOGY. *Current Pos:* RETIRED. *Personal Data:* b San Bernardino, Calif, June 22, 23; m 46; c 2. *Educ:* Univ Calif, Los Angeles, BA, 48. *Prof Exp:* Gen meteorologist, US Weather Bur, Nat Weather Serv, 51-55, forecast meteorologist, 55-57, meteorologist proj analyst, 57-60, quant precipitation meteorologist, 60-64, sect supvr meteorol, 64-68, br chief, 68-69, meteorologist in chg, Weather Serv Off, Washington, DC, 69-80. *Mem:* Am Meteorol Soc; Nat Weather Asn. *Res:* Objective methods adapted to operational meteorology. *Mailing Add:* 5550 Rio Vida Lane Sebastopol CA 95472

LARUE, ROBERT D(EAN), computer graphics, computer aided design, for more information see previous edition

LA RUSSA, JOSEPH ANTHONY, ELECTRO-OPTICS, ENGINEERING PHYSICS. *Current Pos:* PRES, SURG MICROSYST INC, 72- *Personal Data:* b New York, NY, May 10, 25; m 46; c 3. *Educ:* City Col NY, BME, 49; Columbia Univ, MS, 55. *Honors & Awards:* De Florez Award, Am Inst Aeronaut & Astronaut, 68. *Prof Exp:* Sr vpres & tech dir, Farrand Optical Co Inc, 52-88. *Concurrent Pos:* Lectr flight simulation, Univ Dayton, 80; bd mem, Microsurg Res Found, 75- *Mem:* NY Acad Sci; Am Inst Aeronaut & Astronaut. *Res:* Development of many optical systems for spaceflight simulators including Mercury, Gemini, Apollo, LEM, T-27 and for major air force simulators; developed many surgical instruments for ophthalmological surgeons; research on implantable artificial kidney; implantable artificial heart; implantable heart valves; 31 patents in engineering technologies. *Mailing Add:* 451 Rutledge Dr Yorktown Heights NY 10598

LA RUSSO, NICHOLAS F, MEDICINE BIOLOGY. *Current Pos:* PROF & CHMN, DIV GASTROENTEROL & DIR, CTR BASIC RES DIGESTIVE DIS, MAYO MED SCH CLIN & FOUND, 77- *Mailing Add:* Dept Internal Med Div Gastroenterol Mayo Clin 200 First St SW Rochester MN 55905-0001

LASAGA, ANTONIO C, GEOCHEMISTRY, PHYSICAL CHEMISTRY. *Current Pos:* PROF GEOCHEM, YALE UNIV, 84- *Personal Data:* b Havana, Cuba, Dec 17, 49; US citizen; m 73; c 2. *Educ:* Princeton Univ, BA, 71; Harvard Univ, MS, 73, PhD(chem physics), 76. *Honors & Awards:* F W Clarke Medal, Geochem Soc, 79; Award, Mineral Soc Am, 85. *Prof Exp:* Res asst chem, Harvard Univ, 73-76, lectr chem & geol, 76-77; from asst prof to prof geochem, Pa State Univ, 77-84. *Concurrent Pos:* NSF prin investr, 78-85; vis assoc prof, Yale Univ, 81; Guggenheim fel, 88. *Mem:* Geochem Soc; Am Geophys Union; fel Mineral Soc Am. *Res:* Kinetics and thermodynamics of geochemical processes, particularly modeling diagenetic reactions in the oceans; geochemical cycles; diffusion in silicates; non-equilibrium aspects of geothermometry; quantum mechanics of bonding in silicates; structure of silicate melts. *Mailing Add:* Dept Geol & Geophys Yale Univ PO Box 208109 New Haven CT 06520-8109

LASAGNA, LOUIS (CESARE), PHARMACOLOGY. *Current Pos:* acad dean, Med Sch, DEAN, SACKLER SCH GRAD BIOMED SCI TUFTS UNIV, 85-, DEAN SCI AFFAIRS, 95- *Personal Data:* b New York, NY, Feb 22, 23; m 46, Helen; c Nina, David, Maria, Kristin, Lisa, Peter & Christopher. *Educ:* Rutgers Univ, BS, 43; Columbia Univ, MD, 47. *Hon Degrees:* DSc (Hon), Hahnemann Med Sch, 80 & Rutgers Univ, 83. *Honors & Awards:* J Allyn Taylor Int Prize Med; Oscar B Hunter Award; Exp Therapeut Award, Am Soc Pharmacol & Exp Therapeut; Lilly Prize, Brit Pharmacol Soc. *Prof Exp:* Asst & instr pharmacol, Sch Med, Johns Hopkins Univ, 50-52, from asst prof to assoc prof med & from asst prof to assoc prof pharmacol & exp therapeut, 54-70; prof pharmacol, toxicol & med, Univ Rochester, 70-84. *Concurrent Pos:* Vis physician, Columbia Res Serv, Goldwater Mem Hosp, 51, 53 & 54; clin & res fel, Mass Gen Hosp, 52-54; lectr, Sch Med, Boston Univ, 52-54; res assoc, Harvard Univ, 53-54. *Mem:* Inst Med-Nat Acad Sci; Asn Am Physicians; Am Soc Pharmacol & Exp Therapeut; Am Soc Clin Invest; Am Fedn Clin Res. *Res:* Hypnotics; analgesics; psychological responses to drugs; placebos; clinical trials; prescribing patterns. *Mailing Add:* Sackler Sch 136 Harrison Ave Tufts Univ Boston MA 02111. *Fax:* 617-956-0375

LASALA, EDWARD FRANCIS, PHARMACEUTICAL CHEMISTRY, ORGANIC CHEMISTRY. *Current Pos:* RETIRED. *Personal Data:* b Lynn, Mass, June 15, 28; m 53; c 5. *Educ:* Mass Col Pharm, BS, 53, MS, 55, PhD(pharmaceut chem), 58. *Prof Exp:* From instr to prof chem, Mass Col Pharm, 58-91, chmn dept, 77-91. *Mem:* Am Chem Soc; Am Pharmaceut Asn. *Res:* Synthesis and biological studies of medicinal agents, chiefly analgesics and antiradiation agents. *Mailing Add:* 37 Highland Ave Saugus MA 01906

LASALLE, BERNARD, ANIMAL & PUBLIC HEALTH & HYGIENE, MICROBIOLOGY. *Current Pos:* BIOCONSULT, 86- *Personal Data:* b Joliette, Que, Jan 31, 13; US citizen; wid, Anna-Marie E Talbot. *Educ:* Univ Montreal, BSA, 34, DMV, 37. *Prof Exp:* Vet microbiologist, Animal Dis Res Inst, 37; vet meat inspection, Can Dept Agr, 37-40, field vet, Animal Dis Eradication, 40-42; lic mfr vet biol, Accurate Labs, 42-45; vet consult, Lab Hyg, Dept Nat Health & Welfare, Ottawa, 47-52; dir res & prod vet pharmaceut, Arnold Labs, 52-57; area vet, USDA Agr Res Serv, 57-58, vet biol inspector, 58-65, sr staff vet vet biol & stand, 66-86. *Mem:* Am Vet Med Asn; Int Asn Biol Asns; Am Asn Vet Immunologists; Am Asn Avian Pathologists. *Res:* Animal infectious and parasitic diseases; diagnostic, control, immunology and related biotechnologies. *Mailing Add:* 6200 Westchester Park Dr Apt 1212 College Park MD 20740-2840

LASATER, ERIC MARTIN, RETINAL NEUROPHYSIOLOGY. *Current Pos:* res asst prof, Univ Utah, 85-88, dir res, Dept Ophthal, 87-90, assoc prof, 88-92, VCHMN & DIR RES, DEPT OPHTHAL, UNIV UTAH, 91-, PROF OPHTHAL, 92- *Personal Data:* b Stuttgart, Ger, Jan 6, 53; US citizen. *Educ:* Colo State Univ, BS, 75; Univ Calif, Davis, MS, 77; Univ Tex, PhD(physiol & biophys), 80. *Honors & Awards:* William & Mary Greve Int Res Scholar, Res Prev Blindness, Inc, 91. *Prof Exp:* Fel, Harvard Univ, 80-84, lectr biol, 84-85. *Concurrent Pos:* Mem visual sci A2 study sect, Div Res Grants, NIH, 90- *Mem:* Soc Neurosci; Asn Res Vision & Ophthal; Int Soc Eye Res; Sigma Xi; Int Brain Res Orgn. *Res:* How retinal neurons process visual information; study anatomy and connectivity, physiology, and neuropharmacology of individual retinal neurons to understand how these cells function in both health and disease states; technical management. *Mailing Add:* Dept Ophthal Moran Eye Ctr 50 N Medical Dr Salt Lake City UT 84132. *Fax:* 801-581-3357; *E-Mail:* rlasater@jmec.med.utah.edu

LASATER, HERBERT ALAN, MATHEMATICAL STATISTICS, APPLIED STATISTICS. *Current Pos:* EXEC VPRES, TENN ASSOCS INT, INC, 84- *Personal Data:* b Paris, Tenn, Sept 11, 31; m 59, 84; c 2. *Educ:* Univ Tenn, BS, 57, MS, 62; Rutgers Univ, PhD(statist), 69. *Prof Exp:* Instr statist, Univ Tenn, Knoxville, 57-58; assoc statistician, Nuclear Div, Union Carbide Corp, 58-62; asst prof, Univ Tenn, Knoxville, 62-65 & 68-71, assoc prof statist, 71- *Concurrent Pos:* Lectr statist, Univ Tenn, 59-62; ed, J Qual Technol, 71-74. *Mem:* Am Statist Asn; fel Am Soc Qual Control; Sigma Xi. *Res:* Statistical quality control techniques. *Mailing Add:* 452 Wyndahm Hall Way Knoxville TN 37922

LASCA, NORMAN P, JR, QUATERNARY GEOLOGY, GEOARCHAEOLOGY. *Current Pos:* asst prof, Univ Wis-Milwaukee, 66-71, assoc prof geol, 71-76, asst to chancelor, 75-77, assoc dean grad sch, 77-80, chmn dept, 80-81 & 84-88, actg vchancellor, 81-82, PROF GEOL SCI, UNIV WIS-MILWAUKEE, 76- *Personal Data:* b Detroit, Mich, Oct 20, 34; m 65; c 2. *Educ:* Brown Univ, AB, 57; Univ Mich, MS, 61, PhD(geol), 65. *Prof Exp:* Res asst geol, Univ Mich, 60-61; teaching fel, 61-65; NATO res fel, Inst Geol, Univ Oslo, 65-66. *Concurrent Pos:* Assoc scientist, 71-76, sr scientist, Ctr Great Lakes Studies, Univ Wis-Milwaukee, 76-; fel acad admin, Am Coun Educ, 74-75. *Mem:* Fel Geol Soc Am; Am Asn Quaternary Res; Int Asn Quaternary Res; Glaciol Soc; Swedish Soc Anthrop & Geog; Sigma Xi. *Res:* Glacial geology and geomorphology of polar regions; river and lake ice formation and processes; Glacial-Pleistocene geology in Wisconsin, Geoarcheology in upper midwest. *Mailing Add:* Dept Geosci Univ Wis PO Box 413 Milwaukee WI 53201

LASCELLES, JUNE, MICROBIOLOGY, BIOCHEMISTRY. *Current Pos:* prof, 65-89, EMER PROF MICROBIOL, UNIV CALIF, LOS ANGELES, 89- *Personal Data:* b Sydney, Australia, Jan 23, 24. *Educ:* Univ Sydney, BSc, 44, MSc, 47; Oxford Univ, DPhil(microbial biochem), 52. *Prof Exp:* Mem external sci staff, Med Res Coun, Eng, 53-60; lectr microbial biochem, Oxford Univ, 60-65. *Concurrent Pos:* Rockefeller fel, 56-57; consult panel microbial chem, NIH, 73-77; ed, J Bact, 80-89. *Mem:* Am Soc Microbiol; Am Soc Biol Chemists; Brit Biochem Soc; Brit Soc Gen Microbiol. *Res:* Biochemistry of microorganisms; tetrapyrrole synthesis and regulation; bacterial photosynthesis. *Mailing Add:* Dept Microbiol & Molecular Genetics Univ Calif-Los Angeles Los Angeles CA 90024

LASCHEVER, NORMAN LEWIS, ELECTRICAL ENGINEERING. *Current Pos:* RETIRED. *Personal Data:* b Hartford, Conn, July 27, 18; m 42; c 4. *Educ:* Mass Inst Technol, BS, 40; Northeastern Univ, MSEE, 70. *Prof Exp:* Sect chief airborne commun & navig hq, Air Tech Command, Wright-Patterson AFB, Ohio, 46-55; asst dir res eng, Lab Electronics, Mass, 55-62; mgr radar eng, RCA Corp, 62-71, chief engr, Aerospace Systs Div, 71-76, prin scientist, Automated Systs Div, 76-83. *Mem:* Sr mem Inst Elec & Electronics Engrs; Sigma Xi. *Res:* Instrumentation of aircraft dynamics; development of aircraft communication and navigation equipment, airborne Doppler navigators and aerospace radar and transponder equipment. *Mailing Add:* 21310 Millbrook Ct Boca Raton FL 33498

LASEK, RAYMOND J, NEUROBIOLOGY. *Current Pos:* asst prof, 69-73, assoc prof, 74-78, PROF ANAT, CASE WESTERN RES UNIV, 79- *Personal Data:* b Chicago, Ill, Nov 25, 40; m 64; c 3. *Educ:* Utica Col, BA, 61; State Univ NY, PhD(anat), 67. *Prof Exp:* NIH res fel neuropath, McLean Hosp, Harvard Med Sch, 66-68 & neurobiol, Univ Calif, San Diego, 68-69. *Res:* Axonal transport; regulation of growth and differentiation in neurons; evolutionary neurobiology. *Mailing Add:* 23490 Letchworth Rd Beachwood OH 44122

LA SEUR, NOEL EDWIN, METEOROLOGY. *Current Pos:* from asst prof to assoc prof, 53-58, PROF METEOROL, FLA STATE UNIV, 58- *Personal Data:* b Stanhope, Iowa, June 25, 22; m 44; c 3. *Educ:* Univ Chicago, SB, 47, SM, 49, PhD(meteorol), 53. *Prof Exp:* From asst to instr, Univ Chicago, 48-52. *Mem:* AAAS; Am Meteorol Soc; Am Geophys Union; Royal Meteorol Soc. *Res:* Synoptic meteorology of temperature and tropical latitudes. *Mailing Add:* Dept Meteorol Fla State Univ Tallahassee FL 32306-1096

LASFARGUES, ETIENNE YVES, MICROBIOLOGY, ONCOLOGY. *Current Pos:* RETIRED. *Personal Data:* b Milhars, France, May 5, 16; nat US; wid; c 2. *Educ:* Univ Paris, BS, 35, DVM, 41. *Honors & Awards:* Jensen Prize, Fr Acad Med, 46; Silver & Bronze Medal, Pasteur Inst, 69. *Prof Exp:* Roux Found res fel microbiol, Pasteur Inst, France, 42-44, asst virol, 44-47; head lab virol, 50-55; Am Cancer Soc res fel cytol, Inst Cancer Res, Pa, 47-50; assoc microbiol, Col Physicians & Surgeons, Columbia Univ, 55-59, asst prof, 59-66; assoc mem, Dept Cytol Biophys, Inst Med Res, 66-77, head, Dept Tumor Cell Biol, 77-82. *Concurrent Pos:* Mem, Breast Cancer Task Force Comt, Nat Cancer Inst, 79-83. *Mem:* Am Soc Cell Biologists; Tissue Cult Asn; Int Soc Cell Biologists; Am Asn Cancer Res. *Res:* Viral oncology; cell transformation; cytogenetics. *Mailing Add:* 309 Bridgeboro Rd Moorestown NJ 08057

LASH, JAMES (JAY) W, developmental biology, anatomy, for more information see previous edition

LASH, TIMOTHY DAVID, HETEROCYCLIC CHEMISTRY, CHEMISTRY EDUCATORION. *Current Pos:* from asst prof to assoc prof, 84-93, PROF ORG CHEM, ILL STATE UNIV, 93- *Personal Data:* b Salisbury, Eng, Oct 13, 53; m 81, Susan Shirkey. *Educ:* Univ Exeter, BS, 75; Univ Wales, MSc, 77, PhD(org chem), 79. *Prof Exp:* Assoc, Univ Tex, Arlington, 79-81; vis asst prof chem, Univ Wis-River Falls, 81-82; asst prof org chem, Northern State Univ, 82-84. *Concurrent Pos:* Res grant, Petrol Res Fund, 85-, NSF, 90, 92-, NIH, 92-; Camille & Henry Dreyfus scholar, 96- *Mem:* Royal Soc Chem; Am Inst Chemists; Am Chem Soc; Int Soc Heterocyclic Chem; Sigma Xi; AAAS. *Res:* Synthetic and spectroscopic studies of heterocyclic compounds, particularly pyrroles, porphyrins and oxophlorins; synthesis and geochemical origins of petroporphyrins; studies of normal and abnormal heme biosynthesis; published over 60 articles. *Mailing Add:* Dept Chem Ill State Univ Normal IL 61790-4160. *E-Mail:* tdlash@rs6000.cmp.ilstu.edu

LASHEEN, ALY M, PLANT PHYSIOLOGY, HORTICULTURE. *Current Pos:* RETIRED. *Personal Data:* b Cairo, Egypt, Dec 27, 19; nat US; m 54; c 3. *Educ:* Cairo Univ, BS, 42; Univ Calif, Los Angeles, 49; Agr & Mech Col Tex, PhD(plant physiol, hort), 54. *Prof Exp:* Asst hort, Agr & Mech Col Tex, 50-53, res assoc plant physiol, 54-55; jr plant pathologist, Wash State Univ, 55-57, asst prof hort, 57-61; assoc prof plant physiol, AID Contract-Univ Ky, Indonesia, 61-65, prof, 65-67, prof hort, 67-77; prof hort, Aid Contract, Univ Minn, 77-79. *Concurrent Pos:* Hort adv & chief party, Univ Minn proj, Morocco, 70-79. *Mem:* Am Soc Hort Sci; Am Soc Plant Physiol. *Res:* Chemical analysis of macro and micro elements in plants; biochemical analysis of sugars and amino, organic and nucleic acids in plants; dormancy in seeds; effects of additives on plants; cold hardiness in plants; nature of dwarfing in apples. *Mailing Add:* 3607 Salisbury Dr Lexington KY 40510

LASHEN, EDWARD S, MICROBIOLOGY. *Current Pos:* RETIRED. *Personal Data:* b New York, NY, Aug 11, 34; m 57, Marilyn; c Lori (Spector), David & Jennifer (Caplin). *Educ:* Brooklyn Col, BS, 56; Rutgers Univ, MS, 62, PhD(microbiol), 65. *Prof Exp:* Res asst blood res, Jewish Chronic Dis Hosp, Brooklyn, NY, 56-57; res asst hemat & pharmacol, Wallace Labs Div, Carter Prod Inc, 57-61; sr microbiologist, Res Labs, Rohm & Haas Co, 64-75, head proj leader biocides, 75-81, res sect mgr biocides, 81-92. *Mem:* Am Soc Testing & Mat; Am Soc Microbiol; Soc Indust Microbiol. *Res:* Microbial transformation of thiourea and substituted thioureas; biodegradation of surfactants by sewage sludge and river water microflora; broad spectrum anti-microbial agents for application as industrial biocides. *Mailing Add:* 95 Valley Dr Furlong PA 18925

LASHER, GORDON (JEWETT), ASTROPHYSICS. *Current Pos:* assoc physicist, Res Lab, IBM Corp, 55-56, proj physicist, 56-58, RES STAFF MEM, IBM-THOMAS J WATSON RES CTR, 58- *Personal Data:* b Denver, Colo, Feb 1, 26; m 53; c 3. *Educ:* Rensselaer Polytech Inst, BS, 49; Cornell Univ, PhD(theoret physics), 54. *Prof Exp:* Staff physicist, Lawrence Radiation Lab, Univ Calif, 53-55. *Concurrent Pos:* Vis prof, Cornell Univ, 69-70; vis scholar, Stanford Univ, 80. *Mem:* Fel Am Phys Soc; Int Astron Union. *Res:* Applied mathematics with computer applications; solid state physics; superconductivity; theory of liquid crystals; general relativity; cosmology; theory of supernovae; lattice gauge theory; silicon dioxide and its silicon interface. *Mailing Add:* 50 Fuller Rd Briarcliff Manor NY 10510

LASHEWYCZ-RUBYCZ, ROMANA A, SCIENCE EDUCATION. *Current Pos:* Asst prof, 80-86, ASSOC PROF CHEM, HOBART & WILLIAM SMITH COLS, 86-, CHAIR, 89- *Personal Data:* b Newark, NJ, Mar 1, 52; m 81, Taras; c Adriana. *Educ:* Seton Hall Univ, BS, 74; State Univ NY, Buffalo, PhD(inorg chem), 79. *Concurrent Pos:* Vis asst prof, State Univ NY, Buffalo, 79-80, vis assoc prof, 91; vis asst prof, Univ Rochester, 84; mem exec comt, Geneva Chap, Sigma Xi, 87-89, deleg, 89-91. *Mem:* Am Chem Soc; Am Inst Physics; Am Crystallog Asn; Sigma Xi; Coun Undergrad Res. *Res:* Investigation of group VIII transition metal complexes; preparation of mixed-metal ruthenium-rhenium tetranuclear clusters and study of their behavior with acetylenes; kinetics of substitution reactions involving metal ions in metalloporphyrins; photosubstitution behavior of carbonyl complexes. *Mailing Add:* Dept Chem Hobart & William Smith Cols Geneva NY 14456-3397. *Fax:* 315-781-3587; *E-Mail:* rubycz%hws3@hws.bitnet

LASHLEY, GERALD ERNEST, NUMERICAL ANALYSES. *Current Pos:* FAC, DEPT MATH & COMPUT SCI, POINT LOMA NAZARENE COL, CALIF. *Personal Data:* b Johnstown, Pa, Sept 26, 35; m 55; c 3. *Educ:* Eastern Nazarene Col, BS, 57; Boston Univ, AM, 61; Boston Univ, EdD(math educ), 69. *Prof Exp:* High sch teacher, Mass, 58-63; assoc prof math, Eastern Nazarene Col, 64-72, chmn dept, 70-72; chmn, Div Natural Sci, Mt Vernon Nazarene Col, 72-76, dir, Acad Comput Ctr, 77-80, prof comput sci & math, 80- *Concurrent Pos:* Dir & instr, NSF In-Serv Inst Secondary Teachers, 64-72. *Mem:* Asn Comput Mach; Math Asn Am. *Mailing Add:* 3834 Del Mar Ave San Diego CA 92106

LASHMET, PETER K(ERNS), CHEMICAL ENGINEERING. *Current Pos:* ASSOC PROF CHEM ENG, RENSSELAER POLYTECH INST, 65-, DEPT EXEC OFFICER, 77- *Personal Data:* b Ann Arbor, Mich, Aug 28, 29; m 56; c 5. *Educ:* Univ Mich, BSE(chem eng) & BSE(math), 51, MSE, 52; Univ Del, PhD(chem eng), 62. *Prof Exp:* Process design engr, M W Kellogg Co, 52-53; from chem engr to sr chem engr, Air Prod & Chem, Inc, 58-60, mgr cryostat eng, 60-62, sr cryogenic specialist, 62-65. *Mem:* Am Chem Soc; Am Inst Chem Engrs. *Res:* Catalytic properties of ion exchange resins; cryogenic refrigeration processes; miniature and compact heat exchangers; heat exchanger dynamics; computer simulation of chemical processes; chemical separation processes. *Mailing Add:* Dept Chem Eng Rensselaer Polytech Inst Troy NY 12181

LASHMORE, DAVID S, MATERIALS SCIENCE, PHYSICAL METALLURGY. *Current Pos:* Res assoc metallurgist coatings, 77-79, GROUP LEADER ELECTRODEPOSITED COATINGS, NAT BUR STAND, 79- *Personal Data:* b Hempstead, NY, July 9, 46; m 70, Miriam; c 3. *Educ:* Univ Fla, BS, 69; Mich Technol Univ, MS, 70; Univ Va, PhD(mat sci), 77. *Honors & Awards:* Electrodeposition Res Award, Electrochem Soc; Blum Award; Res Award, Am Electroplaters; Bronze Medal, Dept Com. *Concurrent Pos:* Consult, B-08 Comt Aluminum Coatings, Am Soc Testing & Mat, 78-, Int Sci Orgn, TC107. *Mem:* Sigma Xi; Am Soc Metals; Am Electroplaters; Am Soc Testing & Mat; Am Soc Mech Engrs; Electrochem Soc; Int Sci Orgn. *Res:* Surface and interface properties; transmission electron microscopy; diffraction; electrocrystallization; anodizing; powder metallurgy superlattices; magnetic thin films. *Mailing Add:* Sect 855 Dept Com Nat Inst Sci Technol Washington DC 20234. *Fax:* 301-926-7679; *E-Mail:* Cashmore@enh.nist.gov

LASHNER, BRET AUERBACH, GASTROENTEROLOGY, INTERNAL MEDICINE. *Current Pos:* DIR, CTR INFLAMMATORY BOWEL DIS, CLEVELAND CLIN FOUND, 93- *Personal Data:* b Philadelphia, Pa, July 27, 54; m 88, Penny R Sterrn; c Molly & Allison. *Educ:* Haverford Col, AB, 76; NY Univ, MD, 80; Univ Ill, Chicago, MPH, 88. *Prof Exp:* Asst prof med

& gastroenterol, Univ Chicago, 86-93. *Mem:* Am Gastroenterol Asn; Am Col Gastroenterol. *Res:* Clinical epidemiology of gastrointestinal diseases, principally inflammatory bowel diseases. *Mailing Add:* Cleveland Clin Found Desk S-40 9500 Euclid Ave Cleveland OH 44195

LASHOF, JOYCE COHEN, MEDICINE, PUBLIC HEALTH. *Current Pos:* dean, Sch Pub Health, 82-91, prof, 91-94, EMER PROF PUB HEALTH, UNIV CALIF, BERKELEY, 94- *Personal Data:* b Philadelphia, Pa, Mar 27, 26; m 50, Richard K; c Judith, Carol & Daniel. *Educ:* Duke Univ, AB, 46. *Hon Degrees:* DSc, Med Col Pa, 83. *Prof Exp:* Intern, Bronx Hosp, New York, 50-51, asst resident med, 51-52; asst resident med, Montefiore Hosp, 52-53; Nat Found Infantile Paralysis fel, Yale Univ, 53-54; asst med & physician, Student Health Serv, Univ Chicago, 54-56, from instr to asst prof, Sch Med, 56-60; dir, Sect Prev Med & Clin Labs, Rush-Presby-St Luke's Med Ctr, 61-66, dir, Sect Community Med, 66-72, chmn dept prev med, 72-73; dir, Dept Pub Health, State Ill, 73-77; dep asst secy health progs, Dept HEW, 77-78; asst dir, Off Technol Assessment, US Cong, 78-81. *Concurrent Pos:* Staff physician, Union Health Serv, Inc, 60-61; asst attend physician, Presby-St Luke's Hosp, 60-61, assoc attend physician, 61-; clin asst prof med, Sch Med, Univ Ill, 61-64, assoc prof prev med, 64-71; prof, Rush Med Col, 71-77. *Mem:* Inst Med-Nat Acad Sci; fel Am Col Physicians; fel Am Pub Health Asn (pres, 91); Soc Med Adminr; fel Am Teachers Prev Med; fel Am Col Prev Med. *Res:* Internal medicine; medical care; author of numerous articles and publications. *Mailing Add:* Sch Pub Health Univ Calif Berkeley CA 94720

LASHOF, RICHARD KENNETH, MATHEMATICS. *Current Pos:* From instr to prof math, 54-88, chmn dept, 67-70, EMER PROF MATH, UNIV CHICAGO, 88- *Personal Data:* b Philadelphia, Pa, Nov 9, 22; m 50, Joyce Cohen; c Judith, Carol & Daniel. *Educ:* Univ Pa, BS, 43; Columbia Univ, PhD(math), 54. *Concurrent Pos:* NSF fel, 60-61; mem-at-large, Nat Res Coun; vis scholar, Oxford Univ, 64-65, Univ Va Advan Inst, 78-79 & Inst Advan Study, Princeton, NJ, 60, 70; sr res fel, UK, 81; vis prof, Univ Calif, Berkeley, 85-89, Math Sci Res Inst, 90. *Mem:* Am Math Soc; fel AAAS. *Res:* Algebraic topology; differential geometry. *Mailing Add:* 601 Euclid Ave Berkeley CA 94708

LASHOF, THEODORE WILLIAM, PHYSICS. *Current Pos:* RETIRED. *Personal Data:* b Philadelphia, Pa, June 27, 18; m 50, Barbara Hoskin; c Mark, Sheryl & David. *Educ:* Univ Pa, BS, 39, PhD(physics), 42. *Honors & Awards:* Testing Div Medal, Tech Asn Pulp & Paper Indust, 72; Award of Merit, Am Soc Testing & Mat, 75; Silver Medal, US Dept Com; W J Youden Award in Interlab Testing, 88. *Prof Exp:* Mem staff, Radiation Lab, Mass Inst Technol, 42-45; from instr to asst prof physics, Reed Col, 45-49; assoc prof, Mich Col Mining & Technol, 49-50; physicist, Mass Sect, Nat Inst Stand & Technol, 50-54, Paper Sect, 54-62, Appl Polymer Stand Sect, 62-64 & Eval Criteria Sect, 64-67, actg chief, Paper Stand Sect, 67-70, chief, Performance Criteria Sect, 70-74, prog mgr lab performance, 74-78, res assoc, 78-81, guest worker, 81-85. *Mem:* Fel Am Soc Testing & Mat; fel Tech Asn Pulp & Paper Indust. *Res:* Physical properties of paper; interlaboratory standardization; consumer product performance and safety; testing laboratory evaluation. *Mailing Add:* 415 Russell Ave Gaithersburg MD 20877

LASHOMB, JAMES HAROLD, ENTOMOLOGY. *Current Pos:* asst prof, 78-84, ASSOC PROF ENTOM, RUTGERS UNIV, 84- *Personal Data:* b Potsdam, NY, Oct 25, 42; m 69; c 2. *Educ:* Cornell Univ, BS, 70; Univ Md, College Park, MS, 73, PhD(entom), 75. *Prof Exp:* Res assoc entom, Miss State Univ, 75-78. *Mem:* AAAS; Entom Soc Am; Int Orgn Biol Control Noxious Animals & Plants. *Res:* Sampling of insect populations and natural enemies; parasitic insect distribution within plants and parasitic insect biology. *Mailing Add:* Dept Entom Rutgers Univ New Brunswick NJ 08903

LASIA, ANDRZEJ, ELECTROCHEMISTRY. *Current Pos:* asst prof, 83-87, assoc prof, 87-93, PROF, UNIV SHERBROOKE, 93- *Personal Data:* b Warsaw, Poland, Dec 23, 44; Can citizen; m 64, Pazio; c Peter. *Educ:* Univ Warsaw, Poland, MSc, 67, PhD(electrochem), 75. *Prof Exp:* Fel, Univ Guelph, Ont, 75-76, res assoc, 82-83; asst prof, Univ Warsaw, Poland, 77-82. *Concurrent Pos:* Vis prof, Univ Sao Paulo, Sao Carlos, 77, 92 & 93, Yohanns Kepler Univ, Austria, 88. *Mem:* Chem Inst Can; Electrochem Soc; Soc Electroanal Chem. *Res:* Mechanism and kinetics of electrochemical seachous, hydrogen, evolution and water electrolysis; relaxation and AC impedance techniques in electrochemistry; digital simulation of electrode processes. *Mailing Add:* Dept Chem Univ Sherbrooke Sherbrooke PQ J1K 2R1 Can. *Fax:* 819-821-8017; *E-Mail:* alasia@courrier.usherb.ca

LASIECKA, IRENA, APPLIED MATHEMATICS, PARTIAL DIFFERENTIAL EQUATIONS & CONTROL THEORY. *Current Pos:* PROF CONTROL THEORY, UNIV VA, 87- *Personal Data:* b Warsaw, Poland, Feb 4, 48; m 71; c 1. *Educ:* Univ Warsaw, MS, 72, PhD(appl math), 75. *Honors & Awards:* Creativity Exten Award, NSF, 89; Silver Core Award, Int Fedn Info Processes, 92. *Prof Exp:* Asst prof appl math, Polish Acad Sci, Warsaw, 75-78; vis scholar control theory, Univ Calif, Los Angeles, 78-80; from assoc prof to prof differential equation, Math Dept, Univ Fla, Gainesville, 80-87. *Concurrent Pos:* Assoc ed, J Appl Math & Optimization, 84-, Int J Math & Math Sci, 85-, Soc Indust & Appl Math J Control, Inst Elec & Electronics Engrs, Computational Optimization. *Mem:* Int Fedn Info Processes; Am Math Soc; Soc Indust & Appl Math. *Res:* Applied mathematics; control theory and optimization; partial differential equations; numerical analysis; author of approximately 100 research papers published in major journals. *Mailing Add:* Dept Appl Math Univ Va Charlottesville VA 22903

LASINSKI, BARBARA FORMAN, PLASMA PHYSICS. *Current Pos:* PHYSICIST PLASMA PHYSICS, LAWRENCE LIVERMORE LAB, 72- *Personal Data:* b New York, NY, Nov 28, 41; m 71; c 1. *Educ:* Barnard Col, BA, 62; Univ Rochester, PhD(physics), 68. *Prof Exp:* Res assoc high energy physics, Enrico Fermi Inst, Univ Chicago, 68-71. *Mem:* Am Phys Soc. *Res:* Computational simulation of plasmas; laser-plasma interactions; computational physics. *Mailing Add:* L-472 Lawrence Livermore Lab PO Box 808 Livermore CA 94550

LASKA, EUGENE, MATHEMATICS, STATISTICS. *Current Pos:* dir info sci div, Nathan S Kline Inst Psychiat Res, Orangeburg, NY, 63-84, DIR, STATIST SCI & EPI DIV, 84-, WHO COLLABORATING CTR RES & TRAINING, MENT HEALTH PROG MGT, NATHAN S KLINE INST PSYCHIAT RES, ORANGEBURG, NY, 85-; RES PROF PSYCHIAT, NY UNIV MED CTR, 79- *Personal Data:* b New York, NY, Mar 17, 38; m 59; c 3. *Educ:* City Col New York, BS, 59; NY Univ, MS, 61, PhD(math), 63. *Prof Exp:* Asst res scientist, Comput Lab, Res Div, NY Univ, 59-61, res assoc math, Courant Inst Math Sci, 61-62; systs engr, IBM, NJ, 62-63. *Concurrent Pos:* NIMH grants, 67-78; consult comput psychiat, USSR, Israel, Italy, Iran, Peru & Indonesia, China, Chile, Ecuador, Cuba, 68; mem, Comput & Biomath Sci Study Sect, NIH, 72-76; assoc comnr, NY State Dept Ment Hyg, 80. *Mem:* Fel AAAS; Inst Math Statist; fel Am Statist Asn; Am Soc Clin Pharmacol & Therapeut; Biomet Soc. *Res:* Mathematical statistics, including estimation theory; applied statistics, including biostatistics and clinical trial methodology; computers applications in medicine. *Mailing Add:* 34 Dante St Larchmont NY 10538

LASKAR, RENU CHAKRAVARTI, MATHEMATICS. *Current Pos:* assoc prof, 68-76, PROF MATH, CLEMSON UNIV, 76- *Personal Data:* b Bhagalpur, India, Aug 8, 32; m 62; c 2. *Educ:* Univ Bihar, BS, 54; Univ Bhagalpur, MS, 57; Univ Ill, Urbana, PhD(group theory), 62. *Prof Exp:* Lectr math, Ranchi Women's Col, India, 57-59; lectr, Indian Inst Technol, Kharagpur, 62-65; fel, Univ NC, Chapel Hill, 65-68. *Concurrent Pos:* Guest mathematician, Univ Paris, 75-76. *Mem:* Am Math Soc; Math Asn Am. *Res:* Group theory; combinatorial mathematics, especially graph theory. *Mailing Add:* Dept Math Sci Box 341907 Clemson Univ Clemson SC 29634-1907

LASKARIS, EVANGELOS TRIFON, MECHANICAL & ELECTRICAL ENGINEERING. *Current Pos:* Mech engr advan eng, Large Steam-Turbine Generator Dept, 67-73, cryog br, Power Generation & Propulsion Lab, 73-77, MGR APPL SUPERCONDUCTIVITY PROG, ENGR SYSTS LAB, GEN ELEC CO, 77- *Personal Data:* b Cairo, Egypt, Jan 14, 44; US citizen; m 71; c 2. *Educ:* Nat Tech Univ Athens, BS, 66; Rensselaer Polytech Inst, MS, 71, PhD(mech eng), 74. *Honors & Awards:* Gold & Silver Patent Awards, Corp Res & Develop, Gen Elec Co; IR-100 Award, Indust Res Mag, 77. *Mem:* Greek Chamber Engrs. *Res:* Superconductivity; cryogenics; computational fluid dynamics; rotating machinery; intense magnetic fields. *Mailing Add:* Res & Develop Bldg K-1 Rm EP117 Gen Elec Schenectady NY 12301

LASKER, BARRY MICHAEL, ASTROPHYSICS. *Current Pos:* ASTRONR, SPACE TELESCOPE SCI INST, 81- *Personal Data:* b Hartford, Conn, Aug 12, 39; m 70; c 2. *Educ:* Yale Univ, BS, 61; Princeton Univ, MA, 63, PhD(astrophys sci), 64. *Prof Exp:* NSF fel, Mt Wilson & Palomar Observ, 65-67; asst prof astron, Univ Mich, 67-69; staff astronr, Cerro Tololo Interam Observ, Chile, 69-81. *Mem:* Am Astron Soc; Int Astron Union. *Res:* Supernova remnants; interstellar medium in galaxies; astronomical instrumentation; catalogs of stars and galaxies; digitized sky surveys. *Mailing Add:* Space Telescope Sci Inst 3700 San Martin Dr Baltimore MD 21218. *E-Mail:* lasker@stsci.edu

LASKER, GABRIEL (WARD), BIOLOGICAL ANTHROPOLOGY, HUMAN ANATOMY. *Current Pos:* From instr to prof, 46-82, EMER PROF ANAT, SCH MED, WAYNE STATE UNIV, 82- *Personal Data:* b York, Eng, Apr 29, 12; US citizen; m 49, Bernice A Kaplan; c Robert A, Edward M & Anne T. *Educ:* Univ Mich, AB, 34; Harvard Univ, MA, 41, PhD(phys anthrop), 45. *Honors & Awards:* Charles Darwin Award, Am Asn Phys Anthropologists; Franz Boas Award, Human Biol Asn. *Concurrent Pos:* Viking Fund grant, Paracho, Michoacan, Mex, 48; ed, Human Biol, 53-87; mem staff, Dept Anthrop, Univ Wis, 54-55; Fulbright fel, Peru, 57-58; adj prof anthrop, Wayne State Univ, 82-; fel commoner, Churchill Col, Cambridge Univ, 83-84. *Mem:* Fel AAAS (vpres, 68); Am Asn Phys Anthrop (secy-treas, 46-50, vpres, 60-62, pres, 63-64); Am Asn Anat; fel Am Anthrop Asn; hon mem Soc Study Human Biol; Human Biol Coun (pres, 83-84); Soc Mexicana de Antrop Biol. *Res:* Demographic aspects of human biology; human genetics; physical anthropology; physical characteristics of Chinese, Mexicans and Peruvians; population structure Britain; biological aspects of human migration. *Mailing Add:* Dept Anat & Cell Biol Sch Med Wayne State Univ Detroit MI 48201. *Fax:* 313-577-3125

LASKER, GEORGE ERIC, INFORMATION SCIENCES, PSYCHOLOGY. *Current Pos:* PROF COMPUT SCI, UNIV WINDSOR, 68- *Personal Data:* b Prague, Czech; Can citizen. *Educ:* Prague Tech Univ, EC, 57; Charles Univ, Prague, DP, 61. *Prof Exp:* Asst prof math, Univ Sask, 65-66; assoc prof comput sci, Univ Man, 66-68. *Concurrent Pos:* Nat Res Coun Can grant, Univ Man, 66-68; ed bd, Int J Gen Systs, 74-; vis scholar, Dept Comput & Commun Sci, Univ Mich, Ann Arbor, 74-; distinguished vis, Inst Elec & Electronics Engrs Comput Soc Prog, 79-82; pres, Int Cong Appl Systs Res & Cybernet, 80-; chmn, Soc Gen Systs Res Conf, 82-83; dir, Int Inst Advan Studies Systs Res Cybernet, 83; dir, Int Conf Systs Res, Informatics & Cybernet, Baden, WGer, 85. *Mem:* Can Comput Sci Asn; World Orgn Gen Systs & Cybernet; NY Acad Sci. *Res:* Diagnostic methodology; artificial intelligence; biomimetic engineering; expert systems; cerebrometic design of computers;

simulation models; behavioral prediction; computer controlled conditioning; mathematical psychology; forecasting methodology; computer applications; psychotronics; psychocybernetics; quality of life; expert educational systems; systems models of brain; synergetics. *Mailing Add:* Dept Comput Sci Univ Windsor 401 Sunset Ave Windsor ON N9B 3P4 Can

LASKER, HOWARD ROBERT, MARINE BENTHIC ECOLOGY, ECOLOGY OF GORGONIAN CORALS. *Current Pos:* from asst prof to assoc prof, 79-94, PROF BIOL SCI, STATE UNIV NY, BUFFALO, 94- *Personal Data:* b New York, NY, Feb 8, 52; c 2. *Educ:* Univ Rochester, BS, 72, MS, 73; Univ Chicago, PhD(geophys sci), 78. *Prof Exp:* Fel, Rosenstiel Sch Marine & Atmospheric Sci, Univ Miami, 78-79. *Concurrent Pos:* Vis researcher, Smithsonian Trop Res Inst, 79- *Mem:* Ecol Soc Am; Soc Integrative & Comp Biol; Am Soc Naturalists; Int Soc Reef Studies. *Res:* Ecology of corals and coral reefs; reproductive biology of benthic invertebrates ecology of algal-coelenterate symbioses; population biology of benthic invertebrates. *Mailing Add:* Dept Biol Sci State Univ NY Buffalo NY 14260. *Fax:* 716-645-2975; *E-Mail:* hlasker@acsu.buffalo.edu

LASKER, SIGMUND E, PHYSICAL CHEMISTRY, BIOPHYSICS. *Current Pos:* asst prof biophys, NY Med Col, 66-72, asst prof pharmacol, 72-75, assoc prof, 75-82, PROF MED RES, NY MED COL, 82- *Personal Data:* b New York, NY, Sept 5, 23; m 65, Lorraine Rettig; c Johanna. *Educ:* Brooklyn Col, BS, 49; NY Univ, MS, 51; Stevens Inst Technol, PhD(phys chem), 65. *Prof Exp:* Res assoc surg, NY Med Col, 57-60, asst instr biochem, 58-60; res assoc phys chem, Stevens Inst Technol, 60-66. *Concurrent Pos:* Adj assoc prof, Rockefeller Univ, 68-80. *Mem:* Soc Magnetic Resonance Med; Biophys Soc; Am Chem Soc; NY Acad Sci; Am Heart Asn; Sigma Xi; NY Acad Med. *Res:* Magnetic resonance imaging; polyelectrolytes; experimental thermal injuries; anticoagulants. *Mailing Add:* Dept Med NY Med Col Valhalla NY 10595. *Fax:* 914-993-4694

LASKI, BERNARD, PEDIATRICS, HEMATOLOGY. *Current Pos:* PROF PEDIAT, UNIV TORONTO, 77- *Personal Data:* b Ont, Nov 11, 15; m 47; c 2. *Educ:* Univ Toronto, MD, 39, FRCP(C), 49; Am Acad Pediat, FAAP, 49. *Concurrent Pos:* Chief Pediat, Mt Sinai Hosp, 54-; sr physician, Hosp for Sick Children, 49. *Mem:* Am Pediat Soc; Am Soc Pediat Res; Can Pediat Soc; Am Soc Hemat; Am Acad Pediat. *Mailing Add:* 99 Avenue Rd Toronto ON M5S 2G5 Can

LASKIN, ALLEN I, MICROBIAL TRANSFORMATIONS & BIODEGRADATION. *Current Pos:* RES FEL, CHARLES A DANA RES INST, DREW UNIV, 89- *Personal Data:* b Brooklyn, NY, Dec 7, 28; m 54, 73, Barbara Lawrence; c Jared & Amy. *Educ:* City Col New York, BS, 50; Univ Tex, MA, 52, PhD, 56. *Honors & Awards:* Charles A Thom Award, Soc Indust Microbiol, 92; I M Lewis Award, 77; Selman A Waksman Hon Lectr, Theobald Smith Soc, 74. *Prof Exp:* Res scientist, Univ Tex, 53-55; sr res microbiologist, Squibb Inst Med Res, 55-64, res supvr microbiol, 64-67, asst dir microbiol, 67-69; res assoc, 69-74, sr res assoc, 74-84, head, Biosci Res, Exxon Res & Eng Co, 71-85; assoc dir, NJ Ctr Adv Biotechnol & Med, 85-86; vpres res & develop, Matrix Res Labs, 86-88, pres, 88-89; vpres res & develop, Ethigen Corp, 86-89. *Concurrent Pos:* Vis scholar, Rutgers Univ, 92-93. *Mem:* Soc Indust Microbiol (pres, 78-79); Am Soc Microbiol; Am Chem Soc; fel Am Acad Microbiol; fel NY Acad Sci. *Res:* Cell-free protein synthesis; mode of action of antibiotics; mechanisms of bacterial resistance to antibiotics; microbial transformations of steroids; petroleum microbiology; microbial enzymes; transformations and biodegradation of hydrocarbons and related compounds; BIOREMEDIATION. *Mailing Add:* 383 S Middlebush Rd Somerset NJ 08873. *Fax:* 732-873-8618; *E-Mail:* ailaskin@aol.com

LASKIN, DANIEL M, ORAL SURGERY, MAXILLOFACIAL SURGERY. *Current Pos:* clin asst, Col Dent, Univ Ill, 49-50, res asst, 50-51, from instr to assoc prof, 51-60, prof oral & maxillofacial surg, 60-, assoc head dept, 62-73, head dept, 73-83, EMER PROF ORAL & MAXILLOFACIAL SURG, UNIV ILL, 83-; PROF & CHMN, DEPT ORAL & MAXILLOFACIAL SURG, MED COL VA, 84- *Personal Data:* b New York, NY, Sept 3, 24; m 45, Eve Mohel; c Jeffrey, Gary & Marla. *Educ:* Ind Univ, BS & DDS, 47; Univ Ill, MS, 51; Am Bd Oral & Maxillofacial Surg, dipl; FRCS; FRCPS(G). *Honors & Awards:* Res Recognition Award, Am Asn Oral & Maxillofacial Surgeons, 78; W Harry Archer Award, 81; Francis N Reichman Lectr, 71; Simon P Hullihen Mem Award, WVA Univ, 76; Arnold K Maislen Mem Award, 77; William J Gies Oral Surg Award, 79; Cordwainer Lectr, Univ London, 80; Heidbrink Award, Am Dent Soc Anesthesiol, 83; Rene LeFort Medal, Brazilian Col Oral & Maxillofacial Surg & Traumatology, 85; Distinguished Serv Award, Am Soc Oral Surgeons, 72; Arnold K Maislen Mem Award Oral Surg, 77; Hinman Medallion, 81; Edward C Hinds Lectr, 90; Norton M Ross Award Excellence Clin Res, 94. *Prof Exp:* Intern oral surg, Jersey City Med Ctr, 47-48. *Concurrent Pos:* Resident, Cook County Hosp, 50-51, chmn dept oral surg, 67-72, dep chmn, 77-; attend oral surg, Hosps, 52-; clin prof surg, Univ Ill Hosp, 61-83, head, Dept Dent, 78-83; ed, Am Asn Oral Maxillofacial & Surgeons Forum, J Oral & Maxillofacial Surg & Oral & Maxillofacial Implants; dir, Temporamandibular Joint & Facial Pain Res Ctr, 61-83; attend oral surgeon, Skokie Valley Community Hosp, 77-83, Swed Covenant Hosp, 79-83 & Edgewater Hosp, head dept, 70-83; consult oral surgeon, Ill Masonic Hosp, 65-83 & Bethany Methodist Hosp, 78-83; chmn & attnd oral surgeon, Div Oral Surg, Cook County Hosp, 67-76, dep chmn, 76-83; attend oral & maxillofacial surgeon, Richmond Eye & Ear Hosp & Med Col Va Hosps, 84-; head, Dept Dent, Med Col Va Hosps, 86-; ed-in-chief, J Oral & Maxillofacial Surg, 72-; bd dirs, Am Pain Soc, 78-80. *Mem:* Sigma Xi; Int Asn Dent Res; Soc Exp Biol & Med; Am Soc Exp Path; Am Dent Asn; Am Asn Dent Res; fel AAAS; Am Asn Oral & Maxillofacial Surgeons (pres, 76-77); Int Asn Oral & Maxillofacial Surgeons (pres, 83-86, secy-gen, 89-95). *Res:* Temporomandibular joint; metabolism of bone and cartilage; sutural growth; calcification and resorption of bone; over 700 publications in fields of oral and maxillofacial surgery and dental research and co-author of nine books. *Mailing Add:* Dept Oral & Maxillofacial Surg Va Commonwealth Univ PO Box 980566 Richmond VA 23298-0566. *E-Mail:* dlaskin@gems.vcu.edu

LASKOWSKI, EDWARD L, COMPUTER INTEGRATED MANUFACTURING, SENSORS. *Current Pos:* VPRES TECHNOL, ACME CLEVELAND CORP, 86- *Personal Data:* b Cleveland, Ohio, Mar 13, 43; m 72; c 2. *Educ:* Univ Detroit, BEE, 66; Ohio State Univ, MSEE, 68; Cleveland State Univ, DEng, 78. *Prof Exp:* Res engr, Gen Elec Co, 68-79; mgr advan systs, Bendix Corp, 79-85, dir res, 85-86. *Mem:* Inst Elec & Electronics Engrs; Soc Mfg Engrs; Nat Elec Mfrs Asn. *Res:* Intelligent sensors and systems; manufacturing computer systems; systems modeling; analysis of physical processes to be used as component of control system model; marketing new products. *Mailing Add:* 6154 Winchester Dr Independence OH 44131

LASKOWSKI, LEONARD FRANCIS, JR, MEDICAL MICROBIOLOGY, CLINICAL MICROBIOLOGY. *Current Pos:* Instr bact, St Louis Univ, 46-48 & 51-53, sr instr, 53-54, asst prof microbiol, 54-57, from asst prof to prof path, 57-90, assoc prof internal med, 77-90, EMER PROF PATH & INTERNAL MED, SCH MED, ST LOUIS UNIV, 90- *Personal Data:* b Milwaukee, Wis, Nov 16, 19; m 46, Frances Bielinski; c Leonard F III, James & Thomas. *Educ:* Marquette Univ, BS, 41, MS, 48; St Louis Univ, PhD(med bact), 51; Am Bd Med Microbiol, dipl. *Concurrent Pos:* China Med Bd fel, Latin Am, 57; fel trop med, La State Univ, 57; consult, St Mary's Group Hosp, 57-; attend, Vet Admin Hosp, health & tech training coordr, Latin Am Peace Corps Projs, 62-66; dir, Clin Microbiol Sect, St Louis Univ Hosps, 65; consult clin microbiol, John Cochran Vet Hosp, 66-, St Elizabeth's Hosp, Belleville, Ill, 68- & St Louis Co Hosp, 69-; referee mycol, USPHS Commun Dis Ctr Prog Testing Clin Diag Labs, 68-; consult, Jefferson Barracks, Vet Hosp, 72-, Mogul Diag Div, Mogul Corp, 72-79, St Francis Hosp, 74-77, St Elizabeth's Hosp, Granite City, Ill, 78- & St Louis Co & City Med Examr, 78- *Mem:* NY Acad Sci; Am Soc Microbiol; AAAS; fel Am Acad Microbiol; Med Mycol Soc Americas; Sigma Xi. *Res:* Mechanism of intracellular parasitism; mechanism of action of therapeutic compounds. *Mailing Add:* 6229 Robertsville Rd Villa Ridge MO 63089

LASKOWSKI, MICHAEL, JR, BIOCHEMISTRY. *Current Pos:* from asst prof to assoc prof, 57-65, PROF CHEM, PURDUE UNIV, 65- *Personal Data:* b Warsaw, Poland, Mar 13, 30; nat US; m 57, Joan Heyer; c Michael & Marta. *Educ:* Lawrence Col, BS, 50; Cornell Univ, PhD(phys chem), 54. *Honors & Awards:* McCoy Award, Purdue Univ, 75; Alfred Jurzykowski Found Award, 77. *Prof Exp:* Asst chem, Cornell Univ, 50-52, USPHS fel, 52-56, instr, 56-57. *Concurrent Pos:* Chmn, Gordon Res Conf Physics & Phys Chem Biopolymers, 66, Proteolytic Enzymes & Inhibitors, 82; mem, Biophys & Biophys Chem Study Sect, NIH, 67-71; counr, Am Chem Soc, 84-87; vis prof, Yale Univ, 71, Alberta Univ, 81, Osaka Univ, 85 & Univ Calif, San Francisco, 86. *Mem:* AAAS; Am Chem Soc; Am Soc Biol Chemists; Polish Inst Arts & Sci Am; AAAS; Biophys Soc; Protein Soc. *Res:* Protein chemistry; role of individual amino acid residues in proteinase inhibitor-proteinase interaction; evolution; 05388053xic enzymes and their inhibitors. *Mailing Add:* Dept Chem Purdue Univ West Lafayette IN 47907-1393. *Fax:* 765-494-0239; *E-Mail:* cws@omni.cc.purdue.edu

LASKOWSKI, MICHAEL BERNARD, EXPERIMENTAL BIOLOGY. *Current Pos:* PROF PHYSIOL, DEPT BIOL SCI, UNIV IDAHO, 88-, DIR, WAMI PROG, 88- *Personal Data:* b Chicago, Ill, Apr 20, 43. *Educ:* Loyola Univ, BS, 66; Univ Okla, PhD(physiol), 70. *Prof Exp:* Muscular Dystrophy Asn postdoctoral fel, Dept Biol Sci, Northwestern Univ, 70-71, Dept Pharmacol, Vanderbilt Univ, 71-72, instr, 72-74, asst prof, 74-76; from asst prof to prof physiol, St Louis Univ Sch Med, 76-88, asst dean students, 85-88, actg chmn dept, 87-88. *Concurrent Pos:* Andrew Mellon career develop award, 74-76; vis scientist, Dept Physiol & Biophys, Wash Univ, 84-85; dir, Regional Med Educ Prog, Univ Idaho/Wash State Univ, 88. *Mem:* Sigma Xi; Am Physiol Soc; Am Acad Neurol; Soc Neurosci. *Mailing Add:* WAMI Med Prog Univ Idaho Health Ctr Moscow ID 83843

LASKY, JACK SAMUEL, ORGANIC CHEMISTRY, POLYMER CHEMISTRY. *Current Pos:* CONSULT, 95- *Personal Data:* b New York, NY, Mar 14, 30; m 52; c 2. *Educ:* City Col New York, BS, 51; Univ Md, PhD(chem), 55. *Prof Exp:* Res chemist, US Rubber Co, 55-69; dir polymer res, Onkonite Co, 69-70, vpres res, 70-76, vpres res & eng, 76-95. *Mem:* Am Chem Soc; Inst Elec & Electronics Engrs; Power Eng Soc. *Res:* Synthetic polymers; rubber; plastics; stereospecific polymerization; heterogeneous catalysis; kinetics of reactions; electrical insulating and covering materials. *Mailing Add:* 29 Newman Ave Verona NJ 07044

LASKY, LAWRENCE ALAN, MOLECULAR BIOLOGY, CELL ADHESIONS & INFLAMMATION. *Current Pos:* res scientist, 82-85, sr scientist, 85-91, STAFF SCIENTIST, GENENTECH, 91- *Personal Data:* b Los Angeles, Calif, Apr 15, 51. *Educ:* Univ Calif, Los Angeles, BS, 73, PhD(molecular biol), 78. *Prof Exp:* Fel develop biol, Calif Inst Technol, 78-81; sr scientist, Genetics Inst, 81-82. *Mem:* Am Soc Cell Biol; Am Soc Invest Path. *Res:* Molecular biology; cell adhesions and inflammation. *Mailing Add:* Molecular-Oncol Genetech Inc 460 Point San Bruno Blvd South San Francisco CA 94080

LASKY, RICHARD DAVID, ANALYTICAL BIOCHEMISTRY, GLYCOBIOLOGY. *Current Pos:* SCIENTIST IV, CHARACTERIZATION, HYLAND DIV, BAXTER HEALTHCARE CORP, 92- *Personal Data:* b Galesburg, Ill, Aug 23, 50; m, Alice Liberfarb; c Mara & Juliet. *Educ:* Occidental Col, BA, 72; San Francisco State Univ, MA, 81; Univ Calif, Davis, PhD(biochem), 83. *Prof Exp:* Fel, Lab Carbohydrates Res, Harvard Med Sch, 83-85, Dept Biochem, Univ Calif-Berkeley, 85-87; staff scientist, Barnett Inst Chem Analysis, Northeastern Univ, 87-88; res scientist, Imreg, Inc, 88-91. *Mem:* Soc Glycobiol; Am Soc Biochem & Molecular Biol; Protein Soc. *Res:* Characterization of recombinant monoclonal antibodies and recombinant Factor VIII (rAHF); SDS-PAGE analysis, SEC-HPLC, IEF, capillary electrophoresis, peptide mapping, protein sequence analysis and oligosaccharide analysis. *Mailing Add:* Hyland Div Baxter Biotech 1720 Flower Ave Duarte CA 91010. *Fax:* 626-357-8348; *E-Mail:* rickster1@aol.com

LASLETT, LAWRENCE JACKSON, physics; deceased, see previous edition for last biography

LASLEY, BILL LEE, REPRODUCTIVE PHYSIOLOGY. *Current Pos:* RES ENDOCRINOLOGIST, SAN DIEGO ZOOL GARDEN, 75- *Personal Data:* b Ottumwa, Iowa, June 4, 41. *Educ:* Calif State Univ, Chico, BA, 63; Univ Calif, Davis, PhD(physiol), 72. *Prof Exp:* Teacher math & sci, Roseville Union High Sch, 64-67; fel reproductive biol, Rockefeller Found, 72-75. *Mem:* Endocrin Soc; Soc Gyn Invest; Soc Study Reproduction. *Res:* Reproductive endocrinology with emphasis on comparative studies. *Mailing Add:* 301 Del Oro Ave Davis CA 95616

LASLEY, JOHN FOSTER, animal breeding; deceased, see previous edition for last biography

LASLEY, STEPHEN MICHAEL, NEUROTOXICOLOGY, NEUROCHEMISTRY. *Current Pos:* asst prof, 86-94, ASSOC PROF, DEPT BASIC SCI, COL MED, UNIV ILL, PEORIA, 94- *Personal Data:* b Louisville, Ky, Feb 12, 50; m 74, Carolyn J Culver; c Michael & David. *Educ:* Univ Louisville, MEng, 73, PhD(neuropsychopharmacol), 79. *Prof Exp:* Fel neurotoxicol, Col Med Univ Cincinnati, 79-82, res assoc, 82-83; sci assoc pharmacol, Tex Col Osteop Med, Ft Worth, 83-85, res asst prof pharmacol, 85-86. *Concurrent Pos:* Mem placement comt, Soc Toxicol, 92-96, dir, 96-97; chair, Instnl animal care & use comt, 95- *Mem:* AAAS; Soc Neurosci; Soc Toxicol; Am Soc Pharmacol & Exp Therapeut. *Res:* Neurochemical mechanisms involved in epileptogenesis; environmental neurotoxicology of lead exposure. *Mailing Add:* Dept Biomed & Therapeut Scis Univ Ill PO Box 1649 Peoria IL 61656. *Fax:* 309-671-8403; *E-Mail:* SML@uic.edu

LASS, JONATHAN H, CORNEA & EXTERNAL DISEASES, OPHTHALMOLOGY. *Current Pos:* from asst prof to assoc prof, 79-93, actg chmn ophthal, 93-94, CHARLES I THOMAS PROF, DEPT OPHTHAL, CASE WESTERN RES UNIV, 93-, CHMN, DEPT OPHTHAL, 94- *Personal Data:* b Orange, NJ, July 14, 49; m 70, Leah; c Michael & Jessica. *Educ:* Boston Univ, BA, 72, MD, 73. *Honors & Awards:* Honor Award, Am Acad Ophthal, 87. *Prof Exp:* Clin fel ophthal, Mass Eye & Ear Infirmary, 77-79; Active staff ophthal, Winchester Hosp, Mass, 77-80; asst ophthalmologist, MetroHealth Med Ctr, 79-; corneal consult, courtesy staff, Mt Sinai Med Ctr, 81-; assoc ophthalmologist, Univ Hosps, Cleveland, 85-93, ophthalmologist & actg dir ophthal, 93-; dir ophthal, Univ Hosp, 94. *Mem:* Int Soc Refractive Keratoplasty; Asn Res Vision & Ophthal; Am Acad Ophthal; Eye Bank Asn Am; Contact Lens Asn Ophthalmologists. *Res:* Role of cytokines in the pathogenesis of onchocercal keratitis; develop improved methods for corneal preservation. *Mailing Add:* 11100 Euclid Ave Cleveland OH 44106-5068

LASS, NORMAN J(AY), EXPERIMENTAL PHONETICS, SPEECH & HEARING SCIENCES. *Current Pos:* from asst prof to assoc prof, 69-77, chmn dept, 74-83, PROF SPEECH PATH & AUDIOL, WVA UNIV, 77- *Personal Data:* b Brooklyn, NY, Sept 20, 43; m 67, Martha Greenberger; c Laura S & Jonathan E. *Educ:* Brooklyn Col, City Univ NY, BA, 65; Purdue Univ, MA, 66, PhD(speech path, speech & hearing sci), 68. *Prof Exp:* Res fel, Bur Child Res, Univ Kans Med Ctr, Kansas City, 68-69. *Concurrent Pos:* Consult, Audiol & Speech Path Serv, Vet Admin Med Ctr, Martinsburg, WVa, 75-83. *Mem:* Fel Am Speech-Lang Hearing Asn; Acoust Soc Am; Am Asn Phonetic Sci; Int Soc Phonetic Sci; Am Cleft Palate-Craniofacial Asn. *Res:* Listener attitudes toward vocal characteristics and communicative disorders; listener attitudes toward regional dialects, subjects perceptions of and attitudes toward persons with craniofacial anomalies; listener attitudes toward accented English. *Mailing Add:* Dept Speech Path & Audiol WVa Univ PO Box 6122 Morgantown WV 26506-6122. *Fax:* 304-293-7565; *E-Mail:* nlass@wvu.edu

LASSEN, LAURENCE E, FORESTRY. *Current Pos:* RETIRED. *Personal Data:* b Milwaukee, Wis, Dec 16, 32; m 59; c 2. *Educ:* Iowa State Univ, BS, 54, MS, 58; Univ Mich, PhD(forestry), 67. *Prof Exp:* Res forest prod technologist, Forest Prod Lab, Wis, 58-67, proj leader, 67-71; staff asst res admin, US Forest Serv, 71-72; chief forest prod technol res, Washington, DC, 72-74, dep dir, 74-76, dir, Southern Forest Exp Sta, New Orleans, 76-83, dir, Intermountain Res Sta, Ogden, Ut, 83-92. *Mem:* Soc Am Foresters; Sigma Xi; Soc Range Mgt. *Res:* Forestry research. *Mailing Add:* 4882 Knollwood Dr Ogden UT 84403-4424

LASSER, ELLIOTT CHARLES, MEDICINE, RADIOLOGY. *Current Pos:* chmn dept, 68-77, PROF RADIOL, SCH MED, UNIV CALIF, SAN DIEGO, 68- *Personal Data:* b Buffalo, NY, Nov 30, 22; m 44; c 4. *Educ:* Harvard Univ, BS, 43; Univ Buffalo, MD, 46; Univ Minn, MS, 53. *Prof Exp:* Instr radiol, Grad Sch Med, Univ Minn, 52-53; assoc, Sch Med, Univ Buffalo, 53-54, asst prof, 54-56; prof & chmn dept, Sch Med, Univ Pittsburgh, 56-68. *Concurrent Pos:* Consult, Vet Admin Hosp, Pittsburgh, Pa, 57-68. *Mem:* AAAS; Radiol Soc NAm; AMA; Am Col Radiol. *Res:* Radiology of the vascular system. *Mailing Add:* Dept Radiol Univ Calif San Diego San Diego CA 92092-0001

LASSER, HOWARD GILBERT, CHEMICAL ENGINEERING, ELECTROCHEMISTRY. *Current Pos:* OWNER, MAT RES CONSULTS, SPRINGFIELD & ALEXANDRIA, VA, 83- *Personal Data:* b New York, NY, Nov 24, 26; m 50, Barbara Katz; c Cathy, Ellen (LeVee) & Alan. *Educ:* Lehigh Univ, BS, 50; Columbia Univ, ChemE, 51. *Hon Degrees:* Dr Ing, Darmstadt Polytech Inst, Ger, 56. *Honors & Awards:* Sci Res Award, Sigma Xi, 68. *Prof Exp:* Chem engr indust gases, Eng Res & Develop Labs, Army Corps Engrs, 51-53, cryog, Bur Ships, Dept Navy, 53-55, metal prod, Gen Serv Admin, 55-56, metallic & org coatings, Eng Res & Develop Ctr, Army Corps Engrs, 56-68 & electrochem, Electronics Command, 68-73; mat eng consult coatings & electrochem, Naval Facil Eng Command, Dept Navy, 73-83. *Concurrent Pos:* Chmn, Coatings Comt, Dept Defense, 74-82; consult org & electrodeposited coatings & corrosion processes. *Mem:* Fel Oil & Colour Chemists Asn; Am Electroplaters Soc; Am Inst Chem Engrs; fel Am Inst Chemists; fel AAAS; Nat Asn Corrosion Engrs. *Res:* Corrosion prevention through the use of metallic and organic coatings; development of anodic films on aluminum; transport theory as related to corrosion processes; application of lasers to etching semiconductors and other. *Mailing Add:* 5912 Camberly Ave Springfield VA 22150. *Fax:* 703-683-4635

LASSETER, KENNETH CARLYLE, CLINICAL PHARMACOLOGY, INTERNAL MEDICINE. *Current Pos:* fel clin pharmacol, Sch Med, Univ Miami, 70-71, asst prof, 71-74, assoc prof pharmacol & med, 74-81, CLIN ASSOC PROF PHARMACOL, UNIV MIAMI, 81-; VPRES & MED DIR, CLIN PHARMACOL ASSOC. INC, 81- *Personal Data:* b Jacksonville, Fla, Aug 12, 42; m 63, 77; c 2. *Educ:* Stetson Univ, BS, 63; Univ Fla, MD, 67; Am Bd Clin Pharmacol, dipl, 92. *Honors & Awards:* Res Award, Interstate Postgrad Med Asn, 74. *Prof Exp:* From intern to resident med, Univ Ky Hosp, 67-69, USPHS fel cardiol, 69-70. *Concurrent Pos:* Attend physician, Jackson Mem Hosp, 71-; adj assoc prof pharmacol, Barry Univ Sch Podiat Med, 87- *Mem:* Am Soc Pharmacol & Exp Therapeut; Am Soc Clin Pharmacol & Therapeut; Am Col Physicians; Am Col Clin Pharmacol; Sigma Xi. *Res:* Cardiovascular pharmacology. *Mailing Add:* Clin Pharmacol Assoc Inc 2060 NW 22 Ave Miami FL 33142. *Fax:* 305-633-4904

LASSETER, ROBERT H, ENGINEERING. *Current Pos:* from asst prof to assoc prof, 80-85, assoc chmn, 84-85, PROF, UNIV WIS-MADISON, 85- *Personal Data:* b Miami, Fla, Apr 4, 38; m 79, Lucy Taylor; c Courtney M,, Malahn P, Robert M & Lauren L. *Educ:* NC State Univ, BS, 63, MS, 67; Univ Pa, PhD(physics), 71. *Prof Exp:* Postdoctoral, Univ Pa, 71-73; consult engr, Gen Elec Co, Phila, 73-80. *Concurrent Pos:* Sr consult engr, Siemens AG, Ger, 85-86; consult, LA Power & Water, 82-88, Formas Centrais, Brazil, 86-88, Gen Elec NY & Pa, 82-, Elec Power Res Inst, Palo Alto, Calif, 90-; dir, Power Syst Eng Res Ctr, Wis; vis Ershine fel, Univ Caterbury, NZ, 98. *Mem:* Fel Inst Elec & Electronics Engrs. *Res:* Application of power electronics to power systems; technical issues of utility restructuring; harmonic interactions; simulation methods; power electronic circuits and controls; published numerous articles. *Mailing Add:* Dept Elec & Comput Eng Univ Wis 1415 Engineering Dr Madison WI 53506. *E-Mail:* lasseter@engr.wisc.edu

LASSILA, KENNETH EINO, HIGH ENERGY PHYSICS, THEORETICAL NUCLEAR PHYSICS. *Current Pos:* from asst prof to assoc prof physics, 66-69, PROF PHYSICS, IOWA STATE UNIV, 69- *Personal Data:* b Hancock, Mich, Apr 27, 34; m Susan Sulzberger; c 3. *Educ:* Univ Wyo, BS, 56; Yale Univ, MS, 59, PhD(theoret physics), 61. *Honors & Awards:* Fulbright lectr, Univ Oulu, Finland & Univ Oslo, Norway, 73, Fermi Nat Accelerator Lab, 80-81 & 88. *Prof Exp:* Res assoc theoret physics, Case Inst Technol, 61-63; asst prof physics, Iowa State Univ, 63-64; sr res assoc, Res Inst Theoret Physics, Univ Helsinki, 64-66; res assoc, Stanford Univ, 66. *Concurrent Pos:* Fulbright res fel, Res Inst Theoret Physics, Univ Helsinki, 65; inv prof, Nordic Inst Theoret Atomic Physics, 72; organizer, Fifth Int Workshop Weak Interations, 78; docent, Univ Helsinki, 73- *Mem:* AAAS; fel Am Phys Soc; Finnish Phys Soc. *Res:* Nucleon-nucleon interaction; radiation-field theory; elementary particle interactions and quark-gluon interactions in nuclei. *Mailing Add:* Dept Physics Iowa State Univ Ames IA 50011

LASSITER, RAY ROBERTS, ECOLOGY, ENVIRONMENTAL SCIENCE. *Current Pos:* RES ECOLOGIST, ATHENS ENVIRON RES LAB, ENVIRON PROTECTION AGENCY, 83-, BIOGEOCHEMIST EARTH SYSTS MODELLING, 91- *Personal Data:* b Hertford Co, NC, Apr 8, 37; m 60; c 2. *Educ:* NC State Col, BS, 59, MS, 62; NC State Univ, PhD(animal ecol), 71. *Prof Exp:* Instr biol, Campbell Col, NC, 62-63; asst statistician quant ecol, NC State Univ, 63-67; systs analyst environ statist, Pollution Surveillance Br, SE Water Lab, Environ Protection Agency, 67-70; biol statistician environ sci, Freshwater Ecosysts Br, 70-75; chief environ systs, Br Environ Sci, Athens Environ Res Lab, Environ Protection Agency, 75-81; resident res scientist, Inst Ecol, Univ Ga, 81-83. *Concurrent Pos:* Mem, Inst Ecol, Univ Ga, 77-; res grant, Environ Protection Agency, 81. *Res:* Quantitative ecology; population and community dynamics; experimental ecology using laboratory ecosystems; mathematical modeling of ecosystem processes; fate of toxic chemicals in aquatic ecosystems; predicting effects of toxic chemicals on aquatic ecosystem populations and functions. *Mailing Add:* Environ Protection Agency 960 College Station Rd Athens GA 30605-2720

LASSITER, WILLIAM EDMUND, PHYSIOLOGY, NEPHROLOGY. *Current Pos:* from instr to prof, 60-93, EMER PROF MED, SCH MED, UNIV NC, CHAPEL HILL, 93- *Personal Data:* b Wilmington, NC, July 21, 27; m 56, Diane Irving; c William, Susan, David & John. *Educ:* Harvard Univ, AB, 50, MD, 54. *Prof Exp:* Intern & asst resident med, Mass Gen Hosp, Boston, 54-56; sr asst resident, NC Mem Hosp, 56-57; Donner res fel, Mass Gen Hosp, Boston, 57-58; Life Ins Med Res Fund fel, Univ NC, Chapel Hill, 58-60. *Concurrent Pos:* Estab investr, Am Heart Asn, 62-67, mem coun kidney in cardiovasc dis, 71-; vis investr, Physiol Inst, Berlin, 63-64; Markle scholar, 63-68; Nat Inst Arthritis & Metab Dis career develop award, 67-72; mem cardiovasc & pulmonary res A study sect, NIH, 69-73 & gen med B study sect, 78-82; sect ed, Renal & Electrolyte Physiol, Am J Physiol & J Appl Physiol, 74-76; co-dir NIH surv res needs nephrol & urol, 74-78. *Mem:* AAAS; Am Soc Clin Invest; Am Physiol Soc; fel Am Col Physicians; Am Soc Nephrology. *Res:* Micropuncture studies of mammalian kidney function; tubular transport processes in mammalian kidney; calcium and phosphorus metabolism. *Mailing Add:* 303 N Elliott Rd Chapel Hill NC 27514

LASSITER, WILLIAM STONE, ENGINEERING MANAGEMENT, NOISE & POLLUTION CONTROL. *Current Pos:* Facil engr, Langley Res Ctr, NASA, 63-65, mat engr, 65-70, pollution sensing res, 70-75, ENGR, ANALYSIS & TEST ENG BR, AEROSPACE MECH SYSTS DIV, LANGLEY RES CTR, NASA, 76- *Personal Data:* b Spring Hope, NC, July 7, 39; m 71; c 2. *Educ:* NC State Univ, BS, 61, PhD(mech eng), 71; Col William & Mary, MS, 68, MBA, 73. *Concurrent Pos:* Adj instr, George Washington Univ, Christopher Newport Col & Golden Gate Univ. *Mem:* Am Soc Mech Engrs. *Res:* Noise control; pollution sensing; thermal, structural and fluid analysis. *Mailing Add:* Langley Res Ctr NASA Mail Stop 431 Hampton VA 23681-0001

LASSLO, ANDREW, MEDICINAL CHEMISTRY. *Current Pos:* prof med chem & chmn dept, 60-89, alumni distinguished serv prof & chmn dept, 89-90, EMER PROF MED CHEM, COL PHARM, HEALTH SCI CTR, UNIV TENN, MEMPHIS, 90- *Personal Data:* b Mukacevo, Czech, Aug 24, 22; nat US; m 55, Wilma Reynolds; c Millicent (Meeks). *Educ:* Univ Ill, MSc, 48, PhD(pharmaceut chem), 52, MSLS, 61. *Honors & Awards:* Commendation, Sigma Xi, 76. *Prof Exp:* Asst chem, Univ Ill, 47-51, Univ fel, 51-52; res chemist, Org Chem Div, Monsanto Chem Co, 52-54; asst prof med chem, dept pharmacol, Emory Univ, 54-60. *Concurrent Pos:* 1st lieutenant to captain, Med Serv Corps, USAR, 53-62; prin investr, USPHS, 58-64, 66-72 & 82-89, Geschickter Fund Med Res, 59-65, NSF, 64-66, US Army Med Res & Develop Command, 64-67 & Gustavus & Louise Pfeiffer Res Found, 81-87; consult, Gesckickter Fund Med Res, 61-62; dir, postgrad training prog for sci librn, Nat Libr Med, 66-72 & org med chem, US Food & Drug Admin, 71; chmn subcomt, pre and postdoctoral training, Am Soc Pharmacol & Exp Therapeut, 74-78; producer & moderator TV & radio ser, Health Care Perspectives, 76-78; ed, Surface Chem & Dent Integuments, 73, Blood Platelet Function & Med Chem, 84. *Mem:* Fel AAAS; fel Am Inst Chemists; sr mem Am Chem Soc; Am Soc Pharmacol & Exp Therapeut; fel Am Asn Pharmaceut Scientists; fel Acad Pharmaceut Res & Sci. *Res:* Synthesis and study of compounds with pharmacodynamic potentialities; exploration of relationships between the molecular constitution of synthetic entities and their biodynamic response; science information and library resources; 7 US and 11 foreign patents in field; authored numerous articles in leading scientific and professional journals. *Mailing Add:* 5479 Timmons Ave Memphis TN 38119-6932

LAST, JEROLD ALAN, INHALATION TOXICOLOGY, LUNG DISEASE. *Current Pos:* from asst prof to assoc prof, 76-83, PROF, DEPT INTERNAL MED, PULMONARY DIV, MED CTR, UNIV CALIF, DAVIS, 83- *Personal Data:* b New York, NY, June 5, 40; m 75, Elaine Zimelis; c Matthew, Michael & Andrew. *Educ:* Univ Wis, BS, 59, MS, 61; Ohio State Univ, PhD(biochem), 65. *Honors & Awards:* Frank R Blood Award, Soc Toxicol, 80; ICI Travelling Lectureship, Soc Toxicol, 92. *Prof Exp:* Biochemist, Corn Prod Co, Ill, 61-62; sr res scientist, Squibb Inst Med Res, NJ, 67-69 & Rockefeller Univ, 69-70; asst managing ed, Proc Nat Acad Sci, USA, 70-71, managing ed, 71-73; consult, NIH, 71-73; res assoc, Dept Biochem & Molecular Biol, Harvard Univ, 73-76. *Concurrent Pos:* Am Cancer Soc fel biochem, Med Sch, NY Univ, 66-67; Fulbright prof, Montevideo, Uruguay, 83; vis prof, Bishop Col, Dallas, 82; exp lung res, 80-83, toxicol & appl pharmacol, 84, toxicol, 80-84; vis prof, Cath Univ PR, Ponce, 85, Tuskegee Univ, Tuskegee, Ala, 90; prin investr mult grants. *Mem:* Am Soc Biochem & Molecular Biol; Am Fedn Clin Res; Brit Biochem Soc; Soc Toxicol; Am Thoracic Soc. *Res:* Antibiotics biosynthesis and mechanism of action; lung disease; protein biosynthesis; nucleic acids; collagen biosynthesis; mucus glycoproteins; lung biochemistry; pulmonary fibrosis; health effects of air pollutants; health effects of tobacco smoke; lung disease. *Mailing Add:* Dept Med Div Pulmonary Med Univ Calif Davis CA 95616. *Fax:* 530-752-5593; *E-Mail:* jalast@ucdavis.edu

LAST, JOHN MURRAY, EPIDEMIOLOGY, INTERNATIONAL HEALTH. *Current Pos:* prof epidemiol & community med & chmn dept, 70-92, EMER PROF, UNIV OTTAWA, 92- *Personal Data:* b Tailem Bend, Australia, Sept 22, 26; m 57, Janet Wendelken; c Rebecca, David & Jonathan. *Educ:* Univ Adelaide, MB & BS, 49, MD, 68; Univ Sydney, DPH, 60. *Hon Degrees:* MD, Uppsala Univ, Sweden, 93. *Honors & Awards:* Wade Hampton Frost Award, Am Pub Health Asn, 89; Spec Recognition Award, Am Col Prev Med, 91. *Prof Exp:* Australian Postgrad Med Found fel, Social Med Res Unit, Med Res Coun UK, 61-62; lectr pub health, Univ Sydney, 62-63; asst prof epidemiol, Univ Vt, 63-64; sr lectr social med, Univ Edinburgh, 65-69. *Concurrent Pos:* Mem, Nat Health Grant Rev Comt, NIH, 70-76 & Epidemiol Study Sect, 72-76; consult med educ, WHO, 72-73, 74, 76 & environ health, 84, 90-91 & 95-97; sci ed, Can J Pub Health, 81-91, assoc ed, Am J Prev Med, 86-91; fel, Fac Community Med, UK. *Mem:* Int Asn Epidemiol; fel Am Pub Health Asn; fel Royal Australasian Col Physicians; fel Am Col Prev Med (pres, 87-89); fel Am Col Epidemiol. *Res:* Environmental epidemiology; international health; biomedical ethics (history/philosophy of medicine); author of textbooks on public health and epidemiology. *Mailing Add:* Facil Med Univ Ottawa Ottawa ON K1H 8M5 Can. *Fax:* 613-562-5665; *E-Mail:* last@zeus.med.uottawa.ca

LAST, ROBERT L, AMINO ACID BIOSYNTHESIS IN PLANTS, UV-B RESPONSE IN PLANTS. *Current Pos:* ASSOC SCIENTIST, BOYCE THOMPSON INST PLANT RES, CORNELL UNIV, 89-, ASSOC ADJ PROF GENETICS, 90- *Personal Data:* b New York, NY, Nov 10, 58; m 92. *Educ:* Ohio Wesleyan Univ, BA, 80; Carnegie-Mellon Univ, PhD(biol sci), 86. *Honors & Awards:* NSF Presidential Young Investr Award, 90. *Prof Exp:* Fel, Whitehead Inst Biomed Res, 86-89. *Mem:* AAAS; Am Soc Plant Physiologists; Genetics Soc Am. *Res:* Regulation of amino acid biosynthesis in flowering plants using genetics and molecular biology techniques. *Mailing Add:* 405 Snyder Hill Rd Ithaca NY 14850. *Fax:* 607-254-1272; *E-Mail:* rll3@cornell.edu

LASTER, DANNY BRUCE, ANIMAL SCIENCES. *Current Pos:* DIR, ROMAN L HRUSKA MEAT ANIMAL RES CTR, CLAY CTR, NEBR, 88- *Personal Data:* b Scotts Hill, Tenn, Nov 29, 42; m 60; c 2. *Educ:* Univ Tenn, Knoxville, BS, 63; Univ Ky, Lexington, MS, 64; Okla State Univ, PhD(animal breeding), 70. *Prof Exp:* Res specialist, Univ Ky, Lexington, 65-68; asst prof endocrin, Iowa State Univ, 70-71; res leader, Reproduction Res Unit, Clay Ctr, Agr Res Serv, USDA, Nebr, 71-78, nat prog leader & assoc dep adminr, Beef & Sheep, 81-88. *Mem:* Am Soc Animal Sci. *Res:* Twinning, dystocia and embryonic mortality in beef cattle. *Mailing Add:* US Meat Animal Res Ctr Agr Res Serv USDA PO Box 166 Clay Center NE 68933-0166

LASTER, LEONARD, MEDICINE, SCIENCE POLICY. *Current Pos:* PROF MED, SCH MED & PRES, ORE HEALTH SCI UNIV, 78- *Personal Data:* b New York, NY, Aug 25, 28; m 56; c 3. *Educ:* Harvard Univ, AB, 49, MD, 50; Am Bd Internal Med, dipl, 61; Am Bd Gastroenterol, dipl, 66. *Prof Exp:* From intern to resident med, Mass Gen Hosp, 50-53; vis investr purine metab, Pub Health Res Inst, New York, Inc, 53-54; sr clin investr, Nat Inst Arthritis & Metab Dis, 54-58; chief sect gastroenterol, Metab Dis Br, Nat Inst Arthritis & Metab Dis, 59-69; staff mem, Off Sci & Technol, Exec Off of President, 69-71, asst dir human resources, 71-74; vpres acad & clin affairs & dean, Col Med, State Univ NY Downstate Med Ctr, 74-78. *Concurrent Pos:* Res fel gastroenterol, Mass Mem Hosps, 58-59; clin instr, Sch Med, George Washington Univ, 55-58, prof lectr, 66- *Mem:* Am Soc Biol Chemists; Am Fedn Clin Res; Am Gastroenterol Asn; Am Col Physicians; Am Soc Clin Invest. *Res:* Biochemical aspects of human disease; inborn errors of metabolism; disturbances of the gastrointestinal tract. *Mailing Add:* Univ Mass Med Ctr 120 Front St Suite 800 Worcester MA 01608-1404

LASTER, MARION LYNN, TEST & EVALUATION OF AEROSPACE SYSTEMS. *Current Pos:* USAF, 56-, aeronaut engr, Warren Robins AFB, 56-57, Arnold Eng Develop Ctr, 58-61, res engr, 61-71, tech adv res, 71-78, dir testing eng, 78-80, dir technol, 80-87, tech adv corp planning, 87-91, TECH DIR, ARNOLD ENG DEVELOP CTR, USAF, 91- *Personal Data:* m 55, Jeannine Casey; c Carol, Cheryl, Michelle & Casey. *Educ:* Auburn Univ, BS, 56; Ga Inst Technol, MS, 58; Univ Tenn, PhD(aeronaut & mech eng),71. *Concurrent Pos:* US deleg, NATO/Adv Group Aeronaut Res & Develop, 80-87; mem, Ground Test Tech Comt, Am Inst Aeronaut & Astronaut, 90-92. *Mem:* Am Inst Aeronaut & Astronaut. *Res:* Test engineering; aeronautical systems testing. *Mailing Add:* 709 Holt Lane Tullahoma TN 37388. *E-Mail:* mlaster@edge.net

LASTER, RICHARD, CHEMICAL ENGINEERING & AGRICULTURAL BIOTECHNOLOGY, FOOD SCIENCE. *Current Pos:* MGT CONSULT, 94- *Personal Data:* b Vienna, Austria, Nov 10, 23; nat US; m 48, Liselotte L Schneider; c Susan & Thomas. *Educ:* Polytech Inst Brooklyn, BChE, 43. *Honors & Awards:* Food & Bioeng Award, Am Inst Chem Engrs, 72. *Prof Exp:* Asst lab dir eng res & develop, Cent Labs, Gen Foods Corp, 44-54, res mgr, Walter Baker Div, 54-58, mgr mfg & eng, Franklin Baker Div, 58-60, oper mgr, 60-62, oper mgr, Atlantic Gelatin Div, 62-64, opers mgr res & new prod develop, Jello Div, 64-67, dir corp qual assurance, 67, opers mgr, Maxwell House Coffee Div, 67-69, asst gen mgr corp, 69-71, vpres corp & pres, Maxwell House Coffee Div, 71-72, group vpres coffee & food serv, 72-74, exec vpres & dir, 74-82; chmn, DNA Plant Technol Corp, 88-94, pres & chief exec officer, 82-92, dir, 92-94. *Concurrent Pos:* Dir, Bowater Inc, Rice Tec Inc, Peptor Ltd & Sci Port; chmn, Purchase Col Found; trustee, Polytech Univ; chmn, Westchester Educ Coalition. *Mem:* AAAS; Am Chem Soc; Am Inst Chem Engrs; NY Acad Sci; Inst Food Tech. *Res:* Chemical engineering research as applied to food processing; spray drying; atomization and leaching; chemistry of fats and oils; chocolate processing; agricultural biotechnology; genetic engineering of plants. *Mailing Add:* 23 Round Hill Rd Chappaqua NY 10514

LASTER, WILLIAM RUSSELL, JR, VETERINARY MEDICINE, EXPERIMENTAL ONCOLOGY. *Current Pos:* RETIRED. *Personal Data:* b Ala, Oct 20, 26; m 61, Carol Clark; c Susan M (Schneider). *Educ:* Auburn Univ, DVM, 51. *Prof Exp:* Virologist, Southern Res Inst, 51-56, head, Cancer Screening Sect, 56-66, head, Cancer Screening Div, 66-92. *Mem:* Am Asn Cancer Res. *Res:* Cancer chemotherapy; experimental oncology. *Mailing Add:* 5529 Timber Hill Rd Birmingham AL 35242

LASURE, LINDA LEE, MICROBIAL GENETICS, RESEARCH MANAGEMENT. *Current Pos:* PRES, LASURE M CRAWFORD CONSULT CO, 95- *Personal Data:* b Bartlesville, Okla, Nov 23, 46. *Educ:* St Cloud State Col, BS, 68; Syracuse Univ & State Univ NY, PhD(genetics), 73. *Prof Exp:* Res fel, NY Bot Garden, 72-74; res scientist microbiol, Miles Lab Inc, 74-79, sr res scientist, 79-80, supvr mutation & screening, 80-84, dir bioprod res, 84-89; sr dir, US Labs, Panlabs, Inc, 89-90, vpres, 90-93; pres, Worldwide Res & Develop, 93-95. *Mem:* Sigma Xi; AAAS; Genetics Soc Am; Am Soc Microbiol; Mycol Soc Am. *Res:* Studies of mutagenesis, inheritance, and physiological control of sexual reproduction in the lower fungi, fungal spore germination, and selection of strains of fungi with improved yields of enzymes and organic acids; enzyme synthesis and molecular biology of filamentous fungi. *Mailing Add:* 7332 Lake Alice Rd SE Fall City WA 98024

LASWELL, TROY JAMES, GEOLOGY. *Current Pos:* head dept, 62-85, prof, 62-85, EMER PROF GEOL & GEOG, MISS STATE UNIV, 85- *Personal Data:* b Ottawa, Ky, Nov 12, 20; m 43, Dorothy Howard; c David M. *Educ:* Berea Col, AB, 42; Oberlin Col, AM, 48; Univ Mo, PhD(geol), 53. *Prof Exp:* From asst prof to assoc prof, Washington & Lee Univ, 53-57; from assoc prof to prof, La Polytech Inst, 57-62. *Concurrent Pos:* Geologist, Mo Geol Surv, 52-53; consult geologist, Va Mins, Inc, 55-56, South River Mining Co, 57, Humble Oil & Refining Co, 55-58. *Mem:* Geol Soc Am; Am Asn Petrol Geologists; Am Asn Geol Teachers; Sigma Xi. *Res:* Stratigraphy; sedimentation. *Mailing Add:* 202 Bridle Path Starkville MS 39759

LASZEWSKI, RONALD M, EXPERIMENTAL NUCLEAR PHYSICS, ACOUSTICS. *Current Pos:* from res asst prof physics to sr res physicist, 78-90, PRIN RES PHYSICIST, UNIV ILL, URBANA, 90- *Personal Data:* b Chicago, Ill, June 22, 47. *Educ:* Univ Ill, Urbana, BS, 69, MS, 72, PhD(physics), 75. *Prof Exp:* Res assoc physics, Argonne Nat Lab, 75-78. *Mem:* Am Phys Soc. *Res:* Photonuclear physics and medium energy physics. *Mailing Add:* Nuclear Physics Lab Univ Ill 1110 W Green St Urbana IL 61801. *Fax:* 217-333-1215

LASZLO, CHARLES ANDREW, BIOMEDICAL ENGINEERING. *Current Pos:* assoc dir, Div Health Systs, 74-85, PROF, DEPT ELEC ENG, UNIV BC, 80-, DIR, CLIN ENG PROG, 80- *Personal Data:* b July 8, 35; Can citizen; c 2. *Educ:* McGill Univ, BEng, 61, MEng, 66, PhD(biomed eng), 68. *Honors & Awards:* Award of Merit, Can Hard of Hearing Asn, 90. *Prof Exp:* Design engr, Northern Elec Co & RCA Victor Co, Ltd, Montreal, Que, 61-62; biomed engr, OTL Res Labs, Royal Victoria Hosp, Montreal, Que, 62-68; assoc prof, Biomed Eng Unit & Dept Otolaryngol, McGill, 68-74, dir, Biomed Eng Unit, 70-74. *Concurrent Pos:* Mem, Adv Comt Med Devices, Bur Med Devices, Health Protection Br, Health & Welfare Can, 79-, Comt Hearing Aid Stand, 86-, Comt Telecommun Devices, Can Stand Asn, 88, Res Grant Eval Comt, Health Develop Fund Sci Coun, BC, 89-, Assoc Comt Res & Develop Rehab Disabled Persons, Nat Res Coun, 90-; assoc men, Dept Health Care & Epidemiol & Sch Audiol & Speech Sci, Univ BC, 80-; consult, Royal Columbian Hosp, 83-, Royal Jubilee Hosp, Children's Hosp & St Paul Hosp, 84-, G F Strong Rehab Ctr, 86-; chmn, Bd Hearing Aid Dealers & Consult, Ministry Health, BC, 87- *Mem:* Sr mem Inst Elec & Electronics Engrs; sr mem Instrument Soc Am; fel Am Asn Med Systs & Info. *Res:* Over 120 publications; electrical engineering; biomedical engineering. *Mailing Add:* Elec Eng Dept Univ BC 2356 Main Mall Vancouver BC V6T 1Z4 Can

LATA, GENE FREDERICK, BIOCHEMISTRY OF STEROIDS & ANGIOGENESIS. *Current Pos:* from instr to asst prof, Univ Iowa, 50-62, fel med, 65-66, assoc prof, 62-92, EMER ASSOC PROF BIOCHEM, UNIV IOWA, 92- *Personal Data:* b New York, NY, May 17, 22; m 51; c Paul, Matthew, Thomas, Catherine (Manka) & Mary. *Educ:* City Col New York, BS, 42; Univ Ill, MS, 48, PhD(biochem), 50. *Prof Exp:* Jr chemist, Gen Foods Corp, 42, chemist, 46; asst chem, Univ Ill, 47, asst biochem, 48-50. *Concurrent Pos:* Vis lectr, Huntington Labs, Harvard Med Sch, 65-66; consult, Am Dent Asn; chmn, Iowa Sect, Am Chem Soc, 87. *Mem:* Fel AAAS; Am Chem Soc; Am Soc Biol Chemists; NY Acad Sci; Sigma Xi (pres, Iowa Chap, 87). *Res:* Peroxisomal enzymes and their control; hormonal control of enzyme actions; steroid interactions and transport; aging and steroid hormone dynamics; angiogenesis factors. *Mailing Add:* Dept Biochem Univ Iowa Iowa City IA 52242. *Fax:* 319-335-9570; *E-Mail:* glata@vaxa.weeg.uiowa.edu

LATANISION, RONALD MICHAEL, CORROSION ENGINEERING, MATERIALS PROCESSING. *Current Pos:* prof mat sci & eng, 75-83, dir, Mat Processing Ctr, 84-91, DIR, H H UHLIG CORROSION LAB, MASS INST TECHNOL, 75-, PROF MAT SCI, 83- *Personal Data:* b Richmondale, Pa, July 2, 42; m 64, Carolyn Domerig; c Ivan & Sara. *Educ:* Pa State Univ, BS, 64; Ohio State Univ, PhD(metall eng), 68. *Honors & Awards:* Campbell Award, Nat Asn Corrosion Engrs; Krumb Lectr, 84; McFarland Award, Pa State Univ, 86; W R Whitney Award, Nat Asn Corrosion Engrs Int, 94. *Prof Exp:* Actg head, Mat Sci Group, Martin Marietta Labs, Baltimore, Md, 70-74. *Concurrent Pos:* Sci adv, US House Rep Comt Sci & Technol, 82-83; vis prof, Univ Naples, Italy, 89-; mem adv comt, Mass Off, Sci & Technol, 90-91; founder, Altron Mat Eng, 92. *Mem:* Nat Acad Eng; Nat Asn Corrosion Engrs; Am Inst Mining, Metall & Petrol Engrs; Electrochem Soc; Am Soc Metals; Elec Power Res Inst; Am Soc Test & Mats; Inst Elec & Electronics Engrs. *Res:* Corrosion of new materials (composites, magnetic alloys, etc); materials for construction of engineering systems; materials processing. *Mailing Add:* H H Uhlig Corrosion Lab Mass Inst Technol 77 Massachusetts Ave Rm 8-202 Cambridge MA 02139

LATCH, DANA MAY, ALGEBRA, TOPOLOGY. *Current Pos:* asst prof, 76-79, ASSOC PROF MATH, NC STATE UNIV, 79- *Personal Data:* b New York, NY, Aug 29, 43; c 1. *Educ:* Harpur Col, BA, 65; Queens Col, NY, MA, 67; City Univ New York, PhD(math), 71. *Prof Exp:* Teaching asst math, Queens Col, NY, 65-66, lectr, 66-67; asst prof, Douglass Col, Rutgers Univ, 71-74 & Lawrence Univ, 74-76. *Concurrent Pos:* NSF res grant, Rutgers Univ, 72-73 & NC State Univ, 78-80 & 81-83; Carnegie Found fac develop award, Lawrence Univ, 75; study grant, Ger Acad Exchange Serv, Univ Konstanz, Ger, 78; vis prof math, Universitat Konstanz, Ger, 79; vis scholar comput sci, Univ NC, Chapel Hill, 82; Alexander von Humboldt res fel, Munich, Fed Repub Ger, 83. *Mem:* Am Math Soc; Asn Women Math. *Res:* Algebraic topology of small categories; applications of category theory to the theory of program behaviors; applications of categorical methods to homotopy theory and the theory of localizations. *Mailing Add:* Theory Comput Prog NSF 4201 Wilson Blvd Rm 1145 Arlington VA 22230

LATEEF, ABDUL BARI, FORENSIC SCIENCE, CHEMISTRY. *Current Pos:* from instr to asst prof chem, 69-71, from asst prof to assoc prof, 71-81, PROF FORENSIC SCI, YOUNGSTOWN STATE UNIV, 81; DIR, TRI-STATE LABS INC, 81- *Personal Data:* b Faisalabad, Pakistan, Apr 4, 39; m 70. *Educ:* Punjab Univ, Pakistan, BS, 59, MS, 61; Univ Newcastle, PhD(chem), 66. *Prof Exp:* Nat Res Coun Can fel, Univ Calgary, 66-69. *Mem:* Am Acad Forensic Sci; Forensic Soc London; Acad Criminal Justice; Sigma Xi. *Res:* Spectroscopic and chromatographic analytical techniques in forensic science; role of forensic science in criminal justice system. *Mailing Add:* Tri-State Labs 2870 Salt Springs Rd Youngstown OH 44509-1036

LATERRA, JOHN J, NEURO-ONCOLOGY, NEUROLOGY. *Current Pos:* instr, 88-90, asst prof, 90-94, ASSOC PROF NEUROL, JOHNS HOPKINS UNIV SCH MED, 94- *Personal Data:* b Providence, RI, May 18, 55. *Educ:* Washington Univ, St Louis, BS, 77; Case Western Res Univ, PhD(microbiol), 82, MD, 84. *Prof Exp:* Residency neurol, Univ Mich, 84-88. *Mem:* AAAS; Am Soc Neurochem; Am Soc Cell Biol. *Res:* Neuro-oncology; neurology. *Mailing Add:* Dept Neurol Kennedy Kreiger Inst 707 N Broadway Baltimore MD 21205-0001

LATHAM, ALLEN, JR, ENGINEERING, BIOENGINEERING. *Current Pos:* pres, 72-76, chmn bd, 72-82, FOUNDER, HAEMONETICS CORP, 82- *Personal Data:* b Norwich, Conn, May 23, 08; m 33; c 4. *Educ:* Mass Inst Technol, BS, 30. *Honors & Awards:* Mortem Grove-Rasmussen Mem Award, Am Asn Blood Banks. *Prof Exp:* Jr engr, E I du Pont de Nemours & Co, WVa, 30-35; chief empr, Polaroid Corp, Mass, 36-41; sr mech engr, Arthur D Little, Inc, 41-51, vpres, 51-59, sr vpres, 59-67; pres, 500 Inc, 67-68. *Concurrent Pos:* Chmn bd, Cryogenic Technol, 68-72. *Mem:* Nat Acad Eng; Am Soc Mech Engrs; Am Inst Chem Engrs; Instrument Soc Am. *Res:* Cryogenics; blood processing. *Mailing Add:* Haemonetics Corp 400 Wood Rd Braintree MA 02184

LATHAM, ARCHIE J, PLANT PATHOLOGY, MYCOLOGY. *Current Pos:* CONSULT, 85- *Personal Data:* b Blackfoot, Idaho, June 26, 26; m 63; c 3. *Educ:* Idaho State Col, BS, 56; Univ Idaho, MS, 59; Univ Ill, PhD(plant path), 61. *Prof Exp:* Ranger, Yellowstone Park, Wyo, 56; res asst plant path, Univ Idaho, 56-58 & Univ Ill, 58-61; res biologist, Gulf Res & Develop Co, Kans, 61-67; asst prof bot & plant path, Auburn Univ, 67-78, assoc prof, 78-85. *Mem:* Am Phytopath Soc; Mycol Soc Am. *Res:* Fruit and nut diseases. *Mailing Add:* 310 Flowers Circle Auburn AL 36830

LATHAM, DAVID WINSLOW, ASTRONOMY. *Current Pos:* ASTRONR, SMITHSONIAN ASTROPHYS OBSERV, 65-; LECTR ASTRON, HARVARD UNIV, 71- *Personal Data:* b Boston, Mass, Mar 19, 40; m 60, Virginia Tullis; c James, Peter, Andrew, Jonathan & David Jr. *Educ:* Mass Inst Technol, BS, 61; Harvard Univ, MA, 65, PhD(astron), 70. *Mem:* Am Astron Soc; Royal Astron Soc; Sigma Xi; Int Astron Union. *Res:* Searches for planets orbiting other stars; studies of the frequency and orbital characteristics of binary stars in various stellar populations; observational cosmology. *Mailing Add:* 140 Old Littleton Rd Harvard MA 01451-1415. *E-Mail:* dlatham@cfa.harvard.edu

LATHAM, DEWITT ROBERT, PETROLEUM CHEMISTRY. *Current Pos:* RETIRED. *Personal Data:* b Chugwater, Wyo, Oct 26, 28; m 55; c 2. *Educ:* Univ Wyo, BS, 50. *Prof Exp:* Analytical chemist, Rocky Mountain Arsenal, US Army Chem Corps, Colo, 52-54; chemist, Laramie Energy Res Ctr, US Bur Mines, 54-60, res chemist, 60-64, proj leader, Laramie Energy Tech Ctr, Dept Energy, 64-84. *Mem:* Am Chem Soc; Sigma Xi. *Res:* Nitrogen and oxygen compounds in petroleum; development of methods of analysis for petroleum shale, oil and coal liquids; separation and characterization of fossil fuel energy sources. *Mailing Add:* 1467 N 17th St Laramie WY 82070-2308

LATHAM, DON JAY, ATMOSPHERIC SCIENCES. *Current Pos:* res meteorologist & physicist, 75-97, PROJ LEADER FIRE BEHAV, NORTHERN FOREST FIRE LAB, 97- *Personal Data:* b Lewiston, Idaho, Dec 21, 38; m 60; c 3. *Educ:* Pomona Col, BA, 60; NMex Inst Mining & Technol, MS, 64, PhD, 68. *Prof Exp:* Res asst, NMex Inst Mining & Technol, 61-67; sr res scientist, Rosenstiel Sch Marine & Atmospheric Sci, Univ Miami, 67-68, asst prof atmospheric sci, 68-72, assoc prof, 72-75. *Concurrent Pos:* NSF grants, Univ Miami, 72; fac affil, Univ Mont, 75-; mem, Atmospheric Elec Comt, Am Meteorol Soc, 81-83. *Mem:* Am Meteorol Soc; Am Geophys Union. *Res:* Atmospheric electricity; radar meteorology; combustion physics; artificial intelligence. *Mailing Add:* Intermountain Fire Sci Lab Box 8089 Missoula MT 59807

LATHAM, MICHAEL CHARLES, NUTRITION, TROPICAL PUBLIC HEALTH. *Current Pos:* PROF INT NUTRIT & DIR, PROG INT NUTRIT, DIV NUTRIT SCI, CORNELL UNIV, 68- *Personal Data:* b Kilosa, Tanzania, May 6, 28; m 74; c 2. *Educ:* Univ Dublin, BA, 49, MB, BCh & BAO, 52; Univ London, DTM&H, 58; Harvard Univ, MPH, 65. *Hon Degrees:* FFCM, Royal Col Physicians, London, 73. *Honors & Awards:* Food Cycle Trophy Award, Ministry Health, Tanzania, 78. *Prof Exp:* House surgeon, High Wycombe Hosp, Buckinghamshire, Eng, 52-53; rotating physician, Methodist Hosp, Los Angeles, 53-54; sr house officer, NMiddlesex Hosp, London, 54-55; med officer, Tanzania Ministry Health, 55-64, dir nutrit unit, 62-64; res assoc & asst prof nutrit, Harvard Univ, 64-68. *Concurrent Pos:* Vis exchange fel, Methodist Hosp, Los Angeles, 53-54; contrib ed, Nutrit Rev, 68-74; chmn panel, White House Conf Food, Nutrit & Health & vchmn panel, Follow-Up Conf, 69-71; consult, WHO, Manila, 70 & UN Food & Agr Orgn, 64 & Zambia, 70; mem, Nat Acad Sci-Nat Res Coun Int Nutrit Comt, 70-76; UNICEF consult, Thailand & Malaysia, 73; mem exec comt pest control, Nat Acad Sci, 73-78; mem expert adv panel nutrit, WHO, 74-; vis prof, Univ Nairobi, Kenya, 74-75; World Bank consult, Indonesia, 75; US AID consult, Guyana, 77 & 78, Tanzania, 79 & Philippines, 81; mem comt nutrit & infections, Nat Acad Sci, 78-81, Bd Int Health, Nat Acad Sci & Inst Med, 83-88; assoc scientist, Kenya Med Res Inst, Nairobi; adj prof, Inst Agronomique et Veterinaire Hassan II, Morocco, 86-; mem bd dir, Soc Nutrit Ed, 86-, ed bd, Nutrit-Int J Appl & Basic Nutrit Sci, 87, panel collaborators, J Acta Tropica, Switz, 87-, bd dirs, Soc Nutrit Educ, 86-89, Exec Comt, Soc Int Nutrit Res, 90- & World Alliance Breastfeeding Action, 91-; consult, Swed Int Develop Agency, Tanzania, 86, Meals for Millions Found, Calif, 86, UNESCO, Paris, 88 & UNICEF, 91-93; team leader, UNICEF-WHO Rev JNSP, Ethiopia, 87-88 & Swed Int Develop Authority, Tanzania Eval, 91-92; vis scientist & chief res officer, Kenya Med Res Inst, Nairobi, Kenya, 89-90; external examr, Univ Nairobi, Kenya 89-90. *Mem:* Am Inst Nutrit; Brit Nutrit Soc; Am Soc Clin Nutrit; fel Royal Soc Trop Med & Hyg; fel Am Pub Health Asn. *Res:* International nutrition problems; nutrition and health of low income populations; xerophthalmia; infant feeding practices; nutrition and intellectual development; protein-energy malnutrition of children; evaluation of applied nutrition programs; lactose intolerance; nutritional surveillance; nutrition and parasitic infections; author of co-author of over 300 publications including 6 books. *Mailing Add:* Div Nutrit Sci Cornell Univ Ithaca NY 14853-0001

LATHAM, PATRICIA SUZANNE, HEPATOLOGY. *Current Pos:* ASST PROF MED & PATH, UNIV MD HOSP & BALTIMORE VET ADMIN HOSP, 81-; ASSOC PROF, GEORGE WASHINGTON UNIV, 81- *Personal Data:* b Annapolis, Md, Aug 22, 46. *Educ:* Simmons Col, BS, 68; Univ Southern Calif, MD, 72. *Mem:* Am Asn Study Liver Dis; Am Gastroenterol Asn. *Res:* Investigation of liver diseases with emphasis on structure and function; hepatocytes; Kupffer cells; endotoxin; viral pathogenesis. *Mailing Add:* 2300 I St NW Washington DC 20037

LATHAM, ROGER EARL, PLANT COMMUNITY ECOLOGY, CONSERVATION BIOLOGY. *Current Pos:* field investr, Morris Arboretum, 82-83, RES FEL, UNIV PA, 92- *Personal Data:* b Bellefonte, Pa, May 6, 50. *Educ:* Swarthmore Col, BA, 83; Univ Pa, PhD(biol), 90. *Prof Exp:* Environ planner, Fahringer McCarty Grey Inc, 73-80; dir sci & stewardship, Nature Conservancy, 88-90, stewardship ecologist, 90-92. *Mem:* Am Inst Biol Sci; Ecol Soc Am; Natural Areas Asn; Sigma Xi; Soc Conserv Biol. *Res:* Community ecology, biogeochemistry and conservation biology; restore and safeguard biological resources in two large bioreserves; fire ecology and the biogeography of global biodiversity patterns. *Mailing Add:* PO Box 57 Wallingford PA 19086-0057. *Fax:* 215-898-0964; *E-Mail:* rlatham@mail.sas.upenn.edu

LATHAM, ROSS, JR, INORGANIC CHEMISTRY. *Current Pos:* assoc prof, 66-72, PROF CHEM, ADRIAN COL, 72- *Personal Data:* b Chicago, Ill, Dec 18, 32; m 61; c 2. *Educ:* Principia Col, BS, 55; Univ Ill, MS, 57, PhD(inorg chem), 61. *Prof Exp:* Instr chem, Lafayette Col, 59-60; chemist, Esso Res & Eng Co, NJ, 61-66. *Res:* Titanium alkoxide-halide chemistry. *Mailing Add:* Dept Chem Adrian Col 110 S Madison St Adrian MI 49221-2518

LATHEM, WILLOUGHBY, MEDICINE. *Current Pos:* vpres & med dir, 80-85, VPRES SCI AFFAIRS, STERLING INT, STERLING DRUG, INC, 85- *Personal Data:* b Atlanta, Ga, Oct 9, 23; m 51; c 5. *Educ:* Emory Univ, BS, 44, MD, 46; Am Bd Internal Med, dipl, 54. *Prof Exp:* Asst med, Col Physicians & Surgeons, Columbia Univ, 52-53; asst clin prof, Yale Univ, 53-56; from asst prof to assoc prof, Sch Med, Univ Pittsburgh, 56-64; sci rep, Off Int Res, NIH, Eng, 62-66; dep dir biomed sci, Rockefeller Found, 66-72, assoc dir health sci, 72-78, regional officer, Asia, Bangkok & Thailand, 75-77, field staff, Salvador, Bahia & Brazil, 78-80. *Concurrent Pos:* Hon res assoc, Univ Col, Univ London, 62-65; vis prof, Mt Sinai Sch Med, 80. *Mem:* Am Soc Clin Invest; Harvey Soc; Am Fedn Clin Res. *Res:* International health. *Mailing Add:* 122 Old Logging Rd Stamford CT 06903-4805

LATHERS, CLAIRE M, CARDIO-RENAL DRUG PRODUCTS, PHARMACOLOGY. *Current Pos:* PHARMACOLOGIST, CARDIO-RENAL DRUG PROD, FOOD & DRUG ADMIN, 89- *Personal Data:* b Brooklyn, NY, June 9, 69; State Univ NY, Buffalo, PhD (pharmacol), 73. *Prof Exp:* NIH postdoctoral fel, Med Col Pa, 73-75, from instr to assoc prof, Dept Pharmacol, 75-88. *Concurrent Pos:* Pharmacol lectr, Smith Kline & Fr, 75-83, Pa Col Optom, 76-77, Gwynedd Mercy Col, 78-89 & Hoechst-Roussel Med Col Pa, 82-83; mem, Subcomt Women in Phamacol, Pharmacol Soc, 84-92; vis prof, Dept Pharmacol & Toxicol, Philadelphia Col Pharm & Sci, 87, Dept Pharmacol, Schs Med & Dent, State Univ NY, Buffalo, 87-88; vis scientist sabbatical, Johnson Space Ctr, NASA, 88, vis scientist, 89- *Mem:* Aerospace Med Asn; Am Soc Pharmacol & Ex Therapeut; Soc Exp Biol & Med; Sigma Xi; NY Acad Sci; Am Fedn Clin Res; Int Study Group Res Cardiac Metab; Am Col Clin Pharmacol (treas, 90-). *Mailing Add:* Albany Col Pharm Union Univ 106 New Scotland Ave Albany NY 12208

LATHI, BHAGAWANDAS PANNALAL, COMMUNICATION SYSTEMS, SIGNAL PROCESSING. *Current Pos:* PROF ELEC ENG, CALIF STATE UNIV, 79- *Personal Data:* b Bhokar, Maharashtr, India, Dec 3, 33; m 62, Rajani Damodardas Mundada; c Anjali & Shishir. *Educ:* Poona Univ, BEEE, 55; Univ Ill, MSEE, 57; Stanford Univ, PhD(elec eng), 61. *Prof Exp:* Res asst, Univ Ill, 56-57, Stanford Univ, 57-60; res engr, Gen Electric Co, Syracuse, 60-61; assoc prof elec eng, Bradley Univ, 62-69, US Naval Acad, 69-72; prof, Campinas State Univ, Brazil, 72-78. *Concurrent Pos:* Consult semiconductor indust, India, 61-62; vis prof, Univ Iowa, 78-79. *Mem:* Fel Inst Elec & Electronics Engrs. *Res:* Systems and communication; random signals and communication theory; published numerous articles and books. *Mailing Add:* 3021 Scenic Height Way Carmichael CA 95608

LATHROP, ARTHUR LAVERNE, PHYSICS. *Current Pos:* RETIRED. *Personal Data:* b Kittitas, Wash, Nov 21, 18; m 46. *Educ:* Wash State Univ, BS, 43; Univ Ill, MS, 46; Rice Univ, PhD(physics), 52. *Prof Exp:* Instr physics, Wash State Univ, 43-44, Univ Tulsa, 47-49; physicist, Ames Aeronaut Lab, Moffett Field, Calif, 44-45; res engr, Boeing Airplane Co, Wash, 52-53; res asst physics, Inst Paper Chem, Lawrence, 53-58, res assoc, 58-65; from asst prof to prof physics, Western Ill Univ, 65-88. *Mailing Add:* 1739 Center St Walla Walla WA 99362

LATHROP, JAY WALLACE, SOLID STATE PHYSICS, ELECTRICAL ENGINEERING. *Current Pos:* prof, 68-89, dir, Ctr Semiconductor Device Reliability Res, 84-89, EMER PROF ELEC ENG, CLEMSON UNIV, 89- *Personal Data:* b Bangor, Maine, Sept 6, 27; m 48, 85, Sarah Scott; c 6. *Educ:* Mass Inst Technol, BS, 48, MS, 49, PhD(physics), 52. *Honors & Awards:* Cert of Recognition, NASA, 83. *Prof Exp:* Electronic scientist, Nat Bur Stand, 52-58; mgr advan technol, Semiconductor Components Div, Tex Instruments Inc, 58-68. *Mem:* Fel Inst Elec & Electronics Engrs. *Res:* Microelectronics; integrated circuits; solar cells; semiconductor devices reliability. *Mailing Add:* 680 Winston Way West Union SC 29696. *E-Mail:* j.lathrop@ieee.org

LATHROP, KATHERINE AUSTIN, nuclear medicine, for more information see previous edition

LATHROP, KAYE DON, COMPUTER SCIENCE. *Current Pos:* assoc lab dir & prof, Stanford Linear Accelerator Ctr, 84-94, head, Tech Div, 84-94, chair, Environ, Safety & Health Coordr Coun, 94, EMER PROF APPL RES, STANFORD LINEAR ACCELERATOR CTR, 94- *Personal Data:* b Bryan, Ohio, Oct 8, 32; m 57, Judith M Green; c Braxton L & Scott M. *Educ:* US Mil Acad, BS, 55; Calif Inst Technol, MS, 59, PhD(mech eng, physics), 62. *Honors & Awards:* E O Lawrence Mem Award, 76. *Prof Exp:* Staff mem reactor math, Los Alamos Sci Lab, 62-67; staff mem & group leader reactor physics methods develop, Nuclear Analysis & Reactor Physics Dept, Gen Atomic Div, Gen Dynamics Corp, 67-68; T-1 alt group leader, Los Alamos Nat Lab, 68-72, T-1 group leader, 72-75, T-div asst div leader, 73-75, assoc div leader nuclear safeguards, Reactor Safety & Technol Div, 75-77, alt div leader, Energy Div, 77-78, div leader, Comput Sci & Serv Div, 78-79, assoc dir eng sci, 79-84. *Concurrent Pos:* Vis prof, Univ NMex, 64-65, adj prof, 66-67; consult, Gulf Gen Atomic, 68-73 & Sci Applns Inc, 71-74; guest lectr, Int Atomic Energy Agency, Poland, 69; mem, Adv Comt Reactor Physics, US Energy Res & Develop Admin, 73-77; tech prog chmn, Nat Trop Meeting, Am Nuclear Soc, 77; vis comt, Reactor Physics Div, Argonne Nat Lab, 78-83; mgt adv comt, Y-12 Div, Union Carbide Corp, 79-82; mem, Am Nuclear Soc Deleg People's Repub China, 80, Eng Adv Comt, Univ NMex, 80-84, Eng Nat Adv Comt, Univ Mich, 83-92, Steering Comt, Energy Eng Res Prog, Joint Mass Inst Technol-Idaho Nat Eng Lab, 80-90, Study Mat Control & Acct Dept Energy Nuclear Fuel Complex, Nat Acad Sci, 87-88, Energy Res Adv Bd Panel Access Cand Reactor Technologies New Prod Reactor, 88, External Adv Comt, Nuclear Technol & Eng Div, Los Alamos Nat Lab, 88-93, 93, Nat Lab Adv Comt, Dept Energy Strategy, 89-90. *Mem:* Nat Acad Eng; Am Phys Soc; fel Am Nuclear Soc (treas, 77-79). *Res:* Analytic and numerical solutions of equations of neutron and photon transport; reactor safety; computer systems and communications. *Mailing Add:* Stanford Linear Accelerator Ctr Mail Stop 07 PO Box 4349 Stanford CA 94309. *E-Mail:* kdon@slac.stanford.edu

LATHROP, RICHARD C(HARLES), ELECTRICAL & AERONAUTICAL ENGINEERING. *Current Pos:* CONSULT ENGR, 74- *Personal Data:* b Wauwatosa, Wis, Sept 6, 24; m 56, 83. *Educ:* Univ Wis, BS, 48, MS, 50, PhD(elec eng), 51. *Prof Exp:* Res asst, Univ Wis, 51; proj engr, Wright Air Develop Ctr, USAF, 51-55, staff mem Test Pilot Sch, 55-59, commandant, 59-61, assoc prof elec eng, USAF Acad, 61-65, prof & head dept, Pakistan Air Force Col Aeronaut Eng, 65-67, pilot, Fourth Air Commando Squadron, 67-68, exec officer, Cent Inertial Guide Test Facil, Air Force Missile Develop Ctr, Holloman AFB, NMex, 68-70, tech dir, Air Force Flight Test Ctr, 71-74. *Mem:* Sr mem Inst Elec & Electronics Engrs; assoc fel Am Inst Aeronaut & Astronaut; sr mem Simulation Coun. *Res:* Analog and digital computers; automatic controls; aircraft flight testing; aircraft dynamics; microcomputers. *Mailing Add:* 920 St Ann Dr Paso Robles CA 93446

LATHWELL, DOUGLAS J, SOIL SCIENCE. *Current Pos:* From asst prof to prof, 50-89, EMER PROF SOIL SCI, CORNELL UNIV, 89- *Personal Data:* b Mich, Mar 28, 22; m 48, Catherine Earl; c Daniel, Timm & John. *Educ:* Mich State Univ, BS, 47; Ohio State Univ, PhD(soil sci), 50. *Concurrent Pos:*

Fulbright res scholar, Neth, 64; vis prof, Univ Reading, Eng, 79. *Mem:* Soil Sci Soc Am; fel Am Soc Agron; fel AAAS; Int Soc Soil Sci. *Res:* Soil fertility; plant nutrition. *Mailing Add:* 130 Northview Rd Ithaca NY 14850. *Fax:* 607-255-2644

LATIES, ALAN M, OPHTHALMOLOGY. *Current Pos:* resident, Hosp Univ Pa, 60-63, instr, 63-64, assoc, 64-66, asst prof, 66-70, Given prof, 70-83, HAROLD G SCHEIE RES PROF OPHTHAL, MED SCH, UNIV PA, 83- *Personal Data:* b Beverly, Mass, Feb 8, 31; c 2. *Educ:* Harvard Col, AB, 54; Baylor Univ, MD, 59; Am Bd Ophthal, dipl, 65. *Honors & Awards:* Res to Prevent Blindness Professorship Award, 64; Friedenwald Award for Res in Ophthal, 72. *Prof Exp:* Intern, Mt Sinai Hosp, New York, 59-60. *Concurrent Pos:* NIH trainee, 61-63, spec fel, 63-64; assoc ophthal, Children's Hosp Philadelphia, 63-; asst attend physician, Philadelphia Gen Hosp, 63-; attend ophthal, Vet Admin Hosp, 63-; mem vision res & training comt, Nat Eye Inst. *Mem:* AMA; Asn Res Vision & Ophthal; Histochem Soc; Am Asn Anat; Am Acad Ophthal & Otolaryngol. *Res:* Histochemistry; visual pathways; experimental myopia. *Mailing Add:* Scheie Eye Inst 51 N 39th St Philadelphia PA 19104-2640

LATIES, GEORGE GLUSHANOK, PLANT PHYSIOLOGY. *Current Pos:* plant physiologist, Exp Sta & assoc prof hort sci, Univ, 59-63, PROF PLANT PHYSIOL, DEPT BIOL, UNIV CALIF, LOS ANGELES, 63- *Personal Data:* b Sevastopol, Russia, Jan 17, 20; US citizen; m 47. *Educ:* Cornell Univ, BS, 41; Univ Minn, MS, 42; Univ Calif, PhD(plant physiol), 47. *Prof Exp:* Asst, Div Plant Nutrit, Univ Calif, 42-43, sr asst, 43-47; res fel biol, Calif Inst Technol, 47-50, sr res fel, 50-52 & 55-58; asst prof bot, Univ Mich, 52-55. *Concurrent Pos:* Rockefeller Found fel, Sheffield & Cambridge Univs, 49-50; res botanist, Univ Mich, 52-55; mem, Physiol Chem Study Sect, USPHS, 63-65; Guggenheim fel, Commonwealth Sci & Indust Res Orgn, Australia, 66-67. *Mem:* AAAS; Am Soc Plant Physiol (vpres, 64-65); Bot Soc Am; Scand Soc Plant Physiol. *Res:* Respiratory regulatory mechanisms and respiratory pathways in plant tissues; permeability and salt transport; biochemical aspects of growth and development. *Mailing Add:* 1207 N Tigertail Rd Los Angeles CA 90049

LATIES, VICTOR GREGORY, PSYCHOPHARMACOLOGY, BEHAVIOR ANALYSIS. *Current Pos:* assoc prof radiation biol, biophys, pharmacol & psychol, Univ Rochester, 65-71, prof toxicol, pharmacol & psychol, 71-93, dir, toxicol training prog, 78-91 & 95-96, DIR, ENVIRON STUDIES & INDUST HYG PROG, UNIV ROCHESTER, 82-, EMER PROF ENVIRON MED, 93- *Personal Data:* b Racine, Wis, Feb 2, 26; m 56; Martha A Fisher; c Andrew G, Nancy & Claire E. *Educ:* Tufts Univ, AB, 49; Univ Rochester, PhD(psychol), 54. *Prof Exp:* Res assoc, Univ Rochester, 53-54; teaching intern, Brown Univ, 54-55; from instr to asst prof, Sch Med, Johns Hopkins Univ, 55-65. *Concurrent Pos:* Exec ed, J Exp Analytical Behav, 66-, ed, 73-77; mem preclin psychopharmacol res rev comt, NIMH, 67-71; pres, Div Psychopharmacol, Environ Protection Agency, 68-69, Div Exp Anal Behav, 78-82; mem, Nat Res Coun Panel on Carbon Monoxide, Nat Acad Sci, 73-77, mem bd toxicol & environ health hazards, 77-80 mem toxicol info prog comt, 82-85; mem, Sci Rev Panel Health Res, Environ Protection Agency, 68-69, Div Exp Analytical Behav, 78-82; mem bd sci affairs, Am Psy Asn, 83-86. *Mem:* Am Psychol Asn; Am Soc Pharmacol & Exp Therapeut; Behav Pharmacol Soc (pres, 66-68); Soc Toxicol; Asn Behav Analysis; Soc Exp Analysis Behav (secy-treas, 66-). *Res:* Behavioral pharmacology; experimental analysis of behavior; behavioral toxicology. *Mailing Add:* Dept Environ Med Univ Rochester Sch Med & Dent PO Box EHSC Rochester NY 14642. *Fax:* 716-256-2791

LATIMER, BRUCE MILLIKIN, BIOMECHANICS OF LOCOMOTION, HOMINID PALEONTOLOGY. *Current Pos:* From asst cur to assoc cur, 85-88, CUR & HEAD PHYS ANTHROP, CLEVELAND MUS NATURAL HIST, 88-, SUPVR, COLLECTIONS & RES DIV, 93-; ASST PROF ANAT, CASE WESTERN RES UNIV, 88- *Personal Data:* b Hamilton, Ohio, Aug 23, 53; m 86. *Educ:* Univ Ariz, BA, 75; Case Western Res Univ, MA, 78; Kent State Univ, PhD(biomed sci), 88. *Concurrent Pos:* Supvr, Collections & Res Div, Cleveland Mus Natural Hist, 93- *Mem:* Am Asn Phys Anthropologists. *Res:* Pleistocene hominis evolution; comparative primate anatomy. *Mailing Add:* 24737 Highland Rd Cleveland OH 44143

LATIMER, CLINTON NARATH, NEUROPHYSIOLOGY. *Current Pos:* DIR DRUG SAFETY EVAL, DIR, RES DEVELOP PHARMACEUT DIV, PENNWALT CORP, 80- *Personal Data:* b New York, NY, Aug 30, 24; m 56; c 3. *Educ:* Columbia Univ, AB, 48; Syracuse Univ, PhD(physiol), 56. *Prof Exp:* Group leader neuropharmacol, Am Cyanamid Co, 58-76, study dir toxicol, Lederle Labs Div, 76-80. *Concurrent Pos:* Nat Inst Neurol Dis & Blindness res fel neurophysiol, Univ Wash, 56-58. *Mem:* AAAS; Am Soc Pharmacol & Exp Therapeut; Soc Neurosci; Am Physiol Soc; Am Col Toxicol; Sigma Xi. *Res:* Neuropharmacology; function of the central nervous system as delineated by extra and intracellular recordings of neuronal activity under influence of drugs and in control states; psychopharmacology; safety evaluation of all classes of compounds; physiologic toxicology; long-term alteration of function by drugs; computer applications; research administration, toxicology, pathology, drug safety evaluation. *Mailing Add:* 2785 Rush-Mendon Rd Honeoye Falls NY 14472-9312

LATIMER, GEORGE WEBSTER, JR, ANALYTICAL CHEMISTRY. *Current Pos:* chief, Agr Analytical Systs, 86-92, actg state chemist, 88-90, STATE CHEMIST, OFF TEX STATE CHEMIST, 90- *Educ:* George Washington Univ, BS, 55; Princeton Univ, PhD(analytical chem), 61. *Prof Exp:* Group leader analytical serv & sr res chemist, PPG Industs, Corpus Christi, Tex, 62-64 & 67-73; chief nutrit qual control & sr group leader pharm & nutrit qual control, Mead Johnson, Evansville, Ill, 73-78; asst mgr qual assurance, Whitehall Labs, Elkhart, Ind, 78-81; mgr corp qual control, Bulk Chem Div, SFB, 81-84; mgr corp qual control, Norwood Industs, Malvern, Pa, 84-86. *Concurrent Pos:* Asst prof analytical chem & dir lab, Univ Utah, Salt Lake City, 65-67; consult, Kennecott Copper, 66-67, Desert Industs, 66-67, FGIS/USDA CONASUPO Negotiations, 90, USAF, 92; asst prof sci, Univ Evansville, 74-76; admins liaison counr, Hq Air Force Acad, 78-86; lectr, Air Univ, Maxwell AFB, Ala, 81-86; mem, Tex State Legis Comt Naturally Occurring Radioactive Mat, San Antonio, 89, Houston, 90. *Mem:* Am Asn Feed Control; Sigma Xi. *Res:* Research in method for determining deimethysulfoxide in triamptereme. *Mailing Add:* PO Drawer 3160 College Station TX 77841-3160. *Fax:* 409-845-1389

LATIMER, HOWARD LEROY, PLANT GENETICS, PLANT ECOLOGY. *Current Pos:* From asst prof to assoc prof, 58-68, PROF BIOL, CALIF STATE UNIV, FRESNO, 68- *Personal Data:* b Seattle, Wash, July 18, 29; m 57; c 4. *Educ:* Wash State Univ, BS, 51, MS, 55; Claremont Cols, PhD(bot), 59. *Mem:* Soc Study Evolution; Ecol Soc Am. *Res:* Reproductive ecology of plants. *Mailing Add:* 4534 E Rialto Ave Fresno CA 93726

LATIMER, PAUL HENRY, BIOPHYSICS. *Current Pos:* assoc prof, 62-71, PROF PHYSICS, AUBURN UNIV, 71- *Personal Data:* b New Orleans, La, Nov 25, 25; m 52; c 3. *Educ:* Univ Ill, MS, 50, PhD(biophys), 56. *Prof Exp:* Instr physics, Col William & Mary, 50-51; asst bot, Univ Ill, 53-56; res fel plant biol, Carnegie Inst Technol, 56-57; asst prof physics, Vanderbilt Univ, 57-62. *Concurrent Pos:* Investr, Howard Hughes Med Inst, 57-62; consult, Southern Res Inst, Birmingham, 76; contractor, US Army, 77. *Mem:* Biophys Soc; Am Phys Soc; Optical Soc Am. *Res:* Light scattering; biological optics; fluorescence; photosynthesis. *Mailing Add:* Dept Physics Auburn Univ Auburn AL 36830

LATIN, RICHARD, PHYTOPATHOLOGY, BIOLOGY. *Current Pos:* from asst prof to assoc prof, 81-93, PROF, DEPT BOT & PLANT PATH, PURDUE UNIV, 93- *Personal Data:* b Teaneck, NJ, Oct 4, 51; m 75, Barbara Jennings; c Eric W & David R. *Educ:* Waynesburg Col, BS, 73; Pa State Univ, MS, 77, PhD(plant path), 80. *Mem:* Am Phytopath Soc. *Res:* Epidemiology and management of vegetable diseases; development and delivery of decision support systems for managing cucurbit and tomato diseases. *Mailing Add:* Purdue Univ West Lafayette IN 47907-1968

LATORELLA, A HENRY, GENETICS, ALGOLOGY. *Current Pos:* ASSOC PROF BIOL, STATE UNIV NY, COL GENESEO, 70- *Personal Data:* b Winthrop, Mass, Mar 12, 40; m 64; c 2. *Educ:* Boston Col, BS, 61, MS, 64; Univ Maine, Orono, PhD(zool, genetics), 71. *Prof Exp:* Asst prof biol, Salem State Col, 66-68. *Mem:* Am Genetic Asn; Phycol Soc Am; AAAS; Genetics Soc Am; Sigma Xi. *Res:* Algal genetics and physiology; regulation of DNA replication and genetics and biochemistry of salinity adaptation by phytoflagellates. *Mailing Add:* Dept Biol State Univ NY Col Geneseo NY 14454

LATORRE, DONALD RUTLEDGE, MATHEMATICS. *Current Pos:* from asst prof to assoc prof, 67-76, PROF MATH, CLEMSON UNIV, 76- *Personal Data:* b Charleston, SC, May 4, 38; m 60; c 2. *Educ:* Wofford Col, BS, 60; Univ Tenn, MA, 62, PhD(math), 64. *Prof Exp:* Asst prof math, Univ Tenn, 67. *Mem:* Am Math Soc; Math Asn Am. *Res:* Abstract algebra, especially semigroups. *Mailing Add:* Dept Math Sci Clemson Univ Clemson SC 29631-1907

LATORRE, ROBERT GEORGE, SHIP HYDRODYNAMICS, NAVAL ARCHITECTURE. *Current Pos:* assoc prof, 84-87, PROF & CHMN NAVAL ARCHIT & MARINE ENG, UNIV NEW ORLEANS, 89- *Personal Data:* b Toledo, Ohio, Jan 9, 49; m 80. *Educ:* Univ Mich, BScE, 71, MS, 72; Univ Tokyo, MScE, 75, DEng, 79. *Honors & Awards:* Halburton Award Teaching & Res; Medal, Inst Indust Sci, Tokyo Univ. *Prof Exp:* Asst prof naval archit & marine eng, Univ Mich, 79-83; res scientist, Bassin d Essais des Carenes, Paris, 83-84. *Concurrent Pos:* Res scientist, David W Taylor Navel Ship Res & Develop Ctr, 80 & 81; assoc prof, Dept Mech Eng, Univ Tokyo, Japan, 86-87. *Mem:* Am Soc Mech Engrs; Soc Naval Archit & Marine Engrs; Japan Soc Naval Archit; Royal Inst Naval Archit. *Res:* Development of the design of shallow water river pushboats and estimating methods for ship resistance; towed ship safety and towed vessel course stability; design and use of 125 ft by 7 ft deep - offshore model testbasin in deep and shallow water; numerical hydrodynamics; ship design using computer aided engineering; cavitation noise and underwater acoustics. *Mailing Add:* 300 Lake Marina Dr New Orleans LA 70124

LATORRE, V(ICTOR) R(OBERT), electrical engineering, for more information see previous edition

LATOUR, PIERRE RICHARD, CHEMICAL ENGINEERING, PROCESS CONTROL. *Current Pos:* VPRES, DYNAMIC MATRIX CONTROL CORP, TEX, 95-, VPRES, ASPEN TECHNOL INC, TEX, 96-; PRES, SETPOINT RIGHT INC, TEX, 97- *Personal Data:* b Buffalo, NY, Apr 15, 40; m 62; c Michelle & Lisa. *Educ:* Va Polytech Inst, BSChE, 62; Purdue Univ, MS, 64, PhD(chem eng), 66. *Prof Exp:* Res engr, Math Group, Houston Res Lab, Shell Oil Co, Tex, 66, Comput Control Group, 66-67; mathematician, Theory & Analysis Off, Manned Spacecraft Ctr, NASA, Houston, 67, tech asst to chief, Simulation Br, 67-68; sr engr, head off, Mfg Technol Dept, Shell Oil Co, 69; mgr process control eng, Davis Comput Systs, Inc, NY & Tex, 70 & Biles & Assocs, Inc, Tex, 71-77; dir & chmn bd, Setpoint

Japan Inc, 84-90, consult engr & vpres, Setpoint Inc, Tex, 77-95. *Concurrent Pos:* Lectr, Purdue Univ, 66, Houston Res Lab, Shell Oil Co, 66, 67, Univ Houston, 68, Lehigh Univ, 69 & Univ Calif, Santa Barbara, 80, 81, Univ Tex, 84, Univ Houston & Purdue Univ, 85. *Mem:* Am Chem Soc; Am Inst Chem Engrs; Instrument Soc Am; Sigma Xi. *Res:* Automatic process control; applied mathematics; digital computation; crude oil distillation; computer control of petroleum refining; cracking; simulation; process dynamics; plant economics; optimization; process engineering; computer control justification; sales; business development; marketing. *Mailing Add:* 810 Herdsman Dr Houston TX 77079

LATOURETTE, HAROLD KENNETH, ORGANIC CHEMISTRY. *Current Pos:* RETIRED. *Personal Data:* b Seattle, Wash, Apr 10, 24; m 44, Beverly Burgess; c Helen M, Lorene, Marcia S & Stephen. *Educ:* Whitman Col, AB, 47; Univ Wash, PhD(org chem), 51. *Prof Exp:* Res assoc, Univ Wash, 48-51; res chemist, Westvaco Chem Div, FMC Corp, WVa, 51-54, dir pioneering res, Westvaco Chlor-Alkali Div, 54-56, supvr org res, Cent Res Labs, NJ, 56-57, mgr org res & develop, Becco Chem Div, NY, 57-58, mgr org chem res, Inorg Chem Div, NJ, 58-62, Europ tech dir, Chem Div & vpres, FMC Chem, SA, Switz, 62-65, mgr planning & eval, Cent Res Dept, NJ, 65-72, mgr eval, Chem Group, 72-76, environ mgr Toxic Substances, FMC Corp, Pa, 77-83. *Mem:* Sigma Xi; Am Chem Soc. *Res:* Organic reaction mechanisms; aromatic substitution; peroxides; epoxides; isocyanates; phosphorus and sulfur organics; halogenation; industrial processes. *Mailing Add:* 1526 Deception Rd Anacortes WA 98221

LATOURETTE, HOWARD BENNETT, RADIOLOGY. *Current Pos:* prof radiol, Col Med, Univ Iowa, 59-80, head radiation ther, 78-80. *Personal Data:* b Detroit, Mich, Aug 26, 18; m 42; c 4. *Educ:* Oberlin Col, AB, 40; Univ Mich, MD, 43. *Prof Exp:* From instr to assoc prof radiol, Univ Mich, 49-59. *Concurrent Pos:* Mem staff radiation ther sect, Univ Hosps, Univ Iowa. *Mem:* AAAS; Radiol Soc NAm. *Res:* Clinical use of radiation in treatment of cancer and resulting survival studies; tumor registry organization and function alteration of radiosensitivity of tumors. *Mailing Add:* 701 Oakknoll Dr Iowa City IA 52246-5167

LA TOURETTE, JAMES THOMAS, COMPUTER LANGUAGES. *Current Pos:* PROF ELEC ENG & COMPUT SCI, POLYTECH UNIV, 67- *Personal Data:* b Miami, Ariz, Dec 26, 31; m 55, Muriel Ashe; c Mary B, John E, J Thomas & Joanne. *Educ:* Calif Inst Technol, BS, 53; Harvard Univ, MA, 54, PhD(physics), 58. *Prof Exp:* Res fel physics, Harvard Univ, 57-58, lectr, 58-59; NSF fel, Univ Bonn, 59-60; physicist, Gen Elec Res Lab, 60-62; sr supvry scientist, TRG, Inc Div, Control Data Corp, 62-66, sect head gas laser, 66-67; assoc dir, Weber Res Inst, 87-91. *Mem:* AAAS; Inst Elec & Electronics Engrs; Asn Comp Mach. *Res:* Computer languages, systems and applications; gas laser research and applications; saturated resonance spectroscopy and laser frequency stabilization. *Mailing Add:* Dept Comput Sci Polytech Univ Rte 110 Farmingdale NY 11735. *Fax:* 516-755-4404; *E-Mail:* latour@rama.poly.edu

LATSCHAR, CARL ERNEST, PHYSICAL CHEMISTRY. *Current Pos:* Res chemist, 50-62, SR RES CHEMIST, E I DU PONT DE NEMOURS & CO, INC, 62- *Personal Data:* b Newton, Kans, May 24, 19; m 41; c 5. *Educ:* Kans State Univ, BS, 41, MS, 47; Univ Wis, PhD(phys chem), 50. *Mem:* Am Chem Soc. *Res:* Textile fiber process and product development. *Mailing Add:* PO Box 1273 Salina KS 67402-1273

LATSHAW, DAVID RODNEY, ANALYTICAL CHEMISTRY. *Current Pos:* res chemist, Air Prod & Chem Inc, 66-69, group leader, 69-80, mgr analytical serv, 80-87, RES ASSOC SPECTROS, ALLENTOWN LABS, AIR PROD & CHEM INC, 87- *Personal Data:* b Allentown, Pa, Nov 4, 39; m 71, Patricia M Fix; c Jonathan David & Rebekah Ruth. *Educ:* Muhlenberg Col, BS, 61; Lehigh Univ, MS, 63, PhD(chem), 66. *Prof Exp:* Res asst, Lehigh Univ, 63-66. *Mem:* Am Chem Soc; Sigma Xi. *Res:* Infrared spectroscopy. *Mailing Add:* 944 Belford Rd Allentown PA 18103

LATSHAW, J DAVID, ANIMAL SCIENCE & NUTRITION. *Current Pos:* From asst prof to assoc prof, 70-84, PROF POULTRY SCI, OHIO STATE UNIV, 84- *Personal Data:* b Reading, Pa. *Educ:* Pa State Univ, BS, 64; Wash State Univ, PhD(nutrit), 70. *Mem:* Poultry Sci Asn; Am Inst Nutrit. *Res:* Nutritional needs of egg-type and meat-type chickens; nutrients such as selenium, amino acids, and energy; effects of feedstuff processing. *Mailing Add:* Poultry Sci Dept Ohio State Univ, 674 W Lane Ave Columbus OH 43210-1056

LATTA, BRYAN MICHAEL, SOLID STATE THIN FILM ELECTROCHROMICS, PARTICLE SOLID INTERACTION THEORY & MODELING. *Current Pos:* PROF PHYSICS, ACADIA UNIV, 92- *Personal Data:* b Oshawa, Ont, Oct 25, 46; m 95, Suzhen Huang; c Hope. *Educ:* Queen's Univ, BSc, 70, MSc, 75, PhD(physics), 78. *Prof Exp:* Asst prof physics, Acadia Univ, 78-81; Nat Sci & Eng Res Coun Can Univ res fel, Mem Univ Nfld, 81-84, asst prof physics, 85-92. *Concurrent Pos:* Prin investr, Thin Film Lab, Acadia Univ, 88- *Mem:* Can Asn Physicists; Am Phys Soc. *Res:* Use detailed solid state charge distributions to evaluate the electronic and nuclear stopping power; Monte-Carlo and numerical modeling of particle-solid collision phenomena; multiple layer thin film coating and optical performance evaluation; particle solid interaction theory and modeling; electric discharge in gases; electronic instrumentation. *Mailing Add:* Physics Dept Acadia Univ Wolfville NS B0P 1X0 Can. *Fax:* 902-585-1074; *E-Mail:* latta@acadiau.ca

LATTA, HARRISON, PATHOLOGY. *Current Pos:* assoc prof, 54-60, PROF PATH, SCH MED, UNIV CALIF, LOS ANGELES, 60- *Personal Data:* b Los Angeles, Calif, Apr 5, 18; m 41, 85, Lya Gruber; c 4. *Educ:* Univ Calif, Los Angeles, AB, 40; Johns Hopkins Univ, MD, 43. *Prof Exp:* Intern, Church Home & Hosp, Md, 44; from asst resident to resident path, Johns Hopkins Hosp, 44-46, instr, Johns Hopkins Univ, 45-46; res assoc biol, Mass Inst Technol, 49-51; asst prof path, Sch Med, Case Western Res Univ, 51-54. *Concurrent Pos:* Res fel, Children's Hosp, Boston & Harvard Med Sch, 48-49. *Mem:* AAAS; Electron Micros Soc Am; Am Soc Cell Biol. *Res:* Ultrastructure and diseases of the kidney. *Mailing Add:* Dept Path 1P-250 CHS Med Sch UCLA Los Angeles CA 90095-1732

LATTA, JOHN NEAL, COMPUTER SCIENCE, ELECTRICAL ENGINEERING. *Current Pos:* PRES, FOURTH WAVE, INC, 89- *Personal Data:* b Ottumwa, Iowa, Apr 11, 44; m 66; c 3. *Educ:* Brigham Young Univ, BES, 66; Univ Kans, MS, 69, PhD(elec eng), 71. *Prof Exp:* Mem tech staff holography, RCA Labs, NJ, 67; res asst optics, Ctr Res Eng Sci, Univ Kans, 67-68; mem tech staff holography, Bell Tel Labs, NJ, 69; res engr, Radar & Optics Lab, Univ Mich, Ann Arbor, 69-73; sr res engr, Environ Res Inst Mich, 73-77; sr staff scientist, Sci Applns, Inc, 77-83; pres, Adroit Systs, Inc, 83-89. *Mem:* Inst Elec & Electronics Engrs; Asn Comput Mach; Sigma Xi. *Res:* Multimedia computing; digital image processing; visual displays; system engineering; digital system architecture; software engineering; holography; optical design. *Mailing Add:* PO Box 6547 Alexandria VA 22306-0547

LATTA, WILLIAM CARL, FISH BIOLOGY. *Current Pos:* in-charge, Inst Fisheries Res, 66-76, chief res sect, Fisheries Div, 76-92, FISHERY BIOLOGIST, INST FISHERIES RES, STATE DEPT NATURAL RESOURCES, MICH, 55-, EMER CHIEF RES SECT, 92- *Personal Data:* b Niagara Falls, NY, May 18, 25; m 50, Harriet Mabon; c 5. *Educ:* Cornell Univ, BS, 50; Univ Okla, MS, 52; Univ Mich, PhD(fishery biol), 57. *Prof Exp:* Aquatic biologist, State Conserv Dept, NY, 50. *Concurrent Pos:* Adj prof fisheries & wildlife, Sch Natural Resources, Univ Mich, Ann Arbor, 73- *Mem:* Am Fisheries Soc; Am Soc Ichthyol & Herpet; Wildlife Soc; Ecol Soc Am; Am Inst Fishery Res Biologists; Soc Conserv Biol. *Res:* Fish population dynamics; management of freshwater fisheries; biology of endangered and threatened fishes. *Mailing Add:* Inst Fisheries Res Univ Mus Annex Ann Arbor MI 48109

LATTER, ALBERT L, theoretical physics, for more information see previous edition

LATTER, RICHARD, theoretical physics, for more information see previous edition

LATTERELL, JOSEPH J, ANALYTICAL CHEMISTRY. *Current Pos:* from asst prof to assoc prof, 67-78, PROF ANALYTICAL CHEM, UNIV MINN, MORRIS, 78- *Personal Data:* b St Cloud, Minn, Nov 2, 32; m 64; c 4. *Educ:* St John's Univ, Minn, BA, 59; Purdue Univ, MS, 62; Univ Colo, PhD(analytical chem), 64. *Prof Exp:* Instr analytical chem, Univ Wis, 64; asst prof, John Carroll Univ, 64-67. *Concurrent Pos:* Danforth assoc, 81-86. *Mem:* Am Chem Soc. *Res:* Heavy metal migration and plant uptake of phosphorous in soils amended with wastewater and sewage sludge; chemical analyses of the bottom deposits of Minnesota lakes. *Mailing Add:* Dept Chem Univ Minn Morris MN 56267

LATTERELL, RICHARD L, GENETICS. *Current Pos:* from assoc prof to prof biol, 68-91, EMER PROF BIOL, SHEPARD COL, 91- *Personal Data:* b Paynesville, Minn, Mar 14, 28; m 51. *Educ:* Univ Minn, Duluth, BA, 50; Pa State Univ, MS, 55; Cornell Univ, PhD(genetics), 58. *Prof Exp:* Nat Cancer Inst fel genetics, Brookhaven Nat Lab, 58-60; geneticist, Div Radiation & Organisms, Smithsonian Inst, 60-63; geneticist, Union Carbide Res Inst, 63-68. *Concurrent Pos:* Vis assoc prof agron, Colo State Univ, 79-80. *Mem:* Genetics Soc Am; Bot Soc Am; Sigma Xi; Am Inst Biol Sci. *Res:* Radiation genetics of maize; space biology; stress tolerance of higher plants; plant cytogenetics. *Mailing Add:* Dept Biol Shepherd Col Shepherdstown WV 25443

LATTES, RAFFAELE, MEDICINE. *Current Pos:* SR CONSULT SURG PATH, NY PRESBY HOSP, 78- *Personal Data:* b Italy, May 22, 10; nat US; m 36; c 2. *Educ:* Univ Turin, MD, 33; Columbia Univ, MedSciD, 46. *Prof Exp:* Asst gen surg, Univ Turin, 34-38; instr path, Woman's Med Col Pa, 41-43; instr surg & surg path, Columbia Univ, 43-46, asst prof path, Postgrad Hosp, 46-48, asst prof, 48-51, prof surg path, 51-78, emer prof surg path, Col Physicians & Surgeons, 78. *Concurrent Pos:* Consult, Roswell Park Mem Inst, Knickerbocker Hosp, NY, Roosevelt Hosp, St Lukes Hosp, Hosp Joint Dis & Vet Admin Hosp. *Mem:* Harvey Soc; Am Asn Path & Bact; Am Asn Cancer Res; Col Am Path; Asn Am Med Cols; NY Acad Med. *Res:* Surgical pathology. *Mailing Add:* 597 Rutland Ave Teaneck NJ 07666

LATTIME, EDMUND CHARLES, IMMUNOLOGY. *Current Pos:* Fel immunol, 77-79, res assoc, 79-84, INSTR IMMUNOL, GRAD SCH, CORNELL UNIV, SLOAN-KETTERING INST, 81- *Personal Data:* b Newburyport, Mass, Jan 18, 51; m 74. *Educ:* Gettysburg Col, BA, 73; Rutgers Univ, MS, & PhD(zool), 77. *Concurrent Pos:* Scholar, Leukemia Soc Am, 84; lab asst mem immunol, Sloan-Kettering Inst Cancer Res, 85-; mem, Oncol Rev Bd, US Vet Admin, 88- *Mem:* Am Asn Immunologists; Am Asn Cancer Res; Am Chem Soc. *Res:* Natural immunity with emphasis on mechanisms of lytic factor release and actions. *Mailing Add:* Dept Med Div Neoplastic Dis Thomas Jefferson Univ 1025 Walnut St Suite 1014 Philadelphia PA 19107-5005. *Fax:* 215-923-0797

LATTIMER, JAMES MICHAEL, ASTROPHYSICS, COSMOCHEMISTRY. *Current Pos:* from asst prof to assoc prof, 79-88, PROF ASTRON, STATE UNIV NY, STONY BROOK, 88- *Personal Data:* b Marion, Ind, Apr 12, 50; c Jennifer, Judith, Julia & Jonathan. *Educ:* Univ Notre Dame, BS, 72; Univ Tex, Austin, PhD(astron), 76. *Prof Exp:* Res assoc, Univ Chicago, 76; res assoc astron, Univ Ill, Urbana-Champaign, 76-79. *Concurrent Pos:* Alfred P Sloan res fel, 82-84; Ernst F Fullam fel, 85-86; vis prof, Nordita, Copenhagen, Denmark, 85-86. *Mem:* Am Astron Soc; Int Astron Union; Am Phys Soc; Am Geophys Union; Astron Soc Pac. *Res:* Supernovae; neutron stars; equation of state at high densities and temperatures; meteoritics; grain formation in novae and supernovae; nuclear physics; neutrino astrophysics. *Mailing Add:* Dept Earth & Space Sci State Univ NY Stony Brook NY 11794. *Fax:* 516-632-8240; *E-Mail:* lattimer@sbasts.ess.sunysb.edu

LATTIMER, ROBERT PHILLIPS, ANALYTICAL CHEMISTRY, POLYMER CHEMISTRY. *Current Pos:* SR RES & DEVELOP ASSOC ANALYTICAL CHEM, B F GOODRICH CO, 74- *Personal Data:* b Kansas City, Mo, Feb 2, 45; m 82, Mary Downs; c Scott & Paul. *Educ:* Univ Mo-Columbia, BS, 67; Univ Kans, PhD(chem), 71. *Honors & Awards:* Sparks-Thomas Award. *Prof Exp:* Fel chem, Univ Mich, Ann Arbor, 72-74. *Mem:* Am Chem Soc; Am Soc Mass Spectrometry; Sigma Xi. *Res:* Analysis of polymers; mass spectrometry of polymers; degradation of polymers. *Mailing Add:* B F Goodrich Res & Develop Ctr 9921 Brecksville Rd Brecksville OH 44141. *Fax:* 216-447-5249

LATTIN, DANNY L(EE), MEDICINAL CHEMISTRY. *Current Pos:* DEAN & PROF, COL PHARM, SDAK STATE UNIV, BROOKINGS, 95- *Personal Data:* b Smith Ctr, Kans, Jan 9, 42. *Educ:* Univ Kans, BS, 65; Univ Minn, Minneapolis, PhD(med chem), 70. *Prof Exp:* From asst prof to assoc prof med chem, Col Pharm, Univ Ark Med Sch, Little Rock, 70-75, prof, 80-95. *Concurrent Pos:* Vpres, EPSCOR Ark Sci & Technol Authority, 94-95. *Mem:* Am Chem Soc; Am Asn Cols Pharm. *Res:* Synthesis of novel opiate antagonists; synthesis and evaluation of novel opiate receptor affinity labels; study of sterochemical properties of drug receptors. *Mailing Add:* Col Pharm SDak State Univ Box 2202C Brookings SD 57007. *Fax:* 605-688-6232; *E-Mail:* lattind@mg.sdstate.edu

LATTIN, JOHN D, ENTOMOLOGY. *Current Pos:* asst entomologist, Agr Exp Sta, Ore State Univ, 55-61, from instr to assoc prof, 55-68, asst dean sci, 67-73, PROF ENTOM, ORE STATE UNIV, 68- *Personal Data:* b Chicago, Ill, July 27, 27; m 53; c 3. *Educ:* Iowa State Univ, BS, 50; Univ Kans, MA, 51; Univ Calif, Berkeley, PhD(entom), 64. *Honors & Awards:* Loyd Carter Award, Ore State Univ, 61. *Prof Exp:* Aquatic entomologist, Dept Limnol, Acad Natural Hist, Philadelphia, 51; jr vector control specialist, Bur Vector Control, Calif Dept Pub Health, 54-55. *Concurrent Pos:* Cur, Syst Entom Lab, Ore State, 61-66 & 74-; NSF fac fel, Univ Wageningen, 65-66; consult, USDA, 81-82. *Mem:* Entom Soc Am; Soc Syst Zool. *Res:* Systematics of the Pentatomoidea, Leptopododoidea and Miridae; origin, distribution and phylogeny of the Heteroptera; evolution and zoogeography of the insecta; aquatic entomology; scientific education; education of talented students; introduced insects; applied systematic entomology. *Mailing Add:* Dept Entom Ore State Univ 2046 Cordley Hall Corvallis OR 97331-2907

LATTMAN, EATON EDWARD, MOLECULAR BIOPHYSICS. *Current Pos:* from asst prof to prof, 76-96, PROF & CHMN, DEPT BIOPHYS, SCH ARTS & SCI, JOHNS HOPKINS UNIV, 96- *Personal Data:* b Chicago, Ill, May 15, 40; m 66; c Laura Joy. *Educ:* Harvard Col, BA, 62; Johns Hopkins Univ, 69. *Honors & Awards:* Res Career Develop Award, NIH. *Prof Exp:* NIH fel biophys, Johns Hopkins Univ, 69-70, res scientist, 70-73; fel, Max Planck Inst Biochem, 74; NIH fel biophys, Brandeis Univ, 74-76. *Concurrent Pos:* ed-in-chief, Prokins Structure, Function & Genetics; dir, Intercampus Prog Molec Biophys. *Mem:* Am Phys Soc; Am Crystallog Asn. *Res:* Protein crystallography; actin-binding proteins; mutants of staphylococcal nuclease; tissue metalloproteases; physical studies of protein folding; rational drug design; crystallographic methods development. *Mailing Add:* Dept Biophys Johns Hopkins Univ Baltimore MD 21218-2684. *Fax:* 410-516-4118; *E-Mail:* lattman@jhunix.hcf.jhu.edu

LATTMAN, LAURENCE HAROLD, GEOLOGY. *Current Pos:* pres, 83-93, EMER PRES, NMEX INST MINING TECHNOL, 93- *Personal Data:* b New York, NY, Nov 30, 23; m 46, Hanna Cohn; c Martin & Barbara. *Educ:* City Col New York, BChE, 48; Univ Cincinnati, MS, 51, PhD(geol), 53. *Honors & Awards:* Fulbright lectr, Moscow State Univ, 75. *Prof Exp:* Instr geol, Univ Cincinnati 51 & Univ Mich, 52-53; photogeologist, Gulf Oil Corp, 53-56, asst head, Photogeol Sect, 56-57; from asst prof to prof geomorphol, Pa State Univ, 57-70; prof geol & head dept, Univ Cincinnati, 70-75; dean, Col Mines & Mineral Indust & Col Eng, Univ Utah, 75-83. *Concurrent Pos:* Mem, Nat Res Coun, 59-62. *Mem:* Fel Geol Soc Am; Am Soc Photogram; Am Asn Petrol Geologists; Sigma Xi. *Res:* Remote sensing of environment; geomorphology; fracture analysis on aerial photographs. *Mailing Add:* 11509 Penfield Lane NE Albuquerque NM 87111. *Fax:* 505-237-2382

LATTMAN, MICHAEL, MAIN-GROUP CHEMISTRY, HYPERVALENT MOLECULES. *Current Pos:* from asst prof to assoc prof, 79-93, PROF CHEM, SOUTHERN METHODIST UNIV, 93- *Personal Data:* b New York, NY, June 2, 50; m 74, Michele Miller; c Allison & Lauren. *Educ:* City Col New York, BS, 72; City Univ New York, PhD(inorg chem), 77. *Prof Exp:* Fel, Univ Tex, Austin, 76-79. *Concurrent Pos:* Vis res scientist, E I Du Pont de Nemours & Co, 86-87. *Mem:* Am Chem Soc; Sigma Xi; Coun Undergrad Res. *Res:* Synthesis, structure and reactivity of macrocyclic-stabilized hypervalent main-group elements; reactions at coordinated ligands; new ligands which alter reactions at transition-metal centers. *Mailing Add:* Chem Dept Southern Methodist Univ Dallas TX 75275-0314. *Fax:* 214-768-4089; *E-Mail:* mlattman@sun.cis.smu.edu

LATTUADA, CHARLES P, bacteriology, for more information see previous edition

LATZ, HOWARD W, ANALYTICAL CHEMISTRY. *Current Pos:* assoc prof, 66-74, PROF ANALYTICAL CHEM, OHIO UNIV, 74- *Personal Data:* b Rochester, NY, Jan 9, 33; m 53; c 3. *Educ:* Rochester Inst Technol, BS, 59; Univ Fla, MS, 61, PhD(chem), 63. *Prof Exp:* Res specialist, Union Carbide Corp, 63-66. *Mem:* Am Chem Soc; Sigma Xi. *Res:* Luminescence methods of analysis; electrophoresis of organic ions; analytical applications of dye lasers. *Mailing Add:* Dept Chem Ohio Univ Athens OH 45701-2978

LAU, BRAD W C, biochemistry, for more information see previous edition

LAU, CATHERINE Y, MOLECULAR BIOLOGY, IMMUNOLOGY. *Current Pos:* supvr immunopharmacol, Ortho Pharmaceut, Ltd, Can, 77-84, proj mgr immunopharmacol, 85-87, mgr biotechnol res, 87-88, DIR BIOL RES, THE R W JOHNSON PHARMACEUT RES INST, 89- *Personal Data:* b Hong Kong, Feb 11, 51; Can citizen; m 77, Sek L Yuen; c Harold & Heidi. *Educ:* Ind Univ, BS, 72; Yale Univ, MPhil, 74, PhD(biochem), 76. *Honors & Awards:* PRI Discovery Award; Pinnacle Award for Excellence. *Prof Exp:* Res fel immunol, Ont Cancer Inst & Princess Margaret Hosp, Toronto, 76-77. *Concurrent Pos:* Asst prof, Dept Immunol, Univ Toronto, 84- *Mem:* Sigma Xi; Am Asn Immunologists; Int Soc Immunopharmacol. *Res:* Discover immunologically active molecules and develop them into human therapeutics. *Mailing Add:* R W Johnson Pharmaceut Res Inst 19 Green Belt Dr Don Mills ON M3C 1L9 Can

LAU, CHEUK KUN, LEUKOTRIENES, SYNTHETIC METHODS. *Current Pos:* SR RES CHEMIST MED CHEM, MERCK FROSST CAN INC, 80- *Personal Data:* b Hong Kong, Sept 3, 51; Can citizen; m 84. *Educ:* McMaster Univ, BSc, 74; Univ BC, PhD(chem), 78. *Honors & Awards:* Boris Monsaroff Mem Medal, Chem Inst Can, 74. *Prof Exp:* Res fel chem, Wayne State Univ, 78-80. *Mem:* Am Chem Soc; Chem Inst Can. *Res:* Synthesis of leukotrienes and its related products of the lipoxygenase enzymes and the design of inhibitors of this enzyme. *Mailing Add:* 476 Cr Boyer Ile Bizard PQ H9C 9Z7 Can

LAU, CLIFFORD JAMES, POLYURETHANES, POLYMER BLENDS. *Current Pos:* assoc res scientist, 92-96, ASSOC SCIENTIST, BAYER INC, 96- *Personal Data:* b Red Bank, NJ, Apr 9, 55. *Educ:* Ohio State Univ, BS, 77, PhD(org chem), 87; Northeastern Univ, MS, 82. *Prof Exp:* Assoc scientist, Polaroid Corp, 77-82; sr develop chemist, Miles Inc, 87-92. *Mem:* Am Chem Soc; Soc Plastics Engrs. *Res:* Polymer blends, polyurethemers and organic chemistry; modification of thermoplastic polyurethanes, polycarbonates and mylores; development of polyurethane and polyurea materials for application in exterior automotive body panels. *Mailing Add:* 4709 Lakeshore Terr Ft Gratiot MI 48059. *Fax:* 519-339-7719; *E-Mail:* clifford.lau.b@bayer.com

LAU, FRANCIS YOU KING, MEDICINE. *Current Pos:* CLIN PROF MED & RADIOL, SCH MED, UNIV SOUTHERN CALIF, 79- *Personal Data:* b Honolulu, Hawaii, Jan 5, 24; m 48; c 4. *Educ:* Loma Linda Univ, MD, 47. *Prof Exp:* From clin instr to clin asst prof med, Loma Linda Univ, 54-59; asst prof, Sch Med, Univ Calif, San Francisco, 59-60; assoc prof, 60-72, prof med, Loma Linda Univ, 72- *Concurrent Pos:* Assoc prof med, Univ Southern Calif, 64-70, prof, 70-79; mem attend staff & chief, Adult Cardiovasc Catheterization Lab, Los Angeles Co-Univ Southern Calif Med Ctr, 65-79, chief cardiol, 70-79; consult, Vet Admin & Glendale Hosps; fel coun clin cardiol, Am Heart Asn. *Mem:* Fel Am Col Cardiol; fel Am Col Physicians. *Res:* Cardiology; cardiac catheterization, arrhythmias and pacemakers; artificial heart-lung preparations; balloon valvuloplasty. *Mailing Add:* 1313 S Fann Anaheim CA 92804

LAU, JARK CHONG, LASER APPLICATIONS. *Current Pos:* sr res fel, 80-90, PRIN RES FEL, KIMBERLY-CLARK CORP, 90- *Personal Data:* b Singapore, Oct 18, 35; US citizen; wid; c 2. *Educ:* Calif Inst Technol, MS, 63, AE, 64; Univ Southampton, Eng, PhD(fluid mech), 71. *Prof Exp:* Assoc prof fluid & thermodyn, Univ Singapore, 71-75; tech consult fluid & acoust, Lockheed-Ga Co, 75-80. *Mem:* Assoc fel Am Inst Aeronaut & Astronaut. *Res:* Characterize the structure of free shear turbulence; development of better techniques of forming fibrous webs; consultant service to many mills; development of a laser technology base. *Mailing Add:* Kimberly-Clark Corp 1400 Holcomb Bridge Rd Roswell GA 30076. *Fax:* 770-587-8136; *E-Mail:* jlau@kcc.com

LAU, JOHN H, MECHANICAL ENGINEERING, ENGINEERING PHYSICS. *Current Pos:* SR ENGR ELECTRONICS & MECH ENG, HEWLETT PACKARD LABS, 84- *Personal Data:* b China, June 17, 46; US citizen; m 72, Teresa T; c Judy M. *Educ:* Nat Taiwan Univ, BE, 70; Univ BC, MASc, 73; Univ Wis-Madison, MS, 74; Fairleigh Dickinson Univ, MS, 81; Univ Ill-Urbana, PhD(theoret & appl mech), 77. *Prof Exp:* Teaching asst mech, Univ Ill-Urbana, 74-77; engr struct, Exxon Prod & Res Co, 77-78; res assoc paper physics, Int Paper Co Res Ctr, 78-79; sr engr mech eng, Ebasco Serv Inc, 79-81 & nuclear eng, Bechtel Power Corp, 81-83; mem tech staff stress analysis, Sandia Nat Labs, 83-84. *Concurrent Pos:* Session chmn, tech comt mem & workshop speaker, Inst Elec & Electronics Engrs & Am Soc Mech Eng Tech Conf; assoc tech ed, Inst Elec & Electronics Engrs, Trans Components, Hybrids & Mfg Technol, Am Soc Mech Engrs, Trans J Electronic Packaging. *Mem:* Sigma Xi; NY Acad Sci; AAAS; fel Inst Elec & Electronics Engrs. *Res:* Structural engineering; applied mechanics; nuclear engineering; operations research; materials science engineering; mechanical vibrations; electronics packaging and interconnection. *Mailing Add:* Hewlett Packard Co 3500 Deer Creek Rd Palo Alto CA 94304. *Fax:* 650-852-8560

LAU, JOSEPH T Y, GLYCOBIOLOGY. *Current Pos:* ASST RES PROF MOLECULAR BIOL, STATE UNIV NY, 86- *Personal Data:* b Hong Kong, Mar 21, 53; US citizen; m 88. *Educ:* Univ Wash, Seattle, BS, 75; Purdue Univ, PhD(biochem), 81. *Prof Exp:* Postdoctoral fel molecular biol, Johns Hopkins Sch Med, 81-84, res assoc, 84-85; cancer res scientist III, 86-90, cancer res scientist IV, Roswell Park Cancer Inst, 90- *Mem:* Soc Complex Carbohydrates; Am Soc Biol Chemists; AAAS. *Res:* Function and regulation of glycoconjugates; molecular biology of glycosyltransferases; expression of cellular differentiation epitopes. *Mailing Add:* Dept Cell & Molecular Biol Roswell Park Cancer Inst Elm & Carlton Sts Buffalo NY 14203-1190

LAU, KENNETH W, CHEMISTRY, FLUOROPOLYMERS. *Current Pos:* res chemist, E I Du Pont de Nemours & Co, Inc, 69-73, develop supvr, Film Dept, Richmond, Va, 73-76, area supt-tech, Plastic Prod & Resins Dept, 76-79, mkt mgr, Fluoropolymers Div, 79-85, MKT MGR, SPECIALITY POLYMERS DIV, E I DU PONT DE NEMOURS & CO, INC, 85- *Personal Data:* b Lamoure, NDak, Nov 27, 41; m 63, Judith W; c 2. *Educ:* Univ NDak, BS, 63, PhD(chem), 69; Univ Sask, Regina, MSc, 68. *Prof Exp:* Chemist, Rock Island Arsenal Lab, US Army, 63-64. *Mem:* Am Chem Soc; Sigma Xi. *Res:* Ylid chemistry. *Mailing Add:* 3 Briarwood Ct Landenberg PA 19350

LAU, KIN-HING WILLIAM, BONE & MINERAL RESEARCH. *Current Pos:* RES SCIENTIST, JERRY L PETTIS MEM VET ADMIN HOSP, 82-, ASSOC PROF ENZYMOL & KINETICS, LOMA LINDA UNIV, 90- *Personal Data:* b Hong Kong, China, July 4, 53. *Educ:* State Univ NY, Plattsburg, BA, 76; Iowa State Univ, PhD(biochem), 82. *Concurrent Pos:* Res fel, Loma Linda Univ, 82-84, asst prof enzymol & kinetics, 84-90. *Mem:* Am Soc Biochem & Molecular Biol; Am Soc Bone & Mineral Res; Am Soc Cell Biol; Endocrine Soc; Am Fedn Clin Res. *Res:* Bone and mineral research. *Mailing Add:* Jerry L Pettis Mem Vet Admin Hosp MM151 Loma Linda CA 92357-0001

LAU, L(EUNG KU) STEPHEN, HYDROLOGY, HYDRAULIC & SANITARY ENGINEERING. *Current Pos:* from asst prof to prof, Univ Hawaii, 59-92, assoc dir, Water Resources Res Ctr, 64-70, actg dir, 70, dir, 71-90, EMER PROF CIVIL ENG, UNIV HAWAII, 92- *Personal Data:* b Shanghai, China, Sept 9, 29; US citizen; m 59, Virginia M Lew; c Ronald D, Kristina G (Tong) & Melina C (Doong). *Educ:* Univ Calif, Berkeley, BS, 53, MS, 55, PhD(hydraul & sanit eng), 59. *Honors & Awards:* George Warren Fuller Award, Am Waterworks Asn, 89. *Prof Exp:* Res engr sea water intrusion, Univ Calif, Berkeley, 53-54 & ground water pollution, 55-56. *Concurrent Pos:* Ground water consult, Honolulu Bd Water Supply, 60-64; dir, USPHS training grant, Univ Hawaii, 64-65; vis assoc prof, Univ Calif, Berkeley, 65-66; Fulbright vis prof, Univ Malaya, 73-74; adj vis assoc, East-West Ctr, 80-81; consult, Univ Guam, 72 & 75, WHO, 74, AMAX, 78, World Bank, 78 & UN, 81. *Mem:* Am Waterworks Asn; Am Geophys Union; Am Soc Civil Engrs; Water Environ Fedn. *Res:* Water reuse; groundwater; water pollution assessment; hydrologic evaluation of water resources; flood computations; water resources research administration; water resources policies; Hydrology and water resources of the Hawaiian Islands; hydrology instruction. *Mailing Add:* Water Resources Res Ctr Univ Hawaii Honolulu HI 96822. *Fax:* 808-956-5044

LAU, NGAR-CHEUNG, ATMOSPHERIC GENERAL CIRCULATION. *Current Pos:* vis scientist, Geophys Fluid Dynamics Prog, 78-81, mem res staff, 81-84, res meteorologist, 84-92, SR RES METEOROLOGIST, GEOPHYS FLUID DYNAMICS LAB, PRINCETON UNIV, 92-; LEAD SCIENTIST, OBSERVATIONAL STUDIES PROJ, NAT OCEANIC & ATMOSPHERIC ADMIN, US DEPT COM, 96- *Personal Data:* b Hong Kong, July 21, 53; US citizen; m 79, Chih-Ping F HSU; c Michelle. *Educ:* Chinese Univ, Hong Kong, BSc, 74; Univ Wash, PhD(atmospheric sci), 78. *Honors & Awards:* Clarence Leroy Meisinger Award, Am Meteorol Soc, 90; Unusually Outstanding Performance Award, US Dept Com/Nat Oceanic & Atmospheric Admin, 91. *Prof Exp:* Res asst atmospheric sci, Univ Wash, 74-78. *Concurrent Pos:* Res asst atmospheric sci, Nat Ctr Atmospheric Res, 76-77; lectr with rank of assoc prof, prof, atmospheric & oceanic sci, Princeton Univ, 82-; mem, Coun Equatorial Pac Ocean Climate Studies, US Dept Com, 85-94; US deleg, US/China Monsoon Workshop, 87, US/Japan Elnino-Southern Oscillation Workshop, 87; ed, Comt, Dynamics Atmospheres & Oceans, 88-; vis scientist, Bur Meteorol Res Ctr, Melbourne, Australia, 89; mem, Comt Climate Variations, Am Meteorol Soc, 90-93; Int Reviewer, Nat Res Coun Taiwan, 91-94; vis lectr, Nat Res Coun, Taiwan, 92; C N Yang vis fel, Chinese Univ Hong Kong, 93; ed, J Atmospheric Scis, 96-; sci adv, Royal Observ, Hong Kong, 96- *Mem:* Fel Am Meteorol Soc; World Meteorol Orgn; Am Geophys Union; Hong Kong Meteorol Soc. *Res:* Diagnosis of large-scale circulation system in observed and model-simulated atmospheres; processing of meteorological data sets for studying nature and causes of atmospheric variability on different time scales; studying the influences of air-sea interaction on weather and climate. *Mailing Add:* Geophys Fluid Dynamics Lab Nat Oceanic & Atmospheric Admin Princeton Univ PO Box 308 Princeton NJ 08542. *Fax:* 609-987-5063; *E-Mail:* gl@gfdl.gov

LAU, PHILIP T S, ORGANIC CHEMISTRY, PHOTOGRAPHIC SCIENCE. *Current Pos:* sr res chemist, 63-68, res assoc, 68-79, RES FEL, COLOR PHOTOG DIV, RES LABS, EASTMAN KODAK CO, 79- *Personal Data:* b Kuala Lumpur, Malaysia, Feb 13, 35; US citizen; m 59, Harriet Y; c Linda, Steven & David. *Educ:* Alfred Univ, BS, 58; Syracuse Univ, PhD(org chem), 62. *Prof Exp:* Fel & res assoc chem, Univ Calif, Berkeley, 62-63. *Concurrent Pos:* Lectr Photog Chem; chmn, Eastman Kodak Res Coun, 89-91; mem, Eastman Kodak distinguished inventors gallery. *Mem:* Am Chem Soc. *Res:* New synthetic methodologies to novel heterocyclic and aromatic compounds; regioselective and regiospecific reactions, photographic developers, couplers, stabilizers, dyes, polymer synthesis and applications. *Mailing Add:* 345 St Andrews Dr Rochester NY 14626. *Fax:* 716-722-2327; *E-Mail:* plau@kodak.com

LAU, ROLAND, ORGANIC CHEMISTRY. *Current Pos:* MGR PHARMACEUT CHEM, HARDWICKE CHEM CO, SUBSID ETHYL CORP, 80- *Personal Data:* b China, May 5, 43; US citizen; m 67; c 1. *Educ:* Wayne State Univ, BA, 65; Purdue Univ, PhD(chem), 72. *Prof Exp:* Clin chemist, Henry Ford Hosp, 65; res chemist, Ash-Stevens, Inc, 65-66; fel, Syntex Res Div, Syntex Corp, 72-73; res investr org chem, E R Squibb, Inc, 73-77, sr res investr, 77-80. *Mem:* Am Chem Soc. *Res:* Commercial developments of medicinal agents. *Mailing Add:* Interchem Corp 120 Rte 17 N Paramus NJ 07652

LAU, S S, ELECTRONICS ENGINEERING. *Current Pos:* WONG'S ELECTRONICS CO LTD, HONG KONG. *Personal Data:* b Chungking, China, July 31, 41; US citizen. *Educ:* Univ Calif, Berkeley, BS, 64, MS, 66, PhD, 69. *Prof Exp:* Mem staff, Bell Labs, 69-72; mem staff, Calif Inst Technol, 72-80; prof microelectronics, Univ Calif, San Diego, 80- *Mem:* Bohemian Phys Soc; Inst Elec & Electronics Engrs. *Res:* Metal semiconductor interactions; ion-beam processes; Rutherford backscattering spectrometry; electronic materials. *Mailing Add:* Dept Elec Eng & Comput Sci Univ Calif San Diego R-007 La Jolla CA 92093. *Fax:* 619-534-2486

LAU, YIU-WA AUGUST, MATHEMATICS. *Current Pos:* SR RES SPECIALIST, EXXON PROD RES, 85- *Personal Data:* b Aug 22, 48; US citizen. *Educ:* Univ Houston, BS & MS, 68, PhD(math), 71. *Prof Exp:* From asst prof to assoc prof math, NTex State Univ, 71-80; mem staff, Johnson Space Ctr, NASA, 80-81. *Mem:* Am Math Soc. *Res:* Topological semigroups; topology. *Mailing Add:* Exxon Explor Co PO Box 4778 Houston TX 77210-4778

LAU, YUEN-SUM, PHARMACOLOGY, NEUROSCIENCE. *Current Pos:* PROF & CHMN, DIV PHARMACOL, UNIV WIS, 94- *Personal Data:* b Shanghai, China, Dec 24, 50. *Educ:* Univ Hawaii, Honolulu, BS, 73, MS, 77, PhD(pharmacol), 78. *Honors & Awards:* John Kane Res Award, Creighton Univ, 85, Young Investr Award, 86. *Prof Exp:* Fel pharmacol, Univ Mich, Ann Arbor, 78-80; from asst prof to assoc prof neuropharmacol, Creighton Univ Sch Med, 80-90, prof, 90-94. *Mem:* Chinese Bioscientists Am. *Res:* Pharmacology; neuroscience. *Mailing Add:* Div Pharmacol M3-111 Univ Mo Sch Pharm 2411 Holmes St Kansas City MO 64108

LAUB, ALAN JOHN, SCIENTIFIC COMPUTATION, NUMERICAL ANALYSIS. *Current Pos:* DEAN, COL ENG, UNIV CALIF, DAVIS, 96- *Personal Data:* b Edmonton, Alta, Aug 6, 48; US citizen. *Educ:* Univ BC, BSc, 69; Univ Minn, MS, 72, PhD(control sci), 74. *Honors & Awards:* Control Systs Technol Award, Inst Elec & Electronics Engrs Control Systs Soc, 93. *Prof Exp:* Asst prof systs eng, Case Western Res Univ, 74-75; asst prof elec eng, Univ Toronto, 75-77; res scientist control eng, Lab Info & Decision Systs, Mass Inst Technol, 77-79; assoc prof elec eng, Univ Southern Calif, 79-83; prof, Univ Calif, Santa Barbara, 83-86, chmn dept, 89-92. *Concurrent Pos:* Assoc ed, Inst Elec & Electronics Engrs Trans Automatic Control, 79-81, Int J Control, 80-87, J Control & Optimization, Soc Idust & Appl Math, 85-89, Math Control, Signals & Systs, 86- & Linear & Multilinear Algebra, 87-92; dir, Am Automatic Control Coun, Inst Elec & Electronics Engrs, 90-91; pres, Control Systs Soc, 91. *Mem:* Fel Inst Elec & Electronics Engrs; Soc Indust & Appl Math; Asn Comput Mach. *Res:* Numerical analysis; mathematical software; scientific computation; computer-aided control system design; linear and large-scale control and filtering theory. *Mailing Add:* Eng Deans Off Eng II Univ Calif Davis CA 95616

LAUB, RICHARD STEVEN, PALEONTOLOGY, SEDIMENTOLOGY. *Current Pos:* CUR GEOL, BUFFALO MUS SCI, 73- *Personal Data:* b Brooklyn, NY, Nov, 15, 45; m 74; c 1. *Educ:* Queen's Col, NY, BA, 66; Cornell Univ, MS, 68; Univ Cincinnati, PhD(paleont), 76. *Concurrent Pos:* Supvr, Morse Creek Fossil Salvage Proj, 76; adj fac, Empire State Col, 76-78; corresp, Fossil Cnidaria Newsletter, 76-; adj fac geol, State Univ NY Buffalo, 77-; mem, Distinguished Lectureship Comt, Buffalo Soc Natural Sci, 78- *Mem:* Paleont Soc; Paleont Asn; Am Asn Petrol Geologists; Sigma Xi; Paleont Res Inst. *Res:* Early Paleozoic corals, their systematics, morphology, ecology and distribution; axial torsion in rugose corals; systematics and biology of auloporid tabulate corals. *Mailing Add:* 67 Heritage Rd W Humboldt Pkwy Williamsville NY 14221-2313

LAUBACH, GERALD D, PHARMACEUTICAL CHEMISTRY. *Current Pos:* RETIRED. *Personal Data:* b Bethlehem, Pa, Jan 21, 26; m 53; c 3. *Educ:* Univ Pa, AB, 47; Mass Inst Technol, PhD(chem), 50. *Hon Degrees:* Mt Sinai Sch Med, City Univ New York, DHLett, 88; DL, Conn Col, 86; Hofstra Univ, DSc, 79. *Honors & Awards:* Int Palladium Medal, Am Sect, Soc Indust Chem, France, 85. *Prof Exp:* Lab scientist, Pfizer Inc, 50-58, mgr, Med Prods Res, 58-61, dir, Dept Med Chem, 61, group dir med res, 63, vpres, Med Prods Res, 64, pres, Pfizer Pharmaceut, 69-71, exec vpres, 71, pres, Pfizer, Inc, 72-91. *Concurrent Pos:* Ensign, USNR, 44-46. *Mem:* Nat Acad Eng; Inst Med-Nat Acad Sci; NY Acad Sci; hon fel Am Inst Chemists; AAAS; Soc Chem Indust; Am Chem Soc; Am Mgt Asn. *Res:* Industrial chemistry; corporate competition; pharmaceutical manufacturing. *Mailing Add:* 50 E 89th St New York NY 10128

LAUBER, JEAN KAUTZ, ZOOLOGY, PHYSIOLOGY. *Current Pos:* RETIRED. *Personal Data:* b Seattle, Wash, Aug 30, 26; m 56; c 3. *Educ:* Whitman Col, BA, 48; Wash Univ, MA, 51; Univ NMex, PhD(zool), 59. *Prof Exp:* Sr lab technician electron micros, Sch Med, Univ Wash, 51-53, res assoc, 53-56; instr zool, Univ Idaho, 58-60, asst prof, 60-62; asst prof, Wash State Univ, 62-65; from asst prof to assoc prof, Univ Alta, 65-76, hon assoc prof ophthal, 75-76, prof zool, hon prof ophthal & assoc vpres acad, 76-

Concurrent Pos: Assoc vpres, Acad Univ Alta, 76-80. Mem: AAAS; Am Soc Zool; Am Physiol Soc; Soc Exp Biol & Med; Electron Micros Soc Am. Res: Endocrine physiology; photobiology; ophthalmology; electron microscopy; embryology. Mailing Add: Oak Bay Prof Off Suite 20J 2187 Oak Bay Ave Victoria BC V8R 1G1 Can

LAUBER, JOHN K, HUMAN RELATIONS. Current Pos: VPRES CORP SAFETY & COMPLIANCE, DELTA AIR LINES, ATLANTA, 95- Personal Data: b Archbold, Ohio, Dec, 13, 42; m 67, Susan Elizabeth Myers; c Sarah H. Educ: Ohio State Univ, BS, 65, MS, 67, PhD, 69. Honors & Awards: R F Longacre Award, Aerospace Med Asn, 90; Joseph T Nall Mem Award, Nat Air Traffic Controllers Asn, 92; Paul T Hansen Lectr, 93; Forrest & Dominique Bird Award, Civil Aviation Med Asn, 94. Prof Exp: Res psychologist, US Naval Training Equip Ctr, 69-73; chief aeronaut human factors off, NASA Ames Res Ctr, Moffett Field, 73-85; mem, Nat Transp Safety Bd, Washington, 85-95. Concurrent Pos: Mem aeronaut adv comt, NASA, 87; mem, Res Eng & Develop Adv Comt, Fed Aviation Admin, 95- Mem: Fel Aerospace Med Asn; Human Factors Soc. Res: Published numerous articles; safety & compliance. Mailing Add: Delta Air Lines Dept 025 Hartsfield Int Airport Atlanta GA 30320

LAUBER, THORNTON STUART, ELECTRIC POWER ENGINEERING. Current Pos: PROF ELEC POWER ENG, RENSSELAER POLYTECH INST, 69-, S B CRARY PROF ENG, 70- Personal Data: b Cornwall, Ont, Jan 5, 24; US citizen; m 56; c 4. Educ: Cornell Univ, BSEE, 44; Ill Inst Technol, MSEE, 51; Univ Pa, PhD(elec eng), 64. Prof Exp: Engr, Commonwealth Serv, Inc, Mich, 46-50; develop engr, Large Power Transformer Dept, Gen Elec Co, 51-58, sr analytical engr, Power Circuit Breaker Dept, 58-69. Concurrent Pos: Consult, Gen Elec Co & Hydro-Quebec; comt mem, Am Nat Stand Inst; mem, Int Conf Large High Voltage Elec Systs, 70. Mem: Sr mem Inst Elec & Electronics Engrs; Am Soc Mech Engrs; Sigma Xi. Res: Electric power engineering; power system transients; electromagnetic field theory. Mailing Add: 1005 Seminole Rd Scotia NY 12302

LAU-CAM, CESAR A, PHARMACOLOGY, TOXICOLOGY & ANALYTICAL CHEMISTRY. Current Pos: from asst prof to assoc phytochem, 69-80, PROF PHARMACEUT SCI, DEPT PHARMACEUT SCI, COL PHARM & ALLIED HEALTH PROFESSIONS, ST JOHN'S UNIV, NY, 80- Personal Data: b Lima, Peru, Nov 24, 40; m 67, Aurora Angeles; c Cesar Jr & Davis. Educ: San Marcos Univ, Lima, BS, 63; Univ RI, MS, 66, PhD(pharmacog), 69. Prof Exp: Instr pharm bot, San Marcos Univ, Lima, 62-63; lab instr pharmacog, Univ RI, 67. Concurrent Pos: Sci adv, US Food & Drug Admin, 79-; instr-consult, Harlem Med Ctr, NY, 79-96. Mem: AAAS; Am Soc Pharmacog; Am Pharmaceut Asn; Phytochem Soc NAm; NY Acad Sci; Acad Pharmaceut Sci. Res: Analytical methods applied to natural products; clinical chemistry; pharmacology and toxicology of natural products; pharmacology and toxicology of alcohol; pharmaceutical drug analysis. Mailing Add: Dept Pharmaceut Sci St John's Univ 8000 Jamaica NY 11439. Fax: 718-990-5763

LAUCHLE, GERALD CLYDE, ACOUSTICS, FLUIDS ENGINEERING. Current Pos: From res asst to sr res assoc, 68-85, sr scientist, 85-90, MEM GRAD PROG ACOUST, APPL RES LAB, PA STATE UNIV, 90-, PROF ACOUST, 90- Personal Data: b Williamsport, Pa, Sept 20, 45; m 96, Esther E Moravek; c Keith A & Paul M. Educ: Pa State Univ, BS, 68, MS, 70, PhD(eng acoust), 74. Concurrent Pos: Prin investr, Ctr Acoust & Vibration, Pa State Univ. Mem: Fel Acoust Soc Am; Inst Noise Control Eng; Am Inst Aeronaut & Astronaut. Res: Basic and applied research on the noise generated by fluid flow; general acoustics; acoustic noise control and hydrodynamic drag reduction. Mailing Add: Grad Prog Acoust Appl Res Lab PO Box 30 State College PA 16804. Fax: 814-865-3287; E-Mail: gcl1@psu.edu

LAUCK, DAVID R, ENTOMOLOGY. Current Pos: from asst prof to prof zool, 61-94, chmn, Div Biol Sci, 66-72, EMER PROF ZOOL, HUMBOLDT STATE UNIV, 94- Personal Data: b Alton, Ill, June 6, 30; m 53; c 2. Educ: Univ Ill, BS, 55, MS, 58, PhD(entom), 61. Prof Exp: Cur invert entom, Chicago Acad Sci, 59-61. Mem: Entom Soc Am; Entom Soc Can. Res: Aquatic and forest entomology. Mailing Add: Div Biol Sci Humboldt State Univ Arcata CA 95521

LAUD, PURUSHOTTAM WAMAN, MATHEMATICAL STATISTICS, APPLIED PROBABILITY. Current Pos: Asst prof statist, 77-80, ASST PROF MATH, NORTHERN ILL UNIV, 80- Personal Data: b Bombay, India, Nov 25, 48. Educ: Bombay Univ, BSc, 69; Lamar Univ, MS, 71; Univ Mo-Columbia, MA, 73, PhD(statist), 77. Mem: Inst Math Statist. Res: Bayesian nonparametric inference; reliability theory; stochastic processes. Mailing Add: Dept Math Sci Northern Ill Univ De Kalb IL 60115-2854

LAUDE, HORTON MEYER, AGRONOMY, BOTANY. Current Pos: from asst prof & asst agronomist to prof & agronomist, 46-81, EMER PROF AGRON, EXP STA, UNIV CALIF, DAVIS, 81- Personal Data: b Beaumont, Tex, Feb 25, 15; m 46; c 2. Educ: Kans State Univ, BS, 37; Univ Chicago, PhD(bot), 41. Prof Exp: Agent, USDA, Univ Chicago, 40-41. Mem: Fel Am Soc Agron; Am Soc Plant Physiol; Soc Range Mgt; Crop Sci Soc Am; Sigma Xi. Res: Physiology and ecology of dry range plants, irrigated forages and cereals; plant growth substances; seed production; resistance to environmental stresses of heat, cold and drought. Mailing Add: 818 Oeste Dr Davis CA 95616

LAUDENSLAGER, JAMES BISHOP, CHEMICAL PHYSICS. Current Pos: VPRES, LASER SYSTS & ADVAN INT SYSTS, IRVINE, CALIF, 86- Personal Data: b Harrisburg, Pa, June 8, 45. Educ: Temple Univ, AB, 67; Univ Calif, Santa Barbara, PhD(phys chem), 71. Prof Exp: Res assoc space sci, Jet Propulsion Lab, 71-73, sr res sci chem physics, 73-86. Mem: Am Phys Soc; Optical Soc Am; Soc Photoelectronics & Optics. Res: Fundamental properties of charge transfer and metastable rare gas reactions in the gas phase for use in laser development and mass spectrometry. Mailing Add: 230 Granada Ave Long Beach CA 90803

LAUDENSLAGER, MARK LEROY, PSYCHONEUROIMMUNOLOGY, PHYSIOLOGICAL PSYCHOLOGY. Current Pos: asst clin prof, 84-86, asst prof, 86-90, ASSOC PROF, HEALTH SCI CTR, UNIV COLO, 91-; ASST RESEARCHER, DENVER UNIV, 83- Personal Data: b Charlotte, NC, May 13, 47; c Eric & Kristin. Educ: Univ NC, AB, 69; Univ Calif, Santa Barbara, PhD(psychol), 75. Prof Exp: Teaching asst introductory psychol, Univ Calif, Santa Barbara, 70-71, res asst neuropsychol, 71-72, teaching asst physiol psychol, 73, lectr, 74; NIMH fel, Scripps Inst Oceanog, 75-77; asst res psychologist, Univ Calif, Santa Barbara, 77-80; lectr, Denver Univ, 81-83. Concurrent Pos: Dir, Behav Immunol Lab, 86-; counr, Psychoneuroimmunol Res Soc, 93-; numerous NIMH & other res grants. Mem: Int Soc Develop Psychobiol; AAAS; Am Physiol Soc; Soc Neurosci; Psychoneuroimmunol Res Soc. Res: effects of stress and affective disorders on immunocompetence and health, role of emotions, social support and temperament on health. Mailing Add: Dept Psychiat Univ Colo Health Sci Ctr 4200 E 9th Ave Denver CO 80220-3706. Fax: 303-372-3570; E-Mail: laudensm@essex.hsc.colorado.edu

LAUDER, JEAN MILES, CELL BIOLOGY, ANATOMY. Current Pos: assoc prof, Dept Anat, 78-85, PROF, DEPT CELL BIOL & ANAT, SCH MED, UNIV NC, CHAPEL HILL, 85- Personal Data: b Haverhill, Mass, June 29, 45. Educ: Univ Maine, Orono, BA, 67; Purdue Univ, PhD(biol sci), 72. Prof Exp: NIMH staff fel, Lab Neuropharmacol, St Elizabeth's Hosp, Washington, DC, 72-74; res assoc, Lab Neuromorphol, Dept Behav Sci, Univ Conn, Storrs 74-75, asst prof-in-residence, Dept Behav Sci, 76-78. Concurrent Pos: Mem bd dirs & asst treas, Inst Develop Neurosci & Aging, 83-; dir, Prog Develop Neurosci, Div Behav & Neural Sci, NSF, 84-85; vchmn, Gordon Res Conf Cent Nervous Syst-Neural Develop, 85-87, chmn, 87-89 & vchair, Gordon Conf Neural Develop, 87, chair, 89. Mem: Soc Neurosci; Women Neurosci; Int Soc Develop Neurosci (pres-elect, 86-88, pres, 88-90); AAAS; Am Asn Anatomists; Am Soc Cell Biol; Int Soc Psychoneuroendocrinol; Sigma Xi; Int Brain Res Orgn; NY Acad Sci. Mailing Add: Dept Cell Biol & Anat Univ NC Sch Med Chapel Hill NC 27599-0001

LAUDERDALE, JAMES W, JR, REPRODUCTIVE PHYSIOLOGY, ENDOCRINOLOGY. Current Pos: SCIENTIST, UPJOHN CO, 67- Personal Data: b Washington, DC, Dec 21, 37; m 62; c 3. Educ: Auburn Univ, BS, 62; Univ Wis, MS, 64, PhD(reproductive physiol, endocrinol), 68. Honors & Awards: Animal Physiol & Endocrinol Award, Am Soc Animal Sci, 86. Mem: Am Soc Animal Sci; Soc Study Reproduction. Res: Reproductive, growth and endocrinological function of large animals. Mailing Add: 3699 Cloverdale Rd Delton MI 49046

LAUDERDALE, ROBERT A(MIS), JR, SANITARY ENGINEERING. Current Pos: PROF CIVIL ENG, UNIV KY, 58-, DIR, WATER RESOURCES INST, 65- Personal Data: b Harriman, Tenn, July 27, 22; m 48; c 1. Educ: Univ Tenn, BS, 44, MS, 48; Mass Inst Technol, PhD(sanit eng), 58. Prof Exp: Jr chem engr, Tenn Valley Authority, 44-45; assoc health physicist, Oak Ridge Nat Lab, 48-52; res assoc sanit eng, Mass Inst Technol, 52-58, asst prof, 57-58. Mem: Am Chem Soc; Water Pollution Control Fedn. Res: Industrial and radioactive waste treatment. Mailing Add: 3380 Keithshire Way Lexington KY 40503

LAUDISE, ROBERT ALFRED, SOLID STATE CHEMISTRY. Current Pos: ADJ PROF MAT, MASS INST TECHNOL, 88-; ADJ PROF CERAMICS, RUTGERS UNIV, 90-; ADJ DIR CHEM, BELL LABS, 92- Personal Data: b Amsterdam, NY, Sept 2, 30; m 57, Joye De Silvia; c Thomas, Margaret, Joyhn, Mary & Edward. Educ: Union Univ, NY, BS, 52; Mass Inst Technol, PhD(inorg chem), 56. Honors & Awards: Sawyer Award, Conf Frequency Control, 74; Int Award in Crystal Growth, Int Orgn Crystal Growth, 81; Mat Chem Prize, Am Chem Soc, 90, Orton Lect Award, 94; Reduction to Practice Award, Am Ceramic Soc, 95. Prof Exp: Mem tech staff, Bell Labs, 56-60, head, Crystal Chem Res Dept, 60-73, asst dir mat res, 73-76, dir mat res, 76-79, dir physics & inorg chem res, 80-86, dir mat chem res, 86-90, dir mat & processing res, 90-92. Concurrent Pos: Consult, President's Sci Adv Comt, 60-70; panel mem mat adv bd, Nat Acad Sci, 65-70; vis comt, Nat Inst Stand & Technol, 68-75, 86-, mat sci, Mass Inst Technol, 80-; ed, J Crystal Growth, 74-, J Mat Res, 94- Mem: Nat Acad Sci; Nat Acad Eng; Int Orgn Crystal Growth (pres, 77-84); fel Mineral Soc Am; fel Am Ceramic Soc; Fedn Mats Soc (pres 94-96); fel AAAS; Am Asn Crystal Growth (pres, 68-75). Res: Materials research; crystal growth; hydrothermal chemistry; quartz; ferroelectrics; non-linear optical materials; magnetic materials; physical chemistry; industrial ecology. Mailing Add: Bell Labs Lucent Technol Murray Hill NJ 07974. Fax: 908-582-2521; E-Mail: ral@bell_labs.com

LAUDON, THOMAS S, SEDIMENTARY PETROLOGY, GRAVITY. Current Pos: Chmn dept geol, 69-72, PROF GEOL, UNIV WIS-OSHKOSH, 63- Personal Data: b Sac City, Iowa, June 14, 32; m 56; c 5. Educ: Univ Wis, BSc, 55, MSc, 57, PhD(geol), 63. Concurrent Pos: NSF res grants, 62-67, 70-71, 84-85 & Nat Acad Sci res grants, 71-72; consult geol & geophys, 79- Mem: Sigma Xi; Geol Soc Am; Am Asn Petrol Geologists; Am Geophys Union; Nat Assn Geol Teachers. Res: Geologic exploration of Antarctica; gravity, tectonics and sedimentation in modern and ancient mobile belts. Mailing Add: Dept Geol Univ Wis 800 Algoma Blvd Oshkosh WI 54901

LAUENROTH, WILLIAM KARL, PLANT ECOLOGY. *Current Pos:* Sr res ecologist, Nat Resource Ecol Lab, 75-81, PROF, RANGE SCI DEPT, COLO STATE UNIV, 81- *Personal Data:* b Carthage, Mo, July 31, 45. *Educ:* Humboldt State Col, BS, 68; NDak State Univ, MS, 70; Colo State Univ, PhD(plant ecol), 73. *Honors & Awards:* Outstanding Achievement Award, Soc Range Mgt, 89. *Mem:* Ecol Soc Am; Soc Range Mgt; Bot Soc Am; AAAS; Int Soc Ecol Modelling. *Res:* Primary production and water relations of native plant communities, particularly temperate grasslands; ecosystem analysis of natural and agricultural ecosystems including simulation modelling. *Mailing Add:* Dept Range Sci Colo State Univ Ft Collins CO 80523-0001

LAUER, B(YRON) E(LMER), SCIENCE EDUCATION, CHEMICAL ENGINEERING. *Current Pos:* prof, 46-75, head dept, 47-61, EMER PROF CHEM ENG, UNIV COLO, BOULDER, 75- *Personal Data:* b Glencoe, Okla, Apr 14, 07; m 31, Opal Lewis; c Andrea L (Sahlen). *Educ:* Ore State Univ, BS, 27; Univ Minn, MS, 29, PhD(chem eng), 31. *Prof Exp:* Asst instr, Univ Minn, 27-31; res chem engr, Northern Paper Mills, 31-34 & Crown-Zellerbach Corp, 34-35; from asst prof to prof chem eng, NC State Univ, 35-42. *Concurrent Pos:* Consult, Nat Bur Stand, 61-64, PEC Corp, 64-65, Interam Transp, 68-71, Jet Propulsion Lab, 83-84 & Western Interstate Comn Higher Educ, 82-88; ed, Televised Higher Educ, Assoc Western Univs, Inc, 75-82. *Mem:* Am Chem Soc; Am Soc Eng Educ; Tech Asn Pulp & Paper Indust; Am Inst Chem Engrs. *Res:* Pulp and paper; testing methods; heat transfer; oil shale retorting; information storage and retrieval. *Mailing Add:* 546 14th St Boulder CO 80302-7806

LAUER, DAVID ALLAN, SOIL SCIENCE, AGRONOMY. *Current Pos:* RES SOIL SCIENTIST, AGR RES, USDA, 76- *Personal Data:* b Creston, Iowa, Sept 25, 44; m 64; c 2. *Educ:* Iowa State Univ, BS, 66; Colo State Univ, MS, 69, PhD(soil sci), 71. *Prof Exp:* Res assoc agron, Cornell Univ, 71-75; asst prof, Univ Ga, 75-76. *Mem:* Am Soc Agron; Crop Sci Soc; Soil Sci Soc; AAAS; Sigma Xi. *Res:* Application of soil chemical and plant physiological principles to management of crop production systems with emphasis on plant nutrition. *Mailing Add:* 605 Lincoln Ct Prosser WA 99350

LAUER, EUGENE JOHN, PLASMA PHYSICS. *Current Pos:* Asst physics, 46-51, PHYSICIST, LAWRENCE LIVERMORE LAB, UNIV CALIF, 51- *Personal Data:* b Red Bluff, Calif, Apr 11, 20; m 48; c 5. *Educ:* Univ Calif, BS, 42, PhD(physics), 51. *Mem:* Am Phys Soc. *Res:* Discharge through gases; particle accelerator design; nuclear and plasma physics; controlled thermonuclear energy; relativistic beams. *Mailing Add:* 2221 Martin Ave Pleasanton CA 94588

LAUER, FLORIAN ISIDORE, HORTICULTURE. *Current Pos:* From asst prof to assoc prof, 59-66, PROF POTATO BREEDING, UNIV MINN, ST PAUL, 66- *Personal Data:* b Richmond, Minn, Sept 13, 28; m 55, Mary A Lambert; c Sarah, Shelia, Maureen & Paul. *Educ:* Univ Minn, BS, 51, PhD, 57. *Honors & Awards:* Potato Research of Yr, 91. *Mem:* Am Soc Hort Sci; hon mem, Potato Asn Am. *Res:* Potato breeding and genetics. *Mailing Add:* Hort 305 Alderman Hall Univ Minn 1970 Folwell Ave St Paul MN 55108-6007. *Fax:* 612-624-4914

LAUER, GEORGE, PHYSICAL CHEMISTRY. *Current Pos:* SR CONSULT, ATLANTIC RICHFIELD, INC, 88- *Personal Data:* b Vienna, Austria, Feb 18, 36; US citizen; wid; c 2. *Educ:* Univ Calif, Los Angeles, BS, 61; Calif Inst Technol, PhD(chem), 67. *Prof Exp:* Staff assoc, Sci Ctr, NAm Rockwell Corp, 62-66, mem tech staff, 66-71, group leader, Measurement Sci, 71-72, dir air qual monitoring res, 72-75, mgr environ res & technol, 76-78, dir, Environ Monitoring & Serv Ctr, Rockwell Int Sci Ctr, 78-84; pres, EMSI, Inc, 81-88. *Mem:* AAAS; Am Chem Soc; Air & Waste Mgt Asn; Am Meteorol Soc. *Res:* Development of chronocoulometric techniques in electrochemistry; study of electroactive adsorbed species at electrodes; development of computer controlled instrumentation; instrumental methods in air pollution monitoring; air quality simulation modeling; environmental assessment. *Mailing Add:* 6009 Maury Ave Woodland Hills CA 91367-3683. *Fax:* 213-486-2021; *E-Mail:* glauer@is.arco.com

LAUER, GERALD J, AQUATIC ECOLOGY, LIMNOLOGY. *Current Pos:* SR SCIENTIST & VPRES, EA SCI & TECHNOL, 75- *Personal Data:* b Montgomery City, Mo, Oct 18, 34; m 63. *Educ:* Quincy Col, BS, 56; Univ Wash, MS, 59, PhD(zool), 63. *Prof Exp:* Lab aide limnol, Quincy Col, 54-56; asst, Univ Washington, 56-59; teacher high sch, Mo, 59-60; staff biologist, USPHS, 60-62, prin biologist, Southeast Water Lab, 63-66, chief, Training Br, 66; leader, Fisheries Coop Unit & assoc prof fisheries & limnol res, Ohio State Univ, 66-67; assoc cur, Limnol Dept, Acad Natural Sci, Philadelphia, 67-69; asst dir, Lab Environ Studies, Med Ctr, NY Univ, 69-75. *Concurrent Pos:* Adj assoc prof biol, NY Univ, 70- *Mem:* AAAS; Am Soc Limnol & Oceanog; Am Fisheries Soc; Am Littoral Soc; Ecol Soc Am. *Res:* Population dynamics and community diversity of aquatic organisms; effects of pollutants and other environmental stresses on aquatic life. *Mailing Add:* 25 Mine Rd Monroe NY 10950

LAUER, JAMES LOTHAR, MATERIALS SCIENCE, SPECTROSCOPY. *Current Pos:* prof, 78-93, dir, Inst Wear Control & Tribology, 85-93, EMER PROF MECH ENG, RENSSELAER POLYTECH INST, 93- *Personal Data:* b Vienna, Austria, Aug 2, 20; nat US; m 55, Stefanie Blank; c Michael & Ruth. *Educ:* Temple Univ, AB, 42, MA, 44; Univ Pa, PhD(physics), 48. *Honors & Awards:* Innovative Res Award, Soc Mech Engrs. *Prof Exp:* Asst instr org chem, Temple Univ, 42-44; phys chemist, Sun Oil Co, 44-45, res physicist, 47-54, sr res physicist, 54-58, res assoc, 58-62, res scientist, 62-77, *Concurrent Pos:* Lectr, Univ Del, 52-56; asst prof, Univ Pa, 52-54; fel aerospace eng, Univ Calif, San Diego, 64-65, sr res scientist, Ctr Magnetic Rec Res, 93-95, vis scholar, 95-; prin investr, Air Force Off Sci Res & NASA-Lewis Res Ctr, 73-85, Off Naval Res, 78-85, NSF res grant, 87- & US Army Res Off, 86-; lectr, Coblentz, 78; lectr friction & lubrication, Gordon Res Conf, 82; researcher, Surface Sci & Tribology Br, NASA-Lewis Res Ctr, Cleveland, Ohio, 93-95. *Mem:* Am Chem Soc; Am Phys Soc; Soc Appl Spectros; Optical Soc Am; Mat Res Soc. *Res:* Fourier spectroscopy; Raman and infrared spectroscopy; refraction and dispersion; theory of molecular structure; mathematical physics; x-ray spectra of polymers; combustion; shock waves in gases; adsorption and desorption; applications of molecular, mainly infrared emission, spectroscopy to problems of lubrication and tribology; optical methods of non-contacting surface analysis; electrostatics; boundary lubrication, studied by modern methods of surface analysis and applied to machinery at high operating temperatures. *Mailing Add:* 7622 Palmilla Dr No 78 San Diego CA 92122. *Fax:* 619-458-1786

LAUERMAN, LLOYD HERMAN, JR, VETERINARY MICROBIOLOGY, VETERINARY IMMUNOLOGY. *Current Pos:* VET, DIAG LAB, MICRO SECT, STATE ALA, 81- *Personal Data:* b Everett, Wash, Feb 5, 33; m 55, Lucille C Cooper; c Steven W, David A & Susan M (Young). *Educ:* Wash State Univ, BA, 56, DVM, 58; Univ Wis, MS, 59, PhD, 68; Am Col Vet Microbiol, dipl, 74. *Prof Exp:* Res asst vet med, Univ Wis, 58-60, proj asst, 60-63; res dir vet biol, Biol Specialties Corp, 63-68; Colo State Univ-AID prof microbiol, Univ Nairobi, 68-72; assoc prof, Colo State Univ, 72-81, head bact sect, Diag Lab, Dept Path, 73-81. *Concurrent Pos:* Vis assoc prof microbiol, Sch Dent, Univ Colo, Denver, 74-75; affil prof pathobiol, Aubrun Univ, 81- *Mem:* Am Soc Microbiologists; Am Asn Vet Lab Diagnosticians; Am Vet Med Asn; US Am Health Asn; Am Asn Avian Pathologists. *Res:* Diagnosis and prevention of infectious diseases of animals; research and development of laboratory diagnostic techniques and animal vaccines; biotechnology. *Mailing Add:* Vet Diag Lab PO Box 2209 Auburn AL 36831-2209. *Fax:* 334-826-3592; *E-Mail:* lanerll@vetmed.auburn.edu

LAUF, PETER KURT, PHYSIOLOGY, IMMUNOLOGY. *Current Pos:* PROF PHYSIOL & BIOPHYS & CHMN, SCH MED, WRIGHT STATE UNIV, DAYTON, OHIO, 85- *Personal Data:* b Wuerzburg, Ger, Sept 25, 33; US citizen; m, Norma Adragna; c Cornelia, Bettina & Adrian. *Educ:* Univ Freiburg, MD, 60. *Prof Exp:* Res assoc path, Inst Path, Univ Freiburg, 60-62; res fel biochem, Max Planck Inst Immunobiol, Freiburg, 62-64; res assoc path, Inst Path, Univ Marburg, Ger, 64; res assoc biochem, Child Res Ctr Mich, Detroit, 65-67; asst prof biochem, Wayne State Univ, 66-67; from asst prof to prof physiol, Duke Univ Med Ctr, 68-85, asst prof immunol, 70-80. *Concurrent Pos:* NIH res career develop award, 71-75; Golding distinguished prof, Wright State Univ. *Mem:* Soc Gen Physiol; Am Soc Hemat; Biophys Soc; Am Soc Physiol. *Res:* Membrane physiology; modulation of membrane transport processes of active and passive cation by immunological reactions; isolation and identification of membrane transport proteins and functionally associated surface antigens. *Mailing Add:* Dept Physiol & Biophys Wright State Univ Sch Med Dayton OH 45401-0927. *Fax:* 937-873-3769; *E-Mail:* plauf@sirius.wright.edu

LAUFER, ALLAN HENRY, PHOTOCHEMISTRY, CHEMICAL KINETICS. *Current Pos:* chemist & prog mgr, Chem Sci Div, Off Basic Energy Sci, 83-86, BR CHIEF, FUNDAMENTAL INTERACTIONS BR, US DEPT ENERGY, 86- *Personal Data:* b New York, NY, Mar 27, 36; m 59, Sondra Pallant; c Terri M & Andrea J. *Educ:* NY Univ, BA, 56; Lehigh Univ, MS, 58, PhD(phys chem), 62. *Prof Exp:* Res chemist, Gulf Res & Develop Co, 62-64; res chemist, Nat Bur Stand, 64-83. *Mem:* AAAS; Am Chem Soc; Am Phys Soc; Sigma Xi; Inter-Am Photochem Soc. *Res:* Vacuum ultraviolet photochemistry; gas phase radical reactions and kinetics; chemistry of excited states. *Mailing Add:* Chem Sci Div Basic Energy Sci US Dept Energy Washington DC 20545. *Fax:* 301-903-4110; *E-Mail:* allan.laufer@oer.doe.gov

LAUFER, DANIEL A, ORGANIC CHEMISTRY. *Current Pos:* from asst prof to assoc prof, 66-80 PROF CHEM, UNIV MASS, BOSTON, 80- *Personal Data:* b Affula, Israel, May 30, 38; US citizen; m 68; c 3. *Educ:* Mass Inst Technol, BS, 59; Brandeis Univ, PhD(org chem), 64. *Prof Exp:* Res assoc org chem, Columbia Univ, 63-64; res fel biol chem, Harvard Med Sch, 64-66. *Concurrent Pos:* NIH trainee, 65-66, res grant, 67-70, 72-74 & 79-84. *Mem:* Am Chem Soc; AAAS. *Res:* Peptide synthesis; new reagents for organic synthesis macrocyclic complexations analytic applications of NMR. *Mailing Add:* Dept Chem Univ Mass 100 Morrissey Blvd Boston MA 02125-3393

LAUFER, HANS, BIOTECHOLOGY & ENDOCRINOLOGY, MOLECULAR BIOLOGY & CELL BIOLOGY. *Current Pos:* assoc prof biol, 65-72, PROF BIOL, UNIV CONN, 72- *Personal Data:* b Ger, Oct 18, 29; nat US; m 53, Evelyn Green; c Jessica, Marc & Leonard. *Educ:* City Col New York, BS, 52; Brooklyn Col, MA, 54; Cornell Univ, PhD(zool), 58. *Honors & Awards:* Rosenstiel vis scholar, Brandeis Univ, 73; hon prof, Charles Univ, Prague, 74; Lady Davis vis prof, Hebrew Univ, Jerusalem, 88; Sr Res Serv Award Harvard Univ, 89. *Prof Exp:* Asst, Cornell Univ, 55-57; Nat Res Coun fel embryol, Carnegie Inst, 57-59; asst prof biol, Johns Hopkins Univ, 59-65. *Concurrent Pos:* Vis scholar, Case Western Res Univ, 62; Lalor fel, Marine Biol Lab, Woods Hole, Mass, 62-63, staff embryol course, 67-72, mem, Corp Marine Biol Lab, 62-, trustee, 78-82, mem exec comt, 79-80; assoc ed, J Exp Zool, 69-73, 89-; mem nat bd on grad educ, Conf Bd Assoc Res Couns, 71-75; vis prof, Karolinska Inst, Stockholm, 72 & Yale Univ, 80; NATO fel rev panel, NSF, 74 & 76; partic, Nat Acad Sci-Czech Acad Sci Exchange Prog, 74 & 77; chmn, Div Develop Biol, Am Soc Zoologists, 81-82; vis prof, Harvard Univ, 88-89; Dozer fel & vis prof, Ben Gurion Univ, 97. *Mem:* Am Soc Zoologists; Soc Develop Biol; Am Soc Cell Biol; Tissue Cult

Asn; fel AAAS. *Res:* Developmental physiology and biochemistry; molecular interactions in development; proteins and enzymes in ontogeny, regeneration and metamorphosis; chromosomal puffing in Diptera; gene action as related to development; hormone action during invertebrate development and reproduction. *Mailing Add:* Dept Molecular & Cell Biol U-125 Univ Conn 75 N Eagleville Rd Storrs CT 06269-3125. *Fax:* 860-486-4331

LAUFER, IGOR, GASTROINTESTINAL RADIOLOGY, GALLSTONE DIAGNOSIS & TREATMENT. *Current Pos:* assoc prof, 76-80, CHIEF GASTROINTESTINAL RADIOL, HOSP UNIV PA, 76-, PROF RADIOL, SCH MED, 80- *Personal Data:* b Czech, Aug 8, 44; Can citizen; m 67; c 2. *Educ:* Univ Toronto, BSc, 66 MD, 67. *Honors & Awards:* Cannon Medal, Soc Gastrointestinal Radiologists, 89. *Prof Exp:* Intern, New Mt Sinai Hosp, Toronto, 67-68; med resident, Toronto Western Hosp, 68-69; asst resident,diag radiol, 69-71; chief resident, Beth Israel Hosp, Boston, 71-72; staff radiol, McMaster Univ Med Ctr, 72-76. *Concurrent Pos:* Clin fel radiol, Harvard Med Sch, 69-72; co-dir gallstone-lithotripay unit, Hosp Univ Pa, 88-; consult diag radiol, NIH. *Mem:* Soc Gastrointestinal Radiologists (pres, 87); Am Roentgen Ray Soc; Am Col Radiol; Radiol Soc NAm; Am Gastroenterol Asn. *Res:* Early diagnosis of inflammatory and neoplastic disorders of the gastrointestinal tract; double contrast radiology; gallstone lithotripay. *Mailing Add:* Dept Radiol Hosp Univ Pa 3400 Spruce St Philadelphia PA 19104-4219

LAUFER, ROBERT J, ORGANIC CHEMISTRY. *Current Pos:* RETIRED. *Personal Data:* b Pittsburgh, Pa, May 10, 32; m 67; Judith; c Kenneth & Karen. *Educ:* Carnegie Inst Technol, BS, 53, MS, 56, PhD(org chem), 58. *Prof Exp:* Proj supvr res div, Consol Coal Co, 58-68; proj leader, Int Flavors & Fragrances Inc, 68-69, assoc dir fragrance res, 69-72, dir, 72-75; dir aromatic technol, Norda Inc, 75-77, corp dir res & develop, 77-78, vpres aromatics, 79-80, vpres & gen mgr, Orbis Prod Div, 80-81, vpres corp planning, 81-82. *Mem:* AAAS; Am Chem Soc. *Res:* Research management; aroma chemicals; terpenoids; fragrance applications research. *Mailing Add:* 6 Greenhill Rd Colts Neck NJ 07722-1595

LAUFERSWEILER, JOSEPH DANIEL, ECOLOGY, BOTANY. *Current Pos:* from asst prof to assoc prof, 63-95, EMER PROF BIOL, UNIV DAYTON, 95- *Personal Data:* b Columbus, Ohio, Aug 13, 30; m 59, Judith A Wolfe; c Mark J & Juliana M. *Educ:* Univ Notre Dame, BS, 52; Ohio State Univ, MSc, 54, PhD(ecol), 60. *Prof Exp:* Instr bot & ecol, Ohio State Univ, 59-61; asst prof biol, Drake Univ, 61-63. *Concurrent Pos:* Bd trustees, Dayton Mus Natural Hist, 82-92; adv bd & exec comt, Ohio Biol Surv. *Mem:* Bot Soc Am; Ecol Soc Am; Am Inst Biol Sci. *Res:* Reproduction of plant communities; distribution of original vegetation and its influence on man; early history of the US Atomic Energy Commission environmental sciences program. *Mailing Add:* Dept Biol Univ Dayton Dayton OH 45469-2320. *Fax:* 937-229-2021; *E-Mail:* laufersw@neelix.udayton.edu

LAUFF, GEORGE HOWARD, LIMNOLOGY, ZOOLOGY. *Current Pos:* dir, W W Kellogg Biol Sta, 64-90, prof, 64-92, EMER PROF ZOOL, FISHERIES & WILDLIFE, MICH STATE UNIV, 92- *Personal Data:* b Milan, Mich, Mar 23, 27. *Educ:* Mich State Univ, BS, 49, MS, 51; Cornell Univ, PhD(limnol, zool), 53. *Prof Exp:* Fisheries res technician, Mich State Dept Conserv, 50; asst phycol, Point Barrow, Alaska, 51; biol asst, Cornell Univ, 51-52, zool, 52-53; instr zool, Univ Mich, 53-57, from asst prof to assoc prof, 57-62; res coordr, Sapelo Island Res Found, Ga, 62-64. *Concurrent Pos:* Res assoc, Great Lakes Res Inst, 54-59, Oak Ridge Inst Nuclear Studies & Oak Ridge Nat Lab, 60; assoc prof & dir marine inst, Univ Ga, 60-62. *Mem:* AAAS; Am Inst Biol Sci; Am Soc Limnol & Oceanog (treas, 58-61, secy, 58-64, 67-70, vpres, 71-72, pres, 72-73); Ecol Soc Am; Int Asn Theoret & Appl Limnol. *Mailing Add:* 3818 Heights Dr Hickory Corners MI 49060

LAUFFENBURGER, DOUGLAS ALAN, MOLECULAR & CELLULAR BIOENGINEERING. *Current Pos:* PROF CHEM ENG, CELL & STRUCT BIOL, BIOENG & BIOPHYS, UNIV ILL, 90- *Personal Data:* b Des Plaines, Ill, May 6, 53; m 79, Janelle Miller; c Julie & Wendy. *Educ:* Univ Ill, BS, 75; Univ Minn, PhD(chem eng), 79. *Honors & Awards:* Alan P Colburn Award, Am Inst Chem Engrs, 88, Bioeng Div Award, 92; Curtis W McGraw Award, Am Soc Eng Educ, 92. *Prof Exp:* From asst prof to prof chem eng, bioeng & cell biol, Univ Pa, 79-90. *Concurrent Pos:* J S Guggenheim fel, 89. *Mem:* Am Inst Chem Engrs; Biomed Eng Soc; Am Soc Cell Biol. *Res:* Quantitative investigation of receptor-mediated cell phenomena, including growth, adhesion, migration, chemotaxis and trafficking. *Mailing Add:* Chem Eng Dept Mass Inst Technol Bldg 66 Rm 446 Cambridge MA 02139-0001

LAUFFENBURGER, JAMES C, SOLID STATE PHYSICS. *Personal Data:* b Buffalo, NY, Aug 23, 38; m 61; c 5. *Educ:* Canisius Col, BS, 60; Univ Notre Dame, PhD(solid state physics), 65. *Mem:* Sigma Xi; Am Asn Physics Teachers. *Res:* X-rays. *Mailing Add:* Dept Physics Canisius Col 2001 Main St Buffalo NY 14208-1098

LAUFFER, DONALD EUGENE, PHYSICS. *Current Pos:* Sr res physicist, Phillips Petrol Co, 68-76, supvr geophys, 76-84, br mgr geophys, 84-86, explor & prod planning mgr, 86-88, SR RES ASSOC, PHILLIPS PETROL CO, 88- *Personal Data:* b Lebanon, Pa, July 29, 40; m 64, Susan W Wolfe; c Matthew, Steven & Daniel. *Educ:* Ohio State Univ, BS, 64, PhD(physics), 68. *Mem:* Am Phys Soc; Am Chem Soc. *Res:* Geophysics; wave propagation and signal processing; computational chemistry. *Mailing Add:* 205 CPL PRC Phillips Petroleum Co Bartlesville OK 74004. *Fax:* 918-662-1097; *E-Mail:* del@ppco.com

LAUFFER, MAX AUGUSTUS, JR, BIOPHYSICS. *Current Pos:* assoc res prof, Univ Pittsburgh, 44-47, res prof physics & physiol chem, 47-49, chmn dept physics, 47-48, prof biophys, 49-63, head dept, 49-56, chmn dept, 63-67, assoc dean res natural sci, 53-54, dean, Div Natural Sci, 56-63, Andrew Mellon prof biophys, 63-84, chmn dept biophys & microbiol, 71-76, EMER PROF, UNIV PITTSBURGH, 84- *Personal Data:* b Middletown, Pa, Sept 2, 14; m 36, 64, Erika Erskine; c Edward W, Susan K, Max E & John E. *Educ:* Pa State Univ, BS, 33, MS, 34; Univ Minn, PhD(biochem), 37. *Honors & Awards:* Award, Eli Lilly & Co, 45; Priestley Lectr, Pa State Univ, 46; Pittsburgh Award, Am Chem Soc, 58; Gehrmann Lectr, Univ Ill, 51. *Prof Exp:* Asst, Univ Minn, 35-36, instr biochem, 36-37; fel plant path, Rockefeller Inst, 37-38, asst, 38-41, assoc, 41-44. *Concurrent Pos:* Spec lectr, Stanford Univ, 41; prin investr, Comt Med Res, 44-46; vis prof, Theodor Kocher Inst, Bern Univ, 52, Max Planck Inst Virus Res, Tubingen, 65-66 & Univ Philippines, 67; mem, Nat Res Coun Comn Macromolecules, 47-53, mem, Panel Virol & Immunol, Nat Inst Gen Med Sci, Comt Growth, 53-56; mem sci adv comt, Boyce Thompson Inst Plant Res Inc, 53-82; co-ed, Adv Virus Res, 53-85; mem prog proj comt, Nat Inst Gen Med Sci, 61-63, chmn, 62-63, mem adv coun, 63-67; mem sci adv bd, Delta Regional Primate Res Ctr, Tulane Univ, 64-67; ed, Biophys J, 69-73; consult to the provost, Univ Pittsburgh, 84-86; adj prof, Lebanon Valley Col, 88-90. *Mem:* Am Chem Soc; Am Soc Biol Chemists; Biophys Soc (pres elect, 60, pres, 61); Fedn Am Sci; NY Acad Sci. *Res:* Electrokinetics; ultracentrifugation; viscometry; biophysics of viruses; kinetics of virus disintegration; size and shape of macromolecules; polymerization of virus protein; hydration of proteins; entropy-driven processes in biology. *Mailing Add:* 190 Lauffer Rd Middletown PA 17057

LAUFMAN, HAROLD, VASCULAR SURGERY. *Current Pos:* PROF LECTR SURG, MT SINAI SCH MED, 79-; PRES, HLA SYSTS, INC, 79- *Personal Data:* b Milwaukee, Wis, Jan 6, 12; m 40, June Friend Moses; c Dionne Weigert & Laurein Kogut. *Educ:* Univ Chicago, BS, 32, Rush Med Col, MD, 37; Northwestern Univ, MS, 46, PhD(surg), 48; Am Bd Surg, dipl. *Prof Exp:* From clin asst to prof surg, Med Sch, Northwestern Univ, 40-65; prof, Albert Einstein Col Med, 65-77, emer prof surg, 77; prof lectr surg, Mt Sinai Sch Med, 79- *Concurrent Pos:* Assoc attend surgeon, Cook County Hosp, 46-48; attend, Hines Vet Admin Hosp, 48-50; adj attend, Michael Reese Hosp, Chicago, 48-54; attend, Passavant Mem & Vet Admin Res Hosps, 54-65; James IV traveling prof, Israel, 62; dir, Inst Surg Studies, Montefiore Hosp, 65-81, emer dir, 81- *Mem:* Am Surg Asn; Soc Vascular Surg; fel Am Col Surg; Am Med Writers Asn (pres, 69); Asn Advan Med Instrumentation (pres, 74-75); Sigma Xi. *Res:* Surgical physiology, especially mesenteric and peripheral vascular diseases; surgical design and facilities engineering. *Mailing Add:* 31 E 72nd St New York NY 10021. *Fax:* 212-737-4628

LAUGHLIN, ALEXANDER WILLIAM, GEOCHEMISTRY, ECONOMIC GEOLOGY. *Current Pos:* SR SCIENTIST, ICF KAISER ENGRS, 94- *Personal Data:* b Hot Springs, Ark, Nov 9, 36; m 69, Yvonne O Corne; c 3. *Educ:* Mich Technol Univ, BSc, 58; Univ Ariz, MSc, 60, PhD(geol), 69. *Honors & Awards:* Res & Develop 100 Award, 96. *Prof Exp:* Res assoc isotope geochem, Univ Ariz, 66-69; res assoc geol, Univ NMex, 69-70; from asst prof to assoc prof, Kent State Univ, 70-74; mem staff, Los Alamos Nat Lab, Univ Calif, 74-78 & 80-87, group leader, 78-80, dep group leader, 87-94. *Concurrent Pos:* Adj prof, Univ NMex, 75. *Mem:* Am Geophys Union; Int Asn Geochem & Cosmochem; fel Geol Soc Am. *Res:* Geochronology; trace element geochemistry; origin of ultramafic inclusions and basalts; economic geology; geothermal energy extraction from dry hot rock, geothermal exploration techniques, petrology of pre-Cambrian rocks; potassic mafic rocks. *Mailing Add:* Environ & Energy Group ICF Kaiser Engrs 1086 17th St Los Alamos NM 87544

LAUGHLIN, ALICE, biochemistry, analytical chemistry, for more information see previous edition

LAUGHLIN, CHARLES WILLIAM, NEMATOLOGY. *Current Pos:* DIR/PROF, COLO AGR EXP STA, COLO STATE UNIV, 92- *Personal Data:* b Iowa City, Iowa, Dec 9, 39; m 66, Barbara Waln; c Shannon M & Charles T. *Educ:* Iowa State Univ, BS, 63; Univ Md, MS, 66; Va Polytech Inst & State Univ, PhD(plant path & physiol), 69. *Prof Exp:* Asst exten nematologist, Univ Fla, 68-69; from asst prof to prof nematol, Mich State Univ, 69-80, asst dir acad & student affairs, 73-78, dir, 78-80; dept head plant path & weed sci, Miss State Univ, 80-83; prof and dir, Ga Agr Exp Sta, Univ Ga, 83-92. *Concurrent Pos:* coordr, Exp Sta Comm Orgn & Policy, Leadership Develop Prog, Acad Comm Orgn & Policy, 92- *Mem:* Soc Nematologists; Brazilian Soc Nematol; Am Phytopath Soc; AAAS. *Res:* Management of agro-ecosystems with the goal of developing management strategies for the protection of the crop plants from plant parasitic nematodes and associated microorganisms. *Mailing Add:* Colo Agr Exp Sta 16 Admin Bldg Colo State Univ Ft Collins CO 80523-0001

LAUGHLIN, DAVID EUGENE, PHYSICAL METALLURGY, ELECTRON MICROSCOPY. *Current Pos:* from asst prof to assoc prof, 74-82, PROF METALL, CARNEGIE-MELLON UNIV, 82- *Personal Data:* b Philadelphia, Pa, July 15, 47; m 71, Diane Seamdal; c Jonathan, Elizabeth, Andrew & Daniel. *Educ:* Drexel Univ, BSc, 69; Mass Inst Technol, PhD(metall), 73. *Prof Exp:* Res assoc, Nat Bur Stand, 73-74. *Concurrent Pos:* Pres, Trinity Christian Sch Bd Dirs, 78-83; consult, 80-; assoc ed, Metall Trans, 82, 87-; NEDO grant. *Mem:* Fel Am Metals; Am Inst Mining, Metall & Petrol Engrs; Am Soc Eng Educ; Am Sci Affil; Inst Elec & Electronics Engrs. *Res:* X-ray diffraction; innovative teaching; phase transformations; differential scanning calorimetry; electron microscopy; magnetic materials. *Mailing Add:* Dept Metall & Mat Sci Carnegie-Mellon Univ 5000 Forbes Ave Pittsburgh PA 15213-3816. *Fax:* 412-268-7169; *E-Mail:* dlop@andrew.cmu.ed

LAUGHLIN, ETHELREDA R, BIOCHEMISTRY, SCIENCE EDUCATION. *Current Pos:* instr chem, 63-65, prof chem, 68-85, HEAD, DEPT SCI, CUYAHOGA COMMUNITY COL, WESTERN CAMPUS, 65-, EMER PROF CHEM, 90- *Personal Data:* b Cleveland, Ohio, Nov 13, 22; div; c 1. *Educ:* Case Western Res Univ, AB, 42, MS, 44, PhD(sci educ), 62. *Prof Exp:* Instr chem, anat & physiol, St John Col, 49-51; teacher high sch, Ohio, 53-62; assoc prof sci educ & org chem, Ferris State Col, 62-63. *Concurrent Pos:* Vis prof biochem, Case Western Res Univ, 70-71; sci educ res grants, NSF, 76-78. *Mem:* Nat Educ Asn; Am Chem Soc; Audubon Soc; Sigma Xi; Sierra Club. *Mailing Add:* 6486 State Rd No 12 Parma OH 44134-4162

LAUGHLIN, JAMES STANLEY, STATISTICS, OPERATIONS RESEARCH. *Current Pos:* PROF MATH, WOODRIVER HIGH SCH, 91- *Personal Data:* b Guilford, Mo, Sept 23, 36; m 60; c 2. *Educ:* Northwest Mo State Univ, BS, 58; Univ Northern Colo, MA, 61; Univ Denver, PhD(higher educ, math), 68. *Prof Exp:* Teacher chem & math, Grand Community Schs, Boxholm, Iowa, 58-59; teacher math, Denver Pub Schs, Colo, 59-67, res asst, 67-68; assoc prof math, Kans State Teachers Col, 68-75, dir instnl studies, 70-75; dir instnl res, Idaho State Univ, 75-83, asst prof math, 84-91. *Concurrent Pos:* Kans State Dept Educ grant, 69-70. *Mem:* Math Asn Am; Am Educ Res Asn; Nat Coun Teachers Math. *Res:* Teaching of mathematics. *Mailing Add:* Dept Math Wood River High Sch PO Box 948 Hailey ID 83333

LAUGHLIN, JOHN SETH, MEDICAL PHYSICS. *Current Pos:* PROF BIOPHYS, SLOAN-KETTERING DIV, MED COLL, CORNELL UNIV, 55- *Personal Data:* b Canton, Mo, Jan 26, 18; m 79; c 3. *Educ:* Willamette Univ, AB, 40; Haverford Col, MS, 42; Univ Ill, PhD(physics), 47. *Hon Degrees:* DSc, Willamette Univ, 68. *Honors & Awards:* William D Coolidge Award, Am Asn Physicists in Med, 74; John Wiley Jones Lectr, Rochester Inst Technol, 77; Aebersold Award, Soc Nuclear Med, 84; Janeway Lectr, Am Radium Soc, 86; Gold Medal, Am Col Radiol, 88. *Prof Exp:* Asst, Haverford Col, 40-42; asst, Univ Ill, 42-43, res assoc, Off Sci Res & Develop, 44-45, asst, 46; asst prof spec res, 47-48, asst prof radiol, Col Med, 48-51, assoc prof, 51-52; assoc prof biophys, Sloan-Kettering Div, Med Col, Cornell Univ, 52-55; vpres, 66-72, chief, div biophys, Sloan-Kettering Inst Cancer Res, 52- *Concurrent Pos:* Attend physicist, Mem Hosp, 52-, chmn, Dept Med Physics, 52-88. *Mem:* Radiol Soc NAm; Radiation Res Soc (pres, 70-71); Soc Nuclear Med; Am Asn Physicists in Med (pres, 64-65); Health Physics Soc (pres, 60-61). *Res:* Neutron-proton and neutron-deutron interaction; high pressure cloud chamber design; interaction of high energy electrons with nuclei; application of betatron to medical therapy; radiation dosimetry; high energy gamma ray scanning; development of digital and computer controlled scanning; isotope metabolic studies; 3-dimensional photon treatment planning. *Mailing Add:* Mem Hosp 1275 York Ave Box 62 New York NY 10021

LAUGHLIN, R(OBERT) G(ARDINER) W(ILLIS), CHEMICAL ENGINEERING, WASTE MANAGEMENT. *Current Pos:* DIR, WASTE MGT TECHNOL, ENVIRON TECHNOL DIV, ORTECH, 67- *Personal Data:* b London, Eng, Oct 11, 42; m 67, Rosina Fraser; c Robert, Alexandra & Lydia. *Educ:* Univ Col, Univ London, BSc, 64, PhD(chem eng), 67. *Concurrent Pos:* Chair, Ont Minister Environ Hazardous Waste Adv Comt. *Mem:* Can Soc Chem Eng; Asn Prof Engrs Ont. *Res:* Environmental engineering; industrial waste exchange; spontaneous combustion phenomena; industrial and municipal solid waste utilization; industrial waste treatment; biomass to energy conversion systems; waste treatment systems; waste reduction and minimization; environmental technologic assessment and development. *Mailing Add:* Recycling Technol Ortech Sheridan Park Mississauga ON L5K 1B3 Can. *E-Mail:* blaughlin@ortech.on.ca

LAUGHLIN, ROBERT B, PHYSICS. *Current Pos:* assoc prof physics, 85-89, PROF PHYSICS, SCH HUMANITIES & SCI, STANFORD UNIV, 89-, ANNE T & ROBERT M BASS PROF, PROF APPL PHYSICS, 93- *Personal Data:* b Visalia, Calif, Nov 1, 50; m 79, Anita Rhona Perry; c Nathaniel & Todd. *Educ:* Univ Calif, Berkeley, BA, 72; Mass Inst Technol, PhD (physics), 79. *Honors & Awards:* E O Lawrence Award for Physics, 85; Oliver E Buckley Prize, 86; Eastman Kodak Lectr, 89; Van Vleck Lectr, 94. *Prof Exp:* Bell Tel Labs, 79-81; Lawrence Livermore Nat Lab, 81-82. *Mem:* Nat Acad Sci; AAAS; fel Am Phys Soc; fel Am Acad Arts & Sci. *Mailing Add:* Dept Physics Stanford Univ Stanford CA 94305-4060

LAUGHLIN, ROBERT GENE, PHYSICAL ORGANIC CHEMISTRY, PHYSICAL CHEMISTRY. *Current Pos:* res chemist, 56-68, sect head, 68-92, RES FEL, MIAMI VALLEY LABS, PROCTER & GAMBLE CO, 92- *Personal Data:* b Sullivan, Ind, Aug 9, 30; div; c Steven K & Kenneth B. *Educ:* Purdue Univ, BS, 51; Cornell Univ, PhD(org chem), 55, Hickrill Found, PD, 56. *Honors & Awards:* Samuel Rosen Mem Award, Am Oil Chemists Soc, 92. *Prof Exp:* Fel org chem, Hickrill Res Labs, NY, 55-56. *Mem:* Am Inst Chem; Royal Soc Chem; Am Chem Soc. *Res:* Synthesis, phase science, colloid science and technology of surfactant molecules; correlation of molecular structure with aqueous phase equilibria; development of new phase study methods and principles; physical science of carotenoids. *Mailing Add:* 11641 Bank Rd Cincinnati OH 45251. *Fax:* 513-627-1233; *E-Mail:* laughlin.rg@pg.com, laughlin.rg@aol.com

LAUGHLIN, WILLIAM SCEVA, PHYSICAL ANTHROPOLOGY. *Current Pos:* prof biobehav sci, 69-85, PROF ECOL & EVOLUTIONARY BIOL, UNIV CONN, 85- *Personal Data:* b Canton, Mo, Aug 26, 19; m 44, Ruth Finney; c Leslie (deceased) & Sara. *Educ:* Willamette Univ, BA, 41; Haverford Col, MA, 42; Harvard Univ, AM, 48, PhD(anthrop), 49. *Hon Degrees:* DSc, Willamette Univ, 68. *Prof Exp:* Asst anthrop, Harvard Univ, 47-48; asst prof, Univ Ore, 49-53, assoc prof, 53-55; from assoc prof to prof, Univ Wis, 55-69, chmn dept, 60-62. *Concurrent Pos:* Ed, J Am Asn Phys Anthrop, 58-63; mem anthrop study sect, Nat Res Coun, 59-62; fel, Ctr Advan Study Behav Sci, Stanford Univ, 64-65. *Mem:* AAAS; fel Am Soc Human Genetics; Soc Am Archaeol; Am Asn Phys Anthrop; Am Anthrop Asn. *Res:* Population genetics; blood group genetics and skeletal history of human isolates, Indians and Eskimo-Aleut stock; skeletal analysis of Eskimos and Indians; peopling of New World from Siberia on Bering land bridge coast. *Mailing Add:* Dept Ecol & Evolutionary Biol PO Box U-154 3107 Horsebarn Hill Rd Storrs CT 06268

LAUGHLIN, WINSTON MEANS, SOIL SCIENCE. *Current Pos:* SOIL SCIENTIST, ALASKA AGR EXP STA, 49- *Personal Data:* b Fountain, Minn, May 2, 17; m 47, Dorothy Fuelihan; c Ellen, Laurence, Keith & Brian. *Educ:* Univ Minn, BS, 41; Mich State Univ, MS, 47, PhD(soil sci), 49. *Prof Exp:* Soil surveyor, Univ Minn, 40-41; asst, Mich State Univ, 41-42. *Mem:* AAAS; Am Soc Agron; Soil Sci Soc Am; Am Sci Affil; Int Soc Soil Sci. *Res:* Soil fertility, chemistry and classification with emphasis on Arctic conditions. *Mailing Add:* Agr & Forestry Exp Sta 533 E Fireweed Palmer AK 99645

LAUGHNAN, JOHN RAPHAEL, genetics; deceased, see previous edition for last biography

LAUGHNER, WILLIAM JAMES, JR, genetics, molecular biology; deceased, see previous edition for last biography

LAUGHON, ROBERT BUSH, RADIOACTIVE & HAZARDOUS WASTE DISPOSAL, ENVIRONMENTAL MANAGEMENT. *Current Pos:* CONSULT GEOLOGIST, 94- *Personal Data:* b Greensboro, NC, Apr 20, 34; m 57, Barbara A Jinnette; c Francia & Colin. *Educ:* Colo Col, BA, 60; Univ Colo, Boulder, MS, 63; Univ Ariz, PhD(geol), 70. *Prof Exp:* Geologist, US Geol Surv, 62-63 & Anaconda Co, 64-65; instr, Univ Ariz, 66-67; geologist, Manned Spacecraft Ctr, NASA, 67-76; proj mgr, Nuclear Div, Union Carbide Corp, 76-78; mgr, Geol Explor Dept, Batelle Mem Inst, 78-81, chief geoscientist, Proj Mgt Div, 81-90, geotechnol mgr, Mich LLRW Proj, 90-91, res leader, 91-94. *Concurrent Pos:* Lectr, Moody Col, Tex A&M Univ, 74. *Res:* Waste management; mineralogy-crystallography. *Mailing Add:* 657 Indian Mound Rd Columbus OH 43213

LAUGHTER, ARLINE H, IMMUNOLOGY. *Current Pos:* SR RES ASSOC, DEPT IMMUNOL, VET ADMIN MED CTR, 68- *Mailing Add:* Dept Immunol Res Vet Admin Med Ctr Bldg 109 Rm 226 2002 Holcombe Blvd Houston TX 77030-4298

LAUGHTON, PAUL MACDONELL, ORGANIC CHEMISTRY. *Current Pos:* from asst prof to assoc prof chem, 51-65, PROF CHEM, CARLETON UNIV, 65- *Personal Data:* b Toronto, Ont, Sept 8, 23; m 46; c 4. *Educ:* Univ Toronto, BA, 45; Dalhousie Univ, MSc, 47; Univ Wis, PhD(chem), 50. *Prof Exp:* Res assoc, Univ Wis, 50; Nat Res Coun Can fel, Dalhousie Univ, 50-51. *Concurrent Pos:* Vis prof, Stanford Univ, 62 & Kings Col, London, 72-73; Am Chem Soc-Petrol Res Fund fel, Univ Calif, Berkeley, 62-63. *Mem:* Am Chem Soc; fel Chem Inst Can; Royal Soc Chem; Sigma Xi. *Res:* Mechanism studies; isotope effects. *Mailing Add:* 928 Muskoka Ave Ottawa ON K2A 3H9 Can

LAUKHUF, WALDEN LOUIS SHELBURNE, CHEMICAL ENGINEERING. *Current Pos:* from asst prof to assoc prof, 73-86, PROF CHEM ENG, UNIV LOUISVILLE, 86-, CONSULT, 80- *Personal Data:* b Maysville, Ky, July 25, 43; m 67, Lana Schumann; c Heather & Matthew. *Educ:* Univ Louisville, BSChE, 66, MSChE, 67, PhD(chem eng), 69. *Prof Exp:* Engr, Humble Oil & Refining Co, 69; USAF, 69-73, proj engr, Air Force Rocket Propulsion Lab, 69-71, develop eng specialist, Air Force Mat Lab, 71-73. *Mem:* Am Inst Chem Engrs. *Res:* Distillation; process controls; mass transfer and thermodynamics; digital control. *Mailing Add:* 14104 Tree Crest Ct Louisville KY 40245. *Fax:* 502-852-6355; *E-Mail:* wllauk01@ulkyvm.louisville.edu

LAUKONIS, JOSEPH VAINYS, PHYSICS. *Current Pos:* RETIRED. *Personal Data:* b Mich, Apr 1, 25; m 54. *Educ:* Univ Detroit, BS, 51; Univ Cincinnati, PhD, 57. *Prof Exp:* Sr res physicist, Gen Motors Corp, 57-90. *Mem:* Am Phys Soc. *Res:* Iron whiskers; metal surfaces; high temperature oxidation; formability of sheet metals; electron microscopy; ultrahigh vacuums; oxidation-reduction catalysts. *Mailing Add:* 32405 Northampton Warren MI 48093

LAUL, JAGDISH CHANDER, GEOCHEMISTRY, COSMOCHEMISTRY. *Current Pos:* SR RES SCIENTIST CHEM, PHYS SCI DEPT, PAC NORTHWEST DIV, BATTELLE MEM INST, 72- *Personal Data:* b India, Sept 1, 39; m 70; c 3. *Educ:* Punjab Univ, India, BS, 59; Purdue Univ, MS, & PhD(radio geochem), 69. *Honors & Awards:* Group Achievement Award, NASA, 73. *Prof Exp:* Res assoc, Enrico Fermi Inst, Univ Chicago, 69-71 & Radiation Ctr, Ore State Univ, 71-75. *Mem:* Am Chem Soc; Geochem Soc; Meteoritical Soc. *Res:* Studies of trace elements and their implications in lunar, meteorite, terrestrial, environmental, nuclear waste and fossil fuel samples; development of radioanalytical methods and instrumentation in neutron activation area. *Mailing Add:* 607 Cherrywood Lane Richland WA 99352

LAULAINEN, NELS STEPHEN, ATMOSPHERIC SCIENCE. *Current Pos:* sr res scientist atmospheric sci, Battelle-Pac NW Labs, 74-82, mgr, Atmospheric & Precipitation Chem Sect, Earth Sci, 82-87, prog mgr earth sci, 87-94, SR RES SCIENTIST ATMOSPHERIC SCI, BATTELLE-PAC NW LABS, 94- *Personal Data:* b Longview, Wash, Oct 22, 41; div; c David, Frans, Alan, Soren & Kirsten. *Educ:* Univ Wash, BS, 63, MS, 65, PhD(physics), 68. *Prof Exp:* Res scientist physics, First Phys Inst, Heidelberg Univ, 68-70; res assoc med physics, Med Radiation Physics & Radiol, Univ Wash, 70-71; res assoc geophys & astron, Geophys Prog, 71-74. *Concurrent Pos:* Res scientist, Fulbright Travel Stipend, 68-70; lectr physics, Univ Wash, 72-74; tech adv, US Environ Protection Agency, Washington, DC, 81-82; vis scientist, Fraunhofer Inst Atmospheric Environ Res, Garmisch-Partenkirchen, Ger, 89-90. *Mem:* Am Phys Soc; Sigma Xi; Am Geophys Union; Am Asn Aerosol Res. *Res:* Atmospheric aerosol physics; solar radiation and its interaction with atmospheric constituents; atmospheric pollutant transformation and removal processes; climate effects of energy production; acid deposition field studies and modeling. *Mailing Add:* Battelle-Northwest Labs MSIN K9-30 Atmospheric Sci PO Box 999 Richland WA 99352. *E-Mail:* ns_laulainen@ccmail.pnl.gov

LAUNDRE, JOHN WILLIAM, WILDLIFE BEHAVIOR, ECOLOGY. *Current Pos:* ASST PROF ECOL, SOUTHWEST STATE UNIV, 79- *Personal Data:* b Green Bay, Wis, Jan 30, 49; m 73. *Educ:* Univ Wis, Green Bay, BSc, 71; Northern Mich Univ, MA, 74; Idaho State Univ, PhD(ecol), 79. *Prof Exp:* Instr anat, Northeast Wis Tech & Voc Inst, 74-76. *Mem:* Wildlife Soc; Animal Behav Soc; Am Soc Mammalogist; Sigma Xi. *Res:* Ecology and behavior of mammals, including coyotes, deer, cats and small mammals. *Mailing Add:* 1255 Hiline Rd Pocatello ID 83201-2944

LAUNER, PHILIP JULES, INFRARED SPECTROSCOPY, SILICONE TECHNOLOGY. *Current Pos:* pres, 73-87, DIR RES, LAB FOR MAT INC, 87- *Personal Data:* b Philadelphia, Pa, Nov 20, 22; m 47, Arden Elliott; c Donald, Alden & Elizabeth. *Educ:* Drew Univ, AB, 43; Columbia Univ, MA, 47. *Prof Exp:* Teaching asst quant analysis, Columbia Univ, 47-48; proj chemist petrol chem, Res Dept, Stand Oil Co, Ind, 48-55; specialist spectros, Silicone Prod Dept, Gen Elec Co, 55-72. *Mem:* Am Chem Soc; Soc Appl Spectros; fel Am Inst Chemists; Coblentz Soc. *Res:* Infrared spectroscopy; silicone technology; identification of industrial materials. *Mailing Add:* PO Box 2551 Glenville NY 12325

LAUPUS, WILLIAM E, MEDICINE. *Current Pos:* dean, 75-88, EMER DEAN, SCH MED, ECAROLINA UNIV, 88- *Personal Data:* b Seymour, Ind, May 25, 21; m 48; c 4. *Educ:* Yale Univ, BS, 43, MD, 45. *Prof Exp:* Instr pediat, Med Col, Cornell Univ, 50-52; from asst prof to prof, Med Col Ga, 59-63; prof pediat & chmn dept, Med Col Va, 63-75. *Concurrent Pos:* Examr, Am Bd Pediat, 67-91, bd officer, 73-78, pres, 76-77; vchancellor, ECarolina Univ, 83-88, prof prev med, 88-91; pres, Am Bd Med Specialties, 86-87. *Mem:* Fel Am Acad Pediat; Am Fedn Clin Res; AMA; Am Pediat Soc. *Res:* Pediatric medicine. *Mailing Add:* Welco Consult PO Box 20007 Greenville NC 27858-0007

LAURANCE, NEAL L, COMPUTER SCIENCE. *Current Pos:* Res scientist, Sci Lab, Ford Motor Co, 60-73, mgr, Control Systs Dept, 73-79, mgr analytical sci, Eng & Res Staff, 79-85, SR STAFF SCIENTIST, FORD MOTOR CO, 85- *Personal Data:* b Winsted, Minn, Aug 19, 32; m 53; c 4. *Educ:* Marquette Univ, BS, 54, MS, 55; Univ Ill, PhD(physics), 60. *Mem:* Am Phys Soc; fel Inst Elec & Electronics Engrs. *Res:* Simulation systems; manufacturing automation, OSI computer networks; real-time systems. *Mailing Add:* 876 Heather Way Ann Arbor MI 48104

LAURENCE, ALFRED EDWARD, INDUSTRIAL CHEMISTRY. *Current Pos:* CONSULT, 68- *Personal Data:* b Breslau, Ger, Dec 12, 10; nat US; m 49, Lotte Hadda; c Thomas M, Geoffrey F & Virginia M (Wadlow). *Educ:* LLD, Breslau, Ger, 33; dipl, Poitiers, 34, Caen, 36. *Prof Exp:* Chemist, Serv Lab, Am Corn Prod Co, India, 37-38; chem sales technologist, Shell Oil Co, 38-40; chemist & metallurgist, Indian Smelting & Ref Co, 40-41; chemist, Res & Develop Dept, Atlantic Ref Co, Pa, 41-46; chemist & technologist, Shell Chem Corp, Shell Oil Co, Calif & NY, 46-52; export mgr org chem, Propane Co, Eng, 52-54; mgr indust & chem prods, Europ Res Off, Minn Mining & Mfg Co, Ltd, 54-61; dir res, Int Develop & Invest Co, Ltd, Bahamas, 62-63. *Concurrent Pos:* Consult, UN & UNESCO, 64; econ planning adv, Lewis Berger, Gt Brit Ltd, 65-66; researcher, Economist Intel Univ, London, 67-68; vis prof, Univ Utah, 69, 70. *Res:* Organic chemistry; petrochemistry; analytical methods; corporation finance and economics; international and patent law; sociology of industry. *Mailing Add:* La Mer 7 Sisters Rd St Lawrence PO38 1UZ Isle of Wight England

LAURENCE, GEOFFREY CAMERON, fish biology, ecological modelling, for more information see previous edition

LAURENCE, JOHN A, ENVIRONMENTAL STRESS, COMPUTER MODELING & ASSESSMENTS. *Current Pos:* Asst scientist, 77-82, assoc scientist, 82-88, SCIENTIST, BOYCE THOMPSON INST PLANT RES, 88-, PROG DIR, 91- *Personal Data:* b Berea, Ohio, Dec 16, 49; c Zachary & Molly. *Educ:* Pa State Univ, BS, 71; Univ Minn, MS, 73, PhD(plant path), 76. *Concurrent Pos:* Adj prof, Dept Plant Path, Cornell Univ, 83- *Mem:* Am Phytopath Soc; Sigma Xi. *Res:* Assessment of effects of air pollutants and other environmental stresses on plant growth and yield; modeling tree and forest response to the environment. *Mailing Add:* Boyce Thompson Inst Tower Rd Ithaca NY 14853-1801. *Fax:* 607-254-1242; *E-Mail:* jal6@cornell.edu

LAURENCE, KENNETH ALLEN, MICROBIOLOGY. *Current Pos:* RETIRED. *Personal Data:* b Cleveland, Ohio, Nov 4, 28; m 49, Elaine E Addis; c Kirk A & Denise L (Clough). *Educ:* Marietta Col, AB, 51; Univ Iowa, MS, 53, PhD, 56. *Prof Exp:* NIH fel immunol, Univ Iowa, 56-57; instr microbiol & immunol, Med Col, Cornell Univ, 57-59, asst prof, 59-60; asst med dir, Pop Coun Inc, 60-68, assoc dir, Biomed Div, 68-76; prof & head, Dept Biol Sci, Univ Idaho, 76-80, dir grants & contracts, 80-83; prin contact officer & alt trustee, Consortium Int Develop, Tucson, Ariz, 80-83, dep exec dir, 83-85; res develop coordr, Univ Idaho, 85-94. *Concurrent Pos:* Ford Found consult physiol reprod, Egyptian Univs Prog, 66-67 & 70-; proj specialist, Ford Found, Cairo, Egypt, 73-74; consult, Egyptian Univ, Rockefeller Found, 80; Supreme Coun Univ Foreign Relations Unit, Cairo, Egypt, 84; dir, Int Progs Off, Univ Idaho, 90-92. *Mem:* AAAS; Am Soc Microbiol; Soc Study Reproduction; Sigma Xi; Soc Res Adminr; Int Agr Res & Develop. *Res:* Physiology of reproduction; immunology; parasitology; medical bacteriology, immunologic studies of the reproductive processes. *Mailing Add:* 1242 Timber Lane Moscow ID 83844. *Fax:* 208-885-6198

LAURENCE, ROBERT L(IONEL), CHEMICAL ENGINEERING, POLYMER SCIENCE. *Current Pos:* assoc prof, 68-73, head dept, 82-89, PROF CHEM ENG, POLYMER SCI & ENG, UNIV MASS, AMHERST, 73- *Personal Data:* b West Warwick, RI, July 13, 36; m 59, Carol Jolicoeur; c Jonathan, Lisa & Andrew. *Educ:* Mass Inst Technol, BS, 57; Univ RI, MS, 60; Northwestern Univ, PhD(chem eng), 66. *Hon Degrees:* DSc, Inst Nat Polytechnique Toulouse, Univ Toulouse, France, 89. *Prof Exp:* Res engr, Elec Boat Div, Gen Dynamics Corp, Conn, 57-58; engr, Eng Res Lab, E I du Pont de Nemours & Co, Del, 60-61, engr, Elastomers Dept, Tex, 61-63; asst prof chem eng, Johns Hopkins Univ, 65-68. *Concurrent Pos:* Vis prof, Imp Col Sci & Technol, 74-75, Universidad Nac del Sur, Bahia Blanca, Arg, 78 & Col de France, 82, Gen Elec Corp Res & Develop, 89-90, Ecole Nat Superieure du Ingenieurs, Genie Chemique (Toulouse), 90. *Mem:* Fel Am Inst Chem Engrs; Am Chem Soc; fel Am Inst Chemists. *Res:* Fluid mechanics-hydrodynamic stability; polymerization reaction engineering; diffusion in polymers; polymer processing; diffusion inzeolites. *Mailing Add:* Dept Chem Eng Univ Mass Amherst MA 01002

LAURENCOT, HENRY JULES, DRUG METABOLISM, ANIMAL SCIENCE. *Current Pos:* RES INVESTR, HOFFMAN-LA ROCHE, INC, 66- *Personal Data:* b Brooklyn, NY, Dec 14, 29; m 61; c 4. *Educ:* St Peter's Col, NJ, BS, 51; Fordham Univ, MS, 55, PhD(biol), 65. *Prof Exp:* Asst plant physiol. *Mem:* Am Soc Pharmacol & Exp Therapeut; NY Acad Sci; Sigma Xi; AAAS. *Res:* In vivo and in vitro metabolic studies of radioactive experimental drugs. *Mailing Add:* Bldg 735 Rm 117 Hoffmann-La Roche Inc 22-10 Rte 208 S Fair Lawn NJ 07410

LAURENDEAU, NORMAND MAURICE, MECHANICAL ENGINEERING, PHYSICAL CHEMISTRY. *Current Pos:* From asst prof to assoc prof, 72-82, PROF MECH ENG, PURDUE UNIV, 82-, REILLY PROF COMBUST ENG, 99- *Personal Data:* b Lewiston, Maine, Aug 16, 44; m 72, Marlene; c Andre & Jules. *Educ:* Univ Notre Dame, BS, 66; Princeton Univ, MSE, 68; Univ Calif, Berkeley, PhD(mech eng), 72. *Concurrent Pos:* Res engr, Arthur D Little, Inc, 80-81; dir, Coal Res Ctr, Purdue Univ, 81-84; vis prof, Dept Chem, Northwestern Univ, 88; fel, Japan Soc Prom Sci, 92. *Mem:* Am Soc Mech Engrs; Am Chem Soc; Combustion Inst; Optical Soc Am. *Res:* Combustion; chemical kinetics; combustion diagnostics; air pollution; laser-induced fluorescence; engineering ethics. *Mailing Add:* Sch Mech Eng Purdue Univ West Lafayette IN 47907. *Fax:* 765-494-0539; *E-Mail:* laurende@ecu.purdue.edu

LAURENSON, ROBERT MARK, MECHANICAL ENGINEERING. *Personal Data:* b Pittsburgh, Pa, Oct 25, 38; m 61; c 2. *Educ:* Mo Sch Mines, BS, 61; Univ Mich, Ann Arbor, MSE, 62; Ga Inst Technol, PhD(mech eng), 69. *Honors & Awards:* Award, McDonnell Douglas Astronaut Co, McDonnell Douglas Corp, 71. *Prof Exp:* Dynamics engr, McDonnell Aircraft Co, 62-64, sr dynamics engr, McDonnell Douglas Corp, 68-71, group dynamics engr, 71-74, staff engr, 74-75, tech specialist, 75-92. *Concurrent Pos:* Lectr, Dept Eng Mech, St Louis Univ, 69-71. *Mem:* Am Inst Aeronaut & Astronaut; Am Soc Mech Engrs. *Res:* Vibrations of structures and machine elements; response of elastic and flexible structures to transient loadings. *Mailing Add:* 1104 Jasper Ct Crofton MD 21114

LAURENT, PIERRE, ELECTRON MICROSCOPY. *Current Pos:* res fel, CNRS, Paris, 50-56, sr researcher, 57-68, res dir, Col France, 69-73, RES DIR, CNRS, STRASBOURG, 74- *Personal Data:* b Thionville, France, July 25, 25; m 50; c 3. *Educ:* Acad Lille, BSc, 44; Univ Nancy, MSc, 48; Univ Paris, Sorbonne, DSc, 58. *Prof Exp:* Teacher natural sci, Col d'Armentieres, 48-49; asst prof, Univ Lille, 49-50. *Concurrent Pos:* Vis prof, Michael Rease Hosp, Chicago, 68, CVP Div Hosp, Univ Pa, Philadelphia, 76-80; res consult, 80- *Mem:* Am Physiol Soc; Soc Exp Biol; Am Soc Zoologists; Soc Physiol. *Res:* Structural and physiological approach of adaptative processes in vertebrates, more particularly fishes; osmoregulation, circulation and respiration; gill morphology and physiology, acid-base regulation and ion transport; immunocytochimie of carbonic anhydrase, cortisol, prolactine; cell kinetics. *Mailing Add:* 18 Rue de la Sclerie Ittenheim F 67117 France. *Fax:* 33-88 69 08 13

LAURENT, ROGER, GEOLOGY. *Current Pos:* adj prof, 71-73, assoc prof, 73-79, PROF PETROL, LAVAL UNIV, 79- *Personal Data:* b Geneva, Switz, June 23, 38; m 62, Jeannine Pozzo; c John & Philippe. *Educ:* Univ Geneva, Lic es sci, 62, Ing Geol, 64, Dr es Sci(geol & mineral sci), 67. *Prof Exp:* Asst mineral, Univ Geneva, 63-65, res asst geochronol, Sci Res Nat Corp Switz, 65-67; asst prof mineral & petrog, Middlebury Col, 67-71. *Concurrent*

Pos: Vis prof, Univ Nancy, France, 80 & Univ Geneve, Switz, 89. *Mem:* Fel Geol Asn Can; Swiss Soc Mineral & Petrol; Swiss Geol Soc; fel Geol Soc Am. *Res:* Study of ophiolites, asbestos and chromite in the field and in the labs by petrography; petrology; geochronometric determinations and geochemical studies; study of platinum in ultramafic rocks. *Mailing Add:* Dept Geol Laval Univ Quebec PQ G1K 7P4 Can

LAURENT, SEBASTIAN MARC, CATALYSIS, ZEOLITE SCIENCE. *Current Pos:* RETIRED. *Personal Data:* b Wallace, La, Jan 21, 26; m 49; c 7. *Educ:* Loyola Univ, La, BS, 49. *Prof Exp:* Res physicist catalysis, Esso Res Labs, Humble Oil & Refining Co, 57-67; res physicist, Ethyl Corp, 67-77, sr res physicist mat sci, 77-80, sr res physicist, 80-86, res & develop specialist, 86-89, res & develop adv, Zeolite Appl Res, 90-92. *Mem:* Catalysis Soc; Int Zeolite Asn. *Res:* Application of zeolites to improve nutritional responses in animal diets; bone development, egg shell development and physiological responses under heat stress environments; scanning electron microscopy; x-ray crystallography; x-ray fluorescence spectroscopy; adsorption; ion exchange; animal science research. *Mailing Add:* 26590 Greenwells Springs Rd Greenwell Springs LA 70739

LAURENT, TORVARD CLAUDE, BIOCHEMISTRY. *Current Pos:* SCI SECY, WENNER-GREU FOUND, 93- *Personal Data:* b Stockholm, Sweden, Dec 5, 30; m 53, Ulla B G Hellsing; c Birgitta, Claes & Agneta. *Educ:* Karolinska Inst, BM, 50, MD, 58. *Hon Degrees:* MD, Turku Univ, Finland, 93; PharmD, Bologna Univ, Italy, 94. *Prof Exp:* Instr histol & chem, Karolinska Inst, 49-52 & 55-58; res fel & assoc, Retina Found, 53-54 & 59-61; assoc prof, Univ Uppsala, Sweden, 61-66, prof med & physiol chem, 66-96, chair, Dept Med & Physiol Chem, 73-77 & 87-91. *Concurrent Pos:* Mem, Swed Natural Sci Res Coun, 68-70, Swed Med Res Coun, 70-77, Nobel Comt Chem, 92-; vis prof biochem, Monash Univ, Australia, 79-80. *Mem:* Royal Swed Acad Sci (pres, 91-94); Swed Biochem Soc (secy, 67-70). *Res:* Chemistry of connective tissue, physical properties, physiological functions; turnover and medical applications of the polysaccharide hyaluronan; opthalmic biochemistry, physical chemistry of polysaccharide networks; transport processes in polysaccharide solutions, biochemical separation techniques; methods for cell separation. *Mailing Add:* Inst Med/Physiol Chem Univ Uppsala BMC Box 575 Uppsala S-751 23 Sweden

LAURENZI, BERNARD JOHN, CHEMICAL PHYSICS. *Current Pos:* from asst prof to assoc prof, 69-83, PROF CHEM, STATE UNIV NY, ALBANY, 84- *Personal Data:* b Philadelphia, Pa, Dec 23, 38. *Educ:* St Joseph's Col, Pa, BS, 60; Univ Pa, PhD(chem), 65. *Prof Exp:* Res chemist, Rohm & Haas Chem Co, 60-61; NSF fel, Pa State Univ, 65-66; asst prof chem, Univ Tenn, Knoxville, 66-68 & Bryn Mawr Col, 68-69. *Mem:* Am Chem Soc; Am Phys Soc. *Res:* Quantum chemistry; use of Green's functions in atomic and molecular calculations; properties of isoelectronic molecules. *Mailing Add:* 115A Willow St Guilderland NY 12084

LAURENZI, GUSTAVE, MEDICINE. *Current Pos:* assoc prof, 70-75, PROF MED, SCH MED, TUFTS UNIV, 75- *Personal Data:* b Orange, NJ, July 19, 26; c 2. *Educ:* NY Univ, BA, 49; Georgetown Univ, MD, 53; Am Bd Internal Med, dipl; Am Bd Pulmonary Dis, dipl. *Prof Exp:* Intern path, Mallory Inst Path, Boston City Hosp, 53-54; intern med, Yale Med Serv, Grace-New Haven Hosp, Conn, 54-55; asst resident, Columbia Med Serv, Bellevue Hosp, NY, 55-56; chief resident physician chest serv, Bellevue Med Ctr, 58-59; asst prof med & dir respiratory dis, NJ Col Med & Dent, 60-63, assoc prof med, 63-68. *Concurrent Pos:* Res fel, Cardiopulmonary Lab, Columbia-Presby Med Ctr, 56-57; USPHS res fel, 57-58; Nat Found training fel, Am Trudeau Soc, 58-59; Channing res fel bact & immunol, Mallory Inst Path, Harvard Univ & res fel, Am Thoracic Soc, 59-60; Am Thoracic Soc Edward L Trudeau fel, 62-64; consult, Harvard Med Serv, Boston City Hosp, 59-60; chief med, St Vincent Hosp, Worcester, Mass, 68-; dir respiratory care serv, Newton-Wellesley Hosp. *Mem:* Fel Am Col Physicians; Am Thoracic Soc; Am Fedn Clin Res. *Res:* Chest disease; chronic bronchitis and pulmonary emphysema. *Mailing Add:* Newton-Wellesley Hosp 2000 Washington St Newton Lower Falls MA 02162

LAURIE, GORDON WILLIAM, CELL BIOLOGY, EXTRACELLULAR MATRIX. *Current Pos:* asst prof, 88-94, ASSOC PROF, DEPT CELL BIOL, UNIV VA, 94- *Personal Data:* b Hamilton, Ont, Dec 28, 53; m 81; c 2. *Educ:* McMaster Univ, BSc, 76; McGill Univ, MSc, 79, PhD(anat), 82. *Honors & Awards:* Ralph D Lillie Award, Am Histochem, Soc, 82. *Prof Exp:* From vis fel to vis assoc, NIH, 83-88. *Mem:* Am Asn Anatomists; Am Soc Cell Biol; Soc Develop Biol. *Res:* Molecular assembly and sythesis of basement membrane and its relation to cell receptors. *Mailing Add:* Dept Anat & Cell Biol Univ Va Charlottesville VA 22908. *Fax:* 804-982-3912; *E-Mail:* gwl6s@virginia.edu

LAURIE, JOHN SEWALL, EXPERIMENTAL BIOLOGY. *Current Pos:* RETIRED. *Personal Data:* b Gloucester, Mass, May 30, 25. *Educ:* Ore State Univ, BS, 50; Johns Hopkins Univ, ScD, 56. *Prof Exp:* Res fel parasite physiol, Inst Parasitol, McGill Univ, 56-57; instr zool, Tulane Univ, 57-59; asst prof exp biol, Univ Utah, 59-62; mem staff water pollution study, USPHS, 62-63; from assoc prof to prof biol, ECarolina Univ, 63-90. *Mem:* Am Soc Parasitol; Wildlife Dis Asn; Am Soc Zoologists; Sigma Xi. *Res:* Physiology of parasites; physiology, ultrastructure and ecology of helminth parasites. *Mailing Add:* 1900 S Charles Blvd Greenville NC 27858

LAURIE, VICTOR WILLIAM, PHYSICAL CHEMISTRY. *Current Pos:* RETIRED. *Personal Data:* b Columbia, SC, June 1, 35; m 78, Donna Komar; c William & Kathleen. *Educ:* Univ SC, BS, 54; Harvard Univ, AM, 56, PhD(chem), 58. *Prof Exp:* Fel, Nat Res Coun-Nat Bur Stand, 57-59; NSF fel, Univ Calif, 59-60; asst prof chem, Stanford Univ, 60-66; assoc prof chem, Princeton Univ, 66-71, prof, 71-80. *Concurrent Pos:* Alfred P Sloan fel, 63-67; John S Guggenheim fel, 70. *Mem:* Sigma Xi; AAAS; Am Chem Soc; Am Phys Soc. *Res:* Molecular spectroscopy and structure. *Mailing Add:* 109 Kingsway Commons Princeton NJ 08540

LAURIENTE, MIKE, METALLURGY, SPACE ATMOSPHERES. *Current Pos:* RETIRED. *Personal Data:* b Trail, BC, June 26, 22; US citizen; m 56, Alma VanCott; c Michael. *Educ:* Mich Technol Univ, BS, 43, MS, 47; Johns Hopkins Univ, DrEng, 55. *Prof Exp:* Metallurgist, Int Harvester Co, Ill, 47-49; res staff asst metal physics, Johns Hopkins Univ, 49-55; fel engr, Aerospace Div, Westinghouse Elec Corp, Md, 56-62, adv engr, 62-71; asst secy transp, Off Systs Eng, US Dept Transp, Washington, DC, 71-83; tech mgr, Goddard Space Flight Ctr, Nasa, Greenbelt, Md, 83-97. *Concurrent Pos:* Consult, Ballistics Res Lab, Ord Dept, US Army, Aberdeen Proving Ground, 51-55. *Mem:* Am Phys Soc; fel Am Soc Metals; Sigma Xi. *Res:* Magnetic thin films; active and passive electronic devices; radiation damage; electrical insulation; magnetic anisotropic metals; technological advances having application to transportation safety and security; fracture mechanics; nondestructive testing; space environment. *Mailing Add:* 6608 White Gate Rd Clarksville Ridge Clarksville MD 21029. *Fax:* 301-286-1742; *E-Mail:* laurient@envnet.gsfc.nasa.gov

LAURIN, PUSHPAMALA, ELECTROMAGNETISM, TELECOMMUNICATIONS. *Current Pos:* SR PROJ MGR, SATELLITE COMMUN, MOTOROLLA INC, 89- *Personal Data:* b Bangalore City, India; US citizen; m 64; c Nicole & Erik. *Educ:* Gujarat Univ, India, BSc, 56; Karnatak Univ, India, MSc, 58; Univ Mich, Ann Arbor, MSE, 62, PhD(physics), 67. *Prof Exp:* Jr sci asst, Nat Sugar Inst, Kanpur, India, 58-59; sales engr, Toshniwal Bros, Bombay, 59-60; res asst meteorol, Univ Mich, Ann Arbor, 61-62, asst res physicist, Radiation Lab, 62-67; asst prof math, Eastern Mich Univ, 67-68; res scientist physics, McDonnell-Douglas Corp, Mo, 68-69; lectr elec eng & physics, Southern Ill Univ, 70-71; instr electronics & physics, Harper Col, 71-76; dir info resources, Gould Inc, Rolling Meadows, Ill, 76-86; at AT&T Bell Labs, Maperville, Ill, 86-89. *Concurrent Pos:* Vpres, Greame Publ Co, Wilborheim, Mass, 84-86 & AT&T Bell Labs, 86-89; sr resource mgr, Cellular Intrastruct Group, Motorola Inc, 89- *Mem:* Inst Elec & Electronics Engrs. *Res:* Electromagnetic interactions. *Mailing Add:* 1614 W Oakland Chandler AZ 85224

LAURITZEN, PETER O, ELECTRICAL ENGINEERING & POWER ELECTRONICS, SEMICONDUCTOR DEVICE MODELING. *Current Pos:* from asst prof to assoc prof, 65-73, PROF ELEC ENG, UNIV WASH, 73- *Personal Data:* b Valparaiso, Ind, Feb 14, 35; m 63, Helen Janzen; c Beth & Margo. *Educ:* Calif Inst Technol, BS, 56; Stanford Univ, MS, 58, PhD(elec eng), 61. *Prof Exp:* Mem tech staff, Fairchild Semiconductor Div, 61-65. *Concurrent Pos:* Adj prof social mgt technol, Univ Wash, 77-82; eng mgr, Avtech Corp, 79-80; co-dir, NSF-CDADIC Indust-Univ Coop Res Ctr, 95- *Mem:* Inst Elec & Electronics Engrs; Am Soc Eng Educ; AAAS. *Res:* Semiconductor device modeling; power electronics. *Mailing Add:* Dept Elec Eng Box 352500 Univ Wash Seattle WA 98195. *E-Mail:* plauritz@ee.washington.edu

LAURMANN, JOHN ALFRED, global climate change; deceased, see previous edition for last biography

LAURS, ROBERT MICHAEL, OCEANOGRAPHY, FISHERIES. *Current Pos:* Oceanogr, Southwest Fisheries Ctr, La Jolla Lab, Calif, 67-94, LAB DIR, HONOLULU LAB, NAT MARINE FISHERIES SERV, 94- *Personal Data:* b Oregon City, Ore, Jan 27, 39; m 82, Betty A Durence; c Brendan M & Meghan M. *Educ:* Ore State Univ, BS, 61, MS, 63, PhD(oceanog), 67. *Honors & Awards:* Silver Medal, Dept Com, 80. *Concurrent Pos:* Sci adv, Am Fisherman's Res Found, 71-; sci subgroup, Intergov Oceanog Comn, Intergrated Global Ocean Sta Syst, 81- *Mem:* AAAS; Marine Biol Asn UK; Am Soc Limnol & Oceanog; Am Inst Fishery Res Biologists; Eastern Pac Oceanic Conf; Am Fisheries Soc. *Res:* Fishery forecasting; environmental conditions affecting the distribution and abundance of tunas; albacore tuna ecology; vertical distribution and migration of micronektonic organisms; satellite oceanography. *Mailing Add:* Honolulu Lab Nat Marine Fisheries Serv 2570 Dole St Honolulu HI 96822-2396. *E-Mail:* Omnet: m.lars

LAURSEN, E(MMETT) M(ORTON), HYDRAULIC ENGINEERING. *Current Pos:* head dept, 62-68, PROF CIVIL ENG, UNIV ARIZ, 62- *Personal Data:* b Fairmount, NDak, Jan 24, 19; m 51; c 3. *Educ:* Univ Minn, BCE, 41; Univ Iowa, PhD(mech, hydraul), 58. *Honors & Awards:* Hilgard Prize, Am Soc Civil Engrs, 59, Res Prize, 61. *Prof Exp:* Asst, St Anthony Falls Hydraul Lab, Minn, 41-42, asst scientist, 45; jr engr, Al Johnson Construct Co, 42-43; asst, Inst Hydraul Res, Univ Iowa, 45-47, res assoc, 47-48, res engr, 48-58; assoc prof civil eng, Mich State Univ, 58-62. *Concurrent Pos:* Consult, 85- *Mem:* Am Soc Civil Engrs; Am Geophys Union; Int Asn Hydraul Res. *Res:* Sediment transportation; fluid mechanics and its applications. *Mailing Add:* 926 W Comobabi Dr Tucson AZ 85704

LAURSEN, GARY A, MYCOLOGY, ARCTIC ECOLOGY. *Current Pos:* ADJ ASSOC PROF MYCOL, UNIV ALASKA, FAIRBANKS, 83- *Personal Data:* b Seattle, Wash, Aug 13, 42; m 63; c 2. *Educ:* Western Wash Univ, BA, 65; Univ Mont, MST, 70; Va Polytech Inst & State Univ, PhD(bot/mycol),

75. *Honors & Awards:* Sigma Xi Res Award, Va Polytech Inst & State Univ, 77. *Prof Exp:* Biol instr, Toppenish, Wash, Sch Dist, 65-71; res asst mycol, Va Polytech Inst & State Univ, 71-75, res assoc, 75-76; asst dir sci, Naval Arctic Res Lab, 76-80, prin investr, Animal Res Facil, Univ Alaska, 76-; proj officer cold prog, Off Naval Res, Arlington, 80-82. *Concurrent Pos:* Actg tech dir admin & sci, Naval Arctic Res Lab, Univ Alaska, 76-77 & Remote Sensing Prog, 77-78; prof officer cold prog, Off Naval Res, Arlington, 80-82. *Mem:* Mycol Soc Am; Sigma Xi. *Res:* Systematic and ecological treatments of Arctic, Alpine and Meratime tundra fleshy fungi, their role and significance within these environmentally harsh ecosystems. *Mailing Add:* Dept Biol Sci Univ Alaska Fairbanks PO Box 756100 Fairbanks AK 99775

LAURSEN, PAUL HERBERT, GENERAL CHEMISTRY. *Current Pos:* From asst prof to assoc prof chem, 59-64, acad dean, 76-78, PROF CHEM, NEBR WESLEYAN UNIV, 64-, PROVOST, 78- *Personal Data:* b Ord, Nebr, Mar 28, 29; m 59; c 2. *Educ:* Dana Col, BA, 54; Ore State Univ, PhD(org chem), 61. *Honors & Awards:* NSF sci fac fel, Univ Calif, Los Angeles, 67-68. *Mem:* AAAS; Am Chem Soc. *Res:* Synthesis of nitrogen heterocycles; identification of natural products. *Mailing Add:* 3148 N 75th St Ct Lincoln NE 68507-2499

LAURSEN, RICHARD ALLAN, BIO-ORGANIC CHEMISTRY, PROTEIN CHEMISTRY. *Current Pos:* from asst prof to assoc prof, 66-76, PROF CHEM, BOSTON UNIV, 76- *Personal Data:* b Normal, Ill, May 1, 38; m 71, Irene Shulman; c Michael & Sarah. *Educ:* Univ Calif, Berkeley, BS, 61; Univ Ill, PhD(chem), 64. *Honors & Awards:* Pehr Edman Award, 88. *Prof Exp:* NIH fel, Harvard Univ, 64-66. *Concurrent Pos:* NIH res career develop award, 69-74; guest scientist, Max Planck Inst Molecular Genetics, 71; Alfred P Sloan fel, 72-74; mem sci adv comt on clin invest, Am Cancer Soc, 75-79, NSF Biol Instrumentation Prog, 84-88; specialist protein chem, int adv panel, Chinese Prov Univ Develop, World Bank, Changsha, People's Repub China, 90. *Mem:* Fel AAAS; Am Chem Soc; Am Soc Biochem & Molecular Biol; Protein Soc; Peptide Soc. *Res:* Development of new methods for protein sequence analysis and peptide synthesis; structure, function and evolution of proteins; studies on antifreeze proteins. *Mailing Add:* Dept Chem Boston Univ 590 Commonwealth Ave Boston MA 02215. *Fax:* 617-353-6466; *E-Mail:* laursen@bu.edu

LAURSEN, TOD ALAN, COMPUTATIONAL & CONTACT MECHANICS. *Current Pos:* ASST PROF CIVIL ENG, DUKE UNIV, 92- *Personal Data:* b Corvallis, Ore, Mar 3, 64; m 85, Jennifer Savage; c Orin & Colin. *Educ:* Ore State Univ, BS, 86; Stanford Univ, MS, 89, PhD(mech eng), 92. *Honors & Awards:* Career Award, NSF, 97. *Prof Exp:* Engr, Lawrence Livermore Nat Lab, 86-92. *Concurrent Pos:* Consult, Lawrence Livermore Nat Lab, 92-; young investr award, Off Naval Res, 97. *Mem:* Am Soc Mech Engrs; Am Soc Civil Engrs; Am Acad Mech; Sigma Xi; US Asn Comput Mech. *Res:* Continuum and computational mechanics; formulations and numerical descriptions for systems featuring contact and impact phenomena. *Mailing Add:* Dept Civil & Environ Eng Duke Univ Box 90287 Durham NC 27708-0287

LAUSCH, ROBERT NAGLE, IMMUNOBIOLOGY. *Current Pos:* assoc prof, 77-85, PROF MICROBIOL & IMMUNOL, COL MED, UNIV SALA, 85- *Personal Data:* b Chambersburg, Pa, Feb 22, 38; m 68, Marilyn; c 2. *Educ:* Muhlenberg Col, BS, 60; Pa State Univ, MS, 62; Univ Fla, PhD(microbiol), 66. *Prof Exp:* Fel virol, Baylor Col Med, 66-69; asst prof, Col Med, Pa State Univ, 69-75, assoc prof microbiol, 75-77. *Mem:* Am Soc Microbiol; Am Asn Cancer Res; Am Asn Immunologists; Fedn Am Socs Exp Biol; Asn Res Vision Ophthal. *Res:* Virus immunology; Study of mechanisms operative in ocular inflammation. *Mailing Add:* Dept Microbiol & Immunol Col Med Univ SAla Mobile AL 36688-0001. *Fax:* 334-460-7931

LAUSH, GEORGE, MATHEMATICS. *Current Pos:* from asst prof to assoc prof, 49-62, PROF MATH, UNIV PITTSBURGH, 62- *Personal Data:* b Barrackville, WVa, Sept 17, 21; m 56. *Educ:* Univ Pittsburgh, BS, 43; Cornell Univ, PhD, 49. *Prof Exp:* Asst chem, Univ Pittsburgh, 43-44; res assoc, Manhattan Dist, Univ Rochester, 44-46; asst math, Cornell Univ, 46-49. *Mem:* Am Math Soc; Math Asn Am. *Res:* Infinite series; real functions; functional analysis. *Mailing Add:* 181 Pearce Mill Rd Wexford PA 15090-8508

LAUSHEY, LOUIS M(CNEAL), CIVIL ENGINEERING. *Current Pos:* William Thoms prof civil eng & head dept, 58-78, Geier prof eng educ & interim dean, Col Eng, 83-86, EMER PROF & DEAN, UNIV CINCINNATI, 87- *Personal Data:* b Columbia, Pa, May 13, 17; m 49. *Educ:* Pa State Univ, BS, 42; Carnegie Inst Technol, MS, 47, DSc, 51. *Prof Exp:* Struct draftsman, Am Bridge Co, NJ, 42; instr civil eng, Carnegie Inst Technol, 42-44, 46-48, from asst prof to assoc prof, 48-54; prof & head dept, Norwich Univ, 54-58. *Concurrent Pos:* Former partner, D'Appolonia, Laushey & Peck, Consult Engrs; consult to govt & industs. *Mem:* Am Soc Civil Engrs; Soc Am Mil Engrs; Am Soc Eng Educ; Am Geophys Union; Int Asn Hydraul Res. *Res:* Fluid mechanics; structural design and analysis. *Mailing Add:* Dept Civil & Environ Eng Univ Cincinnati Cincinnati OH 45221

LAUSHMAN, ROGER H, POPULATION GENETICS, CONSERVATION BIOLOGY. *Current Pos:* VIS ASST PROF EVOLUTION & ECOL, OBERLIN COL, 89- *Personal Data:* b Ida Grove, Iowa, May 3, 50; m 83; c 2. *Educ:* Univ Kans, BS, 79; Iowa State Univ, MS, 83; Univ Ga, PhD(bot), 88. *Prof Exp:* Postdoctoral fel, Friday Harbor Labs, Univ Wash, 88-89. *Mem:* Bot Soc Am; Ecol Soc Am; Soc Conserv Biol; Soc Study Evol; Am Soc Naturalists. *Res:* Population genetics of aquatic vascular plants, particularly those with water-pollination; conservation biology, particularly of threatened plant species and aquatic habitats. *Mailing Add:* Biol Dept Oberlin Col 135 W Lorain St Oberlin OH 44074-1076

LAUSON, HENRY DUMKE, PHYSIOLOGY. *Current Pos:* chmn dept, 55-78, prof physiol, 55-78, EMER PROF PHYSIOL & BIOPHYS, ALBERT EINSTEIN COL MED, 78- *Personal Data:* b New Holstein, Wis, Aug 20, 12; m 77, Ruth Eckart. *Educ:* Univ Wis, BS, 36, PhD(physiol), 39, MD, 40. *Prof Exp:* Asst med, Univ Wis, 36-39; intern, Univ Kans Hosps, 40-41; asst resident med, Henry Ford Hosp, 41-42; Off Sci Res & Develop fel physiol & med, Col Med, NY Univ, 42-43; instr physiol, 43-46; assoc & assoc physician, Rockefeller Inst, 46-50; assoc prof physiol in pediat, Med Col, Cornell Univ, 50-55. *Concurrent Pos:* Assoc prof physiol, Med Col, Cornell Univ, 51-55; consult prog-proj comt, Nat Inst Arthritis & Metab Dis, 61-65. *Mem:* Am Physiol Soc; Am Soc Exp Biol & Med; Am Soc Clin Invest; Harvey Soc (secy, 52-55); Am Fed Clin Res; Am Soc Nephrology. *Res:* Pituitary-ovary interrelations; blood pressure in human right heart; renal physiology; nephrotic syndrome; metabolism of antidiuretic hormone. *Mailing Add:* 215 Willow Bend Kiel WI 83042-1354

LAUTENBERGER, WILLIAM J, APPLIED STATISTICS, PHYSICAL CHEMISTRY. *Current Pos:* Res chemist, Dye Div, Org Chem & Res & Develop Dept, Jackson Labs, NJ, 67-71, res chemist, Org Chem Dept, Exp Sta, Wilmington, 71-74, statist prog consult, 74-78, develop specialist, indust hyg, Du Pont Fabrics & Finishes Dept, Appl Technol Div, 78-81, RES SUPVR, ELECTRONICS DEPT, E I DU PONT DE NEMOURS & CO, WILMINGTON, 81- *Personal Data:* b Flushing, NY, Mar 11, 43; m 67; c 2. *Educ:* Muhlenberg Col, BS, 64; Univ Pa, PhD(phys chem), 67. *Mem:* Am Chem Soc; Sigma Xi. *Res:* Reaction mechanisms; photochemistry; heterogenous catalysis; mechanisms of dyeing; emulsion science; solid-solid adsorption; consulting in design and analysis of experiments; air sampling; gas diffusion mechanisms; gas adsorption, desorption phenomena, electronic materials, semiconductors and packaging materials PWB laminates, photo polymers. *Mailing Add:* 506 Ott Rd Bala Cynwyd PA 19004-2510

LAUTENS, MARK, ASYMMETRIC SYNTHESIS, ORGANOMETALLIC CATALYSIS. *Current Pos:* from asst prof to assoc prof chem, 87-95, PROF CHEM, UNIV TORONTO, 95- *Personal Data:* b Hamilton, Ont, July 9, 59. *Educ:* Univ Guelph, BSc, 81; Univ Wis-Madison, PhD(chem), 85. *Honors & Awards:* Merck Frosst Awardee, Can Soc Chem, 94; Rutherford Prize, Royal Soc Can, 94. *Prof Exp:* Res assoc, Harvard Univ, 85-87. *Concurrent Pos:* Biomega young investr, 89-93; Alfred P Sloan Found fel, 91; Eli Lilly Awardee, 92-; Steacie res fel, Natural Sci & Eng Res Coun, 94-96. *Mem:* Am Chem Soc; Can Soc Chem. *Res:* Synthesis of biologically active or structurally novel compounds; metal catalyzed reactions for control of stereochemistry; asymmetric synthesis. *Mailing Add:* Dept Chem Univ Toronto Toronto ON M5S 1A1 Can. *Fax:* 416-978-6083; *E-Mail:* mlautens@alchemy.chem.utoronto.ca

LAUTENSCHLAEGER, FRIEDRICH KARL, ORGANIC CHEMISTRY. *Current Pos:* res chemist, NAm Res Ctr, 61-72, group leader, Dunlop Res Ctr, 72-85; SR SCIENTIST, TREMCO RES CTR, DUNLOP CO, LTD, TORONTO, 85- *Personal Data:* b Gefell, Ger, June 27, 34; m 60, Susanne & Martina; c 2. *Educ:* Univ Heidelberg, BA, 56; Univ Toronto, MA, 60. *Prof Exp:* Res asst org chem, Univ Toronto, 57-59. *Mem:* Am Chem Soc. *Res:* Stereochemistry of organic compounds; synthesis of small ring compounds; organic sulfur chemistry; reactive intermediates; vulcanization chemistry and physics; radiation vulcanization/cure for pressure-sensitive products. *Mailing Add:* 2562 Cushing Rd Mississauga ON L5K 1X1 Can

LAUTENSCHLAGER, EUGENE PAUL, BIOMATERIALS. *Current Pos:* from asst prof to assoc prof, 66-74, PROF BIOL MAT, NORTHWESTERN UNIV, 74-, DIV DIR, 88- *Personal Data:* b Chicago, Ill, Apr 5, 37; m 61; c 1. *Educ:* Ill Inst Technol, BS, 58; Northwestern Univ, MS, 60, PhD(mat sci), 66. *Honors & Awards:* F4 Award of Merit, Am Soc Testing & Mat. *Prof Exp:* Res metallurgist, Allis-Chalmers Mfg Co, 60-62. *Concurrent Pos:* NIH career develop award, 71-75; consult, Bioeng Comt, Am Acad Orthop Surgeons, 73-85; vis prof, Free Univ Berlin, 84. *Mem:* Am Soc Testing & Mat; Am Inst Mining, Metall & Petrol Eng; Int Asn Dent Res; Am Soc Metals; Acad Dent Mat. *Res:* Biological and dental materials; medical implant materials; kinetics of cementing media for implant stabilization; computer assisted instruction. *Mailing Add:* 5056 W Morse Skokie IL 60077-3510

LAUTERBACH, GEORGE ERVIN, PHYSICAL CHEMISTRY. *Current Pos:* MGR NEW PRODS RES & DEVELOP, MARINE COLLOIDS INC, 78- *Personal Data:* b Bushnell, Ill, June 13, 27; m 49; c 5. *Educ:* Monmouth Col, BS, 49; Bradley Univ, MS, 53; Purdue Univ, PhD(biochem), 58. *Prof Exp:* Chemist, Starch & Dextrose Div, Northern Regional Res Lab, 49-53; res org chemist, Paper Lab, Kimberly Clark Corp, 57-65 & Pioneering & Advan Develop Lab, 65-78; assoc prof chem & res assoc, Div Natural Mat & Systs, Inst Paper Chem, 65-78. *Mem:* Am Chem Soc; Tech Asn Pulp & Paper Indust; Am Asn Cereal Chemists. *Res:* Polysaccharide chemistry; enzymic and chemical modification of starch; high temperature starch cooking; hemicelluloses; starch in paper coatings; top sizes and internal sizing of paper products. *Mailing Add:* PO Box 213 Thomaston ME 04861-0213

LAUTERBACH, HANS, PHARMACEUTICAL SCIENCE. *Current Pos:* PRES, DIAG DIV, MILES INC, 92- *Personal Data:* b 1934. *Prof Exp:* Staff, Bayer AG, Leverkusen, Ger, 51-91. *Mailing Add:* Bayer Corp 100 Bayer Rd Pittsburgh PA 15205-9741

LAUTERBACH, JOHN HARVEY, CARBOHYDRATE CHEMISTRY, TOBACCO CHEMISTRY. *Current Pos:* analytical res div head, Brown & Williamson Tobacco Corp, 80-87, mgr mat res, 87-89, Mgr Res Serv, 89-93, DIR RES SERV, BROWN & WILLIAMSON TOBACCO CORP, 92-. *Personal Data:* b Jersey City, NJ, Apr 2, 44; div. *Educ:* Worcester Polytech Inst, BS, 66; Ohio State Univ, MSc, 68, PhD(chem), 70. *Prof Exp:* Asst analytical chem, Ohio State Univ, 66-67; chief asst, 67-68 & org chem, 68-69, res assoc, 70-; chemist analytical chem, Union Carbide Chem & Plastics Co, 70-71; proj supvr, Cent Tech Eval, Nat Starch & Chem Corp, 71-73, mgr, 74-78; mgr chem, Pillsbury Co, 78-79; dir chem, Prof Serv Indust, Inc, 79-80. *Concurrent Pos:* Chmn, Environ Comn, Borough Raritan, NJ, 76-78; chmn & bd dirs, Tobacco Inst Testing Lab, Bethesda, Md. *Mem:* Am Chem Soc; fel Am Inst Chemists; fel Royal Soc Chem; Sigma Xi; Am Soc Testing & Mat; Am Mgt Asn; Inst Food Technol. *Res:* Polysaccharide chemistry, particularly structure determinations and modifications; high performance liquid chromatography and nuclear magnetic resonance spectroscopy; new techniques for managing service departments in research and development organizations; tobacco chemistry; gas chromatography, liquid chromatography and mass spectrometry. *Mailing Add:* Brown & Williamson Tobacco 2600 Weaver Rd Macon GA 31298. *Fax:* 502-568-8210

LAUTERBACH, RICHARD THOMAS, POLYMER CHEMISTRY, ORGANIC CHEMISTRY. *Current Pos:* GROUP LEADER, OIL FIELD SERV, RICHARDSON CO, 81-. *Personal Data:* b Rochester, Pa, Dec 29, 46; m 69; c 1. *Educ:* Johns Hopkins Univ, BS, 68; Northwestern Univ, PhD(chem), 75. *Prof Exp:* Group leader water soluble polymers, Daubert Chem Co, 75-80, group leader protective coatings, 80-81. *Mem:* Am Chem Soc; Soc Cosmetic Chem. *Res:* Water soluble polymers for wastewater treatment and paper production additives; corrosion preventive coatings. *Mailing Add:* 632 S Tenth Ave La Grange IL 60525-3036

LAUTERBUR, PAUL CHRISTIAN, PHYSICAL CHEMISTRY, MEDICAL IMAGING. *Current Pos:* prof, 85-90, DISTINGUISHED UNIV PROF, COL MED, UNIV ILL, CHICAGO, 90-; HEAD, DEPT MED INFO SCI & DEPT CHEM, URBANA- CHAMPAIGN, 85-, DIR, BIOMED MAGNETIC RESONANCE LAB, 85-. *Personal Data:* b Sidney, Ohio, May 6, 29; m 58, 84; c 3. *Educ:* Case Inst Technol, BS, 51; Univ Pittsburgh, PhD(chem), 62. *Hon Degrees:* Dr, Univ Liege, Belg, 84, Nicolaus Copernicus Med Acad, Poland, 88; DSc, Carnegie Mellon Univ, 87, Wesleyan Univ, 89, State Univ NY, 90. *Honors & Awards:* Gold Medal, Soc Magnetic Resonance Med, 82; Biol Physics Prize, Am Phys Soc, 83; Jesse Beams Lectr, Univ Va, 83; Smith Kline & Fr Lectr, Univ Col London, 83; Howard N Potts Medal, Franklin Inst, 84; Albert Lasker Clin Res Award, 84; H H Iddles Lectr Chem, Univ NH, 84; Kosar Mem Award, Soc Photog Scientists & Engrs, 85; Charles F Kettering Prize, Gen Motors Cancer Res Found, 85; Gairdner Found Int Award, 85; Distinguished Res Biomed Sci Award, Asn Am Med Col, 86; Roentgen Medal, 87; Medal Honor, Inst Elec & Electronics Engrs, 87; Nat Medal Sci, 87; Nat Medal Technol, 88; Gold Medal Award, Soc Comput Body Tomog, 89; Laufman-Greatbatch Award, Asn Advan Med Instrumentation, 89; Int Soc Magnetic Resonance Award, 92; Kyoto Prize, Inamori Found (Japan), 94. *Prof Exp:* Res asst, Mellon Inst, 51-52, res assoc, 52-53, jr fel, 53, fel, 55-63; from assoc prof to prof chem, State Univ NY, Stony Brook, 63-83, res prof radiol, 78-85, leading prof chem, 83-84, univ prof, 84-85. *Concurrent Pos:* Mem, Sci Coun Galileo Galilei Found, Coun Int Soc Magnetic Resonance; chmn, subcomt E-13.7 Nuclear Magnetic Resonance, Soc Testing & Mat, 60-62; Alfred P Sloan fel, 65-67; vis scholar, Dept Chem, Stanford Univ, 69-70; ed-in-chief, Magnetic Resonance Med, 82-83; adj prof, State Univ NY, Stony Brook, 85-; prof, Ctr Advan Study, Univ Ill, Urbana-Champaign, 87-, prof bioeng, Dept Elect & Comput Eng & prof biophys, Dept Physiol & Biophys, 88-. *Mem:* Nat Acad Sci; fel Am Phys Soc; Am Chem Soc; fel AAAS; Soc Magnetic Resonance Med (pres, 81-83); Sigma Xi; Radiol Soc NAm; assoc mem Inst Elec & Electronics Engrs; Biophys Soc; Soc Neurosci. *Res:* Nuclear magnetic resonance studies of structure and properties of molecules, crystals and biological systems; imaging by magnetic resonance zeugmatography, including biological and medical applications; published numerous articles in various scientific journals. *Mailing Add:* Univ Ill 1307 W Park St Urbana IL 61801-2332. *Fax:* 217-244-1330

LAUTT, WILFRED WAYNE, LIVER FUNCTIONS, HEPATIC CIRCULATION. *Current Pos:* prof pharmacol & therapeut & sect head, 84-89, dept head, Hepatorenal Res Unit, 89-94, PROF PHARMACOL & THERAPEUT, UNIV MAN, 89-. *Personal Data:* b Lethbridge, Alta, Can, June 29, 46; m 68, Melanie L Nicholls; c Kelly F & Mick M. *Educ:* Univ Alta, BSc, 68; Univ Man, MSc, 70, PhD(pharmacol), 72. *Honors & Awards:* First J A F Stevenson Award Contrib Physiol, Can Physiol Soc, 80; Ciba Geigy Award Contrib Pharmacol, Pharmacol Soc Can, 95. *Prof Exp:* Med Res Coun Can fel toxicol, Univ Montreal, 72-74; asst prof & res scholar, Can Liver Found, Univ Sask, 74-78, from assoc prof to prof physiol, 78-82. *Concurrent Pos:* J A F Stevenson vis prof, Can Physiol Soc, 80; mem coun, Can Physiol Soc, 82-85; mem, Med Adv Bd, Can Liver Found, 82-87; sci officer, Grants Comt, Can Heart Found, 82-88; coun mem, Western Pharmacol Soc, 92-94, pres, 94. *Mem:* Can Physiol Soc; Am Physiol Soc; Can Pharmacol Soc; Am Asn Study Liver Dis; Can Asn Study Liver Dis (vpres, 85, pres, 87-88); Am Soc Pharmacol & Exp Therapeut; Can Soc Clin Investr. *Res:* Peripheral vascular physiology and hepatic physiology, pharmacology and toxicology; vascular and metabolic consequences of autonomic nerve activity in the liver; local control of intestinal and hepatic blood flow. *Mailing Add:* Dept Pharmacol & Therapeut Univ Man Fac Med 770 Bannatyne Ave Winnipeg MB R3E 0W3 Can. *Fax:* 204-783-6915; *E-Mail:* wlautt@cc.umaitoba.ca

LAUTZENHEISER, CLARENCE ERIC, METALLURGY. *Current Pos:* sr res engr, Southwest Res Inst, 62-67, mgr metall eng, 67-69, from asst dir to dir spec eng serv, 69-74, vpres, Qual Assurance Systs & Eng Div, 74-85, VPRES EMER, NDE SCI & TECHNOL DIV, SOUTHWEST RES INST, 85-; PRES, INT ENGRS, 86-. *Personal Data:* b Lincoln, Nebr, May 21, 21; m 48; c 3. *Educ:* Mass Inst Technol, BS, 52. *Prof Exp:* Res engr, Dow Chem Co, 52-53, maintenance engr, 52-60, maintenance specialist, 60-62. *Concurrent Pos:* Consult, Reliability & Qual Assurance Div, NASA, 65-67. *Mem:* Am Soc Metals; fel Am Soc Nondestructive Testing (pres, 75-76); Am Welding Soc; fel Am Soc Mech Engrs; Nat Asn Corrosion Engrs; Sigma Xi. *Res:* New methods of magnesium production; corrosion; failure analysis; welding; nondestructive inspection in petrochemical industry fabrication quality control and in-service inspection of nuclear reactor power systems. *Mailing Add:* Int Engrs PO Box 800 Medina TX 78055

LAUVER, DEAN C, AERONAUTICAL & ASTRONAUTICAL ENGINEERING. *Current Pos:* SR PROJ ENGR, AEROSTRUCTURES, INC, 84-. *Personal Data:* b Warren, Pa, June 8, 20; m 46; c 3. *Educ:* Pa State Univ, BS, 42. *Prof Exp:* Jr engr, Mesta Mach Co, Pa, 42; stress analyst, Air Frame Design Div, Bur Aeronaut, Dept Navy, 46-49, head, Struct Design & Analytical Unit, 49-57, tech asst & asst head, Contract Struct Design Sect, 57-59, air craft & missile specialist, Chief of Naval Opers, 59-61; chief, Struct & Mat Br, Fed Aviation Agency, 61-62; tech dir, Air Progs, Off Naval Res, 62-67, dep asst chief technol, 67-80. *Concurrent Pos:* Mem Fed Aviation Agency-Air Force-NASA working groups supersonic transport res progs & Fed Aviation Agency rep on NASA screening comt on mat, 62; Off Naval Res mem Dept Defense res & eng panel supporting res & technol, Aeronaut & Astronaut Coord Bd, 66-; Navy liaison officer, Adv Group Aerospace Res & Develop, NATO, 76-80. *Mem:* Am Inst Aeronaut & Astronaut. *Res:* Naval vehicle and weapon research and technology, including sensors, electronics, acoustics and operational analysis. *Mailing Add:* 6538 Cedarwood Ct Falls Church VA 22041

LAUVER, MILTON RENICK, PLASMA PHYSICS. *Current Pos:* RETIRED. *Personal Data:* b Springfield, Ohio, Sept 14, 20; m 48; c 4. *Educ:* Wittenberg Col, AB, 42; Western Res Univ, MS, 44, PhD(phys chem), 48. *Prof Exp:* Res chemist, Westvaco Div, Food Mach & Chem Corp, 48-53; res chemist chromium chem div, Diamond Alkali Co, 53-58; res chemist, Lewis Res Ctr, NASA, 58-82. *Mem:* Am Chem Soc. *Res:* Gas dynamics; nuclear fusion plasmas; electrochemistry and phosphoric acid fuel cell technology. *Mailing Add:* 28385 Holly Dr North Olmsted OH 44070-5133

LAUVER, RICHARD WILLIAM, PHYSICAL CHEMISTRY. *Current Pos:* Nat Res Coun res assoc, 72-74, RES CHEMIST, LEWIS RES CTR, NASA, 74-. *Personal Data:* b Monmouth, Ill, Mar 15, 43; m 72. *Educ:* Knox Col, AB, 65; Univ Ill, Urbana, PhD(chem), 70. *Mem:* Am Chem Soc; Soc Adv Mat & Process Eng; Soc Plastic Eng; Coblentz Soc. *Res:* Physical and chemical characterization of polymer materials. *Mailing Add:* 20090 Carolyn Ave Rocky River OH 44116-2497

LAUX, DAVID CHARLES, IMMUNOLOGY, BACTERIOLOGY. *Current Pos:* from asst prof to assoc prof, 73-78, PROF IMMUNOL, UNIV RI, 83-, CHMN, DEPT MICROBIOL, 88-. *Personal Data:* b Sarver, Pa, Jan 1 45; m 70; c 1. *Educ:* Washington & Jefferson Col, BA, 66; Miami Univ, Ohio, MS, 68; Univ Ariz, PhD(microbiol), 71. *Prof Exp:* Fel immunol, Dept Microbiol, Sch Med, Pa State Univ, 71-73. *Concurrent Pos:* Res grant, Nat Cancer Inst, 74, 78 & Nat Inst Allergy & Infectious Dis, 80, 83, 86; vis scientist, Oxford Univ, 88 & 95. *Mem:* Am Soc Microbiol; Am Asn Immunol; Am Asn Advan Sci. *Res:* Molecular basis of large intestine colonization; bacterial/mucosal surface interactions. *Mailing Add:* Dept Biochem Microbiol & Molecular Genetics 117 Morrill Hall Univ RI Kingston RI 02881. *Fax:* 401-792-7148

LAUZON, RODRIGUE VINCENT, COLLOID SCIENCE, PAPER CHEMISTRY. *Current Pos:* group leader, 83-90, RES SCIENTIST, HERCULES INC, 83-. *Personal Data:* b Ottawa, Ont, Oct 24, 37; US citizen; m 89, Andrea L Cole; c Alicia, Rod Jr, David & Christian. *Educ:* Univ Toronto, BA, 60; Univ Conn, MS, 62; Clarkson Col Technol, PhD(colloid chem), 71. *Honors & Awards:* Meritorious Award for Eng Innovation; Petrol Engr Int, Offshore Technol Conf, 82. *Prof Exp:* Res specialist latex, Dow Chem Co, 70-74; res assoc colloid chem, Celanese Res Co, 74-75; dir latex res & develop, Dart Industs, 75-78; sr res scientist colloid, NL Baroid, NL Industs, Inc, 78-82. *Concurrent Pos:* Chmn colloid & surface chem group, Southeastern Sect, Am Chem Soc, 79-83, mem, Colloid Div; vis scientist, Indust Res Inst, 82; colloid consult, 82-83. *Mem:* Am Chem Soc; Trade Asn Pulp & Paper Indust; Asn Consult Chemists & Chem Engrs; Nat Homeopathic Soc. *Res:* Inorganic colloids; clays, oxides, halides; polymer colloids: latexes, water-soluble polymers, natural polymers; rheology of disperse systems; drilling muds; foams and emulsions; coagulation; adsorption from solution; electrokinetics; paper and paper chemicals. *Mailing Add:* 63 Quail Hollow Dr Hockessin DE 19707. *Fax:* 302-995-3694

LAVAIL, JENNIFER HART, NEUROANATOMY, NEUROEMBRYOLOGY. *Current Pos:* assoc prof, 76-86, PROF ANAT, UNIV CALIF, SAN FRANCISCO, 83-. *Personal Data:* b Evansville, Ind, Apr 2, 43; c Matthew H & Katherine H. *Educ:* Trinity Col, DC, BA, 65; Univ Wis, PhD(anat), 70. *Honors & Awards:* Charles Judson Herrick Award, Am Asn Anatomists, 75. *Prof Exp:* Woodrow Wilson fel, 65; from instr to asst prof neuropath, Harvard Med Sch, 73-76. *Concurrent Pos:* Vis fel anat, Sch Med, Washington Univ, 68-69, res fel, 69-70; Nat Inst Neurol Dis & Stroke res fel neuropath, Harvard Med Sch, 70-73, spec fel, 73-76; Alfred P Sloan fel, 76-79; mem neurol study sect, NIH, 82-86; bd sci counr, Nat Inst Neurol & Commun Dis & Stroke, 86-. *Mem:* Am Asn Anatomists; Soc Neurosci; Asn Res Vision Ophthl; Soc Cell Biol. *Res:* Development of the central nervous system; anterograde and retrograde axonal transport. *Mailing Add:* Dept Anat Univ Calif San Francisco CA 94143-0452. *E-Mail:* jhci@itsa.ucsf.edu

LAVAIL, MATTHEW MAURICE, NEUROSCIENCES, CELL BIOLOGY. *Current Pos:* actg chmn, 81-82, ASSOC PROF ANAT, MED SCH, UNIV CALIF, SAN FRANCISCO, 76- *Personal Data:* b Abilene, Tex, Jan 7, 43; m 70. *Educ:* NTex State Univ, BA, 65; Univ Tex Med Br, PhD(anat), 69. *Honors & Awards:* Res Award, Sigma Xi, 70; Fight for Sight Citation, 75; Sundial Award, Retina Found, 76; Friedenwald Award, Asn Res Vision & Ophthal, 81. *Prof Exp:* Res fel, Harvard Med Sch, 69-73, asst prof neuropath, 73-76. *Concurrent Pos:* Nat Eye Inst fel neuropath, Harvard Med Sch, 70-73; res assoc neurosci, Children's Hosp Med Ctr, 73-76; Nat Eye Inst res career develop award, 74-79. *Mem:* Asn Res Vision & Ophthal; Soc Cell Biol; AAAS; Am Asn Anat; Soc Neurosci. *Res:* Photoreceptor-pigment epithelial cell interactions; retinal development; inherited retinal degeneration; neuroembryology; retrograde axonal transport. *Mailing Add:* Beckman Vision Univ Calif Sch Med 10 Kirkham St Box 0730 San Francisco CA 94143-0730. *Fax:* 415-476-0709

LAVAL, WILLIAM NORRIS, GEOLOGY. *Current Pos:* chmn div natural sci, 63-75, PROF GEOL & EARTH SCI, LEWIS-CLARK STATE COL, 63- *Personal Data:* b Seattle, Wash, Jan 27, 22; m 63; c 2. *Educ:* Univ Wash, BS, 43, MS, 48, PhD(geol), 56. *Prof Exp:* Field asst, US Geol Surv, 42, geologist, 43-45 & 48-49; geologist, Corps Eng, US Army, 49-51; resident geologist, Yale Dam, Ebasco Serv, Inc, Wash, 51-53; asst prof geol, Colo State Univ, 56-60; assoc prof geol & geol eng, SDak Sch Mines & Technol, 60-62. *Concurrent Pos:* Consult, 54-56 & 62-63. *Mem:* Fel Geol Soc Am; Sigma Xi. *Res:* Stratigraphy, structure and petrology of Columbia Plateau; environmental geology. *Mailing Add:* Lewis-Clark State Col Lewiston ID 83501

LAVALLE, H CLAUDE, chemical engineering, for more information see previous edition

LAVALLE, PLACIDO DOMINICK, GEOMORPHOLOGY. *Current Pos:* ASSOC PROF GEOG, UNIV WINDSOR, 69- *Personal Data:* b New York, NY, May 13, 37; div; c 3. *Educ:* Columbia Univ, BA, 59; Univ Southern Ill, MA, 61; Univ Iowa, PhD(geog), 65. *Prof Exp:* Res asst geog, Univ Iowa, 62-63; asst prof, Univ Calif, Los Angeles, 64-67 & Univ Ill, Urbana, 67-69. *Concurrent Pos:* Vis prof, Keele Univ, Eng, 76; consult, Parks, Can. *Mem:* AAAS; Asn Am Geogrs; Can Asn Geogr; Nat Speleol Soc. *Res:* Soil geography; quantative analysis of karst geomorphology in Kentucky and Puerto Rico; spatial patterns of soil toxin distribution in Lebec, California; dynamics of shoreline change at Point Pelee, Ontario, Canada. *Mailing Add:* Dept Geog Univ Windsor Windsor ON N9B 3P4 Can

LAVALLEE, ANDRE, WHITE PINE BLISTER RUST. *Current Pos:* RETIRED. *Personal Data:* b Joliette, Que, Can, Aug 31, 36; m 60; c 3. *Educ:* Montreal Univ, BA, 56; Laval Univ, BSc, 60, DSc, 69; McGill Univ, MSc, 63. *Prof Exp:* Biologist forest path, Can Forestry Serv, Que, 60-69, res scientist, 70-75, sect head, Forest Inst Dis Surv, 75-78, prog mgr forest protection, 79-84, scientist forest path, 85-91. *Mem:* Can Phytopath Soc; Can Inst Forestry. *Res:* Characterization of white pine plantation sites with respect to white pine blister rust and weevil susceptibility; elaborate and evaluate integrated forest pest control prescriptions within intensive forest management practices. *Mailing Add:* 2250 Robitaille Quebec City PQ G1P 2M3 Can

LAVALLEE, DAVID KENNETH, INORGANIC CHEMISTRY, BIOCHEMISTRY. *Current Pos:* assoc prof, 78-83, PROF CHEM, HUNTER COL, 84- *Personal Data:* b Malone, NY, Oct 1, 45; m 71; c 3. *Educ:* St Bonaventure Univ, BS, 67; Univ Chicago, SM, 68, PhD(inorg chem), 71. *Honors & Awards:* Catalyst Award, Chem Mfrs Asn, 86. *Prof Exp:* USPHS fel, Dept Anat, Univ Chicago, 71-72; asst prof chem, Colo State Univ, 72-78. *Concurrent Pos:* Vis scientist, Argonne Nat Lab, 71-72; mem grad fac biochem & chem, City Univ New York, 78-; res collabr, Brookhaven Nat Lab, 79-; Fulbright fel, 85-86. *Mem:* Am Chem Soc; AAAS; Sigma Xi; NY Acad Sci; Soc Nuclear Med. *Res:* Synthesis, spectroscopy, reaction mechanisms and structural chemistry of metalloporphyrins; applications of porphyrins to medicine. *Mailing Add:* City Col City Univ NY Convent Ave at 138th St New York NY 10031. *Fax:* 212-650-3655; *E-Mail:* dkl@cunyvm.cuny.edu

LAVALLEE, LORRAINE DORIS, MATHEMATICS. *Current Pos:* From instr to prof, 59-93, assoc head, Dept Math & Statist, 71-72 & 77, EMER PROF MATH, UNIV MASS, AMHERST, 93- *Personal Data:* b Holyoke, Mass, May 31, 31. *Educ:* Mt Holyoke Col, AB, 53; Univ Mass, Amherst, MA, 55; Univ Mich, PhD(math), 62. *Mem:* Am Math Soc; Asn Women in Math; Math Asn Am. *Res:* General topology. *Mailing Add:* 123 Granby Rd South Hadley MA 01075-2909

LAVANCHY, ANDRE C(HRISTIAN), MECHANICAL ENGINEERING. *Current Pos:* res engr, Sharples Res Labs, 50-55, chief analytical engr, 56-65, MGR CENTRIFUGE DEVELOP, PENNWALT CORP, 65- *Personal Data:* b Switz, Nov 17, 22; nat US; m 53; c 3. *Educ:* Swiss Fed Inst Technol, ME, 46. *Prof Exp:* Design & test engr, Brown & Boveri, Switz, 46-49. *Concurrent Pos:* Design engr, Am Viscose Corp, 55. *Mem:* Am Soc Mech Engrs; Am Chem Soc. *Res:* Stress and vibration analysis; applied dynamics; powder technology; liquid-liquid and solid-liquid separation; fluid flow; aerodynamics; thermodynamics. *Mailing Add:* 11 Coniston Dr West Chester PA 19382

LAVANISH, JEROME MICHAEL, ORGANIC CHEMISTRY. *Current Pos:* group leader, Am Cyanamid Co, 88-91, Mgr Chem Discovery, 91-95, dir, 95-96, ASST VPRES GLOBAL FORMULATIONS RES, AGR RES DIV, AM CYANAMID CO, 96- *Personal Data:* b Cleveland, Ohio, Mar 10, 40; m 65. *Educ:* Case Inst Technol, BS, 62; Yale Univ, MS, 63, PhD(chem), 66. *Prof Exp:* Res chemist, PPG Industs, 66-81, mgr biochem synthesis, 81-88. *Mem:* Am Chem Soc; Sigma Xi. *Res:* Synthetic organic chemistry; synthesis and action of herbicides and plant growth regulators; design and action of agrochemicals; formulation and process development, agrochemicals. *Mailing Add:* Agr Res Div Am Cyanamid Co PO Box 400 Princeton NJ 08543-0400

LAVE, ROY E(LLIS), JR, INDUSTRIAL ENGINEERING, OPERATIONS RESEARCH. *Current Pos:* DIR & CHMN BD, SYSTAN, INC, 66- *Personal Data:* b Homewood, Ill, Sept 23, 35; m 60, Penelope Reynolds; c 2. *Educ:* Univ Mich, BS & MBA, 58, MS, 60; Stanford Univ, PhD(indust eng), 65. *Honors & Awards:* Outstanding Young Fac, Am Soc Eng Educ, 71. *Prof Exp:* Asst opers res, Univ Mich, 57-60; asst prof indust eng, Stanford Univ, 62-68, assoc prof & assoc chmn dept, 68-72. *Concurrent Pos:* Consult, Rand Corp, 61-65, Coun Int Prog Mgt, 63, Agency Int Develop, 65-67 & Ford Found, 66; assoc prof eng-econ systs & dir fed internships & interdisciplinary projs, Stanford Univ, 67-68; consult, Inter-Am Develop Bank, 68-72 & Unido, 68-70; dir, Phoenix Housing Develop Corp, 69-77 & Consumer Alliance, 71-73; coun mem, City Los Altos, 74-82, mayor, 76-78; comnr, Metrop Transp Comn, San Francisco Bay Area, 80-87; mem, Paratransit Comt, Transp Res Bd, 82-85, chair, 93- *Mem:* Opers Res Soc Am; Inst Mgt Sci; Inst Indust Engrs; Transp Res Bd. *Res:* Systems analysis in international development planning; managements control systems; national and urban transportation planning and policy analysis; decision budgeting; information systems design; project management. *Mailing Add:* 690 University St Los Altos CA 94022-4021. *Fax:* 650-949-3395

LAVELLE, ARTHUR, NEUROCYTOLOGY. *Current Pos:* from instr to prof, 52-88, EMER PROF ANAT, UNIV ILL COL MED, 88- *Personal Data:* b Fargo, NDak, Nov 29, 21; m 47, Faith W; c Audrey. *Educ:* Univ Wash, BS, 46; Johns Hopkins Univ, MA, 48; Univ Pa, PhD(anat), 51. *Prof Exp:* Asst zool, Univ Wash, 44-46; jr instr biol, Johns Hopkins Univ, 46-48; asst instr anat, Sch Med, Univ Pa, 48-51. *Concurrent Pos:* USPHS fel, Univ Pa, 51-52; USPHS-NIH res grant, Univ Ill, 53-70; vis prof dept anat & brain res inst & Guggenheim fel, Univ Calif, Los Angeles, 68-69. *Mem:* AAAS; Am Asn Anat; Biol Stain Comn (pres, 81-86); Soc Develop Biol; Am Soc Cell Biol; Soc Neurosci. *Res:* Neurocytology; cytological development of nerve cells; experimental alteration of development of nerve cells. *Mailing Add:* 462 Highland Ave Elmhurst IL 60126-2208. *E-Mail:* 71513.3101@compuserve.com

LAVELLE, FAITH WILSON, HISTOLOGY, NEUROEMBRYOLOGY. *Current Pos:* RETIRED. *Personal Data:* b St Johnsbury, Vt, Mar 14, 21; m 47, Arthur; c Audrey. *Educ:* Mt Holyoke Col, BA, 43, MA, 45; Johns Hopkins Univ, PhD(biol), 49. *Prof Exp:* Lab instr zool, Mt Holyoke Col, 43-45; admin asst zool, Univ Pa, 48-51, instr anat, Med Sch, 51-52; lectr, Univ Ill Col Med, 52-53, instr, 53-55, res assoc anat, 55-70; from asst prof to prof anat, Stritch Sch Med, Loyola Univ, Chicago, 70-86, actg chmn dept, 84-85. *Concurrent Pos:* USPHS res grant, Univ Ill Col Med, 53-70; emer prof anat, Stritch Sch Med, Loyola Univ, Chicago, 87- *Mem:* Am Asn Anat; Soc Neurosci; Sigma Xi; AAAS. *Res:* Experimental alteration of development of nerve cells; proteins in neural development. *Mailing Add:* 462 Highland Ave Elmhurst IL 60126

LAVELLE, JOHN WILLIAM, GEOLOGICAL OCEANOGRAPHY, PHYSICAL OCEANOGRAPHY. *Current Pos:* Marine geophysicist, 72-73, geol oceanogr, Environ Res Labs, Miami, 73-77, OCEANOGR, PAC MARINE ENVIRON LAB, NAT OCEANOG & ATMOSPHERIC ADMIN, 77- *Personal Data:* b Sacramento, Calif, Apr 26, 43; m 71. *Educ:* Univ Calif, Berkeley, BA, 65; Univ Calif, San Diego, MS, 68, PhD(physics), 71. *Mem:* Am Geophys Union. *Res:* Theoretical studies of centered on particle transport and deposition in marine environments. *Mailing Add:* Pac Marine Environ Lab 7600 Sand Point Way NE Seattle WA 98115

LAVENDEL, HENRY W, CHEMICAL ENGINEERING, METALLURGY. *Current Pos:* RETIRED. *Personal Data:* b Warsaw, Poland, Apr 23, 19; m 51; c 2. *Educ:* Univ Milan, PhD(indust chem), 51. *Prof Exp:* Res scientist powder metall, Am Electro Metal Co, NY, 52-55; res assoc, Sintercast Corp, 55-57; assoc chem engr, Argonne Nat Lab, 57-60; sr staff scientist, Palo Alto Res Labs, Lockheed Missiles & Space Co, Lockheed Aircraft Co, 61-87. *Mem:* Sigma Xi; Am Inst Mining, Metall & Petrol Engrs; Am Soc Metals; Am Chem Soc. *Res:* High temperature materials. *Mailing Add:* 1511 Hamilton Ave Palo Alto CA 94303-2825

LAVENDER, DENIS PETER, PLANT PHYSIOLOGY. *Current Pos:* assoc prof, Ore Forest Res Lab, 63-70, prof, Sch Forestry, 70-, EMER PROF, FOREST PHYSIOL, ORE STATE UNIV; MEM STAFF, UNIV BC, VANCOUVER, CAN. *Personal Data:* b Seattle, Wash, Oct 13, 26; m 57. *Educ:* Univ Wash, BS, 49; Ore State Univ, MSc, 58, PhD, 62. *Prof Exp:* Res asst, Ore State Bd Forestry, 50-57, in charge forest physiol, Forest Res Ctr, 57-63. *Mem:* Sigma Xi. *Res:* Development of hardy coniferous seedlings; nutrition of second growth Douglas fir stands; reduction of the juvenile period of conifers; dormancy in Douglas fir seedlings and conifers; mineral nutrition and precocious flowering in conifers. *Mailing Add:* 3925 Fairhaven Dr SW Corvallis OR 97333

LAVENDER, DEWITT EARL, MATHEMATICS, STATISTICS. *Current Pos:* Asst prof, 66-68, ASSOC PROF MATH, GA SOUTHERN COL, 68-, HEAD DEPT, 70- *Personal Data:* b Jackson Co, Ga, Nov 9, 38; m 58; c 3. *Educ:* Univ Ga, BS, 62, MA, 63, PhD(math, statist), 66. *Mem:* Am Math Soc; Math Asn Am; Inst Math Statist. *Res:* Mathematical statistics. *Mailing Add:* Dept Math & Comput Sci Ga Southern Univ Statesboro GA 30460-0001

LAVENDER, JOHN FRANCIS, VIROLOGY, MICROBIOLOGY. *Current Pos:* sr virologist, 64-72, res virologist, 72-85, RES SCIENTIST MOLECULAR BIOL, ELI LILY & CO, 85- *Personal Data:* b Nov 16, 29; US citizen; m 69, Beske Hopper; c 3. *Educ:* Drake Univ, BA, 51; Univ Ill, Champaign, MS, 53; Univ Calif, Los Angeles, PhD(infectious dis), 62. *Prof Exp:* NIMH fel virol, Univ Calif, Los Angeles, 62-63. *Mem:* Am Soc Microbiol; Sigma Xi; NY Acad Sci. *Res:* Psychological stress and viral disease resistance; drugs and the entry of viruses across the blood brain barrier; development of parainfluenza, rabies, canine distemper and measles vaccines; Herpes Simplex vaccines types 1 and 2; chemotherapy of virus diseases; molecular biology; cell culture for mass production of proteins. *Mailing Add:* 543 West Dr Indianapolis IN 46202

LAVER, MURRAY LANE, ORGANIC CHEMISTRY, WOOD CHEMISTRY. *Current Pos:* ASSOC PROF FOREST PRODS CHEM, ORE STATE UNIV, 69- *Personal Data:* b Warkworth, Ont, Mar 7, 32; m 63; c 2. *Educ:* Ont Agr Col, BScA, 55; Ohio State Univ, PhD(org chem), 59. *Prof Exp:* Res chemist food sci, Westreco Co, 59-63; res chemist wood sci, Rayonier Can, Inc, 63; res scientist, Weyerhaeuser Co, 64-66, prof specialist res div, 66-68; res instr chem, Univ Wash, 68-69. *Concurrent Pos:* Vis lectr biol chem, Harvard Univ, 77-78. *Mem:* Am Chem Soc; NY Acad Sci; Tech Asn Pulp & Paper Ind; AAAS; Am Asn Univ Prof. *Res:* Pulp and paper, carbohydrate, food and wood chemistry. *Mailing Add:* Dept Forest Prods Ore State Univ Corvallis OR 97331-5703

LAVERDIERE, MARC RICHARD, SOIL CONSERVATION, SOIL CHEMISTRY. *Current Pos:* head, Dept Soil Sci & prof soil conserv & land use, 85-89, PROF SOIL & WATER CONSERV, LAVAL UNIV, 89- *Personal Data:* b Coaticook, Que, May 28, 46; m 69; c 3. *Educ:* Laval Univ, BSc, 69, MSc, 71; Cornell Univ, PhD(agron), 76. *Concurrent Pos:* Res Off Pedogenesis, 71-73; res scientist, Clay Miner, Can Dept Agr, 76-85; guest lectr, Fac Agr, Alimentation Dept Soils, Laval Univ, 77. *Mem:* Soil Conserv Soc; Am Soc Agron; Soil Sci Soc Am; Can Soil Sci Soc; Int Soc Soil Sci. *Res:* Soil conservation; control of soil degradation; surface composting. *Mailing Add:* 1291 Nelles Ste Foy PQ G1W 3B4 Can

LAVERGNE, JULIO A, JR, CELLULAR IMMUNOLOGY, MOLECULAR IMMUNOLOGY. *Current Pos:* instr immunol, Sch Med, Univ PR, 79-80, from asst prof to assoc prof, 80-89, dir, Hybridoma Lab, 85-89, from assoc chair to chair, Dept Microbiol, 87-96, DIR, LAB LASER FLOW CYTOMETRY & MED SCI, UNIV PR, 86-, PROF IMMUNOL, SCH MED, 89- *Personal Data:* b Panama City, Repub Panama, Dec 17, 42; m 71; c Kristin Diane & Adriana Isabel. *Educ:* Univ Costa Rica, licenciature, 70; Univ Tex, PhD(immunol & microbiol), 79. *Prof Exp:* Instr biol, Univ Panama, 70-72. *Concurrent Pos:* Sci adv, PR Health Dept, 82-84; guest researcher, Nat Inst Allergy & Infectious Dis, Bethesda, Md, 83; vis scientist, Ctr Dis Control, Ga, 96; mem, Res Comt, HispanoAm Biomed Asn. *Mem:* Am Soc Microbiol; AAAS; Int Soc Analytical Cytol; NY Acad Sci; Am Asn Vet Immunologists; HispanoAm Biomed Asn. *Res:* Apoptosis regulation in HIV-infected cells; role of cytokines, nitric oxide, reactive oxygen species, dehydrogenases, cytochrome oxidases, mitochondrial membrane electron transport and membrane potential; BCL-2, MnSOD and cyclin expression in apoptosis. *Mailing Add:* F20 19th St Fairview San Juan PR 00926. *Fax:* 787-758-4808; *E-Mail:* j_lavergne@rcmaca.upr.clu.edu

LAVERNIA, ENRIQUE JOSE, SOLIDIFICATION PROCESSING, METAL MATRIX COMPOSITES. *Current Pos:* ASSOC PROF, DEPT MECH ENG, UNIV CALIF, IRVINE, 87- *Personal Data:* b Havana, Cuba, July 30, 60; US citizen; m 86. *Educ:* Brown Univ, BS, 82; Mass Inst Technol, MS, 84, PhD(mat eng), 86. *Prof Exp:* Res asst, Mass Inst Technol, 82-86, res assoc, 86-87. *Concurrent Pos:* Prin investr, Naval Air Develop Ctr, Air Force Off Sci Res, Army Res Off, NSF, Off Naval Res & var indusrs, 87-; NSF presidential young investr, 88-91; secy, Synthesis & Analytical Mat Processing Comt, Metall Soc; fac career develop award, Univ Calif, Irvine, 89; presidential young investr, NSF, 89-94; young investr award, Off Naval Res, 90-93; Alumni Co Am fel, 91. *Mem:* Sigma Xi; Am Soc Metals; Mat Res Soc; Metall Soc; Am Powder Indusrs Fedn. *Res:* Structure and mechanical behavior of metals and alloys processed under rapid solidification conditions; spray atomization and deposition of metals and alloys; solidification processing of metal matrix composites; mathematical modeling of solidification. *Mailing Add:* Chem Eng Univ Calif Irvine CA 92717-0001

LAVERTY, JOHN JOSEPH, PLASTIC ENGINEERING. *Current Pos:* Res chemist, Gen Motors Res Labs, 66-71, assoc sr res chemist, 71-78, sr res chemist, Gen Motors Res Labs, 78-81, STAFF RES SCIENTIST, POLYMER DEPT, GEN MOTORS RES LABS, 81- *Personal Data:* b Chicago, Ill, May 27, 38; m 67, Carol Krause; c Kevin & Colleen. *Educ:* Eastern Ill Univ, BS, 64; Univ Ariz, MS, 66. *Mem:* Am Chem Soc; Soc Plastic Engrs. *Res:* Plastic engineering and polymer physics; structure-property relationship of block copolymers and polymer blends; durability of engineering plastics and the recyclability of engineering thermoplastics. *Mailing Add:* 34066 Chatsworth Sterling Heights MI 48312-4604. *Fax:* 313-986-1207

LAVERY, JOHN EDWARD, CURVE & SURFACE FITTING, NUMERICAL SOLUTION OF EQUATIONS. *Current Pos:* assoc dir, 95-97, PROG MGR, MATH & COMPUT SCI DIV, ARMY RES OFF, 95- *Personal Data:* m 95, Monica Hauck; c Kristen. *Educ:* Mich State Univ, BA, 65; Univ Akron, MS, 68; Univ Md, PhD(math), 73. *Prof Exp:* Aerospace technologist, NASA, 68-73 & 86-89; assoc prof math, Tunghai Univ, Taiwan, 73-74, Humboldt Found & Tech Univ Munich, Ger, 80-82, Case Western Res Univ, 82-86; from assoc prof to prof, Soochow Univ, Taiwan, 75-79; math researcher, US Nat Acad Sci & Comput Ctr Siberian Br, Acad Sci, USSR, 79-80; prog mgr, Off Naval Res, 89-91; dir, Bd Math Sci, Nat Res Coun, 91-94. *Concurrent Pos:* Exchange scholar, US Nat Acad Sci & Czech Acad Sci, 74; adj assoc prof, Case Western Res Univ, 87-89; consult, Gen Elec, 84-86 & Endocardial Solutions Inc, 94-; sole proprietor, L1 Assocs, 94- *Mem:* Soc Indust & Appl Math. *Res:* Curve and surface fitting for computer aided design, image analysis, topography and medical imaging; numerical solutions of equations of electromagnetics, acoustics fluid flow and elasticity. *Mailing Add:* Math & Comput Sci Div Army Res Off PO Box 12211 Research Triangle Park NC 27709-2211. *Fax:* 919-549-4354; *E-Mail:* lavery@aro-emh1.army.mil

LAVI, ABRAHAM, ELECTRICAL ENGINEERING, COMPUTER SCIENCE. *Current Pos:* Res asst, 57, from asst prof to assoc prof elec eng, 59-68, PROF ELEC ENG, CARNEGIE-MELLON UNIV, 68- *Personal Data:* b Iran, Jan 12, 34; US citizen; m 59; c 2. *Educ:* Purdue Univ, BScEE, 57; Carnegie Inst Technol, MS, 58, PhD(elec eng), 59. *Concurrent Pos:* Consult, Graphic Arts Technol Found, Pa; mem staff, Dept Energy, Washington, DC, 76-78. *Mem:* Sr mem Inst Elec & Electronics Engrs; Marine Technol Soc; Int Solar Energy Soc. *Res:* System modelling and optimization; low temperature difference energy conversion; control and instrumentation. *Mailing Add:* Dept Elec Eng Carnegie Mellon Univ 5000 Forbes Ave Pittsburgh PA 15213-3815

LAVIA, LYNN ALAN, obstetrics & gynecology, cancer, for more information see previous edition

LA VIA, MARIANO FRANCIS, IMMUNOPATHOLOGY, FLOW CYTOMETRY. *Current Pos:* prof lab med, Med Univ SC, 79-87, dir, Div Diag Immunol, 79-88, prof path & lab med, 87-95, EMER PROF, MED UNIV SC, 95- *Personal Data:* b Rome, Italy, Jan 29, 26; nat US; m 91, June Faulkner; c William, Maria, Charles, Jacqueline, Susan, Christopher & Thomas. *Educ:* Univ Messina, MD, 49. *Prof Exp:* Asst gen path, Univ Palermo, 50-52; asst path, Univ Chicago, 52-57, instr, 57-60; from asst prof to assoc prof, Sch Med, Univ Colo, Denver, 60-68; prof, Bowman Gray Sch Med, 68-71 & Sch Med, Emory Univ, 71-79. *Mem:* Clin Immunol Soc; Am Asn Immunol; Am Soc Invest Path; Soc Leukocyte Biol; Int Soc Analytical Cytol; Clin Cytom Soc. *Res:* Subtype response to stress and its significance in immunomodulation and morbidity. *Mailing Add:* Med Univ SC Dept Path & Lab Med 171 Ashley Ave Charleston SC 29425. *Fax:* 803-792-3814; *E-Mail:* hiotts@pathol.hms.musc.edu

LAVIGNE, DAVID M, BIOLOGY MANAGEMENT OF MARINE MAMMALS. *Current Pos:* from asst prof to assoc prof, 73-87, PROF ZOOL, UNIV GUELPH, 87- *Personal Data:* b Watford, England, Mar 18, 46; Can citizen; m 68; c 3. *Educ:* Univ Western Ont, BSc, 68; Univ Guelph, MSc, 71, PhD(zool), 73. *Concurrent Pos:* Mem, Seal Specialists Group, Int Union Conserv Nature & Natural Resources, 77-; vis scientist, Brit Antarctic Surv, Cambridge, UK, 80-81; chmn, Sect CSZ, Wildlife Biologists, 85-86. *Res:* Population ecology of marine mammals; ecological energetics and life history traits of mammalian populations; management of marine mammal population. *Mailing Add:* PO Box 60 Rockwood ON N0B 2K0 Can

LAVIGNE, MAURICE J, nuclear materials; deceased, see previous edition for last biography

LAVIGNE, ROBERT JAMES, ENTOMOLOGY. *Current Pos:* from asst prof to assoc prof, 59-71, prof, 71-, EMER PROF ENTOM, UNIV WYO. *Personal Data:* b Herkimer, NY, May 30, 30; m 76; c 4. *Educ:* Am Int Col, BA, 52; Univ Mass, MS, 58, PhD(entom), 61. *Prof Exp:* Res instr entom, Univ Mass, 56-59. *Concurrent Pos:* Chief party, Wyo Team, Somalia, 85-88. *Mem:* Entom Soc Am; Pan-Pac Entom Soc; Orthopterist's Soc; NAm Benthological Soc; Australian Entom Soc. *Res:* Insect taxonomy, especially Diptera; insect behavior, especially robber flies, Asilidae; environmental entomology; biocontrol of weeds; forest entomology; rangeland entomology. *Mailing Add:* Box 3354 Univ Sta Laramie WY 82071

LAVIK, PAUL SOPHUS, BIOCHEMISTRY. *Current Pos:* asst prof biochem, 47-52, assoc prof, 52-70, ASSOC CLIN PROF RADIOL, SCH MED, CASE WESTERN RES UNIV, 70- *Personal Data:* b Camrose, Alta, Feb 11, 15; US citizen; m 41; c 4. *Educ:* St Olaf Col, AB, 37; Univ Wis, MS, 41, PhD(biol chem), 43; Western Res Univ, MD, 59. *Prof Exp:* Instr biochem, Sch Med, La State Univ, 43; from instr to asst prof, Baylor Col Med, 43-47. *Concurrent Pos:* Staff physician radiotherapy, Cleveland Clin, 74-81, emergency clin, 81-; pres, Radiation Ther Consults, 82- *Mem:* Am Soc Biol Chemists; Radiation Res Soc; Am Asn Cancer Res; Am Soc Therapeut Radiologists; Am Col Radiol. *Res:* Nucleic acid metabolism; radiation biochemistry; radiation therapy. *Mailing Add:* 2202 Acacia Park Dr 2702 Lyndhurst OH 44124-3858

LAVILLA, ROBERT E, PHYSICAL CHEMISTRY. *Current Pos:* RETIRED. *Personal Data:* b New York, NY, May 8, 26. *Educ:* Bethany Col, BS, 53; Cornell Univ, PhD(phys chem), 60. *Prof Exp:* X-Ray Spectroscoper, Nat Inst Stand & Technol, 60-61; x-ray spectroscoper, Nat Inst Stand & Technol, 88- *Mem:* Am Phys Soc. *Res:* Electron diffraction of solids and gases; optical properties of materials; x-ray absorption and emission; symchrotron radiation. *Mailing Add:* 19164 Roman Way Gaithersburg MD 20879

LAVIN, EDWARD, POLYMER CHEMISTRY. *Current Pos:* RETIRED. *Personal Data:* b Springfield, Mass, Jan 6, 16; m 48, Norma Pollock; c Daniel, Thomas N & James F. *Educ:* Univ Mass, BS, 36; Tufts Col, MS, 37. *Prof Exp:* Res chemist, Shawinigan Resins Corp, 38-53, group leader, 53-56, sect leader, 56-60, dir appln res, 60-63, res mgr, 63-65; mgr res, Monsanto Co, 65-76, mgt technol, 76-82. *Concurrent Pos:* Monsanto Acad Award, Harvard Univ, 49-50. *Mem:* AAAS; Am Chem Soc; Inst Elec & Electronics Engrs; Soc Aerospace Mat & Process Eng. *Res:* Vinyl high polymers; polyvinyl acetal resins; polyimides; adhesives; reprographic polymer coating. *Mailing Add:* 94 Wheelmeadow Dr Longmeadow Springfield MA 01106-1826

LAVIN, J GERARD, MATERIALS SCIENCE ENGINEERING, ENGINEERING PHYSICS. *Current Pos:* Res engr, Pioneering Res Lab, Du Pont Fibers Inc, 63-68, suprv res & develop, Pioneering & Carothers Res Labs, 68-71 & Kingston Plant, NC, 71-73, sr suprv, Camden Plant, SC, 73-76, process supt, Cape Fear Plant, NC, 76-78, tech supt, Old Hickory Plant, Tenn, 78-81, mfg mgr, 82-83, res mgr, Eng Non-Woven Struct Div, 83-85, sr res fel, Pioneering Res Lab, 85-91, DU PONT FEL, CENT RES & DEVELOP, DU PONT CO, 91- *Personal Data:* b Manchester, Eng, Oct 7, 32; US citizen; m 62, Lora Harrer; c Elinor (Hays) & Jennifer. *Educ:* Univ Mich, MScE, 59, ScD(chem eng), 63. *Mem:* Sigma Xi; Am Carbon Soc; Mat Res Soc. *Res:* Man-made fibers; non-woven fabric forms; research and development cultures and their results; carbon nanoparticles. *Mailing Add:* 15 Wellesley Rd Swarthmore PA 19081. *E-Mail:* lavinjg@a1.esvax.umc.dupont.com

LAVIN, PETER MASLAND, GEOPHYSICS. *Current Pos:* From instr to prof, 60-91, EMER PROF GEOPHYS, PA STATE UNIV, 92- *Personal Data:* b Philadelphia, Pa, Apr 16, 35; m 58; c 2. *Educ:* Princeton Univ, BSE, 57; Pa State Univ, PhD(geophys), 62. *Mem:* Soc Explor Geophys; Am Geophys Union. *Res:* Exploration geophysics with emphasis on gravity and magnetic interpretation; time-series analysis; crustal structure and tectonic history; environmental and groundwater geophysics. *Mailing Add:* 497 Orlando Ave State College PA 16803

LAVIN, PHILIP TODD, BIOSTATISTICS. *Current Pos:* from asst prof to assoc prof biostatist, Sch Pub Health, 77-86, ASSOC PROF SURG, MED SCH, HARVARD UNIV, 87-; PRES, BOSTON BIOSTATIST, INC, 83- *Personal Data:* b Rochester, NY, Nov 21, 46; m 70, Mary Saunders; c 2. *Educ:* Univ Rochester, AB, 68; Brown Univ, PhD(appl math), 72. *Prof Exp:* Res asst prof appl math, Brown Univ, 72-74; res asst prof biostatist, State Univ NY, Buffalo, 74-77. *Concurrent Pos:* Biostatistician, US deleg Japan, Sci Exchange Comt Gastric Oncol, Nat Cancer Inst, 75; prin investr, Gastrointestinal Tumor Study Group, 75-79, DITOH Study, 85-89; coord statistician, Eastern Coop Oncol Group, 76-78; biostatistician, Dana-Farber Cancer Inst, 77-84; pres, Consult Statist, Inc, 84-87; co-investr, Nat Cancer Inst, 88-; panel mem ophthalmic, dent & radiologic devices, Food & Drug Admin, 83-86, dermat, Food & Drug Admin, 92-95. *Mem:* Am Statist Asn; Biomet Soc; Drug Info Asn; Regulatory Affairs Prof Soc. *Res:* Biostatistics; clinical trials; pattern analysis; experimental design; statistical computing; health care evaluation; biomarkers in design and analysis of clinical trials for drugs, biologics, and medical devices; research interests in screening studies, longitudinal data bases, and natural history of disease. *Mailing Add:* Boston Biostatist Inc 615 Concord St Framingham MA 01702. *Fax:* 508-875-2165

LAVINE, ADRIENNE GAIL, HEAT TRANSFER. *Current Pos:* asst prof, 84-91, ASSOC PROF MECH ENG, UNIV CALIF, LOS ANGELES, 91- *Personal Data:* b Norristown, Pa, Aug 14, 58; m 82, Gregory D Small; c Elias B & Jacob S. *Educ:* Brown Univ, ScB, 79; Univ Calif, Berkeley, MS, 83, PhD(mech eng), 84. *Honors & Awards:* Taylor Medal, Int Inst Prod Engrs, 90. *Prof Exp:* Assoc engr, Owens-Corning Fiberglas Tech Ctr, Granville, OH, 79-81. *Concurrent Pos:* NSF presidential young investr award, 88. *Mem:* Am Soc Mech Engrs. *Res:* Thermal aspects of manufacturing processes; microscale heat transfer; natural and mixed convection heat transfer; numerical heat transfer. *Mailing Add:* Mech & Aerospace Eng Dept Univ Calif Los Angeles CA 90095-1597. *Fax:* 310-206-2302; *E-Mail:* lavine@seas.ucla.edu

LAVINE, JAMES PHILIP, THEORETICAL & COMPUTATIONAL PHYSICS. *Current Pos:* PHYSICIST, EASTMAN KODAK CO, 76- *Personal Data:* b Syracuse, NY, Dec 3, 44; m 71, Carolyn S Liberatore; c Gregory D. *Educ:* Mass Inst Technol, BS, 66; Univ Md, PhD(physics), 71. *Prof Exp:* Res assoc physics, Univ Liege, 71-73; res asst prof, Laval Univ, 73-74; res assoc physics, Univ Rochester, 74-76. *Concurrent Pos:* Mem, Tech Adv Bd Microstruct Sci, Semiconductor Res Corp, 91- *Mem:* Am Phys Soc; Mat Res Soc; Micros Soc Am; Am Asn Adv Sci; Electrochem Soc. *Res:* Semiconductor device modeling and simulation of semiconductor device fabrication; optical properties of solids; transport in solids; defects in solids. *Mailing Add:* Res Labs Bldg 81 Eastman Kodak Co Rochester NY 14650-2008

LAVINE, LEROY S, ORTHOPEDIC SURGERY. *Current Pos:* from instr to prof, 65-80, EMER PROF ORTHOP SURG, COL MED, DOWNSTATE MED CTR, STATE UNIV NY, 80-; LECTR, HARVARD MED SCH, 82- *Personal Data:* b Jersey City, NJ, Oct 28, 18; m 46; c 2. *Educ:* NY Univ, AB, 40, MD, 43; Am Bd Orthop Surg, dipl, 55. *Prof Exp:* Res instr orthop surg, Col Med, Ind Univ, 51-52. *Concurrent Pos:* Consult, Am Mus Natural Hist, 55- & Brooklyn Vet Admin Hosp, 65-; consult orthop surgeon, Long Island Jewish Hosp, 57-; adj prof biol, Grad Sch, NY Univ, 66-; clin prof, Med Sch, State Univ NY Stony Brook, 72-; vis orthop surgeon, Mass Gen Hosp, 82- *Mem:* Fel Am Col Surg; Am Asn Phys Anthrop; fel Am Acad Orthop Surg; fel NY Acad Sci; fel NY Acad Med. *Res:* Bone growth and metabolism and mechanisms of calcification; clinical research in bone healing and nerve root compression syndromes; physical properties of piezoelectricity in bone; electrical enhancement of bone growth. *Mailing Add:* Spaulding Rehab Hosp 125 Nashua St Boston MA 02114

LAVINE, RICHARD BENGT, MATHEMATICAL ANALYSIS. *Current Pos:* assoc prof, 72-76, PROF MATH, UNIV ROCHESTER, 76- *Personal Data:* b Philadelphia, Pa, June 27, 38; m 65; c 1. *Educ:* Princeton Univ, AB, 61; Mass Inst Technol, PhD(math), 65. *Prof Exp:* Instr math, Aarhus Univ, 65-66; asst prof, Cornell Univ, 66-71; vis prof, Inst Theoret Physics, Univ Geneva, 71; mem staff, Inst Advan Study, 71-72. *Mem:* Am Math Soc. *Res:* Mathematics of quantum mechanics; functional analysis. *Mailing Add:* Univ Rochester Rochester NY 14627-0001

LAVINE, ROBERT ALAN, NEUROPHYSIOLOGY, PSYCHOLOGY. *Current Pos:* From instr to asst prof, 69-75, ASSOC PROF PHYSIOL & NEUROL, SCH MED, GEORGE WASHINGTON UNIV, 80- *Personal Data:* b Chicago, Ill, Feb 18, 41. *Educ:* Univ Chicago, BS, 62, PhD(physiol), 69. *Concurrent Pos:* NIH fel, George Washington Univ, 69-70; guest scientist, NIMH, 73-; int res fel rev, Fogarty & NIH, 83- *Mem:* Soc Neurosci; Soc Psychophysiol Res. *Res:* Human psychophysiology and experimental neuropsychology; clinical applications of averaged evoked potentials; clinical neurophysiology, computer applications in psychology. *Mailing Add:* Dept Physiol George Washington Univ Med Sch 2300 I St NW Washington DC 20037-2337

LA VIOLETTE, PAUL ESTRONZA, SATELLITE OCEANOGRAPHY. *Current Pos:* OCEANOGR REMOTE SENSING, MISS STATE UNIV RES CTR, 90- *Personal Data:* b New York, NY, Apr 11, 30; m 75, Stella M Prucnal; c 2. *Educ:* Univ Ill, BS, 52. *Prof Exp:* Oceanogr descriptive oceanog, Naval Oceanogr Off, 60-76, oceanogr remote sensing, Naval Ocean Res & Develop Activ, 76-90. *Concurrent Pos:* Prin investr, US & Mex Ocean Exp, 71, Little Window II Sahara Upwelling Explor, US & Spain Ocean Exp, 73 & Grand Banks Explor, US & Can Ocean Exp, 79-80, Doude, Va, 84, Western Mediter Circulation Exp, 86-87. *Mem:* Am Geophys Union; AAAS; Marine Technol Soc; Res Soc Am. *Res:* Basic and applied research in satellite oceanography. *Mailing Add:* Heron Labs PO Box 87 Waveland MS 39576. *Fax:* 228-466-4372

LAVIZZO-MOUREY, RISA J, HEALTH POLICY. *Current Pos:* fac, 84-95, DIR, INST AGING, UNIV PA, 94-, SYLVAN EISMAN ASSOC PROF MED & HEALTH CARE SYSTS, 95-, ASSOC EXEC VPRES HEALTH POLICY, 94-, CHIEF, DIV GERIATRIC MED. *Educ:* Harvard Univ, MD, 79; Univ Pa, MBA, 86. *Prof Exp:* Fac, Temple Univ & Harvard Med Sch. *Concurrent Pos:* Med dir, Elmira Jefferies Mem Home, 84; chair, Minority Health Subcomt, Nat Comt Vital & Health Statist, 89-; co-chair, Task Force Minority Health, Am Geriat Soc, 89-92; dep adminr, Agency Health Policy & Res, 92-94; assoc ed, J Gen Internal Med, 94; mem, Adv Comn Consumer Protection & Qual in Health Care Indust, 97-; mem, White House Task Force Health Care Reform, Task Force Aging Res, Off Technol Assessment Panel Prev Serv Medicare Beneficiaries; mem, Panel Dis & Disability Prev Among Older Adults, Inst Med-Nat Acad Sci. *Mem:* Inst Med-Nat Acad Sci. *Res:* Health policy; health promotion for the elderly; quality of care; minority populations. *Mailing Add:* Inst Aging Univ Pa 3615 Chestnut St Philadelphia PA 19104-6006

LAVKULICH, LESLIE MICHAEL, SOIL SCIENCE. *Current Pos:* From asst prof to assoc prof, 66-75, head dept, 80-90, PROF SOIL SCI, UNIV BC, 75- *Personal Data:* b Coaldale, Alta, Apr 28, 39; m 62, Mary A Olah; c Gregory M & Miles A. *Educ:* Univ Alta, BSc, 61, MSc, 63; Cornell Univ, PhD(soil sci), 67. *Concurrent Pos:* Chair, Resource Mgt & Environ Studies, 90- *Mem:* Am Soc Agron; Can Agr Res Coun; Am Soc Soil Sci; Can Soc Soil Sci (pres, 80-81); Int Soc Soil Sci. *Res:* Soil genesis and classification; weathering of minerals; soil clay mineralogy; soil-plant relationships; mine waste characterization; resource allocation; natural resource management. *Mailing Add:* Dept Soil Sci Univ BC Vancouver BC V6T 2A2 Can. *Fax:* 604-822-9250

LAVOIE, ALVIN CHARLES, EMULSION POLYMERIZATION, ACRYLATES. *Current Pos:* Sr scientist, 81-92, RES SECT MGR, ROHM & HAAS CO, 92- *Personal Data:* b Fall River, Mass, Jan 26, 56; m, M Cathy Staab; c Danielle. *Educ:* Southeastern Mass Univ, BS, 77; Univ Wis-Madison, PhD(org chem), 81. *Mem:* Am Chem Soc. *Res:* Utilization of vinyl sulfides as enolonium equivalents in organic synthesis; applications of organosulfer intermediates in organic synthesis; emulsion polymerization of acrylates. *Mailing Add:* 303 Abbey Lane Lansdale PA 19446-6442

LAVOIE, EDMOND J, SYNTHETIC ORGANIC & NATURAL PRODUCTS CHEMISTRY. *Current Pos:* Res assoc, 75-76, assoc, 76-79, HEAD SECT METAB BIOCHEM, DIV ENVIRON CARCINOGENESIS, AM HEALTH FOUND, 77-, ASSOC MEM, 80- *Personal Data:* b New

York, NY, Jan 11, 50; m 71. *Educ:* Fordham Univ, BS, 71; State Univ NY, Buffalo, PhD(med chem), 75. *Concurrent Pos:* Asst res prof, Dept Urol, NY Med Col. *Mem:* Am Chem Soc; Am Asn Cancer Res; Environ Mutagen Soc. *Res:* Experimental and environmental carcinogenesis; environmental analysis; tobacco sciences. *Mailing Add:* Rutgers Univ Col Pharm Rm 326 W Levine Hall Busch Campus Piscataway NJ 08854

LAVOIE, JEAN-MARC, PHYSIOLOGY. *Current Pos:* From asst prof to assoc prof, 79-89, PROF METAB, DEPT PHYS EDUC, UNIV MONTREAL, 89- *Educ:* Univ Wis, BSc, 71; Univ Montreal, MSc, 73, PhD(exercise physiol), 79. *Mem:* Am Physiol Soc; Can Asn Sports Sci; Am Col Sports Med. *Res:* Physiology. *Mailing Add:* Dept Phys Educ Univ Montreal CP 6128 Succ Centre Ville Montreal PQ H3C 3J7 Can

LAVOIE, MARCEL ELPHEGE, ZOOLOGY. *Current Pos:* RETIRED. *Personal Data:* b Manchester, NH, July 16, 17; m 42; c 2. *Educ:* St Anselm's Col, BA, 40; Univ NH, MS, 52; Syracuse Univ, PhD(zool), 56. *Prof Exp:* Instr chem, St Anselm's Col, 46-47; instr biol, Univ NH, 50-52; lectr zool, Syracuse Univ, 52-55; from asst prof to assoc prof zool, Univ NH 55-84. *Res:* Mammalian anatomy and physiology. *Mailing Add:* 43 Madbury Rd Durham NH 03824

LAVOIE, RONALD LEONARD, METEOROLOGY. *Current Pos:* dir, Environ Modification Off, Nat Oceanic & Atmospheric Admin, 73-79, dir, Atmospheric Progs, Off Res Develop, 79-82, chief, Prog Requirements & Develop, Nat Weather Serv, 82-90, DIR, OFF METEOROL, NAT WEATHER SERV, NAT OCEANIC & ATMOSPHERIC ADMIN, 90- *Personal Data:* b Manchester, NH, Apr 21, 33; m 59; c 2. *Educ:* Univ NH, BA, 54; Fla State Univ, MS, 56; Pa State Univ, PhD, 68. *Prof Exp:* Chief observer, Mt Wash Observ, 57-59; asst prof meteorol, Univ Hawaii, 59-68; assoc prof, Pa State Univ, 68-72; assoc dir meteorol prog, NSF, 72-73. *Concurrent Pos:* NSF sci fac fel, 63-64. *Mem:* AAAS; Am Meteorol Soc; Am Geophys Union; Nat Weather Asn. *Res:* Cloud physics and weather modification; numerical modeling on the mesoscale; tropical meteorology. *Mailing Add:* 16905 Briardale Rd Derwood MD 20855

LAVOND, DAVID G, PSYCHOLOGY. *Current Pos:* ASSOC PROF, DEPTS PSYCHOL & BIOL SCI, UNIV CALIF, LOS ANGELES. *Honors & Awards:* Troland Res Award, Nat Acad Sci, 94. *Mailing Add:* Dept Psychol Biol Sci Univ Southern Calif Los Angeles CA 90024

LAVY, TERRY LEE, WEED SCIENCE, SOIL CHEMISTRY. *Current Pos:* DIR, PESTICIDE RESIDUE LAB, UNIV ARK, 78- *Personal Data:* b Greenville, Ohio, Feb 9, 36; m 55; c 3. *Educ:* Ohio State Univ, BS, 58, MS, 59; Purdue Univ, PhD(plant nutrit), 62. *Prof Exp:* Lab supvr soil chem classification, Ohio State Univ, 58-59; from asst prof to prof agron, Univ Nebr-Lincoln, 62-78. *Mem:* Weed Sci Soc Am; Am Soc Agron; Am Chem Soc. *Res:* Factors affecting the mobility and degradation of pesticides in the soil profile; evaluating exposure of pesticide applicators; monitoring irrigation and domestic wells for pesticide contamination. *Mailing Add:* 2208 Sweetbriar Fayetteville AR 72703-7507

LAW, ALAN GREENWELL, APPROXIMATION & COMPUTING, MEDICAL IMAGING. *Current Pos:* DEAN SCI, MEM UNIV NFLD, 94- *Personal Data:* b Seaham, Eng, Aug 21, 36; m 62, Donella Lucas; c Aurelle, Cameron, Kelly & Colin. *Educ:* Univ BC, BA, 58, MA, 61; Ga Inst Technol, PhD(math), 68. *Honors & Awards:* M A Ferst Res Award, Sigma Xi, 68. *Prof Exp:* Instr math, Ga Inst Technol, 61-68; from asst prof to prof, Univ Regina, 68-94, head comput sci, 90-94. *Concurrent Pos:* Vis staff mem, Los Alamos Meson Physics Facil, 76-77; vis prof, Univ Col Swansea, Wales, 84, Univ Minn, Duluth, 85. *Mem:* Math Asn Am; Sigma Xi; Soc Indust & Appl Math; Can Info Processing Soc. *Res:* Numerical analysis and computing; modelling in sciences; digital image processing; large-scale computational problems; interdisciplinary analysis in natural and computational sciences. *Mailing Add:* Fac Sci Mem Univ St John's NF A1B 3X7 Can. *Fax:* 709-737-3316; *E-Mail:* alaw@morgan.ucs.mun.ca

LAW, ALBERT G(ILES), CIVIL ENGINEERING, HYDROLOGY. *Current Pos:* RETIRED. *Personal Data:* b Ottawa, Ill, July 1, 31; m 54; c 4. *Educ:* Univ Ill, Urbana, BS, 54; Univ Wis, MS, 60, PhD(civil eng), 65. *Prof Exp:* Design engr, Warzyn Eng Co, Wis, 56-58; instr civil eng, Univ Wis, 58-62; from asst prof to assoc prof civil eng, Clemson Univ, 62-77; mgr hydrol sci, Rockwell Hanford Opers, 77-94, fel eng hydrol sci, 94. *Concurrent Pos:* Vis assoc prof, Colo State Univ, 71-72; dir water resources engr, Clemson Univ & consult, US Geol Surv, 75-77. *Mem:* Nat Water Well Asn; Soc Mining Engrs; Am Soc Civil Engrs; Am Geophys Union; Am Water Resources Asn. *Res:* Ground water hydrology, ground water flow, radioactive waste disposal. *Mailing Add:* 417 Snyder Rd Richland WA 99352

LAW, AMY STAUBER, CLINICAL BIOCHEMISTRY. *Current Pos:* CLIN BIOCHEMIST, MED CTR DEL, 69- *Personal Data:* b Philadelphia, Pa, June 26, 38; div. *Educ:* Mt Holyoke Col, AB, 59; Univ Del, MS, 63, PhD(chem), 69. *Prof Exp:* Res chemist, AviSun Corp, 61-65; chief lab sect, Meat Inspection Div, Del State Bd Agr, 68-89. *Mem:* AAAS; Am Chem Soc; Am Asn Clin Chemists; Asn Women Sci. *Res:* Development of clinical methods; clinical applications of protein biochemistry; hemoglobinopathies; clinical toxicology. *Mailing Add:* Spec Chem-Christiana Hosp Med Ctr Del PO Box 6001 Newark DE 19718-6001

LAW, BRUCE MALCOLM, CONDENSED MATTER SURFACE PHYSICS, LIGHT SCATTERING. *Current Pos:* ASST PROF, KANS STATE UNIV, 89- *Personal Data:* b Lower Hutt, NZ, June 23, 56; m 83, Beverley Earles; c Olivia & Rebecca. *Educ:* Victoria Univ, BS, 78, BS, 79, PhD(physics), 85. *Prof Exp:* Res assoc, Univ Md, 85-89. *Mem:* Am Phys Soc. *Res:* Condensed matter surface physics/chemistry; application of light scattering techniques to both bulk & surface phases; non-equilibrium steady states. *Mailing Add:* Dept Physics Kans State Univ Cardwell Hall Manhattan KS 66506. *Fax:* 785-532-6806; *E-Mail:* bmlaw@ksuvm.ksu.edu

LAW, CECIL E, OPERATIONS RESEARCH, MICRO COMPUTER APPLICATIONS. *Current Pos:* RETIRED. *Personal Data:* b Vancouver, BC, Nov 27, 22; m 45, Gerarde J Gommers; c Marie C, Patricia I, Robert H, Jane E, Jennifer A & David P. *Educ:* Univ BC, BA, 50. *Honors & Awards:* Coronation Medal, 53; Award Merit, Can Opers Res Soc, 91. *Prof Exp:* Head animal field exp sect, Suffield Exp Sta, Defence Res Bd, 51, head arctic oper res sect, Defence Res Northern Lab, 51-54, head weapons effects & field trials sect, Can Army Oper Res Estab, 55-58, head oper gaming & tactics sect, 58-60; supvr opers res, Can Industs Ltd, 60-61, opers res mgr, 61-62; sr opers res analyst, Can Nat Rwy, 62-64, coordr opers analysis, 64-66; prof oper res, Queen's Univ, Ont, 66-90, prof comput sci, 69-83, exec dir, Can Inst Guided Transport, 71-83, dir, Comput Lab, 84-88, dir, Inst Community & Occup Health, 85-88, emer prof opers, Res Sch Bus, 90-93. *Concurrent Pos:* Lectr, Exten Dept, McGill Univ, 64-66; dir, Visway TPT Inc, 83-88. *Mem:* Opers Res Soc Am; Opers Res Soc UK; Can Int Proc Soc; Can Opers Res Soc (vpres, 66, pres, 67). *Res:* Wildlife ecology and population dynamics, particularly Arctic; operations research, especially military and civil operational gaming and simulation; theoretical and applied critical path analysis and program evaluation and review technique; transportation research; micro-computer applications. *Mailing Add:* Sch Bus Queen's Univ Kingston ON K7L 3N6 Can. *E-Mail:* lawc@qucdn.queensu.ca

LAW, CHUNG KING, AEROSPACE, ASTRONAUTICS. *Current Pos:* PROF MECH & AEROSPACE ENG, PRINCETON UNIV, 88- *Personal Data:* b Shanghai, Peoples Repub China, Sept 21, 47; m 73, Helen Kwan-Mei Chen; c Jonathan, Jennifer & Jeffrey. *Educ:* Univ Alta, BS, 68; Univ Toronto, MS, 70, Univ Calif, San Diego, PhD, 73. *Honors & Awards:* Curtis W McGraw Award, Am Soc Eng Educ, 84; Silver Medal, Combustion Inst, 90; Propellants & Combustion Award, Am Inst Aeronaut & Astronaut, 94. *Prof Exp:* Assoc sr res engr, GM Res Lab, 73-75; res staff, Princeton Univ, 75-76; from assoc prof to prof, Northwestern Univ, 76-84; prof, Univ Calif, Davis, 84-88. *Mem:* Fel Am Inst Aeronaut & Astronaut; fel Am Soc Mech Engrs; Combustion Inst. *Mailing Add:* Eng Quad Dept Mech/Aerospace Eng Princeton NJ 08544-1019

LAW, DAVID H, INTERNAL MEDICINE, GASTROENTEROLOGY. *Current Pos:* ASSOC CHIEF STAFF EDUC, VET ADMIN MED CTR, BAY PINES, 96- *Personal Data:* b Milwaukee, Wis, July 24, 27; m 49, Patricia Thornton; c 5. *Educ:* Cornell Univ, AB, 50, MD, 54. *Prof Exp:* Intern med, NY Hosp, 54-55, asst resident, 55-57, asst physician to outpatients, 57-58, physician to out-patients & dir personnel health serv, 58-60; med dir out-patient dept & chief div gastroenterol, Vanderbilt Univ Hosp, 60-69; prof med, Sch Med, Univ NMex, 69-; chief med serv, Albuquerque Vet Admin Hosp, 69-85; dir med serv, Vet Admin Cent Off, Washington, DC, 85-86; asst chief med dir, Hosp Based Serv, Vet Admin Hq, 86-95, actg chief, Patient Care off, 95-96. *Concurrent Pos:* NIH fel, Nat Cancer Inst, 57-58; spec consult interdept comt nutrit for nat defense, NIH, 62-63; attend physician, Thayer Vet Admin Hosp, 62-69; prof med, George Wash Med Sch, 85-96. *Mem:* Fel Am Col Physicians; Am Soc Clin Nutrit; Am Gastroenterol Asn; Am Inst Nutrit; Western Soc Clin Invest; Western Asn Physicians. *Res:* Inflammatory bowel disease; malabsorption; gastric secretion; medical care; nutrition; out-patient clinics; delivery of health care. *Mailing Add:* Vet Admin Med Cent 11B PO Box 5005 Bay Pines FL 33744. *Fax:* 813-398-9556; *E-Mail:* law.d@bay-pines.va.gov

LAW, ERIC W, DIAGENESIS-METAMORPHISM, NEURAL NETWORK. *Current Pos:* ASST PROF GEOL, MUSKINGUM COL, 84- *Personal Data:* b Taipei, Taiwan, July 14, 49; c 2. *Educ:* Case Western Res Univ, PhD(geol), 83. *Res:* Petrology; geochronology; Taiwan; subduction; slate; K-Ar; computer; neural network; diagenesis; clay minerals; granite; metamorphism; sandstone. *Mailing Add:* Dept Geog & Geol Muskingum Col New Concord OH 43762-1199

LAW, FRANCIS C P, DRUG METABOLISM, TOXICOKINETIC MODELLING. *Current Pos:* assoc prof environ toxicol prog, Dept Biol Sci, 83-87, PROF, SIMON FRASER UNIV, 87- *Personal Data:* b Hong Kong, Oct 12, 41; Can citizen; m 80; c 4. *Educ:* Univ Alta, BS, 66, MS, 69; Univ Mich, PhD(drug metab), 72. *Prof Exp:* Vis fel, Nat Inst Environ Health Sci, 72-75; asst prof drug metab & toxicol, Col Pharm, Dalhousie Univ, 75-81, assoc prof, 81-82. *Concurrent Pos:* Consult Environ Risk Assessment, BC Indust; mem, BC Sci Coun Environ Technol & Waste Comt. *Mem:* Pharmacol Soc Can; Soc Toxicol Can; Am Soc Pharmacol & Exp Therapeut; Soc Environ Toxicol & Chem. *Res:* Disposition, metabolism and toxicity of drugs; environmental pollutants and other chemicals in living organisms including humans; development of physiologically based toxicokinetic models; human health risk assessment; ecological risk assessment. *Mailing Add:* Dept Biol Sci Environ Toxicol Prog Simon Fraser Univ Burnaby BC V5A 1S6 Can. *Fax:* 604-291-3496; *E-Mail:* flaw@sfu.ca

LAW, GEORGE ROBERT JOHN, poultry genetics, for more information see previous edition

LAW, HSIANG-YI DAVID, OPTOELECTRONICS, SEMICONDUCTOR MATERIAL. *Current Pos:* PRES, ARTERNET CORP, 93- *Personal Data:* b Hong Kong, Feb 12, 49; US citizen; m 73, Ruby H Yee; c Jeremy & George. *Educ:* Univ Wash, BSEE, 72; Cornell Univ, MSEE, 75, PhD(elec eng), 77. *Prof Exp:* Mem tech staff, Sci Ctr, Rockwell Int Corp, 77-80; mgr, Semiconductor Device Lab, Technol Res Ctr, TRW Inc, 80-84; vpres technol, PCO, Inc, 84-91. *Concurrent Pos:* Lectr optoelectronic class; technol eval of cos, Total Qual Consult. *Mem:* Sr mem Inst Elec & Electronics Engrs; Am Phys Soc; Am Qual Control Soc. *Res:* III-V alloys material study; avalanche photodiodes; double heterostructure lasers; integrated optoelectronic devices; ionization coefficients of III-V materials; ion implantation, anodic oxidation and other surface passivation methods. *Mailing Add:* 29776 Woodbrook Dr Agoura Hills CA 91301. *Fax:* 818-222-0736; *E-Mail:* hdavidlaw@aol.com

LAW, JIMMY, THEORETICAL PHYSICS, COMPUTATIONAL PHYSICS. *Current Pos:* from asst prof to assoc prof, 69-84, PROF PHYSICS, UNIV GUELPH, 84- *Personal Data:* b Seremban, Malaysia, Sept 23, 42; m 69; c 2. *Educ:* Univ London, BSc, 63, PhD(physics), 68. *Prof Exp:* Teaching fel physics, McMaster Univ, 66-69. *Mem:* Brit Inst Physics; Can Asn Physicists. *Res:* Theoretical calculations in nuclear and hypernuclear physics; inner shell vacancy creation mechanisms in atomic physics; Anyon physics and chaos. *Mailing Add:* Dept Physics Univ Guelph Guelph ON N1G 2W1 Can. *Fax:* 519-836-9967; *E-Mail:* jlaw@physics.uoguelph.ca

LAW, JOHN, POWER SYSTEMS, ELECTRIC MACHINERY. *Current Pos:* assoc prof, 75-79, PROF ELEC ENGR, UNIV IDAHO, 79- *Personal Data:* b Cleveland, Ohio, Dec 8, 30; m 53; c 4. *Educ:* Case Inst Technol, BS, 57; Univ Wis-Madison, MS, 60, PhD(elec eng), 62. *Prof Exp:* Instr, Univ Wis, 57-61; assoc prof elec eng, Mont State Univ, 62-63; sr elec engr, Carrier Corp, 63-65, chief engr, 65-74, sr staff engr, 74. *Concurrent Pos:* Vis assoc prof elec eng, Bogazici Univ, Turkey, 67-71; NSF fel, Elec Power Res Inst, 78; vis engr, Eng Soc Comn Energy, 79; vis prof elec eng, Wash State Univ, 80; planning engr, Idaho Power Co, 81; engr, Idaho Nat Eng Lab, 77; consult, Idaho Power Co, 76; mem, Fac Improvement Comt, NSF, 78. *Mem:* Inst Elec & Electronics Engrs; Nat Soc Prof Engrs. *Res:* Computer methods in power systems analysis; response of AC servomotors with nonsinusoinal and discontinuous impedance source voltage. *Mailing Add:* Elec Eng Dept Univ Idaho Col Eng Buchanan Eng Lab Moscow ID 83844

LAW, JOHN HAROLD, ENTOMOLOGY. *Current Pos:* dept head, 81-86, dir biotechnol, 86-92, REGENTS PROF, BIOCHEM DEPT, UNIV ARIZ, 92-, DIR, CTR INSECT SCI, 93- *Personal Data:* b Cleveland, Ohio, Feb 27, 31; m 56. *Educ:* Case Inst Technol, BS, 53; Univ Ill, PhD(chem), 57. *Hon Degrees:* HC, Sofia Univ, Bulgaria, 95. *Honors & Awards:* Gregor Mendel Medal, J E Purkinje Medal, Czech Acad Sci. *Prof Exp:* Res fel, Harvard Univ, 57-58; instr chem, Northwestern Univ, 58-59; from instr to asst prof, Harvard Univ, 59-65; prof biochem, Univ Chicago, 65-81, prof chem, 67-81. *Concurrent Pos:* Wellcome vis prof, Univ Mass, 93. *Mem:* Nat Acad Sci; Am Soc Biol Chemists; fel AAAS; Am Chem Soc; fel Entom Soc Am. *Res:* Insect biochemistry; lipid metabolism; protein chemistry. *Mailing Add:* Biochem Dept Biosci W Univ Ariz Tucson AZ 85721. *Fax:* 520-621-3243; *E-Mail:* law@biosci.arizona.edu

LAW, LLOYD WILLIAM, ONCOLOGY. *Current Pos:* sr geneticist, Nat Cancer Inst, 47-54, scientist dir, 54-84, mem sci directorate, 71-80, CHIEF, LAB CELL BIOL, 71-89; EMER SCIENTIST DIR, NAT CANCER INST, 90- *Personal Data:* b Ford City, Pa, Oct 28, 10; m 42; c 2 Lloyd W Jr & David B. *Educ:* Univ Ill, BS, 31; Harvard Univ, AM, 35, PhD(biol), 37. *Honors & Awards:* A F Rosenthal Award, AAAS, 58; G H A Clowes Award, Am Asn Cancer Res, 65; Meritorious Serv Award, USPHS, 65, Distinguished Serv Award, 69; Alexander Pascoli Prize, Univ Perugia, 69; G B Mider Lect Award, 70; hon mem Am Asn Cancer Res, 87; hon mem Europe Asn Cancer Res. *Prof Exp:* Instr high sch, Ill, 31-33; asst, Harvard Univ, 36-37; res assoc, Stanford Univ, 37-38; Finney-Howell med res fel physiol genetics, Jackson Mem Lab, 38-41, Commonwealth Fund fel cancer res, 41-42; sci dir, Jackson Mem Lab, 46-47. *Concurrent Pos:* Harvard Univ Parker fel, Stanford Univ, 37-38; trustee, Jackson Mem Lab, 47-; mem study sect cancer chemother, NIH, 56-59, drug eval panel, Nat Serv Ctr, 56-59, sci adv bd, Roswell Park Mem Inst, 57-62, adv bd, Children's Cancer Found, expert adv panel cancer, WHO, 60-65 & adv sci bd, Hektoen Inst Chicago, 64-; mem, US Nat Comt, Int Union Against Cancer, 68-72 & 72-76, & Am Can Soc Rev Bd, 70-74. *Mem:* Am Soc Exp Path; Am Asn Cancer Res (pres, 68-69); Transplantation Soc; Soc Exp Biol & Med; Soc Exp Leukemia; Am Asn Immunologists; Europ Asn Cancer Res. *Res:* Genetics; factors affecting development of leukemia and breast tumors; immunogenetics of the mouse; tumor immunology; chemotherapy of neoplasms; tumor antigens. *Mailing Add:* 9810 Fernwood Rd Bethesda MD 20817. *Fax:* 301-402-8787

LAW, MARGARET ELIZABETH, EXPERIMENTAL HIGH ENERGY PHYSICS. *Current Pos:* res fel, Harvard Univ, 61-67, res assoc, 67-71, sr res assoc high energy physics, 71-78, lectr, 72-78, 83-85, registr, Fac Arts & Sci, 78-89, SR LECTR, HARVARD UNIV, 86-, DIR PHYSICS LAB, 89- *Personal Data:* b Birmingham, Eng, May 6, 34; m 57. *Educ:* Univ Birmingham, Eng, BSc, 55, PhD(high energy physics), 58; Boston Univ, MBA, 84. *Prof Exp:* Nat Res Coun fel nuclear physics, McMaster Univ, 58-60. *Res:* Experimental research in strong interactions. *Mailing Add:* Physics Dept Harvard Univ Cambridge MA 02138

LAW, PAUL ARTHUR, clinical chemistry, for more information see previous edition

LAW, PETER KOI, NEUROMUSCULAR ELECTROPHYSIOLOGY. *Current Pos:* CHMN, CELL THER RES FOUND, 91- *Personal Data:* b Chengsha, China, Feb 25, 46; Chinese & Can citizen; c 2. *Educ:* McGill Univ, BSc, 68; Univ Toronto, MSc, 69, PhD(neurophysiol), 72. *Prof Exp:* Fel, Med Ctr, McMaster Univ, 72-75; asst prof neurol, Sch Med, Vanderbilt Univ, 75-79; assoc prof neurol physiol & biophys, Univ Tenn, 79-88, prof, 88-91. *Concurrent Pos:* Sr investr, Jerry Lewis Neuromuscular Dis Res Ctr, Nashville, Tenn, 75-79; electromyography consult, Vanderbilt Univ Hosp, 75-79; Baptist Hosp, 75-79 & St Thomas Hosp, 75-79; Muscular Dystrophy Asn Can fel, 72-75; Muscular Dystrophy Asn res grant, 75-88, Vanderbilt Univ Res Coun res grant, 75-79; NIH res grant, 78-79; NSF res grant, 79-82, NIH grants, 83-93. *Mem:* Asn Am Med Cols; AAAS; NY Acad Sci; Soc Neurosci; Can Soc Neurosci. *Res:* Developmental membrane biophysics; motor-unit electrophysiology; muscular dystrophy; myogenesis and muscle regeneration; genetic complementation and therapy; acupuncture analgesia; myogenic cell transplant treatment for muscle disease. *Mailing Add:* Cell Ther Res Found 1770 Moriah Woods Suite 18 Memphis TN 38117

LAW, S EDWARD, BIOLOGICAL ENGINEERING, AGRICULTURAL ENGINEERING. *Current Pos:* from asst to assoc prof, Agr Eng Dept, 70-82, prof, 82-88, D W BROOKS DISTINGUISHED PROF, BIOLOG & AGR ENG DEPT, UNIV GA, 88- *Personal Data:* b Sept 10, 39. *Educ:* NC State Col, BSAE, 61; NC State Univ, Raleigh, MSAE, 64, PhD(biol & agr eng), 68. *Honors & Awards:* Tyler Prize Environ Achievement, Electrostatics Soc Am, 94. *Prof Exp:* Res engr, Gourdine Environ Systs Inc, 69-70. *Concurrent Pos:* Nat Acad Sci postdoctoral res assoc, Just Res Lab, USDA-Agr Res Serv. *Mem:* Nat Acad Eng; fel Inst Elec & Electronics Engrs; fel Am Soc Agr Engrs; Electrostatics Soc Am; Int Ozone Asn; Entom Soc Am; Sigma Xi. *Res:* Light-scattering properties of optically dense biological particulate systems; charged-particulate technology and electrogas dynamics; research and development of electrostatics for agriculture and biological applications; granted 14 domestic and foreign patents; published 8 articles in last 5 years. *Mailing Add:* Driftmier Eng Ctr Dept Biol & Agr Eng Univ Ga Athens GA 30602-4435

LAW, WILLIAM BROUGH, PLASMA PHYSICS. *Current Pos:* asst prof, 65-68, ASSOC PROF PHYSICS, COLO SCH MINES, 68- *Personal Data:* b Elko, Nev, Oct 11, 32; m 56; c 3. *Educ:* Univ Nev, BSc, 54; Ohio State Univ, PhD(nuclear physics), 60. *Prof Exp:* Physicist, Armour Res Found, 60; staff mem, Sandia Lab, 60-65. *Mem:* Am Phys Soc. *Res:* Gamma ray spectroscopy; accelerator physics. *Mailing Add:* Dept Physics Colo Sch Mines Golden CO 80401

LAWFORD, GEORGE ROSS, BIOCHEMISTRY, CELL BIOLOGY. *Current Pos:* PRES & CONSULT, ROSS LAWFORD & ASSOC, 93- *Personal Data:* b Toronto, Ont, Feb 27, 41; m 66; c 2. *Educ:* Univ Toronto, BSc, 63, PhD(biochem), 66. *Prof Exp:* Can Med Res Coun fel, 66-68; asst prof biochem, McMaster Univ, 68-73; mem staff, Weston Res Ctr, 73-77, tech dir & gen mgr, 77-89; pres, Ortech Int, 89-93. *Concurrent Pos:* Mem, Nat Biotechnol Adv Comt Can. *Mem:* Can Res Mgt Asn; Can Inst Food Sci & Technol; Am Asn Cereal Chemists. *Res:* Functional significance of interactions between subcellular components; regulation of protein biosynthesis and the adenyl cyclase system; food chemistry; fermentation; research management. *Mailing Add:* 23 Runsey Rd Toronto ON M4G 1N7 Can

LAWING, WILLIAM DENNIS, STATISTICS. *Current Pos:* ASSOC PROF INDUST & EXP STATIST, UNIV RI, 69- *Personal Data:* b Charlotte, NC, Mar 29, 35; m 57; c 3. *Educ:* NC State Col, BS, 57, MS, 59; Iowa State Univ, PhD(statist), 65. *Prof Exp:* Statistician, Res Triangle Inst, 65-69. *Concurrent Pos:* Adj prof, Duke Univ, 66-67; vis lectr, Iowa State Univ, 67-68; adj assoc prof, NC State Univ, 68-69. *Mem:* Am Statist Asn. *Res:* Industrial applications of statistics; quality control; operations research; sequential analysis; decision theory; survey sampling. *Mailing Add:* Dept Comput Sci & Statist Univ RI Kingston RI 02881

LAWLER, ADRIAN RUSSELL, AQUACULTURE, TOXICOLOGY. *Current Pos:* teaching fel, Gulf Coast Res Lab, 71-73, assoc marine biologist, 73-75, co-chmn toxicol prog & head exp organism cult, 76-84, MARINE BIOLOGIST, GULF COAST RES LAB, 75-, AQUARIUM SUPVR, MARINE EDUC CTR, BILOXI, 84- *Personal Data:* b Etowah, Tenn, Nov 25, 40; div; c 2. *Educ:* Univ Rochester, AB, 62; Col William & Mary, Va, MS, 64, PhD(marine biol), 71. *Prof Exp:* NSF summer student, Va Inst Marine Sci, 62, grad asst, 62-71. *Concurrent Pos:* Consult, Nat Aquaculture Info Syst, 75- *Res:* Culture of marine and freshwater organisms, birds and mammals for experimentation; toxicity testing; external parasites of marine and freshwater fishes; larval fish development; display of organisms in Mississippi's marine science aquarium; disease diagnosis and control in captive organisms on public display; aquarium design and maintenance. *Mailing Add:* Aquarium Supvr Marine Educ Ctr & Aquarium 115 E Beach Blvd Biloxi MS 39530

LAWLER, EUGENE L(EIGHTON), applied mathematics, computer science; deceased, see previous edition for last biography

LAWLER, GREGORY FRANCIS, PROBABILITY. *Current Pos:* From asst prof to assoc prof, 79-91, PROF MATH, DUKE UNIV, 91- *Personal Data:* b Alexandria, Va, July 14, 55; m 90, Marcia Curtis. *Educ:* Univ Va, BA, 76; Princeton Univ, MA, 77, PhD(math), 79. *Concurrent Pos:* Vis mem, Courant Inst Math Sci, 81-82 & 86-87; Sloan res fel, 86-88; vis scientist, Univ BC, 94-95. *Mem:* Am Math Soc; Int Asn Math Physics; fel Int Math Statist. *Res:* Random walks; processes from mathematical physics such as self-avoiding walks and random environments. *Mailing Add:* Dept Math Duke Univ PO Box 90320 Durham NC 27708-0320

LAWLER, JACK (JOHN) W, PHYSICS. *Current Pos:* ASSOC PROF PATH, HARVARD MED SCH, 88-; ASSOC PATHOLOGIST, DEPT PATH, BRIGHAM & WOMENS HOSP, BOSTON, 88- *Personal Data:* b Newton, Mass, May 2, 49. *Educ:* Villanova Univ, BS, 71; Boston Col, PhD(physics), 76. *Prof Exp:* Res fel, Dana-Farber Cancer Inst, 76-80; res assoc, Dept Biomed Res, St Elizabeths Hosp, 80-82; from asst prof to assoc prof, Tufts Univ, Sch Med, 82-88. *Concurrent Pos:* Prin investr, NIH, 82-95, 88-90 & 89-94; asst investr, Dept Biomed Res, St Elizabeths Hosp, 82-83; assoc investr, 83-85, investr, 85-88; sci affairs comt, Tufts Univ, Sch Med, 84-88, chmn, 85-86, comt intellectual property, 85-86; vis scientist, Mass Inst Technol, 85-89, res affil, & 92-; health site vis comt, NIH, 85-92; inst biosafety comt, St Elizabeths Hosp, 88; res comput comt, Brigham & Womens Hosp, 92- *Mem:* Int Soc Thrombosis & Hemostasis; NY Acad Sci; Am Soc Hemat; AAAS; Am Soc Cell biol. *Res:* Structural and functional organization of thrombospondin; the role of thrombospondin and its receptor in the normal and abnormal vascular cell function; the function of thrombospondin in tissue genesis and repair; author of over 50 publications. *Mailing Add:* Dept Path Brigham & Women's Hosp LMRC-414 221 Longwood Ave Boston MA 02115-5701

LAWLER, JAMES E, PSYCHOLOGY. *Current Pos:* from asst prof to assoc prof, 75-85, PROF, DEPT PSYCHOL, UNIV TENN, KNOXVILLE, 85-, PROF, DEPT ANAT & NEUROBIOL, CTR HEALTH SCI, 87- *Personal Data:* b Jan 15, 46; c 1. *Educ:* Cornell Col, BA, 67; Wake Forest Univ, MA, 70; Univ NC, Chapel Hill, PhD(physiol psychol), 73. *Prof Exp:* Grad asst, Wake Forest Univ, 67-68; NIH fel neurobiol, Sch Med, Univ NC, 70-72, res asst psychiat, 72-73; res assoc, Cardiovasc Labs, Sch Pub Health, Harvard Univ, 73-75. *Concurrent Pos:* Mem, High Blood Pressure Res Coun, Am Heart Asn, 77- & Sudden Cardiac Death Rev Comt, Nat Heart, Lung & Blood Inst, NIH, 78; consult progs & planning, Am Psychol Asn, 80; vis assoc prof, Dept Med, Cardiovasc Res & Training Ctr, Sch Med, Univ Ala, 83-84; vis scientist, Minority Access Res Career, Fedn Am Socs Exp Biol, 83-; res incentive award, Sci Alliance, Univ Tenn, 85- & chancellor's fac res scholar award, 87. *Mem:* AAAS; Am Physiol Soc; Soc Behav Med; Soc Neurosci; Soc Psychophysiol Res. *Mailing Add:* Psychophysiol Lab Dept Psychol Univ Tenn Austin Peay Bldg Knoxville TN 37996-0900

LAWLER, JAMES EDWARD, SPECTROSCOPY. *Current Pos:* from asst prof to assoc prof, 80-89, PROF PHYSICS, UNIV WIS, 89- *Personal Data:* b St Louis, Mo, June 29, 51; m 73, Katherine A Moffatt; c Emily C & Catherine M. *Educ:* Univ Mo, BS, 73; Univ Wis-Madison, MS, 74, PhD(physics), 78. *Honors & Awards:* W P Allis Prize, Am Phys Soc; Penning Award, Int Conf Phenomena Ionized Gases. *Prof Exp:* Res assoc, Physics Dept, Stanford Univ, 78-80. *Concurrent Pos:* H I Ronnes fac fel, Univ Wis. *Mem:* Fel Am Phys Soc; fel Optical Soc Am; Sigma Xi. *Res:* Physics of gas discharge plasmas and laser interactions with gas discharge plasmas; laser spectroscopy; nonlinear optics; laboratory astrophysics; atomic physics. *Mailing Add:* Dept Physics Univ Wis 1150 University Ave Madison WI 53706. *Fax:* 608-265-2334; *E-Mail:* jelawler@facstaff.wisc.edu

LAWLER, JAMES HENRY LAWRENCE, CHEMICAL ENGINEERING, NUCLEAR ENGINEERING. *Personal Data:* b Detroit, Mich, Jan 31, 36; m 64; c 8. *Educ:* Univ Louisville, BChE, 59, MEngr, 72; Brigham Young Univ, MS, 66; Univ Utah, ME & PhD(chem eng), 69. *Prof Exp:* Radio engr, Louisville Free Pub Libr, 52-54, Radio Sta WKLO, 57-58 & WKYW, 58-59; engr, Wright Patterson AFB, 59-62 & Boeing Co, 62-65; asst prof chem, Dixie Col, 69-73; head nuclear eng technol, Trident Technol Col, SC, 73-77; chmn chem technol, Univ Dayton, 77-80; staff engr, Rockwell Hanford Oper, 80-86; engr, Gen Dynamics Nat Aerospace Plane, 86-91; physics res engr, Super Conducting Super Collider, 91-94. *Concurrent Pos:* AEC fel, Kans State Univ, 72. *Mem:* Am Inst Chem Eng; Am Chem Soc; Inst Elec & Electronics Engrs. *Res:* Materials; cyclic history; socio-mathematics; quantization of space-time; unified theory of gravity, strong and weak nuclear forces, electromagnetic forces, proton theory. *Mailing Add:* 3721 Century Pl No 101 Ft Worth TX 76133-4107

LAWLER, JOHN PATRICK, SANITARY ENGINEERING, MATHEMATICS. *Current Pos:* PARTNER, LAWLER, MATUSKY & SKELLY ENGRS, 77- *Personal Data:* b Brooklyn, NY, Jan 30, 34; m 57; c 7. *Educ:* Manhattan Col, BCE, 55; NY Univ, MCE, 58; Univ Wis, PhD(sanit eng), 60. *Prof Exp:* Civil engr, F G Davidson, Inc, NY, 55-56; instr civil eng, Manhattan Col, 56-58; asst prof, Rutgers Univ, 60-65; partner, Quirk, Lawler & Matusky Engrs, 65-77. *Concurrent Pos:* Consult, Humble Oil & Refining Co, NJ, 61-62; vis assoc prof, Manhattan Col, 63-, lectr summer inst stream analysis, 64-66; assoc, Cosulich & Quirk, Water Resources Engrs, 64-65; lectr summer inst water resources, Clemson Univ, 65 & 66. *Mem:* Am Soc Civil Engrs; Water Pollution Control Fedn; Sigma Xi. *Res:* Mathematical analysis of the transport processes and reaction kinetics associated with stream and estuarine pollution; water resources systems; water and waste treatment operations. *Mailing Add:* Lawler Matusky & Skelly Engrs One Blue Hill Plaza Pearl River NY 10965

LAWLER, MARTIN TIMOTHY, FLUID MECHANICS, HEAT TRANSFER. *Current Pos:* MANAGING PARTNER, LAWLER & ASSOCS, 72- *Personal Data:* b Rochester, Minn, Apr 6, 37; m 59, 81; c 3. *Educ:* Milwaukee Sch Eng, BS, 61; Case Inst Technol, MS, 65, PhD(eng), 67. *Prof Exp:* Instr mech eng & physics, Milwaukee Sch Eng, 59-61; res asst, Fluid, Thermal & Aerospace Sci, Case Inst Technol, 64-67; prin res scientist, Corp Res Ctr, Honeywell Inc, Minn, 67-70; vpres, Swenberg Eng Inc, 70-72. *Concurrent Pos:* Nat Defense fel, Comt Acad Sci & Eng, Inst Technol, 61-64. *Mem:* Am Soc Mech Engrs; Nat Soc Prof Engrs; Am Soc Heating, Refrig & Air Conditioning Engrs; Sigma Xi; Am Asn Energy Engrs. *Res:* Fluid-particle and two-phase flows; heat transfer; solar systems, energy consumption and conservation. *Mailing Add:* Lawler Eng/Div JSA Parkway W & Rte 60 Pittsburgh PA 15244-0508

LAWLER, RONALD GEORGE, PHYSICAL ORGANIC CHEMISTRY. *Current Pos:* from asst prof to assoc prof, 65-73, PROF CHEM, BROWN UNIV, 73- *Personal Data:* b Centralia, Wash, May 19, 38. *Educ:* Calif Inst Technol, BS, 60; Univ Calif, Berkeley, PhD(chem), 64. *Prof Exp:* Res assoc chem, Columbia Univ, 63-65. *Concurrent Pos:* NSF fel, 63-64; Alfred P Sloan res fel, 70-71. *Mem:* Am Chem Soc. *Res:* Theoretical organic chemistry; electron and nuclear magnetic resonance; chemistry of free radicals and radical ions; radiation chemistry; in vivo nmr. *Mailing Add:* Dept Chem Brown Univ Providence RI 02912

LAWLESS, EDWARD WILLIAM, TECHNICAL MANAGEMENT, ENVIRONMENTAL CHEMICALS ASSESSMENT. *Current Pos:* Assoc chemist, Midwest Res Inst, 59-64, sr chemist, 64-66, prin chemist, 66-73, head, Technol Assessment Sect, 73-82, sr adv, Technol & Health Assessment, 82-87, head, Environ Assessment Sect, 87-91, SR ADV ENVIRON SCI, MIDWEST RES INST, 91- *Personal Data:* b Jacksonville, Ill, Apr 9, 31; m 59, Virginia D Fulton; c Donna N (Newell), Kevin W, Vincent A, Sean J, Patrick E & Paul D (deceased). *Educ:* Ill Col, AB, 53; Univ Mo, PhD(phys chem), 60. *Hon Degrees:* DSc, Ill Col, 79. *Concurrent Pos:* Chem prof, Metrop Community Col, Kansas City, Mo, 92- *Mem:* Am Chem Soc; Soc Risk Anal; Int Asn Impact Assessment (pres, 83-84). *Res:* Hazardous waste incineration and management; technology forecast, risk assessment and societal effects analysis; environmental chemistry and pollution control; evaluation of health and environmental hazards of industrial, consumer product and agricultural chemicals; chemistry of pesticides, fluorine, metal hydrides; correlations of chemical structures with properties; analysis of agricultural innovation; chemical kinetics. *Mailing Add:* Appl Eng Dept Midwest Res Inst 425 Volker Blvd Kansas City MO 64110. *Fax:* 816-753-8420

LAWLESS, HARRY THOMAS, PSYCHOLOGY, FOOD SCIENCE. *Current Pos:* asst prof, 89-92, ASSOC PROF, DEPT FOOD SCI, NY STATE COL AGR & LIFE SCI, CORNELL UNIV, 93- *Personal Data:* b Hackensack, NJ, Mar 20, 52. *Educ:* Yale Univ, BA, 74; Brown Univ, ScM, 76, PhD(psychol), 78. *Prof Exp:* Postdoctoral assoc, Food Sci Lab, US Army Natick Res & Develop Command, 78-80; vis scientist, Gen Foods Tech Ctr, 80; asst mem, Monell Chem Senses Ctr, 81-84; asst prof res, Dept Otolaryngol, Thomas Jefferson Med Col, 82-84; sr scientist, Prod Eval Dept, SC Johnson & Son, 84-88. *Concurrent Pos:* Instr, Northeastern Univ, 79-80; asst prof, Dept Food Sci, Univ Del, 82-84; instr, Dept Psychol, Univ Wis, Parkside, 87-88; prof, Dept Foods & Nutrit, Univ Ill, 87-88; mem, Nat Adv Bd, Nat Inst Deafness & Commun Dis; mem, Grad Field Food Sci & Grad Field Psychol, Cornell Univ; Fulbright res fel, Finland, 95; William Evans vis fel, Univ Otago, 95. *Mem:* Sigma Xi; Inst Food Technologists; Psychonomic Soc; Am Soc Testing & Mat; Asn Chemoreception Sci; Soc Consumer Psychol; Soc Study Ingestive Behav; Am Soc Enol & Viticult; Am Psychol Asn. *Res:* Sensory evaluation of foods; advanced concepts in sensory evaluation; sensory evaluation of dairy products; flavors analysis and applications. *Mailing Add:* Dept Food Sci NY State Col Agr & Life Sci Cornell Univ Ithaca NY 14850

LAWLESS, JAMES GEORGE, analytical chemistry, for more information see previous edition

LAWLESS, KENNETH ROBERT, MATERIALS SCIENCE. *Current Pos:* RETIRED. *Personal Data:* b Key West, Fla, Aug 21, 22; m 52, Alois Yowell; c 4. *Educ:* Lynchburg Col, BS, 46; Univ Va, PhD(chem), 51. *Prof Exp:* Fulbright fel, Univ Norway, 51-52; res assoc chem, Univ Va, 52-60, from asst prof to assoc prof, 60-68, prof mat sci, 68-80, chmn dept, 76-86. *Mem:* Electron Micros Soc Am; Am Crystallog Asn; Inst Mining, Metall & Petrol Engrs; Microbeam Anal Soc. *Res:* Chemistry and physics of solids and surfaces; x-ray diffraction; electron diffraction and electron microscopy. *Mailing Add:* Dept Mat Sci & Eng Univ Va Thornton Hall Charlottesville VA 22903. *Fax:* 804-982-5660; *E-Mail:* krl@virginia.edu

LAWLESS, PHILIP AUSTIN, engineering physics, for more information see previous edition

LAWLESS, WILLIAM N, SOLID STATE PHYSICS. *Current Pos:* STAFF, LAKE SHORE CRYOTRONICS, INC, 80- *Personal Data:* b Denver, Colo, Sept 15, 36; m 57; c 3. *Educ:* Colo Sch Mines, EMet, 59; Rensselaer Polytech Inst, PhD(physics), 64. *Prof Exp:* Fel solid state physics, Swiss Fed Inst Technol, 64-66; sr res physicist, Res & Develop Labs, Corning Glass Works, 66-68, res assoc physics, 69-80. *Concurrent Pos:* Guest worker, Cryogenics Div, Nat Bur Stand, Boulder, 73-75. *Mem:* AAAS; Am Inst Physics; Cryogenic Soc Am; Am Phys Soc. *Res:* Ferroelectricity; doped alkali halides; glass-ceramic technology. *Mailing Add:* 921 Eastwind Dr Suite 110 Westerville OH 43081. *Fax:* 614-882-1437

LAWLEY, ALAN, METALLURGY, MATERIALS SCIENCE. *Current Pos:* assoc prof metall eng, 66-69, chmn, Mat Eng Dept, 69-79, PROF METALL ENG, DREXEL UNIV, 79- *Personal Data:* b Birmingham, Eng, Aug 29, 33; m 60, Nancy Kressler; c Carolyn A, Elizabeth A & Jennifer A. *Educ:* Univ Birmingham, BSc, 55, PhD(phys metall), 58. *Honors & Awards:* Krumb Lectr, Am Inst Mining Metall & Petrol Eng, 85; Distinguished Serv Powder Metall Award, Metal Powder Indust Fedn, 91. *Prof Exp:* Res assoc metall, Univ Pa, 58-61; lab mgr phys metall, Res Labs, Franklin Inst, Pa, 61-66. *Concurrent Pos:* Consult, Open Univ, UK, 75, Cabot Corp, 81. *Mem:* Fel Am Soc Metals Int; Am Soc Eng Educ; Am Powder Metall Inst; Inst Mat; Micros Soc Am. *Res:* Powder metallurgy; composite materials; physical and mechanical metallurgy; failure analysis; engineering education; materials engineering design. *Mailing Add:* 336 Hathaway Lane Wynnewood PA 19096-1925

LAWLEY, THOMAS J, DERMATOLOGY. *Current Pos:* PROF & CHMN DERMAT, EMORY UNIV, 89- *Mailing Add:* Dermat Dept Sch Med Emory Univ 5001 Woodruff Mem Bldg PO Drawer SS Atlanta GA 30322

LAWMAN, MICHAEL JOHN PATRICK, EXPERIMENTAL BIOLOGY. *Current Pos:* ASSOC PROF IMMUNOL, DEPT IMMUNOL & MED MICROBIOL, COL MED, UNIV FLA, 88-, ADJ ASSOC PROF & DIR RES, DEPT PEDIAT, DIV HEMAT-ONCOL, 89- *Personal Data:* b Sept 30, 49; Brit citizen. *Educ:* Guildford Co Tech Col, HNC, 72; Ewell Co Tech Col, LIBiol, 73, MIBiol, 75; Univ Surrey, PhD, 79. *Prof Exp:* Asst sci officer, Dept Exp Path, Animal Virus Res Inst, 69-72, sci officer, 72-76, higher sci officer, 76-79; NIH res fel, Dept Microbiol & Immunol, Univ Tenn, 79-80; asst prof virol-immunol, Dept Microbiol, Sch Vet Med, Auburn Univ, 80-81; asst prof immunol, Dept Prev Med, Col Vet Med, Univ Fla, 81-83, Dept Comp & Exp Path, 83-85, asst prof, Dept Immunol & Med Microbiol, Col Med, 82-85; res scientist & prog coordr immunol, Vet Infectious Dis Orgn, Univ Sask, 85-88. *Concurrent Pos:* Prin investr, USDA, 81-84, 82-86 & 84-87, Natural Sci & Eng Res Coun Can, 86-89 & 87-90; NSF travel scholar, Ruminant Immunol Conf, Kenya, 84, Nat Acad Sci travel scholar, 85; consult, Upjohn, 84, Nat Acad Sci, 85 & USAID, 88-90; co-investr & consult porcine immunity to African swine fever virus, USAID, 87-90. *Mem:* Inst Biol; Conf Res Workers Animal Dis; Asn Am Immunologists; Am Soc Microbiol; Am Vet Immunologist Asn; NY Acad Sci. *Res:* Foot-and-mouth disease virus in British deer; epizootic haemorrhagic disease of deer virus in domestic farm animals and in British deer; in vitro characteristics of epizootic haemorrhagic disease of deer virus; pathogenesis of bluetongue virus in sheep; peste des petits ruminants; vertical transmission of bluetongue virus in sheep; electrophoretic studies on the double stranded RNA genome of orbviruses; stimulation and growth of macrophage of various animals species in in vitro culture. *Mailing Add:* Morphogenesis Inc 12085 Research Dr Alachua FL 32615

LAWRASON, F DOUGLAS, INTERNAL MEDICINE. *Current Pos:* CONSULT, 84- *Personal Data:* b St Paul, Minn, July 30, 19; m 44; c 3. *Educ:* Univ Minn, BA, 41, MA & MD, 44. *Prof Exp:* Instr anat, Med Sch, Univ Minn, 41-43; from intern to resident, Sch Med, Yale Univ, 44-49, from instr to asst prof med, 49-50; prof assoc, Nat Res Coun, 50-53; asst prof & asst dean, Sch Med, Univ NC, 53-55; prof internal med, provost med affairs & dean med ctr, Univ Ark, 55-61; exec dir med res, Merck Sharp & Dohme Res Labs, Pa, 61-66, vpres med res, 66-69; prof internal med, Univ Tex Health Sci Ctr Dallas, 69-73, assoc dean acad affairs, 69-72, dean, 72-73; sr vpres, Sci Affairs & pres, Res Div, Schering-Plough Corp, 73-80, sr vpres sci, 80-84. *Concurrent Pos:* James Hudson Brown res fel, Yale Univ, 48-49; mem hemat study sect, NIH, 51-53; comt blood & related probs, Nat Acad Sci, 53-57; inst grant comt, Am Cancer Soc, 55-60; training grant comt, Nat Res Coun, 59-64; mem bd dirs, Morristown Mem Hosp, 80- & NJ State Sci Adv Comt, 80- *Mem:* AAAS; Am Fedn Clin Res; Am Col Cardiologists; NY Acad Sci; Am Soc Internal Med. *Res:* Cancer and leukemia in inbred strains of mice; hematology; medical education and administration; research management. *Mailing Add:* 2 Carriage Hill Dr Morristown NJ 07960-6994

LAWRENCE, ADDISON LEE, SHRIMP FARMING. *Current Pos:* PROF NUTRIT & MARICULT, TEX A&M UNIV, 79- *Personal Data:* b Cape Girardeau, Mo, Dec 19, 35; m 91; c 8. *Educ:* Southeast Mo State Univ, BSc, 56; Univ Mo, MA, 58, PhD(physiol), 62. *Prof Exp:* Asst prof biol, Westminster Col, Fulton, Mo, 61-62; fel physiol, Stanford Univ, 62-64; prof, Univ Houston, 64-79. *Concurrent Pos:* Vis instr, Hopkins Marine Sta, Stanford Univ, 63; assoc dir res, Univ Houston, 75-77, dir, Marine Sci Prog, 77-78; maricult coordr, Tex A&M Sea Grant Prog, 79-86. *Mem:* Am Soc Zoologists; Soc Exp Biol Med; World Aquacult Soc; Nat Shellfish Soc; Western Soc Naturalists; Crustacean Soc. *Res:* Nutrition; physiology; biochemistry; shrimp mariculture; shrimp reproduction; shrimp raceway and pond production; shrimp larviculture; author of over 160 technical publications. *Mailing Add:* PO Box 1725 Port Aransas TX 78373. *Fax:* 512-749-5756

LAWRENCE, ALONZO WILLIAM, ENVIRONMENTAL ENGINEERING. *Current Pos:* vpres environ resources & occup health, 76-81, vpres sci & technol, 81-84, VPRES & GEN MGR, CHEM SYSTS SECTOR, KOPPERS CO, PITTSBURGH, 84- *Personal Data:* b Rahway, NJ, Apr 11, 37; m 60; c 3. *Educ:* Rutgers Univ, BS, 59; Mass Inst Technol, MS, 60; Stanford Univ, PhD(civil eng), 67. *Honors & Awards:* Eng Sci Award, Am Asn Environ Eng Prof, 77. *Prof Exp:* Asst prof civil eng, Drexel Inst Technol, 65-67; from asst prof to assoc prof environ eng, Cornell Univ, 67-76. *Mem:* Am Soc Civil Engrs; Water Pollution Control Fedn. *Res:* Wastewater treatment technology; wastewater reclamation and reuse; biokinetics; solid wastes disposal; occupational safety and health; technological innovation; strategic management of technology. *Mailing Add:* 4299 Old New England Rd Allison Park PA 15101

LAWRENCE, CHRISTINE, HEMATOLOGY, RHEUMATOLOGY. *Current Pos:* Asst prof med, 66-71, assoc prof, 71-86, PROF MED, ALBERT EINSTEIN COL MED, 86-; DIR CLIN HEMAT, JACOBI MED CTR, 72- *Personal Data:* b New York, NY, Oct 18, 30; m 57, Milford Fulop; c Michael Alain & Tamara Ann. *Educ:* Univ Mich, BS, 52; Columbia Univ, MD, 56. *Mem:* Am Col Physicians; Am Fedn Med Res; Am Soc Hemat. *Res:* Clinical hematology, particularly in genetic disorders of erythrocytes and hemoglobin. *Mailing Add:* 630 W 246th St Bronx NY 10471. *Fax:* 718-918-7460; *E-Mail:* chrisl@mem.po.com

LAWRENCE, CHRISTOPHER WILLIAM, GENETICS, RADIOBIOLOGY. *Current Pos:* assoc prof, 70-82, PROF RADIATION BIOL, UNIV ROCHESTER, 82- *Personal Data:* b London, Eng, Oct 2, 34; m 61; c 3. *Educ:* Univ Wales, BSc, 56; Univ Birmingham, PhD(genetics), 59. *Prof Exp:* Sci officer radiation biol, Wantage Labs, UK Atomic Energy Authority, 59-61, sr sci officer, 61-70. *Concurrent Pos:* Vis asst prof radiation biol, Univ Rochester, 69. *Mem:* AAAS; Genetics Soc Am; Biophys Soc. *Res:* Radiation molecular genetics of Saccharomyces cerevisiae. *Mailing Add:* Dept Biophys Univ Rochester Med Sch 601 Elmwood Ave Rochester NY 14642-0001

LAWRENCE, DALE NOLAN, INTERNAL MEDICINE & INFECTIOUS DISEASES, GENETICS OF HUMAN IMMUNE RESPONSES. *Current Pos:* sect chief clin develop, 89-91, SR SCI ADV COORDR FOR AIDS VACCINE, INT STUDIES, VACCINE RES & DEVELOP BR, BASIC RES & DEVELOP PROG, DIV AIDS, NAT INST ALLERGY & INFECTIOUS DIS, NIH, 91- *Personal Data:* b Covington, Ky, Feb 24, 44; m 73; c 2. *Educ:* Duke Univ, MD, 69; Emory Univ, MPH, 89; Am Bd Internal Med, cert, 73; Am Bd Infectious Dis, cert, 75. *Honors & Awards:* Spec Award, Nat Hemophilia Found, 90. *Prof Exp:* Intern, resident & fel internal med & infectious dis, Univ Tex Health Sci Ctr, San Antonio, 69-73; epidemiol intel serv officer, Field Serv Div, Ctr Dis Control, USPHS, Miami, Fla, 73-75, med officer immunol & parasitol, Clin Immunol Lab, Immunochem Br, Parasitol Div, Bur Labs, 75-77, chief immunogeneticist, Clin Med Br, Divs Immunol & Host Factors, Ctr Infectious Dis, 79-82, task force mem & epidemiologist, AIDS Task Force & Div Host Factors, 82-89. *Concurrent Pos:* Resident gen prev med & epidemiol, Ctrs Dis Control, 74-76, physician mem med adv bd, 79-81; med officer, Genetics Res Prog, NSF, Amazonas, Brazil, 76; vis scientist human leukocyte antigen genetics, Genetics Lab, Dept Biochem, Univ Oxford, UK, 78-79; ed consult, J AMA, J Nat Cancer Inst, J Infectious Dis, J AIDS, Sci & Am J Epidemiol, 79-; vis fel, Harvard Inst Health Res, 84-85; field investr team leader, Ctrs Dis Control-Mayo Clin Collab Reinvest: Swine Influenza Vaccine-Guillain Barre Syndrome, 85-87; consult, Global Prog on AIDS, WHO, 91-; prog officer AIDS panel, US-Japan Coop Med Sci Prog, 91- *Mem:* Fel Infectious Dis Soc Am; fel Am Col Epidemiol; Asn Immunologists; fel Am Col Physicians; fel Am Col Prev Med; Am Soc Histocompatibility & Immunogenetics. *Res:* Early infectious disease epidemiologic investigations; studies of human leukocyte antigen genetics; vaccine immunology and development of AIDS vaccine. *Mailing Add:* AIDS NIAID NIH Rm 2A11 6003 Executive Blvd Rockville MD 20892-7620

LAWRENCE, DAVID A, IMMUNOLOGY. *Current Pos:* CHIEF, LAB ENVIRON & CLIN IMMUNOTOXICOL, WADSWORTH CTR, 93- *Personal Data:* b Paterson, NJ, Jan 9, 45; m 67, Georgia Pappas. *Educ:* Rutgers Univ, BA, 66; Boston Col, MS, 68, PhD(biol), 71. *Prof Exp:* USPHS fel, Scripps Clin & Res Found, 71-74; from asst prof to prof microbiol & immunol, Albany Med Col, 74-91, assoc prof med, 84-88, pharm & toxicol, 88-93, path, 89-93. *Concurrent Pos:* NIH Toxicol Study Sect; Epa Health Res Rev Panel. *Mem:* NY Acad Sci; Am Soc Microbiol; Am Asn Immunologists; Soc Toxicol. *Res:* Cellular and subcellular events resulting from antigen activation and regulation of immune response; tumor immunology; immunotoxicology. *Mailing Add:* Wadsworth Ctr NY State Dept Health PO Box 509 Albany NY 12201

LAWRENCE, DAVID JOSEPH, ELECTRONIC MATERIALS, PHOTONIC DEVICES. *Current Pos:* ASSOC PROF, JAMES MADISON UNIV, 93- *Personal Data:* b Johnson City, NY, June 15, 51. *Educ:* Syracuse Univ, BS, 73; Cornell Univ, MS, 75, PhD(electrophys), 77. *Prof Exp:* Develop engr, Western Elec Co, 77-78; res physicist semiconductor mat, Eastman Kodak Res Lab, 78-93. *Mem:* Am Asn Crystal Growth; Inst Elec & Electronics Engrs; Mat Res Soc; Am Soc Eng Educ. *Res:* III-V compounds; epitaxial growth; solid state light emitters and detectors; transparent conductors; oxide films; chemical vapor deposition. *Mailing Add:* James Madison Univ CISAT Bldg Harrisonburg VA 22807. *Fax:* 540-568-2761; *E-Mail:* lawrendj@jmu.edu

LAWRENCE, DAVID M, PREVENTIVE MEDICINE. *Current Pos:* area med dir & vpres opers, NW Permanente Med Group & regional mgr Colo & Northern Calif regions, CHIEF EXEC OFFICER & CHMN BD, KAISER FOUND HEALTH PLAN INC & KAISER FOUND HOSPS. *Educ:* Amherst Col, BA; Univ Ky, MD; Univ Wash, MPH; Am Bd Prev Med, cert. *Prof Exp:* Health officer & dir, Human Serv, Multnomah Co, Ore; mem fac, Sch Pub Health & Community Med & Sch Med, Univ Wash; Peace Corps physician, Dominican Repub & Washington, DC. *Mem:* Inst Med-Nat Acad Sci. *Mailing Add:* Kaiser Found Health Plan Inc 1 Kaiser Plaza Oakland CA 94612. *Fax:* 510-271-5820

LAWRENCE, DAVID REED, GEOLOGY, INVERTEBRATE PALEONTOLOGY. *Current Pos:* asst prof, 66-69, ASSOC PROF GEOL & MARINE SCI, UNIV SC, 69- *Personal Data:* b Woodbury, NJ, Oct 11, 39; m 66. *Educ:* Johns Hopkins Univ, AB, 61; Princeton Univ, PhD(geol), 66. *Prof Exp:* Asst geol, Princeton Univ, 63-64, assoc prof, 66. *Concurrent Pos:* NSF sci fac fel, Univ Tubingen, Ger, 71-72. *Mem:* Int Paleont Union; Geol Soc Am; Paleont Soc. *Res:* Evolutionary, ecologic and biogeographic aspects of fossil invertebrates; taphonomy; historiography of the earth sciences. *Mailing Add:* Geol Dept Univ SC Columbia SC 29208-0001

LAWRENCE, DEBORAH A, MODELS OF DISEASE TRANSMISSION. *Current Pos:* ASST PROF MATH, RUSSELL SAGE COL, 94- *Personal Data:* b Troy, NY, Dec 9, 65; m 96, Sal Scecchitano. *Educ:* Russell Sage Col, BA, 88; State Univ NY, Albany, MA, 90, PhD(dynamical systs), 92. *Prof Exp:* Asst prof math, Clarion Univ Pa, 92-94. *Mem:* Am Math Soc; Asn

Women Math; Asn Women Sci; Math Asn Am; Soc Math Biol. *Res:* Dynamics of disease transmission; human papilloma virus as it is related to cervical cancer. *Mailing Add:* Dept Math & Comput Sci Russell Sage Col Troy NY 12180. *E-Mail:* lawred@sage.edu

LAWRENCE, DONALD BUERMANN, plant ecology, ethnobotany; deceased, see previous edition for last biography

LAWRENCE, DONALD GILBERT, NEUROLOGY, NEUROANATOMY. *Current Pos:* assoc prof neurol & neurosurg, 72-80, ASSOC PROF ANAT, MCGILL UNIV, 72-, PROF NEUROL & NEUROSURG, 80-, ASSOC DEAN, FAC MED, 84- *Personal Data:* b Kingston, Ont, Jan 18, 32; m 56; c 3. *Educ:* Bishop's Univ, BSc, 53; McGill Univ, MDCM, 57; Royal Col Physicians & Surgeons, FRCP(C), 74. *Honors & Awards:* Osler Medal, Am Asn Hist Med, 58. *Prof Exp:* Res fel neuroanat, Western Res Univ, 65-66; Nat Mult Sclerosis Soc fel neurophysiol, Univ Lab Physiol, Oxford Univ, 66-68; from asst prof to assoc prof neuroanat, Erasmus Univ, 68-72; head, lab neuroanat, Montreal Neuro Inst, 72-84. *Concurrent Pos:* Asst physician, Montreal Gen Hosp, 72-77, assoc physician, 77- *Mem:* Cajal Club; Am Asn Hist Med; Am Asn Anat; Soc Neurosci; Am Acad Neurol; Can Asn Neurosci. *Res:* Anatomical, behavioral and clinical investigations of motor pathways in the central nervous system; regeneration in the central nervous system. *Mailing Add:* Neurosci Unit Montreal Gen Hosp 1650 Cedar Ave Montreal PQ H3G 1A4 Can

LAWRENCE, FRANCIS JOSEPH, PLANT BREEDING. *Current Pos:* RETIRED. *Personal Data:* b Glen Arm, Md, May 12, 25; m 51; c 4. *Educ:* Univ Md, BS, 51, MS, 58, PhD(hort, bot), 65. *Prof Exp:* Asst hort, Univ Md, 53-62, from instr to asst prof, 62-65; res horticulturist, Corvallis Res Sta, USDA, 65-90. *Mem:* Am Soc Hort Sci; Am Pomol Soc. *Res:* Breeding of Fragaria and Rubus. *Mailing Add:* 1430 NW 27th St Corvallis OR 97330-2447

LAWRENCE, FRANKLIN ISAAC LATIMER, organic chemistry, commercial development; deceased, see previous edition for last biography

LAWRENCE, FREDERICK VAN BUREN, JR, METALLURGY, CIVIL ENGINEERING. *Current Pos:* PROF METALL & CIVIL ENG, UNIV ILL, URBANA, 68- *Personal Data:* b Hyannis, Mass, May 16, 38; m 62; c 3. *Educ:* Swarthmore Col, BS, 60; Mass Inst Technol, SM, 62, CE, 65, ScD(mat sci), 68. *Concurrent Pos:* Ed, J Mat Civil Eng, Am Soc Civil Engrs. *Mem:* Am Welding Soc; Am Soc Metals; Am Inst Mining, Metall & Petrol Engrs; Sigma Xi; Am Soc Civil Engrs. *Res:* Fatigue strength of welded joints; microstructure of cementitious materials. *Mailing Add:* 205 N Matthews Ave Newark Rm 1110 Urbana IL 61801-2350

LAWRENCE, GEORGE EDWIN, zoology; deceased, see previous edition for last biography

LAWRENCE, GEORGE MELVIN, PHYSICS. *Current Pos:* vis fel, Joint Inst Lab Astrophys-Lab Atmospheric & Space Physics, 70-71, res assoc, 71-74, SR RES ASSOC, LAB ATMOSPHERIC & SPACE PHYSICS, UNIV COLO, BOULDER, 75- *Personal Data:* b Salt Lake City, Utah, Mar 26, 37; m 85, Judith Aver; c 3. *Educ:* Univ Utah, BS, 59; Calif Inst Technol, PhD(physics), 63. *Prof Exp:* Res assoc astrophys ics, Princeton Univ, 63-65, staff physicist, 65-67; res scientist, McDonnell Douglas Advan Res Lab, Calif, 67-70. *Concurrent Pos:* Vis assoc, Calif Inst Technol, 68-70. *Mem:* Fel Am Phys Soc; Am Geophys Union; Am Inst Aeronaut & Astronaut. *Res:* Transition probabilities; cross sections; physical chemistry; detectors; space science; science education. *Mailing Add:* Lab Atmospheric & Space Phys Univ Colo 1234 Innovation Dr Boulder CO 80303-7814. *Fax:* 303-492-6444; *E-Mail:* lawrence@cololasp

LAWRENCE, HENRY SHERWOOD, IMMUNOLOGY, INFECTIOUS DISEASES MEDICINE. *Current Pos:* asst, NY Univ, 47-49, from instr to prof, 49-61, dir, NY Univ Cancer Ctr, 74-79, JEFFREY BERGSTEIN PROF MED, MED SCH, NY UNIV, 79-, HEAD, INFECTIOUS DIS & IMMUNOL DIV, 59-, CO-DIR, NY UNIV-BELLEVUE MED SERV, 64- *Personal Data:* b New York, NY, Sept 22, 16; m 43, Dorothea Wetherbee; c Thea, Victor & Geoffrey. *Educ:* NY Univ, AB, 38, MD, 43; Am Bd Internal Med, dipl; FRCPS(G), 77. *Honors & Awards:* Von Pirquet Gold Medal Award, Annual Forum Allergy, 72; Distinguished Contribs in Sci as Related to Med Award & Bronze Medal, Am Col Physicians, 73; NY Acad Med Sci Medal, 74; Bristol Award, Infectious Dis Soc Am, 74; Sci Achievement Award, Am Col Allergists, 74; Chapin Medal, 75; Lila Gruber Award for Cancer Res, Am Acad Dermat, 75. *Prof Exp:* Intern, 3rd Med Div, Bellevue Hosp, NY, 43-44, from asst resident to chief resident, 46-48. *Concurrent Pos:* Wyckoff fel, NY Univ, 48-49; dir student health serv, NY Univ-Bellevue Med Serv, 50-57; Commonwealth Fund fel, Univ Col, Univ London, 59; USPHS career develop award, 60-65; assoc mem streptococcal comt, Armed Forces Epidemiol Bd, 56-74; consult, Allergy & Immunol Study Sect, USPHS, 60-65, chmn, 63-65, mem, comt cutaneous syst & comt tissue transplantation, Div Med Sci, Nat Res Coun-Nat Acad Sci, chmn, comt tissue transplantation, 63-65, mem, Nat Res Coun, 70-72; ed-in-chief, Cellular Immunol, 70-96; lectr, Harvey Soc, 73; counr, 74-77; consult & chmn, Allergy & Infectious Dis Panel, Health Res Coun City New York, mem, infectious dis prog comt res serv, Vet Admin & res comts, Arthritis Found, Am Cancer Soc & Am Thoracic Soc; dir, NY Univ Ctr AIDS Res, NIH, 89-94. *Mem:* Nat Acad Sci; Am Soc Clin Invest; Am Asn Immunologists; Harvey Soc (secy, 57-60); Asn Am Physicians; hon fel Am Acad Allergy; fel Am Col Physicians; Infectious Dis Soc; Soc Exp Biol & Med; Fr Soc Allergy. *Res:* Infection and immunity; cellular immunology; lymphokine production; purification and characterization of inducer and suppressor factor in dialysates containing transfer factor. *Mailing Add:* Infectious Dis & Immunol Div NY Univ Med Ctr New York NY 10016. *Fax:* 212-263-7369

LAWRENCE, IRVIN E, JR, EMBRYOLOGY, HISTOLOGY. *Current Pos:* assoc prof biol, 64-70, assoc prof, 70-78, PROF ANAT, ECAROLINA UNIV, 78- *Personal Data:* b Raleigh, NC, Apr 18, 26. *Educ:* Univ NC, AB, 50; Univ Wyo, MS, 55; Univ Kans, PhD(anat), 63. *Prof Exp:* Teacher high sch, NC, 51-54; instr biol, Louisburg Col, 55-57; asst prof zool, Univ Wyo, 60-64. *Concurrent Pos:* Univ Res fel, Univ Wyo, 63-64; USPHS res grant, 64-65; NIH res grant, 75- *Mem:* Am Soc Zool; Soc Develop Biol; Sigma Xi; Pan-Am Asn Anat; Soc Study Reproduction. *Res:* Biogenic amines in development; epithelial-mesenchymal interactions in organogenesis of pancreatic islets and of ovary; ovarian nerves and reproductive function. *Mailing Add:* Dept Anat ECarolina Univ Sch Med Greenville NC 27834

LAWRENCE, JAMES FRANKLIN, MATHEMATICS. *Current Pos:* asst prof, 83-86, ASSOC PROF, GEORGE MASON UNIV, 86- *Personal Data:* b Okemah, Okla, Aug 20, 50. *Educ:* Okla State Univ, BS, 72; Univ Wash, PhD(math), 75. *Prof Exp:* Instr math, Univ Tex, Austin, 75-77; res assoc, Nat Bur Stand, 77-79; asst prof, Univ Ky, 79-83. *Concurrent Pos:* Vis asst prof, Univ Mass, Boston, 81-82. *Mem:* Math Asn Am; Am Math Soc; Sigma Xi. *Res:* Field of combinatorics; study of oriented matroids. *Mailing Add:* Dept Math Sci George Mason Univ Fairfax VA 22030-4444

LAWRENCE, JAMES HAROLD, JR, MECHANICAL ENGINEERING. *Current Pos:* From instr to asst prof, Tex Tech Univ, 56-62, assoc prof, 64-71, chmn dept, 72-83, PROF MECH ENG, TEX TECH UNIV, 71-, ASSOC DEAN, 92- *Personal Data:* b Beatrice, Nebr, Feb 9, 32; m 55; c 2. *Educ:* Tex Tech Col, BS, 56, MS, 60; Tex A&M Univ, PhD(mech eng), 65. *Mem:* Am Soc Eng Educ; Am Soc Mech Engrs; Am Soc Heat, Refrig & Air-Conditioning Engrs. *Res:* Conduction; convection; radiation heat transfer; systems engineering. *Mailing Add:* Dept Mech Eng Tex Tech Univ Lubbock TX 79409-0001

LAWRENCE, JAMES NEVILLE PEED, HEALTH PHYSICS, PHYSICS. *Current Pos:* RETIRED. *Personal Data:* b Norfolk, Va, May 29, 29; m 48; c 1. *Educ:* Johns Hopkins Univ, BA, 50; Vanderbilt Univ, MA, 58, PhD(physics), 68. *Prof Exp:* Res asst health physics, Los Alamos Nat Lab, Univ Calif, 51-54; mem staff, 54-68, assoc group leader, 68-80, asst group leader, 80-88, sr scientist, 88-92. *Mem:* Health Physics Soc. *Res:* Theoretical treatment of nuclear fission, especially liquid drop applications; health physics, especially dosimetry, internal exposure calculations and radio-nuclide identification. *Mailing Add:* 206 El Conejo Los Alamos NM 87544

LAWRENCE, JAMES VANTINE, BACTERIOLOGY. *Current Pos:* RETIRED. *Personal Data:* b Middletown, Ohio, July 2, 18; m 42; c 3. *Educ:* Univ Ill, BS, 43; Ohio State Univ, MS, 48, PhD(bact), 50. *Prof Exp:* From asst prof to prof bact, Ohio Univ, 51-80, prof zool microbiol, 80-85. *Concurrent Pos:* Vis prof, WVa Univ, 51 & 52; clin lab dir, Athens State Hosp, 53, 54 & 56. *Mem:* Am Soc Microbiol; Am Pub Health Asn; Sigma Xi. *Res:* General and pathogenic bacteriology and parasitology. *Mailing Add:* 3 Sue Dr Athens OH 45701-3663

LAWRENCE, JEANNE BENTLEY, GENE MAPPING, IN SITU HYBRIDIZATION. *Current Pos:* fel, 82-85, instr cell biol, Dept Anat, 85-88, ASST PROF, DEPT CELL BIOL, UNIV MASS, MED CTR, 88- *Personal Data:* b Sweetwater, Tex, Dec 10, 51; m, John; c John, Matthew & David. *Educ:* Stephens Col, BA, 73; Rutgers Univ, MS, 75; Brown Univ, PhD(molecular & cell biol), 82. *Honors & Awards:* Jr Outstanding Cell Biologist Career Develop Award, Women Cell Biol, 89. *Prof Exp:* Res assoc, Yale Univ, 75-77. *Concurrent Pos:* Res career & develop award, Nat Ctr Human Genome Res, NIH, 90. *Mem:* AAAS; Am Soc Cell Biologists; Am Asn Human Genetics. *Res:* Analysis of genome and nuclear organization using fluorescence in situ hybridization; human gene mapping and the functional relationship of DNA/RNA to nuclear structure. *Mailing Add:* Cell Biol Dept Med Ctr Univ Mass Med Sch 55 Lake Ave N Worcester MA 01655-0106

LAWRENCE, JOHN, FATE & EFFECTS OF POLLUTANTS, ANALYTICAL QUALITY CONTROL. *Current Pos:* res scientist environ toxic contaminants, Nat Water Res Inst, Can, 73-80, res mgr environ anal methodology, 80-87, dir, Res & Appln Br, 87-93, dir, Aquatic Ecosys Protection Br, 93-96, DIR, AQUATIC ECOSYS CONSERV BR, NAT WATER RES INST, CAN, 96- *Personal Data:* b UK, Mar 23, 43; Can citizen; m 65, Margaret David; c Andrew D & Paul J. *Educ:* Bristol Univ, BSc, 64, PhD(chem), 67. *Prof Exp:* Res assoc electrochem, Univ Ottawa, 67-69 & Colo State Univ, 69-71; res chemist semiconductors, Bell-Northern Res, 71-73. *Concurrent Pos:* Adj prof, Carlton Univ, Ottawa, 91-94. *Mem:* Int Asn Great Lakes Res; Can Asn Environ Analysis Labs; Int Soc Environmetrics. *Res:* Water chemistry; water treatment; fate and effects of toxic contaminants; analytical methods; quality assurance; hydraulics; environmental research; climate change; UV-B impacts; ecosystem health assessment. *Mailing Add:* Nat Water Res Inst PO Box 5050 Burlington ON L7R 4A6 Can. *Fax:* 905-336-4989

LAWRENCE, JOHN KEELER, GENERAL RELATIVITY, ASTROPHYSICS. *Current Pos:* asst prof, 73-76, assoc prof physics & astron, 76-80, PROF PHYSICS & ASTRON, CALIF STATE UNIV, 80-, DEPT CHMN PHYSICS & ASTRON, 76- *Personal Data:* b New York, NY, Oct 11, 40; m 67; c 1. *Educ:* Harvard Univ, AB, 62; Northeastern Univ, MS, 64, PhD(physics), 68. *Prof Exp:* Vis asst prof physics & astron, Univ Ga, 67-68; Univ asst physics, Univ Vienna, 68-71; vis res assoc, Northeastern Univ, 71-72; fel, Univ Windsor, 72-73. *Mem:* Am Phys Soc; AAAS; Austrian Phys Soc; Sigma Xi. *Res:* Deflection of null radiation by gravitational fields; cosmological models; cosmological coincidences; galactic structure; active galaxies and quasars. *Mailing Add:* 3380 Country Club Dr Glendale CA 91208

LAWRENCE, JOHN M, PHYSIOLOGY. *Current Pos:* from asst prof to assoc prof, 65-75, PROF DEPT BIOL, UNIV SFLA, 75- *Personal Data:* b Cape Girardeau, Mo, Oct 11, 37. *Educ:* Southeast Mo State Col, BS, 58; Univ Mo, AM, 60; Stanford Univ, PhD(biol), 66. *Prof Exp:* Instr physiol, Stanford Univ, 64-65. *Concurrent Pos:* Fel, Marine Biol Lab, Hebrew Univ Israel, 69-70. *Mem:* Am Soc Zool; Marine Biol Asn UK; Sigma Xi. *Res:* Nutritional and reproductive physiology of marine invertebrates. *Mailing Add:* Dept Biol Univ SFla 4202 Fowler Ave Tampa FL 33620-9951

LAWRENCE, JOHN MCCUNE, BIOCHEMISTRY. *Current Pos:* RETIRED. *Personal Data:* b Carmichaels, Pa, Feb 17, 16; m 38; c 3. *Educ:* Carnegie Inst Technol, BS, 37, MS, 39; Univ Pittsburgh, PhD(biochem), 43. *Prof Exp:* Res asst, Mellon Inst, 39-41; Nutrit Found fel, Dept Dairy Indust, Cornell Univ, 43-45, from instr to asst prof biochem, 45-48; assoc chemist, Wash State Univ, 48-58, agr chemist, 58-81. *Mem:* AAAS; Am Soc Plant Physiol; Sigma Xi. *Res:* Enzymes; proteins; amino acids; biochemistry of seed germination and nutritional quality of seeds. *Mailing Add:* 1225 NE Orchard Dr Pullman WA 99163

LAWRENCE, JOHN MEDLOCK, fisheries; deceased, see previous edition for last biography

LAWRENCE, JOSEPH D, JR, SYSTEMS DESIGN & SYSTEMS SCIENCE, SEMICONDUCTOR BURN-IN & TEST EQUIPMENT. *Current Pos:* RETIRED. *Personal Data:* b Anderson, SC, Nov 6, 24; m 49, Frances Bethel; c Susan E (Finklea), Virginia L (Butts) & Jane (Schenk). *Educ:* Va Polytech Inst, BS, 51. *Prof Exp:* Test engr, Gen Elec, 51-53; sr engr, Sperry Rand, 53-57, engr mgr, 60-66; prog engr, Burroughs, 57-60; engr/mgr, Tex Instruments, 66-70; mgr digital systs eng, Camco, 70-73; vpres, Datac Co, 73-77, pres, 77-78; mgr res & develop, Reliability Inc Tex, 78-82, vpres & dir technol, Reliability Inc, 82-87, pres, Reliability Japan Inc, 87-90, vpres, Reliability Inc, 87-93. *Res:* Pioneered development of burn-in and test equipment for semiconductor memories; designed computers; designed computerized traffic light control systems; granted 13 US Patents. *Mailing Add:* 115 Gershwin Houston TX 77079

LAWRENCE, KELECHI, BIOCHEMISTRY, INTEGRIN SIGNALLING. *Current Pos:* SR RES SCIENTIST, DUPONT MERCK PARM CO, 95- *Personal Data:* b Owerri, Jan 17, 59; US citizen. *Educ:* Southern Conn State Univ, BS, 84; Med Univ SC, PhD(pharmacol), 91. *Prof Exp:* Postdoctoral fel, Columbia Univ, 92-93, res assoc, 93-94. *Mem:* Am Heart Asn; Fedn Am Socs Exp Biol; NY Acad Sci; AAAS; Asn Res Vision & Ophthal; Asn Black Cardiologists. *Res:* Understnding the role of the integrin in angiogenesis; elaboration of angiogenic factors by retinal pigment epithelial cells; degenerative retinal diseases. *Mailing Add:* Cardio Dis Res DuPont Merck Pharm Co Box 80400 Exp Sta E4000/3237 Wilmington DE 19880. *Fax:* 302-695-8210; *E-Mail:* lawrenk@aol.com

LAWRENCE, KENT L(EE), MECHANICAL ENGINEERING, ENGINEERING MECHANICS. *Current Pos:* assoc prof, 61-62 & 64-77, PROF MECH ENG, UNIV TEX, ARLINGTON, 77-, ENG CONSULT, 65- *Personal Data:* b Beatrice, Nebr, Jan 23, 37; m 61, Carol A Burrow; c Doris R, Kent L Jr & Jamie C. *Educ:* Tex Tech Col, BS, 59, MS, 60; Ariz State Univ, PhD(eng mech), 65. *Prof Exp:* Instr mech, Univ Ill, 60-61. *Mem:* Am Soc Mech Engrs; Am Helicopter Soc. *Res:* Vibrations; dynamics; structural mechanics; finite element methods. *Mailing Add:* Univ Tex Arlington PO Box 19023 Arlington TX 76019-0001

LAWRENCE, KURT C, DIELECTRICS. *Current Pos:* AGR ENGR, AGR RES SERV, USDA, 85- *Personal Data:* b Decatur, Ga, July 9, 62; m 85; c 2. *Educ:* Univ Ga, BS, 85, MS, 87. *Mem:* Assoc mem Am Soc Agr Engrs. *Res:* Measurement of dielectric properties of agricultural products; determination of moisture content by dielectric properties measurements. *Mailing Add:* 1241 Fernwood Dr Watkinsville GA 30677

LAWRENCE, MERLE, PHYSIOLOGY OF HEARING. *Current Pos:* assoc prof physiol acoust, Med Sch, Univ Mich, Ann Arbor, 52-57, prof otolaryngol & psychol, 57-85, prof physiol, 59-65, res assoc, Inst Indust Health, 52-85, dir, Kresge Hearing Res Inst, 61-82, EMER PROF UNIV MICH, ANN ARBOR, 85- *Personal Data:* b Remsen, NY, Dec 26, 19; m 42, Roberta Harper; c Linda A, Roberta H (Henderson) & James B. *Educ:* Princeton Univ, AB, 38, MA, 40, PhD(psychol), 41. *Honors & Awards:* Gold Medal, Am Otol Soc; Award of Merit, Am Acad Opthalmol & Otolaryngol; Award of Merit, Asn Res Otolaryngol; Distinguished Lifetime Achievement Award, Am Acad Audiol. *Prof Exp:* Nat Res Coun fel, Johns Hopkins Univ, 41; from asst prof to assoc prof psychol, Princeton Univ, 46-52. *Concurrent Pos:* Consult, Surgeon Gen Off, 53- & Secy Defense, 55-58; mem, Commun Dis Res Training Comt, Nat Inst Neurol Dis & Stroke, 61-65 & Commun Sci Study Sect, NIH, 65-70, Communicative Dis Rev Comt, Nat Inst Neurol & Communicative Dis & Stroke, 72-76, Nat Adv Neurol & Commun Dis & Stroke Coun, 76-80. *Mem:* Fel Acoust Soc Am; Am Laryngol, Rhinol & Otol Soc; Am Otol Soc; Col Oto-Rhino-Laryngol Amicitiae Sacrum; Asn Res Otolaryngol; Soc Univ Otolaryngologist; Am Acad Otolaryngol; Walter P Work Soc. *Res:* Physiology of hearing; fluid circulation in inner ear; mechanics of middle ear as basis for middle ear surgery; analysis of acoustical distortion in inner; effects of noise on inner ear. *Mailing Add:* 1535 Shorelands Dr E Vero Beach FL 32963-2648. *E-Mail:* merlawrn@aol.com

LAWRENCE, PAUL J, BIOCHEMISTRY. *Current Pos:* VPRES, LITMUS CONCEPTS INC, 85- *Personal Data:* b Hazleton, Pa, Dec 18, 40; m 63; c 1. *Educ:* King's Col, Pa, BS, 62; Univ Wis-Madison, MS, 64, PhD(biochem), 67. *Prof Exp:* From asst prof to assoc prof biochem, Col Med, Univ Utah, 68-77; dir immunol res & develop, Smith Kline Instruments, 77-81, dir, diag res & develop, 79-85; pres, Lawrence Assay, Inc. *Concurrent Pos:* Fel biochem, Univ Wis, 67-68; NIH fel, 67-69. *Mem:* AAAS; Am Chem Soc; Fedn Am Socs Exp Biol; Am Soc Microbiol; NY Acad Sci. *Res:* Mechanisms of drug action; development of diagnostic tests. *Mailing Add:* Litmus Concepts Inc 2981 Copper Rd Santa Clara CA 96051-0701

LAWRENCE, PAULINE OLIVE, INSECT ENDOCRINOLOGY & BIOCHEMISTRY, HOST-PARASITE INTERACTIONS. *Current Pos:* grad res fel, Dept Entom, Univ Fla, Gainesville, 69-72, res asst, 72-75, from asst prof to assoc prof, 76-89, prof res & teaching, Dept Zool, 89-93, PROF, DEPT ENTOM & NEMATOL, UNIV FLA, 93- *Personal Data:* b Nov 10, 45; US citizen; m 76. *Educ:* Univ WI, Jamaica, BSc Hons, 68; Univ Fla, Gainesville, MS, 72, PhD(entom), 75. *Honors & Awards:* Career Advan Award Women, NSF, 88. *Prof Exp:* Asst entomologist res, Ministry Agr, Jamaica, WI, 68-69. *Concurrent Pos:* Prin investr, regulatory biol, NSF, 81-84, 85-88 & 90-; vis assoc prof, Dept Entom, Cornell Univ, 84-85; mem & chmn, Nat Res Coun & NSF Minority Grad Fel Eval Panel Biol Sci, Biochem, Biophys & Biomed Sci, 87-89; assoc, Danforth Found; USDA Competitive Grants rev panel; competitive res grants, entom & nematol, USDA, 87-90 & 90-93; McKnight Found fel, 86-87. *Mem:* AAAS; Am Soc Zoologists; Entom Soc Am; Sigma Xi; Tissue Cult Asn; Soc Invert Path; Int Soc Endocrinol. *Res:* Parasite biology and the influence of host hormones on parasite development; role of symbiotic virus in parasite-host interactions; biochemistry and molecular biology of symbiotic viruses in parasitic wasps. *Mailing Add:* Dept Entom & Nematol Univ Fla PO Box 110620 Gainesville FL 32611-0620. *Fax:* 904-392-0190; *E-Mail:* pol@gnv.ifas.ufl.edu

LAWRENCE, PHILIP LINWOOD, GEOPHYSICS, OIL SEARCH. *Current Pos:* staff adv, NY, 63-65, unit supvr, Geophys Serv Ctr, Tex, 66-68, corp geophysicist, 69-81, CONSULT, OIL EXPLORATION, MOBIL OIL CORP, 81- *Personal Data:* b New Bedford, Mass, Mar 27, 23; m 48; c 2. *Educ:* Colo Sch Mines, GeolE, 49, Southern Methodist Univ, MS, 60. *Prof Exp:* Res physicist, Magnolia Petrol Co, Tex, 49-62. *Concurrent Pos:* Lectr elec eng, Southern Methodist Univ, 60-62. *Mem:* Sigma Xi. *Res:* Seismic, magnetic, gravity data gathering, processing and interpretation techniques and development for mineral exploration. *Mailing Add:* 467 Harvest Glen Richardson TX 75081-5550

LAWRENCE, R(AYMOND) JEFFERY, SHOCK WAVE PHYSICS. *Current Pos:* MEM TECH STAFF SHOCK WAVE PHYSICS, SANDIA LABS, 67- *Personal Data:* b Cornwall, NY, Feb 25, 39; m 63, Jane M Whipple; c Janet B (Sanchez) & David J. *Educ:* Lawrence Col, BA, 61; Univ NMex, MS, 70. *Prof Exp:* Res physicist shock wave physics, Air Force Weapons Lab, Kirtland AFB, NMex, 63-67. *Concurrent Pos:* Prog mgr, Defense Nuclear Agency, 93-94. *Mem:* Am Phys Soc. *Res:* Shock wave physics; numerical wave propagation computer code development and application; constitutive model development; application of these fields to various dynamic phenomena; program management for interactions with former Soviet Union. *Mailing Add:* 1308 Kirby St NE Albuquerque NM 87112. *E-Mail:* rjlawre@sandia.gov

LAWRENCE, RICHARD AUBREY, biochemistry, nutrition, for more information see previous edition

LAWRENCE, ROBERT D, GEOLOGY, STRUCTURE & TECTONICS OF HIMALAYA. *Current Pos:* asst prof, 70-77, ASSOC PROF GEOL, ORE STATE UNIV, 77- *Personal Data:* b Ithaca, NY, May 24, 43; m 66; c 2. *Educ:* Earlham Col, BA, 65; Stanford Univ, PhD(geol), 68. *Prof Exp:* Asst prof geol, Earlham Col, 68-70. *Concurrent Pos:* Fulbright prof, Peshawar Univ, Pakistan, 81-82 & 86-87. *Mem:* Geol Soc Am; Geologischen Vereinigung; Am Geophys Union; Khyber Geol Soc. *Res:* Major faults of western North America; tectonics of Pakistan; tectonic history of Pacific Northwest. *Mailing Add:* Dept Geosci Ore State Univ 104 Wilkinson Hall Corvallis OR 97331-5506

LAWRENCE, ROBERT G, ZOOLOGY. *Current Pos:* RETIRED. *Personal Data:* b Wilmington, NY, Feb 14, 21; m 46, Irene E Willwerth; c Robert K & Barry B. *Educ:* Eastern Nazarene Col, AB, 44; Boston Univ, MA, 46; Okla State Univ, PhD, 64. *Hon Degrees:* LHD, Mt Vernon Col, 87. *Prof Exp:* Teacher, Henry Ford's Boys Sch, Mass, 45-46; prof biol & head dept, Bethany Nazarene Col, 47-68; assoc dean, Mid-Am Nazarene Col, 68-71; prof biol sci, 68-75, dir instnl res, 71-74, acad dean, 74-75; prof biol, Mt Vernon Nazarene Col, Ohio, 75-87, acad dean, 75-87, vpres acad affairs, 76-87. *Concurrent Pos:* Chmn div natural sci, Bethany Nazarene Col, 49-68; mem, Am Conf Acad Deans. *Mem:* Am Ornith Union; Nat Audubon Soc; Wilson Soc; Am Asn Higher Educ. *Res:* Ornithology; relation of weather factors to migration of water fowl. *Mailing Add:* 3501 S Stover St 4-75 Ft Collins CO 80525-2798

LAWRENCE, ROBERT MARSHALL, ANESTHESIOLOGY. *Current Pos:* from instr to assoc prof surg & med, 56-68, PROF ANESTHESIOL, SCH MED, UNIV ROCHESTER, 68- *Personal Data:* b Kennecott, Alaska, June 28, 23; m 50; c 9. *Educ:* Univ Rochester, MD, 49. *Prof Exp:* Resident surg, Strong Mem Hosp, 49-54, resident anesthesiol, 54-56. *Concurrent Pos:* Consult, Vet Admin Hosps, Batavia & Canandaigua, 56- *Mem:* Am Soc Anesthesiol; Am Asn Respiratory Ther. *Res:* Oxygen toxicity; respiratory therapy. *Mailing Add:* Univ Rochester Med Ctr Box 604 Rochester NY 14603-0604

LAWRENCE, ROBERT SWAN, INTERNAL MEDICINE, PREVENTIVE MEDICINE. *Current Pos:* PROF HEALTH POLICY & ASSOC DEAN, HOPKINS SCH PUB HEALTH, 95-, PROF MED, SCH MED, 96- *Personal Data:* b Philadelphia, Pa, Feb 6, 38; m 60, Cynthia Starr; c Job S, Matthew S, Hannah S, Jin S & Sang B. *Educ:* Harvard Univ, AB, 60; Harvard Med Sch, MD, 64. *Honors & Awards:* Spec Recognition Award, Am Col Prev Med, 88. *Prof Exp:* Intern & jr resident, Mass Gen Hosp, 64-66; asst surgeon epidemiol, Epidemic Intel Serv, Ctr Dis Control, USPHS, 66-69; sr resident, Mass Gen Hosp, 69-70; from asst prof med to assoc prof, Sch Med, Univ NC, 70-74; from asst prof to assoc prof med, Harvard Med Sch, 74-91, dir, Div Primary Care, 74-91; dir, Health Sci Div, Rockefeller Found, 91-95. *Concurrent Pos:* Chief, Dept Med, Cambridge Hosp, 80-91; chmn bd, Prev Med Div, Inst Med-Nat Acad Sci, 84, chmn, US Prev Serv Task, Dept Health & Human Serv, 84-89; ed, Am J Prev Med, 90-92; adj prof, Sch Med, NY Univ, 92- *Mem:* Inst Med-Nat Acad Sci; fel Am Col Physicians; Soc Res & Educ Primary Care Internal Med (pres, 78-79); Soc Teachers Prev Med; Am Col Prev Med; Am Pub Health Asn. *Res:* Health beliefs of patients; medical sociology; primary care education; manpower issues; public health; author of various publications. *Mailing Add:* Johns Hopkins Sch Pub Health 615 N Wolfe St Baltimore MD 21205

LAWRENCE, SIGMUND J(OSEPH), CHEMICAL ENGINEERING. *Current Pos:* CONSULT ENGR, 91- *Personal Data:* b Chicago, Ill, May 20, 18; div; c Clifford, Keith, Clandia, Karen, Joan & Mary. *Educ:* Ill Inst Technol, BS, 39; Univ Iowa, MS, 42, PhD(chem eng), 43. *Prof Exp:* Apprentice engr, Caterpillar Tractor Co, Ill, 39-40; res chem engr, Armour Res Found, Ill Inst Technol, 40-41; chem engr, Shell Develop Co, Calif, 43-46; chem engr, Gen Elec Co, Wash, 46-48, res assoc, Knolls Atomic Power Lab, 48-51, Res Lab, 51-52, process engr, Chem Div, Silicone Prods Dept, 52-57, chem engr, Gen Eng Lab, 57-59, appln engr, Process Comput Control, Syst Sales & Eng, 60-67, appln engr spec sensors, Instrument Dept, 67, mgr sensor progs, 67-69, consult engr indust process systs, Reentry & Environ Systs Div, 69-73; supv eng design chem plants, Catalytic Inc/United Engrs & Constructors, Philadelphia, 74-91. *Mem:* Am Chem Soc; Am Inst Chem Eng. *Res:* Process instrumentation, automation and control; computer monitoring and control; air, water and waste monitoring; pollution control; instrument development and design; process analysis and design; process design of chemical equipment. *Mailing Add:* 100 Linda Lane Media PA 19063

LAWRENCE, VINNEDGE MOORE, ENTOMOLOGY, ECOLOGY. *Current Pos:* from asst prof to assoc prof, 68-86, PROF BIOL, WASHINGTON & JEFFERSON COL, 86- *Personal Data:* b Bangor, Maine, Feb 19, 40; m 66, Betty J Heinly; c Malinda (Robbin). *Educ:* Miami Univ Ohio, BS, 62, MA, 64; Purdue Univ, PhD(entom), 68. *Prof Exp:* Instr biol, Xavier Univ Ohio, 64-65. *Concurrent Pos:* Vis prof entom, Rice Creek Biol Field Sta, State Univ Col, Oswego, NY, 69, zool, 70; mem citizen's adv coun, Pa Dept Environ Resources, 71-81. *Mem:* AAAS; Am Inst Biol Sci; Sigma Xi; Asn Biol Lab Educ; Soc Conserv Biol. *Res:* Population dynamics of Odonata naiads in farm-pond ecosystems; distribution of Odonata in Pennsylvania; microdistribution of capniid Plecoptera; breeding behavior of Henslow's sparrow. *Mailing Add:* Dept Biol Washington & Jefferson Col Washington PA 15301-4801. *Fax:* 412-223-5271; *E-Mail:* vlawrence@washjeff.edu

LAWRENCE, WALTER, JR, SURGERY. *Current Pos:* chmn div surg oncol, Med Col Va, 66-90, Am Cancer Soc prof clin oncol, 72-77, dir, Massey Cancer Ctr, 74-88, PROF SURG, MED COL VA, 66-, EMER DIR, 88- *Personal Data:* b Chicago, Ill, May 31, 25; m 47, Susan Shryock; c W Thomas, Elizabeth, W Amos & Edward G. *Educ:* Univ Chicago, PhB, 45, SB, 46, MD, 48. *Honors & Awards:* Sloan Award Cancer Res, 64; Horsley Award, 73; Distinguished Serv Award, Univ Chicago, 76. *Prof Exp:* Intern surg, Johns Hopkins Hosp, 48-49, asst resident & asst, Sch Med, Johns Hopkins Univ, 49-50, Halsted fel, Johns Hopkins Hosp, 50; resident, Mem Ctr Cancer & Allied Dis, 51-52 & 54-56; res fel exp surg, Mem Ctr Cancer & Allied Sci, 56; instr surg, Med Col, Cornell Univ, 57-58, asst prof, 58-63, clin assoc prof, 63-66. *Concurrent Pos:* Asst mem, Sloan-Kettering Inst Cancer Res, 57-60, assoc mem & assoc chief div exp surg, 60-66; clin asst attend surgeon, Mem Hosp, 57-59, asst attend surgeon, 59-62, assoc vis surgeon, 62-; asst vis surgeon, James Ewing Hosp, 57-62, assoc vis surgeon, 62-66; mem surg staff, NY Hosp, 57-66. *Mem:* Halsted Soc (pres, 75); fel Am Col Surg; Am Surg Asn; Soc Surg Oncol (pres, 80); Soc Univ Surgeons; Soc Head & Neck Surgeons; Am Cancer Soc (pres, 92). *Res:* Surgery, particularly cancer and clinical cancer research. *Mailing Add:* Box 980011 Dept Surg Med Col Va Richmond VA 23298. *Fax:* 804-828-4808

LAWRENCE, WALTER EDWARD, THEORETICAL SOLID STATE PHYSICS. *Current Pos:* asst prof, 71-77, ASSOC PROF PHYSICS, DARTMOUTH COL, 77- *Personal Data:* b Albany, NY, May 22, 42; m 69. *Educ:* Carnegie Inst Technol, BS, 64; Cornell Univ, PhD(physics), 70. *Prof Exp:* Res assoc physics, Stanford Univ, 69-71. *Mem:* Am Phys Soc. *Res:* Solid state theory, principally superconductivity; transport theory of metals. *Mailing Add:* Dept Physics Dartmouth Col 6127 Wilder Lab Hanover NH 03755. *Fax:* 603-646-1446

LAWRENCE, WILLARD EARL, STATISTICS. *Current Pos:* From instr to assoc prof, Marquette Univ, 53-69, asst chmn dept, 58-63, prof, 69-87, chmn dept math & statist, 73-79, EMER PROF MATH & STATIST, MARQUETTE UNIV, 87- *Personal Data:* b Chassell, Mich, Apr 8, 17; m 43; c 5. *Educ:* Marquette Univ, BS, 51, MS, 53; Univ Wis, MS, 62, PhD(statist), 64. *Concurrent Pos:* Consult, NSF, 66-69; statistician, Oak Ridge Nat Lab, 79-80. *Mem:* Math Asn Am. *Res:* Experimental design; response surface designs which minimize variance and bias errors; designs for mixtures; probability. *Mailing Add:* 13865 Adelaide Lane Brookfield WI 53005

LAWRENCE, WILLIAM CHASE, VIROLOGY, MOLECULAR BIOLOGY. *Current Pos:* From asst prof to assoc prof, 65-82, PROF MICROBIOL, UNIV PA, 82- *Personal Data:* b Cambridge, Mass, July 10, 34; m 55; c 3. *Educ:* Univ Mass, BS, 55; Univ Pa, VMD, 59, PhD(microbiol), 66. *Concurrent Pos:* USPHS res grant, 67-74; USDA Res Grant, 75- *Mem:* AAAS; Am Vet Med Asn; Am Soc Microbiol; NY Acad Sci; Sigma Xi; Am Soc Virol. *Res:* Molecular virology; vaccine development. *Mailing Add:* Dept Pathobiol Sch Vet Med Univ Pa 3800 Spruce St Philadelphia PA 19104

LAWRENCE, WILLIAM HOMER, TOXICOLOGY, PHARMACOLOGY. *Current Pos:* RETIRED. *Personal Data:* b Magnet Cove, Ark, Mar 20, 28; div; c 4. *Educ:* Col Ozarks, BS, 50; Univ Md, MS, 52, PhD(pharmacol), 55. *Prof Exp:* Instr materia medica, Sch Nursing, Univ Md, 51, asst pharmacol, Sch Pharm, 51-54; from asst prof to assoc prof pharmacol & physiol, Col Pharm, Univ Houston, 56-66; from assoc prof to prof toxicol, Univ Tenn Health Sci Ctr, 66-83, asst dir, Mat Sci Toxicol Labs, 67-75, head, Animal Toxicol Sect, 67-85, assoc dir, Mat Sci Toxicol Labs, 75-85, actg chmn, Dept Drug & Mat Toxicol, 81-83, prof med chem, 83-97, vchmn, 90-97. *Concurrent Pos:* Vis scientist, Univ Tex, 63, consult, Drug-Plastic Res & Toxicol Labs, 63-68, vis scientist, Dept Pharmacol & Toxicol, Med Br at Galveston, 65, lectr, 64-67; vis scientist, Dept Pharmacol & Toxicol, Univ Tex Med Br, Galveston, 65; consult, Vet Admin Hosp, Houston, 64-66 & Memphis, 67-72; mem, Gen Toxicity & Screening Task Force, Int Dent Fedn; adv, Neurostimulation Subcomt, Am Asn Med Implants, 74-78; mem ed bd, J Toxicol Environ Heath, 78-, J Pharmacol Sci, 82-88; dipl, Acad Toxicol Sci, 84-, fel, 89. *Mem:* Soc Toxicol; Am Pharmaceut Asn; Sigma Xi. *Res:* Toxicity of biomaterials and medical devices, especially dental materials, blood bags, intravenous administration tubings, extracorporeal devices, implantable devices and carcinogenic studies of plastics; in vivo activity and toxicity of some novel inhibitors of platelet aggregation. *Mailing Add:* 3341 Joslyn Memphis TN 38128

LAWRENCE, WILLIAM MASON, FISHERIES, NATURAL RESOURCES. *Current Pos:* RETIRED. *Personal Data:* b Brooktondale, NY, Oct 2, 18; m 42, Jane Ridgway; c John & Janet (Kearns). *Educ:* Cornell Univ, BS, 38, PhD(fishery biol), 41. *Honors & Awards:* Seth Gordon Award, Int Asn Fish & Wildlife, 76. *Prof Exp:* Biometrician bur game, NY State Conserv Dept, 41-42, sr aquatic biologist, 46-52, chief bur fish, 52-55, dir fish & game, 55-58, asst comnr, 58-64, dep comnr, NY State Dept Environ Conserv, 64-74; consult, 74-85. *Concurrent Pos:* US comnr, Great Lakes Fishery Comn, 65-88; chmn, Atlantic States Marine Fisheries Comn, 71-73. *Mem:* Am Fisheries Soc (pres, 59); Int Asn Fish & Wildlife Agencies (pres, 69). *Res:* Fish and wildlife conservation; water resources. *Mailing Add:* 991 White Church Rd Brooktondale NY 14817

LAWRENZ, FRANCES PATRICIA, EVALUATION, IN-SERVICE TEACHER TRAINING. *Current Pos:* ASST PROF SCI EDUC, ARIZ STATE UNIV, 81- *Personal Data:* b Milwaukee, Wis, Nov 6, 47; c 1. *Educ:* Univ Minn, Minneapolis, BS, 68, MA, 71, PhD(educ, chem & math), 74. *Prof Exp:* Vol, Peace Corps, Ankara, Turkey, 69-70; asst prof chem, St Mary's Jr Col, 71-74; sci consult, Nat Assessment Ed Prog, 74-75; asst prof sci & phys sci educ, State Univ NY, Buffalo, 75-77; proj mgr, NSF, 77-78; consult adult educ, Govt Yukon, 78-79; evaluator health, Area Health Educ Ctr, 79-80. *Concurrent Pos:* Surv researcher, Ariz Dept Energy, 82-83; eval consult, YMCA, 82-, Native Am Sci Educ Asn, 84-, Med Sch, Univ Ariz, 84-, Northern Ariz Univ, 85-; ed, Ariz Health Educ Newsletter & assoc ed, Sch Sci & Math, 83- *Mem:* Am Educ Res Asn; Nat Asn Res Sci Teaching; Asn Educ Teachers Sci; Sch Sci & Math Asn; Eval Network; Am Sch Health Asn. *Res:* Evaluation of in-service teacher training programs in physical science and health, improvement of the quality of training and determination of what variables affect outcomes. *Mailing Add:* 4711 Folwell Dr Minneapolis MN 55406

LAWREY, JAMES DONALD, LICHENOLOGY. *Current Pos:* ASSOC PROF BIOL, GEORGE MASON UNIV, 77- *Personal Data:* b Arlington, Va, Dec 15, 49. *Educ:* Wake Forest Univ, BS, 71; Univ SDak, MA, 73; Ohio State Univ, PhD(bot), 77. *Mem:* Am Bryol & Lichenological Soc; Ecol Soc Am; Brit Lichen Soc; Mycol Soc Am; Bot Soc Am. *Res:* Population and community ecology of lichens; ecological significance of lichen secondary compounds; use of lichens as biological indicators of atmospheric pollution. *Mailing Add:* Biol Dept George Mason Univ 4400 University Dr Fairfax VA 22030-4443

LAWRIE, DUNCAN H, COMPUTER SCIENCE, COMPUTER ENGINEERING. *Current Pos:* Sr res programmer, Univ Ill, Urbana-Champaign, 70-73, vis res asst prof, 73-74, from asst prof to assoc prof, 74-84, PROF COMPUT SCI, UNIV ILL, URBANA-CHAMPAIGN, 84-, HEAD, DEPT COMPUT SCI, 90- *Personal Data:* b Chicago, Ill, Apr 26, 43. *Educ:* DePauw Univ, BA, 66; Purdue Univ, BSEE, 66; Univ Ill, MS, 69, PhD(comput sci), 73. *Mem:* Fel Inst Elec & Electronics Engrs; Asn Comput Mach; Inst Elec & Electronics Engrs Comput Soc (pres, 91). *Res:* Computer system organization; especially very large systems; memory hierarchies. *Mailing Add:* Dept Comput Sci Univ Ill 1304 W Springfield Ave Urbana IL 61801

LAWROSKI, HARRY, CHEMICAL & NUCLEAR ENGINEERING. *Current Pos:* CONSULT, 79-; PRES H LAWROSKI & ASSOC. *Personal Data:* b Dalton, Pa, Oct 10, 28; m 62, Mary A Dewoody. *Educ:* Pa State Univ, BS, 50, MS, 56, PhD(chem eng), 59. *Prof Exp:* Asst, Pa State Univ, 50-56, instr petrol refining, 56-58; assoc chem engr, Idaho Div, Argonne Nat Lab, 58-63, tech mgr, Zero Power Plutonium Reactor, 63-68, supt, EBR II Opers, 68-73; gen mgr environ, Nuclear Serv Corp, 73-76; asst gen mgr, Idaho Chem Progs, Allied Chem Corp, 76-79. *Concurrent Pos:* Instr, Nat Reactor Testing Sta, Univ Idaho, 59-; chmn, Nuclear Div, Am Inst Chem Engrs, 67-68. *Mem:* Fel Am Nuclear Soc (treas, 71-77, vpres, 79-80, pres, 80-81); fel Am Inst Chem Engrs. *Res:* Reactor engineering; petroleum refining. *Mailing Add:* 5135 W Shoshone Dr Wilson WY 83014

LAWROSKI, STEPHEN, NUCLEAR ENGINEERING. *Current Pos:* RETIRED. *Personal Data:* b Scranton, Pa, Jan 17, 14; m 47; c 2. *Educ:* Pa State Univ, BS, 34, MS, 39, PhD(chem eng), 43. *Honors & Awards:* Robert E Wilson Award, 71. *Prof Exp:* From asst to supvr res & develop, Petrol Refining Lab, Pa, 34-43; res chem engr, Stand Oil Develop Co, NJ, 43-44, asst sect chief, 46; group leader, Manhattan Proj, Math Lab, Univ Chicago, 44-46; adv prof trainee, Clinton Lab, Oak Ridge, Tenn, 46-47; dir, Chem Eng Div, Argonne Nat Lab, 47-63, assoc lab dir, 63-70, sr engr, 70-80. *Concurrent Pos:* Consult, US Army Chem Corps, 60-66; mem, Gen Adv Comt, US AEC, 64-70; mem, Adv Comt Reactor Safeguards, US Nuclear Regulatory Comn, 74-81. *Mem:* Nat Acad Eng; AAAS; Am Chem Soc; fel Am Nuclear Soc; Am Inst Chem Engrs. *Res:* Petroleum technology; separations processes in atomic energy field; composition and utilization of several typical hydrocarbon naphthas; nuclear technology. *Mailing Add:* 1700 Robin Lane Apt 345 Lisle IL 60532

LAWS, EDWARD ALLEN, OCEANOGRAPHY. *Current Pos:* asst prof, 74-80, ASSOC PROF OCEANOG, UNIV HAWAII, 80- *Personal Data:* b Columbus, Ohio, Feb 4, 45. *Educ:* Harvard Univ, BA, 67, PhD(chem physics), 71. *Prof Exp:* Instr oceanog, Fla State Univ, 71-74. *Mem:* AAAS; Am Soc Limnol & Oceanog; Ecol Soc Am; Phycol Soc Am. *Res:* Metabolism of carbon and nitrogen by marine phytoplankton; importance of conditioning in regulating growth characteristics and metabolism; response of phytoplankton communities to nutrient enrichments. *Mailing Add:* Dept Oceanog Univ Hawaii Manoa 1000 Pope Rd Honolulu HI 96822-2336

LAWS, EDWARD RAYMOND, JR, NEUROSURGERY. *Current Pos:* PROF NEUROSURG & MED, UNIV VA, CHARLOTTESVILLE, 92- *Personal Data:* b New York, NY, Apr 29, 38; m 62, Margaret Anderson; c Elizabeth, Margaret, Victoria & Eleanor. *Educ:* Princeton Univ, AB, 59; Johns Hopkins Univ, MD, 63. *Prof Exp:* Intern, Johns Hopkins Hosp, 63-64; asst chief toxicol, Commun Dis Ctr, USPHS, Ga, 64-66; asst prof neurol surg & neurol surgeon, Johns Hopkins Hosp, 66-72; from assoc prof to prof neurol surg, Mayo Med Sch, Mayo Clin, 72-87, neurol surgeon, 72-87; prof & chmn, Med Ctr, George Wash Univ, 87-92. *Concurrent Pos:* USPHS res grants, 60-62; Henry Strong Denison fel, 62-63; fel surg, Johns Hopkins Univ, 63-64. *Mem:* Sigma Xi; Am Acad Neurol Surg; Am Col Surgeons; Child Neurol Soc. *Res:* Neurooncology; pituitary surgery; epilepsy surgery. *Mailing Add:* Univ Va Health Sci Ctr PO Box 212 Charlottesville VA 22908

LAWS, KENNETH LEE, METEOROLOGY, ELECTRONICS. *Current Pos:* from asst prof to assoc prof, 62-78, from asst dean to assoc dean, 71-77, PROF PHYSICS, DICKINSON COL, 78- *Personal Data:* b Pasadena, Calif, May 30, 35; m 65, Priscilla Watson; c Kevin A & Virginia. *Educ:* Calif Inst Technol, BS, 56; Univ Pa, MS, 59; Bryn Mawr Col, PhD(physics), 62. *Prof Exp:* Instr physics, Hobart & William Smith Cols, 58-59. *Mem:* Am Asn Physics Teachers; Am Meteorol Soc; Sigma Xi. *Res:* Biomechanics; physics of dance. *Mailing Add:* Dickinson Col Carlisle PA 17013-2896. *E-Mail:* laws@dickinson.edu

LAWS, LEONARD STEWART, MATHEMATICS. *Current Pos:* dean & registr, 53-55, chmn, Natural Sci Div, 55-74, PROF MATH, SOUTHWESTERN COL, KANS, 55- *Personal Data:* b Pocasset, Okla, Dec 29, 17; m 43; c 4. *Educ:* Willamette Univ, AB, 39; Stanford Univ, MA, 41; Mich State Univ, EdD, 53. *Prof Exp:* Asst math, Stanford Univ, 39-41; asst math & mech, Univ Minn, 41-42, from instr to asst prof, 42-52. *Concurrent Pos:* Asst, Mich State Univ, 47 & 53; NSF fel, Stanford Univ, 61-62; mgt consult, 64- *Mem:* Am Soc Qual Control; Am Statist Asn. *Res:* Industrial reliability; design of experiments. *Mailing Add:* 311 Houston St Winfield KS 67156

LAWS, PRISCILLA WATSON, NUCLEAR STRUCTURE, HEALTH PHYSICS. *Current Pos:* from asst prof to assoc prof, 65-79, PROF PHYSICS, DICKSON COL, 79- *Personal Data:* b New York, NY, Jan 18, 40; m 65, Kenneth L; c Kevin & Virginia. *Educ:* Reed Col, BA, 61; Bryn Mawr Col, MA, 63, PhD(physics), 66. *Honors & Awards:* Dana Award, Pioneering Achievement Educ, 93; Milliken Award, Am Asn Physics Teachers, 96. *Prof Exp:* Asst physics, Bryn Mawr Col, 61-63; sr tech aide, Bell Labs, 62. *Concurrent Pos:* Mem med radiation adv comt, Bur Radiation Health, Food & Drug Admin, HEW, 74-78; consult, Off Technol Assessment, US Cong. *Mem:* Am Asn Physics Teachers. *Res:* Nuclear beta decay; environmental radiation; effects of medical x-rays, energy and environment; development of activity-based curriculum materials entered by computer-based research tools for high school and college students. *Mailing Add:* Dept Physics & Astron Dickinson Col Carlisle PA 17013

LAWSON, ANDREW COWPER, II, PHYSICS. *Current Pos:* STAFF MEM, PHYS METALLURGY GROUP, LOS ALAMOS NAT LAB, 83- *Personal Data:* b Chicago, Ill, Oct 21, 46. *Educ:* Pomona Col, BA, 67; Univ Calif, San Diego, MS, 69, PhD(physics), 72. *Prof Exp:* Asst res physicist, Inst Pure & Appl Physics, Univ Calif, San Diego, 72-77; asst prof physics, Pomona Col, 77-82; assoc prof, Mech Engr, Calif State Univ, Long Beach, 82-83. *Mem:* AAAS; Am Phys Soc; Am Asn Physics Teachers; Am Crystallog Asn. *Res:* Superconductivity in relation to crystal structure; behavior of the electrical resistance of metals; occurance of crystallographic transformations at low temperatures; applications of neutron scattering to materials science. *Mailing Add:* 300 Aragon Ave Los Alamos NM 87544. *Fax:* 505-665-2676

LAWSON, ANTON ERIC, SCIENCE EDUCATION. *Current Pos:* asst prof, 77-80, ASSOC PROF SCI EDUC, ARIZ STATE UNIV, 80- *Personal Data:* b Lansing, Mich, Oct 24, 45; m 68; c 3. *Educ:* Univ Ariz, BS, 67; Univ Ore, MS, 69; Univ Okla, PhD(sci educ), 73. *Honors & Awards:* Res in Sci Teaching Award, Nat Asn for Res in Sci Teaching, 76. *Prof Exp:* Teacher math & sci, Ralston Intermediate Sch, Belmont, Calif, 69-71; instr sci educ, Univ Okla, 72-73; res assoc biol educ, Purdue Univ, 73-74; res educr, Univ Calif, Berkeley, 74-77. *Mem:* Nat Asn Res Sci Teaching; Asn Educ Teachers Sci; Sch Sci & Math Asn; Nat Asn Biol Teaching; AAAS. *Res:* Development of formal reasoning; psychology of teaching science and mathematics. *Mailing Add:* 9227 S Juniper St Tempe AZ 85284

LAWSON, BENJAMIN F, oral medicine, periodontology, for more information see previous edition

LAWSON, CHARLES ALDEN, ROCK MAGNETISM, EXPERIMENTAL PETROLOGY. *Current Pos:* SPEC ASST SCI & TECHNOL, US DEPT STATE, 92- *Personal Data:* b Philadelphia, Pa, May 2, 51. *Educ:* Univ Calif, Santa Cruz, BS, 73; Princeton Univ, MA, 76, PhD(geol), 81. *Prof Exp:* Geologist, Bechtel Corp, 73-74; res fel, Geophys Lab, Carnegie Inst Washington, 77-79, Princeton Univ, 81-82 & NASA-Johnson Space Ctr, 82-84; geologist, US Geol Surv, 84-87; prog officer, US Dept State, 87-89; sci attache, US Embassy, Tel Aviv, 89-92. *Concurrent Pos:* Rock magnetism working group comt, Int Asn Geomagnetism & Aeronomy, 83-87; Tellers Comt, Mineral Soc Am, 85-86. *Mem:* Am Geophys Union; Sigma Xi. *Res:* Chemical and physical properties of iron-titanium oxides; correlation of microstructures and magnetic properties of ilmenite-hematite minerals; scanning and transmission electron microscopy of geologic materials; international multilateral negotiations; middle east water resources and environmental issues. *Mailing Add:* NEA/PPR Rm 5256 US Dept State Washington DC 20520. *Fax:* 202-647-7837

LAWSON, CHARLES L, MATHEMATICS. *Current Pos:* SUPVR APPL MATH GROUP, JET PROPULSION LAB, CALIF TECH INST, 60- *Personal Data:* b Idaho, 31. *Educ:* Univ Calif Berkeley, BS, 52; UCLA, PhD(math), 61. *Mem:* Asn Comput Mach; Soc Indust & Appl Math; Math Asn Am. *Res:* Algorithms in numerical linear algebra; development of mathematical software. *Mailing Add:* 1340 Marianna Rd Appl Math Group Jet Propulsion Lab Pasadena CA 91105-2747

LAWSON, DANIEL DAVID, ORGANIC CHEMISTRY, POLYMER CHEMISTRY. *Current Pos:* RETIRED. *Personal Data:* b Tucson, Ariz, Jan 13, 29; m 57, Margaret Schaeffer; c David D & Monica A. *Educ:* Univ Southern Calif, BS, 57, MS, 59. *Prof Exp:* Biomed res fel, Charles Cook Hastings Found, 59-61; res polymer scientist, Polymer Res Sect, Jet Propulsion Lab, Calif Inst Technol, 61-71, mem tech staff, 71- *Mem:* AAAS; Am Chem Soc; Royal Soc Chem; fel Am Acad Forensic Sci; Brit Soc Chem Indust. *Res:* Physical organic chemistry of polymers; synthesis of new biomaterials; use of thermoluminescence as applied to criminalistics; high energy batteries. *Mailing Add:* Calif Inst Technol Jet Propulsion Lab 919 S Golden W Arcadia CA 91007-6567

LAWSON, DAVID EDWARD, SEDIMENTOLOGY. *Current Pos:* lectr, 66-68, asst prof, 68-76, ASSOC PROF SEDIMENTOLOGY, UNIV WATERLOO, 76- *Personal Data:* b Moncton, NB, Sept 17, 39; m 67. *Educ:* Univ NB, BSc, 60, MSc, 62; Univ Reading, PhD(geol), 71. *Prof Exp:* Res geologist, Sedimentology Res Lab, Univ Reading, 62-66. *Mem:* Int Asn Sedimentology; Soc Econ Paleontologists & Mineralogists; fel Geol Asn Can. *Res:* Environmental fluvial sedimentology; nearshore sedimentation; primary sedimentary structures; volcanic sediments; continental shelf sedimentation; Torridonian sediments of northwest Scotland. *Mailing Add:* Dept Earth Sci Univ Waterloo Waterloo ON N2L 3G1 Can

LAWSON, DAVID FRANCIS, POLYMER ORGANIC CHEMISTRY, FLAMMABILITY & SMOKE GENERATION OF POLYMERS, POLYMERIZATION. *Current Pos:* sr res scientist, Cent Res Labs, 75-81, assoc scientist, 82-94, SECT MGR, POLYMER SYNTHESIS, BRIDGESTONE/FIRESTONE RES, INC, 94- *Personal Data:* b Chicago, Ill, June 24, 45; m 85, Nel; c Amy, David & Erin. *Educ:* Lewis Univ, BA, 67; Iowa State Univ, PhD(org chem), 71. *Prof Exp:* Instr chem, Iowa State Univ, 68-69; res scientist, 70-75. *Concurrent Pos:* Vis scholar, Ohio Acad Sci, 90-93. *Mem:* Am Chem Soc; Adhesion Soc; Sigma Xi. *Res:* Organic polymer chemistry; anionic polymerization; combustion, smoke, and flammability of polymers; synthetic and physical organic chemistry; elastomer synthesis; engineering thermoplastics; adhesives; polymer surface chemistry and adhesion; organolithium chemistry. *Mailing Add:* 11621 Garden Lane NW Uniontown OH 44685

LAWSON, DAVID MICHAEL, REPRODUCTIVE ENDOCRINOLOGY, LACTATION. *Current Pos:* res assoc, 71-73, asst prof, 73-79, ASSOC PROF PHYSIOL, SCH MED, WAYNE STATE UNIV, 79- *Personal Data:* b Denver, Colo, Nov 13, 43; m 66; c 3. *Educ:* Va Polytech Inst, BS, 65, MS, 67; Cornell Univ, PhD(physiol), 70. *Prof Exp:* NIH trainee physiol, Cornell Univ, 71. *Mem:* Endocrine Soc; Soc Exp Biol & Med. *Res:* Control of prolactin secretion; molecular nature of prolactin form synthesis through release; endocrine control of mammary gland function. *Mailing Add:* Dept Physiol Wayne State Univ Sch Med 540 E Canfield Detroit MI 48201

LAWSON, DEWEY TULL, ACOUSTICS. *Current Pos:* SR SCIENTIST, RES TRIANGLE INST, 79- *Personal Data:* b Kinston, NC, Feb 6, 44; m 66; Elizabeth Booker; c Jonathan D & Neal B. *Educ:* Harvard Univ, AB, 66; Duke Univ, PhD(physics), 72. *Prof Exp:* Res assoc physics, Lab Atomic & Solid State Physics, Cornell Univ, 72-74; asst prof physics, Duke Univ, 74-79. *Concurrent Pos:* Consult archit & environ acoust & adj prof physics, Duke Univ, 80-, adj prof otolaryngol, 92- *Mem:* Am Phys Soc; Am Asn Physics Teachers; Sigma Xi. *Res:* Signal processing and electrical stimulation for implanted auditory prostheses, musical acoustics, hearing. *Mailing Add:* PO Box 12194 Res Triangle Inst Research Triangle Park NC 27709. *E-Mail:* dtl@tri.org

LAWSON, EDWARD EARLE, PEDIATRICS, NEONATOLOGY. *Current Pos:* from asst prof to assoc prof, Univ NC, Chapel Hill, 78-86, dir, Div Neonatal/Perinatal Med, 88-95, interim chair, Dept Pediat, 93-95, VCHAIR, UNIV NC, CHAPEL HILL, 95- *Personal Data:* b Winston-Salem, NC, Aug 6, 46; m 69, Rebecca Fitts; c Katherine (Tabol) & Robert Barrett. *Educ:* Harvard Univ, BA, 68; Sch Med, Northwestern Univ, MD, 72. *Prof Exp:* Residency pediat, Children's Hosp, Boston, 72-75; fel neonatology, Harvard Med Sch, 75-78, instr pediat, 77-78. *Concurrent Pos:* E L Trudeau fel, Am Lung Asn, 78-81; prin investr, NIH res grants, 79-; attend pediatrician, NC Mem Hosp, 78-; res career develop award, NIH, 82-87; Alexander von Humboldt res fel, WGer, 85-86. *Mem:* Am Thoracic Soc; Soc Pediat Res; Am Physiol Soc; Am Acad Pediat; Am Pediat Soc; Perinatal Res Soc. *Res:* Neural mechanisms of central respiratory control, particularly in newborns. *Mailing Add:* Dept Pediat Univ NC CB-7220 Burnett-Womack Bldg Chapel Hill NC 27599-7220. *Fax:* 919-966-7299

LAWSON, FRED AVERY, entomology; deceased, see previous edition for last biography

LAWSON, HERBERT BLAINE, JR, MATHEMATICS. *Current Pos:* prof, 80-93, DISTINGUISHED PROF MATH, STATE UNIV NY, STONY BROOK, 93- *Personal Data:* b Norristown, Pa, Jan 4, 42; m 64; c 2. *Educ:* Brown Univ, ScB & AB, 64; Stanford Univ, PhD(math), 68. *Honors & Awards:* Steele Prize, Am Math Soc, 75. *Prof Exp:* Lectr math, Univ Calif, Berkeley, 68-70; vis prof, Inst Pure & Appl Math, Rio de Janeiro, Brazil, 70-71; from assoc prof to prof, Univ Calif, Berkeley, 71-80. *Concurrent Pos:* Sloan Found fel, Univ Calif, Berkeley, 70-72; mem, Inst Advan Study, Princeton, 72-73 & IHES, Bures-sur-Yvette, France, 77-78; Guggenheim fel, 83, Sloan fel & JSPS fel, Kyoto Univ, Japan, 86; vis prof, Ecole Polytech, France, 83-84, Tata Inst Fundamental Res, Bombay, India, 87; mem, Coun Am Math Soc, 86-, Nat Comt Math. *Mem:* Nat Acad Sci; Am Math Soc (vpres, 97). *Res:* Minimal surfaces; Riemannian geometry; foliations; several complex variables; mathematical physics; algebraic geometry. *Mailing Add:* Dept Math State Univ NY Stony Brook NY 11794

LAWSON, JAMES EVERETT, ZOOLOGY. *Current Pos:* RETIRED. *Personal Data:* b Derby, Va, Jan 8, 33; m 60; c 2. *Educ:* ETenn State Univ, BS, 58, MA, 59; Va Polytech Inst, PhD(zool), 67. *Prof Exp:* Instr biol, ETenn State Univ, 59-61; instr, Va Polytech Inst, 61-62; from assoc prof to prof, ETenn State Univ, 64-94. *Concurrent Pos:* Dir, Off Preprofessional Advert. *Res:* Ecology and systematics of pseudoscorpions. *Mailing Add:* 1513 Chickees St Johnson City TN 37614-0250

LAWSON, JAMES W, anti-rhythmic drugs, for more information see previous edition

LAWSON, JIMMIE DON, TOPOLOGICAL ALGEBRA. *Current Pos:* from asst prof to assoc prof, 68-75, chmn, 90-92, PROF MATH, LA STATE UNIV, BATON ROUGE, 76- *Personal Data:* b Waukegan, Ill, Dec 6, 42; m 64, Laura Miller; c Michal & John K. *Educ:* Harding Col, BS, 64; Univ Tenn, PhD(math), 67. *Prof Exp:* Asst prof math, Univ Tenn, 67-68. *Concurrent Pos:* Vis assoc prof, Univ Houston, 76; NSF grants, prin investr, 69-94; Alexander von Humboldt fel & hon Fulbright fel, Tech Univ, Darmstadt, WGer, 80-81; vis prof, Oxford Univ, 84 & Tech Univ, Darmstadt, Ger, 92-93; ed, Semigroup Forum, 88-; ed, Am Math Monthly, 96- *Mem:* Am Math Soc; Math Asn Am. *Res:* Topological algebra; algebraic topology and semigroups; topology; continuous lattices; lie semigroups; control theory; topological dynamics; author of various articles; co-author of two research monographs; co-editor of one research monograph. *Mailing Add:* Dept Math La State Univ Baton Rouge LA 70803. *Fax:* 504-388-4276; *E-Mail:* lawson@marais.math.lsu.edu

LAWSON, JOEL S(MITH), PHYSICS, ELECTRONICS. *Current Pos:* RETIRED. *Personal Data:* b New York, NY, July 3, 24; m 46; c 4. *Educ:* Williams Col, BA, 47; Univ Ill, MS, 49, PhD(physics), 53. *Prof Exp:* Res assoc, Control Systs Lab, Univ Ill, 53-55, from res asst prof to res assoc prof, 55-57; sr staff mem, Sci Eng Inst, 58-65; spec asst electronics, Off Asst Secy Navy, 65-67; res & eng consult, Comdr-in-Chief Pac, 67-68; dir, Naval Labs, Washington, DC, 68-74; tech dir, Naval Electronics Systs, 74-81, chief scientist, 81-84; consult, 85-93. *Mem:* Fel AAAS. *Res:* Applications of digital data processing techniques to information handling; communications systems; radar techniques; development of advanced electronic devices for military applications; theory of military command control. *Mailing Add:* 3089 La Pietra Circle Honolulu HI 96815

LAWSON, JOHN DOUGLAS, COMPUTER SCIENCE, NUMERICAL ANALYSIS. *Current Pos:* PRES, ALGOMA UNIV COL, 87- *Personal Data:* b Meaford, Ont, Sept 2, 37; m 60, Jacqueline C Webb; c David, James & Kathryn. *Educ:* Univ Toronto, BASc, 59; Univ Waterloo, MSc, 60, PhD(appl math), 65. *Prof Exp:* Teaching fel math, 59-60, lectr, 60-64, from asst prof to assoc prof, 64-73, assoc dean math, 68-71, chmn dept comput sci, 74-78 & 83-84, prof comput sci, Univ Waterloo, 73-87. *Concurrent Pos:* Asst scientist, Med Div, Oak Ridge Inst Nuclear Studies, 64-65; vis lectr, Univ Dundee, 71-72. *Res:* Numerical solution of ordinary differential equations; programming languages for scientific applications; approximation theory. *Mailing Add:* Pres Algoma Univ Col Sault Ste Marie ON P6A 2G4 Can. *Fax:* 705-949-6583; *E-Mail:* lawson@tbird.on.ca

LAWSON, JOHN EDWARD, MEDICINAL CHEMISTRY. *Current Pos:* GROUP LEADER, MEAD JOHNSON & CO, 58- *Personal Data:* b Detroit, Mich, Feb 25, 31; m 57; c 2. *Educ:* Wayne State Univ, BS, 53; Vanderbilt Univ, MA, 56, PhD(org chem), 57. *Prof Exp:* Fel, Mass Inst Technol, 57-58. *Mem:* Am Chem Soc. *Res:* Pharmaceutical Chemistry; organic synthesis; heterocyclic chemistry; natural products. *Mailing Add:* 5 Old Pasture Ct Wallingford CT 06492-2565

LAWSON, JOHN EDWIN, ANIMAL BREEDING. *Current Pos:* RETIRED. *Personal Data:* b Shoal Lake, Man, Nov 28, 33; m 58; c 1. *Educ:* Univ Man, BSAgr, 56, MSA, 63. *Prof Exp:* Res scientist beef cattle breeding, Res Br, Agr Can Res Sta, 57-88. *Concurrent Pos:* Head, Animal Sci Sect, Agr Can Res Sta. *Res:* Evaluation of cattle breeds and crosses for reproductive performance and efficiency of production in specific environments; investigation of genotype-environment interactions; direct and correlated response to single trait selection. *Mailing Add:* 2843 Lakeview Dr Lethbridge AB T1K 3G2 Can

LAWSON, JUAN (OTTO), PHYSICS. *Current Pos:* RETIRED. *Personal Data:* b Bluefield, WVa, Apr 18, 39; m 63; c 2. *Educ:* Va State Col, BS, 60; Howard Univ, MS, 62, PhD(physics), 66. *Prof Exp:* From asst prof to assoc prof, Univ Tex El Paso, 67-74, asst dean, Grad Sch, 70-71, prof physics, 74-92, dean, Col Sci, 75-80. *Mem:* Am Phys Soc; Sigma Xi. *Res:* Mathematical physics; solid state theory. *Mailing Add:* 8712 Cielo Vista Dr El Paso TX 79925

LAWSON, KENNETH DARE, ELECTRON MICROSCOPY. *Current Pos:* SECT HEAD, MIAMI VALLEY LABS, PROCTER & GAMBLE CO, 63- *Personal Data:* b Clinchport, Va, May 12, 34; m 56; c 1. *Educ:* E Tenn State Univ, BA, 59; Univ Fla, MS, 61, PhD(chem), 63. *Mem:* AAAS; Am Chem Soc. *Res:* Nuclear magnetic resonance spectroscopy; structure of mesomorphic phases; biophysics. *Mailing Add:* 460 Whitestone Ct Cincinnati OH 45231-2716

LAWSON, KENT DELANCE, PHYSICS. *Current Pos:* prof physics, 65-75, distinguished teaching prof, 75-91, EMER DISTINGUISHED TEACHING PROF, STATE UNIV NY COL, ONEONTA, 91- *Personal Data:* b Binghamton, NY, Feb 17, 21; m 42, Jane Hulbirt; c Lee, Nancy & Ardie. *Educ:* Cornell Univ, BA, 43; Rensselaer Polytech Inst, MS, 51, PhD(physics), 56. *Prof Exp:* Instr physics, Rensselaer Polytech Inst, 46-52; mem fac, Bennington Col, 53-66. *Concurrent Pos:* Res & educ prof consult, 56-70; dir, EDUX Prog, 70-91. *Mem:* Am Phys Soc; Am Asn Physics Teachers. *Res:* Education theory: unified theory of physical reality, man and awareness. *Mailing Add:* 53 Center St Oneonta NY 13820

LAWSON, LARRY DALE, LIPID BIOCHEMISTRY, GARLIC ANALYSIS. *Current Pos:* RES & DEVELOP MGR, MURDOCK, MADAUS, SCHWABE CO, 86- *Personal Data:* b Elkhart, Ind, Dec 23, 46; m 73, Carol Poli; c 6. *Educ:* Purdue Univ, BS, 68; Brigham Young Univ, MS, 73; Univ Ill, PhD(nutrit sci), 79. *Prof Exp:* Fel, Hormel Inst, Univ Minn, 78-83; res assoc, Univ NC, 83-85; res scientist, Murdock Healthcare, 86-90. *Mem:* Am Oil Chemists Soc; Sigma Xi; Am Chem Soc; Am Inst Nutrit; Soc Med Plant Res. *Res:* Lipid biochemistry, intestinal prostaglandins and organosulfur biochemistry of garlic. *Mailing Add:* Murdock Healthcare PO Box 4000 Springville UT 84463-9007. *Fax:* 801-489-1563

LAWSON, MERLIN PAUL, CLIMATOLOGY. *Current Pos:* from asst prof to assoc prof climat, Univ Nebr, Lincoln, 68-82, chmn dept geog, 80-87, asst vchancellor res & assoc dean grad studies, 87-92, PROF CLIMAT, UNIV NEBR, LINCOLN, 82-, DEAN GRAD STUDIES, 92- *Personal Data:* b Jamestown, NY, Jan 12, 41; m 64, Nina Rising; c Keith, Kenneth & Kristin. *Educ:* State Univ NY Buffalo, BA, 63; Clark Univ, MA, 66, PhD(geog climat), 73. *Prof Exp:* Instr climat, Northeastern Univ, 67-68. *Concurrent Pos:* Treas, Midwestern Asn Grad Schs. *Mem:* Sigma Xi; Am Meteorol Soc; Asn Am Geogrs. *Res:* Historical climate of the Great American Desert; severe droughts since 1700 in the western United States; descriptive climatic change; dendroclimatology. *Mailing Add:* Rte 9 Lincoln NE 68506. *E-Mail:* mlawson@unl.edu

LAWSON, MILDRED WIKER, MATHEMATICS, COMPUTER SCIENCES. *Current Pos:* RETIRED. *Personal Data:* b New London, Conn, Nov 10, 22; m 63, Albert C Jr. *Educ:* Univ Md, BS, 47, MA, 49. *Prof Exp:* Asst math, Univ Md, 47-49, instr, 49-50; cartog compilation aide, Corps Engrs, Army Map Serv, 50-51, mathematician, 51-55, proj leader math & comput prog, 55-57, asst chief prog, 57-58; from assoc mathematician to sr mathematician, appl physics lab, Johns Hopkins Univ, Laurel, 58-85. *Res:* Analysis and programming of computer solutions of problems arising in scientific projects; computer language training. *Mailing Add:* 5113 Durham Rd E Columbia MD 21044

LAWSON, NEAL D(EVERE), CHEMICAL ENGINEERING. *Current Pos:* RETIRED. *Personal Data:* b 1916; m 41; c 2. *Educ:* Pa State Col, BS, 38, MS, 42, PhD(chem eng), 46. *Prof Exp:* Asst petrol ref lab, Pa State Col, 38-42, instr, 42-47; group leader petrol chem lab, E I Du Pont de Nemours & Co, Inc, 47-50, head chem div, 50-56, additives mgr, Cent Region, 56-58, tech mgr, Ill, 58-56, develop specialist, 65-66, supvr new prod develop, 66-77, spec asst tech info res & develop, 77-80. *Mem:* Am Chem Soc; Soc Automotive Engrs; Am Soc Lubrication Engrs; Am Soc Testing & Mat. *Res:* Stability of petroleum products; additives for lubricating oils and gasoline; fuel oil stabilizers; additives and thickeners for greases. *Mailing Add:* 1005 Chickadee Lane Penn Wood S West Chester PA 19380-7616

LAWSON, NORMAN C, PLANT BREEDING. *Current Pos:* RETIRED. *Personal Data:* b Glasgow, Scotland, Nov 3, 29; Can citizen; m 60; c 3. *Educ:* Glasgow Univ, BSc, 53; Univ Reading, dipl agr, 54; McGill Univ, MSc, 58, PhD, 61. *Prof Exp:* Res off, Exp Farm, Can Dept Agr, BC, 61-65, res scientist, Res Sta, Sask, 65-67; assoc prof agron, McGill Univ, 67-89, dir dipl prog, 73-89. *Mem:* Am Soc Agron; Crop Sci Soc Am; Genetics Soc Can; Agr Inst Can; Can Soc Agron. *Res:* Genetics and breeding of forage and oil crop species. *Mailing Add:* 20826 Lake Shore Rd Baie-D'urfé PQ H9X 1R9 Can

LAWSON, ROBERT BARRETT, PEDIATRICS. *Current Pos:* RETIRED. *Personal Data:* b Oakland, Calif, Aug 24, 11; m 39; c 2. *Educ:* Harvard Univ, BA, 32, MD, 36; Am Bd Pediat, dipl, 41. *Prof Exp:* From asst prof to prof pediat & dir dept, Bowman Gray Sch Med, 40-54; prof & chmn dept, Sch Med, Univ Miami, 54-62, actg dean, Sch Med, 61-62; prof pediat, Sch Med, Northwestern Univ, 62-71, chmn dept, 62-70, vpres health sci, 70-71; chief staff, Variety Children's Hosp, 71-81. *Concurrent Pos:* Pro Sch Pub Health, Univ NC & assoc, Sch Med, Duke Univ, 40-42; pediat consult, State Bd Health, NC, 40-42; Nat Res Coun fel, Univ Calif & Yale Univ, 45; chief staff, Children's Mem Hosp, Chicago, Ill, 62-71; clin prof pediat, Sch Med, Univ Miami, 71- *Mem:* Soc Pediat Res; Am Pediat Soc; AMA; Am Acad Pediat. *Res:* Infectious disease. *Mailing Add:* 5508 Gregor Ct Winston-Salem NC 27106-2899

LAWSON, ROBERT BERNARD, NEGOTIATIONS, PSYCHOLOGY. *Current Pos:* from asst prof to assoc prof, 66-74, PROF PSYCHOL, UNIV VT, 74-, VPRES RES & GRAD DEAN, 78- *Personal Data:* b New York, NY, June 20, 40; div; c 3. *Educ:* Monmouth Col, NJ, BA, 61; Univ Del, MA, 63, PhD(psychol), 65. *Prof Exp:* NASA fel, 62-64. *Concurrent Pos:* Consult, IBM, 74-77; mem bd govs, Univ Press of New Eng, 78-, chmn, 79-80; numerous res grants, NIH, NSF, NASA & USAID. *Mem:* AAAS; NY Acad Sci; Sigma Xi; Am Psychol Asn. *Res:* Human perception and cognition; stereoscopic vision; psychology of negotiation. *Mailing Add:* Dept Psychol Univ Vt Dewey Hall Burlington VT 05405-0134

LAWSON, ROBERT DAVIS, THEORETICAL PHYSICS. *Current Pos:* assoc physicist, 59-66, SR PHYSICIST, ARGONNE NAT LAB, 66- *Personal Data:* b Sydney, Australia, July 14, 26; nat US; m 50; c 3. *Educ:* Univ BC, BASc, 48, MASc, 49; Stanford Univ, PhD, 53. *Prof Exp:* Asst, Univ BC, 47-48; asst, Stanford Univ, 49-53; jr res physicist, Univ Calif, 53-57; res physicist, Enrico Fermi Inst Nuclear Studies, Ill, 57-59. *Concurrent Pos:* Vis physicist, UK Atomic Energy Authority, Harwell, Eng, 62-63; Weizmann sr fel, Weizmann Inst Sci, Israel, 67-68; vis prof, State Univ NY, Stony Brook, 72-73; Nordita fel, Niels Bohr Inst, Copenhagen, 76-77. *Mem:* Am Phys Soc. *Res:* Nuclear physics. *Mailing Add:* Appl Physics MS 316 Argonne Nat Lab Argonne IL 60439

LAWSON, ROGER, HORTICULTURE. *Current Pos:* NAT PROG LEADER HORT & SUGAR CROPS, USDA, 95- *Personal Data:* b Portland, Ore, Jan 21, 37. *Educ:* Ore State Univ, BS, 60, PhD(plant pathol), 63. *Mailing Add:* Nat Prog Staff/USDA BARC-West Bldg 005 Beltsville MD 20705

LAWSON, WILLIAM, FACIAL PLASTIC SURGERY, MAXILLOFACIAL SURGERY. *Current Pos:* PROF OTOLARYNGOL, MT SINAI SCH MED, 82-, ATTEND SURGEON, MT SINAI HOSP, NY, 82- *Personal Data:* b New York, NY, Nov 23, 34; m 65; c 1. *Educ:* NY Univ, BA, 56, DDS, 61, MD, 65. *Concurrent Pos:* chief head & neck surg, Bronx Vet Hosp, 75-; attend surgeon otolaryngol, Elmhurst Gen Hosp, 82- *Mem:* Am Acad Facial Plastic Reconstruct Surg (vpres, 87-89); Am Soc Head & Neck Surgeons; Am Soc Maxillofacial Surgeons; Am Laryngol Soc; Am Rhinologic, Laryngol, Otol Soc; Am Col Surgeons. *Res:* Melanocytic system of head and neck, discovery of melanocytes in larynx, nasal cavity, orbit and dental lamina; experimental proof of the neurocrine nature of glomus cells of the head and neck; paraganglyonic chemoreceptor system; discovery of paraganglia in larynx; author of sourcebook with 3000 references. *Mailing Add:* 19 E 98 St New York NY 10029-6501

LAWSON, WILLIAM BURROWS, ORGANIC CHEMISTRY. *Current Pos:* PROF CHEM, UNAN-LEON, LEON, NICARAGUA, 89- *Personal Data:* b Detroit, Mich, June 8, 29; div; c 1. *Educ:* Wayne State Univ, BS, 51; Univ Md, PhD(chem), 56. *Prof Exp:* Res assoc, Mass Inst Technol, 55-56 & 57-58; Nat Cancer Inst fel, Mass Inst Technol, 56-57, Max Planck Inst Biochem, 60-61; sr asst scientist, NIH, Md, 58-60; sr res scientist, Wadsworth Ctr Labs & Res, NY State Dept Health, 61-66, assoc res scientist, 66-88. *Mem:* Am Chem Soc; Am Soc Biol Chem. *Res:* Amino acids; synthesis and degradation of peptides; chemical modification and inhibition of enzymes; blood coagulation. *Mailing Add:* Excuela De Quimica Unan-Leon Leon Nicaragua

LAWTON, ALEXANDER R, III, MEDICINE. *Current Pos:* FAC, SCH MED, VANDERBILT UNIV, NASHVILLE. *Personal Data:* b Nov 8, 38. *Educ:* Yale Univ, BA, 60; Vanderbilt Univ, MD, 64. *Prof Exp:* Intern, Vanderbilt Univ Hosp, 64-65, asst resident, 65-66; clin assoc, Lab Clin Invest, Nat Inst Allergy & Infectious Dis, 66-68, clin investr, 68-69; from asst prof to assoc prof, 71-76, prof pediat & microbiol, Sch Med, Univ Ala, Birmingham, 76- *Concurrent Pos:* NIH spec fel immunol, Sch Med, Univ Ala, Birmingham, 69-71. *Mem:* Sigma Xi. *Res:* Pediatrics; microbiology; immunology. *Mailing Add:* Sch Med Vanderbilt Univ Med Ctr 1161 21st Ave Nashville TN 37232-2580

LAWTON, ALFRED HENRY, GERIATRICS. *Current Pos:* clin prof community health & family prac, Univ Fla Sch Med & dir gerontol, 78-82, DIR GERONTOL EDUC, ADVENT CHRISTIAN VILLAGE, 82- *Personal Data:* b Carson, Iowa, July 26, 16; m 40, 74, Ruth Strachen; c George W, Dianna M (Fisel) & Lola M (Finch). *Educ:* Simpson Col, AB, 37; Northwestern Univ, MS, 39, BM, 40, MD, 41, PhD(physiol), 43. *Hon Degrees:* ScD, Simpson Col, 58. *Prof Exp:* Intern, Passavant Mem Hosp, Chicago, 40-41; resident, Henry Ford Hosp, Detroit, 41-42; asst prof med, physiol & pharm, Sch Med, Univ Ark, 46-47; dean & prof physiol & pharm, Univ NDak, 47-48; chief res div, US Vet Admin, Washington, DC, 48-51; med res adv, US Dept Air Force, 51-55; asst dir prof serv res & educ & chief intermediate serv, US Vet Admin Ctr, Bay Pines, 55-62; dir study ctr, Nat Inst Child Health & Human Develop, 62-66; from asst to assoc dean acad affairs, Univ SFla, 66-70, actg vpres acad affairs, 70-73; exec dir tech adv comn aging res, US Dept Health, Educ & Welfare, 73-74; dir geriat res, Educ & Clin Ctr & assoc chief staff res & develop, Vet Admin Ctr, 75-78. *Concurrent Pos:* Asst clin prof, Sch Med, George Washington Univ, 48-55; liaison mem coun arthritis & metab dis, USPHS, 50-55; mem exec coun, Nat Res Coun, US Armed Forces Vision Comt & Nat Coun Aging; actg dean, Col Med, Univ SFla, 68-70. *Mem:* Am Physiol Soc; Am Soc Pharmacol & Exp Therapeut; Am Geriat Soc; Geront Soc; Am Pub Health Asn. *Res:* Aging; chronic diseases. *Mailing Add:* Advent Christian Village Dowling Park FL 32060

LAWTON, EMIL ABRAHAM, SYNTHETIC CHEMISTRY, WATER CHEMISTRY. *Current Pos:* CONSULT, 89- *Personal Data:* b Detroit, Mich, Oct 12, 22; m 76, Cynthia Block; c Gil, Ron & Leona. *Educ:* Wayne State Univ, AB, 46; Purdue Univ, PhD(inorg chem), 52. *Honors & Awards:* Civilian Patriotic Award, US Army, 84. *Prof Exp:* Res chemist, Nat Bur Stand, 52-53; proj leader, Battelle Mem Inst, 53-57; prog mgr, Rocketdyne Div, Rockwell Int, 57-72; sect head, Wasatch Div, Thiokol Corp, 72-75; proj mgr, Neus, Inc, 75-76; vpres res & develop, Tech & Mgt Consults, 76-77; mgr advan prog, Shock Hydrodynamics Div, Whittaker Corp, 77-82; mem tech staff, Jet Propulsion Lab, Calif Inst Technol, 83-89. *Concurrent Pos:* Consult chemist, 89- *Mem:* Am Chem Soc; AAAS; Sigma Xi. *Res:* Combustion; explosives and propellants; lubricants; gun-propellants; fluorine. *Mailing Add:* 13025 Hesby St Sherman Oaks CA 91423

LAWTON, JOHN G, ELECTRICAL ENGINEERING. *Current Pos:* PRES, LAWTRONICS, INC, 83- *Personal Data:* b Vienna, Austria, June 3, 23; c 7. *Educ:* City Col New York, BEE, 49; Mass Inst Technol, SM, 51; Cornell Univ, PhD, 60. *Prof Exp:* Jr engr electronics, Stanford Res Inst, 51; from asst engr to prin staff engr, Cornell Aeronaut Lab, Inc, 54-70, staff scientist, 70-78; pres, J & J Technologies, Inc, 78-83. *Mem:* Inst Elec & Electronics Engrs. *Res:* Communications; modulation; information and communications theory; fire control; guidance equipment; computers; statistics. *Mailing Add:* Northstar Aeronaut 8353 Westfield Rd Seville OH 44273

LAWTON, MICHAEL P, TOXICOLOGY. *Current Pos:* INTRAMURAL RES TRAINING AWARD FEL, NAT INST ENVIRON HEALTH SCI, NIH, 91- *Personal Data:* b Tacoma, Wash, June 26, 63; c 1. *Educ:* Univ Calif, Davis, BS, 86; NC State Univ, PhD(toxicol), 91. *Prof Exp:* Lab tech, Lawrence Livermore Nat Lab, 86-87. *Mem:* Am Soc Biochem & Molecular Biol. *Res:* Toxicology. *Mailing Add:* Pfizer Inc Cent Res Div Groton CT 06340

LAWTON, RICHARD G, SYNTHETIC ORGANIC CHEMISTRY, BIO-ORGANIC CHEMISTRY. *Current Pos:* from instr to assoc prof, 62-70, PROF ORG CHEM, UNIV MICH, ANN ARBOR, 70- *Personal Data:* b Berkeley, Calif, Aug 29, 34; m 58; c 5. *Educ:* Univ Calif, Berkeley, BS, 56; Univ Wis, PhD(chem), 62. *Prof Exp:* Asst isolation & identification, Merck Sharp & Dohme Res Labs, 56-57; asst org chem, Univ Wis, 59-62. *Concurrent Pos:* Vis prof, Univ Wis, 70-71; consult, Colgate-Palmolive Res Labs, 70- & German Wool Res Inst, Aachen, WGer, 79-80; John S Guggenheim Found award, 79-80. *Mem:* AAAS; Am Chem Soc. *Res:* Synthetic organic chemistry including peptide chemistry, alkaloids, terpenes and polycyclic aromatic hydrocarbons. *Mailing Add:* Dept Chem 930 N University Ave Ann Arbor MI 48109-1055

LAWTON, RICHARD L, SURGERY. *Current Pos:* MEM STAFF, GEN SURG & SURG ONCOL, FRANKLIN GEN HOSP, 80- *Personal Data:* b Council Bluffs, Iowa, June 18, 18; m 43; c 7. *Educ:* Univ Omaha, AB, 39; Univ Nebr, BS & MD, 43. *Prof Exp:* Intern, St Mary's & St Louis Hosps, Mo, 43-44; resident, US Vet Hosp, Omaha, Nebr, 46-50, asst chief surg, 50-51; pvt pract, 52-53; staff physician, Vet Admin Hosp, 53-58, chief cancer chemother, 58-76, asst chief surg, 63-76, dir renal dialysis, 64-76; chief, Div Transplantation, & actg chief oncol, Sch Med, Tex Tech Univ, 76-78, prof & vchmn, Dept Surg, 76-80, surg, 64-80. dir renal dialysis, 64-80. *Concurrent Pos:* Instr, Creighton Univ, 50-51; from clin asst prof to clin assoc prof, Univ Iowa, 54-64, assoc prof, 64-68, prof surg, 68-; res grant angiol, Univ Iowa, 64-65. *Mem:* Am Asn Cancer Res; Am Soc Artificial Internal Organs; fel Am Col Surg; Soc Exp Biol & Med; Am Soc Clin Oncol. *Res:* Renal dialysis; cancer chemotherapy; transplant and preservation. *Mailing Add:* RR 6 Box 111B Iowa City IA 52240-9806

LAWTON, RICHARD WOODRUFF, PHYSIOLOGY, BIOPHYSICS. *Current Pos:* RETIRED. *Personal Data:* b New York, NY, June 22, 20; m 46; c 2. *Educ:* Dartmouth Col, AB, 42; Cornell Univ, MD, 44. *Prof Exp:* Fel physiol sci, Med Sch, Dartmouth Col, 46-48; from instr to asst prof physiol, Med Col, Cornell Univ, 48-54; assoc prof, Sch Med, Univ Pa, 54-58; mgr bioastronaut sect, Missile & Space Div, Pa, Gen Elec Co, 58-67, mgr bioastronaut sect, Res & Eng Space Systs Orgn, 67-69, Life Systs, 69-70, med res dir, Med Develop Oper, Chem & Med Div, 70-71, mgr ventures develop, Med Ventures Oper, Med Syst Bus Div, 72-74, consult med systs, Corp Res & Develop, 74-85. *Concurrent Pos:* Head physiol sect, Aviation Med Lab, Naval Air Develop Ctr, Pa, 54-58; adj assoc prof, Sch Med, Univ Pa, 58-70. *Mem:* Am Physiol Soc. *Res:* Public health and epidemiology; elasticity of body tissues; aerospace physiology; cardiovascular physiology. *Mailing Add:* 1340 Stanley Lane Schenectady NY 12309-2421

LAWTON, ROBERT ARTHUR, electronics, electrooptics, for more information see previous edition

LAWTON, STEPHEN LATHAM, STRUCTURAL CHEMISTRY. *Current Pos:* Res chemist, Socony Mobil Oil Co, Inc, 66-69, sr res chemist, 69-75, assoc chemist, 75-78, RES ASSOC, MOBIL RES & DEVELOP CORP, 78- *Personal Data:* b Milwaukee, Wis, Nov 12, 39; m 67; c 2. *Educ:* Univ Wis, BS, 63; Iowa State Univ Sci & Technol, MS, 66. *Mem:* Am Chem Soc; Am Crystallog Asn. *Res:* X-ray crystallography; crystal and molecular structures of inorganic and organometallic compounds and zeolites; computer applications in chemistry. *Mailing Add:* 620 Howard Ave Pitman NJ 08071-1833

LAWVERE, FRANCIS WILLIAM, ALGEBRA. *Current Pos:* PROF MATH, STATE UNIV NY BUFFALO, 74- *Personal Data:* b Muncie, Ind, Feb 9, 37; m 66, Fatima Fenaroli; c Marco, John, Philip, Danilo & Silvana. *Educ:* Ind Univ, BA, 60; Columbia Univ, MA & PhD(math), 63. *Prof Exp:* Syst analyst, Litton Industs, Inc, 62-63; asst prof math, Reed Col, 63-64; NATO fel, Swiss Fed Inst Technol, 64-65, res assoc, 65-66; asst prof, Univ Chicago, 66-67; assoc prof, Grad Ctr, City Univ New York, 67-68; Sloan fel, Swiss Fed Inst Technol, 68-69; res prof, Dalhousie Univ, 69-71; vis prof, Aarhus Univ, 71-72 & Nat Res Inst Italy, 72-74. *Mem:* Am Math Soc. *Res:* Foundations of category theory; categorical foundations of mathematics; algebraic theories and equational doctrines; axiomatic theory of topoi; closed categories and metric spaces; synthetic differential geometry; functorial thermodynamics and continuum mechanics. *Mailing Add:* Dept Math State Univ NY 106 Diefendorf Hall Buffalo NY 14214. *Fax:* 716-829-2299; *E-Mail:* wlawvere@ubunix.buffalo.edu

LAWWILL, STANLEY JOSEPH, MATHEMATICS. *Current Pos:* RETIRED. *Personal Data:* b London, Ohio, May 23, 16; m 40, Martha Fulford; c Judith, Patricia, Lois, Lawrence & Kenneth. *Educ:* Univ Cincinnati, AB, 37, MA, 39, PhD(math), 41. *Prof Exp:* Instr math, Northwestern Univ, 41-44; mathematician appl math group, Columbia Univ, 44; gunnery analyst, 2nd & 20th Air Forces, USAF, 44-46, opers analyst, HQ Strategic Air Command, 46-48, dep chief, Opers Analysis Off, 48-50, chief, Atomic Capabilities Div, 50-54, dep chief scientist, 54-58; tech dir, Sci Analytical Off, Melpar, Inc Div, Westinghouse Air Brake Co, 58; pres, Analytical Servs, Inc, 58-81. *Mem:* Opers Res Soc Am; Sigma Xi. *Res:* Orthogonal functions; overconvergence of approximations in terms of rational harmonic functions; operations analysis; weapon systems evaluation. *Mailing Add:* 6532 Copa Ct Falls Church VA 22044

LAWYER, ARTHUR L, EXPERIMENTAL BIOLOGY. *Current Pos:* DIR, STATE AFFAIRS DIV, TECHNOL SERV GROUP, 91- *Educ:* Univ Calif, Davis, BS; Yale Univ, MPhil, 77, PhD(molecular biochem & biophys), 79. *Prof Exp:* Rockefeller Found fel, Calvin Lab, Lawrence Berkeley Labs, Univ Calif, 79-81; res biochemist, Biotechnol Group, Chevron Chem Co, 81-86, regulatory specialist-state liaison, 86-87, sr state regulatory specialist, Valent USA & Chevron Chem Co, 87-89; mgr, State Govt Affairs, Valent USA Corp, 89-90, sr proj mgr, 90; chmn, Calif-Environ Agency Task Force, Western Agr Chem Asn, 91- *Concurrent Pos:* Mem, State Affairs Comt, Nat Agr Chem Asn, 87-90; chmn, Proposition 65 Task Forces, Western Agr Chem Asn, 87-90, Govt Affairs Comt & Calif Rep Comt, 88-90, Environ Initiative Task Force, 89-90. *Res:* Thirteen publications covering enzymatic mechanisms, photosynthetic metabolism, plant biotechnology and prediction of groundwater contamination. *Mailing Add:* Technol Sci Gp Inc 712 Fifth St Suite A Davis CA 95616

LAX, ANNELI, MATHEMATICS EDUCATION. *Current Pos:* MEM-AT-LARGE, COURANT INST. *Personal Data:* b Kattowitz, Ger, Feb 23, 22; nat US; m 48; c 2. *Educ:* Adelphi Col, BS, 42; NY Univ, MA, 45, PhD, 55. *Honors & Awards:* Polya Award, 77. *Prof Exp:* Asst aeronaut, Inst Mech Sci, NY Univ, 43-44, asst math, 45-55, asst res scientist, Wash Sq Col, 55-65, assoc prof math, 65-71, prof, 72- *Concurrent Pos:* Instr, Wash Sq Col, 45-55; ed, New Math Library, 60- *Mem:* AAAS; Am Math Soc; Math Asn Am. *Res:* Mathematical analysis and exposition; partial differential equations. *Mailing Add:* NY Univ Courant 251 Mercer St New York NY 10012-1110

LAX, BENJAMIN, SOLID STATE PHYSICS, PLASMA PHYSICS. *Current Pos:* mem staff, Lincoln Lab, Mass Inst Technol, 51-53, head, Ferrites Group, 53-55 & Solid State Group, 55-57, assoc head, Commun Div, 57-58, head, Solid State Div, 58-64, dir, 60-81, assoc dir, Lincoln Lab, 64-65, prof, 65-86, EMER PROF, MASS INST TECHNOL, 86-, EMER DIR & PHYSICIST, FRANCIS BITTER NAT MAGNETIC LAB, 81- *Personal Data:* b Miskolz, Hungary, Dec 29, 15; nat US; m 42; c 2. *Educ:* Cooper Union, BS, 41; Mass Inst Technol, PhD(physics), 49. *Hon Degrees:* DSc, Yeshiva Univ, 75. *Honors & Awards:* Buckley Prize, Am Phys Soc, 60; Gano Dunn Medal, Cooper Union Alumni Asn, 69. *Prof Exp:* Mech engr, US Eng Off, 41-42; radar officer, Radiation Lab, Mass Inst Technol, 44-46; mem staff, Air Force Cambridge Res Ctr, 46-51. *Concurrent Pos:* Assoc ed, J Appl Physics, 57-59 & Barnes Eng Co, 78-; mem, Coun Am Phys Soc, 63-67, Joint Coun Quantum Electronics, 64-81 & chmn, 66-68, Solid State Sci Panel, Nat Res Coun, 70-81, Assoc Prog Adv Comt & chmn, Physics Panel, 83-84; mem bd dirs, Infrared Indust, 73-76 & Barnes Eng Co, 78-; chmn, 10th Int Conf Physics Semiconductors, & Int Union Pure & Appl Physics Comn Quantum Electronics, 76-; consult, Raytheon Co, 76-, Gen Motors Res Lab, 83- & Amoco Res Ctr, Stand Oil Co, 85-, Lincoln Lab, Mass Inst Technol, 86-; Guggenheim fel, 81-82; adv comt, Am Friends of Jerusalem Col Technol, 82-83; adv bd, EPSCOR, Ky & adv comt, Weber Res Inst, 86- *Mem:* Nat Acad Sci; NY Acad Sci; Sigma Xi; fel Am Phys Soc; fel Am Acad Arts & Sci; fel Optical Soc Am; fel AAAS. *Res:* Nonlinear effects in solids and plasmas; interaction of submillimeter radiation with plasmas and solids; laser produced plasmas; semiconductors and ferrites; radar and millimeter waves. *Mailing Add:* Francis Bitter Mag Lab Mass Inst Technol Bldg NW14-4104 Cambridge MA 02139. *Fax:* 617-253-5405

LAX, EDWARD, CRYOGENICS. *Current Pos:* RETIRED. *Personal Data:* b Toronto, Ont, Aug 29, 31; US citizen; m 60; c 1. *Educ:* Univ Calif, Los Angeles, AB, 52, MA, 59, PhD(physics), 60. *Prof Exp:* Sr physicist, Ultrasonic Systs, Inc, 60-61; mem tech staff, Aerospace Corp, 61-67; mem tech staff, Autonetics Div, Rockwell Int Corp, 67-96. *Mem:* Am Phys Soc; Inst Elec & Electronics Engrs. *Res:* Electron-phonon effects in metals at low temperatures; acoustical-optical effects; cryogenic heat transfer and thermodynamics; hypersonics and delay lines; infra-red systems. *Mailing Add:* 5637 Wilhelmina Ave Woodland Hills CA 91367

LAX, LOUIS CARL, physiology, medicine, for more information see previous edition

LAX, MELVIN, SOLID STATE PHYSICS, QUANTUM OPTICS. *Current Pos:* DISTINGUISHED PROF PHYSICS, CITY COL NEW YORK, 71- *Personal Data:* b New York, NY, Mar 8, 22; m 49, Heckelman; c Laurie, David, Jonathan & Naomi. *Educ:* NY Univ, BA, 42; Mass Inst Technol, SM, 43, PhD(physics), 47. *Prof Exp:* Res physicist, Underwater Sound Lab, Mass Inst Technol, 42-45, res assoc physics, 47; from asst prof to prof, Syracuse Univ, 47-55; mem tech staff, Bell Tel Labs, 55-71, head, Theoret Physics Dept, 62-64. *Concurrent Pos:* Consult, Crystal Br, US Naval Res Lab, 51-55, US Army Res Off, 71-, Bell Labs, 72- & Los Alamos Nat Lab, 76-; lectr, Princeton Univ, 60, Oxford Univ, 61-62, Brandeis Univ, Can Summer Sch & Tokyo Summer Inst, 66, Trieste, 67, Fla State Univ & Varenna, 71, Israel, 73, Kyoto & Repub China, 82, Univ Lausanne, 83 & Univ NMex, 89; chmn, Gordon Res Conf Chem & Physics of Solids, 65, Univ Comt Res, City Univ New York, 88-90; mem basic res adv comt, Nat Acad Sci, 66-69; mem & secy of class III, Eng & Appl Phys & Math Sci, Nat Acad Sci, 89-92, 95-98. *Mem:* Nat Acad Sci; fel Am Phys Soc; fel AAAS; Optical Soc Am. *Res:* Meson creation and absorption; multiple scattering; phase transitions; optical and electrical properties of solids; impurity bands; classical and quantum relaxation and noise; group theory in solids; quantum communication theory; nonlinear optical properties in deforming solids; optics, lasers, continuum mechanics; two-dimensional transport and tunneling in semiconductors. *Mailing Add:* Dept Physics City Col New York New York NY 10031. *Fax:* 908-582-3260; *E-Mail:* laz@sci.ccny.cuny.edu, lax@bell__labs.com

LAX, MELVIN DAVID, RANDOM DIFFERENTIAL EQUATIONS. *Current Pos:* from asst prof to assoc prof, 77-86, PROF MATH, CALIF STATE UNIV, LONG BEACH, 86- *Personal Data:* b Boston, Mass, Mar 20, 47. *Educ:* Rensselaer Polytech Inst, BS, 69, MS, 71, PhD(math), 74. *Prof Exp:* Lectr math, Southern Ill Univ, Carbondale, 74-76; vis asst prof, Okla State Univ, 76-77. *Mem:* Am Math Soc; Soc Indust & Appl Math. *Res:* Approximate solution of random differential equations and random integral equations. *Mailing Add:* Dept Math Calif State Univ Long Beach CA 90840

LAX, PETER DAVID, PARTIAL DIFFERENTIAL EQUATIONS. *Current Pos:* from asst prof to assoc prof math, NY Univ, 51-57, asst to dir, Math Ctr, 59-63, dir, AEC Comput & Appl Math Ctr, 63-72, head, Dept Math & Comput Sci & dir, Courant Inst Math Sci, 72-80, dir, Courant Math & Comput Lab, 80, PROF MATH, NY UNIV, 58- *Personal Data:* b Budapest, Hungary, May 1, 26; nat US; m 48; c 2. *Educ:* NY Univ, AB, 47, PhD, 49. *Hon Degrees:* Numerous from US & foreign univs. *Honors & Awards:* Nat Medal of Sci; Lester R Ford Award, 66 & 73; von Neumann Lectr, Soc Indust

& Appl Math, 69; Hermann Weyl Lectr, 72; Hedrick Lectr, 73; Chauvenet Prize, Math Asn Am, 74; Norberg Prize, Am Math Soc, 75; Wolf Prize, 87; Steele Prize, 92. *Prof Exp:* Mem, Manhattan Proj, Los Alamos Sci Lab, 45-46, staff mem, 50. *Concurrent Pos:* Consult, Los Alamos Sci Lab, 50; mem, Nat Sci Bd, 80-86. *Mem:* Nat Acad Sci; Am Acad Sci; NY Acad Sci; Math Asn Am; Am Math Soc (pres, 79-80); Russ Acad Sci; Fr Acad Sci; Chinese Acad Sci; Hungary Acad Sci; Am Soc Arts & Sci; Soviet Acad Sci; Beijing Acad Sci; Moscow Math Soc. *Res:* Theory of partial differential equations; numerical analysis; scattering theory; functional analysis; fluid dynamics. *Mailing Add:* NY Univ Courant Inst Math Sci 251 Mercer St New York NY 10012

LAXER, CARY, COMPUTER GRAPHICS. *Current Pos:* from asst prof to assoc prof, 81-93, PROF COMPUT SCI, ROSE-HULMAN INST TECHNOL, 93- *Personal Data:* b Brooklyn, NY, July 16, 55; m 90, Norma F Lautman; c Phillip. *Educ:* New York Univ, BA, 76; Duke Univ, PhD(biomed eng), 80. *Prof Exp:* Res asst prof comput sci, Duke Univ, 80-81. *Mem:* Inst Elec & Electronics Engrs; Asn Comput Mach; Am Soc Eng Educ. *Res:* Computer analysis of cardiac electrical signals with relation to myocardial infarct geometry; biomedical computing. *Mailing Add:* Rose-Hulman Inst Technol Campus Box 100 5500 Wabash Ave Terre Haute IN 47803-3999. *Fax:* 812-877-8175; *E-Mail:* laxer@cs.rose-hulman.edu

LAXPATI, SHARAD R, ANTENNAS, ELECTROMAGNETIC THEORY. *Current Pos:* asst prof info eng, 69-73, ASSOC PROF ELEC ENG & COMPUT SCI, UNIV ILL, CHICAGO, 73-, ASSOC HEAD INSTR, ELEC ENG & COMPUT SCI, 93- *Personal Data:* b Bombay, India, July 16, 38; m 83, Maureen A Burns; c Nealen G & Leela J. *Educ:* Gujarat Univ, India, BE, 57; Univ Ill, MS, 61, PhD(elec eng), 65. *Prof Exp:* Jr sci officer, Reactor Control Div, Atomic Energy Estab, India, 58-60; asst prof elec eng, Pa State Univ, 65-69. *Concurrent Pos:* Vis sr assoc, Syst Res Ltd, Richmond, UK, 76-77; dir, Matrix Publ Priv LTD, India, 78-85; consult, Naval Res Lab, Washington, DC, 79-90, Locus, Inc, Alexandria, VA, 84; owner, LMS Eng, Chicago, IL, 85-; consult, Symmetron Inc, 87-, SFA Inc, 93- *Mem:* Inst Elec & Electronics Engrs; Int Union Radio Sci; Inst Elec Engr London. *Res:* Radiation and propagation of electromagnetic waves; applied mathematics; computational electromagnetics; optical communication. *Mailing Add:* Dept Elec Eng & Comput Sci Univ Ill 851 S Morgan St Chicago IL 60607-7042. *Fax:* 312-413-0024; *E-Mail:* laxpati@eecs.uic.edu

LAY, DAVID CLARK, OPERATOR THEORY, LINEAR ALGEBRA. *Current Pos:* from asst prof to assoc prof, 66-77, PROF MATH, UNIV MD, COLLEGE PARK, 77- *Personal Data:* b Los Angeles, Calif, Mar 1, 41; m 70; c 3. *Educ:* Aurora Col, BA, 62; Univ Calif, Los Angeles, MA, 65, PhD(math), 66. *Prof Exp:* Teaching asst math, Univ Calif, Los Angeles, 63-64. *Concurrent Pos:* NSF res grants, Univ Md, College Park, 68-73, 76-77 & 90-92; res grant, Neth Orgn Advan Pure Res, 73; vis prof, Univ Amsterdam, 80; Air Force USR grants, 87-90. *Mem:* Am Math Soc; Math Asn Am; Sigma Xi; Soc Indust & Appl Math. *Res:* Functional analysis; spectral theory of linear operators; operator-valued analytic functions, linear algebra. *Mailing Add:* Dept Math Univ Md College Park MD 20742. *E-Mail:* lay@math.umd.edu

LAY, DOUGLAS M, ANATOMY, ZOOLOGY. *Current Pos:* ASSOC PROF ANAT, UNIV NC, CHAPEL HILL, 73- *Personal Data:* b Jackson, Miss, July 3, 36; m 61; c 2. *Educ:* Millsaps Col, BS, 58; La State Univ, MS, 61; Univ Chicago, PhD(anat), 68. *Prof Exp:* Instr anat, Univ Chicago, 68-69; asst prof zool & cur mammals, Univ Mich, 69-73. *Mem:* Am Soc Mammal; Am Soc Zool; Soc Study Evol; Soc Syst Zool; Soc Vert Palaeont. *Res:* The adaptive significance of specializations of mammals for life in deserts, particularly the structure and function of the ear in desert rodents; origin, evolution, functional anatomy, biology and systematics of rodents. *Mailing Add:* 100 1/2 Moon Pt Chapel Hill NC 27514

LAY, JOHN CHARLES, VETERINARY DIAGNOSTIC PATHOLOGY, PULMONARY PATHOLOGY. *Current Pos:* ASST PROF, DEPT VET PATH, TEX A&M UNIV, 83- *Personal Data:* b Ponca City, Okla, Mar 6, 48; wid; c 3. *Educ:* Univ Mo, Columbia, BS, 71, DVM, 75; Cornell Univ, PhD, 86. *Prof Exp:* Assoc scientist vet med, Inhalation Toxicol Res Inst, Lovelace Found for Med Educ & Res, 75-77; gen vet practr, Lakin, Kans, 77-78; fel trainee exp path, NY State Col Vet Med, Cornell Univ, 78-83. *Mem:* Am Vet Med Asn. *Res:* Bovine Respiratory Disease; pulmonary inflammatory response and mechanisms of deep lung clearance and lung defense. *Mailing Add:* 311 Brandywine Rd Chapel Hill NC 27516

LAY, KENNETH W(ILBUR), CERAMICS, MATERIALS SCIENCE. *Current Pos:* Res scientist, Gen Elec Res & Develop Ctr, 65-73, commun & admin mgr mat sci & engr, 73-75, mgr ceramics processing, 75-87, MAT SCIENTIST, GEN ELEC RES & DEVELOP CTR, 87- *Personal Data:* b Ringgold Co, Iowa, Feb 4, 39; m 64, Anita Rollins; c Douglas, Marla & Kathleen. *Educ:* Iowa State Univ, BS, 61; Northwestern Univ, PhD(mat sci), 66. *Mem:* Fel Am Ceramic Soc; Mat Res Soc. *Res:* Ceramics processing and properties; diffusion; nuclear fuels; non-stoichiometric compounds; oxide superconductors. *Mailing Add:* Gen Elec Res & Develop Ctr PO Box 8 Schenectady NY 12301

LAY, STEVEN R, MATHEMATICS. *Personal Data:* b Los Angeles, Calif, Nov 28, 44; m 71; c 2. *Educ:* Aurora Col, BA, 66; Univ Calif, Los Angeles, MA, 68, PhD(math), 71. *Prof Exp:* Assoc prof, Aurora Univ, 71-80, prof math, 80-90. *Mem:* Am Math Soc; Math Asn Am; Nat Coun Teachers Math. *Res:* Combinatorial geometry and convexity; the separation of convex sets; mathematics education. *Mailing Add:* 80-1517 Tenjin Cho Ono Shi 675-13 Japan

LAY, THORNE, SEISMOLOGY. *Current Pos:* dir, Inst Tectronics, 90-94, PROF SEISMOL, UNIV CALIF, SANTA CRUZ, 89-, DIR, INST TECTONICS, 94- *Personal Data:* b Casper, Wyo, Apr 20, 56; m 93, Susan Schwartz; c Griffin Reedlay. *Educ:* Univ Rochester, BS, 78; Calif Inst Technol, MS, 80, PhD(geophys), 83. *Honors & Awards:* Macelwane Medal, Am Geophys Union, 91. *Prof Exp:* Researcher, Calif Inst Technol, 83; from asst prof to assoc prof seismol, Univ Mich, 84-89, dir, Seismog Sta, 87-89. *Concurrent Pos:* Sloan Found fel, 85-87; Shell fac fel, Shell Found, 85-88; presidential young investr, NSF, 85-90; panelist, US Geol Surv Rev Panel, 88-90, Air Force Geophys Lab Panel, 88-92, Air Force Tech Appln Ctr Panel, 87-, Defense Advan Res Projs Agency Proposal Rev Panel, 91 & NSF Geophys Panel, 90-93; ed, EOS, Am Geophys Union, 89-91; chmn, SEDI Comt, US Am Geophys Union, 90-92; mem, Comt Seismol, Nat Res Coun, 92-, chmn, Panel Seismic Data Requirements, 94-95, Panel CTBT Res, 95-97. *Mem:* Seismol Soc Am; fel Am Geophys Union; fel Royal Astron Soc; AAAS; Soc Explor Geophysicists; Am Asn Prof Geologists. *Res:* Earthquake seismology; structure of the earths interior; author of over 130 papers in professional journals and books. *Mailing Add:* Earth Sci Dept Univ Calif Santa Cruz Santa Cruz CA 95064. *Fax:* 408-459-2127; *E-Mail:* thorne@earthsci.ucsc.edu

LAYBOURNE, PAUL C, PSYCHIATRY. *Current Pos:* Assoc, 49-51, from asst prof to assoc prof, 51-65, PROF PSYCHIAT, MED CTR, UNIV KANS, 65-, ASSOC PROF PEDIAT, 54-, PROF PSYCHIATRY & FAMILY PRACT, 80- *Personal Data:* b Akron, Ohio, Dec 21, 19; m 45; c 3. *Educ:* NY Med Col, MD, 44; Ind Univ, MS, 49. *Concurrent Pos:* Consult, Spofford Home, Kansas City, Mo, 50-; dir, Atchison Co Guid Clin, 51-59; supvr extern prog, State Hosps, 53-55; dir child guid clin, Mercy Hosp, 57-66. *Mem:* AMA; fel Am Psychiat Asn. *Res:* Child psychiatry. *Mailing Add:* 39th & Rainbow Kansas City KS 66103

LAYCHOCK, SUZANNE GALE, PHOSPHOLIPIDS, CYCLIC NUCLEOTIDES & INSULIN. *Current Pos:* PROF PHARMACOL, STATE UNIV NY, BUFFALO, 89- *Personal Data:* b Brooklyn, NY, Apr 28, 49. *Educ:* Brooklyn Col, BS, 71; City Univ NY, MA, 73; Med Col Va, PhD(pharmacol), 76. *Prof Exp:* Res assoc pharmacol, Vanderbilt Univ, 77-78; from asst prof to assoc prof, Med Col Va, 78-89. *Mem:* Endocrine Soc; Am Soc Pharmacol & Exp Therapeut; Am Diabetes Asn. *Res:* Investigation of the signal transduction mechanisms which regulate insulin secretion from islets of Langerhans; role of phospholipid turnover, cyclic nucleotides, eicosanoids and calcium in regulation of metabolism and insulin release in the beta cell. *Mailing Add:* Pharmacol & Therapeut Dept 102 Farber Hall Sch Med State Univ NY Buffalo NY 14214. *Fax:* 716-829-2801; *E-Mail:* slaychoc@ubmed.buffalo.edu

LAYCOCK, MAURICE VIVIAN, NATURAL PRODUCTS, MARINE ALGAE. *Current Pos:* RETIRED. *Personal Data:* b Liverpool, Eng, Sept 3, 38; Can citizen; m 66; c Katherine & Martin. *Educ:* Liverpool Univ, BSc, 62, PhD(plant physiol), 65. *Prof Exp:* Res officer biochem, Nat Res Coun Can, 68-96. *Res:* Protein chemistry; biochemistry of nitrogen compounds in algae; chemistry of marine toxins. *Mailing Add:* Nat Res Coun 1411 Oxford St Halifax NS B3H 3Z1 Can. *Fax:* 902-426-9413; *E-Mail:* maurice@imb.lan.nrc.ca

LAYCOCK, WILLIAM ANTHONY, PLANT ECOLOGY. *Current Pos:* head, Dept Range Mgt, 85-96, EMER PROF, UNIV WYO, 96- *Personal Data:* b Ft Collins, Colo, Mar 17, 30; m 55, Charlotte Pulscher; c Cody & Donice. *Educ:* Univ Wyo, BS, 52, MS, 53; Rutgers Univ, PhD(bot), 58. *Honors & Awards:* Outstanding Achievement Award, Soc Range Mgt, 85, Renner Award, 93. *Prof Exp:* Asst, Rutgers Univ, 55-58; range scientist, Intermountain Forest & Range Exp Sta, 58-74, asst dir, Rocky Mountain Forest Range Exp Sta, US Forest Serv, 74-76, range scientist, Agr Res Serv, USDA, 76-85. *Concurrent Pos:* Collabr range sci, Utah State Univ, 64-74; NZ Nat Res Adv Coun-NZ Forest Serv sr res fel, 69-70; coordr site dir western coniferous biomed, US Int Biol Prog, 71-72; affil fac, Colo State Univ, 74-; mem, continuing comt, Int Rangeland Cong, 91-99, consult, 96- *Mem:* Ecol Soc Am; fel Soc Range Mgt (pres, 88). *Res:* Ecology and management of rangelands; autecology of range species; snow management on rangelands. *Mailing Add:* Dept Range Mgt Box 3354 University Sta Laramie WY 82071

LAYDEN, GEORGE KAVANAUGH, MATERIALS SCIENCE. *Current Pos:* RETIRED. *Personal Data:* b Greenport, NY, Apr 13, 29; m 60; c 3. *Educ:* Lafayette Col, BS, 53; Pa State Univ, MS, 59, PhD(ceramic technol), 61. *Prof Exp:* mat scientist, Unitet Technol Res Ctr, 61- *Mem:* Am Ceramic Soc; AAAS; Sigma Xi. *Res:* Fabrication and characterization of aerospace materials, including fibrilar carbon and graphite, structrural ceramics, nickel based superalloys and fiber and whisker reinforced glass/ceramic matrix composites. *Mailing Add:* 1071 Farmington Ave West Hartford CT 06107

LAYE, RONALD CURTIS, CLINICAL HEALTH PSYCHOLOGY, APPLIED PSYCHOPHYSIOLOGY. *Current Pos:* PROF PSYCHOL, UNIV COL FRASER VALLEY, 77-; CLIN CONSULT PSYCHOL, 82- *Personal Data:* b New York, NY, Nov 27, 45; m 67, Estarisa Polansky; c Aviva, Basya, Shira, Devora & Aaron. *Educ:* Clarkson Col Technol, BS, 67; Univ Alta, MSc, 73, PhD(psychol), 76. *Prof Exp:* Instr psychol & clin psychologist, Univ Alta, 73-76; vis asst prof, State Univ NY, Oswego, 76-77. *Concurrent Pos:* Consult psychol & clin psychologist, Chillwack Ment Health Ctr, 79-93, dept head, 88-96; pvt pract, 82- *Mem:* Soc Behav Med; Asn Appl Psychophysiol & Biofeedback; Can Psychol Asn. *Res:* Psychophysiological profiling in assessment of stress disorders; biofeedback methodology; personality and health; fibromyalgia; psychophysiology of television. *Mailing Add:* Dept Psychol Univ Col Fraser Valley 33844 King Rd Abbotsford BC V2S 7M9 Can. *Fax:* 604-855-7558; *E-Mail:* laye@ucfv.bc.ca

LAYER, ROBERT WESLEY, ORGANIC CHEMISTRY. *Current Pos:* sr tech mgr, B F Goodrich Co, 55-57, sr res chemist, 57-71, res assoc, 71-79, sr res assoc, 79-90, RES FEL, B F GOODRICH CO, 90- *Personal Data:* b Brooklyn, NY, Aug 11, 28; wid, Barabara A Nelson; c Steven R, David N & Caren S. *Educ:* NY Univ, AB, 50; Univ Cincinnati, PhD, 55. *Honors & Awards:* Melvin Mooney Award, Rubber Div, Am Chem Soc, 92. *Prof Exp:* Control chemist, Naugatuck Chem Co, 50-52. *Mem:* Am Chem Soc; Rubber & Polymer Divs, Akron Rubber Group. *Res:* Rubber chemicals; reactions of ozone; chemistry of p-phenylenediamines and of anils; antioxidants; accelerators. *Mailing Add:* 4621 A Cox Dr Stow OH 44224

LAYLOFF, THOMAS, ANALYTICAL CHEMISTRY. *Current Pos:* From asst prof to prof, 64-76, ADJ PROF CHEM, ST LOUIS UNIV, 76; DIR, DIV DRUG ANALYSIS, FOOD & DRUG ADMIN, 76- *Personal Data:* b Granite City, Ill, Jan 29, 37; m; c 3. *Educ:* Wash Univ, AB, 58, MA, 61; Univ Kans, PhD(analytical chem), 64. *Concurrent Pos:* Sci adv, Nat Ctr Drug Analysis, Food & Drug Admin, 67-76. *Mem:* AAAS; Sigma Xi; Am Chem Soc; Asn Off Anal Chem; fel Am Asn Pharmaceut Scientists. *Res:* Data acquisition and processing; chemometrics. *Mailing Add:* PO Box 207 Granite City IL 62040-0207. *Fax:* 314-539-2113

LAYMAN, DALE PIERRE, MEDICAL TERMINOLOGY-TERMINOLOGY OF BIOLOGICAL SCIENCES, EPIDEMIOLOGIC BASIS OF ATHLETIC INJURIES. *Current Pos:* PROF HUMAN ANAT & PHYSIOL, MED TERMINOLOGY, JOLIET JR COL, 75- *Personal Data:* b Niles, Mich, July 3, 48; m 70, Kathleen Jackowiak; c Andrew, Alexis, Allison & Amanda. *Educ:* Univ Mich, BS, 71, MS, 74; Ball State Univ, Eds, 79, Univ Ill, PhD(health & safety studies), 86. *Prof Exp:* Prof anat & physiol, Lake Super State Univ, 74-75. *Mem:* Human Anat Physiol Soc; AAAS. *Res:* Author of textbooks in human anatomy and physiology, medical terminology; research in epidemiology of running injuries; research and authoring in biological order, disorder. *Mailing Add:* 509 Westridge Lane Joliet IL 60431

LAYMAN, DON LEE, ANATOMY. *Current Pos:* ASSOC PROF, DEPT ANAT, MED CTR, LA STATE UNIV, 84- *Personal Data:* b Johnston, Pa, May 20, 38; m 64, Ann Frances King; c Douglas, Richard & Todd. *Educ:* Juniata Col, BS, 61; Syracuse Univ, MS, 65; George Washington Univ, PhD(cell biol), 70. *Prof Exp:* Biologist, Nat Eye Inst & Nat Inst Dent Res, 68-70, res chemist, Lab Biochem, Nat Inst Dent Res, 70-71; NIH spec fel, Dept Path, Univ Wash, Seattle, 71-73; res asst prof, Dept Path, Baylor Col Med, 73-75; asst prof, Dept Med, Ore Health Sci Univ, 75-77 & Dept Anat, 77-84. *Concurrent Pos:* Spec fel, NIH, 71-73. *Mem:* Sigma Xi; Am Soc Cell Biol; NY Acad Sci; AAAS; Tissue Cult Asn; Am Asn Dent Res. *Res:* Periodontitis. *Mailing Add:* Dept Anat La State Univ Med Ctr 1100 Florida Ave New Orleans LA 70119-2714

LAYMAN, DONALD KEITH, HUMAN NUTRITION, EXERCISE PHYSIOLOGY. *Current Pos:* From asst prof to assoc prof, Univ Ill, 78-89, chair, Div Food & Nutrit, 90-91, dir, Sch Human Res & Family Studies, 91-95, PROF NUTRIT, UNIV ILL, 89-; ASSOC DEAN, COL AGR, CONSUMER & ENVIRON SCI, 95- *Personal Data:* b Kewanee, Ill, Feb 15, 50; c 2. *Educ:* Ill State Univ, BS, 72, MS, 74; Univ Minn, PhD(nutrition), 78. *Honors & Awards:* Young Investr Award, NIH, 82, Shannon Award, 92; BioServ Award, Am Inst Nutrit, 86. *Concurrent Pos:* Consult, nutrition, Regional Office Educ, Ill, 79-80, Nat Aeronaut & Space Admin, 83, Shriner's Hosp Barred Children, 86; adj prof, Inst Agron & Vet, Rabat, Morroco, 86-90; bd, Human Sci, 95- *Mem:* Inst Food & Technol; Sigma Xi; Am Soc Nutrit Sci. *Res:* Regulation of protein turnover and energy metabolism on skeletal muscle; amino acid metabolism cellular growth and development of skeletal muscle, nutrition, and exercise. *Mailing Add:* Dept Food Sci & Human Nutrit 260 Bevier Hall Univ Ill 905 S Goodwin Urbana IL 61801. *E-Mail:* d-layman@uiuc.edu

LAYMAN, WILBUR A, ANALYTICAL CHEMISTRY, PHYSICAL CHEMISTRY. *Current Pos:* RETIRED. *Personal Data:* b Blair, Nebr, Jan 9, 29; m 53, Alice Schultz; c Mike, Karen, Judi, Gregg & Rodney. *Educ:* Dana Col, BS, 53; Univ Nebr, MS, 58; Mont State Univ, PhD(analytical chem), 63. *Prof Exp:* Chemist, Harris Labs, 54-58; instr chem, Hastings Col, 58-60 & Dana Col, 62-63; asst prof, SDak State Univ, 63-66; assoc prof, Adams State Col, 66-67; prof chem & chmn, Phys Sci Dept, Easternmost Col, 67-82. *Mem:* Am Chem Soc. *Res:* Stability constants of metal complexes; polarized infrared spectroscopy of thin crystal films. *Mailing Add:* 619 Ave C Billings MT 59102

LAYMAN, WILLIAM ARTHUR, PSYCHIATRY. *Current Pos:* from instr to assoc prof, 59-74, clin prof, 74-77, PROF PSYCHIAT, UNIV MED & DENT NJ, 77- *Personal Data:* b West New York, NJ, Feb 8, 29; m 83, Barbara M LaBelle; c William K. *Educ:* St Peter's Col, NJ, BS, 51; Georgetown Univ, MD, 55; Am Bd Psychiat & Neurol, dipl, 62. *Prof Exp:* Intern, Hackensack Hosp, NJ, 55-56; jr resident psychiat, Vet Admin Hosp, Lyons, 56-57; sr resident, Fairfield Hills Hosp, Newtown, Conn, 57-59. *Concurrent Pos:* Clin fel psychiat, Sch Med, Yale Univ, 58-59. *Mem:* Am Asn Univ Prof; Am Psychiat Asn; Am Acad Forensic Sci. *Res:* Nonverbal communication; psycotherapeutic technique. *Mailing Add:* Dept Psychiat NJ Med Sch Newark NJ 07103

LAYNE, CLYDE BROWNING, APPLIED PHYSICS. *Current Pos:* TECH STAFF, COMBUSTION PHYSICS DIV, SANDIA NAT LAB, LIVERMORE, CALIF, 80-, INITIATIVE MGR, INT SECURITY. *Personal Data:* b El Paso, Tex, Feb 19, 47; m 69; c 1. *Educ:* Princeton Univ, AB, 69; Univ Calif, Davis, MS, 73, PhD(appl sci), 75. *Prof Exp:* Physicist, Div Laser Physics, Lawrence Livermore Lab, Univ Calif, 69-80. *Mem:* Am Phys Soc; Optical Soc Am. *Res:* Relaxation and energy transfer in ions in solids; atomic vapor-laser isotope separation of uranium; lasers applied to combustion diagnostics. *Mailing Add:* Sandia Nat Labs PO Box 5800 MS-1230 Albuquerque NM 87185

LAYNE, DONALD SAINTEVAL, BIOCHEMISTRY. *Current Pos:* VPRES, TORONTO GEN HOSP, 82- *Personal Data:* b Lime Ridge, Que, Apr 5, 31; m 59; c 3. *Educ:* McGill Univ, BSc, 53, MSc, 55, PhD, 57. *Prof Exp:* Fel biochem, Univ Edinburgh, 57-58; res assoc psychiat, Queen's Univ Ont, 58-59; from scientist to sr scientist, Worcester Found Exp Biol, 59-66; head Physiol & Endocrinol Sect, Food & Drug Directorate, Can, 66-68; prof biochem, Univ Ottawa, 68-79; vpres, Connaught Lab, Ltd, 79-82. *Mem:* AAAS; Endocrine Soc; Am Soc Biol Chemists; Royal Soc Can. *Res:* Biochemistry of estrogenic hormones. *Mailing Add:* Toronto Gen Hosp CCRW 1-800 200 Elizabeth St Toronto ON M5G 2C4 Can

LAYNE, JAMES NATHANIEL, MAMMALOGY, VERTEBRATE BIOLOGY. *Current Pos:* res dir, Archbold Biol Sta & Archbold Cur Dept Mammal & mem bd dir, Archbold Expeds, Am Mus Natural Hist, 67-76, exec dir & mem bd dirs, 76-85, sr res biologist, 85-93, EMER SR RES BIOLOGIST, ARCHBOLD BIOL STA, 94- *Personal Data:* b Chicago, Ill, May 16, 26; m 50, Lois V Linderoth; c Linda C, Kimberly, Jamie, Susan & Rachel. *Educ:* Cornell Univ, BA, 50, PhD(zool), 54. *Honors & Awards:* C Hart Merriam Award, Am Soc Mammalogists, 76. *Prof Exp:* Asst vert zool, Cornell Univ, 50-54, asst prof zool, 63-67; asst prof zool, Southern Ill Univ, 54-55; from asst prof to assoc prof biol, Univ Fla, 55-63; assoc prog zool, Cornell Univ, 63-67. *Concurrent Pos:* Vis scientist, Pvt Ecol Sect, Lab Perinatat Physiol, NINDB, 61-62; from asst cur to assoc cur biol sci, Fla State Mus, 55-63, res assoc, 63-65; adj prof, Univ SFla, 68-89; consult, WHO, 69; res assoc, Am Mus Natural Hist, 82-90; res assoc, Fla State Collection Arthropods. *Mem:* Fel AAAS; Am Soc Zoologists; hon mem Am Soc Mammalogists (vpres, 65-70, pres, 70-72); Wildlife Soc; Ecol Soc Am; Orgn Biol Field Stas (vpres, 84-85, pres, 86-87). *Res:* Mammalian ecology, systematics, behavior and morphology; general vertebrate biology and ecology of Florida. *Mailing Add:* Archbold Biol Sta PO Box 2057 Lake Placid FL 33856. *Fax:* 941-699-1927; *E-Mail:* jlayne@ct.net

LAYNE, PORTER PRESTON, BIOCHEMISTRY. *Current Pos:* assoc investr develop, Smith Kline Corp, 80-81, asst dir clin data sci, 82-83, asst dir, Preregis Affairs, 83-84, assoc dir clin info, 85, dir, 85-86, SR INVESTR DEVELOP, SMITH KLINE CORP, 82-, DIR REGULATORY AFFAIRS, 86- *Personal Data:* b Martin, Ky, Sept 20, 45; m 72; c 2. *Educ:* Univ Ky, BS, 66, PhD(biochem), 71; Boston Univ, MBA, 78. *Prof Exp:* Fel protein chem, Sch Med, Tufts Univ, 71-73, asst prof, 74-80. *Concurrent Pos:* Actg chmn, Div Chem, Sch Med, Tufts Univ, 75-76. *Mem:* Sigma Xi; Drug Info Asn; Regulatory Affairs Prof Soc. *Res:* Extra chromosomal inheritance; bacterial physiology; enzyme mechanism (phosphoglucomutase); adenylate cyclase and tuftsin research. *Mailing Add:* RR 4 Pottstown PA 19465-9804

LAYNE, RICHARD C, PLANT BREEDING. *Current Pos:* RETIRED. *Personal Data:* b St Vincent, Wis, Dec 14, 36; Can citizen; m 63, Val R Davis; c Desmond & Carrie. *Educ:* McGill Univ, BSc, 59; Univ Wis, MS, 60, PhD(agron, plant path), 63. *Honors & Awards:* Shepard Award, Am Pomol Soc, 67 & 83, Wilder Medal, 96; Carrol R Miller Award, Am Soc Hort Sci, 77, 78, 82, 85, Outstanding Researcher Award, 93. *Prof Exp:* Res scientist, Res Sta, Agr Can, 63-96. *Concurrent Pos:* Head, Hort Sci Sect, Harrow Res Sta; int consult hort, 96- *Mem:* Can Soc Hort Sci (pres, 77); fel Am Soc Hort Sci; Am Pomol Soc (pres, 91-92); Int Soc Hort Sci. *Res:* Breeding of cultivars and rootstocks of peach, nectarine and apricot; breeding for cold hardiness and disease resistance; environmental and genetic factors affecting cold hardiness; rootstock-scion physiology; peach orchard management systems. *Mailing Add:* PO Box 132 Harrow ON N0R 1G0 Can. *E-Mail:* layne@mnsi.net

LAYNG, EDWIN TOWER, CHEMISTRY. *Current Pos:* RETIRED. *Personal Data:* b Greenville, Pa, Jan 20, 09; m 46; c 2. *Educ:* Allegheny Col, ScB, 30; NY Univ, PhD(chem), 33. *Prof Exp:* Asst, NY Univ, 30-33; res chemist, M W Kellogg Co, NJ, 34-42, assoc dir res, 43; dir res, Hydrocarbon Res, Inc, 43-44, asst to the pres, 44-46, vpres, 47-63, exec vpres, 64-72, pres, 72-74; vpres, Dynalectron Corp, 64-74; consult, 74-77. *Mem:* Am Chem Soc; Am Inst Chem Eng; Am Petrol Inst. *Res:* Reaction kinetics; catalysis in petroleum processes; synthetic fuels; coal gasification; coal liquefaction. *Mailing Add:* 8 Surrey Rd Summit NJ 07901-3255

LAYSON, WILLIAM M(CINTYRE), PHYSICS, MECHANICAL ENGINEERING. *Current Pos:* vpres & mgr, Wash Div, 70-76, VPRES, CONTINUUM MECH DIV, SCI APPLN INC, 76- *Personal Data:* b Lexington, Ky, Sept 24, 34; m 67; c 2. *Educ:* Mass Inst Technol, BS, 56, PhD(physics), 63. *Prof Exp:* Res physicist, Univ Calif, 62-63; lectr physics, 63-64; sr systs engr tech staff, Pan Am World Airways, 64-67; mem tech staff, Gen Res Corp, 67-69, mgr dept, 69-70. *Mem:* Am Phys Soc; Am Inst Aeronaut & Astronaut; Inst Elec & Electronics Engrs. *Res:* Nuclear weapons effects; dust and debris clouds; radiation transport; ground coupling; fireball effects; radar systems; fluid mechanics; electromagnetic propagation; atmospheric physics; systems analysis. *Mailing Add:* 8301 Summerwood Dr McLean VA 22102

LAYTON, DAVID WARREN, RISK ANALYSIS, WATER RESOURCES. *Current Pos:* ENVIRON SCIENTIST RISK ANALYSIS WATER RESOURCES & ENERGY, LAWRENCE LIVERMORE NAT LAB, UNIV CALIF, 75- *Personal Data:* b Woburn, Mass, Sept 19, 48; m 77; c 3. *Educ:* Bridgewater State Col, BA, 70; Univ Ariz, PhD(water resources admin), 75. *Mem:* Am Water Resources Asn; Soc Risk Analysis. *Res:* Risk analysis; environmental studies; pollution control technologies; geothermal energy. *Mailing Add:* 559 Ontario Dr Livermore CA 94550

LAYTON, EDWIN THOMAS, JR, HISTORY OF TECHNOLOGY. *Current Pos:* PROF HIST SCI & TECHNOL, UNIV MINN, 75- *Personal Data:* b Sept 13, 28; m 82; c 1. *Educ:* Univ Calif, Los Angeles, BA, 50, MA, 53, PhD(hist), 56. *Honors & Awards:* Dexter Prize, Soc Hist Technol, 70, Leonardo da Vinci Medal, 90. *Prof Exp:* Instr hist, Univ Wis, 56-57, Ohio State Univ, 57-60; asst prof, Purdue Univ, 60-65; assoc prof hist sci & technol, Case Western Res Univ, 65-75. *Concurrent Pos:* Adv ed, Isis, 79-81, Bus & Prof Ethics J, 81-; mem, Nuclear Manpower Studies Comn, Nat Acad Sci-Nat Res Coun, 81. *Mem:* Soc Hist Technol (pres, 85-86); Hist Sci Soc; fel AAAS; Soc Social Studies Sci. *Res:* Interaction of science and technology in nineteenth century America; nature and role engineering sciences; history of engineering. *Mailing Add:* 2816 Webster Ave SE Minneapolis MN 55416

LAYTON, JACK MALCOLM, PATHOLOGY. *Current Pos:* RETIRED. *Personal Data:* b Ossian, Iowa, Sept 27, 17; m 43; c 2. *Educ:* Luther Col, AB, 39, DSc, 74; Univ Iowa, MD, 43; Am Bd Path, dipl, 50. *Prof Exp:* Intern, Univ Iowa Hosp, 43, asst path, 46-47, instr, 47-49, assoc, 49-50, from asst prof to prof, 50-67; prof path & head dept, Col Med, Univ Ariz, 67-88. *Concurrent Pos:* Actg dean, Col Med & actg dir, Med Ctr, Univ Ariz, 71-73; trustee, Am Bd Path, 74-; dir clin path, Ariz Health Serv, 67-88. *Mem:* Am Soc Clin Path (pres, 73); Col Am Path; Am Asn Path & Bact; Am Soc Exp Path; Int Acad Path (pres, 75-76); Sigma Xi. *Res:* Virology; host-parasite relationships in viral and rickettsial diseases; comparative pathology of inflammation; ultramicroscopic pathologic anatomy of infectious diseases; biological activities of teratomas; influenza and psittacosis-lymphogranuloma groups of viruses. *Mailing Add:* 5815 N Placita Del Baron Tucson AZ 85718

LAYTON, RICHARD GARY, PHYSICS, CLOUD PHYSICS. *Current Pos:* assoc prof, 69-83, chair, Dept Physics & Astron, 85-92, PROF PHYSICS, NORTHERN ARIZ UNIV, 83- *Personal Data:* b Salt Lake City, Utah, Dec 24, 35; m 63, Susan E Brinkman; c Catherine, Paul & Spencer. *Educ:* Univ Utah, BA, 60, MA, 62; Utah State Univ, PhD(physics), 65. *Prof Exp:* Asst physics, Univ Utah, 60-62; asst res physicist electro-dynamics Labs, Utah State Univ, 63-64; from asst prof to assoc prof physics, State Univ NY Col, Fredonia, 65-69. *Concurrent Pos:* Res assoc, Lowell Observ, 71 & 72; sci collabr, Grand Canyon Nat Park, 72-75; interim chair, Physics Dept, Northern Ariz Univ, 85-86, chair, 86-92. *Mem:* Am Asn Physics Teachers; Am Phys Soc; Sigma Xi. *Res:* Ice nucleation surfaces, ellipsometry; atmospheric optics; frost damage prevention for plants; science education. *Mailing Add:* Dept Physics Box 6010 Northern Ariz Univ Flagstaff AZ 86011-6010. *Fax:* 520-523-1371; *E-Mail:* gary.layton@nau.edu

LAYTON, TERRY NORTH, MEDICAL PRODUCT DESIGN, MEDICAL TECHNOLOGY ASSESSMENT. *Current Pos:* DIR BIOMED ENG, PACKER ENG, 91- *Personal Data:* m 69, Catherine S Crawford; c Amy & Terry N II. *Educ:* Univ Wyo, BS, 66; Univ Ill, MS, 72; Univ Va, PhD (biomed eng), 75. *Prof Exp:* Res engr, Kendall Co, 75-76, sr res engr, 76-78, sect head, 78-80, mgr, 80-88; mgr, Baxter, 88-90; chief tech officer, Laytech, 90-91. *Mem:* Inst Elec & Electronics Engrs; Plastics Eng; Urodynamics Soc. *Res:* Design and commercialization of medical products, with expertise in new technologies, design, engineering and manufacturing in the areas of anesthesia, cathetic, intravenous products and urology. *Mailing Add:* 1771 Andrew Ct Lake Zurich IL 60047

LAYTON, THOMAS WILLIAM, PHYSICS. *Current Pos:* RETIRED. *Personal Data:* b Kaysville, Utah, Feb 24, 27; m 47, Jean Wheeler; c Lisa. *Educ:* Calif Inst Technol, BS, 51, PhD(physics, math), 57. *Prof Exp:* Res engr, Jet Propulsion Lab, Calif Inst Technol, 53-55; mem tech staff, Inertial Guid Dept, Thompson-Ramo-Wooldridge, Inc, 55-59, mgr, 59-64, sr staff engr, Defense & Space Systs Group, 64-91, consult, 91-97. *Mem:* Am Phys Soc; Am Inst Aeronaut & Astronaut. *Res:* Cosmic rays; navigation and guidance systems for ballistic missiles and space flight vehicles. *Mailing Add:* 4836 W Elmdale Dr Rolling Hills CA 90274. *Fax:* 310-378-1692

LAYTON, WILLIAM ISAAC, geometry; deceased, see previous edition for last biography

LAYZER, ARTHUR JAMES, THEORETICAL PHYSICS. *Current Pos:* asst prof, 64-67, ASSOC PROF PHYSICS, STEVENS INST TECHNOL, 68-, ASSOC PROF ENG PHYSICS, 77- *Personal Data:* b Cleveland, Ohio, Aug 21, 27; m 64; c 1. *Educ:* Case Western Res Univ, BS, 50; Columbia Univ, PhD(physics), 60. *Prof Exp:* Res scientist, Courant Inst, NY Univ, 60-63. *Concurrent Pos:* Vis res scientist, Brookhaven Nat Lab, 66; resident visitor comput music, Acoust Div, Bell Labs, 67-83; US Dept Educ grant deafness res & reading, 78-80. *Mem:* AAAS; Am Educ Res Asn. *Res:* Quantum mechanical theory of critical phenomena, especially superconductivity; sound-analogic text representations in deafness and language; score-mediated generation of music and text; test measures and analysis in reading and writing; language and art media applications of computer science. *Mailing Add:* 161 W 75th St Apt 5E New York NY 10023

LAYZER, DAVID, ASTRONOMY. *Current Pos:* res assoc, Harvard Univ, 53-55, res fel & lectr, 55-60, prof astron, 60-80, DONALD H MENZEL PROF ASTROPHYS, HARVARD UNIV, 80- *Personal Data:* b Ohio, Dec 31, 25; m 49, 59; c 6. *Educ:* Harvard Univ, AB, 47, PhD(theoret astrophys), 50. *Honors & Awards:* Bok Prize, 60. *Prof Exp:* Nat Res Coun res fel, 50-51; lectr astron, Univ Calif, Berkeley, 51-52; res assoc physics, Princeton Univ, 52-53. *Concurrent Pos:* Consult, Geophys Corp Am, 59-65. *Mem:* Am Acad Arts & Sci; Am Astron Soc; Int Astron Union; Royal Astron Soc. *Res:* Cosmology and cosmogony; theoretical astrophysics and atomic physics; ionospheric physics. *Mailing Add:* Dept Astron Harvard Univ Observ 60 Gordon St MS 16 Cambridge MA 02138-3800

LAZAR, ANNA, METHOD DEVELOPMENT FOR DETECTING DIETHYLSTILBESTROL RESIDUES IN TISSUES, LIQUID CHROMATOGRAPHIC METHOD DEVELOPMENT FOR THE ANALYSIS OF INSULIN. *Current Pos:* CHEMIST, FOOD & DRUG ADMIN, 70- *Personal Data:* b Budapest, Hungary, Jan 10, 31; US citizen; m 55; c Julie A. *Educ:* Eotros Lorand Sci Univ, Budapest, Dipl, 55. *Prof Exp:* Chemist, Harvard Univ, 57-59, Arthur D Little, 59-61, Wilkens Instr & Res, 61-62, Stanford Univ, 62-63, Hercules Inc, 64-69 & Cancer Res Inst, 69-70. *Res:* Analytical method development for the determination and identification of protein hormones, monoclonal antibody purity assessment, and measurements of a variety of pharmaceutical residues in a number of different matrices; analytical method evaluation of new drug applications. *Mailing Add:* 428 Montgomery Ave Haverford PA 19041

LAZAR, BENJAMIN EDWARD, civil engineering, for more information see previous edition

LAZAR, NORMAN HENRY, PLASMA & NUCLEAR PHYSICS. *Current Pos:* RETIRED. *Personal Data:* b Brooklyn, NY, June 21, 29; m 61, Katie W. *Educ:* City Col New York, BS, 49; Ind Univ, MS, 51, PhD(physics), 53. *Prof Exp:* Physicist, Oak Ridge Nat Lab, Union Carbide Nuclear Co, 53-78; TRW Defense & Space Syst, 78-93. *Mem:* Fel Am Phys Soc; fel AAAS. *Res:* Controlled thermonuclear reactions; beta and gamma ray spectroscopy; plasma physics. *Mailing Add:* 38194 S Golf Course Dr Tucson AZ 85737. *E-Mail:* nlazar@juno.com

LAZARCHICK, JOHN, HEMATOLOGY & HEMOSTASIS. *Current Pos:* asst prof, 79-82, ASSOC PROF HEMAT, MED UNIV SC, 82- *Personal Data:* b Pottsville, Pa, Nov 1, 42; m 60; c John J. *Educ:* Lafayette Col, AB, 64; Thomas Jefferson Med Univ, MD, 68. *Prof Exp:* Asst prof hemat, Health Ctr, Univ Conn, 77-79. *Mem:* Am Fedn Clin Res; AAAS; Asn Clin Scientists; World Hemophilia Fedn. *Res:* Role of protein kinase C in platelet function; release reaction and the pathophysiologic basis of fibronectin elevation in preeclampsia. *Mailing Add:* Dept Lab Med Med Univ SC 171 Ashley Ave Charleston SC 29425-0001

LAZARETH, OTTO WILLIAM, JR, SPACE NUCLEAR POWER, REACTOR PHYSICS. *Current Pos:* physics assoc, 67-73, PHYSICIST, BROOKHAVEN NAT LAB, 74- *Personal Data:* b Brooklyn, NY, Sept 16, 38. *Educ:* Wagner Col, BS, 61; Queens Col, MA, 68; City Univ NY, PhD(physics), 73. *Prof Exp:* Asst res physics, Queens Col, 65-67. *Mem:* Am Phys Soc; Am Nuclear Soc. *Res:* Nucleonics; radiation damage and effects in solids; modeling physical systems with computers. *Mailing Add:* Bldg 701 Brookhaven Nat Lab Upton NY 11973

LAZARIDES, ELIAS, pharmacology, cell biology, for more information see previous edition

LAZARIDIS, ANASTAS, ENERGY ENGINEERING, HEAT TRANSFER. *Current Pos:* from asst prof to assoc prof, 83-97, CHMN, DEPT MECH ENG, WIDENER UNIV, 94-, PROF, 97- *Personal Data:* b Istanbul, Turkey, Dec 8, 40; US citizen; m 66; c 2. *Educ:* Robert Col, Turkey, BS, 63; Columbia Univ, MS, 64, EngScD, 69. *Prof Exp:* Res engr, Exxon Res & Eng Co, 65, Heat & Mass Transfer Lab, Columbia Univ, 65-68, Textile Fibers Dept, E I du Pont de Nemours & Co Inc, 69-72; heat transfer specialist-process eng, Day & Zimmermann Inc, Philadelphia, 72-75; regional mkt mgr process control, Control Automation Technol Co, 75-76; pres, Helios Inc, Wilmington, Del, 76-83. *Concurrent Pos:* Fulbright scholar award, Columbia Univ, 63-64, Boese scholar award, 64-65; lectr mech eng, Manhattan Col, 65-67 & Richmond Col, City Univ New York, 67-68; adj prof mech eng, Drexel Univ, 72-75; tech paper reviewer, Heat Transfer J & Solar Energy Eng J, Am Soc Mech Engrs, Int J Heat & Mass Transfer, Int J Numerical Heat Transfer; fac res grants, Am Soc Eng Educ/Dept Energy, 83, US Army, 85 & USAF, 88-90; Fulbright scholar, Democritas Univ, Thrace, Greece, 97-98. *Mem:* Am Soc Eng Educ; Am Soc Mech Eng. *Res:* Energy; heat transfer; thermodynamics of energetic materials; textile engineering; combustion and detonation; mathematical modeling; contributed over 30 articles to professional publications. *Mailing Add:* Sch Eng Widener Univ Chester PA 19013. *Fax:* 215-499-4059

LAZARIDIS, CHRISTINA NICHOLSON, MATERIALS SCIENCE, ELECTRONIC MATERIALS. *Current Pos:* RES ASSOC, E I DU PONT DE NEMOURS & CO INC, 68- *Personal Data:* b New York, NY, Jan 12, 42; m 66, Anastas; c Emmanuel & Nina. *Educ:* Mt Holyoke Col, AB, 62; Columbia Univ, MA, 63, PhD(chem), 66. *Prof Exp:* Res chemist, Colgate-Palmolive Co, 66-68. *Mem:* Am Chem Soc. *Res:* Photosensitive systems, including conventional silver halide as well as novel photopolymeric materials; thick film materials for electronics, polymeric and cermet systems, membrane touch switch inks, ultraviolet curable products, conductors, dielectrics and resistors for screen-printing applications and photoresists; polyimides and photodefinable polyimides. *Mailing Add:* Electronics Mat du Pont Co Exp Sta PO Box 80336 Wilmington DE 19880-0336. *Fax:* 302-695-8196; *E-Mail:* lazaridi@esvax.dnet.dupont.com

LAZARIDIS, NASSOS A(THANASIUS), MECHANICAL METALLURGY, PHYSICAL METALLURGY. *Current Pos:* CONSULT, AUTOMOTIVE PROD APPLN, 94- *Personal Data:* b Athens, Greece, Oct 6, 43; m 73, Linda E Peterson; c Christine & Laura. *Educ:* Nat Tech Univ, Athens, BS & MS, 67; Univ Wis-Madison, MS, 70, PhD(metall eng), 71. *Prof Exp:* Prod engr metal working, Nat Can Corp, Greece, 73-74; lectr & proj assoc, Univ Wis-Madison, 74-75; sr res engr, Inland Steel Co, 75-79, spec consult, Sec Steel Refining & Continuous Casting, 79-80, supvr res engr, Res Lab, 80-85, sect mgr, Mat Eng, Prod Appl Res, 85-88, sect mgr flat prod, Qual Dept, 87-88; metall technol mgr, I/N Kote, Joint Venture Inland Steel Co & Nippon Steel Corp, 89-94. *Concurrent Pos:* Proj assoc, Am Motors Corp, 74-75; adj prof, Purdue Univ, Calumet Campus, 78-86. *Mem:* Am Soc Metals Int; Greek Tech Chamber Prof Engrs; Sigma Xi; Soc Automotive Engrs. *Res:* Fracture toughness; fatigue; product development; formability, effect of metallurgy on machinability; hot deformation of steel and other alloys; materials engineering; hot drip and electrogalvanizing of sheet steel, product testing, corrosion resistance; applications of sheet steels to automotive design; material selection; automotive materials. *Mailing Add:* 15593 Spring Meadow Lane Granger IN 46530-9063. *Fax:* 219-399-6562; *E-Mail:* lazandis@inland. com

LAZARO, ERIC JOSEPH, surgery, for more information see previous edition

LAZAROFF, NORMAN, GEOCHEMICAL ACTIVITIES OF MICROORGANISMS, SCREENING FOR NEW ANTIBIOTICS. *Current Pos:* assoc prof, 66-90, EMER ASSOC PROF BIOL & RES PROF, STATE UNIV NY BINGHAMTON, 90-; OWNER, MICRONOSTIX, 93- *Personal Data:* b Brooklyn, NY, Nov 24, 27; m 58, Sandra Nord; c Alan & Deborah. *Educ:* Syracuse Univ, AB, 50, MS, 52; Yale Univ, PhD(microbiol), 60. *Prof Exp:* Asst enzymol, Res Found, State Univ NY, 55; bacteriologist, Schwarz Labs, Inc, 55-56; proj leader, Evans Res & Develop Corp, 56-57, consult, 57-59; fel microbiol, Brandeis Univ, 60-61; microbiologist, BC Res Coun, 61-62; asst prof biol sci, Univ Southern Calif, 62-64; sr res scientist, Res Corp, Syracuse, 64-66. *Mem:* Am Soc Microbiol; Am Chem Soc; Phycol Soc Am. *Res:* Photophysiology of cyanobacterial differentiation and morphogenesis; anti-adhesin antibiotics; bio and geochemical role of sulfate in chemolithotrophic iron oxidation. *Mailing Add:* Micronostix 312 Front St Vestal NY 13850. *Fax:* 607-785-3093; *E-Mail:* nostoc@bingvmb.cc. binghamton.edu

LAZAROW, PAUL B, CELL BIOLOGY, INTRACELLULAR TRANSPORT & ASSEMBLY. *Current Pos:* PROF & CHMN, DEPT CELL BIOL & ANAT, MT SINAI SCH MED, NEW YORK, NY, 89- *Personal Data:* b May 6, 45. *Educ:* Univ Chicago, AB, 67; Rockefeller Univ, PhD(biochem cytol), 72. *Prof Exp:* NIH int fel, Lab Molecular Embryol, Naples, Italy, 72-73; Damon Runyon fel, Dept Biol Sci, Stanford Univ, Palo Alto, Calif, 73-75; from asst prof to assoc prof, Rockefeller Univ, New York, NY, 75-89. *Concurrent Pos:* Adj prof, Rockefeller Univ, NY, NY, 89- *Mem:* Harvey Soc Am (secy); Soc Cell Biol; Am Soc Biochem & Molecular Biol; Am Soc Human Genetics, Marine Biol Lab Corp. *Res:* Peroxisome biogenesis in yeast (mutants, genes and the cellular roles of gene products in assembling peroxisomes); inherited human diseases caused by defects in peroxisome function or biogenesis. *Mailing Add:* Cell Biol & Anat Dept Mt Sinai Sch Med Fifth Ave & 100th St Box 1007 New York NY 10029. *Fax:* 212-860-1174

LAZARTE, JAIME ESTEBAN, HORTICULTURE & DEVELOPMENT PHYSIOLOGY, PROTEIN PRODUCTION & BIOTECHNOLOGY. *Current Pos:* LECTR, HARVARD MED SCH, 91-, DIR, PROTEIN PROD & CTR BLOOD RES, 91- *Personal Data:* b Lima, Peru, July 26, 43. *Educ:* Agrarian Univ, BS & Ing Agr, 66; Rutgers Univ, MS, 70, PhD(hort), 76. *Prof Exp:* Lab supvr tissue cult, Rutgers Univ, 73-76; res assoc veg crops, Univ Fla, 76-78; asst prof hort, Tex A&M Univ, 78-82, res, 89-91; pres, PRI, 83-88. *Concurrent Pos:* Consult biotechnol; Fulbright scholar, 90 & 91. *Mem:* Am Soc Hort Sci. *Res:* Flower initiation and sex expression; sex modification; morphology and embryology horticultural crops; asparagus officinalis; plant tissue culture; biotechnology; protein production; insect cell-baculovirus; bioreactors; cyclic guanosine monophosphate facility design; cyclic guanosine, monophosphate protein production. *Mailing Add:* 127 Booth St Needham MA 02194. *Fax:* 617-787-7909

LAZARUS, ALLAN KENNETH, CHEMISTRY. *Current Pos:* RETIRED. *Personal Data:* b Bangor, Maine, May 20, 31; m 57, Gloria Berkowitz; c Carol, Martin & Warren. *Educ:* NY Univ, BA, 52, MS, 55, PhD(org chem), 57. *Prof Exp:* Chemist, Cities Serv Res & Develop Co, 57-59, Inorg Chem Div, FMC Corp, 59-65 & Esso Res & Eng Co, 65-66; group leader synthetic lubricants, Intermediates Div, Tenneco Chem, Inc, 66-71; asst prof chem, Trenton State Col, 72-97. *Mem:* Sigma Xi; Sci Res Soc Am. *Res:* Stereochemistry; organic synthesis; product and process development; fuels; automatic transmission fluids; synthetic lubricants. *Mailing Add:* Dept Chem Col NJ PO Box 4700 Hillwood Lakes Trenton NJ 08650-4700

LAZARUS, DAVID, SOLID STATE PHYSICS. *Current Pos:* from instr to prof, 49-87, EMER PROF PHYSICS, UNIV ILL, URBANA, 87- *Personal Data:* b Buffalo, NY, Sept 8, 21; m 43, Betty J Ross; c Barbara, William, Mary Ann & Richard. *Educ:* Univ Chicago, PhD(physics), 49. *Prof Exp:* Instr electronics, Univ Chicago, 42-43; res assoc, Radio Res Lab, Harvard Univ, 43-45; asst physics, Univ Chicago, 46-49, instr, 49. *Concurrent Pos:* Guggenheim fel, 68-69; vis prof, Univ Paris, 68-69, Harvard Univ & Mass Inst Technol, 78-79; chmn, Coun Mat Sci, US Dept Energy, 81-86; ed-in-chief, Am Phys Soc, 80-91; mem gov bd, Am Inst Physics, 81- *Mem:* Fel Am Phys Soc; fel Am Asn Physics Teachers; fel AAAS. *Res:* Defect and electronic properties of solids; high pressure physics. *Mailing Add:* 502 W Vermont Ave Urbana IL 61801

LAZARUS, GERALD SYLVAN, DERMATOLOGY. *Current Pos:* DEAN, SCH MED, UNIV CALIF, DAVIS, 82- *Personal Data:* b New York, NY, Feb 16, 39; m 61; c 4. *Educ:* Colby Col, BS, 59; George Washington Univ, MD, 63. *Hon Degrees:* MA, Univ Pa, 82. *Honors & Awards:* Sultzberger Award, Am Acad Dermat; Montagna Award, Soc Invest Dermat. *Prof Exp:* Med intern, Univ Mich Med Ctr, 63-64, med resident, 64-65; clin assoc, Med Neurol Br, Nat Inst Neurol Dis & Blindness, 65-67; prin investr, Lab Histol & Path, Nat Inst Dent Res, 67-68; clin & res assoc, Dept Dermat, Harvard Med Sch, 68-70, chief resident dermat, 69-70; vis scientist, Strangeways Labs, Univ Cambridge, Eng, 70-72; assoc prof med & co-dir dermat training prog, Albert Einstein Col Med, 72-75; chmn, Div Dermat, Duke Univ Med Ctr, 75-78, prof med, 75-, J Lamar Calloway chair prof dermat, 75-82; Milton B Hartzell prof & chair, Dept Dermat, Univ Pa, 82-93. *Concurrent Pos:* Carl Herzog fel, 70-72; res fel, Arthritis Found, 70-72; sr investr, 72-77; consult dermat, Addenbrookes Hosp, Cambridge, Eng, 70-72; vis fel, Clare Hall, Cambridge; head, Sect Dermat, Dept Med, Montefiore Hosp, 72-75. *Mem:* Am Rheumatism Asn; Soc Invest Dermat (pres-elect, 97-98); Am Fedn Clin Res; fel Am Col Physicians; Royal Soc Med; Am Soc Clin Invest; Asn Am Physicians; Am Dermat Asn. *Res:* Study of the role of proteinases in catabolic processes in skin and evaluation of the mechanisms by which these proteinases can instigate an inflammatory response; role of proteinases in inflammation generally and skin diseases particularly. *Mailing Add:* Off Dean Sch Med Univ Calif Davis CA 95616

LAZARUS, LAWRENCE H, OPIOID PEPTIDES, RECEPTORS. *Current Pos:* RES CHEMIST, NAT INST ENVIRON HEALTH SCI, NIH, 77-, HEAD, PEPTIDE NEUROCHEM SECT, 83- *Educ:* Univ Calif, Los Angeles, PhD(cellular physiol), 66. *Mem:* AAAS; Am Soc Biochem & Molecular Biol; Int Neuropeptide Soc; Am Chem Soc; Am Peptide Soc. *Res:* Peptide biochemistry; peptide mode of action; neuropeptides. *Mailing Add:* Inst Environ Health Sci NIEHS NIH PO Box 12233 Research Triangle Park NC 27709-2233

LAZARUS, MARC SAMUEL, PHYSICAL INORGANIC CHEMISTRY. *Current Pos:* from asst prof to assoc prof, 74-84, PROF CHEM, HERBERT H LEHMAN COL, CITY UNIV NEW YORK, 84- *Personal Data:* b Brooklyn, NY, Sept 9, 46; c 1. *Educ:* City Univ New York, BS, 68; Princeton Univ, MA, 71, PhD(chem), 74. *Prof Exp:* Res assoc chem, Lawrence Berkeley Lab, Univ Calif, 73-74. *Concurrent Pos:* Res collabr, Brookhaven Nat Lab, 74-84. *Mem:* Am Chem Soc; Am Phys Soc. *Res:* Applications of x-ray photoelectron spectroscopy to the study of transition metal compounds and alloys. *Mailing Add:* Dept Chem Bedford Park Blvd W City Univ NY Herbert H Lehman Col Bronx NY 10468

LAZARUS, ROGER BEN, THEORETICAL PHYSICS. *Current Pos:* Mem staff, Los Alamos Sci Lab, 51-58, group leader, 58-68, div leader, 68-73, MEM STAFF, LOS ALAMOS SCI LAB, 73- *Personal Data:* b New York, NY, June 3, 25; m 46; c 5. *Educ:* Harvard Univ, AB, 47, MA, 48, PhD(physics), 51. *Mem:* NY Acad Sci; Am Phys Soc; Asn Comput Mach. *Res:* Simultaneous partial differential equations; computing machines. *Mailing Add:* 2539 35th St Los Alamos NM 87544-1542

LAZARUS, STEVEN S, MARKETING. *Personal Data:* b Rochester, NY, June, 16, 43; m 66, Elissa C; c Michael, Stuart & Jean. *Educ:* Cornell Univ, BS, 66; Polytech Univ NY, MS, 67; Univ Rochester, PhD, 74. *Prof Exp:* Pres, Mgt Systs Analysis Corp, Denver, 77-94. *Concurrent Pos:* Speaker, Med Group Mgt Asn, 75-; consult, State Colo, Denver, 76-81; dir, Sci Appln Intern Corp, Englewood, Colo, 79-84; assoc prof, Metro State Col, Denver, 83-84; sr vpres, Pal Assocs, Inc, Denver, 84-85; mkt consult, Clin Ref Systs, Denver, 86-, IMX, Louisville, Ky, 86-87; assoc & exec dir, Ctr Res, Ambulatory Health Care Admin. *Mem:* Sr mem Inst Indust Eng; Med Group Mgt Asn; Opers Res Soc Am. *Res:* Strategic planning; marketing; industrial engineering. *Mailing Add:* 4949 Syracuse St Denver CO 80237

LAZAR-WESLEY, ELIANE M, PHYSIOLOGY. *Current Pos:* PATENT EXAMR, PATENT & TRADEMARK OFF. *Personal Data:* b Strasbourg, France, Jan 24, 53. *Educ:* Univ Louis Pasteur, France, BSc, 75, PhD, 82. *Prof Exp:* Researcher, Nat Ctr Sci Res, France, 79-82, sr researcher, 82-84, & Lab Molecular Oncol, Inst Sci Cancer Res, 87-89; vis fel, Lab Chemoprev, Nat Cancer Inst, NIH, Bethesda, 84-87, sr staff fel, Lab Physiol & Pharmacol Studies, Nat Inst Alcohol Abuse & Alcoholism, Rockville, Md, 89- *Mailing Add:* Patent & Trademark Off Arlington VA 22202

LAZAY, PAUL DUANE, solid state physics, for more information see previous edition

LAZDA, VELTA ABULS, IMMUNOLOGY, MOLECULAR BIOLOGY. *Current Pos:* asst prof, Dept Surg, 77-91, ADJ ASSOC PROF, UNIV ILL MED CTR, 91-; DIR HISTOCOMPATIBILITY LAB, REGIONAL ORGAN BANK, ILL, 87- *Personal Data:* b Riga, Latvia, Dec 16, 39; US citizen; m 62. *Educ:* Purdue Univ, BS, 62; Northwestern Univ,

PhD(microbiol), 67. *Prof Exp:* Res assoc, Immunol Div, Res Inst, Am Dent Asn Health Found, 69-77. *Concurrent Pos:* Am Cancer Soc fel ribosome struct, Northwestern Univ, 67-69; USPHS career develop award, 72-77. *Mem:* AAAS; Am Asn Immunologists; Am Soc Microbiol; Am Soc Histocompatibility & Immunogenetics. *Res:* Transplantation immunology. *Mailing Add:* Reg Organ Bank Ill 800 S Wells Suite 190 Chicago IL 60607-4529. *Fax:* 312-431-3626

LAZELL, JAMES DRAPER, POPULATION BIOLOGY, BIOGEOGRAPHY. *Current Pos:* PRES, CONSERV AGENCY, 79- *Personal Data:* b New York, NY, Sept 5, 39. *Educ:* Univ South, Sewanee, BA, 61; Univ Ill, MS, 63; Harvard Univ, MA, 66; Univ RI, PhD(biol), 70. *Prof Exp:* Head, Dept Sci, Palfrey Street Sch, 66-74; sci staff, Mass Audubon Soc, 67-76, sanctuary dir, 75-79. *Concurrent Pos:* Collabr, Nat Park Serv, 69-; prin investr, Earthwatch, 73-; assoc, Mus Comp Zool, 77-, Bishop Mus, 87-, Miss Mus Natural Sci, 90-; curatorial affil, Yale Peabody Mus, 82- *Mem:* Am Soc Ichthyologists & Herpetologists; Am Soc Mammalogists; Am Soc Zoologists; Soc Study Amphibians & Reptiles; fel Explorers Club. *Res:* Vertebrate systematics; endangered species conservation; ecology; demographics; distribution of rare and little-known animals; exploration as of 1990; author of 120 scientific papers and three books. *Mailing Add:* 8 Swinburne St Jamestown RI 02835

LAZERSON, EARL EDWIN, ALGEBRA, NUMBER THEORY. *Current Pos:* Actg chmn, Dept Math, Southern Ill Univ, 71-72, chmn, 72-73, dean, Sch Sci & Technol, 73, actg vpres & provost, 76-77, vpres & provost, 77-79, actg pres, 79-80, PROF MATH, SOUTHERN ILL UNIV, 73-, PRES, 80- *Personal Data:* b Detroit, Mich, Dec 10, 30; m 66; c 2. *Educ:* Wayne State Univ, BS, 53; Univ Mich, MA, 54, PhD, 82. *Concurrent Pos:* NSF res grant, 62-67. *Mem:* Am Math Soc; Math Asn Am; London Math Soc; Soc Math de France. *Mailing Add:* 5 Hidden Valley Lane Edwardsville IL 62025-3706

LAZO, JOHN STEPHEN, ONCOLOGY, BIOCHEMICAL PHARMACOLOGY. *Current Pos:* PROF PHARMACOL & CHMN DEPT, UNIV PITTSBURGH, SCH MED, 87- *Personal Data:* b Philadelphia, Pa, Dec 15, 48; m 74, Jacqui Fiske; c Jacquelyn. *Educ:* Johns Hopkins Univ, BA, 71; Univ Mich, Ann Arbor, PhD(pharmacol), 76. *Prof Exp:* Lab asst, Dept Pharmacol, Thomas Jefferson Med Col, 68-69; lab asst, Dept Chem, Johns Hopkins Univ, 71; USPHS-NIH trainee, Dept Pharmacol, Univ Mich, Ann Arbor, 71-76; fel, Yale Univ, 76-78, from asst prof to assoc prof pharmacol, 78-87. *Concurrent Pos:* Vis scientist, Sloan-Kettering Inst Cancer Res, 85-86 & Nat Cancer Res Inst, Tokyo, Japan, 90. *Mem:* Am Soc Pharmacol & Exp Therapeut; Tissue Culture Asn; Am Asn Cancer Res; NY Acad Sci; AAAS; Am Soc Biochem & Molecular Biol. *Res:* Pharmacology and toxicology of antitumor agents; use of cultured cells to study drug actions; action of drugs on lung tissue. *Mailing Add:* 5128 Pembroke Pl Pittsburgh PA 15232. *E-Mail:* lazo@pop.pitt.edu

LAZOWSKA, EDWARD DELANO, COMPUTER SYSTEMS. *Current Pos:* PROF COMPUT SCI, UNIV WASH, 77-, DEPT CHMN, 93- *Personal Data:* b Washington, DC, Aug 3, 50; m 78, Lyndsay C Downs; c Adam & Jeremy. *Educ:* Brown Univ, 72; Univ Toronto, MSc, 74, PhD, 77. *Concurrent Pos:* Vis scientist, DEC Systs Res Ctr, 84-85; mem, adv bd, Microsoft, 91-, bd dirs, Comput Res Asn, 92- *Res:* Computer systems; modelling & analysis; design and implementation; distributed and parallel systems. *Mailing Add:* Comput Sci FR-35 Univ Wash 3900 Seventh Ave NE Seattle WA 98195-0001

LAZZARA, RALPH, MEDICINE. *Current Pos:* PROF MED, SCH MED, UNIV OKLA, 78- *Personal Data:* b Tampa, Fla, Aug 14, 34; m 59; c 3. *Educ:* Univ Chicago, BA, 55; Tulane Univ, MD, 59. *Prof Exp:* Instr med, Tulane Univ, 60-67; asst prof med, Sch Med, Univ Miami, 71-72, assoc prof, 72-77; chief sect cardiol, Vet Admin Hosp, 74-78. *Concurrent Pos:* Asst, Charity Hosp, New Orleans, 60-64; resident, Med Sch, Tulane Univ & Charity Hosp, 63-64; fel, Col Physicians & Surgeons, Columbia Univ, 64-65; staff mem & dir cardiovasc res lab, Ochsner Clin & Ochsner Found Hosp, New Orleans, 65-67; staff cardiologist & chief sect electrophysiol, Mt Sinai Hosp, Miami Beach, 70-72; dir coronary care unit, Vet Admin Hosp, Miami, 72-75; chief sect cardiol, Univ Okla Health Sci Ctr & Vet Admin Hosp, Oklahoma City, 78- *Mem:* Am Physiol Soc; Soc Chem Invest. *Res:* Cardiac electrophysiology. *Mailing Add:* Univ Okla Health Sci Ctr PO Box 26901 Oklahoma City OK 73190-0001

LAZZARINI, ALBERT JOHN, systems engineering, optical systems design, for more information see previous edition

LAZZARINI, ROBERT A, MOLECULAR GENETICS. *Current Pos:* DIR, BROOKDALE CTR MOLECULAR BIOL, MT SINAI SCH MED, NY, 88- *Personal Data:* b New York, NY, Oct 14, 31. *Educ:* Univ Calif, Los Angeles, BS, 55, PhD(biol chem), 60. *Honors & Awards:* Quastel Lectr Molecular Sci, McGill Univ, Can, 85; Pfizer Lectr, Univ Montreal, Can, 85; Meritorious Exec Rank Award Sr Sci Serv, 86. *Prof Exp:* Postdoctoral fel, Johns Hopkins Univ, 60-63; staff fel, Lab Biochem, Nat Inst Dent Res, NIH, 63-64, Lab Molecular Biol, Nat Inst Neurol & Commun Dis & Stroke, 64-65, res scientist, 65-70, head, Sect Regulation Nucleic Acid Synthesis, 70-74, Sect Molecular Virol, 74-81, chief, Lab Molecular Genetics, 81-88. *Concurrent Pos:* Session chmn, Gordon Res Conf, 74 & 75; chmn, Conf Mech Viral Resistance, Mult Sclerosis Soc, Colo, 80; mem, Virol Study Sect, Div Res Grants, NIH, 80 & Neurol C Study Sect, 88-89; chmn, RNA Virus Div, Am Soc Microbiol, 81-83; mem, Adv Coun Basic Sci, Mult Sclerosis Soc, 81-87, Adv Coun Microbiol & Virol, Am Cancer Soc, 82-84 & Alzheimer Dis Adv Bd, Am Health Assistance Found, 89- *Mem:* Am Soc Biol Chemists; Am Soc Microbiol; Am Soc Neurochem; Am Soc Virol. *Mailing Add:* Mt Sinai Sch Med PO Box 1126 New York NY 10029

LE, CHAP THAN, STATISTICS, BIOMETRICS. *Current Pos:* ASST PROF BIOMET, UNIV MINN, 78- *Personal Data:* b Vietnam, Aug 1, 48; m 75. *Educ:* Calif State Univ, BA, BS & MA, 71; Univ NMex, PhD(statist), 78. *Mem:* Biomet Soc. *Res:* Reliability and life testing; nonparametric statistics; survey sampling; theory of survivorship; epidemiology. *Mailing Add:* Pub Health Box 197 Mays Univ Minn Med Sch 420 Delaware St SE Minneapolis MN 55455-0374

LE, GUAN, SPACE PHYSICS. *Current Pos:* ASST RES GEOPHYSICIST, INST GEOPHYS & PLANETARY PHYSICS, UNIV CALIF, LOS ANGELES, 91- *Personal Data:* b Chengdu, China, Sept 14, 62; m, Zhi Wang. *Educ:* Univ Sci & Technol China, BS, 84; Univ Calif, Los Angeles, MS, 89, PhD(geophys & space physics), 91. *Mem:* Am Geophys Union. *Res:* Ultraflow frequency waves upstream of collisionless shocks, the earth's magneto pause and boundary layers, and solar wind-magnetosphere interaction; analysis and interpretation of spacecrafts data and ground-based data as they related to these research areas. *Mailing Add:* Inst Geophysics & Planetary Physics Univ Calif Los Angeles CA 90024-1567. *Fax:* 310-206-3051; *E-Mail:* guan@igpp.ucla.edu

LE, SHU-YUN, BIOINFORMATICS, STRUCTURAL BIOLOGY. *Current Pos:* vis fel, Lab Math Biol, Div Cancer Biol & Diag, Nat Cancer Inst, NIH, 85-88, vis assoc, 88-89, vis scientist, Div Biol Sci, 92-96, STAFF SCIENTIST, NAT CANCER INST, NIH, 97- *Personal Data:* m, Jing-Jing Wang; c Robert Yi. *Educ:* Shanghai Jiaotong Univ, China, cert, 70; Shanghai Inst Biochem, Chinese Acad Sci, China, MS, 81, PhD, 82. *Prof Exp:* Technician, Shanghai Zhong-Hua Chuang Chang, 70-72, asst engr, 72-75, col teacher math, 75-78; res assoc, Shanghai Inst Biochem, Chinese Acad Sci, 82-83, asst prof, 83-85. *Concurrent Pos:* NIH Fogarty vis fel, NIH, 85-89; res assoc, Nat Res Coun, Can, 89-92. *Mem:* Biophys Soc. *Res:* Computational molecular biology; use the sequences of genes, converted to RNA, to predict the secondary and higher order structures of RNA; research on viruses and cells by computational analysis; published more the 60 papers. *Mailing Add:* LECB DBS Nat Cancer Inst Bldg 469 Rm 151 Frederick MD 21702. *Fax:* 301-846-5598; *E-Mail:* shuyun@ncifcrf.gov

LEA, ARDEN OTTERBEIN, ENTOMOLOGY. *Current Pos:* RETIRED. *Personal Data:* b Cleveland, Ohio, Oct 19, 26; m 52; c 2. *Educ:* Univ Rochester, BA, 48; Ohio State Univ, MSc, 50, PhD(entom), 57. *Prof Exp:* Res assoc insecticide testing, Ohio State Univ, 50-51, insect nutrit, 56-58; USPHS med entomologist, Onchocerciasis Proj, Pan Am Sanit Bur, Guatemala, 51-53; chief, Physiol Sect, Entom Res Ctr, State Bd Health, Fla, 58-69; assoc prof entom, Univ Ga, 69-74, prof, 74-92. *Concurrent Pos:* USPHS spec res fel, Denmark, 60-61; mem, Trop Med & Parasitol Study Sect, NIH, 74-78; mem, Sci Adv Panel Onchocerciasis, WHO. *Mem:* AAAS; Am Soc Trop Med & Hyg; Am Mosquito Control Asn. *Res:* Endocrine physiology of Diptera; physiology and behavior of mosquitoes; peptide hormones. *Mailing Add:* 360 Millstone Circle Athens GA 30605

LEA, GEORGE KOO, HIGH PERFORMANCE COMPUTING, FLUID MECHANICS. *Current Pos:* assoc prog dir, 70-72, prog dir fluid mech, 72-85, PROG DIR, COMMUN & COMPUT SYSTS, NSF, 87- *Personal Data:* b Shanghai, China, Oct 20, 38; US citizen; m 63, Anna Tsao; c Irene T, Elaine T & Michelle T. *Educ:* George Washington Univ, BSME, 60; Va Polytech Inst, PhD(eng mech), 66. *Prof Exp:* Asst prof mech eng, George Washington Univ, 65-71; vis res scientist, David Taylor Res & Develop Ctr, 85-86. *Mem:* Am Phys Soc. *Res:* Perturbation and asymptotic methods in mechanics, gasdynamics, radiative heat transfer, nonlinear water waves. *Mailing Add:* NSF ECS Div Rm 670 4201 Wilson Blvd Arlington VA 22230. *Fax:* 703-306-0305; *E-Mail:* glea@nsf.gov

LEA, JAMES DIGHTON, SYSTEMS SCIENCE. *Current Pos:* Sr res scientist physics, Esso Prod Res Co, Stand Oil NJ, 63-69, sr prof systs analyst, Humble Oil & Refining Co, 69-73, explor systs adv, Exxon Co USA, 73-75, RES ASSOC SYSTS, EXXON PROD RES CO, EXXON CORP, 75- *Personal Data:* b Monticello, Ill, Apr 9, 33; m 53; c 2. *Educ:* Tex Western Col, BA, 57; Univ Tex, MA, 60, PhD(physics), 63. *Mem:* Am Math Soc; Am Phys Soc; Soc Explor Geophysicists; Am Asn Petrol Geologists. *Res:* Application of computer science to geological problems. *Mailing Add:* 6230 Bayou Bridge Houston TX 77096-3706

LEA, JAMES WESLEY, JR, TOPOLOGY, ALGEBRA. *Current Pos:* from asst prof to assoc prof, 71-81, PROF MATH, MIDDLE TENN STATE UNIV, 81- *Personal Data:* b Lebanon, Tenn, Mar 17, 41; m 66; c 2. *Educ:* Tenn Polytech Inst, BS, 63, MS, 65; La State Univ, PhD(math), 71. *Prof Exp:* Instr math, Univ Tenn, Martin, 15-66; instr, Tenn Technol Univ, 66-67. *Concurrent Pos:* Vis assoc prof math, Univ Tenn, Knoxville, 76-77. *Mem:* Am Math Soc; Math Asn Am; Sigma Xi. *Res:* Lattice theory. *Mailing Add:* Middle Tenn State Univ Box 222 Murfreesboro TN 37132-0001

LEA, MICHAEL ANTHONY, BIOCHEMISTRY. *Current Pos:* from asst prof to assoc prof, 67-78, PROF BIOCHEM, UNIV MED & DENT NJ, 78- *Personal Data:* b Leeds, Eng, Dec 26, 39; wid; c Gareth D & Catrin J. *Educ:* Univ Birmingham, BSc, 61, PhD(biochem), 64. *Prof Exp:* Res assoc pharmacol, Sch Med, Ind Univ, 64-66, instr, 66-67. *Mem:* AAAS; Am Chem Soc; Am Soc Cell Biol; Am Asn Cancer Res; Am Soc Biochem Molecular Biol. *Res:* Control of nucleic acid synthesis and growth in normal and neoplastic cells. *Mailing Add:* Dept Biochem Univ Med & Dent NJ Newark NJ 07103-2714. *Fax:* 973-982-5594; *E-Mail:* lea@umdnj.edu

LEA, ROBERT MARTIN, PHYSICS. *Current Pos:* Chmn dept, 70-74 & 87-89, PROF PHYSICS, CITY COL NEW YORK, 57- *Personal Data:* b New York, NY, Nov 4, 31; m 53; c 1. *Educ:* Union Col, NY, BS, 53; Yale Univ, PhD(physics), 57. *Concurrent Pos:* Vis physicist, Brookhaven Nat Lab, 59-70; prin investr, NSF res grants, City Col New York, 59-70, dir, NSF Dept Develop Grant, 70-74, NRCSE, 81-88. *Mem:* Am Phys Soc; Am Asn Physics Teachers. *Res:* High energy experimental physics. *Mailing Add:* 130 Newton Ville Ave Newton MA 02158

LEA, SUSAN MAUREEN, ASTROPHYSICS, PHYSICS EDUCATION. *Current Pos:* assoc prof, 80-84, PROF, DEPT PHYSICS & ASTRON, SAN FRANCISCO STATE UNIV, 84- *Personal Data:* b Cardiff, Wales, UK, July 10, 48; m 74, Michael Lampton; c Jennifer. *Educ:* Cambridge Univ, BA, 69, MA, 73; Univ Calif, Berkeley, PhD(astron), 74. *Prof Exp:* Res assoc astrophys, Ames Res Ctr, NASA, 74-76; res fel, Univ Md, College Park, 76-77; asst res astron, Univ Calif, Berkeley, 77-80. *Mem:* Am Astron Soc; Royal Astron Soc; Int Astron Union; Am Phys Soc. *Res:* High energy astrophysics, especially x-ray and radio astronomy; numerical hydrodynamics; compact galactic x-ray sources, clusters of galaxies, intergalactic matter and cosmology. *Mailing Add:* Dept Physics & Astron San Francisco State Univ 1600 Holloway Ave San Francisco CA 94132-1722

LEA, WAYNE ADAIR, COMPUTER RECOGNITION OF SPEECH. *Current Pos:* DIR, SPEECH SCI PUBL, 80-, DIR, SPEECH SCI INST, 85- *Personal Data:* b Helena, Mont, Jan 16, 40; c 7. *Educ:* Mont State Col, BS, 62, MS, 64; Mass Inst Technol, SM & EE, 66, Purdue Univ, PhD, 72. *Prof Exp:* Res assoc, Electronics Res Lab, Mont State Col, 62-64; NSF fel, Electronics Res Lab, Mass Inst Technol, 64-66; proj leader, Electronics Res Ctr, NASA, 66-70; instr elec eng, Res Found, Purdue Univ, 70-72; prin investr, Defense Systs Div, Sperry Univac, 72-77; res scientist, Speech Commun Res Lab, 77-81. *Concurrent Pos:* Adj assoc prof, Dept Ling, Univ Southern Calif, 78-83 & Dept Elec & Comput Eng, Univ Calif, Santa Barbara, 81-83; consult speech recognition var co, 79-; chmn, Acad Forensic Appl Commun Sci, 78-82; sr vpres & dir, Ctr Speech Res & Educ, VCS Corp, 83-84; actg mgr, Speech Group, A I Lab, NYNEX S&T, 87. *Mem:* Sr mem Inst Elec & Electronics Engrs; Acoust Soc Am; Am Acad Forensic Sci; Am Asn Phonetic Sci; Sigma Xi. *Res:* Computer recognition of speech; intonation, linguistic stress and rhythm; acoustic phonetics, forensic phonetics. *Mailing Add:* PO Box 240428 Apple Valley MN 55124

LEABO, DICK ALBERT, APPLIED STATISTICS, ECONOMIC STATISTICS. *Current Pos:* from asst prof to assoc prof statist, Univ Mich, Ann Arbor, 57-63, assoc dean, Grad Sch Bus, 62-65, dir PhD Prog, 65-81, prof, 63-79, Fred M Taylor Distinguished prof, 78-84, EMER FRED M TAYLOR DISTINGUISHED PROF STATIST, UNIV MICH, ANN ARBOR, 84- *Personal Data:* b Walcott, Iowa, Oct 30, 21; m 55; c 1. *Educ:* Univ Iowa, BS, 49, MA, 50, PhD(statist, econ), 53. *Honors & Awards:* Order of Artus, Hon Econs Soc. *Prof Exp:* Res asst econ, Bur Bus & Econ Res, Univ Iowa, 48-49, res assoc, 49-53, asst prof econ & asst dir, 53-56; asst prof econ & asst dir, Bur Econ & Bus Res, Mich State Univ, 56-57. *Concurrent Pos:* Consult, Brookings Inst, 57-59 & NCent Accrediting Asn, 74-84; exchange prof, Rotterdam Sch Econ, 65. *Mem:* Am Statist Asn; Am Econ Asn; Asn Bus Economists. *Res:* Regional economic research and the application of regression and correlation techniques. *Mailing Add:* 2115 Nature Cove Ct No 105 Ann Arbor MI 48104-4977

LEACH, BARRIE WILLIAM, APPLIED MATHEMATICS, ELECTRICAL ENGINEERING. *Current Pos:* Asst res officer, 72-80, ASSOC RES OFFICER, FLIGHT RES, NAT RES COUN CAN, 80- *Personal Data:* b Winnipeg, Man, Nov 25, 45; m 66; c 2. *Educ:* Univ Man, BSc, 67, MSc, 68, PhD(elec eng), 72. *Mem:* Inst Elec & Electronics Engrs. *Res:* Optimal parameter and state estimation; aeromagnetics; geophysical and anti-submarine warfare applications; digital filtering techniques multi-sensor navigation techniques. *Mailing Add:* Nat Res Coun Montreal Rd Bldg U-61 Ottawa ON K1A 0R6 Can

LEACH, BERTON JOE, ZOOLOGY, SCIENCE ADMINISTRATION. *Current Pos:* RETIRED. *Personal Data:* b Tuscola, Ill, Mar 30, 32; m 55, Barbara L English; c Laura A (Weiss) & Berton F. *Educ:* Washington Univ, AB, 57; Univ Mo, MA, 60, PhD(zool), 63. *Prof Exp:* Asst zool, Univ Mo, 58-60, instr, 60-62, USPHS res fel, 62-63; asst prof, George Washington Univ, 63-66; asst prog dir, Undergrad Student Prog, NSF, 66-67, Col Sci Improv Prog, 67-68; prof biol, Cent Methodist Col, 68-70, F H Dearing prof, 70-74, chmn dept biol & geol, 68-74; exec secy, Cardiovasc & Pulmonary Study Sect, Div Res Grants, NIH, 74-76; chief consult, Berton J Leach Assoc, Rockville, Md, 76-78; sr scientist, Capital Syst Group, 78-81. *Concurrent Pos:* NSF res grant, 63-65; assoc prof, George Wash Univ, 66; USPHS res evaluator, 66-67; vis scholar, Harvard Univ, 69; med technol educ adv, Jewish Hosp, St Louis, 72; comput data bases, US Govt Contracts Pvt Indust, 76-81; gen reader, Marine Biol Lab, 85-87; vol lab instr neuroanat, Georgetown Univ Med Sch, 88, adj assoc prof cell biol, 89-97, dir, Human Neurobiol Educr, 94; guest researcher, Brain & Behav Lab, NIH, 91-92. *Mem:* Sigma Xi; Am Soc Mammalogists; AAAS; Int Soc Hist Philos & Social Studies Biol; Marine Biol Lab Asn. *Res:* Cancer construction data base; vertebrate biology computer courseware; mammalian neuroanatomy; mammalian behavior; vocalizations of Talpidae. *Mailing Add:* 12707 Weiss St Rockville MD 20853. *Fax:* 301-929-8467; *E-Mail:* bertjleach@aol.com

LEACH, CHARLES MORLEY, PLANT PATHOLOGY, MYCOLOGY. *Current Pos:* Instr bot, Ore State Univ, 51-57, from asst plant pathologist to assoc plant pathologist, 57-66, prof plant path, 66-89, EMER PROF PLANT PATH, ORE STATE UNIV, 89- *Personal Data:* b Sacramento, Calif, Oct 28, 24; m 49; c 3. *Educ:* Queen's Univ, Ireland, BS, 49, BAgr, 50; Ore State Univ, PhD(plant path), 56. *Concurrent Pos:* NSF fel, Univ Bristol, 62-63; NZ sr sci fel, 73-74 & Cambridge Univ, 84-85. *Mem:* Am Phytopath Soc; Mycol Soc Am; Brit Mycol Soc; Int Soc Plant Path; Can Plant Path Soc; Int Asn Aerobiology. *Res:* Biology of plant pathogenic fungi, especially reproduction and spore discharge; seed-borne diseases of agricultural crops; electrical nature of plant surfaces. *Mailing Add:* 2815 NW Arthur Ave Corvallis OR 97330

LEACH, ERNEST BRONSON, MATHEMATICS. *Current Pos:* From instr to asst prof, Case Western Res Univ, 53-59, assoc prof math, 59-82, prof, 82-88, EMER PROF, CASE WESTERN RES UNIV, 88- *Personal Data:* b Huchow, China, Dec 21, 24; US citizen; div, Taeko Hirayama; c Charles & Cecelia. *Educ:* Case Inst Technol, BS, 49; Mass Inst Technol, PhD(math), 53. *Concurrent Pos:* Partic, Indo-Am Prog, Indian Inst Technol, Kanpur, 63-64; mem staff, Northwestern Univ Proj, Univ Khartoum, 66-67; partic, Inelec Proj, Inst Nat Elec & Electronics, Boumerdes, Algeria, 76-78. *Res:* Algebraic topology; functional analysis. *Mailing Add:* 6312 Eastondale Rd Mayfield Heights OH 44124-4105

LEACH, FRANKLIN ROLLIN, BIOCHEMISTRY. *Current Pos:* res assoc, Okla State Univ, 59-60, from asst prof to assoc prof biochem, 60-68, chmn grad fac genetics, 76-78, PROF BIOCHEM, OKLA STATE UNIV, 68-, ASSOC DEPT HEAD, 90- *Personal Data:* b Gorman, Tex, Apr 2, 33; m 56, 70, Anna B Justus; c Alan, Barry, Carol (Huddle), Carolyn (Proctor), Janet (Weiss) & Barbara (Perkins). *Educ:* Hardin-Simmons Univ, BA, 53; Univ Tex, PhD(chem), 57. *Prof Exp:* Res scientist I, Biochem Inst, 53-56; Nat Acad Sci fel med sci, Univ Calif, 57-59. *Concurrent Pos:* Soc Am Bacteriologists pres fel, Univ Ill, 60; NIH res career develop award, 62-72; res fel, Calif Inst Technol, 65-66. *Mem:* AAAS; Am Soc Microbiol; Am Soc Biochem & Molecular Biol; Am Soc Photobiol; Coun Biol Ed; Protein Soc; Int Soc Biolumin Chemilumin. *Res:* Bioluminescence; analytical biochemistry; enzymology; environmental biochemistry. *Mailing Add:* Dept Biochem & Molecular Biol Okla State Univ Stillwater OK 74078-3035. *Fax:* 405-744-7799; *E-Mail:* firefly@biochem.okstate.edu

LEACH, JAMES L(INDSAY), mechanical engineering, for more information see previous edition

LEACH, JOHN KLINE, CARDIOLOGY, PHYSIOLOGY. *Current Pos:* from asst prof to assoc prof med, 66-76, from asst prof to prof med & physiol, 72-85, EMER PROF MED & PHARMOL, MED SCH, UNIV, NMEX, 86- *Personal Data:* b Buffalo, NY, July 11, 22; m 45, Priscilla Smith; c Barbara, Catherine, David, Elizabeth & William. *Educ:* Baldwin-Wallace Col, BS, 43; Albany Med Col, MD, 47; Am Bd Internal Med, dipl, 68; Am Bd Cardiovasc Dis, dipl, 69. *Prof Exp:* Instr med, Albany Med Col, 55-62, asst prof physiol, 62-63; assoc chief staff res, Vet Admin Ctr, Wadsworth, Kans, 63-64. *Concurrent Pos:* Clin asst & asst attend, Albany Hosp, 55-62; NIH res fel physiol, Albany Med Col, 61-63, res grant cardiol, Univ NMex, 69-72; lectr, Med Ctr, Univ Kans, 63-64; chief cardiol sect, Vet Admin Hosp, Albuquerque, 66-72 & 77-83, assoc chief staff res, 69-73; attend med, Univ Hosp, Albuquerque, NMex, 66-; consult med, Bataan Hosp, Albuquerque, 69-83; consult med & cardiol, St Joseph Hosp, Albuquerque, 69-83; consult cardiol, Presby Hosp, Albuquerque, 69-83; vis assoc prof, Med Ctr, Univ Calif, Los Angeles, 71-72. *Mem:* Fel Am Col Cardiol; Am Fedn Clin Res; Am Heart Asn; fel Am Col Physicians; Am Physiol Soc; Int Soc Heart Res. *Res:* Cardiovascular research; cardiac muscle mechanics and hemodynamics; shortening deactivation of cardiac muscle-mechanisms and significance; cardiac muscle physiology. *Mailing Add:* Sch Med Dept Pharmacol Univ NMex Albuquerque NM 87131. *Fax:* 505-272-8082

LEACH, JOSEPH HENRY, LIMNOLOGY, FISHERIES BIOLOGY. *Current Pos:* RETIRED. *Personal Data:* b Sturgeon Falls, Ont, Feb 20, 31; m 55, Mary Fraser; c Leslie & Catherine. *Educ:* Univ Toronto, BSA, 54; Univ Guelph, MSc, 66; Univ Aberdeen, PhD(marine ecol), 69. *Honors & Awards:* Anderson-Everett Award, Int Asn Great Lakes Res, 92. *Prof Exp:* Res scientist, Ont Ministry Natural Resources, 69-85, sr scientist, 86-96. *Concurrent Pos:* Adj prof, Univ Windsor, 93- *Mem:* Am Fisheries Soc; Int Asn Great Lakes Res (pres, 78-79); Int Asn Theoret Appl Limnol. *Res:* Limnology and fisheries of the Great Lakes; impacts of cultural perturbations, particularly eutrophication and introduced species. *Mailing Add:* 111 Division St S Kingsville ON N9Y 1P5 Can. *Fax:* 519-825-3163

LEACH, KAREN LYNN, CELL BIOLOGY. *Current Pos:* res scientist, 84-89, SR RES SCIENTIST, DEPT CELL BIOL, UPJOHN CO, KALAMAZOO, 90- *Personal Data:* US citizen; c 1. *Educ:* Ohio Wesleyan Univ, BA, 77; Univ Mich, Ann Arbor, PhD(pharmacol), 81. *Prof Exp:* Postdoctoral fel, Lab Cellular Carcinogenesis & Tumor Prom, Nat Cancer Inst, 84. *Concurrent Pos:* Organizer, Sixth Int Symp Cell Endocrinol, Lake Placid, NY, 90; assoc ed, J Immunol, 90-92; reviewer, Cancer Res, J Biol Chem, J Immunol & J Cell Biol; invited lectr, numerous univs. *Mem:* Soc Neurosci; Am Soc Cell Biol; Am Soc Biochem & Molecular Biol. *Mailing Add:* Dept Cell Biol Uphohn Co 301 Henrietta St Kalamazoo MI 49001

LEACH, LEONARD JOSEPH, TOXICOLOGY, ENVIRONMENTAL HEALTH. *Current Pos:* RETIRED. *Personal Data:* b Rochester, NY, Aug 3, 24; m 53; c 3. *Educ:* Brigham Young Univ, BS, 49. *Prof Exp:* Phys chemist, Army Chem Ctr, Md, 51-52; assoc indust hygienist, Atomic Energy Proj, Univ Rochester, 55-57, instr indust hyg, 57-65, asst prof radiation biol & biophys, Sch Med & Dent, 65-86. *Concurrent Pos:* Speaker, Gordon Res Conf Toxicol & Safety Eval, NH, 60. *Mem:* Am Soc Toxicol; Am Acad Indust Hyg; Pan-Am Med Asn; Am Indust Hyg Asn; NY Acad Sci. *Res:* Inhalation toxicity of airborne agents related to air pollution and all aspects of environmental health. *Mailing Add:* 47 Pickdale Dr Rochester NY 14626

LEACH, ROBERT ELLIS, SPORTS MEDICINE, ORTHOPEDIC SURGERY. *Current Pos:* PROF ORTHOP SURG, MED SCH, BOSTON UNIV, 70-; ED-IN-CHIEF, AM J SPORTS MED, 90- *Personal Data:* b Sanford, Maine, Nov 25, 31; m 55, Laurine Seber; c Cathy, Brian, Michael, Craig, Karen & Diane. *Educ:* Princeton Univ, BA, 53; Columbia Univ, MD, 57; Am Bd Orthop Surg, dipl. *Honors & Awards:* Sports Med Man of Yr Award, Sports Med Soc, 88. *Prof Exp:* Chmn orthop, Lahey Clin Found, 67-70. *Concurrent Pos:* Dir orthop serv, Boston City Hosp, 70-76; lectr, Tufts Univ, 70-; Am, Brit & Can traveling fel, 71; head physician, Olympic Team, USA, 80-84, chmn, Sports Med Coun, US Comt, 85-93. *Mem:* Am Orthop Asn (pres, 94); Am Orthop Soc Sports Med (pres, 83); Am Acad Orthop Surgeons. *Res:* Synthetic ligament reconstruction. *Mailing Add:* 230 Calvary St Waltham MA 02154. *Fax:* 781-736-0607

LEACH, ROLAND MELVILLE, JR, INFLUENCE OF NUTRITION & ENDOCRINE SYSTEM ON SKELETAL DEVELOPMENT. *Current Pos:* assoc prof poultry sci, 68-73, PROF POULTRY SCI, PA STATE UNIV, UNIVERSITY PARK, 73- *Personal Data:* b Framingham, Mass, Aug 27, 32; m 54, 92; c 3. *Educ:* Univ Maine, BS, 54; Purdue Univ, MS, 56; Cornell Univ, PhD(nutrit), 60. *Honors & Awards:* Am Feed Mfrs Asn Award, Poultry Sci Assoc, 80. *Prof Exp:* Asst prof animal nutrit, Cornell Univ, 60-68, chemist, Plant Soil & Nutrit Lab, USDA, 59-68. *Mem:* Poultry Sci Asn; Am Inst Nutrit; AAAS; Am Soc Bone and Mineral Res. *Res:* Mineral nutrition of animals; role of trace elements in bone formation; role of autocrine growth factors in skeletal development. *Mailing Add:* 205 Animal Industs Bldg Pa State Univ University Park PA 16802

LEACH, RONALD, SOFTWARE SYSTEMS. *Current Pos:* PROF, HOWARD UNIV, 69- *Personal Data:* b Baltimore, Md, Feb 5, 44; m 65, Mary Moynihan; c John, Anne & David. *Educ:* Univ Md, BS, 64, MA, 66; Johns Hopkins Univ, PhD(comput sci), 71, MS, 83. *Concurrent Pos:* NASA/ Am Soc Eng Educ fel, 84-85. *Mem:* Asn Comput Mach; Comput Soc; Am Math Asn; Inst Elec & Electronics Engrs. *Mailing Add:* 10 E Lee St No 2101 Baltimore MD 21202

LEACH, WILLIAM MATTHEW, CELL BIOLOGY, RADIOBIOLOGY. *Current Pos:* res biologist, Radiation Bio-Effects Prog, Nat Ctr Radiol Health, 66-67, chief radiation cytol lab, Div Biol Effects, Bur Radiol Health, 67-71, chief exp studies br, Bur Radiol Health, 71-84, dir Div Life Sci, 85-86, ASSOC DIR SCI, OFF SCI & TECHNOL, CTR DEVICES & RADIOL HEALTH, FOOD & DRUG ADMIN, 86- *Personal Data:* b Pine Mountain, Ky, June 26, 33; m 60, Marion Elizabeth Drew; c Jennifer Megan, William Marcus, Steven Drew. *Educ:* Berea Col, BA, 56; Univ Tenn, MS, 62, PhD(zool), 65. *Prof Exp:* USAEC res assoc zool & entom, Inst Radiation Biol, Univ Tenn, 64-66. *Concurrent Pos:* Adj prof genetics, George Washington Univ, 72-; Trustee, Environ Educ Ctr, Pine Mountain Settlement Sch, Ky, 67- *Mem:* AAAS; Am Soc Cell Biol; Am Genetic Asn; Sigma Xi. *Res:* Cell responses to radiation in relation to the cell cycle; cell synthetic activities during the cell cycle; behavior of particulates and molecules in cells; developmental biology; microwave radiation research. *Mailing Add:* 1805 Brisbane St Silver Spring MD 20902. *Fax:* 301-443-2296; *E-Mail:* wml@fdadr.cdrh.fda.gov

LEACH-HUNTOON, CAROLYN S, ENDOCRINOLOGY, PHYSIOLOGY. *Personal Data:* b Leesville, La, Aug 25, 40; m 69; c 1. *Educ:* Northwestern State Col, La, BS, 62; Baylor Univ, MS, 66, PhD(physiol), 68. *Honors & Awards:* Louis H Bauer Founder's Award, Aerospace Med Asn; Paul Best Award for Res Aerospace Physiol; Outstanding Woman in Sci, Am Women in Sci, 84. *Prof Exp:* Med technologist, M D Anderson Hosp & Tumor Inst, Univ Tex, Houston, 62-64, spec med technologist, 64-68; head, Endocrine & Biochem Labs, Johnson Space Ctr, NASA, 68-74, chief, Space Metab & Bioichem Br, 74-76, chief, Biomed Labs Br, 76-84, assoc dir, 84-87, dir space & life sci, 87-89. *Concurrent Pos:* Consult, Proj Sea Lab, US Navy, 68-69, Proj Tektite I, US Navy-NASA-Gen Elec-Dept of Interior, 69 & Proj Tektite II, NASA-Dept of Interior, 70; Nat Res Coun-Nat Acad Sci res assoc, Manned Spacecraft Ctr, NASA, 68-70; adj instr physiol, Baylor Col Med, 68-70, adj asst prof, 70-; assoc investr, Inst Environ Med, Sch Med, Univ Pa, 70; mem res staff, Marine Biomed Inst, Univ Tex. *Mem:* Fel Aerospace Med Asn; Int Astronaut Fedn; Endocrine Soc; Am Physiol Soc; Am Soc Med Technol; Am Soc Clin Path; Am Inst Aeronaut & Astronaut. *Res:* The study of the physiological adaptation of man to changing environments, particularly the endocrine mechanisms involved in adaptation; aerospace medicine. *Mailing Add:* 4154 Sue Ellen St Houston TX 77087

LEACOCK, ROBERT A, THEORETICAL PHYSICS, HIGH ENERGY PHYSICS. *Current Pos:* assoc physics, 65-67, from asst prof to assoc prof, & physicist, Ames Lab, 67-87, PROF PHYSICS, IOWA STATE UNIV, 87- *Personal Data:* b Detroit, Mich, Oct 3, 35; m 61; c 3. *Educ:* Univ Mich, BS, 57, MS, 60, PhD(physics), 63. *Prof Exp:* Instr physics, Univ Mich, 63-64; Am-Swiss Found Sci Exchange fel theoret physics, Europ Orgn Nuclear Res, 64-65. *Concurrent Pos:* Corning Glass Works Found fel, 62-63. *Mem:* Am Phys Soc. *Res:* Theoretical physics. *Mailing Add:* Dept Physics & Astron Iowa State Univ Ames IA 50011. *Fax:* 515-294-8712

LEACOCK, ROBERT JAY, ASTRONOMY. *Current Pos:* res asst astron, 63-71, asst prof, 71-76, ASSOC PROF PHYS SCI & ASTRON, UNIV FLA, 76-, ASSOC CHMN, 80- *Personal Data:* b New York, NY, Mar 1, 39; m 64; c 2. *Educ:* Univ Fla, BS, 60, MS, 62, PhD(astron), 71. *Prof Exp:* Instr physics, Pensacola Jr Col, 62-63. *Mem:* AAAS; Am Astron Soc. *Res:* Nonthermal radio observations of the major planets; optical variations of extragalactic radio sources. *Mailing Add:* 3320 NW 27th St Gainesville FL 32605

LEADABRAND, RAY LAURENCE, ELECTRONICS ENGINEERING. *Current Pos:* SR VPRES, SCI APPLNS INT CORP, 85- *Personal Data:* b Pasadena, Calif, Oct 12, 27; m 55; c 1. *Educ:* San Jose State Col, BS, 50; Stanford Univ, MS, 53. *Prof Exp:* Field engr, Philco Corp, 50-52; asst, Stanford Univ, 52-55; res engr, SRI Int, 55-58, head propagation group, 59-60, mgr, Radio Physics Lab, 60-68, sr vpres, Eng Res Group, 80-85, exec dir, Electronics & Radio Sci Div, 68- *Mem:* AAAS; fel Inst Elec & Electronics Engrs; Am Geophys Union; Int Union Radio Sci; Sigma Xi. *Res:* Ionospheric radio propagation; auroral radar; moon and satellite reflection and transmission; propagation studies related to nuclear explosions and missile flight; radio and radar astronomy research of solar systems. *Mailing Add:* 80 Joaquin Rd Portola Valley CA 94028-8115

LEADBETTER, EDWARD RENTON, MICROBIOLOGY. *Current Pos:* prof, Biol Sci Group, Univ Conn, 78-85, head dept, 78-83, head, Dept Microbiol, 84-85, PROF, DEPT MOLECULAR & CELL BIOL, UNIV CONN, 85- *Personal Data:* b Barnesboro, Pa, Jan 26, 34; m 56; c 4. *Educ:* Franklin & Marshall Col, BS, 55; Univ Tex, PhD(bact), 59. *Hon Degrees:* MA, Amherst Col, 70. *Prof Exp:* Instr, Amherst Col, 59-61, from asst prof to assoc prof, 61-70, chmn dept, 67-71, prof biol, 70-78. *Concurrent Pos:* NSF fel, Hopkins Marine Sta, Pac Grove, Calif, 62-63; NIH spec fel, Univ Mass, 66-67; vis prof, Hampshire Col, 71; instr, Marine Biol Lab, Woods Hole, 71-78, mem corp, 71-; NATO sr fel, Univ Seville, 72; Nat Acad Sci-Hungarian Acad Sci Exchange, Szeged, 85, 88; found microbiol lectr, Am Soc Microbiol, 89-90; prog div, Cellular Biochem, NSF, 90-91. *Mem:* AAAS; Am Soc Microbiol. *Res:* Microbial ecology, physiology, and biochemistry; amine metabolism; photosynthesis; myxobacteria; oral microbiology; hydrocarbon oxidation; ultrastructure; gliding motility, sulfonate formation and degradation. *Mailing Add:* Dept Molecular & Cell Biol Univ Conn U-125 75 N Eaglevil Storrs Manfield CT 06269-0002

LEADER, GORDON ROBERT, PHYSICAL CHEMISTRY. *Current Pos:* RETIRED. *Personal Data:* b Milwaukee, Wis, Jan 27, 16; m 46, Helen Kendrick; c Richard, Julie, Malcolm & James. *Educ:* Univ Wis, BS, 37; Univ Minn, PhD(phys chem), 40. *Prof Exp:* Res chemist, Monsanto Chem Co, Mo, 40-42, Nat Defense Res Comt, Northwestern Univ, 42-43 & Manhattan Dist Proj, Univ Chicago, 43-47; asst prof chem, Univ Ky, 47-51; res chemist, Mallinckrodt Chem Works, Mo, 51-53 & Olin Mathieson Chem Corp, 53-58; sr res chemist, Thiokol Chem Corp, 58-64 & Pennwalt Corp, 64-86; consult, Elf Atochem, 86-96. *Mem:* Am Chem Soc. *Res:* Chemical process development; Raman and nuclear magnetic resonance spectroscopy; radiochemistry; conductance and dielectric constants of organic solutions. *Mailing Add:* 1661 Weedon Rd Wayne PA 19087

LEADER, JOHN CARL, STATISTICAL OPTICS, LASER INTERACTIONS. *Current Pos:* Sr engr, McDonnell Aircraft Reconnaissance Lab, McDonnell Douglas Corp, 69-74, sr scientist, 74-81, chief scientist radiation sci, 81-87, dir res, McDonnell Douglas Res Labs, 87-91, proj mgr, 91-96, CONSULT, MCDONNELL DOUGLAS AEROSPACE, MCDONNELL DOUGLAS CORP, 96- *Personal Data:* b St Louis, Mo, Oct 25, 38; m 61, Kay; c Tracy & Susan. *Educ:* Rensselaer Polytech Inst, BS, 60, PhD(nuclear physics), 69. *Concurrent Pos:* Ed, Proc Soc Photo-Optical Instrumentation Engrs, 83; prin investr & prog mgr for var govt sponsored res. *Mem:* Optical Soc Am; Soc Photo-Optical Instrumentation Engrs; Union Radio Sci Int. *Res:* Theoretical research on radiation scattering from rough surfaces; optical propagation through atmospheric turbulence; partial coherence theory; laser radar; charged particle beam propagation; laser interactions with materials. *Mailing Add:* 1016 Julianna Dr Manchester MO 63011. *E-Mail:* jcleader@concentric.nat

LEADER, ROBERT WARDELL, COMPARATIVE PATHOLOGY. *Current Pos:* PROF PATH & CHMN DEPT, MICH STATE UNIV, 75- *Personal Data:* b Tacoma, Wash, Jan 16, 19; m 40, 69; c 3. *Educ:* Wash State Univ, BS & DVM, 52, MS, 55. *Hon Degrees:* DMedSci, Univ Toledo, 76. *Prof Exp:* Instr vet path, Wash State Univ, 52-55; USPHS fel, Univ Calif, 55-56; asst prof vet path, Wash State Univ, 56-60; assoc prof, Rockefeller Univ, 65-71; prof animal path, Univ Conn, 71-75. *Concurrent Pos:* Mem path training comt, NIH, 66-71, mem virol study sect, 71-; mem bd div, Mark Morris Found, 71- *Mem:* Am Vet Med Asn; Am Soc Exp Path; Am Col Vet Path; NY Acad Sci; Int Acad Path; Sigma Xi. *Res:* Studies of model diseases in animals with objective of elucidating pathogenetic mechanisms of similar diseases in man; chronic degenerative and connective tissue diseases. *Mailing Add:* A620 E Fee Hall Mich State Univ East Lansing MI 48824-1316

LEADER, SOLOMON, MATHEMATICS. *Current Pos:* From instr to assoc prof, 52-61, PROF MATH, RUTGERS UNIV, NEW BRUNSWICK, 61- *Personal Data:* b Spring Lake, NJ, Nov 14, 25. *Educ:* Rutgers Univ, BS, 49; Princeton Univ, MA, 51, PhD(math), 52. *Mem:* Am Math Soc; Math Asn Am; Sigma Xi. *Res:* Functional analysis; general topology. *Mailing Add:* Dept Math Rutgers Univ New Brunswick NJ 08903-2101

LEADERS, FLOYD EDWIN, JR, PHARMACOLOGY, RESEARCH ADMINISTRATION. *Current Pos:* PRES, LEADERS GROUP INC, 92-; CONSULT, FOOD & DRUG ADMIN, NIH OFF ALTERNATIVE MED, 94- *Personal Data:* b Denison, Iowa, Dec 11, 31; m 75; c 1. *Educ:* Drake Univ, BS, 55; Univ Iowa, MS, 60, PhD(pharmacol), 62. *Prof Exp:* From instr to asst prof pharmacol, Med Ctr, Univ Kans, 62-67; head pharmacol res, Alcon Labs, Tex, 67-72; dir res serv, Plough, Inc, Tenn, 72-73; dir res & develop labs, Pharmaceut Div, Pennwalt Corp, NY, 73-78; pres, Tech Eval & Mgt Syst, Inc, 78-92. *Concurrent Pos:* NIH res grant, 62-67; consult, Midwest Res Inst, 65-67; adj asst prof, Univ Tex Southwestern Med Sch; adj prof, Purdue Univ, 78-83, lectr & course dir, Inst Appl Pharm Sci. *Mem:* AAAS; Am Soc

Pharmacol & Exp Therapeut; Soc Exp Biol & Med; Drug Info Asn; NY Acad Sci; Licensing Execs Soc. *Res:* Managing all aspects of pharmaceutical drug research and development, both ethical and proprietary, including data management, regulatory compliance and regulatory submissions; drug-vehicle systems; physiology and pharmacology of the eye, cardiovascular system and autonomic nervous systems; use of computers in biomedical data management. *Mailing Add:* Bot Enterprise 15200 Shady Grove Rd No 350 32 Treworthy Rd Rockville MD 20850-3218

LEADON, BERNARD M(ATTHEW), FLUID MECHANICS. *Current Pos:* prof, 64-75, EMER PROF ENG SCI, UNIV FLA, 75- *Personal Data:* b Farmington, Minn, Nov 29, 17; m 46; c 10. *Educ:* Col St Thomas, BS, 38; Univ Minn, MS, 42, PhD(fluid mech), 55. *Prof Exp:* Engr, Pac Gas & Elec Co, Calif, 41; asst aerodyn, Univ Minn, 42, instr, 42-43; aerodynamicist, Curtiss-Wright Corp, NY, 43-44, sr aerodynamicist, 44-45; head propulsion exp sect, Cornell Aeronaut Lab, 45-46; chief aerodynamicist, Rosemount Aeronaut Lab, 46-48, scientist, 48-57; sr staff scientist, Gen Off, Gen Dynamics/Convair, 57-64. *Concurrent Pos:* Instr, Univ Buffalo, 44-45; lectr, Univ Minn, 46-57; consult, Minneapolis-Honeywell Regulator Corp, 56-57, Gen Dynamics/Convair, 64-65, USAF, 66, AMF Beaird, 69, Martinez & Costa & Assocs, 71 & 78 & Pratt & Whitney Aircraft Corp, 74 & 76-82; vis prof, San Diego State Col, 62-64; NATO fel, 72; chmn, Third US Nat Conf Wind Eng, 78. *Mem:* Am Inst Aeronaut & Astronaut; Sigma Xi. *Res:* Heat transfer; aerodynamics; airplane design. *Mailing Add:* 412 NE 13th Ave Gainesville FL 32601-4323

LEADS, DAN, CERAMIC ENGINEERING. *Honors & Awards:* Samuel Geitsbeek Award, Am Ceramic Soc, 94. *Mailing Add:* Artech Inc Hwy 21 & 164 Box 733 Clarksville AR 72830

LEAF, ALEXANDER, INTERNAL MEDICINE. *Current Pos:* assoc, Harvard Univ, 53-56, from asst prof to assoc prof, 56-65, Jackson prof clin med, 66-81, Ridley Watts prof prev med & chmn, Dept Prev Med & Clin Epidemiol, 80-90, JACKSON EMER PROF CLIN MED, SCH MED, HARVARD UNIV, 90- *Personal Data:* b Yokohama, Japan, Apr 10, 20; nat US; m 43, Barbara Louise Kincaid; c Caroline Joan, Rebecca Louise & Tamara Jean. *Educ:* Univ Wash, BS, 40; Univ Mich, MD, 43. *Hon Degrees:* AM, Harvard Univ, 61. *Honors & Awards:* Homer Smith Award Renal Physiol, 81; Kuber Medal, Asn Am Physicians, 95; A N Richards Award, Int Soc Nephrology. *Prof Exp:* Instr med, Univ Mich, 47-49. *Concurrent Pos:* From asst physician to assoc physician, Mass Gen Hosp, 53-62, physician, 62-, chief med serv, 66-81; John Simon Guggenheim Mem Found fel, Balliol Col, Oxford Univ, 71-72; distinguished physician, Vet Affairs, 92-96. *Mem:* Nat Acad Sci; Inst Med-Nat Acad Sci; Am Physiol Soc; Asn Am Physicians; Am Acad Arts & Sci; Am Soc Clin Invest; foreign mem Royal Danish Acad Sci & Lett. *Res:* Ion transport and membrane physiology; kidney physiology; nutrition; certain polyunsaturated fatty acids in fish oils; prevention of fatal ischemia-induced ventricular arrhythmias; free fatty acids; protective fatty acids that stabilize electrically every cardiac myocyte in the heart; modulating the sodium and calcium ion channel currents in the cell membranes. *Mailing Add:* Mass Gen Hosp Boston MA 02114

LEAF, BORIS, STATISTICAL MECHANICS, ELECTRODYNAMICS. *Current Pos:* RETIRED. *Personal Data:* b Yokohama, Japan, Mar 4, 19; nat US; m 47, Genevieve Lukman; c Evelyn M, David A & Michael L. *Educ:* Univ Wash, BS, 39; Univ Ill, PhD(phys chem), 42. *Prof Exp:* Spec asst chem, Univ Ill, 42-43, instr phys chem, 43-44; assoc chemist, Metall Lab, Univ Chicago, 44-45; Jewett fel, Yale Univ, 45-46; assoc prof physics, Kans State Univ, 46-54, prof, 54-65; chmn dept, State Univ NY Col Cortland, 65-67, prof physics, 65-89. *Concurrent Pos:* Spec asst, Nat Defense Res Comt, Univ Ill, 45; res fel, Brussels, 58-60; prof, State Univ NY, Binghamton, 67-71; fac fel & grants-in-aid, Res Found, State Univ NY, 70-72, scholar exchange prof, 74-; vis prof, Cornell Univ, 73-74; assoc ed, Am J Physics, 76-79; partic, State Univ NY-Moscow State Univ fac exchange, USSR, 81. *Mem:* Fel AAAS; fel Am Phys Soc; Am Asn Physics Teachers; NY Acad Sci. *Res:* Thermodynamic theory; transport processes; quantum theory. *Mailing Add:* 11039 39th Ave NE Seattle WA 98125

LEAHEY, DOUGLAS MCADAM, ATMOSPHERIC CHEMISTRY & PHYSICS. *Current Pos:* mgr air qual serv, 71-88, STAFF SCIENTIST, BOVAR ENVIRON SERV, 88- *Personal Data:* b Truro, NS, Aug 23, 42; m 71, Maureen D Neus. *Educ:* Dalhousie Univ, BS, 63; McGill Univ, MS, 66; NY Univ, PhD(air pollution), 71. *Prof Exp:* Meteorologist, Can Govt, 63-68; res assoc, NY Univ, 68-71. *Mem:* Am Meteorol Soc; Can Meteorol & Oceanog Soc; Air & Waste Mgt Asn. *Res:* Atmospheric turbulence, plume dispersion, urban air pollution and wind flow regimes. *Mailing Add:* 3036 Second St SW Calgary AB T2S 1T3 Can

LEAHY, DENIS ALAN, X-RAY ASTRONOMY, SUPERNOVA REMNANTS. *Current Pos:* sessional instr, Univ Calgary, 82-83, res fel physics, 83-88, from asst prof to assoc prof, 88-93, PROF, DEPT PHYSICS, UNIV CALGARY, 93- *Personal Data:* Taber, Alberta, June 13, 52; m 94. *Educ:* Univ Waterloo. BSc, 75; Univ BC, MSc, 76, PhD(physics), 80. *Prof Exp:* Res assoc, Marshall Space Flight Ctr, 80-82. *Mem:* Am Astron Soc; Can Astron Soc; Sigma Xi; Can Asn Physicists; Int Astronaut Union. *Res:* X-ray astronomy, data analysis and interpretation; supernova remnants; x-ray binaries; symbiotic stars; pulsar magnetospheres. *Mailing Add:* Dept Physics Univ Calgary 2500 University Dr NW Calgary AB T2N 1N4 Can. *Fax:* 403-289-3331; *E-Mail:* Leahy@iras.ucalgary.ca

LEAHY, RICHARD GORDON, GEOCHEMISTRY. *Current Pos:* dir labs, Div Eng & Appl Physics, 60-68, asst to pres civic & govt rels, 70-71, ASSOC DEAN FAC ARTS & SCI, HARVARD UNIV, 68- *Personal Data:* b Buffalo, NY, Mar 6, 29; m 53; c 3. *Educ:* Yale Univ, BS, 52; Harvard Univ, AM, 54, PhD(geol), 57. *Prof Exp:* Asst geochem, Yale Univ, 52-53; asst to dir & res assoc geol, Woods Hole Oceanog Inst, 56-60. *Concurrent Pos:* Mem US tech panel geochem, Int Geophys Year, 57-58; chmn, Consortium Sci Comput, 86-88; exec dir, New Eng Consortium Undergrad Sci Educ, 88- *Mem:* AAAS; Am Geophys Union; NY Acad Sci. *Res:* Geochemistry of heavy isotopes in sea water and marine sediments; chemical processes of submarine weathering; variation of carbon dioxide in the atmosphere and its relation to air mass properties. *Mailing Add:* Sci Ctr Harvard Univ Cambridge MA 02138

LEAHY, SR MARY GERALD, INSECT PHYSIOLOGY, ACAROLOGY. *Current Pos:* FAC, ST ANTHONYS CONVENT, 85- *Personal Data:* b San Francisco, Calif, Oct 11, 17. *Educ:* Univ Southern Calif, BA, 45; Cath Univ Am, MA, 47; Univ Notre Dame, PhD(biol), 62. *Prof Exp:* From asst prof to prof biol, Mt St Mary's Col, 47-85, chmn dept, 62-65. *Concurrent Pos:* NSF res grants, 62-64, 65-67 & 70-71; fel trop pub health, Harvard Univ, 66; WHO grant, Israel Inst Biol Res, Ness Ziona & Hebrew Univ Jerusalem, 68-69; sr res scientist, Nairobi, Kenya, 73-74; collab scientist, EAfrican Vet Res Orgn, Kenya, 73-74; prin investr, NIH grant, 74-77; vis scientist, Ga Southern Col, 74-75; exchange scientist tick pheromones & hormones, Poland, Czech & Russia, Nat Acad Sci. *Mem:* AAAS; Entom Soc Am; Am Inst Biol Sci. *Res:* Mosquitoes and ticks; pheromones and reproductive physiology. *Mailing Add:* Carondelet Ctr 11999 Chalon Rd Los Angeles CA 90048

LEAIST, DEREK GORDON, ELECTROCHEMISTRY, DIFFUSION. *Current Pos:* from asst prof to assoc prof, 82-90, PROF, CHEM DEPT, UNIV WESTERN ONT, LONDON, CAN, 90- *Personal Data:* b Akron, Ohio, Jan 5, 55; Can citizen; m 86. *Educ:* Queen's Univ, Kingston, Ont, BSc, 77; Yale Univ, MSc, 78, PhD(phys chem), 80. *Honors & Awards:* Lash Miller Award, Electrochem Soc, 89. *Prof Exp:* Res assoc chem, Nat Res Coun, Ottawa, Can, 81-82. *Res:* Theoretical and experimental studies of diffusion in liquids, with emphasis on coupled transport in multicomponent electrolyte mixtures; micelle solutions; thermal diffusion in liquids. *Mailing Add:* Dept Chem Univ Western Ont London ON N6A 5B7 Can

LEAK, JOHN CLAY, JR, DRUG REGULATION, RADIO PHARMACEUTICALS. *Current Pos:* res chemist, 76-79, RES CHEMIST, FOOD & DRUG ADMIN, 79- *Personal Data:* b Washington, DC, Aug 31, 28; m 54; c John, Janet & Joel. *Educ:* Univ Vt, BS, 49; Univ Ill, PhD(chem), 54. *Prof Exp:* Asst, Univ Ill, 51-54, res assoc animal nutrit, 55-56; Fulbright scholar, Ger, 54-55; chemist, Isotopes Specialties Co, 56-59, dir carbon-14 dept, 59-60; res dir, Cyclo Chem Corp, 60-61; tech dir, ChemTrac Corp, 61-62, vpres, 62-65, oper mgr, Baird-Atomic, Inc, Mass, 62-65; mgr chem dept, Tracerlab, 65-67, sr staff chemist, 67-69; sr staff chemist, ICN Pharmaceut, Inc, 69-75, mgr prod opers, Life Group, 75-76. *Mem:* Sigma Xi. *Res:* Mechanism of organic reactions; metabolic fate of labeled hydroxy-proline in rats; synthesis of labeled compounds; applications for stable and radioactive isotopes; manufacture and control of radiopharmaceuticals; drug analysis. *Mailing Add:* 1326 Bay Ave Annapolis MD 21403-4661

LEAK, LEE VIRN, CELL BIOLOGY, ELECTRON MICROSCOPY. *Current Pos:* chmn dept, 71-81, PROF ANAT, COL MED, HOWARD UNIV, 71-, PROF, GRAD SCH ART & SCI, 76-, RES PROF, 83- *Personal Data:* b Chesterfield, SC, July 22, 32; m 64; c Alice E & Lee V Jr. *Educ:* SC State Col, BS, 54; Mich State Univ, MS, 59, PhD(cell biol), 62. *Honors & Awards:* Adelle Melbourne Holmes Mem Award, Am Heart Asn. *Prof Exp:* Asst prof biol sci, Mich State Univ, 62; res fel electron micros, Mass Gen Hosp & Harvard Med Sch, 62-64; asst surg, Mass Gen Hosp, 64-65; asst biol, Harvard Med Sch, 65-68, from instr to asst prof anat, 67-71. *Concurrent Pos:* USPHS res grant, 66-; consult, Shriners Burns Res Inst, 67-71; mem, Anat Sci Training Comt, 72-73; Am Heart Asn res grant, 67-70; NHBLI res grant, 71-86; founder/dir, EE Just Lab Cellular Biol, 72-; mem, Div Biol & Agr, Nat Res Coun, 72-75; mem, Nat Bd Med Examr, 73-76; mem, Marine Biol Lab Corp, 73-; NIH (NGMS) res grant, 74-84, 94-98, Nat Inst Allergy Infectious Dis, 66-85; mem, Div Cancer Biol, Diag Bd, Nat Cancer Inst, 79; mem panel basic biomed sci, Nat Res Coun, 80; mem adv coun, Pulmonary Dis Br, Nat Heart, Lung & Blood Inst, 82-86; NSF res grant, 90-93; mem bd trustees, St Andrew Episcopal Sch, 92-94; mem, Res Comt, Am Heart Asn. *Mem:* Am Asn Anat; Am Soc Cell Biol; Am Soc Zool; Genetics Soc Am; Sigma Xi; Am Physiol Soc; Int Soc Lymphol; Tissue Cult Asn; NAm Vascular Org; Soc In Vitro Biol. *Res:* Biology of the lymphatic vascular system and its role during the inflammatory response; pulmonary lymphatic drainage; ontogeny of the lymphatic system; pericarditis; chemotaxis; cell adhesion & migration; cell culture of lymphatic endothelium; lymphangiogenesis in vitro. *Mailing Add:* Dept Anat Col Med Howard Univ 520 W St SW Washington DC 20059. *Fax:* 202-265-7055; *E-Mail:* lleak@fac.howard.edu

LEAKE, DONALD L, BIOMATERIALS, BONE GRAFTING. *Current Pos:* assoc prof oral & maxillofacial surg, 70-74, dir, Dent Res Inst, 82-86, PROF ORAL & MAXILLOFACIAL SURG, SCHS MED & DENT, UNIV CALIF, LOS ANGELES, 74-, CHIEF ORAL & MAXILLOFACIAL SURG, HARBOR-UCLA MED CTR, 70- *Personal Data:* b Cleveland, Okla, Nov 6, 31; m 64, Rosemary Dobson; c John, Elizabeth & Catherine. *Educ:* Univ Southern Calif, AB, 53, MA, 57; Harvard Univ, DMD, 62; Stanford Univ, MD, 69. *Honors & Awards:* First Prize, Plastic Surg Educ Found, 83. *Prof Exp:* NIH fel oral surg, Harvard Univ, 64-66, instr, 66-67. *Concurrent Pos:* Foreign prof, Grad Sch, Asn Med Arg, 90; consult, NIH; mem, Comn on Future, Rose-Hulman Polytech Inst, Terre Haute, 92-93. *Mem:* Biomed Eng Soc; Soc Biomat; AAAS; fel Am Col Surgeons; Sigma Xi. *Res:*

Biomaterials for reconstructive surgery; biomechanics and pathophysiology of the temporomandibular joint; clinical research in oral and maxillofacial and reconstructive surgery; bone grafting. *Mailing Add:* 2 Crest Rd W Rolling Hills CA 90274. *Fax:* 310-782-6786

LEAKE, LOWELL, JR, MATHEMATICS EDUCATION. *Current Pos:* from instr to assoc prof math, 60-74, PROF MATH, UNIV CINCINNATI, 74- *Personal Data:* b Denver, Colo, May 25, 28; m 59, Jane Acomb; c Katherine J & L Gregory. *Educ:* Tufts Col, AB, 50; Univ Wis, MS, 56, PhD(math, educ), 62. *Prof Exp:* Traffic chief, Northwestern Bell Tel Co, 50-54; high sch teacher, Ill, 56-58. *Mem:* Math Asn Am; Nat Coun Teachers Math; Am Asn Univ Professors; Consortium Math Appln. *Res:* Training of secondary and elementary mathematics teachers at undergraduate and graduate levels; learning of mathematics; piaget and probability; computers in education; helping teaching assistants learn to teach. *Mailing Add:* Dept Math Sci/0025 Old Chem 819C Univ Cincinnati Cincinnati OH 45221. *Fax:* 513-556-3417; *E-Mail:* leakel@ucbeh.san.ue.edu

LEAKE, NORMAN, forensic chemistry; deceased, see previous edition for last biography

LEAKE, PRESTON HILDEBRAND, ORGANIC CHEMISTRY, AMINO ACIDS. *Current Pos:* RETIRED. *Personal Data:* b Proffitt, Va, Aug 8, 29; m 54, Elizabeth A Kelly; c Luther H & Lawrence A. *Educ:* Univ Va, BS, 50; Duke Univ, MA, 53, PhD(chem), 54. *Honors & Awards:* Distinguished Serv Award, Va Sect, Am Chem Soc, 76. *Prof Exp:* Res supvr org chem, Nitrogen Div, Allied Chem Corp, 54-60; asst res dir, Albemarle Paper Mfg Co, 60-65; asst to managing dir, Res & Develop Dept, Am Tobacco Co, 65-68, asst managing dir, 68-70, asst dir, 70-87, dir res & develop dept, 87-89, vpres res, 89-92. *Concurrent Pos:* Adj prof, Richmond Prof Inst, 63-64. *Mem:* Am Chem Soc; Am Inst Chemists; Tech Asn Pulp & Paper Indust; Sigma Xi. *Res:* Polycyclic aromatic chemistry: Psychorr synthesis; amino acids and cyanuric acid derivatives; polyethylene; sizing; silica fume; specialty and filter papers; tobacco; plant physiology. *Mailing Add:* 401 Delton Ave Hopewell VA 23860-1815

LEAKE, WILLIAM WALTER, ORGANIC CHEMISTRY. *Current Pos:* from asst prof to assoc prof chem, 61-77, assoc dean, 68-80, DEAN ACAD ADMIN, MIL ADV & VET REP & DIR PROGS, WASHINGTON & JEFFERSON COL, 80- *Personal Data:* b Johnstown, Pa, Apr 24, 26; m 57; c 2. *Educ:* Duquesne Univ, BS, 51; Duke Univ, MA, 53; Univ Pittsburgh, PhD(chem), 58. *Prof Exp:* Res chemist, Monsanto Chem Co, 57-60. *Mem:* Am Chem Soc. *Res:* Instrumental methods of analysis. *Mailing Add:* 81 Anchor Dr Washington PA 15301

LEAKEY, JULIAN EDWARD ARUNDELL, BIOCHEMICAL PHARMACOLOGY, PROTEIN CHEMISTRY. *Current Pos:* vis scientist, Develop Toxicol, 83, res biologist, Div Biometry & Risk Assessment, 91, SR STAFF TOXICOL, DIV REP DEV TOXICOL, NAT CTR TOXICOL RES, 85-; ADJ PROF, UNIV ARK, MED SCI, 87- *Personal Data:* b Settle, Yorkshire, UK, June 12, 51; m 79, Linda Perry; c Laura & Sharon. *Educ:* Univ Dundee, UK, PhD, 76. *Prof Exp:* Fel toxicol, Inst Environ Health & Sci, Res Triangle Park, 77-78; res fel, Dept Biochem, Univ Dundee, 78-85. *Mem:* Teratology Soc; Int Soc Xenobiotics; Soc Exp Bld Med. *Res:* Hormonal development, nutrition and environmental regulation of drug metabolizing enzymes in relation to toxicology, pharmacokinetics and carcinogenesis. *Mailing Add:* 4817 Lafayette St Little Rock AR 72205. *Fax:* 870-543-7576; *E-Mail:* jleakey@ntet.nctr.fda.gov

LEAKEY, RICHARD ERSKINE, ANTHROPOLOGY. *Current Pos:* DIR, KENYA WILDLIFE SERV, 89- *Personal Data:* b Nairobi, Kenya, Dec 19, 44; m 70, Meave Epps; c Anna, Louise & Samira. *Hon Degrees:* DSc, Wooster Col, 78, Rockford Col, 83, Univ Aberdeen, 94; LittD, Univ Kent, 87; LhD, Ohio Univ, 90. *Honors & Awards:* Franklin Burr Prize, 65 & 73; Centennial Award, Nat Geog Soc, 88, Hubbard Medal, 94; James Smithson Medal, Smithsonian Inst, 90; Gold Medal, Royal Geog Soc London, 90; Medal, Port Archaeol Soc, 90. *Prof Exp:* Asst dir, Ctr Prehist & Paleont, 66-67; admin dir, Nat Mus Kenya, 68-74, dir & chief exec, 74-89. *Concurrent Pos:* Leader, Exped West Baringo Kenya, 66, Int Omo River Exped SEthiopia, 67, ERudolph Exped, 68; leader & coordr, Koobi Fora Res Proj, Lake Turkana, 69-; vchmn, Environ Prep Group, Kenya, 72-74; mem, Nakali/Suguta Valley Exped, 78, WTurkana Res Prof, 82, 84-86, Buluk-Early Miocene Proj, 82; chmn, EAfrica Wildlife Soc, 85-89; head, Wildlife Conserv Dept, 89-90. *Mem:* Fel Royal Anthrop Inst; fel AAAS; fel Kenya Acad Sci; fel Inst Cultural Res UK; Pan African Asn Prehist Studies; Sigma Xi; EAfrica Wildlife Soc. *Res:* Numerous publications and scholarly lectures in the United States and abroad; author of five books; contributed various chapters to books and articles to professional journals. *Mailing Add:* PO Box 24926 Nairobi Kenya

LEAL, GEORGE D, CIVIL ENGINEERING. *Current Pos:* CHMN, DAMES & MOORE, 81- *Personal Data:* b San Francisco, Calif, Feb 28, 34. *Educ:* Calif Inst Technol, MS, 58; Univ Chicago, MBA, 65. *Mem:* Nat Acad Eng; Am Soc Civil Eng. *Mailing Add:* Dames & Moore 911 Wilshire Blvd Suite 700 Los Angeles CA 90017. *Fax:* 213-683-0401

LEAL, JOSEPH ROGERS, ORGANIC CHEMISTRY. *Current Pos:* PRES, CRESCENT CONSULTS, 83- *Personal Data:* b New Bedford, Mass, Sept 14, 18; m 44, Mary Desmond; c Joseph E, Michael J, Patricia M (Welch) & Victoria A (Bushey). *Educ:* Univ Mass, BS, 49; Ind Univ, PhD(chem), 53. *Prof Exp:* Res asst, Corn Prod Refining Co, 40-42; asst chemist, Revere Copper & Brass Co, 42-43 & 45-46; res chemist, Am Cyanamid Co, 52-57, tech rep govt res liaison, Washington, DC, 57-63, mgr contract rels, 63-67; sr staff assoc, Celanese Res Co, 67-83. *Mem:* AAAS; Am Chem Soc; NY Acad Sci; Am Inst Chemists; Soc Advan Mat Process Eng. *Res:* High temperature resistant aromatic and heterocyclic polymers; nonflammable fibers; high strength, high modulus reinforcement materials. *Mailing Add:* 10 S Crescent Maplewood NJ 07040-2711

LEAL, L GARY, FLUID MECHANICS, POLYMER PHYSICS. *Current Pos:* PROF & CHAIR CHEM & NUCLEAR ENG, UNIV CALIF, SANTA BARBARA, 89- *Personal Data:* b Bellingham, Wash, Mar 18, 43; m 65, Mary Ann Seelye; c 3. *Educ:* Univ Wash, BS, 65; Stanford Univ, MS, 68, PhD(chem eng), 69. *Honors & Awards:* Allan Colburn Award, Am Inst Chem Engrs, 78, William H Walker Award, 93; Allan Colburn Mem Lectr, Univ Del, 78; Stanley Corrsin Lectr, Johns Hopkins Univ, 90; Stanley Katz Mem Lectr, City Col City Univ, NY, 91; Reilly Mem Lectr, Univ Notre Dame, 92; Robert Pigford Lectr, Univ Del, 94; Julian Smith Lectr, Cornell Univ, 95. *Prof Exp:* NSF fel, Cambridge Univ, 69-70; from asst prof to prof chem eng, Calif Inst Technol, 70-86, Chevron prof, 86-89. *Concurrent Pos:* Petrol Res Fund grant, Calif Inst Technol, 70-; prin investr, NSF, 71- & Off Naval Res, 75-; consult, Richards of Rockford, 75-79, Firestone Res, 81-89, Dynamics Technol Inc, 82-91, Dowell-Schlumberger, 85-88 & Univ Okla, 91-; Guggenheim fel, Cambridge Univ, 76-77, sr vis appl math, 76-77; consult ed, J Am Inst Chem Engrs, 85-87; assoc ed, Int J Multiphase Flow, 85-; mem, US Nat Comt Theoret & Appl Math, 91-, chmn, 94-96; US deleg chair, IUTAM Can Assembly, 92-; mem, Nat Res Coun Space Studies Bd Comt, Microgravity Res, 93-; mem, Policy Comt, Nat Acad Eng, 94-; Rothschild vis prof, Cambridge Univ, 95. *Mem:* Nat Acad Eng; Soc Rheol; Brit Soc Rheol; fel Am Phys Soc; Am Inst Chem Engrs; Am Soc Eng Educ. *Res:* Fluid mechanics; suspension mechanics; rheology; mechanical and optical properties of polymeric liquids; multiphase flows; colloid physics. *Mailing Add:* 1560 Hillcrest Rd Santa Barbara CA 93103

LEAMON, TOM B, ERGONOMICS, HUMAN FACTORS & SAFETY. *Current Pos:* VPRES & DIR, RES CTR, LIBERTY MUTUAL INS CO, 91- *Personal Data:* b Ossett, Yorkshire, UK, Apr 16, 40; US citizen; m 67, Geraldine Bland; c Amanda C, Jonathan M & Genevieve E. *Educ:* Univ Manchester, UK, BS, 61; Cranfield Inst Technol, UK, MS, 68, PhD(indust eng), 82; Univ Aston, UK, MS, 70. *Honors & Awards:* Sir Ben Williams Silver Medal, Inst Prod Engrs, 69; Ergonomics Div Award Outstanding Contrib Enhancement Ergonomics, Inst Indust Eng, 93. *Prof Exp:* Mgr ergonomics, Pilkington Glass, UK, 64-70; dir ergonomics, Ergo Lab, Cranfield Inst, 70-75; br head ergonomics, Nat Coal Bd, UK, 75-81; dir, Grad Safety Prog, Univ Ill, Chicago, 81-82; prof & chair indust eng, Northern Ill Univ, 82-87; prof & chair indust eng, Tex Tech Univ, 87-91. *Concurrent Pos:* Chartered eng, Eng Coun Great Brit, 66; Europ eng, Europ Fed Europ Engrs; assoc reader ergonomics, Univ Loughborough, UK; indust secy, Ergonomics Soc, 69-72, conf secy, 71-73, gen secy, 73-79; chair, Tech Interest Group Indust Ergonomics, Human Factors Soc, 83-85; chair, Ergo Div, Inst Indust Engrs, 90-91; consult to var groups; trustee, Am Soc Safety Engrs; lectr, Harvard Univ, Sch Pub Health, 93. *Mem:* Fel Human Factors & Ergonomics Soc; fel Ergonomics Soc; fel Inst Prod Engrs; Inst Indust Eng; Am Soc Safety Eng. *Res:* Ergonomics and human factors considerations in industry and daily living, including slips and falls, computer application, workplace design, equipment design and the human and work performance of the disabled. *Mailing Add:* 4 Hidden Brick Rd Hopkinton MA 01748-2660. *Fax:* 508-435-8136; *E-Mail:* msmail2.leamont1@tsod.lmig.com

LEAMY, HARRY JOHN, PHYSICAL METALLURGY, PHYSICS. *Current Pos:* mem tech staff, Mat Physics Res Group, 69-77, MEM TECH STAFF, ELECTRONIC MAT RES DEPT, BELL LABS, 77- *Personal Data:* b Alton, Ill, Nov 15, 40; c 3. *Educ:* Univ Mo-Rolla, BS, 63; Iowa State Univ, PhD(metall), 67. *Prof Exp:* Res fel metall, Max Planck Inst Metall Res, 67-69. *Concurrent Pos:* Vis scientist, Philips Res Labs, Eindhoven, The Neth, 76-77. *Mem:* Am Soc Metals; Am Inst Mining, Metall & Petrol Eng; Am Asn Crystal Growth; Am Phys Soc; Electron Micros Soc Am; Mat Res Soc. *Res:* Alloy properties and crystal growth; electron microscopy of crystal lattice defects; magnetic materials; metallic glasses; semiconductor defects; laser beam processing of semiconductor materials. *Mailing Add:* Univ NC CC Cameron Appl Res Ctr Hwy 49 Charlotte NC 28223. *Fax:* 704-547-3183

LEAMY, LARRY JACKSON, QUANTITATIVE GENETICS. *Current Pos:* chmn dept, 88-94, PROF BIOL, UNIV NC, CHARLOTTE, 88- *Personal Data:* b Alton, Ill, Nov 15, 40; m 61, Donna Wilcox; c Timothy & David. *Educ:* Eastern Ill Univ, BS, 62; Univ Ill, Urbana, MS, 65, PhD(zool), 67. *Prof Exp:* from asst prof to prof biol, Calif State Univ, Long Beach, 67-88, chmn dept, 78-88. *Concurrent Pos:* Calif State Univ Found new fac grant, Calif State Univ, Long Beach, 67-68, fac grant-in-aid, 69-70, 73, 78-81; NSF grant, 81-82; vis prof entom & genetics, Univ Wis-Madison, fac grant-in-aid, 82-86; vis prof, Wash Univ Sch Med, 95- *Mem:* Genetics Soc Am; Am Genetic Asn; Soc Study Evolution. *Res:* Quantitative genetics of mice. *Mailing Add:* Dept Biol Univ NC UNCC 9201 University City Charlotte NC 28223-0002. *Fax:* 704-547-3128; *E-Mail:* ljleamy@email.uncc.edu

LEAN, DAVID ROBERT SAMUEL, biology, chemistry, for more information see previous edition

LEAN, ERIC GUNG-HWA, acoustics, optics, for more information see previous edition

LEANDER, JOHN DAVID, PSYCHOPHARMACOLOGY. *Current Pos:* res scientist, 81-84, sr res scientist, 85-89, RES ADV, LILLY RES LAB, ELI LILLY & CO, 90- *Personal Data:* b Mt Vernon, Wash, Apr 8, 44; m 65; c 3. *Educ:* Pac Lutheran Univ, BA, 66; Western Wash State Col, MA, 67; Univ Fla, PhD(psychol), 71; Ind Univ, MBA, 85. *Prof Exp:* Fel neurobiol prog, Univ NC, Chapel Hill, 71-73, instr, 73-74, from asst prof to assoc prof pharmacol, 74-81. *Mem:* AAAS; Behav Pharmacol Soc; Am Soc Pharmacol & Exp Therapeut. *Res:* Behavioral pharmacology; effects of drugs on behavior and the interaction of drugs with ongoing behavior. *Mailing Add:* CNS Res DC-0510 Lilly Res Labs Indianapolis IN 46285-0001. *Fax:* 317-276-9276

LEANING, WILLIAM HENRY DICKENS, TECHNICAL MANAGEMENT, PARASITOLOGY. *Current Pos:* dir mkt develop large animal prod, Merck Sharp & Dohme Co, Inc, 69-72, sr dir clin res animal sci res, 72-74, exec dir animal sci res develop res & admin, 75-81, EXEC DIR TECH SERV, MERCK SHARP & DOHME CO, INC, AGVET, 81- *Personal Data:* b Whakatane, NZ, Feb 24, 34; m 56; c 4. *Educ:* Univ Sydney, BVSc, 56. *Prof Exp:* Vet gen pract, Nth Canterbury Vet Club, NZ & Putaruru Vet Club, NZ, 57-62; vet tech dir appl res parasitol, Merck Sharp & Dohme NZ Ltd, 62-69. *Mem:* NZ Vet Asn; Am Asn Vet Parasitologist; World Asn Adv Vet Parasitol; Am Vet Med Asn; Am Asn Indust Vet. *Res:* Concepts of applied preventive medicine on whole herd/flock basis throughout productive life of animal/bird; primary areas helminthology, entomology; innovation in formulation and treatment application; applied parasitology and agri-economic benefits of year-round parasite control programs. *Mailing Add:* 163 Sherwood Lane Stirling NJ 07980

LEAP, DARRELL IVAN, WATER RESOURCES, AQUIFER ANALYSIS. *Current Pos:* ASSOC PROF HYDROGEOL, PURDUE UNIV, 80- *Personal Data:* b Huntington, WVa, Oct 19, 37. *Educ:* Marshall Univ, BS, 60; Ind Univ, MA, 66; Pa State Univ, PhD(geol), 74. *Honors & Awards:* Super Serv Award, USDA, 88. *Prof Exp:* Geologist, SDak State Geol Surv, 66-71; instr geol, Univ SDak, 66-69; hydrologist, US Geol Surv, 74-80. *Concurrent Pos:* Prin investr, Hydrol Nev Test Site, Nev Nuclear Waste-Storage Invest, US Dept Energy, 78-80, Ground Water Contamination Studies, Purdue Univ. *Mem:* Am Geophys Union; AAAS; Sigma Xi; Geol Soc Am; Nat Asn Ground Water Scientists & Engrs. *Res:* Regional aquifer systems for recharge-discharge relationships and water resources; ground-water modeling; ground-water tracers; radioactive-waste disposal; flow in fractured rocks; flow in glaciated terranes; glacial geology; ground water contamination. *Mailing Add:* 5937 Look Out Dr West Lafayette IN 47906

LEAPMAN, RICHARD DAVID, ELECTRON MICROSCOPY, ELECTRON SPECTROSCOPY. *Current Pos:* vis scientist, 80-88, HEAD, ELECTRON BEAM IMAGING & MICROSPECTROS GROUP BIOMED ENG & INSTRUMENTATION PROG, NAT CTR RES RESOURCES, NIH, 88- *Personal Data:* b Bath, Eng, Dec 6, 50; US citizen; m 79, Gisele Gildener; c Neil, Michael & Juliana. *Educ:* Cambridge Univ, Eng, BA, 73, MA, 76, PhD(physics), 77. *Honors & Awards:* Burton Medal, Micros Soc Am, 85; Birks Award, Microbeam Anal Soc, 85, Heinrich Award, 89. *Prof Exp:* Res fel, Dept Metall & Mat Sci, Oxford Univ, 76-77; res assoc, Sch Appl & Eng Physics, Cornell Univ, 77-79. *Concurrent Pos:* Lectr & consult, Philips Electron Optics, 91-93. *Mem:* Am Phys Soc; Micros Soc Am; Microbeam Analysis Soc; NY Acad Sci; Mat Res Soc. *Res:* Development of analytical electron microscopy for application to biological systems; electron-energy-loss spectroscopy; cryo-scanning transmission electron microscopy of cellular organelles and macromolecular assemblies; elemental mapping at nanometer resolution. *Mailing Add:* 11707 Coldstream Dr Potomac MD 20854. *Fax:* 301-496-6608; *E-Mail:* leapman@helix.nih.gov

LEAR, BERT, PLANT PATHOLOGY. *Current Pos:* RETIRED. *Personal Data:* b Logan, Utah, June 10, 17; m 50; c 1. *Educ:* Utah State Univ, BS, 41; Cornell Univ, PhD(plant path), 47. *Prof Exp:* Agt, Exp Sta, USDA, 41-43; Dow Chem Co fel & res assoc, Cornell Univ, 47-48, asst prof plant path, 48-52; nematologist, NMex Exp, 52-53; from asst nematologist to nematologist, Univ Calif, Davis, 53-74, prof nematol, 63-85. *Mem:* Am Phytopath Soc; Soc Nematol; Orgn Trop Am Nematologists. *Res:* Soil treatment for control of nematodes; fate of chemicals in soils and plants when applied for control of nematodes; role of plant parasitic nematodes in diseases of plants. *Mailing Add:* 1036 Fairway Rd Santa Barbara CA 93108-2839

LEARN, ARTHUR JAY, SOLID STATE PHYSICS. *Current Pos:* VPRES, CVD TECHNOL, SILICON VALLEY GROUP INC, 83- *Personal Data:* b Lewistown, Mont, Mar 25, 33; m 59; c 2. *Educ:* Reed Col, BA, 54; Mass Inst Technol, PhD(physics), 58. *Prof Exp:* Mem tech staff, TRW Systs, Calif, 58-67; mem staff, Electronics Res Ctr, NASA, 67-70; sr mem res staff, Fairchild Camera & Instrument Corp, 70-76; prog mgr, Intel Corp, 76-81; eng mgr, Supertex, Inc, 81-83; exec mem tech staff, Anicon, Inc,. *Mem:* Am Phys Soc; Electrochem Soc; Am Vacuum Soc. *Res:* X-ray diffraction; electron microscopy; properties of thin films; thin film superconductor and semiconductor devices; metallization; chemical vapor deposition; thermal oxidation. *Mailing Add:* 10822 Wilkinson Ave Cupertino CA 95014

LEARNED, JOHN GREGORY, NEUTRINO ASTRONOMY, VHE GAMMA ASTRONOMY. *Current Pos:* PROF PHYSICS, DEPT PHYSICS & ASTRON, UNIV HAWAII. *Personal Data:* b Plattsburgh, NY, Apr 12, 40; m 63; c 2. *Educ:* Columbia Col, NY, AB, 61; Univ Pa, Philadelphia, MS, 63; Univ Wash, Seattle, PhD(physics), 68. *Concurrent Pos:* Tech dir, Dumand Proj, Hawaii Dumand Ctr. *Res:* First high energy neutrino telescope for operation in deep ocean; particle astrophysics. *Mailing Add:* 2032 Ala Eloa St Honolulu HI 96821

LEARNED, ROBERT EUGENE, ECONOMIC GEOLOGY, GEOCHEMISTRY. *Current Pos:* RETIRED. *Personal Data:* b Glendale, Calif, July 3, 28; m 56; c 2. *Educ:* Occidental Col, AB, 55; Univ Calif, Los Angeles, MA, 62; Univ Calif, Riverside, PhD(geol), 66. *Prof Exp:* Geologist, Aerogeophys Co, Calif, 55-56; asst prof geol, Chapman Col, 65-67; geologist, US Geol Surv, 67-92. *Mem:* Geol Soc Am; Geochem Soc; Asn Explor Geochemists; Soc Econ Geologists; Asn Geoscientists Int Develop; Sigma Xi. *Res:* Geology and geochemistry of ore deposits; geochemical exploration methods. *Mailing Add:* 825 Windbell Circle Tucson AZ 85745-9671

LEARSON, ROBERT JOSEPH, FISH PROCESSING TECHNOLOGY. *Current Pos:* CONSULT, 95- *Personal Data:* b Boston, Mass, May 6, 38; m 62; c 3. *Educ:* Suffolk Univ, Boston, Mass, BS, 61. *Honors & Awards:* Arthur S Fleming Award, 76. *Prof Exp:* Chemist, Werby Labs Inc, 61-62 & Bur Com Fisheries, 62-69; res chemist, Nat Marine Fisheries Serv, 69-71, res food technologist, 71-78, dep lab dir, 78-82, actg dep ctr dir, 83, lab dir, 83-95. *Concurrent Pos:* Tech adv, Nat Blue Crab Indust Asn, 75-, Mid Atlantic Fishery Develop Found, 80-, New Eng Fishery Develop Found, 80- & Refrig Res Found, 84-; lectr, Salem State Univ, 79-81; tech consult, Morocco Study Team, Nat Marine Fisheries Serv, 82, chmn, Qual Improv Task Force, 82-84; adj prof, Univ Mass, 84- *Mem:* Inst Food Sci; Asn Off Analytical Chem; Atlantic Fisheries Tech. *Res:* Processing and preservation of fishery products; determination of fish quality; new processing concepts; utilization of processing waste, irradiation of seafoods and chemical species identification. *Mailing Add:* R J Learson Assoc 395 Asbury St South Hamilton MA 01982

LEARY, FRANCIS CHRISTIAN, MODULES OVER COMMUTATIVE RINGS, ALGEBRAIC CODING THEORY. *Current Pos:* asst prof, 85-89, ASSOC PROF MATH, ST BONAVENTURE UNIV, 89- *Personal Data:* b West Hartford, Conn, Apr 23, 49; m 76; c 3. *Educ:* Univ Conn, BA, 71; State Univ NY, Albany, MA, 74, PhD(math), 79. *Prof Exp:* Instr & asst prof, Skidmore Col, 79-80; asst prof math, Transylvania Univ, 80-85. *Concurrent Pos:* Lectr math, Waterbury State Tech Col & Post Jr Col, 73; adj asst prof, Union Col, Schenectady, 75-76. *Mem:* Am Math Soc; Sigma Xi; Math Asn Am. *Res:* Rings and modules; algebraic coding theory. *Mailing Add:* St Bonaventure Univ St Bonaventure NY 14778-9999

LEARY, HARVEY LEE, JR, NUTRITION. *Current Pos:* sr scientist, 85-88, SR RES SCIENTIST, MEAD JOHNSON NUTRIT GROUP, BRISTOL-MYERS SQUIBB CO, 88- *Educ:* NC State Univ, BS, 71, MS, 75, PhD(animal sci-immunol), 78. *Prof Exp:* Res asst, Dept Animal Sci, NC State Univ, 72-78; postdoctoral res assoc, Dept Dairy Sci, Univ Ill, Urbana-Champaign, 78-82 & Dept Biochem, Col Health Sci, Univ Kans, 82-84; sr res scientist, Immuno Biotech, Inc, Overland Park, Kans, 83-85. *Mem:* Am Asn Immunologists; Am Soc Microbiol. *Res:* Radiometric and enzyme immunoassay development; Western blotting; gel precipitation analysis; preparation and characterization of radiotracers and antibody-enzyme conjugates; immunization of animals and purification of antibody; enzymatic digestion of immunoglobulias and purification of biologically active fragments; antigen localization methods with both light and electron microscopy; protein and virus purification and characterization. *Mailing Add:* Mead Johnson Res Ctr 2400 W Lloyd Expressway R-10 Evansville IN 47721-0001

LEARY, JAMES FRANCIS, PATHOLOGY. *Current Pos:* asst prof path, 81-85, ASSOC PROF PATH & LAB MED, MED SCH, UNIV ROCHESTER, 85-, ASSOC PROF PEDIAT, 85- *Personal Data:* b Portsmouth, NH, Apr 12, 48; m 78, Rosemary Conrad; c Charles, Elaine, Selena & Michael. *Educ:* Mass Inst Technol, BS(aeronaut & astronaut) & BS(phil & hist), 70; Univ NH, MS, 74; Pa State Univ, PhD(biophys), 77. *Prof Exp:* Res fel biophys & instrumentation, Los Alamos Sci Lab, 77-78, vis staff mem, 78-80. *Concurrent Pos:* Mem, Strong Childrens Res Ctr; dir, Cell Analysis & Sorting Facil. *Mem:* Soc Analytical Cytol; AAAS; NY Acad Sci. *Res:* Development of new automated laser flow cytometric instrumentation and clinically useful diagnostic tests; molecular biology; cell differentiation; molecular genetics; transplantation; breast cancer diagnostics. *Mailing Add:* Dept Path Box 626 Univ Rochester Med Sch 601 Elmwood Ave Rochester NY 14642-0001. *Fax:* 716-273-1027; *E-Mail:* jleary@sorterpathology. rochester.edu

LEARY, JOHN DENNIS, phytochemistry, natural products, for more information see previous edition

LEARY, RALPH JOHN, ORGANIC CHEMISTRY. *Current Pos:* RETIRED. *Personal Data:* b Elizabeth, NJ, Nov 3, 29; m 52; c 6. *Educ:* Seton Hall Univ, BS, 51; Univ Ill, PhD(chem), 57. *Prof Exp:* Jr chemist, Merck & Co, Inc, 51-54; group leader, Esso Res & Eng Co, 57-67, group leader & res assoc, 67-75, lab head, Exxon Chem Co USA, 75-77, res assoc, 78-80, sect head, Exxon Res & Eng Co, 78-87, sr res assoc, 80-87. *Mem:* Am Chem Soc; Sigma Xi. *Res:* Gas chromatography and automation of laboratory instruments; Am Soc Testing & Mat. *Mailing Add:* 211 Oak Lane Cranford NJ 07016

LEARY, RICHARD LEE, PALEOBOTANY, PALEOECOLOGY. *Current Pos:* CUR GEOL, ILL STATE MUS, 61- *Personal Data:* b Portsmouth, Va, Sept 19, 36; m 61, Eleanor M Riehl; c Seth & Sara. *Educ:* Va Polytech Inst, BS, 59; Univ Mich, MS, 61, PhD(geol), 80. *Concurrent Pos:* Adj asst prof environ geol, Sangamon State Univ, 73-78 & 89-; NSF grantee, 81-84, 85, 86, 94; Fulbright res award, Arg & Brazil, 91. *Mem:* Geol Soc Am; Bot Soc Am; Paleobot Sec; Int Orgn Paleobot; Latin-Am Asn Paleobot & Paleonol. *Res:* Late Paleozoic fossil plants, paleoecology, paleoenvironments and plant evolution; comparisons of Southern Hemisphere glossopterids and Northern Hemisphere Lesleya. *Mailing Add:* 387 Roanoke Dr Springfield IL 62702. *Fax:* 217-785-2857

LEARY, ROLFE ALBERT, FOREST MENSURATION. *Current Pos:* mensurationist, 68-72, PRIN MENSURATIONIST FORESTRY, US FOREST SERV, N CENT FOREST EXP STA, 72- *Personal Data:* b Waterloo, Iowa, Mar 5, 38; m 67; c 2. *Educ:* Iowa State Col, BS, 59; Purdue Univ, MS, 61, PhD(forest mgt), 68. *Prof Exp:* Vol forester, US Peace Corps, St Lucia, WI, 61-63; instr forest mensuration, Southern Ill Univ, 64-65. *Mem:* AAAS; Ecol Soc Am; Sigma Xi; Coun Unified Res & Educ. *Res:* Boundary value problem method of calibrating forest growth models; generalized forest growth projection system; philosophy and methods of forest research; multiple-use decision-making. *Mailing Add:* 1992 Folwell Ave St Paul MN 55108

LEAS, J(OHN) W(ESLEY), ELECTRICAL ENGINEERING. *Current Pos:* PRES, J W LEAS & ASSOCS, TRANSP CONSULT, 72- *Personal Data:* b Delaware, Ohio, June 14, 16; m 43. *Educ:* Ohio State Univ, BS, 38. *Prof Exp:* Sales engr, Armstrong Cork Co, Pa, 38-41; electronic engr airborne radar, Airborne Instrument Lab, NY, 46-47; consult engr air navig, Air Transport Asn, DC, 47-49; electronic res scientist, Air Navig Develop Bd, Dept Com, DC, 49-51; chief engr, Electronic Data Processing Div, Radio Corp Am, 51-60, mgr data commun & custom proj dept, Electronic Data Processing Div, 60-63; gen mgr Valley Forge Div, Control Data Corp, 64-72. *Concurrent Pos:* Mem tech staff telecommun res estab, Ministry Aviation, Eng, 42-43; asst head eng, US Naval Res Lab, 43-46; tech adv, US State Dept, 46; consult, Civil Aeronaut Admin, 48-49 & Dept Defense, 58-63; mem adv group comput, Dept Defense, 55. *Mem:* Fel Inst Elec & Electronics Engrs. *Res:* Development, design and management of engineering digital computers; general management of data communications and custom projects in data processing field. *Mailing Add:* J W Leas & Assocs 910 Potts Lane Bryn Mawr PA 19010

LEASK, R(AYMOND) A(LEXANDER), PULP & PAPER. *Current Pos:* RETIRED. *Personal Data:* b Edmonton, Alta, Jan 15, 19; m 42, Barbara J Chinneck; c Barbara E, Susanne J, Sally D & Martha J. *Educ:* Univ Alta, BSc, 41, MSc, 47. *Prof Exp:* Chemist, Brit-Am Oil Co, 41; res chemist, Can Int Paper Co, 42-44; res asst, Res Coun Alta, 45-47; chem engr, Powell River Co, 48-50; supvr pulping sect, Cent Res Div, Abitibi Power & Paper Co, 50-64; dir res, Bauer Bros Co, 64-71; process engr, Sandwell & Co, 71-73; asst res dir, Ont Paper Co, 73-83. *Concurrent Pos:* Consult, 83-93. *Mem:* Fel Tech Asn Pulp & Paper Indust; Can Pulp & Paper Asn; Asn Prof Engrs; Rotary Int. *Res:* Pulping methods on a pilot-plant scale and on a commercial scale; improving paper machine performance and improving newsprint quality. *Mailing Add:* 3 Mayholme Ct St Catharines ON L2N 4C1 Can

LEATH, KENNETH T, PLANT PATHOLOGY, SELECTION FOR DISEASE RESISTANCE. *Current Pos:* CONSULT, 94- *Personal Data:* b Providence, RI, Apr 29, 31; m 55, Marie Andreozzi; c Kenneth, Steven, Kevin & Maria B. *Educ:* Univ RI, BS, 59; Univ Minn, MS & PhD(phytopath), 66. *Honors & Awards:* Merit Cert, Am Forage & Grassland Coun, 83; Res Award, Nat Alfalfa Seed Coun, 93. *Prof Exp:* Res technician cereal rusts, Cereal Rust Lab, Minn, 59-66; plant pathologist, Regional Pasture Res Lab, USDA, 66-94. *Concurrent Pos:* Adj prof, Dept Plant Path, Pa State Univ, 66-94. *Mem:* Am Phytopath Soc; Am Soc Agron; Am Forage & Grassland Coun; Int Soc Root Res; Sigma Xi. *Res:* Clover and alfalfa diseases; host-parasite interaction; biocontrol; disease resistance methodology; develops protocol for selecting plants resistant to diseases; germplasm evaluation; advising on forage, field and turf crops. *Mailing Add:* 1438 Willowbrook Dr Boalsburg PA 16827-1666

LEATH, PAUL LARRY, SOLID STATE PHYSICS. *Current Pos:* from asst prof to assoc prof, Rutgers Univ, New Brunswick, 67-78, assoc dept, 73-75, assoc provost, 78-87, provost, 87-92, PROF PHYSICS, RUTGERS UNIV, NEW BRUNSWICK, 78-, CHAIR, PHYSICS & ASTRON DEPT, 95- *Personal Data:* b Moberly, Mo, Jan 9, 41; m 62, Rosemary Rippel; c 2. *Educ:* Univ Mo, Columbia, BS, 61, MS, 63, PhD(physics), 66. *Prof Exp:* Res assoc theoret physics, Oxford Univ, 66-67. *Mem:* AAAS; Am Phys Soc; Sigma Xi; Brit Inst Physics; NY Acad Sci. *Res:* Theoretical solid state physics; inelastic neutron scattering; vibrational and electronic properties of alloys; anharmonic crystals; disordered and dilute magnets; percolation processes; breakdown phenomena. *Mailing Add:* Dept Physics & Astron Rutgers Univ Piscataway NJ 08855-0849. *Fax:* 732-445-4343; *E-Mail:* leath@physics.rutgers.edu

LEATHEM, WILLIAM DOLARS, MEDICAL NUTRITION, MEDICAL PARASITOLOGY. *Current Pos:* med monitor nutrit, 76-78, MGR NUTRIT RES, ABBOTT LABS, 78- *Personal Data:* b Chicago, Ill, Jan 6, 31; m 52; c 3. *Educ:* Univ Wis, BS, 61, MS, 63, PhD(zool), 65. *Prof Exp:* Asst zool, Univ Wis, 62; asst prof biol, Wis State Univ, Whitewater, 65-66; asst prof, Univ Wis, Waukesha Ctr, 66-69, NSF grants, 67-69; res assoc, Norwich Pharmacal Co, 69-74, asst dir clin nutrit, Eaton Labs, 74-76. *Mem:* AAAS; Am Soc Parasitol; Soc Protozool; Am Soc Trop Med & Hyg; Am Soc Parenteral & Enteral Nutrit; Sigma Xi. *Res:* General parasitology and protozoology. *Mailing Add:* 1488 Camden Dr Gurnee IL 60031

LEATHER, GERALD ROGER, plant physiology, for more information see previous edition

LEATHERLAND, JOHN F, ENDOCRINOLOGY, PHYSIOLOGY. *Current Pos:* from asst prof to assoc prof, 71-83, PROF PHYSIOL, DEPT ZOOL, UNIV GUELPH, CAN, 83- *Personal Data:* b Nottingham, Eng, July 5, 43; Can citizen; m 65, Ann Murphy; c Steven & Rachel. *Educ:* Sheffield, Eng, BSc, 64; Leeds, Eng, PhD(endocrinol), 67. *Hon Degrees:* DSc, Sheffield Univ, Eng, 93. *Honors & Awards:* Excellence in Res, Sigma Xi, 89. *Prof Exp:* Fel endocrinol, Univ BC, 67-69, Univ Hull, UK, 69-71. *Concurrent Pos:* Vis fel, Univ Bath, UK, 79; vis prof, Murdoch Univ, Australia, 80 & 87; ed-in-chief, Fish Physiol & Biochem, 83- *Mem:* Soc Endocrinol; Can Soc Zool; Sigma Xi. *Res:* Endocrine control of metabolism, growth and reproduction of fish, particularly the role of the pituitary, thyroid and adrenal glands. *Mailing Add:* Dept Zool Univ Guelph Guelph ON N1G 2W1 Can. *Fax:* 519-767-1656

LEATHERMAN, ANNA D, plant ecology, botany; deceased, see previous edition for last biography

LEATHERMAN, NELSON E(ARLE), BIOENGINEERING. *Current Pos:* RES ASSOC, DEPT MED, DUKE UNIV. *Personal Data:* b Grand Rapids, Mich, Mar 22, 39; m 68. *Educ:* Univ Mich, BSE, 62, MSE, 63, PhD(bioeng), 67. *Prof Exp:* Res asst physiol, Univ Mich, 67-68; asst prof, Ind Univ, Bloomington, 68-77; res assoc, Vt Lung Ctr, Univ Vt, 77- *Mem:* Biomed Eng Soc. *Res:* Modeling of biological control systems; particularly identification of nonlinear systems. *Mailing Add:* Med Ctr 321 Bell Bldg Box 3861 Durham NC 27710

LEATHERMAN, STEPHEN PARKER, OCEANOGRAPHY, STRATIGRAPHY-SEDIMENTATION. *Current Pos:* from asst prof to assoc prof geog, 81-87, DIR, LAB COASTAL RES, UNIV MD, 87- *Personal Data:* b Charlotte, NC, Nov 6, 47; m 87. *Educ:* NC State Univ, BS, 70; Univ Va, PhD(environ sci), 76. *Prof Exp:* Asst prof geol, Boston Univ, 75-77; dir res unit, Univ Mass, 77-81. *Concurrent Pos:* Mem Nat Acad Sci Comt Sea Level Impacts, 84-87; petrol geologist, Texaco Inc, Houston, Tex, 70-72; sci adv & team leader, Earthwatch Sci Expeds, Belmont, Mass, 76-81; mem, Expert Panel Selection Global Coastal Biospheres, UNESCO, 80; tech consult, US Dept Interior Task Force Barrier Islands, 80-81, consult, Heritage Coast Proj, Wales, UK, 85-; dir bd, Climate Inst, Washington DC, 87-; expert testimony, US Senate, 86, 87 & 88. *Mem:* Soc Econ Paleontogists & Mineralogists; fel Geol Soc Am; corresp mem Int Geol Correlation Prog; AAAS. *Res:* Beaches and barrier islands; has authored/edited 8 books and over 50 refereed journal articles, including Science and Nature. *Mailing Add:* Dept Geog Univ Md Col Park MD 20742-0001

LEATHERS, CHESTER RAY, mycology, for more information see previous edition

LEATHERWOOD, JAMES M, animal nutrition, for more information see previous edition

LEATHRUM, JAMES FREDERICK, COMPUTER SCIENCE, COMPUTER ENGINEERING. *Current Pos:* PROF ELEC & COMPUT ENG, CLEMSON UNIV, 80- *Personal Data:* b Dover, Del, Dec 24, 37; m 60; c 3. *Educ:* Univ Del, BChE, 59; Princeton Univ, MA, 61, PhD(chem eng), 63. *Prof Exp:* Proj scientist, Union Carbide Corp, 65-67; from asst prof to assoc prof comput sci, Univ Del, 67-80. *Concurrent Pos:* Consult, US Army, 68-83 & Burroughs Corp, 69-73. *Mem:* Asn Comput Mach; Am Inst Chem Engrs; Sigma Xi; Inst Elec & Electronics Engrs. *Res:* Programming systems for real time and interactive computers; software engineering. *Mailing Add:* Elec & Comput Eng Dept Clemson Univ Clemson SC 29631

LEAV, IRWIN, PATHOLOGY. *Current Pos:* assoc prof, Sch Med, Vet Med, Tufts Univ, 70-87, assoc dean basic sci, 78-83, assoc dean res, Sch Vet Med, 83-93, PROF PATH, SCH MED, VET MED, TUFTS UNIV, 87-; ASST PATH, HARVARD MED SCH, 68- *Personal Data:* b Brooklyn, NY, July 4, 37; m 61; c 2. *Educ:* Ohio State Univ, BA, 59, DVM, 65; Am Col Vet Pathologists, dipl, 70. *Honors & Awards:* Pfizer Res Award, 95. *Prof Exp:* Res fel path, Harvard Med Sch, 65-68, NIH spec fel, 68-70. *Concurrent Pos:* Res assoc, Steroid Biochem Lab, 69-; assoc dir path, Angell Mem Hosp, 74-76; consult, US Armed Forces Inst Environ Med, 74- & Angell Mem Hosp, 76-; grant, Nat Cancer Inst, 78-81; Nat Cancer Inst, grant, 81- *Mem:* Int Acad Path; Am Col Vet Pathologists; Am Vet Med Asn. *Res:* Mechanisms of action of sex hormones on normal, hyperplastic and neoplastic male accessory sex organs. *Mailing Add:* Dept Path/Anat Tufts Univ Med Sch Dent & Vet Med 136 Harrison Ave Boston MA 02111

LEAVENS, PETER BACKUS, MINERALOGY. *Current Pos:* from asst prof to assoc prof, 67-88, PROF GEOL, UNIV DEL, 88- *Personal Data:* b Summit, NJ, June 20, 39; m 80, Sharon Fitzgerald; c Karla. *Educ:* Yale Univ, BA, 61; Harvard Univ, MA, 64, PhD, 66. *Prof Exp:* Res assoc, Dept Mineral Sci, Smithsonian Inst, 65-67. *Concurrent Pos:* Res assoc, Smithsonian Inst, 67-90; cur minerals, Univ Del, 78-; regist prof geologist, State Del, 87-; assoc ed, Can Min, 96- *Mem:* Fel Mineral Soc Am. *Res:* Crystal structure analysis; description of new mineral species; conditions of mineral occurrence and stability; mineralogy and geochemistry of pegmatites; carbonate metamorphism; asbestos mineralogy. *Mailing Add:* Dept Geol Univ Del Newark DE 19716. *Fax:* 302-831-4158; *E-Mail:* pbl@udel.edu

LEAVENWORTH, HOWARD W, JR, METALLURGY, RESEARCH ADMINISTRATION. *Current Pos:* RETIRED. *Personal Data:* b Waterbury, Conn, June 3, 28; m 55; c 3. *Educ:* Stevens Inst Technol, ME, 51; Yale Univ, MS, 53. *Honors & Awards:* NASA Award, 67; President's Award, Am Soc Microbiol, 70 & 71; Meritorious Serv, 83. *Prof Exp:* Metallurgist, Franklin Inst, 53-55; sr scientist, Pratt & Whitney Aircraft Co, 55-61 & Oak Ridge Nat Lab, 55-57; prog mgr solid state physics, Air Force Off Sci Res, 61-62; asst mgr, Am Mach & Foundry Co, 62-67; metallurgist, Bur Mines, Albany Res Ctr, 67-88, res supvr, 76-88. *Mem:* Fel AAAS; Sigma Xi; Am Inst Mining, Metall & Petrol Engrs. *Res:* Alloy development; corrosion; surface science; wear; extractive metallurgy; concrete; wire rope; powder metallurgy. *Mailing Add:* 20 Bayview Lane Port Townsend WA 98368

LEAVENWORTH, RICHARD S, INDUSTRIAL ENGINEERING & OPERATIONS RESEARCH, QUALITY CONTROL & CAPITAL BUDGETING. *Current Pos:* prof, 66-88, actg chmn dept, 79, EMER PROF, INDUST & SYSTS ENG, UNIV FLA, 88- *Personal Data:* b Oak Park, Ill, Sept 30, 30; m 55, JoAnne Christie. *Educ:* Stanford Univ, BSIE, 61, MSIE, 62, PhD(indust eng), 64. *Prof Exp:* Eng asst, Light Div, Dept Pub Utilities, Tacoma, Wash, 56-59; asst prof indust eng, Va Polytech Inst, 64-66. *Concurrent Pos:* Consult, Off Transp Res, US Dept Com, 65-66, mfg educ serv, Gen Elec Co, NY, 65-67 & Manhattan Industs, 70-73; ed, Eng Economist, 76-80; adv, Eng Soc Comn Energy, 78-79; consult, Off Chief Economist, TVA, 84-88 & expert consult, Temple, Barker & Sloane, 84; consult, Total Qual Mgt, Naval Aviation Depot, Jacksonville, Fla, 88. *Mem:* Fel Inst Indust Engrs (vpres, 77-79 & 82-84); Am Soc Qual Control; Am Soc Eng Educ. *Res:* Engineering economics; statistical quality control; development of process control systems for Naval Aviation depots; author in quality assurance, quality management and engineering economics. *Mailing Add:* 10035 SW 55th Lane Gainesville FL 32608. *Fax:* 904-392-3537

LEAVIS, PAUL CLIFTON, MUSCLE RESEARCH, PROTEIN SCIENCE. *Current Pos:* prin scientist, 86-88, SR SCIENTIST, BOSTON BIOMED RES INST, 88-; ASSOC PROF PHYSIOL, SCHS DENT, MED & VET MED, TUFTS UNIV, 89- *Personal Data:* b May 17, 44; US citizen; m 70, Judith L Pipkins; c Jeremy & Allison. *Educ:* Univ Notre Dame, BS, 66; Tufts Univ, PhD(physiol), 71. *Prof Exp:* Lab instr, Med Sch, Tufts Univ, 69-71; res fel, Dept Muscle Res, Boston Biomed Res Inst, 72-75, res assoc, 75-78, staff scientist, 78-86; asst prof physiol, Sch Dent Med & Sch Vet Med, Tufts Univ, 78-89. *Concurrent Pos:* Res fel, Dept Neurol, Harvard Med Sch, 74-78, res assoc, 78; lectr, Tufts Univ, 74-; estab investr, Am Heart Asn, 78-83, mem, Molecular Aspects Excitable Tissues Res Study Comt, 86-89; pres, Analytical Biotechnol Servs, 91- *Mem:* AAAS; Biophys Soc; NY Acad Sci; Am Soc Biochem & Molecular Biol. *Res:* Biochemistry of contractile and regulatory proteins in mammalian skeletal and cardiac muscle and non-muscle motile cells; structure and function of calcium binding proteins; effects of protein-protein interactions on the metal binding proteins of troponin C; use of rare earth ions as probes of metal binding sites; supramolecular structure of muscle protein complexes; molecular cytoskeleton structure and function; protein structure and characterization. *Mailing Add:* Analytical Biotechnol Serv 20 Staniford St Boston MA 02114. *E-Mail:* leavis@bbri.harvard.edu

LEAVITT, CHRISTOPHER PRATT, PHYSICS. *Current Pos:* from asst prof to prof, 56-95, actg chmn, Dept Physics & Astron, 58-60, EMER PROF PHYSICS, UNIV NMEX, 96- *Personal Data:* b Boston, Mass, Nov 20, 27; m 59; c 5. *Educ:* Mass Inst Technol, BS, 48, PhD(physics), 52. *Prof Exp:* Res assoc physics, Brookhaven Nat Lab, NY, 52-54, assoc physicist, 54-56. *Concurrent Pos:* Consult, Res Directorate, Physics Div, Kirtland AFB, 56-60; directorate res & develop, Air Force Missile Develop Ctr, Holloman AFB, 56-60; mem, Particles & Fields Subcomt, NASA, 65-67; mem, Tech Adv Panel, Los Alamos Meson Physics Facil, 69-71; mem, Nuclear Physics Steering Comt, 70-71. *Mem:* Am Phys Soc. *Res:* Nuclear and high energy physics; cosmic rays; space physics. *Mailing Add:* Dept Physics Univ NMex Main Campus Albuquerque NM 87131-1156

LEAVITT, FRED W, APPLIED MATHEMATICS. *Current Pos:* chem engr, 57-61, group leader, 61-63, SR ENGR, LINDE DIV, UNION CARBIDE CORP, 63- *Personal Data:* b Elizabeth, NJ, Oct 16, 28. *Educ:* Newark Col Eng, BS, 50; Rensselaer Polytech Inst, MS, 55, PhD(chem eng), 57. *Prof Exp:* Chem engr, Biol Labs, US Army, Camp Detrick, 52-54. *Mem:* AAAS; Am Chem Soc. *Res:* Development of adsorptive separation processes; automatic data logging; development of computer systems for reducing, analyzing and correlating data and making design calculations; chemical kinetics and equilibria. *Mailing Add:* 114 Sundridge Dr Apt 4 Amherst NY 14228

LEAVITT, JOHN ADAMS, ION BEAM ANALYSIS, ATOMIC PHYSICS. *Current Pos:* From asst prof to prof, 60-95, EMER PROF PHYSICS, UNIV ARIZ, 95- *Personal Data:* b Lewis, Colo, Dec 8, 32; m 55, Shirley A Boudreau; c Genevieve, Anne, John, Andrew & Matthew. *Educ:* Univ Colo, BA, 54, Harvard Univ, MA, 56, PhD, 60. *Mem:* Am Phys Soc. *Res:* Developing and using new techniques for analyzing thin films using ion beams from a 6 MV Van de Graaff accelerator. *Mailing Add:* 2130 N Norton Ave Tucson AZ 85719. *Fax:* 520-621-4721; *E-Mail:* jleav5@aol.com

LEAVITT, JULIAN JACOB, LICENSING, TECHNOLOGY ACQUISITION. *Current Pos:* vpres, Chemist Group, Inc, 86-95, VPRES, TECHNOL GROUP, INC. 95- *Personal Data:* b Boston, Mass, Sept 4, 18; m 43, Frances Victoria Albert; c Robert M, Phyllis E & Anne I (Matsui). *Educ:* Harvard Univ, AB, 39, AM, 40, PhD(org chem), 42. *Prof Exp:* Res chemist, Nat Defense Res Comt, Harvard Univ, 42 & Univ Pa, 42-44; res chemist, Calco Chem Div, 44-54, Res Div, 54-58, Org Chem Div, 58-64, mgr explor res, 64-69, tech dir, Decision Making Systs Dept, 69-70, asst to mgr com develop, 70-74, mgr licensing & technol, 74-77, dir licensing & technol acquisition chem, 77-81, dir licensing chemicals, Am Cyanamid Co, 81-85. *Concurrent Pos:* Ed, Sect 41, Chem Abstr Serv, 61-95; mem, Adv Bd Mil Personnel Supplies & Comt Textile Dyeing & Finishing, Nat Acad Sci-Nat Res Coun, 63-68. *Mem:* AAAS; Am Chem Soc; Licensing Exec Soc. *Res:* Dyes; applied photochemistry. *Mailing Add:* 227 Silver Hill Lane Stamford CT 06905-3122

LEAVITT, MARC LAURENCE, NEUROSCIENCE, ANIMAL PHYSIOLOGY. *Current Pos:* SR SCIENTIST, NEUROSCI RES LAB, ALLEGHENY-SINGER RES INST, PITTSBURGH, 86-; ASST PROF PSYCHIAT, MED COL PA, ALLEGHENY CAMPUS, 88- *Personal Data:* b St Louis, Mo, Apr 30, 47; m 71, Linda Brunell; c Michelle. *Educ:* Southern Ill Univ, BA, 69, MA, 71; Univ Iowa, PhD(physiol & biophys), 75. *Prof Exp:* Fel, Dept Pharmacol & Med, Col Med, Univ Ky, Lexington, 75-78; asst prof, Biol Dept, Southwest Mo State Univ, Springfield, 78-82, assoc prof, Biomed Sci Dept, 82-86. *Concurrent Pos:* Kroc Found fel, 75-77; vis investr, Dept Anesthesia Res, Michael Reese Hosp & Med Ctr, Chicago, 80; sr res fel hypertension res, Allegheny-Singer Res Inst, 85-86. *Mem:* Am Physiol Soc; Am Soc Hypertension; Soc Neurosci; NY Acad Sci; AAAS; Soc Cryobiol; Int Behav Neurosci Soc. *Res:* Psychopharmacology of behavior-aggression and delerium; techniques for profound hypothermic cardiac arrest in conjunction with blood substitution; pharmacological modulation of intracranial pressure; brain cancer models; neurotrophic factors and Parkinson's disease. *Mailing Add:* Neurosci Res Lab InVitro Techol Inc 1049 Printers Pl Pittsburgh PA 15237. *Fax:* 412-359-6874

LEAVITT, WENDELL WILLIAM, ENDOCRINOLOGY, REPRODUCTIVE BIOLOGY. *Current Pos:* PROF BIOCHEM, HEALTH SCI CTR & PROF OBSTET & GYNEC, SCH MED, TEX TECH UNIV, 83- *Personal Data:* b Conway, NH, Jan 15, 38; m 59; c 4. *Educ:* Dartmouth Col, AB, 59; Univ NH, MS, 61, PhD(zool), 63. *Prof Exp:* Res analyst zool, Agr Exp Sta, Univ NH, 60-63, res assoc endocrinol & instr zool, 63-64; asst prof biol, Univ Cincinnati, 64-67, from asst prof to prof physiol, Col Med, 67-77; sr scientist endocrinol, Worcester Found Exp Biol, 77-83. *Concurrent Pos:* Vis scientist, Univ Wis-Madison, 67-68 & Med Ctr, Vanderbilt Univ, 72-73; mem, regulatory biol panel, NSF, 77-79; prof obstet & gynec, Med Sch, Univ Mass, 78-83; adj prof, Boston Univ, 78-83; mem Pop Res Comn, Nat Inst Child Health & Human Develop, NIH, 83-87. *Mem:* Sigma Xi; Am Soc Zoologists; Endocrine Soc; Soc Study Reproduction; Am Physiol Soc; Am Soc Cell Biol; Am Soc Biol Chemists. *Res:* Mechanism of pituitary function in relation to gonadotrophin secretion; control of female reproductive processes; estrogens and pituitary function; neuroendocrinology and aging of the reproductive system; steroid hormone receptor systems; mechanism of steroid hormone action. *Mailing Add:* Dept Biol Sci Wichita State Univ 1845 Fairmount CB26 Wichita KS 67208

LEAVITT, WILLIAM GRENFELL, ALGEBRA. *Current Pos:* from instr to assoc prof, Univ Nebr, Lincoln, 47-56, chmn dept, 54-64, prof math, 56-86, EMER PROF MATH, UNIV NEBR, LINCOLN, 86- *Personal Data:* b Omaha, Nebr, Mar 19, 16; wid; c Carol (Eveland), Robert, Elizabeth (deceased). *Educ:* Univ Nebr, AB, 37, MA, 38; Univ Wis, PhD(math), 47. *Prof Exp:* Actg instr math, Univ Wis, 46. *Concurrent Pos:* NSF fel, 59-60; Univ Nebr Res Coun vis fel, Leeds, Eng, 73. *Mem:* Am Math Soc; Math Asn Am. *Res:* Ring theory; theory of modules; theory of radicals. *Mailing Add:* Dept Math Univ Nebr Lincoln NE 68588

LEAVY, PAUL MATTHEW, REMOTE SENSING, SELF-REGULATING AUTONOMOUS VEHICLE OPERATION. *Current Pos:* PRES, PAUL LEAVY ASSOCS, 90- *Personal Data:* b Jackson, Mich, Apr 15, 23; m 44, Jeanne; c William & Paula. *Educ:* US Naval Acad, BS, 44. *Prof Exp:* Mgr navy projs, Arma Div, Am Bosch Arma, 54-57; mgr adv progs, Lab Electronics, 57-59; pres, Trident Corp, 59-62; mgr, Radiation Div, Sanders Assocs, 62-72; vpres, ITT EOPD, 72-78; mgr mkt, Western Div, GTE EOO, 78-84; dir, Develop Progs, Teledyne CME, 84-90. *Concurrent Pos:* Consult, Nat Acad Sci, ASW, 59-60; mem, Counter Terrorism, Nat Acad Eng, 72. *Mem:* Soc Photo-Optical Instrumentation Engrs; Am Inst Aeronaut & Astronaut; AAAS; Unmanned Vehicle Asn. *Res:* Original invention and development of various active OCM and IRCM systems; development of C W sensing lasar radar; development of chemical/bio mass spectrometer for rapid sensing of subtoxic levels of CW or biowarfare threat substances. *Mailing Add:* 8388 Riesling Way San Jose CA 95135

LEBARON, FRANCIS NEWTON, NEUROCHEMISTRY, LIPID CHEMISTRY. *Current Pos:* RETIRED. *Personal Data:* b Framingham, Mass, July 26, 22; m 53; c 1. *Educ:* Mass Inst Technol, BS, 44; Boston Univ, MA, 48; Harvard Univ, PhD(biochem), 51. *Prof Exp:* Asst biochemist, McLean Hosp, Mass, 52-53 & 54-57, assoc biochemist, 57-64; from assoc prof to prof biochem, Sch Med, Univ NMex, 64-83, chmn dept, 71-78. *Concurrent Pos:* USPHS fel, McLean Hosp, Waverley, Mass, 51-52 & Maudsley Hosp, 53-54; res assoc, Harvard Med Sch, Harvard Univ, 56-59, assoc, 59-64, tutor, 57-64; vis scholar, Mass Inst Technol, 74-75. *Mem:* AAAS; Am Soc Neurochem; Am Soc Biol Chem; Am Inst Nutrit. *Res:* Biochemistry of the nervous system, especially the chemistry of proteins and lipids and their nervous complexes as they occur in mammalian nervous tissues; role of polyunsaturated fatty acids in nervous tissues. *Mailing Add:* PO Box 779 Mashpee MA 02649-0779

LEBEL, JACK LUCIEN, RADIOLOGY, RADIATION BIOLOGY. *Current Pos:* assoc prof radiol & radiation biol, 68-73, asst dean, Curric Col, 70-72, PROF RADIOL & RADIATION BIOL, COL VET MED & BIOMED SCI, COLO STATE UNIV, 73- *Personal Data:* b Montreal, Que, Sept 16, 33; US citizen; m 60; c 2. *Educ:* Univ Montreal, DVM, 58; Colo State Univ, MS, 66, PhD(radiation biol), 67. *Prof Exp:* Asst prof vet med, Univ Montreal, 61-64, assoc prof radiol, 67-68. *Concurrent Pos:* Consult, Orthop Found Animals, 69-, Rockewell Int, 73- & Wildlife Pharmaceut, 90- *Mem:* Am Vet Med Asn; Am Vet Radiol Soc. *Res:* Bone pathology; biological effects of plutonium contamination; densitometry; pulmonary physiology. *Mailing Add:* 1424 Front Nine Dr Ft Collins CO 80525

LEBEL, JEAN EUGENE, MATHEMATICS. *Current Pos:* ASSOC PROF MATH, UNIV TORONTO, 65- *Personal Data:* b Can, Mar 21, 22. *Educ:* McGill Univ, BSc, 44; Univ Toronto, MA, 50, PhD(appl math), 58. *Prof Exp:* Theoret physicist, Newmont Explor, Ltd, Ariz, 52-54; lectr, McGill Univ, 55-57; from asst prof to assoc prof math, Georgetown Univ, 58-65. *Mem:* Am Math Soc; Can Math Cong. *Res:* Analysis; applied mathematics. *Mailing Add:* 27 Cheston Rd Toronto ON M4S 2X4 Can

LEBEL, NORMAN ALBERT, ORGANIC CHEMISTRY, REACTION MECHANISMS. *Current Pos:* from asst prof to assoc prof, Wayne State Univ, 57-64, chmn dept, 71-78, interim dean, Col Lib Arts, 83-84, PROF CHEM, WAYNE STATE UNIV, 64- *Personal Data:* b Augusta, Maine, Mar 22, 31; m 52, Constance Ouellette; c Mark, Norma & Carl. *Educ:* Bowdoin Col, AB, 52; Mass Inst Technol, PhD, 57. *Prof Exp:* Chemist, Merck & Co, Inc, 52-54. *Concurrent Pos:* Sloan Found fel, 61-65; Welch Found lectr, 74. *Mem:* Fel AAAS; Am Chem Soc; Sigma Xi; Royal Soc Chem. *Res:* Stereochemistry and mechanism of elimination reactions; chemistry of nitrones and nitrogen heterocycles; additions to olefins; bridged polycyclic molecules; new synthetic reactions. *Mailing Add:* 277 Chem Bldg Wayne State Univ Detroit MI 48202

LEBEL, ROLAND GUY, PHYSICAL CHEMISTRY, CHEMICAL ENGINEERING. *Personal Data:* b Edmundston, NB, Feb 10, 32; m 64; c 1. *Educ:* NS Tech Col, BEng, 55; Mass Inst Technol, SM, 56; McGill Univ, PhD(phys chem), 62. *Prof Exp:* Res engr, Fraser Pulp & Paper Co Ltd, 58-59; demonstr, McGill Univ, 59-62; sr develop engr, Anglo Paper Prod Ltd, 63-65; res & develop proj coordr pulp & paper, Reed Inc, 65-69, tech dir, Papeterie Reed Ltd, 69-80, dir res & develop, 80-85; dean, Sch Forest Sci, Univ Moncton, 85-97. *Mem:* Sr mem Can Pulp & Paper Asn. *Res:* Planning, organization and coordination of research and development of projects related to the manufacture of newsprint and other paper products. *Mailing Add:* Sch Forest Sci Univ Moncton 165 Blvd Hebert Edmundston NB E3V 2S8 Can

LEBEL, SUSAN, MOLECULAR BIOLOGY, MOLECULAR IMMUNOLOGY. *Current Pos:* PRES, GENOMICS ONE CORP, 95- *Personal Data:* b July 5, 59; Can citizen; m 89, Steve N Slilaty; c Catherine E. *Educ:* Montreal Univ, Que, BSc, 82, PhD(molecular biol), 87. *Prof Exp:* Fel, Biotechnol Res Inst, Biomira Inc, 87-88, sr scientist, 89-92; vpres, Quantum Biotechnol Inc, 91-95. *Concurrent Pos:* Vis res fel, Natural Sci & Eng Res Coun Can, 87-88. *Res:* Anecoti based expression system and human cell expression system; design and devlopment of molecular biology products, kits for research. *Mailing Add:* 270 Blvd Samson Suite 105 Laval PQ H7X 2Y9 Can

LEBEN, CURT (CHARLES), PLANT PATHOLOGY. *Current Pos:* RETIRED. *Personal Data:* b Chicago, Ill, July 7, 17; m 44; c 2. *Educ:* Ohio Univ, BS, 40; Univ Wis, PhD(plant path), 46. *Prof Exp:* Asst bot, Ohio Univ, 39-40; asst, Univ Wis, 42, asst plant path, 42-46, res assoc, 46-49, asst prof, 49-55; plant pathologist, Eli Lilly & Co, Ind, 55-57, head agr res labs, 57-59; prof bot & plant path & assoc chmn dept, Ohio State Univ, 59-67, actg chmn, 67-68, prof plant path, Agr Res & Develop Ctr, 67-88. *Mem:* AAAS; fel Am Phytopath Soc; Sigma Xi. *Res:* Antibiotics and antibiosis in relation to plant diseases; microbiology; epiphytic microorganisms; bacterial and decay diseases; forest tree diseases; biological control. *Mailing Add:* 923 Thorne Ave Wooster OH 44691

LEBENBAUM, MATTHEW T(OBRINER), ELECTRONICS ENGINEERING. *Current Pos:* RETIRED. *Personal Data:* b Portland, Ore, Nov 29, 17; m 42; c 2. *Educ:* Stanford Univ, BA, 38; Mass Inst Technol, MS, 45. *Prof Exp:* Asst elec eng, Stanford Univ, 38-39 & Mass Inst Technol, 39-41; asst syst planning engr, Am Gas & Elec Corp, 41-42; res assoc, Radio Res Lab, Harvard Univ, 42-45; dir, Appl Electronics Div, Airborne Instruments Lab, Cutler-Hammer, Inc, 45- *Mem:* Fel Inst Elec & Electronics Engrs; Int Union Radio Sci. *Res:* Radio receivers, especially microwave; methods and techniques of noise measurement; intermediate frequency amplifiers; application of electronic methods to power systems; radio astronomy instrumentation; low noise devices. *Mailing Add:* 80 Whitehall Blvd Garden City NY 11530

LEBENSOHN, ZIGMOND MEYER, PSYCHIATRY. *Current Pos:* chief, Dept Psychiat, 57-76, CHIEF EMERGENCY, SIBLEY MEM HOSP, 76-, CLIN PROF PSYCHIAT, GEORGETOWN UNIV MED SCH, 41- *Personal Data:* b Kenosha, Wis, Sept 8, 10; m 40, 79; c 4. *Educ:* Northwestern Univ, BS, 30, MB, 33, MD, 34; Am Bd Psychiat & Neurol, dipl psychiat, 41, dipl neurol, 40. *Honors & Awards:* Kober Lectr, 52; Jacobi Soc Award, 83; Seymour Pollack Distinguished Achievement Award in Forensic Psychiat, 86. *Prof Exp:* Instr neurol, Med Sch, George Washington Univ, 36-41. *Concurrent Pos:* Med officer, St Elizabeth's Hosp, 35-39; mem staff, Doctors Hosp, 41-74; consult, Vet Admin, 46-49, US Naval Hosp, Bethesda, Md, 52-82, US Info Agency, 58-61, Walter Reed Army Hosp, Washington, DC, 58-66, NIMH, 68-72; consult med adv panel, Fed Aviation Agency, 61-66; chief, Dept Psychiat, Sibley Mem Hosp, 57-76. *Mem:* Fel Am Psychiat Asn; fel AMA; Am Psychopath Asn; Asn Res Nerv & Ment Dis. *Res:* Legal aspects of psychiatry; psychiatric hospital design; trans-cultural psychiatry; psychiatric units in general hospitals. *Mailing Add:* 2015 R St NW Washington DC 20009

LEBENTHAL, EMANUEL, GASTROENTEROLOGY, PEDIATRICS. *Current Pos:* assoc prof pediat, 76-80, PROF PEDIAT GASTROENTEROL, STATE UNIV NY, BUFFALO, 80-; CHIEF PEDIAT GASTROENTEROL, CHILDREN'S HOSP BUFFALO, 80-, DIR, INT INST INFANT NUTRIT & GASTROINTESTINAL DIS, 84- *Personal Data:* b Jerusalem, Israel, Apr 12, 36; US citizen; c 5. *Educ:* Hebrew Univ, Israel, MD, 64. *Honors & Awards:* Int Prize Mod Nutrit, Int Dairy Fedn, Switz, 84. *Prof Exp:* Asst med, Children's Hosp, Boston, 72-74, assoc, 74-76; assoc prof pediat, 76-80, prof pediat gastroenterol, State Univ NY, Buffalo, 80- *Concurrent Pos:* Consult to clin staff, Roswell Park Mem Inst, 77- *Mem:* Soc Pediat Res; NAm Soc Pediat Gastroenterol; Am Pancreatic Asn; Am Asn Study Liver Dis; Am Soc Clin Nutrit; Am Inst Nutrit. *Res:* Impact of the ontogeny of the gut on feeding the compromised and premature infant, specifically the ontogeny of the pancreas; determinants that affect acture diarrhea to develop into chronic diarrhea in children. *Mailing Add:* MS 402 Hahnemann Univ Broad & Vine Sts Philadelphia PA 19102

LEBER, PHYLLIS ANN, REACTION MECHANISMS, PLANT GROWTH REGULATORS. *Current Pos:* asst prof, Franklin & Marshall Col, Pa, 82-88, assoc prof, 88-96, chair, Chem Dept, 89-94, PROF, FRANKLIN & MARSHALL COL, PA, 96- *Personal Data:* b Scranton, Pa, 49; c 1. *Educ:* Albright Col, Pa, BS, 76; Univ NMex, PhD(chem), 81. *Prof Exp:* Jr chemist, Am Color & Chem Co, Reading, Pa, 71-76; asst prof org chem, Pomona Col, Claremont, Calif, 81-82. *Concurrent Pos:* Vis asst prof org chem, Univ NMex, 83. *Mem:* Am Chem Soc; Sigma Xi. *Res:* Physical organic chemistry as it relates to the elucidation of reaction mechanisms of thermal unimolecular isomerizations, both uncatalyzed and catalyzed; synthens and biology of autin cholire ester anpyates. *Mailing Add:* Dept Chem Franklin & Marshall Col Lancaster PA 17604. *Fax:* 717-291-4343; *E-Mail:* p_leber@acad.fandm.edu

LEBER, SAM, METALLURGY. *Current Pos:* RETIRED. *Personal Data:* b Rockford, Ill, Nov 15, 25; m 52; c 2. *Educ:* Univ Ill, BS, 48, MS, 49. *Prof Exp:* X-ray crystallographer, Horizons Inc, 50-55; metallurgist, Lamp Metals & Components Dept, Gen Elec Co, 55-66, supvr struct eval unit, 66-71, mgr metals eval subsect, Refractory Metals Dept, 71-86. *Mem:* Am Soc Metals; Am Inst Mining, Metall & Petrol Engrs. *Res:* Physical metallurgy; x-ray, optical and electron metallurgy. *Mailing Add:* 2495 Deborah Dr Beachwood OH 44122

LEBERMAN, PAUL R, UROLOGY. *Current Pos:* Assoc prof clin urol & asst prof urol, Grad Sch Med, 51-66, PROF CLIN UROL, UNIV PA, 66-, CHIEF UROL SURG, OUTPATIENT DEPT, HOSP, 51-, EMER PROF UROL, 72- *Personal Data:* b New York, Mar 1, 04; m 32, Estelle Rosenthal. *Educ:* NY Univ, BS, 25; Univ Pa, MS, 27, MD, 31; Am Bd Urol, dipl, 42. *Concurrent Pos:* Chief urol, Philadelphia Gen Hosp, 59-; consult, US Naval Hosp, Philadelphia, 60- *Mem:* Fel Am Col Surg; fel Royal Soc Med; fel Int Soc Urol; fel Am Acad Pediat; fel Pan-Pac Surg Asn; Sigma Xi. *Res:* Urological surgery. *Mailing Add:* Warwick 17th St & Locust St Philadelphia PA 19103

LEBERMANN, KENNETH WAYNE, FOOD SCIENCES. *Current Pos:* RETIRED. *Personal Data:* b Davenport, Iowa; m 62; c 2. *Educ:* Univ Ill, Urbana, BS, 59, PhD(food sci), 64; Univ Calif, Davis, MS, 61. *Prof Exp:* Scientist, CPC Int, 64-66; group leader cereals, Quaker Oats Co, 66-67, sr group leader bakery prod, 67-69, sect mgr bakery prod, 69-70, sect mgr pet foods, 70-75, mgr pet food res, 75-78, asst dir, 78, dir, 78-79, vpres res, Quaker Oats Co, 79- *Mem:* Inst Food Technologists; Sigma Xi. *Res:* Industrial research related to new product development, pet food research. *Mailing Add:* 250 Monument Ave Barrington IL 60010

LEBHERZ, HERBERT G, BIOCHEMISTRY. *Current Pos:* assoc prof, 76-80, PROF BIOCHEM, SAN DIEGO STATE UNIV, 80- *Personal Data:* b San Francisco, Calif, July 27, 41; div. *Educ:* San Francisco State Univ, BA, 64, MA, 66; Univ Wash, PhD(biochem), 70. *Prof Exp:* From res assoc to sr res assoc cell biol, Swiss Fed Inst Technol, 71-75; cancer res sci biochem, Roswell Park Mem Inst, 75-76. *Mem:* Am Heart Asn; Am Soc Biol Chemists; AAAS. *Res:* Elucidation of the mechanisms involved in the regulation of protein synthesis and protein degradation in developing adult and diseased organisms. *Mailing Add:* Dept Chem San Diego State Univ San Diego CA 92182-0328

LEBIEDZIK, JOZEF, QUANTITATIVE MICROSCOPY, MATERIALS SCIENCE. *Current Pos:* PRES, MODERN INSTRUMENTATION TECHNOL, INC, 80- *Personal Data:* b Feb 13, 40; US citizen; m 69; c 1. *Educ:* Pa State Univ, BS, 70, MS, 72, PhD(solid state sci), 75. *Prof Exp:* Res asst quant micros, Mat Res Lab, Pa State Univ, 70-75, res assoc, 75-76; vpres res & develop quant micros, Lemont Sci Inc, 76-86. *Mem:* Microbeam Analysis Soc; Am Vacuum Soc. *Res:* Microbeam analysis on automated scanning electron microscopes or electron probe systems; laboratory automation; surface analysis systems - instrumentation. *Mailing Add:* Advan Res Inst Co 2434 30th St Boulder CO 80301

LEBIEN, TUCKER W, LABORATORY MEDICINE, PATHOLOGY. *Current Pos:* postdoctoral res fel, Dept Lab Med & Path, Univ Minn, 77-79, from instr to assoc prof, 79-89, assoc dir, Pathobiol Grad Prog, 85-87, DIR GRAD STUDIES, PATHOBIOL GRAD PROG, UNIV MINN, 88-, PROF, DEPT LAB MED & PATH, 89- *Personal Data:* b Minneapolis, Minn, Dec, 8, 48. *Educ:* NDak State Univ, BS, 70, MS, 73; Univ Nebr, PhD(med microbiol-immunol), 77. *Honors & Awards:* McFadden Lectr, Nebr Med Ctr, 87; Stohlman Mem Award, Leukemia Soc Am, 89. *Prof Exp:* Teaching asst, Dept Med Microbiol, Nebr Med Ctr, 74-76. *Concurrent Pos:* New investr award, Nat Cancer Inst, 80-82; organizing fac, Fermentation Biotechnol Ctr, Univ Minn, 83-, dir, NIH Immunol Training Prog, 89-; assoc ed, J Immunol, 84-88, Blood, 91-93; vis assoc prof path, Lab Molecular Immunol, Harvard Med Sch, 86. *Mem:* Am Asn Immunologists; Am Asn Cancer Res; Am Soc Hemat; Am Soc Microbiol; Sigma Xi; Fedn Am Scientists; AAAS. *Res:* Neutral endopeptidase; differentiative programs of lymphoid progenitor cells. *Mailing Add:* Dept Lab Med & Path-UMHC Univ Minn Box 609 Minneapolis MN 55455-0315

LEBLANC, ADRIAN DAVID, RADIOLOGICAL PHYSICS, NUCLEAR MEDICINE. *Current Pos:* ASST PROF MED, BAYLOR COL MED, 72- *Personal Data:* b Salem, Mass, May 21, 40; m 66; c 2. *Educ:* Univ Mass, BA, 62; Iowa State Univ, MS, 66; Univ Kans, PhD(radiation biophys), 72; Am Bd Health Physics, cert; Am Bd Radiol, cert in nuclear med physics. *Prof Exp:* health physicist, hosp & radiol physicist, dept nuclear med, Methodist Hosp, 66- *Concurrent Pos:* Radiation physicist, Vet Admin Hosp, 67- *Mem:* Health Physics Soc; Soc Nuclear Med; Am Asn Physicists in Med; Sigma Xi. *Res:* Coronary blood flow; neutron activation analysis; x-ray fluorescence; health physics. *Mailing Add:* Baylor Col Med One Baylor Plaza Houston TX 77030-3411

LEBLANC, ARTHUR EDGAR, GEOLOGY, PALYNOLOGY. *Current Pos:* proj palynologist, 69-77, SR PROJ GEOLOGIST, GULF OIL RES & DEVELOP CO, 77- *Personal Data:* b Moncton, NB, Sept 29, 23; US citizen; m 52; c 2. *Educ:* Univ Mass, Amherst, BS, 52, MS, 54. *Prof Exp:* Paleontologist, Shell Oil Co, Tex, 54-62 & Calif, 62-65; sr res scientist, Res Ctr, Pan Am Petrol Corp, Okla, 65-69. *Mem:* AAAS; Am Asn Petrol Geologists; Soc Econ Paleontologists & Mineralogists; Am Asn Stratig Palynologists. *Res:* Stratigraphic Paleozoic palynology; Mesozoic and Cenozoic stratigraphic palynology. *Mailing Add:* 11622 Spriggs Way Houston TX 77024

LEBLANC, DONALD JOSEPH, PLASMID BIOLOGY, MICROBIAL PHYSIOLOGY. *Current Pos:* PROF MICROBIOL, MED SCH, UNIV TEX, SAN ANTONIO, 88- *Personal Data:* b Shirley, Mass, July 3, 42; m 66; c 4. *Educ:* St Michael's Col, BA, 64; Fordham Univ, MS, 66; Univ Mass, Amherst, PhD(microbiol), 70. *Honors & Awards:* Dr John C Hartnett Lectr, St Michaels Col, 80. *Prof Exp:* Postdoctoral, Georgetown Univ Sch Med & Dent, 70-72, NIH staff fel, 72-75, sr staff fel, 75-77, res microbiologist, plasmid biol, 77-81, sect head, 81-88. *Concurrent Pos:* Consult, Food & Drug Admin, 78-92; vis scientist, Am Soc Microbiol Minority Student Sci Careers Support Prog & mem, Am Soc Microbiol Culture Collection Subcomt, Pub Affairs Con, 87-92; mem BM2 study sect, NIH, 92- *Mem:* NY Acad Sci; Am Soc Microbiol; AAAS. *Res:* Molecular, genetic, and biochemical techniques to identification and characterization of chromosomal and extrachromosomal genetic traits. *Mailing Add:* Dept Microbiol Med Sch Univ Tex 7703 Floyd Curl Dr San Antonio TX 78284-6200

LEBLANC, FRANCIS ERNEST, NEUROPHYSIOLOGY, NEUROSURGERY. *Current Pos:* CHIEF, DIV NEUROSURG, FOOTHILLS HOSP, CALGARY, 74- *Personal Data:* b North Sydney, NS, June 10, 35; m 61; c 3. *Educ:* St Francis Xavier Univ, BSc, 55; Univ Ottawa, MD, 59; Univ Montreal, MSc, 62, PhD(neurophysiol), 64; FRCS(C), 68. *Prof Exp:* Intern, Montreal Gen Hosp, Que, 59-60, jr asst resident surg, Queen Mary Vet Hosp, Montreal, 60-61; res asst, Neurol Sci Lab, Univ Montreal, 61-62, lectr physiol, Univ, 61-64; demonstr neurol, McGill Univ, 64-67, lectr neurosurg, 67-68, asst prof, 68-70; from asst prof to assoc prof, 71-79, prof surg, Univ Calgary, 80-, assoc dean clin serv, 83- *Concurrent Pos:* Med Res Coun fel, Univ Montreal, 61-64, res fel, 62-64; clin fel & chief resident, Montreal Neurol Inst, 64-67, res scholar, 67-70, asst neurosurgeon, 68; consult, Queen Mary Vet Hosp, Montreal, 67; vis neurosurgeon, Royal Victoria Hosp, Montreal, 68; consult neurosurgeon, Foothills Hosp, 71-74. *Mem:* Can Neurosurg Soc; Cong Neurol Surg; Asn Acad Surg; fel Am Col Surg. *Res:* Cerebrovascular physiology; epilepsy; movement disorders. *Mailing Add:* Ctr Neurosci Univ Calgary Fac Med 3330 Hospital Dr NW Calgary AB T2N 4N1 Can

LEBLANC, GABRIEL, GEOPHYSICS, SEISMOLOGY. *Current Pos:* sr staff consult & sr seismologist, 77-86, CONSULT, WESTON GEOPHYS CORP, 86- *Personal Data:* b Montreal, Que, June 24, 27; m 68, Katherine Scheffley; c Genevieve. *Educ:* Univ Montreal, BA, 52; L'Immaculee-Conception, Montreal, LPh, 53; Boston Col, MSc, 58, SThL, 60; Pa State Univ, PhD(geophys), 66. *Prof Exp:* Res asst seismol, Pa State Univ, 63-66; assoc prof geophys, Laval Univ, 66-71; sr res scientist, Seismol Div, Dept Energy, Mines & Resources, Can, 71-76. *Mem:* Am Geophys Union; Can Geophys Union; Can Asn Physicists; Seismol Soc Am. *Res:* Regional tectonics and local seismicity; seismic hazard analysis; strong motion; induced seismicity; local arrays. *Mailing Add:* Weston Geophys Corp 325 W Main St Northborough MA 01532. *Fax:* 508-366-9197

LEBLANC, JACQUES ARTHUR, PHYSIOLOGY. *Current Pos:* PROF HUMAN PHYSIOL, FAC MED, LAVAL UNIV, 58- *Personal Data:* b Quebec, Que, Aug 23, 21; nat US; m 51; c 3. *Educ:* Laval Univ, BA, 43, BSc, 47, PhD(physiol), 51. *Prof Exp:* Physiologist human physiol, Defence Res Bd, Can Dept Nat Defence, 49-56. *Mem:* AAAS; Am Physiol Soc; Fedn Am Socs Exp Biol; Soc Exp Biol & Med; Fr-Can Asn Advan Sci. *Res:* Amines in stress conditions; tranquilizers; mast cells; basic and applied work in environmental physiology. *Mailing Add:* Dept Physiol Sch Med Laval Univ Pavillon Vandry No 3218 Quebec PQ G1K 7P4 Can

LEBLANC, JERALD THOMAS, PHOTOGRAPHIC SCIENCE, ORGANIC CHEMISTRY. *Current Pos:* SR CHEMIST RES LABS, EASTMAN KODAK CO, 70-, PROF MP TECH STAFF. *Personal Data:* b Baton Rouge, La, Mar 10, 43; m 68. *Educ:* Birmingham-Southern Col, BS, 65; Fla State Univ, PhD(org chem), 70. *Mem:* Soc Photog Scientists & Engr; Royal Photog Soc; Am Chem Soc. *Res:* Silver halide chemistry and physics; organic dye synthesis. *Mailing Add:* PO Box 92988 Rochester NY 14692

LEBLANC, LARRY JOSEPH, TELECOMMUNICATION NETWORKS, OPERATIONS RESEARCH. *Current Pos:* assoc prof, 80-88, PROF MGT, VANDERBILT UNIV, 88- *Personal Data:* b New Orleans, La, July 21, 47; m 69, Marguerite Jarreau; c Aimee & Sara. *Educ:* Loyola Univ, New Orleans, La, BS, 69; Northwestern Univ, Evanston, IL, MS, 71, PhD(opers res), 73. *Honors & Awards:* Japanese Gov Res Award Foreign Specialists, 94. *Prof Exp:* From asst prof to assoc prof opers res, Southern Methodist Univ, 73-80. *Concurrent Pos:* Fel, Nat Defense Educ Act (Northwestern Univ), 69-72; consult, Miss Chem Corp, Dr Pepper Co, Trailways, McDermott, WFAA Radio, Pan Technol, Urban Systs, US Army Inventory Res Off, US Dept Justice, Port Everglades Steel Co, Eaton Corp, Carbon/Graphite Group & John Hamburg & Assoc, Inc, 77-; NSF grants, 80-81 & 82-83; chmn transp sci sect, Opers Res Soc Am, 84-86; vis prof, Linkoping Inst Tech, Sweden, 80, Technion, Israel, 84, Univ Ulm, Ger, 81, 82, 84 & 85, Ecole Centrale Paris, 87, Univ Chile, 78 & 88, Neth Orgn Appl Sci Res, 91, Univ Thessaloniki, Greece, 92, NISTEP, Japan, 92, Univ Ulster, Northern Ireland, 93, Tel Aviv Univ, Israel, 97; coun mem, telecommun spec interest group, Opers Res Soc Am, 88-90; sci adv, France Telecom, 96 4; grant, US Dept Transp. *Mem:* Inst Opers Res & Mgt Sci. *Res:* Computer implementation techniques for telecommunication networks, traffic management, production and inventory control; applied optimization techniques. *Mailing Add:* Owen Grad Sch Mgt Vanderbilt Univ Nashville TN 37203. *Fax:* 615-343-7177; *E-Mail:* leblanc@ctrvax.vanderbilt.edu

LEBLANC, LEONARD JOSEPH, SOLID STATE PHYSICS. *Current Pos:* RETIRED. *Personal Data:* b Moncton, NB, Nov 6, 37; m 59; c 3. *Educ:* St Joseph's Univ, NB, BSc, 59; Univ Notre Dame, PhD(physics), 64. *Prof Exp:* From asst prof to prof physics, Univ Moneton, 64-96, vdean fac sci, 69-74, dean fac sci & eng, 75-80, vpres acad, 80-96. *Mem:* Am Asn Physics Teachers; Can Asn Physicists. *Res:* Optical and photoelectric properties of metals in the vacuum ultraviolet. *Mailing Add:* Dept Physics Univ Moncton Moncton NB E1A 3E9 Can

LE BLANC, MARCEL A R, PHYSICS, SUPERCONDUCTIVITY. *Current Pos:* prof, 68-94, chmn, Dept Physics, 80-86, EMER PROF PHYSICS, UNIV OTTAWA, 94- *Personal Data:* b Gravelbourg, Sask, Mar 25, 29; m 62, Liliane Legault; c Alexandra, Gabrielle & Lionel. *Educ:* Univ Ottawa, BA, 49; Univ Sask, BA, 52, MA, 54; Univ BC, PhD(physics), 58. *Prof Exp:* Res assoc physics, Stanford Univ, 59-63; asst prof elec eng, Univ Southern Calif, 63-68. *Concurrent Pos:* Asst prof, San Jose State Col, 61-62; consult, Varian Assocs, 61-62 & Spectromagnetic Industs, 62-63; mem tech staff & consult, Aerospace Corp, 63-68. *Mem:* Fel Am Phys Soc; Can Asn Physicists. *Res:* Photonuclear cross-sections; nuclear polarization; low temperature physics; superconductivity. *Mailing Add:* Dept Physics Univ Ottawa Ottawa ON K1N 6N5 Can. *Fax:* 613-562-5190; *E-Mail:* 76153.2047@compuserve.com

LEBLANC, MICHAEL H, PEDIATRICS, NEONATOLOGY. *Current Pos:* from asst prof to assoc prof, 81-92, PROF PEDIAT, UNIV MISS SCH MED, 92- *Personal Data:* b Birmingham, Ala, Oct 19, 50; m 75, Janice Kerns; c Arthur, Vivian & Eric. *Educ:* Auburn Univ, BS, 72; Univ Ala, MD, 75. *Honors & Awards:* Young Investr Award, Am Acad Pediat, 82; Earnest G P Spivey Res Award, Am Heart Asn, 87, John P Mallone Res Award, 91. *Prof Exp:* Resident pediat, Univ Cincinnati, 78, fel neonatol, 81. *Concurrent Pos:* Partic infant incubator task force, Am Acad Pediat, Asn Advan Med Instrumentation, Food & Drug Admin, 82; Counr, Southern Soc Pediat Res, 89-91; chmn res comt, Am Heart Asn, 92-94. *Mem:* AMA; Soc Pediat Res; Am Physiol Soc; Southern Soc Pediat Res (secy-treas, 91-95, pres, 96-97); Asn Advan Med Instrumentation; Am Acad Pediat. *Res:* Heat transfer and thermo regulation in infants; effect of polycythemia on the newborn; agents that amelrorate the effect of hypoxic ischemia on the brain in the newborn; use of surfactants in hyaline membrane disease in human infants. *Mailing Add:* Univ Miss Univ Med Ctr 2500 N State St Jackson MS 39216-4505. *Fax:* 601-984-5266; *E-Mail:* leblanc@fiona.umsmed.edu

LEBLANC, NORMAN FRANCIS, SCIENCE ADMINISTRATION, TECHNICAL MANAGEMENT. *Current Pos:* RETIRED. *Personal Data:* b Boston, Mass, June 28, 26; m 52; c 4. *Educ:* Tufts Univ, BS, 47; Mass Inst Technol, PhD(analytical chem), 50. *Prof Exp:* Res chemist, Hercules Aerospace Co, 50-56, res chemist solid rocket res & develop, 56-58, dir progs, 58-68, dir develop, Polymers Dept, 68-73, dir, Fibers Div, 73-81, group dir plastics, Hercules, Inc, 81-83, vpres technol, 84-89. *Mem:* Am Chem Soc. *Mailing Add:* PO Box 426 Chadds Ford PA 19317

LEBLANC, OLIVER HARRIS, JR, PHYSICAL CHEMISTRY. *Current Pos:* RETIRED. *Personal Data:* b Beaumont, Tex, Nov 14, 31; m 56, Ann Jones; c Catherine. *Educ:* Rice Univ, BA, 53; Univ Calif, PhD, 57. *Prof Exp:* Phys chemist, Res & Develop Ctr, Gen Elec Co, 57-94. *Res:* Electrochemistry; inorganic chemistry; membrane biophysics. *Mailing Add:* 1173 Phoenix Ave Schenectady NY 12308

LEBLANC, ROBERT BRUCE, FLAMMABILITY & FLAME RESISTANCE. *Current Pos:* PRES, LEBLANC RES CORP, 70- *Personal Data:* b Alexandria, La, Jan 28, 25; m 96, Donna Ruhlman; c 7. *Educ:* Loyola Univ, BS, 47; Tulane Univ, MS, 49, PhD(chem), 50. *Prof Exp:* Asst prof chem, Tex A&M Univ, 50-52; res specialist, Org Res Dept, Dow Chem Co, 52-63, sr textile specialist, 63-67; textile chem develop mgr, ADM Chem Div, Ashland Oil Co, 67-68; res mgr, Nat Cotton Coun, 68-70. *Concurrent Pos:* Mem, Info Coun Fabric Flammability. *Mem:* Am Chem Soc; Am Asn Textile Chemists & Colorists; Am Soc Testing & Mat; Nat Fire Protection Asn. *Res:* Textile chemistry and phosphorus chemistry; flammability and fire retardance of textiles and plastics. *Mailing Add:* LeBlanc Res Corp PO Box 391 Tallulah LA 71284-0391

LEBLANC, ROGER M, SURFACE CHEMISTRY, BIOLOGICAL MEMBRANES. *Current Pos:* CHMN & PROF PHYS CHEM, DEPT CHEM, UNIV MIAMI, CORAL GABLES, FLA, 93- *Personal Data:* b Trois-Rivieres, Quebec, Jan 5, 42; m 28, Micheline Vrillette; c Daniel, Hugues, Marie-Jose & Nancy. *Educ:* Laval Univ, Can, BSc, 64, DSc(phys chem), 68. *Honors & Awards:* Vincent Award, Fr Can Asn Advan Sci, 78; Noranda Award, Chem Inst Can, 82; Barringer Award, Spectros Soc Can, 83; John Labatt Ltd Award, Can Soc Chem, 92; Medal Gov Can, 93. *Prof Exp:* Fel phys chem, Davy Faraday Res Lab, Royal Inst, London, Eng, 68-70; chmn, Dept Chem-Biol, Univ Que, 71-75, dir, Group Biophys Res, 78-81, chmn, Ctr Photobiophys, 81-91, prof phys chem, Dept Chem-Biol, 70-93, chmn & prof phys chem, Dept Chem, Univ Miami, Coral Gables, Fla. *Concurrent Pos:* Mem, Cell Biol & Genetics Selection Comt, Natural Sci & Eng Res Coun Can, 80-82, chmn, 82-83, Analytical & Phys Chem Selection Comt, 88-90, chmn, 90-91. *Mem:* Chem Inst Can; Am Chem Soc; Biophys Soc; Europ Photochem Asn; Brit Biophys Soc; Am Soc Photobiol. *Res:* The interaction of chlorophyll (a) with itself and with various chloroplast components; the specific interaction in a two dimensional array is being studied with monolayer and photophysics techniques. *Mailing Add:* Chem Dept Univ Miami 1301 Memorial Dr Cox Sci Bldg 315 PO Box 249118 Coral Gables FL 33124-0431. *Fax:* 305-284-4571

LEBLANC, RUFUS JOSEPH, GEOLOGY. *Current Pos:* OWNER, LEBLANC SCH CLASTIC SEDIMENTS, HOUSTON, TX, 86- *Personal Data:* b Erath, La, Oct 12, 17; m 40; c 4. *Educ:* La State Univ, BS, 39, MS, 41. *Honors & Awards:* Sidney Powers Medal, Am Asn Petrol Geologists, 88. *Prof Exp:* Asst geologist, La State Univ, 41-43; geologist, Miss River Comn, US War Dept, 44-46, chief geol sect, 47-48; sr res geologist, Shell Oil Co, 48-52, mgr, Dept Geol Res, 53-56, sr geologist, Tech Serv, 57-60, sr staff geologist, Explor Dept, Offshore Div, 61-65, mem, Staff Explor Training Dept, clastic sediments, 65-86. *Concurrent Pos:* Mem, Comt Fundamental Res Occurrence & Recovery Petrol, Am Petrol Inst, 52-57; assoc ed, J Am Asn Petrol Geologists. *Mem:* Fel Geol Soc Am; hon mem Soc Econ Paleont & Mineral; hon mem Am Asn Petrol Geologists. *Res:* Fundamental research in stratigraphy and sedimentology; exploration for oil and gas; quaternary geology; exploration training; environmental geology gulf coast. *Mailing Add:* 3751 Underwood St Houston TX 77025

LEBLOND, CHARLES PHILIPPE, HISTOLOGY, ENDOCRINOLOGY. *Current Pos:* lectr histol & embryol, McGill Univ, 41-43, from asst prof to assoc prof, 43-48, chmn dept, 57-75, PROF ANAT, MCGILL UNIV, 48- *Personal Data:* b Lille, France, Feb 5, 10; m 36, Gertrude Sternschuss; c Philippe, Paul, Pierre, Marie & Pascale. *Educ:* Univ Nancy, Lic es S, 32; Univ Paris, MD, 34; Univ Montreal, PhD(iodine metab), 42; Univ Sorbonne, DSc, 45. *Hon Degrees:* DSc, Acadia Univ, 72, Mc Gill Univ, 82, Univ Montreal, 85, York Univ, 86. *Honors & Awards:* Wilson Medal, Am Soc Cell Biol, 82. *Prof Exp:* Asst histol, Med Sch Paris, 34-35; Rockefeller fel, Sch Med, Yale Univ, 36-37; asst, Lab de Synthese Atomique, Paris, 38-40. *Mem:* Am Asn Anat; Histochem Soc; fel Royal Soc; fel Royal Soc Can. *Res:* Histological localization of vitamin C; uptake of iodine by thyroid; tracing of radio elements and labelled precursors of nucleic acids, proteins and glycoproteins by means of radioautography; cell dynamics in gastro-intestinal tract; chromosome condensation. *Mailing Add:* Dept Anat & Cell Biol McGill Univ 3640 University St Montreal PQ H3A 2B2 Can. *Fax:* 514-398-5047

LEBLOND, PAUL HENRI, PHYSICAL OCEANOGRAPHY, FISHERIES. *Current Pos:* from asst prof to assoc prof physics, Univ BC, 65-75, prof physics & oceanog, 75-87, head oceanog, 75-87 & 87-92, EMER PROF, UNIV BC, 92- *Personal Data:* b Que, Can, Dec 30, 38; m 63; c 3. *Educ:* Laval Univ, BA, 57; McGill Univ, BSc, 61; Univ BC, PhD(physics), 64. *Hon Degrees:* DSc, Mem Univ, Nfld, 92. *Honors & Awards:* President's Prize, Can Meteorol Oceanog Soc, 81, Tully Medal, 91. *Prof Exp:* Nat Res Coun Can fel, Inst Meereskunde, Kiel, Ger, 64-65. *Concurrent Pos:* Vis assoc prof, Simon Fraser Univ, 70; vis scientist, Inst Oceanol, USSR Acad Sci, Moscow, 73-74; vis prof, Laval Univ, 79-80; dir, Seaconsult Marine Res Ltd; assoc dean, Fac Sci, Univ BC, 83-85; vis prof, Univ Marseille; prog leader, Ocean Prof Enhancement Network, 91-93; Fisheries Resource Conserv Coun, 93- *Mem:* Can Meteorol Oceanog Soc; Am Geophys Union; Am Meteorol Soc; Int Soc Cryptozool; fel Royal Soc Can, 82; Nat Marine Coun, 88-90; Galiano Conservancy Asn. *Res:* Surface, internal, planetary waves; ocean currents; tides; estuarine circulation; cryptozoology; theoretical biology. *Mailing Add:* S42 C7 RR2 Galiano Island BC V0B 1P0 Can. *Fax:* 604-822-6091

LEBO, GEORGE ROBERT, PHYSICS, RADIO ASTRONOMY. *Current Pos:* Res assoc radio astron, 64-65, asst prof, 65-77, ASSOC PROF PHYSICS & ASTRON, UNIV FLA, 77- *Personal Data:* b Chadron, Nebr, Sept 27, 37; m 58; c 2. *Educ:* Wheaton Col, BS, 59; Univ Ill, MS, 60; Univ Fla, PhD(physics), 64. *Mem:* Am Astron Soc; Am Geophys Union; Am Phys Soc. *Res:* Study of decametric radiation from the planets, particularly Jupiter. *Mailing Add:* Dept Astron Univ Fla Gainesville FL 32611-2055

LEBO, ROGER VAN, GENETIC NEUROPATHY, PRENATAL DIAGNOSIS. *Current Pos:* Res biochemist, Dept Med, Univ Calif, San Francisco, 74-76, asst res biochemist, 76-83, res assoc, Howard Hughes Med Inst, 78-80, dir, cell sorting facil & assoc, 80-86, assoc biochemist, Dept Med, 83-86, dir, Molecular Genetics Lab, 87-93, ASSOC PROF DEPT OBSTET & GYNEC & PEDIAT, SCH MED, UNIV CALIF, SAN FRANCISCO, 87-, DIR, CYTOGENETICS LAB, 93- *Personal Data:* b Pottsville, Pa, Mar 1, 48; m 72, Susan Southard; c Franklin & Paul. *Educ:* Pa State Univ, BS, 70; Duke Univ, PhD(genetics), 74. *Concurrent Pos:* Consult, Nat Cert Agency, Med Lab Personnel, Cytogenetic Subcomt, 80-85, Genotype Corp, 91-92; prin investr, Muscular Dystrophy Asn, 84-94, NIH, 88-92; res liaison, Charcot-Marie-Tooth Asn, 90- *Mem:* Am Soc Human Genetics; NY Acad Sci; Human Genome Orgn; Peripheral Neuropathy Asn; Am Fedn Clin Res. *Res:* Human genetic disease studies included positionally cloning the Charcot-Marie-Tooth 1B gene, developing in-situ prenatal diagnostic tests for gene and chromosome aneuploidy and developing gene mapping by chromosome sorting. *Mailing Add:* Obstet Gynec Univ Calif San Francisco Med Sch 513 Parnassus Ave San Francisco CA 94122-2722. *Fax:* 415-476-6145

LEBOFSKY, LARRY ALLEN, PLANETARY SCIENCES. *Current Pos:* from res assoc to assoc planetary sci, 77-89, SR RES SCIENTIST, UNIV ARIZ, 89- *Personal Data:* b Brooklyn, NY, Aug 31, 47; m 80; c 1. *Educ:* Calif Inst Technol, BS, 69; Mass Inst Technol, PhD(earth & planetary sci), 74. *Prof Exp:* Res assoc planetary sci, Jet Propulsion Lab, 75-77. *Mem:* Am Astron Soc; Int Astron Union; Am Geophys Union; Meteoritical Soc; Nat Sci Teachers Asn; Asn Educ Teachers Sci. *Res:* Remote sensing of the visual, near infrared and thermal infrared spectra of asteroids and satellites for the study of composition; related studies of laboratory reflection spectra. *Mailing Add:* Lunar & Planetary Lab Univ Ariz 2333 E Seventh St Tucson AZ 85719-5610

LEBOLD, WILLIAM KERNS, EDUCATIONAL RESEARCH & INFORMATION SYSTEMS IN ENGINEERING, EQUITY RESEARCH & CAREER DEVELOPMENT. *Current Pos:* res asst, Purdue Univ, 54-57, assoc prof, 58-61, asst to dean eng, 58-71, interim dir, Measurement & Res Ctr, 71, PROF ENG, PURDUE UNIV, 62- *Personal Data:* b Chicago, Ill, Aug 23, 23; m 45, Donna Seterduhl; c William Jr, Sandra J & Thomas L. *Educ:* Univ Minn, BS, 45; Northwestern Univ, MS, 53; Purdue Univ, PhD(psychol), 57. *Honors & Awards:* Distinguished Serv Award, Am Soc Eng Educ, 91, Centennial Medallion, 93; Distinguished Serv Award, Inst Elec & Electronics Engrs, 92; Benjamin Dasher Award, Am Soc Eng Educ & Inst Elec & Electronics Engrs, 93; Harold Amrine Visionary Award, Nat Soc Black Engrs, 96. *Prof Exp:* Elec engr, Automatic Elec, 45-47; engr, Commonwealth Edison, 50-51; instr & staff counr, Univ Ill, Chicago, 47-53, asst prof elec eng, 53-54. *Concurrent Pos:* Consult, Gen Elec Co, 55-56, Alfred Sloan Found, 78; examr, NCent Asn Cols & Univs, 57-80; chair, Educ Res & Methods Div, Am Soc Eng Educ, 57-65, Info Systs, 82-83; vis prof, Univ Calif, Los Angeles, 61-65, Univ Minn, 88-89 & 95-96; proj coordr, Am Soc Eng Educ, 63-70; res assoc, Nat Res Coun, 72-73; res dir, Eng Workforce Comn, 84-87, comnr, 90- *Mem:* Fel Am Soc Eng Educ; fel Am Psychol Asn. *Res:* Engineering education research and information systems; survey research, career development, equity research, equal opportunities, engineering retention, self concepts, longitudinal studies of engineers, optimal placement, applied statistics. *Mailing Add:* 3430 List Pl Apt 1105 Minneapolis MN 55416-4549. *Fax:* 765-494-5819; *E-Mail:* lebold@ecn.purdue.edu

LEBOUTON, ALBERT V, MICROSCOPIC ANATOMY, CELL BIOLOGY. *Current Pos:* Asst prof anat, Univ Calif, Los Angeles, 66-72, actg head dept, 72-74, ASSOC PROF ANAT, UNIV ARIZ, 72- *Personal Data:* b La Salle, Ill, July 10, 37; m 59; c 3. *Educ:* San Diego State Col, BS, 60; Univ Calif, Los Angeles, PhD(anat), 66. *Mem:* AAAS; Am Inst Biol Sci; Fedn Am Sci; Am Soc Cell Biol; Am Asn Anat. *Res:* Radioautography, radiobiochemistry, and immunocytochemistry of protein metabolism and growth in the liver. *Mailing Add:* Dept Anat Univ Ariz Col Med 1501 N Campbell Ave Tucson AZ 85724

LEBOVITZ, NORMAN RONALD, APPLIED MATHEMATICS, ASTROPHYSICS. *Current Pos:* from asst prof to assoc prof, 63-69, PROF MATH, UNIV CHICAGO, 69- *Personal Data:* b New York, NY, Sept 27, 35; m 71; c 2. *Educ:* Univ Calif, Los Angeles, AB, 56; Univ Chicago, MS, 57, PhD(physics), 61. *Prof Exp:* Moore instr math, Mass Inst Technol, 61-63. *Concurrent Pos:* Sloan Found fel, 67; Guggenheim Found fel, 77; managing ed, Soc Indust & Appl Math. *Mem:* Am Astron Soc; Am Math Soc; Soc Indust & Appl Math. *Res:* Stability theory; bifurcation theory; rotating fluid masses; singular perturbation theory. *Mailing Add:* Univ Chicago 5734 S University Ave Chicago IL 60637-1514

LEBOVITZ, ROBERT MARK, NEUROPHYSIOLOGY, BIOMATHEMATICS & BIOENGINEERING. *Current Pos:* assoc prof, 70-80, PROF NEUROPHYSIOL, UNIV TEX HEALTH SCI CTR, DALLAS, 80- *Personal Data:* b Scranton, Pa, May 6, 37; c 3. *Educ:* Calif Inst Technol, BS, 59, MS, 60; Univ Calif, Los Angeles, PhD(neurophysiol), 67. *Prof Exp:* Mem tech staff, Hughes Aircraft Co, 59-62; resident consult, Dept Math, Rand Corp, 67; NSF fel, Sch Med, NY Univ, 67-69; res assoc neural models, Ctr Theoret Biol, State Univ NY Buffalo, 69; staff scientist auditory & visual info processing, Recognition Equip, Inc, 69-70. *Concurrent Pos:* Consult, Dept Path & Eng Sci, Rand Corp, 69, Recognition Equip, Inc, 69, Neurosyst, Inc, 71, Dallas Epilepsy Asn, 71, Energy Conversion Devices, 71 & Equitable Environ Health, 71-; chief technical officer, Centra-Guard Inc & Neighborhood Coop Patrol, 69-71; NSF fel, Univ Tex Regents, 70-72; adj prof, Inst Technol, Southern Methodist Univ, 71-74; prof bd, Home Health Serv, Dallas, 74-; NIH grants, 71-, Food & Drug Admin grant, 74-, Nat Inst Environ Health Sci grant, 77- & Off Naval Res Contracts, 78-; Sloan Consortium scholar, 74-75. *Mem:* Am Physiol Soc; NY Acad Sci; Biophys Soc; Inst Elec & Electronics Engrs; Soc Neurosci. *Res:* Neural networks and neural modelling; neurophysiology of epilepsy and behavior; modification and control of behavior via drugs and implanted or extraneous brain stimulating arrays; microwave interactions with the nervous system and behavior; electronic medicine. *Mailing Add:* Dept Physiol Univ Tex SW Med Ctr 5323 Harry Hines Blvd Dallas TX 75235-8570

LEBOW, IRWIN L(EON), ELECTRONICS. *Current Pos:* CONSULT, 87- *Personal Data:* b Boston, Mass, Apr 27, 26; m 51, Grace Hackel; c Judith, William & David. *Educ:* Mass Inst Technol, SB, 48, PhD(physics), 51. *Prof Exp:* Mem staff, Lincoln Lab, Mass Inst Technol, 51-60, assoc group leader, 60-65, group leader, 65-70, assoc div head, 70-75; chief scientist & assoc dir technol, Defense Commun Agency, 75-81; vpres eng, Am Satellite Co, 81-84; vpres, Syst Res & Appln Corp, 84-87. *Concurrent Pos:* Mem, Comt Commun & Info Processing, Inst Elec & Electronics Engrs. *Mem:* Fel Am Phys Soc; fel Inst Elec & Electronics Engrs; AAAS; Sigma Xi. *Res:* Communication systems, including satellite communications, command and control systems and information processing systems; author on information technology. *Mailing Add:* 2800 Bellevue Terr NW Washington DC 20007-1366. *E-Mail:* irwinle@aol.com

LEBOW, MICHAEL DAVID, BEHAVIORAL MEDICINE, HEALTH PSYCHOLOGY. *Current Pos:* assoc prof, 74-79, PROF PSYCHOL, UNIV MAN, 79- *Personal Data:* b Detroit, Mich, June 24, 41; m 69; c 2. *Educ:* Univ Calif, Los Angeles, BS, 64; Univ Utah, MA, 67, PhD(psychol), 69. *Prof Exp:* Asst prof psychol, Univ Man, 69-72; asst prof med psychol, Med Sch Dartmouth, Univ, 72-74. *Concurrent Pos:* Chmn, Psychol Intervention Subcomt, Task Force Treatment Obesity, Can Health & Welfare, 86- *Mem:* Sigma Xi; Am Psychol Asn; Soc Behav Med; Can Psychol Asn; Asn Advan Behav Therap. *Res:* Treatment programs for the obese; attitudes, perceptions and practices of children, adolescents and adults towards the obese. *Mailing Add:* Dept Psychol Univ Manitoba Winnipeg MB R3T 2N2 Can

LEBOWITZ, BARRY D, GERIATRICS. *Current Pos:* CHIEF, MENT DIS AGING RES BR, NAT INST ALCOHOL ABUSE & ALCOHOLISM, NIH, 83- *Personal Data:* b Boston, Mass, Feb 11, 42. *Educ:* McGill Univ, BA, 64; Ind Univ, MA(comp sociol), 67; Cornell Univ, MA(sociol), 67, PhD(sociol), 70. *Honors & Awards:* Meritorious Achievement, Ment Health Serv, 82; Super Serv Award, USPHS, 91. *Mem:* Am Psychiat Asn; Am Asn Geriat Psychiat. *Mailing Add:* NIAAA Clin & Treat Res 5600 Fisher's Lane Rockville MD 20857. *Fax:* 301-594-6784; *E-Mail:* blehowit@nih.gov

LEBOWITZ, JACOB, MOLECULAR BIOLOGY, BIOCHEMISTRY. *Current Pos:* assoc prof, 74-77, PROF MICROBIOL, MED CTR, UNIV ALA, BIRMINGHAM, 77- *Personal Data:* b Brooklyn, NY, Oct 20, 35; m 78, Candace E Ridington. *Educ:* Brooklyn Col, BS, 57; Purdue Univ, PhD(phys chem), 62. *Prof Exp:* Res fel biophys chem, Calif Inst Technol, 62-66; from asst prof to assoc prof biochem, Syracuse Univ, 66-74. *Concurrent Pos:* Career develop award, NIH, 72-77; scholar award, Am Cancer Soc, 82-83. *Mem:* AAAS; Am Chem Soc; Am Soc Microbiol; Am Soc Biol Chem & Molecular Biol; Biophys Soc; Protein Soc. *Res:* Analysis of RNA polymerase-promoter interactions; structural transitions in supercoiled DNA in relation to biological activity; characterization protein-DNA and proteial-protein interactions using analytical ultra centrifugation. *Mailing Add:* Dept Microbiol Univ Ala Med Ctr 520 CHSB Birmingham AL 35294-2041. *E-Mail:* jack_lebowitz@micro.microbio.uab.edu

LEBOWITZ, JACOB MORDECAI, NUCLEAR PHYSICS. *Current Pos:* From instr to asst prof, 59-70, ASSOC PROF PHYSICS, BROOKLYN COL, 70- *Personal Data:* b New York, NY, Mar 21, 36; m 65; c 2. *Educ:* Yeshiva Univ, BA, 57; Columbia Univ, MA, 60, PhD(physics), 65. *Mem:* Am Phys Soc; Sigma Xi. *Res:* Nuclear forces; fission. *Mailing Add:* 138 W Beech St Long Beach NY 11561

LEBOWITZ, JOEL LOUIS, STATISTICAL MECHANICS, MATHEMATICAL PHYSICS. *Current Pos:* GEORGE WILLIAM HILL PROF MATH & PHYSICS & DIR, CTR MATH SCI RES, RUTGERS UNIV, 77- *Personal Data:* b Taceva, Czech, May 10, 30; nat US; m 53. *Educ:* Brooklyn Col, BS, 52; Syracuse Univ, MS, 55, PhD(physics), 56. *Hon Degrees:* Dr Hon Causa, Ecole Polytech Fed Lausanne, 77. *Honors & Awards:* A Cressy Morrison Award in Natural Sci, NY Acad Sci, 86, Heinz R Pagels Human Rights of Scientists Award, 96; Delmar S Fahrney Medal, The Franklin Inst, 95. *Prof Exp:* NSF res fel, Yale Univ, 56-57; asst prof physics, Stevens Inst Technol, 57-59; from asst prof to prof, Grad Sch Sci, Yeshiva Univ, 57-77. *Concurrent Pos:* Vis prof, Sch Med, Cornell Univ; Guggenheim fel, 76-77; mem, Sci Comt Sci Matters, Inst des Hautes Etudes Scientifiques, Bures-sur-Yvette, France, 79-82, Inst Theoret Physics, ed-in-chief, J Statist Physics, 75, ed/co-ed, Annals NY Acad Sci, Collective Phenomena, 80- *Mem:* Fel Nat Acad Sci; NY Acad Sci (pres-elect, 77-79, pres, 79); fel Am Phys Soc; Am Math Soc; fel AAAS; Int Union Pure & Appl Physics (secy, 82-84, pres, 85-87). *Res:* Statistical mechanics of equilibrium and nonequilibrium processes; theory of liquids. *Mailing Add:* Dept Math Hill Ctr Rutgers Univ New Brunswick NJ 08903

LEBOWITZ, MICHAEL DAVID, EPIDEMIOLOGY, PULMONARY DISEASES. *Current Pos:* from asst prof to assoc prof internal med, Col Med, Univ Ariz, 71-80, asst dir, Specialized Ctr Res, 71-97, from asst dir to dir respiratory sci, 74-96, PROF INTERNAL MED, COL MED, UNIV ARIZ, 80-, EXEC COMT, EPIDEMIOL PROG, 90-, CHAIR, EPIDEMIOL GRAD PROG, 94-, DIR, EPIDEMIOL UNIT, ARIZ PREV CTR, 96-, PROF EPIDEMIOL, 96- *Personal Data:* b Brooklyn, NY, Dec 21, 39; m 60, Joyce; c Jon, Kira & Debra. *Educ:* Univ Calif, Berkeley, AB, 61, MA, 65; Univ Wash, PhC, 69, PhD(epidemiol), 71. *Prof Exp:* Pub health statistician, Alameda Co Health Dept, 62-63; biostatistician, Calif Dept Pub Health, 67; res assoc environ health, Univ Wash, 67-71. *Concurrent Pos:* Partic, NSF-Japan Soc Prom Sci Coop Sci Group in Air Pollution, 69-70; prin investr grants, NIH, 71-, Environ Protection Agency, 77-, Food & Drug Admin, 76-81, Elec Power Res Inst, 83-; consult, NIH & Nat Heart & Lung Inst, 72-, Ital Nat Res Coun, 77-, Polish & Hungarian NIH, 81, Sci Adv Bd, Environ Protection Agency, 84-; mem & chmn, Pima Co Air Qual Adv Coun, 75-; mem, epidemiol study sect, NIH, 75-78, behav study sect, 77; assoc prog dir, NIH Inst Training Prog, 77-86; Fogarty sr int fel, 78-79; sr fel, Univ London, Postgrad Cardiothoracic Inst, Brompton, 78-79; vis prof, Harvard, 78 & 83, Univ Wash, 78, Univ Kans, 78, 82 & 85, Univ Pisa, 79, 80, 82 & 85-, Univ Groningen, 79, 85 & 93 Univ Ill, 79, Univ Crakow, 81 & 86, Polish Acad Sci, 81 & 86, Univ London, 82, Univ Utah, 82, Univ Padua, 82, 86 & 88, Univ Rome, 82 & 85, Univ Catania, 82, NY Univ, 84-, Univ Goteborg, 84 & 88, Johns Hopkins, 84, Yale, 85 & 94, Univ Otago, 89, Fed Univ Rio de Janiero, 89, Univ Wageningen, 91, Ill Inst Technol, 92, Univ Basel, 93, Univ Bergen, 93 & 95 & Univ Nottingham, 93; preceptor, NIH fel, Am Thoracic Soc, Fogarty Ctr fel & CNR fel, 78-90; co-chmn, comt indoor pollutants, Nat Res Coun, Nat Acad Sci, 79-81; WHO adv, 79-; WHO/EURO work group, 82-95; Ariz Gov Spec Environ Investr, 87-94; assoc ed, J Expoe Analysis Environ Epidemiol, 92-, J Toxicol Indust Health, 93- *Mem:* Int Epidemiol Asn; Am Epidemiol Soc; Am Thoracic Soc; Europ Respiratory Soc; Soc Epidemiol Res; fel Am Col Chest Physicians; hon mem Hungarian Soc Med Hyg; Int Acad Indoor Air Sci; fel Am Col Epidemiol; Int Soc Environ Epidemiol; Int Acad Indoor Air Sci. *Res:* Pulmonary and chronic disease epidemiology; etiology and natural history of pulmonary diseases and other chronic diseases; air pollution health effects research; environmental exposure assessment. *Mailing Add:* Ariz Health Sci Ctr Arz Prev Ctr & Sect Pulmonary Dis Univ Ariz Col Med 1501 N Campbell Ave Tucson AZ 85724-5163. *Fax:* 520-626-6093; *E-Mail:* lebowitz@resp_sci.arizona.edu

LEBOY, PHOEBE STARFIELD, GENE EXPRESSION, BONE BIOLOGY. *Current Pos:* res assoc, Sch Med, Univ Pa, 63-66, from instr to assoc prof, 65-76, chmn, Dept Biochem, 92-96, PROF BIOCHEM, SCH DENT MED, UNIV PA, 76- *Personal Data:* b Brooklyn, NY, July 29, 36; m 84, Neal Nathanson. *Educ:* Swarthmore Col, AB, 57; Bryn Mawr Col, PhD(biochem), 62. *Hon Degrees:* MA, Univ Pa, 71. *Prof Exp:* Res assoc biochem, Bryn Mawr Col, 61-63. *Concurrent Pos:* NATO fel, Weizmann Inst Sci, 66-67; NIH res grant, Univ Pa, 68-, & NIH res career develop award, 71-76; vis prof, Univ Calif, San Francisco, 79-80; chairperson, Grad Group Molecular Biol, Univ Pa, 84-87; Fogarty fel, Univ Oxford, 89-90. *Mem:* Am Soc Biol Chem; Am Soc Bone Mineral Res; Am Soc Cell Biol. *Res:* Role of gene expression in tissue mineralization; molecular biology of bone formation. *Mailing Add:* Dept Biochem Sch Dent Med Univ Pa Philadelphia PA 19104-6003. *Fax:* 215-898-3695; *E-Mail:* phoebe@research.dental.upenn.edu

LE BRETON, GUY C, PHARMACOLOGY. *Current Pos:* Postdoctoral trainee, Dept Pharmacol, 73-75, from instr to assoc prof, 75-85, PROF, DEPT PHARMACOL, UNIV ILL, 85- *Personal Data:* b Miami, Fla, Oct 1, 46. *Educ:* Univ Chicago, BS, 68, PhD(pharmacol), 73. *Concurrent Pos:* Fac develop award, Pharmaceut Mfrs Asn, 80-82; mem bd trustees, Am Asn Accreditation Lab Animal Care, 82-86; estab investr, Am Heart Asn, 82-87; field ed, J Pharmacol & Exp Therapeut, 82-; mem, Comt Pub Info, Am Soc Pharmacol & Exp Therapeut, 86-88 & Coun Thrombosis, Am Heart Asn. *Mem:* Sigma Xi; Am Soc Pharmacol & Exp Therapeut; AAAS. *Res:* Drug development; thrombosis and anti-thrombotic drugs; blood platelet: aggregating agents, aggregation, prostaglandins, prostaglandin endoperoxides, thromboxanes, thromboxane antagonists, thromboxane receptor, calcium, ion fluxes, cAMP; fluorescent cation probes; cellular secretion; cellular contraction; fatty acid metabolism. *Mailing Add:* Dept Pharmacol Univ Ill Col Med 835 S Wolcott Ave Chicago IL 60612-3796

LEBRETON, PIERRE ROBERT, BIOPHYSICAL CHEMISTRY. *Current Pos:* from asst prof to assoc prof, 73-87, PROF CHEM, UNIV ILL, CHICAGO, 87- *Personal Data:* b Chicago, Ill, Sept 17, 42; m 69, Laura Wessman; c Paul & David. *Educ:* Univ Chicago, BS, 64; Harvard Univ, MA, 66, PhD(chem physics), 70. *Prof Exp:* Fel physics, Phys Inst, Univ Freiburg, Ger, 70-71; fel chem, Jet Propulsion Lab, Calif Inst Technol, 71-73. *Concurrent Pos:* NIH grants, 80-83, 87-90; Am Cancer Soc grants, 76-80, 84 & 91-; res assoc, Nat Ctr Sci Res, Univ Louis Pasteur, Strasbourg, France, 80; Petrol Res Fund Am Chem Soc, grant, 87-94; Blowitz-Ridgeway Found grant, 93-94, bd trustees, Blowitz Ridgeway Found. *Mem:* Am Chem Soc; Int Soc Quantum Biol; Nat Asn Advan Sci; Biophys Soc; Am Asn Cancer Res; Am Inst Chemists. *Res:* Photoelectron, theoretical quantum mechanical, and time-resolved fluorescence probes of nucleic acid electronic structure, and of nucleic acid interactions with alkylating mutagens and carcinogens. *Mailing Add:* Dept Chem M/C 111 Univ Ill 845 W Taylor St Rm 4500 Chicago IL 60607-7061. *Fax:* 312-996-0431; *E-Mail:* lebreton@uic.edu

LEBRUN, ROGER ARTHUR, MEDICAL ENTOMOLOGY, INVERTEBRATE PATHOLOGY. *Current Pos:* PROF INVERT PATH, UNIV RI, 77- *Personal Data:* b Providence, RI, May 26, 46; m 90, Kathleen M Birt. *Educ:* Providence Col, AB, 68; Cornell Univ, MSc, 73, PhD(invert path), 77. *Concurrent Pos:* Fel, Inst Pasteur; Eli Lilly fel. *Mem:* Soc Invert Path; Entom Soc Am; Sigma Xi. *Res:* Protozoan and fungal pathogens of medically important insects; fungal pathogens of ticks (lyme disease); host-parasite relationships; microbial ecology of pathogens. *Mailing Add:* Ctr Vector-Borne Dis Univ RI 230 Woodward Hall Kingston RI 02881. *Fax:* 401-792-4017; *E-Mail:* lebrun@uriacc.uri.edu

LEBSOCK, KENNETH L, AGRONOMY. *Current Pos:* RETIRED. *Personal Data:* b Brush, Colo, Oct 19, 21; m 43; c 2. *Educ:* Mont State Col, BS, 49; NDak State Univ, MS, 51; Iowa State Col, PhD(plant breeding), 53. *Prof Exp:* Wheat breeding & genetics, Agr Res Serv, USDA, 53-72, agr adminr, 72-87. *Mem:* Fel Am Soc Agron. *Mailing Add:* 3045 Shorewood Lane St Paul MN 55113

LEBURTON, JEAN-PIERRE, THEORY & SIMULATION OF SEMICONDUCTOR & ADVANCED QUANTUM DEVICES. *Current Pos:* vis asst prof, 81-83, from asst prof & res asst prof to assoc prof & res assoc prof, 83-91, PROF PHYS ELECTRONICS & RES PROF, UNIV ILL, 91- *Personal Data:* b Mar 4, 49; m 83, Lisette. *Educ:* Univ Liege, Belg, License, 71, PhD(physics), 78. *Honors & Awards:* Chevalier Dans l'Ordre oes Palnes Acadeniques, Fr Govt, 93. *Prof Exp:* Res scientist, Siemens AG, Munich, Ger, 79-81. *Concurrent Pos:* Vis prof phys electronics, Univ Tokyo, 92, Hitachi Ltd Quantum Mat Chair, 92. *Mem:* Fel Inst Elec & Electronics Engrs; NY Acad Sci; Am Phys Soc; Electrochem Soc. *Res:* Research on electronic, transport and optical properties of nanoscale devices and low dimensional structures such as quantum wells, quantum wires and quantum dots. *Mailing Add:* Beckman Inst 405 N Mathews Ave Urbana IL 61801. *Fax:* 217-244-4333; *E-Mail:* leburton@ceg.uiuc.edu

LEBWOHL, MARK GABRIEL, INHERITED DISORDERS OF ELASTIC TISSUE, PSORIASIS. *Current Pos:* Dir, Div Clin Dermat, Mt Sinai Hosp, 83-97; PROF DERMAT, MT SINAI SCH MED, 93-; CHMN, DEPT DERMAT, MT SINAI MED CTR. *Personal Data:* b New York, NY, Apr 27, 52; m 78; c 2. *Educ:* Columbia Col, BA, 74; Harvard Med Sch, MD, 78. *Mem:* Am Acad Dermat; Soc Investigative Dermat; Dermat Found; Am Dermat Asn. *Res:* Genetic disorders of the skin including psoriasis, neurofibromatosis and pseudoxanthoma elasticum. *Mailing Add:* 1 Gustave Levy Pl New York NY 10029

LE CAM, LUCIEN MARIE, MATHEMATICAL STATISTICS. *Current Pos:* instr math & asst, Statist Lab, Univ Calif, Berkeley, 50-52, instr & jr res statistician, 52-53, from asst prof to prof statist, 53-73, chmn dept, 61-65, prof, 73-91, EMER PROF STATIST & MATH, UNIV CALIF, BERKELEY, 91- *Personal Data:* b Croze, France, Nov 18, 24; m 52, Louise E Romig; c 3. *Educ:* Univ Paris, Lic, 45; Univ Calif, PhD, 52. *Hon Degrees:* Dr, Univ Libre Bruxelles, 97. *Prof Exp:* Statistician, Elec of France, 45-50. *Concurrent Pos:* Sloan Found fel, 57-58; dir, Ctr Math Res, Univ Montreal, 72, mem adv comt, 74-80; mem, C Appl Theor Stat, Nat Res Coun, 87-90. *Mem:* Am Math Soc; Inst Math Statist (pres, 72-73); Int Statist Inst; fel Am Acad Arts & Sci; AAAS; Am Statist Asn. *Res:* General statistics; asymptotic methods in statistical decision theory; limit theorems in probability theory. *Mailing Add:* 101 Kensington Rd Kensington CA 94707-1011. *Fax:* 510-642-7892; *E-Mail:* lecam@stat.berkeley.edu

LECAR, HAROLD, BIOPHYSICS. *Current Pos:* PROF, DEPT MOLECULAR & CELL BIOL, UNIV CALIF, BERKELEY. *Personal Data:* b Brooklyn, NY, Oct 18, 35; m 58, Helene Lerner; c Joshua & Matthew. *Educ:* Columbia Univ, AB, 57, PhD(physics), 63. *Prof Exp:* Biophysicist, Lab Biophys, Nat Inst Neurol & Commun Dis & Stroke, 63-85. *Concurrent Pos:* Fel commoner, Churchill Col, Cambridge Univ, 75-76; regents lectr, Univ Calif, San Diego, 82. *Mem:* AAAS; Am Phys Soc; Biophys Soc; Sigma Xi. *Res:* Biophysics of nerve excitation; ion channels; membrane transport mechanisms. *Mailing Add:* Dept Molecular Cell Biol Div Neurobiol Univ Calif 229 Stanley Hall Berkeley CA 94720. *Fax:* 510-643-9290; *E-Mail:* harold___lear@maillink.berkeley.edu

LECAR, MYRON, ASTROPHYSICS. *Current Pos:* ASTRONR, SMITHSONIAN ASTROPHYS OBSERV, 65- *Personal Data:* b Brooklyn, NY, Apr 10, 30. *Educ:* Mass Inst Technol, BS, 51; Case Inst Technol, MS, 53; Yale Univ, PhD(astron), 63. *Prof Exp:* Lectr astrophys, Yale Univ Observ, 62-65; lectr astrophys, col observ, Harvard Univ, 65- *Concurrent Pos:* Astronr, Inst Space Studies, NASA, 62-65. *Mem:* Am Astron Soc; Fedn Am Scientists; Royal Astron Soc; Sigma Xi. *Res:* Dynamics of the solar system; stellar dynamics and galactic structure; cosmology. *Mailing Add:* Ctr Astrophys Harvard Col Observ & Smithsonian Astrophys Observ 60 Garden St Cambridge MA 02138

LECCE, JAMES GIACOMO, MICROBIOLOGY. *Current Pos:* from asst prof to assoc prof microbiol, 55-63, PROF MICROBIOL, NC STATE UNIV, 63-, PROF ANIMAL SCI, 76- *Personal Data:* b Williamsport, Pa, Jan 11, 26; m 50. *Educ:* Dartmouth Col, BA, 49; Pa State Univ, MS, 51; Univ Pa, PhD(microbiol), 53. *Prof Exp:* Instr prev med, Sch Vet Med, Univ Pa, 53-55. *Mem:* Am Soc Microbiol. *Res:* Rotavirus; passive immunity; enteric diseases. *Mailing Add:* 2729 Cambridge Rd Raleigh NC 27608

LECH, JOHN JAMES, PHARMACOLOGY. *Current Pos:* From instr to asst prof, 67-74, assoc prof pharmacol, 74-80, PROF PHARMACOL & TOXICOL, MED COL WIS, 80- *Personal Data:* b Passaic, NJ, June 21, 40. *Educ:* Rutgers Univ, Newark, BS, 62; Marquette Univ, PhD(pharmacol), 67. *Concurrent Pos:* Am Heart Asn grant, Med Col Wis, 72-75, Sea grant, 71-75. *Mem:* AAAS; Soc Toxicol; Am Fisheries Soc; Am Soc Pharmacol & Exp Therapeut. *Res:* Cardiac triglyceride metabolism; metabolism of organic compounds by fish. *Mailing Add:* Dept Pharmacol Med Col Wis PO Box 26509 Milwaukee WI 53226-0509

LECHAGO, JUAN, GASTROINTESTINAL PATHOLOGY, SURGICAL PATHOLOGY. *Current Pos:* PROF, DEPT PATH, BAYLOR COL MED, 90-; DIR, SURG PATH SERV, METHODIST HOSP, TEX, 90- *Personal Data:* b Barcelona, Spain, Aug 2, 42; US citizen; m 66, Lia Epstein; c John P, James B & Sarah A. *Educ:* Nat Col, Monserrat, Arg, BS, 59; Nat Univ Cordoba, Arg, MD, 66; Queen's Univ, Can, MSc, 67, PhD(path), 71. *Prof Exp:* From asst prof to prof path, Sch Med, Univ Calif, Los Angeles, 73-87; chief lab serv, Vet Admin Med Ctr, Dallas, Tex, 87-90. *Concurrent Pos:* Head gastrointestinal path & staff pathologist, Harbor Med Ctr, Univ Calif, Los Angeles, 73-87, head autopsy path serv, 81-87; key investr, Ctr Ulcer Res & Educ, Los Angeles, 74-90, affil mem, 90-; prin investr, NIH, 74-84, 82-86, Nat Cancer Inst, 95-; lectr & consult, Naval Reg Med Ctr, Long Beach, Calif, 82-87; dir morphal core, Ctr Study Inflammatory Bowel Dis, 85-87, Ctr Diabetes Res, Dallas, 88-90; prof & vchair, Dept Path, Southwestern Med Sch, Univ Tex, Dallas, 87-90, A G Gill endowed prof, 89-90; med dir, Sch Histotechnol, Methodist Hosp, Houston, 91-93. *Mem:* US Can Acad Path; Am Gastroenterol Asn; Gastrointestinal Path Soc (pres, 87-88); Latin Am Path Found (pres, 94-96); Endocrine Path Soc; hon mem Cent Am Asn Path; hon mem Argentian Soc Path. *Res:* Biology and pathology of the neuroendocrine cells of the digestive system in man and experimental species; pathobiology and molecular pathology of gastrointestinal neoplasia and precursor conditions. *Mailing Add:* Dept Path Baylor Col One Baylor Plaza Houston TX 77030. *Fax:* 713-793-1473; *E-Mail:* jlechago@bcm.tmc.edu

LECHEVALIER, HUBERT ARTHUR, MICROBIOLOGY. *Current Pos:* From asst prof to prof, 51-91, EMER PROF MICROBIOL, WAKSMAN INST MICROBIOL, RUTGERS UNIV, NEW BRUNSWICK, NJ, 91- *Personal Data:* b Tours, France, May 12, 26; nat US; m 50, Mary Pfeil; c Marc & Paul. *Educ:* Laval Univ, MS, 48; Rutgers Univ, PhD(microbiol), 51. *Hon Degrees:* DSc, Laval Univ, 83. *Honors & Awards:* Lindback Award, 76; Charles Thom Award, 82; Bergey Award, 89. *Concurrent Pos:* Exchange scientist, Acad Sci, USSR, 58-59; USPHS spec fel, Pasteur Inst, Paris, 61-62. *Mem:* Soc Indust Microbiol; hon mem Fr Soc Microbiol. *Res:* Morphology, classification and products of actinomycetes, including antibiotics; history of microbiology. *Mailing Add:* RR 2 Box 2235 Morrisville VT 05661

LECHEVALIER, MARY P, ACTINOMYCETES, CHEMOTAXONOMY. *Current Pos:* res assoc, Rutgers Univ, 62-75, from asst res prof to assoc res prof, 75-85, res prof, 85-91, EMER PROF MICROBIOL, RUTGERS UNIV, PISCATAWAY, 91- *Personal Data:* b Cleveland, Ohio, Jan 27, 28; m 50, Hubert A; c Marc E & Paul R. *Educ:* Mt Holyoke Col, BA, 49; Rutgers Univ, MS, 51. *Honors & Awards:* Charles Thom Award, Soc Indust Microbiol, 82; Waksman Award, Theobald Smith Soc, 91; J Roger Porter Award, US Fed Cult Collections, 92. *Prof Exp:* Res microbiologist, E R Squibb & Sons, 60-61. *Mem:* AAAS; Brit Soc Gen Microbiol; Am Soc Microbiol; Soc Indust Microbiol; NAm Mycological Asn; Sigma Xi. *Res:* Classification, ecology, physiology and natural products of actinomycetes; microbial transformations; nitrogen fixation. *Mailing Add:* RR 2 Box 2235 Morrisville VT 05661

LECHLEIDER, J W, MATHEMATICS, COMPUTER SOFTWARE. *Current Pos:* mem tech staff, Bell Tel Labs, 55-65, supvr transmission studies, Outside Plant & Underwater Systs Div, 65-67, head outside plant eng dept, 67-70, head loop transmission maintenance eng dept, 70-76, HEAD, MDF SOFTWARE DESIGN DEPT, BELL LABS, 76- *Personal Data:* b Brooklyn, NY, Feb 22, 33; m 55; c 2. *Educ:* Cooper Union, BME, 54; Polytech Inst Brooklyn, MEE, 57, PhD(elec eng), 65. *Prof Exp:* Engr, Gen Elec Co, 54-55. *Mem:* Sr mem Inst Elec & Electronics Engrs; Am Math Soc; Sigma Xi. *Res:* Electromagnetic theory; communication theory; transmission theory. *Mailing Add:* 4 Harding Terr Morristown NJ 07960-4204

LECHNER, BERNARD J, RESEARCH MANAGEMENT, TELEVISION SYSTEMS. *Current Pos:* CONSULT, 87- *Personal Data:* b New York, NY, Jan 25, 32; m 53, Joan Mathewson. *Educ:* Columbia Univ, BSEE, 57. *Honors & Awards:* David Sarnoff Award, RCA Corp, 62; Frances Rice Darne Award, Soc Info Display, 71 & Beatrice Winner Award, 83; David Saznoff Gold Medal Award, Soc Motion Picture & TV Engrs, 96. *Prof Exp:* Mem tech staff, RCA Labs, 57-62, group head, 62-77, lab dir, 77-83, staff vpres, 83-87. *Mem:* Fel Inst Elec & Electronics Engrs; fel Soc Info Display (vpres, 76-78, pres, 78-80); fel Soc Motion Picture & TV Engr. *Res:* Video-tape recording; high speed digital computer circuits; tunnel diodes; display devices and systems; ferroelectrics; electroluminescence; magnetic thin films; instrumentation; liquid crystals; digital television systems; TV receivers; TV tuning systems; TV broadcast equipment; cable TV systems; high definition TV. *Mailing Add:* 98 Carson Rd Princeton NJ 08540. *Fax:* 609-924-7547; *E-Mail:* tvbernie@worldnet.att.net

LECHNER, JAMES ALBERT, APPLIED STATISTICS, RELIABILITY. *Current Pos:* MATH STATISTICIAN, STATIST ENG DIV, NAT INST STAND & TECHNOL, 71- *Personal Data:* b Danville, Pa, Aug 6, 33; m 56; c 3. *Educ:* Carnegie Inst Technol, BS, 54; Princeton Univ, PhD(math statist), 59. *Prof Exp:* Instr math, Princeton Univ, 57-58; sr mathematician, Res Labs, Westinghouse Elec Corp, Pa, 60-63, adv mathematician, Aerospace Div, Md, 63-67; mem tech staff, Res Anal Corp, Va, 67-71. *Concurrent Pos:* Instr, Carnegie Tech, Univ Md & George Washington Univ. *Mem:* Am Statist Asn. *Res:* Probability; theory of reliability; systems analysis; stochastic processes. *Mailing Add:* 3801 Chatham Rd Ellicott City MD 21042

LECHNER, JOHN FRED, CELL & MOLECULAR BIOLOGY, TOXICOLOGY. *Current Pos:* ASST DIR CELL & MOLECULAR BIOL, INHALATION TOXICOL RES INST, ALBUQUERQUE, NMEX, 91- *Personal Data:* b Holyoke, Colo, Oct 27, 42. *Educ:* Cornell Univ, BS, 64; Hahnemann Med Col, PhD(microbiol), 70. *Prof Exp:* Grad teaching asst, Ind Univ, Bloomington, Iowa, 64-65; microbiol training fel, 65-66; res asst, Div Genetics, Hahnemann Med Col, Philadelphia, 66-69, from instr to sr instr, 69-71, asst prof, Div Genetics & mem, Grad Sch Fac, 71-73; res assoc, Mass Inst Technol, Cambridge, 73-75; res fel, W Alton Jones Cell Sci Ctr, Lake Placid, NY, 75-76; res investr, Pasadena Found Med Res, 76-78; asst dir, Prostate Cancer Lab, Pasadena, 78-79; chief, Cell Cult & Media Br, Ctr Infectious Dis, Centers Dis Control, Atlanta, 84-85; expert scientist, Nat Cancer Inst, NIH, 79-83, sr staff fel, 83-84, chief, In Vitro Carcinogenesis Sect, Lab Human Carcinogenesis, 85-91, dep lab chief, 90-91. *Concurrent Pos:* Nat res serv award, Pub Health Serv, 75; mem, Handicapped Employee

Adv Comt, NIH, 82 & Cellular Physiol Grant Rev Study Sect, 82-84, Prostate Cancer Task Force, Nat Cancer Inst, 86-89; chmn, Comt Carcinogenesis Initiative, Prostate Cancer Working Group, 86-87 & Tumor Tissue Request Rev Comt, Nat Dis Interchange, 87-90; consult, Organogenesis, Inc, Mass, 88-90 & Clonetics Inc, Calif, 89-91. *Mem:* Am Asn Cancer Res; Am Soc Cell Biol; Tissue Cult Asn; AAAS; Am Asn Pathologists; Fedn Am Socs Exp Biol. *Res:* Cell biology-growth factor, nutritional and hormonal control of growth and differentiation; in vitro carcinogenesis of human epithelial cells. *Mailing Add:* 13712 Crested Butte Dr NE Albuquerque NM 87112

LECHNER, JOSEPH H, DNA SEQUENCE, MAMMALIAN STRUCTURAL PROTEINS. *Current Pos:* from asst prof to assoc prof, 79-87, PROF CHEM, MT VERNON NAZARENE COL, 87-, CHMN, NATURAL SCI DIV, 89- *Personal Data:* b Boston, Mass, Nov 13, 51; m 81, Catherine E Cook; c Paul, Dawn & Sarah. *Educ:* Roberts Wesleyan Col, BS, 72; Univ Iowa, PhD(biochem), 77. *Prof Exp:* Teaching fel, Dent Sch, Northwestern Univ, 78-79. *Mem:* Am Chem Soc; fel Am Sci Affil. *Res:* Determination of nucleic acid sequences at or near sites of radiation-induced mutations. *Mailing Add:* 800 Martinsburg Rd Mt Vernon OH 43050. *E-Mail:* jlechner@mvnc.edu

LECHNER, ROBERT JOSEPH, SOFTWARE ENGINEERING INFORMATION SCIENCE. *Current Pos:* PROF, UNIV MASS, LOWELL. *Personal Data:* b Danville, Pa, Oct 19, 31; m 55; c Marie, Nancy, Amy, David, Stephen, John & Tony. *Educ:* Carnegie Inst Technol, BS, 52, MS, 53; Harvard Univ, PhD(appl math), 63. *Prof Exp:* Sr engr, Sylvania Electronics Corp, 55-57, res engr, 57-59, adv res engr, 59-61, eng specialist, 61-63, sr eng specialist, 63-70; sr engr, Honeywell Info Systs, 70-75 & C S Draper Lab, 75-76; assoc prof elec eng, Northeastern Univ, 76-82. *Mem:* Inst Elec & Electronics Engrs Comput Soc; Asn Comput Mach. *Res:* Software engineering; information modeling object-oriented methods. *Mailing Add:* Comput Sci Dept Univ Mass-Lowell One University Ave Lowell MA 01854. *E-Mail:* lechner@cs.uml.edu

LECHOWICH, RICHARD V, FOOD SCIENCE, FOOD MICROBIOLOGY. *Current Pos:* DIR, NAT CTR FOOD SAFETY & TECHNOL, 89- *Personal Data:* b Chicago, Ill, June 23, 33; m 57, 83, Isabel D Wolf; c 8. *Educ:* Univ Chicago, AB, 52, MS, 55; Univ Ill, PhD(food sci), 58. *Prof Exp:* Microbiologist, Am Meat Inst Found, Ill, 52-55; res asst food sci, Univ Ill, Urbana, 55-58; res microbiologist, Continental Can Co, Inc, Ill, 58-63; from asst prof to prof food sci, Mich State Univ, 63-71; prof food sci & technol & head dept, Va Polytech Inst & State Univ, 71-81; mgr microbiol, Gen Foods Corp, 81-87; exec vpres, ABC Res Lab, Fla, 87-89. *Mem:* AAAS; Int Asn Milk, Food & Environ Sanitarians; fel Inst Food Technologists; Am Soc Microbiologists; Brit Soc Appl Bact; Am Soc Agr Engrs. *Res:* Food safety mechanisms of bacterial spore formation and germination; chemical composition and thermal resistance phenomena of bacterial spores; food poisoning microorganisms, especially Clostridium botulinum; food safety; HACCP programs. *Mailing Add:* Nat Ctr Food Safety & Technol 6502 S Archer Ave Summit IL 60501. *Fax:* 708-563-1873

LECHOWICZ, MARTIN JOHN, PLANT ECOLOGY. *Current Pos:* asst prof, 76-80, assoc prof plant ecol, 81-88, PROF, MCGILL UNIV, 88- *Personal Data:* b Chicago, Ill, Feb 23, 47; m 77, Marcia J Waterway. *Educ:* Mich State Univ, BA, 69; Univ Wis-Madison, MSc, 73, PhD(plant ecol), 75. *Prof Exp:* Lectr ecol, Dept Bot, Univ Wis-Madison, 75. *Concurrent Pos:* Nat Res Coun Can operating grant, 77-93, strategic grant, 80-89; Can J, Bot, 83, Evolutionary Biol, 87, Plant Species Biol, Forestry Can, 92; Environ Can contracts, 79-82; Atmospheric Environ Serv grant, 81- *Mem:* Ecol Soc Am; Can Bot Asn; Soc Study Evolution; Am Soc Naturalists; Europ Soc Evolutionary Biol; Bot Soc Am. *Res:* Physiological ecology and evolutionary ecology of plants, and particularly resource uptake and allocation; plant herbivore interactions; forest ecology; tree growth. *Mailing Add:* Dept Biol 1205 Dr Penfield Ave Montreal PQ H3A 1B1 Can

LECHTENBERG, VICTOR L, AGRONOMY. *Current Pos:* From instr to prof agron, 69-82, assoc dir, Agr Exp Sta, 82-89, EXEC ASSOC DEAN AGR, PURDUE UNIV, WEST LAFAYETTE, 89- *Personal Data:* b Butte, Nebr, Apr 14, 45; m 67; c 4. *Educ:* Univ Nebr, BS, 67; Purdue Univ, PhD(agron), 71. *Honors & Awards:* Ciba-Geigy Award, Am Soc Agron. *Mem:* Fel Am Soc Agron; fel Crop Sci Soc Am (pres); Am Forage & Grassland Coun; AAAS; Coun Agr Sci & Technol. *Res:* Factors that affect forage crop quality and utilization; environmental physiology of forage crops; genetic improvement of crop quality. *Mailing Add:* 3049 Greenbrier Ave West Lafayette IN 47906-4826

LECHTMAN, MAX D, MICROBIOLOGY. *Current Pos:* INDUST CONSULT, 71- *Personal Data:* b Providence, RI, Apr 24, 35; m 62, Dale Rodney; c Alex N, Jay & Risa. *Educ:* Univ RI, AB, 57; Univ Mass, MS, 59; Univ Southern Calif, PhD(microbiol), 68. *Prof Exp:* Microbiologist, Douglas Aircraft Co, Calif, 61-62 & Res & Develop Div, Magna Chem Co, 62-64; instr microbiol, Univ Southern Calif, 64; microbiol consult, Garrett Corp, 64-65, microbiologist, AiRes Mfg Co Div, 65-67; mem tech staff aerospace microbiol, Autonetics Div, NAm, Rockwell Corp, Anaheim, 67-71; instr, Calif Community Col Syst, 71-95. *Mem:* Am Soc Microbiol; Soc Indust Microbiol; AAAS. *Res:* Microbial cytology, cytochemistry and physiology; bioluminescent bacteria for detection of toxic chemicals; laboratory and medical instrumentation; medical device testing. *Mailing Add:* 8641 Delray Circle Westminster CA 92683. *Fax:* 714-897-7759; *E-Mail:* bythemax@aol.com

LECK, CHARLES FREDERICK, ORNITHOLOGY, ECOLOGY. *Current Pos:* dir ecol prog, 74-78, ASSOC PROF ECOL, RUTGERS UNIV, NEW BRUNSWICK, 70- *Personal Data:* b Princeton, NJ, June 20, 44. *Educ:* Muhlenberg Col, BS, 66; Cornell Univ, PhD(vert zool), 70. *Prof Exp:* Vis res assoc, Smithsonian Trop Res Inst, 68-69. *Concurrent Pos:* Vis fac mem, West Indies Lab, Smithsonian Trop Res Inst, 70-73. *Mem:* Wilson Ornith Soc; Cooper Ornith Soc; Am Ornith Union; Sigma Xi; Asn Trop Biologists. *Res:* Avian ecology and landscape ecology and conservation; tropical biology. *Mailing Add:* Dept Biol Sci Rutgers Univ New Brunswick NJ 08903

LECKIE, FREDERICK ALEXANDER, ENGINEERING MECHANICS, MATERIALS ENGINEERING. *Current Pos:* PROF MECH ENG, UNIV CALIF, SANTA BARBARA, 88- *Personal Data:* b Dundee, Scotland, Mar 26, 29; m 57; c 3. *Educ:* Univ St Andrew, BSc, 49; Stanford Univ, MS, 55, PhD(eng mech), 58. *Prof Exp:* Civil engr, Mott, Hay & Anderson, Westminster, London, 49-51; res asst mech, Tech Hochsch, Hannover, Ger, 57-58; lectr, Univ Cambridge, 58-68; prof eng, Univ Leicester, 68-78; prof theoret & appl mech & mech eng, Univ Ill, Urbana-Champaign, 78-88. *Mem:* Am Soc Mech Engrs; Am Acad Mech. *Res:* Properties of load bearing mechanical components operating at elevated temperatures; creep rupture and fractures of materials at elevated temperatures. *Mailing Add:* Dept Mech Eng Univ Calif Santa Barbara 552 University Ave Santa Barbara CA 93106-0002

LECKLITNER, MYRON LYNN, NUCLEAR MEDICINE, MEDICAL ULTRASOUND. *Current Pos:* assoc prof radiol & dir diag imaging, 83-86, PROF, UNIV SALA, 86-, SR SCIENTIST, CANCER CTR, 84- *Personal Data:* b Canton, Ohio, June 16, 42; c 1. *Educ:* Pa State Univ, BS, 64; Univ Ala, Tuscaloosa, BS, 70, Birmingham, MD, 74; Am Bd Nuclear Med, cert, nuclear med, 82. *Prof Exp:* Resident med, Lloyd Noland Hosp, Birmingham, 74-77, nuclear med, 77-79; asst prof radiol, Univ Tex, San Antonio, 79-83. *Concurrent Pos:* Mem, Acad Coun, Soc Nuclear Med, 81-; vis prof, Univ Nuevo Leon, Monterrey, Mex, 83, Univ Oxford, UK, 85, 88, & Royal Postgrad Med Sch, Univ London, UK, 85; Am Col Nuclear Physicians, 86-88 & mem bd regents & treas, chmn finance comt, 86-88. *Mem:* Soc Nuclear Med; Am Col Nuclear Med; Am Inst Ultrasound Med; Am Col Radiol; AMA; Radiol Soc Am; Am Col Nuclear Physicians; fel Am Col Nuclear Med. *Res:* Basic science and clinical investigations involving human biokinetics and quality control of radiotracers; relation of physiology and pathophysiology to nuclear medicine. *Mailing Add:* Dept Radiol Univ SAla 2451 Fillingim St Mastin 301 Mobile AL 36617

LECKONBY, ROY ALAN, PHYSICAL ORGANIC CHEMISTRY, SYNTHETIC ORGANIC CHEMISTRY. *Current Pos:* SR DEVELOP ENGR, SHELL CHEM CO, 92- *Personal Data:* b Bethlehem, Pa, Aug 1, 49; m 71, Janice Tollerton; c Remington, Brian, Christopher & Peter. *Educ:* Hamilton Col, AB, 71; Univ Rochester, MS, 74, PhD(chem), 76. *Prof Exp:* Fel res, Robert A Welch Found, Rice Univ, 76-77; sr res chemist, Goodyear Tire & Rubber Co, Akron, Ohio, 77-82, plant chemist, La Porte, Tex, 82-86, qual assurance mgr, Apple Grove, WVa, 86-92. *Mem:* Soc Plastics Engrs. *Res:* Organic synthesis; age resistors for rubbers and plastics; monomers; oxidation of organic chemicals. *Mailing Add:* Shell Chem Co 130 Johns Ave Akron OH 44305. *E-Mail:* raleckonby@shellus.com

LECKRONE, DAVID STANLEY, ASTROPHYSICS. *Current Pos:* Astrophysicist, 69, SR ASTROPHYSICIST, LAB ASTRON & SOLAR PHYSICS, GODDARD SPACE FLIGHT CTR, NASA, 69- *Personal Data:* b Salem, Ill, Nov 30, 42; m 64; c 2. *Educ:* Purdue Univ, BS, 64; Univ Calif, Los Angeles, MA, 66, PhD(astron), 69. *Mem:* Am Astron Soc; Int Astron Union. *Res:* Ultraviolet stellar spectroscopy and photometry from space vehicles; magnetic and chemically peculiar stars; stellar atmospheres; abundances of the elements in astronomical objects; instrumentation for space astronomy. *Mailing Add:* Code 440 NASA-Goddard Space Flight Ctr Greenbelt MD 20771

LECLAIRE, CLAIRE DEAN, ORGANIC CHEMISTRY. *Current Pos:* RETIRED. *Personal Data:* b Huron, SDak, Aug 26, 10; m 41. *Educ:* SDak State Sch Mines, BS, 33; Univ Minn, PhD(org chem), 39. *Prof Exp:* Chemist, Coal Res Lab, Carnegie Inst Technol, 38-41 & Rohm & Haas Co, Pa, 41-42; rubber fel, Mellon Inst, 42-47; res chemist, Firestone Tire & Rubber Co, 47-49; asst dir rubber res proj, Univ Minn, 49-51; sect leader appl res, Adhesives & Coatings Div, Minn Mining & Mfg Co, 51-58; sr res chemist, Int Latex Corp, 58-69 & Stand Brands Chem Industs, Inc, 69-76; res chemist, Reichhold Polymers Inc, 76-81; consult, Int Playtex Inc, 81-83. *Mem:* AAAS; Am Chem Soc. *Res:* Organic synthesis; structure; polymerization; properties and utilization of high polymers; bituminous coals; elastomers; resins; adhesives. *Mailing Add:* 134 Lakeview Ave Dover DE 19901

LECOURS, MICHEL, COMMUNICATIONS SYSTEMS, SIGNAL PROCESSING. *Current Pos:* head, Elec Eng Dept, 75-77, vdean, Fac Sci & Eng, 77-85, PROF ELEC ENG, UNIV LAVAL, 67- *Personal Data:* b Montreal, Que, Aug 1, 40; m 63; c 3. *Educ:* Univ Montreal, BScA, 63; Univ London, DIC & PhD(electronics), 67. *Honors & Awards:* Can Award, Excellent Technol Transfer, 86; Ann Mert Award, Ecole Polytech Montreal Alumni Asn, 87; John B Stirling Medal, Eng Inst Can, 96. *Prof Exp:* Engr commun, Bell Can, 63. *Concurrent Pos:* Mem sci staff, Bell Northern Res, 71-72; consult, Lab-Volt, Inc, 82-; vis res, NTT-ECL, Japan, 86; Can Labs Telecommun, Inc, Que, Can, 86- *Mem:* Fel Eng Inst Can; sr mem Inst Elec & Electronics Engrs. *Res:* Performance of digital communications systems (including mobile) in non-gaussian noise, interference and fading; signal processing in the radio and audio frequency bands; indoor and personal communications systems; radar signal processing. *Mailing Add:* Fac Sci & Eng Laval Univ Quebec PQ G1K 7P4 Can. *Fax:* 418-656-3159

L'ECUYER, JACQUES, APPLIED & NUCLEAR PHYSICS. *Current Pos:* vpres teaching & res, 88-93, HEAD, COMN EVAL COL EDUC, UNIV QUE, 93- *Personal Data:* b St-Jean, Que, Mar 6, 37; m 59; c 3. *Educ:* Col St Jean, BA, 56; Univ Montreal, BSc, 59, MSc, 61, PhD(physics), 66. *Prof Exp:* Lectr, Univ Montreal, 61-63 & Univ Sherbrooke, 63-64; asst prof physics, Laval Univ, 64-67; Nat Res Coun Can fel, Oxford Univ, 67-69; from asst prof to assoc prof physics, Univ Montreal, 69-73, prof, 73-86; pres, Que Univ Coun, 81-88. *Concurrent Pos:* Mem bd gov, Univ Montreal, 76-79; mem, Que Univs Coun, 77-81 & Hong Kong Coun Acad Accreditation, 88- *Mem:* Can Asn Physicists; Fr-Can Asn Advan Sci. *Res:* Experimental nuclear physics. *Mailing Add:* 10890 Berri Montreal PQ H3L 2H5 Can

L'ECUYER, MEL R, MECHANICAL ENGINEERING, HEAT TRANSFER. *Current Pos:* Res engr, Jet Propulsion Ctr, 60-64, from asst prof to assoc prof, 64-76, PROF MECH ENG, PURDUE UNIV, 76- *Personal Data:* b Concordia, Kans, June 4, 36; m 62. *Educ:* Purdue Univ, BS, 59, MS, 60, PhD(mech eng), 64. *Concurrent Pos:* Sr eng specialist, LTV Aerospace Div, Ling-Temco-Vought, Inc, Tex, 68- *Mem:* Am Inst Aeronaut & Astronaut; Am Soc Mech Engrs; Am Soc Eng Educ. *Res:* Mass transfer cooling; two-phase flow; propulsion gas dynamics. *Mailing Add:* 690 N 400 W West Lafayette IN 47906

LECZYNSKI, BARBARA ANN, HUMAN & ENVIRONMENTAL MONITORING, QUALITY ASSURANCE. *Current Pos:* STAFF, OFF POLLUTION PREV & TOXICS, US ENVIRON PROTECTION AGENCY, 93- *Personal Data:* b Lowell, Mass, Aug 27, 54. *Educ:* Univ Lowell Mass, BS, 76; Univ Conn, MS, 79. *Prof Exp:* Math statistcian, US Dept Labor, Bur Labor Statist, 78-80; appl math, Eastman Kodak Co, 80-84; proj mgr, Battelle Mem Inst, 84-89; proj mgr, Wash Consult Group, 89-90; sr consult, David C Cox & Assocs, 90-93. *Concurrent Pos:* Chairperson, workgroup Leaded Paint Encapsulants, Am Soc Testing Mat. *Mem:* Am Statist Asn; Am Soc Qual Control. *Res:* Participated on several multi-disciplinary projects with applications to environmental monitoring in particular human monitoring exposure, lead paint and asbestos abatement studies; consumer preference and marketing strategies and economic indicators; developed sampling designs for field studies; provided experimental designs for industrial manufactures research projects. *Mailing Add:* 8497 Lazy Creek Ct Springfield VA 22153

LEDBETTER, HARVEY DON, MATERIALS SCIENCIE ENGINEERING. *Current Pos:* dir technol res & develop, 81-83, sr proj mgr, 83-89, RES SCIENTIST, CENT RES, 90- *Personal Data:* b Pierson, Ill, June 26, 26; m 47; c 3. *Educ:* Univ Ariz, BS, 49, MS, 50; Univ Tenn, PhD(chem), 54. *Prof Exp:* Asst gen chem, Univ Tenn, 50-52; res group leader, Dow Chem USA, 53-67, res supvr, 67-71, tech mgr, Designed Prod Dept, 71-76, lab dir, Cent Res Plastics Lab, 76-81. *Mem:* AAAS; Am Chem Soc; Soc Plastics Engrs; Sigma Xi; Soc Advan Math & Process Eng; Fiber Soc. *Res:* Polymer nucleation and stabilization; vacuum processes; preparation and physics of composite structures; fiber processing. *Mailing Add:* Lake Pinehurst Villas No 14 Pinehurst NC 28374

LEDBETTER, JEFFREY A, IMMUNOTHERAPY. *Current Pos:* RES FEL, DEPT IMMUNOTHER, ONCOGEN, 81- *Mailing Add:* Dept Cell Immunol Bristol-Myers Squibb Pharm Res Inst 3005 First Ave Seattle WA 98121-1069. *Fax:* 206-727-3604

LEDBETTER, JOE O(VERTON), ENVIRONMENTAL HEALTH, CIVIL ENGINEERING. *Current Pos:* resident engr, Tex Hwy Dept, 51-56, from instr to assoc prof, 56-71, PROF CIVIL ENG, UNIV TEX, AUSTIN, 71- *Personal Data:* b New Hope, Ala, Feb 1, 27; m 92, Ann D Hagood. *Educ:* Univ Ala, BSCE, 50; Univ Tex, MS, 58, PhD(civil eng), 63. *Prof Exp:* Proj engr, Ala Hwy Dept, 50-51. *Concurrent Pos:* Pres, USPHS, 50- *Mem:* Am Indust Hyg Asn; Health Physics Soc. *Res:* Air pollution control; sampling, evaluation, and abatement; disposal of solid radioactive and hazardous wastes; radiological and industrial health engineering; air pollution from wastewater treatment. *Mailing Add:* 1814 Rockmoor Dr Austin TX 78703

LEDBETTER, MARY LEE STEWART, GAP JUNCTIONS, ION TRANSPORT. *Current Pos:* from asst prof to assoc prof, 80-93, PROF BIOL, COL HOLY CROSS, 93- *Personal Data:* b Monterrey, Mex, Aug 30, 44; US citizen; m 66, Steven; c William & Joanna. *Educ:* Pomona Col, BA, 66; Rockefeller Univ, PhD(genetics), 72. *Prof Exp:* Res assoc microbiol, Dartmouth Med Sch, 72-75, instr, 75-78, res assoc psychiat, 77-79, res asst prof biochem, 79-80; guest scientist, Scripps Research Inst, 94-95. *Concurrent Pos:* USPHS res trainee, Sch Med, NY Univ, 72; Damon Runyon-Walter Winchell fel, 72-73; Leukemia Soc Am Fel, Dartmouth Med Sch, 73-75 & 77-78; USPHS, NCI fel, Dartmouth Med Sch, 75-77; mem cell biol adv panel, NSF, 86-90; vis assoc prof, Tufts Univ, 92; mem rev panel, NSF Investr Award, NASA NSCORT in Gravitational Biol & Howard Hughes Med Inst; guest scientist, Scripps Res Inst, 94-95. *Mem:* Am Soc Cell Biol; AAAS; Sigma Xi; Asn Women Sci. *Res:* Study of metabolic regulation in cultured mammalian cells, particularly cell communication through gap junctions and ion transport and the interactions between them. *Mailing Add:* Dept Biol PO B Col Holy Cross Worcester MA 01610. *E-Mail:* mldbett@holycross.edu

LEDBETTER, MYRON C, CELL BIOLOGY, BOTANY. *Current Pos:* RETIRED. *Personal Data:* b Ardmore, Okla, June 25, 23. *Educ:* Okla State Univ, BS, 48; Univ Calif, MA, 51; Columbia Univ, PhD, 58. *Honors & Awards:* Distinguished Scientist Award, Biol Micros Soc Am, 96. *Prof Exp:* Fel plant physiol, Boyce Thompson Inst, 53-57, asst plant anatomist, 57-60; guest investr & fel, Rockefeller Inst, 60, res assoc, 61; res assoc, Harvard Univ, 61-65; cell biologist, Brookhaven Nat Lab, 65-74, sr cell biologist, 74-89. *Concurrent Pos:* Guest assoc, Brookhaven Nat Lab, 58-60, guest sr biologist; fel training grant prog, USPHS, 60-61; consult, Celanese Res Corp, 81-82; bd mgr, NY Bot Garden, 82-84; adj prof, City Univ NY, 82- *Mem:* AAAS; Am Soc Cell Biol; Bot Soc Am; Electron Micros Soc Am (pres, 78); Am Inst Biol Sci; Torrey Bot Club (pres, 84-85). *Res:* Morphology of physiologically dwarfed tree seedlings; feeding damage to plant tissues by lygus bugs; histopathology of ozone on plants; distribution of fluorine in plants; plant fine structure, microtubules in plants; plant cell walls; electron microscopy; structure of macromolecular complexes by cluster ion bombardment. *Mailing Add:* PO Box 145 Port Jefferson NY 11777-0145

LEDBETTER, STEVEN R, EXPERIMENTAL BIOLOGY. *Current Pos:* SR RES SCIENTIST, CANCER & INFECTIOUS DIS, UPJOHN CO, 84- *Mailing Add:* Dept Cancer/Develop Biol Upjohn Co 301 Henrietta St Kalamazoo MI 49001. *Fax:* 616-385-7373

LEDBETTER, W(ILLIAM) B(URL), CIVIL ENGINEERING. *Current Pos:* From asst prof to assoc prof, 64-71, from asst res engr to assoc res engr, 64-71, PROF CIVIL ENG & RES ENGR, TEX A&M UNIV, 71-; CONSULT. *Personal Data:* b El Paso, Tex, Sept 15, 34; c 4. *Educ:* Tex A&M Univ, BS, 56; Univ Tex, Austin, PhD(civil eng), 64. *Honors & Awards:* K B Woods Award, Transp Res Bd, Nat Acad Sci, 76. *Concurrent Pos:* Chmn, Transp Res Bd Comt, Nat Res Coun-Nat Acad Sci, 70-79. *Mem:* Nat Soc Prof Engrs; Am Soc Civil Engrs; Am Soc Eng Educ; Am Soc Testing & Mat; Am Concrete Inst; Am Soc Qual Control. *Res:* Quality management; project management; construction materials; concrete materials engineering. *Mailing Add:* 1006 Challedon Way Pendleton SC 29670

LEDDY, JAMES JEROME, INDUSTRIAL CHEMISTRY. *Current Pos:* RETIRED. *Personal Data:* b Detroit, Mich, July 28, 29; m 51, Dorothy Weiland; c Christine, James, Kathleen, Karen, Thomas, Ann, Mary, David & Jeanne. *Educ:* Univ Detroit, BS, 51; Univ Wis, PhD(chem), 55. *Honors & Awards:* Herbert H Dow Medal, 87. *Prof Exp:* Chemist inorg res, Dow Chem USA, 55-59, proj leader, 59-60, proj leader, Electrochem & Inorg Res Lab, 60-63, sr res chemist, 63-67, assoc res scientist, 67-71, res scientist, Electrochem & Inorg Res Lab, 71-73, res scientist, Mich Div Inorg Res, 73-80, tech mgr, Chlor-Alkali Technol Ctr, 80-85, sr res scientist, Cent Res, 85-88, dir, Bioprod Lab, 88-92, Dow res fel, Core Res & Develop, 92-95. *Concurrent Pos:* Asst prof, Assumption Univ, 59-60. *Mem:* Fel AAAS; Am Chem Soc; Sigma Xi. *Res:* Chemistry of less familiar elements, especially titanium, zirconium and hafnium; coordination compounds; unfamiliar oxidation states; amalgam chemistry; electrochemistry; inorganic polymers; industrial inorganic and electrochemistry; chlor-alkali; engineering ceramics and material science; biotechnology. *Mailing Add:* 311 Cherryview Dr Midland MI 48640-5559

LEDDY, JOHN PLUNKETT, IMMUNOLOGY. *Current Pos:* sr instr, 62-64, from asst prof to assoc prof med, 64-73, PROF MED & MICROBIOL, MED CTR, UNIV ROCHESTER, 73-; DIR CLIN IMMUNOL UNIT, 70- *Personal Data:* b New York, NY, Sept 10, 31; m 56; c 3. *Educ:* Fordham Univ, BA, 52; Columbia Univ, MD, 56. *Prof Exp:* From intern to resident internal med, Boston City Hosp, Harvard Med Serv, 56-59; USPHS trainee hemat, Med Ctr, Univ Rochester, 59-60. *Concurrent Pos:* Res med officer immunochem, Walter Reed Army Inst Res, 60-62; Nat Found fel, 62-64; NIH res grant, 65-; sr investr, Arthritis Found, 65-70; dir, USPHS Training Grant, 70-; prog dir, NIH Specialized Res Ctr grant immunol, 78- *Mem:* Am Soc Clin Invest; Am Asn Immunologists. *Res:* Biology of complement system in man; erythrocyte autoantibodies in human diseases. *Mailing Add:* Dept Med Univ Rochester Med Ctr Box 695 Rochester NY 14642-8695. *Fax:* 716-473-1482

LEDDY, SUSAN, NURSING. *Current Pos:* dean & prof nursing, 81-84, DEAN, COL HEALTH SCI, UNIV WYO, 84- *Personal Data:* b Jersey City, NJ, Feb 23, 39; m 72; c 2. *Educ:* Skidmore Col, BS, 60; Boston Univ, MS, 65; NY Univ, PhD(nursing), 73. *Prof Exp:* Instr nursing, Mt Auburn Hosp, 62-65 & New Rochelle Hosp, 65-66; asst prof, Columbia Univ, 66-70 & Pace Univ, 73-75; consult nursing educ, Nat League Nursing, 75; chairperson & prof nursing, Mercy Col, 76-81. *Concurrent Pos:* Independent consult, 75- *Mem:* Nat League Nursing (vpres, 85-87). *Res:* Biological rhythms; nursing education and curriculum; health care delivery. *Mailing Add:* Dir Nursing Widener Univ 700 E 14th St Chester PA 19013-5733

LEDEEN, ROBERT, BIOCHEMISTRY, NEUROBIOLOGY. *Current Pos:* PROF NEUROSCI, UNIV MED & DENT NJ, 91- *Personal Data:* b Denver, Colo, Aug 19, 28; m 82, Lydia Hailparn. *Educ:* Univ Calif, Berkeley, BS, 49; Ore State Univ, PhD(org chem), 53. *Honors & Awards:* Jacob Javits Award, 87; Alexander von Humboldt Prize, 88. *Prof Exp:* Fel, Univ Chicago, 53-54; res chemist, Mt Sinai Hosp, New York, 56-59; res chemist, Albert Einstein Col Med, 59-61, from asst prof to assoc prof biochem in neurol, 62-75, prof biochem in neurol, 75-91. *Concurrent Pos:* Dep chief ed, J Neurochem, 82-88; mem, Neurol Sci Study Sect, NIH, 76-80, Nat Mult Sclerosis Soc Study Sect, 89-95. *Mem:* AAAS; Am Chem Soc; Am Soc Biol Chem; Am Soc Neurochem; Int Soc Neurochem; NY Acad Sci. *Res:* Biochemistry of the nervous system; gangliosides and other lipids of the nervous system; myelin lipids; myelin enzymology and pharmacology; neuronal differentiation. *Mailing Add:* 8 Donald Ct Wayne NJ 07470-4608. *Fax:* 973-982-5059; *E-Mail:* ledeenro@umdnv.edu

LEDER, FREDERIC, CHEMICAL ENGINEERING. *Current Pos:* MANAGING DIR, TECH MGT ASSOCS, WESTPORT, CONN, 95-; ASSOC DIR, OFF COOP RES, YALE UNIV, 95- *Personal Data:* b New York, NY, Nov 1, 39; m 71; c 2. *Educ:* Queens Col, BS, 61; Columbia Univ, BS, 61; Yale Univ, MS, 63, PhD(chem eng), 65. *Prof Exp:* Res engr, Esso Res & Eng Co, Exxon Corp, Linden, 65-68, sr res engr, 68-73, gas separations res assoc, 73; dir explor res, Occidental Res Corp, Irvine, 74-76; dir res, Cities Appl Res & Technol Ctr, 76-85, managing partner, Specialty Capital Group, 85-95. *Concurrent Pos:* Pres, Technol Mgt Assocs. *Mem:* Am Inst Chem Eng; Sigma Xi. *Res:* Phase equilibria at high pressure; gas separations; rate processes; energy technology. *Mailing Add:* 2742 Sturges Hwy Westport CT 06880. *Fax:* 918-481-3585

LEDER, IRWIN GORDON, BIOCHEMISTRY. *Current Pos:* BIOCHEMIST, NAT INST ARTHRITIS, METAB & DIGESTIVE DIS, BETHESDA, 54- *Personal Data:* b New York, NY, June 16, 20; m 45; c 3. *Educ:* Brooklyn Col, AB, 42; NY Univ, MS, 47; Duke Univ, PhD(biochem), 51. *Prof Exp:* Res assoc, Duke Univ, 51; USPHS fel, NY Univ, 51-52 & Yale Univ, 52-53; asst, Pub Health Res Inst, Inc, NY, 53-54. *Mem:* Fedn Am Socs Exp Biol. *Res:* Niacin metabolism; pyridine nucleotide synthesis; intermediary carbohydrate metabolism; enzymology. *Mailing Add:* 4004 Wexford Dr Kensington MD 20895-1523

LEDER, LEWIS BEEBE, EXPERIMENTAL PHYSICS. *Current Pos:* RETIRED. *Personal Data:* b Brooklyn, NY, Oct 28, 20; m 48; c 1. *Educ:* Univ Idaho, BS, 43. *Prof Exp:* Instr physics, Williams Col, 43-44; physicist gas flow, Inst Gas Technol, 44-45; physicist, Dielectric Studies, Indust Condenser Corp, 45-46; physicist electron heat controls, Wheelco Instruments Co, 46-48; physicist nuclear physics, Inst Nuclear Studies, 48-51; physicist electron physics, Nat Bur Stand, 51-62; physicist, Appl Res Lab, Philco Corp, 62-65; physicist electron scattering & superconductivity, Ford Sci Lab, 65-69; res scientist, Xerox Corp, 69-83. *Mem:* Am Vacuum Soc; Am Phys Soc; Sigma Xi. *Res:* Electron scattering; superconductivity; thin films preparation and properties; photoreceptors. *Mailing Add:* 1140 Burning Tree Dr No 1505 Chapel Hill NC 27514

LEDER, PHILIP, MOLECULAR GENETICS. *Current Pos:* PROF & CHMN GENETICS, HARVARD MED SCH, 80- *Personal Data:* b Washington, DC, Nov 19, 34; m 59; c 3. *Educ:* Harvard Col, AB, 56, Med Sch, MD, 60. *Hon Degrees:* DSc, Yale Univ, 84, Mt Sinai Col Med, 85. *Honors & Awards:* Richard Lounsberry Award, Nat Acad Sci; Nat Medal Sci,89. *Prof Exp:* Lab chief molecular genetics, Nat Inst Child Health & Human Develop, NIH, 72-80. *Mem:* Nat Acad Sci; Inst Med-Nat Acad Sci; Genetics Soc Am; Am Acad Arts & Sci; Am Soc Biol Chemists. *Res:* Molecular biology and genetics. *Mailing Add:* Dept Genetics Harvard Med Sch 200 Longwood Ave Boston MA 02115

LEDERBERG, ESTHER MIRIAM, GENETICS, MICROBIOLOGY. *Current Pos:* res geneticist, Med Sch, Stanford Univ, 59-68, res assoc, 68-71, sr scientist, 71-74, res prof, 74-85, EMER PROF MED MICROBIOL, STANFORD UNIV, 85- *Personal Data:* b New York, NY, Dec 18, 22; m 46, 68. *Educ:* Hunter Col, AB, 42; Stanford Univ, MA, 46; Univ Wis, PhD(genetics), 50. *Honors & Awards:* Co-recipient, Pasteur Award, Soc Ill Bact, 56. *Prof Exp:* Proj assoc genetics, Univ Wis, 50-59. *Concurrent Pos:* Fulbright fel, Australia, 57; Am Cancer Soc Sr Dernham fel, 68-70; dir, Plasmid Ref Ctr, 76-86; consult, Molecular Biol Comput Res Resource, 96- *Mem:* Fel AAAS; Genetics Soc Am; Brit Soc Gen Microbiol; Sigma Xi. *Res:* Genetics of microorganisms; lysogenicity; bacterial recombination and transformation; DNA repair; phase variation of Flagellar antigens in Salmonella; R plasmids. *Mailing Add:* Dept Med Microbiol No 5402 Stanford Med Sch Stanford CA 94405

LEDERBERG, JOSHUA, GENETICS. *Current Pos:* pres, 78-90, univ prof, 90-95, EMER PROF, SACKLER FOUND SCHOLAR, ROCKEFELLER UNIV, NY, 95- *Personal Data:* b NJ, May 23, 25; m 68, Marguerite Stein Kirsch; c David K & Anne. *Educ:* Columbia Univ, BA, 44; Yale Univ, PhD(microbiol), 47. *Hon Degrees:* ScD, Yale Univ, 60, Columbia Univ, 67, Univ Wis, 67, Albert Einstein Col Med, 70, Mt Sinai, 79, Rutgers Univ, 81 & NY Univ, 84; MD, Univ Turin, 69 & Tufts Univ, 85; LLD, Univ Pima, 79; DLitt, Jewish Theol Sem, 79; DPhil, Tel Aviv, 91. *Honors & Awards:* Nobel Prize, 58; Nat Medal Sci, 89; Allen Newell Award, 96; Maxwell Finland Award, 97. *Prof Exp:* From asst prof to prof genetics, Univ Wis, 47-58, prof med & genetics & chmn dept, 58-59; prof genetics & chmn dept, Med Sch, Stanford Univ, 59-78. *Concurrent Pos:* Bd dir, Inst Sci Info, Philadelphia, 62-93, Chem Indust Inst Toxicol, NC, 80-, US Defense Sci Bd, 81- & Proctor & Gamble, 84-; sci consult, Cetus Corp, Berkeley, Calif, 71-90; mem, Ann Rev, Inc & bd trustees, 72, Natural Resources Def Coun, 72-84; dir, Ctr Advan Study Behav Sci, 75-81; coun mem, Inst Med-Nat Acad Sci, 78-81; adj prof genetics, Cornell Med Col, 79; bd dirs, Chem Indust Inst Toxicol, NC, 80-; mem bd, Dreyfus Found, 83-, Carnegie Corp, 85-93, NYC Partnership, 85-90, Revson Found, 86-93; dir, Corp Nat Res Initiatives, 86-, Coun Foreign Relations, 89-; adj prof bid sci, Columbia Univ, 90- *Mem:* Nat Acad Sci; Inst Med-Nat Acad Sci; foreign mem The Royal Soc; NY Acad Sci (pres, 93); Am Acad Arts & Sci; Am Philos Soc; fel AAAS. *Res:* Molecular genetics and evolution; science policy; computer science; emulation of scientific reasoning. *Mailing Add:* Rockefeller Univ 1230 York Ave New York NY 10021-6399. *Fax:* 212-327-8651; *E-Mail:* lederberg@rockvax. rockefeller.edu

LEDERBERG, SEYMOUR, MICROBIOLOGY, GENETICS. *Current Pos:* from asst prof to assoc prof, Brown Univ, 58-66, chmn microbiol sect, 70-78, coordr, grad progs biol med, 78-85, assoc dean grad studies biol med, 85-95, PROF BIOL, BROWN UNIV, 66- *Personal Data:* b New York, NY, Oct 30, 28; m 59; c 2. *Educ:* Cornell Univ, BA, 51; Univ Ill, PhD(bact), 55. *Prof Exp:* Am Cancer Soc fel, Univ Calif, 55-57, vis asst prof bact, 57-58. *Concurrent Pos:* USPHS fel, Inst Biol Phys Chem, Paris, 65-66; consult, Nat Inst Gen Med Sci, 70-74, Gen Med & Sci Adv Coun, Cystic Fibrosis Found, 72-76, Comt Genetic Screening Cystic Fibrosis, Nat Acad Sci-Nat Res Coun, 74-75 & Nat Inst Arthritis, Metab & Digestive Dis, 75-78; vis scholar, Harvard Law Sch; lectr, Law Sch Ctr Law & Health Sci, Boston Univ, 73-77, adj prof pub health law, 77- *Mem:* Am Soc Microbiol; Genetics Soc Am; Am Soc Human Genetics. *Res:* Human, microbial and viral genetics; cystic fibrosis; yeast and bacterial biochemistry; chromosomal, microtubule and cell surface functions in cell cycles; transfer of genes for drug-resistance and virulence; intracellular pathogens. *Mailing Add:* Biol & Med Box G-J364 Brown Univ Providence RI 02912. *E-Mail:* seymour_lederberg@brown.edu

LEDERER, C MICHAEL, NUCLEAR CHEMISTRY. *Current Pos:* Dir isotopes proj, Lawrence Berkeley Lab, 64-78, head, Info & Data Analysis Dept, 78-80, DEP DIR, RADIATION MEASUREMENT, NUCLEAR ENG DEPT, ENERGY INST, UNIV CALIF, BERKELEY, 80- *Personal Data:* b Chicago, Ill, June 6, 38; m 70, Claudette Evenson; c Laura & Mark. *Educ:* Harvard Univ, AB, 60; Univ Calif, Berkeley, PhD(nuclear chem), 64. *Concurrent Pos:* Mem, US Nuclear Data Comt, 70-78. *Mem:* AAAS; Am Phys Soc; Am Nuclear Soc; Sigma Xi. *Res:* Energy production, use and environmental effects; experimental nuclear structure physics. *Mailing Add:* Energy Inst Univ Calif 2539 Channing Way Berkeley CA 94720-5180. *Fax:* 510-643-5180; *E-Mail:* lederer@cmsa.berkeley.edu

LEDERER, JEROME F, AEROSPACE SAFETY. *Current Pos:* RETIRED. *Personal Data:* b New York, NY, Sept 26, 02; m 35, Sarah Bojarsky; c Nancy (Cain) & Susan. *Educ:* NY Univ, BS, 24, ME, 25. *Honors & Awards:* Arthur Williams Award, 53; Von Baumhauer Medal, 54; Monsanto Award, 57; Guggenheim Medal, 61; Laura Tabor Barbour Medal, 64; Wright Bros Trophy, 65; Amelia Earhart Medal; Gargarin Medal, Soviet Fedn Cosmonauts; Safety & Health Hall of Fame, Int, 89; Dist Pub Serv Award, Aero Space Writers Asn, 89; Int Space Hall of Fame, 92; Trident Award, Am Soc Mech Engrs, 96. *Prof Exp:* Aeronaut engr, US Air Mail Serv, 26-27; dir, Aerotech, Inc, 27-29; chief engr, Aero Ins Underwriters, 29-40 & 44-48; dir safety bur, Civil Aeronaut Bd, 40-42, Airlines War Training Inst, 42-44; tech dir & pres, Flight Safety Found, 48-67; dir manned space flight safety, NASA, 67-70, dir safety, 70-72. *Concurrent Pos:* James Jackson Cabot prof lectr, Norwich Univ, 39; dir, Cornell-Guggenheim Aviation Safety Ctr, 50-68; adj prof, Inst Safety & Systs Mgt, Univ Southern Calif, 74-80; emer pres, Flight Safety Found; pres, Air Mail Pioneers, 74- *Mem:* Nat Acad Eng; fel Soc Automotive Engrs; Am Soc Mech Engrs; fel Royal Aeronaut Soc; hon mem Airline Pilots Asn; Air Traffic Controllers Asn; fel Aviation Med Asn; hon fel Am Inst Aeronaut & Astronaut. *Res:* Aviation and space safety. *Mailing Add:* 468-D Calle Cadiz Laguna Hills CA 92653

LEDERER, WILLIAM JONATHAN, CARDIAC MUSCLE, CELLULAR & MOLECULAR PHYSIOLOGY. *Current Pos:* from asst prof to assoc prof physiol, 79-88, PROF PHYSIOL, UNIV MD, 88- *Personal Data:* US citizen; m 75, Jennie Z Rothschild; c Miriam & Rebecca. *Educ:* Harvard Univ, BA, 70; Yale Univ, PhD(physiol), 75, MD, 76. *Prof Exp:* Intern internal med, Univ Wash, 76-77; fel physiol, Oxford Univ, 77-79. *Concurrent Pos:* Vis researcher, Univ Col London, 81-90; estab investr, Am Heart Asn, 81-86, mem, Basic Sci Coun, Counr, Biophys Soc, 93- *Mem:* Soc Gen Physiologists; Biophys Soc; NY Acad Sci; AAAS; Am Physiol Soc; Physiol Soc London. *Res:* Mammalian heart muscle to determine how it functions at the cellular and molecular level; links between the electrical activity and the ion transport function of cardiac cells and how these properties relate to the force generated by the heart; cellular control of calcium, sodium and pH. *Mailing Add:* Dept Physiol Sch Med Univ Md 660 W Redwood St Baltimore MD 21201

LEDERIS, KAROLIS (KARL), PHARMACOLOGY, ENDOCRINOLOGY. *Current Pos:* prof, 69-89, EMER PROF PHARMACOL & THERAPEUT, MED SCH, UNIV CALGARY, 89- *Personal Data:* b Lithuania, Aug 1, 20; m 52; c 2. *Educ:* Bristol Univ, BSc, 58, PhD(pharmacol), 61, DSc(endocrinol), 68. *Honors & Awards:* UpJohn Award in Pharmacol, 90. *Prof Exp:* Jr fel pharmacol, Bristol Univ, 61-63, lectr, 63-66, sr lectr, 66-68, reader, 68-69. *Concurrent Pos:* Wellcome Trust & Ger Res Asn fel, Univ Kiel, 61-62; NSF fel, Univ Calif, Berkeley, 67-68; ed, Pharmacol, Int J Exp & Clin Pharmacol; vis prof, Vilnius Univ, Lithuania, USSR, 76, Univ Bristol, Eng, 79, Kyoto Univ, Japan, 80 & Univ Santiago & Valdivia, Chile, 82; chmn, grants comt prog grants, Med Res Coun Can, 81-, mem, 83-84, exec, Med Res Coun Can, 83-90; mem, Int Peer Rev Comt, Networks Ctr Excellence, 89-90. *Mem:* Int Brain Res Orgn; Endocrine Soc; Brit Soc Endocrinol; Brit Pharmacol Soc; UK Physiol Soc; Can Physiol Soc; Can Pharmacol Soc; Can Biochem Soc; NY Acad Sci; Am Soc Pharmacol & Exp Therapeut; Fedn Am Socs Exp Biol; fel Royal Soc Can. *Res:* Hypothalamo-neurohypophyseal system, mechanisms of hormone storage and secretion; central nervous system of teleosts and amphibians; chemistry, pharmacology and gene expression of urotensin peptides, corticotropin releasing hormones and neurohypophyseal hormones. *Mailing Add:* 147 Carthew St Comox BC V9M 1T4 Can

LEDERMAN, DAVID MORDECHAI, BIOMEDICAL ENGINEERING. *Current Pos:* PRES & CHIEF EXEC OFFICER & CHMN BD, ABIOMED INC, 81- *Personal Data:* b Bogota, Colombia, May 26, 44; m 67, Natalie Hirsch; c Jonathan & Jeanine. *Educ:* Univ Los Andes, BEng, 66; Cornell Univ, BSc, 66, MEng, 67, PhD(aerospace eng), 73. *Prof Exp:* From prof appl math, Fac Arts & Sci, to dir div biomed eng, Fac Eng, Univ Los Andes, 72-73; sr staff mem, Avco-Everett Res Lab Inc, Avco Corp, 73-76, prin res scientist, 76-79, chmn, Med Res Comt, 79-81, consult, 81-82. *Concurrent Pos:* Dir, North Shore Chamber Com, Danvers, MA, 94- *Mem:* AAAS; NY Acad Sci; Sigma Xi; Am Phys Soc; Am Soc Artificial Internal Organs; Europ Soc Artificial Organs; Int Soc Artificial Organs; Am Heart Asn; Asn Med Biol Environ. *Res:* Development of clinical cardiovascular devices; prosthetic heart valves; blood-compatible biomaterials; hemodynamics and thrombosis; laser physics and applications to medicine; plastics technology; artificial hearts. *Mailing Add:* PO Box 426 Marblehead MA 01945-0426

LEDERMAN, FRANK L, PHYSICS, MATHEMATICS. *Current Pos:* vpres, res & develop, 88-92, SR VPRES TECHNOL, NORANDA INC, 92- *Personal Data:* b Buffalo, NY, Aug 19, 49; m 93, Daphna Kaplansky. *Educ:* Carnegie-Mellon Univ, BS & MS, 71; Univ Ill, Urbana, PhD(physics), 75. *Prof Exp:* Physicist, solid state physics & ultrasonics, Gen Elec Corp Res & Develop Ctr, 75-78, mgr ultrasound imager prog, 78-80, mgr energy systems mgt branch, 81-82, mgr power electronics systsbr, 83-87. *Mem:* Am Phys Soc; Sigma Xi; Indust Res Inst; Can Res Mgt Asn. *Res:* Solid state physics; signal processing; medical imaging; power circuits, integrated power electronics, lighting systems, motor and drives; metallurgy; metals processing; forestry; computing; Research and development. *Mailing Add:* Alcoa Tech Dr ADM-C Aluminum Co of Am 100 Technical Dr Alcoa Center PA 15069. *Fax:* 514-630-9483

LEDERMAN, HOWARD MARK, PEDIATRICS, IMMUNOLOGY & IMMUNODEFICIENCY. *Current Pos:* asst prof, 84-90, ASSOC PROF PEDIAT, JOHNS HOPKINS UNIV SCH MED, 91-; DIR, PEDIAT IMMUNODEFICIENCY CLIN, JOHNS HOPKINS HOSP, 93- *Personal Data:* b Chicago, Ill, Apr 3, 52; m 84; c 3. *Educ:* Univ Mich, BS, 72, MD, 77, PhD(microbiol), 78. *Prof Exp:* Pediat residency training, Johns Hopkins Hosp, 78-81; pediat immunol fel, Hosp Sick Children, Toronto, 81-83. *Mem:* Am Asn Immunologists; Clin Immunol Soc; Soc Pediat Res. *Res:* Defining and treating primary immunodeficiency diseases; investigating the role of fever as a host defense mechanism. *Mailing Add:* Johns Hopkins Hosp CMSC 1102 600 N Wolfe St Baltimore MD 21287-3923. *Fax:* 410-955-0229

LEDERMAN, LEON MAX, NUCLEAR PHYSICS, INSTRUMENTS. *Current Pos:* PROF PHYSICS & FRANK E SULZBERGER PROF, UNIV CHICAGO, 89-; EMER DIR, FERMILAB, BATAVIA, 89- *Personal Data:* b New York, NY, July 15, 22; m 45, 81; c 3. *Educ:* City Col New York, BS, 43; Columbia Univ, AM, 48, PhD(physics), 51. *Hon Degrees:* DSc, City Col New York, 81, 85, Northern Ill Univ, 83, Univ Chicago, 83, Ill Inst Technol, 87, Lake Forest Col, Carnegie-Mellon Univ, 88, Aurora Univ, 89, Univ Ill, 89, Univ Pittsburgh, 90, Bradley Univ, 90; DHL, Columbia & Rush Univ, 89. *Honors & Awards:* Nobel Prize in Physics, 88; Nat Medal of Sci, 65; Wolf Prize, 82. *Prof Exp:* Res assoc, Columbia Univ, 51-52, from asst prof to prof physics, 52-89; dir, Fermilab, Batavia, 79-89. *Concurrent Pos:* Assoc dir, Nevis Labs, 53, dir, 62-79; Guggenheim & Ford Found fel, 58-59, Ernest Kempton Adams fel, 61 & NSF fel, 67; mem, High Energy Physics Adv Panel, Atomic Energy Comn, 67-70; collabr, Res Nevis Lab Prog, Brookhaven Nat Lab, Europ Ctr Nuclear Res, Fermilab & State Univ NY, Stony Brook; US rep, Int Comt Future Accelerators; Higgins chair physics, Columbia Univ, 72; mem bd dirs, Weizmann Inst Sci, Israel, 88-, physics & astron, Nat Acad Sci, 88-, Mus Sci Indust, Chicago, 89-; chmn, Aspen Ctr Physics, Colo, 89-; mem, Secy Energy Adv Bd, Washington, DC, 90-; chmn, AAAS, 91-92; Pritzker prof sci, Ill Inst Technol. *Mem:* Nat Acad Sci; fel Am Phys Soc; fel Am Acad Arts & Sci; fel AAAS (pres-elect, 90, pres, 91-92). *Res:* Properties and interactions of elementary particles; author of over 200 publications. *Mailing Add:* Fermi Nat Accelerator Lab PO Box 500 Batavia IL 60510-0500

LEDERMAN, MARCOS, MAGNETIC RECORDING, MICROSCOPY & METROLOGY. *Current Pos:* SR RES & DEVELOP ENGR, READ-RITE CORP, 95- *Personal Data:* b Bogota, Columbia, Dec 15, 63. *Educ:* Sch Advan Physics & Chem, Paris, BA, 87; Univ Calif, Los Angeles, MS, 87, PhD(physics), 91. *Prof Exp:* Postdoctoral researcher, Univ Calif-San Diego, 91-95. *Mem:* Am Phys Soc. *Res:* Dynamics of single domain ferromagnetic particles; development of devices based on the spin valve and multilayer effects for magnetic recording including materials development and sensor design; failure analysis of magnetoresistive and spin-valve heads. *Mailing Add:* Read-Rite Corp 44100 Osgood Rd Fremont CA 94539-6401. *Fax:* 510-683-7065

LEDERMAN, PETER B, CHEMICAL & ENVIRONMENTAL ENGINEERING. *Current Pos:* DIR, CTR ENVIRON ENG & SCI, NJ INST TECHNOL. *Personal Data:* b Weimar, Ger, Nov 16, 31; US citizen; m 57, Susan Sturc; c 2. *Educ:* Univ Mich, BSE, 53, MS, 57, PhD(chem eng), 61. *Honors & Awards:* Silver Medal, US Environ Protection Agency, 76; Larry K Cecil Award Environ Eng, Am Inst Chem Engrs, 87; Stanley E Kappe Award, Am Acad Environ Engrs. *Prof Exp:* Jr technologist chem eng, Shell Oil Co, 53; technologist, Cent Res Div, Gen Foods Corp, 56; instr, Univ Mich, 59-61; engr, Esso Res Labs, 61-63, engr chem develop, Esso Res & Eng Co, 63-65, sr chem engr, 66; assoc prof chem eng, Polytech Inst Brooklyn, 66-72; dir indust waste treatment, Res & Develop, US Environ Protection Agency, 72-76; mgr tech develop & res, Cottrell Environ Sci, 76-78, vpres & gen mgr, 78-80; vpres hazardous/toxic mats mgt, Roy F Weston, 80-83, vpres & gen mgr, Spill Prev & Emergency Response Div, 83-88, vpres & sr tech adv, 88-93. *Concurrent Pos:* Teaching fel, Univ Mich, 55-59; lectr, Columbia Univ, 65-67; panel arbitrators, Am Arbit Asn. *Mem:* Fel Am Inst Chem Engrs; Am Chem Soc; Am Soc Eng Educ; Nat Soc Prof Engrs; Air & Waste Mgt Asn; dipl Am Acad Environ Engrs; Am Soc Mech Engrs. *Res:* Environmental studies; solid and hazardous material management; computer application; process optimization; polymers; mass transfer; pollution prevention; waste minimization; emergency response. *Mailing Add:* 17 Pittsford Way New Providence NJ 07974-2428. *Fax:* 908-464-0654; *E-Mail:* lederman@admin1.njit.edu

LEDERMAN, SALLY ANN, PHYSIOLOGY OF PREGNANCY & LACTATION. *Current Pos:* fel nutrit, Columbia Univ, 80-82, fel obstet & biochem, Col Physicians & Surgeons, 83, asst prof, 83-90, assoc prof pub health & nutrit, Sch Pub Health, 90-94, ELLA MCCOLLUM VAHLTEICH PROF, HUMAN NUTRIT, TEACHERS COL, COLUMBIA UNIV, 94- *Personal Data:* div; c Evin & Leandra. *Educ:* Brooklyn Col, BS, 57; Columbia Univ, MS, 76, PhD(nutrit), 80. *Prof Exp:* Anal chemist, Food & Drug Admin, 57-62; lectr chem, Brooklyn Col, 62-66 & 73-74. *Concurrent Pos:* Am Inst Nutrit travel award, 85; mem, Subcomt Weight Gain During Pregnancy, Nat Acad Sci, 88-90; prin investr, Bur Maternal & Child Health, Dept Health & Human Serv, 90- *Mem:* Asn Women Sci; NY Acad Sci; Am Inst Nutrit; Am Pub Health Asn; AAAS; Asn Teachers Maternal & Child Health. *Res:* Physiological and psychosocial factors affecting the course/outcome of pregnancy and lactation with special emphasis on issues related to nutrition and to public health. *Mailing Add:* 41 Lake Dr E Wayne NJ 07470. *E-Mail:* sal1@columbia.edu

LEDFORD, BARRY EDWARD, BIOCHEMISTRY, MOLECULAR BIOLOGY. *Current Pos:* from asst prof to assoc prof biochem, 73-84, PROF, DEPT BIOCHEM & MOLECULAR BIOL, MED UNIT SC, CHARLESTON, 84-, ASSOC DEAN, COL GRAD STUDIES & DIR, PROG MOLECULAR & CELL BIOL & PATHOBIOL, 89- *Personal Data:* b Denver, Colo, Feb 27, 42; m 65, Margaret Dauchess; c Brian & Molly. *Educ:* Univ Colo, Boulder, BA, 63, MS, 65; Fla State Univ, Tallahassee, PhD(chem), 71. *Prof Exp:* Teaching asst, Univ Colo, Boulder, 63-64, res asst, 64-65; jr scientist, Lawrence Livermore Nat Lab, 65-66; teaching asst, Fla State Univ, Tallahassee, 66-67, USPHS biochem trainee, Dept Chem, 67-71; USPHS postdoctoral fel, Biol Div, Oak Ridge Nat Lab, 71-73. *Mem:* Am Soc Biochem & Molecular Biol; AAAS; Am Soc Cell Biol; Soc Develop Biol. *Mailing Add:* Dept Biochem & Molecular Biol Med Univ SC 171 Ashley Ave Charleston SC 29425. *Fax:* 803-792-4322

LEDFORD, RICHARD ALLISON, FOOD MICROBIOLOGY. *Current Pos:* from asst prof to assoc prof, Inst Food Sci, 64-80, chmn dept, 72-77, assoc dir, 75-77, PROF FOOD SCI, CORNELL UNIV, 80-, CHMN DEPT, 85-, DIR, INST FOOD SCI, 88- *Personal Data:* b Charlotte, NC, June 30, 31; m 57, Martha Worley; c Richard Jr, Roeby, Ann, Jeanne & Robert. *Educ:* NC State Univ, BS, 54, MS, 56; Cornell Univ, PhD(food sci), 62. *Honors & Awards:* Nordica Award, 87. *Prof Exp:* Dir, NY State Food Lab, NY State Dept Agr & Mkts, 61-64. *Mem:* Am Soc Microbiol; Inst Food Technologists; Am Dairy Sci Asn. *Res:* Microbiological aspects of food science, especially food fermentations and analytical methods. *Mailing Add:* Dept Food Sci Cornell Univ 114 Stocking Ithaca NY 14853-7201. *Fax:* 607-254-4868

LEDFORD, THOMAS HOWARD, ORGANIC CHEMISTRY. *Current Pos:* sr tech develop chemist, 87-93, CHIEF ENVIRON CHEMIST, RUBICON CORP, 93- *Personal Data:* b Macon, Ga, Aug 24, 42; m 65, Joan McDaniel; c Jeff & Scott. *Educ:* Univ Ga, BS, 64; Univ Fla, PhD(chem), 73. *Prof Exp:* Res chemist polymer intermediates, Tenn Eastman Res Labs, Kingsport, Tenn, 64-68; res chemist fuels processing, Exxon Res & Develop, 73-80, sr res chemist, 80-86. *Concurrent Pos:* Adj assoc prof chem, La State Univ, 81- *Mem:* Am Chem Soc. *Res:* Polymers; reactions in strong acids; fuel processing chemistry; sulfur chemistry; isocyanate chemistry; environmental chemistry. *Mailing Add:* 2322 W Highmeadow Ct Baton Rouge LA 70816-2530. *Fax:* 504-673-4720

LEDIAEV, JOHN P, MATHEMATICS. *Current Pos:* Asst prof, 67-71, ASSOC PROF MATH, UNIV IOWA, 71- *Personal Data:* b Goorgan, Iran, Sept 8, 40; US citizen; div; c 1. *Educ:* Occidental Col, BA, 63; Univ Calif, Riverside, MA, 65, PhD(noether lattices), 67. *Mem:* Am Math Soc. *Res:* Structure; representation and embedding of Noether lattices; primary decomposition in multiplicative lattices; semi-prime operations in Noether lattices. *Mailing Add:* Dept Math Univ Iowa Iowa City IA 52240

LEDIG, F THOMAS, EVOLUTION. *Current Pos:* dir, 79-88, SR SCIENTIST, INST FOREST GENETICS, USDA FOREST SERV, 88- *Personal Data:* b Dover, NJ, Aug 13, 38; div; c Colleen B, Sean C & Brendan O. *Educ:* Rutgers Univ, BS, 62; NC State Univ, MS, 65, PhD(genetics), 67. *Honors & Awards:* Barrington Moore Mem Award, 92; Leslie L Schaffer Lectr, Univ BC, 88-89. *Prof Exp:* Lectr, Yale Univ, 66-67, from asst prof to prof forest genetics, 67-80. *Concurrent Pos:* Res geneticist, Inst Trop Forestry, Rio Piedraes, PR, 78, Keystone Nat Policy Dialogue Biodiversity, 89-90; consult, Nat Res Coun, Strategies Manage Forest Genetic Resources, 89; Glaser Distinguished vis prof, Fla Int Univ, 91-92. *Mem:* AAAS; Soc Am Foresters; Soc Conserv Biol; Int Soc Trop Foresters. *Res:* Population genetics and evolution; conservation of genetic resources; genecology, eucalypt biomass fuel breeding. *Mailing Add:* Inst Forest Genetics USDA-Forest Serv 2480 Carson Rd Placerville CA 95667. *Fax:* 530-622-2633

LEDIN, GEORGE, JR, COMPUTER SCIENCE, STATISTICS. *Current Pos:* PROF COMPUT SCI, SONOMA STATE UNIV, 84-, CHAIR, DEPT COMPUT SCI, 94- *Personal Data:* b Seekirchen, Austria, Jan 28, 46; US citizen; m 68, Suzanne Fisher; c Kathryn & Alexander. *Educ:* Univ Calif, Berkeley, BS, 67; Univ San Francisco, JD, 82. *Prof Exp:* Statistician & mathematician, Univ San Francisco, 65-70, lectr math & comput sci, 68-74, sr res assoc, Inst Chem Biol, 70-75, prof comput sci, 75-84, chmn, Sci Dept, 76-82. *Concurrent Pos:* Consult comput sci & statist, 66-; US rep, Int Fedn Info Processing, 72-74. *Mem:* AAAS; Am Math Soc; Asn Comput Mach; Math Asn Am; NY Acad Sci; Am Asn Artificial Intel; Soc Indust & Appl Math. *Res:* Comp security/data mining and knowledge discovery; programming methodology; heuristic programming; pattern recognition; mathematical models for biosciences; number theory; combinatorics; graph theory; game theory; information theory. *Mailing Add:* Sonoma State Univ 1801 E Cotati Ave Darwin 121 Rohnert Park CA 94928-3609. *E-Mail:* george.ledin@sonoma.edu

LEDINKO, NADA, VIROLOGY. *Current Pos:* prof, 71-89, assoc dir, Toolan Inst Med Res, 90-92, EMER PROF BIOL, UNIV AKRON, 90- *Personal Data:* b Girard, Ohio, Dec 16, 25. *Educ:* Ohio State Univ, BS, 46; Pa State Col, MS, 49; Yale Univ, PhD(microbiol), 52. *Prof Exp:* Res asst virol, Yale Univ, 52-53; Nat Found Infantile Paralysis fel, Walter & Eliza Hall Inst, Australia, 53-55; virologist, Pub Health Res Inst, 56-62; USPHS fel, Carnegie Inst Genetics Res Unit & Salk Inst Biol Studies, 63-65; assoc investr & NIH res career develop awardee, Putnam Mem Hosp Inst Med Res, Bennington, Vt, 65-71. *Concurrent Pos:* Res career develop award, NIH, 66-71. *Mem:* AAAS; Am Asn Path & Bact; Tissue Cult Asn; Am Soc Microbiol; Am Asn Cancer Res. *Res:* Genetical and biochemical aspects of viral growth; cancer research. *Mailing Add:* Regwood Dr RR 2 Box 7020 Bennington VT 05201

LEDLEY, FRED DAVID, pediatrics, gene therapy, for more information see previous edition

LEDLEY, ROBERT STEVEN, BIOPHYSICS, COMPUTER SCIENCE. *Current Pos:* PRES & RES DIR, NAT BIOMED RES FOUND, 60- *Personal Data:* b New York, NY, June 28, 26; m 49; c 2. *Educ:* NY Univ, DDS, 48; Columbia Univ, MA, 49. *Honors & Awards:* Nat Inventors Hall of Fame, 90; Nat Medal of Technol, 97. *Prof Exp:* Res physicist, Radiation Lab, Columbia Univ, 48-50, instr physics, 49-50; vis scientist, Nat Bur Stand, 51-52, physicist, External Control Group, Electronic Comput Lab, 53-54; opers res analyst, Opers Res Off, Strategic Div, Johns Hopkins Univ, 54-56; assoc prof elec eng, Sch Eng, George Washington Univ, 57-60; instr pediat, Sch Med, Johns Hopkins Univ, 60-63; prof elec eng, Sch Eng & Appl Sci, George Washington Univ, 68-70; prof physiol, biophys & radiol, med ctr, Georgetown Univ, 70- *Concurrent Pos:* Consult mathematician, Data Processing Systs Div, Nat Bur Stand, 57-60; mem staff, Nat Acad Sci-Nat Res Coun, 57-61; pres, Digital Info Sci Corp, 70-75; affil rep, Pattern Recognition Soc. *Mem:* Soc Math Biophys; Inst Elec & Electronics Engrs; Biophys Soc; NY Acad Sci; Pattern Recognition Soc. *Res:* Applications of computers to medical instrumentation; computer software systems and applications in medicine and biology; computer aids to medical diagnosis; computer information science; medical imaging; pattern recognition; medical informatics. *Mailing Add:* Biomed Res Found Georgetown Univ 3900 Reservoir Rd NW Washington DC 20007-2187

LEDLEY, TAMARA SHAPIRO, EARTH SYSTEM SCIENCE, CLIMATOLOGY. *Current Pos:* Res assoc climat, Rice Univ, 83-85, asst res scientist, 85-90, assoc res scientist, 90, SR FAC FEL CLIMATE/EARTH SYST SCI, RICE UNIV, 90- *Personal Data:* b Washington, DC, May 18, 54; m 76, Fred D; c Miriam E & Johanna S. *Educ:* Univ Md, BS, 76; Mass Inst Technol, PhD(meteorol), 83. *Concurrent Pos:* Prin investr, NSF grants, 85- & Tex Advan Technol Prog grants, 87-92; mem, Alaska SAR Facil Archive Working Team, 88 & McMurdo SAR Facil Sci Working Team, 90; coordr, Nat Week Educ, Union Concerned Scientists, 89; consult, Sci Connection Elem Sci Curric Proj, Houston Mus Natural Sci, 89-90, Broader Perspectives Inc, 90; dir, Weather & Climate Proj, Teacher Training Prog in Observational Sci, George Observ, 90-92; lectr space physics & astron, Rice Univ, 90 & 91, vis lectr geol & geophys, 93, asst dir, Solar Inst, 93; assoc ed, J Geophys Res-Atmospheres, 93-; mem comt, Global & Environ Chg, Am Geophys Union, 93- *Mem:* AAAS; Am Meteorol Soc; Am Geophys Union; Oceanog Soc; Sigma Xi. *Res:* Understanding the role of the polar regions in shaping climate on a wide range of time scales by examining how atmosphere-sea ice-ocean interactions influence climate change. *Mailing Add:* Rice Univ Dept Space Physics 6100 Main St Houston TX 77005-1892. *Fax:* 713-285-5143

LEDNEY, GEORGE DAVID, RADIATION BIOLOGY, HEMATOLOGY. *Current Pos:* head, Div Immunol, 73-88, proj mgr microbiol-immunol, 88-95, TEAM LEADER, RADIATION INJURY TREATMENT, ARMED FORCES RADIOBIOL RES INST, 95, CHMN, RADIATION MED DEPT. *Personal Data:* b Sharon, Pa, June 25, 37. *Educ:* Youngstown Univ, BS, 60; Univ Notre Dame, PhD(biol), 65. *Prof Exp:* Asst prof radiation biol, Med Units, Univ Tenn, Memphis, 65-67, assoc prof, 70-73. *Concurrent Pos:* Nat Cancer Inst fel, 65-67; Am Cancer Soc grants, 68 & 70. *Mem:* Am Asn Lab Animal Sci; Asn Gnotobiotics. *Res:* Radiation biology; radiation and immune functioning; bone marrow transplantation; wound trauma; radiation and susceptibility to infection. *Mailing Add:* Armed Forces Radiobiol Res Inst Dept Radiation Med 8901 Wisconsin Ave Bethesda MD 20889-5603. *Fax:* 301-295-6503

LEDNICER, DANIEL, ORGANIC CHEMISTRY. *Current Pos:* CONSULT, 94- *Personal Data:* b Antwerp, Belg, Oct 15, 29; nat US; m 56; c 2. *Educ:* Antioch Col, BS, 52; Ohio State Univ, PhD(chem), 55. *Prof Exp:* Sr chemist, G D Searle & Co, 55-56; res assoc, Duke Univ, 56-58; Esso Res & Develop Co fel, Univ Ill, 58-59; chemist, Upjohn Co, 59-73, sr scientist, 73-76; dir chem res, Mead Johnson & Co, 76-80; dir Med Chem & Pharm, Adria Labs, 80-84; pharm mgr, ABC Labs, 84-88; chemist, Nat Cancer Inst, 88-94. *Mem:* Am Chem Soc. *Res:* Stereochemistry; medicinal chemistry; hypotensives; analgesics; pharmaceutical analysis. *Mailing Add:* 826 Bowie Rd Rockville MD 20852-1023. *Fax:* 301-738-7035; *E-Mail:* 21113@umail.uml.edu

LEDOUX, ROBERT LOUIS, MINERALOGY. *Current Pos:* RETIRED. *Personal Data:* b Marieville, Que, Apr 19, 33; m 61; c 2. *Educ:* Univ Montreal, BSc, 56; Laval Univ, MScA, 60; Purdue Univ, PhD(mineral), 64. *Prof Exp:* From assoc prof to prof mineral, Laval Univ, 64-94, prof petrol & mineral, 94- *Mem:* Mineral Asn Am; Can Asn Mineral; Geol Asn Can. *Res:* Infrared studies of layered silicates. *Mailing Add:* 711 rue Moreau Ste Foy PQ G1V 3A5 Can

LEDSOME, JOHN R, PHYSIOLOGY, MEDICINE. *Current Pos:* head, 80-91, PROF PHYSIOL, UNIV BC, 68- *Personal Data:* b Bebington, Eng, June 18, 32; m 57, Allsop; c Henry, Mark & Sarah. *Educ:* Univ Edinburgh, MB, ChB, 55, MD, 62, DSc, 89. *Prof Exp:* Lectr physiol, Univ Leeds, 59-68. *Concurrent Pos:* USPHS int fel, 64-65, res grant, 66-68; Med Res Coun Eng res grant, 65-68; Med Red Coun Can res grant, 68-95; BC Heart Found res grant, 72-94. *Mem:* Can Physiol Soc; Brit Physiol Soc; Am Physiol Soc. *Res:* Control of the cardiovascular system; function of left atrial receptors; atrial natriuretic peptide; effects of microgravity. *Mailing Add:* Dept Physiol Univ BC 2146 Health Sci Mall Vancouver BC V6T 1Z3 Can. *Fax:* 604-822-6048

LEDUC, ELIZABETH, CELL BIOLOGY. *Current Pos:* from asst prof to assoc prof, 53-64, PROF BIOL, BROWN UNIV, 64-, DEAN DIV BIOL & MED, 73- *Personal Data:* b Rockland, Maine, Nov 19, 21. *Educ:* Univ Vt, BS, 43; Wellesley Col, MA, 45; Brown Univ, PhD(biol), 48. *Prof Exp:* Res assoc biol, Brown Univ, 48-49; instr & assoc anat, Harvard Med Sch, 49-53. *Concurrent Pos:* Mem adv coun, Nat Inst Gen Med Sci, 72-76. *Mem:* AAAS; Am Soc Cell Biol; Soc Francaise de Microscopie Electronique; Histochem Soc; Am Soc Exp Path. *Res:* Histophysiology and pathology of the liver; cellular mechanism in antibody production; ultrastructural and cytochemical effects of cancer chemotherapeutic compounds on normal and neoplastic cells. *Mailing Add:* Div Biol & Med Sci Brown Univ Providence RI 02912-0001

LEDUC, GERARD, FISHERIES, BIOCHEMISTRY. *Current Pos:* INDEPENDENT RESEARCHER, 90- *Personal Data:* b Verdun, Que, Sept 7, 34; m 59; c 3. *Educ:* Univ Montreal, BSc, 58, MSc, 60; Ore State Univ, PhD(fisheries), 66. *Prof Exp:* Biologist, Que Wildlife Serv, 63-66; from asst prof to prof biol sci, Sir George Williams Univ, 66-90, chmn dept, 69-72. *Res:* Fisheries problems in water pollution, mainly the long-term effects of sublethal concentrations of toxicant; artificial streams. *Mailing Add:* 6 Chemin de l'Equinox RR 3 Mansonville PQ J0E 1X0 Can

LE DUC, J-ADRIEN MAHER, electrochemistry, inorganic chemistry; deceased, see previous edition for last biography

LEDUC, SHARON KAY, STATISTICS, CLIMATOLOGY. *Current Pos:* Nat Environ Satellite, Data & Info Serv, statistician, Ctr Environ Assessment Serv, Nat Ocean & Atmospheric Admin, Mo, 74-88, ENVIRON PROTECTION AGENCY, NC, 88-; ADJ PROF GEOG, UNIV NC, 90-; ADJ PROF, MEA NC STATE UNIV, 95- *Personal Data:* b Hattiesburg, Miss, Apr 28, 43; m 64, Richard; c Brian, Philip & Russell. *Educ:* Eastern Ill Univ, BS, 65; Univ Mo, Columbia, MA, 67, PhD(statist), 71. *Honors & Awards:* Gold Medal, USDOC. *Prof Exp:* Prof atmospheric sci, Univ Mo, 67-89. *Mem:* Am Statist Asn; Am Meteorol Soc; Sigma Xi. *Res:* Statistical analysis of atmospheric data for climate change; evaluation of air quality models; technological transfer methods. *Mailing Add:* US Environ Protection Agency MD-80A Research Triangle Park NC 27711. *E-Mail:* leduc@hpcc.epa.gov

LEDUY, ANH, BIOCHEMICAL ENGINEERING, APPLIED MICROBIOLOGY. *Current Pos:* from asst to assoc prof, 77-85, PROF CHEM ENG, LAVAL UNIV, 85- *Personal Data:* b Vietnam, Feb 6, 46; Can citizen; m 77, Suzanne Roger; c Isabelle & Dominic. *Educ:* Univ Sherbrooke, BScA, 69, MScA, 72; Univ Western Ont, PhD(biochem eng), 75. *Prof Exp:* Res assoc chem eng, Univ Sherbrooke, 75-77. *Concurrent Pos:* Consult, 81- *Mem:* NY Acad Sci. *Res:* Utilization of microorganisms; enzymes systems in the production of biomass and precious metabolites from abundant raw materials, waste materials and industrial agricultural by-products. *Mailing Add:* Dept Chem Eng Laval Univ Ste Foy PQ G1K 7P4 Can. *Fax:* 418-656-5993; *E-Mail:* anh.leduy@gch.ulaval.ca

LEDWELL, THOMAS AUSTIN, MECHANICAL ENGINEERING, ENERGY CONVERSION & ENVIRONMENTAL IMPACTS OF ENERGY. *Current Pos:* CONSULT, 85- *Personal Data:* b PEI, June 13, 38; m 64, Mary Elaine; c 4. *Educ:* NS Tech Col, BE, 60, ME, 65; Univ Waterloo, PhD(mech eng), 68. *Prof Exp:* Res coordr, Nat Res Coun, 75-77; tech adv, Renewable Energy Policy, 77-78, head res coord, 78-80, sr tech adv, Conserv & Renewable Energy, Energy, Mines & Resources, 80-82, chief, Demonstration Prog, 82-85. *Concurrent Pos:* lectr physics environ, Carleton Univ, 87-96, dir, Renewable Energy Policy, 86-94, sr adv, Sci Technol, 94-97. *Mem:* Combustion Inst. *Res:* Thermodynamics; engine design and development; applied mathematics; energy research and development; environmental impacts and health impacts of energy climate change ozone layer. *Mailing Add:* Natural Resources Can 580 Booth St Ottawa ON K1J 8J2 Can. *Fax:* 613-947-4120; *E-Mail:* tomledwell@esnrcan.gc.ca

LEDWITZ-RIGBY, FLORENCE INA, REPRODUCTIVE ENDOCRINOLOGY. *Current Pos:* dir affirmative action, 94-, PROF BIOL, UNIV WIS. *Personal Data:* b New York, NY, Feb 14, 46; m 68; c 2. *Educ:* City Col NY, BS, 66; Case Western Res Univ, MS, 68; Univ Wis-Madison, PhD(endocrinol & reprod physiol), 72. *Prof Exp:* Res fel reprod physiol, Sch Med, Dept Physiol, Univ Pittsburgh, 72-74, vis asst prof physiol, Dept Biol, 74-75; from asst prof to assoc prof physiol, Dept Biol Sci, Northern Ill Univ, 75-87, prof, 87-90; adv, Women & Gender Relations & hon prof obstet & gynec, Univ BC, 90-94. *Concurrent Pos:* Vis res prof, Dept Genetics, Univ Ill, Chicago, 87-88. *Mem:* Am Physiol Soc; Soc Study Reprod; Endocrine Soc. *Res:* Endocrine and physiological control mechanisms of ovarian cell function and differentiation. *Mailing Add:* Biol Dept 340 Phillips Sci Bldg Univ Wis Eau Claire Eau Claire WI 54701-4800

LEE, ALFRED M, TELECOMMUNICATIONS POLICY, TECHNOLOGY ASSESSMENT. *Current Pos:* telecommun policy analyst, 84-90, SR POLICY ADV, OFF POLICY ANALYSIS & DEVELOP, NAT TELECOMMUN & INFO ADMIN, US DEPT COM, 90- *Personal Data:* b Bloomington, Ind, Aug, 23, 51. *Educ:* Univ Ill, BSEE, 73; Cornell Univ, MS, 75, PhD(civil eng & pub policy), 81. *Prof Exp:* Res specialist mobile commun, Cornell Univ, 75-78, res asst electronic message transfer, 78-80, fel, Prog Sci, Technol & Sci, 80-82. *Concurrent Pos:* Mem, Transp Res Bd, Subcomt Telecommun & Transp, Trade-offs, 80-84; assoc ed, Inst Elec & Electronics Engrs Technol & Soc Mag, 81-84. *Mem:* Inst Elec & Electronics Engrs; Sigma Xi. *Res:* Telecommunications policy; transportation-communications trade-offs and the social impact of developments in telecommunications; mobile communications; electronic message transfer. *Mailing Add:* Nat Telecommun & Info Admin H4725 US Dept Comm Washington DC 20230

LEE, ALFRED TZE-HAU, ANALYTICAL CHEMISTRY, ORGANIC CHEMISTRY. *Current Pos:* chmn, 85-90, PROF CHEM, CITY COL SAN FRANCISCO, 68- *Personal Data:* b Hong Kong, July 22, 39; US citizen; m 70, Kitty Ho; c Winnie & Hanson. *Educ:* Univ Calif, Berkeley, BS, 63; Univ Calif, Los Angeles, PhD(chem), 68. *Prof Exp:* Instr chem, East Los Angeles Col, 67-68. *Concurrent Pos:* Res scientist, Jet Propulsion Lab, Pasadena, 68. *Mem:* Am Chem Soc. *Res:* Oxidation-state diagrams; pulse polarography; analytical methods in general, vacuum-ultraviolet spectra of olefins. *Mailing Add:* 154 Hernandez Ave San Francisco CA 94127-1012

LEE, AMY SHIU, MOLECULAR BIOLOGY, BIOCHEMISTRY. *Current Pos:* from asst to assoc prof, 79-87, PROF BIOCHEM, SCH MED, UNIV SOUTHERN CALIF, 88- *Personal Data:* b Canton, China, Aug 5, 47; US citizen; m 72; c 2. *Educ:* Univ Calif, Berkeley, BA, 70; Calif Inst Technol, MSc, 72, PhD(biophys, molecular biol), 75. *Honors & Awards:* Merit Award, NIH, 88. *Prof Exp:* Res asst bact, Univ Calif, Los Angeles, 70-71; teaching asst biol, Calif Inst Technol, 71-74, res fel, 74-77, sr res fel, 78-79. *Concurrent Pos:* Am Cancer Soc fel, Calif Inst Technol, 75-76, sr res fel, 78-69; NIH Pub Health Serv fel, 77-78; NIH study sect, 80-88; fac res award, Am Cancer Soc, 83-88. *Mem:* AAAS. *Res:* DNA sequence organization and gene expression in cell cycle regeneration eukaryotes; recombinant DNA technology. *Mailing Add:* Dept Biochem Univ Southern Calif Med 1441 Eastlake Ave Los Angeles CA 90033

LEE, ANTHONY, PLASMA PHYSICS. *Current Pos:* DIR, ADV ENG, DIV GEN MOTORS, PACKARD ELEC. *Personal Data:* b Canton, China, Dec 8, 41; US citizen; m 69; c 2. *Educ:* Drexel Univ, BS, 66; Stevens Inst Technol, MS, 69, PhD(physics), 71. *Prof Exp:* Fel plasma physics, Univ Sask, 71-73; adj asst prof, Univ SFla, 73-75, vis asst prof physics, 75-76; sr engr, Res & Develop Ctr, Westinghouse Elec Corp, 76- *Mem:* Am Phys Soc; Inst Elec & Electronics Engrs. *Res:* Nonlinear plasma wave theory; linear and nonlinear low frequency waves in plasmas with density, potential and temperature gradients; catalytic turbulent heating of plasmas as supplementary tokamac heating. *Mailing Add:* Packard Elec PO Box 431 Sta 93L Warren OH 44846

LEE, ANTHONY L, CATALYSIS, GAS PROCESSING. *Current Pos:* chem engr, Inst Gas Technol, 61-66, supvr fundamental properties res, 66-69, supvr catalytic processing, 69-78, sr chem engr, 78-85, asst dir, Catalyst Develop, 85-88, ASSOC DIR, GAS PROCESSING & CATALYSIS, INST GAS TECHNOL, 88- *Personal Data:* b Qingdao, China, Nov 16, 34; US citizen; m 62; c 2. *Educ:* Univ Calif, Berkeley, BS, 58; Mo Sch Mines, MS, 61. *Prof Exp:* Res asst, Calif Inst Technol, 58-59; chemist, Stepan Chem Co, 60. *Mem:* Am Inst Chem Engrs. *Res:* Transport and thermodynamic peoperties of hydrocarbons; coal gasification research; methanation, water-gas shift, hydrotreating, hydrocracking, and steam reforming catalysis; C1 chemistry; hydroforming; gas processing. *Mailing Add:* 305 Oak St Glen Ellyn IL 60137. *Fax:* 312-949-3700

LEE, ARTHUR CLAIR, OPHTHALMOLOGY, RADIATION RESEARCH. *Current Pos:* RETIRED. *Personal Data:* b Abilene, Kans, Aug 3, 23; m 51, Margaret Helzer; c Marsha, Lorraine, Douglas, Suzanne & Angela. *Educ:* Colo State Univ, DVM, 52, MS, 63, PhD(radiation biol), 70. *Prof Exp:* Practr vet med, 52-60; Morris Found fel, 60-62; vet radiologist, AEC Proj, Colo State Univ, Foothills Campus, 63-66, vet sect leader, Collab Radiol Health Lab, USPHS, 64-90. *Mem:* AAAS; Am Vet Med Asn; Radiation Res Soc Am; Am Soc Vet Ophthal. *Res:* Radiation effects on canine growth and development; ocular lesions as a result of age at exposure; cataractogenesis from heavy charged particles. *Mailing Add:* 1908 Mohawk St Ft Collins CO 80525-1526

LEE, BENEDICT HUK KUN, MECHANICAL ENGINEERING, AERONAUTICS. *Current Pos:* SR RES SCIENTIST, NAT RES COUN, 67- *Personal Data:* b Hong Kong, Oct 17, 40; Can citizen; m 66, Alice Lau; c Karen & Alexander. *Educ:* McGill Univ, BEng, 63, MEng, 64, PhD(mech eng), 66. *Prof Exp:* Res assoc, McGill Univ, 66-67. *Concurrent Pos:* Adj prof, Dept Mech Eng, Univ Ottawa, Ont, 91- *Mem:* Am Inst Aeronaut & Astronaut; Acoust Soc Am; Can Aeronaut & Space Inst. *Res:* Fluid mechanics; gas dynamics; acoustics and aerodynamics; aeroelasticity; structural dynamics. *Mailing Add:* Nat Res Coun Bldg U66 Montreal Rd Ottawa ON K1A 0R6 Can

LEE, BERNARD S, CHEMICAL ENGINEERING, PHYSICAL CHEMISTRY. *Current Pos:* vpres, 76-77, exec vpres, 77-78, PRES, INST GAS TECHNOL, 78- *Personal Data:* b China, Dec 14, 34; US citizen; m 63; c 3. *Educ:* Polytech Inst Brooklyn, BChE, 56, PhD(chem eng), 60. *Prof Exp:* Mem staff, Arthur D Little, Inc, 60-65; supvr, mgr & dir coal gasification, 65-75, asst vpres process res, 75-76. *Concurrent Pos:* Lectr, Am Inst Chem Engrs, 81. *Mem:* Fel Am Inst Chem Engrs; Am Chem Soc; Am Inst Mining, Metall & Petrol Engrs; Sigma Xi; Am Gas Asn. *Res:* Energy conversion processes for its production of synthetic fuels from coal, lignite, peat, oil shale, biomass, urban and industrial wastes and efficient energy utilization systems involving solar energy and fuel cells. *Mailing Add:* 1700 S Mt Prospect Rd Des Plaines IL 60618

LEE, BURNELL, COATINGS FORMULATIONS, GENERAL FORMULATION. *Current Pos:* Sr res chemist, 87-90, res specialist, 90-93, SR RES CHEMIST, ETHYL CORP, 93- *Personal Data:* b Hearne, Tex, Dec 8, 55; m 78, Katherin H Corlett; c Aaron D & Kristin M. *Educ:* Southwest Mo State Univ, BS, 80; Univ Ill, Champaign-Urbana, PhD(org chem), 87. *Mem:* Am Chem Soc; Soc Cosmetic Chemists; Am Vacuum Soc; Soc Tribologists & Lubrication Engrs. *Res:* Synthesis and application polyimide polymers for coatings, molding, and composite manufacture; applications of proprietary additives in a variety areas including ceramic coatings, cosmetics, agricultural products, and foams. *Mailing Add:* 15133 Seven Pines Baton Rouge LA 70817. *Fax:* 504-768-5607

LEE, BURTRAND INSUNG, ANALYTICAL CHEMISTRY, MATERIALS SYNTHESIS. *Current Pos:* asst prof mat sci, 86-91, ASSOC PROF CERAMIC ENG, CLEMSON UNIV, 91- *Personal Data:* b Seoul, Korea, Jan 20, 52; US citizen; m 79, Connie W Min; c Curtis J. *Educ:* Southern Col, Collegedale, BA, 76; Western Mich Univ, MS, 79; Univ Fla, Gainesville, PhD(mat eng), 86. *Prof Exp:* Chemist, Biospherics Inc, 76-78. *Concurrent Pos:* Lectr, State Univ NY, 80; prin investr, Petrol Res Fund, Am Chem Soc, 87-88 & NSF, 88-; panel comt mem, Nat Sci & Technol Ctr, 87-88; vis prof, Norweg Inst Technol, 89; Fulbright Found Scholar, 89; distinguished vis prof, Pusan Nat Univ, Korea, 90; vis sr researcher, Hitachi Res Lab, Japan, 93; affil staff researcher, Pac NW Nat Lab, 95- *Mem:* Am Chem Soc; Am Ceramic Soc; Mat Res Soc; Sigma Xi. *Res:* Surface interactions of ceramic and polymeric materials; new methods or new materials for engineering and opto-electronic applications; chemical processing or ultrastructure processing of ceramic materials; sol-gel processing. *Mailing Add:* Dept Ceramic & Mat Eng Olin Hall Clemson Univ Clemson SC 29634-0907. *Fax:* 864-656-1453; *E-Mail:* burt.lee@ces.clemson.edu

LEE, BYUNGKOOK, PROTEIN STRUCTURE MODELING. *Current Pos:* expert, 80-87, res chemist, 87-91, CHIEF, MOLECULAR MODELING SECT, NIH, BETHESDA, MD, 91- *Personal Data:* b Korea, Feb 7, 41; m 64; c 1. *Educ:* Seoul Nat Univ, BS, 61; Cornell Univ, PhD(phys chem), 67. *Prof Exp:* USPHS res fel, Yale Univ, 69-70; from asst prof to assoc prof chem, Univ Kans, 70-83. *Mem:* Protein Soc; Biophys Soc. *Res:* Biothermodynamics; computer modeling of biological macromolecules. *Mailing Add:* NIH Nat Cancer Inst LMB Bldg 37 Rm 4B15 Bethesda MD 20892. *Fax:* 301-402-1344; *E-Mail:* bkl@helix.nih.gov

LEE, C(HIA) H(UAN), ELECTRICAL ENGINEERING. *Current Pos:* sr engr specialist, 64-82, ENG CONSULT, AIRESEARCH MFG CO, 83- *Personal Data:* b China, Oct 1, 19; m 53; c 4. *Educ:* Chiao Tung Univ, China, BS, 42; Cornell Univ, MS, 49, PhD(elec eng), 51. *Honors & Awards:* Cert Recognition, NASA, 73. *Prof Exp:* Design engr, Cent Elec Mfg Works, China, 42-47; distrib engr, Canton Power Co, 47-48; develop engr, Reliance Elec & Eng Co, Ohio, 51-55; asst prof elec eng, Polytech Inst Brooklyn, 55-58; fel engr, Westinghouse Elec Corp, 58-64. *Mem:* Inst Elec & Electronics Engrs; Am Soc Naval Engrs; China Elec Eng Soc. *Res:* Electric machinery; electric power systems; electromagnetic devices; electronic components; circuit theory; land, sea and air transportation; electronic power converter; control systems. *Mailing Add:* 30584 Ganado Dr Rancho Palos Verdes CA 90275-6222

LEE, CATHERINE COYLE, BIOINORGANIC CHEMISTRY, CATALYSIS. *Current Pos:* res chemist, Exxon Res & Eng, 79-80, sr chemist, 80-83 & 83-91, PROJ LEADER, EXXON RES & ENG, 90-, SR STAFF CHEMIST, 91- *Personal Data:* b New York, NY, May 16, 52; c 1. *Educ:* Hunter Col, City Univ NY, BS, 74; Calif Inst Technol, PhD(chem), 78. *Prof Exp:* Fel chem, Stanford Univ, 77-79. *Concurrent Pos:* Res award, Sigma Xi, 77; adj asst prof, Hunter Col, City Univ NY, 81-82; Alexander von Humboldt fel, 84-85. *Mem:* Am Chem Soc. *Res:* Bioinorganic chemistry with specific emphasis on the kinetics of metalloprotein reactions; preparation and characterization of transition metal-sulfur complexes as catalysts and lubricant additives. *Mailing Add:* Exxon Res & Eng Rte 22 E Annandale NJ 08801

LEE, CHARLES ALEXANDER, PHYSICS. *Current Pos:* PROF ELEC ENG, CORNELL UNIV, 67- *Personal Data:* b New York, NY, Aug 28, 22; m 53; c 1. *Educ:* Rensselaer Polytech Inst, BEE, 44; Columbia Univ, PhD(physics), 54. *Prof Exp:* Res assoc molecular beam spectros, Columbia Univ, 52-53; mem tech staff semiconductors, Bell Tel Labs, 53-67. *Mem:* Am Phys Soc; Inst Elec & Electronics Engr; Sigma Xi. *Res:* Solid state device physics; molecular beam spectroscopy. *Mailing Add:* 212 Giles St Apt 6 Ithaca NY 14850

LEE, CHARLES NORTHAM, ENGINEERING, FORESTRY. *Current Pos:* asst prof forest mgt, 59-63, assoc prof forest eng, 64-68, PROF FOREST ENG, STATE UNIV NY COL ENVIRON SCI & FORESTRY, 68-, DIR COMPUT CTR, 84- *Personal Data:* b Syracuse, NY, Jan 13, 25; m 52; c 4. *Educ:* Syracuse Univ, BS, 49, BCE, 57, MCE, 59. *Prof Exp:* Instr civil eng, Syracuse Univ, 57-59. *Concurrent Pos:* Consult geotech engr, 57-; NSF fel Sci Fac MIT, 63-65. *Mem:* Am Soc Civil Engrs; Asn Comput Mach. *Res:* Land locomotion under off-highway conditions; modulation techniques applied to roadway design; information coding content and transformations for analysis and design of engineering systems. Mailing Add: Dir Acad Comput 1 Forestry Dr Col Environ Sci & Forestry State Univ NY Syracuse NY 13210-2723

LEE, CHARLES RICHARD, SOIL CHEMISTRY, PLANT NUTRITION. Current Pos: RES SOIL SCIENTIST, US ARMY CORPS ENGRS, ENVIRON LAB, WATERWAYS EXP STA, 73- Personal Data: b Tarrytown, NY, Dec 3, 42; m 65, Nancy Giles; c Laura A, Juliet M & Katherine A. Educ: Univ Tampa, BS, 64; Clemson Univ, MS, 65, PhD(agron), 68. Prof Exp: Res scientist, Can Dept Agr, 68-73. Concurrent Pos: Adj prof, Delta State Univ, Miss State Univ, Univ Miss & La State Univ. Mem: Am Soc Agron; Int Soc Soil Sci. Res: Land treatment of wastewater; heavy metal uptake by marsh plants; soil fertility; minor elements; plant growth in high zinc, aluminum or manganese media; restoration of problem soil; environmental clean-up. Mailing Add: Environ Lab US Army Engr Waterways Exp Sta 3909 Halls Ferry Rd Vicksburg MS 39180-0631. Fax: 601-634-4298

LEE, CHARLOTTE, BIOCHEMISTRY, ORGANIC CHEMISTRY. Current Pos: INSTR CHEM, TRITON COL, 79-, CHAIRPERSON SCI DEPT, 91- Personal Data: b Boligee, Ala, July 13, 30. Educ: Knoxville Col, BS, 53; Tuskegee Univ, MS, 55; Univ Kans, PhD(biochem), 59. Prof Exp: Asst prof chem, Nassau Community Col, 70-71; assoc prof, Southern Ill Univ, Edwardsville, 71-78. Mem: Am Chem Soc; Nat Asn Advan Colored People. Mailing Add: 333 N Cuyler Oak Park IL 60302

LEE, CHE-HUNG R, METABOLISM. Current Pos: PRIN INVESTR, METAB RES DIV, CCRD NAVY MED RES INST, 84- Mailing Add: Septic Shock Res Prog Naval Med Res Inst Bethesda MD 20889

LEE, CHEN HUI, FORESTRY. Current Pos: from asst prof to assoc prof, 66-77, PROF FORESTRY, UNIV WIS-STEVENS POINT, 77- Personal Data: b Taipei, Taiwan, Dec 2, 29; m 62; c 2. Educ: Nat Taiwan Univ, BS, 53; Mich State Univ, MS, 60, PhD(forestry), 66. Honors & Awards: Sigma Xi Spec Sci Res Award, Univ Wis, Stevene Point Club, 93. Prof Exp: Asst, Nat Taiwan Univ, 54-59, instr, 59-62; res asst, Mich State Univ, 62-66. Concurrent Pos: US Forest Serv res grants, 77 & 79; univ scholar award, Univ Wis-Stevens Pt Club, 91, Sigma Xi spec sci res award, 93. Mem: Soc Am Foresters; Chinese Soc Forestry; Japanese Forestry Soc; Sigma Xi. Res: Forest genetics and tree improvement, especially tree physiology, pine leaf anatomy and wood quality. Mailing Add: Col Natural Res Univ Wis Stevens Point WI 54481

LEE, CHENG-CHUN, RENAL TOXICOLOGY, SAFETY EVALUATION. Current Pos: SR SCI ADV, HEALTH & ENVIRON REV DIV, OFF POLLUTION PREV & TOXIC SUBSTANCES, ENVIRON PROTECTION AGENCY, 79- Personal Data: b Youngchow, China, May 24, 22; nat US; m 59, Janice Y Wang; c James P & Ray W. Educ: Nat Cent Univ, China, BS, 45, MS, 48; Mich State Univ, MS, 50, PhD(physiol), 52. Honors & Awards: Bronze Medal & Special Achievement & Contribs, Environ Protection Agency, 80, 81, & 89. Prof Exp: Asst vet med, Nat Cent Univ, China, 45-48; asst physiol, Mich State Univ, 49-51; from pharmacologist to sr pharmacologist, Eli Lilly & Co, 52-62; from sr pharmacologist to prin pharmacologist, Midwest Res Inst, 62-67, head pharmacol & toxicol, 67-76, asst dir, 76-77, assoc dir, 77-78, dep dir, Biol Sci Div, 78-79. Concurrent Pos: Lectr, Univ Mo-Kansas City, 65-66 & Med Ctr, Univ Kans, 66-79; spec consult antimalarials & drug develop, WHO, 80, 81, 89 & 93; prof lectr, Med Ctr, George Washington Univ, 81-92. Mem: Am Physiol Soc; Am Soc Pharmacol & Exp Therapeut; Soc Toxicol; Am Col Toxicol; NY Acad Sci; Am Soc Exp Biol & Med. Res: Safety evaluation; drug metabolism and disposition; antimalarials; antineoplastics; pharmaceuticals; chemicals; drug development; mechanism of drug action and toxicity; liver and renal functions; author or coauthor of over 100 publications. Mailing Add: Health & Environ Rev Div (TS-7403) Environ Protection Agency 401 M St SW Washington DC 20460. Fax: 202-260-1283

LEE, CHENG-SHENG, AQUACULTURE & MARICULTURE, REPRODUCTIVE PHYSIOLOGY. Current Pos: Res assoc, 79-81, shrimp prog mgr, 81-84, FINFISH PROG MGR, OCEANIC INST, 84-, ASST VPRES, 92- Personal Data: US citizen. Educ: Nat Taiwan Univ, BS, 70, MS, 72; Univ Tokyo, PhD(aquacult), 79. Concurrent Pos: Aquatic biologist, Tungkang Marine Lab, 73-76. Mem: World Aquacult Soc; Asian Fisheries Soc; Am Fisheries Soc. Res: Induction of maturation and spawning of marine finfish; evaluating optimal environment conditions for food organisms and early life stages of finfish. Mailing Add: Oceanic Inst PO Box 25280 Honolulu HI 96825. Fax: 808-259-5971

LEE, CHEUK MAN, ORGANIC CHEMISTRY, PHARMACEUTICAL CHEMISTRY. Current Pos: ASSOC RES FEL, ABBOTT LABS, 60 - Personal Data: b China, Feb 22, 29; c 2. Educ: Univ Hong Kong, BSc, 54, MSc, 57; Univ Mich, PhD(pharmaceut chem), 60. Mem: Am Chem Soc. Res: Synthesis of organic compounds of biological activities; heterocyclic chemistry; anti-biotics. Mailing Add: 504 W Golf Rd Libertyville IL 60048

LEE, CHI-HANG, NATURAL PRODUCTS CHEMISTRY, FOOD SCIENCE. Current Pos: RETIRED. Personal Data: b Vinh Long, SVietnam, Jan 1, 39; nat US; m 64; c 2. Educ: Southern Ill Univ, Carbondale, BA, 60; Rutgers Univ, New Brunswick, PhD(natural prod chem), 66. Honors &

Awards: Chairman's Award, Gen Foods Corp, 77; Agr Comn Appreciation Award, Taiwan, Rep China, 89. Prof Exp: Res asst, Rutgers Univ, 61-65, res assoc, 66; sr chemist, Gen Foods Corp, 67-71, from res specialist to sr res specialist, 72-78; sr res scientist, RJR Foods, 78-80; biochem mgr, Del Monte Corp, 80-85, chem dir, 85-87, dir analytical serv, 88-96. Concurrent Pos: Vis prof, King's Col, 73-77; mem, Adv Comt, Econ Affairs, Repub China, 77-89. Mem: Am Chem Soc; Am Sci Affil (pres, 82). Res: Carbohydrates; flavors; sweeteners; food chemistry, biochemistry and chemical analysis. Mailing Add: Del Monte Corp Res Ctr 205 N Wiget Lane Walnut Creek CA 94598

LEE, CHI-HO, pharmacology, for more information see previous edition

LEE, CHI-JEN, BIOCHEMICAL BASIS ON IMMUNOGENICITY OF BACTERIAL POLYSACCHARIDES, BACTERIAL POLYSACCHARIDE VACCINES. Current Pos: SUPVRY RES CHEMIST, CTR BIOLOGICS, FOOD & DRUG ADMIN, 74- Personal Data: b Yi-Lan, Taiwan, Feb 8, 36; US citizen; m 60, Sue-Yuan; c Johns, Lucia & Benjamin. Educ: Nat Taiwan Univ, BS, 57; Johns Hopkins Univ, ScD, 66. Prof Exp: Pharmacist, China Chem & Pharmaceut Co, Taiwan, 59-62; res assoc, Dept Biochem, Johns Hopkins Univ, 66-67; res assoc, Rockefeller Univ, New York City, 67-68, asst prof, 68-73; sr staff fel, Nat Inst Child Health & Human Develop, NIH, Bethesda, Md, 73-74. Concurrent Pos: Mem, Nat Reconstruct Comt Med & Health, 78; chmn, 3rd Pneumococcal Workshop, Food & Drug Admin, Bethesda, Md, 79, chmn, Polysaccharide Vaccine Comt; mem bd dirs, Chinese Med & Health Asn, Washington, DC, 80; mem bd adv, Dept Biochem, Col Med, Nat Cheng Kung Univ, 83-84, vis prof, 84; thesis dir, Dept Microbiol, Med Ctr, George Washington Univ, 83-84 & 87-; referee, CRC Press, Inc, Boca Raton, Fla, 88. Mem: Am Asn Immunologists; Am Soc Biol Chemists. Res: Characterization of group 19 pneumolysins and cloning of their ply genes have been studied to examine the relationship of ply to virulence; inactivated pneumolysin is conjugated to pneumococcal polysaccharide to form a polysaccharide-protein conjugate to develop a more effective pneumococcal vaccine. Mailing Add: FOA CBER 1401 Rockville Pike Rockville MD 20852-1448

LEE, CHIN OK, CARDIAC ELECTROPHYSIOLOGY. Current Pos: from asst prof to assoc prof, 76-86, PROF CARDIAC ELECTROPHYSIOL, CORNELL UNIV MED CAMPUS, 86- Personal Data: b Choong-buk, Korea, June 8, 39; US citizen; m 69; c 2. Educ: Seoul Nat Univ, BS, 65, MS, 67; Ind Univ, PhD(physiol), 73. Honors & Awards: Louis N Katz Basic Sci Res Prize, 74; Pfizer Award Outstanding Res, 86. Prof Exp: Res fel biochem, Atomic Energy Res Inst, 67-68; fel cardiac electrophysiol, Univ Chicago, 72-76. Concurrent Pos: Estab investr, Am Heart Asn; adv consult, Site Visit, NIH, 80; vis prof, Nat Defense Med Ctr, Taipei, Repub China, 88; mem, res peer rev comt, NY Heart Asn, 88-; overseas vis fel, Brit Heart Found, 90. Mem: Am Physiol Soc; Biophys Soc; NY Acad Sci; AAAS. Res: Cardiac cellular electophysiology; regulation of intracellular Na and Ca ions in heart muscle; intracellular application of ion-selective microelectrodes, intracellular application of ion sensitive dyes. Mailing Add: Dept Physiol Cornell Univ Med Campus 1300 York Ave New York NY 10021-4805

LEE, CHIN-CHIU, MICROBIOLOGY, ELECTRON MICROSCOPY. Current Pos: RETIRED. Personal Data: b Hunan, China, Aug 10, 34; m 64; c 1. Educ: Taiwan Norm Univ, BSc, 55; Loyola Univ, MS, 64; La State Univ, PhD(parasitol), 68. Prof Exp: Biol teacher, Taiwan Prov Agr Sch, 55-56 & High Sch, Taiwan, 56-58; asst instr biol, Taiwan Norm Univ, 58-59 & Nanyang Univ, 59-61; res technologist biochem, La State Univ, 63, res assoc parasitol, 64; assoc prof biol, King's Col, Pa, 68-91, chmn dept, 77-91. Mem: Am Soc Parasitol; Electron Micros Soc Am; AAAS. Res: Medical parasitology; studies on the physiological and ultrastructural aspects of parasites, particularly of parasitic nematodes. Mailing Add: 29 Maple Dr Swoyersville PA 18704

LEE, CHING TSUNG, QUANTUM OPTICS, MATHEMATICAL PHYSICS. Current Pos: assoc prof, 69-73, PROF PHYSICS & MATH, ALA A&M UNIV, 73- Personal Data: b Taiwan, July 1, 37; m 67; c 2. Educ: Nat Taiwan Univ, BS, 62; Rice Univ, MA, 65, PhD(physics), 67. Prof Exp: Welch Found fel, Tex A&M Univ, 67-68; NASA fel, Rice Univ, 68-69. Mem: Am Phys Soc; Optical Soc Am. Res: Superradiance; free-electron laser; squeezed states. Mailing Add: Dept Physics Ala A&M Univ PO Box 285 Normal AL 35762-0285

LEE, CHING-TSE, ANIMAL BEHAVIOR, BEHAVIOR MEDICINE. Current Pos: from asst prof to assoc prof, 71-82, PROF PSYCHOL, BROOKLYN COL, CITY UNIV NEW YORK, 82- Personal Data: b Sinchu, Taiwan, China, May 21, 40; m 69; c 2. Educ: Nat Taiwan Univ, BS, 63; Bowling Green State Univ, MA, 67, PhD(psychol), 69. Honors & Awards: Nat Sci Coun Award, 79 & 80. Prof Exp: Fac assoc psychol, Univ Tex-Austin, 69-71. Concurrent Pos: Fac res award, City Univ New York, 71, 73, 74; fel, Dept Health Educ & Welfare, 74. Mem: Animal Behav Soc; Am Psychol Asn; AAAS; Behav Genetics Asn. Res: Investigation of animal communication processes through olfaction and hormonal determinants of the production of olfactory signals; effects of neonatal hormones on behavioral differentiation; mathematical models applied to animal behavior; biofeedback and behavior medicine; Chinese medicine theories; states of consciousness. Mailing Add: Dept Psychol Brooklyn Col City Univ New York 2901 Bedford Ave Brooklyn NY 11210-2813

LEE, CHING-WEN, ENGINEERING MECHANICS, SOLID MECHANICS. *Current Pos:* assoc prof, 62-66, PROF ENG SCI & MECH, UNIV TENN, KNOXVILLE, 66- *Personal Data:* b Yunnan, China, Nov 19, 21; US citizen; m 51; c 1. *Educ:* Nat Inst Technol, Chungking, China, BS, 44; Ill Inst Technol, MS, 56, PhD(mech), 58. *Prof Exp:* Staff mem, Res & Develop Lab, Int Bus Mach Corp, Endicott, NY, 59-60; asst prof eng mech, Case Inst Technol, 60-62. *Mem:* Am Soc Mech Engrs; Am Soc Eng Educ; Am Acad Mech. *Res:* Mechanics of deformable solids; elasticity; plates and shells; thermal stresses. *Mailing Add:* 8300 Bennington Dr Knoxville TN 37909

LEE, CHI-YU GREGORY, EXPERIMENTAL BIOLOGY, OBSTETRICS & GYNECOLOGY. *Current Pos:* DIR ANDROLOGY, ACUTE CARE UNIT, UNIV BC, 81-, PROF OBSTET-GYNEC, 89- *Personal Data:* b Taiwan, China, Apr 19, 45; US citizen; c 2. *Educ:* Nat Taiwan Univ, China, BSc, 67; Calif Inst Technol, MSc, 71, PhD(chem), 72. *Prof Exp:* Res chemist, Dept Chem, Univ Calif, San Diego, 72-75; sr staff fel, Lab Animal Genetics, Nat Inst Environ Health Sci, NIH, Research Triangle Park, NC, 76-81. *Concurrent Pos:* Vis prof, Chem Ctr, Univ Lund, Sweden, 75; res asst prof, Dept Biochem, Univ NC, Chapel Hill, 77-81; mem, Task Force Vaccines Fertil Regulation, WHO, 85-; consult, Beckman Instruments Inc. *Mem:* Sigma Xi; AAAS; NY Acad Sci; Am Soc Biol Chemists; Soc Study Reproduction; Am Fertil Soc; Am Asn Clin Chem. *Res:* Applications of biotechnology; sperm antigen-based immunocontraceptive vaccines; new tumor markers for early diagnosis and monitoring of cancer patients; monoclonal antibodies against human proteins-hormones and clinical applications. *Mailing Add:* Acute Care Unit Rm F107 Univ BC Vancouver BC V6T 2B5 Can

LEE, CHONG SUNG, MOLECULAR BIOLOGY. *Current Pos:* asst prof, 72-78, ASSOC PROF MOLECULAR GENETICS, UNIV TEX, AUSTIN, 78- *Personal Data:* b Seoul, Korea, Sept 4, 39; nat US; m 72, Jacqueline Vaughan; c Christopher & Jennifer. *Educ:* Seoul Nat Univ, BS, 64; Calif Inst Technol, PhD(chem), 70. *Prof Exp:* Grad res asst biophys, Calif Inst Technol, 65-69; fel biochem, Harvard Med Sch, 69-72. *Concurrent Pos:* Jane Coffin Childs Mem Fund for Med Res fel, 70-72; vis assoc prof, Harvard Med Sch, 82-83. *Mem:* Genetics Soc Am; Am Soc Cell Biol; Am Soc Biochem & Molecular Biol; Korean Chem Soc. *Res:* Molecular genetics of the rosy locus in Drosophila melanogaster. *Mailing Add:* 7205 Running Rope Circle Univ Tex Austin TX 78712

LEE, CHOONG WOONG, TELECOMMUNICATION SYSTEMS, EDTV & HDTV SIGNAL PROCESSING. *Current Pos:* Lectr, Dept Electronics Eng, 64-71, from asst prof to assoc prof, 71-81, PROF, DEPT ELECTRONICS ENG, SEOUL NAT UNIV, 81- *Personal Data:* b Pyunganpuk-Do, Korea, May 3, 35; m 64; c 4. *Educ:* Seoul Nat Univ, BS, 58, MS, 60; Univ Tokyo, Dr Eng, 72. *Honors & Awards:* Dongbaik Order of Merit. *Concurrent Pos:* Res assoc, Commun Systs Lab, Nat Res Inst Defense, Korea, 58-64; vis res fel, Dept Elec Eng, Univ Sydney, 63 & Univ Tokyo, 69-71; chmn, Bd Utilization Radio Waves, Ministry Commun, Korea, 86-89; pres, Korean Soc Med & Biol Eng, 88 & Korean Inst Telematics & Electronics Engrs, 89; trustee, Korea Telecommun, 91. *Mem:* Fel Inst Elec & Electronics Engrs; Inst Electronics, Info & Commun Engrs Japan; Korean Inst Telematics & Electronics. *Res:* Communication systems especially wide band am, fm demodulators; edtv and hdtv signal processing; medical electronics. *Mailing Add:* Seoul Nat Univ 56-1 Shinlim 2 Dong Gwanack-Gu Seoul 151 742 South Korea

LEE, CHOUNG MOOK, FLUID MECHANICS, OCEAN ENGINEERING. *Current Pos:* VPRES, POHANG INST SCI & TECHNOL, 86- *Personal Data:* b Pyungtek, Korea, Oct 3, 35; m 65; c 2. *Educ:* Seoul Nat Univ, BS, 58; Univ NDak, BS, 61; Univ Calif, Berkeley, MEng, 63, PhD(naval archit), 66. *Honors & Awards:* Linnard Prize, Soc Naval Architechts & Marine Engrs, 75. *Prof Exp:* Res scientist hydrodyn, David Taylor Res Ctr, 66-82; sci officer fluid mech, Off Naval Res, 82-86. *Concurrent Pos:* Adj prof, George Washington Univ, 72-73; vpres, Korea Res Inst Ships, 78-79. *Mem:* Soc Naval Architects & Marine Engrs; Am Soc Mech Engrs; Soc Naval Architects Japan; Sigma Xi. *Res:* Theoretical, mumerical and experimental investigation of ship hydrodynamics; water waves; stability and dynamics of floating and submerged bodies; body-wave interactions; resistance of ships. *Mailing Add:* San 31 Hyojadong Pohang 790-784 South Korea

LEE, CHUAN-PU, BIOCHEMISTRY, PHYSICAL CHEMISTRY. *Current Pos:* PROF BIOCHEM, SCH MED, WAYNE STATE UNIV, 75-, DISTINGUISHED PROF BIOCHEM, 90- *Personal Data:* b Tsing-Tao, China, Sept 24, 31. *Educ:* Nat Taiwan Univ, BS, 54; Ore State Univ, PhD(biochem), 61. *Hon Degrees:* DPhil, Univ Stockholm, 78. *Honors & Awards:* Silver Medal, Chinese Chem Soc, 55; Merck Index Award, 60. *Prof Exp:* Instr chem, Nat Taiwan Univ, 54-56; res assoc biochem, Ore State Univ, 60-61; Johnson Found res fel, Univ Pa, 61-63; Jane Coffin Childs Mem Fund Med Res fel physiol chem, Wenner-Gren Inst, Stockholm, 63-65, docent, 65-66; mem staff, Johnson Found, Univ Pa, 66-75; from assoc prof to prof biochem, 70-75. *Concurrent Pos:* USPHS career develop award, 68-73; ed, Biochimica et Biophysica Acta & Biochimica et Biophysica Acta Review on Bioenergetics, 73-; ed, Current Topics in Bioenergetics, 81- *Mem:* AAAS; Chinese Chem Soc; Am Soc Biol Chem; Biophys Soc; NY Acad Sci. *Res:* Reaction mechanisms of electron and energy transfer in oxidative phosphorylation; neuromuscular diseases and mitochondrial metabolism. *Mailing Add:* 1359 Nicolett Pl Detroit MI 48207-2803

LEE, CHUNG, REPRODUCTIVE ENDOCRINOLOGY, NUTRITION. *Current Pos:* assoc obstet & gynec, 71-74, from asst prof to assoc prof, 74-85, PROF UROL, MED SCH, NORTHWESTERN UNIV, CHICAGO, 85-, PROF CELL, MOLECULAR & STRUCT BIOL, 87-, DIR, UROL RES LAB, 74- *Personal Data:* b Shanghai, China, Sept 18, 36; US citizen; m 65; c 2. *Educ:* Nat Taiwan Univ, BS, 59; WVa Univ, MS, 66, PhD(nutrit & endocrinol), 69. *Prof Exp:* USPHS fel, Albany Med Col, 69-71. *Concurrent Pos:* Prin investr, Am Cancer Soc grant, 73-74, Nat Inst Child Health & Human Develop, 77-91, Abbott Labs grant, 78-84, Elsa Univ Pardee Found grant, 82-84, Nat Inst Diabetes & Digestive & Kidney Dis grant, 87-92; res consult, Matpath, 78, Abbott Labs, 78-, Travenol-Baxter, 83-86, Upjohn Co, 85, Lilly Res Labs, 88-, NuClin Diag, 90; lectr, Cook Col Grad Med Sch, 77-80; treas & chair, Finance Comt, Soc Basic Urol Res, 88-90; pres, Chicago Chap, Soc Chinese Bioscientists Am, 88-; mem, Cancer Prevention Comt, Ill Div, Am Cancer Soc, 88-; vis scholar, Vets Gen Hosp, Taipei, Taiwan, 89. *Mem:* Endocrine Soc; Soc Study Reproduction; Am Asn Cancer Res; Am Physiol Soc; Am Soc Cell Biol; Am Urol Asn; Nat Kidney Found. *Res:* Hormonal regulation of breast and prostate cancer; mechanism of sex steroid action; cancer and hormones; protein analysis and indexing. *Mailing Add:* Dept Urol Tarry 11-715 Northwestern Univ Med Sch 303 E Chicago Ave Chicago IL 60611-3008

LEE, CHUNG JA, NUTRITION. *Current Pos:* From asst prof to assoc prof, 70-78, PROF NUTRIT, DEPT HOME ECON, KY STATE UNIV, 78-, PROG AREA COORDR HUMAN NUTRIT, 82- *Personal Data:* b Seoul, Korea, Jan 3, 38. *Educ:* Seoul Nat Univ, BS, 61; Univ Mass, MS, 68; Purdue Univ, PhD(human nutrit), 70. *Mem:* Am Inst Nutrit; Am Dietetic Asn; Am Home Econ Asn. *Res:* Nutrition. *Mailing Add:* Dept Home Econ Ky State Univ PO Box 77 Frankfort KY 40602-0077

LEE, CHUNG N, MATHEMATICS. *Current Pos:* From instr to asst prof, 60-68, ASSOC PROF MATH, UNIV MICH, ANN ARBOR, 68- *Personal Data:* b Sinuiju, Korea, Nov 7, 31. *Educ:* Seoul Nat Univ, BA, 54; Univ Va, MA, 57, PhD, 59. *Mem:* Am Math Soc. *Res:* Algebraic topology; transformation groups; topology of manifolds. *Mailing Add:* Sci & Technol Pohang Univ Kyung-Buk Pohang 790-784 South Korea

LEE, CINDY, ORGANIC GEOCHEMISTRY, MARINE CHEMISTRY. *Current Pos:* assoc prof, 86-90, PROF, STATE UNIV NY, STONY BROOK, 90- *Personal Data:* b Columbus, Ohio, Feb 10, 50. *Educ:* Ariz State Univ, BSE & BS, 70; Univ Calif, PhD(oceanog), 75. *Prof Exp:* Postdoctoral investr, Woods Hole Oceanog Inst, 75-77, asst scientist, 77-81, assoc scientist, 81-86. *Concurrent Pos:* Co-vchmn, Gordon Conf Chem Oceanog, 89, chmn, 91; Nat Res Coun scope, 91-93; guest prof, Max Planck Inst Marine Microbiol, Bremen, 93-94; trustee, Bermuda Biol Sta Res, 95- *Mem:* Geochem Soc; Am Soc Limnol & Oceanog; Am Geophys Union; Europ Asn Org Geochemists; AAAS; Oceanog Soc. *Res:* Distribution and behavior of biogenic compounds in sediments and waters of open ocean and coastal areas, salt marshes, and lakes; rates and mechanisms of transformation reactions which occur as organic compounds are affected by biological, geological, and physical processes. *Mailing Add:* MSRC State Univ NY Stony Brook NY 11794-5000

LEE, DAEYONG, MECHANICAL & COMPUTER-AIDED ENGINEERING. *Current Pos:* PROF, RENSSELAER POLYTECH INST, TROY, NY, 83- *Personal Data:* b Ham Nam, Korea, June 16, 33; US citizen; m 62, Youngja Kang; c 3. *Educ:* Ripon Col, BA, 58; Mass Inst Technol, BS, 58, MS, 62, ScD(metall), 65. *Prof Exp:* Res asst metall, Mass Inst Technol, 61-65, staff mem, 65-66; res staff, Gen Elec Res & Develop Ctr, Schenectady, 66-83. *Concurrent Pos:* Mech Metall, Ladish Co, 58-60; adj prof, Rensselaer Polytech Inst, Troy, 81-83. *Mem:* Am Inst Mining, Metall & Petrol Engrs; Am Soc Metals; Am Soc Mech Eng; Am Deep Drawing Res; Soc Plastics Engrs. *Res:* Mechanical metallurgy; plasticity theory, mechanics, constitutive equations, nuclear materials, fracture, friction and lubrication, materials processing; computer-aided engineering. *Mailing Add:* 33 Cobble Hill Rd Albany NY 12211. *Fax:* 518-276-6025; *E-Mail:* leed@rpi.edu

LEE, DAH-YINN, CIVIL ENGINEERING, HIGHWAY MATERIALS. *Current Pos:* from asst prof to assoc prof, 65-78, PROF CIVIL ENG, IOWA STATE UNIV, 78- *Personal Data:* b Tsing-tao, China, June 4, 34; m 62; c 2. *Educ:* Cheng Kung Univ, Taiwan, BSc, 58; Iowa State Univ, PhD(civil eng), 64. *Prof Exp:* Res assoc, Eng Res Inst, 64-65. *Concurrent Pos:* Comt mem, Hwy Res Bd, Nat Acad Sci-Nat Res Coun. *Mem:* Am Soc Testing & Mat; Am Soc Civil Engrs; Am Concrete Inst. *Res:* Asphalt durability; aggregates used for asphalt mixtures; waste materials in construction; pavement recycling; foamed asphalt; sulfur in construction. *Mailing Add:* Iowa State Univ Ames IA 50011-2010

LEE, DAISY SI, PEDIATRICS, ALLERGY. *Current Pos:* pediatrician, Ctr Develop & Learning Dis, 69-72, asst prof, 69-76, dir pediat allergy prog, 72-76, ASST CLIN PROF PEDIAT, MED CTR, UNIV ALA, BIRMINGHAM, 76- *Personal Data:* b Peiping, China, July 21, 34; US citizen; m 66, Herbert C Cheung; c Sharon & Melissa. *Educ:* Okla Baptist Univ, BA, 56; Bowman Gray Sch Med, MD, 61; Am Bd Pediat, dipl; Am Bd Allergy & Immunol, dipl, 75. *Prof Exp:* Intern med, Georgetown Div, Washington Gen Hosp, 61-62; resident pediat, St Luke's Hosp Ctr, New York, 62-64, NY Heart Asn fel med, 64-65; fel, Inst Nutrit Sci, Columbia Univ & Dept Med, St Lukes Hosp Ctr, 65-66; fel pediat, Sch Med, Stanford Univ, 66-69. *Mem:* NY Acad Sci; Sigma Xi; Am Acad Allergy; Am Col Allergists. *Mailing Add:* 1025 S 18th St Suite 303 Birmingham AL 35205

LEE, DANIEL DIXON, JR, ANIMAL NUTRITION. *Current Pos:* head, 87-91, PROF DAIRY SCI, CLEMSON UNIV, 91- *Personal Data:* b Dillon, SC, Sept 27, 35; m 58; c 4. *Educ:* Clemson Univ, BS, 57, MS, 64; NC State Univ, Raleigh, PhD(biochem & nutril), 70. *Prof Exp:* Res supvr biochem, NC State Univ, 67-70; from asst prof to assoc prof mineral metab, Dept Animal Indust, Southern Ill Univ, 70-86, asst dean res, Sch Agr, 76-86. *Mem:* Am Soc Animal Sci. *Res:* Trace mineral metabolism; nonprotein nitrogen utilization; wintering of cattle on crop residues and feeding of recycled animal wastes to ruminants. *Mailing Add:* Dept Animal & Vet Sci Clemson Univ 115 Poole Agr Ctr PO Box 340361 Clemson SC 29634-0363

LEE, DAVID ALLAN, APPLIED MATHEMATICS. *Current Pos:* dir, res & develop/procurement, Cost Analysis Div, 85-93, CONSULT, OFF SECY DEFENSE, 93- *Personal Data:* b Ft Smith, Ark, Nov 7, 37; m 60, Shilah Adams; c 2. *Educ:* Univ Mo, Columbia, BSEE, 59; Brown Univ, ScM, 61; Ill Inst Technol, PhD(mech), 63. *Honors & Awards:* Barchi Prize, 95. *Prof Exp:* Res mathematician, Air Force Aerospace Res Labs, 63-71, dir, Appl Math Res Lab, 71-75, head, Dept Math & Comput Sci, USAF Inst Technol, 75-85. *Concurrent Pos:* Vis prof, von Karman Inst Fluid Dynamics, Rhode-St-Genese, Belg, 69-70; sr exec fel, Sr Exec Fel Prog, J F Kennedy Sch, Harvard Univ, 83. *Res:* Econometrics of forecasting development and procurement costs of major defense acquisitions; air traffic capacity modeling. *Mailing Add:* 5305 Crestedge Lane Rockville MD 20853. *E-Mail:* dalee1@delphi.com

LEE, DAVID ANSON, GLAUCOMA, OCULAR PHARMACOLOGY. *Current Pos:* from asst prof to assoc prof, 86-96, CHIEF, GLAUCOMA DIV, JULES STEIN INST, UNIV CALIF, LOS ANGELES, 90-, PROF OPHTHAL, SCH MED, 96- *Personal Data:* b Pine Ridge, SDak, Jan 28, 56; m 90, Karen Q Cheng; c Scott K & Steven M. *Educ:* Boston Univ, BA, 80, MD, 80; Univ Minn, Minneapolis, MS, 84; Univ Calif, Los Angeles, MBA, 93. *Honors & Awards:* Honor Award, Am Acad Ophthal, 95. *Prof Exp:* Internship & residency ophthal, Mayo Clin, Rochester, Minn, 80-84; asst ophthal, Mass Eye & Ear Infirmary, Harvard Univ, 85-86. *Concurrent Pos:* Glaucoma fel, Mass Eye & Ear Infirmary, Harvard Univ, Boston, 84-86; fel, Heed Ophthalmic Found, 84-86; Judson Daland fel, Am Philos Soc, 85-87; vis prof ophthal, Univ Calif, San Diego & Univ Pittsburg, 87, Univ Minn, 88 & 89, Cleveland Clin & Baylor Col Med, 89, Univ Calif, Irvine, 90, Harvard Med Sch, 92 & Univ Mich, 93. *Mem:* Fel Am Acad Ophthal; fel Am Col Surgeons; Soc Heed Fels; Am Col Physician Execs; Asn Res Vision & Ophthal; AAAS. *Res:* Biochemistry, cell biology, and pharmacology of the ciliary body epithelium, trabecular meshwork, and aqueous humor of the eye; development and testing of new ocular drug delivery systems; modulating ocular wound healing. *Mailing Add:* Sch Med Univ Calif 100 Stein Plaza Rm 2-235 Los Angeles CA 90095-7004. *Fax:* 310-206-3652; *E-Mail:* leeda@jsei.ucla.edu

LEE, DAVID CHARLES, MICROBIOLOGY, IMMUNOLOGY. *Current Pos:* asst prof, 85-91, DIR, NUCLEIC ACID CORE FAC, LINEBERGER COMPREHENSIVE CANCER CTR, UNIV NC, CHAPEL HILL, 89-, ASSOC PROF, DEPT MICROBIOL & IMMUNOL, 91- *Personal Data:* b Manchester, Eng, June 10, 50. *Educ:* Stanford Univ, BS, 73; Univ Wash, PhD(biochem), 79. *Prof Exp:* Postdoctoral fel, Dept Biol Chem, Wash Univ, 79-81, Dept Pharmacol, 81-83, res assoc, 83; sr scientist, Oncogen, Seattle, Wash, 83-85. *Concurrent Pos:* Helen Hay Whitney Found fel, 80-83; core mem, Cancer Cell Biol Prog, Lineberger Comprehensive Cancer Ctr, Univ NC, 85-, mem, Pharm Eng & Molecular Genetics Prog, 91- *Res:* Regulation of transforming growth factors; immunoregulatory effects of the interferons; transgenic expression of TGFa and related growth factors. *Mailing Add:* Lineberger Comprehensive Cancer Ctr 229 Sch Med Univ NC Campus Box 7295 Chapel Hill NC 27599-7295

LEE, DAVID K H, BIOCHEMISTRY. *Current Pos:* mgr, 93-96, DIR PHARMACOL, ALLELIX BIOPHARMACEUT INC, 96- *Educ:* McGill Univ, BSc, 69; Queen's Univ, PhD(biochem), 73. *Prof Exp:* Postdoctoral fel, McGill Univ, 73-76, prof asst, 76-77, assoc scientist, Royal Victoria Hosp, 77; sr scientist, Wyeth-Ayerst Res, 77-80, res assoc, 80-86, group leader, 86-88, sect head, 88-89; res mgr, Dept Biochem & Pharmacol, R W Johnson Pharmaceut Res Inst, 89-93. *Mem:* Am Soc Pharmacol & Exp Therapeut; NY Acad Sci; AAAS; Soc Neurosci; Soc Exp Biol & Med. *Res:* Focus on drug discovery activities including high throughput screens and functional assays; therapeutic areas include central nervous system, obesity and virology. *Mailing Add:* Allelix Biopharmaceut 6850 Goreway Dr Mississauga ON L4V 1V7 Can. *Fax:* 905-677-9595; *E-Mail:* dkhlee@ftn.net

LEE, DAVID LOUIS, CHEMISTRY. *Current Pos:* GROUP SUPVR, ICI AMERICAS, 87- *Personal Data:* b Oakland, Calif, Oct 19, 48; m 75; c 2. *Educ:* Univ Calif, Berkeley, BS, 70, PhD(chem), 76; Univ Ill, Urbana, MS, 72. *Prof Exp:* Res assoc chem, Univ Calif, San Francisco, 76-77; sr chemist, Cordova Chem Co, 77-80, res chemist, Stauffer Chem Co, 80-82, sr res chemist, 83-84, group supvr, 85-87. *Mem:* Am Chem Soc. *Res:* Defining the structure-activity space of new classes of herbicides. *Mailing Add:* Zeneca 1200 S 47th St Richmond CA 94804-4610

LEE, DAVID MALLIN, EXPERIMENTAL NUCLEAR PHYSICS, NUCLEAR SAFEGUARDS. *Current Pos:* MEM STAFF, LOS ALAMOS NAT LAB, 74- *Personal Data:* b Brooklyn, NY, Jan 18, 44; m 66; c 5. *Educ:* Manhattan Col, BS, 66; Univ Va, PhD(physics), 71. *Prof Exp:* Res assoc physics, Univ Va, 71-74. *Concurrent Pos:* US expert, Int Atomic Energy Agency, 80-81. *Mem:* Am Phys Soc; Sigma Xi. *Res:* Medium energy nuclear physics; position sensitive detectors; beam line instrumentation. *Mailing Add:* 126 Picdra Loop Los Alamos NM 87544

LEE, DAVID MORRIS, PHYSICS. *Current Pos:* From instr to assoc prof, 59-68, PROF PHYSICS, CORNELL UNIV, 68- *Personal Data:* b Rye, NY, Jan 20, 31; m 60, Dana Thorangkul; c Eric B & James M. *Educ:* Harvard Univ, AB, 52; Univ Conn, MS, 55; Yale Univ, PhD(physics), 59. *Honors & Awards:* Nobel Prize Physics, 96; Sir Francis Simon Mem Prize, British Inst Physics, 76; Oliver Buckley Prize, Am Phys Soc, 81. *Concurrent Pos:* Guggenheim fel, 66-67 & 74-75; guest assoc physicist, Brookhaven Nat Lab, 66-67; Japan Soc Prom Sci fel, 77; lectr, Peking Univ, 81; vis prof, Univ Fla, 74-75 & 94, Univ Calif, San Diego, 88, Joseph Fourier Univ, France, 94-; chmn, Nat Res Coun Comt Fundamental Constants & Stand, 90-93; Sect B Electorate Nominating Comt, AAAS, 90-93. *Mem:* Nat Acad Sci; fel Am Acad Arts & Sci; fel AAAS; fel Am Phys Soc. *Res:* Low temperature physics with emphasis on quantum fluids and solids, and superconductivity; solid helium three and solid helium four; normal and superfluid phases of liquid helium three; spin polarized hydrogen gas; liquid helium three helium four mixtures; magnetic resonance; ultrasonics; magnetism. *Mailing Add:* Lab Atomic & Solid State Physics Cornell Univ Dept Physics Ithaca NY 14853. *E-Mail:* dml20@cornell.edu

LEE, DAVID OI, HEAT TRANSFER, ELECTRO MAGNETIC-SEISMIC GEOPHYSICS. *Current Pos:* Mem tech staff, 67-90, SR MEM TECH STAFF, SANDIA NAT LABS, 90- *Personal Data:* b Hong Kong, China, Feb 5, 40; US citizen; div; c Andrea. *Educ:* Tex A&M Univ, BS, 62, MS, 64. *Concurrent Pos:* Mem, Subcomt Nuclear Qual Assurance, Am Soch Mech Engrs; vchmn, Subcomt Environ Res & Develop & Energy & Environ Qual Div, Am Soc Qual Control. *Mem:* Soc Petrol Engrs; Sigma Xi; Am Soc Mech Engrs; Am Soc Qual Control. *Res:* Heat transfer and fluid mechanics experimental and analytical research; system analysis including economic analysis of solar systems; instrumentation development for enhanced oil recovery; development of seismic tehniques for small event detection; development of electromagnetic techniques for sensing of tunnels and contamination plumes; quality assurance. *Mailing Add:* 12709 Northern Sky NE Albuquerque NM 87111

LEE, DAVID ROBERT, HYDROLOGY, RADIOECOLOGY. *Current Pos:* RES OFFICER HYDROL & RADIOECOL, ATOMIC ENERGY CAN, CHALK RIVER, ONT, 79- *Personal Data:* b Grand Forks, NDak, May 9, 45; m 75; c 5. *Educ:* Univ NDak, BS, 68, MS, 72; Va Polytech Inst & State Univ, PhD(zool), 76. *Prof Exp:* Res asst prof earth sci & biol, Univ Waterloo, 76-79. *Concurrent Pos:* Adj prof, Dept Earth Sci, Univ Waterloo, Ont, 79- *Mem:* Am Geophys Union; Am Soc Limnol & Oceanog. *Res:* Groundwater contaminant flux to surface waters; soil and groundwater remediation. *Mailing Add:* Environ Res Br Chalk River Labs Chalk River ON K0J 1J0 Can

LEE, DAVID WEBSTER, PLANT EVOLUTION, PLANT STRUCTURE & FUNCTION. *Current Pos:* asst prof, 80-82, ASSOC PROF BIOL, FLA INT UNIV, 82- *Personal Data:* b Wenatchee, Wash, Dec 10, 42; m 72, Carol Rotsinger; c Sylvia & Katherine. *Educ:* Pac Lutheran Univ, BS, 66; Rutgers Univ, MS, 68, PhD(bot), 70. *Prof Exp:* Res assoc bot & microbiol, Ohio State Univ, 70-72; lectr, Univ Malaya, Kuala Lumpur, 73-76; maite de conf assoc, Univ Montpellier II, 77-78. *Concurrent Pos:* Indo-Am fel, 84-85; field res, Cent Am & Southeast Asia. *Mem:* Am Bot Soc; Soc Trop Biol; Ecol Soc Am; Sigma Xi. *Res:* Evolution and adaptation of plants in humid tropical forests. *Mailing Add:* Dept Biol Sci Fla Int Univ Miami FL 33199

LEE, DER-TSAI, COMPUTER SCIENCE, COMPUTATIONAL GEOMETRY. *Current Pos:* from asst prof to assoc prof, 78-86, PROF ELEC & COMPUT ENG, NORTHWESTERN UNIV, 86- *Personal Data:* b Taipei, Taiwan, Apr 5, 49; m 74; c 2. *Educ:* Nat Taiwan Univ, BS, 71; Univ Ill, MS, 76, PhD(comput sci), 78. *Prof Exp:* Res asst comput sci, Univ Ill, 74-78. *Concurrent Pos:* Consult, Gen Elec Co, 77 & 79, IBM Corp, 82 & USDA, 85; prin investr, NSF, 79-; vis prof, Academia Sinica, 84-85,; ed, Algorithmica, 85-; prog dir, Div Comput & Comput Res, NSF, 89-90; managing ed, Int J Computational Geom & Applns, 90- *Mem:* Fel Inst Elec & Electronics Engrs; fel Asn Comput Mach; Soc Indust & Appl Math. *Res:* Design and analysis of algorithms; computational geometry and data structures; very large scale integration systems; computer graphics; visualization tool development. *Mailing Add:* Dept Elec & Comput Eng Northwestern Univ Evanston IL 60208. *Fax:* 847-467-4144; *E-Mail:* dtlee@ece.nwu.edu

LEE, DIANA MANG, LIPOPROTEINS. *Current Pos:* RES ASSOC PROF, RES DIV WOMEN'S HEALTH DEPT OBSTET/GYNEC, HEALTH SCI CTR, UNIV OKLA, 94- *Personal Data:* b Mukden, China; US citizen; m 60, Fu Chu; c Amy J. *Educ:* Nat Taiwan Univ, BS, 55; Utah State Univ, MS, 60; Univ Okla, PhD(biochem), 67. *Prof Exp:* Chemist analytical chem, Yung-Kang Cement Corp, 55-57; univ asst chem eng, Nat Taiwan Univ, 57; supvr chem, Presby-St Luke's Hosp, 61-64, trainee lipoproteins, 64-67; assoc prof biochem, Sch Med, Univ Okla, 76-93; sr investr, Okla Med Res Found, 67-71, asst mem, 71-75, assoc mem lipoproteins, 75-92, assoc mem, Free Radical Biol & Aging Res Prog, 92-94. *Concurrent Pos:* Res assoc, Dept Biochem, Sch Med, Univ Okla, 68-71, asst prof, 72-76, assoc prof, 76-; NIH grant awardee, 71-; mem, Coun Arteriosclerosis, Credential Comt, Am Heart Asn, 73-75; assoc ed, Artery, 75-; reviewer, Biochem & Biophys Act, 77-83, 87-; consult, NIH, 79-81; mem, arteriosclerosis hypertension & lipid metab adv comt, Nat Heart Lung & Blood Inst, NIH, 92-93; numerous grants awarded. *Mem:* Am Chem Soc; Sigma Xi; AAAS; Am Oil Chemists Soc; NY Acad Sci; Am Soc Biol Chemists; Am Heart Asn. *Res:* Structural aspects of human plasma lipoproteins and apolipoproteins, particularly in low density lipoproteins and apolipoprotein B; lipid peroxidation; antioxidants; estrogen and autiatheiosclerosis. *Mailing Add:* Dept Obstet/Gynec 4SP-700 Okla Univ MSC PO Box 26901 Oklahoma City OK 73190

LEE, DO IK, LATEX TECHNOLOGY, POLYMER SCIENCE. *Current Pos:* res chem engr, Dow Chem USA, 67-72, res specialist, 72-75, sr res specialist, 75-79, assoc scientist, 79-82, sr assoc scientist, 82-88, res scientist, 88-96, SR SCIENTIST, DOW CHEM CO, 97- *Personal Data:* b Chinnampo, Korea, Mar 6, 37; nat US; m 70, Ilhae Kim; c Albert K. *Educ:* Seoul Nat Univ, BS, 59; Columbia Univ, MS, 64, EngScD(chem eng), 67. *Honors & Awards:* Coating & Graphic Arts Div Award, Tech Asn Pulp & Paper Indust; Charles W Engelhard Medallion, 86; Midland Sect Award, Am Chem Soc, 89. *Prof Exp:* Meteorol officer, Korean Air Force, 58-61; res asst, Chem Eng Dept, Columbia Univ, 62-67. *Concurrent Pos:* Tech adv, Inst Chang-Gang Paper Technol, Kangwon Nat Univ. *Mem:* Am Inst Chem Engrs; Am Chem Soc; fel Tech Asn Pulp & Paper Indust; Sigma Xi; Korean-Am Scientist & Engrs Asn; Polymer Soc Korea. *Res:* Rheology of disperse systems; coating rheology; colloid science; paper coating technology; emulsion polymerization; inverse emulsion polymerization; suspension polymerization; latex technology; polymer morphology; polymerization kinetics; structured latex polymerization; particle packing; thermal properties of latexes; plastic pigments. *Mailing Add:* Dow Chem Co Emulsion Polymers Res & Develop 1604 Bldg Midland MI 48674. *Fax:* 517-638-6356; *E-Mail:* dil@dow.com

LEE, DO-JAE, PHYSICAL ORGANIC CHEMISTRY. *Current Pos:* RETIRED. *Personal Data:* b Namwon, Korea, Jan 24, 28; US citizen; m 57; c 2. *Educ:* Long Beach State Col, BS, 60; San Diego State Col, MS, 64; Univ Calif, San Diego, PhD(chem), 67. *Prof Exp:* Res chemist, Toms River Chem Corp, 68-90. *Mem:* Am Chem Soc. *Res:* Development of new dyestuff and economic process for plant production. *Mailing Add:* 34 Oakside Dr Toms River NJ 08755

LEE, DONALD GARRY, PHYSICAL CHEMISTRY, ORGANIC CHEMISTRY. *Current Pos:* assoc prof, 67-71, PROF CHEM, UNIV REGINA, 71-, PRES LUTHER COL. *Personal Data:* b Midale, Sask, June 21, 35; m 59, Marilyn Hultgren; c Wendy, Eric & Rebecca. *Educ:* Univ Sask, BA, 58, MA, 60; Univ BC, PhD(chem), 63. *Prof Exp:* Res assoc, Harvard Univ, 65-66, pres, Lutheran Col, Univ Regina. *Concurrent Pos:* Vis scholar, Univ Oslo, 72-73; vis prof, Stanford Univ, 80-81. *Mem:* Chem Inst Can; Am Chem Soc. *Res:* Oxidation mechanisms; protonation studies; heavy oil and coal research; environmental assessment. *Mailing Add:* Dept Chem Univ Regina Regina SK S4S 0A2 Can. *Fax:* 306-585-4894

LEE, DONALD JACK, NUTRITIONAL BIOCHEMISTRY. *Current Pos:* asst dir, Agr Res Ctr, 75-84, team leader, Lesotho Farming Systs Proj, 84-86, DEPT CHAIR, FOOD SCI & HUMAN NUTRIT, WASH STATE UNIV, 86- *Personal Data:* b Goldendale, Wash, Jan 28, 32; m 58; c 3. *Educ:* Wash State Univ, BS, 58, MS, 60; Univ Ill, PhD(nutrit, biochem), 65. *Prof Exp:* Assoc prof food sci & technol, Food Protection Sect, Ore State Univ, 65-75. *Concurrent Pos:* USPHS res grant, 66-75. *Mem:* Inst Food Technologists; Am Inst Nutrit; Sigma Xi; Am Dietetic Asn. *Res:* Nutritional biochemistry, especially lipid metabolism; toxicity and carcinogenicity of natural compounds. *Mailing Add:* Food Sci & Human Nutrit Wash State Univ Pullman WA 99163. *Fax:* 509-335-4815; *E-Mail:* leed@wsuvm1.csc

LEE, DONALD WILLIAM, FLUID MECHANICS, APPLIED MECHANICS. *Current Pos:* res assoc fluid mech, 77-81, res staff mem, 81-89, GROUP LEADER APPL PHYS SCI, OAK RIDGE NAT LAB, 89- *Personal Data:* b Buffalo, NY, Nov 4, 47; m 78; c 2. *Educ:* Clarkson Col, BS, 69, MS, 73; Univ Mich, PhD(appl mech), 77. *Prof Exp:* Engr, Ford Motor Co, 69-70; teaching fel mech eng, Clarkson Col Technol, 70-71; res asst appl mech, Univ Mich, 71-76. *Concurrent Pos:* Instr gen sci, Wayne State Univ, 75-76; adj assoc prof, NC State Univ, 87-; mem, Low-level Radioactive Waste Tech Resource Group for 40CFR 193 & Low-level Radioactive Waste Peer Rev Panel for Dept Energy Order 5820-2A, 88-; secy, Air & Radiation Mgt Comt Environ Eng Div, Am Soc Civil Eng, 89-90, vchmn, 90- *Mem:* Am Soc Civil Engrs; Am Soc Mech Engrs; Sigma Xi. *Res:* Environmental fluid dynamics of surface water and groundwater; environmental impact assessment of energy technologies; low-level radioactive waste management. *Mailing Add:* 6400 Brandywine Dr Lenoir City TN 37772-6847

LEE, DONG HOON, LIE GROUPS & LIE ALGEBRAS, TOPOLOGICAL GROUPS. *Current Pos:* From asst prof to assoc prof, 67-80, PROF MATH, CASE WESTERN RES UNIV, 81- *Personal Data:* b Seoul, Korea, Nov 17, 38; m 68; c 2. *Educ:* Seoul Nat Univ, BS, 61; Tulane Univ, PhD(math), 67. *Concurrent Pos:* Vis prof math, Seoul Nat Univ, 76-77. *Mem:* Am Math Soc. *Res:* Representation theory of lie groups and lie algebras. *Mailing Add:* Math Dept Case Western Res Univ Cleveland OH 44106-4901

LEE, DOUGLAS HARRY KEDGWIN, ENVIRONMENTAL SCIENCES. *Current Pos:* RETIRED. *Personal Data:* b Bristol, Eng, Feb 22, 05; nat US & Australia; m 52, Dorothy Yingling; c Roderick K. *Educ:* Univ Queensland, MSc, 27; Univ Sydney, MB & BS, 29, dipl trop med, 33, MD, 40; FRACP, 40; Am Bd Indust Hyg, dipl. *Hon Degrees:* MD, Univ Queensland, 86. *Honors & Awards:* Cutter Lectr, Sch Pub Health, Harvard Univ, 50; Order of Australia, 95; Bancroft Medal Queenslane, Inst Med Res, 96. *Prof Exp:* Med officer, Commonwealth Dept Health, Australia, 30-33; prof physiol, King Edward VII Col Med, Singapore, 35-36; prof physiol, Univ Queensland, 36-48, dean fac med, 38-42; prof physiol climat & lectr environ med, Johns Hopkins Univ, 48-55; chief, Res Br, Off Qm Gen, 55-58; assoc sci dir res, Qm Res & Eng Command, 58-60; chief occup health res & training facility, USPHS, 60-66, assoc dir, Nat Inst Environ Health Sci, 66-73; fel, Queensland Inst Med Res, 83; emer prof, Univ Queensland, 90. *Concurrent Pos:* Consult, US Qm Corps, 47-55 & Food & Agr Orgn, UN, 47-60, Mt Sinai Med Sch, 74-76; adj prof, NC State Univ, 68-74. *Mem:* Am Physiol Soc; fel NY Acad Sci. *Res:* Climatic physiology, effects of climate on man and animals and application to clothing, housing and tropical development; occupational and environmental health. *Mailing Add:* 211/180 Swan Rd Taringa Qld 4068 Australia

LEE, DOUGLAS SCOTT, DEVELOPMENT & APPLICATION OF MANNED & UNMANNED SUBMERSIBLES FOR BIOGEOCHEMICAL & ECOLOGICAL SAMPLING & RESEARCH, FISH FORAGING ECOLOGY & HABITAT SELECTION. *Current Pos:* FRESHWATER PROG DIR, NAT UNDERSEA RES CTR, UNIV CONN, 89-, ASST PROF MARINE SCI, DEPT MARINE SCI, 89- *Personal Data:* b Eugene, Ore, July 22, 58; m 83, Mary B Haynes; c Kevin S. *Educ:* Ore State Univ, BS, 80, MS, 84; Mich State Univ, PhD(zool-ecol), 89. *Concurrent Pos:* Prin investr, Nat Oceanic & Atmospheric Admin Nat Undersea Res Prog, 85-86, 88, 90 & 92-, Great Lakes Fishery Comn, 85-86, Conn Dept Environ Protection, 92-94; co-prin investr, NSF, 92-94. *Mem:* Int Asn Great Lakes Res; Am Fisheries Soc; Ecol Soc Am; Am Soc Naturalists. *Res:* Administration and development of manned and unmanned submersible research in the Great Lakes; fish feeding ecology, habitat selection and contaminant cycling. *Mailing Add:* 45 Hedge Ave Norwich CT 06360. *Fax:* 860-445-2969; *E-Mail:* dslee@uconnvm.uconn.edu

LEE, E(RNEST) BRUCE, CONTROL ENGINEERING. *Current Pos:* assoc prof, 63-66, head dept, 76-81, PROF ELEC ENG, UNIV MINN, MINNEAPOLIS, 66- *Personal Data:* b Brainerd, Minn, Feb 1, 32; m 54; c 6. *Educ:* Univ NDak, BS, 55, MS, 56; Univ Minn, PhD(mech eng), 60. *Prof Exp:* Sr res scientist, Honeywell Inc, 56-60, vis scientist, Res Inst Advan Studies, 60-61; sr res scientist, Honeywell Inc, 61-63. *Mem:* Soc Indust & Appl Math; Inst Elec & Electronics Engrs. *Res:* Learning systems; differential equations; optimal control theory. *Mailing Add:* Dept Elec Eng Univ Minn 200 Union St Minneapolis MN 55455-0160

LEE, E(UGENE) STANLEY, OPERATIONS RESEARCH, COMPUTER SCIENCE. *Current Pos:* from asst prof to assoc prof chem eng, 66-71, PROF INDUST ENG, KANS STATE UNIV, 71- *Personal Data:* b Hopei, China, Sept 7, 30; US citizen; m 57, 83, Yuan C; c Linda J, Margaret H, Lynn, Jin & Ming. *Educ:* Chieng-Cheng Inst Tech Taiwan, BChE, 53; Univ NC, MS, 57, Princeton Univ, PhD(chem eng), 62. *Prof Exp:* Res engr, Phillips Petrol Co, Okla, 60-66. *Concurrent Pos:* NSF grant, 71-; vis prof, Univ Southern Calif, Los Angeles, 72-76; ed, Energy Sci & Technol, 77-; assoc ed, J Math Analysis & Applin & Math with Appln, assoc ed, Comput & Math with Appln, Off Air Res Grantee, USDA. *Mem:* Soc Indust & Appl Math; Am Inst Chem Engrs; Opers Res Soc Am; Inst Indust Engrs. *Res:* Optimization theory; applied mathematics; quasilinearization and invariant imbedding; systems engineering; set theory; expert systems. *Mailing Add:* Dept Indust Eng Kans State Univ 237 Durland Hall Manhattan KS 66506-5101. *E-Mail:* eslee@ksuvm.ksu.edu

LEE, EDWARD HSIEN-CHI, PLANT PHYSIOLOGY, ENVIRONMENTAL SCIENCE. *Current Pos:* PLANT PHYSIOLOGIST, AGR RES SERV, USDA, 78- *Personal Data:* b Taiwan, Aug 31, 35; m 67, Amy Cheng; c Tony & Michael. *Educ:* Nat Taiwan Univ, BS, 59; Univ Kans, MA, 66; Univ Okla, PhD(bot), 69. *Prof Exp:* Lab instr gen bot & taxon, Nat Taiwan Univ, 61-64; teaching asst gen bot & physiol, Univ Okla, 66-69; assoc prof cellular physiol, genetics & microbiol, Cent Methodist Col, Mo, 69-78. *Concurrent Pos:* Adj prof, Dept Natural Resource Sci & Landscape Archit, Univ Md, Col Park, 85- *Mem:* AAAS; Am Soc Plant Physiol; Plant Growth Regulator Soc Am; Sigma Xi; Scand Soc Plant Physiol; NAm Taiwanese Prof Asn. *Res:* Environmental stress, air pollution, photosynthesis and oxidative stress. *Mailing Add:* Climate Stress Lab Bldg 046A USDA-Agr Res Serv 10300 Baltimore Ave Beltsville MD 20705-2350. *Fax:* 301-504-7521; *E-Mail:* elee@asrr.arsusda.gov

LEE, EDWARD PRENTISS, PHYSICS. *Current Pos:* STAFF PHYSICIST ACCELERATOR PHYSICS, LAWRENCE BERKELEY LAB, 82- *Personal Data:* b Tulsa, Okla, Oct 3, 42. *Educ:* Calif Inst Technol, BS, 64; Univ Chicago, MS, 66, PhD(physics), 68. *Prof Exp:* Mem staff plasma physics, Inst Advan Study, Princeton, NJ, 68-70; staff physicist plasma physics, Lawrence Livermore Lab, 70-82. *Mem:* Fel Am Phys Soc. *Res:* High current charged particle beams; controlled thermonuclear fusion; astrophysics; particle accelerators. *Mailing Add:* 310 Monte Vista Ave Mill Valley CA 94941

LEE, ELHANG HOWARD, PHOTONICS, SEMI CONDUCTOR SCIENCE. *Current Pos:* EXEC DIR & VPRES RES, KOREA ELEC & TELECOMMUN RES INST, 90- *Personal Data:* b Seoul, Korea, Dec 19, 47; m 74, Namsoo Chang; c David & Jennifer. *Educ:* Seoul Nat Univ, BS, 70; Yale Univ, MS, 73, MPhil, 75, PhD(appl physics), 77. *Honors & Awards:* Nat Medal Hon, Pres Korea; Outstanding Acad Contrib Award, Korean Phy Soc. *Prof Exp:* Res staff scientist, Yale Univ, 78-79; res assoc scientist, Princeton Univ, 79-80; res scientist, Monsanto Co, 80-84; sr mem res staff, AT&T Bell Labs, 84-90. *Concurrent Pos:* Vis prof, Korea Advan Inst Sci & Technol, 92; adj prof, Chungham Nat Univ, Korea, 92-; exec dir, Int Soc Optic Engrs (Korea), 92-; chmn, Laser & Electro-Optic Soc, Int Elec & Electronics Engrs (Korea), 94- *Mem:* Fel Korean Phys Soc; Sigma Xi; fel Optic Soc Korea; Am Phys Soc; Optic Soc Am; NY Acad Sci; AAAS. *Res:* Optoelectronics and photonics for light waves, optical communication and information processing; semiconductor physics, materials and devices for electronics, telecommunications and information technology; author of over 250 papers and 2 book publications. *Mailing Add:* ETRI Daeduck Sci Town Yusong PO Box 106 Daejeon City 305600 South Korea. *Fax:* 82-42-860-6836; *E-Mail:* ehlee@ard.etri.re.kr

LEE, ELLEN SZETO, modeling & simulation, design, for more information see previous edition

LEE, EMERSON HOWARD, PHYSICAL CHEMISTRY, SURFACE CHEMISTRY. *Current Pos:* RETIRED. *Personal Data:* b Okmulgee, Okla, Feb 23, 21; m 48, Margaret J; c Stephen, Richard, Don & Thomas. *Educ:* Univ Tex, BS, 52, PhD(chem), 55. *Prof Exp:* Chemist, Darco Div, Atlas Powder Co, 46-50; res engr, Develop & Res Dept, Continental Oil Co, 54-56; res chemist, Monsanto Co, 56-59, res specialist, 59-60, group leader, 60-65, scientist, 65-82; consult, 82-85. *Mem:* Am Chem Soc; Sigma Xi. *Res:* Surface chemistry and catalysis. *Mailing Add:* 48 Beaver Dr St Louis MO 63141

LEE, ENG-HONG, COCCIDIOSIS VACCINES FOR COMMERCIAL CHICKENS & TURKEYS, IMPROVEMENT OF COCCIDIOSIS VACCINE THROUGH BIOTECHNOLOGY. *Current Pos:* PRES, VETECH LABS, INC, 83- *Personal Data:* b Butterworth, Malaysia, Jan 13, 44; Can citizen; m, Marilyn Breazeale; c May M & Alan W. *Educ:* Nanyang Univ, Singapore, BSc, 67; Univ Guelph, MSc, 70; Univ Mass, Amherst, PhD(zool), 74. *Prof Exp:* Fel, Nat Res Coun, Ottawa, 74-75; res assoc, Univ Guelph, 76-81. *Mem:* Am Soc Parisitol; NY Acad Sci. *Res:* Developed, patented and commercialized a live coccidiosis vaccine for chickens and turkeys which appeared to be effective and is in use worldwide; developed a gel-delivery system for vaccines and microingredients. *Mailing Add:* Vetech Labs Inc 131 Malcolm Rd Rockwood ON N1K 1A8 Can. *Fax:* 519-822-9471

LEE, ERASTUS HENRY, PLASTICITY, CONTINUUM MECHANICS. *Current Pos:* RETIRED. *Personal Data:* b Southport, Eng, Feb 2, 16; c 4. *Educ:* Cambridge Univ, UK, BA, 37, MA, 43; Stanford Univ, PhD(mech eng), 40. *Honors & Awards:* Timoshenko Medal, Am Soc Mech Engrs, 76. *Prof Exp:* Exp sci officer, Ordnance Bd, War Off, UK, 41-43 & Armaments Res Dept, Ministry Supply, UK, 43-46; asst dir tech eng, Dept Atomic Energy, UK, 46-48; from assoc prof to prof appl math, Brown Univ, 48-62, chmn, Div Appl Math, 53-58; prof appl mech & aero eng, Stanford Univ, 62-81; Redfern prof eng, Rensselaer Polytech Inst, 81- *Mem:* Nat Acad Eng; fel Am Soc Mech Engrs; fel Inst Mech Eng UK; fel Am Acad Mech; fel Soc Eng Sci. *Res:* plasticity analysis and constitutive equations. *Mailing Add:* 22 Pearce Pl Stanford CA 94305

LEE, ERIC KIN-LAM, CHEMICAL ENGINEERING, POLYMER CHEMISTRY. *Current Pos:* VPRES TECHNOL & ENG, HEMASURE INC, 94- *Personal Data:* b Hong Kong, June 25, 48; m 72; c 1. *Educ:* NC State Univ, BS, 70, MS, 72, PhD(chem eng), 76. *Prof Exp:* Proj mgr, Bend Res, Inc, 77-84; sr res eng, DuPont Co, 84-86; dir membrane res & technol develop, Sepracor Inc, 86-93. *Concurrent Pos:* Res fel, Max Planck Inst Biophys, 76-77. *Mem:* Am Inst Chem Engrs; Am Chem Soc; NAm Membrane Soc. *Res:* Research and development of synthetic membranes and other separation media; design and engineering of devices, systems and processes for medical, biotechnical and industrial applications. *Mailing Add:* Hemasure Inc 140 Locke Dr Marlborough MA 01752. *Fax:* 508-485-6045; *E-Mail:* elee@hemasure.com

LEE, ERNEST Y, BIOCHEMISTRY, MOLECULAR BIOLOGY. *Current Pos:* PROF BIOCHEM, DEPT BIOCHEM & MOLECULAR BIOL, SCH MED, UNIV MIAMI, 67- *Mailing Add:* Biochem & Molecular Biol Dept Sch Med R629 Univ Miami PO Box 016129 Miami FL 33101-6129

LEE, EUN SUL, SURVEY SAMPLING, DEMOGRAPHIC METHODS. *Current Pos:* res biometrician, 69-72, from asst prof to assoc prof, 72-87, PROF BIOMET & DEMOG, SCH PUB HEALTH, UNIV TEX HEALTH SCI CTR, HOUSTON, 87- *Personal Data:* b Gongju, Korea, Sept 19, 34; US citizen; m 64; c 2. *Educ:* Seoul Nat Univ, BA, 57; Univ Ky, MA, 64; NC State Univ, PhD(exp statist & sociol), 70. *Prof Exp:* Res assoc statist analysis, NC Bd Higher Educ, 66-69. *Concurrent Pos:* Vis prof, Dept Sociol, Utah State Univ, 75; UN Fund Pop Activ, Pop & Develop Inst, Seoul Nat Univ, 76; fel hist med, Univ Cincinnati, Nat Endowment Humanities, 80. *Mem:* Biomet Soc; Am Statist Asn; Pop Asn Am; Am Pub Health Asn; Int Union Sci Study Pop. *Res:* Ethnic differentials in mortality, fertility and health behavior; public health policy analysis; changing cardiovascular mortality and morbidity trends; sample survey design. *Mailing Add:* Sch Pub Health Univ Tex Health Sci Ctr PO Box 20186 Houston TX 77225

LEE, FANG-JEN SCOTT, BIOCHEMISTRY, MICROBIOLOGY. *Current Pos:* SR STAFF, LAB CELLULAR METAB, NAT HEART, LUNG & BLOOD INST, NIH, 90- *Personal Data:* b Taipei, Taiwan, Apr 20, 57; US citizen; m 84, Leewen Lin; c Alice & Albert. *Educ:* Nat Taiwan Univ, BS, 80; NC State Univ, MS, 84, PhD(biotechnol & microbiol), 86. *Prof Exp:* Res fel, Dept Genetics, Harvard Med Sch & Dept Molecular Biol, Mass Gen Hosp, 87-90. *Concurrent Pos:* Consult, Yung-Shin Pharmaceut Industs Co Ltd, 86-90. *Mem:* Am Soc Biochem & Molecular Biol; Am Soc Microbiol; AAAS; Protein Soc; Sigma Xi. *Res:* Investigation of protein processing and signal transduction. *Mailing Add:* Inst Molecular Med Sch Nat Taiwan Univ No 7 Chung Shan South Rd Taipei MD 20892 Taiwan

LEE, FLOYD DENMAN, NUCLEAR PHYSICS. *Current Pos:* ASSOC PROF PHYSICS, MONT STATE UNIV, 68- *Personal Data:* b Hays, Kans, Apr 27, 38. *Educ:* Univ Kans, BS, 60, PhD(physics), 66. *Prof Exp:* Instr physics, Univ Kans, 65-66; Nat Acad Sci-Nat Res Coun assoc, 66-68. *Mem:* Am Asn Physics Teachers; Am Phys Soc. *Res:* Low-energy nuclear research with Van-de-Graaf accelerators; nuclear structure. *Mailing Add:* Dept Physics AJM Johnson Hall Mont State Univ Bozeman MT 59717-0001

LEE, FRED C, POWER CONVERSION. *Current Pos:* DIR, TECHNOL DEVELOP CTR POWER ELECTRONICS, 87- *Personal Data:* US citizen; c 2. *Educ:* Nat Cheng Kung Univ, Taiwan, BS, 68; Duke Univ, Durham, MS, 72, PhD(elec eng), 74. *Honors & Awards:* Ralph R Teeter Award, Soc Automotive Eng, 85; William E Newell Power Electronics Award, Inst Elec & Electronics Engrs, Power Electronics Soc, 89. *Prof Exp:* Teaching asst, Duke Univ, 70-72, res asst, Spacecraft Systs Res Lab, 72-77; from asst prof to prof, 77-86, dir, Va Polytech Eng Ctr, Va Polytech Inst & State Univ, 85-, James S Tucker Prof, 86- *Concurrent Pos:* Assoc ed, Inst Elec & Electronics Engrs Trans Power Electronics, 85-; mem, Power Electronics Coun, Inst Elec & Electronics Engrs, 85-87; bd dirs, Zytec Corp, 86- & adv bd, Power Integrations Inc, 88- *Mem:* Fel Inst Elec & Electronics Engrs; Inst Elec & Electronics Engrs Indust Applications Soc; Inst Elec & Electronics Engrs Power Electronics Soc (vpres, 88-89); Brit Inst Elec Engrs. *Res:* Power conversion; power devices; high frequency resonant converters; distributed power systems; power hybrids; space power systems; nonlinear control; design optimization; system modeling; analysis and simulation. *Mailing Add:* 2909 Stradford Lane Blacksburg VA 24060

LEE, FREDERICK STRUBE, PHYSICAL CHEMISTRY. *Current Pos:* prof chem, Baltimore Jr Col, 61-71, dir gen studies, 71-76, dir sci, bus & technol studies, 76-79, PROF MATH, COMMUNITY COL BALTIMORE, 61- *Personal Data:* b Baltimore, Md, Dec 26, 27; m 52; c 3. *Educ:* Johns Hopkins Univ, AB, 50; Brown Univ, PhD(chem), 58. *Prof Exp:* Res chemist, Agr Div, W R Grace & Co, 58-60 & Analysis & Phys Div, 60-61. *Mem:* Sigma Xi. *Res:* X-ray crystallography; inorganic synthesis; physical inorganic chemistry. *Mailing Add:* 9126 Winands Rd Owings Mills MD 21117-4824

LEE, GARRETT, CARDIOVASCULAR RESEARCH, LASER MEDICINE. *Current Pos:* DIR RES, WESTERN HEART INST, SAN FRANCISCO, 84- *Personal Data:* b San Francisco, Calif, June 23, 46. *Educ:* Univ Calif, Berkeley, BA, 68; Univ Calif, Davis, MD, 72. *Prof Exp:* Internship med, Duke Univ Med Ctr, 72-73; residency med, Univ Calif, Davis, 73-75, fel cardiol, 74-76, asst prof med, 76-83; dir, Laser Res Lab, Cedars Med Ctr, Fla, 83-84. *Concurrent Pos:* Med dir, Aspirin Myocardial Infarction Study, Univ Calif, Davis, 75-78; med consult, Calif Comn Peace Officer Stand, 75-80; chmn, cardiovasc Curric, Univ Calif, Davis, 79-83, dir, Cardiac Cath Lab, 78-83; bd dir, Am Heart Assoc, 81-83; counr, Am Fedn Clin Res, 77-81. *Mem:* Am Col Cardiol; Am Soc Laser Med & Surg; Am Col Clin Pharmacol; Am Col Angiol; Am Fedn Clin Res; Am Heart Asn. *Res:* Cardiovascular pharmacology and interventional cardiology including lasers and heart disease, angioscopy, balloon angioplasty and thrombolytic therapy in acute myocardial infarction; pain management with low power lasers. *Mailing Add:* Western Heart Inst 450 Stanyan St San Francisco CA 94117

LEE, GARY ALBERT, WEED SCIENCE. *Current Pos:* asst dir agr res, Univ Idaho, 79-80, head, Dept Plant, Soil & Entom Sci, 80-86, assoc dean res & dir, Idaho Agr Exp Sta, 86-95, PROF WEED SCI, UNIV IDAHO, 75- *Personal Data:* b Scottsbluff, Nebr, May 18, 41; m 62, Georgia Scott; c Michael, Michelle & Megan. *Educ:* Univ Wyo, BS, 64, MS, 65, PhD(agron), 71. *Prof Exp:* Instr weed sci, Univ Wyo, 65-71, from asst prof to assoc prof, 71-75. *Concurrent Pos:* Consult, US Borax Res Corp, 75-; pres, Western Soc Weed Sci; bd dirs, WSSA, 77-79, ICIA, 80-86, WRAC, 86-; secy, WAAESD, 87-88, pres, 90; bd dirs, Ctr Appl Sri Technol, 90; bd dir, Far West Agro Chem Asn, 96- *Mem:* Weed Sci Soc Am; Am Soc Sugarbeet Technologists; Soc Range Mgt; Int Crop Improv Asn; hon mem Western Soc Weed Sci. *Res:* Mechanisms of herbicide selectivity in agronomic crops and perennial weed control; population dynamics of weeds in agronomic crops and rangeland; influence of herbicides on the metabolism of weed species; biological control and integrated weed management systems. *Mailing Add:* 5572 N Eddy Pl Boise ID 83703-6607

LEE, GEORGE C, STRUCTURAL ENGINEERING, BIOMECHANICS. *Current Pos:* asst prof civil eng, State Univ NY, Buffalo, 61-63, assoc prof, 63-67, actg chmn, Dept Civil Eng, 70-71, chmn, 72-77, dir grad studies, 71-78, dir socio-eng prog, 71-78, dir, Health Instrument & Device Inst, 84-85, PROF ENG & APPL SCI, STATE UNIV NY, BUFFALO, 67-, DEAN ENG & APPL SCI, 78-, ASSOC DIR, CALSPAN-STATE UNIV NY, BUFFALO RES CTR, 83- *Personal Data:* b Peiping, China, July 17, 32; m 61; c 2. *Educ:* Nat Taiwan Univ, BSE, 55; Lehigh Univ, MS, 58, PhD(civil eng), 60. *Honors & Awards:* Adams Mem Award, Am Welding Soc, 74; Super Accomplishment Award, NSF, 77. *Prof Exp:* Res fel civil eng, Lehigh Univ, 56-57, from res asst to res assoc, Frit Eng Lab, 57-61. *Concurrent Pos:* Spec eng consult, Struct Dynamics Dept, Bell Aerosysts Co, 65-; NIH grant & sr res fel, Dept Physiol, Harvard Univ, Sch Pub Health, 69-70; head eng mech sect, NSF, 77-78. *Mem:* Am Soc Civil Engrs; Am Soc Eng Educ; Am Welding Soc; Sigma Xi; AAAS. *Res:* Buckling and stability analysis of structural members, frames, plates and shells; ultimate strength design; respiratory mechanics and lung elasticity; earthquake engineering; cold regions engineering. *Mailing Add:* Red Jacket Quad NCEER Box 610025 Buffalo NY 14261-0025

LEE, GEORGE H, II, ENVIRONMENTAL ANALYSIS. *Current Pos:* assoc chief, Forensic & Doc Div, Air Force Drug Testing Lab, 86-88, chief, Volatile Org Function, Occup & Environ Health Directorate, 88-92, analytical chem consult, 92-94, EXEC MGR, ANALYTICAL SERV DIV, ARMSTRONG LAB, AIR FORCE CTR ENVIRON EXCELLENCE, BROOKS AFB, TEX, 94- *Personal Data:* b Ithaca, NY, Feb 26, 39; m 64, June Esther Brown; c David Michael & Daniel Stephen. *Educ:* Rensselaer Polytech Inst, BChE, 61, PhD(phys chem), 65. *Prof Exp:* Res assoc, Cornell Univ, 65-67; res chemist, Res Ctr, Hercules Inc, Del, 67-71; sr res chemist, Dept Phys & Biol Sci, Southwest Res Inst, 71-73; assoc found scientist, Southwest Found Res & Educ, 73-77; sr res scientist fire technol, Southwest Res Inst, 77-81, sr res scientist, US Army Fuels & Lubricants Res Lab, 81-86. *Concurrent Pos:* Adj prof, Earth & Phys Sci, Univ Texas, San Antonio. *Mem:* Sigma Xi; AAAS; Astron Soc Pac. *Res:* Analysis of potable and non-potable waters, soils and tissues for toxic contaminants. *Mailing Add:* 11107 Whispering Wind San Antonio TX 78230. *Fax:* 210-536-9043; *E-Mail:* glee@guardian.brooks.af.mil

LEE, GLENN RICHARD, INTERNAL MEDICINE, HEMATOLOGY. *Current Pos:* RETIRED. *Personal Data:* b Ogden, Utah, May 18, 32; m 69; c 2. *Educ:* Univ Utah, BS, 53, MD, 56. *Prof Exp:* Intern med, Boston City Hosp, 56-57, asst resident, 57-58; clin fel hemat, Univ Utah, 60-61, res fel, 61-63, from instr to assoc prof, 63-73, assoc dean acad affairs, 73-76, prof med, 73-94, dean, Col Med, 78-94. *Mem:* Am Fedn Clin Res; Am Soc Hemat; Am Col Physicians; Am Soc Clin Invest. *Res:* Clinical and experimentally induced abnormalities in heme biosynthesis; physiologic consequences of copper deficiency; iron metabolism. *Mailing Add:* 3781 S Ruth Dr Holladay UT 84124

LEE, GLORIA, NEURONAL CYTOSKELETON. *Current Pos:* ASST PROF NEUROSCI, DEPT NEUROL, BRIGHAM & WOMEN'S HOSP, 86- *Personal Data:* m 85, Craig T Morita; c Stephen & Catherine. *Educ:* Univ Calif, AB, 74; Harvard Univ, PhD, 81. *Mem:* Soc Neurosci; Am Soc Cell Biol. *Res:* Regulation of cytoskeletal changes taking place during neuronal differentiation. *Mailing Add:* Brigham Group Dept Neurol Brigham & Women's Hosp 221 Longwood Ave Boston MA 02115. *Fax:* 617-732-7787; *E-Mail:* glee@cnd.bwh.harvard.edu

LEE, GORDON M(ELVIN), ELECTRICAL ENGINEERING. *Current Pos:* CONSULT, 81- *Personal Data:* b Minneapolis, Minn, Jan 3, 17; m 41, Harriet Malkerson; c Theodore, James, David & Mary. *Educ:* Univ Minn, BEE, 38; Univ Mo, MS, 39; Mass Inst Technol, DSc(elec eng), 44. *Honors & Awards:* Thompson Mem Prize, Inst Elec & Electronics Engrs, 46. *Prof Exp:* Asst elec eng, Univ Mo, 38-39; asst elec engr, Mass Inst Technol, 39-44, mem staff, Div Indust Coop, 44-45; tech dir elec eng & secy-treas, Cent Res Labs, Inc, Sargent Industs, 45-73, pres, 73-81. *Concurrent Pos:* Mem, Nat Defense Res Comt, 44; lectr, Univ Minn, 48. *Mem:* AAAS; Am Nuclear Soc; Inst Elec & Electronics Engrs. *Res:* Remote handling equipment; properties of dielectrics; high-speed oscillography; development of high-speed micro-oscillograph and remote handling equipment. *Mailing Add:* PO Box 308 Brainerd MN 56401. *Fax:* 218-828-0306

LEE, GRETA MARLENE, CELL BIOLOGY, VIDEO MICROSCOPY. *Current Pos:* Lawton Chiles biotechnol fel, Dept Cell Biol & Anat, 89-92, RES ASST PROF, UNIV NC, CHAPEL HILL, 92- *Personal Data:* b El Paso, Tex. *Educ:* Univ Mo, Columbia, BS, 71; ETenn State Univ, MS, 83; Duke Univ, PhD(zool), 89. *Mem:* Am Soc Cell Biol. *Res:* Chondrocyte biology, dynamic structure of pericellular and extracellular matrices; movements of individual molecules on living cells using specific colloidal gold probes and video enhanced light microscopy. *Mailing Add:* Dept Cell Biol & Anat Arthritis Res Ctr Univ NC 5107 Thruston Bldg CB 7280 Chapel Hill NC 27599-7280. *Fax:* 919-966-1856

LEE, GRIFF C, OFFSHORE DESIGN, OFFSHORE CONSTRUCTION. *Current Pos:* PRES, GRIFF C LEE INC, 83- *Personal Data:* b Jackson, Miss, Aug 17, 26; m 50; c 3. *Educ:* Tulane Univ, BE, 48; Rice Univ, MS, 51. *Prof Exp:* Civil engr, Humble Oil & Refining Co, 48-54; prin engr & design engr, 54-66, chief engr, 66-75, group vpres, 75-78, vpres res & develop, McDermott Inc, 78-83. *Concurrent Pos:* Mem, Marine Bd Nat Res Coun, Offshore Comt Am Petrol Inst, comt-Offshore Technol Detnorske Veritas, Welding Res Coun, Tech Panel Offshore Installations for Lloyd's Register Shipping, Comt Offshore Platforms & Bd Adv, Tulane Univ, 80- *Mem:* Nat Acad Eng; hon mem Am Soc Civil Engrs; Am Concrete Inst; Am Welding Soc; Soc Petrol Eng. *Res:* Advanced engineering technology; offshore construction for the petroleum industry. *Mailing Add:* Griff Lee Inc PO Box 70787 New Orleans LA 70172. *Fax:* 504-539-7203

LEE, H(O) C(HONG), MECHANICAL ENGINEERING. *Current Pos:* staff engr, IBM Corp, 68-70, adv engr, 70-77, sr engr, 77-89, SR TECH STAFF MEM, IBM CORP, 89- *Personal Data:* b Seoul, Korea, Aug 2, 33; m 65; c 2. *Educ:* Univ Bridgeport, BS, 57; Rensselaer Polytech Inst, MME, 59, PhD(mech eng), 62. *Prof Exp:* Asst prof mech eng, Rensselaer Polytech Inst, 62-68. *Concurrent Pos:* Consult, Mech Tech, Inc, 62-65 & Gen Elec Co, 65-68; adj assoc prof, Rensselaer Polytech Inst, 68-70. *Mem:* Am Soc Mech Engrs. *Res:* Dynamics of structural elements; rotor dynamics. *Mailing Add:* 8 Tudor Dr Endicott NY 13760

LEE, HAROLD HON-KWONG, DEVELOPMENTAL BIOLOGY, BIOTECHNOLOGY. *Current Pos:* PROF BIOL, UNIV TOLEDO, 75-, DIR, MASTER LIB STUDIES, 88- *Personal Data:* b China, Jan 31, 34; m 66; c 2. *Educ:* Okla Baptist, AB, 56; Univ Tenn, MS, 58, PhD(embryol), 65. *Prof Exp:* USPHS fel, Carnegie Inst, 65-67. *Concurrent Pos:* Am Cancer Soc, NIH grants, Rockefeller, United Nations grants, Lolor Found, res grants. *Mem:* Soc Develop Biologists; AAAS. *Res:* Cell interactions and fertilization development of reproduction; biotechnology; tissue culture. *Mailing Add:* Dept Biol Univ Toledo 2801 W Bancroft St Toledo OH 43606-3328

LEE, HARVEY SHUI-HONG, DYNAMICS OF VEHICLES ON GUIDEWAY. *Current Pos:* MECH ENGR, US DEPT TRANSP, 75- *Personal Data:* b China, Feb 7, 49; US citizen. *Educ:* Newark Col Eng, BSc, 72; Ohio State Univ, MSc, 74. *Mem:* Am Soc Mech Engrs. *Res:* Vehicle dynamics as it relates to safety; response of railroad vehicles to track irregularities that could lead to derailments; safety considerations of magnetically levitated trains. *Mailing Add:* US Dept Transp John A Volpe Nat Transp Systs Ctr DTS-76 Kendall Sq Cambridge MA 02142. *Fax:* 617-494-3616; *E-Mail:* leeh@volpez.dot.gov

LEE, HAYNES A, LASERS, GLASS TECHNOLOGY. *Current Pos:* RETIRED. *Personal Data:* b Johnson City, Tenn, Oct 14, 32; m 59; c 3. *Educ:* Emory & Henry Col, BS, 54; State Univ NY Col Ceramics, Alfred Univ, MS, 61. *Prof Exp:* Glass technologist, Thatcher Glass Mfg Co, NY, 61-63; glass technologist, Owens-Ill Inc, 63-66, glass scientist, 66-68, chief laser scientist, 68-72; gen mgr optical prod, Laser Inst Am, 73-80, gen mgr, 81- *Concurrent Pos:* Bd dir, Laser Inst Am, 75-80. *Mem:* Am Ceramic Soc; Sigma Xi; Laser Inst Am; Optical Soc Am. *Res:* Electronic pheonmena in glasses, particularly laser phenomena. *Mailing Add:* 5845 Viramar Rd Toledo OH 43611

LEE, HENRY C, FORENSIC SCIENCE & CRIMINAL INVESTIGATION, BIOCHEMISTRY. *Current Pos:* Asst prof, 75-76, assoc prof & dir forensic sci, 76-78, DIR, CTR APPL RES, UNIV NEW HAVEN, 76-, DIR, FORENSIC SCI LAB, 77-, PROF FORENSIC SCI, 78-; CHIEF, CONN STATE FORENSIC SCI LAB, 79- *Personal Data:* b China, Nov 22, 38; US citizen; m 63, Margaret Lee; c Sherry & Stanley. *Educ:* John Jay Col NY, BS, 72; NY Univ, MS, 74, PhD(biochem), 75. *Hon Degrees:* DSc, Univ New Haven, 90; LHD, St Jospeh Univ, 96. *Honors & Awards:* Distinguished Criminalist Award, Am Acad Forensic Sci, 88, Distinguished Fel Award, 94; John Dondero Award, Int Asn Identification, 89, Distinguished Sci Serv Medals, 86, 90 & 96. *Concurrent Pos:* Consult, Conn State Police Forensic Lab, 75; vis prof, Seton Hall Univ, 76, Northeastern Univ, 77-79 & Law Sch, Univ Conn, 93; vis fac, Yale Univ, 78; res grant, Univ New Haven, 78 & 79; ed, Forensic Sci, 81-, Forensic Rev, 89- & Am J Forensic Path, 90-; res scientist, Med Ctr, NY Univ. *Mem:* NY Acad Sci; fel Am Acad Forensic Sci; AAAS; Am Soc Testing & Mat; Am Soc Crime Lab Dirs; Int Found Sci; distinguished mem Int Asn Identification; fel Eng Fingerprint Soc. *Res:* Protein biosynthesis; blood individualization; forensic science and crime scene investigation; forensic chemistry; DNA typing; fingepirnt and trace analysis. *Mailing Add:* Forensic Sci Lab 278 Colony St Meriden CT 06451-2098. *Fax:* 203-639-6486

LEE, HENRY JOUNG, ANTI-INFLAMMATORY STEROIDS. *Current Pos:* from asst prof to assoc prof, 73-82, PROF MED CHEM, COL PHARM, FLA A&M UNIV, 82- *Personal Data:* b Seoul, SKorea, Nov 17, 41; US citizen; m 69; c 3. *Educ:* Seoul Nat Univ, BS, 64, MS, 66; Okla State Univ, PhD(biochem), 71. *Prof Exp:* Instr food technol, Seoul Women's Col, 66-67; res asst biochem, Okla State Univ, 67-71 & res assoc, Mt Sinai Sch Med, 71-73. *Concurrent Pos:* Vis scientist, Rockefeller Univ, 79; prin investr, NIH, 79-; grant reviewer, 85; consult, Taisho Pharmaceut Co, 85, Sandoz Pharmaceut Co, 86- *Mem:* Sigma Xi; Am Chem Soc; Am Soc Biol Chemists. *Res:* Chemical synthesis and evaluation of new anti-inflammatory steroids without adverse effects. *Mailing Add:* Dept Med Chem Fla A&M Sch Pharm Pharm Bldg Rm 227 Tallahassee FL 32307

LEE, HOONG-CHIEN, physics, for more information see previous edition

LEE, HSI-NAN, atmospheric science, mathematic numerical techniques, for more information see previous edition

LEE, HSIN-YI, developmental biology, for more information see previous edition

LEE, HUA, ACOUSTIC MICROSCOPY, IMAGING ALGORITHM DESIGN. *Current Pos:* PROF ELEC ENG, UNIV CALIF, SANTA BARBARA, 90- *Personal Data:* b Taipei, Taiwan, Sept 30, 52; m 76; c 2. *Educ:* Nat Taiwan Univ, BS, 74; Univ Calif, Santa Barbara, MS, 78, PhD(elec eng), 80. *Prof Exp:* Asst prof elec eng, Univ Calif, Santa Barbara, 80-83; from asst prof to assoc prof elec eng, Univ Ill, 83-90. *Concurrent Pos:* Presidential young investr award, 85. *Mem:* Inst Elec & Electronics Engrs; Acoust Soc Am. *Res:* All aspects of the imaging technology; high-resolution high-speed imaging techniques; imaging system optimization; radar and sonar imaging; signal analysis and processing; biomedical imaging, high resolution gerome sequencing; computer vision and non-destructive evaluation. *Mailing Add:* Dept Elec & Comput Eng Univ Calif Santa Barbara CA 93106

LEE, HUA-TSUN, MATHEMATICS, LINEAR & INTEGER PROGRAMMING. *Current Pos:* from asst prof to assoc prof, 69-82, PROF MATH, POINT PARK COL, 82- *Personal Data:* b Nanking, China, May 11, 37; m 63; Su Ling; c Amy, Albert, Margaret & Lita. *Educ:* Tunghai Univ, Taiwan, BS, 59; Univ Pittsburgh, PhD(math), 71. *Prof Exp:* Asst physics, Tunghai Univ, Taiwan, 61; asst physics, Univ Pittsburgh, 61-64, asst math, 65-67 & 68-69, instr biostatist, Grad Sch Pub Health, 67-68. *Concurrent Pos:* Assoc prof, Fudan Univ, 80-81. *Mem:* Math Asn Am. *Res:* Summability methods of infinite series; linear programming; integer programming. *Mailing Add:* 8 Coral Dr Pittsburgh PA 15238

LEE, HULBERT AUSTIN, GEOLOGY. *Current Pos:* pres, 69-96, CONSULT GEOLOGIST, LEE GEO-INDICATORS LTD, 69- *Personal Data:* b Chelsea, Que, June 17, 23; m 47, Katherine A Yuill; c Edith, Eleanor, Thomas, Douglas & Barbara. *Educ:* Queen's Univ, Ont, BSc, 49; Univ Chicago, PhD(geol), 53. *Prof Exp:* Geologist, Geol Surv Can, 50-69. *Concurrent Pos:* Vis lectr, Univ NB, 64-65. *Mem:* Fel Geol Soc Am; Can Inst Mining & Metall; Prospectors & Developers Asn. *Res:* Correlation of quaternary events around Hudson Bay, the Tyrrell Sea and Keewatin ice divide; quaternary studies in New Brunswick; esker and till methods of mineral exploration now firmly established and extensively used in the exploration industry; kimberlite petrology, engineering terrain analysis of Ontario; morphology and significance of gold particles. *Mailing Add:* 10 Alexander St Box 68 Stittsville ON K2S 1A2 Can

LEE, HUNG, ENVIRONMENTAL MICROBIOLOGY, CATABOLIC GENES & ENZYMES. *Current Pos:* asst prof, 86-91, ASSOC PROF ENVIRON MICROBIOL, UNIV GUELPH, 91- *Personal Data:* b Kaoshiung, Taiwan, Nov, 1954; Can citizen; m 90, Colleen McCann; c Jeremy & Jasmine. *Educ:* Univ BC, BSc, 77; McGill Univ, PhD(biochem), 82. *Honors & Awards:* Citation for Res Excellence Award, Imp Oil Ltd, 90. *Prof Exp:* Res assoc, Nat Res Coun Can, 83-86. *Concurrent Pos:* Fel, Med Res Coun Can, 84; adj prof, Sch Eng, Univ Guelph, 92-; vis prof, Biotechnol Lab, Univ BC, 92-93. *Mem:* Am Soc Microbiol; Soc Indust Microbiol. *Res:* Biotransformation and biodegradation of environmental pollutants; molecular cloning and characterization of catabolic genes; structure-function and protein engineering studies of catabolic enzymes; detection and monitoring of microorganisms in the environment; metabolism and bioconversion of hemicellulosic sugars. *Mailing Add:* Dept Environ Biol Univ Guelph Guelph ON N1G 2W1 Can. *Fax:* 519-837-0442; *E-Mail:* hlee@uoguelph.ca

LEE, HYUNG MO, MEDICINE, VASCULAR & TRANSPLANT SURGERY. *Current Pos:* res fel, 59-61, from instr to prof, 63-96 EMER PROF SURG, MED COL VA, 96- *Personal Data:* b Tanchon, Korea, Sept 27, 26; US citizen; m 59; c 2. *Educ:* Keijo Imp Univ, BS, 45; Seoul Nat Univ, MD, 49. *Prof Exp:* Res fel surg, Med Col Va, 59-61. *Concurrent Pos:* Dir, Clin Transplant Prog, Med Col Va, 73-94, chmn, Div Vascular & Transplant Surg, 73-94, Div Vascular Surg, 94-96. *Mem:* Am Col Surgeons; Am Soc Nephrology; Transplantation Soc; Am Soc Transplant Surgeons (secy, 81-83, pres, 84-85); Int Cardiovasc Surg Soc; Int Soc Heart Transplantation; Int Soc Nephrology. *Res:* Renal homotransplantation. *Mailing Add:* Dept Surg Med Col Richmond VA 23298-0057. *Fax:* 804-828-2744

LEE, I P, MOLECULAR BIOLOGY, ENDOCRINOLOGY. *Current Pos:* RES PHARMACOLOGIST MOLECULAR TOXICOL, DEPT HEALTH & HUMAN SERV, FOOD & DRUG ADMIN, 85- *Personal Data:* b Rupl Korea, Dec 25, 35; US citizen; m 62; c 4. *Educ:* Pac Lutheran Univ, BA, 59; Univ Wash, MS, 69, PhD(pharmacol), 71. *Prof Exp:* Res pharmacologist, Nat Cancer Inst, NIH, 69-72, Nat Inst Environ Health Serv, 72-85. *Concurrent Pos:* Vis prof, Fed Tech Univ & Univ Zurich, Inst Toxicol, 75-76, Med Sch, Cath Univ, 83, Med Sch, Yonsei Univ, 84, Beijing Polytech Univ, 87. *Mem:* Am Soc Pharmacol & Exp Therapeut; Soc Toxicol; Sigma Xi. *Res:* Metabolism and toxicology of chemical carcinogens in male reproductive tissues. *Mailing Add:* Dept Health & Human Serv & Molecular Toxicol Food & Drug Admin HFF-162 8301 Muirkirk Rd Laurel MD 20708

LEE, ILZOO, PROPULSION, MATERIALS SYNTHESIS & CHARACTERIZATION. *Current Pos:* SR MEM TECH STAFF, AEROSPACE CORP, 97- *Personal Data:* b Seoul, Korea, Jan 12, 58; US citizen. *Educ:* Han Yang Uni, Seoul, Korea, BS, 82; Alfred Univ, MS, 84; Univ Utah, PhD(mat sci & eng), 89. *Prof Exp:* Post-doctoral fel, Mat Sci & Eng, Univ Utah, 90-91; mat scientist, Res Dept, Naval Air Warfare Ctr, 91-97. *Mem:* Am Ceramic Soc; Am Chem Soc; Am Inst Aeronaut & Astronaut. *Res:* Thermomechanical properties of propellant and explosives; synthesis and characterizations of optical and structural ceramics by selgel technology; solid rocket propulsion system. *Mailing Add:* PO Box 92957-M4/969 Los Angeles CA 90009-2957. *E-Mail:* leei@courier4.aero.org

LEE, INSUP, COMPUTER & INFORMATION SCIENCES. *Current Pos:* ASSOC PROF COMPUT SCI, UNIV PA, 83- *Personal Data:* b Seoul, Korea, Mar 15, 55; c 2. *Educ:* Univ NC, Chapel Hill, BS, 77; Univ Wis, Madison, MS, 78 & PhD(comput sci), 83. *Mem:* Inst Elec & Electronics Engrs; Am Comput Mach. *Res:* Distributed real-time computing. *Mailing Add:* Dept Comput & Info Sci 6389 Univ Pa Moore Sch Elec Eng Philadelphia PA 19104

LEE, I-YANG, NUCLEAR PHYSICS. *Current Pos:* physicist, 75-77, STAFF PHYSICIST NUCLEAR PHYSICS, LAWRENCE BERKELEY LAB, 92- *Personal Data:* b Nanking, China, Dec 21, 46; m 72, Eva Hsu; c Helen & Haidy. *Educ:* Nat Taiwan Univ, BSc, 68; Univ Pittsburgh, PhD(physics), 74. *Prof Exp:* Physicist, Oak Ridge Nat Lab, 77-92. *Mem:* Am Phys Soc. *Res:* Nuclear physics. *Mailing Add:* Nuclear Sci Div Bldg 88 Lawrence Berkeley Nat Lab Berkeley CA 94720. *E-Mail:* iylee@lbl.gov

LEE, JA H, PLASMA PHYSICS. *Current Pos:* SR RES SCIENTIST, NASA LANGLEY RES CTR, 83- *Personal Data:* b Hamyang, S Korea, Apr 25, 25; US citizen; m 52, Chang Bok Choi; c Yeunggil, Yeung-Sook, Insook & Yeung W. *Educ:* Kyungpook Nat Univ, Korea, BS, 48; George Peabody Col, Nashville, MS, 61; Vanderbilt Univ, Nashville, MS, 62, PhD(physics), 64. *Honors & Awards:* Group Achievement Awards, NASA, 79, 81, 92, Tech Excellence Award, 88. *Prof Exp:* Prof physics, Kyungpook Nat Univ, Daegu, Korea, 65-67; res assoc physics, NASA/Nat Acad Sci, 67-69; sr res assoc, Vanderbilt Univ, Nashville, 69-73, res assoc prof, 73-78, res prof physics, 78-83. *Concurrent Pos:* Prin investr grants, Langley Res Ctr, NASA, 69-; adj res prof physics, Hampton Univ, 80- *Mem:* Am Phys Soc; Inst Elec & Electronics Engrs. *Res:* Pulsed high beta plasma; high-pulsed power sources, solar pumped laser and laser pumping source development; atomic and molecular spectroscopy. *Mailing Add:* 37 E Governor Dr Newport News VA 23602-7405. *Fax:* 757-864-7730

LEE, JAMES A, HUMAN ECOLOGY, PUBLIC HEALTH. *Current Pos:* PROF SCI & PUB POLICY, WILLIAM & MARY COL, 91- *Personal Data:* b Troy, NY, July 11, 25; m 46; c 1. *Educ:* Union Col, BS, 49; Cornell Univ, MS, 51; George Washington Univ, MPh, 69, PhD, 70; Univ Sarajevu, Dr(med), 78. *Hon Degrees:* LLD, Penn Col, 79. *Prof Exp:* Sr res biologist, NH, 51-56; tech asst dir, State Conserv Dept, Minn, 56-61, from dep comnr to comnr, State Dept Resources Develop, 61-63; scientist adminr, USPHS, Washington, DC, 63-66, asst environ health to asst secy health & sci affairs, Dept HEW, 67-69, dir human ecol, 69-70; dir environ, health & sci, World Bank, 70-90. *Concurrent Pos:* Vis prof, Sch Med, Cornell Univ, 76-; co-chmn, Int Trop Dis Res Prog & Int Diarrheal Dis Control Prog; Woodrow Wilson vis fel, 81-; clin prof, Sch Med, Univ Miami, 84-; exec dir, Olde Towne Med Ctr, 91- *Mem:* Am Col Prev Med; Ecol Soc Am; Am Soc Trop Med & Hyg; Royal Soc Trop Med & Hyg; Royal Medical Soc; Sigma Xi; Am Col Epidemiol. *Res:* Environmental, public health, and socio-cultural aspects of international economic development; human ecology with emphasis on multi-environmental causation of diseases; social anthropology and medical sociology; natural resources planning and management. *Mailing Add:* 112 Cove Rd Williamsburg VA 23185. *Fax:* 757-221-2390

LEE, JAMES B, ENDOCRINOLOGY, METABOLISM. *Current Pos:* PROF MED, SCH MED, STATE UNIV NY, BUFFALO, 71-, CHMN, HUMAN INSTNL REV BD, 82- *Personal Data:* b Ware, Mass, June 30, 30; m 64; c 2. *Educ:* Col Holy Cross, AB, 51; Jefferson Med Col, MD, 56. *Prof Exp:* Intern med, St Vincent Hosp, Worcester, Mass, 56-57; resident, Pa Hosp, Philadelphia, 57-58; resident, Georgetown Univ Hosp, 58-59; USPH res fel renal metab, Peter Bent Brigham Hosp, Boston, 59-62; dir res metab & endocrinol, St Vincent Hosp, Worcester, 62-68; assoc prof med & chief sect exp med, Sch Med, St Louis Univ, 68-71; med dir, Skilled Nursery Fac, Erie Co Med Ctr, 81-87. *Concurrent Pos:* Mass Heart Asn res grant, 62-; USPHS res grant, 62-, develop training grant, 64-; asst prof, Georgetown Univ Hosp, 63-68. *Mem:* Am Physiol Soc; Am Soc Clin Invest; Am Fedn Clin Res; Endocrine Soc; Am Heart Asn. *Res:* Hypertension; in vitro metabolism of kidney cortex and medulla related to sodium excretion; isolation and indentification of the renal prostaglandes, from renal medulla and their deficency as a cause of essential hypertension. *Mailing Add:* 135 Cary Hall State Univ NY Med Sch Buffalo NY 14214

LEE, JAMES C, HUMAN BIOLOGY CHEMICAL & GENETICS. *Current Pos:* PROF & ROBERT A WELCH CHAIR CHEM, DEPT HUMAN BIOL CHEM & GENETICS, UNIV TEX MED BR, GALVESTON, 90- *Personal Data:* b Shanghai, China, Dec, 16, 41; US citizen; m 69, Lucy Wang; c Ching-Wen & Ching-Men. *Educ:* Hope Col, BA, 66; Case Western Res Univ, PhD(biochem), 71. *Prof Exp:* Postdoctoral fel, Grad Dept Biochem, Brandeis Univ, Boston, Mass, 71-76; from asst prof to prof biochem, St Louis Univ, Mo, 76-90. *Concurrent Pos:* Mem, Molecular & Cellular Biophys Study Sect, NIH, 81-85 & spec study sect, 89, 90 & 91; vis prof, State Univ NY, Stony Brook, 86. *Mem:* Am Chem Soc-Div Biol Chem; AAAS; Biophys Soc; Am Soc Biol Chemists; Am Soc Cell Biol. *Res:* Elucidate the regulatory mechanisms of biological functions at the molecular level; gene expressions; supramacromolecular assembly; enzyme activity. *Mailing Add:* Human Biol Chem & Genetics Dept Univ Tex Med Br Galveston TX 77555-1055

LEE, JAMES MOON, BIOCHEMICAL ENGINEERING, PLANT CELL CULTURE. *Current Pos:* assoc prof, 83-88, PROF CHEM ENG, WASH STATE UNIV, 88- *Personal Data:* b Seoul, Korea, Nov 3, 46; US citizen; m 72, Inn-Soo Sohn; c Young-Jean. *Educ:* Yon-Sei Univ, Korea, BS, 70, MS, 72; Univ Ky, PhD(chem eng), 78. *Prof Exp:* Lectr chem, Korea Mil Acad, 73-76; from asst prof to assoc prof chem eng, Cleveland State Univ, 78-83. *Concurrent Pos:* Consult, Zinpro Corp, Edina, Minn, 93-95. *Mem:* Am Chem Soc; Am Inst Chem Engrs. *Res:* Production of secondary metabolites or foreign protein products from large-scale plant suspension cell culture; mass transfer; mixing; fermentation; bioreactor design. *Mailing Add:* Chem Eng Dept Wash State Univ Pullman WA 99164-2710. *Fax:* 509-335-4806; *E-Mail:* jmlee@che.wsu.edu

LEE, JAMES NORMAN, MAGNETIC RESONANCE IMAGING. *Current Pos:* asst prof radiol, 88-93, ADJ ASST PROF BIOENG, UNIV UTAH, 90- *Personal Data:* b Santa Monica, Calif, Dec 20, 56; m 79, Kim Bailey; c Bethany, Jessica & Christina. *Educ:* Univ Utah, BA, 80, MS, 82; Duke Univ, PhD, 86. *Prof Exp:* Res assoc, Duke Univ, 86-88. *Res:* New techniques in magnetic resonance imaging. *Mailing Add:* Med Imaging Res Lab AC 213 Sch Med Univ Utah Salt Lake City UT 84132. *Fax:* 801-585-3592; *E-Mail:* jim@doug.med.utah.edu

LEE, JANG Y, CARDIOVASCULAR. *Current Pos:* RES INVESTR, DEPT CARDIOVASC PHARMACOL, ABBOTT LABS, 84- *Mailing Add:* Dept Cardiovasc Pharmacol Abbott Labs Dept 47-B/AP-9 Abbott Park IL 60064-3500

LEE, JEAN CHOR-YIN WONG, BIOCHEMISTRY. *Current Pos:* group leader, 86-93, DIR SCI SERV, HARRIS LABS, INC, 93-; ADJ ASST PROF, UNIV NEBR, LINCOLN, 87- *Personal Data:* b Canton, China, Aug 26, 41; m 67, Kit Wi; c Garland & Clifford. *Educ:* Chung Chi Col, Hong Kong, dipl, 62; Univ Nebr, Lincoln, PhD(chem), 67. *Honors & Awards:* Lewis E Harris Award for Excellence, 89. *Prof Exp:* Res instr biochem, Col Med, Univ Nebr, Omaha, 67-70; fel chem & res assoc, Univ Nebr, Lincoln, 70-86. *Mem:* Am Chem Soc; Am Asn Pharmaceut Sci; Clin Ligand Assay Soc. *Res:* Biomembranes, structure and transport; analysis of pharmaceuticals. *Mailing Add:* PO Box 80837 Harris Lab Inc Lincoln NE 68501-0837

LEE, JEFFREY STEPHEN, INDUSTRIAL HYGIENE, OCCUPATIONAL HEALTH. *Current Pos:* asst prof, 80-87, DIR INDUST HYG, ROCKY MT CTR ENVIRON HEALTH, UNIV UTAH, 79-, ASSOC PROF, DEPT FAMILY & COMMUNITY MED, MED SCH, 87- *Personal Data:* b Salt Lake City, Utah, Aug 25, 44; m 69; c 2. *Educ:* Univ Utah, BS, 67; Univ Calif, Berkeley, MPH, 71, PhD(environ health), 80. *Prof Exp:* Indust hygienist, Nat Inst Occup Safety & Health, 69-76; dep dir, Health Response Team, Occup Safety & Health Admin, US Dept Labor, 76-79. *Concurrent Pos:* Chmn, Conf Govt Indust Hygienists. *Mem:* Am Acad Indust Hyg; Am Indust Hyg Asn; Am Conf Gov Indust Hyg; Am Pub Health Asn; Int Occup Hyg Asn (pres). *Res:* Industrial hygiene and occupational health; asbestos; quantification and toxicology of particulates specifically cadmium; industrial hygiene problems related to mining and new energy development. *Mailing Add:* Dept Family & Community Med Univ Utah Sch Med 50 N Medical Dr Salt Lake City UT 84132-0001

LEE, JEN-SHIH, ENGINEERING MECHANICS. *Current Pos:* from asst prof to assoc prof, 69-83, PROF BIOMED ENG, UNIV VA, 84-, CHAIR DEPT, 88- *Personal Data:* b Kwangtung, China, Aug 22, 40; nat US; m 66; c Lionel, Grace & Albert. *Educ:* Nat Taiwan Univ, BS, 61; Calif Inst Technol, MS, 63, PhD(aeronaut, math), 66. *Prof Exp:* Asst res engr, Univ Calif, San Diego, 66-69. *Concurrent Pos:* San Diego Co Heart Asn advan res fel, 66-69; USPHS res grant, Univ Va, 71; Nat Heart & Lung Inst res career develop award, 75-80. *Mem:* Am Physiol Soc; Biomed Eng Soc; fel Am Soc Mech Engrs; Inst Elec & Electronics Engrs; Microcirc Soc; fel Am Inst Med & Biol Eng; Biomed Eng Soc (pres-elect, 93-94). *Res:* Hemodynamics; pulmonary mechanics and edema; indicator dilution technique as applied to microcirculation and transcapillary exchange in microvessels. *Mailing Add:* Dept Biomed Eng Univ Va Health Sci Stacey Hall Charlottesville VA 22908-0001

LEE, JOE, TRANSPORTATION ENGINEERING, TRAFFIC ENGINEERING. *Current Pos:* from asst prof to assoc prof civil eng, 71-81, PROF CIVIL ENG, UNIV KANS, 81-, DIR, TRANSP CTR, 77- *Personal Data:* b Shanghai, China, Mar 2, 39; US citizen; m 70; c 2. *Educ:* Nat Taiwan Univ, BSc, 61; Asian Inst Technol, MEng, 66; Ohio State Univ, PhD(transp & traffic eng), 71. *Prof Exp:* Installation officer maintenance, Chinese Air Force, 61-62; field engr construct, BES Eng Corp, 62-64; res asst, Asian Inst Technol, 64-66 & Ohio State Univ, 66-71. *Concurrent Pos:* Prin investr, Ctr Res, Inc, Univ Kans, 74-; consult, UN, 88-; adv prof, Xian Hwy Univ, Tung Chi Univ, Hefei Indust Univ & Shandong Transp Univ. *Mem:* Inst Transp Engrs; Am Soc Civil Engrs; Am Soc Eng Educ; Am Road & Transp Builders Asn; Am Pub Works Asn; NAm Chinese Transp Profs Asn. *Res:* Traffic flow dynamics; highway design; traffic safety; traffic signal operation and general systems theory. *Mailing Add:* Dept Civil Eng Univ Kans Lawrence KS 66045-0001. *Fax:* 785-864-3199

LEE, JOHN A N, PROGRAMMING LANGUAGES, SOFTWARE ENGINEERING. *Current Pos:* PROF COMPUT SCI, VA TECH, 74- *Personal Data:* b Coventry, UK, Dec 23, 34; US citizen; m 88, Delores J Booth; c Andrew, Derek, Jo-Anne, Stuart & Jamie. *Educ:* Univ Nottingham, BSc, 55, PhD(appl sci), 58. *Honors & Awards:* Outstanding Contrib Award, Asn Comput Mach, 81, Distinguished Serv Award, 93; Cert Distinguished Serv, US Dept Defense, 83. *Prof Exp:* Asst engr, Freeman, Fox & Partners, 57-59; asst prof civil eng, Queens Univ, Kingston, Ont, 59-64; prof comput sci, Univ Mass, Amherst, 64-74. *Concurrent Pos:* Dir, Comput Ctr, Queens Univ, Kingston, Ont, 60-64; head, Dept Comput Sci, Univ Mass, Amherst, 64-69, assoc dir, Comput Ctr, 64-74; chair, Stand Comt, Asn Comput Mach, 64-73, coun mem, 82-84; vis prof, Univ Denver, 70-71; head, Dept Comput Sci, Va Tech, 79-80; fac assoc, Santa Teresa Lab, IBM Corp, San Jose, 80-81; ed & ed-in-chief, Am Fedn Info Processing Socs, 80-91; dir, Ctr Innovative Technol, Inst Info Technol, Herndon, Va, 87-91; ed-in-chief, Inst Elec & Electronics Engrs Comput Soc, 91- *Mem:* Fel Asn Comput Mach (vpres, 84-86); Inst Elec & Electronics Engrs Comput Soc (vpres, 95-96); Am Fedn Info Processing Socs. *Res:* Programming languages: history, compilers and design; software engineering: formal specifications, testing, integration, history of computing. *Mailing Add:* Dept Comput Sci Va Tech 133 McBryde Hall Blacksburg VA 24061-0106. *Fax:* 540-231-6075; *E-Mail:* janlee@cs.vt.edu

LEE, JOHN ALEXANDER HUGH, EPIDEMIOLOGY. *Current Pos:* PROF EPIDEMIOL, UNIV WASH, 66- *Personal Data:* b Isle of Wight, Eng, Oct 10, 25; m 49; c 3. *Educ:* Univ Edinburgh, BSc, 47, MB, ChB, 49, MD, 55; Univ London, DPH, 52. *Prof Exp:* Fel epidemiol, London Sch Hyg & Trop Med, 52-55; mem sci staff, Social Med Res Unit, Med Res Coun, London Hosp, 55-66. *Mem:* Am Epidemiol Soc; Brit Soc Social Med; Brit Med Asn; Int Epidemiol Asn. *Res:* Epidemiology of neoplastic disesase. *Mailing Add:* Dept Epidemiol & Int Health Univ Wash SC 36 Seattle WA 98195

LEE, JOHN C, IMMUNOLOGY. *Current Pos:* ASST DIR, DEPT CELL SCI, SMITH KLINE & FR LABS, 89- *Mailing Add:* Dept Biochem Univ Tex Health Sci Ctr 7703 Floyd Curl Dr San Antonio TX 78284-7760

LEE, JOHN CHAESEUNG, NUCLEAR ENGINEERING. *Current Pos:* from asst prof to assoc prof, 74-81, actg chmn, Dept Nuclear Eng, 86, PROF NUCLEAR ENG, UNIV MICH, ANN ARBOR, 81- *Personal Data:* b Seoul, Korea, July 29, 41; US citizen; m 71, Theresa Lee; c Nina. *Educ:* Seoul Nat Univ, BS, 63; Univ Calif, Berkeley, PhD(nuclear eng), 69. *Prof Exp:* Sr engr nuclear eng, Westinghouse Elec Corp, 69-73; sr engr, Gen Elec Co, 73-74. *Concurrent Pos:* Consult, Adv Comt Reactor Safeguards, US Nuclear Regulatory Comn, 75-94 & Los Alamos Nat Lab, 77-88; vis scientist, Ger, 81-82; mem, Panel Separations Technol & Transmutation Systs, Transmutation Subgroup, Nat Acad Sci, 91-96. *Mem:* Fel Am Nuclear Soc; AAAS. *Res:* Nuclear reactor physics; reactor kinetics; fuel management; reactor safety analysis; power plant simulation and control. *Mailing Add:* Dept Nuclear Eng Univ Mich Ann Arbor MI 48109-2104. *Fax:* 313-763-4540; *E-Mail:* jcl@umich.edu

LEE, JOHN CHEUNG HAN, INDUSTRIAL MICROBIOLOGY, INFECTIOUS DISEASES-ANTIBOTICS. *Current Pos:* ASSOC DIR CELL BIOCHEM, SMITH KLINE BEECHAM. *Personal Data:* b China, Dec 1, 45; m 77; c 1. *Educ:* Rutgers Univ, BA, 67; Long Island Univ, MS, 72; St John's Univ, PhD(microbiol), 79. *Prof Exp:* Sect head, Julius Schmid, Inc, 67-73; supvr, Miles Pharmaceut, 79- *Mem:* Am Soc Microbiol; NY Acad Sci; Soc Indust Microbiol; Sigma Xi. *Res:* In vitro activity of new antibiotics; effect of antibiotics on functions of macrophages. *Mailing Add:* Dept UW 2109 At 709 Swedeland Rd King of Prussia PA 19406

LEE, JOHN CHUNG, BIOCHEMISTRY. *Current Pos:* from asst prof to assoc prof, Med Sch, 69-85, PROF BIOCHEM, UNIV TEX HEALTH SCI CTR, SAN ANTONIO, 85- *Personal Data:* b Shanghai, China, Mar 2, 36; US citizen; m 63, June Yamanchi; c Andrew & Nathan. *Educ:* Taylor Univ, AB, 61; Purdue Univ, West Lafayette, MSc, 64, PhD(molecular biol), 67. *Prof Exp:* Res assoc biochem, Mass Inst Technol, 67-69. *Concurrent Pos:* USPHS res grant, Univ Tex Health Sci Ctr, San Antonio, 71- *Mem:* Am Chem Soc; Am Soc Biochem & Molecular Biol; AAAS; Endocrinol Soc. *Res:* Structure and function of nucleic acids and of ribosomes; RNA-protein interactions. *Mailing Add:* Dept Biochem Univ Tex Health Sci Ctr San Antonio TX 78284-7760. *Fax:* 210-567-6595; *E-Mail:* jclee@bioc02.uthscsa.edu

LEE, JOHN D(AVID), aerodynamics, for more information see previous edition

LEE, JOHN DENIS, METEOROLOGY. *Current Pos:* RES ASSOC, PA STATE UNIV, 86- *Personal Data:* b Trinidad, WI, Apr 22, 29; m 58; c 3. *Educ:* Fla State Univ, BS, 70, MS, 71, PhD(meteorol), 73. *Prof Exp:* Fel, Nat Ctr Atmospheric Res, 73-74; asst prof meteorol, Pa State Univ, 74-78; UN expert meteorol educ & training, Saudi Arabia, 82-86. *Concurrent Pos:* Lectr meteorol, UN Develop Prog for Advan Training in Meteorol in Eng-speaking Caribbean Territories, 78-81. *Mem:* Am Meteorol Soc; Sigma Xi; NY Acad Sci. *Res:* Numerical modeling of cooling tower plumes and urban pollution; time series analysis; numerical modeling of flow over obstacles. *Mailing Add:* 447 Kemmerer Rd State College PA 16801

LEE, JOHN HAK SHAN, COMBUSTION, SHOCK WAVES & EXPLOSIONS. *Current Pos:* lectr, 62-64, from asst prof to assoc prof, 64-66, PROF MECH ENG, MCGILL UNIV, 73- *Personal Data:* b Hong Kong, Sept 7, 38; Can citizen; m 62; c 2. *Educ:* McGill Univ, BSc, 60, PhD(eng), 65; Mass Inst Technol, MSc, 62. *Honors & Awards:* Silver Medal, Combustion Inst, 80 & Dioniry Smolenski Medal, 88; Numa Manson Gold Medal, 91. *Mem:* Order Engrs Quebec; Am Phys Soc; Combustion Inst; Am Inst Aeronaut & Astronaut. *Res:* Combustion and detonation phenomena, combustion synthesis of materials; cause, effects, prevention and mitigation of accidental explosions in the production, transport, storage of flammable gases, liquids, organic, metallic and coal dusts; hydrogen combustion and vapor explosion problems pertaining to nuclear reactor accident. *Mailing Add:* Dept Mech Eng Rm 459 McGill Univ 817 Sherbrooke St W Montreal PQ H2A 2K6 Can. *Fax:* 514-398-7365; *E-Mail:* jhslee@mecheng.mcgill.ca

LEE, JOHN JOSEPH, MARINE MICROBIOLOGY, PROTOZOOLOGY. *Current Pos:* from asst prof to assoc prof, 66-72, PROF BIOL, NEW YORK CITY COL, 72- *Personal Data:* b Philadelphia, Pa, Feb 23, 33; m 56; c 2. *Educ:* Queens Col, NY, BS, 55; Univ Mass, MA, 57; NY Univ, PhD(biol), 60. *Prof Exp:* Asst prof, NY Univ, 61-66. *Concurrent Pos:* Res fel & dir, Living Foraminifera Lab, Am Mus Natural Hist, 60-68, res assoc, 70-; dir, Marine Microbiol Ecol Lab, Inst Oceanog, City Univ New York, 68-; res assoc, Lamont-Doherty Geol Observ, 70- & Philadelphia Acad Natural Sci, 85- *Mem:* Fel AAAS; Soc Protozool (pres, 91); Phycol Soc Am; Am Soc Microbiol; Am Micros Soc. *Res:* Cytology, fine structure, life history, ecology, cultivation and characterization of foraminifera; algal endosymbiosis in foraminifera, meiofauna, benthic marine food webs and diatom assemblages. *Mailing Add:* Dept Biol New York City Col 160 Convent Ave New York NY 10031-9101

LEE, JOHN K, CELL & DEVELOPMENTAL BIOLOGY. *Current Pos:* RES INSTR, VANDERBILT UNIV, TENN, 96- *Prof Exp:* Postdoctoral fel, Cell & Develop Biol Dept, Harvard Univ, 89-94 & Univ Calif San Diego, 94-96. *Mailing Add:* Dept Pharm Vanderbilt Univ 454 MRB1 Nashville TN 37232

LEE, JOHN NORMAN, PHYSICS. *Current Pos:* SUPVR RES PHYSICIST, NAVAL RES LAB, 80- *Personal Data:* b Schenectady, NY, Dec 2, 44; m 68, Lina Chan; c Jennifer & John. *Educ:* Union Col, Schenectady, BS, 66; Johns Hopkins Univ, MA, 68, PhD(physics), 71. *Honors & Awards:* Kingslake Medal & Prize, Soc Photo-Optical Instrumentation Engrs. *Prof Exp:* Res asst physics, Johns Hopkins Univ, 69-71; physicist, Electronics Res & Develop Command, Harry Diamond Labs, 71-80. *Mem:* Am Phys Soc; sr mem Inst Elec & Electronics Engrs; Optical Soc Am. *Res:* Signal processing using acousto-optics and surface acoustic wave devices; signal processing in optical materials and components; signal processing for optical sensors; optical devices for signal processing; optical computing. *Mailing Add:* Naval Res Lab Code 5620 Washington DC 20375. *Fax:* 202-767-6370

LEE, JOHN WILLIAM, CHEMICAL PHYSICS, BIOPHYSICS. *Current Pos:* PROF BIOCHEM, UNIV GA, 75- *Personal Data:* b Sydney, Australia, Apr 7, 35; m 60; c 2. *Educ:* Univ NSW, BSc, 56, PhD(phys chem), 60. *Prof Exp:* Res assoc biochem, McCollum-Pratt Inst, Johns Hopkins Univ, 61-63; staff scientist, New Eng Inst Med Res, 63-69; assoc prof, 69-75. *Mem:* Am Chem Soc; Am Phys Soc. *Res:* Positron annihilation in matter; radiation chemistry; energy exchange processes in chemical and biological systems; bioluminescence; chemiluminescence; radiation physics. *Mailing Add:* Dept Biochem Univ Ga Athens GA 30602-7229

LEE, JOHN YUCHU, ORGANIC CHEMISTRY, ORGANOMETALLICS. *Current Pos:* res chemist indust & specialty chem, res & develop, 80-88, sr res chem, 88-89, RES SPECIALIST, NEW PROJ DEVELOP, ETHYL CORP, 89- *Personal Data:* b Tai-Ho, China, Jan 25, 48; nat US; m 76; c 2. *Educ:* Nat Cheng-Kung Univ, Taiwan, BS, 70; SDak State Univ, MS, 74; Vanderbilt Univ, PhD, 78. *Prof Exp:* Asst, SDak State Univ, 73-74 & Vanderbilt Univ, 74-78; res assoc bioorg chem, chem dept, Tex A&M Univ, 78-79, Robert Welch fel organometallics, 79-80. *Concurrent Pos:* Chem reagent officer, Chinese Air Force Acad, 70-71; prin & prog dir, Baton Rouge Chinese Sch, 85-86; pres, Chinese Asn, Baton Rouge, 89-90. *Mem:* Sigma Xi; fel Am Inst Chemists; Am Chem Soc; Royal Soc Chem; Japanese Chem Soc; Chinese Am Chem Asn; AAAS; Soc Francaise Chimie. *Res:* Synthesis, isolation and characterization of pharmaceutical, agricultural, surfactant and detergent intermediates, as well as process improvement; bromine chemicals; chemicals from biomass; alkylation products; flame retardants; catalysis; polymer chemistry; advanced materials. *Mailing Add:* 1524 Stoneleigh Dr Baton Rouge LA 70808-5776

LEE, JON H(YUNKOO), APPLIED MATHEMATICS, COMPUTER SIMULATION. *Current Pos:* Chem engr, USAF Mat Lab, 62-64, res engr, Aerospace Res Labs, 64-75, RES SCIENTIST, FLIGHT DYNAMICS LAB, WRIGHT-PATTERSON AFB, OHIO, 75- *Personal Data:* b Seoul, Korea, Mar 5, 34; US citizen; m 70, Janet Adams; c 4. *Educ:* Seoul Nat Univ, BS, 56; Ohio State Univ, MS, 58, PhD(chem eng), 62. *Honors & Awards:* Gen Foulois Res Award, 87. *Concurrent Pos:* Adj prof, Dept Chem Eng, Univ Dayton, 62; instr, Air Force Inst Technol, 73. *Mem:* Am Phys Soc; Sigma Xi; Am Acad Mech; Soc Indust & Appl Math. *Res:* Fluid dynamics; structural vibration; turbulence; computational mechanics; dynamical systems. *Mailing Add:* 10661 Putnam Rd Englewood OH 45322. *Fax:* 937-255-6684

LEE, JONATHAN K P, NUCLEAR PHYSICS. *Current Pos:* from asst prof to assoc prof, 68-81, PROF NUCLEAR PHYSICS, MCGILL UNIV, 81-, DIR, FOSTER RADIATION LAB, 79- *Personal Data:* b Kiangsu, China, July 13, 37; m 67; c 3. *Educ:* McGill Univ, BEng, 60, MSc, 62, PhD(nuclear physics), 65. *Prof Exp:* Nat Res Coun Can overseas fel, 65-66; res asst, Univ Toronto, 66-68. *Mem:* Can Asn Physicists; Am Phys Soc; Oper Sci Apliquees. *Res:* Nuclear structure studies; laser spectroscopy. *Mailing Add:* Foster Radiol Lab McGill Univ 3610 University St Montreal PQ H3A 2B2 Can

LEE, JONG SUN, MICROBIOLOGY. *Current Pos:* RETIRED. *Personal Data:* b Suwon, Korea, July 10, 32; m 58; c 3. *Educ:* Univ Calif, Berkeley, BA, 58; Ore State Univ, MS, 62, PhD(microbiol), 63. *Prof Exp:* From asst prof to prof food microbiol, Ore State Univ, 63-82; prof food sci & tech, 80-82; Technol Ctr, Fishery Indust, Kodiak, Alaska, 82-93. *Mem:* AAAS; Am Soc Microbiol; Inst Food Technol; Brit Soc Appl Bact; Sigma Xi. *Res:* Microbiology of seafoods. *Mailing Add:* 2695 SW Pickford St Corvallis OR 97333

LEE, JORDAN GREY, experimental biology; deceased, see previous edition for last biography

LEE, JOSEPH CHUEN KWUN, PATHOLOGY, CELL BIOLOGY. *Current Pos:* dean fac med, 86-89, PROF PATH, CHINESE UNIV, HONG KONG, 82-, DEAN FAC MED, 96- *Personal Data:* b Chungking, China, Oct 6, 38; US citizen; m. *Educ:* Univ Hong Kong, MB, BS, 64; Univ Rochester, PhD(path), 70; FRCP(C), 71, Am Bd Path, 72, FRCP(A), 85, MRC(path), 86. *Prof Exp:* Intern, Hong Kong, 64; rotating intern, St Francis Hosp, NY, 66; resident path, New York Hosp-Cornell Med Ctr, 66-67, Toronto Gen Hosp, Univ Toronto, 70-71 & Princess Margaret Hosp, Ont Cancer Inst Can, 71-72; asst prof to assoc prof path & oncol, Univ Rochester Med Ctr, 72-80; vis prof, NIH, 80; res fel, Armed Forces Inst Path, 81. *Mem:* AAAS; Am Soc Cell Biol; Soc Anal Cytol; Am Asn Path; Electron Micros Soc Am. *Res:* Nasopharyngeal carcinoma. *Mailing Add:* Fac Med Chinese Univ Hong Kong Shatin New Territories Hong Kong People's Republic of China. *Fax:* 852-2637-6274; *E-Mail:* joelee@cuhk.edu.hk

LEE, JOSHUA ALEXANDER, GENETICS. *Current Pos:* prof crop sci, 71-93, GENETICIST, AGR EXP STA, NC STATE UNIV, 58-, EMER PROF CROP SCI, 93- *Personal Data:* b Rocky Ford, Ga, Oct 30, 24; m 56; c 2. *Educ:* San Diego State Col, AB, 50; Univ Calif, PhD(genetics), 58. *Prof Exp:* Technician, Univ Calif, 51-53, asst, 54-56. *Mem:* Crop Sci Soc Am; Soc Study Evolution. *Res:* Genetical problems pertaining to the improvement of domesticated cotton species. *Mailing Add:* 118 West Lake Dr Sylvania GA 30467

LEE, JUNE KEY, ENGINEERING MECHANICS. *Current Pos:* from asst prof to assoc prof, 77-86, PROF MECH, OHIO STATE UNIV, 86- *Personal Data:* b Seoul, Korea, Aug 9, 43; US citizen; m 70, Yoon K Chung; c Jane, Judy & Julie. *Educ:* Han-Yang Univ, BS, 65; Tenn Technol Univ, MS, 70; Univ Tex, Austin, PhD(eng mech), 76. *Prof Exp:* Res asst comput mech, Res Inst, Univ Ala, Huntsville, 70-73; asst instr, Univ Tex, 75-76; asst prof eng, Drexel Univ, 76-77. *Concurrent Pos:* Prin investr, NSF & Ohio State Univ, 78-; co-prin investr var grants, Dept Energy, 80-82, Ohio State Univ, 80-83 & NASA, 81-83; consult, 80- *Mem:* Am Acad Mech; Soc Eng Sci; Sigma Xi; Am Soc Mech Eng; Am Soc Metals. *Res:* Theory and application of the finite element method in applied mechanics; numerical methods; geotechnical engineering; sheet metal forming; hygro-thermo-mechanical response of porous media. *Mailing Add:* Dept Eng Mech Ohio State Univ 155 W Woodruff Ave Columbus OH 43210-1117. *E-Mail:* lee.71@osu.edu

LEE, KAH-HOCK, INORGANIC CHEMISTRY. *Current Pos:* PRES, ADVAN INVESTMENT MGT CO, 79- *Personal Data:* b Jan 28, 41; US citizen; m 67; c 3. *Educ:* Nanyang Univ, BS, 64; Georgetown Univ, PhD(inorg chem), 70. *Prof Exp:* Environ chemist, DC Dept Environ Serv, 69-80. *Concurrent Pos:* Res fel, Dept Chem, Grad Sch, Georgetown Univ, 71-73. *Mem:* Am Chem Soc. *Res:* Environmental toxic trace metals; effect of x-ray film developer on radiation protection; heteropoly inorganic anions exchange mechanisms. *Mailing Add:* 947 Cedar Ridge Ct Orange Park FL 32065-6798

LEE, KAI NIEN, ENVIRONMENTAL MANAGEMENT, SCIENCE POLICY. *Current Pos:* PROF & DIR ENVIRON STUDIES, WILLIAMS COL, 91- *Personal Data:* b New York, NY, Oct 19, 45; m 71; c 2. *Educ:* Columbia Univ, AB, 66; Princeton Univ, PhD(physics), 71. *Honors & Awards:* White House Fel, 76; Kellogg Fel, 80. *Prof Exp:* Soc Sci Res Coun res training fel, 71-72; asst res social scientist, Inst Govt Studies, Univ Calif, Berkeley, 72-73; res asst prof, Prog Social Mgt Technol & Dept Polit Sci, Univ Wash, 73-75, from asst prof to assoc prof, Inst Environ Studies & Dept Polit Sci, 75-91. *Concurrent Pos:* Mem int adv bd, Policy Sci, 74-; White House fel, US Dept Defense, 76-77; mem Naval Res adv comt, 78-; mem adv panel radioactive waste disposal, Off Tech Assessment, 78-81; mem, Environ Studies Bd, 80-82, Bd Radioactive Waste Mgt, Nat Acad Sci, 83-; Kellogg Nat fel, 80-83; mem, Northwest Power Planning Coun, 83-87; vis prof, Kyoto Univ, Japan, 90-91. *Mem:* Fel Soc Religion in Higher Educ; AAAS; Am Polit Sci Asn. *Res:* Energy and environmental policy and politics: energy, fish and wildlife, global climate change, environmental conflict and dispute settlement; influence of technological change on American life. *Mailing Add:* Ctr Environ Studies Williams Col PO Box 632 Williamstown MA 01267. *Fax:* 413-597-4088

LEE, KAI-FONG, ANTENNA THEORY & DESIGN, APPLIED ELECTROMAGNETICS. *Current Pos:* PROF & CHMN, ELEC ENG, UNIV TOLEDO, 88- *Personal Data:* July 17, 39; m 71; Shiow-Lie Huang; c Walter, Steven & Amy. *Educ:* Queen's Univ, Can, BSc, 61, MSc, 63; Cornell Univ, PhD(elec eng), 66. *Prof Exp:* Res asst, Nat Radio Astron Observ, 66; fel, Univ Calif, San Diego, 66-67; vis scientist, Nat Ctr Atmospheric Res, 68-69; from asst prof to assoc prof appl phys, Catholic Univ Am, 67-72; sr resident res assoc, Nat Res Coun-Nat Oceanic & Atmospheric Admin, 72-73; lectr electronics, Chinese Univ Hong Kong, 73-77, sr lectr, 77-83, reader, 84-; head dept electronic eng, City Polytech Hong Kong, 84-85; prof elec eng, Univ Akron, 85-88. *Concurrent Pos:* Vis reseacher, Univ Calif, Los Angeles, 75. *Mem:* Sr mem Inst Elec & Electronics Engrs; fel Inst Elec & Electronics Engrs; Chartered Eng UK; Am Phys Soc; Sigma Xi. *Res:* Theory and design of microstrip, helical and reflector antennas; theory of plasma waves and instabilities. *Mailing Add:* Dept Elec Eng Univ Toledo 2801 W Bancroft St Toledo OH 43606-3328. *Fax:* 419-537-2915; *E-Mail:* klee@uoft02.utoledo.edu

LEE, KAI-LIN, BIOCHEMISTRY, ENDOCRINOLOGY. *Current Pos:* Hoffmann-La Roche fel, Biochem, Biol Div, 68-69, res assoc, 69-70, BIOCHEMIST, BIOL DIV, OAK RIDGE NAT LAB, 70- *Personal Data:* b Nanking, China, Sept 16, 35; m 64. *Educ:* Nat Taiwan Univ, BS, 60; Tulane Univ, PhD(biochem), 66. *Prof Exp:* Teaching asst bot, Nat Taiwan Univ, 61-62; res asst biochem, Tulane Univ, 62-66, fel biochem endocrinol, 66-67, instr, 67-68. *Mem:* AAAS; Endocrine Soc; Am Chem Soc; Am Soc Biol Chemists. *Res:* Hormonal regulation of metabolic processes. *Mailing Add:* Environ Sci Div Oak Ridge Nat Lab Oak Ridge TN 37831-2009

LEE, KANG, SMART SENSOR INTERFACE, SENSOR SYSTEM INTEGRATION. *Current Pos:* GROUP LEADER SENSOR INTEGRATION, NAT INST STAND & TECHNOL, 87- *Personal Data:* b Dec 7, 47. *Educ:* Univ Md, MA, 81. *Concurrent Pos:* Chmn, Sensor Technol Comt, Inst Elec & Electronics Engrs, 95- *Mem:* Inst Elec & Electronics Engrs. *Mailing Add:* Nat Inst Stand & Technol Bldg 233 Rm B102 Gaithersburg MD 20899-0001

LEE, KANG IN, SYNTHETIC POLYMER CHEMISTRY, POLYMERIC MATERIALS SCIENCE. *Current Pos:* SR RES SPECIALIST POLYMER SCI, MONSANTO CO, CHEM GROUP, 84- *Personal Data:* b Korea, Nov 2, 46; US citizen; m 75, Miryoung Noh; c Grace & Albert. *Educ:* Murray State Univ, BA, 70; State Univ NY Buffalo, MA, 72; Polytech Inst New York, PhD(polymer sci), 76. *Honors & Awards:* Seymour L Shapiro Award. *Prof Exp:* Res assoc, Inst Polymer Sci, Univ Akron, 76-77; res scientist polymer chem, Cent Res Labs, Firestone Tire & Rubber Co, 77-80; sr mem tech staff polymer sci, Fundamental Res Lab, Gen Tel & Electronics Labs, 80-84. *Concurrent Pos:* Res assoc, Inst Polymer Sci, Univ Akron, 76-77; affil prof mat sci, Washington Univ, 85-86. *Mem:* Am Chem Soc; Sigma Xi; Korean Scientist & Engrs Am; Tech Asn Pulp & Paper Indust. *Res:* Synthesis and characterization of new polymers for microelectronics application; cationic and ziegler natta polymerizations; new photoresist developments; conducting polymers, electron beam sensitive polymers, polymers for optical fiber sensor applications, and polymers for paper surface sizing applications. *Mailing Add:* Monsanto Co 730 Worcester St Springfield MA 01151. *Fax:* 413-730-2506; *E-Mail:* kilee@ccmail.monsanto.com

LEE, KATHRYN ADELE BUNDING, MOLECULE-SURFACE INTERACTIONS, VIBRATIONAL SPECTROSCOPY. *Current Pos:* RES ASSOC, NAT STARCH & CHEM CO, 94- *Personal Data:* b Chicago, Ill; m 86, Shu; c Emily. *Educ:* Univ Chicago, BA, 71; City Univ NY, PhD(phys org chem), 80. *Prof Exp:* Nat Res Coun fel, Nat Bur Stand, 80-82; vis scientist, IBM, 82-84; res asst, Georgetown Univ, 84-85; res chemist, Naval Res Lab, 85-87; sr scientist SC Johnson Wax, 87-94. *Mem:* Am Chem Soc; Sigma Xi; Electrochem Soc; Soc Appl Spectros. *Res:* Molecule-surface interactions and reactions; use of in situ spectroscopic and electrochemical techniques; Raman and Fourier transform infrared spectroscopies; optical second harmonic generation; near infared spectroscopy. *Mailing Add:* National Starch Co 10 Finderne Ave Bridgewater NJ 08807-0500. *Fax:* 908-685-5005; *E-Mail:* kathryn.lee@nstarch.com

LEE, KEENAN, GEOLOGY. *Current Pos:* asst prof, 69-74, ASSOC PROF GEOL, COLO SCH MINES, 74- *Personal Data:* b Huntington, WV, Nov 20, 36; m 66; c 2. *Educ:* La State Univ, Baton Rouge, BS, 60, MS, 63; Stanford Univ, PhD(geol), 69. *Prof Exp:* Geophys trainee, Cuban Stanalind Oil Co, Pan Am Petrol Corp, 57-58; geologist, Mobil Oil Libya, Ltd, 63-66. *Mem:* AAAS; Geol Soc Am; Am Soc Photogram. *Res:* Hydrogeology; remote sensing. *Mailing Add:* 419 Sunshine Pkwy Golden CO 80403

LEE, KEN, FOOD SCIENCE & TECHNOLOGY. *Current Pos:* From asst prof to assoc prof food sci, 80-90, PROF & CHMN, DEPT FOOD SCI & TECHNOL, COL AGR, OHIO STATE UNIV, 90- *Personal Data:* b West Orange, NJ, Sept 5, 53; m; c 1. *Educ:* Rutgers Univ, BS, 75; Univ Mass, Amherst, PhD(food sci & nutrit), 80. *Concurrent Pos:* Conf chmn, Midwest Food Processing Conf, 84; counr, Inst Food Technologists, 84-; chmn, Tech Adv Comt, Ctr Dairy Res. *Mem:* Sigma Xi; Inst Food Technologists; Am Asn Cereal Chemists; Am Inst Nutrit; Am Dairy Sci Asn. *Res:* Over 40 publications in peer-review research journals and over 30 published abstracts; mineral bioavailability from cured meats; analysis of nutrient inhibitors; mineral binding by dietary fiber; oxidized cholesterol compounds in foods; nitrate metabolism and analysis in foods; anti-nutrients in tea; hydrocolloids in dairy foods. *Mailing Add:* Dept Food Sci & Technol Ohio State Univ 2121 Fyffe Rd Columbus OH 43210-1097

LEE, KENNETH, SOLID STATE PHYSICS. *Current Pos:* vpres eng, 90-93, exec vpres, 93-95, CHIEF TECHNOL OFFICER, QUANTUM CORP, MILPITAS, CALIF, 89-; PRES & GEN MGR, WORK STA, SYSTS STORAGE GROUP, 95- *Personal Data:* b San Francisco, Calif, July 3, 37; m 59, Cynthia Chu; c Marcus S & Stephanie D. *Educ:* Univ Calif, Berkeley, AB, 59, PhD(physics), 63. *Honors & Awards:* Centennial Medal, Inst Elec & Electronics Engrs, 84. *Prof Exp:* Res physicist, Varian Assocs, 63-68; mgr & res staff mem, IBM Res Lab, San Jose, Calif, 68-83; dir memory technol, Southwall Technol, Palo Alto, Calif, 83-84; vpres, Domain Technol, Milpitas, Calif, 84-86, sr vpres prod develop, 88. *Concurrent Pos:* Consult, Lawrence Radiation Lab, Univ Calif, 63-68; comt mem, Magnetism & Magnetic Mat Conf, 64-65, prog comt 71 & adv comt, 71-74, 74-77 & 80-83, prog co-chmn, 75, steering comt, 77, 78 & 81, prog comt, 79; gen chmn, Joint Magnetism & Magnetic Mat-Intermag Conf, 88. *Mem:* Fel Am Phys Soc; sr mem Inst Elec & Electronics Engrs; Sigma Xi. *Res:* Antiferromagnetism; crystal defects and motion of nuclei in solids; electron and nuclear magnetic resonance; magnetism in thin films; amorphous magnetism; thin film technology; magnetic recording; author of over 50 technical articles and over 20 reports on magnetic recording technology, storage technologies and magnetic bubble materials. *Mailing Add:* 20587 Debbie Lane Saratoga CA 95070

LEE, KENNETH, PHYSICS OF BEAMS. *Current Pos:* RES SCIENTIST, LOS ALAMOS NAT LAB, 72- *Personal Data:* b China, Oct 9, 43. *Educ:* Ohio State Univ, BS, 66; Univ Calif, Los Angeles, PhD(physics), 72. *Mem:* Am Phys Soc. *Mailing Add:* 575 Totavi Los Alamos NM 87544

LEE, KEUN MYUNG, acoustic emission, software engineering, for more information see previous edition

LEE, KING C, pharmacology, for more information see previous edition

LEE, KIUCK, NUCLEAR PHYSICS. *Current Pos:* from asst prof to assoc prof, 57-68, PROF PHYSICS, MARQUETTE UNIV, 68- *Personal Data:* b Hamhung, Korea, Jan 15, 22; c 5. *Educ:* Seoul Nat Univ, BS, 47, MS, 49; Fla State Univ, PhD(physics), 55. *Prof Exp:* Res assoc physics, Fla State Univ, 55-56 & Argonne Nat Lab, 56-57. *Concurrent Pos:* Res assoc, Argonne Nat Lab, 60. *Mem:* Am Phys Soc. *Res:* Nuclear structure studies on deformed nucleus, fission and the superheavy nucleus. *Mailing Add:* Marquette Univ Dept Physics 1515 W Wisconsin Ave Milwaukee WI 53233

LEE, KOK-MENG, DYNAMIC SYSTEMS & CONTROL, DESIGN & MANUFACTURING AUTOMATION. *Current Pos:* asst prof, 85-90, ASSOC PROF MECH ENG, GA INST TECHNOL, 90- *Personal Data:* b Singapore, Aug 20, 52; m 82; c 1. *Educ:* State Univ NY, Buffalo, BS, 80; Mass Inst Technol, SM, 82, PhD(mech eng), 85. *Honors & Awards:* Int Hall of Fame New Technol Award, 92. *Prof Exp:* Res asst, Fluid Power Control Lab, Mass Inst Technol, 80-85. *Concurrent Pos:* Consult, Milliken Textile Co, 87 & 88; prin investr, NSF, 88-, Ga Tech, Gen Motors & Ford, 89-; NSF Presidential young investr, 89; Sigma Xi Jr, Fac Award, Ga Tech, 89. *Mem:* Am Soc Mech Engrs; Inst Elec & Electronics Engrs; Instrument Soc Am; Am Soc Eng Educ. *Res:* Dynamic system modeling, control and automation; mechatronics and their application to intelligent control systems and manufacturing automation; awarded one patent. *Mailing Add:* 5595 Covena Ct Norcross GA 30092-2073

LEE, KOTIK KAI, MATHEMATICAL PHYSICS, NONLINEAR DYNAMICAL SYSTEMS. *Current Pos:* CHIEF SCIENTIST, QET INC, 93- *Personal Data:* b Chungking, China, May 30, 41; US citizen; c 2. *Educ:* Chung-Yuan Col, BSc, 64; Univ Ottawa, MSc, 67; Syracuse Univ, PhD(physics), 72. *Prof Exp:* Res asst physics, Syracuse Univ, 68-72, instr, 72-73; asst prof, Rio Grande Col, 73-74; asst physics, 65-67, vis prof math, Univ Ottawa, 74-76; scientist, Lab Laser Energetics, Univ Rochester, 77-78; physicist, Santa Barbara Res Ctr, 78-79; scientist, lab laser energetics, Univ Rochester, 79-82; scientist, TRW, 82-84; sr staff scientist, Gen Elec Co, 84-86; sr staff scientist, Perkin-Elmer Co, 86-89; assoc prof, Univ Colo, 89-93. *Concurrent Pos:* Mem, Educ Coun, Optical Soc Am, 89-91; Educ Comt Am Phys Soc, 92-94. *Mem:* Am Math Soc; Am Phys Soc; Can Asn Physicists; Optical Soc Am; Int Soc Gen Relativity & Gravitation; Inst Elec & Electronics Engrs; NY Acad Sci. *Res:* Global structures of spacetimes, singularities in general relativity, mathematical foundations of quantum field theory and statistical mechanics, differential equations, laser physics, astrophysics, nonlinear optics and nonlinear dynamical systems. *Mailing Add:* 5755 Pale Rock Terr No L Colorado Springs CO 80919

LEE, KUEN HUNG, COMPUTER SCIENCE, ENGINEERING. *Current Pos:* PROF MATH, LOS ANGELES TRADE TECHNIC COL, 74- *Personal Data:* b Mar 17, 44; m 73, Wai Kuen Yu; c Elisa Y, Melisa M, Cindy S & Edmund S. *Educ:* Calif State Univ, BS, 71; Univ Southern Calif, MS, 73; Nova Univ, Dr(math educ), 83. *Prof Exp:* Comput syst analyst, Jet Propulsion Lab. *Concurrent Pos:* Adj prof math, Univ Southern Calif, 73-90, Calif State Univ, 75- *Mem:* Math Asn Am; AAAS; Am Statist Asn. *Res:* Writing mathematics textbooks in a unique step-by-step format with side explanations for each step. *Mailing Add:* 5240 Haskell St La Canada Flintridge CA 91011. *Fax:* 818-952-3638

LEE, KUO-HSIUNG, MEDICINAL CHEMISTRY, NATURAL PRODUCTS CHEMISTRY. *Current Pos:* from asst prof to prof med chem, 70-91, DIR, NATURAL PROD LAB, SCH PHARM, UNIV NC, CHAPEL HILL, 83-, KENAN PROF, 92- *Personal Data:* b Taiwan, Jan 4, 40; m 68; c 2. *Educ:* Kaohsiung Med Col, Taiwan, BS, 61; Kyoto Univ, MS, 65; Univ Minn, Minneapolis, PhD(med chem), 68. *Honors & Awards:* Taite O Soine Mem Award, 90; TM Tu's Sci Award, 95; Merit Award, NIH, 96. *Prof Exp:* Postdoctoral scholar chem, Univ Calif, Los Angeles, 68-70. *Concurrent Pos:* USPHS res grants, Univ NC, 71-, Am Cancer Soc grant, 75-81, 86-, US Army Med Res Acquisition Agency contract, 83-87; ad hoc mem, Br Study Sect, Conf & Sem Prog, NIH-Fogarty Int Ctr, 83; mem, Study Sect Psychopharmacol, NIMH, 83-84; Chem Study Sect, NIH, 85, 86, 88 & 89, Bio-org & Natural Prod Study Sect, 86, 90 & Phys Biochem Study Sect, 88; mem, Develop Therapeut Contracts Rev Comt, Nat Cancer Inst, 84-88; reviewer, natural prod related grant appl, NSF, 85; Hollingsworth fac scholar award, 88; consult, Genelabs, Inc, 88-, Sphinx Biotechnol Corp, 90-94 & Nat Res Inst Chinese Med, Taiwan, 89-; mem, Bioorg Natural Prod Study Sect, NIH, 90-94 & NIH Reviewers Res, 94-98; mem, Sci Rev & Sci Coun Comt, Nat Health Res Inst, Taiwan, Repub China, 96. *Mem:* Am Chem Soc; Am Soc Pharmacog; fel Am Asn Pharm Scientists; fel Acad Pharmaceut Sci; fel AAAS; Chem Soc; Soc Synthetic Org Chem Japan; Phytochem Soc NAm. *Res:* Medicinal chemistry of the bioactive natural products and their synthetic analogs including antitumor, antiviral, anti-AIDS, antibiotics anti-inflammatory, anti-fungal agents, and antimalarial agents; insect antifeedants; Chinese medicines; over 350 research articles in various journals. *Mailing Add:* Sch Pharm Univ NC Chapel Hill NC 27599-7360. *Fax:* 919-966-3893; *E-Mail:* khlee@unc.edu

LEE, KWANG, POULTRY NUTRITION & MANAGEMENT. *Current Pos:* PROF POULTRY SCI & NUTRIT, UNIV ARK, PINE BLUFF, 73- *Personal Data:* b Seoul, Korea, Jan 18, 42; m 70, Soon-Ja Kim; c Albert & Susan. *Educ:* Seoul Nat Univ, BS, 64; Southern Ill Univ, MS, 69; Mich State Univ, PhD(poultry sci & nutrit), 73. *Concurrent Pos:* Prin investr, poultry res projs, 74-; consult, Am Soybean Asn, 93. *Mem:* Poultry Sci Asn; Korean Soc Animal Sci; World Poultry Sci Asn; Am Registry Prof Animal Scientists. *Res:* Improve production efficiency and well-being of poultry through management and nutrition. *Mailing Add:* Dept Agr Univ Ark Pine Bluff AR 71601. *Fax:* 870-543-8543

LEE, KWANG SOO, PHARMACOLOGY. *Current Pos:* PROF PHARMACOL, CHUNG-ANG UNIV, SEOUL, REPUB SKOREA, 80- *Personal Data:* b Seoul, Korea, Feb 1, 18; m 40; c 3. *Educ:* Keijo Imp Univ, Korea, MD, 42, PhD, 45; Johns Hopkins Univ, 56. *Honors & Awards:* Pres Award, Repub Korea. *Prof Exp:* Asst prof pharmacol, Seoul Nat Univ, 48-49; instr, Jefferson Med Col, 49-50, assoc, 50-51, from asst prof to assoc prof, 51-56; prof pharmacol, State Univ NY Downstate Med Ctr & Col Physicians & Surgeons, Columbia Univ, 62-80. *Mem:* Am Soc Pharmacol & Exp Therapeut. *Res:* Cardiac metabolism; mechanisms of drug actions. *Mailing Add:* Dept Pharmacol Chung-Ang Univ 221 Heuksuk Dong Dongjak KU Seoul South Korea

LEE, KYU TAIK, MEDICINE, PATHOLOGY. *Current Pos:* assoc prof, 60-66, PROF PATH, ALBANY MED COL, 66-, ASSOC DEAN FOR GRAD STUDIES & RES, 76-, DIR, GEOG PATH DIV, 60-, DIR SECT MOLECULAR BIOL & PATH, 68- *Personal Data:* b Taegu, Korea, Sept 17, 21; m 44; c 2. *Educ:* Severence Union Med Col, MD, 43; Wash Univ, PhD(path), 56. *Prof Exp:* Physician in chief, Presby Gen Hosp, Taegu, Korea, 50-53; prof med & chmn dept, Kyung-Pook Nat Univ, 56-60. *Concurrent Pos:* NIH res grants, 56-; dir, Saratoga Conf Molecular Biol & Path, 68; managing ed, Exp & Molecular Path, 69; mem comt comp path, Nat Res Coun, 69-71, mem comt path, 70-71; mem nutrit study sect, NIH, 69-73. *Mem:* Am Heart Asn; Am Soc Exp Path; Int Acad Path; Am Soc Cell Biol; Int Soc Cardiol. *Res:* Ultrastructural and biochemical aspects of atherosclerosis and thrombosis; geographic aspects of atherosclerosis. *Mailing Add:* Dept Path & Cytol 6605 Heidi Ct McLean VA 22101-1606

LEE, KYUNG NO, BIOCHEMISTRY. *Current Pos:* ASST MEM, OKLA MED RES FOUND, 93- *Personal Data:* May 12, 45; m 73, Chung S Kim; c Steve C & James C. *Educ:* Korea Univ, BS; Am Univ, PhD. *Prof Exp:* From asst scientist to assoc scientist, Biomed Div, Samuel Roberts Noble Found, 85-93. *Mem:* Am Chem Soc; Am Soc Biochem & Molecular Biol; Am Soc Cell Biol. *Res:* Structure and function of transghitaminases and their substrates; role of factor XIII in thrombosis and hemostasis. *Mailing Add:* Dept Med Univ Okla Health Sci Ctr PO Box 26901 BSEB 306 Oklahoma City OK 73190

LEE, L(AWRENCE) H(WA) N(I), ENGINEERING MECHANICS, STRUCTURAL ENGINEERING. *Current Pos:* from asst prof to assoc prof eng mech, Univ Notre Dame, 50-60, prof eng sci, 60-93, prof, 69-93, EMER PROF AEROSPACE & MECH ENG, UNIV NOTRE DAME, 93- *Personal Data:* b Shanghai, China, Jan 5, 23; nat US; m 48, Lydia S; c Lynn Lawrence. *Educ:* La Univ Utopia, China, BS, 45; Univ Minn, MS, 47, PhD(struct eng & mech), 50. *Honors & Awards:* Struct Mech Res Award, Off Naval Res & Am Inst Aeronaut & Astronaut, 71. *Prof Exp:* Engr, Lin-Hu Reconstruct Asn, 45-46; instr math & mech, Univ Minn, 49. *Concurrent Pos:* Consult, Bendix Corp, 53-75, Gen Motors Corp, 60-63 & 73, Rock Island Arsenal, US Army, 76 & Dodge Div, Reliance Elec Corp, 80. *Mem:* Am Soc Mech Engrs; Am Soc Civil Engrs; Soc Eng Sci; Am Soc Eng Educ. *Res:* Inelastic stability; dynamic plasticity; elasticity; experimental stress analysis and dynamic stability. *Mailing Add:* Dept Aerospace & Mech Eng Univ Notre Dame Notre Dame IN 46556. *Fax:* 219-631-8341

LEE, LELA A, DERMATOLOGY. *Current Pos:* PROF DERMAT, HEALTH SCI CTR, UNIV OKLA, 91- *Personal Data:* b Gorman, Tex, Sept 7, 50; m 84, Norman Wikner; c 1. *Educ:* Rice Univ, BA, 72; Univ Tex, MD, 76; Am Bd Internal Med, cert, 79; Am Bd Dermat, cert, 83. *Honors & Awards:* Stelwagon Award, Am Acad Dermat, 83-84. *Prof Exp:* Fel immunodermat, Univ Colo Sch Med, 83-85, asst prof dermat & med, 85-91. *Concurrent Pos:* William Reed travelling fel, Am Acad Dermat & Col Physicians, Philadelphia, 83-84; mem bd dirs, Soc Invest Dermat, 85-87; prin investr biol cutaneous lupus, NIH grant, 85-90, photosens cutaneous lupus, Ven Admin grant, 91-; chief assoc ed, J Invest Dermat, 90-92; mem, Am Bd Dermat Test Comt, 93-97; mem, Imm Study Sch, Vet Admin, 96-97. *Mem:* Am Dermat Asn; Am Fedn Clin Res; Am Acad Dermat. *Res:* Clinical and basic science studies concerning the definition and pathogenesis of neonatal lupus and of cutaneous lupus in adults. *Mailing Add:* Dept Dermat Univ Okla Health Sci Ctr 619 NE 13th St Oklahoma City OK 73104

LEE, LIENG-HUANG, ORGANIC & POLYMER SURFACE CHEMISTRY, ADHESION SCIENCE. *Current Pos:* CONSULT, 94- *Personal Data:* b Fukien, China, Nov 6, 24; m 49, Chiu-Bin Wu; c Muriel (Payne), Daniel, Robert & Grace. *Educ:* Amoy (Xiamen) Univ, BSc, 47; Case Inst Technol, MSc, 54, PhD(chem), 55. *Honors & Awards:* Mabery Prize, 54. *Prof Exp:* Jr chemist, Nantou Sugar Factory, China, 47-48; asst res chemist, Chia-Yee Solvent Works, 48-51 & Rain Stimulation Res Inst, 51-52; res assoc, Case Inst Technol, 55-56; lectr, Tunghai Univ, 56-57; vis prof, Taiwan Prov Norm Univ, 57-58; res org chemist, Dow Chem Co, 58-63, sr res chemist, 63-68; sr scientist, Xerox Corp, 68-94. *Concurrent Pos:* Consult, Union Res Inst, Taiwan, China, 57-58; adv ed, J Adhesion, 71-; invited lectr, Chinese Acad Sci, 79, 86 & 87; course organizer, Fundamentals Adhesion, 81-96; hon adv, Fujian Res Inst light Indust, 86-; Res Ctr Solid Lubrication, Chinese Acad Sci, 87-; mem comt, Reliability of Adhesive Bonds in Severe Environs, Nat Res Coun, 84; vis prof chem, Xiamen Univ, China, 86-; hon prof, Lanzhou Inst Chem Phys, Chinese Acad Sci, 88-; R L Patrick fel, Adhesion Soc; hon trustee, Anglo-Chinese Col, Fuzhou, China, 89-. *Mem:* Am Chem Soc; Sigma Xi; Am Phys Soc; Adhesion Soc; NY Acad Sci. *Res:* Polymer friction and wear; adhesion and surface chemistry; electrophotography; tribology; published 100 papers, edited 12 technical books and granted 31 US patents; invented mobile cloud-seedings with silver iodide from locomotive. *Mailing Add:* 796 John Glenn Blvd Webster NY 14580. *Fax:* 716-872-2915

LEE, LIH-SYNG, BIOCHEMISTRY, BIOPHYSICS. *Current Pos:* STAFF ASSOC CARCINOGENESIS, COLUMBIA UNIV, 76- *Personal Data:* b China, Oct 28, 45; m 74; c 1. *Educ:* Nat Taiwan Univ, BS, 68; Yale Univ, MPh, 71, MS, 72, PhD(chem), 74. *Prof Exp:* Res scientist biochem & fel, Roswell Park Mem Inst, 74-76. *Mem:* NY Acad Sci; AAAS; Am Chem Soc. *Res:* Chemical carcinogenesis; tumor promotion; growth factors; hormone receptors; cell culture; transport; enzymology; DNA metabolism; cell cycle; gene transfer; membrane biophysics; drug design. *Mailing Add:* 22 Van Wyck Dr Princeton Junction NJ 08550-1640

LEE, LILIAN M, CLINICAL & PROTEIN CHEMISTRY. *Current Pos:* HEAD PROTEIN CHEMIST, SPECTRAL DIAG INC, 92- *Personal Data:* b Hong Kong, 1938. *Educ:* McGill Univ, BS, 63; Univ BC, MS, 65; Univ Western Ont, PhD(path chem), 71. *Prof Exp:* Res fel, Clin Chem Training Prog, Univ Wash, Seattle, 73-75; res assoc, Hosp Sick Children, 75-92. *Res:* Clinical and protein chemistry. *Mailing Add:* 18 Hollywood Ave No 1407 North York ON M2N 6P5 Can

LEE, LINDA SHAHRABANI, ENVIRONMENTAL FATE OF ORGANICS, CONTAMINANT HYDROLOGY. *Current Pos:* ASST PROF ENVIRON ORG CHEM, AGRON DEPT, PURDUE UNIV, 93- *Personal Data:* b Dover, Del, July 22, 59; div; c James R & Joshua R. *Educ:* Univ Fla, BS, 83, MS, 89, PhD(soil chem & contaminant hydrol), 93. *Prof Exp:* Chemist I soil water sci dept, Univ Fla, 84-88, chemist III, 88-89, sr chemist, 89-93. *Mem:* Am Asn Agron; Am Chem Soc; Nat Ground Water Asn; AAAS; Sigma Xi. *Res:* The sorption, solubility, degradation and transport of various classes of organic contaminants in aqueous, mixed-solvent and multi-phasic systems. *Mailing Add:* 1150 Lilly Hall Life Sci West Lafayette IN 47907-1150. *Fax:* 765-496-1368; *E-Mail:* llee@dept.agry.purdue.edu

LEE, LIN-SHAN, ELECTRICAL ENGINEERING. *Current Pos:* assoc prof, 79-82, head, Dept Comput Sci & Info Eng, 82-87, PROF, NAT TAIWAN UNIV, 82- *Personal Data:* b Kaohsiung, Taiwan, Sept, 23, 52; m 83, Chia-Ling Mei; c Meng-Heng. *Educ:* Nat Taiwan Univ, BSEE, 74; Stanford Univ, MSEE, 75, PhD, 77. *Honors & Awards:* Medal Distinguished Accomplishment, Chinese Inst Elec Engrs, 91. *Prof Exp:* Tech consult, Edutel Commun & Devels Inc, 77-79. *Current Pos:* Res fel, Academia Sinica, Taipei, 85-, dir inst info sci, 91-; ed, J Selected Areas in Commun, Inst Elec & Electronics Engrs, 94-95. *Mem:* Inst Elec & Electronics Engrs; Inst Elec & Electronics Engrs Commun Soc; Union Radio Sci Int; Chinese Inst Elec Engrs; Computational Linguistic Soc Repub China. *Res:* Contributed various articles to professional journals; contributions in Mandarin dictation technology for input of Chinese text-to-speech systems for synthesizing Mandarin speech from unlimited Chinese texts. *Mailing Add:* 7 3rd Floor 58th Lane Wen-Chou St Taipei 107 Taiwan

LEE, LINWOOD LAWRENCE, JR, NUCLEAR PHYSICS. *Current Pos:* dir, Nuclear Struct Lab, 65-84, PROF PHYSICS, STATE UNIV NY, STONY BROOK, 65- *Personal Data:* b Trenton, NJ, Aug 5, 28; m 57, Dorothy Tutt; c Linwood III. *Educ:* Princeton Univ, AB, 50; Yale Univ, MS, 51, PhD(physics), 55. *Prof Exp:* Asst physicist, Argonne Nat Lab, 54-59, assoc physicist, 60-65; vis asst prof physics, Univ Minn, 59-60. *Mem:* Fel Am Phys Soc; fel AAAS. *Res:* Experimental studies of nuclear structure and spectroscopy; nucleon transfer reactions; near barrier heavy ion reactions. *Mailing Add:* 8 Johns Rd Setauket NY 11733

LEE, LLOYD LIEH-SHEN, STATISTICAL MECHANICS, POLYMER TECHNOLOGY. *Current Pos:* asst prof, 76-80, ASSOC PROF CHEM ENG & MAT SCI, UNIV OKLA, 80- *Personal Data:* b China, Jan 25, 42; US citizen. *Educ:* Nat Taiwan Univ, BS, 63; Northwestern Univ, PhD(chem eng), 71. *Prof Exp:* Res engr polymer, Du Pont Chem Co, 71-72; researcher liquids, Univ Paris, 72; mgr textiles, Tashing Chem Co, 73-75. *Mem:* Am Chem Soc. *Res:* Natural gas properties; electrolyte solutions; perturbation theory for liquid structure and liquid thermodynamics; Monte Carlo and molecular dynamics simulations; turbulence; high-speed spinning of polymeric filaments. *Mailing Add:* Dept Chem Eng EC T335 Univ Okla 100 E Boyd St Norman OK 73019-6623

LEE, LONG CHI, EXPERIMENTAL PHYSICS. *Current Pos:* PROF ELEC & COMPUT ENG, SAN DIEGO STATE UNIV, 82- *Personal Data:* b Kaohsiung, Taiwan, Oct 19, 40; m 67; c Gloria Y & Thomas D. *Educ:* Taiwan Normal Univ, BS, 64; Univ Southern Calif, MA, 67, PhD(physics), 71. *Honors & Awards:* SDSU Meritorious Performance & Prof Award, 86, 88, 90. *Prof Exp:* From res asst to res assoc, 67-72, res staff physicist, 72-77, adj asst prof physics, Univ Southern Calif, 77; physicist, 77-78, sr physicist, Stanford Res Inst Int, 79-81. *Concurrent Pos:* Vis scientist, Univ Kaiserslautern, Ger, 75. *Mem:* Am Phys Soc; Inter-Am Photochemical Soc; Inst Elec & Electronics Engrs; Am Geophys Union; Int Soc Optical Eng. *Res:* Photoionization and photodissociation processes of small molecules and radicals using vacuum ultraviolet radiation; photodestruction processes of atmospheric positive and negative ions; molecular processes in electrical discharges; optical characteristics of small aerosol particles; molecular processes in chemical etching; reaction kinetics. *Mailing Add:* Dept Elec & Comput Eng San Diego State Univ San Diego CA 92182-0190. *Fax:* 619-594-3701; *E-Mail:* llee@mail.sdsu.edu

LEE, LOU-CHUANG, PLASMA PHYSICS, SPACE PHYSICS. *Current Pos:* assoc prof, 78-86, PROF, GEOPHYS INST, UNIV ALASKA, 86- *Personal Data:* b Taiwan, China, Apr 20, 47; c 2. *Educ:* Nat Taiwan Univ, BS, 69; Calif Inst Technol, MS, 72, PhD(physics), 75. *Honors & Awards:* Moore Prize, 87. *Prof Exp:* Res assoc physics, Goddard Space Flight Ctr, NASA, 75-77; vis asst prof, Inst Phys Sci & Technol, Univ Md, 77-78. *Concurrent Pos:* Toray vis scholar, 86; Distinguished Fulbright Scholar, 88. *Mem:* Am Phys Soc; Am Geophys Union; AAAS. *Res:* Magnetospheric physics. *Mailing Add:* Geophys Inst Univ Alaska Fairbanks AK 99775-0800. *E-Mail:* fflcl@alaska.edu

LEE, LU-YUAN, AIRWAY DISEASE, AIR POLLUTANTS & HEALTH. *Current Pos:* from asst prof to assoc prof, 78-92, PROF PHYSIOL, MED CTR, UNIV KY, 92-, RES DIR, 94- *Personal Data:* b June 26, 46; m 78, Hsiao-Hwa Chou; c Stephanie J & Calvin Y. *Educ:* Nat Taiwan Univ, BS, 69; Univ Miss, MS, 72, PhD(physiol), 75. *Prof Exp:* Res fel, Cardiovasc Res Inst, Univ Calif, San Francisco, 75-78. *Concurrent Pos:* Nat res serv award, 77, NIH, Young investr award, 80, sr int award, 92, mem, Respiratory & Appl Physiol Study Sect; vis scientist, Dept Physiol, Univ Tex Med Br, 85; vis prof, Dept Pharmacol, Karolinoka Inst, Sweden, 92. *Mem:* Am Physiol Soc; Am Thoracic Soc; sr mem Biomed Eng Soc. *Res:* Elucidate the neurohumoral mechanisms underlying the airway responses to inhaled irritants in health and in airway diseases; pulmonary reflexes. *Mailing Add:* Dept Physiol & Biophys Univ Ky Med Ctr Lexington KY 40536-0084. *Fax:* 606-323-1070; *E-Mail:* lylee@pop.uky.edu

LEE, LYNDON EDMUND, JR, SURGERY, PHARMACOLOGY. *Current Pos:* SURG, US VET ADMIN, WASHINGTON, DC, 78- *Personal Data:* b Islip, NY, Aug 11, 12; m 43; c 3. *Educ:* Duke Univ, BS, 37, MD, 38. *Prof Exp:* Asst cardiol, Univ Va, 38; resident obstet & gynec, Duke Univ Hosp, 40; intern surg, Med Col Va, 41; instr, Med Sch, Univ Mich, 42-43, instr pharmacol & surg, 42-47; instr post-grad educ comt, State Med Asn, Tenn, 47-49; dir cancer control, PR Dept Health, 49-54; instr pharmacol & surg, Med Sch, Univ Mich, 54-57; coordr res, 57-69, dir surg servs, 65-69, asst chief med dir res & educ, 69-71, asst chief med dir prof serv, 71-76, spec asst chief med dir, US Vet Admin, 76-77, chief staff, Vet Admin Hosp, Richmond, Va

& assoc dean & prof surg, Med Col Va, 76-78. *Concurrent Pos:* Nat Res Coun fel, 38-40 & 41-42; assoc physician, Blue Ridge Sanatorium, Charlottesville, Va, 38; physician, Am Hosp in Brit, Oxford, Eng, 41 & Pondville State Hosp Cancer, Walpole, Mass; assoc surg, Mass Gen Hosp, Boston; prof, Sch Med, Univ PR, 52-54; dir surg, Wayne Co Gen Hosp, 54-57; mem, Med Sci Div, Nat Acad Sci, 69-76 & White House Fed Coun Sci & Technol, 69-76 Consult, Smithsonian Inst, 58-76, Nat Adv Cancer Coun, NIH, 58-76 & Training Grants Rev Bd & Cancer Chemother Nat Serv Ctr, Nat Cancer Inst, 58-76; mem Nat Adv Coun Child Health & Human Develop, NIH. *Mem:* AAAS; Am Pub Health Asn; Pub Health Cancer Asn Am; fel Am Col Surgeons; fel Int Soc Surg. *Res:* Analgesics and sedatives; neoplasms. *Mailing Add:* 4111 Saul Rd Chevy Chase View Kensington MD 20895-3726

LEE, M(ONHE) HOWARD, THEORETICAL PHYSICS. *Current Pos:* from asst prof to assoc prof, 73-85, PROF PHYSICS, UNIV GA, 85- *Personal Data:* b Pusan, Korea, May 21, 37; US citizen; m 67, Margaret F Kendig; c Jennifer K. *Educ:* Univ Pa, BS, 59, PhD(physics), 67. *Prof Exp:* Fel physics, Theoret Physics Inst, Univ Alta, 67-69; res assoc, Dept Physics & Mat Sci Ctr, Mass Inst Technol, 69-71; NIH res grant & investr biomat, Health Sci & Technol, Mass Inst Technol & Harvard Univ, 71-73. *Concurrent Pos:* Guest lectr, Inst Theoret Physics, Univ Leuven, Belg, 76; grants, NATO, 76-78 & 93-94, Air Force Off Sci Res, 77-78, Dept Energy, 77-87, Off Naval Res, 85-89, NSF, 87-96, Army Res Off, 88-95; Fulbright-Hays Sr Res Scholar Award, Univ Louvain, Belg, 78-79; co-chmn, 17th Eastern Theoret Physics Conf, Athens, Ga, 79; vis prof, Dept Physics, Seoul Nat Univ, Korea, 80; vis scientist, Gzech Acad Sci, 90. *Mem:* Am Phys Soc. *Res:* Many-body theory; statistical mechanics; mathematical physics. *Mailing Add:* Dept Physics Univ Ga Athens GA 30602

LEE, MARIETTA Y W T, DNA REPLICATION, DNA REPAIR. *Current Pos:* From asst prof to assoc prof, 81-92, PROF MED, UNIV MIAMI, 93-, PROF BIOCHEM & MOLECULAR BIOL, 94- *Personal Data:* b Canton, China, Mar 3, 43; m 69, Ernest Y; c Patrick. *Educ:* Nazareth Col, BSc, 65; New York Univ, MS, 67; Univ Miami, PhD(biol), 73. *Concurrent Pos:* Estab investr, Am Heart Asn, 84-89; mem, ASBMB Comt Equal Opportunity Women, 88-91; mem, NIH Biochem Study Sect, 90-94. *Mem:* Am Soc Univ Prof; Am Soc Biol Chemists. *Res:* Inhibition of human DNA polymerases by antiviral drugs; mechanisms of DNA replication and DNA repair; over expression of DNA polymerases, PCNA and replication proteins; production of honodonal antibodies to DNA polymerases and replication protein. *Mailing Add:* Dept Med PO Box 016960-R57 Univ Miami Miami FL 33101-6960. *Fax:* 305-547-5819

LEE, MARK, SOLID STATE PHYSICS. *Current Pos:* ASST PROF PHYSICS, UNIV VA, 92- *Personal Data:* b Taipai, Taiwan, Apr 10, 64. *Educ:* Harvard Univ, BA, 86, MA, 86; Stanford Univ, PhD(physics), 91. *Honors & Awards:* Cottrell scholar award, Res Corp, 96. *Mem:* Am Phys Soc; Mat Res Soc. *Mailing Add:* Dept Physics Univ Va McCormick Rd Charlottesville VA 22903. *Fax:* 804-924-4576; *E-Mail:* marklee@virginia.edu

LEE, MARTIN ALAN, ASTROPHYSICS. *Current Pos:* res scientist astrophys, 79-84, res assoc prof, 84-90, PROF PHYSICS, UNIV NH, 90- *Personal Data:* b Bromley, Eng, Oct 9, 45; US citizen. *Educ:* Stanford Univ, BSc, 66; Univ Chicago, PhD(physics), 71. *Prof Exp:* NATO fel astrophys, Max Planck Inst Extraterrestrial Physics, WGer, 71-72, res assoc, 72-73; res assoc, Lab Astrophys & Space Res, Univ Chicago, 73-74; asst prof physics, Washington Univ, 74-79. *Concurrent Pos:* Ed, Advances in Space Res, 84; vis prof extraterrestrial physics, Max Planck Inst, WGer, 85; prin investr, NSF grant. *Mem:* Am Astron Soc; Am Geophys Union. *Res:* Energetic particle transport and plasma processes in the solar-terrestrial environment including ion shock acceleration, solar modulation of galactic cosmic rays, plasma instabilities and wave propagation. *Mailing Add:* Space Sci Ctr Morse Hall 39 College Rd Univ NH Durham NH 03824-3525

LEE, MARTIN J G, CONDENSED MATTER PHYSICS. *Current Pos:* assoc prof, 74-79, PROF PHYSICS, UNIV TORONTO, 79- *Personal Data:* b Kings Lynn, Eng, Mar 16, 42. *Educ:* Cambridge Univ, BA, 63, MA & PhD(physics), 67. *Prof Exp:* Instr, 67-69, asst prof physics, James Franck Inst & Dept Physics, Univ Chicago, 69-74. *Mem:* Can Asn Physicists. *Res:* Experimental and theoretical study of Fermi surfaces and electronic structure of metals; photo field emission phenomena; high temperature superconductivity. *Mailing Add:* Dept Physics Univ Toronto 60 St George St Toronto ON M5S 1A7 Can

LEE, MARTIN JEROME, BIOCHEMISTRY. *Current Pos:* STAFF, ROCKLAND MEDI-LABS. *Personal Data:* b Bayonne, NJ, May 24, 43; m 67; c 1. *Educ:* Rutgers Univ, New Brunswick, BA, 65, MS, 68, PhD(biochem), 69. *Prof Exp:* Nat Inst Gen Med Sci fel, Univ Wis-Madison, 69-70, res assoc biochem, Enzyme Inst, 70-71; sr res assoc, Pharmacia Fine Chem, Inc, 71-73; staff scientist, Technicon Instruments Corp, 73-80; dir appl res, Coulter Diag, 80- *Mem:* Biophys Soc; Am Chem Soc; Sigma Xi; NY Acad Sci. *Res:* Bioenergetics; chromatography; separational techniques and instrumentation; automated cytochemistry, immunology, clinical chemistry and enzymology. *Mailing Add:* Great Smokie Diag Lab 60 Terrace Rd Asheville NC 28801-1539

LEE, MARTIN JOE, ACCELERATOR PHYSICS, MICROWAVES. *Current Pos:* ENG PHYSICIST SLAC, 67-; CONSULT, 87- *Personal Data:* US citizen. *Educ:* Univ Calif, BS, 60; NY Univ, MS, 62; Stanford Univ, PhD(elec eng), 67. *Prof Exp:* Microwave engr commun, Bell Tel Lab, 60-62; microwave engr accelerator eng, Stanford Linear Accelerator Ctr, 62-67; accelerator physicist, Brookhaven Nat Lab, 67-69; accelerator theorist, 69-78, dep chief, Pep Theory Group, Accelerator Physics, Stanford Linear Accelerator Ctr, 78-87. *Concurrent Pos:* Spec consult, Electron Storage Ring Corp, 78- *Mem:* Inst Elec & Electronics Engrs. *Mailing Add:* Stanford Linear Accelerator Ctr MS 26 2575 Sand Hill Rd Stanford Univ Menlo Park CA 94025

LEE, MATHEW HUNG MUN, PHYSICAL MEDICINE & REHABILITATION. *Current Pos:* Resident, Inst Phys Med & Rehab, Med Ctr, NY Univ, 62-64, NY State Health Dept assignee, Rehab Serv, 64-65, from asst prof to assoc prof rehab med, 65-73, dir educ & training, Dept Rehab Med, 66-68, assoc dir, 68, DIR DEPT REHAB MED, GOLDWATER MEM HOSP, 68-, PROF REHAB MED, SCH MED, NY UNIV, 73- *Personal Data:* b Hawaii, July 28, 31; m 58; c 3. *Educ:* Johns Hopkins Univ, AB, 53; Univ Md, MD, 56; Univ Calif, MPH, 62; Am Bd Phys Med & Rehab, dipl, 66. *Concurrent Pos:* Assoc vis physician, Goldwater Mem Hosp, 65-68, vis physician, 68-, chief electrodiag unit, 66-, vpres med bd, 69-70, pres, 71-; asst clin prof, Col Dent, NY Univ, 66-69, clin asst prof, 69-70, clin assoc prof, 70-; consult, Daughters of Israel Hosp, New York, 65-72, Bur Adult Hyg, 65- & Human Resources Ctr, 66-; asst attend physician, Hosp, NY Univ, 68-; World Rehab Fund consult, Gordon Seagrave & Maryknoll Hosps, Korea, 69; attend physician, Bellevue Hosp Ctr, 71-; consult, US Dept Interior. *Mem:* AAAS; fel Am Acad Phys Med & Rehab; fel Am Col Physicians; Pan-Am Med Asn; fel Am Pub Health Asn. *Mailing Add:* Rusk Inst Rehab Med New York NY 10016

LEE, MAY D-MING (LU), NATURAL PRODUCTS ISOLATION, STRUCTURE ELUCIDATION. *Current Pos:* RES CHEMIST, LEDERLE LABS, 77- *Personal Data:* b China, May 12, 49; US citizen; m 74; c 2. *Educ:* Univ BC, BS, 72; Univ Ill, Urbana, MS, 74, PhD(chem), 76. *Prof Exp:* Res fel chem, Harvard Univ, 76-77. *Mem:* Am Chem Soc; AAAS. *Res:* Isolation, screening and structure elucidation of novel antitumor and antibacterial agents from fermentation; screening methodology. *Mailing Add:* 1335 Carvo Ct Los Altos CA 94024

LEE, MELVIN, NUTRITION, BIOCHEMISTRY. *Current Pos:* prof nutrit & dir, Sch Home Econ, 67-74, PROF NUTRIT, SCH FAMILY & NUTRIT SCI, UNIV BC, 74- *Personal Data:* b New York, NY, Jan 5, 26; m 49; c 4. *Educ:* Univ Calif, Los Angeles, BA, 47; Univ Calif, Berkeley, MA, 52, PhD(nutrit), 58. *Prof Exp:* From instr to asst prof prev med, Sch Med, Univ Calif, San Francisco, 58-67, asst prof biochem, 63-67, lectr dent, 61-67. *Concurrent Pos:* USPHS res fel, 66; sci exchange fel, Japan Soc Prom, 81; vis scientist, Gunma Univ, Japan, 86. *Mem:* AAAS; Am Inst Nutrit; Soc Environ Geochem & Health; Soc Nutrit Latin Am; Can Soc Nutrit Sci. *Res:* Relation of diet to metabolic patterns; factors influencing growth; maternal alcohol and fetal development. *Mailing Add:* Sch Family Nutrit Sci Univ BC Vancouver BC V6T 1W5 Can

LEE, MEN HUI, cancer research, for more information see previous edition

LEE, MICHAEL CHING-HSUEH, MATERIAL COMPOSITION PROCESSING & STRUCTURE, FINITE ELEMENT ANALYSIS IN RHEOLOGY. *Current Pos:* sr res engr, Polymers Dept, Gen Motors Res Labs, 78-81, staff res engr, 81-84, sr staff res engr, 84-89, PRIN RES ENGR, POLYMERS DEPT, GEN MOTORS RES & DEVELOP CTR, 89- *Personal Data:* m 72, Amy Hsu; c Benjamin, Josephine, David & John. *Educ:* Nat Cheng-Kung Univ, BS, 70; Univ Calif, MS, 74, PhD(mech eng), 77. *Prof Exp:* Fel, Dept Chem, Univ Calif, Berkeley, 77-78. *Concurrent Pos:* Group leader, Polymers Dept, Gen Motors Res Labs, 83-87, prog mgr, Exec Dept, 86-87, sr tech staff, 87-93. *Mem:* Am Chem Soc; Soc Rheology. *Res:* Unified constitutive equations for materials; rheology; composition, processing, structure and property relationships for materials; mixing rule for elastonic and plastic composites; co-injection molding process; finite element analysis for elastonar and visco elastic materials; polymer tribology and research planning. *Mailing Add:* 480-106-316 Bldg No 1-6 30500 Mound Rd Warren MI 48090-9055. *Fax:* 248-641-7766; *E-Mail:* michael__c._lee@gmrnotes3.gmr.com

LEE, MING T, HYDRAULICS, WATER RESOURCES. *Current Pos:* SR WATER RESOURCES ENGR, GREINER ENG, 93- *Personal Data:* b Taipei, Taiwan, Aug 15, 40; US citizen; m 70; c 2. *Educ:* Nat Taiwan Univ, BS, 63, MS, 66; Univ Cincinnati, MS, 68; Purdue Univ, PhD(civil eng), 72. *Prof Exp:* Res engr, Hydraul Lab, Water Resources Planning Comn, 66-67; hydraul engr, Vogt, Iver & Assoc, Ohio, 68; res engr hydraul, Agr Econ Dept, Univ Ill, 72-75; assoc prof scientist, Ill State Water Surv, 75-91, prof scientist hydraul, 91-93. *Mem:* Am Geophys Union; Soil Conserv Soc Am; Am Soc Civil Engrs; Sigma Xi. *Res:* Soil erosion; sediment transport; lake hydrology; watershed erosion control; hydrologic computer modeling. *Mailing Add:* 1852 Union St Clearwater FL 34623

LEE, MING-LIANG, MEDICAL GENETICS, BIOCHEMISTRY. *Current Pos:* ASSOC PROF MED GENETICS & CHIEF DIV, RUTGERS MED SCH, 77- *Personal Data:* b Tainan, Taiwan, June 26, 36; m 65; c 3. *Educ:* Nat Taiwan Univ, MD, 62; Univ Miami, PhD(biochem), 69. *Prof Exp:* Asst prof, Sch Med, Univ Miami, 72-76; chief fel med genetics, Sch Med, Johns Hopkins Univ, 76-77. *Mem:* Am Soc Biol Scientist; Am Soc Med Genetics. *Mailing Add:* Acad Health Sci Ctr CN-19 Dept Pediat UMDNJ-R W Johnson Med Sch New Brunswick NJ 08903

LEE, MINYOUNG, MATERIALS SCIENCE. *Current Pos:* MEM TECH STAFF MAT, CORP RES & DEVELOP CTR, GEN ELEC CO, 71- *Personal Data:* b Seoul, Korea, Aug 11, 38; US citizen; m 66; c 2. *Educ:* Seoul Nat Univ, BS, 61; Providence Col, MS, 67; Brown Univ, PhD(mat sci), 71. *Concurrent Pos:* Vis scientist, Cavendish Lab, Cambridge Univ, 76. *Mem:* Am Inst Mining, Metall & Petrol Engrs; Soc Mech Engrs. *Res:* Development of very hard materials primarily for cutting tools and wear parts; advanced materials processing technology; tribology; sensors for factory automation. *Mailing Add:* Corp Res & Develop Ctr Gen Elec Co PO Box 8 Schenectady NY 12301. *Fax:* 518-387-7563; *E-Mail:* leem@crd.ge.com

LEE, NANCY L, BIOLOGICAL SCIENCE. *Current Pos:* PROF MICROBIOL, UNIV CALIF, 65- *Mailing Add:* Biol Sci Dept Univ Calif Santa Barbara CA 93106-0001

LEE, NANCY ZEE-NEE MA, PHARMACOLOGY. *Current Pos:* PROF, DEPT PHARMACOL, UNIV MINN MED SCH, MINNEAPOLIS, 89- *Personal Data:* b Shanghai, China, Oct 28, 40; US citizen; m 65; c 2. *Educ:* Southwestern Univ, Georgetown, Tex, BS, 63; Univ Tex, Austin, PhD(biochem), 67. *Prof Exp:* Res asst, Univ Tex, Austin, 63-67; postdoctoral fel, Dept Biochem, Northwestern Univ, Evanston, Ill, 67; res biochemist III-VI, Dept Pharmacol, Univ Calif, San Francisco, 68-72, asst res biochemist, 72-78, assoc res pharmacologist, Dept Pharmacol & Langley Porter Psychiat Inst, 78-84, adj assoc prof, 84-87, prof, 87-89. *Mem:* Sigma Xi; Soc Neurosci; Am Soc Pharmacol & Exp Therapeut; AAAS; Int Asn Women Bioscientist; Soc Chinese Bioscientists Am. *Res:* Pharmacology; Biochemical mechanism for narcotic addiction. *Mailing Add:* Dept Pharmacol Univ Minn 3-249 Millard Hall 435 Delaware St SE Minneapolis MN 55455-0347

LEE, NORMAN K, APPLIED MATHEMATICS. *Current Pos:* Asst prof, 58-66, admin asst dept, 79-82, ASSOC PROF MATH, BALL STATE UNIV, 69- *Personal Data:* b Frankfort, Ind, Feb 3, 34; m 56; c 2. *Educ:* Hanover Col, BA, 56; Vanderbilt Univ, MA, 58; Purdue Univ, PhD(bionucleonics), 69. *Concurrent Pos:* NSF fel, 63-64, partic, Acad Year Inst, 62-63; sr instr, Somerset Community Col, 68-69. *Mem:* AAAS. *Res:* Mathematical models. *Mailing Add:* 401 W Main St Ridgeville IN 47380

LEE, PATRICE ANNE, PHYSIOLOGY, SEPTIC SHOCK & TRAUMATIC SHOCK. *Current Pos:* DIR PEDIAT CRITICAL CARE RES, MED CITY DALLAS HOSP, 90- *Personal Data:* b Baltimore, Md, Feb 24, 60. *Educ:* Univ Miami, BS, 82; Duke Univ, PhD(physiol), 87. *Prof Exp:* Asst res scientist, Okla Med Res Found, 87-90. *Mem:* Am Thoracic Soc; Soc Critical Care Med; Shock Soc; Am Physiol Soc; Wilderness Med Soc. *Mailing Add:* Dept Pharmacol Amgen Boulder Inc 3200 Walnut St MS AB-30 Boulder CO 80301

LEE, PATRICK A, CONDENSED MATTER THEORY. *Current Pos:* PROF PHYSICS, MASS INST TECHNOL, 82- *Personal Data:* b Hong Kong, Sept 8, 46; m 69; c 2. *Educ:* Mass Inst Technol, BS, 66, PhD(physics), 70. *Honors & Awards:* Oliver Buckley Condensed Matter Physics Prize, 91. *Prof Exp:* J W Gibbs instr physics, Yale Univ, 70-72; mem tech staff, Bell Labs, 72-73; asst prof physics, Univ Wash, Seattle, 73-74; mem tech staff, Bell Labs, 74-82. *Mem:* Nat Acad Sci; fel Am Phys Soc; Am Acad Arts & Sci. *Res:* Disordered electronic systems; quantum transport in small structures; theory of high temperature superconductivity. *Mailing Add:* Dept Physics Mass Inst Technol Cambridge MA 02139

LEE, PAUL D, ASTRONOMY, ASTROPHYSICS. *Current Pos:* ASSOC PROF PHYSICS & ASTRON, MIDDLE TENN STATE UNIV, 94- *Personal Data:* b Ina, Ill, Feb 15, 40; m 61; c 2. *Educ:* Univ Ill, BS, 63, MS, 65, PhD, 68. *Prof Exp:* From asst prof to assoc prof physics & astron, La State Univ, Baton Rouge, 68-94. *Mem:* Royal Astron Soc; Am Astron Soc. *Res:* Spectrophotometry of stellar and nonstellar objects; stellar atmospheres and chemical abundances in stars. *Mailing Add:* Dept Physics & Astron Wiser Patten Bldg Middle Tenn State Univ Murfreesboro TN 37132

LEE, PAUL L, MEDICAL IMAGING. *Current Pos:* Res fel physics, Calif Inst Technol, 71-73, lectr physics, Calif State Univ, Long Beach, 73-75, from asst prof to assoc prof, 75-83, PROF PHYSICS, CALIF STATE UNIV, NORTHRIDGE, 83- *Personal Data:* b China, June 12, 44; US citizen; m 72, Amy Shiu; c 2. *Educ:* Calif Inst Technol, BS, 67, PhD(physics), 71. *Concurrent Pos:* Vis assoc, Calif Inst Technol, 76-83; vis fac, Jet Propulsion Lab, Caltech, 83-84, MTS, 85- *Mem:* Am Phys Soc. *Res:* Image processing and medical physics; nuclear magnetic resonance imaging protocols and special hardware; algorithms for analyzing X-ray angiograms; data analysis; numerical methods. *Mailing Add:* Dept Physics & Astron Calif State Univ Northridge CA 91330. *Fax:* 818-677-5234; *E-Mail:* paul.lee@csvn.edu

LEE, PETER CHUNG-YI, ENGINEERING MECHANICS. *Current Pos:* Sloan vis fel, 65-66, from asst prof to assoc prof, 66-76, PROF CIVIL ENG, PRINCETON UNIV, 76- *Personal Data:* b Hankow, Hupei, China, Sept 29, 34; m 61; c 1. *Educ:* Cheng Kung Univ, Taiwan, BS, 57; Rutgers Univ, MS, 61; Columbia Univ, MS, 65, DEngSc(eng mech), 65. *Honors & Awards:* C B Sawyer Mem Award, 80. *Mem:* Am Soc Mech Engrs; assoc mem Am Soc Civil Engrs; Acoust Soc Am; Inst Elec & Electronics Engrs. *Res:* Theory of elasticity; vibrations and wave propagation in elastic solids and pieoelectric crystals; effects of initial stresses and accelerations; temperature changes on the vibrations of elastic and crystal plates. *Mailing Add:* Dept Civil Eng & Opers Res Princeton NJ 08544

LEE, PETER E, PLANT VIROLOGY. *Current Pos:* RETIRED. *Personal Data:* b Trinidad, WI, Oct 18, 30; m 60; c 2. *Educ:* Univ Man, BSc, 58; Univ Wis, MSc, 59, PhD(entom), 61. *Prof Exp:* Jr res entomologist, Univ Calif, Berkeley, 61; res officer virus-vector studies, Can Dept Agr, 61-65; from asst prof to prof biol, Carleton Univ, 65-89. *Mem:* Electron Micros Soc Am. *Res:* Characterization of leafhopper-transmitted viruses and insect viruses; virus purification and electron microscopy. *Mailing Add:* 38 Inuvik Crescent Kanata ON K2L 1A2 Can

LEE, PETER H Y, FLUID MECHANICS, PLASMA. *Current Pos:* SR SCIENTIST, OCEAN TECHNOL DEPT, TRW SPACE & DEFENSE, 91- *Personal Data:* b Chungking, China, Apr 20, 39. *Educ:* Nat Taiwan Univ, BS, 61; Tech Univ Aachen, Ger, dipl, 67; Calif Inst Technol, PhD(aeronaut), 73. *Prof Exp:* Mem tech staff, TRW, 73-76; physicist, Lawrence Livermore Lab, 76-84; staff mem, Los Alamos Nat Lab, 84-91. *Mem:* Am Phys Soc. *Mailing Add:* 1447 Second St Manhattan Beach CA 90266

LEE, PETER VAN ARSDALE, PHARMACOLOGY, MEDICINE. *Current Pos:* asst prof & asst dean, Univ Southern Calif, 55-58, assoc prof pharmacol, 58-67, assoc prof med, 60-67, assoc dean, 58-60, admis officer, 60-65, prof pharmacol, 67-80, PROF MED, SCH MED, UNIV SOUTHERN CALIF, 67-, PROF FAMILY & PREV MED, 80- *Personal Data:* b San Francisco, Calif, Mar 31, 23; m 51; c 4. *Educ:* Stanford Univ, AB, 44, MD, 47. *Prof Exp:* Intern, San Francisco Hosp, 46-47; asst resident path, Stanford Univ Hosps, 49-50, resident med, 50-51; clin asst, Col Med, State Univ NY, 51-52; instr pharmacol, Sch Med, Stanford Univ, 52-54, asst prof, 54-55. *Concurrent Pos:* Resident, King's Co Hosp, NY, 51-52; consult, Commonwealth Fund, 58-59; vis fel, Brit Asn Study Med Educ, 71-72. *Mem:* AAAS; Am Fedn Clin Res; Asn Am Med Cols; Brit Asn Study Med Educ; fel Royal Soc Med. *Res:* Medical education; clinical pharmacology. *Mailing Add:* Dept Family Med Univ Southern Calif 1420 San Pablo St Los Angeles CA 90033

LEE, PETER WANKYOON, POWDER METALLURGY, METAL FORMING & THIN METALLIC COATING PROCESSES. *Current Pos:* res metallurgist, Timken Co, 68-69, from res specialist to sr res specialist, 72-86, res scientist, 86-91, DEVELOP TECHNOLOGIST, TIMKEN CO, CANTON, OHIO, 91- *Personal Data:* b Seoul, Korea, May 30, 39; US citizen; m 67, Lucy Park; c David & Eugene. *Educ:* Seoul Nat Univ, Korea, BS, 61; Marquette Univ, MS, 66, MS, 68; Drexel Univ, PhD(mat eng), 72. *Honors & Awards:* Cert Recognition, NASA, 89. *Prof Exp:* Designer, Dowha Consult, Seoul, Korea, 61-62. *Concurrent Pos:* Chmn, Powder Metall Comt, Am Soc Metals Int, 82-86, Mat Shaping Tech Div, 86-90, mem, Tech Div Bd, 86-96, Conf Comt, Near Net Shape Mfg, 88 & 90; ed, Rapidly Solidified Mat, Proc Am Soc Metals Int Conf, 86 & 88. *Mem:* Fel Am Soc Metals Int; Am Powder Metall Inst; Asn Iron & Steel Engrs; Soc Mfg Engrs. *Res:* Research activities in the areas of metal forming processes, powder metallurgy and surface modifications in order to improve performance and/or to reduce the manufacturing cost. *Mailing Add:* Timken Co Res 07 PO Box 6930 1835 Dueber Ave SW Canton OH 44706-0930. *Fax:* 330-471-2082; *E-Mail:* pwlee@timken.com

LEE, PHILIP RANDOLPH, INTERNAL MEDICINE. *Current Pos:* SR ADV, SCH MED & EMER PROF, UNIV CALIF, SAN FRANCISCO, 97- *Personal Data:* b San Francisco, Calif, Apr 17, 24; m 53; c 4. *Educ:* Stanford Univ, AB, 45, MD, 48; Univ Minn, MS, 55; Am Bd Internal Med, cert, 56. *Hon Degrees:* ScD, MacMurray Col, 67. *Honors & Awards:* Hugo Schaefer Medal, Am Pharmaceut Asn, 76. *Prof Exp:* Asst prof clin phys med & rehab, Sch Med, NY Univ, 55-56; clin instr med, Sch Med, Stanford Univ, 56-59, asst clin prof, 59-67; asst secy health & sci affairs, Univ Calif, San Francisco, 65-69, chancellor, 69-72, prof social med, Med Ctr, 69-93, dir, Inst Health Policy Studies, 72-93; asst secy health, Dept Health & Human Servs, Washington, 93-97. *Concurrent Pos:* Mem, Dept Internal Med, Palo Alto Med Clin, Calif, 56-65; consult, Bur Pub Health Serv, USPHS, 58-63; dir health serv, Off Tech Coop & Res, AID, 63-65; dep asst secy health & sci affairs, Dept HEW, 65, asst secy, 65-69; mem, Nat Coun Smoking & Pub Policy, 77-78, Nat Coun Health Planning & Develop, Dept HEW, 78-80, USPHS Adv Comt, 78; mem adv bd, Scripps Clin & Res Found, 80-; co-dir, Inst Health & Aging, Sch Nursing, Univ Calif, San Francisco, 80-; mem, Comt Pop, Nat Res Coun-Nat Acad Sci, 83-86; pres bd dirs, World Inst Disability, 84-; pres, Health Comn, City San Francisco, 85-89; chair, Physician Payment Rev Comn, 86-93. *Mem:* Inst Med-Nat Acad Sci; AAAS; AMA; Am Pub Health Asn; Am Fedn Clin Res; Am Col Physicians; Am Geriat Soc; Asn Am Med Col. *Res:* Arthritis and rheumatism, especially Rubella arthritis; cardiovascular rehabilitation; academic medical administration; health policy; author of over 10 books and many technical journal articles. *Mailing Add:* Inst Health Policy Studies 1388 Sutter St Suite 1100 San Francisco CA 94109. *Fax:* 415-476-0705

LEE, PING, CELLULAR PHYSIOLOGY. *Current Pos:* from asst prof to assoc prof, 68-77, PROF MED PHYSIOL, DEPT PHYSIOL, WVA UNIV, 77-, INTERIM CHAIR DEPT, 90- *Personal Data:* b Summantra, Indonesia, Apr 17, 36. *Educ:* Nat Univ Taipei, BS, 59; Duke Univ, MS, 61, PhD(physiol), 64. *Prof Exp:* Fel membrane transport, Duke Univ, 64-66, instr med physiol, 66-68. *Mem:* Am Physiol Soc; Biophys Soc. *Mailing Add:* Dept Physiol WVa Univ Sch Med Morgantown WV 26506-0002

LEE, PING-CHEUNG, PEDIATRICS, CELL BIOLOGY. *Current Pos:* RES PROF & DIR, GASTROINTESTINAL LABS, DEPT PEDIAT, MED COL WIS, MILWAUKEE, 89-, PROF PHARMACOL & TOXICOL. *Personal Data:* b Hong Kong, Sept 10, 39. *Educ:* Univ Hong Kong, BSc, 63; Fla State Univ, MS, 65, PhD, 68. *Prof Exp:* Res assoc, Dept Chem, Fla State Univ, Tallahassee, 68-72; res assoc, Dept Biochem, Med Sch, Northwestern Univ,

72-74, instr, Dept Biochem, 74-75; asst prof, Dept Surg & Biochem, Med Col Ohio, Toledo, 75-79; assoc prof, Dept Pediat, State Univ NY, Buffalo, 79-89. *Concurrent Pos:* Res investr, Steroid Hormone Lab, Wesley Mem Hosp, Chicago, Ill, 72-75; vis investr, Digestive Dis Br, Inst Arthritis, Metab & Digestive Dis, NIH, 78; dir, Gastrointestinal & Nutrit Lab, Children's Hosp, Buffalo, NY, 79-89; asst ed, J Pediat Gastroenterol & Nutrit, 82-90. *Mem:* Am Soc Biochem & Molecular Biol; Am Gastroenterol Asn; Soc Exp Biol & Med; Am Pancreatic Asn; Int Soc Study Fatty Acids & Lipids; Int Soc Study Xenobiotics; Soc Toxicol. *Res:* Alternative enzyme supplements for the treatment of pancreatic insufficiency; endocrine and reproductive toxicology of environmental contaminants. *Mailing Add:* Dept Pediat Med Col Wis MACC Fund Res Ctr 8701 Watertown Plank Rd Milwaukee WI 53226. *Fax:* 414-266-8549; *E-Mail:* pelee@post.its.mcw.edu

LEE, PUI KUM, OPTICS. *Current Pos:* RETIRED. *Personal Data:* b Peking, China, June 22, 16; US citizen; m 41; c 4. *Educ:* Lingnam Univ, BS, 40; Columbia Univ, MS, 49. *Honors & Awards:* IR-100 Award, Indust Res Mag, 78. *Prof Exp:* Asst chem, Nat Kwangsi Univ, China, 40-41; res chemist, Inst Indust Res, 41-42; mgr, China Chem Corp, 42-46; res assoc chem, Columbia Univ, 49-56; sr chemist reprography, Cent Res Labs, 3M Co, 56-63, res specialist imaging, 63-67, sr res specialist, 67-82. *Mem:* Am Chem Soc; Soc Photog Sci & Eng; Optical Soc Am. *Res:* Imaging optics. *Mailing Add:* 2240 Midland Grove Rd No 305 St Paul MN 55113

LEE, RALPH EDWARD, COMPUTER SCIENCE. *Current Pos:* RETIRED. *Personal Data:* b Gilliam, Mo, July 1, 21; m 42; c 5. *Educ:* Mo Valley Col, BS, 42; Univ Mo, MS, 49; Ind Univ, MA, 53. *Prof Exp:* From instr to assoc prof math, Sch Mines, Univ Mo, Rolla, 46-59, prof, 59-88, dir, Comput Ctr, 60-88. *Concurrent Pos:* NSF fel, Nat Bur Stand, 59. *Mem:* Data Processing Mgt Asn; Asn Comput Mach; Soc Indust & Appl Math; Asn Educ Data Systs. *Res:* Numerical analysis; matrix computations. *Mailing Add:* 12651 US Hwy 63 S Rolla MO 65401

LEE, RAY H(UI-CHOUNG), ELECTRICAL ENGINEERING, MATHEMATICS. *Current Pos:* RETIRED. *Personal Data:* b Canton, China, Mar 28, 18; nat US; c 4. *Educ:* Nat Cent Univ, China, BS, 41; Stanford Univ, MA, 45, EE, 46, MS, 47. *Prof Exp:* Design engr, Cent Radio Works China, 41-44; founder & prin, Honolulu Trade Sch, 47-51; engr-specialist, Boeing Airplane Co, 51-55; res specialist & chief mathematician, Chromatic TV Labs & Auktometric Corp, 55-63; staff mem, David Sarnoff Res Ctr, Radio Corp Am, NJ, 64-66; staff mem & mgr, Tex Instruments, 66-69; chief engr, Liquid Crystal Display, Backman Instruments, 69-73; consult prod develop & strategic planning, 73- *Mem:* Inst Elec & Electronics Engrs; Soc Info Display. *Res:* Processings; energy; communication. *Mailing Add:* 23203 Park Esperanza Calabasas CA 91302

LEE, RAYMOND CURTIS, physical chemistry; deceased, see previous edition for last biography

LEE, RICHARD FAYAO, ENVIRONMENTAL CHEMISTRY, BIOLOGICAL OCEANOGRAPHY. *Current Pos:* RES PROF OCEANOG, SKIDAWAY INST OCEANOG, 74- *Personal Data:* b Shanghai, China, July 13, 41; US citizen; m 70, Josephine Zaglp; c Elizabeth & Lori. *Educ:* San Diego State Col, BA, 64, MA, 66; Univ Calif, San Diego, PhD(marine biol), 70. *Prof Exp:* Res assoc biochem, Pa State Univ, 71-72 & Scripps Inst Oceanog, 72-73. *Concurrent Pos:* Lectr oceanog, San Diego State Univ, 71-73; mem adv comt, Marine Resources Res Group Biol Accumulators, UN Food & Agr Orgn, 74-; consult, Exxon Corp, 75. *Mem:* Am Chem Soc; Am Soc Limnol & Oceanog; Sigma Xi. *Res:* Fate of petroleum hydrocarbons in the marine food web; role of lipids in the ecology of marine zooplankton; aquatic toxicology; uitellogenesis in marine crustaceans; environmental toxicology; mariculture. *Mailing Add:* Skidaway Inst Oceanog Ocean Sci Circle Savannah GA 31411. *Fax:* 912-598-2310

LEE, RICHARD J, SOLID STATE PHYSICS. *Current Pos:* MEM STAFF, US STEEL CORP, 74-, OWNER, RJ LEE GROUP. *Personal Data:* b Minot, NDak, July 23, 44; m 60. *Educ:* Univ NDak, BSEd, 66; Colo State Univ, PhD(physics), 70. *Prof Exp:* Instr physics, Lake Regional Jr Col, 66; res asst, Colo State Univ, 68-70; asst prof, Purdue Univ, Ft Wayne, 70-74. *Mem:* Am Phys Soc; Am Asn Physics Teachers; Am Chem Soc. *Res:* Theory of quantum solids; phase transition; light scattering. *Mailing Add:* 350 Hochbery Rd Monroeville PA 15146

LEE, RICHARD K C, PUBLIC HEALTH. *Current Pos:* dir pub health & med activ, Univ Hawaii, 62-65, dean, Sch Pub Health, 65-69, prof, 62-69, exec dir, Res Corp, 70-80, EMER PROF PUB HEALTH & EMER DEAN, SCH PUB HEALTH, UNIV HAWAII, 69-; RES FEL, E W POP INST, E W CTR, 80- *Personal Data:* b Honolulu, Hawaii, Oct 2, 09; m 52; c 3. *Educ:* Tulane Univ, MD, 33; Yale Univ, DrPH, 38. *Hon Degrees:* DSc, Tulane Univ, 73. *Honors & Awards:* Samuel J Crumbine Award, Kans State Univ Interfraternity Coun, 63; Diamond Jubilee Award, Univ Hawaii, 82. *Prof Exp:* Instr anat, Sch Med, Tulane Univ, 33-35; intern, Hotel Dieu Hosp, New Orleans, 35-36; dep comnr health, Territory Hawaii, 36-43, dir pub health, 43-53; pres, Hawaii Bd Health, 53-60; dir health, Hawaii Dept Health, 60-62. *Concurrent Pos:* Lectr, Univ Hawaii, 37-55; WHO fel, 52; mem US deleg, Western Pac Regional Comt Meetings, WHO, 52-65, chief US rep, Manila, 66 & Taiwan, 67, mem US deleg, Assembly Meetings, 57-61; Dept State specialist, Int Educ Exchange Prog, Far East, 55; mem, Western Interstate Comn Higher Educ, Western Ment Health Coun, 60-; coordr-consult health & med prog, East-West Ctr Inst Tech Interchange, 62-; mem task force pub health & med educ, World Affairs of New York & Food Found, 65-; consult, WHO, Manila,
67, Alexandria, UAR, 69, Am Pub Health Asn, Korea, 69, People's Repub China, 78 & Bangkok, 79; chief div environ health & occup med & med coord dept commun med, Straub Clin, 69-71; consult, Water Qual Mgt Prog, City & Co of Honolulu, 69-71 & Southern Calif Coastal Water Res Proj, 69-; actg dir, Cancer Ctr Hawaii, 71-73; mem, Nat Adv Coun, Nat Inst Aging, NIH, 75-77; chmn adv bd, Health Manpower Planning Proj, Hawaii, 75-77; prof dir geront develop prog, Hawaii, 78-; coordr, US-Japan Conf Agr, Hawaii, 83, Tokyo, Japan, 84, Honolulu, 85 & Japan, 86; consult, Peoples Repub China, 86, Indonesia, 87, Washington, DC, 88, Taiwan, 89; mem ctr aging, Univ Hawaii, 87. *Mem:* AAAS; AMA; Am Pub Health Asn (vpres, 62-63). *Res:* Public health administration; international health activities in the Pacific and Asian areas of the world. *Mailing Add:* E W Pop Inst 1777 E W Cent Rd Honolulu HI 96848

LEE, RICHARD NORMAN, ATMOSPHERIC CHEMISTRY. *Current Pos:* RES SCIENTIST, ATMOSPHERIC SCI DEPT, BATTELLE PAC NORTHWEST LABS, 72- *Personal Data:* b Waukegan, Ill, Nov 3, 39; m 64; c 2. *Educ:* Park Col, BA, 61; Univ Kans, PhD(chem), 68. *Prof Exp:* Asst prof chem, St Norbert Col, 66-72. *Mem:* Am Chem Soc. *Res:* Reaction kinetics; environmental chemistry; chemical analysis; atmospheric pollutants and tracers. *Mailing Add:* 1864 Marshall Ave Richland WA 99352-2460

LEE, ROBERT BUMJUNG, TRANSPORTATION & CIVIL ENGINEERING. *Current Pos:* vpres consult engr, 80-81, pres, 81-, TREAS, URBITRAN ASSOCS INC. *Personal Data:* b Seoul, Korea, Jan 24, 37; US citizen; m 65; c 2. *Educ:* Seoul Nat Univ, BSCE, 61; Polytech Inst Brooklyn, MSTP, 69, PhD(transp eng), 73. *Prof Exp:* Hwy engr civil, Madigan-Hyland Eng Co, 64-67; traffic engr, Port of NY Authority, 67-69; res assoc traffic & transp, Polytech Inst Brooklyn, 69-73, asst prof, 73-75; sr traffic engr, Louis Berger Int Inc, 75-80. *Mem:* Am Soc Civil Engrs; Sigma Xi. *Res:* Transportation; transit; environmental impacts. *Mailing Add:* Urbitran Assocs Inc 71 W 23rd St New York NY 10010

LEE, ROBERT E, electrical & biomedical engineering, for more information see previous edition

LEE, ROBERT E, JR, PHYSICAL CHEMISTRY, AIR POLLUTION. *Current Pos:* RES CHEMIST, US ENVIRON PROTECTION AGENCY, 64-, BR CHIEF, EAB. *Personal Data:* b Albany, NY, Sept 21, 36; m 60; c 2. *Educ:* Siena Col, BS, 58; George Washington Univ, MEA, 64; Univ Cincinnati, MS, 67, PhD(phys chem), 69. *Prof Exp:* Chemist, US Army Biol Labs, Md, 58-62; scientist, Melpar, Inc, Va, 62-64. *Mem:* AAAS; Air Pollution Control Asn; Am Chem Soc. *Res:* Air pollution chemistry. *Mailing Add:* US EPA Mail Code 7406 401 M St SW Washington DC 20460

LEE, ROBERT EDWARD, PHYCOLOGY, CRYOBIOLOGY. *Current Pos:* MGR ANAT SERV, COLO STATE UNIV, 81- *Personal Data:* b Worcester, Mass, Sept 15, 42; m 68, Patricia A Grasso; c Nicole, Alana & Christian. *Educ:* Cornell Univ, BSc, 64; Univ Mass, PhD(biol), 71. *Prof Exp:* Lectr, Univ Witwatersrand, 71-77; assoc prof, Shiraz Univ, 77-79; fel, Boston Biomed Res Inst & Harvard Med Sch, 79-81. *Res:* Systematics of algae; electron microscopy and freeze-fracture of biological systems; neuronal growth and development; preservation of tissues using rapid freezing. *Mailing Add:* Dept Anat & Neurobiol Colo State Univ Ft Collins CO 80523. *Fax:* 970-491-7907

LEE, ROBERT GUM HONG, MINING. *Current Pos:* RES ENGR, CAN LIQUID AIR LTD, MONTREAL, 47- *Personal Data:* b Montreal, Que, May 22, 24; m, Maude Toye; c Peter, Patricia & Catherine. *Educ:* McGill Univ, Montreal, BS, 47. *Honors & Awards:* Airey Award, Can Inst Mining & Metall, 74, Falconbridge Innovation Award, 92. *Concurrent Pos:* Mem bd dirs, Montreal Chinese Hosp, 75-82. *Mem:* Soc Cryobiol; Am Inst Mining & Metall; Am Chem Soc; Can Inst Mining & Metall. *Mailing Add:* Can Liquid Air Ltd 1155 Sherbrooke St W Montreal PQ H3A 1H8 Can

LEE, ROBERT JEROME, veterinary medicine; deceased, see previous edition for last biography

LEE, ROBERT JOHN, medical physiology, for more information see previous edition

LEE, ROBERT MAUNG KYAW WIN, HYPERTENSION, VASCULAR SMOOTH MUSCLE. *Current Pos:* fel entom, McMaster Univ, 76-78, res assoc, 78-79, MRC Centennial fel hypertension, 79-80, Rose-Levy Rosenstadt fel, 80-82, from asst prof to assoc prof anaesthesia, 80-89, Ont Ministry Health Career Scientists, 82-92, DIR, SMOOTH MUSCLE RES PROG, MCMASTER UNIV, 88-, PROF ANAESTHESIA, 89- *Personal Data:* b Burma, Nov 7, 43; Can citizen; m 75, Nancy Y Mar; c Frederick J & Andrew J. *Educ:* Univ Mandalay, Burma, BSc(Hons), 66; Univ Rangoon, Burma, MSc, 69, Univ Alta, PhD(entom), 75. *Honors & Awards:* Lo Yuk Tong Found Lectr, Univ Hong Kong, 93. *Prof Exp:* Lectr histol, Univ Regina, 75, fel entom, 75-76. *Concurrent Pos:* Distinguished speaker, Kunming Med Col, China, 85 & 88; mem, Circulation Coun, Am Heart Asn, 87- *Mem:* Am Physiol Soc; Am Heart Asn; Can Hypertension Soc (secy-treas, 90-93); Can Asn Anatomists; Inter-Am Soc Hypertension; Pharmacol Soc Can. *Res:* Role of structural changes of blood vessels in the development of high blood pressure (hypertension) in humans; biology of vascular smooth muscle cells; structure and function of airway cilia in health and in disease. *Mailing Add:* Dept Anesthesia McMaster Univ 1200 Main St W Hamilton ON L8N 3Z5 Can. *Fax:* 905-523-1224; *E-Mail:* rmkwlee@fhs.mcmaster.ca

LEE, ROBERT W, EXPERIMENTAL PHYSICS. *Current Pos:* RETIRED. *Personal Data:* b Cedar Rapids, Iowa, Feb 28, 31; m 51; c 3. *Educ:* Mich State Univ, BS, 53, MS, 55. *Honors & Awards:* AIP Award, Indust Applns Physics, 85. *Prof Exp:* Sr res physicist, Res Labs, Gen Motors Corp, 55-88. *Mem:* Sigma Xi. *Res:* Permanent magnets; electro-optics; gas diffusion in solids. *Mailing Add:* 3090 Myddleton Dr Troy MI 43084

LEE, ROBERT WILLIAM, PHYSICAL PHARMACEUTICAL CHEMISTRY, PHYSICAL BIOORGANIC CHEMISTRY. *Current Pos:* res investr, 91-93, SR RES INVESTR, STERLING WINTHROP PHARMACEUT RES DIV, 93- *Personal Data:* b Honolulu, Hawaii, July 16, 60. *Educ:* Univ Wash, BS(chem) & BS(biol), 82; Univ Calif, Santa Barbara, PhD(phys bioorg chem), 90. *Concurrent Pos:* Adj assoc prof, Univ Kans, 92-94. *Mem:* Am Chem Soc; Am Asn Parmaceut Scientists. *Res:* Development and implementation of novel technologies and computer modeling paradigms to expedite the discovery and development of pharmaceutics. *Mailing Add:* 1335 Roberts Rd Collegeville Rd Gilbertsville PA 19525. *Fax:* 610-983-7910

LEE, ROBERTO, CHEMICAL ENGINEERING. *Current Pos:* sr res chem engr & prin engr specialist, Monsanto Co, 63-76, engr supt, 77-79, engr mgr, 80-82, ENGR GROUP CONSULT, MONSANTO CO, 82- *Personal Data:* b Shanghai, China, Jan 10, 37; m 63; c 2. *Educ:* Univ Ill, BS, 58; Purdue Univ, MS, 60, PhD(chem eng), 64. *Prof Exp:* Engr, Corning Glass Works, 60; res engr, E I du Pont de Nemours & Co, 61. *Mem:* Fel Am Inst Chem Engrs; Am Chem Soc. *Res:* Reaction engineering; biochemical and chemical process design; chemical process research and development. *Mailing Add:* Assoc Chem Eng Serv 11304 Ladue Rd St Louis MO 63141

LEE, ROLAND ROBERT, DIAGNOSTIC RADIOLOGY, MAGNETIC RESONANCE IMAGING & SPECTROSCOPY. *Current Pos:* ASSOC PROF RADIOL & DIR MAGNETIC SOURCE IMAGING UNIV NMEX, ALBUQUERQUE, 97- *Personal Data:* b Cleveland, Ohio, July 18, 54. *Educ:* Calif Inst Technol, BS, 75; Univ Calif, Berkeley, MA, 77; Univ Calif, Los Angeles, MD, 85. *Prof Exp:* Physicist laser fusion & teaching asst physics, Lawrence Livermore Nat Lab, Univ Calif, Berkeley, 75-77; res asst superconductivity, 77-81; intern, Los Angeles Med Ctr, Harbor-Univ Calif, 85-86; resident diag radiol, Harvard Med Sch, Brigham & Women's Hosp, 86-90; clin & res fel magnetic resonance imaging spectros, Long Beach Mem Magnetic Resonance Ctr, Huntington Mem Med Res Inst, 90-91; clin instr & res tel neuroradiol, Dept Radiol, Univ Calif, San Francisco, 91-92; asst prof radiol, Johns Hopkins Hosp, 92-97. *Mem:* Am Col Radiol; Am Soc Neuroradiol; Radiol Soc NAm; AMA. *Res:* Clinical diagnostic radiology; neuroradiology and magnetic resonance imaging; magnetic resonance spectroscopy; medical image processing; magnetoencephalography and magnetic source neuroimaging; spinal imaging. *Mailing Add:* Dept Radiol Sch Med Univ NMex Albuquerque NM 87131. *Fax:* 505-256-5708

LEE, RONALD NORMAN, SURFACE PHYSICS, MATERIALS SCIENCE. *Current Pos:* physicist, US Naval Ord Lab, 68-74, PHYSICIST, MATS DIV, NAVAL SURFACE WARFARE CTR, 74-, TECH LEADER, SURFACE SCI GROUP, 79- *Personal Data:* b Springfield, Mo, Oct 21, 35; m 59; c 1. *Educ:* Univ Ill, BS, 58, MS, 60; Brown Univ, PhD(physics), 65. *Prof Exp:* Res assoc physics, Coord Sci Lab, Univ Ill, 60 & Brown Univ, 64-65; fel phys chem, Battelle Mem Inst, Ohio, 65-68. *Mem:* Am Phys Soc; Am Vacuum Soc; AAAS; Sigma Xi. *Res:* Surface science; composite materials interface properties, carbon fiber surface properties, corrosion, bio-corrosion; physics of electron spectroscopies; physics of scanning tunneling; microscopy, battery electrode chemistry; energetic materials. *Mailing Add:* Naval Surface Warfare Ctr 10901 New Hampshire Ave Silver Spring MD 20903. *Fax:* 301-394-4472

LEE, RONALD S, SHOCK COMPRESSION OF SOLIDS, DETONATION PHYSICS. *Current Pos:* physicist, 87-92, GROUP LEADER, LAWRENCE LIVERMORE LAB, 92- *Personal Data:* b Ames, Iowa, Dec 29, 38; m 66, Jean A Hanson; c Elizabeth & Karin. *Educ:* Luther Col, Iowa, BA, 61; Iowa State Univ, PhD(physics), 67. *Prof Exp:* From asst prof to prof physics, Kans State Univ, 64-87. *Mem:* Am Phys Soc; Am Defense Preparedness Asn. *Res:* Shock waves in chemically reacting media; radiation effects in solids. *Mailing Add:* 1822 Vancouver Way Livermore CA 94550. *Fax:* 510-422-2382

LEE, RONNIE, TOPOLOGY. *Current Pos:* asst prof, 70-73, ASSOC PROF MATH, YALE UNIV, 73-, DIR UNDERGRAD STUDIES, 77- *Personal Data:* b China, Nov 6, 42. *Educ:* Chinese Univ Hong Kong, BS, 65; Univ Mich, PhD(math), 68. *Prof Exp:* Mem, Inst Advan Studies, 68-70. *Concurrent Pos:* Sloan Found fel, 73. *Res:* Differential topology. *Mailing Add:* Dept Math Yale Univ Box 2155 Yale Sta New Haven CT 06520-2155

LEE, SAMUEL C, ELECTRICAL ENGINEERING, COMPUTER SCIENCE. *Current Pos:* PROF ELEC ENG & COMPUT SCI, UNIV OKLA, 75- *Personal Data:* b Hong-Chow, China, May 4, 37; US citizen. *Educ:* Nat Taiwan Univ, BS, 60; Univ Calif, Berkeley, MS, 63; Univ Ill, Urbana, PhD(elec eng), 65. *Prof Exp:* Mem tech staff elec eng, Bell Labs, Murray Hill, 65-67; assoc prof, NY Univ, 67-70 & Univ Houston, 70-75. *Concurrent Pos:* Consult, Bell Labs, 67-70 & NAm Aircraft Co, Conn, 68-69; vis assoc prof, Baylor Col Med & asst neurophysiologist, Methodist Hosp, Houston, 72-75. *Mem:* Inst Elec & Electronics Engrs; Asn Comput Mach; Am Soc Eng Educ. *Res:* Digital systems; logical design; pattern recognition; artificial intelligence. *Mailing Add:* Elec Eng & Comput Sci Univ Okla Main Campus 900 Asp Ave Norman OK 73019-4050

LEE, SHAW-GUANG LIN, biochemistry, for more information see previous edition

LEE, SHIH-SHUN, MOLECULAR GENETICS, CANCER CHEMOTHERAPY. *Current Pos:* RETIRED. *Personal Data:* b Taiwan, May 25, 36; US citizen; m 69; c 2. *Educ:* Nat Taiwan Univ, BS, 59, MS, 64; Mont State Univ, PhD(genetics), 69. *Prof Exp:* Instr agron, Prov Taiwan Agr Col, 64-66; res asst genetics, Mont State Univ, 66-69; res assoc cancer res, Stehlin Found, 73-74, assoc dir cancer res, 75-81; chmn tissue cult dept, Burzynski Res Inst, 81-93. *Concurrent Pos:* Fels, Indiana Univ, 69-70 & M D Anderson Hosp & Tumor Inst, 70-73. *Mem:* Sigma Xi. *Res:* Tumor tissue culture; tumor chemotherapy; induction of cancer cell differentiation. *Mailing Add:* 2707 Cane Field Dr Sugar Land TX 77479

LEE, SHIH-YING, MECHANICAL ENGINEERING, ENGINEERING EDUCATION. *Current Pos:* CHMN & CHIEF EXEC OFFICER, SETRA SYSTS INC, 96- *Personal Data:* b Peking, China, Apr 30, 18. *Educ:* Mass Inst Technol, ScD, 45. *Prof Exp:* Res engr, Mass Inst Technol, 47-52, fac mem, 52-74, prof mech eng, 66-74, emer prof, 74-96. *Mem:* Nat Acad Eng. *Mailing Add:* Setra Systs Inc 159 Swanson Rd Boxborough MA 01719. *E-Mail:* leesy@setra.com

LEE, SHUI LUNG, organic chemistry, for more information see previous edition

LEE, SHUISHIH SAGE, EXPERIMENTAL PATHOLOGY, ANATOMIC PATHOLOGY. *Current Pos:* PATHOLOGIST, PARKVIEW MEM HOSP, 79-; CLIN ASST PROF, DEPT PATH, MED SCH, IND UNIV, 89- *Personal Data:* b Soo-chow, China, Jan 5, 48; m 73, Chung Seng; c Yvonne & Michael. *Educ:* Nat Taiwan Univ, MD, 72; Univ Rochester, PhD(path), 76. *Prof Exp:* Intern path, Med Ctr, Univ Rochester, 76-77, resident, 77-78; resident path, Northwestern Mem Hosp, 78-79. *Mem:* Int Acad Pathol; Am Asn Pathologists; Am Soc Clin Pathologists; Col Am Pathologists; Int Acad Cytol; Electron Micros Soc Am. *Res:* Synthesis of ferritin in rat liver and hepatoma cells; cytopathology. *Mailing Add:* Dept Path 5728 Prophet's Pass Ft Wayne IN 46845-9659

LEE, SHUNG-YAN LUKE, ORGANIC CHEMISTRY. *Current Pos:* RES CHEMIST PHOTOG SYST, E I DU PONT DE NEMOURS & CO, INC, 66-, SCIENTIST. *Personal Data:* b China, Sept 10, 38; US citizen; m 62; c 2. *Educ:* Univ Wis, BS, 59; Ohio State Univ, MS, 62, PhD(phys org chem), 66. *Mem:* Am Chem Soc. *Res:* Investigations of photopolymerization systems. *Mailing Add:* 714 Foxdale Rd Wilmington DE 19803-1604

LEE, SHWU-LUAN, molecular biology, gene regulation, for more information see previous edition

LEE, SHYH-YUAN, ACCELERATOR PHYSICS, NUCLEAR PHYSICS. *Current Pos:* PROF PHYSICS, IND UNIV, 90- *Personal Data:* b Yuinin, Taiwan, Nov 17, 43. *Educ:* Univ Taiwan, BS, 63; State Univ NY, Stony Brook, MS, 69 & PhD(physics), 72. *Prof Exp:* Res assoc, Univ Paris Orsay, 76-77 & Univ Wash Seattle, 77- 78; asst prof physics, State Univ NY, Stony Brook, 78-84; assoc physicist, Brookhaven Nat Labs, 84-85, physicist, 85-90. *Mem:* Am Phys Soc; Nat Geog Soc. *Res:* Nonlinear physics; accelerator and spin physics. *Mailing Add:* Dept Physics Ind Univ Swain Hall W117 Bloomington IN 47405

LEE, SI DUK, ENVIRONMENTAL SCIENCES, BIOLOGICAL CHEMISTRY, TOXICOLOGY. *Current Pos:* SR SCI HEALTH ADV, US ENVIRON PROTECTION AGENCY, 73- *Personal Data:* b Ham Hung, Korea, Jan 2, 32; US citizen; m 57; c 3. *Educ:* Seoul Nat Univ, BS, 55; Univ Md, MS, 59, PhD(biochem), 62. *Honors & Awards:* Bronze Medal, US Environ Protection Agency, 80 & 84. *Prof Exp:* Res assoc biochem, Med Ctr, Duke Univ, 61-62, NIH fel, 62-63, Am Heart Asn adv res fel, 63-64; res chemist, USPHS, 64-65, supvry res chemist, 65-67, chief biochem unit, 67-69, chief biochem sect, Nat Air Pollution Control Admin, 69-71; dep chief, biol effects br, Nat Environ Res Ctr, Environ Protection Agency, 71-73. *Concurrent Pos:* Adj asst prof, Dept Biol, Col Med, Univ Cincinnati, 67-80 & Dept Environ Health, 75-80; adj assoc prof, Duke Univ Med Sch, 82-87; vis scholar, Harvard Univ, 87- *Mem:* AAAS; Am Chem Soc; Am Col Toxicol; Air Pollution Control Asn; Sigma Xi; Soc Toxicol. *Res:* Effects of air pollutants on metabolism; lipid metabolism; effects of pollutants on aging; effects of sulfur dioxide on subcellular metabolism; environmental management. *Mailing Add:* US Environ Protection Agency NCEA MD-52 Research Triangle Park NC 27711-0001

LEE, SIDNEY, chemical engineering, physical chemistry, for more information see previous edition

LEE, SIN HANG, SURGICAL PATHOLOGY, HISTOCHEMISTRY. *Current Pos:* assoc prof, 71-73, ASSOC CLIN PROF PATH, YALE UNIV, NEW HAVEN, CONN, 73-; PATHOLOGIST, HOSP ST RAPHAEL, NEW HAVEN, CONN, 73- *Personal Data:* b Hong Kong, Nov 17, 32; US citizen; m 58, Kee H Hau; c Emil & Karen. *Educ:* Wuhan Med Col, China, MD, 56. *Prof Exp:* Postgrad bact, Sichuan Med Col, Chengou, China, 56-57, asst lectr, 57-61; demonstr path, Univ Hong Kong, 61-63; intern clin, South Baltimore Gen Hosp, 63-64; resident path, NY Hosp, Cornell Med Ctr, 64-67; fel, Mem Hosp Cancer & Allied Dis, 67-68; asst prof, McGill Univ, Montreal, Can, 68-71. *Concurrent Pos:* Guest prof, Tongji Med Univ Hankow, Wuhan, China, 84- *Mem:* Col Am Pathologists; Int Acad Path; Am Asn Pathologists; NY Acad Sci; AAAS; Royal Col Physicians & Surgeons Can. *Res:* Histochemical localization of enzyme activities; cytochemical assays of steroid receptors in breast cancer and other target cells; mycoplasma pneumoniae antigen for the detection of specific membrane antibodies in patients for early diagnosis of infection; awarded two patents. *Mailing Add:* Dept Path Hosp St Raphael 1450 Chapel St New Haven CT 06511

LEE, SIU-LAM, INSECT ECOLOGY, EVOLUTION. *Current Pos:* ASSOC PROF BIOL, UNIV MASS, LOWELL, NORTH CAMPUS, 75- *Personal Data:* b Macao, China, Oct 3, 41; m 82, Felicia Tsang; c Terence, Timothy & Serena. *Educ:* Chung Chi Col, Chinese Univ, Hong Kong, BSc, 62; Oberlin Col, AM, 63; Cornell Univ, PhD(entom), 67. *Prof Exp:* NSF res grant, 69-72. *Mem:* Am Entom Soc; Animal Behav Soc; Bee Res Asn; Sigma Xi. *Res:* Learning ability of fruit fly; behavioral ecology of the leaf-cutter bee; effects of ginseng, Panax ginseng, on mamalian blood cells and malaria infecton; the flora of temperate deciduous forests. *Mailing Add:* Dept Biol Univ Mass Lowell North Campus Lowell MA 01854. *Fax:* 978-934-3044; *E-Mail:* lees@woods.uml.edu

LEE, SOOHEE, HUMAN CELL BLOOD GROUPS. *Current Pos:* ASST MEM, NY BLOOD CTR, 87- *Personal Data:* b Seoul, Korea, Apr 15, 44. *Educ:* Univ Ewha, Korea, BS, 67; Univ Tex, MS, 71; Univ Utah, PhD(pharmaceut), 85. *Prof Exp:* Fel molecular biol, Univ Med & Dent NJ, 85-87. *Mem:* Am Soc Cell Biol. *Res:* Calcium binding proteins. *Mailing Add:* NY Blood Ctr 310 E 67th St New York NY 10021

LEE, STANLEY L, INTERNAL MEDICINE, HEMATOLOGY. *Current Pos:* from assoc prof to prof, Downstate Med Ctr, State Univ NY, 59-90, dean fac, 78-79, actg pres, 79-81, dean, Col Med & vpres acad affairs, 81-82, EMER PROF MED, DOWNSTATE MED CTR, STATE UNIV NY, 90-; EMER DIR HEMAT & ONCOL, BROOKDALE HOSP MED CTR, 96- *Personal Data:* b Newburgh, NY, Aug 27, 19; m 47, Ann Rosenthal; c Nancy, Edward J & Kenneth R. *Educ:* Columbia Univ, AB, 39; Harvard Univ, MD, 43. *Prof Exp:* Intern, Mt Sinai Hosp, NY, 43-44, resident med, 46-48, Georg Escherich fel path, 48-49, asst, 49-53, asst attend hematologist, 53-59; dir hemat & oncol, Brookdale Hosp Med Ctr, 82-96. *Concurrent Pos:* Dir hemat, Maimonides Med Ctr, Brooklyn, 59-71; treas, Int Cong Hemat, NY, 65-68; dir med, Jewish Hosp & Med Ctr, Brooklyn, 71-77. *Mem:* Am Soc Hemat; Am Rheumatism Asn; Soc Human Genetics; Am Fedn Clin Res; fel Am Col Physicians; Am Soc Clin Oncol. *Res:* Systematic lupus erythematosus; leukemia. *Mailing Add:* Dept Hemat Brookdale Hosp Brooklyn NY 11212. *Fax:* 718-240-6034; *E-Mail:* s.lee@worldnet.att.net

LEE, STEPHEN, SOLID STATE CHEMISTRY. *Current Pos:* asst prof, 88-93, assoc prof, 93-97, PROF CHEM, UNIV MICH, 97- *Personal Data:* b New York, NY, Oct 25, 55; m 85, Kim Keery. *Educ:* Yale Univ, BA, 78; Univ Chicago, PhD(chem), 85. *Honors & Awards:* John D & Catherine T MacArthur Fel, MacArthur Found, 93- *Prof Exp:* NATO fel, Univ Nantes, 85-86, Humboldt res fel, Univ Munster, 87 & 95. *Concurrent Pos:* Alfred P Sloan fel, Alfred Sloan Found, 93-95. *Res:* Solid state chemistry synthesis; structural characterization and electronic structure of solids; materials chemistry; author of numerous publications. *Mailing Add:* Dept Chem Univ Mich 930 N University Ave Ann Arbor MI 48109-1055

LEE, STEVE S, HERBAL PROCESS, TRADITIONAL FOLK MEDICINE. *Current Pos:* PLANT MGR, SUNRIDER INT, 87- *Personal Data:* b Taiwan, Nov 2, 48; US citizen; m 79, Rosa Chen; c Peter & Katherine. *Educ:* Kaohsiung Med Col, Taiwan, BS, 72; Duquesne Univ, MS, 84. *Prof Exp:* Lab mgr, Grad Sch Pub Health, Univ Pittsburgh, 85-87. *Concurrent Pos:* Mgr, Prod Develop, Nature's Sunshine, 93- *Mem:* Inst Food Technologies; Asn Cosmetic Chemists; Asn Traditional Med. *Res:* Extraction of Chinese folk medicinal herbs; evaluation of the extract particularly in antitumor and antibacteria. *Mailing Add:* 1742 Misty Meadows Sandy UT 84093

LEE, STEVEN HUNTER, ANALYTICAL CHEMISTRY. *Current Pos:* PROF CHEM, WALLA WALLA COL, 83- *Personal Data:* b Battle Creek, Mich, June 17, 53; m 76, Heather Luchak; c Derek. *Educ:* Andrews Univ, BS, 76; Univ Wis-Madison, PhD(analytical chem), 81. *Prof Exp:* Assoc, Ind Univ, 81-83. *Mem:* Am Chem Soc. *Res:* Laser excited fluorescence and non-linear spectroscopy. *Mailing Add:* 1148 SW Bade Ave College Place WA 99324-1559

LEE, STUART M(ILTON), MATERIALS SCIENCE. *Current Pos:* RETIRED. *Personal Data:* b New York, NY, Apr 14, 20; m 48, Miriam Drucker; c Gary, Scott & Randy. *Educ:* Long Island Univ, BS, 41; Univ Nev, MS, 47; Fla State Univ, PhD(org chem), 53. *Honors & Awards:* Nat Meritorious Bronze Award, Soc Advan Mat & Process Eng, 82, Space Award, 95. *Prof Exp:* Chemist analysis & testing, NY Testing Labs, 41-42; chemist analytical develop, Gen Dyestuffs Corp, 42-43; chief chemist org synthesis, Trinity Res Found, 49-50; sr res chemist & proj leader org res, Allied Signal Corp, 52-59; res chemist, Aerojet-Gen Corp, 59-61; mgr chem res & develop, Electro-Optical Systs, Inc, Xerox Corp, 61-64; sr tech specialist, Autonetics Div, NAm Rockwell Int Corp, Calif, 64-71; sr staff scientist, Ford Aerospace & Commun Corp, 71-85; res polymer batteries, SRI Int, 85-86; int tech dir, Soc Advan Mat & Process Eng, 89-90. *Concurrent Pos:* Ed, Soc Advan Mat & Process Eng J, 79-95; ed-in-chief, Technomic Publ Co, 83-90, ed, Encycl Composites, 85-92; consult, SRI Int, GTE, Siemens, Teledyne & others; emer ed, Mat & Design. *Mem:* Emer mem Am Chem Soc; fel Soc Advan Mat & Process Eng. *Res:* Electronic materials, bioengineering materials and satellites; composites, coatings, encapsulants and sealants; instrumental failure analysis; materials and processes used for thick and thin films, dielectrics, high voltage and corona, bonding, joining, laser and electronic organics, polymer batteries and plastic packaging; systems for withstanding space environments; electronic and laser organics; high temperature and organic polymers; Sterilization and decontamination effects; approximately 80 technical publications including 13 patents; contributing author or editor of 23 books; granted 13 US and foreign patents. *Mailing Add:* 3718 Cass Way Palo Alto CA 94306. *Fax:* 650-493-4085

LEE, SUE YING, VERTEBRATE MORPHOLOGY. *Current Pos:* RETIRED. *Personal Data:* b Schenectady, NY, Jan 11, 40; m 73, Archie Mossman; c Mathew. *Educ:* State Univ NY Albany, BS, 61, MS, 63; Univ Ill, Urbana, PhD(zool), 68. *Prof Exp:* Instr vert morphol & human anat, Univ Ill, Chicago, 67-69; from asst prof to prof vert morphol & human anat, Humboldt State Univ, 69-96. *Concurrent Pos:* Consult, Int Union Conserv Nature & Natural Resources, World Wildlife Fund, 74-75. *Mem:* AAAS; Am Soc Zool; Am Inst Biol Sci; Western Soc Naturalists; Soc Vert Paleont; Am Asn Anatomists; Am Soc Mammal. *Res:* Reproductive biology; ultrastructure of fetal membranes. *Mailing Add:* Dept Biol Sci Humboldt State Univ Arcata CA 95521. *Fax:* 707-826-3201; *E-Mail:* sylt@axe.humboldt.edu

LEE, SUK YOUNG, SOIL SCIENCE, ENVIRONMENTAL CHEMISTRY. *Current Pos:* RES SCIENTIST ENVIRON SCI, OAK RIDGE NAT LAB, 77- *Personal Data:* b Seoul, Korea, June 18, 40; US citizen; m 66; c 2. *Educ:* Univ Sask, MS, 68; Univ Wis, PhD(soil sci), 73. *Prof Exp:* Fel, Univ Wis, 74-75, Univ SFla, 75-76 & Tex A&M Univ, 76-77. *Mem:* Am Soc Agron; Soil Sci Soc Am; Clay Minerals Soc. *Res:* Transport of trace elements and radio nuclides, such as plutonium and uranium, in environment. *Mailing Add:* 12 Monaco Lane Oak Ridge TN 37830-8304

LEE, SUN, SURGERY. *Current Pos:* assoc prof surg, 68-74, PROF EXP SURG, UNIV CALIF, SAN DIEGO, 74-; ASSOC, SCRIPPS CLIN & RES FOUND, 64- *Personal Data:* b Seoul, Korea, June 2, 20; US citizen; m 45; c 6. *Educ:* Seoul Nat Univ, MD, 45. *Honors & Awards:* Gold Medal, Pioneer Exp Microsurg, Ger; Gold Medal, Lombardo Surg, Italy. *Prof Exp:* From instr to asst prof, Univ Pittsburgh, 57-64. *Concurrent Pos:* Surg fel, Univ Pittsburgh, 55-57. *Mem:* Int Microsurg Soc; Int Proctol Soc. *Res:* Development of organ transplant in the rat to study transplantation immunology and associated physiology; techniques of heart-lung, liver, spleen, pancreas, testicle, kidney and stomach transplantation and allied microsurgical techniques in rats. *Mailing Add:* 6462 Cardeno Dr La Jolla CA 92038

LEE, SUNG MOOK, THEORETICAL MECHANICS, SNOW & COLD ENVIRONMENTAL RESEARCH. *Current Pos:* from asst prof to assoc prof, 65-72, dean res & grad sch, 88-91, PROF PHYSICS, MICH TECHNOL UNIV, 72-, DIR, KEWEENAW RES CTR, 76-, VPROVOST RES & DEAN, GRAD SCH, 91- *Personal Data:* b Seoul, Korea, Mar 2, 33; wid; c Peter, Patricia & Janet. *Educ:* Yonsei Univ, BSc, 55; Ohio State Univ, MSc, 59, PhD(crystal dynamics), 65. *Prof Exp:* Teacher, Hansung Boy's High Sch, Korea, 54-55; asst prof physics, Denison Univ, 61-65. *Concurrent Pos:* NATO sr fel sci, 74; vis sr res fel, Inst Sound & Vibration Res, Univ Southampton, Eng, 80 & 81. *Mem:* Am Phys Soc. *Res:* Vibrational analysis of periodic systems, crystal lattices, and molecules; wave propagation in solids; mechanical properties of solids; mechanics; acoustics; optics; snow and ice. *Mailing Add:* Grad Sch Mich Technol Univ Houghton MI 49931. *Fax:* 906-487-2245; *E-Mail:* smlee@mtu.edu

LEE, SUNGGYU, PROCESS DEVELOPMENT, FUEL SCIENCE. *Current Pos:* From asst prof to assoc prof, 80-88, ROBERT IREDELL PROF CHEM ENG & DEPT HEAD, UNIV AKRON, 88- *Personal Data:* b Kangjin-Kun, Korea, Mar 11, 52; m 80, Kyung Paik; c Tracy Y, Jo Jo Y & Leroy J. *Educ:* Seoul Nat Univ, BS, 74, MS, 76; Case Western Res Univ, PhD(chem eng), 80. *Honors & Awards:* Louis A Hill Award, 87. *Concurrent Pos:* Prin investr, Univ Akron, 80-, dir, Process Res Ctr, 90-; prof consult, 80- *Mem:* Am Inst Chem Engrs; Am Chem Soc; Sigma Xi; Am Soc Elec Eng. *Res:* Process development for the manufacture of clean liquid and solid fuels; coal desulfurization and characterization; manufacture of enzymes; manufacture specialty and reactive polymers and polymerization; oxygenates; author of 6 books, 103 journal articles and 131 papers; granted 14 patents. *Mailing Add:* Dept Chem Eng Univ Akron Akron OH 44325-3906. *Fax:* 330-972-5856

LEE, SUNGSOO C, FOOD SCIENCE. *Current Pos:* assoc res scientist, Kellogg Co, 83-84, assoc res chemist, 84-86, res chemist, 86-88, sr res chemist, 89-90 & 90-93, SR SCIENTIST, KELLOGG CO, 93- *Educ:* Ewha Univ, BS, 72, MS, 74; Univ Wis, MS, 78, PhD(food sci), 83. *Concurrent Pos:* Mem, Food Nutrit Methods Comt, Asn Official Analytical Chemists, 92-; vchair sub comt dietary fiber/complex carbohydrates & food nutrit & safety comt, Int Life Sci Inst, 93- *Mem:* Int Life Sci Inst; Am Asn Cereal Chemists; Asn Off Anal Chemists (pres elect, 91-92, pres, 92-93); Inst Food Technologists; assoc mem Am Inst Nutrit. *Res:* Food scientist with special expertise in dietary fiber and carbohydrates; proficient in development of worldwide nutrition labelling, product improvements, laboratory quality control and new business opportunity programs; author of 10 publications. *Mailing Add:* Kellogg Co 235 Porter St Battle Creek MI 49016-3423

LEE, T(IEN) P(EI), ELECTRICAL ENGINEERING. *Current Pos:* MEM TECH STAFF, BELL TEL LABS, 63- *Personal Data:* b Nanking, China, Sept 8, 33; m 63; c 2. *Educ:* Taiwan Norm Univ, BS, 57; Ohio State Univ, MS, 59; Stanford Univ, PhD(elec eng), 63. *Mem:* Inst Elec & Electronics Engrs; Sigma Xi. *Res:* Microwave electronics; microwave solid state devices; varactor diodes; parametric amplifiers; semiconductor lasers and related optical communication. *Mailing Add:* 5 Marion Dr Holmdel NJ 07733

LEE, T(HOMAS) S(HAO-CHUNG), ELECTRICAL ENGINEERING. *Current Pos:* From instr to asst prof, 57-66, ASSOC PROF ELEC ENG, UNIV MINN, MINNEAPOLIS, 66- *Personal Data:* b Soochow, China, Nov 18, 31; m 60; c 2. *Educ:* Nat Taiwan Univ, BS, 54; Univ Minn, Minneapolis, MS, 56, PhD(elec eng), 61. *Concurrent Pos:* Consult, mil prod group, Honeywell Regulator Co, 61-62, aero div, 63-64 & US Naval Res Lab, 65- *Mem:* Am Phys Soc; Am Geophys Union. *Res:* Acoustics; explosive phenomena; gas-dynamics; systems; electromagnetism; interplanetary phenomena. *Mailing Add:* Dept Elec Eng 139 Elec Eng Bldg Univ Minn Rm 4-178 200 Union St Minneapolis MN 55455

LEE, TED C K, PROTEIN PURIFICATION, PROTEIN DRUG DEVELOPMENT. *Current Pos:* RES GROUP LEADER, DADE INT INC, 92- *Personal Data:* b Seoul, Korea, Dec 3, 40; US citizen; m 66, Sue J Moon; c Shirley, Charles & Michelle. *Educ:* Korea Univ, BS, 65; Okla State Univ, PhD(biochem), 71. *Prof Exp:* Res assoc, Rockefeller Univ, 71-73; asst prof, Howard Univ Med Col, 73-78; vis prof, Cornell Univ, 78-81; sr res scientist, Rhone-Poulene Rorer Inc, prin scientist, sect mgr, 81-92. *Mem:* Am Soc Biochem & Molecular Biol; Am Chem Soc. *Res:* Protein drug development; purification, refolding and formulation of proteins; assay development. *Mailing Add:* PO Box 520672 Dade Int Inc MS W-708 Miami FL 33152-0672

LEE, TEH HSUN, BIOCHEMISTRY. *Current Pos:* RETIRED. *Personal Data:* b Shaoshin, China, Mar 25, 17; m 52, Mang Sheklee; c Robert. *Educ:* Chekiang Univ, BS, 38; Univ Mich, PhD, 54. *Prof Exp:* Res assoc, Sch Med, Univ Ore, 54-55; res assoc, Sch Med, Yale Univ, 55-60, asst prof exp med, 60-62; sr biochemist, Merck, Sharp & Dohme, 62-64; asst dir, Vet Admin Human Protein Hormone Bank, Vet Admin Hosp, 64-66, chief, Protein Hormone Res Lab, 66-84; vis assoc prof biochem, Albert Einstein Col Med, 67-84. *Concurrent Pos:* Assoc prof, Sch Med, Univ Colo, Denver, 64-66. *Mem:* Am Chem Soc; Am Soc Biol Chem; Endocrine Soc. *Res:* Pituitary hormones. *Mailing Add:* 196 Bradley Rd Scarsdale NY 10583

LEE, TEH-HSUANG, SOLID STATE PHYSICS. *Current Pos:* SR PHYSICIST, RES LABS, EASTMAN KODAK CO, 67- *Personal Data:* b Shanghai, China, Aug 15, 36; m 61; c 2. *Educ:* Nat Taiwan Univ, BS, 58; Purdue Univ, West Lafayette, PhD(physics), 67. *Mem:* Am Phys Soc. *Res:* Optical properties of solids; semiconductors; magnetic semiconductors. *Mailing Add:* Eastman Kodak Co 343 State St Rochester NY 14650

LEE, TEN CHING, MEMBRANES, PHOSPHOLIPIDS. *Current Pos:* BIOCHEMIST, UNIV TENN. *Educ:* Tulane Univ, New Orleans, PhD(biochem), 67. *Mailing Add:* Med/Health Sci Div Oak Ridge Assoc Univ PO Box 117 Oak Ridge TN 37831-0117

LEE, THERESA, RECOMBINANT DNA, BIOTECHNOLOGY. *Current Pos:* PROG OFF, DIV PRECLIN RES, NAT INST DRUG ABUSE, 88- *Personal Data:* b Beijing, China; US citizen; m 70; c 1. *Educ:* Nat Taiwan Univ, BS, 62; Univ Pittsburgh, MS, 64; Wash Univ, PhD(biochem), 68. *Prof Exp:* Fel biochem, Med Sch, Univ Wis, 68, Harvard Univ, 68-70; fel, Johns Hopkins Univ, 70-71, prof staff microbiol, Med Sch, 71-77; res chemist molecular biol, Nat Cancer Inst, NIH, 77-84; chemist, Chem Div, Food & Drug Admin, 84-88. *Mem:* Am Soc Biol Chemists; AAAS; Am Soc Microbiologists; NY Acad Sci; Am Chem Soc. *Res:* Recombinant DNA techniques; molecular biology; proteins; biochemistry; virology. *Mailing Add:* Div Preclin Res Parklawn Nat Inst Drug Abuse 1709 Sunrise Dr Rockville MD 20854-2666

LEE, THOMAS HENRY, PHYSICS. *Current Pos:* vis res prof, Mass Inst Technol, 79-80, prof elec eng & assoc dir, Energy Lab, 80-82, dir, Lab Electromagnetic & Electronic Systs, 82-84, co dir, 84, dir, Int Inst Appl Systs Analysis, 84-87, Philip Sporn prof, 82-88, EMER PROF ENERGY PROCESSING, MASS INST TECHNOL, 88-; PRES, CTR QUAL MGT, 89- *Personal Data:* b Shanghai, China, May 11, 23; nat US; m 48; c 3. *Educ:* Nat Chiao-Tung Univ, China, BS, 46; Union Col, MS, 50; Rensselaer Polytech Inst, PhD(elec eng, physics), 54. *Prof Exp:* Eng analyst, Gen Elec Co, Pa, 54-55, sr res engr, 55-59, mgr eng res, 59-67, mgr lab opers, 67-71, mgr tech resources, 71-74, mgr strategic planning opers, 74-77, staff exec power systs technol oper, 77-80. *Concurrent Pos:* Adj prof, Rensselaer Polytech Inst, 54-55; lectr, Univ Pa, 59-61 & Lehigh Univ, 61-62. *Mem:* Nat Acad Eng; Am Phys Soc; fel Inst Elec & Electronics Engrs; Power Eng Soc (pres); Am Vacuum Soc; Sigma Xi; Swiss Acad Eng Sci; fel AAAS. *Res:* Electron physics; gaseous discharges; magnetohydrodynamics; ultra high vacuum technology; electrical systems; plasma physics; systems theory; management science. *Mailing Add:* Beacon Hill 44 Chestnut St Boston MA 02108

LEE, THOMAS J, ENGINEERING. *Current Pos:* PVT CONSULT, 94- *Personal Data:* b Wedowee, Ala, 1935; m, Jean Gullatt; c Kevin & Patrick. *Educ:* Univ Ala, BS, 58, PhD, 93. *Honors & Awards:* Exec Excellence Distinguished Serv Award, Sr Execs Asn Prof Develop League, 92. *Prof Exp:* Aerospace res engr, Ballistic Missile Agency, US Army, Redstone Arsenal, Ala, 58-60; syst engr, Marshall Space Flight Ctr, NASA, 60-69, from tech asst to tech dep dir, 79-73, mgr, Sortie Lab Task Team, 73-74, mgr, 74-80, dep dir, 80-89, dir, 89-94. *Mem:* Fel Am Inst Aeronaut & Astronaut. *Mailing Add:* 230 Walden Lane New Market AL 35761

LEE, TIEN-CHANG, GEOPHYSICS, HYDROGEOLOGY. *Current Pos:* asst prof, 74-79, assoc prof, 79-87, PROF GEOPHYS, UNIV CALIF, RIVERSIDE, 87- *Personal Data:* b Nantou, Taiwan, July 1, 43; m 69, Zora M Yen; c Cin-T, Cin-Y. *Educ:* Nat Taiwan Univ, BS, 65; Univ Southern Calif, PhD(geophys), 74. *Prof Exp:* Fel marine geophys, Woods Hole Oceanog Inst, 73-74. *Mem:* Am Geophys Union; Soc Explor Geophysicists. *Res:* Terrestrial heat flow; hydrogeology; fault zone characterization. *Mailing Add:* Dept Earth Sci Univ Calif Riverside CA 92521. *Fax:* 909-787-4509; *E-Mail:* tien.lee@ucr.edu

LEE, TONG-NYONG, PLASMA PHYSICS, ATOMIC PHYSICS. *Current Pos:* PROF PHYSICS, POHANG INST SCI & TECHNOL, 88- *Personal Data:* b July 22, 27; US citizen; m 59; c 3. *Educ:* Seoul Nat Univ, BS, 50; Univ London, PhD(physics), 59. *Prof Exp:* Asst prof physics, Seoul Nat Univ, 60-63; assoc prof appl physics, Cath Univ Am, 64-70; res physicist plasma physics & optical sci, Naval Res Lab, 70-88. *Mem:* Am Phys Soc. *Res:* Short wavelength laser generation; plasma physics and spectroscopy of high temperature; high density plasma and solar flare study. *Mailing Add:* Pohang Inst Sci & Technol PO Box 125 Pohang City Kyungbuk 790-784 South Korea

LEE, TONY JER-FU, PHARMACOLOGY. *Current Pos:* From asst prof to assoc prof, 75-87, PROF PHARMACOL, SCH MED, SOUTHERN ILL UNIV, SPRINGFIELD, 87- *Personal Data:* b Hualien, Taiwan, Nov 10, 42; US citizen; m 78; c 2. *Educ:* Taipei Med Col, Taiwan, BS, 67; WVa Univ, PhD(pharmacol), 73. *Concurrent Pos:* Fel, Univ Calif, Los Angeles, 73-75; mem, High Blood Pressure Coun, Am Heart Asn & Stroke Coun, Soc Neurol Sci; Am Heart Asn grant, NIH. *Mem:* Am Soc Pharmacol & Exp Therapeut; Soc Neurosci. *Res:* Cerebral vessel innervation in health and disease. *Mailing Add:* S Ill Univ Sch Med 801 N Rutledge St Springfield IL 62708-3926

LEE, TSUNG DAO, THEORETICAL PHYSICS. *Current Pos:* ENRICO FERMI PROF PHYSICS, COLUMBIA UNIV, 63-, UNIV PROF, 84- *Personal Data:* b China, Nov 25, 26; m 50; c 2. *Educ:* Univ Chicago, PhD(physics), 50. *Hon Degrees:* DSc, Princeton Univ, 58; LLD, Chinese Univ Hong Kong, 69; ScD, City Col New York, 78, Bard Col, 84, Peking Univ, 85, Drexel Univ, 86, Univ Bologna, 88, Columbia Univ, 90, Adelphi Univ, 91. *Honors & Awards:* Nobel Prize in Physics, 57; Loeb Lectr, Harvard Univ, 64; Order of Merit, Grande Ufficiale, Repub Italy, 86; Ettore Majorana-Erice Sci Peace Prize, 90. *Prof Exp:* Res assoc astrophys, Univ Chicago, 50; res assoc physics, Univ Calif, 50-51; mem, Inst Advan Study, 51-53; from asst prof to prof, Columbia Univ, 53-60; prof, Inst Advan Study, 60-63. *Concurrent Pos:* Hon prof, Univ Sci & Technol, China, 81, Jinan Univ & Fudan Univ, 82, Quinghua Univ, 84, Peking Univ & Nanjing Univ, 85, Nankai Univ, 86, Shanghai Jiao Univ & Suzhou Univ, 87 & Zhejiang Univ, 88. *Mem:* Nat Acad Sci; Acad Sci China; Am Acad Arts & Sci; Am Philos Soc. *Res:* Field theory; statistical mechanics; gravity; particle physics. *Mailing Add:* Dept Physics Bldg 538 Columbia Univ Morningside Heights W 120th St New York NY 10027

LEE, TSUNG TING, PLANT HORMONE, GROWTH REGULATION. *Current Pos:* RETIRED. *Personal Data:* b Anhwei, China, Mar 21, 23; m 50; c 3. *Educ:* Nat Cent Univ, China, BS, 47; Univ Wis, MS, 59, PhD(plant physiol), 62. *Prof Exp:* Plant physiologist, London Res Ctr, Can Dept Agr, 68-88. *Concurrent Pos:* Hon lectr, Univ Western Ont, 76- *Mem:* Am Soc Plant Physiol; Plant Growth Regulator Soc Am; Sigma Xi; Int Asn Plant Tissue Cult; Can Soc Plant Physiol. *Res:* Plant growth regulators; auxin metabolism, concerning regulation of conjugation and oxidation of IAA. *Mailing Add:* 30 Runnymede London ON N6G 1Z8 Can

LEE, TSUNG-SHUNG HARRY, NUCLEAR PHYSICS. *Current Pos:* res assoc physics, Argonne Nat Lab, 75-77, asst physicist, 77-81, physicist, 81-93, SR PHYSICIST, ARGONNE NAT LAB, 93- *Personal Data:* b Taipei, Taiwan, June 7, 43; m 68, Chinmei C; c Thomas S. *Educ:* Taiwan Norm Univ, BS, 65; Nat Tsing-Hua Univ, MS, 67; Univ Pittsburgh, PhD(physics), 73. *Prof Exp:* Res assoc physics, Bartol Res Found, 73-75. *Mem:* Fel Am Phys Soc. *Res:* Intermediate-energy and high-energy nuclear physics. *Mailing Add:* Physics Div Argonne Nat Lab Argonne IL 60439

LEE, TUNG-CHING, FOOD SCIENCE & TECHNOLOGY, FOOD SAFETY. *Current Pos:* from asst prof to assoc prof, 72-79, PROF FOOD SCI, UNIV RI, 79- *Personal Data:* b Szechwan, China, Oct 28, 41; US citizen; m 70; c 2. *Educ:* Tung-Hai Univ, Taiwan, BS, 63; Univ Calif, Davis, MS, 66, PhD(agr chem), 70. *Prof Exp:* Res asst, Univ Calif, 65-70; sr food technologist, Hunt-Wesson Foods, Inc, 70-72. *Concurrent Pos:* Vis prof, Inst Biochem, Cluj, Romania, 75 & Grad Inst Food Sci, Nat Taiwan Univ, 78-79; adv, Food Indust Res & Develop Adv Comt, Repub China, 76-; consult, many US & int food co, 76- *Mem:* Fel Inst Food Technologists; Am Chem Soc; Am Inst Nutrit; Am Soc Microbiol. *Res:* Nutritional and safety aspects of food processing; Maillard browning reaction; carotenoids and vitamins; food extrusion; marine food technology; biotechnological applications in food technology; fish nutrition; fishfeed technology. *Mailing Add:* Dept Food Sci & Nutrit Rutgers State Univ PO Box 231 New Brunswick NJ 08903-0235

LEE, TZOONG-CHYH, ORGANIC CHEMISTRY, BIO-ORGANIC CHEMISTRY. *Current Pos:* RES MGR, LEA RONAL, INC, 80- *Personal Data:* b Taiwan, Jan 2, 36; m 62; c 3. *Educ:* Yamagata Univ, Japan, BSc, 63; Tohoku Univ, Japan, MSc, 65; Australian Nat Univ, PhD(med chem), 68. *Prof Exp:* USPHS fel, Sloan-Kettering Inst Cancer Res, 68-71, Damon Runyon Res fel, 69-70, res assoc org chem, 71-75, assoc, 75-80. *Mem:* Am Chem Soc. *Res:* Nitrogen heterocyclic chemistry; organic synthesis; structure-activity relationship; imaging chemicals. *Mailing Add:* 6 Villa Lane Larchmont NY 10538-1249

LEE, VING JICK, CHEMISTRY, NATURAL PRODUCTS CHEMISTRY. *Current Pos:* VPRES CHEM, MICROCIDE PHARMACEUT. *Personal Data:* b Columbus, Ohio, July 28, 51; m 74; c 2. *Educ:* Ohio State Univ, BA, 71; Univ Ill, Urbana, MS, 73, PhD(chem), 75. *Prof Exp:* Res assoc chem, Univ Ill, Urbana, 71-75, teaching assoc, 71-73; NIH res assoc, Harvard Univ, 75-77; res chemist, Lederle Labs, Am Cyanamid Co, 77-, sr res group leader, 87-89, head, Dept Chem, Infectious Dis & Molecular Biol Res, 90- *Concurrent Pos:* Mem, Med Chem Study Sect, NIH. *Mem:* Am Chem Soc; Int Soc Heterocyclic Chem. *Res:* Antibiotics, antivirals and natural products. *Mailing Add:* Microcide Pharmaceut 850 Maude Ave Mountain View CA 94043

LEE, VIN-JANG, HETEROGENEOUS CATALYSIS, QUANTUM THEORY. *Current Pos:* PRES, CYBERDYNE, INC, 81- *Personal Data:* b Honan, China, Feb 14, 37; div; c 1. *Educ:* Ord Eng Col, Taiwan, Dipl eng, 53; Notre Dame Univ, MS, 58; Univ Mich, PhD(chem eng), 63. *Prof Exp:* Chem engr, 26th Arsenal, Repub China, 52-57; res specialist, Monsanto Chem Co, 64-65; res specialist, Univ Mo, Columbia, 65-68, assoc prof chem eng, 68-74; vis prof, Dept Chem, Univ Calif, Los Angeles, 72-73; consult catalysis, Libby Corp, 74-77; pres, Lee Securities & Investment Co, 75-80 & Econo Trading Corp, 80-81. *Mem:* Am Phys Soc; Am Chem Soc; Am Inst Chem Eng. *Res:* Surface physics; catalysis and kinetics; tunneling in catalysis; physical foundations of quantum theory. *Mailing Add:* Cyberdyne Inc 1045 Ocean Ave Suite 2 Santa Monica CA 90403

LEE, VIRGINIA ANN, biochemistry, for more information see previous edition

LEE, WAI-HON, OPTICAL PHYSICS, COMMUNICATIONS SCIENCE. *Current Pos:* PRES, HOETRON INC, SUNNYVALE, CALIF, 89- *Personal Data:* b Haiphong, Vietnam, Apr 29, 42; US citizen; m 68; c 2. *Educ:* Mass Inst Technol, BSc, 65, MSc, 67, DSc, 69. *Prof Exp:* Assoc prin eng coherent optics, Electronic Syst Div, Harris Corp, 69-73; staff mem res optical sci, Palo Alto Res Ctr, Xerox Corp, 73-81; mgr laser imaging systs, Xidex Corp, 81- *Mem:* Inst Elec & Electronics Engrs; Optical Soc Am; Soc Photo-Optical Instrumentation Engrs; Soc Photog Scientists & Engrs. *Res:* Applications of grating structures for testing optical surfaces and scanning laser beam; optical methods for storing digital information at high density. *Mailing Add:* Hoetron Inc 776 Palomar Ave Sunnyvale CA 94086

LEE, WARREN FORD, AGRICULTURAL ECONOMICS. *Current Pos:* assoc prof agr finance, 70-80, prof agr econ & rural sociol, 80-, PROF AGR ECON, OHIO STATE UNIV, 80- *Personal Data:* b Harriston, Ont, Aug 25, 41; m 66; c 3. *Educ:* Univ Toronto, BSA, 63; Univ Ill, MS, 67; Mich State Univ, PhD(agr econ), 70. *Prof Exp:* Credit adv, Farm Credit Corp, 63-65. *Concurrent Pos:* Economist, Econ Br, Agr Can, 75-76. *Mem:* Am Agr Econ Asn. *Res:* Agricultural credit and finance; farm firm growth; rural capital markets; bank structure and performance; financial institutions. *Mailing Add:* Dept Agr Econ 103 Agr Admin Bldg Main Campus Ohio State Univ Columbus OH 43210

LEE, WEI-KUO, PETROCHEMICAL SEPARATIONS, SOLID FLUIDIZATION TECHNOLOGY. *Current Pos:* TECH STAFF MEM, UNION CARBIDE CHEM & PLASTICS CO, 88- *Personal Data:* b Hopei, China, Apr 29, 43; US citizen; m. *Educ:* Nat Taiwan Univ, BS, 65; Univ Houston, PhD(chem eng), 71. *Prof Exp:* Unidel fel, Univ Del, 72-73; res engr, Celanese Res Co, 73-77; staff engr, Exxon Res & Eng Co, 77-86; sr res engr, Shell Develop Co, 86-88. *Concurrent Pos:* Adj prof, Chem Eng Dept, NJ Inst Technol, 75-81. *Mem:* Am Inst Chem Engrs; Soc Plastics Engrs; Soc Rheology; Am Inst Physics; Sigma Xi. *Res:* Applications of fluid mechanics and rheology in various plastics technology and petrochemical engineering problems, including fibers, films, wire and cable insulations, oil field fluids, solid suspensions, composites, multiphase dispersions, fluidized solids and powders. *Mailing Add:* 328 Eileen Way Bridgewater NJ 08807. *Fax:* 732-271-7886

LEE, WEI-LI S, BIOCHEMISTRY. *Current Pos:* instr dermat med, 75-82, ASST PROF DERMAT, STATE UNIV NY DOWNSTATE MED CTR, 83-, DIR, LAB EXP DERMAT, 93- *Personal Data:* b Kiangsi, China, Feb 14, 45; m 70; c 2. *Educ:* Tunghai Univ, BS, 66; State Univ NY, Buffalo, MA, 69, PhD(biol), 72. *Prof Exp:* Asst biol sci, State Univ NY, Buffalo, 66-72; res assoc immunochem, Col Physicians & Surgeons, Columbia Univ, 72-75. *Concurrent Pos:* Dermat Found grant, Soc Investigative Dermat, 79, Benjamin Zohn Res, Cult Fund grant, 83, Johnson & Johnson grant, Estee Lauder grant. *Mem:* Sigma Xi; NY Acad Sci; Soc Investigative Dermat; Am Fedn Clin Res; Skin Pharmacol Soc. *Res:* Identification of specific extracellular and cell surface factors (enzymes) derived from major skin microflora, propionibacterium acnes and studies of their role in leukocytes chemotaxis and chemiluminescence in order to elucidate the mechanisms of inflammation in acne; development of a in vitro model system to elucidate the mechanism of skin inflammation and testing of potential irritants and anti-irritants. *Mailing Add:* Dept Dermat State Univ NY Downstate Med Ctr 450 Clarkson Ave Brooklyn NY 11203

LEE, WEI-MING, physical chemistry, polymer chemistry, for more information see previous edition

LEE, WILLIAM CHIEN-YEH, ELECTRICAL ENGINEERING. *Current Pos:* vpres, Pactel Cellular, 85-, VPRES, AIRTOUCH. *Personal Data:* b London, Eng, July 20, 32; m 64; c 2. *Educ:* Chinese Naval Acad, Taiwan, BSc, 54; Ohio State Univ, MS, 60, PhD(elec eng), 63. *Prof Exp:* Mem tech staff commun, Bell Labs, 64-79; sr scientist & mgr, Defense Commun Div, ITT, 79-84. *Concurrent Pos:* Publ chmn, Inst Elec & Electronics Engrs Transactions on Vehicular Technol, 79-; mem, Nat Commun Forum Overseas Coun, 85-, affil mem, Univ Calif, Irvine, 85-; affil mem, Univ Calif, Davis, 85- *Mem:* Brit Inst Elec Engrs; fel Inst Elec & Electronics Engrs; Sigma Xi. *Res:* Wave propagation in anisotropic medium; antennas; signal fading; communication systems, particularly those relating to the ultrahigh frequency and x-band regions; author of three books on mobile communications and more than one hundred technical articles. *Mailing Add:* Airtouch Commun Corp Tech Group 1340 Treat Blvd Suite 500 Walnut Creek CA 94596

LEE, WILLIAM HUNG KAN, geophysics, for more information see previous edition

LEE, WILLIAM JOHN, PRESSURE TRANSIENT TESTING, RESERVOIR PERFORMANCE ANALYSIS. *Current Pos:* Samuel Roberts Noble chair, 87-92, PROF PETROL ENG, TEX A&M UNIV, 77-, L F PETERSON CHAIR, 92-; EXEC VPRES TECHNOL, S A HOLDITCH & ASSOC, 80- *Personal Data:* b Lubbock, Tex, Jan 16, 36; m 61; c Anne P (Widdison) & Mary D. *Educ:* Ga Inst Technol, B Che, 59, MS, 61, PhD(chem eng), 63. *Honors & Awards:* Reservoir Eng Award, Soc Petrol Engrs, 86, Distinguished Serv Award, 92, John Franklin Carll Award, 95. *Prof Exp:* Sr res specialist, Exxon Prod Res Co, 62-68; assoc prof petrol eng, Miss State Univ, 68-71; tech adv, Exxon Co, USA, 71-77. *Concurrent Pos:* Lectr, Soc Mining, Metall & Petrol Engrs, 70- & Am Asn Petrol Geologists, 77-; distinguished lectr, Soc Petrol Engrs, 78. *Mem:* Nat Acad Eng; Soc Petrol Engrs; Sigma Xi. *Res:* Pressure transient testing; low permeability gas well analysis; petroleum reservoir engineering; tight gas applications; reservoir rock and fluid properties. *Mailing Add:* Dept Petrol Eng Tex A&M Univ College Station TX 77843. *Fax:* 409-845-1307

LEE, WILLIAM ORVID, FIELD CROPS. *Current Pos:* RETIRED. *Personal Data:* b Brigham City, Utah, July 2, 27; m 51; c 4. *Educ:* Utah State Univ, BS, 50, MS, 54; Ore State Univ, PhD(farm crops), 65. *Prof Exp:* Soil scientist, Bur Reclamation, US Dept Interior, 50-51; agronomist, Sci & Educ Admin, Agr Res, USDA, Utah, 51-54 & Wyo, 54-56, res agronomist, 56-83. *Mem:* Weed Sci Soc Am. *Res:* Crop science; control of weeds in forage and turf seed crops; legumes and grasses. *Mailing Add:* 1538 NW 12th Corvallis OR 97701

LEE, WILLIAM ROSCOE, GENETICS. *Current Pos:* assoc prof, 67-73, PROF ZOOL & PHYSIOL, LA STATE UNIV, BATON ROUGE, 73- *Personal Data:* b Little Rock, Ark, Feb 14, 30; m 53; c 3. *Educ:* Univ Ark, BSA, 53; Univ Wis, MS, 53, PhD(genetics, entom), 56. *Prof Exp:* Asst, Univ Wis, 52-56; from asst prof to assoc prof entom, Univ NH, 56-63; asst prof zool, Univ Tex, Austin, 63-67. *Concurrent Pos:* Res exec for H J Muller, Ind Univ, 62-63; dir, Inst Mutagenesis, La State Univ, Baton Rouge. *Mem:* Genetics Soc Am; Radiation Res Soc; Environ Mutagen Soc. *Res:* Radiation genetics; mechanisms of mutagenesis; recombinant DNA; southern blot experiments with both cloned and synthetic probes; relation between DNA adducts in the germ cells of Drosophila melanogaster and changes in DNA of induced mutants. *Mailing Add:* Dept Zool & Physiol La State Univ Baton Rouge Baton Rouge LA 70803-0001

LEE, WILLIAM STATES, engineering; deceased, see previous edition for last biography

LEE, WILLIAM THOMAS, MICROBIOLOGY. *Current Pos:* ASST INSTR, DEPT MICROBIOL, UNIV TEX HEALTH SCI CTR, DALLAS, 87- *Personal Data:* b Hartford, Conn, July 18, 58; m. *Educ:* George Washington Univ, BA, 80, MForensic Sci, 82; Johns Hopkins Univ, PhD(immunol), 86. *Mem:* Am Asn Immunologists. *Mailing Add:* Lab Immunol David Axelrod Inst Pub Health Wadsworth Ctr Labs & Res NY State Dept Health PO Box 2202 Albany NY 12201-2002

LEE, WILLIAM WAI-LIM, resource management, environmental engineering, for more information see previous edition

LEE, WILLIAM WEI, MEDICINAL CHEMISTRY. *Current Pos:* RETIRED. *Personal Data:* b San Francisco, Calif, May 17, 23; m 47, Pauline Lee; c Peter H, Kerwin J & Roderick M. *Educ:* Univ Calif, BS, 47; Univ Minn, PhD(org chem), 52. *Prof Exp:* Jr chemist org analytical chem, Shell Develop Co, 47-48; asst org chem, Univ Minn, 48-51; org res chemist, Cent Res Dept, Monsanto Chem Co, 52-54; assoc chemist org chem, SRI INT, 54-56, sr org chemist, 56-77, prog dir, Synthetic Cancer Drugs, 78-87. *Mem:* Am Chem Soc; Sigma Xi; Radiation Res Soc. *Res:* Allylic and acetylenic compounds; nucleosides, amino acids and alkylating agents; enzyme chemistry; active halogen compounds; folic acid antagonists; heterocyclic chemistry; chemotherapy, particularly cancer chemotherapy; radiosensitizing agents. *Mailing Add:* 991 N California Ave Palo Alto CA 94303-3407

LEE, WONYONG, HIGH ENERGY PHYSICS. *Current Pos:* res assoc, 62-64, from asst prof to assoc prof, 64-72, PROF PHYSICS, COLUMBIA UNIV, 72- *Personal Data:* b Korea, Dec 29, 30; m 61; c 1. *Educ:* Calif Inst Technol, BS, 57; Univ Calif, Berkeley, PhD(physics), 61. *Prof Exp:* Res assoc physics, Lawrence Radiation Lab, Univ Calif, 61-62. *Concurrent Pos:* Sloan Found fel, 65-67. *Mem:* Am Phys Soc. *Res:* High energy experimental physics. *Mailing Add:* Dept Physics Columbia Univ New York NY 10027

LEE, WOONG MAN, PATHOLOGY. *Current Pos:* PATHOLOGIST, GLEN FALLS HOSP, NY, 79- *Personal Data:* b Seoul, Korea, Dec 3, 38; US citizen; m 68, Young-Sook; c Danny, Francis & Peggy. *Educ:* Seoul Nat Univ, BS, 60, MD, 64; Am Bd Path, cert, 76. *Prof Exp:* From instr to asst prof path, Albany Med Col, NY, 70-79. *Concurrent Pos:* Asst residency, Albany Med Ctr Hosp, 67-70, residency, 70-72, asst attend pathologist, 74-79; attend pathologist, Vet Admin Hosp, Albany, NY, 74-79. *Mem:* Col Am Path; Am Soc Clin Path; Am Acad Path; Can Acad Path. *Res:* Anatomical aspects and drug treatment of atherosclerosis. *Mailing Add:* Dept Path Glens Falls Hosp Glens Falls NY 12801

LEE, WOOYOUNG, POLYMER MANUFACTURING. *Current Pos:* res engr, Mobil Res & Develop Corp, 66-69, sr res engr, 69-74, res assoc, 74-77, mgr, reforming & spec process develop, 77-80, synthetic fuels develop, 80-84, mgr, Chem Prods Dept, 84-85, mgr polyolefins process, 85-86, MGR, EDISON RES LAB, MOBIL CHEM CO, 86- *Personal Data:* b Pusan, Korea, Jan 2, 38; m 66, June J Moon; c Marjorie & Christina. *Educ:* Seoul Nat Univ, BS, 61; Univ Wis-Madison, MS, 64, PhD(chem eng), 66. *Prof Exp:* Fel chem eng, Univ Wis, 66. *Mem:* Am Inst Chem Engrs; Am Chem Soc; Soc Polymer Engrs. *Res:* Conversion of oxygenates to hydrocarbons; aromatics and olefin upgrading process development; fluid bed catalytic cracking; kinetics and reaction engineering; lube additives and synthetic hydrocarbon fluids; polyethylene process product. *Mailing Add:* Mobil Chem Res & Develop Corp PO Box 3029 Edison NJ 08818-3029. *Fax:* 732-321-6343

LEE, Y C, DATABASES, COMPUTATIONAL GEOMETRY. *Current Pos:* Asst prof, 77-91, ASSOC PROF GIS, DEPT SURV ENG, UNIV NB, 91- *Personal Data:* b Hong Kong, Mar 30, 48; Can citizen; m 81; c 2. *Educ:* Simon Fraser Univ, BSc, 77; Univ NB, MSc, 80, PhD(surv eng), 86. *Honors & Awards:* Bauch & Lomb Photogram Award, Can Inst Surv & Mapping, 82, ACDS Graphics Award, 91. *Concurrent Pos:* Consult, Universal Systs Ltd, Fredericton, NB, 87-, Can Int Develop Agency, 88-, NB Geog Info Corp, 90-; mem, working group GIS, Int Soc Photogram & Remote Sensing, 89-, Comn Urban Cartog, Int Cartog Asn, 89-, Tech Comt Geomatics, Can Gen Stand Bd, 89-. *Mem:* Can Inst Surv & Mapping; Can Cartog Asn; Inst Elec & Electronics Engrs Comput Soc. *Res:* Geographic information systems and automated cartography, particularly in areas of data models, data structures, geometric processing, visualization, user interfaces and spatial search algorithms. *Mailing Add:* Dept Surv Eng Univ NB PO Box 4400 Fredericton NB E3B 5A3 Can

LEE, YIEN-HWEI, PHARMACOLOGY. *Current Pos:* MED DIR, LIBERTY REHAB & MED CTR, PHILADELPHIA, PA, 93- *Personal Data:* b Taiwan, Oct 20, 37; m 68, Shan-guang Lin; c Yishane, Yiying & Yiking. *Educ:* Nat Taiwan Univ, MD, 63; Univ Calif, Los Angeles, PhD(pharmacol), 68. *Prof Exp:* Res asst pharmacol, Univ Calif, Los Angeles, 64-66, res pharmacologist, 66-68, res assoc, Neuropsychiat Inst, 66-68; sr investr pharmacol, Searle Res Lab, G D Searle & Co, 68-72; sect head, Abbott Labs, 72-76; staff, Chicago Med Sch Hosp, 76-77; staff physician, St Joseph Hosp, Chicago, 77-78; fel sect hemat, Rush-Presby & St Luke's Hosp, Chicago, 78-80; Am Cancer Soc fel clin onocol, Sect Hemat & Oncol, Cook Co Hosp, Chicago, 80-81; consult specialist, Bethesda Res Lab, Gaithersburg, 81-82; attend hematologist, Georgetown Univ, Washington, DC, 82-83; attend hematologist oncologist, Shady Grove Adventist Hosp, Rockville, Md, 82-85; pres, L&L Clin, Inc, Rockville, Md, 83-85; med dir, Lee Clin, Villanova, Pa, 85-93. *Concurrent Pos:* Attend hematologist oncologist, Greater Beltsville Laurel Med Ctr, Md, 83-85 & Leland Hosp, Riverdale, Md, 84-85; attend physician, Jefferson Park Hosp, Philadelphia, Pa, 85-92 & Thomas Jefferson Univ Hosp, 92-; consult physician, Spruce Med Ctr, Philadelphia, Pa, 85-91. *Mem:* AAAS; Am Soc Pharmacol & Exp Therapeut; Sigma Xi; Am Chem Soc; Am Ctr Chinese Med Sci. *Res:* Gastrointestinal pharmacology and physiology; biochemical pharmacology; cancer chemotherapy; experimental leukemia; hematology; oncology. *Mailing Add:* 155 S Spring Mill Rd Villanova PA 19085-1408. *Fax:* 215-923-7320

LEE, YIM TIN, ATOMIC PROCESS IN PLASMA, LAB X-RAY LASER RESEARCH. *Current Pos:* RES PHYSICIST, LAWRENCE LIVERMORE NAT LAB, 79- *Personal Data:* b Canton, China, June 14, 50. *Educ:* Univ Calif, Berkeley, BA, 72; Univ Calif, San Diego, PhD(physics), 77. *Prof Exp:* Fel physics, Univ Calif, San Diego, 77-79. *Concurrent Pos:* Consult, Phys Dynamics Inc, 76-77. *Mem:* Am Phys Soc; AAAS; Fusion Energy Asn. *Res:* Atomic processes in laser produced plasma and soft x-ray lasing. *Mailing Add:* Lawrence Livermore Lab PO Box 808 L-298 Livermore CA 94550

LEE, YING KAO, POLYMER CHEMISTRY. *Current Pos:* res chemist, E I du Pont de Nemours & Co, Inc, 65-68, staff chemist, 68-70, res assoc, 70-76, res fel, 76-87, sr res fel, 86-89, dept fel, 89-90, DUPONT FEL, MARSHALL RES & DEVELOP LAB, E I DU PONT DE NEMOURS & CO, INC, 90- *Personal Data:* b Shanghai, China, Dec 14, 32; US citizen; m 61, Theresa Tai; c Arthur, Annette & Angela. *Educ:* Tai Tung Univ, BSc, 52; Univ Cincinnati, PhD(chem), 61. *Honors & Awards:* Achievement Award, Chinese Inst Engrs, US, 94. *Prof Exp:* Res chemist, Tex-US Chem Co, 60-63, proj leader, 65. *Concurrent Pos:* Hon prof, Inst Chem, Beijing, 94; Dupont fel & chief scientist, Dupont Automotive, 96; distinguished scientist & Dupont fel, E I Du Pont de Nemours & Co, Inc, 96. *Mem:* Am Chem Soc; Sigma Xi. *Res:* Polymers or polymeric systems used in coating field; high temperature polymer for electronics applications; crosslinking chemistries. *Mailing Add:* Marshall Res & Develop Lab E I du Pont de Nemours & Co Inc Philadelphia PA 19146. *Fax:* 215-339-6114

LEE, YONG YUNG, ACCELERATOR PHYSICS. *Current Pos:* PHYSICIST ACCELERATOR PHYSICS, BROOKHAVEN NAT LAB, 71- *Personal Data:* b Kyungpook, Korea, Feb 12, 36; US citizen; m 63; c 2. *Educ:* Kyung-Pook Nat Univ, BS, 58, MS, 60; Univ Mich, PhD(physics), 64. *Prof Exp:* Res assoc physics, Univ Wis, 64-67; asst prof, State Univ NY, Stony Brook, 67-71. *Mem:* Fel Am Phys Soc. *Res:* Accelerator physics. *Mailing Add:* Bldg 911B Brookhaven Nat Lab Upton NY 11973

LEE, YOUNG HIE, CHEMICAL ENGINEERING, BIOCHEMICAL ENGINEERING. *Current Pos:* PROF CHEM ENG, DREXEL UNIV, 78- *Personal Data:* b Seoul, Korea, Jan 12, 46; m 72; c 2. *Educ:* Seoul Nat Univ, BS, 71; Purdue Univ, MS, 74, PhD(chem eng), 77. *Concurrent Pos:* Prin investr, NSF proj, 78-90. *Mem:* Am Inst Chem Engrs; Am Chem Soc. *Res:* Transport phenomena; gas liquid reaction; waste water treatment; biomass utilization. *Mailing Add:* Dept Chem Eng Drexel Univ 3141 Chestnut St Philadelphia PA 19104-2816

LEE, YOUNG JACK, STATISTICS. *Current Pos:* MATH STATISTICIAN, NIH, 79- *Personal Data:* b Seoul, Korea, Feb 25, 42; m 67; c 3. *Educ:* Seoul Nat Univ, BSE, 64; Ohio State Univ, MS, 72, PhD(statist), 74. *Prof Exp:* Instr electronics eng, Korean Air Force Acad, 67-69; asst prof statist, Univ Md, College Park, 74-79. *Mem:* Am Statist Asn; Biomet Soc. *Res:* Nonparametric/robust design of experiment and statistical analysis in hypothesis testing, ranking and selection and estimation; applications of statistics to social science and life science; method in clinical trial, statistical design and analysis for carcinogenesis and mutagenesis bioassays. *Mailing Add:* NIH 6100 Executive Blvd Rm 7B13 Bethesda MD 20892

LEE, YOUNG-HOON, SEMICONDUCTOR DEVICES. *Current Pos:* MEM RES STAFF, IBM THOMAS J WATSON RES CTR, 78- *Personal Data:* b Korea, Sept 18, 35; m 65, Kim Poong-mee; c Benjamin S. *Educ:* Dong-Guk Univ, BS, 61, MS, 63; State Univ NY Albany, PhD(physics), 72. *Prof Exp:* Sr asst physics, Dong-Guk Univ, 63-66; fel physics, State Univ NY, Albany, 73-78. *Mem:* Am Phys Soc; Am Vacuum Soc. *Res:* Defects in solids and electron spin resonance; electronics engineering; microelectronics fabrication techniques; plasma processings. *Mailing Add:* IBM T J Watson Res Ctr PO Box 218 Yorktown Heights NY 10598. *E-Mail:* ylee@watson.ibm.com

LEE, YOUNG-ZOON, TOXICOLOGY, FISHERIES TECHNOLOGY. *Current Pos:* DIR, EGG BIOLOGICS RES, STOLLE RES & DEVELOP CORP, 90- *Personal Data:* b Korea, Oct 1, 43; Can citizen; m 75, Sung-ae; c Yohan, Eric & Ruthann. *Educ:* Dongguk Univ, Seoul, Korea, BSc, 66, MSc, 69; Kyushu Univ, Fukuoka, Japan, PhD(enzym), 74. *Prof Exp:* Lectr microbiol, Dept Agrobiol, Dongguk Univ, Seoul, Korea, 75; Nat Res Coun res fel, Fisheries Marine Serv, Nfld Biol Sta, Can, 75-77; univ res fel, Biochem Dept, mem Univ Nfld, 78-80, asst prof res, 80-84; res assoc, Poultry Sci Dept, Univ BC, 84-85, Food Sci Dept, 86-89. *Mem:* Inst Food Technologists; Poultry Sci Asn; Am Asn Avian Pathologists; Korean Scientist & Engrs Asn Am; Soc Toxicol Can; Japan Soc Biosci Biotechnol & Agrochem. *Res:* Identification and isolation of biological factors in avian eggs, animal bloods, marine products and microorganisms using supercritical fluid chromatography and extraction, affinity, high-performance liquid chromatography, gas chromatography-mass spectrometry, ultrafiltration and immunological techniques for developing pharmaceutical and functional food compounds to control human, animal and fish diseases. *Mailing Add:* Stolle Res & Develop Co 6954 Corner Rd Cincinnati OH 45242. *Fax:* 513-247-3645

LEE, YUAN CHUAN, BIOCHEMISTRY. *Current Pos:* from asst prof to assoc prof, 65-74, PROF BIOL, JOHNS HOPKINS UNIV, 74- *Personal Data:* b Taiwan, China, Mar 30, 32; m 58; c 1. *Educ:* Nat Taiwan Univ, BS, 55, MS, 57; Univ Iowa, PhD(biochem), 62. *Honors & Awards:* Merit Award, NIH. *Prof Exp:* Res assoc biochem, Univ Iowa, 62 & Univ Calif, Berkeley, 62-65. *Concurrent Pos:* Vis prof, Kyoto Univ, Academia Sinica, Taipei & Beijing Med Univ. *Mem:* Am Chem Soc; Am Soc Biol Chem; Japanese Biochem Soc; Chinese Biochem Soc; Am Soc Cell Biol. *Res:* Complex carbohydrates; carbohydrate receptors. *Mailing Add:* Dept Biol Johns Hopkins Univ 3400 N Charles St Baltimore MD 21218-2699

LEE, YUAN TSEH, CHEMISTRY. *Current Pos:* prof, 74-91, Univ prof, 91-94, GRAD PROF, DEPT CHEM, UNIV CALIF, BERKELEY, 94-; PRIN INVESTR, CHEM SCI DIV, LAWRENCE BERKELEY LAB, 74- *Personal Data:* b Hsinchu, Taiwan, Nov 29, 36; m 63, Bernice; c Ted, Sidney & Charlotte. *Educ:* Nat Taiwan Univ, BS, 59; Nat Tsing Hua Univ, Taiwan, MS, 61; Univ Calif, Berkeley, PhD(chem), 65. *Hon Degrees:* Dr, Univ Waterloo, Can, 86, Chinese Acad Sci, 87, Chinese Univ Hong Kong, 89, Ariz State Univ, 90, Univ Rome, 92, Univ Southern Calif, 93, Chenkuna Univ, Taiwan, 94, Hong Kong Baptist Univ, 94, Providence Univ, 95, Univ Md, 96, Int Tech Univ, San Jose, Calif, 96. *Honors & Awards:* Nobel Prize in Chem, 86; numerous named lectrs, US & foreign univs, 73-; Ernest O Lawrence Award, US Dept Energy, 81; Harrison Howe Award, Rochester Sect, 83; Peter Debye Award, Am Chem Soc, 86; Nat Medal of Sci, 86 & 90; Michelson Award, 87; Faraday Medal, Royal Soc Chem, 92. *Prof Exp:* From asst prof to prof chem, Univ Chicago, 68-74. *Concurrent Pos:* Alfred P Sloan fel, 69-71; John Simon Guggenheim fel, 76-77; hon prof, Inst Chem Chinese Acad Sci, 80, Fudan Univ, 80, Chinese Univ, Sci & Technol, 86, Nanjing Univ, 87, Nankai Univ, 87, Nat Lab Chem Kinetics & Reaction Dynamics, Beijing Univ, 88, Xiamen Univ, 88, Fuzou Inst, 88, Bilkent Univ, 93, Nat Taiwan Univ, 94; vis prof, Univ Perugia, 89; pres, Acad Sinica, 94- *Mem:* Nat Acad Sci; fel Am Phys Soc; fel Am Acad Arts Sci; Am Chem Soc; fel AAAS; hon mem Int Acad Sci; corresp mem Gottingen Acad Sci. *Res:* Chemical kinetics, reaction dynamics, laser chemistry and molecular interaction. *Mailing Add:* Dept Chem Univ Calif B38 Hildebrand Hall No 1460 Berkeley CA 94720

LEE, YUEN SAN, FOODS, BIOCHEMISTRY. *Current Pos:* chairperson, Dept Food Sci, 89-92, PROF, UNIV DC, 77- *Personal Data:* b Taipei, Taiwan, Oct 13, 39; m 67, Helen Fung Ping; c James & May. *Educ:* Nat Taiwan Univ, BS, 62; Utah State Univ, MS, 65; Univ Md, College Park, PhD(food sci, biochem), 68. *Prof Exp:* Chemist, Comn Pub Health, DC Govt, 68-77. *Mem:* Inst Food Technol; Am Chem Soc; Am Dietetic Asn. *Res:* Method development in the determination of pesticides in meat, milk and water; quality control of detecting adulteration in meat and meat products for consumer protection; heavy metals in foods. *Mailing Add:* 5 Maplewood Ct Greenbelt MD 20770

LEE, YUE-WEI, ORGANIC CHEMISTRY, MEDICINAL CHEMISTRY. *Current Pos:* SR RES CHEMIST SYNTHESIS RES TRIANGLE INST, 78-,. *Personal Data:* b San-Tung, China, Mar 9, 46; m 72; c 3. *Educ:* Calif State Univ, Sacramento, MS, 73; Columbia Univ, MS, 75, PhD(chem), 78. *Prof Exp:* Res grad asst, Columbia Univ, 74-78. *Mem:* Am Chem Soc. *Res:* Synthesis of steroidal hormone for contraceptive purpose; isolation and structure determination of medicinal component from natural resources; countercurrent chromatography and its applications in natural products and recombinant protein research; isolation of bio-active components from Chinese herbal medicine. *Mailing Add:* 105 Highland Dr Chapel Hill NC 27514-6624

LEE, YUNG, MECHANICAL ENGINEERING. *Current Pos:* from asst prof to assoc prof, 67-73, PROF MECH ENG, UNIV OTTAWA, 73-; DIR, OTTAWA-CARLETON INST MECH & AERONAUT ENG, 84- *Personal Data:* b Inchon, Korea, May 11, 32; Can citizen; m 60; c 1. *Educ:* Seoul Nat Univ, BEng, 59, MEng, 61; Univ Liverpool, PhD(mech eng), 64. *Prof Exp:* Lectr mech eng, Liverpool Polytech Inst, 64-65; res officer, Chalk River Nuclear Lab, Atomic Energy Can, Ltd, 65-67. *Mem:* Can Soc Mech Engrs; Eng Inst Can; Asn Prof Engrs Ont. *Res:* Fluid flow; heat transfer. *Mailing Add:* Dept Mech Eng Univ Ottawa Ottawa ON K1N 6N5 Can

LEE, YUNG-CHANG, PHYSICS. *Current Pos:* ASSOC PROF PHYSICS, STATE UNIV NY, BUFFALO, 67 - *Personal Data:* b Canton, China, Nov 7, 35; US citizen. *Educ:* Nat Taiwan Univ, BSc, 55; Univ Md, PhD(physics), 63. *Prof Exp:* Mem tech staff, Bell Tel Lab, 61-67. *Concurrent Pos:* Vis prof, Nat Tsing Hua Univ & Nat Taiwan Univ, 73-74; physicist, Lawrence Livermore Lab, 78-79. *Mem:* Am Phys Soc. *Res:* Solid state physics and quantum optics, including superradiance in thin crystal films; excitons in thin films; Anderson localization and Thouless' maximum resistance; interaction of electromagnetic radiation with plasmas; parametric coupling in plasmas; two dimensional crystalline order; high temperature superconductivity; meissner attractive forces on dirty superconductors; density functional theory; clustered hubbard model. *Mailing Add:* Physics Dept State Univ NY Buffalo Amherst NY 14260

LEE, YUNG-CHENG, ELECTRONIC PACKAGING, HEAT TRANSFER. *Current Pos:* ASST PROF, DEPT MECH ENG, UNIV COLO, BOULDER, 89- *Personal Data:* b Taiwan, Repub China, Feb 5, 56; US citizen; m 83; c 1. *Educ:* Nat Taiwan Univ, BS, 78; Univ Minn, MS, 82, PhD(mech eng), 84. *Prof Exp:* Res asst, Univ Minn, 80-84; mem tech staff, AT&T Bell Labs, Murray Hill, 84-89. *Concurrent Pos:* NSF presidential young investr award, 90. *Mem:* Am Soc Mech Engrs; Soc Mfg Engrs. *Res:* Low-cost prototyping and manufacturing of electronic multichip modules; three dimensional packaging for portable supercomputers; optoelectronic packaging; mechatronics; plasma-aided manufacturing. *Mailing Add:* Dept Mech Eng Univ Colo Cb 427 Boulder CO 80309

LEE, YUNG-KEUN, NUCLEAR PHYSICS. *Current Pos:* from asst prof to assoc prof, 64-71, PROF PHYSICS, JOHNS HOPKINS UNIV, 71- *Personal Data:* b Seoul, Korea, Sept 26, 29; m 58, Ock-Kyung Pai; c Ann, Arnold, Sara, Sylvia & Clara. *Educ:* Johns Hopkins Univ, BA, 56; Univ Chicago, MS, 57; Columbia Univ, PhD(physics), 61. *Prof Exp:* Res scientist, Columbia Univ, 61-64. *Mem:* Am Phys Soc. *Res:* Nuclear beta decay; nuclear reactions; Mossbauer effects; intermediate energy physics. *Mailing Add:* Dept Physics John Hopkins Univ 34th & Charles St Baltimore MD 21218. *Fax:* 410-516-7239; *E-Mail:* yklee@jhuvms.hcf.jhu.edu

LEECH, GEOFFREY BOSDIN, RESEARCH ADMINISTRATION. *Current Pos:* RETIRED. *Personal Data:* b Montreal, Que, Aug 28, 18; m 46, Jean Winters; c Joan (Edwards). *Educ:* Univ BC, BASc, 42; Queen's Univ, Ont, MSc, 43; Princeton Univ, PhD(petrol, econ geol), 49. *Prof Exp:* Field asst, Geol Surv Can, 40-41 & 42; geologist, Int Nickel Co Can, Ltd, Ont, 43-46; chief party, BC Dept Mines, 47-48; geologist, Geol Surv Can, Dept Energy, Mines & Resources, 49-72, head, Econ Geol Subdiv, 73-78, dir, Econ Geol Div, 79-82. *Concurrent Pos:* Assoc secy gen, Int Asn on Genesis of Ore Deposits, 78-84. *Mem:* Fel Geol Soc Am; fel Soc Econ Geol; fel Royal Soc Can; Can Inst Mining & Metall; fel Geol Asn Can. *Res:* Regional metallogeny; mineral resource evaluation; problems of resource adequacy. *Mailing Add:* 1113 Greenlawn Crescent Ottawa ON K2C 1Z4 Can

LEECH, H(ARRY) WILLIAM, PHYSICS, COMPUTER SCIENCE. *Current Pos:* PROF PHYSICS, WLIBERTY STATE COL, 90-, CHMN, 92- *Personal Data:* b Triadelphia, WVa, Apr 28, 40; m 66, 88, Carolyn C Bumpas; c Albert B, Amy J, Alan J, William J & Julia L. *Educ:* WVa Univ, BS, 62, MS, 64; Univ Md, PhD(physics), 75. *Prof Exp:* From instr to asst prof physics & math, WLiberty State Col, 64-68; mem tech staff comput sci, Comput Sci Corp, 73-77; asst prof physics, Southern Conn State Col, 77-78; asst prof physics, Bethany Col, 78-80; from assoc prof to prof eng technol, Jefferson Tech Col, 80-90, chmn, 84-86, dean technol & commun, 86-90. *Mem:* Am Asn Physics Teachers. *Res:* Cosmic ray astrophysics; celestial mechanics; orbit determination; scientific applications of computer science. *Mailing Add:* West Liberty State Col West Liberty WV 26074

LEECH, STEPHEN H, INTERNAL MEDICINE, CLINICAL IMMUNOLOGY. *Current Pos:* DIR IMMUNOL, GENETICS LAB, TEMPLE UNIV, 93-, PROF PATH & LAB MED, MED SCH, 93- *Personal Data:* b Mar 27, 42; m; c 4. *Educ:* Univ Edinburgh, MB, 65; Univ London, PhD(immunol), 76; FRCP(C), 71. *Prof Exp:* House surgeon, Edinburgh Royal Infirm, Scotland, 65-66; internship, Mem Res Ctr & Hosp, Univ Tenn, Knoxville, 66-67; resident internal med, Univ Minn, Mayo Clin, 67-69, Minneapolis, 69-70; fel allergy & immunol, Royal Victoria Hosp, Montreal, 70-72; clin res fel, Tumor Immunol Unit, Univ Col Hosp, London, 72-76; chief, Sect Allergy & Clin Immunol, Med Ctr, La State Univ, New Orleans, 76-87, from asst prof to prof med statist, Dept Med, 76-87; dir, Immunol Lab, Sentara Norfolk Gen Hosp, Va, 87-, dir, Sentara Serol Lab, 88-; prof clin immunol, Dept Immunol & Microbiol, Eastern Va Med Sch, 88-93. *Concurrent Pos:* House physician, St Mary's Hosp, Knoxville, 67; dir, Allergy Clin, Charity Hosp, La State Univ, New Orleans, 76-87, dir, B Cell Clin, 81-87; dir, Immunocytogenetics Lab, Med Ctr, La State Univ, 79-87, assoc prof, Dept Biomet & Genetics, 85-87; mem, Nat Histocompatability Comt, United Network Organ Sharing. *Mem:* Am Acad Allergy & Immunol; Am Soc Histocompatability & Immunogenetics; Am Fedn Clin Res; Am Asn Immunologists; Am Soc Transplant Physicans; Clin Immunol Soc. *Mailing Add:* Temple Univ Hosp 2 PAP/Clin Labs Broad & Ontario Sts Philadelphia PA 19140. *Fax:* 215-707-2053, 804-628-4171; *E-Mail:* flybo442@vm.temple.edu

LEED, RUSSELL ERNEST, NUCLEAR CHEMISTRY, CHEMICAL PLANT ENGINEERING. *Current Pos:* RETIRED. *Personal Data:* b Denver, Pa, Dec 24, 15. *Educ:* Franklin & Marshall Col, BS, 37; Univ Md, MS, 40, PhD(phys chem), 41. *Prof Exp:* From instr to asst prof chem, Va Mil Inst, 41-48; assoc prof, Va Polytech Inst, 48-51; chemist, Prod Div, Oak Ridge Opers, 51-73, dep dir, 58-73, asst to asst mgr, Uranium Enrichment Prog, Dept Energy, 73-80. *Concurrent Pos:* chem warfare serv, US Army, US & Europe, 43-46. *Mem:* Am Chem Soc. *Res:* Solutions; war gases; physical properties of alloys; thermal conductivity; phase diagrams; process development; nuclear weapons and separation of uranium isotopes; gas centrifuge and gaseous diffusion processes. *Mailing Add:* 360 Laboratory Rd Oak Ridge TN 37830

LEEDER, JOSEPH GORDEN, DAIRY PRODUCTS MANUFACTURE, CONSULTANT IN ICE CREAM MANUFACTURE. *Current Pos:* RETIRED. *Personal Data:* b Oil City, Pa, July 4, 16; m 39, Roma A Krumm; c 2. *Educ:* Ohio State Univ, BS, 38; Univ Vt, MS, 40; Pa State Univ, PhD, 44. *Prof Exp:* Instr dairy mfg, Univ Vt, 39-41, Pa State, 42-44; dir labs & supvr zone qual control, Nat Dairy Prod Co, Cleveland, Ohio, 44-46, chief res chemist, Ramsey Labs, 46-48; from assoc prof to prof dairy indust, Dept Animal Sci, Rutgers Univ, New Brunswick, NJ, 48-65, res prof food sci, Dept Food Sci, 65-81. *Mem:* Am Dairy Sci Asn; Inst Food Technologists; Sigma Xi. *Res:* Immobilized enzymes for whey utilization; food emulsions; chemistry of butter oil used in deep-fat frying; fat demulsification in ice cream; use of corn syrup in ice cream; trace hydroginated butteroil in candy; dairy chemistry. *Mailing Add:* 687B Yarborough Way N Jamesburg NJ 08631

LEEDHAM, CLIVE D(OUGLAS), AUTOMOTIVE ELECTRONICS, COMPUTERS. *Current Pos:* RETIRED. *Personal Data:* b London, Eng, Nov 1, 28; m 55, June R McAlmond; c Alexander Clive & Barry Scott. *Educ:* Univ London, BSc, 49; Mass Inst Technol, SM, 55; Purdue Univ, PhD(elec eng), 63. *Prof Exp:* Asst lectr elec eng, Univ London, 48-49; apprentice, Metrop Vickers Elec Co Ltd, 49-51, jr engr, 51-52; teaching asst, Mass Inst Technol, 53-55; instr, Purdue Univ, 58-62; asst prof, Univ Calif, 62-65; consult, Delco Electronics Corp, 63-65, staff engr, 65-76, bus develop mgr digital systs, 76-83 & 90-93, regional mgr int sales, 83-90. *Concurrent Pos:* Consult, USAF, 61-62. *Res:* Automatic control; signal processing; acoustics; digital computers. *Mailing Add:* 1811 El Faro Santa Barbara CA 93109-1903. *Fax:* 805-966-2605; *E-Mail:* 72537.3153@compuserve.com

LEEDOM, JOHN MILTON, INTERNAL MEDICINE, INFECTIOUS DISEASES. *Current Pos:* from asst prof to assoc prof, 62-76, HASTINGS PROF MED, SCH MED, UNIV SOUTHERN CALIF, 76-, CHIEF, DIV INFECTIOUS DIS, DEPT MED, 75- *Personal Data:* b Peoria, Ill, Oct 18, 33; m 56; c 2. *Educ:* Univ Ill, BA, 55, BS, 56, MD, 58; Am Bd Internal Med, dipl, 67 & 74. *Prof Exp:* Resident med, Univ Ill Res & Educ Hosps, 59-60 & 61-62. *Concurrent Pos:* Res fel, Univ Ill Res & Educ Hosps, 60-61; officer res proj, Epidemic Intel Serv, USPHS, Infectious Dis Lab, Univ Southern Calif, 62-64, consult health facil construct div, Health Serv & Ment Health Admin. *Mem:* Am Fedn Clin Res; Am Soc Microbiol; Infectious Dis Soc Am; Western Soc Clin Invest; Western Asn Physicians. *Res:* Infectious disease, particularly viral and bacterial diseases of the central nervous system; AIDS and AIDS treatment. *Mailing Add:* Dept Med Univ Southern Calif 2025 Zonal Ave Los Angeles CA 90033

LEEDS, J VENN, JR, ELECTRICAL ENGINEERING, ENVIRONMENTAL ENGINEERING. *Current Pos:* asst prof elec eng, Rice Univ, 63-65, from asst prof to prof elec & environ eng, 65-90, master, Sid W Richardson Col, 70-76, EMER PROF ELEC & ENVIRON ENG, RICE UNIV, 90- *Personal Data:* b Wharton, Tex, Oct 26, 32; m 56, Jan Norvell; c David V & Elizabeth (Nuchia). *Educ:* Rice Univ, BA, 55, BSEE, 56; Univ Pittsburgh, MSEE, 60, PhD(elec eng), 63; JD, Univ Houston, 72. *Prof Exp:* Sr engr, Bettis Atomic Lab, Westinghouse Elec Corp, 56-63. *Concurrent Pos:* Consult, Esso Prod Res Co Div, Exxon, 63-68 & Geospace Corp, 68-72; mem safety & licensing panel, US Nuclear Regulation Comn, 71-78; consult, var ins co and law firms, 72- *Mem:* Inst Elec & Electronics Engrs; Sigma Xi. *Res:* Design and analysis of large, complex systems; applied mathematics; interactions of law and engineering; applied mathematics; electrical events; fire and explosions; artificial intelligence. *Mailing Add:* 10807 Atwell Houston TX 77096-4439. *Fax:* 713-723-3902

LEEDS, MORTON W, ORGANIC CHEMISTRY, PHARMACOLOGY. *Current Pos:* EXEC DIR, MED-CHEM ASSOC, 82- *Personal Data:* b Brooklyn, NY, Dec 18, 16; m 45, Norma Sterne; c Valerie. *Educ:* Polytech Univ NY, BS, 38, MS, 39, PhD(org chem), 44. *Prof Exp:* Chemist, Bio-Med Res Lab, NY, 35-39; sr chemist, Res Lab, Interchem Corp, 39-45, head develop dept amino acids, Biochem Div, NJ, 45-48; sr chemist, E I du Pont de Nemours & Co, Inc, 48-50; asst chief chemist, Schwarz Labs, NY, 50-52; head appln & develop, Res Labs, Air Reduction Co, 52-56, supvr org chem develop & res, 56-60, from asst dir to assoc dir chem res, 60-71; mgr clin develop, Ciba-Geigy Pharmaceut Co, 71-77, asst dir med prods mgt, Med Res Div, 77-82. *Concurrent Pos:* Permanent adj prof, Kean Col, 71-80. *Mem:* Am Chem Soc; fel Am Inst Chem; NY Acad Sci; Sigma Xi. *Res:* Organic synthesis and development; acetylene and pharmaceutical chemistry; petrochemicals; clinical pharmacology research. *Mailing Add:* 6 Sunningdale Ct Maplewood NJ 07040

LEEDS, NORMA S, ISOLATION & CHEMICAL CHARACTERIZATION OF NATURAL PRODUCTS, ORGANIC & GENERAL CHEMISTRY. *Current Pos:* from assoc prof to prof, 64-91, dept chmn, 70-72, EMER PROF ORG CHEM, KEAN COL, 91- *Personal Data:* m 50, Morton W Leeds; c Valerie A. *Educ:* Hunter Col, BA, 40; Rutgers Univ, PhD(org chem), 50. *Prof Exp:* Sr chemist, Gen Aniline & Film, 53-58; res assoc, Sloan Kettering Inst, 55; instr chem, Fairleigh Dickinson Univ, 58-60; asst prof, Caldwell Col, 60-64. *Mem:* Sigma Xi; Am Chem Soc. *Res:* Partial synthesis in steroid hormone field of compounds with possible carcinogenic properties; synthesis of surfactants; isolation and characterization of natural products; history of chemistry; publications. *Mailing Add:* 6 Sunningdale Ct Maplewood NJ 07040

LEEDY, CLARK D, SOILS SCIENCE. *Current Pos:* RETIRED. *Personal Data:* b Chicago, Ill, June 3, 33; m 56; c 5. *Educ:* Purdue Univ, BS, 55; NMex State Univ, MS, 64, MA, 66; Tex A&M Univ, PhD(educ), 74. *Prof Exp:* Exten soils specialist, NMex State Univ, 57-71; div leader, WVa Univ, 73-76; assoc soil scientist, Univ Nev, Reno, 76. *Mem:* Sigma Xi. *Res:* Forms, rates, methods and timing of phosphorous fertilizer application on alfalfa yield and quality. *Mailing Add:* 10405 Red Rock Rd Reno NV 89506

LEEDY, DANIEL LONEY, URBAN WILDLIFE, OUTDOOR RECREATION & ECOLOGY. *Current Pos:* RETIRED. *Personal Data:* b North Liberty, Ohio, Feb 17, 12; m 45, 89, Virginia S Biltenbender; c Robert & Kathleen. *Educ:* Miami Univ, AB, 34, BSc, 35; Ohio State Univ, MSc, 38, PhD(wildlife mgt), 40. *Honors & Awards:* Conserv Award, Am Motors Corp, 58; Aldo Leopold Award, Wildlife Soc, 83. *Prof Exp:* Lab asst geol & zool, Miami Univ, 34-35; asst leader, Ohio Wildlife Res Unit, Ohio State Univ, 40-42; leader, Ohio Unit, US Fish & Wildlife Serv, 45-48, coordr, Coop Wildlife Res Unit Prog, 49-57, chief br wildlife res, 57-63; chief div res & educ, Bur Outdoor Recreation, 63-65, water resources res scientist, Off Water Resources Res, US Dept Interior, 65-74; sr scientist, Nat Inst Urban Wildlife, 75-94. *Concurrent Pos:* Mem, res coun comts & panels, Nat Acad Sci, 57-74 & surface mining panel, 78-79. *Mem:* Wildlife Soc (pres, 53, exec secy, 54-57); Am Fisheries Soc; Am Ornithologists Union; Wilson Ornith Soc; Sigma Xi. *Res:* Wildlife ecology; socioeconomics of fish and wildlife and recreation; natural resources training and employment; wildlife-land use relationships; water resources; urban wildlife and ecology; ecologic impacts of water development, surface mining, highways, and electric utilities in relation to wildlife. *Mailing Add:* 12401 Ellen Ct Silver Spring MD 20904

LEEF, AUDREY V, MATHEMATICS. *Current Pos:* assoc prof math, 66-90, CHAPLAIN, MONTCLAIR STATE COL, UPPER MONTCLAIR, NJ, 90- *Personal Data:* b Hoboken, NJ, July 15, 22; m 47; c 4. *Educ:* Montclair State Col, BA, 43; Stevens Inst Technol, MS, 47; Rutgers Univ, EdD, 76; Drew Univ, MDiv, 85. *Prof Exp:* Teacher & dept chairperson math, Millburn High Sch, NJ, 43-48. *Mem:* Nat Coun Teachers Math; Asn Women Math; Asn Women Educ; Am Asn Univ Women. *Res:* Mathematics education; math anxiety. *Mailing Add:* 24 Overlook Rd Mountain Lakes NJ 07046

LEEF, JAMES LEWIS, CRYOBIOLOGY, IMMUNOLOGY. *Current Pos:* EXEC DIR, BIOMED RES INC, 82- *Personal Data:* b San Francisco, Calif, Mar 6, 37; m 64; c 4. *Educ:* Univ Calif, San Francisco, BA, 67; Univ Tenn, PhD(biol), 74. *Prof Exp:* sr investr cryobiol & head Malaria Res Dept, 76-82, DIR, BIOMED RES INST, 82- *Concurrent Pos:* Consult, Sci & Indust Res & Develop Co, 67-69; fel, Univ Ill, 73-76; guest scientist, Navy Med Res Inst, 76- *Mem:* Soc Cryobiol; Tissue Cult Asn; Am Asn Tissue Banks; NY Acad Sci; AAAS. *Res:* Malariology; mechanisms of freezing injury; study of various developmental stages of malaria and schistosomiasis parasites as antigens in developing a malaria and schistosomiasis vaccine and preservation of these forms at low temperatures. *Mailing Add:* Biomed Res Inst 12111 Parklawn Dr Rockville MD 20852

LEE-FRANZINI, JULIET, experimental physics, for more information see previous edition

LEE-HAM, DOO YOUNG, PHARMACOLOGY, TOXICOLOGY. *Current Pos:* PHYSIOLOGIST, DIV ONCOL & RADIOPHARM DRUG PROD, FOOD & DRUG ADMIN, 69- *Personal Data:* b Seoul, Korea, Mar 31, 32; US citizen; m 66, Euiyoung; c Thomas & Deanna. *Educ:* Mercer Univ, BA, 57; Cath Univ Am, MS, 61, PhD(physiol), 66. *Prof Exp:* Res scientist, Microbiol Assoc, Inc 62-66; spec lectr physiol & biochem, Sungshin Womans Univ & Ewha Womans Univ, 66-67; sr scientist, Melpar, Inc, 67-69. *Mem:* NY Acad Sci. *Res:* Basic and applied cell physiology; in vitro and in vivo testing of drugs and chemicals for their carcinogenic potential, mutagenicity and cell transformation. *Mailing Add:* Food & Drug Admin HFD-150 Parklawn Bldg 5600 Fishers Lane Rockville MD 20857. *Fax:* 301-594-0499

LEEHEY, PATRICK, APPLIED MECHANICS. *Current Pos:* assoc prof mech eng, Mass Inst Technol, 64-67, from assoc prof to prof naval archit, 64-71, prof appl mech, 71-79, PROF MECH & OCEAN ENGR, MASS INST TECHNOL, 79- *Personal Data:* b Waterloo, Iowa, Oct 27, 21; m 44; c Patrick M, David J, Christopher M, Jonathan R, Susan E (Guare) & Jennifer A. *Educ:* US Naval Acad, BSc, 42; Brown Univ, PhD(appl math), 50. *Honors & Awards:* Gold Medal, Am Soc Naval Eng, 62. *Prof Exp:* Proj officer, US Off Naval Res, DC, 51-53, prog officer, David Taylor Model Basin, 53-56, design supt, Puget Sound Naval Shipyard, Wash, 56-58, head, Ship Silencing Br, Bur Ships, DC, 58-63, head, Acous & Vibration Lab, David Taylor Model Basin, 63-64; liaison scientist, Off Naval Res, London, 84-85. *Concurrent Pos:* Fulbright lectr, Austria, 77-78, Berlin, Ger, 93. *Mem:* Am Math Soc; fel Acoust Soc Am; Am Soc Naval Eng. *Res:* Hydrodynamics; hydrofoil craft development, unsteady airfoil theory; supercavitating flow theory; acoustics; ship silencing, underwater acoustics, boundary layer noise; mathematics; hyperbolic partial differential equations; singular integral equations; boundary layer stability. *Mailing Add:* 48 Bellevue Rd Swampscott MA 01907

LEE-HUANG, SYLVIA, BIOCHEMISTRY, MOLECULAR BIOLOGY. *Current Pos:* res scientist, 66-67, from instr to asst prof, 67-70, res assoc prof, 70-71, ASSOC PROF BIOCHEM, SCH MED, NY UNIV, 71- *Personal Data:* b Shanghai, China, July 14, 30; US citizen; m 57; c 3. *Educ:* Nat Taiwan Univ, BS, 52; Univ Idaho, MS, 57; Univ Pittsburgh, PhD(biophys), 61. *Prof Exp:* NIH fel microbiol, Sch Med, Univ Pittsburgh, 61-62; res assoc chem physics, Sloan-Kettering Inst, 62-64; instr biochem, Med Col, Cornell Univ, 64-66. *Concurrent Pos:* Prin investr, 72- *Mem:* AAAS; Am Soc Biol Chemists; Biophys Soc; Harvey Soc; NY Acad Sci. *Res:* Molecular mechanism of transmission and expression of genetic information; control and mechanism of differentiation and development; erythropoietin and the regulation of red cell production; mechanism of anti-HIV action of plant proteins and polycyclic compounds. *Mailing Add:* Dept Biochem NY Univ Sch Med 550 First Ave New York NY 10016

LEELA, SRINIVASA (G), MATHEMATICS. *Current Pos:* assoc prof, 68-73, PROF MATH, STATE UNIV NY COL GENESEO, 73- *Personal Data:* b Mysore, India. *Educ:* Osmania Univ, India, BSc, 55, MSc, 57; Marathwada Univ, India, PhD(math), 65. *Prof Exp:* Lectr math, Women's Col, Kurnool, India, 59-65; instr, Calgary Univ, 65-66; asst prof, Univ RI, 66-68. *Mem:* Am Math Soc; Math Asn Am. *Res:* Qualitative analysis in differential equations; stability theory. *Mailing Add:* Dept Math State Univ NY Col Geneseo Geneseo NY 14454

LEELING, JERRY L, pharmacology; deceased, see previous edition for last biography

LEEMAN, SUSAN EPSTEIN, PHYSIOLOGY, ENDOCRINOLOGY. *Current Pos:* PROF PHARMACOL, BOSTON UNIV SCH MED, 92- *Personal Data:* b Chicago, Ill, May 9, 30; m 57; c 3. *Educ:* Goucher Col, BA, 51; Radcliffe Col, MA, 54, PhD, 58. *Hon Degrees:* DSc, State Univ NY, Utica/Rome, 92; Dr, Goucher Col, Towson, Md, 93. *Honors & Awards:* Astwood Award, 81; Van Dyke Award, 82; Louis & Bert Freedman Found Award, 82. *Prof Exp:* Instr physiol, Harvard Med Sch, 58-59; fel neurochem, Brandeis Univ, 59-62, sr res assoc biochem, 62-66, adj asst prof, 66-68, asst res prof, 68-71; from asst prof to assoc prof physiol, Lab Human Reprod & Reprod Biol, Harvard Med Sch, 72-80; prof physiol, Med Sch, Univ Mass, 80-92, dir, Interdepartmental Neurosci Prog, 84-92. *Concurrent Pos:* USPHS career develop award, 62-; mem, Endocrinol Study Sect, Div Res Grants, NIH, 81; Albert Heritage med res vis prof, 81; dir, Intramural Res Sci Comt, NIMH & ad hoc comt, Recent Prog Hormone Res; Fogarty scholar, 94. *Mem:* Nat Acad Sci; Endocrine Soc; Soc Neurosci; AAAS; Am Physiol Soc. *Res:* Neuroendocrinology. *Mailing Add:* Dept Pharmacol Boston Univ Sch Med 80 E Concord St Boston MA 02118. *Fax:* 617-638-4374; *E-Mail:* sleeman@bu.edu

LEEMANN, CHRISTOPH WILLY, EXPERIMENTAL & ACCELERATOR PHYSICS. *Current Pos:* fel, 70-72, fel accelerator physics, 72-73, STAFF SCIENTIST ACCELERATOR PHYSICS, LAWRENCE BERKELEY LAB, UNIV CALIF, 73- *Personal Data:* b Basel, Switz, Jan 12, 39; m 69; c 2. *Educ:* Univ Basel, PhD(nuclear physics), 69. *Prof Exp:* Res asst nuclear physics, Univ Basel, 63-69, res assoc, 69-70. *Concurrent Pos:* Sabbatical leave, Europ Orgn Nuclear Res, Geneva, Switz, 80-81. *Mem:* AAAS. *Res:* Design and development of particle accelerators and related devices; beam cooling techniques; colliding beam devices; relativistic heavy ion accelerators. *Mailing Add:* CEBAF 12000 Jefferson Ave Newport News VA 23606

LEEMANS, WIM PIETER, PHYSICS. *Current Pos:* STAFF SCIENTIST, LAWRENCE BERKELEY LAB, CALIF, 91- *Personal Data:* b Gent, Belg, June 7, 63. *Educ:* Free Univ, Brussels, BS, 85; Univ Calif, Los Angeles, MS, 87, PhD(elec eng), 91. *Honors & Awards:* Simon Ramo Award, Am Phys Soc, 92. *Concurrent Pos:* Grad scholar, Inst Elec & Electronics Engrs Nuclear & Plasma Soc, 87; mem, Francqui Found. *Mem:* Int Soc Optical Eng; Am Phys Soc; Inst Elec & Electronics Engrs; Royal Flemish Engrs Soc. *Res:* High-intensity laser-plasma interaction in pre-formed and laser-produced plasmas; plasma beat-wave acceleration of electrons, driven density fluctuations using collective thomson scattering of visible laser probe beam; analysis of forward and backward scattered spectra of the pump beam and hole-coupled resonator mode analysis. *Mailing Add:* Lawrence Berkeley Lab Div Accelerator Fusion Res One Cyclotron Rd MS 71-259 Berkeley CA 94720

LEEMING, DAVID JOHN, MATHEMATICS. *Current Pos:* From instr to assoc prof, 63-86, 75-86, PROF MATH, UNIV VICTORIA, BC, 86- *Personal Data:* b Victoria, BC, June 8, 39; m 66, Yvonne Muir; c Heather, Graeme & Robert. *Educ:* Univ BC, BSc, 61; Univ Ore, MA, 63; Univ Alta, PhD(math), 69. *Concurrent Pos:* Course writer, Open Learning Inst, 79; mem, Acad Coun, Open Learning Agency, Burnaby, BC. *Mem:* Math Asn Am; Can Math Soc. *Res:* Approximation theory; error bounds for interpolation schemes; rational approximation. *Mailing Add:* Dept Math Univ Victoria PO Box 3045 Victoria BC V8W 3P4 Can. *Fax:* 250-721-8962; *E-Mail:* leeming@uvvm.bitnet

LEENEN, FRANS H H, CARDIOLOGY, HYPERTENSION. *Current Pos:* PROF MED & PHARMACOL, UNIV OTTAWA, 89-, DIR, HYPERTENSION UNIT, HEART INST, 89- *Personal Data:* b Linne, Neth, Sept 16, 43; Can citizen; m 86, Mindy B Fein; c Arjan, Bob-Willen, Sarah C, David A & Peter M. *Educ:* Univ Utrecht, PhD(renal hypertension), 71, MD, 73; FRCP(C), 86. *Honors & Awards:* Young Investr Award, Can Hypertension Soc, 82; Career Investr Award, Heart & Stroke Found Ont, 89. *Prof Exp:* Res fel clin pharmacol, Univ Pittsburgh Sch Med, 72-73; Resident inter med & cardiol, Univ Utrecht, Neth, 74-78; from asst prof to assoc prof, Hypertension Unit, Univ Toronto, 79-89. *Concurrent Pos:* Fel, Coun High Blood Pressure Res, Am Heart Asn; dir, Hypertension Unit, Toronto Western Hosp, 79-88; prin investr, Heart & Stroke Found Ont, 82- & Med Res Coun Can, 85-; coordr, Clin Pharmacol Training Prog, Univ Toronto, 85-88. *Mem:* Fel Am Physiol Soc; fel Am Heart Asn; Inter-Am Soc Hypertension; Int Soc Hypertension. *Res:* Pharmacology; cardiology; brain ouabain and sympathetic hyperactivity in salt sensitive hypertension and heart failure; effects of antihypertensive drugs on the heart in both animal models and humans. *Mailing Add:* Dept Med & Pharmacol Univ Ottawa Heart Inst 1053 Carling Ave Ottawa ON K1Y 4E9 Can. *Fax:* 613-761-4521; *E-Mail:* fleenen@ohi-net.heartinst.on.ca

LEEP, HERMAN ROSS, MANUFACTURING, ENGINEERING ECONOMY. *Current Pos:* Asst prof graphics, 73-79 & indust eng, 79-83, ASSOC PROF INDUST ENG, UNIV LOUISVILLE, 83-; MECH ENGR, E I DU PONT DE NEMOURS, 63- *Personal Data:* b Louisville, Ky, Oct 21, 40; m 75. *Educ:* Univ Louisville, BSME, 63, Univ Del, MMAE, 67; Purdue Univ, PhD(indust eng), 79. *Concurrent Pos:* Lectr, GE, 86-88. *Mem:* Am Soc Metals Int. *Res:* Machining of composite materials; machining of titanium alloys; measurement of tool wear; measurement of cutting forces; measurement of surface finish. *Mailing Add:* 4707 Valley Station Rd Louisville KY 40272

LEEPER, DENNIS BURTON, RADIATION BIOLOGY, HYPERTHERMIC ONCOLOGY CANCER. *Current Pos:* From asst prof to assoc prof, 70-80, PROF RADIATION ONCOL, THOMAS JEFFERSON UNIV HOSP, 80- *Personal Data:* b Glendale, Calif, May 3, 41; m; c 5. *Educ:* Univ Iowa, BS, 64, PhD(radiation biol), 69. *Honors & Awards:* Sci Award, Am Cancer Soc, 86. *Concurrent Pos:* AEC fel, Colo State Univ, 69-70, affil grad fac, 70-72; prin investr, NIH Res Grants, 72-; consult radiation biol, Franklin Inst, Pa, 76-82; adj assoc prof biomed eng, Univ Pa, 72-80; chmn, NAm Hyperthermia Group, 81-85; mem, Training Grant Study Sect, NCI, 82-83, Diag Radiol & Nuclear Med Study Sect, NIH, 83-87; counr biol, Radiation Res Soc, 83-86; assoc ed, Int J Radiation Biol, 83-86, Int J Hyperthermia, 85- *Mem:* Radiation Res Soc; Am Asn Cancer Res; Cell Kinetics Soc; AAAS; Am Soc Thermalapeut Radiol Oncol; NAm Hyperthermia Group; Sigma Xi; NY Acad Sci. *Res:* Interaction of radiation, hyperthermia, and anti-cancer drugs in mammalian cells in culture and in normal and tumor tissues in vivo; cell cycle kinetics; experimental radiation oncology. *Mailing Add:* Dept Radiation Oncol Thomas Jefferson Univ Hosp 1020 Sansom St Philadelphia PA 19107-5004. *Fax:* 215-955-2052

LEEPER, HAROLD MURRAY, POLYMER CHEMISTRY. *Current Pos:* CONSULT, 91- *Personal Data:* b Akron, Ohio, July 14, 20; m 42, Mildred Pollak; c Sheryl L (Glotzer), David G & Mark R. *Educ:* Univ Akron, BS, 42, MS, 47. *Prof Exp:* Rubber technologist, US Eng Bd, 42-44; polymer chemist rubber, Govt Rubber Labs, 44-47; res chemist polymers, Wm Wrigley Jr Co, 47-54; group leader, Monsanto Co, 54-70; res scientist, Alza Corp, 70-80, prin scientist polymers, 80-91. *Mem:* Am Chem Soc; Soc Plastics Engrs; AAAS. *Res:* Chemistry, physics, and technology of rubbers and plastics; drug delivery systems. *Mailing Add:* Alza Corp 1040 Gest Dr Mountain View CA 94040. *Fax:* 650-968-4736; *E-Mail:* hal1920@aol.com

LEEPER, HERBERT ANDREW, JR, SPEECH PATHOLOGY, COMMUNICATIVE DISORDERS. *Current Pos:* assoc prof, 77-94, PROF OTOLARYNGOL, FAC MED, UNIV WESTERN ONT, 88-, PROF SPEECH PATH, 94- *Personal Data:* b Lewistown, Pa, Nov 5, 42; m 77; c William R & Terrence J. *Educ:* Bloomsburg State Univ, BS, 63; Purdue Univ, MS, 66, PhD(speech path), 69. *Prof Exp:* Speech pathologist, Jewish Hosp, St Louis, 69-71; asst prof, Med Ctr, Univ Okla, 71-74; assoc prof, Okla State Univ, 74-77. *Concurrent Pos:* Lectr, Fac Dent, Univ Western Ont, 79-; consult, Cleft Palate Team, Thames Valley Children's Ctr, 79- *Mem:* fel Am Speech Lang Hearing Asn; Am Cleft Palate Asn (secy, 74-77); Acoust Soc Am; Am Asn Phonetic Sci; Can Asn Speech Lang Pathologists & Audiologists; Sigma Xi. *Res:* Description of the physiological, acoustical, and perceptual characteristics of the speech produced by children and adults with cranio-facial anomalies, laryngeal dysfunction and deafness. *Mailing Add:* Dept Commun Dis Elborn Col Univ Western Ont London ON N6G 1H1 Can. *E-Mail:* hleeper@julian.uwd.ca

LEEPER, JOHN ROBERT, ENTOMOLOGY. *Current Pos:* sr res biologist, Du Pont Exp Sta, Du Pont Inc, 80-85, licensing prod mgr, New Bus Ventures, 85-88, mgr US prod develop, rice herbicides, Agr Prod Dept, 88-89, mgr, Agr Sci Lab, Tsukuba, Japan, 89-92, res asst, Appln Technol, 92-94, TECHNOL LEADER, ASIA PAC, DU PONT INC, 94- *Personal Data:* b Hackensack, NJ, July 12, 47; m 73, Catherine Lindburg; c Schuyler R & Michael Thomas. *Educ:* Carthage Col, BA, 69; Univ Hawaii, MS, 71, PhD(entom), 75. *Prof Exp:* Res assoc entom, Tree Fruit Res Ctr, Wash State Univ, 75-77; asst prof entom, NY State Agr Exp Sta, Cornell Univ, 77-80. *Mem:* Entom Soc Am. *Res:* Managing collaborative research projects throughout Asia Pacific. *Mailing Add:* Stine Haskell Lab 215/304A 1094 Elkion Rd Newark DE 19713. *Fax:* 302-366-5236

LEEPER, RAMON JOE, PLASMA PHYSICS, HIGH ENERGY NUCLEAR PHYSICS. *Current Pos:* mem tech staff Plasma Physics, 76-86, SUPVR DIAGNOSTICS DIV, SANDIA NAT LABS, 86- *Personal Data:* b Princeton, Mo, Apr 1, 48; m 76; c 1. *Educ:* Mass Inst Technol, SB, 70; Iowa State Univ, PhD(high energy nuclear physics), 75. *Prof Exp:* Res assoc high energy nuclear physics, Ames Lab, US Dept of Energy, 75-76. *Concurrent Pos:* Guest scientist, Argonne Nat Lab, 71-76. *Mem:* Am Phys Soc; Sigma Xi. *Res:* Particle beam induced controlled thermonuclear fusion; neutron physics; fusion plasma diagnostic techniques; neutron production of inertially confined high temperature fusion plasmas; high intensity pulsed neutron sources; high current ion beams; meson spectroscopy. *Mailing Add:* Diagnostics Target Experiment Div 9577 Box 5800 Sandia Nat Labs Albuquerque NM 87185-1196

LEEPER, ROBERT WALZ, organic chemistry; deceased, see previous edition for last biography

LEERBURGER, BENEDICT ALAN, SCIENCE WRITING, JOURNALISM. *Current Pos:* CONSULT COMPUT SCI, PHYS SCI & GEN SCI COMMUN, 79- *Personal Data:* b New York, NY, Jan 2, 32; m 58, Julie Lees; c Ellen & Marian. *Educ:* Colby Col, BA, 54. *Prof Exp:* Asst ed Prod Eng Mag, 54-59; sci ed, Grolier, Inc, 59-61; ed, Cowles Ed Corp, 61-68; proj dir, CCM Info Sci, Inc, 68-70; vpres & ed dir, Nat Micro-Publ Corp, 70-72; dir publ, NY Times, 72-74; publ, Kraus-Thomson Org, Ltd, 74-76. *Concurrent Pos:* Consult, Sci Digest, 59-61, Cross, Hinshaw & Lindberg, Inc, 65-67, Storrington Printing & Pub Co, Inc, 67-70 & NSF Deep Freeze Prog, Antarctica, 67; ed-in-chief, McGraw-Hill Book Co, 76-79; free lance writer, 80- *Mem:* Nat Asn Sci Writers; Am Hist Asn; Nat Sci Teachers Asn; Am Soc Journalists & Authors. *Res:* Physical science; Antarctica; American scientific history. *Mailing Add:* 338 Heathcote Rd Scarsdale NY 10583

LEE-RUFF, EDWARD, CHEMISTRY. *Current Pos:* from asst prof to assoc prof, 74-84, PROF CHEM, YORK UNIV, 85- *Personal Data:* b Shanghai, China, Jan 4, 44; Can citizen; m 69, Claudette Grondin; c Daniel, Caroline & Stephane. *Educ:* McGill Univ, BSc, 64, PhD(org chem), 67. *Prof Exp:* Nat Res Coun fel, Columbia Univ, 67-69. *Mem:* Am Chem Soc; Chem Inst Can. *Res:* Organic photochemistry; reactions of strained molecules; organic chemistry. *Mailing Add:* Dept Chem York Univ Downsview ON M3J 1P3 Can. *Fax:* 416-736-5936; *E-Mail:* fs300073@sol.yorku.ca

LEES, ALISTAIR JOHN, PHOTOCHEMISTRY, SPECTROSCOPY. *Current Pos:* asst prof, 81-86, ASSOC PROF INORG CHEM, STATE UNIV NY, BINGHAMTON, 86- *Personal Data:* b Preston, Eng, July 12, 55; m 79; c 2. *Educ:* Univ Newcastle, BSc, 76, PhD(chem), 79. *Prof Exp:* Fel phys chem, Univ Southern Calif, 79-81. *Concurrent Pos:* Consult, IBM Corp, 85-86, Int Paper Corp, 85- *Mem:* Am Chem Soc; Royal Soc Chem. *Res:* Photochemistry and spectroscopy of transition metal compounds; organometallic chemistry; homogeneous catalysis; kinetics and mechanism; low-temperature spectroscopy and photochemistry. *Mailing Add:* Dept Chem State Univ NY Binghamton NY 13902

LEES, ANDREW, BIOCONJUGATE CHEMISTRY, VACCINE DEVELOPMENT. *Current Pos:* res instr, 88-93, ASST RES PROF, DEPT MED, UNIFORMED SERVS, UNIV HEALTH SCI, 93-; SR RES SCIENTIST, VIRION SYSTS, INC, 93- *Personal Data:* b Boston, Mass, Feb 9, 53; m 87, Julie Pierson; c Adam E & Elizabeth M. *Educ:* Harvey Mudd Col, BS, 76; Johns Hopkins Univ, PhD(biophys), 84. *Prof Exp:* Fel, Johns Hopkins Univ, 85-88. *Mem:* AAAS; Am Chem Soc. *Res:* Developing new chemistries for convalently coupling proteins to carbohydrates with the goal of enhanced vaccine capabilities to stimulate better responses to both the carbohydrate and protein components; developing combination vaccines to minimize the total number of necessary immunizations. *Mailing Add:* Dept Med Uniformed Servs Univ Health Sci 4301 Jones Bridge Rd Bethesda MD 20814

LEES, DAVID ERIC BERMAN, OPTICAL MEASUREMENT TECHNOLOGY. *Current Pos:* CONSULT, DEBL ASSOCS, 93- *Personal Data:* b Boston, Mass, July 22, 50; m 77; c 3. *Educ:* Oakland Univ, BS, 72; Univ Rochester, MS, 74, PhD(optics), 79. *Prof Exp:* Prin develop engr, Honeywell, 79-82; systs engr, Automatrix, Inc, 82-86; prin investr, Sparta, Inc, 86-93. *Concurrent Pos:* Prin investr, NSF Phase I Small Bus Innovation Res Award, 84, ONR Phase I, 89. *Mem:* Optical Soc Am (secy, 90-91); Soc Photo-Optical Instrumentation Engrs. *Res:* Machine vision for industrial applications; vision guided robots; optical gauging; speckle imaging; imaging laser radan development. *Mailing Add:* Four Militia Dr Lexington MA 02173. *Fax:* 781-861-0941; *E-Mail:* debl@world.std.com

LEES, GEORGE EDWARD, VETERINARY INTERNAL MEDICINE, VETERINARY NEPHROLOGY & UROLOGY. *Current Pos:* assoc prof, 80-86, PROF SMALL ANIMAL MED, COL VET MED, TEX A&M UNIV, 86- *Personal Data:* b Pittsburgh, Pa, Feb 7, 48; m 80, Kathleen K Schultze. *Educ:* Colo State Univ, BS, 70, DVM, 72; Univ Minn, MS, 79. *Prof Exp:* Intern small animal med & surg, Sch Vet Med, Univ Calif, Davis, 75-76; resident small animal med, Col Vet Med, Univ Minn, St Paul, 76-79, clin asst prof small animal med, 79-80. *Concurrent Pos:* Chmn bd, Am Col Vet Internal Med, 91-92. *Mem:* Am Col Vet Internal Med (vpres, 88-90, pres-elect, 89-90, pres, 90-91). *Res:* Diagnosis, treatment and prevention of spontaneous diseases of the urinary system in dogs and cats. *Mailing Add:* 200 Lampwick Circle College Station TX 77840-1853

LEES, GRAHAM, BIOPHYSICS. *Current Pos:* ED DIR LIFE & MED SCI, ACADEMIC PRESS, 93- *Personal Data:* b Pemburg, Eng, Feb 17, 53. *Educ:* Univ Cambridge, BA, 74, MA, 76, PhD(neurophysiol), 78. *Prof Exp:* Res fel biophys, Gif-Sur-Yvelle, France, 78-80; ed, Elsevier Sci Publ, 80-86, ed mgr, 86-88; ed in chief, Raven Press, 88-93. *Mem:* Soc Neurosci; Am Acad Sci. *Res:* Biophysics. *Mailing Add:* Academic Press 525 B St Suite 1900 San Diego CA 92101

LEES, MARJORIE BERMAN, NEUROCHEMISTRY, NEUROIMMUNOLOGY. *Current Pos:* prof, 85-93, EMER PROF BIOCHEM, NEUROL DEPT, MED SCH, HARVARD UNIV, 93-; BIOCHEMIST, EUNICE KENNEDY SHRIVER CTR, 76-, DIR, BIOCHEM DIV, 90-, ASSOC DIR, MENT RETARDATION RES CTR, 93- *Personal Data:* b New York, NY, Mar 17, 23; m 46, Sidney; c David, Andrew & Eliot. *Educ:* Hunter Col, BA, 43; Univ Chicago, MS, 45; Harvard Univ, PhD(med sci), 51. *Prof Exp:* Asst, Univ Chicago, 43-45; asst, Col Physicians & Surgeons, Columbia Univ, 45-46; Am Cancer Soc res fel, 51-53; res asst, McLean Hosp, 53-55; asst biochemist, 55-58, assoc biochemist, 58-62; sr res assoc pharmacol, Dartmouth Med Sch, 62-66; assoc biochemist, McLean Hosp, 66-76. *Concurrent Pos:* Instr neuropath, Harvard Med Sch, 55-59, assoc neurosci, 59-62 & 66-71, prin res assoc, 71-75, sr res assoc, 75-85; biochem, Neurol Div, Mass Gen Hosp, 58; prin investr, NIH grants, 62-; mem, Nat Adv Coun, Nat Inst Neurol & Communicative Disorders & Stroke, 79-82; Javits invest award, NIH, 84-91, 91-97; chief ed, J Neurochem, 86-90; mem, Panel Biomed & Biol Behav Res, NASA & NIH, 93- *Mem:* Am Soc Biol Chem; Am Soc Neurochem (treas, 75-81, pres, 83-85); Soc Neurosci; Am Asn Neuropath; Int Soc Neurochem; Int Soc Neuroimmunol. *Res:* Chemistry of the nervous system; myelin and demyelinating diseases; neuroimmunology; brain proteins. *Mailing Add:* E K Shriver Ctr 200 Trapelo Rd Waltham MA 02254. *Fax:* 781-893-4824; *E-Mail:* mleea@shriver.org

LEES, MARTIN H, PEDIATRICS, CARDIOLOGY. *Current Pos:* Assoc prof, 62-71, PROF PEDIAT, MED SCH, UNIV ORE, 71- *Personal Data:* b London, Eng, May 11, 29; m 59, Elizabeth; c Deborah, Jacqueline & Christina. *Educ:* Univ London, MB, BS, 55, MD, 62. *Hon Degrees:* FRCP, 80. *Concurrent Pos:* Chief, pediat cardiol, Emanuel Hosp, Portland, Ore. *Mem:* Am Pediat Soc; Am Heart Asn; Royal Col Physicians London. *Res:* Pediatric cardiology; newborn and infant cardiopulmonary physiology and pathophysiology. *Mailing Add:* Dept Pediat Univ Ore Med Sch Portland OR 97201. *Fax:* 503-280-4134

LEES, NORMAN DOUGLAS, MICROBIOLOGY, MOLECULAR BIOLOGY. *Current Pos:* asst prof, 73-80, ASSOC PROF BIOL, IND UNIV-PURDUE UNIV, INDIANAPOLIS, 80- *Personal Data:* b Providence, RI, Sept 16, 45; m 81; c 3. *Educ:* Providence Col, AB, 67; Northwestern Univ, PhD(microbiol), 73. *Prof Exp:* Teaching asst biol sci, Northwestern Univ, 67-73. *Concurrent Pos:* Grants, Ind Univ-Purdue Univ, Indianapolis, 74 & Biomed Sci Res, 75 & 77. *Mem:* Am Soc Microbiol; Sigma Xi. *Res:* Role of sterols in biological membranes. *Mailing Add:* Dept Biol SL-2306 Indiana Univ-Purdue Univ 723 W Michigan St Indianapolis IN 46202-5132

LEES, ROBERT S, MEDICINE, BIOCHEMISTRY. *Current Pos:* dir, Clin Res Ctr, 69-74, assoc prof, 69-71, PROF HEALTH SCI TECHNOL, HARVARD UNIV & MASS INST TECHNOL, 71-; PRES, BOSTON HEART FOUND, 91- *Personal Data:* b New York, NY, July 16, 34; m 60; c 4. *Educ:* Harvard Univ, AB, 55, MD, 59; Am Bd Internal Med, dipl. *Prof Exp:* Intern med, Mass Gen Hosp, Boston, 59-60, asst resident med, 61-62; hon asst registr cardiol, Nat Heart Hosp, Eng. 62-63; staff assoc & attend physician med, Nat Heart Inst, 63-66; asst prof med & attend physician, Rockefeller Univ, 66-69. *Concurrent Pos:* USPHS res fel med, 60-61; Dalton scholar, Harvard Med Sch, 60; USPHS fel, 62-63; fel coun arteriosclerosis, Am Heart Asn, 65-; assoc in med, Peter Bent Brigham Hosp; asst in med, Mass Gen Hosp. *Mem:* Am Heart Asn; Am Fedn Clin Res; Am Soc Clin Invest; Am Soc Pharmacol & Exp Therapeut. *Res:* Cardiology, especially ischemic heart disease; lipid and lipoprotein metabolism. *Mailing Add:* Boston Heart Found 139 Main St Cambridge MA 02142. *E-Mail:* vsl@mit.edu

LEES, RONALD EDWARD, OCCUPATIONAL MEDICINE. *Current Pos:* FROM ASST PROF TO PROF EPIDEMIOL, QUEEN'S UNIV, 69-, PROF FAMILY MED, 75-, DIR, OCCUP MED, 78- *Personal Data:* b Carlisle, UK, Feb 14, 35; Can citizen; m 62; c 2. *Educ:* Glasgow Univ, MBChB, 58, DPM, 62, MD, 67. *Prof Exp:* Med officer health, Govt St Lucia, Wis, 62-65; field med officer, Rockefeller Found, NY, 65-68. *Res:* Tropical health-infant malnutrition, schistosomiasis, parasitic and infectious disease control; environmental and occupational health-epidemiologic studies in effect of toxins, noise induced hearing loss, effects of shift work and stress; occupational health problems in underdeveloped countries. *Mailing Add:* Dept Community Health & Epidemiol Queen's Univ Kingston Kingston ON K7L 3N6 Can

LEES, RONALD MILNE, MOLECULAR SPECTROSCOPY. *Current Pos:* assoc prof, 68-77, dept chmn, 81-88, PROF PHYSICS, UNIV NB, FREDERICTON, 77- *Personal Data:* b Sutton, Eng, Oct 28, 39; Can citizen; m 62; c 2. *Educ:* Univ BC, BSc, 61, MSc, 65; Bristol Univ, PhD(physics), 67. *Prof Exp:* Nat Res Coun Can fel, Nat Res Coun, Ottawa, 66-68. *Concurrent Pos:* Nat Res Coun Can grant, Univ NB, Fredericton, 68-, vis assoc prof, Physics Dept, Univ BC, Vancouver, 74-75; prin investr, Centres of Excellence in Molecular & Interfacial Dynamics, Fed Networks of Centres Excellence Prog. *Mem:* Can Asn Physicists; Am Asn Physics Teachers; Optical Soc Am; Soc Photo-Optical Instrumentation Engrs. *Res:* Atomic and molecular physics; molecular spectroscopy. *Mailing Add:* Dept Physics Univ NB Fredericton NB E3B 5A3 Can

LEES, SIDNEY, ENGINEERING. *Current Pos:* SR STAFF MEM & HEAD BIOENG DEPT, FORSYTH DENT CTR, BOSTON, 66- *Personal Data:* b Philadelphia, Pa, Apr 17, 17; m 46, Marjorie Berman; c David E, Andrew P & Eliot J. *Educ:* City Col New York, BS, 38; Mass Inst Technol, SM, 48, ScD, 50. *Prof Exp:* Observer, US Weather Bur, 38-40; engr, US Signal Corps, 40-43; res assoc aeronaut, Mass Inst Technol, 47-50, asst prof, 50-57; consult instrumentation, 57-59; vpres, United Res Inc, 59; pres, Lees Instrument Res Inc, 59-63; prof eng, Dartmouth Col, 62-66. *Concurrent Pos:* Chmn, Joint Automatic Control Conf, 65 & Res Conf Instrumentation Sci, 71; vis scientist, Univ Amsterdam Dent Sch, 75; chmn, Conf Ultrasonics, 78; joint chmn, NE Doppler Conf, 81; adj prof, Northeastern Univ. *Mem:* Emer mem Am Phys Soc; emer mem Sigma Xi; emer mem Inst Elec & Electronics Engrs; emer mem Am Acoust Soc. *Res:* Ultrasonics; bioinstrumentation; measurement systems and components; control systems; geophysical instrumentation. *Mailing Add:* 50 Eliot Mem Rd Newton MA 02158. *Fax:* 617-262-4021

LEES, THOMAS MASSON, ANALYTICAL CHROMATOGRAPHY, FERMENTATION PRODUCTION. *Current Pos:* RETIRED. *Personal Data:* b New York, NY, June 16, 17; m 43, Nola Winters; c David & Christine. *Educ:* Long Island Univ, BS, 39; Iowa State Univ, MS, 42, PhD(biophys chem), 44. *Prof Exp:* Res chemist, Am Distilling Co, 44-46; from produn supvr to sr res chemist, Pfizer, Inc, 46-80. *Mem:* Am Chem Soc. *Res:* Fermentative production of glycerol; antibiotics development, production and identification; analysis of medicinal compounds. *Mailing Add:* 35 Woodridge Circle Gales Ferry CT 06335

LEES, WAYNE LOWRY, EXPERIMENTAL PHYSICS, ENGINEERING PHYSICS. *Current Pos:* RETIRED. *Personal Data:* b Washington, DC, July 18, 14; m 39; c 2. *Educ:* Swarthmore Col, BA, 37; Harvard Univ, MA, 40, PhD(physics), 49. *Prof Exp:* Asst, Bartol Res Found, Pa, 39-40; physicist, Geophys Lab, Wash, DC, 42-44, Nat Bur Standards, 44-46, Tracerlab, Inc, 49-50, Metall Proj, Mass Inst Technol, 50-54, Nuclear Metals, Inc, 54-58, Instrumentation Lab, Mass Inst Technol, 58-65 & Electronics Res Ctr, NASA, Cambridge, 65-70; assoc prof math, Wash Tech Inst, 71-72; proj engr, Design Automation, Inc, Lexington, Mass, 72-73; staff mem, lab phys sci, P R Mallory & Co, Inc, Burlington, Mass, 74-80; mem staff, Duracell Int, Inc, 80-82. *Mem:* AAAS; Am Phys Soc; Fedn Am Sci; Inst Elec & Electronics Engrs. *Res:* Quasistatic electrical systems and dielectric properties; physics of high pressures and metals; electrode phenomena; electron and ion transport; engineering physics. *Mailing Add:* 29 Tower Rd Lexington MA 02173

LEESE, JOHN ALBERT, REMOTE SENSING, NUMERICAL MODELING. *Current Pos:* VIS SCIENTIST, GLOBAL ENERGY WATER CYCLE EXP, WORLD CLIMATE RES PROG, UNIV CORP ATMOSPHERIC RES, 93- *Personal Data:* b Manchester, Md, Dec 6, 32; m 59; c 4. *Educ:* Pa State Univ, BS, 57; Fla State Univ, MS, 59; Univ Mich, PhD(meteorol), 64. *Prof Exp:* Meteorologist res & develop, Air Force Cambridge Labs, 59-61; lectr, Univ Mich, 61-64; dept mgr res & develop, Atmospheric Sci Dept, IBM Corp, 64-69; div chief res & develop, Nat Environ Satellite Serv, 69-75, assoc dir data processing, 75-78, dep dir admin, 78-82; sr scientist admin, World Meteorol Orgn, Geneva, Switz, 82-88; dir res, Inst Naval Oceanog, 88-92; Dept Meteorol, Univ Md, 92-93. *Concurrent Pos:* Meteorologist, USNR, 58-78. *Mem:* Am Meteorol Soc; Oceanog Soc. *Res:* Digital data processing and quantitative information extraction techniques of environmental satellite data for input to numerical models of the atmosphere and the oceans. *Mailing Add:* 9411 Caroline Ave Silver Spring MD 20901. *Fax:* 301-427-2222

LEESER, DAVID O(SCAR), FORENSIC MATERIALS ENGINEERING. *Current Pos:* CONSULT ENGR, 87- *Personal Data:* b El Paso, Tex, Aug 3, 17; m 45; c 2. *Educ:* Univ Tex, BS, 43; Ohio State Univ, MS, 50. *Honors & Awards:* Award, Off Sci Res & Develop; Award, Nat Adv Comt Aeronaut, 44; Apollo Achievement Award, NASA, 69. *Prof Exp:* Metallurgist, Bradley Mining Co, Idaho, 43-44; res engr, Battelle Mem Inst, 44-50; assoc metallurgist, Argonne Nat Lab, 50-54; staff metallurgist & chief mat sect, Atomic Power Develop Assocs, Inc, 54-61; chief scientist, Missile Div, Chrysler Corp, 61-68, chief metallurgist, Amplex Div, 68-75; mgr, Eng Mat Lab, Burroughs Corp, 75-86. *Concurrent Pos:* Reactor mat engr, Nuclear Power Dept, Detroit Edison Co, 54-61; mem, Atomic Indust Forum; mem welding forum, US AEC, 54-64, high temperature nuclear fuel comt, 57-61; US del, World Metall Cong, 57, Int Conf Peaceful Uses of Atomic Energy, Geneva, 58 & Int Atomic Energy Agency Conf, Vienna, 61. *Mem:* Am Soc Testing & Mat; Sigma Xi; Am Soc Mech Engrs; Am Mgt Asn; Am Soc Metals; Am Soc Metals Int. *Res:* Evaluation of aerospace designs with regard to conventional and nonconventional materials applications and advanced aerospace requirements; ground and launch support equipment; materials for high-speed computer and electromechanical business machine systems under development; failure analysis in each category. *Mailing Add:* 11515 N 91st St Suite 151 Scottsdale AZ 85260

LEESON, CHARLES ROLAND, ANATOMY. *Current Pos:* prof, anat, Sch Basic Med Sci, EMER PROF ANAT, SCH MED, UNIV ILL, 88- *Personal Data:* b Halifax, Eng, Jan 26, 26; m 54; c 5. *Educ:* Cambridge Univ, BA, 47, MB, BChir, 50, MA, 50, MD, 59, PhD(anat), 71. *Prof Exp:* Lectr anat, Univ Col SWales, 55-58; assoc prof, Dalhousie Univ, 58-61; assoc prof anat & histol, Queen's Univ, Ont, 61-63; prof anat, Univ Iowa, 63-66; prof anat & chmn dept, Univ Mo, Columbia, 66-78. *Concurrent Pos:* Vis prof anat, London Hosp Med Col, Eng, 73-74. *Mem:* Anat Soc Gt Brit & Ireland; Am Asn Anat. *Res:* Post natal development, particularly in marsupials and rodents and with reference to certain organ systems. *Mailing Add:* 19810 SW 95th St Dunnellon FL 34432

LEESON, DAVID BRENT, EDUCATION. *Current Pos:* chmn, chief exec officer & founder, 68-93, EMER CHMN, CALIF MICROWAVE INC, 93-; CONSULT, PROF, DEPT ELEC ENG, STANFORD UNIV, 94- *Personal Data:* b Cleveland, Ohio, Apr 12, 37; m 80, Barbara Splane; c Hugh L & Melinda A. *Educ:* Calif Inst Technol, BS, 58; Mass Inst Technol, MS, 59; Stanford Univ, PhD(elec eng), 62. *Prof Exp:* Dir microwave lab, Applied Tech Inc, Palo Alto, 64-68. *Concurrent Pos:* Bd dirs, Am Electronics Asn, 80-82; bd govs, Electronics Indust Asn, 83-84. *Mem:* Fel Inst Elec & Electronics Engrs; Am Electronics Asn; Electronics Indust Asn. *Res:* Author of numerous articles. *Mailing Add:* Calif Microwave Inc 985 Almanor Ave Sunnyvale CA 94086-2903

LEESON, LEWIS JOSEPH, BIOPHARMACEUTICS, PHARMACO-KINETICS. *Current Pos:* PRES, LJL ASSOCS INC, 93- *Personal Data:* b Paterson, NJ, Apr 26, 27; m 53; c 3. *Educ:* Rutgers Univ, BS, 50, MS, 54; Univ Mich, PhD(pharmaceut chem), 57. *Honors & Awards:* Lou Busse lectr, Univ Wis. *Prof Exp:* Intern pharm, Mack Drug Co, 50-51; pharmacist, Silver Rod Drugs, 51-52; asst, Rutgers Univ, 52-54 & Univ Mich, 55-56; res chemist, Lederle Labs, Am Cyanamid Co, 57-67; proj leader pharmaceut, Union Carbide Res, 67-69; asst dir pharmaceut develop, Geigy Chem Corp, 69-71, asst dir, 71-73, dir, 73-78, sr dir pharm res & develop, 78-80, sr res fel biopharm, 80-84, distinguished res fel, biopharm, Ciba-Geigy Pharmaceut Co, 84-93. *Concurrent Pos:* Relief pharmacist, Frieds Pharm, 52-54. *Mem:* Controlled Release Soc; Am Pharmaceut Asn; fel Acad Pharmaceut Sci; Sigma Xi; fel Am Asn Pharmaceut Sci; Int Pharmaceut Fedn. *Res:* Pharmaceutical product development; application of physical chemical techniques for developing various pharmaceutical dosage forms; biopharmaceutics; pharmacokinetics. *Mailing Add:* 134 Ridge Dr Montville NJ 07045

LEESON, THOMAS SYDNEY, ANATOMY. *Current Pos:* head dept, 63-82, PROF ANAT, UNIV ALTA, 82- *Personal Data:* b Halifax, UK, Jan 26, 26; m 52; c 3. *Educ:* Cambridge Univ, BA, 46, MA, 49, MD & BCh, 50, MD, 59, PhD, 71. *Prof Exp:* Asst lectr anat, Univ Wales, 55-57; from asst prof to assoc prof, Univ Toronto, 57-63. *Mem:* Am Asn Anat; Brit Asn Clin Anatomists; Anat Soc Gt Brit & Ireland; Electron Microscopy Soc Am. *Res:* Electron microscopy, histology and embryology; pancreatic centroacinar cells as they relate to acinar and ductular cells and to insular cells the latter associated with paracrine secreatin and hormonal control of exocrine secretion. *Mailing Add:* No 45 903 109th St Edmonton Edmonton AB T6J 6R1 Can

LEESTMA, JAN E, PATHOLOGY, NEUROPATHOLOGY. *Current Pos:* ASSOC MED DIR, CHICAGO NEUROSURG CTR & CHICAGO INST NEUROSURG & NEURORESEARCH, 87- *Personal Data:* b Flint, Mich, Nov 30, 38; m 61; c 2. *Educ:* Hope Col, BA, 60; Univ Mich, MD, 64; Northwestern Univ, MBA, 85. *Prof Exp:* Resident & intern path, Univ Colo Med Sch, Denver, 64-67; fel neuropath, Einstein Med Col & instr path, Univ Colo Med Sch, Denver, 67-68; from asst prof to assoc prof path, Sch Med, Northwestern Univ, 71-86; prof path & neurol, Univ Chicago, 86-87. *Concurrent Pos:* Consult, DC Gen Hosp, Washington, DC, 69-71; Nat Naval Med Ctr, Bethesda, Md, 69-70, Vet Admin Lakeside Hosp & Vet Admin North Chicago Hosp, Ill, 71-, Baxter-Travenol Labs, Morton Grove, Ill, 73-76, Great Lakes Naval Hosp, Ill, 74- & 80 W Suburban Hosp, Oak Park, Ill, 76-85; attend physician, Northwestern Mem Hosp, Chicago, 71-, Children's Mem Hosp, 82-; asst med examr, Cook Co Off Med Examr, Chicago, 77-; dean student, Div Biol Sci, Pritzker Sch Med, Univ Chicago, 86-87. *Mem:* Am Asn Neuropathologists; Sigma Xi; AAAS; NY Acad Sci. *Res:* Experimental neurology; neurological degenerative disease; central nervous system tissue; brain tumors; computerized data analysis; electron microscopy forensic medicine; electron microscopy, forensic neuropathology. *Mailing Add:* Chicago Neurosurgical Ctr Chicago Inst Neurosurg & Neuroresearch 5841 S Maryland Ave Box 69 Chicago IL 60690-0069

LEET, RICHARD HALE, HEALTH PHYSICS. *Current Pos:* RETIRED. *Personal Data:* b Maryville, Mo, Oct 11, 26; m 49, Phyllis J Combs; c Richard H II, Alan C & Dana E. *Educ:* NW Mo State Col, BS, 48; Ohio State Univ, PhD(phys chem), 52. *Prof Exp:* Res chemist, Stand Oil Co, 53-64; dir, Mktg Dept, Am Oil Co, 64-68, mgr, Mfg Dept, 69-70, regional vpres, Atlanta, 70-71, vpres supply, 71-74; vpres planning & admin, Amoco Chems Corp, 74-75, vpres mktg, 75-77, exec vpres, 77-78, pres, 78-83; dir, Amoco Corp, 83-91, vchmn, 91-92. *Mem:* Am Chem Soc; Soc Chem Indust; Am Indust Health Coun. *Mailing Add:* 3631 Lantern Dr Gainesville GA 30504-5420

LEETCH, JAMES FREDERICK, MATHEMATICS. *Current Pos:* From asst prof to assoc prof, 61-71, prof, 71-85, EMER PROF MATH, BOWLING GREEN STATE UNIV, 85- *Personal Data:* b Butler, Pa, Sept 27, 29; m 58, Nancy Wikoff; c Alic & Elaine. *Educ:* Grove City Col, BS, 51; Ohio State Univ, MA, 57, PhD(math), 61. *Mem:* Math Asn Am. *Res:* Mathematical analysis. *Mailing Add:* 19 Darlyn Dr Bowling Green OH 43402. *E-Mail:* leetch@banet.bgsu.edu

LEETE, EDWARD, ORGANIC CHEMISTRY. *Current Pos:* from asst prof to assoc prof, 58-63, PROF ORG CHEM, UNIV MINN, MINNEAPOLIS, 63- *Personal Data:* b Leeds, Eng, Apr 18, 28; nat US; m 54, 76; c 7. *Educ:* Univ Leeds, BSc, 48, PhD(chem), 50, DSc, 65. *Honors & Awards:* First Phytochem Prize & Medal, 90. *Prof Exp:* Goldsmith fel, Nat Res Coun Can, 51-52, res fel, 52-54; from instr to asst prof org chem, Univ Calif, Los Angeles, 54-58. *Concurrent Pos:* Mem med chem study sect, NIH, 62-65; Alfred P Sloan fel, 62-65; Guggenheim fel, Univ Oxford Eng, 65; consult, Philip Morris Res Ctr, Richmond, Va, 74-; vis prof agr, Univ Kyoto, 90. *Mem:* Am Chem Soc; Am Soc Pharmacog; fel Royal Soc Chem; Soc Pharmaceut Bottling Res; Sigma Xi; fel AAAS; Phytochem Soc NAm. *Res:* Biosynthesis of natural substances, especially alkaloids; synthesis of heterocyclic compounds; isolation of enzymes from plants; use of radioactive and stable isotopes. *Mailing Add:* 399 Otis Ave St Paul MN 55104-4929. *Fax:* 612-626-7541

LEEVY, CARROLL M, MEDICINE, NUTRITION. *Current Pos:* assoc prof, NJ Med Sch, 59-62, dir, Div Hepatic Metab & Nutrit, 59-91, actg chmn, Dept Med, 66-68, chmn & physician in chief, 75-91, PROF MED, COL MED NJ, 62-, DIR, LIVER CTR, 90-; SCI DIR, SAMMY DAVIS JR NAT LIVER INST, 84- *Personal Data:* b Columbia, SC, Oct 13, 20; m 56, Ruth S Barboza; c Carroll B & Maria S. *Educ:* Fisk Univ, AB, 41; Univ Mich, MD, 44. *Hon Degrees:* DSc, NJ Inst Technol, 73; DHH, Dr Hum, Fisk Univ, 81; BSc, Univ Nebr, 89. *Honors & Awards:* Mod Med Award, 72; Achievement Award, Nat Med Asn, 87; Distinguished Serv Award, Am Asn Study Liver Dis, 91. *Prof Exp:* Intern med, Jersey City Med Ctr, 44-45, resident, 45-48, dir Clin Invest & Outpatient Dept, 48-58; res assoc, Harvard Univ, 58-59. *Concurrent Pos:* USPHS spec res fel, 58-59; consult, US Naval Hosp, St Albans, 48; consult & mem med adv comt, Vet Admin Hosp, East Orange, NJ, 64; physician-in-chief, Martland Hosp, 66-68; mem dean's comt, East Orange Vet Admin Hosp, 66-68, chief med, 66-71; mem clin cancer training comt, NIH, 69-73; consult, Food & Drug Admin, 70-78 & Nat Med Libr, 80-84; chmn bd trustees, Asn Acad Minority Physicians, 88- *Mem:* Soc Exp Biol & Med; Nat Med Asn; Master Am Col Physicians; Asn Am Physicians; Am Asn Study Liver Dis (pres, 70); Int Assoc Study Liver (pres, 72-76); Asn Acad Minority Physicians (pres, 86-88). *Res:* Pathogenesis and treatment of end stage liver disease; factors which control hepatic nucleic acid and collagen synthesis; mechanism and treatment of portal hypertension, nutrition and liver disease; immunology and genetic of liver disease. *Mailing Add:* Sammy Davis Jr Nat Liver Inst NJ Med Sch 100 Bergen St Newark NJ 07109

LEE-WHITING, GRAHAM EDWARD, CHARGED-PARTICLE OPTICAL SYSTEMS, PHYSICAL BOUNDARY-VALUE PROBLEMS. *Current Pos:* RETIRED. *Personal Data:* b Iroquois Falls, Ont, Can, Mar 2, 26; m 52. *Educ:* Univ Toronto, BASc, 48, MA, 49; Bristol Univ, PhD (theoret physics), 52. *Prof Exp:* Theoret physicist, Atomic Energy Can Res Co, 52-69, head, Theoret Physics Br, 69-91, emer researcher, 91- *Mem:* Can Asn Physicists; Am Phys Soc. *Res:* The theory of focusing and dispersive systems for charged particles; beta spectrometers using magnetic and or electric fields. *Mailing Add:* Chalk River Labs AECL Res Chalk River ON K0J 1J0 Can

LEFAR, MORTON SAUL, organic chemistry, for more information see previous edition

LEFCOE, NEVILLE, PHYSIOLOGY. *Current Pos:* PVT PRACT, 94- *Personal Data:* b Montreal, Que, July 19, 25; m 54; c 4. *Educ:* McGill Univ, BSc, 46; Vanderbilt Univ, MD, 50; FRCP(C), 56. *Prof Exp:* From instr to assoc prof med, Univ Western Ont, 57-72, prof, 72-94. *Mem:* Am Fedn Clin Res; Can Soc Clin Invest. *Res:* Pulmonary physiology, chiefly exercise physiology, cellular mechanisms in bronchial smooth muscle and the domestic microenvironment. *Mailing Add:* 219 Oxford St W Suite 201 London ON N6H 1S5 Can

LE FEBVRE, EDWARD ELLSWORTH, ENVIRONMENTAL CHEMISTRY, ANALYTICAL CHEMISTRY. *Current Pos:* CHEMIST, VA DIV CONSOL LABS. *Personal Data:* b Great Falls, Mont, Mar 9, 33; m 53; c 4. *Educ:* Univ Wash, BA, 54; Univ Tex, San Antonio, MS, 75. *Prof Exp:* Chemist, State Health Dept, Helena, Mont, 58-62; USAF, 62-, chief, Analytical Div, Environ Health Lab, McClellan AFB, Calif, 62-66, res chemist, Sch Aerospace Med, Brooks AFB, Tex, 66-68, chief, Environ Studies Br, Environ Health Lab, Kelly AFB, Tex, 68-74, dep chief, Analytical Div, 74-76, chief, Anal Serv Div, Occup & Environ Health Lab, USAF, 76- *Concurrent Pos:* Comnr, Nat Cert Comn in Chem & Chem Eng, 77-81. *Mem:* Am Chem Soc; Am Indust Hyg Asn; Am Inst Chemists; Am Conf Govt Indust Hygenists. *Mailing Add:* 12915 Red Chestnut Dr Midlothian VA 23112

LE FEBVRE, EUGENE ALLEN, CONSERVATION ECOLOGY. *Current Pos:* from asst prof to assoc prof, 66-91, EMER PROF ZOOL, SOUTHERN ILL UNIV, 91- *Personal Data:* b St Paul, Minn, Oct 18, 29; m 66; c 2. *Educ:* Univ Minn, BS, 52, AP, 53, MS, 58, PhD(zool), 62. *Prof Exp:* Teaching asst ornith & zool, Univ Minn, Minneapolis, 53-59, res fel ornith, Mus Natural Hist, 60-61, res assoc, 61-66. *Concurrent Pos:* Res assoc, NIH grant, 60-65, co-prin investr, 63-65; grantee, NSF, Midway Island, 69-73 & 80-83, Int Documentation & Commun Ctr, 81-82, Nat Register Archives, 86, Southern Ill Univ, Carbondale, 86-87; co-prin investr, Nat Register Archives. *Mem:* AAAS; Am Ornith Union; Cooper Ornith Soc; Ecol Soc Am; Am Inst Biol Sci; Brit Ornith Union; Sigma Xi. *Res:* Conservation biology; habitat requirements of birds; environmental toxicology; biological diversity. *Mailing Add:* Dept Zool Southern Ill Univ Carbondale IL 62901. *E-Mail:* glefebur@siu.edu

LEFEBVRE, MARIO, STOCHASTIC PROCESSES, STOCHASTIC CONTROL THEORY. *Current Pos:* asst prof, 85-90, ASSOC PROF MATH, ECOLE POLYTECH MONTREAL, 90- *Personal Data:* b Montreal, Que, Sept 20, 57. *Educ:* Univ Montreal, BSc, 79, MSc, 80; Univ Cambridge, Eng, PhD(math), 84. *Prof Exp:* Lectr math, Royal Mil Col St-Jean, 84-85. *Mem:* Soc Indust & Appl Math; Can Statist Soc. *Res:* Applied probability and stochastic control theory; electrical engineering applications; pure science, such as biology, chemistry and physics. *Mailing Add:* Dept Appl Math Ecole Polytech Montreal PQ H3C 3A7 Can. *Fax:* 514-340-4463; *E-Mail:* d500@music.polymtl.ca

LEFEBVRE, PAUL ALVIN, DEVELOPMENTAL BIOLOGY. *Current Pos:* asst prof, 82-88, ASSOC PROF GENETICS & CELL BIOL, UNIV MINN, 88- *Personal Data:* b Washington, DC, Mar 12, 50; m 81. *Educ:* Univ Va, BA, 72; Yale Univ, MPhil, 78, PhD(biol), 80. *Prof Exp:* Fel, Mass Inst Technol, 80-81. *Mem:* Genetics Soc Am; Am Soc Microbiol. *Res:* Regulation of expression of genes for flagellar proteins in Chlamydomonas; genetics and molecular biology of nitrate reductase. *Mailing Add:* 2230 Marion Rd St Paul MN 55113

LEFEBVRE, RENE, medicine, for more information see previous edition

LEFEBVRE, RICHARD HAROLD, SCIENCE EDUCATION. *Current Pos:* from asst prof to assoc prof, 67-73, chmn dept, 70-75 & 85-88, PROF GEOL, GRAND VALLEY STATE UNIV, 75- *Personal Data:* b Detroit, Mich, Dec 11, 33; m 59, Sandra Beck; c Lauryl, Jeffrey & W Curtis. *Educ:* Univ Mich, BS, 57; Univ Kans, MS, 61; Northwestern Univ, PhD(geol), 66. *Prof Exp:* Asst prof geol, Univ Ga, 65-67; geologist, US Geol Surv, 75-85. *Mem:* Geol Soc Am; Nat Asn Geol Teachers; Nat Sci Teachers Asn. *Res:* Flood basalts of the northwestern United States; remote sensing of Holocene basaltic lava flows, especially Craters of the Moon National Monument, Idaho. *Mailing Add:* Dept Geol Grand Valley State Univ Allendale MI 49401

LEFEBVRE, XAVIER P, BIOCHEMICAL ENGINEERING. *Current Pos:* SR SCIENTIST, ABIOMED, 92- *Personal Data:* b Montee Notre Dame, France, Jan 16, 66. *Educ:* Nat Upper Sch Chem Eng, France, BS, 88; Ga Inst Technol, PhD(biochem eng), 92. *Prof Exp:* Teaching asst, Ga Inst Technol, 87-92. *Mem:* Biomed Eng Soc. *Mailing Add:* 40 Homsy Lane Needham MA 02194

LEFER, ALLAN MARK, CARDIOVASCULAR PHYSIOLOGY, PHARMACOLCOGY. *Current Pos:* PROF PHYSIOL & CHMN DEPT, JEFFERSON MED COL, THOMAS JEFFERSON UNIV, 74- *Personal Data:* b New York, NY, Feb 1, 36; m 59, Mary E Indoe; c Debra L, David J, Barry L & Leslie A. *Educ:* Adelphi Univ, BA, 57; Western Reserve Univ, MA, 59; Univ Ill, PhD(physiol), 62. *Prof Exp:* Instr physiol, Case Western Res Univ, 62-64; from asst prof to prof, Sch Med, Univ Va, 64-72. *Concurrent Pos:* USPHS fel, 62-64; estab investr, Am Heart Asn, 68-73; vis prof & USPHS sr fel, Hadassah Med Sch, Hebrew Univ, Israel, 71-72; mem comt pub affairs, Fedn Am Socs Exp Biol; ed, Circulatory Shock; consult, Task Group on Shock, NIH; mem, Int Study Group Res Cardiac Metab & Pancreatic Study Group; mem coun basic sci, Circulation Coun, Am Heart Asn; mem, Study Sect Pharmacol, NIH; vis prof, Wellcome Found, 85-86; managing ed, Eicosanoids, 88- *Mem:* Am Physiol Soc; Am Heart Asn; Soc Exp Biol & Med; Am Soc Pharmacol & Exp Therapeut; Soc Leukocyte Biol; Shock Soc (pres, 83-84); Int Soc Heart Res. *Res:* Cardiovascular effects of adrenal hormones; humoral regulation of myocardial contractility; nitric oxide biology; experimental myocardial infarction; atherosclerosis pathophysiology; pathogenesis of circulatory shock; prostaglandins and thromboxanes; pharmacology of coronary circulation; PAF and other lipid mediators; endothelial function; adhesion molecules. *Mailing Add:* Jefferson Med Col Thomas Jefferson Univ 102 Locust St Philadelphia PA 19107-6799

LEFEVER, ROBERT ALLEN, SOLID STATE CHEMISTRY, MATERIALS SCIENCE. *Current Pos:* RETIRED. *Personal Data:* b York, Pa, May 29, 27; m 46; c 3. *Educ:* Juniata Col, BS, 50; Mass Inst Technol, PhD(inorg chem), 53. *Prof Exp:* Res chemist, Linde Co, 53-56; sr scientist, Va Inst Sci Res, 56-58; mem tech staff, Hughes Res Labs, 58-59, head chem physics group, 59-61; staff mem, Gen Tel & Electronics Labs, Inc, 61-63; supvr, Mat Res Div, Sandia Labs, 63-74; dir mat preparation, Sch Eng, Univ Southern Calif, 74-77; mgr, Process Eng Dept, Ampex Corp, 77-80, plant mgr, Ferrite Memory Core Plant, 80- *Concurrent Pos:* Consult, Spectrotherm Corp, 74-77 & Luxtron Corp, 77- *Mem:* Am Phys Soc; Am Chem Soc; Am Ceramic Soc; fel Am Inst Chemists; Sigma Xi; Am Asn Crystal Growth. *Res:* Single crystal growth; growth mechanisms and characterization; sintering processes and mechanisms; ferrites; garnets; metal and rare earth oxides; semiconductors; phosphors; thermoelectrics. *Mailing Add:* 1940 S Broadway Grand Junction CO 81503

LEFEVRE, GEORGE, JR, GENETICS, CYTOGENETICS. *Current Pos:* RETIRED. *Personal Data:* b Columbia, Mo, Sept 13, 17; m 43, 72; c 3. *Educ:* Univ Mo, AB, 37, AM, 39, PhD(genetics), 49. *Prof Exp:* Asst zool, Columbia Univ, 41-42; res biologist, Oak Ridge Nat Lab, 46-47; instr zool, Univ Mo, 47-48; from asst prof to assoc prof biol, Univ Utah, 49-56; prog dir genetic biol, NSF, 56-59; dir biol labs, Harvard Univ, 59-65; chmn, Calif State Univ, Northridge, 65-79, prof, 65-84, emer prof biol, 84-90. *Concurrent Pos:* Consult, NSF, 59-62 & NIH, 62-66, 79-83; ed, Genetics, 76-81. *Mem:* Genetics Soc Am (treas, 72-75); Sigma Xi. *Res:* Radiation genetics of Drosophila melanogaster; comparative mutagenetics; cytogenetics. *Mailing Add:* 10132 Eton Ave Chatsworth CA 91311

LEFEVRE, HARLAN W, NUCLEAR PHYSICS. *Current Pos:* assoc prof, 61-71, PROF PHYSICS, UNIV ORE, 71- *Personal Data:* b Great Falls, Mont, May 19, 29; div; c 8. *Educ:* Reed Col, BA, 51; Univ Idaho, MS, 57; Univ Wis, PhD(physics), 61. *Prof Exp:* Physicist, Hanford Atomic Prod Oper, Gen Elec Co, Wash, 51-58. *Concurrent Pos:* Consult, Lawrence Livermore Lab, Univ Calif, 62-; vis physicist, Australian Nat Univ, 68-69, Lawrence Livermore Nat Lab, 76-77 & Univ Melbourne, 88-89. *Mem:* Am Phys Soc. *Res:* Experimental nuclear physics; nuclear reactions; fast neutron spectrometry; scanning microscopy and analysis. *Mailing Add:* Dept Physics Univ Ore Eugene OR 97403

LEFEVRE, MARIAN E WILLIS, PHYSIOLOGY. *Current Pos:* RETIRED. *Personal Data:* b Washington, DC, Jan 21, 23; m 48, Paul G; c Louise V, Vanessa F & Ralph S. *Educ:* Iowa State Univ, BS, 44; Univ Pa, MS, 47; Univ Louisville, PhD(physiol), 69. *Prof Exp:* Assoc, Mt Sinai Sch Med, 68-73, asst prof physiol, 73-78; scientist, Brookhaven Nat Lab, 78-85. *Concurrent Pos:* Res collabr, Brookhaven Nat Lab, 68-75, assoc scientist, 75-78. *Mem:* Am Physiol Soc; Am Gastroenterol Asn; Am Soc Cell Biol; Soc Exp Biol & Med. *Res:* Structure and function of multicellular membranes; ion transport and metabolism; intestinal barrier function. *Mailing Add:* 15 Agassiz Rd Woods Hole MA 02543

LEFEVRE, PAUL GREEN, CELL PHYSIOLOGY. *Current Pos:* prof, 68-83, EMER PROF PHYSIOL & BIOPHYS, HEALTH SCI CTR, STATE UNIV NY, STONY BROOK, 84- *Personal Data:* b Baltimore, Md, Dec 27, 19; m 48, Marian E Willis; c Bradley P (deceased), Louise V (Fine), Vanessa F (Lerman) & Ralph S. *Educ:* Johns Hopkins Univ, AB, 40; Univ Pa, PhD(physiol, zool), 45. *Prof Exp:* Asst zool, Univ Pa, 43-45; from instr to asst prof physiol, Col Med, Univ Vt, 45-49, assoc prof physiol & biophys, 49-52; asst to chief med br, AEC, 52-55; scientist, Med Res Ctr, Brookhaven Nat Lab, 55-60; prof pharmacol, Sch Med, Univ Louisville, 60-68. *Concurrent Pos:* Bd gov, bio-sci info exchange, 53-55. *Mem:* AAAS; Soc Gen Physiol; Am Physiol Soc; Biophys Soc; Am Soc Cell Biol. *Res:* Mechanisms, kinetics and model systems for cell membrane mediated transport; phospholipid-carbohydrate complexing. *Mailing Add:* 15 Agassiz Woods Hole MA 02543

LEFF, ALAN R, MEDICINE. *Current Pos:* asst prof med, Pulmonary Sect, Pritzer Sch Med, Univ Chicago, 79-85, asst prof, Comt Clin Pharmacol, Div Biol Sci, 83-85, dir, Pulmonary Med Serv, Dept Med, Sect Pulmonary & Crit Care Med, 84-87, assoc prof med & Comt Clin Pharmacol, 85-89, assoc prof anesthesia & crit care, 88-89, PROF MED, ANAESTHESIA & CRIT CARE & COMT PHARMACOL, UNIV CHICAGO, 89-, HEAD SECT PULMONARY & CRIT CARE MED, 89- *Personal Data:* b Pittsburgh, Pa, May 23, 45. *Educ:* Oberlin Col, AB, 67; Univ Rochester, MD, 71; Am Bd Internal Med, cert, 76. *Prof Exp:* Med officer, Tuberc Br, Ctr Dis Control, USPHS, 72-74; intern internal med, Univ Mich Hosp, 71-72 & House Off II, III internal med, 74-76; clin fel pulmonary dis, Cardiovasc Res Inst, Univ Calif, San Francisco, 76-77, postdoctoral res fel, 77-79. *Concurrent Pos:* Asst tuberc control officer, Bd Health, Chicago, 72-74; assoc attend physician, Cook Co Hosp, 73-74; consult, Tuberc Prog, Dept Pub Health, San Francisco, 77-79 & adv respiratory dis, Dept Pub Health, Chicago, 80-84; dir, Pulmonary Function Labs, Univ Chicago Hosps & Clins, 79-87, Pulmonary Exercise Lab, 83-87; dir, Respiratory Serv, Hyde Park Community Hosp, 82-89; standing counr, Am Fedn Clin Res, 83-87; mem prog comt, Am Thoracic Soc, 86-, chmn, Program Struct & Function Assembly, 88-89; head, Sect Pulmonary & Crit Care Med, Univ Chicago & Michael Reese Hosps, 87-89; mem joint prog comt, Am Thoracic Soc-Am Physiol Soc, 88-89. *Mem:* Am Soc Clin Invest; Cent Soc Clin Invest; Am Thoracic Soc; Am Col Physicians; Sigma Xi; Am Soc Internal Med; Int Union Tuberc; Am Fedn Clin Res; Am Physiol Soc; Am Soc Pharmacol & Exp Therapeut. *Mailing Add:* Dept Med Univ Chicago M/C 6076 5841 S Maryland Ave Chicago IL 60637-1463

LEFF, HARVEY SHERWIN, THERMAL PHYSICS. *Current Pos:* PROF & CHAIR, PHYSICS DEPT, CALIF STATE POLYTECH UNIV, POMONA, 83- *Personal Data:* b Chicago, Ill, July 24, 37; m 58, Ellen Wine; c Lisa, Robyn, Jordan & Jeremy. *Educ:* Ill Inst Technol, BS, 59; Northwestern Univ, MS, 60; Univ Iowa, PhD(physics), 63. *Prof Exp:* Res assoc physics, Case Inst Technol, 63-64, from asst prof to assoc prof, 64-71; assoc prof & chmn, Dept Phys Sci, Chicago State Univ, 71-75, prof physics, 75-79; scientist, Oak Ridge Assoc Univ, 79-83. *Concurrent Pos:* Vis prof physics, Col Sci & Eng, Harvey Mudd Col, 77-78; workshop leader, Pre-Col Teachers Energy Ideas & Physics of Toys, 86-; physic coordr, Inst Teaching & Learning, Calif State Univ; assoc ed, Am J Physics, 92- *Mem:* Am Asn Physics Teachers; Am Phys Soc; Sigma Xi. *Res:* Foundations of thermodynamics; thermal efficiency of heat engines; Maxwell's Demon; physics of light bulbs; physics of toys; analysis of energy-related topics relevant to energy policymaking. *Mailing Add:* 538 E Bishop Pl Claremont CA 91711. *Fax:* 909-869-4396; *E-Mail:* hsleff@csupomona.edu

LEFF, JUDITH, MICROBIOLOGY, BIOTECHNOLOGY. *Current Pos:* SR CONSULT FOOD TECHNOL, JLN ASSOCS, 83- *Personal Data:* b Vienna, Austria, July 6, 35; US citizen; m 61, Nathaniel; c Auraham, Anne & David. *Educ:* Sorbonne, Lic natural sci, PhD(photobiol), 61. *Prof Exp:* Jr researcher photobiol seed germination, Nat Ctr Sci Res, Paris, 60-61, res assoc photobiol, 61; fel biol, Brandeis Univ, 62-63; fel pharmacol, Sch Med, Tufts Univ, 65, res assoc, 66-67; res assoc plant morphogenesis, Manhattan Col, 67-71, NY Univ, 71-72 & Hebrew Univ, Jerusalem, 72-73; NIH spec res fel, Albert Einstein Col Med, 74-79; appln chemist, Farrand Optical, 79-82. *Concurrent Pos:* Nat Res Serv award, Albert Einstein Col Med, 76-77. *Mem:* Sigma Xi; Am Soc Microbiol; Inst Food Technol. *Res:* Photobiology; chloroplast development; molecular biology; microbiology; nucleic acids as tools for solving physiological or developmental questions; microbiology of crown gall; replication of mitochondrial DNA in yeast; fluorescence spectroscopy; food and ingredient technology for the Kosher market. *Mailing Add:* 302 Howard Ave Passaic NJ 07055. *Fax:* 973-471-8389

LEFF, TODD, MOLECULAR BIOLOGY. *Current Pos:* SR RES ASSOC, PARKE-DAVIS PHARMACEUT, 91- *Personal Data:* b Iowa City, Iowa, June 10, 54. *Educ:* Univ Iowa, BA, 76; Ind Univ, PhD(molecular biol), 82. *Honors & Awards:* Young Investr Award, Int Atherosclerosis Soc, 89; Estab Investr Award, Am Heart Asn, 90. *Prof Exp:* Fel molecular biol, Univ Louie Pasteur, France, 82-85; asst prof biochem genetics & metab, Rockefeller Univ, 85-91. *Mem:* AAAS; NY Acad Sci; Am Soc Biochem & Molecular Biol. *Res:* Molecular biology. *Mailing Add:* Dept Biotechnol Parke-Davis Pharmaceut Inc Ann Arbor MI 48105

LEFFAK, IRA MICHAEL, BIOCHEMISTRY. *Current Pos:* ASST PROF BIOCHEM, WRIGHT STATE UNIV, 70- *Personal Data:* b New York, NY, Oct 13, 47; m 69; c 1. *Educ:* City Col New York, BS, 69; City Univ New York, PhD(biochem), 76. *Prof Exp:* Res fel biochem, Princeton Univ, 76-78. *Concurrent Pos:* NIH fel, 76-78. *Mem:* AAAS. *Res:* Molecular biology of development; cell differentiation. *Mailing Add:* Dept Biol Chem Wright State Univ Dayton OH 45435

LEFFALL, LASALLE DOHENY, JR, SURGICAL ONCOLOGY. *Current Pos:* from asst prof to assoc prof surg, Howard Univ, 62-70, asst dean, 64-70, actg dean, 70, prof surg & chmn dept, 70-96, CHARLES R DREW PROF SURG, COL MED, HOWARD UNIV, 96- *Personal Data:* b Tallahassee, Fla, May 22, 30; m 56; c 1. *Educ:* Fla A&M Univ, BS, 48; Howard Univ, MD, 52; Am Bd Surg, dipl, 58. *Hon Degrees:* DSc, Georgetown Univ, 84, Fla A&M Univ, 87, Clark Univ, 89; LHD, Meharry Med Col, 88. *Honors & Awards:* William H Sinkler Mem Award, Nat Med Asn, 72; St George Medal, Am Cancer Soc, 77; Thomas Wyatt Turner Award, 82; Florence Nightingale Award, 82; W Montague Cobb Mem Lectr, Nat Med Asn, 84; James H Jackson Award, 84; Roger L Brooke Distinguished Lectr, Brooke Army Med Ctr, 86; Robert Wilson Kitchen, Jr Award, Am Cancer Soc, 86; James Ewing Lectr & Medal, Soc Surg Oncol, 87. *Prof Exp:* Intern, Homer G Phillips Hosp, St Louis, 52-53; resident, Freedmen's Gen Hosp, Washington, DC, 53-57 & Mem Sloan Kettering Cancer Ctr, NY, 57-59. *Concurrent Pos:* Asst ed, J Nat Med Asn, 55-57, actg co-ed, 64-65, consult ed, 73-; pvt pract med, Washington, DC, 62-; mem staff, Howard Univ Hosp; consult, St Elizabeth's Hosp, 66-76, Walter Reed Army Med Ctr, 71-, Nat Cancer Inst, 72- & Am Cancer Soc, 76-77; prof lectr surg, Georgetown Univ, 70-; mem, Med & Sci Comt, Am Cancer Soc, 70, Surg Training Comt, Nat Inst Gen Med Sci, 71-72, Diag Res Activ Group, Nat Cancer Inst, 72-75, Comt Study Surg Serv US, Am Col Surgeons & Am Surg Asn, 72-74, Tissue & Organ Biol Sect, President's Panel Biomed Res, 75, US Comt & Nat Orgn Comt, 13th Int Cancer Cong, 79 & Nat Cancer Adv Bd, 80; vis prof & lectr, numerous US & foreign univs, 71- *Mem:* Inst Med-Nat Acad Sci; Soc Surg Oncol (secy, 74-76, pres, 78-79); Am Cancer Soc (pres, 78-79); Am Surg Asn; Am Chem Soc; AMA; fel Am Col Surgeons (secy, 83-). *Res:* Cancer diseases; polyps and cancer of the coloectum; breast cancer; head and neck cancer; soft tissue sarcomas; author of more than 100 technical publications. *Mailing Add:* Dept Surg Howard Univ Hosp Tower Bldg Suite 4000 Washington DC 20060

LEFFEK, KENNETH THOMAS, PHYSICAL ORGANIC CHEMISTRY, HISTORY OF CHEMISTRY. *Current Pos:* RETIRED. *Personal Data:* b Nottingham, Eng, Oct 15, 34; Can citizen; m 58, Janet M Wallace; c Katharine H & Geoffrey K. *Educ:* Univ London, BSc, 56, PhD(chem), 59. *Prof Exp:* Nat Res Coun Can fel, 59-61; from asst prof to assoc prof, Dalhousie Univ, 61-72, dean grad studies, 72-90, prof chem, 72- *Concurrent Pos:* Leverhulme vis fel, Univ Kent, Canterbury, 67-68; pres, Atlantic Can Chap, Royal Soc Arts, 88-91. *Mem:* Fel Chem Inst Can (vpres, 85-86, pres, 86-87); Royal Soc Chem; Royal Soc Arts. *Res:* Kinetics and mechanisms of organic reactions; primary and secondary kinetic deuterium isotope effects. *Mailing Add:* 980 Kentwood Terr Victoria BC V8Y 1A6 Can. *Fax:* 902-494-1310

LEFFEL, CLAUDE SPENCER, JR, PHYSICS. *Current Pos:* RETIRED. *Personal Data:* b Pearisburg, Va, Dec 21, 21; m 80; c 2. *Educ:* St John's Col, Md, BA, 43; Johns Hopkins Univ, PhD(physics), 60. *Prof Exp:* Tutor math & physics, St John's Col, Md, 46-50; sr physicist, Appl Physics Lab, Johns Hopkins Univ, 60-83. *Mem:* AAAS; Am Phys Soc; Sigma Xi. *Res:* Plasma physics; nuclear physics; applied physics; atmospheric physics; cryogenics. *Mailing Add:* 7200 Third Ave CO69 Sykesville MD 21784

LEFFEL, ROBERT CECIL, PLANT BREEDING, GENETICS. *Current Pos:* RETIRED. *Personal Data:* b Woodbine, Md, Apr 26, 25; m 59; c 2. *Educ:* Univ Md, BS, 48; Iowa State Univ, MS, 50, PhD, 52. *Prof Exp:* Res agronomist, Agr Res Serv, 52-57; assoc prof agron, Univ Md, 57-62; investigations leader, Agr Res Serv, 62-72, chief, Plant Nutrit Lab, 72-75, chief, Cell Cult & Nitrogen Fixtion Lab, 75-76; staff scientist oilseed crop prod, Nat Prog Staff, USDA, 76-83, res agronomist, agr Res Serv, 83-94. *Concurrent Pos:* Exec secy, Soybean Res Adv Inst, 82-84; FAO consult on soybeans, Yugoslavia, 83 & India, 87. *Mem:* Crop Sci Soc Am; Am Soybean Asn. *Res:* Soybean, forage crop and clover genetics; breeding and production; enhancing nitrogen metabolism of soybean; high protein soybeans. *Mailing Add:* PO Box 7 Brogue PA 17309

LEFFELL, MARY S, IMMUNOGENETICS, IMMUNOLOGY. *Current Pos:* ASSOC PROF MED, SCH MED & MOLECULAR MICROBIOL & IMMUNOL, SCH HYG, JOHNS HOPKINS UNIV, 89-, CO DIR, IMMUNOGENETIC LAB, 89- *Personal Data:* b Knoxville, Tenn, Oct 12, 46. *Educ:* Univ Tenn, BS, 68; Univ NC, PhD(immunol), 73. *Prof Exp:* Asst prof surg, EVa Med Sch, 79-85; assoc prof surg, Med Col Ga, Univ Ga, 85-89. *Mem:* Am Soc Histocompatability & Immunogenetics (pres 95); Am Asn Immunologists; Am Soc Transplant Physicians; United Network Organ Sharing (vpres, 92-93). *Res:* Immunogenetics & transplantation immunology. *Mailing Add:* Johns Hopkins Univ Sch Med 2041 E Monument St Baltimore MD 21205. *Fax:* 410-955-0431; *E-Mail:* msleffel@welchlink.welch.jhu.edu

LEFFELL, W(ILL) O(TIS), ELECTRICAL ENGINEERING. *Current Pos:* Asst, 36-39, from instr to prof, 40-77, EMER PROF ELEC ENG, UNIV TENN, KNOXVILLE, 77- *Personal Data:* b Tazewell Co, Va, Dec 11, 12; m 41; c 2. *Educ:* Washington & Lee Univ, BS, 34; Univ Tenn MS, 39. *Mem:* Inst Elec & Electronics Engrs. *Res:* Physics; mathematics; magnetism; power generation; transmission and distribution; electrical apparatus and machinery. *Mailing Add:* 3539 Miser Station Rd Louisville TN 37777

LEFFERT, CHARLES BENJAMIN, ENERGY CONVERSION, CHEMICAL PHYSICS. *Current Pos:* res asst, Res Inst Eng Sci, 70-74, ASSOC PROF CHEM ENG, WAYNE STATE UNIV, 74-, DIR COL ENG ENERGY CTR, 74- *Personal Data:* b Logansport, Ind, May 22, 22; m 45. *Educ:* Purdue Univ, BS, 43; Univ Pittsburgh, MS, 57; Wayne State Univ, PhD(chem eng), 74. *Prof Exp:* Chem engr, Res Dept, Union Oil Co Calif, 43-49; chem engr, Pittsburgh Consol Coal Co, 49-52; asst physics, Univ Pittsburgh, 52-56; sr res physicist, Res Labs, Gen Motors Corp, 57-70. *Mem:* Am Phys Soc; Am Inst Chem Engrs; Sigma Xi. *Res:* Chemical engineering. *Mailing Add:* 1302 Wrenwood Dr Troy MI 48084-2688

LEFFERT, HYAM LERNER, CELL BIOLOGY, ANIMAL CELL GROWTH CONTROL. *Current Pos:* assoc prof med, 80-82, assoc prof pharmacol, 82-90, PROF PHARMACOL & CTR MOLECULAR GENETICS, SCH MED, UNIV CALIF, SAN DIEGO, 90- *Personal Data:* b New York, NY, May 11, 44; m 87, Katherine S Koch; c 3. *Educ:* Univ Rochester, BA, 65; Brandeis Univ, MA, 67; Albert Einstein Col Med, MD, 71. *Prof Exp:* Fel, Salk Inst Biol Studies, 71-72, res assoc, 72-73, asst res prof cell biol, 73-80. *Concurrent Pos:* Res grant, Nat Cancer Inst, NSF & Diabetes Asn Southern Calif, 74; consult cell biol, Dept Nutrit Path, Mass Inst Technol, 76, Nat Heart & Lung Inst, 73- & Dept Med, Vet Admin Hosp, Dallas, 74-; res grant, Nat Cancer Inst, 76-80, Nat Inst Arthritis, Metab & Digestive Dis, 80, Nat Inst Alcohol Abuse & Alcoholism, 80- & NIH 96-; John Simon Guggenheim fel, 87-88; Morton Grossman scholar, Am Gastroenterol Asn, 87-88. *Mem:* Int Study Group Carcinoembryonic Proteins. *Res:* Mechanism of liver regeneration, differentiation, gene expression and gene therapy. *Mailing Add:* Dept Pharmacol & Ctr Molecular Genetics Univ Calif San Diego Med Sch La Jolla CA 92093-0636. *E-Mail:* hleffert@ucsd.edu

LEFFEW, KENNETH W, CHEMICAL ENGINEERING, POLYMER ENGINEERING. *Current Pos:* RES ASSOC, E I DU PONT DE NEMOURS & CO, 73- *Personal Data:* b Louisville, Ky, Nov 5, 50; m 69; c 3. *Educ:* Univ Louisville, BS, 73, MEng, 73, PhD(chem eng), 81. *Concurrent Pos:* Adj prof, Univ Louisville, 78-80. *Mem:* Am Inst Chem Engrs. *Res:* Application of advanced process control to new process developments in large industrial projects. *Mailing Add:* Du Pont Exp Sta Bldg 304 Wilmington DE 19880

LEFFINGWELL, JOHN C, ORGANIC CHEMISTRY. *Current Pos:* VPRES, FRANCHISE BEVERAGE PROD, DEL MONTE CORP, 85-; EXEC VPRES, FOXFIRE FARMS, INC-; PRES, LEFFINGWELL & ASSOCS, 90- *Personal Data:* b Evanston, Ill, Feb 16, 38; m 60; c 3. *Educ:* Rollins Col, BS, 60; Emory Univ, MS, 62, PhD(org chem), 63. *Honors & Awards:* Philip Morris Award for Distinguished Achievement in Tobacco Sci, Philip Morris Inc & Tobacco Sci, 74. *Prof Exp:* Res assoc org chem, Columbia Univ, 63-64; res chemist, Org Chem Div, Glidden Co, Fla, 64-65 & R J Reynolds Tobacco Co, 65-70; head flavor res, R J Reynolds Industs Inc, 70-73, head flavor develop, R J Reynolds Tobacco Co, 73-75; vpres, Aromatics Int, 75-77; vpres res & develop, Sunkist Soft Drinks, sr vpres, 78-85. *Concurrent Pos:* NIH fel, 63-64; dir, Foxfire Farms, Inc, 85- *Mem:* Am Chem Soc; Royal Soc Chem; NY Acad Sci; Inst Food Technologists; AAAS; Soc Soft Drink Technologists. *Res:* Natural products; flavor chemistry; olfaction; consumer products. *Mailing Add:* 4699 Arbor Hill Rd Canton GA 30115-8162

LEFFLER, AMOS J, INORGANIC CHEMISTRY, PHYSICAL CHEMISTRY. *Current Pos:* assoc prof, 65-75, PROF CHEM, VILLANOVA UNIV, 75- *Personal Data:* b New York, NY, Sept 9, 24; m 49; c 3. *Educ:* Brooklyn Col, BS, 49; Univ Chicago, PhD(inorg chem), 53. *Prof Exp:* Chemist, Callery Chem Co, 53-55; res chemist, Stauffer Chem Co, 55-60; res assoc chem, Arthur D Little, Inc, 60-65. *Concurrent Pos:* Am Inst Chemists Award, Brooklyn Col, 49; sr res assoc, Nat Acad Sci-Nat Res Coun, 73. *Mem:* Am Chem Soc; Royal Soc Chem. *Res:* Inorganic and physical chemistry, especially boron and metallorganic chemistry, catalysis and metal oxides and fluorine chemistry. *Mailing Add:* Dept Chem Villanova Univ Villanova PA 19085-1699

LEFFLER, CHARLES WILLIAM, CARDIOVASCULAR PHYSIOLOGY, PERINATAL PHYSIOLOGY. *Current Pos:* from asst prof to assoc prof, 77-86, PROF PHYSIOL & BIOPHYS, HEALTH SCI CTR, UNIV TENN, MEMPHIS, 86-, PROF PEDIAT, 89, DIR, LAB RES NEONATAL PHYSIOL, 90- *Personal Data:* b Cleveland, Ohio, May 21, 47; m 68, Robin Burke; c Noelle. *Educ:* Univ Miami, BS, 69; Univ Fla, MS, 71, PhD(zool), 74. *Prof Exp:* Teaching asst zool, Univ Fla, 69-73, coun fel, 73-74, fel, 74-76; asst prof physiol & biophys, Univ Louisville, 76-77. *Concurrent Pos:* Estab investr, Am Heart Asn, 82-87. *Mem:* Am Physiol Soc; Soc Exp Biol & Med; AAAS; Sigma Xi; Am Heart Asn; Soc Pediat Res. *Res:* Vascular biology; paracrine/autocrine mediators in control of perinatal circulation; cerebral hemodynamics in the newborn; lipid mediators. *Mailing Add:* Dept Physiol & Biophys 894 Union Ave NA427 Memphis TN 38163

LEFFLER, ESTHER BARBARA, PHYSICAL CHEMISTRY. *Current Pos:* CONSULT, 88- *Personal Data:* b Clearfield, Pa, Feb 1, 25. *Educ:* Pa State Univ, BS, 45; Univ Va, PhD(chem), 50. *Prof Exp:* Asst chemother, Stanford Res Labs, Am Cyanamid Co, 45-46; instr chem, Randolph-Macon Woman's Col, 49-53; from asst prof to prof chem, Sweet Briar Col, 53-66, chmn dept, 56-59 & 60-66; from asst prof to prof chem, Calif State Polytech Univ, 67-88, actg chmn dept, 73-74, assoc dean, Sch Sci, 78-84. *Concurrent Pos:* Res assoc & vis lectr, Stanford Univ, 66-67; res assoc, Oxford Univ, 74-75; resident dir, Calif State Univ Int Prog in UK, 74-75. *Mem:* Sigma Xi. *Res:* Software development for science education. *Mailing Add:* 19950 Esquiline Ave Walnut CA 91789

LEFFLER, HARRY REX, PLANT PHYSIOLOGY, PLANT GENETICS. *Current Pos:* AGRON CONSULT, 92- *Personal Data:* b Rensselaer, Ind, Sept 20, 42; m 71; c 3. *Educ:* Iowa State Univ, BS, 64; Purdue Univ, MS, 67, PhD(plant physiol), 70. *Prof Exp:* Res assoc agron, Univ Ill, 70-71; res assoc hort, Purdue Univ, 71-72; plant physiologist, Cotton Physiol & Genetics Unit, Agr Res Serv, USDA, 72-85, DeKalb Pfizer Genetics Co, 85-92. *Concurrent Pos:* Assoc ed, Agron J, 82-85, Dekalb-Pfizer, 85-88. *Mem:* Am Soc Agron; Am Soc Plant Physiologists; Crop Sci Soc Am. *Res:* Physiological genetics of seed development. *Mailing Add:* 15 Golfview Pl Dekalb IL 60115

LEFFLER, JOHN EDWARD, CHEMISTRY. *Current Pos:* from asst prof to assoc prof, 50-59, PROF CHEM, FLA STATE UNIV, 59- *Personal Data:* b Brookline, Mass, Dec 27, 20; m 52, Nell Foust. *Educ:* Harvard Univ, BS, 42, PhD(org chem), 48. *Prof Exp:* Res assoc chem, Harvard Univ, 42-44 & Univ Chicago, 44-45; res assoc rocket fuels, USN Proj, Mass Inst Technol, 45-46; du Pont fel, Cornell Univ, 48-49; mem fac, Brown Univ, 49-50. *Mem:* Am Chem Soc; fel AAAS. *Res:* Reaction rate theory; polar and radical reactions; reactive intermediates of organic chemistry; peroxides; reactions of adsorbed organic compounds. *Mailing Add:* Dept Chem Fla State Univ Tallahassee FL 32306-1096. *Fax:* 850-644-8281

LEFFLER, MARLIN TEMPLETON, ORGANIC CHEMISTRY. *Current Pos:* RETIRED. *Personal Data:* b College Corner, Ind, Feb 28, 11; m 33; c 3. *Educ:* Miami Univ, AB, 32; Univ Ill, MA, 33, PhD(org chem), 36. *Prof Exp:* Asst chemist, Univ Ill, 33-35; res chemist, Abbott Labs, Ill, 36-46, head, Org Dept, 46-49, asst dir res, 49-50, assoc dir, 50-57, dir chem & agr res, 57-59, dir res liaison, 59-71; consult, 71-80. *Mem:* Am Chem Soc. *Res:* Local anesthetics; antiseptics; chemotherapy; optical activity of organic deuterium compounds; organic medicinal chemistry; biochemistry; overseas technological advances. *Mailing Add:* 200 Laurel Lake Dr Apt 173 Hudson OH 44236-2133

LEFFORD, MAURICE J, IMMUNOLOGY, MICROBIOLOGY. *Current Pos:* assoc prof, 79-85, PROF, DEPT IMMUNOL & MICROBIOL, SCH MED, WAYNE STATE UNIV, 85- *Personal Data:* b London, Eng, Nov 27, 30; US citizen. *Educ:* Univ London, Eng, BS, 55. *Prof Exp:* Resident internal med, Royal Victoria Hosp, Bournemouth, 57-59 & path, St Bartholomew's Hosp, London, 59-63; mem, Unit Lab Studies Tuberc, Brit Med Res Coun, Royal Postgrad Med Sch, 63-71; asst mem, Trudeau Inst, NY, 71-75, assoc mem, 75-79. *Concurrent Pos:* Mem, Sci Group Leprosy, Nat Inst Allergy & Infectious Dis, 76, Sci Working Group Immunol Leprosy, WHO, 76-80 & US Tuberculosis Panel, US-Japan Coop Med Sci Prog, 84-88; chmn Mycobact Div, Am Soc Microbiol, 84. *Mem:* Am Asn Immunologists; Am Soc Microbiol; Int Leprosy Asn. *Mailing Add:* Immunol & Microbiol Dept Wayne State Univ Sch Med 540 E Canfield Ave Detroit MI 48201-1908

LEFKOWITZ, BONNIE, PUBLIC HEALTH. *Current Pos:* dir, Div Health Resources & Servs Anal, 77-82, ASSOC BUR DIR EVAL, ANALYSIS & RES, BUR PRIMARY HEALTH CARE, DEPT HEALTH & HUMAN SERVS, USPHS, 83- *Educ:* Univ Md, BA, 60; Harvard Univ, MPA, 75. *Prof Exp:* Dir substance abuse & health servs anal, NY City Health Servs Admin, 70-74; prin analyst, Cong Budget Off, 75-77. *Concurrent Pos:* Fed exec fel, Brookings Inst, 81; prog dir, Interagency Comt Infant Mortality, Health Resources & Servs Admin, Dept Health & Human Servs, USPHS, 90-92; co-chair, White House Task Force Health Care Reform, 93. *Res:* strategic planning health systems; change and its impact on safety net providers; development of need criteria; state-based planning. *Mailing Add:* Bur Primary Health Care Eval Analysis & Res Health Resources & Serv Admin Rockville MD 20857

LEFKOWITZ, DORIS LYNNE, CELLULAR IMMUNOLOGY, MACROPHAGE ACTIVATION. *Current Pos:* Asst prof, 86-92, ASSOC PROF BIOL SCI, TEX TECH UNIV, 92- *Personal Data:* b Ellenville, NY, June 27, 43; m 79, Stanley S; c Michael S. *Educ:* Univ Miami, BS, 66; Tex Tech Univ, MS, 78, PhD(med microbiol), 86. *Mem:* Am Soc Microbiol; Soc Exp Biol Med; Asn Med Lab Immunologists. *Res:* Myeloperoxides as an endogenous immunoregulatory substance; cocaine effects on leukocyte functions. *Mailing Add:* 3801 67th St Lubbock TX 79413. *Fax:* 806-742-2712

LEFKOWITZ, IRVING, SYSTEMS & CONTROL ENGINEERING. *Current Pos:* res assoc instrumentation eng, Case Western Res Univ, 53-58, from asst prof to assoc prof eng, 58-65, dir, Control Indust Systs Prog, 58-65, prof systs eng & chmn dept, 65-87, chmn, Dept Systs Eng, 70-74 & 80-83, EMER PROF SYSTS ENG, CASE WESTERN RES UNIV, 87-; CHIEF CONSULT, CONTROL SOFT, INC, 87- *Personal Data:* b New York, NY, July 8, 21; m 55, Madelyn Moinester; c Deborah & Daniel. *Educ:* Cooper Union Sch Eng, BChE, 43; Case Inst Technol, MS, 55, PhD(control eng), 58. *Honors & Awards:* Control Heritage Award, Am Automatic Control Coun. *Prof Exp:* Instrument engr, Calvert Distilling Co, 44-47; instrument engr, J E Seagram & Sons, Inc, 47-51, head instrumentation res, 51-53. *Concurrent Pos:* NATO fel, 62-63; res fel, Int Inst Appl Systs Anal, 74-75; chmn, Systs Eng Comt, Int Fedn Automatic Control, 78-81; chmn, Comt Indust Systs Control, Control Systs Soc, 84-85. *Mem:* Fel AAAS; fel Inst Elec & Electronics Engrs; Int Fedn Automatic Control. *Res:* Hierarchical computer control; control of industrial processes; energy conservation through integrated systems control. *Mailing Add:* Dept Systs Eng Case Western Res Univ University Circle Cleveland OH 44106

LEFKOWITZ, LEWIS BENJAMIN, JR, MEDICINE. *Current Pos:* from asst prof to assoc prof, 65-78, PROF PREV MED, SCH MED, VANDERBILT UNIV, 78-, ASST PROF MED, 71- *Personal Data:* b Dallas, Tex, Dec 18, 30; m 61; c David H, Gerald L & Paul L. *Educ:* Denison Univ, BA, 51; Univ Tex Southwest Med Sch Dallas, MD, 56. *Prof Exp:* USPHS res fel med, Univ Tex Southwest Med Sch Dallas, 59-60, instr, 60-61; USPHS res fel, Univ Ill, 61-62, USPHS trainee infectious dis, 62-65. *Concurrent Pos:* Asst clin prof internal med, Meharry Med Col, 66-78, clin prof family & community med, 78-81, assoc clin prof internal med, 78-85; consult, US Army Hosp, Ft Campbell, Ky, 69-85. *Mem:* Am Col Prev Med; Am Pub Health Asn. *Res:* Epidemiology and pathogenesis of infectious diseases; health care delivery. *Mailing Add:* Dept Prev Med Vanderbilt Univ Sch Med Nashville TN 37232. *Fax:* 615-343-8722

LEFKOWITZ, ROBERT JOSEPH, MOLECULAR PHARMACOLOGY, MEDICAL SCIENCE. *Current Pos:* assoc prof med & asst prof biochem, 73-77, prof med, Med Ctr, 77-82, JAMES B DUKE PROF MED, DUKE UNIV MED CTR, 82-, PROF BIOCHEM, 85- *Personal Data:* b New York, NY, Apr 15, 43; m 91, Lynn Tilley; c David, Larry, Cheryl, Mara, Joshua. *Educ:* Columbia Univ, BA, 62, MD, 66; Am Bd Internal Med, dipl. *Honors & Awards:* Janeway Prize, 66; John J Abel Award, Am Soc Pharmacol & Exp Therapeut, 78; Ernst Oppenheimer Mem Award, Endocrine Soc, 82; Gordon Wilson Medal, Am Clin & Climatol Asn, 82; Lita Annenberg Hazen Award, 83; Outstanding Res award, Int Soc Heart Res, 85; Goodman & Gilman Award, Am Soc Pharmacol & Expert Therapeut, 86; Gairdner Found Int Award, 88; Novo Nordisk Biotechnol Award, 90; Res Award, Asn Am Med Col, 90; Basic Res Prize, Am Heart Asn, 90; Giovanni Lorenzini Prize, 92. *Prof Exp:* From intern to jr asst resident, Columbia Presby Med Ctr, NY, 66-68; clin & res assoc, Nat Inst Arthritis & Metab Dis, 68-70; sr asst resident, Mass Gen Hosp, Harvard Univ, 70-71, fel cardiol, 71-73. *Concurrent Pos:* Estab investr, Am Heart Asn, 73-76; investr, Howard Hughes Med Inst, 76- *Mem:* Nat Acad Sci; Inst Med-Nat Acad Sci; Asn Am Physicians; Am Heart Asn; Am Soc Pharmacol & Exp Therapeut; Am Soc Clin Invest; Am Acad Arts & Sci; Endocrine Soc; Am Soc Biol Chem. *Res:* Molecular pharmacology of drug and hormone receptors; author of numerous articles. *Mailing Add:* Duke Univ Med Ctr PO Box 3821 Durham NC 27710. *Fax:* 919-684-8875

LEFKOWITZ, RUTH SAMSON, mathematics, for more information see previous edition

LEFKOWITZ, STANLEY A, PHYSICAL INORGANIC CHEMISTRY. *Current Pos:* VPRES FALCONWOOD CORP & MOCATTA METALS CORP, 75- *Personal Data:* b Philadelphia, Pa, Aug 5, 43; m 94, Debra Kaplan. *Educ:* Temple Univ, AB, 65; Princeton Univ, PhD(chem), 70. *Prof Exp:* Asst to vchancellor Urban Affairs, City Univ New York, 70-73; asst dir instruct develop, Queens Col, 73-75. *Concurrent Pos:* Environ consult, NY State Temp Comn Powers Local Govt, 72-73; consult, Prof Exam Serv, 74-75 & Guana Island Hotel Corp, 76-; dir, Iron Mountain Depository Corp, 79-87. *Res:* Alternative techniques for the extraction, refining and analysis of precious metals; the development and design of a solar-wind energy installation on Guana Island in the British Virgin Islands. *Mailing Add:* 60 E Eighth St Apt 22J New York NY 10003. *Fax:* 212-984-1442; *E-Mail:* stan@pipeline.com

LEFKOWITZ, STANLEY S, MICROBIOLOGY, VIROLOGY. *Current Pos:* assoc prof, 72-78, assoc dean, 75-81, actg chairperson, Microbiol Dept & res coordr, 78-81, PROF VIROL, SCH MED, TEX TECH UNIV, 78- *Personal Data:* b New York, NY, Nov 26, 33; m 78; c 3. *Educ:* Univ Miami, BS, 55, MS, 57; Univ Md, PhD(plant path), 61; Am Bd Med Microbiol, dipl, 74. *Prof Exp:* Fel viral oncol, Variety Childrens Res Found, 61-64, res assoc, 64-65; from asst prof to assoc prof virol, Med Col Ga, 65-69. *Concurrent Pos:* Assoc scientist, Sloan Kettering Inst Cancer Res, 77-81; mem, Clin Cancer Educ Comt, NIH, 78-81. *Mem:* AAAS; fel Am Acad Microbiol; Am Soc Microbiol; Tissue Cult Asn; Soc Exp Biol & Med; Reticuloendothelial Soc (treas); NY Acad Sci; Am Asn Immunol. *Res:* Effects of highly abused drugs on immunity; cocaine alteration of macrophage functions; myeloperoxidase as an immunoregulatory agent; effects of highly abused drugs on immunity. *Mailing Add:* Dept Microbiol Tex Tech Univ Health Sci Ctr 3601 Fourth St Lubbock TX 79430

LEFORT, HENRY G(ERARD), CERAMICS ENGINEERING. *Current Pos:* ASSOC PROF CERAMIC ENG, CLEMSON UNIV, 62- *Personal Data:* b Mineola, NY, Apr 4, 28; m 55; c 3. *Educ:* Clemson Col, BCerE, 52; Univ Ill, MS, 57, PhD(ceramic eng), 60. *Prof Exp:* Ceramic engr, Nat Bur Standards, 52-55; res assoc ceramic eng, Univ Ill, 55-60; chemist, Lawrence Radiation Lab, Univ Calif, 60-62. *Mem:* Am Ceramic Soc; Nat Inst Ceramic Engrs. *Res:* Ceramic structural adhesives for high temperature use; ceramic coatings; procelain enamels; nuclear ceramics. *Mailing Add:* PO Box 65 Clemson SC 29631

LEFRAK, EDWARD ARTHUR, CARDIAC, VASCULAR & THORACIC SURGERY. *Current Pos:* DIR CARDIAC SURG, FAIRFAX HOSP, VA, 77-, MED DIR CARDIAC TRANSPLANTATION PROG, 86- *Personal Data:* b Newark, NJ, Apr 21, 43; m 73; c 5. *Educ:* State Univ NY, Buffalo, BA, 65; Ind Univ Sch Med, MD, 69; Am Bd Surg, cert, 76; Am Bd Thoracic Surg, cert, 78. *Prof Exp:* Intern surg, Baylor Col Med Affil Hosp, Houston, Tex, 69-70, resident gen surg, 70-75; resident cardiopulmonary surg, Univ Ore Med Sch, Portland, 75-77. *Concurrent Pos:* Asst clin prof surg, Georgetown Univ Sch Med, 78-; mem Coun Cardiovasc Surg, Am Heart Asn, 82. *Mem:* Fel Am Col Cardiol; fel Am Col Surgeons; AMA; fel Am Col Chest Physicians; fel Int Col Surgeons; Int Soc Heart Transplantation; Am Asn Thoracic Surg. *Res:* Cardiac & vascular surgery; heart transplantation. *Mailing Add:* 3301 Woodburn Rd No 301 Annandale VA 22003

LEFRANCOIS, LEO, EXPERIMENTAL BIOLOGY. *Current Pos:* res scientist, 86-90, SR RES SCIENTIST III, DEPT CELL BIOL, UPJOHN CO, 90- *Personal Data:* b Bristol, Conn, Jan 6, 56. *Educ:* Colo State Univ, BS, 78; Wake Forest Univ, PhD(immunol), 82. *Prof Exp:* Med technologist, Bristol Hosp, Conn, 78-79; teaching asst, Dept Microbiol & Immunol, Bowman Gray Sch Med, Winston-Salem, NC, 81-82; res assoc, Dept Immunol, Scripps Clin & Res Found, La Jolla, Calif, 82-86. *Concurrent Pos:* Assoc ed, J Immunol; adv coun mem, Midwest Autumn Immunol Conf. *Mailing Add:* Dept Med Div-Rheumatology Univ Conn Health Ctr 263 Farmington Ave Farmington CT 06030-1310

LEFTIN, HARRY PAUL, PHYSICAL ORGANIC CHEMISTRY, INDUSTRIAL CHEMISTRY. *Current Pos:* res chemist, Pullman Kellogg, 59-60, supvr chem res, 60-67, sr res assoc, Res & Develop Lab, 67-73, MGR RES, PULLMAN KELLOGG, 73-, CONSULT. *Personal Data:* b Beverly, Mass, Oct 23, 26; m 54, Selma Gordon; c Lori (Starr), Debra (Carnes) & Alyson (Leftin). *Educ:* Boston Univ, AB, 50, PhD(chem), 55. *Prof Exp:* Res fel, Mellon Inst, 54-59. *Concurrent Pos:* Instr, Fairleigh Dickinson Univ, 60-75; ed, Catalysis Rev, 67-85; assoc dir res, M W Kellogg Co, 85-86; consult, 86- *Mem:* Am Chem Soc; Catalysis Soc NAm; Sigma Xi. *Res:* Heterogeneous catalysis; chemisorption; electronic infrared and nuclear magnetic resonance spectra of molecules in the adsorbed state; petroleum and petrochemical process development; gas phase kinetics. *Mailing Add:* M W Kellogg Technol Co Technol Develop Ctr 16200 Bark Row Houston TX 77084-5195

LEFTON, LEW EDWARD, NONLINEAR DIFFERENTIAL EQUATIONS, NONLINEAR ANALYSIS. *Current Pos:* ASST PROF MATH, UNIV NEW ORLEANS, 89- *Personal Data:* b Albuquerque, NMex, Sept 24, 60; m 88. *Educ:* NMex Inst Mining & Technol, BS, 82; Univ Ill, Urbana, MS, 86, PhD(math), 87. *Prof Exp:* Vis asst prof math, Univ Calif, Riverside, 87-89. *Mem:* Am Math Soc; Math Asn Am. *Res:* Existence, multiplicity, and qualitative behavior of solutions to nonlinear ordinary and partial differential equations; applying both numerical techniques and analytic methods from functional analysis; elliptic partial differential equations. *Mailing Add:* Dept Math Univ New Orleans New Orleans LA 70148-2900

LEFTON, PHYLLIS, MATHEMATICS, NUMBER THEORY. *Current Pos:* asst prof, 77-82, assoc prof math, 82-87, PROF MATH & COMPUT SCI, MANHATTANVILLE COL, 87- *Personal Data:* b Neptune, NJ, Feb 10, 49; m 79; c 1. *Educ:* Barnard Col, BA, 71; Columbia Univ, MA, 72, MPhil & PhD(math), 75; Jewish Theol Sem, BHL, 75. *Prof Exp:* Teaching asst calculus, Columbia Univ, 70-73; instr math, Belfer Grad Sch & Stern Col, Yeshiva Univ, 75-77. *Mem:* Am Math Soc; Math Asn Am; Asn Women in Math; Nat Coun Teachers Math. *Res:* Algebraic number theory; analytic number theory; group representation theory; theory of polynomials and field theory. *Mailing Add:* Dept Math Manhattanville Col 2900 Purchase St Purchase NY 10577

LEGAL, CASIMER CLAUDIUS, JR, inorganic chemistry; deceased, see previous edition for last biography

LEGAN, SANDRA JEAN, REPRODUCTIVE PHYSIOLOGY, NEUROENDOCRINOLOGY. *Current Pos:* from asst prof to assoc prof, 79-92, PROF PHYSIOL, UNIV KY, LEXINGTON, 92- *Personal Data:* b Cleveland, Ohio, Sept 10, 46. *Educ:* Univ Mich, BS, 67, MS, 70, PhD(physiol), 74. *Prof Exp:* Lab asst, Geigy Co, Basel, Switz, 67-68; instr physiol, Univ Mich, 71-72, teaching fel, 72-73; NIH fel physiol, Emory Univ, 74-75; NIH fel, Reproductive Endocrinol Prog, Univ Mich, Ann Arbor, 75-77, res assoc, 77-79. *Mem:* Am Physiol Soc; Endocrine Soc; Soc Study Reproduction; Soc Neurosci; Soc Study Fertil. *Res:* Neuroendocrine control of gonadotrophin secretion, specifically how modulations in steroid concentrations, environmental stimuli and neural input are transduced into endocrine events in the hypothalamo-hypophyseal axis. *Mailing Add:* Dept Physiol Univ Ky Lexington KY 40536-0084. *Fax:* 606-323-1070; *E-Mail:* legans@pop.uky.edu

LEGARE, RICHARD J, POLYMER CHEMISTRY, CHEMICAL KINETICS. *Current Pos:* Sr res chemist, Allegany Ballistics Lab, Md, 62-71, staff scientist, Bacchus Works, 71-76 & Fibers Technol Ctr, Research Triangle Park, NC, 76-78, STAFF SCIENTIST, FIBERS TECHNOL CTR, HERCULES INC, 78- *Personal Data:* b Central Falls, RI, Dec 27, 34; m 57; c 2. *Educ:* Providence Col, BS, 56; Univ Minn, MS, 60, PhD(phys chem), 62. *Mem:* Am Chem Soc. *Res:* High speed kinetics; biophysical and polymer chemistry; rocket propellants; high temperature resins; composite materials. *Mailing Add:* 2619 Country Club Dr Conyers GA 30208

LEGASPI, ADRIAN, ONCOLOGY. *Current Pos:* ASST PROF SURG, UNIV MIAMI SCH MED, 87- *Personal Data:* b Mexico City, Mex, Jul 13, 52; m 80; c 1. *Educ:* Army Med Sch, Mex, MD, 76. *Prof Exp:* Res fel, surgery, Cornell Univ NY Hosp, 83-85; clin fel, surgery oncol, mem Sloan Kettering Cancer Ctr Med Col, 85-87. *Mem:* Europ Soc Parenteral & Enteral Nutrit; Asn Acad Sug. *Res:* Treatment of cancer by means of surgery; nutritional aspects of patient support before and after surgery; injury and hospitalization on protein metabolism. *Mailing Add:* 1500 Bricknell Ave Miami FL 33129

LEGATES, JAMES EDWARD, ANIMAL GENETICS. *Current Pos:* from asst prof to prof animal indust, NC State Univ, 49-56, actg head dairy husb sect, 55-58, head animal breeding sect, 58-70, William Neal Reynolds prof animal sci & genetics, 56-86, dean sch agr & life sci, 71-86, EMER WILLIAM NEAL REYNOLDS PROF & DEAN, NC STATE UNIV, 86- *Personal Data:* b Milford, Del, Aug 1, 22; m 44; c 4. *Educ:* Univ Del, BS, 43; Iowa State Col, MS, 47, PhD, 49. *Honors & Awards:* Borden Award, Am Dairy Sci Asn, 67, Award of Honor, 89; J Rockefeller Prentice Animal Breeding & Genetics Award, Am Soc Animal Sci, 77. *Prof Exp:* Asst, Iowa State Col, 48-49. *Concurrent Pos:* Consult agr prog, Rockefeller Found, Colombia, 59; consult, Exp Sta Div, USDA, 59-65; vis prof, Nat Inst Animal Sci, Copenhagen, 63 & State Agr Univ, Wageningen, 71. *Mem:* AAAS; Biomet Soc; Am Soc Animal Sci; Am Dairy Sci Asn. *Res:* Selection in dairy cattle; genetics of mastitis resistance; quantitative inheritance in mice. *Mailing Add:* 1717 Wayside Farm Rd Franklinton NC 27525

LEGAULT, ALBERT, SYSTEMATIC BOTANY, PHYTOGEOGRAPHY. *Current Pos:* RETIRED. *Personal Data:* b Hull, Que, June 7, 19; m 57. *Educ:* Univ Montreal, BA, 48, BPed, 53, BSc, 55, MSc, 58; Yale Univ, MSc, 59. *Prof Exp:* Teacher biol, Montreal-St Louis Col, Montreal, 50-57; researcher palynol, Serv Biogeog, Prov Que, 61-62; from asst prof to assoc prof, Univ Sherbrooke, 62-76, prof bot, 76- *Mem:* Can Bot Asn; Int Asn Plant Taxon; Fr-Can Asn Advan Sci. *Res:* Floristics of southeastern, arctic and subarctic Quebec. *Mailing Add:* 2531 Verdun Sherbrooke PQ J1K 1Y3 Can

LEGECKIS, RICHARD VYTAUTAS, PHYSICAL OCEANOGRAPHY, REMOTE SENSING. *Current Pos:* SCIENTIST OCEANOG, NAT ENVIRON SATELLITE SERV, NAT OCEANIC & ATMOSPHERIC ADMIN, 75- *Personal Data:* b Panevezys, Lithuania, Jan 28, 41; US citizen; m 67; c 2. *Educ:* City Univ New York, BS, 65; Fla Inst Technol, MS, 68; Fla State Univ, PhD(phys oceanog), 74. *Prof Exp:* Space engr, Grumman Corp, 65-70; res assoc sci, Fla State Univ, 74; assoc oceanog, Nat Res Coun, 74-75. *Concurrent Pos:* Nat Res Coun grant, 74. *Mem:* Am Geophys Union. *Res:* Ocean currents and temperature fronts; application of satellite remote sensing to ocean studies. *Mailing Add:* 15004 Whitegate Rd Silver Spring MD 20905

LEGENDRE, LOUIS, BIOLOGICAL OCEANOGRAPHY, NUMERICAL ECOLOGY. *Current Pos:* res assoc, Laval Univ, 73-74, asst prof, 74-77, assoc prof, 77-81, PROF OCEANOG, LAVAL UNIV, 81- *Personal Data:* b Montreal, Que, Feb 16, 45. *Educ:* Univ Montreal, BSc, 67; Dalhousie Univ, PhD(oceanog), 71. *Honors & Awards:* Leo-Pariseau Award, Fr-Can Asn Advan Sci, 85, Michel-Jurdant Award, 86. *Prof Exp:* NATO fel oceanog, Marine Sta Villefranche-sur-Mer, Univ Paris, 71-73. *Concurrent Pos:* Secy gen interuniv group res oceanog, Que, Laval & McGill Univs, 77-79, res coordr, 80-86, vpres, 89-; mem Can nat comt for sci, comt oceanog res, Nat Res Coun Can, 78-79; mem Pop Biol Comt, Nat Sci Eng Res Coun Can, 80-83; mem Comt Perfect, Inst Ocean Paris Monaco, 81-; mem, working group 73, Sci Comt Oceanic Res, 83-87, working group 86, Sci Comt Oceanic Res, 88-, mem, Strategic Panel Oceans, Natural Sci & Eng Res Coun Can, 85-87, chmn, 88-89; group chair Life Sci, 89-92; mem, Comt Res Centres, FCAR Fund Que, 88-89, & 95-96, chair Comt Actions struct, 90; mem, Int Exec Comt, Group on Aquatic Productivity, 88-92, Sci Cultural Coun, Fr Univ Pac, 90-; chair, Sci Coord Group Int Arctic Polymya Programme, 89-; mem, bd Environ Policy, Royal Soc, 90-92; mem, task team photosynthesis measurements, Joint Global Ocean Flux Study, 93-; vpres, Modelenviron, Univ Liege, Belg, 93-; Killam Res fel, Can Coun, 97- *Mem:* Am Soc Limnol & Oceanog; fel Royal Soc Can. *Res:* Marine primary production; physiological ecology of photosynthesis in marine phytoplankton; numerical analysis of ecological data sets. *Mailing Add:* Dept Biol Laval Univ Quebec PQ G1K 7P4 Can. *Fax:* 418-656-2339; *E-Mail:* pouis.pegendre@bio.upavap.ca

LEGENDRE, PIERRE, NUMERICAL ECOLOGY, COMMUNITY ECOLOGY. *Current Pos:* assoc prof, 80-84, PROF BIOL, UNIV MONTREAL, 84- *Personal Data:* b Montreal, Que, Oct 5, 46; m 69; c 2. *Educ:* Univ Montreal, BA, 65; McGill Univ, MSc, 69; Univ Colo, PhD(biol), 71. *Honors & Awards:* Michel-Jurdant Prize Environ Sci, Asn Canadienne-Francaise pour l'Advan des Sci, 86. *Prof Exp:* Postdoctoral genetics, Genetiska Institutionen, Lunds Universitat, Lund, Sweden, 71-72; res assoc environ sci, Univ Que, Montreal, 72-73, res dir environ sci, 73-80, prof physics, 80. *Concurrent Pos:* Res assoc, Nat Sci & Eng Res Coun, 77-80; expert, Environ Training & Mgt Africa, USA, Workshop in Togo, 83; invited prof, Montpellier, France, 85, Louvain-la-Neuve, Belg, 87, 88 & 89; chmn, Theme 5, ECOTHAU Res Prog, Montpellier, France, 85-90 & Grant Selection Comt Pop Biol-18, Nat Sci & Eng Res Coun, 89-90; dir, Advan Res Workshop Numerical Ecol, France, 86; mem bd dirs, Classification Soc NAm, 86-89; res fel, Killam Prog, Can Coun, 89-91, selection comt mem, 90-93. *Mem:* Classification Soc NAm. *Res:* Mathematically analyzing the organization of ecological communities through space and integrating spatial structures into population and community models in order to increase their predictive power; application to several types of ecosystems (aquatic and terrestrial); author of several textbooks on numerical ecology, that have established the foundations of this new sub-discipline. *Mailing Add:* Dept Biol Sci Univ Montreal CP 6128 Succursale A Montreal PQ H3C 3J7 Can. *Fax:* 514-343-2293

LEGER, ROBERT M(ARSH), ELECTRICAL ENGINEERING. *Current Pos:* RETIRED. *Personal Data:* b Foochow, China, June 3, 21; US citizen; m 44, 78, Alicia M Olsen; c Carol A, Betsy J & James R. *Educ:* Antioch Col, BS, 44; Ill Inst Technol, MS, 50, PhD(elec eng), 55. *Prof Exp:* Final test foreman, Collins Radio Co, 43-44, qual control engr, 44-46; asst elec eng, Ill Inst Technol, 47-48, instr, 48-52, asst prof, 52-53; from electronics engr to mgr info systs, Convair Astronaut Div, Gen Dynamics/Convair, 53-70, eng specialist, Gen Dynamics Electronics, 71-86. *Mem:* Sr mem Inst Elec & Electronics Engrs; Sigma Xi. *Res:* Information handling systems; guidance and tracking systems. *Mailing Add:* 6517 Altair Ct San Diego CA 92120

LEGERTON, CLARENCE W, JR, gastroenterology; deceased, see previous edition for last biography

LEGG, DAVID ALAN, MATHEMATICAL ANALYSIS. *Current Pos:* From asst prof to assoc prof, 74-80, PROF MATH, IND UNIV-PURDUE UNIV, FT WAYNE, 84- *Personal Data:* b Elwood, Ind, Sept 7, 47; m 79; c 1. *Educ:* Purdue Univ, BS, 69, MS, 70, PhD(math), 73. *Mem:* Am Math Soc; Math Asn Am; Sigma Xi. *Res:* Approximation theory. *Mailing Add:* 11310 St Joe Rd Ft Wayne IN 46835-9737

LEGG, IVAN, BIOINORGANIC CHEMISTRY. *Current Pos:* PROVOST, MEMPHIS STATE UNIV, 92- *Personal Data:* b New York, NY, Oct 15, 37; m 62; c 2. *Educ:* Oberlin Col, BA, 60; Univ Mich, MS, 63, PhD(inorg chem), 65. *Prof Exp:* Res assoc inorg chem, Univ Pittsburgh, 65-66; from asst prof to prof chem, Wash State Univ, 66-78, assoc biochem, 75-78, chmn, Dept Chem, 78-87; dean, Col Sci & Math, Auburn Univ, 87-92. *Concurrent Pos:* NIH spec fel, Harvard Med Sch, 72-73. *Mem:* Am Chem Soc. *Res:* Use of metal ions to probe structure-function relationships in metalloenzymes; development of models for metal ions binding sites in proteins. *Mailing Add:* Provost Univ 360 Admin Bldg Campus Box 526653 Memphis TN 38152-6653

LEGG, JAMES C, ATOMIC PHYSICS, NUCLEAR PHYSICS. *Current Pos:* assoc prof, 67-73, dir, Nuclear Sci Lab, 72-83, PROF PHYSICS, KANS STATE UNIV, 73-, HEAD DEPT, 87- *Personal Data:* b Kokomo, Ind, Sept 17, 36; m 73, Marilyn Gilliland; c Robert, Ted & Thomas. *Educ:* Ind Univ, BS, 58; Princeton Univ, MA, 60, PhD(physics), 62. *Prof Exp:* Instr physics, Princeton Univ, 61-62; res assoc, Rice Univ, 62-63, asst prof, 63-67. *Mem:* Am Phys Soc; AAAS; Am Asn Physics Teachers. *Res:* Atomic and molecular collisions. *Mailing Add:* Dept Physics Kans State Univ Cardwell Hall Manhattan KS 66506. *Fax:* 785-532-6806; *E-Mail:* legg@ksuvm.ksu.edu

LEGG, JOHN WALLIS, PHYSICAL CHEMISTRY. *Current Pos:* assoc prof, 64-71, PROF CHEM, MISS COL, 71-, HEAD DEPT, 82- *Personal Data:* b Minter City, Miss, Sept 20, 36; m 56, Betty Tullos; c David, Diane & Linda. *Educ:* Miss Col, BS, 58; Univ Fla, MS, 60, PhD, 64. *Prof Exp:* Chemist, Shell Oil Co, Tex, 58; asst, Univ Fla, 58-60; asst prof, Miss Col, 60-62; asst, Univ Fla, 62-64, instr, 63. *Concurrent Pos:* Vis prof, George Peabody Col, 66. *Mem:* Am Chem Soc; Am Sci Affil. *Res:* Adsorption at solid surfaces and heterogeneous catalysis, specifically reactions over thorium oxide catalysts, primarily of the alcohols; dielectric properties of freon hydrates; coal powders and slurries. *Mailing Add:* Dept Chem Miss Col Box 4064 Clinton MS 39058. *Fax:* 601-925-3933; *E-Mail:* legg@mc.edu

LEGG, JOSEPH OGDEN, SOIL SCIENCE. *Current Pos:* RETIRED. *Personal Data:* b Tex, Oct 16, 20; m 44. *Educ:* Univ Ark, BS, 50, MS, 51; Univ Md, PhD(soil fertil), 57. *Prof Exp:* Soil scientist, USDA, 51-79. *Concurrent Pos:* USDA exchange scientist to USSR, 63-64; adj prof, Agron Dept, Univ Ark, 80- *Mem:* Fel AAAS; Soil Sci Soc Am; Am Soc Agron; Int Soc Soil Sci; Coun Agr Sci & Technol. *Res:* Nitrogen transformations in soils; biological nitrogen fixation; soil organic matter. *Mailing Add:* 2400 W New Hope Rd Rogers AR 72758-1324

LEGG, KENNETH DEARDORFF, ANALYTICAL CHEMISTRY. *Current Pos:* DIR RES, ALLIED HEALTH & SCI PRODS, 83- *Personal Data:* b Ogdensburg, NY, Feb 19, 43; m 67. *Educ:* Union Col, BS, 64; Mass Inst Technol, PhD(chem), 69. *Prof Exp:* Vis prof chem, Univ Southern Calif, 74-75; asst prof chem, Calif State Univ, Long Beach, 69-74, assoc prof, 75-78; prin scientist, Instrumentation Lab Inc, 78-81, mgr, anal res, 81-82, dir res, 82-83. *Mem:* Am Asn Clin Chem; Am Chem Soc; Electrochem Soc. *Res:* Study of fast photophysical processes using laser excitation; biomedical instrumentation; electrogenerated chemiluminescence; ion selective electrodes, amperometric sensors and biomedical instrumentation. *Mailing Add:* 29 Jefferson Rd Wellesley MA 02181-5400

LEGG, MERLE ALAN, PATHOLOGY. *Current Pos:* asst resident & resident path, New Eng Deaconess Hosp, 53-55, clin assoc path, Harvard Med Sch, 66-70, asst clin prof, 70-74, chmn, Dept Path, 75-78 & 79-88, ASSOC PROF PATH, HARVARD MED SCH, NEW ENG DEACONESS HOSP, 74-, EMER CHMN, DEPT PATH, 88- *Personal Data:* b San Francisco, Calif, Feb 26, 26. *Educ:* Univ Puget Sound, BS, 48; McGill Univ, MD, 52; Am Bd Path, dipl, 57. *Honors & Awards:* Distinguished Serv Award, Am Soc Clin Pathologists, 81, Commissioner's Medal, 88. *Prof Exp:* Intern, Michael Reese Hosp, Chicago, 52-53; resident & chief resident path, Mallory Inst Path, Boston City Hosp, 55-57; instr path, Boston Univ Med Sch, 55-57, Harvard Med Sch, 56-57 & 58-66. *Concurrent Pos:* Assoc staff pathologist, New Eng Deaconess Hosp, 57-60, staff pathologist, 61-; assoc staff pathologist, New Eng Baptist Hosp, 60-63, staff pathologist, 63-, chmn, Dept Path, 74-76 & 79-88, pres med staff, 80-81 & 82-83; consult-lectr path, US Naval Hosp, Chelsea, 62-74; assoc path, Peter Bent Brigham Hosp, Boston, 73-77; mem, Coun Anat Path, Am Soc Clin Pathologists, 74-80, chmn, 78-80; consult path, Cambridge Hosp, 75-87, Children's Hosp Med Ctr, Boston, 76-, Boston Vet Admin Hosp, 77-, West Roxbury Vet Admin Med Ctr, 81-, Waltham Hosp, 84-87; mem, Comt Anat Path, Col Am Pathologists, 78-80, Cancer Comt, 80-81 & Path Comt, Radiation Ther Oncol Group, 82-90; chief path, Brooks Hosp, Boston, 79-80; assoc staff path, Hahnemann Hosp, Brighton, 81-82; hon prof, Xi'an Med Univ, People's Repub China, 88, hon spec consult, 89; referring consult staff, Champlain Valley Physicians Hosp Med Ctr, Plattsburgh, NY, 90- *Mem:* AMA; AAAS; Am Soc Clin Pathologists; fel Col Am Pathologists; Int Acad Path; Am Asn Pathologists. *Res:* Pancreatic endocrine and exocrine tumors; pathology of diabetes mellitus; pulmonary interstitial disease; definitions of pulmonary tumors and their behavior; biliary tract tumors. *Mailing Add:* New Eng Deaconess Hosp 185 Pilgrim Rd Boston MA 02215-5399

LEGG, THOMAS HARRY, PHYSICS, RADIO ASTRONOMY. *Current Pos:* SR RES OFFICER, HERZBERG INST ASTROPHYS, NAT RES COUN CAN, 60- *Personal Data:* b Kamloops, BC, May 4, 29; m 57; c 2. *Educ:* Univ BC, BASc, 53; McGill Univ, MSc, 56, PhD(physics), 60. *Prof Exp:* Radar engr, Can Aviation Electronics Ltd, 53-54; sci officer radio physics, Defense Res Bd Can, 56-57. *Mem:* AAAS; Am Astron Soc; Can Asn Physicists; Royal Astron Soc Can; Inst Elec & Electronics Engrs; Sigma Xi. *Res:* Microwave diffraction; electronic circuitry; radio interferometry. *Mailing Add:* Herzberg Inst Astrophys Nat Res Coun Can 100 Sussex Dr Ottawa ON K1A 0R6 Can

LEGGE, NORMAN REGINALD, THERMOPLASTIC ELASTOMERS, SYNTHETIC ELASTOMERS. *Current Pos:* CONSULT POLYMER RES & DEVELOP, 79- *Personal Data:* b Edmonton, Alta, Apr 20, 19; US citizen; m 42; c 5. *Educ:* Univ Alta, BSc, 42, MSc, 43; McGill Univ, PhD(phys chem), 45. *Honors & Awards:* Charles Goodyear Medalist, Rubber Div, Am Chem Soc, 87. *Prof Exp:* Proj leader, Polysar, Sarnia, Can, 45-51; dir res & develop, Ky Synthetic Rubber Corp, 51-55; mgr, Elastomers Res, Shell Develop, 55-61; dir, Elastomers Res Lab, Rubber Div, Shell Chem Co, 61-64, mgr res & develop, 65-69, mgr res & develop, Polumer Div, 69-71, mgr, Shell Chem Co, 72-78. *Concurrent Pos:* Tech ed, 85- *Mem:* Fel AAAS; Am Chem Soc; Soc Plastic Engrs. *Res:* Elastomers, thermoplastic elastomers, polymerization systems for polydienes and polystyrenes, elastomer latices; initiating and high energy explosives, technological forecasting. *Mailing Add:* 19 Barkentine Rd Palos Verdes Peninsula CA 90275-5822

LEGGE, RAYMOND LOUIS, APPLIED ENZYMOLOGY, SOIL BIOREMEDIATION. *Current Pos:* assoc prof chem eng, 85-96, ASSOC PROF & ASSOC CHAIR CHEM ENG & GRAD STUDIES, UNIV WATERLOO, 96-, COORDR, BIOSEPARATIONS GROUP, BIOTECH RES CTR, 96- *Personal Data:* b Calgary, Alta, June 9, 54. *Educ:* Univ Calgary, BSc, 76; Univ Waterloo, PhD(biol), 83. *Honors & Awards:* Lionel Cinq Mars Award, Can Bot Asn, 82. *Prof Exp:* Lab technician, Univ Calgary, 76-77, res assoc, 77-78; jr res officer, Whiteshell Nuclear Res Est, 78-79; NATO fel, Univ Tex, Austin, 83-85. *Concurrent Pos:* Res fel, Nat Sci & Eng Res Coun Can, 85-95. *Mem:* Chem Inst Can; Can Soc Chem Eng (secy, 92-94); Am Chem Soc; Can Soc Chem; AAAS. *Res:* Protein and biomimetic engineering; purification of enzymes; use of enzymes in novel reaction media; enzyme immobilization; enzyme stability; reaction kinetics; design and analysis of multienzyme reaction systems; soil bioremediation with Phanerochaete chrysosporum; plant cell culture. *Mailing Add:* Dept Chem Eng Univ Waterloo Waterloo ON N2L 3G1 Can. *Fax:* 519-746-4979; *E-Mail:* rllegge@chemical.watstar.uwaterloo.ca

LEGGE, THOMAS NELSON, ZOOLOGY, LIMNOLOGY. *Current Pos:* from asst prof to assoc prof, 67-70, dept chmn, 85-87, PROF BIOL, EDINBORO UNIV PA, 70- *Personal Data:* b Erie, Pa, Sept 23, 36; m 60; c 2. *Educ:* Edinboro State Col, BS, 59; Miami Univ, MAT, 62; Univ Vt, PhD(zool), 69. *Prof Exp:* Instr biol, Northwestern Mich Col, 62-64. *Mem:* Am Soc Limnol & Oceanog; Int Asn Gt Lakes Res. *Res:* Physical and biological limnology, especially the distribution and ecology of calanoid copepods; ecology of small reservoirs. *Mailing Add:* Dept Biol & Health Sci Edinboro Univ Pa 219 Meadville St Edinboro PA 16444-0001

LEGGETT, ANTHONY J, THEORETICAL PHYSICS. *Current Pos:* PROF, DEPT PHYSICS, UNIV ILL, 83- *Personal Data:* b UK. *Educ:* Oxford Univ, BA, 59, BS, 61, PhD(physics), 64. *Prof Exp:* Prof, Dept Physics, Univ Sussex, UK, 78-83. *Mem:* Foreign assoc Nat Acad Sci; Am Phys Soc. *Mailing Add:* Dept Physics Univ Ill 1110 W Green St Urbana IL 61801

LEGGETT, ROBERT DEAN, METALLURGICAL ENGINEERING, NUCLEAR FUELS & MATERIALS. *Current Pos:* RETIRED. *Personal Data:* b Midvale, Ohio, Aug 2, 29; m 51, Lillian Simpson; c Dean, Mark, John, Beth (Bailey), Ben & Matt. *Educ:* Ohio State Univ, BMetE & MSc, 52; Carnegie Inst Technol, PhD(metall eng), 59. *Prof Exp:* Engr, Bettis Lab, Westinghouse Elec Corp, 52-55; res asst, Metals Res Lab, Carnegie Inst Technol, 58-59; sr engr, Hanford Labs, Gen Elec Co, 59-64, tech specialist, 64-65; res assoc irradiation effects in metals, Pac Northwest Labs, Battelle Mem Inst, 65-70 & WADCO Corp, 70-71; res assoc, Westinghouse-Hanford Co, 72-76, mgr, LMR fuel develop, 76-88, LMR Progs, 88-89. *Concurrent Pos:* Pvt consult, 89- *Mem:* Am Soc Metals; fel Am Nuclear Soc. *Res:* Basic mechanisms of irradiation behavior of materials, especially fissionable metals; corrosion of single crystals and bi crystals of stainless steel; hot water corrosion of uranium base alloys and stainless steel; irradiation behavior of nuclear fuels, materials and core components. *Mailing Add:* 2113 Harris Ave Richland WA 99352

LEGGETT, WILLIAM C, FISH & MARINE ECOLOGY, POPULATION DYNAMICS. *Current Pos:* PROF BIOL, QUEEN'S UNIV, 94-, PRIN & VCHANCELLOR, 94- *Personal Data:* b Orangeville, Ont, June 25, 39; m 64, Claire L Holman; c David S & John W. *Educ:* Waterloo Univ Col, BA, 62; Univ Waterloo, MSc, 65; McGill Univ, PhD(zool), 69. *Hon Degrees:* DSc, Univ Waterloo, 92, Laval Univ, 96; LLD, Wilfrid Laurier Univ, 94. *Honors & Awards:* Stevenson Lectr, 87; Fry Medal, Can Soc Zoologists, 90; D Webster Prof Award Merit, Am Fisheries Soc, 86, Award Excellence Fisheries Educ, 90, Oscar E Sette Award, 96; Outstanding Biologist Award, Can Coun Biol Chmn, 93. *Prof Exp:* Res scientist fisheries, Essex Marine Lab, 65-70, res assoc, 70-78; from asst prof to prof biol, McGill Univ, 70-94, chmn dept, 81-85, dean fac sci, 86-91, vprin acad, 91-94. *Concurrent Pos:* Assoc ed, J Am Fisheries Soc, 76-78 & Am J Fisheries Aquatic Sci, 80-85; mem, Comt Prof Cert, Am Fisheries Soc, 76-78; mem bd dirs, Memphremagog Conserv Inc, 76-80; mem, Grants Adv Comt, Can Nat Sportsmans Fund, 77-81; mem, Grant Selection Comt Pop Biol, Natural Sci & Eng Res Coun Can, 78-81, chmn, 81-82, mem, Grant Selection Comt Oceans, 84-86, chmn, 85-86; pres & chmn bd, Huntsman Marine Lab, 80-83, chmn bd, 86-91; pres, Group Interuniv Oceanog Res Que, 86-91; adj prof biol, McGill Univ, 94- *Mem:* Can Soc Zoologists; Am Fisheries Soc; Am Soc Limnol & Oceanog; Am Soc Naturalists. *Res:* Life history strategies in fishes; reproductive ecology of fish; environmental regulation of migration in fish; larval fish ecology; regulation of mortality in fish; lake ecosystem ecology; fish migrations and distributions; fish population dynamics; marine ecology. *Mailing Add:* Dept Biol Richardson Hall Rm 206 Queens Univ Kingston ON K7L 3N6 Can. *Fax:* 613-545-6838; *E-Mail:* wcl@post.queensu.ca

LEGLER, DAVID M, REMOTE SENSING, CLIMATE VARIABILITY. *Current Pos:* DEP DIR & RES ASSOC, FLA STATE UNIV, 92- *Personal Data:* b Louisville, Ky, Apr 14, 60; m 82. *Educ:* Fla State Univ, BS, 82, MS, 84, PhD(meteorol), 92. *Concurrent Pos:* Co-prin investr, Fla State Univ/Nat Oceanic & Atmospheric Admin, 85-94; consult, Nat Oceanic & Atmospheric Admin, 93; mem, Atlantic Ocean Climate Studies Panel, World Meteorol Orgn, 94- *Mem:* Am Geophys Union; Am Meteorol Soc; Oceanog Soc. *Res:* Remote sensing of ocean surface conditions; variability of the ocean-atmosphere system and global climate variability. *Mailing Add:* COAPS 235 E Dirac Suite 200 Johnson Bldg Fla State Univ Tallahassee FL 32306-3041. *Fax:* 850-644-4841; *E-Mail:* legler@masig.fsu.edu

LEGLER, DONALD WAYNE, IMMUNOLOGY, PHYSIOLOGY. *Current Pos:* DEAN, COL DENT, UNIV FLA, 83- *Personal Data:* b Minneapolis, Minn, Oct 2, 31; m 57; c 4. *Educ:* Univ Minn, BS, 54, DDS, 56; Univ Ala, PhD(physiol), 66. *Prof Exp:* From instr pedodont to assoc prof oral biol, Sch Dent, Univ Ala, Birmingham, 63-71,asst dean, 71-74, prof oral biol & chmn dept, 71-80, asst dean admin affairs, 74-80; assoc dean, advan educ & res, Sch Dent, Univ Minn, 80-83. *Concurrent Pos:* NIH trainee, 62-66; Swed Med Res Coun fel, 67-68. *Mem:* Am Dent Asn; fel Am Col Dent; Am Soc Microbiol. *Res:* Comparative immunology; germ free research; preventive dentistry. *Mailing Add:* 6426 SW 37th Way Gainesville FL 32608

LEGLER, JOHN MARSHALL, ZOOLOGY. *Current Pos:* from asst prof to assoc prof, 59-69, PROF BIOL, 59-, CUR HERPET, 59-, PROF ZOOL, UNIV UTAH, 69-; CUR REPTILES & AMPHIBIANS, UTAH MUS NATURAL HIST, 69- *Personal Data:* b Minneapolis, Minn, Sept 9, 30; m 52; c 3. *Educ:* Gustavus Adolphus Col, BA, 53; Univ Kans, PhD(zool), 59. *Prof Exp:* Asst human anat, Gustavus Adolphus Col, 52-53; asst zool, Univ Kans, 53-57, asst cur herpet, Mus Natural Hist, 55-59, asst instr zool, 58; res asst physiol excise lab, Univ Kans, 58-59, asst instr herpet, 59; vis prof zool, Univ New Eng, Armidale, NSW, Australia, 72-74, 76-77 & 80. *Concurrent Pos:* Var individual res grants, 59-; res assoc, Gorgas Mem Lab, Panama, 64- & Los Angeles County Mus Natural Hist, 75- *Mem:* Soc Study Evolution; Am Soc Ichthyologists & Herpetologists; fel Herpetologists League (pres, 68-70); Sigma Xi; Brit Herpet Soc. *Res:* Herpetology; the biology of chelonians, the turtles of Middle America and Australia; biosystematics; evolution; ecology and morphology. *Mailing Add:* Dept Biol Univ Utah 201 S Biol Bldg Salt Lake City UT 84112-1196

LEGLER, WARREN KARL, COMPUTER SCIENCE, ELECTRICAL ENGINEERING. *Current Pos:* SYSTS ANALYST, DIT-MCO INT, 80- *Personal Data:* b Hiawatha, Kans, Apr 28, 30; m 52; c 3. *Educ:* Univ Kans, BS, 52, PhD(elec eng), 69; Mass Inst Technol, MS, 60. *Prof Exp:* Physicist, US Naval Ord Test Sta, 52-63; instr elec eng, Med Ctr, Univ Kans, 63-68, instr comput sci, 68-70, asst prof physiol, 70-80. *Mem:* Inst Elec & Electronics Engrs; Asn Comput Mach; Sigma Xi. *Res:* Application of computers to medical research, practice and teaching. *Mailing Add:* 1630 Illinois St Lawrence KS 66044-4040

LEGNER, E FRED, ENTOMOLOGY, ECOLOGY. *Current Pos:* from asst entomologist to assoc entomologist, 62-75, ENTOMOLOGIST, 75-, ASSOC PROF ENTOM, 70-, PROF BIOL CONTROL, UNIV CALIF, RIVERSIDE, 73- *Personal Data:* b Chicago, Ill, Oct 17, 32; m 60; c 1. *Educ:* Univ Ill, Urbana, BS, 54; Utah State Univ, MS, 58; Univ Wis, PhD(entom), 61. *Prof Exp:* Asst entom, Univ Wis, 61-62. *Concurrent Pos:* Consult, Africa, Australasia, SAm, Mid-E, Micronesia, WI & Europe, 62, 63 & 65-75; USPHS grants, 64-70 & NSF, 72-74. *Mem:* Entom Soc Am; Int Orgn Biol Control; Entom Soc Can; Am Mosquito Control Asn; Sigma Xi. *Res:* Population dynamics of arthropods and their biological control; behavior of parasitic hymenoptera. *Mailing Add:* 6158 Oswego Dr Riverside CA 92506

LEGOFF, EUGENE, ORGANIC CHEMISTRY. *Current Pos:* assoc prof, 65-78, PROF ORG CHEM, MICH STATE UNIV, 78- *Personal Data:* b Passaic, NJ, Aug 18, 34; m 60; c 2. *Educ:* Rutgers Univ, BS, 56; Cornell Univ, PhD(org chem), 59. *Prof Exp:* Fel, Harvard Univ, 59-60; fel org chem, Mellon Inst, 60-65. *Mem:* Am Chem Soc. *Res:* Synthesis of pseudoaromatics, non-benzenoid aromatics, heteroannulenes organic conductors, porphyrins new synthetic methods. *Mailing Add:* Dept Chem Mich State Univ 320 Chem Bldg East Lansing MI 48824-1322

LEGRAND, DONALD GEORGE, PHYSICAL CHEMISTRY. *Current Pos:* RES CHEMIST, RES LABS, GEN ELEC CO, 59- *Personal Data:* b Springfield, Mass, Apr 3, 30; m 51; c 4. *Educ:* Boston Univ, BA, 52; Univ Mass, PhD(chem), 59. *Prof Exp:* Res chemist, Mallinckrodt Chem Works, 52; asst prof chem, Univ Mass, 58-59. *Mem:* Am Chem Soc; Am Phys Soc; Soc Rheol. *Res:* Polymer physics; surface physics; rheo-optics. *Mailing Add:* Gen Elec Res Lab PO Box 1088 Schenectady NY 12301

LEGRAND, FRANK EDWARD, GENETICS, ECOLOGY. *Current Pos:* Exten agronomist, 63-79, dir, Okla Pedigreed Seed Serv, 79-95, PROF AGRON, OKLA STATE UNIV, 74- *Personal Data:* b Mayfield, Okla, Dec 18, 26; m 49; c 5. *Educ:* Okla State Univ, BS, 59; NDak State Univ, PhD(plant breeding), 63. *Concurrent Pos:* Mem, Okla Crop Improv Asn, 95- *Mem:* Am Soc Agron. *Res:* Genetic studies of wheat in relation to the inheritance of several quantitative and qualitative characters. *Mailing Add:* RR 5 Box 164 Stillwater OK 74074

LEGRAND, HARRY E, HYDROGEOLOGY. *Current Pos:* CONSULT HYDROLOGIST, 74- *Personal Data:* b Concord, NC, May 19, 17; m 45; c 2. *Educ:* Univ NC, BS, 38. *Prof Exp:* Geol aide, US Geol Surv, 38-40, geologist, Ground Water Br, 46-49, dist geologist, 49-56, consult geologist, 56-59, res geologist, 59-60, chief radiohydrol sect, 60-62, res geologist, 62-74. *Mem:* AAAS; Geol Soc Am; Am Inst Prof Geologists; Am Geophys Union; Am Water Works Asn; Nat Water Well Asn. *Res:* Contamination and geochemistry of ground water; ground water geology; ground water in igneous and metamorphic rocks; pollution and ground waste disposal. *Mailing Add:* 331 Yadkin Dr Raleigh NC 27609

LEGROW, GARY EDWARD, ORGANIC CHEMISTRY. *Current Pos:* PRIN SCIENTIST, PCR, INC, 95- *Personal Data:* b Toronto, Ont, Mar 9, 38; m 63, Lynda Sloper; c Stephen, Lisa & Michael. *Educ:* Univ Toronto, BA, 60, MA, 62, PhD(organosilicon chem), 64. *Prof Exp:* Res assoc metall organosiloxanes, Dept Chem, Univ Sussex, 64-65; res chemist, Dow Corning Corp, 65-68, group leader organo-functional silicon chem, 68-70, group leader resins res, 73-77, assoc res scientist resins res, 77-80, assoc res scientist basic mat res, 80-83, assoc res scientist, 83-85, res scientist advan ceramics, 85-88, develop scientist, 88-95. *Concurrent Pos:* Lectr, Mich State Univ, 66-68. *Mem:* Am Chem Soc; Sigma Xi; Soc Cosmic Chemists. *Res:* Creation and development of novel silicone-organic hybrid materials for use in a wide spectrum of market segments including personal care, automotive, electronic and coatings. *Mailing Add:* 13707 SW First Lane Newberry FL 32669. *Fax:* 904-418-1509; *E-Mail:* gelegrow@concentric.net

LEGTERS, LLEWELLYN J, PREVENTIVE MEDICINE, TROPICAL PUBLIC HEALTH. *Current Pos:* PROF & CHMN, DEPT PREV MED & BIOMED, UNIFORMED SERV UNIV HEALTH SCI, BETHESDA, MD, 80- *Personal Data:* b Clymer, NY, May 23, 32; m 91; c 2. *Educ:* Univ Buffalo, BA & MD, 56; Harvard Univ, MPH, 61. *Honors & Awards:* Gorgas Medal. *Prof Exp:* Rotating intern, Akron Gen Hosp, Ohio, 56-57; surgeon, 82nd Airborne Div, US Army, 57-58, 504th Infantry, Ger, 58-59, prev med officer, 8th Infantry Div, Ger, 59-60 & John F Kennedy Ctr Mil Assistance, 63-66, chief, Walter Reed Amy Inst Res Field Epidemiol Surv Team, Vietnam, 66-68, prev med officer, US Army Training Ctr, Ft Ord, Calif, 68-70, command & gen staff col, Ft Leavenworth, Kans, 70-71, chief, Volar Eval Group, Training Ctr, Infantry & Ft Ord, 71-72, chief, Ambulatory Health Serv, Silas B Hays Army Hosp, Ft Ord, 72-74, US Army War Col, Carlisle Barracks, Pa, 74-75, chief, Health & Environ Div, Off Surg Gen, 75-77, comdr surg US Army Med Dept Activ XVIII Airborne Corps, Ft Bragg, NC, 77-78; sr med consult, Enviro Control Inc, 79-80. *Concurrent Pos:* La State Univ fel trop med & parasitol, Cent Am, 63. *Mem:* AAAS; fel Am Col Prev Med; Am Soc Trop Med & Hyg; Am Pub Health Asn; NY Acad Sci. *Res:* Epidemiology of infectious diseases, especially malaria, other tropical infectious diseases. *Mailing Add:* Uniformed Serv Univ Health Sci 4301 Jones Bridge Rd Bethesda MD 20814. *Fax:* 301-295-1933; *E-Mail:* legters@usuhsb.usuhs.mil

LEHAN, FRANK W(ELBORN), ELECTRICAL ENGINEERING. *Current Pos:* RETIRED. *Personal Data:* b Los Angeles, Calif, Jan 26, 23; m 44; c 1. *Educ:* Calif Inst Technol, BSEE, 44. *Prof Exp:* Chief, Telemetry Sect, Jet Propulsion Lab, Calif Inst Technol, 44-49, Telecommun Sect, 49-52 & electronics res, 53-54; sr staff mem, Ramo-Wooldridge Corp, 54-56, assoc dir electronics res & develop staff, Guided Missile Res Div, 56-58; exec vpres & pres, Space Gen Corp, Calif, 58-66; consult, 66-67; asst secy res & technol, Dept Transp, Washington, DC, 67-69; dir, Syst Develop Corp, 71-83. *Concurrent Pos:* Mem, Res & Develop Bd, Dept Defense, 48-52, Gov Coun Ocean Resources, 65-66, President's Health Manpower Comt, 65-67 & Naval Warfare Panel, President's Sci Adv Group, 65-; consult, 69-; chmn, Elec Intel Panel, Defense Sci Bd, 70-71. *Mem:* Nat Acad Eng; fel Inst Elec & Electronics Engrs. *Res:* Technical management. *Mailing Add:* 1696 E Valley Rd Santa Barbara CA 93108

LEHENY, ROBERT FRANCIS, APPLIED PHYSICS. *Current Pos:* PROG MGR, DEPT DEFENSE ADVAN RES PROJS AGENCY, 93- *Personal Data:* b New York, Ny, Dec 8, 38; m 62, Ann D Lynch; c Ann R & Robert. *Educ:* Univ Conn, BS, 60; Columbia Univ, MS, 63, DrEngrSc, 66. *Honors & Awards:* Lasers & Electro-Optics Soc Traveling Lectr Inst Elec & Electronics Engrs, 87-88. *Prof Exp:* Engr electronic systs, Sperry Gyroscope Co, 60-61; res asst, Columbia Univ, 62-66, asst prof, 66-67; mem tech staff semiconductor res & optical properties semiconductors, Bell Labs, Inc, 67-84; dist res mgr, High Speed Device Res Group, 84-87, Bell Commun Res, Inc, div mgr, Electronic Sci & Technol Res, 87-93. *Concurrent Pos:* Mem bd dirs, Laser Electrooptic Soc, Inst Elec & Electronics Engrs. *Mem:* AAAS; Am Phys Soc; fel Inst Elec & Electronics Engrs, 91; Sigma Xi; NY Acad Sci; Optical Soc Am. *Res:* Optical properties of semiconductors; plasma physics; electromagnetic radiation; carrier transport in semiconductor; optoelectronic device research. *Mailing Add:* 2101 Connecticut Ave NW Apt 76 Washington DC 20008-1761. *E-Mail:* rleheny@arpa.mil

LEHISTE, ILSE, SPEECH PERCEPTION, GENERAL PHONETICS. *Current Pos:* assoc prof Slavic ling, Ohio State Univ, 63-65, chmn, Dept Ling, 65-71, prof ling, 65-87, chmn ling, 85-87, EMER PROF LING, OHIO STATE UNIV, 87- *Personal Data:* b Tallinn, Estonia, Jan 31, 22. *Educ:* Univ Hamburg, Ger, PhD, 48; Univ Mich, Ann Arbor, PhD(ling), 59; Univ Lund, Sweden, PhD(philos), 82. *Hon Degrees:* Dr, Univ Essex, Eng, 77; PhD, Univ Lund, Sweden, 82, Univ Tartu, Estonia, 89. *Prof Exp:* Lectr ling, Univ Hamburg, Ger, 48-49; assoc prof, Kans Wesleyan Univ, Salina, 50-51 & Detroit Inst Technol, 51-56; res assoc phonetics, Commun Sci Lab, Univ Mich, 57-63. *Concurrent Pos:* Vis prof ling, Univ Cologne, 65, Univ Calif, Los Angeles, 66, Univ Vienna, Austria, 74 & Tokyo Univ, 80; Guggenheim fel, 69-70 & 75-76. *Mem:* Ling Soc Am (pres, 80); fel Acoust Soc Am; Int Soc Phonetic Sci; Asn Advan Baltic Studies (pres, 74-76); Mod Lang Asn; fel Am Acad Arts & Sci. *Res:* Acoustic analysis of spoken language; acoustic manifestation of syntactic structure; suprasegmental structure of various languages. *Mailing Add:* Dept Ling Ohio State Univ 1712 Neil Ave Columbus OH 43210. *E-Mail:* ilsele@ling.ohio__state.edu

LEHMAN, ALFRED BAKER, MATHEMATICS. *Current Pos:* vis prof, 65-67, prof, 67-96, EMER PROF MATH & COMPUT SCI, UNIV TORONTO, CAN, 96- *Personal Data:* b Cleveland, Ohio, Mar 21, 31. *Educ:* Ohio Univ, BS, 50; Univ Fla, PhD(math), 54. *Honors & Awards:* Delbert Ray Fulkerson Award, Am Math Soc, 91. *Prof Exp:* Instr math, Tulane Univ, 54; mem staff, Acoust Lab & Res Lab Electronics, Mass Inst Technol, 55-57; asst prof, Case Inst Technol, 57-61; vis mem, Res Ctr, Univ Wis, 61-63; res assoc, Rensselaer Polytech Inst, 63; res mathematician, Walter Reed Army Inst Res, 64-67. *Concurrent Pos:* Res assoc, Rensselaer Polytech Inst, 63. *Mem:* Math Asn Am; Soc Indust & Appl Math. *Res:* Combinatorial network theory. *Mailing Add:* Comput Sci 10 Kings College Rd Toronto ON M5S 3G3 Can. *E-Mail:* lehman@cs.toronto.edu

LEHMAN, AUGUST F(ERDINAND), HYDRODYNAMICS, FLUID MECHANICS. *Current Pos:* PRES, A F LEHMAN ASSOCS INC, 77- *Personal Data:* b Waukesha, Wis, July 10, 24; c 3. *Educ:* Agr & Mech Col, Tex, BS, 50; Pa State Univ, MS, 54. *Prof Exp:* Engr, Ord Res Lab, Pa State Univ, 51-53, group leader, 53-54, proj leader, 54-62, asst prof, 55-59, assoc prof, 59-62; head water tunnel div, Oceanics, Inc, 62-77. *Mem:* Sigma Xi. *Res:* Hydrodynamics and low speed aerodynamics; marine propulsion; flow visualization; cavitation; tip vortices; drag reduction: polymers, suction, heating, body shape; design and construction of water and wind tunnels and special instrumentation and equipment. *Mailing Add:* A F Lehman Assocs Inc PO Box 27 Centerport NY 11721-0027

LEHMAN, DENNIS DALE, CHEMICAL INSTRUMENTATION, PHYSIOLOGICAL CHEMISTRY. *Current Pos:* From asst prof to assoc prof, 68-81, PROF CHEM, LOOP COL, 81- *Personal Data:* b Youngstown, Ohio, July 14, 45; div; c 2. *Educ:* Ohio State Univ, BSc, 67; Northwestern Univ, MS, 68, PhD(chem), 73. *Concurrent Pos:* Vis scholar, Dept Chem, Northwestern Univ, 73-, vis assoc prof, 77-81, vis prof, 81- & lectr, Med Sch, 81-89. *Mem:* Am Chem Soc; Sigma Xi; AAAS. *Res:* The use of organometallic complexes as catalyst for a variety of inorganic reactions; the reaction of transition metal complexes with small molecules and structural studies on the resulting products. *Mailing Add:* 13780 Elm Lane PO Box 241 Wadsworth IL 60083

LEHMAN, DONALD RICHARD, THEORETICAL NUCLEAR PHYSICS. *Current Pos:* dept chmn, George Washington Univ, 87-93, dir, Ctr Nuclear Studies, 90-93, assoc vpres res & grad studies, 93-96, from asst prof to PROF PHYSICS, GEORGE WASHINGTON UNIV, 82-, VPRES ACAD AFFAIRS, 96- *Personal Data:* b York, Pa, Dec 13, 40; m 62, Elyse J Brauch. *Educ:* Rutgers Univ, BA, 62; Air Force Inst Technol, MS, 64; George Washington Univ, PhD(physics), 70. *Prof Exp:* Proj scientist nuclear physics, Air Force Off Sci Res, 64-68; instr physics, George Washington Univ, 69-70; Nat Acad Sci-Nat Res Coun res assoc nuclear physics, Nat Bur Standards, 70-72. *Concurrent Pos:* Guest worker, Nat Bur Stand, 72-89; vis staff mem & collabr, Los Alamos Nat Lab, 74-; co-prin investr, Energy Dept Contract/Grant, George Washington Univ, 79-86 & 96, prin investr, 86-96; vis sr scientist, Duke Univ & Triangle Univ Nuclear Lab, 93. *Mem:* Fel Am Phys Soc. *Res:* Nuclear few-body problem; photonuclear physics; intermediate energy physics; hypernuclei; scattering theory. *Mailing Add:* Acad Affairs George Washington Univ Washington DC 20052. *Fax:* 202-994-0907; *E-Mail:* lehman@gwis2.circ.gwu.edu

LEHMAN, DUANE STANLEY, INORGANIC CHEMISTRY. *Current Pos:* res mgr high impact polystyrene, 76-78, DIR, RES & DEVELOP RECRUITING & RES DEVELOP, 78- *Personal Data:* b Berne, Ind, Jan 18, 32; m 55; c 3. *Educ:* Wheaton Col, Ill, BS, 54; Ind Univ, PhD(chem), 59. *Prof Exp:* Res chemist, 58-65, proj leader, Chem Dept Res Lab, 65-67, group leader, Chem Eng Lab, lab dir, chem eng lab, Dow Chem Co, 71-76. *Mem:* Am Chem Soc; Sigma Xi. *Res:* Coordination chemistry; brine chemistry; inorganic process research; basic refractories; new product development. *Mailing Add:* 704 Linwood Dr Midland MI 48640-3474

LEHMAN, ERNEST DALE, BIOCHEMISTRY. *Current Pos:* sr res biochem, 74-78, res fel, 78-87, SR RES FEL, DEPT VIRUS & CELL BIOL RES, MERCK, SHARP & DOHME RES LABS, 87- *Personal Data:* b Woodward, Okla, Mar 2, 42; m 65; c 3. *Educ:* Northwestern State Col, Okla, BS, 65; Okla State Univ, PhD(biochem), 71. *Prof Exp:* Res assoc biochem, Okla State Univ, 71-72; NIH fel, Case Western Res Univ, 72-74. *Mem:* AAAS; Soc Complex Carbohydrates. *Res:* Biochemistry and function of glycoproteins; isolation and identification of bacterial and viral antigens. *Mailing Add:* Dept Virus & Cel Biol Res Merck & Co WP26B-1123 PO Box 4 West Point PA 19486

LEHMAN, EUGENE H, MATHEMATICAL STATISTICS. *Current Pos:* PROF MATH, CEGEP DU QUEBEC, 81- *Personal Data:* b New York, NY, Jan 26, 13; m 61; c 4. *Educ:* Yale Univ, BA, 33; Columbia Univ, MA, 37; NC State Univ, PhD(math statist), 61. *Prof Exp:* Res assoc math, Univ Alaska, 49-51; asst prof, Univ Fla, 55-57 & Univ San Diego, 57-58; consult statistician, Los Angeles, 61-64; consult biostatistician, Cedars of Lebanon Hosp, 64-66; assoc prof math, Northern Mich Univ, 66-69; prof math, Mo Southern Col, 69-70; prof statist, Univ Que, Trois-Rivieres, 70-76; prof math, Univ Nat du Rwanda, 76-78; prof statist, Concordia Univ, Montreal, 78-79. *Concurrent Pos:* Corresp abstractor, Math Rev, 60-; referee, La Rev Can de Statist; teaching Dumai, Indonesia, 83-84. *Mem:* Am Math Soc; Am Statist Asn; Asn Can-French Advan Sci; Soc Statist Can; World Coun Gifted & Talented Children. *Res:* Children in mathematics. *Mailing Add:* Four Viburnum Ave Pointe Claire PQ H9R 5A7 Can

LEHMAN, GRACE CHURCH, ZOOLOGY, ENDOCRINOLOGY. *Current Pos:* USPHS fel, Univ Mich, Ann Arbor, 67 & 68-70, univ fel, 70-71, res assoc, 71-74, RES INVESTR ZOOL, UNIV MICH, ANN ARBOR, 74- *Personal Data:* b Mt Holly, NJ, June 10, 41. *Educ:* Drew Univ, AB, 63; Ind Univ, Bloomington, PhD(zool), 67. *Mem:* Am Soc Zool. *Res:* Endocrine interactions; influence of thyroid activity on reproduction; comparative and developmental endocrinology; reproductive biology of the amphibia. *Mailing Add:* 400 Maynard Ann Arbor MI 48104

LEHMAN, GUY WALTER, THEORETICAL PHYSICS. *Current Pos:* PROF PHYSICS, UNIV KY, 70- *Personal Data:* b Walkerton, Ind, Sept 21, 23. *Educ:* Purdue Univ, BSEE, 48, MS, 50, PhD(physics), 54. *Prof Exp:* Jr engr electronics, Eastman Kodak Co, 48; asst physicist, Cornell Aeronaut Lab, 51; asst physics, Purdue Univ, 51-54; res specialist, Res Dept, Atomics Int Div, NAm Aviation, Inc, 54-62, group leader theoret physics, Sci Ctr, 63-67, mem tech staff, 67-70. *Mem:* Fel Am Phys Soc. *Res:* Solid state; mathematical physics; electronic structure; statistical mechanics; electromagnetic theory; lattice dynamics. *Mailing Add:* Dept Physics Univ Ky Lexington KY 40506

LEHMAN, HARVEY EUGENE, DEVELOPMENTAL BIOLOGY, EMBRYOLOGY. *Current Pos:* From asst prof to assoc prof, 48-59, chmn dept, 62-67, PROF ZOOL, UNIV NC, 59-, CHMN DEPT, 76- *Personal Data:* b Yuhsien, China; US citizen; m 58. *Educ:* Maryville Col, Tenn, BA, 41; Univ NC, MA, 44; Stanford Univ, PhD(embryol), 48. *Concurrent Pos:* Fel, Univ Berne, 52-53; chg exp embryol course, Bermuda Biol Sta, 60-75; vis prof zool, Univ Vienna, 76. *Mem:* AAAS; Soc Develop Biol; Am Soc Zoologists; Am Micros Soc; Am Soc Cell Biol. *Res:* Rhabdocoele parasitology; amphibian pigmentation; nuclear transplantation in Triton; hybridization in Echinoderms; tissue culture; cell migration and differentiation of the neural crest; invertebrate larvae and metamorphosis; cytochemistry of embryonic differentiation. *Mailing Add:* Dept Biol Wilson Hall Box 3280 Univ NC Chapel Hill NC 27599

LEHMAN, HUGH ROBERTS, CHEMICAL ENGINEERING, PHYSICS. *Current Pos:* RETIRED. *Personal Data:* b Ft Leavenworth, Kans, Jan 25, 21; m 45; c 3. *Educ:* The Citadel, BS, 41; Ohio State Univ, MSc, 47; Univ Calif, Berkeley, PhD(chem eng), 51. *Prof Exp:* Proj officer, Power Plant Lab, Wright Field, USAF, 45-46, Air Proving Ground, Fla, 47-48 & Armed Forces Spec Weapons Proj, 51-52; staff mem nuclear weapons, Los Alamos Sci Lab, 52-55, dep chief, Analytical Div, Air Force Spec Weapons Ctr, 55-58; br chief, Air Force Intel Ctr, 58-62; staff asst nuclear disarmament, US AEC, 62-64; staff mem nuclear weapons, Los Alamos Nat Lab, 64-91. *Concurrent Pos:* Mem, Consult Panel, Ballistics Missile Re-entry Systs, 66-68 & Defense Technol Steering Group, AEC. *Mem:* Am Nuclear Soc; Am Inst Aeronaut & Astronaut. *Res:* Employment and effects of nuclear weapons; vulnerability of targets, nuclear and conventional. *Mailing Add:* 331 Potrillo Dr White Rock NM 87544

LEHMAN, I ROBERT, BIOCHEMISTRY. *Current Pos:* from asst prof to assoc prof, 59-66, chmn dept, 74-79 & 84-86, PROF BIOCHEM, SCH MED, STANFORD UNIV, 66- *Personal Data:* b Tauroggen, Lithuania, Oct 5, 24; US citizen; m 59, Sandra L Teper; c Ellen R, Deborah & Samuel M. *Educ:* Johns Hopkins Univ, AB, 50, PhD(biochem), 54. *Hon Degrees:* MD, Univ Gothenberg, 87; DSc, Univ Paris, 92. *Honors & Awards:* Merck Award, Am Soc Biochem & Molecular Biol. *Prof Exp:* Am Cancer Soc fel, 55-57; instr microbiol, Wash Univ, 57-59. *Concurrent Pos:* Assoc ed, J Biol Chem, 71-74, 81-83, 89-; William Hume prof, Sch Med, Stanford Univ, 79. *Mem:* Nat Acad Sci; fel Am Acad Arts & Sci; Am Soc Biol Chem. *Res:* Nucleic acid metabolism; biochemistry of virus infection. *Mailing Add:* Dept Biochem Sch Med Stanford Univ Stanford CA 94305

LEHMAN, JOE JUNIOR, ORGANIC CHEMISTRY. *Current Pos:* RETIRED. *Personal Data:* b Versailles, Mo, July 1, 21; m 43; c 4. *Educ:* Bethel Col, Kans, AB, 43; Wash State Univ, MS, 47, PhD, 49. *Prof Exp:* From instr to assoc prof, Colo State Univ, 49-64, prof chem, 63-92. *Concurrent Pos:* Res fel, Midwest Res Inst, 58-59; vis prof, US Naval Acad, 61-62. *Mem:* AAAS; Am Chem Soc; Am Soc Microbiol. *Res:* Organic synthesis; modification of compounds by microorganisms; steric acceleration of hydrolytic reactions. *Mailing Add:* 906 E Elizabeth St Ft Collins CO 80524

LEHMAN, JOHN MICHAEL, EXPERIMENTAL PATHOLOGY, VIROLOGY. *Current Pos:* PROF & CHMN, DEPT MICROBIOL & IMMUNOL, ALBANY MED COL. *Personal Data:* b Abington, Pa, June 19, 42; m, Elizabeth Bowen; c Deborah & Eric. *Educ:* Philadelphia Col Pharm & Sci, BS, 64; Univ Pa, PhD(path), 70. *Prof Exp:* NIH fel, Wistar Inst Anat & Biol, 70; NIH fel, 70-71, from instr to assoc prof, 71-80, prof path, Med Sch, Univ Colo Med Ctr, Denver. *Concurrent Pos:* Vis staff mem, Los Alamos Nat Lab, 72-92; mem study sect, NIH & NSF. *Mem:* Am Soc Microbiol; Tissue Cult Asn; Am Asn Cancer Res; Am Asn Exp Path; Am Soc Cell Biol. *Res:* Tumor biology and virus transformation with oncogenic DNA viruses. *Mailing Add:* Dept Microbiol Immunol A-68 & Molecular Genetics Albany Med Col 47 New Scotland Ave Albany NY 12208-3479

LEHMAN, JOHN THEODORE, LIMNOLOGY, ECOLOGY. *Current Pos:* Asst prof limnol, 78-80, asst prof biol, 80-88, PROF BIOL, UNIV MICH, 88-, MEM, GREAT LAKES RES DIV, 80- *Personal Data:* b Taylor, Pa, Oct 13, 52; m 74, Donna Alieni; c Jeffrey & Elizabeth. *Educ:* Yale Univ, BS & MS, 74; Univ Wash, PhD(zool), 78. *Mem:* Am Soc Limnol & Oceanog (pres); Int Asn Theoret & Appl Limnol; Phycol Soc Am; Sigma Xi. *Res:* Aquatic ecology; population dynamics of phytoplankton and zooplankton; mathematical models and numerical simulations of biological and chemical processes. *Mailing Add:* Div Biol Sci Natural Sci Bldg Univ Mich Ann Arbor MI 48109

LEHMAN, MEIR M, SOFTWARE ENGINEERING, SOFTWARE DEVELOPMENT PROCESS. *Current Pos:* prof comput sci, 72-84, head dept, 79-84, EMER PROF, IMP COL, 84-, SR RES FEL, 89- *Personal Data:* b Karlsruhe, Ger, Jan 24, 25; UK citizen; m 53, Chava Robinson; c Machla L, Benjamin M, Yonathan D, Rafi D & Esti D. *Educ:* Imp Col, BSc Hons, 53, PhD(math), 57; London Univ, DSc(comput sci), 87. *Prof Exp:* Logic designer, Ferantti Ltd, 54-57; head, digital comput, Sci Dept, Israel Ministry Defense, 57-66; res staff mem & mgr, Res Div, IBM, 66-72. *Concurrent Pos:* Head dept, ICT&N, 79-84, dir proj, 91-94, prin invest project FEAST/1, 96-; chmn, dir & consult, Imp Software Technol Ltd, 82-87. *Mem:* Fel Inst Elec & Electronics Engrs; fel Brit Comput Soc; fel Asn Comput Mach; fel Royal Acad Eng; fel Inst Elec Engrs UK. *Res:* Software engineering; software development process and its support; evolution in software technology; scientific framework for software technology. *Mailing Add:* Dept Comput Imp Col 180 Queens Gate London SW7 2BZ England. *Fax:* 44-171-594-8215; *E-Mail:* mml@doc.ac.ic.uk

LEHMAN, R SHERMAN, MATHEMATICS. *Current Pos:* from asst prof to prof, 58-94, EMER PROF MATH, UNIV CALIF, BERKELEY, 94- *Personal Data:* b Ames, Iowa, Jan 25, 30; div; c Clifford, Anne, John, Helen, Andrew & Irene. *Educ:* Stanford Univ, BS, 51, MS, 52, PhD, 54. *Prof Exp:* Prob analyst, Comput Lab, Ballistic Res Labs, Aberdeen Proving Ground, 55-56; Fulbright res grant, Univ Gottingen, 56-57. *Concurrent Pos:* Consult, Rand Corp, 54-65. *Mem:* Am Math Soc; Math Asn Am; Asn Symbolic Logic. *Res:* Numerical analysis and computing; number theory. *Mailing Add:* Dept Math Univ Calif Berkeley CA 94720. *E-Mail:* lehman@math.berkeley.edu

LEHMAN, RICHARD LAWRENCE, BIOPHYSICS, ENVIRONMENTAL HEALTH. *Current Pos:* dept dir Off Ecol, 71-81, PHYS SCIENTIST, CLIMATE PREDICTION CTR, NAT WEATHER SERV, NAT OCEANIC & ATMOSPHERIC ADMIN, 81- *Personal Data:* b Portland, Ore, Nov 7, 29; m 63, Eva Simmel; c Gordon, Dale, Debra & Sandra. *Educ:* Univ Ore, BS, 51, MA, 53; Univ Calif, Berkeley, PhD(biophys), 63. *Honors & Awards:* Wellcome Trust Award, 66. *Prof Exp:* High sch instr math & sci, Calif, 53-56; physicist, Lawrence Radiation Lab, Univ Calif, 57-64; asst prof biophys & nuclear med, med ctr, Univ Calif, Los Angeles, 64-68; res physicist, lab nuclear sci, Mass Inst Technol, 68-71. *Concurrent Pos:* Vis scientist, Am Inst Biol Sci, 61-81; vis scientist, Swiss Fed Inst Technol, 63 & Cambridge Univ, 66. *Mem:* AAAS; Am Meteorol Soc; Am Geophys Union; Health Physics Soc. *Res:* Climate data applications; definition of forecast; contigent probability distributions; climate impact assessment; software systems. *Mailing Add:* Climate Prediction Ctr Nat Oceanic & Atmospheric Admin Washington DC 20233

LEHMAN, ROBERT HAROLD, PHYSIOLOGY, ECOLOGY. *Current Pos:* Asst prof biol, Longwood Col, 66-70, assoc prof bot, 70-74, asst dean, 74-79, dean, continuing studies, 79-86, ASSOC PROF BIOL, LONGWOOD COL, 74-, DEAN, GRAD SCH, 86- *Personal Data:* b Duncannon, Pa, Nov 15, 29; m 52; c 1. *Educ:* Bloomsburg State Col, BS, 60; Univ Okla, MNS, 65, PhD(physiol, ecol), 70. *Concurrent Pos:* Consult; environ waste mgt & planning. *Mem:* Sigma Xi. *Res:* Allelopathic effects of caffeoylquinic acids and scopolin on vegetational patterning; land reclamation; use of sledge as fertilizers; biochemistry. *Mailing Add:* 230 Reed Rd New Market AL 35761

LEHMAN, ROGER H, MEDICINE, OTOLARYNGOLOGY. *Current Pos:* PROF OTOLARYNGOL, MED COL WIS, 66- *Personal Data:* b Neosho, Wis, Apr 24, 21; m 57; c 3. *Educ:* Univ Wis, BA, 42, MD, 44. *Prof Exp:* Resident otolaryngol, Vet Admin Ctr, Wood, Wis, 48-51; resident ophthal, Milwaukee Co Gen Hosp, 51-52; consult, Vet Admin Ctr, Wood, 54-78. *Concurrent Pos:* Chief otolaryngol, Vet Admin Med Ctr, Milwaukee Co Hosp, Wis, 60-88, Milwaukee Children's Hosp, 71-88 & Froedtept Mem Lutheran Hosp, 80-88. *Mem:* AMA; Am Col Surg; Am Laryngol, Rhinol & Otolaryngol Soc; Soc Univ Otolaryngol; Am Acad Otolaryngol; Sigma Xi. *Mailing Add:* Vet Admin Med Ctr Milwaukee WI 53193

LEHMAN, THOMAS ALAN, CHEMICAL EDUCATION. *Current Pos:* assoc prof, 73-81, PROF CHEM, BETHEL COL, 81- *Personal Data:* b Berne, Ind, Jan 12, 39; m 61; c 2. *Educ:* Bluffton Col, BS, 61; Purdue Univ, PhD(chem), 67. *Prof Exp:* Asst prof chem, Bluffton Col, 66-69; assoc prof chem & physics, Nat Univ Zaire, 71-73. *Concurrent Pos:* Res assoc, Univ NC Chapel Hill, 69-70; vis scientist, Nat Inst Environ Health Sci, 79-80. *Mem:* Am Chem Soc; Am Soc Mass Spectrometry. *Res:* Gaseous ion/molecule reactions; ion cyclotron resonance spectrometry; author and co-author scientific publications and book. *Mailing Add:* 1824 S Lakeshore Dr Chapel Hill NC 27514

LEHMAN, WILLIAM JEFFREY, MUSCLE BIOCHEMISTRY & BIOPHYSICS, ELECTRON MICROSCOPY. *Current Pos:* from asst prof to assoc prof, 73-90, PROF PHYSIOL, DEPT PHYSIOL, BOSTON UNIV SCH MED, 90- *Personal Data:* b June 20, 45; m 82, Diana Martin; c Frank Martin & John Marshall Lisle. *Educ:* State Univ NY, Stony Brook, BS, 66; Princeton Univ, PhD(biol), 69. *Prof Exp:* Postdoctoral res fel, Biol Dept, Brandeis Univ, 69-72; higher sci officer, Zool Dept, Oxford Univ, 73. *Concurrent Pos:* Estab investr, Am Heart Asn, 82; Whitaker award, 83-84. *Mem:* Am Heart Asn; Soc Gen Physiologists; Biophys Soc; Biochem Soc. *Res:* Mechanism of regulation of muscle contraction. *Mailing Add:* Dept Physiol Boston Univ Sch Med 80 E Concord St Boston MA 02118-2394. *Fax:* 617-638-4273; *E-Mail:* lehman@med_rana.bu.edu

LEHMANN, A(LDO) SPENCER, CHEMISTRY, CHEMICAL ENGINEERING. *Current Pos:* RETIRED. *Personal Data:* b Los Angeles, Calif, Sept 23, 16; m 53, Rosalie Lowther; c Larry & Bruce. *Educ:* Stanford Univ, AB, 38; Brown Univ, PhD(chem), 41. *Honors & Awards:* Cert of Appreciation, Am Petrol Inst. *Prof Exp:* Res chemist, Brown Univ, 40-42, 43-45 & Naval Res Lab, 42-43; sr engr, Tenn Eastman Corp, Oak Ridge, Tenn, 45-46; chemist, Shell Develop Co, 46-50, supvr develop, 50-52, tech rep, 52-53, asst to pres, 53-54, mgr, Tech Dept, Wood River Refinery, Shell Oil Co, 54-58, asst mgr, NY Tech Dept, 58-62, process supt, 62-63, chief technologist, 63-64, refinery supt, Houston Refinery, 64-66, refinery mgr, Wilmington Refinery, Calif, 66-68, gen mg, Tech Depts, 68-73, gen mgr, Res Orgn & Facil, 73-76. *Concurrent Pos:* Dir, Fallbrook Pub Utilites Dist, 83-, ACWA/Joint Powers Ins Authority, 86-; bd pres, San Diego Blood Bank, 87. *Mem:* Am Petrol Inst; Am Chem Soc; Sigma Xi; Am Inst Chem Engrs. *Res:* Infrared spectroscopy; development of reaction for producing metallic potassium; chemistry of uranium; design of special equipment for uranium recovery and processing; development of processes for production of petrochemicals; petroleum process design; research laboratory design and construction. *Mailing Add:* 1050 Ridge Heights Dr Fallbrook CA 92028-3671. *E-Mail:* slehmann@alumni.stanford.org

LEHMANN, ELROY PAUL, RESOURCE MANAGEMENT, PETROLEUM GEOLOGY. *Current Pos:* PETROL CONSULT, 86- *Personal Data:* b Tigerton, Wis, June 22, 28; m 51; c 2. *Educ:* Univ Wis, BS, 50, MS, 51, PhD(geol), 55. *Prof Exp:* Asst prof geol, Wesleyan Univ, 52-59, actg chmn, 55-57; paleontologist, Mobil Oil Can, Libya, 59-60, sr paleontologist, 60-61, geol lab supvr, 61-63, staff geologist, Mobil Oil Libya Ltd, 63-65, sr staff geologist, Mobil Latin Am Inc, 65-67, sr res geologist, Mobil Res & Develop Corp, 67-69, chief geoscientist, Int Div, Mobil Oil Corp, 69-72, sr staff explorationist, 72-74, explor mgr, Mobil Oil Libya Ltd, 74-78; explor mgr new areas, Mobil Explor & Producing Serv, Inc, 78-79; pres & gen mgr, Mobil Explor Egypt, Inc, 79-83, gen mgr, Mobil Alaska Explor, 83-86. *Concurrent Pos:* Mem educ comt, Am Geol Inst, 55-57; Fulbright lectr, Karachi, 58-59. *Mem:* AAAS; fel Geol Soc Am; Am Asn Petrol Geologists; Soc Econ Paleontologists & Mineralogists; Libya Petrol Explor Soc (treas, 64, pres, 65); Sigma Xi. *Res:* Geoscience aspects of energy resource identification and evaluation. *Mailing Add:* PO Box 700367 Dallas TX 75370. *Fax:* 972-732-8942

LEHMANN, ERICH LEO, MATHEMATICAL STATISTICS. *Current Pos:* From asst prof to assoc prof math, 42-54, prof, 54-89, chmn dept, 73-76, EMER PROF STATIST, UNIV CALIF, BERKELEY, 89- *Personal Data:* b Strasbourg, France, Nov 20, 17; nat US; m 77, Juliet Popper; c Stephen, Barbara & Fia. *Educ:* Univ Calif, MA, 42, PhD(math statist), 46. *Hon Degrees:* DSc, Univ Leiden, 85 & Univ Chicago, 91. *Honors & Awards:* R A Fisher Award, 88; SS Wilks Award, 96. *Concurrent Pos:* Vis assoc prof, Columbia Univ, 50 & Stanford Univ, 51; vis lectr, Princeton Univ, 51; ed, Ann

Math Statist, 53-55; Guggenheim fel, 55, 66 & 79. *Mem:* Nat Acad Sci; Am Statist Asn; Inst Math Statist; Int Statist Inst; Am Acad Arts & Sci; hon fel Royal Statist Soc. *Res:* Theories of testing hypotheses and of estimation; nonparametric statistics. *Mailing Add:* Dept Statist Univ Calif Berkeley CA 94720

LEHMANN, GILBERT MARK, GAS DYNAMICS, HEAT TRANSFER. *Current Pos:* Dean, Col Eng, 72-79, PROF MECH ENG, VALPARAISO UNIV, 56- *Personal Data:* b Libertyville, Ill, Aug 4, 33; m 58, Marilyn A Hoffman; c Susan H & Christopher M. *Educ:* Valparaiso Univ, BS, 55; Ill Inst Technol, MS, 57; Purdue Univ, PhD(jet propulsion), 66. *Mem:* Am Soc Mech Engrs; Am Soc Eng Educ. *Res:* Internal ballistics of solid propellant rockets. *Mailing Add:* 205 Mayfield Ave Valparaiso IN 46383

LEHMANN, HEINZ EDGAR, PSYCHIATRY, PSYCHOPHARMACOLOGY. *Current Pos:* From asst prof to prof, 52-81, chmn dept, 70-74, EMER PROF PSYCHIAT, McGILL UNIV, 81- *Personal Data:* b Berlin, Ger, July 17, 11; nat Can; m 40, Annette Toyal; c Francois. *Educ:* Univ Berlin, MD. *Hon Degrees:* LLD, Univ Calgary. *Honors & Awards:* Lasker Award, Am Pub Health Asn, 57; McNeill Award, Can Psychiat Asn, 69, 70 & 74; Officer of the Order of Can, 76; Heinz Lehmann Award for Excellence in Psychiat, Que Psychiat Asn, 86. *Concurrent Pos:* Dir med educ & res, Douglas Hosp, 48-; vis prof, Univ Cincinnati, 58-; dep commr res, Off Mental Health, State NY, 81-, Heinz Lehmann res award, 90. *Mem:* Life fel Am Psychiat Asn; Can Psychiat Asn; Can Ment Health Asn; fel Am Col Neuropharmacol; fel Int Col Neuropsychopharmacol; fel Royal Soc Can. *Res:* Diagnosis and therapy of psychotic conditions; effects of drugs on mental processes. *Mailing Add:* Dept Psychiat McGill Univ 1033 Pine Ave W Montreal PQ H3A 1A1 Can. *Fax:* 514-398-4370

LEHMANN, HERMANN PETER, CLINICAL BIOCHEMISTRY. *Current Pos:* from asst prof to assoc prof, 71-82, PROF PATH, LA STATE UNIV MED CTR, NEW ORLEANS, 82- *Personal Data:* b London, Eng, June 24, 37. *Educ:* Univ Durham, BSc, 59, PhD(phys chem), 64. *Honors & Awards:* Distinguished Serv Award, Am Soc Clin Path, 87-; Outstanding Contrib Educ Award, Am Asn Clin Chem, 90. *Prof Exp:* Weizmann Fel, Weizmann Inst Sci, 65-66; Volkswagen Found fel, Max Planck Inst, Mulheim Ruhr, WGer, 66-67; res assoc, Radiation Lab, Univ Notre Dame, 67-69; NIH sr fel biochem, Univ Wash, 69-71. *Concurrent Pos:* Vis scientist, Charity Hosp La, New Orleans, 71-; consult, Vet Admin Hosp, New Orleans, 73-; clin chemist, LA State Univ, Clin Lab, New Orleans, 75-; dir, Radionuclide Lab, Med Ctr La, New Orleans, 77- *Mem:* Am Chem Soc; The Chem Soc; Am Asn Clin Chem; Brit Asn Clin Biochem; Am Soc Clin Path. *Res:* Clinical chemistry; molecular pathology. *Mailing Add:* Dept Path La State Univ Med Ctr 1901 Perdido St New Orleans LA 70112-1328

LEHMANN, JOHN R(ICHARD), COMPUTER SYSTEMS DESIGN, RESEARCH ADMINISTRATION. *Current Pos:* Asst-assoc prog dir, Eng Systs Prog, Div Eng, NSF, 63-67, prog dir, Develop Computer Uses Prog, Off Comput Activ, 67-70, prog dir, Computer Systs Design Prog, Div Computer Res, 70-86, prog dir, Computer Res Equip Prog, Div Computer Res, 82-86, prog dir, Microelectronic Systs Archit Prog, 86-87, DEP DIV DIR, MICROELECTRONIC INFO PROCESSING SYSTS DIV, NSF, 87- *Personal Data:* b Oak Park, Ill, Mar 24, 34; m 56, Barbara Lowis; c Nancy Jane & Richard Allen (deceased). *Educ:* Univ Ill, BS, 56, MS, 58, PhD(elec eng), 64. *Concurrent Pos:* Mem, Simulation Coun, 65-75. *Mem:* Inst Elec & Electronics Engrs; Am Soc Eng Educ; Inst Elec & Electronics Engrs Comput Soc; Sigma Xi. *Res:* Computer systems design; microcomputer applications; electronics. *Mailing Add:* Microelectronic Info Processing Div NSF 4201 Wilson Blvd Arlington VA 22230. *Fax:* 703-706-0610

LEHMANN, JUSTUS FRANZ, PHYSICAL MEDICINE. *Current Pos:* PROF PHYS MED & CHMN DEPT PHYS MED & REHAB, UNIV WASH, 57- *Personal Data:* b Koenigsberg, Ger, Feb 27, 21; nat US; m 43; c 3. *Educ:* Univ Frankfurt, MD, 45. *Prof Exp:* Asst physician internal med, Univ Frankfurt, 45-46; res asst, Max Planck Inst Biophys, 46-48; asst physician internal med, Univ Frankfurt, 48-51; asst prof med, Mayo Clinic, 51-55; asst prof & assoc dir dept, Ohio State Univ, 55-57. *Concurrent Pos:* Fel phys med, Mayo Clin, 51-55. *Mem:* Biophys Soc; AMA; Am Asn Electromyog & Electrodiag; Am Acad Phys Med & Rehab; Am Cong Rehab Med. *Res:* Biophysics of physical agents used in medicine; rehabilitation. *Mailing Add:* Univ Wash RJ-30 Seattle WA 98195

LEHMANN, PAUL F, MEDICAL MYCOLOGY, MYCOLOGY. *Current Pos:* from asst prof to assoc prof, 79-93, PROF MICROBIOL, MED COL OHIO, 93- *Personal Data:* b Kampala, Uganda, June, 49; m 80, Carol B Cook; c Hannah, Esther & Sophie. *Educ:* Univ Cambridge, UK, BA(Hons), 70, PhD(bot), 74; Univ Birmingham, UK, MSc, 76. *Prof Exp:* Vis scientist, Ctr Dis Control, Atlanta, Ga, 78-81; fel, Univ Cambridge, 78. *Mem:* Am Soc Microbiol; Med Mycol Soc Am; Mycol Soc Am. *Res:* Fungi causing human disease including yeasts, molds and poisonous mushrooms. *Mailing Add:* Med Col Ohio PO Box 10008 Toledo OH 43699-0008. *Fax:* 419-381-3002

LEHMANN, WILMA HELEN, VERTEBRATE MORPHOLOGY. *Current Pos:* RETIRED. *Personal Data:* b Chicago, Ill, Nov 14, 29. *Educ:* Mundelein Col, BA, 51; Northwestern Univ, MS, 54; Univ Ill, PhD(zool), 61. *Prof Exp:* Res asst allergy, Med Sch, Northwestern Univ, 54-56; asst prof zool, Pa State Univ, 61-64; asst prof natural sci, Mich State Univ, 64-67; from asst prof to prof biol, Northeastern Ill Univ, 67-91, chairperson, Dept Biol, 83-91. *Concurrent Pos:* Indexer, Evolution, 60-66; NSF instnl res grant, 63-64; vis res assoc, Argonne Nat Lab, 69-70. *Mem:* Fel AAAS; Soc Study Evolution; Am Soc Zool; Sigma Xi. *Res:* Comparative vertebrate anatomy; adaptive radiation of primates and rodents; functional mammalian anatomy; functional morphology, gross and microscopic, of bone; glaucoma. *Mailing Add:* 5859 N Kenneth Ave Chicago IL 60645

LEHMBERG, ROBERT HENRY, NON-LINEAR OPTICS, LASER-PLASMA PHYSICS. *Current Pos:* RES PHYSICIST, NAVAL RES LAB, WASHINGTON, DC, 72- *Personal Data:* b Philadelphia, Pa, Dec 4, 37; m 66, Norma Geder; c Karl Robert. *Educ:* Pa State Univ, BSc, 59; Univ Ariz, MSc, 61; Brandeis Univ, PhD(physics), 68. *Honors & Awards:* Excellence in Plasma Physics Res Award, Am Phys Soc, 93. *Prof Exp:* Res physicist, Naval Air Develop Ctr, Warminster, Pa, 66-72. *Concurrent Pos:* Chmn prog comt, Conf Lasers & Electro-Optics, 91. *Mem:* Fel Am Phys Soc; AAAS; Sigma Xi; affil Inst Elec & Electronics Engrs. *Res:* Development of optical beam smoothing techniques for laser fusion; optical design of the Naval Research Laboratory's Nike laser facility; nonlinear optics and laser-plasma interaction physics; contributed articles to professional journals; patentee in field. *Mailing Add:* 4502 Hadrian Ct Alexandria VA 22310-1420. *Fax:* 202-767-0046; *E-Mail:* lehmberg@this.nrl.navy.mil

LEHMKUHL, DENNIS MERLE, ENTOMOLOGY, ECOLOGY. *Current Pos:* From asst prof to assoc prof, 74-80, PROF BIOL, UNIV SASK, 80- *Personal Data:* b Pierre, SDak, Aug 22, 42; m 65; c 3. *Educ:* Univ Mont, BA, 64, MS, 66; Ore State Univ, PhD(entom), 69. *Concurrent Pos:* Ecol & taxon consult. *Mem:* NAm Benthological Soc; Entom Soc Can. *Res:* Taxonomy and biology of Ephemeroptera; ecology of rivers; arctic and northern aquatic insects, especially ecological adaptations and limiting factors and the resulting zoogeographical implications. *Mailing Add:* Dept Biol Univ Sask 112 Science Pl Saskatoon SK S7N 5E2 Can

LEHMKUHL, L DON, CLINICAL NEUROPHYSIOLOGY, HEAD INJURY REHABILITATION. *Current Pos:* asst prof, 76-92, ASSOC PROF, BAYLOR COL MED, 92-; DIR BRAIN INJURY RES, INST REHAB & RES, 90- *Personal Data:* b Lodgepole, Nebr, Jan 2, 30; m 53; c Pamela K, Sandra S & Linda D. *Educ:* Univ Nebr, BS, 53; Univ Iowa, MS, 58, PhD, 59. *Honors & Awards:* Lucy Blair Award, Am Phys Ther Asn, 83; Worthingham Fel, Am Phys Ther Asn, 84; McMillan lectr, Am Phys Ther Asn, 90; Outstanding Clinician Award, Nat Head Injury Found, 91. *Prof Exp:* Instr physiol, Univ Iowa, 59-60; sr instr, Case Western Res Univ, 60-66, asst prof phys ther, 60-68, assoc prof, 68-70, asst prof physiol, 66-70; asst dir, Am Med Assoc, Dept Allied Med Prof & Serv, Chicago, 70-76. *Concurrent Pos:* Mem voc rehab admin adv panel phys ther, HEW, 64-68; assoc ed, J Am Phys Ther Asn, 82-85; sci & clin ed, Head Injury Update, 86- *Mem:* Sigma Xi; Am Phys Ther Asn; AAAS; Am Physiol Soc; Int Soc Electromyographic Kinesiology; Soc Behav Kinesiology (pres, 77-81); Am Cong Rehab Med; Nat Head Injury Found. *Res:* Functional capacity of peripheral circulation by venous occlusion plethysmography; spread of excitation in cardiac muscle and pacemaker electrophysiology using cultured heart cells; physiological effects of heat and cold; neurophysiologic profile of patients with brain injury or spinal cord injury; disorders of motor control; costs and outcomes of head injury rehabilitation. *Mailing Add:* Dept Brain Injury 4007 Bellaire Suite EE Houston TX 77030-3405. *Fax:* 713-668-5210

LEHN, JEAN-MARIE PIERRE, CHEMISTRY. *Current Pos:* PROF, COL FRANCE, 79- *Personal Data:* b Rosheim, France, Sept 30, 39; m 65, Sylvie Lederer; c 2. *Educ:* Univ Strasbourg, PhD, 63. *Hon Degrees:* PhD, Univ Jerusalem, 84, Univ Autonoma, 85, Univ Gottingen, 87, Univ Bruxells, 87, Univ Herakliou, 89, Univ Bologna, 89, Charles Univ, 90, Univ Twente, 91, Univ Sheffield, 91, Univ Athens, 92, Univ Polytech Athens, 92, Polytech Univ Bucharest, 94, Ill Wesleyan Univ, 95 & Univ Montreal, 95. *Honors & Awards:* Nobel Prize Chem, 87; Bronze, Silver & Gold Medals, Ctr Nat Sci Res; Gold Medal, Pontifical Acad Sci, 81; Paracelsus Prize, Swiss Chem Soc, 82; von Humboldt Prize, 83; Karl-Ziegler Prize, 89; Bonner Chemiepreis, 93; Ettore Majorana-Erice-Sci Peace Prize, 94; Gold Medal, Soc Acad Arts, Sci Letters, 95. *Prof Exp:* Staff, Nat Ctr Sci Res, 60-66; asst prof, Univ Strasbourg, 66-69; assoc prof, Univ Louis Pasteur Strasbourg, 70, prof chem, 70-79. *Concurrent Pos:* Postdoctoral res assoc, Harvard Univ, 63-64; vis prof chem, Harvard Univ, 72 & 74, Switz, 77, Cambridge Univ, 84, Barcelona Univ, 85 & Frankfurt Univ, 85-86; Heinrich-Hertz Gast prof, Karlsruhe Univ, 89. *Mem:* Nat Acad Sci; hon mem AAAS; Royal Neth Acad; Am Philos Soc; Acad Europaea; Yougoslav Acad Arts & Sci; Indian Acad Sci; Polish Acad Sci; Royal Acad Sci Lett & Fine Arts; Korean Acad Sci & Technol; Acad Sci Ukraine; Acad Roumaine; Royal Soc. *Res:* Contributed over 470 articles to scientific publications. *Mailing Add:* 6 rue des Pontonniers Strasbourg 67000 France

LEHN, WILLIAM LEE, MATERIALS ENGINEERING, CHEMISTRY. *Current Pos:* CONSULT, 91- *Personal Data:* b Spring Valley, Ill, Mar 17, 32; m 54, Joan Schur; c Karen S, Michael J, Andrea J & Linda M. *Educ:* Univ Ill, BS, 54; Univ Rochester, PhD(chem), 58. *Honors & Awards:* Sky Lab Achievement Award, NASA, 74; R T Schwartz Eng Award, 87. *Prof Exp:* Chemist polymers, E I du Pont de Nemours, 58-60; res chemist, Air Force Mat Lab, 60-81, group leader, 61-67, tech area mgr, 67-81, mat engr coatings, 81-90. *Mem:* Am Chem Soc; Res Soc Am; Am Inst Aeronaut & Astronaut; Sigma Xi. *Res:* Materials; coatings; protective and functional coatings and materials for aircraft and spacecraft; spacecraft survivability. *Mailing Add:* 450 Deauville Dr Dayton OH 45429-5933

LEHNE, RICHARD KARL, ORGANIC CHEMISTRY. *Current Pos:* RETIRED. *Personal Data:* b Newark, NJ, Nov 18, 20; m 45; c 4. *Educ:* Muhlenberg Col, BS, 41; Yale Univ, PhD(org chem), 49. *Prof Exp:* Process develop chemist, Gen Aniline & Film Co, 49-52; from assoc dir to dir res &

LEHNER, GUYDO R, TOPOLOGY. *Current Pos:* from instr to assoc prof, 58-68, PROF MATH, UNIV MD, COLLEGE PARK, 68- *Personal Data:* b Chicago, Ill, Apr 14, 28. *Educ:* Loyola Univ, Ill, BS, 51; Univ Wis, MS, 53, PhD, 58. *Prof Exp:* Instr math, Univ Wis-Milwaukee, 57-58. *Mem:* Am Math Soc; Math Asn Am. *Res:* Abstract spaces; continua; point set topology. *Mailing Add:* Dept Math Univ Md College Park MD 20742-0001

LEHNER, PHILIP NELSON, ANIMAL BEHAVIOR, ECOLOGY. *Current Pos:* from asst prof to assoc prof, 69-83, PROF ANIMAL BEHAV, COLO STATE UNIV, 83- *Personal Data:* b NH, July 5, 40; m 67; c 2. *Educ:* Syracuse Univ, BS, 62; Cornell Univ, MS, 64; Utah State Univ, PhD(animal behav), 69. *Prof Exp:* Biologist, Bur Sport Fisheries & Wildlife, 62; res asst, Cornell Univ, 62-64 & Smithsonian Inst, 64-65; biologist, USPHS, 65. *Concurrent Pos:* NIH grant, Colo State Univ, 69-; consult, Stearns-Roger Corp, 70-80; pres, Animal Behav Assocs, Inc, 83- *Mem:* AAAS; Animal Behav Soc; Soc Exp Anal Behav; Wildlife Soc; Am Vet Soc Animal Behav. *Res:* Animal behavior, its description, analysis and the effects of environmental variables; wild and domestic species; fish and wildlife; zoology. *Mailing Add:* Dept Biol Colo State Univ Ft Collins CO 80523-0001

LEHNERT, SHIRLEY MARGARET, RADIOBIOLOGY. *Current Pos:* asst prof therapeut radiol, 74-82, assoc prof radiation oncol, 82-97, PROF RADIATION ONCOL, MCGILL UNIV, 97- *Personal Data:* b London, Eng, June 2, 34; m 61; c 2. *Educ:* Univ Nottingham, BSc, 55; Univ London, MSc, 58, PhD(biophys), 61. *Prof Exp:* Fel, Univ Rochester, 61-63; res biophysicist, Montreal Gen Hosp, 63-65; sci serv officer, Defence Bd Can, 65-67; res assoc phys biol, Sloan-Kettering Inst Cancer Res, 68-71; asst prof radiol, Radiol Res Lab, Col Physicians & Surgeons, Columbia Univ, 71-74. *Concurrent Pos:* Vis scientist, Inst Gustav Roussy, Paris, France, 85. *Mem:* AAAS; Radiation Res Soc; Am Asn Cancer Res. *Res:* Biological and biochemical effects of ionizing radiation; delivery systems for radio and chemo-sensitizing drugs. *Mailing Add:* Dept Radiation Oncol Montreal Gen Hosp 1650 Cedar Ave Montreal PQ H3Q 1A4 Can. *Fax:* 514-934-8220; *E-Mail:* mdle@musica.mcgill.ca

LEHNHOFF, TERRY FRANKLIN, MECHANICAL ENGINEERING, ENGINEERING MECHANICS. *Current Pos:* from asst prof to assoc prof mech eng, 68-77, res assoc, Rock Mech Res Ctr, 70-80, PROF MECH & AEROSPACE ENG, UNIV MO, ROLLA, 77- *Personal Data:* b St Louis, Mo, July 7, 39; m 60, Donna Hoecker; c Mark, Lori, Stephen & Hope. *Educ:* Univ Mo, Rolla, BS, 61, MS, 62; Univ Ill, Urbana, PhD(theoret & appl mech), 68. *Prof Exp:* Res engr, Caterpillar Tractor Co, 62-65. *Concurrent Pos:* Consult, Detroit Tool, 76-85, Eaton Corp, 80-82 & Rockwell Int, 81-82, CMI, 89-93 & Paul Mueller Co, 90-94; pres, Enmeco, 83-; legal consult, mech design & failure anal. *Mem:* Sigma Xi; Am Soc Mech Engrs. *Res:* Stress analysis by conventional and finite element methods; stress analysis of bolted and welded joints; solid mechanics; pressure vessel design. *Mailing Add:* Dept Mech Aerospace Eng & Eng Mech Univ Mo Rolla MO 65401

LEHOCZKY, JOHN PAUL, STATISTICS, REAL-TIME COMPUTER SYSTEMS & COMPUTATIONAL FINANCE. *Current Pos:* From asst prof to prof statist, 69-87, prof statist & math, 88-96, DEPT HEAD, CARNEGIE MELLON UNIV, 84-, THOMAS LORD PROF STATIST, 97- *Personal Data:* b Columbus, Ohio, June 29, 43; m 66, Mary L Zimmerman; c Jennifer L (Elliott) & Jessica A. *Educ:* Oberlin Col, BA, 65; Stanford Univ, MS, 67, PhD(statist), 69. *Concurrent Pos:* Assoc ed, J Real-Time Systs, Inst Elec & Electronics Engrs Trans Comput. *Mem:* Fel Inst Math Statist; fel Am Statist Asn; Inst Mgt Sci; AAAS; Inst Elec & Electronics Engrs; Int Statist Inst; Info Optimum Resource Mgt. *Res:* Applied probability theory; stochastic processes and their application to computer and communication systems; real-time computer systems; mathematical finance and space biostatistics. *Mailing Add:* Dept Statist Carnegie Mellon Univ Pittsburgh PA 15213. *Fax:* 412-268-7828; *E-Mail:* jpl@stat.cmu.edu

LEHOUX, JEAN-GUY, BIOCHEMISTRY, ENDOCRINOLOGY. *Current Pos:* from asst prof to assoc prof obstet & gynec, Sherbrooke Univ, 71-81, head clin endocrinol, 74-86, head, Dept Biochem, 80-92, PROF, DEPT BIOCHEM, OBSTET & GYNEC, SHERBROOKE UNIV, 81- *Personal Data:* b St Severin, Que, Jan 9, 39; m 63; c Nathalie, Caroline & Martine. *Educ:* Univ Montreal, BSc, 63, MSc, 67, PhD(biochem), 69. *Prof Exp:* Chief chemist, Cyanamid Can Ltd, 63-65; res asst biochem, Univ Montreal, 65-69; lectr med, 69-71. *Concurrent Pos:* Biochemist, Hosp Maisonneuve, 69-70; Med Res Coun Can fel, Fac Med, Univ Montreal, 69-70 & Dept Zool, Univ Sheffield, 70-71; Med Res Coun Que & Med Res Coun Can grant, Univ Sherbrooke, 71-74; Med Res Coun Can scholar, 74. *Mem:* Brit Soc Endocrinol; Soc Endocrinol; NY Acad Sci. *Res:* Studies on steroid hydroxylation with a special interest to aldosterone regulation. *Mailing Add:* Fac Med Dept Biochem Univ Sherbrooke Sherbrooke PQ J1H 5N4 Can. *Fax:* 819-564-5340; *E-Mail:* jilehoux@courrier.nsherb.ca

LEHOVEC, KURT, SEMI-CONDUCTING DEVICES, OPTO-ELECTRONICS. *Current Pos:* PRES, INVENTORS & INVESTORS, 67-; EMER PROF ELECTRONICS, UNIV SOUTHERN CALIF, 88- *Personal Data:* b Ledvice, Czech, June 12, 18; US citizen; m 52; c 4. *Educ:* Prague Charles Univ, BS, 38, MS, 40, PhD(physics), 41. *Prof Exp:* Head res lab, Physics Inst, Prague Univ, 42-45, res fel, 45- 46; res fel, US Signal Corps, Ft Monmouth, NJ, 47-52; dir semiconductor res & develop, Sprague Elec Co, 52-66. *Concurrent Pos:* Prof electronics, Univ Southern Calif, 71-88; adj prof, Williams, Col, 67, Univ Calif, Irvine, 80; consult, var co, 67- *Mem:* Fel Am Phys Soc; fel Inst Elec & Electronics Engrs. *Res:* Crystal structure; phase diagrams; defects; energy levels; transistors; solar cells. *Mailing Add:* Univ Southern Calif Univ Park MC 0483 Seaver Sci Ctr 522 Los Angeles CA 90089

LEHR, CARLTON G(ORNEY), ELECTRICAL ENGINEERING. *Current Pos:* RETIRED. *Personal Data:* b Boston, Mass, Sept 11, 21; m 47, Elizabeth Durkee; c Janet, Judith & Betsy. *Educ:* Mass Inst Technol, BS, 43, MS, 48. *Prof Exp:* Mem staff, Div Indust Coop, Mass Inst Technol, 46-47, asst elec eng, 47-48; sr engr, Microwave & Power Tube Div, Raytheon Co, 48-54, mem staff, Microwave Group, Res Div, 54-58, mgr, 58-64; staff engr, Smithsonian Astrophys Observ, 64-76; consult, 76-79; sr radar & optical engr, Ford Aerospace & Commun Corp, 79-86. *Concurrent Pos:* Lectr, Northeastern Univ, 63-70. *Res:* Satellite tracking; lasers; mathematics. *Mailing Add:* Five Childs Rd Lexington MA 02173-4501

LEHR, DAVID, CARDIOVASCULAR PHARMACOLOGY, MEDICINE. *Current Pos:* from instr to assoc prof pharmacol, NY Med Col, 41-54, prof & chmn, Dept Physiol & Pharmacol, 56-64, prof & chmn, Dept Pharmacol, 64-79, ASSOC PROF MED, NY MED COL, 49-, EMER PROF PHARMACOL, 80- *Personal Data:* b Sadagura, Austria, Mar 22, 10; US citizen; div; c 2. *Educ:* Univ Vienna, Austria, BA, 29, MD, 35. *Prof Exp:* Asst pharmacol, Univ Vienna, 34-48; instr, Univ Lund, 38-39; pharmacologist & res assoc, Path Dept, Newark Beth Israel Hosp, NJ, 39-42. *Concurrent Pos:* Asst vis physician, Metrop Hosp, Welfare Island, NY, 42-54, vis physician, 54-75; asst attend physician, Flower & Fifth Ave Hosps, 44-49, assoc attend physician, 49-75; vis physician, Bird S Coler Hosp, 54-75; Claud Bernard prof, Inst Exp Med & Surg, Univ Montreal, 61; mem rev comt, Health Res Coun New York, 61-65, vchmn, Panel Neurol & Psychiat Dis, 61-65; chmn ad hoc comt, Use New Therapeut Agents & Procedures Human Beings, Assoc Med Schs, NY, 67-; mem, Coun Arteriosclerosis, Am Heart Asn; co-chmn, Coun Drugs, Am Col Nutrit, 80-; consult ed, J Am Col Nutrit, 82. *Mem:* Fel AAAS; fel Am Col Physicians; fel Am Col Cardiol; Soc Exp Biol & Med; Am Soc Pharmacol & Exp Therapeut; Am Soc Arteriosclerosis; Am Soc Exp Path; Sigma Xi; NY Acad Sci; Harvey Soc; Int Soc Heart Res. *Res:* Cardiology; hypertension; arteriosclerosis; toxicity of sulfonamides; sulfonamide mixtures; chemotherapy; experimental cardiovascular necrosis; parathyroid hormone interrelations; tissue electrolytes. *Mailing Add:* 125 W 96th St New York NY 10025-6419. *Fax:* 212-666-1726

LEHR, GARY FULTON, NEW TECHNOLOGY EXPLORATION & EVALUATION. *Current Pos:* staff scientist res, Cent Res & Develop Dept, 81-84, staff specialist, Comput Consult, 84-89, TECH LEADER, PROTOTYPING GROUP, DU PONT FIBERS, E I DU PONT DE NEMOURS & CO, INC, 89- *Personal Data:* b Rockville Centre, NY, July 16, 52; m 81; c 3. *Educ:* Manhattanville Col, AB, 75; Brown Univ, PhD(chem), 81. *Prof Exp:* Res assoc, Dept Chem, Columbia Univ, 79-81. *Mem:* Am Chem Soc; AAAS. *Res:* Study of reaction mechanisms involving free radical and carbene intermediates, including radical-radical, radical-molecule photochemical, organometallic and autoxidation reactions. *Mailing Add:* 122 Chatham Pl Wilmington DE 19810

LEHR, HANNS H, PHARMACEUTICAL CHEMISTRY. *Current Pos:* RETIRED. *Personal Data:* b Sadagora, Austria, Jan 1, 08; nat US; m 34, Friederike Gross; c Judith, Ruth & Michael. *Educ:* Univ Vienna, PhD(chem), 31, MPharm, 32. *Prof Exp:* Asst org chem, Univ Vienna, 30-32; managing dir, Pharmaceut Lab, Salvatorapotheke, Vienna, 33-38; asst pharmacol, Paris, 38-40 & Fr Pub Health Serv, 40; asst biochem, Univ Aix Marseille, 40-42; asst org chem, Univ Basle, Switz, 43-46; sr res chemist, Hoffmann-La Roche, Inc, 46-66, asst to vpres chem res, 66-68, asst dir, 68-73, consult, 73-76. *Mem:* AAAS; Am Chem Soc; fel Am Inst Chemists. *Res:* Organic chemistry; biochemistry; chemotherapy; antibiotics; synthetic drugs; research administration. *Mailing Add:* 180 Walnut St Montclair NJ 07042

LEHR, JAY H, hydrology, groundwater geology, for more information see previous edition

LEHR, MARVIN HAROLD, POLYMER PHYSICS, POLYMER CHEMISTRY. *Current Pos:* Res chemist, B F Goodrich Res Ctr, 59-61, sr res chemist, 61-66, res assoc, 66-73, sr res assoc, 73-78, RES FEL CORP RES, B F GOODRICH RES & DEVELOP CTR, 78- *Personal Data:* b Brooklyn, NY, Mar 17, 33; m 56, Susan Quenk; c Mike, Ted, Steve & Bob. *Educ:* Reed Col, BA, 54; Yale Univ, MS, 55, PhD(chem), 59. *Res:* Viscoelastic-fracture behavior; polymer morphology; relation of polymer structure to properties; structure-property studies on polymer blends and composites; relationships of physical, mechanical and rheological properties to composition, microstructure and morphology of miscible and immiscible mixtures. *Mailing Add:* 1252 Briarhill Spur Akron OH 44333. *Fax:* 216-447-5249

LEHR, ROLAND E, ORGANIC CHEMISTRY. *Current Pos:* From asst prof to assoc prof chem, Univ Okla, 68-80, actg chair, 87-88, interim dean, Col Arts & Sci, 89-90, PROF CHEM, UNIV OKLA, 80-, DAVID ROSS BOYD PROF CHEM & BIOCHEM, 91- *Personal Data:* b Quincy, Ill, Nov 7, 42; m 70, Karen A Kruse; c Quincy & Amy. *Educ:* Princeton Univ, AB, 64; Harvard Univ, AM, 66, PhD(chem), 69. *Concurrent Pos:* Res grants, NASA, 68-69, Am Chem Soc, 68-70 & NIH, 77- *Mem:* Am Chem Soc; Am Asn

Cancer Res; Sigma Xi. *Res:* Chemical carcinogenesis of polycyclic aromatic hydrocarbons and their DNA adducts; neurotoxins. *Mailing Add:* Dept Chem 1516 Oakwood Dr Norman OK 73069-4445. *Fax:* 405-325-6111; *E-Mail:* relehr@voknor.edu

LEHRER, GERARD MICHAEL, NEUROLOGY. *Current Pos:* NEUROLOGIST, CHIEF GRADE, PALO ALTO VET ADMIN HEALTH CARE SYST, 94- *Personal Data:* b Vienna, Austria, May 29, 27; US citizen; m 94, Suzanne Macahilig; c 2. *Educ:* City Col New York, BS, 50; NY Univ, MD, 54. *Prof Exp:* Res asst neurol, Col Physicians & Surgeons, Columbia Univ, 53-54; asst neurol, Sch Med, Wash Univ, 58-60; intern, Mt Sinai Hosp, NY, 54-55, asst resident neurologist, 55-57, resident, 58, from asst attend neurologist to assoc attend neurologist, 60-68, assoc prof, 66-67, dir, Div Neurochem, 66-74, prof neurol, Mt Sinai Sch Med, 67-94, attend neurologist, 68-94. *Concurrent Pos:* NIH trainee, Mt Sinai Hosp, NY, 56-58; NIH spec trainee neurochem & res fel pharmacol, Sch Med, Wash Univ, 58-61; consult, Preclin Psychopharmacol Res Rev Comt, NIMH, 65-69; res collabr, Brookhaven Nat Lab, NY, 67-69; consult neurologist, Vet Admin Hosp, Bronx, NY, 67-75; sr staff neurologist, Bronx Vet Affairs Med Ctr, 76-94; attend neurologist, St Vincent Hosp, Nev, 76- *Mem:* Fel Am Acad Neurol; NY Acad Med; Int Soc Neurochem; Am Neurol Asn; Am Soc Neurochem; Asn Res Nervous & Ment Disease. *Res:* Brain maturation and metabolism; molecular mechanisms of central nervous system differentiation and disease, especially demyelination; neuroimmunology. *Mailing Add:* Neurol Palo Alto Vet Admin Health Care Syst PO Box 2575 Carmel CA 93921-2575. *Fax:* 408-624-9577; *E-Mail:* plorre@ix.netcom.com

LEHRER, HAROLD Z, RADIOLOGY. *Current Pos:* ASSOC PROF NEURORADIOL, NY MED COL, 68-; DIR DEPT RADIOL, BIRD S COLER HOSP, NY, 73- *Personal Data:* b New York, NY, Aug 22, 27. *Educ:* Columbia Univ, AB, 47; NY Univ, MD, 53; Am Bd Radiol, dipl, 60. *Prof Exp:* Am Cancer Soc fel, 58; asst adj radiologist, Beth Israel Hosp & Med Ctr, NY, 59-63; instr neuroradiol, NY Univ-Bellevue Med Ctr, 63-65; from asst to assoc prof, Sch Med, Tulane Univ, 65-67. *Concurrent Pos:* NIH spec fel neuroradiol, NY Univ-Bellevue Med Ctr, 63-65. *Mem:* AAAS; Radiol Soc NAm; Am Roentgen Ray Soc; Am Soc Neuroradiol. *Res:* Neuroradiology, especially analysis of clinical data mathematicly. *Mailing Add:* 89 River St Box M705 Hoboken NJ 07030-0705

LEHRER, HARRIS IRVING, biochemistry, immunochemistry, for more information see previous edition

LEHRER, PAUL LINDNER, PHYSICAL GEOGRAPHY. *Current Pos:* assoc prof, 66-69, PROF GEOG, UNIV NORTHERN COLO, 69- *Personal Data:* b Chicago, Ill, Feb 9, 28; m 53; c 4. *Educ:* Univ Cincinnati, BS, 49; Ohio State Univ, MA, 51; Univ Nebr, PhD(geog), 62. *Prof Exp:* Instr geog, Ohio Univ, 56-59; from instr to asst prof, Univ Wis-Milwaukee, 60-66. *Concurrent Pos:* NSF sci fac fel, Univ Witwatersrand, 64-65. *Mem:* Asn Am Geogr; Sigma Xi. *Res:* Soils and regional geography of Subsaharan Africa. *Mailing Add:* 1617 Fair Acres Dr Greeley CO 80631-5319

LEHRER, PAUL MICHAEL, RELAXATION THERAPY, PSYCHOPHYSIOLOGY. *Current Pos:* from asst prof to assoc prof, 72-86, PROF PSYCHIAT, ROBERT WOOD JOHNSON MED SCH, 86- *Personal Data:* b New York, NY, Aug 30, 41; m 65, Phyllis Alpert; c 2. *Educ:* Columbia Col, AB, 63; Harvard Univ, PhD(clin psychol), 69. *Prof Exp:* Clin instr psychol, Tufts Univ Sch Med, 68-70; asst prof psychol, Rutgers Univ, 70-72. *Concurrent Pos:* Vis prof, Univ London, 80-81. *Mem:* Am Psychol Asn; Biofeedback Soc Am; Soc Psychophys Res; Soc Behav Med; Asn Adv Behav Ther. *Res:* Psychophysiological research on the effects of relaxation therapy on psychosomatic disease; psychophysiology of asthma, headache, back pain and anxiety; nature and treatment of stage fright. *Mailing Add:* Dept Psychiat UMD R W Johnson Med Sch 675 Hoes Lane Piscataway NJ 08854-5635. *Fax:* 732-297-1413; *E-Mail:* lehrer@rwja.umdnj.edu

LEHRER, ROBERT N(ATHANIEL), INDUSTRIAL & SYSTEMS ENGINEERING. *Current Pos:* assoc dir, Sch Indust & Systs Eng, Ga Inst Technol, 63-66, prof indust eng, 63-81, dir, 66-78, EMER PROF & EMER DIR, GA INST TECHNOL, 81- *Personal Data:* b Sandusky, Ohio, Jan 17, 22; m 45, Patricia Lee Martin; c Joan E. *Educ:* Purdue Univ, BS, 45, MS, 47, PhD(indust eng), 49. *Honors & Awards:* Outstanding Indust Eng Award, Am Inst Indust Engrs, 57; Frank & Lillian Gilbreath Indust Eng Award, Inst Elec & Electronics Engrs, 87. *Prof Exp:* Asst & instr indust eng, Purdue Univ, 46-49; asst prof, Ore State Col, 49-50; assoc prof, Ga Inst Technol, 50-54, prof, 54-58, res assoc, 50-58; prof & chmn dept, Technol Inst, Northwestern Univ, Ill, 58-63; UNESCO expert, Guadalajara & Guanajuato, 62-63. *Concurrent Pos:* Consult opers res, 50-; ed-in-chief, J Indust Eng, 53-62; adv indust & systs eng sem, Japan, 59 & 62; adv indust eng, Eindhoven & Dutch Ministry Educ, 62-; Nat Acad Sci workshop panel indust & technol res, Indonesia, 71; consult ed indust eng & mgt sci ser, Reinhold Publ Corp; mem adv bd mil personnel supplies, Nat Acad Sci-Nat Res Coun; assoc & vis sr adv, Am Productivity Ctr, 78-79. *Mem:* Nat Acad Sci; Am Soc Eng Educ; fel Am Inst Indust Engrs (vpres, 60); Inst Mgt Sci; Sigma Xi; Opers Res Soc Am. *Res:* Work simplification; operations research and management science; management of improvement; author of numerous publications. *Mailing Add:* 248 Bolton Sta 765 First Dr PO Box 180 Atlanta GA 30318

LEHRER, SAMUEL BRUCE, ALLERGY, IMMUNOLOGY. *Current Pos:* from asst prof to assoc prof, 75-83, PROF MED, SCH MED, TULANE UNIV, 83- *Personal Data:* b New Britain, Conn, Apr 1, 43; m 71; c 4. *Educ:* Upsala Col, BS, 66; Temple Univ, PhD, 71. *Prof Exp:* Lab technician, Microbiol Dept, State Lab Hartford, 65; researcher, Univ Lausanne, Switz, 69; fel, Scripps Clin & Res Found, La Jolla, 71-75. *Concurrent Pos:* NIH fel, 74; Nat Inst Allergy & Infectious Dis young investr award, 78-81; Am Lung Asn grant, 78-80; consult, Food & Drug Admin, 78-80, Nat Heart Lung & Blood Inst, 83; adj assoc prof microbiol & immunol, Tulane Univ, 80-, adj prof environ health sci, 96-; res award, Cander Asn New Orleans, 81-82; scholar grant, Nat Fisheries Inst, 84-95; chmn, Stand Comt, Am Acad Allergy, Asthma & Immunol, 90-95; Exec Comt, Int Union Immunol Sci, 91, co-chmn, Allergen Stand Comt, 93- *Mem:* Am Soc Microbiol; Am Acad Allergy; Am Asn Immunologists; Am Thoracic Soc; Col Int Allergologicum; Am Acad Allergy Asthma & Immunol; Int Union Immunol Sci. *Res:* Pathogenesis of allergic diseases including: seafood allergy, immunopathogenesis of food allergy, allergenicity of transgenic crops, mold allergy, occupational allergies and effects of indoor allergens and pollutants. *Mailing Add:* Tulane Univ Sch Med 1700 Perdido St New Orleans LA 70112. *Fax:* 504-584-3686

LEHRER, SHERWIN SAMUEL, MUSCLE PROTEIN INTERACTIONS. *Current Pos:* SR STAFF SCIENTIST BIOCHEM, BOSTON BIOMED RES INST, 70- *Personal Data:* b New York, NY, Apr 2, 34; m 60, Liane Reif; c Damon & Erica. *Educ:* Univ Pittsburgh, BS, 56; Univ Calif, Berkeley, PhD(chem), 61. *Prof Exp:* Staff scientist thin magnetic films, Lincoln Lab, Mass Inst Technol, 61-62; fel biochem, Brandeis Univ, 63-66; res assoc, Retina Found, Mass, 66-70. *Concurrent Pos:* Prin assoc, Harvard Med Sch, 68- *Mem:* AAAS; NY Acad Sci; Am Soc Biol Chem; Am Chem Soc; Biophys Soc; Protein Soc. *Res:* Application of fluorescence techniques to muscle protein conformation and interactions; muscle protein interactions. *Mailing Add:* Muscle Res Lab Boston Biomed Res Inst 20 Staniford St Boston MA 02114. *E-Mail:* lehrer@bbri.harvard.edu

LEHRER, WILLIAM PETER, JR, ANIMAL SCIENCE, ANIMAL NUTRITION. *Current Pos:* RETIRED. *Personal Data:* b Brooklyn, NY, Feb 6, 16; m 45, Lois L Meister; c Sharon. *Educ:* Pa State Univ, BS, 41; Univ Idaho, MS, 46 & 54; Wash State Univ, PhD(animal nutrit, chem), 51; Blackstone Sch Law, LLB, 72, JD, 74; Pepperdine Univ, MBA, 75. *Honors & Awards:* WAP Award, Agr-Bus Award, 64. *Prof Exp:* Mgt trainee, Swift & Co, WVa, 41-42; US Army Air Corps, 42-43; mgr livestock farm, NY, 44-45; from asst prof & asst animal husbandman to prof animal husb & animal husbandman, Univ Idaho, 46-60, prof, 60; dir nutrit, Albers Milling Co, 60-62, dir nutrit & res, 62-74, dir, albers Milling Co & John W Eshelman & Sons, 74-76; dir, Milling Div, Carnation Co, 76-81. *Concurrent Pos:* Mem, Comt Animal Nutrit & Comt Dog Nutrit, Nat Acad Sci-Nat Res Coun & Tech Comt, Western Livestock Range Livestock Nutrit, USDA; mem, Nutrit Coun, Am Feed Mfrs, 62-81, chmn, 69-70; mem, Res Adv Coun, US Brewers Asn, 69-81 & Adv Coun, Calif State Polytech Univ, Pomona, 69-81. *Mem:* Fel AAAS; Am Inst Nutrit; Sigma Xi; fel Am Soc Animal Sci; Inst Food Technologists; Coun Agr Sci & Technol; Am Soc Agr Engrs; Am Registry Prof Animal Scientists. *Res:* Animal production and nutrition; reproduction and growth of beef cattle and dairy cattle, dogs, horses, sheep and swine; author of 115 scientific journal articles. *Mailing Add:* Rocking L Ranch 12180 Rimrock Rd Hayden ID 83835

LEHRMAN, GEORGE PHILIP, PHARMACY ADMINISTRATION. *Current Pos:* asst dean, Col Pharm, 75-89, EMER PROF, UNIV NMEX, 89- *Personal Data:* b New York, NY, Nov 28, 26; m 48, Natalie Mortensen; c Philip, Paul & Peter. *Educ:* Univ Conn, BS, 50, PhD, 55; Purdue Univ, MS, 52. *Prof Exp:* Asst pharm, Purdue Univ, 50-52, instr chem, 52-53; mkt analyst, Mead Johnson & Co, 55-57; res chemist, Am Cyanamid Co, 57-59; head develop, Cent Pharmacal Co, Ind, 59-61; pharmaceut develop mgr, Baxter Labs, 61-62; dir labs, Conal Pharmaceut, 62-64; vpres, Owen Labs, 64-67; assoc prof pharm, Univ Okla, 67-75. *Concurrent Pos:* Res fel, Univ Conn, 53-55. *Mem:* Am Chem Soc; Am Pharmaceut Asn; Soc Cosmetic Chemists. *Res:* Natural products; pharmaceutics. *Mailing Add:* 8431 Palo Duro NE Albuquerque NM 87111

LEHRSCH, GARY ALLEN, SOIL PHYSICS, SOIL MANAGEMENT. *Current Pos:* soil scientist, Nat Sedimentation Lab, Oxford, Miss, 86-87, SOIL SCIENTIST, SOIL & WATER MGT RES UNIT, AGR RES SERV, USDA, KIMBERLY, IDAHO, 87- *Personal Data:* b Altoona, Pa, June 16, 54; m 81, Cynthia G Williams; c Benjamin, Zachary & William. *Educ:* Pa State Univ, BS, 76, MEPC, 79, MS, 81; Miss State Univ, PhD(soil physics), 85. *Prof Exp:* Res assoc, Miss State Univ, 80-86. *Concurrent Pos:* Grad res asst, Pa State Univ, 80; affil prof soil sci, Univ Idaho, 88-; res asst prof, Utah State Univ, 88- *Mem:* Am Soc Agron; Am Soc Surface Mining & Reclamation; Soil Sci Soc Am; Soil & Water Conserv Soc. *Res:* Quantification of effects of tillage, compaction, freezing, thawing, water content, climate and time on soil aggregate stability; improvement of crop and irrigation management systems; estimation of soil interrill erodibility from properties of original soil matrix. *Mailing Add:* 642 Navajo Loop Twin Falls ID 83301

LEHTO, MARK R, HUMAN FACTORS ENGINEERING, SAFETY ENGINEERING. *Current Pos:* ASSOC PROF INDUST ENG, PURDUE UNIV, 86- *Personal Data:* b Longview, Wash, Sept 29, 56. *Educ:* Ore State Univ, BS, 78; Purdue Univ, MSIE, 80; Univ Mich, PhD(eng), 85. *Prof Exp:* Sr res engr, J M Miller, Inc, 83-86. *Concurrent Pos:* Vis asst prof indust eng, Univ Mich, 89-90; lectr, Nordic Inst Advan Training Occup Health, Turkey & Finland, 89; NSF presidential young investr award, 89; NEC fac fel, 91; vis assoc prof psychol, Univ Western Australia, 93. *Mem:* Sr mem Human Factors Soc; Indust Eng Soc. *Res:* Safety engineering; human factors; computer aided design methods that address product safety problems early in the design process; author of several books. *Mailing Add:* Sch Indust Eng Purdue Univ West Lafayette IN 47907-1968. *E-Mail:* lehto@ecn.purdue.edu

LEI, DAVID KAI YUI, NUTRITION. *Current Pos:* assoc prof, 80-88, PROF NUTRIT, UNIV ARIZ, 88- *Personal Data:* b Macau, July 30, 44; m 66, Polin Tong; c Hestia. *Educ:* Univ London, BS, 68; Univ Guelph, MS, 70; Mich State Univ, PhD(human nutrit), 73. *Prof Exp:* Res asst nutrit, Mich State Univ, 70-73; res assoc hemat, Wayne State Univ, 74-75; from asst prof to assoc prof nutrit, Miss State Univ, 75-80. *Concurrent Pos:* Grants, NIH, 77, Am Heart Asn, 81, 92 & USDA NRI, 84, 86, 89, 92 & 96; fel, Pew Nat Fac Sch Nutrit, 91. *Mem:* Am Inst Nutrit; Am Dietetic Asn; Sigma Xi; Am Heart Asn; AAAS. *Res:* Trace mineral metabolism; lipoprotein metabolism; nutrients on gene expression. *Mailing Add:* Dept Nutrit Sci Univ Ariz Tucson AZ 85721. *Fax:* 520-621-9446

LEI, KUAN-SHAUR, COMPUTER ENGINEERING. *Current Pos:* SR MEM TECH STAFF, ADVAN TECHNOL DEPT, COMPAQ COMPUT CORP, 90- *Personal Data:* b Taipei, Taiwan, Nov 25, 55; US citizen; m, Yuying Liu; c Tiffany & Timothy. *Educ:* Nat Tsung-Hua Univ, Taiwan, BS, 77; Va Tech Inst, MS, 81; Ohio State Univ, PhD(metal eng), 85. *Prof Exp:* Sr scientist, Geo-Centers Inc, 86-88; staff engr, Cortest Labs Inc, 88-90. *Mem:* Inst Elec & Electronics Engrs; Am Soc Metals Inc; Surface Mount Technol Asn. *Res:* Advanced materials and manufacturing technologies involving computer/electronics including printed circuit boards, integrated circuits, packaging, soldering flux processes. *Mailing Add:* PO Box 692000 M/S 060105 Houston TX 77269

LEI, SHAU-PING LAURA, AGRICULTURAL & FOOD CHEMISTRY. *Current Pos:* DIR PROTEIN PURIFICATION, XOMA CORP, 90- *Personal Data:* b Taipei, Taiwan, Oct 7, 53; US citizen; m 80, Hun-Chi Lin; c Victoria & Benita. *Educ:* Nat Taiwan Univ, BS, 76, MS, 80; Univ Calif, Los Angeles, PhD(molecular biol), 85. *Prof Exp:* Teaching assoc anal chem, Nat Taiwan Univ, 76-78; proj dir, Int Genetic Eng Inc, 86-89 & Trigen Inc, 89-90. *Res:* Host-vector development for recombinant DNA; gene cloning and expression in bacteria system and chimeric antibody, fab fragment; fabs and Igg purification from mammalian; yeast and bacteria systems in pilot scale. *Mailing Add:* 11452 Clarkson Rd Los Angeles CA 90064

LEIBACH, FREDRICK HARTMUT, BIOCHEMISTRY, ENDOCRINOLOGY. *Current Pos:* assoc prof endocrinol, 76-79, assoc prof biochem, 67-91, PROF CELL & MOLECULAR BIOL, MED COL GA, 79-, PROF & CHMN, BIOCHEM & MOLECULAR BIOL, 91- *Personal Data:* b Kitzingen, Ger, Sept 21, 30; US citizen; wid; c John, Maria & James. *Educ:* Southwest Mo State Col, BS, 59; Emory Univ, PhD(biochem), 64. *Prof Exp:* Nat Acad Sci-Nat Res Coun res assoc, Ames Res Ctr, NASA, 64-67. *Mem:* AAAS; Am Chem Soc; Am Soc Biol Chemists; Am Physiol Soc; Sigma Xi; Am Soc Nephrology. *Res:* Enzymes in protein and amino acid metabolism; peptidases; protein turnover; membrane transport of organic solutes; regulation of membrane transport systems by hormones and second messengers; cloning of membrane transporters from intestine, kidney and placenta. *Mailing Add:* Dept Biochem & Molecular Biol Med Col Ga Augusta GA 30912-2100. *Fax:* 706-721-6608

LEIBACHER, JOHN W, ASTROPHYSICS, RESEARCH ADMINISTRATION. *Current Pos:* dir, 88-93, ASTROPHYS, NAT SOLAR OBSERV, 82- *Personal Data:* b Chicago, Ill, May 28, 41; m 76, Lise Ouvrard. *Educ:* Harvard Univ, PhD(astron), 71. *Prof Exp:* Postdoctoral, Univ Colo, 70-72; res scientist astrophys, Laboratorie de Physique Stellaire at Planetaire, 72-75; res scientist astrophys, Lockheed Res Labs, 75-82. *Mem:* Am Astron Soc; Int Astron Union. *Res:* Solar physics; helioseismology. *Mailing Add:* Nat Solar Observ 950 N Cherry Ave Tucson AZ 85719. *Fax:* 520-325-9278

LEIBBRANDT, VERNON DEAN, ANIMAL NUTRITION. *Current Pos:* asst prof, 78-80, ASSOC PROF ANIMAL NUTRIT, UNIV WIS-MADISON, 80- *Personal Data:* b McCook, Nebr, Oct 31, 44; m 67; c 2. *Educ:* Univ Nebr, BS, 66; Iowa State Univ, PhD(animal nutrit), 72. *Prof Exp:* Asst prof animal nutrit, Univ Fla, 75-78. *Concurrent Pos:* Fel, Res Div, Cleveland Clin Found, 72-75. *Mem:* Am Soc Animal Sci. *Res:* Husbandry and nutritional aspects of swine production. *Mailing Add:* 7317 Branford Lane Madison WI 53717

LEIBEL, WAYNE STEPHAN, EVOLUTIONARY GENETICS, MOLECULAR SYSTEMATICS. *Current Pos:* ASSOC PROF BIOL, LAFAYETTE COL, 83- *Personal Data:* b Aug 5, 51; US citizen. *Educ:* Dartmouth Col, AB, 73; Yale Univ, MPhil, 75, PhD(biol), 79. *Mem:* Soc Study Evolution; Am Soc Ichthyologists & Herpetologists; Am Soc Zoologists; Sigma Xi. *Res:* Evolution at the molecular level; speciation and diversification of neotropical freshwater fishes. *Mailing Add:* Biol Dept Lafayette Col Easton PA 18042-1786

LEIBHARDT, EDWARD, SPECTROSCOPY. *Current Pos:* PRES, DIFFRACTION PROD, INC, 51- *Personal Data:* b New Rome, Wis, Oct 13, 19; m 61; c 2. *Educ:* Northwestern Univ, BA, 54, PhD(astron), 59. *Mem:* Optical Soc Am. *Res:* Developed ruling engine for producing interferometrically ruled diffraction gratings; holographic gratings. *Mailing Add:* PO Box 1030 Woodstock IL 60098

LEIBHOLZ, STEPHEN W, INFORMATION & COMMUNICATION SCIENCES. *Current Pos:* FOUNDER, CHMN & CHIEF EXEC OFFICER, TECHNOL LABS, 91- *Personal Data:* b Berlin, Ger, Jan 28, 32; US citizen; m 58; c 3. *Educ:* NY Univ, AB, 52. *Prof Exp:* Res asst & teaching fel physics, NY Univ, 52-53; tutor, Queens Col, 53-54; res assoc electronics, Adv Group Electron Devices, US Dept Defense, 54-56; prin engr, Repub Aviation Corp, 57-60; sr mem tech staff, Auerbach Corp, 60-64, prog mgr opers res & anal, 64-66, mgr syst design & anal, 66-67; pres & chief exec officer, Analytics, 67-91. *Concurrent Pos:* Mem var ad panels, Dept Defense, 70-; mem, Simulation Coun; ed, Mil Oper Res Monogra. *Mem:* Inst Elec & Electronics Engrs; Soc Indust & Appl Math; Opers Res Soc Am; Mil Oper Res Soc. *Res:* Applied mathematics and operations research in areas of information systems and military systems, especially statistical problems; systems architecture and engineering in areas of information, communications, automation control and surveillance systems for industry and government. *Mailing Add:* Technol Labs 2333 Huntington Pike Huntington Valley PA 19006

LEIBMAN, KENNETH CHARLES, BIOCHEMICAL PHARMACOLOGY. *Current Pos:* from instr to assoc prof, 56-68, PROF PHARMACOL, COL MED, UNIV FLA, 68- *Personal Data:* b New York, NY, Aug 7, 23; m 46; c 2. *Educ:* Polytech Inst Brooklyn, BS, 43; Ohio State Univ, MSc, 48; NY Univ, PhD(biochem), 53. *Prof Exp:* Org res chemist, Nat Lead Co, 43-44; asst chem, Ohio State Univ, 46-48; instr, Univ Louisville, 48-49; fel oncol, Univ Wis, 53-54, proj assoc, 54-55; specialist tracer techniques, US Tech Coop Mission, India, 55-56. *Concurrent Pos:* Ed, Drug Metab & Disposition, 72- *Mem:* AAAS; Am Soc Pharmacol & Exp Therapeut. *Res:* Drug metabolism; enzymology; toxicology. *Mailing Add:* 15413 SW 107th St Archer FL 32618

LEIBMAN, LAWRENCE FRED, ORGANIC CHEMISTRY. *Current Pos:* MEM STAFF, BASF WYANDOTTE CORP, 80- *Personal Data:* b Bronx, NY, Sept 10, 47. *Educ:* City Univ New York, PhD(chem), 76. *Prof Exp:* Fel org biochem, Columbia Univ, 75-76; chemist, Am Cyanamid Co, 76-80. *Mem:* Am Chem Soc; Sigma Xi. *Res:* Organic reaction mechanisms. *Mailing Add:* BASF Corp 36 Riverside Ave Rensselaer NY 12144-2928

LEIBO, STANLEY PAUL, CRYOBIOLOGY, EMBRYOLOGY. *Current Pos:* RES PROF, DEPT BIOMED SCI, UNIV GUELPH. *Personal Data:* b Pawtucket, RI, Apr 8, 37; m 61; c 2. *Educ:* Brown Univ, AB, 59; Univ Vt, MS, 61; Princeton Univ, MA, 62, PhD(biol), 63. *Prof Exp:* Res assoc, Oak Ridge Nat Lab, 63-64, USPHS res fel, 64-65, staff biologist, Biol Div, 65-80; vpres, Res & Develop Div, Rio Vista Int, 81-88; res assoc prof obstet/gynec, Baylor Col Med. *Concurrent Pos:* Lectr, Oak Ridge Grad Sch Biomed Sci, Univ Tenn, 69-80; mem adv bd, Am Type Cult Collection, 71-74; vis scientist health sci & technol, Mass Inst Technol, 74; mem fac, UNESCO-ICLA-ICRO Training Course & Roving Seminars on Deep Freeze Preserv Mouse Strains, Neth, 75, Denmark, Hungary & Poland, 76 & Czech, Italy & Yugoslavia, 77; mem sci staff, Inst Immunol, Basel, Switz, 77-78, vis scientist, 80, 82 & 84; adj prof, Health Sci Ctr, Univ Tex, 83-; adv mem, Colombian Ctr Fertil & Steril, 85-; adj assoc sci, SW Found Biomed Res, Tex, 86-88; bd dirs & exec comt, Hubbs-Sea World Res Inst, Calif, 86-88; adj prof biomed eng, Univ Tex, Austin, 87-; consult, UN Food & Agr Orgn, Rome, 87-; mem, Comt Basic Sci Found Med Assisted Conception, Inst Med-Nat Acad Sci, 87-88; adj res prof, Ctr Cryobiol Res, State Univ NY, Binghamton, 88-90; mem fac, Univ Wis, 88. *Mem:* Soc Study Reproduction; Soc Cryobiol (vpres, 78-80 & 83-85, pres, 85-87); Int Embryo Transfer Soc (pres, 90-91); Am Fertility Soc. *Res:* Cryobiology and physiology of mammalian spermatozoa and oocytes and embryos, erythrocytes, lymphocytes and tissue-culture cells; bovine reproduction and embryology; micromanipulation of bovine embryos; immunology and cytogenetics of bovine embryos; biology of bacteriophage; cryobiology of bacteriophage, proteins and algae. *Mailing Add:* Dept Biomed Sci Univ Guelph Bldg 165 Guelph ON N1G 2W1 Can

LEIBOLD, MATHEW ALBERT, COMMUNITY ECOLOGY, EVOLUTIONARY ECOLOGY. *Current Pos:* ASSOC PROF ECOL & EVOLUTION, UNIV CHICAGO, 91- *Personal Data:* b Seville, Spain, Sept 7, 56; US citizen. *Educ:* Univ Ariz, BS, 80, MS, 81; Mich State Univ, PhD(zool), 88. *Prof Exp:* Res assoc, Kellogg Biol Sta, Mich State Univ, 88-89, Zool Dept, Duke Univ, 89-90. *Mem:* Ecol Soc Am. *Res:* Theoretical and experimental approaches to understanding how species interactions act to regulate the evolution, abundances distributions and species diversity of organisms in natural communities, especially in ponds and lakes. *Mailing Add:* 1101 E 57th St Chicago IL 60637. *E-Mail:* mleibold@pondside.uchicago.edu

LEIBOVIC, K NICHOLAS, NEUROSCIENCES, BIOPHYSICS. *Current Pos:* RETIRED. *Personal Data:* b Plunge, Lithuania, June 14, 21; m 43, Marianne Karpf; c 3. *Educ:* Cambridge Univ, 43; London Univ, 52. *Prof Exp:* Mathematician, Dulwich Col, Eng, 46-53 & Courtaulds, 53-56; proj leader indust math, Brit Oxygen Res & Develop Co, 56-60; sr mathematician, Westinghouse Res Labs, 60-63; prin mathematician, Cornell Aeronaut Lab, 63-64; from assoc prof to prof biophys, State Univ NY, Buffalo, 64-74, asst dir, Ctr Theoret Biol, 67-68. *Concurrent Pos:* Lectr, Norwood Col, Eng, 52-53; mem math adv coun, Battersea Col Technol, 59-60; vis prof, Univ Calif, Berkeley, 69, Hadassah Med Sch, Hebrew Univ, 71 & Inst Ophthal, London, 78; prog dir, Neurosci Res Prog, Mass Inst Technol, 78-79; vis scholar, Harvard Univ, 79-80. *Mem:* AAAS; Soc Neurosci; Biophys Soc; Asn Res Vision & Ophthal. *Res:* Information processing in the nervous system; electrophysiology and psychopyhsics of vision; nervous system theory; mathematical models in biology. *Mailing Add:* 105 High Park Blvd State Univ NY Buffalo NY 14226. *Fax:* 716-446-0637; *E-Mail:* bphknl@ubvms.cc.bufflo.edu

LEIBOVICH, SIDNEY, FLUID DYNAMICS, APPLIED MATHEMATICS. *Current Pos:* from asst prof to assoc prof thermal eng, 66-78, prof, 78-88, SAMUEL B ECKERT PROF MECH & AEROSPACE ENG, CORNELL UNIV, 88- *Personal Data:* b Memphis, Tenn, Apr 2, 39;

m 62; c 2. *Educ:* Calif Inst Technol, BS, 61; Cornell Univ, PhD(theoret mech), 65. *Prof Exp:* NATO fel, London, 65-66. *Concurrent Pos:* Sr vis fel, Math Inst, Univ St Andrews, 77; assoc ed, Soc Indust & Appl Math J Appl Math, 72-75, J Appl Mech, 76-83, J Fluid Mech, 82-; adv, Mech Eng & Appl Mech, NSF, 84-85; chmn, Appl Mech Div, Am Soc Mech Engrs, 87-88; chmn, Div Fluid Dynamics, Am Phys Soc, 88-89; US Nat Comt Theoret & Appl Mech, 91-93. *Mem:* Nat Acad Eng; Soc Indust & Appl Math; fel Am Soc Mech Engrs; Am Geophys Union; fel Am Phys Soc; fel Am Acad Arts & Sci. *Res:* Fluid mechanics, particularly dynamics of vortex flows, geophysical fluid dynamics, hydrodynamic stability, and wave propagation phenomena in fluids. *Mailing Add:* 22 Smugglers Path Ithaca NY 05850

LEIBOVITZ, BRIAN, NUTRITION. *Current Pos:* ED-IN-CHIEF, J OPTIMAL NUTRIT, NUTRIT CONSULT, TWINLABS, 85- *Personal Data:* Dec 16, 51. *Educ:* Univ Wyo, PhD(zool & physiol). *Mem:* AIN; NY Acad Sci; Sigma Xi; Oxygen Soc; Am Col Nutrit. *Res:* Nutritional supplements are effective for the prevention and treatment of disease as well as the maintenance of optimal health. *Mailing Add:* 440 Clearview Pl Petaluma CA 94952. *Fax:* 707-762-7365

LEIBOWITZ, GERALD MARTIN, MATHEMATICAL ANALYSIS. *Current Pos:* ASSOC PROF MATH, UNIV CONN, 69- *Personal Data:* b New York, NY, Feb 17, 36; m 63; c 4. *Educ:* City Col New York, BS, 57; Mass Inst Technol, SM, 59, PhD(math), 63. *Prof Exp:* Instr math, Mass Inst Technol, 63; from instr to asst prof, Northwestern Univ, 63-68; assoc dir, Comt on Undergrad Prog in Math, Math Asn Am, Calif, 68-69. *Concurrent Pos:* Asst engr, Ford Instrument Co, 57. *Mem:* Am Math Soc; Math Asn Am. *Res:* Functional analysis; Banach algebras. *Mailing Add:* Dept Math Univ Conn Storrs CT 06269-3009

LEIBOWITZ, JACK RICHARD, LOW TEMPERATURE PHYSICS, SUPERCONDUCTIVITY. *Current Pos:* assoc prof physics, Cath Univ Am, 69-73, chmn, Dept Art, 82-86, assoc dean grad studies, 88-93, prof, 74-95, EMER PROF PHYSICS, CATH UNIV AM, 95- *Personal Data:* b Bridgeport, Conn, July 21, 29; m 54, 89, Ariel McQuillen; c Jane & Jon. *Educ:* NY Univ, BA, 51, MS, 55; Brown Univ, PhD(physics), 62. *Prof Exp:* Res physicist, Lincoln Labs, Mass Inst Technol, 56-61 & Westinghouse Res Lab, 61-64; asst prof physics, Univ Md, College Park, 64-69. *Concurrent Pos:* Consult, Nat Broadcasting Co, 79-93. *Mem:* Fel Am Phys Soc; Sigma Xi. *Res:* Superconductivity; ultrasonic interactions in solids; intermediate and mixed states; Fermi surfaces; electron-phonon interaction; excitation spectra of inhomogeneous superconductors; physical acoustics of solids. *Mailing Add:* Dept Physics Cath Univ Am Washington DC 20064. *Fax:* 202-319-4448; *E-Mail:* leibowitz@cua.edu

LEIBOWITZ, JULIAN LAZAR, VIROLOGY, PATHOLOGY. *Current Pos:* asst prof, 83-85, ASSOC PROF PATH, UNIV TEX, HEALTH SCI CTR, HOUSTON, 85- *Personal Data:* b New York, NY, Dec 14, 47. *Educ:* Alfred Univ, BA, 68; Albert Einstein Col Med, PhD(cell biol), 74, MD, 75. *Prof Exp:* Med scientist trainee virol, Albert Einstein Col Med, 70-74, med scientist trainee med, 74-75; path resident, Univ Calif, San Diego, 75-77, USPHS fel neuropath & virol, 77-79, asst prof, 79-83. *Mem:* AAAS; Am Soc Microbiol; Am Soc Virol. *Res:* Animal virology; virus induced demyelinating disease. *Mailing Add:* Dept Path Lab Med Tex A & M Univ Health Sci Ctr 208 Reynolds Med Bldg College Station TX 77843-1114

LEIBOWITZ, LEONARD, THERMOPHYSICAL PROPERTIES. *Current Pos:* asst chemist, Argonne Nat Lab, 58-61, assoc chemist, 61-72, chemist, 72-88, SR CHEMIST, CHEM TECHNOL DIV, ARGONNE NAT LAB, 88- *Personal Data:* b New York, NY, Feb 5, 31; m 76, Stephanie M Melkin; c Michael G, Naomi C & Zoe R. *Educ:* NY Univ, AB, 51, MS, 54, PhD(chem), 56. *Prof Exp:* Chemist, Pigments Dept, E I du Pont de Nemours & Co, 56-58. *Mem:* Am Chem Soc; Sigma Xi; AAAS. *Res:* Thermophysical properties; alloy phase diagrams; application of synchrotron radiation to materials science. *Mailing Add:* Chem Technol Div Argonne Nat Lab Argonne IL 60439. *E-Mail:* leibowitz@cmt.anl.gov

LEIBOWITZ, LEWIS PHILLIP, ADVANCED SPACE SYSTEMS, LARGE OPTICAL SYSTEMS. *Current Pos:* ADVAN SYSTS LEADER, LOCKHEED MISSLES & SPACE CO, 85- *Personal Data:* b Chicago, Ill, June 22, 42; m 67; c 3. *Educ:* Northwestern Univ, BS, 64; Univ Calif, San Diego, MS, PhD(eng sci), 69. *Honors & Awards:* New Technol Award, NASA, 76. *Prof Exp:* Mem tech staff atmospheric entry technol, Calif Inst Technol, Jet Propulsion Lab, 69-75, team leader geothermal energy, 75-77, mgr advan solar technol, 77-80; prob mgr, NASA, Dept Defense Exploratory Technol, 80-83; mgr, Technol Appl, Int Power Technol, Inc, 83-85. *Concurrent Pos:* Team leader, oil explor assessment, Jet Propulsion Lab, Calif Inst Technol, 77. *Mem:* Am Phys Soc; Sigma Xi. *Res:* Dynamic performance of distributed communication and data processing networks, system definition and performance analysis of advanced space systems for communications, space surveillance, astrophysics investigation and robotic applications; developed experiments for the testing of large antennas and deployable optical systems in space; energy systems; solar and thermal technology; developed comprehensive system/cost effectiveness model that permits trade-off of advanced technology, reliability and maintenance. *Mailing Add:* Dept M120 Bldg 158 PO Box 3504 Sunnyvale CA 94088-3504

LEIBOWITZ, MARTIN ALBERT, APPLIED MATHEMATICS, OPERATIONS RESEARCH. *Current Pos:* RETIRED. *Personal Data:* b New York, NY, Oct 15, 35. *Educ:* Columbia Univ, BA, 56; Harvard Univ, MA, 57, PhD(appl math), 61. *Prof Exp:* Staff scientist, Int Bus Mach Res Ctr, 60-63; mem tech staff, Bellcomm, Inc, Washington, DC, 63-66; assoc prof eng, State Univ NY Stony Brook, 66-73, assoc prof appl math & statist, 73-82. *Mem:* Opers Res Soc Am; Asn Comput Mach. *Res:* Random processes with application to control theory; guidance and communications; scientific programming. *Mailing Add:* 15 Charles St New York NY 10014

LEIBOWITZ, MICHAEL JONATHAN, VIROLOGY, PLASMIDS & RIBOZYMES. *Current Pos:* from asst prof to assoc prof, 82-86, PROF MOLECULAR GENETICS & MICROBIOL, ROBERT WOOD JOHNSON MED SCH, UNIV MED & DENT NJ, 86-, ACTG ASSOC DEAN, GRAD SCH BIOMED SCI, 92- *Personal Data:* b Brooklyn, NY, May 14, 45; m 66; c 2. *Educ:* Columbia Univ, AB, 66; Albert Einstein Col Med, PhD(molecular biol), 71, MD, 73. *Prof Exp:* Intern, Barnes Hosp, Wash Univ, St Louis, 74; res assoc, Nat Inst Gen Med Sci & guest worker, Lab Biochem Pharmacol, Nat Inst Arthritis, Metab & Digestive Dis, NIH, 74-76, sr staff fel, Lab Biochem Pharmacol, 76-77. *Concurrent Pos:* Dir, Core Curric Molecular & Cell Biol, Rutgers Univ & Univ Med & Dent NJ; Alexandrine & Alexander L Sinsheimer Scholar, 80-83; dir, DNA Synthesis Lab, Robert Wood Johnson Med Sch, Univ Med & Dent NJ, 86-; sci adv comt, Am Found AIDS Res, 93- *Mem:* Am Soc Cell Biol; Am Chem Soc; Genetics Soc Am; Am Soc Microbiol; Am Soc Virol; AAAS. *Res:* Molecular basis of the interaction of viruses with eukaryotic host cells, mainly in Saccharomyces cevevisiae; molecular genetics of Pneumocystis carinii; ribozymes. *Mailing Add:* Dept Molecular Genetics & Microbiol UMDNJ Robert Wood Johnson Med Sch 675 Hoes Lane Piscataway NJ 08854-5635. *Fax:* 732-235-5223; *E-Mail:* leibowitz@mbcl.rutgers.edu

LEIBOWITZ, SARAH FRYER, PSYCHOPHARMACOLOGY, NUTRITION. *Current Pos:* USPHS fel & guest investr, 68-70, asst prof, 70-78, ASSOC PROF NEUROPHARMACOL, ROCKEFELLER UNIV, 78- *Personal Data:* b White Plains, NY, May 23, 41; m 66; c 3. *Educ:* NY Univ, BA, 64, PhD(physiol psychol), 68. *Honors & Awards:* First Prize, Div Psychopharmacol, Am Psychol Asn, 69. *Concurrent Pos:* Alfred P Sloan found award, 77-79. *Mem:* AAAS; fel Am Psychol Asn; NY Acad Sci; Am Soc Pharmacol & Exp Therapeut; Soc Neurosci; Asn Res Neurol & Ment Dis; Sigma Xi; fem Am Psychol Soc; fel Acad Behav Med Res. *Res:* Study of neurochemical mechanisms in the brain which regulate behavioral and physiological responses. *Mailing Add:* Rockefeller Univ 1230 York Ave New York NY 10021-6399

LEIBSON, IRVING, CHEMICAL ENGINEERING. *Current Pos:* mgr process & environ sci develop, 75-78, VPRES & MGR RES & ENG, BECHTEL GROUP INC, 78- *Personal Data:* b Wilkes Barre, Pa, Sept 28, 26; m 50. *Educ:* Univ Fla, BChE, 45, MS, 47; Carnegie Inst Technol, 49, DSc(chem eng), 52. *Prof Exp:* Chem engr, Humble Oil & Refining Co, 52, staff engr, 57-59, supv engr, 59-61; mgr process engr, Rexall Chem Co, 61-63, develop mgr, 63-65, dir res & develop, 65-67, dir com develop, 67, gen mgr Acrylonitrile-Butadiene-Styrene Plastic Div, 67-69; vpres, Dart Indust Chem Group, 69-74, mgr com ventures & investment dept, 74-75. *Concurrent Pos:* Lectr, Univ Md; prof, Rice Univ, 58; mem, Eng Manpower Comn; assoc, Coal Indust Adv Bd, Int Energy Agency, 80- & World Coal Study, 79-80. *Mem:* Am Chem Soc; Am Inst Chem Eng; fel Am Inst Chem. *Res:* Unit operations. *Mailing Add:* 2920 SE Dunes Dr Apt 410 Stuart FL 34996-0917

LEIBSON, PAUL JOSEPH, IMMUNOLOGY. *Current Pos:* ASST PROF, DEPT IMMUNOL, MAYO CLIN, 86- *Personal Data:* b Chicago, Ill, June 15, 52; m; c 1. *Educ:* Univ Ill, Urbana, BS, 74; Univ Chicago, PhD(immunol), 79, MD, 81; Am Bd Pediat, cert, 86. *Honors & Awards:* Henry Kaplan Award, 88. *Prof Exp:* Intern & resident, Health Sci Ctr, Univ Colo, Denver, 81-84; fel, Nat Jewish Hosp & Res Ctr, Denver, 84-86. *Concurrent Pos:* Course chmn immunol, Mayo Med Sch. *Mem:* Am Asn Immunologists; Soc Leukocyte Biol. *Res:* Author of numerous publications. *Mailing Add:* Dept Immunol Mayo Clin 200 First St SW Rochester MN 55905-0001

LEIBU, HENRY J, CHEMISTRY. *Current Pos:* RETIRED. *Personal Data:* b Schlesiengrube, Ger, Apr 22, 17; c 2. *Educ:* Swiss Fed Inst Technol, ChemE, 42, ScD(chem), 45. *Prof Exp:* Instr & res assoc indust chem, Swiss Fed Inst Technol, 45-49; chemist res plant develop, Polychem Dept, E I du Pont de Nemours & Co, Inc, 49-59, sales develop, Europe, SAm & Australia, 59-66, sr res chemist Res & Develop Elastomers, 66-73, tech sales & develop, 73-85. *Concurrent Pos:* Consult, elastomers, med prod, high performance liquid chromatography. *Mem:* Am Chem Soc. *Res:* Elastomers; urethanes. *Mailing Add:* 4905 Threadneedle Rd Wilmington DE 19807-2527

LEIBY, CLARE C, JR, GRAVITATION & ELECTROMAGNETISM, BLACK-HOLES. *Current Pos:* RES PHYSICIST, ROME AIR DEVELOP CTR, 76- *Personal Data:* b Ashland, Ohio, May 4, 24; m 52; c 5. *Educ:* Mass Inst Technol, SB, 54; Univ Ill, MS, 58. *Prof Exp:* Physicist, Air Force Cambridge Res Labs, 54-56; res physicist, Univ Ill, 60-61 & Sperry Rand Res Ctr, 61-64; res physicist, Air Force Cambridge Res Labs, 64-76. *Concurrent Pos:* Consult, Leghorn Labs. *Mem:* Sigma Xi. *Res:* Gravitation theory, gravitation and its relationship to electromagnetism; extremely dense astrophysical objects, such as black holes, neutron and white dwarf stars; experimental and theoretical research in laser interactions with molecules; molecular beams; atomic clocks; neutron/white dwarf stars. *Mailing Add:* 229 Old Billerica Rd Bedford MA 01730-1275

LEIBY, ROBERT WILLIAM, ORGANIC CHEMISTRY. *Current Pos:* ASST PROF CHEM, SOUTHERN ILL UNIV, 87- *Personal Data:* b Allentown, Pa, Apr 2, 49; m 74. *Educ:* Albright Col, BS, 71; Lehigh Univ, MS, 73, PhD(org chem), 75. *Prof Exp:* Res assoc org chem, Dartmouth Col, 75-76;

med chemist, Purdue Frederick Co, 76-77; vis asst prof chem, Hampden-Sydney Col, 77-78; vis asst prof chem, Duke Univ, 78-80; mem fac, Dept Chem, Univ Wis-Whitewater, 80-85; Univ RI, 85-87. *Mem:* Am Chem Soc; Sigma Xi. *Res:* Organic mass spectroscopy; heterocyclic synthesis; synthesis of pharmaceutical agents particularly central nervous system agents and antineoplastic agents: organic rearrangements and mechanisms; development of new synthetic techniques and reagents. *Mailing Add:* 97 First St Danville PA 17821-1169

LEICH, DOUGLAS ALBERT, NUCLEAR COSMOCHEMISTRY, MASS SPECTROMETRY. *Current Pos:* dep div leader, 86-89, CHEMIST NUCLEAR CHEM, LAWRENCE LIVERMORE LAB, UNIV CALIF, 76- *Personal Data:* b Paterson, NJ, Jan 26, 47; m 72; c 1. *Educ:* Colgate Univ, BA, 68; Calif Inst Technol, PhD(physics), 74. *Prof Exp:* Asst res physicist, Univ Calif, Berkeley, 73-76. *Concurrent Pos:* Mem, Lunar & Planetary Sample Team, Lunar & Planetary Inst, 81-83. *Mem:* Meteoritical Soc; Am Phys Soc; Am Chem Soc. *Res:* Isotopic abundance variations in materials and their uses in interpreting natural and anthropagenic processes. *Mailing Add:* L-195 LLNL UCL PO Box 808 Livermore CA 94551

LEICHNER, GENE H(OWARD), electrical engineering, for more information see previous edition

LEICHNER, PETER K, dosimetry, tomography, for more information see previous edition

LEICHNETZ, GEORGE ROBERT, NEUROANATOMY. *Current Pos:* from asst prof to assoc prof, 70-85, PROF ANAT, MED COL VA, VA COMMONWEALTH UNIV, 85- *Personal Data:* b Buffalo, NY, Oct 15, 42; m 67, Athalie Archibald; c Keri, Geoffrey & Joel. *Educ:* Wheaton Col, Ill, BS, 64; Ohio State Univ, MS, 66, PhD(anat), 70. *Prof Exp:* Instr anat, Ohio State Univ, 69-70. *Concurrent Pos:* A D Williams res grant, Med Col Va, Va Commonwealth Univ, 71-72; NSF grant, 78-86 & 90-93. *Mem:* Am Asn Anatomists; Soc Neurosci; Am Sci Affil. *Res:* Comparative neuroanatomy of primates; connections from cerebral cortex and cerebellum to brainstem pre-oculomotor nuclei and their role in the control of eye movement. *Mailing Add:* Dept Anat Med Col Va PO Box 709 Va Commonwealth Univ Richmond VA 23298-0709. Fax: 804-786-9477

LEICHTER, JOSEPH, NUTRITION, FOOD SCIENCE. *Current Pos:* from asst prof to assoc prof, 69-82, PROF NUTRIT, UNIV BC, 82- *Personal Data:* b Feb 4, 32; US citizen. *Educ:* Cracow Col, Poland, BS, 56; Univ Calif, Berkeley, MS, 66, PhD(nutrit), 69. *Prof Exp:* Chemist, Pharmaceut Plant, Cracow, Poland, 56-57, Ministry Com & Indust, Haifa, Israel, 57-60 & Anresco Lab, Calif, 60-65. *Mem:* Am Inst Nutrit; Can Soc Nutrit Sci. *Res:* Folic acid metabolism; effect of protein-calorie malnutrition on carbohydrate digestion and absorption; effect of dietary lactose on intestinal lactase activity; effect of maternal alcohol consumption and cigarette smoking on growth and development of offspring. *Mailing Add:* Human Nutrit Div Sch Family & Nutrit Sci Univ BC Vancouver BC V6T 1Z4 Can. Fax: 604-822-5143

LEID, R WES, INFLAMMATION, BIOCHEMICAL MECHANISMS OF VIRAL SUPPRESSION OF ALVEOCAR MACROPHAGE FUNCTION. *Current Pos:* assoc prof, 80-85, PROF MICROBIOL & PATH, WASH STATE UNIV, 85- *Personal Data:* b Walla Walla, Wash, May 25, 45; m 66; c 2. *Educ:* Cent Wash Univ, BA, 68 & MS, 70; Mich State Univ, PhD(microbiol), 73. *Prof Exp:* Fel immunol, Harvard Med Sch, 73-76, instr med, 76-77; asst prof path, Mich State Univ, 77-80. *Concurrent Pos:* Consult, WHO, 78; reviewer, Am J Vet Res, 80-83; vis prof, Walter & Eliza Hall Inst, Melbourne, 85. *Mem:* Am Asn Immunol; Am Asn Pathologists; AAAS; Reticuloendothelial Soc; Am Soc Biochem & Molecular Biol. *Res:* Pulmonary inflammation; immediate hypersensitivity; eosinophil, neutrophil, alveolar macrophage and mast cell and basophilic function; platelet biochemistry, molecular interactions of the complement cascade. *Mailing Add:* Dept Vet Microbiol & Path Lab Molecular & Cellular Inflammation Wash State Univ Dept Animal Sci Pullman WA 99164-6320

LEIDER, HERMAN R, SOLID STATE CHEMISTRY, PHYSICAL CHEMISTRY. *Current Pos:* SCIENTIST, M H CHEW & ASSOC, INC, 92- *Personal Data:* b Detroit, Mich, Jan 14, 29; m 60, Marjorie R Johnson Von Egidy; c Karen (Fichman) & Amy. *Educ:* Wayne State Univ, BS, 51, PhD(chem), 54. *Prof Exp:* Asst, Wayne State Univ, 51-52, res assoc, 52-54; aeronaut res scientist, Solid State Physics Br, Chem Mat Sec, Nat Adv Comt Aeronaut, 54-56; chemist, Lawrence Livermore Lab, Univ Calif, 56-70, group leader, Hydrides Group, 70-76 & Chem Compatibility Group, 76-81, sect leader phys chem, 81-88, task leader, Yucca Mountain Proj, 88-91. *Concurrent Pos:* Consult, Clean Sci Inc. *Mem:* Am Phys Soc; Am Chem Soc; AAAS; Am Defense Preparedness Asn. *Res:* Alkali halides; compatibility of materials; color center; luminescence; radiation effects; hydrides; dissolution of uranium oxides. *Mailing Add:* 1091 Batavia Ave Livermore CA 94550

LEIDERMAN, P HERBERT, PSYCHIATRY. *Current Pos:* assoc prof, 63-68, PROF PSYCHIAT, MED SCH, STANFORD UNIV, 68- *Personal Data:* b Chicago, Ill, Jan 30, 24; m 47; c 4. *Educ:* Calif Inst Technol, MS, 49; Univ Chicago, MA, 49; Harvard Med Sch, MD, 53. *Prof Exp:* Asst psychol, Univ Chicago, 48-49; intern med, Beth Israel Hosp, 53-54; resident neurol, Boston City Hosp, 54-56; resident psychiat, Mass Gen Hosp, 56-57; res fel, Mass Ment Health Ctr, 57-58; assoc, Harvard Med Sch, 58-63. *Concurrent Pos:* Consult, USPHS & Nat Res Coun. *Mem:* AAAS; Am Psychosom Soc; Soc Res Child Develop; Am Acad Child Psychiat; Sigma Xi. *Res:* Child development; psychology; transcultural psychiatry; psychophysiology. *Mailing Add:* 828 Lathrop Dr Stanford CA 94305

LEIDERSDORF, CRAIG B, COASTAL ENGINEERING, ARCTIC ENGINEERING. *Personal Data:* b Mineola, NY, Mar 12, 50; m 84. *Educ:* Stanford Univ, BS, 72; Univ Calif, Berkeley, MS, 75. *Prof Exp:* Res assoc hydraul res, Univ Calif, Berkeley, 75-76; coastal engr, Swan Wooster Eng Co Ltd, 76-77 & Tetra Tech, Inc, 77-80; exec vpres coastal eng, Tekmarine, Inc, 80-86. *Concurrent Pos:* Guest lectr, Univ Calif, Berkeley, 82, 84, 85, Univ Tokyo, 83. *Mem:* Am Soc Civil Engrs; Asn Environ Prof; Am Shore & Beach Preserv Asn; Permanent Int Asn Navig Cong. *Res:* Coastal engineering and coastal oceanography, including field data acquisition, assessment of coastal stability and design of slope protection; arctic engineering relating to offshore structures and sea ice. *Mailing Add:* Coastal Frontiers Corp 9420 Topanga Canyon Blvd Suite 101 Chatsworth CA 91311-5759

LEIDHEISER, HENRY, JR, PHYSICAL CHEMISTRY. *Current Pos:* RETIRED. *Personal Data:* b Union City, NJ, Apr 18, 20; m 44, Virginia Townsend; c Margaret F (LeBaron) & Henry III. *Educ:* Univ Va, BS, 41, MS, 43, PhD(phys chem), 46. *Honors & Awards:* Award, Oak Ridge Inst Nuclear Studies, 48; J Shelton Horsley Res Prize, Va Acad Sci, 49; Young Auth Prize, Electrochem Soc; Silver Medal, Am Electroplaters' Soc, 78; Arch T Colwell Award, Soc Automotive Engrs, 78; Whitney Award, Nat Asn Corrosion Engrs, 83; Humboldt Award, 85; Silver Medal, SAfrican Corrosion Inst, 86; Electrodeposition Div Res Award, Electrochem Soc, 87; Mattiello Award, Fedn Socs Coatings Technol, 90; Uhlig Award, Electrochem Soc, 91. *Prof Exp:* Res worker, Nat Adv Comt Aeronaut Proj, Univ Va, 43-45, res assoc, Cobb Chem Lab, 46-49; proj dir, Va Inst Sci Res, 49-52, mgr lab, 52-58, dir res, Lab, 58-60, dir res, Inst, 60-68; prof chem & dir, Zettlemoyer Ctr Surface Studies, Lehigh Univ, 68-83; chair prof, Alcoa, 83-90, dept chmn, 88-89. *Concurrent Pos:* Mem adv comt, Oak Ridge Nat Lab; chmn, Gordon Conf Corrosion, 64; NATO sr scientist fel, Cambridge Univ, 69; consult, Marshall Space Flight Ctr, NASA, 71-; Von Humboldt Award, 85-86. *Mem:* Am Chem Soc; Electrochem Soc; Nat Asn Corrosion Engrs; fel AAAS. *Res:* Corrosion; surface science; electrodeposition; Mossbauer spectroscopy; polymer coatings; long-term food storage; paint adherence. *Mailing Add:* 822 Carnoustie Dr Venice FL 34293

LEIDY, BLAINE I(RVIN), MECHANICAL ENGINEERING. *Current Pos:* RETIRED. *Personal Data:* b Conemaugh, Pa, Aug 15, 23; m 57, Arlene Shevel; c Bruce K. *Educ:* Univ Pittsburgh, BS, 51, MS, 57, PhD(mech eng), 62. *Prof Exp:* From instr to asst prof, Univ Pittsburgh, 51-62, assoc prof mech eng, 62-90. *Concurrent Pos:* Consult, Westinghouse Elec Corp, 54-57 & 69-73. *Mem:* Am Soc Eng Educ; Am Soc Mech Engrs. *Res:* Heat transfer; fluid mechanics; thermodynamics; energy conservation in small industries under federally supported grant. *Mailing Add:* 440 Pacific Ave Pittsburgh PA 15221

LEIDY, ROSS BENNETT, AGRICULTURAL & FOOD CHEMISTRY. *Current Pos:* sr res scientist, 74-92, assoc prof, Dept Toxicol, 90-95, DIR, PESTICIDE RESIDUE RES LAB, NC STATE UNIV, 92-, PROF, 95- *Personal Data:* b Newark, Ohio, June 1, 39; m 71, Nancy Antoine; c Marsha & Karl. *Educ:* Tex A&M Univ, BS, 63, MS, 66; Auburn Univ, PhD(biochem), 72. *Prof Exp:* Res asst radiation biol, Radiation Biol Lab, Tex A&M Univ, 65-66; instr & lab supvr, Biol Br, Microbiol Lab, US Army Chem Ctr & Sch, Ft McClellan, Ala, 66-68; supvr pesticide residues, Lab Div, NC Dept Human Resources, 73-74. *Concurrent Pos:* NIH res assoc, Dept Animal Sci, NC State Univ, 72-73, assoc mem, Dept Entom, 96-; consult, pesticide residues in air, soils & surfaces in home & working environ. *Mem:* Sigma Xi; NY Acad Sci; Am Chem Soc. *Res:* Methodology and analyses of pesticide residues on plant products, soil, water, and indoor air related to the laboratory's research projects. *Mailing Add:* Pesticide Residue Res Lab 3709 Hillsborough St NC State Univ Raleigh NC 27607. Fax: 919-515-5462; E-Mail: ross_leidy@ncsu.edu

LEIER, CARL V, MEDICAL DEVICES DIAGNOSTICS, MEDICAL PHYSICS. *Current Pos:* Intern, 69-70, instr med, 71-73, chief instr, 73-74, clin instr, Div Cardiol, 74-76, from asst prof to assoc prof, 76-84, PROF MED & PHARMACOL, OHIO STATE UNIV COL MED, 84-, DIR, DIV CARDIOL, 86- *Personal Data:* b Bismarck, NDak, Oct 20, 44; m 70; c 3. *Educ:* Creighton Univ, BS, 65; Creighton Univ Col Med, MD, 69; Am Bd Internal Med, cert & dipl, 73; cardiovasc subspecialty, Am Bd Internal Med, cert, 78. *Concurrent Pos:* Mem, Internship Selection Comt, Dept Med, Ohio State Univ Col Med, 73-74, hosp procedures; comt, Ohio State Univ Hosps, 73-74, pharmacol & therapeut comt, 76-80; res comt, Cent Ohio Heart Chapter, Am Heart Asn, 77-84, mem, bd trustees, 79-; fac mem, grad sch, Ohio State Univ Col Med, 80-, dir res, Div Cardiol, 80-83, James W Overstreet prof med, 83- *Mem:* Am Col Physicians; fel Am Col Clin Pharmacol; Am Fed Clin Res; Am Col Cardiol; AAAS; Am Soc Clin Invest; Int Soc Heart Res. *Res:* Pharmacology. *Mailing Add:* Div Cardiol Col Med Ohio State Univ Hosp Rm 669 1654 Upham Dr Columbus OH 43210

LEIES, GERARD M, NUCLEAR WEAPON PHENOMENOLOGY. *Current Pos:* RETIRED. *Personal Data:* b Chicago, Ill, Aug 19, 18. *Educ:* Loyola Univ, Ill, BS, 40; Univ Calif, MA, 53; Georgetown Univ, PhD(physics), 62. *Prof Exp:* Asst tech dir, Air Force Tech Appln Ctr, 62-73, command tech dir, 73-88. *Concurrent Pos:* Consult. *Mem:* Am Phys Soc; Am Geophys Union. *Res:* Nuclear weapon test detection. *Mailing Add:* 23427 Melmore Pl Middleburg VA 20117

LEIF, ROBERT CARY, IMMUNOHEMATOLOGY, BIOMEDICAL ENGINEERING. *Current Pos:* VPRES, ADA-MED, 93- & NEWPORT INSTRUMENTS, 93- *Personal Data:* b New York, NY, Feb 27, 38; m 63; c 2. *Educ:* Univ Chicago, BS, 59; Calif Inst Technol, PhD(chem), 64. *Prof Exp:* Fel, Univ Calif, Los Angeles, 64-66; res assoc microbiol, Sch Med, Univ

Southern Calif, 66-67; asst prof chem & biochem, Fla State Univ, 67-71; assoc scientist, Papanicolaou Cancer Res Inst, 71-72, sr scientist, 72-81; corp fel, mgr adv concepts, Coulter Electronics, 81-93. *Concurrent Pos:* Consult, Int Equip Corp, 65-73, Xerox Corp, 66-67, Damon Eng, 69-73, Solid State Radiation, Calif, 67-73, Coulter Electronics, 75- & Photometrics, 75-; res scientist, Dept Microbiol, Univ Miami, 71-72, adj asst prof microbiol, 73-76 & adj asst prof biomed eng, 74-76, assoc prof microbiol & biomed eng, 76-, assoc prof oncol, 80- *Mem:* AAAS; Sigma Xi; Biomed Eng Soc; Am Chem Soc; Am Soc Cytol; sr mem Inst Elec & Electronics Engrs. *Res:* Cellular differentiation; cytology automation; clinical chemistry instrumentation; cytology specimen preparation; computer based instrumentation; cytophysical and histochemical techniques to separate, purify and analyze heterogeneous cell populations; identification of biological activities with cell morphology. *Mailing Add:* 5648 Toyon Rd San Diego CA 92115-1022. *E-Mail:* 76137.2164@compuserve.com

LEIFER, CALVIN, experimental pathology, electron microscopy, for more information see previous edition

LEIFER, HERBERT NORMAN, SOLID STATE PHYSICS. *Current Pos:* RETIRED. *Personal Data:* b New York, NY, Jan 30, 25; m 48; c 3. *Educ:* Univ Calif, Los Angeles, BA, 48, PhD(physics), 52. *Prof Exp:* Asst physics, Univ Calif, Los Angeles, 48-51, res engr, 51-52; res assoc, Res Lab, Gen Elec Corp, 52-55; staff scientist, Lockheed Missiles & Space Co, 55-59, mgr solid state electronics dept, 61-62; mgr basic physics, Fairchild Semiconductor Corp, 62-65; staff scientist, Electro optical Lab, Autonetics Div, NAm Aviation, Inc, Calif, 65-67 & High Energy Laser Lab, TRW Systs Group, 68-72; sr staff scientist, Rand Corp, 72-79; sr staff scientist, Rocketdyne Div, Rockwell Int, 79-90. *Concurrent Pos:* Mem staff, Physics Lab, Ecole Normale Superieure, Paris, 60. *Mem:* Am Phys Soc. *Res:* Semiconductors; thermoelectric effects; electron-acoustic interactions; electrooptic effects; lasers. *Mailing Add:* 16557 Park Lane Circle Los Angeles CA 90049

LEIFER, LARRY J, BIOMEDICAL ENGINEERING. *Current Pos:* assoc prof, 76-82, PROF MECH ENG & DIR, CTR DESIGN RES, STANFORD UNIV, 82- *Educ:* Stanford Univ, BS, 62, MS, 63, PhD(biomed eng), 69. *Prof Exp:* Staff mem, Ames Res Ctr, NASA, 69-72; NASA res exchange fel, Man-Vehicle Lab, Mass Inst Technol, 73; asst prof biomed systs anal, Swiss Fed Inst Technol, Zurich, 73-76. *Concurrent Pos:* Co-founder, Ohlone Int Corp, 89- *Res:* Developed laboratory and curriculum for programmable electromechanical systems design; develop basic design theory and methodology through application of knowledge-based engineering technology to a wide range of industrial machine design problems. *Mailing Add:* Mech Eng Design Div Stanford Univ Stanford CA 94305. *Fax:* 650-725-8475

LEIFER, LESLIE, PHYSICAL CHEMISTRY. *Current Pos:* PROF CHEM, MICH TECHNOL UNIV, 66- *Personal Data:* b New York, NY, Apr 13, 29; m 57; c 1. *Educ:* City Col New York, BS, 50; Univ Kans, PhD(phys chem), 59. *Prof Exp:* Res assoc nuclear & inorg chem, Mass Inst Technol, 56-59; asst prof chem, Clark Univ, 59-60; res assoc & staff mem, Lab Nuclear Sci, Mass Inst Technol, 61-63; assoc prof, Boston Col, 63-66. *Concurrent Pos:* Travel awards, US AEC, Stockholm, 62, Australia, 63, Stockholm, 71; res award, Mich Technol Univ, 70. *Mem:* AAAS; Am Chem Soc; Sigma Xi. *Res:* Solution physical chemistry; Mossbauer spectroscopy; quantum chemistry; energy storage materials. *Mailing Add:* Dept Chem Mich Technol Univ Houghton MI 49931

LEIFER, ZER, GENETIC TOXICOLOGY, POLYAMINE BIOSYNTHESIS. *Current Pos:* res asst prof, 76-81, RES ASSOC PROF MICROBIOL, NY MED COL, 81- *Personal Data:* b Brooklyn, NY, May 24, 41; m 72; c 5. *Educ:* Yeshiva Univ, BA, 63; Harvard Univ, MA, 65; NY Univ, PhD(microbiol), 72. *Prof Exp:* Fel microbiol, NY Univ, 72-74; Queens Col, City Univ NY, 74-76. *Concurrent Pos:* Mem, DNA Repair Deficient Bacterial Assay Work Group, Genetic Toxicol Prog, Environ Protection Agency, 78-81. *Mem:* Am Soc Microbiol; Am Chem Soc; AAAS; Environ Mutagen Soc; Sigma Xi. *Res:* Development and utilization of microbial assay systems for the detection of environment mutagens and carcinogens; biosynthesis and biological role of polyamines. *Mailing Add:* Dept Basic Sci NY Col Podiatric Med 53 E 124th St New York NY 10035

LEIFIELD, ROBERT FRANCIS, INORGANIC CHEMISTRY. *Current Pos:* PRES, LEIFIELD INC, 86- *Personal Data:* b St Louis, Mo, Jan 29, 28; m 52; c 7. *Educ:* St Louis Univ, BS, 52, MS, 59. *Prof Exp:* Chemist, Great Lakes Carbon Co, 52-56; chemist, Mallinckrodt Chem Works, 56-58, supvr metall & ceramics, 58-61, group leader process develop, 61-62, res chemist, 62-66, assoc mgr res, 66-69, res & develop mgr, Calsicat Div, 69-70, tech mgr, 70-77, dir res & develop, chem div, 77-85, dir new prod develop, Catalysts & Performance Chem Div, Mallinckrodt Inc, 85-86. *Mem:* Catalysis Soc; Am Chem Soc; Licensing Execs Soc. *Res:* Column and thin layer chromatography; analytical reagents; product and process research and development; uranium metallurgical chemistry; heterogeneous catalysis; licensing consultation. *Mailing Add:* 7433 Hibbard Lane St Louis MO 63123-2015

LEIGA, ALGIRD GEORGE, PHYSICAL CHEMISTRY. *Current Pos:* CONSULT IMAGING MAT TECHNOL & MFG, 95- *Personal Data:* b New York, NY, Mar 25, 33; m 55, Ann Dumig; c 4. *Educ:* NY Univ, BA, 55, MS, 60, PhD(phys chem), 63. *Prof Exp:* Res scientist, Dept Chem, NY Univ, 62-64; sr scientist, Mat Sci Lab, NY, 64-73, mgr mat develop, Xeroradiography, Pasadena, 73-77; corp res & develop staff, Xerox Corp, Palo Alto, 77-81, mgr mat technol opers, Xerox Med Systs, Monrovia, Calif, 81-87, mgr, Supplies Bus Ctr, 88-89, mgr mat technol & mfg, 89-95. *Concurrent Pos:* Councilman, City Claremont, Calif, 90-94, mayor, 94-97. *Mem:* Am Chem Soc; Soc Photog Scientists & Engrs; Am Phys Soc. *Res:* Vacuum ultraviolet photochemistry and spectroscopy; decomposition reactions of solids; materials development for electrophotography. *Mailing Add:* 3790 Elmira Ave Claremont CA 91711

LEIGH, CHARLES HENRY, re-entry physics & chemistry, technical management & consulting; deceased, see previous edition for last biography

LEIGH, DONALD C, CONTINUUM MECHANICS. *Current Pos:* assoc prof eng mech & math, 65-68, chmn dept eng mech, 72-80, PROF ENG MECH, UNIV KY, 68-, ASSOC DEAN ENG, 83- *Personal Data:* b Toronto, Ont, Feb 25, 29; nat US; m 52; c 3. *Educ:* Univ Toronto, BASc, 51; Cambridge Univ, PhD(math), 54. *Prof Exp:* Sr aerophys engr, Gen Dynamics/Ft Worth, 54-56; supvr tech comput, Curtiss-Wright Corp, 56-57; lectr mech eng, Princeton Univ, 57-58, asst prof aerospace & mech sci, 58-65. *Mem:* Soc Natural Philos; Soc Rheol; Am Acad Mech; Am Soc Mech Engrs; Nat Soc Prof Engrs. *Res:* Continuum mechanics; systems engineering; pressure vessels. *Mailing Add:* 1213 Trumpeter Row Lexington KY 40502-2891

LEIGH, EGBERT GILES, JR, TROPICAL ECOLOGY, EVOLUTIONARY POPULATION GENETICS. *Current Pos:* BIOLOGIST, SMITHSONIAN TROP RES INST, 69- *Personal Data:* b Richmond, Va, July 27, 40; m 68, Elizabeth M Hodgson; c John M & Mary B. *Educ:* Princeton Univ, AB, 62; Yale Univ, PhD(biol), 66. *Prof Exp:* Actg instr biol, Stanford Univ, 66; asst prof, Princeton Univ, 66-72. *Mem:* Ecol Soc Am; Am Soc Naturalists; Paleont Res Inst; Brit Ecol Soc. *Res:* Role of mutualism in evolution; what circumstances lend effectiveness to the common interest of members in the good of their group or community; ecology of tropical forest. *Mailing Add:* Smithsonian Trop Res Inst Unit 948 APO AA 34002-0948. *Fax:* 507-52-3065

LEIGH, RICHARD WOODWARD, ENERGY TECHNOLOGY, ELECTRIC UTILITY ANALYSIS. *Current Pos:* CONSULT, ENERGY CONSERV & UTILITY ANALYSIS, US & DEVELOP COUNTRIES. *Personal Data:* b New York, NY, Apr 26, 42. *Educ:* Oberlin Col, AB, 65; Columbia Univ, PhD(physics), 73. *Prof Exp:* Res assoc physics, City Col New York, 72-73, adj asst prof, 73-75; res fel, Lab Spectros Hertzienne, Ecole Normale Superieure, Paris, 75-77; asst scientist, Brookhaven Nat Lab, 77-80, assoc scientist energy syst, 80-87; assoc prof physics, Pratt Inst, 87-93. *Concurrent Pos:* Consult energy conserv & utility anal, US and developing countries; sr res assoc, Brookhaven Nat Lab, 94-96. *Mem:* AAAS; Am Phys Soc. *Res:* Energy technologies, especially heat exchanger materials and design; energy efficiency, storage and solar; technical, economic and infrastructural requirements and benefits; electric utility planning methods and systems; coherent optics. *Mailing Add:* 415 Central Park W 12C New York NY 10025-4807. *Fax:* 212-866-4560

LEIGH, THOMAS FRANCIS, entomology, pest management; deceased, see previous edition for last biography

LEIGHLY, HOLLIS PHILIP, JR, PHYSICAL METALLURGY. *Current Pos:* assoc prof, 60-70, PROF METALL ENG, UNIV MO-ROLLA, 70- *Personal Data:* b St Joseph, Ill, May 28, 23; m 51, Elizabeth Petersen; c Karen & David. *Educ:* Univ Ill, BS, 48, MS, 50, PhD(metall eng), 52. *Prof Exp:* Res metallurgist, Bendix Aviation Corp, 52-54; res metallurgist, Denver Res Inst, 54-60, asst prof metall & chmn dept, Univ Denver, 58-60. *Concurrent Pos:* Sabbatical, Dept Phys Metall, Birmingham Univ, 67-68 & Oak Ridge Nat Lab, 74-75; NATO fel, Univ Guelph, 74; res fel, Univ East Anglia, Norwich, Eng, 79-80 & 87; Benjamin Meaker fel, Univ Bristol, UK, 91. *Mem:* AAAS; Am Soc Metals; Am Inst Mining, Metall & Petrol Engrs; fel Inst Metallurgists; Sigma Xi. *Res:* Recrystallization; nuclear reactor materials; radiation damage; electron microscopy; positron annihilation. *Mailing Add:* Dept Metall Eng Univ Mo Rolla MO 65401-0249. *Fax:* 573-341-6934; *E-Mail:* hpl@umr.edu

LEIGHLY, KAREN MARIE, X-RAY ASTRONOMY, ACTIVE GALACTIC NUCLEI. *Current Pos:* ASSOC RES SCIENTIST, COLUMBIA ASTROPHYS LAB, 97- *Personal Data:* b Denver, Colo, Apr 30, 59. *Educ:* NMex Inst Mining & Technol, BS(physics) & BS(math), 83; Mont State Univ, MS, 87, PhD(physics), 91. *Prof Exp:* Nat Res Coun fel, Goddard Space Flight Ctr, NASA, 92-94; Sci & Technol Agency fel, Inst Phys & Chem Res, 94-96. *Concurrent Pos:* Prin investr, NASA/HST, ELIVE, IVE, ROSAT, GINGA, ASCA, XTE, SAX, 92- *Mem:* Am Astron Soc; Int Astron Union. *Res:* X-ray emission from active galactic nuclei; x-ray spectrum and the variability of these objects; analysis of data from various orbiting observatories; the x-ray emission from active galactic nuclei is important because very rapid variability observed implies the emission comes from close to the black hole believed to power these objects. *Mailing Add:* Columbia Astrophys Lab 538 W 120th St New York NY 10027. *Fax:* 212-854-8121; *E-Mail:* leighly@ulisse.phys.columbia.edu

LEIGHT, WALTER GILBERT, OPERATIONS RESEARCH, STANDARDS ENGINEERING. *Current Pos:* DEP DIR, OFF STANDS SERV, NAT INST STANDS & TECHNOL, 89- *Personal Data:* b New York, NY, Nov 19, 22; m 48, Frances Edgal; c Claudia R & K Adam. *Educ:* City Col NY, BS, 42. *Honors & Awards:* Bronze Medal, Dept Com, 79, Silver Medal, 95; Meritorious Service Award, Am Nat Stand Inst, 96. *Prof Exp:* High sch instr, NY, 42; res meteorologist, US Weather Bur, 46-53; from sci analyst to dir opers anal div, Opers Eval Group & sr sci analyst, Systs Eval Group, Ctr Naval Anal, 53-70; prog mgr decision systs, Tech Anal Div, Nat Bur Stands, 71-74, chief, Off Consumer Prod Safety, Nat Inst Stands & Technol, 74-78, chief, Prod Safety Technol Div, 78-81, chief, Off Stands Info Anal & Develop, 81- 82, prog mgr, Stands Code & Info, 82-86, asst assoc dir indust & stands, 87-88. *Concurrent Pos:* Govt mem coun, Am Nat Stand Inst, Z-21 comt. *Mem:* Fel AAAS; Opers Res Soc Am; Am Metrol Soc. *Res:* Decision systems; criminal justice; search and rescue; nuclear safeguards; military systems; extended forecasting; consumer product safety; standards and trade; laboratory accreditation; conformity assessment. *Mailing Add:* 9416 Bulls Run Pkwy Bethesda MD 20817. *Fax:* 301-963-2871; *E-Mail:* walter.leight@nist.gov

LEIGHTON, ALEXANDER HAMILTON, PSYCHIATRIC EPIDEMIOLOGY, CULTURAL ANTHROPOLOGY. *Current Pos:* prof social psychiat & head, Dept Behav Sci, 66-75, EMER PROF SOCIAL PSYCHIAT, HARVARD SCH PUB HEALTH, 75-; PROF PSYCHIAT & COMMUNITY HEALTH EPIDEMIOL, DALHOUSIE UNIV, 75- *Personal Data:* b Philadelphia, Pa, July 17, 08; m 37, 66, Jane Murphy; c Doreen (Walker) & Fredrick A. *Educ:* Princeton Univ, BA, 32; Cambridge Univ, MA, 34; Johns Hopkins Univ, MD, 36. *Hon Degrees:* AM, Harvard Univ, 66; SD, Acadia Univ, 74; SD, Univ Laval, 91. *Honors & Awards:* Human Rels Award, Am Soc Advan Mgt, 46; La Pouse Award, Am Pub Health Asn, 75; Ment Health Asn Res Achievement Award, 75; Malinowski Award, Soc Appl Anthrop, 84; Jubin Award, Am Psychopath Asn, 94. *Prof Exp:* Social Sci Res Coun fel field work among Navajos & Eskimos, Columbia Univ, 39-40; Guggenheim fel, 46-47; prof sociol & anthrop, Col Arts & Sci, Cornell Univ, 47-66, dir, SW Proj, 48-53, dir, Prog Social Psychiat, 55-66; prof social psychiat, Med Col, 56-66. *Concurrent Pos:* Prof, Sch Indust & Labor Rels, 47-52; consult, Bur Indian Affairs, US Dept Interior, 48-50; Surgeon Gen Adv Comt Indian Affairs, 56-59 & Peace Corps, 61-63; mem bd dirs, Social Sci Res Coun, 48-58, chmn comt psychiat & social sci, 50-58; dir, Stirling Co Proj, 48-75; tech adv, Milbank Mem Fund, 56-63; fel, Ctr Advan Study Behav Sci, 57-58; mem expert adv panel ment health, WHO, 57-75; Thomas W Salmon Mem lectr, NY Acad Med, 58; mem sub-panel behav sci, President's Sci Adv Comt, 61-62; reflective fel, Carnegie Corp NY, 62-63; vis lectr, Cath Univ Louvain, 71; mem comt effects of herbicides in Vietnam, Nat Acad Sci, 71-73; Nat Health Scientist Award, Can, 75-84; mem, Consult Comt Ment Health Res, Dept Nat Health & Welfare, Can, 82- *Mem:* Fel AAAS; fel Am Psychiat Asn; Am Philos Soc; fel Am Anthrop Asn; Am Psychopath Asn; hon fel Royal Col Psychiatrists, UK. *Res:* Social and cultural change; social psychiatry; psychiatric epidemiology. *Mailing Add:* PO Box 71 Smiths Cove NS B0S 1S0 Can

LEIGHTON, ALVAH THEODORE, JR, GENETICS, PHYSIOLOGY. *Current Pos:* assoc prof, 59-71, PROF POULTRY SCI, VA POLYTECH INST & STATE UNIV, 71- *Personal Data:* b Portland, Maine, Apr 17, 29; m 53; c 4. *Educ:* Univ Maine, BS, 51; Univ Mass, MS, 53; Univ Minn, PhD(poultry genetics & physiol), 60. *Prof Exp:* Asst poultry genetics, Univ Mass, 51-52 & Univ Minn, 55-59. *Mem:* Sigma Xi; World Poultry Sci Asn; Am Genetic Asn; Poultry Sci Asn. *Res:* Reproductive physiology and management of turkey populations. *Mailing Add:* Dept Poultry Sci Va Polytech Inst & State Univ PO Box 0306 Blacksburg VA 24063-0001

LEIGHTON, FREDERICK ARCHIBALD, VETERINARY MEDICINE. *Current Pos:* student asst wildlife dis studies, Dept Vet Path, Western Col Vet Med, Univ Sask, 75-78, instr, 79-80, assoc prof, 84-88, PROF & HEAD, DEPT VET PATH, WESTERN COL VET MED, UNIV SASK, 88-, SUPVR, ELECTRON MICROS LAB, 85- *Personal Data:* b Nov 4, 48. *Educ:* Cornell Univ, AB, 70; Univ Sask, DVM, 79; NY State Col Vet Med, PhD(exp path), 84. *Prof Exp:* Teacher, Crescent Collegiate, Robert's Arm, Nfld, 72-73; res asst wildlife ecol, Bald Eagle Proj, Besnard Lake, Sask, 74. *Concurrent Pos:* Hon vis res fel, Dept Biochem, Mem Univ Nfld, St John's, 83, hon vis assoc prof, 85; mem mgt comt, Wildlife Health Fund, 84-, chmn, 87-; mem, Toxicol Group, Univ Sask, 84-, Comput Coord Comt, Western Col Vet Med, 85-87, 88-89 & Electron Micros User's Comt, 86-90; co-dir Can Coop Wildlife Health Ctr, 92- *Mem:* Wildlife Dis Asn; Am Col Vet Pathologists; AAAS; Am Asn Vet Pathologists; Can Vet Med Asn; Can Asn Vet Pathologists (vpres, 87-88, pres, 88-89). *Res:* Wild animal diseases-pathology and surveillance; toxicopathology of petroleum oils and pesticides in wild birds. *Mailing Add:* Vet Path Dept Western Col Vet Med Univ Sask 52 Campus Dr Saskatoon SK S7N 5B4 Can

LEIGHTON, FREEMAN BEACH, geology, for more information see previous edition

LEIGHTON, HENRY GEORGE, METEOROLOGY. *Current Pos:* res assoc, 71-72, asst prof, 72-80, ASSOC PROF METEOROL, MCGILL UNIV, 80- *Personal Data:* b London, Eng, May 2, 40; Can citizen; m 62; c 3. *Educ:* McGill Univ, BS, 61, MS, 64; Univ Alta, PhD(nuclear physics), 68. *Prof Exp:* Res assoc nuclear physics, R J van de Graaff Lab, Holland, 68-70; vis asst prof, Univ Ky, 70-71. *Mem:* Can Meteorol Soc; Am Meteorol Soc. *Res:* Atmospheric radiation; cloud physics and cloud chemistry. *Mailing Add:* Dept Atmospheric & Oceanogr Sci McGill Univ 805 Sherbrooke St Montreal PQ H3A 2K6 Can

LEIGHTON, JOSEPH, PATHOLOGY, ONCOLOGY. *Current Pos:* PATHOLOGIST, AERON BIOTECHNOL, INC, 89- *Personal Data:* b New York, NY, Dec 13, 21; m 46; c 2. *Educ:* Columbia Univ, AB, 42; Long Island Col Med, MD, 46. *Prof Exp:* From assoc prof to prof path, Sch Med, Univ Pittsburgh, 46-71; chmn dept, Med Col Pa, 71-87, prof, 71-89. *Concurrent Pos:* Intern, Mt Sinai Hosp, NY, 46-47; resident path anat, Mass Gen Hosp, Boston, 48-49; resident clin path, USPHS Hosp, Baltimore, 50, exp pathologist, Path Lab, Nat Cancer Inst, 51-56, consult, Nat Serv Ctr, 59-; chmn, Gordon Res Conf Cancer, 63, mem coun, Gordon Res Confs, 63-66. *Mem:* Am Soc Exp Path; Soc Develop Biol; Am Asn Path & Bact; Tissue Cult Asn; Am Asn Cancer Res. *Res:* Experimental surgical pathology; development of matrix methods and histophysiologic gradient methods for tissue culture; pathogenesis of tumor invasion and metastasis; cancer research; tissue culture; cancer matastasis. *Mailing Add:* Aeron Biotechnol Inc 1933 Davis St No 310 San Leandro CA 94577

LEIGHTON, MORRIS WELLMAN, EXPLORATION GEOLOGY, BASIN STUDIES. *Current Pos:* chief, 83-94, EMER CHIEF, ILL STATE GEOL SURV, 94- *Personal Data:* b Champaign, Ill, June 17, 26; m 47, Jean Bosley; c Randi, Kathryn & Kari. *Educ:* Univ Ill, BS, 47; Univ Chicago, MS, 48, PhD(geol), 51. *Honors & Awards:* John T Galey Sr Mem Pub Serv Award, Am Inst Prof Geologists, 94; George V Cohee Pub Serv Award, Am Asn Petrol Geologists, 94; Gaylord Donnelley Award, Nature Ill Found, 94. *Prof Exp:* Res geologist, Jersey Prod Res Co, 51-58, geol sect head, 58-61, geologist-in-chg Europ study group, Esso Mediter, 61-63, sr res geologist, Jersey Prod Res Co, 63-64, geol adv, Esso Explor Inc, 64-68, asst explor mgr, Esso Stand Oil Ltd, Australia, 69-70, explor mgr, Esso Australia Ltd, 70-72, div mgr, Esso Prod Res Co, 72-74, chief geologist, Esso InterAmerica, 74-83. *Concurrent Pos:* Emer adj prof, Univ Ill, 94-; distinguished lectr, Am Asn Petrol Geologists, 90. *Mem:* Am Asn Petrol Geologists (pres, 90); fel Geol Soc Am; hon mem Asn Am State Geologists. *Res:* Petroleum geology; basin studies; basin and play assessment; earth sciences, general; carbonate rocks. *Mailing Add:* 302 E Sherwin Dr Urbana IL 61802. *Fax:* 217-244-7004; *E-Mail:* leighton@geoserv.isgs.uiuc.edu

LEIGHTON, ROBERT BENJAMIN, telescope design, millimeter-wave astronomy; deceased, see previous edition for last biography

LEIGHTON, TERRANCE J, BIOCHEMISTRY. *Current Pos:* from asst prof to prof microbiol, 74-88, PROF BIOCHEM & MOLECULAR BIOL, DEPT MOLECULAR & CELL BIOL, UNIV CALIF, BERKELEY, 89- *Personal Data:* b Twin Falls, Idaho, Oct 14, 44. *Educ:* Ore State Univ, BSc, 66; Univ BC, PhD, 70. *Prof Exp:* Postdoctoral fel, Dept Biochem & Biophys, Univ Calif, Davis, 70-72; asst prof, Dept Microbiol, Med Sch, Univ Mass, Worcester, 72-74. *Concurrent Pos:* Guest Ger Govt, Max Planck Inst Molecular Genetics, Berlin, WGer, 76; Alexander von Humboldt-Stiftung fel, 80-83; sr fel, Max Planck Inst, 84- *Mem:* AAAS; Sigma Xi; Biophys Soc; Am Soc Biochem & Molecular Biol; Am Chem Soc; Am Soc Microbiol; fel Am Inst Chem; Soc Indust Microbiol. *Res:* Genetic engineering of high performance bioprocess systems; molecular genetic regulation of Bacillus subtilis development; molecular genetic regulation of Bacillus subtilis translational initiation and termination; environmental mutagenesis, carcinogenesis and the role of flavonols and flavonol glycosides as dietary anticarcinogens. *Mailing Add:* Biochem Dept 3589 Walnut St Unit F Lafayette CA 94549-4245

LEIKIN, JERROLD BLAIR, TOXICOLOGY, EMERGENCY MEDICINE. *Current Pos:* ATTEND MED TOXICOL, COOK CO HOSP, 85-; ASSOC PROF MED, RUSH MED COL, 88-, MED DIR, RUSH POISON CONTROL CTR, ASSOC DIR, RUSH EMERGENCY SERVS. *Personal Data:* b Chicago Ill, Aug 28, 54; m 82, Robin E Goldman; c Scott & Eryn. *Educ:* Univ Iowa, BS 76; Univ Chicago, MD, 80. *Concurrent Pos:* Asst prof med, Univ Ill, 84-88; chmn, Res & Educ, Am Col Emergency Physicians, 87- *Mem:* AMA; Am Acad Clin Toxicol; Am Col Physicians; Am Col Emergency Physicians; Am Col Med Toxicol. *Res:* Toxicology and emergency medicine; drugs of abuse and inhalation toxins. *Mailing Add:* 1037 Edgebrook Lane Glencoe IL 60022. *Fax:* 312-421-1832

LEIMGRUBER, RICHARD M, PHYSICAL SCIENCE. *Current Pos:* SR RES SPECIALIST, PHYS SCI CTR, MONSANTO CO, 83- *Mailing Add:* Anal Sci Ctr Monsanto Co 700 Chesterfield Pkwy N BB3K St Louis MO 63198

LEIMKUHLER, FERDINAND F, INDUSTRIAL ENGINEERING, OPERATIONS RESEARCH. *Current Pos:* assoc prof, 61-66, head, Sch Indust Eng, 69-74 & 81-93, PROF INDUST ENG, PURDUE UNIV, 66- *Personal Data:* b Baltimore, Md, Dec 31, 28; m 56; c 6. *Educ:* Loyola Col, Md, BS, 50, Johns Hopkins Univ, BEng, 52, Dr Eng, 62. *Honors & Awards:* Distinguished lectr, Am Soc Info Sci, 71-72. *Prof Exp:* Engr, E I du Pont de Nemours & Co, 52-57; res assoc & instr indust eng, Johns Hopkins Univ, 57-61. *Concurrent Pos:* Vis prof, Univ Calif, Berkeley, 68-69, 90-91; Fulbright prof, Univ Ljubjana, Yugoslavia, 74-75. *Mem:* Opers Res Soc Am; Inst Mgt Sci; fel Am Inst Indust Engrs; Am Soc Eng Educ. *Res:* Library operations research; engineering economic analysis; transportation of highly radioactive materials; stochastic system theory; manufacturing systems. *Mailing Add:* Sch Indust Eng Purdue Univ West Lafayette IN 47907-1968

LEIN, ALLEN, ANIMAL PHYSIOLOGY. *Current Pos:* assoc dean & prof med, Univ Calif, San Diego, 68-73, prof reprod med, 73-84, assoc dean grad studies health sci, 74-77 & 81-82, prog dir med scientist training, 75-77, prog dir health professions hon prog, 79-80, actg assoc dean acad affairs, 80-82, EMER PROF REPROD MED, UNIV CALIF, SAN DIEGO, 84- *Personal Data:* b New York, NY, Apr 15, 13; m 41, Teresa R LaFratta; c Laura & David. *Educ:* Univ Calif, Los Angeles, BA, 35, MA, 38, PhD(endocrinol), 40. *Prof Exp:* Instr surg res, Sch Med, Ohio State Univ, 41-42, res assoc aviation physiol, Res Found, 42-43; from asst prof to prof physiol, Med Sch, Northwestern Univ, 47-68, dir student affairs, 60-63, dir honors prog med educ, 62-68, asst dean, Med Sch & dir med scientist training prog, 64-68, asst dean, Grad Sch, 66-68. *Concurrent Pos:* Asst prof physiol, Med Sch, Vanderbilt Univ, 46-47; vis prof chem, Calif Inst Technol, 54-55; Guggenheim fel, Col France, Paris, 58-59; consult, Vet Admin Res Hosp, Chicago, Ill, 64-68, Dept Reprod Med, Univ Calif, San Diego, 84-94; Scholar in residence, Bellagio Study Ctr, Rockefeller Found, 77. *Mem:* Am Physiol Soc; AAAS; Am Inst Biol Sci; Soc Exp Biol & Med; Endocrine Soc; Fedn Am Soc Exp Biol; Sigma Xi. *Res:* Endocrine regulation of reproductive function, thyroid function and carbohydrate and fat metabolism. *Mailing Add:* 8653 Dunaway Dr La Jolla CA 92037

LEIN, PAMELA J, NEUROSCIENCES. *Current Pos:* ASST PROF BIOL, CANISIUS COL, 93- *Personal Data:* b Buffalo, NY, Apr 16, 59; m 81, Richard Meigs. *Educ:* Cornell Univ, BS, 81; ETenn State Univ, MSEH, 83; State Univ NY, PhD(pharmacol), 90. *Prof Exp:* Fel molecular immunol, Roswell Park Cancer Inst, 91-92; environ health analyst, Dames & Moore, 92-93. *Concurrent Pos:* Adj assist prof, Dept Pharmacol, State Univ NY, Buffalo. *Mem:* Soc Neurosci; Am Soc Cell Biol; Am Pub Health Asn. *Res:* Epigenetic specification of neuronal form. *Mailing Add:* Dept Biol Canisius Col 2001 Main St Buffalo NY 14208. *Fax:* 716-888-3157; *E-Mail:* leinp@canisius.edu

LEINBACH, F HAROLD, PHYSICS. *Current Pos:* RETIRED. *Personal Data:* b Ft Collins, Colo, Jan 7, 29; wid; c 2. *Educ:* SDak State Univ, BS, 49; Calif Inst Technol, MS, 50; Univ Alaska, PhD(geophys), 62. *Prof Exp:* Geophysicist, Geophys Inst, Alaska, 50-53 & 56-62; asst prof physics, Univ Iowa, 62-66; instr, Space Environ Lab, Nat Oceanog, Atmospheric Admin, Univ Colo, 78-79, physicist, 66-93. *Concurrent Pos:* Actg dir, Space Environ Lab, 82-86. *Mem:* Am Astron Soc; Am Geophys Union; Am Asn Physics Teachers; Sigma Xi. *Res:* High latitude ionospheric absorption of cosmic radio noise; solar cosmic rays and their interaction with the ionosphere; solar physics; space physics; laboratory plasma physics. *Mailing Add:* 2015 Kohler Dr Boulder CO 80303

LEINBACH, RALPH C, JR, ALLOYS. *Current Pos:* RETIRED. *Personal Data:* b Esterly, Pa, Nov 24, 28; m 51; c 4. *Educ:* Lehigh Univ, BS, 54. *Honors & Awards:* Regional Tech Award, Am Iron & Steel Inst, 63, Spec Achievement Cert, 67; Bradley Stoughton Award, Am Soc Metals, 77. *Prof Exp:* Metallurgist, Atomic Power Div Res Ctr, Babcock & Wilcox Co, Alliance, Ohio, 54; metallurgist, Res & Develop Lab, Electronics & Magnetics, Carpenter Technol Corp, Reading, Pa, 55, melting metallurgist, 56, melting metallurgist, Bridgeport, Conn plant, 57-61, plant metallurgist, 61-65, mgr, Mill Metallurgy, 65-68, chief metallurgist, 68-70, asst vpres metall, Carpenter Technol Corp, 70-71, vpres metall, 71-75, vpres tech, 75-76, div vpres tech, 76-79, group vpres, Carpenter Steel Div, 79-82, sr vpres technol, eng & purchasing, 82-87. *Concurrent Pos:* Mem bd dirs, Metal Prop Coun Inc, 80; Mem, Interim Core Group Mkt Develop Comt, Am Iron & Steel Inst, 85. *Mem:* Fel Am Soc Metals; Am Inst Metall Engrs; Am Iron & Steel Inst; Soc Automotive Engrs; Soc Metall Engrs; Am Welding Soc; Metals Soc; Am Vacuum Soc. *Res:* Stainless steel making utilizing vacuum treatment; vacuum induction melting of specialty steels and alloys; specialty steel melting; US and Canadian patents; technical publications. *Mailing Add:* 2404 Bell Dr Reading PA 19609

LEINEN, MARGARET SANDRA, PALEOCEANOGRAPHY, PALEOCLIMATE. *Current Pos:* Marine scientist, Univ RI, 80-82, from asst res prof to assoc res prof, 82-88, prof & assoc dean, 88-92, VPROVOST MARINE PROGS & DEAN, UNIV RI, 92- *Personal Data:* b Chicago, Ill, Sept 20, 46; m; c Daniel W. *Educ:* Univ Ill, BS, 69; Ore State Univ, MS, 75; Univ RI, PhD(oceanog), 80. *Mem:* Geochem Soc; fel Geol Soc Am; Am Geophys Union; Oceanog Soc (pres, 94-). *Res:* Deep sea sedimentary processes; history of atmospheric circulation. *Mailing Add:* Univ RI 15 S Ferry Rd Narragansett RI 02882-1197. *Fax:* 401-792-6889; *E-Mail:* mleinen@gsosun1.gsc.uri.edu

LEININGER, HAROLD VERNON, MICROBIOLOGY. *Current Pos:* CONSULT MICROBIOL, FOOD, DRUGS & COSMETICS, 80- *Personal Data:* b Baton Rouge, La, June 18, 25; m 50; c 1. *Educ:* La State Univ, BS, 48, MS, 51. *Prof Exp:* Lab technician, Dairy Improv Ctr, La State Univ, 51; food & drug inspector, Food & Drug Admin, 51, from bacteriologist to dir biol warfare proj, 52-63, res microbiologist, 63-71, dir, Minneapolis Ctr Microbiol Invest, 71-80. *Concurrent Pos:* Proj officer, Test Site, AEC, Nev, 57. *Mem:* Asn Off Analytical Chemists; Am Soc Microbiologists; Inst Food Technologists; Int Asn Milk, Food & Environ Sanit. *Res:* Microbiological research in food toxicity, decomposition, natural flora, and sanitation. *Mailing Add:* 3200 Voss Dr El Paso TX 79936

LEININGER, PAUL MILLER, physical chemistry; deceased, see previous edition for last biography

LEININGER, ROBERT IRVIN, BIOMEDICAL ENGINEERING, POLYMER CHEMISTRY. *Current Pos:* CONSULT BIOMAT, 86- *Personal Data:* b Cleveland, Ohio, May 11, 19; m 42; c Karen (Kaplan), Christine (Furlanette), Nels & Eric. *Educ:* Cleveland State Univ, BChE, 40; Case Western Res, MS, 41, PhD, 43. *Honors & Awards:* IR-100 Indust Res Award, 72; Clemson Award, Soc Biomat, 81. *Prof Exp:* Instr chem eng, Fenn Col, 40-43; res chemist, Monsanto Chem Co, 43-48; prin chemist, Battelle Mem Inst, 48-51, asst chief, Rubber Plastics Div, 51-60, chief polymer Res Sect, 60-65, mgr, 65-69; tech adv, Korean Inst Sci & Technol, Seoul, 69-70; prof dir biomat, Dept Biol, Environ & Chem, 70-73, mem res coun, 74-80, dir res coun, Columbus Labs, Battelle Mem Inst, 80-84; dir, Nat Ctr Biomed Infrared Spectros, 83-85. *Concurrent Pos:* Mem adv comt, Div Technol Devices, Nat Heart & Lung Inst, 72-73; mem adv comt, Nuclear Powered Artificial Heart Prog, Energy Res & Develop Admin, 75-76; mem, Surg & Bioeng Study Sect, 76-79; mem, Small Bus Admin, NIH, 82- *Mem:* Int Soc Artificial Organs; Am Soc Artificial Internal Organs; Soc Biomat; Am Chem Soc; NY Acad Sci; Sigma Xi. *Res:* Biomaterials; biomedical engineering; polymer chemistry. *Mailing Add:* 1973 Milden Rd Columbus OH 43221-1937

LEINROTH, JEAN PAUL, JR, SEPARATION PROCESSES. *Current Pos:* PRES, LEINROTH ASSOC, 88- *Personal Data:* b Utica, NY, July 4, 20; m 46; c 3. *Educ:* Cornell Univ, BMechEng, 41; Mass Inst Technol, SM, 48, ScD(chem eng), 63. *Prof Exp:* Trainee, Stand Oil Co, Ohio, 41-42; asst job engr, M W Kellogg Co, NY, 42-43; proj engr, Union Carbide Chem Co, 48-56, proj leader, 56-59; instr thermodyn, Mass Inst Technol, 60-61, vis assoc prof, 63-64; assoc prof chem eng, Cornell Univ, 64-71; vis prof, Mass Inst Technol, 71-72; process dir, John Brown E&C, 72-80, mgr spec projs, 80-85; vis prof, Univ Conn, 86-88 & Mass Inst Technol, 88-89. *Concurrent Pos:* Consult, Union Carbide Chem Co, 64-68, Develop Sci, 71-72, Gen Elec, Sterling Org, Nycomed John Brown E&C, Vanderbilt Chem Corp, Syntex, Velsicol Westex, Rohm & Haas, Clean Harbors, Mass Inst Technol Energy Lab, CPI Plants, Great Lakes Citem, Cabot Corp, 87- *Mem:* Am Inst Chem Engrs. *Res:* Chemical kinetics; thermodynamics; staged operations; computer applications. *Mailing Add:* 33 Millstone Rd PO Box 475 Wilton CT 06897

LEINWAND, LESLIE, IMMUNOLOGY. *Current Pos:* PROF, UNIV COLO, 85- *Personal Data:* b New York, NY, Nov 18, 50. *Educ:* Cornell Univ, BS, 72; Yale Univ, PhD(biol), 78. *Prof Exp:* Fel immunol, Rockefeller Univ, 78-81; from asst prof to assoc prof immunol, Albert Einstein Col Med, 81-85. *Mailing Add:* Dept Cellular & Develop Biol Univ Colo Campus Box 347 Boulder CO 80309-0347

LEINWEBER, FRANZ JOSEF, DRUG METABOLISM. *Current Pos:* SR SCIENTIST, HOFFMANN-LA ROCHE INC, 77- *Personal Data:* b Berlin, Ger, Jan 18, 31; US citizen; m 60; c 2. *Educ:* Univ Tuebingen, Dr rer nat(biol), 56. *Prof Exp:* Fel biochem, Tex A&M Univ, 57-60 & Johns Hopkins Univ, 60-63; res assoc, Univ Tenn, 63-65; sr scientist, McNeil Labs, Inc, 65-69; sr scientist, Warner-Lambert Res Inst, 69-77. *Mem:* Am Soc Pharmacol & Exp Therapeut. *Res:* Photoperiodism and biological clocks; enzymology, intermediary metabolism and metabolic regulation of sulfur amino acid biosynthesis in bacteria and molds; drug metabolism and separation methods; enzymatic mechanisms of drug biotransformation. *Mailing Add:* 3 Georgian Rd Randolph NJ 07869-1205

LEIPNIK, ROY BERGH, NON-LINEAR PARTIAL DIFFRENTIAL EQUATIONS, STOCHASTIC PROCESSES AND CLASSICAL ANALYSIS. *Current Pos:* PROF APPL MATH & MEM ALGEBRA INST, UNIV CALIF, SANTA BARBARA, 75- *Personal Data:* b Los Angeles, Calif, May 6, 24; m 44, Joan Hagist; c Karl, Erik & Mark. *Educ:* Univ Chicago, SB, 45, SM, 48; Univ Calif, Berkeley, PhD(math), 50. *Prof Exp:* Asst math statist & econ, Univ Chicago, 45-46; from asst to assoc math, Univ Calif, 46-48; fel, Sch Math, Inst Advan Study, Princeton, 48-50; asst prof, Univ Wash, 50-57; sr res scientist, Naval Weapons Ctr, Calif, 57-75. *Concurrent Pos:* Fulbright res prof, Univ Adelaide, 55, 63 & 68; lectr, Univ Calif, Los Angeles, 59-; prof, Univ Fla, 61-62, 64-65 & 70; pres, Idactic Co. *Mem:* Am Math Soc; Math Asn Am; Inst Math Statist; Inst Elec & Electronics Engrs; Soc Indust & Appl Math. *Res:* Operator analysis; mathematical physics; control systems; stochastic processes; information theory; plasma physics; transportation theory; recursive algorithms; differential equations; engineering mechanics; hydrologic and climatic equations; fluid mechanics, micro-economics; statistical distributions. *Mailing Add:* Math Dept Univ Calif Santa Barbara CA 93106. *E-Mail:* leipnik@math.ucsb.edu

LEIPOLD, MARTIN H(ENRY), ceramics, for more information see previous edition

LEIPPER, DALE F, SEA-AIR INTERACTION. *Current Pos:* chmn, 68-80, chmn, Dept Oceanogr, 80-89, DESERT RES INST, NAVAL POSTGRAD SCH, MONTEREY, 89- *Personal Data:* b Salem, Ohio, Sept 8, 14; m 42; c 4. *Educ:* Wittenberg Univ, BS 37; Ohio State Univ, MA, 39; Univ Calif, PhD(oceanog), 50. *Hon Degrees:* DSc, Wittenberg Univ, 68. *Prof Exp:* Weight & balance engr, Consol Aircraft, Calif, 40; sch teacher, Calif, 40-41; oceanogr, Scripps Inst, Univ Calif, 46-49; from assoc prof to prof oceanog & head dept, Tex A&M Univ, 49-68. *Concurrent Pos:* Head dept, Tex A&M Univ, 50-64, assoc exec dir, Tex A&M Found, 53-54, trustee, Univ Corp Atmospheric Res, 59-65; dir, World Data Ctr Oceanog, 57-60; consult, Comt Sci & Astronaut, US House Rep, 60; mem joint panel sea-air interaction, Nat Acad Sci, 60-62; adj prof oceanog, Naval Postgrad Sch, 80-88. *Mem:* Am Meteorol Soc; Am Soc Limnol & Oceanog (pres, 58); Am Soc Oceanog (pres, 67); Am Geophys Union; Oceanog Soc. *Res:* Coastal fog forecasting; analysis of sea temperature variations; use of the bathythermograph; interaction between ocean and atmosphere; physical oceanography; marine meteorology. *Mailing Add:* 716 Terra Ct Reno NV 89506-9606

LEIPUNER, LAWRENCE BERNARD, HIGH ENERGY & ELEMENTARY PARTICLE PHYSICS. *Current Pos:* SR RES PHYSICIST, BROOKHAVEN NAT LAB, 55- *Personal Data:* b Long Beach, NY, May 27, 28; m 48; c 3. *Educ:* Univ Pittsburgh, BS, 50; Carnegie Inst Technol, MS, 54, PhD(physics), 62. *Concurrent Pos:* Vis prof, Yale Univ, 67-68. *Mem:* Fel Am Phys Soc. *Res:* Lepton and quark experiments. *Mailing Add:* Dept Physics Bldg 510A Brookhaven Nat Lab Upton NY 11973

LEIPZIGER, FREDRIC DOUGLAS, ANALYTICAL CHEMISTRY. *Current Pos:* PRES, NORTHERN ANALYTICAL LAB, INC, 82- *Personal Data:* b New York, NY, Aug 26, 29; m 51; c 2. *Educ:* Univ Conn, BA, 51; Univ Mass, MS, 53, PhD(chem), 56. *Prof Exp:* Res assoc chem, Gen Elec Co, 55-62; head anal chem dept, Sperry Rand Res Ctr, 62-66; mgr anal serv, Ledgemont Lab, Kennecott Copper Corp, 66-81. *Mem:* Am Chem Soc; Soc Appl Spectros; Am Soc Mass Spectrometry; Am Asn Crystal Growth. *Res:* Electron microscopy; mass spectrometry; atomic absorption; automated analyses; process control. *Mailing Add:* 21 Donovan Ct Merrimack NH 03054

LEIS, BRIAN NORMAN, FRACTURE MECHANICS, DAMAGE MECHANICS. *Current Pos:* Scientist appl mech, Battelle Columbus Lab, 74-79, staff scientist, 79-81, sr scientist, 81-85, RES LEADER APPL MECH, BATTELLE COLUMBUS LAB, 85- *Personal Data:* b Kitchener, Ont, Oct 25, 47; m 69, Linda Cook; c Shawn, Craig & Shannon. *Educ:* Univ Waterloo, BASc, 71, MASc, 72, PhD(civil eng), 79. *Concurrent Pos:* Adj prof mech eng, Ohio State Univ, 80-83; subcomt chmn, Am Soc Testing & Mat, 81-85. *Mem:* Am Soc Testing & Mat; Am Soc Mech Engrs; Am Inst Metall Engrs. *Res:* Damage mechanics in materials and structures, including model simulation, with emphasis on fatigue, fracture and environmental degradation; granted one patent. *Mailing Add:* Battelle Columbus Lab Columbus OH 43201. *Fax:* 614-424-3457

LEIS, DONALD GEORGE, ORGANIC CHEMISTRY. *Current Pos:* group leader, 55-63, mgr mkt develop-cellular prod, 63-71, com mkt mgr, 71-75, SR MKT CONSULT, SILICONES & URETHANES DIV, UNION CARBIDE CORP, 75- *Personal Data:* b Jeannette, Pa, Aug 26, 19; m 45; c 3. *Educ:* St Vincent Col, BS, 41; Univ Notre Dame, MS, 42, PhD(org chem), 45. *Prof Exp:* Chemist, Carbide & Carbon Chem Co, 46-55. *Mem:* AAAS; Nat Fire Protection Asn; Soc Plastics Engrs; Am Chem Soc; Soc Plastics Indust. *Res:* Urethane products; polyethers; polyglycols; alkylene oxides; alkylene oxide derivatives; ethylene oxide; propylene oxide; urethanes; surfactants; lubricants and coatings. *Mailing Add:* 11 Coulter St No 28 Old Saybrook CT 06475-2349

LEIS, JONATHAN PETER, NUCLEIC ACID ENZYMOLOGY, VIROLOGY. *Current Pos:* assoc prof, 79-86, PROF BIOCHEM, MED SCH, CASE WESTERN RES UNIV, 86- *Personal Data:* b Brooklyn, NY, Aug 17, 44; m 70; c 2. *Educ:* Hofstra Univ, BA, 65; Cornell Univ, PhD(biochem), 70. *Prof Exp:* Fel develop biol & cancer, Albert Einstein Col Med, 70-73; asst prof surg, microbiol & immunol, Med Ctr, Duke Univ, 74-79. *Concurrent Pos:* Damon Runyon res fel, 71; res career develop awards, NIH, 74-79. *Mem:* Am Soc Biol Chemists; Am Soc Microbiol; Am Soc Virol. *Res:* Control of expression of eukaryotic genes; biochemical mechanisms of replication of Retro viruses; author of over 87 publications. *Mailing Add:* Dept Biochem Med Sch Case Western Res Univ 2119 Abington Rd Cleveland OH 44106. *Fax:* 216-368-4544; *E-Mail:* jxl8@po.cwru.edu

LEISE, ESTHER M, INVERTEBRATE NEUROANATOMY, LARVAL NEUROBIOLOGY. *Current Pos:* ASST PROF NEUROBIOL, DEPT BIOL, UNIV NC, GREENSBORO, 91- *Personal Data:* b Washington, DC, May 13, 53. *Educ:* Univ Md, BS, 75; Univ Wash, PhD(zool), 83. *Prof Exp:* Teaching asst, Dept Zool, Univ Wash, 75-83; postdoctoral res assoc, Dept Zool, Univ Calif, Davis, 83-88; postdoctoral res assoc, Dept Biol, Ga State Univ, 88-90; asst researcher, Pac Biomed Res Ctr, Univ Hawaii, Honolulu, 90-91. *Mem:* Soc Neurosci; AAAS; Am Soc Zoologists; Int Soc Neuroethol. *Res:* Neuroendocrine control of settlement and metamorphosis in marine invertebrate larvae, particularly molluscan veligers. *Mailing Add:* Dept Biol Univ NC Greensboro NC 27412-5001

LEISERSON, LEE, ORGANIC CHEMISTRY, PHYSICAL CHEMISTRY. *Current Pos:* RETIRED. *Personal Data:* b Toledo, Ohio, Mar 30, 16; m 43, 71, Marion J Blackburn; c Jay L, Margery J (Spinney), Ellen J, Jo A(Williams), Jan C(Furman) & Jody L(Graham). *Educ:* Antioch Col, BS, 37; Univ NC, MA, 40, PhD(org chem), 41. *Prof Exp:* Res chemist, Eastman Kodak Co, NY, 41-45; fel, Va Smelting Co, NC, 45-47; chemist, Am Cyanamid Co, NJ, 47-51; chief org chemist, Liggett & Myers Tobacco Co, 51-55; chemist & res adminr, Air Force Off Sci Res, Washington, DC, 55-62; chief, Chem Div, Off Saline, 62-74, consult, 74-76; field serv coordr, Environ Protection Agency, 76-80. *Concurrent Pos:* Consult. *Mem:* Fel AAAS; Am Chem Soc; Sigma Xi. *Res:* Surface active agents; organic synthesis; development of natural products; turpentine and tall oil separation processes; reactions in liquid sulfur dioxide; tobacco; water and aqueous solutions; environmental chemistry. *Mailing Add:* 200 Tabernacle Rd F-46 Black Mountain NC 28711-2592

LEISMAN, GERALD, NEUROPSYCHOLOGY, CONTROL THEORY. *Current Pos:* PROF BIOMED ENG, BIOBEHAV & NEUROSCI, TOURO COL, 91-, ASSOC DEAN & DIR, INST BIOMED ENG & REHAB SERVS, 92- *Personal Data:* b London, Eng, Oct 18, 47; US citizen; c Yael M, Akiba J & Daniel E. *Educ:* Queens Col, BA, 68; Univ Manchester, MSc, 70, MB ChB, 72; Union Inst, PhD(biomed eng & neuropsych), 79; Int Univ Complementary Med, MD, 90. *Honors & Awards:* Outstanding Contrib Vision Sci, Am Optometric Asn, 82. *Prof Exp:* Assoc prof health sci & comput sci, City Univ NY, 72-79; assoc prof psychiat, neurol & ophthal, Univ Med & Dent NJ-NJ Med Sch, 72-79; vpres res & develop, Trans Am Power Corp, 79-82, Am Electromedics Corp, 82-84, Hai Surg Corp, 84-87; prof neurosci, NY Chiropractic Col, 86-90, dean res & dir, Cons Health Care Res Inst, 86-90; pres & chief sci officer, Nat Inst Complementary Med, 90-92. *Concurrent Pos:* Adj prof comput sci & psychol, Pace Univ, 81-82, neurol & biomed eng, Harvard Univ Med Sch, 82-86, life sci & elec eng, NY Inst Technol, 86-91; mem, Comt Emerging Biomed Technol, Eng Med Biol Soc, 90-; vis scholar, Palmer Col Chiropract, 90; distinguished lectr biomed eng, Inst Elec & Electronics Engrs, 92. *Mem:* Fel Am Psychol Soc; NY Acad Sci; Am Col Forensic Examrs; sr mem Inst Elec & Electronics Engrs Eng Med & Biol Soc; Int Neuropsychol Soc; AAAS. *Res:* Neurosciences, neuroimaging, and electrophysiology applied to brain organization, vision, neuropsychology, systems science, neurophysics, and related areas; brain cognition; forensic examination. *Mailing Add:* 16 Cortelyou Rd Merrick NY 11566. *Fax:* 516-427-2703; *E-Mail:* drgersh@aol.com

LEISMAN, GILBERT ARTHUR, BOTANY. *Current Pos:* from asst prof to assoc prof, 55-64, PROF BIOL, EMPORIA STATE UNIV, 64- *Personal Data:* b Washington, DC, May 12, 24; m 52. *Educ:* Univ Wis, BS, 49; Univ Minn, MS, 52, PhD, 55. *Prof Exp:* Asst plant physiol, Univ Wis, 49-50; asst bot, Univ Minn, 50-55. *Concurrent Pos:* Mem, World Orgn Paleobot, Int Union Biol Sci. *Mem:* AAAS; Bot Soc Am; Nat Asn Biol Teachers; Int Asn Plant Taxon. *Res:* Coal ball plants; morphology of pteridosperm leaves and fructifications; plant succession and soil development of mine dumps. *Mailing Add:* 66 SO 1 Emporia KS 66801

LEISS, ERNST L, HIGH-PERFORMANCE COMPUTING, DATA SECURITY. *Current Pos:* from asst prof to assoc prof, 79-92, dir, Res Comput Lab, 85-93, PROF COMPUT SCI, UNIV HOUSTON, 92- *Personal Data:* b Ger, July 7, 52; m 79, Benigna Cortes; c Ernst A. *Educ:* Univ Waterloo, Can, MMath, 74; Tech Univ Vienna, Austria, Dipl Ing, 75, Dr Techn, 76. *Prof Exp:* Fel, Univ Waterloo 76-77; mem fac, Univ Chile, 78 & Univ Ky, 79. *Concurrent Pos:* Vis prof, var univs, Europe & Latin Am; Nat lectr, Asn Comput Mach, 91-97. *Mem:* Sr mem Inst Elec & Electronics Engrs; Asn Comput Mach; Soc Explor Geophysicists. *Res:* Vector and parallel computing; seismic data processing; data security; databases; automata theory. *Mailing Add:* Dept Comput Sci Univ Houston Houston TX 77204-3475. *E-Mail:* coscel@cs.uh.edu

LEISS, JAMES ELROY, PHYSICS. *Current Pos:* RETIRED. *Personal Data:* b Youngstown, Ohio, June 2, 24; m 45, Wilma Dindore; c 4. *Educ:* Case Inst Technol, BS, 49; Univ Ill, MS, 51, PhD(physics), 54. *Prof Exp:* Lab asst, Gen Elec Co, 48-49; asst physics, Univ Ill, 49-54; dir, Ctr Radiation Res, Nat Bur Stand, 54-78; dir, Off High Energy & Nuclear Physics, Dept Energy, 78-85. *Mem:* Am Phys Soc; AAAS; Sigma Xi. *Res:* Nuclear physics, especially photonuclear reactions and photomeson reactions; design of particle accelerators; scientific research management. *Mailing Add:* Rte 2 Box 142C Broadway VA 22815

LEISSA, A(RTHUR) W(ILLIAM), VIBRATIONS, BUCKLING. *Current Pos:* res assoc, Res Found, 55-56, from instr to assoc prof, 56-64, PROF ENG MECH, OHIO STATE UNIV, 64-, RES FOUND SUPVR, 62- *Personal Data:* b Wilmington, Del, Nov 16, 31; m 53; c 2. *Educ:* Ohio State Univ, BME & MSc, 54, PhD(eng mech), 58. *Prof Exp:* Assoc engr, Sperry Gyroscope Co, 54-55. *Concurrent Pos:* Mech engr, Ralph & Curl Engrs, 54-58; fac assoc, Boeing Airplane Co, 57; consult, NAm Aviation, Inc, 58-64, Battelle Mem Inst, 64-, Kaman Nuclear, 68-70, & Medtronic, Inc, 84-85; vis prof, Swiss Fed Inst Technol, 72-73; assoc ed, Appl Mech Reviews, 85-93, J Vibration Acoust, 89-93; vis prof, USAF Acad, 85-86; chmn, Orgn Comt, Pan Am Congress Appl Mech, 86-89; res fel, Japan Soc Prom Sci, 90; ed-in-chief, Appl Mech Reviews, 93- *Mem:* Assoc fel Am Inst Aeronaut & Astronaut; Am Soc Eng Educ; Int Asn Shell Struct; fel Am Soc Mech Engrs; fel Am Acad Mech (pres 87-88). *Res:* Elasticity; plates and shells; vibration of continuous systems; buckling; numerical methods for solving boundary value and eigenvalue problems; composite structures. *Mailing Add:* Dept Eng Mech Ohio State Univ 155 W Woodruff Columbus OH 43210-1117

LEISTER, HARRY M, PHYSICAL CHEMISTRY. *Current Pos:* sr chem, 82-83, group lab mgr, 83-88, DIR, QUAKER CHEM CORP, 88- *Personal Data:* b Quakertown, Pa, Mar 3, 41; m 62, Marie Mascola; c 4. *Educ:* Pa State Univ, BS, 63; Drexel Univ, MS, 65; Temple Univ, PhD(phys chem), 70. *Prof Exp:* Res chemist, E I Du Pont de Nemours & Co, 69-70; chemist, Amchem Div, Union Carbide Corp, 71-73; group leader, Amchem Prod, Inc, 73-81, scientist, 81-82. *Mem:* Am Chem Soc; Immunochemiluminometric Assay. *Res:* Organic coatings; inorganic coatings; formulation of specialty products for metal process industry; emulsification. *Mailing Add:* 1206 Prospect Ave Ft Washington PA 19034

LEISURE, ROBERT GLENN, SOLID STATE PHYSICS. *Current Pos:* from asst prof to assoc prof, 70-78, chmn, Dept Physics, 84-90, PROF PHYSICS, COLO STATE UNIV, 78- *Personal Data:* b Cromwell, Ky, Jan 29, 38; m 62, Jeanine Smith. *Educ:* Western Ky Univ, BS, 60; Wash Univ, PhD(physics), 67. *Honors & Awards:* US-France Exchange Scientist Award; Sci & Eng Res Coun Award, UK 83 & 87. *Prof Exp:* Res scientist, Boeing Sci Res Lab, 67-70. *Concurrent Pos:* Vis scientist, Univ Paris VI, 78-79; sr vis fel, St Andrews Univ, Scotland, 83 & 87; collabr, Los Alamos Nat Lab, 90-94; mem operating bd, Colo Advan Mat Inst; vis prof, Tokushima Univ, 91. *Mem:* Am Phys Soc; Sigma Xi; Acoust Soc Am. *Res:* Ultrasonics; elastic and anelastic properties of solids; phase transformations; hydrogen-metal systems. *Mailing Add:* Dept Physics Colo State Univ Ft Collins CO 80523. *Fax:* 970-491-7947; *E-Mail:* leisure@lamar.colostate.edu

LEITCH, CRAIG H B, EARTH SCIENCE, ECONOMIC GEOLOGY. *Honors & Awards:* Barlow Medal, Can Inst Mining & Metall, 91. *Mailing Add:* c/o Xerox Tower Suite 120 3400 de Maissonneuve Blvd W Montreal PQ H3Z 3B8 Can

LEITCH, GORDON JAMES, GASTROINTESTINAL PHYSIOLOGY. *Current Pos:* PROF MED PHYSIOL, MOREHOUSE SCH MED, 77-, CHMN DEPT, 78- *Educ:* Univ Chicago, PhD(physiol), 64. *Res:* Diarrhea pathophysiology; alcohol pathophysiology. *Mailing Add:* Dept Physiol Morehouse Sch Med 720 Westview Dr SW Atlanta GA 30310-1495

LEITCH, JAY A, ENVIRONMENTAL & RESOURCE ECONOMICS, PUBLIC FINANCE. *Current Pos:* PROF AGR ECON, NDAK STATE UNIV, 81- *Personal Data:* b Fergus Falls, Minn, Sept 20, 48; m 90, Rebecca L Bekkerus; c Philip, Forrest & Rachel. *Educ:* Moorhead State Univ, Minn, BA, 74; NDak State Univ, MS 76; Univ Minn, PhD(agr & appl econ), 81. *Concurrent Pos:* Naval intel officer, USNR, 80-92; sci adv, Secy Army, 85-86, spec asst, Off Asst, 86-88; sr economist off policy anal, Off Secy, Dept Interior, 86; dir, Tri-Col Univ Ctr Environ Studies, 86-92; assoc dir, NDak Water Resources Res Inst, 87-90. *Mem:* Soc Wetland Scientists (pres, 89-90); Am Water Resources Asn; Can Water Resources Asn; Am Agr Econs Asn; Asn Environ Prof; Int Impact Assessment Asn. *Res:* Wetland economics and policy at all levels from local to global. *Mailing Add:* Agr Econ NDak State Univ Fargo ND 58105-5636. Fax: 701-237-7400; E-Mail: coa-nrm@ndsuext.nodak.edu

LEITE, RICHARD JOSEPH, PRELIMINARY DESIGN OF SPACECRAFT & SPACEFLIGHT PAYLOADS, DEVELOPMENT OF MINIATURIZED SENSORS & INSTRUMENTS. *Current Pos:* RETIRED. *Personal Data:* b Fremont, Ohio, Mar 8, 23; m 55, Barbara M Higgins; c Mark R, Jeffrey H & Mary L (Berlew). *Educ:* Univ Notre Dame, BNS, 45, BSE, 47; Univ Mich, MSE, 48, PhD(aero eng), 56. *Prof Exp:* Res assoc, Univ Mich, Ann Arbor, 48-56, res engr, 58-71; sr engr, Booz-Allen Appl Res, Inc, 56-58; sr staff engr, Bendix Aerospace Corp, 71-72; sr scientist, KMS Fusion, Inc, 72-77; staff mgr, Eng & Test Div, TRW Inc, Redondo Beach, Calif, 77-92. *Concurrent Pos:* Lectr, Univ Mich, Ann Arbor, 58-60, prin investr, 63-71, res consult, 68-71. *Mem:* Sigma Xi. *Res:* Electrical systems design and development of spacecraft; qualification testing and electrical integration of systems components and systems; laser fusion fuel pellet development and insertion technology; spaceflight mass spectrometer development; upper atmosphere composition measurement pioneer; experimental demonstration of stability criteria for tube flow; one United States patent. *Mailing Add:* 6742 Abbottswood Dr Rancho Palos Verdes CA 90275-3018

LEITER, EDWARD HENRY, CELL BIOLOGY. *Current Pos:* from assoc staff scientist to staff scientist, 74-89, SR STAFF SCIENTIST, JACKSON LAB, 90- *Personal Data:* b Columbus, Ga, Apr 17, 42; m 64, Susan Shaw. *Educ:* Princeton Univ, BS, 64; Emory Univ, MS, 66, PhD(biol), 68. *Prof Exp:* NIH trainee, Univ Tex, Austin, 68-71; asst prof biol, Brooklyn Col, 71-74. *Concurrent Pos:* Nat Inst Arthritis & Metab Dis res grant, 74-; Juvenile Diabetes Found grant, 76- *Mem:* Endocrine Soc; Am Diabetes Asn; Am Asn Immunologists. *Res:* Function of normal and diabetic pancreatic endocrine cells in vitro; genetic, viral, and environmental parameters producing pancreatic pathologies in the mouse; immunology of type 1 diabetes. *Mailing Add:* Jackson Lab Bar Harbor ME 04609. E-Mail: ehl@aretha.jax.org

LEITER, HOWARD ALLEN, PHYSICS. *Current Pos:* RETIRED. *Personal Data:* b Mt Gilead, Ohio, Feb 16, 18; m 52; c 3. *Educ:* Miami Univ, AB, 40; Univ Ill, AM, 42, PhD(physics), 49. *Prof Exp:* Asst physics, Univ Ill, 40-42; mem staff, Radiation Lab, Mass Inst Technol, 42-45; asst physics, Univ Ill, 45-48, res assoc, 48-49; physicist, Res Labs, Westinghouse Elec Corp, 49-58; sr engr, Labs, Int Tel & Tel Corp, 58-69; assoc prof physics, Tri-State Col, 70-75; instr, Inventive Indust, 75-77; instr, Int Tel & Tel Corp, 78-83. *Concurrent Pos:* Guest lectr, Off-campus Grad Prog, Purdue Univ, 59-60. *Mem:* Am Phys Soc. *Res:* Charged particle scattering; microwave components; interaction of electromagnetic radiations with matter; infrared detectors and systems; image tubes; cryogenic equipment; field emission microscopy; satellite instrumentation. *Mailing Add:* 2703 Capitol Ave Ft Wayne IN 46806

LEITER, JOSEPH, BIOCHEMISTRY. *Current Pos:* CONSULT, 83- *Personal Data:* b New York, NY, May 14, 15; m 39; c 2. *Educ:* Brooklyn Col, BS, 34; Georgetown Univ, PhD(biochem), 49. *Prof Exp:* Jr chemist org & fibrous mat, Nat Bur Stands, 35-38; carcinogenesis, Nat Cancer Inst, 38-40, asst chemist, 40-42, assoc chemist chemother, 46-47, chemist, 47-49, from sr chemist to sr scientist & chief biochem sect, Lab Chem Pharmacol, 49-55, scientist dir & asst chief lab activ, Cancer Chemother Nat Serv Ctr, 55-63, chief, Ctr, 63-65, assoc dir libr opers, Nat Libr Med, 65-83. *Mem:* AAAS; Soc Pharmacol & Exp Therapeut; Am Chem Soc; Am Asn Cancer Res. *Res:* Carcinogenesis, production of tumors with chemical agents, air dust; chemotherapy of cancer; drug metabolism, effect of chemical agents on enzymes in normal and malignant tissues; biomedical library and information systems. *Mailing Add:* 5101 Ridge Field Rd Bethesda MD 20816

LEITH, ARDEAN, BIOLOGICAL COMPUTING. *Current Pos:* RES SCIENTIST, HEALTH RES INC, ALBANY, NY, 85- *Personal Data:* b Warsaw, NY, Mar 21, 47; m 82, Meeli Chew; c Eric Weiming. *Educ:* Rensselaer Polytech Inst, BS, 68, MS, 86; Univ Rochester, PhD(biol), 72. *Prof Exp:* Fac mem biophys, Nat Univ Malaysia, 72-76 & cell biol, Univ Pertanian Malaysia, 78-82; sr res assoc cell biol, Worcester Polytech Inst, Mass, 76-78; asst prof cell biol, Univ Guam, USA, 82-85. *Mem:* Am Comput Mach; Inst Elec & Electronics Engrs; Am Chem Soc; AAAS. *Res:* Visualization of cellular structure; display techniques for tomographic and confocal microscopy data; mathematical modeling of biological processes; computer graphics applications in biology. *Mailing Add:* Wadsworth Labs Empire State Plaza PO Box 509 Albany NY 12201. E-Mail: leith@wadsworth.org

LEITH, CARLTON JAMES, GEOLOGY. *Current Pos:* RETIRED. *Personal Data:* b Madison, Wis, Sept 24, 19; m 41, Marian Pollensky; c Carol J (Kurumada) & Ronnie S. *Educ:* Univ Wis, BA, 40, MA, 41; Univ Calif, PhD(geol), 47. *Prof Exp:* Asst geol, Univ Calif, 41-42; from jr mineral economist to asst mineral economist, Mineral Prod & Econ Div, US Bur Mines, 42-43; geologist, Stand Oil Co, Tex, 46; asst geol, Univ Calif, 46-47; from instr to asst prof geol, Univ Ind, 47-49; chief petrog unit, US Engrs Testing Lab, 49-51; geologist, Stand Oil Co, Calif, 51-60 & Holmes & Narver, Inc, 60-61; assoc prof, 61-65, prof geol eng, 65-80, emer prof geosci, NC State Univ, 80, Head dept, 67-80. *Mem:* Am Asn Petrol Geol. *Res:* Engineering geology; sedimentary petrology; areal geology; gravity and magnetics. *Mailing Add:* 17960 Tanleaf Lane Salinas CA 93907

LEITH, CECIL ELDON, JR, TURBULENCE, ATMOSPHERIC SCIENCES. *Current Pos:* physicist, 83-90, EMER PHYSICIST, LAWRENCE LIVERMORE NAT LAB, DEPT ENERGY, 90- *Personal Data:* b Boston, Mass, Jan 31, 23; m 42, Mary Henry; c Ann, John & Paul. *Educ:* Univ Calif, Berkeley, AB, 43, PhD(math), 57. *Honors & Awards:* Meisinger Award, Am Meteorol Soc, 67, Carl-Gustaf Rossby Res Medal, 81. *Prof Exp:* Physicist, Lawrence Radiation Lab, Univ Calif, 46-68; sr scientist, Nat Ctr Atmospheric Res, 68-78, dir, Atmospheric Anal & Prediction Div, 78-81, sr scientist, 81-83. *Concurrent Pos:* Mem, Int Comn Dynamic Meteorol, Int Asn Meteorol & Atmospheric Physics, 72-80 & Int Comn Climate, 78-80; mem joint organizing comt, Global Atmospheric Res Prog, World Meteorol Orgn & Int Counc Sci Unions, 76-80, officer, Joint Sci Comt, World Climate Res Prog, 81-83; chmn, Comt Atmospheric Sci, Nat Res Coun, 78-80. *Mem:* Fel AAAS; fel Am Phys Soc; fel Am Meteorol Soc; Am Math Soc. *Res:* Computational fluid dynamics; statistical hydrodynamics; turbulence. *Mailing Add:* 627 Carla St Livermore CA 94550-2316. E-Mail: leith1@llnl.gov

LEITH, DAVID W G S, HIGH ENERGY PHYSICS. *Current Pos:* assoc prof, 66-70, PROF PHYSICS, LINEAR ACCELERATOR CTR, STANFORD UNIV, 70-, DIR RES, 91- *Personal Data:* b Glasgow, Scotland, Sept 5, 37; m 62, Doveen; c 3. *Educ:* Univ Glasgow, BSc, 59, PhD(natural philos), 62. *Prof Exp:* Res fel pyisics, Glasgow Univ, Europ Orgn Nuclear Res, Geneva, Switz, 62-63, staff physicist, 63-66. *Mem:* Fel Am Phys Soc; Brit Inst Physics & Phys Soc. *Res:* Strong interaction physics with emphasis on scattering experiments and investigations of resonance properties, their classification and the associated phenomenological analysis; study of electroweak interaction via the production and decay of z boson. *Mailing Add:* 754 Mayfield Ave Stanford Univ Stanford CA 94305. Fax: 650-926-4500; E-Mail: leith@slac.stanford.edu

LEITH, EMMETT NORMAN, ELECTRO-OPTICS. *Current Pos:* asst eng res inst, Univ Mich, Ann Arbor, 52-56, res assoc, 56-59, assoc res engr, 59-65, assoc prof, 65-68, PROF ELEC ENG, UNIV MICH, ANN ARBOR, 68- *Personal Data:* b Detroit, Mich, Mar 12, 27; m 56, Lois June Neswold; c Kim & Pam. *Educ:* Wayne State Univ, BS, 49, MS, 52, PhD, 79. *Hon Degrees:* DSC, Univ Aberdeen, Scotland, 96. *Honors & Awards:* Gordon Mem Award, Soc Photo-Optical Instrumentation Eng, 65, Liebmann Award, Inst Elec & Electronics Engrs, 67; Daedalion Award, 68; Stuart Ballantine Medal, Franklin Inst, 69; R W Wood Prize, Optical Soc Am, 75; Holly Medal, Am Soc Chem Engrs, 76; Inventor Year Award, Asn Adv Invention & Innovation, 76; Nat Medal Sci, 79; Ivestr Medal, Optical Soc Am; Dennis Gabor Medal, Soc Photo-Optical Instrumentation Eng, 84, Gold Medal, 89. *Prof Exp:* Lab instr physics, Wayne State Univ, 51-52. *Mem:* Nat Acad Eng; fel Optical Soc Am; fel Inst Elec & Electronics Engrs; fel Soc Photo-Optical Instrument Engrs. *Res:* Wavefront reconstruction; electronic physics; electromagnetics; radar; resonant cavity design; data processing; optical system design; coherent optics; interferometry; holography. *Mailing Add:* Dept Elec & Comput Eng Univ Mich Ann Arbor MI 48109-2122. Fax: 313-647-2718

LEITH, JOHN DOUGLAS, PATHOLOGY. *Current Pos:* RETIRED. *Personal Data:* b Grand Forks, NDak, Apr 20, 31; m 57; c 2. *Educ:* Lehigh Univ, BA, 52; Univ Pa, MD, 56; Univ Wis, PhD(cytol), 64; Am Bd Path, cert anat & clin path, 74, cert radioisotopic path, 75. *Prof Exp:* Intern, Med Ctr, Univ Calif, San Francisco, 56-57; asst zool, Univ Wis, 59-60, NSF fel, 60-63; Nat Cancer Inst spec fel, 63-64; asst prof anat & cell biol, Med Sch, Univ Pittsburgh, 64-67; from asst prof to assoc prof biol, Univ Wis-Oshkosh, 67-71; resident path, Peter Bent Brigham Hosp, Boston, 71-74; assoc pathologist, Brockton Hosp, 75-91, actg chief pathologist, 91-93. *Concurrent Pos:* Am Cancer Soc Inst res grant, 65-66, Health Res Serv Found res grant, 66-67, NSF grant, 68-70, Univ Wis res grants 68-70. *Mem:* Col Am Path; Am Soc Clin Path; Sigma Xi. *Mailing Add:* 162 Islington Rd Auburndale MA 02166

LEITH, WILLIAM CUMMING, MECHANICAL ENGINEERING, POLLUTION CONTROL. *Current Pos:* CONSULT, 90- *Personal Data:* b Kimberley, BC, Apr 15, 25; m 50, Marian Mills; c James, Brenda & Hope. *Educ:* Univ BC, BAppSc, 48, MAppSc, 49; McGill Univ, PhD(mech eng), 60. *Honors & Awards:* Duggan Prize & Medal, Eng Inst Can, 59. *Prof Exp:* Jr engr, Dom Eng Works, Que, 49-50 & Cominco-Trail, BC, 51-52; mech res engr, Dom Eng Works, Que, 53-61; sr res scientist, Hydronautic Inc, Md, 61-62; design engr, Cominco-Trail, BC, 62-64 & H G Acres Co, Ont, 64-67; res assoc prof nuclear eng, Univ Wash, 67-73; mech engr, Cominco Ltd, 73-90. *Prof Exp:* Consult, wood chip refining. *Mem:* Am Soc Mech Engrs. *Res:* Design of devices for access to blood circulatory systems such as cannulas, fistulas and catheters; pollution control; scrubbing of gases; uranium enrichment by gas centrifuge; cavitation correlated to vibration white finger in loggers' hands and minimum energy model of wood chip refining pulp/paper making. *Mailing Add:* PO Box 157 Trail BC V1R 4L4 Can

LEITMAN, MARSHALL J, APPLIED MATHEMATICS, CONTINUUM PHYSICS. *Current Pos:* asst prof, 66-71, assoc prof, 71-81, PROF MATH, CASE WESTERN RES UNIV, 81- *Personal Data:* b Yonkers, NY, Jan 16, 41. *Educ:* Rensselaer Polytech Inst, BS, 62; Brown Univ, PhD(appl math), 65. *Prof Exp:* Res assoc appl math, Brown Univ, 65-66. *Concurrent Pos:* Vis asst prof, Cath Univ Louvain, 70-71. *Mem:* Soc Natural Philos; Soc Indust & Appl Math. *Res:* Mechanics; viscoelasticity. *Mailing Add:* Dept Math & Statist Case Western Res Univ University Circle Cleveland OH 44106-1749

LEITMANN, G(EORGE), MECHANICS, SYSTEMS & CONTROL. *Current Pos:* from asst prof to prof eng sci, Univ Calif, Berkeley, 57-91, chmn, Div Appl Mech, 71-72, Univ Ombudsman, 68-70, assoc dean, Col Eng, 81-94, Hughes Chair Mech Eng, 90-91, EMER PROF ENG SCI, UNIV CALIF, BERKELEY, 91-, CHAIR, FAC ENG, 94-, PROF GRAD SCH, 95- *Personal Data:* b Vienna, Austria, May 24, 25; nat US; m 55, Nancy Lloyd; c Josef L & Elaine M (Parker). *Educ:* Columbia Univ, BS, 49, MA, 50; Univ Calif, PhD(eng sci), 56. *Hon Degrees:* DSc, Technische Univ, Vienna, 88, Univ Paris, 89; DIng, Technische Univ, Darmstadt, 89. *Honors & Awards:* Pendray Aerospace Lit Award, Am Inst Aeronaut & Astronaut, 77; Levy Medal, Franklin Inst, 81; Mech & Control of Flight Award, Am Inst Aeronaut & Astronaut, 80; Alexander von Humboldt Sr Scientist Award, 81; Alexander von Humboldt Medal, 91; Oldenburger Medal, Am Soc Mech Engrs, 95; Bellman Award, 95. *Prof Exp:* Physicist, Naval Ord Test Sta, 50-55, head aeroballistics anal sect, 55-57. *Concurrent Pos:* Consult, Martin Co, 57-58 & Lockheed Missiles & Space Co, 58-66; ed, J Math Anal Appl; assoc ed, J Optimal Theory Appln; pres, Alexander von Humboldt Asn Am, 94- *Mem:* Nat Acad Eng; Int Acad Astronaut; Acad Sci Bologna; fel Am Inst Aeronaut & Astronaut; Arg Acad Eng; Russ Acad Natural Sci; Bavarian Acad Sci. *Res:* Exterior ballistics of rockets and astrodynamics; variational problems in mechanics and astronautics; optimal control of dynamic systems; game theory; control of uncertain systems; applications to economics, engineering; resource management. *Mailing Add:* Dept Mech Eng Univ Calif Berkeley CA 94720. *Fax:* 510-642-6216; *E-Mail:* gleit@hera.eecs.berkeley.edu

LEITNER, ALFRED, MATHEMATICAL THEORY OF WAVE PROPAGATION, DEMONSTRATION EXPERIMENTS. *Current Pos:* prof, 67-87, EMER PROF PHYSICS, RENSSELAER POLYTECH INST, 87- *Personal Data:* b Vienna, Austria, Nov 3, 21; m 48, Marzia O'Neil; c Kathleen, Deborah (Matulis) & David. *Educ:* Univ Buffalo, BA, 44; Yale Univ, MS, 45, PhD(physics), 48. *Prof Exp:* Res scientist, Courant Inst, NY Univ, 47-51; from asst prof to prof physics, Mich State Univ, 51-67. *Concurrent Pos:* Vis prof physics & Guggenheim fel, Aachen Technische Hochschule, Ger, 58-59; vis prof physics, Rensselaer Polytech Inst, 64 & US Mil Acad, West Point, 83-85; res assoc, Proj Physics, Harvard Univ, 65-66, consult, 66-67; Ger exchange fel, Deutsches Mus, Munich, 77-78. *Mem:* Fel Am Phys Soc; Am Asn Physics Teachers. *Res:* Mathematical theory of wave propagation, boundary value problems and special functions; production of educational films demonstrating physical phenomena for students of physics; history of physics. *Mailing Add:* 1201 Eighth Terr N Naples FL 34102-5411

LEITNER, PHILIP, VERTEBRATE ZOOLOGY. *Current Pos:* from instr to assoc prof, 62-76, chmn dept, 70-76, PROF BIOL, ST MARY'S COL, CALIF, 76- *Personal Data:* b Peking, China, June 16, 36; US citizen; m 60; c 2. *Educ:* St Mary's Col, Calif, BS, 58; Univ Calif, Los Angeles, MA, 60, PhD(zool), 61. *Prof Exp:* Jr res zoologist, Univ Calif, Los Angeles, 61-62. *Concurrent Pos:* NIH res grant, 63-65, NSF res grants, 65-70. *Mem:* AAAS; Am Soc Zoologists; Soc Study Evolution; Am Soc Mammalogists. *Res:* Environmental physiology of mammals, especially physiological responses to temperature and photoperiod. *Mailing Add:* Dept Biol St Marys Col 1928 St Marys Rd Moraga CA 94556-8144

LEITZ, FRED JOHN, JR, PHYSICAL CHEMISTRY, NUCLEAR CHEMISTRY. *Current Pos:* CONSULT, 84- *Personal Data:* b Portland, Ore, Feb 2, 21; m 45, Kathryn Kauper; c Fred, Robert & Steven. *Educ:* Reed Col, BA, 40; Univ Calif, PhD(phys chem), 43. *Prof Exp:* Instr chem, Univ Calif, 43-44; sr res chemist, Monsanto Chem Co, Ohio, 44-46; sr chemist, Oak Ridge Nat Lab, Tenn, 46-48; chemist, Radiochem & Reactor Metall Res, Hanford Works, Gen Elec Co, Wash, 48-56; nuclear engr, Atomic Power Develop Assocs, Mich, 56-58; develop proj engr, Atomic Power Equip Dept, Gen Elec Co, 58-64, mgr fast reactor core eng & test, Advan Prod Oper, 64-66, mgr steam reactor technol, 66-68; consult to dir, Battelle Northwest Lab, 69-70; sr staff scientist, Westinghouse Hanford Co, 70-76, mgr planning & anal, 76-79, staff mgr technol, 79-84. *Mem:* Am Chem Soc; Am Nuclear Soc. *Res:* Heavy element and fission product chemistry; nuclear fuel cycle development; fast and steam cooled reactor design and technology. *Mailing Add:* 10411-140th Ave E Puyallup WA 98374

LEITZ, FREDERICK HENRY, pharmacology, for more information see previous edition

LEITZ, VICTORIA MARY, BIOCHEMISTRY, LABORATORY MEDICINE. *Current Pos:* PRIN, INT BIOMED CONSULT, 94- *Personal Data:* b Yorkshire, Eng. *Educ:* Oxford Univ, BA, 64, DPhil(clin chem), 68. *Prof Exp:* Res scientist human genetics, Med Res Coun, Oxford, Eng, 67-68; chemist neurochem, Sect Child Neurol, Nat Inst Neurol Dis & Stroke, NIH, 68-70; mgr develop chem & clin chem, Becton-Dickinson, NJ, 71-72; mgr diag chem & clin chem, Electro-Nucleonics, Inc, 74-79, dir tech serv, 79-81, dir mkt, 81-84, vpres int sales & mkt, 84-89, dir clin chem, Pharmacia plug, 90-94. *Mem:* Am Asn Clin Chem; Nat Comt Clin Lab Stand; Biomed Mkt Asn. *Mailing Add:* 55 Peninsula Dr Hilton Head Island SC 29926

LEITZEL, JAMES ROBERT C, MATHEMATICS. *Current Pos:* asst prof, 65-69, ASSOC PROF MATH, OHIO STATE UNIV, 69- *Personal Data:* b Shenandoah, Pa, May 27, 36; m 65; c 2. *Educ:* Pa State Univ, BA, 58, MA, 60; Ind Univ, PhD(math), 65. *Prof Exp:* Asst prof math, Bloomsburg State Col, 59-63. *Concurrent Pos:* Chair, Comt Math Educ Teachers, Math Asn Am. *Mem:* Am Math Soc; Math Asn Am; AAAS; Nat Coun Teachers Math; Asn Women Math. *Res:* Algebra, especially class field theory and algebraic function fields. *Mailing Add:* Kingsbury Hall Univ NH Durham NH 03824-3591

LEITZEL, JOAN PHILLIPS, MATHEMATICS. *Current Pos:* from asst prof to assoc prof, 65-83, PROF MATH, OHIO STATE UNIV, 83- *Personal Data:* b Valparaiso, Ind, July 2, 36; m 65; c 2. *Educ:* Hanover Col, AB, 58; Brown Univ, AM, 61; Univ Ind, PhD(algebra), 65. *Prof Exp:* Instr math, Oberlin Col, 61-62. *Concurrent Pos:* Vchmn Math Dept, Ohio State Univ, 73-, assoc provost, 85-90, pres; div dir, NSF, 90- *Mem:* Am Math Soc; Math Asn Am. *Res:* Field theoretical proofs for cohomological results in class field theory. *Mailing Add:* Off of Pres Univ N H Thompson 105 Main St Durham NH 03824

LEITZMANN, CLAUS, BIOCHEMISTRY, NUTRITION. *Current Pos:* assoc, 74-78, PROF INST NUTRIT, UNIV GIESSEN, 78-, DIR INST NUTRIT, 90- *Personal Data:* b Dahlenburg, Ger, Feb 6, 33; m 57; c 4. *Educ:* Capital Univ, BS, 62; Univ Minn, MS, 64, PhD(biochem), 67. *Honors & Awards:* Zabel prize, 87. *Prof Exp:* Nat Inst Gen Med Sci res asst molecular biol inst, Univ Calif, Los Angeles, 67-69; vis prof biochem, Mahidol Univ, Thailand, 69-71; chief labs, Anemia & Malnutrit Res Ctr, Thailand, 71-74. *Concurrent Pos:* Mem, Trop Inst, Univ Giessen, 74- *Mem:* AAAS; Inst Soc Nutrit; Am Soc Clin Nutrit; Am Inst Nutrit. *Res:* Nutrition in developing countries; interaction of nutrition and infection; adaptations to changes in food intake; hunger and satiety; obesity; dietary fibers; vegetarianism. *Mailing Add:* Inst Nutrit Justus-Liebig-U Wilhelmstr 20 35392 Giessen Germany

LEIVO, WILLIAM JOHN, PHYSICS. *Current Pos:* PROF PHYSICS, OKLA STATE UNIV, 55- *Personal Data:* b New Castle, Pa, Sept 11, 15; m 39; c 2. *Educ:* Carnegie Inst Technol, BS, 39, MS, 45, DSc(physics), 48. *Prof Exp:* Supt bldg construct, Matthew Leivo & Sons, Inc, Pa, 33-35 & 39-42; from instr to asst prof physics, Carnegie Inst Technol, 42-55. *Mem:* Fel Am Phys Soc; Am Asn Physics Teachers. *Res:* Color centers in crystals; radiation effects in solids; optics; solid state physics; semiconducting diamond; ESR studies of blood cell membranes. *Mailing Add:* Dept Physics Okla State Univ Stillwater OK 74074

LEJA, J(AN), SURFACE CHEMISTRY, METALLURGY. *Current Pos:* prof, 65-83, EMER PROF METALL, UNIV BC, 83- *Personal Data:* b Grodzisko, Poland, May 27, 18; m 47; c 6. *Educ:* Univ London, BSc, 45; Univ Krakow, dipl Ing, 47; Cambridge Univ, PhD(surface chem), 54. *Hon Degrees:* Dr, Marie Curie-Sklodowska Univ, Poland, 76. *Prof Exp:* Res metallurgist, Southwest Africa Co, Eng, 47-49, reduction officer, SAfrica, 49-52; res fel colloid sci, Cambridge Univ, 54-57; from asst prof to prof metall, Univ Alta, 57-65. *Mem:* Brit Inst Mining & Metall; fel Can Inst Chem; Can Inst Mining & Metall. *Res:* Surface chemistry; infrared spectroscopy of adsorption; effluent control; dissolution of metals; corrosion. *Mailing Add:* 32741 Richards Ave RR 5 Mission BC V2V 5X4 Can

LEJA, STANISLAW, MATHEMATICS. *Current Pos:* asst prof, 57-67, EMER PROF MATH, WESTERN MICH UNIV, 82- *Personal Data:* b Grodzisko, Poland, Jan 3, 12; nat US; m 39, 87; c 4. *Prof Exp:* Teacher high schs, Palestine & Eng, 45-51; from asst to instr, Cornell Univ, 53-57. *Mem:* Am Math Soc; Math Asn Am. *Res:* Real variable; Fourier analysis. *Mailing Add:* 2205 Thurber Ct Orlando FL 32837-6785

LEKEUX, PIERRE MARIE, VETERINARY PHYSIOLOGY, BOVINE & EQUINE DISEASES. *Current Pos:* PROF PHYSIOL, UNIV LIEGE, 86-; DIR, LAB FUNCTIONAL INVEST, 88- *Personal Data:* b Liege, Belg, Apr 7, 54; m 78, Delogne Odette; c Max & David. *Educ:* Univ Liege, Belg, DVM, 78; Univ Utrecht, Neth, PRD 84. *Honors & Awards:* Peter Bridge Award, 91. *Prof Exp:* Pres, Comp Respiratory Soc, 88-89. *Concurrent Pos:* Assoc ed-in-chief, Annals of Med, 86 & Pratipue Vet Equine, 91; pres equine, Equine Res Funds, 88-; secy gen bovine, World Asn Buiatrics, 90-; chmn meeting comt, World Eprine Vet Asn, 91-; bd mem, Int Comt Eprine Exercise Physiol, 94- *Mem:* Comp Respiratory Soc; Am Physiol Soc; World Asn Buiatrics; World Equine Vet Asn. *Res:* Physiological, pathophysiological and pharmacological studies of the cardio-pulmonary function in large animals; exercise physiology. *Mailing Add:* Univ Liege Bat B42 Sart Tilman Liege B-4000 Belgium. *Fax:* 32-41-562935

LEKLEM, JAMES ERLING, NUTRITION. *Current Pos:* from asst prof to assoc prof, 75-85, PROF NUTRIT, ORE STATE UNIV, 85- *Personal Data:* b Rhinelander, Wis, Aug 1, 41; m 67; c 2. *Educ:* Univ Wis, BS, 64, MS, 66, PhD(nutrit), 73. *Honors & Awards:* Borden Award, Am Home Econ Found, 85. *Prof Exp:* Proj assoc clin oncol, Univ Wis, 66-71, res assoc, 73-75. *Mem:* Sigma Xi; Am Inst Nutrit. *Res:* Vitamin B6; metabolism of tryptophan; nutrient relationship to cancer etiology; obesity; diabetes. *Mailing Add:* Dept Nutrit/Food Ore State Univ Milam 108 Corvallis OR 97331-5103

LELACHEUR, ROBERT MURRAY, PHYSICS. *Current Pos:* RETIRED. *Personal Data:* b Ottawa, Ont, Oct 12, 20; US citizen; m 46; c 4. *Educ:* Mt Allison Univ, BSc, 42; Dalhousie Univ, MSc, 47; Univ Va, PhD(physics), 49. *Prof Exp:* Physicist, Nat Res Coun Can, 49-53; mem tech staff, Bell Labs, NJ,

53-58; asst supt eng, Western Elec Co, Inc, 58-62, dir mat & chem processes res & develop, NY, 62-66, mgr develop & mfg eng, Reading, 66-91. *Mem:* Am Phys Soc; Inst Elec & Electronics Engrs; Sigma Xi. *Res:* Materials properties and processing; semiconductor device engineering. *Mailing Add:* 1005 Wyomissing Blvd Wyomissing PA 19610-2509

LELAND, FRANCES E(LBRIDGE), PHYSICAL CHEMISTRY. *Current Pos:* RETIRED. *Personal Data:* b Chicago, Ill, Apr 22, 32. *Educ:* Swarthmore Col, BA, 54; Northwestern Univ, PhD(phys chem), 59. *Prof Exp:* Instr chem, Brooklyn Col, 59-61; from asst prof to assoc prof chem, MacMurray Col, 62-73, prof, 73-94. *Mem:* Am Chem Soc. *Res:* Molecular quantum mechanics. *Mailing Add:* 950 Goltra Ave Jacksonville IL 62650

LELAND, HAROLD R(OBERT), ELECTRICAL ENGINEERING, SYSTEMS ANALYSIS. *Current Pos:* Var res & supvry positions, Cornell Aeronaut Lab,Inc, 58-63, staff scientist, 63-66, asst head, Syst Res Dept, 66-70, head, 70-71, vpres & dir elec syst group, 71-73, vpres com develop group, 73-76, pres, 74-76, vpres electronics & systs group, 76-78, vpres & gen mgr, Advan Technol Ctr, 78-83, PRES, CALSPAN CORP, 83- *Personal Data:* b Eau Claire, Wis, Apr 18, 31; m 58; c 2. *Educ:* Univ Wis, BS & MS, 54, PhD(elec eng), 58. *Mem:* Am Inst Aeronaut & Astronaut; Inst Elec & Electronics Engrs. *Res:* Automatic controls and pattern recognition; electronic warfare; military systems analysis; mathematical modeling of large systems. *Mailing Add:* 198 Bridle Path Williamsville NY 14221-4536

LELAND, STANLEY EDWARD, JR, PARASITOLOGY. *Current Pos:* actg head dept infectious dis, 70-72, EMER PROF PARASITOL, KANS STATE UNIV, 67-, EMER ASSOC DIR AGR EXP STA, 75- *Personal Data:* b Chicago, Ill, Aug 1, 26; m 50, Jeanne L Melby; c Stanley B, Steven B & Clayton B. *Educ:* Univ Ill, BS, 49, MS, 50; Mich State Univ, PhD(parasitol), 53. *Honors & Awards:* Col Vet Med Res Award, Kans State Univ, 71 & *Prof Exp:* Asst parasitol, Mich State Univ, 50-53; from assoc parasitologist to parasitologist, Univ Ky, 53-60, prof animal path, 60-63; assoc parasitologist, Univ Fla, 63-67. *Concurrent Pos:* Coop agent animal dis & parasite res div, USDA, 53-59; consult, Eli Lilly Co, 62-66; vis prof parasitol, Ahmadu Bello, Univ, Zaria, Nigeria, 72-73; USDA Comt of Nine, 85-88. *Res:* Electrophoresis; drug testing; pathology; physiology; biochemistry; in vitro cultivation; immunology as related to parasitology published in over 120 scientific papers and nine book chapters. *Mailing Add:* 420 Shelle Rd Manhattan KS 66502-3833

LELAND, WALLACE THOMPSON, LASERS. *Current Pos:* MEM STAFF NUCLEAR RES, LOS ALAMOS NAT LAB, 50- *Personal Data:* b Minn, Jan 21, 22; m 43; c 4. *Educ:* Univ Minn, BEE, 43, PhD(physics), 50. *Prof Exp:* Head, Instrument Develop Dept, Carbide & Carbon Chem Corp, 46-47. *Mem:* Am Phys Soc; Sigma Xi. *Res:* Mass spectroscopy and nuclear reactions; high energy lasers. *Mailing Add:* 233 Andanada Los Alamos NM 87544

LELE, PADMAKAR PRATAP, BIOMEDICAL ULTRASONICS. *Current Pos:* assoc prof, 69-71, PROF EXP MED, MASS INST TECHNOL, 72-; PROF, HARVARD-MASS INST TECHNOL HEALTH SCI & TECHNOL, 78- *Personal Data:* b Chanda, India, Nov 9, 27; m 59, Chrla M Top128; c Martin & Malcolm. *Educ:* Bombay Univ, BS, 49, MD, 50; Oxford Univ, DPhil(biophys), 55. *Honors & Awards:* Hist Med Ultrasound Pioneer Award, World Fedn Ultrasound Med & Biol, 88; Joseph H Holmes Pioneer Award, Am Inst Ultrasound Med, 88. *Prof Exp:* Vis scientist, NIH, 58-59; tech dir med acoust & neurosurg assoc, Mass Gen Hosp, Boston, 59-69. *Concurrent Pos:* Physiol assoc, Harvard Med Sch, 59-69; consult, NIH, 60- & Harvard Univ Hosps, 70-; mem, Diag Radiol Study Sect, NIH; assoc ed, Ultrasound in Med & Biol, 78-, In Vivo, 86-; Rockefeller Found fel. *Mem:* Fel Am Inst Ultrasound Med; fel Acoust Soc Am; Am Soc Clin Hyperthermic Oncol; Inst Elec & Electronics Engrs; NAm Hyperthermia Group-Radiation Res Soc; Bioelectromagnetics Soc; Int Clin Hyperthermic Soc; Europ Soc Hyperthermic Oncol; Am Soc Physicists Med. *Res:* Non-ionizing radiations; ultrasound and microwaves; applications in diagnostic and therapeutic medicine, industry and home, and safety; development and evaluation of local hyperthermia in cancer therapy, ultrasonic surgery and diagnosis, safety; biomedical engineering; heat transfer. *Mailing Add:* 5820 Ravenwood Rd La Jolla CA 92037

LELE, SHREEDHAR G, ELECTRICAL ENGINEERING, PHYSICS. *Current Pos:* DIR, ENG PROG, UNIV MASS, BOSTON, 85- *Personal Data:* b Varanasi, India, Apr 19, 31; m 66; c 2. *Educ:* Banaras Hindu Univ, India, MSc, 52; Univ Mich, MSE, 62, PhD(elec eng), 66. *Prof Exp:* Lectr physics, Banaras Hindu Univ, India, 52-60; res asst elec eng, Univ Mich, 61-66. *Concurrent Pos:* Consult, 80- *Mem:* Inst Elec & Electronics Engrs. *Res:* Ionospheric physics; microwave tubes; design of electron guns and solid-state devices. *Mailing Add:* Boston Harbor Campus Univ Mass Sci Bldg Rm S/3/110 Boston MA 02125

LELEIKO, NEAL SIMON, PEDIATRIC GASTROENTEROLOGY, HEPATOLOGY-NUTRITION. *Current Pos:* Dir, Gen Clin Res Ctr, 87-90, ASSOC PROF PEDIAT, MT SINAI, 87- *Personal Data:* b Brooklyn, NY, Oct 26, 46; m 67; c 2. *Educ:* Brooklyn Col, BS, 67; NY Med Col, MD, 71; Mass Inst Technol, PhD(biochem & metab), 79. *Mem:* AAAS; Am Acad Pediat; NAm Soc Pediat Gastroenterol; Soc Pediat Res; Am Fedn Clin Res. *Res:* Molecular biology of gene nutrient interactions; cost of illness in children and adults; treatment and cause of inflammatory bowel disease. *Mailing Add:* Div Pediat Gastroenterol Mt Sinai Hosp Fifth Ave & 100th St New York NY 10029

LE LEVIER, ROBERT ERNEST, THEORETICAL PHYSICS. *Current Pos:* RETIRED. *Personal Data:* b Los Angeles, Calif, Nov 7, 23; m 45; c 3. *Educ:* Univ Calif, Los Angeles, PhD(physics), 51. *Prof Exp:* Mem staff, Lawrence Radiation Lab, Univ Calif, 51-57 & Rand Corp, 57-71; mem staff, R & D Assocs, 71-80, chief scientist, 80-83; chief scientist & bd mem, Ros Technologies, 83-93. *Mem:* Am Phys Soc. *Res:* Ionospheric physics; nuclear physics; geophysics. *Mailing Add:* 961 Jacon Way Pacific Palisades CA 90272

LELEWER, DEBRA ANN, DATA COMPRESSION, SOFTWARE ENGINEERING. *Current Pos:* lectr math & comput sci, 82-85, from asst to assoc prof comput sci, 85-92, PROF & CHAIR COMPUT SCI, CALIF STATE POLYTECH UNIV, POMONA, 92- *Personal Data:* m 72, Steven A. *Educ:* Mich State Univ, BS, 73; Calif State Polytech Univ, Pomona, MS, 76, MS, 85; Univ Calif, Irvine, PhD(info & comput sci), 91. *Prof Exp:* Teacher & dept chair math, Glendora High Sch, 73-82. *Concurrent Pos:* Lectr, Nat Technol Univ, 92-93. *Mem:* Asn Comput Mach; Inst Elec & Electronics Engrs Comput Soc; Am Asn Univ Women; Asn Women Sci. *Res:* Design and analysis of algorithms, with algorithms for data compression being a particular interest; software engineering: software metrics and software testing, mutation testing in particular; artificial intelligence, specifically natural language processing and genetic algorithms. *Mailing Add:* Comput Sci Dept Calif State Polytech Univ Pomona CA 91768. *Fax:* 909-869-4396; *E-Mail:* dalelewer@csupomona.edu

LELKES, PETER ISTVAN, ENDOTHELIAL CELL BIOLOGY, STIMULUS-SECRETION-SYNTHESIS COUPLING. *Current Pos:* assoc prof, 88-93, PROF LAB CELL BIOL, UNIV WIS MED SCH, 93- *Personal Data:* b Budapest, Hungary, Feb 28, 49; Ger & Israeli citizen; m 78, Iris Goren; c Tamar, Efrat, Nadar & Yphtach. *Educ:* Univ Aacheu, MS, 74, PhD(cell biol), 77. *Prof Exp:* Scientist, Weizmann Inst Sci, 77-83; vis scientist, NIH, 83-88. *Mem:* Am Heart Asn; AAAS; Am Soc Cell Biol; Biophys Soc; Am Soc Artificial Internal Organs; Int Soc Appl Vascular Biol. *Res:* Endothelial cell biology; heterogeneity and adaptation to mechanical stimuli, signal transduction mechanisms; endothelialization of artificial blood pickups; neuroendocrine development and differentiation. *Mailing Add:* Univ Wisc 950 N 12th St Mt Sinai Med Ctr Milwaukee WI 53201-0342

LELLINGER, DAVID BRUCE, TAXONOMIC BOTANY. *Current Pos:* CUR FERNS, US NAT HERBARIUM, SMITHSONIAN INST, 63- *Personal Data:* b Chicago, Ill, Jan 24, 37; wid; c 2. *Educ:* Univ Ill, AB, 58; Univ Mich, MS, 60, PhD(bot), 65. *Concurrent Pos:* Ed-in-chief, Am Fern Soc, 66-84; Nat Geog Soc & Smithsonian Res Found explor & res grantee, 71 & 74; hon assoc cur pteridophytes, Mus Nat Costa Rica; ed, Pteridologia, 85- *Mem:* Int Asn Plant Taxon; Brit Pterid Soc; Am Fern Soc. *Res:* Taxonomy of ferns and fern allies, especially those of the New World tropics. *Mailing Add:* US Nat Herbarium NHB 166 Smithsonian Inst Washington DC 20560

LELLOUCHE, GERALD S, THERMAL PHYSICS, NUCLEAR ENGINEERING. *Current Pos:* PRES, TECH DATA SERV, 90- *Personal Data:* b New York, NY, June 21, 30; m 81, Mary V Crain. *Educ:* Purdue Univ, BS, 52; NC State Col, PhD(nuclear eng), 60. *Prof Exp:* Jr engr, Brookhaven Nat Lab, 52-55, asst nuclear eng, 60-64, assoc physicist, 64-68, physicist, 68-74; prog mgr, Probabilistics & Statist, Elec Power Res Inst, 74- 80, sr prog mgr code develop & validation, 80-86; mgt consult, S Levy Inc, 86-90. *Mem:* Am Chem Soc; Am Inst Chem Eng; Am Nuclear Soc. *Res:* Reactor kinetics, nonlinear dynamics; thermal hydraulics, two-phase flow; probabilistics, risk analysis. *Mailing Add:* 6252 N Lakewood Chicago IL 60660

LELONG, MICHEL GEORGES, PLANT TAXONOMY. *Current Pos:* Assoc prof, 65-77, PROF BIOL, UNIV S ALA, 77- *Personal Data:* b Casablanca, Morocco, Mar 20, 32; US citizen; m 59; c 3. *Educ:* Univ Algiers, baccalaureat, 50; Northwestern State Col, La, BS, 59, MS, 60; Iowa State Univ, PhD(syst bot), 65. *Mem:* Am Soc Plant Taxon; Int Asn Plant Taxon. *Res:* Systematics of Panicum subgenus Dichanthelium of North America; flora of the Mobile Bay region. *Mailing Add:* Dept Biol Sci Univ SAla 307 Univ Blvd Mobile AL 36688

LEM, KWOK WAI, POLYMER SYNTHESIS, MOLECULAR COMPOSITE. *Current Pos:* res engr, gas separation membrane, Corp Technol, Allied-Signal Inc, 85-86, res engr, polymer blends, 86-87, sr res engr, polymer alloys & composites, Corp Technol, 87-89, sr res engr, Armors & Composites Corp Res & Technol, 89-93, RES SCIENTIST, ALLIED-SIGNAL, INC, 93- *Personal Data:* b Canton, China, July 14, 52; US citizen; m 86, Margaret Yun-Ming; c Paul C & Richard C. *Educ:* Univ Toronto, Ont, Can, 76; Polytech Inst NY, MSc, 80; PhD(polymer sci eng), 83. *Honors & Awards:* Melvin M Gerson Award, 80 & 81. *Prof Exp:* Chem specialist, Can Hanson Ltd, Toronto, Ont, 76-77; polymer chemist, Schenectady Chem Can, Ont, 77-78; res engr, Corp Technol, Allied Corp, 83-85. *Concurrent Pos:* Adj prof, Polytech Univ, NY, 91. *Mem:* Soc Plastics Engrs; Soc Physics; Soc Rheology; Sigma Xi. *Res:* Polymer processing and rheology; reactive extrusion and injection molding; advanced polymer blends and synthesis; electrochemical and membrane technologies; processing-structure-property relations in polymer materials; advanced armor materials; dynamic behavior of advanced materials; impact dynamics; degradation and stability of materials; flammability materials. *Mailing Add:* 11 Old Coach Rd Randolph NJ 07869

LEMAIRE, IRMA, PHARMACOLOGY. *Current Pos:* PROF, DEPT PHARMACOL, UNIV OTTAWA, 90- *Mailing Add:* Pharmacol Dept Health Sci Ctr Sch Med Univ Ottawa 451 Smyth Rd Ottawa ON K1H 8M5 Can

LEMAIRE, PAUL J, OPTICAL FIBER RESEARCH & DEVELOPMENT. *Current Pos:* RES SCIENTIST, AT&T BELL LABS, 80- *Personal Data:* b Colchester, Vt, Aug 11, 53; m 86; c 2. *Educ:* Mass Inst Technol, BS, 75, PhD(ceramics), 80. *Honors & Awards:* Purdy Award, Am Ceramic Soc, 84. *Mem:* Am Ceramic Soc; Mat Res Soc. *Res:* Optical fiber research and development; optical loss; defects in glasses; waveguide design; optical fiber processing and manufacturing; hermetic coatings; fiber reliability and hydrogen-glass reactions. *Mailing Add:* 18 Ferndale Rd Madison NJ 07940

LEMAISTRE, CHARLES AUBREY, INTERNAL MEDICINE, EPIDEMIOLOGY. *Current Pos:* pres, 78-96, EMER COUN PHYSICIAN, UNIV TEX, M D ANDERSON CANCER CTR, 96- *Personal Data:* b Lockhart, Ala, Feb 10, 24; m 52; c 4. *Educ:* Univ Ala, BA, 43; Cornell Univ, MD, 47. *Hon Degrees:* LLD, Austin Col, 70 & Univ Ala, 71; DSc, Univ Dallas, 78 & Southwestern Univ, 81. *Prof Exp:* From instr to asst prof internal med, Med Col, Cornell Univ, 51-54; assoc prof, Sch Med, Emory Univ, 54-59, prof prev med & chmn dept, 57-59; prof, Univ Tex Southwestern Med Sch, Dallas, 59-66, assoc dean, 65-66; vchancellor health affairs, Univ Tex, Austin, 66-68; from exec vchancellor to chancellor-elect, Univ Tex Syst, 68-70, chancellor, 71-78. *Concurrent Pos:* Mem, Human Ecol Study Sect, NIH, 62-65; mem, Surgeon Gen Adv Comt Smoking & Health, 63-64; mem, Gov Comt Eradication Tuberc, 63-64; mem, Comt Res Tobacco & Health, AMA Educ & Res Found, 64-66; mem, Nat Citizens Comn Int Coop, 65-; mem, Surgeon Gen Emergency Health Preparedness Adv Comt, Dept Health, Educ & Welfare, 67, consult, Div Physician Manpower, 67-70; mem, President's Comn White House fel, 71; mem, Comn Non-Traditional Study, 71-73; mem joint task force continuing competence pharm, Am Pharmaceut Asn-Am Asn Col Pharm, 73-74; mem bd comnr, Nat Comn Accrediting, 73-76; trustee, Biol Humanics Found, Dallas, 73-; mem, Nat Coun Educ Res, 73-75, consult, 75; chmn, Subcomt Diversity & Pluralism, Nat Coun Educ Res, 73-75; mem, United Negro Col Fund Develop Coun, 74-78; mem, Nat Adv Coun, Inst Serv Educ, 74-77. *Mem:* Am Cancer Soc (pres, 86-87). *Res:* Chest diseases. *Mailing Add:* 13104 Travis View Loop Austin TX 78732-1741

LE MAISTRE, CHRISTOPHER WILLIAM, AUTOMATION & ROBOTICS. *Current Pos:* MANAGING DIR, SCH TECHNOL CTR SUPERCONDUCTIVITY, UNIV ILL, URBANA-CHAMPAIGN, 93- *Personal Data:* b Moradabad, India, Aug 20, 38; Australian citizen; m 63; c 2. *Educ:* Univ Adelaide, BS, 63 & 64; Rensselaer Polytech Inst, PhD(mat eng), 72. *Prof Exp:* Exp officer, Australian Defence Sci, 64-72, sr res scientist, 72-79; assoc dir, Mfg Ctr, Rensselaer Polytech Inst, 79-84, dir, Ctr Indust Innovation, 84-92, asst dean eng, 84-92. *Concurrent Pos:* Res & develop rep, Australian High Comn, London, 74-77; head int progs, Australian Defense Sci, Canberra, 77-78, head lab progs, 78-79. *Mem:* Am Ceramic Soc; Am Soc Metals; Am Soc Eng Educ. *Res:* Near net shape (sintering); structural studies of carbon fibers; composite design and fabrication; automation and robotics; intellectual property. *Mailing Add:* 1022 Mat Res Lab 104 S Goodwin Ave Urbana IL 61801. *Fax:* 217-244-8544; *E-Mail:* clem@uluc.edu

LEMAL, DAVID M, ORGANIC CHEMISTRY. *Current Pos:* from assoc prof to prof, 65-81, dept chair, 76-79, ALBERT W SMITH PROF CHEM, DARTMOUTH COL, 81- *Personal Data:* b Plainfield, NJ, Feb 20, 34; m 63, 94, Lee Gabriel; c Anne-Marie, Marielle, Richard J & Corinne. *Educ:* Amherst Col, AB, 55; Harvard Univ, PhD, 59. *Honors & Awards:* Catalyst Award, Chem Mfrs Asn, 87. *Prof Exp:* From instr to asst prof chem, Univ Wis, 58-65. *Concurrent Pos:* Vis lectr, Harvard Univ, 67; A P Sloan Found res fel, 68-70; trustee, Gordon Res Conf, 73-79 & chmn bd, 77-78; sabbaticals, ETH, Zurich, 74, Univ Utah, 81 & Harvard Univ, 94; mem exec comt, Fluorine Div, Am Chem Soc, 80-83, alt coun, Org Div, 81-93, chmn, Fluorine Div, 90. *Mem:* Sigma Xi; Am Chem Soc. *Res:* Organofluorine chemistry; unusual species, stable and short-lived, in organic chemistry; organic reaction mechanisms; organic photochemistry. *Mailing Add:* Dept Chem Dartmouth Col Hanover NH 03755-1477. *E-Mail:* david.m.lemal@dartmouth.edu

LEMAN, ROBERT B, ARRHYTHMIA MANAGEMENT. *Current Pos:* intern internal med, Med Univ SC, 76-77, resident, 77-79, fel cardiol, 79-81, instr internal med & cardiol, 81-82, asst prof med, 83-89, ASSOC PROF MED, MED UNIV SC, 89- *Personal Data:* b Upper Darby, Penn, Dec 23, 47; m 73, Patti R Pennington; c Brian & Heather. *Educ:* Ursinus Col, BS, 69; Univ Ark, Little Rock, MD, 76. *Prof Exp:* Instr phys sci, Gloucester County Col, 69-70. *Concurrent Pos:* Dir, Charleston Vet Admin Cardiac Catherization Lab, Vet Admin Hosp, 86-92; dir, Pacemaker Surveillance, Med Univ SC, 82-, Adult Electrophysiol, 88- *Mem:* Fel Am Heart Asn; Am Col Physicians; Am Col Cardiol; NAm Soc Pacing & Electrophysiol. *Res:* Arrhythmia management, devices, medicine, ablation. *Mailing Add:* 171 Ashley Ave Musc-816 CSB Charleston SC 29425-2220. *Fax:* 803-792-7771; *E-Mail:* lemanrb@musc.edu

LEMANN, JACOB, JR, EXPERIMENTAL BIOLOGY. *Current Pos:* assoc prof, 70-71, CHIEF NEPHROLOGY DIV, MED COL WIS, MILWAUKEE, 70-, PROF MED, 71- *Personal Data:* b New Orleans, La, Aug 31, 29; m; c 3. *Educ:* Univ Calif, Berkeley, AB, 50; Univ Buffalo, MD, 54; Am Bd Internal Med, cert, 63 & 74. *Prof Exp:* Intern, Mass Mem Hosp, Boston, 54-55, res fel med, renal & metabol dis, 57-59 & clin fel, 60-61; asst resident, New Eng Med Ctr, Boston, 59-60; instr med, Boston Univ Sch Med, 61-63; from asst prof to assoc prof med, Marquette Sch Med & assoc dir, Clin Res Ctr, 63-68; assoc prof, Boston Univ Sch Med, 68-70. *Concurrent Pos:* Chief, Renal Sect, Boston Univ Sch Med, 68-70; mem, Gen Med B Study Sect, NIH, 70-74 & 82-84; mem, Coun Med Adv Comt, Kidney Found Wis, 70- *Mem:* AAAS; fel Am Col Physicians; Am Fedn Clin Res; AMA; Am Physiol Soc; Am Soc Clin Invest; Am Soc Bone & Mineral Res; Am Soc Nephrology; Asn Am Physicians; Int Soc Nephrology. *Res:* Medicine. *Mailing Add:* Nephrology Sect 2601 St Charles Ave New Orleans LA 70130-5927

LEMANSKI, LARRY FREDERICK, DEVELOPMENT BIOLOGY, IMMUNOELECTRON MICROSCOPY. *Current Pos:* PROF & CHMN ANAT & CELL BIOL, STATE UNIV NY, 83- *Personal Data:* b Madison, Wis, June 5, 43; m 66, Sharon L Wulf; c Scott F & Jennifer L. *Educ:* Univ Wis, BS, 66; Ariz State Univ, MS, 68, PhD(zool), 71. *Honors & Awards:* Presidential Award, Electron Micros Soc Am; Louis N Katz Basic Sci Res Prize, Am Heart Asn. *Prof Exp:* Fel biol & biochem, Univ Pa, 71-75; asst prof anat, Univ Calif, San Francisco, 75-77; from assoc prof to prof anat, Univ Wis, 77-83. *Concurrent Pos:* Prin investr, NIH, 76-; estab investr award, Am Heart Asn, 76-81, Louis Katz res prize, 78; distinguished sci examr, Bhopal Univ, India, 84-; dir, Cell & Molecular Training Prog, 87-90. *Mem:* Am Soc Cell Biol; AAAS; Asn Anat Chairmen; NY Acad Sci; Soc Develop Biol; Sigma Xi; Am Heart Asn. *Res:* Embryonic heart development using cellular and molecular biology approaches to study; the initiation and maintenance of normal heart function in vertebrates. *Mailing Add:* Dept Anat & Cell Biol State Univ NY Health Sci Ctr 750 E Adams St Syracuse NY 13210. *Fax:* 315-464-8535

LEMANSKI, MICHAEL FRANCIS, HETEROGENEOUS CATALYSIS. *Current Pos:* RES SCIENTIST, BP AM CORP, 78- *Personal Data:* b Cleveland, Ohio, Nov 16, 46. *Educ:* Univ Dayton, BS, 69; Ohio State Univ, MS, 72, PhD(inorg chem), 75. *Prof Exp:* Sr res chemist, Diamond Shamrock Corp, 75-78. *Concurrent Pos:* Vis researcher, Ctr Catalytic Sci & Technol, Univ Del, 80. *Mem:* Am Chem Soc. *Res:* Heterogeneous catalysis, including selective oxidation and selective reduction of small molecules. *Mailing Add:* Shell Chem C1341 3333 Hwy 6 S Houston TX 77082

LEMASTER, EDWIN WILLIAM, SOLID STATE PHYSICS. *Current Pos:* PROF PHYS SCI & CHMN, ENG DEPT, UNIV TEX, PAN AM, 88- *Personal Data:* b Perryton, Tex, Apr 27, 40; m 64, Jane Rohr; c Annie & Matthew. *Educ:* West Tex Tech Univ, BS, 62; Tech Tech Univ, MS, 66; Univ Tex, PhD(physics), 70. *Prof Exp:* Asst prof physics, Gen Motors Inst, 64-66; asst prof, Pan Am Univ, 70-, chmn, Phys Sci Dept, 73-; dean sci & technol, NMex Highlands Univ, 86-88. *Mem:* Am Phys Soc; Am Asn Physics Teachers. *Res:* Metalammonia solution properties; amorphous semiconductors; remote sensing of vegetative canopies; mathematical modeling. *Mailing Add:* Eng Dept Univ Tex Pan Am 1201 W University Dr Edinburg TX 78539

LEMASTERS, JOHN J, CELL BIOLOGY, ANATOMY. *Current Pos:* from asst prof to assoc prof, 77-85, PROF CELL BIOL & ANAT, LAB CELL BIOL, SCH MED, UNIV NC, CHAPEL HILL, 85- *Personal Data:* b Newark, Ohio, May 29, 47; m 80; c 3. *Educ:* Yale Univ, BA, 69; Johns Hopkins Univ, MD, 75, PhD(cell biol & anat), 75. *Prof Exp:* Teaching asst, Dept Anat, Sch Med, Johns Hopkins Univ, 71-72; teaching asst neuroanat, Dept Cell Biol, Southwestern Med Sch, Univ Tex Health Sci Ctr, 73, asst prof, 75-77. *Concurrent Pos:* Dir, Grad Studies in Anat, Univ NC, 77-84, Electron Microscope Lab, 83-90, Confocal Imaging Facil, 89-; estab investr, Am Heart Asn, 82-87; vis profs, Div Gastroenterol & Sect Transplantation Surg, Mayo Grad Sch Med, 87; prin investr, Off Naval Res, 88-91, USPHS, 89-94 & 90-94, NSF, 90-92; mem, Coun Circulation, Am Heart Asn. *Mem:* AAAS; Am Asn Study Liver Dis; Am Asn Anatomists; Am Heart Asn; Am Soc Biochem & Molecular Biol; Biophys Soc; Electron Micros Soc Am. *Res:* Rescue of injured myocytes; liver preservation for transplantation; laser scanning confocal microscope; mechanisms of cell death in hepatocytes. *Mailing Add:* Lab Cell Biol Dept Cell Biol & Anat Univ NC Sch Med Campus Box 7090 236 Taylor Hall Chapel Hill NC 27599-7090

LEMASURIER, WESLEY ERNEST, GEOLOGY. *Current Pos:* assoc prof, 68-76, PROF GEOL, DIV NAT & PHYS SCI, UNIV COLO, DENVER, 76- *Personal Data:* b Wash, DC, May 3, 34; m 63; c 3. *Educ:* Union Col, BS, 56; Univ Colo, MS, 62; Stanford Univ, PhD(geol), 65. *Prof Exp:* Geologist, US Geol Surv, 61-64; asst prof geol, Cornell Univ, 64-68. *Mem:* AAAS; Geol Soc Am; Am Geophys Union; Int Asn Volcanol & Chem Earth's Interior; Sigma Xi. *Res:* Subglacial volcanism; petrology and tectonic relationships of volcanism in Antarctica. *Mailing Add:* Geol Dept Univ Colo Box 173364 Denver CO 80217-3364

LEMAY, CHARLOTTE ZIHLMAN, PHYSICS, SOLID STATE PHYSICS. *Current Pos:* from asst prof to assoc prof sci, 63-69, prof physics & chmn dept, 69-77 & 85-89, EMER PROF PHYSICS, WESTERN CONN STATE UNIV, 90-; OWNER, SESAME STUDIOS, 89- *Personal Data:* b Ft Worth, Tex, June 30, 19; m 44, Jack Evans; c Douglas Russell, Lawrence Bruce & Caroline (Salvati). *Educ:* Tex Christian Univ, AB, 40; Mt Holyoke Col, MA, 41; La State Univ, PhD(physics), 50. *Prof Exp:* Res physicist, Monsanto Chem Co, 43-44; instr physics, Mt Holyoke Col, 45-46; instr physics, La State Univ, 46-48, res asst, 48-50; engr, Tex Instruments, Inc, 52-53, 55-57; res physicist, Stanford Res Inst, 53-54; engr, Westinghouse Elec Corp, 58-60 & Int Bus Mach Corp, 60-63. *Concurrent Pos:* Otis Skinner fel physics, 40-41. *Mem:* Am Phys Soc; Am Asn Physics Teachers; sr mem Inst Elec & Electronics Engrs; Sigma Xi; Am Soc Eng Educ; sr mem Soc Women Engrs; Optical Soc Am. *Res:* Dielectric liquids; transistors; fiber optics; invention world's first silicon and silicon carbide transistors; electro-optic telecommunications. *Mailing Add:* 1516 Casey Key Rd Nokomis FL 34275

LEMAY, HAROLD E, JR, CHEMICAL EDUCATION. *Current Pos:* From asst prof to assoc prof, Univ Nev, Reno, 66-78, vchmn dept, 74-76, chmn dept, 84-85, assoc chmn, 85-90, PROF CHEM, UNIV NEV, RENO, 78- *Personal Data:* b Tacoma, Wash, May 28, 40; m 64; c 2. *Educ:* Pac Lutheran, BS, 62; Univ Ill, MS, 64, PhD(inorg chem), 66. *Concurrent Pos:* Vis prof, Univ NC, Chapel Hill, 77-78, Univ Col Wales, 78 & Univ Calif Los Angeles, 89-90. *Mem:* Am Chem Soc; Sigma Xi. *Res:* Preparation and characterization of coordination compounds; reactions of coordination compounds in the solid phase; writer of chemistry textbooks. *Mailing Add:* Dept Chem Univ Nev Reno NV 89557-0001

LEMAY, JEAN-PAUL, ANIMAL PHYSIOLOGY, ANIMAL BREEDING. *Current Pos:* PROF ANIMAL SCI, LAVAL UNIV, 62- *Personal Data:* b St Hyacinthe, Que, July 4, 23; m 52; c 2. *Educ:* Classical Col St Hyacinth, BA, 45; Univ Montreal, BSA, 49; Univ Mass, MSc, 51; Laval Univ, PhD, 67. *Prof Exp:* Mem artificial insemination unit, Classical Col St Hyacinthe, 48-49; from instr to prof animal sci, Res Sta La Pocatiere, Que, 51-62. *Mem:* Am Soc Animal Sci; Can Soc Animal Prod. *Res:* Early weaning of sheep; histophysiology of sperm atogenesis and ovogenesis in sheep; sterility in dairy cattle; physiology of reproduction in dairy cattle, sheep and goat. *Mailing Add:* Dept Animal Sci Laval Univ Fac Agr Ste Foy PQ C1K 7P4 Can

LEMBACH, KENNETH JAMES, MONOCLONAL ANTIBODIES, CELL REGULATION. *Current Pos:* DIR PRECLIN RES, PHARMACEUT DIV, BIOTECHNOL GROUP, BAYER CORP, 95- *Personal Data:* b Rochester, NY, June 16, 39; m 65, Regis Mann; c Lara & Aimee. *Educ:* Mass Inst Technol, BS, 61; Univ Pa, PhD(biochem), 66. *Prof Exp:* USPHS fel, Mass Inst Technol, 66-68, res assoc biochem, 68-69; from asst prof to assoc prof, Sch Med, Vanderbilt Univ, 69-79; plasma prod res sect head, Miles Inc, 79-82, prin staff scientist, 82-86, mgr cell physiol res, 86-88, mgr cell & molecular biol res cutter biol, 81-91, dir cell & mollecular biol, 91-93, dir preclin biol, Pharmaceut Div, 93-95. *Concurrent Pos:* US Nat Cancer Inst res grants, 71-74 & 75-79. *Mem:* AAAS; Am Soc Biochem & Molecular Biol. *Res:* Cytokines; immune regulation and therapies. *Mailing Add:* Preclin Res Bayer Corp Pharmaceut Div Biotechnol Berkeley CA 94710. *Fax:* 510-705-5558

LEMBECK, WILLIAM JACOBS, MICROBIOLOGY, ACADEMIC ADMINISTRATION. *Current Pos:* asst prof bot, Baton Rouge, La State Univ, 66-68, assoc prof biol & head sci, 68-75, prof, 75-92, EMER PROF BIOL, LA STATE UNIV, EUNICE, 92- *Personal Data:* b Kansas City, Mo, Aug 29, 28; m 60, Jean Dyess; c Nancy Mae (Smith). *Educ:* La State Univ, BS, 50, MS, 56, PhD(bact), 62. *Prof Exp:* Supvry bacteriologist, US Army Chem Corps, Pine Bluff Arsenal, Ark, 57-59; from asst prof to assoc prof biol, Ark Agr & Mech Col, 61-62; asst prof bact, McNeese State Col, 62-65, assoc prof microbiol, 65-66. *Mem:* Am Inst Biol Sci; Sigma Xi. *Res:* Effects of herbicides on normal soil microflora; biological catalysis of herbicides in soil; effects of herbicides on cellulose decomposition by Sporocytophaga myxococcoides. *Mailing Add:* 110 University Pl PO Box 1129 Eunice LA 70535-6810. *Fax:* 318-546-6620

LEMBERG, HOWARD LEE, BROADBAND NETWORKS, FIBER OPTIC NETWORKS. *Current Pos:* mem tech staff, Bell Labs, 78-81, supvr, 81-84, dist mgr, 84-91, DIR, BELLCORE, 92- *Personal Data:* b Queens, NY, July 29, 49; m 70, Christine Van Ullen; c 2. *Educ:* Columbia Univ, BA, 69; Univ Chicago, PhD(chem physics), 73. *Prof Exp:* Res chem physics, Bell Labs, 73-75; asst prof chem, Univ NC, 75-78. *Mem:* Inst Elec & Electronics Engrs; Soc Cable TV Engrs; Soc Photo Instrument Engr. *Res:* Communications networks; optical networks; optical fiber-subscriber loop networks and broadband access video networks. *Mailing Add:* Bell Commun Res Rm Mve 2-M-289 445 South St Morristown NJ 07962. *Fax:* 973-829-5886

LEMBERG, LOUIS, ELECTROCARDIOGRAPHY, CARDIOLOGY. *Current Pos:* PROF CLIN CARDIOL, SCH MED, UNIV MIAMI, 69- *Personal Data:* b Chicago, Ill, Dec 27, 16; m 39, Miriam Weintraub; c Jerry & Laura. *Educ:* Univ Ill, BS, 38, MD, 40; Am Bd Internal Med, dipl, 50, recert, 74 & 88; Am Bd Cardiovasc Dis, dipl, 55. *Honors & Awards:* Luis Guerrero Mem Award, Philippines. *Prof Exp:* Intern, Mt Sinai Hosp, Chicago, Ill, 40-41, res, 45-48. *Concurrent Pos:* Dir cardiol, Dade County Hosp, 55-57; attend specialist, Vet Admin Hosp, 55-64; chief staff, Nat Children's Cardiac Hosp, Miami, 55-66; attend cardiologist, Mercy & Cedars of Lebanon Hosp; chief chief div electrophysiol, 76-74, dir coronary care unit, Jackson Mem Hosp, 68-74; chief div cardiol, Mercy Hosp, 76- mem coun clin cardiol, Am Heart Asn; ed-in-chief, Accel for Nurses, 81-85, Current Concepts Cardiovasc Dis, 85-87; Louis Lemberg endowed chair cardiol, Sch Med, Univ Miami. *Mem:* Hon mem Philippine Med Asn; fel Am Col Physicians; Am Col Chest Physicians; Am Col Cardiol; NY Acad Sci. *Res:* Cardiology; pioneer in the development of the demand pacemaker. *Mailing Add:* Div Cardiol (D39) Univ Miami PO Box 016960 Miami FL 33101. *Fax:* 305-547-3516

LEMBERGER, AUGUST PAUL, PHARMACEUTICS. *Current Pos:* PROF PHARM & DEAN, SCH PHARM, UNIV WIS-MADISON, 80- *Personal Data:* b Milwaukee, Wis, Jan 25, 26; m 47; c 7. *Educ:* Univ Wis, BS, 48, PhD(pharm), 52. *Honors & Awards:* Kiekhofer Award, Univ Wis, 57. *Prof Exp:* Sr chemist pharmaceut res, Merck & Co, Inc, 52-53; from instr to prof pharm, Univ Wis-Madison, 53-69, coordr exten serv, 65-69; prof pharm & dean, Col, Univ Ill Med Ctr, 69-80. *Concurrent Pos:* Mem & secy, Wis Pharm Internship Comn, 65-69; consult, Dept Health, Educ & Welfare, 72-74; mem, Am Coun Pharmaceut Educ, 78-84, bd trustees, Am Pharmaceut Soc, 85-88; mem, Tech Adv Coun Ill Dept Pub Health Drug Substitution law, 78-80. *Mem:* Am Pharmaceut Asn; fel Acad Pharm Res & Sci; fel AAAS; fel Am Asn Pharmaceut Scientists; Am Asn Cols Pharmacy; Am Soc Hosp Pharmacists. *Mailing Add:* 7439 Cedar Creek Trail Madison WI 53717

LEMBERGER, LOUIS, CLINICAL PHARMACOLOGY. *Current Pos:* PROF PHARM MED & PSYCHIATRY, SCH MED, IND UNIV, 93- *Personal Data:* b Monticello, NY, May 8, 37; m 59; c 2. *Educ:* Long Island Univ, BS, 60; Albert Einstein Col Med, PhD(pharmacol), 64, MD, 68. *Hon Degrees:* DSc, Long Island Univ, 94. *Honors & Awards:* Award, Am Soc Pharmacol & Exp Therapeut, 85; Rawls Palmer Prog Med Award, 86; Henry Elliott Award, 92; Harry Gold Award, 93. *Prof Exp:* Fel pharmacol, Albert Einstein Col Med, 64-68; med intern, Metropolitan Hosp Ctr-NY Med Col, 68-69; pharmacol & toxicol res assoc clin pharmacol, Lab Clin Sci, NIMH, 69-71; clin pharmacologist, 71-75, chief, 75-78; dir clin pharmacol, Lilly Lab Clin Res, Lilly Res Labs 78-89, clin res fel, 89-93. *Concurrent Pos:* Dir, Clin Pharmacol Training Prog, Sch Med, Ind Univ, 72-75, asst prof pharmacol & med, 72-73, assoc prof, 73-77, prof pharmacol, med & psychiat, 77-; assoc prof, Grad Fac, 75-77, prof, 77-; adj prof clin pharmacol, Ohio State Univ, 75-86; chmn, Second World Conf Clin Pharmacol, Int Union Clin Pharmacol. *Mem:* Am Soc Pharmacol & Exp Therapeut (pres, 87-88); Am Soc Clin Pharmacol & Therapeut (pres, 83-84); fel Am Col Neuro Psychopharm; fel Am Col Physicians; Sigma Xi. *Res:* Drug metabolism and drug-drug interactions; synthesis and metabolism of biogenic amines; biochemical mechanisms of drug action; clinical psychopharmacology; pharmacology of marihuana and cannabinoids. *Mailing Add:* 3315 Walnut Creek Dr N Carmel IN 46032. *Fax:* 317-873-3921

LEMBKE, ROGER ROY, PHYSICAL CHEMISTRY, RADIATION CHEMISTRY. *Current Pos:* assoc prof, 76-78, PROF CHEM & CHMN DEPT, CENT METHODIST COL, 78- *Personal Data:* b Clayton Co, Iowa, Apr 24, 40; m 69; c 2. *Educ:* Luther Col, AB, 62; Univ Nebr, Lincoln, MS, 66; Wayne State Univ, PhD(phys chem), 73; Univ Evansville, Ind, MCSE, 84. *Prof Exp:* Instr chem, Hastings Col, 65-69; guest scientist, Hahn-Meitner Inst, Berlin, 73-74; res assoc, Univ Fla, 75; asst prof, Cornell Col, 75-76. *Mem:* Am Chem Soc; Asn Comput Mach. *Res:* Radiolysis and photolysis; rate constants and mechanisms. *Mailing Add:* Dept Chem Cent Methodist Col Fayette MO 65248-1198

LEMCOE, M M(ARSHALL), CIVIL ENGINEERING. *Current Pos:* CONSULT, 83- *Personal Data:* b St Louis, Mo; m 51; c 2. *Educ:* Wash Univ, BS, 43, MS, 49; Univ Ill, PhD(civil eng), 57. *Honors & Awards:* Award, Curtiss-Wright Corp, 45; IR-100 Award, 76. *Prof Exp:* Struct engr, Curtiss-Wright Corp, 43-46; mem staff, Res Found & Dept Civil Eng, Wash Univ, 47-51; supvr aeroelasticity & spec consult, Southwest Res Inst, 51-52, mgr, Strength Anal Sect, Dept Struct Res, 52-61; supvr exp mech & sr tech specialist, Atomics Int Div, NAm Rockwell Corp, Calif, 61-71; tech adv, Columbus Div, Battelle Mem Inst, 71-83. *Mem:* Soc Exp Stress Anal; Sigma Xi. *Res:* Experimental stress analysis; structures; pressure vessels; high temperature materials technology and strain gage technology; high temperature behavior of structures. *Mailing Add:* 12990 Camino Ramillette San Diego CA 92128

LE MEE, JEAN M, ENGINEERING, DESIGN EDUCATION. *Current Pos:* assoc prof, 64-80, PROF MECH ENG, COOPER UNION SCH ENG & SCI, 80-, CHMN MECH ENG, 86- *Personal Data:* b June 4, 31; US citizen; m 64, Katharine H Wilbur; c Hannah-Therese. *Educ:* Carnegie-Mellon Univ, MS, 59, PhD(mech eng), 63. *Prof Exp:* Design engr, James Gordon & Co Ltd, Eng, 55-58; teaching asst eng, Carnegie-Mellon Univ, 59-61; res engr, Lawrence Radiation Lab, Univ Calif, Berkeley, 60 & Westinghouse Res Labs, 62-64. *Mem:* Inst Elec & Electronics Engrs; Sigma Xi; Am Soc Mech Engrs. *Res:* Control systems; semiconductor devices; design process; engineering education. *Mailing Add:* 16 Mevan Ave Tributary Woods Englewood NJ 07631-3863

LE MEHAUTE, BERNARD J, HYDRODYNAMICS, COASTAL ENGINEERING. *Current Pos:* prof & chmn ocean eng, 78-83, prof appl marine physics, 83-92, EMER PROF APPL MARINE PHYSICS, ROSENSTIEL SCH MARINE ENG, UNIV MIAMI, 92- *Personal Data:* b St Brieuc, France, Mar 29, 27; m 91, Marie Josseline; c Anne & Patrick. *Educ:* Univ Rennes, Baccalaureat, 47; Univ Toulouse, lic es sc, 51; Univ Grenoble, Dr es Sc(hydrodyn), 57. *Honors & Awards:* Int Coastal Eng Award, Am Soc Civil Engrs, 79; Creative Award, NSF, 81. *Prof Exp:* Res engr, Neyrpic-Sogreah, France, 53-57; assoc prof hydrodyn, Polytech Sch, Montreal, 57-59; res prof, Queen's Univ, Ont, 59-61; mem tech staff, Nat Eng Sci Co, 61-62; mem sr staff, 62-64, assoc dir hydrodyn, 64-66; vpres, Tetra Tech, Inc, 66-70, sr vpres, 66-78, mem bd, 66-84. *Concurrent Pos:* Mem, Nat Sea Grant Rev Panel, 70-78; mem, Coastal Eng Res Bd, Dept Defense, 82-88;

mem, Marine Bd, exec comt, Nat Res Coun, 89-92. *Mem:* Nat Acad Eng; Am Soc Civil Eng; Marine Technol Soc; Int Asn Hydraul Res. *Res:* Hydrodynamics and hydraulic and coastal engineering, ranging from theoretical fluid mechanics to physical oceanography applied to the design of engineering structures for water power, coastal harbors and offshore drilling. *Mailing Add:* 7320 Southwest Terr Miami FL 33157

LEMENT, BERNARD S, FAILURE ANALYSIS, ACCIDENT RECONSTRUCTION. *Current Pos:* MAT ENG CONSULT, LEMENT & ASSOCS, 67- *Personal Data:* b Boston, Mass, Feb 11, 17; m 42; c 3. *Educ:* Mass Inst Technol, BS, 38, ScD(metall), 49. *Prof Exp:* Metallurgist testing, NY Testing Labs, 38-39; res asst tool steels, Mass Inst Technol, 40; assoc metallurgist army ord, Watertown Arsenal, 40-46; instr physics, Univ Mass, 46-47; res staff mem dimensional stability, Mass Inst Technol, 47-49; asst prof metall, Univ Notre Dame, 49-51; mem res staff electron microscopy, Mass Inst Technol, 51-57; proj dir res & develop, ManLabs, Inc, 57-67. *Mem:* Fel Am Soc Metals; Am Inst Metall Engrs; Am Welding Soc; Am Soc Testing & Mat; Am Soc Safety Engrs. *Mailing Add:* 24 Graymore Rd Waltham MA 02154

LEMESHOW, STANLEY ALAN, SAMPLING, EXPERIMENTAL DESIGN. *Current Pos:* asst prof, 76-80, ASSOC PROF BIOSTATISTS, UNIV MASS, AMHERST, 80- *Personal Data:* b Brooklyn, NY, Jan 29, 48; m 72; c 2. *Educ:* City Col New York, BBA, 69; Univ NC, Chapel Hill, MSPH, 70; Univ Calif, Los Angeles, PhD(biostatist), 76. *Prof Exp:* Res asst, Dept Prev Med, NY Med Col, 68-69; statist supvr, Health Res Training Prog, New York City Dept Health, 69; anal statistician, Comn Off, Nat Ctr Health Statist, USPHS, 70-72; sr statisticin, Sch Pub Health, Univ Calif, Los Angeles, 74-75. *Concurrent Pos:* Dir, Coord Ctr for Multicenter Clin Trial of Hyperbaric Oxygen in Treatment of Burn Injuries, Univ Mass, 77-78; prog dir, Biopharmceut Res Unit, Div Pub Health, Univ Mass, Amherst, 78- *Mem:* Am Statist Asn; Soc Epidemiol Res; Am Pub Health Asn. *Res:* Sampling; variance estimation in complex sampling designs; sample size determination and logistic regression analysis; medical and other applied health sciences. *Mailing Add:* Sch Pub Health Univ Mass Amherst Amherst MA 01003-0002

LEMESSURIER, WILLIAM JAMES, STRUCTURAL ENGINEERING. *Current Pos:* Founder, Goldberg-LeMessurier, 52-61, founder & partner, LeMessurier Assoc, Inc, 61-73, chmn & chief exec officer, Sippican Consult Int, Inc, 73-85, EMER CHMN, LEMESSURIER CONSULT, INC, 85- *Personal Data:* b Pontiac, Mich, June 12, 26; m 53; c 3. *Educ:* Harvard Univ, AB, 47; Mass Inst Technol, MS, 53. *Honors & Awards:* Spec Award, Am Inst Steel Construct, 72; George Winter Award, Am Soc Civil Engrs, Pres Medal, 96. *Concurrent Pos:* Asst prof, Mass Inst Technol, 52-56, assoc prof, 64-67, sr lectr, 76-77; assoc prof, Harvard Grad Sch Design, 56-61, lectr, 73-, adj prof, 82-; Masonry Res Adv Coun, Sci Adv Comt, Nat Ctr Earthquake Eng Res 500 Allied Prof Medal, Am Inst Architects, 68. *Mem:* Nat Acad Eng; fel Am Soc Civil Engrs; fel Am Concrete Inst; hon mem Am Inst Architects. *Res:* Structural engineering design; precast concrete high rise housing system; staggered truss system for high rise steel structures; tuned mass damper system used to reduce tall building motion; structural stability. *Mailing Add:* LeMessurier Consult Inc 675 Massachusetts Ave Cambridge MA 02139

LEMIEUX, CLAUDEL, WEED SCIENCE, WEED BIOLOGY & ECOLOGY. *Current Pos:* Biologist, 83-86, RES SCIENTIST, AGR & AGR-FOOD CAN, 86-; ASSOC PROF WEED SCI, LAVAL UNIV, 91- *Personal Data:* b Montmagny, Que, Aug 31, 55; m 77, Christiane Paquet. *Educ:* Laval Univ, BSc, 79, MSc, 83; McGill Univ, PhD(agron), 86. *Concurrent Pos:* Dir, Que Soc Protection Plants, 87-89; chmn, Provintial Weed Comt, 90-; chmn, Expert Comt Weeds, 91; assoc ed, Phytoprotection, 89- *Mem:* Weed Sci Soc Am; Can Soc Agron; Int Weed Sci Soc. *Res:* Develop integrated weed management programs to meet economic and environmental sustainability; reduce herbicide dependency. *Mailing Add:* Sta Agr Can 2560 Hochelaga Blvd Ste-Foy PQ G1V 2J3 Can. *Fax:* 418-648-2402; *E-Mail:* lemieuxc@qcrssf.agr.ca

LEMIEUX, RAYMOND URGEL, VIROLOGY, PHYSIOLOGY. *Current Pos:* prof, 61-85, EMER & UNIV PROF ORG CHEM, UNIV ALTA, 85- *Personal Data:* b Lac la Biche, Alta, June 16, 20; m 48; c 6. *Educ:* Univ Alta, BSc, 43; McGill Univ, PhD(org chem), 46. *Hon Degrees:* DSc, Univ NB, 67, Laval Univ, 70, Univ Ottawa, 75, Waterloo Univ, 80, Mem Univ, 81, Univ de Que, 82, Queens Univ, 83, McGill Univ, 84, Univ de Sherbrooke, 86, McMaster Univ, 86, Univ Alta, Edmonton, 91; Doctorate, Univ de Provence, France, 72; LLD, Univ Calgary, 79, Univ Sask, Saskatoon, 93; Dr Philos, Univ Stockholm, 88. *Honors & Awards:* Merck lectr, 56; Folkers lectr, 58; Medal, Chem Inst Can, 64; C S Hudson Award, Am Chem Soc, 66; Medal of Serv, Order of Can, 68; Karl Pfister lectr, 68; Purves lectr, 70; Haworth Medal, Chem Soc, Eng, 78; Killam Prize, Can Coun, 81; Medal Hon, Can Med Asn, 85; Gairdner Found Int Award, 85; Rhone-Poulenc Award, Royal Soc Chem, 89; LeSueur Award, Soc Chem Indust, 89; King Faisal Int Prize Sci, 90; Can Gold medal for Sci & Eng, 91; E C Manning Nat Award Sci, 92; Albert Einstein World Award of Sci, 92; Medal Honor, PMAC Res Found, 92; Spec Alta Sci & Technol Found Award, Alta Pioneer, 93. *Prof Exp:* Res assoc carbohydrate chem, Ohio State Univ, 46-47; asst prof org chem, Univ Sask, 47-49; res officer chem natural prod, Prairie Regional Lab, Nat Res Coun, 49-54; prof chem, chmn dept & vdean fac pure & appl sci, Ottawa Univ, Can, 54-61. *Concurrent Pos:* Pres & dir res, Raylo Chem Ltd, Alta, 66-76; pres, Chembiomed Ltd, 77-78, mem bd, 77-78 & 83-84, hon bd mem, 86-, chmn, Sci Adv Comt, 90- *Mem:* Royal Soc Chem; fel Chem Inst Can; fel Royal Soc Can. *Res:* Stereochemistry; conformational analysis; carbohydrate chemistry; synthesis and conformation; especially antibiotics and blood group determinants. *Mailing Add:* Dept Chem Univ Alberta Edmonton AB T6G 2G2 Can

LEMING, CHARLES WILLIAM, PHYSICS. *Current Pos:* PROF PHYSICS, HENDERSON STATE UNIV, 70- *Personal Data:* b Cutler, Ill, Nov 5, 43; m 65; c 1. *Educ:* Eastern Ill Univ, BS, 65; Mich State Univ, MS, 67, PhD(physics), 70. *Concurrent Pos:* Res assoc, Fac Develop Prog, NSF, 77 & Student Sci Training Prog, 78, proj dir, 79; res assoc, Carbondale Mining Technol Ctr, 81; mem proj staff, NSF Consortium upper level physics software. *Mem:* AAAS; Am Asn Physics Teachers. *Res:* Optical devices; radon detection; science museum programs for teacher enhancement; textbooks which integrate computer methods into undergraduate physics courses. *Mailing Add:* One Ranch Rd Arkadelphia AR 71923

LEMIRE, ROBERT JAMES, ACTINIDE CHEMISTRY, SOLUTION CHEMISTRY. *Current Pos:* researcher, Whiteshell Nuclear Res Estab, 77-92, RES CHEM, CHALK RIVER LAB, ATOMIC ENERGY CAN LTD, 92- *Personal Data:* b Toronto, Ont, Mar 12, 45. *Educ:* Univ Toronto, BSc, 68, MSc, 71, PhD(chem), 75. *Prof Exp:* Researcher fel chem, Univ Ky, 75-77. *Mem:* Chem Inst Can; Am Chem Soc. *Res:* Properties of aqueous solutions; complexation; octinide chemistry; compilation of chemical thermodynamic databases. *Mailing Add:* Atomic Energy Can Ltd Chalk River ON K0J 1J0 Can

LEMIRE, RONALD JOHN, TERATOLOGY, PEDIATRICS. *Current Pos:* from asst prof to assoc prof, 68-77, PROF PEDIAT, UNIV WASH, 77- & DIR INPATIENT SERV, CHILDREN'S HOSP & MED CTR, SEATTLE. *Personal Data:* b Portland, Ore, Apr 20, 33; m 93, Kathy Brazeau; c Gregory, Suzanne, Jennifer, Anne & Alisa. *Educ:* Univ Wash, MD, 62. *Prof Exp:* Intern, King Co Hosp, Seattle, Wash, 62-63; NIH fel teratology & embryol, Univ Wash, 63-65, asst resident pediat, 65-67; chief resident, Children's Orthop Hosp & Med Ctr, 67-68. *Mem:* Soc Pediat Res; Teratology Soc; Japanese Teratology Soc; Europ Teratology Soc. *Res:* Neuroembryology; neuroteratology. *Mailing Add:* Dir Inpatient Serv Childrens Hosp & Med Ctr Mail Stop CH-41 4800 Sand Pt Way NE PO Box 5371 Seattle WA 98105. *Fax:* 206-527-3836; *E-Mail:* rlemir@chmc.org

LEMISH, JOHN, ECONOMIC GEOLOGY, GEOCHEMISTRY. *Current Pos:* CONSULT, 91- *Personal Data:* b Rome, NY, July 4, 21; m 46; c 5. *Educ:* Univ Mich, BS, 47, MS(geol), 48, PhD, 55. *Prof Exp:* Geologist, US Geol Surv, 48, 49-51; instr geol, Univ Mich, 53-55; from asst prof to prof geol, Iowa State Univ, 55-91. *Concurrent Pos:* Mem comts, Hwy Res Bd, Nat Acad Sci-Nat Res Coun, 58-70; chmn, State Mining Bd, 64-73, chmn publ comt, Am Geol Inst; mem adv comt, Iowa Coal Proj, 74-79; mem tech adv comt, Nat Gas Surv, Fed Power Comn, 75-81; NSF fel, 52-53. *Mem:* AAAS; fel Geol Soc Am; Geochem Soc; Am Asn Petrol Geol; Am Inst Mining, Metall & Petrol Eng. *Res:* Weathering studies of concrete; behavior of carbonate aggregates in Portland cement concrete; aggregate-cement reactions; physical and chemical phenomena related to ore deposition; structural geology; trace elements in Pennsylvania shales; occurrence of coal deposits in Iowa; coal exploration; occurrence of deep coal in Iowa; geology of Forest City Basin; pore properties of carbonate rocks in Iowa suitable for desulfurization by burning coal in fluidized bed combustion. *Mailing Add:* Dept Geol Sci Iowa State Univ Ames IA 50011

LEMKE, CALVIN A(UBREY), CIVIL ENGINEERING. *Current Pos:* asst prof, 56-65, ASSOC PROF CIVIL ENG, LA TECH UNIV, 65- *Personal Data:* b Waco, Tex, Aug 25, 21; m 48, Wanda Wilkes; c Steve W. *Educ:* Agr & Mech Col, Tex, BS, 43, MS, 61, PhD, 88. *Prof Exp:* Instr math, Baylor Univ, 52-56. *Res:* Structures and highways; highway culverts; soils. *Mailing Add:* 516 Glendale Dr Ruston LA 71270

LEMKE, CARLTON EDWARD, MATHEMATICS. *Current Pos:* from asst prof to prof math, 56-67, FORD FOUND PROF MATH, RENSSELAER POLYTECH INST, 67- *Personal Data:* b Buffalo, NY, Oct 11, 20; m 55; c 2. *Educ:* Univ Buffalo, BA, 49; Carnegie Inst Technol, MA, 51, PhD(math), 53. *Prof Exp:* Instr math, Carnegie Inst Technol, 52-54; res assoc anal, Knolls Atomic Power Lab, Gen Elec Co, NY, 54-55; engr Radio Corp Am, NJ, 55-56. *Mem:* Am Math Soc; Soc Indust & Appl Math; Opers Res Soc Am; Economet Soc; Math Asn Am. *Res:* Algebra; mathematical programming; probability and statistics; operations research. *Mailing Add:* 10 Burke Dr Troy NY 12180-3590

LEMKE, DONALD G(EORGE), MECHANICAL ENGINEERING. *Current Pos:* asst prof eng mech, Mich Technol Univ, 65-68, asst prof mech eng, 68-77, ASSOC PROF MECH ENG, UNIV ILL, CHICAGO CIRCLE, 77- *Personal Data:* b Chicago, Ill, Mar 25, 32; m 55; c 4. *Educ:* Ill Inst Technol, BS, 55; Univ Pa, MS, 60, PhD(mech eng), 70. *Prof Exp:* Engr, Teletype Corp, 55-58 & Westinghouse Elec Corp, 58-59; appl mech specialist, Dyna/Struct, Inc, 60-61; res engr, Advan Space Proj Dept, Gen Elec Co, 62-63; assoc scientist, Missile Div, Chrysler Corp, 63-64, res mgr aero ballistics & mech, 64-65. *Mem:* Am Soc Mech Engrs; Am Inst Aeronaut & Astronaut. *Res:* Machine mechanics; dynamics; structural mechanics. *Mailing Add:* Dept Civil Eng Univ Ill Chicago IL 60612-3796

LEMKE, JAMES UNDERWOOD, MAGNETIC RECORDING, MAGNETIC MATERIALS. *Current Pos:* CHIEF EXEC OFFICER & FOUNDER, REC ORDING PHYSICS INC, 86- *Personal Data:* b Grand Rapids, Mich, Dec 26, 29; m 53; c 3. *Educ:* Ill Inst Technol, BS, 59; Northwestern Univ, MS, 60; Univ Calif, Santa Barbara, PhD, 66. *Honors & Awards:* Reynold Johnson Medal, Inst Elec & Electronic Engrs Magnetic Soc, 95. *Prof Exp:* Electronics engr prod develop, Temco, 51-53; vpres eng, AV Mfg Co, 53-56; assoc to tech vpres, Armour Res Found, 57-60; dir magnetic res, Bell & Howell Res Labs, 60-68; pres & founder, Spin Physics

Inc, 68-82; res fel, Eastman Kodak Res Labs, 82-86. *Concurrent Pos:* Adj prof, Univ Calif, San Diego, 84- *Mem:* Nat Acad Eng; Inst Elec & Electronics Engrs; Am Phys Soc; AAAS; Am Asn Physics Teachers. *Res:* Physics of magnetic recording process; development of related components, materials, processes, devices and circuits. *Mailing Add:* 4251 Tenth Ave San Diego CA 92103. *Fax:* 619-220-0808; *E-Mail:* 73163.1371@compuserve.com

LEMKE, PAUL ARENZ, GENETICS, MICROBIOLOGY. *Current Pos:* prof bot, plant path, microbiol & head dept, 79-85, PROF MOLECULAR GENETICS, AUBURN UNIV, 85- *Personal Data:* b New Orleans, La, July 14, 37; div; c Paul III & Anne. *Educ:* Tulane Univ, BS, 60; Univ Toronto, MA, 62; Harvard Univ, PhD(biol), 66. *Honors & Awards:* Porter Award, Soc Indust Microbiol. *Prof Exp:* Instr biol, Tulane Univ, 62-63; sr microbiologist, Eli Lilly & Co, Ind, 66-72; assoc prof biol sci, Carnegie-Mellon Univ, 72-79. *Concurrent Pos:* Instr, Franklin Col, 67; sr fel, Carnegie-Mellon Inst Res, 72-79; Alexander von Humboldt Award, 77-78; vis prof, Ruhr Univ, WGer, 77-78 & Emory Univ, 85-86; Woodrow Wilson fel. *Mem:* Am Soc Microbiol; Genetics Soc Am; Mycol Soc Am; Bot Soc Am; Soc Indust Microbiol (treas, 76-78, pres-elect, 78-79, pres, 79-80); fel Am Acad Microbiol. *Res:* Genetics and viruses of fungi; plasmid DNA in fungi; immunochemistry of fungal viruses and double-stranded RNA; biosynthesis of antibiotics; cytoplasmic inheritance in fungi; flourescent staining of fungal nuclei and chromosomes; gene cloning in fungi. *Mailing Add:* Dept Bot Auburn Univ Auburn AL 36849-3501. *Fax:* 334-844-1645

LEMKE, RONALD DENNIS, THERMAL MODELS USED TO QUANTIFY COOKING METHODS, PSYCHOMETRIC MODELS. *Current Pos:* STAFF MEM, CHECKER ENG, MINN, 90- *Personal Data:* b St Paul, Minn, Apr 27, 41; m 67; c 2. *Educ:* Mankato State Univ, BS, 66; Col St Thomas, MBA, 80. *Prof Exp:* Engr, Honeywell, 66-69; eng mgr, Thermoking Div, Westinghouse, 69-80; res & develop mgr, Despatch Inc, 80-85; vpres eng & opers, Appl Vision Systs, 85-87; dir eng, Stein Inc, 87-90. *Mem:* Am Soc Heating Refrig & Air Conditioning Engrs. *Res:* Development of products that utilize different heat transfer methods for the preparation of food products; forced convection, latent heat and liquid immersion heat transfer. *Mailing Add:* 2701 Nevada Ave Minneapolis MN 55427

LEMKE, THOMAS FRANKLIN, ORGANIC CHEMISTRY, CORROSION. *Current Pos:* tech serv specialist, 72-80, MEM STAFF MKT DEVELOP, INCO ALLOYS INT INC, 80- *Personal Data:* b Tremont, Pa, July 28, 42; m 65. *Educ:* Wake Forest Univ, BS, 64; Marshall Univ, MS, 66; Lehigh Univ, PhD(chem), 68. *Prof Exp:* Biochemist, Med Res Labs, Edgewood Arsenal, 68-70; asst prof chem, Marshall Univ, 70-72. *Mem:* Am Chem Soc; Nat Assn Corrosion Engrs; Sigma Xi; Am Soc Metals. *Res:* Synthesis of heterocyclic compounds of medicinal interest; corrosion of nickel base alloys. *Mailing Add:* 7 Pinecrest Dr Huntington WV 25705-3439

LEMKE, THOMAS LEE, MEDICINAL CHEMISTRY. *Current Pos:* from asst prof to assoc prof, 70-84, PROF PHARM, UNIV HOUSTON, 84- *Personal Data:* b Waukesha, Wis, June 1, 40; m 63; c 3. *Educ:* Univ Wis, BS, 62; Univ Kans, PhD(med chem), 66. *Prof Exp:* Res assoc org chem & patent liaison, Upjohn Co, Mich, 66-70. *Mem:* Am Chem Soc; Am Pharmaceut Asn; Am Asn Col Pharm; Am Asn Pharmaceut Scientists. *Res:* Heterocyclic chemistry; anticancer agents; Favorskii rearrangement; drugs for mental disease; cardiovascular agents. *Mailing Add:* Col Pharm Univ Houston 4800 Calhoun Rd Houston TX 77204-5511

LEMKEY, FRANKIN DAVID, MATERIALS SCIENCE ENGINEERING, METALLURGY & PHYSICAL METALLURGICAL ENGINEERING. *Current Pos:* VIS PROF METALL ENG MAT, UNIV CONN, 88- *Personal Data:* b Oak Park, Ill, Jan 6, 37; m 78; c 3. *Educ:* Univ Mich Ann Arbor, BSE, 60; Univ Oxford, Eng, DPhil, 73. *Honors & Awards:* Grossman Author's Award, Am Soc Metals Int, 70. *Prof Exp:* Adj prof eng, Dartmouth Col, 82-88. *Concurrent Pos:* Sr consult scientist, United Technologies Res Ctr, 60-; counr, Mat Res Soc, 78-82; chmn, Exec Bd Rev, Metall Trans, Am Inst Mech Engrs, 80-81; expert, DWG mem, Univs Space Res Asn, 80-88; vis, Accreditation Bd Eng & Technol, 85-; dir, Microgravity Sci & Appln Div, NASA Hq, 88-89; pres exec exchange fel, White House, 88. *Mem:* Fel Am Soc Metals Int; Mat Res Soc; Am Inst Mech Engrs. *Res:* Melt grown metallic and ceramic composites for high temperature applications; discovered Raney type nickel catalysts from RSR atomization of powders; shock compaction of ferrous alloy powders; high temperature austenitic stainless steel alloys for stirling engine components; high temperature oxidation and corrosion of alloys together with thermochemical properties evaluations. *Mailing Add:* 122 Eastview Dr Windsor CT 06095

LEMLICH, ROBERT, CHEMICAL ENGINEERING, BUBBLES & FOAM. *Current Pos:* from asst prof to prof, 52-85, EMER PROF CHEM ENG, UNIV CINCINNATI, 85- *Personal Data:* b Brooklyn, NY, Aug 22, 26; m 76, Elizabeth A Murphy. *Educ:* NY Univ, BChE, 48; Polytech Inst Brooklyn, MChE, 51; Univ Cincinnati, PhD(chem eng), 54. *Honors & Awards:* Sigma Xi award, 69. *Prof Exp:* Chem res engr, Gen Chem Div, Allied Chem & Dye Corp, 48-49. *Concurrent Pos:* Res grants, Res Corp, Procter & Gamble, USPHS, HEW & NSF, 54-81, 85-88; Fulbright lectr, Israel Inst Technol, 58-59, Univ Arg, 66 & Moscow Aviation Inst, 91; fel, Grad Sch, Univ Cincinnati, 71-, chmn fels, 76-78. *Mem:* Fel AAAS; Am Chem Soc; Am Soc Eng Educ; fel Am Inst Chem Engrs; Sigma Xi. *Res:* Foam fractionation and properties; convective heat transfer. *Mailing Add:* Dept Chem Eng Univ Cincinnati Cincinnati OH 45221-0171. *Fax:* 513-556-3473

LEMM, ARTHUR WARREN, NEW MATERIALS DEVELOPMENT. *Current Pos:* SUPVR, ANALYTICAL LAB, COOPER POWER SYSTS, 86- *Personal Data:* b Biloxi, Miss, Mar 9, 52; m 72; c 5. *Educ:* Marquette Univ, BS, 74; Univ Wis-Milwaukee, MS, 90. *Prof Exp:* Supv chemist, Cerac Inc, 74-77; lab technician, RTE Corp, 77-81, res & develop mat engr, 81-86. *Mem:* Am Chem Soc; Inst Elec & Electronics Engrs; Am Soc Testing & Mat; Soc Plastics Engrs; Am Soc Metals; Mat Res Soc. *Res:* Investigation of new materials development and how their utilization can be used to improve and optimize the performance and reduce costs for products of the electrical and electronic industries. *Mailing Add:* W281 S 3696 Waukesha WI 53188-9760

LEMMERMAN, KARL EDWARD, PHYSICAL CHEMISTRY. *Current Pos:* RETIRED. *Personal Data:* b Willoughby, Ohio, May 30, 23; m 46; c 3. *Educ:* Oberlin Col, AB, 47; Cornell Univ, PhD(chem), 51. *Prof Exp:* Asst gen chem, Cornell Univ, 47-50; res chemist, Procter & Gamble Co, 51-88. *Mem:* Am Chem Soc. *Res:* Kinetics of gas-phase photochemical reactions; complex inorganic electrolytes; surfactant solutions; colloids. *Mailing Add:* 1952 Compton Rd Mt Healthy OH 45231-4206

LEMMING, JOHN FREDERICK, NUCLEAR PHYSICS. *Current Pos:* SR PHYSICIST NUCLEAR SPECTROS, MONSANTO RES CORP, MOUND LAB, 74- *Personal Data:* b Dayton, Ohio, Oct 31, 43. *Educ:* Univ Dayton, BS, 66; Ohio Univ, MS, 68, PhD(physics), 72. *Prof Exp:* Fel physics, Ohio Univ, 72-74. *Concurrent Pos:* Nuclear infor res assoc, Nat Acad Sci, Nat Res Coun Comt Nuclear Sci, 72-74. *Mem:* Am Inst Physics; Am Phys Soc. *Res:* Nuclear safeguards. *Mailing Add:* 4408 Van Winkle Amarillo TX 79121

LEMMON, DONALD H, SPECTROSCOPY. *Current Pos:* SR SCIENTIST, DHL LAB, 91- *Personal Data:* b Sugar Grove, Pa, Oct 19, 35; m 56; c 1. *Educ:* Univ Pittsburgh, PhD(chem), 66. *Prof Exp:* Fel, State Univ NY, Stony Brook, 66-67; sr engr, Westinghouse Res Ctr, 67-91. *Mem:* Am Chem Soc; Coblentz Soc. *Res:* Infrared, Raman and nuclear magnetic resonance spectroscopy; mass spectrometry. *Mailing Add:* 1415 Homestead Rd Verona PA 15147-2439. *Fax:* 412-798-9636; *E-Mail:* wavenumber@msn.com

LEMMON, RICHARD MILLINGTON, RADIATION CHEMISTRY. *Current Pos:* RES CHEMIST, LAWRENCE BERKELEY LAB, UNIV CALIF, 51- *Personal Data:* b Sacramento, Calif, Nov 24, 19; m 49, Marguerite Hayward; c Janet, Marilyn & Brian. *Educ:* Stanford Univ, AB, 41; Calif Inst Technol, MS, 43; Univ Calif, PhD(chem), 49. *Honors & Awards:* Mosher Award, Am Chem Soc, 89. *Prof Exp:* Res chemist, Calif Inst Technol, 43-45; fel, Med Sch, Univ Calif, 49-50; USPHS fel, Fed Inst Tech, Switz, 50-51. *Concurrent Pos:* Guggenheim fel, Helsinki, 65; assoc dir, Lab Chem Biodynamics, Univ Calif, 57-84. *Mem:* AAAS; Am Chem Soc; Radiation Res Soc. *Res:* Radiochemistry; hot-atom chemistry; radiation decomposition of organic compounds; chemical evolution. *Mailing Add:* 298 Los Altos Dr Berkeley CA 94708

LEMNIOS, A(NDREW) Z, AERONAUTICAL ENGINEERING, APPLIED MECHANICS. *Current Pos:* DIR ROTORCRAFT TECHNOL CTR, RENSSELAER POLYTECH INST, 93- *Personal Data:* b Newburyport, Mass, Nov 23, 31; m 54, Aspasia Hanos; c Karen & Keith. *Educ:* Mass Inst Technol, BS, 53, MS, 54; Univ Conn, PhD (appl mech), 67, Harvard Univ, Cert, 83. *Prof Exp:* Asst, Aeroelastic Struct & Res Labs, Mass Inst Technol, 53-54; res engr, Res Labs, United Aircraft Corp, 54-61; sr anal engr, Kaman Corp, 61-63, res proj mgr, 63-65, chief fluid mech res, 65-69, chief res engr, 69-76, dir res & technol, 76-89, asst vpres res & technol, Kaman Aerospace Corp, Bloomfield, Conn, 90-93. *Concurrent Pos:* Instr, Western New Eng Col, 57-; adj fac, Univ Mass, 77-; mem aeronaut adv comt, NASA, 78-84; mem adv comt, Rotary Wing Technol, Rennselaer Polytech Inst, Univ Md & Ga Inst Tech, 83-92. *Mem:* Am Inst Aeronaut & Astronaut; Am Helicopter Soc. *Res:* Aeroelastic behavior of rotating structures; structural dynamics and vibrations; structures and structural mechanics; computer modeling; applied mathematics; research administration. *Mailing Add:* 144 Primrose Dr Longmeadow MA 01106

LEMNIOS, WILLIAM ZACHARY, PHYSICS, ELECTRICAL ENGINEERING. *Current Pos:* Staff mem systs anal, 52-65, asst group leader, 64-65, group leader, 65-69, assoc div head, 69-83, DIV HEAD RADAR MEASUREMENTS DIV, LINCOLN LAB, MASS INST TECHNOL, 83- *Personal Data:* b Athens, Greece, Sept 13, 25; US citizen; m 54; c 4. *Educ:* Mass Inst Technol, BS, 49; Univ Ill, MS, 51. *Mem:* AAAS; Am Phys Soc; sr mem Inst Elec & Electronics Engrs; Sigma Xi; Am Inst Aeronaut & Astronaut. *Res:* Computer systems and simulation; radar systems. *Mailing Add:* Mass Inst Technol 36 Independence Ave Lexington MA 02173-5945

LEMOINE, ALBERT N, JR, ophthalmology; deceased, see previous edition for last biography

LEMON, EDGAR ROTHWELL, SOIL SCIENCE. *Current Pos:* RETIRED. *Personal Data:* b Buffalo, NY, Aug 22, 21; m 44, Donna V Deline; c Wilfred T, R Bruce & Robert J. *Educ:* Cornell Univ, BS, 43, MS, 49; Mich State Univ, PhD(soil physics), 54. *Honors & Awards:* Soil Sci Award, Am Soc Agron, 72; Biometeor Award, Am Meterol Soc, 94. *Prof Exp:* Prof agron, Tex A&M Univ, 51-56; prof agron, Cornell Univ, 56-80; soil scientist, Agr Res Serv, USDA, 51-80. *Concurrent Pos:* Guggenheim & Fulbright fel, Australia, 62-63; USSR-US exchange scientist, 69; Dept Sci & Indust Res fel, NZ, 70-71; consult, Univ Guelph, 83-85. *Mem:* Fel AAAS; fel Am Soc Agron; Soil Sci Soc Am. *Res:* Applied physics, particularly physical processes in the environment of agricultural crops. *Mailing Add:* 67 Ricardo Niagara-on-the-Lake ON L0S 1J0 Can

LEMON, LESLIE ROY, METEOROLOGICAL RADAR SYSTEMS DESIGN, SEVERE CONVECTIVE STORM METEOROLOGY. *Current Pos:* mgr, Nexrad Opers Compatibility Assurance Soc, Nexrad Radar Develop, Unisys Surveillance & Fire Control Systs, 81-91, mgr, Weather Systs Bus Develop, Paramax, 91-93, MGR, WEATHER RES & OPER, ADV WEATHER SYSTS, UNISYS GOVT SYSTS GROUP, UNISYS CORP, 94- *Personal Data:* b Greenville, SC, Jan 19, 47; m 68, Betty Vest; c Kristen, Allison & Jonathan. *Educ:* Univ Okla, BS, 70. *Honors & Awards:* Special Achievement Award for Discovery of the Doppler Weather Radar. *Prof Exp:* Meteorologist, Severe Storms Res, Nat Severe Storms Lab, Nat Oceanic & Atmospheric Admin Comn Corps, 69-70, mem staff oceanog data collection, 70-73, res meteorologist, 73-76, meteorologist, Nat Severe Storms Forecast Ctr, 76, res meteorologist, Tech Develop Unit, 76-81. *Concurrent Pos:* Consult & lectr severe storms; training instr, Severe Storm Structure. *Mem:* Am Meteorol Soc; Nat Weather Asn. *Res:* Understanding and documenting severe storm structure and evolution and tornado genesis, as well as operational application of conventional and meteorological Doppler radar to the warning services; radar and visual severe storm identification. *Mailing Add:* 16416 Cogan Dr Independence MO 64055

LEMON, PETER WILLIAN REGINALD, EXERCISE PHYSIOLOGY, NUTRITION. *Current Pos:* From asst prof to assoc prof, 79-87, PROF EXERCISE PHYSIOL, KENT STATE UNIV, 87- *Personal Data:* b London, Ont, Mar 15, 51; m 79, Mary E Nageotte; c Kristina & Kimberly A. *Educ:* McMaster Univ, BA & BPE, 73; Univ Windsor, MS, 75; Univ Wis- Madison, PhD(exercise physiol), 79. *Honors & Awards:* Biomed Sci Award, Int Olympic Comt Pres, 91. *Concurrent Pos:* Vis scientist, McMaster Univ, 89. *Mem:* Fel Am Col Sports Med; Am Physiol Soc; Can Soc Exercise Physiol. *Res:* Protein/amino acid metabolism during both heavy resistance and endurance exercise; quantify the protein/amino acid requirements of active individuals and to identify the mechanisms responsible for any increased needs. *Mailing Add:* Appl Physiol Res Lab Kent State Univ Kent OH 44242-0001. *Fax:* 330-672-4106; *E-Mail:* plemon@kentum

LEMON, ROY RICHARD HENRY, GEOLOGY. *Current Pos:* PROF GEOL, FLA ATLANTIC UNIV, 68-, CHMN DEPT, 77- *Personal Data:* b Birmingham, Eng, July 13, 27; Can citizen; m 59. *Educ:* Univ Wales, BSc, 51; Univ Toronto, MA, 53, PhD, 55. *Prof Exp:* Geologist, Ghana Geol Surv, 56-57; asst cur invert paleont, Royal Ont Mus, 57-58, 59-61, assoc cur, 61-67; staff geologist, Texaco Oil Co, Trinidad, WI, 67-68. *Concurrent Pos:* Nat Res Coun res grant, 63-66; asst prof, Queen's Univ, Ont, 58-59; assoc prof, Univ Toronto, 62-67. *Mem:* Geol Soc Am; Am Asn Petrol Geol. *Res:* Pliocene and Pleistocene geology and faunas of the west coast of South America and the Caribbean; world wide Pleistocene sea level changes; origin of sedimentary phosphates. *Mailing Add:* Dept Geol Fla Atlantic Univ PO Box 3091 Boca Raton FL 33431-0991

LEMONDE, ANDRE, BIOCHEMISTRY, PHYSIOLOGY. *Current Pos:* from asst prof to assoc prof, 52-66, prof, 66-, head dept, 76-81, EMER PROF BIOCHEM, SCH MED, LAVAL UNIV. *Personal Data:* b Saint-Liboire, Que, May 30, 21; m 53; c 2. *Educ:* Univ Montreal, BA, 42; Laval Univ, BS, 47, ScD(biol), 51. *Prof Exp:* Demonstr physiol, Laval Univ, 47-51; hon fel biochem & entom, Cornell Univ, 51-52. *Mem:* AAAS; Am Physiol Soc; Can Biochem Soc; Nutrit Soc Can. *Res:* Comparative biochemistry and physiology. *Mailing Add:* Dept Biochem Laval Univ Sch Med Quebec PQ J1K 7P4 Can

LEMONE, DAVID V, INVERTEBRATE PALEONTOLOGY, PALEOBOTANY. *Current Pos:* asst prof, 64-67, assoc prof, 67-77, PROF GEOL, UNIV TEX, EL PASO, 77- *Personal Data:* b Columbia, Mo, Apr 16, 32; m 55; c 2. *Educ:* NMex Inst Mining & Technol, BS, 55; Univ Ariz, MS, 59; Mich State Univ, PhD(geol), 64. *Prof Exp:* Geologist, Stanolind Oil & Gas Co, 55-56 & Tex Co, 58-59; assoc prof geol, SMiss Univ, 61-64. *Concurrent Pos:* Dir, SW Biostratig Inst. *Mem:* Fel AAAS; Am Paleont Soc; Soc Econ Paleontologists & Mineralogists; Geol Soc Am; Am Nuclear Soc; Mat Res Soc. *Res:* Paleophycology; stratigraphic paleontology; systematic invertebrate paleontology and paleobotany; nuclear waste management; paleoecology. *Mailing Add:* Univ Tex PO Box 3 El Paso TX 79968. *E-Mail:* lemone@belle.utep.geo.edu

LEMONE, MARGARET ANNE, CONVECTIVE STORMS, ATMOSPHERE BOUNDARY LAYER. *Current Pos:* fel, Advan Study Prog, 72-73, scientist, 73-92, SR SCIENTIST, NAT CTR ATMOSPHERIC RES, 92- *Personal Data:* b Columbia, Mo, Feb 21, 46; m 76, Peter A Gilman; c Patrick & Sarah. *Educ:* Univ Mo, AB, 67; Univ Wash, PhD(atmospheric sci), 72. *Mem:* Nat Acad Eng; fel AAAS; Am Geophys Union; fel Am Meteorol Soc. *Res:* Structure and dynamics of atmospheric boundary layer; structure and dynamics of cumulus and cumulonimbus clouds and mesoscale convective systems and their interaction with the environment, the boundary layer and larger-scale flow. *Mailing Add:* Nat Ctr Atmospheric Res PO Box 3000 Boulder CO 80307. *Fax:* 303-497-8181; *E-Mail:* lemone@ucar.edu

LEMONICK, AARON, HIGH ENERGY PHYSICS. *Current Pos:* assoc prof, Princeton Univ, 61-64, assoc dir, Princeton-Pa Accelerator, 61-67, assoc chmn dept, 67-69, dean grad sch, 69-73, dean fac, 73-89, PROF PHYSICS, PRINCETON UNIV, 64- *Personal Data:* b Philadelphia, Pa, Feb 2, 23; m 50; c 2. *Educ:* Univ Pa, BA, 50; Princeton Univ, MA, 52, PhD, 54. *Prof Exp:* Instr physics, Princeton Univ, 53-54; asst prof, Haverford Col, 54-57, assoc prof & chmn dept, 57-61. *Concurrent Pos:* NSF sci fac fel, Univ Calif, Berkeley, 60-61. *Mem:* Fel Am Phys Soc; Am Asn Physics Teachers. *Mailing Add:* 22 Jefferson Rd Princeton NJ 08540

LEMONS, JACK EUGENE, BIOMATERIALS, MATERIALS ENGINEERING. *Current Pos:* from instr to assoc prof, 71-73, prof eng & chmn dept, 77-90, PROF, BIOMAT & SURG, DIV RES, UNIV ALA, BIRMINGHAM, 90- *Personal Data:* b St Petersburg, Fla, Jan 20, 37; m 62; c 2. *Educ:* Univ Fla, BS, 63, MS, 64, PhD(metall, chem, physics), 68. *Honors & Awards:* I Lew Mem Award, Am Acad Implant Dent, 85. *Prof Exp:* Owner & operator, J E Lemons Gen Repair & Mach Shop, 55-60; res assoc metall & mat, Univ Fla, 63-64, asst, 64-68; res metall & head, Phys Metall, Eng Div, Southern Res Inst, Ala, 68-70; asst prof interdisciplinary studies, Clemson Univ, 70-71. *Concurrent Pos:* NIH spec fel, Med Sch, Univ Ala, 71-73. *Mem:* Am Soc Metals; Am Inst Mining, Metall & Petrol Engrs; Soc Biomat; Int Asn Dent Res; Orthod Res Soc. *Res:* Properties of materials for applications in physiological environments; interfacial interactions between synthetic biomaterials and tissues. *Mailing Add:* 229 Richmar Dr Birmingham AL 35213-4415

LEMONS, THOMAS M, REFLECTOR DESIGN, LIGHTING PRODUCT DESIGN. *Current Pos:* PRES, TLA-LIGHTING CONSULTS, INC, 70- *Personal Data:* b Indianapolis, Ind, Sept 15, 34; m 59; c 2. *Educ:* Purdue Univ, BS, 56. *Honors & Awards:* Distinguished Serv Award, Illum Eng Soc, 83. *Prof Exp:* Mgr appln eng, GTE-Sylvania Lighting Prods, 56-70. *Concurrent Pos:* Co-founder & vpres, ARC Sales, Inc, 79-, lectr, TLA Lighting Consults, Inc, 80- & Mass Inst Technol, 84-94; group mgr, design & applications, Illum Eng Soc, 82-84; expert witness, Tech Adv Serv for Attorneys, 84-; consult, Qualite Sports Lighting, Inc, 85- & Wilmette Park Dist, Ill, 86-95. *Mem:* Illum Eng Soc; Nat Soc Prof Engrs; Int Comn Illum; Soc Motion Picture & TV Engrs; fel US Inst Theatre Technol. *Res:* Energy efficient products and lighting systems; combine the latest light sources with improved optical systems to achieve unique results; author of over sixty technical papers; awarded 12 patents. *Mailing Add:* 7 Pond St Salem MA 01970-4819

LEMONTT, JEFFREY FIELDING, MOLECULAR GENETICS, TUMOR CELL DRUG RESISTANCE. *Current Pos:* SR SCIENTIST, GENZYME CORP, 89- *Personal Data:* b New York, NY, July 1, 44; m 70; c 2. *Educ:* Rensselaer Polytech Inst, BS, 65; Univ Calif, Berkeley, MBiorad, 67, PhD(biophys), 70. *Prof Exp:* Res fel genetics, Nat Res Coun Can, 70-72 & Nat Inst Med Res, 73-74; res staff mem yeast genetics, Oak Ridge Nat Lab, 74-81; sr scientist, Integrated Genetics, Inc, 82-89. *Concurrent Pos:* Lectr, Oak Ridge Grad Sch Biomed Sci, Univ Tenn, 74-81. *Mem:* Genetics Soc Am. *Res:* Yeast genetics and molecular biology; mechanisms of mutagenesis and DNA repair in yeast; expression of foreign genes in yeasts; yeast transformation; recombinant DNA technology; detection of pathogenic fungi; mechanisms of multidrug resistance in human tumor cell lines; bacterial and mammalian protein expression systems. *Mailing Add:* 165 Fairway Dr West Newton MA 02165

LEMOS, ANTHONY M, theoretical physics, solid state physics, for more information see previous edition

LEMP, JOHN FREDERICK, JR, VIROLOGY, CELL BIOLOGY. *Current Pos:* SR SCIENTIST, ADVAN BIOTECHNOL, INC, COLUMBIA, MD, 89- *Personal Data:* b Alton, Ill, May 25, 28; m 53, Barbara; c George, Vicki & Joel. *Educ:* Univ Ill, BS, 51; Nat Registry Microbiologists, Regist. *Prof Exp:* Bacteriologist, Com Solvents Corp, Ind, 51, fermentation supt & microbiologist, Ill, 53-57; microbiologist, Pilot Plants Div, US Army Biol Labs, Ft Detrick, Md, 57-61, prin investr, Process Develop Div, 61-63; sr microbiologist & asst br chief, Biol Ctr, 63-71; proj mgr retrovirus, dir cell sci lab, Electro-Nucleonics, Inc, 71-88. *Concurrent Pos:* Bd dir, Advan Biotechnol Inc, Columbia, Md, 90- *Mem:* Am Soc Microbiol; Sigma Xi. *Res:* Fermentation, purification microbial products, B-12, riboflavin and penicillin; bacitracin, alcohols, fungal amylase, continuous sterilization and culture, pH control, polarographic dissolved oxygen; mammalian tissue culture; virus propagation and purification; electrophoresis; human interferons; human lymphokines; acquired immunodeficiency syndrome virus diagnostic tests; HIV-1, HIV-2 and HHV-6,-7,-8 research and development. *Mailing Add:* 14 W Broad Way Lovettsville VA 22080. *Fax:* 540-497-9773; *E-Mail:* jlemp@abionline.com

LEMPERT, JOSEPH, MAGNETOHYDRODYNAMICS. *Current Pos:* RETIRED. *Personal Data:* b North Adams, Mass, July 3, 13; m 41, Jean Handler; c Eugene, Judith (Springer) & Larry. *Educ:* Mass Inst Technol, BS, 35; Stevens Inst Technol, MS, 42. *Prof Exp:* Engr, Lamp Div, Westinghouse Res & Develop Ctr, 36-44, sect engr, 44-53, mgr, Eng Sect, Electronic Tube Div, 53-56, adv develop, 56-58, sect mgr camera tubes, 58, res engr, 58-66, adv engr, 66-78, consult, 78-83. *Mem:* Am Phys Soc; fel Inst Elec & Electronics Engrs. *Res:* Photoemission; photoconductivity; secondary emission; thin films; vacuum tube electronics; electronic imaging; x-ray image intensification; x-rays; storage techniques; electron beams; electron beam welding; thermionic emission; magnetohydrodynamics. *Mailing Add:* 140 Spring Grove Rd Pittsburgh PA 15235

LEMPERT, NEIL, BIOLOGY, CHEMISTRY. *Current Pos:* From asst instr to instr, 60-68, from asst prof to assoc prof, 68-78, PROF SURG, ALBANY MED COL, 78- *Personal Data:* b New York, NY, Nov 25, 33; m 62; c 5. *Educ:* Hamilton Col, BS, 54. *Concurrent Pos:* Resident exp surg, Albany Med Ctr, 60-61; res fel surg, Mary Imogene Bassett Hosp & Clin, Cooperstown, NY, 63-64; consult surg, Vet Admin Med Ctr, 67-; dir, Histocompatibility Lab, Albany Med Col, 72- *Mem:* Am Surg Asn; Asn Acad Surg; Transplantation Soc; Am Soc Transplant Surgeons; Cent Surg Asn. *Res:* Transplantation and preservation of tissues and organs; basic immunology of organ transplantation. *Mailing Add:* Dept Surg Albany Med Col 47 New Scotland Ave Albany NY 12208-3412. *Fax:* 518-262-5571

LEMPICKI, ALEXANDER, PHYSICS. *Current Pos:* RES PROF, CHEM & PHYSICS DEPT, BOSTON UNIV. *Personal Data:* b Warsaw, Poland, Jan 26, 22; nat US; m 52; c 2. *Educ:* Imp Col, Univ London, MSc, 52, PhD, 60. *Prof Exp:* Res physicist, Electronic Tube Co, Ltd, Eng, 49-54; head quantum physics group, 65-72, mgr electrooptics lab, Govt Technol Ctr, Gen Tel & Electronics Labs, Inc, 73- *Concurrent Pos:* Mem adv subcomt electrophys, NASA, 69-71. *Mem:* Fel Am Phys Soc; fel Optical Soc Am. *Res:* Electroluminescence; optical properties of solids; spectroscopy and molecular structure of organo metallic complexes; optical maser materials, particularly liquid luminescence; luminescence and structure of glasses; luminescent solar collectors; semiconductors; spectroscopy of transition metal ions; scintillator materials. *Mailing Add:* 590 Commonwealth Ave Boston MA 02115

LEMPKE, ROBERT EVERETT, SURGERY. *Current Pos:* RETIRED. *Personal Data:* b Dover, NH, Nov 27, 24; m 49, Mary Baker; c Robert E Jr, Paul D, Martha B & Kari. *Educ:* Yale Univ, MD, 48. *Prof Exp:* Intern surg, Johns Hopkins Hosp, Baltimore, 48-49; resident, Med Ctr, Ind Univ, Indianapolis, 49-51; med officer, Army Med Res Lab, Ft Knox, Ky, 51-53; resident, Med Ctr, Ind Univ, Indianapolis, 53-55; assoc chief of staff med res, Vet Admin Hosp, Indianapolis, 56-71; from instr to assoc prof, surg, Sch Med, Ind Univ, Indianapolis, 56-65, prof, 65-93; chief surg, Vet Admin Hosp, Indianapolis, 59-93. *Concurrent Pos:* Vis prof surg, Jinnah Postgrad Med Ctr, Karachi, Pakistan, 64-65. *Mem:* Soc Surg Alimentary Tract; Cent Surg Asn; Am Col Surg; Asn Vet Admin Surgeons. *Res:* Diseases of the alimentary tract. *Mailing Add:* 4029 Roland Rd Indianapolis IN 46208

LEMYRE, C(LEMENT), ELECTRICAL ENGINEERING. *Current Pos:* secy fac sci & eng, Univ Ottawa, 70-73, chmn dept, 71-78, dir, Coop Educ Progs, 80-83, asst dean acad affairs, 86-88, ASSOC PROF ELEC ENG, UNIV OTTAWA, 69- *Personal Data:* b Shawinigan, Que, Apr 2, 34; m 62; c 4. *Educ:* Laval Univ, BScEng, 57; Univ London, PhD(transistors), 62. *Prof Exp:* From asst prof to assoc prof, Laval Univ, 62-69. *Concurrent Pos:* Am Orgn Stages France fel, 65-66. *Mem:* Sr mem Inst Elec & Electronics Engrs; fel Eng Inst Can; Can Soc Elec & Computer Eng; Am Soc Eng Educ. *Res:* Characterization of transistors. *Mailing Add:* Dept Elec Eng Univ Ottawa Ottawa ON K1N 6N5 Can

LENA, ADOLPH J, metallurgy; deceased, see previous edition for last biography

LENARD, ANDREW, MATHEMATICAL PHYSICS. *Current Pos:* PROF MATH PHYSICS, IND UNIV, BLOOMINGTON, 66- *Personal Data:* b Balmazujvaros, Hungary, July 18, 27; US citizen; m 53; c 2. *Educ:* State Univ Iowa, BA, 49, PhD(physics), 53. *Prof Exp:* Res assoc mathematician, Columbia Univ, 55-57; res staff mem, Plasma Physics Lab, Princeton Univ, 57-65. *Concurrent Pos:* Mem, Inst Haute Etudes Sci, 79-80. *Mem:* Am Phys Soc; Am Math Soc. *Res:* Kinetic theory; statistical mechanics; fundamental problems of quantum physics; mathematical problems related to physics. *Mailing Add:* Dept Physics & Math Ind Univ Bloomington IN 47405

LENARD, JOHN, VIROLOGY, PHYSIOLOGY. *Current Pos:* assoc prof, 73-76, PROF PHYSIOL & BIOPHYS, RUTGERS MED SCH, UNIV MED & DENT NJ, 76- *Personal Data:* b Vienna, Austria, May 17, 37; US citizen; m 59; c 4. *Educ:* Cornell Univ, BA, 58, PhD(biochem), 64. *Prof Exp:* Res assoc biochem, Cornell Univ, 63-64; fel biol, Univ Calif, San Diego, 64-65; Am Heart Asn advan res fel, 65-67; asst prof biochem, Albert Einstein Col Med, 67-68; assoc, Sloan-Kettering Inst Cancer Res, 68-72. *Concurrent Pos:* Am Heart Asn estab investr, 70-72; adj asst prof biol, Hunter Col, 70-73. *Mem:* Am Soc Biol Chemists; Am Soc Cell Biol; Am Soc Microbiol; Biophys Soc; Am Soc Virol. *Res:* Structures of biological membranes and enveloped viruses; entry and assembly of enveloped viruses; function of viral glycoproteins; endocrinology of lower eukaryotes; insulin action. *Mailing Add:* Dept Physiol & Biophys Univ Med & Dent NJ-Robert Wood Johnson Med Sch 675 Hoes Lane Piscataway NJ 08854-5635

LENARZ, WILLIAM HENRY, FISH BIOLOGY, BIOSTATISTICS. *Current Pos:* Fishery biologist, La Jolla, 68-76, FISHERY BIOLOGIST, SOUTHWEST FISHERIES CTR, MARINE FISHERIES SERV, TIBURON, 76- *Personal Data:* b Sacramento, Calif, Sept 18, 40; m. *Educ:* Humboldt State Univ, BS, 63; Univ Wash, MS, 66, PhD(fisheries), 69. *Concurrent Pos:* Sci adv, US Deleg Int Comn Conserv of Atlantic Tunas, 70-74 & Pac Fisheries Mgt Coun, 77-88. *Mem:* Am Statist Asn; Biometric Soc; Sigma Xi; AAAS; Ecol Soc Am; Am Inst Fishery Res Biologists. *Res:* Dynamics of exploited populations of fish. *Mailing Add:* Nat Marine Fisheries Serv PO Box 251 Kentfield CA 94914-0251

LENCHNER, NATHANIEL HERBERT, PROSTHODONTICS. *Current Pos:* DENT CONSULT, COLTENE/WHALEDENT, 77- *Personal Data:* b New York, NY, Aug 28, 23; m 59, Florence Smith; c Jonathan, Michael & Debra (Kane). *Educ:* NY Univ, BA, 43, DDS, 50. *Prof Exp:* Instr dent, Col Dent, NY Univ, 50-55; asst clin prof prev dent, Sch Dent & Oral Surg, Columbia Univ, 74-78. *Concurrent Pos:* Asst attend dentist, Long Island Col Hosp, 64-65; assoc ed, J Prosthetic Dent, 77-88; adj assoc prof biomed eng, Sch Eng & Archit, Univ Miami, 80-90. *Mem:* Study Group Advan Dent Diag (pres, 68-69); Am Prosthodontic Soc; Am & Int Asn Dent Res; life mem Am Dent Asn; fel Acad Gen Dent; fel Northeastern Gnathological Soc (pres, 66-70). *Res:* Biomedical engineering relative to dental devices; electrosurgery; the true effect of wave forms on cutting and coagulation. *Mailing Add:* 104-20 Queens Blvd Forest Hills NY 11375

LENDARIS, GEORGE G(REGORY), SYSTEMS SCIENCE, SYSTEMS DESIGN FACILITATOR. *Current Pos:* PROF SYSTS SCI, SYSTS SCI PHD PROG, PORTLAND STATE UNIV, 71- *Personal Data:* b Helper, Utah, Apr 2, 35; m 58; c 2. *Educ:* Univ Calif, Berkeley, BS, 57, MS, 58, PhD(elec eng), 61. *Prof Exp:* Sr staff scientist adaptive flight control systs, Gen Motors Defense Res Labs, 61-63, sr res engr, 63-69; assoc prof systs sci & chmn fac, Ore Grad Ctr Study & Res, 69-71. *Concurrent Pos:* NSF fel, 60-61; mem, Gov Tech Adv Comt, Ore, 70-72; consult to pres, Ore State Senate, 71; mem, Ore State Senate Task Force Econ Develop, 72-73; vis scientist, Johnson Space Ctr, NASA, 73-74; Nat Acad Sci res fel, 73-74; vis scholar, Eng & Econ Systs Dept, Stanford Univ, 78. *Mem:* Fel Inst Elec & Electronics Engrs; Soc Gen Systs Res; Pattern Recognition Soc; Asn Transpersonal Psychol; Sigma Xi; Int Neural Network Soc. *Res:* Developing methodologies for assisting teams of people to carry out systems design, engineering; analysis of social and human systems; models for complex systems; structural modeling; artificial intelligence; neural networks with application to conceptual graph knowledge systems. *Mailing Add:* Systs Sci Portland State Univ 2204 SW Hoffman Ave Portland OR 97201-3144

LENDER, ADAM, DIGITAL COMMUNICATIONS, SPEECH COMPRESSION. *Current Pos:* RETIRED. *Personal Data:* US citizen; c 2. *Educ:* Columbia Univ, BS, 54, MS, 56; Stanford Univ, PhD(elec eng), 72. *Honors & Awards:* Centennial Medal, Inst Elec & Electronics Engrs, 84. *Prof Exp:* Mem tech staff, Bell Tel Labs, Murray Hill, NJ, 54-60; proj engr, Int Tel & Tel Labs, 60-61; head, Advan Develop, Gen Tel Lenkurt Labs, San Carlos, 61-84; sr consult scientist, Lockheed Palo Alto Res Labs, 84-93. *Concurrent Pos:* Chmn, Data Commun Systs Comt, Inst Elec & Electronics Engrs, Commun Soc, 72-76, mem bd gov, 77-79 & 82-84; adj prof elec eng, Santa Clara Univ, 76-91; ed-in-chief, Trans Commun, Inst Elec & Electronics Engrs, 78-84, J Selected Areas Commun, 83-84, sr tech ed, Commun Mag, 87- *Mem:* Fel Inst Elec & Electronics Engrs; assoc fel Am Inst Aeronaut & Astronaut. *Res:* Digital communications; invented correlative, duobinary or partial response used worldwide for efficient, fast digital communications applied to high density magnetic disk recording for computers; 30 US patents. *Mailing Add:* Lockheed Palo Alto Res Labs Org 91-50 Bldg 251 3251 Hanover St Palo Alto CA 94304

LENEL, FRITZ (VICTOR), METALLURGY. *Current Pos:* RETIRED. *Personal Data:* b Kiel, Ger, July 7, 07; nat US; m 43; c 5. *Educ:* Univ Heidelberg, PhD, 31. *Honors & Awards:* Powder Metall Pioneer Award, Am Powder Metall Inst, 84. *Prof Exp:* Fel, Univ Goettingen, 31-33; metallurgist, Charles Hardy, Inc, NY, 33-37 & Delco-Moraine Div, Gen Motors Corp, Ohio, 37-47; from asst prof to prof, Rensselaer Polytech Inst, 47-73, chmn dept, 65-69, emer prof metall eng, 73-75. *Mem:* Fel Am Soc Metals; Am Inst Mining, Metall & Petrol Engrs; Brit Inst Metals; fel Am Soc Testing & Mat. *Res:* Powder metallurgy. *Mailing Add:* 2218 Burdett Ave Troy NY 12180

LENER, WALTER, ENTOMOLOGY. *Current Pos:* PROF BIOL, NASSAU COMMUNITY COL, 64- *Personal Data:* b New York, NY, Mar 20, 25. *Educ:* NY Univ, BA, 48, MA, 50, PhD(biol), 57; Rutgers Univ, MS, 60. *Prof Exp:* Instr biol, State Univ NY Col Oneonta, 50-51, sci consult, New Paltz, 51-52, from instr to prof biol, Geneseo, 52-64, coordr biol sci, 62-64. *Concurrent Pos:* Res grant, Res Found, State Univ NY, 63-64, 65-67; fel trop med, Sch Med, La State Univ, 64; NSF res grant, 66-68; consult. *Mem:* AAAS; Ecol Soc Am; Animal Behav Soc; NY Acad Sci; Sigma Xi; Entom Soc Am. *Res:* Investigating the physiology, genetics and ethology of large milkweed bug, Oncopeltus fasciatus. *Mailing Add:* 682F Front St Hempstead NY 11550-4528

LENES, BRUCE ALLAN, HEMATOLOGY. *Current Pos:* ASST PROF MED & PATH, SCH MED, UNIV MIAMI, 81- *Personal Data:* b White Plains, NY, April 4, 49; m 74; c 3. *Educ:* Union Col, Union Univ, BS, 71; Albany Med Col, Union Univ, MD, 75. *Prof Exp:* Resident int med, Shands Teaching Hosp & Clin, Univ Fla, 75-78; fel hematol, Georgetown Univ Hosp, Washington, DC, 78-80; fel blood banking, NIH, Bethesda Md, 80-81; MED DIR, AM RED CROSS BLOOD SERV, MIAMI, 81- *Concurrent Pos:* Clin asst prof med, Sch Med, Georgetown Univ, 80- *Mem:* Sigma Xi; Am Med Asn; Am Asn Blood Banks. *Res:* Clinical research in hematology and blood banking; special emphasis on pheresis and hemolytic anemia. *Mailing Add:* Am Red Cross Blood Serv SFla Region PO Box 013201 Miami FL 33101

LENEY, LAWRENCE, WOOD SCIENCE, MICROSCOPY. *Current Pos:* RETIRED. *Personal Data:* b New York, NY, Dec 14, 17; m 45; c 5. *Educ:* State Univ NY Col Forestry, Syracuse, BS, 42, MS, 48, PhD, 60. *Prof Exp:* Instr wood tech, State Univ NY Col Forestry, Syracuse, 46-52; asst prof, Univ Mo, 52-60; from assoc prof to prof wood & fiber sci, Col Forest Resources, Univ Wash, 60-83. *Mem:* AAAS; Forest Prod Res Soc; Tech Asn Pulp & Paper Indust; Int Asn Wood Anat; Soc Wood Sci & Technol. *Res:* Wood anatomy; microtechnique; machining wood; photomicrography of woody tissue; seasoning and preservation of wood; pulp and paper fiber analysis. *Mailing Add:* 2101 E First Ave Ellensburg WA 98926

LENFANT, CLAUDE J M, PHYSIOLOGY. *Current Pos:* assoc dir lung progs & actg assoc dir collab res & develop prog, Nat Heart & Lung Inst, NIH, 70-72, actg chief, Pulmonary Res Br, 72-74, dir, Div Lung Dis, Nat Heart, Lung & Blood Inst, 72-80, dir, Fogarty Int Ctr & assoc dir, Int Res, 81-82, DIR, NAT HEART, LUNG & BLOOD INST, NIH, 82- *Personal Data:* b Paris, France, Oct 12, 28; US citizen; m 49; c 5. *Educ:* Univ Rennes, BS, 48; Univ Paris, MD, 56; FRCP, 92. *Hon Degrees:* DSc, State Univ NY, Buffalo, 88. *Honors & Awards:* Distinguished Serv Award, Am Heart Asn, 83; Forrest M Bird Contributory Award, Am Respiratory Ther Found, 85; Breath of Life Award, Cystic Fibrosis Found, 88; Brotherhood Award, Asn Black

Cardiologists, 90; Presidential Distinguished Exec Award, 91; Surgeon Gen Exemplary Award, 93; Laura Graves Award, Nat Morrow Donor Prog, 95. *Prof Exp:* From res asst to dir res, Ctr Marie Lannelongue, France, 54-57; res fel, Univ Buffalo, 57-58; res fel, Columbia Univ, 58-59; asst prof physiol, Univ Lille, 59-60; from instr to prof med, physiol & biophys, Univ Wash, 61-72. *Concurrent Pos:* Fulbright fel, 56-58; assoc dir, Inst Respiratory Physiol & staff physician, Firland Sanitorium, Seattle, 61-68; mem, Physiol Study Sect, NIH, 69-70; hon prof, Nat Yang-Ming Med Col, Taipei, Taiwan, 80, Peruvian Univ, Lima, Peru, 81; bd gov, US Israel Binat Sci found, 90-93. *Mem:* Inst Med-Nat Acad Sci; Am Physiol Soc; Am Fedn Clin Res; Fr Physiol Soc; Asn Am Physicians; hon fel Am Col Chest Physicians; hon fel Am Heart Asn; hon mem Royal Soc Med; USSR Acad Med Sci; hon mem Cardiol Soc; Am Soc Clin Invest; Int Fedn Med Electronics; Am Soc Zoologists; Soc Exp Med & Biol; Undersea Med Soc; NY Acad Sci; fel Royal Col Physicians; hon fel Poland Soc Hypertension. *Res:* Respiratory physiology, especially in gas exchange; comparative physiology related to the development and environmental adaptation of the respiratory system; author or co-author of 228 scientific publications. *Mailing Add:* Nat Heart Lung & Blood Inst NIH 31 Center Dr Bethesda MD 20892-2486. *Fax:* 301-402-0818; *E-Mail:* lefantc@gwgate.nhlbi.nih.gov

LENG, DOUGLAS E, CHEMICAL ENGINEERING. *Current Pos:* RETIRED. *Personal Data:* b Kitchener, Ont, May 28, 28; m 55, Marguerite Lambert; c Ronald, Janet & Douglas. *Educ:* Queen's Univ, Ont, BSc, 51, MSc, 53; Purdue Univ, PhD(chem eng), 56. *Honors & Awards:* H H Dow Gold Medal; NAm Mixing Forum Award. *Prof Exp:* Chem engr, Benzene Prod Lab, Cent Res Eng Lab, 56-61, res engr, Process Fundamentals Lab, 62-63, sr res engr, 63-70, assoc scientist, Dow Interdisciplinary Groups Eng, 70-74, res scientist, 75-82, dir, 82-89, sr res scientist, 89-96. *Concurrent Pos:* Mem panel M, bd assessment, Nat Bur Stand, Nat Res Coun, 85-88 & 92-98. *Mem:* Am Chem Soc; fel Am Inst Chem Engrs. *Res:* Multiphase behavior; coalescence and dispersion; mixing, micromixing. *Mailing Add:* 1714 Sylvan Lane Midland MI 48640. *Fax:* 517-832-2624; *E-Mail:* lengde@aol.com

LENG, EARL REECE, GENETICS, RESEARCH ADMINISTRATION. *Current Pos:* prof, 58-77, EMER PROF AGRON, UNIV ILL, URBANA, 77- *Personal Data:* b Williamsfield, Ill, June 12, 21; m 44; c 3. *Educ:* Univ Ill, BS, 41, MS, 46, PhD(agron), 48. *Prof Exp:* Spec asst agron, 41-42, asst plant genetics, 46-48, from asst prof to assoc prof, 48-58, from asst dir to assoc dir int prog, 69-73, crop specialist, USAID, 75-77. *Concurrent Pos:* Fulbright sr res fel, Max Planck Inst, Ger, 61; consult, Fed Govt Yugoslavia & USAID, 60-61; res adv, USAID & Uttar Pradesh Agr Univ, India, 64-66; adv, USAID & Midwest Univs Consortium for Int Activities, Indonesia, 71; consult, Food & Agr Organ, Thailand, 71; consult, Int Coffee Orgn, 72; consult, UNDP-FAO, Yugoslavia, 73, 75; consult, World Bank, Malaysia, 74, USAID & Pac Consults, Sudan, Jamaica & Mauretania, 77-78; prof dir, INTSORMIL, Univ Nebr, Lincoln, 79-84. *Mem:* Crop Sci Soc Am; Am Soc Agron. *Res:* Comparative international agriculture; genetics and breeding of maize; breeding systems; evolution of maize and relatives; international soybean improvement; international agricultural development, emphasis on major cereal crops. *Mailing Add:* SE 181 Arcadia Shores Rd Shelton WA 98584

LENG, MARGUERITE LAMBERT, AGRICULTURAL BIOCHEMISTRY, ANALYTICAL BIOCHEMISTRY. *Current Pos:* PRES, LENG ASSOCS (CONSULTS), MIDLAND, MICH, 91- *Personal Data:* b Edmonton, Alta, Can, Sept 25, 26; m 55, Douglas E; c Ronald B, Janet (Dumas) & Douglas L. *Educ:* Univ Alta, BSc, 47; Univ Sask, MSc, 50; Purdue Univ, PhD(biochem), 56. *Prof Exp:* Ed asst chem & physics, Nat Res Coun Can, 47-48, anal chemist, 48-49; sr chemist, Allergy Res Lab, Univ Mich Hosp, Ann Arbor, 50-53; anal chemist, Dow Chem Co, Midland, Mich, Agr Dept, 56-59, registr specialist, Agr-Org Dept, 66-73, sr regist specialist, 73-80, res assoc int regulatory affairs, Health & Environ Sci, 80-86; mgr int regulatory affairs, Agr Chem, 86-90. *Concurrent Pos:* Chmn, Div Pesticide Chem, Am Chem Soc, 80. *Mem:* Fel Am Chem Soc; Sigma Xi; fel Am Inst Chemists; Int Soc Study Xenobiotics; NY Acad Sci. *Res:* Pesticides, their toxicology, metabolism, residues, analytical methods and realistic evaluation of hazard to the environment; meaningful communication of scientific information; international regulation of hazardous chemicals. *Mailing Add:* Leng Assoc 1714 Sylvan Ln Midland MI 48640-2538

LENG, WAI-CHOI, molecular biology & medicine, for more information see previous edition

LENGEL, ROBERT CHARLES, vibroacoustic measurement & analysis, measurement system engineering & development, for more information see previous edition

LENGEMANN, FREDERICK WILLIAM, PHYSICAL BIOLOGY. *Current Pos:* assoc prof, 59-67, prof phys biol, 67-88, EMER PROF PHYSIOL, NY STATE VET COL, CORNELL UNIV, 88- *Personal Data:* b New York, NY, Apr 8, 25; m 50; c 2. *Educ:* Cornell Univ, BS, 50, MNS, 51; Univ Wis, PhD(dairy husb), 54. *Prof Exp:* Res assoc radiation biol, Univ Tenn, 54-55, asst prof chem, 55-59. *Concurrent Pos:* Biochemist, Div Biol & Med, US AEC, 62; consult, FAD-IAEA, Vienna, 66 & 76. *Mem:* Fel AAAS; Am Dairy Sci Asn; Am Inst Nutrit; Coun Agr Sci & Technol. *Res:* Environmental contamination; fission product and mineral metabolism; milk secretion; mineral absorption; bone calcification. *Mailing Add:* PO Box 217 Rome PA 18837

LENGYEL, BELA ADALBERT, LASERS, MATHEMATICAL PHYSICS. *Current Pos:* RETIRED. *Personal Data:* b Budapest, Hungary, Oct 5, 10; US citizen; m 42, 62, Birgit Holmquist; c Judith A & Thomas E. *Educ:* Pazmany Univ Budapest, PhD (math), 35. *Prof Exp:* Res fel, Harvard Univ, 35-36; asst actuary, Astra Insurance Co, Budapest, 37-38; asst statistician, Worcester State Hosp, Mass, 38-39; instr math, Rensselaer Polytech Inst, NY, 39-42; instr phys, City Col New York, 42-43; asst prof phys, Univ Rochester, NY, 43-46; physicist, Navy Dept, Washington, DC, 46-52; sr staff physicist, Hughes Res Labs, Calif, 52-63; prof, 63-77, emer prof physics, State Univ, Northridge, 77. *Concurrent Pos:* Vis prof, Universidad Nat LaPlata, Arg, 70, Lund Tech Univ, Sweden, 71, Eidgenossiche Tech Hochschule, Zurich, Switz, 72; independent indust consult, 78-85. *Mem:* Am Math Soc; Am Phys Soc; Inst Elec & Electronics Engrs. *Res:* Functional analysis; math statistics; engineering applications of electromagnetic theory; author of three books on lasers. *Mailing Add:* 28 Sequoia Tree Lane Irvine CA 92612

LENGYEL, G(ABRIEL), ELECTRICAL ENGINEERING, OPTICAL COMMUNICATIONS. *Current Pos:* assoc prof, 66-76, PROF ELEC ENG, UNIV RI, 76- *Personal Data:* b Budapest, Hungary, Apr 30, 27; US citizen. *Educ:* Budapest Tech Univ, BASc, 49; Univ Toronto, PhD(elec eng), 63. *Prof Exp:* Demonstr math, Budapest Tech Univ, 49-50; res engr, Elec Power Res Inst, Budapest, 50-56; proj engr, E B Eddy Co, Que, 56-58; develop engr, Sangamo Co, Ont, 58-59; sr res fel appl, Ont Res Found, 59-66. *Concurrent Pos:* Res asst, Univ Toronto, 60-63; mem assoc comt elec insulation, Nat Res Coun Can, 60-64; guest scientist, Res Labs, Siemens Corp, Munich, 72- *Mem:* Inst Elec & Electronics Engrs; Am Phys Soc; Optical Soc Am. *Res:* Semiconductor lasers and optical modulations. *Mailing Add:* Dept Elec Eng Kelley Hall Univ RI Kingston RI 02881. *Fax:* 401-782-6422

LENGYEL, ISTVAN, ORGANIC CHEMISTRY, HISTORY OF SCIENCE. *Current Pos:* from asst prof to assoc prof, 67-73, chmn dept, 85-91, PROF CHEM, ST JOHN'S UNIV, NY, 73- *Personal Data:* b Kaposvar, Hungary, July 12, 31; US citizen. *Educ:* Lorand, Univ Budapest, dipl, 55; Mass Inst Technol, PhD(org chem), 64. *Honors & Awards:* Sr Awardee, Alexander Von Humboldt Found, Ger, 73-74. *Prof Exp:* Res chemist, G Richter Pharmaceut Co, 54-55; sci co-worker geochem, Geophys Res Inst Hungary, 55-56; lab chemist, Kundl Tirol Austria Pharmaceut Co, 57-58; res asst biochem, Sch Med, Johns Hopkins Univ, 58-59; res assoc org synthesis, Mass Inst Technol, 59-64; fel, Munich Tech Univ, 64-65; res assoc mass spectrometry, Mass Inst Technol, 65-67. *Concurrent Pos:* NAS vis scholar, Univ Budapest, 73; vis prof, Tech Univ Munich, 73-74. *Res:* History of organic chemistry. *Mailing Add:* Dept Chem St John's Univ 81-50 Utopia Pkwy Jamaica NY 11439

LENGYEL, JUDITH ANN, DEVELOPMENTAL BIOLOGY, MOLECULAR BIOLOGY. *Current Pos:* from asst prof to assoc prof, 76-87, PROF BIOL, UNIV CALIF, LOS ANGELES, 87- *Personal Data:* b Rochester, NY, May 15, 45; m 83, Frederick Eiserling; c 2. *Educ:* Univ Calif, Los Angeles, BA, 67, MA, 68; Univ Calif, Berkeley, PhD(molecular biol), 72. *Prof Exp:* Fel molecular biol, Univ Calif, Berkeley, 72-73; fel cell biol, Mass Inst Technol, 73-75. *Concurrent Pos:* Prin investr, NIH, 76-, NSF, 81-90 & Am Cancer Soc, 90-; mem NSF Develop Biol Panel, 80-84; mem comt coun affairs & coun deleg, AAAS, 93-; mem sci adv comt, March Dimes & Am Cancer Soc, 93- *Mem:* Sigma Xi; Soc Develop Biol; Am Soc Cell Biol; Genetics Soc Am; fel AAAS; Am Cancer Soc. *Res:* Molecular and genetic analysis of genes required to establish the body plan during embryogenesis in Drosophila. *Mailing Add:* Dept Biol Univ Calif Box 951606 Los Angeles CA 90095-1606

LENGYEL, PETER, BIOCHEMISTRY. *Current Pos:* assoc prof molecular biophys, 65-69, PROF MOLECULAR BIOPHYS & BIOCHEM, YALE UNIV, 69- *Personal Data:* b Budapest, Hungary, May 24, 29; US citizen; m 56; c 2. *Educ:* Budapest Tech Univ, Dipl, 51; NY Univ, PhD(biochem), 62. *Prof Exp:* Instr biochem, Sch Med, NY Univ, 62-63, asst prof, 63-65. *Concurrent Pos:* NIH spec fel, Pasteur Inst, Paris, 63-64. *Mem:* Am Soc Virol; Am Soc Biolchem & Molecular Biol. *Res:* Protein biosynthesis; nucleic acid and protein metabolism of animal cells and viruses; interferon defense mechanism; oncogenes. *Mailing Add:* Dept Molecular Biophys & Biochem Yale Univ C-139 SHM 33 Cedar St New Haven CT 06520-8025

LENHARD, JAMES M, CELL BIOLOGY, PHYSIOLOGY. *Current Pos:* RES ASST, MED SCH, WASH UNIV, 89- *Mailing Add:* Dept Immun/Physiol Glaxo Wellcome Res & Develop 5 Moore Dr Res Triangle Park NC 27709

LENHARD, JOSEPH ANDREW, HEALTH PHYSICS, NUCLEAR PHYSICS. *Current Pos:* MGT & TECH CONSULT, 89- *Personal Data:* b Detroit, Mich, June 18, 29; m 83, Crissy Thompson; c Andrea & Michelle. *Educ:* Vanderbilt Univ, BA, 53, MS, 57; Am Bd Health Physics, dipl, 60. *Prof Exp:* Health physicist radiation protection, Oak Ridge Opers Off, 57-61, sr health physicist broad nuclear safety, US Atomic Energy Coun, 61-67, dir safety & environ control div, 67-72, dir res, energy res & develop admin, 72-77, dir res, Dept Energy, 77-89. *Concurrent Pos:* Charter mem, Sr Exec Serv US Govt, 79. *Mem:* Health Physics Soc. *Res:* Research administration; physical, life and engineering sciences. *Mailing Add:* 125 Newell Lane Oak Ridge TN 37830

LENHARDT, MARTIN LOUIS, AUDIOLOGY, SPEECH & HEARING SCIENCES. *Current Pos:* asst prof, 71-75, ASSOC PROF OTORHINOLARYNGOL, MED COL VA, VA COMMONWEALTH UNIV, 71-, ASSOC PROF PEDIAT DENT, 76- *Personal Data:* b Elizabeth,

NJ, Dec 14, 44; m 66; c 11. *Educ:* Seton Hall Univ, BS, 66, MS, 68; Fla State Univ, PhD(audiol, speech sci), 70. *Prof Exp:* Nat Inst Neurol Dis & Stroke fel, Johns Hopkins Univ, 70-71. *Concurrent Pos:* Mem staff adj fac, Va Inst Marine Sci, Col William & Mary, 80- *Mem:* Acoust Soc Am; Am Audiol Soc; Animal Behav Soc; Asn Res Otolaryngol. *Res:* Psychological and physiological acoustics; speech communication; bioacoustics and linguistics. *Mailing Add:* Med Col Va Box 168 MCV Sta 23298 Richmond VA 23298-0168

LENHART, JACK G, FLUID CONTROLS, THERMODYNAMIC SYSTEMS. *Current Pos:* DIR ENG, TELEDYNE REPUB MFG, 78- *Personal Data:* b Bremen, Ohio, May 6, 29; m 51; c 3. *Educ:* Case Inst Technol, BSME, 51. *Prof Exp:* Mat res engr, NAm Aviation, 51-54; proj eng, TRW Equip Lab, 56-67; sr proj engr, chief engr, mgr ground support dept, mgr contracts admin, Accessories Div, Parker-Hannifin, 67-75; chief engr, Scott & Fetzer-Meriam Instrument, 75-78. *Mem:* Nat Fluid Power Asn; Am Met Soc; Am Soc Mech Eng. *Mailing Add:* 2000 Winchester Rd Cleveland OH 44124

LENHERT, ANNE GERHARDT, ORGANIC CHEMISTRY. *Current Pos:* ASST PROF CHEM, KANS STATE UNIV, 67- *Personal Data:* b Lynchburg, Va, Apr 1, 36; m 67; c 2. *Educ:* Hollins Col, BA, 58; Univ NMex, MS, 63, PhD(chem), 65. *Prof Exp:* Res fel, Univ NMex, 64-65; asst prof chem, Cent Mo State Univ, 65-67. *Mem:* Am Chem Soc; Sigma Xi; Int Heterocyclic Chem. *Res:* Synthesis of heterocyclic ring systems as potential purine and pteridine antagonists; anti-cancer agents and anti-radiation drugs. *Mailing Add:* Dept Chem Kans State Univ 111 Willard Hall Manhattan KS 66506-3701

LENHERT, DONALD H, COMPUTER ENGINEERING. *Current Pos:* from asst prof to assoc prof elec eng, 66-81, PROF ELEC & COMPUT ENG, KANSAS STATE UNIV, 81- *Personal Data:* b Winfield, Kans, Nov 25, 34; m 67; c 2. *Educ:* Kans State Univ, BS, 56; Syracuse Univ, MS, 58; Univ NMex, PhD(elec eng), 66. *Prof Exp:* Syst engr, Gen Elec Co, NY, 56-58; res engr, Dikewood Corp, NMex, 60-62; res & teaching assoc elec eng, Univ NMex, 62-66. *Concurrent Pos:* Consult Air Force Spec Weapons Ctr, NMex, 60-62 & Am Inst Prof Educ, 77-83; vis prof, Intel Corp, 83-84, Teletronix, 83, Motorola, 84 & Delco Electronics, 84. *Mem:* Inst Elec & Electronics Engrs; Nat Soc Prof Engrs. *Res:* Microprocessor systems; microprocessor applications; testing of digital systems; testing of analog to digital converters. *Mailing Add:* Dept Elec & Comput Eng Kans State Univ Durland Hall Manhattan KS 66506

LENHERT, P GALEN, CRYSTALLOGRAPHY, COMPUTER SCIENCE. *Current Pos:* from asst prof to assoc prof, 64-82, PROF PHYSICS, VANDERBILT UNIV, 82- *Personal Data:* b Dayton, Ohio, July 31, 33; m 56; c 2. *Educ:* Wittenburg Univ, AB, 55; Johns Hopkins Univ, PhD(biophys), 60. *Prof Exp:* USPHS res fel chem crystallog, Oxford Univ, 60-61; asst prof physics, Wittenburg Univ, 61-64. *Concurrent Pos:* USPHS grants, 62-63, 64-75, NSF grants, 72-76, 78-81; vis scientist, WPAFB Mats Lab, 82-90. *Mem:* AAAS; Am Crystallog Asn. *Res:* Determination of molecular structures by x-ray crystallographic methods; phase changes and modulated structures; polymer fiber diffraction. *Mailing Add:* 3109 Overlook Dr Nashville TN 37212

LENHOFF, HOWARD MAER, INVERTEBRATE ZOOLOGY, HISTORY & PHILOSOPHY OF SCIENCE. *Current Pos:* assoc dean sch biol sci, 69-71, dean grad div, 71-73, prof develop & cell biol, 69-92, EMER PROF, UNIV CALIF, IRVINE, 93- *Personal Data:* b North Adams, Mass, Jan 27, 29; m 54, Sylvia Grossman; c Gloria & Bernard. *Educ:* Coe Col, BA, 50; Johns Hopkins Univ, PhD(biol), 55. *Hon Degrees:* DSc, Coe Col, 76. *Honors & Awards:* Hon mem, Soc Phys & Nat Hist, Geneva Swiss Acad Sci, 90. *Prof Exp:* USPHS fel, Loomis Lab, Nat Cancer Inst, 54-56; actg chief, Biochem Sect, Armed Forces Insts Path, 56-57; assoc consult res, George Washington Univ, 57-58; fel, Dept Terrestrial Magnetism, Carnegie Inst Technol, 58; assoc prof biol, Univ Miami, Fla, 59-65, prof, 66-69, dir lab quant biol, 63-69. *Concurrent Pos:* Vis lectr, Howard Univ, 57-58; investr, Biochem Labs, Howard Hughes Med Inst, 58-63; USPHS career develop award, 65-69; vis scientist, Polymer Lab, Weizmann Inst Sci, Israel, 68-69; vis prof, Hebrew Univ Jerusalem, 70, 71, 77-78; vis prof chem eng, Israel Inst Technol, 73-74, social ecol, Ben Gurion Univ, Beersheba, Israel, 81; vis sr res fel, Jesus Col, Oxford Univ, 88; distinguished fel, Iowa Acad Sci, 86. *Mem:* Am Soc Biol Chem; Am Soc Cell Biol; Am Chem Soc; Biophys Soc; Soc Develop Biol; Hist Sci Soc. *Res:* Invertebrate biology; chemoreception; symbiosis; cellular differentiation; immobilized enzymes; enzyme immunoassays; history of experimental biology; folklore and medicine. *Mailing Add:* 304 Robin Hood Lane Univ Calif Costa Mesa CA 92627-2134. *E-Mail:* hmlenhof@uci.edu

LENIART, DANIEL STANLEY, PHYSICAL CHEMISTRY. *Current Pos:* IMMUNOL DIAG INSTRUMENTATION, TECHNICON INSTRUMENT CORP, 86- *Personal Data:* b Norwich, Conn, Jan 5, 43; m 71. *Educ:* The Citadel, BS, 64; Cornell Univ, PhD(phys chem), 69. *Prof Exp:* Fel, Varian Assocs, 69-70, appln engr, 70-75, mgr EPR res & develop, 75-80; Gas Chromatography-Mass Spectros, Hewlett Packard, 81-85. *Mem:* Am Phys Soc. *Res:* Study of relaxation phenomena using the techniques of electron spin resonance, electron nuclear double resonance and electron-electron double resonance. *Mailing Add:* Six Guernsey Rd Brookfield CT 06804

LENKE, ROGER RAND, MATERNAL FETAL MEDICINE, MEDICAL GENETICS. *Current Pos:* RETIRED. *Personal Data:* b Brooklyn, NY, April 6, 46. *Educ:* Columbia Univ, MD, 71. *Prof Exp:* Intern med, Roosevelt Hosp, 71-72; resident obstet & gynec, Columbia Presby, NY, 72-76; fel neurol, Mass Gen Hosp, 79; fel maternal & fetal med, Univ Southern Calif, Los Angeles, 79-81; dir prenatal diag, Univ Wash, Seattle, 82-85; dir maternal & fetal med, Med Col Ohio, Toledo & prof obstet & gynec, 85-89; prof obstet & gynec, Univ Colo, 89-94; dir mat fetal med, St Vincent's Hosp & Health Servs, 94-96. *Mem:* Am Col Obstetricians & Gynecologists; Am Inst Ultrasound Med; Am Soc Human Genetics; Soc Perinatal Obstets; AMA; Int Soc Fetal Med & Surg. *Res:* High risk obstetrics and prenatal diagnosis. *Mailing Add:* 8801 N Meridian St Suite 209 Indianapolis IN 46260

LENKER, SUSAN STAMM, MATHEMATICAL LOGIC, STATISTICS. *Current Pos:* asst prof oper res, 76-88, assoc prof software systs, Dept Info Systs & Anal 89-91, ASSOC PROF MATH, DEPT MATH, CENT MICH UNIV, 91- *Personal Data:* b Bridgeport, Conn, Nov 13, 45; m 68, Terry; c Scott & Carl. *Educ:* Western Conn State Col, BS, 69; Univ Colo, MA, 70; Univ Mont, PhD(math), 75. *Prof Exp:* Asst prof math, Univ Louisville, 75-76. *Mem:* Am Statist Asn; Opers Res Soc Am; Am Inst Decision Sci; Am Math Soc; Sigma Xi. *Res:* Data base theory; decision theory including fuzzy sets; statistics; category theory. *Mailing Add:* Dept Math Cent Mich Univ 100 W Preston Rd Mt Pleasant MI 48859-0001. *E-Mail:* 3c5agcj@cmuvm.csv.cmich.edu

LENKOSKI, L DOUGLAS, MEDICINE, PSYCHIATRY. *Current Pos:* chmn dept, 70-86, PROF PSYCHIAT, SCH MED, CASE WESTERN RES UNIV, 69-, ASSOC DEAN, 82- *Personal Data:* b Northampton, Mass, May 13, 25; m 52; c 4. *Educ:* Harvard Univ, AB, 48; Western Res Univ, MD, 53. *Prof Exp:* Fel psychiat, Yale Univ, 55-56; teaching fel, 57-60, from instr to assoc prof, 60-69, dir dept, Cleveland Metrop Gen Hosp, 69-76. *Concurrent Pos:* Consult, DePaul Maternity & Infant Home, 58-67, & Cleveland Ctr on Alcoholism, 58-61; actg dir dept psychiat, Univ Hosps Cleveland, 62-66, assoc dir dept, 66-69, dir dept, 69-86; consult, Cleveland Vet Admin Hosp, 65-; chief of staff, Univ Hosps Cleveland, 82-90; dir, Substance Abuse Ctr, Case Western Reserve Univ, 90- *Mem:* AAAS; Am Col Psychiat; fel Am Psychiat Asn; Am Psychoanal Asn. *Res:* Psychiatric education; community mental health planning. *Mailing Add:* One Bratenahl Pl Cleveland OH 44108

LENLING, WILLIAM JAMES, THERMAL SPRAY COATINGS. *Current Pos:* RES MGR, THERMAL SPRAY TECHNOLOGIES, 91- *Personal Data:* b Madison, Wis, Jan 16, 61; m 87. *Educ:* Univ Wis-Madison, BS, 85, MS, 87. *Prof Exp:* Mat engr plasma coating res & develop, Fisher-Barton, Inc, 87-90, Sandia Nat Labs, 88-90; mat engr plasma coating res & develop, Fisher-Barton, Inc, 87-90. *Concurrent Pos:* Mem, Mat Sci Comt, Thermal Spray Div, Am Soc Metall, 90-, chmn, Publicity Comt, 93- *Mem:* Am Soc Metall; Tech Asn Pulp & Paper Indust. *Res:* Material science coating development of thermal spray coatings; develop coatings for a wide variety of industrial applications; author of four publications and two patents. *Mailing Add:* 2141 Lakeland Ave Madison WI 53704. *Fax:* 608-825-2737

LENN, NICHOLAS JOSEPH, NEUROLOGY, ANATOMY. *Current Pos:* PROF NEUROL, SCH MED, STATE UNIV NY, 90- *Personal Data:* b Chicago, Ill, Nov 26, 38; m 64; c 3. *Educ:* Univ Chicago, SB, 59, MS & MD, 64, PhD(anat), 67. *Prof Exp:* Res assoc neuroanat, NIH, 64-66; asst prof pediat & med, Univ Chicago, 70-74; from asst prof to assoc prof neurol, Univ Calif, Davis, 74-80, from asst prof to assoc prof pediat, 74-80. *Mem:* AAAS; Am Asn Anat; Am Acad Neurol; Child Neurol Soc; Am Neurol Asn. *Res:* Developmental plasticity of mammalian brain. *Mailing Add:* Dept Neurol State Univ NY HSC T12-20 Stony Brook NY 11794-8121. *E-Mail:* nlenn@neuro.som.sunysb.edu

LENNARTZ, MICHELLE R, MEDICINE. *Current Pos:* DIR MED, WASH UNIV, 91- *Mailing Add:* Physiol & Cell Biol Albany Med Col 47 New Scotland Ave Albany NY 12208-3412

LENNARZ, WILLIAM J, BIOCHEMISTRY, CELL BIOLOGY. *Current Pos:* LEADING PROF & CHMN, DEPT BIOCHEM & CELL BIOL, STATE UNIV NY, STONY BROOK, 89-, DIR, INST CELLULAR & DEVELOP BIOL, 90- *Personal Data:* b New York, NY, Sept 28, 34; m; c 3. *Educ:* Pa State Univ, BS, 56; Univ Ill, PhD(chem), 59. *Prof Exp:* Postdoctoral fel, Harvard Univ, 59-62; from asst prof to prof, Dept Biol Chem, Sch Med, Johns Hopkins Univ, 62-83; Robert A Welch prof chem & chmn, Dept Biochem & Molecular Biol, M D Anderson Cancer Ctr, Univ Tex, 83-89, prof, 84-89. *Concurrent Pos:* NSF fel, 69-60, NIH fel, 60-62; mem, Physiol Chem Study Sect, NIH, 74-78, ad hoc mem, Molecular Biol Study Sect, 80-81, mem, Pathobiol Chem Study Sect, 82-86; vis prof biochem, Sch Med, WVa Univ, 82, Burroughs Wellcome vis prof, State Univ, NY, 83, Univ PR, 88; mem, Grad Prog Cell & Develop Biol, Genetics Prog, 89- & Acad Standards Coun, 90- *Mem:* Am Chem Soc; Am Soc Biochem & Molecular Biol (pres-elect, 88-89); Am Soc Microbiol; Sigma Xi; Am Soc Cell Biol; Soc Complex Carbohydrates; Am Soc Zoologists. *Res:* Cancer research; author of numerous scientific publications. *Mailing Add:* Dept Biochem & Cell Biol State Univ NY 450 Life Sci Bldg Stony Brook NY 11794-5215

LENNETTE, EDWIN HERMAN, EPIDEMIOLOGY, EXPERIMENTAL PATHOLOGY. *Current Pos:* chief biomed lab, 73-78, chief, 47-78, interim dir, Walton Jones Cell Sci Ctr, 81, EMER CHIEF VIRAL & RICKETTSIAL DIS LAB, CALIF STATE DEPT HEALTH SERV, 78- *Personal Data:* b Pittsburgh, Pa, Sept 11, 08; m 30; c 2. *Educ:* Univ Chicago, BS, 31, PhD(hyg & bact), 35; Rush Med Col, MD, 36. *Honors & Awards:* Bronfman Award &

Prize Achievement Pub Health, Am Pub Health Asn, 69; Wyeth Award Clin Microbiol & Prize, Am Soc Microbiol, 76. *Prof Exp:* Instr bact, Univ Chicago, 36-37, res assoc, 37-38; instr path, Wash Univ, 38-39; mem staff, Int Health Div, Rockefeller Found, 39-46; chief med-vet div, Camp Detrick, Md, 46-47. *Concurrent Pos:* Lectr, Sch Pub Health, Univ Calif, 47-78, lectr, Univ, 48-58; consult physician, Highland-Gen Hosp, 48-80; consult, Sixth Army Surgeon, 48-; assoc mem comn influenza, Armed Forces Epidemiol Bd, 48-51, mem, 51-73; mem comn rickettsial dis, 51-73; dep dir & chief lab serv prog, Calif State Dept Health, 72-73; mem, Armed Forces Epidemiol Bd, Off Surgeon Gen, 70-76, pres, 73-76; mem adv panel, Naval Biol Lab, 48-56; dir regional lab, Influenza Study Prog, WHO, 49-75, mem expert adv panel virus dis, 51-, mem expert adv panel zoonoses, 52-62, mem WHO sci group on virus dis, 66-75, mem sci adv comt to WHO team, EAfrican Virus Res Inst, 71-; mem viral rickettsial registry, Am Type Cul Collection, 49-65; coordr sect XII, sect res prog, NIH, 51-56; mem virus & rickettsia study sect, NIH, 51-53, chmn, 52-53, mem board sci adv comt, 68-72; consult, NIH, 51-, co-chmn microbiol & immunol study sect, Div Res Grants & Fels, 53-54, chmn, 55-56; mem adv comt, Poliomyelitis Vaccine Eval Ctr, Nat Found Infantile Paralysis, 53-61; chmn bd sci counsr, Nat Inst Allergy & Infectious Dis, 57-61, mem training grant comt, 60-61, chmn, 62, mem panel respiratory & related viruses, 60-63, mem comt vaccine develop, 63-68, mem & chmn subcomt rubella virus, 65-66, mem nat adv allergy & infectious dis coun, 63-66; consult physician, Peralta Hosp, 57-; mem microbiol panel study manpower needs in basic health sci, Fedn Am Soc Exp Biol, 60-61; chmn ad hoc comt rubella vaccine, Nat Inst Neurol Dis & Blindness, 63-64; mem microbiol panel, Wooldridge Comt, White House, 64; mem & chmn panel virus dis, US-Japan Coop Med Sci Prog, Off Sci & Technol, White House & Off Int Res, 65-69, mem US del, US Dept State, 70-76; mem sci adv comt, Hastings Found, 66-76; consult, Univ Tex, MD Anderson Hosp & Tumor Inst, 66-77; mem solid tumor-virus segment, Spec Virus-Cancer Prog, Nat Cancer Inst, 66-72, consult Nat Cancer Inst, 67-73; founding mem, Am Biol Coun, 68-70; mem bd dir, Rush Med Col, 70-74; consult, Bur Biologics, Fed Drug Admin & mem, Bur Panel Viral & Rickettsial Vaccines, 73- *Mem:* Fel Am Pub Health Asn, 61-77; hon fel Am Soc Clin Path, 72; Soc Gen Microbiol; Tissue Cult Asn (pres, 76-78); fel Royal Soc Trop Med & Hyg. *Res:* Virology; clinical, epidemiologic and immunologic research on viral and rickettsial diseases, including poliomyelitis, enteroviruses, respiratory disease, Q fever and virus-cancer relationships. *Mailing Add:* Calif Pub Health Found 6605 Ascot Dr Oakland CA 94611-1710

LENNEY, JAMES FRANCIS, BIOCHEMISTRY. *Current Pos:* assoc prof, 64-74, PROF PHARMACOL, UNIV HAWAII, 74- *Personal Data:* b St Louis, Mo, Oct 11, 18; m 42, 73, Ruth Kleinfeld; c Ann & Ellen. *Educ:* Wash Univ, BA, 39; Mass Inst Technol, PhD(gen physiol), 46. *Honors & Awards:* Fel, AAAS. *Prof Exp:* Asst zool, Wash Univ, 41; asst, Mass Inst Technol, 42-43; res chemist, 44-45; res biochemist, Fleischmann Labs, 46-49, head, Enzyme Dept, 49-56; sect head, Union Starch & Ref Co, 56-63. *Mem:* Am Soc Pharmacol & Exp Therapeut; AAAS; Am Chem Soc. *Res:* Biochemical pharmacology; enzyme and protein chemistry. *Mailing Add:* Dept Pharmacol Univ Hawaii Sch Med 1960 East-West Rd Honolulu HI 96822. *Fax:* 808-732-8468

LENNON, EDWARD JOSEPH, internal medicine; deceased, see previous edition for last biography

LENNON, GERARD PATRICK, CIVIL ENGINEERING. *Current Pos:* Asst prof, 80-86, actg dir, Environ Studies Ctr, 89-91, ASSOC PROF, LEHIGH UNIV, BETHLEHEM, PA, 86-; CONSULT, WOODWARD-CLYDE CONSULTS & PLYMOUTH MEETING, PA, 85- *Personal Data:* b New York, NY, Nov, 15, 51; m 76, Linda More; c Elizabeth, Brian & Marianne. *Educ:* Drexel Univ, BS, 75; Cornell Univ, MS, 77, PhD, 80. *Mem:* Am Soc Chem Engrs. *Res:* Design of fluidization systems for coastal applications; boundary element method for solving groundwater flow problems. *Mailing Add:* Civil Eng Lehigh Univ 27 Memorial Dr W Bethlehem PA 18015-3044

LENNON, JOHN W(ILLIAM), CERAMIC ENGINEERING. *Current Pos:* RETIRED. *Personal Data:* b Columbus, Ohio, Oct 21, 17; m 44; c 7. *Educ:* Ohio State Univ, BCerE, 40, MSc, 43. *Prof Exp:* Ceramic engr, Stupakoff Ceramic & Mfg Co, Pa, 40-42; asst ceramic eng, Ohio State Univ, 42-43; ceramic engr, Isolantite Inc, NJ, 43-44; fel, Mellon Inst, 45-46; ceramic engr, Orefraction, Inc, 46-49; eng exp sta, Ohio State Univ, 49-51; res engr, Battelle Mem Inst, 51-82. *Mem:* Am Ceramic Soc; Mineral Soc Am. *Res:* High frequency electrical insulation; special oxide compositions; high dielectrics; heat shock compositions; enamels; refractory coatings; glass; ceramic microstructure; electrodeposition of ceramic coatings; ferroelectric and ferromagnetic ceramics. *Mailing Add:* 942 Lambeth Rd Columbus OH 43220

LENNON, PATRICK JAMES, HOMOGENEOUS CATALYSIS, MACROCYCLIC CHEMISTRY. *Current Pos:* sr res chemist, Monsanto Co, 80-84, res specialist, 84-87, sr res specialist, 87-92, SYNTHETIC CHEM CONSULT, MONSANTO CO, 92- *Personal Data:* b Amsterdam, NY, July 24, 50. *Educ:* State Univ NY, Binghamton, BA, 72; Brandeis Univ, PhD(org chem), 77. *Prof Exp:* Res fel, Oxford Univ, 77-79. *Mem:* Am Chem Soc; Royal Soc Chem. *Res:* Homogeneous catalysis of organic reactions by transition metal complexes; organosilicon chemistry; design and synthesis of enzyme inhibitors; syntheses of macrocycles; inorganic and organic phosphorus chemistry. *Mailing Add:* 50 Wilshire Terr Webster Groves MO 63119. *E-Mail:* pjlenn@ccmail.monsanto.com

LENNON, VANDA ALICE, NEUROIMMUNOLOGY. *Current Pos:* CONSULT NEUROL & IMMUNOL, MAYO CLINIC, 78-, assoc prof neurol & immunol, Mayo Grad Sch Med, 78-83, PROF NEUROL & IMMUNOL, MAYO GRAD SCH MED, 83- *Personal Data:* b Sydney, Australia, Aug 1, 43; m 75. *Educ:* Univ Sydney, MB, BS, 66; Univ Melbourne, PhD(immunol), 73. *Prof Exp:* Res asst nuclear med, Univ Sydney, 66; from jr intern to asst med resident, Montreal Gen Hosp, 66-68; fel immunol, Walter & Eliza Hall Inst Med Res, 68-72; res assoc, Salk Inst Biol Studies, 72-73, asst res prof, 73-77. *Concurrent Pos:* Assoc adj prof, Dept Neurosci, Univ Calif, San Diego, 77-78. *Mem:* Am Acad Neurol; Sigma Xi; Am Asn Immunol; Soc Neurosci; Am Soc Clin Invest; Am Asn Neuropath. *Res:* Autoimmunity to antigens of central and peripheral nervous systems and muscle; identification of neural antigens on small cell lung cancer; immunologic studies of patients with neurological and paraneoplastic diseases of presumed autoimmune basis. *Mailing Add:* Neuroimmunol Lab Depts Neurol & Immunol Mayo Clin 200 First St Guggenheim Bldg 828 Rochester MN 55905-0001

LENNON-THOMPSON, DORIS, EXERCISE PHYSIOLOGY. *Current Pos:* assoc dir, Nutrit & Health Sci & Sci Rels, 91-93, SR SCIENTIST PROD DEVELOP, DESSERTS DIV, KRAFT GEN FOODS DEPT, GEN FOODS USA, TARRYTOWN, NY, 93- *Educ:* City Univ New York, BA, 73, MS, 75; Univ Wis-Madison, PhD(exercise physiol). *Prof Exp:* Marie L Carns res fel, Dept Phys Educ & Dance, Univ Wis-Madison, 80-81, res assoc, Clin Nutrit Ctr, 81-82, lectr & lab specialist, Biodynamics Lab, 82-84, adj asst prof, 84-86; sr staff scientist, Med Dept, Chem & Biol Med Sci Div, Hazelton Labs Am, Inc, 84-85; scientist nutrit & health sci, Gen Foods Tech Ctr, 85-87, tech supvr, 88-89; mgr consumer nutrit affairs, Nutrit & Health Serv, 89-91. *Concurrent Pos:* Dir exercise physiol & res, Cardiopulmonary Rehab Corp, 82; chair, Indust Liaison Comt, Am Inst Nutrit, 90-, Task Force on Dis; adj asst prof community & prev med, NY Med Col, 91- *Mem:* Am Inst Nutrit; Inst Food Technol; Sigma Xi; fel Am Col Sports Med; Am Alliance Health, Phys Educ, Recreation & Dance. *Res:* Nutrition; exercise physiology; co-author of numerous scientific publications. *Mailing Add:* Kraft Gen Foods Tarrytown Tech Ctr 555 S Broadway T33-1 Tarrytown NY 10519

LENNOX, ARLENE JUDITH, MEDICAL PHYSICS, ELEMENTARY PARTICLE PHYSICS. *Current Pos:* staff physicist, 80-86, DEPT HEAD, FERMILAB NEUTRON THERAPY FACIL, 86- *Personal Data:* b Cleveland, Ohio, Dec 3, 42. *Educ:* Notre Dame Col, Ohio, BS, 63; Univ Notre Dame, MS, 73, PhD(physics), 74. *Prof Exp:* Teacher, Marymount High Sch, 63-64, Regina High Sch, 64-65 & Shrine High Sch, 65-69; res assoc physics, Fermilab, 74-77; prof physics, NCent Col, 77-80. *Concurrent Pos:* Vis physicist, Fermilab, 78-80; assoc prof, Dept Radiation Oncol, Rush Med Ctr; mem-at-large, Forum on Educ, Am Phys Soc. *Mem:* Am Phys Soc; AAAS; Am Asn Physics Teachers; Am Asn Physicists Med; Am Soc Therapeut Radiol & Oncol. *Res:* Experiments to study backward peak in pi-p elastic scattering; experiments to measure pion form factor; p-p colliding beams; neutron therapy physics; medical uses for proton linacs. *Mailing Add:* Fermilab MS 301 PO Box 500 Batavia IL 60510-0500

LENNOX, DONALD HAUGHTON, HYDROLOGY. *Current Pos:* RETIRED. *Personal Data:* b Toronto, Ont, June 7, 24; m 47; c David M & Patricia A. *Educ:* Univ Toronto, BA, 49; Univ Alta, MSc, 60. *Prof Exp:* Tech Off, Occup Health Lab, Dept Nat Health & Welfare Can, 50-57; asst res officer, Res Coun Alta, 57-61, head, Groundwater Div, 61-68; maritime res sect, 68-70, head, Groundwater Subdiv, 70-72; chief, Hydrol Res Div, Environ Can, 72-79, dir, Nat Hydrol Res Inst, 79-85, spec adv, Inland Waters Directorate, 85-88. *Mem:* Geol Soc Am; Geol Asn Can; Nat Water Well Asn. *Res:* Application of geophysical techniques to shallow groundwater exploration; investigation of analytical methods for the determination of aquifer and well characteristics. *Mailing Add:* 18 Glendenning Dr Nepean ON K2H 7Y9 Can

LENNOX, ROBERT BRUCE, BIOELECTROCHEMISTRY, INTERFACIAL CHEMISTRY. *Current Pos:* asst prof, 87-93, ASSOC PROF CHEM, MCGILL UNIV, 93- *Personal Data:* b New Orleans, La, June 5, 57; Can citizen; m 85; c 1. *Educ:* Univ Toronto, BSc, 79, MSc, 81, PhD(chem), 85. *Prof Exp:* Res assoc chem, Imp Col, Univ London, 85-87. *Mem:* Electrochem Soc; Chem Inst Can; Amer Chem Soc. *Res:* Interfacial reactivity, organized assembly chemistry, bioelectrochemistry, organic thin films, bioelectrocatolysis; Monolayers; Bioorganic mechanisms; Biosensors; Organic chemistry. *Mailing Add:* Dept Chem McGill Univ 801 Sherbrooke St W Montreal PQ H3A 2K6 Can. *Fax:* 514-398-3793

LENNOX, WILLIAM C(RAIG), MECHANICS. *Current Pos:* From asst prof to assoc prof, 66-71, chmn dept, 76-77 & 79-82, PROF CIVIL ENG, UNIV WATERLOO, 71-, DEAN ENG, 82- *Personal Data:* b Mount Forest, Ont, May 22, 37; m 61. *Educ:* Univ Waterloo, BASc, 62, MSc, 63; Lehigh Univ, PhD(mech), 66. *Concurrent Pos:* Vis prof, Col Petrol & Minerals, Saudi Arabia, 70-71 & Harvey Mudd Col, 77-79. *Mem:* Am Inst Aeronaut & Astronaut; Am Soc Eng Educ; Am Acad Mech. *Res:* Stochastic processes; nonlinear mechanisms; stochastic processes; nonlinear mechanics; ice research. *Mailing Add:* Dept Civil Eng E23314 Univ Waterloo Waterloo ON N2L 3G1 Can

LE NOBLE, WILLIAM JACOBUS, organic chemistry, for more information see previous edition

LENOIR, WILLIAM BENJAMIN, GEOPHYSICS, ELECTRICAL ENGINEERING. *Current Pos:* SCIENTIST, BOOZ-ALLEN & HAMILTON, 84- *Personal Data:* b Miami, Fla, Mar 14, 39; m 64; c 1. *Educ:* Mass Inst Technol, SB, 61, SM, 62, PhD(elec eng), 65. *Prof Exp:* Asst elec eng, Mass Inst Technol, 62-64, instr, 64-65, asst prof, 65-67, Ford fel eng, 65-66; scientist-astronaut, Johnson Space Ctr, NASA, 67-84. *Mem:* AAAS; Am Geophys Union. *Res:* Microwave studies of planetary atmospheres; propagation of partially polarized waves. *Mailing Add:* Booz-Allen & Hamilton Inc 8251 Grensboro Dr Mc Lean VA 22102

LENOIR, WILLIAM CANNON, JR, botany, for more information see previous edition

LENON, HERBERT LEE, FISH BIOLOGY. *Current Pos:* Asst prof, 67-74, ASSOC PROF FISHERIES BIOL & ICHTHYOL, CENT MICH UNIV, 74- *Personal Data:* b Battle Creek, Mich, June 8, 39; m 62; c 3. *Educ:* Albion Col, AB, 61; Wayne State Univ, MS, 64; Mich State Univ, PhD(fisheries), 68. *Mem:* Am Fisheries Soc; Nat Audubon Soc; Nat Wildlife Fedn. *Res:* Freshwater fish population dynamics; management evaluation. *Mailing Add:* Dept Biol Cent Mich Univ 150 W Prestone Dr Mt Pleasant MI 48859-0021

LENOX, RONALD SHEAFFER, POLYMER CHEMISTRY, FIRE RETARDANT CHEMISTRY. *Current Pos:* res unit mgr, 79-90, SR PRIN SCIENTIST, ARMSTRONG WORLD INDUSTS, 90- *Personal Data:* b Lancaster, Pa, Jan 25, 48; m 71, Barbara Claar; c Jason Frederic. *Educ:* Juniata Col, BS, 69; Univ Ill, PhD(org chem), 73. *Prof Exp:* Asst prof chem, Wabash Col, Crawfordsville, Ind, 73-79. *Mem:* Am Chem Soc. *Res:* Sulfonyl azide chemistry; polymer blends and alloys; fire retardant chemistry; corosion chem, elastomeric foams. *Mailing Add:* Innovation Ctr Armstrong World Indust Lancaster PA 17604

LENSCHOW, DONALD HENRY, METEOROLOGY. *Current Pos:* SCIENTIST, NAT CTR ATMOSPHERIC RES, 66- *Personal Data:* b LaCrosse, Wis, July 17, 38; m 64, Janette L Chin; c Christine & Audrey. *Educ:* Univ Wis, BS, 60, MS, 62, PhD(meteorol), 66. *Prof Exp:* Affil prof, Colo State Univ, 74-85 & Univ Colo, 89-94. *Mem:* Fel Am Meteorol Soc. *Res:* Atmospheric boundary layer; airborne turbulence measurements and airplane research instrumentation f; air/surface exchange measurements and biogeochemical cycles. *Mailing Add:* 95 Pawnee Dr Boulder CO 80303

LENSKI, RICHARD E, POPULATION BIOLOGY MICROORGANISMS. *Current Pos:* HANNAH PROF MICROBIAL ECOL, MICH STATE UNIV, 91- *Personal Data:* b Ann Arbor, Mich, Aug 13, 56. *Educ:* Oberlin Col, BA, 77; Univ NC, PhD(zool), 82. *Honors & Awards:* Pres Award, Am Soc Naturalists, 86 & 92; MacArthur Fel, John D & Catherine T MacArthur Found, 96. *Prof Exp:* Res assoc, Univ Mass, 82-85; from asst prof to assoc prof ecol & evol biol, Univ Calif, Irvine, 85-91. *Concurrent Pos:* Vis asst prof biol sci, Dartmouth Col, 84; pres young investr, NSF, 88-93; mem, Comt Life Sci, Nat Res Coun, 90-, Bd Biol, 90-; fel, J S Guggenheim Mem Found, 92-93; vis fel, All Souls Col, Oxford, 92-93. *Mem:* Am Soc Microbiol; Am Soc Naturalists; Ecol Soc Am; Genetics Soc Am; Soc Study Evol. *Res:* Experimental study of ecological and evolutionary dynamics using microorganisms; coevolution of parasites and hosts; causes and consequences of mutation. *Mailing Add:* Ctr Microbial Ecol Mich State Univ East Lansing MI 48824

LENSTRA, HENDRIK W, NUMBER THEORY. *Current Pos:* PROF MATH, UNIV AMSTERDAM, 78- *Personal Data:* b Zaaadax, Neth, Apr 16, 49. *Educ:* Univ Amsterdam, PhD(math), 77. *Honors & Awards:* Fulkerson Prize, AMS & Parisenne Soc, 85; Royal Dutch Acad Ser Prize. *Mem:* Am Math Soc; Dutch Math Soc. *Res:* Algorithmic number theories which interface with computer sciences and algebraic number theories. *Mailing Add:* Dept Math Univ Calif Berkeley No 3840 Berkeley CA 94720-3840

LENTINI, EUGENE ALFRED ANTHONY, PATHOLOGY. *Current Pos:* CONSULT BIOHAZARD MED, 85-; DIR, VASCAR RES CONSULT. *Personal Data:* b Boston, Mass, July 6, 29; m 51; c Eugene Jr, J Blaise, Mark & Dirk. *Educ:* Boston Univ, AB, 51, MA, 55, PhD(myocardial metab), 58. *Prof Exp:* Instr physiol, Med Sch, Univ Ore, 58-64; asst prof, Med Col Va, 64-68; assoc prof physiol, Albany Col Pharm, 68-75; assoc prof, Dept Physiol & Pharmacol, Philadelphia Col Osteopath Med, 77-81; scientist, Vet Admin Hosp, Philadelphia, 81-82; res assoc prof surg, Pa Med Col, 82-83. *Concurrent Pos:* Nat Heart & Lung Inst fel, 56-58; Heart & Lung res awards, 60-65 & 69-72; vis prof, Mass State Col & Univ Lowell, 75-77; adj prof physiol, Sch Vet Med, Univ Penn, 81-84; grant awards, Nat Heart, Lung & Blood Inst, Am Heart Asn, Ore Heart, Va Heart, Am Osteop Asn, AMA & NIH. *Mem:* Sigma Xi; NY Acad Sci; AAAS; Am Physiol Soc; Am Heart Asn; Am Asn Univ Prof. *Res:* Bioelectronics, electronic micrometer, chart viewer; biophysics determination of oxygen diffusion coefficient through heart muscle; biochemical interrelation between ventricular dynamics and oxidative metabolism; effects of metabolic inhibitors on endogenous substrate; analysis of endogenous lipids and glycogens; physiological myocardial contract as related to substrate utilization; myocardial infarct model; vascular effects of catheterization; oncology and smooth muscle dynamics; 40 publications. *Mailing Add:* 221 Canterbury Dr Broomall PA 19008

LENTON, PHILIP A(LFRED), CHEMICAL ENGINEERING. *Current Pos:* RETIRED. *Personal Data:* b Detroit, Mich, Aug 13, 19; m 42, Lois Rosevear; c Carol & May Kay. *Educ:* Wayne State Univ, BSChE, 41; Mich State Col, MSChE, 43. *Prof Exp:* Chem engr res, Girdler Corp, 43-44; prod supvr gas mfr, Houdaille Hershey Corp, 44-45; mem staff chem eng res, Wyandotte Chem Corp, 45-49, sect head, BASF Wyandotte Corp, 49-56, develop engr, 56-63, acquisition specialist, 63-69, corp planning coordr, 69-77, sr indust engr, 77-80. *Mem:* Am Chem Soc; Am Inst Chem Engrs. *Res:* Process for manufacturing of lubricating grease; development of various organic and inorganic processes, including sodium carboxymethylcellulose and sodium alkyl aryl sulfonate; evaluation of business opportunities, including possible corporate acquisitions; long-range corporate planning. *Mailing Add:* 1920 Dacosta St Dearborn MI 48128

LENTZ, BARRY R, BLOOD COAGULATION, CELLULAR FUSION. *Current Pos:* from asst prof to assoc prof, 75-88, PROF, DEPT BIOCHEM, UNIV NC, CHAPEL HILL, 88- *Personal Data:* b Philadelphia, Pa, Sept 2, 44; m 66; c 3. *Educ:* Univ Pa, BA, 66; Cornell Univ, PhD, 73. *Prof Exp:* Vis scientist biophysics, Weitmann Inst Sci, 72; NIH fel biophys, Dept Biochem, Univ Va Sch Med, 73-75. *Concurrent Pos:* Estab investr, Am Heart Asn, 79-84. *Mem:* Am Chem Soc; Am Heart Asn; Am Soc Biochem & Molecular Biol; AAAS; N Am Thermal Anal Soc; Biophys Soc. *Res:* Physical chemistry used for the solution of biologically relevant problems; platelet-derived membranes in blood coagulation; poly ethylene glycol induced cellular fusion. *Mailing Add:* Dept Biochem Univ NC 418 FLOB CB-7260 Chapel Hill NC 27599-7260

LENTZ, CHARLES WESLEY, CHEMISTRY, SILICON CHEMISTRY. *Current Pos:* RETIRED. *Personal Data:* b Mt Pleasant, Mich, May 6, 24; m 47, Elinor Jessup; c Stephan, James, Joseph, Anthony, Christopher, Mary & Deanne. *Educ:* Mich State Univ, BS, 46. *Honors & Awards:* Sigma Xi Award, 65. *Prof Exp:* Chemist, Mich Chem Corp, 46-52 & Columbia-Southern Div, Pittsburgh Plate Glass Co, 52-55; chemist, Dow Corning Corp, 55-61, supvr develop, 61-68, mgr develop, 68-70, mgr res, 70-75, mgr life sci res & develop, 75- 77, dir health & environ sci, 77-86. *Concurrent Pos:* Mem comt MC-B5, Hwy Res Bd, Nat Acad Sci-Nat Res Coun, 67-80; chmn, Sci Affairs Comt, Chem Specialities Mfg Asn, 79-81; bd dir, Chippewa Nature Ctr, 89-95. *Res:* Study of silica as a reinforcing agent for silicone rubber, silicate minerals and the silicate structure changes that occur in portland cement during hydration. *Mailing Add:* 5105 Foxcroft Midland MI 48642

LENTZ, DAVID LEWIS, MESOAMERICAN ARCHAEOLOGICAL BOTANY, ETHNOBOTANY. *Current Pos:* DIR, GRAD STUDIES PROG, NY BOT GARDEN, 73- *Personal Data:* b Lima, Ohio, Sept 25, 51. *Educ:* Washington & Jefferson Col, BA, 73; Eastern NMex Univ, MA, 79; Univ Ala, PhD(biol & bot), 84. *Concurrent Pos:* Adj asst prof anthrop, Columbia Univ, 96-; vis prof biol, NY Univ, 96-; asst prof adj, Sch Forestry, Yale Univ, 96- *Res:* Substistance and medicinal plant use practices of Central American people, both past and present. *Mailing Add:* NY Bot Garden Bronx NY 10458

LENTZ, GARY LYNN, ECONOMIC ENTOMOLOGY. *Current Pos:* asst prof, 74-80, ASSOC PROF ENTOM, AGR EXP STA, UNIV TENN, 80- *Personal Data:* b Hollywood, Calif, July 15, 43; m 65, Aneita Meddress; c Carol, Jeffrey, Ann, Jonathan, Janeita & Shellaine. *Educ:* Univ Mo-Columbia, AB, 65; Iowa State Univ, PhD(entom), 73. *Prof Exp:* Res assoc entom, Iowa State Univ, 68-72; asst prof, Univ Ariz, 72-74. *Mem:* Entom Soc Am. *Res:* Pest management of cotton and soybean insects. *Mailing Add:* WTenn Exp Sta 605 Airways Blvd Jackson TN 38301. *Fax:* 901-425-4760; *E-Mail:* g115405@erc.jscc.cc.tn.us

LENTZ, MARK STEVEN, ENERGY CONSERVATION, SPECIALTY ENVIRONMENT DESIGN. *Current Pos:* PRES, LENTZ ENG ASSOC, INC, 95- *Personal Data:* b Madison, Wis, July 3, 49; m 80, Duyuan Tremelling. *Educ:* Univ Wis-Madison, BSME, 78. *Honors & Awards:* Energy Award, Am Soc Heating, Refrigerating & Air Conditioning Engrs, 88. *Prof Exp:* Proj engr, Affil Engrs, Inc, 76-81 & Stanley Consults, 81-83; sr mech engr, Donohue & Assocs, Inc, 83-91; sr proj engr, PSJ Eng, Inc, 91-95. *Concurrent Pos:* Chmn, TC 9.8-Large Bldg Air Conditioning Appln, Am Soc Heating, Refrigerating & Air Conditioning Engrs, Inc, 84-88, corresp mem, 88-; mem, TC 9.2-Indust Air Conditioning, Am Soc Heating, Refrigerating & Air Conditioning Engrs, Inc, 85-89. *Mem:* Am Soc Heating, Refrigerating & Air Conditioning Engrs; Nat Fire Protection Asn. *Res:* Advanced systems design for high-tech laboratory and specialty environment employing variable-volume ventilation and evaporative cooling; author of three publications. *Mailing Add:* 437 Center Walk Kohler WI 53044. *Fax:* 920-459-9767

LENTZ, PAUL JACKSON, JR, BIOCHEMISTRY, X-RAY CRYSTALLOGRAPHY. *Current Pos:* MED PRACT, 87- *Personal Data:* b Niagara Falls, NY, Oct 10, 44; m 68; c 2. *Educ:* Univ Alaska, BS, 66; Purdue Univ, PhD(molecular biol), 71; Univ Miami, MD, 84. *Prof Exp:* Fel biol, Wallenberg Lab, Uppsala Univ, Sweden, 71-75; scholar chem, Univ Mich, 75-78; asst prof biol, Kings's Col, 78-82; med resident, Univ Mich Hosps, 84-87. *Concurrent Pos:* NIH grant, 71-73; lectr chem, Univ Mich, 76-78. *Mem:* AMA; Am Acad Family Phys. *Res:* X-ray crystallographic structure determination of proteins, nucleic acids and viruses. *Mailing Add:* 304 State St Adrian MI 49221

LENTZ, PAUL LEWIS, MYCOLOGY. *Current Pos:* RETIRED. *Personal Data:* b Indianapolis, Ind, May 26, 18; m 43; c 2. *Educ:* Butler Univ, AB, 40; Univ Iowa, MS, 42, PhD(mycol), 53. *Prof Exp:* Asst bot lab, Butler Univ, 38-40, bact lab, 40; asst mycol, Univ Iowa, 40-42, 46-47; assoc mycologist, Plant Indust Sta, USDA, 47-56, mycologist, Plant Sci Res Div, 56-72, instr advan educ sci, Grad Sch-Found, 58-71, chief, Mycol Lab, Sci & Educ

Admin-Age Res, 72-83. Mem: Bot Soc Am; Mycol Soc Am; Int Soc Plant Taxon; Sigma Xi. Res: Basidiomycete taxonomy, anatomy, morphology and biology; Aphyllophorales; National Fungus Collections. Mailing Add: Five Orange Ct Greenbelt MD 20770-1609

LENTZ, THOMAS LAWRENCE, ACETYLCHOLINE RECEPTOR, RABIES VIRUS. Current Pos: From instr to asst prof anat, Sch Med, Yale Univ, 64-69, assoc prof cytol, 69-74, assoc prof cell biol, 74-85, PROF CELL BIOL, SCH MED, YALE UNIV, 85-, ASST DEAN ADMIS, 76-, VCHMN CELL BIOL, 92- Personal Data: b Toledo, Ohio, Mar 25, 39; m 61, Judith Pernaa; c Stephen, Christopher & Sarah. Educ: Yale Univ, MD, 64. Mem: AAAS; Am Soc Cell Biol; Soc Neurosci; NY Acad Sci. Res: Characterization of functional domains on the acetylcholine receptor; identification of cellular receptors for rabies virus. Mailing Add: Dept Cell Biol Yale Univ Sch Med 333 Cedar St New Haven CT 06510. Fax: 203-785-7226; E-Mail: thomas.lentz@yale.edu

LENTZNER, HAROLD, PUBLIC HEALTH & EPIDEMIOLOGY. Current Pos: SPEC ASST CHRONIC DIS & AGING STUDIES, OFF ANALYSIS, EPIDEMIOL & HEALTH PROM, 93- Personal Data: b Chicago, Ill, May 1, 43. Educ: Occidental Col, BA, 65; Univ Wis, MA, 67; Univ Pa, PhD(demog), 87. Prof Exp: Epidemiologist, Ctr Dis Control & Prev, 89-93. Mem: Pop Asn Am; Am Pub Health Asn. Mailing Add: Off Analysis Epidemiol & Health Prom Rm 790 6525 Belcrest Rd Hyattsville MD 20782. Fax: 301-436-8459; E-Mail: hrl1@cdc.gov

LENZ, ALFRED C, GEOLOGY. Current Pos: from asst prof to assoc prof, 64-75, prof paleont & stratig, 75-80, PROF GEOL, UNIV WESTERN ONT, 80- Personal Data: b Olds, Alta, Jan 6, 29; m 54; c 2. Educ: Univ Alta, BSc, 54, MSc, 56; Princeton Univ, PhD(paleont), 59. Prof Exp: Paleontologist, Calif Standard Co, 59-64. Concurrent Pos: Lectr, Univ Alta, 60-61. Mem: Int Palaeont Asn; Paleont Soc; Can Palaeont Asn. Res: Lower Paleozoic biostratigraphy; Devonian stratigraphy and paleontology; graptolite biostratigraphy; Upper Silurian and Lower Devonian brachiopods. Mailing Add: Dept Geol Univ Western Ont Middlesex Coll London ON N6A 5B7 Can

LENZ, CHARLES ELDON, ENGINEERING, MATHEMATICS. Current Pos: ENG CONSULT & AUTHOR, 88- Personal Data: b Omaha, Nebr, Apr 13, 26. Educ: Mass Inst Technol, SB, 51, SM, 53; Cornell Univ, PhD, 57; Univ Calif, MS, 71. Prof Exp: Engr, Gen Elec Co, 49-56; consult, Assoc Univs, 56; sr engr design engr, Avco Corp, 58-60; mem tech staff, Armour Res Found, 60-62; sr scientist, Autonetics Div, NAm Aviation, Inc, 62-69; consult lectr, Univ Nebr, 73-77; sr engr, Control Data Corp, 77-80; staff develop engr, USAF, Offutt AFB, 80-84; res engr, Union Pac Syst, 84-87. Concurrent Pos: Prof, Univ Hawaii, 66-68; guest lectr, Univs Hawaii & Minn, Cornell Univ & Col Aeronaut, Cranfield, Eng; lectr, Univ Calif; mem, Nat Feedback-Control Comt, Inst Elec & Electronics Engrs. Mem: Inst Elec & Electronics Engrs; Instrument Soc Am; Am Soc Civil Engrs; NY Acad Sci; Sigma Xi. Res: Solving significant electronic, economic and other engineering problems with simulation, novel hardware and new mathematical techniques later incorporated into computer programs of broad utility. Mailing Add: 5016 Western Ave Omaha NE 68132

LENZ, GEORGE H, NUCLEAR PHYSICS. Current Pos: assoc prof, 71-76, WHITNEY-GUION PROF PHYSICS, SWEET BRIAR COL, 76-, CHMN DEPT, 71- Personal Data: b Irvington, NJ, Oct 9, 39; m 61; c 2. Educ: Rutgers Univ, AB, 61, MS, 63, PhD(physics), 67. Prof Exp: Asst prof physics, Univ Va, 67-71. Mem: Am Phys Soc; Am Asn Physics Teachers. Res: Analogue states; compound nucleus and direct reactions; Coulomb energy systematics. Mailing Add: Box D Sweet Briar Col Sweet Briar VA 24595

LENZ, GEORGE RICHARD, RESEARCH ADMINISTRATION, BIOENGINEERING & BIOMEDICAL. Current Pos: DIR HEALTH CARE RES & DEVELOP, BOC GROUP TECH CTR, MURRAY HILL, NJ, 85- Personal Data: b Chicago, Ill, Nov 22, 41; m 70; c 3. Educ: Ill Inst Technol, BS, 63; Univ Chicago, MS, 65, PhD(chem), 67; Northwestern Univ, MBA, 83. Prof Exp: Nat Cancer Inst fel, Yale Univ, 67-69; res investr, 69-71, sect head, G D Searle & Co, 71-85. Mem: AAAS; Am Chem Soc; Royal Soc Chem. Res: Photochemistry; medicinal chemistry. Mailing Add: Grlen Res & Develop Assoc 6 Apple Blossom Rd Andover MA 01810

LENZ, PAUL HEINS, PHYSIOLOGY, ENDOCRINOLOGY. Current Pos: Asst prof, 66-70, assoc prof phyiol, 70-80, PROF BIOL SCI, FAIRLEIGH DICKINSON UNIV, 80- Personal Data: b Newark, NJ, Mar 29, 38; m 60; c 4. Educ: Franklin & Marshall Col, BS, 60; Rutgers Univ, MS, 64, PhD(endocrinol), 66. Concurrent Pos: Univ res grants, 67-68, Eli Lilly grant, 70; Ciba grants, 70-71. Mem: Endocrine Soc; Am Oil Chemists' Soc; Am Asn Clin Chemists; Am Heart Asn. Res: Development of micro-chemical techniques; hormonal and biochemical control of lipid metabolism; platelet aggregation and its control. Mailing Add: PO Box 5877 Bethesda MD 20824

LENZ, ROBERT WILLIAM, ORGANIC CHEMISTRY. Current Pos: from assoc prof to prof, 66-95, EMER PROF POLYMER SCI & ENG, UNIV MASS, AMHERST, 95- Personal Data: b New York, NY, Apr 28, 26; m 53, Madeleine Leblanc; c Kathleen, Douglas, Cynthia & Suzanne. Educ: Lehigh Univ, BS, 49; Inst Textile Technol, MS, 51; State Univ NY, PhD(polymer chem), 56. Honors & Awards: Sr Humboldt Prize, 79; Am Chem Soc Award in Polymer Chem, 92. Prof Exp: Res chemist, Chicopee Mfg Corp, 51-53; res chemist, Polymer Res Lab, Dow Chem Co, 55-61, Eastern Res Lab, 61-63; asst dir, Fabric Res Labs, Inc, 63-66. Concurrent Pos: Vis prof, Univ Mainz, Ger, 72-73; Royal Inst Technol, Stockholm, Sweden, 75, Univ Freiburg, Ger, 79-80, Japan Soc Prom Sci, 79, Univ Pisa, Italy, 87, Univ Montpelier, France, 94 & Univ Paris, 95; ed-in-chief, Macromolecules, 95- Mem: Am Chem Soc; Bio/Environ Degradable Polymer Soc; Am Inst Chem Eng. Res: Monomer and polymer synthesis; kinetics and mechanism of polymerization; structure-property relations of polymers; reactions of polymers; bacterial polyesters; biodegradation of polymers. Mailing Add: Polymer Sci & Eng Dept Univ Mass Amherst MA 01003. Fax: 413-545-2595; E-Mail: rwlenz@polysci.umass.edu

LEO, ALBERT JOSEPH, MEDICAL CHEMISTRY. Current Pos: Res assoc med chem, 68-71, DIR, MED CHEM PROJ, POMONA COL, 71-, ADJ ASST PROF, 81- Personal Data: b Winfield, Ill, Sept 29, 25; m 47; c 3. Educ: Pomona Col, BA, 48; Univ Chicago, MS, 49, PhD(chem), 52. Mem: Sigma Xi; Am Chem Soc. Res: Database of parameters useful in drug design, toxicological and environmental fate studies. Mailing Add: 311 Armsley Sq Ontario CA 91762-1606

LEO, GERHARD WILLIAM, GEOCHEMISTRY, MINERALOGY-PETROLOGY. Current Pos: RETIRED. Personal Data: b Frankfurt, WGer, Jan 31, 30; US citizen; m 68; c 2. Educ: Stanford Univ, BS, 51, PhD(geol), 61. Prof Exp: Actg mineral, Stanford Univ, 56; geologist, US geol surv, Menlo Park Calif, 57-59; vis lectr, Univ Bahia, Salvador, 59-61; res geologist, US Geol Surv, Washington, DC, 61-92. Mem: Fel Geol Soc Am; Am Geophys Union; Am Soc Testing & Mat. Res: Investigations of early paleozoic; metamorphosed plutonic and volcanic rocks in the northern Appalachians. Mailing Add: 1417 Crowell Rd Vienna VA 22182

LEOF, EDWARD B, CELL BIOLOGY. Current Pos: fel, 83-85, ASSOC PROF MOLECULAR BIOL, MAYO CLIN, 92- Personal Data: b Pittsburgh, Pa, May 9, 54. Educ: Purdue Univ, BS, 76; Univ NC, PhD(cell biol), 82. Prof Exp: From asst prof to assoc prof molecular biol, Vanderbilt Univ, 85-92. Mem: Am Soc Cell Biol; Am Asn Cancer Res; AAAS; Sigma Xi. Res: Cell biology. Mailing Add: Mayo Clin & Found Guggenheim 6 Rochester MN 55905

LEON, ARTHUR SOL, MEDICAL RESEARCH, NUTRITION. Current Pos: assoc prof, 73-80, dir appl physiol, Nutrit Sect, 73-91, PROF, LAB PHYSIOL HYG, DIV EPIDEMIOL, SCH PUB HEALTH, UNIV MINN, MINNEAPOLIS, 80-, HENRY L TAYLOR PROF & DIR, LAB PHYSIOL HYG & EXERCISE SCI, DIV KINESIOLOGY, COL EDUC. Personal Data: b Brooklyn, NY, Apr 26, 31; m 56, Gloria Rakita; c Denise, Harmon & Michelle. Educ: Univ Fla, BS, 52; Univ Wis-Madison, MS, 54, MD, 57. Honors & Awards: William G Anderson Award, Am Alliance & Health Phys Educ, 81; Citation Award, Am Col Sports Med, 95. Prof Exp: Intern, Henry Ford Hosp, Detroit, 57-58; fel internal med, Lahey Clin, Boston, 58-60; fel cardiol, Sch Med, Univ Miami & Jackson Mem Hosp, 60-61; chief gen med & cardiol, 34th Gen Hosp, US Army, France, 61-64, cardiol consult, US Armed Forces, France, 61-64, res cardiologist, Dept Cardiorespiratory Dis, Walter Reed Army Inst Res, 64-67; mem med eval team, Gemini & Apollo Projs, 66-67; dir clin pharmacol, Roche Spec Treatment Unit, Newark Beth Israel Med Ctr, 67-73. Concurrent Pos: Res assoc, Dept Clin Pharmacol, Hoffmann-La Roche Inc, 67-73; from instr to assoc prof, Col Med & Dent NJ, 67-73; chief med serv, 322nd Gen Hosp, USAR, Newark, 67-73; sr investr mult coronary risk factor intervention & lipid res clin trials, Univ Minn, Minneapolis, 73-; chief med cardiol & prof serv, 551st Army Hosp, Ft Snelling, Minn, 73-86; pres, Hennepin Div, Am Heart Asn, 83-84. Mem: Am Col Cardiol; Am Col Chest Physicians; Am Physiol Asn; Am Soc Preventive & Exp Therapeut; Am Col Sports Med (vpres, 77-79); Am Asn Cardiac & Pulmonary Rehab; Am Heart Asn. Res: Prevention of coronary heart disease by risk factor modification; metabolic and cardiovascular effects of exercise; exercise testing; effects of exercise conditioning; evaluation of new cardiovascular and lipid-lowering drugs. Mailing Add: Div Kinesiology 202 Cooke Hall Univ Minn 1900 Univ Ave SE Minneapolis MN 55455. Fax: 612-626-7701; E-Mail: arthurs.leon-1@tc.umn.edu

LEON, B(ENJAMIN) J(OSEPH), ELECTRICAL ENGINEERING, TELECOMMUNICATIONS. Current Pos: PROF ELEC & COMPUT ENG, UNIV SOUTHWESTERN LA, 90- Personal Data: b Austin, Tex, Mar 20, 32; m 54, Maxine Murphy; c Nathaniel J, Victoria (Morris), Jennifer A & Theresa A. Educ: Univ Tex, BS, 54; Mass Inst Technol, SM, 57, ScD, 59. Honors & Awards: Centennial Medal, Inst Elec & Electronics Engrs. Prof Exp: Mem staff, Lincoln Lab, Mass Inst Technol, 54-59; tech staff, Hughes Aircraft Co, 59-62; from assoc prof to prof elec eng, Purdue Univ, W Lafayette, 62-80; chmn dept, Univ Ky, Lexington, 80-84, prof elec eng, 80-88; sr staff officer, Nat Res Coun, 88-90. Concurrent Pos: Ed, Trans Circuit Theory, Inst Elec & Electronics Engrs, 67-69; consult ed, Holt, Rinehart & Winston Series Elec Eng, Electronics & Systs, 67-73; Rome Air Develop Ctr fel & vis prof, Cornell Univ, 68-69; elec engr, Defense Commun Agency, 75-76; Consult, Westinghouse Telecommun, 80; vis prof, Southern Methodist Univ, 86-87. Mem: Nat Soc Prof Engrs; fel AAAS; fel Inst Elec & Electronics Engrs (vpres, Educ Div, 79-80). Res: Communications systems; circuit and system theory; telecommunications management and policy. Mailing Add: 200 Cherry St Lafayette LA 70506-3626. Fax: 318-231-6687; E-Mail: bleon@usl.edu

LEON, HENRY A, ENVIRONMENTAL PHYSIOLOGY, AEROSPACE BIOLOGY. Current Pos: res scientist aerospace biol, 62-81, PAYLOAD PROJ SCIENTIST, AMES RES CTR, NASA, 81- Personal Data: b San Francisco, Calif, Sept 25, 28; m 58; c 3. Educ: Univ Calif, Berkeley, BS, 52, PhD(physiol), 60. Prof Exp: Nat Cancer Inst fel, Wenner-Gren Inst,

Stockholm, Sweden, 60-61; Milton res fel path, Harvard Med Sch, 61-62. *Concurrent Pos:* Mem staff, Mass Gen Hosp, Boston, 61-62. *Mem:* Am Physiol Soc; Aerospace Med Asn. *Res:* Effect of space cabin environments on blood elements; stress and the control of liver protein synthesis; nutrition and stress. *Mailing Add:* 2371 Richland Ave San Jose CA 95125-3644

LEON, KENNETH ALLEN, FISH BIOLOGY. *Current Pos:* RETIRED. *Personal Data:* b New York, NY, Nov 19, 37; m 63; c Susan & David. *Educ:* Ohio State Univ, BS, 60; Col William & Mary, MS, 63; Univ Wash, PhD(fisheries mgt), 70. *Prof Exp:* Biol consult, Ichthyol Assocs, 70-71; res biologist, Tunison Lab Fish Nutrit, US Bur Sport Fisheries & Wildlife, 71-74; prin biologist, Fish Rehab, Enhancement & Develop Div, Alaska Dept Fish & Game, Juneau, 75-88, regional biologist, Fisheries Rehab Enhancement Div, Douglas, 88-92. *Mem:* Am Fisheries Soc. *Res:* Enhancement and rehabilitation of salmonid species, specialty salmon incubation and hatchery design. *Mailing Add:* 5251 Myakka Valley Trail Sarasota FL 34241. *E-Mail:* ihunter@prodigy.com

LEON, MELVIN, EXOTIC ATOMS, MUON SPIN ROTATION. *Current Pos:* AT LOS ALAMOS NAT LAB. *Personal Data:* b Brooklyn, NY, Sept 2, 36; m 63, Allison Kinsman; c Jennifer & David. *Educ:* Univ Md, BS, 57; Cornell Univ, PhD(physics), 61. *Prof Exp:* Imp Chem Industs res fel & NSF fel theoret physics, Univ Birmingham, 61-63; res physicist, Carnegie Inst Technol, 63-66; asst prof physics, Rensselaer Polytech Inst, 66-72; mem staff, Los Alamos Nat Lab, 72-93. *Mem:* Fel Am Phys Soc. *Res:* Exotic atoms; muon spin rotation; muon-catalyzed fusion. *Mailing Add:* 283 El Conejo Los Alamos NM 87544. *Fax:* 505-665-7920; *E-Mail:* leon@lampf.lanl.gov

LEON, MICHAEL ALLAN, EARLY LEARNING, NEUROBIOLOGY. *Current Pos:* assoc prof, 80-84, PROF PSYCHOBIOL, UNIV CALIF, IRVINE, 84- *Personal Data:* b New York, NY, Nov 23, 47; m 70; c 2. *Educ:* Brooklyn Col, BS, 68; Univ Chicago, PhD(biopsychol), 72. *Prof Exp:* From asst prof to assoc prof psychol, McMaster Univ, 72-80. *Concurrent Pos:* Assoc ed, Develop Psychobiol, 85- *Mem:* Soc Neurosci; Int Soc Develop Psychobiol; Asn Chemoreception Sci. *Res:* Neurobiology of early learning. *Mailing Add:* Dept Psychobiol Univ Calif Irvine Irvine CA 92717-0001

LEON, MYRON A, IMMUNOLOGY. *Current Pos:* PROF IMMUNOL, SCH MED, WAYNE STATE UNIV, 74- *Personal Data:* b Troy, NY, July 13, 26. *Educ:* Columbia Univ, BS, 50, PhD(biochem), 54. *Prof Exp:* Assoc surg res, St Luke's Hosp, 53-64, assoc head path res, 64-74. *Concurrent Pos:* Fel, Univ Lund, Sweden, 58. *Mem:* Am Asn Immunol; AAAS; Am Soc Microbiol. *Res:* Immunochemistry; mechanisms of natural resistance to infection; complement; myeloma proteins; lymphocyte stimulation. *Mailing Add:* Dept Immunol Wayne State Univ Sch Med 7374 Scott Hall 540 E Canfield Detroit MI 48201-1998

LEON, RAMON V, RELIABILITY THEORY, STOCHASTIC INEQUALITIES. *Current Pos:* ASSOC PROF, UNIV TENN, 81- *Personal Data:* b Holguin, Oriente, Cuba, Sept 29, 48; div. *Educ:* Fla State Univ, BS, 72, MS, 76, PhD(statist), 79; Tulane Univ, MS, 75. *Honors & Awards:* Ralph A Bradley Award, Fla State Univ, 79. *Prof Exp:* Vis instr statist, Fla State Univ, 78-79; asst prof statist, Rutgers Univ, 79-81. *Mem:* Inst Math Statist; Am Statist Asn; Am Soc Quality Control. *Res:* Reliability; robust design; statistical process control. *Mailing Add:* 205 Whittington Dr Knoxville TN 37923-5558

LEON, ROBERT LEONARD, MEDICINE, PSYCHIATRY. *Current Pos:* prof psychiat & chmn dept, 67-96, ASHBEL SMITH PROF, UNIV TEX HEALTH SCI CTR SAN ANTONIO, 90- *Personal Data:* b Denver, Colo, Jan 18, 25; m 47, Willena Lee; c Alexis Kay (Sigurani), Mark Robert, Jeffrey Clayton & Stacey Lee. *Educ:* Univ Colo, MD, 48. *Prof Exp:* Intern, Univ Hosp, Ann Arbor, Mich, 48-49; resident psychiat, Med Ctr, Univ Colo, 49-52; resident child psychiat, State Dept Health, Conn, 52-53; asst dir & act dir child psychiat, Greater Kansas City Ment Health Found, 53-54; from asst prof to prof psychiat, Southwest Med Sch, Univ Tex, 57-67. *Concurrent Pos:* Chief ment health serv, USPHS, Mo, 54-57; consult, Bur Indian Affairs, 62-67; consult regional off VI, NIMH, 57-73, mem psychiat training rev comt, 70-74; consult, Audie Murphy Mem Vet Hosp, 73- *Mem:* Fel Am Psychiat Asn; fel Am Col Psychiatrists (pres, 87-88); fel Am Orthopsychiat Asn; fel Am Acad Child Psychiat; AMA; fel Am Asn Soc Psychiatrists (pres 90-92). *Res:* Social psychiatry; transcultural psychiatry. *Mailing Add:* Dept Psychiat Univ Tex Health Sci Ctr 7703 Floyd Curl Dr San Antonio TX 78284-7792. *Fax:* 210-567-6941; *E-Mail:* leon@uthscsa.edu

LEON, SHALOM A, BIOCHEMISTRY, RADIOBIOLOGY. *Current Pos:* MEM BIOSCI STAFF, 68-, DIR, RADIATION RES LAB, ALBERT EINSTEIN MED CTR, 79-; ASSOC PROF RADIOBIOL, SCH MED, TEMPLE UNIV, 79- *Personal Data:* b Sofia, Bulgaria, Apr 7, 35; m 62; c 3. *Educ:* Hebrew Univ, Jerusalem, MSc, 60, PhD(pharmacol), 64. *Prof Exp:* Jr res asst pharmacol, Med Sch, Hebrew Univ, Jerusalem, 60-64; res assoc biochem, Ind Univ, 65-67. *Mem:* Am Asn Cancer Res; AAAS; Radiation Res Soc; Am Chem Soc; NY Acad Sci; Am Asn Immunol. *Res:* Mechanism of antibiotic action; biosynthesis of nucleic acids and proteins; use of radioactive isotopes in clinical research and diagnosis; relationship between structure and biological activity of toxins from microorganisms; effect of radioprotective agents against ionizing radiation. *Mailing Add:* Radiation Res Lab Albert Einstein Med Ctr York & Tabor Rd Philadelphia PA 19141-3098

LEONARD, A(NTHONY), ENGINEERING. *Current Pos:* PROF AERONAUT ENG, CALIF INST TECHNOL, 85- *Personal Data:* b June 2, 38; US citizen; m 60; c 2. *Educ:* Calif Inst Technol, BS, 59; Stanford Univ, MS, 60, PhD(nuclear eng), 63. *Honors & Awards:* Edward Teller Award, 63. *Prof Exp:* Mem tech staff, Rand Corp, 63-66; from asst prof to assoc prof mech eng, Stanford Univ, 66-73; res scientist, NASA Ames Res Ctr, 75-85. *Concurrent Pos:* Lectr, Calif Inst Technol, 65-66; consult, Gen Elec Co; NASA Ames Res Ctr sr fel, 73-75. *Mem:* Am Phys Soc; Soc Indust & Appl Math. *Res:* Nuclear reactor theory; particle transport theory; turbulence theory; numerical fluid mechanics. *Mailing Add:* 301-46 Grad Aeronaut Labs Calif Inst Technol Pasadena CA 91125

LEONARD, ARNOLD S, SURGERY. *Current Pos:* Univ fel, 56-63, from asst prof to assoc prof, 63-73, PROF SURG, UNIV MINN, MINNEAPOLIS, 73- *Personal Data:* b Minneapolis, Minn, Oct 26, 30; m 50; c 4. *Educ:* Univ Minn, Minneapolis, BA, 52, BS, 53, MD, 55, PhD(surg path), 63. *Mem:* Am Soc Artificial Internal Organs; Am Soc Exp Path; Int Soc Hist Med; Soc Univ Surg; Am Pediat Surg Asn; Sigma Xi. *Res:* Gastrointestinal physiology; hypothalamic stimulation and study of gastric secretion; transplantation; extracorporeal organ perfusion; pediatric surgery; computer technology. *Mailing Add:* Dept Surg Univ Minn Hosp 420 Delaware St SE PO Box 82 Mayo Minneapolis MN 55455-0082

LEONARD, B(ENJAMIN) F(RANKLIN), (III), MINERALOGY & PETROLOGY. *Current Pos:* from jr geologist to geologist, 43-93, geologist-in-charge, 62-93, EMER GEOLOGIST, ORE MICROS LAB, US GEOL SURV, 93- *Personal Data:* b Dobbs Ferry, NY, May 12, 21; m 50, Eleanor Vandewater; c 2. *Educ:* Hamilton Col, BS, 42; Princeton Univ, MA, 47, PhD(geol), 51. *Honors & Awards:* Meritorious Serv Award, US Dept Interior, 88. *Prof Exp:* Geol field asst, Geol Surv Nfld, 42. *Concurrent Pos:* Vis prof, 67-68, adj prof, Colo Sch Mines, 90-; mem, Int Comn Ore Micros, 68-70, vchmn, 82-86; regional counr NAm, Int Asn Genesis Ore Deposits, 84-89. *Mem:* Fel Mineral Soc Am; fel Geol Soc Am; fel Soc Econ Geol; Soc Geol Appl Mineral Deposits; Mineral Asn Can; Asn Explor Geochemists. *Res:* Ore deposits, especially gold, iron and tungsten; geology of central Idaho and northwest Adirondacks; ore minerals; rock-forming minerals; geochemical and biogeochemical exploration. *Mailing Add:* 2907 Sunset Dr Golden CO 80401-2587

LEONARD, BILLIE CHARLES, instructional behavior, instructional technology, for more information see previous edition

LEONARD, BOWEN RAYDO, JR, PHYSICS. *Current Pos:* RETIRED. *Personal Data:* b Houston, Tex, Mar 7, 26; div; c 2. *Educ:* Tex Western Col, BS, 47; Univ Wis, MS, 49, PhD(physics), 52. *Prof Exp:* Asst, Univ Wis, 47-51; physicist, Hanford Labs, Gen Elec Co, 52-53, sr scientist, 53-57, mgr exp physics res, 57-64; mgr exp physics res, Pac Northwest Lab, Battelle Mem Inst, 65-67, sr staff scientist, 67-82. *Concurrent Pos:* Mem, nuclear cross sect adv group, Atomic Energy Comn, 57-63, ad-hoc mem, 69-, mem cross sect eval working group, 66- *Mem:* Fel Am Phys Soc; Am Nuclear Soc; Sigma Xi. *Res:* Neutron cross section measurements; nuclear physics; x-ray scattering; slow neutron in-elastic scattering studies of solids and liquids. *Mailing Add:* 212 S Morain St Kennewick WA 99336

LEONARD, BRIAN PHILLIP, PLASMA PHYSICS, FLUID MECHANICS. *Current Pos:* PROF MECH ENG, UNIV AKRON, 82- *Personal Data:* b Melbourne, Australia, June 4, 36; m 64; c 2. *Educ:* Univ Melbourne, BMechE, 58; Cornell Univ, MAeroE, 61, PhD(aerospace eng), 65. *Prof Exp:* Asst aerospace eng, Cornell Univ, 61-64, asst elec eng, 64-65, vis asst prof, 65-66; sr lectr aeronaut eng, Royal Melbourne Inst Technol, 67; lectr appl math, Monash Univ, Australia, 67-68; Air Force Off Sci Res assoc plasma physics, Columbia Univ, 69-70; asst prof eng sci, Richmond Col NY, 70-76; assoc prof, City Univ New York, 76-82. *Mem:* Am Phys Soc; Am Inst Aeronaut & Astronaut; Am Nuclear Soc. *Res:* High temperature gas dynamics; shock wave structure; magnetically driven shock waves; applied mathematics; control systems; hydrodynamics and ship stability and control; thermonuclear fusion. *Mailing Add:* Dept Mech Eng Univ Akron Leigh Hall Rm 201F Akron OH 44325

LEONARD, BYRON PETER, PHYSICS. *Current Pos:* dir satellite-missile observation syst prog, 60-65, vpres & gen mgr, Man Orbiting Lab, Systs Eng Off, 65-68, VPRES & GEN MGR EL SEGUNDO TECH OPERS & GROUP VPRES, PROGS GROUP, AEROSPACE CORP, 68- *Personal Data:* b Morgan City, La, Feb 26, 25; m 46. *Educ:* Southwestern La Univ, BS, 43; Univ Tex, MA, 52, PhD, 53. *Prof Exp:* Proj engr, US Naval Ord Test Sta, 46-47; instr physics, Southwestern La Univ, 48-50 & Univ Tex, 50-53; chief nuclear res & develop, Gen Dynamics Corp, 53-59; sr staff engr, Space Technol Labs, 59-60. *Mem:* Am Nuclear Soc; Am Inst Aeronaut & Astronaut; Am Chem Soc. *Res:* Nuclear shielding; radiation effects to materials and operating components; radiation hazards of fission products released to the atmosphere; design of research reactors; design and use of satellite systems, particularly for surveillance applications. *Mailing Add:* 2600 W Farwell Ave Chicago IL 60645-4523

LEONARD, CHARLES BROWN, JR, BIOCHEMISTRY. *Current Pos:* Asst, Univ Md, Baltimore, 55-58, from instr to assoc prof, 58-76, dir off admis, 75-77, asst dean recruitment & admis, 77-85, chmn dept, 85-93, PROF BIOCHEM, DENT SCH, UNIV MD, BALTIMORE, 76-, PROF GALLAUDET UNIV WASH, 93- *Personal Data:* b Woodbury, NJ, May 28, 34; m 55; c 2. *Educ:* Rutgers Univ, AB, 55; Univ Md, MS, 57, PhD(biochem), 63. *Concurrent Pos:* Consult, Dr H L Wollenweber, clin pathologist, 59-61.

Mem: AAAS; Am Chem Soc; NY Acad Sci; Am Inst Chem; Am Asn Dent Sch; Sigma Xi. Res: Amino acid incorporation into rat liver ribosomes; effect of divalent ions on structure of rat liver RNA; effect of o,p'-DDD on cellular metabolism; metabolic products of o,p'-DDD. Mailing Add: 9202 Furrow Ave Ellicott City MD 21042

LEONARD, CHRISTIANA MORISON, NEUROANATOMY, PSYCHOLOGY. Current Pos: assoc prof, 76-86, PROF NEUROSCI, COL MED, UNIV FLA, 86- Personal Data: b Boston, Mass, Jan 22, 38; m 59, 82, John M Kuldau; c Andrew W, Amy E, Gretchen A Kuldau & J Gustav Kuldau. Educ: Radcliffe Col, BA, 59; Mass Inst Technol, PhD(psychol), 67. Prof Exp: USPHS trainee, Rockefeller Univ, 67-70, res assoc, 70-71, asst prof neuropsychol, 71-74; asst prof anat, Mt Sinai Sch Med, 74-76. Mem: AAAS; Soc Neurosci; Sigma Xi; Am Anat Asn; Animal Behav Soc. Res: Neurological basis of language and thought; development of language; learning disabilities and schizophrenia; functional imaging. Mailing Add: Dept Neurosci Box 100244 JHM Health Ctr Col Med Univ Fla Gainesville FL 32610

LEONARD, CLAIRE MARIE, DIABETES RESEARCH, DIABETIC COMPLICATIONS. Current Pos: SR SCIENTIST, ALTEON INC, 90- Personal Data: b New York City, NY, Feb 18, 55. Educ: Iona Col, BS, 77; NY Med Col, MS, 86, PhD(cell biol), 87. Prof Exp: Fel gene regulation during development, Dept Genetics, Albert Einstein Col Med, NY, 87-89; res assoc prof, NY Med Col, 89-90. Mem: AAAS; Am Soc Cell Biol. Res: Diabetes, diabetic complications. Mailing Add: Alteon Inc 170 Williams Dr Ramsey NJ 07446

LEONARD, DAVID E, ENTOMOLOGY. Current Pos: PROF, DEPT ENTOM, UNIV MASS, AMHERST, & ACTG DEAN, COL FOOD NAT RESOURCES. Personal Data: b Greenwich, Conn, Dec 28, 34; m 57; c Linda & Robyn. Educ: Univ Conn, BS, 56, MS, 60, PhD(entom), 64. Prof Exp: From asst to assoc entomologist, Conn Agr Exp Sta, 64-70; from assoc prof to prof entom, Univ Maine, Orono, 70-80; assoc dir, Maine Agr Exp Sta, 79-82 & Mass Agr Exp Sta, 82-85. Concurrent Pos: Co-ed, Annals Entom Soc Am, 78-83. Mem: Entom Soc Am; Entom Soc Can; Ecol Soc Am; AAAS. Res: Biosystematics, biology and ecology of insects; host-parasite relationships; biology of lymantriidae. Mailing Add: Dept Entom Univ Mass Amherst Fernald Hall Amherst MA 01003-0002

LEONARD, EDWARD (FRANCIS), CHEMICAL ENGINEERING. Current Pos: from asst prof to assoc prof, 58-67, CHMN BIOENG COMN, 65-68, 91-, PROF CHEM ENG, 67-, DIR ARTIFICIAL ORGANS RES LABS, COLUMBIA UNIV, 68- Personal Data: b Paterson, NJ, July 6, 32; m 55, Gerarda S van Geel; c Mary, Edward Jr, Gerald, Louise & Joseph. Educ: Mass Inst Technol, BS, 53; Univ Pa, MS, 55, PhD(chem eng), 60. Honors & Awards: Allan P Colburn Award, Am Inst Chem Engrs, 69. Prof Exp: Res engr, Barrett Div, Allied Chem Corp, 53-55; instr chem eng, Univ Pa, 55 & 57-58. Concurrent Pos: Resident eng pract, Ford Found, 64-65; consult, Mt Sinai & St Luke's Hosp, NY, & Baxter Healthcare Corp, Am Red Cross, Medigene Corp, Cytotherapeutics Inc; mem bd, Assoc Univs Inc, 71-78. Mem: Fel Am Inst Chem Engrs; Am Soc Artificial Internal Organs (pres, 72); Biomed Eng Soc; fel Am Inst Med & Biol Engrs. Res: Heat, mass, momentum transport in fluid systems; distributed parameter chemical systems; transient behavior of chemical process systems; design of transport devices in medicine, particularly for immunotherapy and cell separation. Mailing Add: 351 Engineering Terr New York NY 10027. Fax: 212-854-8362; E-Mail: leonard@columbia.edu

LEONARD, EDWARD CHARLES, JR, POLYMER CHEMISTRY. Current Pos: PRES & CHIEF EXEC OFFICER, HUME CO INC, 93- Personal Data: b Burlington, NC, Aug 21, 27; m 52; c 1. Educ: Univ NC, BS, 47, PhD(chem), 51; Univ Chicago, MBA, 74. Prof Exp: Asst, Univ NC, 47-50; sr res chemist, Res Dept, Bakelite Co, 51-56, group leader, Union Carbide Plastic Co, 56-64; res mgr, Borden Chem Co, 64-67; mgr indust chem prod lab, Res & Develop Div, Kraft, Inc, 67-73; tech dir, Humko Sheffield Chem Co Div, 73-77, vpres res & develop, Humko Sheffield Chem Co Div, 77-80, vpres res & develop, Humko Chem Div, Witco Chem Corp, 80-, gen mgr, vpres & officer, 83-93. Concurrent Pos: Vpres & mem Bd Dirs, Enenco, Inc, 74- Mem: Am Chem Soc. Res: Synthetic surface active agents; ionic polymerizations; graft polymers; fatty acids; homogeneous catalysis; chemical economics. Mailing Add: 40 Twelve Oaks Circle Memphis TN 38117

LEONARD, EDWARD H, ANALYTICAL CHEMISTRY. Current Pos: ASSOC PROF PHYSICS & NATURAL SCI, WORCESTER STATE COL, 64- Personal Data: b Berwick, Maine, Feb 21, 19; m 51; c 1. Educ: Dartmouth Col, AB, 42; Tufts Univ, MA, 54; Univ NH, MS, 61. Prof Exp: Res & develop engr, Elec Res Lab, Simplex Wire & Cable Co, 42-46; Eng Dept, 46-51; head sci dept high sch, NJ, 51-60, sci coord, 60-64. Mem: AAAS; Am Chem Soc; Am Asn Physics Teachers; Nat Sci Teachers Asn. Res: Design and development of apparatus and aids for the teaching of physical science. Mailing Add: 184 Holden St Holden MA 01520-1738

LEONARD, EDWARD JOSEPH, MEDICINE. Current Pos: investr, 69-73, head tumor antigen sect, Biol Br, 73-76, HEAD IMMUNOPATH SECT, LAB IMMUNOBIOL, NAT CANCER INST, 76- Personal Data: b Boston, Mass, Mar 20, 26; m 56; c 3. Educ: Harvard Med Sch, MD, 49. Prof Exp: Investr, Nat Heart Inst, 53-69. Concurrent Pos: From instr to assoc clin prof, George Washington Univ, 57-74. Mem: Am Fedn Clin Res; Soc Gen Physiologists; Am Asn Immunol. Res: Tumor immunology. Mailing Add: Immunopath Sect Nat Cancer Inst FCRDC Bldg 560 Rm 12-71 Frederick MD 21702

LEONARD, ELLEN MARIE, PLASMA PHYSICS, NUCLEAR ENGINEERING. Current Pos: tech staff mem. 73-93, GROUP LEADER, LOS ALAMOS NAT LAB, 93- Personal Data: b New York, NY, Nov 28, 44; m 75, John Kammerdiener; c Susan & Michael. Educ: Univ Mich, BS, 66, MS, 68, PhD(plasma physics), 73. Mem: Am Phys Soc; Am Nuclear Soc; AAAS; Inst Elec & Electronics Engrs. Res: Nuclear nonproliferation; technology security. Mailing Add: 102 Monte Rey Dr N Los Alamos NM 87544. Fax: 505-665-3456; E-Mail: eleonard@lanl.gov

LEONARD, HENRY SIGGINS, JR, MATHEMATICS. Current Pos: asst chmn, Dept Math Sci, 75-78, PROF MATH, NORTHERN ILL UNIV, 68-, DIR GRAD STUDIES, 93- Personal Data: b Needham, Mass, Oct 12, 30; m 54; c 1. Educ: Mich State Univ, BS, 52; Harvard Univ, AM, 53, PhD(math), 58. Prof Exp: From asst prof to assoc prof math, Carnegie Inst Technol, 58-68. Concurrent Pos: Prin investr, NSF grants, 59-70; vis assoc prof, Univ Ill, Urbana, 67-68; vis fel, Yale Univ, 73-74; vis scholar, Univ Chicago, 80-81; vis, Univ Manchester, Eng, 87-88. Mem: Am Math Soc; Math Asn Am. Res: Theory of groups of finite order. Mailing Add: Dept Math Northern Ill Univ DeKalb IL 60115-2888

LEONARD, JACK E, CHEMISTRY. Current Pos: PRES, ENVIRON MGT INST, 90- Personal Data: b Chickasha, Okla, Feb 6, 43; m 65; c 3. Educ: Harvard Univ, AB, 65; Southern Methodist Univ, BD, 67; Calif Inst Technol, PhD(chem & biol), 71. Prof Exp: Asst prof chem, State Univ NY, 61-75 & Tex A&M Univ, 75-81, assoc res scientist, 82-83; sr environ scientist, Indianapolis Ctr Advan Res, Inc, 85-90. Concurrent Pos: Sr res chemist, Allied Corp, 80; vis assoc prof chem, Univ Tex, El Paso, 81-82; fac mem, Blinn Col, 83-85. Mem: Am Chem Soc; AAAS. Res: Physical organic chemistry from mechanisms of photochemical and electrochemical reactions to laser synthesis of catalysts to mathematical group and graph theory; environmental chemical policy. Mailing Add: Environ Mgt Inst 5610 Crawfordsville Rd Suite 15 Indianapolis IN 46224. Fax: 317-248-4846

LEONARD, JACQUES WALTER, POLYMER CHEMISTRY, PHYSICAL CHEMISTRY. Current Pos: from asst prof to assoc prof chem, Laval Univ, 66-75, dept dir, 78-81, vdean res, Fac Sci & Eng, 87-89, Dept Dir, 91-94, PROF CHEM, LAVAL UNIV, 75- Personal Data: b Montreal, Que, Aug 7, 36; m 63, Marthe-Andree Roberge; c Anne & Simon. Educ: Univ Montreal, BSc, 60, MSc, 61, PhD(chem), 64. Prof Exp: Can Nat Res Coun fel, Univ Leeds, 64-66. Concurrent Pos: Vis prof, Univ Sussex, Eng, 77-78; vis fel, Inst Charles Sadron, Nat Sci Res, Strasbourg, France, 90, Univ De Bordeaux, France, 91. Mem: Fel Chem Inst Can; Am Chem Soc. Res: Kinetics and thermodynamics of polymerizations in solution; effect of the medium on the equilibrium of reversible cyclizations, homo- and copolymerizations; thermodynamics of polymer solutions and binary liquid mixtures. Mailing Add: Dept Chem Laval Univ Quebec PQ G1K 7P4 Can. Fax: 418-656-7916; E-Mail: jacques.leonard@chm.ulaval.ca

LEONARD, JAMES JOSEPH, INTERNAL MEDICINE, CARDIOLOGY. Current Pos: PROF MED & CHMN DEPT, UNIV HEALTH SCI, 77- Personal Data: b Schenectady, NY, June 17, 24; m 54, Helen Mitchel; c James J, W Jeffrey, Paul M & Kathleen M. Educ: Georgetown Univ, MD, 50. Prof Exp: From intern to jr asst resident med, Georgetown Univ Hosp, 50-52; asst resident med serv, Boston City Hosp, Mass, 52-53; resident, Pulmonary Dis Div, DC Gen Hosp, 54-55; instr, Sch Med, Georgetown Univ, 55-56; instr, Med Sch, Duke Univ, 56-57; asst prof & dir, Div Cardiol, Georgetown Univ Serv, DC Gen Hosp, 57-59; from asst prof to assoc prof med, Univ Tex Med Br, 59-62; dir cardiopulmonary lab, 61-62; assoc prof med & dir cardiac diag lab, Ohio State Univ, 62-63; assoc prof med & dir cardiol, Sch Med, Univ Pittsburgh, 63-67, actg chmn dept med, 70-71, prof med, 67-77, chmn dept, 71-77. Concurrent Pos: Washington Heart Asn fel cardiol, Georgetown Univ Hosp, 53-54; Am Trudeau Soc fel, Pulmonary Dis Div, DC Gen Hosp, 54-55; NIH cardiac trainee, Duke Univ Hosp, 56-57; med officer, DC Gen Hosp, 55-56, chief cent heart sta, 57-59; attend cardiol, Mt Alto's Vet Hosp, DC, 57-59. Mem: Asn Am Physicians; Asn Prof Med; Asn Univ Cardiologists; Sigma Xi; Am Col Physicians; Am Clin & Climat Asn; master Am Col Physicians. Res: Cardiopulmonary physiology. Mailing Add: Dept Med Uniformed Serv Univ 4301 Jones Bridge Rd Bethesda MD 20814

LEONARD, JANET LOUISE, neuroethology, invertebrate zoology, for more information see previous edition

LEONARD, JOHN ALEX, INDUSTRIAL CHEMISTRY. Current Pos: res adv, C-I-L, Inc, 74-77, technol & agreement mgr, 77-84, Ventures Mgr, 84-88, CHEM BUS MGR, ICI CAN, 88- Personal Data: b Swindon, Eng, Dec 13, 37; m 61; c 2. Educ: Univ London, BSc, 59, PhD(chem), 62. Prof Exp: Res chemist polymers, Shell Develop Co, Calif, 63-66; from sr scientist catalysis to bus planning, Imperial Chem Indust, UK & USA, 66-74. Concurrent Pos: Fel, Harvard Univ, 62-63. Mem: Am Chem Soc; Chem Soc Can; Royal Soc Chem. Res: Catalytic, electrochemical and biological processes and research management. Mailing Add: ICI Can 90 Shepppard Ave E PO Box 200 North York ON M2N 6H2 Can

LEONARD, JOHN EDWARD, ORGANIC CHEMISTRY, PHYSICAL CHEMISTRY. Current Pos: RETIRED. Personal Data: b Great Falls, Mont, Apr 18, 18; div; c 2. Educ: Antioch Col, BS, 42; Ohio State Univ, PhD(chem), 49. Prof Exp: Res engr, Battelle Mem Inst, 42-46; res fel, Calif Inst Technol, 49-52; res scientist, Beckman Instruments Inc, 52-56, chief proj engr, 56-62, sr scientist, 62-66, mgr appl res, Med Chemical Activ, 66-69; chief scientist, Int Biophys Corp, 69-71; consult electrochem sensors & instrumentation, 71-78; res dir, Broadley-James Corp, Santa Ana, 78-86. Mem: Am Chem Soc;

AAAS; NY Acad Sci. *Res:* Analytical instruments, particularly electrochemical, for chemical research and industrial use; biomedical engineering; medical instrumentation research. *Mailing Add:* PO Box 278 Freeland WA 98249

LEONARD, JOHN JOSEPH, PHYSICAL ORGANIC CHEMISTRY. *Current Pos:* sr res chemist, Arco Chem Co, 73-78, supvr catalyst res, 78-79, mgr catalyst res, 79-85, mgr res & develop, 85-89, MGR CORP PLANNING, ARCO CHEM CO, DIV ATLANTIC RICHFIELD CO, 89- *Personal Data:* b Philadelphia, Pa, Feb 12, 49; m 72; c 2. *Educ:* Drexel Univ, BS, 72, PhD(phys org chem), 72. *Prof Exp:* Res assoc chem, Univ Pa, 72-73. *Concurrent Pos:* Adj prof math, Drexel Univ Evening Div, 73-80. *Mem:* Am Chem Soc; Int Catalysis Soc; AAAS. *Res:* Kinetics and mechanisms of organic reactions especially catalysis of organic oxidation reactions(heterogeneous and homogeneous catalysis); spectroscopy of organic molecules. *Mailing Add:* 37 S Hillcrest Springfield PA 19064-2413

LEONARD, JOHN LANDER, MATHEMATICS. *Current Pos:* asst prof math, 66-76, LECTR MATH, UNIV ARIZ, 76- *Personal Data:* b Jamaica, NY, Oct 20, 35; m 65, Cecilia Luschak; c Allegra. *Educ:* Carnegie Inst Technol, BS, 57; Univ Calif, Santa Barbara, MA, 63, PhD(math), 66. *Honors & Awards:* Fulbright Lectr, Peru, 73, Intercountry Fulbright Lectr, Columbia, 73. *Prof Exp:* Opers analyst, Comput Dept, Gen Elec Co, 59-60, mem tech staff, Tech Mil Planning Oper, 60-61; asst math, Univ Calif, Santa Barbara, 61-63, 64-66. *Mem:* Math Asn Am; Sigma Xi. *Res:* Graph theory, extremal problems, connectivity; real function theory; mathematical analysis. *Mailing Add:* Dept Math Bldg 89 Univ Ariz Tucson AZ 85721. *Fax:* 520-621-8322; *E-Mail:* jleonard@math.arizona.edu

LEONARD, JOHN W, SCIENCE ADMINISTRATION. *Current Pos:* RETIRED. *Personal Data:* b Washington, DC, Jan 19, 25. *Educ:* Mass Inst Technol, BS. *Honors & Awards:* Beavers Award, 85. *Prof Exp:* Engr, Morrison Knudsen Co Inc, 47-50, proj engr, 58-61, chief engr, 68-75, vpres eng, 75-84, sr vpres eng, 85-87, sr exec, 87-91; owner, H&W Construct Co Pac NW, 50-53. *Concurrent Pos:* Visual aide, Sch Eng, Gonzaga Univ; mem, US Comt Large Dams, 75-88; arbitor, Am Arbitration Asn, 80-93; indust mem, US Nat Comt Tunneling Technol, 82-85. *Mem:* Nat Acad Eng; fel Am Soc Civil Engrs; Sigma Xi; Soc Am Mil Engrs. *Mailing Add:* 1012 Wyndemere Dr Boise ID 83702-1367

LEONARD, JOSEPH THOMAS, FUEL SCIENCE. *Current Pos:* RES CHEMIST FUELS, NAVAL RES LAB, WASHINGTON, DC, 59- *Personal Data:* b Scranton, Pa, Aug 8, 32; m 58; c 4. *Educ:* Univ Scranton, BS, 54; Pa State Univ, University Park, PhD(fuel technol), 59. *Prof Exp:* Res asst chem, Pa State Univ, University Park, 54-59. *Mem:* Am Chem Soc. *Res:* Electrostatic charging of hydrocarbon liquids and fuels; suppression of evaporation of hydrocarbons and smoke abatement techniques. *Mailing Add:* 6424 Rotunda Ct Springfield VA 22150-1342

LEONARD, JOSEPH WILLIAM, MINERAL PROCESSING ENGINEERING. *Current Pos:* chmn, 82-86, prof, 82-92, DISTINGUISHED MINING ENG FOUND PROF, UNIV KY, 92- *Personal Data:* b Pottsville, Pa, Dec 24, 30; m 52, Josephine Sunday; c 4. *Educ:* Pa State Univ, BS, 52, MS, 58. *Honors & Awards:* Howard N Eavenson Award, Am Inst Mining Engrs, 69, Erisline Ramsay Medal, 89. *Prof Exp:* Asst to div supt coal mining, Philadelphia & Reading Coal & Iron, Pottsville, Pa, 52-54; asst pre engr, United Elec Coal Co, Chicago, Ill, 54-56; res asst coal prep, Pa State Univ, 56-58; res engr coal mining, US Steel Corp, Monroeville, Pa, 58-61; dir bur, WVa Univ, 61-81, prof mining, 74-81, dean, 78-81, William N Poundstone res prof, 81-82. *Concurrent Pos:* Consult, numerous countries, 62-, Pa Elec Co, Johnstown, 71- Cortix, Bochum, WGer, 78-82. *Mem:* Fel Am Inst Chemists; distinguished mem Am Inst Mining Engrs; Am Mining Cong; Sigma Xi; distinguished mem Soc Mining Engrs. *Res:* Mining; coal reserve analysis; coal preparation including design; coal utilization. *Mailing Add:* Dept Mining Eng Univ Ky Lexington KY 40506-0107

LEONARD, KATHLEEN MARY, GROUND WATER STUDIES, FATE OF CONTAMINANTS. *Current Pos:* ASST PROF CIVIL ENG, UNIV ALA, HUNTSVILLE, 91- *Personal Data:* b Grand Rapids, Mich, Aug 14, 54. *Educ:* Univ Wis-Milwaukee, BS, 83, MS, 85; Univ Ala, Huntsville, PhD(environ eng), 90. *Honors & Awards:* Engr of the Yr, Soc Am Mil Engrs, 96. *Prof Exp:* Vpres, Optechnol, Inc, 89- *Mem:* Am Soc Civil Engrs; Soc Women Engrs; Water Environ Fedn; Soc Am Mil Engrs; Int Asn Water Qual. *Res:* Using optical fibers for remote chemical sensing of environmental systems, specializing in ground water and hazardous waste applications. *Mailing Add:* Dept Civil & Environ Eng Univ Ala Huntsville AL 35899. *Fax:* 205-890-6724

LEONARD, KURT JOHN, PLANT DISEASE EPIDEMIOLOGY, PLANT HOST-PARASITE GENETICS. *Current Pos:* DIR, CEREAL RUST LAB, AGR RES SERV-USDA, UNIV MINN, 88- *Personal Data:* b Holstein, Iowa, Dec 6, 39; m 61, Maren Simonsen; c Maria C, Mary A & Benjamin A. *Educ:* Iowa State Univ, BS, 62; Cornell Univ, PhD(plant path), 68. *Prof Exp:* Res plant scientist, Agr Res Serv-USDA, NC State Univ, 68-88. *Concurrent Pos:* Mem coun, Am Pythopathol Soc, 82-85; ed, Phytopath, 82-85, APS Pr, 94-97; counr, Int Soc Plant Path, 83- *Mem:* Fel Am Phytopath Soc; Int Soc Plant Path; Mycol Soc Am. *Res:* Epidemiology and genetics of cereal rust diseases; population genetics of host-parasite interactions in plant diseases. *Mailing Add:* 693 Birch Lane N St Paul MN 55126-1207

LEONARD, LAURENCE, PHYSICAL METALLURGY, MATERIALS SCIENCE. *Current Pos:* PRIN SCIENTIST, FRANKLIN RES CTR, 71- *Personal Data:* b New York, NY, Jan 9, 32; m 58; c 4. *Educ:* Mass Inst Technol, SB, 54, SM, 56, ScD(metall), 62. *Prof Exp:* Asst prof metall, Case Western Res Univ, 62-69; group supvr, SKF Industs, Inc, 69-71. *Concurrent Pos:* Adj assoc prof, Drexel Univ, 78-; adj assoc prof, Great Valley Grad Ctr, Pa State Univ, 90- *Mem:* Am Soc Metals. *Res:* Materials failure analysis; physical metallurgy of rolling contact bearings; scanning electron microscopy; metal embrittlement; x-ray diffraction; residual stresses; phase transformations; heat treatment; nondestructive testing; wear monitoring by oil analysis. *Mailing Add:* 505 Princeton Dr King of Prussia PA 19406

LEONARD, MARTHA FRANCES, PEDIATRICS, CHILD DEVELOPMENT. *Current Pos:* fel, Child Study Ctr, 60-62, from instr to prof, 79-86, SR RES SCIENTIST & EMER PROF PEDIAT, YALE UNIV, 86- *Personal Data:* b New Brunswick, NJ, May 10, 16. *Educ:* NJ Col Women, BSc, 36; Johns Hopkins Univ, MD, 40. *Hon Degrees:* MS, Yale Univ, 79. *Honors & Awards:* Winslow Award, 88. *Prof Exp:* Intern, Baltimore City Hosp, 40-41; asst resident med, Vanderbilt Univ Hosp, 42-43; asst resident pediat, NY Hosp, 43-46; pvt pract, 46-60. *Concurrent Pos:* Consult, Area Coop Educ Serv, Village St Sch, North Haven. *Mem:* Am Acad Pediat; Ambulatory Pediat Asn; Am Pub Health Asn. *Res:* Normal and deviant child development; effects of deprivation; failure to thrive; child abuse; developmental impact of conditions such as genetic, metabolic and endocrine disorders. *Mailing Add:* Child Study Ctr Yale Univ New Haven CT 06510. *Fax:* 203-488-9429; *E-Mail:* ewmfl@aol.com

LEONARD, MICHAEL STEVEN, HEALTH CARE SYSTEMS DESIGN, QUALITY ENGINEERING. *Current Pos:* head, 90-95, PROF INDUST ENG, CLEMSON UNIV, 90- *Personal Data:* m 69, Mary E Stewart; c Dorothy E, Amanda B & Gabrielle F. *Educ:* Univ Fla, BE, 70, ME, 72, PhD(syst eng), 73. *Prof Exp:* Asst prof, Health Syst Res Ctr, Ga Inst Technol, 73-75; from asst prof to assoc prof indust eng, Univ Mo, 75-82, prof, 82-90, chmn, 85-90. *Concurrent Pos:* Eval visitor, Accreditation Bd Eng & Technol, 88-94; mem, Eng Accreditation Comn, Accreditation Bd Eng & Technol, 94- *Mem:* Fel Inst Indust Engrs; Soc Health Syst; Inst Opers Res & Mat Sci. *Res:* Health care and information systems design; inventory control; production scheduling; facility location; quality engineering. *Mailing Add:* 204 Freeman Hall Clemson SC 29634. *Fax:* 864-656-0795; *E-Mail:* mike.leonard@eng.clemson.edu

LEONARD, NELSON JORDAN, ORGANIC BIOCHEMISTRY. *Current Pos:* fel & res asst chem, Univ Ill, Urbana, 42-43, instr, 43-44, assoc, 44-47, from asst prof to prof chem, 47-86, head, Div Org Chem, 54-63, prof chem & biochem, 73-86, Reynold C Fuson prof chem & mem, Ctr Advan Study, 81-86, REYNOLD C FUSON EMER PROF, UNIV ILL, 86-; FAC ASSOC, CALIF INST TECHNOL, 92- *Personal Data:* b Newark, NJ, Sept 1, 16; m 92, Peggy Phelps; c Kenneth Jan, Marcia Louise, James Nelson & David Anthony. *Educ:* Lehigh Univ, BS, 37; Univ Oxford, BSc, 40, DSc, 83; Columbia Univ, PhD(org chem), 42. *Hon Degrees:* ScD, Lehigh Univ, 63; Dr, Adam Mickiewicz Univ, 80; DSc, Univ Ill, 88. *Honors & Awards:* Synthesis Award, Am Chem Soc, 63, Edgar Fahs Smith Award, 75, Roger Adams Award, 81; Medal Creative Res Synthetic Org Chem, Synthetic Org Chem Mfrs Asn, 70; George W Wheland Award, Univ Chicago; Paul G Gassman Distinguished Service Award, Am Chem Soc, 94. *Prof Exp:* Sci consult & spec investr, Field Intel Agency Tech, US Army & US Com, Europ Theatre, 44-46. *Concurrent Pos:* Mem, Comt Med Res, 44-46; ed, Org Syntheses, 51-58, ed-in-chief, 56, pres, Bd Dirs, 80-88; Am-Swiss Found lectr, 53, 70; Guggenheim Mem Found fel, 59, 67; mem prog comt basic phys sci, Alfred P Sloan Found, 61-66; Stieglitz lectr, 62; mem educ adv bd & bd of selection, John Simon Guggenheim Mem Found, 69-88; Edgar Fahs Smith Mem lectr, Univ Pa, 75; Arapahoe lectr, Univ Colo, 79; Calbiochem-Beohring lectr, Univ Calif, San Diego, 81; Fogarty scholar-in-residence, NIH, Bethesda, Md, 89-90; Sherman Fairchild distinguished scholar, Div Chem & Chem Eng, Calif Inst Technol, Pasadena, 91, fac assoc, 92- *Mem:* Nat Acad Sci; fel Am Acad Arts & Sci (vpres, 90-93); Am Chem Soc; Royal Soc Chem; Swiss Chem Soc; AAAS; hon mem Pharmaceut Soc Japan. *Res:* Structure, synthesis and biological activity of cytokinins; modification of nucleic acid bases; fluorescent probes of coenzyme, enzyme binding and nucleic acid structures; intramolecular interactions. *Mailing Add:* 389 California Terr Pasadena CA 91105

LEONARD, RALPH AVERY, SOIL CHEMISTRY. *Current Pos:* RES SOIL SCIENTIST, USDA, 66- *Personal Data:* b Louisburg, NC, Mar 2, 37; m 58; c 3. *Educ:* NC State Univ, BS, 59, PhD(soil chem), 66; Purdue Univ, MS, 62. *Prof Exp:* Instr soil sci, NC State Univ, 62-66. *Mem:* Am Chem Soc; Soil Sci Soc Am; Am Soc Agron; Sigma Xi. *Res:* Physical chemistry of soils; fate of pesticides in soil and water; soil chemical aspects of waste disposal and utilization on the land. *Mailing Add:* 224 Franklin Ave River Forest IL 60305-2116

LEONARD, REID HAYWARD, CHEMISTRY. *Current Pos:* RETIRED. *Personal Data:* b Littleton, NH, Aug 28, 18; m 46; c 3. *Educ:* Univ Vt, BS, 40; Univ WVa, MS, 42; Univ Wis, PhD(biochem), 47. *Prof Exp:* Asst, Exp Sta, Univ WVa, 40-42; asst, Univ Wis & Forest Prod Lab, US Forest Serv, 43-45; res chemist, Salvo Chem Corp, Wis, 46-47; res chemist, Newport Industs, 47-56; consult biochemist, 56- *Mem:* Am Chem Soc. *Res:* Chemistry of wood; sugars from wood; lignin; levulinic acid; kidney stones; blood lipids; gas chromatography. *Mailing Add:* 537 Brent Lane Pensacola FL 32503

LEONARD, ROBERT F, PHOTOLITHOGRAPHY, MICROLITHOGRAPHY. *Current Pos:* DIR RES, PROD DEVELOP, OCG MICROELECTRONICS MAT, INC, 90- *Personal Data:* b Oceanside, NY, Aug 21, 34; m 64; c 3. *Educ:* Hofstra Univ, BA, 66; Worchester Polytech Inst, MS, 81. *Prof Exp:* Dir res, Litho Chem & Supply Co, 68-69; mgr printing prod, Rogers Corp, 69-76; res mgr printing prod, 76-79 & photopolymer applns, 79-84, dir res, prod develop, Philip A Hunt Chem Corp, 84- *Mem:* Am Chem Soc; Am Inst Chemists; Am Soc Testing Mat; Electrochem Soc; Soc Photographer Scientists & Engrs; Soc Photo-Optical Instrumentation Engrs. *Res:* Photolithographic chemicals and processes; microelectronics. *Mailing Add:* 24 Lens Ave Dayville CT 06241-2219

LEONARD, ROBERT GRESHAM, mechanical engineering, control engineering, for more information see previous edition

LEONARD, ROBERT STUART, GEOPHYSICS, AERONOMY. *Current Pos:* RETIRED. *Personal Data:* b Berkeley, Calif, Jan 20, 30; m 56, Kathryn Freeman; c Karen & Carl. *Educ:* Univ Nev, BS, 52, MS, 53; Univ Alaska, PhD(geophys), 61. *Prof Exp:* Res asst auroral studies, Geophys Inst, Univ Alaska, 53-58, instr, 58-60; radio physicist, SRI Int, 61-62, sr ionospheric physicist, 62-69, prog mgr, 69-72, asst dir, 72-77, dir, Radio Physics Lab, 77-80, dep div dir, 80-86; exec dir, Geosci & Eng Ctr, 86-87; Consult, 87-95. *Mem:* Int Union Radio Sci; Am Geophys Union; Am Phys Soc; Inst Elec & Electronics Engrs. *Res:* Chemical seeding in the ionosphere; transionospheric propagation; ionospheric disturbances; radio wave propagation. *Mailing Add:* 12837 Old Oregon Trail Redding CA 96003

LEONARD, ROBERT THOMAS, PLANT PHYSIOLOGY. *Current Pos:* DEPT HEAD PLANT SCI, UNIV ARIZ, 94- *Personal Data:* b Providence, RI, Dec 18, 43; div, Christine A; c 1. *Educ:* Univ RI, BS, 65, MS, 67; Univ Ill, Urbana, PhD(biol), 71. *Prof Exp:* Fel plant physiol, Univ Ill & Purdue Univ, 71-73; res asst prof to prof plant physiol, Univ Calif, Riverside, 73-82, vchmn dept, 78-82, assoc dean, Grad Div & Res Develop, 85-88, dept chmn, 88-94. *Mem:* Am Soc Plant Physiologists; Am Inst Biol Sci; AAAS. *Res:* Physiology and biochemistry of ion transport in plants. *Mailing Add:* Dept Plant Sci Forbes Bldg Rm 303 Univ Ariz Tucson AZ 85721-0001. *Fax:* 909-787-4437

LEONARD, ROY J, GEOTECHNICAL ENGINEERING. *Current Pos:* PROF CIVIL ENG, UNIV KANS, 66- *Personal Data:* b Central Square, NY, Aug 17, 29; c 2. *Educ:* Clarkson Col Technol, BSCE, 52; Univ Conn, MS, 54; Iowa State Univ, PhD(civil eng), 58. *Prof Exp:* Asst prof civil eng, Univ Del, 57-59; from asst prof to assoc prof, Lehigh Univ, 59-66. *Concurrent Pos:* NSF res grants, 59 & 62, sci fac fel, 63-65; pres, Alpha-Omega Geotech, Inc, Kansas City, Kans. *Mem:* Am Eng Geologists; Soc Mining Engrs; Am Soc Testing Mats; Int Soc Found Eng & Soil Mechanics; fel Am Soc Civil Engrs. *Res:* Applied soil and rock mechanics; foundation engineering; tunnels; earth dams and conduits. *Mailing Add:* 25003 MacKey Rd Lawrence KS 66044. *Fax:* 913-371-6710

LEONARD, STANLEY LEE, PLASMA PHYSICS. *Current Pos:* mem tech staff, 60-64, head, plasma radiation dept, Plasma Res Lab, 64-73, head, chem physics dept, Chem & Physics Lab, 73-74, DIR PHOTOVOLTAIC SYSTS, ENERGY SYSTS DIRECTORATE, AEROSPACE CORP, 74- *Personal Data:* b Oakland, Calif, Aug 27, 26; wid; c 4. *Educ:* Principia Col, BS, 47; Univ Calif, PhD(physics), 53. *Prof Exp:* Physicist, Radiation Lab, Univ Calif, 52-53; instr physics, Principia Col, 53-55, asst prof, 55-56; mem tech staff, Ramo-Wooldridge Corp, 56-59 & Space Technol Labs, Inc, 59-60. *Mem:* Am Phys Soc; Int Solar Energy Soc. *Res:* Analysis of terrestrial photovoltaic applications. *Mailing Add:* 2617 Via Carrillo Palos Verdes Estates CA 90274-2801

LEONARD, THOMAS JOSEPH, DEVELOPMENTAL GENETICS. *Current Pos:* PROF & CHMN BIOL, CLARK UNIV, 94- *Personal Data:* b Watertown, Mass, July 27, 37; m 65; c 1. *Educ:* Clark Univ, AB, 62; Ind Univ, PhD(microbiol), 67. *Prof Exp:* NIH fel, Harvard Univ, 67-68; assoc prof mycol, Univ Ky, 68-74; prof bot & genetics, Univ Wis-Madison, 74-94. *Mem:* AAAS; Genetics Soc Am; Mycol Soc Am; Brit Mycol Soc. *Res:* Physiology and genetics of fungi as applied to development; genetics and physiological aspects of cell differentiation. *Mailing Add:* Dept Biol Clark Univ 950 Main St Worcester MA 01610

LEONARD, WALTER RAYMOND, zoology, physiology, for more information see previous edition

LEONARD, WARREN J, CELL BIOLOGY. *Current Pos:* sr staff fel, Metab Br, Nat Cancer Inst, NIH, 81-85, sr staff fel, Cell Biol & Metab Br, Nat Inst Child Health & Human Develop, 85-87, med officer res, Cell Biol & Metab Br, 87-91, CHIEF, SECT PULMONARY & MOLECULAR IMMUNOL, OFF DIR, INTRAMURAL RES PROG, NAT HEART, LUNG & BLOOD INST, NIH, BETHESDA, 91- *Personal Data:* b Washington, DC, Feb 28, 52; m; c 2. *Educ:* Princeton Univ, AB, 73; Stanford Univ, MD, 77; Am Bd Internal Med, dipl, 80; Am Bd Allergy & Immunol, dipl, 83. *Prof Exp:* Residency internal med, Barnes Hosp, St Louis, 78-80; res assoc, Sch Med, Wash Univ, 80-81. *Mem:* Sigma Xi; Am Asn Immunologists; Am Soc Clin Invest. *Res:* Cell biology; two patents; numerous publications. *Mailing Add:* Nat Heart, Lung & Blood Inst NIH Bldg 10 Rm 7N244 MS 1674 Bethesda MD 20892-0001

LEONARD, WILLIAM WILSON, MATHEMATICS. *Current Pos:* from asst prof to assoc prof, 65-74, PROF MATH, GA STATE UNIV, 74-, MEM, URBAN LIFE FAC, 77- *Personal Data:* b Portland, Maine, May 1, 34; m 61; c 2. *Educ:* Univ Tampa, BS, 60; Univ SC, MS, 63, PhD(math), 65. *Prof Exp:* Asst prof math, Susquehanna Univ, 64-65. *Mem:* Am Math Soc; Math Asn Am; Math Soc France. *Res:* Module theory; homological algebra. *Mailing Add:* 156 Cleve Tripp Rd Poland Spring ME 04274

LEONARDS, G(ERALD) A(LLEN), civil engineering; deceased, see previous edition for last biography

LEONARDS, KENNETH STANLEY, BIOCHEMISTRY, BIOPHYSICS. *Current Pos:* res scientist III, 90-94, STAFF SCIENTIST, CIBA-GEIGY, 94- *Personal Data:* b Detroit, Mich, July 19, 50. *Educ:* Kalamazoo Col, BS, 72; Mich State Univ, MS, 75, PhD(biophys), 80. *Prof Exp:* Fel membrane biol, State Univ NY, Buffalo, 80-82; fel membrane transport, Univ Va, 82-84; asst prof res, Cardiovasc Res Lab, Dept Physiol, Univ Calif, Los Angeles Sch Med, 84-90. *Mem:* Biophys Soc; Am Chem Soc; Oxygen Soc; Am Physiol Soc. *Mailing Add:* Ciba-Geigy Mail Stop 2115 LSB 556 Morris Ave Summit NJ 07901

LEONBERGER, FREDERICK JOHN, INTEGRATED OPTICS, FIBER OPTICS. *Current Pos:* VPRES/CHIEF TECHNOL OFFICER, UNIPHASE TELECOMMUN PROD, 95- *Personal Data:* b Washington, DC, Sept 25, 47; m 70, Janet M Bueche; c Gregory & Katharine. *Educ:* Univ Mich, BSE, 69; Mass Inst Technol, MS, 71, PhD(elec eng), 75. *Honors & Awards:* Quantum Electronics Award, Inst Elec & Electronics Engrs, 93. *Prof Exp:* Staff mem, Lincoln Lab, Mass Inst Technol, 75-81, group leader, 81-84; mgr photonics, United Technol Res Ctr, 84-90, gen mgr, United Technol Photonics, 91-95. *Mem:* Fel Optical Soc Am; fel Inst Elec & Electronics Engrs; Inst Elec & Electronics Engrs Laser & Electrooptics Soc (pres, 88). *Res:* Photonic device research, with emphasis on integrated optics, fiber optics and optoelectronic devices and their applications to communication, sensing and signal processing. *Mailing Add:* Uniphase Telecommun Prod 1289 Blue Hills Ave Bloomfield CT 06002

LEONE, CHARLES ABNER, IMMUNOLOGY, RADIATION BIOLOGY. *Current Pos:* vpres & vprovost, 75-79, vpres res & grad studies, 79-81, PROF ZOOL, UNIV ARK, FAYETTEVILLE, 81- *Personal Data:* b Camden, NJ, July 13, 18; m 41; c 3. *Educ:* Rutgers Univ, BS, 40, MS, 42, PhD, 49. *Prof Exp:* Asst zool, Rutgers Univ, 40-42, instr, 46-49; from asst prof to prof, Univ Kans, 49-68; prof biol & dean grad sch, Bowling Green State Univ, 68-71, vprovost res & grad studies, 71-75. *Concurrent Pos:* Resident res assoc, Argonne Nat Lab, 55, consult, 55-60; adj prof, Med Col Ohio, Toledo, 69-75. *Mem:* Fel AAAS; Am Asn Immunologists; Sigma Xi. *Res:* Immunochemistry; radiation biophysics; comparative serology among arthropods, mollusks and mammals. *Mailing Add:* 1923 E Joyce St Fayetteville AR 72703-2919

LEONE, FRED CHARLES, STATISTICS. *Current Pos:* exec dir & secy-treas, 73-83, EXEC DIR & SECY, AM STATIST ASN, 84- *Personal Data:* b New York, NY, Aug 3, 22; m 45; c 7. *Educ:* Manhattan Col, BA, 41; Georgetown Univ, MS, 43; Purdue Univ, PhD(math statist, educ), 49. *Prof Exp:* Instr, Georgetown Univ, 42-43; instr, Purdue Univ, 43-44 & 46-49; from instr to prof math, Case Western Res Univ, 49-66, dir statist lab, 51-65, actg chmn dept, 63-65; prof statist & indust eng, Univ Iowa, 66-73. *Concurrent Pos:* Fulbright prof, Univ Sao Paulo, Brazil, 68-69; ed, Technometrics, 63-68; NAm ed, Statist Theory & Methods Abstracts, 69-73. *Mem:* Fel AAAS; fel Am Soc Qual Control; fel Am Statist Asn; Sigma Xi; Math Asn Am. *Res:* Experimental design and statistics applied to engineering; order statistics, especially in analysis of variance. *Mailing Add:* 201 E Wayne Ave Silver Spring MD 20901

LEONE, IDA ALBA, POLLUTION BIOLOGY. *Current Pos:* Asst plant path, Col Agr, Rutgers Univ, 46-50, res assoc, 50-58, asst res specialist, 58-70, assoc res prof, 70-76, prof plant biol, 76-87, prof II, 87-88, EMER PROF DEPT PLANT PATH, COOK COL, RUTGERS UNIV, 88- *Personal Data:* b Elizabeth, NJ, Apr 28, 22. *Educ:* Rutgers Univ, BS, 44, MS, 46. *Concurrent Pos:* Consult, NY State Environ Protection Bur, 75-76, US Dept Interior, NY State Dept Transp, Pa Power & Light Co, Niagara Mohawk Power Co, Rohm & Haas, Cambridge Mass Landfill Revegetation Comn, Cabot Corp; lectr, univ & inst, India, 77, China, 85; dir, NJ Jr Acad Sci. *Mem:* Sigma Xi; Am Phytopath Soc; Am Soc Plant Physiologists; Air Pollution Control Asn; NY Acad Sci; Indian Soc Air Pollution Control. *Res:* Effect of air pollution; nutritional, physiological and environmental factors on plant growth; plants as sources of air pollution; undergraduate and graduate courses in air pollution effects; effect of cooling-tower or de-icing salt spray on crops; phytotoxicity of anaerobic landfill gases; role of mycorrhizae in adapting woody species to landfill conditions. *Mailing Add:* 876 Rayhon Terr Rahway NJ 07065-2107

LEONE, JAMES A, PHYSICAL CHEMISTRY, INSTRUMENTATION. *Current Pos:* from asst prof to assoc prof phys chem, 67-74, dir med technol, 74-77, ASSOC PROF CHEM & COMPUT SCI, CANISIUS COL, 77- *Personal Data:* b Braddock, Pa, Dec 11, 37; m 61; c 1. *Educ:* Univ Cincinnati, BS, 61; Johns Hopkins Univ, MA, 63, PhD(phys chem), 65. *Prof Exp:* Res assoc, Univ Notre Dame, 65-67. *Concurrent Pos:* Vis assoc prof, Va Polytech Inst & State Univ, 75-76. *Mem:* Am Chem Soc; Sigma Xi; Soc Appl Spectros. *Res:* Radiation chemistry; ESR; on-line minicomputers; minicomputer and microprocessor interfacing; minicomputers and microprocessors in instrumentation automation. *Mailing Add:* 15 Summit Ave Buffalo NY 14214-2305

LEONE, LUCILE P, HEALTH ADMINISTRATION. *Current Pos:* RETIRED. *Personal Data:* b Ohio, 1902; m 52, Nicholas Choone. *Educ:* Univ Del, BA, 24; Johns Hopkins Univ, BS, 27; Teachers Col, Columbia, MS, 29. *Prof Exp:* Staff nursing, Johns Hopkins, 27-29 & Univ Minn, 29-47; comt mem, Student Nursing Serv, USPHS, 41-42, dir, Cadet Corp Prog, 42-48, chief nurse officer & asst surgeon gen, 48-66; assoc dean nursing, Tex Womans Col, 77-82; adv int students, Sch Nursing, Univ Calif, San Francisco, 78-83. *Mem:* Inst Med-Nat Acad Sci. *Mailing Add:* 1400 Geary Blvd San Francisco CA 94109

LEONE, RONALD EDMUND, ORGANIC CHEMISTRY. *Current Pos:* sr res chemist, 71-91, RES ASSOC, EASTMAN KODAK CO, 91- *Personal Data:* b New York, NY, Aug 11, 42. *Educ:* Northwestern Univ, BA, 64; Princeton Univ, MA, 67, PhD(org chem), 70. *Prof Exp:* Fel org chem, Yale Univ, 69-71. *Mem:* Am Chem Soc; Sigma Xi. *Res:* Aspects of physical organic chemistry including organic reaction mechanisms and nuclear magnetic resonance spectroscopy; synthesis of compounds for photographic applications including sensitizing dyes, silver halide fogging agents; image couplers, development inhibitor releasing couplers, bleach accelerator releasing couplers, interlayer scavengers, and latent image stabilizers. *Mailing Add:* 755 Corwin Rd Rochester NY 14610. *Fax:* 716-588-7611; *E-Mail:* releone.vivanet.com

LEONE, STEPHEN ROBERT, CHEMICAL PHYSICS. *Current Pos:* adj asst prof chem, 76-81, adj assoc prof, 81-82, ADJ PROF CHEM, UNIV COLO, 82-; FEL, NAT INST STAND & TECHNOL, 86- *Personal Data:* b New York, NY, May 19, 48. *Educ:* Northwestern Univ, BA, 70; Univ Calif, Berkeley, PhD(phys chem), 74. *Honors & Awards:* Silver Medal Award, Dept Com, 80, Gold Medal; Pure Chem Award, Am Chem Soc, 82, Nobel Laureate Signature Award, 83; Coblentz Award, 84; Arthur S Flemming Award, 86; Herbert P Broida Prize, Am Phys Soc, 89; Samuel Wesley Stratton Award, Nat Inst Stand & Technol, 92; Bourke Medal, Faraday Div, Royal Soc Chem, 95. *Prof Exp:* Asst prof chem, Univ Southern Calif, 74-76; physicist, Nat Bur Stand, 76-86. *Concurrent Pos:* Lectr, Dept Physics, Univ Colo, 76-, fel, Joint Inst Lab Astrophys, 78-, chair, 91-92; Alfred P Sloan Found fel, 77; John Simon Guggenheim fel, 88; vis Miller res prof, Univ Calif, 90; vis prof, Chem Res Prom Ctr, Taiwan, 92. *Mem:* Nat Acad Sci; Fel Am Phys Soc; Am Chem Soc; Am Inst Physics; Sigma Xi; fel Optical Soc Am; fel AAAS; fel Japan Soc Prom Sci. *Res:* Laser-excited chemical reactions; kinetics and spectroscopic investigations of excited states using specific laser excitation; energy transfer and dynamical processes of small gas phase molecules; photodissociation; new laser development; ion molecule reaction dynamics; surface dynamics; granted 3 US patents; author of 4 publications. *Mailing Add:* Joint Inst Lab Astrophys Univ Colo Boulder CO 80309-0440. *Fax:* 303-492-5504; *E-Mail:* srl@jila.colorado.edu

LEONG, JO-ANN CHING, VIROLOGY. *Current Pos:* from asst prof to assoc prof, Ore State Univ, 75-85, distinguished prof, 93, dept chair, 96, PROF MICROBIOL, ORE STATE UNIV, 85- *Personal Data:* b Honolulu, Hawaii, Mar 15, 42; c 2. *Educ:* Univ Calif, Berkeley, BA, 64; Univ Calif, PhD(microbiol), 71. *Honors & Awards:* Res Award, Sigma Xi, 90. *Prof Exp:* Sr res asst virol, Dept Surg, Stanford Univ Sch Med, 65-67; from teaching assoc microbiol to res biochemist, Univ Calif, San Francisco, 71-73, res fel biochem, 73-75. *Concurrent Pos:* Dernham fel, Am Cancer Soc, Calif Div, 73-75; Giannini Found fel,73; pres, Fish Health Sect, Am Fisheries Soc. *Mem:* Am Soc Microbiologists; AAAS; Soc Gen Microbiol; NY Acad Sci; Am Asn Cancer Res; Am Soc Virol. *Res:* Virus-cell interactions; tumor virology; development of recombinant DNA based vaccines for fish and shellfish. *Mailing Add:* Dept Microbiol Ore State Univ Nash Hall Corvallis OR 97331

LEONG, KAM CHOY, BIOCHEMISTRY, POULTRY NUTRITION. *Current Pos:* RETIRED. *Personal Data:* b Honolulu, Hawaii, Dec 17, 20; m 50; c 3. *Educ:* Wash State Univ, BS, 49, MS, 50; Univ Wis, PhD(biochem, poultry), 58. *Prof Exp:* Asst, Wash State Univ, 48-50; jr animal husbandman, Univ Hawaii, 51-54; asst, Univ Wis, 54-57; fel, Wash State Univ, 57-58; jr poultry scientist, 58-61; res chemist, Bur Com Fisheries, 61-65; nutritionist, Milling Co Div, Carnation Co, 65-81, asst dir nutrit, 81-86. *Mem:* Am Poultry Sci Asn; Am Inst Nutrit. *Res:* Amino acids; enzymes; vitamins; protein; metabolizable energy. *Mailing Add:* 410 S Las Flores Dr Nipomo CA 93444

LEONG, KAM W, MATERIALS SCIENCE & ENGINEERING. *Current Pos:* asst prof, 86-91, ASSOC PROF, DEPT BIOMED ENG & DEPT MAT SCI & ENG, JOHNS HOPKINS UNIV SCH MED, 91-, DIR, MASTER PROG BIOMED ENG, 90- *Personal Data:* b Nov 13, 55; nat US. *Educ:* Univ Calif, Santa Barbara, BS, 77; Univ Pa, Philadelphia, PhD(chem eng),82. *Prof Exp:* Res assoc, Whitaker Col Health Sci & Technol & Dept Appl Biol Sci, Mass Inst Technol, 82-85. *Concurrent Pos:* Johnson & Johnson fel biomed res, Mass Inst Technol, 83-85. *Mem:* Am Chem Soc; Am Inst Chem Engrs; Sigma XI; Controlled Release Soc. *Res:* Biomaterials design; controlled drug delivery; tissue engineering. *Mailing Add:* Dept Biomed Eng Johns Hopkins Univ Sch Med 3400 N Charles St Baltimore MD 21218-2608

LEONG, WILLIAM, PROCESS DEVELOPMENT. *Current Pos:* sr scientist, 90-92, assoc prin scientist, 92-94, PRIN SCIENTIST, SCHERING-PLOUGH RES INST, 94- *Personal Data:* b Dec 26, 61; m, Fina Liotta. *Educ:* Univ San Francisco, BS, 83; Univ Calif, Davis, PhD(chem), 88. *Prof Exp:* Fel, Iowa State Univ, 88-90. *Concurrent Pos:* Mem, Chem Safety Comt, Am Chem Soc, 95- *Mem:* Am Chem Soc; Sigma Xi. *Res:* Development of chemical processes for the synthesis of molecular entities of biological and medicinal interest; asymmetric synthesis and transition metal mediated catalysis. *Mailing Add:* Schering-Plough Res Inst 1011 Morris Ave Union NJ 07083. *Fax:* 908-820-6772; *E-Mail:* william.leong@spcorp.com

LEONHARD, WILLIAM E, CIVIL & ELECTRICAL ENGINEERING. *Current Pos:* RETIRED. *Personal Data:* b Middletown, Pa, Dec 9, 14. *Educ:* Pa State Univ, BS, 36; Mass Inst Technol, MS, 40. *Hon Degrees:* LLD, Pepperdine Univ, 87. *Honors & Awards:* George Washington Award, Inst Advan Eng, 84. *Prof Exp:* From lt to lt colonel, US ACE, 36-51; dir construct, USAF, 52-56, dep commdr, Missile & Space Div, 56-61, chief staff-brigadier gen, Hq Systs Command, 61-64; dir, Tittan III prog, United Technol Corp, 64-66; sr vpres & gen mgr, Parsons Corp, 66-74, pres, 74-75, pres & chief exec officer, 75-78, chmn, pres & chief exec officer, 78-90. *Mem:* Nat Acad Eng. *Mailing Add:* 455 Windmere Dr Apt 5B State College PA 16801. *Fax:* 814-231-2965

LEONHARDT, EARL A, MATHEMATICS. *Current Pos:* RETIRED. *Personal Data:* b Council Bluffs, Iowa, Apr 18, 19; m 41; c 3. *Educ:* Union Col, Nebr, BA, 50; Univ Nebr, ME, 52, PhD(sec educ, math), 62. *Prof Exp:* High sch instr, Nebr, 51-52; from instr to prof math, Union Col, Nebr, 52-90. *Concurrent Pos:* Mem, Nat Coun Teachers Math. *Mem:* Math Asn Am. *Mailing Add:* 5300 Cooper Ave Lincoln NE 68506

LEONORA, JOHN, ENDOCRINOLOGY. *Current Pos:* from instr to assoc prof, 59-69, PROF MED, SCH MED, LOMA LINDA UNIV, 69-, CO-CHMN DEPT PHYSIOL & PHARMACOL, 74- *Personal Data:* b Milwaukee, Wis, Jan 30, 28; m 52; c 2. *Educ:* Univ Wis, BS, 49, MS, 54, PhD(zool), 57. *Honors & Awards:* Res Award Sigma Xi. *Prof Exp:* Asst endocrinol, Univ Wis, 52-57. *Concurrent Pos:* NIH fel, Univ Wis, 57-59. *Mem:* AAAS; NY Acad Sci; Endocrine Soc; Sigma Xi. *Res:* Hypothalamic-parotid endocrine axis; relationship of dentinal fluid movement to dental caries. *Mailing Add:* Dept Physiol Loma Linda Univ Sch Med 25027 Mound St Loma Linda CA 92350-0001

LEONOV, VIKTOR, STRUCTURE OPTIMIZATION OF REAL-TIME MICROPROCESSOR SYSTEMS, STRUCTURE SYNTHESIS. *Current Pos:* DESIGN ENGR, 3COM CORP, 95- *Personal Data:* b Russia, Feb 22, 56; m 79, Veronika Khatala; c Yelena. *Educ:* Moscow Inst Telecommun, BSEE, 83, PhDEE(telecommun), 92. *Prof Exp:* Chief engr res lab, Telecommun Networks & Informatics Sci Res Ctr, Moscow Univ, Telecommun & Informatics, 83-94. *Concurrent Pos:* Assoc prof, Moscow Univ Telecommuns & Informatics, 92-94. *Mem:* Inst Elec & Electronics Engrs. *Res:* Development methodology of the analysis and synthesis structure of the real time microprocessor control systems in the field of telecommunications. *Mailing Add:* 2128A Rugen Rd Glenview IL 60025. *Fax:* 847-676-7312; *E-Mail:* vleonov@usr.com

LEON-PORTILLA, MIGUEL, PHILOSOPHY. *Current Pos:* PROF FAC PHILOS, NAT UNIV MEX, 57- *Personal Data:* b Mexico City, Mex, Feb 22, 26; m 65, Ascension Hernandez Trevino; c Marisa. *Educ:* Loyola Univ, BA, 48, MA, 51; Nat Univ Mex, PhD, 56. *Hon Degrees:* DHL, Southern Meth Univ, 80; PhD, Southern Meth Univ, 80; Univ Tel Aviv, 87, Southern Calif Univ, 89, Toulouse Univ, 90, Colima Univ & Univ La Paz, 94. *Honors & Awards:* Nat Prize in Soc Sci, Govt Mex, 81; Gamio Award, 83; Ralphael Heliodoro Valle Prize in Hist, 84. *Concurrent Pos:* Secy, Interam Indian Inst, Mex City, 55-58, asst dir, 58-60, dir, 60-66; dir, Inst Hist Res, 66-76; Guggenheim fel, 69; distinguished lectr, Am Anthrop Asn, 74; Fulbright fel, 75. *Mem:* Foreign mem Nat Acad Sci; Mex Acad Hist (pres, 96); hon mem Am Hist Asn; Inst Different Civilizations; Soc Mex Anthrop; Am Anthrop Asn. *Mailing Add:* Coyoacan 103 Alberto Zamora Mexico City 04000 Mexico

LEONTE, OANA MARIANA, ELECTROCHEMISTRY, CATALYSIS. *Current Pos:* SR RES CHEMIST, EKC TECHNOL, CALIF, 96- *Personal Data:* m 64, Dinu Ioan; c Laura L. *Educ:* Polytech Inst Bucharest, Romania, MS, 67, PhD, 86. *Honors & Awards:* Nicolae Teclu, Romanian Acad, 78; Outstanding Contrib to Design & Technol, Inst Indust Technol Chem Indust, 88. *Prof Exp:* Chem engr, Drugs Co Bucharest, 67-71; res & develop scientist & chem engr, Ctr Chem Timivoarz, Romanian Acad, 71-76, sr res & develop scientist & chem engr, Inst Phys Chem, 76-90; postdoctoral res, Lawrence Berkeley Lab, 90-91; sr chemist, Balazy Anal Lab, 91; sr res & develop scientist, Berkeley Polymer Technol, 91-92; sr res & develop chem engr/ scientist, Space Systs, 92-94; sr res & develop scientist, Pinnacle Res Inst, Ga, 95. *Concurrent Pos:* Vis scholar, Univ Calif, Berkeley, 90-91. *Mem:* Am Chem Soc; Electrochem Soc; Catalysis Soc; AAAS; Am Inst Chem Engrs. *Res:* Chemicals and materials with emphasis on chemical process, engineering, synthesis, formulation, characterization, technology as applied to materials science, semiconductors, storage energy materials technology, catalysis, polymers and organic synthesis. *Mailing Add:* 1137 Walpert St No 69 Hayward CA 94171. *Fax:* 510-537-9442, 784-9181; *E-Mail:* odleonte@ix.netcom.com

LEONTIEF, WASSILY, ECONOMICS. *Current Pos:* founder, Inst Econ Anal, 78-85, mem res staff, 86, PROF ECONS, NY UNIV, 75-, UNIV PROF, 83- *Personal Data:* b Leningrad, Russia, Aug 5, 06; m 32, Estelle Helena Marks; c Svetlana Eugenia Alpers. *Educ:* Univ Berlin, PhD, 28. *Hon Degrees:* PhD, Univ Bruxelles, 62, Univ York, 67, Univ Louvain, 71, Univ Paris, 72, Univ Pa & Univ Lancaster, 76; Dr, Adelphi Col, 88, Univ Cordoba, 90, Humboldt Univ Berlin, 95; LHD, Rensselaer Polytech Inst, 88. *Honors & Awards:* Nobel Prize in Econs, 73; Takemi Mem Award, Inst Seizon & Life Sci, 91. *Prof Exp:* Res economist, Inst Weltwirtschaft, Univ Kiel, Ger, 27-28 & 30; econ adv, Chinese Govt, 29; staff, Nat Bur Econ Res, 31; instr econs, Harvard Univ, 32-33, from asst prof to prof, 33-75, dir, Econ Proj, 48-72, Henry Lee prof, 53-75. *Concurrent Pos:* Guggenheim fel, 40 & 50; consult, Dept Labor 41-47, Off Statist Stand, 43-45, UN, 61-62, Dept Com, 66-82, Econ Price Adjust, 75-80 & UN, 80- *Mem:* Nat Acad Sci; fel Econometric

Soc; fel Royal Statist Asn; AAAS; Int Statist Inst; Am Econ Asn; Am Statist Asn; USSR Acad Sci; Royal Econ Soc; Brit Asn Advan Sci. *Res:* Contributed various articles to science journals and periodicals in the US and abroad. *Mailing Add:* Dept Econs NY Univ 269 Mercer St New York NY 10003-6633

LEONTIS, T(HOMAS) E(RNEST), PHYSICAL METALLURGY, MAGNESIUM. *Current Pos:* RETIRED. *Personal Data:* b Plainfield, NJ, Mar 13, 17; m 54, Anna Pavlatos; c Neocles, Artemis & Helen (Cleo). *Educ:* Stevens Inst Technol, ME, 38; Carnegie Inst Technol, MS, 42, DSc(phys metall), 46. *Prof Exp:* Instr chem, Stevens Inst Technol, 38-39; res metallurgist, Vanadium Corp Am, 39-41; grad fel, Carnegie Inst Technol, 41-44; metallurgist, Dow Chem Co, 44-51, sect chief metall lab, 51-57, asst to dir metall labs, 57-62, proj planning mgr, Dow Metal Prod Co Div, 62-65, mgr govt bus, 65-68, mgr tech & govt laison, 68-71; sr tech adv & assoc mgr, Battelle-Columbus, 71-75, mgr, Magnesium Res Ctr, 75-82. *Mem:* AAAS; fel Am Soc Metals (secy, 66-68, vpres, 70, pres, 71); Am Inst Mining, Metall & Petrol Engrs; Am Soc Metals Found Educ & Res (pres, 72). *Res:* Oxidation of metals; age hardening; powder metallurgy extrusion; extrusion of metals; high temperature magnesium alloys; magnesium alloy development; melting, casting and solidification; die casting; metal protection; surface finishing. *Mailing Add:* 3590 Hythe Ct Columbus OH 43220

LEOPOLD, ALDO CARL, PLANT PHYSIOLOGY, AGRONOMY. *Current Pos:* distinguished scientist, 77-78, William C Crocker Scientist, 78-90, EMER WILLIAM C CROCKER SCIENTIST, BOYCE THOMPSON INST, ITHACA, NY, 90- *Personal Data:* b Albuquerque, NMex, Dec 18, 19; c 3. *Educ:* Univ Wis, BA, 41; Harvard Univ, MA, 47, PhD(biol), 48. *Prof Exp:* Plant physiologist, Hawaiian Pineapple Co, Hawaii, 48-49; from asst prof to prof hort, Purdue Univ, 49-75; grad dean & asst vpres res, Univ Nebr, 75-77. *Concurrent Pos:* Carnegie vis prof, Univ Hawaii, 62; mem panel regulatory biol, NSF, 65, sr policy analyst, 74-75; bd govs, Am Inst Biol Sci & Am Soc Gravitational Space Biol, 84; mem bd agr & renewable resources, Nat Res Coun, 75-78; adj prof, Cornell Univ, 78-, Univ Fla, 88- *Mem:* Fel AAAS; Am Soc Plant Physiol (vpres, 59, pres, 65); Am Soc Gravitational Space Biol (vpres, 88, pres, 89). *Res:* Plant growth and development; seed viability; desiccation tolerance. *Mailing Add:* Cornell Univ Boyce Thompson Inst Ithaca NY 14853

LEOPOLD, DANIEL J, ELECTRONIC & OPTICAL MATERIALS. *Current Pos:* RES ASSOC PROF, WASH UNIV, 94- *Personal Data:* b NY. *Educ:* Rochester Inst Technol, BS, 77; Wash Univ, MA, 79, PhD(physics), 83. *Prof Exp:* Postdoctoral fel physics, Harvard Univ, 83-84; scientist physics, McDonnell Douglas Res Labs, 84-94. *Concurrent Pos:* Adj assoc prof, Physics Dept, Wash Univ, 90-94. *Mem:* Am Phys Soc; Mat Res Soc. *Res:* Optical and electronic properties of semiconductor quantum wells; molecular beam epitaxy; thin film amorphous semiconductors and conductive polymers; photonic devices. *Mailing Add:* Dept Physics Wash Univ St Louis MO 63130

LEOPOLD, DONALD JOSEPH, FOREST ECOLOGY, DENDROLOGY. *Current Pos:* ASSOC PROF DENDROL, COL ENVIRON SCI & FORESTRY, STATE UNIV NY, SYRACUSE, 85- *Personal Data:* b Ft Thomas, Ky, July 13, 56; m 80; c 2. *Educ:* Univ Ky, BS, 78, MSF, 81; Purdue Univ, PhD(forest ecology), 84. *Prof Exp:* Res assoc, Univ Ga, Athens, 85. *Mem:* Ecol Soc Am; Soc Am Foresters; Torrey Bot Club; Soc Conserv Biologists; Int Asn Veg Sci. *Res:* Vegetation responses to disturbance (natural or man-induced); restoration techniques for disturbed plant communities; rare plant management. *Mailing Add:* Environ Studies State Univ NY Col Environ Sci 320 Bray Hall Syracuse NY 13210-2723

LEOPOLD, DOREEN GELLER, SPECTROSCOPY OF GAS PHASE IONS & RADICALS. *Current Pos:* asst prof, 86-93, ASSOC PROF CHEM, UNIV MINN, 93- *Personal Data:* b Brooklyn, NY, Oct 25, 51; m 80; Kenneth R; c Karen S. *Educ:* Cornell Univ, BA; Mass Inst Technol, BS, 78; Harvard Univ, AM, 80, PhD(chem), 83. *Honors & Awards:* Presidential Young Investr Award, NSF, 88. *Prof Exp:* Res assoc, Joint Inst Lab Astrophysics, 83-86. *Mem:* Am Chem Soc; Am Phys Soc. *Res:* Study ions and radicals in the gas phase using the technique of negative ion photoelectron spectroscopy; small transition metal complexes. *Mailing Add:* Dept Chem Univ Minn 207 Pleasant St SE Minneapolis MN 55455-0431. *Fax:* 612-626-7541; *E-Mail:* dleopold@chemsun.chem.umn.edu

LEOPOLD, ESTELLA (BERGERE), BOTANY. *Current Pos:* prof bot & forest resources & dir, Quaternary Res Ctr, Univ Wash, Seattle, 76-82, prof, Dept Bot & Col Forest Resources, 82-89, prof environ studies, 89-94, PROF BOT, UNIV WASH, SEATTLE, 89- *Personal Data:* b Madison, Wis, Jan 8, 27. *Educ:* Univ Wis, PhB, 48; Univ Calif, Berkeley, MS, 50; Yale Univ, PhD(bot), 55. *Honors & Awards:* Co-recipient, Conservationist of Yr Award, Colo Wildlife Fedn, 69; Keep Colo Beautiful Ann Award, 79. *Prof Exp:* Asst res hydrologist, Tree Ring Res Lab, Univ Ariz, 51; teaching asst, Dept Plant Sci, Yale Univ, 52-53, Dept Zool, 54; res botanist, Paleont & Stratig Br, US Geol Survey, Denver, Colo, 55-76. *Concurrent Pos:* Res asst, Genetics Exp Sta, Smith Col, 52; mycologist, Forest Prod Labs, Madison, Wis, 52; Jr Sterling scholar, Yale Univ, 53-54; Sheffield Sci Sch scholar, 54-55; NSF travel grant to Spain, 57, Poland, 61, Eng, 76, USSR, 82, Can, 87; adj prof, Dept Biol, Univ Colo, 67-76; NSF grants, 68-69, 79-81, 82-83 & 91; vis prof, Dept Bot & Inst Environ Studies, Univ Wis-Madison, 71-72; mem, McIntyre Stennis Coop Forestry Res Adv Comt, 74-82; mem, US Nat Comt, Int Union Quaternary Res, 76-78, vchmn, 78-82, chmn, 82-87; mem, Environ Studies Bd, Nat Acad Sci, 77-80, Climate Res Bd, 83; assoc ed, Quaternary Res, 80-83; mem, Comt on Climate, AAAS, 83-84; mem, Mt St Helens Sci Adv Bd, US Forest Serv, 86-89; mem bd, Friends of the Earth Found, 87-89; Zucker environ fel, Univ Cornell, 93. *Mem:* Nat Acad Sci; fel AAAS (pres-elect, 94-); Am Quaternary Asn (pres-elect, 80-82, pres, 82-84); Bot Soc Am; Ecol Soc Am; fel Geol Soc Am; Sigma Xi. *Res:* Late Cenozoic paleobotany, palynology, paleoecology and paleoclimate; pollen and spore floras of late Cenozoic age in Wyoming, Idaho, Washington, Colorado and Alaska; palynology research in late quaternary deposits of Connecticut, Washington & California; Upper Cretaceous pollen and spore floras of Alabama and Wyoming; history of western grasslands; forest history of Washington; history of Pacific Northwest forest associations; climate and vegetation patterns since glaciation. *Mailing Add:* Bot Dept Univ Wash Box 355325 Seattle WA 98195-5325. *Fax:* 206-685-1728; *E-Mail:* eleopold@u.washington.edu

LEOPOLD, LUNA BERGERE, GEOMORPHOLOGY. *Current Pos:* PROF GEOL, UNIV CALIF BERKELEY, 72- *Personal Data:* b Albuquerque, NMex, Oct 8, 15; m 40; c 2. *Educ:* Univ Wis, BS, 36; Harvard Univ, PhD(geol), 50; Univ Calif, Los Angeles, MA, 45. *Hon Degrees:* DrGeog, Univ Ottawa, 70; DSc, Iowa Wesleyan Univ, 72, Univ Wis, 80, St Andrews Univ, Scotland, 81, Univ Murcia, Spain, 88. *Honors & Awards:* Nat Medal of Sci, 91; Dept Interior Distinguished Serv Award, 58; Bryan Award, Geol Soc Am, 58; Veth Medal, Royal Neth Geog Soc, 63; Liege Univ Medal, 66; Cullum Medal, Am Geog Soc, 68; Rockefeller Pub Serv Award, 71; Busk Medal, Royal Geog Soc, London, 84. *Prof Exp:* From jr engr to assoc engr, Soil Conserv Serv, USDA, NMex, 36-40; assoc engr, US Eng Off, Los Angeles, 41-42; assoc engr, Bur Reclamation, US Dept Interior, Washington, DC, 46-47; head meteorologist, Pineapple Res Inst, 47-50; hydraul engr, US Geol Surv, 50-56, chief hydrologist, 56-66, sr res hydrologist, 66-72. *Mem:* Nat Acad Sci; Am Soc Civil Eng; Geol Soc Am (pres, 71); Am Philos Soc; Am Acad Arts & Sci. *Res:* Hydrology of arid regions; rainfall characteristics; river morphology, erosion and sedimentation. *Mailing Add:* Dept Geol Univ Calif Berkeley CA 94720

LEOPOLD, REUVEN, OCEAN ENGINEERING & HYDRODYNAMICS, SHIP DESIGN & GAS TURBINES. *Current Pos:* CHMN BD & PRES SYNTEK TECHNOL INC, 86- *Personal Data:* b Arad, Rumania, May 5, 38; US citizen; m 62; c 3. *Educ:* Mass Inst Technol, BS, 61, MS, 63, Marine Mech Engr, 65, PhD(eng), 77; George Washington Univ, MBA, 77. *Honors & Awards:* Harold E Saunders Award, Am Soc Naval Engrs, 86; Albert Michaels Award, Navy League, 92. *Prof Exp:* Res scientist hydrodyn, Hydronautics Inc, 61-62; res engr, Mass Inst Technol, 62-66; dir ship eng & design, Shipbldg Div, Litton Industs, 66-71; tech dir surface ship & submarine design, Naval Ship Eng Ctr, 72-78; vpres advan systs aerospace, Govt Prod Div, Pratt & Whitney Aircraft Group, 78-81; mgr bus develop & strategic plan, Mil Engines Oper, Gen Elec Co, 81-84; chmn bd & chief exec officer, N K F Engr Inc, 84-87. *Concurrent Pos:* Mem vis comt, Mass Inst Technol, 73-76 & 87-; assoc mem, Defense Sci Bd, 75-84; task force mem, Atlantic Coun US, 76-78; mem, Chief Naval Opers Sr Adv Bd, 79- *Mem:* Fel Soc Naval Architects & Marine Engrs; Am Soc Naval Engrs; Sigma Xi; Am Defense Preparedness Asn; Royal Acad Eng. *Res:* Computers; materials; ship design; marine engineering. *Mailing Add:* 4301 N Fairfax Dr Suite 850 Arlington VA 22203

LEOPOLD, ROBERT SUMMERS, organic chemistry; deceased, see previous edition for last biography

LEOPOLD, ROGER ALLEN, CRYBIOLOGY, EMBRYOLOGY. *Current Pos:* res leader, 76-78, lead scientist, 86-88, RES ENTOMOLOGIST, BIOSCI RES LAB, AGR RES SERV, USDA, 67- *Personal Data:* b Redwood Falls, Minn, Mar 23, 37; m 88, Dana Bologna; c 2. *Educ:* Concordia Col, Minn, BA, 62; Mont State Univ, PhD(entom), 67. *Prof Exp:* Res asst stress physiol, Mont State Univ, 62-67. *Concurrent Pos:* Adj prof zool, NDak State Univ, 71-; Sir Frederick McMaster fel, Canberra, Australia, 96. *Mem:* AAAS; Entom Soc Am; Am Soc Zoologists; Soc Cryobiol. *Res:* Insect reproductive physiology and development; cryobiology. *Mailing Add:* Bio Sci Res Lab USDA Agr Res Serv PO Box 5674 Fargo ND 58105. *Fax:* 701-239-1348; *E-Mail:* leopoldr@fargo.ars.usda.gov

LEOPOLD, WILBUR RICHARD, III, EXPERIMENTAL CHEMOTHERAPY, TUMOR BIOLOGY. *Current Pos:* scientist, Cancer Res Inst, Parke-Davis Pharmaceut, 82-83, sr scientist, 83-85, res assoc 85-86, sr res assoc 86-88, sect dir tumor biol, 88-90, dir cancer res, 90-94, SR DIR, CANCER RES INST, PARKE-DAVIS PHARMACEUT, 94- *Personal Data:* b Paterson, NJ, July 26, 49; m 89, Judith Sebolt; c Matt, Aaron, Justin, Megan & John. *Educ:* Univ Ill, BS, 71, MS, 73; Univ Wis, PhD(oncol), 81. *Prof Exp:* Chem engr, Exxon Co, 71-72 & 73-75; res oncologist, Southern Res Inst, 81-82. *Mem:* Am Chem Soc; AAAS; Am Assoc Cancer Res. *Res:* Model development for cancer therapy; evaluation of anticancer drugs; chemical carcinogenesis and toxicological evaluations. *Mailing Add:* Parke-Davis Pharmaceut 2800 Plymouth Rd Ann Arbor MI 48105. *E-Mail:* leopolw@aa.wl.com

LEOPOLDE, CARL, ENGINEERING EDUCATION. *Current Pos:* PROF ENG, BOYCE THOMPSON INST, CORNELL UNIV. *Honors & Awards:* Charles Reid Barnes Life Mem Award, Am Soc Plant Physiol, 94. *Mem:* Am Soc Plant Physiol. *Mailing Add:* Boyce Thompson Inst Cornell Univ Ithaca NY 14853

LEOSCHKE, WILLIAM LEROY, NUTRITION OF FUR ANIMALS. *Current Pos:* RETIRED. *Personal Data:* b Lockport, NY, May 2, 27; m 56, Marjorie A Kovell; c Peter & Anna. *Educ:* Valparaiso Univ, BA, 50; Univ Wis, MS, 52, PhD(biochem), 54. *Prof Exp:* Proj assoc biochem, Univ Wis, 54-59;

from asst prof to prof chem, Valparaiso Univ, 57-95. Concurrent Pos: Consult, Mink Specialties Co, Ill, 55-; mem, Nat Res Coun Sub-comt Fur Animal Nutrit. Mem: Am Chem Soc; Am Asn Univ Professors; Sigma Xi. Res: Biochemistry and nutrition of mink; fundamental nutritional requirements of mink; mink diseases of nutritional origin; composition of blood and urine of mink. Mailing Add: 278 W 100th St Valparaiso IN 46383

LEOVY, CONWAY B, METEOROLOGY. Current Pos: assoc prof atmospheric sci, 69-74, dir, 86-89, PROF ATMOSPHERIC SCI & GEOPHYS & ADJ PROF ASTRON, UNIV WASH, 74- Personal Data: b Hermosa Beach, Calif, July 16, 33; m 58; c 4. Educ: Univ Southern Calif, BA, 54; Mass Inst Technol, PhD(meteorol), 63. Honors & Awards: NASA Outstanding Sci Achievement Award, 72. Prof Exp: Meteorologist, Rand Corp, Calif, 63-69. Concurrent Pos: Mem, Comt on Atmospheric Sci, Nat Acad Sci, 72-75 & comt on Lunar & Planetary Exploration, 74-76; ed, J Atmos Sci; Solar Syst Explor Comt, NASA, 84-87. Mem: Am Meteorol Soc; Am Geophys Union; AAAS. Res: Dynamics, radiation and photochemistry of earth and planetary atmospheres. Mailing Add: Dept Atmospheric Sci Univ Wash Seattle WA 98195

LEPAGE, RAOUL, RANDOM PROCESSES, SEQUENTIAL ANALYSIS. Current Pos: assoc prof, 72-76, PROF STATIST & PROBABILITY, MICH STATE UNIV, 77- Personal Data: b Detroit, Mich, Mar 5, 38; m 61; c 2. Educ: Mich State Univ, BS, 61, MS, 62; Univ Minn, PhD(math statist), 67. Prof Exp: Instr statist & probability, Columbia Univ, 65-66; asst prof statist & probability, Columbia Univ, NY, 67-70; vis assoc prof statist & probability, Univ Colo, 71. Concurrent Pos: Consult statist. Mem: Inst Math Statist. Res: Isolating and proving significant properties of random processes; nonstandard statistical questions of an applied character and the interface between probability, statistics and computing. Mailing Add: A413 Wells Hall-Statist Mich State Univ East Lansing MI 48824-1020

LE PAGE, WILBUR R(EED), ELECTRICAL ENGINEERING. Current Pos: assoc prof, 47-50, chmn dept, 56-74, PROF ELEC & COMPUTER ENG, SYRACUSE UNIV, 50- Personal Data: b Kearney, NJ, Nov 16, 11; c 1. Educ: Cornell Univ, EE, 33, PhD(elec eng), 41; Univ Rochester, MS, 39. Prof Exp: Instr elec eng, Univ Rochester, 33-38; res engr advan develop sect, Photophone Div, Radio Corp Am Mfg Co, 41-42; res physicist radiation lab, Johns Hopkins Univ, 42-46; sr res engr, Stromberg-Carlson Co, 46-47. Mem: Fel Inst Elec & Electronics Engrs; Asn Comput Mach. Res: Network theory; applied mathematics; education; computer applications. Mailing Add: Dept Elec & Comput Eng Syracuse Univ Syracuse NY 13210

LEPESKA, BOHUMIR, THERMOSET RESINS, RESIN STRUCTURE ANALYSIS. Current Pos: SR RES CHEMIST, PLASTICS ENG CO, 72- Personal Data: b Humpolec, Czech, Nov 7, 39. Educ: Inst Chem Technol, Czech, BS, 62; Czech Acad Sci, PhD(organometallic chem), 67. Prof Exp: Res assoc, Inst Chem Technol, 68-69; assoc org chem, Univ Notre Dame, 69-72. Concurrent Pos: Vis prof advan org chem, Univ Wis, 74-75. Mem: Am Chem Soc; Soc Plastics Eng; Sigma Xi. Res: Synthesis of new and improved thermosetting resins (polymers); structure-properties relationship of these resins; physical properties testing of molded test specimens. Mailing Add: 3234-B W Meadows Ct Sheboygan WI 53081. Fax: 920-458-1923

LE PICHON, XAVIER, GEOPHYSICS, OCEANOGRAPHY. Current Pos: DIR, DEPT GEOL, STAND SUPERIOR SCH, FRANCE, 84-, PROF & CHAIR GEODYNAMICS, COL FRANCE, 86- Personal Data: b Quinhon, Viet-Nam, June 18, 37; French citizen; c 6. Honors & Awards: Silver Medal, Nat Ctr Sci Res, 73; Maurice Ewing Medal, Am Geophys Union, 84; A G Huntsman Prize Oceanog Inst, Can, 87; Wollaston Medal Geol Soc, London, 91. Prof Exp: Res asst, Univ Columbia, NY, 63-68; sci counr, Ctr Nat Exploitation Oceans, 68-69; sci adv to pres, 73-78; chief, Dept Marine Geol, Ctr Oceanic Brit, Brest, 69-73; prof, Univ P&M Curie, Paris, 78-84. Concurrent Pos: Vis prof, Oxford Univ, 94 & Ocean Res Inst, Tokyo Univ, 95; distinguished vis lectr, Nigerian Mining & Geosci Soc, 94. Mem: Nat Acad Sci. Res: Plate tectonics. Mailing Add: Ecole Normale Superieure Lab de Geol 24 rue Lhomond Paris 75231 Cedex 05 France. Fax: 33-01-44-32-20-00; E-mail: lepichon@sphene.ens.fr

LEPIE, ALBERT HELMUT, PHYSICAL CHEMISTRY. Current Pos: RES CHEMIST, NAVAL WEAPONS CTR, 64- Personal Data: b Malapane, Ger, Aug 6, 23; US citizen; m 56; c 1. Educ: Aachen Tech Univ, MS, 58; Munich Tech Univ, PhD(chem), 61. Honors & Awards: Jannaf Cert of Recognition, 85; William B McLean Award, 88. Prof Exp: Res chemist, Ger Inst Res Aeronaut, 61-63 & US Naval Propellant Plant, Md, 63-64. Concurrent Pos: Mem, Interagency Chem Rocket Propulsion Group; fel, Naval Weapons Ctr, 90. Mem: AAAS; Sigma Xi; Am Chem Soc. Res: Performance calculations of propellants; hypergolic ignitions; mechanical behavior of polymers; advanced testing methods. Mailing Add: 121 Desert Candles St Ridgecrest CA 93555-4218

LEPINE, FRANCOIS, MASS SPECTROMETRY, ANALYSIS OF MICROBIAL METABOLITES. Current Pos: PROF ANAL CHEM, INST ARMAND-FRAPPIER, 87- Personal Data: b Montreal, Que, Mar, 1955. Educ: Univ Que, Montreal, BSc, 79, MSc, 81; McGill Univ, PhD(chem), 85. Prof Exp: Assoc, McGill Univ, 86-87. Mem: Am Soc Mass Spectrometry. Res: Mass spectrometry as a tool to study the decomposition of various organic compounds under physical treatment such as ultraviolet or gamma ray irradiation or microbial degradation. Mailing Add: Inst Armand-Frappier 531 Des Prairies Blvd Laval PQ H7N 4Z3 Can. Fax: 514-686-5501; E-Mail: francois___lepine@iaf.uquebec.ca

LEPLAE, LUC A, THEORETICAL SOLID STATE PHYSICS. Current Pos: res assoc, 66-67, vis asst prof, 67-68, asst prof, 68-77, ASSOC PROF PHYSICS, UNIV WIS-MILWAUKEE, 77- Personal Data: b Hammemille, Belgium, Nov 27, 30; m 59; c 4. Educ: Cath Univ Louvain, Lic en Theoret Physics, 55; Univ Md, PhD(physics), 62. Prof Exp: Res assoc physics, Inst Theoret Physics, Naples, Italy, 62-66. Res: Application of the Boson method to superconductivity, superfluidity, magnetism and phase transitions; many body problem; solid state physics. Mailing Add: 3714 N Prospect Ave Milwaukee WI 53211

LEPLEY, ARTHUR RAY, PHYSICAL ORGANIC CHEMISTRY. Current Pos: QUAL ASSURANCE OFFICER, LABS ADMIN, MD DEPT HEALTH & MENT HYG, DIV QUAL ASSURANCE, SAFETY & TRAINING, 88- Personal Data: b Peoria, Ill, Nov 1, 33; m 85; c 4. Educ: Bradley Univ, AB, 54; Univ Chicago, SM, 56, PhD(chem), 58. Prof Exp: Res assoc org chem, Univ Munich, 58-59 & Univ Chicago, 59-60; asst prof chem, State Univ NY Stony Brook, 60-65; from assoc prof to prof chem, Marshall Univ, 68-88. Concurrent Pos: NSF fel, 58-59; USPHS gen med fel, 60; vis prof, Univ Utah, 69-71; guest worker, Lab Chem Phys, Nat Inst Arthritis, Metabolism & Digestive Dis, Md, 75-76; consult, Interox Res & Develop Labs, Widnes, Eng, 85; Resources Conserv, Bellevue, Wash, 86. Mem: AAAS; Am Chem Soc; Am Inst Chem; Sigma Xi. Res: Flow nuclear magnetic resonance; microprocessor application in chemistry; total quality management; molecular rearrangements; free radical intermediates; continuing quality improvement; laboratory information systems; instrument interfaces; quality assurance; laboratory database. Mailing Add: Labs Admin PO Box 2355 Baltimore MD 21203. E-Mail: lepleyar@juno.com

LEPOCK, JAMES RONALD, BIOPHYSICS, PROTEINS & MEMBRANES. Current Pos: from asst prof to assoc prof, 77-87, PROF PHYSICS, UNIV WATERLOO, 87-, CHAIR, 93- Personal Data: b Fairmont, WVa, Oct 20, 48; m 70, Elizabeth Kahle; c 3. Educ: WVa Univ, BS, 70, MS, 72; Pa State Univ, PhD(biophys), 76. Prof Exp: Fel radiobiol, New Eng Med Ctr, Tufts Univ, 76-77. Concurrent Pos: Med Res Coun Can grants, 82-85; Nat Sci & Eng Res Coun Can grant, 78-, NIH grant, 85- Mem: AAAS; Biophys Soc; Radiation Res Soc; NAm Hyperthermia Soc; Biophys Soc Can; Can Asn Physicists. Res: Protein stability; differential scanning calorimetry; mammalian cell tissue culture; hypothermia and hyperthermia, radiation biology; fluorescence spectroscopy. Mailing Add: Dept Physics Univ Waterloo Waterloo ON N2L 3G1 Can. Fax: 519-746-8115; E-Mail: lepock@sciborg.uwaterloo.ca

LEPOFF, JACK H, PHYSICS. Current Pos: RETIRED. Personal Data: b Portland, Maine, July 22, 23; m 47; c 2. Educ: Univ NH, BS, 43; Columbia Univ, MA, 48. Prof Exp: Electronic scientist, Nat Bur Stands, 49-50, Naval Res Lab, 50-51, Nat Bur Stands, 51-53 & Naval Ord Lab, 53-54; sr staff mem, Motorola, Inc, 54-59; eng specialist, Sylvania Electronic Defense Lab, Gen Tel & Electronics Corp, 59-65; diode appln mgr, HPA Div, Hewlett Packard Co, 65-73, appln engr, 73-92. Mem: Sigma Xi; Inst Elec & Electronics Engrs. Res: Microwaves; semiconductors. Mailing Add: 850 Del Mar Downs Rd Apt 420 Solana Beach CA 92075

LEPORE, JOHN A(NTHONY), CIVIL ENGINEERING, APPLIED MECHANICS. Current Pos: asst prof civil eng, Dept Civil & Urban Eng, Univ Pa, 68-71, Winterstein asst prof, 71-78, from assoc prof to prof, 78-86, PROF & UNDERGRAD CHAIR, DEPT SYST, UNIV PA, 87- Personal Data: b Philadelphia, Pa, Feb 19, 35; m 59, Patricia A Luning; c 4. Educ: Drexel Inst, BSCE, 57; Univ Pa, MS, 61, PhD(appl mech), 67. Prof Exp: Nuclear engr, NY Ship Bldg Corp, 57-61; supv engr missile & space div, Gen Elec Co, 61-68. Concurrent Pos: Danforth assoc. Mem: Am Soc Civil Engrs; Am Soc Eng Educ; Am Acad Mech; Earthquake Eng Res Inst. Res: Stability of dynamic systems; applied mathematics; random processes; earthquake, wind and ocean engineering; disaster mitigation; solar energy applications. Mailing Add: 229 Towne Bldg Univ Pa Philadelphia PA 19104. Fax: 215-573-2065; E-Mail: lepore@seas.upenn.edu

LEPOUTRE, PIERRE, POLYMER CHEMISTRY, PAPER SCIENCE. Current Pos: PROF CHEM ENG, OBER CHAIR, UNIV MAINE, 91- Personal Data: b Roubaix, France, July 28, 33; Can citizen; m 62; c 3. Educ: Sch Advan Indust Studies, Lille, BS, 57; NC State Univ, MSc, 60, PhD(chem eng), 68. Honors & Awards: Coating & Graphic Arts Div Award, Tech Asn Pulp & Paper Indust. Prof Exp: Chem engr, Olegum, France, 57-58, Rohm & Haas France, 60-63; res engr, Int Cellulose Res, 63-66; res engr, Consol Bathurst, 68-71; res engr, Pulp & Paper Res Inst, 71-78, head, Polymer Sect, 78-82, dir, Appl Surface Sci Div, 82-91. Mem: Fel Tech Asn Pulp & Paper Indust; Can Tech Asn Pulp & Paper Indust. Res: Chemical modification of cellulose; adhesion; polymer latexes; paper coating. Mailing Add: Univ Maine Jenness Hall Orono ME 04469-5737

LEPOW, MARTHA LIPSON, PEDIATRICS, INFECTIOUS DISEASES. Current Pos: dir clin studies ctr, 78-87, vchmn dept, 82-95, PROF PEDIAT, ALBANY MED COL, 78-, CHMN DEPT, 95- Personal Data: b Cleveland, Ohio, Mar 28, 27; wid; c Lauren, David & Daniel. Educ: Oberlin Col, BA, 48; Case Western Res Univ, MD, 52. Prof Exp: Intern & resident pediat, Case Western Res Univ, 52-56, sr instr & asst prof, 58-67; fel infectious dis, Cleveland Metro Gen Hosp, 56-58; from assoc prof to prof pediat, Sch Med, Univ Conn, 67-78. Concurrent Pos: Mem study sects, NIH, 72-76; mem comt infectious dis, Am Acad Pediat, 85-91. Mem: Am Pediat Soc; Am Asn Immunol; Infectious Dis Soc Am; emer mem Soc Pediat Res; Am Acad Pediat; Am Soc Microbiol. Res: Clinical vaccine evaluation. Mailing Add: Albany Med Col Dept Pediat 47 New Scotland Ave A-88 Albany NY 12208-3478

LEPOWSKY, JAMES IVAN, MATHEMATICAL CONFORMAL FIELD THEORY. *Current Pos:* assoc prof, 77-80, PROF MATH, RUTGERS UNIV, 80- *Personal Data:* b New York, NY, July 5, 44; m, Lael Leslie. *Educ:* Harvard Univ, AB, 65; Mass Inst Technol, PhD(math), 70. *Prof Exp:* Lectr & res assoc math, Brandeis Univ, 70-72; asst prof math, Yale Univ, 72-77. *Concurrent Pos:* Mem, Sch Math, Inst Advan Study, 75-76, 80, 85, 87-88 & 92; Alfred P Sloan fel, 76-78; vis assoc prof math, Univ Paris, 78; assoc ed, Am Math Soc, 80-85; mem, Math Sci Res Inst, 83-84; Guggenheim fel, 87-88. *Mem:* Am Math Soc; Math Asn Am; Am Phys Soc. *Res:* Conformal field theory; vertex operator algebra theory; interactions with other branches of mathematics and physics; finite group theory; string theory; infinite-dimensional lie theory; combinatorics. *Mailing Add:* Hill Ctr Busch Campus Rm 303 Rutgers Univ New Brunswick NJ 08903

LEPP, CYRUS ANDREW, CLINICAL BIOCHEMISTRY, DRUG ANALYSIS. *Current Pos:* DIR TECHNOL, OLYMPUS AM INC, 91- *Personal Data:* b Brooklyn, NY, Aug 11, 46; m 72, Faye C Zuckerman; c Darius H & Marcus D. *Educ:* Syracuse Univ, BS, 68, PhD(biochem), 74. *Prof Exp:* Lab technician clin chem, Nassau Hosp, 68-69; sr biochemist clin chem & biochem, Corning Glass Works, 74-80, mgr develop, Corning Med & Sci, 80-85, mgr, Reagent Systs Res & Develop, Ciba-Corning Diag, 85-91. *Mem:* Am Asn Clin Chem; Am Chem Soc. *Res:* Electrophoretic separations of isoenzymes and hemoglobins; development of specific isoenzyme assay procedures; development of immunologic assays, clinical chemistry reagents, clinical chemistry controls, bloodgas reagents & controls. *Mailing Add:* Olympus Am Inc 2 Corporate Dr Melville NY 11747. *Fax:* 516-544-6405

LEPPARD, GARY GRANT, CELL BIOLOGY, LIMNOLOGY. *Current Pos:* RES SCIENTIST BIOL, CAN DEPT ENVIRON, 71- *Personal Data:* b Medicine Hat, Can, Aug 6, 40; m 70, Kristine Krassich; c Enrico & Desiree. *Educ:* Univ Sask, BA, 62, BA hons, 63, MA, 64; Yale Univ, MS, 66, MPhil, 67, PhD(biol), 68. *Honors & Awards:* NATO Sci Award, 81; Japan Inst Res Innovative Technol for Earth Award, 93. *Prof Exp:* NATO Sci fel, Fac Med, Univ Paris, 68, Inst Pharmacol, Univ Milan, 69; Nat Res Coun Sci fel, Fac Sci, Univ Laval, 69-70, Biochem Lab, Nat Res Coun Can, 70-71. *Concurrent Pos:* Sci res exec mem, Prof Inst Pub Serv Can, 71-73; adj prof, Dept Biol, Univ Ottawa, 74-75; NATO sci award, 81; Comn Europ Communities award, 82; prof biol, McMaster Univ, Hamilton, Ont, 88-; mem, Comn Environ Anal Chem, Int Union Pure & Appl Chem, 89-95 & Comn Fundamental Environ Chem, 96-97. *Mem:* Sigma Xi; Int Asn Great Lakes Res. *Res:* Physico-chemical and ecotoxicological relationships between living cells, nutrients and contaminants in aquatic ecosystems; technology transfer from biomedical sciences into aquatic sciences for analyzing the behaviour of aquatic colloid systems and flocs. *Mailing Add:* 226 Simon Dr Burlington ON L7N 1X9 Can. *Fax:* 905-336-4420

LEPPELMEIER, GILBERT WILLISTON, physics, for more information see previous edition

LEPPI, THEODORE JOHN, ANATOMY, MEDICAL SCHOOL ADMINISTRATION. *Current Pos:* ASSOC DEAN ADMIS & PROF ANAT & CELL BIOL, HEALTH SCI CTR, UNIV NTEX, FT WORTH, 90- *Personal Data:* b Mountain Iron, Minn, May 30, 33; m 59; c 3. *Educ:* Albion Col, BA, 59; Yale Univ, PhD(anat), 63. *Prof Exp:* From asst prof to assoc prof anat, Sch Med, Univ NMex, 66-71; assoc dean, Sch Med, Univ Minn, Duluth, 71-77, prof Biomed Anat & Chmn Dept, 71-88, dir admis, 71-77 & 83-89. *Concurrent Pos:* Staff fel, Lab Exp Path, Nat Inst Arthritis & Metab Dis, 63-66; guest lectr, Sch Med, Georgetown Univ, 63-64,; asst prof lectr, Sch Med, George Washington Univ, 65-66; Lederle Med Fac Award, 68-71; vis scientist, Pac Biomed Res Ctr, Univ Hawaii, 78-79; vis prof, Sch Med Univ Hawaii, 88. *Mem:* Am Asn Clin Anat. *Res:* Anatomical basis for the sectional imaging modalities. *Mailing Add:* 108 Sundance Ct Weatherford TX 76087

LEPPLA, STEPHEN HOWARD, BACTERIAL TOXINS, PROTEIN PURIFICATION. *Current Pos:* RES CHEMIST, NAT INST DENT RES, 89- *Personal Data:* b Oak Park, Ill, Feb 1, 41; m 80. *Educ:* Calif Inst Technol, BS, 63; Univ Wis-Madison, PhD(biochem), 69. *Prof Exp:* NIH fel dept molecular biol, Univ Calif, Berkeley, 69-71; res assoc, div biol & med sci, Brown Univ, 71-73; res chemist, US Army Med Res Inst Infectious Dis, 74-89. *Mem:* Am Soc Microbiol; Am Chem Soc; Am Soc Cell Biol. *Res:* Study of bacterial protein toxins to discover mechanisms of action, structure-function relationships; vaccine design; employment of methods of protein purification; immunochemical characterizations using monoclonal antibodies; gene cloning, and eukaryotic cell culture. *Mailing Add:* Bldg 30 Rm 309 NIH Bethesda MD 20892-0030. *Fax:* 301-402-0396; *E-Mail:* leppla@irp.nidr.nih.gov

LEPPLE, FREDERICK KARL, CHEMICAL OCEANOGRAPHY, GEOCHEMISTRY. *Current Pos:* PROG MGR, SHIP SAFETY & SURVIVABILITY, CHIEF NAVAL OPERS, 89- *Personal Data:* b Newark, NJ, July 1, 44; m 75; c 2. *Educ:* Univ Miami, BS, 67, MS, 71; Univ Del, PhD(marine studies), 75. *Prof Exp:* Res chemist org polymers, Air Reduction Corp, 67-68; res assoc, Nat Acad Sci-Nat Res Coun, Naval Res Lab, 74-76, res chemist marine aerosols, 76-89. *Mem:* AAAS; Am Chem Soc; Am Geophys Union. *Res:* Chemistry, transport and effects of aerosols in the marine environment; marine geochemistry and oceanography; fire protection applied to navy ships. *Mailing Add:* 2613 Woodlawn Lane Alexandria VA 22306

LEPS, THOMAS MACMASTER, CIVIL ENGINEERING, GEOTECHNICAL ENGINEERING. *Current Pos:* CONSULT CIVIL ENGR DAMS & POWER PLANTS, THOMAS M LEPS, INC, 63- *Personal Data:* b Keyser, WVa, Dec 3, 14; m 40; c 1. *Educ:* Stanford Univ, AB, 36; Mass Inst Technol, MS, 39. *Honors & Awards:* Cert of Appreciation, Am Soc Civil Engrs, 61. *Prof Exp:* Jr engr dams, US Corps Engrs, 39-41; asst engr dams, US Bur Reclamation, 41-42; chief civil engr dams & power plants, Southern Calif Edison Co, 46-61; chief engr dams & found, Shannon & Wilson, 61-63. *Concurrent Pos:* Mem & chmn exec comt, Soil Mech & Found Div, Am Soc Civil Engrs, 55-61; mem, Peer Group Mem Comt, Nat Acad Eng, 75-77; mem, Exec Comt, US Comt Large Dams, 76-, vchmn, 78-80. *Mem:* Nat Acad Eng; Am Soc Civil Engrs. *Res:* Soil mechanics and seismologic engineering. *Mailing Add:* PO Box 217 Dinuba CA 93618-0217

LEPSE, PAUL ARNOLD, ORGANIC CHEMISTRY. *Current Pos:* from asst prof to assoc prof, 63-72, PROF CHEM, SEATTLE PAC UNIV, 72- *Personal Data:* b Seattle, Wash, Mar 18, 37; m 61; c 2. *Educ:* Seattle Pac Col, BS, 58; Univ Wash, PhD(org chem), 62. *Prof Exp:* NSF fel, Univ Munich, 62. *Mem:* AAAS; Am Chem Soc; Sigma Xi. *Res:* Organic reaction mechanisms; carbene chemistry. *Mailing Add:* Dept Chem Seattle Pac Univ Seattle WA 98119-1899

LEPSELTER, MARTIN P, ENGINEERING. *Current Pos:* PRES, BELL TELEPHONE LABS FELLOWS INC, 93- *Personal Data:* b New York, NY, Nov 24, 29. *Educ:* City Univ New York, BME, 51. *Honors & Awards:* Daniel C Hughes Jr Mem Award, Int Soc Hybrid Microelectronics; Jack A Morton Award, Inst Elec & Electronics Engrs, 79. *Prof Exp:* Dir, Advan Very Large Scale Integration Develop Lab, AT&T Bell Labs, Murray Hill, NJ, 57-86; chmn, pres & chief exec officer, Lepton Inc, 86-93. *Mem:* Nat Acad Eng; fel Inst Elec & Electronics Engrs; Am Soc Mech Engrs. *Res:* Engineering; granted 47 US patents. *Mailing Add:* 25 Sweetbriar Rd Summit NJ 07901. *Fax:* 908-273-9109

LEPSON, BENJAMIN, MATHEMATICAL ANALYSIS, COMPUTATIONAL MATHEMATICS. *Current Pos:* EMER PROF MATH, CATH UNIV AM, WASHINGTON, DC, 94- *Personal Data:* b New York, NY, Mar 4, 24; m 48; c 1. *Educ:* Yale Univ, BS, 43, MS, 44; Columbia Univ, PhD(math), 50. *Prof Exp:* Lab asst physics, Yale Univ, 43-44; math physicist, Naval Ord Lab, 44-46; lectr math, Columbia Univ, 46-48; mem, Inst Advan Study, 50-52; mathematician, Off Naval Res, 52-53; asst prof math, Cath Univ Am, 53-54; head, Res Comput Ctr, US Naval Res Lab, 54-61, Numerical Anal Br, 61-65, math consult, Nucleonics Div, 65-66, Nuclear Physics Div, 66-67, Math & Info Sci Div, 67-69, Space Sci Div, 69-74, res mathematician, Math Res Ctr, 74-75, res mathematician & actg head, appl math staff, 75-76, consult, Res Comput Ctr, 76-79, mathematician & comput sci consult, Mgt Info Div, 79-83, chief, Staff Off, 83-87, Command Support Div, 87-90. *Concurrent Pos:* Asst instr math, Stanford Univ, 47, Univ Ill, 48; lectr, Univ Md, 52-53 & Am Univ, 52-53, 56-57; lectr & res assoc, Cath Univ Am, 54-64; adj prof, 64-74; vis prof math & statist, Univ Md, 74-75. *Mem:* Am Math Soc; Math Asn Am; Inst Math Statist; Inst Elec & Electronics Engrs; Comput Soc; Sigma Xi; fel AAAS. *Res:* Complex function theory, especially entire and meromorphic functions; Dirichlet type series; real function theory; potential theory; computer science; numerical analysis; applied mathematics; probability; mathematical statistics; application of mathematics, computers and statistics to physical sciences. *Mailing Add:* 9429 Curran Rd Silver Spring MD 20901-2806

LE QUESNE, PHILIP WILLIAM, ORGANIC CHEMISTRY. *Current Pos:* assoc prof org chem, Northeastern Univ, 73-78, chmn dept, 79-87, interim vprovost res & grad educ, 92-93, PROF CHEM & MED CHEM, NORTHEASTERN UNIV, 78-; ASSOC DIR, BARNETT INST, 93- *Personal Data:* b Auckland, NZ, Jan 6, 39; m 65, 90; c 2. *Educ:* Univ Auckland, MSc, 61, PhD(chem), 64. *Hon Degrees:* DSc, Univ Auckland, 79. *Prof Exp:* Res assoc org chem, Oxford Univ, 64-65; res assoc, Univ BC, 65-66, teaching fel, 66-67; asst prof, Univ Mich, Ann Arbor, 67-73. *Mem:* Am Chem Soc; Phytochem Soc NAm; Royal Soc Chem; assoc NZ Inst Chem; Am Soc Pharmacog. *Res:* Natural product chemistry, especially steroids, alkaloids, terpenoids, fungal metabolites; comparative phytochemistry; physiologically active compounds. *Mailing Add:* Dept Chem & Barnett Inst Northeastern Univ Boston MA 02115-5096

LEQUIRE, VIRGIL SHIELDS, PATHOLOGY. *Current Pos:* PROF PATH & CELL BIOL, SCH MED, VANDERBILT UNIV, 66- *Personal Data:* b Maryville, Tenn, June 15, 21; m 46; c 4. *Educ:* Maryville Col, BA, 42; Vanderbilt Univ, MD, 46. *Honors & Awards:* Thomas Jefferson Award. *Prof Exp:* NIH res asst, 49-50, from asst prof to assoc prof anat, 50-66, actg chmn dept path, 71-73. *Concurrent Pos:* USPHS sr fel. *Mem:* AAAS; Am Asn Anat; Am Fedn Clin Res; Am Soc Exp Path; Sigma Xi; NY Acad Sci. *Res:* Lipoprotein transport; fat embolization; membrane structure. *Mailing Add:* Vanderbilt Univ 698 Sneed Rd Franklin TN 37069-7085

LERBEKMO, JOHN FRANKLIN, GEOLOGY. *Current Pos:* Asst prof geol, Univ Alta, 56-59, from assoc prof to prof, 59-91, EMER PROF SEDIMENTARY GEOL, UNIV ALTA, 91- *Personal Data:* b Alta, Can, Dec 8, 24; m 49; c Craig, Janice, Todd & Mona. *Educ:* Univ BC, BASc, 49; Univ Calif, Berkeley, PhD(geol), 56. *Mem:* Geol Soc Am; Geol Asn Can; Can Soc Petrol Geologists. *Res:* Sedimentary petrology; detrital sediments; magnetostratigraphy. *Mailing Add:* Dept Geol 1-26 Earth Sci Bldg Univ Alta Edmonton AB T6G 2E3 Can. *Fax:* 403-492-2030

LERCH, IRVING A, medical physics, for more information see previous edition

LERCHE, RICHARD ALLAN, LASER FUSION DIAGNOSTICS. *Current Pos:* RES SCIENTIST, LASER ENG DIV, LAWRENCE LIVERMORE NAT LAB, 84- *Personal Data:* b Chicago, Ill, Feb 6, 43. *Educ:* Univ Ill, BS, 66, MS, 67, PhD(nuclear eng), 72. *Mem:* Am Phys Soc; Inst Elec & Electronics Engrs. *Res:* Laser fusion diagnostics. *Mailing Add:* 1561 Bluebell Ct Livermore CA 94550

LERCHER, BRUCE L, MATHEMATICAL LOGIC. *Current Pos:* asst prof, 62-67, ASSOC PROF MATH, STATE UNIV NY, BINGHAMTON, 67- *Personal Data:* b Milwaukee, Wis, June 7, 30; m 60; c 2. *Educ:* Univ Wis, BS, 51, MS, 52; Pa State Univ, PhD(math), 63. *Prof Exp:* Instr math, Univ Rochester, 59-62. *Mem:* Math Asn Am; Asn Symbolic Logic. *Res:* Combinatory logic. *Mailing Add:* Dept Math State Univ NY Binghamton NY 13902

LE RICHE, WILLIAM HARDING, MEDICINE. *Current Pos:* res assoc pub health, 57-59, prof, 59-62, prof & head Dept Epidemiol & Biomet, Sch Hyg, 62-75, prof epidemiol, 75-81, EMER PROF EPIDEMIOL, DEPT PREV MED, FAC MED, UNIV TORONTO, 82- *Personal Data:* b Dewetsdorp, SAfrica, Mar 21, 16; Can citizen; m 43; c 5. *Educ:* Univ Witwatersrand, BSc, 37, MB, BCh, 43, MD, 49; Harvard Univ, MPH, 50; FRCP(C), 72. *Honors & Awards:* Defries Medal, Can Pub Health Asn, 81. *Prof Exp:* Med officer, Union Health Dept, 44-49, epidemiologist, 50-52; consult epidemiol, Dept Nat Health & Welfare, Ottawa, Can, 52-54; res med officer, Physicians Serv, Inc, 54-57. *Concurrent Pos:* Carnegie fel, Bur Educ & Social Res, SAfrica, 37-39; consult, Physicians Serv Inc, 57-66, Toronto & Can Forces Med Coun, 69- *Mem:* Can Med Asn; fel Am Col Physicians. *Res:* Child growth, nutrition and infectious diseases; medical care studies; epidemiology; cardiovascular disease; education in public health and preventive medicine; hospital infections. *Mailing Add:* 169 Crinbrooke Ave Toronto ON M5M 1M6 Can

LERMAN, ABRAHAM, TECHNICAL MANAGEMENT. *Current Pos:* assoc prof, 71-75, PROF GEOL SCI, NORTHWESTERN UNIV, 75- *Personal Data:* b Harbin, China, Nov 14, 35; US citizen; c 1. *Educ:* Hebrew Univ, Israel, MSc, 60; Harvard Univ, PhD(geol), 64. *Prof Exp:* Lectr geol, Johns Hopkins Univ, 64, asst prof, 64-65; asst prof, Univ Ill, Chicago, 65-66; sr scientist, Weizmann Inst, Israel, 66-69; res scientist chem limnol, Can Centre Inland Waters, Can Dept Environ, 69-71. *Concurrent Pos:* Guggenheim fel, 72; vis prof, Inst Aquatic Sci, Swiss Fed Inst Technol, Duebendorf, 76-77 & Univ Karlsruhe, 79, 81 & 87; consult, Basalt Waste Isolation Proj, US Dept Energy, 81-87, mem, Mat Rev Bd, 85-88; mem, peer rev panels nuclear repository projs, Argonne Nat Lab, 83-; underground injection controls, US Environ Protection Agency, 89- *Mem:* AAAS; Geochem Soc; Am Chem Soc; fel Geol Soc Am; Am Geophys Union; Sigma Xi. *Res:* Global biogeochemical cycles; water and sediment geochemistry; transport processes; nuclear wastes; surface and ground water quality. *Mailing Add:* Dept Geol Sci Northwestern Univ Evanston IL 60208

LERMAN, CHARLES LEW, BIO-ORGANIC CHEMISTRY. *Current Pos:* SR RES CHEMIST, ZENECA PHARMACEUT, 81- *Personal Data:* b Elizabeth, NJ, Apr 23, 48; div; c 1. *Educ:* Yale Univ, BS, 69; Harvard Univ, AM, 70, PhD(org chem), 74. *Prof Exp:* Asst prof chem, Juniata Col, 74-76 & Haverford Col, 76-81. *Mem:* Am Chem Soc; AAAS; Sigma Xi. *Res:* Enzyme mechanisms and model systems; specificity of molecular interactions; mechanism of 5-aminolevulinic acid dehydratase; model for the active site of ribonuclease; NMR studies of biochemical systems; protein modeling. *Mailing Add:* Zeneca Pharmaceut 1800 Concord Pike Wilmington DE 19850. *Fax:* 302-886-2577; *E-Mail:* lerman@zen.com

LERMAN, LEONARD SOLOMON, MOLECULAR BIOLOGY. *Current Pos:* SR LECTR, DEPT BIOL, MASS INST TECHNOL, 87- *Personal Data:* b Pittsburgh, Pa, June 27, 25; div; c Averil, Lisa & Alexander. *Educ:* Carnegie Inst Technol, BS, 45; Calif Inst Technol, PhD(chem), 50. *Prof Exp:* Asst org chem & explosives, Explosives Res Lab, Carnegie Inst Technol, 45; asst chem, Calif Inst Technol, 45-49; Schenley fel, Univ Chicago, 49-51; instr pediat, Univ Colo, 51-52, asst prof, 52-53, from asst to prof biophys, 53-65; prof molecular biol, Vanderbilt Univ, 65-77; prof & chmn dept biol sci, State Univ NY, Albany, 77-84; dir diagnostics, Genetics Inst, 84-87. *Concurrent Pos:* USPHS res career award, 63-65, mem, NSF Adv Panel, 65-68; NIH study sect, 69-73; Guggenheim fel, 71-72; mem, Health & Environ Adv Bd, Dept Energy, 87-92; bd, Radiation Effects Res, Nat Res Coun, 88-96; subcomt Human Genome, Dept Energy-NIH, 89-93; ed, Genomics, 90-94. *Mem:* Nat Acad Sci; AAAS; Soc Human Genetics. *Res:* Aspects of the physical nature of DNA as related to human genetics; mutagenesis; structure of the nucleus; recognition of genetic variations. *Mailing Add:* Dept Biol Rm 68-630 Mass Inst Technol Cambridge MA 02139. *E-Mail:* islerman@mit.edu

LERMAN, MANUEL, COMPUTABILITY THEORY. *Current Pos:* assoc prof, 73-76, PROF MATH, UNIV CONN, 76- *Personal Data:* b New York, NY, Feb 5, 43; m 75; c 2. *Educ:* City Col New York, BS, 64; Cornell Univ, PhD(math logic), 68. *Prof Exp:* Instr math, Mass Inst Technol, 68-70; asst prof, Yale Univ, 70-73. *Concurrent Pos:* Vis prof, Univ Ill, Chicago Circle, 75-76 & Univ Chicago, 80; mem, Math Sci Res Inst, Berkeley, 90. *Mem:* Am Math Soc; Asn Symbolic Logic. *Res:* Recursive function theory; recursive model theory. *Mailing Add:* Dept Math Univ Conn Storrs CT 06269. *Fax:* 860-486-4238; *E-Mail:* mlerman@math.uconn.edu

LERMAN, MICHAEL ISAAC, MOLECULAR CLONING OF HUMAN TUMOR SUPPRESSOR GENES & GENES CAUSING ALZHEIMERS DISEASE. *Current Pos:* vis scientist, 80-87, expert, 87-90, RES CHEMIST, LAB IMMUNOL, NAT CANCER INST, FCRDC, NIH, 90- *Personal Data:* b Korosten, USSR, Sept 21, 32; US citizen; m 75, Eugenia Miniovicke; c Eugene M & Leah V. *Educ:* First Moscow Med Sch, MD, 57; Acad Med Sci, Moscow, PhD(biochem), 61, DSc(molecular biol), 68. *Honors & Awards:* Director's Award, NIH, 92. *Prof Exp:* Asst prof biochem, Dept Biochem, First Moscow Med Sch, 60-62; sr scientist, Inst Molecular Biol, Acad Sci, Moscow, 62-64 & Bach Inst Biochem, 64-66; sr scientist, Inst Biol Med Chem, Acad Med Sci, Moscow, 66-78, dir, Lab Molecular Pathobiol, 68-79. *Concurrent Pos:* Consult, Diag Div, Abbott Labs, 89-93. *Mem:* Am Soc Biol Chemists; AAAS; Am Soc Human Genetics; Genetic Soc Am; Int Mammalian Genome Soc; Am Asn Cancer Res. *Res:* Molecular biology of protein biosynthesis; molecular biology of aging; molecular genetics of human cancers; molecular cloning of disease genes. *Mailing Add:* Nat Cancer Inst-FCRDC Bldg 560 Rm 12-26 Frederick MD 21702. *Fax:* 301-846-6145; *E-Mail:* lerman@heiferf.gov

LERMAN, SIDNEY, OPHTHALMOLOGY, CHEMISTRY. *Current Pos:* PROF OPHTHAL, NY MED COL, 88- *Personal Data:* b Montreal, Can, Oct 6, 27; m 57; c 2. *Educ:* McGill Univ, BSc, 48, MD, CM, 52; Univ Rochester, MS, 61. *Honors & Awards:* Award in Ophthal & J B Cramer Mem Award, Rochester Acad Med, 58; Parker Heath Mem Award, 85. *Prof Exp:* Dir ophthalmic res, Univ Rochester, 57-68, asst prof biochem, 61-68, assoc prof ophthal, 62-68; prof ophthal & biochem & dir exp ophthal, McGill Univ, 68-73; prof ophthal, Sch Med, Emory Univ, 75-88. *Concurrent Pos:* Chmn, Int Conf Ophthalmic Biochem, Woods Hole, Mass, 64-72; consult, Bausch & Lomb, 66-69, Nat Patent Develop Corp, 68-73 & Alza Corp, 69-72; adj prof chem, Ga Inst Technol, 75- *Mem:* Am Asn Res Vision & Ophthal; Am Chem Soc; Am Soc Biol Chem; Am Soc Photobiol; Int Soc Ocular Toxicol (pres, 91). *Res:* Ophthalmic biochemistry and photobiology. *Mailing Add:* Dept Ophthal NY Med Col 12 E 12th St Apt 5SE New York NY 10003

LERMAN, STEPHEN PAUL, IMMUNOLOGY. *Current Pos:* ASSOC PROF IMMUNOL & MICROBIOL, WAYNE STATE UNIV SCH MED, 78-, DIR FLOW CYTOMETRY LAB, 86- *Personal Data:* b Philadelphia, Pa, Oct 3, 44; m; c 1. *Educ:* Philadelphia Col Pharm & Sci, BS, 66; Hahnemann Med Col, MS, 70, PhD(microbiol), 73. *Prof Exp:* Fel, 72-74, asst res scientist, 74-75, res asst scientist path, Sch Med, NY Univ, 75-78. *Concurrent Pos:* Spec fel, Leukemia Soc Am, 76-78. *Mem:* Am Asn Immunologists; Am Soc Microbiol; fel Am Acad Microbiol. *Res:* Tumor immunology. *Mailing Add:* Wayne State Univ Sch Med Dept Immunol & Microbiol 540 E Canfield Ave Detroit MI 48201-1908

LERMAN, STEVEN I, OCCUPATIONAL SAFETY & HEALTH, ASBESTOS. *Current Pos:* CONSULT CHEM, SIL CONSULT, 88- *Personal Data:* b Bronx, NY, Nov 14, 44; m 65, Ruth J Mandle; c Craig, Tracy & Erica. *Educ:* Queen's Col, City Univ New York, BS, 65; Adelphi Univ, MS, 72. *Honors & Awards:* Outstanding Serv Award, Am Soc Testing & Mat, 88. *Prof Exp:* Chemist, Con Edison NY, 65-86; sr chemist, NY Power Authority, 86-88. *Concurrent Pos:* Cong sci counr, Am Chem Soc, 81-83; subcomt chmn, Am Soc Testing & Mat, 83-; instr, Inst Asbestos Awareness, 88-90, Tall Oaks Publ, 89- & FED Training Ctr, 91-; consult, Nat Inst Stand & Technol, US Dept Com, 88- *Mem:* Fel Am Inst Chemists; Environ Info Asn; Am Chem Soc; Am Soc Testing & Mat. *Res:* Environmental laboratories; quality assurance programs for compliance; industrial health and safety; computer systems. *Mailing Add:* SIL Consult Three Allan Gate Plainview NY 11803. *Fax:* 516-433-3412; *E-Mail:* prodigy: fctf29a

LERMAN, ZAFRA MARGOLIN, SCIENCE FOR NON-SCIENCE MAJORS, TEACHER PREPARATION & TRAINING. *Current Pos:* dir sci prog, Inst Sci Educ & Sci Commun, 77-81, chair & founder, Dept Sci & Math, 81-91, distinguished prof sci & pub policy, 91, HEAD, INST SCI EDUC & SCI COMMUN, COLUMBIA, COL, 91- *Personal Data:* b Haife, Israel, Jan 24, 37; US citizen. *Educ:* Technion-Israel Inst Technol, BS, 60, MS, 64; Weizmann Inst Sci, PhD(chem), 69. *Honors & Awards:* Natural Catalyst Award, Chem Manufacturers Asn, 90. *Prof Exp:* Fel, Dept Chem, Cornell Univ, 69-72; res assoc, Dept Chem, Northwestern Univ, 72-76; vis scholar, Tech Chem Lab, ETH, Zurich, Switz, 76-77. *Concurrent Pos:* Prin investr, NSF, 79-81 & 87-, USN, 91-; vis scholar, Grad Prog Sci, Technol & Pub Policy, George Washington, Univ, 84-85. *Mem:* AAAS; Am Chem Soc; Int Coun Asn sci Educ; Int Union Pure & Appl Chem; Nat Sci Teachers Asn; NY Acad Sci; fel Am Inst Chemists; Royal Soc Chem. *Res:* College science course for non-science majors future communicators; courses for pre-service teachers; teacher enhancement workshops; community-based workshops for teachers and parents together. *Mailing Add:* Columbia Col Sci Inst 600 S Michigan Ave Chicago IL 60605

LERNER, AARON BUNSEN, DERMATOLOGY, BIOCHEMISTRY. *Current Pos:* assoc prof, Sch Med, Yale Univ, 55-57, chmn dept, 58-85, prof, 58-95, EMER PROF, DEPT DERMAT, SCH MED, YALE UNIV, 95- *Personal Data:* b Minneapolis, Minn, Sept 21, 20; m 45; c 4. *Educ:* Univ Minn, BA, 41, MS, 42, MB & PhD(physiol chem), 45, MD, 45; Am Bd Dermat, dipl, 53. *Honors & Awards:* Myron-Gordon Award, 69; Stephen Rothman Award, 71; Dome Lectr, 80; Lita Annenberg Hazen Award, 81. *Prof Exp:* Asst physiol chem, Univ Minn, 41-45; Am Cancer Soc fel, Sch Med, Western Res Univ, 48-49; asst prof dermat, Med Sch, Univ Mich, 49-52; assoc prof, Univ Ore, 52-55. *Mem:* Sr mem Inst Med-Nat Acad Sci; Soc Invest Dermat; Am Acad Dermat; Am Soc Biol Chemists; Sigma Xi. *Res:* Plasma proteins associated with disease; metabolism of phenylalanine and tyrosine; biochemistry of melanin pigmentation; mechanism of endocrine control of pigmentation; malignant melanomas; cryoglobulins; biochemistry of skin; author or co-author of numerous publications. *Mailing Add:* Dept Dermat Yale Univ Sch Med PO Box 208059 New Haven CT 06520-8059. *Fax:* 203-785-7234; *E-Mail:* aaron.lerner@yale.edu

LERNER, ALBERT MARTIN, INTERNAL MEDICINE. *Current Pos:* prof med, 67-82, chief, Hutzel Hosp Med Unit, 70-82, CLIN PROF MED, COL MED, WAYNE STATE UNIV, 82- *Personal Data:* b St Louis, Mo, Sept 3, 29; div; c 4. *Educ:* Wash Univ, BA, 50, MD, 54; Am Bd Internal Med, dipl, 61. *Prof Exp:* Intern, Barnes Hosp, St Louis, Mo, 54-55; lab investr, Nat Inst Allergy & Infectious Dis, 55-57; asst resident, Harvard Med Serv, Boston City Hosp, Mass, 57-58; sr asst resident, Barnes Hosp, Mo, 58-59; res assoc biol, Mass Inst Technol, 62-63; assoc prof med & assoc microbiol & path, Col Med, Wayne State Univ, 63-67; assoc med & path & dir bact lab, Detroit Gen Hosp, 64-69, clin consult bact lab, 69- *Concurrent Pos:* Res fel med, Thorndike Mem Lab, Boston City Hosp & Harvard Med Sch, 59-62; fel, Med Found Greater Boston, Inc, 60-63; consult, Vet Admin Hosp, Allen Park, Mich, 63-82. *Mem:* Fel Am Col Physicians; Am Soc Clin Invest; Inf Dis Soc Am; dipl mem Pan-Am Med Asn; Asn Am Physicians; Am Fedn Clin Res. *Res:* Infectious diseases. *Mailing Add:* 31000 Lahser Birmingham MI 48025

LERNER, B(ERNARD) J, CHEMICAL ENGINEERING. *Current Pos:* PRES, BECO ENG CO, 70- *Personal Data:* b Brooklyn, NY, Apr 28, 21; m 51; c 3. *Educ:* Cooper Union, BChE, 43; Univ Iowa, MS, 51; Syracuse Univ, PhD(chem eng), 49. *Prof Exp:* Instr chem eng, Univ Iowa, 46-47; res engr, Inst Indust Res, Syracuse Univ, 47-48; asst prof, Univ Tex, 49-54; group leader, Gulf Res & Develop Co, 54-59; consult, Dominion Gulf Co, 59-63; pres, Patent Develop Assocs, Inc, Pa, 63-68; vpres res & dir chem eng res, MK Res & Develop Co, Pa, 68-70. *Concurrent Pos:* Consult, Monsanto Chem Co, 52-53 & Maurice A Knight Co, 63-68; pvt consult chem engr, 59-80. *Mem:* Am Chem Soc; Am Inst Chem Engrs; Air Pollution Control Asn. *Res:* Mass transfer; two-phase fluid flow; air pollution control. *Mailing Add:* Beco Eng Co PO Box 443 Oakmont PA 15139-0443. *Fax:* 412-828-6144

LERNER, DAVID EVAN, MATHEMATICAL PHYSICS, SCIENTIFIC COMPUTING. *Current Pos:* asst prof, 75-79, ASSOC PROF MATH, UNIV KANS, 80- *Personal Data:* b Kansas City, Mo, Mar 21, 44. *Educ:* Haverford Col, BA, 64; Univ Pittsburgh, PhD(math), 72. *Prof Exp:* Instr math, Univ Pittsburgh, 72-73; res assoc physics, Syracuse Univ, Relativity Group, 73-75. *Concurrent Pos:* Math Inst, Univ Oxford, 76-77. *Mem:* Am Phys Soc; Am Math Soc. *Res:* Geometric visualization; applications and theory of nonlinear dynamics. *Mailing Add:* Dept Math Univ Kans Lawrence KS 66045. *E-Mail:* lerner@math.ukans.edu

LERNER, EDWARD CLARENCE, theoretical physics, for more information see previous edition

LERNER, JOSEPH, BIOCHEMISTRY. *Current Pos:* PROF CHEM, COL ARTS & SCI, TENN TECH UNIV, COOKEVILLE, 84-, DEAN, 84- *Personal Data:* b Wilkes-Barre, Pa, Jan 16, 42; m 63, Linda Dell; c Michael & Michele. *Educ:* Rutgers Univ, BS, 63, PhD(biochem), 67. *Prof Exp:* Sr res investr biochem, Eastern Utilization Res & Develop Div, USDA, 67-68; from asst prof to assoc prof biochem, Univ Maine, Orono, 68-77, prof, 77-, chmn dept, 78-83. *Concurrent Pos:* Coe Res Fund grant, 68-69; Hatch Fund grant, 69-83; NIH res grant, 74-83; res assoc, Dept Avian Sci, Univ Calif, Davis, 74; fac fel acad higher admin, Univ NH, 82-83; pres, Tenn Coun Arts & Sci Deans, 88. *Mem:* Am Chem Soc; Am Inst Nutrition; NY Acad Sci; Sigma Xi; AAAS. *Res:* Intestinal absorption of amino acids in chicken; metabolism of small intestine; genetic aspects of transport processes; separation of nucleotide derivatives by column chromatography. *Mailing Add:* Tenn Technol Univ Box 5055 Cookeville TN 38505-0001

LERNER, JULES, GENETICS, CYTOLOGY. *Current Pos:* Asst prof, 67-71, assoc prof, 71-77, PROF BIOL, NORTHEASTERN ILL UNIV, 77- *Personal Data:* b Englewood, NJ, Oct 24, 41; m 69, Joyce Wallace. *Educ:* Bowdoin Col, BA, 63; Johns Hopkins Univ, PhD(biol), 67. *Mem:* AAAS. *Res:* Developmental biology and genetics. *Mailing Add:* Dept Biol Northeastern Ill Univ 5500 N Saint Louis Ave Chicago IL 60625

LERNER, LAWRENCE ROBERT, ORGANIC CHEMISTRY. *Current Pos:* group leader, Harmon Colors Corp, 72-73, supvr org pigments, 73-81, mgr process control & develop, 81-85, TECH MGR, MOBAY CHEM CORP, 85- *Personal Data:* b New York, NY, Mar 17, 43; m 64; c 2. *Educ:* City Col New York, BS, 64; Mich State Univ, PhD(org chem), 68. *Prof Exp:* Res chemist org pigments, E I du Pont de Nemours & Co, 68-72. *Concurrent Pos:* Adj asst prof, County Col Morris, NJ, 73-74. *Mem:* Sigma Xi; Am Chem Soc; AAAS; Inter-Soc Color Coun. *Res:* Synthesis of colored organic pigments; study of the effects of structure on the photostability, color and physical properties of organic pigments. *Mailing Add:* 176 Grove Terr Livingston NJ 07039-4113

LERNER, LAWRENCE S, CONDENSED MATTER PHYSICS, HISTORY OF SCIENCE. *Current Pos:* assoc prof, 69-73, dir, Gen Honors Prog, 76-80, PROF PHYSICS & ASTRON, CALIF STATE UNIV, LONG BEACH, 73- *Personal Data:* b New York, NY, Mar 10, 34; m 59. *Educ:* Univ Chicago, AB, 53, MS, 55, PhD(physics), 62. *Prof Exp:* Staff mem, Labs Appl Sci, Univ Chicago, 58-60; physicist, Hughes Res Labs, 62-65 & Hewlett-Packard Labs, Calif, 65-67; res scientist, Lockheed Palo Alto Res Lab, 67-69. *Concurrent Pos:* Danforth Assoc, 75-; mem, Nat Sci Humanities Arts & Sci 78-; foreign mem, Ctr Hist Ideas Anglo-Am World Sorbonne; mem, Calif Curric Framework & Criteria Comt Sci, 88-89. *Mem:* AAAS; Am Phys Soc; Am Asn Physics Teachers; Hist Sci Soc; Sigma Xi. *Res:* Fermi surfaces of metals and semimetals; preparation and properties of ternary compound semiconductors; semiconductor physics; influence of non-scientific philosophical movements on early scientific revolution. *Mailing Add:* Dept Physics & Astron Calif State Univ Long Beach CA 90840. *Fax:* 562-985-7924; *E-Mail:* lslerner@csulb.edu

LERNER, LEON MAURICE, BIOCHEMISTRY. *Current Pos:* from instr to assoc prof, 65-80, PROF BIOCHEM, STATE UNIV NY HEALTH SCI CTR, BROOKLYN, 80- *Personal Data:* b Chicago, Ill, Feb 2, 38; m 59, 96, Fern Loevsky; c Linda, Marcia & Gary. *Educ:* Ill Inst Technol, BS, 59, MS, 61; Univ Ill, PhD(biochem), 64. *Prof Exp:* Res assoc biochem, Col Med, Univ Ill, 64-65. *Mem:* AAAS; Am Chem Soc; Sigma Xi. *Res:* Potential nucleic acid antimetabolites; nucleoside analogs; chemistry and biochemistry of carbohydrates. *Mailing Add:* 450 Clarkson Ave Brooklyn NY 11203

LERNER, LEONARD JOSEPH, CANCER, REPRODUCTION & FERTILITY. *Current Pos:* res prof, Depts Obstet & Gynec & Pharmacol, 71-89, HON PROF, DEPT PHARMACOL, THOMAS JEFFERSON MED COL, 89- *Personal Data:* b Roselle, NJ, Sept 26, 22. *Educ:* Rutgers Univ, BSc, 43, AB, 51, MS, 53, PhD(zool), 54. *Honors & Awards:* Cain Mem Award, Am Asn Cancer Res, 89. *Prof Exp:* Pharmacist, 46-51; assoc, Bur Biol Res, Rutgers Univ, 53-54; endocrinologist, William S Merrell Co, 54-58; head endocrine res, Squibb Inst Med Res, 58-71; dir endocrinol, Gruppo Lepetit Spa, 71-77. *Concurrent Pos:* Assoc mem, Bur Biol Res, Rutgers Univ; vis prof obstet & gynec, Hahnemann Med Sch; mem, Steering Comt Int Study Group, Steroid Hormones; mem, Breast Cancer Task Force Comt & Concept Rev Comt, Nat Cancer Inst; consult, pharmaceut co; mem, Animal Res & Experimentation Comt, NY Acad Sci; Comt Animals in Res, Soc Study Reprod, co-ed res steroids; chmn & vchmn sect Biol & Med, NY Acad Sci; mem bd dirs, Am Diabetes Soc, NJ affil; adj prof, Sch Nursing, Univ Pa, 90- *Mem:* Endocrine Soc; Am Physiol Soc; fel NY Acad Sci; Am Soc Reproductive Med; Soc Study Reproduction; Am Asn Cancer Res; Soc Exp Biol Med; fel AAAS. *Res:* Hormone antagonists; fertility control; pregnancy, ova transport and reproduction; placenta; prostaglandins; ovulation; steroids; endocrine-tumor relationships and anti-cancer research; hormone treatment pre- and post- natally effects on hormonal and behavior responses; endocrine biochemistry; central nervous system-endocrine system relationship; adrenal physiology; growth and development; diabetes, atherosclerosis and endocrine in relation to stress, hormone, blood lipids; anti-inflammation; diabetes and reproduction, diabetes and cardiovascular system; awarded 35 patents; author of numerous publications. *Mailing Add:* Thomas Jefferson Univ Med Col Dept Pharmacol 1020 Locust St Philadelphia PA 19107. *Fax:* 215-923-7145, 923-7144

LERNER, LOUIS L(EONARD), COSMETIC CHEMISTRY, MEDICAL & HEALTH SCIENCES. *Current Pos:* RETIRED. *Personal Data:* b Chicago, Ill, Feb 25, 15; m 49, Jean M Sailing; c David L. *Educ:* Cent YMCA Col, BS, 42. *Prof Exp:* Chem asst, Universal Merchandise Co, 34, assoc chemist, 35-37; chief chemist, Russian Duchess Labs, 37; pres & dir res, LaLerne Labs, 37-40; dir res & prod, Consol Royal Chem Corp, 40-46; exec vpres & dir res & prod, Allied Home Prods Corp, 46-49; vpres & dir res, Kalech Res Labs, 49-50; vpres & dir res & new prod develop, Bymart, Inc, 50-52; sr scientist, Personal Care Div, Gillette Co, 52-74; consumer protection specialist, Fed Trad Comn, US Govt, 74, phys scientist, 75-95. *Concurrent Pos:* Dir, Brokers, Inc, 37-40; instr, Cent YMCA Col, 42-44; dir, AD Prods Corp, 64-66; consult, Seaquist Valve Co, 74-; ed, Chem Bull, Am Chem Soc, 71-77, consult ed, 78-80, ed, 91. *Mem:* Fel AAAS; Am Chem Soc; Soc Cosmetic Chem; NY Acad Sci; Nat Asn Sci Writers. *Res:* Product development, exploratory research; pharmaceuticals, proprietaries, cosmetics, detergents, emulsions, waving compositions, dyes and pigments; chemistry of polymers, proteins and enzymes; mechanical devices; surface chemistry; consumer products; environmental sciences; biology. *Mailing Add:* 900 N Lake Shore Dr Chicago IL 60611

LERNER, MELVIN, analytical chemistry; deceased, see previous edition for last biography

LERNER, MICHAEL PAUL, VIROLOGY, CELL BIOLOGY. *Current Pos:* SR SCI DEAN, McGEE EYE INST, 84- *Personal Data:* b Los Angeles, Calif, May 2, 41; m 65; c 2. *Educ:* Univ Calif, Los Angeles, BA, 63; Kans State Univ, MS, 67; Northwestern Univ, PhD(microbiol), 70. *Prof Exp:* Nat Inst Neurol Dis & Stroke fel, Univ Calif, Los Angeles, 70-71, asst res biologist neurochem, Ctr Health Sci, 72-73; assoc prof microbiol, Health Sci Ctr, Univ Okla, 73-84. *Concurrent Pos:* Fel, NATO Advan Study Inst, Italy, 72. *Mem:* Am Soc Microbiol. *Res:* Mammalian cell biochemistry and development. *Mailing Add:* 3136 Willow Brook Rd Oklahoma City OK 73120

LERNER, MOISEY, SOFTWARE LEGACY SYSTEMS, ELECTRICAL ENGINEERING & CHAOS ENGINEERING. *Current Pos:* PRES, TOMIN CORP, 82-, PATENT AGENT. *Personal Data:* b Kiev, USSR, May 15, 31; US citizen; wid; c Julia & Vladislav. *Educ:* Polytech Inst, USSR, MS, 53; Pedagogical Inst, BA, 54; Power Eng Inst, USSR, MS, 57, PhD(elec eng), 61. *Hon Degrees:* Docent, Supreme Cert Comn, Moscow, USSR, 64. *Prof Exp:* Asst prof physics, Inst Elec Commun, USSR, 62-68; asst prof elec eng, Air Force Mil Eng Acad, USSR, 68-73. *Concurrent Pos:* Dir res & develop, Sanford Process Corp, 75-80. *Mem:* Am Electroplaters Soc; Inst Elec & Electronics Engrs. *Res:* Low voltage hardcoating of aluminum; designing and maintaining large electrical and software systems; bottom line double entry accounting system; heat dissipation at non-sinusoidal voltages; taming chaos in product development and maintenance. *Mailing Add:* Tomin Corp PO Box 812206 Wellesley MA 02181. *Fax:* 781-449-8923

LERNER, NARCINDA REYNOLDS, CHEMICAL KINETICS. *Current Pos:* RES SCIENTIST, AMES RES CTR, NASA, 70- *Personal Data:* b Brooklyn, NY, Oct 10, 33; m 59, Lawrence S. *Educ:* Hofstra Univ, BA, 56; Univ Chicago, MS, 59, PhD(chem), 62. *Prof Exp:* Mem tech staff, Hughes Res Labs Labs, Calif, 62-63; res scientist, Lockheed Palo Alto Res Lab, 66-70. *Mem:* AAAS; Am Phys Soc. *Res:* Paramagnetic resonance; electron nuclear double resonance; crystalline field theory; crystal preparation; electrical properties of polymers; polymer degradation; abiotic synthesis of organic compounds. *Mailing Add:* Ames Res Ctr NASA MS 239-4 Moffett Field CA 94035

LERNER, NORMAN CONRAD, ENGINEERING ECONOMICS, INVESTMENT FEASIBILITY ANALYSIS. *Current Pos:* PRES, TRANSCOMM, INC, 69- *Personal Data:* b New York, NY, Feb 13, 36; wid; c Sheila & Julie. *Educ:* Mass Inst Technol, BS, 57; Columbia Univ, MBA, 61; Am Univ, PhD(math econ), 68. *Prof Exp:* Proj mgr, ITT/RCA Corp, 57-65 & Mitre Corp, 65-68; dir, Command Systs Div, Comput Sci Div, 68-71. *Concurrent Pos:* Spec asst to dir, Exec Off Pres, US Off Telecommun Policy, 71-72; assoc prof mgt sci, George Washington Univ; rep, US-Peoples Repub China Telecommun Protocol; partic, World Admin Radio Conf, Presidential Task Force Commun Policy, Cong Off Technol Assessment-Int Telecommun, NASA Joint Study Group-Satellite Commun Underdevelop Countries & FCC Cable TV Adv Panel; mem, US State Dept Comt Ctr Telecommun Develop, Int Telecommun Union. *Mem:* Nat Soc Prof Engrs; Am Econ Asn; Inst Elec & Electronics Engrs; Nat Asn Bus Economists. *Res:* Economic, financial and market development aspects of high technology industries in the US and overseas, particularly telecommunications and energy; Extensive writing addresses the privatization of telecommunications in developing countries. *Mailing Add:* 4527 Pickett Rd Fairfax VA 22042

LERNER, PAULINE, NEUROCHEMISTRY. *Current Pos:* CHEMIST, FOOD & DRUG ADMIN, 80- *Personal Data:* b Baltimore, Md, July 4, 48; div. *Educ:* Goucher Col, BA, 69; Univ Md, PhD(chem), 73. *Prof Exp:* Chemist, NIH, 74-80. *Mem:* AAAS; Asn Women Sci; Am Chem Soc; Am Soc Neurochem; Soc Neurosci. *Res:* Regulatory work in the area of nutrition and health. *Mailing Add:* 5202 Crossfield Ct Apt 9 Rockville MD 20852-2153

LERNER, RICHARD ALAN, IMMUNOLOGY. *Current Pos:* assoc immunol, 70-71, assoc mem, 71-73, PROF, DEPT CHEM & DIR, RES INST, SCRIPPS CLIN, LA JOLLA, CALIF, 74-, PRES, 91- *Personal Data:* b Chicago, Ill, Aug 26, 38; m 66; c 3. *Educ:* Stanford Univ, MD, 64. *Prof Exp:* Intern med, Stanford Univ, 64-65; USPHS grant, Scripps Clin & Found, 65-68; assoc cell biol, Wistar Inst, 68-70. *Concurrent Pos:* Consult, Nat Cancer Inst, 72- *Mem:* Nat Acad Sci; Am Soc Path; Biophys Soc; Am Soc Microbiol; Am Soc Immunol. *Res:* Molecular medicine; differentiation. *Mailing Add:* Dept Molecular Biol Res Inst Scripps Clin 10550 N Torrey Pines Rd La Jolla CA 92037

LERNER, RITA GUGGENHEIM, information science; deceased, see previous edition for last biography

LERNER, ROBERT GIBBS, HEMATOLOGY, HEMOSTASIS. *Current Pos:* from asst prof to assoc prof, 67-80, PROF MED & CHIEF HEMAT, NY MED COL, 80-, PROF PATH, 93-, ACTG CHMN, DEPT MED, 96- *Personal Data:* b Brooklyn, NY, Mar 3, 36; m 58; c 3. *Educ:* NY Univ, AB, 56, MD, 60. *Prof Exp:* Teaching asst, Sch Med, NY Univ, 61-62; instr, Sch Med, Univ Southern Calif, 65-67. *Concurrent Pos:* Prin investr var grants & projs, NY Med Col, 70-; consult, Food & Drug Admin, 75-78; bd dirs, Island Peer Rev Orgn, 90-; mem, Coun Thrombosis, Am Heart Asn. *Mem:* Fel Am Col Physicians; Am Soc Hemat; Nat Hemophilia Found. *Res:* Hematology, specifically hemostasis and thrombosis; clinical aspects of the diagnosis and treatment of hemorrhagic and thrombotic. *Mailing Add:* NY Med Col Valhalla NY 10595. *Fax:* 914-285-1156; *E-Mail:* lerner@nymc.edu

LEROI, GEORGE EDGAR, CHEMICAL PHYSICS. *Current Pos:* assoc prof, 67-72, PROF CHEM, MICH STATE UNIV, 72- *Personal Data:* b London, Eng, June 23, 36; US citizen; m 73; c 4. *Educ:* Univ Wis, BA, 56; Harvard Univ, AM, 58, PhD(chem), 60. *Honors & Awards:* Coblentz Prize, 72. *Prof Exp:* Res assoc chem, Univ Calif, Berkeley, 60-62; lectr, Princeton Univ, 62-64, asst prof, 64-67. *Concurrent Pos:* Guest prof, Lab Phys Chem, Swiss Fed Inst Technol, 74-75; Japan Soc Prom Sci vis prof, 77; Syncrotron Ultraviolet Radiation Facil fel, US Nat Bur Stand, 81-82; guest res, Brookhaven Nat Lab, 85; Ford Found fel, 52-56; mem, Phys Chem Div, Am Chem Soc. *Mem:* Am Phys Soc; Am Chem Soc. *Res:* Molecular spectroscopy and structure; vacuum ultraviolet, visible, infrared, far infrared, Raman; ion/molecule chemistry; laser spectroscopy and photochemistry. *Mailing Add:* Col Natural Sci Mich State Univ 103 Natural Sci Univ East Lansing MI 48824

LEROITH, DEREK, MEDICINE, DIABETES. *Current Pos:* vis scientist diabetes, 79-83, SR INVESTR DIABETES, NIH, 84- *Personal Data:* b Cape Town, SAfrica, Jan 3, 45; m 79; c 3. *Educ:* Univ Cape Town, MB, ChB, 67, PhD(med), 73. *Prof Exp:* Registr med, Univ Cape Town, SAfrica, 72-75; sr registr med, Middlesex Med Sch, London, England, 75; sr lectr med, Univ Ben Gurion, Israel, 76-79; assoc prof med, Univ Cincinnati, 83-84. *Mem:* Fel Am Col Physicians; Am Endocrine Soc. *Res:* Evolutionary origins of the vertebrate endocrine systems; hormonal substances in invertebrates; brain insulin receptors. *Mailing Add:* Diabetes Br NIH Bldg 10 Rm 8S239 Bethesda MD 20892-1770

LEROUX, EDGAR JOSEPH, INSECT ECOLOGY, ENTOMOLOGY. *Current Pos:* RETIRED. *Personal Data:* b Ottawa, Ont, Jan 23, 22; m 44, Ardis M Andrew; c Estelle, Pierre & Elizabeth. *Educ:* Carleton Univ, Can, BA, 50; McGill Univ, MSc, 52, PhD(entom), 54. *Hon Degrees:* DSc, McGill Univ, 73; DU, Univ Ottawa, 86. *Honors & Awards:* Grace Griswold lectr, Cornell Univ, 71; Jubilee Medal, Governor Gen Can, 77; Armand Frappier Medal, 84; Gold Medal, Entom Soc Can, 86; Golden Award, Can Feed Indust Asn, 86; Merit Award, Pub Serv Can, 87; Officer Order Can, Gov Gen Can, 88, Commemorative Medal Confederation Can, 92. *Prof Exp:* Asst entomologist, Fruit Insect Invests, Sci Serv, 49-50; res scientist, Res Br, Can Dept Agr, 50-62, res coordr, 65-68, asst dir gen, 68-75, dir gen, 75-78, asst dep minister res, 78-87. *Concurrent Pos:* Demonstr, MacDonald Col, McGill Univ, 50-51, asst, 53-54, lectr, 58-62, assoc prof, 62-65, hon prof, 70-71; mem orchard protection comt, Info & Res Serv, Que Dept Agr, 59-63, adv comt entom probs, Defense Res Bd, Dept Nat Defense, 64-67, panel experts integrated pest control, Food & Agr Orgn, 66-71; sci ed, Can J Plant Sci, 65-68; dir, Biol Coun Can, 66-70, pres, 70-71; off cor entom, Commonwealth Inst Biol Control, 67-73; Can rep, Int Soc Hort Sci, 67-73; mem, World Hort Coun, 68-70; pres Biol Coun Can, 70-71, Entom Soc Can, 69-70 & Entom Soc Que, 65-66; dir, Can Soc Zool, 68-70; negotiated grants comt & adv comt biol, Nat Res Coun, 73-78; vchmn, Agr Stabilization Bd & Agr Prod Bd, 77-80, Can Agr Res Coun, 77-87; Co-chmn, Can/USSR Agr Working Group & Can/Romania Comt Cooperation Agr, 81-87; chmn, comt agr, Orgn Environ Coop & Develop, 78-80, Fed Interdept Comt Pesticides, 78-87, assoc comt biotechnol, Nat Res Coun, 83-87; mem, coord comt, Can Agr Servs, 75-87, interdept comt, Can Ministry State Sci & Technol, 78-84, indept panel, Energy Mines & Resources Can, 78-87; mem, Nat Res Coun Can, 80-86, Nat Biotechnol Adv Comt, 83-87. *Mem:* Emer mem Entom Soc Can (pres, 69-70); Can Seed Grower's Asn; fel Agr Inst Can; Asn Advan Sci Can (hon treas, 70-72). *Res:* Insect ecology; integrated pest control; morphology; toxicology; author of over 100 publications and three memoirs books; quantitative population (dynamics) ecology studies of some key orchard, field and forest insect pests resulting in improved crop protection programs via integrated pest control approaches with heavy emphasis on use of beneficial species that feed on these crop pests. *Mailing Add:* 27 Keppler Cres Nepean ON K2H 5Y1 Can

LEROUX, EDMUND FRANK, HYDROLOGY. *Current Pos:* RETIRED. *Personal Data:* b Muskegon Heights, Mich, Mar 8, 25; m 49; c 3. *Educ:* Mich State Univ, BS, 48. *Prof Exp:* Geologist, US Geol Surv, 49-60, chief, Manpower Sect, 61-64, asst dist chief hydrol, 64- *Mem:* Am Geophys Union; Int Asn Hydrogeologists; AAAS. *Res:* Ground water temperature; hydrology of glacial terrain in a semiarid climate. *Mailing Add:* 1675 Illinois Ave SW Huron SD 57350-2469

LEROUX, PIERRE, MATHEMATICS. *Current Pos:* PROF MATH, UNIV QUE, MONTREAL, 71-, DIR, COMBINATORICS & MATH INFO LAB, 90- *Personal Data:* b Quebec City, Can, Aug 18, 42; m 64; c 2. *Educ:* Univ Montreal, BSc, 64, MSc, 66, PhD(math), 70. *Mem:* Can Math Soc; Am Math Soc; Soc Indust & Appl Math. *Res:* Enumerative combinatorics and special functions. *Mailing Add:* Math Dept Univ Que CP8888 Suce Centre-ville Montreal PQ H3C 3P8 Can

LEROY, ANDRE FRANCOIS, ANALYTICAL CHEMISTRY, PHYSICAL CHEMISTRY. *Current Pos:* CHIEF, ANALYTICAL METHODS, BIOMED ENG & INSTRUMENTATION BR, DIV RES SERV, NIH, 80- *Personal Data:* b Philadelphia, Pa, Sept 30, 33. *Educ:* Yale Univ, BE, 56; Calif Inst Technol, MS, 57; Harvard Univ, AM, 65, PhD(eng), 67. *Honors & Awards:* Clemens Herschel Prize; Commendation Medal, Pub Health Serv, 87. *Prof Exp:* Engr, Radiol Health Res Activ, USPHS, 58-60, res chemist, Northeastern Radiol Health Lab, Mass, 63-68; engr, NIH, Md, 69-78; mem staff, Sci Off, Am Embassy, Paris, France, 78-80. *Concurrent Pos:* Dir, Tech Equip Seminars, US Dept Com, France, 80, Spain, Italy, Greece, 81 & France & Belg, 83; coordr, Instrumentation & Biomed Eng Sci Res, NIH-Nat Inst Health & Med Res, France, 83-; div res serv rep, Fogarty Int Ctr, 84-; mem, Bd Sci Counrs, Life Sci Div, French AEC, 85-86; coordr, NIH-CGR Collab Res Prog in Magnetic Resonance Imaging, 86- *Mem:* Am Chem Soc; Am Inst Chem Engrs; Sigma Xi. *Res:* Physical chemistry of transition metal complexes; analytical chemical and ultra-trace level isolation, characterization and quantitation of metal complex species and kinetics of protein binding and their transformations in biological systems and natural waters; high spatial resolution analysis of elements by instrumental micro analysis (electron- probe); WDX and EDX, chromatography, neutron activation analysis. *Mailing Add:* 11705 College View Dr Wheaton MD 20902-2432

LEROY, CLAUDE, NUCLEAR PHYSICS, PARTICLE PHYSICS. *Current Pos:* attache res, dir, Nuclear Physics Lab, 91-94, 78-80, TITULAR PROF PHYSICS, UNIV MONTREAL, 90- *Personal Data:* b Charleroi, Hainaut, Belg, Sept 30, 47. *Educ:* Faculte St Louis, Brussels, Mathematique Speciale, 67; Univ Louvain, Belg, Lic en Sci, 71, DSc, 76. *Honors & Awards:* Rutherford Prize, Royal Soc Can, 88. *Prof Exp:* Res assoc, McGill Univ, Montreal, 77-80, Northwestern Univ, Evanston, Ill, 80-81; researcher, Dept Develop Sci, Univ Louvain, 81-83; res scientist, Inst Particle Physics, Montreal, 83-90. *Concurrent Pos:* Vis res fel, Univ Southampton, Eng, 76-77; sci assoc, Ctr Europ Res Nuclear Physics, Geneva, Switz, 80-, Dept Energetics, Univ Florence, 95-; assoc prof, McGill Univ, 83-90; Killam res fel, Can Coun, 93-95; hon prof, Nat Univ Peru, 94- *Mem:* Fel Royal Soc Can; Inst Particle Physics Can; Can Inst Physicists; Acad Sci III; Royal Soc. *Res:* Nuclear physics; particle physics; instrumentation, high energy physics; author & co-author of over 300 scientific journals and reviews. *Mailing Add:* Nuclear Physics Lab Univ Montreal CP 6128 Succursale Ave Montreal PQ H3C 3J7 Can. *Fax:* 514-343-6215; *E-Mail:* leroyzp@lps.umontreal.ca

LEROY, EDWARD CARWILE, RHEUMATOLOGY. *Current Pos:* chmn, Dept Phys Med & Rehab, 82-91, prof med & dir, Div Rheumatology & Immunol, Dept Med, 75-95, PROF & CHMN, DEPT MICROBIOL & IMMUNOL, MED UNIV SC, CHARLESTON, 95- *Personal Data:* b Elizabeth City, NC, Jan 19, 33; m 60, Garnette; c DeFord & Carwile. *Educ:*

Wake Forest Univ, Winston-Salem, BS, 55; Univ NC, Chapel Hill, MS, 58, MD, 60; Am Bd Internal Med, dipl, 67. *Prof Exp:* Med internship & asst residency, Presby Hosp, Columbia-Presby Med Ctr, NY, 60-62; clin assoc, Nat Heart Inst, Bethesda, Md, 62-65; fel arthritis, Columbia Univ Col Physicians & Surgeons, 65-66, assoc, 66-67, from asst prof to assoc prof, Dept Med, 67-75, dir, Div Rheumatic Dic, 71-75. *Concurrent Pos:* NIH spec fel, 65-67; asst attend physician, Presby Hosp, NY, 67-70, assoc attend physician & dir, Edward Daniels Faulkner Arthritis Clin, 70-75, mem & chmn, var comts, Am Rheumatism Asn, 67-, Am Col Rheumatology, 89- & Am Col Physicians, 75-80; vis prof & lectr, numerous US & foreign univs, 69-91; Fogarty sr int fel endothelial cell biol, US Dept Health & Human Serv, 82-83; sabbatical, Corpus Christi Col, Cambridge Univ, Eng, 82-83. *Mem:* Sigma Xi; fel Am Rheumatism Asn; Am Col Rheumatology; fel Am Col Physicians; AAAS; Am Asn Immunologists. *Res:* Mechanisms involved in human connective tissue diseases; immunology; molecular and cellular mechanisms of fibrosis in the context of autoimmune disease, especially scleroderma; author of numerous medical publications. *Mailing Add:* Dept Microbiol & Immunol Med Univ SC 171 Ashley Ave Charleston SC 29425. *Fax:* 803-792-2464

LEROY, ROBERT FREDERICK, NEUROLOGY, ELECTROENCEPHALOGRAPHY. *Current Pos:* ASST PROF & DIR CLIN NEUROPHYSIOL, DEPT NEUROL, HEALTH SCI CTR, SOUTHWESTERN MED SCH, UNIV TEX, 82- *Personal Data:* b Passaic, NJ, July 24, 50; m 74; c 2. *Educ:* Brown Univ, AB, 72; Pa State Univ, MD, 77. *Prof Exp:* Intern, Dept Med, Baltimore City Hosp, 77-78; resident neurol, Dept Neurol, Sch Med, Yale Univ, 78-81, fel, Merritt Pulnam Epilepsy Found Am, 81-82. *Concurrent Pos:* Consult, Dallas Tex Vet Admin, Med Ctr, 82. *Mem:* Am Acad Neurol. *Res:* Electroencephalography and general clinical neurophysiology as it pertains to epilepsy and its treatments. *Mailing Add:* 5323 Harry Hines Arlington TX 75235-7200

LEROY, ROBERT JAMES, INTERMOLECULAR FORCES, MOLECULAR CLUSTERS. *Current Pos:* From asst prof to assoc prof, 72-82, PROF CHEM, UNIV WATERLOO, 82- *Personal Data:* b Ottawa, Ont, Sept 30, 43; m 67, Virginia T; c 4. *Educ:* Univ Toronto, BSc, 65, MSc, 67; Univ Wis-Madison, PhD(chem), 71. *Honors & Awards:* Rutherford Mem Medal, Royal Soc Can, 84. *Concurrent Pos:* A P Sloan Found fel, 74, sr vis fel, Sci Res Coun UK, 76 & J S Guggenheim Mem Found fel, 79; invited prof, Univ Paris-S Orsay, France, 82; dir, Guelph-Waterloo Ctr Grad Work Chem, 82-85. *Mem:* Can Asn Physicists; fel Chem Inst Can; Am Phys Soc; Am Chem Soc. *Res:* Empirical methods for determining intermolecular forces in simple systems; understanding and predicting the properties of simple molecules and molecular clusters. *Mailing Add:* Guelph-Waterloo Ctr Grad Work Chem Univ Waterloo Waterloo ON N2L 3G1 Can. *Fax:* 519-746-0435; *E-Mail:* leroy@theochem.uwaterloo.ca

LEROY, RODNEY LASH, PHYSICAL CHEMISTRY, ELECTROCHEMISTRY. *Current Pos:* MGR ENERGY & PROD APPLICATIONS LAB, NORANDA TECHNOL CTR, 88- *Personal Data:* b Ottawa, Ont, Nov 15, 41; m 83; c 6. *Educ:* Univ Toronto, BSc, 64, MA, 65, PhD(phys chem), 68; McGill Univ, dipl 78, MBA, 83. *Prof Exp:* Fel phys chem, Univ Colo & Yale Univ, 68-70; assoc scientist chem, Noranda Res Ctr, 70-72, group leader electrochem, 72-78, prin scientist electrochem, 78-79, prog mgr res, 78-79; tech dir, Electrolyser Inc, 80-85, exec vpres, 85-88. *Mem:* Fel Chem Inst Can; Electrochem Soc; Nat Asn Corrosion Engrs; Int Asn Hydrogen Energy; Soc Petrol Engrs; Soc Explor Geophysicists; Petrol Soc. *Res:* Corrosion research; electrometallurgy of non-ferrous metals, especially copper and zinc; hydrogen production by electrolysis of water; petroleum engineering. *Mailing Add:* Noranda Advan Mat 4950 Levy St Ste-Laurent PQ H4R 2P1 Can

LERSTEN, NELS R, BOTANY. *Current Pos:* From asst prof to assoc prof, 63-70, PROF BOT, IOWA STATE UNIV, 70- *Personal Data:* b Chicago, Ill, Aug 6, 32; m 58; c 3. *Educ:* Univ Chicago, BS, 58, MS, 60; Univ Calif, Berkeley, PhD(bot), 63. *Mem:* Bot Soc Am; Sigma Xi. *Res:* Systematic and developmental anatomy of angiosperms; embryology of flowering plants. *Mailing Add:* Dept Bot Iowa State Univ Ames IA 50011-1020

LERTORA, JUAN J L, PHARMACOLOGY, INTERNAL MEDICINE. *Current Pos:* PROF PHARMACOL & MED, TULANE UNIV, SCH MED, 70-, HEAD, SECT CLIN PHARMACOL, 74- *Res:* Pharmacology; internal medicine. *Mailing Add:* Tulane Univ Sch Med 1430 Tulane Ave New Orleans LA 70112-2699

LES, DONALD HENRY, AQUATIC ANGIOSPERM SYSTEMATICS, ANGIOSPERM EVOLUTION. *Current Pos:* ASSOC PROF PLANT SYSTS, UNIV CONN, 92- *Personal Data:* b Detroit, Mich, Mar 26, 54; m 78, Jane E Rohn; c Katherine R & Angela M. *Educ:* Eastern Mich Univ, BS, 76, MS, 80; Ohio State Univ, PhD(bot), 86. *Prof Exp:* Asst prof biol, Univ Wis, Milwaukee, 86-92, assoc prof, 92. *Mem:* Am Soc Plant Taxonomists; Bot Soc Am; Soc Study Evolution; Int Asn Plant Taxonomists. *Res:* Systematics, evolution, conservation and ecology of aquatic angiosperms using morphological, biochemical and molecular data. *Mailing Add:* Dept Ecol & Evolutionary Biol Univ Conn U-42 Storrs CT 06269-3042. *Fax:* 860-486-4320; *E-Mail:* les@uconnvm.uconn.edu

LES, EDWIN PAUL, LABORATORY ANIMAL SCIENCE. *Current Pos:* RETIRED. *Personal Data:* b Adams, Mass, Dec 28, 23; m 67; c 2. *Educ:* Northeastern Univ, BS, 52; Ohio State Univ, MS, 53; PhD(genetics), 59. *Prof Exp:* Assoc staff scientist, Jackson Lab, 59-60; biologist, Biol Div, Oak Ridge Nat Lab, 60-62; staff scientist, Jackson Lab, 62-75, sr staff scientist, 75-90. *Mem:* Am Asn Lab Animal Sci. *Res:* Effect of environment on reproduction, growth and survival of laboratory mice; mouse husbandry techniques and practices; laboratory animal ecology. *Mailing Add:* Indian Point Rd Bar Harbor ME 04609

LESAGE, LEO G, NUCLEAR ENGINEERING, REACTOR PHYSICS. *Current Pos:* Nuclear engr, Fast Breeder Reactor Develop, 66-81, dir, Appl Physics Div, 81-88, DIR, ENG PHYSICS DIV, ARGONNE NAT LAB, 88- *Personal Data:* b Concordia, Kans, Apr 15, 35; m 58, Carolyn Bailey; c Annette G & Marietta L. *Educ:* Univ Kans, BS, 57; Stanford Univ, MS, 62, PhD(nuclear eng), 66; Univ Chicago, MBA, 81. *Concurrent Pos:* US mem, Comt on Reactor Physics, Nuclear Energy Agency, 81- *Mem:* Fel Am Nuclear Soc. *Res:* Fast reactor physics; fast reactor critical experiments; research management. *Mailing Add:* 303 N Third St Watseka IL 60970. *Fax:* 630-252-5318

LESAGE, SUZANNE, REMEDIATION TECHNOLOGIES FOR GROUNDWATER CONTAMINATED WITH SOLVENTS OR PETROLEUM, ANALYTICAL METHODS FOR HAZARDOUS WASTES. *Current Pos:* res chemist, 86-89, RES SCIENTIST GROUNDWATER, NAT WATER RES INST, ENVIRON CAN, 89- *Personal Data:* b Quebec City, Que, Mar 23, 52; div; c Francois Patrinieri & Bruno Paltrinieri. *Educ:* Univ Ottawa, BSc, 73; McGill Univ, PhD(chem), 77. *Prof Exp:* Fel, Agr Can, 77-78, res scientist, 78-80; head, Org Chem Lab, Wastewater Technol Ctr, 80-86. *Concurrent Pos:* Conf chair, In-situ Bioremediation, 90-92. *Mem:* Am Chem Soc; Soc Environ Toxicol & Chem; Am Soc Testing & Mat. *Res:* Remediation of groundwater contaminated with solvents, petroleum or landfill leachate, using biological or biochemical methods; methods and apparatus for the analysis of organic contaminants in groundwater and soil. *Mailing Add:* Groundwater Remediation NWRI Environ Can Burlington ON L7R 4A6 Can. *Fax:* 905-336-4972

LESCARBOURA, JAIME AQUILES, PETROLEUM ENGINEERING. *Current Pos:* res assoc, 84-90, SR STAFF ENGR, CONOCO, INC, 91- *Personal Data:* b Barcelona, Spain, Aug 29, 37; US citizen; m 57; c 2. *Educ:* Univ Kans, BS, 59, PhD(chem eng), 67; Univ Wis-Madison, MS, 61. *Prof Exp:* Engr, Cardon Refinery, Shell Oil Co Venezuela, 61-63; res scientist, Continental Oil Co, 67-76, sr res scientist, 76-82, staff eng, 82-84. *Concurrent Pos:* Am Oil Found fel, 66-67. *Mem:* Soc Petrol Engrs; Soc Rheology. *Res:* Flow of Newtonian and non-Newtonian fluids; falling cylinder viscometer for non-Newtonian fluids; turbulent flow drag reduction by addition of polymers; well testing; formation evaluation; rheology of crosslinked gels, drilling muds, waxy crudes and viscous crudes; well stimulation by blasting. *Mailing Add:* 3606 Wildwood Dr San Angelo TX 76904

LESER, ERNST GEORGE, ORGANIC CHEMISTRY. *Current Pos:* Res chemist, Jackson Lab, 69-74, prod supvr, Chamber Works, 74-84, sr res chemist, Jackson Lab, 84-90, RES ASSOC, JACKSON LAB, E I DU PONT DE NEMOURS & CO, INC, 90- *Personal Data:* b Mineola, NY, May 3, 43; m 69; c 3. *Educ:* Bucknell Univ, BS, 65; Fordham Univ, PhD(org chem), 70. *Mem:* Am Chem Soc. *Res:* Supervision of dyes and intermediates production; fluorochemical research; tetraethyl lead process assistance. *Mailing Add:* Zorioles Nest Glen Farms Elkton MD 21921-2039

LESER, RALPH ULRICH, INTERNAL MEDICINE. *Current Pos:* RETIRED. *Personal Data:* b Bloomington, Ind, Dec 31, 05; m 66; c 2. *Educ:* Ind Univ, AB, 27, MD, 30; Am Bd Internal Med, dipl, 44. *Prof Exp:* Intern, Philadelphia Gen Hosp, Pa, 30-32; fel internal med, Mayo Clin, 34-37; from instr to assoc med, Ind Univ, Indianapolis, 38-50, asst prof, 50-67, assoc prof med, Sch Med, 67-88. *Concurrent Pos:* Vis physician, Marion Co Gen Hosp, 38-, chief, Diag Clin, 46-58; vis physician, Methodist, St Vincents & Community Hosps. *Mem:* AMA; fel Am Col Physicians. *Res:* Cardiology; diseases of metabolism; gastroenterology. *Mailing Add:* 5434 Ashurst St Indianapolis IN 46220

LESH, THOMAS ALLAN, PHYSIOLOGY. *Current Pos:* asst prof, 72-77, ASSOC PROF PHYSIOL & HEALTH SCI, BALL STATE UNIV & MUNCIE CTR MED EDUC, 77- *Personal Data:* b Chicago, Ill, Aug 6, 29; m 79. *Educ:* Mich State Univ, BS, 51; Ind Univ, PhD(physiol), 68. *Prof Exp:* Assoc ed, Howard W Sams & Co, Inc, Ind, 55-63; USPHS cardiovasc trainee, Bowman Gray Sch Med, 68-70; asst prof physiol, Med Ctr, Univ Ark, Little Rock, 70-72. *Mem:* Asn Am Physiol Soc; Sigma Xi. *Res:* Control of blood flow. *Mailing Add:* 15803 Massey Rd Hagerstown IN 47346-9736

LESHER, DEAN ALLEN, clinical pharmacology, nephrology; deceased, see previous edition for last biography

LESHER, GARY ALLEN, PHARMACOLOGY, DRUG METABOLISM. *Current Pos:* ASST PROF PHARMACOL, SCH PHARM, UNIV MD, 77- *Personal Data:* b Chicago, Ill, June 29, 50; m 73; c 2. *Educ:* Carroll Col, Wis, BS, 72; Purdue Univ, West Lafayette, MS, 75, PhD(pharmacol), 77. *Mem:* Am Asn Col Pharm. *Res:* Narcotic drug dependence and drug interactions in narcotic dependent animals, effects of narcotics on drug metabolism; effects of environmental contaminants on drug metabolism; toxicology. *Mailing Add:* Dept Basic & Health Sci Ill Col Optom 3241 S Michigan Ave Chicago IL 60616-3816

LESH-LAURIE, GEORGIA ELIZABETH, DEVELOPMENTAL BIOLOGY. *Current Pos:* VCHANCELLOR ACAD AFFAIRS, UNIV COLO. *Personal Data:* b Cleveland, Ohio, July 28, 38; m 69. *Educ:* Marietta Col, BS, 60; Univ Wis, MS, 61; Case Western Res Univ, PhD(biol), 66. *Prof Exp:* Instr biol, Case Western Res Univ, 65-66; asst prof biol sci, State Univ NY Albany, 66-69; from asst prof to assoc prof biol, Western Res Col, Case Western Res Univ, 69-77, asst dean, 73-76; chmn, Dept Biol, Cleveland State Univ, 77-81,prof biol, 77-, dean, Col Grad Studies, 81-86, dean, Col Arts & Sci, 86-, interim provost, 89-90. *Concurrent Pos:* NY State Res Found res fel, 66-67; USPHS instnl grant, 70-71; Am Cancer Soc grants, 68-71 & 77-80; Res Corp grant, 71; Am Cancer Soc instnl grant, 73; Am Heart Asn Grant, 82-83; Wright fel, Bermuda Biol Sta, 84. *Mem:* AAAS; Am Soc Zool; Soc Develop Biol; NY Acad Sci; Am Soc Cell Biol. *Res:* Study of the neural control of developmental events in cnidarian systems and the role of nematocyst products on the mammalian cardiovascular system. *Mailing Add:* VChancellor Acad Affairs Univ Colo Campus Box 137 Denver CO 80217-0001

LESHNER, ALAN IRVIN, PSYCHOPHYSIOLOGY. *Current Pos:* dep dir, 88-90, actg dir, 90-94, DIR, NAT INST DRUG ABUSE, NIMH, 94- *Personal Data:* b Lewisburg, Pa, Feb 11, 44; m 69; c 2. *Educ:* Franklin & Marshall Col, AB, 65; Rutgers Univ, MS, 67, PhD(psychol), 69. *Prof Exp:* From asst prof to prof psychol, Bucknell Univ, 69-81; proj mgr, NSF, 80-82, dep exec dir, NSB comn on precol educ, 82-83, dep dir, Div Behav & Neurol Sci, 83-85, exec dir, Behav & Social Sci, 85-87; dir, Off S & T Ctrs Develop, 88. *Concurrent Pos:* NIMH res grant, 70-71 & 78-80; NSF res grant, 70-72 & 75-77; Fulbright lectr, Weizmann Inst, Israel, 77-78; vis scientist, Wis Regional Primate Res Ctr, 76-77. *Mem:* AAAS; fel Am Psychol Asn; Soc Neurosci; fel NY Acad Sci. *Res:* Biological basis of behavior; current and emerging science and technology policy issues; precollege and college level mathematics and science education. *Mailing Add:* Dir Nat Inst Drug Abuse NIH 5600 Fishers Lane Rm 10-05 Rockville MD 20857

LESHT, BARRY MARK, PHYSICAL LIMNOLOGY, ENVIRONMENTAL SYSTEMS ANALYSIS. *Current Pos:* asst physicist, 79-84, physicist & group leader, 85-92, ASSOC DIV DIR, ARGONNE NAT LAB, 93- *Personal Data:* b Chicago, Ill, Nov 29, 48; m 80, Kay L Schichtel; c Alison & Deanna. *Educ:* Wash Univ, St Louis, BS, 71; Univ Chicago, MS, 73, PhD(geophys scis), 77. *Honors & Awards:* Anderson-Everett Award, Int Asn Great Lakes Res, 94. *Prof Exp:* Res assoc, Grad Sch Oceanog, Univ RI, 77; Nat Res Coun resident fel, Atlantic Oceanog & Meteorol Labs, 78. *Concurrent Pos:* Consult, S Fla Water Mgt Dist, NY Great Lakes Res Consortium & Int Joint Comn, 92. *Mem:* Int Asn Great Lakes Res (treas, 89-92, secy, 93-); Am Geophys Union; Am Meteorol Soc; Int Asn Math Geol. *Res:* Systems analysis modeling of environmental systems; applications of non-parametric statistical analysis to environmental data; design and optimization of environmental sampling networks; analysis of satellite remote sensing data for studies of the Great Lakes. *Mailing Add:* 9700 S Cass Ave Argonne IL 60439. *Fax:* 630-252-2959; *E-Mail:* bmlesht@anl.gov

LESIEUTRE, BERNARD CHARLES, POWER SYSTEM ENGINEERING. *Current Pos:* ASST PROF ELEC ENG, MASS INT TECHNOL, 93- *Personal Data:* b Detroit, Mich, Jan 19, 64. *Educ:* Univ Ill, BS, 86, MS, 88, PhD(elec eng), 93. *Mem:* Inst Elec & Electronics Engrs. *Res:* Modeling, monitoring and analysis of large scale power systems. *Mailing Add:* Mass Inst Technol 10-091 77 Massachusetts Ave Cambridge MA 02139

LESIKAR, ARNOLD VINCENT, CHEMICAL PHYSICS, PHYSICS. *Current Pos:* PROF PHYSICS, ST CLOUD STATE UNIV, 66- *Personal Data:* b Galveston, Tex, Nov 3, 37; m 76. *Educ:* Rice Univ, BS, 58; Calif Inst Technol, PhD(physics), 65. *Prof Exp:* Res asst physics, Calif Inst Technol, 60-65; asst physics, Tech Univ, Munich, Ger, 65-66. *Concurrent Pos:* Vis prof chem physics, Cath Univ Am, 78- *Mem:* Sigma Xi; Am Chem Soc; Am Asn Physics Teachers; Am Phys Soc. *Mailing Add:* 1708 Red Fox Rd St Cloud MN 56301

LESK, MICHAEL E, COMPUTER & INFORMATION SCIENCE. *Current Pos:* mem staff, Comput Sci Res Lab, Bell Labs, 69-83, exec dir, Comput Sci Res Dept, 83-95, CHIEF RES SCIENTIST, INFO SCI RES LAB, BELLCORE, 95- *Personal Data:* b Brooklyn, NY, May 21, 45; m 68. *Educ:* Harvard Univ, BA, 64, MA, 66, PhD(chem phys), 69. *Concurrent Pos:* Adj lectr comput sci, Columbia Univ, 83-85; sr res fel, Univ Col London, 87. *Mem:* Fel Asn Comput Mach; Am Soc Info Sci. *Res:* Word processing; programming languages; computer systems; information retrieval. *Mailing Add:* Bell Commun Res Lab 435 South St Rm 2A-385 Morristown NJ 07960. *Fax:* 973-829-5981

LESKO, KEVIN THOMAS, FISSION PROPERTIES. *Current Pos:* fel, 85-87, STAFF SCIENTIST II & PHYSICIST, NUCLEAR SCI DIV, LAWRENCE BERKELEY LAB, 87- *Personal Data:* b Apr 30, 56. *Educ:* Leland Stanford, Jr Univ, BS, 78; Univ Wash, PhD(physics), 83. *Prof Exp:* Postdoctoral fel, Argonne Nat Lab, 83-85. *Concurrent Pos:* Tandem Accelerator Operator, Stanford Nuclear Physics Lab, 76-78; teaching asst, Stanford Physics Dept, Stanford Univ, 77-78; res asst, Nuclear Physics Lab, Univ Wash, 78-83, Accelerator Operator Instr, 81-83. *Mem:* Am Phys Soc. *Res:* Author of several scientific journals. *Mailing Add:* Univ Calif Lawrence Berkeley Lab Bldg 88 One Cyclotron Rd 50-208 LBL Berkeley CA 94720

LESKO, PATRICIA MARIE, POLYMER CHEMISTRY. *Current Pos:* chemist polymer chem, Res Labs, 75-91, RES FEL, ROHM & HAAS CO, 91- *Personal Data:* b Oakland, Calif, Jan 19, 47; m 93, Ronald W Novak. *Educ:* Rice Univ, BA, 68, MS, 72, PhD(org chem), 73. *Prof Exp:* Fel org chem, Syntex Corp, 73-75. *Mem:* AAAS; Am Chem Soc. *Res:* Emulsion polymers; coatings; leather chemistry; latex film formation. *Mailing Add:* Rohm & Haas Co 727 Norristown Rd Spring House PA 19477. *E-Mail:* rsspml@rohvm1

LESKO, STEPHEN ALBERT, BIOCHEMISTRY. *Current Pos:* Instr, Johns Hopkins Univ, 65-68, res assoc, 68-73, asst prof, 73-82, assoc prof biophys, 82-90, ASSOC PROF ENVIRON HEALTH SCI, JOHNS HOPKINS UNIV, 82-, ASSOC PROF BIOCHEM, 90- *Personal Data:* b Cassandra, Pa, Dec 30, 31; m 81. *Educ:* Ind Univ, Pa, BS, 59; Univ Md, PhD(biochem), 65. *Mem:* AAAS; Am Chem Soc; Am Asn Cancer Res. *Res:* Chemical carcinogenesis; nucleic acid chemistry and biology; oxygen toxicity; chromosome topography in interphase nuclei; relationship between DNA damage and cellular responses in the carcinogenic process; quantification of gene expression at the single cell level; gene mapping. *Mailing Add:* Dept Biochem 3rd Floor Johns Hopkins Univ Baltimore MD 21205-2191

LESLEY, FRANK DAVID, ANALYSIS. *Current Pos:* From asst prof to assoc prof, 70-77, PROF MATH, SAN DIEGO STATE UNIV, 77- *Personal Data:* b El Paso, Tex, Dec 20, 44; m 67; c 2. *Educ:* Stanford Univ, BS, 66; Univ Calif, San Diego, MA, 68, PhD(math), 70. *Mem:* Am Math Soc. *Res:* Boundary behavior of conformal mappings, including minimal surfaces and approximation theory. *Mailing Add:* Dept Math San Diego State Univ San Diego CA 92182-0001

LESLIE, CHARLES MILLER, MEDICAL ANTHROPOLOGY. *Current Pos:* prof, 76-91, EMER PROF, CTR SCI & CULT, UNIV DEL, 91- *Personal Data:* b Lake Village, Ark, Nov 8, 23; m 46, Zelda Solda; c Mario, Mira & Sam. *Educ:* Univ Chicago, PhB, 49, MA, 50, PhD(anthrop), 59. *Prof Exp:* Instr anthrop, Southern Methodist Univ, 50-51; instr, Univ Minn, 54-56; from instr to assoc prof, Pomona Col, 56-65; vis prof, Univ Wash, 65; assoc prof, Case Western Res Univ, 66-67; chmn, Anthrop Dept, Univ Col, NY Univ, 67-71, prof, 67-76. *Concurrent Pos:* NSF fel, Sch Oriental & African Studies, Univ London, 62-63; res assoc, Dept Anthrop, Univ Chicago, 74-75; NSF res grant, 74 & 76; med anthrop ed, Social Sci & Med, 77-89; vis prof, Univ Calif, Berkeley, 87 & Harvard Med Sch, 92; vis prof anthrop, McGill Univ, 93 & Univ Calif, Berkeley, 95. *Mem:* Fel AAAS; fel Am Anthrop Asn; fel Royal Anthrop Inst Gt Brit & Ireland; Am Ethnological Soc; Soc Med Anthrop; Soc Latin Am Anthrop. *Res:* World view and social change in India and Latin America; comparative study of medical systems. *Mailing Add:* Med Scholars Prog Univ Del Newark DE 19716

LESLIE, GERRIE ALLEN, IMMUNOLOGY, IMMUNOCHEMISTRY. *Current Pos:* PRES, IMMUNOL CONSULTS LAB INC, 77- *Personal Data:* b Red Deer, Alta, Nov 19, 41; m 65, Anna Ladefoged; c Kirsten & John G. *Educ:* Univ Alta, BSc, 62, MSc, 65; Univ Hawaii, PhD(microbiol), 68. *Prof Exp:* From asst prof to assoc prof microbiol, Sch Med, Tulane Univ, 70-74; assoc prof microbiol & immunol, Ore Health Sci Univ, 74-81, prof, 81-86. *Concurrent Pos:* USPHS fel, Col Med, Univ Fla, 68-70; adj assoc prof microbiol, Sch Med, Tulane Univ, 74-80; res affil, Delta Regional Primate Res Ctr, Covington, La; NL Tartat res fel, 77 & 82. *Mem:* Am Asn Immunol; Am Soc Microbiol; Am Hereford Asn. *Res:* Phylogeny of immunoglobulin structure and function; regulation of the immune response; secretory immunologic system; immunoglobulin D. *Mailing Add:* Immunol Consults Lab Inc 23891 Warbler Pl Sherwood OR 97140

LESLIE, JAMES, PHARMACEUTICAL CHEMISTRY. *Current Pos:* asst prof, 63-66, assoc prof med chem, 66-79, ASSOC PROF PHARM, SCH PHARM, UNIV MD, BALTIMORE, 79- *Personal Data:* b Belfast, Ireland, Apr 25, 34; m 64, Louisa; c Ethel, Thyra & David. *Educ:* Queen's Univ, Belfast, BSc, 56, PhD(chem), 59. *Prof Exp:* Fel, Okla State Univ, 59-61, asst prof & res assoc, 61-62; asst prof chem, Wash Col, 62-63. *Concurrent Pos:* NIH res grant, 64, vis, Dept Clin Physics & Bioeng, Western Regional Hosp Bd, Glasgow, Scotland, 71-72. *Mem:* Am Chem Soc; Am Asn Cols Pharm. *Res:* Kinetics of processes of biological interest; drug analysis. *Mailing Add:* Univ Md Sch Pharm 100 Penn St No 540 Baltimore MD 21201-1082. *Fax:* 410-706-6580

LESLIE, JAMES C, MANUFACTURING TECHNOLOGY, ADVANCED COMPOSITE MATERIALS. *Current Pos:* DIR ENG, PRES & CHIEF EXEC OFFICER, ADVAN COMPOSITES & TECHNOL INC, 80- *Personal Data:* b Berlin, Pa, July 14, 33; m, Dayle K Hess; c James C II, Lori E, Leanne M, John C & Nicole (Hansen). *Educ:* Pa State Univ, BSc, 56; Ohio State Univ, MSc, 58, PhD(chem eng), 64. *Honors & Awards:* Judd Hall Award Outstanding Contrib to Composites Mfg, Can Mfrs Asn/Soc Mfg Engrs, 97. *Prof Exp:* Asst chem anal, Pa State Univ, 55-56; eng exp sta, Ohio State Univ, 56-57, Dept Chem Eng, 57-58, fel, 58-59, res asst chem eng, Res Found, 59-62; sr res engr, Adv Develop Dept, Hercules Inc, 62-64, group leader, Thermal Anal & High Temp Res & Develop, 64-65, supvr, Rocket Nozzle, Case Bond & Insulation Groups, 65-66, group supvr, Composite Struct Group, 66-68; mgr, Advan Composite Prods, Reliable Mfg, 75-76; contractor, Jim Leslie Consults, 76-80. *Concurrent Pos:* Instr, Frostburg State Col, 62-63 & WVa Univ Exten Serv, Allegany Ballistics Lab, 64-65; mgr mkt & eng, Advan Composite Pipe & Tube, 77-81; mem nat bd adv, Composites Mfg Asn-SME, 91- *Mem:* Fel Soc Mfg Engrs; Soc Advan Mat & Process Eng (first vpres, 73, pres, 74). *Res:* Research and development; consultant; prototype and process development in many areas of advanced composite materials fabrication; tracer techniques; development of graphite fibers; advanced composite materials & manufacturing techniques. *Mailing Add:* Advan Composite Prods & Technol Inc 15602 Chemical Lane Huntington Beach CA 92649-1507. *Fax:* 714-895-7766

LESLIE, JAMES D, SOLID STATE PHYSICS. *Current Pos:* Asst prof, 63-68, PROF PHYSICS, UNIV WATERLOO, 68- *Personal Data:* b Toronto, Ont, July 6, 35; m 64; c 3. *Educ:* Univ Toronto, BASc, 57; Univ Ill, MS, 60, PhD(physics), 63. *Mem:* Am Phys Soc; Can Asn Physicists. *Res:* Low temperature physics; far infrared spectroscopy; superconductivity; electron tunneling. *Mailing Add:* Dept Physics Univ Waterloo 200 Univ Ave W Waterloo ON N2L 3G1 Can

LESLIE, JEROME RUSSELL, WORD PROCESSING & ELECTRONIC DELIVERY OF NEWS RELEASES, PHOTOGRAPHY. *Current Pos:* AGR NEWS ED, SDAK STATE UNIV, 78- *Personal Data:* b Luverne, Minn, Oct 11, 39; m 64; c 3. *Educ:* SDak State Univ, BS, 62, MS, 90. *Prof Exp:* Reporter-photogr, Watertown Pub Opinion, SDak, 62-63; reporter-photogr & deskman, Sioux City J, Iowa, 63-73; state ed, Brookings Daily Reporter, SDak, 73-78. *Mem:* Int Agr Commun Educ. *Res:* Evaluating electronic transfer and other news delivery methods; articles on plant science, animal science, veterinary science, dairy science and economics. *Mailing Add:* 206 Eighth St Brookings SD 57006. *Fax:* 605-688-4018

LESLIE, JOHN FRANKLIN, FUNGAL GENETICS. *Current Pos:* from asst prof to assoc prof, 84-96, PROF PLANT PATH, KANS STATE UNIV, MANHATTAN, 96- *Personal Data:* b Dallas, Tex, July 2, 53; m 76, Ingelin Lono; c Timothy F & Inger J. *Educ:* Univ Dallas, BA, 75; Univ Wis-Madison, MS, 77, PhD(genetics), 79. *Prof Exp:* Fel trainee, NIH, Lab Genetics, Univ Wis-Madison, 76-79; fel res affil, Dept Biol Sci, Stanford Univ, Calif, 79-81; res microbiologist genetics, Int Mineral & Chem Corp, 81-84. *Concurrent Pos:* Tech adv, Inst Christian Resources, San Jose, Calif, 81-; sr res assoc, Dept Biol Sci, Stanford Univ, Stanford, Calif, 92-93; assoc ed, Mycologia, 94-97; vis prof, Dept Microbiol, Nat Univ Rio Cuaito, Arg, 96; ed, Appl & Environ Microbiol, 97- *Mem:* Genetics Soc Am; Mycol Soc Am; Am Soc Microbiol; Brit Mycol Soc; Soc Gen Microbiol; Am Phytopath Soc. *Res:* Molecular, classical and population genetics of filamentous fungi, especially Neurospora and Fusarium; stability of transformed DNA in fungi, genetics of mycotoxins in F-moniliforme; genetics of nit mutants and vegetative compatibility. *Mailing Add:* Dept Plant Path 4002 Throckmorton Plant Sci Ctr Kans State Univ Manhattan KS 66506-5502. *Fax:* 785-532-2414; *E-Mail:* jfl@plantpath.pp.ksu.edu

LESLIE, PAUL WILLARD, POPULATION GENETICS, DEMOGRAPHY. *Current Pos:* ASST PROF ANTHROP, STATE UNIV NY, BINGHAMTON, 78- *Personal Data:* b Peekskill, NY, Apr 23, 48. *Educ:* Bucknell Univ, BA, 70; Pa State Univ, MA, 72, PhD(anthrop), 77. *Prof Exp:* Asst prof anthrop, Univ Tex, Austin, 76-78. *Mem:* AAAS; Am Asn Phys Anthropologists; Human Biol Coun; Pop Asn Am; Soc Study Social Biol. *Res:* Population genetics, demography of small populations, mathematical modeling and computer simulation; interactions among the social, demographic, and genetic structures of human populations. *Mailing Add:* 182 Nature Trail Chapel Hill NC 27514

LESLIE, STEPHEN HOWARD, MEDICINE. *Current Pos:* Clin asst, Sch Med, NY Univ, 46-49, clin instr med, 49-54, asst prof, 54-69, ASSOC PROF CLIN MED, SCH MED, NY UNIV, 69- *Personal Data:* b New York, NY, Nov 6, 18; m 43, Lilliam Osimoff; c Bruce & Barbara. *Educ:* NY Univ, BS, 38, MD, 42. *Concurrent Pos:* Fel, Sch Med, NY Univ, 44-46. *Mem:* Endocrine Soc; Am Diabetes Asn; Am Fedn Clin Res. *Res:* Metabolic diseases; endocrinology. *Mailing Add:* 160 E 38th St 33B New York NY 10016-2651

LESLIE, STEVEN WAYNE, PHARMACOLOGY. *Current Pos:* Asst prof, 74-81, ASSOC PROF PHARMACOL, UNIV TEX, AUSTIN, 81- *Personal Data:* b Franklin, Ind, Jan 23, 46; m 70; c 1. *Educ:* Purdue Univ, BS, 69, MS, 72, PhD(pharmacol), 74. *Mem:* Sigma Xi; AAAS. *Res:* Investigations concerning the role of cellular organelles in calcium-mediated termination mechanisms in secretory tissues and the effects of various drugs on these termination mechanisms. *Mailing Add:* Dept Pharmacol Univ Tex Col Pharm Austin TX 78712-1074

LESLIE, THOMAS M, PHOTOCHEMISTRY, SYNTHETIC ORGANIC CHEMISTRY. *Current Pos:* STAFF SCIENTIST, CELANESE RES CO, 85- *Personal Data:* b Philadelphia, Pa, Nov 11, 54; m 82. *Educ:* Rider Col, BS, 76; Univ Notre Dame, PhD(chem), 80. *Prof Exp:* Mem tech staff, Bell Tel Labs, 80-85. *Mem:* Am Chem Soc; NY Acad Sci. *Res:* Mechanism of photochemical reactions via reaction intermediates produced in laser flash photolysis; study of the effect of subtle changes in chemical constitution on materials exhibiting liquid crystal phases; liquid crystal side chain polymers; nonlinear optical materials. *Mailing Add:* Dept Chem Univ Ala Huntsville AL 35899

LESLIE, WALLACE DEAN, ANALYTICAL CHEMISTRY. *Current Pos:* RETIRED. *Personal Data:* b Dacoma, Okla, Nov 9, 22; m 48; c 3. *Educ:* Northwestern State Col, Okla, BS, 47; Okla State Univ, MS, 50. *Prof Exp:* Asst chem, Okla State Univ, 47-49; instr, Northwestern State Col, Okla, 49-51; anal chemist, Mfg Dept, Continental Oil Co, 51-52, from assoc res chemist to sr res chemist, 52-62, res group leader, res & develop dept, 62-77, dir, anal res sect, 77-85. *Mem:* Am Chem Soc. *Res:* Analytical research and development; petroleum and petroleum products; petrochemicals. *Mailing Add:* 11 Forest Rd Ponca City OK 74604

LESLIE, WILLIAM C(AIRNS), METALLURGY. *Current Pos:* prof mat eng, 73-85, EMER PROF MAT ENG, UNIV MICH, 85- *Personal Data:* b Dundee, Scotland, Jan 6, 20; nat US; m 48, Florence Hall; c Barbara (Putney). *Educ:* Ohio State Univ, BMetE, 47, MSc, 48, PhD(metall), 49. *Honors & Awards:* Krumb Lectr, Am Inst Mining, Metal & Petrol Engrs, 67 & Howe Lectr, 82; Andrew Carnegie Lectr, Am Soc Metals, 70, Campbell Lectr, 71, Sauveur Lectr & Jeffries Lectr, 75; Garofalo Lectr, Northwestern Univ, 77; Sorby Award, Int Metallog Soc, 91; Barret Medal, Am Soc Metals Int, 92, Gold Medal, 95. *Prof Exp:* Res assoc, Res Found, Ohio State Univ, 47-49; metallurgist, US Steel Corp, 49-53; assoc dir res, Thompson Prod Inc, 53-54; metallurgist, US Steel Corp, 54-57, sr scientist, Fundamental Res Lab, 57-63, asst dir phys metall, 63-69, mgr, E C Bain Lab Fundamental Res, 69-73. *Concurrent Pos:* Battelle vis prof, Ohio State Univ, 64-65; chmn, Int Conf Strength Metals & Alloys, Calif, 70; vis prof Melbourne Univ, Australia, 79; mem, Coun Sci & Indust Res exchange scientist, NSF, India, 81; distinguished alumnus lectr, Ohio State Univ, 84. *Mem:* Fel & hon mem Am Soc Metals; fel Am Inst Mining Metall & Petrol Engrs (vpres, 75); fel Inst Mat Gt Brit. *Res:* Physical metallurgy, especially of steels; studies of the physical and mechanical behavior of steels through fundamental research on the relationships between composition, microstructure and ferrous alloy properties; failure analysis. *Mailing Add:* RR 7 Box 7416 Palmyra VA 22963

LESNAW, JUDITH ALICE, VIROLOGY, MOLECULAR BIOLOGY. *Current Pos:* from asst prof to assoc prof, 74-88, PROF BIOL SCI, UNIV KY, 88- *Personal Data:* b Chicago, Ill, July 30, 40. *Educ:* Univ Ill, BS, 62, MS, 64, PhD(cell biol), 69. *Prof Exp:* Res assoc virol, Univ Ill, 69-74. *Concurrent Pos:* Mem, Med Biochem Study Sect, NIH. *Mem:* Am Soc Microbiol; Am Soc Virol; Am Soc Biochem & Molecular Biol. *Res:* Structure and function of viral proteins and RNA; replication of RNA viruses; defective interfering particles; expression of recombinant proteins. *Mailing Add:* 124 Combs Markey Cancer Ctr Univ Ky Sch Biol Sci 800 Rose St Lexington KY 40536-0096. *Fax:* 606-257-7648; *E-Mail:* biojal@ukcc.uky.edu

LESNER, SHARON A, REHABILITATIVE AUDIOLOGY. *Current Pos:* PROF AUDIOL, UNIV AKRON, 79- *Personal Data:* b Lorain, Ohio, Apr 1, 51. *Educ:* Hiram Col, BA, 73; Kent State Univ, MA, 75; Wayne State Univ, MA, 76; Ohio State Univ, PhD(audiol), 79. *Mem:* Am Speech, Lang & Hearing Asn; Acad Rehab Audiol; Acoust Soc Am; Alexander Graham Bell Asn Deaf; Am Auditory Soc; Am Acad Audiol. *Res:* Visual, auditory and audio-visual reception of speech; evoked potentials including auditory and visual; hearing aid use; central auditory processing. *Mailing Add:* Common Disorders Univ Arkon 302 Buchtel Mall Akron OH 44325-0001. *Fax:* 330-972-7884

LESNIAK, LINDA, GRAPH THEORY. *Current Pos:* assoc prof, 85-91, PROF MATH, DREW UNIV, 91- *Personal Data:* b Gary, Ind, Aug 14, 48; m 83, Mark Kraal. *Educ:* Western Mich Univ, BA, 70, MA, 71, PhD(math), 74. *Honors & Awards:* Fulbright Award, 91. *Prof Exp:* Asst prof, La State Univ, Baton Rouge, 74-78; asst prof to assoc prof math, Western Mich Univ, 78-85. *Mem:* Am Math Soc; Sigma Xi; Math Asn Am; NY Acad Sci; Asn Women in Math; Soc Indust Appl Math. *Res:* Extremal problems in graph theory; generalized degree conditions. *Mailing Add:* Dept Math & Comput Sci Drew Univ Madison NJ 07940

LESPERANCE, PIERRE J, INVERTEBRATE PALEONTOLOGY. *Current Pos:* from asst prof to assoc prof, 61-71, chmn dept, 75-79, PROF GEOL, UNIV MONTREAL, 71- *Personal Data:* b Montreal, Que, Aug 16, 34; m 60; c 3. *Educ:* Univ Montreal, BSc, 56; Univ Mich, MS, 57; McGill Univ, PhD(geol), 61. *Prof Exp:* Geologist, Dept Natural Resources, Que, 60-61. *Mem:* Geol Soc Can; Am Asn Petrol Geol; Soc Econ Paleont & Mineral; Paleont Soc; Brit Palaeont Asn. *Res:* Low and middle Paleozoic field mapping in Quebec; paleontology and biostratigraphy of Upper Ordovician to Lower Devonian trilobites and brachiopods. *Mailing Add:* Dept Geol Univ Montreal Sta Sucre Centre Ville PO Box 6128 Montreal PQ H3C 3J7 Can

LESSARD, JAMES LOUIS, BIOCHEMISTRY. *Current Pos:* assoc prof, 72-79, assoc prof res pediat, 79-86, PROF MOLECULAR GENETICS, MICROBIOL & BIOCHEM, MED SCH, UNIV CINCINNATI, 74-, PROF PEDIAT, 86- *Personal Data:* b Eau Claire, Wis, Mar 9, 43; m 65; c 2. *Educ:* Marquette Univ, BS, 65, PhD(biochem), 70. *Prof Exp:* Fel, Roche Inst Molecular Biol, Nutley, NJ, 69-71; res scholar biochem, Children's Hosp Res Found, 71-72. *Concurrent Pos:* Fel pharmacol-morphol, Pharmaceut Mfrs Asn Found, Cincinnati, Ohio, 72-74. *Mem:* Am Chem Soc; AAAS; Sigma Xi. *Res:* Regulatory processes in development; cell motility; immunochemistry. *Mailing Add:* Children's Hosp Res Found 3333 Burnet Ave Cincinnati OH 45229-3039

LESSARD, JEAN, ORGANIC ELECTROCHEMISTRY. *Current Pos:* from asst prof to assoc prof, 69-76, PROF ORG CHEM, UNIV SHERBROOKE, 76- *Personal Data:* b East-Broughton, Que, Apr 29, 36; m 93, Francine Duguay; c Francois & Ivan. *Educ:* Laval Univ, BA, 56, BSc, 60, PhD(org chem), 65. *Prof Exp:* Nat Res Coun Can fel, Imp Col, Univ London, 65-67; asst res officer org chem, Nat Res Coun Can, 67-69. *Mem:* Chem Inst Can; Royal Soc Chem; Am Chem Soc; Electrochem Soc; AAAS; Can Soc Chem; Fr Soc Chem; Int Union Pure & Appl Chem. *Res:* Electrochemistry and photochemistry used to study new methods of effecting organic reactions or new organic reactions, investigation of the mechanism, scope and synthetic utility of these reactions. *Mailing Add:* Dept Chem Univ Sherbrooke Sherbrooke PQ J1K 2R1 Can. *Fax:* 819-821-8017; *E-Mail:* jlessard@courrier.usherb.ca

LESSARD, RICHARD R, PETROLEUM PRODUCTS RESEARCH. *Current Pos:* Proj staff engr, Exxon Res & Eng Co, 70-76, sect head, 76-79, lab dir res & develop, 80-82, res coordr, 82-84, mgr, 84-89, OIL SPILL TECHNOL CONSULT, EXXON RES & ENG CO, 89- *Personal Data:* b Lowell, Mass, Mar 15, 43; m 66; c 2. *Educ:* Lowell Technol Inst, BS, 66; Univ Maine, MS, 68, PhD(chem eng), 70. *Concurrent Pos:* Mem, Fossil Energy Res Working Group III, Dept Energy, 80. *Mem:* Am Inst Chem Engrs; Sigma Xi. *Res:* Coordinator of technical studies in support of Alaska oil spill cleanup. *Mailing Add:* 12 Witherspoon Ct Morristown NJ 07960

LESSARD, ROGER ALAIN, optics, for more information see previous edition

LESSELL, SIMMONS, NEUROLOGY, OPHTHALMOLOGY. *Current Pos:* assoc prof neurol, 67-70, PROF ANAT, NEUROL & OPHTHAL, SCH MED, BOSTON UNIV, 70- *Personal Data:* b Brooklyn, NY, May 25, 33; m 55; c 4. *Educ:* Amherst Col, BA, 54; Cornell Univ, MD, 58. *Prof Exp:* Intern med, Cornell Univ, 58-59; resident neurol, Univ Vt, 59-60; resident ophthal, Mass Eye & Ear Hosp, 63-66. *Concurrent Pos:* Physician, NIH, 59-60; lectr, Sch Med, Tufts Univ, 66-; vis surgeon & dir dept ophthal, Boston City Hosp; vis surgeon, Univ Hosp; consult ophthal, Vet Admin Hosp & Tufts-New Engl Med Ctr. *Mem:* Asn Res Vision & Ophthal. *Res:* Optic neuropathies, clinical and experimental; histochemistry and experimental pathology of the optic nerve. *Mailing Add:* Mass Eye & Ear Inst 243 Charles St Boston MA 02114

LESSEN, MARTIN, FLUID MECHANICS, SOLID MECHANICS. *Current Pos:* prof mech & aerospace sci & chmn dept, 60-70, Yates mem prof eng, 68-83, EMER YATES MEM PROF ENG, UNIV ROCHESTER, 83- *Personal Data:* b New York, NY, Sept 6, 20; m 48, Elizabeth Scher; c Margot, Deborah & David. *Educ:* City Col New York, BME, 40; NY Univ, MME, 42; Mass Inst Technol, ScD(mech eng), 48. *Prof Exp:* Mech engr, Navy Dept, 41-46; asst fluid mech, Mass Inst Technol, 48; aeronaut res scientist, Nat Adv Comt Aeronaut, 48-49; prof aero eng, Pa State Col, 49-53; prof appl mech, Univ Pa, 53-60. *Concurrent Pos:* NSF sr fel shock waves & instabilities, Cambridge Univ, 66-67; Nat Acad Sci exchange visitor, USSR, 67; IBM Corp pure sci div grant; consult, RCA Corp, NJ, Rochester Appl Sci Assocs, GE Corp, Philadelphia & Adv Comt Energy Div, Oak Ridge Nat Lab; liaison scientist, US Off Naval Res, London, 76-79; Vollmer Fries fel, Rensselaer Polytech Inst, 78; founding chmn, Energetics Prof Div, Am Soc Mech Engrs, 63, 67. *Mem:* Fel Am Phys Soc; fel Am Soc Mech Engrs; Am Soc Eng Educ; Ger Soc Appl Math & Mech; Am Inst Aeronaut & Astronaut; fel AAAS. *Res:* Fluid mechanics; thermodynamics and heat transfer; vibrations; hydrodynamic stability and transition to turbulence; continuum mechanics; thermoelasticity; biomechanics; biophysics; plasma dynamics; field theory. *Mailing Add:* 12 Country Club Dr Rochester NY 14618

LESSEPS, ROLAND JOSEPH, developmental biology, for more information see previous edition

LESSER, MICHAEL PATRICK, EFFECTS OF ULTRA-VIOLET RADIATION ON ALGAE-INVERTEBRATE SYMBIOSES, EFFECTS OF WATER FLOW TEMPERATURE & FOOD OF THE BIOGENETICS OF MARINE INVERTEBRATES. *Current Pos:* RES ASST PROF ZOOL, UNIV NH, 93- *Personal Data:* b Bangor, Maine, Oct 15, 54. *Educ:* Univ NH, BA, 83, MA, 85; Univ Maine, PhD(zool), 89. *Prof Exp:* Assoc, Bigelow Lab for Ocean Sci, 89-91; res scientist, 91-93. *Concurrent Pos:* Instr, Shoals Marine Lab, 89-93, East-West Prog, Northeastern Univ, 91, Hawaii Inst Marine Biol, 91, 93; chief scientist, Sea Educ Asn, 91-93; consult, Pittsburgh Zoo, 93. *Mem:* Am Soc Limnol & Oceanog; Am Soc Zool; Oceanog Soc; Int Soc Study Coral Reefs; Western Soc Naturalists; Nat Shellfisheries Asn. *Res:* Effects of ultraviolet radiation on corals; ultraviolet radiation effects on phytoplankton and the biogenetics of sessile suspension-feeding marine invertebrates. *Mailing Add:* Dept Zool Univ NH Bigelow Lab Ocean Sci Durham NH 03824

LESSIE, THOMAS GUY, MICROBIAL PHYSIOLOGY. *Current Pos:* asst prof, 68-74, assoc prof, 74-81, PROF MICROBIOL, UNIV MASS, AMHERST, 81- *Personal Data:* b New York, NY, Dec 14, 36; m 62; c 3. *Educ:* Queens Col, NY, BS, 58; Harvard Univ, AM, 61, PhD(biol sci), 63. *Prof Exp:* Res asst microbiol, Haskins Labs, NY, 58-59; NIH fels biochem, Oxford Univ, 63-65 & biol sci, Purdue Univ, 65-67; res assoc microbiol, Univ Wash, 67-68. *Concurrent Pos:* Numerous grants from US govt, 68-90; vis prof, dept biol sci, Purdue Univ, 74, dept microbiol, Med Col Va, 81, dept biol, Yale Univ, 88; Cystic Fibrosis Found, 90-91; Dept Engergy, 91-95; Elec Power Res Inst, 95-97. *Mem:* Am Soc Microbiol; Am Chem Soc. *Res:* Biochemical genetics of Pseudomonas cepacia with emphasis on regulatory mechanisms governing carbohydrate and amino acid metabolism; roles of transposable gene-activating elements in evolution of new metabolic functions. *Mailing Add:* Dept Microbiol Univ Mass Amherst MA 01003. *Fax:* 413-545-1578; *E-Mail:* tlessie@microbio.umass.edu

LESSIN, LAWRENCE STEPHEN, HEMATOLOGY, ONCOLOGY. *Current Pos:* assoc prof, 70-74, PROF MED PATH & DIR HEMAT & ONCOL, SCH MED, GEORGE WASHINGTON UNIV, 74- *Personal Data:* b Washington, DC, Oct 14, 37; m 62; c 3. *Educ:* Univ Chicago, MD, 62. *Prof Exp:* Intern med, Univ Pa, 61-67; Nat Heart Inst spec fel hematol med, Inst Cell Path, Paris, France, 67-68; asst prof med, Sch Med, Duke Univ, 68-70. *Concurrent Pos:* Consult, Nat Heart, Lung & Blood Inst & US Naval Med Ctr, 74- & Walter Reed Army Med Ctr, 75- *Mem:* Am Col Physicians; Am Soc Hemat; Am Fedn Clin Res; Int Soc Hemat; Am Soc Clin Oncol; Sigma Xi. *Res:* Red cell membrane structure in hemolytic anemias; red cell rheology; hematologic neoplasia; preleukemia (myelodysplasia). *Mailing Add:* Cancer Inst Wash Hosp Ctr 110 Irving St NW Washington DC 20010

LESSING, PETER, ENVIRONMENTAL GEOLOGY. *Current Pos:* environ geologist, WVa Geol Surv, 71-73, chief, Geol Div, 80-85, head, Environ Geol Sect, 73-89, SR RES GEOLOGIST, WVA GEOL SURV, 89- *Personal Data:* b Englewood, NJ, June 15, 38; m 65, Katherine B Burry; c 2. *Educ:* St Lawrence Univ, BS, 61; Dartmouth Col, MA, 63; Syracuse Univ, PhD(geol), 67. *Prof Exp:* Asst prof geol, St Lawrence Univ, 66-71. *Concurrent Pos:* Adj prof, WVa Univ, 73- *Mem:* Geol Soc Am; Asn Earth Sci Ed; Hist Earth Sci Soc. *Res:* Geologic field mapping; environmental geology investigations; history of geology; landslide evaluation; geologic hazard studies; hydrology and water use. *Mailing Add:* WVa Geol Surv PO Box 879 Morgantown WV 26507-0879. *E-Mail:* lessing@geosrv.wvnet.edu

LESSIOS, HARILAOS ANGELOU, EVOLUTION. *Current Pos:* STAFF BIOLOGIST, SMITHSONIAN TROP RES INST, 79- *Personal Data:* b Thessaloniki, Greece, Mar 4, 51; m 83, Kristin Neva; c Nicolas & Anna. *Educ:* Harvard Univ, BA, 73; Yale Univ, MPhil, 76, PhD(biol), 79. *Honors & Awards:* John Spangler Nicholas Prize, Yale Univ. *Mem:* Soc Study Evolution; Soc Syst Biol. *Res:* Evolution and ecology of marine organisms. *Mailing Add:* Smithsonian Trop Res Inst Unit 948 APO AA 34002-0948. *Fax:* 507-28-0516

LESSLER, JUDITH THOMASSON, SURVEY RESEARCH METHODS. *Current Pos:* SR RES LEADER & CTR DIR, BATTELLE MEM INST, 92- *Personal Data:* b Charlotte, NC, Oct, 10, 43; m 70; c 2. *Educ:* Univ NC, Chapel Hill, AB, 66, PhD(biostatist), 74; Emory Univ, Ga, MAT, 67. *Prof Exp:* Statistician, Res Triangle Inst, 74-78, dept mgr, 80-84, sr statistician, 78-92. *Concurrent Pos:* Prin investr, NSF grant, 79-81; adj asst prof, Biostatist Dept, Univ NC, 81-; serv fel, Nat Ctr Health Statist, 84-85; bd mem, Am Statist Asn, 85-87. *Mem:* Am Statist Asn; Am Pub Health Asn; AAAS. *Res:* Survey research methods; statistical treatment of nonsampling errors and multiframe-multiplicity estimators; application of cognitive psychology to survey design. *Mailing Add:* PO Box 12194 Research Triangle Park NC 27709

LESSMAN, CHARLES ALLEN, OOCYTE MEIOTIC MATURATION, CYTOSKELETON IN DEVELOPMENT. *Current Pos:* PROF, DEPT BIOL, MEMPHIS STATE UNIV, 88- *Personal Data:* b St Paul, Minn, June 18, 48; m 71, Mary E Heille; c Shaun T & Damian C. *Educ:* Univ Minn, Minneapolis, BA, 70, MS, 75; Univ Minn, St Paul, PhD(cell biol), 80. *Prof Exp:* Fel, Johns Hopkins Univ, 78-81; asst prof, St Francis Xavier Univ, 81-85, assoc prof, 85-88. *Concurrent Pos:* Adj prof, Delhousie Univ, 84-87; vis prof, Univ Iowa, 87-88. *Mem:* Am Soc Cell Biol; AAAS; Soc Study Reproduction; Am Soc Zoologists; Soc Develop Biol; Sigma Xi. *Res:* Ovarian physiology, especially oocyte meiotic maturation in lower vertebrates; steroid (progesterone) mode of action in oocyte maturation and the cytoskeletal changes. *Mailing Add:* Dept Microbiol & Molecular Cell Sci Univ Memphis Memphis TN 38152. *Fax:* 901-678-4457, 678-3299

LESSMAN, GARY M, SOIL FERTILITY. *Current Pos:* asst prof, 69-77, ASSOC PROF AGRON, UNIV TENN, KNOXVILLE, 77- *Personal Data:* b Hillsboro, Ill, July 15, 38. *Educ:* Southern Ill Univ, BS, 60, MS, 62; Mich State Univ, PhD(soil sci), 67. *Prof Exp:* Exten agronomist, Purdue Univ, 67-68. *Mem:* Sigma Xi; Am Soc Agron. *Res:* Micronutrient nutrition. *Mailing Add:* Dept Plant & Soil Sci Univ Tenn Knoxville 1345 Circle Park Knoxville TN 37996-0001

LESSMANN, RICHARD CARL, MECHANICAL ENGINEERING, FLUID MECHANICS. *Current Pos:* Asst prof, 69-75, ASSOC PROF MECH ENG & APPL MECH, UNIV RI, 75- *Personal Data:* b New York, NY, Oct 14, 42; m 65; c 3. *Educ:* Syracuse Univ, BSME, 64; Brown Univ, ScM, 66, PhD(eng), 69. *Mem:* Am Inst Aeronaut & Astronaut; Am Phys Soc; Sigma Xi. *Res:* Turbulent flows; boundary layer theory; heat transfer. *Mailing Add:* 35 Courtland Dr Narragansett RI 02882-1215

LESSNER, HOWARD E, INTERNAL MEDICINE, ONCOLOGY. *Current Pos:* from instr to prof med, 59-75, PROF ONCOL, UNIV MIAMI, 74- *Personal Data:* b Philadelphia, Pa, Feb 28, 27; m 57; c 3. *Educ:* Univ Pa, MD, 53. *Prof Exp:* Jr asst resident, Jackson Mem Hosp, 54-55, sr asst resident, 55-56, clin fel, 56-57; res fel, Nat Heart Inst, Barnes Hosp, 57-58, clin fel, Nat Cancer Inst, 58-59. *Concurrent Pos:* Dir, Comprehensive Cancer Ctr, 72-74, clin dir, 74- *Mem:* Am Col Physicians; AMA; Am Soc Clin Oncol; Am Asn Cancer Res; AAAS. *Mailing Add:* 8950 N Kendall Dr No 410 Miami FL 33176

LESSO, WILLIAM GEORGE, OPERATIONS RESEARCH. *Current Pos:* assoc prof mech eng, 67-72, PROF MECH ENG, UNIV TEX, AUSTIN, 72- *Personal Data:* b Cleveland, Ohio, Mar 23, 31; m 52; c 5. *Educ:* Univ Notre Dame, BSME, 53; Xavier Univ, Ohio, MBA, 63; Case Inst Technol, MS, 66, PhD(opers res), 67. *Prof Exp:* Design engr, Clevite Corp, 53-58; proj engr, Flight Propulsion Div, Gen Elec Co, 58-64. *Mem:* Opers Res Soc Am; Inst Mgt Sci. *Res:* Application of operations research to industrial and economic problems. *Mailing Add:* 2505 Roxmoor Dr Austin TX 78723

LESSOFF, HOWARD, SOLID STATE SCIENCE. *Current Pos:* ADJ PROF CHEM, MONTGOMERY COL, 92- *Personal Data:* b Boston, Mass, Sept 23, 30; m 59, Veva Schlosberg; c Victor & Steven. *Educ:* Northeastern Univ, BS, 53, MS, 57. *Prof Exp:* Staff engr, Radio Corp Am, Mass, 57-60, sr staff mem, 61-64; staff mem, Bell Tel Labs, 60-61; aerospace technologist, Electronic Res Ctr, NASA, 64-70; supvry physicist, Naval Res Lab, 70-75, br head electronic mat, 75-92. *Concurrent Pos:* Lectr, Lincoln Col,

Northeastern Univ, 57-70; consult, Datacove Corp, NJ, 69- *Mem:* AAAS; Inst Elec & Electronics Engrs; Sigma Xi. *Res:* Crystal growth; semiconductor materials; microwave and optic properties; solid state physics; magnetic materials. *Mailing Add:* 11811 Enid Dr Potomac MD 20854. *Fax:* 301-299-0506; *E-Mail:* vlessoff@umds.umd.edu

LESSOR, DELBERT LEROY, PHYSICS, APPLIED MATHEMATICS. *Current Pos:* sr res scientist phys sci, 67-80, sr res scientist eng physics, 80-89, STAFF SCIENTIST, APPL PHYSICS CTR, PAC NORTHWEST LABS, BATTELLE MEM INST, 89- *Personal Data:* b 1941; US citizen; m 62; c 2. *Educ:* Ft Hays State Univ, BS, 62; Kans State Univ, PhD(physics), 67. *Prof Exp:* Temp asst prof physics, Kans State Univ, 66-67. *Mem:* Am Phys Soc; Sci Res Soc NAm; Sigma Xi; Bioelectromagnetics Soc; Am Vacuum Soc. *Res:* Electromagnetic field computation in industrial and instrument configurations; air filtration theory; nuclear particle transport; nuclear reaction theory; nuclear reactor instrumentation; geothermal chemistry; fluid flow calculation; optics theory; bioelectromagnetics effects; low energy electron diffraction analysis. *Mailing Add:* K7-15 ISB-1 Pac NW Lab Richland WA 99352

LESSOR, EDITH SCHROEDER, ANALYTICAL CHEMISTRY, GENERAL CHEMISTRY. *Current Pos:* from asst prof to assoc prof, Mt St Mary Col, NY, 67-76, chmn, Div Natural Sci & Math, 73-84, chmn dept, 68-88, prof, 76-93, chmn Div Natural Sci, 88-91, EMER PROF CHEM, MT ST MARY COL, NY, 93- *Personal Data:* b Chicago, Ill, Aug 5, 30; wid; c Ralph & Karen L (Moran). *Educ:* Valparaiso Univ, BS, 52; Ind Univ, Bloomington, PhD(anal chem), 55. *Prof Exp:* Instr chem, Ulster Community Col, 64-65; lectr, Harpur Col, State Univ NY, Binghamton, 65-67. *Mem:* AAAS; Am Chem Soc; Sigma Xi. *Res:* Spectrophotometry of organic analytical reagents and analytical chemistry of water pollution control. *Mailing Add:* 7F Knightsbridge Rd Poughkeepsie NY 12603

LESTER, CHARLES TURNER, ORGANIC CHEMISTRY. *Current Pos:* from asst prof to assoc prof, 42-50, chmn, Dept Chem, 54-57, vpres grad studies, 70-74, vpres arts & sci, 74-78, PROF CHEM, EMORY UNIV, 50-, DEAN GRAD SCH, 57-, EXEC VPRES & DEAN FAC, 78- *Personal Data:* b Covington, Ga, Nov 10, 11; m 36; c 2. *Educ:* Emory Univ, AB, 32, MA, 34; Pa State Univ, PhD(org chem), 41. *Honors & Awards:* Herty Medal, 65. *Prof Exp:* Teacher high sch, Ga, 34-35; instr chem, Emory Jr Col, 35-39; res chemist, Calco Div, Am Cyanamid Corp, NJ, 41-42. *Concurrent Pos:* Coun mem, Oak Ridge Assoc Univs, 58-62, 70-79, mem bd dirs, 62-65; mem, Ga Sci & Technol Comn, 63-72; mem bd dirs, Atlanta Speech Sch, 65-71; mem exec comt, Coun Grad Schs US, 65-68; mem bd dirs, Southeastern Educ Lab, 66-68; bd trustees, Reinhardt Col, 66-72; vchmn, Ocean Sci Ctr, Atlantic Comn, 67-72; mem bd trustees, Huntingdon Col, 68; chief acad progs br, Bur Higher Educ, 69-70; chmn elect, Coun Grad Sch, 73, chmn, 74. *Mem:* Am Chem Soc; Sigma Xi; Am Inst Chem. *Res:* Sterically hindered ketones; indigosol dyes; biphenyl mercaptan; oxetanones; alkyl aryl ketones; anti-microbial compounds. *Mailing Add:* 1800 Clairmont Lake No 512 Decatur GA 30033

LESTER, DAVID SIMON, FLUORESCENCE MICROSCOPY, VIBRATIONAL SPECTROSCOPY IMAGING MICROSCOPY. *Current Pos:* STAFF SCIENTIST, FOOD & DRUG ADMIN, 93- *Personal Data:* b Sydney, Australia, Feb 23, 55; m 80, Janice; c Adam & Daniel. *Educ:* Univ NSW, Australia, BSc Hons, 77; Hebrew Univ Jerusalem, Israel, MSc, 79; Northwestern Univ, PhD(biol). *Honors & Awards:* Outstanding Researcher, Israel Cancer Soc, 87. *Prof Exp:* Res asst, Hebrew Univ Jerusalem, 78-79; teaching asst, Northwestern Univ, 79-81; res assoc, Univ NC, 81-83; fel, Harvard Univ Med Sch, 83-85, Weizmann Inst Sci, 85-86, staff scientist, 86-90; vis assoc, NIH, 90-93. *Concurrent Pos:* Fel, Muscular Dystrophy Asn, 84-85. *Mem:* Int Soc Neurochem; Am Soc Neurosci; Int Brain Res Orgn; Am Asn Anatomists. *Res:* Development of alternative procedures to monitor biochemical activities in simple and complex neuronal systems; new approaches to noninvasive analyses of brain function. *Mailing Add:* Food & Drug Admn/DAPR MOD1 8301 Muirkirk Rd Rm 2009 Laurel MD 20708. *Fax:* 301-594-3037; *E-Mail:* lesterd@cder.fda.gov

LESTER, DONALD THOMAS, FORESTRY. *Current Pos:* SUPVR, FOREST BIOL, FORESTRY RES DIV, CROWN ZELLERBACH CORP, 77- *Personal Data:* b New London, Conn, Aug 26, 34; m 62; c 2. *Educ:* Univ Maine, BS, 55; Yale Univ, MF, 57, PhD(forest genetics), 62. *Prof Exp:* From asst prof to prof forestry, Univ Wis-Madison, 62-77. *Mem:* Sigma Xi. *Res:* Tree breeding; genecology. *Mailing Add:* 1424 N Beach Rd Salt Spring Island BC V8K 1B2 Can

LESTER, GEORGE RONALD, AIR PURIFICATION, CATALYSIS. *Current Pos:* PRES, GEORGE LESTER INC, 96- *Personal Data:* b War Eagle, WVa, Sept 6, 34; m 56, 93, Patricia P; c Julia, Kay, Brooke & David. *Educ:* Berea Col, BA, 54; Univ Ky, MS, 56, PhD(chem), 58. *Prof Exp:* Chemist, Universal Oil Prod Co, 58-63, assoc res coordr, UOP, Inc, 63-74, mgr appl catalysis, 74-76, dir mat sci res, 76-83; sr res scientist, Allied-Signal Engineered Mat Res Ctr, 83-90; res fel, Allied-Signal Res & Technol, 90-92, sr res fel, 92-96. *Concurrent Pos:* Chair, Gordon Res Conf Catalysis, 91; adj prof, Catalysis & Surface Sci Ctr, Northwestern Univ. *Mem:* AAAS; Am Chem Soc; Faraday Soc; Sigma Xi; Catalysis Soc; fel Soc Automotive Engrs. *Res:* Conductivity of nonaqueous solutions; adsorption of gases on solids; heterogeneous catalysis; petrochemical processes; material science; automotive exhaust catalysis; solar systems; energy conservation; catalytic combustion; automotive gas turbine engines; electric power plant catalytic combustion; electrocatalysis for fuel cells for power plants; catalytic destruction of chemical warfare agents; catalytic incineration of hazardous pollutants. *Mailing Add:* 1200 Pickwick Lane Salem VA 24153-1714. *Fax:* 540-387-2787

LESTER, HENRY ALLEN, NEUROBIOLOGY, BIOPHYSICS. *Current Pos:* PROF BIOL, CALIF INST TECHNOL, 73- *Personal Data:* b New York, NY, July 4, 45; c 2. *Educ:* Harvard Col, AB, 66; Rockefeller Univ, PhD(biophys), 71. *Prof Exp:* Res fel molecular neurobiol, Inst Pasteur, 71-73. *Concurrent Pos:* Res grants, NIH Res Career Develop Award, 77-82, Alfred P Sloan Res fel, 74-76, & Sen Jacob Javits investr, NIH, 85-; vis prof, Dept Biol Chem, Hebrew Univ, Israel, 80-81; mem, Physiol Study Sect, 85-89. *Mem:* Soc Neurosci; Biophys Soc; Soc Gen Physiologists; fel AAAS. *Res:* Excitable membranes; molecular neuroscience. *Mailing Add:* Div Biol Calif Inst Technol MC 156-29 Pasadena CA 91125

LESTER, JOHN BERNARD, ASTRONOMY, ASTROPHYSICS. *Current Pos:* asst prof, 76-81, ASSOC PROF ASTRON, UNIV TORONTO, 81- *Personal Data:* b San Diego, Calif, Mar 11, 45; m 72; c 2. *Educ:* Northwestern Univ, BA, 67; Univ Chicago, MS, 69, PhD(astron), 72. *Prof Exp:* Lectr physics, Univ Wis-Milwaukee, 69-71; presidential intern astron, Smithsonian Astrophys Observ, 72-73, physicist, 73-76. *Mem:* Am Astron Soc; Astron Soc Pac; Int Astron Union. *Res:* High dispersion stellar spectroscopy; stellar abundances; ultraviolet astronomy; infrared spectroscopy. *Mailing Add:* 1014 Fleet St Mississauga ON L5H 4C6 Can

LESTER, JOSEPH EUGENE, PHYSICAL CHEMISTRY. *Current Pos:* ADVAN ENG SPECIALIST, OSRAM-SYLVANIA, INC, 89- *Personal Data:* b Bay City, Tex, July 2, 42; m 59; c 2. *Educ:* Rice Univ, BA, 64; Univ Calif, Berkeley, PhD(chem), 68. *Prof Exp:* Asst prof chem, Northwestern Univ, Evanston, 67-74; mem staff, GTE Labs, 73-77, sr res chemist, 78-81, res assoc, Gulf Sci & Technol, 81-85, mgr mat characterization, 85-89. *Mem:* Am Chem Soc; Am Phys Soc; Mat Res Soc. *Res:* Kinetics and mechanisms of surface reactions; kinetics of high temperature transport reactions; thermodynamics. *Mailing Add:* Osram Sylvania 71 Cherry Hill Dr Beverly MA 01915. *E-Mail:* lester@osi.sylvania.com

LESTER, LARRY JAMES, POPULATION GENETICS. *Current Pos:* From asst prof to assoc prof, 75-91, PROF BIOL, UNIV HOUSTON-CLEAR LAKE, 91- *Personal Data:* b Bay City, Tex, July 15, 47; m 69, 78, 83; c 1. *Educ:* Univ Tex, Austin, BA, 69, PhD(pop genetics), 75. *Mem:* Sigma Xi; World Aquacult Soc; Crustacean Soc. *Res:* Genetics of aquaculture species. *Mailing Add:* Natural Sci Univ Houston Clearlake 2700 Bay Area Blvd Houston TX 77058-1002

LESTER, RICHARD GARRISON, RADIOLOGY. *Current Pos:* prof, 84-93, dean, 84-89, EMER PROF RADIOL, EASTERN VA MED SCH, 93- *Personal Data:* b New York, NY, Oct 24, 25; m 53, M Louise Kurtz; c 2. *Educ:* Princeton Univ, AB, 46; Columbia Univ, MD, 48. *Hon Degrees:* LHD, Meharry Med Col, 93. *Honors & Awards:* Gold Medal, Raidol Soc NAm, 88. *Prof Exp:* From instr to assoc prof radiol, Univ Minn, 54-61; prof & chmn dept, Med Col Va, 61-65; prof radiol & chmn dept, Duke Univ, 65-76; prof radiol, Univ Tex Med Sch, 76-84. *Concurrent Pos:* Mem comt acad radiol, Nat Acad Sci, 66; mem steering comt, Soc Chmn Acad Radiol Dept, 67; mem bd trustees, Am Bd Radiol, Meharry Med Col, 75-92; interim pres, Meharry Med Col, 81-82. *Mem:* AMA; Am Roentgen Ray Soc; Am Col Radiol; Soc Pediat Radiol (secy-treas, 58-62); Am Col Chest Physicians; Radiol Soc NAm (pres, 82-83). *Res:* Cardiovascular radiology; mammography & diagnosis of breast diseases. *Mailing Add:* Box 1980 Norfolk VA 23501

LESTER, ROBERT LEONARD, BIOCHEMISTRY. *Current Pos:* from asst prof to prof, 60-95, chmn dept, 74-83, EMER PROF BIOCHEM, MED SCH, UNIV KY, 95- *Personal Data:* b New Haven, Conn, Aug 21, 29; m 54, Elizabeth Land; c Henry A & Ellen M (Stonecipher). *Educ:* Yale Univ, BS, 51; Calif Inst Technol, PhD(biochem), 56. *Prof Exp:* Asst prof biochem, Univ Wis, 58-60. *Concurrent Pos:* Res fel, Inst Enzyme Res, Univ Wis, 55-58; NIH res grants, 60-; vis res biologist, Univ Calif, San Diego, 69-70; Nat Bd, Med Examiners, 82-85; consult, Merck & Co, 87-92. *Mem:* AAAS; Am Soc Biol Chemists; Am Chem Soc; Am Soc Microbiol; Fedn Am Sci. *Res:* Lipid metabolism in yeast. *Mailing Add:* Univ Ky Med Sch Lexington KY 40536

LESTER, ROGER, MEDICINE. *Current Pos:* PROF GASTROENTEROL & CHIEF DIV, SCH MED, UNIV PITTSBURGH, 73- *Personal Data:* b Brooklyn, NY, Dec 26, 29; m 54; c 2. *Educ:* Princeton Univ, AB, 50; Yale Univ, MD, 55. *Prof Exp:* From intern to resident med, Col Med, Univ Utah, 55-57, resident, 59-60; NIH fel, 56-59; fel Thorndike Mem Lab, Harvard Univ, 60-62; asst prof med, Sch Med, Univ Chicago, 62-65; from asst prof to prof med, Sch Med, Boston Univ, 65-73. *Concurrent Pos:* NIH career develop award, 63-73, res grant, 65- *Mem:* Am Fedn Clin Res; Am Asn Study Liver Dis; Am Soc Clin Invest; Am Gastroenterol Asn; Int Asn Study Liver. *Res:* Fetal hepatic and intestinal function; effect of alcohol and liver disease on sexual function. *Mailing Add:* Div Gastroenterol Emory Univ Sch Med 525 Mt Paran Rd NW Atlanta GA 30327

LESTER, WILLIAM ALEXANDER, JR, QUANTUM MONTE CARLO. *Current Pos:* assoc dean, 91-95, PROF CHEM, UNIV CALIF, 81- *Personal Data:* b Chicago, Ill, Apr 24, 37; m 59, Rochelle Reed; c William A III & Allison K. *Educ:* Univ Chicago, BS, 58, MS, 59; Cath Univ, PhD(chem), 64. *Honors & Awards:* Percy L Julian Award, Nat Orgn Black Chemists & Chem Engrs, 79, Outstanding Teacher Award, 86. *Prof Exp:* Proj asst physics, lab molecular struct & spectra, Univ Chicago, 57-59; asst chem, Wash Univ, 59-60 & Cath Univ, 60-62; phys chemist, Phys Chem Div, Nat Bur Stand, 61-64; proj assoc, Theoret Chem Inst, Univ Wis-Madison, 64-65, asst dir, 65-68; mem permanent prof staff, IBM Res Lab, 68-75, mem tech planning staff, T J Watson Res Ctr, IBM Corp, Yorktown Heights, NY, 75-76; mgr molecular interactions group, IBM Res Lab, San Jose, Calif, 76-78; dir, Nat

Resource Comput Chem, Lawrence Berkeley Lab, assoc dir, 78-81; sr fel sci & eng & asst to dir human resource develop, NSF, 95-96. *Concurrent Pos:* Lectr, Univ Wis-Madison, 66-68; secy & treas, Wis Sect, Am Chem Soc, 67-68, treas, Div Comput Chem, 74-77, vchmn, Div Phys Chem, 77, chmn elec, 78, chmn, 79; ed, Proc Conf on Potential Energy Surface in Chem, 71; mem, res eval panel, Off Sci Res, USAF, 74-78, US Nat Comt, Int Union Pure & Appl Chem, 76-79, Nat Res Coun Panel for Chem physics, Nat Bur Stand, 80-83, comt to survey chem sci, Nat Acad Sci, 82-84, exec bd, Nat Orgn Black Chemists & Chem Engrs, 84-87, comt on recommendations, US Army Basic Sci Res, 84-87; consult, NSF, 76-; exec bd, Nat Orgn Black Chemists & Chem Engrs, 84-87; vchmn, div chem physics, Am Phys Soc, 85, chmn, 86; mem, Sci Yr adv bd, World Bk, Inc, 89-, external adv comt, Sci & Technol Ctr Res in Parallel Comput, NSF, 89- & Fed Networking Adv Comt, 91-; consult, Teltech, Inc, 91-95, Educ Testing Serv, 91 & Blue Ribbon Panel on High Performance Comput, NSF, 93; mem, Comt High Performance Comput & Commun, Nat Res Coun, 94-95, Comt Math Challenges Theoret/Comput Chem, 94-95, Army Res Lab Tech Assessment Bd, 96- *Mem:* Am Chem Soc; fel Am Phys Soc; Sigma Xi; Nat Orgn Black Chemists & Chem Engrs; fel AAAS. *Res:* Molecular quantum mechanics and molecular collision theory. *Mailing Add:* Dept Chem Univ Calif Berkeley CA 94720. *E-Mail:* walester@cchem.berkeley.edu

LESTER, WILLIAM LEWIS, MICROBIOLOGY. *Current Pos:* from asst to assoc prof, 70-79, PROF MICROBIOL HUMBOLDT STATE UNIV, 79- *Personal Data:* b Webster City, Iowa, July 21, 32; m 64; c 5. *Educ:* San Jose State Col, BA, 58; Univ Calif, Davis, PhD(microbiol), 68. *Prof Exp:* Lab technician pharmacol, Univ Calif, Davis, 62-66; supvr res & develop, Cutter Labs, 68-70. *Concurrent Pos:* Nat Oceanic & Atmospheric Admin sea grant, Samoa & Calif, 70-73; bd dirs, Redwood Health Consortium, 73-75; univ rep, Conf Assist Undergrad Sci Educ, 75-; health manpower coordr, Humboldt State Univ, 76-83, mem Acad Senate, 89- *Mem:* AAAS; Am Soc Microbiol; Wildlife Soc; Am Soc Allied Health Prof. *Res:* Biodegradation of kraft pulp mill effluent; microbial ecology; marine bioassays utilizing echino embryo. *Mailing Add:* Dept Biol Humboldt State Univ 1 Harps St Arcata CA 95521-8299

LESTINGI, JOSEPH FRANCIS, ENGINEERING MECHANICS, STRUCTURAL ENGINEERING. *Current Pos:* DEAN ENG & PROF MECH ENG, MANHATTAN COL, RIVERDALE, NY, 83- *Personal Data:* b Long Island, NY, Apr 24, 35; m 57; c 4. *Educ:* Manhattan Col, BCE, 57; Va Polytech Inst, MS, 59; Yale Univ, DEng(solid mech), 66. *Honors & Awards:* Western Elec Fund Award, Am Soc Eng Educ, 75. *Prof Exp:* Instr eng mech, Va Polytech Inst, 57-59 & Pa State Univ, 59-60; struct res engr, Elec Boat Div, Gen Dynamics Corp, Conn, 60-65; sr mech engr, Battelle Mem Inst, Ohio, 65-67; from asst prof to prof civil eng, Univ Akron, 67-78; prof eng mech & chmn, Dept Math & Eng Mech, 78-79, Gen Motors Inst, 78-79, prof mech eng & head dept, 79-83. *Concurrent Pos:* Res fel, Am Soc Civil Engrs; consult eng staff, Gen Motors Corp, Warren, Mich, 79-; Danforth assoc. *Mem:* Fel Am Soc Civil Engrs; fel Am Soc Mech Engrs; Am Soc Eng Educ; Am Acad Mech; Sigma Xi; Soc Automotive Engrs. *Res:* Computer assisted design; computer assisted manufacturing; finite element methods; shock and vibration analysis; computer methods. *Mailing Add:* 181 Crossridge Dr Kettering OH 45429-1563

LESTON, GERD, ORGANIC CHEMISTRY. *Current Pos:* CONSULT, 85- *Personal Data:* b Germany, Sept 19, 24; nat US; m 50, Gloria Kohnberg; c Laura & Jeffrey. *Educ:* City Col New York, BS, 48; Purdue Univ, MS, 49, PhD(chem), 52; Univ Pittsburgh, BS, 81. *Honors & Awards:* Pittsburgh Award, Pittsburgh Sect, Am Chem Soc, 96. *Prof Exp:* Chemist, Koppers Co Inc, 52-54, sr chemist, 54-58, group mgr, 58-66, sr group mgr, 67-72, sr proj scientist, 72-85. *Mem:* Am Chem Soc; Sigma Xi. *Res:* Synthetic organic chemistry, particularly phenol chemistry, aromatic substitution; aromatic alkylation and dealkylation; hydrogenation; aromatic acylation; ultraviolet stabilizers; antioxidant synthesis and testing; homogenous and heterogenous catalysis; pesticides; drugs; separation techniques; organics-salt complexes. *Mailing Add:* 1219 Raven Dr Pittsburgh PA 15243-1241

LESTOURGEON, WALLACE MEADE, MOLECULAR BIOLOGY. *Current Pos:* From asst prof to assoc prof, 78-86, PROF MOLECULAR BIOL, VANDERBILT UNIV, 86- *Personal Data:* b Alexandria, La, Jan 16, 43; m 86; c 2. *Educ:* Univ Tex, Austin, BS, 66, PhD(cell biol), 70. *Prof Exp:* NIH fel oncol, McArdle Lab Cancer Res, 70-74, asst scientist, 74-78. *Concurrent Pos:* Prin investr, NSF grants, 75, 78, 81, 85 & 88, NIH grants, 93-; dir, Cell Biol Prog, NSF, 83-84. *Mem:* AAAS; Am Soc Cell Biol; Sigma Xi. *Res:* Molecular biological, biochemical and physical chemical studies on the structure of 40's nuclear ribonucleoprotein particles and their role in RNA splicing and in the modulation of information flow in eucaryotes; gene regulation. *Mailing Add:* Dept Molecular Biol Vanderbilt Univ Nashville TN 37235-0001

LESTRADE, JOHN PATRICK, HIGH-ENERGY ASTROPHYSICS, MATH PHYSICS. *Current Pos:* from asst prof to assoc prof, 84-93, PROF PHYSICS, MISS STATE UNIV, 93- *Personal Data:* b New Orleans, La, Mar 25, 49; m 74; c 2. *Educ:* La State Univ, New Orleans, BS, 71; Purdue Univ, MS, 72; Rice Univ, MS, 76, PhD(space physics), 78. *Hon Degrees:* French Lang Master, Univ Aix-Marseille, France, 68. *Prof Exp:* Design scientist nuclear reactors, Westinghouse-Bettis Labs, 73-74; res assoc planetary atmospheres, Rice Univ, 78-80; asst prof physics, Tex A&M Univ, 80-84. *Mem:* Am Astron Soc. *Res:* High-energy astrophysics; gamma-ray burster modelling; fractal analysis of astrophysical phenomena. *Mailing Add:* Dept Physics Miss State Univ PO Box 5167 Mississippi State MS 39762. *Fax:* 601-325-8898; *E-Mail:* lestrade@ra.msstate.edu

LESTZ, SIDNEY J, FUEL ENGINEERING, ENGINE LUBRICATION. *Current Pos:* RETIRED. *Personal Data:* US citizen; m 63, Darlene Bresslow. *Educ:* Pa State Univ, BS, 57, MS, 59. *Prof Exp:* Asst, Dept Petrol & Natural Gas Eng, Pa State Univ, 58-59; asst proj engr, Wright Aeronaut Div, Curtiss Wright Corp, 61-64; sr res engr, Exxon Res & Eng Co, 64-70; sr res engr, US Fuels & Lubricants Res Lab, Southwest Res Inst, 70-71, mgr fuels & lubricants eng, 71-78, dir, 78-96, dir, Army Fuels & Lubricants Prog, 76-96. *Mem:* Combustion Inst; Soc Automotive Engrs; Coord Res Coun; Sigma Xi. *Res:* Wider boiling range fuels; synthetic fuels; alternate fuels; synthetic lubricants; universal hydraulic power transmission fluid development; safety fuels and fluids technology. *Mailing Add:* 622 Briar Oak San Antonio TX 78216

LESURE, FRANK GARDNER, GEOLOGY. *Current Pos:* RETIRED. *Personal Data:* b Camden, SC, Jan 28, 27; m 63; c 2. *Educ:* Va Polytech Inst, BS, 51; Yale Univ, MS, 52, PhD(geol), 55. *Honors & Awards:* Meritorious Serv Award, US Dept Interior, 85. *Prof Exp:* Geologist, US Geol Surv, 55-92. *Mem:* Soc Econ Geol; Geol Soc Am. *Res:* Genealogy. *Mailing Add:* 304 Upper College Terr Frederick MD 21701-4869

LE SURF, JOSEPH ERIC, PHYSICAL CHEMISTRY. *Current Pos:* CONSULT, 95- *Personal Data:* b London, Eng, July 21, 29; Can citizen; m 52; c 3. *Educ:* Univ London, BSc, 50 & 51. *Prof Exp:* Sci officer corrosion, Royal Naval Sci Serv, 51-57; sr sci officer, UK Atomic Energy Authority, 57-64; head, Syst Mat Br, Atomic Energy Can Ltd, 64-78; tech dir, London Nuclear Ltd, 78-84, pres & chief exec officer, London Nuclear Ltd & Johnson Nuclear Serv Inc, 84-88; prin scientist, Vectra Tech Inc, 88-95. *Mem:* Nat Asn Corrosion Engrs; Am Nuclear Soc; Can Nuclear Asn; Can Nuclear Soc. *Res:* Marine corrosion; corrosion, material selection, for nuclear decontamination processing plants and nuclear power plants. *Mailing Add:* 3529 Yale Cres Niagara Falls ON L2J 3C4 Can

LESYNA, LARRY, PHYSICS. *Current Pos:* SCIENTIST, NORTHROP GRUMMAN, 86- *Personal Data:* b Schenectady, NY, Mar 20, 58. *Educ:* Calif Inst Technol, BS, 78; Stanford Univ, PhD(appl physics), 87. *Concurrent Pos:* Adj assoc prof physics & astron, Hofstra Univ, 92- *Res:* Remote sensing; low temperature physics; infrared and submillimeter astronomy. *Mailing Add:* 13 Charlotte Pl Plainview NY 11803

LETARTE, JACQUES, PEDIATRICS, ENDOCRINOLOGY. *Current Pos:* dir govt affairs, 90-96, DIR EXTERNAL AFFAIRS, SCHERING CAN INC, 96- *Personal Data:* b Montreal, Que, Aug 19, 34; m 60; c 2. *Educ:* Univ Montreal, BA, 57, MD, 62. *Prof Exp:* Resident med, Notre Dame Hosp, Montreal, 62; resident pediat, St Justine Hosp, 63-64; resident, Royal Postgrad Med Sch, London, 68; assoc prof pediat, Univ Montreal, 69-80, prof, 80-90. *Concurrent Pos:* Mead-Johnson fel pediat, Univ Montreal, 63-64; res fel biochem, Children's Hosp, Zurich, 64-65; Queen Elizabeth II res fel, Can, 64-68; res fel, Clin Biochem Inst, Geneva, 65-67; res fel metab, Royal Postgrad Med Sch, London, 68-69; Med Res Coun Can fel, 68-69, scholar, 69-74; dir, Pediat Res Ctr, Hosp Ste-Justine, 82-86, med dir, 87-89; assoc med dir, Schering Can Inc, 89- *Mem:* AAAS; Can Soc Clin Invest; Soc Pediat Res; Endocrine Soc. *Res:* Hormonal regulation of carbohydrate metabolism; hyperammonemia in children; lipid and carbohydrate metabolism in children. *Mailing Add:* Schering Can Inc 3535 Trans-Can Pointe Claire PQ H9R 1B4 Can

LETARTE, MICHELLE, MOLECULAR IMMUNOLOGY, LEUKEMIA. *Current Pos:* From asst prof to assoc prof, 75-86, PROF, DEPT IMMUNOL, MED BIOPHYS & PEDIAT, UNIV TORONTO, 87-; SR SCIENTIST & SR INVESTR, RES INST, HOSP SICK CHILDREN, 80-; TERRY FOX RES SCIENTIST, NAT CANCER INST, 85- *Personal Data:* b Quebec, Oct 12, 47. *Educ:* Laval Univ, BSc, 68; Univ Ottawa, PhD(biochem), 72. *Concurrent Pos:* Nat Cancer Inst scholarship, Med Res Coun Can, 75-81, associateship, 81-85. *Mem:* Am Asn Histocompatibility Testing; Am Asn Immunologists; Can Soc Immunol (pres, 97-); Can Soc Biochem; NY Acad Sci. *Res:* Structure/function of endoglin its role in vascular biology and its role in the pathology of hereditary haemorrhagic telangiectasia for which it is a target gene. *Mailing Add:* Hosp Sick Children 555 University Ave Toronto ON M5G 1X8 Can. *E-Mail:* mablab@sickkids.on.ca

LETAW, HARRY, JR, TECHNOLOGY. *Current Pos:* PRES, SEVERN COMMUN CORP, 65-; PRES, INTELLINET CORP, 83-; CHMN, PRES, CHIEF EXEC OFFICER & BD DIRS, ESSEX CORP, 88- *Personal Data:* b Miami, Fla, Aug 7, 26; m 47, Joyce Winston Brown; c Anne Winston, Kaye Lynn, John Robert, Mary Jane, Amelia Elizabeth & James Brown. *Educ:* Univ Fla, BS, 49, MS, 51, PhD, 52. *Prof Exp:* Res asst prof, Dept Elec Eng, Univ Ill, 52-55; mkt mgr, Raytheon, 55-61; dir advan progs, Elec Div, Martin Marietta, 61-64; vpres & gen mgr, Eastern Tech Ctr, Inc, Bunker-Ramo Corp, 64-65; pres, Logos Ltd, 68-72; chmn & pres, Radiation Systs, Inc, 74-78. *Concurrent Pos:* Partic, DOD Joint Civilian Orientation Conf, Dept Defense, 58 & 95; adj assoc prof bus admin, Drexel Inst, 63-64; consult, Compagnie Int Pour L'Informatique, St German-en-Laye, France, 66-68; bd dirs, Econ Opportunity Comt, Anne Arundel Co, 69-71; chmn adv comt, Md State Dept Educ, 69-73; pres, Greater Severna Park Coun, 72-73. *Mem:* Sr mem Inst Elec & Electronics Engrs; Am Phys Soc; Security Affairs Support Asn; Sigma Xi. *Res:* Contributed articles to professional journals; patentee in field. *Mailing Add:* Essex Corp 9150 Guilford Rd Columbia MD 21046-1891. *E-Mail:* hletaw@essexcorp.com

LETCHER, DAVID WAYNE, DATABASE MANAGEMENT, BUSINESS INFORMATION SYSTEMS. *Current Pos:* PROF INFO SYSTS, SCH BUS, COL NJ, 87- *Personal Data:* b Dover, NJ, May 5, 41; m 63; c 4. *Educ:* Rutgers Univ, BS, 63; Newark NJ, MS, 65; Cornell Univ, PhD(meteorol), 71. *Prof Exp:* From asst prof to assoc prof meteorol, Trenton State Col, 68-81, coordr acad comput, 81-85, assoc prof meteorol, Physics Dept, 85-86. *Concurrent Pos:* Vis prof, Pub Serv Elec & Gas Co, Newark, NJ, 77-78; co-adj prof atmospheric sci, Rutgers Univ & Mercer Co Community Col; adj prof info systs, Mercer City Community Col. *Mem:* Asn Info Systs; Int Bus Sch Comput Asn. *Res:* Development of ways to incorporate computer technology into the college business curriculum. *Mailing Add:* Sch Bus Trenton State Col Hillwood Lakes Cn4700 Trenton NJ 08650. *Fax:* 609-771-2845; *E-Mail:* letcher@tscvm.trenton.edu

LETCHER, JOHN HENRY, III, PHYSICS, COMPUTER SCIENCE. *Current Pos:* PRES, SYNERGISTIC CONSULTS, INC, 70- *Personal Data:* b Wilkes-Barre, Pa, July 18, 36; m 60; c 2. *Educ:* Univ Tulsa, BS, 57 & 58; Univ Mo, MS, 59, PhD(physics), 63. *Hon Degrees:* DEng Tech, Toulane Col, 62. *Prof Exp:* Mem staff, Advan Electronics Techniques Div, McDonnell Corp, 63-64; mem staff, Cent Res Dept, Monsanto Co, 64-68; vpres systs & res, Data Res Corp, 68-70. *Concurrent Pos:* Mem staff, Dept Comput Sci, Southern Methodist Univ, Dallas, 75-79; prof comput sci, Univ Tulsa. *Mem:* Sigma Xi. *Res:* Computer software; hardware systems development; quantum physics and chemistry; medical physics-magnetic resonance imaging. *Mailing Add:* 7421 S Marion Ave Tulsa OK 74136

LETCHER, STEPHEN VAUGHAN, PHYSICS. *Current Pos:* From asst prof to assoc prof, 63-75, PROF PHYSICS, UNIV RI, 75- *Personal Data:* b Chicago, Ill, Dec 13, 35; m 59, Bettina Havens; c Benjamin & Abby. *Educ:* Trinity Col, BS, 57; Brown Univ, PhD(physics), 64. *Mem:* Am Phys Soc; Fel Acoust Soc Am; Int Soc Optical Eng. *Res:* Physical acoustics; physics of fluids; fiber-optic sensors. *Mailing Add:* Dept Physics Univ RI Kingston RI 02881. *E-Mail:* sletcher@uriacc.uri.edu

LETEY, JOHN, JR, RESEARCH, ADMINISTRATION. *Current Pos:* asst prof soil physics, Univ Calif, Los Angeles, 59-61, from asst prof to assoc prof, Riverside, 61-68, chmn, Dept Soil & Environ Sci, 75-80, dir, Kearney Found Soil Sci, 80-85, PROF SOIL PHYSICS, UNIV CALIF, RIVERSIDE, 68-, ASSOC DIR WATER & WILDLAND RESOURCES, 93- *Personal Data:* b Carbondale, Colo, June 13, 33; m 55; c Laura (Petersen), Donald & Lisa (Smith). *Educ:* Colo State Univ, BS, 55; Univ Ill, PhD(soil sci), 59. *Honors & Awards:* Soil Sci Res Award, Soil Sci Soc Am, 73. *Prof Exp:* Asst agron, Univ Ill, 55-59; asst prof soil physics, Univ Calif, Los Angeles, 59-61. *Concurrent Pos:* Consult, UN Food & Agr Orgn, Bulgaria, 73, India, 87; deleg, People to People Soil Sci Deleg, China, 83. *Mem:* Fel Am Soc Agron; fel Soil Sci Soc Am; fel AAAS. *Res:* Various transport phenomena, including water movement, gas movement, ionic diffusion, pesticide and other organic chemical interaction and movement through soil. *Mailing Add:* 435 Campus View Riverside CA 92507. *Fax:* 909-787-3993

LETKEMAN, PETER, CHEMISTRY. *Current Pos:* lectr, Brandon Univ, 63-66, from asst prof to assoc prof, 66-76, dept head, 72-80, dean sci, 82-93, PROF CHEM, BRANDON UNIV, 76- *Personal Data:* b Winkler, Man, Feb 12, 38; m 64; c 3. *Educ:* Univ Man, BSc, 60, MSc, 61, PhD(chem), 69. *Prof Exp:* Teacher high sch, Man, Can, 61-63. *Concurrent Pos:* Mem sci curric coun, Dept Educ, Man, 68-; grant, Univ Calif, Riverside, 70; consult, Christie Sch Supplies, Man, 70-; mem bd gov & senate, Brandon Univ, 73-77; pres, Western Man Sci Fair, 76; judge-in-chief, Can Wide Sci Fair, 75; mem staff, Tex A&M Univ, 77-78 & Univ Ariz, 93-94. *Mem:* Fel Chem Inst Can; AAAS. *Res:* The polarography and nuclear magnetic resonance of metal complexes in aqueous media; environmental research with regard to water and soil analysis; determination of stability constants of metal complexes; metal speciation in blood via computer modelling. *Mailing Add:* Dept Chem Brandon Univ Brandon MB R7A 6A9 Can

LETO, SALVATORE, ANDROLOGY, CLINICAL CHEMISTRY. *Current Pos:* DIR, CLIN LAB WASHINGTON FERTIL STUDY CTR, 73- *Personal Data:* b Borgetto, Sicily, Nov 28, 37; US citzen; m 64; c 2. *Educ:* City Col New York, BS, 61; Georgetown Univ, PhD(biol), 67. *Prof Exp:* Staff res fel, Nat Inst Child Health & Human Develop, NIH, 67-71; supvr clin lab, Idant Corp, NY, 71-72; dir clin lab, Baltimore, 72-73. *Mem:* Am Fertil Soc; Am Physiol Soc; Am Soc Andrology; Sigma Xi; Am Asn Tissue Banks; AAAS. *Res:* Human male fertility; sperm cryo-preservation; immuno-infertility; endocrinology of reproduction. *Mailing Add:* Washington Fertil Study Ctr 2600 Virginia Ave NW Suite 500 Washington DC 20037-1905

LETO, THOMAS L, MOLECULAR BIOLOGY & IMMUNOLOGY, CELL BIOLOGY. *Current Pos:* STAFF SCIENTIST, NIH, 88- *Personal Data:* b Bridgeport, Conn, Oct 5, 53. *Educ:* Western Conn State, BA, 75; Univ Va, PhD(biochem), 80. *Prof Exp:* NIH fel protein struct & function, Dept Pathol & Hemat, Yale Univ, 80-88, res assoc, 83-88. *Mem:* Am Soc Cell Biol; Am Fedn Clin Res. *Mailing Add:* Nat Inst Allergy & Infectious Dis NIH Bldg 10 Rm 11 N106 Bethesda MD 20892-1886

LETOURNEAU, DUANE JOHN, PLANT BIOCHEMISTRY. *Current Pos:* asst prof agr chem & asst agr chemist, Univ Idaho, 53-58, assoc prof & assoc agr chemist, 58-63, actg head, Dept Agr Biochem & Soils, 61-62, prof agr biochem & agr biochemist, 63-73, prof biochem & biochemist, 73-91, asst dept head, 89-90, secy fac, 90-91, EMER PROF BIOCHEM & EMER SECY FAC, UNIV IDAHO, 91- *Personal Data:* b Stillwater, Minn, July 12, 26; m 47; c Bruce Duane, Diane Elaine & Keith George. *Educ:* Univ Minn, BS, 48, MS, 51, PhD(agr bot), 54. *Prof Exp:* Asst, Univ Minn, 48-53. *Concurrent Pos:* Resident res assoc, USDA, 64-65; vis prof, Bot Dept, Univ Sheffield, Eng, 73; vis scientist, Nat Res Coun, Saskatoon, Can, 81. *Mem:* Fel AAAS; Am Soc Plant Physiol; Am Chem Soc; Am Phytopath Soc; Mycol Soc Am. *Res:* Plant biochemistry; plant cell culture techniques. *Mailing Add:* 479 Ridge Rd Moscow ID 83843. *Fax:* 208-885-6518

LETOURNEUX, JEAN, THEORETICAL NUCLEAR PHYSICS. *Current Pos:* from asst prof to assoc prof, 66-74, PROF PHYSICS, UNIV MONTREAL, 74- *Personal Data:* b Que, Mar 23, 35; m 70. *Educ:* Laval Univ, BSc, 59; Oxford Univ, DPhil(physics), 62. *Prof Exp:* Ciba fel, Inst Theoret Physics, Copenhagen, 62-64; res assoc physics, Univ Va, 64-65, asst prof, 65-66. *Mem:* Am Phys Soc; Can Asn Physicists. *Res:* Nuclear theory. *Mailing Add:* Dept Physics Univ Montreal PO Box 6128 Centre Ville Sta Montreal PQ H3C 3J7 Can

LETSINGER, ROBERT LEWIS, ORGANIC CHEMISTRY. *Current Pos:* from instr to prof, Northwestern Univ, 46-88, chmn dept, 72- 75, C H Hall prof, 88-91, EMER C H HALL PROF CHEM, NORTHWESTERN UNIV, 91- *Personal Data:* b Bloomfield, Ind, July 31, 21; m 43; c 3. *Educ:* Mass Inst Technol, BS, 43, PhD(org chem), 45. *Hon Degrees:* DSc, Acadia Univ, Can, 93. *Honors & Awards:* Rosenstiel Award, 85; Humboldt Sr Scientist Award, 88; Arthur C Cope, Am Chem Soc, 93. *Prof Exp:* Asst, Mass Inst Technol, 43-45, res assoc, 45-46; res chemist, Tenn Eastman Corp, 46. *Concurrent Pos:* Guggenheim fel, 56; mem, NIH Fel Rev Panel, 65-69; med chem study sect, NIH, 71-75. *Mem:* Nat Acad Sci; Am Soc Biol Chemists; AAAS; fel Japan Soc Prom Sci; Am Chem Soc; Am Acad Arts & Sci. *Res:* Bioorganic chemistry; synthesis of polynucleotides and nucleotide analogs; photochemistry; organoboron and organoalkali metal compounds. *Mailing Add:* 316 Third St Wilmette IL 60091

LETT, GREGORY SCOTT, SCIENTIFIC COMPUTING, OPTIMIZATION. *Current Pos:* sr consult, 89-91, SR CONSULT ASSOC, SCI SOFTWARE-INTERCOMP, INC, 91- *Personal Data:* b Denver, Colo, Apr 20, 58; m 83, Elizabeth A McAvoy; c Michael, Patrick & Bryan. *Educ:* Univ Colo, BA, 82, PhD(comput math), 91. *Prof Exp:* Sr engr, Martin Marietta Astronaut Group, 83-85 & 86-89; consult, Software Develop Lab, 85-86. *Mem:* Soc Indust & Appl Math. *Res:* Numerical linear algebra; simulation; numerical analysis of petroleum reservoir flow; numerical analysis of groundwater flow; modelling of fluid flow in porous media; applied and computational math; numerical partial differential equations. *Mailing Add:* 13892 W Virginia Dr Lakewood CO 80228. *E-Mail:* slett@ssii.com

LETT, JOHN TERENCE, BIOPHYSICS, RADIATION BIOLOGY. *Current Pos:* PROF RADIOL & RADIATION BIOL, GRAD SCH, COLO STATE UNIV, 68- *Personal Data:* b London, Eng, Dec 23, 33; m 56; c 1. *Educ:* Univ London, BSc, 56, PhD(phys org chem), 60. *Prof Exp:* Sr lectr, Inst Cancer Res, Univ London, 56-67. *Concurrent Pos:* Res assoc, Univ Calif, 61; vis scientist, Oak Ridge Nat Lab, 64. *Mem:* Radiation Res Soc; Brit Biophys Soc; Biophys Soc; Brit Asn Radiation Res. *Res:* DNA structure of the chromosome; repair of radiation damage to cellular DNA; radiation and aging. *Mailing Add:* Dept Radiol Health Sci Colo State Univ Ft Collins CO 80523

LETT, PHILIP W(OOD), JR, MECHANICAL SYSTEMS DESIGN. *Current Pos:* PRES, PWL INC, 87- *Personal Data:* b Newton, Ala, May 4, 22; m 48, Katy Howell; c Kathy, Warren & Lisa. *Educ:* Auburn Univ, BME, 43; Univ Ala, MS, 47; Univ Mich, PhD(mech eng), 50; Mass Inst Technol, ScM, 61. *Honors & Awards:* Cheonsu Medal, Repub Korea; Silver Medal, Am Defense Preparedness Asn; Ben Gilmer Award; Distinguished Eng Award, Auburn Univ. *Prof Exp:* Instr, Univ Mich, 48-50; proj engr, Eng Div, Chrysler Corp, 50-54, asst chief engr, 54-58, chief engr, 58-61, operating mgr, Chrysler Defense Eng, 61-73, prog mgr, MI Tank Prog, 73-76, gen mgr, Sterling Defense Div, 76-79, vpres eng, Chrysler Defense Div, 79-82; vpres res & eng, Gen Dynamics Land Systs, Warren, Mich, 82-87. *Concurrent Pos:* Mem, Eng Coun, Auburn Univ, contrib author to the Int Defense Rev, US Army; chmn, Vehicle Technol Sect, Tank-Automotive Div, Am Defense Preparedness Asn; consult, Gen Dynamics & US Army; mem bd trustees Univ Ala Colt Eng; distinguished eng fel, Univ Ala. *Mem:* Nat Acad Eng; Soc Automotive Engrs; Asn US Army; Am Defense Preparedness Asn. *Res:* Analytical and experimental studies of dynamic stability of surface vehicles employing models in wind tunnels and full scale instrumented vehicles on roads; computer simulation of business systems using industrial dynamics techniques; combat and tactical vehicle systems research and development; research on armored combat vehicle system. *Mailing Add:* PWL Inc 1330 Oxford Bloomfield Hills MI 48304

LETTENMAIER, DENNIS P, ENVIRONMENTAL & CIVIL ENGINEERING. *Current Pos:* PROF CIVIL ENG, UNIV WASH, 78- *Personal Data:* b Dec 7, 48. *Educ:* Univ Wash, BS, 70, PhD(civil eng), 75; George Washington Univ, MS, 72. *Honors & Awards:* Exceptional Achievement Award, US Geol Surv, 86; Sci & Technol Achievement Award, US Environ Protection Agency, 89; Huber Res Prize, Am Soc Civil Engrs, 90. *Mem:* Fel Am Geophys Union; Am Meteorol Soc; Europ Geophys Soc; Am Soc Civil Engrs; Am Water Resource Asn. *Mailing Add:* Civil Eng Dept Univ Wash Box 352700 Seattle WA 98195

LETTERMAN, GORDON SPARKS, surgery, plastic surgery, for more information see previous edition

LETTERMAN, HERBERT, ANALYTICAL CHEMISTRY, LABORATORY MANAGEMENT. *Current Pos:* DIR, ANALYTICAL TECHNOL, WARNER LAMBERT PHARMACEUT CO, 95- *Personal Data:* b Brooklyn, NY, Oct 8, 36; m 57, Barbara Bershad; c Sherel, Mitchell, Allison & David. *Educ:* City Col New York, BS, 58; Brooklyn Col, MA, 62; Seton Hall Univ, MS, 67, PhD(anal chem) 73. *Prof Exp:* Anal chemist, Brooklyn Jewish Hosp, NY, 58-59, Ciba Pharmaceut Co, NJ, 59-63; group leader phys chem res & develop, Bristol Myers Prod Div, 63-66, head qual control, 66-78, mgr qual serv, 78-86, mgr prod stability develop, 86-94. *Concurrent Pos:* Consult, 94-95. *Mem:* Sigma Xi; Am Chem Soc; Acad Pharmaceut Sci; fel Am Soc Qual Control. *Res:* Quality control; analytical method development. *Mailing Add:* 44 Delaware Ave New Providence NJ 07974. *Fax:* 973-540-5265

LETTIERI, THOMAS ROBERT, OPTICS, MICROMETROLOGY. *Current Pos:* physicist optics, 79-93, PROG MGR, ADVAN TECHNOL PROG, NAT INST STANDS & TECHNOL, 93- *Personal Data:* b Scranton, Pa, Sept 19, 52; m 94, May Ajam. *Educ:* Univ Miami, BS, 73; Univ Rochester, MS, 76, PhD(optics), 78; Univ Md, MGA, 87. *Honors & Awards:* IR-100 Award, 86. *Prof Exp:* Physicist high pressure, Nat Bur Stand, 78-79. *Concurrent Pos:* Consult, Develop Proj, Chinese Univ; tech monitor, Agency Int Develop Projs, Egypt & India. *Mem:* AAAS; Am Soc Testing & Mat; Optical Soc Am. *Res:* Optical science and technology; surface finish; microparticle measurements; light scattering; dimensional metrology. *Mailing Add:* 14313 Duvall Hill Ct Burtonsville MD 20866

LETTON, JAMES CAREY, PHARMACEUTICAL CHEMISTRY, ORGANIC SYNTHESIS. *Current Pos:* ORG CHEMIST, PROCTER & GAMBLE CO, 76- *Personal Data:* b Paris, Ky, June 9, 33; m 56; c 3. *Educ:* Ky State Col, BS, 55; Univ Ill, Chicago Med Ctr, PhD(chem), 71. *Hon Degrees:* LHD, Ky State Univ. *Honors & Awards:* Percy L Julian Award, Nat Orgn Prof Advan Black Chemists & Chem Engrs, 89. *Prof Exp:* Prod foreman, Julian Labs, 57-62, supt prod, Smith Kline & French Labs, 62-64, res & develop chemist, Julian Res Inst, 64-69; instr org chem, Triton Col, 68-70; assoc prof org chem, Ky State Univ, 70-73, chmn, Dept Chem, 71-75, prof org chem, 73-75. *Concurrent Pos:* Nat pres, Ky State Univ Alumni Asn, 78-84; bd dirs, Ky State Univ Found, 85-; Victor Mills Soc res fel, Procter & Gamble Co, 92- *Mem:* Fel Am Inst Chemists; Am Chem Soc; hon Soc Pharmaceut Sci. *Res:* Medicinal chemistry, especially beta amino ketones and analgesic properties; morphine-like compounds; steroid synthesis-carbohydrate chemistry; surface active and nonionics-synthesis; sugar derived surfactants; fat substitutes/sucrose esters. *Mailing Add:* 1247 Jeremy Ct Cincinnati OH 45240-2914

LETTS, LINDSAY GORDON, RESEARCH ADMINISTRATION. *Current Pos:* VPRES RES, NITROMED, INC, 94- *Personal Data:* b Warragul, Australia, Jan 9, 48; m 69, Barbara Hawkey; c Michelle, Kathryn & David. *Educ:* Monash Univ, BSc, 71; Sydney Univ, PhD(pharmacol), 80. *Prof Exp:* Tutor pharmacol, Sydney Univ, 76-80; res scientist, Royal Col Surgeons Eng, 80-82; sr res fel pharmacol, Merck Frosst Can Inc, 82-87; dir, Boehringer Ingelheim Pharmaceut, 87-94. *Concurrent Pos:* Sect ed, Prostaglandins, 86-; mem bd, Nat Inst Community Health Educ, Quinnipiac Col, Conn, 90-94; adj assoc prof, Yale Univ Sch Med, 91-94; mem bd, Conn United Res Excellence, 90-94, Inflammation Res Asn, 92- *Mem:* Am Thoracic Soc; Soc Leukocyte Biol; NY Acad Sci; Am Heart Asn; Inflammation Res Asn. *Res:* Inflammation research, including arachidonic acid metabolites, especially prostaglandins and leukotrienes; pulmonary inflammation including cellular influx, mediator release, airway responsiveness, asthma; elucidation of role of integrins during inflammatory responses; author of numerous publications. *Mailing Add:* 12 Abbott Rd Dover MA 02030. *Fax:* 617-638-5601; *E-Mail:* gletts@nitromed.com

LETTVIN, JEROME Y, NEUROPHYSIOLOGY. *Current Pos:* NEUROPHYSIOLOGIST, LAB ELECTRONICS, MASS INST TECHNOL, 51-, PROF COMMUN PHYSIOL, DEPTS BIOL, ELEC ENG & COMPUT SCI, 66-, EMER PROF. *Personal Data:* b Chicago, Ill, Feb 23, 20; m 47; c 3. *Educ:* Univ Ill, BS, 42, MD, 43. *Prof Exp:* Intern neurol, Boston City Hosp, 43-44; physiologist, Dept Psychol, Univ Rochester, 47-48; neuropsychiatrist & physiologist, Manteno State Hosp, 48-51. *Concurrent Pos:* Lectr neurol, Harvard Med Sch, 75- *Mem:* Am Physiol Soc. *Res:* Experimental epistemology. *Mailing Add:* Dept 20A002 77 Massachusetts Ave Cambridge MA 02139

LEU, MING C, ROBOTICS, MANUFACTURING AUTOMATION. *Current Pos:* PROF & CHAIR ROBOTICS & AUTOMATION, NJ INST TECHNOL, 87- *Personal Data:* b Taoyuan, Taiwan, Apr 27, 51; US citizen; m 78; c 3. *Educ:* Nat Univ Taiwan, BS, 72; Pa State Univ, MS, 77; Univ Calif, Berkeley, PhD(mech eng), 81. *Honors & Awards:* Wood Award, Forest Prod Res Soc, 81. *Prof Exp:* Res asst surface friction, Pa State Univ, 75-77; res asst vibration & control, Univ Calif, Berkeley, 77-81; asst prof robotics & automation, Cornell Univ, 81-87. *Concurrent Pos:* Consult, Moog Inc, 81-87, AT&T, 88-; presidential young investr award, NSF, 85; exec comt mem, Prod Eng Div, Am Soc Mech Engrs, 86-89, chmn, 89-90; prog chmn, Japan-US Symp on Flexible Automation, 90- *Mem:* Am Soc Mech Engrs; Inst Elec & Electronics Engrs; Soc Automotive Engrs; Soc Mfg Engrs; Int Soc Prod Engrs. *Res:* Motion planning and control; sensors and actuators; geometric modeling; robotics; automated assembly; author of over 100 technical publications. *Mailing Add:* Dept Mech Eng NJIT-MEC 204 200 Central Ave Newark NJ 07103-3918

LEU, RICHARD WILLIAM, MICROBIOLOGY, IMMUNOLOGY. *Current Pos:* MEM STAFF, NOBLE FOUND, 74-, HEAD IMMUNOL SECT, 76- *Personal Data:* b Argonia, Kans, Jan 5, 35; m 60; c 2. *Educ:* Northwestern State Col, Okla, BS, 60; Univ Okla, MS, 63, PhD(microbiol, immunol), 70. *Prof Exp:* USPHS res training fel pediat & path, Med Sch, Univ Minn, Minneapolis, 70-74. *Res:* Cellular immunity; effector molecules associated with macrophage inhibition, proliferation and activation; role of cytophilic antibody in cellular immunity; localized immunity in the lung. *Mailing Add:* Immunol Sect Bell Bldg Okla Res Found 825 NE 13th St Oklahoma City OK 73104

LEUBNER, GERHARD WALTER, ORGANIC CHEMISTRY. *Current Pos:* RETIRED. *Personal Data:* b Walton, NY, Aug 31, 21; m 44; c 3. *Educ:* Union Col, BS, 43; Univ Ill, PhD(chem), 49. *Prof Exp:* Chemist, Winthrop Chem Co, 43-45; asst, Univ Ill, 45-46; res assoc, Eastman Kodak Co, 48- *Mem:* Am Chem Soc. *Res:* Patent information storage and retrieval systems. *Mailing Add:* 151 Upland Dr Rochester NY 14617

LEUBNER, INGO HERWIG, PHYSICAL CHEMISTRY. *Current Pos:* SR RES CHEMIST, RES LABS, EASTMAN KODAK CO, 69- *Personal Data:* b Prittlbach, Ger, Apr 9, 38; div; c 2. *Educ:* Munich Tech Univ, Dipl, 63, PhD(phys chem), 66. *Honors & Awards:* Lieven Gevaert Medal, Soc Imaging Sci & Technol, 95. *Prof Exp:* Ger Res Asn res fel phys chem, Munich Tech Univ, 66-68; Welch Found fel & lectr photochem, Tex Christian Univ, 68-69. *Mem:* Fel Soc Imaging Sci & Technol; Am Chem Soc; Sigma Xi. *Res:* Photochemistry of organic and inorganic compounds; crystal formation (nucleation); photographic and imaging science. *Mailing Add:* 23 Willowview Dr Penfield NY 14526

LEUCHTAG, H RICHARD, MEMBRANE BIOPHYSICS, ION CHANNEL THEORY. *Current Pos:* from asst prof to assoc prof, 82-91, PROF BIOL, TEX SOUTHERN UNIV, 91- *Personal Data:* b Breslau, Ger, June 2, 27; US citizen; m 55, Alice Kesner; c Clyde R. *Educ:* Univ Calif, Los Angeles, BA, 50, MA, 55; Ind Univ, PhD(physics), 74. *Prof Exp:* Instr, Don Bosco Tech High Sch, 61-62, Univ San Diego Col Men, 62-63, San Diego State Col, 63-65 & Ind Univ-Purdue Univ, Indianapolis, 65-70; res assoc, Biophys Lab, Phys Dept, NY Univ, 72-74; assoc ed, Physics Today, Am Inst Physics, 74-78; res scientist, Dept Physiol & Biophys, Univ Tex Med Br, 78-82. *Concurrent Pos:* Physicist, Western Elec Co, 66; consult, Dept Physiol & Biophys, NY Univ Med Ctr, 78; secy, Int Conf Struct & Function Excitable Cells, 81; vis scientist, Mat Res Lab, Pa State Univ, 90. *Mem:* Am Phys Soc; Biophys Soc; Sigma Xi. *Res:* Physical basis of excitability in channels and membranes; ferroelectric transition hypothesis; measurement of noise, admittance and impedance in axons; monitored retrievable disposal of high-level radioactive waste; electrostatics, instability, effects of tilt and chirality and transitions in electrically charged segments of channels. *Mailing Add:* Dept Biol Tex Southern Univ 3100 Cleburne Ave Houston TX 77004. *E-Mail:* leuchtag@tsu.edu

LEUCK, EDWINE E, II, PLANT SYSTEMATICS. *Current Pos:* PROF BIOL, CENTENARY COL, LA, 80- *Personal Data:* b June 21, 51; m 73, Beth E Eldridge; c Nicholas E & Victor R. *Educ:* Mich State Univ, BS, 73; Univ Okla, MS, 75, PhD(bot), 80. *Mem:* Sigma Xi. *Res:* Floristic studies in northwest Louisiana and on the Beaver Island Archipelago in northeast Lake Michigan. *Mailing Add:* Dept Biol Centenary Col Shreveport LA 71104. *Fax:* 318-869-5795

LEUNG, ALBERT YUK-SING, PHARMACOGNOSY, BIOMEDICAL INFORMATION SERVICES. *Current Pos:* CONSULT NATURAL PRODS, 77- *Personal Data:* b Hong Kong, May 24, 38; nat US; m 68; c 2. *Educ:* Nat Taiwan Univ, BS, 61; Univ Mich, Ann Arbor, MS, 65, PhD(pharmacog), 67. *Prof Exp:* NIH res chemist, Med Ctr, Univ Calif, 67-69; res supvr microbial protein prod, Bohna Eng & Res, Inc, 69-71; tech dir chem & microbiol consult, Sci Res Info Serv, Inc, 71-74; dir res & develop, Dr Madis Labs, Inc, 74-77. *Concurrent Pos:* Lily Found fel, 63-67. *Mem:* Am Chem Soc; Am Soc Pharmacog; NY Acad Sci; Sigma Xi. *Res:* isolation of active principles from plants and microorganisms; retrieval and dissemination of biomedical information, especially from Chinese sources. *Mailing Add:* 35 Cumberland Rd Glen Rock NJ 07452-2603

LEUNG, ALEXANDER KWOK-CHU, GENERAL PEDIATRICS. *Current Pos:* clin asst prof, 82-90, CLIN ASSOC PEDIAT, UNIV CALGARY, 90-; CONSULT PEDIAT, FOOTHILLS PROV HOSP & ALTA CHILDRENS HOSP, 80- *Personal Data:* b Hong Kong, Oct 1, 48; Can citizen; m 75, Rita; c 5. *Educ:* Univ Hong Kong, MBBS, 73; Royal Col Physicians London & Royal Col Surgeons Eng, DCH, 77; Royal Col Physicians & Surgeons Ireland, DCH, 79, MRCPI, 78; MRCP(UK), 80; FRCP(C), 79, FAAP, 80, Am Bd Pediat Endocrinol & Pediat, dipl, 86; World Univ, PhD, 88, FRCP(G), 89, FRCPCE, 90, FRCPI, 90. *Honors & Awards:* Gold Medal Award, ABI, 87; Physician Recognition Award, AMA, 87, 90 & 93; Prep Fel Award, Am Acad Pediat, 87 & 90. *Prof Exp:* Intern, Univ Hong Kong, 73-74, lectr surg, 74; lectr pediat, Univ Queensland, 77; endocrine fel, Univ Calgary, 78-80. *Concurrent Pos:* Consult pediat, Calgary Gen Hosp, 80-81 & Grace Hosp, 80-82. *Mem:* Fel Royal Soc Med; fel Royal Soc Health; fel Can Pediat Soc; fel Am Acad Pediat; fel Royal Col Physicians Can; fel Royal Col Physicians Ireland; fel Royal Col Physicians Edinburgh; fel Royal Col Physicians Glasgow; fel Royal Acad Med. *Res:* General pediatrics; author of over 350 publications in various fields of pediatrics. *Mailing Add:* 233 16th Ave NW Plaza 162 Calgary AB T2M 0H5 Can. *Fax:* 403-242-6734

LEUNG, BENJAMIN SHUET-KIN XERJEN, ENDOCRINOLOGY, ONCOLOGY. *Current Pos:* assoc prof & dir, Hormone Res Lab, 78-83, chief, Div Cel Biol, 84-95, dir grad studies, 90-96, PROF, DEPT OBSTET & GYNEC, UNIV MINN, 84- *Personal Data:* b Hong Kong, June 30, 38; US citizen; m 64, Helen Hsu; c Kay, Titus & Steven. *Educ:* Seattle Pac Col, BS, 63; Colo State Univ, PhD(biochem), 69. *Prof Exp:* Res asst steroid hormones, Pac Northwest Res Found, 63-66; from asst prof to assoc prof surg, Med Sch, Univ Ore, dir, Hormone Receptor Lab, Clin Res Ctr Lab, 71-76; sr res scientist, Dept Surg, Cedars-Sinai Med Ctr, Los Angeles, 76-78. *Concurrent Pos:* NIH & Ford Found res fel reprod endocrinol, Med Sch, Vanderbilt Univ, 69-71; Med Res Found Ore grant, Med Sch, Univ Ore, 71-72; Am Cancer Soc Ore Div res grants, 72-74; Cammack Trust Fund grant, 74-75; NIH grants, 75-79; assoc oncologist, Div Surg Oncol, Univ Calif, Los Angeles, 76-78; Med Res Found Ore res grant, 76-77; Nat Cancer Inst res grant, 77-91; Minn Med Found res grant, 78-79; ad hoc consult & grant rev, NSF, NIH, Nat Cancer Inst, Nat Inst Alcohol Abuse & Alcoholism; ad hoc ed & referee sci manuscripts, J Nat Cancer Inst, J Biol Chem & J Steroid Biol; from assoc prof to prof, Dept Animal Physiol, Univ Minn, 82-; vis prof minority insts, Fedn Am Socs Exp Biol. *Mem:* Am Soc Biol Chemists; AAAS; Endocrine Soc; Soc Gynec Invest; Am Asn Cancer Res; Soc Chinese Bioscientists Am. *Res:* Growth factors, oncogenes and steroid hormone action in regulating fetal and cancer growth; cell biology; recipient of over 36 grants. *Mailing Add:* Dept Obstet & Gynec PO Box 395 UMHC Minneapolis MN 55455. *Fax:* 612-626-0665.

LEUNG, CHARLES CHEUNG-WAN, SEMICONDUCTOR PROCESSING, DEVICE PHYSICS. *Current Pos:* PRES & CHMN, BIPOLARICS, 88- *Personal Data:* b Hong Kong, June 27, 46; US citizen; m 73; c 1. *Educ:* Univ Hong Kong, BSc, 69; Univ Chicago, MS, 71, PhD(physics), 76. *Prof Exp:* Sr scientist, Corning Glass Works, 76-80; sr staff engr, Motorola, 80-81; sr mem tech staff, Avantek, 81-88. *Mem:* Am Phys Soc; Am Chem Soc; Am Vacuum Soc; Soc Info Display. *Res:* Electro-optic materials; glassification; carbon; vacuum deposition; thin film; surface science. *Mailing Add:* Bipolarics 108 Albright Way Los Gatos CA 95030.

LEUNG, CHRISTOPHER CHUNG-KIT, EMBRYOLOGY, IMMUNOLOGY. *Current Pos:* ASSOC PROF ANAT, NJ MED SCH, 85- *Personal Data:* b Hong Kong, Jan 3, 39; m 70, Stella M Tang; c Jacquelyn & Therese. *Educ:* Howard Univ, BSc, 64; Jefferson Med Col, PhD(anat, embryol), 69. *Prof Exp:* Res asst, Sch Med, Univ Rochester, 64-65; from instr to assoc prof pediat, Jefferson Med Col, Thomas Jefferson Univ, 69-74, instr anat, 69-75, instr, Col Allied Health Sci, 70-75, res assoc prof pediat, 74-75; asst prof anat, Univ Kans Med Ctr, 75-79; assoc prof anat, Sch Med, La State Univ, 79-85. *Concurrent Pos:* NIH fel, Stein Res Ctr, Thomas Jefferson Univ, 65-69; NIH res grant, 79-89; mem Ad Hoc Study Sect, NIH, 85. *Mem:* Teratol Soc; Am Asn Anatomists; Am Asn Immunologists; Am Soc Cell Biol. *Res:* Teratology; immunopathology; cell biology; anatomy. *Mailing Add:* Dept Anat NJ Med Sch Univ Med & Dent Newark NJ 07103. *Fax:* 973-982-7489.

LEUNG, CHUNG NGOC, THEORETICAL PHYSICS, ELEMENTARY PARTICLE PHYSICS. *Current Pos:* asst prof, 89-95, ASSOC PROF, UNIV DEL, 95- *Personal Data:* b Macao, May 12, 56; m. *Educ:* Univ Minn, BS, 77, PhD(physics), 83. *Prof Exp:* Res assoc, Fermi Nat Accelerator Lab, 83-85, Purdue Univ, 85-86 & 87-89 & Max Planck Inst Physics & Astrophys, 86-87. *Mem:* Am Phys Soc. *Res:* Elementary particle theory; dynamical symmetry breaking in gauge theories; fermion mass problem; neutrino physics; phenomenology of elementary particles. *Mailing Add:* Dept Physics & Astron Univ Del Newark DE 19716. *Fax:* 302-831-1637.

LEUNG, DONALD YAP MAN, KAWASAKI DISEASE, ATOPIC DERMATITIS. *Current Pos:* ASSOC PROF PEDIAT, UNIV COLO, 89- *Personal Data:* b New York, NY, Oct 1, 49; m 78; c 2. *Educ:* Johns Hopkins Univ, BA, 70; Univ Chicago, PhD(biochem), 75, MD, 77. *Prof Exp:* Intern pediat, Children's Hosp, Boston, 77-78, resident pediat, 78-79, fel allergy-immunol, 79-81; clin fel pediat, Harvard Med Sch, 77-79, instr pediat, 81-85, from asst prof to assoc prof pediat, 83-89. *Concurrent Pos:* Dir allergy, Children's Hosp, 87-89; head, Div Allergy-Immunol, Nat Jewish Ctr Immunol & Respiratory Med, 89- *Mem:* Am Fedn Clin Res; Am Acad Allergy & Immunol; Am Asn Immunologists; Soc Pediat Res; AAAS. *Res:* Mechanisms of allergic diseases including atopic dermatitis, asthma and food allergy, IgE responses; immunopathogenesis of Kawasaki disease; use of immunomodulatory agents in the treatment of allergic disorders. *Mailing Add:* Dept Pediat K926 Nat Jewish Ctr Immunol & Resp Med 1400 Jackson St Denver CO 80206-2762.

LEUNG, FREDERICK C, MOLECULAR BIOLOGY, ZOOLOGY. *Current Pos:* SR RES SCIENTIST CELL BIOL, DEPT BIOL & CHEM, BATTELLE, PAC NORTHWEST LABS, 85- *Personal Data:* b Hong Kong, Dec 1, 52; US citizen; m 78; c 2. *Educ:* Univ Calif, Berkeley, BA, 74, PhD(endocrinol), 78. *Prof Exp:* Fel neuroendocrinol, dept physiol, Mich State Univ, 78-80; sr res biochemist animal physiol, Merck, Sharp & Dohme Res Labs, 80-84, res fel, 84-85. *Concurrent Pos:* Adj prof, dept animal sci, Rutgers Univ, 82-85. *Mem:* Am Endocrinol Soc; Am Physiol Soc; NY Acad Sci; Am Soc Zool. *Res:* Hormonal regulation of growth; hypothalamic regulation of anterior pituitary function; structure & function of growth hormone and its receptor; eukaryotic cell expression and gene insertion. *Mailing Add:* 714 Redwood Lane Richland WA 99352.

LEUNG, IRENE SHEUNG-YING, MINERALOGY. *Current Pos:* asst prof, 71-77, ASSOC PROF GEOL, LEHMAN COL, 77- *Personal Data:* b Hong Kong, July 10, 34. *Educ:* Univ Hong Kong, BA, 57; Ohio State Univ, MA, 63; Univ Calif, Berkeley, PhD(geol), 69. *Prof Exp:* Res staff geologist, Yale Univ, 69-71. *Mem:* Sigma Xi; Mineral Soc Am; Am Geophys Union; Geochem Soc; Asian Environ Soc. *Res:* X-ray investigation of mineral inclusions in natural diamonds; magmatic crystallization and sector-zoning in crystals; deformation structures and glide mechanisms in deformed minerals. *Mailing Add:* Dept Geol & Geog City Univ NY Lehman Col 250 Bedford Park W Bronx NY 10468-1589.

LEUNG, JOSEPH YUK-TONG, SCHEDULING THEORY, COMPLEXITY THEORY. *Current Pos:* chmn dept comput sci & eng, 90-96, PROF DEPT COMPUT SCI & ENG, UNIV NEBR, LINCOLN, 90- *Personal Data:* b Hong Kong, June 25, 50; m 73, Maria Mo; c Jonathan. *Educ:* Southern Ill Univ, Carbondale, BA, 72; Pa State Univ, PhD(comput sci), 77. *Prof Exp:* Asst prof comput sci, Va Polytech Inst & State Univ, 76-77; asst prof elec eng & comput sci, Northwestern Univ, Evanston, 77-81, assoc prof, 81-85; prof comput sci prog, Univ Tex, Dallas, 85-90, assoc prog head, 87-90. *Mem:* Asn Comput Mach; Inst Elec & Electronics Engrs; AAAS; NY Acad Sci. *Res:* Operating systems; scheduling theory; analysis of algorithms; real-time systems; computational complexity. *Mailing Add:* Dept Comput Sci & Eng Univ Nebr-Lincoln Lincoln NE 68588-0115.

LEUNG, JULIA PAULINE, MONOCLONAL ANTIBODY, CANCER BIOLOGY. *Current Pos:* Sr Res Mgr, Dept Cell Biol, 81-90, RES MGT & ADMIN, CANCER RES CTR, HYBRITECH, INC, 90- *Educ:* Univ Wash, PhD(cell biol), 74. *Mailing Add:* Cancer Res Ctr Hawaii Univ Hawaii 1236 Lauhala St Honolulu HI 96813.

LEUNG, KAM-CHING, ASTRONOMY, ASTROPHYSICS. *Current Pos:* asst prof physics, 70-72, assoc prof, 72-78, PROF PHYSICS & ASTRON, UNIV NEBR, LINCOLN, 78- *Personal Data:* b Hong Kong, June 16, 35; m 63; c 2. *Educ:* Queen's Univ, Ont, BSc, 61; Univ Western Ont, MA, 63; Univ Pa, PhD(astron), 67. *Prof Exp:* Nat Acad Sci-Nat Res Coun res fel astron, Inst Space Studies, NASA, 68-70. *Concurrent Pos:* NSF res grant, Univ Nebr, Lincoln, 70-71, 75, 81-82, 85-87 & 87-89, NASA grant, 86-87, dir observ, 72-75; staff assoc astron sect, NSF, 75; mgt specialist, Off Nuclear Energy, ERDA, 77; sr assoc, Off Energy Res, Dept Energy. *Mem:* Fel AAAS; Int Astron Union; Am Astron Soc. *Res:* Stellar photometry and spectroscopy; intrinsic variable stars; binary stars. *Mailing Add:* 1953 B St Lincoln NE 68502.

LEUNG, KA-NGO, ELECTRICAL ENGINEERING, SYSTEMS DESIGN. *Current Pos:* staff physicist, 78-88, SR STAFF PHYSICIST, LAWRENCE BERKELEY LAB, 88- *Personal Data:* b Canton, China. *Educ:* Chinese Univ Hong Kong, BS, 68; Univ Akron, MS, 71; Univ Calif, Los Angeles, PhD(physics), 75. *Prof Exp:* Asst prof physics, James Madison Univ, Va, 75-78. *Mem:* Fel Am Phys Soc; Sigma Xi. *Res:* Development of positive and negative ion sources for neutral beam heating in fusion reactors and particle accelerators. *Mailing Add:* Lawrence Berkeley Lab Bldg 4 Univ Calif One Cyclotron Rd Berkeley CA 94720.

LEUNG, LAI-WO STAN, NEUROPHYSIOLOGY, BEHAVIOR & NEURAL ACTIVITY. *Current Pos:* from asst prof to assoc prof clin neurol sci, physiol & psychol, 80-93, PROF PHYSIOL & CLIN NEUROL SCI, UNIV WESTERN ONT, LONDON, CAN, 93- *Personal Data:* b Macau, Can, July 21, 52; m 79; c 1. *Educ:* Calif State Univ, Northridge, BSc, 73; Univ Calif, Berkeley, PhD(biophys), 78. *Prof Exp:* Teaching assoc physiol & biophys, Univ Calif, Berkeley, 77-78; fel physiol psychol, Univ Western Ont, London, Can, 78-79, fel brain res, Int Brain Res Orgn & UNESCO fel, Inst Med Physics, Utrecht, Holland, 79-80. *Concurrent Pos:* Univ res fel, Natural Sci & Eng Res Coun, 80-90; mem, Biopsychol Study Sect, NIH, 87-91; staff mem, Neurosci Prog, Univ Western Ont, London, Can. *Mem:* Soc Neurosci; AAAS. *Res:* Analyses of normal and abnormal neuronal activities in the cerebral cortex in vivo and in vitro; neural plasticity after seizures, brain rhythms; experimental epilepsy, neural plasticity. *Mailing Add:* Dept Clin Neurol Sci Univ Western Ont London ON N6A 5C5 Can. *Fax:* 519-661-3827.

LEUNG, PAK SANG, COLLOID CHEMISTRY. *Current Pos:* ASST PROF, ORANGE CO COL, MIDDLETOWN, NY, 93- *Personal Data:* b Shanghai, China, June 8, 35; US citizen; m 65, Priscilla Chan; c Kent & Ross. *Educ:* Nat Taiwan Univ, BSc, 57; Columbia Univ, MA, 62, PhD(phys chem), 67. *Prof Exp:* Dyes lab asst, Imp Chem Industs, 57-59; demonstr chem, Hong Kong Baptist Col, 59-61; res scientist, Brookhaven Nat Lab-Columbia Univ, 66-67; sr res scientist, Union Carbide Corp, Tarrytown, 67-93. *Concurrent Pos:* Mem chem adv bd, Harriman Col, 74- *Mem:* Sigma Xi; Am Chem Soc. *Res:* Surface and collidal chemistry; polymer composite; polymer processing; clinical chemistry. *Mailing Add:* 15 Woodland Rd Highland Mills NY 10930. *E-Mail:* pleung@mail.sunyorange.edu.

LEUNG, PETER, DRUG METABOLISM, PHARMACOKINETICS. *Current Pos:* staff toxicologist, 91-96, SR TOXICOLOGIST, DEPT PESTICIDE REGULATION, MED TOXICOL BR, CALIF ENVIRON PROTECTION AGENCY, 96- *Personal Data:* b New York, NY, Apr 12, 55; M 92, Bernice C Low. *Educ:* Johns Hopkins Univ, BA, 77; State Univ NY, PhD(pharmacol), 83; Am Bd Toxicol, dipl, 87. *Honors & Awards:* Travel Award, Am Soc Pharmacol & Exp Therapeut, 84. *Prof Exp:* Fel, Col Med, Tex A&M Univ, 83-86; sr scientist, Schering-Plough Corp, 86-89; staff toxicologist, Med Toxicol Br, Calif Dept Food & Agr, 89-96. *Mem:* Soc Toxicol; Am Col Toxicol; Am Soc Pharmacol & Exp Therapeut. *Res:*

Metabolism and disposition of cyanide in the presence and absence of cyanide antagonists; new prophylactic and therapeutic treatments for cyanide intoxication; erythrocytes as drug carriers for purified enzymes. *Mailing Add:* Dept Pesticide Regulation-Med Toxicol Br Rm 234 Calif Environ Protection Agency 1020 N St Sacramento CA 95814

LEUNG, PHILIP MAN KIT, MEDICAL PHYSICS, BIOPHYSICS. *Current Pos:* SR PHYSICIST, ONT CANCER INST, 68- *Personal Data:* b Hong Kong, June 22, 33; Can citizen; m 59; c 2. *Educ:* Univ Toronto, BASc, 60; McMaster Univ, MSc, 61; Univ Toronto, PhD(biophys), 67. *Prof Exp:* Lectr, Ryerson Inst Technol, Can, 61-62; physicist, BC Cancer Inst, Can, 67-68. *Concurrent Pos:* Fel, Univ BC, 67-68; consult physicist, Orillia Soldier Mem Hosp, Can, 69-70 & Can Soc Radiol Technicians, 69-78; ed, Physics in Med & Biol, 72-75; investr, Children's Cancer Study Group, Nat Cancer Inst, USPHS, 76-77 & 77-78; lectr, Dept Med Biophys, Univ Toronto, 79- *Res:* Radiation dosimetry; radiotherapy treatment techniques and new equipment associated with radiation oncology. *Mailing Add:* Ont Cancer Inst 610 University Ave 1B738 Toronto ON M5G 2M9 Can

LEUNG, SO WAH, dentistry, physiology, for more information see previous edition

LEUNG, WAI YAN, PHYSICS. *Current Pos:* ASSOC PROF, DEPT CHEM, AMES LAB, IOWA STATE UNIV, 91- *Prof Exp:* Asst prof, Dept Chem, Fla Int Univ, 89-91. *Mem:* Am Phys Soc. *Res:* Service structures. *Mailing Add:* 5326 Schubert St Ames IA 50014

LEUNG, WAI YAN, MOLECULAR BIOLOGY. *Current Pos:* FAC MEM, DEPT PATH, TULANE UNIV SCH MED, 92- *Personal Data:* b Hong Kong, China, May 23, 48. *Educ:* Chinese Univ, Hong Kong, BS, 70; Baylor Col Med, PhD(virol), 74. *Prof Exp:* Fac, Dept Med, Univ Ark Sch Med Sci, 89-92. *Mem:* Am Chem Soc; Am Phys Soc. *Mailing Add:* Dept Path Tulane Univ Sch Med 1430 Tulane Ave New Orleans LA 70112-2699

LEUNG, WING HAI, SURFACE CHEMISTRY. *Current Pos:* asst prof, Hampton Inst, 78-82, ASSOC PROF CHEM, HAMPTON UNIV, 82- *Personal Data:* b Hong Kong, July 29, 37; m 65; c 3. *Educ:* Univ Hong Kong, BSc, 63; Univ Miami, MS, 70, PhD(phys chem), 74. *Prof Exp:* Res assoc, State Univ NY, Buffalo, 74-76; sr chemist res, GAF Corp, Binghamton, NY, 76-77; res scientist, Clinton Corn Corp, Iowa, 77-78. *Mem:* Am Chem Soc; Sigma Xi; Am Geophys Union. *Res:* Surface phenomena and kinetic studies of crystal growth; the structure and interaction at solid-solution interfaces. *Mailing Add:* Hampton Univ Hampton VA 23668

LEUNG, WOON FONG (WALLACE), FLUID DYNAMICS, SOLID-LIQUID SEPARATION. *Current Pos:* sr res scientist centrifuge dynamics & fluid/particle separation, 86-93, DIR PROCESS TECHNOL, BIRD MACH CO, 93- *Personal Data:* b Hong Kong, Jan 25, 54; m 78, Stella Cheng; c Jessica W & Jeffrey K. *Educ:* Cornell Univ, BS, 77; Mass Inst Technol, MS, 78, ScD(mech eng), 81. *Honors & Awards:* Cedric Ferguson Medal, Soc Petrol Engrs, 87; Eng Merit Award, Am Filtration & Separation Soc, 91; Baker Hughes Tech Achievement Award, 92. *Prof Exp:* Res engr flow in porous media, Gulf Res & Develop Co, 81-84; proj leader flow near well-bore & transient testing, Schlumberger, 84-86. *Concurrent Pos:* Chmn, Centrifuge Network; tech session chmn, Am Filtration & Separation Soc Ann meetings, 90, 91, dir & conf chmn, 93; course dir, Ctr prof advan, NJ; dir, Am Filtration & Separation Soc, 95, chmn, Awards Comt, 95-; sci comt, 8th World Filtration Cong 2000, UK. *Mem:* Soc Mech Engrs; Soc Petrol Engrs; Am Filtration & Separation Soc; Am Inst Aeronaut & Astronaut; Soc Rheology. *Res:* Physical-chemical hydrodynamics for industrial applications, solid-liquid separation in industrial centrifuges, suspension and dense cake rheology, membrane filtration and inclined lamella settlers; fluid flow and compaction-consolidation in porous media; oil and gas production through wellbore perforations; petroleum reservoir engineering; develop and use computer models and experimental test rigs in research and developmental study; develop innovative dynamic balancing methods for rotating machinery under process condition; eighteen published technical papers and over 800 in-house technical reports; author of one publication; granted over 15 US patents. *Mailing Add:* 100 Neponset Rd South Walpole MA 02071. Fax: 508-668-6855

LEUNG, YIU M, PARALLEL PROCESSING, PROGRAMMING LANGUAGES. *Current Pos:* MEM TECH STAFF, LUCENT TECHNOL, 96- *Personal Data:* b Canton, China, July 29, 51; US citizen. *Educ:* Chinese Univ Hong Kong, BS, 74; Syracuse Univ, MS, 83, PhD(comput eng), 92. *Prof Exp:* Lead programmer, IBM Corp, 79-92, res staff, 92-96. *Concurrent Pos:* Adj fac parallel prog, State Univ NY, Binghamton, 93- *Res:* Parallel processing, in particular, parallel programming languages, parallel programming environment, communications, parallel computer architecture. *Mailing Add:* 19 Exeter Pass Colts Neck NJ 07722-1768. *E-Mail:* leungym@unet.ibm.com

LEUPOLD, HERBERT AUGUST, PHYSICS, MATERIALS SCIENCE. *Current Pos:* RES PHYSICIST, ELECTRONICS RES DEVELOP COMMAND, US ARMY, 67- *Personal Data:* b Brooklyn, NY, Jan 6, 31. *Educ:* Queens Col, NY, BS, 53; Columbia Univ, AM, 58, PhD(physics), 64. *Honors & Awards:* Commendation, Inst for Explor Res, US Army, 69 & Electronics Technol & Devices Lab, US Army, 72; Harold Jacobs Award, 87. *Prof Exp:* Fel physics, Lawrence Radiation Lab, Livermore, Calif, 64-67. *Concurrent Pos:* Lectr physics, Queens Col, NY, 57 & Monmouth Col, 67-70, 84-85, & Univ Dayton 84, 86, 88 & lectr chem, Trenton State Col, 83. *Mem:* Am Phys Soc; Sigma Xi; fel Inst Elec & Electronics Engrs; Inst Elec & Electronics Engrs Magnetics Soc. *Res:* Magnetism; semiconductors; superconductivity; thermodynamics; cryogenics; magnetic circuit design; magnetic materials. *Mailing Add:* 26 B Stony Hill Gardens Eatontown NJ 07724

LEUSCHEN, M PATRICIA, PERINATOLOGY, NEUROENDOCRINOLOGY. *Current Pos:* CLIN ASSOC PROF, CREIGHTON UNIV, OMAHA, 89-; ASSOC PROF, MED CTR, UNIV NEBR, OMAHA, 91- *Personal Data:* b Iowa, June 3, 43; m 63; c 4. *Educ:* Creighton Univ, BS, 65, MS, 67; Med Ctr, Univ Nebr, Omaha, MS, 74, PhD(anat), 76. *Prof Exp:* Res asst pediat, Med Ctr, Univ Nebr, Omaha, 80-82, asst prof pediat & res dir, Div Newborn Med, 82-91. *Concurrent Pos:* Chair, Med Sci Interdepartmental Area Grad Prog, Univ Nebr Med Ctr, 89-, Exec Grad Comt, Univ Nebr Syst, 90-91. *Mem:* Am Asn Anatomists; Am Soc Cell Biol; Soc Neurosci. *Res:* Cerebral microvasculature and intracranial hemorrhage in premature infants; B-endorphin and related neurohormones and stress in neonates, ultrastructural studies including morphometry; association with perinatal asphyxia and/or apnea; interaction between prostaglandin synthesis and neuroendocrine axis; Chloride changes and astrocyte swelling. *Mailing Add:* Univ Nebr Med Ctr 600 S 42nd St Omaha NE 68198-1205

LEUSSING, DANIEL, JR, ANALYTICAL CHEMISTRY. *Current Pos:* from asst prof to assoc prof, 62-70, PROF CHEM, OHIO STATE UNIV, 70- *Personal Data:* b Cincinnati, Ohio, Oct 8, 24; m 57; c 3. *Educ:* Univ Cincinnati, BA, 45; Univ Ill, MS, 47; Univ Minn, PhD(chem), 53. *Prof Exp:* Instr anal chem, Univ Minn, 51-52; chemist, Am Cyanamid Co, 53; instr anal chem, Mass Inst Technol, 53-55; from instr to asst prof, Univ Wis, 55-60; chemist, Nat Bur Stands, 60-62. *Mem:* Am Chem Soc. *Res:* Physical chemistry of aqueous solutions; coordination chemistry; metal mercaptide complexes; Schiff base complexes; kinetics. *Mailing Add:* Dept Chem Ohio State Univ Columbus OH 43210

LEUTENEGGER, WALTER, BIOLOGICAL ANTHROPOLOGY, PRIMATOLOGY. *Current Pos:* from asst prof to assoc prof, 71-83, PROF BIOL ANTHROP, UNIV WIS-MADISON, 83- *Personal Data:* b Winterthur, Switz, Oct 18, 41; US citizen. *Educ:* Univ Zurich, PhD(biol anthrop), 69. *Prof Exp:* Anthropologist, Bern Natural Mus Hist, Switz, 67-69; sci res asst biol anthrop, Univ Zurich, 69-71. *Concurrent Pos:* Affil scientist, Wis Regional Primate Res Ctr, 71- *Mem:* Am Asn Phys Anthropologists; Am Soc Naturalists; Am Soc Primatologists; Soc Vert Paleont. *Res:* Functional anatomy of the primate locomotor apparatus; determinants of behavioral and morphological sexual dimorphism; reconstruction of early hominid social organization and behavior. *Mailing Add:* Dept Anthrop Univ Wis Madison 1180 Observatory Dr Madison WI 53706-1393

LEUTHEUSSER, H(ANS) J(OACHIM), FLUID MECHANICS, TRIBOLOGY. *Current Pos:* instr fluid mech, Dept Mech Eng, Univ Toronto, 55-57, lectr, 57-62, from asst prof to prof fluid mech, 63-92, assoc chmn dept, 77-79, assoc chmn dept & coordr grad studies, 84-88, EMER PROF, DEPT MECH ENG, UNIV TORONTO, 92- *Personal Data:* b Eisenach, Ger, Feb 1, 27; Can citizen; m 55, Gudrun E P nee Bege; c Michael J, Doris E & Suzanne M. *Educ:* Karlsruhe Univ, Dipl Ing, 52; Univ Toronto, MASc, 57, PhD(mech eng), 61. *Prof Exp:* Asst hydraul eng, Theodor-Rehbock Lab, Karlsruhe Univ, 51-52; field engr, Oulujoki Oy, Helsinki, Finland, 52-53; sr engr, Friedrich Buchner, Wuerzburg, Ger, 53-54. *Concurrent Pos:* Consult engr, 57-; sabbatical leaves, Inst Mech Statist of Turbulence, Univ Aix Marseille, 66-67, Inst Hydromech, Karlsruhe Univ, 75-76, Univ Santiago & Aristotle Univ, Thessaloniki, 81, Univ Victoria, BC, 89, Univ Shanghai & Tokyo, 90. *Mem:* Am Soc Civil Engrs; Int Asn Hydraul Res; Gesellschaff fuer angewandle Math & Mech (GAMM). *Res:* Fundamental fluid mechanics and applications; turbulence; fluid elasticity and transients; biomechanics; building aerodynamics; tribology. *Mailing Add:* Dept Mech & Indust Eng Univ Toronto Toronto ON M5S 3G8 Can. Fax: 416-978-7753; *E-Mail:* leutheu@mie.utoronto.ca

LEUTZE, WILLARD PARKER, geology; deceased, see previous edition for last biography

LEUTZINGER, RUDOLPH L(ESLIE), MECHANICAL ENGINEERING, AEROSPACE ENGINEERING. *Current Pos:* assoc prof mech eng, 76-79, EMER PROF MECH ENG, UNIV MO-COLUMBIA, 79-; DIR, AERO TURB MFG, 79-; CONSULT ENGR, LEUTZINGER CONSULT ASSOCS, 79- *Personal Data:* b Dallas Center, Iowa, June 17, 22; m 50; c 6. *Educ:* Iowa State Univ, BS, 43; Univ Mich, MS, 52; Univ Iowa, PhD(mech eng), 76. *Prof Exp:* Stress analyst, Douglas Airplane Co, 44-46 & McDonnell Airplane Co, 46 & 47; instr aeronaut eng, Iowa State Univ, 47-50; res assoc dynamics, Aeronaut Res Ctr, Univ Mich, 51; res engr, Midwest Res Inst, Mo, 51-53; asst prof aeronaut eng & appl mech, Univ Kans, 54-56; assoc prof aerodyn, Agr & Mech Col Tex, 56-58; assoc prof thermodyn, Univ Mo-Rolla, 58-60; assoc prof eng & chmn dept, Univ Mo-Kansas City, 62-76. *Concurrent Pos:* Consult, Boeing Airplane Co, 57, Gas Turbine Div, Westinghouse Elec Corp, 56 & McDonnell Aircraft Corp, 58, 59 & 62; assoc mem grad fac & eng admin coun, Agr & Mech Col Tex, 58; mem grad fac, Univ Mo, 59; NSF inst res grants, 61, 62 & 64; Kans City Regional Coun Higher Educ grant, 64-65; vis lectr, Col Eng, Univ Iowa, 69-; NASA fel propulsion, 73 & 77. *Mem:* Soc Eng Sci; Am Inst Aeronaut & Astronaut (secy-treas, 42 & 75-78); Am Soc Eng Educ; Nat Soc Prof Engrs; Am Soc Mech Engrs; Sigma Xi. *Res:* Structural mechanics and dynamics; gas dynamics; flow fields in turbomachinery, especially three-dimensional and boundary layers; vehicle design and analysis; internal and external aerodynamics of ducts and bodies; granted 2 patents. *Mailing Add:* 1521 N Holder Rd Independence MO 64050

LEUZE, REX ERNEST, RADIOCHEMICAL PROCESS DEVELOPMENT, RADIOCHEMICAL PLANT OPERATION & SAFETY. *Current Pos:* RETIRED. *Personal Data:* b Sabetha, Kans, Mar 7, 22; m 48, Ruth Morris; c Michael R, Robert M & Thomas E. *Educ:* Kans State Univ, BS, 44; Univ Tenn, Knoxville, MS, 56. *Honors & Awards:* IR-100 Award Indust Res Fabrication Process for Nuclear Fuel (Gel-Sphere-Pac Process). *Prof Exp:* Anal chemist, Monsanto Chem Co, Ill, 44-45; anal chemist, Clinton Labs, 45-47; chem engr, Tech Div, Oak Ridge Nat Lab, 47-49, develop group leader inorg fluorides, Chem Tech Div, 49-54, develop group leader transuranium element chem, 54-63, asst chief, Chem Develop Sect, 63-72, asst chief, Pilot Plant Sect, 72-76, sect head, Exp Eng Sect, 76-81, head, Pilot Plant, 81-87. *Concurrent Pos:* Consult, radiochem opers safety, 89-94. *Mem:* Am Nuclear Soc; Am Chem Soc; fel Am Inst Chem; Sigma Xi; AAAS. *Res:* Ion exchange and solvent extraction, especially of the transuranium elements, neptunium through fermium; preparation and properties of concentrated colloids of metal oxides and hydroxides; nuclear fuel reprocessing and waste treatment. *Mailing Add:* 517 W Fifth Ave Lenoir City TN 37771

LEVA, JAMES ROBERT, ELECTRIC UTILITIES. *Current Pos:* CHMN, CHIEF EXEC OFFICER & BD DIRS, GEN PUB UTILITIES, 92- *Personal Data:* b Boonton, NJ, May 10, 32; m 50, Marie Marinaro; c James, Daniel, Linda, Michael & Christopher. *Educ:* Fairleigh Dickinson Univ, BSEE, 60; Seton Hall Law Sch, JD, 80. *Prof Exp:* Elec engr, Jersey Cent Power & Light, 60-62, personnel rep, 62-68, mgr employee rels, 68-69, vpres personnel & serv, 69-79, vpres consumer affairs, 79-82, dir, 76-82, pres & chief oper officer, 86-92; pres & chief oper officer & dir, Pa Elec Co, Johnstown, 82-86. *Concurrent Pos:* Chmn, pres, chief exec officer & bd dirs, GPU Serv Corp; chmn & bd dirs, GPU Nuclear Corp; chmn, chief exec officer & bd dirs, Met Edison Co, Pa Elec Co Utilities Mutual Ins Co, NJ Utilities Asn; chmn, St Clares Health Care Found; bd overseers, NJ Inst Technol; trustee, Tri-County Scholar Fund, Fairleigh Dickinson Univ; chmn, Sch Planning & Pub Policy, Rutgers Univ. *Mailing Add:* Gen Pub Utilities 100 Interpace Pkwy Parsippany NJ 07054-1149

LEVAN, MARIJO O'CONNOR, MATHEMATICS. *Current Pos:* assoc prof, Eastern Ky Univ, 69-74, actg chmn, 78-79, chmn, 79-84, prof math, 74-93, vpres, 95-96, ACTG ASSOC, EASTERN KY UNIV, 96- *Personal Data:* b Detroit, Mich, Oct 27, 36; m 59, Jerome H; c Mary Kathryn, Mary Michelle (Shevely) & Jerome Michael. *Educ:* Spring Hill Col, BS, 59; Univ Ala, MA, 61; Univ Fla, PhD(math), 64. *Prof Exp:* From instr to asst prof math, Univ Fla, 62-67; asst prof, Southeast Mo State Col, 67-69. *Mem:* Am Math Soc. *Res:* Number theory; partition functions; translated geometric progressions; pseudo perfect numbers; additive distributive functions. *Mailing Add:* Dept Math Eastern Ky Univ Richmond KY 40475

LEVAN, MARTIN DOUGLAS, JR, ADSORPTION, FLUID MECHANICS. *Current Pos:* from asst prof to assoc prof, 78-89, PROF CHEM ENG, UNIV VA, 89- *Personal Data:* b Chattanooga, Tenn, Aug 30, 49; m 77; c 2. *Educ:* Univ Va, BS, 71; Univ Calif, Berkeley, PhD(chem eng), 76. *Prof Exp:* Sr res engr, Amoco Prod Co, Stand Oil Co, 76-78. *Concurrent Pos:* Mem, Nat Prog Comt Adsorption & Ion Exchange, Am Inst Chem Engrs, 80-, vchmn, 83-85 & chmn, 85-87, mem, Nat Prog Comt Interfacial Phenomena, 82-; Fulbright sr scholar, Univ Porto, Portugal, 85-86 & LIMSI, Nat Ctr Sci Res, France, 93-94; chmn, Group I, Eng Sci & Fundamentals, 89-91; dir, Int Adsorption Soc, 92- *Mem:* Am Inst Chem Engrs; Am Chem Soc; Int Adsorption Soc. *Res:* Adsorption and fluid mechanics; fixed-bed adsorption; adsorption equilibria; low Reynolds number hydrodynamics; free surface flows; computer applications in chemical engineering. *Mailing Add:* Dept Chem Eng Vanderbilt Univ Box 1604 Sta B Nashville TN 37235

LEVAN, NHAN, ELECTRICAL ENGINEERING. *Current Pos:* from asst prof to assoc prof syst sci, 67-79, PROF ELEC ENG, SCH ENG & APPL SCI, UNIV CALIF, LOS ANGELES, 79- *Personal Data:* b Quang Yen, Vietnam, Nov 6, 36; m 60; c 2. *Educ:* Univ New Eng, Australia, BSc, 60; Univ NSW, MSc, 62; Monash Univ, Australia, PhD(elec eng), 66. *Honors & Awards:* Excellence in Eng Educ, Am Soc Eng Educ Award, 79. *Prof Exp:* Lectr elec eng, Monash Univ, Australia, 65-66. *Mem:* AAAS; Inst Elec & Electronics Engrs; Sigma Xi. *Res:* System theory; signal processing; distributed parameter systems; applied functional analysis and scattering systems; control theory and applications. *Mailing Add:* Dept Eng 56-125B Univ Calif Los Angeles CA 90024. *Fax:* 310-206-8495; *E-Mail:* levan@ee.ucla.edu

LEVAND, OSCAR, ORGANIC CHEMISTRY, BIOCHEMISTRY. *Current Pos:* asst prof, 74-80, ASSOC PROF CHEM, UNIV GUAM, 80- *Personal Data:* b Parnu, Estonia, Nov 3, 27; US citizen; div; c 1. *Educ:* Miss State Col, BS, 54; Purdue Univ, MS, 58; Univ Hawaii, PhD(org chem), 63; Univ Minn, Minneapolis, MPH, 70. *Prof Exp:* Jr res chemist, Mead Johnson Co, Ind, 54-56; res chemist, Knoll Pharmaceut Co, NJ, 58-59; fel NIH, 62-63; res chemist, Dole Co, Hawaii, 63-68; consult, Air Pollution Control Prog, Govt of Guam, 70-74. *Mem:* Am Chem Soc; Sigma Xi. *Res:* Air and water chemistry. *Mailing Add:* 3809 Fishing Trail Sarasota FL 34235

LEVANDER, ORVILLE ARVID, NUTRITION. *Current Pos:* res chemist, 69-94, RES LEADER, USDA HUMAN NUTRIT RES CTR, 94- *Personal Data:* b Waukegan, Ill, Apr 6, 40; m 81; c 2. *Educ:* Cornell Univ, BA, 61; Univ Wis-Madison, MS, 63, PhD(biochem), 65. *Honors & Awards:* Osborne & Mendel Award, Am Inst Nutrit, 86; Klaus Schwarz Medal, 95. *Prof Exp:* Res fel biochem, Col Physicians & Surgeons, Columbia Univ, 65-66; res assoc, Sch Public Health, Harvard Univ, 66-67; res chemist, Food & Drug Admin, 67-69. *Concurrent Pos:* Mem, Nat Res Coun Comt Biol Effects Environ Pollutants, 74-77, mem subcomt nutrit, Safe Drinking Water Comt, 77-79; temp adv, Environ Health Criteria Doc on Selenium, WHO, 77-87; mem, Comt Animal Nutrit, Agr Bd, Nat Res Coun, 79-83, Comt Dietary Allowances, Food & Nutrit Bd, 80-85; William Evans vis fel, Univ Otago, Dunedin, NZ, 82; mem, US Nat Comt Int Union of Nutrit Sci, 85-; travel fel, Danish Med Res Coun, 87; Burroughs Wellcome vis prof nutrit, Ore State Univ, Corvallis, 87; WHO/FAO consult trace elements human nutrit, 88-93; mem, comn Mil Nutrit Res, Inst Med, 94- *Mem:* AAAS; Am Inst Nutrit; Am Chem Soc; Am Soc Clin Nutrit. *Res:* Toxicology and nutrition of selenium; pharmacology of heavy metals; trace mineral nutrition; vitamin E; drug metabolism; lead poisoning; tropical parasitic diseases; malaria; coxsackic virus. *Mailing Add:* USDA Agr Res Ctr Beltsville MD 20705

LEVANDOWSKI, DONALD WILLIAM, geology; deceased, see previous edition for last biography

LEVANDOWSKY, MICHAEL, MARINE ECOLOGY, BEHAVIOR. *Current Pos:* asst prof biol, 70-71, RES SCIENTIST, HASKINS LABS, PACE UNIV, 70- *Personal Data:* b Knoxville, Tenn, Aug 15, 35. *Educ:* Antioch Col, AB, 61; Columbia Univ, MA, 65, PhD(biol), 70; NY Univ, MS, 73. *Prof Exp:* Instr biol, Bard Col, 67-69; instr, Bronx Community Col, 69-70. *Concurrent Pos:* Nat Sci Found sci fac fel, Courant Inst Math Sci, NY Univ, 71-72; asst prof biol, York Col, NY, 73-74; mem citizens' adv comt on resource recovery for borough of Brooklyn, 81-89; distinguished lectr, NE Algal Soc, 86; secy, Environ Scientists Global Survival, 88-91; bd dir, The River Proj, 89. *Mem:* Soc Protozool; Phycol Soc Am; Water Environ Fedn; Am Soc Limnol & Oceanog; Am Soc Microbiol; Am Chem Soc. *Res:* Mathematical models in ecology; microbial ecology; marine biology; sensory physiology and behavior of Protista; environmental problems and bioremediation; environmental education. *Mailing Add:* Haskins Labs Pace Univ 41 Park Row New York NY 10038

LEVASSEUR, KENNETH M, GRAPH THEORY, ALGEBRA. *Current Pos:* Asst prof, 80-85, ASSOC PROF MATH, UNIV MASS, LOWELL, 85- *Personal Data:* m 77, Karen Mazur; c Joseph, Kathryn & Matthew. *Educ:* St Anselm Col, BA, 71; Univ RI, MS, 73, PhD(math), 80. *Concurrent Pos:* Vis lectr math, AT&T Bell Labs, 89; lectr math, Rivier Col, 90- *Mem:* Math Asn Am; Sigma Xi. *Res:* Interplay between graph theory and algebra. *Mailing Add:* Dept Math Sci Univ Mass Lowell MA 01854. *E-Mail:* levasseur@woods.uml.edu

LEVASSEUR, MAURICE EDGAR, OCEANOGRAPHY. *Current Pos:* Biologist, 85-90, RESEARCHER, FISHERIES & OCEANS, CAN, 90- *Personal Data:* b Rivière-du-Loup, Que, June 30, 53; m 82; c 2. *Educ:* Univ Laval, Can, BS, 79, MS, 84; Univ BC, PhD(oceanog), 90. *Mem:* Am Soc Limnol & Oceanog. *Res:* Ecological and physiological aspects of marine algae; physiological effects of different N sources upon microalgae. *Mailing Add:* Fisheries & Oceans Can Maurice-Lamontagne Inst PO Box 1000 Mont-Joli PQ G5H 3Z4 Can. *Fax:* 418-775-0546

LEVCHUK, JOHN W, PARENTERAL TECHNOLOGY, HOSPITAL PHARMACY. *Current Pos:* CONSUMER SAFETY OFFICER, OFF COMPLIANCE, DIV MFG PROD QUAL, STERILE DRUGS BR, US FOOD & DRUG ADMIN, 87- *Personal Data:* b Hudson, NY, Jan 13, 42; m 66; c 2. *Educ:* Philadelphia Col Pharm & Sci, BS, 63, MS, 68; Univ Ariz, MEd, 73, PhD(pharm), 77. *Prof Exp:* Pharmacist, USPHS Indian Hosp, Gallup, NMex, 64-66, comn officer, USPHS, 64; asst prof drug info & poison control, State Univ NY, Buffalo, 67-69; dir, Poison Control & Drug Info Ctr, Buffalo Children's Hosp, 67-69; from asst prof to assoc prof hosp pharm & sterile prod, Univ NMex, 69-79; assoc prof sterile prod & hosp pharm, Univ Alta, 79-83; assoc prof sterile prod, Univ Tenn, 83-87. *Concurrent Pos:* Regional coordr residency progs, Can Soc Hosp Pharmacists, 79-83; mem, Training Comt, Parenteral Drug Asn, 83- *Mem:* Parenteral Drug Asn; Am Soc Hosp Pharmacists. *Res:* Microbiological quality of pharmaceutical processing facilities, activities and dosage forms; experimental aerobiology; packaging of sterile dosage forms. *Mailing Add:* 6056 Wild Ginger Ct Columbia MD 21044

LEVEAU, BARNEY FRANCIS, PHYSICAL MEDICINE, BIOMECHANICS. *Current Pos:* chmn, 92-96, PROF, DEPT PHYS THER, GA STATE UNIV, 92- *Personal Data:* b Denver, Colo, Oct 2, 39; m 61, Nancy Robinson; c Wendy, David & Stephen. *Educ:* Univ Colo, BS, 61, MS, 66; Mayo Clin, RPT, 65; Pa State Univ, PhD(phys educ), 73. *Prof Exp:* Teacher math & sci, Colorado Springs Sch Dist, 61-63; from asst prof to assoc prof phys educ, WChester State Col, 66-70; from asst prof to assoc prof phys ther, Sch Med, Univ NC, Chapel Hill, 72-85; prof & chair, Dept Phys Ther, Southwestern Med Ctr, Dallas, 85-92. *Mem:* Am Phys Ther Asn; Am Col Sports Med; Int Soc Biomech. *Res:* Biomechanics as it applies to physical therapy and physical education; sports medicine. *Mailing Add:* Dept Phys Ther Univ Plaza Ga State Univ Atlanta GA 30303. *Fax:* 404-651-1584

LEVECK, MARY D, NURSING. *Current Pos:* SCI PROG ADMINR, NAT INST NURSING RES, NIH, 90- *Personal Data:* b Olney, Ill, Jan 19, 45. *Educ:* Univ Evansville, BSN, 63; Univ Colo, MS, 74; Univ Tex, Austin, PhD(nursing), 83. *Prof Exp:* Assoc prof, Univ Ky, 71-83 & Univ SC Col Nursing, 83-90. *Mem:* Am Nursing Asn. *Mailing Add:* NINR NIH Bldg 45 Rm 3AN12 MSC 6300 Bethesda MD 20892-6300. *Fax:* 301-480-8260; *E-Mail:* mleveck@ep.ninr.nih.gov

LEVEEN, HARRY HENRY, SURGERY. *Current Pos:* prof, 79-89, EMER PROF SURG, MED UNIV SC, 89- *Personal Data:* b Woodhaven, NY, Aug 10, 16; c 2. *Educ:* Princeton Univ, BA, 36; NY Univ, MD, 40; Univ Chicago, MS, 47; Am Bd Surg, dipl. *Prof Exp:* Instr & res assoc, Univ Chicago, 45-47; instr surg, Col Med, NY Univ, 47-50; assoc prof physiol, Sch Med, Loyola Univ, Ill, 50-55; assoc prof surg, Chicago Med Sch, 55-56; assoc prof surg, Col Med, State Univ NY, Downstate Med Ctr, 57-59, prof, 60-79. *Concurrent Pos:* Assoc prof, NMex Mil Inst, 52-55; chief surgeon, Vet Admin Hosp, 57-78. *Mem:* Soc Exp Biol & Med; Am Physiol Soc; Int Soc Surg; fel Am Col Surg; NY Acad Med. *Res:* Surgical physiology; radiofrequency thermotherapy; cirrhosis. *Mailing Add:* 2173 St James Dr Charleston SC 29412

LEVEILLE, GILBERT ANTONIO, NUTRITION, BIOCHEMISTRY. *Current Pos:* VPRES RES & TECH SERV, NABISCO BISCUIT CO, 86- *Personal Data:* b Fall River, Mass, June 3, 34; m 81; c 3. *Educ:* Univ Mass, BVA, 56; Rutgers Univ, MS, 58, PhD(nutrit), 60. *Honors & Awards:* Res Award, Poultry Sci Asn, 65; Mead Johnson Res Award, Am Inst Nutrit, 71. *Prof Exp:* Biochemist, US Army Med Res & Nutrit Lab Colo, 60-66; assoc prof nutrit biochem, Univ Ill, Urbana, 66-69, prof, 69-71; prof food sci & human nutrit & chmn dept, Mich State Univ, 71-80; dir nutrit & health sci, Gen Foods Corp, 80-86. *Mem:* AAAS; Am Inst Nutrit; Am Soc Clin Nutrit; Am Chem Soc; Poultry Sci Asn; Inst Food Technologists. *Res:* Lipid metabolism; protein and amino acid nutrition and metabolism; atherosclerosis; obesity. *Mailing Add:* VPres Res & Tech Serv Nabisco Food Group 200 Deforest Ave PO Box 1944 East Hanover NJ 07936-1944

LEVELTON, B(RUCE) HARDING, CHEMICAL ENGINEERING. *Current Pos:* VPRES, CHATTERTON PETROCHEM CORP, 84- *Personal Data:* b Bella Coola, BC, June 18, 25; m 50; c 3. *Educ:* Univ BC, BASc, 47, MASc, 48; Tex A&M Univ, PhD(chem eng), 51. *Prof Exp:* Asst res engr, BC Res Coun, 51-54; assoc res engr, 54-58, res engr, 58-64, assoc head div appl chem, 64-66; prin, B H Levelton & Assocs Ltd, 66-, pres, 66- *Concurrent Pos:* Spec lectr, Univ BC, 57-65. *Mem:* Am Inst Chem Engrs; Nat Asn Corrosion Engrs; Air Pollution Control Asn; Chem Inst Can; Forest Prod Res Soc; Am Water Works Asn. *Res:* Treatment and beneficiation of industrial minerals; utilization of wood wastes by carbonization; corrosion of metals in chemical industry and in marine service; corrosion of copper in potable waters; environmental technology; solid waste disposal; toxic and hazardous waste disposal. *Mailing Add:* 5531 Cornwall Dr No 48 Richmond BC V7C 5N7 Can

LEVEN, ROBERT MAYNARD, CELL BIOLOGY, HEMATOLOGY. *Current Pos:* ASST PROF ANAT & MED, RUSH MED COL, CHICAGO, ILL, 90-, DIR DISABILITY SERVS, 96- *Personal Data:* b Chicago, Ill, Nov 7, 55; m 82; c 2. *Educ:* Wash Univ, BA, 77; Univ Pa, PhD(anat), 82. *Prof Exp:* Postdoctoral fel thrombosis, Med Sch, Temple Univ, 82-84; staff scientist res med, Lawrence Berkeley Lab, 84-90. *Concurrent Pos:* Instr anat, Univ Calif, San Francisco, 86; prin investr, Nat Heart Lung & Blood Inst, NIH, 88-94, Am Cancer Soc, 94-97; consult, Amgen, Inc, 89-90. *Mem:* Am Soc Cell Biol; Int Soc Exp Hemat. *Res:* Hormonal and microenvironmental factors that control the formation of blood platelets from megakaryocytes using in vitro cell culture models. *Mailing Add:* Dept Anat Rush Presby-St Luke's Med Col 1653 W Congress Pkwy Chicago IL 60612-3833

LEVENBERG, MILTON IRWIN, MASS SPECTROMETRY, COMPUTER SCIENCE. *Current Pos:* Sr chem physicist, Abbott Labs, 65-73, assoc res fel, 73-84, sect head, 84-90, MGR, ABBOTT LABS, 90- *Personal Data:* b Chicago, Ill, Nov 5, 37; div; c 2. *Educ:* Ill Inst Technol, BS, 58; Calif Inst Technol, PhD(chem), 65. *Mem:* Am Chem Soc; Sigma Xi; Am Soc Mass Spectrometry. *Res:* Computer applications to instrumentation; instrumentation; electronics; mass spectrometry; nuclear magnetic resonance spectroscopy. *Mailing Add:* Abbott Labs D-418 AP-9 Abbott Park IL 60064-3500

LEVENBOOK, LEO, BIOCHEMISTRY. *Current Pos:* RETIRED. *Personal Data:* b Kobe, Japan, Dec 29, 19; nat US; m 50; c 1. *Educ:* Univ London, BSc, 41; Cambridge Univ, PhD(biochem), 49. *Prof Exp:* Asst insect biochem, Cambridge Univ, 46-50; fel, Harvard Univ, 50-51; res assoc biochem genetics, Inst Cancer Res, Philadelphia, 51-54; asst prof biochem, Jefferson Med Col, 54-58; biochemist, Nat Inst Diabetes, Metab & Digestive Dis, NIH, 58-86. *Concurrent Pos:* Lectr, Haverford Col, 53-54. *Mem:* Am Soc Biol Chemists. *Res:* Insect physiology and biochemistry. *Mailing Add:* NIAMS NIH Bldg 6 Rm 137 Bethesda MD 20892-0001

LEVENE, CYRIL, ANATOMY. *Current Pos:* assoc prof, 69-74, prof anat, Div Morphol Sci, 74-88, EMER PROF ANAT, DEPT ANAT, FAC MED, UNIV CALGARY, 88- *Personal Data:* b Gateshead, Eng, May 27, 26; m 52; c 3. *Educ:* Queen's Univ Belfast, MB, BCh & BAO, 48, MD, 60. *Prof Exp:* Demonstr anat, Queen's Univ Belfast, 51-52, asst lectr, 52-54; lectr human anat, Univ Col WI, 54-65, sr lectr anat, 65-67; assoc prof, Univ Western Ont, 67-69. *Concurrent Pos:* WHO fel human genetics, 66. *Mem:* Hon mem Can Asn Anat. *Res:* Medical education. *Mailing Add:* Dept Anat Univ Calgary 3330 Hospital Dr NW Calgary AB T2N 4N1 Can

LEVENE, HOWARD, MATHEMATICAL STATISTICS. *Current Pos:* Exten lectr zool & math statist, Columbia Univ, 47-48, from instr to prof math statist & biomet, 48-70, prof math statist & genetics, 70-82, chmn, Dept Statist, 76-82, EMER PROF MATH STATIST & SPECIAL LECTR, COLUMBIA UNIV, 82- *Personal Data:* b New York, NY, Jan 17, 14. *Educ:* NY Univ, BA, 41; Columbia Univ, PhD(math statist), 47. *Mem:* AAAS; Am Math Soc; Soc Study Evolution; Biomet Soc; Am Soc Human Genetics (vpres, 63); Am Soc Naturalists (pres, 76); Inst Math Statist; Am Statist Soc. *Res:* Mathematical genetics; nonparametric tests; biometrics; population genetics and evolution. *Mailing Add:* 22 E 88th St New York NY 10128

LEVENE, RALPH ZALMAN, OPHTHALMOLOGY. *Current Pos:* PROF OPHTHAL, UNIV ALA, BIRMINGHAM, 73- *Personal Data:* b Winnipeg, Man, May 17, 27; nat US; m 54, Roslyn Bearman; c Douglas & Carina. *Educ:* Univ Man, MD, 49; NY Univ, DSc(ophthal), 57; Am Bd Ophthal, dipl, 55. *Prof Exp:* Intern, Winnipeg Gen Hosp, Can, 49-50, resident ophthal, 51-55; from instr to assoc prof, Med Sch, NY Univ, 55-73. *Mem:* AMA; Asn Res Vision & Ophthal; Am Acad Ophthal & Otolaryngol; NY Acad Med; Sigma Xi; Am Ophthal Soc. *Res:* Clinical and basic science aspects of glaucoma. *Mailing Add:* 2008 Brookwood Med Ctr Dr Suite 209 Birmingham AL 35209. *Fax:* 205-877-2958

LEVENSON, ALAN IRA, PSYCHIATRY. *Current Pos:* head dept, 69-89, PROF PSYCHIAT, COL MED, UNIV ARIZ, 69- *Personal Data:* b Boston, Mass, July 25, 35; m 94, Linda A Nadell. *Educ:* Harvard Univ, AB, 57, MD, 61, MPH, 65; Am Bd Psychiat & Neurol, dipl, 67. *Prof Exp:* Intern, Univ Hosp, Ann Arbor, 61-62; resident in psychiat, Mass Ment Health Ctr, Boston, 62-65; staff psychiatrist, NIMH, 65-66, dir servs div, 67-69. *Concurrent Pos:* Chief exec officer, Palo Verde Ment Health Serv, 71-91, chief med officer, 91-93. *Mem:* Fel Am Psychiat Asn; fel Am Col Psychiat; Group Advan Psychiat; fel Am Col Mental Health Admin. *Res:* Organization and delivery of mental health services; malpractice issues in psychiatry. *Mailing Add:* 75 N Calle Resplendor Tucson AZ 85716

LEVENSON, HAROLD SAMUEL, FOOD SCIENCE. *Current Pos:* RETIRED. *Personal Data:* b Allentown, Pa, July 12, 16; m 38, Alice Nathan; c Eric O, Jenifer A & Laura E. *Educ:* Lehigh Univ, BSChE, 37, MS, 39, PhD(chem physics), 41. *Prof Exp:* Asst chem, Lehigh Univ, 37-41; res chemist, Gen Foods Corp, NJ, 41-46, chief chemist, Maxwell House Div, Calif, 46-51, res mgr, NJ, 51-64, dir coffee res, Tech Ctr, NY, 65-78. *Mem:* Am Chem Soc; Inst Food Technol; Sigma Xi. *Res:* Antioxidants; food spoilage; kinetics of saponification; hydrocaffeic acid and esters as antioxidant for edible materials; coffee technology. *Mailing Add:* 5577 Inverness Ave Santa Rosa CA 95404-9724

LEVENSON, JAMES B, PLANT ECOLOGY, GEOGRAPHIC INFORMATION SYSTEMS. *Current Pos:* asst environ sci, 79-84, ECOLOGIST, ARGONNE NAT LAB, 84- *Personal Data:* b San Francisco, Calif, Aug 22, 44; m 92, Dee Seymour; c Lori & Brian. *Educ:* Ind State Univ, Terre Haute, BS, 71, MA, 73; Univ Wis-Milwaukee, PhD(bot), 76. *Prof Exp:* Res assoc, Univ Wis-Milwaukee, 76-77; asst prof ecol, Saginaw Valley State Col, 77-79. *Concurrent Pos:* Co-investr, NSF grant, 78-80. *Mem:* AAAS; Am Inst Biol Sci; Ecol Soc Am; Sigma Xi. *Res:* Interactions and resultant impacts of man-dominated systems on remnant ecosystem patches; identification, description and quantification of natural areas; application of ecological concepts to regional assessments. *Mailing Add:* 22136 S Eastcliff Dr Joliet IL 60436-9684. *Fax:* 630-252-6414; *E-Mail:* levensoj@smtplink.eid.anl.gov

LEVENSON, LEONARD L, PHYSICS. *Current Pos:* chmn dept, 81-84, PROF, DEPT PHYSICS & ENERGY SCI, UNIV COLO, COLORADO SPRINGS, 84- *Personal Data:* b San Francisco, Calif, Sept 18, 28; m 57; c 3. *Educ:* Univ Calif, Berkeley, AB, 52, MS, 55; Univ Paris, PhD(physics), 68. *Prof Exp:* Physicist, US Naval Ord Test Sta, 52; res engr, Univ Calif, Berkeley, 52-58, physicist, Lawrence Radiation Lab, 58-62; physicist, Nuclear Res Ctr, Saclay, France, 62-68; from asst prof to assoc prof physics, Univ Mo-Rolla, 68-76, prof, 76-81, dir grad ctr mat res, 75-81. *Concurrent Pos:* Vis prof, Kyoto Univ, Japan, 86-87 & 88-89, Univ Houston, 89. *Mem:* Inst Elec & Electronics Engrs; Am Phys Soc; Am Vacuum Soc; Sigma Xi. *Res:* Gas-surface interactions; thin films; surface physics; electronics materials. *Mailing Add:* 975 Point of the Pines Dr Colorado Springs CO 80919-8143

LEVENSON, MARC DAVID, LASERS, QUANTUM ELECTRONICS. *Current Pos:* RETIRED. *Personal Data:* b Philadelphia, Pa, May 28, 45; m 71. *Educ:* Mass Inst Technol, BS, 67; Stanford Univ, MS, 68, PhD(physics), 72. *Honors & Awards:* Adolph Lomb Award, Optical Soc Am, 76. *Prof Exp:* Res fel non-linear optics, Gordon McKay Lab, Harvard Univ, 71-74; asst prof physics, Univ Southern Calif, 74-77, assoc prof physics & elec eng, 77-79; head mgr optical storage, IBM Res Lab, 87-88, mem res staff, 79-84. *Concurrent Pos:* Alfred P Sloan fel, 75-77; Joint Inst Lab Astrophys vis fel, Univ Colo, 78-79. *Mem:* Am Phys Soc; Inst Elec & Electronics Engrs; Optical Soc Am. *Res:* Development and application of new techniques of laser spectroscopy to problems in atomic, molecular and condensed matter physics; application of optical and laser techniques to electronics manufacturing; quantum optics; optical memories; photolithography. *Mailing Add:* 19868 Bonnie Ridge Way Saratoga CA 95070

LEVENSON, MILTON, CHEMICAL ENGINEERING. *Current Pos:* CONSULT, 90- *Personal Data:* b St Paul, Minn, Jan 4, 23; m 50, Mary Novick; c James, Barbara, Richard, Scott & Janet. *Educ:* Univ Minn, BChE, 43. *Honors & Awards:* Robert E Wilson Award, Am Inst Chem Engrs, 75; Source Term Award, Am Nuclear Soc, 88. *Prof Exp:* Jr engr, Houdaille-Hershey Corp, 44; asst engr, Oak Ridge Nat Labs, 44-48; from assoc engr to assoc lab dir energy & environ, Argonne Nat Lab, 48-73; dir nuclear power, Elec Power Res Inst, 73-81; exec eng, Bechtel Power Corp, San Francisco, 81-90, vpres, Bechtel Int, 83-90. *Concurrent Pos:* Nuclear Soc Int (past pres). *Mem:* Nat Acad Eng; fel Am Inst Chem Engrs; fel Am Nuclear Soc (pres); AAAS. *Res:* Water reactor technology; fuel cycle technology; breeder reactor development; nuclear safety. *Mailing Add:* 21 Politzer Dr Menlo Park CA 94025

LEVENSON, MORRIS E, mathematics, for more information see previous edition

LEVENSON, ROBERT, cell biology, for more information see previous edition

LEVENSON, STANLEY MELVIN, SURGERY, SURGICAL RESEARCH. *Current Pos:* PROF SURG, ALBERT EINSTEIN COL MED, 61-, DEP DIR RES SURG, COL MED, 67- *Personal Data:* b Dorchester, Mass, May 25, 16; m 42; c 2. *Educ:* Harvard Univ, AB, 37, MD, 41; Am Bd Nutrit, dipl, 52; Am Bd Surg, dipl, 57. *Honors & Awards:* Jonathan E Rhoads lectr, Am Soc Parenteral & Enteral Nutrit, 78; Arnold M Seligman Mem, Sinai Hosp Baltimore, 79; McCollum Award, Am Soc Clin Nutrit, 83. *Prof Exp:* Surg house officer, Beth Israel Hosp, Boston, Mass, 41-42; resident burn serv & res assoc surg, Boston City Hosp, 42-43; surg scientist, Med Nutrit Lab, Univ Chicago, 47-49; from asst resident to sr asst resident surg, Med Col Va, 50-52; chief dept surg metab & physiol, Walter Reed Army Inst Res, 56-61, from assoc dir to dir dept germfree res, 56-61, dir div basic surg res, 61. *Concurrent Pos:* Res fel med, Thorndike Mem Lab, Harvard Univ, 44-47; NIH res career award, 62-; chmn subcomt burns & radiation injury, Food & Nutrit Bd, Nat Res Coun, 49-50, comt on trauma, 56-; dir surg metab lab & clin assoc prof, Georgetown Univ, 59-61; res assoc physiol, Sch Pub Health, Harvard Univ, 41-; consult, Walter Reed Army Inst Res, 61-63; Am Surg Asn rep, Nat Res Coun-Nat Acad Sci, 71-75. *Mem:* Am Surg Asn; Am Burn Asn; Am Inst Nutrit; Am Soc Clin Nutrit; Am Col Surgeons; Am Soc Parenteral & Enteral Nutrit. *Res:* Metabolic and clinical response to trauma; wound healing; germfree life; infection; burns; neoplasia; nutrition; radiation. *Mailing Add:* ICU-Burn Unit Albert Einstein Col Med 1300 Morris Park Ave Bronx NY 10461-1975

LEVENSPIEL, OCTAVE, CHEMICAL ENGINEERING. *Current Pos:* prof, 68-91, EMER PROF CHEM ENG, ORE STATE UNIV, 91- *Personal Data:* b Shanghai, China, July 6, 26; nat US; m 52, Mary J Smiley; c Bekki, Barney & Morris. *Educ:* Univ Calif, BS, 47; Ore State Col, MS, 49, PhD(chem eng), 52. *Hon Degrees:* Dr, ENSIC, Nancy, France, 87. *Honors & Awards:* 3M Lectureship Award, Am Soc Eng Educ, 66; Wilhelm Award, Am Inst Chem Engrs, 79; Danckwerts Award, London, 88. *Prof Exp:* Jr res engr, Inst Eng Res, Univ Calif, 51-52; asst prof chem eng, Ore State Col, 52-54; asst & assoc prof, Bucknell Univ, 54-58; assoc & prof, Ill Inst Technol, 58-68. *Concurrent Pos:* NSF sr fel, Cambridge Univ, 63-64, Fulbright fel, 68-69; vis prof, Univ NSW, Australia, 76, Denmarks Tech Univ, 77, Univ Groningen, Neth, 84, Univ Sydney, Australia, 85. *Mem:* Am Chem Soc; Am Inst Chem Engrs. *Res:* Chemical reactor design; fluidization. *Mailing Add:* Dept Chem Eng Gleason Hall Rm 301A Ore State Univ Corvallis OR 97331. *Fax:* 541-737-4600

LEVENSTEIN, HAROLD, LASER RADAR SYSTEMS, FIRE CONTROL SYSTEMS. *Current Pos:* CONSULT, ELECTROOPTICS, 88- *Personal Data:* b Philadelphia, Pa, June 28, 23; m 47, Gloria Potasnick; c Paula B, Marcia (Weisman) & Alissa (Onigman). *Educ:* Cooper Union Sch Eng, BEE, 43; Polytech Inst Brooklyn, MS, 49; Columbia Univ, MS, 79. *Prof Exp:* Engr mgr radar & control systs, various co, 43-64; dept head systs & opers res, Div Cutler Hammer, Ail, 64-71; prog mgr radar systs, Missile & Surface Radar Div, RCA, 71-73; tech dir electrooptics systs, Military Systs Div, Perkin Elmer Corp, 73-88. *Concurrent Pos:* Mem, ASW Comt, Navy/NSIA, 56-60; adj asst prof statist models, Dept Marine Sci, C W Post Ctr, Long Island Univ, 68-71; consult radar, Electronics Div, W L Maxson, 71; lectr statist, Univ Conn, Storrs, 83; speaker, NAS/AF Study Hi Energy Laser Optics, 84; mem adv bd, Defense Intel Agency, 88- *Mem:* Inst Elec & Electronics Engrs; Opers Res Soc Am; Am Statist Asn; Soc Indust & Appl Math; Am Inst Aeronaut & Astronaut; Int Soc Optical Eng. *Res:* Design development of radar and control systems for guidance and navigation; network theory for multivariable systems; modular optical (laser) radar for space applications; decision theory studies. *Mailing Add:* 12 Arrowhead Rd Westport CT 06880. *Fax:* 203-259-1058; *E-Mail:* zvilev@aol.com

LEVENTHAL, CARL M, NEUROLOGY, NEUROPATHOLOGY. *Current Pos:* RETIRED. *Personal Data:* b New York, NY, July 28, 33; m 62; c 4. *Educ:* Harvard Univ, AB, 54; Univ Rochester, MD, 59. *Prof Exp:* Intern med, Johns Hopkins Hosp, 59-60, asst res physician, 60-61; asst resident neurol, Mass Gen Hosp, 61-62, fel neuropath, 62-63, resident, 63-64; assoc neuropathologist, Nat Inst Neurol Dis & Blindness, 64-66, neurologist, Nat Cancer Inst, 66-68, asst to dep dir sci, NIH, 68-74, actg dep dir sci, 73-74; dep dir, Bur Drugs, Food & Drug Admin, 74-77; dep dir, Nat Inst Arthritis, Metab & Digest Dis, 77-81; div dir, Nat Inst Neurol Dis & Stroke, 81-96. *Concurrent Pos:* Fel, Johns Hopkins Univ, 59-61; fel, Harvard Univ, 61-64; instr, Georgetown Univ, 64-66, asst prof, 67-74; med officer, USPHS, 64-96. *Mem:* Am Acad Neurol; Am Asn Neuropath; Am Neurol Asn; Asn Res Nervous & Ment Dis. *Res:* Government research administration; clinical neuropathology. *Mailing Add:* 10924 Brewer House Rd Rockville MD 20852-3422

LEVENTHAL, EDWIN ALFRED, SOLID STATE PHYSICS. *Current Pos:* DIR, MKT INFO SYSTS, AM MED INT, 84- *Personal Data:* b Brooklyn, NY, Jan 26, 34; m 56; c 2. *Educ:* Cornell Univ, BEng Phys, 56; Polytech Inst Brooklyn, MS, 59; NY Univ, PhD(physics), 63. *Prof Exp:* Sr physicist, Philips Labs Div, NAm Philips Co, 61-70; ed & publ, Med Instrument Reports, 70-74; dir, systs planning, Friesen Int, 74-84. *Mem:* Am Phys Soc; Asn Advan Med Instrumentation; NY Acad Sci. *Res:* Materials handling and information processing in hospital management and design; medical equipment planning. *Mailing Add:* 23723 Kivik St Woodland Hills CA 91367

LEVENTHAL, HOWARD, HUMAN EMOTION, HEALTH PSYCHOLOGY. *Current Pos:* PROF PSYCHOL, RUTGERS UNIV, 88- *Personal Data:* b Brooklyn, NY, Dec 7, 31; m 54, Elaine A Silverman; c Edith (Burns) & Sharan. *Educ:* City Univ New York Queens Col, BS, 52; Univ NC Chapel Hill, MS, 54, PhD(psychol), 56. *Honors & Awards:* Outstanding Contrib to Health Psychol Award, Div Health Psychol, Am Psychol Asn, 87. *Prof Exp:* Sr asst sci psychol, USPHS, 56-58; asst prof psychol, Yale Univ, 58-64, assoc prof psychol, 64-67; prof psychol, Univ Wis-Madison, 67-88. *Concurrent Pos:* Prof sociol, Univ Wis-Madison, 74-, assoc, Clin Cancer Ctr, 80-; mem, Behav Med Study Sect, NIH, 86-; chair, Dept Psychol, Univ Wis-Madison, 87-88; mem adv bd, Acad Behav Med Res, 88- *Mem:* Sr mem Inst Med-Nat Acad Sci; fel Am Psychol Asn; Acad Behav Med Res; fel Am Psychol Soc; Am Psychosom Asn; fel AAAS. *Res:* Focus on common sense views of illness and how these representations affect health and illness behaviors and emotional reactions to health crises; effects of stress on immune function in elderly persons. *Mailing Add:* Inst Health Policy & Aging Rutgers Univ 30 College Ave New Brunswick NJ 08903. *Fax:* 732-932-6872

LEVENTHAL, JACOB J, ATOMIC PHYSICS, MOLECULAR PHYSICS. *Current Pos:* from asst prof to assoc prof, 68-77, PROF PHYSICS, UNIV MO-ST LOUIS, 77- *Personal Data:* b Brooklyn, NY, Dec 18, 37; m 62. *Educ:* Wash Univ, BS, 60; Univ Fla, PhD(physics), 65. *Prof Exp:* Res assoc physics & chem, Brookhaven Nat Lab, 65-67, assoc chemist, 67-68. *Mem:* Am Phys Soc. *Res:* Interactions of positive ions with neutral molecules; spectroscopic observations of excited state production in low energy atomic and molecular collision processes. *Mailing Add:* Dept Physics Univ Mo St Louis MO 63121

LEVENTHAL, JOEL STEPHEN, GEOCHEMISTRY. *Current Pos:* res chemist, GS-12 Energy Br, US Geol Surv, 74-77, GS-13 sect leader, Energy Br, 78-81, GS-14 proj chief, Minerals Br, 81-87, GS-15 PROJ CHIEF, MINERALS BR, US GEOL SURV, 88- *Personal Data:* b Saginaw, Mich, Nov 23, 41; m 67, 84; c 4. *Educ:* Calif State Univ, Los Angeles, BS, 68; Univ Ariz, Tucson, MS, 70, PhD(geochem), 72. *Prof Exp:* Asst res biogeologist fel, Univ Calif, Santa Barbara, 72-74. *Concurrent Pos:* Co-prin investr collab res travel grant, NATO, 90 & 91; US prin investr, Civilian Res & Develop Found, 96- *Mem:* AAAS; Geochem Soc; Am Geophys Union; fel Soc Econ Geologists; Soc Wetland Scientists. *Res:* Organic and inorganic geochemistry of metalliferous black shales and sedimentary ore deposits; environmental radioactivity, natural nuclear reactors and tritium hydrology; environmental arsenic related to mining and coal ash; global change in coastal wetlands and methane emissions. *Mailing Add:* US Geol Surv Fed Ctr MS 973 Denver CO 80225. *Fax:* 303-236-3200; *E-Mail:* jleventh@usgs.gov

LEVENTHAL, LEON, RADIOCHEMISTRY, CHEMICAL ENGINEERING. *Current Pos:* RETIRED. *Personal Data:* b New York, NY, Jan 25, 22; wid; c 4. *Educ:* Univ Calif, BS, 42; Va Polytech Inst, BS, 44; Univ Calif, Los Angeles, MS, 48. *Prof Exp:* Control chemist, Richfield Oil Corp, Calif, 42-43; res chemist, Metall Lab, Chicago, 44-45; jr chem engr, Oak Ridge Nat Lab, 45; chem engr, Atomic Bomb Lab, Los Alamos Sci Lab, 45-46; res chemist, Radiol Defense Lab, San Francisco Naval Shipyard, 47-49; res radiochemist, Tracerlab, Inc, 49-50, sr chemist, 50-57, dept head, 57-59, div mgr tech serv, 59-67, vpres, 75-81, gen mgr, LFE Environ Anal Labs, Div LFE Corp, 67-90, tech dir, EAL Corp, 81-90; tech dir, TMA/Norcal, 88-90. *Concurrent Pos:* Prof engr, State Calif Nuclear Eng; consult, 90- *Mem:* Am Chem Soc; fel Am Health Phys Soc; fel Am Nuclear Soc; fel Am Inst Chem. *Res:* Nuclear, plutonium and semimicro chemistry; plutonium metallurgy; complex compounds of zinc with zinc 65; general radiochemistry of radiological defense and radioactive waste problems; fission products; environmental and fallout studies; particle analysis; mass spectrometry of plutonium and uranium; applications of radioisotopes to science and industry; transuranium nuclides in the environment; decontamination and decommissioning; radioactive and hazardous waste disposal. *Mailing Add:* 1511 Arch St Berkeley CA 94708

LEVENTHAL, MARVIN, ASTROPHYSICS, ATOMIC PHYSICS. *Current Pos:* CHMN, ASTRON DEPT, UNIV MD, 93- *Personal Data:* b New York, NY, Dec 4, 37; m 61; c 2. *Educ:* City Col New York, BS, 58; Brown Univ, PhD(physics), 64. *Prof Exp:* Res assoc physics, Yale Univ, 63-67, asst prof, 67-68; mem tech staff, Bell Labs, 68-93. *Mem:* Fel Am Phys Soc; Am Astron Soc. *Res:* Precision measurements of atomic physics quantities which have bearing on quantum electrodynamics; experimental and theoretical gamma ray astronomy; laboratory astrophysics. *Mailing Add:* Dept Astron Univ Md Space Sci Bldg Stadium Dr College Park MD 20742-2421

LEVENTHAL, STEPHEN HENRY, NUMERICAL ANALYSIS, RESERVOIR SIMULATION. *Current Pos:* staff res, 85-89, SR STAFF RES MATH, SHELL DEVELOP CO, SHELL OIL, 89- *Personal Data:* b New York, NY, Apr 2, 49; m 71, Ellen Warach; c Daniel & Seth. *Educ:* Rutgers Univ, BA, 69; Univ Md, MA, 71; PhD(math), 73. *Prof Exp:* Res math, Naval Surface Weapons Ctr, 73-77; res math, Gulf Res & Develop Co, Gulf Oil, 77-79, sr res math, 79-81, supvr math, 81-83, dir reservoir simulation, 83-85. *Mem:* Soc Indust & Appl Math; Soc Petrol Engrs. *Res:* Development of high order numerical methods and state of the art reservoir simulation; founder of OCI method; principal developer of Gulf Oil's Black Oil Simulator; one of the principal developers of Shell Oil's multi-purpose simulator. *Mailing Add:* Shell Develop Co PO Box 481 Houston TX 77001. *Fax:* 713-245-7990; *E-Mail:* shl@shell.com

LEVENTIS, NICHOLAS, ELECTROCHEMISTRY OF CONDUCTING POLYMERS, MICROELECTROCHEMICAL DEVICES & ELECTROCHROMICS. *Current Pos:* PROF CHEM, UNIV MO-ROLLA, 94- *Personal Data:* b Athens, Greece, Nov 12, 57; m 88, Chariklia Sotiriou. *Educ:* Univ Athens, Greece, BS, 80; Mich State Univ, PhD(org chem), 85. *Honors & Awards:* Arthur K Doolittle Award, Am Chem Soc, 93. *Prof Exp:* Res assoc, Mass Inst Technol, 85-88; vpres res, Molecular Displays, Inc, 88-93. *Concurrent Pos:* Consult, Igen, Inc, 87-93, Hyperion Catalysis, Inc, 89-93, Delta F Corp, 92-93. *Mem:* Am Chem Soc; Electrochem Soc; Int Union Pure & Appl Chem. *Res:* Development of electrode surface confined electrochromic polymers for large area transmittance control for application in smart windows; new concepts in the area of microelectrochemical immunochemical sensors based on conducting polymers synthetically modified at the monomer level to introduce specificity. *Mailing Add:* 1604 McCutchen Dr Rolla MO 65401. *Fax:* 573-341-6033; *E-Mail:* leventis@umr.edu

LEVEQUE, RANDALL J, MATHEMATICS, APPLIED MATHEMATICS. *Current Pos:* From asst prof to assoc prof, 85-90, PROF, MATH & APPL MATH, UNIV WASH, 90- *Personal Data:* b Ann Arbor, Mich, Sept 30, 55. *Educ:* Univ Calif, BA, 77; Stanford Univ, PhD(comput sci), 82. *Prof Exp:* NSF fel, Courant Inst Math Sci, NY Univ, 82-83; Hedrick asst prof math, Univ Calif, Los Angeles, 83-85. *Concurrent Pos:* NSF Grad fel, 77-80; Hertz Found grad fel, 80-82; vis scientist, Inst Comput Appln Sci & Eng, NASA Langley Res Ctr, 83, 84, 86, consult, 86-; vis lectr, Inst Math, ETII Zurich, 89, prof, 90-91; vis mem, Courant Inst, NY Univ, 90. *Res:* Author of book, 28 journal publications and 15 conference proceedings. *Mailing Add:* Dept Appl Math Univ Wash Box 352420 Seattle WA 98195-2420

LEVEQUE, WILLIAM JUDSON, MATHEMATICS. *Current Pos:* RETIRED. *Personal Data:* b Boulder, Colo, Aug 9, 23; m 49, 70; c 1. *Educ:* Univ Colo, BA, 44; Cornell Univ, MA, 45, PhD(math), 47. *Prof Exp:* Benjamin Peirce instr math, Harvard Univ, 47-49; from instr to prof, Univ Mich, Ann Arbor, 49-70, chmn dept, 67-70; prof math, Claremont Grad Sch, 70-77; exec dir, Am Math Soc, 77-88. *Concurrent Pos:* Fulbright res scholar, 51-52; Sloan res fel, 57-60; exec ed, Math Rev, 65-69; chmn, Conf Bd Math Sci, 73-74. *Mem:* Am Math Soc; Math Asn Am; fel AAAS. *Res:* Theory of numbers. *Mailing Add:* 12684 Sunrise Dr Bainbridge Island WA 98110

LEVER, ALFRED B P, INORGANIC CHEMISTRY. *Current Pos:* assoc prof, 67-72, PROF CHEM, YORK UNIV, 72- *Personal Data:* b London, Eng, Feb 21, 36; m 63, 87; c 4. *Educ:* Univ London, BSc & ARCS, 57, dipl, Imp Col & PhD(chem), 60. *Honors & Awards:* Alcan Lecture Award, 81. *Prof Exp:* Hon res asst, Univ Col, London, 60-61, hon res assoc, 61-62; lectr chem, Inst Sci & Tech, Univ Manchester, 62-66; vis lectr, Ohio State Univ, 67. *Concurrent Pos:* Ed, Coord Chem Rev, 66-; prog chmn, XIVth Int Conf Coord Chem, Toronto, 72; vis prof, Calif Inst Technol, 76-77, Sydney Univ, 78, Univ Calabria, 83 & Univ Pavia, 89. *Mem:* Am Chem Soc; Chem Inst Can; Royal Soc Chem; fel Jan Prom Sci. *Res:* Inorganic electronic spectroscopy; solar energy conversion; phthalocyanine chemistry; electrochemistry; alternate energy; electronic structure; chemical sensors. *Mailing Add:* Dept Chem CCB124 York Univ 4700 Keele St North York ON M3J 1P3 Can. *Fax:* 416-736-5936; *E-Mail:* blever@sol.yorku.ca

LEVER, ALVIN, ARCHITECTURE, PSYCHOLOGY. *Current Pos:* dir membership & fin, 90-92, exec dir, 92-95, EXEC VPRES & CHIEF EXEC OFFICER, AM COL CHEST PHYSICIANS, 95- *Personal Data:* b St Louis, Mo, Jan 29, 39; m 63, Norine S Schwedt; c Daniel J & Michael L. *Educ:* Wash Univ, BS, 61, BArch, 63; Univ Santa Monica, MA, 92. *Prof Exp:* Proj designer, Sir Basil Spence Archits, Edinburgh, Scotland, 63-65; sr proj designer, 65-68, Hellmuth, Obata & Kassabaum, St Louis, vpres proj mgr, 65-68; vpres facil develop, Michael Reese Med Ctr, 72-74; vpres & gen mgr, Apelco Int Ltd, 74-90. *Mem:* Am Soc Med Soc Execs. *Mailing Add:* Am Col Chest Physicians 3300 Dundee Rd Northbrook IL 60062-2303

LEVER, CYRIL, JR, ORGANIC CHEMISTRY. *Current Pos:* Asst treas & asst dir res, 53-57, pres & dir res, 57-90, PRES & CHIEF EXEC OFFICER, C LEVER CO, INC, 90- *Personal Data:* b Abington, Pa, June 5, 29; m 61, Norma; c Scott & Ruth. *Educ:* Pa Mil Col, BS, 53. *Mem:* Am Asn Textile Chemist & Colorist; Tech Asn Pulp & Paper Indust; Am Chem Soc. *Res:* Dyes and colors for paper. *Mailing Add:* C Lever Co Inc Lever Bldg 736 Dunks Ferry Rd Bensalem PA 19020-6575

LEVER, JOHN, CHEMISTRY, NEUROSCIENCE. *Current Pos:* CHEMIST, DEPT ENVIRON HEALTH SCI, SCH HYG, JOHNS HOPKINS UNIV, 83- *Personal Data:* b Owensboro, Ky, Nov 7, 53. *Educ:* Univ SC, BS, 75; NC State Univ, PhD(chem), 81. *Mem:* Am Chem Soc; Soc Nuclear Med. *Mailing Add:* Dept Environ Health Sci Sch Hyg John Hopkins Univ Baltimore MD 21205

LEVER, JULIA ELIZABETH, BIOCHEMISTRY, MOLECULAR BIOLOGY. *Current Pos:* from asst prof to assoc prof, 79-86, PROF, DEPT BIOCHEM & MOLECULAR BIOL, MED SCH, UNIV TEX, 86- *Personal Data:* b Montreal, Que, Nov 23, 45. *Educ:* McGill Univ, BS, 66; Univ Calif, PhD(biochem), 71. *Prof Exp:* Vis res scientist, Roche Inst Molecular Biol, 74; vis scientist staff, Dept Cell Regulation, Imp Cancer Res Fund Lab, 74-77; asst res prof, Salk Inst Biol Studies, 77-79. *Concurrent Pos:* Prin investr, Nat Cancer Inst, 76-77; mem fac, Grad Sch Biomed Sci, Univ Tex, 79- *Mem:* Soc Biol Chemists; Am Physiol Soc. *Res:* Biochemistry; molecular biology; numerous publications in the area of cell and molecular biology of membrane transport. *Mailing Add:* Biochem & Molecular Biol Dept Univ Tex Med Sch PO Box 20708 Houston TX 77225-0708. *Fax:* 713-794-4150; *E-Mail:* jlever@utmmg.med.uth.tmc.edu

LEVERANT, GERALD ROBERT, MATERIALS SCIENCE ENGINEERING. *Current Pos:* mgr metall, Southwest Res Inst, 77-81, asst dir, 81-85, dir mat sci, 85-90, dir mat & mech, 90-94, DIR POWER GENERATION MAT, SOUTHWEST RES INST, 94- *Personal Data:* b Hartford, Conn, June 18, 40; m 62, Michele DuBrow; c Debra & Lori. *Educ:* Rensselaer Polytech Inst, BMetE, 62, PhD(metall), 66. *Honors & Awards:* Henry Marion Howe Gold Medal, Am Soc Metals, 70. *Prof Exp:* Sr res scientist, Res Lab, United Aircraft Corp, 66, res assoc, Mat Eng & Res Lab, Pratt & Whitney Aircraft Div, 66-68, sr res assoc, 68-74, group leader, 74-77. *Mem:* Fel Am Soc Metals Int; Am Inst Mining, Metall & Petrol Engrs. *Res:* Relation of metallurgical structure to mechanical properties; gas turbine materials. *Mailing Add:* Southwest Res Inst PO Drawer 28510 San Antonio TX 78228-0510. *Fax:* 210-522-5122; *E-Mail:* gleverant@swri.org

LEVERE, RICHARD DAVID, INTERNAL MEDICINE, HEMATOLOGY. *Current Pos:* SR VPRES MED AFFAIRS, BROOKLYN HOSP CTR, 94-; PROF MED & ASSOC DEAN, NY UNIV SCH MED, 94- *Personal Data:* b Brooklyn, NY, Dec 13, 31; m 78; c Scott M, Elyssa C & Colinne G. *Educ:* State Univ NY, MD, 56. *Prof Exp:* From intern to asst resident med, Bellevue Hosp, 56-58; resident, Kings Co Hosp, 60-61; instr med, State Univ NY, 62-63; res assoc biochem, Rockefeller Inst, 62-63, asst prof, 64-65; from asst prof to prof med, State Univ NY Downstate Med Ctr, 65-77, chief hemat sect, 70-77; prof med & chmn dept, NY Med Col, 77-93. *Concurrent Pos:* Fel hemat, State Univ NY, 61-62; NIH grant, 65-82; adj prof, Rockefeller Univ, 73-; dir med serv, Westchester Co Med Ctr, 78-93. *Mem:* AAAS; Am Soc Clin Invest; Am Fedn Clin Res; Am Soc Hemat; Am Col Physicians; Sigma Xi. *Res:* Control mechanisms in heme and porphyrin synthesis; metabolism of normal and abnormal hemoglobins; diseases of porphyrin metabolism. *Mailing Add:* Med Affairs Brooklyn Hosp Brooklyn NY 11201. *Fax:* 718-250-6606

LEVERE, TREVOR HARVEY, HISTORY OF CHEMISTRY, SCIENCE & ARCTIC EXPLORATION. *Current Pos:* Lectr, Univ Toronto, 68-69, from asst prof to assoc prof, 69-81, dir, Inst Hist & Philos Sci, 81-86, PROF HIST SCI, UNIV TORONTO, 81-, DIR, INST HIST & PHILOS SCI, 93- *Personal Data:* b London, Eng, March 21, 44; Can & Brit citizen; m 66; c 2. *Educ:* Oxford Univ, BA, 66, MA, 69, DPhil(mod hist & hist sci), 69. *Concurrent Pos:* Killam fel, Can Coun, 75-77; John Simon Guggenheim Found fel, 83; vis fel, Clare Hall & vis scholar, Scott Polar Res Inst, Cambridge Univ, 83-84; resident fel, Dibner Inst, Mass Inst Technol, 95. *Mem:* Foreign mem Dutch Soc Sci; Can Soc Hist & Philos Sci; corresp mem Int Acad Hist Sci; fel Royal Soc Can; Hist Sci Soc. *Res:* History of chemistry; social and cultural contexts; science and Romanticism; science and Arctic exploration; history of sciences from eighteenth to twentieth centuries. *Mailing Add:* Inst Hist & Philos Sci Victoria Col Univ Toronto 73 Queen's Park Crescent E Toronto ON M5S 1K7 Can. *Fax:* 416-978-3003

LEVERENZ, HUMBOLDT WALTER, SOLID STATE SCIENCE. *Current Pos:* RETIRED. *Personal Data:* b Chicago, Ill, July 11, 09; m 40, Edith Langmuir; c David, Edith, Julia & Ellen. *Educ:* Stanford Univ, AB, 30. *Honors & Awards:* Brown Medal, Franklin Inst, 54. *Prof Exp:* Res chemico-physicist, Radio Corp Am, 31-54, dir phys & chem lab, 54-57, asst dir res, 57-59, dir, 59-61, assoc dir, RCA Labs, 61-66, staff vpres, Res & Bus Eval, 66-68, staff vpres & chmn educ aid comt, RCA Corp, 68-74. *Concurrent Pos:* Advan mgt prog, Bus Sch, Harvard Univ, 58; mem, Mat Adv Bd, Nat Acad Sci, 64-68; mem conf comt, Nat Conf Admin Res, 64-68. *Mem:* Nat Acad Eng; fel AAAS; Am Chem Soc; fel Am Phys Soc; fel Inst Elec & Electronic Engrs; fel Optical Soc Am. *Res:* Syntheses and applications of solids used in electronics; phosphors; secondary-emitters; photoconductors; semiconductors; nonmetallic magnetic materials; scotophors; crystals used in electronics. *Mailing Add:* 2240 Gulf Shore Blvd N Apt K4 Naples FL 34102

LEVERETT, DENNIS HUGH, DENTISTRY, CLINICAL RESEARCH. *Current Pos:* PROF DENT RES, SCH MED & DENT, UNIV ROCHESTER, 84- *Personal Data:* b Cleveland, Ohio, June 22, 31; c 7. *Educ:* Ohio State Univ, DDS, 56; Harvard Univ, MPH, 68; Am Bd Dent Pub Health, dipl. *Prof Exp:* Intern dent, USPHS, 56-57, dent officer, 57-60; pvt pract gen dent, 60-66; pub health dentist, NMex Dept Pub Health, 66-67; res fel ecol dent, Sch Dent Med, Harvard Univ, 67-69; resident dent pub health, Mass Dept Pub Health & Sch Dent Med, Harvard Univ, 68-69; exec dir, Ctr Community Dent Health, Portland, Maine, 69-73; chmn dept community dent, Eastman Dent Ctr, 73- *Concurrent Pos:* Consult, Bio-Dynamics, Inc, Mass, 68, Maine Dept Health & Welfare, 69-70, Mass Dept Pub Health, 69, Southern Maine Comp Health Asn, Inc, 70-73, Genesee Valley Group Health Asn, 73, Rochester Regional Med Prog, 76-77 & Health Econ Group, Inc, 78-; lectr dent ecol, Sch Dent Med, Harvard Univ, 69-73; clin instr social dent, Sch Dent Med, Tufts Univ, 70-73; clin assoc prof prev med & community health & clin dent, Sch Med & Dent, Univ Rochester, 73-84; adj prof dent hyg, Monroe Community Col, 73-82; dir dent care progs, Portland, Maine Model Cities, 69-73, chmn health task force, 70-72; mem prof adv comt, Portland City Health Dir, 69-73; mem med adv comt, Southern Maine Comprehensive Health Asn, 69-73; mem attend staff, Maine Med Ctr, Portland; mem courtesy staff, Mercy Hosp, Portland, Maine, 70-73; mem bd dirs, Smilemobile, Monroe County, NY, 73-77; mem dent hyg adv comt, Monroe Community Col, 73-85; dent dir, Monroe County Health Dept, 73-; mem bd dir, Westside Health Serv, Rochester, NY, 75-, chmn prog comt, 76-; co-prin investr, USPHS res grants, 74-77 & 77-81; prin investr, Nat Inst Dent Res grants, 75-79, 77-81 & 82-; lectr dent, var hosps & orgn, 73-81; ed, J Pub Health Dent, 87- *Mem:* Am Asn Pub Health Dent; Int Asn Dental Res; Am Asn Dental Res; Am Pub Health Asn; Europ Orgn Caries Res. *Res:* Clinical trials of therapeutic and preventive agents, including adhesive sealants and fluorides; evaluation of third party payment mechanisms, dental care delivery systems and post-doctoral dental education. *Mailing Add:* 28 Chasewood Circle Rochester NY 14618

LEVERETT, M(ILES) C(ORRINGTON), NUCLEAR ENGINEERING. *Current Pos:* RETIRED. *Personal Data:* b Danville, Ill, Dec 18, 10; m 38. *Educ:* Kans State Col, BS, 31; Univ Okla, MSE, 32; Mass Inst Technol, ScD(chem eng), 38. *Honors & Awards:* Robert E Wilson Award, Am Inst Chem Engrs, 76. *Prof Exp:* Asst chemist, Marathon Paper Mills Co, Wis, 32-33 & Phillips Petrol Co, Okla, 33-35; sr res engr, Humble Oil & Ref Co,

Tex, 38-42; assoc div dir, Metall Lab, Univ Chicago, 42-43; div dir, 43-48; res assoc, Humble Oil & Ref Co, 48-49; tech dir, Nuclear Engine Propulsion Aircraft Proj, Fairchild Eng & Airplane Corp, 49-51; mgr eng, Aircraft Nuclear Propulsion Dept, Gen Elec Co, 51-56 & Develop Labs, 56-61, mgr res & eng, Nuclear Reactor Dept, 61-67, safety & qual mgr, Nuclear Energy Div, 67-71 & Nuclear Safety & Boiling Water Reactor Qual Assurance, 71-76; nuclear consult engr, 76-93. *Concurrent Pos:* Div dir, Monsanto Chem Co & Carbide & Chem Co, Tenn, 43-48; leader US deleg, Int Stand Orgn Meeting Reactor Safety Stand, 58 & 60; mem, Res Adv Comt Nuclear Energy Processes, NASA, 59-60. *Mem:* Nat Acad Eng; fel Am Nuclear Soc (vpres, 59-60, pres, 60-61). *Res:* Petroleum emulsions; flow of fluids in porous solids; nuclear reactors; reactor materials; reactor safety; nuclear physics. *Mailing Add:* 800 Blossom Hill Rd Unit M255 Los Gatos CA 95032-3572

LEVERT, FRANCIS EDWARD, NUCLEAR REACTOR NOISE ANALYSIS, RADIATION DETECTION. *Current Pos:* VPRES, KEMP CORP, 85- *Personal Data:* b Tuscaloosa, Ala, Mar 28, 39; m 65, Faye Burnett; c Francis, Gerald & Lisa. *Educ:* Tuskegee Inst, BS, 64; Univ Mich, MS, 66; Pa State Univ, PhD(nuclear eng), 71. *Prof Exp:* From asst prof to assoc prof nuclear eng & mech eng, Tuskegee Inst, 66-72, head, Mech Eng Dept, 72-73; indust fel reactor anal, Commonwealth Edison Elec Co, 73-74; nuclear engr, Appl Physics Div, Argonne Nat Lab, 74-79; chief scientist, Technol Energy Corp, 79-85. *Concurrent Pos:* Mem, Currie Comt Eng Educ Disadvantaged, Pa State Univ, 69-71, Am Nuclear Soc-Nuclear Educ & Comt Disadvantaged Youth, 72-74; Ford Found fel Am Soc Eng Educ, Commonwealth Edison Co, 73-74; radiation safety officer, Technol Energy Corp, 85-96. *Mem:* Am Soc Mech Engrs; Nat Soc Prof Engrs; Am Nuclear Soc; Am Soc Mech Engrs. *Res:* Nuclear reactor noise analysis, neutron and gamma ray detector development; thermionic converters and instrumentation development for the fossil power fuel power industry; author of 77 technical papers and two books; granted twenty patents. *Mailing Add:* 1725 E Magnolia Ave Knoxville TN 37917-7827. *Fax:* 423-544-0840; *E-Mail:* tec.engr@ix.netcom.com

LEVERTON, WALTER FREDERICK, SOLID STATE PHYSICS, MATERIALS SCIENCE. *Current Pos:* CONSULT, 79- *Personal Data:* b Imperial, Sask, Dec 24, 22; m 48; c 2. *Educ:* Univ Sask, BS, 46, MS, 48; Univ BC, PhD(physics), 50. *Prof Exp:* Asst prof elec eng, Univ Minn, 50-51; asst div mgr semiconductors, Res Div, Raytheon Co, 51-60; group vpres develop, Aerospace Corp, 60-79. *Concurrent Pos:* Mem, Defence Commun Agency Sci Adv Group, 74-79. *Mem:* Am Phys Soc; fel Inst Elec & Electronics Engrs. *Res:* Cathode materials; semiconductors; 1061 Glenhaven Dr. *Mailing Add:* 1061 Glenhaven Dr Pacific Palisades CA 90272

LEVESON, NANCY, COMPUTER SCIENCE. *Current Pos:* PROF, UNIV WASH, 93- *Educ:* Univ Calif, Los Angeles, PhD, 80. *Prof Exp:* Prof, Univ Calif, Irvine. *Concurrent Pos:* Ed-in-chief, Inst Elec & Electronic Engrs Transactions Software Eng; bd dirs, Comput Res Asn, Int Coun Systs Eng; mem, Comn Eng Tech Systs, Nat Res Coun, Comt Comput Pub Policy, Asn Comput Mach; chair, Nat Res Coun. *Mem:* Fel Asn Comput Mach. *Res:* Demonstration of a safety assessment on part of the US Air Traffic Control System. *Mailing Add:* Dept Comput Sci & Eng Univ Wash Box 352350 Seattle WA 98195-2350

LEVESQUE, ALLEN HENRY, communication theory, communication systems development, for more information see previous edition

LEVESQUE, CHARLES LOUIS, ORGANIC CHEMISTRY. *Current Pos:* RETIRED. *Personal Data:* b Manchester, NH, Feb 16, 13; m 38; c 3. *Educ:* Dartmouth Col, AB, 34, AM, 36; Univ Ill, PhD(org chem), 39. *Prof Exp:* Instr anal chem, Dartmouth Col, 34-36; sr chemist, Resinous Prod & Chem Co, 39-41, group leader, 41-45, lab head, 45-48; res supvr, Rohm & Haas Co, 48-69, asst dir res, 69-71; prof appl sci & dir, Eve Sch, Ursinus Col, 71-79, dean continuing educ, 79-81. *Mem:* Am Chem Soc; Sigma Xi. *Res:* Structures of vinyl polymers; polyester resins and raw materials; new organic synthesis; surface active agents; pharmaceuticals. *Mailing Add:* Normandy Farms Estates Box 1108 Apt F-304 Blue Bell PA 19422

LEVESQUE, RENE J A, NUCLEAR PHYSICS. *Current Pos:* RETIRED. *Personal Data:* b St-Alexis, Que, Oct 30, 26; div; c 3. *Educ:* Sir George Williams Col, BSc, 52; Northwestern Univ, PhD(physics), 57. *Honors & Awards:* Queen Elizabeth Jubilee Medal. *Prof Exp:* Res assoc physics, Univ Md, 57-59; from asst prof to assoc prof, Univ Montreal, 59-67, dir, Lab Nuclear Physics, 65-69, prof physics, 67-87, dir, Dept Physics, 68-73, vdean res fac arts & sci, 73-75, dean fac arts & sci, 75-78, vpres res, 78-85, vpres res & planning, 85-87, emer prof, 87; pres, Atomic Energy Control Bd, 87-93. *Concurrent Pos:* Asst ed, Can J Physics, 73-75; vpres, Can-France-Hawaii Telescope Corp, 79, pres, 80; pres, Asn Sci, Eng & Technol Community Can, 80. *Mem:* Can Asn Physicists (pres, 76-77); Natural Sci & Eng Res Coun Can (vpres, 81-86). *Res:* Nuclear spectroscopy; nuclear reactions at low energy. *Mailing Add:* 190 Willowdale PH 1 Outremont PQ H3T 1G2 Can

LEVETIN AVERY, ESTELLE, MYCOLOGY, BOTANY. *Current Pos:* asst prof, 72-78, ASSOC PROF BOT, UNIV TULSA, 78- *Personal Data:* b Boston, Mass, Mar 24, 45; m 74, Allan; c Deborah & Jason. *Educ:* State Col Boston, BS, 66; Univ RI, PhD(bot & mycol), 71. *Prof Exp:* Lab instr & teaching asst bot, Univ RI, 69-71, asst prof, Exten Div, 71-72, fel res assoc, Dept Plant Path, 71-72; asst prof physiol, Mt St Joseph Col, 72. *Concurrent Pos:* Consult, Joint Res Prog, Allergy Clin Tulsa, Inc, 75-76. *Mem:* Mycol Soc Am; Bot Soc Am; Int Asn Aerobiol; Brit Mycol Soc; Pan Am Aerobiol Asn. *Res:* Fungal allergens; distribution of fleshy fungi in Oklahoma; distribution of air-borne fungi and pollen in Tulsa County; allergenic spores and pollen; indoor air bioaerosols. *Mailing Add:* Fac Biol Sci Univ Tulsa 600 S College Tulsa OK 74104. *Fax:* 918-631-2764; *E-Mail:* biol_el@utulsa.edu

LEVEY, DOUGLAS J, ECOLOGY, BEHAVIOR-ETHOLOGY. *Current Pos:* Archie Carr fel zool, 87-88, ASST PROF ORNITH, UNIV FLA, 88- *Personal Data:* b Boston, Mass, Sept 20, 57; m 88. *Educ:* Earlham Col, BA, 79; Univ Wis, MS, 82, PhD(zool), 86. *Mem:* Ecol Soc Am; Am Ornithologists Union; Asn Trop Biol; Animal Behav Soc. *Res:* Community structure and co-evolution of fruit eating birds and fruiting plants in the tropics; digestive physiology of frugivores; seed dispersal systems. *Mailing Add:* Dept Zool Univ Fla PO Box 118525 Gainesville FL 32611-8525

LEVEY, GERALD SAUL, INTERNAL MEDICINE, ENDOCRINOLOGY. *Current Pos:* CHMN, DEPT MED, SCH MED, UNIV PA, PHILADELPHIA. *Personal Data:* b Jersey City, NJ, Jan 9, 37; m 61; c 2. *Educ:* Cornell Univ, AB, 57; NJ Col Med, MD, 61. *Prof Exp:* Intern med, Jersey City Med Ctr, 61-62, resident, 62-63; resident, Mass Gen Hosp, Boston, 65-66; clin assoc endocrinol, Nat Inst Arthritis & Metab Dis, 66-68; sr investr endocrinol, Nat Heart & Lung Inst, 69-70; assoc prof med, 70-73, Sch Med, Univ Miami, Fla, prof, 73- *Concurrent Pos:* NIH fel biochem, Med Sch, Harvard Univ, 63-65; consult med, Vet Admin Hosp, Miami, Fla, 70-; investr, Howard Hughes Med Inst, 71-; lecture, Channel 10, WTLG. *Mem:* Am Soc Clin Invest; Am Col Physicians; Am Thyroid Asn; Am Fedn Clin Res; Soc Exp Biol & Med. *Res:* Mechanism of hormone action; cyclic adenosine monophosphate. *Mailing Add:* Univ Pittsburgh Sch Med 1218 Scaife Hall Pittsburgh PA 15261

LEVEY, HAROLD ABRAM, ENDOCRINE PHYSIOLOGY. *Current Pos:* from instr to assoc prof, 56-64, ASSOC PROF PHYSIOL, COL MED, STATE UNIV NY DOWNSTATE MED CTR, 64- *Personal Data:* b Boston, Mass, Aug 14, 24; m 59; c 2. *Educ:* Harvard Univ, AB, 47; Univ Calif, Los Angeles, PhD(zool), 53. *Prof Exp:* Jr & asst res physiol chemist, Univ Calif, Los Angeles, 53-56. *Concurrent Pos:* USPHS fel, 53-; China Med Bd vis prof physiol, Fac Med, Univ Singapore, 66-67. *Mem:* AAAS; Am Physiol Soc; Endocrine Soc; NY Acad Sci; Harvey Soc. *Res:* Pituitary chemistry and physiology; pituitary-thyroid interrelationships; factors influencing metabolism of endocrine organs; electrophysiology of thyroid. *Mailing Add:* Dept Physiol Box 31 160 Columbia Hts Apt 9B Brooklyn NY 11201

LEVI, ANTHONY FREDERIC JOHN, electronic & opto-electronic development, for more information see previous edition

LEVI, BARBARA GOSS, ARMS CONTROL, ENERGY & ENVIRONMENT. *Current Pos:* from assoc ed to sr assoc ed, 87-93, SR ED, PHYSICS TODAY, 93- *Personal Data:* b Washington, DC, May 5, 43; m 66, Ilan M; c Daniel S & Sharon R. *Educ:* Carleton Col, BA, 65; Stanford Univ, MS, 67, PhD(physics), 71. *Prof Exp:* Lectr physics, Fairleigh Dickinson Univ, 70-76, lectr, Ga Inst Technol, 76-80; mem res staff, Ctr Energy & Environ Studies, Princeton Univ, 80-82 & 83-87; mem tech staff, Bell Labs, 81-82. *Concurrent Pos:* Consult eed, Physics Today, 70-87 & 88-89; mem task force energy, Am Asn Univ Women, 75-77; consult, Off Technol Assessment, US Cong, 76-95; vis prof, Rutgers Univ, 88-89; chair, Forum Physics & Soc, Am Phys Soc, 88-89, mem educ comt, 89-91, counr, 92-95, mem exec bd, 94-96. *Mem:* Fel Am Phys Soc; Am Asn Physics Teachers; fel AAAS. *Res:* Writing news of current physics research; problems of science and society; arms control; global warming. *Mailing Add:* 1616 La Vista del Oceano Santa Barbara CA 93109

LEVI, DAVID WINTERTON, POLYMER CHEMISTRY. *Current Pos:* SUPVRY CHEMIST, PICATINNY ARSENAL, DOVER, 59- *Personal Data:* b Berryville, Va, Sept 2, 21; m 47; c 2. *Educ:* Randolph-Macon Col, BS, 43; Va Polytech Inst, MS, 51, PhD(chem), 54. *Prof Exp:* From instr to assoc prof chem, Va Polytech Inst, 46-59. *Mem:* Am Chem Soc. *Res:* Solution properties of high polymers; polymer-energetic compatibility; adhesives; thermal degradation of polymers. *Mailing Add:* 17533 Victory Blvd Van Nuys CA 91406

LEVI, ELLIOTT J, ORGANIC CHEMISTRY, PHYSICAL CHEMISTRY. *Current Pos:* RETIRED. *Personal Data:* b Brooklyn, NY, June 12, 40; m 64; c 2. *Educ:* City Col New York, BS, 61; Univ Cincinnati, PhD(chem), 66. *Prof Exp:* Chief chemist, Apollo Chem Corp, 66-68; group leader, Chem Systs Inc, 68-70; res mgr chem, Drew Chem Corp, 70-80, dir res & develop, 81-87; dir res planning, Ashland Chem Corp, 85-87. *Concurrent Pos:* Adj asst prof, Upsala Col, 67-71. *Mem:* Sigma Xi. *Mailing Add:* 1307 Mercedes St Teaneck NJ 07666-2130

LEVI, ENRICO, ENERGY CONVERSION, PLASMA PHYSICS. *Current Pos:* from assoc prof to prof, 58-88, EMER PROF ELECTROPH, POLYTECH UNIV NY, 88-; PRES & TREAS, ENRICO LEVI, INC, 76- *Personal Data:* b Milano, Italy, May 20, 18; US citizen; m 41, Nechama B Froimberg. *Educ:* Israel Inst Technol, BSc, 41, Ing, 42; Polytech Inst Brooklyn, MEE, 56, DEE, 58. *Honors & Awards:* Charles J Hirsch Award, Inst Elec & Electronics Engrs, 80. *Prof Exp:* Foreman elec shop, Shipwrights & Engrs Ltd, Israel, 42-44; mech engr, Palestine Elec Co, 44-45; sect head elec eng, Mouchly Eng Co, 45-48; lectr, Israel Inst Technol, 48-55; fel, Microwave Res Inst, Polytech Inst Brooklyn, 56-57; sr scientist, Elec & Electronic Res Found, Westbury, 57-58. *Concurrent Pos:* Consult, Lever Bros, Israel, 48-55, Hudson Paper Mill Co, 54-55, Am Mach & Foundry Co, 60-62, Westinghouse Elec Astronuclear Labs, Pa, 62-64, Gen Appl Sci Labs, 65, Van Karman Inst Fluid Dynamics, 66, Consol Edison Co, New York, 72, Long Island Lighting Co, 73-74, US Dept Energy, 76-78, Lawrence Livermore Lab, 78, Argonne Nat Lab, 78, Nasa Lewis Res Ctr, 80 & North-Hills Electronics, 84-; mem, Israel Govt Comt, 50-51 & Elec Wire Stand Comt, Israel, 50-55; Technion vis prof, 80-81 & 84; Lady Davis fel award, 80. *Mem:* Inst Elec & Electronics Engrs; Sigma Xi. *Res:* Electromechanical power conversions; magnetic amplifiers; automatic control; linear electric propulsion; variable speed drives, electric power. *Mailing Add:* Dept Elec Eng Polytech Univ 6 Metrotech Ctr Brooklyn NY 11201. *Fax:* 718-260-3906

LEVI, HERBERT WALTER, ARACHNOLOGY, SYSTEMATICS. *Current Pos:* from asst cur to assoc cur, Mus, 55-66, mem fac educ, Univ, 64-66, lectr biol, 64-70, prof biol, 70-72, Agassiz prof zool, 72-91, cur Arachrol, Mus Comp Zool, 66-91, EMER PROF BIOL, HARVARD UNIV, 91- *Personal Data:* b Frankfurt am Main, Ger, Jan 3, 21; nat US; m 49, Lorna Rose; c Frances. *Educ:* Univ Conn, BS, 46; Univ Wis, MS, 47, PhD(zool), 49. *Hon Degrees:* AM, Harvard Univ, 70. *Prof Exp:* From instr to assoc prof bot & zool, Exten Div, Univ Wis, 49-56. *Concurrent Pos:* Secy, Rocky Mountain Biol Lab, 59-65; vpres, Ctr Int Document Arachnol, 65-68, pres, 80-83; vis prof, Hebrew Univ Jerusalem, 75; hon cur, Univ Panama Mus Invert. *Mem:* Fel AAAS; Am Arachnol Soc (pres, 79-81); Soc Syst Zool; Am Ecol Soc; Am Inst Biol Sci; Am Micros Soc; Soc Study Evolution; Soc Syst Biol; Am Soc Zool; Centre Int de Doc Arachnologique. *Res:* Evolution; systematic zoology; spiders and other arachnids; animal transplantation; systematic studies of orb-weaving spiders in the family Araneidae and Tetragnathidae. *Mailing Add:* Mus Comp Zool Harvard Univ Cambridge MA 02138-9706. *E-Mail:* mczarach@oeb.harvard.edu

LEVI, IRVING, MEDICINAL CHEMISTRY. *Current Pos:* PRES, ALMEDIC DIV, RHOING LTD, 68- *Personal Data:* b Winnipeg, Man, Dec 15, 14; m 44; c 4. *Educ:* Univ Man, BSc, 38, MSc, 39; McGill Univ, PhD(chem), 42. *Prof Exp:* Carnegie Corp res fel, McGill Univ, 42-43, res assoc, 44-46, lectr, 46-47; sr res chemist, Charles E Frosst & Co, 48-68. *Concurrent Pos:* Civilian with Can Govt, 40-44. *Mem:* Am Chem Soc; fel Chem Inst Can. *Res:* Organic synthesis; carbohydrates; synthetic analgesics and sedatives; antibiotic and cancer chemotherapy; amino acids and derivatives; steroids and hormones; medicinal applications of natural products and derivatives. *Mailing Add:* 22 Glenmore Rd Hampstead PQ H3X 3M6 Can

LEVI, MICHAEL PHILLIP, FOREST PRODUCTS. *Current Pos:* assoc prof forestry, 71-77, PROF WOOD PAPER SCI, NC STATE UNIV, 77- *Personal Data:* b Leeds, Eng, Feb 5, 41; m 66; c 2. *Educ:* Univ Leeds, BS, 61, PhD(biophys), 64. *Prof Exp:* Fulbright travel scholar & res fel wood prod path, Sch Forestry, Yale Univ, 65; res fel, NC State Univ, 65-66; Sci Res Coun-NATO res fel, Univ Leeds, 66-67; sr biologist, Timber Res & Develop Lab, Hickson & Welch, Eng, 67-68, head res wood preservation, 68-71. *Mem:* Forest Prod Res Soc; Royal Soc Chem; Am Phytopath Soc. *Res:* Wood preservation; mode of action of fungicides; wood deterioration by fungi; wood as fuel. *Mailing Add:* 4909 Lites Rd Raleigh NC 27606

LEVI, ROBERTO, PHARMACOLOGY, CARDIOVASCULAR IMMUNOPHARMACOLOGY. *Current Pos:* from asst prof to assoc prof, 66-77, PROF PHARMACOL, MED COL, CORNELL UNIV, 77- *Personal Data:* b Milano, Italy, Mar 2, 34; m 62; c 2. *Educ:* Univ Florence, MD, 60. *Honors & Awards:* Pfizer Lect, Clin Pharmacol, Univ Minn Med Sch, 87; Geoffrey B West Mem Lect, Europ Histamine Res Soc, 93. *Prof Exp:* Asst pharmacol, Univ Florence, 60-61. *Concurrent Pos:* Fulbright travel fel pharmacol & exp therapeut, Sch Med, Johns Hopkins Univ, 61-63; sr res fel electrophysiol, Univ Florence, 63-66; prin investr, USPHS grant, 67-68; co-investr, NIH grant, 67-69; prin investr, NY Heart Asn grant, 68-71, 71-73 & 74-76; Nat Inst Gen Med Sci grant, 74-81; vis prof pharmacol, Col Physicians & Surgeons, Columbia Univ, 77-78; Sterling Drug vis prof, Med Sch, Ore Health Sci Univ, 87; conf co-chmn, Biol Leukotrienes, NY Acad Sci, 87; vis prof, Dept Anesthesiol, Sch Med, Emory Univ, 90. *Mem:* Am Soc Pharmacol & Exp Therapeut; Am Asn Immunologists; Am Asn Pathologists; Int Soc Heart Res. *Res:* Cardiovascular pharmacology; heart electrophysiology; neuropharmacology; immunopharmacology; autonomic pharmacology; pharmacology of mediators of immediate hypersensitivity; role of histamine in cardiac function and dysfunction; synthesis, release, actions of EDRF/nitric oxide in the heart and vasculature. *Mailing Add:* Dept Pharmacol Cornell Univ Med Col 1300 York Ave New York NY 10021-4896

LEVIALDI, STEFANO, PARALLEL PROCESSING, MULTICOMPUTER ARCHITECTURES. *Current Pos:* PROF COMPUT SCI, UNIV ROME, 83- *Personal Data:* b Rome, Italy, Nov 6, 36; m 85; c 3. *Educ:* Marconi Col, cert advan electronics, 61. *Prof Exp:* Lectr electronics, Univ Genoa, 61-65 & Univ Naples, 66-68; sr researcher image processing, Ital Nat Coun Res, 68-81; prof comput sci, Univ Bari, Italy, 81-83. *Concurrent Pos:* Assoc ed, Computer Vision, Graphics & Image Processing & Signal Processing, 79-, Pattern Recognition, 80-, Pattern Recognition Lett, 82-, Image & Vision Comput, 83- & J Parallel & Distrib Comput, 84-; co-ed, J Visual Lang & Comput, 89- *Mem:* Fel Inst Elec & Electronics Engrs; Int Asn Pattern Recognition (vpres, 90-). *Res:* Image analysis and understanding, algorithms, languages, architectures; visual languages; iconic interfaces; scientific visualization; computational metaphors. *Mailing Add:* Scienze Dell' Informazione Univ Di Roma La Sapienza via Salaria 113 Rome 00198 Italy

LEVICH, CALMAN, RADIATION BIOPHYSICS, AUTOMOBILE ACCIDENT ANALYSIS. *Current Pos:* prof, 70-83, chmn dept, 75-83, EMER PROF PHYSICS, CENT MICH UNIV, 83-; PRES, CALEB ASSOCS, 83- *Personal Data:* b Iowa City, Iowa, May 26, 21; m 46, Eva B Lindas; c Judith, David, Rebecca & Miriam. *Educ:* Morningside Col, BS, 49; Cath Univ Am, PhD(physics), 66. *Prof Exp:* Biophysicist, Naval Med Res Inst, 50-61; proj dir, Armed Forces Radiobiol Res Inst, 61-67; assoc prof physics, Cent Mich Univ, 67-68; chmn dept, Seton Hall Univ, 68-70. *Concurrent Pos:* Mem, legislative off of sci adv, State Mich, 80-81, radiation adv bd, 82-90, governor's task force on high level radiation waste, 83-86; mem, Mich Indoor Radon Task Force, 87-90. *Mem:* AAAS; Biophys Soc; Radiation Res Soc; Am Asn Physics Teachers; Sigma Xi. *Res:* Radiation biophysics; reactor operator education; radiation safety and transport of radioactive materials. *Mailing Add:* PO Box 546 Pentwater MI 49449-0546. *E-Mail:* clevich@aol.com

LEVIE, HAROLD WALTER, SURFACE PHYSICS. *Current Pos:* MAT SCIENTIST SURFACE TECHNOL, INORG MAT DIV, LAWRENCE LIVERMORE LAB, 75- *Personal Data:* b Augusta, Ga, Jan 17, 49. *Educ:* William Marsh Rice Univ, BA, 71, MS, 73, PhD(mat sci), 76. *Prof Exp:* Physicist, Phys Sci Lab, US Army Missile Command, 71. *Concurrent Pos:* Instr corrosion eng, Nat Asn Corrosion Engrs, 75. *Mem:* Nat Asn Corrosion Engrs; Sigma Xi. *Res:* Analysis and characterization of solid surfaces; kinetics of surface reactions and interface formation. *Mailing Add:* 4279 Amherst Way Livermore CA 94550-4901

LEVIEN, LOUISE, PETROPHYSICS, CRYSTALLOGRAPHY. *Current Pos:* res geologist, Exxon Prod Res Co, 81-84, res specialist, 84-91, sr res specialist, 91-92, sr planning asst, 92-94, RES SUPVR, EXXON PROD RES CO, 94- *Personal Data:* b New York, NY, Mar 23, 52; m 84, Robert G Eby; c David A & Allison E. *Educ:* Brown Univ, ScB, 74; State Univ NY, Stony Brook, MS, 75, PhD(geochem), 79. *Prof Exp:* Weizmann fel, Calif Inst Technol, 79-81. *Concurrent Pos:* Mem, Am Geol Inst Women Geoscientists Comt, 78-80, chmn, 80; mem educ & human resources comt, Am Geophys Union, 80-84. *Mem:* Am Asn Petrol Geologists; Am Geophys Union; Mineral Soc Am; Soc Prof Well Log Analysts; Soc Petrol Engrs. *Res:* Geochemistry and geophysics of hydrocarbon reservoirs; relationship of elastic properties and crystal chemistry of minerals. *Mailing Add:* Exxon Prod Res Co PO Box 2189 Houston TX 77252-2189

LEVIEN, ROGER ELI, INFORMATION SCIENCE, TECHNOLOGY STRATEGY. *Current Pos:* dir strategic systs anal, Xerox, 82-85, vpres, Strategy Off, 85-92, VPRES, TECHNOL & MARKET DEVELOP, 92-95, VPRES, STRAT & INNOVATION, XEROX CORP, 95-, VPRES, XEROX 2005, 96- *Personal Data:* b Brooklyn, NY, Apr 16, 35; m 60, Carla Johanna Sherow; c Alisa T & Royce A. *Educ:* Swarthmore Col, BS, 56; Harvard Univ, MS, 58, PhD(appl math), 62. *Honors & Awards:* Austrian Ehrenkreuz First Class, Sci & Art. *Prof Exp:* Mem, res staff, Rand Corp, 60-67, head, Syst Sci Dept, 67-71, mgr, Wash Domestic Progs, 71-74; proj leader, Int Inst Appl Systs Anal, Austria, 74-75, dir, 75-81. *Concurrent Pos:* Adj prof, Univ Calif, Los Angeles, 70-74. *Mem:* Asn Comput Mach; Inst Elec & Electronics Engrs; AAAS; Asn Pub Policy Anal & Mgt. *Res:* Policy analysis; research and development management; information sciences; strategic planning; tehnology strategy; document processing technology. *Mailing Add:* 28 Fresh Meadow Rd Weston CT 06883. *Fax:* 203-968-4301; *E-Mail:* rlevien@aol.com

LEVI-MONTALCINI, RITA, GROWTH FACTORS. *Current Pos:* res assoc, Inst Zool, 47-51, from assoc prof to prof, Inst Biol, 51-81, EMER PROF NEUROBIOL, INST BIOL, WASH UNIV, 77-; FAC MEM, INST NEUROBIOL, DEPT BIOL, COMN NATURAL RESOURCES, NAT RES COUN, ROME, 89- *Personal Data:* b Torino, Italy, Apr 22, 09; Italian & US citizen. *Educ:* Univ Turin, MD, 40. *Hon Degrees:* Dr, Univ Uppsala, Sweden, 77, St Mary's & Notre Dame's Col, 80; PhD, Wash Univ Med Sch, St Louis, Mo, 82, Univ London, Eng, 87, Univ Buenos Aires, 87, Loyola Univ, Chicago, 87 & Biophys Inst, Univ Brazil, 87, Harvard Univ, 89 & Univ Urbino, Italy, 90. *Honors & Awards:* Nobel Prize Med/Physiol, 86; Max Weinstein Award, Cerebral Palsy Found, 62; Harvey Lectr, 65; Feltrinelli Int Prize Med, 69; Golden Plate Award, Am Acad Achievement, 70; Ibico-Reggino Award Biol Sci, 70; Int St Vincent Award, 79; Knights of Humanity Award, Int Philanthrop Soc, 79; Gold Medal Sci, Rome, 86; Albert Lasker Med Res Award, 86; Thudicum Award & Lectr, Eng, 87; US Nat Medal Sci, 87; Gold Medal, Ministry Pub Health, Rome, 88. *Prof Exp:* Asst prof anat, Univ Turin, 45-47. *Concurrent Pos:* Dir, Neurobiol Res Ctr, Comn Natural Resources, Nat Res Coun, 61-69, dir, Cellular Biol Lab, 69-79, researcher/guest prof, 79-89, guest prof, Inst Neurobiol, 89; Fogarty scholar, Washington, DC, 78; mem, Int Sci Adv Bd, Int Acad Biomed & Drug Res, Belgium, 90, Nat Comt Bioethics, Italy, & Nat Comn Unesco, Italy, 90. *Mem:* Nat Acad Sci; AAAS; Soc Develop Biol; Am Asn Anatomists; hon mem Tissue Cult Asn; Sigma Xi; Am Acad Arts & Sci; Am Philos Soc; hon mem Am Soc Zoologists; hon mem Am Med Women's Asn; Nat Acad Sci Italy; Belg Royal Acad Med; Europ Acad Sci; Acad Arts & Sci Florence; Nat Acad die Lineei; Pontifical Acad. *Res:* Experimental neurology; effect of a nerve growth factor isolated from the mouse salivary gland on the sympathetic nervous system and of an antiserum to the nerve growth factor; specific growth factors. *Mailing Add:* Inst Neurobiol Nat Res Coun Viale Marx 15 Rome 00156 Italy

LEVIN, AARON R, PEDIATRICS, CARDIOLOGY. *Current Pos:* PROF PEDIAT, NY MED COL, 94- *Personal Data:* b Johannesburg, SAfrica, Mar 19, 29; m 55; c 3. *Educ:* Univ Witwatersrand, BSc, 48, MBBCh, 53, MD, 68; Royal Col Physicians & Surgeons, dipl child health, 60; FRCP, 81. *Prof Exp:* Intern, Edenvale Hosp, SAfrica, 54-55; sr intern, Johannesburg Fever Hosp, 55; pediat intern, Coronation Hosp, 55-56; pediat registr, 56-60; pediat registr, Charing Cross Hosp, Eng, 61; gen pract, 62-63; instr pediat, Med Ctr, Duke Univ, 64-66; from asst prof to prof pediat, Med Ctr, Cornell Univ, 66-94. *Concurrent Pos:* NIH fel cardiol, Med Ctr, Duke Univ, 64-66; attend physician, Pediat Intensive Care Unit, NY Hosp-Cornell Med Ctr. *Mem:* Fel Royal Col Physicians; Soc Pediat Res; Am Pediat Soc; Am Heart Asn; Am Col Cardiol. *Res:* Pediatric cardiology, specifically related to studies of pressure-flow dynamics in various forms of congenital heart disease; extra cardiac factors in congenital heart disease; right ventricular hypertrophy at cellular level. *Mailing Add:* Pediat Cardiol Sect NY Med Col 618 Munger Pavilion Valhalla NY 10595

LEVIN, ALAN EDWARD, FISSION REACTOR THERMAL-HYDRAULICS, NUCLEAR REACTOR SAFETY. *Current Pos:* reactor engr, 90-92, SR REACTOR ENGR, US NUCLEAR REGULATORY COMN, 90- *Personal Data:* b Baltimore, Md, May 17, 53; m 88, Bonnie S Richter; c Ariel L & Jonathan M. *Educ:* Mass Inst Technol, SB, 75, ScD(fission reactor eng), 80. *Prof Exp:* Staff mem, Oak Ridge Nat Lab, 80-86; assoc prof nuclear eng, Ga Inst Technol, 86-90. *Concurrent Pos:* Prof engr, 83-; summer fac fel, Oak Ridge Assoc Univs, 89. *Mem:* Am Nuclear Soc; Am Soc Mech Engrs. *Res:* Regulatory review of reseach in nuclear reactor thermal-hydraulics and safety; testing related to advanced power reactor designs. *Mailing Add:* 12410 Rousseau Terr North Potomac MD 20878

LEVIN, ALFRED A, RESEARCH ADMINISTRATION, AGRICULTURAL & FOOD CHEMISTRY. *Current Pos:* RETIRED. *Personal Data:* b Chicago, Ill, May 18, 28; m 56; c 4. *Educ:* Univ Ill, Urbana, BS, 51; Loyola Univ, Chicago, MS, 62. *Prof Exp:* Chemist, Leaf Brands Inc, 51-53 & Wallace A Erickson & Co, 53-55; res chemist, Velsicol Chem Corp, 55-70, mgr, labels & petitions, 70-75, dir govt compliance, 76-78, dir staff & support progs, 78-80, dir toxic substances control, 80- *Mem:* Am Chem Soc; Am Inst Chemists. *Res:* Synthesis of chemicals with intended pesticidal properties. *Mailing Add:* 8242 Ridgeway Skokie IL 60076

LEVIN, ANDREW ELIOT, EXPERIMENTAL BIOLOGY. *Current Pos:* FOUNDER & PRES, IMMUNETICS, INC, 87- *Personal Data:* b Newton, Mass, Mar 9, 54; m. *Educ:* Princeton Univ, AB, 76; Univ Wis-Madison, 84. *Prof Exp:* Res technician, Genetics Unit, Mass Gen Hosp, 76-77; fel, Dept Cellular & Develop Biol, Harvard Univ, 84-87. *Concurrent Pos:* Consult ed, Encycl Sci Instruments; adv bd mem, Am Chem Soc; consult, Soviet biotechnol & biomed res technol. *Mem:* Am Soc Cell Biol. *Res:* Immunochemistry and immunoassays; protein purification and characterization; cell culture; monoclonal antibodies and hybridoma production; immunofluorescence microscopy; four patents. *Mailing Add:* Immunetics Inc 63 Rogers St Cambridge MA 02139

LEVIN, BARBARA CHERNOV, TOXICOLOGY, FIRE SCIENCES. *Current Pos:* res biologist, Nat Bur Stand, 78-82, group leader, 82-85, proj leader fire toxicol, Nat Inst Stand & Technol, 85-92, RES BIOLOGIST BIOTECHNOL, NAT INST STAND & TECHNOL, 93- *Personal Data:* b Providence, RI, May 5, 39; m 61, Ira W; c David M & Jordan J. *Educ:* Brown Univ, BA, 61; Georgetown Univ, PhD(microbial genetics), 73. *Prof Exp:* Res asst endocrinol, Sch Med, Johns Hopkins Univ, 62-63; teaching asst biol, Georgetown Univ, 68-73; fel molecular biol, NIH, 73-75, staff fel, 75-78. *Concurrent Pos:* Mem, comt develop toxicity test method to assess combustion prod, Nat Bur Standards, 78-82, sci officer numerous grants, Extramural Res, 78-92; lectr environ toxicol, grad sch, NIH, 83-91; mem, comt toxicity complex mixtures, Nat Acad Sci, 84-88; chmn, Tech Adv Group to Int Standards Orgn on Toxic Hazards in Fire, 84-94; counr, Am Col Toxicol, 89-91; adj prof, Fire Protection Eng Dept, Univ Md, College Park, 91-; consult, Fire Toxicol & Inhalation Toxicol, 92-; mem, Comt Improved Fire & Smoke Resistant Mat for Com Aircraft Interiors. *Mem:* Soc Toxicol; Am Chem Soc; Sigma Xi; Am Col Toxicol; Asn Govt Toxicologists; Am Soc Testing & Mat. *Res:* Toxicology of combustion products; assessment of acute inhalation toxicity; development of model to predict toxicity; mutagenesis and repair of DNA; DNA technology. *Mailing Add:* Bldg 222 Rm A353 Nat Inst Stand & Technol Gaithersburg MD 20899. *Fax:* 301-330-3447

LEVIN, BARRY EDWARD, NEUROBIOLOGY, NEUROLOGY. *Current Pos:* ASSOC PROF NEUROSCI, COL MED NJ, 77- *Personal Data:* b Brooklyn, NY, May 1, 42. *Educ:* Emory Univ, MD, 67; Am Bd Psychiat & Neurol, dipl. *Prof Exp:* Instr & chief resident neurol, Cornell Med Sch, 71-72; clin assoc, Nat Inst Neurol Dis & Blindness, 72-74; asst prof neurol & psychiat, Dartmouth Med Sch, 74-77. *Concurrent Pos:* Grantee, Vet Admin Res & Educ grant, 74-; dir lab of neuropharmacol & dept neurosci, Col Med NJ, 77-; staff neurologist, Vet Admin Hosp, East Orange, NJ, 77-; attend neurologist, Martland Hosp, Col Med NJ, 78- *Mem:* Soc Neurosci; Am Acad Neurol. *Res:* Metabolism, axonal transport and rhythms of catecholamines in health and disease. *Mailing Add:* Neurol Serv Vet Admin Med Ctr East Orange NJ 07019

LEVIN, BRUCE, MATHEMATICAL STATISTICS. *Current Pos:* prof math statist & biostatist, 74-83, assoc prof clin pub health biostatist, 83-92, ASSOC PROF PUB HEALTH BIOSTATIST, COLUMBIA UNIV, 92- *Personal Data:* b New York, NY, Mar 14, 48; m 70, Betty Wolder; c Joel & Laura. *Educ:* Columbia Univ, AB, 68; Harvard Univ, MA, 72, PhD(appl math), 74. *Prof Exp:* Data analyst & comput programmer, Albert Einstein Col Med, 66-72. *Concurrent Pos:* Consult, Statistica, Inc, 78-; consult ed, Am J Pub Health. *Mem:* Am Statist Asn; Inst Math Statist; Sigma Xi. *Res:* Statistical inference and data analysis. *Mailing Add:* 39 Claremont Ave No 42 New York NY 10027-6824. *Fax:* 212-305-9408; *E-Mail:* blg@columbia.edu

LEVIN, EDWIN ROY, SOLID STATE SCIENCE. *Current Pos:* RETIRED. *Personal Data:* b Philadelphia, Pa, Nov 4, 27; m 51; c 3. *Educ:* Temple Univ, AB, 49, MA, 51, PhD(physics), 59. *Prof Exp:* Asst physics, Temple Univ, 49-51; physicist, Frankford Arsenal, US Army, 51-63; mem tech staff, RCA Labs, 63-87; consult, Electron Micros Applications, 87-92. *Concurrent Pos:* Secy Army res & study fel, Cavendish Lab, Cambridge Univ, 61-62; guide prof, World Univ, 73- *Mem:* AAAS; Am Phys Soc; Electron Micros Soc Am. *Res:* Solid state physics; theory of dielectrics; photoconductivity; quantum electronics; analysis of solid materials for electronics, including electron microscopy and related methodologies. *Mailing Add:* 37 Pineknoll Dr PO Box 3263 Lawrenceville NJ 08648-3143

LEVIN, EUGENE (MANUEL), PHYSICS. *Current Pos:* PROF PHYSICS, YORK COL, NY, 67- *Personal Data:* b New York, NY, Aug 14, 34; m 60; c 3. *Educ:* Univ Vt, BA, 56; Columbia Univ, MA, 59; NY Univ, PhD(physics), 67. *Mem:* Am Asn Physics Teachers. *Res:* Excited states and fluorescence properties of organic molecules; applications of fluorescence techniques to charged particle dosimetry. *Mailing Add:* Dept Physics York Col City Univ NY Jamaica NY 11451. *E-Mail:* levin@ycvax.york.cuny.edu

LEVIN, EUGENE G, BIOCHEMISTRY. *Current Pos:* Fel plasminogen activators, 78-83, asst mem, 84-90, ASSOC PROF, SCRIPPS & RES INST, 90- *Personal Data:* b Philadelphia, Pa, May 29, 48. *Educ:* Pa State Univ, BS, 69; Univ Calif, Irvine, PhD(biochem), 77. *Mem:* Am Heart Asn; Am Soc Cell Biol; Int Soc Fibrinolysis. *Mailing Add:* Dept Molecular & Exp Med SBR 13 Scripps & Res Inst 10550 N Torrey Pines Rd La Jolla CA 92037. *Fax:* 619-784-2174; *E-Mail:* tcglenn@scripps.edu

LEVIN, FRANK S, NUCLEAR PHYSICS, FEW-BODY PHYSICS. *Current Pos:* assoc prof, 67-77, PROF PHYSICS, BROWN UNIV, 77- *Personal Data:* b Bronx, NY, Apr 14, 33; m 55, 73; c 4. *Educ:* Johns Hopkins Univ, AB, 55; Univ Md, PhD(physics), 61. *Honors & Awards:* Alexander von Humboldt Sr US Scientist Award, 79-80. *Prof Exp:* Res assoc physics, Rice Univ, 61-63 & Brookhaven Nat Lab, 63-65; temp res assoc, Atomic Energy Res Estab, Eng, 65-67. *Concurrent Pos:* Exchange scientist, US-India Exchange Scientists Prog, 73; sr vis fel, UK Sci Res Coun, 74; founder, Topical Group Few Body Systs & Multiparticle Dynamics, Am Phys Soc. *Mem:* Fel Am Phys Soc. *Res:* Nuclear reaction theory; scattering theory; few-body problems; molecular structure. *Mailing Add:* Dept Physics Brown Univ Providence RI 02912. *E-Mail:* fsl@brownvm.brown.edu

LEVIN, FRANKLYN KUSSEL, EXPLORATION GEOPHYSICS. *Current Pos:* CONSULT, 87- *Personal Data:* b Terre Haute, Ind, June 28, 22; m 46; c 3. *Educ:* Purdue Univ, BS, 43; Univ Wis, PhD(physics), 49. *Honors & Awards:* Robert Earll McConnell Award, 81; Reginald Fessenden Award, Soc Explor Geophys, 84; Maurice Ewing Medal, Soc Explor Geophys, 88. *Prof Exp:* Physicist, Sam Labs, Columbia Univ, 43-44, Carbide & Carbon Chem Corp, 44-46; asst physics, Univ Wis, 46-47; physicist, Carter Oil Co, 49-53; asst dir, Hudson Labs, Columbia Univ, 53-54; physicist, Carter Oil Co, 54-58; physicist, Jersey Prod Res Co, Standard Oil Co, 58-59, res assoc, 59-63, sr res assoc, 63-64, sr res assoc, Esso Prod Res Co, 65-67, res scientist, 67-73, sr res scientist, Exxon Prod Res Co, 73-86. *Concurrent Pos:* Lectr, Univ Tulsa, 58-63; ed, Geophys, 69-71. *Mem:* AAAS; Seismol Soc Am; Am Geophys Union; Acoust Soc Am; Soc Explor Geophys; Europ Asn Explor Geophys; Inst Elec & Electronics Engrs. *Mailing Add:* 802 W Forest Dr Houston TX 77079-3324

LEVIN, GEOFFREY ARTHUR, PLANT SYSTEMATICS. *Current Pos:* asst prof scientist, 94-96, ASSOC PROF SCIENTIST, ILL NATURAL HIST SURV, 96-, DIR, CTR BIODIVERSITY, 96- *Personal Data:* b Los Alamos, NMex, Dec 7, 55; m 81, Renee Papini; c Tobias & Madeline. *Educ:* Pomona Col, BA, 77; Univ Calif, Davis, MS, 80, PhD(bot), 84. *Honors & Awards:* Jesse M Greenman Award, 87. *Prof Exp:* Asst prof bot, Ripon Col, 82-84; cur bot, San Diego Natural Hist Mus, 84-93; dir res & collections, 93. *Concurrent Pos:* Adj prof bot, San Diego State Univ, 85-93; vis prof biol, Univ San Diego, 87, 89-90; res assoc, Mo Bot Garden, 94-; adj prof, Univ Ill, 95- *Mem:* Bot Soc Am; Am Soc Plant Taxonomists; Sigma Xi; Am Inst Biol Sci; Soc Syst Biol. *Res:* Systematics of Euphorbiaceae; Mexican flora; midwestern flora. *Mailing Add:* Ctr Biodiversity Ill Natural Hist Surv 607 E Peabody Dr Champaign IL 61820. *Fax:* 217-333-4949; *E-Mail:* levin1@uiuc.edu

LEVIN, GERSON, MATHEMATICS. *Current Pos:* STAFF MEM, PRUDENTIAL INS CO, 85- *Personal Data:* b Philadelphia, Pa, Oct 27, 39; m 69. *Educ:* Univ Pa, AB, 61; Univ Chicago, MS, 62, PhD(math), 65. *Prof Exp:* NSF fel, Univ Ore, 66, vis asst prof math, 66-67; asst prof, NY Univ, 67-74; asst prof, Brooklyn Col, 74-76, assoc prof math, 76-85. *Res:* Commutative rings and homological algebra. *Mailing Add:* 470 First St Brooklyn NY 11215

LEVIN, GIDEON, PHYSICAL ORGANIC CHEMISTRY, PHOTOCHEMISTRY. *Current Pos:* AT DEPT MAT RES, WEIZMANN INST SCI. *Personal Data:* b Mazkeret Ratia, Israel, Apr 6, 36; US citizen; m 63; c 2. *Educ:* Israel Inst Technol, BSc, 60; Purdue Univ, West Lafayette, MSc, 65; State Univ NY Col Environ Sci & Forestry, PhD(chem), 71. *Prof Exp:* Chemist polymers, Dow Corning Corp, 65-67; res assoc photochem, Upsala Univ, 72; res assoc photochem, Col Environ Sci & Forestry, State Univ NY, 72-75, sr res assoc, 75- *Concurrent Pos:* Vis scientist, Weizmann Inst Sci, 78- *Mem:* Am Chem Soc. *Res:* Mechanism of photochemical reaction initiated by flash of light which includes conversion of light energy to chemical energy and photo-reduction and photoreduction of organic and organo metallic molecules which have biological significance. *Mailing Add:* Dept Mat Res Weizmann Inst Sci Rehovot 76100 Israel

LEVIN, GILBERT VICTOR, ENVIRONMENTAL HEALTH, ENGINEERING. *Current Pos:* PRES, BIOSPHERICS INC, 67- *Personal Data:* b Baltimore, Md, Apr 23, 24; m 53, Marian K Bloomquist; c Ron, Henry & Carol. *Educ:* Johns Hopkins Univ, BE, 47, MS, 48, PhD(sanit eng), 63. *Honors & Awards:* IR-100 Indust Res Mag, 75; Necomb Cleveland Prize, AAAS, 77. *Prof Exp:* Jr asst sanit engr, State Dept Health, Md, 48-50; asst sanit engr, Dept Pub Health, Calif, 50-51; pub health engr, DC, 51-56; vpres, Resources Res, Inc, 56-63; dir spec res, Hazleton Labs, Inc, 63-65, dir, Life Systs Div, 65-67. *Concurrent Pos:* Res asst biochem, Schs Med & Dent, Georgetown Univ, 52-61, clin asst prof, 53-60; biochemist, Dept Sanit Eng,

DC, 62-63; consult, Dept Interior, 63-71; NASA planetary quarantine adv, 65-74; NASA experimenter, Mariner 9, 71 & Viking Mission to Mars, 76; trustee, Johns Hopkins Univ, 82-85. *Mem:* Am Soc Civil Eng; fel Am Pub Health Asn; Water Pollution Control Fedn; NY Acad Sci; Am Inst Biol Sci; AAAS; Am Water Works Asn. *Res:* Inventor PhoStrip process for wastewater phosphorus removal; Lev-o-cal L-sugar noncaloric sweetener; D-tegatose nonfattening sweetener; life sciences; applied biology; water supply; waste disposal; sanitary biology; environmental sanitation; life detection techniques; public health and medical microbiology; low caloric sweeteners instrumentation; space biology. *Mailing Add:* Biospherics Inc 12051 Indian Creek Ct Beltsville MD 20705

LEVIN, HAROLD LEONARD, GEOLOGY, PALEONTOLOGY. *Current Pos:* from asst prof to assoc prof, Washington Univ, 61-71, chmn, Dept Earth & Planetary Sci, 73-76, assoc dean, Col Arts & Sci, 76-94, PROF PALEONT, WASHINGTON UNIV, 71- *Personal Data:* b St Louis, Mo, Mar 11, 29; m 54, Kay H Tamarkin; c Linda, Stephen & Janet. *Educ:* Univ Mo, AB, 51, MA, 52; Washington Univ, PhD(paleont), 56. *Prof Exp:* Res geologist, Stand Oil Co Calif, 56-61. *Concurrent Pos:* Res grants, Washington Univ, 61-72; consult ecol serv, Mo Bot Garden, 73-75. *Mem:* AAAS; Soc Econ Paleont & Mineral; Paleont Soc; Geol Soc Am. *Res:* Foraminifera, Coccolithophoridae and related microfossils; biostratigraphy of microorganisms; geological education; author of physical and historical geology and paleontology textbooks. *Mailing Add:* Dept Earth & Planetary Sci Washington Univ St Louis MO 63130

LEVIN, HARVEY STEVEN, NEUROPSYCHOLOGY. *Current Pos:* from asst prof to assoc prof, 74-84, PROF NEUROPSYCHOL, UNIV TEX MED BR, 84- *Personal Data:* b New York, NY, Dec 12, 46; m 68; c 1. *Educ:* City Col, Univ NY, BA, 67; Univ Iowa, MA, 71, PhD(clin psychol), 72. *Honors & Awards:* Caveness Award, Nat Head Injury Found, 85. *Prof Exp:* Fel, Dept Neurol, Univ Iowa, 72-73; intern clin psychol, Ill Masonic Med Ctr, 73-74. *Concurrent Pos:* Consult, Dept Neurol, Univ Hosps, Iowa, 73-74; vis lectr, dept psychol, Univ Mo, Columbia, 81; vis prof, dept neurosurg, Univ Pa, 81-; prin investr, Neuropsychol Sect, Nat Inst Neurol & Commun Dis & Stroke Prog Proj, 75-; investr, Int Study Group Pharmacol Memory, 78-; ed, Cortex, 81-, J Clin & Exp Neuropsychol, 83-, Develop Neuropsychol, 84- & Brain Injury, 85-; mem, Vet Admin Merit Rev Bd, 84-; mem, med prof adv bd, Nat Head Injury Found, 85-; Jacob K Javits Neurosci Investr Award, 84. *Mem:* AAAS; fel Am Psychol Asn; Soc Neurosci; Acad Aphasia. *Res:* Recovery from brain injury in children and adults; cholinergic augmentation in dementia of the Alzheimer type; visual perception in patients with focal brain lesions. *Mailing Add:* Div Neurosurg E17 Univ Tex Med Br Galveston TX 77550

LEVIN, IRA WILLIAM, BIOPHYSICS, CHEMICAL PHYSICS. *Current Pos:* guest worker, NIH, 63-65, staff fel, 65-66, res chem, Phys Biol Lab, 66-72, actg chief, Lab Chem Physics, 84-85, RES CHEMIST, LAB CHEM PHYSICS, NIH, 72-, DEP CHIEF, 87-, CHIEF, SECT MOLECULAR BIOPHYS, 79- *Personal Data:* b Washington, DC, Sept 20, 35; m 61; c 2. *Educ:* Univ Va, BS, 57; Brown Univ, PhD(chem), 61. *Honors & Awards:* Lippincott Award, 85; Meggers Award, 93; Iddles lectr, 93. *Prof Exp:* Res instr chem, Univ Wash, 61-62. *Concurrent Pos:* Lectr, Georgetown Univ, 64-65, assoc mem grad fac chem, 74-75. *Mem:* Coblentz Soc (pres, 77-78); fel Am Phys Soc; Biophys Soc; Am Soc Biol Chemists. *Res:* Vibrational spectroscopy; absolute intensities; molecular dynamics and structure; spectra; spectroscopy of biomembranes. *Mailing Add:* 612 Smallwood Rd Rockville MD 20850

LEVIN, IRVIN, physical chemistry; deceased, see previous edition for last biography

LEVIN, JACK, INTERNAL MEDICINE, HEMATOLOGY. *Current Pos:* PROF LAB MED & MED, UNIV CALIF SCH MED, SAN FRANCISCO, 82-, ATTEND PHYSICIAN, LAB MED & INTERNAL MED, MED CTR, 86- *Personal Data:* b Newark, NJ, Oct 11, 32; m 75. *Educ:* Yale Univ, BA, 53, MD, 57; Am Bd Internal Med, dipl, 65, recert, 74. *Honors & Awards:* Frederik B Bang Award, 86. *Prof Exp:* Chief resident & instr, Yale Univ, 64-65; from instr to assoc prof, Johns Hopkins Univ, 65-78, prof med, div hemat, 78-82; dir, Hemat Lab & Blood Bank, Vet Admin Med Ctr, San Francisco, 82-93. *Concurrent Pos:* Fel med, Sch Med, Johns Hopkins Univ, 62-64; mem corp, Marine Biol Lab, 65-; physician chg hemat out-patient clin, Johns Hopkins Hosp, 67-71, 76-82; Markle scholar acad med, 68-73; consult, Vet Admin Hosp, Baltimore, Md, 68-82; res career develop award, USPHS, 70-75; atten physician Lab Med & Internal Med, Univ Calif Med Ctr, San Francisco, 86-; dir, Flow Cytometry Facil, Vet Admin Med Ctr, San Francisco, 87-90; mem, bd trustees, Marine Biol Lab, Woods Hole, Mass, 88-93. *Mem:* Int Soc Hemat; Int Soc Exp Hemat; fel Am Col Physicians; Am Soc Hemat; Am Soc Clin Invest; Sigma Xi. *Res:* Blood coagulation, platelets; thrombopoiesis; endotoxin and endotoxemia; thrombocytosis; invertebrate blood coagulation; megakaryocytopoiesis; transfusion medicine. *Mailing Add:* Hemat 111H2 Vet Admin Hosp 4150 Clement St San Francisco CA 94121-1598. Fax: 415-221-7542

LEVIN, JACOB JOSEPH, MATHEMATICAL ANALYSIS. *Current Pos:* assoc prof, 63-66, PROF MATH, UNIV WIS-MADISON, 66- *Personal Data:* b New York, NY, Dec 21, 26; m 52; c 3. *Educ:* City Col New York, BEE, 49; Mass Inst Technol, PhD, 53. *Prof Exp:* Instr math, Mass Inst Technol, 52-53; instr, Purdue Univ, 53-55; vis lectr, Mass Inst Technol, 55-56, staff mem, Lincoln Lab, 56-63. *Concurrent Pos:* NSF sr fel, Univ Calif, Los Angeles, 70-71; vis prof, Univ BC, 77-78. *Mem:* Am Math Soc; Soc Indust & Appl Math. *Res:* Differential equations; integral equations. *Mailing Add:* Dept Math Univ Wis Madison WI 53706

LEVIN, JEROME ALLEN, MEDICAL INFORMATICS. *Current Pos:* asst prof, Med Col Ohio, 68-74, interim chmn, 73-75, assoc prof pharmacol, 74-79, PROF PHARMACOL, MED COL OHIO, 79-, ASSOC DEAN ACAD RESOURCES, 87-, DIR COMPUTER LEARNING RESOURCE CTR, 88- *Personal Data:* b Washington, DC, Aug 25, 39; m; c 3. *Educ:* Philadelphia Col Pharm & Sci, BSc, 61; Univ Mich, PhD(pharmacol), 66. *Prof Exp:* Res assoc pharmacol, State Univ NY Downstate Med Ctr, 66-68. *Concurrent Pos:* USPHS fel, State Univ NY Downstate Med Ctr, 66-68; Am Heart Asn res grant, Med Col Ohio, 69-75, USPHS res grant, 70-76. *Mem:* AAAS; Am Heart Asn; Am Soc Pharmacol & Exp Therapeut. *Res:* Computer applications in medicine. *Mailing Add:* Dept Pharmacol Med Col Ohio CS 10008 Toledo OH 43699-0008

LEVIN, JOSEPH DAVID, INDUSTRIAL MICROBIOLOGY. *Current Pos:* RETIRED. *Personal Data:* b New York, NY, Feb 7, 18; m 47, Carol Silverman; c 2. *Educ:* Queens Col, NY, BS, 41. *Prof Exp:* Tech aide, E R Squibb & Sons, 47-50, res asst, 50-53, res asst supvr, Squibb Div, Olin Mathieson Chem Corp, 53-59, res scientist, 59-64, sr res scientist, 64-69, lab supvr, Inst Med Res, Squibb Corp, New Brunswick, 68-82. *Mem:* NY Acad Sci; Am Soc Microbiol. *Res:* Analytical microbiology; test and develop microbiological assays of antibiotics including traces in mammalian tissues; test and development methods for pharmaceutical preservative efficacy; co-patentee, diagnostic aid for fungal infection. *Mailing Add:* 30 S Adelaide Ave No 8C Highland Park NJ 08904

LEVIN, JUDITH GOLDSTEIN, VIROLOGY, MOLECULAR GENETICS. *Current Pos:* Sr scientist molecular biol viruses, Nat Cancer Inst, 69-73, sr scientist, Lab Molecular Genetics, 73-92, HEAD, UNIT VIRAL GENE REGULATION, NAT INST CHILD HEALTH & HUMAN DEVELOP, 92- *Personal Data:* b Brooklyn, NY, Nov 8, 34; m 57, Jonathan; c Joshua & Daniel. *Educ:* Barnard Col, Columbia Univ, BA, 55; Harvard Univ, MA, 57; Columbia Univ, PhD(biochem), 62. *Concurrent Pos:* Nat Heart Inst res fel biochem genetics, 62-69; USPHS fel, 63-65; Am Heart Asn advan res fel, 66-68; consult lab path, Nat Cancer Inst, 69; estab investr, Am Heart Asn, 69-74. *Mem:* AAAS; Am Soc Biochem & Molecular Biol; Am Chem Soc; Am Soc Microbiol; Am Soc Virol. *Res:* Molecular genetics of retrovirus (e.g. HIV) replication correlation of gene structure with functional activity reverse transcription and role of accessory proteins; regulated expression of viral genetic information. *Mailing Add:* Lab Molecular Genetics Nat Inst Child Health & Human Develop NIH Bldg 6B Rm 216 Bethesda MD 20892. *Fax:* 301-496-0243; *E-Mail:* jlevin@longvax.nichd.nih.gov

LEVIN, KATHRYN J, SOLID STATE PHYSICS THEORY. *Current Pos:* asst prof, 75-85, PROF PHYSICS, UNIV CHICAGO, 85- *Personal Data:* b Lawrence, Kans, Feb 25, 44; m 69. *Educ:* Univ Calif, Berkeley, BA, 66; Harvard Univ, PhD(physics), 70. *Prof Exp:* Res assoc physics, Univ Rochester, 70-72; asst res physicist, Univ Calif, Irvine, 72-75. *Mem:* Fel Am Phys Soc. *Res:* Exotic superconductivity disordered systems. *Mailing Add:* James Franck Inst Univ Chicago 5640 Ellis Ave Chicago IL 60637

LEVIN, LEONID A, ALGORITHMIC COMPLEXITY. *Current Pos:* PROF MATH & COMPUT SCI, BOSTON UNIV, 80- *Personal Data:* b USSR, Nov 2, 48. *Educ:* Moscow Univ, 72; Mass Inst Technol, PhD(math), 79. *Concurrent Pos:* Vis scientist comput sci, Mass Inst Technol, 78-; vis MacKey prof, UC Berkeley, 86; vis prof, Calif Inst Technol, 87. *Res:* Foundations of mathematics, statistics and computer science; algorithmic complexity with applications to randomness and information theories, inductive inference, functional analysis, combinatorics and graph theory, mathematical logic, theory of computations; randomness and information. *Mailing Add:* Comput Sci Boston Univ 111 Cummington St Boston MA 02215-2411

LEVIN, MARTIN ALLEN, ELECTRON MICROSPY, CELL ULTRASTRUCTURE. *Current Pos:* from asst prof to assoc prof, 78-88, PROF BIOL, EASTERN CONN STATE COL, 88- *Personal Data:* b Philadelphia, Pa, Aug 14, 49; m 77, Mary G Hanzel; c Andrew, Daniel & Rachael. *Educ:* Rutgers Univ, BA, 71, MS, 73; Ohio Univ, PhD(zool), 77. *Prof Exp:* Teaching asst biol, Rutgers Univ, 71-73; teaching assoc biol, Ohio Univ, 74-77. *Concurrent Pos:* news-ed, Micros Soc Conn Newsletter. *Mem:* Micros Soc Am. *Res:* Ultrastructural studies of the abdominal muscles of terrestrial and semiterrestrial amphipods: correlating structure to locomotory function; ultrastructural and histochemical studies of the walking legs of brachyuran crabs. *Mailing Add:* Dept Biol Eastern Conn State Univ 83 Windham St Willimantic CT 06226-2211. *Fax:* 860-465-5213; *E-Mail:* levin@ecsuc.ctstateu.edu

LEVIN, MICHAEL H(OWARD), ENVIRONMENTAL SCIENCES & ENGINEERING, ECOLOGY. *Current Pos:* PRES, ENVIRON RES ASSOCS, INC, 70-, DIR RES, 73- *Personal Data:* b New York, NY, Sept 25, 36; m 86, Lorna MacDonald; c Eleanor M. *Educ:* Univ Vt, BS, 58; Rutgers Univ, MS, 60, PhD(bot), 64. *Prof Exp:* Res assoc taxon, NY Bot Garden, 64; cur, Greene-Nieuwland Herbarium & asst prof biol, Univ Notre Dame, 64-66; asst prof bot & cur herbarium, Univ Man, 66-68; asst prof landscape archit & regional planning, Univ Pa, 68-73. *Concurrent Pos:* Adj prof agr & natural resources, Del State Col, 79- *Mem:* Fel AAAS; Ecol Soc Am; Sigma Xi. *Res:* Environmental sciences and geotechnical investigations; ecology of altered communities and ecosystems; ecological management; application of gradient analysis to terrestrial communities; wetlands ecology; hydrobiology, hydrology and water resources; wood science; research and testing of natural and man made materials; health and safety evaluations; environmental studies and surveys; testing and laboratory services; engineering and planning. *Mailing Add:* Environ Res Assocs Inc 414 Mill Rd Havertown PA 19083-3740

LEVIN, MORRIS A, MICROBIOLOGY. *Current Pos:* MICROBIOLOGIST HEALTH EFFECTS, ENVIRON PROTECTION AGENCY, 70- *Personal Data:* b New York, NY, May 15, 34; m 57; c 2. *Educ:* Univ Chicago, BS, 59; Univ RI, PhD(microbiol), 70. *Prof Exp:* Microbiologist aerobiol, Dept Defense, 57-66; microbiologist marine microbiol, Dept Health Educ & Welfare, 66-70. *Concurrent Pos:* Adj prof civil eng & microbiol, Univ RI, 75. *Mem:* Sigma Xi. *Res:* Quantitating of microorganisms in the environment, dose-response relationships and epidemiological considerations correlating the public health effects of exposure to microbial populations under natural conditions; forecasting, trend analysis of environmental problems, genetic engineering. *Mailing Add:* 14405 Woodcrest Dr Rockville MD 20853

LEVIN, MORTON LOEB, preventive medicine, public health; deceased, see previous edition for last biography

LEVIN, MURRAY LAURENCE, INTERNAL MEDICINE, NEPHROLOGY. *Current Pos:* assoc, Northwestern Univ, 66-69, from asst prof to assoc prof, 69-80, chief, Sect Nephrol, Med Ctr, 86-91, PROF MED, MED SCH, NORTHWESTERN UNIV, CHICAGO, 80-, CHIEF, PATTERSON TEACHING FIRM, 90- *Personal Data:* b Boston, Mass, Nov 14, 35; m 61, Joan E Solomon; c Russell J & Cynthia A. *Educ:* Harvard Col, AB, 57; Tufts Univ, MD, 61. *Prof Exp:* Intern med, Beth Israel Hosp, Boston, Mass, 61-62, resident, 62-64; res fel renal dis, Univ Tex Southwestern Med Sch Dallas, 64-66. *Concurrent Pos:* NIH res fel, 65-66; Chicago Heart Asn res grants, 66-70 & 73-75; Nat Inst Arthritis & Metab Dis res grant, 67-70; attend physician, Vet Admin Lakeside Hosp, Chicago, Ill, 66-, chief renal sect, 72-76, chief med serv, 76-85; adj staff, Passavant Mem Hosp, 68-, assoc attend physician, 75-80; attending physician, Northwestern Mem Hosp, 80-; secy-treas, Cent Soc Clin Res, 82-87; chief, Sect Nephrology/Hypertension, Northwestern Univ Med Ctr, 86- *Mem:* AAAS; Am Fedn Clin Res; Int Soc Nephrol; Am Soc Nephrol; Cent Soc Clin Res; Nat Kidney Found. *Res:* Salt and water metabolism; uremia; membrane transport; calcium and phosphorus metabolism. *Mailing Add:* Sect Nephrol Dept Med Northwestern Mem Hosp Rm 446 250 E Superior St Chicago IL 60611. *Fax:* 312-908-5232

LEVIN, NORMAN LEWIS, ZOOLOGY, PARASITOLOGY. *Current Pos:* from instr to prof, 60-96, EMER PROF BIOL, BROOKLYN COL, 96-, DEP CHMN DEPT, 82- *Personal Data:* b Hartford, Conn, Mar 31, 24; m 50, Shirley A Ginsberg; c Faye D & Alan J. *Educ:* Univ Conn, BS, 48, MS, 49; Univ Ill, PhD(zool, parasitol), 56. *Prof Exp:* Asst zool, Univ Ill, 53-56, instr, 56-57; asst prof biol, Westminster Col, Mo, 57-60. *Concurrent Pos:* Fel trop med, Sch Med, La State Univ, 59. *Mem:* Fel AAAS; Am Soc Zool; Am Soc Parasitol; Am Soc Trop Med & Hyg; Am Micros Soc; Am Inst Biol Sci. *Res:* General taxonomy; morphology; life cycles; interrelationship of larval trematodes and marine snails. *Mailing Add:* Dept Biol Brooklyn Col Brooklyn NY 11210

LEVIN, ROBERT AARON, CLINICAL CHEMISTRY. *Current Pos:* Res toxicologist, Norwich Pharmacal Co, 55-58, sr researcher clin path & toxicol, 58-62, unit leader clin path, 62-80 & 80-89, MGR PATH, ANATOMIC & CLIN PATH SECT, NORWICH-EATON PHARMACEUT, 90- *Personal Data:* b New York, NY, July 25, 29; m 55; c 4. *Educ:* St John's Univ, NY, BS, 51, MS, 55. *Concurrent Pos:* Sci adv, Med Technol Dept, State Univ NY Agr & Tech Col Morrisville, Broome Tech Col, State Univ NY, Canton; adj prof, State Univ NY, Utica. *Mem:* Am Chem Soc; Am Asn Clin Chem; Am Soc Vet Clin Pathologists. *Res:* Automation and computerization of chemical technics; drug safety assessment; establishing effects on clinical pathology parameters; veterinary hematology. *Mailing Add:* 25 Hillview Dr Norwich NY 13815

LEVIN, ROBERT E, MICROBIOLOGY, FOOD SCIENCE. *Current Pos:* from asst prof to assoc prof, 64-77, PROF FOOD SCI, UNIV MASS, AMHERST, CHEENOWTH LAB, 77- *Personal Data:* b Boston, Mass, Dec 1, 30; c 2. *Educ:* Los Angeles State Col, BS, 52; Univ Southern Calif, MS, 54; Univ Calif, Davis, PhD(microbiol), 63. *Prof Exp:* Asst prof microbiol, Ore State Univ, 63-64. *Concurrent Pos:* NIH res grant, 65-68. *Mem:* Am Soc Microbiol; Inst Food Technologists; Soc Cryobiol. *Res:* Microbiological sulfate reduction; yeast cytology; psychophilic bacteria; enzymology; molecular taxonomy. *Mailing Add:* Dept Food Sci Univ Mass Amherst Chenoweth Lab Amherst MA 01003-0002

LEVIN, ROBERT EDMOND, LIGHT & RADIOMETRIC OPTICS. *Current Pos:* SR SCIENTIST LIGHT & RADIATION, GTE SYLVANIA INC, 63- *Personal Data:* b Orange, Calif, Oct 11, 31; m 58, Karen N Andree; c Kristen & Erik. *Educ:* Stanford Univ, BS, 53, MS, 54, Engr, 56, PhD(elec eng), 60. *Honors & Awards:* Illuminating Eng Soc NAm Medal, 95. *Prof Exp:* Assoc prof elec eng, Calif State Univ, San Jose, 58-63. *Concurrent Pos:* Consult engr, 58-63; instr continuing educ, Northeastern Univ, 68-82; contrib ed, McGraw-Hill, 71-75; adj prof elec eng, Univ NH, 83-; adj assoc prof archit, Rensselaer Polytech Inst, 90- *Mem:* Optical Soc Am; sr mem Inst Elec & Electronics Engrs; fel Illum Eng Soc; Am Soc Photobiol; Am Soc Eng Educ; Soc Motion Picture & TV Engrs; Sigma Xi. *Res:* Control and application of non-ionizing radiation in photobiological, photochemical and visual systems; radiometric optics. *Mailing Add:* Osram Sylvania Inc 71 Cherry Hill Dr Beverly MA 01915. *Fax:* 978-750-1794; *E-Mail:* levin@osi.sylvania.com

LEVIN, ROBERT HAROLD, ORGANIC CHEMISTRY. *Current Pos:* RES/MGT CONSULT, 78- *Personal Data:* b Chicago, Ill, Nov 1, 15; m 43; c 4. *Educ:* Univ Ill, AB, 37; Univ Wis, PhD(org chem), 41. *Prof Exp:* Chem libr asst, Univ Ill, 34-36; asst chem, Univ Wis, 37-41; res chemist, Upjohn Co, Mich, 41-46, group leader chem res, 46-52, head dept chem, 52-58, asst dir res, 58-68; vpres res, Richardson-Merrell, Inc, 68-78. *Concurrent Pos:* Mem subcomt steroid nomenclature, Nat Res Coun, 50-55; mem coun, Gordon Res Conf. *Mem:* AAAS; Am Chem Soc; Sigma Xi. *Res:* Chemistry of steroids, especially the cortical hormones; biomedical research and new drug development long range planning for pharmaceutical research; international pharmaceutical product licensing. *Mailing Add:* 11127 Jardin Pl Cincinnati OH 45241-6629

LEVIN, ROBERT MARTIN, PHARMACOLOGY. *Current Pos:* PROF PHARMACOL & DIR RES, DEPT BIOL SCI, ALBANY COL PHARM, 96- *Personal Data:* b New York, NY, Apr 6, 45; m 67, Sheila S; c Sharon & Michelle. *Educ:* Albright Col, BS, 67; Univ Pa, MS, 69, PhD(pharmacol), 74. *Prof Exp:* Fel, Dept Pharmacol, Med Col Pa, 74-76, instr pharmacol, 76-78; res assoc, Div Urol, Univ Pa, 78-79, res asst prof, 79-83, from res assoc prof to res prof pharmacol & urol, 83-96. *Concurrent Pos:* Dir urol res, Univ Pa, 78-; pharmacologist term appt, Vet Admin Med Ctr 84- *Mem:* Int Continence Soc; Am Urol Asn; Am Soc Pharmacol & Exp Therapeut; Basic Urol Res Soc; Urodynamics Soc; Urol Res Soc; Int Soc Impotence Res. *Res:* Smooth muscle plasticity in response to pathological situations. *Mailing Add:* Albany Col Pharm 106 New Scotland Ave Albany NY 12208-3492. *Fax:* 518-445-7202

LEVIN, ROGER L(EE), MATERIALS SCIENCE. *Current Pos:* RETIRED. *Personal Data:* b Clearfield, Pa, Mar 21, 36; m 60; c 3. *Educ:* Pa State Univ, BS, 58; Yale Univ, MEng, 61; Northwestern Univ, PhD(mat sci), 63. *Prof Exp:* Sonar proj officer, Accoust Warfare Proj Off, Naval Ship Systs Command, DC, 56-70, USN, 58-70, anal officer, sonal opers anal, Naval Test & Eval Detachment, Fla, 63-65; mgr undersea warfare progs, Hydrospace Res Corp, 70-72; pres, Mar Inc, 72-92, tech dir, 77-92. *Mem:* Am Soc Naval Engrs; Am Oceanic Orgn; Am Defense Preparedness Asn; US Naval Inst. *Res:* Underwater acoustics. *Mailing Add:* 4 Cleveland Ct Rockville MD 20850

LEVIN, RONALD HAROLD, ORGANIC CHEMISTRY. *Current Pos:* MEM STAFF, IBM CORP, 78- *Personal Data:* b San Francisco, Calif, Sept 26, 45; m 69; c 2. *Educ:* Case Western Res Univ, BS, 67; Princeton Univ, PhD(chem), 70. *Prof Exp:* Fel chem, Univ Freiburg, 70-71 & Calif Inst Technol, 71-72; asst prof chem, Harvard Univ, 72-77. *Mem:* Am Chem Soc; Chem Soc London; Sigma Xi. *Res:* Reactive intermediates; thermal and photochemical transformations; applications of magnetic resonance; electrophotography. *Mailing Add:* Lexmark Int Inc 6555 Monarch Rd PO Box 9042 Boulder CO 80301

LEVIN, ROY, PROGRAMMING ENVIRONMENT, DISTRIBUTED SYSTEMS & OPERATING SYSTEMS. *Current Pos:* Mem tech staff, 84-88, SR CONSULT ENGR, SYSTS RES CTR, DIGITAL EQUIP CORP, 88- *Personal Data:* b New York, NY, 1948. *Educ:* Yale Univ, BS, 70; Carnegie Mellon Univ, PhD(computer sci), 77. *Concurrent Pos:* Chmn, Spec Interest Group Oper Systs, Asn Comput Mach, 87-91. *Mem:* Asn Comput Mach; Inst Elec & Electronics Engrs. *Mailing Add:* Systs Res Ctr Digital Equip Corp 130 Lytton Palo Alto CA 94301

LEVIN, S BENEDICT, REMOTE SENSING, TECHNOLOGY TRANSFER. *Current Pos:* RETIRED. *Personal Data:* b New Orleans, La, July 9, 10; m 36; c 2. *Educ:* Columbia Univ, AB, 31, BS, 32, EM, 33, PhD(geol), 48. *Honors & Awards:* Medal, Antarctic Serv, NSF, 65. *Prof Exp:* Mining geologist, Central Am Mines, 34-37; instr geol, Hunter Col, 37-42; geol engr mineral explor, US Bur Mines, 42-45; res dir, US Army Electronics Command, 45-60; dir, Inst Explor Res, 60-68; asst dir res, Off Secy Defense, 68-70; exec vpres, Earth Satellite Corp, 70-76; prof eng & appl sci, George Washington Univ, 76-79. *Concurrent Pos:* Mem, Solid State Sci Panel, Nat Acad Sci, 49-68, chmn Panel, Space Info, Nat Acad Eng, 74-75; chmn, Defense Ctr Res, 69-70; mem, Fed Coun Sci & Technol, Acad Sci & Eng, 69-70 & adv coun, Technol Transfer, NASA, 78-80; consult, earth resources, 79- *Mem:* Fel Geol Soc Am; fel Am Geophys Union; Sigma Xi; fel Am Soc Photogram & Remote Sensing; fel Mineral Soc Am. *Res:* Application of remote sensing from earth satellites and aircraft to resource exploration and development; solid state physics. *Mailing Add:* Lake Waramaug New Preston CT 06777

LEVIN, SAMUEL JOSEPH, BIOCHEMISTRY. *Current Pos:* ASST PROF, PATH, UNIV ILL,CHICAGO, COL MED, 89- *Personal Data:* b Detroit, Mich, Sept 19, 35; m 63; c 2. *Educ:* Wayne State Univ, BA, 58, PhD(chem), 61; Am Bd Clin Chem, dipl. *Prof Exp:* Res assoc chem, Col Med, Wayne State Univ, 55-61; scientist, Warner Lambert Pharmaceut Co, 61-62; from instr to asst prof biochem, Div Grad Studies, Med Col, Cornell Univ, 63-66; from asst prof to assoc prof biochem, Sch Dent, Univ Mo-Kansas City, 67-74, from asst prof to assoc prof, Sch Med, 68-74; asst dir clin path, Michael Reese Hosp, 74-76, mem, Michael Reese Inst, 74-76, dir, div biochem, Michael Reese Hosp, 77-, assoc dir, clin path, 83- *Concurrent Pos:* Asst attend biochemist, Mem Hosp Cancer & Allied Dis, 62-66; assoc, Sloan-Kettering Inst, 63-66; chief biochemist, Dept Path, Kansas City Gen Hosp, 66-74. *Mem:* AAAS; Am Asn Clin Chem; Clin Lab Mgt Asn; Sigma Xi. *Res:* Clinical biochemistry. *Mailing Add:* Pathol M/C 847 Univ Ill Chicago Col Med 1819 W Polk St Chicago IL 60612-7331

LEVIN, SEYMOUR A(RTHUR), CHEMICAL ENGINEERING. *Current Pos:* RETIRED. *Personal Data:* b Newark, NJ, Sept 16, 22; m 48; c 4. *Educ:* Johns Hopkins Univ, BE, 43. *Prof Exp:* Res asst, Columbia Univ, 43-45; dept head, Union Carbide Nuclear Co Div, Uniion Carbide Corp, 45-68, head long range planning, Nuclear Div, 68-89. *Mem:* Am Chem Soc; AAAS; Nat Soc Prof Engrs. *Res:* Design and analysis of isotope separation process. *Mailing Add:* 956 W Outer Dr Oak Ridge TN 37830

LEVIN, SEYMOUR R, INTERNAL MEDICINE. *Current Pos:* PROF MED, UNIV CALIF, LOS ANGELES, 81- *Personal Data:* b Chicago, Ill, Apr 27, 34; m 57; c 3. *Educ:* Univ Ill, BS, 56, MD, 61; Am Bd Internal Med, dipl internal med, 70 & endocrinol, 73. *Prof Exp:* Intern, Cook Co Hosp, Chicago, 61-62; resident, Wadsworth Vet Admin Hosp, Los Angeles, 62-65; physician, US Army Hosp, Ft Carson, 65-67; res fel endocrinol, Univ Calif, San Francisco, 67-69; asst res physician, 69-73; dir diabetes clin & chief metab unit, Wadsworth Vet Admin Hosp, 73- *Concurrent Pos:* Endocrine Div, Univ Calif, Los Angeles, 73-; assoc prof med, Univ Calif, Los Angeles, 75-81; grants, Vet Admin, 73-91 & NIH Tug grant assoc inv, 83-92. *Mem:* Fel Am Col Physicians; Am Fedn Clin Res; Am Diabetes Asn; Endocrine Soc. *Res:* Studies of insulin secretion and mechanisms of secretion by the endocrine pancreas. *Mailing Add:* Wadsworth Vet Admin Hosp 691/111K Los Angeles CA 90073

LEVIN, SIDNEY SEAMORE, physiology, pharmacology, for more information see previous edition

LEVIN, SIMON ASHER, MATHEMATICS, BIOLOGY. *Current Pos:* GEO M MOFFETT PROF BIOL, PRINCETON UNIV, 92-, DIR ENVIRON INITIATIVES, 92-, ASSOC FAC APPL & COMPUTATINAL MATH, 92- *Personal Data:* b Baltimore, Md, Apr 22, 41; m 64, Carole Leiffer; c Jacob E & Rachel S Klopfer. *Educ:* Johns Hopkins Univ, BA, 61; Univ Md, PhD(math), 64. *Hon Degrees:* DSC, Eastern Mich Univ, 90. *Honors & Awards:* lansdowne Lectr, Univ Victoria, BC, 81; Grace Kimball Mem lectr, Wilkes Col, Pa, 86; H J Oosting Mem lectr, Duke Univ, 87; MacArthur Award, Ecol Soc Am, 88. *Prof Exp:* Asst math, Univ Md, 61-62; NSF fel biomath, Univ Calif, Berkeley, 64-65; asst prof math, Cornell Univ, 65-70, assoc prof appl math, 71-77, assoc prof ecol & systs & theoret & appl math, 72-77, chmn sect ecol & systs, 74-79, dir, Ecosysts Res Ctr, 80-87, dir, Ctr Environ Res, 87-90, prof appl math & ecol, 77-92, Charles A Alexander prof biol sci, 85-92, dir & prof theoret & comput biol, 90-92. *Concurrent Pos:* Res assoc, Univ Md, College Park, 64; co-chmn biomath, Gordon Res Conf, 70, chmn theoret biol & biomath, 71; vis prof, Univ Md, College Park, 68, Univ Wash, Seattle, 73- 74, Weizmann Inst, Rehovot, Israel, 77 & 80, Univ BC, Vancouver, 79-80, Stanford Univ, 88; assoc ed, Ecol & Ecol Monographs, Ecol Soc Am, 73-75, ed, 75-77; assoc ed, Theoret Pop Biol, 76-84; managing ed, Lecture Notes Biomath, 73-, J Appl Math, Soc Indust & Appl Math, 75-79 & Biomathematics, 76-; adv ed, J Math Biol, 73-76, ed, 76-79, managing ed, 79-; ed, Lect on Math in Life Sci, 74-79; mem US comt, Israel Environ, 75-; adv ed, J Theoret Biol, 76-; consult ed, Evolutionary Theory, 76-, Math Intelligencer, 77-84 & Math & Comput Modelling, 79-; mem adv comt, Environ Sci Div, Oak Ridge Nat Lab, 78-81; Guggenheim fel, 79-80; vchmn math, Comt Concerned Scientists, 79-; chair, comt Human Rights Math Scientist, 80-83; co-dir, autumn course on ecol, Trieste, Italy, Inter Atomic Energy Agency, UNESCO, 82, 86, 90 & 92; sci panel, Hudson River Found, 82-, chmn, 85-86, bd dir, 86, mem, Prog Comt, 89, chair, 92; mem, Comn Life Sci, Nat Res Coun, Nat Acad Sci, 83-89, Comt Release Genetically Eng Organisms into Environ, 86-87, bd biol, 83-89, chmn, Subcomt Ecol & Ecosyst, 86-87; mem ed adv coun, Nat Res Modeling, 84-; mem, Health & environ res Adv Comt, Dept Energy, 86-90; mem, bd dir, Hudson River Found, 86-Dept Energy, 86-90; dir, Ctr Environ Res, 87-; mem, Comn Ecol, Int Union Conserv Nature & Natural Resources, 87-91, Santa Fe Inst Sci Bd, 91-94, Comt Environ Res, Nat Acad Sci, 91-93, US Nat Comt for Man & Biosphere Prog, 93-94. *Mem:* Soc Math Biol (pres, 87-89, vpres, 89-91); Am Math Soc; Am Soc Naturalists; Ecol Soc Am (pres-elect, 89-90, pres, 90-91); Soc Indust & Appl Math; Brit Ecol Soc. *Res:* Theoretical ecology; mathematical and computational models of ecological and evolutionary processes; biological growth and spread; landscape models in relation to disturbance and global change; terrestrial, intertidal, and marine ecosystems. *Mailing Add:* Princeton Univ Dept Ecol & Evolutionary Biol 203 Eno Hall Princeton NJ 08544-1003

LEVIN, SIMON EUGENE, TOXICOLOGY, INDUSTRIAL HYGIENE. *Current Pos:* RETIRED. *Personal Data:* b Philadelphia, Pa, Nov 29, 20; m 48; c 2. *Educ:* Philadelphia Col Pharm, BS, 41; Pa State Col, MS, 42, PhD, 49. *Prof Exp:* Bacteriologist, La Wall & Harrison Res Labs, 38-41; lab asst bact, Pa State Col, 41-42; bioassayist, La Wall & Harrison Res Labs, 42-43 & 46; asst bact, Pa State Col, 46-49; res assoc chemother, E R Squibb & Sons, 49-50; head div biol, La Wall & Harrison Res Labs, 50-56; pres, Huntingdon Farms, Inc, West Conshohocken, 57-74; dir, Life Sci Div, Am Stand Testing Bur, 74-77; occup health consult, NJ State Dept Labor & Indust, 77-91. *Concurrent Pos:* Dir, Syndot Labs, 57-74; consult, Decker Corp, 59-70; comn radiation protection, State NJ, 78- *Mem:* AAAS; Am Indust Hyg Asn; Toxicol Soc; Am Chem Soc; NY Acad Sci. *Res:* Medical and industrial pharmacology and toxicology. *Mailing Add:* Beaver Hill Apts N205 309 Florence Ave Jenkintown PA 19046-2602

LEVIN, VICTOR ALAN, CANCER, NEUROLOGY. *Current Pos:* PROF & CHMN, DEPT NEURO-ONCOL, UNIV TEX, 88- *Personal Data:* b Milwaukee, Wis, Nov 22, 41; m 63; c 2. *Educ:* Univ Wis-Madison, BS, 63, MD, 66. *Honors & Awards:* Fac Res Award, Am Cancer Soc, 77-81; Ann & Jason Faber Award, 88; David A Frommer Mem Lectr Neuro-Oncol, Harvard Med Sch, 90; Fred Plum Lectr, Sch Med, Univ Wash, 91. *Prof Exp:* Intern med, St Louis City Hosp, Washington Univ, 66-67; staff assoc chem pharm, Nat Cancer Inst, 67-69; resident neurol, Mass Gen Hosp, 69-71, Nat Inst Neurol Dis & Stroke fel, 71-72; from instr to assoc prof neurol, Univ Calif, San Francisco, 72-81, prof neuro-oncol & pharmacol, 81-88 & chem, 81-88. *Mem:* Am Acad Neurol; Am Asn Cancer Res; Am Soc Clin Oncol; AAAS; Soc Neuro-Oncol. *Res:* Development of new therapeutic approaches for the treatment of brain tumors. *Mailing Add:* Dept Neuro-Oncol M D Anderson Cancer Ctr 1515 Holcombe Blvd PO Box 100 Houston TX 77030

LEVIN, WAYNE, PROTEIN CHEMISTRY, CHEMICAL CARCINOGENESIS. *Current Pos:* biochemist, Dept Biochem, Hoffmann-La Roche Inc, 70-71, sr scientist, 71-74, group chief, 74-78, sect head, 78-85, mem, Roche Inst Molecular Biol, 85-87, distinguished res leader, Dept Protein Biochem, 87-90, dir, Dept Protein Biochem, 90-92, DISTINGUISHED RES LEADER, DEPT INFLAMMATION/ AUTOIMMUNE DIS, HOFFMANN-LA ROCHE INC, 92- *Personal Data:* b New York, NY, Feb 29, 40; m 62, Rosemary Barnello; c Kira & Darryl. *Educ:* Ithaca Col, BA, 62; Univ Ill, MS, 64. *Hon Degrees:* DSc, Rutgers Univ, 93. *Honors & Awards:* Achievement Award, Acad Pharmaceut Sci, 79; Bernard B Brodie Award, Am Soc Pharmacol & Exp Therapeut, 88. *Prof Exp:* Biochemist, Burroughs Wellcome & Co, 65-70. *Concurrent Pos:* Mem, Study Sect Chem Path, NIH, 77-79; distinguished lectr, Col Vet Med, Tex A&M Univ, 85-86; vis prof, Univ BC, 89-90; adj prof, Rutgers Univ, 89- *Mem:* Am Soc Biochem & Molecular Biol; Am Soc Pharmacol & Exp Therapeut; Am Asn Cancer Res; Soc Toxicol; NY Acad Sci; AAAS. *Res:* Purification and characterization of soluble and membrane-bound proteins, structure-activity relationships and immunochemical characterization of proteins. *Mailing Add:* Dept Inflammation/Autoimmune Dis Hoffmann-La Roche Inc Bldg 123/3 340 Kingsland St Nutley NJ 07110-1199. *Fax:* 973-235-8104

LEVIN, WILLIAM COHN, INTERNAL MEDICINE, HEMATOLOGY. *Current Pos:* From instr to assoc prof internal med, Univ Tex Med Br, Galveston, 44-65, dir, Hemat Res Lab & Blood Bank, 46-74, pres, 74-87, PROF INTERNAL MED, UNIV TEX MED BR, GALVESTON, 65- *Personal Data:* b Waco, Tex, Mar 2, 17; m 41; c 2. *Educ:* Univ Tex, BA, 38, MD, 41. *Hon Degrees:* Dr, Univ Montpellier, 80. *Honors & Awards:* Ordre des Palmes Academiques, 81. *Mem:* Am Fedn Clin Res; Am Soc Hemat; AMA; fel Am Col Physicians; fel Int Soc Hemat. *Res:* Hematology; immunology; oncology. *Mailing Add:* PO Box 1259 Galveston TX 77553. *Fax:* 409-766-4662

LEVIN, ZEV, ATMOSPHERIC SCIENCES, CLOUD PHYSICS. *Current Pos:* head, Dept Geophys & Planetary Sci, 85-87, vpres res & develop & dean res, 87-92, PROF ATMOSPHERIC SCI, TEL AVIV UNIV, ISRAEL, 71- *Personal Data:* b Haifa, Israel, Dec 17, 40; US citizen; m 65, Susan M Warshaw; c Rami & Tamar. *Educ:* Calif State Univ, Los Angeles, BS, 66; Univ Wash, PhD(atmospheric sci), 70. *Prof Exp:* Res meteorologist, Univ Calif, Los Angeles, 70-71. *Concurrent Pos:* Vis sr scientist atmospheric sci, Nat Ctr Atmospheric Res, 76-77; sr res assoc, Nat Res Coun, Ames Res Ctr, NASA, 81, fac fel, 85 & Goddard Space Flight Ctr, 92-93. *Mem:* Am Meteorol Soc; Am Geophys Union; Sigma Xi; Europ Geophys Soc; Israel Aerosol Orgn. *Res:* Formation of clouds and precipitation; cloud electrifications; atmospheric aerosols; ice nucleation. *Mailing Add:* Dept Geophys & Planetary Sci Tel Aviv Univ Ramat Aviv 69978 Israel. *Fax:* 972-3-6408274; *E-Mail:* zev@hail.tau.ac.il

LEVINE, AARON WILLIAM, PHYSICAL CHEMISTRY, POLYMER CHEMISTRY. *Current Pos:* mem tech staff, David Sarnoff Res Ctr, Subsid SRI Int, 69-84, head org mat & lithography res, RCA Labs, 84-87, head thin film & org mat res, 87-89, & Advan Mat Res, 90-92, mem tech staff, 92-96, SR MEM TECH STAFF, DAVID SARNOFF RES CTR, SUBSID SRI INT, 96- *Personal Data:* b New York, NY, July 14, 43; m 64, Rhoda Mausneq; c Jonathan M, Daniel J & Sharon J. *Educ:* Yeshiva Univ, BA, 63; City Col New York, MA, 66; Seton Hall Univ, PhD(org chem), 70. *Prof Exp:* Teacher, High Schs, NY, 63-66; res chemist, M&T Chem, Inc, 66-69. *Mem:* Am Chem Soc; fel Am Inst Chemists. *Res:* Materials science and processing, materials selection, characterization and specification; polymers/plastics degradation and stabilization. *Mailing Add:* David Sarnoff Res Ctr CN 5300 201 Washington Rd Princeton NJ 08543-5300. *Fax:* 609-734-2599; *E-Mail:* alevine@sarnoff.com

LEVINE, ALAN E, TUMOR BIOLOGY, CELL BIOLOGY. *Current Pos:* ASSOC PROF BIOCHEM, HEALTH SCI CTR, UNIV TEX, 91- *Personal Data:* b Los Angeles, Calif, May 5, 52. *Educ:* Univ Calif, Irvine, BA, 74; Univ Wash, PhD(biochem), 79. *Prof Exp:* Fel, Dept Neurobiol, Stanford Univ Med Sch, 79-82; from asst prof to assoc prof pharmacol & growth factors, Baylor Col Med, 82-91. *Mem:* Am Soc Cell Biol; Am Asn Cancer Res; AAAS. *Res:* Tumor biology; cell biology. *Mailing Add:* Health Sci Ctr Univ Tex PO Box 20068 Houston TX 77225

LEVINE, ALAN STEWART, HEMATOLOGY, BIOCHEMISTRY. *Current Pos:* from staff fel to sr staff fel, NIH, 72-77, health scientist adminr & dep br chief, 77-86, chief, Blood Dis Br, 86-91, chief, Cellular Hemat Br, 91-94, DIR, BLOOD DIS PROG, NAT HEART LUNG BLOOD INST, NIH, 94- *Personal Data:* b New York, NY, Aug 11, 44; m 67, Irene Solowey; c Lisa & Scott. *Educ:* Monmouth Col, NJ, BS, 66; Univ Del, PhD(chem), 71. *Prof Exp:* Teaching asst chem, Univ Del, 66-71; res assoc, Sch Pharm, Univ Kans, 71-72. *Mem:* Am Soc Hemat; AAAS; NY Acad Sci; Int Soc Exp Hemat. *Res:* Molecular mechanism of human red blood cell sickling; diseases of the red blood cell; thalassemia; hematopoietic stem cell biology and transplantation; in utero stem cell therapy; gene therapy. *Mailing Add:* Nat Heart Lung & Blood Inst NIH Rockledge II MSC 7950 Bethesda MD 20892. *Fax:* 301-496-9940

LEVINE, ALFRED MARTIN, QUANTUM OPTICS & DISSAPATIVE SYSTEMS. *Current Pos:* PROF ENG SCI, COL STATEN ISLAND, CITY UNIV NEW YORK, 70-, MEM DOCTORAL FAC PHYSICS, CITY UNIV, 71- *Personal Data:* b Brooklyn, NY, Apr 5, 41; m 65; c 2. *Educ:* Cooper Union, BEE, 61; Princeton Univ, MA, 64, PhD(elec eng), 66. *Prof Exp:* Mem res staff, Plasma Physics Lab, Princeton Univ, 66; scientist, Gas Lab, Ionizatti, Frascati, Italy, 66-68; mem tech staff, Bell Labs, 68-70. *Concurrent Pos:* Vis scientist, Weizmann Inst, Israel, 86. *Mem:* Am Phys Soc; Inst Elec & Electronics Engrs; Optical Soc Am; Fulbright Fel, 86. *Res:* noise in laser systems; quantum optics; four wave mixing; computer modelling of environmental systems; dissipation in quantum mechanical systems. *Mailing Add:* Dept Appl Sci Col Staten Island 2800 Victory Blvd Staten Island NY 10314

LEVINE, ALLEN STUART, FOOD INTAKE, NUTRIENT ABSORPTION. *Current Pos:* ASSOC DIR RES, VET ADMIN MED CTR, 87- *Personal Data:* b Newark, NJ, Aug 1, 49; m 73; c 1. *Educ:* Rutgers Univ, BA, 70; Univ Minn, MS, 73 & PhD(nutrit), 77. *Honors & Awards:* Mead Johnson Award, Am Inst Nutrit, 85. *Prof Exp:* from asst prof to assoc prof, 81-86, prof food sci & nutrit, Univ Minn, 86-, prof surg, 87- *Concurrent Pos:* Res chemist, Vet Admin Med Ctr, 78-87. *Mem:* Am Inst Nutrit; Soc Neurosci. *Res:* Regulation of food intake; investigation of the interactions of neuropeptides and monoamines in the control of feeding; emphasis on the role of the endogenous opioids in the initiation of feeding; importance of specific opiate receptors; role of regulatory peptides in energy expenditure. *Mailing Add:* Neuroendocrine Res Lab Vet Admin Med Ctr 151 One Veterans Dr Minneapolis MN 55417-2399

LEVINE, ALVIN SAUL, VIROLOGY. *Current Pos:* ASST DEAN, SCH MED, IND UNIV, 80-, EMER PROF MICROBIOL & IMMUNOL, 92- *Personal Data:* b Hamlet, NC, Aug 29, 25; m 51; c Richard M, Steven E, James H & Lawrence M. *Educ:* Wake Forest Col, BS, 48; Univ NC, MSPH, 50; Rutgers Univ, PhD(microbiol), 54. *Prof Exp:* Res asst biochem, Duke Univ, 50-51; instr bact & immunol, Harvard Med Sch, 56-58; from asst prof to assoc prof microbiol, Sch Med, Ind Univ, Indianapolis, 58-64, prof microbiol & immunol, 64-71; prof life sci & dir, Terre Haute Ctr Med Educ, Ind State Univ, Terre Haute, 71-80. *Concurrent Pos:* Res fel microbiol, Rutgers Univ, 51-54; teaching fel bact & immunol, Harvard Med Sch, 54-56; Fulbright vis prof, Univ WI, 67-68. *Mem:* Fel Am Soc Microbiol; Am Asn Path; Am Asn Immunol; Am Asn Cancer Res. *Res:* Infectious diseases; viral oncology; RNA viruses; biochemical, biophysical and immunological studies. *Mailing Add:* 308 Hickory Hill Dr Terre Haute IN 47802-4911

LEVINE, ARNOLD DAVID, THEORETICAL PHYSICS. *Current Pos:* from asst prof to assoc prof, 62-71, PROF PHYSICS, WVA UNIV, 71- *Personal Data:* b Brooklyn, NY, Oct 24, 25; m 62. *Educ:* Columbia Univ, PhD(physics), 58. *Prof Exp:* Asst prof physics, WVa Univ, 57-60; asst prof, Wayne State Univ, 60-62. *Concurrent Pos:* Consult, Columbia Liquified Natural Gas Corp, 71-73; consult, Am Gas Asn, currently. *Mem:* Combustion Inst; Am Phys Soc; Am Asn Physics Teachers; Sigma Xi. *Res:* Meson physics; quantum field theory; non-equilibrium thermodynamics; fluid dynamics; combustion. *Mailing Add:* Dept Physics WVa Univ PO Box 6315 Morgantown WV 26506

LEVINE, ARNOLD J, BIOLOGY. *Current Pos:* chmn, Dept Biol, 84-96, HARRY C WIESS PROF MOLECULAR BIOL, DEPT BIOL, PRINCETON UNIV, 84- *Personal Data:* b Brooklyn, NY, July 30, 39; m, Linda H Lavine; c Samantha & Alison. *Educ:* State Univ NY, BA, 61; Univ Pa, PhD(microbiol), 66. *Honors & Awards:* Merit Award, Nat Cancer Inst, 89; Susan Swerling lectr, Harvard Med Sch, 90; Lila Gruber Cancer Res Award, Am Acad Dermat, 92; Solomon Berson Mem lectr, Mt Sinai Sch Med, 92. *Prof Exp:* From asst prof to prof biochem, Princeton Univ, 68-79; chmn & prof microbiol, Sch Med, State Univ NY, Stony Brook, 79-83. *Concurrent Pos:* Mem, Human Cell Biol Panel, NSF, 71-72, Genetics & Biol Panel, 72-73; Camille & Henry Dreyfus Found teacher-scholar, 72-77; assoc ed, Virol, 73-74, ed, 74-84; mem, Virus Cancer Prog Sci Rev Comt, Nat Cancer Inst, 76-77, bd sci counr, Div Cancer Biol & Diag, 86-90; panel mem, Basic Virol-Cell Biol Task Force, Nat Inst Allergy & Infectious Dis, 77, mem, Papovirus Study Group, Int Comt Taxonomy of Viruses, 77-; mem, Biochem-Cell Biol Panel, Am Heart Asn, 78-80; mem, Microbiol Sect, Nat Bd Med Examnrs, 83-84; assoc ed, J Cellular & Molecular Biol, 84-88; ed-in-chief, J Virol, 84-; alt counr, Div S, DNA Viruses, Am Soc Microbiol, 86-87; Gen Motors vis prof, Univ Southern Calif Cancer Ctr, 89; Am Cancer Soc scholar, 90-91; Rosie & Max Varon vis prof, Dept Immunol, Weizmann Inst, Rehovot, Israel, 90-91; John Simon Guggenheim mem fel, 91; sci consult, Mem Sloan-Kettering Cancer Ctr, 92- *Mem:* Nat Acad Sci; Inst Med-Nat Acad Sci; Fedn Am Socs Exp Biol; Am Soc Biol Chemists; Sigma Xi; Am Soc Microbiol; AAAS; NY Acad Sci. *Res:* DNA replication; animal virology; tissue culture systems for the study of gene expression and the regulation of the cell cycle; genetics of higher organisms; viral oncogenesis; testicular teratomas. *Mailing Add:* Dept Molecular Biol Princeton Univ Princeton NJ 08544-1014

LEVINE, ARNOLD MILTON, COMMUNICATION ENGINEERING. *Current Pos:* RETIRED. *Personal Data:* b Preston, Conn, Aug 15, 16; m 41, Bernice E Levich; c Mark J, Michael M & Kevin L. *Educ:* Tri-State Col, BS, 39; Univ Iowa, MS, 40. *Hon Degrees:* DSc, Tri-State Univ, 60. *Prof Exp:* Head, Sound Dept, Columbia Broadcasting Co, 40-42; from asst engr to vpres & dir missile & space systs, IT&T Corp, 42-71, vpres & gen mgr, ITT Aerospace, 71, vpres & tech dir, ITT Gililan Inc, 71-74, sr scientist, IT&T Corp, 74-86. *Mem:* Fel Inst Elec & Electronics Engrs; Am Inst Navig; fel Inst Advan Eng; Soc Motion Picture Technol Engrs. *Res:* Research and development in communication and missile guidance navigation; time division systems; pulse code modulation; pseudo noise modulation; pulse and continuous wave missile guidance; radar research and development; fiber optics; granted 52 patents. *Mailing Add:* 10828 Fullbright Ave Chatsworth CA 91311

LEVINE, ARTHUR SAMUEL, MOLECULAR VIROLOGY, ONCOLOGY. *Current Pos:* staff fel oncol, Div Cancer Treatment, Nat Cancer Inst, NIH, 67-70, sr investr molecular virol & oncol, 70-75, chief, Pediat Br, 75-82, SCI DIR, NAT INST CHILD HEALTH & HUMAN DEVELOP, NIH, 82- *Personal Data:* b Cleveland, Ohio, Nov 1, 36; m 59; c 3. *Educ:* Columbia Univ, AB, 58; Chicago Med Sch, MD, 64, Am Bd Pediat, dipl, 70; Am Bd Hemat-Oncol, dipl, 76. *Honors & Awards:* Karon Mem Lectr, Univ Southern Calif, Los Angeles, 83; Seham Lectr, Univ Minn, Minneapolis, 83; Meritorious Serv Medal, USPHS, 87. *Prof Exp:* Intern & resident pediat Univ Minn Hosps, 64-66, USPHS fel hemat & genetics, Univ Minn, Minneapolis, 66-67. *Concurrent Pos:* Vis lectr, Cold Spring Harbor Lab, NY, 73; vis prof, Benares Hindu Univ, India, 74, Univ Minn, Minneapolis, 74, Hebrew Univ, Israel, 81, Univ Bologna, Italy, 89 & Univ Calabria, Italy, 90; prof pediat, Uniformed Servs Univ of Health Sci, 83-; prof med & pediat, Georgetown Univ, 75-; ed-in-chief, New Biologist, 88- *Mem:* Am Soc Clin Invest; Soc Pediat Res; Am Asn Cancer Res; Am Soc Hemat; AAAS; Am Soc Microbiol. *Res:* Molecular genetics of SV40 and adenovirus-SV40 hybrids; mechanism of viral oncogenesis; DNA repair and mutagenesis; oncology. *Mailing Add:* NIH Bldg 31 Rm 2A50 Bethesda MD 20892

LEVINE, BARRY FRANKLIN, LASERS. *Current Pos:* PHYSICIST, BELL LABS, 68-, DEPT HEAD, 77- *Personal Data:* b Brooklyn, NY, Sept 5, 42; m 68. *Educ:* Polytech Inst Brooklyn, BS, 63; Harvard Univ, PhD(physics), 69. *Mem:* Am Phys Soc. *Res:* Experimental and theoretical nonlinear optics of crystals and liquids; coherent Raman scattering; optical picosecond spectroscopy of surfaces; novel high speed semiconductor devices (phototransistors, functional element tests, lasers, photodetectors). *Mailing Add:* AT&T Bell Labs 600 Mountain Ave Murray Hill NJ 07974

LEVINE, BERNARD BENJAMIN, IMMUNOLOGY, MEDICINE. *Current Pos:* From asst prof to assoc prof, 62-70, PROF MED, MED CTR, NY UNIV, 70-, DIR ALLERGY, 62- *Personal Data:* b New York, NY, Nov 8, 28. *Educ:* City Col New York, BS, 50; NY Univ, MD, 54. *Concurrent Pos:* Res fel path, Med Ctr, NY Univ, 60-62. *Mem:* Am Asn Immunol; Soc Exp Biol & Med; Am Soc Clin Invest; Am Acad Allergy. *Res:* Immunopathology; hypersensitivity; antigenicity; immune response; allergy. *Mailing Add:* NY Univ Sch Med 566 First Ave New York NY 10016

LEVINE, BRUCE MARTIN, STATISTICAL OPTICS, ADAPTIVE OPTICS. *Personal Data:* b Lakewood, NJ, Mar 26, 50. *Educ:* Rochester Inst Technol, BS, 72; Colo State Univ, MS, 76; Univ Rochester, PhD(optics), 86. *Prof Exp:* Tech specialist, Xerox Corp, 76-80; tech staff, Riverside Res Inst, 86-90; mem tech staff, Spatial Interferometry Group, Jet Propulsion Lab, 90-94. *Concurrent Pos:* Consult imaging sci, Xerox Corp, 80-81, scanned imaging, 84; Fulbright travel fel, 88; vis fac investr, Air Force Phillips Lab, 88 & 89. *Mem:* Optical Eng Soc; Optical Soc Am. *Res:* Analysis of imaging optical systems such as adaptive optics and other forms of wavefront reconstruction; data analysis and theoretical analysis of laser beam propagation experiments. *Mailing Add:* Jet Propulsion Lab 4800 Oak Grove Dr M/X 306-388 Pasadena CA 91109. *Fax:* 626-447-2402; *E-Mail:* marty@huey.jpl.nasa.gov

LEVINE, CHARLES (ARTHUR), PHYSICAL CHEMISTRY, ELECTROCHEMISTRY. *Current Pos:* SR SCIENTIST, OMNI-TECH, INT, 86- *Personal Data:* b Des Moines, Iowa, Dec 25, 22; m 48, Beverly Damlos; c Alice & Dan. *Educ:* Iowa State Col, BS, 47; Univ Calif, PhD(chem), 51. *Prof Exp:* Asst, Univ Calif, 48-49, asst, Radiation Lab, 49-51; res chemist, Dow Chem Co, 51-65, assoc scientist, 65-86. *Mem:* AAAS; Electrochem Soc; Am Chem Soc; Am Phys Soc. *Res:* Nuclear chemistry; radiation chemistry; electrochemistry. *Mailing Add:* 124 Buena Vista Ave Santa Cruz CA 95062

LEVINE, D(ONALD) J(AY), ELECTRICAL ENGINEERING, TELECOMMUNICATIONS. *Current Pos:* electronics engr, 89-90, CONSULT, USN TELCOM, 90- *Personal Data:* b Brooklyn, NY, Oct 10, 21; m 46, Gloria Lerner; c Judith E (Duvall) & Nancy B (Intrator). *Educ:* City Col NY, BEE, 43; Polytech Inst Brooklyn, MEE, 52. *Honors & Awards:* Scott Helt Mem Award, Outstanding Contrib Inst Elec & Electronics Engrs Broadcast Tech Trans, 89. *Prof Exp:* Sr asst, Microwave Res Inst, Polytech Inst Brooklyn, 46-48; dir, Radio Transmission & Anti-Submarine Warfare Lab, Int Tel & Tel Corp, 48-65; vpres & mgr, Transmission Systs Div, Commun Systs Inc, Comput Sci Corp, 65-67; dept head, Network Eng & Anal Dept, Commun Div, Mitre Corp, 67-73; dir systs eng, Page Commun Eng, Vienna, Va, 73-74; dir commun systs, Litton-Amecom, College Park, 74-75; dir commun eng, Aerospace Corp, Washington, DC, 75-76; vpres eng, Kings Electronics Co, Inc, Tuckahoe, NY, 76-82 & Am Nucleonics Corp, Westlake Village, Calif, 82-83; chief, Broadcast Syst Eng Div, USIA/Voice Am (SES-4), Washington, DC, 84-86; consult, USIA/Voice Am (SES-4), Washington, DC, 86-88 & Int Broadcast Syst, Inc, 88-89; pres, Int Broadcast Systs, Inc, 88. *Concurrent Pos:* Consult to indust & govt, 86-93; res vol, Nat Air & Space Mus, Smithsonian Inst, 88-94; vol, Adv Technol Prog, Nat Inst Space Technol, 94. *Mem:* Nat Soc Prof Engrs; sr mem Inst Elec & Electronics Engrs; Armed Forces Commun & Electronics Asn; AAAS. *Res:* Microwave components, systems, antennas and antenna systems; radio communications; line of sight and troposcatter systems; switched telecommunications systems; network management planning and analysis; systems engineering for fixed, mobile, surface, air, space and submarine environments; operations analysis; shortwave/mediumwave broadcast systems engineering; avionics. *Mailing Add:* 7155 Summer Tree Dr Boynton Beach FL 33437. *E-Mail:* djlinfl@juno.com

LEVINE, DANIEL, electrical engineering, for more information see previous edition

LEVINE, DAVID MORRIS, BEHAVIORAL SCIENCES, HEALTH EDUCATION. *Current Pos:* resident prev med, 68-70, assoc prof pub health, med educ & internal med, 72-81, PROF BEHAV SCI, HEALTH EDUC, JOHNS HOPKINS UNIV, 81-, DIR MANPOWER STUDIES, CTR HEALTH SERV RES & DEVELOP, 72- *Personal Data:* b Boston, Mass, Dec 15, 39; m 65; c 2. *Educ:* Brandeis Univ, AB, 59; Univ Vt, MD, 64; Johns Hopkins Univ, MPH, 69, SCD, 72; Nat Bd Med Examr, dipl, 65; Am Col Prev Med, dipl, 71; Pan Am Med Assoc, dipl. *Prof Exp:* Intern, Montefiore Hosp, Pittsburgh, 64-65; resident, Waltham Hosp, Mass, 65-66; US Army Med Corp, 66-68. *Concurrent Pos:* Fel pub health serv, Sch Hyg & Pub Health, Johns Hopkins Univ, 68-71; consult, Nat Ctr Health Serv Res, 72- & Am Asn Med Col, 73-; mem study sect, Nat Heart-Lung Inst, NIH, 75-, Vet Admin Mert Rev, 80- *Mem:* AAAS; Am Pub Health Asn; Am Fedn Clin Res; Am Col Prev Med; Pan Am Med Asn. *Res:* Health behavior, health education and health promotion; health care manpower-services, health education strategies in managing chronic disease process and outcome of medical education. *Mailing Add:* 5806 Greenspring Rd Baltimore MD 21209

LEVINE, DONALD MARTIN, ZOOLOGY, PARASITOLOGY. *Current Pos:* assoc prof, 62-74, PROF BIOL SCI, WILLIAM PATERSON COL NJ, 74- *Personal Data:* b Boston, Mass, Oct 17, 29. *Educ:* Univ Vt, BA, 51; Univ RI, MS, 53; Univ Pa, PhD(zool), 58. *Prof Exp:* USPHS fel, 58-60; helminthologist, Liberian Inst, Am Found Trop Med, 60-62. *Mem:* Am Soc Trop Med & Hyg; Am Inst Biol Sci. *Res:* Immunology and ecology of parasitic infections. *Mailing Add:* Dept Biol Sci William Paterson Col 300 Pompton Rd Wayne NJ 07470-2103

LEVINE, DUANE GILBERT, CHEMISTRY, PHYSICS. *Current Pos:* Combustion, electrochem & petrol researcher, Exxon Res & Eng Co, 59-68, head air pollution control res & develop, Automotive Emission Res Sect, 68-70, adv logistics, Exxon Corp, 70-71, mgr petrol fuels res & develop, Fuels Prod Qual Res Lab, Exxon Res & Eng Co, 71-74, mgr petrol process eng, Gasoline & Lubes Process Eng Div, 74-76, gen mgr synthetic fuels res & develop, Baytown Res & Develop Div, 76-78, exec dir, Corp Res-Sci Labs, 78-89, MGR SCI & STRATEGY DEVELOP, EXXON CORP, 89- *Personal Data:* b Baltimore, Md, July 5, 33; m 57; c 6. *Educ:* Johns Hopkins Univ, BES, 56, MS, 58. *Concurrent Pos:* Mem, Eng & Tech Res Comt, Am Petrol Inst, 71-74; mem, Air Pollution Res Adv Comt, joint comt US Govt, Petrol Indust & Automotive Indust, 71-74; participant UN/Indust-Sponsored Conf Environ Mgt, Versailles, France, 84; chmn, Rene Dubos Int Forum Managing Hazardous Mat, New York, 87, Forum Global Urbanization, 88; mem, Adv Comt, Calif Inst Technol, Johns Hopkins Univ, Rene Dubos Ctr. *Mem:* AAAS; fel Am Inst Chemists; Am Inst Chem Engrs; Am Chem Soc; Int Combustion Inst; Sigma Xi; NY Acad Sci. *Res:* Solid state sciences; surface sciences; optics; catalysis; materials; theoretical and mathematical sciences; biosci; engineering sciences; laser chemistry; polymer sciences; emulsion chemistry; chemical physics. *Mailing Add:* 8959 Los Colinas Irving TX 75039

LEVINE, ELISSA ROBIN, SOIL PROCESS MODELING. *Current Pos:* RES SCIENTIST, BIOSPHERIC SCI BR, NASA-GODDARD SPACE FLIGHT CTR, 86- *Personal Data:* b New York, NY, Dec 10, 52; c 2. *Educ:* Kans State Univ, BS, 78; Pa State Univ, MS, 81, PhD(soil genesis), 84. *Prof Exp:* Fel, Univ Conn, 85-86, Nat Res Coun, 86. *Concurrent Pos:* Soil consult, pvt firm, 84-86; lectr, Am Women Geoscientists, 90-; vis prof, NC Agr & Tech Univ, 92-; mem, Soil Subcomt, Fed Geog Data Comt, 92- *Mem:* Am Soc Agron; Soil Sci Soc Am; Asn Women Soil Scientists. *Res:* Modelling of processes related to the genesis of soils in response to environmental conditions using simulation models, artificial intelligence, techniques and remote sensing. *Mailing Add:* NASA-Goddard Space Flight Ctr Code 923 Greenbelt MD 20771. *Fax:* 301-286-1757; *E-Mail:* elissa@lichen.gsfc.nasa.gov

LEVINE, ELLIOT MYRON, CELL BIOLOGY, CELL CULTURE. *Current Pos:* coordr res training, Wistar Inst, 74-80, from asst prof to assoc prof,72-84, assoc dir, Sci Admin, 94-96, PROF, WISTAR INST, 84- *Personal Data:* b Brooklyn, NY, June 16, 37; m 59, Marian C Levy; c Bruce L, Eric S & Carolyn J. *Educ:* Queens Col, NY, BS, 57; Yale Univ, PhD(biochem), 61. *Prof Exp:* Sr asst scientist biochem, Nat Inst Arthritis, Metab & Digestive Dis, 61-63; from assoc to asst prof cell biol, Albert Einstein Col Med, 63-72. *Concurrent Pos:* NIH fel, Albert Einstein Col Med, 63-64, NIH spec res fel, 64-65, NIH career develop award, 68-72; NSF res grants, Albert Einstein Col Med & Wistar Inst, 70-; NIH res grants, Wistar Inst, 72-; mem grad groups cell biol, genetics & pathol, Univ Pa, 75-, Lung Cell Comt, Am Type Cult Col, 76-; staff mycoplasma detection course, W Alton Jones Cell Sci Ctr, 77-; mem, Cell Biol Study Sect, NIH, 78-82, chmn, 80-82; mem bd dirs, Am Type Cult Collection; adj prof med, Med Sch, Univ Pa, 96- *Mem:* Fel AAAS; Tissue Cult Asn (pres, 90-92); Sigma Xi; Soc In Vitro Biol. *Res:* Proliferation and differentiation in cultured cells, especially vascular endothelial and smooth muscle cells. *Mailing Add:* Wistar Inst 3601 Spruce St Philadelphia PA 19104-4268. *Fax:* 215-898-0847; *E-Mail:* levine@wista.wistar.upenn.edu

LEVINE, EUGENE, ANALYTICAL STATISTICS, OPERATIONS RESEARCH. *Current Pos:* PROF, GRAD SCH NURSING, UNIFORMED SERV UNIV HEALTH SCI, 93- *Personal Data:* b Brooklyn, NY, Jan 11, 25; m 48, Barbara Stevenson; c Gary M, Jeffrey H & Douglas E. *Educ:* City Col New York, BBA, 48; NY Univ, MPA, 50; Am Univ, PhD(pub admin), 60. *Prof Exp:* Statistician, New York City Dept Health, 47-50; chief, Manpower Anal & Resources Br, Div Nursing, USPHS, 50-78, dep dir, Div Health Prof Anal, 78-80; assoc, Levine Assoc, 80-93. *Concurrent Pos:* Res consult, Sch Nursing, Georgetown Univ, 84- *Mem:* Am Pub Health Asn; Nat League Nursing; Am Statist Asn; Am Asn Health Serv Res. *Res:* Health manpower analysis; problems of health services organization and delivery; psychometric analysis into problems of job satisfaction; career choice and motivation; evaluation of health care programs; nursing research. *Mailing Add:* 8135 Inverness Ridge Rd Potomac MD 20854. *Fax:* 301-295-1994; *E-Mail:* elevine666@aol.com

LEVINE, FREDERIC M, PAIN MANAGEMENT & RESEARCH. *Current Pos:* asst prof, 67-73, ASSOC PROF PSYCHOL, STATE UNIV NY, STONY BROOK, 73-; PVT PRACTICE. *Personal Data:* b New York, NY, May 20, 37; m 65, Marilyn Wehrmann; c Samuel & Max. *Educ:* City Col NY, BA, 61; Northwestern Univ, MA, 63, PhD(psychol), 65. *Prof Exp:* Res assoc psychol, Harvard Med Sch, 65-67. *Mem:* Am Psychol Asn; Am Pain Asn. *Res:* Social and psychological factors that influence pain report; models of psychotherapeutic intervention. *Mailing Add:* 120 Bleeker St Port Jefferson NY 11777. *Fax:* 516-473-6622

LEVINE, GEOFFREY, NUCLEAR PHARMACY, HEALTH PHYSICS. *Current Pos:* clin asst prof pharmaceut, Univ Pittsburgh, 72-80, coord, prog radiopharm, 72-83, asst prof radiol, 72-83, assoc prof, Sch Pharm, 85, ASSOC PROF RADIOL, SCH MED, UNIV PITTSBURGH, 83-; CLIN PROF NUCLEAR MED, ALLEGHENY CO COMMUNITY COL, 84- *Personal Data:* b Washington, DC, Sept 2, 42; m 70; c Julie, Karen & Lisa. *Educ:* Temple Univ, BS, 65, MS, 67; Northwestern Univ, PhD(civil eng & environ health), 78. *Prof Exp:* Pharmacist, 65-67; at Abbott Lab, NChicago, 66-68. *Concurrent Pos:* Grants, Am Cancer Soc, Union Carbide Corp, Soc Nuclear Med & others, 74-; dir nuclear pharm, Univ Health Ctr, Presby-Univ Hosp, 72-87, radiopharm adv nuclear pharm, 72-, radiation safety comt, 75-, radiopharmacist, 72-, clin asst med staff, 73-83, assoc med staff, 84-, nuclear med res comt, 85-; consult, Shadyside Hosp, 74-75, Ames Labs, 75, Charleston Area Med Ctr, 79-80, NEN-Dupont Radiopharm Div, 84, Am Pharm Asn, 86-, Mallinckrodt-NeoRx Monoclonal Antibody Develop Prog, 88-90; pharm staff, Montefiore Hosp, 75-, radiation res comt, 78-; mem, Human Use Subcomt Radiation Safety Comt, Univ Pittsburgh, 85-, Radioactive Drug Res Comt, 85-; dir nuclear pharm, Cent Imaging Serv, Inc, 85-91; assoc mem, Pittsburgh Cancer Inst, 87-, clin dir, Monoclonal Antibody Ctr, 93- *Mem:* Health Physics Soc; Soc Nuclear Med (secy-treas, 74); Sigma Xi; Am Pharmaceut Asn; AAAS; Health Physics Soc; Am Soc Hosp Pharmacists. *Res:* Drug interactions; radioactive pharmaceuticals and radioactive monoclonal antibodies for tumor detection; author of numerous publications; cost-benefit risk analysis; inventory control modeling of radiopharmaceuticals; radiopharmacology. *Mailing Add:* Dept Radiol Univ Pittsburgh Sch Med Pittsburgh PA 15261-0001

LEVINE, HAROLD, APPLIED MATHEMATICS. *Current Pos:* RETIRED. *Personal Data:* b New York, NY, Mar 24, 22; m 47. *Educ:* City Col New York, BS, 41; Cornell Univ, PhD(physics), 44. *Prof Exp:* Res fel physics, Harvard Univ, 45-54; assoc prof math, Stanford Univ, 55-70, prof, 70-92. *Concurrent Pos:* Lectr, Harvard Univ, 52-54; consult, Lawrence Radiation Lab, Univ Calif. *Mem:* Am Phys Soc. *Res:* Boundary value problems of classical field theories, particularly acoustics, electrodynamics and hydrodynamics. *Mailing Add:* Dept Math Stanford Univ Stanford CA 94305-2125

LEVINE, HAROLD, MATHEMATICS. *Current Pos:* from asst prof to assoc prof, 60-70, PROF MATH, BRANDEIS UNIV, 70- *Personal Data:* b Lynn, Mass, Dec 14, 28; m 61. *Educ:* Univ Chicago, PhD(math), 57. *Prof Exp:* Fulbright fel & Ger Res Asn grant, Univ Bonn, 57-59; instr math, Yale Univ, 59-60. *Mem:* Am Math Soc; Math Asn Am. *Res:* Differential topology. *Mailing Add:* 32 Grande Rue 45360 Chatillon-Sur-Loire France

LEVINE, HARRY, POLYMER SCIENCE OF FOODS. *Current Pos:* sr prin scientist, Nabisco Brands, 87-91, RES FEL, NABISCO FOODS GROUP, 91- *Personal Data:* b New York, NY, Dec 16, 47; m 81, Louise Slade. *Educ:* Rensselaer Polytech Inst, BS, 68, PhD(polymer chem), 75. *Prof Exp:* Fel, Roswell Park Mem Inst, 74-76; sr polymer chemist, Gen Foods Corp, 76-87. *Concurrent Pos:* Course dir, Ctr Prof Advan, Am Asn Cereal Chem & Am Chem Soc, 87- *Mem:* Fel Am Inst Chemists; Am Chem Soc; Am Asn Cereal Chemists; Sigma Xi. *Res:* Polymer science approach to foods; glasses and glass transitions in foods; water relations in foods; water as plasticizer. *Mailing Add:* Nabisco Brands Inc PO Box 1943 East Hanover NJ 07936-2897

LEVINE, HARRY, III, ALZHEIMERS DISEASE, MEMBRANE BIOLOGY. *Current Pos:* ASSOC RES FEL, WARNER-LAMBERT PARKE-DAVIS PHARM, 91- *Personal Data:* b Utica, NY, July 12, 49; m 72, Melissa Dixon; c Julia C. *Educ:* Cornell Univ, BS, 71; Johns Hopkins Univ, PhD(physiol chem), 75. *Prof Exp:* Postdoctoral Wellcome Res Labs, 75-77, res scientist, 72-87; res investr, Glaxo Res Labs, 87-91. *Concurrent Pos:* Adj asst prof, Dept Neurobiol, Duke Univ, 89-91; adj asst res scientist, Dept Biol, Univ Mich, 93- *Mem:* Fedn Am Socs Exp Biol; Soc Neurosci. *Res:* Development of strategies to treat neurodegenerative diseases such as Alzheimer's disease; study of signal transduction mechanisms and the relationship of protein structure/function to pathophysiology. *Mailing Add:* Parke-Davis Pharmaceut Res Warner-Lambert Co 2800 Plymouth Rd Ann Arbor MI 48105

LEVINE, HARVEY ROBERT, PARASITOLOGY, MEDICAL ENTOMOLOGY. *Current Pos:* chmn Dept Biol, 68-76, asst dean Acad Affairs, Sch Sci, 71-72, PROF BIOL, QUINNIPIAC COL, 68- *Personal Data:* b New York, NY, Sept 15, 31; m 56, Rosalyn Freides; c David & Nancy (Fichman). *Educ:* City Col New York, BS, 53; Univ Mass, MS, 55, PhD(entom), 58. *Prof Exp:* Instr entom, Univ Mass, 55; from asst prof to prof biol, Bemidji State Col, 58-68. *Concurrent Pos:* Consult, Trout Unlimited; mem, Mus Natural Hist; bd trustees, Quinnipiac Col, 84-93; dir Title II Math, Sci Inst, 89-92. *Mem:* Am Inst Biol Sci; Am Asn Lab Animal Sci; Soc Vector Ecol; Entom Soc Am; Sigma Xi; Am Fedn Teachers. *Res:* Acaptatious of freshwater insects; medical entomology (aquatic vectors); lyme disease diagnosis. *Mailing Add:* Dept Biol Sci Quinnipiac Col 275 Mt Carmel Ave Hamden CT 06518-1961

LEVINE, HERBERT JEROME, CARDIOLOGY. *Current Pos:* sr instr, 61-63, from asst prof to assoc prof, 63-70, PROF MED SCH MED, TUFTS UNIV, 70- *Personal Data:* b Boston, Mass, July 22, 28; m 58; c 2. *Educ:* Harvard Univ, AB, 50; Johns Hopkins Univ, MD, 54; Am Bd Internal Med, dipl, 63. *Prof Exp:* Intern med, Peter Bent Brigham Hosp, 54-55, sr resident, 58-59; resident, Mass Gen Hosp, 57-58; res fel, Harvard Med Sch, 59-61; chief cardiol serv, New Eng Med Ctr Hosps, 61-88. *Concurrent Pos:* Res fel cardiol, Peter Bent Brigham Hosp, 56-61; consult, Vet Admin Hosp, Mass, 66-; lectr, US Naval Hosp, Mass, 67- *Mem:* Fel Am Fedn Clin Res; fel Asn Univ Cardiol; fel Am Col Cardiol; fel Am Soc Clin Invest; Asn Am Physicians. *Res:* Clinical cardiology; physiology of congestive heart failure; muscle mechanics and energetics in the intact heart. *Mailing Add:* New Eng Med Ctr Hosp 750 Washington St Boston MA 02111

LEVINE, HERMAN SAUL, PHYSICAL CHEMISTRY, HIGH TEMPERATURE CHEMISTRY. *Current Pos:* RETIRED. *Personal Data:* b Jeannette, Pa, Feb 11, 22; m 47; c 3. *Educ:* Univ Pittsburgh, BS, 43; Univ Ill, PhD(phys chem), 48. *Prof Exp:* Res asst, Ill State Geol Surv, 44-46; staff mem, NY State Col Ceramics, Alfred Univ, 48-51 & USPHS, R A Taft Sanit Eng Ctr, 51-57; mem tech staff, Sandia Labs, 57-89. *Mem:* Am Chem Soc. *Res:* X-ray spectroscopy. *Mailing Add:* 8874 Ahmed Ave Elk Grove CA 95624

LEVINE, HOWARD ALLEN, MATHEMATICS. *Personal Data:* b St Paul, Minn, Jan 15, 42; m 74, Elyse Misbin; c 2. *Educ:* Univ Minn, Duluth, BA, 64; Cornell Univ, MA, 67, PhD(math), 69. *Prof Exp:* Asst prof math, Univ Minn, Minneapolis, 69-73; from asst prof to assoc prof, Univ RI, 73-78; from assoc prof to prof math, Iowa State Univ, 78-89, dept chair, 89-92. *Concurrent Pos:* Vis scientist, Battelle Advan Studies Ctr, Switz, 71 & 72; Sci Res Coun Gt Brit grant, Univ Dundee, 72; NSF res grant, 74-77 & 78-79; part-time res consult, Naval Underwater Systs Ctr, 77-78; assoc prof, Iowa State Univ, 78-79, Consiglio Nazionale delle Recerche, Italy & Math Sci Res Inst, 83. *Mem:* Am Math Soc; Sigma Xi. *Res:* Partial differential equations; numerical analysis. *Mailing Add:* Dept Math Iowa State Univ Ames IA 50011. *Fax:* 515-294-5454; *E-Mail:* levine@pollux.math.iastate.edu

LEVINE, HOWARD BERNARD, COMPUTER LANGUAGES, SCIENTIFIC SOFTWARE. *Current Pos:* SR SOFTWARE ENGR, TELEDYNE RYAN AERONAUT, 89- *Personal Data:* b Brooklyn, NY, Apr 15, 28; m 67, Helene Yura; c Stefanie & Jessica. *Educ:* Univ Ill, BS, 50; Univ Chicago, MS, 52, PhD(chem), 55. *Prof Exp:* Res fel chem, Inst Atomic Res, Iowa State Univ, 55-56; chemist, Lawrence Radiation Lab, Univ Calif, 56-62; mem tech staff, NAm Aviation Sci Ctr, 62-70; proj assoc, Theoret Chem Inst & Space Sci & Eng Ctr, Univ Wis, 70-71; prof chem eng, Va Polytech Inst & State Univ, 71-73; prog mgr chem systs, Systs, Sci & Software, 73-76; prin scientist, Jaycor, 76-82; pres, 21st Century Data, Inc, 82-89. *Concurrent Pos:* Consult, Tech Adv Bd Supersonic Transport, Dept Com; mem ad hoc comt ozone & environ studies bd, Nat Acad Sci. *Mem:* Am Chem Soc; fel Am Phys Soc; Am Inst Chem Eng. *Res:* Thermodynamics; embedded real time computer systems; spectroscopy; atmospheric chemistry; molecular physics; applied mathematics; chemical kinetics; computer languages. *Mailing Add:* 2817 Luciernaga St Carlsbad CA 92009-5927. *Fax:* 619-260-5400

LEVINE, IRA NOEL, PHYSICAL CHEMISTRY. *Current Pos:* from instr to assoc prof, 64-77, PROF CHEM, BROOKLYN COL, 78- *Personal Data:* b Brooklyn, NY, Sept 8, 37. *Educ:* Carnegie Inst Technol, BS, 58; Harvard Univ, AM, 59, PhD(chem), 63. *Prof Exp:* Res assoc chem, Univ Pa, 63-64. *Concurrent Pos:* Am Chem Soc Petrol Res Fund starter grant, 65-66. *Mem:* Am Chem Soc. *Res:* Quantum chemistry. *Mailing Add:* Dept Chem Brooklyn Col Brooklyn NY 11210. *E-Mail:* inlevine@brooklyn.cuny.edu

LEVINE, J(OSEPH) S(AMUEL), PETROLEUM ENGINEERING. *Current Pos:* RETIRED. *Personal Data:* b San Antonio, Tex, Sept 14, 15; m 55, Doris Hughes; c Susan & Charles J. *Educ:* Univ Tex, BS, 36; Pa State Col, MS, 38, PhD(petrol eng), 41. *Prof Exp:* Asst & instr petrol eng, Pa State Col, 36-42; sr chemist fluid flow res, Shell Develop Co Div, Shell Oil Co, 46-60, sr exploitation engr, 60-64, staff engr, 64-65, staff res engr, 65-83. *Mem:* Am Inst Mining, Metall & Petrol Engrs; Soc Petrol Engrs. *Res:* Fluid flow; hydrodynamics; fluid flow through porous media; mechanism of displacement of oil by water; secondary recovery of oil. *Mailing Add:* 5614 Jackwood St Houston TX 77096-1106

LEVINE, JACK, MATHEMATICS. *Current Pos:* from instr to assoc prof, 35-47, PROF MATH, NC STATE UNIV, 47- *Personal Data:* b Philadelphia, Pa, Dec 15, 07; m 38. *Educ:* Univ Calif, Los Angeles, AB, 29; Princeton Univ, PhD(math), 34. *Prof Exp:* Asst math, Univ Calif, Los Angeles, 29-30; instr, Princeton Univ, 30-35. *Concurrent Pos:* Res analyst, US Dept War, 42-43. *Mem:* Am Math Soc; Math Asn Am. *Res:* Differential geometry; tensor analysis; combinatorial analysis; particle dynamics. *Mailing Add:* 801 Dixie Trail Raleigh NC 27607

LEVINE, JEFFREY, MATHEMATICS. *Current Pos:* MEM STAFF, MCDONNELL DOUGLAS CORP, 80- *Personal Data:* b Brooklyn, NY, Feb 7, 45; m 66. *Educ:* State Univ NY Stony Brook, BS, 66; Rutgers Univ, New Brunswick, PhD(math), 70. *Prof Exp:* Asst prof math, Monmouth Col, NJ, 69-71; asst prof math, State Univ NY Col Geneseo, 71-80. *Mem:* Am Math Soc; Math Asn Am. *Res:* Ring theory. *Mailing Add:* 761 La Feil Dr Ballwin MO 63021

LEVINE, JEROME PAUL, TOPOLOGY. *Current Pos:* assoc prof, 66-69, chmn dept, 74-76 & 88-90, PROF MATH, BRANDEIS UNIV, 69- *Personal Data:* b New York, NY, May 4, 37; m 58; c 3. *Educ:* Mass Inst Technol, BS, 58; Princeton Univ, PhD(math), 62. *Honors & Awards:* Humboldt Prize, Ger. *Prof Exp:* Instr math, Mass Inst Technol, 61-63; NSF fels, 63-64; from asst prof to assoc prof math, Univ Calif, Berkeley, 64-66. *Concurrent Pos:* NSF postdoctoral fel, 63-64; Sloan Found fel, 66-68. *Mem:* Am Math Soc. *Res:* Differential topology; knot theory. *Mailing Add:* Dept Math Brandeis Univ Waltham MA 02254-9110

LEVINE, JERRY DAVID, ENVIRONMENTAL PROTECTION. *Current Pos:* nuclear-environ engr, Plasma Physics Lab, 87-91, head, Environ & Health Br, 91-95, HEAD, ENVIRON & SAFETY DIV, PRINCETON UNIV, 95- *Personal Data:* b Mount Vernon, NY, June 27, 52; m 77, Ronnie Freedman; c Audrey. *Educ:* State Univ NY, Stony Brook, BS, 74; Polytech Inst NY, MS, 76. *Honors & Awards:* Nat Environ Policy Act Compliance Officer Award, US Dept Energy, 95. *Prof Exp:* Asst engr, Ebasco Ser, Inc, 76-77, assoc engr, 77-78, engr, 78-80, sr engr, 80-84, prin engr, Envirosphere Co, 84-87. *Concurrent Pos:* Chmn environ rev comt, Plasma Physics Lab, Princeton Univ, 92-96; chmn, Safety Rev Comt, Plasma Physics Lab, 95-; mem, Comt Occup Safety & Health, Princeton Univ, 95- & Radiation Safety Comt, 95- *Mem:* Am Nuclear Soc. *Res:* Nuclear fusion safety studies; review of nuclear safety and environmental aspects of design and operation of Tokamak devices, including the Tokamak Fusion Test Reactor and the planned; national spherical toms experiment; develop national standard for fusion safety. *Mailing Add:* One Ivy Way Dayton NJ 08810-1420. *E-Mail:* jlevine@pppl.gov

LEVINE, JOEL S, GEOCHEMISTRY, GEOPHYSICS. *Current Pos:* Res scientist atmospheric sci, Goddard Inst Space Studies, 64-70, SR RES SCIENTIST, ATMOSPHERIC SCI DIV, LANGLEY RES CTR, NASA, 70- *Personal Data:* b Brooklyn, NY, May 14, 42; m 68, Arlen Spielholz; c Lisa K. *Educ:* Brooklyn Col, BS, 64; NY Univ, MS, 67; Univ Mich, MS, 73, PhD, 77. *Honors & Awards:* Halpern Award Photochem, NY Acad Sci, 82; Medal Except Sci Achievement, NASA, 83. *Concurrent Pos:* Instr physics & dir astron observ, Brooklyn Col, 64-70; res scientist atmospheric sci, Geophys Sci Lab, NY Univ, 64-70; consult, Mars Aeronomy, Viking Proj NASA, 72-76, Comt Planetary Biol & Chem Evolution, Space Sci Bd, Nat Res Coun-Nat Acad Sci, 78-81 & Va Dept Ed Sci Dir, 85-; prin guest investr, Orbiting Astron Observ-Copernicus, 74-76, Int Ultraviolet Explorer, 81-83; res adv, Sch Eng, Old Dominion Univ, 77-81, adj assoc prof, Dept Geol Sci, 85-88; lectr, Col William & Mary, 76-92 & Tidewater Ctr, Univ Va, 82-85; prin investr, Global Tropospheric Chem Photochem Processes, 77-89, Atmospheric Chem Exp, NASA Storm Hazards Proj, 79-82 & Photochem & Geochem Early Earth, 83-93, Global Biomass Burning, 87-; mem NASA Life Sci Adv Comt, 85-88, Sci Steering Comt, Origins Solar Systs Prog, 87-90, Space Sci & Appln Adv Comt, 88-90, Ctr Explor Prog Scientists, 88-92; ed, Photochem of Atmospers: Earth, Other Planets & Comets, 85, Space Opportunities for Tropospheric Chem Res, 87, Global Biomass Burning: Atmospheric, Climate & Biospheric Implications, 91; co-dir, Global Emissions Inventory Biomass Burning, Int Global Atmospheric Chem Proj, 90-, mem, Burning Exp, 90- & Biosphere-Atmosphere Trace Gas Exp, 90-; prin investr, SAfrica Fire-Atmosphere Res Initiative, 90-; dir, Atmospheric Sci Prog, Col William & Mary, Williamsburg, Va, 92-, adj prof appl sci & physics, 92-; co-prin investr, Boreal Forest Res Exp, 93- *Mem:* Am Geophys Union; Int Soc Study Origin Life. *Res:* Origin, evolution, physics and chemistry of planetary atmospheres; atmospheric photochemistry; biogeochemical cycling; global climate change; origin & evolution of life. *Mailing Add:* 205 William Claiborne Williamsburg VA 23185. *Fax:* 757-864-6326; *E-Mail:* j.s.levine@lare.nasa.gov

LEVINE, JON DAVID, MEDICAL SCIENCES, INTERNAL MEDICINE. *Current Pos:* FEL RHEUMATOL & CLIN IMMUNOL, UNIV CALIF, SAN FRANCISCO, 81-, FEL CLIN PHARMACOL & THERAPEUT, 82- *Personal Data:* b New York, NY, Mar 20, 45. *Educ:* Univ Mich, BS, 66; Yale Univ, PhD(neurobiol), 72; Univ Calif, San Francisco, MD, 78. *Concurrent Pos:* Asst prof med, Univ Calif, San Francisco, 84-; Hartford Found fel. *Mem:* Am Soc Clin Invest. *Res:* Mechanisms of pain and analgesia and application of research in this area to the diagnosis and mangement of clinical pain; pathophyisology of inflammatory joint disease; rheumatology; neurobiology; clinical pharmacology. *Mailing Add:* Dept Med & Neurosci Box 0452 Univ Calif DMFS 513 Parnassus Ave Rm S-1334 San Francisco CA 94143-0452

LEVINE, JON HOWARD, ENDOCRINOLOGY. *Current Pos:* from asst prof to assoc prof endocrinol, 78-82, PROF MED, MED UNIV SC, 82- *Personal Data:* b Toronto, Ont, July 13, 41; m 64; c 3. *Educ:* Univ Toronto, MD, 65, MSc, 69; Royal Col Physicians & Surgeons Can, FRCP(C), 71; Am Bd Internal Med, cert endocrinol, 77. *Prof Exp:* Instr, Vanderbilt Univ, 71-73. *Concurrent Pos:* Fel, Med Res Coun Can, 71-73. *Mem:* Am Fedn Clin Res; Endocrine Soc; Can Soc Endocrin & Metab. *Res:* Medical education; pituitary regulation of adrenal steroidogenesis; clinical problem solving techniques by physicians. *Mailing Add:* 2222 State St Nashville TN 37203

LEVINE, JOSEPH H, RISK MANAGEMENT, PRODUCT ASSURANCE. *Current Pos:* OWNER, ENG CONSULT SERV, 86- *Personal Data:* b Mineral Wells, Tex, Apr 16, 26; m 50; c Edward. *Educ:* Southern Methodist Univ, BS, 50, MS, 58. *Prof Exp:* Proj engr, Gen Dynamics Corp, 56-62; chief, Reliability Div, Johnson Space Ctr, NASA, 62-86. *Concurrent Pos:* Mem, Nuclear Regulation Comn Invest Group, 86. *Mem:* Assoc fel Am Inst Aeronaut & Astronaut; Nat Asn Consults. *Res:* Manufacturing processes relative to risk; process failure modes and effects analysis technique applied to solid propulsion improvement program and advanced solid propulsion program. *Mailing Add:* 3722 Montvale Houston TX 77059

LEVINE, JUDAH, PHYSICS. *Current Pos:* PROF, DEPT PHYSICS, UNIV COLO, 74- *Personal Data:* b New York, NY, Nov 17, 40. *Educ:* Yeshiva Col, AB, 60; New York Univ, MS, 63, PhD(physics), 66. *Honors & Awards:* Bronze Medal, Dept Com, 80; Gold Medal, Dept Com, 83. *Prof Exp:* Teaching asst, Physics Dept, New York Univ, 60-62, res asst, 62-63; fel, NSF, 63-66; NATO fel, Claredon Lab, Oxford Univ, Eng, 66-67; physicist, Quantum Electronics Div, Nat Inst Stand & Technol, 69-73. *Concurrent Pos:* Mem, Joint Inst Lab Astrophys, 69-75, fel, 76-; physicist, Time & Frequency Div, Nat Inst Stand & Technol, 74- *Mem:* Fel Am Phys Soc; Am Asn Physics Teachers; Am Geophys Union. *Res:* Physics. *Mailing Add:* Univ Colo Campus Box 440 Boulder CO 80309

LEVINE, JULES DAVID, MATERIALS SCIENCE ENGINEERING. *Current Pos:* BR MGR SOLAR CELL DEVELOP, TEX INSTRUMENTS, 79- *Personal Data:* b New York, NY, June 24, 37; m 66; c 2. *Educ:* Columbia Univ, BS, 59; Mass Inst Technol, PhD(physics, nuclear eng), 63. *Prof Exp:* Mem tech staff surface & mat res, David Sarnoff Res Ctr, RCA Labs, 63-73, proj mgr flat panel TV, 73-76, proj mgr cathode res & develop, 76-79. *Concurrent Pos:* Vis lectr elec eng, Princeton Univ, 71-72 & 74-75. *Mem:* Fel Inst Elec & Electronics Engrs; sr mem Am Vacuum Soc. *Res:* Physical processes and engineering of surfaces; thin films; semiconductors; electron emitters; display and power tubes; thermionic energy conversion; high voltage phenomena; electron beams; varistors; vacuum science and technology; fabricates novel solar cells made from miniature single crystal silicon spheres mounted in a planar matrix. *Mailing Add:* Tex Instruments MS 8207 PO Box 655303 Dallas TX 75265

LEVINE, JULES IVAN, HEALTH SCIENCES, MEDICAL ADMINISTRATION. *Current Pos:* From asst prof to assoc prof pediat, 72-86, asst vpres health affairs, 78-86, PROF HEALTH AFFAIRS & ASSOC VPRES HEALTH SCI, UNIV VA, 86- *Personal Data:* b Brooklyn, NY, Apr 17, 38; m 62; c 2. *Educ:* Univ Va, BEE, 60, PhD(biomed eng), 72; Johns Hopkins Univ, MS, 68. *Prof Exp:* Sr engr aerospace electronics, Westinghouse Elec Corp, 63-68. *Concurrent Pos:* Consult, NIH; assoc dean, Sch Med, Univ Va, 74-78. *Mem:* Soc Col & Univ Planning; Am Asn Med Cols. *Res:* Planning and evaluation of health resources and the health care delivery system. *Mailing Add:* Univ Va Med Ctr Box 492 Charlottesville VA 22908

LEVINE, LAURENCE, cell biology; deceased, see previous edition for last biography

LEVINE, LAWRENCE, IMMUNOCHEMISTRY. *Current Pos:* from asst prof to assoc prof, 57-70, PROF BIOCHEM, BRANDEIS UNIV, 70- *Personal Data:* b Hartford, Conn, July 18, 24. *Educ:* Univ Conn, BA, 48; Univ Mich, MS, 50; Johns Hopkins Univ, DSc(microbiol), 53. *Prof Exp:* Instr microbiol, Johns Hopkins Univ, 53-54; res scientist, Div Labs & Res, State Dept Health, NY, 54-57. *Res:* Blood proteins and their immunol properties. *Mailing Add:* Dept Biochem Brandeis Univ 415 South St Waltham MA 02254-2700. *Fax:* 781-736-2349

LEVINE, LAWRENCE ELLIOTT, APPLIED MATHEMATICS. *Current Pos:* From asst prof to assoc prof, 68-77, Head, Dept Pure & Appl Math, 91-96, PROF MATH, STEVENS INST TECHNOL, 97. *Personal Data:* b Chelsea, Mass, June 23, 41; m 65; c 6. *Educ:* Rensselaer Polytech Inst, BS, 63; Univ Md, PhD(appl math), 68, Stevens Inst Technol, MEng, 77. *Mem:* Am Math Asn. *Res:* Fluid dynamics; partial differential equations; perturbation methods; CAI in mathematics; computer education. *Mailing Add:* Dept Math Sci Stevens Inst Technol Hoboken NJ 07030. *Fax:* 201-216-8321; *E-Mail:* llevine@vaxc.stevens-tech.edu

LEVINE, LEO MEYER, MATHEMATICS. *Current Pos:* assoc prof, 70-81, PROF MATH, QUEENSBOROUGH COMMUNITY COL, 81- *Personal Data:* b Brooklyn, NY, May 26, 22; m 49; c 3. *Educ:* City Col New York, BS, 42; NY Univ, PhD(math), 60. *Prof Exp:* Asst physicist, Signal Corps Labs, Eatontown, NJ, 42-43; sr physicist, Mat Lab, NY Naval Shipyard, 47-59; from asst res scientist to assoc res scientist, Courant Inst Math Sci, NY Univ, 59-63, from asst prof to assoc prof, 63-70. *Concurrent Pos:* Consult, Radio Corp Am, 61-62. *Mem:* Am Math Soc; Math Asn Am. *Res:* Applied mathematics; ordinary and partial differential equations; acoustics; electromagnetic theory. *Mailing Add:* 138-21 77th Ave Flushing NY 11367

LEVINE, LEON, POLYMER CHEMISTRY. *Current Pos:* sr chemist, 92-95, CONSULT CHEMIST, DYMAX CORP, 95- *Personal Data:* b Brooklyn, NY, Jan 6, 34; m 66; c 2. *Educ:* Brooklyn Col, BS, 56; Polytech Inst New York, PhD(org chem), 63. *Prof Exp:* Res & develop chemist polymers, Foster Grant Co, 63-66, Gaylord assoc, 66-67; res & develop chemist polymers, Sun Chem Co, 67-68, Nat Patent Develop Corp, 72-76, Loctite Corp, 76-80; res & develop chemist dent mat, Warner Lambert Co, 68-72; sr chemist, Coats & Levine, Inc, 81-82, Richardson Polymer Corp, 82-89. *Concurrent Pos:* Consult, L&E Assocs, 82. *Mem:* Am Chem Soc. *Res:* Adhesives; photopolymerizations; do it yourself products; dental materials; hydrophilic polymers; suspension polymerization. *Mailing Add:* 109 S Main St No B1 West Hartford CT 06107-2526

LEVINE, LEONARD, NEUROPHYSIOLOGY. *Current Pos:* PROF PHYSIOL, PAC UNIV, 66-, PROF PHARMACOL, 76- *Personal Data:* b Atlantic City, NJ, Jan 28, 29; m 52; c 2. *Educ:* Rutgers Univ, BS, 50; Columbia Univ, PhD(physiol), 59. *Prof Exp:* Instr physiol, Columbia Univ, 57-60; from asst prof to assoc prof, Univ Va, 61-66. *Concurrent Pos:* USPHS fel physiol, Columbia Univ, 59-60; fel biophys, Univ Col, Univ London, 60-61; USPHS res grants, 62-65, 67-68 & 70-72; res grant proposal evaluator, Regulatory Biol Prog, NSF, 78- *Mem:* AAAS; Am Physiol Soc; Biophys Soc; Am Soc Zool; Am Soc Pharmacol & Exp Therapeut; Sigma Xi. *Res:* Electrophysiology and pharmacology of ocular tissues; trophic interrelations between nerve and muscle tissues. *Mailing Add:* 246 Forest Dr Lake Jackson TX 77566-4649

LEVINE, LEONARD P, HUMAN-COMPUTER INTERFACING. *Current Pos:* dir comput ctr, 67-70, PROF ELEC ENG & COMPUT SCI, UNIV WIS-MILWAUKEE, 66- *Personal Data:* b Newark, NJ, July 24, 32; m 54, Marilyn Gordon; c David. *Educ:* Queens Col, NY, BS, 54; Syracuse Univ, MS, 56, PhD(physics), 60. *Prof Exp:* Engr, Sperry-Gyroscope Co, 59-60; sr scientist, Honeywell Res Ctr, 60-64, prin res scientist, 64-66. *Mem:* Asn Comput Mach. *Res:* Human and machine interfacing; system to system interfacing; small machine system design; computer teaching techniques. *Mailing Add:* Dept Elec Eng & Comput Sci Univ Wis Milwaukee WI 53201. *Fax:* 414-229-6958; *E-Mail:* levine@cs.uwm.edu

LEVINE, LOUIS, POPULATION & FORENSIC GENETICS. *Current Pos:* From instr to assoc prof, 55-67, PROF BIOL, CITY COL NEW YORK, 68- *Personal Data:* b New York, NY, May 14, 21. *Educ:* City Col New York, BS, 42, MS, 47; Columbia Univ, MA, 49, PhD(zool), 55. *Concurrent Pos:* NSF grants, 60-; AEC grant, 63- *Mem:* Fel AAAS; Animal Behav Soc; Am Genetic Asn; Genetics Soc Am; Am Soc Naturalists. *Res:* Population genetics of both humans and drosophila. *Mailing Add:* Dept Biol City Col NY New York NY 10031. *Fax:* 212-650-8585

LEVINE, LOUIS DAVID, ARCHAEOLOGY. *Current Pos:* ASST COMNR & DIR, NY STATE MUS, ALBANY, 90- *Personal Data:* b New York, NY, June 4, 40; div; c Sarra L & Samuel E. *Educ:* Univ Pa, BA, 62, PhD, 69. *Prof Exp:* Instr, Hebrew Univ, Pa, 66-69; from asst prof to prof, Univ Toronto, 69-90. *Concurrent Pos:* Asst cur, Royal Ont Mus, Toronto, Can, 69-75, assoc cur, 75-80, cur, 81, assoc dir, 87-90; dir, Seh Gabi Explor, Western Iran, 71-73 & Mahidasht Proj, 75-79; vis sr lectr, Hebrew Univ, Jerusalem, 75-76; vis prof, Univ Copenhagen, 85. *Mem:* Fel Inst Advan Studies; Brit Inst Persian Studies; Am Asn Mus; Am Oriental Soc. *Res:* Archaeology. *Mailing Add:* NY State Mus Cult Educ Ctr Rm 3099 Albany NY 12230

LEVINE, MAITA FAYE, MATHEMATICS. *Current Pos:* From instr to assoc prof, 63-85, PROF MATH, UNIV CINCINNATI, 85- *Personal Data:* b Cincinnati, Ohio, Oct 17, 30. *Educ:* Univ Cincinnati, BA, 52, BE, 53, MAT, 66; Ohio State Univ, PhD(math educ), 70. *Prof Exp:* Teacher, High Sch, Ohio, 53-63. *Concurrent Pos:* NSF res grant, 74, 85 & 93. *Mem:* Math Asn Am; Am Educ Res Asn; Nat Coun Teachers Math; Asn Women Math; Am Asn Univ Prof (vpres, 86-88); Sigma Xi. *Res:* Relationship between mathematical competence and mathematical confidence; mathematical modeling; reasons why qualified women do not pursue mathematical careers; applications of computers and graphics calculators in the undergraduate curriculum; applications of mathematics to politics. *Mailing Add:* 1106 Lois Dr Cincinnati OH 45237. *Fax:* 513-556-3417

LEVINE, MARK DAVID, ENERGY ANALYSIS. *Current Pos:* prog leader, 78-97, DIV DIR, LAWRENCE BERKELEY LAB, 97- *Personal Data:* b Cleveland, Ohio, May 26, 44; m, Irma D Herrera; c Tony Levine. *Educ:* Princeton Univ, BA, 66; Univ Calif, Berkeley, PhD(chem), 75. *Prof Exp:* Staff scientist, Ford Found Energy Policy Proj, 72-73; sr policy analyst, Stanford Res Inst, 74-78. *Concurrent Pos:* Fulbright scholar; Woodrow Wilson Found scholar; mem bd dirs, Ctr Clean Air Policy Adv Bd, Int Inst Energy Conserv; bd dirs, Am Coun Energy Efficient Econ. *Mem:* Int Asn Energy Economists; Am Soc Heating, Refrig & Air Conditioning Engrs; AAAS. *Res:* Comprehensive analysis of energy efficiency and energy policy options for the People's Republic of China; analysis of energy efficiency standards and guidelines for commericial buildings with application in developing countries; development of techniques to improve energy demand forecasting in the US, particularly for the building sector; analysis of energy issues related to global climate change. *Mailing Add:* Lawrence Berkeley Lab Bldg 90 Rm 90-3026 Berkeley CA 94720. *Fax:* 510-486-6996; *E-Mail:* mdlevine@lbl.gov

LEVINE, MARTIN, ENGINEERING, EDUCATION. *Current Pos:* RETIRED. *Personal Data:* b Brooklyn, NY, Oct 27, 25; m 60; c 2. *Educ:* City Col New York, BSEE, 50; Univ Pittsburgh, MLitt, 50, MEd, 60; Univ Md, PhD(higher educ), 69. *Prof Exp:* Proj engr, Air Res & Develop, 50-53; mem fac, Pa State Univ, 53-63 & Harrisburg Area Community Col, 65-68; prof elec technol, Va West Community Col, 68-96. *Mem:* Inst Elec & Electronics Engrs; Am Soc Eng Educ. *Res:* Student-work interface. *Mailing Add:* 2269 Maiden Ln SW Roanoke VA 24015

LEVINE, MARTIN DAVID, COMPUTER VISION. *Current Pos:* From asst prof to assoc prof, 65-77, PROF ELEC ENG, McGILL UNIV, 77-, DIR, CTR INTELLIGENT MACH. *Personal Data:* b Montreal, Que, Mar 30, 38; m 61; c 2. *Educ:* McGill Univ, BEng, 60, MEng, 63; Univ London, DIC & PhD(control theory), 65. *Concurrent Pos:* Vis prof comput sci, Hebrew Univ, Jerusalem, Israel, 79-80; Am Soc Eng Educ-Ford Found fel, 72; assoc ed, Comput Vision, Graphics & Image Processing; tech staff mem, Image Processing & Jet Propulsion Labs, Pasadena, Calif, 72-73; assoc ed, Trans Pattern Anal & Mach Intel, Inst Elec & Electronics Engrs. *Mem:* Fel Inst Elec & Electronics Engrs; Pattern Recognition Soc; Int Asn Pattern Recognition. *Res:* Computer vision; biomedical image processing; artificial intelligence; intelligent robotics. *Mailing Add:* Dept Elec Eng McGill Univ 3480 University St Montreal PQ H3A 2A7 Can

LEVINE, MELVIN MORDECAI, NUCLEAR ENGINEERING & REACTOR PHYSICS. *Current Pos:* RETIRED. *Personal Data:* b Richmond, Va, Nov 20, 25; m 50, Lilo Guggenheim; c Susan (Fox), Wendy (Dunn) & David. *Educ:* Mass Inst Technol, BS, 46; Univ Va, PhD(physics), 55. *Prof Exp:* Instr physics, Pa State Univ, 46-48; physicist, Babcock & Wilcox Co, 55-59; physicist, Brookhaven Nat Lab, 59-88. *Mem:* Fel Am Nuclear Soc. *Res:* Nuclear reactor safety research and applications, including neutronics and thermal-hydraulic phenomena; computational methods for reactor physics and engineering problems. *Mailing Add:* Two Meadow Lane Saranac Lake NY 12983. *E-Mail:* mlevine@northnet.org

LEVINE, MICHAEL S, ANIMAL PHYSIOLOGY. *Current Pos:* Fel neurophysiol, Brain Res Inst, 70-72, asst res neurophysiologist, 72-76, lectr psychol, 75-76, from asst prof to assoc prof psychiat, 76-85, PROF PSYCHIAT, UNIV CALIF, LOS ANGELES, 85- *Personal Data:* b Brooklyn, NY, Sept 22, 44; c 1. *Educ:* Queens Col, BA, 66; Univ Rochester, PhD(physiol psychol), 70. *Concurrent Pos:* Consult neuropsychologist, Hereditary dis Found, 75. *Mem:* Soc Neurosci; Am Psychol Asn; Am Asn Anatomists; Sigma Xi. *Res:* Neurophysiology and neuroanatomy of basal ganglia in mature, developing and aging animals; role of basal ganglia in regulation of behavior; development and prediction of learning ability in developing animals. *Mailing Add:* Ment Retardation Res Ctr Dept Psychiat Univ Calif 760 Westwood Plaza Los Angeles CA 90024

LEVINE, MICHAEL STEVEN, DEVELOPMENTAL BIOLOGY. *Current Pos:* prof biol, 91-96, PROF GENETICS, UNIV CALIF, SAN DIEGO, 96- *Personal Data:* b Los Angeles, Calif, Mar 5, 55; m 85; c 1. *Educ:* Univ Calif, Berkeley, BA, 76; Yale Univ, PhD(molecular biol), 81. *Prof Exp:* Fel, Univ Basel, Switz, 82-83 & Univ Calif, Berkeley, 83-84; from asst prof to prof biol, Columbia Univ, 84-91. *Concurrent Pos:* Sloan fel, 85. *Res:* Control of gene expression during early embryonic development; DNA binding proteins and regulatory switch genes; the developmental regulation of eukaryotic promoters by crudely localized positional cues and morphogen gradients. *Mailing Add:* Dept MCB Univ Calif 401 Barker Hall Berkeley CA 94720

LEVINE, MICHAEL W, VISUAL SCIENCE, SENSORY PROCESSES. *Current Pos:* from asst prof to assoc prof, 72-85, PROF PSYCHOL, UNIV ILL, CHICAGO, 85- *Personal Data:* b New York, NY, Mar 10, 43; m 69, Jane Freeman; c Matthew & Andrea. *Educ:* Mass Inst Technol, BS, 65, MS, 67; Rockefeller Univ, PhD(biophysics), 72. *Prof Exp:* Res asst mech eng, Mass Inst Technol, 65-67; proj engr, Lion Res Corp, Newton, Mass, 67; grad fel biophysics, Rockefeller Univ, 67-72. *Concurrent Pos:* Assoc prof bioeng, Univ Ill Chicago, 81-84; vis scholar, Northwestern Univ, 81; vis prof, Univ Sydney, Australia, 87-88. *Mem:* AAAS; Asn Res Vision & Ophthal; Sigma Xi; Soc Neurosci. *Res:* Visual system; firing patterns of retinal ganglion cells; statistics of neural discharges; sensation and perception; author of various publications. *Mailing Add:* Dept Psychol M/C 285 Univ Ill Chicago 1007 W Harrison St Chicago IL 60607-7137. *E-Mail:* mikel@uic.edu

LEVINE, MICHEAL JOSEPH, PHYSICS, DATA ACQUISITION. *Current Pos:* SR PHYSICIST NUCLEAR PHYSICS, BROOKHAVEN NAT LAB, 68- *Personal Data:* b Oak Park, Ill, Dec 1, 40; m 69, Dreania Lev; c Dana N. *Educ:* Yale Univ, BS, 62, MS, 64, PhD(physics), 68. *Prof Exp:* Consult, High Voltage Eng Corp, 72-75; guest physicist, Max Planck Inst Nuclear Physics, Heidelberg, Ger, 75 & Ctr d'Etudes Nucleaires, Saclay, France, 80-81; sci assoc, CERN, Geneva, Switz. *Mem:* Am Phys Soc; Inst Elec & Electronics Engrs. *Res:* Study of nuclear reactions induced by relativistic heavy ions; development of magnetic spectrometers and associated focal plane detectors; development of data acquisition architectures. *Mailing Add:* Brookhaven Nat Lab Bldg 510A Upton NY 11973-5000. *Fax:* 516-344-4206; *E-Mail:* levine@bnl.gov

LEVINE, MYRON, GENETICS, VIROLOGY. *Current Pos:* from assoc prof to prof, 61-96, EMER PROF HUMAN GENETICS, SCH MED, UNIV MICH, ANN ARBOR, 96- *Personal Data:* b Brooklyn, NY, July 28, 26; m 50, Barbara R Kohn; c Sura & Peter. *Educ:* Brooklyn Col, BA, 47; Ind Univ, PhD(zool), 52. *Prof Exp:* Res assoc microbiol, Univ Ill, 54-56; asst to assoc biologist, Brookhaven Nat Lab, 56-61. *Concurrent Pos:* Am Cancer Soc fel, Johns Hopkins Univ, 53-54; Commonwealth Fund fel, Univ Geneva, 66-67; ed, J Virol, 72-75; vis scientist, Imp Cancer Res Fund, London, 73-74 & Cambridge Univ, 82; chmn grad prog cell & molecular biol in health sci, Univ Mich, 74-90; mem & chmn genetic basis of dis rev comt, Nat Inst Gen Med Sci, NIH, 75-79; sr fel, Soc Fels, Univ Mich, 82-85; Claire Hall life fel, Cambridge Univ, 82-; chmn, educ comt, Genetics Soc Am, 86-89; vis scientist, Weizmann Inst Sci, Israel, 83 & Inst Sci Res Cancer, France, 83; vis prof, Biol Dept, Harbin Normal Univ, Harbin, People's Repub China, 86. *Mem:* Genetics Soc Am; Am Soc Microbiol; Am Soc Virol; AAAS. *Res:* Genetics and regulation of gene expression of animal viruses; herpesvirus genetics, latency and biology; gene therapy for the central nervous system; molecular genetics. *Mailing Add:* Dept Human Genetics Univ Mich Sch Med Ann Arbor MI 48109-0618. *Fax:* 313-763-3784; *E-Mail:* mylevine@umich.edu

LEVINE, MYRON MAX, TROPICAL PEDIATRICS. *Current Pos:* instr, Dept Pediat, Univ Md Sch Med, 71-72, from asst prof to prof, 72-83, act head, Div Infectious Dis, 84-85, DIR, CTR VACCINE DEVELOP, UNIV MD SCH MED, 74-; HEAD, DIV GEOG MED, 84-, HEAD, DIV INFECTIOUS DIS & TROP PEDIAT, 85- *Personal Data:* b Riverdale, NY, Feb 11, 44; m, Suzanne; c Orin, Rachel & Rebecca. *Educ:* City Col NY, BS, 63; Med Col Va, MD, 67; London Sch Hyg & Trop Med, DTPH, 74. *Honors & Awards:* Howard Fiorey Mem Lectr, Univ Adelaide, SAustralia, 87; Bazely Oration, Australian Soc Microbiol, 92; Colonel George W Hunter III Award, Walter Reed Army Inst Res, 95. *Prof Exp:* Intern pediat, Bronx Munic Hosp Ctr, Albert Einstein Col Med, 67-68, from asst resident to sr resident, 68-70, fel, Div Pediat Infectious Dis Immunol, 70-72. *Concurrent Pos:* Vis prof, Fac Med, Univ Peruana Cayetano Heredia, Peru, 80-; sr assoc, Dept Epidemiol, Johns Hopkins Univ Sch Hyg & Pub Health, 85-; fel, Sackler Inst Adv Studies, Tel Aviv Univ, 87-88; Lederle-Praxis vis prof vaccinology, Oxford Univ. *Mem:* Inst Med-Nat Acad Sci; fel Infectious Dis Soc Am; Am Soc Trop Med & Hyg; Am Epidemiol Soc; Royal Soc Trop Med & Hyg; Am Soc Microbiol; Soc Epidemiol Res; Soc Intestinal Microbiol Ecol & Dis; Asn Am Physicians; fel Am Acad Pediat. *Mailing Add:* Ctr Vaccine Develop Univ Md 685 W Baltimore St Rm 480 Baltimore MD 21201. *Fax:* 410-706-6205; *E-Mail:* mlevine@umppa1.ab.umd.edu

LEVINE, NATHAN, COMMUNICATIONS ENGINEERING. *Current Pos:* Mem tech staff, Bell Tel Labs, 57-61, supvr re-entry physics, 61-64, dept head, 64-83, dir anti-missile systs res, 68-71, dir toll transmission eng ctr, 71-83, dir educ ctr, 83-86, dir transmission facil planning, 86-89, DIR, NETWORK SERV PERFORMANCE, BELL TEL LABS, 89- *Personal Data:* b Brooklyn, NY, Aug 7, 30; m 53; c 2. *Educ:* Mass Inst Technol, BS, 52; Univ Ill, MS, 54, PhD(physics), 57. *Mem:* Inst Elec & Electronics Engrs. *Res:* System studies and design of integrated network planning tools for the evolution of communication networks; network services performance evaluation. *Mailing Add:* 2 Burr Dr Princeton NJ 08540

LEVINE, NORMAN DION, PARASITOLOGY, PROTOZOOLOGY & HUMAN ECOLOGY. *Current Pos:* asst animal parasitologist, Univ Ill, 37-41, assoc animal path, 41-42, from asst prof to assoc prof vet parasitol, 46-53, asst to dean Col Vet Med, 47-57, prof, 53-83, EMER PROF VET PARASITOL & VET RES, COL VET MED, UNIV ILL, URBANA, 83- *Personal Data:* b Boston, Mass, Nov 30, 12; wid. *Educ:* Iowa State Col, BS, 33; Univ Calif, PhD(zool), 37; Am Bd Med Microbiol, cert pub health & med lab parasitol. *Hon Degrees:* DSc, Univ Ill, Urbana, 89. *Prof Exp:* Asst zool, Univ Calif, 33-37. *Concurrent Pos:* Mem, Nat Res Coun, 56-62; mem bd gov, Am Bd Microbiol, 59-64; sr mem, Ctr Zoonoses Res, 60-74, prof zool, 65-73, dir, Ctr Human Ecol, Univ Ill, Urbana, 68-74; vis prof, Univ Hawaii, 62, Santa Catalina Marine Biol Lab, 72 & J Hopkins Marine Sta, 80; mem comt health sci achievement award prog, NIH, 65-66, mem trop med & parasitol study sect, 65-69, chmn, 66-69, mem natural resources adv comt, 71-75; ed, J Protozool, 65-71. *Mem:* AAAS; Am Soc Parasitol; hon mem Soc Protozool (secy, 52-58, vpres, 58-59, pres, 59-60, actg secy, 60-62); hon mem Micros Soc Am (pres, 69-70); fel Am Acad Microbiol; Sigma Xi; hon mem, World Asn Advan Vet Parasitol. *Res:* Protozoan and roundworm parasites of domestic and wild animals; malaria and other insect-borne diseases. *Mailing Add:* Manor Care 309 E Springfield Ave Champaign IL 61820

LEVINE, O ROBERT, EXPERIMENTAL BIOLOGY. *Current Pos:* PROF PEDIAT, UNIV MED & DENT NJ, 72- *Mailing Add:* Dept Pediat UMDNJ NJ Med Sch Newark NJ 07103

LEVINE, OSCAR, PHYSICAL CHEMISTRY. *Current Pos:* RETIRED. *Personal Data:* b Brooklyn, NY, Feb 6, 23; m 48; c 2. *Educ:* City Col New York, BS, 43; Columbia Univ, AM, 48; Georgetown Univ, PhD(chem), 57. *Prof Exp:* Nat Adv Comt Aeronaut, Ohio, 48-52; chemist, USN Res Lab, 52-58; chemist, chem & mat res, Gillette Safety Razor Co, Boston, 58-85. *Concurrent Pos:* Vpres res & develop lubricant coatings, Ro-59, Inc, 85- *Mem:* Am Chem Soc. *Res:* Chemistry and physics of solid and liquid surfaces and interfaces; lubrication; adhesion. *Mailing Add:* 43 Connolly St Randolph MA 02368-1510

LEVINE, PAUL HERSH, THEORETICAL PHYSICS, APPLIED PHYSICS. *Current Pos:* CONSULT PHYSICIST, 82- *Personal Data:* b New York, NY, Sept 27, 35; m 63, Lea Walker. *Educ:* Mass Inst Technol, BS, 56; Calif Inst Technol, MS, 57, PhD(theoret physics), 63. *Prof Exp:* Sr scientist, Jet Propulsion Lab, Calif Inst Technol, 63-64; chief scientist, Astrophys Res Corp, 64-72 & Megatek Corp, 72-82. *Res:* Ionospheric physics; over-the-horizon radar; quantum many-body problem; exploding wire phenomena; electron field emission; radiative transport; electromagnetic propagation; navigation and communication systems analysis; minicomputer applications; electroencephalography; psychobiology of consciousness. *Mailing Add:* PO Box 8827 Incline Village NV 89452

LEVINE, PAUL HOWARD, VIRAL ONCOLOGY, INTERNAL MEDICINE. *Current Pos:* RES INVESTR VIRAL ONCOL, NAT CANCER INST, 68- *Personal Data:* b New York, NY, Sept 11, 37; m 60; c 3. *Educ:* Cornell Univ, BA, 59; Univ Rochester, MD, 63. *Prof Exp:* Intern internal med, Strong Mem Hosp, 63-64; resident fel oncol, Roswell Park Mem Inst, 64-66; resident internal med, Univ Colo, 66-68. *Concurrent Pos:* Co-chmn immunol group, Nat Cancer Inst, 71-72, chmn immunol-epidemiol segment, Virus Cancer Prog, 72-75, head clin studies sect, Viral Leukemia & Lymphoma Br, 74-75, chmn clin adv group, Div Cancer Cause & Prev, 76-81, head clin studies sect, Lab Viral Carcinogenesis, 78-82, sr investr, Epidemiol & Biostatists, 82-; clin asst prof med, George Washington Univ, Med Ctr, 78- *Mem:* Am Asn Cancer Res; Am Col Physicians; Am Col Epidemiol; AAAS. *Res:* Epidemiology of oncogenic viruses, particularly Epstein-Barr virus and HTLV-I; viral immunol, application of assays to cancer etiology, diagnosis, treatment. *Mailing Add:* Epidemiol & Biostatists EPN 434 Nat Cancer Inst Bethesda MD 20892

LEVINE, PHILLIP J, PHARMACY. *Current Pos:* from asst prof to assoc prof, 63-70, PROF PHARM, COL PHARM, DRAKE UNIV, 70-, COORDR CONTINUING EDUC PROG PHARM, 77- *Personal Data:* b Providence, RI, Jan 7, 34; m 55; c 2. *Educ:* Univ RI, BS, 55; Univ Md, MS, 57, PhD(pharm), 63. *Prof Exp:* Instr pharm, Sch Pharm, Univ Md, 57-63. *Concurrent Pos:* Consult, Dr Salsbury's Labs, Charles City, Iowa, 65-70; dir, Coop IV Additive Proj, 67-69; chmn, Mayor's Task Force on Drugs, Des Moines, Iowa, 69-70; consult, Gov, State of Iowa, 70-72. *Mem:* Am Pharmaceut Asn. *Res:* Development of topical anesthetic suspensions to test their applicability to long duration of anesthesia in dental patients; product development in area of suspension and formulations. *Mailing Add:* Dept Pharm Drake Univ 2507 University Ave Des Moines IA 50311

LEVINE, RACHMIEL, ENDOCRINOLOGY. *Current Pos:* med dir, 70-78, EMER MED DIR, CITY OF HOPE MED CTR, 82- *Personal Data:* b Poland, Aug 26, 10; nat US; m 43; c 2 Judith L (Feldman) & Daniel S. *Educ:* McGill Univ, BA, 32, MD, 36. *Hon Degrees:* MD, Univ Ulm, 69; ScD, Northwestern, 85, McGill, 87. *Honors & Awards:* Thompson Award, Am Geriat Soc, 71; Gairdner Found Award, 71. *Prof Exp:* Asst dir, Dept Metab & Endocrine Res, Michael Reese Hosp, 39-42, dir, 42-58, chmn, Dept Med & dir med educ, 52-60; prof & chmn dept, NY Med Col, 60-70. *Concurrent Pos:* Williams fel, Michael Reese Hosp, 36-37, res fel, 37-39; consult, NSF, 56-59 & 70-; Endocrine Soc Upjohn scholar, 57; pres, Int Fedn Diabetes, 67-70; Guggenheim Found fel, 71-72; mem bd dirs, Found Fund Psychiat Res. *Mem:* Nat Acad Sci; Am Physiol Soc; Soc Exp Biol & Med; Endocrine Soc; Am Diabetes Asn (pres, 64-65); fel Am Acad Arts & Sci. *Res:* Hormonal control of metabolism; mode of action of insulin; diabetes. *Mailing Add:* 2024 Canyon Rd Arcadia CA 91006

LEVINE, RANDOLPH HERBERT, ASTROPHYSICS, SOLAR PHYSICS. *Current Pos:* sr scientist & dir comput, atmospheric & environ res, 81-82, mgr software eng, 82-85, MKT EXEC, DIGITAL EQUIP CORP, 85- *Personal Data:* b Denver, Colo, Nov 20, 46; m 70; c 2. *Educ:* Univ Calif, Berkeley, AB, 68; Harvard Univ, AM, 69, PhD(physics), 72. *Prof Exp:* Vis scientist solar physics, High Altitude Observ, Nat Ctr Atmospheric Res, Boulder, Colo, 72-74; Res fel solar physics, Ctr Astrophys, Harvard Col Observ, 74-75, res assoc solar physics, 75-81, lectr astron, 77-81. *Mem:* Am Astron Soc; Am Geophys Union; Int Astron Union; Am Phys Soc; Inst Elec & Electronics Engrs. *Res:* Scientific computing; design and development of products. *Mailing Add:* 50 Carver Rd Newton MA 02161

LEVINE, RAPHAEL DAVID, MOLECULAR REACTIONS. *Current Pos:* PROF THEORET CHEM, HEBREW UNIV, JERUSALEM, 69-, CHMN, RES CTR MOLECULAR DYNAMICS, 81-, MAX BORN PROF, NATURAL PHILOS, 85- *Personal Data:* b Alexandria, Egypt, Mar 29, 38; Israeli citizen; m 62, Gillian T Ephraty; c Ornah T. *Educ:* Hebrew Univ, Jerusalem, MSc, 59; Nottingham Univ, Eng, PhD(math), 64; Oxford Univ, Eng, DPhil, 66. *Hon Degrees:* PhD, Univ Liege, Belg, 91; Tech Univ Munich, 96. *Honors & Awards:* Ann Award, Int Acad Quantum Molecular Sci, 68; Landau Prize, 72; Israel Prize Exact Sci, 74; Weizman Prize, 79; Wolf Prize, 88; Rothschild Prize, 92; Max Planck Prize for Int Cooperation, Humboldt Found, 96. *Prof Exp:* Vis asst prof, Univ Wis, 66-68. *Concurrent Pos:* Ramsay mem fel, 64-66; Alfred P Sloan fel, 70-72; Battelle prof chem & math, Ohio State Univ, 70-74; Brittingham vis prof, Univ Wis, 73; adj prof, Tel Aviv Univ, 74-80, Mass Inst Technol, 80-88, Univ Calif, Los Angeles, 89; Miller res prof, Univ Calif, Berkeley, 89; A D White prof-at-large, Cornell Univ, 89- *Mem:* Fel Am Phys Soc; Am Philos Soc; Israel Acad Sci; Max Planck Soc; Acad Europe; Am Acad Arts & Sci. *Res:* Author of various articles and books. *Mailing Add:* Dept Chem & Biochem Univ Calif Los Angeles CA 90095

LEVINE, RHEA JOY COTTLER, CELL BIOLOGY, CYTOCHEMISTRY. *Current Pos:* from asst prof to assoc prof, 69-80, PROF ANAT, MED COL PA, 80- *Personal Data:* b Brooklyn, NY, Nov 26, 39; m 60, Stephen M; c Elizabeth (Kennedy), Michael G & Zachary T. *Educ:* Smith Col, AB, 60; NY Univ, MS, 63, PhD(biol), 66. *Prof Exp:* Lab instr biol, Sch Com, Acct & Finance, Wash Sq Col, NY Univ, 63-64; res assoc neuropath, Sch Med, Univ Pa, 68-69. *Concurrent Pos:* A H Robins Co fel biochem res, Manhattan State Hosp, Ward's Island, 66; USPHS fel, Sch Med, Yale Univ, 66-68; grantee, Nat Heart & Lung Inst, Pa Muscle Inst, 73-, Nat Inst Gen Med Sci, 75-81, NSF, 79-80, 80-81, 85-86 & 91-94; Nat Inst Arthritis & Metab Dis, 84-87, Biol Instrumentation, 87 & Am Heart Asn, 95-97; Nat Inst Neurol Commun Dis & Stroke career develop award, 74-79; reviewer, J Cell Biol, Am J Physiol Sci & Biophys J, 75-; mem, Cardiovasc & Pulmonary Study Sect, Div Res Grants, NIH, 80-84; co-ed, Basic biol Muscle; coun mem, Biophys Soc, 90-94, chair, Pub Policy Comt, 93-94; chair, bd trustees, Richard Stockton Col, NJ, 91-94. *Mem:* AAAS; Histochem Soc; Am Asn Anat; NY Acad Sci; Soc Gen Physiol; Biophys Soc; Am Soc Cell Biol; Sigma Xi. *Res:* Ultrastructure; muscle structure and function; comparative aspects of muscle immunohistochemistry and cytochemistry; electron microscopic analysis of thick filament structure by 3D reconstruction. *Mailing Add:* Dept Neurobiol & Anat/EPPI Div MCP Hahnemann Sch Med 3200 Henry Ave Philadelphia PA 19129. *Fax:* 215-843-9082

LEVINE, RICHARD JOSEPH, OCCUPATIONAL MEDICINE, EPIDEMIOLOGY. *Current Pos:* expert, 91-94, RES MED OFFICER, NIH, 94- *Personal Data:* b New York, NY, Nov 12, 39; m 69; c 2. *Educ:* Princeton Univ, AB, 60; Calif Inst Technol, MS, 64, St Louis Univ, MD, 76; Harvard Univ MPH, 76. *Prof Exp:* Intern med, Grady Mem Hosp, 71-72; epidemiologist, Ctr Dis Control, Epidemic Intell serv, 72-75; sr med scientist, Ctr Occup & Environ Health, Stanford Res Inst, 76-77; chief epidemiol, Chem Indust Inst Toxicol, 77-92. *Concurrent Pos:* Asst state epidemiologist, Ala State Health Dept, 72-73; epidemiologist, Cholera Res Lab, Dacca, Bangladesh, 73-75; partic, Working Group Asbestos, Int Agency Cancer Res, 77; adj asst prof, Dept Family Commun Med, Div Occup Med, Duke Univ, 78-, assoc prof, 83-; adj assoc prof, Dept Epidemiol, Univ NC Sch Pub Health, 84- *Mem:* Soc Epidemiol Res; Am Occup Med Asn; fel Am Col Occup Med. *Res:* Epidemiology of cholera and mass hysteria; effects of occupation on male reproduction; preeclampsia. *Mailing Add:* NIH 6100 Executive Bldg Rm 7B03 Bethesda MD 20892

LEVINE, RICHARD S, CORROSION CONTROL & WATER TREATMENT, ENVIRONMENTAL TESTING. *Current Pos:* PRES, INDUST CORROSION MGT, INC, 73- *Personal Data:* b Pittsburgh, Pa, Jan 14, 47; m 69; c 1. *Educ:* Carnegie-Mellon Univ, BS, 68; Univ Ill, MS, 71. *Prof Exp:* Chemist, Univ Ill, 71-73. *Mem:* Am Chem Soc; Am Soc Testing & Mat; Am Water Works Asn; Asn Off Anal Chemists. *Res:* Corrosion control and water treatment in central air conditioning and heating systems; environmental testing; author of numerous publications. *Mailing Add:* Indust Corrosion Mgt Inc 1152 Rte 10 Randolph NJ 07869

LEVINE, ROBERT, ORGANIC CHEMISTRY. *Current Pos:* from instr to assoc prof, 46-59, PROF CHEM, UNIV PITTSBURGH, 59- *Personal Data:* b Boston, Mass, July 30, 19; m 50; c 3. *Educ:* Dartmouth Col, BA, 40, MA, 42; Duke Univ, PhD(org chem), 45. *Prof Exp:* Asst, Dartmouth Col, 40-42; asst, Duke Univ, 42-45; chemist, Mathieson Chem Corp, NY, 45-46. *Concurrent Pos:* Consult, Monsanto Co, 52-62, Schering Corp, 59-63, Reilly Tar & Chem Corp, 64-66, FMC Corp, 65-67, Columbia Org Chem Co, 70-73, Pressure Chem Co, 70-75, Fike Chem Inc, 71-74 & Mallinckrodt Chem Works, 74-75. *Mem:* Am Chem Soc; Int Asn Heterocyclic Chem; NY Acad Sci; Israel Chem Soc; Sigma Xi. *Res:* Heterocyclic nitrogen chemistry, including pyridine, pyrazine, pyrimidine and triazine; synthesis of organic fluorine compounds; chemistry of organometallic compounds; synthesis of potential medicinals. *Mailing Add:* 121 Virginia Rd Pittsburgh PA 15237-3710

LEVINE, ROBERT, PEDIATRIC CARDIOLOGY. *Current Pos:* PROF PEDIAT & DIR PEDIAT CARDIOL, NJ MED SCH, COL MED & DENT NJ, 72- *Personal Data:* b New York, NY, Nov 10, 26; m 54; c 2. *Educ:* City Col New York, BS, 48; Western Res Univ, MD, 54. *Prof Exp:* From intern to resident pediat, State Univ NY Upstate Med Ctr, 54-57; from instr to assoc prof, Col Physicians & Surgeons, Columbia Univ, 62-72. *Concurrent Pos:* NIH trainee pediat cardiol, Col physicians & Surgeons, Columbia Univ, 59-61 & NIH fel cardiorespiratory physiol, 61-62; NY City Health Res Coun career scientist award, 62-72; John Polachek Found fel, 68-69; prin investr, NIH Grad Training Prog Pediat Cardiol, Columbia Univ, 70-72, responsible investr, Nat Heart & Lung Inst-SCOR, Col Physicians & Surgeons, 71-72. *Mem:* Am Acad Pediat; Am Pediat Soc; Am Physiol Soc. *Res:* Cardiorespiratory physiology. *Mailing Add:* Univ Med & Dent NJ Med Sch Rm F 576 Newark NJ 07130-2714

LEVINE, ROBERT ALAN, MEDICINE, PHARMACOLOGY. *Current Pos:* PROF MED, STATE UNIV NY UPSTATE MED CTR, 71-, CHIEF DIV GASTROENTEROL, STATE UNIV HOSP, 71- *Personal Data:* b New York, NY, June 12, 32; m 56; c 3. *Educ:* Cornell Univ, AB, 54, MD, 58; Am Bd Gastroenterol, cert. *Prof Exp:* Intern med, NY Hosp-Cornell Med Ctr, 58-59, asst resident, 59-60; clin fel med, Liver Study Unit, Sch Med, Yale Univ, 61-62, res fel, 62-63; from asst chief to chief metab div, Army Med Res & Nutrit Lab, Fitzsimons Gen Hosp, 63-65; chief div gastroenterol, Brooklyn-Cumberland Med Ctr, 65-71, assoc prof med, 69-71. *Concurrent Pos:* Clin fel gastroenterol, NY Hosp-Cornell Med Ctr, 60-61. *Mem:* Am Soc Pharmacol & Exp Therapeut; Am Fedn Clin Res; Am Gastroenterol Asn; Am Asn Study Liver Dis. *Res:* Basic and clinical research in gastroenterology, metabolism and pharmacology; cyclic adenosine 3', 5'-monophosphate in vivo and in vitro; isolated perfused rat liver; chronic hepatitis; hormone regulation of gastrointestinal function. *Mailing Add:* Dept Med State Univ NY Healty Sci Ctr 750 E Adams St Syracuse NY 13210. *Fax:* 315-464-5784

LEVINE, ROBERT JOHN, INTERNAL MEDICINE, MEDICAL ETHICS. *Current Pos:* from instr to assoc prof internal med & pharmacol, Yale Univ, 64-73, chief, Sect Clin Pharmacol, 66-74, dir, Physician's Assoc Prog, 73-75, PROF INTERNAL MED & LECTR PHARMACOL, SCH MED, YALE UNIV, 73- *Personal Data:* b New York, NY, Dec 29, 34; m 87, Jeralea F Hesse; c John G & Elizabeth H (Braun). *Educ:* George Washington Univ, MD, 58; Am Bd Internal Med, dipl, 65. *Prof Exp:* Intern internal med, Peter Bent Brigham Hosp, Boston, Mass, 58-59, asst resident, 59-60; clin assoc clin pharmacol, Nat Heart Inst, 60-62; resident internal med, Vet Admin Hosp, West Haven, Conn, 62-63; investr clin pharmacol, Nat Heart Inst, 63-64. *Concurrent Pos:* Clin asst, Yale-New Haven Hosp, 64-65, asst attend physician, 65-68, attend physician, 68-; clin investr, Vet Admin Hosp, West Haven, Conn, 64-66, attend physician, 66-; mem myocardial infarction comt, Nat Heart & Lung Inst, 69-72; ed, Clin Res, Am Fedn Clin Res, 71-76; consult, Nat Comn Protection Human Subj Biomed & Behav Res, 74-78; mem lipid metab adv comt, Nat Heart, Lung & Blood Inst, 77-79; ed, IRB: Rev Human Subjects Res, 79-; vchmn, Comn Fed Drug Approval Process, 81-82; mem, Adv Comt Acquired Immune Deficiency Syndrome Prog, US Dept Health & Human Serv, 89-95. *Mem:* Am Soc Pharmacol; Am Soc Clin Invest; fel Am Col Physicians; Am Soc Law, Med & Ethics (pres, 89-90, 94-95); fel Hastings Ctr; fel AAAS. *Res:* Writing, teaching and consulting in the field of medical ethics; concentrating on research involving human subjects; the doctor-patient relationship and care of the dying patient. *Mailing Add:* Dept Internal Med Yale Univ Sch Med New Haven CT 06520. *Fax:* 203-785-2847

LEVINE, ROBERT PAUL, GENETICS. *Current Pos:* PROF GENETICS, MED SCH, WASHINGTON UNIV, 78- *Personal Data:* b Brooklyn, NY, Dec 18, 26; m 69. *Educ:* Univ Calif, Los Angeles, AB, 49, PhD(genetics), 51. *Hon Degrees:* AM, Harvard Univ, 57. *Prof Exp:* Instr biol, Amherst Col, 51-53; from asst prof to prof, Harvard Univ, 53-78, chmn dept, 67-70. *Concurrent Pos:* NSF sr fel, 63-64. *Mem:* AAAS; Genetics Soc Am; Sigma Xi; Soc Gen Physiol; Am Soc Cell Biol. *Res:* Genetic specification of membrane structure. *Mailing Add:* Hopkins Marine Sta Oceanview Blvd Pacific Grove CA 93950

LEVINE, ROBERT S(IDNEY), FIRE RESEARCH, FIRE PROTECTION ENGINEERING. *Current Pos:* chief, Fire Res Resources Div, 74-80, SR ENGR, NAT INST SCI & TECHNOL, 80- *Personal Data:* b Des Moines, Iowa, June 4, 21; m 47, 70, Sharon White; c Michelle, James, George & Gail. *Educ:* Iowa State Col, BS, 43; Mass Inst Technol, SM, 46, ScD(chem eng), 49. *Prof Exp:* Assoc res dir, Rocketdyne Div, Rockwell Int, 49-66; chief liquid rocket res & technol, Off Advan Res & Technol, NASA, 66-74. *Concurrent Pos:* Mem subcomt combustion, Nat Adv Comt Aeronaut, 58; asst prof heat & mass transfer, Univ Calif, Los Angeles, 70-74; prof combustion, George Washington Univ, 77-78. *Mem:* Am Chem Soc; Am Inst Aeronaut & Astronaut; Nat Fire Protection Asn; Combustion Inst (vpres, 70, pres, 74-78); Soc Fire Protection Engrs. *Res:* Combustion and combustion stability in liquid rocket engines; combustion phenomena and heat transfer in liquid rocket engines; mathematical modeling of growth of unwanted fire in buildings. *Mailing Add:* 19017 Threshing Pl Gaithersburg MD 20879

LEVINE, RUTH R, PHARMACOLOGY. *Current Pos:* from asst prof to prof, Boston Univ, 58-65, Univ prof pharmacol, Sch Med, 72-96, chmn, Div Med & Dent Sci, Grad Sch, 64-69, assoc dean, Sch Med, 81-89, ASSOC DEAN & EMER PROF, BOSTON UNIV, 96- *Personal Data:* b New York, NY; m 53. *Educ:* Hunter Col, BA, 38; Columbia Univ, MA, 39; Tufts Univ, PhD(pharmacol), 55. *Prof Exp:* From instr to asst prof pharmacol, Sch Med, Tufts Univ, 55-58. *Mem:* Am Soc Pharmacol & Exp Therapeut (secy-treas, 75); Biophys Soc; Acad Pharmaceut Sci; Am Chem Soc; fel AAAS; Sigma Xi. *Res:* Pharmacokinetics mechanisms of transport of drugs across biological barriers, particularly the intestinal epithelium; biochemical, histological and physiological factors influencing intestinal absorption; environmental toxicology. *Mailing Add:* Div Med & Dent Sci Boston Univ Sch Med 80 E Concord St Boston MA 02118-2394. *Fax:* 617-638-4248

LEVINE, SAMUEL, PHYSICAL CHEMISTRY. *Current Pos:* PROF CHEM & DEAN, SAGINAW VALLEY STATE COL, 64- *Personal Data:* b Brooklyn, NY, Jan 21, 21; m 53; c 3. *Educ:* Brooklyn Col, BA, 46; Columbia Univ, MA, 52, PhD(chem), 55. *Prof Exp:* Electrochemist, Arc Anodying & Plating Co, 46-47; phys chemist thermodyn, Nat Bur Stand, 47-51, proj leader, Macromolecular Properties Unit, Northern Regional Res & Develop Div, 55-58; assoc prof chem, Western Ill Univ, 58-59; chemist, Dow Chem Co, 59-61; prof chem & dir sci, Delta Col, 61-64. *Mem:* AAAS; Am Chem Soc; Sigma Xi. *Res:* Physical chemistry of polymers; thermodynamics; kinetics. *Mailing Add:* 1604 E Canterbury Trail Mt Pleasant MI 48858-2597

LEVINE, SAMUEL GALE, ORGANIC CHEMISTRY. *Current Pos:* assoc prof, 64-68, PROF CHEM, NC STATE UNIV, 68- *Personal Data:* b Malden, Mass, Nov 1, 28; m 53, Pearl Halperin; c Cynthia, Amy, Beth & Kenneth. *Educ:* Tufts Univ, BS, 50; Harvard Univ, MA, 52, PhD(org chem), 54. *Prof Exp:* Res assoc, Forrestal Res Ctr, Princeton Univ, 53-54; res chemist, Walter Reed Army Inst Res, 54-56 & Eastern Regional Res Br, USDA, 56-60; sr chemist, Natural Prod Lab, Res Triangle Inst, 60-64. *Concurrent Pos:* Consult, Res Triangle Inst, 64-; Weizmann fel, Weizmann Inst Sci, 71-72. *Mem:* Am Chem Soc. *Res:* New methods in organic synthesis; stereochemistry and conformational analysis; structure determination and synthesis of natural products; chemical education; new experiments for undergraduate organic laboratory. *Mailing Add:* Dept Chem NC State Univ Raleigh NC 27695

LEVINE, SAMUEL HAROLD, NUCLEAR ENGINEERING & REACTOR PHYSICS, NEUTRON RADIOGRAPHY & RADIATION DETECTION. *Current Pos:* dir nuclear reactor facil, 68, prof, 68-91, EMER PROF NUCLEAR ENG, PA STATE UNIV, UNIVERSITY PARK, 91- *Personal Data:* b Hazlehurst, Ga, Nov 30, 25; m 55; c 3. *Educ:* Va Polytech Inst, BS, 47; Univ Ill, MS, 48; Univ Pittsburgh, PhD(physics), 54. *Honors & Awards:* Invention Award, NASA, 73. *Prof Exp:* Instr physics, Va Polytech Inst, 49-50; sr scientist, Bettis Atomic Power Lab, Westinghouse Elec Corp, 54-55, supv scientist, 55-57, mgr, 57-59; physicist in charge, Gen Atomic Div, Gen Dynamics Corp, 59-61; group physicist, Rocketdyne Div, NAm Aviation, Inc, 61-62; lab head nuclear sci, Northrop Space Labs, 62-68. *Concurrent Pos:* Lectr, Univ Calif, Los Angeles, 64-68; consult, Int Atomic Energy Agency, 77-, PP&L, 88- *Mem:* Am Phys Soc; fel Am Nuclear Soc. *Res:* In-core fuel management; neutron detection; experimental reactor physics; neutron radiography; nuclear reactor fuel management; dosimetry. *Mailing Add:* 231 Sackett Bldg PA State Univ University Park PA 16802

LEVINE, SAMUEL W, PHYSICAL CHEMISTRY. *Current Pos:* RETIRED. *Personal Data:* b Dallas, Tex, May 15, 16; m 44; c 1. *Educ:* Agr & Mech Col Tex, BS, 38, MS, 41; Mass Inst Technol, PhD(phys chem), 48. *Prof Exp:* Combustion engr, Lone Star Gas Co, Tex, 38-39; instr thermodyn, Agr & Mech Col Tex, 40-41; assoc chemist, Atlantic Refining Co, 48-51; dir develop labs, Fisher Sci Co, 51-53; assoc dir res & develop, Fairchild Camera & Instrument Corp, 53-55, dir res & eng, Graphic Equip Div, 55-59, dir res & eng, Defense Prod Div, 59-61, tech dir, Corp, NY, 61-70; vpres technol, Varadyne, Inc, Calif, 70-72; vpres corp develop, Datel Systs, 72-76, vpres Semi Alloys, 76-85. *Mem:* Am Chem Soc; Optical Soc Am; Inst Elec & Electronics Engrs; NY Acad Sci; fel Am Inst Chemists. *Res:* X-ray spectroscopy; emission spectroscopy; petroleum reservoir characteristics; thermodynamic properties of hydrocarbons; radar systems research and development; instrumentation physics; radioactive tracers; photogrammetry instrumentation; corporate technical management; semiconductors; integrated circuits. *Mailing Add:* 11 Melby Lane Roslyn NY 11576

LEVINE, SEYMOUR, PATHOLOGY, NEUROPATHOLOGY. *Current Pos:* EMER PROF PATH, NY MED COL, 56- *Personal Data:* b New York, NY, Mar 13, 25; m 45, Lillian Konigsberg; c Linda & Sandra. *Educ:* NY Univ, BA, 46; Chicago Med Sch, MB, 47, MD, 48. *Prof Exp:* Pathologist, St Francis Hosp, Jersey City, NJ, 56-64; pathologist & chief labs, Ctr Chronic Dis, Bird S Coler Hosp, 64-77; chief neuropath, Westchester Co Med Ctr, 77-87. *Concurrent Pos:* Consult, Vet Admin Hosp, Montrose, NY, 77-87. *Mem:* Soc Exp Biol & Med; Am Asn Neuropath (pres, 68-69). *Res:* Demyelinating diseases; mechanisms of lithium action; muscle pathology. *Mailing Add:* Nathan Kline Inst Psychiat Res 140 Old Orangeburg Rd Orangeburg NY 10962

LEVINE, SEYMOUR, VIROLOGY. *Current Pos:* from assoc prof to prof, 71-89, EMER PROF MICROBIOL, SCH MED, WAYNE STATE UNIV, 89- *Personal Data:* b Chicago, Ill, Apr 30, 22; wid; c 2. *Educ:* Univ Chicago, BS, 43; Univ Ill, MS, 45, PhD(bact), 49. *Prof Exp:* Asst bact, Med Sch, Univ Ill, 45-49; from instr to asst prof biophys, Univ Colo, 51-56; res biologist, Lederle Labs, Am Cyanamid Co, 56-65; sr res scientist, Upjohn Co, Mich, 65-71. *Concurrent Pos:* Nat Res Coun AEC fel, Univ Colo, 49-50; Case Western Res Univ, 50-51. *Mem:* Am Soc Microbiol; Tissue Cult Asn; Am Acad Microbiol; Soc Exp Biol & Med; Am Soc Virol. *Res:* Viral-host cell interactions; tissue culture; viral replication; viral interference and interferon. *Mailing Add:* 34223 Hillside Dr Paw Paw MI 49079-9555

LEVINE, SEYMOUR, BEHAVIOR. *Current Pos:* assoc prof, 62-69, PROF, STANFORD UNIV, 69- *Personal Data:* b Brooklyn, NY, Jan 23, 25; m 49, Barbara L McWilliams; c Robert T, Leslie I & Alicia M. *Educ:* Univ Denver, BA, 48; New York Univ, MA, 50, PhD(psychol), 52. *Honors & Awards:* Hoffheimer Res Award, 61; Res Career Develop Award, NIMH, 62, Res Scientist Award, 67. *Prof Exp:* Asst prof, Boston Univ, 52-53, Ohio State Univ, 56-60. *Concurrent Pos:* Dir, Biol Sci Res Training Prog, Stanford Univ, 71-, dir, Stanford Primate Facil, 76-; consult, Found Human Develop, Dublin, Ireland, 73- *Mem:* Fel Am Psychol Asn; fel AAAS; Int Soc Develop Psychobiol (pres, 75-76); Int Soc Psychoneuroendocrinol (pres, 90-93); Am Soc Primatologists; Int Primatology Soc. *Mailing Add:* Dept Psychol & Behav Sci Stanford Univ Sch Med Stanford CA 94305

LEVINE, SIMON P, PHYSICAL MEDICINE & REHABILITATION. *Current Pos:* Res assoc, Univ Mich, 78-80, sr res assoc & actg dir rehab eng, 80-83, asst prof, 83-90, DIR, REHAB ENG PROG, DEPT PHYS MED & REHAB, UNIV MICH, 83-, ASSOC PROF PHYS MED & REHAB, 90- *Personal Data:* b Los Angeles, Calif, Feb 7, 52; m, Julie A Stotesbury; c Evan M & Hannah R. *Educ:* Univ Calif, Los Angeles, BA, 73; Univ Mich, MA, 75, MS, 76, PhD(bioeng), 83. *Concurrent Pos:* Prin investr, Kenny Mich Found, 79-82 & 87-88, NIMH, 79-85, Vet Admin, 85-, Univ Space Res Asn, 86-87, Mich Consortium Enabling Technol, 88-89, Univ Mich, 91-92, NIH, 91-; proj dir, Nat Inst Occup Safety & Health, 79-81, Nat Inst Handicapped Res, 81-83 & WHO, 89-90; co-investr, Kenny Mich Found, 83-85, Univ Mich, 86-87 & 88-89, Robert Wood Johnson Found, 87-90 & Nat Inst Disability & Rehab Res, 93-; clin consult, Rehab Med Servs, Ann Arbor Vet Admin Med Ctr, 84-, Res Servs, 85-; co-chmn, Elec Stimulation Spec Interest Group, Rehab Eng Soc NAm, 86-87; chmn, Rehab Eng Comt, Inst Elec & Electronics Engrs Eng Med & Biol Soc, 86-88; consult, NIMH, 87-88; dir, Rehab Technol Servs, Univ Mich, 87- *Mem:* Rehab Eng Soc NAm; Am Cong Rehab Med; Inst Elec & Electronics Engrs; Inst Elec & Electronics Engrs Eng Med & Biol Sci; AAAS; Am Asn Univ Profs; Math Asn Am. *Res:* Computerized and robotic assistive technology systems; etiology and prevention of pressure sores; specialized needs of people with disability. *Mailing Add:* Univ Mich Med Ctr 1500 E Med Ctr Dr 1C335 Ann Arbor MI 48109-0032. *Fax:* 313-936-7515; *E-Mail:* silevine@umich.edu

LEVINE, SIMON ROCK, membrane transport phenomena, bioelectric phenomena, for more information see previous edition

LEVINE, SOLOMON LEON, ELECTRODEPOSITION. *Current Pos:* PROF, NC INST TECHNOL, 94- *Personal Data:* b Schenectady, NY, Jan 7, 40; m 60, Sheila Korkin; c Stuart, Stephen & Lisa. *Educ:* Rensselaer Polytech Inst, BS, 61; Univ RI, PhD(anal chem), 66. *Prof Exp:* Sr assoc engr, Components Div, IBM Corp, 65-66, sr assoc chemist, 66-68, staff chemist, 68-69, proj chemist, 69-72, develop chemist, 72-74, adv chemist, 74-79, sr chemist, 79-93. *Concurrent Pos:* Adj fac, Durham Tech Community Col, 94- *Mem:* Sigma Xi; Soc Electroanal Chem; Am Chem Soc. *Res:* Spectroscopy, absorption and emission; electroanalytical chemistry; electrodeposition. *Mailing Add:* 110 Skylark Way Raleigh NC 27615

LEVINE, STEPHEN ALAN, ORGANIC CHEMISTRY, INFORMATION SYSTEMS. *Current Pos:* chemist, 66-67, sr chemist, 67-73, res chemist, 73-79, SR RES CHEMIST, TEXACO RES CTR, 79- *Personal Data:* b Brooklyn, NY, Dec 24, 38; m 61; c 4. *Educ:* City Col New York, BS, 61; Purdue Univ, PhD(org chem), 66; Marist Col, MS(info systs), 87. *Prof Exp:* Res chemist, Acme Shellac Prod Co, 61. *Concurrent Pos:* Adj Prof, Marist Col, 88- *Mem:* Fel Am Inst Chem; Sigma Xi; NY Acad Sci. *Res:* Polymer chemistry; computer information system design and development; process research; lubricant additive synthesis. *Mailing Add:* 2274 Sierra Blvd Apt A Sacramento CA 95825-4710

LEVINE, STEVEN RICHARD, STROKE, ANTIPHOSPHOLIPID ANTIBODIES. *Current Pos:* Fel cerebrovascular dis, 85-87, DIR CLIN STROKE SERV & ACUTE STROKE UNIT, CTR STROKE RES, HENRY FORD HOSP, 87-; CLIN ASSOC PROF NEUROL, UNIV MICH MED SCH, 89- *Personal Data:* m 83, Joanne M Traurig; c Aaron M, David B & Aliza R. *Educ:* Univ Mich, BS, 77; Med Col Wis, MD, 81. *Honors & Awards:* Co-recipient, Harold G Wolff Award Headache Res, 89 & 91. *Concurrent Pos:* Course dir, Am Acad Neurol, 89-; prin investr, NIH-Nat Inst Neurol Dis & Stroke, 90-, Antiphospholipid Antibodies & Stroke Study, 93-; chmn, Stroke Comt, Am Heart Asn Mich, 92- *Mem:* Assoc Am Acad Neurol; fel Am Heart Asn; AMA. *Res:* Antiphospholipid antibodies and their significance in cerebrovascular disease; cocaine associated stroke; thrombolytic therapy for acute stroke; magnetic resonance in stroke. *Mailing Add:* 2799 W Grand Blvd Detroit MI 48202. *Fax:* 313-876-3014

LEVINE, SUMNER NORTON, PHYSICAL CHEMISTRY. *Current Pos:* chmn dept, 61-67, PROF MAT SCI, STATE UNIV NY STONY BROOK, 61- *Personal Data:* b Boston, Sept 5, 23; m 52; c 1. *Educ:* Brown Univ, BS, 46; Univ Wis, PhD(phys chem), 49. *Honors & Awards:* Clemson Award, Soc Biol Mats Res, 73; Dan Forth Lectureship, Am Res Col, 64. *Prof Exp:* Instr phys chem, Univ Chicago, 49-50; sr res fel, Columbia Univ, 50-54; dir res labs, US Vet Admin Hosp, East Orange, NJ, 54-56; mgr chem & physics lab, Gen Eng Labs, Am Mach & Foundry Co, 56-58; sr staff scientist, Surface Commun Div, Radio Corp Am, 58-60, head Solid State Devices & Electronics, 60-61. *Concurrent Pos:* Childs fel, Univ Chicago, 49; Runyan fel, Columbia Univ, 52; lectr, Atomic Instrument Forum, 56, Albert Einstein Med Col, 57 & Grad Div, Univ Conn, 57-58; instr, Grad Div, Brooklyn Col, 60 & City Col New York, 60; vis prof & dir urban res, Grad Ctr, City Univ New York, 67-68; ed-in-chief, Advan in Biomed Eng & Med Physics, J Socio-Econ Planning Sci & J Biomed Mat Res; NSF guest lectr, Berlin Acad Sci. *Mem:* Am Chem Soc; Electrochem Soc; Sigma Xi; sr mem Inst Elec & Electronics Engrs; Inst Mgt Sci. *Res:* Biophysical investigation of reaction mechanisms and isotopes; semiconductor physics; solid state high frequency devices; thermoelectric materials and devices; energy conversion techniques; superconductors. *Mailing Add:* PO Box 2118 Setauket NY 11733-0883

LEVINE, WALTER (GERALD), PHARMACOLOGY. *Current Pos:* from asst prof to assoc prof, 61-76, PROF PHARMACOL, ALBERT EINSTEIN COL MED, 76- *Personal Data:* b Detroit, Mich, Dec 18, 30; m 55; c 3. *Educ:* Wayne State Univ, BS, 52, MS, 54, PhD(physiol, pharmacol), 58. *Prof Exp:* Res assoc physiol & pharmacol, Wayne State Univ, 54-56 & 57-58, asst, 56-57. *Concurrent Pos:* Fel pharmacol, Albert Einstein Col Med, 58-61; USPHS career develop award. *Mem:* Am Soc Pharmacol & Exp Therapeut; NY Acad Sci; AAAS; Int Soc Study Xenobiotics. *Res:* Biochemical pharmacology; drug metabolism and disposition; regulation of the hepatic metabolism of azo dye carcinogens. *Mailing Add:* Dept Molecular Pharmacol Albert Eisnstein Col Med 1300 Morris Park Ave Bronx NY 10461-1975

LEVINE, WILLIAM SILVER, ELECTRICAL ENGINEERING. *Current Pos:* from asst prof to assoc prof, 69-81, PROF ELEC ENG, UNIV MD, COLLEGE PARK, 81- *Personal Data:* b Brooklyn, NY, Nov 19, 41; m 63; c 2. *Educ:* Mass Inst Technol, SB, 62, SM, 65, PhD(elec eng), 69. *Honors & Awards:* Distinguished Mem, Inst Elec & Electronics Engrs Control Systs Soc, 90. *Prof Exp:* Asst, Mass Inst Technol, 65-69. *Concurrent Pos:* Sr res engr, Data Technol Inc, Mass, 62-64; consult, BTS Inc, 82-; vis scientist, Nat Inst Res in Informatics & Automation, France, 85-86 & 93; vis researcher, Univ Newcastle, Australia, 89. *Mem:* Fel Inst Elec & Electronics Engrs; Soc Ind & Appl Math. *Res:* Optimal controls and systems with special emphasis on the theories of optimal feedback control and system identification and the application of this theory to biological and transportation systems. *Mailing Add:* 5546 Phelps Luck Dr Columbia MD 21045-2555. *E-Mail:* wsl@eng.umd.edu

LEVINGER, BERNARD WERNER, MATHEMATICS. *Current Pos:* ASSOC PROF MATH, COLO STATE UNIV, 68- *Personal Data:* b Berlin, Ger, Sept 3, 28; late US; m 54; c 3. *Educ:* Lehigh Univ, BS, 48; Mass Inst Technol, MS, 50; NY Univ, PhD(math), 60. *Prof Exp:* Asst metallurgist, Armour Res Found, Ill Inst Technol, 51-52; res metallurgist, Tung-Sol Elec, Inc, 52-57; res engr, Labs, Gen Tel & Electronics Corp, 57-62; asst prof math, Case Western Res Univ, 62-68. *Mem:* Am Math Soc; Math Asn Am; Soc Indust & Appl Math. *Res:* Matrix theory; numerical analysis; group theory. *Mailing Add:* Math & Statist Dept Colo State Univ Ft Collins CO 80523-0001

LEVINGER, JOSEPH S, FEW-BODY SYSTEMS. *Current Pos:* prof, 64-92, EMER PROF PHYSICS, RENSSELAER POLYTECH INST, 92- *Personal Data:* b New York, NY, Nov 14, 21; m 43, Gloria Edwards; c Sam, Laurie, Louis & Joe. *Educ:* Univ Chicago, BS, 41, MS, 44; Cornell Univ, PhD(physics), 48. *Prof Exp:* Jr physicist, Metall Lab, Univ Chicago, 42-44; physicist, Franklin Inst, 45-46; asst, 46-48, instr physics, Conell Univ, 48-51; from asst prof to prof, La State Univ, 51-61; Avco vis prof, Cornell Univ, 61-64. *Concurrent Pos:* Guggenheim fel, 57-58; Fulbright travel grant, 72-73; assoc prof, Univ Paris, 72-73. *Mem:* Fel Am Phys Soc. *Res:* Theoretical physics: specialities, the few-nucleon problem and nuclear photoeffect. *Mailing Add:* Dept Physics Rensselaer Polytech Inst Troy NY 12180. *Fax:* 518-276-6680; *E-Mail:* levinj@rpi.edu

LEVINGS, CHARLES SANDFORD, III, GENETICS. *Current Pos:* Res instr, 62-64, from asst prof to assoc prof, 64-72, prof, 72-, DISTINGUISHED UNIV & WILLIAM NEAL REYNOLDS EMER PROF GENETICS, NC STATE UNIV. *Personal Data:* b Madison, Wis, Dec 1, 30; c 4. *Educ:* Univ Ill, BS, 53, MS, 56, PhD(agron), 63. *Concurrent Pos:* Assoc ed, Current Genetics, 80-, Develop Genetics, 80-85, Maydica, 80-86, Plant Physiol, 80-87, Plant Molecular Biol, 86, Sci, 88-92. *Mem:* Nat Acad Sci; Am Genetic Asn; Genetics Soc Am; Am Soc Plant Physiologists; Am Soc Agron; AAAS; Int Soc Molecular Biol; Crop Sci Soc Am. *Res:* Autotetraploid genetics; maize biochemical genetics; higher plants; extrachromosomal inheritance; mitochondria and mitochondrial genomes; molecular genetics. *Mailing Add:* 3726 Swift Dr Raleigh NC 27606

LEVINGS, COLIN DAVID, BIOLOGICAL OCEANOGRAPHY, FISHERIES ECOLOGY. *Current Pos:* res scientist & prog head, 72-83, SECT HEAD, SCI BR, COASTAL & MARINE HABITAT SCI, 83- *Personal Data:* b Victoria, BC, May 23, 42; m 68; c 2. *Educ:* Univ BC, BSc Hons, 65, MSc, 67; Dalhousie Univ, PhD(oceanog), 72. *Prof Exp:* Field biologist technician marine fish soci, Int Pac Halibut Comn, Seattle, Wash, 62-63; scientist, Fisheries Res Bd Can, Pac Biol Sta, Nanaimo, BC, 67-68. *Concurrent Pos:* Res assoc, Dept Zool, Univ BC; vis scientist, Inst Marine Res, Bergen, Norway, 89; assoc ed, Can J Fish Aquat Sci, 89-; vis lectr, Univ Tsukuba, Japan, 90; vis scientist, Norweg Inst Nature Res, Trondheim, Norway, 92. *Mem:* Can Soc Zoologists; Pac Estuarine Res Soc (pres, 88-); Estuarine Res Fedn. *Res:* Ecology of marine and estuarine benthos; community structure at disrupted habitats; ocean dumping and dredging; coastal fish habitats and food webs; ecology of fjords; juvenile salmonid ecology; river habitats of fishes; aquaculture siting in coastal areas. *Mailing Add:* Dept Fisheries & Oceans 2645 Dollarton Hwy Pac Environ Sci Ctr North Vancouver BC V7V 1V2 Can. *Fax:* 604-924-2555; *E-Mail:* levings@mailhost c.dfo.ca

LEVINS, RICHARD, POPULATION BIOLOGY, MATHEMATICAL BIOLOGY. *Current Pos:* JOHN ROCK PROF POP SCI, SCH PUB HEALTH, HARVARD UNIV, 75- *Personal Data:* b New York, NY, June 1, 30; m 50, Rosario Morales; c Aurora, Ricardo & Alejandro. *Educ:* Cornell Univ, AB, 51; Columbia Univ, PhD(zool), 65. *Hon Degrees:* MPH, Harvard Univ, 75. *Honors & Awards:* Edinburgh Sci Medal, 96. *Prof Exp:* Res assoc pop genetics, Univ Rochester, 60-61; assoc prof biol, Univ PR, 61-66; from assoc prof to prof math biol, Univ Chicago, 67-75. *Concurrent Pos:* Farmer, 51-56; NIH res grant, 63-66; consult agr ecol prog, Cuban Acad Sci, 64-65; NSF res grant, 64-66. *Mem:* Am Acad Arts & Sci; Am Soc Naturalists; Int Soc Ecosyst Health. *Res:* Ecology and genetics; complex systems; agriculture; epidemiological ecology and evolution. *Mailing Add:* Dept Pop Sci Harvard Sch Pub Health Boston MA 02115

LEVINSKAS, GEORGE JOSEPH, TOXICOLOGY, ENVIRONMENTAL HEALTH. *Current Pos:* RETIRED. *Personal Data:* b Tariffville, Conn, July 8, 24; m 46, Ruth Hublitz; c Robert, Nancy (Armstrong) & Edward. *Educ:* Wesleyan Univ, AB, 49; Univ Rochester, PhD(pharmacol), 53; Am Bd Toxicol, dipl, 80. *Prof Exp:* Res assoc biol sci, USAEC, Univ Rochester, 52-53; dept occup health, Grad Sch Pub Health, Univ Pittsburgh, 53-54, res assoc & lectr, 54-56, asst prof appl toxicol, 56-58; res pharmacologist, Cent Med Dept, Am Cyanamid Co, 58, chief indust toxicologist & dir environ health lab, 59-71; mgr prod eval, Dept Med & Health Sci, Monsanto Co, 71, mgr environ assessment & toxicol, 72-77, dir, 78-85, sr toxicol consult, 86-91. *Mem:* Soc Toxicol; Am Chem Soc; Am Indust Hyg Asn; Environ Mutagen Soc; Am Soc Pharmacol & Exp Therapeut; fel AAAS; Sigma Xi; fel Acad Toxicol Sci (pres, 90). *Res:* Pharmacology and toxicology of boron compounds; organic phosphates; industrial chemicals; food additives; insecticides; chemistry of bone mineral. *Mailing Add:* 526 Fairways Circle Creve Coeur MO 63141-7554

LEVINSKY, NORMAN GEORGE, ANIMAL PHYSIOLOGY, NEPHROLOGY. *Current Pos:* from instr to assoc prof, Boston Univ, 60-68, Wesselhoeft prof, 68-72, wade prof med & chmn div, Sch Med, 72-97, ASSOC PROVOST, MED CAMPUS, BOSTON UNIV, 97- *Personal Data:* b Boston, Mass, Apr 27, 29; m 56, Elena Sartori; c H Robb, Andrew & Nancy (Safran). *Educ:* Harvard Univ, AB, 50, MD, 54. *Honors & Awards:* Distinguished Teacher Award, Am Col Physicians, 92. *Prof Exp:* Intern & resident med, Beth Israel Hosp, Boston, Mass, 54-56; clin assoc, Nat Heart Inst, 56-58; NIH spec fel med, Boston Univ Hosp, 58-60, dir Evans Mem Dept Clin Res, prev med & physicians-in-chief, 72-97; chief med, Boston City Hosp, 68-72 & 93-97. *Concurrent Pos:* Asst dir, Univ Med Serv, Boston City Hosp, 61-68. *Mem:* Inst Med-Nat Acad Sci; Am Soc Clin Invest; Asn Am Physicians; Am Soc Nephrol; Asn Prof Med (secy-treas, 84-87 pres, 88-89); Am Col Physicians; Am Fedn Clin Res. *Res:* Renal physiology and medical research. *Mailing Add:* 20 Kenwood Ave Newton MA 02159-1439. *Fax:* 617-638-7179

LEVINSKY, WALTER JOHN, MEDICINE. *Current Pos:* resident path, Univ Hosp, 48-49, resident internal med, 49-52, instr, Sch Med, 52-54, assoc, 54-58, from asst prof to assoc prof internal med, 58-74, CLIN PROF MED, SCH MED, TEMPLE UNIV, 74- *Personal Data:* b Meadville, Pa, Sept 16, 20; m 48; c 4. *Educ:* Allegheny Col, BS, 42; Temple Univ, MD, 45, MS, 52; Am Bd Internal Med, dipl, 54 & 74. *Prof Exp:* Intern med, Hamot Hosp, Erie, Pa, 45-46. *Concurrent Pos:* Chief dept med, Northeastern Hosp, Philadelphia, Pa, 54-58. *Mem:* Sr mem Am Fedn Clin Res; fel Am Col Physicians; fel Royal Soc Med. *Res:* Internal medicine; clinical research. *Mailing Add:* 3401 N Broad St Philadelphia PA 19140-5103

LEVINSON, ALFRED ABRAHAM, EXPLORATION GEOCHEMISTRY. *Current Pos:* PROF GEOL, UNIV CALGARY, 67- *Personal Data:* b Staten Island, NY, Mar 31, 27. *Educ:* Univ Mich, BS & MS, 49, PhD(mineral), 52. *Prof Exp:* Asst, 50-52, res assoc, Univ Mich, 52-53; asst prof mineral, Ohio State Univ, 53-56; mineralogist, Dow Chem Co, 56-62; sr res geologist, Gulf Res & Develop Co, 62-67. *Concurrent Pos:* Lectr, Univ Houston, 57-59; exec ed, Geochimica et Cosmochimica Acta, 67-70; ed, Proc Apollo 11 & Second

Lunar Sci Conf. *Mem:* Fel Mineral Soc Am; Geochem Soc; fel Geol Soc Am; Mineral Asn Can; Sigma Xi. *Res:* General mineralogy and geochemistry with industrial application; environmental geochemistry; relation of geochemistry to health; exploration geochemistry. *Mailing Add:* Dept Geol Univ Calgary Calgary AB T2N 1N4 Can

LEVINSON, ALFRED STANLEY, ORGANIC CHEMISTRY. *Current Pos:* from asst prof to prof, 63-94, EMER PROF CHEM, PORTLAND STATE UNIV, 94- *Personal Data:* b Portland, Ore, Aug 27, 32; m 58, Amy Perlstein; c Ellen E, Mark R & Rebecca Anne (deceased). *Educ:* Reed Col, BA, 54; Wesleyan Univ, MA, 57; Ind Univ, PhD(org chem), 63. *Prof Exp:* Res assoc chem, Ind Univ, 62-63. *Mem:* AAAS; Am Chem Soc. *Mailing Add:* Dept Chem Portland State Univ Box 751 Portland OR 97207. *E-Mail:* al@sbiisb2.pdx.edu

LEVINSON, ARTHUR DAVID, MOLECULAR BIOLOGY. *Current Pos:* sr scientist, Genentech, Inc, 80-83, staff scientist, 83-83, dir, Dept Cell Genetics, 87-89, vpres res technol, 89-90, vpres res technol, 90-93, sr vpres, 93-95, PRES & CHIEF EXEC OFFICER, GENENTECH, INC, 95- *Personal Data:* b Seattle, Wash, Mar 31, 50; m 78; c 2. *Educ:* Univ Wash, BS, 72; Princeton Univ, PhD(biochem), 77. *Prof Exp:* NIH predoctoral fel, 72-77; NIH res fel, Univ Calif, San Francisco, 77-78; sr res fel, Am Cancer Soc, 78-80. *Mem:* AAAS; Am Soc Microbiol; Am Soc Biochem & Molecular Biol. *Res:* Role of cellular genes in tumor development; regulation of mammalian gene expression; molecular genetics. *Mailing Add:* Genentech Inc 460 Pt San Bruno Blvd South San Francisco CA 94080

LEVINSON, BARRY L, CENTRAL NERVOUS SYSTEM DISORDERS, ENDOCRINOLOGY & FERTILITY CONTROL. *Current Pos:* scientist, 89-92, sr analyst, 92-94, MGR, PRECLIN TECHNOL DEVELOP, BERLEX LABS, INC, 94- *Personal Data:* b Camden, NJ, July 2, 55; m 81, Marcia Wagner; c Eliron & Ayiyam. *Educ:* Princeton Univ, AB, 77; Yale Univ, MPhil, 80, PhD(molecular biol, biophys & biochem), 83. *Prof Exp:* Res asst, Fox Chase Inst Cancer Res, 76-77; vis scientist, Weizmann Inst, Israel, 77-78; fel, Univ Southampton, UK, 83-85; res scientist, Ecogen Inc, 85-89, sr res scientist, 89. *Mem:* AAAS; Am Chem Soc; Am Soc Biochem & Molecular Biol; Asn Univ Technol Mgrs; NY Acad Sci. *Res:* Identify and develop new technologies and pharmaceuticals in central nervous system, autoimmune disease and female healthcare; author of 8 publications; granted 1 US patent. *Mailing Add:* Off Technol 300 Fairfield Rd Wayne NJ 07470-7358. *Fax:* 973-292-8770; *E-Mail:* barry_levinson@berlex.com

LEVINSON, CHARLES, CELL PHYSIOLOGY. *Current Pos:* assoc prof, 68-72, PROF PHYSIOL, MED SCH, UNIV TEX, SAN ANTONIO, 72- *Personal Data:* b San Antonio, Tex, Dec 31, 36; m 67; c 2. *Educ:* Univ Tex, BA, 58; Trinity Univ, MA, 60; Rutgers Univ, PhD(physiol), 64. *Prof Exp:* Nat Cancer Inst fel, Med Col, Cornell Univ, 65-66; sr cancer res scientist, Roswell Park Mem Inst, 66-68. *Mem:* Biophys Soc; Soc Gen Physiol; Am Physiol Soc; Sigma Xi. *Res:* Membrane phenomena; ion transport in tumor cells. *Mailing Add:* Dept Physiol Univ Tex Health Sci Ctr 7703 Floyd Curl Dr San Antonio TX 78284-7756

LEVINSON, DAVID ALAN, SPACECRAFT ATTITUDE DYNAMICS, DYNAMICS OF MULTIBODY SYSTEMS. *Current Pos:* Sr assoc scientist, Lockheed Missiles & Space Co, 77-79, scientist, 79-82, sr scientist, 82-85, res scientist, 85-89, staff scientist, 89-91, staff engr, 91-96, STAFF AEROSPACE ENGR, ADVAN TECHNOL CTR, LOCKHEED MARTIN MISSILES & SPACE, 96- *Personal Data:* b Meadville, Pa, Apr 6, 50. *Educ:* Cornell Univ, BS, 72; Stanford Univ, MS, 73. *Honors & Awards:* Outstanding Young Engr Award, Am Inst Aeronaut & Astronaut, 84; Engr Yr Award, 89 & 97; Outstanding Achievement Award, Am Astronaut Soc, 85; Distinguished Mech Engr Award, Am Soc Mech Engrs, 89. *Concurrent Pos:* Lectr dynamics & spacecraft dynamics, Dept Mech Eng, Stanford Univ, 81, 84, 88 & 93-94; mem, Astrodyn Tech Comt, Am Inst Aeronaut & Astronaut, 81-84, Astrodyn Tech Comt Stand, 92-94; managing ed, J Astronaut Sci, 83-85; chmn, Discover "E" Eng Outreach Prog, Silicon Valley Eng Coun, 93-94. *Mem:* Fel Am Astronaut Soc; fel Am Soc Mech Engrs; assoc fel Am Inst Aeronaut & Astronaut; Am Acad Mech. *Res:* Apply computerized symbol manipulation to the formulation of exact, explicit equations of motion of complex multibody systems, such as spacecraft, mechanisms and robots. *Mailing Add:* 3375 Alma St No 172 Palo Alto CA 94304-1121

LEVINSON, DAVID W, PHYSICAL METALLURGY, FAILURE ANALYSIS. *Current Pos:* assoc head, Dept Mat Eng, Univ Ill, Chicago Circle, 64-67, actg dean col eng, 67-69, prof, 64-87, EMER PROF METALL, UNIV ILL, CHICAGO CIRCLE, 87- *Personal Data:* b Chicago, Ill, Feb 24, 25; m 49, Betty Sachnoff; c Louis E, Joseph P & Jeanne L. *Educ:* Ill Inst Technol, BS, 48, MS, 49, PhD(metall eng), 53. *Prof Exp:* Res metallurgist, Armour Res Found, 53-57, supvr non-ferrous metall res, 57-59, asst dir metals res, 59-62, sci adv, Metals & Ceramics Div, IIT Res Inst, 62-64. *Concurrent Pos:* Consult, Triodyne Inc, 87-; adj prof, Univ Ariz, Tucson, 90- *Mem:* Am Soc Mat Int; Am Inst Mining, Metall & Petrol Engrs; Am Soc Eng Educ; Sigma Xi. *Res:* High temperature alloy development; coatings for thermal control of surfaces; metallurgical transformations in alloys in thin film form; binary and ternary phase equilibria in metallic systems; stress relaxation in high carbon steels, fatigue and fracture toughness of resulfurized steels. *Mailing Add:* Dept Mat Sci & Eng Univ Ariz Tucson AZ 85712. *Fax:* 520-621-8059; *E-Mail:* mandm13@juno.com

LEVINSON, GILBERT E, MEDICINE, CARDIOLOGY. *Current Pos:* CHIEF MED, ST VINCENT HOSP, WORCESTER, MASS, 76-85 & 91-; PROF MED, MED SCH, UNIV MASS, 76- *Personal Data:* b New York, NY, Jan 25, 28; m 50, Sally Stone; c Nancy & Alex. *Educ:* Yale Univ, AB, 48; Harvard Med Sch, MD, 53. *Prof Exp:* Intern med, Harvard Med Serv, Boston City Hosp, 53-54, asst resident, 54-55, chief resident, Thorndike Mem Ward, 58-59; from asst prof to prof med, Univ Med & Dent NJ, NJ Med Sch, 59-76; chief med, Worcester City Hosp, 85-91. *Concurrent Pos:* Teaching fel, Harvard Med Sch, 54-55; Nat Heart Inst res fel, Thorndike Mem Lab, Boston City Hosp, 57-59; Nat Heart & Lung Inst res career develop award, 67-70; assoc dir, T J White Cardiopulmonary Inst, B S Pollak Hosp, Jersey City, NJ, 61-71; consult, USPHS Hosp, Staten Island, NY, 63-; estab investr, Union Co Heart Asn, NJ, 61-66 & 70-75. *Mem:* Am Fedn Clin Res; fel Am Col Cardiol; Am Physiol Soc; Am Soc Clin Invest; fel Am Col Physicians. *Res:* Hemodynamics in valvular heart disease; indicator-dilution theory and methodology; cardiopulmonary blood volumes; relations between myocardial performance and metabolism. *Mailing Add:* Dept Med Univ Ma Med Sch St Vincent Hosp 15 Westwood Dr Worcester MA 01609-1245. *Fax:* 508-798-1798

LEVINSON, HERBERT S, TRANSPORTATION. *Current Pos:* PRIN, HERBERT S LEVINSON, TRANSP CONSULT, 80- *Personal Data:* b Sept 25, 24; m 77, Sally Farver. *Educ:* Ill Inst Technol, BS, 49. *Honors & Awards:* Presidential Design Award; Theordore M Matson Award, Inst Transp Engrs. *Prof Exp:* Jr traffic engr, Chicago Park Dist, 49-51; from assoc, prin assoc & vpres to sr vpres, Wilbur Smith & Assoc, 52-80. *Concurrent Pos:* Vis lectr city planning, Yale Univ, 61-80; prof civil eng, Univ Ct, 80-86; prof transp eng, Polytech Univ, 86-88, res prof, 88-90. *Mem:* Nat Acad Eng; Am Soc Civil Engrs; Inst Transp Engrs; Am Inst Planners; Transp Res Bd. *Res:* Public transportation; transportation, engineering and planning; parking; transportation policy. *Mailing Add:* 40 Hemlock Rd New Haven CT 06515

LEVINSON, LIONEL MONTY, ELECTRONIC MATERIALS, CERAMIC ENGINEERING. *Current Pos:* MGR, ELECTRONIC & OPTICAL MAT, GE CORP RES, 80- *Personal Data:* b Johannesburg, SAfrica, Mar 12, 43. *Educ:* Univ Witwatersrand, BSc, 65, MSc, 66; Weizmann Inst Sci, PhD(solid state physics), 70. *Honors & Awards:* IR 100 Award; Dashman Award. *Prof Exp:* Physicist, Gen Elec Corp Res & Develop, 70-79. *Mem:* Nat Res Soc; fel, Am Ceramic Soc (vpres). *Res:* Electronic ceramics; varistors; electronic packaging; thermoelectrics transparent ceramics; current limiters; voltage limiters; scintillators; phyosphors. *Mailing Add:* One Linda Lane Schenectady NY 12309. *Fax:* 518-387-6204; *E-Mail:* levinson@crd.ge.com

LEVINSON, MARK, HISTORY OF TECHNOLOGY, MECHANICS. *Current Pos:* PVT RES. *Personal Data:* b Brooklyn, NY, June 12, 29; m 53, Suzanne Josephson; c 2. *Educ:* Polytech Inst Brooklyn, BAeroE, 51, MS, 60; Calif Inst Technol, PhD, 64. *Prof Exp:* Asst appl mech, Polytech Inst Brooklyn, 51-52, instr math, 56, sr asst appl mech, 59; stress analyst, Foster-Wheeler Corp, 57-58; asst prof mech eng, Ore State Col, 60-61; assoc prof, Clarkson Col Technol, 64-66; assoc prof theoret & appl mech, WVa Univ, 66-67; prof eng mech, McMaster Univ, 67-80; A O Willey prof mech eng, Univ Maine, Orono, 80-85, dir, Technol & Soc Proj, 85-90. *Concurrent Pos:* A W Mellon fel, 84-85; sr fel, NSF, 88-89; vis prof aeronaut & astronaut, Univ Wash, 91- *Mem:* AAAS; Am Soc Mech Engrs; Am Inst Aeronaut & Astronaut; Soc Indust & Appl Math; Soc Hist Technol. *Res:* Theory of elasticity; continuum mechanics; elastic stability; structural dynamics; theory of plates; history of early aviation. *Mailing Add:* 630 Giltner Lane Edmonds WA 98020

LEVINSON, RACHEL E, BIOCHEMISTRY, SCIENCE POLICY. *Current Pos:* ASST DIR, LIFE SCI, OFFICE SCI & TECHNOL POLICY, 93- *Personal Data:* b Hornell, NY, Apr 16, 52. *Educ:* Univ Md, BS, 75; George Washington Univ, MA, 85. *Mem:* AAAS. *Mailing Add:* Off Sci & Technol Policy Old Exec Off Bldg NW Rm 436 Washington DC 20502

LEVINSON, SIDNEY BERNARD, CHEMISTRY, CHEMICAL ENGINEERING. *Current Pos:* OWNER, SIDLEV ASSOCS, 83- *Personal Data:* b Russia, July 4, 11; nat US; m 65; c 2. *Educ:* City Col New York, BS(chem) & BS(eng), 32, Chem Engr, 33. *Honors & Awards:* PaVaC Award & lectr; Roy H Kienle Award, NY Soc Coating Technol. *Prof Exp:* Consult, Protective Coatings, Joachim Res Labs, 33-36; pres, Indust Consult Labs, 36-42; vpres & tech dir, Adco Chem Co, 42-48; supt & tech dir, Garland Co, 48-52; vpres & tech dir, D H Litter Co, 52-73, pres, David Litter Labs, Inc, DBA D/L Labs, 74-83. *Concurrent Pos:* dir, Artists Tech Res Inst, 65-74. *Mem:* Am Chem Soc; hon mem, Am Soc Testing & Mat; Nat Asn Corrosion Engrs; Fedn Socs Coatings Technol. *Res:* Protective coatings; thermosetting and reinforced plastics, sealants and allied products; evaluation of raw materials; formulation; testing of finished products; certification; preparation of specifications and manuals, personnel training, industry surveys, investigation of failures and legal assistance. *Mailing Add:* 20B John Adams St Cranbury NJ 08512-4605

LEVINSON, STANLEY S, PATHOLOGY. *Current Pos:* DIR CLIN CHEM & IMMUNOL, LAB SERV, VET ADMIN MED CTR, UNIV LOUISVILLE, 89-, ASST PROF, DEPT PATH, 89- *Personal Data:* m; c 3. *Educ:* Boston Univ, BA, 64; Univ Calif, MS, 67, PhD(physiol), 70; Am Bd Clin Chem, cert. *Prof Exp:* Res assoc, Dept Nutrit, Mass Inst Technol, 70-73; res fel med, Clin Chem Lab, Mass Gen Hosp, 73-74; adj asst prof, Dept Path & assoc, Dept Biochem, Sch Med, Wayne State Univ, 81-86, adj assoc prof, Dept Path & assoc, Dept Biochem, 88-89. *Concurrent Pos:* Lectr clin chem, Grad Sch Pharm & Health, Northeastern Univ, 78-80; dir clin lab, Joslin Found Diabetic Unit, Brookline Hosp, 74-80. *Mem:* Am Asn Immunol; Nat

Acad Clin Biochem; Clin Ligand Assay Soc; AAAS; Am Asn Clin Chem; Soc Complex Carbohydrates. *Res:* Methods of assay of antigens via immunochemical techniques; methods of assaying circulating immune complexes, rheumatoid factors and idiotypic antibodies; regulation of the immune response through molecules that stimulate and inhibit the synthesis of circulating immune complexes and rheumatoid factors by affecting lymphocytes; clinical correlates with measurement of circulating immune complexes and complement function tests; testing for apolipoproteins and clinical studies related to lipid metabolism as risk factors for cardiovascular disease; numerous publications. *Mailing Add:* Dept Path Va Med Ctr Univ Louisville Sch Med Louisville KY 40292

LEVINSON, STEPHEN, SPEECH PROCESSING, AUTOMATIC SPEECH. *Current Pos:* ELEC ENGR, BELL LAB, 76- *Personal Data:* b New York, NY, Sept 27, 44; m 76, Diana E Sheets. *Educ:* Harvard Univ, BA, 66; Univ RI, MS, 72, PhD(elec eng), 74. *Prof Exp:* Instr comput sci, Yale Univ, 74-76. *Mem:* Fel Inst Elec & Electronics Engrs; fel Acoust Soc Am. *Mailing Add:* Ling Res Dept 2D-446 Bell Lab 600 Mountain Ave Murray Hill NJ 07974

LEVINSON, STEVEN R, ANALYTICAL CHEMISTRY, PHOTOGRAPHY. *Current Pos:* SR RES CHEMIST, PHOTOG RES DIV, KODAK RES LABS, EASTMAN KODAK CO, 73- *Personal Data:* b Brooklyn, NY, Oct 13, 47. *Educ:* Rensselaer Polytech Inst, BS, 68, PhD(anal chem), 73. *Concurrent Pos:* Instr, Rochester Inst Technol, 76- *Mem:* Am Chem Soc; Sigma Xi; Soc Photog Scientists & Engrs. *Res:* Research and development of photographic materials. *Mailing Add:* 102 Mountain Rd Rochester NY 14625-1819

LEVINSON, STUART ALAN, PALEONTOLOGY, GEOLOGY. *Current Pos:* PRES, MICROCOMPUT SERV, INC. *Personal Data:* b Detroit, Mich, Oct 29, 20; m 47; c 3. *Educ:* Wayne State Univ, BS, 47; Wash Univ, AM, 49, PhD(geol), 51. *Prof Exp:* Asst geol, Wash Univ, 47-51; sr geologist, Humble Oil & Refining Co, 51-64; res supvr, Esso Prod Res Co, 64-66, res assoc, 66-90. *Concurrent Pos:* Instr, Wash Univ, 50-51. *Mem:* AAAS; Paleont Soc; Soc Econ Paleontologists & Mineralogists (vpres, 57); Geol Soc Am; Am Asn Petrol Geologists. *Res:* Invertebrate paleontology, micropaleontology and zoology. *Mailing Add:* 5050 Woodway Dr No 5G Houston TX 77056-0806

LEVINSON, WARREN E, MICROBIOLOGY, IMMUNOLOGY. *Current Pos:* Assoc prof, 65-70, PROF MICROBIOL, MED CTR, UNIV CALIF, SAN FRANCISCO, 70- *Personal Data:* b Brooklyn, NY, Sept 28, 33; m 65, Barbara Boykin. *Educ:* Cornell Univ, BS, 53; Univ Buffalo, MD, 57; Univ Calif, Berkeley, PhD(virol), 65. *Concurrent Pos:* Am Cancer Soc fel tumor viruses, Univ Col, Univ London, 65-67; R W Johnson Health Policy fel, 80-81. *Res:* Tumor viruses. *Mailing Add:* Dept Microbiol Univ Calif Med Ctr San Francisco CA 94143

LEVINTHAL, CHARLES F, NEUROSCIENCES. *Current Pos:* From asst prof to assoc prof, 71-87, PROF PSYCHOL, HOFSTRA UNIV, 87- *Personal Data:* b Cincinnati, Ohio, July 6, 45; m 73; c 2. *Educ:* Univ Cincinnati, AB, 67; Univ Mich, MA, 68, PhD(exp psychol), 71. *Mem:* Am Psychol Asn; Soc Neuroscience; Soc Psychophysiol Res; NY Acad Sci. *Res:* Studies of hemisphere specialization among bilingual individuals. *Mailing Add:* Dept Psychol Hofstra Univ 1000 Fulton Ave Hempstead NY 11550-1091

LEVINTHAL, ELLIOTT CHARLES, PHYSICS. *Current Pos:* prof & assoc dean res, 83-90, EMER PROF MECH ENG, SCH ENG, STANFORD UNIV, 91- *Personal Data:* b Brooklyn, NY, Apr 13, 22; m 44, Rhoda Arons; c David, Judith, Michael & Daniel. *Educ:* Columbia Univ, BA, 42; Mass Inst Technol, MS, 43; Stanford Univ, PhD(physics), 49. *Prof Exp:* Proj engr, Sperry Gyroscope Co, NY, 43-46; res assoc nuclear physics, Stanford Univ, 46-48; res physicist, Varian Assocs, 49-50, res dir, 50-52; chief engr, Century Electronics & Instruments, Inc, 52-53; pres, Levinthal Electronic Prod, Inc, 53-61; assoc dean res affairs, Sch Med, Stanford Univ, 71-74, dir Instrumentation Res Lab, 61-81, adj prof genetics, Sch Med 74-80; dir, defense sci off, Defense Advan Res Agency, Dept Defense, 81-83; dir, Sch Eng, Inst Mfg & Automation, 83-90. *Concurrent Pos:* Co-investr, Mariner Mars Photo Interpretation Team, 70; prin investr & dep team leader, Viking Lunar Imaging Sci Team, 75. *Mem:* AAAS; fel Am Phys Soc; sr mem Inst Elec & Electronics Eng; Optical Soc Am; Biomed Eng Soc; Sigma Xi. *Res:* Measurements of nuclear moments; applications of computers to image processing and medical instrumentation; exobiology and planetary sciences; manufacturing and automation systems. *Mailing Add:* 59 Sutherland Dr Atherton CA 94027-6430. *Fax:* 650-723-6792

LEVINTHAL, MARK, MICROBIAL GENETICS, MOLECULAR EVOLUTION. *Current Pos:* ASSOC PROF BIOL, PURDUE UNIV, 72- *Personal Data:* b Brooklyn, NY, Mar 3, 41; m 62, 90, Donna Osborn; c Peter S & Sarita. *Educ:* Brooklyn Col, BS, 62; Brandeis Univ, PhD(biol), 66. *Prof Exp:* Fel genetics, Johns Hopkins Univ, 66-68; staff fel genetics lab molecular biol, Nat Inst Arthritis & Metal Dis, 68-72. *Concurrent Pos:* NIH fel, 66-68 & 72-77. *Mem:* Am Soc Microbiol; Sigma Xi; Genetics Soc Am; AAAS; Italian Molecular Biol Soc; Soc Study Evolution. *Res:* Regulation of enzyme synthesis of biosynthetic pathways and its relationship to general metabolic controls in bacteria; regulatory mechanisms-their evolution and contribution to general evolutionary theory. *Mailing Add:* Dept Biol Sci Purdue Univ West Lafayette IN 47907. *Fax:* 765-474-0876; *E-Mail:* marklev@bilbo.bio.purdue.edu

LEVINTON, JEFFREY SHELDON, ECOLOGY, PALEONTOLOGY. *Current Pos:* From instr to assoc prof paleoecol, 70-83, PROF ECOL & EVOLUTION, STATE UNIV NY, STONY BROOK, 83- *Personal Data:* b New York, NY, Mar 20, 46; m 79, Joan Miyazski; c 2. *Educ:* City Col New York, BS, 66; Yale Univ, MPhil, 69, PhD(paleoecol), 71. *Concurrent Pos:* State Univ NY, Stony Brook Res Found fel & grant-in-aid, 71; managing ed, Am Naturalist, 74-75; vis prof, Uppsala Univ, Sweden, 81 & Univ Cambridge, 84; Guggenheim fel, 84-85; chmn, Dept Ecol & Evolution, Univ Wash, 85-93, vis prof, 90-91; chmn, Panel Hudson River Found, 86-90, assoc ed Ecol, 86-89, assoc ed Ecol Appln, 90-93. *Mem:* Ecol Soc Am; Am Soc Naturalists; Soc Study Evolution; AAAS. *Res:* Marine benthic ecology; paleoecology; fossil population dynamics; benthic deposit feeder-detritus-microbial interactions; evolutionary biology of marine invertebrates. *Mailing Add:* Friday Harbor Labs 620 University Rd Friday Harbor WA 98250. *Fax:* 516-632-7626; *E-Mail:* levinton@sbbiovm.sunysb.edu

LEVINTOW, LEON, BIOCHEMISTRY, VIROLOGY. *Current Pos:* PROF MICROBIOL, SCH MED, UNIV CALIF, SAN FRANCISCO, 65-, CHMN, DEPT MICROBIOL & IMMUNOL, 80- *Personal Data:* b Philadelphia, Pa, Nov 10, 21; m 46; c 4. *Educ:* Haverford Col, AB, 43; Jefferson Med Col, MD, 46. *Prof Exp:* Intern, Jefferson Hosp, Philadelphia, Pa, 46-47; chief of lab, US Army Hepatitis Res Ctr, Ger, 47-49; biochemist, Nat Cancer Inst, 49-56, asst chief lab cell biol, Nat Inst Allergy & Infectious Dis, 56-61, asst chief lab biol viruses, 61-65. *Concurrent Pos:* Res fel, Biochem Res Lab, Mass Gen Hosp, Boston, 51-52. *Mem:* Am Soc Microbiol; Am Chem Soc; Am Soc Biol Chemists. *Res:* Biochemistry of viruses. *Mailing Add:* Dept Microbiol & Immunol Univ Calif Sch Med Rm HSW 1542 Box 0552 San Francisco CA 94143-0552

LEVIS, ALEXANDER HENRY, COMMAND & CONTROL. *Current Pos:* PROF ELEC, COMPUTER & SYST ENG, GEORGE MASON UNIV, 90-, CHAIR, SYSTS ENG DEPT, 92- *Personal Data:* b Yannina, Greece, Oct 3, 40; wid; c Livia & Philip. *Educ:* Ripon Col, BA, 63; Mass Inst Technol, BS & MS, 65, ME, 67, ScD(mech eng), 68. *Prof Exp:* Res asst control systs, Eng Projs Lab, Mass Inst Technol, 63-65, res asst, Electronics Systs Lab, 65-68; from asst prof to assoc prof elec eng, Polytech Inst NY, 68-74; sr engr, Systs Control Inc, 73-76, dept mgr, 76-81; sr res scientist, Mass Inst Technol, 79-91. *Concurrent Pos:* Engr, Christina Lab, E I du Pont de Nemours & Co, Inc, 65; dir, Am Automatic Control Coun, 86-87; consult, Sweet Assocs Ltd, 86-91, Control Syst Soc, Inst Elec & Electronics Engrs, 87, distinguished mem, 87. *Mem:* Fel Inst Elec & Electronics Engrs; fel AAAS; Sigma Xi; Am Inst Aeronaut & Astronaut; distinguished mem Control Systs Soc; Armed Forces Commun & Electronics Asn. *Res:* Mathematical organization theory, distributed intelligence systems, command and control. *Mailing Add:* 10607 Springvale Ct Great Falls VA 22066. *E-Mail:* alevis@gmu.edu

LEVIS, C(URT) A(LBERT), RADIOWAVE PROPAGATION & ANTENNAS. *Current Pos:* res assoc, Antenna Lab, Ohio State Univ, 50-56, assoc supvr, 56-61, from asst prof to prof elec eng, 56-85, dir, Antenna Lab, 61-69, EMER PROF, OHIO STATE UNIV, 85- *Personal Data:* b Ger, Apr 16, 26; nat US; m 58, Katharine Slaven; c Alan P, Linda K (Volkovitsch) & Susan I (Groseclose). *Educ:* Case Inst Technol, BS, 49; Harvard Univ, AM, 50; Ohio State Univ, PhD(elec eng), 56. *Prof Exp:* Studio engr, Radio Sta WSRS, Inc, 48-49. *Concurrent Pos:* Sr fel, Nat Ctr Atmospheric Res, 76-77; guest vis, Inst Telecommun Sci, 85-86. *Mem:* Fel Inst Elec & Electronics Engrs. *Res:* Radiowave propagation; antennas; electromagnetic theory; satellite communications. *Mailing Add:* Dept Elec Eng Ohio State Univ 2015 Neil Ave Columbus OH 43210-1272. *Fax:* 614-292-7596; *E-Mail:* levis.i@osu.edu

LEVIS, DONALD J, CLINICAL PSYCHOLOGY, BEHAVIORAL THERAPY. *Current Pos:* from asst prof to assoc prof clin psychol, 65-72, PROF CLIN PSYCHOL, STATE UNIV NY, BINGHAMTON, 72- *Personal Data:* b Cleveland, Ohio, Sept 19, 36; c 2. *Educ:* John Carroll Univ, BSS, 58; Kent State Univ, MA, 60; Emory Univ, PhD(psychol), 64. *Prof Exp:* USPHS fel clin psychol, Lafayette Clin, Detroit, 64-65, res psychologist psychobiol, 65-66. *Concurrent Pos:* Lectr, Emory Univ, 63-64; adj asst prof, Wayne State Univ, 65-66; dir res & training clin, Univ Iowa, 70-72; dir & developer clin psychol training prog, State Univ NY, Binghamton, 72-81, dir & developer psychol res & training clin, 73-76; adj prof, Col Med, Upstate Med Ctr, Syracuse, 79- *Mem:* Fel Am Psychol Asn; Psychonomic Soc; Asn Advan Behavior Ther; Soc Psychophysiol Res; Sigma Xi. *Res:* Developing the theoretical model and applied therapeutic behavioral technique of implosive (flooding) therapy; decoding of traumatic memories motivating psychopathology; author of over 80 scientific articles. *Mailing Add:* Psychol Dept Binghamton Univ Box 6000 Binghamton NY 13902-0600

LEVIS, WILLIAM WALTER, JR, ORGANIC CHEMISTRY. *Current Pos:* RETIRED. *Personal Data:* b Chicago, Ill, May 14, 18; m 41; c 2. *Educ:* Univ Fla, BS, 41. *Prof Exp:* Res chemist, Fla Chem Indust, 41-42; sr res chemist, Sharples Chem, Inc, 42-52; sr res chemist, BASF Wyandotte Corp, 52-55, sect head, 55-56, res supvr, 56-84, sr res assoc, 84-86. *Mem:* Am Chem Soc. *Res:* Organic synthesis; catalysis; hydrogenation; amination; oxyalkyation. *Mailing Add:* 2069 SE 37th Ct Circle Ocala FL 34471

LEVI-SETTI, RICCARDO, ION MICROSCOPY, SECONDARY ION MASS SPECTROMETRY. *Current Pos:* asst prof, 57-62, assoc prof, 62-65, PROF PHYSICS, UNIV CHICAGO, 65-, DIR, ENRICO FERMI INST, 92- *Personal Data:* b Milan, Itlay, July 11, 27; m 59, 77, Nike Semkoff; c Emile & Matteo. *Educ:* Univ Pavia, Dr(physics), 49; Univ Rome, Libera Docenza(physics), 55. *Prof Exp:* Asst prof, Univ Pavia, Italy, 49-51 & Univ Milan, 57-64. *Concurrent Pos:* Angelo della Riccia fel, Ital Phys Soc, 54; res mem, Nat Inst Nuclear Res, Univ Milan, 51-56; res assoc, Enrico Fermi Inst, Univ Chicago, 56-57; John Simon Guggenheim fel, Europ Orgn Nuclear Res, Geneva, 63; hon res assoc, Field Mus Natural Hist, Chicago, 76. *Mem:* Fel Am Phys Soc. *Res:* Imaging microanalysis of material by secondary ion mass spectrometry at high lateral resolution; studies of metal alloys, ceramics, minerals, biomaterials; development of new microanalytical instrumentatiom. *Mailing Add:* Enrico Fermi Inst 5640 S Ellis Ave Chicago IL 60637-1433

LEVISON, MATTHEW EDMUND, MEDICAL SCIENCE, HEALTH SCIENCES. *Current Pos:* from asst prof to assoc prof med & chief, 70-77, prof med & chief infectious dis div, Med Col Pa, 77-95, PROF MED & CHIEF INFECTIOUS DIS DIV, ALLEGHANY UNIV HEALTH SCI, MCP HAHEMANN SCH MED, 95- *Personal Data:* b New York, NY, May 18, 37; m 66, Sandra Peltz; c Daniel P & Julie H. *Educ:* Columbia Univ, BA, 58; State Univ NY, MD, 62. *Prof Exp:* Asst instr med, Downstate Med Ctr, State Univ NY, 65-67; asst physician, NY Hosp, 67-69; instr, Med Col, Cornell Univ, 68-69; instr, Downstate Med Ctr, State Univ, NY, 69-70. *Concurrent Pos:* Attend physician & chief infectious dis unit, Queens Hosp Ctr, Long Island Jewish Med Ctr affil, 69-70; attend staff, Philadelphia Vet Admin Hosp, 70- *Mem:* Am Soc Microbiol; Am Fedn Clin Res; Infectious Dis Soc Am; fel Am Col Clin Pharmacol; fel Am Col Physicians; Soc Healthcare Epidemiol Am. *Res:* Anaerobic bacteria, the pathogenesis of the renal concentrating defect in experimental pyelonephritis and the pathogenesis of experimental endocarditis; antimicrobial pharmacodynamics. *Mailing Add:* Allegheny Univ Health Sci MCP Hahnemann Sch Med 3300 Henry Ave Philadelphia PA 19129

LEVISON, SANDRA PELTZ, NEPHROLOGY. *Current Pos:* from instr to assoc prof med, Med Col Pa, 70-81, dir, Hypertension Ctr, 74, Nephrology Fel Training Prog, 76 & Hemodialysis Serv, 78, chief hypertension, renal & dialysis, 78, PROF MED, MED COL PA, 81-, ASSOC CHAIR, DEPT MED, DIR WOMEN'S HEALTH EDUC PROG. *Personal Data:* b New York, NY, Apr 20, 41; m 66; c 2. *Educ:* Hunter Col, NY, BA, 61; NY Univ, MD, 65. *Prof Exp:* Asst instr med, State Univ NY, Downstate, 66-67 & 68-70; asst instr med, Med Ctr, NY Univ, 67-68. *Concurrent Pos:* Bd mem, Am Diabetes Asn; consult, Food & Drug Admin; co-chair, Nat Acad Women's Health Med Educ; chief, Div Nephrology, Hahnenann Univ & MCP Hosps; clin serv chief, Dept Med, MCP Hosps. *Mem:* Am Soc Nephrology; Int Soc Nephrology; fel Am Col Physicians. *Res:* Elucidation of the renal concentrating defect in experimental infective Pyelonephritis; effects of exercise on blood pressure of adolescents; comparing blood pressures in infants and children of toxemic, hypertensive and normal mothers; geriatric renal disease; women's health. *Mailing Add:* Med Col Pa 3300 Henry Ave Philadelphia PA 19129

LEVISON, WILLIAM H(ENRY), ENGINEERING PSYCHOLOGY, MAN-MACHINE SYSTEMS. *Current Pos:* CONSULT, 96- *Personal Data:* b Cincinnati, Ohio, Mar 21, 36; m 66, Helen Hanessian; c Jeffrey W & Carl H. *Educ:* Mass Inst Technol, BS, 58, MS, 60, ScD, 64. *Prof Exp:* Sr scientist, Bolt Beranek & Newman Inc, 64-88, div scientist, BBN Corp, 88-96. *Mem:* Inst Elec & Electronics Engrs; Transp Res Bd; Human Factors & Ergonomics Soc. *Res:* Modeling and measurement of human operator performance. *Mailing Add:* 19 Phinney Rd Lexington MA 02173. *E-Mail:* levinson@tiac.net

LEVIT, EDITHE J, MEDICINE, MEDICAL ADMINISTRATION. *Current Pos:* asst dir, 61-67, secy & assoc dir, 67-75, vpres & secy, 75-77, pres & chief exec officer, 77-86, EMER PRES & LIFE MEM BD, NAT BD MED EXAMR, 87- *Personal Data:* b Wilkes-Barre, Pa, Nov 29, 26; m 52; c 2. *Educ:* Bucknell Univ, BS, 46; Woman's Med Col Pa, MD, 51. *Hon Degrees:* DMS, Med Col Pa, 78; DSc, Wilkes Univ, 90. *Honors & Awards:* Commonwealth Comt of Woman's Med Col Award, 70; Distinguished Serv Award, Fedn State Med Bds, 87. *Prof Exp:* Intern med, Philadelphia Gen Hosp, 51-52, fel endocrinol, 52-53, clin instr, 53-57, dir med educ, 57-61. *Concurrent Pos:* Bd dirs, Philadelphia Elec Co, 80-, Germantown Savings Bank, Philadelphia, 79-; consult, women in med, Josiah Macy Jr Found, 66-76, Comt Pract Fed Ct, US Judiciary, 77, Off Technol Assessment, US Cong, 78-79; mem sci coun, Nat Lib Med Bd, 81-, adv coun Inst Nuclear Power Opers, Atlanta, 88- *Mem:* Inst Med-Nat Acad Sci; AMA; master Am Col Physicians; Asn Am Med Cols. *Res:* Evaluation of professional competence in medicine. *Mailing Add:* 210W Rittenhouse Sq Philadelphia PA 19103

LEVIT, LAWRENCE BRUCE, PHYSICS. *Current Pos:* MKT MGR, DIV HIGH ENERGY PHYSICS, LECROY RES SYST CORP, 74- *Personal Data:* b Cleveland, Ohio, Sept 24, 42; m 67; c 1. *Educ:* Case Western Res Univ, BS, 64, PhD(physics), 71. *Prof Exp:* Res assoc physics, Case Western Res Univ, 66-69; asst prof, La State Univ, Baton Rouge, 69-74. *Mem:* Am Phys Soc; Am Inst Physics. *Res:* Ultrahigh energy physics research using cosmic rays as a particle source. *Mailing Add:* Jandel Sci 2591 Kerner Blvd San Rafael CA 94901

LEVIT, ROBERT JULES, LOGIC, COMPUTER SCIENCE. *Current Pos:* from asst prof to prof, 57-72, EMER PROF MATH, SAN FRANCISCO STATE UNIV, 72- *Personal Data:* b San Francisco, Calif, Aug 17, 16; m 43, 55, Jean Bernasconi; c Linga Manette, Arthur Frank & Miles Theodore. *Educ:* Calif Inst Technol, BS, 38, MS, 39; Univ Calif, PhD(math), 41. *Prof Exp:* Instr math, Univ Calif, 40-41; from asst prof to assoc prof, Univ Ga, 46-53; vis asst prof, Mass Inst Technol, 54-55; mem staff, Appl Sci Div, Int Bus Mach Corp, 55-57. *Mem:* Am Math Soc; Math Asn Am; Asn Symbolic Logic. *Res:* Foundations of mathematics; algebra; number theory, analysis. *Mailing Add:* 100 Bay Pl No 1902 Oakland CA 94610

LEVITAN, ALEXANDER ALLEN, MEDICAL ONCOLOGY, MEDICAL HYPNOSIS. *Current Pos:* PVT PRACT, INTERNAL MED & ONCOL, MINNEAPOLIS & FRIDLEY, MINN. *Personal Data:* b Boston, Mass, Oct 19, 39; m 67, Lucy K Albree; c Lara, Denise & Karen. *Educ:* Cornell Univ, BA, 59; Univ Rochester, MD, 63; Univ Minn, MPH, 70; Am Bd Internal Med, dipl, 71 & 77, dipl oncol, 73. *Prof Exp:* Med resident, Harvard Med Serv, Boston City Hosp, 64-65 & med br, Nat Cancer Inst, NIH, Bethesda, MD, 65-67; instr microbiol, Univ Minn, Minneapolis, 68-70, clin assoc prof, Dept Family Pract, 75-89. *Mem:* Am Fedn Clin Res; fel Am Soc Clin Hypnosis; fel Am Col Physicians; Am Soc Prev Oncol; fel Soc Clin & Exp Hypnosis. *Res:* Hypnosis and pain control for use in surgery with anesthesia. *Mailing Add:* 7260 University Ave NE Suite 235 Minneapolis MN 55432. *Fax:* 612-572-1393; *E-Mail:* levit008@maroon.tc.umn.edu

LEVITAN, HERBERT, NEUROBIOLOGY, MEMBRANE BIOPHYSICS. *Current Pos:* assoc prof, 72-83, PROF, DEPT ZOOL, UNIV MD, COL PARK, 83- *Personal Data:* b Brooklyn, NY, Apr 25, 39; m 64; c 2. *Educ:* Cornell Univ, BEE, 62, PhD(phys biol), 65. *Prof Exp:* NIH fel neurophysiol, Brain Res Inst, Univ Calif, Los Angeles, 65-67, anatomist, Anat Dept, 67; NIH fel, Lab Neurophysiol Cellulaire Ctr Etude Physiol Nerveuse, Paris, France, 68-70, Lab Neurophysiol, NIMH, 70, Lab Neurobiol, Nat Inst Child Health & Human Develop, 70-72. *Concurrent Pos:* Instr neurobiol, Marine Biol Lab, Woods Hole, 74; neurophysiologist, Lab Neurosci Gerontol Res Ctr, Nat Inst Aging, 79-82; Fulbright Hayes Fel, 87-88; prog dir, NSF, Washington, DC, 90-92. *Mem:* Soc Neurosci; Am Physiol Soc; Soc Gen Physiologists; Am Soc Cell Biol. *Res:* Physico-chemical and biophysical mechanisms underlying the effects of drugs on the physiology of nerves and muscles. *Mailing Add:* 6000 Fourth St N Arlington VA 22203

LEVITAN, MAX, GENETICS, ANATOMY. *Current Pos:* assoc prof, 68-70, PROF ANAT, MT SINAI SCH MED, CITY UNIV NY, 70-, PROF HUMAN GENETICS, 95- *Personal Data:* b Tverai, Lithuania, Mar 1, 21; nat US; m 47, Beth German; c Eve L (Gerber), Sara A & Marjorie R (Gross). *Educ:* Univ Chicago, AB, 44; Univ Mich, MA, 46; Columbia Univ, PhD(zool), 51. *Honors & Awards:* Just Lectr, Howard Univ, 68; Res Career Develop Award, USPHS, 63. *Prof Exp:* Statistician, USPHS, 44-45; asst zool, Columbia Univ, 46-49; assoc prof genetics, Va Polytech Inst, 49-55; from asst prof to assoc prof anat, Woman's Med Col Pa, 55-62, prof anat & med genetics, 62-66; prof biol & chmn dept, George Mason Col, Univ Va, 66-68. *Concurrent Pos:* Seminar assoc, Columbia Univ, 58-; spec lectr, Univ Pa, 62-63; adj prof anat & genetics, George Wash Univ & Sch Med, Univ Va, 66-68, assoc ed, Evolution, 77-79; auth. *Mem:* Am Asn Anatomists; Am Soc Naturalists; Am Soc Human Genetics; Genetics Soc Am; Soc Study Evolution; AAAS. *Res:* Cytogenetics; population genetics of linked loci; chromosome breakage; cytoplasmic inheritance; medical genetics; author of textbook. *Mailing Add:* 1212 Fifth Ave New York NY 10029. *Fax:* 212-860-1174

LEVITAN, MICHAEL LEONARD, MATHEMATICS. *Current Pos:* asst prof, 70-74, ASSOC PROF MATH, VILLANOVA UNIV, 74- *Personal Data:* b Brooklyn, NY, Sept 12, 41; m 92, Mary J Davis; c Cheryl, Eric, Benjamin & Laura. *Educ:* Rensselaer Polytech Inst, BS, 62; Univ Minn, MS, 66, PhD(math), 67. *Prof Exp:* Asst prof math, Drexel Univ, 67-70. *Mem:* Am Math Soc; Math Asn Am; Am Asn Univ Professors. *Res:* Probability theory; Markov processes; operations research; statistics; math anxiety. *Mailing Add:* Dept Math Sci Villanova Univ Villanova PA 19085-1699. *Fax:* 610-519-6928; *E-Mail:* levitan@ucis.vill.edu

LEVITAN, RUVEN, INTERNAL MEDICINE, GASTROENTEROLOGY. *Current Pos:* assoc prof, 68-70, PROF MED, ABRAHAM LINCOLN SCH MED, UNIV ILL MED CTR, 70- *Personal Data:* b Kaunas, Lithuania, Mar 12, 27; US citizen; m 49; c 3. *Educ:* Hebrew Univ, Israel, MD, 53; Am Bd Internal Med, dipl & cert gastroenterol. *Prof Exp:* Resident, Mt Sinai Hosp, NY, 56-57; resident, Beth Israel Hosp, Boston, 58-59; dir gastroenterol res, New Eng Med Ctr Hosps, 64-68. *Concurrent Pos:* Spec fel med neoplasia, Mem Ctr Cancer & Allied Dis, NY, 57-58; fel gastroenterol & res fel med, Mass Mem Hosps & Sch Med, Boston Univ, 59-61, sr res fel, Mass Mem Hosps, 61-62; from asst prof to assoc prof, Sch Med, Tufts Univ, 64-69; lectr, Sch Med, Boston Univ, 65-68; pres, Chicago Soc Gastroenterol; chief gastroenterol sect, Vet Admin West Side Hosp, 68-77. *Mem:* Fel Am Col Physicians; Am Physiol Soc; Am Gastroenterol Asn; Am Asn Study Liver Dis; Am Soc Clin Invest. *Res:* Water electrolyte absorption from the intestine; hormonal influences on absorption; lymphomas, including involvement of liver and gastrointestinal tract. *Mailing Add:* Dept Med Gastroenterol Univ Ill Abraham Lincoln Sch Med 4709 Golf Rd Suite 1000 Skokie IL 60076

LEVITAS, ALFRED DAVE, PHYSICS. *Current Pos:* RETIRED. *Personal Data:* b New York, NY, Mar 27, 20; m 43; c 1. *Educ:* Syracuse Univ, BA, 47, MS, 50, PhD(physics), 58. *Prof Exp:* Res engr solid state physics, Sylvania Elec Corp, 53-55 & Sprague Elec Corp, 55-56; physicist, Honeywell Res Ctr, 56-58; prof physics, State Univ NY, Albany, 58- *Concurrent Pos:* Consult, Naval Res Lab, 60-63. *Mem:* Am Phys Soc. *Res:* Solid state and statistical physics; thermodynamics. *Mailing Add:* 420 Sand Creek Rd Albany NY 12205

LEVITICUS, LOUIS I, TRACTOR-OFF ROAD VEHICLE DEVELOPMENT, ENGINE DEVELOPMENT. *Current Pos:* chief engr, Tractor Test Lab, 75-87, assoc dir, Ctr Agr Equip, 87-90, PROF AGR ENG, UNIV NEBR, 75-, SUPV TEST & DEVELOP, NEBR POWER LAB, 90- *Personal Data:* b Aalten, Neth, July 4, 31; Dutch & US citizen; m 82, Rose Mitchell; c Melanie & Joanna. *Educ:* Technion, Israel Inst Technol, BSc, 60, MSc, 63; Purdue Univ, PhD(agr eng), 69. *Prof Exp:* Sr res engr, Stevens Inst

Technol, 69-71; consult & instr agr eng, Technion, Israel Inst Technol & Israel Defense Forces, 71-75. *Mem:* Int Soc Terrain Vehicle Systs; Soc Automotive Engrs; Am Soc Agr Engrs; Asian Asn Agr Engrs. *Res:* Off-road locomotion, oriented on agricultural and military soil-wheel interaction; alternate fuel use in diesel engines, alcohol, ethanol, ETBE, natural gas, vegetable oils; instrumentation for handicapped farmers; renewable energy; safety on farm. *Mailing Add:* Rm 207 L W Chase Hall Univ Nebr Lincoln NE 68583-0726. *Fax:* 402-472-8367; *E-Mail:* bsen011@unlvm.unl.edu

LEVITIN, LEV BEROVICH, ENGINEERING SCIENCE. *Current Pos:* prof, 82-86, DISTINGUISHED PROF ENG SCI, BOSTON UNIV, 86- *Personal Data:* b Moscow, Sept 25, 35; div; c Boris M. *Educ:* Acad Sci USSR, PhD, 69. *Prof Exp:* Sr res scientist, Inst Transmission Prob, USSR Acad Sci, 61-73; sr lectr, Tel Aviv Univ, 74-80; vis prof, Bielefeld Univ, 80-81 & Syracuse Univ, 81-82. *Concurrent Pos:* Ed, Prin Cybern, 67; consult, Vishay Israel Ltd, 79; vis scientist, Heinrich-Hertz Inst, 80 & Inst Optoelektronik, 81. *Mem:* Fel Inst Elec & Electronics Engrs; Am Asn Univ Prof; Am Math Soc; Asn Comput Mach; Soc Indust & Appl Math; Am Soc Eng Educ; Math Asn Am; AAAS; NY Acad Sci. *Mailing Add:* Boston Univ Col Eng 44 Cummington St Boston MA 02215-2407

LEVITON, ALAN, PUBLIC HEALTH, EPIDEMIOLOGY. *Current Pos:* teaching fel epidemiol, Sch Pub Health, 70-71, from instr to assoc prof, 71-96, PROF NEUROL, HARVARD MED SCH, 96- *Personal Data:* b Brooklyn, NY, June 17, 38; m 63; c 2. *Educ:* NY Univ, AB, 59; State Univ NY, MD, 63; Harvard Univ, SM, 71. *Prof Exp:* Intern, Kings Co Hosp, Brooklyn, 63-64, resident, 64-65; officer epidemiol, Epidemic Intel Serv, Ctr Dis Control, USPHS, 65-67; resident neurol, Washington Univ, St Louis, 67-70. *Concurrent Pos:* Dir, Neuroepidemiol Unit, Children's Hosp, Boston. *Mem:* Soc Epidemiol Res; Am Pub Health Asn; Am Neurol Asn; Child Neurol Soc; Am Col Epidemiol. *Res:* Using epidemiological techniques to search for antecedents of neurologic disabilities in children. *Mailing Add:* Children's Hosp 300 Longwood Ave Boston MA 02115-5737

LEVITON, ALAN EDWARD, SYSTEMATIC ZOOLOGY, ZOOGEOGRAPHY. *Current Pos:* From asst cur to assoc cur, Calif Acad Sci, 57-62, chmn dept, 62-83, cur herpet & chmn comput serv, 83-92, CURATOR HERPET & ED, SCI PUBL, CALIF ACAD SCI, 93- *Personal Data:* b Brooklyn, NY, Jan 11, 30; m 52, Gladys Robertson; c 2. *Educ:* Stanford Univ, AB, 49, AM, 53, PhD, 60. *Concurrent Pos:* Assoc cur div syst biol, Stanford Univ, 62-63, lectr, 62-70; adj prof biol sci, San Francisco State Univ, 67-; exec dir, Pac Div AAAS, 79-97. *Mem:* Fel AAAS; Soc Study Amphibians & Reptiles; Am Soc Ichthyol & Herpet; fel Geol Soc Am; Hist Sci Soc; Hist Earth Sci Soc. *Res:* Herpetology of Asia; Tertiary paleogeography; phylogeny and taxonomy of reptiles. *Mailing Add:* Dept Herpet Calif Acad Sci San Francisco CA 94118. *E-Mail:* leviton@sfsu.edu

LEVITSKY, DAVID A, CONTROL OF BODY WEIGHT, EFFECTS OF NUTRITION IN DEVELOPMENT. *Current Pos:* NIMH fel nutrit, Cornell Univ, 68-70, asst prof nutrit & psychol, 70-76, assoc prof, 76-86, PROF NUTRIT & PSYCHOL, DIV NUTRIT SCI, CORNELL UNIV, 88- *Personal Data:* b Philadelphia, Pa, Oct 15, 42; m 85, Barbara J Strupp; c Steven, Sandy, Susan, Michael & Sarah. *Educ:* Rutgers Univ, BA, 64, MS, 66, PhD(feeding behav), 68. *Honors & Awards:* Outstanding Res Award, Soc Nutrit Educ, 94. *Concurrent Pos:* Career Develop Award, Nat Inst Child Health & Human Develop, 74-79; traveling fel, NY State Col Agr & Life Sci, Israel, 80 & France, 88. *Mem:* Am Inst Nutrit; Am Psychol Asn; Am Asn Univ Professors. *Res:* Control of food intake; techniques for changing food preference; role of drugs to control energy intake and energy expenditure; role of macronutrients in the control of energy intake. *Mailing Add:* Div Nutrit Sci Cornell Univ Ithaca NY 14853-0001

LEVITSKY, LYNNE LIPTON, ENDOCRINOLOGY, PEDIATRICS. *Current Pos:* from asst prof to assoc prof, 73-85, PROF, PEDIAT PRITZKER SCH MED, UNIV CHICAGO, 55- *Personal Data:* b Columbia, SC, May 14, 42; m 67; c 3. *Educ:* Bryn Mawr Col, BA, 62; Yale Univ, MD, 66. *Prof Exp:* Intern pediat, Bronx Munic Hosp Ctr, 66-67; resident, Childrens Hosp Philadelphia, 67-68; fel endocrinol & metab, Sch Med, Univ Md, 68-70; asst prof pediat, Sch Med, Univ Ill, 70-73; dir pediat endocrinol, Michael Reese Hosp Med Ctr, 73-86. *Mem:* Soc Pediat Res; Endocrine Soc; Lawson Wilkins Pediat Endocrine Soc. *Res:* Carbohydrate metabolism; diabetes; fetal and neonatal metabolism and endocrinology. *Mailing Add:* Wyler Childrens Hosp 5841 Maryland Ave Chicago IL 60637

LEVITSKY, MYRON, MECHANICAL ENGINEERING. *Current Pos:* RETIRED. *Personal Data:* b New York, NY, June 22, 30. *Educ:* Cooper Union, BME, 51; NY Univ, MS, 64, PhD(mech eng), 69. *Prof Exp:* Res engr, Heat & Mass Flow Analyzer Lab, Columbia Univ, 51-53; instr mech eng, NY Univ, 53-54; proj engr, Consumer's Union, 62-63; lectr & assoc prof mech eng, City Col New York, 65-91. *Concurrent Pos:* Assoc res scientist, NY Univ, 65-70, vis mem, Courant Inst, 77-78; NSF res grant, City Col New York, 71-72. *Mem:* AAAS; Am Soc Mech Engrs; Am Phys Soc; Am Soc Eng Educ; Am Acad Mech. *Res:* Elasticity theory; heat transfer; thermal stresses in chemically hardening media; applications to concrete and plastic molding. *Mailing Add:* 392 Central Park W New York NY 10025

LEVITSKY, SIDNEY, CARDIOVASCULAR SURGERY, SURGERY. *Current Pos:* assoc prof surg, Col Med, Univ Ill, 70-75, lectr surg, Cook Co, Grad Sch, 70-89, PROF SURG & PHARMACOL, COL MED, UNIV ILL, 75-, CHIEF, DIV CARDIOTHORACIC SURG, MED CTR, 74-, CHIEF SURG, 89- *Personal Data:* b New York, NY, Mar 3, 36; m 67; c 3. *Educ:* Albert Einstein Col Med, MD, 60; Am Bd Surg & Bd Thoracic Surg, dipl, 68. *Prof Exp:* Instr surg, Sch Med, Yale Univ, 64-66; chief surg, Third Hosp Vietnam, 66-67; thoracic surgeon, Valley Forge Army Hosp, 67-68; sr invstr cardiac surg, Nat Heart Inst, NIH, 68-70. *Concurrent Pos:* Estab invstr, Am Heart Asn, 71; attend surgeon, Cook Co Hosp, 73-; sr consult, West Side Vet Hosp, 75- *Mem:* Soc Univ Surgeons; Am Physiol Soc; Soc Thoracic Surgeons; Am Asn Thoracic Surg; Asn Acad Surg; Sigma Xi; Am Surg Asn. *Res:* Thoracic surgery; non-invasive methods of monitoring myocardial contractility; intra-operative protection of myocardium; myocardial ischemia and metabolism. *Mailing Add:* Dept Surg Univ Ill Med Ctr 1740 W Taylor St PO Box 6998 Chicago IL 60612

LEVITT, ALBERT P, materials science, mechanical engineering, for more information see previous edition

LEVITT, BARRIE, PHARMACOLOGY, INTERNAL MEDICINE. *Current Pos:* CARDIOLOGIST PVT PRACT. *Personal Data:* b Brooklyn, NY, Aug 19, 35; m 68; c 1. *Educ:* State Univ NY Downstate Med Ctr, MD, 59. *Prof Exp:* Rotating intern, Mt Sinai Hosp, NY, 59-60, resident med, 60-63; fel pharmacol, Downstate Med Ctr, State Univ NY, 63-64; fel, Med Col, Cornell Univ, 64-65, from instr to asst prof pharmacol, 65-69; asst prof med, NY Med Col, 69-70, assoc prof med & pharmacol & dir, Div Clin Pharmacol, 70-80; prof med & cardiol, Albert Einstein Col Med, 80- *Concurrent Pos:* NY Heart Asn sr invstr, Med Col, Cornell Univ, 66-69; consult, Bur Drugs, US Food & Drug Admin, 71-; clin prof med, Albert Einstein Col Med. *Mem:* Am Soc Pharmacol & Exp Therapeut; Am Heart Asn; Sigma Xi. *Res:* Clinical and cardiovascular pharmacology; cardiology. *Mailing Add:* 1199 Park Ave New York NY 10128

LEVITT, DAVID GEORGE, PHYSIOLOGY. *Current Pos:* Assoc prof, 68-77, PROF PHYSIOL, UNIV MINN, MINNEAPOLIS, 77- *Personal Data:* b Minneapolis, Minn, May 9, 42; m 64; c 2. *Educ:* Univ Minn, BS, 66, MD & PhD(physiol), 68. *Res:* Theoretical transport processes across membranes and in capillary beds; intestinal absorption; microcirculation in skeletal muscle. *Mailing Add:* Physiol 6-255 Millard Hall Univ Minn Med Sch 435 Delaware St S E Minneapolis MN 55455. *Fax:* 612-625-5149

LEVITT, GEORGE, ORGANIC CHEMISTRY, PESTICIDES. *Current Pos:* RETIRED. *Personal Data:* b Newburg, NY, Feb 19, 25; m 50, Julie Zeto; c Barbara (Klein), Jeffrey, David & Gregory (deceased). *Educ:* Duquesne Univ, BS, 50, MS, 52; Mich State Univ, PhD, 57. *Honors & Awards:* Quadriennial Award Pesticide Res, Swiss Soc Chem Industs, 82; Nat Agr Award Excellence, Nat Agr Mkt Asn, 87 & 88; Am Chem Soc Award Creative Invention, Corp Assocs Am Chem Soc, 89; Kenneth Spencer Award, Outstanding Achievement Agr Chem, Am Chem Soc, 91; Nat Medal Technol, 93. *Prof Exp:* Res chemist, Exp Sta, E I du Pont de Nemours & Co, Inc, 56-63, res chemist, Stine Lab, 63-66, res chemist, Exp Sta, 66-68, sr res chemist, 68-80, res assoc, 81-86. *Concurrent Pos:* Instr, Del Tech & Community Col, 75-80. *Mem:* Am Chem Soc; Int Union Pure & Appl Chem; AAAS; Sigma Xi. *Res:* Organic synthesis; herbicides, fungicides, medicinals; pesticides; heterocyclic compounds; synthesis, characterization and identification of novel organic compounds for biological evaluation; developed programs to define and optimize chemical structure- biological activity relationships; sulfonylurea herbicides; heterocyclics; exploratory process research. *Mailing Add:* 110 Downs Dr Greenville DE 19807-2556

LEVITT, ISRAEL MONROE, ASTRONOMY. *Current Pos:* RETIRED. *Personal Data:* b Philadelphia, Pa, Dec 19, 08; m 37, Alice Gross; c Peter L & Nancy B. *Educ:* Drexel Univ, BS, 32; Univ Pa, MA, 37, PhD(astron), 48. *Hon Degrees:* DSc, Temple Univ, 58, Drexel Univ, 58, Philadelphia Col Pharm, 63. *Honors & Awards:* Cert Recognition, NASA, 77; Joseph Priestly Award, Spring Garden Inst, 63; Samuel S Fels Medal, 70. *Prof Exp:* Engr, Abrasive Co, 29-30; astronr, Franklin Inst, 33-39, asst dir, Fels Planetarium, 39-48, dir, 48-70, vpres, Inst, 70-72; exec dir, Mayor's Sci & Technol Coun, Philadelphia, Pa, 72-93. *Concurrent Pos:* Engr, Eclipse Exped, Franklin Inst, 32, asst assoc dir astron, photog & seismol, 38-48 & assoc dir astron & seismol, 49-70; astronr, Cook Observ, Univ Pa, 35-46; mem, Air Pollution Control Bd, Philadelphia, 64-, chmn, 66- *Mem:* Fel AAAS; fel Am Astronaut Soc; Am Inst Aeronaut & Astronaut; Am Astron Soc; Brit Astron Soc. *Res:* Lunar studies; scientific museum and planetarium operation; technology transfer. *Mailing Add:* 3900 Ford Rd Apt 19-D Philadelphia PA 19131

LEVITT, LEROY P, PSYCHIATRY. *Current Pos:* RETIRED. *Personal Data:* b Plymouth, Pa, Jan 8, 18; m 71; c 4. *Educ:* Pa State Univ, BS, 39; Chicago Med Sch, MD, 43; Inst Psychoanal, cert, 59. *Honors & Awards:* Chicagoan Year Award in Med, 71; Laughlin Award, Am Col Psychoanalysts. *Prof Exp:* Pvt pract, 49-66; prof psychiat & dean, Chicago Med Sch, 66-73; dir dept ment health, State of Ill, 73-76; vpres med affairs, Mt Sinai Hosp Med Ctr, 76-81, chmn, Dept Psychiat, 81-88, dir, Med Educ, 88-; prof psychiat, Rush Med Col, 76- *Concurrent Pos:* Consult, Chicago Am Red Cross, 50-54, Asn Family Living, 50- 54 & Nat Coun Aging, 52-; mem, Mayor's Comn Aging, 60- & Gov Comn Ment Health Planning Bd, 66-; pres, Chicago Bd Health, 78-82. *Mem:* Fel Am Psychiat Asn; fel Am Psychoanal Asn; fel Acad Psychoanal; Am Col Psychiat; Am Col Psychoanal (1st vpres, 81-82, pres, 84-85). *Res:* Process of aging; medical education and administration and study of personality of medical students; psychoanalysis; geriatric psychiatry; mental health. *Mailing Add:* 222 Harbour Dr Apt 201 Naples FL 33940

LEVITT, MARVIN FREDERICK, NEPHROLOGY. *Current Pos:* prof med, 68-95, CHIEF, DIV NEPHROL, DEPT MED, MT SINAI SCH MED, 60-, DISTINGUISHED SERV PROF, 95- *Personal Data:* b New York, NY, Dec 9, 20; c 2. *Educ:* Cornell Univ, BA, 41; NY Univ, MD, 44. *Prof Exp:* Res asst med, Mt Sinai Sch Med, 50-53; asst attend physician, Mt Sinai Hosp, 53-60. *Concurrent Pos:* Mem cardio-vascular renal panel, Mayor's Res Coun, 69-72; mem sci adv bd, NY State Kidney Dis Inst, 69-72; emer mem, Nat Heart Inst Training Comt; chmn med adv bd, NY Kidney Dis Found. *Mem:* NY Acad Sci; Am Soc Clin Invest; Am Fedn Clin Res; fel Am Col Physicians; Asn Am Physicians. *Mailing Add:* Mt Sinai Sch Med Ctr 19 E 98th St Suite 7A New York NY 10029

LEVITT, MELVIN, NEUROBIOLOGY. *Current Pos:* RETIRED. *Personal Data:* b Chicago, Ill, Mar 13, 25; div; c 1. *Educ:* Roosevelt Univ, BS, 49, MA, 53; Mich State Univ, PhD(psychol), 58. *Prof Exp:* Res asst neurol & psychiat, Med Sch, Northwestern Univ, 52-54; res assoc neurophysiol, Rockefeller Inst, 61; assoc anat, Sch Med, Univ Pa, 61-65, asst prof anat & mem, Inst Neurol Sci, 65-70; assoc prof physiol, Bowman Gray Sch Med, 70-90. *Concurrent Pos:* USPHS fel, Inst Neurol Sci, Sch Med, Univ Pa, 57-61. *Mem:* Am Physiol Soc; Am Asn Anat; Soc Neurosci; Int Asn Study Pain. *Res:* Dysesthesias of central neural origin in subhumans. *Mailing Add:* 724 Chester Rd Winston-Salem NC 27104-1706

LEVITT, MICHAEL D, GASTROENTEROLOGY. *Current Pos:* from asst prof to assoc prof, 68-74, PROF MED, MED SCH, UNIV MINN, 74- *Personal Data:* b Chicago, Ill, May 10, 35; m 56; c 3. *Educ:* Univ Minn, BS, 58, MD, 50. *Prof Exp:* Intern, Univ Minn Hosp, 60-61; resident, Boston Univ Hosp, 61-64; resident, Beth Israel Hosp, Boston, 64-65; fel gastroenterol, Boston City Hosp, 65-68. *Concurrent Pos:* Guest lectr, Gastroenterol Res Group, 72; counr, Am Fedn Clin Res, 74-76; consult med, Minneapolis Vet Admin Hosp, 74- *Mem:* Am Fedn Clin Res; Am Soc Clin Invest; Am Gastroenterol Soc. *Res:* Studies employing gas to investigate gastrointestinal physiology and studies of serum and urinary isoamylases. *Mailing Add:* 150 Malcolm Ave SE Minneapolis MN 55414

LEVITT, MORTON, NEUROCHEMISTRY. *Current Pos:* SR RES ASSOC, NY STATE PSYCHIAT INST, 81- *Mailing Add:* 32 Fenimore Rd Scarsdale NY 10583

LEVITT, SEYMOUR H, RADIOTHERAPY. *Current Pos:* PROF THERAPEUT RADIOL & HEAD DEPT, UNIV MINN, MINNEAPOLIS, 70- *Personal Data:* b Chicago, Ill, July 18, 28; div; c 3. *Educ:* Univ Colo, BA, 50, MD, 54. *Prof Exp:* Instr radiation ther & radiol, Med Sch, Univ Mich, 61-62; asst radiotherapist, Sch Med & Dent, Univ Rochester, 62-63; assoc prof radiation ther & chief div, Sch Med, Univ Okla, 63-66; prof radiol & chmn div radiation ther, Med Col Va, 66-70. *Concurrent Pos:* Consult radiother, Vet Admin Hosp, Minneapolis; trustee, Am Bd Radiol; mem, Am Joint Comt; pres, Soc Chmn Acad Radiol Oncol Prog, 74-76; mem bd dirs, 76-78. *Mem:* Fel Am Col Radiol; Am Radium Soc (pres, 83); Soc Nuclear Med; Radiol Soc NAm; Am Soc Therapeut Radiol (pres, 78-79). *Res:* Experimental and clinical radiation therapy; radiation biology. *Mailing Add:* Dept Therapeut Radiol Univ Minn Hosps Minneapolis MN 55455

LEVITZ, HILBERT, MATHEMATICS, COMPUTER SCIENCE. *Current Pos:* assoc prof math, 69-84, PROF COMPUT SCI, FLA STATE UNIV, 84- *Personal Data:* b Lebanon, Pa, Nov 13, 31; m 80. *Educ:* Univ NC, BA, 53; Pa State Univ, PhD(math), 65. *Prof Exp:* Instr math, Williams Col, 65; asst prof, NY Univ, 65-69. *Mem:* Am Math Soc; Asn Symbolic Logic; Asn Computing Mach. *Res:* Mathematical logic; concrete systems of ordinal notations. *Mailing Add:* Dept Comput Sci Fla State Univ 600 W College Ave Tallahassee FL 32306-1096

LEVITZ, MORTIMER, BIOCHEMISTRY, ENDOCRINOLOGY. *Current Pos:* res assoc, 52-56, from asst prof to assoc prof, 56-67, PROF OBSTET & GYNEC, MED CTR, NY UNIV, 67- *Personal Data:* b New York, NY, May 11, 21; m 47; c 2. *Educ:* City Col New York, BS, 41; Columbia Univ, MA, 47, PhD(org chem), 51. *Prof Exp:* Res assoc steroid biochem, Col Physicians & Surgeons, Columbia Univ, 51-52. *Concurrent Pos:* NIH res career award, 62-72; consult, Endocrine Study Sect, NIH, 66-70 & 73-75, Clin Sci Study Sect, 81-85, chmn, 83-85; ed, Endocrinol, 83-87, assoc ed-in-chief, 86-87. *Mem:* Am Chem Soc; Am Soc Biol Chemists; Endocrine Soc; Soc Gynec Invest. *Res:* Estrogen metabolism and mechanisms of action in pregnancy and cancer. *Mailing Add:* NY Univ Med Ctr 550 First Ave New York NY 10016-6402. *Fax:* 212-263-7184

LEVITZKY, MICHAEL GORDON, PULMONARY PHYSIOLOGY, CARDIOVASCULAR PHYSIOLOGY. *Current Pos:* from asst prof to assoc prof, 75-85, PROF PHYSIOL, MED CTR, LA STATE UNIV, 85- *Personal Data:* b Elizabeth, NJ, Jan 3, 47; m 85, Elizabeth Gouaux; c Edward B & Sarah E. *Educ:* Univ Pa, BA, 69; Albany Med Col, PhD(physiol), 75. *Prof Exp:* Instr physiol, Albany Med Col, Union Univ, 74-75. *Concurrent Pos:* Consult, NIH grants, 74-76 & 79-80, prin investr, 76-81 & 82-86; chmn, Acad Studies Comt, La State Univ, 81-89, Curric Comt, 82-88, 90-; mem, Basic Sci Coun, Am Heart Asn; adj prof pediat & physiol, Tulane Univ Med Ctr, 90- *Mem:* Am Physiol Soc; Sigma Xi; Soc Exp Biol & Med; NY Acad Sci; Am Thoracic Soc. *Res:* Cardiopulmonary physiology, particularly in those factors that control pulmonary blood flow. *Mailing Add:* Dept Physiol Med Ctr La State Univ 1901 Perdido St New Orleans LA 70112-1393. *Fax:* 504-568-6158

LEVKOV, JEROME STEPHEN, PHYSICAL CHEMISTRY, FORENSIC SCIENCES. *Current Pos:* asst prof, 70-80, PROF GEN & PHYS CHEM, IONA COL, 80- *Personal Data:* b New York, NY, June 12, 39. *Educ:* City Col New York, BS, 61; Univ Pa, PhD(phys chem), 67. *Prof Exp:* Swiss Copper Inst fel, Swiss Fed Inst Technol, 67-68; asst prof gen & phys chem, Drexel Univ, 68-69. *Mem:* Am Chem Soc; AAAS. *Res:* Forensic chemistry; computers in chemistry education. *Mailing Add:* 715 North Ave New Rochelle NY 10801. *Fax:* 914-633-2279; *E-Mail:* jlevkov@iona.edu

LEVOW, ROY BRUCE, COMPUTER SCIENCE. *Current Pos:* from asst prof to assoc prof math, Fla Atlantic Univ, 70-80, chmn dept, 74-78, assoc prof comput & info syst, 80-87, spec asst comput & commun planning, 85-86, assoc prof comput sci, 87-93, PROF COMPUT SCI & ENG, FLA ATLANTIC UNIV, 93- *Personal Data:* b Richmond, Va, June 3, 43; m 62, Esther Shanes; c 2. *Educ:* Univ Pa, AB, 64, PhD(appl math), 69. *Prof Exp:* Sci programmer, Atlantic-Richfield Co, 64-65; asst prof math, Univ Hawaii, 69-70. *Concurrent Pos:* Consult comput aids, classification & retrieval, 75- & prof develop & comput personnel, 79- *Mem:* Asn Comput Mach; Inst Elec & Electronics Engrs. *Res:* Software engineering; object-oriented systems; data communications; operating systems; computer science education; programming languages and programming environments; information retrieval. *Mailing Add:* Dept Comput Sci & Eng Fla Atlantic Univ Boca Raton FL 33431. *Fax:* 561-367-2800; *E-Mail:* roy@cse.fau.edu

LEV-RAN, ARYE, DIABETES, INTERNAL MEDICINE. *Current Pos:* RES SCIENTIST, DEPT DIABETES & ENDOCRINOL, CITY HOPE MED CTR, DUARTE, CA, 81- *Personal Data:* b Leningrad, USSR, June 7, 30; US citizen; m 68; c 4. *Educ:* First Leningrad Med Sch, MD, 53; Cand Sci, Inst Physiol, Acad Sci, Leningrad, 59, DSci, 64. *Prof Exp:* Jr res scientist, 56-64, sr res scientist endocrinol, Dept Gen Endocrinol, Inst Ob/Gyn, Acad Med Sci, Leningrad, USSR, 64-67; dir Central Endocrinol Lab of Sick Fiend, Tel Aviv, Israel, 67-75, sr lectr, Tel Aviv Univ Sch Med, 69-75; staff physician, Scripps Clin, La Jolla, CA, 77-81. *Concurrent Pos:* Clin prof med, Univ Southern Calif, 82- *Mem:* Am Diabetes Asn; Endocrine Soc; Europ Asn Study Diabetes; fel Am Col Physicians; AAAS. *Res:* Pathogenesis of diabetes; epidemial growth factor in pathology; EGF receptors in carcinogenosis. *Mailing Add:* 1500 Duarte Rd Duarte CA 91010

LEVY, ALAN B, ORGANOMETALLIC CHEMISTRY. *Current Pos:* sr res chemist, Allied Corp, 80-85, res assoc, 85-90, RES SCIENTIST, ALLIED-SIGNAL CORP, 91- *Personal Data:* b San Francisco, Calif, Apr 12, 45; m 69, Ellen Jacobs; c 2. *Educ:* Univ Calif, Berkeley, BS, 67; Univ Colo, Boulder, PhD(chem), 71. *Prof Exp:* Fel chem, Purdue Univ, 71-74; asst prof chem, State Univ NY Stony Brook, 74-80. *Mem:* Am Chem Soc; Sigma Xi; AAAS. *Res:* The use of organoboranes and organocopper reagents for the development of new synthetic methods; the total synthesis of natural products; homogenous and heterogenous catalysis in organic synthesis; process control and the modeling of chemical processes. *Mailing Add:* 9 Southview Rd Randolph NJ 07869-4812

LEVY, ALAN C, PHYSIOLOGY, TOXICOLOGY. *Current Pos:* AT MICROBIOL ASSOCS INC. *Personal Data:* b Baltimore, Md, Feb 24, 30; m 56; c 2. *Educ:* Univ Md, BS, 52; George Washington Univ, MS, 56; Georgetown Univ, PhD(physiol), 58. *Prof Exp:* Instr physiol, Sch Med, Howard Univ, 58-60; sect head, Dept Endocrinol, William S Merrell Co, 60-67; dir labs, Woodard Res Corp, 67-69; group chief, Hoffmann-La Roche Inc, 69-74; sect head, dept toxicol & path, 74- *Mem:* Am Physiol Soc; Reticuloendothelial Soc; Endocrine Soc; NY Acad Sci; Soc Toxicol; Sigma Xi. *Res:* Inflammation; anti-inflammation; adrenal cortex; neuroendocrinology; lipid metabolism; acute and chronic toxicology; teratology. *Mailing Add:* US EPA 7509C 401 M St SW Washington DC 20460-0001

LEVY, ALAN JOSEPH, ELASTICITY & MICROMECHANICS, MECHANICAL BEHAVIOR OF MATERIALS. *Current Pos:* Asst prof, 82-88, assoc dept chair, 95-96, ASSOC PROF MECH, SYRACUSE UNIV, 88- *Personal Data:* b New York, NY, Oct 30, 55; m 91, Janice Salpeter. *Educ:* State Univ NY, BS, 77; Columbia Univ, MS, 79, MPhil, 81, PhD(eng mech), 82. *Concurrent Pos:* Fac res fel mech, Mat Technol Lab, US Army, 87 & 88. *Mem:* Am Soc Mech Eng; Soc Indust & Appl Math; Am Acad Mech; Sigma Xi. *Res:* Micromechanics of cavity formation in solid media; effective properties of composites; phenomenological and physically based constitutive modelling. *Mailing Add:* 127 Link Hall Dept Mech Aerospace & Mfg Eng Syracuse Univ Syracuse NY 13244. *E-Mail:* ajlevy@mailbox.syr.edu

LEVY, ALLAN HENRY, COMPUTER SCIENCES, MEDICAL EDUCATION. *Current Pos:* head, Dept Med Info Sci, Col Med, 83-95, PROF CLIN SCI & PROF COMPUT SCI, UNIV ILL, URBANA, 75- *Personal Data:* b New York, NY, Nov 2, 29; m 61; c 2. *Educ:* Columbia Univ, AB, 49; Harvard Med Sch, MD, 53. *Prof Exp:* From intern to asst resident, Harvard Med Serv, Boston City Hosp, 53-55; clin assoc, Nat Cancer Inst, 55-57; from instr to asst prof microbiol, Johns Hopkins Univ, 59-65; assoc prof virol & comput sci, Baylor Col Med, 65-71, prof comput sci, 71-73, prof virol & epidemiol, 73-75. *Concurrent Pos:* Res fel, Sch Med, Johns Hopkins Univ, 57-59; USPHS res career develop award, 60-65; consult div hosp & med facil, Bur State Serv, USPHS, 65-70; mem, adv comt to dir, Div Res Grants, NIH. *Mem:* Am Fedn Clin Res; Am Med Info Asn; Am Col Med Informatics. *Res:* Artificial intelligence in medicine; hospital information systems; general applications of digital computers to medicine and biology; hypertext and information retrieval techniques in medicine; uses of computers in medical student education and in biomedical research. *Mailing Add:* 190 Med Sci Bldg Univ Ill Urbana IL 61801. *Fax:* 217-333-8868; *E-Mail:* a_levy@uiuc.edu

LEVY, ARTHUR, COMBUSTION KINETICS, ATMOSPHERIC CHEMISTRY. *Current Pos:* RETIRED. *Personal Data:* b New York, NY, Sept 29, 21; m 49, Rita V Hoch; c Mark, Patricia, Paul & Richard. *Educ:* Queen's Col, BS, 43; Univ Minn, MS, 48. *Prof Exp:* Chemist, Los Alamos Nat Lab, 44-46; aeronaut res scientist, Nat Adv Comt Aeronaut, 48-50; phys chemist, Brookhaven Nat Lab, 50-51; prin phys chemist, Columbus Labs, Battelle Mem Inst, 51-59, asst chief, 56-69, fel, 69-71, sr fel, 71-73, sr res leader, 73-76, mgr combustion, 76-79, res leader, 79-85. *Concurrent Pos:* Consult, 85-, Ohio Coal Develop Off, 92- *Mem:* Am Chem Soc; Combustion Inst; Air Pollution Control Asn. *Res:* Kinetics of hydrogen and hydrocarbon oxidation; combustion chemistry; kinetics of radiation and ionic reactions; boron hydride chemistry; induced reactions; flame structure; air pollution kinetics; coal-oil combustion and environmental assessments; synthetic fuel combustion; clean coal technology. *Mailing Add:* 614 Farrington Dr Worthington OH 43085. *Fax:* 614-466-6532; *E-Mail:* alevy929@aol.com

LEVY, ARTHUR LOUIS, ANALYTICAL CHEMISTRY, CLINICAL CHEMISTRY. *Current Pos:* chemist, Hodgkins Dis Res Lab, 54-58, CHIEF CHEMIST, ST VINCENT'S HOSP, 58- *Personal Data:* b Bridgeport, Conn, Aug 2, 17; m 43; c 1. *Educ:* Univ Mo, AB, 38; Yale Univ, PhD(phys chem), 48. *Honors & Awards:* Van Slyhe Award, Am Asn Clin Chem, 87. *Prof Exp:* From instr to asst prof phys chem, Rensselaer Polytech Inst, 48-54. *Concurrent Pos:* Ford Found fel, 53-54; dir labs, New York Dept Health, 64- *Mem:* AAAS; Am Asn Clin Chem; Am Chem Soc; NY Acad Sci; Asn Clin Sci. *Res:* Electrolyte solutions; immunochemistry of Hodgkins disease; enzymes; standards and methodologies in clinical chemistry including automation and data processing. *Mailing Add:* 15 La Mesa Ave East Chester NY 10709

LEVY, ARTHUR MAURICE, CARDIOLOGY. *Current Pos:* resident, 58-59, from instr to assoc prof med, Col Med, 63-76, asoc prof pediat, 69-77, PROF MED, COL MED, UNIV MT, 76-, PROF PEDIAT, 77- *Personal Data:* b New York, NY, Nov 20, 30; c 3. *Educ:* Harvard Univ, BA, 52; Cornell Univ, MD, 56; Am Bd Internal Med, dipl, 66. *Prof Exp:* Intern, Cornell Med Div, Bellevue Hosp, 56-57, resident med, 57-58. *Concurrent Pos:* NIH fel cardiol, Col Med, Univ Vt, 59-60; Nat Heart Inst res fel, 59-60; trainee cardiol, Harvard Med Sch, Boston Children's Hosp, 62-63; teaching scholar, Am Heart Asn, 66-71; fel coun clin cardiol, Am Heart Asn, 69- *Mem:* Am Fedn Clin Res; fel Am Col Physicians; fel Am Col Cardiol. *Res:* Clinical electrophysiology. *Mailing Add:* Cardiol Dept Med Ctr Hosp Vt Burlington VT 05401

LEVY, BERNARD, JR, MECHANICAL ENGINEERING. *Current Pos:* RETIRED. *Personal Data:* b New Orleans, La, Oct 27, 24; m 51; c 3. *Educ:* Univ Nebr, BS, 45, MS, 48. *Prof Exp:* Engr, Westinghouse Elec Corp, 48-57, mgr var activ, 57-82, mgr, Steam Generator Prog, Advan Reactors Div, 80-86. *Mem:* Am Soc Mech Engrs; Sigma Xi. *Res:* Design and development of nuclear reactor plants for naval application. *Mailing Add:* 2669 Strathmore Lane Bethel Park PA 15102

LEVY, BERNARD C, STATISTICAL SIGNAL PROCESSING, MULTIDIMENSIONAL SIGNAL PROCESSING. *Current Pos:* PROF, DEPT ELEC & COMPUT ENG, UNIV CALIF, DAVIS, 87-, CHAIR, 96- *Personal Data:* b Princeton, NJ, July 31, 51; m 90, Chuc K Thanh; c Daniel. *Educ:* Nat Sch Advan Mines, Paris, ingenieur civil, 74; Stanford Univ, PhD(elec eng), 79. *Prof Exp:* From asst prof to assoc prof elec eng, Mass Inst Technol, 79-87. *Concurrent Pos:* Consult, Draper Lab, 86-89; vis researcher, Nat Inst Info & Automat Res, France, 93. *Mem:* Fel Inst Elec & Electronics Engrs; Soc Indust & Appl Math; Acoust Soc Am. *Res:* Signal estimation and detection, image analysis and processing and acoustic imaging. *Mailing Add:* Dept Elec & Comput Eng Univ Calif Davis CA 95616

LEVY, BORIS, PHOTOGRAPHIC CHEMISTRY, PHOTOCATALYSIS. *Current Pos:* RES PROF CHEM, BOSTON UNIV, 89- *Personal Data:* b New York, NY, Nov 24, 27; m 56, Ann Reiter; c 3. *Educ:* NY Univ, BA, 48, MS, 50, PhD(phys chem), 55. *Prof Exp:* Res chemist, Sylvania Elec Co, 50-51; sr res chemist, Radio Corp Am, 55-56; sr scientist, Westinghouse Elec Corp, 56-60; sr res chemist, Socony Mobil Oil Co, 60-65; mgr, Imaging Mat Res & Develop, Polaroid Corp, 65-89. *Concurrent Pos:* Assoc prof, Trenton Jr Col, 62-65; assoc ed, Photog Sci & Eng, 75. *Mem:* Am Chem Soc; fel Soc Photog Scientists & Engrs. *Res:* Radiotracers; surface chemistry; electrokinetics; photoconductivity; photoelectron emission from semiconductors; spectral sensitization; energy and electron transfer reactions across phase boundaries; photographic emulsion preparation and characterization; preparation of novel image rector layers in diffusion transfer photography; kinetics of photo-induced processes; photovoltaic solar energy conversion. *Mailing Add:* 14 Waltham Rd Wayland MA 01778-1112. *Fax:* 617-353-6466; *E-Mail:* levy@bu_chem.bu.edu

LEVY, CHARLES KINGSLEY, RADIATION ECOLOGY. *Current Pos:* assoc prof radiol & biol, 62-70, PROF BIOL, BOSTON UNIV, 70- *Personal Data:* b Boston, Mass, Dec 25, 24; div; c 3. *Educ:* George Washington Univ, BSc, 48, MSc, 51; Univ NC, Chapel Hill, PhD(physiol), 56. *Prof Exp:* Instr physiol, Vassar Col, 56-58; staff scientist, Worcester Found Exp Biol, 58-62. *Concurrent Pos:* Res collabr, Brookhaven Nat Lab, 57-61; Am Physiol Soc fel, Boston Univ, 58; staff scientist, Worcester Found Exp Biol, 58-62; consult, Mass Gen Hosp, 62-; consult bioinstrumentation, NASA, 67-; Fulbright prof zool, Univ Nairobi, 69-70; proj dir avian radioecol nuclear reactor site, AEC, Dept Energy, 73-78. *Mem:* Am Physiol Soc; Radiation Res Soc; Soc Gen Physiol. *Res:* Effect of high energy particulate radiation mammalian systems; dose-rate phenomena and responses of sensory and neural tissues to ionizing radiation; biological impact of reactor effluents on free ranging populations of wild birds; kinship in voles by radionuclide tagging and whole-body gamma spectroscopy. *Mailing Add:* Dept Biol Boston Univ Boston MA 02215

LEVY, DANIEL, BIOCHEMISTRY, MEMBRANES. *Current Pos:* assoc prof, 74-80, PROF BIOCHEM, SCH MED, UNIV SOUTHERN CALIF, 80- *Personal Data:* b New York, NY, Nov 27, 40; m 68. *Educ:* City Col New York, BS, 61; Brandeis Univ, MS, 63, PhD(chem), 65. *Prof Exp:* Res biochemist, Univ Calif, Berkeley, 67-68. *Concurrent Pos:* NIH fel biochem, Univ Calif, Berkeley, 65-67; NIH res grant, 73-; vis prof biochem, Univ Basel, Switzerland, 77-78. *Mem:* AAAS; Am Soc Biol Chem; Am Chem Soc. *Res:* Membrane structure and function; mechanism of hormone action. *Mailing Add:* Dept Biochem Univ Southern Calif Los Angeles CA 90033

LEVY, DAVID ALFRED, ALLERGY. *Current Pos:* CONSULT, PHARMACEUT INDUST, 90-; SCI ADV, CENTRE D'ALLERGIE HOSP, ROTHSCHILD, PARIS, 91- *Personal Data:* b Washington, DC, Aug 27, 30; m 51, 85, Anne Badoux; c Jill, William & Stanley. *Educ:* Univ Md, BS, 52, MD, 54; Am Bd Internal Med, cert, 62; Am Bd Allergy & Immunol, cert, 74. *Prof Exp:* From intern to chief resident med, Univ Hosp, Baltimore, Md, 54-59; physician, Pulmonary Dis Serv, Fitzsimons Gen Hosp, Denver, 59-61; staff physician, Chest Serv, Vet Admin Hosp, Baltimore, 61-62; USPHS fel, Sch Med, Johns Hopkins Univ, 62-66, asst prof radiol sci, 66-68, from assoc prof to prof radiol sci & epidemiol, 68-73, prof biochem & epidemiol, Sch Hyg & Pub Health, 73-85, prof immunol & infectious dis, 80-85; adj dir, Centre d'Immunologie et de Balogie Pierre Fabre, 85-90. *Concurrent Pos:* Fogarty Sr Int fel, Col de France, Paris, 76; vis scientists, Inst Pasteur, Paris, 84-85. *Mem:* Am Asn Immunol; fel Am Acad Allergy; Fr Soc Allergy & Clin Immunol; Europ Acad Allergol & Clin Immunol. *Res:* Mechanisms of allergic reactions; mechanisms of immunotherapy for allergic diseases; allergy to latex. *Mailing Add:* 11 Quai Saint Michel 75005 Paris France. *Fax:* 33-01-40-19-33-64

LEVY, DAVID EDWARD, NEUROLOGY. *Current Pos:* fel & instr, 72-75, asst prof, 75-80, ASSOC PROF NEUROL, MED COL, CORNELL UNIV, 80- *Personal Data:* b Washington, DC, May 10, 41; m 67. *Educ:* Harvard Univ, AB, 63; Harvard Med Sch, MD, 68; Am Bd Internal Med, dipl, 72; Am Bd Psychiat & Neurol, dipl, 75. *Honors & Awards:* Teacher-Scientist Award, Andrew W Mellon Found, 75. *Prof Exp:* From intern to resident, New York Hosp, 68-72. *Concurrent Pos:* Asst attend neurologist, New York Hosp, 75-80, assoc attend neurologist, 80-; estab investr, Am Heart Asn, 78. *Mem:* Soc Neurosci; fel Am Col Physicians; Am Acad Neurol; Am Neurol Asn; Fel Am Heart Asn. *Res:* Brain carbohydrate and energy metabolism in cerebral ischemia; prediction of outcome from stroke and coma. *Mailing Add:* 30 N Jefferson Whippany NJ 07981

LEVY, DEBORAH LOUISE, PSYCHOLOGY. *Current Pos:* CO-DIR, PSYCHOL LAB, MCLEAN HOSP, 90-; ASSOC PROF, DEPT PSYCHIAT, HARVARD MED SCH, 94- *Personal Data:* b Minneapolis, MN, Nov 3, 50. *Educ:* Univ Chicago, BA, 72, PhD(psychol), 76. *Honors & Awards:* Karl Menninger Sci Day Award, Menninger Found, 79. *Prof Exp:* Res assoc, Univ Chicago, 72-76; intern clin psychol, NY Hosp, Cornell Med Ctr, 76-77; fel, Menninger Found, 77-79; asst unit chief, Ill State Psychiat Inst, 79-81, res scientist & supvr clin teaching, 79-87; dir psychophysiol, Hillside Hosp, Glen Oaks, NY, 87-90. *Concurrent Pos:* Res assoc, Dept Psychiat, Univ Chicago, 80-87; prin investr, res scientist develop award, 81-86. *Mem:* AAAS; Am Psychol Asn; NY Acad Sci; Am Psychopath Asn; Soc Neurosci; Sigma Xi. *Res:* Genetics of the major psychoses. *Mailing Add:* McLean Hosp 115 Mill St Belmont MA 02178. *Fax:* 617-855-2778; *E-Mail:* levy@isr.harvard.edu

LEVY, DONALD HARRIS, CHEMICAL PHYSICS, SPECTROSCOPY. *Current Pos:* From asst prof to assoc prof, 67-78, chmn dept, 83-85, PROF CHEM, DEPT CHEM & PHYS SCIS, UNIV CHICAGO, 78-, RALPH & MARY OTIS ISHAM PROF. *Personal Data:* b Youngstown, Ohio, June 30, 39; m 64, Susan Miller; c Jonathan, Michael & Alexander. *Educ:* Harvard Univ, BA, 61; Univ Calif, Berkeley, PhD(chem), 65. *Honors & Awards:* Albert Noyes Lectr, Rochester Univ; H H King Lectr, Kans State; Plyler Prize, Am Phys Soc, 87; Bourke Lectr, Royal Soc Chem. *Concurrent Pos:* NIH fel, Cambridge Univ, 65-66; NATO fel, 66-67; Alfred P Sloan fel, 67-73; DuPont fac fel, 69-70; Guggenheim fel, 75-76; mem rev panel chem physics, Nat Bur Stand, 81-84 & chem adv comt, NSF, 82-85; Sigma Xi nat lectr, 81-83; chmn molecular spectros tech group, Optical Soc Am, 82-84; assoc ed, J Chem Physics, 83-; chmn, Molecular Electronic Spectros Gordon Conf, 91. *Mem:* Nat Acad Sci; fel AAAS; fel Am Phys Soc; fel Am Acad Arts & Sci. *Res:* Optical spectroscopy in supersonic molecular beams; spectroscopy and photochemistry of van der Waals molecules; energy transfer; spectroscopy of porphyrin and related molecules; spectroscopy of gas phase amino acids and peptides. *Mailing Add:* James Franck Inst Univ Chicago 5640 S Ellis Ave Chicago IL 60637. *Fax:* 773-702-5863; *E-Mail:* levy@dilly.uchicago.edu

LEVY, DONALD M(ARC), DIGITAL SIGNAL PROCESSING, COMMUNICATION SYSTEMS. *Current Pos:* SR STAFF ENG, LOCKHEAD MISSLES & SPACE CORP, 90- *Personal Data:* b Lynbrook, NY, Mar 27, 35; m 57; c 2. *Educ:* Univ Wis, BS, 56, PhD(elec eng), 65; Mass Inst Technol, MS, 58. *Prof Exp:* Mem tech staff, Hycon Eastern, Inc, 56-57; res asst & staff mem, Instrumentation Lab, Mass Inst Technol, 57-58; instr elec eng, Univ Wis, 59-61; staff engr, Commun Systs Dept, IBM Corp, 61-63; instr elec eng, Univ Wis, 63-65; from asst prof to assoc prof info eng, Univ Iowa, 65-79; supvr signal processing syst, Western Develop Labs, Ford Aerospace & Commun Corp, 79-87. *Mem:* Inst Elec & Electronics Engrs. *Res:* Statistical communication theory; topological network theory; bioengineering; digital signal processing. *Mailing Add:* 755 Newell Rd Palo Alto CA 94303

LEVY, EDWARD KENNETH, ENERGY CONVERSION, POWER GENERATION. *Current Pos:* PROF MECH ENG, LEHIGH UNIV, 67-, DIR, ENERGY RES CTR, 80- *Educ:* Univ Md, BS, 63; Mass Inst Technol, SM, 64, ScD, 67. *Concurrent Pos:* Prof assoc, Nat Acad Eng. *Mem:* Am Soc Mech Engrs; Am Inst Chem Engrs; Am Nuclear Soc. *Res:* Fluid mechanics, heat transfer and applied thermodynamic aspects of energy with emphasis on power generation systems. *Mailing Add:* Energy Res Ctr Lehigh Univ 117 Atlss Dr Bethlehem PA 18015

LEVY, EDWARD ROBERT, ORGANIC CHEMISTRY. *Current Pos:* RETIRED. *Personal Data:* b New York, NY, Oct 3, 27; m 51; c 4. *Educ:* City Col New York, BS, 49; Univ Kans, PhD(org chem), 63. *Prof Exp:* Asst instr chem, Univ Kans, 49-50 & 51-53; res chemist, Glyco Prod, Inc, 53-57; process chemist, Chemagro Corp, 57-65, asst supvr, Process Develop Lab, 65-66, supvr, 66-68, asst mgr, 68-70, mgr, 70-73, prin chemist, Agr Div, Mobay Chem Corp, 73-93. *Mem:* AAAS; Am Chem Soc; Sigma Xi. *Res:* Organophosphorus insecticides; carbamates; chelating agents; synthesis and process development. *Mailing Add:* 3645 Somerset Dr Shawnee Mission KS 66208

LEVY, ELINOR MILLER, IMMUNE REGULATION, PSYCHONEUROIMMUNOLOGY. *Current Pos:* res assoc, 75-76, from instr to asst prof, 76-84, ASSOC PROF IMMUNOL, SCH MED, BOSTON UNIV, 84- *Personal Data:* b New York, NY, Mar 18, 42; m 62, Charles; c Benjamin & Rebecca. *Educ:* Brandeis Univ, BA, 63; Emory Univ, PhD(biophysics), 72. *Prof Exp:* Res asst biophys, Univ BC, 73-75. *Concurrent Pos:* Study sect mem, Nat Inst Alcohol Abuse & Alcoholism, 90-93. *Mem:* Am Asn Immunologists; AAAS; Psychoneuroimmunology Res Soc. *Res:* Immune suppression and T-cell differentiation defects in the acquired immunodeficiency syndrome; psychosocial and neuroendocrine modulation of the immune response in humans. *Mailing Add:* Sch Med Boston Univ 80 E Concord St Boston MA 02118. *Fax:* 617-638-4286; *E-Mail:* emlevy@bu.edu

LEVY, EUGENE HOWARD, ASTROPHYSICS, PLANETARY GEOPHYSICS. *Current Pos:* from asst prof to prof planetary sci, Univ Ariz, 75-94, assoc dept head, 81-83, dir, Lunar & Planetary Lab, 83-94, head, Dept Planetary Sci, 83-94, MEM FAC APPL MATH, UNIV ARIZ, 81-, DEAN, COL SCI, 93-, PROF PHYSICS, 95- *Personal Data:* b New York, NY, May 6, 44; c Roger, Jonathan & Benjamin. *Educ:* Rutgers Univ, AB, 66; Univ Chicago, PhD(physics), 71. *Honors & Awards:* Distinguished Pub Serv Medal, NASA, 83; Alexander von Humboldt-Stiftung Sr Scientist Award, Fed Repub Ger, 89. *Prof Exp:* Fel physics & astron, Univ Md, 71-73; asst prof, Bartol Res Found, Franklin Inst, 73-75. *Concurrent Pos:* fel, Ctr Theoret Physics, Univ Md, 71-73; mem, Comt Planetary & Lunar Explor, Nat Acad Sci, 76-79, chmn, 78-82; partic, Comet Halley Sci Working Group, NASA, 77-78; co-chmn bd study, Explor Primitive Solar Syst Bodies, Nat Acad Sci, 78, mem, Space Sci Bd, 79-82, chmn Comt Planetary & Lunar Explor, 79-82; sci consult, Rockwell Corp, 80; mem, Solar Syst Explor Comt, 80-83, Solar Syst Explor Div Mgt Coun, 83-85 & Space & Earth Sci Adv Comt, 85-88; chmn, Fields & Particles Panel, Int Comet Mission Rev Comt, NASA, mem, Theory Panel & Rev Panel Origins of Plasmas Earth's Neighborhood, 80; mem, Comprehensive & Coord Sci Prog Int Tech Panel on Comets, 80-82; mem, NASA deleg, Int Coop Invest of Halley's Comet, Italy, 81, Joint Working Group Near-Earth Space, Moon & Planets, USSR, 81 & head, US deleg, Nat Acad Sci-Europ Sci Found Joint Working Group Coop in Planetary Explor, 82-84; mem exec comt, Univs Space Sci Working Group, Asn Am Univs, 82-; mem adv bd, Int Conf Cometry Explor, Budapest, 82; mem, Study Panel Renewing US-Soviet Coop Space Sci, 84; mem, NASA-LPI Comt Future Space-Sta Sci Projs, 85- & NASA Space-Sta Sci User's Working Group, 85-88; distinguished vis scientist, Jet Propulsion Lab, Calif Inst Technol, 85-91; mem, Ariz Theoret Astrophs Prog, 85-; Mars Explor Strategy Advan Group, NASA, 86; chmn, Comet Rendezvous & Asteroid Flyby Rev Panel, NASA, 86, mem, Mars Rover Sample Return Sci Working Group, 87-89, Planetary Systs Sci Working Group, 88-, Lunar & Planetary Geophys Rev Panel, 88-90, Origins Solar Systs Progs Rev Panel, 90-91; chmn, Adv Comt Int Coop Mars Sample Return, Space Sci Bd, Nat Acad Sci, 86-88, mem, Comt Coop USSR Planetary Sci, 88-89, Astron & Astrophys Surv Comt, Sci Opportunities Panel, 89-90; mem, Study Panel Robotic Explor Moon & Mars, Off Technol Assessment, US Cong, 91; mem, Comt Pub Educ, Am Astron Soc, 94- *Mem:* Am Astron Soc; Int Astron Union; Sigma Xi; AAAS. *Res:* Theoretical astrophysics and solar system studies; magnetohydrodynamics; space and solar physics; planetary and geophysics; magnetic field generation; physical processes associated with the origin of the solar system; techniques for the observational discovery and study of other planetary systems. *Mailing Add:* Col Sci Gould-Simpson Bldg 1025 Univ Ariz Tucson AZ 85721. *Fax:* 520-621-8389; *E-Mail:* ehl@m.arizona.edu

LEVY, GABOR BELA, CHEMISTRY. *Current Pos:* CONSULT, 82- *Personal Data:* b Budapest, Hungary, July 16, 13; nat US; m 38, Friedel Kotljar; c Michal B & Margaret E (Rouse). *Educ:* Karlsruhe Tech Univ, Dipl Ing, 38; Inst Divi Thomae, PhD(chem), 53. *Prof Exp:* Asst physics, NY Univ, 38-41; sr res chemist & sect head, Schenley Labs, Inc, 42-50, head anal & phys chem res, 50-55; head chem div, Consumers Union US, 55-57; asst to pres, Photovolt Corp, 57-64, sr vpres, 64-82; adj prof, Polytech Inst NY, 68-82. *Concurrent Pos:* Consult ed, Int Sci Commun. *Mem:* AAAS; Am Chem Soc; Am Asn Clin Chem; Sigma Xi. *Res:* Applied colloid chemistry; spectrophotometry; polarography; electron microscopy; swelling of casein; determination of antibiotics; physical methods in organic chemistry; enzymes; optical rotation. *Mailing Add:* 11 Bossy Lane Wilton CT 06897-4601

LEVY, GEORGE CHARLES, COMPUTER METHODS. *Current Pos:* PROF CHEM, SYRACUSE UNIV, 81-, PROF SCI & TECHNOL, 85- *Personal Data:* b Brooklyn, NY, June 4, 44; m 79, Linda Fink; c Lauren & Natalie. *Educ:* Syracuse Univ, AB, 65; Univ Calif, Los Angeles, PhD(chem), 68. *Honors & Awards:* Thomas L Saaty Prize, 90. *Prof Exp:* Mem res staff, Gen Elec Corp, 68-73; from assoc prof to prof chem, Fla State Univ, 73-81. *Concurrent Pos:* Alfred P Sloan res fel, 75-77; Camille & Henry Dreyfus teacher-scholar, 76-81; John van Geuns prof, Univ Amsterdam, 79; dir res resource multi-nuclear, Nuclear Magnetic Resonance & Data Processing, NIH, 81-90; ed, Comput Enhanced Spectros J, 82-87; adj prof radiol, State Univ NY Upstate Med Ctr, 84-; founder & chmn, New Methods Res Inc, 83-91. *Mem:* Am Chem Soc; Sigma Xi. *Res:* Nuclear magnetic resonance spectroscopy and computer methods in chemistry; chemical and biophysical applications of carbon-13, nitrogen-15, and other nuclei nuclear magnetic resonance; statistical expert systems. *Mailing Add:* 1614 Brooklyn Ave Ann Arbor MI 48104-4421. *Fax:* 315-443-1022; *E-Mail:* glevy@cat.syr.edu

LEVY, GERALD FRANK, ECOLOGY. *Current Pos:* from asst prof to assoc prof biol & ecol, 67-77, PROF BIOL SCI, OLD DOM UNIV, 78- *Personal Data:* b Paterson, NJ, June 20, 38; m 60, Paula Rosenberg; c Linda, David, Deborah & Karen. *Educ:* Bowling Green State Univ, BS, 60, MA, 61; Univ Wis, PhD(bot), 66. *Honors & Awards:* Pres Award, Va Wildlife Fedn, 79. *Prof Exp:* Tech asst, Univ Wis, 63-65; asst prof bot & zool, Univ Wis, Marinette Campus, 65-67. *Concurrent Pos:* Bot consult, Animal Ecol Proj, 68-69; vpres, Environ Consult, Inc, 73-81, chmn bd, 81-82; mem sci adv bd, Va Mus Nat Hist, 85-87; secy & bd mem, Norfolk Bot Garden Soc. *Res:* Phytosociology; longleaf pine regeneration; fire ecology; history and natural history Great Dismal Swamp. *Mailing Add:* Dept Biol Sci Old Dom Univ Norfolk VA 23529. *E-Mail:* gfl100f@viper.mgb.odu.edu

LEVY, GERHARD, PHARMACOLOGY. *Current Pos:* DISTINGUISHED PROF PHARMACEUT, SCH PHARM, STATE UNIV NY, BUFFALO, 72- *Personal Data:* b Wollin, Ger, Feb 12, 28; nat US; m 58; c 3. *Educ:* Univ Calif, BS, 55, PharmD, 57. *Hon Degrees:* Dr, Univ Uppsala, 75, Phila Col Pharm & Sci, 79, Long Island Univ, 81; DSc, Univ Ill, 86, Hoshi Univ, Tokyo, 96. *Honors & Awards:* Richardson Pharm Award, 57; McKeen Cattell Distinguished Achievement Award Clin Pharmacol, Am Col Clin Pharmacol, 78; Host-Madsen Medal, Int Pharmaceut Fedn, 78; Oscar B Hunter Mem Award, Am Soc Clin Pharmacol & Therapeut, 82; Volwiler Res Achievement Award, Am Asn Col Pharm, 82; Sidney Riegelman lectr, Univ Calif, San Francisco, 83; Am Col Clin Pharm Therapeut Frontiers Lectr Award, 83; Takeru Higuchi Res Prize, Acad Pharmaceut Sci, 83; Lifetime Achievement Award, Int Pharmaceut Fedn, 94. *Prof Exp:* Res pharmacist, Med Ctr, Univ Calif, 57-58, from asst prof to assoc prof pharm, 58-64, prof biopharmaceut, 64-72, actg chemn dept, 59-60, chmn, 66-70. *Concurrent Pos:* Vis prof, Hebrew Univ Jerusalem, 66- & Univ Rochester, 72-73; consult, Bur Drugs, Food & Drug Admin, 71-73; mem, Comt Probs Drug Safety, Nat Acad Sci-Nat Res Coun, 71-75; grad prof, Victorian Col Pharm, Melbourne, Australia, 73-; vis prof, Basic Med Sci, 85-86. *Mem:* Inst Med-Nat Acad Sci; Am Chem Soc; fel Am Pharmaceut Asn; Am Soc Pharmacol & Exp Therapeut; fel AAAS. *Res:* Biopharmaceutics; clinical pharmacology; pharmacokinetics. *Mailing Add:* Dept Pharmaceut State Univ NY Sch Pharm Rm 206 Amherst NY 14260. *Fax:* 716-645-3693

LEVY, HANS RICHARD, ENZYMOLOGY. *Current Pos:* from asst prof to assoc prof, 63-71, PROF BIOCHEM, SYRACUSE UNIV, 71-, CHMN, DEPT BIOL, 93- *Personal Data:* b Leipzig, Ger, Oct 22, 29; nat US; m 60, Betty Samuels; c Karen. *Educ:* Rutgers Univ, BSc, 50; Univ Chicago, PhD(biochem), 56. *Prof Exp:* USPHS fel, Ben May Lab, Univ Chicago, 56-58 & Hammersmith Hosp, London, Eng, 58-59; from instr to asst prof biochem, Ben May Lab, Univ Chicago, 59-63. *Mem:* AAAS; Am Soc Biol Chem; Am Chem Soc; Am Asn Univ Prof; Protein Soc. *Res:* Mechanisms of action and regulation of enzymes; protein structural features that determine pyridine nucleotide dehydrogenase coenzyme specificity, especially for various glucose 6-phosphate dehydrogenases. *Mailing Add:* Biol Res Labs Dept Biol Syracuse Univ Syracuse NY 13244-1220

LEVY, HARVEY LOUIS, BIOCHEM GENETICS, PEDIATRICS. *Current Pos:* from instr to asst prof, 68-77, ASSOC PROF NEUROL, HARVARD MED SCH, 77- *Personal Data:* b Augusta, Ga, Oct 3, 35; m 61, Barbara Montag; c Larni & Vicki. *Educ:* Med Col Ga, MD, 60. *Prof Exp:* Intern pediat, Boston City Hosp, 60-61; asst resident path, Columbia-Presby Med Ctr, 61-62; asst resident pediat, Johns Hopkins Hosp, 64-65; chief resident, Boston City Hosp, 65-66. *Concurrent Pos:* NIH fel neurol, Harvard Med Sch, 66-68; consult, Walter E Fernald Sch Ment Retardation, 67-; lectr, Grad Sch Dent, Boston Univ, 68-; prin investr, Mass Dept Pub Health, 69-75; dir, Mass Metab Dis Prog, 75-; assoc, Ctr Human Genetics, Harvard Med Sch, 71-; assoc neurologist & pediatrician, Mass Gen Hosp, 77-; sr assoc med & genetics & dir, Inborn Errors of Metab-Phenylketonuria Prog, Children's Hosp Med Ctr, 78- *Mem:* Fel Am Acad Pediat; Soc Pediat Res; Am Pediat Soc; Soc Inherited Metab Disorders; Am Soc Human Genetics. *Res:* Inborn errors of metabolism; biochemical and genetic disorders; pathogenesis of inborn errors of metabolism. *Mailing Add:* Children's Hosp Boston MA 02115. *Fax:* 617-730-0461

LEVY, HARVEY MERRILL, BIOCHEMISTRY, PHYSIOLOGY. *Current Pos:* RETIRED. *Personal Data:* b Pittsburgh, Pa, May 12, 28; m 57; c 1. *Educ:* Univ Calif, Los Angeles, BA, 50, PhD(biochem), 55. *Prof Exp:* Asst res biochemist, Army Med Res Lab, Ky, 54-56; assoc res biochemist, Brookhaven Nat Lab, 56-58; asst prof pharmacol, Sch Med, NY Univ, 58-60, from asst prof to prof physiol & biophys, 60-71; prof physiol & biophys, State Univ NY Stony Brook, 71-91. *Mem:* Am Chem Soc; Am Soc Biol Chemists; Harvey Soc; Biophys Soc; Soc Gen Physiol. *Res:* Muscle biochemistry; enzymology; kinetics. *Mailing Add:* 242 Christian St Stony Brook NY 11790

LEVY, HILTON BERTRAM, VIROLOGY. *Current Pos:* HEAD SECT MOLECULAR VIROL, NAT INST ALLERGY & INFECTIOUS DIS, 52- *Personal Data:* b New York, NY, Sept 21, 16; m 42; c 2. *Educ:* City Col New York, BS, 35; Columbia Univ, MA, 36; Polytech Inst Brooklyn, PhD(biochem), 46. *Prof Exp:* Chief chemist, Gen Sci Labs, NY, 37-41; res biochemist, Mem Hosp Cancer & Allied Dis, 41-46; res biochemist, Overly Biochem Res Found, 46-52. *Concurrent Pos:* Prof, Med Sch, Howard Univ. *Mem:* Soc Exp Biol & Med; Am Asn Immunol; Soc Gen Physiol; Am Soc Biol Chem; Infectious Dis Soc; Soc Biol Response Modifiers. *Res:* Cancer; nucleic acid metabolism; infectious diseases; virus reproduction; interferon action and induction; treatment of neoplastic and viral diseases. *Mailing Add:* 12441 Park Lawn Dr Rockville MD 20852

LEVY, JACK BENJAMIN, ORGANIC CHEMISTRY. *Current Pos:* From asst prof to prof, Univ NC, 68-86, Will S Deloach prof chem, 86-91, chmn dept, 75-92, PROF CHEM, UNIV NC, WILMINGTON, 91- *Personal Data:* b Savannah, Ga, Jan 17, 41; m 63, Doris Levy; c Rachel & Matthew. *Educ:* Duke Univ, AB, 62, NC State Univ, MS, 64, PhD(chem), 67. *Mem:* Am Chem Soc; Sigma Xi. *Res:* Synthesis and spectral properties of new phenoxaphosphine derivatives and related compounds. *Mailing Add:* Dept Chem Univ NC Wilmington Wilmington NC 28403-3297

LEVY, JERRE MARIE, PSYCHOBIOLOGY. *Current Pos:* assoc prof, 77-82, PROF BIOPSYCHOL, UNIV CHICAGO, 82- *Personal Data:* b Birmingham, Ala, Apr 7, 38; m 69; c 2. *Educ:* Univ Miami, BA, 62, MS, 66; Calif Inst Technol, PhD(psychobiol), 70. *Prof Exp:* Res tech neuropsychol, Vet Admin Hosp, Denver, 69-70; fel psychol, Univ Colo, 70-71; fel biochem, Ore State Univ, 71-72; from asst prof to assoc prof psychol, Univ Pa, 72-77. *Concurrent Pos:* Prin investr, NSF grant, 75-77 & NIH grant, 77-79 & Spencer Found grant, 79-88; consult ed, J Exp Psychol: Human Perception & Performance, 75-84; bd assoc eds, Brain & Cognition, 82-, Neuropsychol, 88-, J Neurosci, 90- *Mem:* Soc Exp Psychologists; Int Neuropsychol Symp. *Res:* Cerebral asymmetry and cognitive function; evolution and genetics of human brain, especially hemispheric lateralization and correlated behaviors; variations in human lateralization patterns. *Mailing Add:* Dept Psychol Univ Chicago 5848 S University Ave Chicago IL 60637-1515

LEVY, JOSEPH, organic chemistry; deceased, see previous edition for last biography

LEVY, JOSEPH BENJAMIN, PHYSICAL CHEMISTRY, ORGANIC CHEMISTRY. *Current Pos:* PROF CHEM, GEORGE WASHINGTON UNIV, 65- *Personal Data:* b Manchester, Eng, Feb 23, 23; nat US; m 48; c 3. *Educ:* Univ NH, BS, 43; Harvard Univ, MA, 45, PhD(chem), 48. *Prof Exp:* Mem sci staff, Columbia Univ, 47-49; res chemist, US Naval Ord Lab, 49-56 & Atlantic Res Corp, 56-65. *Mem:* Am Chem Soc. *Res:* Thermal decomposition of nitrate esters; reactions of free radicals; chemistry of rocket propellants; fluorine chemistry. *Mailing Add:* 7610 Honestway Bethesda MD 20817-5520

LEVY, JOSEPH VICTOR, PHYSIOLOGY, PHARMACOLOGY. *Current Pos:* assoc prof, Sch Med Sci, Univ Pac, 69-77, assocc prof, Sch Dent, 72-85, clin prof physiol & pharmacol, Sch Dent 85-91, PHARMACOL COURSE DIR, SCH DENT UNIV PAC, 81-, PROF & CHMN PHYSIOL, 91- *Personal Data:* b Los Angeles, Calif, Apr 7, 28; m 54, Joanne Presley; c Virginia R & Suzanne (Garrett Jr). *Educ:* Stanford Univ, BA, 50; Univ Calif, Los Angeles, MS, 56; Univ Wash, PhD(pharmacol), 59. *Prof Exp:* Asst physiol, Stanford Univ, 51-53, asst pharmacol, 54-56; asst, Univ Wash, 56-57; pharmacologist, Surg Res Labs, Presby Hosp, 60; sr res pharmacologist, Res Labs, Presby Med Ctr, 60-65; dir, Lab Pharmacol & Exp Therapeut, Pac Presby Med Ctr, 61-89. *Concurrent Pos:* NIH res trainee pharmacol, 57-58 & anesthesiol, 58-59; res fel, Am Heart Asn, 59-60; res career prog scientist, Nat Heart Inst, 65-70; mem drug interaction panel, Am Pharmaceut Asn, 73-85; mem, Coun Basic Res, Am Heart Asn; mem res comt, Calif Heart Asn, 75-77; mem, Hypertenison Task Force, Nat Heart Inst, NIH, 76-77; consult, WHO & UN Develop Prog, 81; mem expert adv panel geriat drugs, US Pharmacopea, 85-95; mem, Pharmacol & Therapeut Comt, Calif, Pac Med Ctr, 72- *Mem:* Soc Exp Biol & Med; Cardiac Muscle Soc; Am Soc Clin Pharmacol & Therapeut; Am Soc Pharmacol & Therapeut; Am Chem Soc; Am Physiol Soc. *Res:* Physiology and pharmacology; hypertension; central nervous systems prostaglandins; inflammation; vascular; analgesia; thrombosis; platelets. *Mailing Add:* Dept Physiol & Pharmacol Sch Dent Univ Pac 2155 Webster St San Francisco CA 94115

LEVY, JULIA GERWING, MICROBIOLOGY. *Current Pos:* From instr to assoc prof, 58-74, PROF MICROBIOL, UNIV BC, 74-, MEM CANCER RES UNIT, 77- *Personal Data:* b Singapore, May 15, 34; nat Can; m 55, 69; c 3. *Educ:* Univ BC, BA, 55; Univ London, PhD(bact), 58. *Hon Degrees:* Doctorate, Univ Ottawa, 89; Doctorate, Mt St Vincents Univ, 90. *Honors & Awards:* Killiam Sci Prize; Biely Sci Award. *Concurrent Pos:* Vpres, Res & Develop, Quadralogic Technol Inc. *Mem:* Am Asn Immunologists; fel Royal Soc Can. *Res:* Characterization of antigenic determinants on natural antigens and the effect of these determinants on the cellular immune response; photoimmunotherapy; a study of immunotoxins to which photosensitizers have been conjugated. *Mailing Add:* QLT PhotoTherapeut Inc 520 W Sixth Ave Suite 200 Vancouver BC V5Z 4H5 Can

LEVY, LAWRENCE S, ALGEBRA. *Current Pos:* from asst prof to assoc prof, 61-71, PROF MATH, UNIV WIS-MADISON, 71- *Personal Data:* b Cleveland, Ohio, Oct 2, 33; m 61; c 2. *Educ:* Juilliard Sch Music, BS, 54, MS, 56; Univ Ill, MA, 58, PhD(math), 61. *Prof Exp:* Instr math, Univ Ill, 61. *Mem:* Am Math Soc. *Res:* Structure of associative rings and their modules. *Mailing Add:* Math Dept Univ Wis-Madison 480 Lincoln Dr Madison WI 53706-1388. *Fax:* 608-263-8891

LEVY, LEO, PSYCHOLOGY, PREVENTIVE MEDICINE. *Current Pos:* asst prof psychiat, Univ Ill Med Ctr, 65-69, assoc prof prev med, 69-75, prof pub health & prev med, 75-89, EMER PROF PUB HEALTH, UNIV ILL MED CTR, 89- *Personal Data:* b New York, NY, July 11, 28; m 57, Annika Ameen; c Stephanie & Anna. *Educ:* City Col New York, BS, 50, MA, 51; Univ Wash, PhD(psychol), 58; Harvard Univ, SMHyg, 64. *Prof Exp:* Instr psychol, Univ Mich, 58-60; adminr & chief psychologist, Pueblo Guid Ctr, Pueblo, Colo, 60-63; dir planning & eval, Ill Dept Ment Health, 64-69. *Concurrent Pos:* NIMH fels, Univ Mich, 58-60 & Harvard Univ, 63-64; Fulbright Hays res grant, State Univ Leiden, 72-73; vis assoc prof psychiat, McMaster Univ, 69-71; Fogerty Sr Int fel, Inst Psychiat, London, 79-80; vis prof, St George's Hosp Med Sch, London, 79-80; clin fac psychiat, Univ NMex, 94- *Mem:* Am Asn Univ Prof; Am Psychol Asn. *Res:* Promotion and maintenance of mental health; social planning; drug abuse; social ecology; psychosocial epidemiology; problems of urban mental health. *Mailing Add:* 4804 Mariah Rd NW Albuquerque NM 87107

LEVY, LEON BRUCE, INDUSTRIAL ORGANIC CHEMISTRY. *Current Pos:* SR RES ASSOC, TECH CTR, HOECHST CELANESE CORP, 90- *Personal Data:* b New York, NY, July 20, 37; m 68, Cornelia Y Gonzalez; c Elizabeth & Joseph. *Educ:* NY Univ, BA, 58; Harvard Univ, AM, 59, PhD(chem), 62. *Prof Exp:* Res chemist, Clarkwood Res Lab, Celanese Chem Co, 62-65, sr res chemist, Tech Ctr, 65-71, res assoc, 72-90. *Mem:* Catalysis Soc. *Res:* Kinetics and mechanisms of homolytic organic reactions; vapor phase oxidations of hydrocarbons; heterogeneous catalysis; monomer stability. *Mailing Add:* Hoechst Celanese Chem Group Box 9077 Corpus Christi TX 78469-9077. *E-Mail:* lbl@corhcc1.hcc.com

LEVY, LEON SHOLOM, computer science, for more information see previous edition

LEVY, LEONARD ALVIN, PODIATRIC DERMATOLOGY, AGING. *Current Pos:* Dean & vpres podiat med, Calif Col Podiat Med, 67-74, dean podiat med, State Univ NY, Stony Brook, 74-76, consult podiat med, Univ Tex Health Sci Ctr, 76-81, interim vpres planning & research, 93, DEAN PODIAT MED, UNIV OSTEOPATH MED & HEALTH SCI, 81- *Personal Data:* b New York, NY, Aug 19, 35; m 60, Eleanore Autrbach; c Sarilyn J & Andrew L. *Educ:* NY Univ, BA, 56; NY Col Podiat Med, DPM, 61; Columbia Univ Sch Pub Health, MPH, 67. *Concurrent Pos:* Mem review comt, USPHS Adv Comt, 68-72, clin assoc prof, Dept Dermat, Stanford Univ Sch Med, 70-74, chmn & mem test comt, Nat Bd Podiat Med examrs, 77-, governing coun mem, Am Pub Health Asn, 78-80 & 84-86, mem test comt dermat, Nat Bd Podiat Med Examrs, 81-; mem spec med adv group, Dept Vet Admin, 90- *Mem:* Am Pub Health Asn; Am Pub Health Asn; Am Acad Dermat; Am Asn Col Podiat Med; Asn Am Med Col; Nat Rural Health Asn. *Res:* Podiatric medical education; public health dermatological problems of the foot and ankle; health promotion and prevention; geriatrics; rural health primary care. *Mailing Add:* 7114 Franklin Ave Des Moines IA 50322. *Fax:* 515-271-1532

LEVY, LOUIS, PHARMACOLOGY. *Current Pos:* STAFF TOXICOLOGIST, DEPT HEALTH SERVS, STATE CALIF, 88- *Personal Data:* b Brooklyn, NY, Feb 1, 23; m 54; c 5. *Educ:* Univ Iowa, BS, 49, MS, 51, PhD(pharmacol), 54. *Prof Exp:* Asst chem, Syracuse Univ, 49-50; asst pediat, Univ Iowa, 50-52, instr pharmacol, 53-54; asst prof, Med Sch, Georgetown Univ, 54-55; asst prof, Col Med, Univ Cincinnati, 55-59; sr pharmacologist, Riker Labs, Calif, 59-71; from assoc prof to prof pharmacol, Sch Med, Univ Calif, Los Angeles, 71-85; consult, 85-88. *Concurrent Pos:* Res collabr, Brookhaven Nat Lab, 53-55. *Mem:* AAAS; Am Soc Pharmacol & Exp Therapeut; NY Acad Sci. *Res:* Biochemical pharmacology. *Mailing Add:* 4961 Edlerton Ave Encino CA 91436

LEVY, LOUIS A, ORGANIC CHEMISTRY. *Current Pos:* scientist, Nat Air Pollution Control Admin, USPHS, 66-67, scientist, Lab Environ Chem, 67-, RES CHEMIST, NAT INST ENVIRON HEALTH SCI. *Personal Data:* b New York, NY, Mar 6, 41; m 67; c 1. *Educ:* City Col New York, BS, 61; Univ Colo, PhD(chem), 66. *Prof Exp:* Proj leader synthesis, Int Flavors & Fragrances, Inc, 65-66. *Mem:* Am Chem Soc; The Chem Soc. *Res:* Chemistry and synthesis of chemicals of environmental concern; Nuclear Magnetic Resonance spectroscopy. *Mailing Add:* Nat Inst Environ Health Sci Lab Struct Biol PO Box 12233 Research Triangle Park NC 27709

LEVY, M(ORTON) FRANK, ORGANIC CHEMISTRY. *Current Pos:* RETIRED. *Personal Data:* b New York, NY, May 31, 25; m 90; c Brooke (Greene), Drew (Irvin) & Alisa. *Educ:* Queens Col, NY, BS, 50; Columbia Univ, MA, 51; Yale Univ, PhD(chem), 56. *Prof Exp:* Group leader org synthesis & anal develop, Argus Chem Co, 55-60; group leader org synthesis, Harchem Div, Wallace & Tiernan, NJ, 60-64; sr chemist, Mat Sci Lab, IBM Corp, San Jose, 64-90. *Concurrent Pos:* Res assoc, Univ Calif, Berkeley, 75-76. *Mem:* Am Chem Soc; AAAS. *Res:* Utilization of new raw materials in organic synthesis; photosensitive materials; dibasic acids; dye chemistry; preparation of radiolabeled compounds; new polymers; application of computers to chemistry. *Mailing Add:* 101 Pinta Ct Los Gatos CA 95032-6331

LEVY, MARILYN, PHOTOGRAPHIC ENGINEERING, CHEMISTRY. *Current Pos:* CONSULT, 80- *Personal Data:* b New York, NY, Apr 3, 22. *Educ:* Hunter Col, AB, 42. *Prof Exp:* Chemist anal-drugs, NY Quinine & Chem Co, 42-43; chemist lacquer formulation, Roxalin Flexible Finishes, 43-46, chemist lacquer mfg, Valspar Corp, 46-48; inspector chem, NY Quartermaster Proc Agency, 51-52; res chemist photog process, US Army Electronics Command, 53-74; chief photog optics div, Photog Eng, US Army

Combat & Surveillance Lab, 75-80. *Concurrent Pos:* Mem & US Army rep, Am Nat Standards Inst, 62-; chmn, Processing Sect, Soc Photog Scientists & Engrs, 73-74; US Army adv, NATO Photog Standards Comt & Air Standardization Coord Comt, 78- *Mem:* Fel Soc Photog Scientists & Engrs; Am Chem Soc. *Res:* Photographic processing; non-conventional photographic systems; aerial photography; photographic sensitometry; color photography; rapid processing; 26 patents and 20 papers in photo science field. *Mailing Add:* 56 Cheshire Sq Little Silver NJ 07739

LEVY, MARK B, MATHEMATICS. *Current Pos:* Sr prof, 83-85, SYST ENG, FED AVIATION ADMIN, 85- *Personal Data:* b Hong Kong, China, June 19, 51. *Educ:* Cooper Union, BA, 74. *Mem:* Am Math Soc; Am Comput Mach. *Res:* Multi parallel computing operating systems. *Mailing Add:* AIT-400 800 Independance Ave Washington DC 20591

LEVY, MARTIN J LINDEN, medical sciences, research administration, for more information see previous edition

LEVY, MATTHEW NATHAN, PHYSIOLOGY, BIOMEDICAL ENGINEERING. *Current Pos:* CHIEF DEPT INVESTIGATIVE MED, MT SINAI HOSP, 67- *Personal Data:* b New York, NY, Dec 2, 22; m 46, Ruth Joseph; c Donald J, Garry E & James R. *Educ:* Western Res Univ, BS, 43, MD, 45. *Honors & Awards:* Lederle Med Fac Award, 55-57; Shanes Mem Lectureship, 72; Wiggers Award, Am Physiol Soc, 83; Merit Award, NIH, 86; Distinguished Scientist Award, 88; Mikamo Lectr, Kyoto, 91; Gordon Moe Lectr, 94. *Prof Exp:* From instr to asst prof physiol, Western Res Univ, 49-53; from asst prof to assoc prof, Albany Med Col, 53-57; dir res, St Vincent Charity Hosp, Cleveland, Ohio, 57-67; assoc prof, 61-68, prof, physiol & biomed eng, Case Western Res Univ, 68- *Concurrent Pos:* Res fel, Western Res Univ, 48-49; assoc prof, Case Inst Technol, 63-67; assoc ed, Circulation Res, 70-74; sect ed, Am J Physiol, 75-, ed, Am J Physiol, Heart & Circulatory Physiol, 76-81. *Mem:* Am Physiol Soc; Am Heart Asn. *Res:* Cardiovascular physiology. *Mailing Add:* Dept Investigative Med Mt Sinai Med Ctr Cleveland OH 44106. *Fax:* 216-421-5111; *E-Mail:* mnl@po.cwru.edu

LEVY, MATTHYS P, STRUCTURAL DESIGN IN ARCHITECTURE. *Current Pos:* staff, 56-64, prin, 64-86, EXEC VPRES & DIR STRUCT DIV, WEIDLINGER ASSOCS, 86- *Personal Data:* b Basle, Switz. *Educ:* City Col NY, BSCE, 51; Columbia Univ, MSCE, 56, CE, 62. *Honors & Awards:* Lincoln Arc Welding Award, 61, 81 & 91; Prestressed Concrete Inst Award, 63, 71 & 92; Medal of Excellence, Eng News Record, 92; Innovation in Civil Eng Award, Am Soc Civil Engrs, 94. *Prof Exp:* Struct consult, New York, NY & Chicago, Ill, 51-55; asst opers officers, 453rd Eng Construct Battalion, US Army, Korea, 52-54. *Concurrent Pos:* Vis critic archit, Yale Univ, 60-65; adj prof, Sch Archit, Columbia Univ, 62-80; distinguished prof, Pratt Inst, NY, 80-81; lectr, Univ Idaho, Rutgers Univ, Princeton Univ, Harvard Univ, Cath Univ & Univ Fla. *Mem:* Nat Acad Eng; fel Am Inst Civil Engrs; Am Concrete Inst; Nat Acad Forensic Engrs; Int Asn Shell & Spatial Struct; Int Asn Bridge & Struct Eng; fel Am Soc Civil Engrs; Am Inst Architects. *Mailing Add:* Weidlinger Assocs 333 Seventh Ave New York NY 10001. *Fax:* 212-564-2279

LEVY, MOISES, LOW TEMPERATURE SOLID STATE PHYSICS, PHYSICAL ACOUSTICS. *Current Pos:* assoc prof, 71-73, chmn dept, 75-78, PROF PHYSICS, UNIV WIS-MILWAUKEE, 73- *Personal Data:* b Panama, Apr 8, 30; US citizen; m 83. *Educ:* Calif Inst Technol, BS, 52, MS, 55; Univ Calif, Los Angeles, PhD(physics), 63. *Prof Exp:* Res chemist, Speciality Resins, Inc, 53-54; mem tech staff, Semiconductor Div, Hughes Aircraft Co, 56-58; asst prof solid state physics, Univ Pa, 64-65; asst prof ultrasonic invest solid state, Univ Calif, Los Angeles, 65-70. *Concurrent Pos:* NATO postdoc fel, 63-64; chmn, Ultrasonics Symp, 74 & 83, prog comt mem, 72-; vis prof, Int Vis Info Serv, 72, 76 & 82, Univ Sao Paolo, 79 & 83, Techmon Univ, 85-86; Lady Doris fel, 85-86. *Mem:* Fel Am Phys Soc; Acoustical Soc Am; Ultrasonic, Ferroelec & Frequency Control Soc. *Res:* Experimental investigation of electron phonon interaction in superconductors and normal metals; spin phonon in magnetic superconductors and rare earth metals; surface wave investigation of superconducting films and magnetic films. *Mailing Add:* Dept Physics Univ Wis Milwaukee WI 53201

LEVY, MORRIS, BIOSYSTEMATICS. *Current Pos:* Asst prof, 73-79, ASSOC PROF BIOL SCI, PURDUE UNIV, 79- *Personal Data:* b Chicago, Ill, May 22, 44; m 74; c 1. *Educ:* Univ Ill, Chicago Circle, 67; Yale Univ, MPh, 72, PhD(ecol, evolution), 73. *Concurrent Pos:* Dir, Kriebel Herbarium, Purdue Univ, 73-; NSF grant, Res Prog Biomed Sci, 75; NSF grant, 78 & 79. *Mem:* Bot Soc Am; Soc Study Evolution; Soc Am Naturalists; AAAS. *Res:* Systematics and biochemical ecology of plants; evolution of hybrid and polyploid species; population biology of weeds; host plant-fungal pathogen co-evolution; pollination ecology. *Mailing Add:* Dept Biol Sci Purdue Univ West Lafayette IN 47907-1968

LEVY, MORTIMER, RESEARCH ADMINISTRATION. *Current Pos:* RETIRED. *Personal Data:* b Rochester, NY, July 7, 24; m 50; c 2. *Educ:* Cornell Univ, BSEE, 49; Columbia Univ, MA, 51. *Prof Exp:* Physicist, Xerox Corp, 54-57, sect leader, 58-61; dir appl res, Mat Res Corp, 61-63; res scientist, Xerox Corp, 63-64, sr scientist, 64-67, mgr explor res, 67-73, mgr process sect, 73-75, mgr, Process Element Sect, 75-78, mgr mat, Processes & Corp Staff, 78- *Mem:* Soc Photog Sci & Eng. *Res:* Electrostatic photography. *Mailing Add:* 105 Towpath Lane Rochester NY 14618

LEVY, NELSON LOUIS, PHARMACEUTICAL RESEARCH & DEVELOPMENT. *Current Pos:* CHIEF EXEC OFFICER & CHMN, CORETECHS CORP, 84- *Personal Data:* b Somerville, NJ, June 19, 41; m 74, Louisa Stiles; c Scott, Erik, Jonathan, Michael, Andrew & David. *Educ:* Yale Univ, BA & BS, 63; Columbia Univ, MD, 67; Duke Univ, PhD(immunol), 73. *Prof Exp:* Intern surg, Univ Colo Med Ctr, 67-68; res assoc virol & immunol, NIH, 68-70; resident neurol, Duke Univ Med Ctr, 71-72, from asst prof to assoc prof immunol, 76-80; vpres, Pharmaceut Res, Abbott Labs, 81-84; pres, Fujisawa Pharmaceut Co, 92-93; chief exec officer, Ill Tech Develop Corp, 93-94. *Concurrent Pos:* Study sects, NIH, Nat Mult Sclerosis Soc, 75-80; bd dir, Bionica Pty, Ltd, Intek Diagnostics, SASHA, Inc, Heybach Enterprises, MedVac, Inc, Quantum Group, Inc, Anthra Pharmaceut, Inc, Myotech Corp, Chem Bridge Corp, Mei-Rui Pharma, Ltd, Horizon Quest, Inc, Ligand Pharmaceut. *Mem:* Am Asn Cancer Res; Am Asn Immunologists; Soc Neuroscience; Pharmaceut Mfrs Asn; Drug Info Asn; Licensing Execs Soc. *Res:* Immunologic and non-immunologic defenses against human cancer; pathogenesis and etiology of multiple sclerosis; neurologic control of the immune system; molecular modeling of pharmaceuticals. *Mailing Add:* Coretechs Corp 1391 Concord Dr Lake Forest IL 60045

LEVY, NEWTON, JR, INORGANIC CHEMISTRY, TECHNICAL MANAGEMENT. *Current Pos:* RETIRED. *Personal Data:* b Tampa, Fla, Oct 10, 35; m 61; c 2. *Educ:* Univ Fla, BSCh, 61, PhD(kinetics), 64. *Prof Exp:* Res chemist, Wash Res Ctr Div, W R Grace & Co, 64-67, sr chemist, 67-69, res supvr, 69-72; sect head refractories, Martin Marietta Labs, Martin Marietta Chem, 72-74, mgr fuel additives, Refractories Div, 74-76, mgr prod develop, 77-81, vpres sales-chem, 81-91. *Res:* Preparation, fabrication, characterization and applications of reactive, fine sized ceramic oxide powders; properties and uses of magnesium oxide; chemical treatment of oils for combustion; chemical market studies; marketing specialty chemicals. *Mailing Add:* 23 Skye Dr Brevard NC 28712

LEVY, NORMAN B, PSYCHIATRY, PSYCHOSOMATIC MEDICINE. *Current Pos:* PROF PSYCHIAT, MED & SURG, NY MED COL & DIR, LIAISON PSYCHIAT DIV, WESTCHESTER CO MED CTR & NY MED COL, 80- *Personal Data:* b New York, NY, May 28, 31; m 58, 70, Carol L Spiegel; c Karen, Susan, Joanne & Robert B. *Educ:* NY Univ, BA, 52; State Univ NY Downstate Med Ctr, MD, 56. *Prof Exp:* Res physician & teaching fel med, Sch Med, Univ Pittsburgh, 57-58; dir med serv, USAF Hosp, Ashiya, Japan, 58-60; resident physician psychiat, Kings Co Hosp Ctr, Brooklyn, NY, 60-63; from instr to asst prof med & psychiat, State Univ NY Downstate Med Ctr, 63-73, dir continuing educ psychiat, 74-76, presiding officer fac, Col Med, 75-76, assoc prof, 73-79, prof psychiat, 79-80, assoc dir, Med Psychiat Liaison Serv, 72-80. *Concurrent Pos:* NIMH career teacher award, 66; consult psychiat educ, NIMH, 74-; examr psychiat, Am Bd psychiat & Neurol, 74-; assoc ed, Int J Psychiat Med, 77-78; assoc ed, General Hosp Pschiat & ed of sect, Liaison Rounds, 79-; vis prof psychiat & med, Univ Hawaii, 81. *Mem:* Fel Am Col Physicians; fel Am Psychiat Asn; fel Int Col Psychosom Med; Sigma Xi; fel Am Col Psychiatrists; Am Psychosom Soc. *Res:* Effects of psychological stresses on kidney transplant rejections; psychological adaptation to hemodialysis; psychiatry and the changing role of males in society; attitudes of students and physicians on informing patients of their fatal diagnosis; use of fluoxetine in renal failure; use of fluoxetine in depressed patients with medical illnesses. *Mailing Add:* Dept Psychiatr Mhc 145 Coney Island Hosp Brooklyn NY 11235

LEVY, NORMAN STUART, OPHTHALMOLOGY, GLAUCOMA. *Current Pos:* Asst prof ophthal & pediat, 72-75, CO-CLIN ASSOC PROF FAMILY MED, UNIV FLA, 81- *Personal Data:* b Detroit, Mich, July 17, 40; m 64; c 4. *Educ:* Case Western Res, MD, 65; Univ Chicago, PhD(ophthal), 75. *Honors & Awards:* Paleologos Award, 95. *Concurrent Pos:* Chief ophthal, Vet Admin Hosp, Gainesville, 73-75 & Vet Admin Med Ctr, Lake City, 76-89; dir, Kerato Refractive Soc, 80-94. *Mem:* Am Acad Ophthal; Asn Res Vision & Ophthal; Am Col Surgeons; Kerato Refractive Soc; Contemp Soc Ophthal (pres, 92-94). *Res:* Mechanism of damage in the disease, glaucoma, and method of diagnosis and early treatment; pharmaceutical glaucoma research. *Mailing Add:* 7106 NW 11th Pl Gainesville FL 32605-3157

LEVY, PAUL, APPLIED MATHEMATICS. *Current Pos:* ASST PROF MATH, STATE UNIV NY MARITIME COL, 77- *Personal Data:* b New York, NY, May 25, 41; m 65; c 1. *Educ:* Rensselaer Polytech Inst, BS, 63, MS, 65, PhD(math), 68. *Prof Exp:* Asst prof math, NY Univ, 67-74; asst prof math, NY Inst Technol, 74-77. *Mem:* Am Math Soc; Soc Indust & Appl Math. *Res:* Investigation of problems in wave propagation and elasticity. *Mailing Add:* Brookhaven Nat Lab Bldg 480 PO Box 5000 Upton NY 11973-5000

LEVY, PAUL F, ANALYTICAL CHEMISTRY, INSTRUMENTATION. *Current Pos:* proj engr, E I DuPont De Nemours & Co, 65-68, sr proj engr, 68-69, supvr appln lab, 69-73, prod mgr thermal anal, 73-75, prod mgr liquid chromatog, 75-78, develop mgr, 78-85, MKT DEVELOP MGR, BIOMED PROD DEPT, E I DU PONT DE NEMOURS & CO, 85- *Personal Data:* b New York, NY, Dec 9, 34; m 59, 73; c 4. *Educ:* City Col New York, BS, 59; Columbia Univ, MA, 61, PhD(anal chem), 65. *Prof Exp:* Lectr chem, City Col New York, 59-65. *Mem:* Am Chem Soc; Am Asn Clin Chemists. *Res:* Theory, applications, design and development of thermal analysis and other material characterization instrumentation; coulostatic impulse-chain and other forms of polarography; electrochemical instrumentation; clinical and biomedical instrumentation; development management. *Mailing Add:* 4818 Hogan Dr 20381 Wilmington DE 19808-1715

LEVY, PAUL W(ARREN), SOLID STATE PHYSICS. *Current Pos:* assoc physicist, 52-58, PHYSICIST RADIATION DAMAGE INSULATORS REACTIVE MAT & MINERALS, BROOKHAVEN NAT LAB, 58- *Personal Data:* b Chicago, Ill, Mar 17, 21; m 44; c 4. *Educ:* Univ Chicago, BS, 43; Carnegie Inst Technol, PhD, 54. *Prof Exp:* Jr physicist, Metall Lab, Univ Chicago, 43-44; physicist beta-ray spectros, Oak Ridge Nat Lab, 44-48. *Concurrent Pos:* Consult to indust, civilian & mil agencies, 55-; adj prof, Adelphi Univ, 66-; adj prof geol, Univ Pa, 76- *Mem:* Fel Am Phys Soc; Optical Soc Am; Mat Res Soc. *Res:* Nuclear physics; luminescence of solids; optical and defect properties of solids; optical spectrophotometry; radiation effects in glasses, insulators, scintillators, metals, explosives and propellants; minerals, especially for radioactive waste applications; crystal growth; geoscience applications of solid state physics; thermoluminescence of solids and applications to dosimetry, mineralogy, mineral exploration and archaeology. *Mailing Add:* Bldg 480 Brookhaven Nat Lab Upton NY 11973

LEVY, PETER MICHAEL, ELECTRON TRANSPORT IN MAGNETIC METALS. *Current Pos:* assoc prof, 70-75, chmn dept, 76-82 & 91-97, PROF PHYSICS, NY UNIV, 75- *Personal Data:* b Frankfurt, Ger, Jan 10, 36; US citizen; m 65, Darline Gay Shapiro; c Erik & Serge. *Educ:* City Col New York, BME, 58; Harvard Univ, MA, 60, PhD(appl physics), 63. *Honors & Awards:* Vermeil Medal, Soc Advan Progress, Paris, 78. *Prof Exp:* Res assoc physics, Lab Electrostatics & Physics of Metals, Grenoble, France, 63-64; res assoc, Univ Pa, 64-66; asst prof, Yale Univ, 66-70. *Concurrent Pos:* NSF fel, 58-62; fel, Nat Ctr Sci Res, France, 63-64; Air Force Off Sci Res grant, Yale Univ & NY Univ, 67-72; NSF grants, NY Univ, 72-75, 75-79, 79-82, 82-86 & 87; Fulbright-Hays res scholar, France, 75-76; res exchange scientist, NSF-Nat Ctr Sci Res, France, 75-76 & 83-84. *Mem:* Fel Am Phys Soc; Mat Res Soc. *Res:* The magneto-transport properties of metallic multilayered structures (superlattices); magnetoresistivity of rare earth metallic compounds; orbital effects in rare earth compounds; anisotropy in disordered magnetic systems; spin glasses; long range interactions between local movements in metals; spin-dependent tunneling in ferromagnetic tunnel junctions. *Mailing Add:* Dept Physics NY Univ 4 Washington Pl New York NY 10003. *E-Mail:* levy@nyu.edu

LEVY, RALPH, MICROWAVE THEORY, CIRCUIT THEORY. *Current Pos:* INDEPENDENT CONSULT, 89- *Personal Data:* b London, Eng, Apr 12, 32; US citizen; m 59, Barbara Nee Dent; c Mark S & Sharon E (Armad). *Educ:* Cambridge Univ, MA, 53; Univ London, PhD(appl sci), 66. *Honors & Awards:* Microwave Career Award, Inst Elec & Electronics Engrs, Microwave Theory & Techniques Soc, 97. *Prof Exp:* Mem sci staff microwave eng, Gen Elec Co, Stanmore, Eng, 53-59, Mullard Res Labs, Redhill, 59-64; lectr elec eng, Univ Leeds, 64-67; vpres res microwave eng, Microwave Develop Labs, KW Microwave Inc, 67-84, vpres eng, 84-89. *Concurrent Pos:* Consult, Decca Radar Ltd & Gen Elec Co, 64-67, Weinschel Eng, 65-66. *Mem:* Fel Inst Elec & Electronics Engrs. *Res:* Microwave passive components; distributed circuit theory; military microwave systems; author of over 60 papers & 3 books; granted 12 US patents. *Mailing Add:* R Levy Assoc 1897 Caminito Velasco La Jolla CA 92037. *Fax:* 619-459-6752; *E-Mail:* rlevy@ieee.org

LEVY, RAM LEON, SEPARATION SCIENCE, CHEMICAL INTRUMENTATION. *Current Pos:* SCIENTIST, POLYMER CHEMISTRY, MCDONNELL DOUGLAS RES LABS, MCDONNELL DOUGLAS CORP, 68- *Personal Data:* b Samokov, Bulgaria, Oct 7, 33; US citizen; m 58; c 3. *Educ:* Israel Inst Technol, BSc, 61, MSc, 63; Univ Man, PhD(anal chem), 67. *Prof Exp:* Res assoc, Dept Plant Sci, Univ Man, 63-67; assoc chemist, Midwest Res Labs, Kansas City, 67-68. *Concurrent Pos:* Affil dir, Sch Continuing Prof Educ, Washington Univ, 70-72; vis lectr, Chem Dept, St Louis Univ, 75. *Mem:* Am Chem Soc; Am Mass Spectrometry. *Res:* Chemical mechanisms of polymer aging; detection of stress and fatigue induced molecular phenomena in polymers by infrared spectroscopy; chemluminescence of polymers; chromatographic characterization of oligimers; incorporation of molecular probes in polymer networks; thermal degradation of polymers. *Mailing Add:* 1622 Parquet Ct St Louis MO 63146-4319

LEVY, RENE HANANIA, PHARMACODYNAMICS. *Current Pos:* asst prof pharm, Col Pharm, 70-74, assoc prof, 74-77, PROF PHARMACEUT, SCH PHARM & PROF NEUROL SURG, SCH MED, UNIV WASH, 77- *Personal Data:* b Casa Blanca, Morocco, Sept 30, 42; US citizen; m 64; c 3. *Educ:* Univ Bordeaux, Baccalaureat, 60; Univ Paris, Pharm, 65; Univ Calif, San Francisco, PhD(pharm, pharmaceut chem), 70. *Prof Exp:* Intern, Hosps of Paris, Hopital Corentin Celton, 64-66. *Mem:* Am Epilepsy Soc; Fedn Int Pharmaceutique; Am Pharmaceut Asn; Acad Pharmaceut Sci. *Res:* Pharmacokinetic evaluation of anticonvulsants prior to efficacy testing in primates; clinical pharmacology of new antiepileptic drugs; kinetics of drug metabolites. *Mailing Add:* Dept Pharm Univ Wash Box 357610 Seattle WA 98195-7610

LEVY, RICARDO BENJAMIN, SURFACE CHEMISTRY, CHEMICAL ENGINEERING. *Current Pos:* vpres, 74-77, EXEC VPRES CONSULT RES & DEVELOP, CATALYTICA ASSOCS, INC, 77- *Personal Data:* b Quito, Ecuador, Jan 11, 45; US citizen; m 67; c 2. *Educ:* Stanford Univ, BSc, 66, PhD(chem eng), 72; Princeton Univ, MA, 67. *Prof Exp:* Gen mgr mfg, Sudam Cia Ltda, 67-69; res eng chem physics, Exxon Res & Eng Co, 72-74. *Concurrent Pos:* Prof chem eng, Inst Politecnico Nac, Quito, Ecuador, 67-69. *Mem:* Am Inst Chem Engrs; Am Chem Soc; Faraday Soc; Catalysis Soc. *Res:* Reactivity of solid surfaces in catalytic reactions; new materials for catalysis; chemical vapor transport. *Mailing Add:* Catalytica Assocs Inc 430 Ferguson Dr Bldg 3 Mountain View CA 94043-5214

LEVY, RICHARD, MEDICAL ENTOMOLOGY, CONTROLLED RELEASE TECHNOLOGY. *Current Pos:* RES ENTOMOLOGIST MED ENTOM COORDR, LEE CO MOSQUITO CONTROL DIST, 75- *Personal Data:* b Brooklyn, NY, June 29, 44; m 69, Diane Durrenberger; c Jonathan. *Educ:* Univ Fla, BS, 67 & BS, 68, MS, 69, PhD(entom), 71. *Prof Exp:* Res asst med entom, Dept Entom & Nematol, Univ Fla, 71-74; tech & training consult pest control, Orkin Exterminating Co, 74; res entomologist med entom, WFla Arthropod Res Lab, 74-75. *Concurrent Pos:* Consult, US & overseas. *Mem:* Am Registry Prof Entomologists; Entom Soc Am; Am Mosquito Control Asn; Am Chem Soc; Soc Invert Path; Controlled Release Soc; AAAS; Am Soc Testing Mats. *Res:* Biological and chemical control of insects of medical and veterinary importance; US patents; overseas patents. *Mailing Add:* Lee Co Mosquito Control Dist PO Box 06005 Ft Myers FL 33906

LEVY, RICHARD ALLEN, MEDICATION MANAGEMENT. *Current Pos:* VPRES SCI AFFAIRS, NAT PHARMACEUT COUN, 81- *Educ:* Univ Del, PhD(pharmacol), 70. *Mailing Add:* Nat Pharmaceut Coun 1894 Preston White Dr Reston VA 20191

LEVY, RICHARD PHILIP, DIABETES, THROID DISEASE. *Current Pos:* from assoc prof to prof, 68-78, CLIN PROF MED, CASE WESTERN RES UNIV SCH MED, 79-; PROF INTERNAL MED, NORTHEASTERN OHIO UNIVS COL MED, 78- *Personal Data:* b Hempstead, NY, Nov 3, 23; m 45, Barbara Quint; c Donald M, Ellen (Raper) & Charles M. *Educ:* Yale Univ, BS, 44, MD, 47; Am Bd Internal Med, cert internal med, 55, cert endocrinol & metab, 72. *Prof Exp:* Med consult, Cleveland State Hosp, 53-55; instr med, Western Med Univ, 56-58, sr instr, 58-61, asst prof, 61-68. *Concurrent Pos:* Teaching fel, Univ Hosps, Cleveland, Ohio, 52-52; teaching fel med, Western Res Univ, 53-54, 54-55, Zakraschefska fel med, 55-56; dir health serv, Univ Hosps, Cleveland, Ohio, 53-60; asst prof radiol, Case Western Res Univ, 68-75, assoc prof, 75-78; dir, Thyroid Ctr, Dept Med, Univ Hosps, 75-78; prog dir, Internal Med, Canton Med Educ Found, 78-85; dir, Div Med, Northeastern Ohio Univs Col Med, 78-85, chmn Internal Med, 83-89, chmn Inst Rev Bd, 85-89; chmn, Dept Endocrinol, Med Ctr, St Thomas Hosp, 85- *Mem:* Am Col Physicians; Am Diabetes Asn; Am Fedn Clin Res; Am Thyroid Asn; Endocrine Soc. *Res:* Novel approaches to the treatment of insulin-requiring patients with diabetes; author of numerous scientific publications. *Mailing Add:* 444 N Main St Akron OH 44310. *Fax:* 330-253-2829

LEVY, ROBERT, biochemistry, clinical chemistry, for more information see previous edition

LEVY, ROBERT AARON, SOLID STATE PHYSICS, ACCIDENT RECONSTRUCTION. *Current Pos:* CONSULT PHYS PROB ENERGY & ENVIRON, 69- *Personal Data:* b El Paso, Tex, Nov 15, 26; m 56, Phyllis Bargman; c David A, Robin L, Carolyn L (Opegard) & Teresa L. *Educ:* Univ Tex, BS, 47, MA, 48; Univ Calif, Berkeley, MA, 50, PhD(physics), 55. *Prof Exp:* Physicist, US Naval Radiol Defense Lab, 50-53; asst physics, Univ Calif, 53-55; physicist, Tex Instruments, Inc, 55-57; proj engr, Motorola, Inc, 57-59; mem tech staff, Hughes Aircraft Co, 59-60; physicists, Nat Co, 61-62; assoc prof, Univ Cincinnati, 63-69. *Concurrent Pos:* Assoc fac mem, Ariz State Univ, 58-59 & Univ Southern Calif, 60-61; consult, US Naval Radiol Defense Lab, 59; fel, Israel AEC, 62-63. *Mem:* AAAS; fel Am Phys Soc; Am Asn Univ Prof. *Res:* Magnetic resonance spectroscopy; quantum electronics; solar energy. *Mailing Add:* 1617-D N Mesa St El Paso TX 79902-3527. *Fax:* 915-533-4327

LEVY, ROBERT EDWARD, TECHNOLOGY PLANNING, ADVANCED PROCESS CONTROL. *Current Pos:* VPRES GOVT & REGULATORY AFFAIRS, ENERGY BIOSYST CORP, 93. *Personal Data:* b Cincinnati, Ohio, May 23, 39; m 70, Candace Wolfe; c Brian & Jessica. *Educ:* Cornell Univ, BChE, 62; Univ Calif, Berkeley, PhD(chem eng), 67. *Prof Exp:* Actg instr process control, Univ Calif, Berkeley, 65-66; engr & mgr, Exxon Corp, 67-86; independent consult, 86-87; vpres & dir technol develop, M W Kellogg Co, 87-93. *Mem:* Am Inst Chem Engrs; Sigma Xi; Indust Res Inst. *Res:* Manage the scaleup and commercialization of breakthrough biocatalytic processes for oil refining. *Mailing Add:* 3911 Arnold St Houston TX 77005

LEVY, ROBERT I, MEDICINE, BIOCHEMISTRY. *Current Pos:* PRES, WYETH-AYERST RES, 92- *Personal Data:* b Bronx, NY, May 3, 37; m 58; c 4. *Educ:* Cornell Univ, BA, 57; Yale Univ, MD, 61. *Honors & Awards:* Arthur S Flemming Award, 75; Humanitarian Award, Assoc Health Found, 76; Am Asn Clin Chem Award, 79; Donald D Van Slyke Award Clin Chem, 80; Albert Lasker Spec Pub Health Award, 80; Roger J Williams Award Prev Nutrit, 85; Humana Heart Found Award, 88. *Prof Exp:* Intern med, Yale-New Haven Med Ctr, 61-62, resident, 62-63; clin asst med res, Nat Heart Lung & Blood Inst, 63-65, chief resident med, 65-66, inst dir, 66-81, dep clin dir, 68-69, chief clin serv, Molecular Dis Br, 69-73, chief, Lipid Metab Br, 70-74, dir, Div Heart & Vascular Dis, 73-75, head, Sect Lipoproteins, 75-81; prof med, dean & vpres, Sch Med, Tufts Univ, 81-83; vpres health sci, Columbia Univ, 83-84, prof med, Col Physicians & Surgeons, 83-87, sr adv to Univ, 84-87; pres, Sandoz Res Inst, 88-92. *Concurrent Pos:* Mem, Coun Arteriosclerosis, Am Heart Asn; surgeon, USPHS, 63-66; mem & chmn numerous comts, councils & bd, 70-; spec consult anti-lipid drugs, Food & Drug Admin, 73-83; coordr, Cardiovasc Portion, US-USSR Agreement Health & Med Sci, 75-81; adj prof med, Col Physicians & Surgeons, Columbia Univ, 89- *Mem:* Inst Med-Nat Acad Sci; fel NY Acad Sci; Am Soc Clin Invest; fel Am Col Cardiol; Am Fedn Clin Res; fel Soc Behav Med; Am Inst Nutrit; Am Soc Clin Pharmacol & Therapeut; Asn Am Physicians; Int Soc Cardiol; Asn Univ Cardiologists; Int Soc Hypertension; Am Heart Asn; Am Soc Clin Nutrit. *Res:* Lipid metabolism; lipid transport; atherosclerosis; hyperlipoproteinemia; lipoproteins; preventive cardiology; clinical nutrition; nutrition education. *Mailing Add:* Wyeth-Ayerst Res PO Box 8299 Philadelphia PA 19101. *Fax:* 610-995-4884

LEVY, ROBERT S(AMUEL), ENGINEERING. *Current Pos:* ADJ ASSOC PROF, AIRCRAFT DESIGN, POLYTECHNIC UNIV, 85- *Personal Data:* b New York, NY, May 28, 20; m 54; c 2. *Educ:* City Col New York, BME, 40; Polytech Inst Brooklyn, MME, 43, DrAeroEng, 46. *Prof Exp:* Mech Engr, NY Naval Shipyard, 41-46; struct engr, Repub Aviation Div, Fairchild-Hiller Corp, 46-59, develop engr, Fairchild Industs, 59-65, proj eng manned spaced vehicles, 65-66, eng prog mgr supersonic transp, 66-71, mgr design eng, 71-75, dir eng, 75, mgr tech eng, 76, mgr new systs res, 77-78, tech specialist, Fairchild Repub Co, 79-85. *Concurrent Pos:* Civilian with Nat Adv Comt Aeronaut, 44. *Mem:* Assoc fel Am Inst Aeronaut & Astronaut; Sigma Xi. *Res:* Aircraft structures. *Mailing Add:* 11 Brookside Dr Huntington NY 11743

LEVY, ROBERT SIGMUND, BIOCHEMISTRY, BIOLOGICAL PSYCHIATRY. *Current Pos:* RETIRED. *Personal Data:* b Fresno, Calif, Nov 3, 21; m 52; c 1. *Educ:* Univ Calif, Berkeley, AB, 48, AM, 52; Univ Southern Calif, PhD(biochem, nutrit), 57. *Prof Exp:* Asst zool, Univ Calif, Berkeley, 49-52; asst biochem & nutrit, Sch Med, Univ Southern Calif, 55-57; from asst prof to prof biochem, Sch Med, Univ Louisville, 57-72, dir, Lab-Biol Psychiat, 78- *Concurrent Pos:* Assoc psychiat & emergency med, Sch Med, Univ Louisville; fel, Coun Arteriosclerosis, Am Heart Asn. *Mem:* Asn Multidiscipline Educ Health Sci; Sigma Xi; Am Chem Soc; Am Soc Biol Chem; Soc Neurosci. *Res:* Isolation of unusual peptides from blood and hemodialysates of schizophrenic patients; detection of enkephalins and endorphins in biological fluids by radioimmunoassay and radioreceptor assay; biochemistry of brain function and role of neuropeptides; reversal of atherosclerosis by lipoproteins in cell culture. *Mailing Add:* Dept Psychiat Univ Louisville Health Sci Ctr Louisville KY 40292. *Fax:* 502-588-6222

LEVY, RONALD, MEDICINE. *Current Pos:* MEM FAC, STANFORD UNIV, CALIF, 75-, ASSOC PROF, DEPT MED-ONCOL. *Personal Data:* b Carmel, Calif. *Educ:* Harvard Univ, BS; Stanford Univ, MD, 68; Am Bd Internal Med, dipl. *Prof Exp:* Intern, Mass Gen Hosp, Boston, 68-69, researcher, 69-70; Helen Hay Whhitney Found fel, Dept Chem Immunol, Weizmann Inst Sci, Rehovot, Israel, 73-75. *Mem:* Am Col Physicians; Am Soc Clin Oncol. *Res:* Cancer research; oncology; medicine. *Mailing Add:* Dept Med-Oncol Stanford Univ Stanford CA 94305-5306

LEVY, RONALD FRED, TOPOLOGY. *Current Pos:* asst prof, 76-81, ASSOC PROF MATH, GEORGE MASON UNIV, 81- *Personal Data:* b St Louis, Mo, Dec 11, 44; m 66; c 1. *Educ:* Wash Univ, AB, 66, AM, 70, PhD(math), 74. *Prof Exp:* Asst prof math, Goucher Col, 74-75; instr math, Wash Univ, 75-76. *Mem:* Am Math Soc; Math Asn Am. *Res:* Compact Hausdorff spaces; almost-P-spaces; linearly ordered topological spaces. *Mailing Add:* Dept Math Sci George Mason Univ 4400 Univ Dr Fairfax VA 22030

LEVY, SALOMON, MECHANICAL ENGINEERING. *Current Pos:* CONSULT, LEVY & ASSOCS, 94- *Personal Data:* b Jerusalem, Apr 4, 26; US citizen; m 51; c 2. *Educ:* Univ Calif, Berkeley, BS, 49, MS, 51, PhD(mech eng), 53. *Honors & Awards:* Heat Transfer Mem Award, Am Soc Mech Engrs, 66; Thermal Hydraul Div Tech Achievement Award, Am Nuclear Soc, 87, Walter H Zinn Award, 89; Donald Q Kern Award, Am Inst Chem Engrs, 93. *Prof Exp:* Mgr systs eng, Gen Elec Co, 66-68, mgr design eng dept, 68-71, gen mgr nuclear fuel dept, 71-73, gen mgr boiling water reactor systs dept, 73-75, gen mgr boiling water reactor opers, 75-77; pres, S Levy Inc, Eng Consult, 77-94. *Concurrent Pos:* Consult, Assoc Midwestern Univ, 76-81, Brookhaven Nat Lab, 77- & Elec Power Res Inst, 77-84 & Elec Power Res Inst, 77-85; dir, Iowa Elec, 85- *Mem:* Nat Acad Eng; fel Am Soc Mech Engrs; fel Am Nuclear Soc. *Res:* Heat transfer and fluid flow, particularly two-phase flow and boiling heat transfer; nuclear reactor power plant design and analysis; authored over 50 publications. *Mailing Add:* Levy & Assocs 3880 S Bascom Ave Suite 112 San Jose CA 95124. *Fax:* 408-369-8720

LEVY, SAMUEL C, ELECTROCHEMISTRY, ELECTROANALYTICAL CHEMISTRY. *Current Pos:* RETIRED. *Personal Data:* b Far Rockaway, NY, Jan 5, 37; m 58, Cecile Peltz; c June & Robert. *Educ:* Hofstra Col, BA, 58; Iowa State Univ, PhD(inorg chem), 62. *Prof Exp:* staff mem, Sandia Nat Labs, 62-93, distinguished mem tech staff, 93-96. *Concurrent Pos:* Treas, Battery Div, Electrochem Soc, 90-92, vchmn, 92-94. *Mem:* Am Chem Soc; Electrochem Soc. *Res:* Chemical to electrical energy conversion; mechanism of electrochemical reactions; lithium and lithium-ion battery research and development. *Mailing Add:* Sandia Labs Div 2223 PO Box 5800 Albuquerque NM 87185-0614

LEVY, SAMUEL WOLFE, CLINICAL CHEMISTRY. *Current Pos:* CONSULT, ST ANNE D'BELLEVUE HOSP, 96- *Personal Data:* b Montreal, Que, Feb 26, 22; m 67; c 2. *Educ:* McGill Univ, BSc, 49, PhD(physiol), 54; Univ Sask, MSc, 51. *Honors & Awards:* Ames Award, Can Soc Clin Chem, 75. *Prof Exp:* Multiple Sclerosis Soc Can res fel biochem, McGill-Montreal Gen Hosp Res Inst, 54-56; res assoc, Hotel-Dieu Hosp, Montreal, 56-61; dir, Dept Biochem, Queen Mary Vet Hosp, Montreal, 61-79; dir, Dept Biochem, Queen Elizabeth Hosp, Montreal, 79-96. *Concurrent Pos:* Dom-Prov Health grant, 56-61; Dept Vet Affairs grant, 64-71. *Mem:* Chem Inst Can; Can Soc Clin Chem (pres, 70-71); Am Asn Clin Chem. *Res:* Lysosomal enzymes in blood in inflammation disease; effects of heparin in vivo on enzymes and lipid in blood; serum ribonuclease; assay, properties and alterations in disease. *Mailing Add:* 5629 W Lake Ave Cote St Luc PQ H4W 2N3 Can

LEVY, SANDER ALVIN, METALLURGY. *Current Pos:* res scientist, Metall Lab, Reynolds Metals Co, 68-70, supvr, Ingot Casting Technol Sect, 70-78, mgr, Dept Ingot Casting Technol & Metall Serv, 78-82, mgr, Dept Mfg Technol, 82-86, tech specialist, 87-90, SR METALLURGIST, METALL LAB, REYNOLDS METALS CO, 90- *Educ:* Lehigh Univ, BS & BA, 62, PhD(metal eng), 65. *Prof Exp:* Mem tech staff, Bell Tel Labs, Murray Hill, NJ, 65-66; casting res, Pittman Dun Res Labs, Frankford Arsenal, US Army & teacher welding metall, Drexel Inst Technol, 66-68. *Res:* Metallurgy; ingot casting technology; molten metal quality for aluminum alloys; diamond machine of aluminum. *Mailing Add:* 2215 Aspen Way Richmond VA 23233

LEVY, STUART B, MOLECULAR BIOLOGY, MICROBIOLOGY. *Current Pos:* from asst prof to assoc prof, 71-80, PROF MED, MOLECULAR BIOL & MICROBIOL, MED SCH, TUFTS UNIV, BOSTON, 80-, DIR, CTR ADAPTATION GENETICS & DRUG RESISTANCE, 92- *Personal Data:* b Wilmington, Del, Nov 21, 38; m 83, Cecile Pastel; c 3. *Educ:* Williams Col, AB, 60; Univ Pa, MD, 65. *Honors & Awards:* Hoechst-Roussel Award, Am Soc Microbiol. *Prof Exp:* Intern & med resident, Mt Sinai Hosp, NY, 65-67, res fel, Dept Cellular Biol, 66-67; staff assoc, Nat Inst Arthritis & Metab Dis, NIH, Bethesda, Md, 67-70; fel hemat, New Eng Med Ctr, Boston, Mass, 70-71. *Concurrent Pos:* Res fel, Dept Microbiol, Univ Milan, Italy, 62 & Dept Microbiol, Keio Univ, Tokyo, 64; publiker nutrit fel, Kenyatta Nat Hosp, Nairobi, Kenya, 64; vis prof, Dept Path, Univ Padua, Italy, 70 & Pasteur Inst, Paris, France, 76; collabr, EAfrican Viral Inst, Entebbe, Uganda, 71; res career develop award, 72-77; staff physician, NE Med Ctr Hosp, Boston, Mass, 76-; staff scientist, Cancer Res Ctr, Med Sch, Tufts Univ, 76-; sci adv, Biomed Res Ctr, Univ Nat Pedro Henriquez Urena, Santo Domingo, DR, 77-83; consult, Food & Drug Admin, Washington, DC, 78-80 & 85-87; adv, Fate of the Earth, Inc, 81-; pres, Alliance for the Prudent Use of Antibiotics, 81- & Boston Blood Club, 1984 overseas vis, Bd Postgrad Med Educ, Royal Melbourne Hosp, Australia, 83-84; gen chmn, Int Task Forces on Use of Antibiotics Worldwide, Fogarty Int Ctr, NIH, 83-86; mem, subcomt, Gram-Negative Facultatively Anaerobic Rods, Am Soc Metals, 85-88, Subcomt on Plasmid Ref Ctr Collection, Comt on Genetic & Molecular Microbiol, Am Soc Microbiol, 86, Subcomt Health & Antibiotic Resistance, Environ Protection Agency, 88- & Comt Environ Microbiol, Am Soc Microbiol, 89-; lectr, Am Soc Microbiol Found, 89-90, Australian Soc Microbiol, 90-; mem, Sci Eval Comt, Pasteur Inst, Paris, 90. *Mem:* Am Asn Cancer Res; Am Soc Biochem & Molecular Biol; Am Soc Clin Invest; Am Soc Hemat; Am Soc Microbiol; Infectious Dis Soc Am. *Res:* Resistance to antibiotics and anticancer drugs. *Mailing Add:* Molecular Biol & Microbiol Dept Sch Med Tufts Univ 136 Harrison Ave Boston MA 02111. *Fax:* 617-636-0458; *E-Mail:* slevy@opal.tufts.edu

LEW, CHEL WING, CHEMISTRY. *Current Pos:* RETIRED. *Personal Data:* b San Antonio, Tex, Dec 9, 35; m 59; c 4. *Educ:* Tex A&M Univ, BS, 60. *Prof Exp:* Technician chem, Southwest Res Inst, 60-61, from asst res chemist to sr res chemist, 61-94. *Mem:* Sigma Xi. *Res:* Microencapsulation. *Mailing Add:* 9218 Old Homestead San Antonio TX 78230

LEW, GLORIA MARIA, BIOCHEMISTRY & NEUROCHEMISTRY, PHARMACOLOGY. *Current Pos:* from asst prof to assoc prof, 72-92, PROF ANAT, MICH STATE UNIV, 92- *Personal Data:* b Kingston, Jamaica, March 7, 34; US citizen. *Educ:* Mt St Vincent Col, BA, 56; Boston Col, MS, 58; Univ Calif, Berkeley, PhD(zool), 72. *Prof Exp:* Chmn, Sci Dept, Alpha Jr Col, 64-66; instr biol, Cardinal Cushing Col, 66-68, asst prof, 68-69. *Mem:* Am Soc Zoologists; Am Soc Neurosci; Am Physiol Soc; Int Soc Chronobiol; Am Asn Anatomists; Am Soc Neurochem. *Res:* Circadian rhythms in catecholamine metabolism; effects of estrogen on catecholamine metabolism in genetic hypertension; biochemistry and ultrastructure of pineal gland effects of cocaine and PCP on neurochemistry of developing rats; molecular effects of drugs & hormones on neuroblastomas. *Mailing Add:* Dept Anat Mich State Univ East Lansing MI 48824

LEW, HIN, PHYSICS. *Current Pos:* assoc & sr res officer atomic beams & molecular spectros, 49-85, GUEST SCIENTIST, NAT RES COUN CAN, 85- *Personal Data:* b Vancouver, BC, Apr 18, 21; m 59, Marion Lim; c Stephen Ning, Clifford Wei & Melvin Ken. *Educ:* Univ BC, BA, 40; Univ Toronto, MA, 42; Mass Inst Technol, PhD(physics), 48. *Prof Exp:* Jr res physicist acoust, Nat Res Coun Can, 42-45; res assoc atomic beams, Mass Inst Technol, 48-49. *Mem:* Am Phys Soc; Can Asn Physicists. *Res:* Hyperfine structure of atoms and molecules by the atomic beam magnetic resonance method; spectra and structure of molecular ions. *Mailing Add:* 28 Parkridge Crescent Gloucester ON K1B 3E7 Can

LEW, JOHN S, APPLIED MATHEMATICS. *Current Pos:* RES STAFF MEM MATH SCI, T J WATSON RES CTR, IBM CORP, 70- *Personal Data:* b New York, NY, Sept 9, 34; m 63, 75; c 2. *Educ:* Yale Univ, BS, 55; Princeton Univ, PhD(physics), 60. *Prof Exp:* C L E Moore instr math, Mass Inst Technol, 62-64; asst prof appl math, Brown Univ, 64-70. *Mem:* Math Asn Am; Soc Indust & Appl Math; Sigma Xi. *Res:* Applied analysis, especially asymptotic expansions; lattice points. *Mailing Add:* 122 Morningside Dr Ossining NY 10562-3010

LEWANDOS, GLENN S, ORGANIC CHEMISTRY, ORGANOMETALLIC CHEMISTRY. *Current Pos:* from asst prof to assoc prof 77-85, PROF CHEM, CENT MICH UNIV, 85- *Personal Data:* b Dallas, Tex, Feb 23, 45; m 68, Pamela Scaggs; c Margo. *Educ:* Southern Methodist Univ, BS, 67; Univ Tex, Austin, PhD(chem), 72. *Prof Exp:* Asst prof chem, Sul Ross State Univ, 72-76; vis asst prof, Univ Tex, Austin, 76-77. *Concurrent Pos:* Res Corp grant, 78-80, Am Chem Soc grant, 81-84, 88-91. *Mem:* Am Chem Soc; Royal Soc Chem. *Res:* Synthesis and reactivity of organometallic pi complexes; catalysis by transition metals; crown ethers. *Mailing Add:* Dept Chem Cent Mich Univ Mt Pleasant MI 48859. *Fax:* 517-774-3883; *E-Mail:* 36jiyyz@cmich.edu

LEWANDOWSKI, GORDON A, BIOLOGICAL TREATMENT OF HAZARDOUS WASTE. *Current Pos:* from asst prof to assoc prof, 77-86, dept chmn chemeng, chem & environ sci, 88-93, PROF CHEM ENG, NJ INST TECHNOL, 86- *Personal Data:* b Brooklyn, NY, Feb 3, 45. *Educ:* Polytech Inst Brooklyn, BS, 65, MS, 66; Columbia Univ, DEngSci, 70. *Prof Exp:* Res engr, FMC Corp, 70-73; proj engr, Exxon Res & Eng Co, 73-76; sr proj engr, Jacobs Eng Co, 76-77. *Mem:* Am Inst Chem Engrs; Am Chem Soc. *Res:* Biological treatment of hazardous waste (theoretical and experimental); in-situ treatment; sequencing batch reactors; reactor engineering. *Mailing Add:* Dept Chem NJ Inst Technol 323 High St Newark NJ 07102

LEWANDOWSKI, JOHN JOSEPH, STRUCTURE PROPERTY RELATIONSHIPS, MECHANICAL BEHAVIOR OF METALS, DEFORMATION PROCESSING. *Current Pos:* from asst prof to assoc prof, 86-93, PROF MAT SCI & ENG, CASE WESTERN RES UNIV, 94- *Personal Data:* b Pittsburgh, Pa, Dec 17, 56; m 83, Amy Cook; c John R & Mark E. *Educ:* Carnegie Mellon Univ, BS, 79, ME, 81, PhD(metall eng & mat sci), 83. *Honors & Awards:* Bradley Stoughton Award, Am Soc Metals Int, 89; Ralph R Teetor Educ Award, Soc Automotive Engrs, 92. *Prof Exp:* Co-op metall engr, Chevron, USA, 76-79; Allegheny int fel metall eng & mat sci, Carnegie Mellon Univ, 79-81, Hertz Found fel, 81-83; NATO fel, Univ Cambridge, UK, 84-86. *Concurrent Pos:* Vis scientist, Univ Cambridge, UK, 86 & Wright Patterson AFB, 87; mem, Star-Bast Nat Comt, Nat Acad Sci, 89-91 & Long Term Aging Effects Panel, 94-96; NSF presidential young investr award, 89-94; mem, NRC fel panel, 97-99. *Mem:* Fel Am Soc Metals Int; Metall Soc; Mat Res Soc; Soc Advan Mat & Process Eng; Soc Automotive Engrs; Sigma Xi. *Res:* Effects of microstructure on deformation and fracture of materials, including metals, intermetallics, ceramics, and composites; effects of high pressure on deformation and fracture, including deformation processing, failure analysis, environmental effects, fracture and fatigue. *Mailing Add:* 3636 Traynham Rd Shaker Heights OH 44122. *Fax:* 216-368-3209; *E-Mail:* jjl3@po.cwru.edu

LEWANDOWSKI, MELVIN A, CHEMICAL ENGINEERING. *Current Pos:* RETIRED. *Personal Data:* b Chicago, Ill, Dec 8, 30; m 54, Margaret S Szatkowski; c Cynthia M (Adam). *Educ:* Northwestern Univ, BS, 54; Univ Chicago, MBA, 74. *Prof Exp:* Res engr, Int Minerals & Chem Corp, 57-61, purchasing agt, 61-65, mgr eng & distrib, 65-74; exec vpres, Chinhae Chem Co, Seoul, Korea, 75-78; corp staff vpres res & develop, Int Minerals & Chem Corp, 78-80, vpres chem group, 80-83, develop fertilizer group, 83-85; consult, Lindsay Int Sales, 85-86; vpres & gen mgr, Richmond Lox, 86-88. *Mem:* Am Inst Chem Engrs; Am Chem Soc. *Res:* Administration. *Mailing Add:* 9917 N Calle Loma Linda Oro Valley AZ 85737. *Fax:* 847-394-5226

LEWARS, ERROL GEORGE, ORGANIC CHEMISTRY. *Current Pos:* fel, 72-73, from asst prof to assoc prof, 73-85, PROF CHEM, TRENT UNIV, 86- *Personal Data:* Can citizen. *Educ:* LondonUniv, BSc, 64; Univ Toronto, PhD(chem), 68. *Prof Exp:* Fel chem, Harvard Univ, 68-70, Univ Western Ont, 70-72. *Mem:* Am Chem Soc. *Res:* Synthetic organic chemistry; compounds of theoretical interest. *Mailing Add:* Dept Chem Trent Univ Peterborough ON K9J 7B8 Can

LEWBART, MARVIN LOUIS, BIOCHEMISTRY. *Current Pos:* RETIRED. *Personal Data:* b Philadelphia, Pa, May 28, 29; m 57; c 4. *Educ:* Philadelphia Col Pharm & Sci, BSc, 51, MSc, 53; Jefferson Med Col, MD, 57; Univ Minn, PhD(biochem), 61. *Prof Exp:* Intern pharm, Jefferson Med Col, 51-52, res assoc biochem, 53-57; intern med, Lankenau Hosp, 57-58; fel biochem, Mayo Found, Univ Minn, 58-61; USPHS spec res fel, Univ Basel, 61-62; res assoc, Jefferson Med Col, 62-67, from asst prof to assoc prof med, 67-75; assoc med dir, Franklin Mint Corp, 74-82; dir, Steroid Lab, Crozer-Chester Med Ctr, 75-90. *Concurrent Pos:* USPHS res fel, 59-61; clin assoc prof med, Hahnemann Med Col, 75-90. *Mem:* AMA; Am Chem Soc; AAAS. *Res:* Steroid chemistry and metabolism. *Mailing Add:* 333 Lancaster Ave Malvern PA 19355

LEWELLEN, ROBERT THOMAS, GENETICS, PLANT BREEDING. *Current Pos:* RES GENETICIST, AGR RES SERV, USDA, 66- *Personal Data:* b Nyssa, Ore, Apr 27, 40; m 62, Priscilla Stark. *Educ:* Ore State Univ, BS, 62; Mont State Univ, PhD(genetics), 66. *Honors & Awards:* Meritorious Award, Am Soc Sugar Beet Technol. *Prof Exp:* Asst agronomist, Mont State Univ, 65-66. *Concurrent Pos:* Appointment, Exp Sta, Univ Calif, Davis. *Mem:* Fel Am Soc Agron; Crop Sci Soc Am; Am Phytopath Soc; Am Soc Sugar Beet Technol. *Res:* Genetics of disease resistance in sugar beet, Beta vulgaris, and development of resistant lines; germplasm enhancement of beta genetic resources. *Mailing Add:* Agr Res Sta USDA 1636 E Alisal St Salinas CA 93905. *Fax:* 408-753-2866

LEWELLEN, WILLIAM STEPHEN, FLUID DYNAMICS. *Current Pos:* RES PROF, WVA UNIV, 93- *Personal Data:* b Reedy, WVa, Aug 7, 33; m 58; c 2. *Educ:* WVa Univ, BS, 57; Cornell Univ, MAeroE, 59; Univ Calif, Los Angeles, PhD(eng), 64. *Prof Exp:* Mem tech staff, Space Tech Labs, Inc, 59-60; mem tech staff, Aerospace Corp, 60-64, mgr fluid dynamics sect, 64-66; vis assoc prof aeronaut & astronaut, Mass Inst Technol, 66-67, assoc prof, 67-72, sr consult, Aeronaut Res Assoc Princeton, Inc, 72-79, vpres fluid mech, 79-82, sr vpres, 82-86; sr consult, CRT Inc, 87-92. *Concurrent Pos:* Consult, Aerojet Gen Corp, 68-70; assoc ed, Am Inst Aeronaut & Astronaut J, 78-79; adv comt, Mech & Aerospace Eng, WVa Univ, 81- *Mem:* AAAS; Am Inst Aeronaut & Astronaut; Am Meteorol Soc. *Res:* Energy conversion; fluid dynamics of vortex flows; micrometeorology; computer modeling of turbulent transport; pollutant dispersal. *Mailing Add:* Mech & Aerospace Eng Dept WVa Univ PO Box 6106 Morgantown WV 26506

LEWENZ, GEORGE F, ORGANIC CHEMISTRY. *Current Pos:* RETIRED. *Personal Data:* b Berlin, Ger, Aug 29, 20; US citizen; m 49, Bess Levy; c David, Steven, Thomas & Susan. *Educ:* Western Res Univ, BS, 47, MS, 52. *Prof Exp:* Aeronaut res scientist, NASA, 48-53; chemist, Texaco, Inc, 53-58 & Esso Res & Eng Co, NJ, 59-68; res logician, 68-71, sr info chemist, 71-73, res specialist, Dow Chem Co, 73-86. *Mem:* Am Chem Soc; fel Am Inst Chemists. *Res:* Organic synthesis; abstracting, indexing and information science. *Mailing Add:* 2305 Burlington Dr Midland MI 48642

LEWERT, ROBERT MURDOCH, MEDICAL PARASITOLOGY, IMMUNOLOGY. *Current Pos:* instr parasitol, Dept Bact & Parasitol, 48-52, asst prof, 52-54, microbiol, 54-56, assoc prof, 57-61, prof microbiol, 61-83, prof molecular genetics & cell biol, 83-85, EMER PROF, UNIV CHICAGO, 86- *Personal Data:* b Scranton, Pa, Sept 30, 19; wid; c Philip (deceased) & Barbara. *Educ:* Univ Mich, BS, 41; Lehigh Univ, MS, 43; Johns Hopkins Univ, ScD(parasitol), 49. *Prof Exp:* Asst instr biol, Lehigh Univ, 42-43; instr zool, Cols Seneca, 43-44. *Concurrent Pos:* Fulbright res fel, Philippines, 61; Guggenheim fel, 61; vis prof, Inst Hyg, Univ Philippines, 61 & 63-65; consult, Surg Gen, US Army, 59-75 & clin parasitol, Hines Vet Admin Hosp, 75-80; mem, Comn parasitic diseases, Armed Forces Epidemiol Bd, 59-66, parasitol study sect, NIH Trop Med, 65-69, Am Bd Microbiol, 65-68. *Mem:* AAAS; fel Am Acad Microbiol; Am Soc Parasitol; Sigma Xi; Royal Soc Trop Med & Hyg; Am Soc Trop Med & Hyg. *Res:* Host parasite relationships with emphasis on immunity, tolerance and immunopathology of schistosomiasis; histochemical and cytochemical studies of parasite effects on host; immunity and invasiveness of helminths; schistosomiasis. *Mailing Add:* 37 Henry Mtn Rd Brevard NC 28712

LEWETT, GEORGE P, SYSTEMS DESIGN & SYSTEMS SCIENCE, OPERATIONS RESEARCH. *Current Pos:* prog mgr opers res, 73-76, DIR, OFF TECH INNOVATION, NAT INST STAND & TECHNOL, 76- *Personal Data:* b June 5, 26; m 51, Therese A Mulveahy; c George, Linda, John, Jeanne, Susan & Stephen. *Educ:* Syracuse Univ, BS, 50; Rutgers Univ, MA, 55. *Prof Exp:* Dept chief opers res mfg & eng, Western Elec, 51-63; prog mgr, Tech Oprs Inc, 63-68, Matrix Res Corp, 65-78 & CRU Inc, 72-73. *Mem:* Technol Transfer Soc; Am Inst Indust Engrs. *Res:* Manage an evaluation service providing assessments of technical and commercial feasibility of inventions and new technological applications. *Mailing Add:* Nat Inst Stand & Technol Bldg 820 Rm 264 Gaithersburg MD 20899-0001. *E-Mail:* george.lewett@nist.gov

LEWIN, ALFRED S, MITOCHONDRIA, RNA CATALYSIS. *Current Pos:* assoc prof immunol & med microbiol, 87-95, PROF MOLECULAR GENETICS & MICROBIOL, UNIV FLA, 95- *Personal Data:* b Chicago, Ill, Apr 25, 51; m 72; c 3. *Educ:* Univ Chicago, AB, 73, PhD(biol), 78. *Honors & Awards:* Jr Fac Res Award, Am Cancer Soc, 82; Established Investr, Am Heart Asn, 87. *Prof Exp:* Acad asst biochem, Biocenter Univ, Basel, 78-81; asst prof chem, Ind Univ, 81-87. *Concurrent Pos:* Europ Molecular Biol Orgn fel, 78-; jr fac res award, Am Cancer Soc, 82; vis prof, Univ Paris-South, 85. *Mem:* Am Soc Biol Chemists; Am Soc Microbiol; Genetics Soc Am; AAAS; Sigma Xi. *Res:* Biosynthesis of mitochondrial enzymes; RNA catalysis-mechanisms and applications. *Mailing Add:* Dept Molecular Genetics & Microbiol Univ Fla Col Med PO Box 100266 Gainesville FL 32610-0266. *E-Mail:* lewin@college.med.ufl.edu

LEWIN, ANITA HANA, PHYSICAL ORGANIC CHEMISTRY, MOLECULAR MODELLING. *Current Pos:* fel, 74-75, SR CHEMIST, RES TRIANGLE INST, 75- *Personal Data:* b Bucarest, Rumania, Oct 27, 35; m 56, Arie Yehuda; c Tal M & Oren C. *Educ:* Univ Calif, Los Angeles, BS, 59, PhD(phys org chem), 63. *Prof Exp:* Res asst prof chem, Univ Pittsburgh, 64-66; from asst prof to assoc prof, Polytech Inst Brooklyn, 66-74. *Mem:* Am Chem Soc. *Res:* Reaction mechanisms; conformational analysis; hindered rotation; retinoids-synthesis and properties; organic synthesis; synthesis of radiolabeled compounds; molecular modeling; receptor binding; alkaloid synthesis; structure activity correlations; peptide synthesis. *Mailing Add:* Chem & Life Sci Group PO Box 12194 Research Triangle Park NC 27709

LEWIN, JOYCE CHISMORE, MICROBIOLOGY. *Current Pos:* RETIRED. *Personal Data:* b Ilion, NY, Nov 13, 26; m 50. *Educ:* Cornell Univ, BS, 48; Yale Univ, MS, 50, PhD(bot, microbiol), 53. *Prof Exp:* Guest res worker, Biol Lab, Nat Res Coun Can, 52-55; res assoc marine biol, Woods Hole Oceanog Inst, 56-60; asst res biologist, Scripps Inst, Univ Calif, San Diego, 60-65; from asst prof to prof, Univ Wash, 65-74, res prof oceanog, 74- *Mem:* Am Soc Limnol & Oceanog; Phycol Soc Am; Am Inst Biol Sci; Marine Biol Asn UK; Int Phycol Soc. *Res:* Culture of marine microalgae, especially diatoms; physiology and nutrition of marine diatoms; physiology and ecology of surf diatom blooms. *Mailing Add:* Sch Oceanog WB-10 Univ Wash Seattle WA 98195

LEWIN, KLAUS J, PATHOLOGY, GASTROENTEROLOGY. *Current Pos:* assoc prof, 77-80, PROF PATH, MED SCH, UNIV CALIF, LOS ANGELES, 80-, PROF, DEPT MED, DIV GASTENTEROL, 86- *Personal Data:* b Jerusalem, Israel, Aug 10, 36; m 64, Patricia C Milne; c David, Nicola & Brumo. *Educ:* Westminster Med Sch, London, Eng, MB & BS, 59; Univ London, MD, 66; Am Bd Path, dipl. *Honors & Awards:* Chesterfield Medal, Inst Dermat, 66; Arris & Gale lectr, Royal Col Surgeons, 68. *Prof Exp:* Resident pathologist clin chem, bact, hemat, blood transfusion & serology, Westminster Hosp, Med Sch, 61-62, registr, Dept Morbid Anat, 62-64; rotating sr registr morbid anat, Royal Devon Exeter Hosp, 64-68; vis asst prof path, Stanford Univ Med Sch, 68-70, asst prof, 70-76. *Concurrent Pos:* Mem, Curric Comt, Univ Calif, Riverside, 77-84, vchmn path, Los Angeles, 79-86; pres, Los Angeles Soc Pathologists Inc, 85-86; consult, Wadsworth Vet

Affairs Hosp, Nat Cancer Inst, Sepulveda Vet Affairs Hosp. *Mem:* Fel Royal Col Pathologists; Path Soc Gt Brit; Am Gastenterol Soc; Gastrointestinal Path Soc (pres, 85-86); US Acad Path; Can Acad Path; Asn Clin Pathologists; Path & Bact Soc Gt Brit; Int Acad Path. *Res:* Gastrointestinal pathology; cancer research; bacteriology; hematology; structure, function and pathologic disorders of gastrointestinal tract and liver. *Mailing Add:* Univ Calif Sch Med Dept Path 10833 Le Conte Ave Los Angeles CA 90024. *Fax:* 310-206-5178; *E-Mail:* klewin@pathlogy.medsch.ucla.edu

LEWIN, LEONARD, ELECTRICAL ENGINEERING, MATHEMATICS & EDUCATION. *Current Pos:* prof, 68-86, coordr telecommun prog, 74-86, EMER PROF ELEC ENG, UNIV COLO, BOULDER, 87- *Personal Data:* b Southend, Eng, July 22, 19; US citizen; m 43, Daphne Smith; c David I & Wendy P. *Hon Degrees:* DSc, Univ Colo, 67. *Honors & Awards:* Premium Awards, Brit Inst Elec Engrs, 52 & 60; Microwave Prize & W G Baker Award, Inst Elec & Electronics Engrs, 62; Prestige Lectr, Nat Inst Elec Eng, NZ, 87; Microwave Career Award, Microwave Theory & Techniques Soc, 93. *Prof Exp:* Sci officer radar, Brit Admiralty, 41-45; sr engr microwaves, Stand Telecommun Labs, 46-50, dept head, 50-60, asst mgr transmissions, 60-66, sr prin res electromagnetic theory, 67-68. *Concurrent Pos:* Consult, Stand Telecommun Labs, 68-90, Medion Ltd, 70-90, Westinghouse Corp, 71, Nat Bur Stand, 78-90, Mass Inst Technol Lincoln Labs, 85-93; Sci Res Coun grants, UK, 73 & 75; Fulbright fel, 82. *Mem:* Fel Brit Interplanetary Soc; Brit Inst Elec Engrs; fel Inst Elec & Electronics Engrs. *Res:* Electromagnetic theory; wave propagation; waveguides and antennas; mathematics; mathematical applications to engineering; history and properties of the polylogarithmic functions. *Mailing Add:* Dept Elec Eng Campus Box 425 Univ Colo Boulder CO 80309

LEWIN, RALPH ARNOLD, PHYCOLOGY. *Current Pos:* assoc prof marine biol, 59-67, PROF EXP PHYCOL, SCRIPPS INST OCEANOG, UNIV CALIF, 67- *Personal Data:* b London, Eng, Apr 30, 21; m 69, Lanna Cheng. *Educ:* Cambridge Univ, BA, 42, MA, 46, ScD, 72; Yale Univ, MSc, 49, PhD, 50. *Honors & Awards:* Darbaker Prize, Bot Soc Am, 58. *Prof Exp:* Spec lectr phycol, 50-51, instr bot, Yale Univ, 51-52; asst res off biol, Maritime Regional Lab, Nat Res Coun Can, 52-55; investr phycol, NIH grant, Marine Biol Lab, Woods Hole, 55-59. *Concurrent Pos:* Mem, Corp Marine Biol Lab, Woods Hole. *Mem:* Int Phycol Soc; Marine Biol Asn UK; Brit Phycol Soc; Phycol Soc Am (pres, 70); Sigma Xi. *Res:* Experimental phycology; microbiology; microbial genetics; marine biology. *Mailing Add:* Scripps Inst Oceanog Univ Calif La Jolla CA 92093-0202. *Fax:* 619-534-7313; *E-Mail:* rlewin@ucsd.edu

LEWIN, SEYMOUR Z, PHYSICAL & ANALYTICAL CHEMISTRY. *Current Pos:* RETIRED. *Personal Data:* b New York, NY, Aug 16, 21; m 43, Pearl Goldman; c David & Jonathan. *Educ:* City Col New York, BS, 41; Univ Mich, MS, 42, PhD(chem), 50. *Honors & Awards:* A Cressy Morrison Prize, NY Acad Sci, 56; Kasimir Fajans Prize, 58. *Prof Exp:* Lectr chem, Univ Mich, 47; from instr to prof chem, NY Univ, 51-91. *Concurrent Pos:* Belg-Am Educ Found fel, 62; hon prof, Chem Inst, Inst Quimico Sarria, Barcelona, Spain, 62; ed, Art & Archeol Tech Abstr, 66-69; consult, US Army Chem Corp, Smithsonian Inst, Food & Drug Admin & Warner-Lambert Co; instrumentation ed, J Chem Educ, 60-68. *Mem:* AAAS; Am Chem Soc; Soc Appl Spectros; Am Inst Chemists; fel NY Acad Sci; fel Am Inst Chemists. *Res:* Crystal growth; spectroscopy; instrumentation; materials of art and archaeology; polymorphism; solid state chemistry; stone decay and preservation; food chemistry. *Mailing Add:* 4231 N Walnut Ave Arlington Heights IL 60004-1302

LEWIN, VICTOR, ECOLOGY. *Current Pos:* from asst prof to prof, Univ Alta, 58-87, dir, 58-80, cur herpet, Mus Zool, 80-87, EMER PROF ZOOL, UNIV ALTA, 87- *Personal Data:* b San Francisco, Calif, Sept 8, 30; m 50; c 3. *Educ:* Univ Calif, AB, 53, PhD(zool), 58. *Honors & Awards:* Painton Award, Cooper Ornith Soc, 65. *Prof Exp:* Asst zool, Univ Calif, 54-58. *Concurrent Pos:* Asst cur, Mus Vert Zool, Univ Calif, 55-56. *Mem:* Wildlife Soc; Am Soc Mammalogists; Cooper Ornith Soc; Am Ornithologists Union; Can Soc Wildlife & Fishery Biol. *Res:* Wildlife ecology; ecology of game birds and mammals, particularly reproductive anatomy and physiology of gallinaceous birds; effects of chlorinated hydrocarbon residues on birds; ecology of exotic game bird species. *Mailing Add:* PO Box 97 Heriot Bay BC V0P 1H0 Can

LEWIN, WALTER H G, HIGH ENERGY ASTROPHYSICS. *Current Pos:* fel space res & asst prof, 66, assoc prof, 68-74, PROF PHYSICS, MASS INST TECHNOL, 74- *Personal Data:* b The Hague, Netherlands, Jan 29, 36; c 4. *Educ:* Univ Delft, Ir, 60, Dr(physics), 65. *Honors & Awards:* Outstanding Sci Achievement Award, NASA, 78. *Prof Exp:* Res assoc physics, Univ Delft, 59-66. *Concurrent Pos:* Recipient Guggenheim Fel, 84; Alexender von Humboldt award, 84 & 91; distinguished Spring Lectr, Princeton Univ, 86. *Mem:* Int Astron Union; Am Astron Soc; Am Phys Soc; Royal Dutch Acad Sci; corresp mem Neth Nat Royal Acad Sci. *Res:* Radioactive isotope applications; nuclear and atomic physics; x-ray astronomy; high-altitude ballooning; satellite observations, orbital solar observatory-7, small astronomy satellite-3, high energy astronomy observatory-1; astrophysics; ginga, rosat & gro; Ginga. *Mailing Add:* Mass Inst Technol 37-627 Cambridge MA 02139. *Fax:* 617-253-0861; *E-Mail:* lewin@space.mit.edu

LEWINSON, VICTOR A, OPERATIONS RESEARCH. *Current Pos:* RETIRED. *Personal Data:* b New York, NY, 1918; m 57; c 2. *Educ:* Harvard Col, AB, 39; Columbia Univ, MA, 45, PhD(chem), 50. *Prof Exp:* fel chem, Columbia Univ, 39-42; res scientist & sect leader, Manhattan Proj, 42-45; res fel chem, Calif Inst Technol, 50-51; fel, Mellon Inst, 51-54; analyst opers res, Nat Acad Sci, 54-61; mem prof staff, Arthur D Little, Inc, 61-86. *Res:* Freight transportation, especially maritime and railroad. *Mailing Add:* Arthur D Little Inc 25 Acorn Park Cambridge MA 02140-2390

LEWIS, A(LBERT) D(ALE) M(ILTON), CIVIL ENGINEERING, STRUCTURAL ENGINEERING. *Current Pos:* assoc prof, 54-85, EMER PROF STRUCT ENG, PURDUE UNIV, WEST LAFAYETTE, 85- *Personal Data:* b Paoli, Ind, May 20, 20; m 46, Eleanora G Irons; c Linda L (Raney). *Educ:* Purdue Univ, BS, 41, MS, 51. *Prof Exp:* Field engr oil refinery construct, M W Kellogg Co, 41-44, 46-47 & Gulf Oil Corp, 47-49; instr struct eng, Purdue Univ, 51-52; design engr, Stand Oil Co, Calif, 52-54. *Concurrent Pos:* Consult, Truss Bridge Res Proj, Northwestern Univ; vis assoc prof struct eng, Univ Calif, Los Angeles, 71. *Mem:* Am Soc Civil Engrs; Am Soc Eng Educ; Am Concrete Inst; Am Rwy Eng Asn; Asn Comput Mach; Soc Exp Mech; Nat Soc Prof Engrs. *Res:* Structural analysis; structural design; design optimization; digital computers; experimental mechanics. *Mailing Add:* 107 Sylvia St West Lafayette IN 47906

LEWIS, AARON, BIOPHYSICS. *Current Pos:* NIH fel, 70-72, instr, 71-72, asst prof, 72-76, ASSOC PROF BIOPHYS, CORNELL UNIV, 76- *Personal Data:* b Calcutta, India, Oct 14, 45; US citizen. *Educ:* Univ Mo, BS, 66; Case Western Reserve Univ, PhD(phys chem), 70. *Prof Exp:* Instr phys chem, Case Western Reserve Univ, 70. *Concurrent Pos:* Sloan fel, 74-76; vis prof, Calif Inst Technol, 77 & Hebrew Univ, 79-80; Guggenheim fel, 79-80. *Mem:* AAAS; Am Chem Soc; Biophys Soc; Asn Res Vision & Ophthal; Am Photobiol Soc. *Res:* Molecular mechanism of ion gates and pumps, specifically bacteriorhodopsin and rhodopsin. *Mailing Add:* Dept Appl Physics Sch Appl Sci Bergmann Bldg Hebrew Univ Jerusalem Israel

LEWIS, ALAN ERVIN, MEDICINE. *Current Pos:* from instr to sr instr internal med, Hahnemann Med Col & Hosp, 67-71, from asst prof to assoc prof med, 71-87. *Personal Data:* b Milwaukee, Wis, Feb 1, 36; m 61; c 2. *Educ:* Univ Wis-Madison, BS, 57; Marquette Univ, MD, 60. *Prof Exp:* Intern, Hosp Univ Pa, 60-61; resident, Med Ctr, Univ Mich, 61 & 63-65. *Concurrent Pos:* Fel endocrinol, Sch Med, Tufts Univ, 65-67. *Mem:* Am Diabetes Asn; Am Fedn Clin Res; Am Col Physicians; Endocrine Soc. *Mailing Add:* 1450 S Dobson Rd Suite 202-A Mesa AZ 85202-4774

LEWIS, ALAN GRAHAM, BIOLOGICAL OCEANOGRAPHY, ZOOLOGY. *Current Pos:* from asst prof to assoc prof, 64-76, PROF OCEANOG & ZOOL, UNIV BC, 76- *Personal Data:* b Pasadena, Calif, Mar 14, 34; m 57; c 2. *Educ:* Univ Miami, BSc, 56, MSc, 58; Univ Hawaii, PhD(zool), 61. *Prof Exp:* Asst prof zool, Univ NH, 61-64. *Mem:* Am Geophys Union; Sigma Xi. *Res:* Ecology of marine plankton. *Mailing Add:* Dept Earth & Ocean Sci Univ BC 6270 Univ Blvd Vancouver BC V6T 1Z4 Can

LEWIS, ALAN JAMES, ISLAND BIOGEOGRAPHY, FLORISTIC BIOGEOGRAPHY. *Current Pos:* PROF ECOL, UNIV MAINE, MACHIAS, 78- *Personal Data:* b Green Bay, Wis, June 2, 43; m 75; c 1. *Educ:* Wis State Univ-Eau Claire, BS, 68; Rutgers Univ, PhD(plant ecol), 71. *Prof Exp:* Teaching asst gen biol, Rutgers Univ, New Brunswick, 68-69; NSF fel, 69-70, teaching asst gen biol & plant ecol, 70-71; asst prof biol, Kean Col NJ, 71-74; vis prof, Swarthmore Col, 75-76; asst prof, Mercyhurst Col, 76-78. *Concurrent Pos:* NSF fel, Rutgers Univ, 69; res assoc, Univ Houston, 72; Fulbright scholar, Univ Papua, New Guinea, 85. *Mem:* AAAS; Am Inst Biol Sci; Ecol Soc Am; Sigma Xi. *Res:* Floristic distributions of Maine; island biogeography of Maine. *Mailing Add:* Div Sci & Math Univ Maine Machias Nine O Ave Machias ME 04654-1321

LEWIS, ALAN JAMES, PHARMACOLOGY. *Current Pos:* PRES, CHIEF EXEC OFFICER & CHIEF OPERS OFFICER, SIGNAL PHARMACEUT, INC, SAN DIEGO, 94- *Personal Data:* b Newport, Gwent, UK; m 68, Judith Royle; c Nina, Huw & Victoria. *Educ:* Southampton Univ, Hampshire, BSc, 67; Univ Wales, Cardiff, PhD(pharmacol), 70. *Prof Exp:* Fel biomed sci, Univ Guelph, Ont, Can, 70-72; res assoc, Lung Res Ctr, Yale Univ, 72-73; sr pharmacologist, Organon Labs, Ltd, Lanarkshire, Scotland, 73-79; res mgr immunoinflammation, Wyeth-Ayerst Res, 79-82, assoc dir exp therapeut, 82-85, dir exp therapeut, 85-87, asst vpres exp therapeut, 87-89, vpres res, Am Home Prod, 89-93. *Concurrent Pos:* Ed, Allergy Sect, Agents & Actions & Int Arch Pharmacodyn Ther; reviewer, J Petrol Technol, Biochem Pharmacol, Can J Physiol Pharmacol, Europ J Pharmacol & J Pharmaceut Sci; pres, Mid-Atlantic Pharmacol Soc, 93-, Int Asn Inflammation Soc. *Mem:* Pulmonary Res Asn; Inflammation Res Asn (pres, 86-88); Am Soc Pharmacol & Exp Therapeut; Pharmaceut Mfrs Asn; Am Rheumatism Asn. *Res:* Mechanisms and treatment of inflammatory diseases including arthritis and asthma; cardiovascular pharmacology; metabolic disorders; central nervous system pharmacology; osteoporosis. *Mailing Add:* 5555 Oberlin Dr San Diego CA 92121. *Fax:* 619-555-7513

LEWIS, ALAN LAIRD, OPTOMETRY. *Current Pos:* DEAN, COL OPTOM, FERRIS STATE UNIV, 91- *Personal Data:* b Holyoke, Mass, Sept 1, 42; m 83, Barbara George; c Evan & Keith. *Educ:* Mass Col Optom, BSc, 65, OD, 70; Ohio State Univ, MSc, 71, PhD(physiol optics), 71. *Prof Exp:* Optometrist, USN, 65-68; from asst prof to prof, physiol optics, Col Optom, State Univ NY, 72-91. *Concurrent Pos:* Pres, Ophthalmic Res Inst, 85-90; vpres, US Nat Comt, Comn Int L'Eclairage, 91- *Mem:* Fel Am Acad Optom; fel Illum Eng Soc; Asn Res Vision & Opthal; Optical Soc Am; Am Optom Asn. *Res:* Visual performance; color vision; environmental effects on vision. *Mailing Add:* Dean,s Off Mich Col Optom Ferris State Univ Big Rapids MI 49307. *Fax:* 616-592-2394; *E-Mail:* yb14@music.ferris.edu

LEWIS, ALLEN ROGERS, BEHAVIORAL ECOLOGY. *Current Pos:* from asst prof to assoc prof, 78-86, PROF BIOL, UNIV PR, 86-, ASSOC DEAN RES & EXTERNAL FUNDING, 91- *Personal Data:* b Ithaca, NY, Aug 11, 47; m 69, Laurie J Irvine; c Jessica & Kenneth. *Educ:* Cornell Univ, BS, 69;

Univ Del, MS, 71; Univ Rochester, MS, 77, PhD(biol), 79. *Prof Exp:* Marine exten specialist, Col Marine Studies, Univ Del, 71-74. *Concurrent Pos:* Ed, Carribean J Sci, 81-90. *Mem:* AAAS; Asn Trop Biol; Ecol Soc Am; Soc Study Amphibians & Reptiles; Animal Behav Soc; Am Soc Naturalists. *Res:* Analysis of social behavior and ecology of tropical lizards. *Mailing Add:* Univ PR Mayaguez Contract Station Univ PR Mayaguez PR 00680. *Fax:* 787-265-2205; *E-Mail:* a__lewis@rumac.upr.clu.edu

LEWIS, ALVIN EDWARD, BIOSTATISTICS, PHYSIOLOGY. *Current Pos:* RETIRED. *Personal Data:* b New York, NY, Nov 21, 16; m 43; c 2. *Educ:* Univ Calif, Los Angeles, AB, 38; Stanford Univ, AM, 39, MD, 44. *Prof Exp:* Asst path, Stanford Univ, 47-48; clin instr & chief path sect, AEC Proj, Univ Calif, Los Angeles, 49-53; dir labs, Mt Zion Hosp, 53-66; prof path, Mich State Univ, 66-72; prof path & chmn dept, Med Sch, Univ SAla, 72-74; from prof to emer prof path, Univ Calif, 74-87. *Concurrent Pos:* Am Cancer Soc fel, Stanford Univ, 48-49; vis physician, Los Angeles County Harbor Hosp, 49-53; attend physician, Wadsworth Gen Hosp, 50-53; asst clin prof, Med Ctr, Univ Calif, San Francisco, 59-66. *Mem:* AAAS; Am Physiol Soc; AMA; fel Col Am Path. *Res:* Hepatic function tests; plasma volume and distribution. *Mailing Add:* 21 Woodgreen Ct Santa Rosa CA 95405

LEWIS, ARMAND FRANCIS, PHYSICAL CHEMISTRY, MATERIALS SCIENCE. *Current Pos:* VIS LECTR, TEXTILE SCI DEPT, UNIV MASS DARTMOUTH, 93- *Personal Data:* b Fairhaven, Mass, May 22, 32; m 58, Joan Doyle; c Jeffrey & Kent. *Educ:* Southeastern Mass Univ, BS, 53; Okla State Univ, MS, 55; Lehigh Univ, PhD(chem), 58. *Honors & Awards:* Union Carbide Award, Am Chem Soc, 63. *Prof Exp:* Res asst rheology, Lehigh Univ, 58-59; res chemist, Cent Res Div, Am Cyanamid Co, 59-63, sr res chemist, Plastics & Resins Div, 63-64, group leader polymer physics & adhesion, 64-69, proj leader noise control mat, 70-71; sr res assoc, Lord Corp, 71-73, sr mat scientist, 73-81; res assoc, Kendall Co, 84-89. *Mem:* Am Chem Soc; Soc Rheology (treas, 66-). *Res:* Polymer physics; rheology; surface chemistry and adhesion; dynamic mechnical properties of polymers; glass transition phenomena in polymeric systems; polymer to metal adhesion and fracture of adhesive joints; vibration and noise control materials; rubber chemicals; engineering composites; marine materials. *Mailing Add:* Textile Sci Dept Univ Mass Dartmouth North Dartmouth MA 02747

LEWIS, ARNOLD D, ANALYTICAL CHEMISTRY. *Current Pos:* RETIRED. *Personal Data:* b Philadelphia, Pa, May 6, 20; m 45, Helen Miller; c Janet A & Simon D. *Educ:* Philadelphia Col Pharm, BS, 40; Polytech Inst Brooklyn, MS, 47. *Prof Exp:* Control chemist, Hance Bros & White, 40-41; pilot plant chemist, United Gas Improv Corp, 41-43; asst scientist to Dr E A H Friedheim, 43-44; jr scientist, G D Res Inst, 44-47; scientist, Dept Org Chem, Warner-Lambert Co, 47-54, sr scientist, 54-63, sr res assoc, Chem Res Div, 63-64, dir anal & phys chem, Prof Prod Group, 64-77; consult, 78-81; dir tech affairs, S S T Corp, 81-86. *Mem:* Am Chem Soc. *Res:* Organic synthesis of heterocycles; infrared and ultraviolet absorption spectrophotometry; microanalysis; gas, paper, thin-layer and column chromatography; chemical safety; proton magnetic resonance spectroscopy. *Mailing Add:* 42 Intervale Rd Livingston NJ 07039-2756

LEWIS, ARNOLD LEROY, II, instrumentation, spectroscopy, for more information see previous edition

LEWIS, ARTHUR B, PHYSICS, SOLID STATE PHYSICS. *Current Pos:* from assoc prof to prof physics, Univ Miss, 36-57, from assoc prof to prof math, 36-47, chmn, dept physics & astron, 52-57, prof astron, 52-57, dean, Col Liberal Arts, 69-71, prof math, 69-71, EMER PROF PHYIICS & ASTRON & DEAN, COL LIB ARTS, UNIV MISS, 71- *Personal Data:* b Forest, Miss, Nov 21, 01; m 30; c 4. *Educ:* Univ Miss, BA, 23, MA, 25; Johns Hopkins Univ, PhD(physics), 30. *Prof Exp:* Asst prof math & physics, Univ Miss, 25-26; jr physicist, Nat Bur Standards, 26-30, asst physicist, 30-36. *Concurrent Pos:* Consult, Solid State Div, Oak Ridge Nat Lab, 51-68. *Mem:* Am Phys Soc; Am Asn Physics Teachers; AAAS. *Res:* Electrical instruments and measuring techniques; effects of neutron bombardment on the resistivity of precipitation-hardening alloys. *Mailing Add:* 301 Washington Ave W Oxford MS 38655-2024

LEWIS, AUSTIN JAMES, ANIMAL NUTRITION. *Current Pos:* from asst prof to assoc prof, 77-85, PROF ANIMAL NUTRIT, UNIV NEBR, 85- *Personal Data:* b Poole, Eng, Nov 29, 45; m 73; c 1. *Educ:* Univ Reading, BSc, 67; Univ Nottingham, PhD(nutrit), 71. *Prof Exp:* Assoc animal nutrit, Iowa State Univ, 71-74; res assoc, Univ Nebr, 74-75; asst prof, Univ Alta, 75-77. *Mem:* Am Soc Animal Sci; Am Inst Nutrit. *Res:* Nutritional requirements of swine, especially proteins and amino acids. *Mailing Add:* Dept Animal Sci Univ Ne C206 Animal Sci Lincoln NE 68583-0908

LEWIS, BARBARA-ANN GAMBOA, ENVIRONMENTAL RADIOACTIVITY, CLAY CHEMISTRY. *Current Pos:* ASSOC PROF ENVIRON ENG, NORTHWESTERN UNIV, 79- *Personal Data:* b Manila, Philippines, Jan 9, 34; US citizen; m 66, Roy S; c Gilita (Star), Marya (Curie) & Stephen Berkeley. *Educ:* Philippine Women's Univ, BS, 53; Univ Calif, Berkeley, MS, 63, PhD(soil sci), 71. *Honors & Awards:* Palladium Medal, Nat Asn Eng Soc & Nat Audubon Soc, 84. *Prof Exp:* Staff res assoc soils, Dept Forestry, Univ Calif, Berkeley, 71-72; postdoctoral, Argonne Nat Lab, 72-73, environ scientist, 73-79. *Mem:* Soil Sci Soc Am; Am Soc Agron; Am Chem Soc; Sigma Xi. *Res:* Soil-contaminant-vegetation interactions; reclamation of distrubed land; soil-clay chemistry; radon and radium in soils; transport of contaminants in soil. *Mailing Add:* 923 Asbury Ave Evanston IL 60202. *Fax:* 847-491-4011; *E-Mail:* b__lewis@nwu.edu

LEWIS, BENJAMIN MARZLUFF, physiology; deceased, see previous edition for last biography

LEWIS, BERNARD, CHEMICAL ENGINEERING, COMBUSTION SCIENCE. *Current Pos:* CONSULT, ENERGY SYSTS ASSOCS, 87- *Personal Data:* b London, Eng, Nov 1, 1899; nat US; m 34; c 1. *Educ:* Mass Inst Technol, BS, 23; Harvard Univ, MA, 24; Cambridge Univ, PhD(phys chem), 26. *Hon Degrees:* ScD, Cambridge Univ, 53. *Honors & Awards:* Lewis Gold Medal, Combustion Inst, 58; Gold Medal, Ital Thermotech Asn, 61; Pittsburgh Award, Am Chem Soc, 74; Orleans Medal, France, 75; Bordeaux Medal, France, 81; Tecknior Israel Medal, 82. *Prof Exp:* Demonstr phys chem, Cambridge Univ, 25-26; Nat Res Coun fel, Univ Berlin & Univ Minn, 26-29; phys chemist, US Bur Mines, 29-42, chief, Explosives & Phys Sci Div, 46-53; pres, Combustion & Explosives Res, Inc, 53-87. *Concurrent Pos:* Dir res powder & explosives, Ord Dept, US Army, 51-52; consult, US Army, USN, USAF & Nat Bur Standards; mem, Sci Adv Comt, Ord Corps, Aberdeen Proving Ground, Md, Combustion Comt, Nat Adv Comt Aeronaut & Fire Res Conf, Nat Acad Sci; pres, Comt high temperature, Int Union Pure & Appl Chem; US ed, J Combustion & Flame; co-ed, Phys Measurements in Gas Dynamics & Combustion, 54 & Combustion Processes, 56; consult, tech adv comt, US Dept Interior, numerous industs & res insts. *Mem:* Emer mem, Am Chem Soc; Am Phys Soc; fel Am Inst Aeronaut & Astronaut; Combustion Inst (pres, 54-66, hon pres, 66-); fel NY Acad Sci; fel Inst Chem. *Res:* Chemical kinetics of gas reactions; thermodynamics of explosives; flame propagation; ignition; combustion in jet propulsion; propellants; detonation; internal combustion engines; oxidation of hydrocarbons; fuels, interior ballistics; combustion and flame phenomena; explosion hazard prevention in industry; nuclear power plant safety; author of book on combustion. *Mailing Add:* 5863 Marlborough Ave Pittsburgh PA 15217-1415

LEWIS, BERNARD LEROY, RADAR SIGNAL PROCESSING. *Current Pos:* RADAR CONSULT, BERNARD L LEWIS ASSOC, 84- *Personal Data:* b Storm Lake, Iowa, Dec 19, 23; m 90; c David L, Michael P, Patrick D & Timothy M. *Educ:* Tulane Univ, BS, 47, MS, 48. *Prof Exp:* Sect head, Naval Res Lab, 48-57; consult, Systs Inc, 57-60; prin engr, Radiation Inc, 60-61; design engr, Martin Marietta Co, 61; chief engr, Airtronics, 61-63; prin engr, Harris Intertype, 63-69; bus partner, McDowell Assoc, 69-72; sr scientist, Nval Res Lab, 72-84. *Concurrent Pos:* Adj prof, Fla Test Technol, 84-89; consult, Sperry Rand, 84-87; Naval Res Lab, 87-88. *Mem:* Inst Elec & Electronics Engrs. *Res:* Contributed over 72 technical papers to professional journals; patentee in field. *Mailing Add:* 817 Villa Dr Melbourne FL 32940-7037

LEWIS, BERTHA ANN (BETTY), CARBOHYDRATE CHEMISTRY, FOOD CHEMISTRY. *Current Pos:* assoc prof design & environ anal, 67-70, assoc dean, Col Human Ecol & asst dir, Cornell Agr Exp Sta, 74-80, ASSOC PROF, DIV NUTRIT SCI, CORNELL UNIV, 70- *Personal Data:* b Lewisville, Minn, Oct 21, 27. *Educ:* Univ Minn, BChem, 49, MS, 54, PhD(biochem), 57. *Prof Exp:* Res fel biochem, Univ Minn, St Paul, 57-65, res assoc, 65-67. *Concurrent Pos:* Prin investr, NIH, 71-74 & 80-82, Nat Cancer Inst, 78-89 & NSF, 79-82; mem, US Dept Agr Comt Regional Res & Home Econ Sub-Comt Agr Exp Stas Comt on Policy, 76-79, & Nat Agr Res Comt, 80-85; vis prof, Dept Chem, Univ BC, 84 & 85. *Mem:* Am Chem Soc; Inst Food Technologists; Soc Glycobiol; Fiber Soc; Am Asn Cereal Chemists; AAAS. *Res:* Carbohydrate chemistry and biochemistry; chemistry of glycoproteins; protein structure and functionality; dietary fiber; anti-nutrients in food; phytochemicals. *Mailing Add:* Div Nutrit Sci Cornell Univ 116 Savage Hall Ithaca NY 14853-6301. *Fax:* 607-255-1033

LEWIS, BRIAN KREGLOW, HUMAN PHYSIOLOGY, COMPUTER BASED INSTRUCTION. *Current Pos:* OWNER, LEWIS & ASSOCS, 84- *Personal Data:* b SAfrica, Sept 2, 32; US citizen; m 53, Helen Kidwell; c Brian E, James A, Charles A, Carol J, Robert E & Sharon H. *Educ:* Ohio State Univ, BS, 54; Tufts Univ, PhD(physiol), 71. *Prof Exp:* res assoc physiol, Sch Med, Tufts Univ, 71, May Inst Med Res, Jewish Hosp Cincinnati, 71-74 & Col Med, Univ Cincinnati, 74-75; from asst prof to assoc prof health sci, Grand Valley State Col, 75-81; assoc prof physiol, Ponce Sch Med, 81-84, prof & chmn, Dept Physiol & dir comput sci, 87-91. *Concurrent Pos:* Adj asst prof physiol, Col Med, Univ Cincinnati, 72-75; instr, Sarasota Co Tech Inst, 95- *Mem:* Endocrine Soc; Soc; Study Reprod; Study Fertil; Sigma Xi. *Res:* Developing computer simulations for use in physiology instruction for medical and PhD students; develop software and training for small businesses. *Mailing Add:* 6423 Caracara St Sarasota FL 34241-9104. *E-Mail:* bklew@ix.netcom.com

LEWIS, BRIAN MURRAY, GALAXIES, RADIO ASTRONOMY MEASUREMENTS. *Current Pos:* STAFF SCIENTIST RES, ARECIBO OBSERV, PR, 82- *Personal Data:* b Oxford, UK, June 20, 43; UK & NZ citizen; m 67; c 2. *Educ:* Adelaide Univ, Australia, BS, 65; Australian Nat Univ, PhD(astron), 70. *Prof Exp:* Res asst astron, Jodrell Bank, Univ Manchester, UK, 69-71; dir teaching-pub rels-res, Carter Observ, Wellington, NZ, 73-81. *Concurrent Pos:* Secy, Nat Comt Astron, NZ, 73-80; vis fel, Nat Radio Astron Observ, 79-80; vis prof, Cornell Univ, 84, 87. *Mem:* Australian Astron Soc; Am Astron Soc; Int Astron Union. *Res:* Properties of galaxies, the precision of velocity estimates and their use in Tully-Fisher relation; missing mass in galaxies; identification of OH-IR stars; properties of circumstellar envelopes. *Mailing Add:* Arecibo Observ PO Box 995 Arecibo PR 00613

LEWIS, C S, JR, INTERNAL MEDICINE. *Current Pos:* DIR INT STUDIES INTERNAL MED, MED COL, UNIV OKLA, TULSA. *Personal Data:* b Muskogee, Okla, July 19, 20. *Mem:* Inst Med-Nat Acad Sci. *Mailing Add:* Dept Internal Med Univ Okla Med Col Tulsa OK 74129

LEWIS, CAMERON DAVID, organic chemistry; deceased, see previous edition for last biography

LEWIS, CARMIE PERROTTA, HISTOLOGY. *Current Pos:* assoc prof, 67-74, PROF BIOL, SUFFOLK CO COMMUNITY COL, 74- *Personal Data:* b New Castle, Pa, June 9, 29; m 65. *Educ:* Thiel Col, BS, 51; Univ NH, MS, 53; Univ Wis, PhD(anat, zool), 56. *Prof Exp:* Res asst, Univ Wis, 53-56; Am Asn Univ Women res fel, Cambridge Univ, 56-57; lectr embryol & histol, Fac Med, Queen's Univ, Ont, 57-58; instr anat, Sch Med, Yale Univ, 58-61; asst radiobiologist, Brookhaven Nat Lab, 61-64, res collabr, 64-67. *Concurrent Pos:* USPHS res fel, 61-64; asst prof, Queens Col, NY, 64-67; Mellon fel, Ctr Univ NY-Community Col Proj, 88. *Mem:* Am Asn Anat. *Res:* Radiobiology; endocrines of reproduction. *Mailing Add:* 107 Alden Dr Port Jefferson NY 11777

LEWIS, CHARLES E, MEDICINE, PREVENTIVE MEDICINE. *Current Pos:* head, Div Pres & Occup Med, Med Sch & dir, Health Servs Res Ctr, 91-93, PROF PUB HEALTH, UNIV CALIF, LOS ANGELES, 70-, PROF MED, 72-, PROF NURSING, 74-, DIR, CTR HEALTH PROM & DIS PREV, 91- *Personal Data:* b Kansas City, Mo, Dec 28, 28; m 63, Mary A Gurera; c 4. *Educ:* Harvard Med Sch, MD, 53; Univ Cincinnati, MS, 57, ScD(prev med), 59. *Honors & Awards:* Ginsberg Prize, 74; Glasier Award, 88. *Prof Exp:* House officer med, Univ Kans Hosps, 53-54; resident occup med, Eastman Kodak Co, 58-59, plant physician, Tex Div, 59-60; asst prof epidemiol, Col Med, Baylor Univ, 60-61; assoc prof med, Med Ctr, Univ Kans, 61-62; prof prev med, 62-69; prof social med, Harvard Med Sch, 69-70. *Concurrent Pos:* Fel prev med, Kettering Lab, Univ Cincinnati, 56-58; USPHS trainee, 57-58; dir, Kans Regional Med Prog, 67-69; mem, Regent Am Col Physicians, 88-; comnr, Joint Comn Accreditation Health Care Orgn, 90- *Mem:* Am Pub Health Asn; Asn Am Physicians; Am Col Physicians. *Res:* Medical care and education. *Mailing Add:* 221 S Burlingame Ave Los Angeles CA 90049

LEWIS, CHARLES J, ANIMAL SCIENCE. *Current Pos:* RETIRED. *Personal Data:* b Park River, NDak, May 20, 27; m 50, Norma McLaughlin; c Patrick J & Susan L. *Educ:* Utah State Univ, BS, 52; Iowa State Univ, MS, 54, PhD(animal nutrit), 56. *Prof Exp:* Dir nutrit, Kent Feeds, Inc, 56-58, vpres & nutritionist, 58-67, mem, Bd Dirs, 60-67; prof animal sci & head dept, SDak State Univ, 67-68; exec vpres, Grain Processing Corp & Kent Feeds, Inc, 68-93. *Concurrent Pos:* Dir & pres, Friend Agr & Iowa State Univ Res Found. *Mem:* AAAS; Am Inst Biol Sci; Am Soc Animal Sci; Inst Food Technologists; Poultry Sci Asn Am. *Res:* Animal nutrition and research. *Mailing Add:* 7 Colony Dr Muscatine IA 52761

LEWIS, CHARLES WILLIAM, PHYSICAL CHEMISTRY. *Current Pos:* RETIRED. *Personal Data:* b New York, NY, Oct 29, 20; wid, Barbara Medzerian; c 1. *Educ:* City Col New York, BS, 41; Polytech Inst New York, PhD(chem), 50. *Prof Exp:* Res chemist, Res Labs, Westinghouse Elec Corp, 49-58; assoc dir basic res, Int Resistance Co, 58-65; staff scientist, PPG Industs, Inc, 65-84. *Mem:* Am Chem Soc. *Res:* Polymer chemistry; solid and liquid dielectrics; kinetics and mechanism of organic reactions; physics of thin films; mechanical behavior of polymers. *Mailing Add:* 2400 McGinley Rd Monroeville PA 15146-3546

LEWIS, CLARK HOUSTON, FLUID MECHANICS, GAS DYNAMICS. *Current Pos:* PRES, VRA, INC, 84- *Personal Data:* b McMinnville, Tenn, Nov 6, 29; m 58; c 2. *Educ:* Univ Tenn, BSME, 51, MS, 59, PhD(viscous flow), 68. *Prof Exp:* Supvr theoret gas dynamics, Aerophys Div, Aro Inc, Arnold Eng Develop Ctr, Tenn, 51-68; prof aerospace eng, Va Polytech Inst & State Univ, 68-84. *Mem:* Assoc fel Am Inst Aeronaut & Astronaut; Am Phys Soc; Am Soc Mech Engrs. *Res:* Physical gas dynamics; high-speed viscous flows; chemically reacting flows; thermophysical gas properties; numerical methods in engineering. *Mailing Add:* VRA Inc PO Box 50 Blacksburg VA 24063-0050

LEWIS, CLAUDE IRENIUS, ANALYTICAL CHEMISTRY. *Current Pos:* res chemist, 65-66, sr res chemist, 66-70, supvr anal develop, 70-76, DIR QUAL ASSURANCE, LORILLARD CORP, 70- *Personal Data:* b Stanley, NC, Apr 21, 35; m 56; c 2. *Educ:* Duke Univ, BS, 57; Va Polytech Inst, MS, 59, PhD(chem), 62. *Prof Exp:* Res chemist, Texaco, Inc, 61-62 & E I du Pont de Nemours & Co, 62-65. *Concurrent Pos:* Instr, Guilford Col, 67-70. *Mem:* AAAS; Am Chem Soc; Am Inst Chem Eng; Am Soc Qual Control; Sigma Xi. *Res:* Cigarette tobacco technology; tobacco smoke chemistry; polyester fiber technology; alkyl benzene synthesis; synthesis of polycyclic aromatic compounds. *Mailing Add:* 3001 Shadylawn Dr Greensboro NC 27408-2620

LEWIS, CLIFFORD JACKSON, INORGANIC CHEMISTRY, METALLURGICAL ENGINEERING. *Current Pos:* environ consult, 73-80, DIR ENVIRON SERV, NAT LIME ASN, 80-; TECH DIR, STEEL BROS CAN, LTD, 85-; STAFF MEM, CONTINENTAL LIME INC, SALT LAKE CITY, UTAH. *Personal Data:* b Altoona, Pa, Aug 18, 12; m 39, Katherine E Kissick; c Jean, Joan & Ann. *Educ:* Franklin & Marshall Col, BS, 33; Univ Pittsburgh, BS, 44; Pa State Univ, MA, 37. *Prof Exp:* Tech dir, Warner Co, 45-51; sr res fel, Mellon Inst, 51-54; res dir, Res Inst, Colo Sch Mines, 55-70; environ consult indust wastes & sulfur oxides control, 70-73. *Mem:* Am Chem Soc; Am Inst Chem Engrs; Air Pollution Control Asn. *Res:* Municipal waste treatment; control of sulfur oxides emission by wet scrubbing and metals recovery by hydrometallurgical processes. *Mailing Add:* Nat Lime Asn 2446 Otis Ct Edgewater CO 80214

LEWIS, CORNELIUS CRAWFORD, AGRONOMY, SOIL SCIENCE. *Current Pos:* PROF AGRON & NUCLEAR SCI, VA STATE COL, 63- *Personal Data:* b Appomattox, Va, May 24, 21; m 49. *Educ:* Va State Col, BS, 42; Mich State Univ, MS, 45; Univ Mass, PhD(agron), 48. *Prof Exp:* Prof agron, Ft Valley State Col, 47-48; head dept agr, WVa State Col, 48-49; prof agron, Univ Md, 49-50; anal chemist, New York Testing Lab, 50-51; soil specialist, USDA For Serv, Liberia, WAfrica, 51-53; head dept plant industs, Agr & Tech Col, NC, 54-56; head dept agr, Grambling Col, 56-63. *Mem:* AAAS; Am Chem Soc; Am Soc Agron; Soil Sci Soc Am; Sigma Xi. *Res:* Field crops; soil fertility; plant nutrient relationship, particularly fertility levels and nutrient requirements for economic crops. *Mailing Add:* 20412 Woodpecker Rd Petersburg VA 23803

LEWIS, CRISTINA T, ENZYMOLOGY. *Current Pos:* res scientist, 93-96, SR SCIENTIST, AGOURON PHARMACEUT, 96- *Personal Data:* b West Palm Beach, Fla, Nov 11, 62. *Educ:* Univ SFla, BS, 83; Univ Tenn, PhD(biochem), 89. *Prof Exp:* Jane Coffin Childs fel, Scripps Res Inst, 90-93. *Mem:* Am Chem Soc; Am Soc Biochem & Molecular Biol. *Res:* Enzymological characterization and purification of pharmaceutically relevant proteins; application of structure based drug design; detailed characterization of enzyme structure-function relationships. *Mailing Add:* Agouron Pharmaceut 3565 Gen Atomics Ct San Diego CA 92121-1121. *Fax:* 619-622-7999; *E-Mail:* clewis@agouron.com

LEWIS, CYNTHIA LUCILLE, invertebrate biology, developmental biology, for more information see previous edition

LEWIS, DANIEL MOORE, ALLERGIES & HYPERSENSITIVITY DISEASES, PULMONARY IMMUNOLOGY. *Current Pos:* CHIEF, IMMUNOL SECT, NIOSH, MORGANTOWN, WVA, 91- *Personal Data:* b Barnesville, Ohio, Oct 1, 45; m 70; c 3. *Educ:* Ohio State Univ, BS, 67; WVa Univ, MS, 69, PhD(microbiol), 74. *Prof Exp:* Res fel immunol, Mayo Clin & Found, Rochester, Minn, 74-76; res asst prof immunol, Ohio State Univ, Columbus, 76-80; immunologist, USPHS, Morgantown, 80-91. *Concurrent Pos:* From adj asst prof to adj assoc prof microbiol, WVa Univ, Morgantown, 82-89, adj prof, 89- *Res:* Immunologic aspects of occupational lung diseases with special interest in allergy and occupational asthma; development of assays to evaluate the inflammatory potential of organic dusts found in agricultural work sites and development of assays for the measurement of airborne allergens in the worksite. *Mailing Add:* Immunol Sect Nat Inst Occup Safety & Health 1095 Willowdale Rd Morgantown WV 26505

LEWIS, DANIEL RALPH, MATHEMATICS. *Current Pos:* AT DEPT MATH, TEX A&M UNIV. *Personal Data:* b Camden, Ark, Oct 31, 44. *Educ:* La State Univ, Baton Rouge, 66, MS, 68, PhD(math), 70. *Prof Exp:* Asst prof math, Va Polytech Inst & State Univ, 70-72; asst prof math, Univ Fla, 72-77; assoc prof math, Ohio State Univ, 77- *Mem:* Am Math Soc. *Res:* Functional analysis. *Mailing Add:* Tex A&M Univ College Station TX 77843-3368

LEWIS, DANNY HARVE, POLYMER CHEMISTRY. *Current Pos:* VPRES NEW PROD DEVELOP, STOLLE RES & DEVELOP CORP, 82- *Personal Data:* b Decatur, Ala, Apr 9, 48; m 68; c 2. *Educ:* Univ NAla, BS, 69; Univ Ala, PhD(chem), 73. *Prof Exp:* Res chemist textile fibers, E I du Pont de Nemours & Co Inc, 73-75; sr chemist polymer chem, Southern Res Inst, 75-77, head, Biomat Sect, 77-80, head, Biosysts Div, 80-82. *Concurrent Pos:* Consult, NIH. *Mem:* Sigma Xi; Controlled Release Soc (pres-elect). *Res:* Controlled-release delivery systems; biomaterials for dental and orthopedic use; synthesis and characterization of new polymers; physical properties of polymers; polymers for fiber spinning, polymers as adhesives and membranes. *Mailing Add:* Stolle Res 383 Wynn Wallace Rd Hartselle AL 35640-7960

LEWIS, DAVID EDWIN, DEVELOPMENT OF SYNTHETIC METHODOLOGY, DEVELOPMENT OF NOVEL PHOTOCHEMICALLY ACTIVATED ANTIVIRAL COMPOUNDS. *Current Pos:* PROF & CHAIR, UNIV WIS-EAU CLAIRE, 97- *Personal Data:* b Tailem Bend, SAustralia, Nov 21, 51; m 78, Deborah A Schurtz; c Graeme A & Veronica A. *Educ:* Univ Adelaide, BSc, 72, PhD(org chem), 80. *Prof Exp:* Res assoc chem, Univ Ark, 77-78, lectr, 79-80; vis asst prof, Univ Ill, Urbana-Champaign, 80-81; from asst prof to assoc prof, Baylor Univ, 81-88; from assoc prof to prof, SDak State Univ, 89-97. *Concurrent Pos:* Dir res, Chem Div, Micro Bio Med Corp; vis distinguished scholar, Univ Adelaide, 88. *Mem:* Royal Australian Chem Inst; Am Chem Soc; Am Soc Photobiol. *Res:* Asymmetric synthesis; development of new bornane-based chiral auxillaries; photochemical inactivation of enveloped viruses and cells; development of novel photochemically-activated chemotherapeutic agents. *Mailing Add:* Univ Wis Eau Claire WI 54702-4004. *Fax:* 605-688-6364

LEWIS, DAVID HAROLD, CARDIOLOGY. *Current Pos:* guest investr, 78-80, CHIEF CLIN RES, CLIN RES CTR, UNIV HOSP, LINKOPING UNIV, 80- *Personal Data:* b New York, NY, Dec 22, 25; m 47, 63; c 2. *Educ:* Columbia Univ, AB, 44, MD, 47. *Prof Exp:* Intern med, Bellevue Hosp, New York, 47-48; intern, Kings County Hosp, 48-49, resident, 49-50; from instr to asst prof physiol, Sch Med, Univ Pa, 50-57, assoc cardiol, Grad Sch Med, 55-63; guest investr, First Surg Dept, Univ Goteborg, 63-78. *Concurrent Pos:* Chief hemodynamics sect, Div Cardiol, Philadelphia Gen Hosp, 55-63; estab investr, Am Heart Asn, 57-62. *Mem:* Am Physiol Soc; Am Fedn Clin Res; Am Heart Asn. *Res:* Cardiovascular physiology. *Mailing Add:* Clin Res Ctr Univ Hosp Linkoping Univ Grangatan 7 S-58245 Linkoping Sweden. *Fax:* 46-13-127465

LEWIS, DAVID KENNETH, PHYSICAL CHEMISTRY. *Current Pos:* From asst prof to prof chem, 69-88, assoc dean fac, 85-86, chmn chem, 87-88, CHARLES A DANA PROF CHEM, COLGATE UNIV, 88-, DIR, DIV NAT SCI & MATH, 82-85 & 88- *Personal Data:* b Poughkeepsie, NY, Feb

11, 43; m 64; c 3. *Educ:* Amherst Col, AB, 64; Cornell Univ, PhD(phys chem), 70. *Concurrent Pos:* Vis sr res fel, Univ Colo/Nat Oceanic & Atmospheric Admin, 77-78; environ mgt coun, Madison County, NY, 81-86; mem Cent NY Task Force Hazardous & Toxic Waste, 82-84; vis prof chem, Syracuse Univ, 86, Univ NC, 87. *Mem:* Am Chem Soc; Sigma Xi. *Res:* Chemical kinetics and energy transfer in gases at high temperatures; ultra-high resolution molecular spectroscopy; atmospheric chemistry and physics; innovative teaching methods. *Mailing Add:* Dept Chem Wynn Hall Colgate Univ Hamilton NY 13346

LEWIS, DAVID KENT, FOREST MANAGEMENT, FOREST ECONOMICS. *Current Pos:* ASSOC PROF FORESTERY, OKLA STATE UNIV, 82- *Personal Data:* b Madison, Wis, June 11, 38; m 62, Judith Grover; c Lynn R (Ross), Anoc E (Badger) & Evan D. *Educ:* Univ Minn, BS, 60; Yale Univ, MF, 66; Univ Oxford, D Phil, 76. *Prof Exp:* Forester, Ore, 63-65; silviculturist, Forestry Res Ctr, 67-76; forest economist, Res & Develop, Weyerhaeuser Co, Wash, 76-82. *Mem:* Soc Am Foresters; Am Econ Asn. *Res:* Economics of producing timber crops; economic of global climate change; impact of forest resources on reginal economics. *Mailing Add:* Dept Forestry Rm 008C Agr Hall Okla State Univ Stillwater OK 74078. *E-Mail:* dklewis@okway.okatate.edu

LEWIS, DAVID S(LOAN), JR, AERONAUTICAL ENGINEERING. *Current Pos:* RETIRED. *Personal Data:* b North Augusta, SC, July 6, 17; m 41; c 4. *Educ:* Ga Tech Univ, BS, 39. *Hon Degrees:* DSc, Clarkson Col Technol, 71; LLD, St Louis Univ. *Honors & Awards:* Collier Trophy, Pres Ford, 76; Wright Bros Trophy; Sands of Time Award, 77; Distinguished Achievement Award, Wings Club, 83. *Prof Exp:* Aerodynamicist, Martin Co, 39-46; chief aerodyn, McDonnell Aircraft Corp, 46-52, chief preliminary design, 52-55, mgr sales, 55-56, mgr all projs, 56-57, vpres, 57-59, sr vpres, 59-61, sr vpres opers, 60-61, exec vpres, 61-62, pres, 62-67, pres, McDonnell Douglas Corp, 67-70; chmn bd & chief exec officer, Gen Dynamics Corp, 70-86, dir, 86-92. *Concurrent Pos:* Mem, Subcomt Highspeed Aerodyn & Subcomt Stability & Control, Nat Adv Comt Aeronaut, 51-57. *Mem:* Nat Acad Eng; fel Am Inst Aeronaut & Astronaut. *Res:* Aerodynamics; high speed flight characteristics; space mechanics. *Mailing Add:* 19 Tradd St Charleston SC 29401-2537. *Fax:* 803-577-9634

LEWIS, DAVID THOMAS, AGRONOMY, SOIL MORPHOLOGY. *Current Pos:* instr agron, 67-71, from asst prof to assoc prof, 75-80, PROF SOIL CLASSIFICATION, DEPT AGRON, UNIV NEBR, 80- *Personal Data:* b Downing, Mo, Sept 27, 35; m 68; c 1. *Educ:* Univ Maine, BS, 60, MS, 62; Univ Nebr, PhD(agron), 71. *Prof Exp:* Instr soil sci, Dept Agron, Univ Maine, 60-62; soil scientist, Soil Conserv Serv, USDA, 62-67. *Mem:* Soil Sci Soc Am; Soil Conserv Soc Am; Sigma Xi. *Res:* Studies relating to the genesis and classification of soils and to the solution of problems that relate to proper correlation of survey mapping units. *Mailing Add:* Dept Agron E Campus Univ Nebr 279 Plant Sci PO Box 830915 Lincoln NE 68583-0915

LEWIS, DAVID W(ARREN), MECHANICS. *Current Pos:* assoc prof mech eng, 63-71, PROF MECH ENG & BIOMED ENG, UNIV VA, 71- *Personal Data:* b Salem, Ohio, June 16, 30; m 53; c 4. *Educ:* Rice Univ, BA, 52, BS, 53, MS, 55; Northwestern Univ, PhD(mech), 58. *Prof Exp:* Instr mech eng, Northwestern Univ, 55-57; asst prof, US Naval Postgrad Sch, 58-60; staff engr, IBM Corp, 60-63. *Mem:* Am Soc Eng Educ; Am Soc Mech Engrs. *Res:* Mechanics, especially elasticity and kinematics. *Mailing Add:* Dept Mech & Aerospace Eng Univ Va McCormick Rd Charlottesville VA 22901

LEWIS, DEBRA A, CARDIOVASCULAR PHYSIOLOGY & PHARMACOLOGY, VASCULAR INJURY. *Current Pos:* Fel cardiovasc physiol & pharmacol, 88-90, ASST PROF & RES ASSOC, MAYO CLIN, 94- *Personal Data:* b Burlington, Vt, Nov 13, 53. *Educ:* Univ NH, BS, 75; Pa State Univ, MS, 82, PhD(physiol), 88. *Concurrent Pos:* Minn affil res fel, Am Heart Asn, 93-95; res comt, Dept Surg, Mayo Clin. *Mem:* Am Physiol Soc; NAm Vascular Biol Orgn. *Res:* Vascular injury and the mechanisms that promote medial growth; transplant accelerated atherosclerosis in a porcine model. *Mailing Add:* Dept Surg & Cardiol Mayo Clin Alfred 2 Cavbi Rochester MN 55905. *Fax:* 507-284-5075; *E-Mail:* lewis.debra@mayo.edu

LEWIS, DENNIS ALLEN, ORGANIC CHEMISTRY. *Current Pos:* asst prof, 72-76, ASSOC PROF CHEM, ROSE-HULMAN INST TECHNOL, 76- *Personal Data:* b Morristown, NJ, Dec 25, 42; m 70; c 2. *Educ:* St Peters Col, BS, 64; Univ Conn, PhD(org chem), 72. *Prof Exp:* Instr & sr instr, Nuclear Weapons Employ Div, Ft Sill, Okla, 70-71. *Concurrent Pos:* Instr, US Army Reserve Sch, Ft Benjamin Harrison, Ind, 73- *Mem:* Am Chem Soc; Sigma Xi. *Res:* Synthesis of small-ring compounds via photochemical reactions involving carbene and nitrene intermediates; investigation of chemiluminescent systems. *Mailing Add:* Dept Chem Rose-Hulman Inst Technol 5500 Wabash Ave Terre Haute IN 47803-3999

LEWIS, DONALD EVERETT, BIOCHEMISTRY, SCIENCE EDUCATION. *Current Pos:* assoc prof, 66-68, PROF CHEM, ABILENE CHRISTIAN COL, 68- *Personal Data:* b Paducah, Tex, July 3, 31; m 68, Marian Crowson; c Donna M & Paul A. *Educ:* Abilene Christian Col, BS, 52; Fla State Univ, MS, 54, PhD(biochem), 57. *Prof Exp:* From assoc prof to prof chem, Queen's Col, NC, 57-66. *Concurrent Pos:* Vis assoc prof, Abilene Christian Col, 63-64; vis prof chem, Univ Tex, Austin, 80-81. *Mem:* Am Chem Soc. *Res:* Synthesis and biological assay of amino acid analogues. *Mailing Add:* 2541 Campus Courts Abilene TX 79601. *Fax:* 915-674-6988

LEWIS, DONALD HOWARD, FISH PATHOLOGY, MICROBIOLOGY. *Current Pos:* Res assoc, 66-68, asst prof, 69-75, assoc prof, 75-79, PROF MICROBIOL, TEX A&M UNIV, 79-, ACTG HEAD VET MICROBIOL & PARASITOL, 81- *Personal Data:* b Stamford, Tex, May 31, 36; m 60; c 3. *Educ:* Univ Tex, Austin, BA, 59; Southwest Tex State Univ, MA, 64; Tex A&M Univ, PhD(vet microbiol), 67. *Concurrent Pos:* Consult, TerEco Corp, 75. *Mem:* AAAS; Am Soc Microbiol; Am Fisheries Soc; Soc Invert Path; World Maricult Soc. *Res:* Microbial diseases and immune mechanisms of aquatic animals; role of microflora upon host welfare; antibiotic resistance; molecular biology. *Mailing Add:* Dept Vet Microbiol Col Vet Med Tex A&M Univ College Station TX 77843-4467

LEWIS, DONALD JOHN, MATHEMATICS, NUMBER THEORY. *Current Pos:* assoc prof, 61-63, chmn, 84-94, PROF MATH, UNIV MICH, ANN ARBOR, 63-; DIR, DIV MATH SCI, NSF, 95- *Personal Data:* b Adrian, Minn, Jan 25, 26; m 53, Carolyn D Hauf. *Educ:* Col St Thomas, BS, 46; Univ Mich, MS, 49, PhD(math), 50. *Honors & Awards:* Humboldt Stiftung Sr Award, 80 & 82. *Prof Exp:* Instr math, Ohio State Univ, 50-52; NSF fel, Inst Adv Study, 52-53; from asst prof to assoc prof, Univ Notre Dame, 53-61. *Concurrent Pos:* NSF sr fel, Manchester & Cambridge Univs, 59-61; sr vis fel, Cambridge Univ, 65-69; vis fel, Brasenose Col, Oxford, 69; guest prof, Heidelberg Univ, 79-80 & 83. *Mem:* Am Math Soc; Math Asn Am. *Res:* Diophantine equations; finite fields; algebraic number theory. *Mailing Add:* Dept Math E Hall Univ Mich Main Campus Ann Arbor MI 48109-1003

LEWIS, DONALD RICHARD, ISOTOPE GEOCHEMISTRY, ARCHAEOLOGICAL CHEMISTRY. *Current Pos:* FAC ASSOC, CTR ARCHAEOL RES, UNIV TEX, SAN ANTONIO, 80-, LECTR, ISOTOPE GEOCHEM, 87-, FAC ASSOC, CTR WATER RES, 87- *Personal Data:* b New Leipzig, NDak, May 18, 20; m 43, Evelyn Schwingel; c Donna & Jeff. *Educ:* Univ Wis-Madison, BS, 42, MS, 47, PhD(chem), 48. *Prof Exp:* Ballistics supvr, Hercules Powder Co, 42-46; asst, Univ Wis, 46-48; res chemist, Shell Develop Co, div Shell Oil Co, 48-58, staff res chemist, 58-70, group leader, 70-75, proj leader, 75-80. *Concurrent Pos:* Exchange scientist, Shell Develop Co & Royal Dutch Shell, Amsterdam, Neth, 56-57; assoc ed, Comt Clay Minerals, Nat Acad Sci-Nat Res Coun, 57-59; prin scientist, USAF-Advan Res Proj Agency, 65-66; consult & dir, Nuclear Monitoring Syst & Mgt Corp, 80-92; lectr archaeometry, chem & geochem, Div Earth & Phys Sci & Div Behav & Dult Sci, Univ Tex, San Antonio, 80-; res fel, Tex Archaeol Res Lab, Univ Tex, Austin, 88- *Mem:* Fel AAAS; Am Chem Soc; Am Phys Soc; fel Mineral Soc Am; Geochem Soc; Geol Soc Am. *Res:* Thermoluminescence dating; anthrosol land use; trace element and stable isotope studies for environmental characterization and paleodiet studies; trace element geochemistry; isotope geochemistry and geochronology; groundwater geochemistry. *Mailing Add:* 9219 Lasater San Antonio TX 78250-2418. *Fax:* 210-458-4469

LEWIS, DOUGLAS SCOTT, ANIMAL PHYSIOLOGY. *Current Pos:* asst res scientist, 80-86, assoc res scientist, 87-92, ASSOC PROF FOOD SCI, SOUTHWEST FOUND BIOMED RES, 92- *Personal Data:* b Dayton, Ohio, Aug 10, 51; m 80; c 4. *Educ:* Univ Ga, BS, 73; Mich State Univ, PhD(biochem), 78. *Prof Exp:* Postdoctoral physiol, Univ Tex Health Sci Ctr, San Antonio, 78-80. *Concurrent Pos:* Asst prof, Dept Physiol, Univ Tex Health Sci Ctr, San Antonio, 84- *Mem:* Am Physiol Soc; Am Heart Asn. *Res:* Mechanisms by which nutritional factors regulate lipid metabolism during growth and development; investigate endocrine regulation of fat cell and hepatic metabolism in preweaning infants using a non-human primate. *Mailing Add:* Dept Food Sci Iowa State Univ 1127 Human Nutrit Sci Bldg Ames IA 50011

LEWIS, EDWARD B, GENETICS. *Current Pos:* From instr to assoc prof genetics, Calif Inst Technol, 46-56, prof biol, 56-66, Thomas Hunt Morgan prof, 66-88, EMER THOMAS HUNT MORGAN PROF BIOL, CALIF INST TECHNOL, 88- *Personal Data:* b Wilkes-Barre, Pa, May 20, 18; m 46, Pamela Harrah; c Hugh H & Keith D. *Educ:* Univ Minn, BA, 39; Calif Inst Technol, PhD(genetics), 42. *Hon Degrees:* Dr, Univ Umea, Sweden, 81; DSc, Univ Minn, 93. *Honors & Awards:* Nobel Prize Med, 95; Morgan Medal, Genetics Soc Am, 83; Gairdner Found Int Award, 87; Wolf Found Prize in Med, 89; Rosenstiel Award, 90; Nat Medal Sci, 90; Albert Lasker Basic Med Res Award, 91; Louisa Gross Horwitz Prize, 92. *Concurrent Pos:* Rockefeller Found fel, Sch Bot, Cambridge Univ, 47-48; mem, Nat Adv Comt Radiation, 58-61; guest prof, Univ Copenhagen, 75-76. *Mem:* Nat Acad Sci; AAAS; Am Acad Arts & Sci; Genetics Soc Am (secy, 62-64, vpres, 66, pres, 67); Am Philos Soc; foreign mem Royal Soc London; hon mem Genetical Soc Gt Brit. *Res:* Developmental genetics; somatic effects of ionizing radiation. *Mailing Add:* Biol Div 156-29 Calif Inst Technol Pasadena CA 91125. *Fax:* 626-564-9685

LEWIS, EDWARD LYN, OCEANOGRAPHY. *Current Pos:* res scientist, 62-95, EMER SCIENTIST, OCEAN SCI & SURV, DEPT FISHERIES & OCEANOG, CAN, 95- *Personal Data:* b Aberystwyth, UK, Oct 9, 30; m 59; c 3. *Educ:* Univ London, BSc, 51, MSc, 58, PhD(physics), 62. *Prof Exp:* Physicist, Mullard Res Labs, 52-56; Harwell res fel, Univ London, 56-59; res assoc microwave electronics, Univ BC, 59-62. *Mem:* Am Geophys Union; Glaciol Soc. *Res:* Arctic oceanography; ice physics; energy exchange ocean-atmosphere; arctic instrument development. *Mailing Add:* 3904 Bedford Rd Victoria BC V8N 4K5 Can

LEWIS, EDWARD SHELDON, CHEMISTRY, CHEMICAL DYNAMICS. *Current Pos:* from asst prof to prof, 48-90, chmn dept, 80-85, EMER PROF CHEM, RICE UNIV, 90- *Personal Data:* b Berkeley, Calif, May 7, 20; m 55, Fofo Catsinas; c Richard & Gregory. *Educ:* Univ Calif, BS, 40; Harvard Univ,

MA, 47, PhD(chem), 47. *Honors & Awards:* Southwest Regional Award, Am Chem Soc. *Prof Exp:* Nat Res Coun fel, Univ Calif, Los Angeles, 47-48. *Concurrent Pos:* Vis prof, Univ Southampton, 57; chmn, Dept Chem, Rice Univ, 65-67 & 81-86; Guggenheim fel, 67; vis prof, Phys Chem Lab, Oxford Univ, 67-68, Univ Col, Dublin, 78. *Mem:* Am Chem Soc; Royal Soc Chem; AAAS. *Res:* Mechanism of reactions of organic compounds, especially diazonium salts, hydrogen isotope effects, methyl transfers and organo-phosphorus chemistry. *Mailing Add:* Dept Chem MS 60 Rice Univ 6100 Main St Houston TX 77005-1892. *Fax:* 713-285-5155

LEWIS, EDWIN REYNOLDS, BIOENGINEERING. *Current Pos:* PROF BIOENG, UNIV CALIF, BERKELEY, 67- *Personal Data:* b Los Angeles, Calif, July 14, 34; m 60; c 2. *Educ:* Stanford Univ, AB, 56, MS, 57, PhD(elec eng), 62. *Prof Exp:* Mem res staff neural modeling, Lab Automata Res, Gen Precision, 61-67. *Mem:* Fel Inst Elec & Electronics Engrs; Acoust Soc Am; Soc Neurosci; AAAS; Asn Res Otolaryngol; Sigma Xi. *Res:* Applications of engineering analytical tools to problems in neurobiology; network models of dynamical biological systems; morphology and physiology of vestibular and auditory systems. *Mailing Add:* 1047 Overlook Rd Berkeley CA 94708-1711

LEWIS, FORBES DOWNER, COMPUTER SCIENCE. *Current Pos:* assoc prof comput sci & chmn dept, 78-82, PROF COMPUT SCI, UNIV KY, 83- *Personal Data:* b New Haven, Conn, Apr 15, 42. *Educ:* Cornell Univ, BS, 67, MS, 69, PhD(comput sci), 70. *Prof Exp:* Asst prof, Harvard Univ, 70-75; assoc prof, State Univ NY, Albany, 75-78. *Mem:* Asn Comput Mach; Soc Indust & Appl Math; Inst Elec & Electronics Engrs. *Res:* CAD algorithms for very-large-scale integration; computational complexity. *Mailing Add:* Dept Comput Sci Univ Ky 971 Patterson Off Tower Lexington KY 40506

LEWIS, FRANK HARLAN, BOTANY. *Current Pos:* from asst prof to prof, 48-82, EMER PROF BOT, UNIV CALIF, LOS ANGELES, 82- *Personal Data:* b Redlands, Calif, Jan 8, 19; m 45, 68, 84, Margaret R Ensign; c Donald A & Frank M. *Educ:* Univ Calif, Los Angeles, BA, 41, MA, 42, PhD(bot), 46. *Honors & Awards:* Award of Merit, Bot Soc Am, 72. *Prof Exp:* Asst instr bot, Univ Calif, Los Angeles, 42-44, instr, 46-47; Nat Res Coun fel, John Innes Hort Inst, London, 47-48. *Concurrent Pos:* Teaching fel, Calif Inst Technol, 43-44; Guggenheim fel, 54-55; consult, NSF, 58-69; chmn, Dept Bot, Univ Calif, Los Angeles, 59-62, dean, Div Life Sci, 62-82; vpres, Int Orgn Biosyst, 64-69, pres, 69-75; ed, Evolution, 72-74. *Mem:* Fel AAAS; Am Inst Biol Sci; Am Soc Naturalists (pres, 71); Am Soc Plant Taxonomists (pres, 69); Soc Study Evolution (secy, 53-58, vpres, 59, pres, 61); Bot Soc Am; Genetics Soc Am. *Res:* Mechanisms of evolution; systematics of flowering plants. *Mailing Add:* Dept Biol Univ Calif Los Angeles CA 90024

LEWIS, FRANK LEROY, ELECTRICAL ENGINEERING. *Current Pos:* PROF & MONCRIEF-O'DONNELL ENDOWED CHAIR ELEC ENG, UNIV TEX, ARLINGTON, 90- *Personal Data:* b Wurzburg, Ger, May 11, 49; m 86, Theresa Maldonado; c Christopher Mario Shirley. *Educ:* Rice Univ, BA & MEE, 71; Univ WFla, MS, 77; Ga Inst Technol, PhD(elec eng), 81. *Honors & Awards:* Monie A Ferst Award for Outstanding Doctoral Res in Eng, Sigma Xi, 81; Frederick E Terman Award, Am Soc Eng Educ, 89. *Prof Exp:* From asst prof to prof, Ga Inst Technol, Atlanta, 81-90. *Concurrent Pos:* Sigma Xi res award, 81, 84, 90; assoc ed, J Circuits, Systs, Signal Processing, 86; Fulbright res award, 88; adj prof, Ga Inst Technol, Atlanta, 90-; invited consult-lectr, UN Umbrella Proj, Warsaw, Poland, 91; bd govs, Inst Elec & Electronics Engrs Control Systs Soc, 95. *Mem:* Fel Inst Elec & Electronics Engrs Control Systs Soc; Soc Indust & Appl Math; AAAS; Sigma Xi; sr mem Inst Elec & Electronics Engrs. *Res:* Intelligent control; nonlinear control; robotics; discrete event systems; manufacturing control; optimal control systems; neural networks and fuzzy logic; author of various publications; manufacturing. *Mailing Add:* Automation & Robotics Res Inst Univ Tex Arlington 7300 Jack Newell Blvd S Ft Worth TX 76118

LEWIS, FRANK M, ORTHOPEDICS, BIOMEDICAL ENGINEERING. *Current Pos:* PRES & CHIEF EXEC OFFICER, INNERVISION INC, 92-; VPRES CORP DEVELOP, BUGEYE INC, 94-; CONSULT, HOLOMEDICA INC, 96- *Educ:* Univ Fla, BS, 73, MS, 74. *Prof Exp:* Proprietor, Gainsville Bicycle Distribrs, 70-72; proj engr, Codman & Shurtleff Inc, 75-76; tech dir, Dow Corning Wright, 76-82; dir eng, Richards Med Co Inc, 82-88; vpres res & develop,Danek Med Inc, 88-91; vpres corp develop, K Plus A Med Int, 91-92; vpres develop spine & arthroscopy, Wright Med Technol Inc, 94-95. *Concurrent Pos:* Adj assoc prof mech eng, Memphis State Univ; instr biomech, Campbell Clin, Memphis; lectr total knee prosthesis, Univ Wash, Seattle & Univ Ky, Lexington; vis prof, Univ Philippines, 86. *Mem:* Soc Biomat; Am Soc Testing & Mat; Orthop Surg Mfrs Asn (secy-treas, 76-86); Am Soc Artificial Internal Organs; Orthop Res Soc; Knee Soc; Scoliosis Res Soc. *Res:* Gustilo metal base tibial prosthesis. *Mailing Add:* 6258 Shady Grove Rd E Memphis TN 38120

LEWIS, FRED A, SCHISTOSOMIASIS, MICROBIOLOGY. *Current Pos:* SR SCIENTIST, BIOMED RES INST, 77- *Personal Data:* b Atlanta, Tex, Dec 9, 44; m 70, Maureen B; c Matthew R & Elizabeth A. *Educ:* La Tech Univ, BS, 66; Northwestern State Univ, MS, 71, PhD(microbiol), 75. *Mem:* Am Soc parasitologists; Am Soc Trop Med & Hyg; Am Asn Immunologists. *Res:* Disease schistosomiasis; parasitology. *Mailing Add:* Biomed Res Inst 12111 Parklawn Dr Rockville MD 20852-1784

LEWIS, FRED P, METEOROLOGY. *Current Pos:* USAF, 72-, automated prog designer, Global Weather Ctr, Offutt AFB, Nebr, 73-76, asst chief Numerical Forecast Sect, 79-81, officer-in-charge, Weather Forecasts Models Unit, 81-82, officer-in-charge operating location B, Detachment 15, 30th Weather Squadron, Suwon AFB, S Korea, 83-89; asst chief Environ Servs Br, Hq Military Airlift Command, Scott AFB, Ill, 84-86, vice comdr, Environ Tech Appln Ctr, Scott AFB, 86-87, comdr 26th Weather Squadron, Barksdale AFB, La, 87-89, dep chief staff automation support, Airlift Commun Div, 90, comdr, 1500th Comput Systs Group, Scott AFB, Ill, 90-92, chief, Weather Div, US Transp Command, Scott AFB, Ill, 92-94, dir, Joint Transp Corp Info Mgt Ctr, US Transp Command, SCOTT AFB, ILL, 94-96, DIR WEATHER, DEP CHIEF STAFF PLANS & OPERS, HQ USAF, WASHINGTON, DC, 96- *Personal Data:* b Cottonwood, Ariz, Mar 2, 49; m, Christine E Soltis; c Fred. *Educ:* Univ Ariz, BS, 72; Univ Utah, PhD(meteorol), 79. *Res:* Developing doctrine, policy, requirements and standards for weather support to the Air Force and Army. *Mailing Add:* Directorate Weather HQ USAF XOW 1490 Air Force Pentagon Washington DC 20330-1490

LEWIS, FREDERICK D, PHOTOCHEMISTRY. *Current Pos:* from asst prof to assoc prof, 69-79, assoc dean, 89-92, PROF, NORTHWESTERN UNIV, 79- *Personal Data:* b Boston, Mass, Aug 12, 43; m 68, Susan Rice; c Gordon & Katherine. *Educ:* Amherst Col, BA, 65; Rochester Univ, PhD(chem), 68. *Prof Exp:* USPHS res fel chem, Columbia Univ, 68-69. *Concurrent Pos:* Fel, Dreyfus Found, 73-78 & Sloan Found, 75-77; consult, 3M Corp; assoc ed, J Phys Org Chem, 87-95, Int Union Pure & Appl Chem Comm Photochem, 90-96, J, Am Chem Soc, 95- *Mem:* Am Chem Soc; InterAm Photochem Soc; Europ Photochem Asn. *Res:* Organic photochemistry; radical ions; free radicals; cycloaddition reactions; exciplexes; nucleic acids. *Mailing Add:* Dept Chem Northwestern Univ Evanston IL 60208-3113. *Fax:* 847-467-2184; *E-Mail:* lewis@chem.nwu.edu

LEWIS, GEORGE CAMPBELL, JR, OBSTETRICS & GYNECOLOGY, ONCOLOGY. *Current Pos:* PROF GYNEC ONCOL & DIR DIV, JEFFERSON MED COL, 73- *Personal Data:* b Williamsburg, Ky, Mar 25, 19; m 45; c 6. *Educ:* Haverford Col, BS, 42; Univ Pa, MD, 44; Am Bd Obstet & Gynec, dipl, 53; Gyn Oncol, 80. *Prof Exp:* Intern med, Hosp Univ Pa, 44-45, resident obstet & gynec, 47-50, instr, Sch Med, Univ Pa, 50-53, instr radium ther, 51-63, res asst, 53-56, asst prof obstet & gynec, 56-63; prof obstet & gynec & chmn dept, Hahnemann Med Col & Hosp, 62-73, dir div gynec oncol, 71-73. *Concurrent Pos:* Am Cancer Soc fel gynec oncol, Hosp Univ Pa, 50-52; consult lectr, US Naval Hosp Philadelphia, 56-77; consult, Lankenau Hosp & Philadelphia Gen Hosp, 62-, Am Oncol Hosp, 63- & Magee Mem Hosp Rehab Ctr, 68-; mem div gynec oncol, Am Bd Obstet & Gynec; chmn, Gynec Oncol Grp, 75-89. *Mem:* Am Cancer Soc; Soc Gynec Oncol (pres, 69); Am Gynec Soc; Am Asn Obstet & Gynec; Am Col Obstet & Gynec. *Res:* Etiology, early diagnosis and evaluation of modes of therapy of gynecologic oncology. *Mailing Add:* Thomas Jefferson Univ 1025 Walnut St Philadelphia PA 19107-5001

LEWIS, GEORGE EDWARD, CONTINENTAL STRATIGRAPHIC PALEONTOLOGY, STRATEGIC & TERRAIN INTELLIGENCE. *Current Pos:* RETIRED. *Personal Data:* b Lorain, Ohio, Oct 27, 08; m 37, 61, Jane M DeChant; c Maria I (Minick), John E & Elizabeth M. *Educ:* Yale Univ, PhB, 30, PhD, 37. *Prof Exp:* Instr geol, Yale Univ, 38-43, asst prof, 43-45, geologist, US Geol Surv, 44-79. *Concurrent Pos:* Cur, Peabody Mus, Yale Univ, 39-45; vis prof, Univ Guayaquil, Ecuador, 42-43; comdr, USNR, 49-79; res assoc, Denver Mus Natural Hist. *Mem:* Fel Geol Soc Am; Soc Vert Paleont. *Res:* Continental stratigraphy; Permo-Triassic vertebrates; Cenozoic mammals, primates; strategic and terrain intelligence. *Mailing Add:* 155 Brentwood St Lakewood CO 80226

LEWIS, GEORGE EDWIN, ORGANIC CHEMISTRY. *Current Pos:* assoc prof, 66-80, PROF CHEM, JACKSONVILLE UNIV, 80- *Personal Data:* b Decatur, Ga, Jan 6, 33; m 56. *Educ:* Emory Univ, AB, 52, MS, 53; Fla State Univ, PhD(chem), 58. *Prof Exp:* Res asst, Ga Inst Technol, 58-59; asst prof chem, La State Univ, 59-66. *Mem:* Am Chem Soc; The Chem Soc. *Res:* Mechanisms of organic reactions. *Mailing Add:* Div Sci & Math Jacksonville Univ Jacksonville FL 32211-3393

LEWIS, GEORGE MCCORMICK, GEOMETRY. *Current Pos:* Asst prof, 67-72, assoc prof, 72-79, PROF MATH, CALIF POLYTECH STATE UNIV, SAN LUIS OBISPO, 79- *Personal Data:* b Los Angeles, Calif, Sept 14, 40; m 64; c Melanie, Heather & Alice (Gray). *Educ:* Stanford Univ, BA, 61; Univ Southern Calif, MA, 64, PhD(math), 70. *Mem:* Am Math Soc; Math Asn Am. *Res:* Synthetic differential geometry. *Mailing Add:* Dept Math Calif State Polytech Univ San Luis Obispo CA 93407. *Fax:* 805-756-6537; *E-Mail:* glewis@calpoly.edu

LEWIS, GEORGE R(OBERT), CHEMICAL ENGINEERING. *Current Pos:* CONSULT, 88- *Personal Data:* b Kansas City, Mo, June 26, 24; m 54; c 3. *Educ:* Ohio State Univ, BChE, 48, MSc, 49, PhD(chem eng), 51. *Prof Exp:* Res engr cellophane process, E I du Pont de Nemours & Co, 51-53, chem develop supvr, Film Dept, 53-55; res engr, Paperboard Res Labs, Mead Corp, Dayton, 55-60, staff consult, 60-64, prod mgr, 64-69, tech dir, Paperboard Prod Div, 69-88. *Mem:* Tech Asn Pulp & Paper Indust; Am Inst Chem Engrs. *Res:* Industrial wastes; cellophane process; pulp and paper; recycled paperboard; paperboard products. *Mailing Add:* 9450 Sugar Bend Trail Dayton OH 45458-3863

LEWIS, GLENN C, SOIL CHEMISTRY. *Current Pos:* RETIRED. *Personal Data:* b Oakley, Idaho, July 13, 20; m 56; c 6. *Educ:* Univ Idaho, BS, 46, MS, 49; Purdue Univ, PhD(soils), 62. *Prof Exp:* Anal agr chem, Univ Idaho, 47-52, from asst prof agr chem to prof soils, 52-85. *Mem:* Soil Sci Soc Am; Int Soc Soil Sci; AAAS. *Res:* Chemical and mineralogical studies on slick spot soils; water quality, including effects of irrigation water quality on soil characteristics; phosphorus reactions in calcareous soils; mineralogical studies on loess. *Mailing Add:* 1012 S Howard St Moscow ID 83843

LEWIS, GORDON, CERAMIC ENGINEERING. *Current Pos:* assoc prof ceramic eng, 64-73, PROF CERAMIC ENG, UNIV MO, ROLLA, 73- *Personal Data:* b Cincinnati, Ohio, Apr 7, 33; m 58; c 3. *Educ:* Alfred Univ, BS, 56, PhD(ceramics), 63. *Prof Exp:* Ceramic engr, Carborundum Co, NY, 57-58; res assoc chem, Univ Kans, 62-64. *Mem:* Am Ceramic Soc; Nat Inst Ceramic Engrs; Am Soc Eng Educ. *Res:* High temperature chemistry; phase equilibria and vaporization behavior in oxide systems; thermogravimetric behavior and phase identification of high alumina refractory cements. *Mailing Add:* Dept Ceramic Eng Clemson Univ 110 Olin Hall Clemson SC 29632-0001

LEWIS, GORDON DEPEW, FOREST ECONOMICS, POLICY. *Current Pos:* RETIRED. *Personal Data:* b Charlottesville, Va, July 22, 29; m 54. *Educ:* Va Polytech Inst, BS, 51; Duke Univ, MFor, 57; Mich State Univ, PhD(forest econ), 61. *Prof Exp:* Asst prof forest econ, Univ Mont, 59-62; proj leader, Southeastern Forest Exp Sta, US Forest Serv, 62-66, economist, Washington, DC, 66-67, br chief, 68-71, proj leader, Rocky Mountain Forest Exp Sta, 71-77, prog mgr, western environ forestry res, Rocky Mountain Forest Exp Sta, 77-81, asst dir, 81-92. *Mem:* Soc Am Foresters; Am Econ Asn. *Res:* Economic evaluations of alternative methods of exploiting natural resources for regional development consistent with the maintenance of the quality of rural and wildlife environments. *Mailing Add:* Three Weston Heights Dr Asheville NC 28803-8518

LEWIS, GWYNNE DAVID, PLANT PATHOLOGY. *Current Pos:* from asst prof to assoc prof, 58-70, PROF PLANT PATH, RUTGERS UNIV, NEW BRUNSWICK, 70- *Personal Data:* b Hackensack, NJ, June 12, 28; m 60; c 1. *Educ:* Rutgers Univ, BS, 51; Purdue Univ, MS, 53; Cornell Univ, PhD, 58. *Honors & Awards:* Bronze Medal, Am Rhododendron Soc, 75. *Prof Exp:* Asst plant path, Purdue Univ, 51-53 & Cornell Univ, 53-58. *Mem:* Am Phytopath Soc. *Res:* Diseases of vegetable crops; plant nematology; control of plant and vegetable diseases. *Mailing Add:* Dept Plant Path Rutgers Univ New Brunswick NJ 08903

LEWIS, H(ERBERT) CLAY, chemical engineering, for more information see previous edition

LEWIS, H(AROLD) RALPH, PHYSICS, PLASMA & COMPUTATIONAL PHYSICS. *Current Pos:* PROF PHYSICS, DARTMOUTH COL, 91- *Personal Data:* b Chicago, Ill, June 7, 31; m 61, Renate J Wenzel; c Beata C & Annette K. *Educ:* Univ Chicago, AB, 51, SB, 53; Univ Ill, MS, 55, PhD(physics), 58. *Hon Degrees:* MA, Dartmouth Col, 93. *Prof Exp:* Res assoc physics, Univ Heidelberg, 58-60; instr, Princeton Univ, 60-63; mem staff, Los Alamos Nat Lab, 63-75, assoc group leader, 75-81, dep group leader, 81-83, lab fel, 83-91. *Concurrent Pos:* Ger Acad Exchange Serv fel, Univ Heidelberg, 58-59; prof physics, Dartmouth Col, 91- *Mem:* Fel Am Phys Soc. *Res:* Plasma physics; nulcear spectroscopy; superconductivity; computational physics. *Mailing Add:* Dept Physics & Astron Dartmouth Col Hanover NH 03755-3528

LEWIS, HAROLD WALTER, NUCLEAR PHYSICS. *Current Pos:* Vis instr & res assoc, Duke Univ, 46-49, from asst prof to prof, 49-86, vprovost, 63-80, dean fac, 69-80, chmn dept, 81-86, univ distinguished serv prof, 80-86, EMER PROF PHYSICS, DUKE UNIV, 86- *Personal Data:* b Keene, NH, May 7, 17; m 46; c 2. *Educ:* Middlebury Col, BS, 38; Univ Buffalo, AM, 40; Duke Univ, PhD(physics), 50. *Concurrent Pos:* Dean arts & sci, Duke Univ, 63-69. *Mem:* Fel Am Phys Soc; Am Asn Physics Teachers. *Mailing Add:* Dept Physics Duke Univ Durham NC 27706

LEWIS, HAROLD WARREN, PHYSICS. *Current Pos:* PROF PHYSICS, UNIV CALIF, SANTA BARBARA, 64- *Personal Data:* b New York, NY, Oct 1, 23; m 47; c 2. *Educ:* NY Univ, AB, 43; Univ Calif, AM, 44, PhD(physics), 48. *Prof Exp:* Asst prof physics, Univ Calif, 48-53; mem tech staff, Bell Tel Labs, NJ, 51-56; from assoc prof to prof physics, Univ Wis, 56-64. *Concurrent Pos:* Mem staff, Inst Advan Study, 47-48 & 50-51; dir, Quantum Inst, Univ Calif, Santa Barbara, 69-73. *Mem:* Am Phys Soc; Sigma Xi. *Res:* Theoretical physics. *Mailing Add:* Dept Physics Univ Calif Santa Barbara Santa Barbara CA 93106. *E-Mail:* hlewis@physics.ucsb.edu

LEWIS, HARVYE FLEMING, NUTRITION. *Current Pos:* RETIRED. *Personal Data:* b Hodge, La, Dec 24, 17. *Educ:* La Polytech Inst, BS, 38; Univ Tenn, MS, 42; Iowa State Col, PhD(nutrit), 50. *Prof Exp:* Teacher high sch, La, 38-40; nutritionist, State Dept Pub Health, Tenn, 42; res assoc, Agr Exp Sta, La State Univ, 43-47, asst nutritionist, 50-52; assoc prof food & nutrit, Fla State Univ, 52-65; prof food & nutrit, sch home econ, La State Univ, 65-82. *Mem:* AAAS; Am Dietetic Asn; Am Home Econ Asn; Inst Food Technologists; Am Inst Nutrit; Sigma Xi. *Res:* Vitamin content of foods; nutritional requirements; food patterns and nutritional health of children. *Mailing Add:* 11275 Mollylea Dr Baton Rouge LA 70815-5247

LEWIS, HENRY RAFALSKY, PHYSICS. *Current Pos:* RETIRED. *Personal Data:* b Yonkers, NY, Nov 19, 25; m 57; c 3. *Educ:* Harvard Univ, AB, 48, MA, 49, PhD(physics), 56. *Prof Exp:* Mem staff opers res, Opers Eval Group, Mass Inst Technol, 51-53, 56; group head quantum electronics, David Sarnoff Res Ctr, RCA Corp, 57-66, dir, electronic res lab, 66-70; vpres res & develop, Itek Corp, 70-73; pres, Optel Corp, 73-74; group vpres & dir, Dennison Mfg Corp, 74-82, sr vpres & dir, 82-85, vchmn & dir, 86-91. *Concurrent Pos:* Dir, Delphany Syst, Randolph, Mass, 80, AOI Inc, Lowell, Mass, 87-, Genzyme Corp, Cambridge, Mass, 87- *Mem:* Am Phys Soc; Inst Elec & Electronics Engrs; NY Acad Sci; Sigma Xi. *Res:* Paramagnetic resonance; quantum electronics; operations research; molecular beams. *Mailing Add:* 35 Clover St Belmont MA 02178

LEWIS, HERMAN WILLIAM, GENETICS, ZOOLOGY. *Current Pos:* RETIRED. *Personal Data:* b Chicago, Ill, July 10, 23; c 2. *Educ:* Univ Ill, BS, 47, MS, 49; Univ Calif, PhD(genetics), 53. *Honors & Awards:* Mendel Medal. *Prof Exp:* USPHS res fel, Univ Calif, 52-54; asst prof biol, Mass Inst Technol, 54-61; prof life sci & chmn dept, Mich State Univ, 61-62; prog dir genetic biol, NSF, 62-66, head, Cellular Biol Sect, 66-77, sr scientist, 77-84, dep dir, Div Molecular Biosci, 84-86, dep exec dir, US-Israel Binat Sci Found, 86-89. *Mem:* AAAS; Biophys Soc; Genetics Soc Am; Am Soc Cell Biol. *Res:* Biochemical, physiological and molecular genetics; biophysics and cytology of genetic material; human cell biology. *Mailing Add:* One Gristmill Ct Apt 204 Baltimore MD 21208

LEWIS, HOMER DICK, METALLURGY, NUCLEAR ENGINEERING. *Current Pos:* RETIRED. *Personal Data:* b Covington, Ky, Oct 4, 26; m 48, Marjorie Louise Hacker; c Homer Daniel, Holly Joanna, Laurel Marion & Heather Eileen. *Educ:* Univ Cincinnati, MetE, 52; Univ NMex, MS, 64, MSc, 71. *Prof Exp:* Staff mem uranium casting, Los Alamos Sci Lab, Univ Calif, 52-57; res engr, Boeing Airplane Co, 57-58; staff mem, Los Alamos Sci Lab, Univ Calif, 58-86. *Concurrent Pos:* Co-prin investr, Liquid Metal Fast Breeder Reactor Fuels Properties, 75-78, mem, Nat Task Group, Los Alamos Lab Rep, 77-81; sect leader, Solidification Tech, 81-86. *Mem:* Am Soc Metals. *Res:* Packing behavior of particulate solids; small particle statistics; physics of particulate systems; powder metallurgy; carbon and graphite research and development; electrical and thermal transport properties of plutonium and plutonium alloys and compounds; solidification process; thermochemistry of uranium, plutonium compounds; solidification processes. *Mailing Add:* PO Box 644 Bayfield CO 81122

LEWIS, IRA WAYNE, CONTINUUM THEORY, GEOMETRIC TOPOLOGY. *Current Pos:* Vis lectr, 77-79, from asst prof to assoc prof, 79-89, PROF MATH, TEX TECH UNIV, 89- *Personal Data:* b Hillsboro, Tex, Sept 22, 50. *Educ:* Univ Houston, BSc, 72; Tex A&M Univ, MSc, 74; Univ Tex, Austin, PhD(math), 77. *Concurrent Pos:* Vis asst prof, Tulane Univ, 79-80, Univ Tex, Austin, 80, Univ Ala, Birmingham, 81, Univ Ky, 82 & vis assoc prof, Auburn Univ, 84-85; Nat Acad Sci exchange scientist, Inst Math, Polish Acad Sci, 81 & Stephan Banach Ctr, 84-85; invited lectr, Inst Math, Hanoi, S R Vietnam, 86. *Mem:* Am Math Soc; Am Inst Aeronaut & Astronaut; Astron Soc Pac; AAAS; Sigma Xi; Am Math Asn. *Res:* Continuum theory and geometric topology including indecomposable continua, classification of homogeneous continua, embeddings of tree-like continua, continuous decompositions and homogeneous embeddings of continua in manifolds; manifolds. *Mailing Add:* Dept Math Tex Tech Univ Lubbock TX 79409-0001

LEWIS, IRVING JAMES, HEALTH & PUBLIC POLICY. *Current Pos:* prof, 70-86, EMER PROF COMMUNITY HEALTH, ALBERT EINSTEIN COL MED, 86- *Personal Data:* b Boston, Mass, July 9, 18; m 41; c 3. *Educ:* Harvard Univ, AB, 39; Univ Chicago, AM, 40. *Honors & Awards:* Except Serv Award, Bur Budget, 64; Career Serv Award, Nat Civil Serv League, 69. *Prof Exp:* Res fel, Brookings Inst, 41; with US Govt, 42 & 46-55, dep chief, Int Div, Bur Budget, 55-57, dept head, Inter-govt Comn Europ Migration, Geneva, Switz, 57-59, dep chief, Int Div, Bur Budget, 59-65, chief, Health & Welfare Div, 65-67, dep admnr health serv & ment health admin, Dept HEW, 68-70. *Mem:* Inst Med-Nat Acad Sci; Am Pub Health Asn. *Res:* Public health and epidemiology. *Mailing Add:* 3310 N Leisure World Blvd Apt 623 Silver Spring MD 20906

LEWIS, IRWIN C, PYROLYSIS CHEMISTRY, CARBON & GRAPHITE. *Current Pos:* CORP FEL, UNION CARBIDE CORP, 60-, SR CORP FEL, VCAR CARBON CO. *Personal Data:* b New York, NY. *Educ:* City Col New York, BS, 53; Univ Kans, PhD(org chem), 57. *Honors & Awards:* Charles Pettinos Int Award in Carbon Sci, Am Carbon Soc, 87, Graffin Lectr, 86. *Prof Exp:* Assoc phys-org, Pa State Univ, 58-60. *Mem:* Am Chem Soc; Sigma Xi; Am Carbon Soc. *Res:* Studies of pyrolysis of aromatic hydrocarbons, characterization and reactions of carbonaceos materials, coal and petroleum chemistry, electron spin resonance of aromatic radicals, liquid crystal and polymerization in pitch, carbon fibers. *Mailing Add:* VCAR Carbon Corp PO Box 6116 Cleveland OH 44101-1116

LEWIS, J(OHN) E(UGENE), ELECTRICAL ENGINEERING. *Current Pos:* from asst prof to assoc prof, 74-80, chmn dept, 80-89, PROF ELEC ENG, UNIV NB, FREDERICTON, 80- *Personal Data:* b St John, NB, Apr 11, 41; m 64; c 3. *Educ:* Univ NB, Fredericton, BScE, 64; Univ BC, PhD(elec eng), 68. *Prof Exp:* Nat Res Coun Can fel, Univ Southampton, 68-69. *Concurrent Pos:* Dir, Cadmi Microelectronics, Inc, 86- *Mem:* Inst Elec & Electronics Engrs; Brit Inst Elec Engrs; Int Microwave Power Inst. *Res:* Industrial applications of microwaves to materials processing and process control; microwave measurement of nonelectrical quantities; low-loss waveguides. *Mailing Add:* Elec Eng Dept Univ NB PO Box 4400 Fredericton NB E3B 5A3 Can

LEWIS, J(ACK) R(OCKLEY), metallurgy, for more information see previous edition

LEWIS, JAMES, SYSTEM ENGINEERING, PROJECT MANAGEMENT. *Current Pos:* mem tech staff, TRW Systs Group, 69-75, head, Signal Design Sect, TRW Defense & Space Systs Group, 75-77, SPACE SYST MGR, TRW DEFENSE & SPACE SYSTS GROUP, 78- *Personal Data:* b Nashville, Tenn, Sept 17, 42; m 69; c 3. *Educ:* Vanderbilt Univ, BE, 63; Princeton Univ, MSE, 65; Purdue Univ, PhD(elec eng), 69. *Prof Exp:* Instr elec eng, Purdue Univ, 66-67. *Concurrent Pos:* Japan Soc Prom Sci fel,

Kyoto Univ, 71-72; lectr, Loyola Marymount Univ, 77-81. *Mem:* Inst Elec & Electronics Engrs; Inst Math Statist. *Res:* Systems engineering; communication theory; stochastic processes; optical communications. *Mailing Add:* TRW SPACE & ELECTRONICS GROUP 1 Space Park Redondo Beach CA 90278. *E-Mail:* jim.lewis@trw.com

LEWIS, JAMES CHESTER, WILDLIFE ECOLOGY. *Current Pos:* RETIRED. *Personal Data:* b Kalamazoo, Mich, Jan 31, 36; m 57; c 3. *Educ:* Univ Mich, BS, 57; Mich State Univ, MS, 63; Okla State Univ, PhD(wildlife ecol), 74. *Prof Exp:* Biologist aide, Mich Game Div, 57-59; dist biologist, Tenn Game Div, 59-60, res proj leader game mgt, 60-64, res supvr, 64-67; asst unit leader, Okla Coop Wildlife Res Unit, 67-77, from asst prof to assoc prof life sci, Sch Biophys Sci, 67-77; tech ed, US Fish & Wildlife Serv, Colo State Univ, 77-97. *Concurrent Pos:* Consult, Nat Audubon Soc, 80. *Mem:* Wildlife Soc. *Res:* Endangered species research; deer and turkey management; ecology of wildlife rabies; mourning dove and sandhill crane behavior and ecology. *Mailing Add:* 7712 Midge NE Albuquerque NM 87109

LEWIS, JAMES CLEMENT, biochemistry, for more information see previous edition

LEWIS, JAMES KELLEY, RANGE SCIENCE. *Current Pos:* RETIRED. *Personal Data:* b Waco, Tex, Oct 24, 24; m 49; c 4. *Educ:* Colo State Univ, BS, 48; Mont State Univ, MS, 51. *Prof Exp:* Asst prof animal sci, SDak State Univ, 50-58, assoc prof, 58-85. *Mem:* Soc Range Mgt; Am Soc Animal Sci; Ecol Soc Am; Wildlife Soc; Brit Grassland Soc. *Res:* Structure, function, measurement, manipulation, uses and systems analysis of range ecosystems; range animal nutrition and management; coupling of range and agronomic ecosystems. *Mailing Add:* RR 5 Box 341A Carthage MO 64836

LEWIS, JAMES PETTIS, LIQUEFIED NATURAL GAS & CRYOGENIC TECHNOLOGY, FACILITY SAFETY FOR HAZARDOUS MATERIALS. *Current Pos:* PRES, PROJ TECH LIAISON ASSOCS, 78- *Personal Data:* b Omaha, Nebr, Apr 21, 33; m 85, Peggy J Freed; c Margo A (Carnegie), Sterling F, Cameron R & Justin W. *Educ:* Calif Inst Technol, BSME, 55. *Prof Exp:* Dist engr, Richfield Oil Corp, 55-62; asst chief engr, Cosmodyne Corp, 62-69; tech dir, Distrigas Corp, 69-72; proj mgr, Transco Energy Co, 72-78. *Mem:* Am Soc Mech Engrs; Am Inst Chem Engrs; Seismol Soc Am; Earthquake Eng Res Inst; Nat Fire Protection Asn; NY Acad Sci. *Res:* Life limiting mechanisms and life extension measures for hazardous facilities; non destructive composite material testing; failure mechanisms in brittle insulating materials; liquefied natural gas as vehicle fuel. *Mailing Add:* 7803 Aleta Dr Spring TX 77379. *Fax:* 281-251-5625; *E-Mail:* ptla@mail.net

LEWIS, JAMES VERNON, ENVIRONMENTAL SCIENCES. *Current Pos:* assoc prof, 53-80, EMER PROF MATH, UNIV NMEX, 80- *Personal Data:* b Neligh, Nebr, May 2, 15; div; c Alfred Bruce, Aleta & Lance Eric. *Educ:* Univ Calif, AB, 37, MA, 39, PhD(math), 42; Univ NMex, MCRP, 84. *Prof Exp:* Asst, Univ Calif, 39-42; jr physicist, USN, Calif, 42-43; mathematician, Radiation Lab, Univ Calif, 43-45 & Aberdeen Proving Ground, 45-53. *Concurrent Pos:* Asst prof, Univ Nev, 46-47. *Mem:* Am Planning Asn; Math Asn Am; Sigma Xi; Fedn Am Scientists. *Res:* Urban planning; iterative methods for decision making in urban planning; calculuc of variations. *Mailing Add:* 3401 Mars Rd NE Albuquerque NM 87107

LEWIS, JAMES W L, MOLECULAR PHYSICS, FLUID PHYSICS. *Current Pos:* PROF PHYSICS, SPACE INST, UNIV TENN, 77-; PHYSICIST, CALSPAN, INC, 81- *Personal Data:* b Natchez, Miss, May 3, 38; m 6?; c 3. *Educ:* Univ Miss, BS, 60, MS, 64, PhD(physics), 66. *Prof Exp:* Physicist, US Naval Weapons Lab, 61-62 & ARO, Inc, 66-68; UK Sci Res Coun fel physics, Queen's Univ, Belfast, 68-69; assoc prof physics, Space Inst, Univ Tenn, 66-77; physicist, Aro, Inc, 69-80. *Mem:* Am Inst Aeronaut & Astronaut; Am Phys Soc. *Res:* Vibrational relaxation processes in gases; molecular processes in hypersonic flow phenomena; molecular and atomic beam collision processes using high temperature shock tube source; raman-rayleigh scattering in gases; condensation processes in gases; nonlinear optics. *Mailing Add:* Dept Physics Univ Tenn Space Inst 411 B H Goethert Pkwy Tullahoma TN 37388

LEWIS, JASPER PHELPS, chemistry, biochemistry, for more information see previous edition

LEWIS, JERRY PARKER, MEDICINE. *Current Pos:* assoc prof, 67-69, chief div hemat & oncol, 67-80, lectr clin path & vet med, 68-74, chief staff, Med Ctr, 79-80, actg chmn, Dept Int Med, 80-82, PROF MED, UNIV CALIF, DAVIS, 69-, PROF PATH, 78-, CHIEF DIV HEMAT & ONCOL, 82- *Personal Data:* b Terre Haute, Ind, Sept 20, 31; m 56; c 4. *Educ:* James Millikin Univ, 52; Univ Ill, BS, 53, MD, 56. *Prof Exp:* Asst prof med, Univ Ill, 64-67. *Concurrent Pos:* NIH fel hemat, Presby-St Luke's Hosp, Chicago, 61-63, res fel, 63-65; actg chief clin hemat & chief spec hemat, Presby-St Luke's Hosp, Chicago, 65-67; consult, David Grant Hosp Travis, AFB, Calif, 68- *Mem:* Am Soc Hemat; Am Soc Clin Oncol; fel Am Col Physicians; Soc Exp Hemat; Am Soc Human Genetics. *Res:* Leukemia; cytogenetics; toxicity of laetrile; molecular biology of oncogenes. *Mailing Add:* Sch Med Univ Calif 1508 Alhambra Blvd Davis CA 95616-6510

LEWIS, JESSE C, MATHEMATICS, COMPUTER SCIENCES. *Current Pos:* VPRES ACAD AFFAIRS, NORFOLK STATE UNIV, 84- *Personal Data:* b Vaughan, Miss, June 26, 29; m 59, Emma Goldman; c Valerie. *Educ:* Univ Ill, MS, 55, MA, 59; Syracuse Univ, PhD(math), 66. *Prof Exp:* Instr math, Southern Univ, 55-57 & Prairie View Agr & Mech Col, 57-58; asst prof, Jackson State Col, 59-61; res asst, Comput Ctr, Syracuse Univ, 63-66; dir, Comput Ctr & chmn, Dept Comput Sci, Jackson State Univ, 66-80, prof math & chmn Div Natural Sci, 67-80, assoc dean comput serv & prof comput sci, 80- 84. *Concurrent Pos:* Consult, Comt Undergrad Prog Math, Jackson State Col; mem eval panel sci comput, Nat Bur Stands, 80-83; deleg leader, People to People Citizen Ambassador Prog, Western Europ & Russia, 82, Korea & Hong Kong, 84. *Mem:* Math Asn Am; Am Math Soc; Asn Comput Mach; Asn Educ Data Systs. *Res:* Computer study of permanents of n-square (0,1)-matrices with k l's in each row and column. *Mailing Add:* Norfolk State Univ Acad Affairs Norfolk VA 23504

LEWIS, JESSICA HELEN, MEDICINE, HEMATOLOGY. *Current Pos:* res assoc med, Univ Pittsburgh, 55-58, res assoc prof, 58- 70, res prof med, 70-77, prof med, 75-85, vpres, Cent Blood Bank, 75-85, med dir, 85-90, sr vpres, 85-92, sci dir, 87-92, EMER SCI DIR, UNIV PITTSBURGH & CENT BLOOD BANK, 92- *Personal Data:* b Harpswell, Maine, Oct 26, 17; m 46, Jack D Myers; c Judith D (deceased), John L, Jessica R, Elizabeth R & Margaret A. *Educ:* Goucher Col, AB, 38; Johns Hopkins Univ, MD, 42. *Prof Exp:* Intern, Hosp Women, Baltimore, Md, 42-43; asst resident, Univ Calif Hosp, 43-44; res fel, Thorndike Mem Lab & Harvard Univ, 44-46; res assoc physiol, Univ NC, 48-55. *Concurrent Pos:* USPHS res fel, Univ NC, 47-48; asst med, Boston City Hosp, 44-46; res assoc, Med Sch, Emory Univ, 46-47; assoc med, Med Sch, Duke Univ, 51-55; staff mem, Presby-Univ Hosp, 55-; dir res, Cent Blood Bank Pittsburgh, 69-75, vpres, 75- *Mem:* Am Soc Hemat; World Fedn Hemophilia; Am Physiol Soc; Am Soc Clin Invest; Am Fedn Clin Res; Am Asn Blood Banks. *Res:* Blood coagulation; enzyme and protein chemistry; comparative hematology in vertebrates. *Mailing Add:* Dept Med Univ Pittsburgh Cent & Blood Bank 220 N Dithridge Pittsburgh PA 15213

LEWIS, JOHN BRADLEY, MARINE BIOLOGY. *Current Pos:* dir, Bellairs Res Inst, 54-71, assoc prof, 61-69, dir, Pedpath Mus, 71-83, PROF MARINE SCI, MCGILL UNIV, 69-, DIR, INST OCEANOG, 83- *Personal Data:* b Ottawa, Ont, Jan 12, 25; m 80; c 3. *Educ:* McGill Univ, BSc, 40, MSc, 50, PhD(zool), 54. *Prof Exp:* Asst marine biol, Inst Marine Sci, Univ Miami, 51-54. *Mem:* Can Soc Zool; Int Soc Reef Studies. *Res:* Tropical marine ecology and physiology; tropical marine organisms and coral reef ecology. *Mailing Add:* Dept Biol McGill Univ Sherbrooke St W Montreal PQ H3A 2M5 Can

LEWIS, JOHN E, AUTOMATIC TEST. *Current Pos:* CONSULT, 90- *Personal Data:* b Riverside, Calif, Mar 30, 39; m 66; c 2. *Educ:* Calif State Univ, BS, 64; Univ Southern Calif, MS, 75. *Prof Exp:* Qual mgr, Interstate Electronics, 65-67; sr engr, USN, 67-90. *Mem:* Sr mem Inst Elec & Electronics Engrs; fel Inst Automotive Engrs. *Res:* Automatic test and test software. *Mailing Add:* Nine Alcoba Irvine CA 92714

LEWIS, JOHN HUBBARD, GEOLOGY. *Current Pos:* CONSULT, 80- *Personal Data:* b Jamestown, NY, Apr 13, 29; m 56, 83; c Patricia, Mark, David & Timothy. *Educ:* Allegheny Col, BS, 56; Univ Colo, PhD(geol), 65. *Prof Exp:* From instr to assoc prof geol, Colo Col, 58-74, chmn dept, 70-78, prof, 74-81. *Concurrent Pos:* Lectr, Exten Div, Univ Colo, 58-66; dir, NSF Sec Sci Training Prog, Colo Col, 65-67; US Antarctic res partic, Tex Tech Col, 67-68. *Res:* Sedimentary petrology; petrology and diagenesis of upper Cambrian rocks of Colorado; structural geology. *Mailing Add:* 918 N Royer Colorado Springs CO 80903. *E-Mail:* jhlrkdk@aol.com

LEWIS, JOHN L, JR, OBSTETRICS & GYNECOLOGY. *Current Pos:* assoc prof, 68-71, PROF OBSTET & GYNEC, MED COL, CORNELL UNIV, 71-, ATTEND SURGEON, GYNEC SERV, MEM HOSP CANCER & ALLIED DIS & JAMES EWING HOSP, 90- *Personal Data:* b San Antonio, Tex, June 5, 29; m 55; c 3. *Educ:* Harvard Univ, BA, 52, MD, 57; Am Bd Obstet & Gynec, dipl, 67, cert, 79. *Prof Exp:* Clin assoc endocrinol br, Nat Cancer Inst, 59-61, sr investr surg br, 65-67. *Concurrent Pos:* Sr investr clin ctr, NIH, 65-67; assoc attend gynecologist, Francis Delafield Hosp, 67; assoc attend obstetrician & gynecologist, Presby Hosp, NY, 67; assoc attend obstetrician & gynecologist, New York Lying-in Hosp, 68-71, attend obstetrician & gynecologist, 71-; attend surgeon, Mem Hosp Cancer & Allied Dis, 68-, chief gynec serv, 68-90; assoc, Sloan-Kettering Inst Cancer Res, 68-73, mem, 73-; assoc prof, Col Physicians & Surgeons, Columbia Univ, 67, lectr, 68-; dir, Am Bd Obstet & Gynec, 70-76 & Div Gynec Oncol, 70-76; consult Am joint comt cancer staging & end result reporting. *Mem:* Soc Gynec Invest; AMA; Soc Surg Oncol; Am Radium Soc; Am Asn Cancer Educ. *Res:* Gynecologic cancer; hormonal, immunologic and therapeutic aspects of gestational trophoblastic neoplasms. *Mailing Add:* Mem Sloan-Kettering Cancer Ctr 1275 York Ave New York NY 10021-6007

LEWIS, JOHN MORGAN, ANIMAL HUSBANDRY, ANIMAL SCIENCE & NUTRITION. *Current Pos:* RETIRED. *Personal Data:* b Joliet, Ill, June 5, 20; m 44; c 3. *Educ:* Univ Ill, BS, 43. *Prof Exp:* Asst supt, Univ Ill, Urbana, 43-59, actg supt, 59-62, assoc prof animal sci, Dixon Springs Exp Sta, 62-81. *Mem:* Am Soc Animal Sci. *Res:* Sheep breeding, feeding and management. *Mailing Add:* RR 2 Box 305 Metropolis IL 62960-9655

LEWIS, JOHN RAYMOND, POLYMER CHEMISTRY, ACQUISITION & MERGERS. *Current Pos:* RETIRED. *Personal Data:* b Philadelphia, Pa, July 25, 18; m 42, Rachel E Brinard; c Sondra L (Sperati). *Educ:* Franklin & Marshall Col, BS, 42. *Prof Exp:* Chemist, Naval Stores Div, Res Ctr, Hercules Inc, 42-44, shift supvr, Explosives Dept, Sunflower Ord Works, Kans, 44-45, chemist, Naval Stores Div, 45-49, res chemist, 49-55, res supvr, 55-59, res mgr, Plastics & Elastomers Div, 59-64, res assoc, Cent Res Div, 64, mgr develop, Res Dept, 64-69, venture projs, New Enterprise Dept, 69-75, mgr planning & acquisitions, 75-77, mgr corp acquisitions, 77-83. *Concurrent Pos:* Consult, 83-85. *Mem:* Am Chem Soc; Financial Analysts Asn; Sigma Xi; Com Develop Asn. *Res:* Commercial development; polymers, energy and raw materials; acquisitions. *Mailing Add:* 118 Dickinson Lane West Park Wilmington DE 19807-3138

LEWIS, JOHN REED, pharmacology, for more information see previous edition

LEWIS, JOHN SIMPSON, GEOCHEMISTRY, METEORITICS. *Current Pos:* PROF PLANETARY SCI, UNIV ARIZ, 82-, CO-DIR, UA/NASA SPACE ENG RES CTR, 86- *Personal Data:* b Trenton, NJ, June 27, 41; m 64, Ruth M Adams; c John V, Margaret (Martell), Christopher F, Katherine R, Elizabeth A & Peter M. *Educ:* Princeton Univ, AB, 62; Dartmouth Col, MA, 64; Univ Calif, San Diego, PhD, 68. *Honors & Awards:* J B Macelwayne Award, Am Geophys Union, 76. *Prof Exp:* From asst prof to assoc prof chem, earth & planetary sci, Mass Inst Technol, 68-80, prof planetary sci, 80-82. *Concurrent Pos:* Mem, Working Group Outer Planet Probe Sci, NASA-Ames Res Ctr, 74-, NASA Phys Sci Comt, 75-78 & Space Sci Bd spec panels outer solar syst & explor Venus, Nat Acad Sci-Nat Res Coun; Guggenheim lectr, Nat Air & Space Mus, Smithsonian Inst, 73; sci lectr, Div Planetary Sci, Am Astron Soc, 74, Space Sci Bd, Nat Acad Sci, 80-82; chmn, Uranus Sci Adv Comt, NASA-Jet Propulsion Lab, 74-75, mem, Sci Adv Group Outer Solar Syst; mem, Working Group Outer Planet Probe Sci, Ames Res Ctr, NASA, 74-, Phys Sci Comt, 75-78 & Space Sci Bd Spec Panels Outer Solar Syst & Explor Venus, Nat Acad Sci-Nat Res Coun. *Mem:* AAAS; Am Chem Soc; Int Astron Union; Am Astron Soc. *Res:* Composition, structure and origin of planetary atmospheres; atmosphere-lithosphere interactions; application of thermodynamics to problems of composition and origin of meteorites; exploitation of extraterrestrial resources. *Mailing Add:* LPL Univ Ariz Tucson AZ 85721. *Fax:* 520-621-4933; *E-Mail:* ssl@u.arizona.edu

LEWIS, JON C, CELLULAR BIOLOGY, ELECTRON MICROSCOPY. *Current Pos:* PROF PATH, BOWMAN GREY SCH MED, WAKE FOREST UNIV, 90- *Res:* Cellular and chemical aspects of athrosclorosis platelette membrane receptors; hemostasis and thrombosis; cell biology; electron microscopy. *Mailing Add:* Dept Pathol Wake Forest Univ Bowman Gray Sch Med Med Ctr Blvd Winston-Salem NC 27157-1092

LEWIS, JONATHAN JOSEPH, GROWTH FACTOR SIGNAL TRANSDUCTION. *Current Pos:* postdoctoral assoc surg & cell biol, 87-90, CHIEF RESIDENT SURG, YALE UNIV SCH MED, 90- *Personal Data:* b Johannesburg, SAfrica, May 23, 58; m 90. *Educ:* Witwatersrand Univ, MB Bch, 82, PhD(cell biol), 90; FRCS(E), 87. *Prof Exp:* Resident surg, Witwatersrand Univ Sch Med, 83-87. *Mem:* Am Soc Cell Biol; Am Asn Cancer Res; AAAS; AMA; NY Acad Sci. *Res:* Growth factor signal transduction; parietal cell signal transduction. *Mailing Add:* 7 Harbor St Branford CT 06405

LEWIS, KATHERINE, carcinogenesis, intermediary metabolism, for more information see previous edition

LEWIS, L GAUNCE, JR, MATHEMATICS, ALGEBRAIC TOPOLOGY. *Current Pos:* from asst prof to assoc prof, 81-93, PROF MATH, SYRACUSE UNIV, NY, 93- *Personal Data:* b Boston, Mass, Sept 14, 49; m 84, Kathleen Edwards. *Educ:* Harvard Col, AB, 71; Univ Chicago, MS, 76, PhD(math), 78. *Prof Exp:* Asst prof, Univ Mich, Ann Arbor, 78-81. *Concurrent Pos:* Alexander von Humboldt fel, 89-90. *Mem:* Am Math Soc; Math Asn Am; Sigma Xi. *Res:* Equivariant homotopy theory; generalized cohomology theories; stable category; group actions on rings; representation theory. *Mailing Add:* 116 W Eighth St Oswego NY 13126-1410. *Fax:* 315-443-1475; *E-Mail:* gaunce@ichthus.syr.edu

LEWIS, LAURENCE A, HUMAN ECOLOGY, LAND DEGRADATION. *Current Pos:* PROF PHYS GEOG, CLARK UNIV, 70- *Personal Data:* b 1939; c 2. *Educ:* Antioch Co, BA, 61; Northwestern Univ, MS, 63, PhD(geog), 65. *Honors & Awards:* Honor Award, Soil & Water Conserv Soc, 89. *Res:* Environmental sciences; author of publications; relations between the human and physical environments with regard to sustainability. *Mailing Add:* Grad Sch Geog Clark Univ Worcester MA 01610-1477. *Fax:* 508-793-8881; *E-Mail:* llewis@clarku.edu

LEWIS, LAWRENCE GUY, MATHEMATICS, INFORMATION SCIENCE. *Current Pos:* PRES, SOFTWARE FIRST INC, 83-; VPRES, INFO TECHNOL PARTNERS, 91- *Personal Data:* b Logan, Utah, July 28, 41; m 64; c 4. *Educ:* Univ Utah, BA, 65; Ind Univ, PhD(math), 69. *Prof Exp:* Fel math, Grad Ctr, City Univ New York, 69-70; asst prof math, Univ Utah, 70-73; mgr licensees, Ireco Chem, 73-78, dir, Mgt Info Serv, 78-82. *Concurrent Pos:* Adj assoc prof math, Univ Utah, 86- *Mem:* AAAS; Data Processing Mgt Asn; Planning Exec Group. *Res:* Ideal boundaries and information systems. *Mailing Add:* 3859 Park Saddle Circle Park City UT 84098

LEWIS, LEROY CRAWFORD, PROCESS ANALYTICAL CHEMISTRY. *Current Pos:* BR MGR, WESTINGHOUSE IDAHO NUCLEAR CO, 84- *Personal Data:* b Pocatello, Idaho, Mar 18, 40; m 62; c 2. *Educ:* Col Idaho, BS, 62; Ore State Univ, PhD(phys chem), 68. *Prof Exp:* Sr res chemist, Idaho Nuclear Corp, 68-71; sr res chemist, Allied Chem Corp, 71-72, group supvr, 72-74, sect leader, 74-76, br mgr, 76-79; br mgr, Exxon Nuclear Idaho Co, 79-84. *Mem:* Am Chem Soc; Sigma Xi. *Res:* Nuclear fuel reprocessing chemistry; chemical waste handling chemistry; actinide chemistry; electrochemistry; analytical chemistry. *Mailing Add:* 3774 S Fifth W Idaho Falls ID 83404-7983

LEWIS, LESLIE ARTHUR, GENETICS, MICROBIOLOGY. *Current Pos:* from lectr to assoc prof, 69-85, PROF BIOL, YORK COL, NY, 85- *Personal Data:* b Castries, St Lucia, WI, May 17, 40; m 68; c 2. *Educ:* Univ Toronto, BSA, 63, MSA, 64; Columbia Univ, PhD(genetics), 68. *Prof Exp:* NIH fel, Mich State Univ, 68-69. *Concurrent Pos:* Univ Paris, France, 72-73. *Mem:* Genetics Soc Am; AAAS; Am Soc Microbiol. *Res:* Non-reciprocal recombination in the fungus Sordaria; genetic basis of resistance to aminoglycoside antibiotics. *Mailing Add:* York Col 9420 Guy R Brewer Blvd Jamaica NY 11433-1101

LEWIS, MARC SIMON, BIOPHYSICS, BIOCHEMISTRY. *Current Pos:* biophysicist biomed eng & instrumentation, 78-96, DIR ANALYTICAL ULTRACENTRIFUGATION RESOURCE, BIOMED ENG & INST PROG, NAT CTR RES RESOURCES, NIH, 96- *Personal Data:* b Cleveland, Ohio, Oct 30, 26; m 92, Anne C Guffey; c 6. *Educ:* Western Res Univ, BS, 46, MS, 47; Georgetown Univ, PhD(biochem), 55. *Prof Exp:* Guest scientist, Nat Inst Arthritis & Metab Dis, 52-55; USPHS fel, 55-57; biochemist, Nat Inst Arthritis & Metab Dis, 57-58, biochemist, Nat Inst Dent Res, 58-62, head, Sect Ophthal Chem, Nat Inst Neurol Dis & Blindness, 62-70, sr res investr, Lab Vision Res, Nat Eye Inst, 70-78. *Concurrent Pos:* Adj prof, Dept Biochem & Molecular Biol, Sch Med, Georgetown Univ. *Mem:* Am Chem Soc; Biophys Soc; Am Soc Biochem & Molecular Biol; AAAS. *Res:* Applications of analytical ultracentrifugation to physical biochemistry and biophysics, particularly to the thermodynamics of the interactions of molecules of biological interest; mathematical modeling for the study of such systems. *Mailing Add:* Biomed Eng & Instrumentation Prog NIH Bethesda MD 20892. *Fax:* 301-496-6608; *E-Mail:* mslewis@helix.nih.gov

LEWIS, MARGARET NAST, PHYSICS. *Current Pos:* res fel, 61-70, ASSOC, HARVARD COL OBSERV, 70- *Personal Data:* b Baltimore, Md, Aug 20, 11. *Educ:* Goucher Col, AB, 31; Johns Hopkins Univ, PhD(physics), 37. *Prof Exp:* Asst physics, Vassar Col, 37-38; Am Asn Univ Women Berliner fel, Univ Calif, 38-39, fel, Crocker Radiation Lab, 39-40, Howell fel, 40-42; instr, Vassar Col, 42-43; instr physics, Univ Pa, 43-48, assoc physics res, 53-54; lectr, Boston Univ, 48-50; physicist, Nat Bur Stands, 50-52; asst prof res, Brown Univ, 54-58; assoc prof, Univ Mass, 58-61. *Concurrent Pos:* Radioisotopes res, Mass Mem Hosp, 48-49 & Haverford Col, 52-54; nat consult, Schlesinger Libr, Radcliffe Col. *Mem:* Am Phys Soc; Sigma Xi. *Res:* Spectroscopy; atomic structure. *Mailing Add:* 10 Fernald Dr No 21 Cambridge MA 02138-1430

LEWIS, MARIAN L MOORE, EXPERIMENTAL BIOLOGY. *Current Pos:* CHIEF, BIOREACTOR LAB, KENNETH E JOHNSON RES CTR, UNIV ALA, 89- *Personal Data:* b Decatur, Ga, Mar 5, 37. *Educ:* Ga State Col Women, BA, 59; Univ Ariz, MS, 68; Univ Houston, PhD(biophys sci), 79. *Prof Exp:* Technician & res asst, Commun Dis Ctr, 59-64; res scientist, Dept Virol & Epidemiol, Col Med, Baylor Univ, Tex Med Ctr, 64-66, res asst, Dept Virol, M D Anderson Hosp & Tumor Inst, 68-71; res analyst, Dept Virol, Northrop Serv, Inc, 71-73. *Mem:* Assoc fel Am Inst Aeronaut & Astronaut; Am Soc Microbiol; NY Acad Sci; AAAS; Sigma Xi; Int Soc Thrombosis & Haemostasis; Am Heart Asn; Am Soc Cell Biol; Am Soc Space & Gravitational Biol; Inst Advan Studies Life Support. *Res:* Experimental biology; numerous publications. *Mailing Add:* BioReactor Lab Univ Ala Johnson Res Ctr Sci Bldg Rm 360 4701 Univ Dr NW Huntsville AL 35899. *Fax:* 205-539-7622, 539-7620

LEWIS, MARILYN WARE, PUBLIC UTILITIES. *Current Pos:* BD DIRS & CHMN, AM WATER WORKS CO, INC. *Personal Data:* b 1943. *Prof Exp:* Pres, Solano Publ Co. *Concurrent Pos:* Bd dirs, Pa Fuel Gas Co, Cigna Corp. *Mailing Add:* 2 E Main St Strasburg PA 17579

LEWIS, MARION JEAN, IMMUNO-HAEMATOLOGY, MAPPING THE HUMAN GENOME. *Current Pos:* From asst prof to assoc prof, 73-84, prof immunohemat, Dept Pediat, 84-93, SCIENTIST IMMUNOHEMAT, RH LAB, DEPT PEDIAT, UNIV MAN, 44- *Personal Data:* b Windsor, Ont, Sept 21, 25. *Educ:* Univ Man, BA, 60. *Hon Degrees:* DSc, Univ Winnipeg, 86. *Honors & Awards:* Karl Landsteiner Mem Award, Am Asn Blood Banks, 71; La Medaille de la Ville de Paris, Paris, France, 87. *Concurrent Pos:* Mem, Med Adv Comt, Children's Hosp Winnipeg Res Found, 82-; chmn, Int Soc Blood Transfusion, Working Party Terminol Red Cell Surface Antigens, 83-90; prof immunogenetics, Dept Human Genetics, Univ Man, 86- *Mem:* Human Genome Orgn; hon fel Can Col Med Geneticists; Int Soc Blood Transfusion; fel Royal Soc Can Acad Sci. *Res:* Description, distribution, expression, inheritance of red cell antigens; genetic linkage and mapping of blood group genes; red cell immunization in haemolytic disease of the newborn; international reference laboratory; author of 160 publications. *Mailing Add:* Rh Lab 735 Notre Dame Ave Winnipeg MB R3E 0L8 Can

LEWIS, MARK HENRY, PSYCHOPHARMACOLOGY. *Current Pos:* STAFF MEM, UNIV FLA, 85- *Personal Data:* b Boston, Mass, Feb 5, 50; m 77; c 1. *Educ:* Bowdoin Col, BA, 72; Western Mich Univ, MA, 75; Vanderbilt Univ, PhD(psychol), 80. *Prof Exp:* Fel, Biol Sci Res Ctr, Med Sch, Univ NC, 80-85. *Mem:* Sigma Xi; Soc Neurosci. *Res:* Neuropharmacology of oxidative metabolitics of pherothiazine anti-psychotic drugs both in vivo and in vitro; dopamine receptor supersensitivity; function ascorbic acid in brain. *Mailing Add:* Univ Fla 1600 SW Archer Rd Box 10025 Gainesville FL 32610

LEWIS, MICHAEL EDWARD, NEUROPHARMACOLOGY, HISTOCHEMISTRY. *Current Pos:* BIODILIGENCE PARTNERS, 96- *Personal Data:* b Chicago, Ill, Nov 9, 51; m 81. *Educ:* George Washington Univ, BA, 73; Clark Univ, MA, 75, PhD(psychol), 77. *Prof Exp:* Guest worker neurochem, Sect Intermediary Metab, Lab Develop Neurobiol, Nat Inst Child Health & Human Develop, NIH, 77; fel behav neurochem, Psychol Lab, Cambridge Univ, 77-79; instr, Europ Div, Univ Col, Univ Md, 79; res psychologist, Sect Biochem & Pharmacol, Biol Psychiat Br, NIMH & Nat Inst Drug Abuse, 80-81; res investr, Ment Health Res Inst, Univ Mich, 81-85; prin scientist, E I Dupont Co, 85-87; dir pharmacol, Cephalon Inc, 88-93; vpres res, Symphony Pharmaceut Inc, 93-96. *Concurrent Pos:* Felix & Elizabeth Brunner fel, Ment Health Found, London, 77-79; Twinning grant, Europ Training Prog in Brain & Behav Res, Europ Sci Found, Strasbourg, 79-; Wellcome res fel, The Wellcome Trust, London, 79; John G Searle clin pharmacol fel, 81; vis assoc prof pharmacol, Col Pa, 86-; mem, Div Med Chem, Am Chem Soc. *Mem:* Soc Neurosci. *Res:* Histochemical and biochemical analysis of receptors and endogenous ligands; pharmacology of neuropeptides and psychoactive drugs; recovery of function after brain damage; neuropsychology. *Mailing Add:* Biodiligence Partners 1007 Saber Rd Westchester PA 19382

LEWIS, MILTON, NUCLEAR ENGINEERING. *Current Pos:* RETIRED. *Personal Data:* b New York, NY, Dec 30, 21; m 43, Rhonda S; c 3. *Educ:* Univ Wash, BS; Univ Calif, PhD(chem), 50. *Prof Exp:* Field serv consult, Off Sci Res Develop, 43-46; asst, Univ Calif, 46-48; chemist, Gen Elec Co, 48-51, chg pile coolant studies, 51-54, supvr, Nonmetallic Mat Develop, 54-56, sr engr prog, 56-62, mgr chem & metall, 62-67; mgr chem & metall, Douglas United Nuclear, Inc, 67-68, fuel & target technol, 68, asst chief, Mat Br, Donald W Douglas Labs, 68-70, mgr, Betacel Prog, 70-74; pres, Columbia Engrs Serv, Inc, Wash, 74-80; sr res scientist, Battelle Pac NW Labs, 82-86. *Concurrent Pos:* Vis lectr, Univ Calif, Los Angeles, 60-61; consult, 80-94. *Mem:* Am Nuclear Soc. *Res:* Mechanism of irreversible reactions; analytical chemistry of fission products; corrosion in aqueous media; radiation effects on materials; safety of nuclear processes. *Mailing Add:* 2600 Harris Ave Richland WA 99352

LEWIS, MORTON, organic chemistry, adhesives & coatings, for more information see previous edition

LEWIS, NATHAN SAUL, ELECTROCHEMISTRY, PHOTOELECTROCHEMISTRY. *Current Pos:* assoc prof, 88-90, PROF CHEM, CALIF INST TECHNOL, 91- *Personal Data:* b Los Angeles, Calif, Oct 20, 55. *Educ:* Calif Inst Technol, BS, 77, MS, 77, Mass Inst Technol, PhD(inorg chem), 81. *Honors & Awards:* Am Chem Soc Award in Pure Chem, 90; Fresenius Award, 90. *Prof Exp:* Res asst chem, Mass Inst Technol, 77-81; from asst prof to assoc prof, Stanford Univ, 81-88. *Concurrent Pos:* Div ed, J Electrochem Soc, 84-90; Alfred P Sloan Found fel, 85-87; consult, Inst Defense Anal, 85-90. *Mem:* Am Chem Soc; Electrochem Soc; Int Soc Electrochem. *Res:* Electrochemistry of semiconductor surfaces; scanning tunneling microscopy in electrochemistry; inorganic complexes use as electrocatalyst. *Mailing Add:* 127-72 Dept Chem Calif Inst Technol Pasadena CA 91125

LEWIS, NEIL JEFFREY, MEDICINAL CHEMISTRY, ORGANIC CHEMISTRY. *Current Pos:* VPRES RES, JACOBUS PHARMACEUT CO, 88-; ADJ PROF, BUR BIOL RES, RUTGERS UNIV, 89- *Personal Data:* b New York, NY, Feb 10, 45; m, Nancy E Strauss; c Anne R & Adam B. *Educ:* City Col New York, BS, 66; Univ Kans, PhD(med chem), 72. *Prof Exp:* NIH res assoc, Ohio State Univ, 72, from asst prof to assoc prof med chem, Div Med Chem, Col Pharm, 72-82, dir, Environ Chem Anal Lab, 77-82; dir drug develop & assoc dir res, Muscular Dystrophy Asn, 82-87, dir res develop, 87-88. *Concurrent Pos:* Lady Davis vis prof, 79-80; mem, US Environ Protection Agency Human Health Effects Study Sect, 81-85, Int Comt Neuromuscular Dis Drug Develop, 84-88, NJ Munic Environ Adv Comt, 91- *Mem:* Am Chem Soc; Am Pharmaceut Asn; Sigma Xi; NY Acad Sci; Soc Clin Trials; AAAS. *Res:* Chemotherapeutics; environmental carcinogenesis and toxicology; immunochemotherapy; antiviral agents; drug development; neuromuscular diseases; clinical trials. *Mailing Add:* Xeno Biotic Labs Inc 107 Morgan Lane Plainsboro NJ 08536

LEWIS, NINA ALISSA, COMPUTER SECURITY. *Current Pos:* SR TECH STAFF, ORACLE CORP, 92- *Personal Data:* b Princeton, NJ, Oct 5, 54; m 92, Davis Barch; c Brian R Barch. *Educ:* Univ Calif, Santa Barbara, BS, 75, MS, 85. *Prof Exp:* Prin software engr, Unisys Defense Systs, Inc, 85-92. *Mem:* Asn Comput Mach; Inst Elec & Electronics Engrs; Inst Elec & Electronics Engrs Comput Soc. *Res:* Computer penetration analysis; network security; database security. *Mailing Add:* 1716 Monticello Rd San Mateo CA 94402. *Fax:* 650-573-0804; *E-Mail:* nlewis@oracle.com

LEWIS, NITA ARIES, HIGH PRESSURE SOLUTION REACTIONS, ELECTRON TRANSFER CHEMISTRY. *Current Pos:* ASSOC PROF CHEM, UNIV MIAMI, 82- *Personal Data:* b Guelph, Ont, Apr 14, 49; m 85; c Reisa & Carl. *Educ:* Univ Waterloo, BSc, 72; Univ Guelph, PhD(chem), 77. *Prof Exp:* Nat Res Coun fel, Stanford Univ, 77-79; from asst prof to assoc prof, Univ New Brunswick, 79-85; Alexander Von Humboldt fel, Univ Frankfurt, 86-87. *Concurrent Pos:* Prin investr, Res Corp, 80, Nat Sci & Eng Res Coun, Can, 80-85, NIH, 83-89, Sigma Xi, 86, NSF, 90-91; vis assoc, Calif Inst Technol, 85; vis scientist, Toronto Sick Childrens Hosp, 93-94. *Mem:* Am Chem Soc; fel Am Inst Chemists; Can Inst Chemists; Royal Soc Chem; Sigma Xi; NY Acad Sci. *Res:* High pressure solution chemistry; chemistry in supercritical fluids; long distance electron transfer reactions; metobolic errors in epileptic children; cytochrome P450 chemistry; inorganic complexes and proteins. *Mailing Add:* Dept Chem Univ Miami Coral Gables FL 33124

LEWIS, NORMAN G, PLANT CELL WALL SYNTHESIS, PHENYLPROPANOID METABOLISM. *Current Pos:* DIR, INST BIOL CHEM, WASH STATE UNIV, 90-; EISIG-TODE DISTINGUISHED PROF, 90- *Personal Data:* b Scotland, Sept 16, 49; Brit & Can citizen; div; c Fiona & Kathryn. *Educ:* Univ Strathclyde, Glasgow, Scotland, BSc, 73; Univ BC, Vancouver, PhD(chem), 77. *Prof Exp:* Res chemist, Imp Chem Industs, 69-73; Nat Res Coun fel, Univ Cambridge, Eng, 78-80; asst scientist, Pulp & Paper Res Inst Can, 80-82, group leader, 82-85; assoc prof, Va Polytech Inst & State Univ, 85-90. *Concurrent Pos:* Res assoc, Nat Res Coun Can, 80; consult, Am Inst Biol Sci, 90-; chmn, Plant Biol Group, Gravitational Biol Facil for Space Sta Freedom, 92-; mem, US-Russia Shuttle-MIR Collab, 93-; assoc ed, Phytochem, 93-, NAm ed; chair, grad prog plant physiol, Wash State Univ, 93-; consult, Am Soc Gravitational & Space Biol, 93- *Mem:* Hon mem Russ Asn Space & Mankind; Phytochem Soc NAm; Am Chem Soc; Am Soc Plant Physiologists; Chem Inst Can; Can Pulp & Paper Asn; Am Soc Gravitational & Space Biol. *Res:* Defining biochemical pathways to the phenylpropanoid metabolites, the lignins, lignans, and neolignans as well as phenylpropanoid-acetate products, the suberins; define how microgravity effects plant growth and development; biochemical pathway to antitumor alkaloids (taxol) and the lignans (podophyllotoxin); lignin and lignan biosynthesis and function. *Mailing Add:* Wash State Univ Inst Biol Chem 467 Clark Hall Pullman WA 99164-6340. *Fax:* 509-335-7643; *E-Mail:* lewisn@wsuvm1.csc.wsu.edu

LEWIS, PAUL HERBERT, PHYSICAL CHEMISTRY. *Current Pos:* RETIRED. *Personal Data:* b New York, NY, Jan 19, 24; m 55, Miriam Blander; c Debra, Richard & Nancy. *Educ:* Columbia Univ, AB, 47, MA, 48; Iowa State Col, PhD(chem), 52. *Prof Exp:* Chemist paints, E I du Pont de Nemours & Co, Inc, 48; petrol chemist, Texaco Inc, 52-85. *Mem:* Am Chem Soc. *Res:* X-ray analysis; catalysts. *Mailing Add:* 1600 Tawakoni Lane Plano TX 75075-6728

LEWIS, PAUL KERMITH, JR, MEAT SCIENCE. *Current Pos:* from asst prof to prof animal sci, 57-95, EMER PROF ANIMAL SCI, UNIV ARK, FAYETTEVILLE, 95- *Personal Data:* b Monticello, Ark, Jan 24, 31; m 55; c 3. *Educ:* Okla State Univ, BS, 53; Univ Wis, MS, 55, PhD, 58. *Prof Exp:* Res asst animal husb & biochem, Univ Wis, 53-57. *Mem:* AAAS; Am Soc Animal Sci; Am Meat Sci Asn; Inst Food Technologists; Coun Agr Sci & Technol. *Res:* Pre-slaughter stress and storage life of beef and pork; sensory characteristics of beef and pork; cholestral comparatives of beef. *Mailing Add:* 750 Weaver Dairy Rd Apt 3107 Chapel Hill NC 27514-1438

LEWIS, PAUL OLLIN, POPULATION GENETICS, PLANT SYSTEMATICS & PHYLOGENETICS. *Current Pos:* ASST PROF BIOL, UNIV NMEX, 96- *Personal Data:* b Louisville, Ky, Dec 29, 61; m 86, Louise A Wawrzyniak. *Educ:* Georgetown Col, Ky, BS, 82; Memphis State Univ, MS, 84; Ohio State Univ, PhD(plant sci), 91. *Prof Exp:* Res assoc, NC State Univ, 91-94; molecular evolution fel, Smithsonian Inst, 94-95. *Mem:* Soc Study Evolution; Soc Syst Biologists; Bot Soc Am; Am Soc Plant Taxonomists. *Res:* Analysis of population structure, plant systematics and biogeography, statistical genetics and phylogeny reconstruction. *Mailing Add:* Dept Biol Univ NMex Albuquerque NM 87131-1091. *E-Mail:* lewisp@unm.edu

LEWIS, PAUL WELDON, MATHEMATICS. *Current Pos:* Asst prof, 70-74, ASSOC PROF MATH, NTEX STATE UNIV, 74- *Personal Data:* b Dallas, Tex, Jan 31, 43; m 65; c 2. *Educ:* NTex State Univ, BA, 65, MS, 66; Univ Utah, PhD(math), 70. *Mem:* Am Math Soc. *Res:* Vector measures; functional analysis; operators on function spaces. *Mailing Add:* Univ N Tex Denton TX 76203-6737

LEWIS, PETER A, ELECTRICAL ENGINEERING, ELECTRONICS ENGINEERING. *Current Pos:* MGR DIR EDUC ACTIV, INST ELEC & ELECTRONICS ENGRS, 92- *Personal Data:* b Somerville, NJ, Feb 18, 38; m 58, Gretchen Gunkel; c Sharon L (Ransom), Jeffrey S & Timothy B. *Educ:* Lehigh Univ, BSEE, 59; Newark Col Eng, MS, 69. *Prof Exp:* Engr, Pub Serv Elec Gas Co, 63-71, sr engr, 71, asst mgr res & develop, 71-78, mgr energy utilization res & develop, 78-88, mgr res & develop planning, 88-92. *Concurrent Pos:* Consult, Elec Power Res Inst, 73-86, Gas Res Inst Chicago, 88-; chmn tech comt, Fuel Cell Users Group, 79-87; vchmn, Comn Tech Educ NJ, 87-95. *Mem:* Fel Inst Elec & Electronics Engrs; Electrochem Soc; Nat Soc Prof Engrs. *Mailing Add:* Inst Elec & Electronics Engrs PO Box 1331 Piscataway NJ 08855-1331

LEWIS, PETER ADRIAN WALTER, STATISTICS. *Current Pos:* PROF STATIST & OPERS RES, NAVAL POSTGRAD SCH, 71- *Personal Data:* b Johannesburg, SAfrica, Oct 3, 32; US citizen; m 60; c 2. *Educ:* Columbia Univ, BA, 54, BS, 55, MS, 57; Univ London, PhD(statist), 64. *Prof Exp:* Res staff mem statist, Int Bus Mach Res Labs, 55-71. *Concurrent Pos:* NIH spec fel, Imp Col, Univ London, 69-70. *Mem:* Inst Math Statist; Royal Statist Soc; Am Statist Asn. *Res:* Stochastic process; applications of statistics in computer applications. *Mailing Add:* Dept Oper Res Naval Postgrad Sch Code OR/LW Monterey CA 93943-5000

LEWIS, PHILIP M, COMPUTER SCIENCE. *Current Pos:* LEAD PROF & CHAIR, COMPUT SCI DEPT, STATE UNIV NY, STONY BROOK, 87- *Personal Data:* b New York, NY, May 30, 31; m 53; c 2. *Educ:* Rensselaer Polytech Inst, BEE, 52; Mass Inst Technol, SM, 54, ScD, 56. *Prof Exp:* From instr to asst prof elec eng, Mass Inst Technol, 54-59; mem tech staff, Gen Elec Res & Develop Ctr, 59-69, consult automata theory & software design, 59, mgr, 69-78, mgr, Comput Sci Br, 78-87. *Concurrent Pos:* Consult, Epsco, Inc, 55, Lincoln Labs, Mass Inst Technol, 55-56, Hycon Eastern Inc, 56-57 & Sanders Assocs, Inc, 58; adj prof, Rensselaer Polytech Inst, 60-; managing ed, J Comput, Soc Indust & Appl Math, 71-; Coolidge fel, Gen Elec Res & Develop Corp, 77- *Mem:* Asn Comput Mach; Soc Indust & Appl Math; fel Inst Elec & Electronics Engrs. *Res:* Theory of information processing, including compiler design, retrieval and self organization; automata theory; abstract languages. *Mailing Add:* Comput Sci Dept State Univ NY Stony Brook NY 11794

LEWIS, RALPH WILLIAM, THEORIES & STRUCTURE OF KNOWLEDGE. *Current Pos:* From instr to prof, 37-80, EMER PROF BIOL, MICH STATE UNIV, 80- *Personal Data:* b Marion, Mich, May 21, 11; m 37, Olive Watrous; c Cornelia & Susan. *Educ:* Mich State Col, BS, 34, MS, 37, PhD(plant path), 45. *Concurrent Pos:* Res fel, Calif Inst Technol, 47; NIH spec res fel, Instituto Superiore Sanita, Rome, 58-59. *Mem:* Fel AAAS; Am Soc Naturalists; Nat Sci Teachers Asn; Nat Asn Biol Teachers; Inst Biol. *Res:* Study of the theories and structure of biological knowledge. *Mailing Add:* Col Natural Sci Mich State Univ East Lansing MI 48824-1031

LEWIS, RANDOLPH VANCE, ENDOCRINOLOGY, PROTEIN CHEMISTRY. *Current Pos:* from asst prof to assoc prof biochem, 80-89, head molecular biol, 86-91, PROF MOLECULAR BIOL, UNIV WYO, 89- *Personal Data:* b Powell, Wyo, Apr 8, 50; m 72, Lorrie Emery; c Brian & Karren. *Educ:* Calif Inst Technol, BS, 72; Univ Calif, San Diego, MS, 74, PhD(biochem), 78. *Prof Exp:* Asst, Roche Inst Molecular Biol, 78-80. *Mem:* Am Chem Soc; Am Soc Biol Chemists; Protein Soc. *Res:* Peptide hormones of adrenal medulla; protein sequencing; chemical structures of spider silks; protein and peptide purification methods. *Mailing Add:* Univ Wyo PO Box 3944 Laramie WY 82071-3944. *E-Mail:* silk@uwyo.edu

LEWIS, RICHARD THOMAS, CARBON CHEMISTRY, THERMAL ANALYSIS. *Current Pos:* SR RES ASSOC, UCAR CARBON CO, 96- *Personal Data:* b East Cleveland, Ohio, Jan 9, 43; div; c Gregory. *Educ:* Case Western Res Univ, BS, 64; Univ Chicago, PhD(phys chem), 70. *Prof Exp:* Staff scientist chem, Carbon Prod Div, Union Carbide Corp, 70-74, group leader, 74-78, res scientist, 78-80, sr res scientist, 80-82, res assoc, 82-96. *Mem:* Am Chem Soc; NAm Thermal Anal Soc. *Res:* Surface chemistry; physical chemistry and chemistry of carbonization. *Mailing Add:* UCAR Carbon Co 12900 Snow Rd Parma OH 44130. *Fax:* 216-676-2423

LEWIS, ROBERT ALLEN, ORGANIC CHEMISTRY. *Current Pos:* res assoc, Chevron Res Co, Richmond, 70-82, prod develop mgr, Chevron Cent Labs, Rotterdam, Neth, 82-86, tech mgr, Orogil, Nevilly-Seine, France, 86-90, UNIT MGR, CHEVRON RES & TECHNOL CTR, CHEVRON CORP, RICHMOND, CALIF, 90- *Personal Data:* b Dunkirk, NY, July 27, 43; m 69. *Educ:* Carnegie Inst Technol, BS, 65; Princeton Univ, MS, 67, PhD(org chem), 69. *Prof Exp:* Postdoctoral, Mass Inst Technol, 69-70. *Mem:* Am Chem Soc; Soc Automotive Engrs. *Res:* Synthesis, evaluation and chemical process definition of fuel and lubricant additives. *Mailing Add:* 1298 Grizzly Peak Blvd Berkeley CA 94708-2128

LEWIS, ROBERT ALLEN, experimental biology, for more information see previous edition

LEWIS, ROBERT EARL, ENTOMOLOGY, VERTEBRATE ZOOLOGY. *Current Pos:* from assoc prof to prof, 67-96, EMER PROF ENTOM, IOWA STATE UNIV, 97- *Personal Data:* b Richmond, Ind, Dec 1, 29; m 52, Nancy A Bailie. *Educ:* Earlham Col, AB, 52; Univ Ill, MS, 56, PhD(entom), 59. *Prof Exp:* From asst prof to assoc prof zool, Am Univ, Beirut, 59-67. *Concurrent Pos:* Consult, US Naval Med Res Unit, Egypt, 63-; grants, Off Naval Res, 66-71 & NIH, 64-67; ARS, 67- *Mem:* Entom Soc Am; Am Entom Soc; Am Soc Mammal; Soc Syst Zool; Royal Entom Soc London. *Res:* Siphonaptera of the world, their host relationships and zoogeography. *Mailing Add:* 3906 Stone Brook Circle Ames IA 50010-4174. *Fax:* 515-233-1851; *E-Mail:* relewis@iastate.edu

LEWIS, ROBERT EDWIN, JR, IMMUNOPATHOLOGY, PATERNITY TESTING. *Current Pos:* Instr path & anesthesiol, Univ Miss Med Ctr, 76-77, asst prof anesthesiol, 77-85, asst prof path, 77-84, assoc prof path, 84-91, CO-DIR, TISSUE TYPING LAB & CLIN IMMUNOPATH LAB & DIR, PATERNITY TESTING LAB, UNIV MISS MED CTR, 81-, PROF PATH, 91- *Personal Data:* b Meridian, Miss, Mar 11, 47. *Educ:* Univ Miss, Oxford, BA, 69, MS, 73; Univ Miss, Jackson, PhD(immunol & path), 76. Concurrent *Pos:* Sr ed, Path & Immunopath Res & Immunol Res & Transgene; dep ed-in-chief, Pathobiol. *Mem:* Fel Royal Soc Health (UK); Am Asn Pathologists; Am Asn Immunologists; Can Soc Immunol; Reticuloendothelial Soc; Am Soc Microbiol. *Res:* Cellular immunology; natural killer cell morphology, levels and function in human patients with leukemias, lymphomas and in renal allotransplant recipients; mechanisms of Natural Killer and natural cytotoxicity cell actions in allograft rejection and antitumor immunity; Interleukin-2 in immunomodulation of tumors in man and animals. *Mailing Add:* Dept Path Univ Miss 2500 N State St Jackson MS 39216-4505. *Fax:* 601-984-1531

LEWIS, ROBERT GLENN, ENVIRONMENTAL CHEMISTRY & PHYSICS. *Current Pos:* sect chief, 71-79, chief, Methods Develop Br, 79-94, SR SCI ADV, ENVIRON PROTECTION AGENCY, 94- *Personal Data:* b Morehead City, NC, Nov 11, 37; m 60, Sue Muirhead; c Michael R, David G & Steven J. *Educ:* Univ NC, BS, 60; Univ Wis, PhD(org chem), 64. *Honors & Awards:* Merit Award, Am Soc Testing & Mat. *Prof Exp:* Res chemist, Chemstrand Res Ctr, Inc, 64-69, group leader & res specialist, 69-71. *Concurrent Pos:* NSF fel, 61; NIH fel, 61-64. *Mem:* Am Chem Soc; Sigma Xi; AAAS; fel Am Soc Testing & Mat; Air & Waste Mgt Asn. *Res:* Environmental chemistry; environmental toxicology; air pollution analysis; human exposure assessment; organic photochemistry; ultraviolet-visible absorption and luminescence spectroscopy; organic analyses; pesticide chemistry and analysis; mass spectrometry. *Mailing Add:* Nat Exposure Res Lab US Environ Protection Agency Triangle Park NC 27711. *Fax:* 919-541-3527; *E-Mail:* lewis.bob-dr@epamail.epa.gov

LEWIS, ROBERT MILLER, IMMUNOLOGY. *Current Pos:* PROF PATH, NY STATE COL VET MED, CORNELL UNIV, 75- *Personal Data:* b Flushing, NY, May 20, 37; m 58; c 2. *Educ:* Wash State Univ, DVM, 61. *Honors & Awards:* Mary Mitchell Award Outstanding Res, 61. *Prof Exp:* Intern, Angell Mem Animal Hosp, 61-62; res fel, Harvard Med Sch, 62-65; from instr to sr instr surg, Sch Med, Tufts Univ, 65-67, from asst prof to assoc prof, 67-75, dir, Lab Animal Sci, 69-75. *Concurrent Pos:* Res assoc path, Angell Mem Animal Hosp, 62-63, assoc pathologist, 65-67, affil in med, 68-75; consult surg res, New Eng Med Ctr Hosp, 62-65, mem spec sci staff, 66-75, chief vet serv, 70-75; asst path, Harvard Med Sch, 65-68, clin asst, 68-76. *Mem:* Am Vet Med Asn; Am Col Vet Pathologists; Int Acad Path; Am Asn Lab Animal Sci; Am Soc Vet Clin Pathologists; Sigma Xi. *Res:* Investigations on the etiology and pathogenesis of spontaneous immunologic diseases of animals which mimic human diseases. *Mailing Add:* Dept Path Col Vet Med Cornell Univ VRT, T4D19B Ithaca NY 14853

LEWIS, ROBERT RICHARDS, JR, THEORETICAL PHYSICS. *Current Pos:* from asst prof to prof, 58-92, EMER PROF PHYSICS, UNIV MICH, ANN ARBOR, 93- *Personal Data:* b New Haven, Conn, Mar 7, 27; m 50; c 4. *Educ:* Univ Mich, BS, 50, MS, 53, PhD(physics), 54. *Prof Exp:* Asst prof physics, Univ Notre Dame, 54-58. *Concurrent Pos:* Mem, Inst Advan Study, 56-58. *Mem:* Fel Am Phys Soc. *Res:* Quantum theory; angular correlation theory; parity nonconservation in atoms; partial coherence theory. *Mailing Add:* Dept Physics Univ Mich Ann Arbor MI 48109

LEWIS, ROBERT WARREN, ELECTRICAL ENGINEERING, OPTICS. *Current Pos:* ADJ PROF, OAKLAND COMMUNITY COL, 90- *Personal Data:* b Mansfield, Ohio, Feb 4, 43; m 78; c 2. *Educ:* Univ Cincinnati, BSEE, 66; Univ Mich, MSE, 68, MA, 69, PhD(elec eng), 73. *Prof Exp:* Res asst coherent optics, Willow Run Labs, Univ Mich, 69-72; res assoc radar, Environ Res Inst Mich, 72-73; assoc sr res scientist optics & computerized tomography, Gen Motors Res Labs, 78-87. *Concurrent Pos:* Educ consult & imaging consult. *Mem:* Optical Soc Am; Inst Elec & Electronics Engrs; Sigma Xi. *Res:* Optics and electrical engineering; computerized tomographic mapping of temperature induced refractive index fields in combusting mixtures. *Mailing Add:* McComb Comm Col Math Dept 44575 Garfield Rd Clinton Township MI 48038

LEWIS, ROGER ALLEN, BIOCHEMISTRY. *Current Pos:* from asst prof to assoc prof, 69-82, PROF BIOCHEM, UNIV NEV, RENO, 82- *Personal Data:* b Wellington, Kans, June 1, 41; m 62; c 3. *Educ:* Phillips Univ, BA, 63; Ore State Univ, PhD(biochem), 68. *Prof Exp:* Res assoc pyrimidine nucleotide metab, Stanford Univ, 68-69. *Mem:* Am Chem Soc; Sigma Xi; AAAS; Am Soc Pharmacol & Exp Therapeut; Am Soc Biochem Molecular Biol. *Res:* Purine deoxynucleotide biosynthesis and its control; toxicology of pesticides with respect to nucleotide metabolism and DNA and/or RNA synthesis. *Mailing Add:* Dept Biochem Univ Nev Reno NV 89557-0901

LEWIS, ROGER T, DIFFERENTIAL EQUATIONS, MATHEMATICAL PHYSICS. *Current Pos:* from asst prof to assoc prof, 75-81, chair, Dept Math, 84-87, PROF MATH, UNIV ALA, BIRMINGHAM, 81- *Personal Data:* b Apr 22, 42; m, Barbara A Lewis; c Ronald D & Pamela J. *Educ:* Univ Tenn, AB, 64, PhD, 72; Fla Inst Technol, MS, 68. *Prof Exp:* Mathematician, Ballistics Res Lab, Aberdeen Proving Grounds, 64-66 & RCA Serv Corps, Patrick AFB, 66-67; engr, Radiation Inc, Fla, 67-68; asst prof, Slippery Rock State Col, Pa, 72-75. *Concurrent Pos:* Grantee, NSF, 80-, NATO, 92-94; prin investr math, Exp Proj Stimulate Competitive Res, NSF, Ala, 86-91, asst proj dir, 92-; Fulbright Found lectr/researcher, Univ Oslo, Norway, 95. *Mem:* Am Math Soc; Int Asn Math Physics. *Res:* Authored numerous professional publications. *Mailing Add:* Dept Math Univ Ala Birmingham AL 35294

LEWIS, ROY STEPHEN, METEORITICS. *Current Pos:* SR RES ASSOC METEORITICS, DEPT CHEM, UNIV CHICAGO, 73- *Personal Data:* b Oakland, Calif, Aug 10, 44; m 66; c 3. *Educ:* Univ Calif, Berkeley, AB, 67, PhD(atmospheric & space sci), 73. *Honors & Awards:* Except Sci Achievement Medal, NASA. *Mem:* Meteoritical Soc; fel AAAS. *Res:* Isotopic composition and elemental abundances of noble gases in meteorites and other samples. *Mailing Add:* Enrico Fermi Inst Univ Chicago 5630 S Ellis Ave Chicago IL 60637

LEWIS, RUSSELL J, SOIL CHEMISTRY. *Personal Data:* b Liberty Road, Ky, Jan 23, 29; m 54, Mineko Shiroishi; c Jon M & Robert M. *Educ:* Univ Ky, BS, 56, MS, 57; NC State Col, PhD(soils), 61. *Prof Exp:* Int Atomic Energy Agency fel chem, Univ NC, 61-62; from asst prof to prof soil chem, Univ Tenn, Knoxville, 62-93. *Mem:* Am Soc Agron; Soil Sci Soc Am; Clay Minerals Soc; Sigma Xi. *Res:* Surface chemistry of colloids; ion exchange, fixation and nutrient availability; pedoarchaeology; wetlands. *Mailing Add:* 1124 Burton Rd Knoxville TN 37919. *Fax:* 423-974-7997

LEWIS, RUSSELL M(ACLEAN), TRAFFIC ENGINEERING, HIGHWAY SAFETY. *Current Pos:* CONSULT ENGR, 80- *Personal Data:* b New York, NY, June 20, 30; m 57, Nancy Hinsdill; c Jeffrey, Cynthia, Roger & Susan. *Educ:* Trinity Col, Conn, BS, 52; Rensselaer Polytech Inst, BCE, 53, MCE, 54; Purdue Univ, PhD, 62. *Prof Exp:* From instr to assoc prof civil eng, Rensselaer Polytech Inst, 57-68; assoc, Byrd, Tallamy, MacDonald & Lewis, Div Wilbur Smith & Assocs, 68-70, partner, 71-72, sr assoc, 72-80. *Concurrent Pos:* Ford Found fel, Purdue Univ, 60-62; affil, Transp Res Bd, Nat Res Coun-Nat Acad Sci; mem, Construct & Maintenance Subcomt, Nat Comt Uniform Traffic Control Devices, 79- *Mem:* Am Soc Civil Engrs; Inst Traffic Engrs. *Res:* Highway accident analysis; highway safety research; traffic and parking studies; expert witness testimony in accident cases; training programs for transportation agencies. *Mailing Add:* 8313 Epinard Ct Annandale VA 22003-4441

LEWIS, SHELDON NOAH, PHYSICAL CHEMISTRY, ORGANIC CHEMISTRY. *Current Pos:* PRES, SNL INC, TECHNOL CONSULT INDUST, 91- *Personal Data:* b Chicago, Ill, July 1, 34; m 57, Suzanne Goldberg; c Sara, Matthew & Rachel. *Educ:* Northwestern Univ, BA & MS, 56; Univ Calif, Los Angeles, PhD(phys & org chem), 59. *Prof Exp:* NSF fel, Univ Basel, 59-60; sr chemist, Rohm & Haas Co, 60-61, group leader org chem, 61-63, lab head, 63-68, res supvr, 68-73, dir specialty chem res, 73-74, gen mgr, DCL Lab AG, Switz, 74-75, dir, Europ Labs, France, 75-76, corp dir res polymers, resins & monomers worldwide, 76-78; vpres res & develop, Clorox Co, 78, group vpres & dir, 78-84, exec vpres & dir, 84-91. *Mem:* Am Chem Soc; Indust Res Inst; Soc Chem Indust. *Res:* Reaction mechanisms; organic synthesis; process development; agricultural chemicals; polymers and surface coatings; leather, paper, textile, cosmetic and petroleum chemicals; plastics and modifiers; ion exchange resins; adhesives; building products; biocides, detergents, bleaches and household cleaning products. *Mailing Add:* 3711 Rose Ct Lafayette CA 94549. *Fax:* 510-283-6465; *E-Mail:* shel@aol.com

LEWIS, SHERRY M, NUTRITION, NUTRITIONAL BIOCHEMISTRY. *Current Pos:* dep contract mgr, 90-93, diet prep proj mgr, 92-93, ANALYTICAL NUTRITIONIST, NAT CTR TOXICOL RES, 87- *Personal Data:* b June 12, 44; c Lisa & Bradley. *Educ:* Southern Ill Univ, BSc, 77, MSc, 79; Ohio State Univ, PhD, 83. *Prof Exp:* Researcher, Ohio State Univ & Eli Lilly Corp, 84; res instr, Univ Ill, 85-87. *Mem:* Am Asn Lab Animal Sci; Am Inst Nutrit; Am Registry Prof Animal Sci. *Res:* Scientific research and development to improve data bases, standards, methods and technologies; adjunct researcher Program on Nurtritional Modulation of Risk and Toxicity; technol dietary process development. *Mailing Add:* Nat Ctr Toxicol Res Bionetics Corp Nat Ctr Toxicol Res Jefferson AR 72079. *Fax:* 870-543-7065, 541-4382; *E-Mail:* slewis@fdant.nctr.fda.gov

LEWIS, SILAS DAVIS, ORGANIC CHEMISTRY. *Current Pos:* RETIRED. *Personal Data:* b Gastonia, NC, June 26, 30; m 62, Ruth M Krause; c Anna J (Greiner). *Educ:* Wake Forest Col, BS, 52; Ga Inst Technol, PhD(org chem), 59. *Prof Exp:* Sr chemist, Atlast Chem Industs, Inc, 59-63; assoc prof chem, Del Valley Col, 63-66; assoc prof chem, Augusta Col, 66-88. *Mem:* Am Chem Soc; Sigma Xi. *Res:* Polyphenyls; Ullmann reaction; nitro and nitrato compounds and explosives. *Mailing Add:* 1760 Kissing Bower Rd Augusta GA 30904

LEWIS, SIMON ANDREW, EPITHELIAL TRANSPORT, ELECTROPHYIOLOGY. *Current Pos:* PROF PHYSIOL & BIOPHYS, UNIV TEX, 87- *Personal Data:* b Welling Kent, Eng, Apr 18, 48; Can citizen; m 76. *Educ:* Univ BC, BSc, 70, MSc, 71; Univ Calif, Los Angeles, PhD(physiol), 75. *Prof Exp:* Res assoc physiol, Univ Calif, Los Angeles, 75-76; res assoc physiol, Med Br, Univ Tex, 76-77; from asst prof to assoc prof physiol, Yale Med Sch, 77-87. *Mem:* Biophys Soc. *Res:* Mechanisms of salt and water transport across epithelial cells membranes using electrophysiological methods. *Mailing Add:* Dept Physiol & Biophys Univ Tex Med Br Basic Sci Bldg Galveston TX 77555-0641

LEWIS, STANDLEY EUGENE, ENTOMOLOGY, PALEONTOLOGY. *Current Pos:* from asst prof to assoc prof biol, 68-78, PROF BIOL, ST CLOUD STATE COL, 78- *Personal Data:* b Twin Falls, Idaho, Nov 15, 40; m 65; c 2. *Educ:* Univ Nebr, Omaha, BA, 62, MA, 64; Wash State Univ, PhD(entom), 68. *Prof Exp:* Teaching asst biol, Univ Nebr, Omaha, 63-64; teaching asst zool-entom, Wash State Univ, 64-68. *Concurrent Pos:* Res asst mosquito control, Adams County Abate Dist, 65-; res consult, N States Power Co, 75-77; res assoc, Sci Mus Minn; Sigma Xi, Geol Soc Am & St Cloud instnl grants, 68, 70, 75, 77, 83 & 85. *Mem:* Sigma Xi; Paleont Soc Am; Entom Soc Am. *Res:* Paleobiology, specifically paleoentomology; tertiary insect site in US; fossil insect studies, Miocene sites: Wash And Idaho, Oligocene sites: Mont, Cretaceous sites: Minn; fossil bison kill site in Central Minn. *Mailing Add:* 1226 Kilian Blvd SE St Cloud MN 56304

LEWIS, STEPHEN ALBERT, PLANT NEMATOLOGY. *Current Pos:* asst prof, 73-77, ASSOC PROF NEMATOL, DEPT PLANT PATH & PHYSIOL, CLEMSON UNIV, 77- *Personal Data:* b Sodus, NY, Sept 9, 42; m 68; c 1. *Educ:* Pa State Univ, BS, 64; Rutgers Univ, MS, 69; Univ Ariz, PhD(plant path), 73. *Prof Exp:* Sales rep, Stand Oil Calif, 65-66. *Mem:* Soc Nematologists; Sigma Xi. *Res:* Host-parasite relations of the phytoparasitic nematodes, Hoplolaimus columbus and Criconemoides xenoplax on field crops and peach trees, respectively; nematode-mycorrhizae-rhizobium relationships; gnotobiotic culture of nematodes. *Mailing Add:* Dept Plant Path Clemson Univ Clemson SC 29632-0001

LEWIS, STEPHEN B, ENVIRONMENTAL MEDICINE. *Current Pos:* CAPT, US NAVAL MED CORPS, 79- *Personal Data:* b Berkeley, Calif, Mar 9, 40; m 72; c 3. *Educ:* Univ Calif, Berkeley, BA, 62; Wash Univ, MD, 66. *Prof Exp:* Intern med serv & chmn, Dept Med, Michael Reese Hosp, Chicago, 66-67, asst resident med, 67-69; fel, Dept Physiol, Sch Med, Vanderbilt Univ, 69-72, instr, Dept Med & res assoc, Dept Physiol, 71-72; endocrinologist & asst dir, Clin Invest Ctr & head, Endocrinol & Metab Br, Med Serv, Naval Regional Med Ctr, Oakland, Calif, 72-78, dir, Clin Invest Ctr & head, Endocrinol Br, 78-83; clin asst prof med, Univ Calif, San Francisco, 77-83 & Tissue Bank Stem Cell Res, Naval Med Res Inst, 83-86; dep dir, Environ Med Dept, 86-90. *Concurrent Pos:* Spec res fel, NIH, 71-72. *Mem:* Am Diabetes Asn (pres, 81-83); Am Fed Clin Res; Soc Exp Biol & Med; Endocrine Soc; AAAS; Am Physiol Soc; Europ Asn Study Diabetes. *Res:* Blood and blood substitutes; wounds, sepsis and shock; hypothermia and non-freezing cold injury; readiness planning and material; post injury enhancement. *Mailing Add:* 2550 Almond Ave Suite 4-3 Concord CA 94520

LEWIS, STEPHEN ROBERT, plastic surgery, for more information see previous edition

LEWIS, STEVEN CRAIG, CHEMICAL CARCINOGENESIS, RISK ASSESSMENT & COMMUNICATION. *Current Pos:* toxicologist, Exxon Biomed Sci, Inc, 75-79, sr toxicologist & unit head, 79-82, toxicol assoc, 82-96, SR TOXICOL ASSOC, EXXON BIOMED SCI, INC, 96- *Personal Data:* b Anderson, Ind, Dec 30, 43; m 69, Sandra Sue Hahneri. *Educ:* Ind Univ, BA, 70, PhD(toxicol), 75; Am Bd Toxicol, dipl, 80, recert, 85 & 90. *Prof Exp:* Res asst biochem, Med Sch, Ind Univ, 65-71, res fel toxicol, 71-75, supvr, Statist Cancer Res Unit, 72-75. *Concurrent Pos:* Mem bd dir, Toxicol Forum, 82-84; vchmn & chmn, Toxicol Comt, Am Petrol Inst, 83-; mem sci rev group, NY Dept Environ Conserv, 85-; consult, US Environ Protection Agency Sci Adv Bd, 89-92; chair sci policy, Am Indust Health Coun, 96- *Mem:* Soc Risk Anal; Inter Soc Regulatory Toxicol & Pharmacol; Soc Toxicol. *Res:* Chemical carcinogenesis; biostatistics; risk analysis; neurotoxicology; toxicology; product safety; non-cancer risk assessment; risk communication. *Mailing Add:* Mettlers Rd CN2350 East Millstone NJ 08875-2350. *Fax:* 732-873-6009; *E-Mail:* steven.lewis@ere.exxon.sprint.com

LEWIS, STEVEN M, RESPIRATORY PHYSIOLOGY, SIMULATION. *Current Pos:* MEM TECH STAFF, AEROSPACE CORP, 89- *Personal Data:* b Washington, DC, June 9, 48. *Educ:* Calif Inst Technol, BS, 69; Univ Wash, PhD(biophys), 74. *Prof Exp:* From asst prof to assoc prof biomed eng, Univ Southern Calif, University Park, 76-89. *Mem:* Biomed Eng Soc; Am Physiol Soc; Inst Elec & Electronics Engrs; Asn Comput Mach. *Mailing Add:* 2350 E El Segundo Blvd El Segundo CA 90245

LEWIS, SUSAN ERSKINE, IN VIVO MUTOGENESIS, DEVELOPMENTAL GENETICS. *Current Pos:* sr res geneticist, 79-90, SR PROG DIR, RES TRIANGLE INST, 90- *Personal Data:* b Philadelphia, Pa, Mar 10, 41; m 65; Carl M; c Andrew & Karen. *Educ:* Bryn Mawr Col, AB, 63; NY Univ, MS, 67; Albert Einstein Col Med, PhD(genetics), 75. *Prof Exp:* Res assoc, Albert Einstein Col Med, 75-76; fel, Univ Mich, 76-79. *Mem:* Genetics Soc Am; Environ Mutagen Soc; Am Soc Human Genetics. *Res:* Explore mechanism of action of toxic chemicals on the germ line; genetic control of mammalian development; in particular genes acting in the early embryo. *Mailing Add:* Rte 1 PO Box 12194 Research Triangle Park NC 27709-2194. *Fax:* 919-541-7237

LEWIS, SUSANNA MAXWELL, DNA RECOMBINATION. *Current Pos:* ASSOC PROF IMMUNOL, UNIV TORONTO, 95-; SCIENTIST, HOSP FOR SICK CHILDREN RES INST, 95- *Personal Data:* b Boston, Mass; m 86, Howard D Lipshitz; c Sarah. *Educ:* Tufts Univ, BS, 76; Mass Inst Technol, PhD(biol), 85. *Prof Exp:* Postdoctoral fel biochem, Stanford Univ, 85-86; staff fel, Lab Molecular Biol, NIH, 86-88; sr res fel biol, Calif Inst Technol, 88-95. *Concurrent Pos:* Helen Hay Whitney fel, 85-88; res grant, Am Cancer Soc, 90- *Mem:* Am Asn Immunologists. *Res:* Mechanism of immunoglobulin and T cell receptor gene rearrangement. *Mailing Add:* Immunol Dept Med Sci Bldg Univ Toronto 1 Kings Col Circle Toronto ON M5S 1A8 Can. *Fax:* 626-564-8709; *E-Mail:* lewiss@starbase1.caltech.edu

LEWIS, T(HOMAS) SKIPWITH, ELECTRICAL ENGINEERING. *Current Pos:* RETIRED. *Personal Data:* b Bluefield, WVa, Nov 21, 36; m 62; c 2. *Educ:* Va Polytech Inst, BS, 59; Univ Va, MS, 64, ScD(elec eng), 67. *Prof Exp:* Engr, Air Arm Div, Westinghouse Elec Corp, 59-62; instr elec eng, Univ Va, 64-67; sr res engr, United Aircraft Res Labs, 67-70; adj asst prof elec eng, Univ Hartford, 67-70, assoc prof, 70-81, dean, Col Eng, 71-81; from asst vpres to vpres, Hartford Steam Boiler, 81-85, sr vpres, 85- *Mem:* Inst Elec & Electronics Engrs. *Res:* Microwave engineering and antennas; microwave properties of materials. *Mailing Add:* 41 N Parker Rd Marlborough CT 06447

LEWIS, THEODORE, CHEMICAL ENGINEERING, POLYMER CHEMISTRY. *Current Pos:* INDUST, GOVT & UNIV CONSULT, 74- *Personal Data:* b New York, NY, Apr 9, 24. *Educ:* Rensselaer Polytech Inst, BChE, 46, MChE, 48; Princeton Univ, PhD(chem eng), 55; NY Univ, MBA, 71. *Prof Exp:* Res engr chem & chem eng, Esso Res Eng Co, Stand Oil Co, NJ, 54-59, sr mkt develop engr, Enjay Chem Co, 59-65, assoc synthetic elastomers dept, 65-71; assoc prof, Col Bus, Fairleig Dickinson Univ, Rutherford, pharmaceut/chem prog & admin asst to dean, 71-74. *Concurrent Pos:* Adj fac, Fairleigh Dickinson Univ & Adelphi Univ, 74- *Mem:* Am Chem Soc; Am Inst Chem Engrs. *Res:* Textile fibers; synthetic elastomers; petrochemicals; products and process research; market development of thermosets, synthetic elastomers and special industries; granted 25 patents. *Mailing Add:* PO Box 486 Toms River NJ 08754-0486

LEWIS, TREVOR JOHN, GEOPHYSICS. *Current Pos:* RES SCIENTIST GEOTHERMAL STUDIES, DEPT ENERGY MINES & RESOURCES, GEOL SURV CAN, 64- *Personal Data:* b Vancouver, BC, Jan 19, 40; m 64; c 3. *Educ:* Univ BC, BASc, 63, MSc, 64; Univ Western Ont, PhD(geophys), 75. *Mem:* Geol Asn Can; Can Geophys Union; Am Geophys Soc; Can Geothermal Energy Asn; Int Heat Flow Comt. *Res:* Geothermal studies, thermal structure of the earth. *Mailing Add:* Pac Geosci Ctr PO Box 6000 Sidney BC V8L 4B2 Can

LEWIS, URBAN JAMES, ENDOCRINOLOGY. *Current Pos:* RETIRED. *Personal Data:* b Flagstaff, Ariz, Apr 28, 23; m 50; c 2. *Educ:* San Diego State Col, BA, 48; Univ Wis, MS, 50, PhD(biochem), 52. *Prof Exp:* NIH fel, Med Nobel Inst, Stockholm, 52-53; instr biochem & biochemist, Am Meat Found, Univ Chicago, 53-54; sr biochemist, Merck & Co, Inc, 54-61; mem, Scripps Clin & Res Found, 61-82; mem, Whittier Inst, 82-93. *Mem:* Am Soc Biol Chem; Am Chem Soc; Endocrine Soc. *Res:* Proteolytic enzymes; pituitary hormones. *Mailing Add:* 5733 Skylark Pl La Jolla CA 92037

LEWIS, VANCE DE SPAIN, PHYSICS, EDUCATIONAL ADMINISTRATION. *Current Pos:* From asst prof to prof, 46-64, EMER PROF PHYSICS, CALIF POLYTECH STATE UNIV, SAN LUIS OBISPO, 72- *Personal Data:* b Los Angeles, Calif, June 26, 09; m 36, Marjorie Sieghold; c Linda (Harmon) & Diane (Martin). *Educ:* Univ Calif, Berkeley, BA, 33, MA, 40; Univ Southern Calif, PhD(educ), 54. *Concurrent Pos:* Assoc dean, Col Sci & Math, Calif Polytech State Univ, San Luis Obispo, 68-72. *Mem:* Am Phys Soc. *Res:* Optics; statistical analysis. *Mailing Add:* 17050 Arnold Dr F-113 Riverside CA 92518

LEWIS, VICTOR L, PLASTIC & RECONSTRUCTIVE SURGERY. *Current Pos:* ASSOC PROF CLIN SURG, NORTHWESTERN UNIV MED SCH, 77- *Personal Data:* b Evanston, Ill, Sept 22, 42; m 72, Jayne; c Torrey & Michael. *Educ:* Yale Univ, BA, 64; Northwestern Univ, MD, 68. *Mem:* Am Soc Maxillofacial Surgeons (pres, 92-93); Am Soc Plastic & Reconstructive Surgeons; Am Col Surgeons; Am Asn Plastic Surgeons; Am Asn Surg Trauma. *Res:* Role of nerves in wound healing; healing of soft tissue complications of chronic spine trauma. *Mailing Add:* 707 N Fairbanks Ct Suite 1210 Chicago IL 60611-3042. *Fax:* 312-335-9848

LEWIS, W DAVID, HISTORY OF TECHNOLOGY. *Current Pos:* Hudson prof hist & eng, 71-, DISTINGUISHED UNIV PROF, AUBURN UNIV. *Personal Data:* b Towanda, Pa, June 24, 31; m 86; c 3. *Educ:* Pa State Univ, BA, 52, MA, 54; Cornell Univ, PhD(hist), 61. *Prof Exp:* Instr pub speaking, Hamilton Col, 54-57; fel coordr, Eleutherian Mills-Hagley Found, Inc, Wilmington & lectr hist, Univ Del, 59-65; from assoc prof to prof, State Univ NY, Buffalo, 65-71. *Concurrent Pos:* Dir, Nat Endowment Humanities Proj Technol, Human Values & Southern Future, Auburn Univ, 74-; fel, Nat Humanities Inst, Univ Chicago, 78-; grants, State Univ NY, Auburn Univ, Eleutherian Mills Hist Libr, Nat Endowment for the Humanities & Delta Airlines Found. *Mem:* Soc Hist Technol. *Res:* History of technology, particularly history of iron and steel industry and aerospace history. *Mailing Add:* Dept Hist 310 Thach Hall Auburn Univ Auburn AL 36849-3501

LEWIS, WALLACE JOE, ENTOMOLOGY. *Current Pos:* ENTOMOLOGIST, SOUTHERN GRAIN INSECTS RES LAB, ENTOM RES DIV, AGR RES SERV, USDA, 67- *Personal Data:* b Smithdale, Miss, Oct 30, 42; m 65; c 2. *Educ:* Miss State Univ, BS, 64, MS, 65, PhD(entom), 68. *Concurrent Pos:* Asst prof, Univ Fla, 70- *Mem:* Entom Soc Am; Sigma Xi. *Res:* Ecological and physiological relationships between parasitic insects and their hosts; development of methods for the use of parasitic insects for control of insect pests. *Mailing Add:* USDA Agr Res Serv IBPMRL PO Box 748 Tifton GA 31793

LEWIS, WALTER HEPWORTH, BOTANY. *Current Pos:* assoc prof, 64-69, PROF BIOL, WASH UNIV, 69- *Personal Data:* b Carleton Place, Ont, June 26, 30; m 57; c 2. *Educ:* Univ BC, BA, 51, MA, 54; Univ Va, PhD(bot), 57. *Honors & Awards:* Horsley Res Award, Va Acad Sci, 57. *Prof Exp:* Asst prof biol & dir herbarium, Stephen F Austin State Col, 57-61, assoc prof biol, 61-64. *Concurrent Pos:* Guggenheim fel, 63-64; dir herbarium, Mo Bot Garden, 64-72, sr botanist, 72- *Mem:* Bot Soc Am; Am Soc Plant Taxon; Asn Trop Biol; Int Asn Plant Taxon; Int Orgn Biosyst; fel Linnean Soc London. *Res:* Cytotaxonomy of Rosa, the Rubiaceae, palynotaxonomy of angiosperms and southern flora; medical plants; allergy. *Mailing Add:* Dept Biol Campus Box 1137 Wash Univ One Brookings Dr St Louis MO 63130-4862

LEWIS, WILLIAM E(RVIN), COMPUTER PERFORMANCE EVALUATION, ANALYTICAL MODELING. *Current Pos:* Assoc prof, 65-80, chmn dept, 80-85, PROF COMPUT SCI, ARIZ STATE UNIV, 80-, ASST DEAN ENG, 85- *Personal Data:* b Hagerstown, Md, Sept 10, 40; m 58; c 5. *Educ:* Johns Hopkins Univ, BES, 62; Northwestern Univ, Evanston, MS, 64, PhD(indust eng), 66. *Concurrent Pos:* Consult, Good Samaritan Hosp, 66-68, Gen Elec Info Systs, 69-71, Honeywell Info Systs, 71-79; eval analyst, Phoenix Alcohol Safety Action Proj, 71-73; staff mem, Intel, 79-80; staff mem, Ariz Dept Health Serv, 87- *Mem:* Am Inst Indust Engrs; Asn Comput Mach. *Res:* Application of operations research and computer techniques to industrial problems; computer systems design. *Mailing Add:* 1213 E Loyola Tempe AZ 85282-3945

LEWIS, WILLIAM JAMES, MATHEMATICS. *Current Pos:* from asst prof to assoc prof, 71-93, vchmn dept, 80-83, CHAIR, UNIV NEBR-LINCOLN, 88-, PROF MATH, 93- *Personal Data:* b Talahassee, Fla, Feb 11, 45; m 82, Doris Hitz; c Michael, Tanya & Steven. *Educ:* La State Univ, Baton Rouge, BS, 66, PhD(math), 71. *Prof Exp:* Instr math, La State Univ, 71. *Mem:* Am Math Soc; Math Asn Am; Am Asn Univ Profs. *Res:* Commutative algebra; mathematics education. *Mailing Add:* Dept Math Univ Nebr Lincoln NE 68588-0323. *E-Mail:* jlewis@unl.edu

LEWIS, WILLIAM MADISON, FISHERIES. *Current Pos:* RETIRED. *Personal Data:* b Faison, NC, Nov 26, 22; m 43; c 4. *Educ:* NC State Col, BS, 43; Iowa State Col, MS, 48, PhD(zool), 49. *Prof Exp:* Sci bact aide, USDA, 42; asst prof, Southern Ill Univ, 49-60, dir, Coop Fisheries Lab, 49-, prof zool, 60-, chmn, Dept Zool, 72- *Mem:* Am Fisheries Soc. *Res:* Aquaculture and fish management. *Mailing Add:* 7500 Pine Ridge Faison NC 78341

LEWIS, WILLIAM MASON, WEED SCIENCE. *Current Pos:* RETIRED. *Personal Data:* b Ithaca, NY, Aug 13, 29; m 57, Marie Blackwell; c Karl, Keith, Karen, Kaye & Kirsten. *Educ:* Tex A&M Univ, BS, 52; Univ Minn, MS, 56, PhD(plant genetics), 57. *Honors & Awards:* Outstanding Exten Worker Award, Weed Sci Soc Am, 88. *Prof Exp:* Asst agron & plant genetics, Univ Minn, 52-56; from instr to assoc prof, NC State Univ, 56-69, prof crop sci & weed sci ext specialist, 69- *Concurrent Pos:* Vis prof, Univ Ill, 74. *Mem:* Am Soc Agron; Crop Sci Soc Am; Weed Sci Soc Am; Int Turf Grass Soc; Southern Weed Sci Soc. *Res:* Agronomy; turf weed control. *Mailing Add:* Dept Crop Sci NC State Univ Raleigh NC 27695-7620. *Fax:* 919-515-5315; *E-Mail:* wlewis@wolf.ces.ncsu.edu

LEWIS, WILLIAM PERRY, MEDICAL MICROBIOLOGY. *Current Pos:* RETIRED. *Personal Data:* b Swatow, China, Aug 12, 29; US citizen; m 51; c 2. *Educ:* Univ Redlands, BS, 51; Univ Calif, Los Angeles, PhD(infectious dis), 62. *Prof Exp:* Asst res parasitologist & instr parasitol, Sch Pub Health, Univ Calif, Los Angeles, 62-69; assoc prof path, Sch Med, Univ Southern Calif & chief med microbiologist, Los Angeles County-Univ Southern Calif Med Ctr, 69-94. *Concurrent Pos:* Pres, W M Lewis Info Serv. *Mem:* AAAS; Am Soc Trop Med & Hyg; Am Soc Microbiol; Am Soc Parasitol. *Res:* Immunology of parasitic diseases, especially toxoplasmosis, amebiasis and filariasis; diagnostic bacteriology, parasitology and immunology. *Mailing Add:* 24301 Friar St Woodland Hills CA 91367-1126

LEWONTIN, RICHARD CHARLES, GENETICS, POPULATION BIOLOGY. *Current Pos:* PROF BIOL, HARVARD UNIV, 73- *Personal Data:* b New York, NY, Mar 29, 29; m 47; c 4. *Educ:* Harvard Univ, AB, 51; Columbia Univ, MA, 52, PhD(zool), 54. *Prof Exp:* Reader biomet, Columbia Univ, 53-54; asst prof genetics, NC State Col, 54-58; from asst prof to prof biol, Univ Rochester, 58-64; prof biol, Univ Chicago, 64-73. *Concurrent Pos:* NSF fel, 54-55, sr fel, 61-62 & 71-72; lectr, Columbia Univ, 59, sem assoc, 59-61; Fulbright fel, 61-62; co-ed, Am Naturalist, Am Soc Nat, 65. *Mem:* AAAS; fel Am Acad Arts & Sci; Genetics Soc Am; Soc Study Evolution (pres, 70). *Res:* Population genetics, ecology and evolution. *Mailing Add:* Mus Comp Zool Harvard Univ Cambridge MA 02138

LEWY, ALFRED JAMES, PSYCHIATRY, NEUROSCIENCE. *Current Pos:* PROF PSYCHIAT & OPHTHAL, ORE HEALTH SCI UNIV, 86-, PROF PHARMACOL, 88-, PROF PHYSIOL & PHARMACOL, 96- *Personal Data:* b Chicago, Ill, Oct 12, 45; m, Colleen Shannon. *Educ:* Univ Chicago, MD, 73, PhD(pharmacol), 73. *Mem:* Sigma Xi; Am Psychiat Asn; Am Col Neuropsychopharmacol; Sleep Res Soc; Soc Biol Rhythm. *Res:* Chronobiology research in psychiatry; bright light treatment of sleep and mood disorders; clinical and basic pineal melatonin research. *Mailing Add:* Ore Health Sci Univ Portland OR 97201. *Fax:* 503-494-5329; *E-Mail:* lewy@ohsu.edu

LEX, R(OWLAND) G(ARBER), JR, ELECTRICAL ENGINEERING. *Current Pos:* RETIRED. *Personal Data:* b Philadelphia, Pa, Dec 29, 24; m 52; c 2. *Educ:* Univ Pa, BS, 49, MS, 50. *Prof Exp:* Elec engr, Leeds & Northrup Co, 49-55, group chief, 55-58, sect head, 58-62, mgr, Develop Div, 62-68, gen mgr, Digital Equip Div, 68-69, mgr, Eng Coord & Serv Dept, 69-72, gen mgr, Recorder & Test Instrument Div, 72-76, dir, Develop & Eng Dept,

Instrument Group, 76-87, vpres res develop & eng, 87-90. *Mem:* Inst Elec & Electronics Engrs; fel Instrument Soc Am. *Res:* Application of digital techniques including computers to measurement and control of processes. *Mailing Add:* 914 Remington Rd Wynnewood PA 19096

LEY, ALLYN BRYSON, MEDICINE. *Current Pos:* RETIRED. *Personal Data:* b Springfield, Mass, Dec 5, 18; m 43, 67, Barbara Goble; c 6. *Educ:* Dartmouth Col, AB, 39; Columbia Univ, MD, 42; Am Bd Internal Med, dipl. *Prof Exp:* asst med, Med Col, Cornell Univ, 47-49, instr, 51-52, asst dir, Sloan-Kettering Div, 54-55, cancer coord, 54-63, from asst prof to assoc prof, 54-63, prof med, 63-93, clin dir, Univ Health Serv, 71-87. *Concurrent Pos:* Asst, Boston City Hosp, 49-51; dir blood bank, Mem Hosp, 51-63, dir hemat labs, 55-63; asst attend physician, NY Hosp, 54-63, attend physician & dir ambulatory serv, 63-69; consult, Manhattan Vet Admin Hosp, 58-60, Hosp Spec Surg, 58-71 & Mem Sloan Kettering Cancer Ctr, 71-87; assoc vis physician, Bellevue Hosp, 60-67; chief staff, SS Hope, 69-70; attend physician, Tompkins Community Hosp, 71-90. *Mem:* AAAS; Am Soc Hemat; Am Col Physicians. *Res:* Immunohematology; erythrocyte biochemistry; medical education and care. *Mailing Add:* Cornell Univ Health Serv 10 Central Ave Ithaca NY 14853

LEY, HERBERT L, JR, EXPERIMENTAL BIOLOGY. *Current Pos:* PRES CONSULT FIRM, HERBERT LEY FIRM, 70- *Mailing Add:* 4816 Camelot St Rockville MD 20853-3018

LEY, KENNETH D, BIOMEDICAL RESEARCH. *Current Pos:* RES SCIENTIST, LOVELACE INST, 86- *Personal Data:* b Gallop, NMex, July 28, 41. *Educ:* NMex State Univ, BS, 65; Wash State Univ, PhD(microbiol), 69. *Prof Exp:* Fel cell biol, Univ Calif, Los Angeles, 69-71; asst prof vet sci, Univ Fla, 71-77; mem tech staff, Sandia Nat Labs, 77-80. *Mem:* Am Soc Biochem & Molecular Biol; AAAS. *Mailing Add:* 28 Rael Rd Sandia Park NM 87047

LEYBOURNE, A(LLEN) E(DWARD), III, CHEMICAL ENGINEERING. *Current Pos:* DIR ENG, INTERPINE LUMBER CO, 80- *Personal Data:* b Jacksonville, Fla, Aug 26, 34; m 54, Cecile Fuller; c 2. *Educ:* Univ Fla, BS, 56, PhD(chem eng), 61; Pa State Univ, MS, 58. *Prof Exp:* Res Assoc petrol res, Pa State Univ, 56-58, instr chem, Univ Fla, 58-59; res chemist, Atlantic Refining Co, 60; sr engr, Am Oil Co, 61-62; supvr textile develop, Textile Div, Monsanto Co, 63-71; plant mgr, Texfi Industs, Inc, 71-77, dir prod eng, 77-80. *Concurrent Pos:* Prof, Eng Technol, Univ Southern Miss. *Mem:* Am Inst Chem Eng; Soc Mfg Engrs; Am Asn Eng Educ. *Res:* Polymer textiles, ocean acoustics and signal processing. *Mailing Add:* Eng Tech SS Univ Southern Miss PO Box 5137 Hattiesburg MS 39406-5137

LEYDA, JAMES PERKINS, PHARMACY, PHARMACEUTICAL CHEMISTRY. *Current Pos:* mgr new prod develop, Merrell Int Div, Richardson-Merrell, 69-76, dir, 76-81, head, Dept Pharm Res & Develop, Merrell Dow Res Inst, 81-84, dir com develop, US area, 84-89, assoc dir drug reg affairs, 90-92, MGR, STRATEGIC RES ALLIANCE, MARION MERRELL DOW PHARM, 92- *Personal Data:* b Youngstown, Ohio, Oct 2, 35; m 67, Barbara Dykstra; c Jason, Jeffrey & Justin. *Educ:* Ohio Northern Univ, BS, 57; Ohio State Univ, MS, 59, PhD(pharm), 62. *Honors & Awards:* Lunsford Richardson Award, 60. *Prof Exp:* Develop chemist, Lederle Labs Div, Am Cyanamid Co, 62-66, mgr prod develop, Int Med Res & Develop, 66-69. *Concurrent Pos:* Operating chmn, Sci Affairs Comt, Nat Pharmaceut Coun. *Mem:* AAAS; Am Pharmaceut Asn; NY Acad Sci; Am Asn Pharm Scientist; Sigma Xi; Am Soc Hosp Pharmacists; Am Soc Microbiol. *Res:* Drug delivery systems; antibiotics; cardiovascular agents and commercial liaison; biotechnology. *Mailing Add:* 10597 Tanagerhills Dr Cincinnati OH 45249-3634. *Fax:* 513-948-7982

LEYDEN, DONALD E, ANALYTICAL CHEMISTRY. *Current Pos:* ASSOC PRIN SCIENTIST, PHILIP MORRIS USA, 88- *Personal Data:* b Gadsden, Ala, June 26, 38; m 61; c 2. *Educ:* Kent State Univ, BS, 60; Emory Univ, MS, 61, PhD, 64. *Prof Exp:* Res assoc, Univ NC, 64-65; from asst prof to assoc prof chem, Univ Ga, 65-76; Phillipson prof chem, Univ Denver, 76-81; prof chem, Colo State Univ, 82-88. *Mem:* Am Chem Soc; Soc Appl Spectros; Mat Res Soc. *Res:* Chemically modified surfaces; ion-exchange; applications of nuclear magnetic resonance to the study of chemical systems of analytical importance. *Mailing Add:* Philip Morris USA Res & Develop PO Box 26583 Richmond VA 23261-6583

LEYDEN, RICHARD NOEL, ORGANOMETALLIC CHEMISTRY, POLYMER CHEMISTRY. *Current Pos:* TECH STAFF POLYMER RES, HUGHES AIRCRAFT CO, 77- *Personal Data:* b Santa Monica, Calif, Nov 14, 48. *Educ:* Univ Calif, Los Angeles, BS, 71, PhD(chem), 75. *Prof Exp:* Res asst polymer res, Univ Witwatersrand, 75-76; res asst inorg chem, Calif Inst Technol, 76-77. *Mem:* Am Chem Soc; Sigma Xi. *Res:* Polymers, especially with semiconducting or electrical properties; organometallic polymers; organic metals; ultra high pressure chemistry. *Mailing Add:* 22024 Alta Dr Topanga CA 90290-9755

LEYDORF, GLENN E(DWIN), ELECTRONICS. *Current Pos:* from instr to assoc prof elec eng, 46-57, PROF ELEC ENG, US NAVAL ACAD, 57- *Personal Data:* b Perrysburg, Ohio, June 7, 14; m 43; c 2. *Educ:* Univ Toledo, BE, 42; Univ Md, MS, 54. *Prof Exp:* Instr elec eng & physics, Univ Toledo, 42-44. *Mem:* Inst Elec & Electronics Engrs; Am Soc Eng Educ. *Res:* Electronic circuit applications to metastable atom studies. *Mailing Add:* 8310 River Crescent Dr Annapolis MD 21401

LEYH, GEORGE FRANCIS, CIVIL ENGINEERING. *Current Pos:* EXEC VPRES, AM CONCRETE INST, 75-, ED JOUR, 75- *Personal Data:* b Utica, NY, Oct 1, 31; m 55, Mary A Mosher; c Timothy G & Kristin A. *Educ:* Cornell Univ, BCE, 54, MS, 56. *Honors & Awards:* Bloem Distinguished Serv Award, Am Concrete Inst, 72. *Prof Exp:* Struct engr, Eckerlin & Klepper, 56-59; assoc dir eng, Martin Marietta Corp, 59-63; struct engr, Portland Cement Asn, 63-67; dir mkt, Concrete Reinforcing Steel Inst, 67-75. *Concurrent Pos:* Bd dirs, Am Nat Stand Inst, 86- & Am Soc Concrete Construct, 84- *Mem:* Am Soc Civil Engrs; Nat Inst Bldg Scientists; Am Rwy Eng Asn; Am Nat Stand Inst; Am Soc Concrete Construct. *Mailing Add:* Am Concrete Inst PO Box 9094 Farmington Hills MI 48333

LEYMASTER, GLEN RONALD, MEDICINE. *Current Pos:* RETIRED. *Personal Data:* b Aurora, Nebr, Aug 7, 15; m 42; c 3. *Educ:* Univ Nebr, AB, 38; Harvard Univ, MD, 42; Johns Hopkins Univ, MPH, 50; Am Bd Prev Med, dipl. *Prof Exp:* Intern, Boston City Hosp, 42-43, asst resident, 43, resident, 44; clin instr, Sch Med, Johns Hopkins Univ, 44-46; from instr to asst prof bact, Sch Hyg & Pub Health, 46-48; assoc prof pub health & prev med, Sch Med, Univ Utah, 48-50, prof prev med & head dept, 50-60; assoc secy, Coun Med Educ & Hosps, AMA, 60-63; pres, dean, prof prev med & assoc prof med, Med Col, Pa, 64-70; dir dept undergrad med educ, AMA, 70-75; exec dir, 75-81, exec vpres, Am Bd Med Specs, 81-82. *Concurrent Pos:* Clin asst, Harvard Med Sch, 42-44; asst prof & dir univ health serv, Univ Utah, 50-60; med educ adv, US Dept State, Int Coop Admin, Thailand, 57-58. *Mem:* AMA; Am Col Prev Med. *Res:* Clinical and epidemiological character of influenza and of data regarding encephalitis; experimental immunity and epidemiology of mumps; industrial toxicology; epidemiology of gastroenteritis; medical education. *Mailing Add:* 154 Kendal at Longwood Kennet Square PA 19348-2331

LEYON, ROBERT EDWARD, ANALYTICAL CHEMISTRY, SPECTROSCOPY. *Current Pos:* from asst prof to assoc prof, 69-92, chmn dept, 79-83, 88-90 & 94-97, PROF CHEM, DICKINSON COL, 92- *Personal Data:* b Newton, Mass, July 28, 36; m 62; c 2. *Educ:* Williams Col, BA, 58; Princeton Univ, MA, 60, PhD(chem), 62. *Prof Exp:* Instr chem, Princeton Univ, 61-62; from instr to asst prof, Swarthmore Col, 62-69. *Concurrent Pos:* Res assoc, Univ NC, 67-68, Colo State Univ, 75-76, Univ Tex, Austin, 83-84. *Mem:* Soc Appl Spectros. *Res:* Graphite furnace spectroscopy; trace metal analysis by atomic absorption. *Mailing Add:* Dept Chem Dickinson Col Carlisle PA 17013-2846

LEYSE, CARL F(ERDINAND), SPACE NUCLEAR PROPULSION & POWER, NUCLEAR REACTOR TECHNOLOGY & DESIGN. *Current Pos:* CONSULT, 85- *Personal Data:* b Kewaunee, Wis, Feb 11, 17; m 46, Rhodora Stearns; c Karen E & Dale R. *Educ:* Univ Wis, BS, 48. *Prof Exp:* Phys sci aide rocket res, Naval Res Lab, 48; mech eng, Argonne Nat Lab, 48-51; chief eng res sect, Atomic Energy Div, Phillips Petrol Co, 51-56; tech dir, Internuclear Co, 56-59; asst mgr, Nuclear Dept, Res Div, Curtiss-Wright Corp, 59-60; mem staff, Gen Atomics Div, Gen Dynamics Corp, 60-61; pres, Internuclear Co, 61-63; mgr, Nuclear & Radiation Safety Dept, Reon Div, Aerojet Gen Corp, 63-67; mgr, Nuclear Safety, Aerojet Nuclear Systs Co, 67-72, dir prog develop, Aerojet Nuclear Co, 72-76; mgt tech develop, Idaho Nat Engr Lab, 76-84. *Mem:* Am Nuclear Soc; Am Inst Aeronaut & Astronaut; Nat Space Soc. *Res:* Development of technology, concepts and designs for nuclear reactors for research, materials and component testing, electrical power generation, space propulsion and space power. *Mailing Add:* 2860 Holly Pl Idaho Falls ID 83402-4632

LEYSIEFFER, FREDERICK WALTER, MATHEMATICS, PROBABILITY. *Current Pos:* From asst prof to assoc prof, 64-82, assoc head dept, 69-76, chmn dept, 81-87 & 90-93, actg dean, Col Arts & Sci, 94-95, PROF STATIST, FLA STATE UNIV, 82-, ASSOC DEAN, COL ARTS & SCI, 94- *Personal Data:* b Milwaukee, Wis, Jan 30, 33; m 64, Annelise Carlsen; c Kirsten, Suzanne & Beth. *Educ:* Univ Wis-Madison, BA, 55, MA, 56; Univ Mich, PhD(math), 64. *Concurrent Pos:* Vis lectr, Sheffield Univ, Sheffield, Eng, 73-74, Leverhulme Commonwealth-Am fel, 73. *Mem:* Am Math Soc; Am Statist Asn; Math Asn Am; Inst Math Statist; AAAS; Sigma Xi. *Res:* Probability theory; stochastic processes; sampling theory; environmental statistics. *Mailing Add:* Dept Statist Fla State Univ Tallahassee FL 32306-3033. *E-Mail:* fleysief@mailer.fsu.edu

LEYSON, JOSE FLORANTE JUSTININANE, HUMAN SEXUALITY, URODYNAMICS. *Current Pos:* fel spinal cord, 76-77, CLIN CHIEF, SPINAL CORD INJURY UNIT, VET ADMIN HOSP, ORANGE, NJ, 77-; ASSOC PROF UROL, NJ MED SCH, 88- *Personal Data:* b Philippines, Aug 17, 36; m 89, Karen Sullivan; c Meghan M & Erin E. *Educ:* Cebu Inst Technol, BS, 65, MD, 70; Am Bd Urol, dipl, 79. *Hon Degrees:* MS, US Army Comdr & Gen Staff Col, Kans, 92. *Honors & Awards:* Cert Achievement, Am Asn Phys Therapists, 88. *Prof Exp:* Fel entom, US Agency Int Develop, 70-71; fel sexuality, Johns Hopkins Hosp, 76. *Concurrent Pos:* Fel urodynamics, Yale Univ Hosp, 78; Vis prof urodynamics, Yale Univ Hosp, 79; fel sex educ & parenthood, Am Univ, Washington, DC, 81; consult, Urodynamics, Bronx Vet Admin Hosp, NY, 79, Forum, Essence & MS Quarterly Mag, 78- & AMA Archives Internal Med; dir, Urodynamics & Sex Clin, Vet Admin Hosp, NJ, 79- & Sexual Dysfunction Ctr, Newark, NJ, 80-; prof sexuality, Fairleigh Dickinson Univ, NJ, 80-85; chief, Urol Hosp Ctr Essex Co, Cedar Groves, NJ. *Mem:* Philippines Asn Sexologists (am pres, 80-82); Philippine Med Asn Am; Am Urol Asn Inc; Am Col Surg; Laser Soc; Am Col Clin Sexologists. *Res:* Sexuality for both abled-bodied and disabled persons; drugs or electrical stimulations to produce erection in impotent patients; ways to produce urination in patients with paralysis and spinal defects due to injury or birth defects; laser erectiometer; erection pacemaker; author of two books; ointment for erection or orgasm. *Mailing Add:* Spinal Cord Injury Unit Vet Admin Hosp Med Ctr East Orange NJ 07019

LEZNOFF, CLIFFORD CLARK, ORGANIC CHEMISTRY, PHTHALOCYANINES. *Current Pos:* from asst prof to assoc prof, 67-79, PROF ORG CHEM, YORK UNIV, 80-, CHAIR CHEM, 90- *Personal Data:* b Montreal, Que, May 30, 40; m 63; c 3. *Educ:* McGill Univ, BSc, 61, PhD(org chem), 65. *Prof Exp:* Fel org chem, Northwestern Univ, 64-65; Nat Res Coun Can overseas fel, Cambridge Univ, 65-67. *Concurrent Pos:* Vis prof, Weizmann Inst Sci, 73-74, Australian Nat Univ, 80-81 & Univ BC, 87-88. *Mem:* Am Chem Soc; Chem Inst Can. *Res:* Polymer supports in organic synthesis; synthesis of chiral compounds, pheromones, phthalocyanines and flourinated heterocyclic compounds; phthalocyanines in photodynamic therapy of cancer, multinuclear phthalocyanines. *Mailing Add:* Dept Chem York Univ Downsview ON M3J 1P3 Can. *Fax:* 416-736-5936; *E-Mail:* leznoff@yorku.ca

L'HEUREUX, JACQUES (JEAN), COSMIC RAY PHYSICS, ASTROPHYSICS. *Current Pos:* SR RES ASSOC, UNIV CHICAGO, 78- *Personal Data:* b Trois-Rivieres, Que, Dec 20, 39; div; c 3. *Educ:* Univ Montreal, BSc, 61; Univ Chicago, MSc, 62, PhD(physics), 66. *Prof Exp:* Res assoc physics, Univ Chicago, 66-69; asst prof physics, Univ Ariz, 69-77. *Mem:* Fel Am Phys Soc; Am Geophys Union. *Res:* Primary cosmic ray electrons; solar modulation of cosmic rays; primary heavy nuclei at high energies. *Mailing Add:* Univ Del Bartol Res Inst Newark DE 19716

L'HEUREUX, MAURICE VICTOR, BIOCHEMISTRY. *Current Pos:* assoc, 46-49, from asst prof to prof, 49-79, EMER PROF BIOCHEM, STRITCH SCH MED, LOYOLA UNIV CHICAGO, 79- *Personal Data:* b Lewiston, Maine, May 23, 14; m 46, Patricia M St Pierre; c Victor, Pierre, David, Paul & Claude. *Educ:* Col Holy Cross, BS, 36, MS, 37; Yale Univ, PhD(biochem), 44. *Prof Exp:* Control chemist, Stokely Bros-Van Camp, Inc, Ind, 40-41. *Mem:* Am Soc Biochem & Molecular Biol. *Res:* Lipid metabolism; modifying and regulatory effects of parathyroid hormone, calcitonin and vitamin D upon calcium metabolism. *Mailing Add:* 304 W Kenilworth Ave Villa Park IL 60181-2524

LHILA, RAMESH CHAND, PRESSURE SENSITIVE ADHESIVES, POLYMER BLENDS. *Current Pos:* DIR RES, TESA TUCK INC, ROCHELLE, NY, 88- *Personal Data:* b Rangoon, Burma, India. *Educ:* Calcutta Univ, BS, 72, BTech, 75; Univ Akron, PhD(polymer sci), 83. *Prof Exp:* Res chemist, Tuck Industs, New Rochelle, NY, 82, group leader res & develop, 82-83, asst dir res & develop, 83-87, tech dir gen prod, 87-88. *Concurrent Pos:* Hon instr, St Xavier's Col, Calcutta, India, 72. *Mem:* Am Chem Soc; Am Chem Soc Polymer Chem Div; Am Chem Soc Rubber Div; fel Plastics & Rubber Inst; Soc Plastics Engrs. *Res:* Pressure sensitive adhesive tapes based on rubber, acrylics and silicones by various methods including solution, hot melt and water-based coatings; coating technology; emulsion and solution polymerisation; polymer blends and rubber-modified high impact plastics. *Mailing Add:* 127 Gorski Dr South Windsor CT 06074

LHOTKA, JOHN FRANCIS, histochemistry, microanatomy; deceased, see previous edition for last biography

LI, C(HING) C(HUNG), PATTERN RECOGNITION & IMAGE PROCESSING, BIOCYBERNETICS. *Current Pos:* Asst prof, 59-60, 61-62, assoc prof, 62-67, PROF ELEC ENG, UNIV PITTSBURGH, 67-, PROF COMPUT SCI, 77- *Personal Data:* b Changshu, China, Mar 30, 32; m 61, Hanna Wu; c William Wei-Lin & Vincent Wei-Tsin. *Educ:* Nat Taiwan Univ, BS, 54; Northwestern Univ, MS, 56, PhD(elec eng), 61. *Honors & Awards:* Cert Merit, Radiol Soc NAm, 79. *Concurrent Pos:* Vis assoc prof, Univ Calif, Berkeley, 64, vis prin scientist, Alza Corp, Palo Alto, Calif, 70; chmn, Biocybernetics Tech Comt, Inst Elec & Electronics Engrs Systs, Man & Cybernetics Soc, 72-79, admin comt, 77-79; prin investr NSF Res Grants, 75-81, 85-87, Commonwealth Pa, Dept Health, 77-79, Western Pa Advan Technol Ctr, 83-84, 86-88, Health Res & Serv Found, 85-86 & DARPA/AFOSR, 90-93; Chmn, Cybernetics Standing Comt, 79-93; exec comt, Pattern Anal & Mach Intel Tech Comt, Inst Elec & Electronics Engrs, Comput Soc, 81-84; consult, Westinghouse Res Develop Ctr, 81; fac res partic, Dept Energy, Pittsburgh Energy Technol Ctr, 82, 83, 85, 88 & 89; Biomed Pattern Recognition Tech Comt, Int Asn Pattern Recognition, 83-, chmn, 87-90; assoc ed, Pattern Recognition, 85-; sabbatical leave, Lab Info & Decision Systs, Mass Inst Technol, 88. *Mem:* AAAS; fel Inst Elec & Electronics Engrs; Pattern Recognition Soc; Biomed Eng Soc; NY Acad Sci; Sigma Xi. *Res:* Application of wavelet transform to image processing; computer vision; biomedical pattern recognition; artificial neural networks and intelligent systems; biocybernetics. *Mailing Add:* Dept Elec Eng Univ Pittsburgh Pittsburgh PA 15261. *Fax:* 412-624-8003; *E-Mail:* ccl@vms.cis.pitt.edu

LI, CHE-YU, MATERIALS SCIENCE & ENGINEERING. *Current Pos:* Res assoc, 60-62, from asst prof to assoc prof, 62-72, PROF MAT SCI & ENG, CORNELL UNIV, 72-, DIR, ELECTRONIC PACKING PROG, 90-, DIR, DEPT MAT SCI & ENG, 93- *Personal Data:* b Honan, China, Nov 15, 34; m 61; c 3. *Educ:* Nat Taiwan Univ, BSE, 54; Cornell Univ, PhD(chem eng), 60. *Concurrent Pos:* Mem staff, US Steel Res Ctr, 65-66; mem staff, Argonne Nat Lab, 69-71, consult, Nuclear Mat, Electronic Packaging. *Mem:* Am Phys Soc; Am Inst Mining, Metall & Petrol Engrs. *Res:* Mechanical behavior; radiation damage; surface and interface; development of a state variable description of mechanical properties of crystalline solids; micro-mechanical testing; nuclear materials, electronic packaging, high-temperature engineering alloys. *Mailing Add:* Bard Hall Cornell Univ Ithaca NY 14853. *Fax:* 607-255-6575; *E-Mail:* alliance@msc.cornell.edu

LI, CHI, polymer physics, multiphase polymer systems, for more information see previous edition

LI, CHIA-CHUAN, MATERIALS SCIENCE, MICROELECTRONICS. *Current Pos:* PROG MGR, ELECTRO-OPTICAL CTR, ROCKWELL INT CORP, 85- *Personal Data:* b Taipei, Taiwan, Dec 29, 46; US citizen; m 83, Clemencia Vasquez; c Angie & Andrew. *Educ:* Nat Taiwan Univ, BS, 69; Rutgers Univ, MS, 74; Univ Mich, PhD(mat eng), 77; Pepperdine Univ, MBA, 86. *Prof Exp:* Sr engr, Gen Atomic Co, 77-84; syst engr, Electro-Optical & Data Systs, Hughes Aircraft Co, 84-85. *Concurrent Pos:* Lectr, San Diego City Col, 80-83. *Mem:* Metall Soc; Sigma Xi; Am Soc Metals. *Res:* Metallurgy, friction and wear; high temperature materials and coatings; infrared focal plane array materials; signal processing electronics; electro-optical systems. *Mailing Add:* 11 Meadow Wood Dr Trabuco Canyon CA 92679

LI, CHIA-YU, ELECTROANALYTICAL CHEMISTRY. *Current Pos:* from asst prof to assoc prof, 73-84, PROF CHEM, E CAROLINA UNIV, 84- *Personal Data:* b Shanghai, China, May 5, 41; m 69; c 3. *Educ:* Taiwan Normal Univ, BS, 63; Univ Louisville, MS, 67; Wayne State Univ, PhD(anal chem), 72. *Prof Exp:* Res fel electrochem, Univ Ariz, 72-73. *Mem:* Am Chem Soc; Sigma Xi. *Res:* Electrochemistry of organic and biological model compounds; computer-controlled electrochemical instrumentation; electrochemical detecting techniques for high performance liquid chromatography; electrochemical detection of trace elements. *Mailing Add:* Dept Chem E Carolina Univ Greenville NC 27858

LI, CHING CHUN, POPULATION GENETICS, BIOMETRICS. *Current Pos:* RETIRED. *Personal Data:* b Tientsin, China, Oct 27, 12; nat US; m 41, Clara Lem; c Carol & Steven. *Educ:* Nanking Univ, BS, 36; Cornell Univ, PhD(plant breeding), 40. *Prof Exp:* Plant breeder, Agr Exp Sta, Yenching Univ, 36-37; asst prof, Agr Col, Nat Kwangsi Univ, 42-43; prof genetics & biomet, Agr Col, Nanking Univ, 43-46; prof agron & head dept, Peking Univ, 46-50; from res fel to asst prof, Univ Pittsburgh, 51-58, from assoc prof to prof, 58-75, head dept, 69-75, univ prof human genetics, Grad Sch Pub Health, 75-82. *Mem:* Am Soc Human Genetics (pres, 60); AAAS; Int Statist Inst; Biomet Soc; fel Am Statist Asn; Academia Sinica. *Res:* Biometry; design of experiments; population genetics; path analysis. *Mailing Add:* Dept Human Genetics Univ Pittsburgh Grad Sch Pub Health Pittsburgh PA 15261

LI, CHIN-HSIU, ENGINEERING MECHANICS, THERMAL TECHNOLOGY. *Current Pos:* assoc sr res engr, Gen Motors Res Labs, 72-76, sr res engr, eng mech, 76-81, staff res engr, Mech Res Dept, 81-85, sr staff res engr, Eng Mech Dept, 85-88, Engine Res Dept, 88-94, PRIN RES ENGR & SECT MGR, ENGINE RES DEPT, RES & DEVELOP CTR, GEN MOTORS RES LABS, 94- *Personal Data:* b Taiwan, China, Jan 3, 38; m 69; c 2. *Educ:* Nat Cheng Kung Univ, BS, 61; Nat Cent Univ, MS, 64; Brigham Young Univ, MS, 66; Univ Mich, PhD(eng mech), 68. *Honors & Awards:* McCuen Award, Gen Motors Labs, 84. *Prof Exp:* Res assoc fluid mech, Case Western Res Univ, 69-71; vis assoc prof, Nat Cheng Kung Univ, 71-72; res assoc, Univ Mich, 72. *Mem:* Soc Automotive Engrs; Am Soc Mech Engrs. *Res:* Hydrodynamic stability; fluid flow and heat transfer; lubrication theory; rotor dynamics; mechanics of automotive components; computer-aided engine design, ceramic engines; engine thermostructure. *Mailing Add:* Engine Res Dept Gen Motors Res Labs Warren MI 48090

LI, CHI-TANG, PHYSICAL CHEMISTRY, CRYSTALLOGRAPHY. *Current Pos:* SR ANALYTICAL SPECIALIST, ANALYTICAL SCI, DOW CORNING, 83- *Personal Data:* b Ningtu, Kiangsi, China, Oct 16, 34; m 62, Yen L Lee; c Mary, Florence, Albert & Thomas. *Educ:* Nat Taiwan Univ, BS, 55; Univ Louisville, MS, 59; Mont State Univ, PhD(chem), 64. *Prof Exp:* Scientist, Adv Mat Res Sect, Owens-Ill Tech Ctr, 64-67, sr scientist, 67-78; supvr fuel-cell mat res, Inst Gas Technol, 78-80, prin engr, 80-82. *Mem:* Am Chem Soc; Am Crystallog Asn; Am Ceramic Soc. *Res:* Crystal structure and chemistry; studies of glass ceramic materials, research on high temperature materials; fuel cell research; fiber and composite development; x-ray diffraction of silicone materials. *Mailing Add:* Mat Res 1510 Timber Dr Midland MI 48642

LI, CHOU H(SIUNG), PHYSICAL METALLURGY, STATISTICS. *Current Pos:* PRES, LINTEL TECHNOL, INC, 81- *Personal Data:* b Haining, China, June 8, 23; US citizen; m 53; c 2. *Educ:* Chiao Tung Univ, BS, 44; Purdue Univ, MS, 49, PhD(phys metall), 51. *Honors & Awards:* David Gessner Prize, Am Soc Eng Educ, 55 & 56; NASA New Technol Innovation Award, 77. *Prof Exp:* Metallurgist, RCA, 51-59; sr scientist, Shockley Transistor Corp, 59-60; mgr semiconductors, Gen Instrument Corp, 60-62;

930 / LI

sr res scientist, Grumman Aerospace Corp, 62-77; staff technologist, Singer Co, 78-79; dir, Res & Develop, Semi-Alloys, 80-81. *Concurrent Pos:* Ed, Chinese Inst Engrs J, 65-68; NASA Skylab consult specialist, 72-75; adj prof mat sci, State Univ NY, Stony Brook, 77-85; consult, 77-82; prin investr, 84-91. *Mem:* Sr mem Inst Elec & Electronics Engrs; sr mem Am Soc Qual Control; Am Inst Mining, Metall & Petrol Engrs; Am Phys Soc; Chinese Inst Engrs. *Res:* self-optimizing automation; ceramic bonding and coating; very large scale integration and ultralarge scale integration microcircuits; intelligent manufacturing, servicing, training and education; automatic generation of optimized knowledge bases, expert systems and computer software; friction; physics of failures; reliability; computer programming; artificial intelligence. *Mailing Add:* 379 Elm Dr Roslyn NY 11576

LI, CHUNG-HSIUNG, heat transfer, fluid mechanics, for more information see previous edition

LI, CHUNG-SHENG, DIGITAL LIBRARY, MULTIMEDIA DATABASE. *Current Pos:* researcher, 90-91, RES STAFF MEM, IBM T J WATSON RES CTR, 91-, MGR, 96- *Personal Data:* b Nantou, Taiwan, Sept 26, 62; US citizen. *Educ:* Nat Taiwan Univ, BSEE, 84; Univ Calif, Berkeley, MS, 89, PhD(elec eng & comput sci), 91. *Prof Exp:* Programmer, Data Processing Ctr, Ministry Finance, Taiwan, 82; teaching asst, Dept Elec Eng, Nat Taiwan Univ, 83-84; instr electronics & commun theory, Air Force Comm & Electronics Acad, Taiwan, 85-86; instr spectrum anal, Dept Elec Eng & Comput Sci Univ Calif, 86-87; researcher, Univ Calif, Berkeley, Elec Res Lab, 87-90. *Mem:* Inst Elec & Electronics Engrs. *Res:* Development of protocols, system architectures and innovative devices for high-bandwidth hybrid- and all-optical networks for local area networks, metropolitan area networks and wide area network applications; development of optical interconnects for short-distance computer applications. *Mailing Add:* IBM T J Watson Res Ctr PO Box 704 Yorktown Heights NY 10598. *Fax:* 914-784-7455; *E-Mail:* csli@watson.ibm.com

LI, FREDERICK P, CANCER ETHOLOGY. *Current Pos:* PROF CLIN CANCER EPIDEMIOL, HARVARD SCH PUB HEALTH, 80-, PROF MED. *Personal Data:* b China, May 7, 40; US citizen; m 72, Elaine Shiang; c 3. *Educ:* Univ NY, Rochester, BA, 60, MD, 65; Georgetown Univ, MA, 69. *Hon Degrees:* MA Harvard Univ. *Honors & Awards:* Mott Prize, General Motors Cancer Res Found, 95. *Prof Exp:* Epidemiologist, Nat Cancer Inst, 67-80. *Mem:* Am Soc Clin Oncol; Am Asn Cancer Res. *Res:* Identification of persons at high risk of cancer; genetic and environmental causes of cancer susceptability. *Mailing Add:* 44 Binney St Boston MA 02115. *Fax:* 617-632-3161

LI, GEORGE SU-HSIANG, ORGANIC CHEMISTRY. *Current Pos:* sr res chem, 74-77, res assoc, 77-86, RES SCIENTIST II, POLYMER RES, BP CO, OHIO, 87- *Personal Data:* b Chunking, China, Oct 24, 43; m 71, Tung-Chia Wang; c Kenneth C. *Educ:* Cheng Kung Univ, BS, 65; Purdue Univ, PhD(org chem), 71. *Prof Exp:* Res assoc, Med Chem Dept, Purdue Univ, 71-73. *Mem:* Am Chem Soc. *Res:* Synthesis of latex based polymers; exploration of novel polymers with high heat resistance and barrier characteristics; polymer modification and alloying; granted 50 patents. *Mailing Add:* 4440 Warrensville Ctr Rd Cleveland OH 44128-2837

LI, GUANG CHAO, SOIL CHEMISTRY, SURFACE ANALYSIS. *Current Pos:* grad asst, 87-92, assoc, 92, SCI AID, UNIV IDAHO, 93- *Personal Data:* b Lin-tong, Shaanixi, China, Nov 30, 61; m 86, Xiao Y Yao; c Rebecca Y. *Educ:* Northwestern Agr Univ, BS, 83; Univ Idaho, MS, 89, PhD(soil sci), 92. *Prof Exp:* Instr soil sci, Northwestern Agr Univ, China, 83-87. *Mem:* Soil Sci Soc China; Soil Sci Soc Am; Am Soc Agron. *Res:* Soil nutrient availability in soils; effects of soil and environmental factors on soil nutrients in soils; the use of statistic analysis method in soil fertility research. *Mailing Add:* Soil Sci Div Univ Idaho Moscow ID 83844. *E-Mail:* guangcha@idui1.csrv.uidaho.edu

LI, HAIZHANG, OPTOELECTRONICAL INSTRUMENTS, PRECISION ENGINEERING. *Current Pos:* SR ENGR, CONTINENTAL OPTICAL CORP, 93- *Personal Data:* b Shanghai, China, Feb 10, 46; m 90, Xiaodan; c Ying. *Educ:* Nanjing Univ Sci & Technol, BS, 78; Beijing Univ Sci & Technol, MS, 82; Univ Minn, MS, 89, PhD(cad/cae), 93. *Honors & Awards:* Space Act Award, NASA. *Prof Exp:* Instr optics, Nanjing Univ Sci & Technol, 82-84; hon fel, Univ Minn, 84-85, res asst, 85-93. *Concurrent Pos:* Prin investr, Marshall Space Flight Ctr, NASA, 94-95 & 96- *Mem:* Soc Photo-Optical Instrumentation Engrs. *Res:* X-ray mirror metrology; SR mirror metrology; pencil laser beam interferometry; laser beam focusing and steering drives; fiber optics; polarization optics; digital image processing; holographic interferometry; acoustic imaging. *Mailing Add:* 15 Power Dr Hauppauge NY 11788. *Fax:* 516-582-1054; *E-Mail:* haizhang@mindspring.com

LI, HENG-CHUN, BIOCHEMISTRY. *Current Pos:* From asst prof to assoc prof, 71-81, PROF BIOCHEM, MT SINAI MED CTR, 86- *Personal Data:* b Canton, China, Oct 22, 38. *Educ:* Nat Taiwan Univ, BS, 62; Cornell Univ, PhD(biochem), 68. *Mem:* AAAS; Am Soc Biochem & Molecular Biol. *Mailing Add:* Dept Biochem Mount Sinai Med Ctr 5th Ave & 100th St PO Box 1020 New York NY 10029

LI, HONG, SURFACE SCIENCE, THIN FILMS. *Current Pos:* SR SCIENTIST, GROUP TECH CTR, BOC GROUP, INC, 91- *Personal Data:* b China, Feb 25, 62. *Educ:* Zhejiang Univ, China, BS, 82; Univ Wis, MS, 84, PhD(physics), 88. *Prof Exp:* Res asst surface sci, Lab Surface Studies, Univ Wis, 84-88; res assoc, Dept Math Sci & Eng, State Univ NY, Stony Brook, 88-91. *Mem:* Am Phys Soc; Am Vacuum Soc. *Res:* Surface science; structure of surfaces, interfaces and thin films; processing and characterization of epitaxially grown thin films on metals, semiconductors and polymers; development and application of surface analytical spectroscopies and microscopies. *Mailing Add:* Intel Corp F9-07 4100 Sara Rd Rio Rancho NM 87124

LI, HSIN LANG, polymer science, for more information see previous edition

LI, HSUEH MING, POLYMER CHEMISTRY. *Current Pos:* res chemist polymer res, 73-79, sr res chemist, 79-85, RES ASSOC, ETHYL CORP, 85- *Personal Data:* b Taiwan, Rep China, Oct 25, 39; US citizen; m 63; c 2. *Educ:* Tunghai Univ, Taiwan, BS, 62; Southern Methodist Univ, MS, 66; Polytech Inst Brooklyn, PhD(polymer chem), 71. *Prof Exp:* Fel x-ray diffraction, Polytech Inst Brooklyn, 70-72; res assoc polymer chem, Midland Macromolecular Inst, 72-73. *Mem:* Am Chem Soc. *Res:* Opacifying plastic pigment; polymeric flame retardants based on phosphazene-synthesis and evaluation; synthesis, characterization and mechanism of linear and cyclic phosphonitrillic chloride oligomers; advanced composites, specialty glasses, high-tech ceramics. *Mailing Add:* Albemarie Corp 8000 GSRI Ave Baton Rouge LA 70820-7497

LI, HUA, SEMICONDUCTOR LASERS, NONLINEAR DYNAMICS IN OPTICAL SYSTEMS. *Current Pos:* sr res engr, 90-96, instr optoelectronics, 95, RES SCIENTIST, CTR HIGH TECHNOL MAT, UNIV NMEX, 97- *Personal Data:* b Xiam, China, Sept 28, 45; div; c Jie L. *Educ:* Beijing Univ, MS, 81; Hannover Univ, PhD, 90. *Prof Exp:* Instr optics, Physics Dept, Northwestern Univ, China, 81-88. *Concurrent Pos:* Vis scholar, Phys Tech Inst Ger, 85-90. *Mem:* Optical Soc Am; Inst Elec & Electronics Engrs. *Res:* Semiconductor laser systems including noise properties, modulation characteristics, mode structure and polization properties; different routes to chaos in edge emitting laser diodes; vertical cavity surface emitting lasers; unstable resonator high power laser diodes; optical feedback on external injections. *Mailing Add:* 1419 Girard NE No 5 Albuquerque NM 87106. *Fax:* 505-277-6433; *E-Mail:* huali@chtm.unm.edu

LI, HUNG CHIANG, statistics, analytical mathematics, for more information see previous edition

LI, J(AMES) C(HEN) M(IN), MATERIALS SCIENCE, MECHANICAL ENGINEERING. *Current Pos:* ALBERT ARENDT HOPEMAN PROF ENG, UNIV ROCHESTER, 71- *Personal Data:* b Nanking, China, Apr 12, 25; m 50; c 3. *Educ:* Nat Cent Univ, China, BS, 47; Univ Wash, MS, 51, PhD, 53. *Honors & Awards:* Mathewson Gold Medal, Metall Soc, 72; Robert Mehl Gold Medal, Am Inst Mining, Metall & Petrol Engrs & Inst Metals lectr, 78; Lu Tse-Hon Medal, Chinese Soc Mat Sci, 88; Acta Metallurgica Gold Medal, Am Soc Metals Int, 90. *Prof Exp:* Res chemist, Sch Med, Univ Wash, 51-53; res chemist & fel, Univ Calif, 53-55; supvr res proj, Mfg Chemists Asn, Carnegie Inst Technol, 55-56; phys chemist, Res Labs, Westinghouse Elec Corp, 56-57; scientist, Fundamental Res Lab, US Steel Corp, 57-60, sr scientist, 60-64, staff scientist, 64-69; mgr strength physics dept, Mat Res Ctr, Allied Chem Corp, 69-71. *Concurrent Pos:* Vis prof, Columbia Univ, 64-65, adj prof, 65-71; consult, Mat Res Ctr, Allied Chem Corp, 71-79, NSF, 75-77 & US Steel Corp, 76; vis prof, Ruhr Universitat Bochum, Ger, 78-79; vis scientist, Naval Res Lab, 84-85, 88; Alexander von Humboldt sr award, 78-79. *Mem:* Fel Am Phys Soc; fel Am Inst Mining, Metall & Petrol Engrs; fel Am Soc Metals; Mat Res Soc; Am Soc Mech Engrs. *Res:* Dislocations and defects; plastic deformation; amorphous and polymeric materials; microstructural interactions; equilibirum and non-equilibrium phenomena. *Mailing Add:* Dept Mech Eng Univ Rochester Rochester NY 14627

LI, JACK H, PHARMACOLOGY. *Current Pos:* res pharmacologist, 82-88, PRIN PHARMACOLOGIST, ZENECA PHARMACEUT CORP, 88-, GROUP LEADER, 90- *Personal Data:* b Shanghai, China, Aug 27, 42. *Educ:* Univ Calif, Berkeley, BS, 67; Tufts Univ, PhD(physiol), 73. *Prof Exp:* Researcher membrane physiol, Boston Med Sch, 73-74; med asst prof, Univ Geneva, Switz, 74-77; res assoc, Univ Hamburg, Ger, 77-82. *Mem:* Am Soc Pharmacol & Exp Therapeut; Biophys Soc; NY Acad Sci. *Mailing Add:* Zeneca Pharmaceut Corp 1800 Concord Pike Wilmington DE 19850-5437

LI, JAMES CC, MEDICINE. *Current Pos:* PRIN ASSOC, DEPT MED, HARVARD MED SCH, 84- *Educ:* Nat Taiwan Univ, BS, 61, MS, 63; Boston Univ Sch Med, PhD(biochem), 71. *Prof Exp:* Asst res fel, Academia Sinica, Taiwan, China, 63-67; res fel microbiol & molecular genetics, Harvard Med Sch, 70-72; res assoc exp biol, Worcester Found, 72-74; res chemist, Dept Microbiol & Molecular Genetics, Harvard Med Sch, 74-76, prin assoc, 76-79; clin chemists, Dept Path, New Eng Deaconess Hosp, 80-82; ASSOC DIR, MED RES LAB, HEBREW REHAB CTR AGED, 82- *Res:* Biochemistry and cell biology in medical research; all types cell culture including cultivation of cells from primary and secondary cultures; experienced in cell culture techniques such as growing cells in monolayer; roller bottle or spinner bottle; semisolid agar colonizing; cell volume determination. *Mailing Add:* 26 Alton Ct Brookline MA 02146-6535

LI, JANE CHIAO, APPLIED STATISTICS. *Current Pos:* mgr, 81-86, sr mgr data anal & processing, 86-95, SR MGR STATIST & COMPUT APPLNS, UOP INC, 95- *Personal Data:* b Shanghai, China, May 1, 39; US citizen; m 63, Norman N; c Rebecca H & David. *Educ:* Hunter Col, BS, 63; Rutgers Univ, MS, 65, PhD(statist), 71. *Prof Exp:* Res chemist, Endo Labs, Long Island, NY, 61-63; statist consult comput sci & statist, Rutgers Univ, 74-78; sr statistician, Paramins Div, Exxon Chem Co, 78-79, sect head world-wide product testing, 79-81. *Concurrent Pos:* Course dir, Ctr Prof Achievement, 86-; co-chair, Am Inst Chem Engrs Symposium 87 & 88. *Mem:* Sigma Xi; Am Statist Asn; Inst Math Statist; Am Soc Qual Control. *Res:* Design and analysis of mixture experiments with process variables; statistical design of experiments and analysis of data for research and manufacturing; statistical process control for continuous and batch chemical processes; database management for petroleum and chemical processes; total quality management. *Mailing Add:* 620 Rolling Lane Arlington Heights IL 60004

LI, JEANNE B, ANALYTICAL CHEMISTRY, BIOCHEMISTRY. *Current Pos:* asst prof physiol, 73-79, res assoc pediat, 79-95, SR APPL CHEMIST, WATERS DIV, HERSHEY MED CTR, PA STATE UNIV, 93- *Personal Data:* b New York, NY, Apr 15, 44. *Educ:* Vassar Col, AB, 66; Harvard Univ, PhD(biochem), 71. *Prof Exp:* Res fel physiol, Harvard Med Sch, 71-73. *Concurrent Pos:* Nat Cancer Inst & Muscular Dystrophy Asn fels, Harvard Med Sch, 71-73; Am Diabetes Asn grant, Hershey Med Ctr, Pa State Univ, 74-76. *Mem:* Am Physiol Soc; AAAS. *Res:* Applied research instrumentation. *Mailing Add:* Prin Scientist Waters Corp 34 Maple St Milford MA 01757-2437

LI, JOHN KONG-JIANN, CARDIOVASCULAR DYNAMICS & INSTRUMENTATION. *Current Pos:* from asst prof to assoc prof, 79-89, dir biomed eng, 86, PROF BIOMED ENG, RUTGERS UNIV, 89- *Personal Data:* b Taiwan, China, Aug 28, 50; US citizen; m 74, Evangeline Sim; c Michael & Christopher. *Educ:* Univ Manchester, BSc, 72; Univ Pa, MSEng, 74, PhD(bioeng), 78. *Prof Exp:* Instr physics, Cent Found High Sch, London, 72; res fel bioeng, Univ Pa, 73-77, thesis supvr, 78-79. *Concurrent Pos:* Chief biomed engr cardiol, Presby Univ Pa Med Ctr, 77-79; prin investr, Rutgers Univ, NSF, 80-; chmn, Eng Med & Biol, Princeton Sect, Inst Elec & Electronics Engrs, 85-; vis scientist, Fedn Am Soc Exp Biol, 81-; adj prof surg & bioeng, Univ Med & Dent NJ, Rutgers Med Sch, 81- *Mem:* Inst Elec & Electronics Engrs; Am Physiol Soc; Am Heart Asn; fel Am Col Angiol; Am Soc Hypertension; Biomed Eng Soc. *Res:* Cardiovascular dynamics; biomedical instrumentation; diagnostic cardiology; comparative physiology; physiological controls; hypertension and myocardial ischemia; controlled drug delivery. *Mailing Add:* Dept Biomed Eng Rutgers Univ New Brunswick NJ 08903. *Fax:* 732-932-3753; *E-Mail:* jli@biomed.rutgers.edu

LI, JONATHAN J, HORMONAL CARCINOGENESIS, PHARMACOLOGY & TOXICOLOGY. *Current Pos:* VPRES SCI AFFAIRS, PHYTOSYN, INC, 92-; DIR, DIV ETIOLOGY & PREV HORMONAL CANCERS, CANCER CTR, MED CTR, UNIV KANS, 93-, PROF, DEPT PHARMACOL, TOXICOL & THERAPEUTICS, SCH MED, 93- *Personal Data:* b New York, NY; m, Sara A; c Christopher I & Stephanie S. *Educ:* Brown Univ, AB, 62; State Univ NY, PhD(pharmacol & biochem), 71. *Prof Exp:* Res fel, Dept Biol Chem, Lab Human Reproduction & Reproductive Biol, Harvard Med Sch, 71-74; asst dir, SDTU, Med Res Labs, Res & Endocrine Sect, Vet Admin Med Ctr, Minneapolis, 74-76, sr res scientist, 76-90, dir, Hormonal Carcinogenesis Lab, 83-90; Dorothy Otto Kennedy distinguished prof pharmaceut sci, Sch Pharm, Wash State Univ, 90-93, dir, Hormonal Carcinogenesis Lab, 90-93, assoc, Prog Genetics & Cell Biol, 91-93; dir, Cancer Prev Res Ctr, 92-93. *Concurrent Pos:* Co-founder & co-chmn, First Biennial Gordon Res Conf Hormonal Carcinogenesis, New Hampton Sch, NH, 85, chmn, Second Bienniel Gordon Res Conf, 87; vis prof, Inst Pharmacol & Toxicol, Univ Wurzburg, Ger, 89; sr lectr, Dept Pharmacol, Univ Minn, Minneapolis, 89-90; chmn, Int Symp Hormonal Carcanogenesis, Cancun, Mex, 91-, Stockholm, Sweden, 94, Seattle, WA, 98. *Mem:* Histochem Soc; AAAS; Am Asn Cancer Res; Am Soc Biochem & Molecular Biol; Endocrine Soc; Soc Toxicol; NY Acad Sci. *Res:* Etiology and prevention of hormonal cancers; pharmacology, toxicology and therapeutics; education of the biologic, cellular and molecular processes involved in hormonal carcinogenesis of the kidney, liver, breast and prostate; cell cycle and cell proliferation, aneuploidy, genomic instability, photo-oncogene and suppressor gene expression. *Mailing Add:* Div Etiology & Prev Hormonal Cancers Univ Kans Cancer Ctr 3901 Rainbow Blvd Suite 5008 Kansas City KS 66160-7312. *Fax:* 913-588-4740

LI, KAM W(U), MECHANICAL ENGINEERING. *Current Pos:* from asst prof to assoc prof mech eng, 67-73, assoc dean, Eng Col, 89-91, PROF MECH ENG, NDAK STATE UNIV, 73-, INTERIM CHMN MECH ENG DEPT, 93- *Personal Data:* b China, Feb 16, 34; m 56, Margaret; c Christopher & Charles. *Educ:* Chu Hai Col, Hong Kong, BSME, 57; Colo State Univ, MSME, 61; Okla State Univ, PhD, 65. *Prof Exp:* Asst prof, Tex A&I Univ, 65-67. *Concurrent Pos:* Consult engr, Scott Eng Sci Corp, 67-68; NSF Instnl Fund grants, NDak State Univ, 67-68 & 71; Dept Defense grant, 69; Am Soc Eng Educ-Ford Found resident fel, Northern States Power Co, Minneapolis, Minn, 71-72; eng consult, Chas T Main Inc, Boston, 73-80; USDA res grants, 74-78 & 76-78; consult, Ctr Prof Advan, NJ, 82-83. *Mem:* Am Soc Mech Engrs; NY Acad Sci. *Res:* Heat transfer; fluid dynamics; thermodynamics; power generation; thermal system design; applied mathematics; energy models; new power generation systems. *Mailing Add:* 2516 18th St S Moorhead MN 56560-4811

LI, KELVIN K, PHYSICS. *Current Pos:* PHYSICIST, BROOKHAVEN NAT LAB, 65- *Personal Data:* b Kwantung, China, Mar 25, 34; US citizen; m 65; c 4. *Educ:* McGill Univ, BEng, 58; Mass Inst Technol, PhD(physics), 64. *Mem:* Am Phys Soc. *Res:* Elementary particle interactions. *Mailing Add:* Dept Physics Brookhaven Nat Lab Upton NY 11973

LI, KUANG-PANG, ANALYTICAL CHEMISTRY. *Current Pos:* ASSOC PROF, DEPT CHEM, UNIV LOWELL, 80- *Personal Data:* b Kwang-tung, China, Oct 11, 38; c 3. *Educ:* Nat Taiwan Univ, BS, 61; Univ Ill, MS, 68, PhD(anal chem), 70. *Prof Exp:* Lectr chem, Kaohsiung Prov Inst Technol, Taiwan, 64-65; res assoc, Ariz State Univ, 70-72; res assoc, Univ Ill, 72-73; asst prof chem, Univ Fla, 73-80. *Mem:* Am Chem Soc; NY Acad Sci; AAAS. *Res:* Metallic ion transport in biomembranes; membrane interactions of carcinogenic polynuclear aromatics; theoretical and practical developments of chromatographic methods; excitation mechanism in inductively coupled plasma (ICP). *Mailing Add:* Dept Chem Univ Lowell 1 University Ave Lowell MA 01854-2881

LI, KUN, CHEMICAL ENGINEERING. *Current Pos:* assoc prof chem eng, 62-64, PROF CHEM ENG, CARNEGIE-MELLON UNIV, 64- *Personal Data:* b Kunming, China, Nov 20, 23; m 51; c 2. *Educ:* Nat Southwest Assoc Univ, China, BEng, 45; Carnegie Inst Technol, MS, 49, DSc, 52. *Prof Exp:* Res chemist, Petrol Res Lab, Carnegie Inst Technol, 52-55, supvr & sr res chemist, 55-56; sr res engr, Jones & Laughlin Steel Corp, 56-58, res assoc, 58-62. *Concurrent Pos:* Consult, Jones & Laughlin Steel Corp. *Mem:* Am Chem Soc; Am Inst Chem Engrs; Am Inst Mining, Metall & Petrol Engrs. *Res:* Fluid flow; kinetics of high-temperature processes. *Mailing Add:* 112 Alpine Circle Pittsburgh PA 15215-1902

LI, LI-HSIENG, BIOCHEMISTRY. *Current Pos:* sr res scientist, 65-73, SR SCIENTIST, UPJOHN CO, 88- *Personal Data:* b Peking, China, Dec 31, 33; m 60; c 2. *Educ:* Nat Taiwan Univ, BS, 55; Va Polytech Inst, MS, 62, PhD(biochem), 64. *Prof Exp:* Res assoc, Ind Univ, 64-65. *Mem:* Am Asn Cancer Res; Am Asn Biol Chemists. *Res:* mechanism of action of anticancer agent; immmunity and cancer; cell biology; experimental therapeutic and pharmacology. *Mailing Add:* 5128 Grosse Pointe St Kalamazoo MI 49008

LI, LING-FONG, THEORETICAL HIGH ENERGY PHYSICS. *Current Pos:* from asst prof to assoc prof, 74-83, PROF PHYSICS, CARNEGIE-MELLON UNIV, 83- *Personal Data:* b Fukien, China, Apr 17, 44; m 77; c Victor W & Herman W. *Educ:* Nat Taiwan Univ, BS, 65; Univ Pa, MS, 67, PhD(physics), 70. *Prof Exp:* Res assoc physics, Rockefeller Univ, 70-72; res assoc, Stanford Linear Accelerator Ctr, Stanford Univ, 72-74. *Mem:* Fel Am Phys Soc; Sigma Xi. *Res:* Unified theories of weak and electromagnetic interactions in relation to the fundamental structure of the elementary particles. *Mailing Add:* Dept Physics Carnegie-Mellon Univ Pittsburgh PA 15213. *Fax:* 412-681-0648; *E-Mail:* lfli@cmphys.phys.cmu.edu

LI, LU KU, biochemistry, protein chemistry, for more information see previous edition

LI, LUYUAN, enzymatic reaction mechanisms, protein structure-function relationships, for more information see previous edition

LI, MING CHIANG, PHYSICS, MATHEMATICS. *Current Pos:* asst prof, 68-72, ASSOC PROF PHYSICS, VA POLYTECH INST & STATE UNIV, 72- *Personal Data:* b Ningpo, China, June 18, 35; US citizen; m 65; c 2. *Educ:* Peking Univ, BS, 58; Univ Md, PhD(physics, math), 65. *Prof Exp:* Lectr physics, Norm Col Inner Mongolia, China, 58-61; res asst, Univ Md, 64-65; fel & mem sci, Inst Advan Study, 65-67. *Concurrent Pos:* Sr tech staff, Mitre Coop, 82-83; sr physicist, 83-88, group leader, Naval Res Lab, 88- *Mem:* Am Phys Soc; Inst Elec & Electronics Engrs. *Res:* Atomic and molecular physics; interferometry; laser optics; electronics counter measures radar development. *Mailing Add:* 11415 Bayard Dr Bowie MD 20721

LI, NORMAN N, MATERIALS SCIENCE & POLYMER ENGINEERING. *Current Pos:* CHIEF EXEC OFFICER, NL CHEM TECHNOL, INC, 95- *Personal Data:* b Shanghai, China, Jan 14, 33; US citizen; m 63, Jane C; c Rebecca H & David H. *Educ:* Taiwan Nat Univ, BS, 54; Wayne State Univ, MS, 57; Stevens Inst Technol, ScD(chem eng), 63. *Honors & Awards:* Am Chem Soc Award in Separation Sci & Technol, 88; Res Award, Am Inst Chem Eng Award, 88, Ernest Thiele Award, 95. *Prof Exp:* Chem engr, Shinlin Paper

& Pulp Co, 53 & Parke-Davis & Co, 56; instr chem, Newark Col Eng, 61-63; res engr, Exxon Res & Eng Co, 63-66, sr res engr, 66-70, res assoc, 70-77, sr res assoc, 77-81, head, Separation Sci Group, 76-81; dir separations res, UOP Inc, 81-84; dir separation sci & technol, Allied Signal Inc, 84-88, dir eng prod & process technol, 88-92, dir res & technol, 92-95. *Concurrent Pos:* Vis lectr, Newark Col Eng, 63-67; consult, Bell Aerosysts Co, 67; chmn, Gordon Res Conf Separations & Purification, 73, Gordon Res Conf Transport Phenomena in Membranes, 75, Eng Found Int Conf Separations, 84 & 87, Int Cong Membranes & Membrane Processes, 90. *Mem:* Nat Acad Eng; fel Am Inst Chem Engrs; Am Chem Soc; NAm Membrane Soc (pres, 91-93); Acad Sinica. *Res:* Mass transfer; surface chemistry; interfacial phenomena; transport through membranes; separation techniques; catalysis; material engineering. *Mailing Add:* 620 Rolling Lane Arlington Heights IL 60004. *Fax:* 847-398-7278

LI, PEI-CHING, CHEMICAL ENGINEERING. *Current Pos:* RETIRED. *Personal Data:* b Kiangsu, China, Nov 2, 19; m 45, Al-Juel Hsiao; c Robert Y, Lilian & Richard. *Educ:* Nat Southwest Assoc Univ, China, BE, 45; Univ Rochester, MS, 55, PhD(chem eng), 59. *Prof Exp:* Asst chem eng, Nat Southwest Assoc Univ, China, 44-46; teacher sci, Chungking Women's Norm Sch, 46-47; chemist & engr, Taiwan Sugar Corp, 47-53; asst chem eng, Univ Rochester, 54-57, res assoc glass, 58-59; mem res staff, Raytheon Co, 59-64; res scientist, Am Stand Corp, 64-65; res scientist ceramics div, IIT Res Inst, 65-68; adv engr, IBM Corp, 68-90. *Mem:* Sigma Xi. *Res:* Physical properties of molten glass, particularly enamel glass and binary system of borates; solid state reactions of ferrites; pyrolytic high temperature materials; chemical vapor deposition and plasma enhanced chemical vapor deposition of dielectric films. *Mailing Add:* 12466 Beechgrove Ct Moorpark CA 93021-3108

LI, PEN H (PAUL), HORTICULTURE, PLANT PHYSIOLOGY. *Current Pos:* PROF HORT & PLANT PHYSIOL, UNIV MINN, 63- *Personal Data:* b China, May 4, 33; US citizen; m 63; c 2. *Educ:* Ore State Univ, PhD(hort & plant physiol), 63. *Honors & Awards:* Dow Chem Co Award, Am Soc Hort Sci, 65, Alex Laurie Award, 66. *Concurrent Pos:* Vis prof, Int Potato Ctr, 73, Inst Low Temperature Sci, Hookkaido Univ, 76, Peking Agr Univ, 80 & Inst Plant Physiol, USSR Acad Sci, 87. *Mem:* Fel Am Soc Hort Sci; Am Soc Plant Physiologists; Potato Asn Am; Soc Cryobiol; Am Soc Agron. *Res:* Plant hardiness and stress physiology. *Mailing Add:* Dept Hort Sci Univ Minn St Paul 305 Alderman Hall 1970 Folwell Ave St Paul MN 55108-6007

LI, PETER WAI-KWONG, GEOMETRIC ANALYSIS, PARTIAL DIFFERENTIAL EQUATION. *Current Pos:* PROF MATH, UNIV CALIF, IRVINE, 91-, CHAIR, 93- *Personal Data:* b Hong Kong, Apr 18, 52; m 82, Glenna Seaver; c 3. *Educ:* Calif State Univ, BA, 74; Univ Calif, Berkeley, MA, 77, PhD(math), 79. *Prof Exp:* Res mem, Inst Advan Study, 79-80; asst prof math, Stanford Univ, 80-83; assoc prof, Purdue Univ, 83-85; prof, Univ Utah, 85-89 & Univ Ariz, 89-91. *Concurrent Pos:* Prin investr, NSF, 80-; vis asst prof, Univ Calif, San Diego, 80 & 81; Sloan fel, Alfred P Sloan Found, 82; res mem, Math Sci Res Inst, 83; Guggenheim fel, John Simon Guggenheim Found, 89; ed, Rocky Mountain J Math, 89-91 & Proc Am Math Soc, 91-; ed-in-chief, Commun Anal & Geom, 92- *Mem:* Am Math Soc. *Res:* Interplay between the geometry, topology and the analysis of geometrical objects. *Mailing Add:* Dept Math Univ Calif Irvine CA 92697-3875. *Fax:* 714-824-7993; *E-Mail:* pli@math.uci.edu

LI, ROUNAN, BIO-MATERIAL IMPLANTS. *Current Pos:* SR RES ENGR, NORTON CO. *Educ:* Univ Fla, PhD(mat sci), 91. *Mem:* Am Ceramic Soc. *Res:* Suprabrasive vitrified products and process research and development in order to improve performance, product consistency and grinding efficiency. *Mailing Add:* 32 Monroe St Shrewsbury MA 01545

LI, SAN, MOLECULAR SPECTROSCOPY, ANALYTICAL-PHYSICAL CHEMISTRY. *Current Pos:* RES SCIENTIST, BLACKLIGHT POWER CORP, MALVERN, PA, 97- *Personal Data:* b Chengdu, China, Sept 28, 62; m 87, Mei; c Hansen. *Educ:* Nankai Univ, China, BS, 83; Memphis State Univ, PhD(phys chem), 91. *Prof Exp:* Asst lectr chem, Chengdu Univ Sci & Technol, 83-86; res assoc, Univ Fla, 91-96; postdoctoral fel, Pac NW Nat Lab, 96-97. *Mem:* Am Chem Soc; Coblentz Soc Spectros. *Res:* Molecular spectroscopy studies of molecular structure, magnetic properties and photochemical reactions; new material designs, syntheses and characterizations. *Mailing Add:* 2500 George Washington Way No 209 Richland WA 99352. *E-Mail:* li@pine.circa.ufl.edu

LI, SARA ANTONIA, HORMONAL CARCINOGENESIS, GENE EXPRESSION. *Current Pos:* ASSOC PROF, DEPT PHARMACOL, KANS UNIV MED CTR, 93- *Personal Data:* b Monterrey, Mex, Aug 28, 42; US citizen; m 72, Jonathan J; c Christopher & Stephanie. *Educ:* Univ Labastida, Mex, BS, 63; State Univ NY, PhD(pharmacol), 69. *Prof Exp:* Res asst prof, Dept Pharmacol, Univ Minn, 77-90; assoc prof, Dept Pharmacol Sci, Wash State Univ, 90-93. *Mem:* Am Asn Cancer Res; Endocrine Soc. *Res:* Estrogen and its role in cancer; estrogen-induced kidney tumor of the Syrian hamster as a model system. *Mailing Add:* 12328 Catalina Leawood KS 66209. *Fax:* 913-588-4740; *E-Mail:* sli@kumc.edu

LI, SHENG-SAN, ELECTRICAL ENGINEERING. *Current Pos:* from asst prof to assoc prof, 68-78, PROF ELEC ENG, UNIV FLA, 78- *Personal Data:* b Hsin-Chu, Taiwan, Dec 10, 38; m 64, Chen Bih-Jean; c Jim, Grace & Jeanette. *Educ:* Cheng Kung Univ, Taiwan, BS, 62; Rice Univ, MS, 66, PhD(elec eng), 68. *Prof Exp:* Engr, China Elec Mfg Co, Taiwan, 63-64; teaching asst elec eng, Rice Univ, 64-67. *Concurrent Pos:* Electronic engr, Nat Bur Stands, 75-76; consult, Battelle Columbus Labs, Ohio, 75-77 & Harris Semiconductors Inc, Fla, 78-, Hughes Res Labs, 85-; vis prof, Nat Chiao-Tung Univ, Taiwan, 95. *Mem:* Am Phys Soc; sr mem Inst Elec & Electronics Engrs; Am Soc Testing & Measurements; Electrochem Soc. *Res:* Semiconductor device physics; transport phenomena in semiconductors; photoelectric effects in semiconductors and devices; defect and recombination properties in semiconductor materials and devices; solar cells and photodetectors; high-speed devices; quantum well infrared defectors; defects in scientific and optical instruments, materials and devices; silicon-on-insulator materials and devices. *Mailing Add:* 231 Benton Hall Univ Fla Gainesville FL 32611. *Fax:* 352-392-8671; *E-Mail:* shengli@eng.ufl.edu

LI, SHIN-HWA, CHEMICAL VAPOR DEPOSITION, III-V & GROUP IV SEMICONDUCTORS. *Current Pos:* ENGR, SGS-THOMSON MICROELECTRONICS, 94- *Personal Data:* b Taipei, Taiwan, Apr 8, 58; m 83, Yina Gan; c Crystal & Jason. *Educ:* Nat Cent Univ, Taiwan, BS, 80; Univ SWLa, Lafayette, MS, 85; Univ Utah, Salt Lake City, ME, 87, PhD(mat sci eng), 91. *Prof Exp:* Liaison officer, Repub China Marine Corps, 80-82; qual control engr, Ko-sheng Enterprises, Ltd, Taiwan, 82-83; res asst, Univ SWLa, Lafayette, 83-85; res asst, Univ Utah, Salt Lake City, 85-90, res assoc, 90-91; res scientist, Univ Mich, Ann Arbor, 91-94. *Concurrent Pos:* Res fel, Air Force Off Sci Res, 91-94. *Mem:* Inst Elec & Electronics Engrs; Minerals, Metals & Mat Soc; Mat Res Soc. *Res:* Organometallic vapor-phase epitaxy reaction mechanisms; decomposition of the precursors for epitaxy of many III-V materials; mass spectrometric methods used to analyze the reaction mechanisms; gas-source molecular beam epitaxy of group IV semiconductors, materials characterization, devices fabrication; chemical-mechanical polishing; photoluminescence; phase diagrams; velocity-field measurement. *Mailing Add:* SGS Thomson Microelectronics 1000 East Bell Rd Phoenix AZ 85022-2649. *Fax:* 520-485-2955; *E-Mail:* shinhwa.li-phx@st.com

LI, SHU, CATALYSIS CHEMISTRY, ELECTROCHEMISTRY. *Current Pos:* sr res scientist, 92-93, RES & DEVELOP MGR, POLYTRONIX, INC, 93- *Personal Data:* b Changchun, China, Mar 11, 58; m, Fang Ma; c James. *Educ:* Jilin Univ, China, BS, 82, MS, 85; Rutgers Univ, PhD(solid state chem), 90. *Prof Exp:* Res fel, Calif Inst Technol, 91-92. *Mem:* Am Chem Soc; Mat Res Soc; Soc Info Displays. *Res:* Materials issues related to liquid crystal displays; correlations between liquid crystal physical properties and performance of liquid crystal displays; developing new types of liquid crystal displays. *Mailing Add:* 44 Cedar Lane Apt C Highland Park NJ 08904. *Fax:* 972-644-0805

LI, STEVEN SHOEI-LUNG, GENETICS, BIOCHEMISTRY. *Current Pos:* RES GENETICIST, NAT INST ENVIRON HEALTH SCI, NIH, 77- *Personal Data:* b Taiwan, China, Oct 20, 38; m 67, Pearl Chen; c Michael & Nancy. *Educ:* Nat Taiwan Univ, BS, 61, MS, 63; Univ Mo, PhD(genetics), 68. *Prof Exp:* Res assoc, Univ Tex, Austin, 68-70; res assoc, Stanford Univ, 70-74; assoc prof, Mt Sinai Sch Med, 74-77. *Concurrent Pos:* Adj prof biochem & chem, Univ NC, Chapel Hill, 87- *Mem:* AAAS; Am Soc Biochem & Molecular Biol; Genetics Soc Am. *Res:* Biochemical genetics; structure, regulation and evolution of eukayotic genes and proteins. *Mailing Add:* Nat Inst Environ Health Sci NIH Research Triangle Park NC 27709

LI, SU-CHEN, BIOCHEMISTRY. *Current Pos:* From asst prof to assoc prof, 72-80, PROF BIOCHEM, SCH MED, TULANE UNIV, 80- *Personal Data:* b Taipei, Taiwan, June 8, 35; US citizen; m 62; c 2. *Educ:* Nat Taiwan Univ, BS, 58; Univ Okla, PhD(biochem), 65. *Concurrent Pos:* Career Develop Award, NIH, 75-80. *Mem:* Am Soc Biol Chemists; AAAS; Soc Complex Carbohydrates. *Res:* Biochemical studies of glycoconjugates and glycosidases. *Mailing Add:* Dept Biochem Med Sch Tulane Univ 1430 Tulane Ave New Orleans LA 70112-2699

LI, TAO PING, ORGANIC CHEMISTRY. *Current Pos:* RETIRED. *Personal Data:* b Szechwan, China, Nov 16, 20; m 48, Grace; c William, Kenneth & Linda. *Educ:* Nat Szechwan Univ, China, BS, 41; Univ Tex, Austin, MA, 59, PhD(org chem), 60. *Prof Exp:* Fel, Univ Tex, Austin, 60-61; sr proj chemist, Am Oil Co, Ind, 61-64; res specialist, Monsanto Co, 64-66, from group leader to sr group leader, 66-82, sci fellow, 82-87. *Mem:* AAAS; Am Chem Soc; Catalysis Soc; NY Acad Sci. *Res:* Chemical kinetics, heterogeneous catalysis and chemistry of metal organic compounds. *Mailing Add:* 295 Heather Crest Dr Chesterfield MO 63017-2855

LI, THOMAS M, experimental biology, for more information see previous edition

LI, TIEN-YIEN, MATHEMATICS. *Current Pos:* from asst prof to assoc prof, 76-82, PROF MATH, MICH STATE UNIV, 82- *Personal Data:* b Hunan, China, June 28, 45; c Teddy. *Educ:* Nat Tsing-Hua Univ, BS, 68; Univ Md, PhD(math), 74. *Prof Exp:* Instr math, Univ Utah, 74-76. *Concurrent Pos:* Vis assoc prof math, Res Ctr, Univ Wis, 78-79; vis prof, Res Inst Math Sci, Kyoto Univ, Japan, 87-88; hon prof, Tsing-Hua Univ & Jilin Univ, People's Repub China; Guggenheim fel, 95-96. *Mem:* Am Math Soc; Soc Indust & Appl Math. *Res:* Differential equations, dynamical systems and numerical analysis. *Mailing Add:* Dept Math Mich State Univ East Lansing MI 48824. *Fax:* 517-432-1562; *E-Mail:* li@math.msu.edu

LI, TING KAI, MEDICINE, BIOCHEMISTRY. *Current Pos:* prof, 71-80, John B Hickam prof, 80-85, DISTINGUISHED PROF MED & BIOCHEM, SCH MED, IND UNIV, INDIANAPOLIS, 85- *Personal Data:* b Nanking, China, Nov 13, 34; US citizen; m 60; c 2. *Educ:* Northwestern Univ, AB, 55;

Harvard Med Sch, MD, 59; Mass Inst Technol, 60-61. *Honors & Awards:* Res Excellence Award, Res Soc on Alcoholism; Jellinck Award; James B Isaacson Award, Res Substance Abuse. *Prof Exp:* House officer, Peter Bent Brigham Hosp, 59-60, asst med, 60-63, jr assoc, 63-65; instr med, Harvard Med Sch, 65-67, assoc, 67-69; dep dir div biochem, Walter Reed Army Inst Res, 69-71. *Concurrent Pos:* Helen Hay Whitney Found fel, 60-64; Med Found Boston fel, 64-68; Markle scholar acad med, 67-73; asst med, Harvard Med Ach, 60-63, res assoc biochem, 63-65; chief med resident, Peter Bent Brigham Hosp, 65-66; guest scientist, Nobel Med Inst, Sweden, 68. *Mem:* Am Chem Soc; Am Soc Clin Invest; Endocrine Soc; Am Soc Biol Chem; Am Inst Nutrit; Asn Am Physicians. *Res:* Enzymology; metabolism; chemical basis of biological specificity; alcohol metabolism. *Mailing Add:* Dept Med Emerson Hall 421 Ind Univ Sch Med 545 Barnhill Dr Indianapolis IN 46202-5124

LI, TINGYE, ELECTRICAL ENGINEERING, OPTOELECTRONICS. *Current Pos:* Mem tech staff, AT&T Bell Labs, 57-67, head, Repeater Tech Res Dept, 67-76, head, Lightwave Media Res Dept, 76-84, head, Lightwave Systs Res Dept, 84-96, HEAD, LIGHTWAVE NETWORKS RES DEPT, AT&T LABS, 96- *Personal Data:* b Nanjing, China, July 7, 31; m 56, Edith Wu; c Deborah (Chunroh) & Kathryn (Dairoh). *Educ:* Univ Witwatersrand, BSc, 53; Northwestern Univ, MS, 55, PhD(elec eng), 58. *Hon Degrees:* DEng, Nat Chiao Tung Univ, Hsinchu, Taiwan, 91. *Honors & Awards:* W R G Baker Prize, Inst Elec & Electronics Engrs, 75, David Sarnoff Award, 79, John Tyndall Award, 95; Achievement Award, Chinese Inst Engrs-USA, 78; Achievement Award, Chinese Am Acad & Prof Asn, 83. *Mem:* Nat Acad Eng; fel Optical Soc Am; fel AAAS; Chinese Inst Engrs-USA; fel Inst Elec & Electronics Engrs; fel Photonic Soc Chinese Americans; Chinese Acad Eng. *Res:* Optical communications; lasers and coherent-wave optics; electromagnetic field theory; antennas and propagation; microwave theory and techniques; high-speed techniques and systems for lightwave transmission and networking; commercial application of optical fiber communications; author of over 90 publications; granted 16 patents. *Mailing Add:* AT&T Labs Res 791 Holmdel-Keyport Rd Holmdel NJ 07733. *E-Mail:* tli@research.att.com

LI, TONGCHUAN, RESEARCH & DEVELOPMENT OF NEW ANTIBIOTICS, PRECLINICAL PHARMACOLOGY & TOXICOLOGY STUDIES OF ANTIMICROBIALS. *Current Pos:* PROJ MGR, CUBIST PHARMACEUT, INC, 95- *Personal Data:* b Yongtai, China, Oct 11, 55; m 82, Xingxian Yan; c Bing, Scion, Louisa & Mark. *Educ:* Zhangzhou Health Sch, China, dipl, 75; Fujian Med Col, China, MD, 82; Univ Minn, PhD(pharmacol), 90. *Prof Exp:* Postdoctoral scientist, Boehringer Ingelheim Pharmaceut, 90-93; sr scientist, CytoMed Inc, 93-94. *Mem:* Am Soc Pharmacol & Exp Therapeut; AAAS; NY Acad Sci. *Res:* New antimicrobial drugs effective against resistant pathogens. *Mailing Add:* Cubist Pharmaceut 24 Emily St Cambridge MA 02139

LI, WEN-CH'ING WINNIE, COMBINATURICS & FINITE MATHEMATICS, NUMBER THEORY. *Current Pos:* assoc prof, 79-84, PROF MATH, PA STATE UNIV, 84- *Personal Data:* b Taiwan, Dec 25, 48; c Jaline & Ylaine. *Educ:* Nat Taiwan Univ, BS, 70; Univ Calif, Berkeley, PhD(math), 74. *Prof Exp:* Asst prof math, Harvard Univ, 74-78 & Univ Ill, Chicago, 78-79. *Concurrent Pos:* Mem, Inst Advan Study, Princeton, 78 & 84; Alfred Sloan fel, 81-83; vis prof, Univ Paris, Orsay, 85-86, Univ Pa, 91-92, Nat Taiwan Univ, Taipei, Taiwan, 92-93; consult, Bell Labs. *Mem:* Am Math Soc. *Res:* Automorphic forms; representation theory; number theory; combinatorics. *Mailing Add:* Dept Math University Park PA 16802. *Fax:* 814-865-3735; *E-Mail:* wli@math.psu.edu

LI, WEN-HSIUNG, EVOLUTIONARY GENETICS, MOLECULAR EVOLUTION. *Current Pos:* from asst prof to assoc prof, 73-84, PROF POP GENETICS, UNIV TEX, HOUSTON, 84- *Personal Data:* b Ping-Tung, Taiwan, Sept 22, 42; US citizen; m 75, Sue-Jean Hsu; c Vivian, Herman & Joyce. *Educ:* Chung-Yuang Col Sci & Eng, Taiwan, BE, 65; Nat Cent Univ, Taiwan, MS, 68; Brown Univ, PhD(appl math), 72. *Prof Exp:* Proj assoc, Univ Wis-Madison, 72-73. *Concurrent Pos:* Assoc ed, Genetics, 86-; Betty Wheless Trotter prof. *Mem:* Genetics Soc Am; AAAS; Am Soc Human Genetics; Soc Study Evolution. *Res:* Molecular evolution; biomathematics; human population genetics; evolution of DNA sequences, duplicate genes and pseudogenes; mathematical theory of population genetics; molecular evolutionary genetics of color vision. *Mailing Add:* Human Genetics Ctr Univ Tex PO Box 20334 Houston TX 77225. *Fax:* 713-500-0900; *E-Mail:* li@hgc.sph.uth.tmc.edu

LI, WU-SHYONG, PHYSICAL ORGANIC CHEMISTRY. *Current Pos:* sr chemist, 78-80, res specialist, 80-88, SR RES SPECIALIST, 3M CO, 89- *Personal Data:* b Taipei, Taiwan, Aug 20, 43; m 75; c 2. *Educ:* Nat Taiwan Univ, BS, 66; Kent State Univ, MS, 69; Univ Minn, PhD(org chem), 73. *Prof Exp:* Fel, Ohio State Univ, 73-75; sr chemist plastic, Rohm & Haas Co, 75-78. *Mem:* Am Chem Soc. *Res:* Reaction mechanism, kinetics, polymers and UV curing. *Mailing Add:* 3M Co 3M Ctr Bldg 201-1C-18 St Paul MN 55144

LI, XIAO FENG, REPRODUCTIVE MEDICINE, GYNECOLOGICAL ENDOCRINOLOGY. *Current Pos:* SR RES FEL, MED COL WIS, 96- *Personal Data:* b Zhejiang, China, Oct 17, 57; m 85, Xian Wu He; c Yao He. *Educ:* Wenzhou Med Col, BMed, 80, MD, 84, MSc, 87; Birmingham Univ, PhD(human reproductive med), 94. *Prof Exp:* Postdoctoral fel, Birmingham Univ, UK, 89-91 & 94-96. *Concurrent Pos:* Prin investr, Zhejiang Acad Med, China, 87-89; mem steering comt, Human Reproductive Prog, WHO, 90-96. *Res:* Human reproductive biology including mechanism of menstruation, conception, contraception and placental physiology. *Mailing Add:* Dept Physiol Med Col Wis Milwaukee WI 53226. *E-Mail:* lixteng@its.post.mcw.edu

LI, XIAO JIAN, BONE HISTOMORPHOMETRY, ANIMAL MODEL DEVELOPMENT. *Current Pos:* PRIN SCIENTIST & HEAD, HISTOPATH LAB, GENETICS INST, 95- *Personal Data:* b Guangdong, China, June 18, 54; US citizen; m 83, Katie Zhuo; c Heidi & George. *Educ:* Guangdong Med Col, China, MD, 82. *Prof Exp:* Res fel, Radiobiol Div, 84-87; dir, Bone Biol Lab, Radiobiol Div, Univ Utah, 87-90; scientist bone histomorphometrist, Proctor & Gamble Pharmacol, 90-95. *Mem:* Am Soc Bone & Mineral Res; Int Chinese Hard Tissue Soc (secy, 94-96). *Res:* Conducting in vivo preclinical research which employ/develop appropriate animal models and histological methodologies to discover and develop therapeutic agents for the prevention and treatment of osteoporosis or for enhancing fracture healing. *Mailing Add:* 117 Howe St Methuen MA 01844. *Fax:* 978-623-1389; *E-Mail:* jli@genetics.com

LI, XIEZHANG, ITERATIVE METHOD, EIGEN VALVE PROBLEMS FOR TOEPLITE & QUASITOEPLITE MATRICES. *Current Pos:* asst prof, 90-95, ASSOC PROF MATH & COMPUT SCI, GA SOUTHERN UNIV, 95- *Personal Data:* b Junming Wang; c Ying. *Educ:* Shanghai Normal Univ, BS, 66, MS, 81; Kent State Univ, PhD(numerical anal), 90. *Prof Exp:* Instr math, Shanghai Normal Univ, 81-84; vis prof, Kent State Univ, 84-85. *Mem:* Soc Indust & Appl Math. *Res:* Develop near optimal iterative methods for solving a large system of linear equations; determine or estimate an upper bound of errors by function theory; approximation theory and conformat mapping theory. *Mailing Add:* Dept Math & Comput Sci Ga Southern Univ Statesboro GA 30460. *E-Mail:* xli@gsu.cs.gasou.edu

LI, YAO TZU, SCIENCE EDUCATION. *Current Pos:* chmn & treas, 68-96, HON CHMN & TREAS, SETRA SYSTS, INC, 96-; CHMN, Y T LEE ENG, 82- *Personal Data:* b Beijing, China, Feb 1, 14. *Educ:* Mass Inst Technol, ScD, 39. *Concurrent Pos:* Prof control & guidance, Mass Inst Technol, 70-79, dir, Innovation Ctr, 72-79. *Mem:* Fel Nat Acad Eng. *Mailing Add:* Setra Systs Inc 159 Swanson Rd Boxborough MA 01719

LI, YAO-EN, HETEROGENOUS CATALYSIS, GAS PURIFICATION. *Current Pos:* scientist, 88-90, SR SCIENTIST, AIR LIQUIDE AM CORP, 90- *Personal Data:* b Shanghai, China, Oct 24, 58; m 85, Yi-Yin Ku; c Kory & Katherine. *Educ:* Univ Ill, Chicago, BS, 84, MS, 86, PhD(chem eng), 88. *Concurrent Pos:* Student res award, Am Inst Chemists, 84. *Mem:* Am Chem Soc; Am Inst Chem Engrs. *Res:* Research on gas separation, purification technologies; characterize noble metal supported catalysts; develop new process for chemical industry; contamination-free manufacture processes. *Mailing Add:* Air Liquide Am Corp 5230 S East Ave Countryside IL 60525. *E-Mail:* david.li@airliguide.com

LI, YI, PLANT MOLECULAR BIOLOGY & PHYSIOLOGY. *Current Pos:* ASST PROF, DIV BIOL, KANS STATE UNIV, 93- *Personal Data:* b Sichuan, China, Apr 27, 58; m 85, Yan-Hong Wu; c Kevin Y & Jessica. *Educ:* Beijing Forestry Col, BS, 82; State Univ NY, Syracuse, PhD(plant physiol), 89. *Prof Exp:* Fel, Dept Biochem, Univ Mo, 89-91, res asst prof, 91-93. *Mem:* Am Soc Plant Physiologists; Am Soc Gravitational & Space Biol; Int Soc Plant Molecular Biol. *Res:* Mechanisms of hormone action and gravitropism in higher plants using molecular, physiological and biochemical approaches. *Mailing Add:* Div Biol Kans State Univ Manhattan KS 66506. *Fax:* 785-532-6653

LI, YING SING, STRUCTURAL CHEMISTRY, MOLECULAR SPECTROSCOPY. *Current Pos:* ASSOC PROF RES & TEACHING, MEMPHIS STATE UNIV, 82- *Personal Data:* b Kwangtung, China, July 26, 38; US citizen; m 68; c 4. *Educ:* Cheng Kung Univ, BS, 60; Univ Kanas, PhD(chem), 68. *Prof Exp:* Res asst, Taiwan Sugar Exp Sta, 61-63; res assoc, Princeton Univ, 68-70 & Univ SC, 70-75 & 76-82; assoc prof, Benedict Col, 78-82. *Concurrent Pos:* Oak Ridge Nat Lab, 90-91. *Mem:* Am Chem Soc; Sigma Xi. *Res:* Microwave infrared and Raman spectra conformations; structures of cyclic, fluoro, and organometalic compounds; chemical bonding; intermolecular interactions; matrix isolations infrared; surface-enhanced Raman scattering. *Mailing Add:* Dept Chem Memphis State Univ Memphis TN 38152

LI, YUAN, SOLID STATE PHYSICS, HIGH ENERGY PHYSICS. *Current Pos:* ASSOC PROF PHYSICS, RUTGERS UNIV, 77- *Personal Data:* b Ningpo, China, Sept 15, 36. *Educ:* Nat Taiwan Univ, BS, 58; Ind Univ, PhD(physics), 66. *Prof Exp:* Res assoc physics, Rutgers Univ, 65-68, asst prof, 65-77; assoc prof, Tuskegee Inst, 75-77. *Concurrent Pos:* NSF res grant, 76-77. *Mem:* Am Phys Soc; Am Asn Physics Teachers. *Res:* Crystallography and lattice dynamics. *Mailing Add:* Dept Physics NCAS Rutgers Univ 101 Warren St Rm 211 Newark NJ 07102

LI, YUANJING, ELECTRONMICROSCOPIES, LASER TRIM OF THIN FILMS. *Current Pos:* PROCESS RELIABILITY ENGR, ANALOG DEVICES INC, 95- *Personal Data:* b Nanjing, China, May 31, 60; m 86, Yiping Xu; c 1. *Educ:* Nanjing Inst Technol, BS, 82; Univ Calif, Santa Barbara, MS, 89, PhD(elec eng), 92. *Prof Exp:* Sr staff engr, Motorola Corp, 94-95. *Res:* Process optimization for effective laser trim of thin film resistors. *Mailing Add:* 20094 Merritt Dr Cupertino CA 95014. *E-Mail:* yuanjing.li@analog.com

LI, YU-TEH, BIOCHEMISTRY. *Current Pos:* chief, Delta Regional Primate Res Ctr, 66-85, PROF BIOCHEM, SCH MED, TULANE UNIV, 74- *Personal Data:* b Hsin-Chu City, Formosa, Apr 1, 34; m 62; c 2. *Educ:* Nat Taiwan Univ, BS, 57, MS, 60; Univ Okla, PhD(biochem), 63. *Prof Exp:* From instr to asst prof biochem, Sch Med, Univ Okla, 63-66. *Concurrent Pos:* Fel biochem, Sch Med, Univ Okla, 63-64; Nat Cancer Inst grant, 64-66; NSF grant, 68-; NIH grant, 71-; USPHS res career develop award, 71-76; Javits Neurosci Investr Award, 84-91, 91-98. *Mem:* Am Soc Neurochem; Am Soc Biol Chem. *Res:* Biochemical studies on glycoconjugates and various glycosidases. *Mailing Add:* Dept Biochem Tulane Univ Sch Med New Orleans LA 70112-2699. *Fax:* 504-584-1611

LI, YUYING, SCIENTIFIC COMPUTING OPTIMIZATION. *Current Pos:* Res assoc, Cornell Univ, 89-95, lectr, 90, 92, 93 & 95, SR RES ASSOC, CORNELL UNIV, 95- *Personal Data:* m 92, Thomas F Coleman; c Lena V. *Educ:* Sichuan Univ, China, BS, 82; Univ Waterloo, Can, MS, 85, PhD(comput sci), 88. *Honors & Awards:* Six Fox Prize, Oxford Univ. *Mem:* Soc Indust & Appl Math. *Res:* Numerical optimization and scientific computing applying optimization techniques to many application problems, such as medical imaging and financial optimization. *Mailing Add:* Dept Comput Sci Cornell Univ Upson Ithaca NY 14850. *Fax:* 607-255-4428; *E-Mail:* yuying@cs.cornell.edu

LI, ZHENG, SEMICONDUCTOR HIGH ENERGY PARTICLE DETECTORS, RADIATION DAMAGE & HARDNESS OF SEMICONDUCTOR DETECTORS. *Current Pos:* Asst physicist, 86-88, ASSOC PHYSICIST, BROOKHAVEN NAT LAB, 89- *Personal Data:* b Xiangtan, China, Nov 10, 58; US citizen; m, Yan-Xia Liu; c Michael & Katie. *Educ:* Beijing Univ, BS, 81; Pa State Univ, PhD(physics), 86. *Mem:* Inst Elec & Electronics Engrs. *Res:* Designing, developing and processing of silicon position sensitive particle detectors; radiation damage effects and radiation hardness study on silicon detectors. *Mailing Add:* 3211 Ave I Apt 6-0 Brooklyn NY 11210-3912. *E-Mail:* zhengl@bnlcl1.bnl.gov

LI, ZHONGSHAN, COMBINATORIAL MATRIX ANALYSIS, SIGN PATTERN MATRICES & THEIR GENERALIZATIONS. *Current Pos:* instr, 91-92, ASST PROF MATH, GA STATE UNIV, 92- *Personal Data:* b Lanzhou, China, Apr 22, 63; US citizen; m 88, Joan Liang; c Angela C & Andrew T. *Educ:* Lanzhou Univ, China, BSc, 83; Beijing Normal Univ, China, MSc, 86; NC State Univ, PhD(math), 90. *Prof Exp:* Asst prof math, Hebei Normal Col, China, 86; instr, NC State Univ, 90-91. *Mem:* Am Math Soc; Int Linear Algebra Soc. *Res:* Matrix theory, especially combinatorial matrix theory and qualitative matrix theory, in which sign patterns and graphs are used extensively. *Mailing Add:* Dept Math & Comput Sci Ga State Univ Atlanta GA 30303-3083. *Fax:* 404-651-2246; *E-Mail:* matzli@panther.gsu.edu

LI, ZI-CAI, numerical methods, image transformation, for more information see previous edition

LIAN, ERIC CHUN-YET, HEMATOLOGY. *Current Pos:* asst prof med, Sch Med, 73-76, assoc prof med, Sch Med, 78-87, COMPREHENSIVE HEMOPHILIA CTR, UNIV MIAMI, 76-, DIR HEMOSTASIS LAB, 76-, PROF MED, SCH MED, 87- *Personal Data:* b Tainan Hsien, Taiwan, Nov 11, 38; m 73; c Elizabeth & Alexander. *Educ:* Nat Taiwan Univ, MD, 64. *Prof Exp:* Res fel hemat, Univ Miami, 69-71; res assoc hemostasis, Harvard Med Sch, 71-73. *Concurrent Pos:* Prin investr biochem, immunol & physiol of antihemophilic factor, 76- & pathogenesis of thrombotic thrombocytopenic purpura, 78- *Mem:* Fel Am Col Physicians; AAAS; Am Fedn Clin Res; Am Soc Hemat; Am Heart Asn; Int Soc Thrombosis & Hemostasis; Am Soc Biochem & Molecular Biol. *Res:* Thrombosis and hemostasis; hematology; thrombotic thrombocytopanic purpura. *Mailing Add:* Vet Admin Hosp 1201 NW 16th St Miami FL 33125. *Fax:* 305-324-3375; *E-Mail:* elian@mednet.med.miami.edu

LIAN, JANE B, CELL BIOLOGY. *Current Pos:* PROF CELL BIOL, UNIV MASS, MED CTR, 88- *Educ:* Boston Univ, PhD(biochem), 72. *Res:* Cellular biology. *Mailing Add:* Dept Cell Biol Univ Mass Med Ctr 55 Lake Ave N Worcester MA 01655-0001

LIAN, SHAWN, materials science engineering, for more information see previous edition

LIANG, CHANG-SENG, CARDIOLOGY. *Current Pos:* assoc prof med, 82-86, PROF MED, UNIV ROCHESTER MED CTR, 86- *Personal Data:* b Fukien, China, Jan 6, 41; US citizen; m 68; c 3. *Educ:* Nat Taiwan Univ, MD, 65; Boston Univ, PhD(pharmacol), 71. *Prof Exp:* Instr med, Boston Univ Sch Med, 73-74, from asst prof to assoc prof med & pharmacol, 73-82. *Concurrent Pos:* Prin investr, NIH res grants, 77-, study sect reviewer, NIH, 81-85. *Mem:* Am Physiol Soc; Am Soc Pharmacol & Exp Therapeut; Am Heart Asn; Am Soc Clin Invest; Am Fedn Clin Res. *Res:* Circulatory control and neurohumoral regulation of the cardiovascular system in heart failure; receptor pharmacology; changes of membrane signal transduction; hemodynamic measurements. *Mailing Add:* Cardiol Unit 601 Elmwood Ave Box 679 Rochester NY 14642. *Fax:* 716-271-2184

LIANG, CHARLES C, PHYSICAL CHEMISTRY, ANALYTICAL CHEMISTRY. *Current Pos:* MGT & TECHNOL CONSULT, CHEM POWER SOURCES INDUST, 95- *Personal Data:* b Nanking, China, June 9, 34; m 61, Anna R Juan; c Anita, Bertrand & Bryan. *Educ:* Nat Taiwan Univ, BS, 56; Baylor Univ, PhD(phys chem), 62. *Honors & Awards:* IR 100 Award, Indust Res Mag, 71. *Prof Exp:* Res chemist, Houdry Process & Chem Co, 62-63; from asst prof to assoc prof phys chem, WVa Inst Technol, 63-65; sr staff mem electrochem, P R Mallory Co, Inc, 65-73, assoc tech dir batteries, Lab Phys Sci, 73-77; dir, VP Technol, Wilson Greatbatch, Ltd, 77-79; pres, Electrochem Industs, Inc, 79-82 & Omnion Enterprises, Inc, 82-93; vpres rechargeable systs, Ultralife Batteries, Inc, 93-94. *Mem:* Am Chem Soc; Electrochem Soc. *Res:* Mechanisms and kinetics of electrode processes; high energy density battery systems. *Mailing Add:* 95 Waterford Way Fairport NY 14450

LIANG, CHARLES SHIH-TUNG, AERONAUTICAL & ASTRONAUTICAL ENGINEERING. *Current Pos:* ENG STAFF SPECIALIST, FT WORTH DIV, GEN DYNAMICS CORP, 69- *Personal Data:* b Peking, China, Dec 10, 40; US citizen; m 65; c 2. *Educ:* Univ Ill, BS, 62, PhD(elec eng), 68; Harvard Univ, SM, 63. *Prof Exp:* Asst elec eng, Univ Ill, 63-68. *Mem:* AAAS; Inst Elec & Electronics Engrs; Int Union Radio Sci. *Res:* Electromagnetic scattering research as related to radar signature analysis and target identification; radar antenna design and development; advanced technology aircraft design and development; radar cross-section measurement techniques. *Mailing Add:* Lockheed Martin Tactical Aircraft Systs MZ 4205 PO Box 748 Ft Worth TX 76101

LIANG, EDISON PARK-TAK, ASTROPHYSICS, PLASMA RADIATION. *Current Pos:* PROF SPACE PHYSICS & ASTRON, RICE UNIV, 91- *Personal Data:* b Canton, China, July 22, 47; nat US; m 71, Lily; c Olivia, James & Justin. *Educ:* Univ Calif, Berkeley, BA, 67, PhD(physics), 71. *Prof Exp:* Res assoc, Univ Tex, Austin, 71-73; res assoc & assoc instr astrophys & relativity, Univ Utah, 73-75; asst prof astrophys, Mich State Univ, 75-76; asst prof physics, Stanford Univ, 76-79; group leader, Physics Dept, Lawrence Livermore Nat Lab, 83-90, assoc div leader, 88-90, physicist, 80-93. *Concurrent Pos:* Lectr & vis scholar, Ctr Space Sci & Astrophys, Stanford Univ, 80-90. *Mem:* Sigma Xi; Am Astronom Soc; fel Am Phys Soc; Int Astron Union. *Res:* Plasma radiation; astrophysics of compact objects (x-ray and gamma ray sources); laser-plasma interactions; relativity and cosmology; supernova remnants. *Mailing Add:* Dept Space Physics & Astron Rice Univ MS 108 Houston TX 77005-1892. *Fax:* 713-285-5143; *E-Mail:* liang@spacsun.rice.edu

LIANG, GEORGE H, PLANT GENETICS, SOMATIC CELL GENETICS. *Current Pos:* from asst prof to assoc prof, 64-76, PROF PLANT GENETICS & CYTOGENETICIST, KANS STATE UNIV, 77-, CHMN, GENETICS PROG, 82- *Personal Data:* b Beijing, China, Oct 1, 34; m 63, Yun-Teh Shen; c J May & Roy C. *Educ:* Taiwan Prov Col Agr, BS, 56; Univ Wyo, MS, 61; Univ Wis, PhD(agron), 65. *Honors & Awards:* Int Agr Coop Award, Ministry Agr, 93. *Prof Exp:* Agronomist, Taiwan Prov Res Inst Agr, 58-59. *Concurrent Pos:* Sabbatica, Univ Calif-Davis, 81; consult, World Bank, 83; tech consult, UN Develop Prog, 91 & 93; Germplasm Resources, Chinese Acad Agr Sci, 93; distinguished prof, Chinese Acad Agr Sci, Jiangsu Agr Univ & Henan Agr Univ. *Mem:* Am Soc Agron; Crop Sci Soc Am; Am Genetic Asn; Sigma Xi; Genetics Soc Can. *Res:* Quantitative genetics in plant species; cytogenetics and breeding aspects in cultivated crops; somatic cell genetics; biotechnology; plant transformation. *Mailing Add:* Dept Agron Kans State Univ 2004 Throckmorton Manhattan KS 66506. *Fax:* 785-532-6094; *E-Mail:* ytlaing@ksuvm.ksu.edu

LIANG, ISABELLA Y S, CARDIAC VASCULAR DISEASES. *Current Pos:* HEALTH SCI ADMINR, NIH, 90- *Personal Data:* b Kwellin, China; US citizen. *Educ:* Hong Kong Chinese Univ, BS, 66; Hong Kong Univ, PhD(physiol), 79. *Mem:* Am Heart Asn; Sigma Xi; Am Physiol Soc; Am Soc Molecular Biol & Med. *Mailing Add:* Heart & Vascular Dis NIH Fed Bldg Rm 9142 6701 Rockledge Dr Bethesda MD 20817

LIANG, JACK N, PROTEIN CHEMISTRY. *Current Pos:* BIOCHEMIST, BRIGHAM & WOMEN'S HOSP, 82- *Personal Data:* b Taiwan, China, Feb 4, 42. *Educ:* Taiwan Normal Univ, BS, 68; McMaster Univ, PhD(biophys chem), 77. *Prof Exp:* Fel, Brown Univ, 79-81; res assoc, Mass Eye & Ear Infirmary, 81-82. *Mem:* Biophys Soc; Am Chem Soc. *Res:* Conformation of polypeptides and polysaccharides. *Mailing Add:* Dept Ophthal Brigham & Women's Hosp 221 Longwood Ave Boston MA 02115-5817

LIANG, JOSEPH JEN-YIN, MATHEMATICS. *Current Pos:* From asst prof to assoc prof, 70-77, PROF MATH, UNIV SFLA, 78- *Personal Data:* b China; US citizen; m 65; c 2. *Educ:* Nat Taiwan Univ, BA, 58; Univ Detroit, MA, 62; Ohio State Univ, PhD(math), 69. *Prof Exp:* Res fel math, Calif Inst Technol, 69-70. *Concurrent Pos:* Vis asst prof, Ohio State Univ, 72; vis assoc, Calif Inst Technol, 75 & 77; vis res prof, Nat Tsing Hua Univ, Taipei, Taiwan, Repub China, 83. *Mem:* Am Math Soc; Math Asn Am. *Res:* Number theory; coding theory; algorithms. *Mailing Add:* Dept Math Phys 114 Univ SFla 4202 Fowler Ave Tampa FL 33620-9951

LIANG, KENG-SAN, MATERIALS SCIENCE, SOLID STATE PHYSICS. *Current Pos:* STAFF PHYSICIST MAT SCI, CORP RES LABS, EXXON RES & ENG CO, 78- *Personal Data:* b Tainan, Taiwan, Dec 17, 43; m 69; c 2. *Educ:* Nat Taiwan Univ, BS, 66; Stanford Univ, MS, 70, PhD(appl physics), 73. *Prof Exp:* From assoc scientist to scientist mat sci, Xerox Corp, 73-78. *Mem:* Am Phys Soc; Am Vacuum Soc. *Res:* Amorphous solids, x-ray diffraction, x-ray photoelectron spectroscopy, electronic structure, thin films. *Mailing Add:* Exxon Corp Res Rte 22 E Annandale NJ 08801

LIANG, SHOU CHU, CHEMISTRY. *Current Pos:* gen mgr, 70-85, consult, 85-88, PVT RES, COMINCO ELECTRONIC MAT INC, 88- *Personal Data:* b Foochow, China, May 14, 20; m 50, Chi-Chan Woo; c Pitur & Maurice. *Educ:* Cent Univ, China, BS, 42; Princeton Univ, MA, 46, PhD(chem), 47. *Prof Exp:* Instr, Teacher High Sch, China, 42; anal chemist, China Match Raw Mat Mfg Co, 42-44; asst, Princeton Univ, 45-47, Int Nickel Co fel, 47-48; res chemist, Merck & Co, NJ, 48-49; fel, Nat Res Coun Can, 49-51, asst res officer II, 51-53; group leader, Res Lab, Dom Tar & Chem Co, 53-56; res engr, Consol Mining & Smelting Co Can, Ltd, 56-64, head gen metall res, 64-70. *Mem:* Am Chem Soc; NY Acad Sci; Chem Inst Can; AAAS. *Res:* Flotation of ores; preperation of inorganic reagents; chemical method of analysis; surface catalysis; heterogeneity of catalyst surfaces for chemisorption; fast drying paint; metallurgy; semiconductors. *Mailing Add:* S 4206 Helena St Spokane WA 99203

LIANG, SHOUDAN, CORRELATED CONDENSED MATTER SYSTEMS, COMPUTATIONAL PHYSICS. *Current Pos:* ASST PROF PHYSICS, PA STATE UNIV, 90- *Personal Data:* b Fuzhou, China, Feb 10, 61. *Educ:* Peking Univ, BS, 82; Univ Chicago, PhD(physics), 86. *Prof Exp:* Res assoc physics, Princeton Univ, 86-88 & Univ Ill, Urbana-Champaign, 88-90. *Mem:* Am Phys Soc. *Res:* Theoretical condensed matter physics include quantum antiferromagnets, new algorithms for overcoming slow dynamics in spin glasses and simulated annealing, random growth and computational physics. *Mailing Add:* 104 Davey Lab Pa State Univ University Park PA 16802. *E-Mail:* liang@phys.psu.edu

LIANG, SHOUDENG, VACUUM TECHNOLOGY & APPLICATIONS, SURFACE CHARACTERIZATIONS & PROPERTY ANALYSIS. *Current Pos:* res asst surface sci, Chem Dept, 89, proj asst, 89-90, RES ASST X-RAY LITHOGRAPHY, CTR X-RAY LITHOGRAPHY, UNIV WIS, 90- *Personal Data:* b Yantai, China, Mar 9, 59. *Educ:* Qufu Normal Univ, China, BS, 81; Univ Ill-Chicago, MS, 87; Univ Wis-Madison, MS, 90. *Prof Exp:* Researcher catalysis & phys chem, Dalian Inst Chem Physics, China, 82-85; res asst surface chem, Chem Dept, Univ Ill, Chicago, 86-88. *Mem:* Am Vacuum Soc; Mat Res Soc. *Res:* Surface chemistry of thin films and interfaces of metals/semiconductors and gas/metals; application of synchrotron radiation to materials research and scanning x-ray spectromicroscopy; x-ray lithography from synchrotron radiation sources. *Mailing Add:* 951 Clopper Rd Gaithersburg MD 20878

LIANG, SHU-MEI, CYTOKINE RESEARCH, STRUCTURE-FUNCTION STUDIES. *Current Pos:* mgr, 92-93, DIR, PROTEIN CHEM & MOLECULAR BIOL, AMVAX INC, 93- *Personal Data:* b Taiwan, Feb 4, 49; US citizen; m; c 1. *Educ:* Nat Taiwan Univ, BS, 71; Univ Ark, PhD(biochem), 78. *Prof Exp:* Vis fel res, Div Bact Prod, BOB, Food & Drug Admin, 77-80, staff fel, Div Biochem & Biophysics, 80-83, res chemist res & regulatory work, Div Virol, CBER, 86-88; res chemist, Div Virol, Food & Drug Admin, 86-88, Div Cytokine Biol, CBER, 88-92. *Concurrent Pos:* scientist res & develop, Dept Protein Chem, Biogen, SAm, 83-85. *Mem:* Am Soc Biochem & Molecular Biol; Protein Soc; Chinese Biochem Soc. *Res:* Structure-function relationships of cytokines especially interleukin-2 and the regulation of immune response by thiol compounds; purification and characterization of proteins especially membrane proteins and recombinant DNA derived proteins; expression of bacterial membrane proteins in E coli. *Mailing Add:* 12031 Indian Creek Ct Beltsville MD 20705

LIANG, TEHMING, BIOCHEMISTRY. *Current Pos:* ASSOC PROF, DEPT DERMAT, WRIGHT STATE UNIV SCH MED, 92-, ASSOC PROF, DEPT DERMAT, VET ADMIN MED CTR, DAYTON, OHIO, 92- *Personal Data:* b Taiwan, Apr 14, 45; m; c 1. *Educ:* Nat Taiwan Univ, BS, 68; Univ Chicago, PhD(biochem), 73; Univ Miami, MD, 87. *Prof Exp:* Res assoc biochem, Ben May Lab Cancer Res, Univ Chicago, 73-76, res asst prof, 76-77; sr res biochem, Merck Inst Therapeut Res, 77-81, res fel, 81-87; resident internal med, Robert Wood Johnson Med Sch, Univ Chicago, 88-89, resident dermat, 89-91. *Mem:* Am Soc Biol Chemists; Endocrine Soc; Soc Neurosci; Am Med Asn; Am Acad Dermat; Soc Investigative Dermat. *Res:* Molecular mechanism of hormone action. *Mailing Add:* Dept Dermat Wright State Univ Sch Med PO Box 927 Dayton OH 45401-0927. *Fax:* 937-262-0211

LIANG, TUNG, OPERATIONS RESEARCH, AGRICULTURAL ENGINEERING. *Current Pos:* Assoc prof, 68-76, PROF AGR ENG, UNIV HAWAII, 76- *Personal Data:* b Peking, China, June 7, 32; m 58; c 2. *Educ:* Nat Taiwan Univ, BS, 56; Mich State Univ, MS, 63; NC State Univ, PhD(biol eng), 67. *Mem:* Am Soc Agr Engrs. *Res:* Agricultural system modeling and optimization; development of natural resource information system. *Mailing Add:* Dept Agr Eng Univ Hawaii 3050 Maile Way Honolulu HI 96822-2270

LIANG, WEI CHUAN, ORGANIC CHEMISTRY, PROCESS DEVELOPMENT SAFETY. *Current Pos:* SR PRIN SCIENTIST, RHONE POULENC INC, 87- *Personal Data:* b Shanghai, China, Nov 23, 36; m 70, Yu-Lan Wang; c Elan & Emay. *Educ:* Kalamazoo Col, BA, 61; Case Western Res Univ, MS, 66; Ohio State Univ, PhD(org chem), 72. *Prof Exp:* Res chemist, Lubrizol Corp, 61-67; fel org chem res, Ga Inst Technol, 72-74; res chemist, Union Carbide Corp, 74-77, group leader process develop, 77-87, res scientist, 82-87. *Mem:* Am Chem Soc; Am Inst Chem Engrs. *Res:* Exploratory syntheses; pesticide process research; process research and development; process safety. *Mailing Add:* Rhone Poulenc Inc CN 7500 Cranbury NJ 08512. *Fax:* 609-860-0218

LIANG, YOLA YUEH-O, ANALYTICAL CHEMISTRY, GOOD LABORATORY PRACTICE. *Current Pos:* RES ASSOC ANALYTICAL CHEM, DOW CHEM CO, 81- *Personal Data:* b Taiwan, Feb 12, 47; m 75; c 2. *Educ:* Nat Taiwan Normal Univ, BS, 70; Univ Kans, PhD(chem), 78. *Mem:* Am Chem Soc; Asn Women Sci. *Res:* Analytical chemistry; organic electrochemistry; neurochemistry; enzyme kinetics; analytical separations using gas chromatography and liquid chromatography. *Mailing Add:* 386 Mt Sequoia Pl Clayton CA 94517. *Fax:* 510-432-5105

LIANG, ZHI-PEI, ELECTRICAL ENGINEERING, INTELLIGENT SYSTEMS. *Current Pos:* postdoctoral fel, Nat Ctr Supercomput Appln, 89-91, res asst prof, Biomed Magnetic Resonance Lab, 91-93, ASST PROF, DEPT ELEC & COMPUT ENG, BECKMAN INST ADVAN SCI & TECHNOL, COORD SCI LAB, BIOENG PROG & DEPT MED INFO SCI, COL MED, UNIV ILL, URBANA, CHAMPAIGN, 93- *Personal Data:* b Guangdong, China, Dec 25, 61; m 86, Bo Liu; c Annie Han. *Educ:* SChina Inst Technol, BS, 82; Case Western Res Univ, MS, 85, PhD, 89. *Honors & Awards:* RIA Award, NSF, 94, Career Award, 95. *Concurrent Pos:* Whitaker biomed eng res grantee, 91; assoc ed, Trans on Med Imaging, Inst Elec & Electronics Engrs; reviewer, NSF, 94, NIH, 95, 96 & 97. *Mem:* NY Acad Sci; Inst Elec & Electronics Engrs; Int Soc Magnetic Resonance Med. *Res:* Magnetic resonance imaging; superresolution image reconstruction using a priori constraints; statistical, scale-space, and neural network approaches to image analysis; multimodality image registration and fusion. *Mailing Add:* Beckman Inst Urbana IL 61801. *Fax:* 217-244-0105; *E-Mail:* z-liang@uiuc.edu

LIANIDES, SYLVIA PANAGOS, PHYSIOLOGY, BIOCHEMISTRY. *Current Pos:* RETIRED. *Personal Data:* b Lynn, Mass, Sept 2, 31; div; c 3. *Educ:* Tufts Univ, BS, 53, PhD(physiol), 59. *Prof Exp:* Res biologist, US Naval Radiol Defense Lab, 59-60; lectr biol, Col Notre Dame, Calif, 62-71; instr biol sci, De Anza Col, 71-73; instr ecol, Chabot Col, 73-75; prof anat & physiol, W Valley Col, Calif, 75-96, chmn, Biol Dept, 81-83. *Mem:* AAAS; Sigma Xi; Nat Asn Biol Teachers; Nat Sci Teachers Asn. *Res:* Hormonal and environmental influences upon mitochondrial oxidative phosphorylation; effects of environmental cold on lipid and carbohydrate metabolism; radiation physiology; anatomy. *Mailing Add:* PO Box 2334 Saratoga CA 95070

LIAO, HSUEH-LIANG, ANALYTICAL CHEMISTRY. *Current Pos:* GROUP LEADER & SCIENTIST, LEDERLE LABS, AM CYANAMID CO, 77- *Personal Data:* b Silo, Taiwan, Jan 24, 41; US citizen; m 52; c 2. *Educ:* Cheng Kong Univ, BS, 65; Drexel Univ, MS, 69; Georgetown Univ, PhD(chem), 72. *Prof Exp:* Sr res assoc chem, Northeastern Univ, 72-74; sr res chemist, Norwich Pharmacal Co, Morton-Norwich Prod Inc, 74-76; sr res scientist, Bristol Myers Co, 76-77. *Mem:* Am Chem Soc; Am Inst Chem Eng. *Res:* Analytical methods development; chromatographic methods of separation (HPLC, GC & TLC) and quantitation; analytical and physical chemistry of drug compounds; solution thermodynamics. *Mailing Add:* 83 Ridge Rd New City NY 10956-6824

LIAO, MARTHA, SOMATIC CELL GENETICS, RECOMBINANT DNA. *Current Pos:* AT DEPT MOLECULAR GENETICS, ALBERT EINSTEIN COL MED. *Personal Data:* b Leeds, Eng, Feb 9, 48; US citizen; m 91. *Educ:* Bryn Mawr Col, BA, 70; Univ Pa, PhD(chem), 74. *Prof Exp:* Fel chem, Univ Denver, 74-75; fel, Health Sci Ctr, Eleanor Roosevelt Inst Cancer Res, Univ Colo, 75-79, inst fel, 79-86, sr fel genetics, 86- *Concurrent Pos:* Am res scholar, Comt Scholarly Commun with People's Republic China, Nat Acad Sci, 81-82; NIH fel, 76-79; assoc prof, Dept Pediat, Univ Colo Health Sci Ctr, 86- *Mem:* Am Cell Biol; Am Soc Human Genetics; AAAS. *Res:* Human gene mapping using chinese hamster/human cell hybrids; using recombinant DNA techniques to obtain DNA markers from specific human chromosome. *Mailing Add:* Dept Molecular Genetics ULM 1217 Albert Einstein Col Med 1300 Morris Park Ave Bronx NY 10461-1975

LIAO, MEI-JUNE, INTERFERON SCIENCE. *Current Pos:* sr scientist, Bioresponse Modifier Group, Interferon Sci, Inc, 83-84, head, Cellular Immunol Group, 84-85, dir cell biol, 85-86, DIR, RES & DEVELOP, INTERFERON SCI, INC, 87- *Personal Data:* b Nat Tsing-Hua Univ, BS, 73; Yale Univ, MPh, 77, PhD(phys biochem), 80. *Prof Exp:* Assoc biochem & biophys, Mass Inst Technol, 80-83. *Mem:* Am Soc Biochem & Molecular Biol; Int Soc Inteferon & Cytokine Res; Soc Chinese Bioscientists Am. *Res:* Purification and characterization of natural and recombinant human interferon proteins; natural interferon induction systems; mechanism of interferon action; interferon receptor purification and characterization; production of monoclonal and polyclonal antibodies; development of immunochemical assay systems; state of the art protein chemistry techniques and cytokine assays and cDNA cloning and expression of human cytokines; preparation of PLA and response to the Food and Drug Administration for the approval of natural and recombinant interferon product. *Mailing Add:* Interferon Sci Inc 783 Jersey Ave New Brunswick NJ 08901-3660

LIAO, PAUL FOO-HUNG, ENGINEERING PHYSICS. *Current Pos:* div mgr physics & optical sci res, Bellcore, 84-87, div mgr photonic sci & tech res, 87-89, asst vpres solid state sci & tech, 89-90, asst vpres, 90-93, GEN MGR, NETWORK FOUNDATIONS, ARCHIT & PLANNING, NETWORK SYSTS RES, BELLCORE, 93- *Personal Data:* b Philadelphia, Pa, Nov 10, 44; m 68; c 2. *Educ:* Mass Inst Technol, BS, 66; Columbia Univ, PhD(physics), 73. *Prof Exp:* Res assoc, Radiation Lab, Columbia Univ, 72-73; mem tech staff physics, Bell Labs, 73-80, head Quantum Electronics Res Dept, 80-83. *Concurrent Pos:* Chmn, Joint Coun Quantum Electronics, 66; ed Acad Press, Quantum Electronics; ed, J Optical Soc Am, 88. *Mem:* Fel Am Phys Soc; fel Optical Soc Am; fel Inst Elec & Electronics Engrs. *Res:* Communications systems; nonlinear optics. *Mailing Add:* Bellcore 331 Newman Springs Rd Rm 1A209A Red Bank NJ 07701-5699

LIAO, PING-HUANG, SANITARY & ENVIRONMENTAL ENGINEERING, OTHER ENVIRONMENTAL EARTH & MARINE SCIENCES. *Current Pos:* Fel, 75-78, RES SCIENTIST, UNIV BC, 78- *Personal Data:* b Taipei, Taiwan, Jan 16, 46; Can citizen; m 71, Hsiu-mei Hsieh; c Marrin, Perry & Justin. *Educ:* Tunghai Univ, BSc, 69; Univ Neb, MS, 73 & PhD(chem), 76. *Concurrent Pos:* Instr, Columbia Col, 81. *Mem:* Int Asn Water Qual. *Res:* Fermentation biotechnology, biomass utilization and bioenergy production from renewable resources; waste management; biological treatment; composting technology. *Mailing Add:* Dept Bio-Resource Eng Univ BC 2357 Main Hall Vancouver BC V6T 1Z4 Can. *Fax:* 604-822-5704

LIAO, SHU-CHUNG, physical-analytical chemistry; deceased, see previous edition for last biography

LIAO, SHUEN-KUEI, CANCER, IMMUNOLOGY. *Current Pos:* lectr, Dept Pediat, 74-76, asst prof, 76-80, ASSOC PROF PATH & PEDIAT, SCH MED, MCMASTER UNIV, 80- *Personal Data:* b Morioka, Japan, June 27, 40; Can citizen; m 72; c 2. *Educ:* Tunghai Univ, Taiwan, BSc, 64; McMaster Univ, PhD(immunol), 71. *Prof Exp:* Demonstr, fel histol, Univ Toronto, 70-73; prof asst cancer, Hamilton Clin, Ont Cancer Found, 73-74. *Concurrent Pos:* Mem staff lab med, Henderson Gen Hosp, Hamilton, 74-; res grants, Med Res Coun Can, Ont Cancer Treatment & Res Found, 74 & Nat Cancer Inst Can, 81-; Ont Cancer Fund res associateship, 74-84. *Mem:* AAAS; Can Soc Cell Biol; Am Asn Cancer Res; Can Soc Immunol; NY Acad Sci; Int Soc Pigment Cell. *Res:* Cancer immunology; cell biology. *Mailing Add:* 36 Mountain Brow Blvd Hamilton ON L8T 1A3 Can

LIAO, SHUTSUNG, BIOCHEMISTRY, ENDOCRINOLOGY. *Current Pos:* From asst prof to assoc prof, 64-71, PROF DEPT BIOCHEM & MOLECULAR BIOL, BEN MAY INST, UNIV CHICAGO, 72- *Personal Data:* b Tainan, Taiwan, Jan 1, 31; m 60, Shuching Kuo; c Jane, Tzufen, Tzuming & May. *Educ:* Nat Taiwan Univ, BSc, 54, MSc, 56; Univ Chicago, PhD(biochem), 61. *Honors & Awards:* Sci Achievement Award, Taiwanese-Am Found; Pfizer Lectr Award, Clin Res Inst Montreal; Gregory Pincus Medal & Award, Worcester Found; Tsung Ming Tu Award, Formosan Med Asn. *Concurrent Pos:* NIH res grant, 63-; Am Cancer Soc res grant, 74-82; mem study sect, NIH; assoc ed, Cancer Res, 82-89. *Mem:* Am Soc Biol Chem; Endocrine Soc; Am Asn Cancer Res; NAm Taiwanese Prof Asn (pres, 80-81). *Res:* Mechanism of hormone action; control of gene expression; nuclear receptors enzymology; prevention and suppresion of cancers. *Mailing Add:* Ben May Inst Univ Chicago 5841 S Maryland Chicago IL 60637. *Fax:* 773-702-6260

LIAO, SUNG JUI, PHYSICAL MEDICINE. *Current Pos:* clin assoc prof rehab med, 71-82, clin prof oral & maxillo facial surg, 78-92, CLIN PROF SURG SCI, NY UNIV COL DENT, 92- *Personal Data:* b Changsha, China, Nov 15, 17; nat US; m 53, Karin Agren; c Thomas, Elizabeth, Margaret & John. *Educ:* Hsiang Ya Med Col, China, MD, 42; Nat Cent Univ, China, MPH, 44; London Sch Hyg & Trop Med, Univ London, DPH, 46; dipl bact, 47; Am Bd Phys Med & Rehab, dipl, 58. *Prof Exp:* Asst prof prev med, Sch Med, Yale Univ, 50-54; res assoc & assoc res prof bact, Col Med, Univ Utah, 49-50; dir phys med & rehab, Waterbury Hosp, 57-73; lectr rehab med, Boston Univ Sch Med, 73-93. *Concurrent Pos:* Milbank Mem fel prev med, Sch Med, Yale Univ, 47-49; clin fel phys med, Mass Gen Hosp, Boston, 55-57; consult physiatrist, Middlesex Mem Hosp, Middletown, Conn, 57-60 & St Raphael Hosp, New Haven, Conn, 72-82; med dir, Waterbury Area Rehab Ctr, 57-62; dir phys med & rehab, St Mary's Hosp, 57-67 & Danbury Hosp, 57-69; attend physiatrist, Waterbury Hosp, 57-90, hon physiatrist, 91-; med consult, Waterbury & Danbury, Conn State Div Voc Rehab, 63-72, chief admin med consult, 69-73; assoc clin prof, Sch Med, Boston Univ, 67-73; hon consult biomech, NY Univ Inst Rehab Med, 69-76; chmn ad hoc comt acupuncture, Conn State Med Soc; secy, Am Acad Acupuncture, Inc; pres, Res Inst Acupuncture & Chinese Med; consult, Rhode Island State Bd Acupuncture, 80-84. *Mem:* Sr fel Am Col Physicians; sr fel Royal Soc Med; sr fel Am Acad Phys Med & Rehab; sr mem Sigma Xi. *Res:* Excitability and conduction nerve and muscle; biomedical engineering; acupuncture; themography; pain. *Mailing Add:* 66 Skyline Dr Middlebury CT 06762-1717

LIAO, TA-HSIU, PROTEIN CHEMISTRY, ENZYMOLOGY. *Current Pos:* PROF BIOCHEM, INST BIOCHEM, NAT TAIWAN UNIV, 85- *Personal Data:* b Taipei, Taiwan, Feb 22, 42; m; c 2. *Educ:* Nat Taiwan Univ, BS, 64; Univ Calif, Los Angeles, PhD(biol chem), 69. *Prof Exp:* Postdoctoral biochem, Moore-Stein Lab, Rockefeller Univ, 72-73; asst prof biochem, 73-74; from asst prof to prof biochem, Biochem Dept, Okla State Univ, 74-85. *Concurrent Pos:* Vis prof, A Kornberg's Lab, Stanford Univ, 81. *Mem:* Am Soc Biochem & Molecular Biol. *Res:* Protein chemistry; enzymology; deoxyribonuclease; structure and function relationships of proteins; physical methods of characterization of biological macromolecules. *Mailing Add:* Biochem Dept Nat Taiwan Univ Col Med No 1 Jen Ai Rd 1st Sect Taipei Taiwan. *Fax:* 886-2-391-5295, 2-393-8354

LIAO, TSUNG-KAI, ORGANIC CHEMISTRY, PHARMACEUTICAL CHEMISTRY. *Current Pos:* SR CHEMIST, MIDWEST RES INST, 87-, CHEM CONSULT, 87- *Personal Data:* b Chiayi, Taiwan, Aug 1, 23; m 63; c 3. *Educ:* Nat Taiwan Univ, BS, 52; Wesleyan Univ, MA, 57; Univ Kans, PhD(chem), 60. *Prof Exp:* Asst chem, Nat Taiwan Univ, 53-55; fel, Wesleyan Univ, 55-57; res assoc, Univ Kans, 57-60; res assoc, Univ Mich, 60-61; assoc chemist, Midwest Res Inst, 61, sr chemist, 61-77; dir, molecular electronics, Carnegie-Mellon Inst Res, Carnegie-Mellon Univ, 78-87. *Concurrent Pos:* Fel, Res Inst, Univ Mich, 60-61; vis prof, Midwest Res Inst, vis specialist of Nat Sci Coun, Repub China & Lectr of Sixth Tamkang Chair, Tamkang Col, 76; mem, Contract Develop Therapeut Comt, Nat Cancer Inst, 85-87. *Mem:* Am Chem Soc; Sigma Xi. *Res:* Synthesis of biologically active organic compounds; organic semiconductors; chemistry of nitrogen heterocyclic compounds; polymer chemistry, reverse osmosis composite membranes; high temperature lubricants; zeroshrink thermosetting polymers; polymer chemistry. *Mailing Add:* 1317 E 101 Terr Kansas City MO 64131

LIAU, GENE, VASCULAR BIOLOGY. *Current Pos:* res scientist I, 87-92, RES SCIENTIST II, DEPT MOLECULAR BIOL, AM RED CROSS, 92- *Personal Data:* b Hsing-Chu, Taiwan, Nov 28, 54. *Educ:* Univ NC, BS, 77; Vanderbilt Univ, PhD(biochem), 82. *Prof Exp:* Fel collagen gene regulation, NIH, 82-85; assoc mem, Dept Cell Biol, Revlon Biotechnol Res Ctr, 85-87. *Concurrent Pos:* Established investr, Am Heart Asn; res career develop award, NIH, 90- *Mem:* Am Soc Biochem & Molecular Biol; AAAS; Soc Chinese Biochemists. *Res:* Vascular biology. *Mailing Add:* Dept Molecular Biol Am Red Cross 15601 Crabbs Branch Way Rockville MD 20855-2743

LIAU, ZONG-LONG, SEMICONDUCTOR LASERS & MATERIALS, INTEGRATED OPTOELECTRONICS. *Current Pos:* STAFF MEM, LINCOLN LAB, MASS INST TECHNOL, 78- *Personal Data:* b Taipei, Taiwan, Aug 25, 50; US citizen; m 79, Jane J Chen; c Albert & Brian. *Educ:* Nat Taiwan Univ, BS, 72; Calif Inst Technol, PhD(appl physics), 79. *Prof Exp:* Vis scientist, Bell Labs, 77-78. *Mem:* Optical Soc Am; Bohmische Phys Soc. *Res:* Physics and technology of semiconductor devices; materials science and engineering; atomic phenomena in compound semiconductor surfaces; fabrication of diode lasers, miniature mirrors, microlenses, integrated micro-optical and optoelectronic systems; issued 9 patents. *Mailing Add:* Lincoln Lab Mass Inst Technol Lexington MA 02173-9108. *Fax:* 781-981-5793; *E-Mail:* liau@ll.mit.edu

LIAUW, KOEI-LIANG, ORGANIC CHEMISTRY. *Current Pos:* PROJ LEADER CENT RES, TECH CTR, WITCO CHEM CORP, 69- *Personal Data:* b Indonesia, May 4, 35; US citizen; m 61; c 1. *Educ:* Nanyang Univ, Singapore, BSc, 60; Univ Calif, Berkeley, MS, 62, PhD(chem), 64. *Prof Exp:* Res chemist, Gen Chem Div, Allied Chem Corp, 64-66; sr res chemist, Mobil Chem Co, Div Mobil Oil Corp, 66-68. *Mem:* Sigma Xi; Am Chem Soc. *Res:* Textile treating agents; paper sizings; process development; synthetic organic chemistry; organotin chemistry; stabilizers for polyvinyl chloride and polyolefins; flame retardants; vapor phase catalysis. *Mailing Add:* 285 W Steven Ave Wyckoff NJ 07481

LIAW, HANG MING, MATERIALS SCIENCE ENGINEERING, ELECTRONICS ENGINEERING. *Current Pos:* prin staff engr, 78-81, mem tech staff, 81-84, SR MEM TECH STAFF, MOTOROLA INC, 84- *Personal Data:* b Taichung, Taiwan, Feb 1, 36; US citizen; m, Chau Yi; c Tsui, Lucy & Sally. *Educ:* Cheng Kung Univ, BS, 59; Pa State Univ, MS, 67, PhD(solid state sci), 70. *Mem:* Inst Elec & Electronics Engrs; Japan Soc Appl Physics. *Res:* Development of piezoelectric aluminum nitride films; effect of sputtering parameters on the characteristics of acoustic wave transducers and resonators fabricated from the sputtered aluminum nitride films. *Mailing Add:* 11540 N 104th St Scottsdale AZ 85260. *Fax:* 602-897-4477; *E-Mail:* rwd720@e.email.mot.com

LIAW, JYE REN, NUCLEAR ENGINEERING, RADIATION PHYSICS. *Current Pos:* mem staff, Appl Physics Div, 80-89, MEM STAFF, REACTOR ANAL DIV, ARGONNE NAT LAB, 90- *Personal Data:* b Hsin-Chu, Taiwan, May 12, 46; m 72; c 2. *Educ:* Nat Tsing Hua Univ, Taiwan, BS, 68; Univ Ore, Eugene, MS, 71; Ore State Univ, PhD(nuclear eng), 75. *Prof Exp:* Res asst physics, Univ Ore, Eugene, 71-73; res asst nuclear eng, Ore State Univ, 73-75; asst prof nuclear eng, Univ Okla, 75-80; consult, Los Alamos Sci Lab, 77-80. *Mem:* Am Phys Soc; Am Nuclear Soc; Sigma Xi; Nat Soc Prof Engrs. *Res:* Nuclear reactor design and analysis; radiation transport and dosimetry; nuclear fission product data evaluation; Van de Graff accelerator and nuclear reactor experiments; high vacuum technology; nuclear fuel reprocessing. *Mailing Add:* 1502 Terrance Dr Naperville IL 60565

LIBAN, ERIC, APPLIED MATHEMATICS. *Current Pos:* assoc prof, 67-71, PROF MATH, YORK COL, 71-, CHMN DEPT, 75- *Personal Data:* b Vienna, Austria, June 20, 21; nat US; m 54; c 3. *Educ:* NY Univ, BA, 48, MS, 49, PhD(math), 57. *Prof Exp:* Instr math, Long Island Univ, 49 & NY Univ, 49-50; asst, Ind Univ, 50-51; mathematician, Naval Res Lab, 51-52; assoc mathematician, Proj Cyclone, Reeves Instrument Corp, NY, 52; sr dynamics engr, Repub Aviation Corp, 52-55; staff mem analog comput & consult ctr, Dian Labs, Inc, 55-58; assoc prof eng sci, Pratt Inst, 58-61; res scientist, Grumman Aircraft Eng Corp, 61-67. *Concurrent Pos:* Lectr, Univ Md, 50; consult, Avco Res & Develop Corp, Mass, 59-60 & Comput Systs, Inc, NJ, 59-61; adj lectr, Polytech Inst Brooklyn, 62-65; adj prof, Adelphi Univ, 66-67; adj assoc prof, Queens Col, 67-68. *Mem:* Am Math Soc; Asn Comput Mach. *Res:* Applications and methods of simulation on analog computers; logical design of computing systems; automata studies; theory of servo and feedback systems; information and communication theory; operations research. *Mailing Add:* Dept Math CUNY York Col 94-20 Guy Brewer Blvd Jamaica NY 11452-0001

LIBBEY, LEONARD MORTON, FOOD SCIENCE. *Current Pos:* From asst prof to assoc prof, 61-81, PROF FOOD SCI & TECHNOL, ORE STATE UNIV, 81- *Personal Data:* b Boston, Mass, Apr 17, 30; m 71. *Educ:* Univ Mass, BVA, 53; Univ Wis, MS, 54; Wash State Univ, PhD(food technol), 61. *Mem:* AAAS; Inst Food Technologists; Am Chem Soc; Am Oil Chemists Soc; Sigma Xi; Am Soc Mass Spectrometry. *Res:* Food chemistry; chromatographic and spectrometric analysis, especially gas chromatography and mass spectrometry. *Mailing Add:* Dept Food Sci & Technol Wiegand Hall Ore State Univ Corvallis OR 97331. *Fax:* 541-737-1877; *E-Mail:* libbeyl@bcc.orst.edu

LIBBEY, WILLIAM JERRY, POLYOLEFINS, ENGINEERING PLASTICS. *Current Pos:* RETIRED. *Personal Data:* b Grand Rapids, Minn, Mar 18, 42; m 64, June Hanson; c William B & Daniel. *Educ:* Carleton Col, BA, 64; Univ Wis, PhD(org chem), 69. *Prof Exp:* Res chemist, Continental Oil Co, 68-72; sr chemist, 72-76, res group leader, Conoco, Inc, 77-81, sect dir, 82-85; sr res assoc, E I Du Pont De Nemours & Co Inc, 85-92, res fel, 92-96. *Mem:* Am Chem Soc. *Res:* Carbonium ion chemistry; thermal rearrangements; alkyl halide chemistry; Fischer-Tropsch chemistry; polyolefins; Ziegler-Natta catalysis; hydrocarbon pyrolysis; high density polyethylene; engineering plastics. *Mailing Add:* 837 Baltimore Pike Chadds Ford PA 19317. *Fax:* 302-695-1513

LIBBRECHT, KENNETH, ASTRONOMY. *Current Pos:* PROF, CALIF INST TECHNOL. *Honors & Awards:* Newton Lacy Pierce Prize, Am Astron Soc, 91. *Mem:* Am Astron Soc. *Res:* Astronomy. *Mailing Add:* Physics 103-33 Calif Inst Technol 1201 E California Pasadena CA 91125-0001

LIBBY, CAROL BAKER, ENZYMOLOGY. *Current Pos:* ASST PROF CHEM, COLBY COL, 85- *Personal Data:* b South Kingstown, RI, Apr 20, 49; m 69; c 1. *Educ:* Pa State Univ, BS, 71, PhD(org chem), 75. *Prof Exp:* Asst prof chem, Oberlin Col, 74-75; vis asst prof chem, Kenyon Col, 75-77; asst prof chem & physics, Skidmore Col, 77-79; mem staff, A E Staley Mfg Co, 79-82; mem staff, Best Foods, Res & Engr Ctr, 83-85; vis asst prof, Univ Maine, Farmington, 86-87. *Concurrent Pos:* Res assoc, State Univ NY, 78. *Mem:* Am Chem Soc; AAAS; Asn Women Sci. *Res:* Enzyme catalyzed reactions, especially mechanism and isolation of enzymes with emphasis on carbohydrate hydrolases and glycoproteins. *Mailing Add:* 384 Pine Top Trail Bethlehem PA 18017-1767

LIBBY, PAUL A(NDREWS), AERONAUTICAL ENGINEERING. *Current Pos:* assoc dean grad studies, 67-72, PROF FLUID MECH, UNIV CALIF, SAN DIEGO, 64- *Personal Data:* b Mineola, NY, Sept 4, 21; m 55; c 2. *Educ:* Polytech Inst Brooklyn, BAE, 42, MS, 47, PhD, 49. *Honors & Awards:* Royal Soc Guest Fel, 82-83. *Prof Exp:* Design engr, Chance Vought Aircraft Co, Conn, 42-43; instr aeronaut eng, Polytech Inst Brooklyn, 43-44, 46-49, from asst prof to prof, 49-64, asst dir aerodyn lab, 59-64. *Concurrent Pos:* Consult, Gen Bronze Corp, 48, NAm Aviation, Inc, 55, Gen Elec Co, 56, Gen Appl Sci Labs, Inc, 56-72, Avco, 76 & Systs Sci & Software, 76-; mem, Fluid Dynamics Panel, Adv Group Aerospace Res & Develop, NATO, 60-72, Fluid Mech Adv Comn, NASA, 63-69, Air Force Systs Command Scramjet Panel, 64-65 & Nat Acad Sci Adv Comn on Scramjet, 65-; corresp mem, Eng Sci Sect, Int Acad Astronaut, Int Astronaut Fedn, 66-; Guggenheim fel, 72-73. *Mem:* Fel Am Inst Aeronaut & Astronaut; Am Phys Soc. *Res:* Combustion theory; turbulent flow; turbulent combustion. *Mailing Add:* Dept AMES 0310 Univ Calif San Diego La Jolla CA 92093

LIBBY, PAUL ROBERT, BIOCHEMISTRY. *Current Pos:* RETIRED. *Personal Data:* b Torrington, Conn, Sept 2, 34; m 59; c 3. *Educ:* Yale Univ, BS, 56; Univ Chicago, PhD(biochem), 62. *Prof Exp:* Fel biochem, Univ Calif, Davis, 62-63; sr cancer res scientist, Roswell Park Mem Inst, 63-72, assoc cancer res scientist, 72-91. *Concurrent Pos:* Res prof, Niagara Univ, NY, 78-; from asst to assoc res prof, Dept Physiol, State Univ NY, 71-80, assoc res prof, Dept Pharmacol, 80-91. *Mem:* AAAS; Am Asn Cancer Res; Endocrine Soc; Am Chem Soc; Am Soc Cell Biol; Sigma Xi. *Res:* Biochemical mechanisms of chemical carcinogenesis. *Mailing Add:* 93 Melody Lane Tonawanda NY 14150

LIBBY, PETER, CELL BIOLOGY, CARDIOVASCULAR MEDICINE. *Current Pos:* PHYSICIAN & DIR, VASCULAR MED & ATHEROSCLEROSIS UNIT, CARDIOVASC DIV, DEPT MED BRIGHAM & WOMEN'S HOSP, 90-; PROF MED, HARVARD MED SCH. *Personal Data:* b Berkeley, Calif, Feb 13, 47; m 75; c 2. *Educ:* Univ Calif, Berkeley, BA, 69; Univ Calif, San Diego, MD, 73. *Hon Degrees:* MA, Harvard Univ, 96. *Honors & Awards:* Merit Award, Nat Heart, Lung & Blood Inst. *Prof Exp:* Res physician, Peter Bent Brigham Hosp, 73-76; res fel physiol, Med Sch, Harvard Univ, 76-79; cardiol fel, Brigham & Women's Hosp, 79-80; from asst prof to assoc prof med, Sch Med, Tufts Univ, 80-90, assoc prof physiol, 88-90. *Concurrent Pos:* S A Levine fel, Am Heart Asn, 76-77; nat res serv award, Nat Heart, Lung & Blood Inst, 76-77; fel, Med Found, 80-82; estab investr, Am Heart Asn; assoc prof med, Harvard Med Sch. *Mem:* Am Heart Asn; Am Soc Cell Biol; AAAS; Am Fedn Clin Res; Am Soc Physiol; Am Soc Clin Invest; Am Col Cardiol; Am Asn Pathologists; Am Asn Immunologists; Asn Am Physicians. *Res:* Cellular, molecular, and inflammatory aspects of cardiovascular diseases; atherogenesis; arterial wall biology. *Mailing Add:* Vascular Med Unit Brigham & Women's Hosp 75 Francis St Boston MA 02115. *Fax:* 617-732-6961

LIBBY, R DANIEL, ENZYMOLOGY, BIO-ORGANIC CHEMISTRY. *Current Pos:* ASSOC PROF & CHAIR CHEM, MORAVIAN COL, 92- *Personal Data:* b Waterville, Maine, Feb 5, 46; m 69, Carol Baker; c Lisa K. *Educ:* Colby Col, AB, 68; Pa State Univ, PhD(chem), 74. *Prof Exp:* Vis asst prof chem, Oberlin Col, 74-75; Kenyan Col, 75-77; asst prof chem, Skidmore Col, 77-80, Barnard Col, 82-85, Colby Col, 85-92; res assoc biochem, Univ Ill, 80-82. *Mem:* Am Chem Soc; Nat Col Sci Teachers Asn. *Res:* Develop an understanding of the interplay among the pathways of the many reactions catalyzed by the enzyme chloroperoxidase. *Mailing Add:* Dept Chem Moravian Col 1200 Main St Bethlehem PA 18018-6650. *Fax:* 610-861-1595; *E-Mail:* rdlibby@moravian.edu

LIBBY, WILLIAM JOHN, (JR), FORESTRY, GENETICS. *Current Pos:* CONSULT, CENTRE ADVAN FOREST BIOTECHNOL, TE TEKO, NZ, 94- *Personal Data:* b Oak Park, Ill, Sept 10, 32; m 56, 91, Iris C Glaesner; c Lisa (Albert), Eric L & Sara (Wampler). *Educ:* Univ Mich, BS, 54; Univ Calif, Berkeley, MS, 59, PhD(genetics), 61. *Prof Exp:* NSF fel genetics, NC State Col, 61-62; asst prof forestry, Univ Calif, Berkeley, 62-67, assoc prof forestry & genetics, 67-72, prof forestry & genetics, 72-94. *Concurrent Pos:* Pack lectr, Yale Univ, 67; L T Murray distinguished vis lectr forest resources, Univ Wash, 68; Fulbright res scholar, NZ Forest Res Inst, Univ Canterbury, Australian Forest Res Inst, 71, Univ Zagreb, 79; sr fel, Norweg Forest Res Inst, 80; lectr, Swed Agr Univ, Garpenberg, Umea, 85; HR MacMillan lectr, Univ BC, 87; vis scientist, NZ Forest Res Inst, 92-93. *Mem:* Soc Am Foresters. *Res:* Quantitative genetics of forest trees; genetic conservation; vegetative propagation of conifers; maturation of woody plant meristems; clonal forestry. *Mailing Add:* 28 Valencia Rd Orinda CA 94563

LIBCHABER, ALBERT JOSEPH, PHYSICS. *Current Pos:* DETLEV W BRONK PROF, ROCKEFELLER UNIV, 95- *Personal Data:* b Paris, France, Oct 23, 34; m 55, Irene Gelman; c Jacques, Remy & David. *Educ:* Univ Paris, BS, 56; Univ Ill, MS, 59; Sch Normale Super, Paris, PhD, 65. *Honors & Awards:* Silver Medal, Fr Phys Soc, 71; Prix Richard, 79; Wolf Prize, Wolf Found, 86. *Prof Exp:* Master res, Nat Ctr Sci Res, Sch Normale, Paris, 67-74, dir, 74-83; prof, Univ Chicago, 83-91, Paul Snowden distinguished serv prof physics, 87-91; prof, Dept Physics, Princeton Univ, NY, 91-94. *Concurrent Pos:* MacArthur Found fel, 86-91; ed, J nonlinearity, 87-93; fel, NEC Res Inst, Princeton, 91- *Mem:* Am Phys Soc; Fr Phys Soc; Am Acad Arts & Sci; NY Acad Sci; corresp mem French Acad Sci. *Res:* Physics; implications of nonlinear dynamics on the physical world, including the biological sciences; the evolution of fluids from laminar states, with emphasis on plate tectonics-like problems, coexistence of convections and solidification. *Mailing Add:* Rockefeller Univ Box No 265 1230 York Ave New York NY 10021-6399. *Fax:* 212-327-7406; *E-Mail:* libchbr@rockvax. rockefeller.edu

LIBELO, LOUIS FRANCIS, THEORETICAL PHYSICS. *Current Pos:* RES PHYSICIST, HARRY DIAMOND LAB, ARMY RES LAB, 80- *Personal Data:* b Brooklyn, NY, Oct 12, 30; m 54; c 4. *Educ:* Brooklyn Col, BS, 53; Univ Md, MS, 56; Rensselaer Polytech Inst, PhD(physics), 64. *Honors & Awards:* Hinman Award, 87. *Prof Exp:* Engr physics, Md Electronics Co, 54; proj engr, Ahrendt Instrument Co, 55; physicist, Opers Res Off, Johns Hopkins Univ, 57-58; asst prof physics, Am Univ, 65-68, adj prof, 68-73; adj prof, State Univ NY, Albany, 73-79. *Concurrent Pos:* Res physicist, US Naval Surface Weapons Ctr, 64-80; consult physicist, L & L Assocs, 76-, Entron Inc & Lutech Inc, 78-81; vis scholar, Rensselaer Polytech Inst, 96-; guest res, US Naval Res Lab, 96-; fel-elect, Summa Found 96; delegate, Nat Asn Acad Sci, 97. *Mem:* Inst Elec & Electronic Engrs; Am Phys Soc; Electromagnetic Soc; Sigma Xi; NY Acad Sci. *Res:* Scattering theory for finite size targets and by apertures; theory of cooperative phenomena in solids; theory of nonlinear phenomena in insulators; microwaves and electromagnetic theory; interaction, coupling and generation. *Mailing Add:* L&L Assocs 9413 Bulls Run Pkwy Bethesda MD 20817

LIBERA, RICHARD JOSEPH, MATHEMATICS. *Current Pos:* from asst prof to assoc prof, 62-73, PROF MATH, UNIV DEL, 73- *Personal Data:* b Thorndike, Mass, Aug 26, 29; m 54; c 2. *Educ:* Am Int Col, BA, 56; Univ Mass, MA, 58; Rutgers Univ, PhD(math), 62. *Prof Exp:* Instr math, Rutgers Univ, 60-62. *Mem:* Am Math Soc; Math Asn Am; Polish Math Soc. *Res:* Geometric function theory. *Mailing Add:* 402 Apple Rd Newark DE 19711-5118

LIBERATORE, FREDERICK ANTHONY, PROTEIN BIOCHEMISTRY. *Current Pos:* MEM STAFF, DUPONT/NEW ENG NUCLEAR CORP, 78- *Personal Data:* b Framingham, Mass, Dec 11, 44; m 68, Jeannine; c 4. *Educ:* Mass State Col Framingham, BA, 70; Univ NH, PhD(biochem), 74. *Prof Exp:* Fel, Ohio State Univ, 74-76; mem staff, Sigma Chem Co, 76-78. *Mem:* AAAS; Sigma Xi; Am Chem Soc. *Res:* Labeling proteins with radioactive isotopes including iodine; protein cross-linking; bifunctional chelators; protein purification and characterization; ELISA and RIA; protein purification; industrial scale-up. *Mailing Add:* 49 Liberty Dr North Billerica MA 01862-3276. *E-Mail:* liberafa@wmvx.dnet.dupont.com

LIBERMAN, ALLEN HARVEY, ELECTRICAL ENGINEERING. *Current Pos:* PARTNER, TRADE QUOTES INC, 81- *Personal Data:* b Memphis, Tenn, Sept 15, 43. *Educ:* Rensselaer Polytech Inst, BEE, 65; Carnegie Inst Technol, MSEE, 66; Univ Detroit, DEng(elec eng), 68. *Prof Exp:* Asst prof comput design, Univ Detroit, 67-69, assoc dir comput eng, 69; vpres comput res & develop, Mgt Sci Inc, 69-70; vpres & dir comput res & develop, Nat Info Serv, Inc, 69-74; vpres finance, DBX Inc, Newton, 74-81. *Concurrent Pos:* Technician, Digital Electronics Inc, 62-63; engr, Fairchild Camera & Instrument Corp, 64-67 & Hell Corp, 65; consult, Burroughs Corp, 68-69; adj prof & grant, Univ Detroit, 69-70. *Mem:* Am Soc Eng Educ; Inst Elec & Electronics Engrs. *Res:* Digital computer applications in personal identification and high density photographic memories; multi-user/multi-task minicomputer operating systems. *Mailing Add:* V P Trade Quotes Inc 675 Massachusetts Ave Cambridge MA 02139

LIBERMAN, ARTHUR DAVID, HIGH ENERGY PHYSICS, NUCLEAR WELL LOGGING. *Current Pos:* AT SCHLUMBERGER-DOLL RES CTR, 80- *Personal Data:* b Newark, NJ, Oct 13, 40; m 68; c 2. *Educ:* Dartmouth Col, AB, 62; Harvard Univ, MA, 63, PhD(physics), 69. *Prof Exp:* Res assoc high energy physics, Linear Accelerator Lab, Univ Paris, 69-70; adj asst prof particle physics, Univ Calif, Los Angeles, 70-74; res physicist, High Energy

Physics Lab, Stanford Univ, 74-80. *Mem:* Am Phys Soc. *Res:* The study of gamma rays and entirely neutral final states in the annihilation interactions at electron-positron storage rings by utilizing the Crystal Ball, a large solid angle, good energy resolution, highly modularized NaI(Tl) detector. *Mailing Add:* Schlumberger-Doll Res Ctr Old Quarry Rd Ridgefield CT 06877. *Fax:* 203-438-3819; *E-Mail:* Liberman@sdr.slb.com

LIBERMAN, IRVING, LASERS, OPTICAL PROCESSING & DEVICES. *Current Pos:* MGR MICROSYSTS, NORTHROP GRUMMAN SCI & TECHNOL CTR, 63- *Personal Data:* b New York, NY, June 24, 37. *Educ:* City Col New York, BEE, 58; Northwestern Univ, MSEE, 60, PhD(elec eng), 65. *Concurrent Pos:* Indust staff mem, Los Alamos Nat Lab, 74-80. *Mem:* Am Phys Soc; Optical Soc Am; Sigma Xi. *Res:* Development of optically pumped solid state lasers and transverse electrically excited gas lasers; design, installation, alignment, and evaluation of optical systems; development of miniature atomic clocks; development of electro-optical components and devices. *Mailing Add:* Northrop Grumman Sci Technol Ctr 1350 Beulah Rd Pittsburgh PA 15235. *Fax:* 412-256-1661

LIBERMAN, MARTIN HENRY, ANALYTICAL & POLYMER CHEMISTRY. *Current Pos:* CHEMIST, US CUSTOMS SERV, 74- *Personal Data:* b Los Angeles, Calif, Oct 5, 36; m 67; c 1. *Educ:* Univ Calif, Los Angeles, BS, 58; Fla State Univ, PhD(phys chem), 68. *Prof Exp:* Asst, US Army Med Res & Nutrit Lab, Denver, Colo, 60-62; res assoc, Stanford Univ, 68-72. *Mem:* Am Chem Soc; Royal Soc Chem; AAAS. *Res:* Analytical chemistry; polymer chemistry. *Mailing Add:* 145 Lundy Lane Palo Alto CA 94306-4563

LIBERMAN, ROBERT PAUL, PSYCHIATRY, CLINICAL PSYCHOLOGY. *Current Pos:* PROF PSYCHIAT RESIDENCE, SCH MED, UNIV CALIF, LOS ANGELES, 77-; PRIN INVESTR & DIR, MENT HEALTH CLIN RES CTR SCHIZOPHRENIA & PSYCHIAT REHAB. *Personal Data:* b Newark, NJ, Aug 16, 37; m 61, 73; c 5. *Educ:* Dartmouth Col, AB, 59; Dartmouth Med Sch, dipl med, 60; Univ Calif, MS, 61; Johns Hopkins Univ, MD, 63. *Honors & Awards:* First Prize, Int Rehab Film Festival, 83; Silvano Arieti Award, Am Acad Psychoanal, 86; Samuel Hibbs Award Innovations Treat, Am Psychiat Asn, 88, Arnold Van Ameringen Award Psychiat Rehab, 89; Howard Davis Mem Award, Knowledge Transfer Soc, 89. *Prof Exp:* Intern internal med, Bronx Munic Hosp Ctr, Albert Einstein Col Med, 63-64; res scientist, NIMH, 68-70; from asst prof to assoc prof, 70-76, prof psychiat, Sch Med, Univ Calif, Los Angeles, 77-; dir, prog clin res, Camarillo-Neuropsychiat Inst Res Prog, 70-; chief rehab med serv, Brentwood VA Med Ctr, 80. *Concurrent Pos:* NIMH res grants, 67-; consult various insts & govt, 70-; consult, Ventura Co, Los Angeles Co Ment Health Dept & Calif State Dept Ment Health, 72-; Fogarty sr res int fel, NIH, 75-76; assoc ed, J Appl Behav Anal, 76-77 & Schizophrenia Bull, 80-86; mem med staff, var hosps, 70-; prin investr, Mental Health Clin Res Ctr, 77- & proj dir, Rehab Res & Training Ctr, 80-85; mem, Res Rev Comt, NIMH, 79-81; consult, Charter Pac Hosp, 84-87; pres, Psychiat Rehab Consults, 85-; co-prin investr, Ctr Improving Ment Health Servs, 91-96. *Mem:* Fel Am Psychiat Asn; Asn Advan Behav Ther; Physicians Social Responsibility; Int Physicians Against Nuclear War- *Res:* Experimental analysis of behavior in clinical psychiatry and psychology; interactions between drug effects and behavior modification; community mental health; behavior therapy; schizophrenia; author of numerouus publications. *Mailing Add:* Community & Rehab Psychiat W Los Angeles VA Med Ctr 11301 Wilshire Blvd Los Angeles CA 90073

LIBERTA, ANTHONY E, MYCOLOGY. *Current Pos:* RETIRED. *Personal Data:* b La Salle, Ill, May 17, 33; m 60, Susan Fitch; c Marc R & Valerie S. *Educ:* Knox Col, Ill, AB, 55; Univ Ill, Urbana, MS, 59, PhD(bot), 61. *Prof Exp:* Res mycologist, Ill State Natural Hist Surv, 61; from assoc prof to prof mycol, Ill State Univ, 61-90, distinguished prof, 90-93. *Concurrent Pos:* NSF grants, 63-71 & 81-87. *Mem:* Mycol Soc Am. *Res:* Effects of soil disturbance and surface-mining on endomycorrhizae; ecological relationships of prairie plants and endomycorrhizae; antifungal/antitumor activity of thiosemicarbazones. *Mailing Add:* 905 Ruston Ave Normal IL 61761-2817

LIBERTI, FRANK NUNZIO, POLYMER CHEMISTRY, PHYSICAL CHEMISTRY. *Current Pos:* Develop chemist, Gen Elec Co, 67-69, specialist prod develop, 69-73, mgr qual assurance, 73-75, specialist advan develop, 75-76, specialist prod develop, 76-79, mgr process technol, 79-85, mgr prod develop progs, Plastics Bus Group, 85-88, mgr, Lexan Core Prod Technol, 88-90, prog commercialization leader, 90-93, SITE RAW MAT PROGS LEADER, GEN ELEC PLASTICS, 93- *Personal Data:* b Warsaw, NY, Nov 2, 39; m 66, Margaret P Curley; c Patricia & Michael. *Educ:* Rensselaer Polytech Inst, BChE, 61, PhD(phys chem), 67. *Mem:* Soc Plastics Engrs. *Res:* Stabilization of polymers; flame retardant polymers; solid state of polymers; polymer crystallinity; thermal analysis of polymers. *Mailing Add:* Gen Elec Plastics One Lexan Lane Mt Vernon IN 47620. *Fax:* 812-831-7189; *E-Mail:* frank.liberti@gep.ge.com

LIBERTI, JOSEPH POLLARA, CELL BIOLOGY. *Current Pos:* from asst prof to assoc prof, 67-75, PROF BIOCHEM, MED COL VA, RICHMOND, 75- *Personal Data:* b Passaic, NJ, Nov 2, 37. *Educ:* Fairleigh Dickinson Univ, BS, 59; Loyola Univ, MS, 62, PhD(biochem), 64. *Prof Exp:* Res fel biochem, Univ Minn, 64-65; res fel endocrinol, Mem Sloan-Kettering Cancer Inst, 65-66, res assoc, 66-67. *Concurrent Pos:* Instr biochem, Cornell Univ Med Ctr, 66-67; vis prof, Oxford Univ, 77-78; vis scientist, Sloan-Kettering Cancer Inst, 83-84. *Mem:* Endocrine Soc; Am Chem Soc; Am Soc Biochem & Molecular Biol. *Res:* Regulation of cell growth and proliferation: molecular actions of lactogenic hormones, particularly post-receptor signalling events. *Mailing Add:* Dept Biochem Box 614 Med Col Va Sta Med Col Va Richmond VA 23298

LIBERTI, PAUL A, MAGNETIC LIQUIDS. *Current Pos:* pres & chief scientist, 83-94, CHIEF EXEC OFF IMMUNICON CORP, 94- *Personal Data:* b Lyndhurst, NJ, Mar 18, 36; m 96, Rae Francis; c Paul P, Theodore, Roseanne & Joseph. *Educ:* Columbia Col, AB, 59; Loyola Univ, Ill, MS, 61; Stevens Inst Technol, PhD(phys chem), 66. *Honors & Awards:* Ottens Res Award, 69. *Prof Exp:* From instr to prof biochem, Jefferson Med Col, 67-84. *Concurrent Pos:* Lectr, Fairleigh Dickenson Univ, 64-67 & Temple Univ, 67-; res fel phys chem, Stevens Inst Technol, 66; Nat Inst Allergy & Infectious Dis res career develop award, 73; adj prof biochem, Jefferson Med Col, 84- *Mem:* Am Asn Immunol; Am Asn Biol Chem; Am Soc Hemat. *Res:* Discovery and development of magnetic liquids and their application to tumor cell detection, cell ethergy and immuno assay. *Mailing Add:* Immunicon Corp 1310 Masons Mill Bus Park Huntingdon Valley PA 19006

LIBERTINY, GEORGE ZOLTAN, MECHANICAL ENGINEERING, MATERIALS SCIENCE. *Current Pos:* sr res engr, 71-73, prin res eng assoc, Advan Testing Methods Dept, 73-78, PRIN RES ENG ASSOC, AUTOMOTIVE SAFETY OFF, FORD MOTOR CO, 78- *Personal Data:* b Szolnok, Hungary, June 14, 34; m 56, Anna; c Thomas & Karen. *Educ:* Univ Strathclyde, BSc, 59; Bristol Univ, PhD(mech eng), 64. *Honors & Awards:* R R Teetor Award, Soc Automotive Engrs, 67, Forest R McFarland Award, 83. *Prof Exp:* Res & develop engr, English Elec Co Ltd, Eng, 59-60; from asst prof to assoc prof mech eng, Univ Miami, 63-68; assoc prof, Ill Inst Technol, 68-71. *Concurrent Pos:* Mem, US Adv Comt, Int Stand Orgn Fluid Power, 68-71, Eng Educ Comt, Soc Automotive Engrs, 73-86, chmn, 84-86, Am Soc Mech Engrs, 74-, chmn, 87-; assoc ed, J Vibration, Stress & Reliability in Design, 82-86; adj prof mech eng, Univ Mich, 83-; consult, safety, mfg & design. *Mem:* Fel Am Soc Mech Engrs; Sigma Xi; Soc Automotive Engrs; Soc Exp Stress Anal; Am Soc Eng Educ. *Res:* Fatigue of metals; static and dynamic fractures due to multiaxial stress-strain systems; nondestructive testing; experimental stress analysis; high pressure engineering; design; safety risk analysis; special transducer. *Mailing Add:* 24637 Rockford St Dearborn MI 48124. *Fax:* 313-594-2268

LIBET, BENJAMIN, PHYSIOLOGY. *Current Pos:* from asst to prof physiol, 62-84, EMER PROF PHYSIOL, MED SCH, UNIV CALIF, SAN FRANCISCO, 84- *Personal Data:* b Chicago, Ill, Apr 12, 16; m 39, Fay Evans; c Julian, Moreen, Ralph & Gayla. *Educ:* Univ Chicago, BS, 36, PhD(physiol), 39. *Prof Exp:* Asst physiol, Univ Chicago, 37-39; instr, Albany Med Col, 39-40; res assoc physiol & biochem, Inst Pa Hosp, 40-43; instr physiol, Sch Med, Univ Pa, 43-44; mat engr, Personal Equip Lab, USAF, Ohio, 44-45; from instr to asst prof physiol, Univ Chicago, 45-48; staff physiologist, Kabat-Kaiser Inst, 48-49. *Concurrent Pos:* Consult, Mt Zion Neurol Inst, 56-; vis scientist, Japan Soc for Promotion of Sci, 79; fel, Commonwealth Fund, 56-57 & 64; scholar, Bellagio Study, Ctr Rockfeller Found, 77. *Mem:* Fel AAAS; Am Physiol Soc; Soc Neurosci; Int Brain Res Orgn. *Res:* Neurophysiology; electrical and metabolic aspects of neural function; synaptic mechanisms; cerebral mechanisms in conscious experience. *Mailing Add:* Dept Physiol S-762 Sch Med Univ Calif San Francisco CA 94143-0444

LIBOFF, ABRAHAM R, MEDICAL PHYSICS, BIOPHYSICS. *Current Pos:* PROF PHYSICS & CHMN DEPT, OAKLAND UNIV, 72-, DIR MED PHYSICS PROG, 73- *Personal Data:* b Paterson, NJ, Aug 27, 27; m 52; c 1. *Educ:* Brooklyn Col, BS, 48; NY Univ, MS, 52, PhD(physics), 64. *Prof Exp:* Jr physicist, Naval Ord Lab, Md, 48-50; sr physicist, Metall Res Lab, Sylvania Elec Prod, Inc, 51-58; res asst cosmic ray lab, NY Univ, 59-64, assoc res scientist, 64-68, assoc dir environ radiation lab, 68-69, sr res scientist & proj coordr, Biophys Res Lab, 69-72. *Concurrent Pos:* Adj assoc prof physics, Hunter Col, NY, 68-72. *Mem:* Am Phys Soc; Biophys Soc; Am Geophys Union; Am Asn Physicists in Med; Bioelec Repair & Growth Soc (secy, 81). *Res:* Physics of collagenous tissues; biophysics of growth and development; electrically induced osteogenesis; sea-level cosmic ray ionization; environmental radiation; acoustic detection of nucleonic cascades; pyroelectric properties of bone. *Mailing Add:* Dept Physics Oakland Univ Rochester MI 48309-4401

LIBOFF, RICHARD L, THEORETICAL PHYSICS. *Current Pos:* assoc prof, 64-69, PROF ELEC ENG & APPL PHYSICS, CORNELL UNIV, 69- *Personal Data:* b New York, NY, Dec 30, 31; m 54; c 2. *Educ:* Brooklyn Col, AB, 53; NY Univ, PhD(physics), 61. *Prof Exp:* Res asst appl math, Courant Inst Math Sci, NY Univ, 56-61, asst prof physics, NY Univ, 62-64. *Concurrent Pos:* Chief consult, NRA, Inc, 63-65; prin investr, Off Naval Res contract, 66-76, Air Force Off Sci Res, 77-81 & Army Res Off, 83-; Solvay fel, Univ Brussels, 71; vis prof physics, Univ Paris, Orsay, 79 & Tel Aviv Univ, 84 & 85; consult, Battelle Columbus Lab, 83 & 85; Fulbright scholar, 84. *Mem:* AAAS; fel Am Phys Soc; sr mem Inst Elec & Electronics Engrs. *Res:* Kinetic theory; quantum mechanics; short wavelength lasing; fusion physics; dense recombining plasma; strongly coupled plasmas and fluids; condensed-matter theory; semiconductor transport and superlattice theory; applied mathematics with emphasis on classical and quantum chaos; author of 3 technical books. *Mailing Add:* Dept Elec Eng Cornell Univ Ithaca NY 14850

LIBONATI, JOSEPH PETER, CLINICAL MICROBIOLOGY. *Current Pos:* From instr to asst prof med clin microbiol, Sch Med, 68-77, SPEC LECTR MICROBIOL, SCH DENT, UNIV MD, BALTIMORE, 69-; CHIEF, DIV MICROBIOL, LABS ADMIN, MD STATE DEPT HEALTH & MENT HYG, 77- *Personal Data:* b Philadelphia, Pa, Nov 16, 41; m 69; c 3. *Educ:* St Joseph's Col, Pa, BS, 63; Duquesne Univ, MS, 65; Univ Md, Baltimore, PhD(microbiol), 68. *Mem:* AAAS; Am Soc Microbiol. *Res:* Enteric bacterial diseases; pathophysiology; immunologic response and vaccine development. *Mailing Add:* 3801 Juniper Rd Baltimore MD 21218

LIBOVE, CHARLES, STRUCTURES, FAILURE ANALYSIS. *Current Pos:* from instr to assoc prof, 58-67, PROF MECH & AEROSPACE ENG, SYRACUSE UNIV, 67- *Personal Data:* b New York, NY, Nov 7, 23; m 51, Rosa G; c Joel & Fred. *Educ:* City Col NY, BCE, 44; Univ Va, MS, 52; Syracuse Univ, PhD(mech eng), 62. *Prof Exp:* Aeronaut res scientist, Nat Adv Comt Aeronaut, 44-53; appl mathematician, Brush Labs, 53-55; assoc prof aeronaut eng, Tri-State Col, 55-58. *Concurrent Pos:* Fel, NSF, Nottingham Univ, 67-68; consult, Pratt & Whitney Aircraft Co, 79 & 80. *Mem:* Am Soc Civil Engrs; assoc fel Am Inst Aeronaut & Astronaut; fel Am Soc Mech Engrs; Struct Stability Res Coun. *Res:* Stress analysis of swept wings, sandwich plates, composite thin-walled beams, corrugated plates and microelectronic packaging; elastic stability. *Mailing Add:* Dept Mech & Aerospace Eng Syracuse Univ Syracuse NY 13244-1240. *Fax:* 315-443-9099

LIBOW, LESLIE S, GERIATRICS, INTERNAL MEDICINE. *Current Pos:* CLIN DIR LONG TERM CARE DEPT, GERIAT & ADULT DEVELOP, MT SINAI SCH MED & CHIEF MED SERV, JEWISH HOME & HOSP AGED, NY. *Personal Data:* b New York, NY; m 73; c 2. *Educ:* Brooklyn Col, BA, 54; Chicago Med Sch, MD, 58. *Honors & Awards:* Kent Award, Geront Soc Am, 81; Mascher-Manning Award, Am Geriat Soc, 87. *Prof Exp:* Intern, Mt Sinai Hosp New York, 58-59, resident, 63-64; resident, Bronx Vet Admin Hosp, 59-60; clin assoc bio-med psychiat, NIH, 60-62, res assoc, 62-63; chief geriat med, Mt Sinai City Hosp Ctr, Elmhurst, NY, 64-75; from asst prof to assoc prof med, Mt Sinai Sch Med, NY, 67-75; assoc prof, 75-78, prof med, State Univ NY Stony Brook, 78-; med dir, Jewish Inst Geriat Care, New Hyde Park, NY & chief geriat med, Long Island Jewish Hillside Med Ctr, NY, 75- *Concurrent Pos:* Consult to dir, Nat Inst Aging, Bethesda, 76-; consult, NIH, 75- *Mem:* Geront Soc; Am Geriat Soc; Am Col Physicians; AAAS. *Res:* Diseases of late life; brain and behavioral changes; human aging; thyroid disease; health care delivery. *Mailing Add:* Dept Geriat & Adult Develop Mt Sinai Sch Med One Gustave L Levy Pl New York NY 10029

LIBOWITZ, GEORGE GOTTHART, SOLID STATE CHEMISTRY, MATERIALS SCIENCE. *Current Pos:* CONSULT, G G LIBOWITZ, INC, 86- *Personal Data:* b Brooklyn, NY, June 18, 23; m 49, 86, Jeannette Julian; c Skona (Brittain) & Steven. *Educ:* Brooklyn Col, BA, 45, MA, 50; Cornell Univ, PhD(phys chem), 54. *Prof Exp:* Chemist, Chromium Corp Am, 45-46, R Kann Chem Lab, 47-48 & Picatinny Arsenal, US Army, 49; asst physics, Cornell Univ, 49-53; sr engr chem, Sylvania Elec Prod, Inc, 54; res assoc, Tufts Univ, 54-57; res supvr, Atomics Int Div, NAm Aviation, Inc, 57-61; sect head, Mat Sci Lab, Aerospace Corp, 61-63; staff scientist, Ledgemont Lab, Kennecott Copper Corp, 63-73; mgr, Solid State Chem Dept, Mat Res Ctr, Allied-Signal Corp, 73-78, mgr, Inorg & Solid State Chem Dept, Corp Res Ctr, 78-80, sr scientist, 80-86. *Concurrent Pos:* Lectr, Dept Metall, Univ Denver, 65; assoc ed, Solid State Ionics, 80-84, Mat Letters, 82-88; co ed, Mat Sci & Technol Series, 80-86; consult, Dept Energy & Environ, Brookhaven Nat Lab, 81-82; chmn, Gordon Res Conf Metal Hydrides, 83. *Mem:* AAAS; Am Chem Soc; fel Am Phys Soc; Sigma Xi; NY Acad Sci; Int Asn Hydrogen Energy; Mat Res Soc. *Res:* Solid state chemistry; metal hydrides and metal-hydrogen systems; nonstoichiometric compounds; thermodynamic properties of solids. *Mailing Add:* G G Libowitz Inc PO Box 392 Morristown NJ 07963. *Fax:* 973-984-1691; *E-Mail:* 75037.3144@compuserve.com

LIBURDY, ROBERT P, EXPERIMENTAL BIOLOGY. *Current Pos:* RES STAFF SCIENTIST, LAWRENCE BERKELEY LAB, RES MED & RADIATION BIOPHYS DIV, BIOELECTROMAGNETIC RES FACIL, 84- *Personal Data:* b Detroit, Mich, Oct 23, 47; m. *Educ:* Brown Univ, PhD(biochem), 75; Univ Northern Colo, MBA, 80. *Prof Exp:* Grad teaching fel introductory biol, molecular biophysics & biochem pharmacol, Dept Biol & Med Sci, Brown Univ, 69-74; chief, Environ Health Serv, USAF Clin, Electronic Syst Div, Hanscom AFB, Mass, 80-81; asst prof environ med, Inst Environ Med, NY Univ Med Ctr, New York, NY, 81-84. *Concurrent Pos:* Prin investr, Electromagnetic Radiation Bioeffects Res Prog, Radiation Sci Div, USAF Sch Aerospace Med, Brooks AFB, 75-80; prin investr, USAF Proj, 75-80, Off Naval Res Proj, 81-87, Div Res Resources, NIH, 84-85, Liposome Technol, Inc, Menlo Park, Calif, 86-; Dept Energy Proj, 88- & NIH Proj, High-Field NMR Bioeffects, 91-; prog environ health sci, Grad Sch Arts & Sci, NY Univ, Washington Sq, New York, 81-84; course instr, Health Effects of Nonionizing Electromagnetic Radiation, Prog Environ Health Sci & Grad Sch Arts & Sci, NY Univ, Washington Sq, New York, 83-84; adj prof mech eng, Col Eng, Clemson Univ, SC, 87-; co-prin investr, Dept Energy Proj, Off Health & Environ Res, 88- *Mem:* Am Asn Immunologists; Am Chem Soc; Am Heart Asn; Am Soc Biochem & Molecular Biol; Bioelectromagnetics Soc; Biophys Soc; Inst Elec & Electronics Engrs; NY Acad Sci; Radiation Res Soc; Sigma Xi. *Res:* Electromagnetic field interactions with biological systems; liposome drug delivery; response of cellular systems to hyperthermia; atherogenesis. *Mailing Add:* Lawrence Berkeley Lab Res Med & Radiation Biophys Univ Calif Bioelectromagnetics Res Facil Lbl-Bldg 934 One Cyclotron Rd Berkeley CA 94720-0001

LICARI, JAMES JOHN, ORGANIC CHEMISTRY. *Current Pos:* RETIRED. *Personal Data:* b Norwalk, Conn, July 22, 30; m 48. *Educ:* Fordham Univ, BS, 52; Princeton Univ, PhD, 55. *Prof Exp:* Res chemist, Am Cyanamid Co, 55-57; res proj chemist, Am Potash & Chem Corp, 57-59; sr res engr, NAm Aviation, Inc, 59-61, supvr org chem, 61-67, group scientist, Res & Eng Div, NAm Rockwell Corp, 67-70, supvr chem lab, 70-72, mgr, Microcircuit Eng Labs, Rockwell Int Corp, Anaheim, 72-88. *Concurrent Pos:* Asst prof, Fordham Univ, 55-56; lectr, Cal State Univ, Fullerton. *Mem:* Am Chem Soc; Int Soc Hybrid Microelec. *Res:* Materials and processes for microelectronics. *Mailing Add:* 15711 Arbela Dr Whittier CA 90603

LICEAGA, CARLOS ARTURO, RELIABILITY MODELING, FAULT-TOLERANT COMPUTING. *Current Pos:* RES COMPUT ENGR, NASA-LANGLEY RES CTR, 79- *Personal Data:* b San Juan, PR, Nov 20, 58; m 80, Marisol Pina; c Juan, Camil & Mariel. *Educ:* Univ PR, BS, 81; Col William & Mary, MS, 84; Carnegie-Mellon Univ, PhD, 92. *Concurrent Pos:* Instr, Electronics Col & Comput Prog, 81; asst instr comput eng, Carnegie-Mellon Univ, 85; comput sci instr, Thomas Nelson Community Col, 87-88; consult comput engr, Compass Consults Corp, 90; asst prof comput sci, Col William A Mary, 93 & comput eng, Old Dominion, 93. *Mem:* Inst Elec & Electronics Engrs; Digital Equip Comput Users Soc. *Res:* Automation of reliability and availability modeling of life-critical fault-tolerant computer systems; software reliability engineering and modeling; fault-tolerant hardware and software research and design. *Mailing Add:* 935 Elton Hall Circle Newport News VA 23608

LI-CHAN, EUNICE, FOOD PROTEIN CHEMISTRY, CHEMICAL MODIFICATION. *Current Pos:* res asst, Univ BC, 82-83, res assoc food chem, Dept Food Sci, 83-91, asst prof, 92-94, ASSOC PROF, UNIV BC, 94- *Personal Data:* b Hong Kong, 23, 53; Can citizen; m 76, Michael; c Timothy & Nicholas. *Educ:* Univ BC, BSc, 75, PhD(food sci), 81; Univ Alta, MSc, 77. *Prof Exp:* Killam fel food chem, Can Coun, 80-82. *Mem:* Am Chem Soc; Inst Food Technologists; Can Inst Food Sci & Technol; Am Oil Chemists Soc. *Res:* Properties of food proteins, including the relationship of molecular structure to function; improvement in nutritional and functional properties by chemical or enzymatic modification; utilization of yolk antibodies; raman spectroscopy of food proteins. *Mailing Add:* Dept Food Sci Univ BC 6650 NW Marine Dr Vancouver BC V6T 1Z4 Can. *Fax:* 604-822-3959

LICHENS-PARK, ANN ELIZABETH, RISK ASSESSMENT OF ENVIRONMENTAL INTRODUCTIONS OF BIOTECHNOLOGY PRODUCTS, DEVELOPER OF BIOMONITORING DATABASE ON CD-ROM. *Current Pos:* PROG DIR, COOP STATE EDUC & EXTEN SERV, USDA, 92- *Personal Data:* b Oakland, Calif, Sept 7, 58; m 87, Samuel L Park; c Shirley & Christina. *Educ:* Pomona Col, BA, 80; Harvard Univ, PhD(microbiol & molecular genetics), 88. *Prof Exp:* Res technician, Vet Admin, 80-81; fel, Harvard Univ, 88-89 & Dartmouth Med Sch, 89-90. *Mem:* AAAS. *Res:* Developed a database on CD-ROM containing information pertaining to the safety/risk of field testing biotechnology products. *Mailing Add:* Coop State Educ & Exten Serv USDA Stop 2241 1400 Independence Ave SW Washington DC 20250-2241. *Fax:* 202-401-4888; *E-Mail:* lichenspark@csrs.esusda.gov

LICHSTEIN, HERMAN CARLTON, microbiology, medical education; deceased, see previous edition for last biography

LICHT, ARTHUR LEWIS, PHYSICS. *Current Pos:* ASSOC PROF, DEPT PHYSICS, UNIV ILL, CHICAGO CIRCLE, 70- *Personal Data:* b Hartford, Conn, Dec 18, 34; m 58. *Educ:* Brown Univ, BSc, 57; Univ Md, PhD(physics), 63. *Prof Exp:* Physicist, Nat Bur Stands, 57-59; res physicist, NASA, 59-61 & US Naval Ord Lab, 61-70. *Concurrent Pos:* Asst prof, Univ Md, 63-65; mem sch math, Inst Adv Study, 65-66. *Mem:* Am Phys Soc. *Res:* Space physics; quantum field theory. *Mailing Add:* Physics Dept Univ Ill Chicago 845 W Taylor St #2236 Chicago IL 60607-7059

LICHT, PAUL, ZOOLOGY, ENDOCRINOLOGY. *Current Pos:* From asst prof to assoc prof, 64-73, PROF ZOOL & CHMN DEPT, UNIV CALIF, BERKELEY, 73-, DEAN, DIV BIOL. *Personal Data:* b St Louis, Mo, Mar 12, 38; m 63. *Educ:* Washington Univ (Mo), AB, 59; Univ Mich, MS, 61, PhD(zool), 64. *Honors & Awards:* Grace Pickford Award. *Concurrent Pos:* USF grants, 64-90; Lalor Found grant, 67-68; consult ed, Col Div, McGraw-Hill Book Co, 68-; chmn, Comp Endocrinol Div, Am Soc Zoologists. *Mem:* Fel AAAS; Soc Study Reproduction; Soc Integrative Comp Biol; Am Soc Ichthyologists & Herpetologists. *Res:* Comparative physiology and evolution of pituitary hormones with special reference to reproduction; endocrinology of thyroid hormone bindings and sexual development in hyenas. *Mailing Add:* Dept Integrative Biol Univ Calif Berkeley CA 94720. *Fax:* 510-642-2286; *E-Mail:* licht@garnet.berkeley.edu

LICHT, STUART LAWRENCE, SOLAR ENERGY & ENERGY STORAGE, ELECTROCHEMISTRY & ANALYTICAL CHEMISTRY. *Current Pos:* CARLSON CHAIR & ASSOC PROF CHEM, CLARK UNIV, 88- *Personal Data:* b Boston, Mass, July 24, 54. *Educ:* Wesleyan Univ, BA(chem) & BA(physics), 76, MA, 80; The Weizmann Inst Sci, PhD(chem), 86. *Honors & Awards:* Delek Energy Award, Delek Corp, 83; Elad Res Excellence Award, Weizmann Inst, 85; Weizmann-Bantrell Award, Bantrell Found of Israel, 86. *Concurrent Pos:* Vis asst prof chem, Northeastern Univ, 85-86; vis scientist & fel chem, Mass Inst Technol, 85-86. *Mem:* Am Chem Soc; Electro Chem Soc; Sigma Xi; Mat Res Soc. *Res:* Highest efficiency photoelectrochemical solar cells, novel materials for electrochemical energy storage, sulfur chemistry, analytical and environmental methods, and fundamental studies in the structure of electrolytes (pH, conductivity, and microelectrochemistry) and in electron correlation. *Mailing Add:* Dept Chem Technion Israel Inst Technol Haifa 32000 Israel

LICHT, W(ILLIAM), JR, CHEMICAL ENGINEERING. *Current Pos:* RETIRED. *Personal Data:* b Cincinnati, Ohio, Sept 29, 15; m 42. *Educ:* Univ Cincinnati, ChE, 37, MS, 39, PhD(chem eng), 50. *Honors & Awards:* Award, Am Inst Chem Engrs, 72. *Prof Exp:* Asst, Univ Cincinnati, 37-39, from instr to prof, 39-85, head dept, 54-68, emer prof chem eng, 85-86. *Concurrent Pos:* Consult govt & var indust concerns, 42-; vis prof, Univ Minn, 68 & 72. *Mem:* Am Soc Eng Educ; fel Am Inst Chem Engrs; Air Pollution Control Asn. *Res:*

Properties of azeotropic mixtures; drying of gases and refrigerants; adsorption in dessicant beds; dewpoint indicators; mechanics of drops; air pollution control; dust collection; design of systems; mathematical modelling particulate collection; fuel ethanol production. *Mailing Add:* 3580 Shaw Ave Cincinnati OH 45208

LICHTBLAU, IRWIN MILTON, CHEMICAL ENGINEERING. *Current Pos:* Sr res engr, Chevron Res Corp, 63-69, asst mgr systs develop & appln, Western Opers Inc, 69-71, mgr comput opers, Comput Serv Dept, 71-74, sr eng assoc, Chevron Res Corp, sr staff econ analyst, Anal Div, 76-80, CONSULT, CORP DEVELOP, STAND OIL CALIF, 80- *Personal Data:* b Woodmere, NY, May 11, 36; m 65. *Educ:* Princeton Univ, BSE, 58; Yale Univ, MEng, 60, DEng, 63. *Mem:* Am Inst Chem Engrs; Sigma Xi. *Res:* Petroleum process design; high pressure technology; compressibility of gas mixtures at high pressures and temperatures. *Mailing Add:* 1096 Upper Happy Valley Rd Lafayette CA 94549

LICHTEN, WILLIAM LEWIS, PHYSICS. *Current Pos:* dir undergrad studies, 69-71, PROF PHYSICS, YALE UNIV, 64-, PROF PHYSICS & ENG & APPL SCI, 75- *Personal Data:* b Philadelphia, Pa, Mar 5, 28; m 50, Susan Larie; c Michael, Stephen & Julia. *Educ:* Swarthmore Col, BA, 49; Univ Chicago, MS, 53, PhD(physics), 56. *Prof Exp:* NSF fel, 56-57; res physicist, Radiation Lab, Columbia Univ, 57-58; from asst prof to assoc prof physics, Univ Chicago, 58-64. *Concurrent Pos:* Mem bd dirs, Nat Asn Metric Educ. *Mem:* Fel Am Phys Soc; Am Asn Physics Teachers. *Res:* Psychology of perception; biophysics; chemical physics; optics; laser spectroscopy; atomic physics; science education; educational research. *Mailing Add:* Dept Physics Yale Univ Box 6666 New Haven CT 06520

LICHTENBAUM, STEPHEN, NUMBER THEORY. *Current Pos:* chmn, Dept Math 94-97, PROF MATH, BROWN UNIV, 90- *Personal Data:* b Brooklyn, NY, Aug 24, 39; m 61, Marilyn Harris; c Karen, Peter, Erica, Roger & Amy. *Educ:* Harvard Univ, AB, 60, AM, 61, PhD(math), 64. *Prof Exp:* Lectr math, Princeton Univ, 64-67; from asst prof to assoc prof, Cornell Univ, 67-73, chmn, Dept Math, 79-82, prof math, 73-90. *Concurrent Pos:* Guggenheim fel, John Simon Guggenheim Mem Found, 73-74. *Mem:* Am Math Soc. *Res:* Algebraic number theory and algebraic geometry, particularly the study of the values of zeta and L-functions. *Mailing Add:* Dept Math Brown Univ Providence RI 02912. *Fax:* 401-863-9013; *E-Mail:* slicht@math.brown.edu

LICHTENBERG, ALLAN J, NON-LINEAR DYNAMICS. *Current Pos:* From asst prof to assoc prof, 61-72, PROF ELEC ENG & COMP SCI, UNIV CALIF, BERKELEY, 72- *Personal Data:* b Passaic, NJ; m 59, Elizabeth Lind. *Educ:* Harvard Univ, AB, 52; Mass Inst Technol, MS, 54; Oxford, DPhil, 61. *Concurrent Pos:* Chmn energy & resources group, Univ Calif, Berkeley; Guggenheim fel, 65, NSF fel, 84. *Mem:* Fel Am Phys Soc. *Res:* Plasma physics and engineering; non-linear dynamics; energy conservation and related problems. *Mailing Add:* Elec Eng & Comput Sci Dept Univ Calif Berkeley CA 94720

LICHTENBERG, BYRON KURT, BIOENGINEERING, BIOMEDICAL ENGINEERING. *Current Pos:* PRES, OMEGA AEROSPACE INC, 91- *Personal Data:* b Stroudsburg, Pa, Feb 19, 48; m 70; c 2. *Educ:* Brown Univ, ScB, 69; Mass Inst Technol, MS, 75, ScD, 79. *Hon Degrees:* DSc, Westminster Univ, 93. *Honors & Awards:* Haley Spaceflight Award, Aerospace Indust Asn Am; Spaceflight Award, NASA, 83 & 92; Komarov Award, Int Aeronaut Fedn, 84. *Prof Exp:* Res scientist, Mass Inst Technol, 78-84; pres, Payload Syst, 84-89, chief scientist, 89-91. *Concurrent Pos:* Res affil, Mass Inst Technol. *Mem:* Sigma Xi; Asn Space Explorers. *Res:* Human adaptation to spaceflight particularly in the field of the inner ear system; human-machine interface, performance and habitation in spaceflight. *Mailing Add:* PO Box 15-3605 Irving TX 75015-3605

LICHTENBERG, DON BERNETT, THEORETICAL PHYSICS. *Current Pos:* from assoc prof to prof, 63-93, EMER PROF PHYSICS, IND UNIV, BLOOMINGTON, 94- *Personal Data:* b Passaic, NJ, July 2, 28; m 54, Rita Kalter; c Naomi & Rebecca. *Educ:* NY Univ, BA, 50; Univ Ill, MS, 51, PhD(physics), 55. *Prof Exp:* Res assoc physics, Ind Univ, 55-57; guest prof, Univ Hamburg, 57-58; from asst prof to assoc prof, Mich State Univ, 58-63; physicist, Linear Accelerator Ctr, Stanford Univ, 62-63. *Concurrent Pos:* Vis prof, Tel-Aviv Univ, 67-68, Imp Col, Univ London, 71 & Oxford Univ, 79-80, Univ Wash, 86-87, Univ Turin, 87-88; sr fel, Sci Res Coun, UK, 79-80; Fulbright travel grant, Italy, 87-88. *Mem:* Fel Am Phys Soc. *Res:* Physics of the elementary particles. *Mailing Add:* Dept Physics Ind Univ Bloomington IN 47405. *Fax:* 812-855-5533; *E-Mail:* lichten@indiana.edu

LICHTENBERGER, DENNIS LEE, SURFACE SCIENCE, CATALYSIS. *Current Pos:* from asst prof to assoc prof, 76-87, PROF CHEM, UNIV ARIZ, TUCSON, 87- *Personal Data:* b Elkhart, Ind, Sept 30, 47; m 68, Mina D Campbell; c Jeffifer A & Kathryn D. *Educ:* Ind Univ, BS, 69; Univ Wis-Madison, PhD(chem), 74. *Honors & Awards:* Sci Award, Eastman Kodak, 74. *Prof Exp:* Fel, Univ Ill, Champaign-Urbana, 74-76. *Concurrent Pos:* Alfred P Sloan fel, 79; counr, Am Chem Soc, 89- *Mem:* AAAS; Am Chem Soc; NY Acad Sci; Am Vacuum Soc; Am Phys Soc. *Res:* Study of the behavior of organometallic molecules, molecules on surfaces, and catalysts through the development of high resolution gas phase photoelectron spectroscopy, ultra high vacuum surface spectroscopy and scanning tunneling microscopy. *Mailing Add:* Dept Chem Univ Ariz Tucson AZ 85721. *Fax:* 520-621-8407; *E-Mail:* dlichten@ccit.arizona.edu

LICHTENBERGER, GERALD BURTON, MEDICAL DEVICE TECHNOLOGIES, MEDICAL IMAGING. *Current Pos:* PRES & CHIEF EXEC OFFICER, ISIGHT, INC, 90- *Personal Data:* b St Louis, Mo, Jan 14, 45; m 73; c 3. *Educ:* Mass Inst Technol, BS, 66, MS, 67; Yale Univ, PhD(elec eng), 72. *Prof Exp:* Consult appln statist, IBM Res, 70-72; mem tech staff ocean systs res, Bell Labs, 72-75; prin scientist, dir & co-founder comput systs, Xybion Corp, 75-79; pres & founder, Systs of the Future, Inc, 79-86; vpres, strategic planning, Pentax, 86-90. *Mem:* Inst Elec & Electronics Engrs. *Res:* Application of state of the art computer technology to diverse disciplines such as interactive data management and analysis in medical research; signal and information processing; array processing; random process modeling, electronic imaging. *Mailing Add:* 11 Heather Hill Way Mendham NJ 07945

LICHTENBERGER, LENARD MICHAEL, PATHOGENESIS OF PEPTIC ULCERS. *Current Pos:* from asst prof to assoc prof, 76-87, PROF PHYSIOL & CELL BIOL, UNIV TEX MED SCH, 87- *Personal Data:* b New York, NY, Apr 26, 47. *Educ:* Washington Univ, St Louis, BS, 68; Rutgers Univ, MS, 70; Univ Okla Med Sch, PhD(endocrinol), 72. *Prof Exp:* Fel gastrointestinal endocrinol, Univ Calif, Los Angeles, 72-74; fel gastrointestinal cell biol, Harvard Univ, 74-76. *Mem:* Am Physiol Soc; Am Gastroenterol Soc. *Mailing Add:* Dept Physiol & Cell Biol MSMB 4-402 Univ Tex Med Sch PO Box 20708 Houston TX 77225-0708

LICHTENFELS, JAMES RALPH, PARASITOLOGY, TAXONOMY. *Current Pos:* ZOOLOGIST, ANIMAL PARASITOL INST, AGR RES SERV, USDA, 67-, CUR NAT PARASITE COLLECTION, 71- *Personal Data:* b Robinson, Pa, Feb 14, 39; m 61; c 2. *Educ:* Ind Univ Pa, BS, 62; Univ Md, MS, 66, PhD(zool), 68. *Concurrent Pos:* Instr, USDA Grad Sch, 71-77; res assoc, Div Worms, Mus Natural Hist, Smithsonian Inst, Washington, DC, 72-; res affiliate, Div Parasitol, State Mus, Univ Nebr, Lincoln, 72-; mem coun resources, Asn Syst Collections, 75-77; ed, Proc Helm Soc Wash, 83-87, asst ed, Systematic Parasitol, 87-; chair, Fed Soc Parasitol, 95-96. *Mem:* Am Soc Parasitol (vpres, 87); Wildlife Dis Asn; Am Micros Soc; Sigma Xi; Am Asn Zool Nomenclature (pres, 86). *Res:* Intra and interspecific variation in parasitic nematodes; effects of host on morphology of parasitic nematodes; identification, classification and description of parasitic nematodes of vertebrates especially of domestic animals. *Mailing Add:* 12311 Whitehall Dr Bowie MD 20715. *E-Mail:* rlichtech@ggpl.arsusda.gov

LICHTENSTEIN, ALICE HINDA, LIPO PROTEIN METABOLISM, LIPO PROTEIN KINETICS. *Current Pos:* asst prof, 88-94, ASSOC PROF, SCH NUTRIT, TUFTS UNIV, 94-, ASSOC PROF, DEPT FAMILY MED & COMMUNITY HEALTH, 95- *Personal Data:* m, Barry R Goldin; c 2. *Educ:* Cornell Univ, BS, 71; Pa State Univ, MS, 73; Harvard Univ, MS, 75, DSc(nutrit), 79. *Prof Exp:* Teaching asst, Pa State Univ, 71-73; instr, Queens Col, 73-74; lectr, Tufts Univ, 78-82; fel, Sch Med, Boston Univ, 79-82, asst prof med & biochem, 82-88. *Concurrent Pos:* Scientist I, USDA Human Nutrit Res Ctr Aging, Tufts Univ, 95- *Mem:* Am Heart Asn; Am Inst Nutrit; Am Soc Clin Nutrit. *Res:* Kinetic behavior of lipo protein particles in order to elucidate mechanisms responsible for changes in blood lipid levels induced by alterations in dietary fat and cholesterol intake. *Mailing Add:* Tufts Univ 711 Washington St Boston MA 02111. *Fax:* 617-556-3103; *E-Mail:* lichtenst.li@hnrc.tufts.edu

LICHTENSTEIN, E PAUL, ENTOMOLOGY. *Current Pos:* proj assoc, 54-56, asst prof, 56-65, PROF ENTOM, UNIV WIS-MADISON, 65-, ASSOC DIR, CTR ENVIRON TOXICOL, 72- *Personal Data:* b Selters, WGer, Feb 24, 15; nat US; m 51; c 2. *Educ:* Hebrew Univ, Israel, MSc, 41, PhD(entom, biochem), 48. *Prof Exp:* Lectr biol, Sch Educ, Israel, 41-53; asst prof physiol & anat, Ill Wesleyan Univ, 53-54. *Mem:* Entom Soc Am; Am Chem Soc; Soc Toxicol. *Res:* Pesticidal residues and their effect on the biological complex on our environment; factors affecting persistence and breakdown of pesticides in soils, crops and water; naturally occurring toxicants. *Mailing Add:* Dept Entom Univ Wis Madison WI 53706

LICHTENSTEIN, HARRIS ARNOLD, ANALYTICAL CHEMISTRY, MOLECULAR BIOLOGY. *Personal Data:* b Houston, Tex, May 7, 41; div; c Jill & Gregg. *Educ:* Tulane Univ, BA, 63; Univ Houston, BS, 66, MS, 67, PhD(biol), 70. *Prof Exp:* Pres, Spectrix Corp, 69-86; vpres, Keystone Environ Inc, Subsid Koppers Co Inc, 86-88. *Concurrent Pos:* Chief exec officer & chmn, Intrepid Technol Inc. *Mem:* AAAS; Am Chem Soc; Sigma Xi. *Mailing Add:* 4600 Post Oak Place Dr Suite 152 Houston TX 77057

LICHTENSTEIN, LAWRENCE M, MEDICINE, IMMUNOLOGY. *Current Pos:* Intern med, 60-61, fel microbiol, 61-65, resident, 65-66, from asst prof to assoc prof, 66-75, PROF MED, SCH MED, JOHNS HOPKINS UNIV, 75- *Personal Data:* b Washington, DC, May 31, 34; m 56; c 3. *Educ:* Univ Chicago, BA, 54, MD, 60; Johns Hopkins Univ, PhD(immunol), 65. *Mem:* Am Acad Allergy; Am Asn Immunol; Am Fedn Clin Res; Am Soc Clin Invest; Am Asn Physicians. *Res:* Mechanisms of reactions of immediate hypersensitivity and relationship to clinical problems. *Mailing Add:* Johns Hopkins Asthma & Allergy Ctr 5501 Hopkins Bayview Circle Baltimore MD 21224-6801. *Fax:* 410-550-1733

LICHTENWALNER, HART K, CHEMICAL ENGINEERING. *Current Pos:* RETIRED. *Personal Data:* b Easton, Pa, Oct 1, 23; m 45; c 3. *Educ:* Lafayette Col, BS, 43; Lehigh Univ, MS, 49, PhD(chem eng), 50. *Prof Exp:* Org chemist, Res Labs, Gen Motors Corp, 43-48; chem engr, Silicone Prod Dept, Gen Elec Co, 50-61, eng leader, 61-62, mgr process develop, 62-66, mgr room-temp vulcanising rubber develop, 66-68, mgr res & develop, 68-70, mgr var prod sect, 70-77, managing dir, Gen Elec Silicones-Europe, 77-80, mgr strategic planning & venture develop, 80-87. *Mem:* Am Chem Soc; fel Am Inst Chem Engrs; NY Acad Sci. *Res:* Chemical process technology of organosilanes and siloxanes. *Mailing Add:* 24 Via Da Vinci Clifton Park NY 12065-2097

LICHTER, BARRY D(AVID), MATERIALS SCIENCE, CORROSION & STRESS-CORROSION. *Current Pos:* assoc prof mat sci, 68-72, PROF MAT SCI & MGT TECHNOL, VANDERBILT UNIV, 72- *Personal Data:* b Boston, Mass, Nov 29, 31. *Educ:* Mass Inst Technol, SB, 53, SM, 55, ScD(metall), 58. *Prof Exp:* Asst, Mass Inst Technol, 52-58; metallurgist, Air Force Cambridge Res Ctr, 58-61 & Oak Ridge Nat Lab, 61-62; fel, Lawrence Radiation Lab, Univ Calif, Berkeley, 62-64; assoc prof metall eng, Univ Wash, 64-68. *Concurrent Pos:* Tech consult, Boeing Co, 66; centennial fel, Vanderbilt Univ, 74-75; NSF fac fel, 75-76; consult, Off Technol Assessment, 76-78 & Oak Ridge Nat Lab, 78-79; vis prof, Fac Chem Eng & Mat Sci, Delft Univ Technol, Neth, 91- *Mem:* Minerals Metals & Mat Soc; NY Acad Sci; Nat Asn Corrosion Engrs; Electrochem Soc; Am Soc Metals. *Res:* Corrosion; oxidation & alloys; technology and human values; philosophy and engineering ethics; thermodynamics of alloys; stress-corrosion cracking. *Mailing Add:* Mat Vanderbilt Univ 2201 W End Ave Nashville TN 37240-0001. *Fax:* 615-343-8730; *E-Mail:* lichter@vuse.vanderbilt.edu

LICHTER, EDWARD A, PREVENTIVE MEDICINE, COMMUNITY HEALTH. *Current Pos:* assoc prof, Univ Ill, 66-68, prof prev med & head dept, 68-86, prof health care serv & head dept, Sch Pub Health, 72-79, PROF COMMUNITY HEALTH SCI, SCH PUB HEALTH, UNIV ILL, 80-, PROF MED, COL MED, 86-, ACTG CHIEF GEN INTERNAL MED, 96- *Personal Data:* b Chicago, Ill, June 5, 28; m 52; c Michael & Jay. *Educ:* Univ Chicago, PhB, 47; Roosevelt Univ, BS, 49; Univ Ill, MS, 51, MD, 55. *Honors & Awards:* Distinguished Serv Award, Am Col Prev Med. *Prof Exp:* Asst physiol, Col Med, Univ Ill, 50-51, resident internal med, 58-61, instr med, 60-61; USPHS fel immunochem, Nat Inst Allergy & Infectious Dis, 61-63, mem staff, 63-66. *Mem:* Am Pub Health Asn; Cent Soc Clin Res; fel Am Col Prev Med; fel Am Col Physicians; Am Col Epidemiol. *Res:* Radiation effects on peripheral circulation; chronic pulmonary infections; clinical pharmacology and therapeutic evaluation of antibiotics; immunochemistry; immunogenetics of immunoglobulins and other serum proteins; structure and function of health care services. *Mailing Add:* Dept Med Col Med MC 787 Univ Ill Med Ctr 8405 Wood St Chicago IL 60612

LICHTER, JAMES JOSEPH, ECONOMIC ANALYSIS OF ENVIRONMENTAL REGULATIONS. *Current Pos:* ANALYST, CALIF TRADE & COM AGENCY, 95- *Personal Data:* b Algona, Iowa, Apr 29, 39. *Educ:* Loras Col, BS, 61; Fordham Univ, MS, 63; Duke Univ, PhD(physics), 69; Univ Calif, Santa Barbara, MBE, 86. *Prof Exp:* From physicist to res physicist, US Naval Ord Lab, Md, 60-65; res asst, Duke Univ, 65-69; assoc scientist, ITT Fed Elec Corp, 69-77; software specialist, 77-83; energy specialist, Calif Energy Comn, 87-95. *Mem:* Am Phys Soc. *Res:* Economic analysis of regulations, computable general equilibrium models of California's economy. *Mailing Add:* 2348 American River Dr No 206 Sacramento CA 95825

LICHTER, PAUL RICHARD, OPHTHALMOLOGY. *Current Pos:* From asst prof to assoc prof, 71-78, PROF & CHMN, DEPT OPHTHAL, UNIV MICH, ANN ARBOR, 78- *Personal Data:* b Detroit, Mar 7, 39; m 60, Carolyn Goode; c Laurie & Susan. *Educ:* Univ Mich, BA, 60, MD, 64, MS, 68; Am Bd Ophthal, dipl. *Concurrent Pos:* Bd dirs, Am Acad Ophthal, 81-, Pan Am Asn Ophthal, 88-; mem, Mich State Med Soc, Washtenaw Co Med Soc & Mich Ophthal Soc; ed-in-chief, Ophthal J, 86-; pres, Mich Ophthal Soc, 93- *Mem:* AMA; Pan Am Asn Ophthal; Asn Univ Profs Ophthal (pres, 91-92). *Res:* Ophthalmology; medicine. *Mailing Add:* Univ Mich Med Sch Kellogg Eye Ctr 1000 Wall St Ann Arbor MI 48105-1912

LICHTER, ROBERT (LOUIS), ORGANIC CHEMISTRY, EDUCATION ADMINISTRATOR. *Current Pos:* EXEC DIR, CAMILLE & HENRY DREYFUS FOUND INC, 89- *Personal Data:* b Cambridge, Mass, Oct 26, 41; m 91; c 2. *Educ:* Harvard Univ, AB, 62; Univ Wis-Madison, PhD(chem), 67. *Prof Exp:* USPHS fel, Brunswick Tech Univ, 67-68; res fel chem, Calif Inst Technol, 68-70; from asst prof to prof chem, Hunter Col, 70-83, chmn dept, 77-82; regional dir grants, Res Corp, 83-86; vprovost res & grad studies, staff Univ New York Stony Brook, 86-89. *Concurrent Pos:* Vis scientist, Sandoz Res Lab, 81, Exxon Res & Eng Co, 82; adj prof, Hunter Col, City Univ NY, 83-86. *Mem:* Am Chem Soc; Sigma Xi; fel AAAS. *Res:* Organonitrogen chemistry; nuclear magnetic resonance spectroscopy; application of carbon and nitrogen nuclear magnetic resonance to organic chemistry. *Mailing Add:* Camille & Henry Dreyfus Found Inc 555 Madison Ave New York NY 10022. *E-Mail:* rlichter@panix.com

LICHTI, ROGER L, EXPERIMENTAL SOLID STATE PHYSICS, MAGNETIC RESONANCE. *Current Pos:* from asst prof to assoc prof, 79-92, PROF PHYSICS, TEX TECH UNIV, 92- *Personal Data:* b Milford, Nebr, Aug 27, 45; m 70; c 2. *Educ:* Ottawa Univ, BSc, 67; Univ Ill, MS, 69, PhD(physics), 72. *Prof Exp:* Vis asst prof, Univ Kans, 72-73, res assoc, 73-74; res assoc, Univ Mass, 74-77, vis asst prof, 78-79. *Mem:* Am Phys Soc; Math Res Soc. *Res:* Magnetic resonance of dilute paramagnetic systems; muonium/hydrogen in semiconductors; muon spin rotation/resonance. *Mailing Add:* Physics Dept Tex Tech Univ Lubbock TX 79409. *Fax:* 806-742-1182; *E-Mail:* xbrll@ttu.edu

LICHTIG, LEO KENNETH, CLINICAL & FINANCIAL INFORMATION SYSTEMS, HEALTH SERVICES RESEARCH. *Current Pos:* case mix economist, 90-92, vpres res & develop, 92-95, SR VPRES & CHIEF INFO OFFICER, NETWORK INC, 95- *Personal Data:* b Brooklyn, NY, Oct 20, 53; m 77, Susan Walsh; c Brielle J & Danica J. *Educ:* Rensselaer Polytech Inst, BS & MS, 74, PhD(commun res), 76. *Prof Exp:* Res asst commun res, Rensselaer Polytech Inst, 74-76; asst prof commun, State Univ NY Albany, 76-77; asst proj mgr, NJ State Dept Health, 77-82, assoc proj mgr, 82; policy res specialist, Blue Cross Northeastern, NY, 82-83; vpres, Health Care Res Found, 82-90; dir, Utilization Econ & Res, Empire Blue Cross Blue Shield, 83-90. *Concurrent Pos:* Mem, Ad-hoc Comt, US Dept Health, Educ & Welfare, 79-81; mem, Comt Privacy & Confidentiality, Am Statist Asn, 81-84; mem, tech adv comt, NY Statewide Planning & Res Coop Syst, 82-, tech rev comt & reimbursement adv group, NY State Long Term Care Case Mix Reimbursement Proj, 84-86; contrib ed, Nat Report Compt & Health, 82-85; chairperson, Inst Rev Bd, Health Care Res Found, 83-90; mem, Tech Adv Group, Health Info Reporting Co, 87-90, Tech Adv Comt, NY State Off Mental Health Case Mix Classification Proj Steering, 86-89, Health Care Financing, 85-87; adj fac, Grad Prog Health Admin, Russell Sage Col, 86-94, Union Col, 91-92; subcomt Qual & Productivity Measures in Health Care, Am Statist Asn, 88-90. *Res:* Integration of clinical and financial information to address issues affecting the cost and management of health services and public health policy; development of case mix classification systems for specialized patient populations; numerous published articles and book. *Mailing Add:* 57 Fairlawn Latham NY 12110. *Fax:* 518-782-1848; *E-Mail:* lichtl@rpi.edu

LICHTIN, J LEON, PHARMACEUTICAL CHEMISTRY, COSMETIC CHEMISTRY. *Current Pos:* RETIRED. *Personal Data:* b Philadelphia, Pa, Mar 5, 24; m 50; c 2. *Educ:* Philadelphia Col Pharm, BS, 44, MS, 47; Ohio State Univ, PhD(pharmaceut chem), 50. *Prof Exp:* From asst prof to assoc prof pharm, Cincinnati Col Pharm, 50-55; from assoc prof to prof, Univ Cincinnati, 55-71, Andrew Jergens prof pharm, 72-92. *Mem:* AAAS; fel Soc Cosmetic Chem. *Res:* Dermatologicals; formulation of pharmaceutical products; cosmetics. *Mailing Add:* 801 Cloverview Ave Cincinnati OH 45231

LICHTIN, NORMAN NAHUM, PHOTO CHEMISTRY, CATALYTIC CHEMISTRY. *Current Pos:* lectr, Boston Univ, 47, from instr to prof, 48-93, chmn dept, 73-84, univ prof, 73-93, dir, Div Eng & Appl Sci, 83-87, EMER PROF CHEM, BOSTON UNIV, 93-, EMER UNIV PROF, 93- *Personal Data:* b Newark, NJ, Aug 10, 22; m 47, Phyllis Wasserman; c Harold H, Sara M (Boyd) & Daniel A. *Educ:* Antioch Col, BS, 44; Purdue Univ, MS, 45; Harvard Univ, PhD(phys org chem), 48. *Honors & Awards:* Coochbehar lectr, Soc Cult Sci, India, 80. *Prof Exp:* Teaching fel, Harvard Univ, 45-47. *Concurrent Pos:* Vis chemist, Brookhaven Nat Lab, 57-58, res collab, 58-70; resident consult, Atomics Int, 61; NSF sr fel, 62-63; guest scientist, Weizmann Inst, 62-63; vis prof, Hebrew Univ Jerusalem, 62-63, 70-71, 72, 73, 76 & 80; consult, Solar Energy Conv Unit, Exxon Res & Eng Co, 71-78; vis prof, Inst Physics & Chem Res, Wako, Saitama, Japan, 80; sabbatical vis, Solar Energy Res Inst, Golden, Colo, 80; consult, Arco Solar, Inc, 80-88, Clearflow Inc, 93-94, Photox Corp, 94-96, Zentox Corp, 97-; chief scientist, Proj Sunrise, Inc, 87-93. *Mem:* Fel AAAS; Am Chem Soc; Sigma Xi; Int Solar Energy Soc. *Res:* Radiation chemistry; atomic nitrogen chemistry; photochemical conversion of solar energy; physical photochemistry; photo-assisted solid catalysis; chemical reaction mechanism. *Mailing Add:* 195 Morton St Newton Centre MA 02159-1522. *Fax:* 617-353-6466; *E-Mail:* lichtin@bu-chem.bu.edu

LICHTMAN, DAVID, SURFACE PHYSICS. *Current Pos:* assoc prof, 67-70, PROF PHYSICS, UNIV WIS-MILWAUKEE, 70- *Personal Data:* b New York, NY, Feb 7, 27; m 48; c 3. *Educ:* City Col New York, BS, 49; Columbia Univ, MS, 50. *Prof Exp:* Physicist, Airborne Instruments Lab, 50-56; res engr, Sperry Gyroscope Co, 56-62; sr prin res scientist, Honeywell Res Ctr, 62-67. *Concurrent Pos:* NATO sr sci fel, 71. *Mem:* AAAS; Am Phys Soc; Am Vacuum Soc. *Res:* Mass spectrometry; beam-surface interactions; thin films; metal-ceramic seals; dark trace tubes; gaseous discharge phenomena; high and ultra-high vacuum; surface physics; electron spectroscopy; photodesorption. *Mailing Add:* 7510 N Crossway Rd Milwaukee WI 53217

LICHTMAN, HERBERT CHARLES, INTERNAL MEDICINE, CLINICAL PATHOLOGY. *Current Pos:* PROF MED, BROWN UNIV, 70 - *Personal Data:* b New York, NY, Sept 6, 21; m 46; c 3. *Educ:* Brooklyn Col, BA, 42; Long Island Col Med, MD, 45; Am Bd Internal Med, dipl, 53; Am Bd Clin Path, dipl, 73. *Prof Exp:* Intern, Long Island Col Serv, Kings Co Hosp Ctr, 45-46; asst resident path, Montefiore Hosp, Bronx, NY, 48-49; asst resident med, Long Island Col Div, Kings Co Hosp Ctr, 49-50; from instr to prof med, Col Med, State Univ NY Downstate Med Ctr, 51-70. *Concurrent Pos:* Res fel clin med, Long Island Col Med, 50; clin fel hemat, Col Med, Univ Utah, 50-51; clin asst vis physician, Kings Co Hosp, 51-53, assoc attend physician, 53-59, attend physician, 59 -; chief hemat & blood bank, State Univ NY Hosp, 66-70; dir div clin path, Dept Lab Med & chief div lab med, Miriam Hosp, 70-74, physician-in-chief, 74-86. *Mem:* AAAS; Am Soc Hemat; Soc Exp Biol & Med; Am Fedn Clin Res; Harvey Soc; Sigma Xi. *Res:* Hematology; leukemia and malignant lymphona; heme synthesis. *Mailing Add:* Univ Physicians Found 165 Summit Ave Providence RI 02906

LICHTMAN, IRWIN A, SURFACE CHEMISTRY, SCIENCE EDUCATION. *Current Pos:* RETIRED. *Personal Data:* b New York, NY, Nov 3, 20; m 48; c 1. *Educ:* City Col New York, BS, 43; NY Univ, MS, 48, PhD(phys chem), 51. *Prof Exp:* Instr chem, Seton Hall Col, 47-48; asst prof, Community Col, NY, 48-52; sr res chemist, Lever Bros Res Ctr, 52-55; group leader phosphates & detergents, Food Mach & Chem Co, 55-60; sr res chemist, Shell Chem Co, 60-64; mgr phys chem lab, 64-77, group mgr res &

develop, process chem div, Diamond Shamrock Chem Co, Morristown, 77-82. *Concurrent Pos:* Vis prof, NJ Inst Technol, Chem Eng Dept, 82-84; consult surface chem, 84- *Mem:* Am Chem Soc; Am Inst Chem. *Res:* Surface and colloid chemistry; defoamers; insecticide decomposition mechanisms; reaction kinetics; mechanism of defoamer action, particularly role of hydrophobic particles; volatile insecticides in polymeric matrix; phosphate glasses. *Mailing Add:* 24 Wenzel Lane Stony Point NY 10980-2310

LICHTMAN, MARSHALL A, HEMATOLOGY, BIOPHYSICS. *Current Pos:* instr med, Sch Med & chief resident, Med Ctr, Univ Rochester, 65-66, sr instr med, Sch Med, 66-67, from asst prof to assoc prof med, radiation biol & biophys, 71-74, chief hemat unit, 75-77, cochief, hemato unit, 77-89, assoc dean. *Personal Data:* b New York, NY, June 23, 34; m 57, Alice Jo Maisel; c Susan, Joanne & Pamela. *Educ:* Cornell Univ, AB, 55; Univ Buffalo, MD, 60; Am Bd Internal Med, dipl, 67. *Prof Exp:* Resident internal med, Med Ctr, Univ Rochester, 60-63; res assoc epidemiol, Sch Pub Health, Univ NC, 63-65. *Concurrent Pos:* USPHS res fel, Univ Rochester, 67-69; Leukemia Soc scholar, 69-74; from asst physician to sr assoc physician, Strong Mem Hosp, 65-71, sr physician, 74-; exec vpres, Res & Med Affairs, Leukemia Soc Am, 96- *Mem:* Master Am Col Physicians; Am Soc Hemat (vpres, 87, pres, 89); Am Soc Clin Invest; Asn Am Physicians; Am Physiol Soc; Am Soc Cell Biol. *Res:* Biochemical and biophysical studies of human erythrocytes and leukocytes. *Mailing Add:* Dept Hematol Univ Rochester Med Ctr PO Box 610 610 Elmwood Ave Rochester NY 14642. *Fax:* 716-276-1876; *E-Mail:* mal@medicine.rochester.edu

LICHTON, IRA JAY, NUTRITION. *Current Pos:* from assoc prof to prof, 62-92, EMER PROF NUTRIT, UNIV HAWAII, 92- *Personal Data:* b Chicago, Ill, Sept 18, 28; m 49, Marilyn Mendel; c Alex I. *Educ:* Univ Chicago, PhB, 47; Univ Ill, BS, 50, MS, 51, PhD(physiol), 54. *Prof Exp:* Res assoc obstet & gynec, Univ Chicago, 54-56; Am Heart Asn res fel cardiovasc physiol, Med Res Inst, Michael Reese Hosp, Chicago, Ill, 56-58; instr physiol, Stanford Univ, 58-62. *Concurrent Pos:* Vis prof, Hebrew Univ, 88-89. *Mem:* AAAS; Am Physiol Soc; Soc Study Reprod. *Res:* Water and electrolyte metabolism in pregnancy; growth; nutritional status. *Mailing Add:* 9 Kaapuni Dr Univ Hawaii Kailua HI 96734-2323. *Fax:* 808-956-3842; *E-Mail:* x002760@uhccmvs

LICHTWARDT, ROBERT WILLIAM, MYCOLOGY. *Current Pos:* from asst prof to prof, 57-95, EMER PROF BOT, UNIV KANS, 95- *Personal Data:* b Rio de Janeiro, Brazil, Nov 27, 24; US citizen; m 51, Elizabeth Thomas; c Ruth E & Robert T. *Educ:* Oberlin Col, AB, 49; Univ Ill, MS, 51, PhD(bot), 54. *Honors & Awards:* Distinguished Mycologist Award, Mycol Soc Am, 91. *Prof Exp:* Fel, NSF, 54-55; res assoc bot, Iowa State Univ, 55-57. *Concurrent Pos:* NSF sr fel, 63-64; ed-in-chief, Mycologia, 65-70; chmn, Dept Bot, Univ Kans, 71-74 & 81-84. *Mem:* AAAS; Bot Soc Am; Mycol Soc Am (pres, 72-73); Mycol Soc Japan; Brit Mycol Soc. *Res:* Fungi association with arthropods, particularly those inhabiting their guts. *Mailing Add:* Dept Bot Univ Kans Lawrence KS 66045-2106. *Fax:* 785-864-5321; *E-Mail:* licht@kuhub.cc.ukans.edu

LICINI, JEROME CARL, QUANTUM TRANSPORT, SEMICONDUCTOR DEVICES. *Current Pos:* asst prof, 87-93, ASSOC PROF PHYSICS, LEHIGH UNIV, 93- *Personal Data:* b 1958; m 85. *Educ:* Princeton Univ, AB, 80; Mass Inst Technol, PhD(condensed matter physics), 87. *Prof Exp:* Res asst, IBM Corp, Tucson, 81; vis researcher, AT&T Bell Labs, 84-85; assoc, Mass Inst Technol, 87. *Concurrent Pos:* Consult, Valley Technol, Inc, 91-93, Leighton Electronics, Inc, 96- *Mem:* Am Phys Soc; Sigma Xi. *Res:* New quantum phenomena in ultra-small semiconductor devices; fabrication of sub-micron silicon and gallium-arsenide sub- micron devices; measurement of quantum transport phenomena at ultra-low temperatures. *Mailing Add:* Physics Dept Lehigh Univ 16 Memorial Dr E Bethlehem PA 18015-3182. *Fax:* 610-758-5730; *E-Mail:* jcl3@lehigh.edu

LICK, DALE W, PURE MATHEMATICS, APPLIED MATHEMATICS. *Current Pos:* prof math & pres, 91-93, UNIV PROF, FLA STATE UNIV, 93-, DIR, LEARNING SYST INST. *Personal Data:* b Marlette, Mich, Jan 7, 38; m 56, Marilyn K Foster; c Kitty, Diana & Ronald. *Educ:* Mich State Univ, BS, 58, MS, 59; Univ Calif, Riverside, PhD(math, partial differential equations), 65. *Prof Exp:* Instr math & chmn dept, Port Huron Jr Col, 59-60; asst to comptroller, Mich Bell Tel Co, 60-61; from instr to asst prof math, Univ Redlands, 61-63; from asst prof to assoc prof math, Univ Tenn, 65-69; asst res mathematician, Dept Appl Math, Brookhaven Nat Lab, 67-68; vpres acad affairs, Russell Sage Col, 72-74; prof math & dean, Sch Sci & Health Professions, Old Dom Univ, 74-78; prof math & comput sci & pres, Ga Southern Col, 78-86; prof math & pres, Univ Maine, 86-91. *Concurrent Pos:* Consult, Union Carbide Corp, AEC, Oak Ridge Nat Lab, 66-67; adj assoc prof, Med Sch, Temple Univ; assoc prof & head dept, Drexel Univ, 69-72. *Mem:* AAAS; Am Math Soc; Asn Comput Mach; Math Asn Am; Soc Indust & Appl Math; Sigma Xi. *Res:* Singular non-linear hyperbolic second order partial differential equations; non-linear Dirichlet problems; systems of non-linear boundary and initial value problems; partial differential equations and their numerical solution. *Mailing Add:* 348 Remington Run Loop Tallahassee FL 32312-1402. *Fax:* 850-644-3783; *E-Mail:* klick@mailer.fsu.edu

LICK, DON R, MATHEMATICS. *Current Pos:* PROF & HEAD MATH, EASTERN MICH UNIV, 85- *Personal Data:* b Marlette, Mich, Sept 3, 34; m 61; c 2. *Educ:* Mich State Univ, BS, 56, MS, 57, PhD(math), 61. *Prof Exp:* Asst prof math, Purdue Univ, 61-63 & NMex State Univ, 63-66; vis assoc prof, Western Mich Univ, 65-66, from assoc prof to prof math, 72-85. *Concurrent Pos:* NSF res grant, 69-70; US Army Res Off Conf grant, 71-72; vis prof, Univ Calif, Irvine, 72-73 & Calif State Univ, Los Angeles, 72-73. *Mem:* Math Asn Am; Am Math Soc; Am Asn Univ Prof. *Res:* Complex analysis; sets of convergence of series; representation of measurable functions by series; graph theory; connectivity; structural problems; coloring problems. *Mailing Add:* Dept Math Eastern Mich Univ Ypsilanti MI 48197. *Fax:* 313-487-2489; *E-Mail:* lick@emich.edu

LICK, THOMAS ARTZ, PHYSICS. *Current Pos:* From asst prof to assoc prof, 68-83, chmn, Physics Dept, 82-95, PROF PHYSICS, STETSON UNIV, 83- *Personal Data:* b Stillwater, Okla, Sept 22, 40; m 66, Miriam Ruble; c Deborah Lynn (Chiders) & Rodney Artz. *Educ:* Muhlenberg Col, BS, 62; Ohio Univ, PhD(physics), 69. *Concurrent Pos:* Vis res prof, Univ NC, Chapel Hill, 81-82. *Mem:* Sigma Xi; Am Phys Soc. *Res:* Investigation of electric field effects using an electron spin echo spectrometer; thermoluminescence and x-ray stimulated luminescence in insulating crystals; computerized data acquisition and analysis in introductory physics laboratories. *Mailing Add:* Unit 8267 Stetson Univ DeLand FL 32720. *Fax:* 904-822-8910; *E-Mail:* lick@stetson.edu

LICK, WILBERT JAMES, ENVIRONMENTAL ENGINEERING, MARINE SCIENCES. *Current Pos:* chmn dept, 82-84, PROF MECH & ENVIRON ENG, UNIV CALIF, SANTA BARBARA, 79- *Personal Data:* b Cleveland, Ohio, June 12, 33; c James & Sarah. *Educ:* Rensselaer Polytech Inst, BA, 55, MA, 57, PhD(aeronaut eng), 58. *Prof Exp:* Res fel & lectr mech eng, Harvard Univ, 59-61, asst prof, 61-66; sr res fel aeronaut, Calif Inst Technol, 66; assoc prof eng, Case Western Res Univ, 66-69, chmn dept earth sci, 73-76, prof geophys & eng, 69-79. *Concurrent Pos:* Guggenheim fel, 65; Fulbright fel, 78. *Mem:* Am Geophys Union; Am Soc Mech Eng; Int Asn Great Lakes Res; Soc Indust Appl Math; Int Asn Sediment Water Sci. *Res:* Environmental engineering and applied mathematics. *Mailing Add:* Dept Mech Eng Univ Calif Santa Barbara CA 93106. *Fax:* 805-893-8651

LICKO, VOJTECH, MATHEMATICAL BIOLOGY. *Current Pos:* CONSULT, 92- *Personal Data:* b Banska Stiavnica, Czech, Aug 30, 32; US citizen; m 59; c 1. *Educ:* Slovak Univ Bratislava, MS, 54; Czech Acad Sci, CSc(biophys), 63; Univ Chicago, PhD(math biol), 66. *Prof Exp:* Chief radioisotope lab, Inst Endocrinol, Slovak Acad Sci, Bratislava, 54-63; fel math biol, Univ Chicago, 63-66; scientist & assoc prof biophys, Inst Physics, Comenius Univ, Bratislava, 66-68; res fel biomath, Dept Biochem & Biophys, Cardiovasc Inst, Univ Calif, San Francisco, 68-71, res asst, 73-74, res asst biomath, 74-78, assoc adj prof, 78-90, adj prof biomath, 90-92. *Concurrent Pos:* Assoc adj prof biomath, Dept Med, Univ Calif, San Francisco, 80-90, dir, Biomath Core Fac, Liver Ctr, 80-92. *Mem:* Biophys Soc; AAAS; Soc Math Biol; NY Acad Sci. *Res:* Pharmacokinetics and pharmacodynamics; mathematical modeling of biochemical and physiological processes; theory of secretory mechanisms; dynamics of glucose-insulin control in man; kinetics of transport of substances through epithelia. *Mailing Add:* 1786 Fell St San Francisco CA 94117-2027

LIDDELL, CRAIG MASON, EPIDEMIOLOGY OF PLANT DISEASE, ECOLOGY OF SOIL FUNGI. *Current Pos:* ASST PROF PLANT PATH, NMEX STATE UNIV, 89-, PRIN INVESTR, COMPUT RES LAB, 90-, FAC MEM, MOLECULAR BIOL GRAD PROG, 92- *Personal Data:* b Sydney, NSW, Australia, June 10, 58; c Scott & Alexandra. *Educ:* Univ Sydney, BSc, 79, Dipl plant path, 81, PhD(plant path), 86. *Prof Exp:* Res asst plant path, Univ Calif, Davis, 86-87 & Univ Wis-Madison, 88-89. *Concurrent Pos:* Chmn, Regional Res Proj, USDA, 93-94; sr ed, J Phytopath. *Mem:* Am Phytopath Soc; Mycol Soc Am; Australian Plant Path Soc; Brit Mycol Soc; AAAS; Ecol Soc Australia. *Res:* Physical ecology of soil fungi; computer modelling of fungal growth and development; computer modelling of plant disease epidemiology; biological control of soilborne diseases of crop plants. *Mailing Add:* Dept Entom Plant Path & Weed Sci NMex State Univ Las Cruces NM 88003. *Fax:* 505-646-8087

LIDDELL, ROBERT WILLIAM, JR, ORGANIC CHEMISTRY, BIOCHEMISTRY. *Current Pos:* CONSULT, 78- *Personal Data:* b Pittsburgh, Pa, Sept 11, 13; m 40, 90, Mary M Moore; c 3. *Educ:* Univ Pittsburgh, BS, 34, PhD(chem), 40. *Prof Exp:* Chem engr, Swindell-Dressler Corp, 34-35; chemist, Hall Labs, 35-36; res chemist, Hagan Chem & Controls, Inc, 40-55, asst res mgr, 55-63; mgr prod eng, Calgon Corp, 63-70, mgr pilot res & develop, 70-78. *Concurrent Pos:* Bd dirs, Community Water Co, 90- *Mem:* Am Chem Soc. *Res:* Water treatment; phosphate chemicals. *Mailing Add:* 20 Calle Lecho Green Valley AZ 85614-1999

LIDDELL, WILLIAM DAVID, PALEOECOLOGY. *Current Pos:* ASST PROF GEOL & PALEONT, GEOL DEPT, UTAH STATE UNIV, 81- *Personal Data:* b Dayton, Ohio, Sept 17, 51; m 77. *Educ:* Miami Univ, BA, 73; Univ Mich, MS, 75, PhD(geol), 80. *Prof Exp:* Asst prof geol & paleont, Earth Sci Dept, Univ New Orleans, 79-81. *Mem:* AAAS; Ecol Soc Am; Int Palaeont Asn. *Res:* Paleoecology of ancient, primarily Paleozoic, communities; geology and ecology of modern coral reefs. *Mailing Add:* 5080 W 3400 S Logan UT 84321

LIDDICOAT, RICHARD THOMAS, JR, GEMOLOGY, MINERALOGY. *Current Pos:* instr, Gemological Inst Am, 40-41, dir ed, 41-42, 46-49, asst dir, 49-52, exec dir, 52-83, pres, 70-83, CHMN BD, GEMOLOGICAL INST AM, 83- *Personal Data:* b Kearsage, Mich, Mar 2, 18; m 39. *Educ:* Univ Mich, BS, 39, MS, 40; dipl, Gemol Inst Am, 41; Calif Inst Technol, MS, 44. *Honors & Awards:* Robert M Shipley Award, Am Gem Soc, 76; Hanneman Award, 78. *Prof Exp:* Asst mineral, Univ Mich, 37-40. *Concurrent Pos:* US deleg, Int Gem Conf, 60-81; hon res staff, Los Angeles Mus Nat Hist, 68. *Mem:* Sigma Xi; fel AAAS; fel Geol Soc Am; fel Mineral Soc Am; hon fel Gemol Asn Gt Brit; Gemol Asn Australia (hon vpres); Am Gem Soc. *Res:* Gem identification and grading. *Mailing Add:* 1660 Stewart St Santa Monica CA 90402

LIDDLE, CHARLES GEORGE, VETERINARY MEDICINE, RADIATION BIOLOGY. *Current Pos:* RETIRED. *Personal Data:* b Detroit, Mich, Mar 22, 36; m 60; c 4. *Educ:* Mich State Univ, BS, 58, DVM, 60; Univ Rochester, MS, 63. *Prof Exp:* Vet, Pvt Pract, Mich, 60-61; chief biophys unit, Twinbrook Res Lab, Environ Protection Agency, 70-73, res vet, Exp Biol Div, Health Effects Res Lab, Environ Res Ctr, 73-92. *Mem:* Am Vet Med Asn. *Res:* The effects of microwaves on the immunological competence of laboratory animals. *Mailing Add:* 21870 Hancock Lane Nathrop CO 81236

LIDE, DAVID REYNOLDS, JR, CHEMICAL PHYSICS, SCIENCE INFORMATION. *Current Pos:* ED-IN-CHIEF, CRC HANDBOOK CHEM & PHYSICS, 88-; CO-ED, HANDBOOK DATA ORG COMPOUNDS, 92- *Personal Data:* b Gainesville, Ga, May 25, 28; m 55, 88, Bettijoyce Breen; c David A, Vanessa G (Whitcomb), James H & Quentin R. *Educ:* Carnegie Inst Technol, BS, 49; Harvard Univ, AM, 51, PhD(chem physics), 52. *Honors & Awards:* Silver Medal, US Dept Com, 65, Gold Medal, 68; Stratton Award, Nat Bur Standards, 68; Presidential Rank Award Meritorious Fed Exec, 86; Herman Skolnik Award, Am Chem Soc, 88; Patterson-Crane Award, Am Chem Soc, 91. *Prof Exp:* Fulbright scholar & Ramsay mem fel, Oxford Univ, 52-53; res fel, Harvard Univ, 53-54; physicist, Nat Bur Stands, 54-63, chief, Infrared & Microwave Spectros Sect, 63-68, dir, Off Stand Ref Data, 68-88. *Concurrent Pos:* Lectr, Univ Md, 56-66; NSF sr fel, Univ London, 59-60 & Univ Bologna, 67-68; ed, J Phys & Chem Ref Data, 72-92; US nat deleg, Comt Data Sci & Technol, Int Coun Sci Unions, 73-81, secy gen, 82-86, pres, 86-90; counr, Am Phys Soc, 76-83; chmn, Comn Symbols, Terminology & Units, Int Union Pure & Appl Chem, 77-81, pres, Phys Chem Div, 83-87 & Comt Chem Databases, 85-89; chmn, Am Inst Physics Publ Bd, 78-80; mem, adv bd, Chem Abstracts Serv, 78-83, Petrol Res Fund, 82-84, adv comt, Eng Info, Inc, 84-88 & bd gov, Mat Properties Data Network, Inc, 89-93; US Adv Comt Int Coun Sci Unions, 87-89; Comt on Atomic & Molecular Sci, NAS, NRC, 80-84; vchmn, Joint Comt Atomic & Molecular Phys Data, 89-93; guest scientist, Nat Inst Stands & Technol, 89-93; chmn, US Nat Comt, CODATA, 94-97. *Mem:* Am Chem Soc; fel Am Phys Soc; AAAS. *Res:* Free radicals, high temperature, microwave and infrared spectroscopy; molecular structure and spectroscopy; critical data evaluation in the physical sciences; molecular lasers; scientific databases; thermodynamics. *Mailing Add:* 13901 Riding Loop Dr Gaithersburg MD 20878. *Fax:* 301-738-7147; *E-Mail:* dlide@earthlink.net

LIDE, ROBERT WILSON, NUCLEAR PHYSICS. *Current Pos:* Asst prof, 57-65, ASSOC PROF PHYSICS, UNIV TENN, KNOXVILLE, 65- *Personal Data:* b Hwanghsien, Shantung, China, June 27, 22; US citizen; m 55; c 3. *Educ:* Wake Forest Col, BS, 43; Univ Mich, MS, 50, PhD, 59. *Mem:* Am Phys Soc. *Res:* Low-energy nuclear physics; gamma-gamma angular correlation; gamma-ray spectroscopy. *Mailing Add:* 309 Irwin Rd Powell TN 37849

LIDGARD, GRAHAM PETER, CANCER DIAGNOSTICS. *Current Pos:* VPRES PROD & DEVELOP, DEPT RES & DEVELOP, MARITECH, INC, 88-, DEPT GEN PROBE BIOTEC, 88- *Personal Data:* b Hull, Eng, Dec 23, 48. *Educ:* Univ Manchester, Eng, BA, 70, PhD(biol chem), 74. *Prof Exp:* Leader, Protein Chem Lab, Regional Hormone Lab, Univ Edenboro, Scotland, 73-77; prod mgr, Cieba-Corning, 77-84, prog mgr, 84-88. *Mem:* AAAS. *Res:* Cancer diagnostics. *Mailing Add:* 12838 Stebick St San Diego CA 92130

LIDIAK, EDWARD GEORGE, GEOLOGY. *Current Pos:* from asst prof to assoc prof geol, 64-80, PROF GEOL & PLANETARY SCI, UNIV PITTSBURGH, 76-, CHMN, DEPT GEOL, 71- *Personal Data:* b La Grange, Tex, Mar 14, 34. *Educ:* Rice Univ, BA, 56, MA, 60, PhD(geol), 63. *Prof Exp:* Res scientist, Univ Tex, 62-64. *Concurrent Pos:* Geologist, US Geol Surv, Pa, 65- *Mem:* AAAS; Geochem Soc; Geol Soc Am. *Res:* Petrology of island are volcanic rocks; geology of buried Precambrian rocks of United States; phase equilibria in mineral systems. *Mailing Add:* Dept Geol Univ Pittsburgh 321 Old Engineering Pittsburgh PA 15260-3303

LIDICKER, WILLIAM ZANDER, JR, POPULATION BIOLOGY, MAMMALOGY. *Current Pos:* From instr to assoc prof, Univ Calif, 57-69, from asst cur to assoc cur, Mus, 57-69, vchmn, Dept Zool, 66-67 & 81-83, assoc dir, Mus Vert Zool, 68-81, prof zool, 69-89, cur mammals, 69-94, actg dir, 74-75, prof integrative biol, 89-94, EMER PROF INTEGRATIVE BIOL CUR MAMMALS, UNIV CALIF, BERKELEY, 94- *Personal Data:* b Evanston, Ill, Aug 19, 32; m 56, 89; c Jeffrey R & Kenneth P. *Educ:* Cornell Univ, BS, 53; Univ Ill, MS, 54, PhD(zool), 57. *Honors & Awards:* C Hart Marriam Award, Am Soc Mammalogists, 86. *Concurrent Pos:* Vis scholar, Dept Zool, Sydney Univ & Div Animal Genetics, CSIRO, Sydney, Austrailia, 63-64; assoc res prof, Miller Inst Basic Res Sci, 67-68; hon res fel, Dept Animal Genetics, Univ Col London, 71-72; hon lectr, Dept Biol, Royal Free Hosp Sch Med, London, 71-72; NAm rep steering comt, Int Theriological/ Mammalogical Coun, 78-89; co-chmn, rodent specialist group, Species Survival Comn, Int Union Conserv Nature & Natural Resources, 80-84 & chmn, 84-89; Bd of Trustees, Biosciences Info Serv Inc, 87-92; vis scholar, Savannah River Ecol Lab, Univ Ga, 89-90, div zool, Univ Oslo, Norway, 90; fac mem, Inst Ecol. *Mem:* Hon mem Am Soc Mammal (2nd vpres, 74-76, pres, 76-78); Ecol Soc Am; Soc Study Evolution; Am Soc Naturalists; Soc Integration & Comp Biol; fel AAAS; Soc Conser Biol. *Res:* Ecology and evolution of mammals; landscape ecology. *Mailing Add:* Mus Vert Zool Univ Calif Berkeley CA 94720. *Fax:* 510-643-8238; *E-Mail:* lidicker@violet.berkeley.edu

LIDIN, BODIL INGER MARIA, microbiology, for more information see previous edition

LIDMAN, WILLIAM G, METALLURGY, CERAMICS. *Current Pos:* mgr Hazleton, Pa Plant & Yonkers NY Div, Cabot Corp, 71-74, group mgr metall res & develop, Kawecki Berylco Industs, 74-80, tech sales mgr develop prods, KBI Div, 80-84, prod mgr, Aluminum Master Alloys, 84-86, DIR, PROD MGT, KB ALLOYS, CABOT CORP, READING, PA, 86- *Personal Data:* b Rochester, NY, Nov 22, 21; m 43, Sheila Gluck; c Bonnie (Fox), Edward & Debra (Steinfeld). *Educ:* Univ Mich, BS, 43. *Prof Exp:* Res scientist, NASA, Ohio, 43-52; eng sect head, Sylcor Div, Gen Tel & Electronics Corp, 52-57, eng dept head, 57-60, proj mgr nuclear fuel elements, 60-61; tech dir beryllium mfg, Gen Astrometals Corp, 61-71. *Mem:* Sigma Xi; Am Soc Metals (treas, 55-57); Am Inst Metall Engrs. *Res:* Sintering mechanism of powder metallurgy products; production methods for manufacturing fuel elements for nuclear reactors and beryllium products; chemical specialty metals and beryllium; non-ferrous materials; refractory metals and ceramics. *Mailing Add:* 354 Pennsylvania Ave Shillington PA 19607

LIDOFSKY, LEON JULIAN, NUCLEAR ENGINEERING, COMPUTER SCIENCE. *Current Pos:* res asst, 49-52, res assoc, 52-59, from asst prof to assoc prof nuclear sci & eng, 59-64, PROF APPL PHYSICS & NUCLEAR ENG, COLUMBIA UNIV, 64- *Personal Data:* b Norwich, Conn, Nov 8, 24; m 48; c 2. *Educ:* Tufts Univ, BS, 45; Columbia Univ, MA, 47, PhD(physics), 52. *Prof Exp:* Instr physics, NY State Maritime Col, 48-49. *Concurrent Pos:* Res scholar, Inst Nuclear Physics, Amsterdam, 68-69; consult, Mt Sinai Sch Med, 70-77 & Am Phys Soc Study Group, 76-77. *Mem:* Am Nuclear Soc; Am Phys Soc. *Res:* Radiation transport; nuclear physics. *Mailing Add:* Appl Physics Columbia Univ 2960 Broadway New York NY 10027-6902

LIDOW, ERIC, ELECTRICAL ENGINEERING, SOLID STATE PHYSICS. *Current Pos:* PRES & CHMN BD, INT RECTIFIER CORP, 47- *Personal Data:* b Vilnius, Lithuania, Dec 9, 12; US citizen; m 52; c 4. *Educ:* Tech Univ, Berlin, MS, 37. *Prof Exp:* Chief engr, Selenium Corp Am, 41-44, vpres in charge res & eng, 44-46. *Mem:* Sr mem Inst Elec & Electronics Engrs. *Res:* Photoelectric phenomena; selenium photocells; selenium rectifiers; silicone power devices. *Mailing Add:* Int Rectifier Corp 233 Kansas St El Segundo CA 90245

LIDTKE, DORIS KEEFE, COMPUTER SCIENCE EDUCATION, SOCIAL & ETHICAL ISSUES IN COMPUTING. *Current Pos:* asst prof comput sci & math, 68-81, assoc prof, 81-90, PROF COMPUT SCI, TOWSON STATE UNIV, 90- *Personal Data:* b Bottineau Co, NDak, Dec 6, 29; m 51, Vernon L Lidtke. *Educ:* Univ Ore, BS, 52, PhD(comput sci educ), 79; Johns Hopkins Univ, MEd, 74. *Honors & Awards:* Outstanding Educr Award, Asn Educ Data Systs, 86; Distinguished Serv Award, Am Chem Soc. 95; Golden Care, Inst Elec & Electronics Engrs Comput Soc, 96. *Prof Exp:* Jr mathematician, Shell Develop Co, 55-59; programmer, Univ Calif, Berkeley, 60-62; asst prof comput, Lansing Community Col, 63-67; educ specialist, Johns Hopkins Univ, 68. *Concurrent Pos:* Vis assoc prof, Univ Ore, 81-83, 85; assoc prog dir, NSF, 84, prog dir, 92-93; Software Productivity Consortium, 87-88. *Mem:* Asn Comput Mach; Inst Elec & Electronics Engrs Comput Soc; Nat Educ Comput Conf. *Res:* Impact of computer on society; computer literacy and computer awareness; computers and education; computer and information sciences curriculum. *Mailing Add:* Dept Comput & Info Sci Towson State Univ Baltimore MD 21204. *E-Mail:* lidtke@towson.edu

LIDZ, THEODORE, PSYCHIATRY, PSYCHOANALYSIS. *Current Pos:* prof, 51-77, Sterling prof, 77-78, EMER STERLING PROF PSYCHIAT, YALE UNIV, 78- *Personal Data:* b New York, NY, Apr 1, 10; m 39, Ruth Wilmanns; c Victor M, Charles W & Jerome S. *Educ:* Columbia Univ, AB, 31, MD, 36; Am Bd Psychiat & Neurol, dipl. *Hon Degrees:* MA, Yale Univ, 51. *Honors & Awards:* Frieda Fromm-Reichmann Award, Acad Psychoanal, 61; William C Menninger Award, Am Col Physicians, 72; Stanley R Dean Award, Am Col Psychiat, 73; Laughlin Award, Am Col Psychoanalysts, 82; Spec Award, Am Family Ther Asn, 88. *Prof Exp:* From instr to assoc prof psychiat, Johns Hopkins Univ, 40-51. *Concurrent Pos:* Capt to Lt Colonel, US Army Med Corps, 42-46; examr, Am Bd Psychiat & Neurol, 46-51; psychiatrist-in-chief, Grace-New Haven Hosp, 51-61 & Yale Psychiat Inst, 51-61; chmn, Comt Educ, Am Psychiat Asn, 52-55; mem, Study Sect Res Grants, NIMH, 52-56, Training Grants Comt, 59-63, career investr, 61-78, mem, Ment Health Prog-Proj Comt, 63-67; consult, Off Surgeon Gen, 58-72; fel, Ctr Advan Study Behav Sci, 65-66; chmn, Dept Psychiat, Sch Med, Yale Univ, 67-69. *Mem:* Am Psychosom Soc (secy-treas, 52-56, pres, 57-58); fel Am Psychiat Asn; fel Am Col Psychoanal (pres-elect, 90, pres, 91); fel Am Col Psychiat; Am Psychoanal Asn; Sigma Xi; fel AAAS. *Res:* Etiology and treatment of Schizophrenia disorders; pioneer work in family and psychopathology; studies of cultures of Papua/New Guinea. *Mailing Add:* 200 Leeder Hill Dr Hamden CT 06517

LIE, WEN-RONG, MOLECULAR IMMUNOLOGY, IMMUNOGENETICS. *Current Pos:* RES SCIENTIST, SEARLE, ST LOUIS, 94- *Personal Data:* b Taiwan, Repub China, Sept 27, 57; m 86, Jen S Chan; c Jonathan C. *Educ:* Tunghai Univ, BS, 79; Iowa State Univ, PhD(immunobiol), 87. *Prof Exp:* Fel, Sch Med, Washington Univ, St Louis, 87-92; sr res biologist, Monsanto, St Louis, 92-94. *Concurrent Pos:* Am Asn Immunologists travel award, 89. *Mem:* Am Asn Immunologists. *Res:* Molecular biology of class I major histocompatibility complex molecules. *Mailing Add:* Dept Immunol AA4G Searle Res & Develop Seaarle Monsanto 700 Chesterfield Pkwy N St Louis MO 63198-0001

LIEB, CARL SEARS, HERPETOLOGY. *Current Pos:* Asst cur, Lab Environ Biol, Univ Tex, El Paso, 81-87, assoc cur, 87-89, interim dir, Centennial Mus, 89-90, assoc prof & coordr, Introd Biol Labs, 90-92, dir, Indio Mountains Res Sta, 91-96, MEM, GRAD FAC, LAB ENVIRON BIOL, UNIV TEX, EL

PASO, 83- *Personal Data:* b San Antonio, Tex, May 27, 49; m 80, Joyce K Belkin; c David, Eric & Joseph. *Educ:* Tex A&M Univ, BS, 71, MS, 73; Univ Calif, Los Angeles, PhD(biol), 81. *Concurrent Pos:* Mus assoc, Natural Hist Mus Los Angeles Co, 73-82, res assoc, 82-; vis fac, Brigham Young Univ, 84-85; herpetology ed, Southwestern Naturalist, 87-89. *Mem:* Am Soc Ichthyologists & Herpetologists; Herpetologists' League; Soc Study Amphibians & Reptiles; Southwestern Asn Naturalists; Sigma Xi; Soc Molecular Biol & Evolution. *Res:* Evolution, biosystematics and evolutionary genetics of vertebrate animals, particularly amphibians and reptiles. *Mailing Add:* Dept Biol Sci Univ Tex 500 W University Ave Rm 202 El Paso TX 79968-0519. *Fax:* 915-747-5808; *E-Mail:* elieb@mail.utep.edu

LIEB, ELLIOTT HERSHEL, MATHEMATICAL PHYSICS. *Current Pos:* PROF MATH & PHYSICS, PRINCETON UNIV, 75- *Personal Data:* b Boston, Mass, July 31, 32; m 75, Christiane Fellbaum; c Alexander & Gregory. *Educ:* Mass Inst Technol, BSc, 53; Univ Birmingham, PhD(physics), 56. *Hon Degrees:* DSc, Univ Copenhagen, 79, Fed Polytech Inst, Lausanne, 95. *Honors & Awards:* Boris Pregel Award, NY Acad Sci, 70; Heineman Prize, Am Phys Soc & Am Inst Physics, 78; Sci Prize, UAP, 85; Birkhoff Prize, Am Math Soc & Soc Indust Appl Math, 88; Max-Planck Medal, Ger Phys Soc, 92. *Prof Exp:* Fulbright fel physics, Kyoto Univ, 56-57; res assoc, Univ Ill, 57-58; lab nuclear studies, Cornell Univ, 58-60; staff physicist, Res Lab, IBM Corp, 60-63; assoc prof physics, Belfer Grad Sch Sci, Yeshiva Univ, 63-66; prof, Northeastern Univ, 66-68; prof math, Mass Inst Technol, 68-75. *Concurrent Pos:* Sr lectr, Univ Col Sierra Leone, 61-62; consult, IBM Corp, 63-65; guest prof, Inst Advan Sci Studies, France, 72-73; Guggenheim Found fel, 72 & 78; vis prof, Inst Advan Study, NJ, 82; ed, Commun Math Phys, Studies Appl Math, Lett Math Phys & Rev Mod Phys; mem bd gov, Inst Math & Applns, 83-87; mem bd trustees, Math Sci Res Inst, 85-89; coun mem, Am Math Soc, 92- *Mem:* Nat Acad Sci; fel Am Phys Soc; Austrian Acad Sci; Int Asn Math Physics (pres, 81-84); Royal Danish Acad Sci & Letts; Am Acad Arts & Sci. *Res:* Statistical mechanics; field theory; solid state physics; atomic physics; analysis; mathematical physics. *Mailing Add:* Dept Physics Princeton Univ PO Box 708 Jadwin Hall Princeton NJ 08544-0708. *Fax:* 609-258-6360; *E-Mail:* lieb@math.princeton.edu

LIEB, MARGARET, GENETICS. *Current Pos:* vis assoc prof, 60-62, assoc prof, 62-67, PROF MICROBIOL, SCH MED, UNIV SOUTHERN CALIF, 67- *Personal Data:* b Bronxville, NY, Nov 28, 23. *Educ:* Smith Col, BA, 45; Ind Univ, MA, 46; Columbia Univ, PhD, 50. *Prof Exp:* Asst prof biol, Brandeis Univ, 55-60. *Concurrent Pos:* USPHS fel, Calif Inst Technol, 50-52, Nat Found Infantile Paralysis fel, 52-53; fel, Inst Pasteur, 53-54; French Govt fel, Inst Radium, 54-55; NIH res career award, 62-72; prog dir genetic biol, NSF, 72-73. *Mem:* Fel AAAS; Genetics Soc Am; Am Soc Microbiol. *Res:* Bacteriophage genetics; DNA repair; spontaneous mutation. *Mailing Add:* Dept Molecular Microbiol & Immunol Sch Med Univ Southern Calif Los Angeles CA 90033. *Fax:* 213-342-1721

LIEBE, DONALD CHARLES, PHYSICAL CHEMISTRY. *Current Pos:* SECT MGR, PACKAGE DEVELOP, S C JOHNSON & SON, INC, 83- *Personal Data:* b Cleveland, Ohio, Nov 16, 42; m 64. *Educ:* Case Western Reserve Univ, BA, 66, MA, 68, PhD(phys chem), 70. *Prof Exp:* Res assoc chem, Yale Univ, 70-71, NIH res fel, 71-73, asst instr, 74; res investr, G D Searle & Co, 74-79, sect head, Res & Develop Div, 79-83. *Mem:* Am Chem Soc. *Res:* Physical chemistry of nucleic acids, protein-nucleic acid interactions; binding to nucleic acids; mechanism of animal virus replication; growth factors; physical pharmacy in pharmaceutical development; emulsion science; novel drug delivery systems; polyene macrolide antibiotic physical chemistry; polymer physical chemistry; packaging science. *Mailing Add:* Schering Plough Corp 2000 Galloping Hill K-11-1 I-2 Kenilworth NJ 07033

LIEBE, RICHARD MILTON, GEOLOGY. *Current Pos:* PROF GEOL, STATE UNIV NY COL BROCKPORT, 67- *Personal Data:* b Norwalk, Conn, May 26, 32; m 55; c 3. *Educ:* Bates Col, BS, 54; Univ Houston, MS, 59; Univ Iowa, PhD(geol), 62. *Prof Exp:* Assoc prof geol, Col Wooster, 61-67. *Mem:* Paleont Soc; Nat Asn Geol Teachers. *Res:* Stratigraphic paleontology of the Paleozoic era using conodonts; shallow water sedimentology and coral reef ecology. *Mailing Add:* Dept Earth Sci State Univ NY 350 New Campus Dr Brockport NY 14420-2915

LIEBELT, ANNABEL GLOCKLER, MICROSCOPIC ANATOMY, CANCER. *Current Pos:* fel expert, 87-92, SPEC VOL, NAT CANCER INST, 92- *Personal Data:* b Washington, DC, June 27, 26; div; c Ralph A, Laurie A, Erica L & Nancy L (Guthrie). *Educ:* Western Md Col, BA, 48; Univ Ill, Col Med, MS, 55; Baylor Col Med, PhD(anat), 60. *Prof Exp:* Biologist, Path Sect, Nat Cancer Inst, 49-52; asst anat, Col Med, Univ Ill, 52-54; asst, Col Med, Baylor Univ, 54-58, from instr to assoc prof, 58-71; assoc prof cell & molecular biol, Med Col Ga, 71-74; prof anat, Northeastern Ohio Univs Col Med, 74-86. *Concurrent Pos:* Dir, Kirschbaum Mem Lab, Col Med, Baylor Univ, 62-71, coordr, Micros Anat Teaching Prog, 77, dir, 78-79, chmn, 79-81; bd dirs, Augusta Radiation Ctr, 72-74, Portage Co Children's Serv Ctr, 79-82; bd dirs, Am Cancer Soc, Portage Co Unit, 74-82, vpres, 76-77, pres, 77-78, chair, Prof Educ Comt, 74-78; consult, Breast Cancer Task Force, Nat Cancer Inst, NIH, 76-80; vis prof, Univ Tokushima Med Sch, Japan, 90. *Mem:* NY Acad Sci; life mem Am Cancer Soc; Am Asn Path; Am Asn Lab Animal Sci; Soc Toxicol Path; Am Asn Cancer Res; Sigma Xi; Am Asn Women Sci; Am Asn Anatomists; Soc Toxicol Path; US & Can Acad Path. *Res:* Carcinogenesis, aging and pathology in inbred mice of several organ systems, especially the endocrine and reproductive (emphasis on mammary gland); biology histopathology; etiology; metastasis, environmental influences; animal models; educational materials or study sets of microscopic slides and accompanying syllabi. *Mailing Add:* Registry Exp Cancers 830 Quince Orchard Blvd #202 Gaithersburg MD 20878-0736. *Fax:* 301-402-1829

LIEBELT, ROBERT ARTHUR, ANATOMY, ALCOHOLISM. *Current Pos:* charter dean, 74-79, provost/dean, 79-82, PROF ANAT, NORTHEASTERN OHIO UNIV COL MED, 74- *Personal Data:* b Chicago, Ill, Feb 3, 27; m 80; c 5. *Educ:* Loyola Univ, Ill, BS, 50; Wash State Univ, MS, 52; Baylor Univ, PhD(anat), 57, MD, 58. *Prof Exp:* Asst, Wash State Univ, 50-52; asst, Col Med, Baylor Univ, 54-57, from instr to prof anat & chmn dept, 57-71; prof cell & molecular biol & exp med & assoc dean curriculum, Med Col Ga, 71-72, provost, 72-74. *Concurrent Pos:* Vis prof, Okayama Univ, 61; dir med educ, St Thomas Hosp, Akron, Ohio & dir, Ignatia Hall Alcoholism Ctr, 82. *Mem:* AAAS; Soc Exp Biol & Med; Am Asn Anat; Am Asn Cancer Res; NY Acad Sci. *Res:* Adipose tissue in obesity; relationship between nutrition and neoplasia; hypothalamus and appetite control; hypothalmic-pituitary relationships in experimental neoplasia; effects of pressure on food intake and body composition; biostereometric analysis for breast cancer; medical education; alcoholism. *Mailing Add:* Dept Anat Northeastern Ohio Univs Col Med 4209 State Rte 44 PO Box 95 Rootstown OH 44272-9698

LIEBENAUER, PAUL (HENRY), EXPERIMENTAL NUCLEAR PHYSICS. *Current Pos:* asst prof, 68-70, ASSOC PROF PHYSICS, STATE UNIV NY COL OSWEGO, 70- *Personal Data:* b Cleveland, Ohio, Sept 21, 35; m 62; c 2. *Educ:* Case Western Reserve Univ, BS, 57, MS, 60, PhD(physics), 71. *Prof Exp:* Instr physics, Clarkson Col Technol, 60-62. *Concurrent Pos:* Consult, NASA, 71-; NSF grant, 72. *Mem:* Am Phys Soc; Am Asn Physics Teachers; Sigma Xi. *Res:* Low energy nuclear physics. *Mailing Add:* Dept Physics State Univ Col Oswego NY 13126

LIEBENBERG, DONALD HENRY, LOW TEMPERATURE PHYSICS, HIGH PRESSURES. *Current Pos:* RETIRED. *Personal Data:* b Madison, Wis, July 10, 32; m 57, Norma Malmanger; c Karl H & Kira J. *Educ:* Univ Wis, BS, 54, MS, 56, PhD, 71. *Prof Exp:* Asst, Univ Wis, 54-61; staff mem physics, Los Alamos Nat Lab, 61-87; staff mem, NSF, 81-88; staff mem & sci officer condensed matter physics, Off Naval Res, 88-95, adj prof physics. *Concurrent Pos:* Solar-terrestrial res prog dir, NSF, 67-68; app liaison to Geophys Res Bd, Nat Acad Sci & US Comt Solar Terrestrial Res; US coordr, Solar Eclipse 70; sabbatical leave, prog dir low temp physics, on leave from NSF to Dept of Energy, 86-87. *Mem:* AAAS; Am Astron Soc; fel Am Phys Soc; Am Geophys Union. *Res:* Low temperature physics, especially superfluidity and helium films; solar physics; magneto optics; high pressure physical measurements; high pressure physics, superconductivity. *Mailing Add:* 49 Starboard Tack Dr Salem SC 29676-4026. *Fax:* 703-696-2611

LIEBER, BARUCH B, BIOMEDICAL ENGINEERING. *Current Pos:* Researcher, 85-87, ASST PROF BIOENG, STATE UNIV NY, BUFFALO, 87- *Personal Data:* b Tel Aviv, Israel, Aug 6, 52. *Educ:* Tel Aviv Univ, BS, 79; Ga Inst Technol, MS, 83, PhD(biomed), 85. *Mem:* Biomed Eng Soc; Am Inst Aeronaut & Astronaut; Sigma Xi; Am Soc Med Eng. *Mailing Add:* Dept Mech & Aerospace Eng 324 Jarvis Hall State Univ NY Buffalo NY 14260-0001

LIEBER, CHARLES SAUL, INTERNAL MEDICINE, NUTRITION. *Current Pos:* assoc prof, 68-69, PROF MED, MT SINAI SCH MED, 69-; CHIEF SECT LIVER DIS & NUTRIT, VET ADMIN HOSP, 68-; DIR, ALCOHOLISM RES & TREAT CTR, 77- *Personal Data:* b Antwerp, Belg, Feb 13, 31; US citizen; m 74; c 3. *Educ:* Univ Brussels, MD, 55. *Honors & Awards:* Laureate, Belg Govt, 56; McCollum Award, Am Soc Clin Nutrit, 73, Herman Award, 93; Distinguished Achievement Award, Am Gastroent Asn, 73, Hugh R Butt Award Liver/Nutrit, 92; E M Jellinek Mem Award, 77; W S Middleton Award, US Vet Admin, 77; Sci Excellence Award, Res Soc Alcoholism, 80, Distinguished Serv Award, 92; Achievement Award, Am Soc Addictive Med, 89; Outstanding Achievement Award, Am Col Nutrit, 90. *Prof Exp:* Asst resident med, Univ Hosp Brugmann Brussels, Belg, 55-56; instr med, Harvard Med Sch, 61-62, assoc, 62-63; assoc prof, Med Col, Cornell Univ, 63-68. *Concurrent Pos:* Belg Coun Sci Res fel internal med, Med Found Queen Elizabeth, 56-58; Belg-Am Found res fel med, Harvard Med Sch, 58-60; mem fat comt, Food & Nutrit Bd, Nat Acad Sci-Nat Res Coun, 61-67; dir liver dis & nutrit unit, Bellevue Hosp, 63-68; NIH res career develop award, 64-68. *Mem:* Am Soc Clin Invest; Am Med Soc Alcoholism (pres, 75); Am Soc Clin Nutrit (pres, 75); Asn Am Physicians; Res Soc Alcoholism (pres, 79). *Res:* Diseases of the liver; nutrition and intermediary metabolism, especially alcoholic cirrhosis, fatty liver, hyperlipemia, hyperuricemia, pathogenesis and treatment of hepatic coma and ascites, and pathophysiology of liver regeneration and drug abuse. *Mailing Add:* Alcohol Res Ctr Bronx Vet Admin Med Ctr Mt Sinai Sch Med 130 W Kingsbridge Rd Bronx NY 10468-3904

LIEBER, MICHAEL, THEORETICAL PHYSICS. *Current Pos:* chmn dept, 83-86, from asst prof to assoc prof, 70-83, PROF PHYSICS, UNIV ARK, 83- *Personal Data:* b Brooklyn, NY, Dec 28, 36; m 64, Eileen Saffron; c Kenneth, Laura & Deborah. *Educ:* Cornell Univ, AB, 57; Harvard Univ, AM, 58, PhD(physics), 67. *Prof Exp:* Sr scientist, Res & Advan Develop Div, Avco Corp, 63-66, chief sci probs, 66-67; assoc res scientist & adj asst prof physics, NY Univ, 67-70. *Concurrent Pos:* Prin investr, Dept Energy, 80-85; vis mem, Inst Theoret Physics, Univ Calif, Santa Barbara, 88; planetarium lectr, Univ Ark, 72-83, dir, Reach Kit Proj, 74-78. *Mem:* Am Phys Soc; Am Asn Physics Teachers; Sigma Xi. *Res:* Quantum scattering theory; few body problems; quantum electrodynamics and field theory; mathematical methods; atomic collisions; cosmic rays; elementary particles; general relativity and cosmology. *Mailing Add:* Dept Physics Univ Ark Fayetteville AR 72701. *Fax:* 501-575-4580; *E-Mail:* mlieber@comp.uark.edu

LIEBER, RICHARD L, MUSCLE MECHANICS & REHABILITATION. *Current Pos:* res assoc, Univ Calif, Davis, 81-82, res physiologist, San Diego, 82-85, asst prof surg, Dept Surg-Orthop & Rehab, 85-89, ASSOC PROF, DEPT ORTHOP, UNIV CALIF, SAN DIEGO, 89-; BIOMED ENGR, DEPT ORTHOP RES, VET ADMIN MED CTR, 83- *Personal Data:* b Walnut Creek, Calif; m 80; c 2. *Educ:* Univ Calif, Davis, BS, 78, PhD, 82. *Honors & Awards:* Talbot Award, Biophys Soc, 81. *Prof Exp:* Fel, NIH, 78-81. *Concurrent Pos:* Invited speaker, Frontiers Eng Health Care, Inst Elec & Electronic Engrs, 84; lectr, Skelatal Muscle Plasticity Series, Univ Calif, San Diego, Statist in Exp Biol, 85 & 86 & Bioeng Lab, 87 & 88. *Mem:* Biophys Soc; Inst Elec & Electronics Engrs; Orthop Res Soc; Rehab Eng Soc NAm; Soc Neurosci; Am Acad Orthop Surgeons. *Res:* Characterize skeletal muscle adaptation to altered use; elucidate mechanisms of torque generation during normal. *Mailing Add:* Div Orthop Univ Calif San Diego San Diego CA 92161

LIEBERBURG, IVAN M, NEUROSCIENCE, ENDOCRINOLOGY. *Current Pos:* staff scientist, Dept Cell Biol, Athena Neurosci, Inc, 87-88, sr scientist, Dept Molecular Biol, 88-90, vpres Alzheimer's res, 90-94, VPRES RES, ATHENA NEURO SCI, INC, 94-; CLIN PROF MED, UNIV CALIF HOSPS, SAN FRANCISCO, 94- *Personal Data:* b June 18, 49. *Educ:* Cornell Univ, AB, 71; Rockefeller Univ, PhD(neurobiol), 76; Univ Miami, MD, 80; Am Bd Internal Med, cert, 83, cert endocrinol & metab, 85. *Prof Exp:* Med resident, Univ Calif Hosps, San Francisco, 80-82, res fel endocrine, Univ, 82-84; asst prof endocrinol & med, Albert Einstein Col Med, 84-87; assoc prof neurobiol & psychiat, Mt Sinai Sch Med, 87; assoc clin prof med, Univ Calif Hosps, San Francisco, 90-94. *Mem:* Fel Orgn Trop Studies; Endocrine Soc; Soc Neurosci; Am Asn Cancer Researchers; Am Soc Cell Biol; Am Asn Neuropathologists. *Res:* Neuroscience; endocrinology. *Mailing Add:* Athena Neurosci Inc 800F Gateway Blvd South San Francisco CA 94080-7021

LIEBERMAN, ABRAHAM N, NEUROLOGY. *Current Pos:* Instr, 70-71, from asst prof to assoc prof, 71-80, PROF NEUROL, NY UNIV MED CTR, 80- *Personal Data:* b Brooklyn, NY, July 8, 38; c 4. *Educ:* Cornell Univ, AB, 59; NY Univ Med Sch, MD, 63. *Concurrent Pos:* Staff neurologist, US Air Force Hosp, Tachikawa, Japan, 67-69; asst chief neurol, Manhattan Vet Admin Hosp, 70-72; attend physician, Univ Hosp, NY Univ Sch Med, 70-; grants & contracts from var univs, cols & insts, 71-85; dir, Neurol Clin, Bellevue Hosp, 73-; consult, AMA Drug Evaluations, Chicago, Ill, 79- *Mem:* Asn Res Nervous & Ment Disease; Am EEG Soc; Am Soc Clin Pharmacol & Therapeut; fel Am Col Clin Pharmacol; Am Neurol Asn. *Mailing Add:* Neurol Group Ltd 222 W Thomas Rd Suite 401 Phoenix AZ 85013

LIEBERMAN, ALVIN, CHEMICAL ENGINEERING. *Current Pos:* RETIRED. *Personal Data:* b Chicago, Ill, June 14, 21; m 47, Tillie B Lavin; c Gary & Harold. *Educ:* Cent YMCA Col, BS, 42; Ill Inst Technol, MS, 49. *Honors & Awards:* Hausner Award, Fine Particle Soc, 84; Whitfield Award, Inst Environ Sci, 85; Seligman Award, Inst Environ Sci, 96. *Prof Exp:* Res assoc metal-ceramics, Alfred Univ, 49-51; res chem engr, IIT Res Inst, 51-63, sect mgr fine particles res, 63-68; dir res, Pac Sci Co, 68-74, vpres, Royco Instruments, Inc, 74-80, vpres, adv develop, HIAC/ROYCO Instrument Div, 80-83; Tech Specialist Particle Measuring Systs, 83-92. *Concurrent Pos:* Regional ed, Powder Technol, 69-; tech spec, Particle Measuring Systs, 83-85, 87-; chief scientist, HIAC/ROYCO instr div, Pac Sci Co, 85-87. *Mem:* AAAS; Am Chem Soc; Am Inst Chem Engrs; Am Asn Contamination Control (vpres, 62-63); Fine Particle Soc (pres, 77-78); Sigma Xi; Am Asn Aerosol Res; Inst Environ Sci. *Res:* Aerosol studies and application of electronic techniques; cloud physics; dust-free assembly area control and procedures; particle technology for gas/liquid suspensions. *Mailing Add:* 1943 Mt Vernon Ct 309 Mountain View CA 94040. *Fax:* 510-490-8213

LIEBERMAN, ARTHUR STUART, REGIONAL LANDSCAPE PLANNING & LANDSCAPE ECOLOGY. *Current Pos:* STAFF MEM, DEPT OVERSEAS STUD PROGS, UNIV HAIFA. *Personal Data:* b Brooklyn, NY, Feb 24, 31; m 56; c 3. *Educ:* Cornell Univ, BS, 52, MS/LD, 58. *Prof Exp:* Teacher high sch, NY, 52-53; from instr to prof environ qual, Cornell Univ, 58-86, emer prof, 86- *Concurrent Pos:* Adv, Nature Reserves Authority & Ministry Agr, Israel, 71-72; res fel, Technion Israel Inst Technol, Haifa, 75-76, Lady Davis vis prof award, 80-81, prof, Technion, 80-81; chmn & coordr, Cornell Tree Crops, Cornell Univ, 78-86, res proj coordr, Multidisciplinary Int Land-Use Planning Prog, 79-86; consult, UN Food & Agr Orgn, Bangalore, India, 85; res dir, Cornell (Abroad) Prog Israel, 87- *Mem:* Int Asn Landscape Ecol; Israel Soc Ecol & Environ Qual Sci. *Res:* Physical environmental quality; ecology-based regional land-use planning; regional landscape inventories and information systems for physical planning; analysis and use of vegetation in comprehensive land planning; tree crops (agroforestry) for food and forage on rough marginal lands. *Mailing Add:* Dept Overseas Stud Progs Univ Haifa Mt Carmel Haifa 31905 Israel. *Fax:* 972-4-8240391

LIEBERMAN, BURTON BARNET, MATHEMATICS. *Current Pos:* Asst prof, 65-69, actg chmn math dept, 90, ASSOC PROF MATH, POLYTECH UNIV, 69-, ADMIN OFFICER, MATH DEPT, 91- *Personal Data:* b Boston, Mass, Sept 28, 38; m 63, Miriam Smith; c Bruce S & Jenny M. *Educ:* Harvard Univ, BA, 60; NY Univ, MS, 62, PhD(math), 67. *Concurrent Pos:* Prin investr & consult, US Golf Asn, 79- *Mem:* Am Math Soc; Sigma Xi; Inst Math Stat; Am Stat Asn; Math Asn Am. *Res:* Ordinary differential equations; robust statistical methods; sports science. *Mailing Add:* 451 W Broadway New York NY 10012-3104. *E-Mail:* blieberm@vm.poly.edu

LIEBERMAN, DANIEL, PSYCHIATRY. *Current Pos:* dir, Jefferson Community Ment Health-Ment Retardation Ctr, Thomas Jefferson Univ, 67-74, prof & actg chmn, Dept Psychiat & Human Behav, 74-76, prof & dir, Psychosom Serv, 76-83, prof & chmn, 83-89, EMER PROF, DEPT PSYCHIAT & HUMAN BEHAV, JEFFERSON MED COL, THOMAS JEFFERSON UNIV, 89- *Personal Data:* b Gunnison, Utah, Feb 21, 19; c Janine (Vogel). *Educ:* Univ Calif, AB, 42, MD, 46. *Prof Exp:* Chief hosp serv, Sonoma State Hosp, Calif, 49-54; supt & med dir, Mendocino State Hosp, 54-60; from chief dep dir to dir, State Dept Ment Health, 60-63; pvt pract, 63-64; comnr ment health, Del Dept Ment Health, 64-67. *Concurrent Pos:* Consult forensic psychiat, Calif Superior Courts, 54-63; consult ment hosp serv, Am Psychiat Asn, 60-62; consult forensic psychiat, US Fed Court, 61-; consult, Ment Health Res Inst, Palo Alto, Calif, Nat Inst Alcohol Abuse & Acoholism, 63-64; consult state ment progs, NIMH, 65-68, consult, Alcohol Rev Comt, 67-70, consult, Nat Coun Community Health Ctrs, 72-73; consult, Vet Admin Hosp, Coatesville, Pa, 67-89; med dir, Medco Corp, 91-94. *Mem:* Fel AAAS; Am Col Psychiat; fel Am Asn Ment Deficiency; fel Acad Psychosom Med; fel Am Psychiat Asn; fel Am Asn Social Psych; Sigma Xi. *Res:* Chronic pain; psychosomatic medicine; treatment of stress disorders. *Mailing Add:* Thomas Jefferson Univ Curtis Bldg Rm 327F 11th & Walnut St Philadelphia PA 19107. *Fax:* 215-923-8219

LIEBERMAN, DIANA DALE, POPULATION BIOLOGY, TROPICAL FOREST ECOLOGY. *Current Pos:* from asst prof to assoc prof, 81-92, PROF BIOL, DEPT BIOL, UNIV NDAK, 92-; RESIDENT DIR, SAN LUIS BIOL STA, COSTA RICA, 95- *Personal Data:* b Los Angeles, Calif, Jan 19, 49; m 68, Milton; c Sarah. *Educ:* Univ Ghana, Legon, BSc, 76, PhD(bot), 79. *Prof Exp:* Demonstr plant ecol, Dept Bot, Univ Ghana, 76-79; vis scholar forest ecol & trop biol, Dept Environ Sci, Univ Va, 80-81. *Concurrent Pos:* NSF res grants, 81-86, 92-; NASA, res grant, 87-90; Mellon Found res grant, 94-96. *Mem:* Ecol Soc Am; Sigma Xi; Asn Trop Biologists; Int Soc Trop Foresters. *Res:* Tree growth rates, age-size relationships and tropical forest dynamics; plant population biology, phenology and seed dispersal; community ecology; tropical forest conservation and restoration. *Mailing Add:* Apdo 35 Santa Elena Monteverde Punts Costa Rica. *Fax:* 506-645-5277, 380-3255

LIEBERMAN, EDWARD MARVIN, PHYSIOLOGY. *Current Pos:* PROF PHYSIOL, SCH MED, E CAROLINA UNIV, 78- *Personal Data:* b Lowell, Mass, Feb 10, 38; m 60; c 3. *Educ:* Tufts Univ, BS, 59; Univ Mass, MA, 61; Univ Fla, PhD(physiol), 65. *Prof Exp:* Res assoc physiol, Col Med, Univ Fla, 66; asst prof, 68-72, assoc prof, Bowman Gray Sch Med, 72-76; assoc prof, 76-78. *Concurrent Pos:* Swed Med Res Coun fel, Col Med, Univ Uppsala, 66-68. *Mem:* Soc Neurosci; Biophys Soc; Am Heart Asn; Am Physiol Soc; NY Acad Sci. *Res:* Cellular nerve physiology; membrane ion and water transport and metabolism; ultraviolet radiation effects on membranes; Schwann cell axon interactions. *Mailing Add:* Dept Physiol ECarolina Univ Sch Med Greenville NC 27858-4354

LIEBERMAN, EDWIN JAMES, PSYCHIATRY, SCIENCE COMMUNICATIONS. *Current Pos:* CLIN PROF PSYCHIAT, SCH MED, GEORGE WASH UNIV, 90- *Personal Data:* b Milwaukee, Wis, Nov 21, 34; m 59, 88, Carol Silverman; c Karen L (Troccoli) & Daniel. *Educ:* Univ Calif, Berkeley, AB, 55; Univ Calif, San Francisco, MD, 58; Harvard Univ, MPH, 63; Am Bd Psychiat & Neurol, dipl, 66. *Prof Exp:* Psychiat fel, Mass Ment Health Ctr, Boston, 59-61; child psychiat fel, Putnam's Children Ctr, Boston, 61-62; psychiatrist & chief, Ctr Child & Family Ment Health, NIMH, 63-70; dir family ther, Hillcrest Children's Ctr, DC, 71-74, dir ment health proj, 72-75, dir family planning proj, Am Pub Health Asn, 75-77; clin assoc prof psychiat, Sch Med, George Washington Univ, 77-87; adj prof, Family & Community Develop, Univ Md, 87-90. *Concurrent Pos:* Child psychiat fel, Hillcrest Children's Ctr, DC, 65-66; mem bd dirs, Sex Info & Educ Coun US, 66-69 & 73-76; clin asst prof psychiat, Sch Med, Howard Univ, 67-76; mem bd dirs, Nat Coun Family Rels, 69-73; vis lectr maternal & child health, Harvard Sch Pub Health, 69-73. *Mem:* AAAS; fel Am Psychiat Asn; fel Am Pub Health Asn; fel Am Asn Marriage & Family Therapists; Esperanto League NAm (pres, 72-75). *Res:* Mental health; preventive psychiatry; family planning; nonviolence; Esperantic studies; international language planning; Otto Rank (1884-1939); evolution of psycho therapy. *Mailing Add:* 3900 Northampton St NW Washington DC 20015. *Fax:* 202-363-6899; *E-Mail:* ejl@gwis2.circ.gwu.edu

LIEBERMAN, GERALD J, OPERATIONS RESEARCH, STATISTICS. *Current Pos:* from asst prof to prof statist & indust eng, Stanford Univ, 53-67, chmn, Dept Opers Res, 67-75, assoc dean, Sch Humanities & Sci, 75-77, dean res, 77-80, vprovost,77-85, actg vpres & provost, 79, dean, grad studies & res, 80-85, provost, 91-93, PROF STATIST & OPERS RES, STANFORD UNIV, 67- *Personal Data:* b New York, NY, Dec 31, 25; m 50, Helen Herbert; c Janet A, Joanne, Michael & Diana. *Educ:* Cooper Union, BME, 48; Columbia Univ, AM, 49; Stanford Univ, PhD(statist), 53. *Honors & Awards:* Shewhart Medal, Am Soc Qual Control, 72; Kimball Medal, Inst Opers Res & Mgt Sci. *Prof Exp:* Math statistician, Nat Bur Stand, 49-50. *Concurrent Pos:* Mem, Maritime Transp Res Bd, Nat Res Coun, 66-71, Panel Appl Math Alternatives for Navy, 77-89, Comt Appl & Theoret Statist, 78-81 & Panel Appl Math, Nat Bur Stand, 83-89, chmn, 85-89; mem, Adv Panel Math Sci, NSF, 68-73; mem bd dirs, Am Statist Asn, 74-76; mem bd adv, Naval Postgrad Sch, 76-85; mem, Grad Record Exam Bd, 84-88, panel, Qual Control Family Assistance Progs, Nat Res Coun, 86-88, bd math sci, 88-, bd trustees, Ctr Advan Study Behav Sci, 90-; fel, Ctr Advan Study Behav Sci, 85-86. *Mem:* Nat Acad Eng; Opers Res Soc Am; fel Am Soc Qual Control (teas, 60-64); fel Am Statist Asn (vpres, 63-64); fel Inst Math Statist; Int Statist Inst; Inst Mgt Sci (pres, 80-87); Inst Opers Res & Mgt Sci. *Res:* Industrial statistics; quality control; reliability; applied probability models. *Mailing Add:* Dept Opers Res Stanford Univ Stanford CA 94305-4022. *E-Mail:* hk.gjl@.forsythe.stanford.edu

LIEBERMAN, HERBERT A, PHARMACEUTICAL CHEMISTRY. *Current Pos:* RETIRED. *Personal Data:* b New York, NY, Aug 6, 20; m 49, Helen Oken; c Bruce Alan & Robert Adam. *Educ:* Univ Ark, BS, 40; Columbia Univ, AM, 48, BS, 51, MS, 52; Purdue Univ, PhD(pharmaceut chem), 55. *Honors & Awards:* Pres Citation Distinguished Serv, 76. *Prof Exp:* Res fel biochem, Beth Israel Hosp, New York, 40-41; chemist, Pine Bluff Arsenal, Ark, 41-43; instr & assoc anal chem, Col Pharm, Columbia Univ, 46-52, res pharmacist, Res Inst, Wyeth Labs, 54-57; mgr pharmaceut prod develop, Isodine Pharmacal Co, 57-61; sr res assoc, Warner Lambert Co, Inc, 61-63, dir pharmaceut res & develop, 63-72, vpres, Personal Prods Div, 72-77, dir develop consumer prods, 77-85; pres, Lieberman Assocs Inc, Livingston, NJ, 85-94. *Concurrent Pos:* Ed, var pharmaceut journals. *Mem:* Am Chem Soc; Am Asn Pharmaceut Scientists; fel Acad Pharmaceut Sci; Sigma Xi; fel Acad Pharmaceut Sci, 72; fel Am Asn Pharmaceut Scientists, 86. *Res:* Industrial pharmacy; pharmaceutical technology, particularly process and product development; analytical methods development for pharmaceutical products. *Mailing Add:* 4 Browning Dr Livingston NJ 07039

LIEBERMAN, HILLEL, ORGANIC CHEMISTRY, MICROBIAL BIOCHEMISTRY. *Current Pos:* Var admin & sci asst dir res, 73-76, asst vpres res, 76-79, vpres res, 79-82, vpres res & develop, 82-86, CHMN, BETZ INC, TREVOSE, 86-, SR VPRES, 87- *Personal Data:* b Philadelphia, Pa, Jan 24, 42; m 66; c 2. *Educ:* Temple Univ, BS, 63, MS, 65, PhD(med org chem), 70. *Mem:* Am Soc Microbiol; Am Chem Soc; Sigma Xi; Tech Asn Pulp & Paper Indust. *Res:* Development of chemical agents of an antimicrobial and/ or antipollution nature to be employed in industrial water systems; development of conceptual information to aid in application of the aforementioned. *Mailing Add:* 3782 Midvale Lane Huntingdon Valley PA 19006

LIEBERMAN, JACK, pulmonary diseases, enzymology, for more information see previous edition

LIEBERMAN, JAMES, PUBLIC HEALTH. *Current Pos:* DIR, DEPT HEALTH, GREENWICH, CONN, 76- *Personal Data:* b New York, NY, June 2, 21; m 43, Lucille Goldstein; c Margaret A. *Educ:* Middlesex Univ, DVM, 44; Univ Minn, MPH, 47. *Honors & Awards:* Cert Commendation, UNRRA, 46; Letter of Commendation, Surgeon Gen, US Navy, 52; Citation, Nat League Nursing, 62; Citation, Nat AV Asn, 67; Brenda Award, Theta Sigma Phi, 68; Myrtle Wreath Award, Hadassah, 69. *Prof Exp:* Sr consult vet, UNRRA, 46; regional milk & food consult, USPHS, Kansas City, 48-50, asst to the chief, Milk & Food Br, DC, 50-51, from asst chief to chief spec proj br, Bur State Serv, 51-52, liaison officer to USN, 52, consult, spec regulatory prog, 52-54, detailed epidemiologist, Div Epidemiol & Commun Dis Control, NY State Health Dept, 54-55, training consult, Training Br, Commun Dis Ctr, asst chief training br & chief AV sect, 59-62, chief med AV br dir, Pub Health Serv AV Fac, Commun Dis Ctr, 62-67, dir, Nat Med AV Ctr & assoc dir AV & telecommun, Nat Libr Med, 67-70, asst surgeon gen, USPHS, 68-70; vpres, Med Div, Videorec Corp Am, 70-73; consult health sci educ & commun, 73-76. *Concurrent Pos:* Secy, Conf Pub Health Vets, 53-57; consult, WHO, Geneva, 55; chmn, Fed Adv Coun Med Training Aids, 60; mem task force sci commun, Surgeon Gen Conf Health Commun, 62; secy AV Conf Med & Allied Sci, 62-70; pres, Metrop Atlanta Commun Coun, 65; chmn conf biomed commun, NY Acad Sci, 67; mem comt bio-technol, Ga Sci & Technol Comn, 69-70; mem prof adv coun, Nat Easter Seal Soc Crippled Children & Adults, 69-75; vis prof, Sch Med, Hahnemann Univ, 73-; mem bd gov & pres-elect, Conn Inst Health Manpower Resources, 74-78; mem, adv coun, Pub Understanding Sci Prog, NSF, 78-80 & bd gov, US Conf Local Health Officers, 79-87; chairperson, Ment Health Consortium, Darien, Greenwich, New Canaan & Stamford, Inc, 86-87; mem, Conn Alcohol & Drug Policy Coun, 96- *Mem:* Fel Am Pub Health Asn; Asn Mil Surg US; Am Vet Med Asn; NY Acad Sci; Sigma Xi; Am Col Epidemiol. *Res:* Biomedical communication and education; public health practice-policy and epidemiology; training and administration; comparative medicine. *Mailing Add:* 12 Silver Brook Rd Westport CT 06880. *Fax:* 203-622-7770

LIEBERMAN, JAMES S, NEUROLOGY, PHYSICAL & REHABILITATION MEDICINE. *Current Pos:* SR ASSOC DEAN, CLIN SERV, COLUMBIA UNIV, 96-, ASST VPRES HEALTH SCI, 96- *Personal Data:* b Minneapolis, Minn, Apr 24, 38. *Educ:* Univ Calif, BS, 60, MD, 63. *Prof Exp:* Instr & asst prof neurol, NY State Univ, 67-71; vis asst prof to prof, Columbia Univ, 70-72; from asst prof to prof, Univ Calif, Davis, 72-91, prof & chmn phys med, 82-91. *Mem:* Inst Med-Nat Acad Sci; Am Acad Clin Neurophysiol; Am Acad Neurol; Am Acad Phys Med & Rehab. *Mailing Add:* Dept Rehab Med Loc 38 Columbia Univ 630 W 168th St New York NY 10032

LIEBERMAN, LESLIE SUE, BIOLOGICAL ANTHROPOLOGY. *Current Pos:* asst prof anthrop, 76-81, grad coordr, Ctr Geront Studies, 79-82, ASSOC PROF ANTHROP & PEDIAT, UNIV FLA, 81-, RES EPIDEMIOLOGIST, DIABETES RES, EDUC & TREAT CTR, 79- *Personal Data:* b Rockville Ctr, NY, June 23, 44; c 1. *Educ:* Univ Colo, BA, 65; Univ Ariz, MA, 71; Univ Conn, PhD(biobehav sci), 75. *Prof Exp:* Proj assoc body composition, Human Performance Res Lab, Pa State Univ, University Park, 75-76. *Concurrent Pos:* Fel, Nat Inst Gen Med Sci Human Performance Res Lab & Dept Anthrop, Pa State Univ, 74-75; mem, Coun Nutrit Anthrop, vpres, 80-82; prin investr, NSF grant, 81-83; vis lectr, Am Anthrop Asn, 81, Fla State Univ, London, 85, Univ Zagreb, Yugoslavia, 88; exec comt, Am Anthrop Asn, 87-88; pres, Coun Nutrit Anthrop, 96-; bd dirs, Nat Asn Acad Sci, 96- *Mem:* AAAS; Am Anthrop Asn; Am Asn Phys Anthropologists; Human Biol Asn; Sigma Xi. *Res:* Study of body composition and the effects of nutritional behavior and diet on adaptation and microevolution in human populations; epidemiology of diabetes mellitus especially in US minority populations. *Mailing Add:* Dept Anthrop Univ Fla 1350 Tur PO Box 117305 Gainesville FL 32611

LIEBERMAN, MAURY L, OCCUPATIONAL MENTAL HEALTH, COMMUNITY DEVELOPMENT. *Current Pos:* CHIEF, SPEC PROGS, SUBSTANCE ABUSE & MENT HEALTH ADMIN, 94- *Personal Data:* b Chicago, Ill, Apr 29, 42. *Educ:* Univ Wis, BS, 60; Rutgers Univ, MSW, 66; Univ Pittsburgh, MURP, 70. *Mailing Add:* Ctr Ment Health Servs 18C-07 5600 Fishers Lane Rockville MD 20857. *Fax:* 301-443-7912; *E-Mail:* nlieberman@samhsa.gov

LIEBERMAN, MELVYN, PHYSIOLOGY. *Current Pos:* res assoc, Div Biomed Eng, Sch Eng & Dept Physiol & Pharmacol, Duke Univ, 67-68, from asst prof to prof physiol, 68-88, PROF CELL BIOL, DUKE UNIV, 88-, ASSOC PROF, DEPT MED, 89-, PROF, DEPT BIOMED ENG, 93- *Personal Data:* b Brooklyn, NY, Feb 4, 38; m 61, Rochelle Beller; c Eric N & Marc E. *Educ:* Cornell Univ, BA, 59; State Univ NY, PhD(physiol), 65. *Honors & Awards:* Cecil Hall Award, Electron Micros Soc Am, 89. *Prof Exp:* Instr biol, Queen's Col, NY, 60; asst physiol, State Univ NY Downstate Med Ctr, 60-64. *Concurrent Pos:* Nat Heart Inst fel, 64-65; Carnegie Inst fel, 65; Nat Heart Inst fel, Biophys Inst, Brazil, 65-67; Nat Heart Inst spec fel, Med Ctr, Duke Univ, 67-68; lectr, Queen's Col, NY, 63-64; vis investr, Jan Swammerdam Inst, Neth, 75; Soc Gen Physiol secy, 69-71, Nat Res Coun rep, 71-75, pres, 81-82; chmn res rev comt, NC Heart Asn, 75-76 & mem res rev comt, NY Heart Asn, 80-85; co-coordr, US Japan Coop Sci Prog, 74, 88 & US Brazil Coop Sci Prog, 80; Porter Develop Prog, Am Physiol Soc, 74-77, educ mat rev bd, 75-77, int comt chmn, 93-; assoc ed, Am J Physiol, 81-, Experientia, 82-90, Physiol Rev, 85-91 & Molecular Cell Biochem 91-; consult, Macy Found, Nat Heart Lung & Blood Inst, NSF, Vet Admin & Am Heart Asn; Estab Investr Award, Am Heart Asn, 71-76, mem physiol study sect, 80-84, Cardiovasc Res Study Comt, 87-90, Fel Rev Comt, 89-93 & Res Training Study Sect, 90-; coun, cell & gen physiol sect, Am Physiol Soc, 84-86, chmn, 86-87, 91-; mem, Task Force Govt-Univ-Indust Collab Res, Nat Res Coun, 91-93, Howard Hughes Fel Prog Bio Sci, 94-; co unr, Am Sect, Int Soc Heart Res, 93- *Mem:* Am Heart Asn; Am Physiol Soc; Biophys Soc; Cardiac Muscle Soc; Int Soc Heart Res; NY Acad Sci; Soc Gen Physiol; Physiol Soc; AAAS; Am Soc Cell Biol; Sigma Xi. *Res:* Electrophysiology of cardiac muscle; regulation of ion transport; cultured heart cells as a model to study myocardial ischemia; mechanisms of cardiac cell injury; cardiotoxicity; cell volume regulation. *Mailing Add:* Dept Cell Biol Div Physiol Duke Univ Med Ctr Box 3709 Durham NC 27710-0001

LIEBERMAN, MICHAEL A, MOLECULAR GENETICS. *Current Pos:* ASSOC PROF, DEPT MOLECULAR GENETICS, BIOCHEM & MICROBIOL, COL MED, UNIV CINCINNATI, 83- *Personal Data:* b New York, NY, Aug 22, 50; m; c 2. *Educ:* Mass Inst Technol, SB, 72; Brandeis Univ, PhD(biochem), 78. *Prof Exp:* Fel, Dept Biol Chem, Sch Med, Wash Univ, 77-79, res assoc, 79-80; asst prof biochem, Dept Nutrit, Harvard Sch Pub Health, 81-83. *Concurrent Pos:* Jr fac award, Am Cancer Soc, 81-84; mem, Study Sect Cellular Biol & Physiol II, NIH, 86-89. *Mem:* Am Soc Biochem & Molecular Biol; Am Soc Cell Biol. *Res:* Numerous publications; molecular genetics. *Mailing Add:* Molecular Genetics Biochem & Microbiol Dept Univ Cincinnati Col Med 231 Bethesda Ave Cincinnati OH 45267-0524

LIEBERMAN, MICHAEL A, PLASMA PHYSICS. *Current Pos:* FAC MEM, DEPT ELEC ENG & COMPUT SCI, UNIV CALIF, BERKELEY, 66- *Personal Data:* b Oct 3, 40. *Educ:* Mass Inst Technol, BS, 62, PhD(physics), 66. *Mem:* Fel Inst Elec & Electronics Engrs; fel Am Phys Soc. *Mailing Add:* Dept Elec Eng & Comput Sci 189M Cory Hall Univ Calif Berkeley CA 94720

LIEBERMAN, MICHAEL MERRIL, CELLULAR IMMUNOLOGY, HUMORAL IMMUNOLOGY. *Current Pos:* RES ASSOC, DEPT CHEM, UNIV HAWAII, MANOA, 96- *Personal Data:* b Chicago, Ill, June 10, 44; div; c Ted. *Educ:* Univ Chicago, BS, 66, PhD(microbiol), 69; Am Bd Med Lab Immunol, dipl. *Prof Exp:* Nat Res Coun res assoc, Ames Res Ctr, Calif, NASA, 69-71; sr res microbiologist, Cutter Labs, Inc, 71-75 & Brooke Army Med Ctr, Tex, 76-83; chief microbiol serv, Dept Clin Invest, Tripler Army Med Ctr, Hawaii, 83-87; chief microbiol & immunol, dept path, Wm Beaumont Army Med Ctr, El Paso, Tex, 87-91; chief immunol serv, Fitzsimons Army Med Ctr, 91-96. *Mem:* Am Soc Microbiol; Am Asn Immunol; Clin Cytometry Soc; fel Asn Med Lab Immunologists. *Res:* Bacterial vaccine development; enzymology of halophilic bacteria; biochemical genetics and metabolic regulation; bacterial antigen and toxin purification; clinical and diagnostic immunology. *Mailing Add:* Dept Chem 2545 The Mall Univ Hawaii Manoa Honolulu HI 96822. *Fax:* 808-956-5908; *E-Mail:* michaell@gold.chem.hawaii.edu

LIEBERMAN, MICHAEL WILLIAMS, EXPERIMENTAL PATHOLOGY, MOLECULAR BIOLOGY. *Current Pos:* RETIRED. *Personal Data:* b Pittsburgh, Pa, Apr 20, 41; m 68; c 2. *Educ:* Yale Univ, BA, 63; Univ Pittsburgh, MD, 67, PhD(biochem), 72; Am Bd Path, cert anat path, 72. *Honors & Awards:* Warner-Lambert & Parke-Davis Award, Am Asn Pathologists, 81. *Prof Exp:* Sarah Mellon Scoife fel, 69-70; res assoc, Fels Inst, Temple Health Sci Ctr, 70-72 & Exp Path Br, Nat Cancer Inst,74-76; head, Somatic Cell Genetics Sect, Nat Inst Environ Health Sci, 74-76; assoc prof, Sch Med, Wash Univ, 76-80, prof, dept path & dir grad studies, div biol & biomed sci, 80-84; chmn, dept path, Fox Chase Cancer Ctr, Philadelphia, PA, 84-88. *Concurrent Pos:* Adj asst & assoc prof, dept path, Med Sch, Univ NC, 74-76; assoc pathologist, Barnes Hosp, St Louis, 76-84; mem, Chem Path Study Sect, NIH, 78-; mem, Bd Toxicol, & Environ Health Hazards, Nat Res Coun, 80-84; vchmn, US Nat Comt Int Coun Soc Path, 87-90, counr, Am Asn Pathologists, 88-90. *Mem:* Am Asn Cancer Res; AAAS; Am Asn Pathologists; Environ Mutagen Soc; Am Soc BioChemists & Molecular Biologists. *Res:* Molecular analysis of disease; molecular biology and gene expression, especially the role of oncogenes in the modulation of cellular gene expression in vitro and in carcinogenesis; chemical carcinogenesis. *Mailing Add:* Dept Path Baylor Col Med One Baylor Plaza Houston TX 77030-3498. *Fax:* 713-798-5555

LIEBERMAN, MILTON EUGENE, TROPICAL & QUANTITATIVE ECOLOGY. *Current Pos:* RES PROF, DEPT BIOL, UNIV NDAK, 81-; RESIDENT DIR, SAN LUIS BIOL STA, COSTA RICA, 95- *Personal Data:* b Chicago, Ill, Aug 30, 34; m 68, Diana D Smith; c Sarah. *Educ:* Univ Calif, Berkeley, AB, 62; Ariz State Univ, MS, 66; Univ Calif, Irvine, PhD(biol scis), 69. *Prof Exp:* Sr lectr ecol, Dept Zool, Univ Ghana, 74-79; vis prof, Dept Environ Sci, Univ Va, 80-81. *Concurrent Pos:* NSF res grants, 81-86, 92-; res assoc, Mo Bot Garden, St Louis, 80-; sr res assoc, Nat Res Coun, 85-86; res grant, NASA, 87-90; Mellon Found res grant, 94-96. *Mem:* Ecol Soc Am; Sigma Xi; Asn Trop Biologists; Int Soc Trop Foresters. *Res:* Ecology of new world tropical forests, tropical marine benthic algal assemblages; reproductive phenology of temperate and tropical fleshy-fruited plants; plant-animal interactions; tropical forest conservation and restoration. *Mailing Add:* Apdo 35 Santa Elena Monteverde Punts Costa Rica. *Fax:* 506-645-5277, 380-3255

LIEBERMAN, MORTON LEONARD, PHYSICAL CHEMISTRY. *Current Pos:* STAFF MEM TECH RES, SANDIA LABS, 68- *Personal Data:* b Chicago, Ill, Nov 22, 37; m 62, Elaine Sterling; c Laura Amy & Neal Reid. *Educ:* Ill Inst Technol, BS, 59, MS, 63, PhD(phys chem), 65. *Prof Exp:* Sr chemist, Res & Develop Labs, Corning Glass Works, 65-68. *Mem:* Am Chem Soc. *Res:* High-temperature chemistry, thermodynamics; phase transitions; thin films; optical properties; fossil fuels; pyrotechnics and explosives; carbon research. *Mailing Add:* 1316 Paisano Northeast Albuquerque NM 87112-4524. *E-Mail:* mlliebe@sandia.gov

LIEBERMAN, RICHARD BARRY, OLEFIN POLYMERIZATION PROCESS DEVELOPMENT & CATALYSIS. *Current Pos:* DIR MFG TECHNOL, MONTELL, DEL, 95- *Personal Data:* b New York, NY, July 18, 50. *Educ:* Cooper Union, BE, 70; Princeton Univ, PhD(chem eng), 76. *Prof Exp:* Sr res engr, Res Ctr, Hercules Inc, 75-84; res scientist, Rev Develop Ctr, Himont USA Inc, 84-87, mgr res, 87-89, assoc dir, 89-92, dir technol strategy, 92-95,. *Mem:* Am Chem Soc; Indust Res Inst. *Res:* Direction of process and product development activities for the production of polyolefins, including research involving Ziegler-Natta catalysts. *Mailing Add:* Montell NAm 3 Little Falls Ctr 2801 Centerville Rd PO Box 5437 Wilmington DE 19850. *Fax:* 410-996-1805

LIEBERMAN, ROBERT, RADIOCHEMISTRY. *Current Pos:* chief phys sci br, Eastern Environ Radiation Lab, 71-74, chief qual assurance sect, 74-79, RES & DEVELOP CHEMIST, EASTERN ENVIRON RADIATION FACIL, ENVIRON PROTECTION AGENCY, 74- *Personal Data:* b Columbus, Ohio, Apr 9, 24; m 62; c 3. *Educ:* Ohio State Univ, BA, 48, MSc, 52. *Prof Exp:* Chemist, Plastics Div, Battelle Mem Inst, 55-58, res scientist, Chem Physics Div, 58-64, sr chemist, 64-67, chief bioassay sect, Southeastern Radiol Health Lab, USPHS, 67-69, chief chem & biol, 69-71. *Res:* Polyurethane foams; fission gas release; neutron dosimetry; radiation effects on plastics; use of radiotracers on wear studies; measurement of radionuclides in environmental samples. *Mailing Add:* 3707 Laconia Lane Montgomery AL 36111

LIEBERMAN, ROBERT ARTHUR, OPTICAL SENSORS-PHYSICAL & CHEMICAL, GUIDED WAVE OPTICAL DEVICES. *Current Pos:* dir adv fiber optics, 91-94, vpres res & develop sensor systs, 94-95, VPRES & GEN MGR RES & DEVELOP, PHYS OPTICS CORP, 96- *Personal Data:* b Grand Rapids, Mich, May 22, 50; m 88, Jaye C; c Sam & Lee. *Educ:* Rensselaer Polytech Inst, BS, 71, MS, 73; Univ Mich, PhD(physics), 81. *Prof Exp:* Fel, Univ Mich, 81; mem tech staff, AT&T Bell Labs, 81-91. *Concurrent Pos:* Chair, fibersensors conf, Int Soc Optical Engrs, 87-; prin investr, NSF, 91-, USAF, 91-, Defense Advan Res Prog Agency, 92-, NASA, 92-, DOE, 92-, Navy, 92-, NIH, 94- *Mem:* AAAS; Am Phys Soc; Am Stand Testing Mat; sr mem Inst Elec & Electronics Engrs; Optical Soc Am; Int Soc Optical Engrs. *Res:* Fiberoptic sensors for gases, liquids and physical properties; development of distributed and multiplexed sensor configuration; planar-waveguide and surface plasmon devices; protein biophysics research; scientific project management; biosensors; environmental sensors; biological spectroscopy. *Mailing Add:* Phys Optics Corp 20600 Gramercy Pl Torrance CA 90501-1821. *Fax:* 310-320-4667; *E-Mail:* rlieberman@aol.com

LIEBERMAN, SAMUEL VICTOR, CHEMISTRY. *Current Pos:* RETIRED. *Personal Data:* b Philadelphia, Pa, Nov 3, 14; m 38; c 2. *Educ:* Univ Pa, BS, 36, MS, 37, PhD(chem), 48. *Prof Exp:* Asst, Sharp & Dohme, Inc, 41-42; res chemist, Wyeth Inst Med Res, 45-47, sr res chemist, 48-55; scientist in charge, Phys Analysis Dept, Prod Div, Mead Johnson Co, 55-57, dir develop & phys sci, 57-60; consult pharmaceut prod, 61-79. *Mem:* AAAS; Sigma Xi. *Res:* Research, development and testing of pharmaceutical products. *Mailing Add:* 3400 N Ocean Dr No 508 Singer Island FL 33404

LIEBERMAN, SEYMOUR, BIOCHEMISTRY. *Current Pos:* PRES, ST LUKE'S-ROOSEVELT INST HEALTH SCI, 81-, EMER PROF, OFF SCI & TECHNOL, COLUMBIA COL PHYSICIANS & SURGEONS, 87-, ASSOC DIR, 91- *Personal Data:* b New York, NY, Dec 1, 16; m 44; c 1. *Educ:* Brooklyn Col, AB, 36; Univ Ill, MS, 37; Stanford Univ, PhD(chem), 41. *Honors & Awards:* Ciba Award, Endocrine Soc, 52 & Koch Award, 70, Roussel Prize, 84, Dale Medal, 86. *Prof Exp:* Chemist, Schering Corp, 38-39; Rockefeller Found asst, Stanford Univ, 39-41; spec res assoc, Harvard Univ, 41-45; assoc, Sloan-Kettering Inst, 45-50; from asst prof to emer prof biochem, Col Physicians & Surgeons, Columbia Univ, 50-87, assoc dean, 84-90, assoc vprovost, 87-90. *Concurrent Pos:* Mem, Panel Steroids, Comt Growth, Nat Res Coun, 46-50 & Panel Endocrinol, 55-56; traveling fel from Mem Hosp, NY to Basel, Switz, 46-47; mem, Endocrinol Study Sect, NIH, 58-63, mem, Insts, 59-65, chmn, 63-65, mem, Gen Clin Res Ctrs Comn, 67-70; mem, Med Adv Comt, Pop Coun, 61-74; assoc ed, J Clin Endocrinol & Metab, 63-67; prog officer, Ford Found, 74-75. *Mem:* Nat Acad Sci; Am Chem Soc; Am Soc Biol Chem; fel NY Acad Sci; Endocrine Soc (vpres, 67, pres, 74). *Res:* Steroid chemistry and biochemistry; biogenesis and metabolism of steroid hormones; steroid hormone-protein conjugates; steroid sulfates and lipoidal derivatives of steroids. *Mailing Add:* 515 E 72nd St New York NY 10021. *Fax:* 212-523-7442

LIEBERMANN, HOWARD HORST, THERMODYNAMICS & MATERIAL PROPERTIES, ELECTROMAGNETISM. *Current Pos:* sr metallurgist, Allied Corp Metglas Prod, 82-84, MGR RES & DEVELOP, ALLIED SIGNAL AMORPHOUS METALS, 85- *Personal Data:* b Ger, Nov 27, 49; m 79, Lynda Kobuskie; c Daniel & Amanda. *Educ:* Polytech Inst New York, BS, 72; Univ Pa, MS, 75, PhD(metall & mat sci), 77. *Prof Exp:* Staff metallurgist, Corp Res & Develop, Gen Elec Co, 77-81. *Mem:* Sigma Xi; Inst Elec & Electronics Engrs Magnetics Soc; Am Soc Metals; Am Inst Mining, Metall & Petrol Engrs; Iron & Steel Soc. *Res:* Materials processing; amorphous alloys; magnetic materials; electronic soldering alloys. *Mailing Add:* 11 Cynthia Dr Succasunna NJ 07876

LIEBERMANN, LEONARD NORMAN, PHYSICS. *Current Pos:* res assoc, Marine Phys Lab, 46-48, assoc prof geophys, 48-54, prof physics, 54-82, EMER PROF PHYSICS, 82- *Personal Data:* b Ironwood, Mich, May 14, 15; m 41, Miller; c 3. *Educ:* Univ Chicago, BS, 37, MS, 38, PhD(physics), 40. *Prof Exp:* Instr physics, Wash Univ, 40-41; instr, Univ Kans, 41-43, asst prof, 43-44; prin physicist bur ships, Woods Hole Oceanog Inst, Mass, 44-46. *Concurrent Pos:* Guggenheim Found fel, 52-53; vis prof, Yale Univ, 52-53 & Imp Col, 69-70; dir, Proj Sorrento, 59; US sci rep, NATO, Italy, 62-63. *Mem:* Fel Am Phys Soc; fel Acoust Soc Am. *Res:* Ultrasonics; underwater sound; hydrodynamics; properties of liquids; electromagnetic propagation; solid state. *Mailing Add:* Univ Calif San Diego Physics-0319 9500 Gillman Dr La Jolla CA 92093-0319

LIEBERMANN, ROBERT C, GEOPHYSICS. *Current Pos:* ASSOC PROF, STATE UNIV NY, STONY BROOK, 76- *Personal Data:* b Ellwood City, Pa, Feb 6, 42; m 64; c 3. *Educ:* Calif Inst Technol, BS, 64; Columbia Univ, PhD(geophys), 69. *Prof Exp:* Res scientist, Lamont-Doherty Geol Observ, 69-70; res fel geophys, Calif Inst Technol, 70; mem fac, Australian Nat Univ, 70-76. *Concurrent Pos:* Assoc ed, J Geophys Res, 73-76. *Mem:* Fel Royal Astron Soc; Am Geophys Union; Seismol Soc Am. *Res:* Relative excitation of seismic waves by earthquakes and underground explosions; elastic properties of minerals and rocks as a function of pressure and temperature; composition and mineralogy of earth's mantle. *Mailing Add:* 2 Cornwallis Rd East Setauket NY 11733

LIEBERT, JAMES WILLIAM, ASTRONOMY, ASTROPHYSICS. *Current Pos:* Res assoc, 76-79, asst prof, 79-86, PROF ASTRON, STEWARD OBSERV, UNIV ARIZ, 86- *Personal Data:* b Coffeyville, Kans, June 19, 46. *Educ:* Univ Kans, BA, 68; Univ Calif, Berkeley, MA, 70, PhD(astron), 77. *Honors & Awards:* Trumpler Prize, Astron Soc Pac, 77. *Concurrent Pos:* Prin investr, NSF grant, Univ Ariz, 77-80. *Mem:* Am Astron Soc; Int Astron Union; Astron Soc Pac. *Res:* Observational stellar astronomy and astrophysics; white dwarf stars. *Mailing Add:* 2302 E Hampton St Tucson AZ 85719

LIEBES, SIDNEY, JR, PHYSICS. *Current Pos:* AT HEWLETT-PACKARD CO. *Personal Data:* b San Francisco, Calif, Dec 13, 29; m 58; c 2. *Educ:* Princeton Univ, BSE, 52; Stanford Univ, PhD(physics), 58. *Prof Exp:* Instr physics, Princeton Univ, 57-61, asst prof, 61-64; res assoc-physicist, dept genetics, Med Ctr, 64-80, MEM STAFF, DEPT COMPUT SCI, STANFORD UNIV, 80- *Mem:* Am Phys Soc; Am Asn Physics Teachers. *Res:* Experimental atomic and electron physics; gravitation experiments; mass spectrometry; physical microanalysis; techniques applied to bio-medical research; computer imagery processing; Martian Lander imagery. *Mailing Add:* Hewlett-Packard Co 1501 Page Mill Rd 4 U 1 Palo Alto CA 94304

LIEBESKIND, HERBERT, PHYSICAL CHEMISTRY. *Current Pos:* from instr to prof, Cooper Union, 45-88, asst dean, 68-72, dir admissions & registr, 70-87, dean admissions & records, 72-87, EMER PROF CHEM, COOPER UNION, 88- *Personal Data:* b New York, NY, Nov 24, 21; m 43, 83; c 2. *Educ:* NY Univ, BS, 41. *Prof Exp:* Asst instr chem, NY Univ, 43-45. *Concurrent Pos:* Vis lectr, Stevens Inst Technol, 52-54; vis assoc prof, Yeshiva Univ, 61-62. *Mem:* Am Chem Soc; Am Soc Eng Educ; NY Acad Sci. *Mailing Add:* 1464 E 91st St Brooklyn NY 11236-4906

LIEBESKIND, JOHN C, PSYCHOLOGY. *Current Pos:* from asst prof to prof, 65-78, PROF PSYCHOL & ANESTHESIOL & MEM, BRAIN RES INST, UNIV CALIF, LOS ANGELES, 78- *Personal Data:* b Waterbury, Conn, Feb 2, 35. *Educ:* Harvard Univ, BA, 57; Univ Mich, MS, 59, PhD(psychol), 62. *Honors & Awards:* Jacob K Javits Neurosci Investr Award, NIH, 85. *Prof Exp:* Instr, Dept Psychol & asst res psychol biologist, Ment Health Res Inst, Univ Mich, 62-63; NIMH postdoctoral fel, Inst Marey, Paris, France, 63-65. *Concurrent Pos:* Mem, Sci Prog Comt, Am Pain Soc, 78-80 & Res Comt, 80-81; vis scientist, Vis Scientists Minority Inst Prog, NMex Highland Univ, Fedn Am Socs Exp Biol, 84; mem bd dirs, Found Advan Brain Studies, 84-87; founding pres & bd dirs, Int Pain Found, 86-94. *Mem:* Nat Acad Sci; Int Brain Res Orgn; Am Pain Soc (pres, 90-91); fel Am Psychol Asn; fel Am Psychol Soc; Soc neurosci. *Res:* Authored and co-authored over 300 professional research publications. *Mailing Add:* Dept Psychol Univ Calif 405 Hilgard Ave Los Angeles CA 90095-1563

LIEBESKIND, LANNY STEVEN, ORGANIC CHEMISTRY, ORGANOMETALLIC CHEMISTRY. *Current Pos:* FAC DEPT CHEM, EMORY UNIV. *Personal Data:* b Buffalo, NY, Sept 5, 50. *Educ:* State Univ NY, Buffalo, BS, 72; Univ Rochester, MS, 74, PhD(chem), 76. *Prof Exp:* NSF fel chem, Mass Inst Technol, 76-77; NIH fel, Stanford Univ, 77-78; asst prof chem, Fla State Univ, 78- *Mem:* Am Chem Soc. *Res:* Application of organotransition metal chemistry to the solution of problems in synthetic organic chemistry. *Mailing Add:* Dept Chem Emory Univ Atlanta GA 30322-0001

LIEBHARDT, WILLIAM C, SOILS, SUSTAINABLE AGRICULTURE. *Current Pos:* DIR, SUSTAINABLE AGR RES & EDUC PROG, DEPT AGR & RANGE SCI, UNIV CALIF, DAVIS, 87- *Personal Data:* b Duluth, Minn, Feb 16, 36; m 61; c 4. *Educ:* Univ Wis-Madison, BS, 58, MS, 64, PhD(soils), 66. *Prof Exp:* Agronomist, Stand Fruit Co, 66-68; sr agronomist, Allied Chem Corp, 68-69; from asst prof to assoc prof plant sci, Univ Del, 70-81; from assoc dir to dir res, Rodale Res Ctr, 81-87. *Res:* Soil fertility; plant nutrition; sustainable agriculture; farming systems. *Mailing Add:* Dept Agr & Range Sci Univ Calif Davis CA 95616-8580

LIEBLEIN, SEYMOUR, AEROSPACE ENGINEERING. *Current Pos:* RETIRED. *Personal Data:* b New York, NY, June 17, 23. *Educ:* City Col New York, BS, 44; Case Inst Technol, MS, 52. *Honors & Awards:* Gas Turbine Award, Am Soc Mech Engrs, 61; Goddard Award, Am Inst Aeronaut & Astronaut, 67. *Prof Exp:* Researcher, Nat Adv Comt Aeronauts, Lewis Res Ctr, NASA, 44-57, chief, Flow Anal Br, 57-65, chief, Vertical Takeoff & Landing Propulsion Br, 65-70, div tech asst, Short Takeoff, Landing & Noise Div, 70-74; mgr & owner, Tech Report Serv, 77- *Mem:* Am Soc Mech Engrs; assoc fel Am Inst Aeronaut & Astronaut. *Res:* Fluid flow and design in axial flow compressors; aerodynamic performance and design of vertical takeoff and landing propulsion systems; waste-heat systems, space power; technical report writing; wind turbine blades and flow. *Mailing Add:* 3400 Wooster Rd Rocky River OH 44116

LIEBLING, RICHARD STEPHEN, MINERALOGY. *Current Pos:* asst prof, 68-73, ASSOC PROF GEOL, HUNTER COL, 73- *Personal Data:* b Brooklyn, NY, Aug 31, 38; m 70. *Educ:* Columbia Univ, BA, 60, MA, 61, PhD(mineral), 63. *Prof Exp:* Sr ceramist, Carborundum Co, 63-68. *Mem:* Mineral Soc Am; Sigma Xi. *Res:* Clay mineralogy of sediments. *Mailing Add:* Dept Geol-Geog CUNY Hunter Col 695 Park Ave New York NY 10021-5024

LIEBMAN, ARNOLD ALVIN, ORGANIC CHEMISTRY, RADIOCHEMISTRY. *Current Pos:* RETIRED. *Personal Data:* b St Paul, Minn, Mar 5, 31; m 55, 77; c 4. *Educ:* Univ Minn, BS, 56, PhD(pharmaceut chem), 61. *Prof Exp:* Asst prof biochem, Loyola Univ, La, 61-63; Nat Inst Gen Med Sci res fel chem, Univ Calif, Berkeley, 63-66; asst prof chem, Sch Pharm, Univ Md, 66-68; sr chemist, Hoffman-LaRoche Inc, 68-72, res group chief, 72-80, sr res group chief, 80-81, res sect chief, 82-85, res investr, 85-93. *Mem:* AAAS; Am Chem Soc; Int Isotope Soc. *Res:* Heterocyclic chemistry of natural products; isotopic synthesis, heterocyclic chemistry. *Mailing Add:* 144 Red Cedar Lane Johns Island SC 29455

LIEBMAN, FREDERICK MELVIN, PHYSIOLOGY. *Current Pos:* Asst, 53-56, from instr to assoc prof, 56-65, PROF PHYSIOL & BIOPHYS, COL DENT, NY UNIV, 65-, CHMN DEPT, 69- *Personal Data:* b New York, NY, July 26. 22; m 48, Grace Heinman; c 3. *Educ:* NY Univ, BA, 42, PhD, 56; Univ Pa, DDS, 47. *Concurrent Pos:* Int Asn Dent Res rep, Int Cong Physiol, Buenos Aires, Arg, 59; dir, Basic Med Sci (Dent), Grad Sch Arts & Sci, NY Univ. *Mem:* AAAS; Am Physiol Soc; Harvey Soc; NY Acad Sci; fel Am Col Dent. *Res:* Peripheral circulation; control of circulation in the dental pulp and oral cavity; functional activity of the muscles of mastication; control of posture and movement; pain; analgesics; narcotic-antagonists; opioid agonists. *Mailing Add:* Dept of Physiol Ny Univ Col Dent 550 Scarsdale Rd Tuckahoe NY 10707

LIEBMAN, JEFFREY MARK, CELL BIOLOGY, OSTEOARTHRITIS. *Current Pos:* sr staff scientist psychopharmacol, 76-83, mgr behav neurosci, 83-87, SR RES FEL, CIBA-GEIGY PHARMACEUT, 88- *Personal Data:* b Milwaukee, Wis, Nov 7, 46; m 74, Anita Epstein; c 3. *Educ:* Oberlin Col, BA, 68; Univ Calif, Los Angeles, PhD(psychol), 73. *Prof Exp:* Res assoc fel psychopharmacol, Sch Med, Univ Calif, San Diego, 73-76. *Concurrent Pos:* Res fels, Sloan Found, 73-74 & Alcoholism, Drug Abuse & Ment Health Admin, 74-76; vis scientist, NIH, 89-91. *Mem:* Soc Neurosci; Sigma Xi; Am Soc Pharmacol & Exp Therapeut. *Res:* Molecular biological aspects of osteoarthritis and inflammation. *Mailing Add:* 14 Tall Oaks Dr Summit NJ 07901. *Fax:* 908-277-4739; *E-Mail:* jeffrey.liebman@ussu.mhs.ciba.com

LIEBMAN, JOEL FREDRIC, THEORETICAL CHEMISTRY, INORGANIC CHEMISTRY, ORGANIC CHEMISTRY. *Current Pos:* from asst prof to assoc prof, 72-82, PROF, DEPT CHEM, UNIV MD, BALTIMORE CO, 82- *Personal Data:* b Brooklyn, NY, May 6, 47; m 70, Deborah Van Vechten. *Educ:* Brooklyn Col, BS, 67; Princeton Univ, MA, 68, PhD(chem), 70. *Prof Exp:* NATO fel, Depts Phys & Theoret Chem, Cambridge Univ, 70-71; Nat Res Coun & Nat Bur Stand fel, Inorg Chem Sect, Nat Bur Stand, 71-72. *Concurrent Pos:* Ramsay hon fel, Ramsay Mem Fel Trust, 70; consult & contractor, Nat Bur Stand, 72-; unofficial consult, Argonne Nat Lab, 72-75; guest scientist, 75-82; German Acad Exchange Serv Fac fel, 76; co-ed, Molecular Struct & Energetics, 84-91; mem ed adv bd, Methods Stereochem Anal, 85-; consult ed, Struct Chem, 90-; consult, Energetics & Reactivity Chem, 91-; Norwegian Marshall Fund Fac Travel grantee, 92 & 94; Luro-Am Fund Develop (Portugal), Faculty Travel Grantee, 92. *Mem:* Am Chem Soc; Am Phys Soc; Sigma Xi. *Res:* Chemical bonding theory, rules and regularities of molecular geometry and energetics; strain and resonance energy of alicyclic and aromatic hydrocarbons; noble gas and fluorine compounds; thermochemistry of molecular ions; mathematical chemistry; structural chemistry. *Mailing Add:* Dept Chem & Biochem 1000 Hilltop Circle Univ Md Baltimore County Baltimore MD 21250. *Fax:* 410-455-2608; *E-Mail:* jliebman@umbc2.umbc.edu

LIEBMAN, JON C(HARLES), ENVIRONMENTAL SYSTEMS ANALYSIS. *Current Pos:* assoc head dept civil eng, 76-78, head, Dept Civil Eng, 78-84, prof environ eng, 72-96, EMER PROF ENVIRON ENG, UNIV ILL URBANA-CHAMPAIGN, 96- *Personal Data:* b Cincinnati, Ohio, Sept 10, 34; m 58, Judith Stenzel; c 3. *Educ:* Univ Colo, BS, 56; Cornell Univ, MS, 63, PhD(sanit eng), 65. *Prof Exp:* From asst prof to assoc prof environ eng, Johns Hopkins Univ, 65-72. *Mem:* Fel AAAS; Inst Mgt Sci; Am Soc Civil Engrs; Sigma Xi. *Res:* Applications of operations research to the field of environmental engineering. *Mailing Add:* Dept Civil Eng Univ Ill Urbana-Champaign Urbana IL 61801-2397. *E-Mail:* jcl@uiuc.edu

LIEBMAN, JUDITH STENZEL, ENGINEERING OPTIMIZATION. *Current Pos:* from asst prof to prof, opers res, 72-96, vchancellor, Res & Dean Grad Col, 87-92, EMER PROF OPERS RES, UNIV ILL, URBANA, 96- *Personal Data:* b Denver, Colo, July 2, 36; m 58; c 3. *Educ:* Univ Colo, BA, 58; Johns Hopkins Univ, PhD(opers res), 71. *Honors & Awards:* George E Kimball Medal, Inst Opers Res & Mgt Sci. *Prof Exp:* Engr data anal, Convair Astronaut, Gen Dynamics, 58-59; programmer eng syst, Gen Elec Co, 63-64; programmer chem, Cornell Univ, 64-65; res asst opers res, Johns Hopkins Univ, 65-71, asst prof & health serv res scholar, 71-72. *Concurrent Pos:* Pres, bd dir, E Cent Ill Health Systs Agency, 80-82. *Mem:* Opers Res Soc Am (pres, 87-88); Sigma Xi; Inst Mgt Sci; Am Asn Univ Profs; AAAS; Inst Opers Res & Mgt Sci. *Res:* Mathematical optimization; model building; applications of operations research in civil and military infrastructure management. *Mailing Add:* 140 Mech Eng Bldg Univ Ill Urbana IL 61801

LIEBMAN, PAUL ARNO, BIOPHYSICS, PHYSIOLOGY. *Current Pos:* res assoc physiol, 63-65, asst prof, 65-69, assoc prof, 69-76, PROF ANAT, UNIV PA, 76-, PROF OPHTHALMOL, 77- *Personal Data:* b Pittsburgh, Pa, Aug 1, 33; m; c 1. *Educ:* Univ Pittsburgh, BS, 54; Johns Hopkins Univ, MD, 58. *Prof Exp:* Intern internal med, Barnes Hosp, St Louis, Mo, 58-59. *Concurrent Pos:* Fel biophys, Univ Pa, 59-63. *Mem:* Biophys Soc; Asn Res Vision & Ophthal; Am Soc Neurosci. *Res:* Vision; microspectrophotometry of single visual receptors; transducer mechanism of photoreceptors in vision. *Mailing Add:* Dept Neurosci Univ Pa 143 Anat/Chem Bldg Philadelphia PA 19104-6058

LIEBMAN, SUSAN WEISS, MOLECULAR GENETICS. *Current Pos:* from asst prof to assoc prof, 77-87, PROF BIOL, UNIV ILL, CHICAGO CIRCLE, 87- *Personal Data:* b New York, NY, Dec 2, 47; m 69, Alan; c Judith & Michael. *Educ:* Mass Inst Technol, BS, 68; Harvard Univ, MA, 69; Univ Rochester, PhD(biophys), 74. *Prof Exp:* Am Cancer Soc fel, Sch Med & Dent, Univ Rochester, 74-76. *Concurrent Pos:* USPHS career develop award. *Mem:* AAAS; Genetics Soc Am; Am Soc Microbiol. *Res:* Molecular genetics of yeast, including nonsense suppression, mutators, transposable elements; ribosomal RNA; prions. *Mailing Add:* Molecular Biol Res Facil Lab Molecular Biol M/C 567 Univ Ill 900 S Ashland Ave Chicago IL 60607

LIEBMANN, JEFFREY MITCHELL, GLAUCOMA. *Current Pos:* Clin instr, 87-88, asst clin prof, 89-92, ASSOC CLIN PROF OPHTHAL, NY MED COL, 92- *Personal Data:* b New York, NY, Mar 10, 58; m 85, Cindy Geller; c 3. *Educ:* Boston Univ, BA & MD, 83. *Concurrent Pos:* Assoc dir glaucoma serv, NY Eye & Ear Infirmary, 88- *Mem:* AMA; Am Acad Ophthal; Asn Res Vision & Ophthal; Am Glaucoma Soc. *Res:* Evaluation of new ophthalmic laser technologies and ocular imaging modalities such as ultrasound biomicroscopy. *Mailing Add:* 310 E 14th St New York NY 10003. *Fax:* 212-260-1002

LIEBNER, EDWIN J, RADIOLOGY. *Current Pos:* DIR RADIOTHER DIV, ILL RES & EDUC HOSPS, 61- *Personal Data:* b Chicago, Ill, July 12, 21; m 63; c 2. *Educ:* Univ Ill, BS, 44, MD, 46. *Prof Exp:* Resident radiol, Ill Res Hosps, 53-56; from asst prof to assoc prof, 56-66, PROF RADIOL, UNIV ILL HOSP, 66-, ACTG HEAD DEPT RADIOL, UNIV ILL COL MED, 71- *Concurrent Pos:* Consult radiol, Vet Admin Hosp, Hines, 64- *Mem:* Am Radium Soc; Roentgen Ray Soc; Am Soc Therapeut Radiol; Radiol Soc NAm. *Res:* Therapeutic lymphography; refrigeration and irradiation; therapeutic pediatric radiology. *Mailing Add:* 1107 Jackson River Forest IL 60305-1419

LIEBNITZ, PAUL W, MATHEMATICS. *Current Pos:* Asst prof, 61-67, ASSOC PROF MATH, UNIV MO, KANSAS CITY, 67- *Personal Data:* b Kansas City, Mo, Jan 18, 35; m 61, Jennifer McGonigle; c Philip, Karl, John, David & Kathryn. *Educ:* Rockhurst Col, BS, 55; Univ Kans, MA, 57, PhD(math), 64. *Mem:* Math Asn Am. *Res:* Topology, theory of retracts. *Mailing Add:* Dept Math Univ Mo Kansas City MO 64110

LIEBOVITCH, LARRY S, FRACTALS, CHAOS. *Current Pos:* ASSOC PROF, FLA ATLANTIC UNIV, 93- *Personal Data:* b New York, NY. *Educ:* City Col NY, BS, 72; Harvard Univ, AM, 73, PhD(astron), 78. *Prof Exp:* Postdoctoral, Mt Sinai Sch Med, NY, 78-79; postdoctoral asst prof, Columbia Col Physicians & Surgeons, 79-93. *Concurrent Pos:* Chair, Biophys Sect, NY

Acad Sci, 91-92. *Mem:* AAAS; fel Am Phys Soc; Asn Acads Sci; Asn Res Vision & Ophthal; Math Asn Am; Am Acad Allergy & Immunol. *Res:* Applying ideas from mathematics and physics to analysis, model and understand biomedical systems. *Mailing Add:* Ctr Complex Systs Fla Atlantic Univ Boca Raton FL 33431

LIEBOW, CHARLES, ONCOLOGY, PANCREATOLOGY. *Current Pos:* PROF, DEPT ORAL & MAXILLOFACIAL SURG, SCH DENT MED, STATE UNIV NY, BUFFALO, 84-, PROF, DEPT OTOLARYNGOL, 91-, DIR, LASER SURG CTR, 92-, PROF, DEPT PHYSIOL, 95- *Personal Data:* b Brooklyn, NY, June 17, 44; m 68, Roslyn Raskin; c Bradley, Adam & Lisa. *Educ:* NY Univ, AB, 66; Harvard Univ, DMD, 70; Univ Calif, San Francisco, PhD(physiol), 73. *Prof Exp:* Asst prof physiol, Cornell Univ Med Sch, 73-80; assoc sci dir, Nat Pancreatic Cancer Proj, Div Nat Cancer Inst, 80-84; assoc prof surg & physiol, La State Univ Med Sch, 80-84. *Concurrent Pos:* Assoc sci dir, Nat Pancreatic Cancer Proj, La State Univ, 80-84, Roswell Park Cancer Inst, 84-86. *Res:* How cells regulate intracellular functions; studied why cancer cells grow more rapidly than normal cells; how receptors can activate tyrosine phosphatase to slow growth; used hormone analogues activating these phosphatases to treat cancer; lasers and photodynamic therapy to treat cancers. *Mailing Add:* Dept Oral & Maxillofacial Surg State Univ NY Buffalo NY 14214. *Fax:* 716-829-3019; *E-Mail:* charles_liebow@sdm.buffalo.edu

LIEBOWITZ, HAROLD, MECHANICS, AERONAUTICAL ENGINEERING. *Current Pos:* dean & prof, 68-90, L STANLEY CRANE PROF ENG & APPL SCI, GEORGE WASHINGTON UNIV, 90-, EMER DEAN, 93- *Personal Data:* b Brooklyn, NY, June 25, 24; m 51; c 3. *Educ:* Polytech Inst Brooklyn, BAEE, 44, MAEE, 46, DAEE, 48. *Honors & Awards:* Nilakantan Mem Lectr, 69; Albert Einstein Prize, 91. *Prof Exp:* Res asst, Polytech Inst Brooklyn, 45-46, res assoc, 46-47, sr res assoc, 47-48; aeronaut engr, Off Naval Res, 48-50, eng mech scientist, 50-51, physicist, 51-54, aeronaut res engr & tech consult, 54-56, chief tech eng consult & coordr struct mech, 56-59, head, Struct Mech Br, 59-69, eng consult, 60-61, eng adv & coordr, Polaris Prog & dir, Prog Solid Propellant Mech, 62-68. *Concurrent Pos:* Vis prof aeronaut eng, actg asst dean grad sch & exec dir exp sta, Univ Colo, 60-61, dir eng curricula study, NSF grant, 60-61; res prof, Cath Univ Am, 62-68; tech adv, US House of Rep, founder & ed-in-chief, J Eng Fracture Mech, & prin investr, NASA res grants, 68-; consult, NATO, 68-84; ed-in-chief, J Comput & Struct, 72-; consult, Acad Press, Advan Eng Res & Develop Co, CASA/GIFTS, Inc, ESDU Int, Ltd, Pergamon Press, Pratt Whitney Aircraft Co, Reynolds Metals Co; lectr, Asn Govt Civil Engrs, Philippines, 65, Asn Struct Engrs, 65, Pac Meeting Joint Am Soc Mech Engrs & Am Soc Testing Mats, Seattle, 65, Am Inst Aeronauts & Astronauts, Chicago, 66, Am Inst Mining, Metall & Petrol Engrs, Los Angeles, 66, Univ Cincinnati, 66, Univ Md, 66, NY Univ, 67, Syracuse Univ NSF prog, 67, Princeton Univ, 67, Aeronaut Soc India, 69, Am Soc Metals, 69, Duke Univ, 69; mem, NSF Eng Progs Comt, Metal Composites Panel Mat Res Bd, Comput Mech Comt & Mat Adv Bd Struct Mat Design Comt, Nat Res Coun. *Mem:* Nat Acad Eng (pres, 95); fel AAAS; fel Am Inst Aeronaut & Astronaut; hon fel Soc Eng Sci (pres, 72-80); Am Soc Mech Engrs; Soc Eng Sci (pres, 74-75); Eng Acad Japan; Arg Nat Acad Sci; Soc Exp Stress Anal; Am Inst Metall Eng; fel Am Acad Mech (pres, 74-75); fel Am Soc Metals; hon mem Hungarian Acad Sci; Acad Sci Ukraine; hon fel Japanese Soc Strength & Fracture Mat; Sigma Xi. *Res:* Applied mechanics; engineering curricula; astronautics and aeronautics; materials engineering; solid mechanics; solid propellant propulsion; rheology; dynamics; aeronautical missile, space and ship structures; weapons and weapons systems; fundamental engineering research; fracture mechanics; computers and structures; author of more than 130 technical publications. *Mailing Add:* Sch Eng & Appl Sci George Washington Univ 801 22nd St Suite 704 Washington DC 20006

LIEBOWITZ, STEPHEN MARC, PHARMACEUTICAL CHEMISTRY. *Current Pos:* ASST PROF ANALYSIS PHARMACEUT CHEM, UNIV TEX, AUSTIN, 81- *Educ:* State Univ NY, Buffalo, BS, 74; Va Commonwealth Univ, PhD(med chem), 80. *Prof Exp:* Fel, Ohio State Univ, 80 & Adria Labs, 80-81; fel, Adria Labs, 80-81. *Concurrent Pos:* Prin investr, Robert A Welch Found, 82- *Mem:* Am Chem Soc; NY Acad Sci; AAAS. *Res:* Synthesis of organic molecules to aid in a basic understanding of biochemical processes on a molecular level; new synthetic methodology. *Mailing Add:* Schering Plough K-2-1 F31A 2000 Galloping Hill Rd Kenilworth NJ 07033-1310

LIEBSON, SIDNEY HAROLD, PHYSICS. *Current Pos:* CONSULT, 83- *Personal Data:* b New York, NY, July 9, 20; m 47, Jeannette Burman; c Alice R & Gail A. *Educ:* City Col New York, BS, 39; Univ Mich, MS, 40; Univ Md, PhD(physics), 47. *Prof Exp:* Physicist, Naval Res Lab, 40-49, head electromagnetics br, 49-55; mgr res & develop, Nuclear Develop Corp Am, 55-59; asst dir physics, Armour Res Found, Ill Inst Technol, 59-60; mgr phys res, Nat Cash Register Co, 60-66; mgr xerographic technol, Xerox Corp, 66-69, sr corp planner, 69-74, mgr mfg Res & Develop, 74-83. *Mem:* Fel Am Phys Soc; Inst Elec & Electronics Engrs. *Res:* Solid state phenomena; Geiger counters; electronic circuit analysis and design; discharge mechanism of self-quenching Geiger-Miller counters; scintillation and fluorescence of organics; photoconductivity; manufacturing technologies; research administration. *Mailing Add:* 15 Forestwood Dr Stamford CT 06903

LIECHTY, RICHARD DALE, ENDOCRINE SURGERY. *Current Pos:* assoc dean grad med educ, 84-88, PROF SURG, MED SCH, UNIV COLO, 71- *Personal Data:* b Lake Geneva, Wis, Oct 20, 25; m 52; c 3. *Educ:* Yale Univ, BA, 50; Northwestern Univ, MD, 54. *Prof Exp:* Instr med to prof surg, Med Sch, Univ Iowa, 61-71. *Mem:* Fel Am Col Surgeons; Am Thyroid Asn; Am Asn Endocrine Surgeons; Western Surg Asn (pres, 86). *Res:* Endocrinology; surgery of Grave's disease; anatomy of parathyroid glands. *Mailing Add:* 4200 E Ninth Ave B-192 Denver CO 80262

LIEDL, GERALD L(EROY), MATERIALS SCIENCE, METALLURGICAL ENGINEERING. *Current Pos:* From instr to assoc prof, 58-73, asst head dept, 69-78, PROF METALL ENG, PURDUE UNIV, WEST LAFAYETTE, 73-, HEAD DEPT, 78- *Personal Data:* b Fergus Falls, Minn, Mar 2, 33; m 57; c 2. *Educ:* Purdue Univ, BS, 55, PhD(metall eng), 60. *Mem:* Am Soc Eng Educ; fel Am Soc Metals; Metals Soc; Mat Res Soc; Am Ceramics Soc. *Res:* Diffraction; electron microscopy; correlations among structure, texture, and properties of crystalline solids and thin films. *Mailing Add:* Sch Mat Eng Purdue Univ MSEE Bldg West Lafayette IN 47907-1968. *Fax:* 765-494-1204; *E-Mail:* liedl@ecn.purdue.edu

LIEDTKE, CAROLE M, CELLULAR BIOLOGY. *Current Pos:* ASSOC PROF CELL PHYSIOL, DEPT PEDIAT, CHILDRENS HOSP, CASE WESTERN RES UNIV, 90- *Personal Data:* b Cleveland, Ohio, 1944. *Educ:* Case Western Res Univ, PhD(anat), 80. *Res:* Cellular biology. *Mailing Add:* Dept Pediat Rainbow Babies & Children's Hosp Case Western Res Univ 10900 Euclid Ave Cleveland OH 44106-4948

LIEF, HAROLD ISAIAH, MARITAL & SEX THERAPY & RESEARCH. *Current Pos:* dir, Div Family Study, 67-81, dir, Marriage Coun Philadelphia & Ctr Study Sex Educ in Med, 68-81, prof, 67-82, EMER PROF PSYCHIAT, SCH MED, UNIV PA, 82- *Personal Data:* b New York, NY, Dec 29, 17; m 61; c 5. *Educ:* Univ Mich, AB, 38; NY Univ, MD, 42; Columbia Univ, cert psychoanal, 50. *Hon Degrees:* MA, Univ Pa, 71. *Honors & Awards:* Ann Award Soc Sci, Am Asn Sex Educrs, Counrs & Therapists, 80 & 90. *Prof Exp:* Intern, Queens Gen Hosp, Jamaica, NY, 42-43; resident psychiat, Long Island Med Col, 46-48; res asst, Col Physicians & Surgeons, Columbia Univ, 49-51; from asst prof to prof psychiat, Sch Med, Tulane Univ, 51-67. *Concurrent Pos:* Vis prof, Sch Med, Univ Va, 58; pres, Sex Info & Educ Coun of US, 68-70; consult, HEW, 69-76, WHO, 71 & 74, AMA, 70-78 & Psychiat Educ Br, NIMH, 74-75; assoc psychiatrist, 81-83, psychiatrist, Pa Hosp, 83-87, emer psychiatrist, 87-; hon co-pres, World Cong Sexology, 81. *Mem:* Fel Am Acad Psychoanal (pres, 67-68); fel Am Psychiat Asn; fel Am Col Psychiat; fel Am Col Psychoanal; Am Psychosomatic Soc; Soc Sex Therapists & Researchers; World Asn Sexology (secy, 81-85, vpres, 85-89). *Res:* Marital and sexual relations; sex education in medicine; adult development; psycho-endocrinological-pharmacologic aspects human sexuality; adolescent sexuality. *Mailing Add:* 987 Old Eagle School Rd Wayne PA 19087

LIEGEY, FRANCIS WILLIAM, MICROBIOLOGY. *Current Pos:* RETIRED. *Personal Data:* b Frenchville, Pa, Jan 4, 23; m 47; c 6. *Educ:* St Bonaventure Univ, BS, 47, MS, 50, PhD(microbiol), 59. *Prof Exp:* From instr to assoc prof biol, St Bonaventure Univ, 48-64; prof biol, Ind Univ Pa, 64-, chmn dept, 72-90. *Mem:* Am Soc Microbiol. *Res:* Microbial ecology of acid mine streams. *Mailing Add:* 23 Elm St Indiana PA 15701

LIEHR, JOACHIM G, CANCER RESEARCH, HORMONAL CARCINOGENESIS. *Current Pos:* asst prof, Univ Tex Med Sch, Houston, 76-85; PROF PHARMACOL, UNIV TEX MED BR, GALVESTON, 85- *Personal Data:* b Namslay, Ger, June 20, 42; US citizen; m 88, Katherine Meakin; c Christopher J. *Educ:* Univ Munster, Ger, Vordiplom, 65; Univ Del, PhD, 68. *Prof Exp:* Vis asst prof, Inst Lipid Res, Baylor, 72-74; res chemist, Ciba-Geigy Ltd, Switz, 74-76. *Concurrent Pos:* Mem, Chem Pathol Study Sect, Nat Cancer Inst, 86-90. *Mem:* Am Asn Cancer Res; AAAS; Am Soc Mass Spectroscopy; Endocrine Soc; Am Soc Biol Chemists. *Res:* Mechanism of estrogen-induced cancer; tumor-preventing action of vitamin C; synthesis of non-carcinogenic estrogens; biochemical and clinical applications of mass spectroscopy. *Mailing Add:* Pharmacol & Toxicol Br Univ Tex Med Br 301 University Blvd Galveston TX 77555-1031. *E-Mail:* jliehr@marlin.utmb.edu

LIELMEZS, JANIS, CHEMICAL ENGINEERING. *Current Pos:* from asst prof to prof, 63-91, EMER PROF CHEM ENG, UNIV BC, 91- *Personal Data:* b Riga, Latvia, June 1, 26; US citizen; m 70, Alna M Blaus. *Educ:* Univ Denver, BS, 54; Northwestern Univ, MS, 56. *Honors & Awards:* Sci & Technol Award, World Fedn Free Latvians, 81. *Prof Exp:* Engr, Snow, Ice & Permafrost Res Estab, US Army CEngrs, 56; engr, Shell Develop Co, 57-58, 59, consult chem eng, 58-59; res engr, Inst Mineral Res, Mich Col Mining & Technol, 60-63, asst of chem eng, 62-63. *Concurrent Pos:* Ed chem, Tech Rev, Latvian Engrs Asn, 74-; ed sci & technol, Latvian Encycl, 76- *Mem:* Fel NY Acad Sci; fel Chem Inst Can. *Res:* Applied and theoretical thermodynamics; applied mechanics; fluid flow; magnetism and phase transformations; magnetocatalytic effect in chemical reactions; transport properties of fluids. *Mailing Add:* Dept Chem Eng Univ BC Vancouver BC V6T 1W5 Can. *Fax:* 604-822-6003

LIEM, KAREL F, VERTEBRATE MORPHOLOGY. *Current Pos:* HENRY BRYANT BIGELOW PROF, CUR ICHTHYOL & PROF BIOL, HARVARD UNIV, 72- *Personal Data:* b Java, Indonesia, Nov 24, 35; m 65. *Educ:* Indonesia Univ, BSc, 57, MSc, 58; Univ Ill, PhD(zool), 61. *Prof Exp:* Asst prof zool, Leiden Univ, 62-64; from asst prof to assoc prof anat, Univ Ill Col Med, 64-72. *Concurrent Pos:* Head, Div Vert Anat, Chicago Natural Hist Mus, Ill, 65-72; mem comt Latimeria, Nat Acad Sci, 67; Guggenheim fel, 70-71; mem vis comt, New Eng Aquarium, 74-; trustee, Cohosset Marine Biol Sta, 74-; ed, Copeia & assoc ed, J Morphol, 74- *Mem:* Am Soc Zool; Am Soc Ichthyol & Herpet; Soc Syst Zool; fel Zool Soc London; Neth Royal Zool Soc. *Res:* Evolution of chordate structure; functional anatomy of teleosts; morphology and hydrodynamics of air-breathing teleost blood circulations; sex reversal in teleosts; functional anatomy and evolution of African cichlid fishes. *Mailing Add:* Organ Evol Biol Harvard Univ 26 Oxford St Cambridge MA 02138-2902

LIEM, RONALD KIAN HONG, NEUROBIOLOGY. *Current Pos:* assoc prof, 87-90, PROF PATH, ANAT & CELL BIOL, COL PHYSICIANS & SURGEONS, COLUMBIA UNIV, 91- *Personal Data:* b Lombok, Indonesia, Feb 8, 46; US citizen. *Educ:* Amherst Col, AB, 67; Cornell Univ, MSc, 69, PhD(chem). *Prof Exp:* Assoc prof pharmacol, NY Univ Sch Med, 78-87. *Mem:* Am Soc Cell Biol; Am Soc Neurosci; Am Soc Neurochem. *Res:* Biochemical studies on the neuronal cytoskeleton, especially with regard to the assembly of neurofilaments and their interactions with other cytoskeletal elements, both in vivo and in vitro. *Mailing Add:* Dept Path Columbia Univ 630 W 168th St New York NY 10032-3702. *Fax:* 212-305-5498

LIEMOHN, HAROLD BENJAMIN, SPACECRAFT-ENVIRONMENT INTERACTIONS, SPACE-PLASMA WAVES. *Current Pos:* MGR SPACE PHYSICS, ENG TECHNOL, BOEING AEROSPACE CO, 77-, MGR, SPACE STA ENVIRON, BOEING DEFENSE & SPACE GROUP, 91- *Personal Data:* b Minneapolis, Minn, Feb 2, 35; m 57, Clarice Johnson; c Kimberley, Jeffrey, Thomas, Michael & Michelle. *Educ:* Univ Minn, BA, 56, MS, 59; Univ Wash, PhD(physics), 62. *Prof Exp:* Teaching asst physics, Univ Minn, 56-59; staff mem geo-astrophys, Sci Res Labs, Boeing Co, 59-63; asst prof atmospheric & space sci, Southwest Ctr Advan Studies, 63-66; staff mem, Geo-Astrophys Sci Res Labs, Boeing Co, 66-72; res staff math-physics, Pac Northwest, Battelle Mem Inst, 72-77. *Concurrent Pos:* Adj asst prof, Southern Methodist Univ, 64-65; affil assoc prof, Univ Wash, 68-; chmn & secy local arrangements, Ann Meeting, Comt Space Res, Seattle, 71; reporter particle-wave interactions, Comn V, Int Asn Geomag & Aeronomy, 71-73. *Res:* Theoretical research in radiation belt physics, electromagnetic waves in magnetoplasma, hydromagnetic waves in magnetosphere, and spacecraft charging and contamination; ionizing radiation effects; sunlight reflections from space craft. *Mailing Add:* 2320 Fairwind Rd Houston TX 77062

LIEN, ERIC JUNG-CHI, PHARMACEUTICAL CHEMISTRY. *Current Pos:* from asst prof to assoc prof, 68-76, coordr, 78-84, PROF PHARMACEUT & BIOMED CHEM, SCH PHARM, UNIV SOUTHERN CALIF, 76- *Personal Data:* b Kaohsiung, Taiwan, Nov 30, 37; m 65, Linda L Chen; c Raymond & Andrew Y. *Educ:* Taiwan Univ, BS, 60; Univ Calif, San Francisco, PhD(pharmaceut chem), 66. *Prof Exp:* Teaching fel, Univ Calif, San Francisco Med Ctr, 66-67; res assoc bio-org chem, Pomona Col, 67-68; sci adv, Nat Lab Food & Drugs, Dept Health, exed, Yuam, Taipei, Taiwan, Repub China, 92-94. *Concurrent Pos:* Mem comt, Develop Therapeut Contract Rev, Nat Cancer Inst, 83-87; consult, Ariz Dis Control Res Comn, Phoenix, Ariz, 86- *Mem:* Fel AAAS; Am Pharmaceut Asn; Am Chem Soc; Am Asn Cols Pharm; Am Asn Cancer Res; fel Am Asn Pharmaceut Sci. *Res:* Structure-activity relationship and bioorganic chemistry; physical organic chemistry; natural products; antiviral and antitumor agents. *Mailing Add:* Sch Pharm 1985 Zonal Ave Los Angeles CA 90033. *Fax:* 213-342-1390

LIEN, ERIC LOUIS, NUTRITIONAL BIOCHEMISTRY. *Current Pos:* sr biochemist, Wyeth-Ayerst Labs, 75-83, mgr, Metab Disorders Sect, 83-87, assoc dir, nutrit res & develop, 87-90, dir, 90-93, SR DIR NUTRIT RES, WYETH-AYERST LABS, 93- *Personal Data:* b Hammond, Ind, Apr 9, 46; m 87, Winifred Latham; c Steven, Janet, Elizabeth, Jeffrey, Alison & Caroline. *Educ:* Col Wooster, BA, 68; Univ Ill, Urbana-Champaign, MS, 71, PhD(biochem), 72. *Prof Exp:* Fel biochem, Sch Med, Univ Pa, 72-75. *Mem:* AAAS; Am Inst Nutrit; Am Soc Parenteral & Enternal Nutrit. *Res:* Infant nutrition; triglyceride absorption; amino acid analysis. *Mailing Add:* Wyeth-Ayerst Labs PO Box 8299 Philadelphia PA 19101. *Fax:* 215-989-4586

LIEN, HWACHII, TURBULENT FLOWS, ENGINEERING INSTRUMENTATION. *Current Pos:* GEN MGR ADMIN, HOPAX CO, 74- *Personal Data:* b Taipei, Taiwan, Nov 10, 30; US citizen; m 64, Mei-shien Ho; c Lyndon, Leslie & Lester. *Educ:* Nat Taiwan Univ, BS, 53; Kans State Univ, MS, 56; Univ Pa, PhD(appl mech), 62. *Prof Exp:* Staff scientist, Avco Missile Syst Div, 62-67; tech supvr, Gen Appl Sci Lab, 67-68; asst mgr, Avco Syst Div, 68-70, prin scientist, 71-74. *Concurrent Pos:* Vis prof, Nat Taiwan Univ, 70-71; tech dir, Yuen Foong Yu Paper Mfg Co, 70-71; consult, Anathon Corp, 79-; pres, Financial Scis Inc, 74-; chmn, Liberty Bank & Trust Co, 77- *Mem:* Am Inst Aeronaut & Astronaut. *Res:* Fluid dynamics and its related diagnostic instrumentation in general; turbulence; chemically reacting flows; magnetohydrodynamics; mechanics of multiphase fluids; electrostatic probes. *Mailing Add:* 26 Berkshire Dr Winchester MA 01890

LIENER, IRVIN ERNEST, BIOCHEMISTRY, NUTRITION. *Current Pos:* From instr asst prof to prof, 49-59, EMER PROF BIOCHEM, UNIV MINN, ST PAUL, 89- *Personal Data:* b Pittsburgh, Pa, June 27, 19; m 46, Dorothy J Claysmith; c 2. *Educ:* Mass Inst Technol, BS, 41; Univ Southern Calif, PhD(biochem, nutrit), 49. *Honors & Awards:* Spencer Award Outstanding Achievement Agr & Food Chem, Am Chem Soc, 77 & 82; Fulbright Award, 90. *Concurrent Pos:* Guggenheim fel, Carlsberg Lab, Copenhagen, Denmark, 57; Welcome vis prof nutrit, 79; ed, J Agr & Food Univ, 83-; pres, Int Lectin Soc, 87-92. *Mem:* Fel Venezuelan Asn Advan Sci; Am Chem Soc; Am Soc Biol Chem; Am Inst Nutrit; Sigma Xi. *Res:* Isolation and characterization of antinutritional factors in legumes; structure and mechanism of action of proteolytic enzymes and their naturally-occurring inhibitors. *Mailing Add:* Dept Biochem Col Biol Sci Univ Minn St Paul MN 55108. *Fax:* 612-624-5358; *E-Mail:* liene001@maroon.tc.umn.edu

LIENHARD, GUSTAV E, BIOCHEMISTRY. *Current Pos:* assoc prof, 72-75, PROF BIOCHEM, DARTMOUTH MED SCH, 75- *Personal Data:* b Plainfield, NJ, June 21, 38; m 60; c 2. *Educ:* Amherst Col, BA, 59; Yale Univ, PhD(biochem), 64. *Prof Exp:* From asst prof to assoc prof biochem & molecular biol, Harvard Univ, 65-72. *Concurrent Pos:* Res fel biochem, Brandeis Univ, 63-65. *Mem:* Am Soc Biochem & Molecular Biol. *Res:* Mechanisms of insulin action; regulation of transport by hormones. *Mailing Add:* Dept Biochem Dartmouth Med Sch Hanover NH 03755-3844

LIENHARD, JOHN H(ENRY), HISTORY, MECHANICAL ENGINEERING. *Current Pos:* PROF MECH ENG, UNIV HOUSTON, 80- *Personal Data:* b St Paul, Minn, Aug 17, 30; m 59, Carol Bratton; c John H V & Andrew J. *Educ:* Ore State Col, BS, 51; Univ Wash, Seattle, MS, 53; Univ Calif, Berkeley, PhD(mech eng), 61. *Honors & Awards:* Charles Russ Richards Mem Award, Am Soc Mech Engrs, 80, Heat Transfer Mem Award, 81, Ralph Coats Roe Medal, 89. *Prof Exp:* Design engr, Boeing Airplane Co, 51-52; instr mech eng, Univ Wash, Seattle, 55-56; assoc, Univ Calif, Berkeley, 56-61; assoc prof, Wash State Univ, 61-67; prof mech eng, Univ KY, 67-80. *Mem:* Fel Am Soc Mech Engrs; Am Soc Eng Educ; fel AAAS; Soc Hist Technol. *Res:* Statistical mechanical modeling of macroscopic systems; thermal systems with emphasis on boiling and other two-phase problems; nuclear thermohydraulics; history of technology; equations of state. *Mailing Add:* Dept Mech Eng Univ Houston Houston TX 77201-4792. *Fax:* 713-743-4503; *E-Mail:* jhl@jetson.uh.edu

LIENTZ, BENNET PRICE, INFORMATION SYSTEMS, REENGINEERING. *Current Pos:* PROF GRAD SCH MGT, UNIV CALIF, LOS ANGELES, 77- *Personal Data:* b Hollywood, Calif, Oct 24, 42. *Educ:* Claremont Men's Col, BA, 64; Univ Wash, MS, 66, PhD(math), 68. *Prof Exp:* Instr math, Univ Wash, 65-68; sr res scientist, Syst Develop Corp, 68-70; assoc prof indust eng & Air Force Off Sci Res grant, Univ Southern Calif, 70-72. *Concurrent Pos:* Dir, Off Admin Info Serv, 78-81. *Mem:* Opers Res Soc Am (secy-treas, 71); Inst Math Statist; Am Statist Asn; Am Math Soc; Asn Comput Mach; Inst Elec & Electronics Engrs. *Res:* Communication and network analysis; computers and systems analysis; computer security networks; re-engineering; distributed systems. *Mailing Add:* Grad Sch Mgt Univ Calif 405 Hilgard Los Angeles CA 90024. *Fax:* 310-858-1615

LIEPA, GEORGE ULDIS, LIPID METABOLISM. *Current Pos:* PROF NUTRIT, TEX WOMAN'S UNIV, 79- *Personal Data:* b Oldenburg, Germany, Oct 4, 46; US citizen; m 79, Candice; c Arlanne & Marisa. *Educ:* Drake Univ, BA, 68, MA, 70; Iowa State Univ, PhD(molecular biol), 76, Am Bd Nutrit, dipl. *Prof Exp:* Asst instr med & grad physiol, Univ Tex Health Sci Ctr, San Antonio, 76-77, NIH fel, 77-78. *Concurrent Pos:* Assoc ed, J Am Oil Chemists Soc, 85- *Mem:* Sigma Xi; Am Oil Chemists Soc; Am Inst Nutrit; Latvian-Am Asn Univ Profs & Scientists; Am Soc Clin Nutrit. *Res:* Lipid metabolism; dietary care of trauma patient; metabolism during trauma; diet and cancer; diet and kidney disease. *Mailing Add:* 314 Stone Cliff Ct Saline MI 48176-1569

LIEPINS, ATIS AIVARS, STRUCTURAL ENGINEERING, APPLIED MECHANICS. *Current Pos:* ASSOC, SIMPSON GUMPERTZ & HEGER INC, 77- *Personal Data:* b Aloja, Latvia, Apr 17, 35; m 60; c 2. *Educ:* Mass Inst Technol, SB, 57, SM, 60, Engr, 60. *Prof Exp:* Res engr appl mech, Res Labs, United Aircraft Corp, 60-61; prin engr, Dynatech Corp, 61-68; sr staff engr, Littleton Res & Eng Corp, 68-77. *Mem:* Am Inst Aeronaut & Astronaut; Am Soc Mech Engrs; Am Soc Civil Engrs. *Res:* Static and dynamic response of thin shell structures; propeller induced ship vibration; soil-structure interaction. *Mailing Add:* Simpson Gumpertz & Heger, Inc 297 Broadway Arlington MA 02174

LIEPINS, RAIMOND, POLYMER ENGINEERING, SUPERCONDUCTORS. *Current Pos:* sect leader mat sci & technol, 77-91, assoc group leader, 86-87, TECH COORDR, LOS ALAMOS NAT LAB, 87- *Personal Data:* b Plavinas, Latvia, May 19, 30; m 61, Leila Zayas; c Elsa, Ilze, Rebecca & Otto. *Educ:* Southern Ill Univ, BA, 54; Univ Minn, MS, 56; Kans State Univ, PhD(org chem), 60. *Prof Exp:* Res chemist, B F Goodrich Co, 60-64; res assoc polymer res, Univ Ariz, 64-66; sr chemist, Res Triangle Inst, 66-77. *Concurrent Pos:* Lectr, NC State Univ, 76, Clemson Univ, 76, State Univ NY, New Paltz, 77 & Brookhaven Nat Lab, 85; prin investr, Indust Org Chem Indust, Res Triangle Inst, Environ Protection Agency, 70-77; consult, 85- *Mem:* Soc Advan Mat & Process Eng; Am Chem Soc; fel Am Inst Chem; Am Soc Metals Int. *Res:* Coatings for laser fusion targets; gas phase coating techniques; flame retardance; low pressure plasma applications; high temperature polymers; piezoelectric polymers; organometallic polymers; conducting polymers; liquid crystal polymers; tamper proof packages; magnetic processing; buckminsterfullerenes; super conductors. *Mailing Add:* 2303 North Ct Santa Fe NM 87505

LIEPMAN, H(ANS) P(ETER), AEROSPACE ENGINEERING. *Current Pos:* AEROSPACE CONSULT, 87- *Personal Data:* b Kiel, Ger, Oct 24, 13; nat US; m 46; c 4. *Educ:* Swiss Fed Inst Technol, Dipl, 37; Harvard Univ, MS, 39; Univ Mich, PhD(aeronaut), 53. *Prof Exp:* From instr to asst prof aeronaut eng, Univ Cincinnati, 39-44; sr aerodynamicist, Goodyear Aircraft Corp, 44-46, chief aerodynamicist, 46-49; lectr aeronaut eng, Univ Mich, 49-55, assoc prof, 56-59, dir supersonic wind tunnel, 49-59; asst mgr, Systs Develop Dept & asst prog mgr, Aerosci Lab, TRW Systs Group, Calif, 59-71; educ & technol admin & develop consult, 71-73; mem res staff, Inst for Defense Anal, 73-78; aerospace eng, Dept Defense, 81-87. *Concurrent Pos:* Consult, Space Technol Labs, 57-59, Appl Physics Lab, Johns Hopkins Univ, 78-80 & Inst Defense Anal, 78-80; vis prof aerospace eng, Iowa State Univ, 80-81. *Mem:* Assoc fel Am Inst Aeronaut & Astronaut. *Res:* Reentry system performance and penetration aids system studies; multiple nozzle plume interactions; rocket exhaust interactions; base heating; supersonic nozzle design; system engineering of space and missile systems; comparative analysis and evaluation of tactical and strategic weapons systems and test data. *Mailing Add:* 672 Serrano Dr #1 San Luis Obispo CA 93405

LIEPMANN, H(ANS) WOLFGANG, AERONAUTICS. *Current Pos:* fel aeronaut, Calif Inst Technol, 39-45, from asst prof to prof, 45-76, Charles Lee Powell prof fluid mech & thermodyn, 76-83, Theodore von Karman prof aeronaut, 83-85, dir, Grad Aeronaut Labs, 72-85, EMER THEODORE VON KARMAN PROF AERONAUT, CALIF INST TECHNOL, 85- *Personal Data:* b Berlin, Ger, July 3, 14; nat US; m 39, 54; c 2. *Educ:* Univ Zurich, PhD(physics), 38. *Hon Degrees:* DEng, Tech Univ, Aachen, 85. *Honors & Awards:* Ludwig-Prandtl-Ring, Ger Soc Aeronaut & Astronaut, 68; Worcester Reed Warner Medal, Am Soc Mech Engrs, 69; Monie A Ferst Award, Sigma Xi, 78; Fluid Dynamics Prize, Am Phys Soc, 80 & Otto Laporte Award, 85; Fluids Eng Award, Am Soc Mech Engrs, 84; Nat Medal Sci, 86; Guggenheim Medal, 86; Nat Medal Technol, 93. *Prof Exp:* Fel physics, Univ Zurich, 38-39. *Concurrent Pos:* Foreign fel, Max-Planck Inst, 88. *Mem:* Nat Acad Sci; Nat Acad Eng; AAAS; hon fel Am Inst Aeronaut & Astronaut; fel Am Acad Arts & Sci; hon fel Indian Acad Sci; hon mem Am Soc Mech Engrs. *Res:* Laminar instability, transition and turbulence; shock wave boundary layer interaction; transonic flow; aerodynamic noise; fluid mechanics of Helium II. *Mailing Add:* Dept Aeronautics Calif Inst Technol Pasadena CA 91125

LIEPSCH, DIETER W, BIOFLUID MECHANICS, FLUID MECHANICS. *Current Pos:* PROF FLUID MECH, HEAT TRANSFER, FACHHOCHSCHULE MUNCHEN & TECH UNIV, 72-, HEAD, LAB BIO FLUID MECH, 89- *Personal Data:* m 82; c Stephen & Eva. *Educ:* Tech Univ, Munchen, dipl-Ing, 66, Dr-Ing, 74, Dr-habil, 86. *Prof Exp:* Guest prof, Univ Houston, 83-84; sr scientist, Hal B Wallis Res Facil, Eisenhower Med Ctr, 86-87, dir cardiovasc res, 87-89. *Concurrent Pos:* Adj prof, Univ Southern Calif, San Diego, 87-89. *Mem:* Am Soc Mech Engrs; Biomed Eng Soc; Europ Soc Biorheology; Europ Soc Microcirculation; Soc Ger Engrs; Soc App Math & Mech; Int Soc Optical Eng; Am Phys Soc. *Res:* Flow visualization and laser doppler ancinometer studies in models of human blood vessels to find out specifically causes for athero clerosis and aging; blood flow studies coagulation, cell-cell and cell-vessel wall interactions; air conditioning and air flow in buildings. *Mailing Add:* Am Buchen Wald 29 82340 Feldafing Germany

LIER, FRANK GEORGE, BOTANY, ECOLOGY. *Current Pos:* Asst bot, Columbia Univ, 46-47, lectr, Sch Gen Studies, 47-50, from asst prof to prof bot, 50-77, prof biol sci, 77-80, EMER PROF BIOL SCI, SCH GEN STUDIES, COLUMBIA UNIV, 80- *Personal Data:* b New York, NY, Feb 19, 13; m 37. *Educ:* Columbia Univ, PhD, 50. *Mem:* Bot Soc Am; Torrey Bot Club (pres, 64); Am Inst Biol Sci; NY Acad Sci; Am Bryol & Lichenological Soc. *Res:* Plant morphology; developmental anatomy. *Mailing Add:* 2 Cambridge Ct E Old Saybrook CT 06475

LIER, JOHN, regional climatology, tropospheric meteorology, for more information see previous edition

LIES, THOMAS ANDREW, ORGANIC CHEMISTRY. *Current Pos:* RETIRED. *Personal Data:* b Oak Park, Ill, Jan 16, 29; m 59; c 2. *Educ:* John Carroll Univ, BS, 49; Univ Chicago, SM, 51; Univ Wis-Madison, PhD(org chem), 58. *Prof Exp:* Res chemist, Wyandotte Chem Corp, 58-59, Am Cyanamid Co, 59-91. *Mem:* Am Chem Soc. *Res:* Synthesis of pesticides. *Mailing Add:* 893 Cherry Hill Rd Princeton NJ 08540-7712

LIESCH, JERROLD MICHAEL, NATURAL PRODUCTS STRUCTURE DETERMINATION, MASS SPECTROMETRY. *Current Pos:* SR INVESTR, MERCK & CO, INC, 77- *Personal Data:* b Chicago, Ill, Dec 12, 49. *Educ:* Ill Inst Technol, BS, 71; Univ Ill, MS, 73, PhD(org chem), 75. *Prof Exp:* NIH fel org chem, Mass Inst Technol, 76-77. *Mem:* Am Chem Soc; Am Soc Mass Spectrometry. *Res:* Structure elucidation; mass spectrometry; proton and carbon magnetic resonance spectrometry. *Mailing Add:* Merck Res Labs PO Box 2000 R50-105 Rahway NJ 07065-0900. *E-Mail:* jerry_liesch@merck.com

LIESE, HOMER C, MINERALOGY, PETROLOGY. *Current Pos:* ASSOC PROF GEOL, UNIV CONN, 62- *Personal Data:* b New York, NY, Oct 25, 31; m 55. *Educ:* Syracuse Univ, BS, 53; Univ Utah, MS, 57, PhD(mineral), 62. *Prof Exp:* X-ray technician, Kennecott Copper Inc, 60-61. *Mem:* Geol Soc Am; Mineral Soc Am; Soc Appl Spectros. *Res:* Spectroscopy of minerals. *Mailing Add:* Dept Geol Univ Conn Main Campus U-45 354 Mansfield Storrs CT 06269-0002

LIETH, HELMUT HEINRICH FRIEDRICH, GEOECOLOGY, ECOLOGICAL MODELLING. *Current Pos:* prof, 77-91, EMER PROF BIOL & ECOL, UNIV OSNABRUECK, 91- *Personal Data:* b Kuerten-Steeg, Ger, Dec 16, 25; m 52; c 4. *Educ:* Univ Cologne, DrPhil, 53; Univ Stuttgart-Hohenheim, PD, 60. *Honors & Awards:* Biometerol Res Found Award, 82; Biometeorol Award, Am Meteorol Soc, 87. *Prof Exp:* Asst bot, Univ Cologne, 54-55, Agr Univ, Stuttgart-Hohenheim, 55-66; prof, Univ Hawaii, 66-67; from assoc prof to prof bot & ecol, Univ NC, Chapel Hill, 67-77. *Concurrent Pos:* Nat Res fel bot & ecol, Univ Montreal, 60-61; guest prof bot, Cent Univ, Caracas, Venezuela, 61, Univ Tolima, Ibague, Colombia, 63; guest scientist ecol & biophys, Nuclear Res Lab, Julich, Ger, 73-74; govt adv ecol, Portugal, 74; adj prof ecol, Univ NC, Chapel Hill, 77-; guest prof, Waseda Univ, Tokyo, 88- & United Arab Emirates, Univ AC Ain, 90; ed-in-chief, Int J Biometeorol, 87-93, Vegetatio, 90-92, Task for Veg Sci, 81-; adv Hum Univ Irkutsk, 94- *Mem:* Int Biometeorol Soc (pres, 79-84); Int Soc Trop Ecol (pres, 85-91); Inst Asn Ecol (treas, 86-90); Ecol Soc Am. *Res:* Systems ecology, geoecology; inter-disciplinary modelling ecology, economy, sociology, climate and atmosphere, plant relations, net primary productivity, phenology and seasonality; high salinity ecosystems. *Mailing Add:* AG Systs Univ Osnabrueck 49069 Osnabrueck Germany. *Fax:* 49-54-969-2570

LIETMAN, PAUL STANLEY, CLINICAL PHARMACOLOGY. *Current Pos:* Asst prof pediat, 68-72, asst prof pharmacol, 69-72, assoc prof med, pediat & pharmacol, 72-80, WELLCOME PROF CLIN PHARMACOL & PROF MED, PEDIAT & PHARMACOL, JOHNS HOPKINS UNIV, 80- *Personal Data:* b Chicago, Ill, Mar 24, 34; m 56; c 3. *Educ:* Western Reserve Univ, AB, 55; Columbia Univ, MD, 59; Johns Hopkins Univ, PhD(physiol chem), 68. *Concurrent Pos:* Investr, Howard Med Inst, 68-72. *Mem:* Am Soc Pharmacol & Exp Therapeut; Soc Microbiol; Am Pediat Soc; Soc Pediat Res; Am Acad Pediat. *Res:* Developmental pharmacology; antibiotics; antiviral agents. *Mailing Add:* Johns Hopkins Hosp Univ Med Sch Baltimore MD 21287-5554

LIETZ, GERARD PAUL, NUCLEAR PHYSICS. *Current Pos:* asst prof, 67-77, ASSOC PROF PHYSICS, DEPAUL UNIV, 77- *Personal Data:* b Chicago, Ill, Dec 10, 37; m 64; c 5. *Educ:* DePaul Univ, BS, 59; Univ Notre Dame, PhD(nuclear physics), 64. *Prof Exp:* Exchange asst nuclear physics, Univ Basel, 66-67. *Mem:* Am Phys Soc; Am Asn Physics Teachers; Sigma Xi. *Res:* Energy levels in nuclei. *Mailing Add:* Dept Phys DePaul Univ 2219 N Kenmore Chicago IL 60614

LIETZKE, DAVID ALBERT, PEDOLOGY, CLAY MINERALOGY. *Current Pos:* INDEPENDENT SOIL CONSULT, 86- *Personal Data:* b Pontiac, Mich, Apr 20, 40; m, Elaine Scott; c 2. *Educ:* Mich State Univ, BS, 62, MS, 68, PhD(clay mineral geomorphol), 72. *Prof Exp:* Soil scientist, Soil Conserv Serv, Mich, 62-68 & 71-73, Mich Agr Exp Sta, 68-71; asst prof & urban soils specialist, Va Polytech Inst & State Univ, 73-79; assoc prof soils, Univ Tenn, Knoxville, 79-86. *Concurrent Pos:* Consult, soil mapping, soil invests, 85. *Mem:* Nat Soc Consult Soil Scientists (secy-treas, 88-90, pres-elect, 93). *Res:* Processes of soil formation, soil-geomorphic relationships, soil-climatic relationships and fundamental weathering processes of earth materials to form soil parent materials. *Mailing Add:* Rte 3 Box 607 Rutledge TN 37861. *Fax:* 423-828-5336

LIETZKE, MILTON HENRY, PHYSICAL CHEMISTRY. *Current Pos:* prof, 63-89, EMER PROF CHEM, UNIV TENN, 89- *Personal Data:* b Syracuse, NY, Nov 23, 20; m 43, 65, Jean Hawkins; c Kathryn A, Susan L, Lindl, Carol L & Milton H Jr. *Educ:* Colgate Univ, BA, 42; Univ Wis, MS, 44, PhD(chem), 49. *Prof Exp:* Asst, Univ Wis, 42-43, instr chem, 43-44; lab foreman, Tenn Eastman Corp, 44-47; asst, Univ Wis, 47-49; res chemist, Oak Ridge Nat Lab, 49-57, group leader, 58-74, sr scientist, 75-83. *Mem:* Am Chem Soc; fel NY Acad Sci; fel Am Inst Chemists; Sigma Xi; Sci Res Soc Am. *Res:* Electrochemistry, electrodeposition; potential measurements; high temperature solution thermodynamics; corrosion research; phase studies; application of high speed computing techniques to chemical problems; author or coauthor of over 150 publications in the areas of thermodynamics, electrochemistry, reactor chemistry, chemical kinetics, ion exchange and organic chemistry. *Mailing Add:* Dept Chem Univ Tenn Knoxville TN 37916

LIEUX, MEREDITH HOAG, PALYNOLOGY, BOTANY. *Current Pos:* ATTY, OFF LEGAL AFFAIRS & ENFORCEMENT, LA DEPT ENVIRON QUAL, 91- *Personal Data:* b Morgan City, La, Nov 9, 39; m 68. *Educ:* La State Univ, Baton Rouge, BS, 60, PhD(bot), 69, JD, 86; Univ Miss, MS, 64. *Prof Exp:* Teacher pub schs, Lake Charles & Monroe, La, 60-71; fel geol, La State Univ, Baton Rouge, 71-72, from instr to assoc prof bot, 72-82. *Concurrent Pos:* Law clerk, 19th Juducial Dist Ct, La, 86-87; asst atty gen, Dept Justice, 87-90. *Mem:* Am Asn Stratig Palynologists; Int Bee Res Asn; Bot Soc Am; Sigma Xi; Asn Women Sci; Am Bar Asn. *Res:* Holocene spore and pollen studies in the Gulf of Mexico Region; pollen morphology involving light, scanning electron and transmission electron microscopy; applied insect-pollen related studies, or melissopalynology. *Mailing Add:* 1627 Louvay Dr Baton Rouge LA 70808

LIEW, CHOONG-CHIN, MOLECULAR BIOLOGY & PROTEIN CHEMISTRY OF CARDIOVASCULAR SYSTEM. *Current Pos:* from asst prof to assoc prof biochem, 70-78, assoc prof med, 78-79, PROF CLIN BIOCHEM & MED, UNIV TORONTO, 79- *Personal Data:* b Malaysia, Sept 2, 37; Can citizen; m 64, Gik E Ng; c Gailina J, Allan S & Victor S. *Educ:* Nanyang Univ, Singapore, BSc, 60; Univ Toronto, MA, 64, PhD(path chem), 67. *Honors & Awards:* Hoffman Mem Prize, 67. *Prof Exp:* Guest investr, Rockefeller Univ, 69-70. *Concurrent Pos:* Hon prof biochem, Peking Union Med Col, Zhongshan Med Col, W China Med Univ, Zheijiang Med Univ, Shanghai Second Med Col, Xian Med Univ, Harabin Med Sci Univ, Shihezi Med Col, Xinjiang Med Col, Chinese Univ Hong Kong. *Mem:* Can Biochem Soc; Biochem Soc; Am Soc Cell Biol; Am Heart Asn. *Res:* Gene regulation in eukaryotes; chromosomal proteins; structure and function of cardiac myosin heavy chain genes; correlation of chromatin proteins and genetically determined heart diseases; catalogue of genes in the cardiovascular system. *Mailing Add:* Dept Clin Biochem 100 College St Toronto ON M5G 1L5 Can. *Fax:* 416-978-5650

LIFKA, BERNARD WILLIAM, METALLURGICAL ENGINEERING. *Current Pos:* RETIRED. *Personal Data:* b Chicago, Ill, Apr 8, 31; m 56; c 4. *Educ:* Purdue Univ, BS, 58. *Honors & Awards:* AR 100 Award, 87; Arthur Vining Davis Award, 88. *Prof Exp:* Engr corrosion, Alcoa Labs, 58-62, sr engr, 63-77, sr engr alloy develop, 77-79, staff engr, 80-81, tech supvr, 81-85, tech consult, 85-93. *Mem:* Am Soc Metals; Nat Asn Corrosion Engrs; Sigma Xi; Am Soc Testing & Mat. *Res:* Alloy development, increased plant production and resistance to corrosion of high-strength, heat-treatable aluminum alloys for aerospace and automotive applications. *Mailing Add:* 2750 Iowa Dr New Kensington PA 15068

LIFSCHITZ, MEYER DAVID, NEPHROLOGY, EICOSINOID PHYSIOLOGY. *Current Pos:* From asst prof to assoc prof, 73-84, PROF MED, UNIV TEX HEALTH SCI CTR, SAN ANTONIO, 84- *Personal Data:* b Patchogue, NY, Jan 9, 42; m 70; c 3. *Educ:* Mass Inst Technol, BS, 63; Boston Univ, MS, 66, MD, 67. *Concurrent Pos:* NIH fel, 71, NIH, Vet Admin & NASA res grants, 73-; chief, Renal Sect, Audie Murphy Vet Admin Hosp, 76-85, actg chief, SDTU, 78-81, assoc chief staff res & develop, 84-; consult, Brooke Army Med Ctr, 79- & St Lukes Lutheran Hosp, 84-; actg chief, Div Nephrology, Univ Tex Health Sci Ctr, San Antonio, 89-91; mem, Kidney & Hypertension Coun, Am Heart Asn. *Mem:* Am Soc Nephrology; Am Physiol Soc; Am Soc Clin Invest; Am Heart Asn. *Res:* Inter-relationships of hormones and kidney function. *Mailing Add:* Dept Med Audie Murphy Vet Admin Hosp 7703 Floyd Curl Dr San Antonio TX 78284. *Fax:* 210-567-6550; *E-Mail:* lifschitz@uthscsa.edu

LIFSHITZ, KENNETH, NEUROPSYCHIATRY, PSYCHOBIOLOGY. *Current Pos:* res assoc prof, 79-87, RES PROF PSYCHIAT, NY UNIV MED CTR, 87-; HEAD NEUROPHYSIOL DIV, NATHAN S KLINE INST PSYCHIAT RES, 86- *Personal Data:* b New York, NY, Aug 16, 30. *Educ:* Syracuse Univ, AB, 51; State Univ NY, MD, 55. *Prof Exp:* Capt, USAF Med Corp, 56-58; chief investr psychobiol, Nathan Kline Inst, 58-86; chief psychiat res, Rockland Res Inst, 76-81. *Concurrent Pos:* Consult psychiat, Good Samaritan Hosp, Suffern, 61-87. *Mem:* Fel Am Psychiat Asn; fel Am EEG Asn; AAAS; Soc Biol Psychiat; Int Pharmaco-EEG Group. *Res:* Major psychopathologies, their treatment, differential diagnostic issues, the effect of psychotropic medications; usefulness of computer analyzed electroencephalographs and non-human primate models. *Mailing Add:* Nathan Kline Inst Orangeburg NY 10962

LIFSON, WILLIAM E(UGENE), CHEMICAL ENGINEERING. *Current Pos:* RETIRED. *Personal Data:* b Newark, NJ, Apr 17, 21; m 46; c 2. *Educ:* Mass Inst Technol, BS, 41, MS, 42. *Prof Exp:* Res engr petrol prod res, Exxon Res & Eng Co, 46-51, group head, 51-54, sect head, 54-56, asst dir, 56-62, dir, Prod Res Div, 62-64, dir, Chem Res Div, 64-65, dir, Enjay Chem Labs, 65-66, mgr chem planning & coord, 66-69, asst gen mgr, Exxon Eng Technol Dept, 69-80, relocation mgr, 80-81, new facil proj exec, 81-84. *Mem:* Am Chem Soc; Soc Automotive Engrs. *Res:* Petroleum products and petrochemicals; engineering research and development process industries. *Mailing Add:* 365 Long Hill Dr Short Hills NJ 07078-3399

LIGGERO, SAMUEL HENRY, PHYSICAL ORGANIC CHEMISTRY. *Current Pos:* sr lab supvr film develop, Polaroid Corp, 70-71, res group leader film develop, 72-76, mgr process eng, 77-78, sr tech mgr, 79-82, plant mgr, 82-85, mktg dir, 85-87, DIR, IMAGING APPLN, POLAROID CORP, 87- *Personal Data:* b Amsterdam, NY, Apr 17, 42; m 66; c 2. *Educ:* Fordham Univ, BS, 64; Georgetown Univ, PhD(chem), 69. *Honors & Awards:* Chuck Hall Award, 87. *Prof Exp:* NIH fel, Princeton Univ, 69-70. *Mem:* The Chem Soc; AAAS; Soc Photog Scientists & Engrs; Am Chem Soc; Sigma Xi. *Res:* Application of physical organic chemistry principles to the development of instant color photographic transparencies employing diffusion transfer processes; application of chemistry, physics and engineering to the manufacture and development of the polaroid 35mm instant slide system. *Mailing Add:* 69 Sheridan Rd Wellesley Hills MA 02181-5419

LIGGETT, JAMES ALEXANDER, CIVIL ENGINEERING. *Current Pos:* PROF HYDRAUL, CORNELL UNIV, 61- *Personal Data:* b Los Angeles, Calif, June 29, 34; m 60, Carole Lattus. *Educ:* Tex Tech Col, BS, 56; Stanford Univ, MS, 57, PhD(civil eng), 59. *Honors & Awards:* Rouse Award & Torrens Award, Am Soc Civil Engrs. *Prof Exp:* Engr, Chance Vought Aircraft Corp, 59-60; asst prof hydraul, Univ Wis, 60-61. *Mem:* Am Soc Civil Engrs; Int Asn Hydraul Res. *Res:* Hydraulics; fluid mechanics; free surface flow; circulation and temperature distribution in lakes; groundwater flow; numerical methods. *Mailing Add:* Sch Civil & Environ Eng Cornell Univ 220 Hillister Hall Ithaca NY 14853-3501. *Fax:* 607-255-9004; *E-Mail:* jim_liggett@cornell.edu

LIGGETT, LAWRENCE MELVIN, ANALYTICAL CHEMISTRY, ORGANIC CHEMISTRY. *Current Pos:* RETIRED. *Personal Data:* b Denver, Colo, June 22, 17; m 43, Edith Harris; c Pamela J (Schwartz) & Betty S (El Gammal). *Educ:* Cent Col, Iowa, AB, 38; Iowa State Col, PhD(chem), 43. *Prof Exp:* Res chemist, Nat Defense Res Comt, Iowa State Col, 41-43; plant supt, Alkali Chlorates & Perchlorates Cardox Corp, 43-48; supvr inorg res, Wyandotte Chems Corp, 48-55; dir res, Speer Carbon Co, 55-64, vpres & tech dir, 65-67, vpres & gen mgr, Airco Speer Electronics, 67-70, pres, Airco Speer Electronics Div, 70-75, pres, Vacuum Equip & Systs, Airco Temescal Div, Airco Inc, 75-82. *Concurrent Pos:* Bus & tech consult, 82- *Mem:* Am Chem Soc; Electrochem Soc. *Res:* Alkali perchlorate production; nonblack pigments for rubber and paper; carbon and graphite technology; resistors; capacitors and electronic components; technical management. *Mailing Add:* 1856 Piedras Circle Danville CA 94526-1329

LIGGETT, THOMAS MILTON, INTERACTING PARTICLE SYSTEMS. *Current Pos:* From asst prof to assoc prof, 69-76, PROF MATH, UNIV CALIF, LOS ANGELES, 76- *Personal Data:* b Danville, Ky, Mar 29, 44; m 72, Christina Goodale; c Timothy J & Amy A. *Educ:* Oberlin Col, AB, 65; Stanford Univ, MS, 66, PhD(math), 69. *Concurrent Pos:* Sloan fel, 73; ed, Annals of Probability, 85-87. *Mem:* Am Math Soc; Math Asn Am; fel Inst Math Statist; Bernoulli Soc. *Res:* Probability theory; interacting particle systems. *Mailing Add:* Dept Math Univ Calif 405 Hilgard Ave Los Angeles CA 90095-1555. *E-Mail:* tml@math.ucla.edu

LIGGETT, WALTER STEWART, JR, EXPERIMENTAL DESIGN, APPLIED STATISTICS. *Current Pos:* MATH STATISTICIAN, STATIST ENG DIV, NAT INST STANDS & TECHNOL, 79- *Personal Data:* b Abington, Pa, Aug 27, 40; m 62; c 3. *Educ:* Rensselaer Polytech Inst, BS, 61, MS, 64, PhD(math), 67. *Prof Exp:* Prin engr, Submarine Signal Div, Raytheon Co, Portsmouth, 65-73; mathematician, Rand Inst, New York, 73-75; statistician, Div Environ Planning, Tenn Valley Authority, 75-79. *Concurrent Pos:* Mem, Am Statist Asn, Comt Statist & Environ, 80- *Mem:* Inst Math Statist; Soc Indust & Appl Math; Am Statist Asn. *Res:* Statistical planning of studies that involve physical mesaurements having non-standard error properties such as multiple components, a non constant variance, a non-normal distribution, or serial correlation. *Mailing Add:* 20418 Shadow Oak Ct Gaithersburg MD 20879-1128

LIGGITT, H DENNY, PATHOLOGY. *Current Pos:* PROF, DEPT COMP MED, SCH MED, UNIV WASH, 89- *Personal Data:* b Denver, Colo, Feb 19, 48. *Educ:* Colo State Univ, BS, 70, DVM, 72, PhD(path), 79. *Prof Exp:* Assoc vet, Anchorage & Denver, 72-75; teaching assoc, Dept Path & Hyg, Univ Ill, Urbana, 75-76; res asst, Dept Path, Colo State Univ, 76-79; asst prof, Dept Vet Microbiol & Path, Col Vet Med, Wash State Univ, 79-84, assoc prof, 84-87; actg assoc dir, Dept Pharmacol Sci, Pathobiol Res Lab, Genentech, Inc, 85-86, assoc dir & sr exp pathologist & head, Path Sect, 87-89. *Res:* Pathogenesis of disease. *Mailing Add:* Dept Comp Med Sch Med Univ Wash T-150 Health Sci SB-42 Seattle WA 98195

LIGH, STEVE, MATHEMATICS. *Current Pos:* PROF MATH, SOUTHEASTERN LA UNIV, 90- *Personal Data:* b Canton, China, Nov 12, 37; US citizen. *Educ:* Univ Houston, BS, 61; Univ Mo-Columbia, MA, 62; Tex A&M Univ, PhD(math), 69. *Prof Exp:* Instr math, Ohio Univ, 62-64, Houston Baptist Col, 65-66 & Tex A&M Univ, 68-69; asst prof, Univ Fla, 69-70; from assoc prof to prof math, Univ Southwestern La, 72-90. *Mem:* Math Asn Am; Am Math Soc. *Res:* Algebra; generalizations of rings; near rings. *Mailing Add:* Southeastern La Univ Hammond LA 70402-0687

LIGHT, ALBERT, BIOCHEMISTRY. *Current Pos:* from assoc prof to prof, 65-92, head, Div Biochem, 78-82, EMER PROF, PURDUE UNIV, 92- *Personal Data:* b Brooklyn, NY, June 19, 27; m 52; c 2. *Educ:* City Col New York, BS, 48; Yale Univ, PhD(biochem), 55. *Prof Exp:* Fel biochem, Cornell Univ, 55-57; asst res prof, Univ Utah, 57-63; assoc prof, Univ Calif, Los Angeles, 63-65. *Mem:* AAAS; Am Chem Soc; Am Soc Biochem & Molecular Biol. *Res:* Protein chemistry and enzymology; protein folding; relationship of structure to function of biologically active proteins. *Mailing Add:* Dept Chem Purdue Univ BRWN Bldg Lafayette IN 47907-1393

LIGHT, DONALD W, SOCIAL & BEHAVIORAL MEDICINE, SOCIOLOGY. *Current Pos:* PROF COMP HEALTH CARE & DIR, DIV SOC BEHAV MED, UNIV MED & DENT NJ, 80- *Personal Data:* m, Nancy; c Holly & Peter. *Educ:* Stanford Univ, BA, 63; Univ Chicago, MA, 67; Brandeis Univ, PhD(sociol), 70. *Prof Exp:* Asst prof, Princeton Univ, 69-75; assoc prof, City Col NY, 75-80. *Concurrent Pos:* Sr fel, Leonard Davis Inst Health Econs, 84-; vis fel, Oxford Univ, 90 & 92; sr consult, Carnegie Found, 91-; DeCamp fel, Princeton Univ, 92-93. *Mem:* Fel Royal Soc Med. *Res:* Comparative analysis and design of health care systems; social aspects of economic and professional behavior. *Mailing Add:* 10 Adams Dr Princeton NJ 08540. *Fax:* 609-921-7293

LIGHT, DOUGLAS B, ION CHANNEL REGULATION, OVERWINTERING ADAPTATIONS. *Current Pos:* ASST PROF BIOL, RIPON COL, 89- *Personal Data:* b New York, NY, Apr 9, 56; m 77; c 3. *Educ:* Colby Col, BA, 78; Univ Minn, MS & PhD(physiol), 86. *Honors & Awards:* Award for Res Excellence, Am Physiol Soc, 87, Caroline tum Suden Award, 88. *Prof Exp:* Biol teacher, Winslow High Sch, 78-81; teaching asst physiol, Univ Minn, 81-84, res asst physiol, 84-86; postdoctoral fel physiol, Dartmouth Med Sch, 86-88, res asst, assoc, 88-89. *Concurrent Pos:* Instr biol, Sch Life Long Learning, 88. *Mem:* Sigma Xi; Biophys Soc; Am Soc Zoologists; Am Physiol Soc; Soc Gen Physiol & Cryobiol. *Res:* Ion channel regulation, cell volume regulation and overwintering adaptations of invertebrates. *Mailing Add:* Dept Biol Ripon Col 300 Seward St Ripon WI 54971-0248

LIGHT, IRWIN JOSEPH, PEDIATRICS. *Current Pos:* from asst prof to assoc prof pediat, 65-73, from asst prof to assoc prof obstet & gynec, 68-73, dir newborn clin serv, 73-83, PROF PEDIAT, OBSTET & GYNEC, UNIV CINCINNATI, 73- *Personal Data:* b Montreal, Que, July 21, 34; m 72; c 2. *Educ:* McGill Univ, BS, 55, MD, 59. *Prof Exp:* Intern med, Royal Victoria Hosp, 59-60; resident, 60-61; resident pediat, Montreal Children's Hosp, 61-63. *Concurrent Pos:* Clin fel pediat, Cincinnati Gen Hosp & res fel, Univ Cincinnati, 63-65; res assoc pediat, Children's Hosp Res Found, 63-; chmn, Inst Rev Bd, Children's Hosp Med Ctr, 84- *Mem:* AAAS; Am Acad Pediat; Soc Pediat Res; Am Pediat Soc; Am Fedn Clin Res. *Res:* Neonatal infectious diseases; newborn metabolism. *Mailing Add:* Univ Cincinnati Col Med 231 Bethesda Ave Cincinnati OH 45267-0541. *Fax:* 513-558-7770

LIGHT, JOHN CALDWELL, CHEMICAL PHYSICS. *Current Pos:* from instr to assoc prof chem, Univ Chicago, 61-70, dir, Mat Res Lab, 70-73, chmn, Dept Chem, 80-82, PROF CHEM, UNIV CHICAGO, 70- *Personal Data:* b Mt Vernon, NY, Nov 24, 34; m 58, Phyllis Kittel; c 3. *Educ:* Oberlin Col, BA, 56; Harvard Univ, PhD(chem), 60. *Prof Exp:* NSF fel, Brussels, 59-61. *Concurrent Pos:* Sloan fel, 66; vis fel, Joint Inst Lab Astrophys, Univ Colo, 76-77; ed, J Chem Phys, 82- *Mem:* AAAS; fel Am Phys Soc; Am Chem Soc; Int Acad Quantum Molecular Sci. *Res:* Theoretical studies of elementary gas phase reactions; quantum mechanics and chemical kinetics; scattering theory; computational methods for theoretical chemistry; theoretical spectroscopy. *Mailing Add:* Dept Chem Univ Chicago Chicago IL 60637

LIGHT, JOHN HENRY, mathematics, for more information see previous edition

LIGHT, KENNETH FREEMAN, mechanical engineering, for more information see previous edition

LIGHT, KIM EDWARD, biogenic amines, receptors, for more information see previous edition

LIGHT, ROBLEY JASPER, BIOCHEMISTRY, ORGANIC CHEMISTRY. *Current Pos:* instr, Fla State Univ, 62-63, from asst prof to assoc prof, 62-72, chmn, 83-90, PROF BIOCHEM, FLA STATE UNIV, 72- *Personal Data:* b Roanoke, Va, Nov 8, 35; m 60, D Jeanne Kosko; c George E. *Educ:* Va Polytech Inst, BS, 57; Duke Univ, PhD(org chem), 61. *Honors & Awards:* Alexander von Humboldt US Sr Scientist Award, 77. *Prof Exp:* NSF fel biochem, Harvard Univ, 60-62. *Concurrent Pos:* USPHS res career develop award, 67-72; prog dir biol instrumentation, NSF, 90-91. *Mem:* Am Chem Soc; Am Soc Biochem & Molecular Biol. *Res:* Lipid metabolism, structure, and function; polyketides and other secondary metabolites of microorganisms. *Mailing Add:* Dept Chem Fla State Univ Tallahassee FL 32306. *Fax:* 850-644-8281; *E-Mail:* rlight@sb.fsu.edu

LIGHT, THOMAS BURWELL, PRINTER TECHNOLOGY, MATERIALS SCIENCE. *Current Pos:* mem res staff, Thomas J Watson Res Ctr, 65-81, DEVELOP CONSULT, IBM US DEVELOP STAFF, IBM CORP, 81- *Personal Data:* b Dayton, Ohio, July 9, 28; m 51; c 4. *Educ:* Antioch Col, BS, 51; Ill Inst Technol, MS, 54; Yale Univ, PhD(mat sci), 66. *Prof Exp:* Mem tech staff, Bell Tel Labs, 53-62. *Mem:* AAAS; Am Phys Soc; Inst Elec & Electronics Engrs. *Res:* Deposition, structure and properties of thin films; structure of and crystallization in amorphous materials; structure of oxide layers and interface reactions. *Mailing Add:* 94 Eastwood Dr Portsmouth NH 03801

LIGHT, TRUMAN S, ANALYTICAL CHEMISTRY, ELECTRO-ANALYTICAL METHODS. *Current Pos:* CONSULT, 88-; ADJ PROF CHEM, AQUINAS COL, 94- *Personal Data:* b Hartford, Conn, Dec 16, 22; m 46, 80, Arlene Wick; c Edward N, Stuart L (Licht) & Joel M. *Educ:* Harvard Univ, SB, 43; Univ Minn, MS, 49; Univ Rome, DrChem, 61. *Honors & Awards:* James L Waters, Award, 96. *Prof Exp:* Asst prof chem, Boston Col, 49-59; staff scientist, Res & Adv Develop Div, Avco Corp, 59-64; sr res chemist, Foxboro Co, 64-72, mgr, Chem Anal & Mat Lab, 72-80, prin res scientist, 80-88; adj prof chem, Boston Col, 87-88; adj prof chem, Suffolk Univ, 91-92. *Concurrent Pos:* NSF fel, Chem Inst, Univ Rome, Italy, 60-61; consult, Children's Med Ctr, Boston, Mass, 56-60 & Watertown Arsenal, 51-55. *Mem:* Am Chem Soc; Electrochem Soc; Soc Appl Spectros; Instrument Soc Am; Sigma Xi; Soc Elecroanal Chem. *Res:* Instrumental methods of analysis; electrochemistry; physical chemistry; materials sciences, water quality and pollution controls. *Mailing Add:* 4 Webster Rd Lexington MA 02173-8222. *E-Mail:* tslight@aol.com

LIGHTBODY, JAMES JAMES, IMMUNOLOGY, BIOCHEMISTRY. *Current Pos:* asst prof, 72-76, ASSOC PROF BIOCHEM, SCH MED, WAYNE STATE UNIV, 76-, ASSOC IMMUNOL, 73-, CLIN ASSOC PROF INTERNAL MED, 76- *Personal Data:* b Detroit, Mich, Mar 1, 39; m 64; c 2. *Educ:* Wayne State Univ, BA, 61, BS, 64, PhD(biochem), 66. *Prof Exp:* Res assoc biochem & NIH trainee, Brandeis Univ, 67-69; instr pediat & Swiss Nat Sci Found grant, Univ Bern, 69-70; sr res assoc immunol, Basel Inst Immunol, 70-71; res assoc, Univ Wis, 71-72. *Concurrent Pos:* Vis prof, Mem Sloan-Kettering Cancer Ctr, 73; lectr, Cancer Inst, Cairo Univ, 74. *Mem:* AAAS; Am Asn Immunol; Transplantation Soc. *Mailing Add:* Dept Biochem Wayne State Univ Sch Med 540 E Canfield Detroit MI 48230

LIGHTERMAN, MARK S, COMPUTER PROGRAMMING. *Current Pos:* VPRES, HMMM CORP, 82- *Personal Data:* b New York, NY, Jan 17, 60. *Educ:* Syracuse Univ, BS & BA, 82; Univ Miami, MS, 85. *Concurrent Pos:* Mem bd, Fla Alliance Technol Educ, 89-91, pres, 91- *Mem:* NY Acad Sci; Asn Comput Mach; Am Math Soc; Inst Elec & Electronics Engrs; Am Med Info Asn; Soc Motion Picture & TV Engrs. *Res:* Curriculum enhancement by bringing technology back into the classroom. *Mailing Add:* 9230 SW 59th St Miami FL 33173-1660

LIGHTFOOT, DONALD RICHARD, BIOCHEMICAL GENETICS. *Current Pos:* ASSOC PROF BIOL & DIR BIOCHEM/BIOTECHNOL, EASTERN WASH UNIV, 80- *Personal Data:* b Los Angeles, Calif, Aug 8, 40; m 72. *Educ:* Univ Redlands, BA, 62; Univ Ariz, MS, 67, PhD(biochem), 72. *Prof Exp:* Teacher, Philippine High Sch, Peace Corps, 62-64; res trainee biochem, Med Sch, Univ Ore, 69-71; fel, Univ Calif, Riverside, 71-74; asst prof biochem & nutrit, Va Polytech Inst & State Univ, 74-79. *Concurrent Pos:* DNA diagnostics consult, Sacred Heart Med Ctr. *Mem:* AAAS; Am Chem Soc; Soc Exp Biol & Med; Sigma Xi. *Res:* Plant virology; tobacco mosaic virus infection process; gene titration in tobacco species; minor nucleosides; transfer RNA, messenger RNA 5.85 ribosomal RNA and viral RNA NMR structure and function; biotechnology education, turnip yellow mosaic virus structure/function; polymerase chain reaction applications. *Mailing Add:* 1405 E Woodcliff Rd Spokane WA 99203-3855

LIGHTFOOT, E(DWIN) N(IBLOCK), JR, SEPARATIONS, BIOTECHNOLOGY. *Current Pos:* from asst prof to prof biochem eng, 53-80, Hilldale prof chem eng, 80-95, EMER PROF CHEM ENG, UNIV WIS-MADISON, 95- *Personal Data:* b Milwaukee, Wis, Sept 25, 25; m 49; c 5. *Educ:* Cornell Univ, BS, 47, PhD(chem eng), 51. *Hon Degrees:* Dr, Tech Univ Norway. *Honors & Awards:* William H Walker Award, Am Inst Chem Engrs, 75, Food, Pharm & Bioeng Award, 79, Warren K Lewis Award, 91; Lacey lectr, Calif Inst Technol, 84; Van Winkle lectr, Univ Tex, 84; Stanley Katz lectr, City Col, City Univ NY, 86; Goff Smith lectr, Univ Mich, 87; Kloor Mem lectr, Indian Inst Sci, Bangalore, 87; Reilly lectr, Univ Notre Dame, 88; Benjamin Smith Reynolds Award , Univ Wis Col Eng, 88; Kelly lectr, Purdue Univ, 89; Harry G Fair lectr, Univ Okla, 91; Hilldale Award, Univ Wis, 92; E V Murphree Award, Am Chem Soc, 92. *Prof Exp:* Chem engr, Chas Pfizer & Co, 50-53. *Concurrent Pos:* Tech consult, 53-88; vis prof, Tech Univ Norway, 62, Stanford Univ & Tech Univ Denmark, 71, Univ Canterbury, NZ, 72; Erskine fel, Univ Canterbury, NZ, 72. *Mem:* Nat Acad Sci; Nat Acad Eng; Royal Norweg Soc Sci & Lett; Am Inst Chem Engr; Am Chem Soc. *Res:* Physical separation techniques; mass transfer; biomedical engineering; author of 14 books and technical articles. *Mailing Add:* Dept Chem Eng Univ Wis 1415 Eng Dr Madison WI 53706

LIGHTFOOT, RALPH B(UTTERWORTH), AERONAUTICAL ENGINEERING. *Current Pos:* CONSULT ENGR, 74- *Personal Data:* b Fall River, Mass, June 19, 13; m 37, Beatrice Walsh; c William E & Thomas R. *Educ:* Univ RI, BS & ME, 35. *Honors & Awards:* Merit Award, Am Helicopter Soc, 48; Bell Award, 61; Sperry Award, 64; Gold Medal, NY Acad Sci & Cierva Prize, Royal Aeronaut Soc, 65. *Prof Exp:* Wind tunnel engr, Sikorsky Aircraft Div, United Technologies Corp, 35-37, chief wind tunnel engr, 38-40, chief flight test engr, 40-43, chief wind tunnel res, 44-57, chief engr, 57-66, engr mgr, 66-67, sr staff engr, 68-74. *Concurrent Pos:* Instr, Univ Bridgeport, 39, 77, lectr, 63-65; instr, Bullard Havens Tech Inst, 41-43; lectr, NY Univ, 43; designated eng rep, Fed Aviation Agency, 55-60, mem airworthiness stand eval comt, 66; mem, NASA, 56-68; mem adv coun, Bridgeport Eng Inst, Univ Bridgeport, Housatonic Community Col & Adv Group Aerospace Res & Develop, NATO, 59, 62; navigator, US Power Squadron; lectr, Univ Conn, 62; USCG Auxil, 79-95; mem adv coun, Univ RI, 81-96. *Mem:* Nat Soc Prof Engrs; hon fel Am Helicopter Soc (vpres, 50, pres, 51); fel Am Inst Aeronaut & Astronaut; fel NY Acad Sci; fel Royal Aeronaut Soc. *Res:* Aerodynamics; wind tunnel; analytical flight test; flying boats; helicopters; management; airplanes; accident litigation. *Mailing Add:* 55 Eliphamets Lane Chatham MA 02633

LIGHTMAN, ALAN PAIGE, THEORETICAL ASTROPHYSICS, THEORETICAL PHYSICS. *Current Pos:* PROF SCI & WRITING, MASS INST TECHNOL, 88-, JOHN E BURCHARD PROF, 95- *Personal Data:* b Memphis, Tenn, Nov 28, 48; m 76, Jean Greenblatt; c Elyse & Kara. *Educ:* Princeton Univ, AB, 70; Calif Inst Technol, MA, 73, PhD(physics), 74. *Honors & Awards:* Andrew Gemant Prize, Am Inst Physics, 96. *Prof Exp:* Res assoc physics, Calif Inst Technol, 74; res assoc astrophysics, Cornell Univ, 74-76; asst prof astron, Harvard Univ, 76-79, lectr astron & phys, 79-88. *Mem:* Fel Am Phys Soc; Am Astron Soc; fel AAAS; Soc Lit & Sci; fel Am Acad Arts & Sci. *Res:* Theoretical frameworks for analyzing modern gravitation theories; relativistic astrophysics, x-ray astronomy; stellar dynamics; radiation processes; philosophy of science. *Mailing Add:* Dept Physics Mass Inst Technol Cambridge MA 02139

LIGHTNER, DAVID A, BIOORGANIC CHEMISTRY, STEREOCHEMISTRY. *Current Pos:* assoc prof, Univ Nev, Reno, 74-76, dept chmn, 85-88, found prof, 87-90, PROF CHEM, UNIV NEV, RENO, 76-, RC FUSON PROF, 84- *Personal Data:* b Los Angeles, Calif, Mar 25, 39; m 74, Renne Kirk; c Mikah & Derek. *Educ:* Univ Calif, Berkeley, AB, 60; Stanford Univ, PhD, 63. *Prof Exp:* NSF fels, Stanford Univ, 63-64 & Univ Minn, 64-65; asst prof chem, Univ Calif, Los Angeles, 65-72; assoc prof, Tex Tech Univ, 72-74. *Concurrent Pos:* Assoc ed, Photochem Photobiol, 83-86; fel, Ctr Advan Study, Univ Nev; adj prof biochem, Univ Nev, Reno, 84-; counr, Am Soc Photobiol, 90-93. *Mem:* Fel AAAS; Am Chem Soc; Royal Soc Chem; Am Soc Photobiol; Inter-Am Photochem Soc. *Res:* Photochemistry of biological materials; molecular recognition; synthesis and stereochemistry; circular dichroism and optical rotatory dispersion; phototherapy and jaundice. *Mailing Add:* Dept Chem Univ Nev Reno NV 89557-0020. *Fax:* 702-784-6804; *E-Mail:* lightner@chem.unr.edu

LIGHTNER, JAMES EDWARD, MATHEMATICS, EDUCATION. *Current Pos:* from instr to assoc prof math, Western Md Col, 62-77, chmn dept, 68-73, dir Jan term, 69-83, dir math proficiency, 83-95, PROF MATH & EDUC, WESTERN MD COL, 77-, FAC ASST ADMIN, 95- *Personal Data:* b Frederick, Md, Aug 29, 37. *Educ:* Western Md Col, AB, 58; Northwestern Univ, AM, 62; Ohio State Univ, PhD(math, educ), 68. *Prof Exp:* Teacher, Frederick County Bd Educ, Md, 58-62. *Concurrent Pos:* Fed Liaison Rep, Western Md Col, 73-78, coordr int studies, 80-83; consult sch systs & Md State Dept Educ; exec secy, Md Coun Teachers Math, 88- *Mem:* Nat Coun Teachers Math; Math Asn Am; Sigma Xi. *Res:* Undergraduate mathematics curricula; secondary mathematics curricula and methodology; secondary school geometry; history of mathematics. *Mailing Add:* Dept Math Western Md Col 2 College Hill Westminster MD 21157

LIGHTON, JOHN R B, ECOLOGICAL PHYSIOLOGY, WATER RELATIONS. *Current Pos:* ASST PROF ECOPHYSIOL, UNIV UTAH, 91- *Personal Data:* b Johannesburg, SAfrica, Aug 25, 52. *Educ:* Univ Cape Town, BA, 75, BSc, 81, MSc, 84; Univ Calif, Los Angeles, PhD(physiol), 87. *Honors & Awards:* David & Lucille Packard Award. *Prof Exp:* Hollaender distinguished postdoctoral fel ecophysiol, Univ Calif, Los Angeles, 87-89, adj asst prof, 89-90. *Concurrent Pos:* Guest prof ecophysiol, Univ Zurich, 90.

Mem: AAAS; Am Soc Zoologists. *Res:* Ecological physiology of animals, concentrating on insects, their respiratory and ventilatory physiology. *Mailing Add:* Biol Dept Univ Utah 201 S Biology Bldg Salt Lake City UT 84112-1196. *Fax:* 801-581-4668; *E-Mail:* lighton@bioscience.utah.edu

LIGHTSEY, PAUL ALDEN, AERONAUTICAL & ASTRONAUTICAL ENGINEERING, ATMOSPHERIC CHEMISTRY & PHYSICS. *Current Pos:* prin systs engr, 86-94, STAFF CONSULT, BALL AEROSPACE SYSTS GROUP, 95- *Personal Data:* b Wray, Colo, Aug 25, 44; m 65; c 1. *Educ:* Colo State Univ, BS, 66; Cornell Univ, MS, 69, PhD(physics), 72. *Prof Exp:* Res aide atmospheric physics, Colo State Univ, 62-66; physicist, surface physics, Dow Chem-Rocky Flats Div, 66; res asst solid state physics, Cornell Univ, 66-72; lectr physics, Beloit Col, 72-73; asst prof physics & math, Univ Dallas, 73-75; electrician, Great Western Sugar Co, 75-76; assoc prof physics & math, Colo Mountain Col, 76-77; assoc prof & chmn dept physics, Univ Northern Colo, 77-86. *Concurrent Pos:* Instr, Frontiers Sci Inst, Univ Northern Colo, 80-82; physicist, Nat Oceanic & Atmospheric Admin, 82-84; scientist, Nat Ctr Atmospheric Res, 86- *Mem:* Am Asn Physics Teachers; Sigma Xi; Int Soc Biomechanics in Sports; Soc Photo Instrumentation Engrs; Optical Soc Am; Nat Sci Teachers Asn. *Res:* Use of laser radar for remote sensing characteristics of atmosphere; biomechanical analysis of sports; optical propagation through atmospheric turbulence; electro-optical systems engineering; atmospheric optics; Hubble space telescope instrumentation. *Mailing Add:* Ball Aerospace PO Box 1062 Boulder CO 80306-1062

LIGHTY, JOANN SLAMA, WASTE REMEDIATION, INCINERATION. *Current Pos:* ASST PROF CHEM ENG, UNIV UTAH, 88- *Personal Data:* b Weehawken, NJ, Jan 5, 60. *Educ:* Univ Utah, BS, 82, PhD(chem eng), 88. *Prof Exp:* Proj engr, NW Pipeline Corp, 82-84. *Concurrent Pos:* Sr scientist, Reaction Eng Int, 90- *Mem:* Am Inst Chem Eng; Soc Women Engrs; Combustion Inst; Air & Waste Mgt Asn. *Res:* Remediation of contaminated solids by thermal treatment; MSW incineration; fate of metals during incineration; circulating fluidized bed combustion. *Mailing Add:* Dept Chem Eng Univ Utah 3290 Merrill Eng Salt Lake City UT 84112-1107

LIGHTY, RICHARD WILLIAM, PLANT GENETICS, HORTICULTURE. *Current Pos:* assoc prof plant sci & coordr Longwood prog ornamental hort, 67-82, DIR MT CUBA CTR STUDY PIEDMONT FLORA, UNIV DEL, 83- *Personal Data:* b Freeport, Ill, Nov 8, 33; m 55; c 2. *Educ:* Pa State Univ, BS, 55; Cornell Univ, MS, 58, PhD(genetics), 60. *Honors & Awards:* A H Scott Medal & Award; Silver Medal, Mass Hort Soc; Eloise Payne Lequer Medal, Garden Club Am. *Prof Exp:* Geneticist, Longwood Gardens, Pa, 60-67. *Mem:* AAAS; Am Asn Bot Gardens & Arboretums. *Res:* Plant breeding; cytotaxonomy; horticultural taxonomy; floriculture. *Mailing Add:* Mt Cuba Ctr PO Box 3570 Greenville DE 19807

LIGLER, FRANCES SMITH, BIOSENSORS. *Current Pos:* SR SCIENTIST, NAVAL RES LAB, 85-, HEAD, BIOSENSORS & BIOMAT LAB, 93- *Personal Data:* b Louisville, Ky, June 11, 51; m 72; George T; c Amy E & Adam G. *Educ:* Furman Univ, BSc, 72; Oxford Univ, Eng, DPhil. *Honors & Awards:* Am Asn Med Instrumentation Ann Meeting Manuscript Award, 3M; Policy Technol Transfer Award, Nat Drug Control; Hillebrand Award, Am Chem Soc. *Prof Exp:* Fel biochem, Univ Tex Health Sci Ctr, San Antonio, 75-76; asst instr immunol, Southwestern Med Sch, 76-78, instr, 78-80; primary scientist immunol, E I du Pont de Nemours & Co, Inc, 80-84, group leader cellular immunol, 84-85. *Concurrent Pos:* From adj asst prof to adj assoc prof, Hahnemann Univ, 81-85. *Mem:* Am Asn Immunologists; AAAS; Am Asn Pathologists; Am Chem Soc; Soc Photooptical & Instrumentation Engrs. *Res:* Biosensors; immunoassay development; fluorescence. *Mailing Add:* Naval Res Lab Code 6900 Washington DC 20375-5348

LIGOMENIDES, PANOS ARISTIDES, SYNERGETIC & NEURAL COMPUTERS, EXPERIMENTAL KNOWLEDGE ENGINEERING. *Current Pos:* RETIRED. *Personal Data:* b Pireus, Greece, Apr 3, 28; US citizen; m 73; c 2. *Educ:* Univ Athens, Greece, dipl physics, 51, MSc, 52; Stanford Univ, MSc, 56, PhD(elec eng & physics), 58. *Prof Exp:* Radio engr radiotel, Greek Tel & Tel Co, 54-55; res & staff engr elec eng & comput, IBM, 58-64; asst prof elec eng, Univ Calif, Los Angeles, 64-69; adj prof, Stanford Univ, 69-70; prof comput eng, Elec Eng Dept, Univ MdD, 71-93. *Concurrent Pos:* Tech consult indust & govt, 64-; Orgn Econ Coop & Develop fel, Greece, 65 & 74; Ford Found fel, SAm, 66 & 68; vis prof, Univ Ceara, Brazil, 66, Stanford Univ, 67, Univ Athens, Greece, 68-69 & Polit Univ Madrid, Spain, 82-84; prin investr grants & contracts from indust & govt, 68-; Fulbright prof univs in Greece, 70-71; Salzburg Sem fel, Salzburg Sem Am Studies, 71; distinguished prof, Elec Eng Dept, Univ Md, 71-72; pres & owner, Comput Eng Consults, 75-81; vpres res, Caelum Res Corp, 87-93. *Mem:* Sr mem Inst Elec & Electronics Engrs; Int Soc Optical Eng. *Res:* Applied artificial intelligence; neural networks; decisions support technologies; pattern recognition; computer architectures; microcomputer-based systems; synergetic computer applications. *Mailing Add:* 8802 Magnolia Dr Lanham MD 20742

LIGON, JAMES DAVID, ZOOLOGY. *Current Pos:* from asst prof to assoc prof, 68-77, PROF BIOL, UNIV NMEX, 77- *Personal Data:* b Wewoka, Okla, Feb 2, 39; m 67; c 1. *Educ:* Univ Okla, BS, 61; Univ Fla, MS, 63; Univ Mich, PhD(zool), 67. *Prof Exp:* Asst prof biol, Idaho State Univ, 67-68. *Mem:* Am Ornith Union; Cooper Ornith Soc. *Res:* Avian ecology and behavior. *Mailing Add:* Dept Biol Univ NMex Main Campus One Univ Campus Albuquerque NM 87131-0001

LIGON, JAMES T(EDDIE), SOILS & SOIL SCIENCE. *Current Pos:* assoc prof, 66-71, chmn directorate, Water Resources Res Inst, 75-78, actg head, Agr Eng Dept, 84-85, PROF AGR ENG, CLEMSON UNIV, 71- *Personal Data:* b Easley, SC, Feb 20, 36; m 58; c 3. *Educ:* Clemson Univ, BS, 57; Iowa State Univ, MS, 59, PhD(agr eng, soil physics), 61. *Prof Exp:* Asst prof agr eng, Univ Ky, 61-66. *Mem:* Am Soc Agr Engrs; Am Geophys Union; Sigma Xi; Am Soc Eng Educ. *Res:* Soil drainage and physics; soil, water and plant relationships; hydrologic modeling. *Mailing Add:* 1331 Milwee Creek Rd Pendleton SC 29670

LIGON, WOODFIN VAUGHAN, JR, ORGANIC MASS SPECTROMETRY & CHEMISTRY. *Current Pos:* STAFF SCIENTIST ORG MASS SPECTROMETRY, GEN ELEC CORP RES & DEVELOP, 73- *Personal Data:* b Farmville, Va, Apr 24, 44. *Educ:* Longwood Col, BS, 66; Univ Va, PhD(org chem), 70. *Prof Exp:* Vis asst prof org chem, Univ Ill, 72-73. *Concurrent Pos:* NIH fel, Univ Ill, Urbana, 71-72. *Mem:* Am Soc Mass Spectrometry. *Res:* New modes of ionization for mass spectrometry; secondary ion mass spectrometry; multidimensional gas chromatography. *Mailing Add:* 2251 Van Antwerp Rd Schenectady NY 12309

LIGUORI, FRED, MAINTENANCE TESTING, WEAPON SYSTEMS SUPPORT. *Current Pos:* head, Automatic Test Equip Br, Naval Air Eng Ctr, 71-88, dir, Advan Develop Res & Develop Lab, 88-91, sr technologist, 91-95, HEAD, SYSTS SUPPORTABILITY BR, NAVAL AIR ENG CTR, 95- *Personal Data:* b Somerville, Mass, Dec 21, 30; m 57, Ebba L Knudson; c Victor & Carol. *Educ:* Tufts Univ, BSEE, 57; Hofstra Univ, MB, 60. *Honors & Awards:* Distinguished Serv Award, Inst Elec & Electronics Engrs, 85. *Prof Exp:* Sr engr, Sperry Gyroscope Co, 57-60; proposal mgr, Epsco Inc, 60; asst tech dir, Gen Commun Co, 61; sr proj engr, RCA, 61-68; mgr, Automatic Test Equip Lab, Emerson Elec Co, 68-71. *Concurrent Pos:* Ed, Trans Instrumentation Soc Elec & Electronics Engrs, 81-85; chair tech meetings, Comput Soc Inst Elec & Electronics Engrs, 93-94, chair testing tech comt, 95-96. *Mem:* Fel Inst Elec & Electronics Engrs; Soc Logistics Engrs; Inst Elec & Electronics Engrs Instrument & Measurement Soc (pres, 85); Inst Elec & Electronics Engrs Comput Soc. *Res:* Automatic test equipment; authored 45 technical papers on automatic testing. *Mailing Add:* 38 Clubhouse Rd Browns Mills NJ 08015-3207

LIGUORI, VINCENT ROBERT, MARINE MICROBIOLOGY. *Current Pos:* RETIRED. *Personal Data:* b Brooklyn, NY, Dec 15, 28; m 49, 52; c 5. *Educ:* St Francis Col, NY, BS, 51; Long Island Univ, MS, 58; NY Univ, PhD(microbiol), 67. *Prof Exp:* Res asst cancer chemother, Sloan-Kettering Inst Cancer Res, 55-56; supvr, Oncol Lab, Vet Admin Hosp, NY, 56-62; staff scientist microbiol, NY Aquarium, 62-65; asst prof biol & marine sci, Long Island Univ, 65-66; res assoc microbiol, Osborn Labs Marine Sci, NY Aquarium, 66-71; lectr, Kingsborough Community Col, City Univ NY, 66-68, assoc prof biol & dep chmn, Dept Biol Sci, 71-73, prof biol, 73-95. *Concurrent Pos:* Lectr, Nassau Co Mus Natural Hist, 65-68, Richmond Col, 67-70 & Queens Col, 68-69; mem bd dir, Mid Atlantic Natural Sci Coun, Inc, 75-78; mem, Bermuda Biol Sta Res, 75-78. *Mem:* Am Soc Microbiol; Sigma Xi. *Res:* Biological effects of natural products and the mechanism of adhesion in marine invertebrates; role of marine microorganisms in the disease processes of marine animals; aquaculture; invertebrates. *Mailing Add:* 173 Edgewood Ave PO Box 359 Oakdale NY 11769

LIH, MARSHALL MIN-SHING, CHEMICAL ENGINEERING. *Current Pos:* prog dir, Thermodyn & Mass Transfer, NSF, 73-76, sect head, Eng Chem & Energetics, 76-79, div dir chem & process eng, 79-87, dir cross disciplinary res, 87-92, US SR EXEC SERV, ENG CTRS, NSF, 79-, DIR, DIV ENGR ED & CTRS, 92- *Personal Data:* b Nanking, China, Sept 15, 36; m 62; c 3. *Educ:* Nat Taiwan Univ, BS, 58; Univ Wis-Madison, MS, 60, PhD(chem eng), 62. *Prof Exp:* Res engr, E I du Pont de Nemours & Co, 62-64; mem fac chem eng, Cath Univ Am, 64-74; sr res scientist, Nat Biomed Res Found, 66-76. *Concurrent Pos:* Dir, Inst Creative Eng Methodology, 68-70; NSF vis prof & chmn, Dept Chem Eng, Nat Taiwan Univ, 70-71; adj lectr, Georgetown Univ Med Sch, 83- *Mem:* Fel Am Inst Chem Engrs; Sigma Xi. *Res:* Kinetics and catalysis; transport processes; color technology; application of mathematics in chemical engineering; biomedical engineering. *Mailing Add:* NSF EEC Div Suite 585 4201 Willson Blvd Arlington VA 22230. *Fax:* 703-306-0326; *E-Mail:* mlih@nsf.gov

LIIMATAINEN, T(OIVO) M(ATTHEW), ENGINEERING PHYSICS, MATHEMATICS. *Current Pos:* RETIRED. *Personal Data:* b Gloucester, Mass, Nov 14, 10; m 50. *Prof Exp:* Engr, Gen Elec Co, 41-46 & Sylvania Elec Prod Co, 46-48; proj engr, Nat Bur Standards, 48-53; asst br chief electron devices, Diamond Ord Fuze Labs, US Dept Army, 53-59, br chief microelectronics, 59-63; aerospace engr, Goddard Space Flight Ctr, NASA, Md, 63-66 & Electronics Res Ctr, Cambridge, 66-70; gen engr, Transp Systs Ctr, Dept Transp, Mass, 70-71; consult, 71-80. *Mem:* AAAS; sr mem Inst Elec & Electronics Engrs; NY Acad Sci. *Res:* Semiconductor devices; integrated circuits; microelectronics; high vacuum and gas discharge devices. *Mailing Add:* 1004 Union St Schenectady NY 12308

LIIMATTA, ERIC WILHO, SURFACTANTS. *Current Pos:* RES & DEVELOP SPECIALIST, ALBEMARLE CORP, 89- *Personal Data:* b Two Harbors, Minn, July 25, 62. *Educ:* Macalester Col, BA, 84; Northwestern Univ, PhD(inorg chem), 88. *Prof Exp:* Postdoctoral fel, Univ Calif, Los Angeles, 88-89. *Mem:* Am Chem Soc; Am Soc Testing & Mat. *Res:* Formulation and efficacy testing of consumer cleaning products. *Mailing Add:* PO Box 14799 Baton Rouge LA 70898. *Fax:* 504-768-5990; *E-Mail:* eric_liimatta@albemarle.com

LIITTSCHWAGER, JOHN M(ILTON), OPERATIONS RESEARCH, INDUSTRIAL ENGINEERING. *Current Pos:* chmn dept, 74-81, PROF INDUST & MGT ENG, UNIV IOWA, 61- *Personal Data:* b Alden, Iowa, Oct 24, 34; m 55, Virginia Idso; c Jeffrey S, Fonda L (Weber), Robert J & Jean C (Matteson). *Educ:* Iowa State Univ, BS, 55; Northwestern Univ, MS, 61. *Prof Exp:* Engr, foods div, Anderson Clayton & Co, 55-56; consult pub utility, Mid West Serv Co, 56-60. *Mem:* Am Soc Qual Control; Int Ref Orgn Forensic Med & Sci; Inst Indust Eng. *Res:* Legislative districting by computer; mathematical programming; reliability theory. *Mailing Add:* 4104 Eng Bldg Univ Iowa Iowa City IA 52242

LIJEWSKI, LAWRENCE EDWARD, MISSILE AERODYNAMICS, COMPUTATIONAL FLUID DYNAMICS. *Current Pos:* AEROSPACE ENGR, AIR FORCE ARMAMENT LAB, 77- *Personal Data:* b Milwaukee, Wis, Mar 12, 48; m 75; c 2. *Educ:* Univ Notre Dame, BSAE, 70, MSAE, 72, PhD(aerospace), 74. *Prof Exp:* Mech engr, Army Aviation Systs Command, 74-77. *Mem:* Am Inst Aeronaut & Astronaut. *Res:* Aerodynamics of aircraft and missiles; computational fluid dynamics and experimental methods to obtain aerodynamic characteristics and fundamental understanding of basic aerodynamic phenomena. *Mailing Add:* USAF Armament Lab MNAU Eglin AFB FL 32542

LIJINSKY, WILLIAM, environment carcinogenesis, for more information see previous edition

LI KAM WA, PATRICK, ultrashort pulse generation from solid state lasers, semiconductor optoelectronic devices, for more information see previous edition

LIKE, ARTHUR A, PATHOLOGY. *Current Pos:* PROF PATH, MED SCH, UNIV MASS, 75- *Personal Data:* b New York, NY. *Mailing Add:* Path Dept Med Sch Univ Mass 55 Lake Ave N Worcester MA 01655-0125

LIKENS, GENE ELDEN, AQUATIC ECOLOGY, LIMNOLOGY. *Current Pos:* DIR, INST ECOSYST STUDIES, 83-, PRES, 93- *Personal Data:* b Pierceton, Ind, Jan 6, 35; m 83, Phyllis Craig; c Kathy S, Gregory G & Leslie D. *Educ:* Manchester Col, BS, 57; Univ Wis, MS, 59, PhD(zool), 62. *Hon Degrees:* DSc, Manchester Univ, 79, Rutgers Univ, 85, Plymouth State Col, 89, Miami Univ, 90, Marist Col, 93; LHD, Union Col, 91; Dr, Inst Bodenkultur, Vienna, Austria, 92. *Honors & Awards:* Am Motors Conserv Award, 69; First G E Hutchinson Award, Am Soc Limnol & Oceanog, 82; NY Acad Sci Award, 86; Int Ecol, Limnetic Ecol, 88; Distinguished Serv Award, Am Inst Biol Sci, 90; Tyler Prize, 93; Naumann-Thienemann Medal, Int Soc Limnol, 95. *Prof Exp:* Asst zool, Univ Wis, 57-61; from instr to assoc prof biol sci, Dartmouth Col, 61-69; from proj asst to res assoc, Univ Wis, 62, res assoc meteorol, 62-63; from assoc prof to prof ecol & syst, Cornell Univ, 69-83, chmn, 73-74. *Concurrent Pos:* Vis lectr, Univ Wis, 63; mem, US Nat Comt Int Hydrol Decade, 66-70; vis assoc ecologist, Brookhaven Nat Lab, 68; NATO sr fel, Eng & Sweden, 69; mem adv panel, US Senate Comt Pub Works, 70-73; US Nat Rep, Int Asn Theoret & Appl Limnol, 70-; Guggenheim fel, 72-73; mem, Comt Water Qual Policy, Nat Acad Sci, 73-76, mem, Assembly Life Sci, 77-82; mem, Ecol Adv Comt & Sci Adv Bd, Environ Protection Agency, 74-78; mem, Biol Res Comt, Edmund Niles Huyck Preserves & resource adv, NY State Dept Environ Conserv, 74-79; vis prof, Ctr Advan Sci, Dept Environ Sci, Univ Va, 78-79; assoc ed, Am Water Resources Asn, 83-88; adj prof, Sect Ecol & Syst, Cornell Univ, 83-; vpres, NY Bot Garden & dir, Mary Flagler Cary Arboretum, 83-93; sr adv, Ctr Energy & Environ Res, Univ PR, 83-88; prof, Dept Biol, Yale Univ, 84-; mem, US Environ Protection Agency Steering Comt, State Univ NY, Albany, 84-85; adv, White House, Spec Envoy for Acid Rain to Pres, 85; prof, Grad Field Ecol, Rutgers Univ, 85- *Mem:* Nat Acad Sci; Am Polar Soc; Am Soc Limnol & Oceanog (vpres, 75-76, pres, 76-77); Ecol Soc Am (vpres, 78-79, pres, 81-82); Int Asn Theoret & Appl Limnol; hon mem Am Water Resource Asn; Am Acad Arts & Sci; Int Water Resource Asn; fel AAAS; Am Inst Biol Sci; foreign mem Royal Danish Acad Sci & Lett; foreign mem Royal Swed Acad Sci; hon mem Brit Ecol Soc. *Res:* Circulation in lakes using radioactive tracers; meromictic lakes; biogeochemistry and analysis of ecosystems; Antarctic and Arctic limnology; precipitation chemistry; acid rain. *Mailing Add:* Inst Ecosyst Studies PO Box AB Millbrook NY 12545. *Fax:* 914-677-5976; *E-Mail:* pkhg32a@prodigy.com

LIKES, CARL JAMES, PHYSICAL CHEMISTRY. *Current Pos:* prof, 58-82, EMER DISTINGUISHED PROF CHEM, COL CHARLESTON, 82- *Personal Data:* b Charleston, SC, Sept 11, 16; m 43. *Educ:* Col Charleston, BS, 37; Univ Va, PhD(phys chem), 41. *Hon Degrees:* LHD, Col Charleston, 95. *Prof Exp:* Instr chem, Univ Va, 41-43; asst prof, Tulane Univ, 43, asst prof, 44-46; prof & head dept, Hampden-Sydney Col, 47-52; proj supvr, Va Inst for Sci Res, 52-58. *Mem:* Am Chem Soc. *Res:* Electrophoretic and ultracentrifugal analysis of proteins. *Mailing Add:* 2280 Shore Line Dr Johns Island SC 29455

LIKHAREV, KONSTANTIN K, SUPERCONDUCTOR AND LOW-TEMPERATURE ELECTRONICS. *Current Pos:* PROF PHYSICS, STATE UNIV NY, STONY BROOK, 91- *Personal Data:* b Moscow, Russia, Nov 6, 43; m 63, Lioudmila N Korotina; c Sergei & Natasha. *Educ:* Moscow State Univ, MS, 66, PhD(sci), 69, Dr Sci, 79. *Prof Exp:* Jr scientist, Moscow Univ, 69-73, sr scientist, 73-87, head, Lab Cryoelectronics, 88-91. *Concurrent Pos:* Adj maj scientist, Moscow Univ, 91-; mem sci adv bd, Hypres Inc, 91- *Mem:* Am Phys Soc; Res & Develop Asn Future Electronic Devices (Japan); Inst Elec & Electronics Engrs. *Res:* Josephson effect physics; Josephson junction dynamics, superconductor electronics (analog and digital), nonlinear dynamics (classical and quantum), correlated single-electron tunneling and its applications. *Mailing Add:* Dept Physics State Univ NY Stony Brook NY 11794. *Fax:* 516-632-8774; *E-Mail:* klikharev@ccmail.sunysb.edu

LIKINS, PETER WILLIAM, DYNAMICS, CONTROL SYSTEMS. *Current Pos:* PRES, LEHIGH UNIV, 82- *Personal Data:* b Tracy, Calif, July 4, 36; m 55; c 6. *Educ:* Stanford Univ, BS, 57, PhD(eng mech), 65; Mass Inst Technol, SM, 58. *Prof Exp:* Develop engr, Jet Propulsion Lab, Calif Inst Technol, 58-60; from asst prof to prof eng, Univ Calif, Los Angeles, 64-76, from asst dean to assoc dean, 74-76; from prof & dean to provost, Columbia Univ, 76-82. *Concurrent Pos:* Baker scholar; consult var industs & govt res agencies, 66-; mem, US Pres Coun Adv Sci & Technol; mem, Adv Comt Health Univ, White House; mem bd, Comsat Corp, Consol Edison Co, Dynacs Eng Co, Parker-Hannifen Inc, St Lukes Hosp, & Safeguard Sci Inc. *Mem:* Nat Acad Eng; fel Am Inst Aeronaut & Astronaut. *Res:* Problems of space vehicle dynamics, stability and control; author of numerous articles and texts. *Mailing Add:* Alumni Mem Bldg Lehigh Univ 27 Mem Dr W Bethlehem PA 18015-3089

LIKUSKI, ROBERT KEITH, BIOMEDICAL ENGINEERING, LIQUID CHROMATOGRAPHY. *Current Pos:* GROUP LEADER, BIO-RAD LABS, 92- *Personal Data:* b Hillcrest, Alta, Oct 16, 37; m 71, Ines Levy; c David & Andrew. *Educ:* Univ Alta, BS, 59; Univ Ill, MS, 61, PhD(elec eng), 64. *Prof Exp:* Asst prof elec eng, Univ Tex, Austin, 65-70; staff engr comput memories, Micro-Bit Corp, 70-76; chief engr biomed eng, 76-80, dir res & develop, Berkeley Bio-Eng, Inc, 80-81; adv develop mgr, Beckman Instr, 81-92. *Mem:* Inst Elec & Electronics Engrs; Sigma Xi. *Res:* Development of instrumentation for analytical & medical use; capillary electrophorisis. *Mailing Add:* 4430 School Way Castro Valley CA 94546. *E-Mail:* bob_likuski@b10_rad.com

LILENFELD, HARVEY VICTOR, PHYSICAL CHEMISTRY. *Current Pos:* scientist chem, McDonnell Douglas Corp, 72-80. *Personal Data:* b Brooklyn, NY, Aug 25, 45. *Educ:* Polytech Inst Brooklyn, BS, 66; Mass Inst Technol, PhD(phys chem), 71. *Prof Exp:* Res assoc, Brookhaven Nat Lab, 71-72. *Mem:* Am Chem Soc; Sigma Xi. *Res:* Laser chemistry; kinetics of gas phase reactions. *Mailing Add:* McDonnell Douglas MS1111-041 PO Box 516 St Louis MO 63166-0516. *Fax:* 314-777-1328

LILES, JAMES NEIL, COMPARATIVE PHYSIOLOGY, HUMAN PHYSIOLOGY. *Current Pos:* from asst prof to assoc prof, 60-71, PROF ENTOM, UNIV TENN, 71- *Personal Data:* b Akron, Ohio, Apr 25, 30; m 55; c 3. *Educ:* Miami Univ, BA, 51; Ohio State Univ, MSc, 53, PhD(insect physiol), 56. *Prof Exp:* Asst prof biol, Univ SC, 56-58; res assoc entom, Ohio State Univ, 58-60. *Mem:* Am Inst Biol Sci; Am Soc Zool; Geront Soc; Entom Soc Am; Am Col Sports Med; Sigma Xi. *Res:* Aging in insects; insect nutrient utilization. *Mailing Add:* 2142 Cherokee Blvd Knoxville TN 37919

LILES, SAMUEL LEE, PHYSIOLOGY. *Current Pos:* Instr, 68-70, asst prof, 70-75, ASSOC PROF PHYSIOL, LA STATE UNIV MED CTR, NEW ORLEANS, 75- *Personal Data:* b Texas City, Tex, June 24, 42; m 86; c 1. *Educ:* McNeese State Col, BS, 64; La State Univ Med Ctr, New Orleans, PhD(physiol), 68. *Concurrent Pos:* Nat Inst Neurol Dis & Stroke grant, La State Univ Med Ctr, New Orleans, 70- *Mem:* AAAS; Am Physiol Soc; NY Acad Sci; Soc Neurosci; Sigma Xi. *Res:* Regional neurophysiology; electrophysiological correlates between brain neuronal activity and voluntary motor and sensory function. *Mailing Add:* Dept Physiol La State Univ Med Ctr 1100 Florida Ave New Orleans LA 70119-2799

LILEY, NICHOLAS ROBIN, ZOOLOGY. *Current Pos:* Nat Res Coun Can fel zool, 63-65, from asst prof to assoc prof, 65-78, PROF ZOOL, UNIV BC, 78- *Personal Data:* b Halifax, Eng, Dec 17, 36; m 61. *Educ:* Oxford Univ, BA, 59, DPhil(zool), 64. *Prof Exp:* Animal Behav Soc; Can Soc Zool. *Res:* Comparative ethology and the evolution of behavior; endocrine mechanisms in control of behavior. *Mailing Add:* Dept Zool Univ BC 6270 University Blvd Vancouver BC V6T 1Z4 Can

LILEY, PETER EDWARD, PHYSICS, CHEMICAL ENGINEERING. *Current Pos:* from asst prof to assoc prof, 57-72, PROF MECH ENG, PURDUE UNIV, WEST LAFAYETTE, 72- *Personal Data:* b Barnstaple, Eng, Apr 22, 27; m 63, Elaine E Kull; c Elizabeth E & Rebecca A. *Educ:* Univ London, BSc, 51, PhD(physics), 57; Imp Col, Univ London, dipl, 57. *Prof Exp:* Chem engr, Brit Oxygen Eng, Ltd, 55-57. *Concurrent Pos:* Mem, Thermophysical Properties comt, Am Soc Mech Engrs, 60-87 & chmn, 71-73. *Res:* Thermodynamic and transport properties of matter, principally fluids; cryogenic engineering; high pressure. *Mailing Add:* Sch Mech Eng Purdue Univ West Lafayette IN 47907-1288. *Fax:* 765-494-0539

LILIEHOLM, ROBERT JOHN, LAND USE PLANNING, RISK & UNCERTAINTY. *Current Pos:* asst prof forest mgt & econs, 88-94, honors prof, 94-95, ASSOC PROF, FOREST MGT & ECONS, UTAH STATE UNIV, 94- *Personal Data:* b Morristown, NJ, Apr 9, 60; m 85; c 1. *Educ:* Utah State Univ, BS, 83; La State Univ, MS 84; Univ Calif, Berkeley, PhD(forestry), 88. *Prof Exp:* Expert witness US Dept Justice; consult bus govt. *Concurrent Pos:* Baker-Bidwell res fel Univ Calif, Berkeley, 86 & 87; vis fac, Orgn Trop Studies, 90; fac assoc Lincoln Inst Land Policy, vis fel, 94-95. *Mem:* Soc Am Foresters; Opers Res Soc Am; Int Soc Trop Foresters; Am Econ Asn. *Res:* Integrate economic and ecological approaches to resource management to meet diverse management objectives on a landscape level. *Mailing Add:* Dept Forestry Utah State Univ Logan UT 84322-5215. *Fax:* 435-750-4040

LILIEN, OTTO MICHAEL, GENITOURINARY SURGERY. *Current Pos:* RETIRED. *Personal Data:* b New York, NY, Apr 26, 24; c 6. *Educ:* Jefferson Med Col, MD, 49; Columbia Univ, MA, 60. *Prof Exp:* Lectr zool, Columbia Univ, 56-58; from asst prof to prof urol, State Univ NY Upstate Med Ctr, 61-88, chmn dept, 63-88. *Concurrent Pos:* Nat Cancer Inst trainee, 56-58. *Mem:* AMA; Am Urol Asn; fel Am Col Surg. *Res:* Renal and cell physiology. *Mailing Add:* 5164 NW 26th Circle Boca Raton FL 33496

LILIENFIELD, LAWRENCE SPENCER, MEDICINE, PHYSIOLOGY. *Current Pos:* instr med, Med Sch, Georgetown Univ, 55-57, instr physiol, 56-57, from asst prof to assoc prof med, physiol & biophys, 57-64, chmn, 63-93, PROF PHYSIOL & BIOPHYS, SCHS MED & DENT, GEORGETOWN UNIV, 64- *Personal Data:* b New York, NY, May 5, 27; m 50, Eleanor Russ; c Jan, Adele S & Lisa. *Educ:* Villanova Col, BS, 45; Georgetown Univ, MD, 49, MS, 54, PhD, 56; Am Bd Internal Med, dipl, 57, 74. *Prof Exp:* Intern med, Georgetown Univ Hosp, 49-50, from jr asst resident to sr asst resident, 50-53, asst chief cardiovasc res lab & attend physician, 56; base surgeon, USAF, 51-52. *Concurrent Pos:* Am Heart Asn res fel, 57; USPHS sr res fel, 59 & res career award, 63; attend physician, DC Gen Hosp, 56 & Vet Admin Hosp, 57; estab investr, Am Heart Asn, 58; consult, USPHS, 65-72; vis prof, Univ Saigon; vis prof, Univ Tel-Aviv, 67-68; assoc, Comt Int Exchange Persons, 71-76. *Mem:* AAAS; Biophys Soc; Am Physiol Soc; Soc Exp Biol & Med; Am Soc Clin Invest. *Res:* Transcapillary exchange; hemodynamics; blood distribution in organs; renal concentrating mechanisms; medical education. *Mailing Add:* Dept Physiol Sch Med Georgetown Univ Washington DC 20007-2187

LILL, PATSY HENRY, IMMUNOLOGY, PATHOLOGY. *Current Pos:* ASST PROF PATH, SCH MED, UNIV SC, 77- *Personal Data:* b Mesa, Ariz, July 6, 43. *Educ:* Northwestern Univ, BS, 66; Univ Wis, MST, 72; Chicago Med Sch-Univ Health Sci, PhD(path), 75. *Prof Exp:* Teacher biol, Highland Park High Sch, Ill, 66-70; lab supvr cancer res, Dept Exp Path, Mt Sinai Hosp Med Ctr, 70-75; fel tumor immunology & cancer biol, Frederick Cancer Res Ctr, 75-77. *Concurrent Pos:* Prin investr, Univ SC Res & Prod Scholarship grant, 79 & Nat Cancer Inst grant, 79-82; mem, Charles Louis Davis Doctor Vet Med Found. *Mem:* AAAS; Am Asn Pathologists; Am Asn Cancer Res. *Res:* Tumor immunology; effect of physical and chemical carcinogens on syngeneic tumor growth. *Mailing Add:* Dept Path Univ SC Sch Med Columbia SC 29208-0001

LILLARD, DORRIS ALTON, FOOD CHEMISTRY, BIOCHEMISTRY. *Current Pos:* assoc prof, 68-80, PROF FOOD SCI, UNIV GA, 80- *Personal Data:* b Thompson Station, Tenn, July 17, 36. *Educ:* Middle Tenn State Univ, BS, 58; Ore State Univ, MS, 61, PhD(food sci), 64. *Prof Exp:* Res fel lipid autoxidation, Ore State Univ, 58-64; asst prof food flavor chem, Iowa State Univ, 64-68. *Mem:* AAAS; Am Chem Soc; Am Oil Chem Soc; Inst Food Technol; Am Meat Sci Asn. *Res:* Flavor chemistry of foods; autoxidation of lipids; mycotoxins in foods; food microbiology. *Mailing Add:* Dept Food Sci Univ Ga Athens GA 30602

LILLEGRAVEN, JASON ARTHUR, PALEONTOLOGY, PALEOGEOGRAPHY. *Current Pos:* assoc prof, 76-78, PROF GEOL, UNIV WYO, 78- *Personal Data:* b Mankato, Minn, Oct 11, 38; m 64, 83, Linda E Thompson; c Ture A & Brita A (Crowe). *Educ:* Calif State Col Long Beach, BA, 64; SDak Sch Mines & Technol, MS, 64; Univ Kans, PhD(zool), 68. *Honors & Awards:* Alexander von Humboldt Sr US Scientist Award, 88 & 89. *Prof Exp:* Instr zool, Calif State Col Long Beach, summer, 64; NSF fel paleont, Univ Calif, Berkeley, 68-69; from asst prof to prof zool, San Diego State Univ, 69-75. *Concurrent Pos:* Prog dir, syst biol prog, NSF, 77-78; co-ed, Contrib to Geol, 76-88; assoc dean, Col Arts & Sci, Univ Wyo, 84-85; assoc ed, J Vert Paleo, 93-; co-ed, Rocky Mountain Geol, 96- *Mem:* Paleont Soc; Soc Vert Paleont (vpres & pres, 84-86); Am Soc Mammal; fel Linnean Soc London; Soc Mammalian Evolution; Sigma Xi. *Res:* Paleogeography; Mesozoic and early Cenozoic mammalian paleontology, comparative anatomy and evolution of mammalian reproduction; stratigraphy and structural geology. *Mailing Add:* Dept Geol & Geophys Univ Wyo Laramie WY 82071-3006. *Fax:* 303-766-6679; *E-Mail:* bagpipe@uwyo.edu

LILLEHOJ, EIVIND B, PLANT PHYSIOLOGY, BIOCHEMISTRY. *Current Pos:* RETIRED. *Personal Data:* b Kimballton, Iowa, Aug 11, 28; m 48; c 4. *Educ:* Iowa State Univ, BS, 60, MS, 62, PhD(plant physiol), 64. *Prof Exp:* NIH fel, Carlsberg Lab, Copenhagen, Denmark, 64-65; microbiol, Northern Regional Res Lab, USDA, 65-79 & Southern Regional Res Lab, 79-89; pres, La Jolla Cancer Res Found, 76-89, dir, Cancer Res Ctr, 81-89; Southern Res Lab, Dept Agr New Orleans, 89-90. *Mem:* Fel AAAS; Am Soc Microbiol. *Res:* Fungal physiology; mycotoxins; fermentation; microbial products. *Mailing Add:* PO Box 22 Kimballton IA 51543-0022

LILLEHOJ, HYUN SOON, IMMUNOGENETICS, IMMUNOPARASITOLOGY. *Current Pos:* RES IMMUNOLOGIST, USDA, 84- *Personal Data:* b Seoul, Korea, Mar 1, 49; m 79; c 2. *Educ:* Univ Hartford, BS, 74; Univ Conn, MS, 76; Wayne State Univ, PhD(immunol), 79. *Prof Exp:* Staff fel, Nat Inst Allergy & Infectious Dis, NIH, 81-84. *Concurrent Pos:* Assoc ed, Poultry Sci, 88; adj prof, Univ Del, 89. *Mem:* Am Asn Immunologists; Poultry Sci Asn; Am Asn Avian Vet Pathologists. *Res:* Vaccine against Eimeria; monoclonal antibodies detecting avian lymphocytes and lymphokines; immunopathology and immunogenetics of avian coccidiosis; molecular cloning of avian lymphokines. *Mailing Add:* BARC-E Bldg 1040 PDL LPSI USDA Beltsville MD 20705

LILLELAND, OMUND, pomology; deceased, see previous edition for last biography

LILLELEHT, L(EMBIT) U(NO), THERMAL SCIENCES, ENERGY CONVERSION. *Current Pos:* from assoc prof to prof chem eng, 66-95, EMER PROF CHEM ENG, UNIV VA, 95- *Personal Data:* b Parnu, Estonia, Mar 9, 30; US citizen; m 60, Karen Van Doren; c Erica & Mark L. *Educ:* Univ Del, BChE, 53; Princeton Univ, MSE, 55; Univ Ill, PhD(chem eng), 62. *Prof Exp:* Engr process develop & res, E I du Pont de Nemours & Co, Inc, 54-57; from asst prof to assoc prof chem eng, Univ Alta, 60-66. *Concurrent Pos:* Partner, Assoc Environ Consults, 72-; vis assoc prof, Solar Energy Res Inst, 78-79; lectr solar energy, US Int Comn Agency, 78-79; vis sr scientist, Goddard Space Flight Ctr, NASA, 91-92. *Mem:* Am Inst Chem Engrs; Am Chem Soc; Int Solar Energy Soc; Sigma Xi; AAAS; Am Solar Energy Soc. *Res:* Multiphase flows; air pollution control; nucleation and condensation of refractory vapors in microgravity environment; heat transfer; utilization of solar and other alternative energy resources. *Mailing Add:* Dept Chem Eng Thornton Hall Univ Va Charlottesville VA 22903-2442. *Fax:* 804-982-2658; *E-Mail:* lul@virginia.edu

LILLER, WILLIAM, ARCHAEOASTRONOMY. *Current Pos:* chmn, dept astron, 60-66, prof, 60-70, ROBERT WHEELER WILLSON PROF APPL ASTRON, HARVARD UNIV, 70- *Personal Data:* b Philadelphia, Pa, Apr 1, 27; m 85; c 3. *Educ:* Harvard Univ, AB, 49; Univ Mich, AM, 50, PhD(astron), 53. *Prof Exp:* Mem meteor exped, Harvard Univ, 47-48, supt, 52-53; asst, McMath-Hulbert Observ, Univ Mich, 52, from instr to assoc prof astron, 53-60. *Concurrent Pos:* Guggenheim fel, 64-65; master, Adams House, Harvard Univ, 68-73, head tutor, astron dept, 77-80; vis comnr, Bartol Found, 68-, chmn, 76-79; sr res fel, Isaac Newton Inst, Santiago, Chile, 81- *Mem:* Am Astron Soc; Royal Astron Soc Can; fel AAAS; Am Acad Arts & Sci; Int Astron Union; Brit Astron Asn. *Res:* Photoelectric photometry of planetary nebulae and hot stars; investigation of x-ray sources; spectrophotometry; globular clusters; archaeoastronomy (easter I). *Mailing Add:* Vina del Mar Casilla 5022 Renaca Chile

LILLESAND, THOMAS MARTIN, REMOTE SENSING. *Current Pos:* PROF REMOTE SENSING, UNIV WIS-MADISON, 82- *Personal Data:* b Laurium, Mich, Oct 1, 46; m 68, Theresa Hofmeister; c Mark, Kari & Michael. *Educ:* Univ Wis-Madison, BS, 69, MS, 70, PhD(civil eng), 73. *Honors & Awards:* Alan Gordon Award, Am Soc Photogram & Remote Sensing, 79 & 93, Talbert Abrams Award, 84, Fennell Award, 88. *Prof Exp:* Prof remote sensing, State Univ NY, Syracuse, 73-78 & Univ Minn, 78-82. *Concurrent Pos:* Consult, 73- *Mem:* Fel Am Soc Photogram & Remote Sensing; Am Soc Civil Engrs; Soc Am Foresters; Am Congr Surveying & Mapping; Asn Am Geo. *Res:* Remote sensing and image processing of satellite data for application in agriculture, forestry, water resources and environmental monitoring; space policy; image interpretation; commercial applications of remote sensing. *Mailing Add:* Environ Remote Sensing Ctr Rm 1239 1225 W Dayton St Madison WI 53706. *E-Mail:* tlillesand@facstaff.wisc.edu

LILLEVIK, HANS ANDREAS, BIOCHEMISTRY. *Current Pos:* from instr to assoc prof chem & biochem, 46-70, PROF BIOCHEM, MICH STATE UNIV, 70- *Personal Data:* b Sherman, SDak, Feb 4, 16; m 46; c 4. *Educ:* St Olaf Col, BA, 38; Univ Minn, MS, 40, PhD(biochem), 46. *Prof Exp:* Instr biochem, Univ Minn, 42-44; res chemist, Minn Mining & Mfg Co, 44-45. *Concurrent Pos:* Am Scand Found fel, Carlsberg Lab, Denmark, 47-48. *Mem:* AAAS; Am Chem Soc; Am Soc Biol Chemists; Am Dairy Sci Asn. *Res:* Chemical properties and biological function of proteins and enzymes. *Mailing Add:* 708 Knoll Rd East Lansing MI 48823-2826

LILLEY, ARTHUR EDWARD, astronomy, for more information see previous edition

LILLEY, DAVID GRANTHAM, COMBUSTION AERODYNAMICS, FIRE MODELING. *Current Pos:* assoc prof, 78-82, PROF MECH ENG, OKLA STATE UNIV, 82- *Personal Data:* b Shipley, Eng; US citizen. *Educ:* Sheffield Univ, Eng, BSc, 66, MSc, 67, PhD(chem eng), 70. *Prof Exp:* Lectr math, Sheffield Polytech, Eng, 70-73; sr res assoc, Cranfield Inst Technol, Eng, 73-75; vis assoc prof combustion, Univ Ariz, 75-76; assoc prof mech eng, Concordia Univ, Montreal, 76-78. *Mem:* Assoc fel Am Inst Aeronaut & Astronaut; Am Soc Mech Engrs; Inst Fuel; assoc fel Inst Math & Applns. *Res:* Theoretical combustion aerodynamics; computational fluid dynamics; swirling flows; combustor design; numerical methods; finite difference methods; turbulent reacting flows; heat transfer, fires, flames, and computer simulation. *Mailing Add:* Dept Eng Sci Okla State Univ Main Campus Stillwater OK 74078-0002. *Fax:* 405-744-6487

LILLICH, THOMAS TYLER, BACTERIAL PHYSIOLOGY, HOST PARASITE RELATIONS. *Current Pos:* Asst prof oral & cell biol, Univ Ky, 72-75, act chair oral biol, 75, assoc prof oral biol & microbiol & immunol, 75-81, chair, dept oral biol, 80-88, MEM MICROBIOL GRAD FAC, UNIV KY, 74-, PROF ORAL BIOL & MICROBIOL & IMMUNOL, 81-, CHAIR DEPT ORAL HEALTH SCI, 88- *Personal Data:* b Cincinnati, Ohio, Sept 8, 43; m 65; c 2. *Educ:* Miami Univ, AB, 65; NC State Univ, MS, 68, PhD(microbiol), 70. *Concurrent Pos:* NIH res fel, Univ Ky, 70-72, & Agr Res Serv contractee, 73-76; vis prof, Roy Dent Col, Arhus Denmark, 78; consult, Div Educ Res Prog, Am Asn Med Sch, 77-85, Bd Educ Training, Am Soc Microbiol, 77-79, Univ Tex Dent Br San Antonio, Ohio State Univ Col Dent, 87; comt, Dent Accreditation, Am Dent Asn, 90-91, SIII Univ Grad Sch, 91. *Mem:* Am Soc Microbiol; Am Asn Dent Sch (chair elect, 75-76, 88-89, chair, 76-77, 89-90); Int Asn Dent Res; Sigma Xi; Am Asn Dent Res. *Res:* Effects of antimicrobials on the oral microflora; emphasis on oral microflora of medically comprised patients; identification and ratios of organisms; control with tropical antimicrobials to reduce systematic disease; host response to microbial challenge. *Mailing Add:* Dept Oral Health Sci Col Dent Univ Ky Lexington KY 40536-0084

LILLIE, CHARLES FREDERICK, AERONAUTICAL ENGINEERING, ASTRONAUTICAL ENGINEERING. *Current Pos:* sr systs engr, Fed Systs Div, 79-, ADVAN PROG PROJ MGR, CIVIL & INT SYSTS DIV, TRW SPACE & ELECTRONICS GROUP. *Personal Data:* b Indianola, Iowa, Feb 20, 36; wid; c 3. *Educ:* Iowa State Univ, BS, 57; Univ Wis, Madison, PhD(astrophys), 68. *Prof Exp:* Instr eng, NASA Flight Res Ctr, Edwards, Calif, 60-62; teaching asst, Dept Astron, Univ Wis, 62-64, res asst, Washburn Observ, 64-68, proj assoc, Space Astrophys Lab, 68-70; from asst prof to assoc prof physics & astrophys, Univ Colo, 70-77, assoc prof astrogeophys, Attendant Rank & fel Lab Atmospheric & Space Physics, 77-79. *Concurrent Pos:* Prin investr, Voyager Photopolarimeter Exp, 72-79; co-investr, Apollo 17 Ultraviolet Spectrometer Exp, 72-74; team mem, Large Space Telescope Inst Definition Team High Resol Spectrograph, 73-75. *Mem:* Am Astron Soc; AAAS; Soc Photo-Optical Instrumentation Engrs; Int Astron Union; Am Inst Aeronaut & Astronaut; Air Force Asn. *Res:* Surface brightness of the night sky, zodiacal light, diffuse galactic light, interstellar radiation density, extragalactic light; cometary physics, ultraviolet spectroscopy of stars and nebulae; spacecraft design, RF environment, contamination; spacecraft operations and on orbit servicing; optics. *Mailing Add:* TRW Space & Electronics Group One Space Park MS-2978 Redondo Beach CA 90278

LILLIE, JOHN HOWARD, ANATOMY, DENTISTRY. *Current Pos:* PROF ANAT, SCH MED & ASSOC PROF, SCH DENT, UNIV MICH, ANN ARBOR, 72-, STAFF MEM, DENT RES INST, 72- *Personal Data:* b Oak Park, Ill, Dec 16, 40; m 63; c 2. *Educ:* Univ Mich, DDS, 66, PhD(anat), 72. *Concurrent Pos:* Admin, Sch Dent. *Mem:* Am Soc Cell Biol; Am Asn Anat. *Res:* Cellular control mechanisms in exocrine secretion and epithelia-connective tissue interactions; features of synthesis and control in the production of basal lamina constituents. *Mailing Add:* Dept Anat & Cell Biol Univ Mich Rm 4818 Med Sch 11 Ann Arbor MI 48109-0616

LILLIE, ROBERT JONES, POULTRY NUTRITION. *Current Pos:* RETIRED. *Personal Data:* b Rochester, Minn, Apr 15, 21; m 46, Mary Guers; c Elizabeth & Kathryn. *Educ:* Pa State Col, BS, 44; Univ Md, MS, 46, PhD(poultry nutrit), 49. *Honors & Awards:* Am Poultry Sci Asn Award, 50; Commission Award, US Civil Serv, 76. *Prof Exp:* Asst, Poultry Dept, Univ Md, 45-47; poultry husbandman, Animal & Poultry Husb Res Br, USDA, 47-72, res animal scientist, Nonruminant Animal Nutrit Lab, Nutrit Inst, Sci & Educ Admin Agr Res, 72-78. *Concurrent Pos:* Mem stand diet subcomt, Nat Res Coun, 54. *Mem:* Am Poultry Sci Asn; Am Inst Nutrit; Worlds Poultry Cong. *Res:* Vitamins, antibiotics, surfactants, arsenicals, unidentified factors, proteins and amino acids; pesticides; reproductive efficiency; air pollutants affecting poultry; trace minerals in swine. *Mailing Add:* Cornwall Manor PO Box 125 Cornwall PA 17016-0125

LILLIEFORS, HUBERT W, STATISTICS. *Current Pos:* from instr to assoc prof, 62-67, PROF STATIST, GEORGE WASHINGTON UNIV, 67- *Personal Data:* b Reading, Pa, June 14, 28; m 80; c 2. *Educ:* George Washington Univ, BA, 52, PhD(statist), 64; Mich State Univ, MA, 53. *Prof Exp:* Mathematician, Diamond Ord Fuze Labs, 53-55; sr scientist opers res, Lockheed Missile Systs Div, 55-56, opers analyst, Opers Eval Group, 56-57; mathematician opers res, Appl Physics Lab, Johns Hopkins Univ, 57-64. *Mem:* Am Statist Asn; Inst Math Statist. *Res:* Nonparametric statistics; statistical inference. *Mailing Add:* Dept Statist George Washington Univ 2201 G St NW Washington DC 20052-4211

LILLIEN, IRVING, ORGANIC CHEMISTRY, COMPUTER SCIENCES. *Current Pos:* RETIRED. *Personal Data:* b New York, NY, Feb 2, 29. *Educ:* Univ Denver, BS, 50; Purdue Univ, MS, 52; Polytech Inst NY, PhD(org chem), 59. *Prof Exp:* Fel org chem, Wayne State Univ, 59-61; asst prof, Georgetown Univ, 61-62; asst prof, Univ Miami, 62-65, Sch Med, 65-67; assoc prof, Marshall Univ, 67-69; from assoc prof to prof org chem, Miami-Dade Community Col, 69-96. *Concurrent Pos:* Air Force Off Sci & Res grant, 63-65. *Mem:* AAAS; Am Chem Soc; Royal Soc Chem; Inst Elec & Electronics Engrs. *Res:* Physical-organic chemistry; mechanisms of organic reactions; chemistry and conformation of small and medium size rings; science education and administration. *Mailing Add:* Dept Chem Miami-Dade Community Col 11011 SW 104 St Miami FL 33176. *E-Mail:* irvlillien@worldnet.att.net

LILLINGTON, GLEN ALAN, PULMONARY MEDICINE, CONTINUING MEDICAL EDUCATION. *Current Pos:* PROF MED, SCH MED, UNIV CALIF, DAVIS, 73- *Personal Data:* b Winnipeg, Can, Oct 20, 26; m 57; c Karlin, Peter & Barry. *Educ:* Univ Manitoba, BSc, 46, MD, 51; Univ Minn, MS, 57; FRCP, 59; FACP, 67. *Prof Exp:* Asst staff med, Mayo Clin & Found, 57-58; lectr, Univ Manitoba Fac Med, 58-60; asst clin prof, Sch Med, Stanford Univ, 60-73. *Concurrent Pos:* Res assoc, Palo Alto Med Res Found, 65-73; consult, Rand Corp, Santa Monica, 69-70; med dir respiratory therapy, Sch Respiratory Therapy, Foothill Col, 72-73; travelling fel, Webb-Waring Inst, Denver, 73-74; actg chmn, Dept Med, Med Sch, Univ Calif, Davis, 79-80, chief staff, 79-80, dir residency med, Med Ctr, 79-80, prof med, 75-81, chief pulmonary, critical care div, 75-87. *Mem:* Am Col Physicians. *Res:* Experimental emphysema; pulmonary mechanics; differential diagnosis of pulmonary diseases based on roentgenographic patterns; decision analysis in medicine. *Mailing Add:* Med Ctr Univ Calif 4301 X St Sacramento CA 95817. *Fax:* 916-734-7924

LILLWITZ, LAWRENCE DALE, INDUSTRIAL ORGANIC CHEMISTRY, INDUSTRIAL PROCESS CHEMISTRY. *Current Pos:* res chemist, 77-79, staff res chemist, 79-81, sr res chemist, 81-86, ASSOC RES CHEMIST, AMOCO CHEM CO, 86- *Personal Data:* b Hinsdale, Ill, June 1, 44; m 68; c 5. *Educ:* Ill Benedictine Col, BS, 66; Univ Notre Dame, PhD(org chem), 70. *Prof Exp:* Group leader, Chem Div, Quaker Oats Co, 70-77. *Mem:* Am Chem Soc. *Res:* Monomer synthesis; organic reaction mechanisms; homogeneous and heterogeneous catalysis. *Mailing Add:* 773 Crescent Blvd Glen Ellyn IL 60137-4263

LILLY, ARNYS CLIFTON, JR, PHYSICS. *Current Pos:* res physicist, Phillip Morris Res Ctr, 65-67, sr scientist, Physics Div, 67-74, assoc prin scientist, 74-81, prin scientist, 81-84, res fel, 84-96, VPRES, TECHNOL ASSESSMENT, PHILLIP MORRIS RES CTR, 96- *Personal Data:* b Beckley, WVa, June 3, 34; m 56, Agnes Micou; c Greg, Diane & Jim. *Educ:* Va Polytech Inst, BS, 57, PhD, 89; Carnegie Inst Technol, MS, 63; Va Polytech Inst, PhD, 89. *Prof Exp:* Res physicist, Gulf Res & Develop Co, Pa, 57-65. *Mem:* Am Phys Soc; Sigma Xi. *Res:* Ion & electron optics; dielectric theory and experiment; electrostatics and organic conduction; space charge in insulators; thermal physics; combustion; laser processing; fluid mechanics; quantum chemistry; theoretical physics; theory of liquids. *Mailing Add:* Vpres Technol Assessment Philip Morris Res Ctr PO Box 26583 Richmond VA 23261

LILLY, DOUGLAS KEITH, MESOSCALE DYNAMICS. *Current Pos:* RETIRED. *Personal Data:* b San Francisco, Calif, June 16, 29; m 54; c 3. *Educ:* Stanford Univ, BS, 50; Fla State Univ, MS, 54, PhD(meteorol), 59. *Honors & Awards:* Rossby Medal, Am Meteorol Soc, 86; Symons Mem Medal, Royal Meteorol Soc, UK, 93. *Prof Exp:* Res meteorologist, US Weather Bur, 58-65; prog scientist, Nat Ctr Atmospheric Res, 65-73, sr scientist, 73-82; dir, Ctr Anal & Prediction Storms, Univ Okla, 89-94, Robert Lowrey Prof Meteorol, 92-95. *Mem:* Fel Am Meteorol Soc; Royal Meteorol Soc. *Res:* Atmospheric convection, turbulence and gravity waves; numerical simulation of meteorological flows. *Mailing Add:* Sch Meteorol Univ Okla Main Campus Norman OK 73019. *Fax:* 405-325-7689; *E-Mail:* dlilly@ou.edu

LILLY, FRANK, genetics, oncology; deceased, see previous edition for last biography

LILLY, JOHN RUSSELL, pediatric surgery; deceased, see previous edition for last biography

LILLY, PERCY LANE, PLANT TAXONOMY. *Current Pos:* RETIRED. *Personal Data:* b Spanishburg, WVa, July 14, 27; m 51; c 4. *Educ:* Concord Col, BS, 50; Univ WVa, MS, 51; Pa State Univ, PhD, 57. *Prof Exp:* Instr biol, Salem Col, WVa, 51-53; from asst prof to prof biol, Heidelberg Col, 56-, chmn dept, 65- *Concurrent Pos:* Spec field staff mem, Rockefeller Found, Colombia, 68-69. *Mem:* AAAS; Bot Soc Am. *Res:* Plant genetics and microbiology; nitrogen fixation in Azotobacter; tropical botany. *Mailing Add:* 110 Mohawk St Tiffin OH 44883

LILLYA, CLIFFORD PETER, ORGANIC CHEMISTRY. *Current Pos:* Staff assoc, 63-64, from asst prof to assoc prof, 64-73, PROF CHEM, UNIV MASS, AMHERST, 73- *Personal Data:* b Chicago, Ill, May 23, 37; m 62; c 2. *Educ:* Kalamazoo Col, AB, 59; Harvard Univ, PhD(chem), 64. *Concurrent Pos:* Fel, Woodrow Wilson, 59, NSF, 59-63, Alfred P Sloan Found, 69-71; vis scholar, Univ Calif, Los Angeles, 70-71, Stanford Univ, 78. *Mem:* Am Chem Soc; AAAS. *Res:* Organic polymers; liquid crystals; nitramines. *Mailing Add:* Dept Chem Lederle GRC Tower Univ Mass Box 34510 Amherst MA 01003-4510

LILLYWHITE, HARVEY B, COMPARATIVE PYHSIOLOGY, PHYSIOLOGICAL ECOLOGY. *Current Pos:* PROF ZOOL, UNIV FLA, GAINESVILLE, 84- *Personal Data:* b Nogales, Ariz, Dec 1, 43; m 67, Jamie Johnson; c Steven M & Shauna R. *Educ:* Univ Calif, Riverside, BA, 66; Univ Calif, Los Angeles, MA, 67, PhD(zool), 70. *Prof Exp:* Fel zool, Univ Calif, Berkeley, 70-71; from asst prof to prof physiol, Univ Kans, Lawrence, 71-84. *Concurrent Pos:* Vis lectr, Monash Univ, Clayton, Victoria, Australia, 75-76; sect ed, Copeia, 78-82, Ecol & Ecol Monographs, 82-86; secy nominating comt, Ecol Soc Am, 78-79; vis scientist, Scripps Inst Oceanog, La Jolla, Calif, 79-80; res fel, San Diego Zoo & Wild Animal Park, 79-80; mem publ policy comt, Am Soc Ichthyologists & Herpetologists, 80-82; res fel, Univ New Eng, Armidale, NSW, Australia, 91; Fulbright fel, India, 92-93; Nat Res Coun sr res assoc, NASA-Ames Res Ctr, 92-97. *Mem:* Soc Integrative & Comp Biol; Am Physiol Soc; Ecol Soc Am; Am Soc Ichthyologists & Herpetologists; Soc Study Amphibians & Reptiles; AAAS. *Res:* Comparative and ecological physiology of vertebrates, especially amphibians and reptiles; cardiovascular adaptations of reptiles; functional morphology of vertebrate integument; water and thermal relations; ecology of fire disturbance and animal coloration. *Mailing Add:* Dept Zool Univ Fla Bartram Hall Gainesville FL 32611. *Fax:* 352-392-3704; *E-Mail:* hbl@zoo.ufl.edu

LIM, ALEXANDER TE, HEAT TRANSFER & THERMAL SCIENCES, AIR CONDITIONING & REFRIGERATION. *Current Pos:* DIR TECHNOL, 87-93, DIR QUAL ASSURANCE & TECHNOL, INTER CITY PROD CORP, 93- *Personal Data:* b Manila, Philippines, June 17, 42; US citizen; m 71; c Gregory & Karen. *Educ:* Univ St Thomas, BS, 64; Duke Univ, MS, 69. *Prof Exp:* Instr, Col Eng, Ateneo de Manila Univ, 64-66; teaching asst undergrad eng, Mech Eng Dept, Duke Univ, 66-69; sr engr, Res & Develop Div, Carrier Corp, 69-76, mgr develop eng, Room Air Opers, 76-80, dir eng, Light Residential Div, 80-85; dir res & develop, ICG Keeprite Corp, 85-86, vpres, 86-87. *Concurrent Pos:* comt mem, Am Soc Heating, Refrig & Air Conditioning Engrs, Comt, 74-79; comt mem, Am Home Appliance Mfrs Eng Comt, 78-83 & 88-91; comt mem, Air Conditioning &

Refrig Inst Packaged Terminal Air Conditioning Eng Comt, 85-91, mem, Res & Technol Comt, 89-91; chmn, Air Conditioning & Refrig Inst Packaged Terminal Air- Conditioning Eng Comt, 93- *Mem:* Am Soc Mech Engrs; Am Soc Heating, Refrig & Air Conditioning Engrs; Air Conditioning & Refrig Inst. *Res:* Air-side and refrigerant-side heat and mass transfer as applied to air-conditioning and refrigeration; new concepts and cycles for air-conditioning application; granted four patents. *Mailing Add:* 1214 Choctaw Trail Brentwood TN 37027

LIM, DANIEL V, PATHOGENIC MICROBIOLOGY, ENVIRONMENTAL MICROBIOLOGY. *Current Pos:* from asst prof to assoc prof microbiol, Univ SFla, 76-87, actg chmn biol, 83-85, dir, Inst Biomolecular Sci, 88-93, PROF MICROBIOL, UNIV SFLA, 87- *Personal Data:* b Houston, Tex, Apr 15, 48; m 73, Carol Lee. *Educ:* Rice Univ, BA, 70; Tex A&M Univ, PhD(microbiol), 73. *Honors & Awards:* Searle/Donald Richardson Mem Award, Am Col Obstet & Gynec, 87; Fla Gov's Award for Outstanding Contrib in Sci & Technol, 90. *Prof Exp:* Fel, Baylor Col Med, 73-76. *Concurrent Pos:* Consult, Pharmacia Diag-Pharmacia AB, 79-86, Life Technols, Inc-Gibco Labs, 82-86, The Conservancy, 80-84, Tilly & Graves, PA, 90-92; assoc fac mem, Tampa Gen Hosp, 82-88; pres, Micro Concepts Res Corp, 86-; grad fel panel, Nat Res Coun/NSF, 89-92; pres, southeastern br, Am Soc Microbiol, 90-91. *Mem:* Am Soc Microbiol; Inter-Am Soc Chemother (vpres, 83-88); AAAS; Sigma Xi; fel Am Acad Microbiol. *Res:* The virulence of bacteria and rapid diagnosis of bacterial diseases; group B streptococci, Neisseria gonorrhoeae, and environmental pathogens; invented Lim group B strep broth; author of two books. *Mailing Add:* Dept Biol LIF136 Univ SFla Tampa FL 33620-5150. *Fax:* 813-974-3263; *E-Mail:* lim@chuma.cas.usf.edu

LIM, DAVID J, OTOLARYNGOLOGY, ELECTRON MICROSCOPY. *Current Pos:* CHIEF OTOLARYNGOL BIOL, NIDCD, NIH, ROCKVILLE, MD. *Personal Data:* b Seoul, Korea, Nov 27, 35; US citizen; m 66; c 2. *Educ:* Yonsei Univ, Korea, AB, 55, MD, 60. *Honors & Awards:* First Award Scientific Exhibit, Am Acad Ophthal & Otolaryngal, 72. *Prof Exp:* Intern, Nat Med Ctr, Seoul, Korea, 60-61; resident otolaryngol, 61-64; res assoc, Col Med, Ohio State Univ, 66-67; from asst prof to assoc prof, 67-76, prof otolaryngol, 76- & emer prof anat, 77- *Concurrent Pos:* Spec fel otol res, Mass Eye & Ear Infirmary & Harvard Med Sch, 65-66; dir, Otol Res Labs, Ohio State Univ, 67-; mem task force, Am Acad Ophthal & Otolaryngol & Am Bd Otolaryngol, 69-72; consult comt res otolaryngol, Am Acad Ophthal & Otolaryngol, 77-; mem ad hoc adv comt, Commun Disorders Prog, Nat Inst Neurol & Commun Disorders & Stroke, 76-79; mem sci rev comt, Deafness Res Found, 77-80; mem commun sci study sect, NIH, 77; mem, Nat Adv Neurol & Commun Disorders & Stroke Coun, NIH, 79-83; adv-at-large, Comt Hearing, Bioacoust & Biomech, Nat Res Coun, 80-; mem bd dir, Deafness Res Found, 80-; prin investr, various grants & contracts, 69-; Fogarty sr Int & vis scientist, Swed Med Res Coun, Karolinska Inst, 82. *Mem:* Am Acad Otolaryngol; Soc Neurosci; Am Otol Soc; Asn Res Otolaryngol (secy-treas, 73-75, pres, 76-77, past pres & prog chair, 77-78, ed hist, 80-); Barany Soc; Histochem Soc; Am Soc Cell Biol; Soc Mucosal Immunol. *Res:* Investigation of the ear as to the normal function and disorders of hearing and balance with the use of light and electron microscopy; immunocytochemistry; immunochemistry and microbiology. *Mailing Add:* House Ear Inst 2100 W Third St Los Angeles CA 90057

LIM, EDWARD C, PHYSICAL CHEMISTRY. *Current Pos:* GOODYEAR PROF CHEM, UNIV AKRON, 89- *Personal Data:* b Seoul, Korea, Nov 17, 32; nat US; m 58, Bee Tuan Uy; c Diane M & Janice C. *Educ:* St Procopius Col, BS, 54; Okla State Univ, MS, 57, PhD(chem), 59. *Prof Exp:* Instr phys chem, Loyola Univ, Ill, 58-60, from asst prof to prof, 60-68; prof chem, Wayne State Univ, 68-89. *Concurrent Pos:* Ed, Excited States, 74-; ed-in-charge, Lasers in Chem, 92- *Mem:* Fel Am Phys Soc; Am Chem Soc. *Res:* Molecular electronic spectroscopy; molecular photophysics. *Mailing Add:* Dept Chem Univ Akron Akron OH 44325-3601. *Fax:* 330-972-6407; *E-Mail:* elim@uakron.edu

LIM, H(ENRY) C(HOL), CHEMICAL & BIOCHEMICAL ENGINEERING. *Current Pos:* PROF & CHMN, CHEM & BIOCHEM ENG & PROF MICROBIOL & MOLECULAR GENETICS, UNIV CALIF, IRVINE, 87- *Personal Data:* b Seoul, Korea, Oct 24, 35; US citizen; m 59, Sun Boo; c David, Carol & Michael. *Educ:* Okla State Univ, BS, 57; Univ Mich, MSE, 59; Northwestern Univ, PhD(chem eng), 67. *Honors & Awards:* Food Pharmaceut & Bioeng Award, Am Inst Chem Eng, 87. *Prof Exp:* Process develop engr, Pfizer, Inc, 59-63; from asst prof to prof chem eng, Purdue Univ, 66-87. *Concurrent Pos:* Vis scholar, Calif Inst Technol, 77. *Mem:* Am Inst Chem Engrs; Am Soc Microbiol; Am Chem Soc; Inst Food Technologists. *Res:* Modelling, optimization and control of chemical and biochemical processes; biological reactor engineering; cellular growth kenetics; optimal operating strategies for fed-batch bioreactors of recombinant cells with regulated promoters; on-line optimization of continuous flow bioreactors with little prior knowledge; engineering of recombinant cell product expression and secretion. *Mailing Add:* Chem Eng Univ Calif Irvine CA 92717-0001. *Fax:* 714-725-2541

LIM, HONG SEH, IMAGE PROCESSING, COMPUTER VISION. *Current Pos:* PRES, MIL KERED INC, 92- *Personal Data:* b Hong Kong, Aug 5, 58; m 84; c 3. *Educ:* Univ Hong Kong, BSc, 81; Stanford Univ, MS(elec eng) & MS(opers res), 83, MS & PhD(elec eng), 87. *Prof Exp:* Res asst, Stanford Univ, 82-87; staff mem, Los Angeles Sci Ctr, IBM, 87-90 & Palo Alto Sci Ctr, 90-91; lang mgr, Calera Recognition Systs, 91-92. *Concurrent Pos:* Prin investr, AKM Assocs, 85-87; lectr, Univ Calif, Los Angeles, 89; consult, Univ Calif, San Francisco, 90-91. *Mem:* Sr mem Inst Elec & Electronics Engrs; Asn Comput Mach; Optical Soc Am; Opers Res Soc Am; Inst Mgt Sci. *Res:* Application of image processing and computer vision to target identification, object recognition, industrial parts identification and manufacturing inspection; character recognition; multimedia, video compression. *Mailing Add:* Mil Kered Inc 101 First St Suite 552 Los Altos CA 94022. *E-Mail:* lim@btr.com

LIM, JAMES KHAI-JIN, PHARMACEUTICS. *Current Pos:* From asst prof to assoc prof, 66-76, PROF PHARM, SCH PHARM, WVA UNIV, 76- *Personal Data:* b Batavia, Java, March 11, 33; US citizen; m 62; c 3. *Educ:* Univ Malaya, Singapore, BPharm, 58; Univ NC, MS, 62, PhD(pharmaceut), 65. *Concurrent Pos:* Res fel, Biochem Dept, Univ NC, 65-66; vis scientist, Lipid Dept, Mend Div, Oak Ridge, 65-66; dent res, Inst Advan Educ Dent Res, 71. *Mem:* Am Pharmaceut Asn; Am Asn Pharmaceut Sci; Am Asn Col Pharm; Am Asn Dent Res; Malayan Pharmaceut Asn; Soc Cosmetic Chemists. *Res:* Pharmaceutical formulations for solubilization and stability of drugs; caries research involving in vitro pellicle and streptococci plaque; blood cholesterol and triglyceride levels with fiber diets; viscosity measurements of semisolids; tableting formulations. *Mailing Add:* Sch Pharm Health Sci Ctr WVa Univ Morgantown WV 26506

LIM, JOHNG KI, GENETICS. *Current Pos:* From asst prof to assoc prof, 63-69, PROF BIOL, UNIV WIS-EAU CLAIRE, 69- *Personal Data:* b Seoul, Korea, Feb 12, 30. *Educ:* Univ Minn, BS, 58, MS, 60, PhD(genetics), 64. *Concurrent Pos:* Vis prof, Dept of Med Genetics, Univ Wis-Madison, 77-78. *Mem:* AAAS; Genetics Soc Am; Environ Mutagen Soc; Sigma Xi. *Res:* Chemical mutagenesis; cytogenetics. *Mailing Add:* Dept Biol Univ Wis Eau Claire WI 54701

LIM, RAMON (KHE SIONG), NEUROCHEMISTRY. *Current Pos:* PROF & DIR NEUROL & NEUROCHEM, UNIV IOWA, 81- *Personal Data:* b Cebu, Philippines, Feb 5, 33; m 61, Victoria Sy; c Jennifer, Wendell & Caroline. *Educ:* Univ Santo Tomas, Manila, MD, 58; Univ Pa, PhD(biochem), 66. *Prof Exp:* Intern, Long Island Col Hosp, NY, 59-60; USPHS trainee & fel, Univ Pa, 60-66; asst res biochemist, Ment Health Res Inst, Univ Mich, 66-69; asst prof neurosurg & biochem, Brain Res Inst & Sect Neurosurg, Univ Chicago, 69-76, assoc prof neurochem, 76-81. *Concurrent Pos:* NIMH spec res fel, 68-69; Int Soc Neurochem lectureship, China, 86; vis prof, Univ Santo Tomas, Manila, 74, Cent Univ Venezuela, Caracas, 78, Nat Yang-Ming Med Col, Taipei, 87. *Mem:* AAAS; Am Soc Neurochem; Int Soc Neurochem; Am Soc Biochem & Molecular Biol; Soc Neurosci; Am Soc Cell Biol; Int Soc Develop Neursci. *Res:* Brain proteins and peptides; tissue culture; growth and maturation of brain cells; signal transduction; molecular biology. *Mailing Add:* 118 Richards St Iowa City IA 52246-3516. *Fax:* 319-356-4505

LIM, SOON-SIK, GAS LASERS, NUCLEAR PUMPED GAS LASERS. *Current Pos:* from asst prof to assoc prof, 81-91, PROF CHEM ENG, YOUNGSTOWN STATE UNIV, 91- *Personal Data:* b Kaesung, Korea, Mar 2, 44; US citizen; m 73, Jae Yeon You; c Steve & Anna. *Educ:* Yonsei Univ, BS, 71; Wayne State Univ, MS, 75, PhD(chem eng), 81. *Prof Exp:* Res engr, Pac Chem Co, 70-73. *Mem:* Am Inst Chem Engrs; Am Chem Soc; Am Soc Eng Educ; Sigma Xi. *Res:* Hazardous waste incineration calculation. *Mailing Add:* 3166 Hummingbird Youngstown OH 44514. *E-Mail:* sslim@cc.ysu.edu

LIM, SUNG MAN, PLANT PATHOLOGY. *Current Pos:* PLANT PATHOLOGIST, USDA, 77- *Personal Data:* US citizen; m 68; c 2. *Educ:* Seoul Univ, Korea, MS, 59; Miss State Univ, MS, 63; Mich State Univ, PhD(crop sci & plant path), 66. *Honors & Awards:* Soybean Researcher's Award, Am Soybean Asn; Distinguished Sci Award, Minist Sci & Technol, Korea. *Prof Exp:* Agronomist, Crop Exp Sta, Suwon, Korea, 60-61; res asst, Miss State Univ, 61-63 & Mich State Univ, 63-66; res assoc, Univ Ill, 67-71, asst prof, plant path, 71-77, assoc prof, 77-83, prof, 83- *Concurrent Pos:* Assoc ed, Plant Dis; mem, Soybean Germplasm Adv Comt, USDA; assoc ed & sr ed, Phytopath. *Mem:* Fel Am Phytopath Soc; Am Genetic Asn; Am Soc Agron; Crop Sci Soc Am; fel AAAS. *Res:* Epidemics of plant diseases; genetics of host-pathogen interactions. *Mailing Add:* 1782 Rockwood Trail Univ Ark PTSC217 Fayetteville AR 72701-1202

LIM, TECK-KAH, THEORETICAL NUCLEAR PHYSICS, THEORETICAL ATOMIC & MOLECULAR PHYSICS. *Current Pos:* asst prof physics, 70-75, assoc prof, 75-82, PROF PHYSICS & ATMOSPHERIC SCI, DREXEL UNIV, 82- *Personal Data:* b Malacca, Malaysia, Dec 1, 42; m 66, Nyok-Kheng Liew; c Kian-Tat & Al-Li. *Educ:* Univ Adelaide, BS, 64, PhD(nuclear physics), 68. *Prof Exp:* Lectr math, Univ Malaya, 68; res assoc nuclear physics, Fla State Univ, 68-70. *Concurrent Pos:* Secy-treas, Topical Group, few-body systs, Am Phys Soc; consult, UN Develop Prog, 85. *Mem:* Fel Am Phys Soc. *Res:* Few-nucleon problem; spin-polarized quantum systems; chemical physics; molecular physics; computers in education. *Mailing Add:* Dept Physics Drexel Univ Philadelphia PA 19104. *Fax:* 215-895-5934; *E-Mail:* limtk@duvm.ocs.drexel.edu

LIM, TEONG CHENG, APPLIED PHYSICS, ELECTRICAL ENGINEERING. *Current Pos:* PRES, AMERASIA TECHNOL, INC. *Personal Data:* b Penang, Malaysia, Oct 4, 39; m 66. *Educ:* Nat Taiwan Univ, BSc, 63; Ottawa Univ, MSc, 64; McGill Univ, PhD(elec eng), 68. *Prof Exp:* Elec engr, Malayan Racing Asn, 62-63; res asst elec eng, Ottawa Univ, 63-64; electronic engr, Can Marconi Co, Montreal, 65; res asst elec eng, McGill Univ, 65-68; Nat Res Coun Can fel, Imp Col, Univ London, 68-70; mem tech staff, Sci Ctr, NAm Rockwell Corp, 70-74, group leader, 75-80, mgr, Sci Ctr, Rockwell Int, 80- *Mem:* Sr mem Inst Elec & Electronics Engrs; Brit Inst Elec Engrs. *Res:* Physics of ferroelectric and display materials and devices. *Mailing Add:* Amerasia Technol Inc 2307 Townsgate Rd Westlake Village CA 91361

LIM, YOUNG WOON (PETER), SURFACE CHEMISTRY, COLLOID CHEMISTRY. *Current Pos:* UNION CAMP, FRANKLIN, 92- *Personal Data:* b Seoul, Korea, Oct 25, 35; m 68; c 3. *Educ:* Ohio Wesleyan Univ, AB, 57; Univ Dayton, MS, 63; State Univ NY Col Forestry, Syracuse, PhD(polymer chem), 69. *Prof Exp:* Res chemist, Paper Res Dept, NCR Corp, 69-71; group leader analytical chem, Appleton Papers Div, 71-74; res assoc chem, Tissue & Towel Res & Develop, Am Consumer Prod, Am Can Co, Neenah, Wis, 74-77; proj leader, Crown Zellerbach Cent Res, Camas, Wash, 77-82; Boise Cascade, 82-92. *Mem:* Am Chem Soc; Tech Asn Pulp & Paper Indust. *Res:* Application of surface and colloid chemistry to pulp and paper research and development; morphology of cellulose and synthetic fibers; functional coatings; microencapsulation. *Mailing Add:* 1318 Meade Dr Suffolk VA 23434

LIMA, GAIL M, INVERTEBRATE ZOOLOGY. *Current Pos:* ASST PROF BIOL, ILL WESLEYAN UNIV, 87- *Personal Data:* b Cambridge, Mass, July 2, 57. *Educ:* Wash Univ, St Louis, AB, 79; Tufts Univ, Medford, Mass, MS, 83; Rutgers Univ, New Brunswick, PhD(zool), 87. *Concurrent Pos:* Res assoc, Boshe Inst, 91- *Mem:* Am Soc Zoologists; Am Malacological Union; Sigma Xi; Nat Asn Biol Teachers; Asn Biol Lab Educ. *Res:* Invertebrate reproduction and development; larval biology; ecological and developmental implications of molluscan shell morphology; zebra mussel biology. *Mailing Add:* 68 Lincoln St Dover Foxcroft ME 04426. *Fax:* 309-556-3411; *E-Mail:* limag@vmd.cso.uiuc.edu

LIMA, JOHN J, CLINICAL PHARMACOKINETICS. *Current Pos:* RETIRED. *Personal Data:* b New Bedford, Mass, June 19, 40; c 2. *Educ:* Bridgewater State Col, BSEd, 62; Mass Col Pharm, BS, 67; Univ Mich, PharmD, 77. *Prof Exp:* Pharm dir, Al Jordan Health Ctr, 72-75; fel, State Univ NY, Buffalo, 76-77, res assoc, 77-78; assoc prof pharm, Ohio State Univ, 79-93. *Mem:* Am Asn Pharmaceut Scientist; Am Col Clin Pharm; Am Asn Cols Pharm. *Res:* Modelling time course; extent and mechanisms associated with drug/hormone induced adaptations, specifically hypersensitivity to adrenergic stimulation folling chronic treatment with certain drugs. *Mailing Add:* 1525 Bethel Rd Apt 100 Columbus OH 43220

LIMB, JOHN ORMOND, communications, electrical engineering, for more information see previous edition

LIMBERT, DAVID EDWIN, DYNAMIC SYSTEMS, CONTROL ENGINEERING. *Current Pos:* Asst prof to assoc prof, 69-83, PROF MECH ENG, UNIV NH, 83- *Personal Data:* b Omaha, Nebr, Oct 21, 42; m 72; c 2. *Educ:* Iowa State Univ, BS, 64; Case Inst Technol, MS, 65; Case Western Res Univ, PhD(control eng), 69. *Honors & Awards:* Rail Transp Award, Am Soc Mech Engrs, 91. *Concurrent Pos:* Dir, DEL Eng, 71- *Mem:* Am Soc Mech Engrs; Inst Elec & Electronics Engrs; Air Brake Asn; Sigma Xi. *Res:* Modeling and computer simulation of freight train air brake systems including piping and valves; boundary element simulation of electric fields for electroplating; communication aids for handicapped; electric wheel chair controller design. *Mailing Add:* Dept Mech Eng Kingsbury Hall Univ NH Durham NH 03824

LIMBERT, DOUGLAS A(LAN), INSTRUMENTED SYSTEM & COMPONENT TESTING, SYSTEM DYNAMICS. *Current Pos:* managing engr, 84-90, SR MANAGING ENGR, FAILURE ANALYSIS ASSOCS, INC, 90- *Personal Data:* b Council Bluffs, Iowa, Feb 6, 48. *Educ:* Mass Inst Technol, SB & SM, 70, ScD, 77. *Prof Exp:* Instr mech eng, Mass Inst Technol, 74-76; asst prof mech eng, Ariz State Univ, 77-84. *Concurrent Pos:* Assoc ed, Am Soc Mech Engrs Trans: J Dynamic Systs & Control, 84-87. *Mem:* Sigma Xi; Am Soc Mech Engrs; Inst Elec & Electronic Engrs; Soc Automotive Engrs. *Res:* Modeling, dynamics and control of physical systems; advanced ground transportation suspensions; test engineering; instrumentation; automotive engineering; failure analysis. *Mailing Add:* 501 W Tonopah Dr Phoenix AZ 85027

LIMBIRD, LEE EBERHARDT, SIGNAL TRANSDUCTION, MOLECULAR BASIS HORMONE & DRUG ACTION. *Current Pos:* PROF & CHAIR, DEPT PHARMACOL, VANDERBILT UNIV, 83- *Personal Data:* b Philadelphia, Pa, Nov 27, 48; m 70, Thomas James; c Eric & Jessica. *Educ:* Col Wooster, BA, 70; Univ NC, Chapel Hill, PhD(biochem), 73. *Honors & Awards:* John Jacob Abel Award. *Res:* alpha-adrenergic receptors as a model system for understanding signal transduction via G-protein coupled receptors; structure function relationships of individual receptors; evaluating mechanisms for receptor targeting to partial or microdomains in cells; homologous recombination to introduce intentionally modified alpha receptor structures into the mouse genome. *Mailing Add:* Dept Pharmacol Vanderbilt Univ Sch Med 476 MRB Nashville TN 37232

LIMBURG, WILLIAM W, ORGANIC POLYMER CHEMISTRY. *Current Pos:* From sr chemist to assoc scientist, 65-66, scientist, 67-73, sr scientist, 73-80, TECH SPECIALIST & PROJ MGR, XEROX CORP, 80- *Personal Data:* b Buffalo, NY, Nov 9, 35; m 66. *Educ:* Univ Buffalo, BA, 59, MA, 62; Univ Toronto, PhD(organosilicon chem), 65. *Mem:* Am Chem Soc; Royal Soc Chem; Soc Photog Scientists & Engrs. *Res:* Synthesis of organometallic compounds; mechanistic and stereochemical studies of molecular rearrangements of carbon-functional silicon-containing compounds; non-silver halide imaging methods; synthesis of organic photoconductive materials; synthesis of novel polysiloxanes. *Mailing Add:* 66 Clearview Dr Penfield NY 14526-2433

LIMERICK, JACK MCKENZIE, SR, CHEMISTRY. *Current Pos:* CONSULT, 72- *Personal Data:* b Fredericton, NB, July 16, 10; m 37. *Educ:* Univ NB, BSc, 31, MSc, 34. *Honors & Awards:* Award, Tech Asn Pulp & Paper Indust, 59, 82 & 90. *Prof Exp:* Res chemist, Fraser Co, 34-37; chief chemist, Bathurst Paper Co, 37-41, supt, Control Dept, 41-44, tech & res dir, Bathurst Paper Co Ltd, 44-67, assoc dir res & develop, Consol-Bathurst Ltd, 67-71. *Concurrent Pos:* Lectr, Royal Tech Inst, Sweden, 52; consult, Iran, 72-78; pulp, paper & container indust, Brazil, 73- & US & Can, 80- *Mem:* Fel Tech Asn Pulp & Paper Indust; Can Pulp & Paper Asn; fel Chem Inst Can; Pulp & Paper Res Inst Can. *Res:* Pulp; paper; containers; author of over 100 publications. *Mailing Add:* 36 E St PH4 Oakville ON L6L 5K2 Can

LIMPERT, FREDERICK ARTHUR, HYDROLOGY. *Current Pos:* RETIRED. *Personal Data:* b Frankfort, NY, Feb 4, 21; m 44, Patricia Cheney. *Educ:* Wash State Univ, BSCE, 43. *Honors & Awards:* Meritorious Serv Award, US Dept Interior. *Prof Exp:* Civil engr, Columbia Basin Proj, Wash Bur Reclamation, 46-61; head hydrol sect & chief hydrologist, Bonneville Power Admin, 61-77. *Concurrent Pos:* Mem, Interagency Adv Comt Water Data, 72- & Coord Coun Water Data Acquisition Methods, 74- *Mem:* Fel Am Soc Civil Engrs; Nat Soc Prof Engrs; Western Snow Conf. *Res:* Use of satellite data for determining areal snow cover and cloud classification for areal precipitation. *Mailing Add:* 10701 Pinion Lane Sun City AZ 85373-1831. *E-Mail:* fritzlimpert@juno.com

LIMPERT, RUDOLF, MECHANICAL ENGINEERING. *Current Pos:* CONSULT, MOTOR VEHICLE SAFETY, 81- *Personal Data:* b Neuhaldensleben, Ger, Mar 19, 36; US citizen; m 62; c 6. *Educ:* Wolfenbuettel Univ, Ger, Ing, 58; Brigham Young Univ, BES & MS, 68; Univ Mich, Ann Arbor, PhD(mech eng), 72. *Prof Exp:* Proj engr, Alfred Teves Corp, Ger, 63-65; res asst, Hwy Safety Res Inst, Univ Mich, Ann Arbor, 69-72; safety stand engr, Nat Hwy Traffic Safety Admin, Dept Transp, 72-73; res prof, Univ Utah, 73-81. *Mem:* Soc Automotive Engrs. *Res:* Motor vehicle accident reconstruction and cause analysis; product liability research; automotive systems design. *Mailing Add:* 280 Woodland Dr Park City UT 84098

LIN, ALICE LEE LAN, SPACE PHYSICS, ELECTRO-OPTICS & ACOUSTO-OPTICS. *Current Pos:* physicist, Nondestructive Eval Br, 80-82, PHYSICIST, MECH MAT DIV, US ARMY MAT TECHNOL LAB, WATERTOWN, MASS, 82- *Personal Data:* b Shanghai, China, Oct 28, 37; US citizen; m 62; c Peter A. *Educ:* Univ Calif, Berkeley, AB, 63; George Washington Univ, MA, 74. *Honors & Awards:* Mencius Educ Award. *Prof Exp:* Res asst physics, Cavendish Lab, Cambridge, Eng, 65-66; info anal specialist, Nat Acad Sci, Washington, DC, 70-71; teaching fel physics, George Washington Univ, Washington, DC, 72-74; physicist, Goddard Space Flight Ctr, NASA, Greenbelt, Md, 75-80. *Concurrent Pos:* Physicist & instr, Nondestructive Testing Sch, Army Res Lab, Watertown, Mass. *Mem:* Am Phys Soc; Am Soc Nondestructive Testing; Soc Exp Stress Anal; Am Ceramic Soc; NY Acad Sci; AAAS. *Res:* Nondestructive methods to detect flaws in materials. *Mailing Add:* 28 Hallett Hill Rd Weston MA 02193. *Fax:* 781-899-6751; *E-Mail:* plinmarcus@gis.net

LIN, ANTHONY T, PLASMA PHYSICS. *Current Pos:* FAC MEM, DEPT PHYSICS, UNIV CALIF, LOS ANGELES, 73- *Personal Data:* b Taiwan, June 25, 41. *Educ:* Nat Taiwan Univ, BS, 63; ETenn State Univ, MS, 66; Univ Mich, PhD(elec eng), 70. *Mem:* Fel Am Phys Soc. *Mailing Add:* Dept Physics Univ Calif Los Angeles CA 90024

LIN, BENJAMIN MING-REN, COMPUTER NETWORKING, REAL-TIME SYSTEMS. *Current Pos:* PROF COMPUT SCI, MOORHEAD STATE UNIV, 73- *Personal Data:* US citizen; m 70; c 2. *Educ:* Taipei Inst Technol, dipl, 61; Univ Wyo, MS, 67; Univ Iowa, PhD(elec eng), 73. *Prof Exp:* Engr, Radio Wave Res Labs, 62-65; design & develop engr, Collins Radio Co, 67-68; engr, Addressograph Multigraph Corp, 68-69. *Concurrent Pos:* Dir, Grad Sch Info Eng, Tamkang Univ, Taiwan, 80-81; vis prof, Shandong Inst Mining & Technol, China, 88. *Mem:* Sigma Xi; Asn Comput Mach; Inst Elec & Electronics Engrs; Comput Soc. *Res:* Application of microprocessors in consumer products and data communications; fault-tolerant computing systems design; computer architecture in artificial intelligence; real-time signature verification. *Mailing Add:* Moorhead State Univ Moorhead MN 56560

LIN, BOR-LUH, MATHEMATICS. *Current Pos:* From asst prof to assoc prof, 63-72, PROF MATH, UNIV IOWA, 72- *Personal Data:* b Fukien, China, Mar 4, 35; m 63; c 3. *Educ:* Nat Taiwan Univ, BS, 56; Univ Notre Dame, MS, 60; Northwestern Univ, PhD(math), 63. *Concurrent Pos:* Vis assoc prof, Ohio State Univ, 70-71; vis prof, Univ Calif, Santa Barbara. *Mem:* Am Math Soc. *Res:* Functional analysis, Banach spare theory; minimax theorems. *Mailing Add:* Univ Iowa Iowa City IA 52242-0001

LIN, CHENTAO, PLANT DEVELOPMENT BIOLOGY, PHOTOSENSORY SIGNAL TRANSDUCTION. *Current Pos:* ASST PROF, UNIV CALIF, LOS ANGELES, 96- *Personal Data:* m 87, Hongyun Yang; c Marysa D & Sophia D. *Educ:* Iowa State Univ, MS, 88; Mich State Univ, PhD(genetics), 92. *Prof Exp:* NIH postdoctoral fel, Univ Pa, 92-96. *Mem:* AAAS; Am Soc Plant Physiologists. *Res:* Molecular mechanism of the function and signal transduction of photosensory receptors in higher plants. *Mailing Add:* Dept MCDB Univ Calif Los Angeles CA 90095-1606. *Fax:* 310-206-3987; *E-Mail:* clin@mcdb.ucla.edu

LIN, CHIA CHIAO, APPLIED MATHEMATICS. *Current Pos:* from assoc prof to inst prof, 47-87, EMER INST PROF MATH, MASS INST TECHNOL, 87- *Personal Data:* b Foochow, China, July 7, 16; US citizen. *Educ:* Nat Tsing Hua Univ, China, BSc, 37; Univ Toronto, MA, 41; Calif Inst Technol, PhD(aeronaut), 44. *Hon Degrees:* LLD, Chinese Univ Hong Kong, 73. *Honors & Awards:* John Von Neumann lectr, Soc Indust & Appl Math-Am Math Soc, 67; Otto Laporte Mem lectr, Am Phys Soc, 73; DSD Prize, 79; Timoshenko Medal, Am Soc Mech Engrs, 75; Award Appl Math & Numerical Anal, Nat Acad Sci, 77; Fluid Dynamics Prize, Am Phys Soc & US Off Naval Res, 79. *Prof Exp:* Asst, Tsing Hua Univ, China, 37-39; from asst to res engr, Calif Inst Technol, 43-45; from asst prof to assoc prof appl math, Brown Univ, 45-47. *Concurrent Pos:* Guggenheim fels, 53 & 60; mem, Inst Advan Study, Princeton, NJ, 59-60 & 65-66; mem, Comt on Support Res in Math Sci, Nat Acad Sci, 66-68. *Mem:* Nat Acad Sci; Am Astron Soc; Soc Indust & Appl Math (pres, 72-74); Am Math Soc; fel Am Acad Arts & Sci; Am Philos Soc; Am Phys Soc; fel Inst Aerospace Sci. *Res:* Hydrodynamics; stellar dynamics; astrophysical problems; spiral structure of galaxies; density wave theory developed in great mathematical detail with predictions checked against various astronomical observations. *Mailing Add:* Dept Math Mass Inst Technol Cambridge MA 02139

LIN, CHII-DONG, ATOMIC PHYSICS. *Current Pos:* from asst prof to assoc prof, 76-80, PROF, KANS STATE UNIV, 84- *Personal Data:* b Taiwan. *Educ:* Nat Taiwan Univ, BS, 69; Univ Chicago, MS, 73, PhD(physics), 74. *Prof Exp:* Fel astrophys, Ctr Astrophys, Harvard Col Observ, 74-76. *Concurrent Pos:* Sloan fel, 79-83. *Mem:* fel, Am Phys Soc. *Mailing Add:* Dept Physics Kans State Univ Cardwell Hall Manhattan KS 66506

LIN, CHIN-CHUNG, BIOCHEMICAL PHARMACOLOGY. *Current Pos:* Sr scientist, 69-75, prin scientist, 75-79, res fel, 79-82, ASSOC DIR, SCHERING CORP, 83- *Personal Data:* b Taipei, Taiwan, Oct 8, 37; c 2. *Educ:* Chung Hsing Univ, Taiwan, BS, 60; Tuskegee Inst, MS, 65; Northwestern Univ, PhD(biochem), 69. *Concurrent Pos:* Res fel biochem, Med Sch, Northwestern Univ, 69. *Mem:* AAAS; Am Chem Soc; Am Soc Pharmacol & Exp Therapeut; NY Acad Sci. *Res:* Drug metabolism and the mechanism of enzymatic hydroxylation. *Mailing Add:* 95 Pheasant Way Florham Park NJ 07932

LIN, CHING Y, ANIMAL BREEDING, QUANTITATIVE GENETICS. *Current Pos:* RES SCIENTIST, AGR CAN, 80- *Personal Data:* b Taiwan, May 22, 40; Can citizen; m 65; c 2. *Educ:* Nat Chung-Hsing Univ, Taiwan, BS, 63; Iowa State Univ, MS, 71; Ohio State Univ, PhD(dairy sci), 76. *Prof Exp:* Jr specialist agr exten, Taiwan Prov Dept Agr & Forestry, 64-68; res assoc poultry breeding, Dept Animal Sci, Univ Guelph, Can, 76-80. *Concurrent Pos:* Vis res fel, Japan, 89-90. *Mem:* Am Soc Animal Sci; Am Dairy Sci Asn; Can Soc Animal Sci. *Res:* Dairy cattle breeding; quantitative genetics; statistical analysis as applied to animal breeding. *Mailing Add:* Cent Exp Farm Agr & Agr Food Can 930 Carling Ave Bldg 34 Rm 23 Ottawa ON K1A 0C5 Can. *Fax:* 613-759-1355

LIN, CHINLON, BROADBAND OPTICAL FIBER COMMUNICATIONS, CABLE TELEVISION & DIGITAL VIDEO DISTRIBUTION SYSTEMS. *Current Pos:* Mem tech staff, Laser Sci Res, Bell Labs, Holmdel, 74-85, DIR, BROADBAND LIGHTWAVE SYSTS, BELL COMMUN RES, 86- *Personal Data:* b Taiwan, Rep of China, Jan 19, 45; m 69, Helen Chou; c Thomas Yichiao & Daniel Yibin. *Educ:* Nat Taiwan Univ, BS, 67; Univ Ill, MS, 70; Univ Calif, Berkeley, PhD(elec eng), 74. *Concurrent Pos:* Assoc ed, J Appl Optics, Optical Soc Am, 82-84 & J Lightwave Technol, Inst Elec & Electronics Engrs, 91-94; vis guest prof, Tech Univ Denmark, 84. *Mem:* Fel Inst Elec & Electronics Engrs; fel Optical Soc Am; fel Photonics Soc Chinese Am. *Res:* Lasers and quantum electronics; optical fibers and lightwave communications; advanced photonics technologies and applications to broadband optical fiber telecommunications; high-capacity video distribution systems. *Mailing Add:* Broadband Lightwave Syst Res Bellcore 3X255 Red Bank NJ 07701. *Fax:* 732-758-4372; *E-Mail:* chinlon@bellcore.com

LIN, CHIN-TARNG, CELL BIOLOGY, NEUROBIOLOGY. *Current Pos:* RES FEL, INST BIOMED SCI, ACAD SINICA, TAIPEI, TAIWAN, ROC, 87- *Personal Data:* b Chu-Nan, Taiwan, Dec 11, 38; US citizen; m 83; c 1. *Educ:* Nat Taiwan Univ, DDS, 63; Med Br, Univ Tex, Galveston, PhD(cell biol), 75. *Prof Exp:* Doctor & teaching asst path, Dept Path, Col Med, Nat Taiwan Univ, 64-69, instr, 69-75; teaching asst, Div Cell Biol, Med Br, Univ Tex, Galveston, 71-75; assoc prof path, Dept Path, Col Med, Nat Taiwan Univ, 75-78; res assoc, Dept Cell Biol, Baylor Col Med, 78-80, res instr, 80-83; asst prof, Dept Physiol, Col Med, Pa State Univ, 83-87. *Concurrent Pos:* Vis prof, Dept Pathol, Col Med, Nat Taiwan Univ, 87-89, PROF PATHOL, 89- *Mem:* Histochem Soc; AAAS; Am Soc Cell Biol; Soc Neurosci. *Res:* Immunochemical approaches to protein synthesis and transport in normal and cancer cells; cell biology; neurobiology; neurotransmitter synthesizing enzymes; immunohistochemistry; immunoelectron microscopy; in situ nucleic acid hybridization; monoclonal hybridoma technique; nasopharyngeal carcinoma tumor biology; stroke animal model. *Mailing Add:* Nat Taiwan Univ Hosp Taipei 10007 Taiwan

LIN, CHI-WEI, CANCER, BIOCHEMISTRY. *Current Pos:* DIR, UROL RES LAB & STAFF MEM, DEPT UROL, MASS GEN HOSP, 79- *Personal Data:* b Hong Kong, May 16, 37; m 69; c 1. *Educ:* Nat Taiwan Univ, BS, 61; Univ Wis-Madison, MS, 65, PhD(biochem), 69. *Prof Exp:* Fel cancer res, Sch Med, Tufts Univ, 69-71, res assoc, 71-72, asst prof path, 72-80. *Mem:* Biochem Soc; AAAS; Histochem Soc; Am Asn Cancer Res; Sigma Xi. *Res:* Biochemical characteristics of cancer, specifically, the studies of tumor-associated enzymes and isozymes, including histaminase, acid phosphatase and alkaline phosphatase; processes of synthesis and distribution of acid hydrolases and the biogenesis of lysosomes. *Mailing Add:* Dept Urol Mass Gen Hosp Fruit St Boston MA 02114

LIN, CHUN CHIA, ATOMIC & MOLECULAR COLLISIONS, ELECTRONIC ENERGIES OF SOLIDS. *Current Pos:* PROF PHYSICS, UNIV WIS, 68-, JOHN & ABIGAIL VAN VLECK PROF PHYSICS, 91- *Personal Data:* b Canton, China, March 7, 30; US citizen. *Educ:* Univ Calif, Berkeley, BS, 51, BA, 52; Harvard Univ, PhD(chem), 55. *Honors & Awards:* Will Allis Prize Am Phys Soc, 96. *Prof Exp:* From asst prof to prof physics, Univ Okla, 55-68. *Concurrent Pos:* Consult & univ retainee, Tex Instruments, Inc, 60-68; Alfred P Sloan fel, 62-66; secy, Gaseous Electronics Conf, 73, chmn, 90-92; secy-treas, Div Electron & Atomic Physics, Am Phys Soc, 74-77; consult, Sandia Labs, 76-81; vchmn, Div Atomic Molecular & Optical Physics, Am Phys Soc, 92-93; chmn elect, 93-94, chmn, 94-95. *Mem:* Am Phys Soc. *Res:* Atomic and molecular collision processes; radiation of atoms and molecules excited by electron impact and laser irradiation; electronic energy band theory of crystalline solids, impurity atoms in solids, amorphous solids. *Mailing Add:* Dept Physics Univ Wis Madison WI 53706

LIN, CHUN-WEL, NEUROSCIENCE. *Current Pos:* pharmacologist, Abbott Labs, 82-84, sr pharmacologist, 84-87, res investr, 87-90, assoc res fel, 90-92, GROUP LEADER, ABBOTT LABS, 92- *Personal Data:* b Taipei, Taiwan, Dec 30, 53. *Educ:* City Col New York, BS, 76; Mt Sinai Med Ctr, MS, 79, PhD(neuropharmacol), 81. *Prof Exp:* Researcher, New York Med Sch, 81-82. *Mem:* Soc Neurosci; Am Soc Pharmacol & Exp Therapeut. *Res:* Nuero peptide receptors. *Mailing Add:* Neurosci Area Abbott Labs D-47U AP10 Abbott Park IL 60064-3500

LIN, DENIS CHUNG KAM, ANALYTICAL CHEMISTRY, MASS SPECTROMETRY. *Current Pos:* AT ETC CORP, 80- *Personal Data:* b Hong Kong, July 7, 44; Can citizen; m 69; c 1. *Educ:* Univ Man, BSc, 68, MSc, 70, PhD(chem), 72. *Prof Exp:* Fel, Univ Montreal, 72-74; staff chemist, Battelle Mem Inst, 74-80. *Mem:* Am Chem Soc; Am Soc Mass Spectrometry; Int Asn Forensic Toxicologists. *Res:* Identification and quantification of low levels of drugs and their metabolites in biological samples by mass spectrometry and other techniques; nucleic acid and protein sequencing; pyrolytic reactions. *Mailing Add:* 214 Deepdale Dr Middletown NJ 07748-3057

LIN, DIANE CHANG, CELL BIOLOGY, CELL MOTILITY. *Current Pos:* RES SCIENTIST BIOPHYS, JOHNS HOPKINS UNIV, 74- *Personal Data:* b China, Aug 6, 44; US citizen; m 69, Shin; c Howe & Payton. *Educ:* Nat Taiwan Univ, BS, 66; Univ Calif, Los Angeles, PhD(biol), 71. *Prof Exp:* Asst res scientist pharmacol, Univ Calif, San Francisco, 71-74. *Concurrent Pos:* Prin investr, Johns Hopkins Univ, 78- *Mem:* Am Soc Biochem & Molecular Biol; Am Soc Cell Biol. *Res:* Actin-binding proteins from chicken muscles. *Mailing Add:* Dept Biophys Johns Hopkins Univ 3400 N Charles St Baltimore MD 21218-2699. *Fax:* 410-516-5170

LIN, DONG LIANG, PHYSICS, ELECTRICAL ENGINEERING. *Current Pos:* MEM STAFF, BELL LABS, HOLMDEL, NJ, 80- *Personal Data:* b Taiwan, China, Mar 5, 47; m 71; c 3. *Educ:* Nat Taiwan Univ, BS, 69; Columbia Univ, MS, 72, PhD(physics), 75. *Prof Exp:* Res fel physics, Johns Hopkins Univ, 75-77; staff scientist physics, Sci Appln Inc, 77-80. *Mem:* Am Phys Soc; Nat Soc Prof Engrs. *Res:* Atomic physics; plasma physics; solid state physics. *Mailing Add:* Lucent Technols Bell Labs Coter Rd Princeton NJ 08542-0900

LIN, DUO-LIANG, THEORETICAL PHYSICS, CONDENSED MATTER PHYSICS. *Current Pos:* from asst prof to assoc prof, 64-90, PROF PHYSICS, STATE UNIV NY, BUFFALO, 90- *Personal Data:* b Juian, China, May 16, 30; m 63, Sharon Chien; c Jennifer & Kenneth. *Educ:* Taiwan Norm Univ, BSc, 56; Tsing Hua Univ, China, MSc, 58; Ohio State Univ, PhD(physics), 61. *Prof Exp:* Res assoc physics, Yale Univ, 61-64. *Concurrent Pos:* Sr vis, Oxford Univ, 70-71; vis prof, Nat Taiwan Univ, 71; Tsing Hua Univ, Peking, 78, Liao Ning Univ, Shen Yang, 81 & Jiaotong Univ, Shanghai, 85; hon prof, Neimonggu Univ, China, 85-; Tokten consult, UN Develop Prog, 86-92; adj prof, Univ Sci & Technol China, Hefei, 87-, Shandong Univ, Jinan, 88-, Sichuan Univ, Chengdu, 90-; adv prof, Chengdu Univ Sci & Technol, 86-, Southwestern Jiao, Tong Univ, Chengdu, 87-, Chongqing Univ, 85-, Lanzhou University, Lanzhou, 91. *Mem:* Am Phys Soc. *Res:* Quantum transport theory; electronic and optical properties of semiconductor heterostructures; nonlinear optical response and ultrafast processes in polymers photonics materials; critical phenomena and phase transitions in magnetic films. *Mailing Add:* Dept Physics State Univ NY Buffalo NY 14260. *Fax:* 716-645-2507; *E-Mail:* dll@acsu.buffalo.edu

LIN, EDMUND CHI CHIEN, BIOCHEMISTRY. *Current Pos:* Instr biochem, 57-60, assoc, 60-63, from asst prof to assoc prof, 63-69, PROF MICROBIOL & MOLECULAR GENETICS, HARVARD MED SCH, 69- *Personal Data:* b Peking, China, Oct 28, 28; nat US. *Educ:* Univ Rochester, AB, 52; Harvard Univ, PhD, 57. *Concurrent Pos:* Vis prof, Univ Calif, Berkeley, 72; Guggenheim fel, Pasteur Inst Paris, 69; prof chmn dept, Harvard Med Sch, 73-75; Fogarty Sr Int fel, Univ Paris, VI, 77-78; vis prof biol, Univ Konstanz, Ger, 81; hon res prof, Inst Plant Physiol, Academia Sinica, Shanghai, 80- *Mem:* Am Soc Microbiol; Am Soc Biol Chem. *Res:* Bacterial physiology and genetics and biochemical evolution. *Mailing Add:* Microbiol & Molecular Genetics Harvard Med Sch Boston MA 02115

LIN, FU HAI, MOLECULAR BIOLOGY, NEUROSCIENCES. *Current Pos:* sr res scientist, 69-70, assoc res scientist, 70-76, RES SCIENTIST V & HEAD LAB VIRAL BIOCHEM, INST BASIC RES DEVELOP DISABILITY, 76- *Personal Data:* b Fukien, China, Feb 15, 28; US citizen; m 56, Ruth Chen; c Nancy, Alan, Boris, Calvin & David. *Educ:* Nat Taiwan Univ, BS, 53; Univ WVa, MS, 59; Rutgers Univ, PhD(bact), 65. *Prof Exp:* Asst, Univ WVa, 58-59; tech asst biochem, Boyce Thompson Inst, 59-61; res asst, Rutgers Univ, 61-65; asst mem biochem, Albert Einstein Med Ctr, 65-69. *Mem:* AAAS; Am Soc Microbiol; Am Chem Soc; Sigma Xi; NY Acad Sci. *Res:* Mitochondrial mutation in Alzheimer disease and related neurodegenerative syndromes; gene expression of animal RNA viruses of slow infection; biochemistry and function of proteins of slow viruses. *Mailing Add:* Inst Basic Res Developmental Disability 1050 Forest Hill Rd Staten Island NY 10314. *Fax:* 718-698-3803

LIN, GEORGE HUNG-YIN, GENERAL TOXICOLOGY & ENVIRONMENTAL TOXICOLOGY. *Current Pos:* prog specialist, Xerox Corp, 74-76, staff toxicologist, 74-84, sr scientist, 84-91, PRIN SCIENTIST, XEROX CORP, 91- *Personal Data:* b Shantung, China, Mar 9, 38; m 69, Margaret Y; c Benjamin. *Educ:* Tunghai Univ, Taiwan, BS, 60; Univ Nev, MS, 65; Univ Calif, Davis, PhD(chem), 69; Am Bd Toxicol, dipl, 82-87, 87-92, 92- *Prof Exp:* NSF fel biochem, Univ Wis-Madison, 69-71; Rockefeller fel chem, Univ Calif, Riverside, 71-74. *Concurrent Pos:* Adj fac toxicol, Univ Rochester, 80-82. *Mem:* Soc Toxicol; Environ Mutagen Soc. *Res:* Industrial toxicology; inhalation toxicology; biometrics; chemical carcinogenesis; x-ray crystallography; general toxicology; carcinogen risk assessment; structure-activity relationships; environmental toxicology; environmental mutagenesis. *Mailing Add:* Xerox Corp PUID Bldg 843 Webster NY 14580. *Fax:* 716-422-6449; *E-Mail:* lin:wbst843:xerox

LIN, GLORIA C, biochemistry, for more information see previous edition

LIN, GRACE WOAN-JUNG, NUTRITIONAL BIOCHEMISTRY. *Current Pos:* asst res specialist, 74-83, ASSOC RES SPECIALIST, RUTGERS UNIV, 83- *Personal Data:* b Taipei, Taiwan; US citizen; m. *Educ:* Nat Taiwan Univ, BS, 59; Tex Woman's Univ, MS, 64; Univ Calif, Berkeley, PhD(nutrit), 71. *Prof Exp:* Res asst, US Naval Med Res Unit 2, 59-62 & Thorndike Mem Lab, Med Sch, Harvard Univ, 64; res fel, Columbia Univ, 69-70. *Mem:* Res Soc Alcoholism; Am Inst Nutrit; Int Soc Biomed Res Alcoholism. *Res:* Effects of ethanol on absorption and metabolism of nutrients (amino acids and water soluble vitamins) and on fetal development. *Mailing Add:* 9365 Wickham Way Orlando FL 32836-5518

LIN, H(UA), AERONAUTICAL ENGINEERING. *Current Pos:* RETIRED. *Personal Data:* b Peiping, China, Nov 25, 19; nat US; m 47; c 2. *Educ:* Nat Tsing Hua Univ, China, BS, 40; Univ Mich, MS, 44; Mass Inst Technol, ScD(aeronaut eng), 55. *Prof Exp:* Engr, aeronaut dept, Cent Aircraft Mfg Co, China, 40-42; instr, Nat Tsing Hua Univ, 42-43; stress analyst, Stinson Div, Consol Vultee Aircraft Corp, Mich, 44-45; engr, Cincinnati Milling Mach Co, Ohio, 45-47; asst mgr, Far East Develop Corp, NY, 47-49; res aeronaut engr, aeroelastic & structural res lab, Mass Inst Technol, 49-56; res specialist, struct dynamics staff, 56-58, chief dynamics, systs mgt off, 58-59, chief struct tech unit, Aerospace Div, 59-64, mgr, Struct & Mat Tech Dept, Aerospace Group Div, Boeing Co, 65-66, chief missile tech, Missile & Info Systs Div, 66-68, chief engr, minuteman prog, Missile Div, 68-70, dep prog mgr, minuteman prog, Aerospace Group, 70-71, prog mgr hardsite defense, 71-73, prod develop mgr, Boeing Airplane Co, 73-75; dir offensive systs, US Directorate Res & Eng, Dept Defense, 75-78; chief scientist, Boeing Aerospace Co, 78-90. *Concurrent Pos:* Partic, sr exec prog, Sloan Sch Indust Mgt, Mass Inst Technol, 69. *Mem:* Sr mem Am Astron Soc; fel Am Inst Aeronaut & Astronaut; Fel Brit Interplanetary Soc; Am Soc Mech Engrs. *Res:* Aeroelasticity; structural dynamics; structural analysis; steady-state and unsteady aerodynamics; aerodynamic heating and thermal analysis; stability and control; structural flexibility and servo-control interaction. *Mailing Add:* 3212 90th Pl SE Mercer Island WA 98040

LIN, HO-MU, SUPERCRITICAL FLUID TECHNOLOGIES, FUEL TECHNOLOGIES. *Current Pos:* res engr, 75-79, tech dir & sr engr, Thermodynamics Res Lab, 79-87, SR RES FEL, PURDUE UNIV, 88-; SR SCI ADVISER, BIOS INT, 87- *Personal Data:* b Kaohsiung, Taiwan, July 12, 38; m 72, Su-Jung Wang; c Eugene T & Jeffrey E. *Educ:* Nat Taiwan Univ, BS, 62; Tokyo Inst Technol, 66; Okla State Univ, PhD(chem eng), 70. *Prof Exp:* Teaching & res asst, Nat Taiwan Univ, 63-65, lectr, 66-67; UNESCO fel, Tokyo Inst Technol, 65-66; grad teaching & res asst, Okla State Univ, 67-70, sr lectr & res assoc, 70-73; staff researcher, Rice Univ, 74-75. *Concurrent Pos:* Consult, Great Lakes Chem, 80, Exxon, 82, Biotechnol Serv Int, 84-85; co-prin investr, Elec Power Res Inst, 75-86, Am Inst Chem Engrs, 82-87, US Dept Energy, 85-87. *Mem:* Am Inst Chem Engrs; Am Chem Soc; Sigma Xi; AAAS; fel Int Biog Asn. *Res:* Explosion pretreatment of cellulosic materials for enhanced glucose production and supercritical fluid in utilization of cellulosic materials; author of over 100 technical publications. *Mailing Add:* 3303 Hunter Rd West Lafayette IN 47906

LIN, HSIU-SAN, RADIATION ONCOLOGY, MICROBIOLOGY. *Current Pos:* From asst prof to assoc prof, 71-84, PROF RADIOL, WASHINGTON UNIV, ST LOUIS, 84-, ASSOC PROF MICROBIOL, 85- *Personal Data:* b Nagoya, Japan, March 15, 35; US citizen; m 62, Su-chiung Chen; c Kenneth, Bertha & Michael. *Educ:* Nat Taiwan Univ, MD, 60; Univ Chicago, PhD(microbiol), 68. *Honors & Awards:* Res Career Develop Award, Nat Cancer Inst, 74. *Concurrent Pos:* Vis scientist, Univ Oxford, Eng, 77-78 & Harvard Med Sch, 93; consult ed, J Leukocyte Biol. *Mem:* Am Soc Microbiologists; Am Soc Therapeut Radiol & Oncol; Am Asn Cancer Res; Reticuloendothelial Soc; Sigma Xi; fel Am Col Radiol. *Res:* Differentiation of monocytes and macrophages; radiobiology of mononuclear phagocytes. *Mailing Add:* Mallinckrodt Inst Radiol Washington Univ Sch Med St Louis MO 63110. *Fax:* 314-362-8521; *E-Mail:* lin@roc.wustl.edu

LIN, HUNG CHANG, ELECTRONICS. *Current Pos:* MGR ADVAN DEVELOP, MOLECULAR ELECTRONICS DIV, WESTINGHOUSE CORP, LINTHICUM HEIGHTS, 63-, SR ADV ENGR, AEROSPACE DIV, BALTIMORE, 69- *Personal Data:* b Shanghai, China, Aug 8, 19; US citizen; m 59; c 2. *Educ:* Chiao Tung Univ, BSEE, 41; Univ Mich, MS, 48; Polytech Inst Brooklyn, DEE(elec eng), 56. *Honors & Awards:* Ebers Award, Inst Elec & Electronics Engrs Electron Device Soc, 78. *Prof Exp:* Engr, Cent Radio Works of China, 41-44 & Cent Broadcasting Admin of China, 44-47; res engr, RCA, 48-56; mgr appln, CBS Semiconductor Opers, 56-59; adv engr, Res Lab, Westinghouse Corp, Baltimore, 59-63. *Concurrent Pos:* Adj prof, Univ Pittsburgh, 59-63; vis lectr, Univ Calif, Berkeley, 65-66; lectr, Univ Md, College Park, 66-69, vis prof elec eng, 69-71, prof elec eng, 71-90, emer prof, 90-. *Mem:* Fel Inst Elec & Electronics Engrs; Sigma Xi. *Res:* Semiconductor and integrated circuits. *Mailing Add:* 8 Shindler Ct Silver Spring MD 20903

LIN, JAMES C H, GENETICS, CELL PHYSIOLOGY. *Current Pos:* from asst prof to assoc prof, 65-75, PROF BIOL, NORTHWESTERN STATE UNIV, 75- *Personal Data:* b Macao, Aug 12, 32; wid; c David, Gilbert & Bruce. *Educ:* Taiwan Prov Norm Univ, BS, 54; Rice Univ, MA, 60; NC State Univ, PhD(genetics), 65. *Prof Exp:* Lab instr zool, Nat Taiwan Univ, 55-57; res asst nuclear med, Methodist Hosp, Houston, Tex, 59-60 & Hermann Hosp, 60. *Concurrent Pos:* Vis prof, Univ Tex, M D Anderson Hosp & Tumor Inst, 80-81. *Mem:* Genetics Soc Am; Sigma Xi; Tissue Cult Asn. *Res:* Chemical mutagenesis; cholinesterase in fire ants; crossing over in Drosophila; nucleolar organizing regions of Chinese hamster ovary cells; DNA methylation in drosophila. *Mailing Add:* Dept Biol Sci Northwestern State Univ Natchitoches LA 71497. *Fax:* 318-357-4518; *E-Mail:* linj@alpha.nsula.edu

LIN, JAMES CHIH-I, BIOENGINEERING, ELECTRICAL ENGINEERING. *Current Pos:* dir robotics & automation lab, Univ Ill, Chicago, 82-89, prof elec eng & head bioeng, 80-92, DIR SPEC PROJ ENG, UNIV ILL, & PROF ELEC ENG, BIOENG, PHYSIOL & BIOPHYS, 92- *Personal Data:* b Dec 29, 42; m 70, Mei Fei; c Janet, Theodore & Erik. *Educ:* Univ Wash, Seattle, BS, 66, MS, 68, PhD(elec eng), 71. *Prof Exp:* Elec engr, Crown Zellerbach Corp, 66-67; teaching & res asst elec eng, Univ Wash, Seattle, 67-71, asst prof rehab med, 71-74, asst dir, Bioelectromagnetic Res Lab, 74; prof elec eng, Wayne State Univ, Detroit, 74-80; dir robotics & automation lab, Univ Ill, Chicago, 82-89, prof elec eng & head bioeng, 80-92, dir spec proj eng, 92- *Concurrent Pos:* Consult, Walter Reed Army Inst Res, 73-75, Battelle Mem Inst, 76-80, SRI Int, 78-79, Arthur D Little, Inc, 80-82 & Ga Tech Res Inst, 84-86; URS Corp, 86-87, CBS, Inc, 88, ACS, Inc, 88-89, Luxtron, Inc, 90-; appointee, Diag Radiol Study Sect, NIH, 81-85, Nat Acad Sci & Int Union Radio Sci, 80-82, Presidential Young Investr Award Panel, NSF, 84-89; vis prof, Nat Yang Ming Med Col, Taipei, 81, Chung Yuan Univ, Taiwan, 81 & 88, Univ Rome, 85 & 88, Shangdong Univ, China, 88; chair, US Am Comn Man & Radiation, Inst Elec & Electronic Engrs, 90-91; vchair comn K, Int Union Radio, Sci, 96-99; chair, Nat Coun Radio Protection & Measurement, secy, 89-95 & 95-98; Nat Res Coun Nat Acad Sci Comt ELF Monitoring, 95-96; ed, Advances in Fam Field Living Systs. *Mem:* Fel Inst Elec & Electronics Engrs; Bioelectromagnetic Soc; Biomed Eng Soc; fel AAAS; Nat Coun Radiation Protection & Measurements; Am Soc Engr Educ; Nat Soc Prof Engr; fel Int Asn Med & Biol Environ. *Res:* Biological effects and medical applications of electromagnetic fields; hyperthermia for cancer therapy; visual and nonvisual robotic sensing; microwave technology for minimally invasive surgery; bioelectromagnetics; telemedicine. *Mailing Add:* Col Eng MC154 Univ Ill 851 S Morgan St Chicago IL 60607-7053. *Fax:* 312-413-0024; *E-Mail:* u45339@uic.edu

LIN, JAMES PEICHENG, ALGEBRAIC TOPOLOGY. *Current Pos:* From asst prof to assoc prof, 74-86, PROF MATH, UNIV CALIF, SAN DIEGO, 86- *Personal Data:* b New York, NY, Sept 30, 49. *Educ:* Univ Calif, Berkeley, BS, 70; Princeton Univ, PhD(math), 74. *Concurrent Pos:* Vis prof math, Princeton Univ, 76-77; Sloan Found fel, 77-78; mem, Inst Advan Studies, Hebrew Univ, Jerusalem, Israel, 81-82; vis scholar, Univ Calif, Berkeley, 82, Mass Inst Technol, 83-84 & Univ Neuchatel, Switz, 84; Prin invest, NSF grant. *Mem:* Am Math Soc. *Res:* Algebraic topology, concentrating on finite H-spaces. *Mailing Add:* Dept Math MS 0112 Univ Calif San Diego 9500 Gilman Dr La Jolla CA 92093-0112

LIN, JANE HUEY-CHAI, ATHEROSCLEROSIS, ENDOTHELIA ACTIVATION. *Current Pos:* Res assoc, 86-90, res asst prof, 90-93, ASST PROF, DEPT EXP PATH, NY MED COL, 93- *Personal Data:* b Taipei, Taiwan. *Educ:* Univ Ill, PhD(microbiol), 86. *Res:* Molecular mechanisms for endothelial activation by native low density lipo protein at atherogenic levels. *Mailing Add:* Dept Exp Path NY Med Col Valhalla NY 10595. *Fax:* 914-993-4679

LIN, JIA DING, FLUID MECHANICS, HYDROLOGY AND WATER RESOURCES. *Current Pos:* asst prof, 62-64, assoc prof, 64-81, PROF CIVIL ENG, UNIV CONN, 81- *Personal Data:* b Fuzhou, China, Dec 24, 31; US citizen; m 58; c 3. *Educ:* Nat Taiwan Univ, BS, 53, Univ Ill, MS, 56; Mass Inst Technol, ScD(hydromech), 61. *Prof Exp:* Res scientist, Hydronautics Inc, 60-62. *Concurrent Pos:* Vis prof, Taiwan Univ, 79-80. *Mem:* Asn Hydrol Res; Am Geophys Union. *Res:* hydrodynamics; hydrology. *Mailing Add:* Dept Civil Eng & Environ Univ Conn Main Campus U-37 261 Glenbrook Rd Storrs CT 06269-2037

LIN, JIAN, MARINE GEOPHYSICS, TECTONOPHYSICS. *Current Pos:* asst scientist, 88-92, ASSOC SCIENTIST GEOPHYS, WOODS HOLE OCEANOG INST, 92- *Personal Data:* b Fuzhou, Fujian. *Educ:* Univ Sci & Technol, China, BS, 82; Brown Univ, MS, 84, PhD(geophys), 88. *Prof Exp:* Vis scientist res geophys, US Geol Surv, Menlo Park, Calif, 88; vis fel, Southern Calif Earthquake Ctr, NSF, 91-92. *Concurrent Pos:* Mem, Steering Comt & Crustal Accretion Variables Working Group, US Ridge Prog, 89-97; prog chmn, Tectonophysics Sect, Am Geophys Union, 92-93; assoc ed, J Geophys Res, 92-94; mem, Earthquake Geol & Crustal Deformation Working Group, Southern Calif Earthquake Ctr, 92-; panelist, NSF US Geol Surv Ocean Drilling Prog, 93-97. *Mem:* Am Geophys Union; Sigma Xi; Geol Soc Am; AAAS. *Res:* Mid-ocean ridge dynamics; thermal evolution of the lithosphere; mantle hotspots; crustal deformation; earthquake mechanisms. *Mailing Add:* Dept Geol & Geophys Woods Hole Oceanog Inst Woods Hole MA 02543. *Fax:* 508-457-2187

LIN, JIANN-TSYH, PLANT LIPIDS & HORMONES, GIBBERELLINS. *Current Pos:* RES CHEMIST, WESTERN REGIONAL RES CTR, USDA, 77- *Personal Data:* b Taoyuan, Taiwan, Jan 15, 40; US citizen; m 69, Cheng-Ling Lin; c Robert C & Jeffrey C. *Educ:* Chung-Hsing Univ, Taiwan, BS, 63; Univ Miss, MS, 67; Drexel Univ, Philadelphia, PhD(biochem), 71. *Prof Exp:* Res assoc, Univ Tenn Med Ctr, 71-72, Hormel Inst, Univ Minn, 72-76 & Harborview Med Ctr, 76-77. *Mem:* Am Chem Soc; Am Soc Plant Physiologists; Am Oil Chemists Soc. *Res:* Biochemistry and analytical chemistry of steroids, lipids and enzymes; biochemistry and analysis of plant hormone, gibberellins, in wheat and apple; biochemistry and analysis of plant lipids. *Mailing Add:* USDA Western Regional Res Ctr 800 Buchanan St Albany CA 94710. *Fax:* 510-559-5777

LIN, JIUNN H, DRUG METABOLISM. *Current Pos:* ASSOC DIR, MERCK SHARP & DOHME, 88- *Personal Data:* b Taiwan, 1943. *Mailing Add:* Merck Res Labs WP 44-B100 West Point PA 19486

LIN, KUANG-FARN, POLYMER SCIENCE. *Current Pos:* chemist, Hercules Res Ctr, 63-67, res chemist, 69-73, proj leader, 73-75, sr res chemist, 74-78, venture mgr, 89-94, RES SCIENTIST, HERCULES RES CTR, 78-, TECH MGR, 79-, RES ASSOC, 84-, BUSINESS DEVELOP MGR, 95- *Personal Data:* b Taiwan, China, Feb 25, 36; m 58, Grace nee Yang; c 2. *Educ:* Cheng Kung Univ, Taiwan, BSc, 57; NDak State Univ, MS, 63, PhD(polymers, coatings), 69. *Prof Exp:* Asst instr chem, Chinese Naval Acad, 57-59; supt synthetic resins, Yung Koo Paint & Varnish Mfg Co, 59-61. *Concurrent Pos:* Asst, NDak State Univ, 63 & 67. *Mem:* Am Chem Soc; Sigma Xi; Tech Asn Pulp & Paper Indust; fel Am Inst Chemists; Am Inst Mining, Metall & Petrol Engrs. *Res:* Structure-property relationship; mineral processing; adhesion, coatings and polymer synthesis; elastomers. *Mailing Add:* Hercules Inc Wilmington DE 19894. *Fax:* 302-995-4448; *E-Mail:* klin@herc.com

LIN, KUANG-TZU DAVIS, BIOCHEMISTRY, BIOCHEMICAL GENETICS. *Current Pos:* ASSOC PROF PEDIAT, MEHARRY, 88- *Personal Data:* b Nantou, Taiwan, Aug 12, 40; m 68; c 2. *Educ:* Nat Taiwan Univ, BM, 66; Univ Wis-Madison, PhD(physiol chem), 71. *Prof Exp:* Surg officer, Tainan Air Force Hosp, 66-67; res asst physiol chem, Univ Wis-Madison, 67-71, proj assoc, 71-74; asst prof, 74-82, assoc prof med biol, mem res ctr, Univ Tenn, 82-86. *Concurrent Pos:* Med staff, Dept Pediat, William Beaumont Hosp, 85-86, Meharry Hubbard Hosp; dir, Biochem Genetic Lab, Meharry Hubbard Hosp. *Mem:* Soc Exp Biol Med; Am Soc Biochem & Molecular Biol; Am Bd Med Genetics. *Res:* Structure and function, especially carbonic anhydrase, hemoglobin, protease inhibitors and erythropoietin; amino acid metabolic disorder; pediatrics; genetic disorder. *Mailing Add:* Dept Pediat Meharry Med Col 1005 D B Todd Jr Blvd Nashville TN 37208-3599. *Fax:* 615-327-5989; *E-Mail:* linkut45@ccvax.mmc.edu

LIN, KWAN-CHOW, BIOLOGICAL WASTEWATER TREATMENT, WATER QUALITY STUDIES. *Current Pos:* res assoc, Univ NB, 69-70, lectr, 74, from asst prof to assoc prof, 74-83, PROF, UNIV NB, 83- *Personal Data:* b Hong Kong; Can citizen; m 69, Kwok Yee. *Educ:* Chu Hai Col Hong Kong, BSc, 66; Univ NB, MScE, 69; Univ Toronto, PhD(environ eng), 74. *Prof Exp:* Civil engr, Domtar Newsprint Ltd, 66-67. *Concurrent Pos:* Design engr, Environ Resources Consult Ltd, 69-70; consult, WHO, Copenhagen, 76, var eng firms & munic in Can, 78-; lectr, Univ Hong Kong, 80. *Mem:* Can Soc Civil Eng; Eng Inst Can; Water Environ Fedn; Can Asn Water Qual; Overseas Chinese Environ Engrs & Scientists Asn. *Res:* Aerobic, anoxic and anaerobic biological wastewater treatment; field and laboratory water quality studies; mathematical modeling of biological processes and surface and ground water quality and transport. *Mailing Add:* Dept Civil Eng Univ NB PO Box 4400 Fredericton NB E3B 5A3 Can. *Fax:* 506-453-3568; *E-Mail:* lin@unb.ca

LIN, LARRY Y H, CIVIL ENGINEERING. *Current Pos:* MEM STAFF, ROY WESTON INC, 66- *Personal Data:* b China. *Educ:* Nat Taiwan Univ, BS, 57; WVa Univ, MS, 63, PhD(civil eng), 66; Am Acad Environ Engrs, dipl. *Prof Exp:* Teaching asst, Nat Taiwan Univ, 59-61; res asst assoc, WVa Univ, 61-64. *Mem:* Water Pollution Control Fedn. *Res:* Process design of industrial and municipal wastewater treatment facilities; physical, chemical and biological aspects of water pollution; air and solid waste problems; data analysis and computer programming; energy conservation. *Mailing Add:* 19 Montbard Dr Chadds Ford PA 19317

LIN, LAWRENCE I-KUEI, STATISTICS, DATA MANAGEMENT. *Current Pos:* res statistician, 79-87, sr res statistician, 87-95, SR RES SCIENTIST STATIST, BAXTER HEALTHCARE CO, 95- *Personal Data:* b Fuchou, China, May 21, 48; m 71, Sha-Li Yen; c Juintu, Buortau & Shintau. *Educ:* Nat Chengchi Univ, Taiwan, BC, 70; Univ Iowa, MS, 73, PhD(statist), 79. *Prof Exp:* Res asst, Dept Prev Med, Univ Iowa, 73, statistician, Iowa Epidemiol Study Pesticides, 73-79. *Mem:* Am Statist Asn; Biomet Soc; Drug Info Asn. *Res:* Discriminant analysis; risk assessment; M-estimator; pharmacokinetics; generalized Linear model. *Mailing Add:* Baxter Healthcare Co Rte 120 & Wilson Round Lake IL 60073. *Fax:* 847-270-5449

LIN, LEEWEN, MOLECULAR BIOLOGY, PROTEIN CHEMISTRY. *Current Pos:* Staff fel, 90-92, SR STAFF FEL, CBER FOOD & DRUG ADMIN, 92- *Personal Data:* b Taipei, Taiwan; m 84, Fang-Jen S Lee; c Alice & Albert. *Educ:* BS, Nat Taiwan Univ, 80, MS, 82; PhD, NC State Univ, 87. *Prof Exp:* Res Fel, Mass Gen Hosp, 87-90. *Mem:* Am Soc Biochem & Molecular Biol. *Res:* Molecular biology and genetics of parasites; vaccines against parasitic diseases. *Mailing Add:* Div Allergenic Prod & Parasitol CBER Food & Drug Admin 8800 Rockville Pike Bldg 29 Rm 511 Bethesda MD 20892. *Fax:* 301-496-4681

LIN, LEU-FEN HOU, protein chemistry, neurotrophic factor, for more information see previous edition

LIN, MAO-SHIU, ELECTRICAL ENGINEERING. *Current Pos:* from asst prof to assoc prof elec eng, 66-72, chmn, elec & comput eng dept, 76-87, PROF ELEC ENG, SAN DIEGO STATE UNIV, 72- *Personal Data:* b Tainan, Taiwan, June 20, 31. *Educ:* Nat Taiwan Univ, BSE, 55; Univ Mich, MSE, 58, PhD(elec eng), 64. *Prof Exp:* Asst engr elec mach, Ta-Tung Elec Mfg Co, Taiwan, 55-56; assoc res engr, Electron Physics Lab, Univ Mich, 64-66. *Mem:* Inst Elec & Electronics Engrs; Am Soc Eng Educ. *Res:* Material science; solid state electronics; quantum electronics; power engineering. *Mailing Add:* Dept Elec Eng San Diego State Univ 5402 College Ave San Diego CA 92182-0190

LIN, MICHAEL C, HORMONE REGULATION, CELLULAR DIFFERENTIATION. *Current Pos:* RES CHEMIST, NIH, 75- *Personal Data:* b 1938. *Educ:* Med Col Ga, PhD(biochem), 66. *Mem:* Am Soc Biochem & Molecular Biol; Am Chem Soc. *Mailing Add:* NHLBI-NIH 6701 Rockledge Dr Suite 10193 Bethesda MD 20892-7956

LIN, MING CHANG, CHEMICAL KINETICS, LASER APPLICATIONS. *Current Pos:* ROBERT W WOODRUFF PROF PHYS CHEM, EMROY UNIV, 88- *Personal Data:* b Hsinpu, Hsinchu, Taiwan, Oct 24, 36; US citizen; m 65, J H Chern; c Karen & L Hsinjih & Ellena J. *Educ:* Taiwan Normal Univ, BSc, 59; Univ Ottawa, Can, PhD(phys chem), 65. *Honors & Awards:* Alexander von Humboldt Award, 82. *Prof Exp:* Res fel, Univ Ottawa, 65-67; res assoc, Cornell Univ, 67-69; res chemist, Naval Res Lab, 70-74, supvry res chemist, 74-82, sr scientist, 82-88. *Concurrent Pos:* Adj prof, Dept Chem, Catholic Univ, Washington, DC, 81-88; Guggenheim fel, 82-83; dist vis prof, Inst Atomic & Molecular Sci, Taipei, Taiwan, 94; Prize Sci & Technol, Taiwanese Am Found, 89- *Mem:* Am Chem Soc; Combustion Inst; Sigma Xi; Am Vacuum Soc; Mat Res Soc. *Res:* Kinetics of chemical reactions are studies with modern diagnostic tools such as lasers with special emphasis on the elucidation of mechanisms of combustion and planetary reactions, heterogeneous catalytic processes and microelectronic processing chemistry. *Mailing Add:* Dept Chem Emory Univ Atlanta GA 30322. *Fax:* 404-727-6586

LIN, MING-FONG, CANCER RESEARCH, SIGNAL TRANSDUCTION IN CELL GROWTH REGULATION. *Current Pos:* ASST PROF, UROL & CANCER CTR, UNIV SOUTHERN CALIF, MED CTR, 88- *Personal Data:* b Taiwan, Oct 9, 51; US citizen; m 79, Fen-Fen Yang; c Frank & Jamie. *Educ:* Kaohsiung Med Col, Taiwan, BS, 74; Nat Tsing Hua Univ, MS, 76; Roswell Park Mem Inst, Buffalo, NY, PhD(exp pathol), 83. *Honors & Awards:* Best Proj Award, Nat Cancer Inst, 89. *Prof Exp:* Fel, La State Univ, Med Ctr, 83-86, res asst prof, 86; res asst prof, Ore Health Sci Univ, 87-88. *Mem:* Am Asn Cancer Res; Am Soc Cell Biol; Am Soc Microbiol; AAAS; NY Acad Sci; Sigma Xi. *Res:* Cell growth regulation, the approach is to delineate the regulation of phosphotyrosine level in cells; dephosphorylation by a protein tryosine phosphatase, a tissue-specific differentiation antigen, the results will provide clues to understand the carcinogenesis of male prostate cancer it will also lead us to understand the biological significance of differentiation-associated phosphatases in cell growth regulation. *Mailing Add:* Dept Biochem & Molecular Biol Univ Nebr Med Ctr 600 S 42nd St Omaha NE 68198. *Fax:* 213-342-2498

LIN, MOW SHIAH, BIOCHEMISTRY, ORGANIC CHEMISTRY. *Current Pos:* res assoc enzyme, 75-77, assoc chemist, 77-91, CHEMIST, BROOKHAVEN NAT LAB, 91- *Personal Data:* b Kwangtung, China, June 18, 41; US citizen; m 68; c 3. *Educ:* Tamkang Col, BS, 65; Univ Wyo, PhD(chem), 73. *Prof Exp:* Fel vision, NIH, 73-75. *Mem:* AAAS; Am Chem Soc; Sigma Xi. *Res:* Chemistry of vision; isomerase and bacteriorhodopsin; nuclear engineering; nuclear wastes. *Mailing Add:* Brookhaven Nat Lab Bldg 318 Upton NY 11973

LIN, OTTO CHUI CHAU, POLYMER CHEMISTRY, RHEOLOGY. *Current Pos:* DIR GENERAL, MAT RES LAB, ITRI, 83-, VPRES, 85- *Personal Data:* b Kwongtang, China, Aug 8, 38; m 63; c 3. *Educ:* Nat Taiwan Univ, BS, 60; Columbia Univ, MA, 63, PhD(phys chem), 67. *Prof Exp:* Res chemist, E I Dupont de Nemours & Co, Inc, 67-69, staff chemist, 69-71, res assoc, Marshall Res Lab, Fabrics & Finishes Dept, 71- *Concurrent Pos:* Vis prof, Inst Polymer Sci & actg dean, Col of Eng, Nat Tsing Hua Univ, 78-80; bd dir, China Tech Consult, Inc, 84-; bd dir, Feng Chia Univ, 86- *Mem:* AAAS; Am Chem Soc; Am Inst Chem Engrs; NY Acad Sci; Soc Rheol; Chinese Soc Mat Sci (pres, 86-). *Res:* Physical chemical characterization of polymers; rheological properties of polymers; sedimentation; viscometry; organic coatings; ecological impacts of polymer applications; polymers for electronics applications. *Mailing Add:* 103 Clementi Rd Singapore 129788 Singapore

LIN, P(EN) M(IN), ELECTRICAL ENGINEERING. *Current Pos:* from asst prof to prof, 61-94, EMER PROF ELEC ENG, PURDUE UNIV, 94- *Personal Data:* b China, Oct 17, 28; nat US; m 62, Louise S; c Marian, Margaret & Janice. *Educ:* Taiwan Univ, BS, 50; NC State Col, MS, 56; Purdue Univ, PhD(elec eng), 60. *Prof Exp:* From instr to asst prof elec eng, Purdue Univ, 56-60; mem tech staff, Bell Tel Labs, NJ, 60-61. *Concurrent Pos:* Assoc ed, Trans Circuit Theory, Inst Elec & Electronics Engrs, 71-73. *Mem:* Life fel Inst Elec & Electronics Engrs. *Res:* Circuit theory; computer-aided circuit analysis. *Mailing Add:* Sch Elec Eng Purdue Univ Lafayette IN 47907

LIN, PAUL C S, HILBERT & BANACH SPACES, ALGEBRAS. *Current Pos:* from asst prof to assoc prof, 81-89, PROF MATH, BISHOP'S UNIV, 89- *Personal Data:* b Taiwan; Can citizen; m 76, Margaret P M Aw; c Angela. *Educ:* Nat Taiwan Norm Univ, BSc, 63; McMaster Univ, MSc, 65; Univ NB, PhD(math), 73. *Honors & Awards:* Res Award, Nat Res Coun Can & Natural Sci & Eng Res Coun Can. *Prof Exp:* Asst prof math, St Thomas Univ, 78-81. *Concurrent Pos:* Res fel, Res Inst Can Math Cong, 75; hon res assoc, Univ NB, 77-85; chmn, Dept Math, St Thomas Univ, 79-81 & Bishop's Univ, 89-90 & 92- *Mem:* Am Math Asn; Math Asn Am; Can Math Soc. *Res:* Normed linear spaces; Hilbert and Banach spaces; operators on Hilbert spaces. *Mailing Add:* Bishop's Univ Lennoxville PQ J1M 1Z7 Can. *Fax:* 819-822-9661; *E-Mail:* plin@hera.ubishops.ca

LIN, PAUL KUANG-HSIEN, EXPERIMENTAL DESIGN, QUALITY ENGINEERING. *Current Pos:* asst prof, 84-87, ASSOC PROF STATIST, UNIV MICH, DEARBORN, 87- *Personal Data:* b Tung-Shih, Taiwan, Nov 12, 46; m 78, Cathy Jen; c Elizabeth & John. *Educ:* Fu-Jen Univ, Taiwan, BS, 70; Brigham Young Univ, 75; Wayne State Univ, PhD(statist), 80. *Prof Exp:* Asst prof statist, Oakland Univ, 80-82; asst prof statist, Western Mich Univ, 82-84. *Concurrent Pos:* Consult, Qual Improv. *Mem:* Am Statist Asn; Inst Math Statist; Am Soc Quality Control; Sigma Xi. *Res:* Experimental design; interval estimation and hypothesis testing; Taguchi's methods for quality improvement. *Mailing Add:* Dept Math Statist Univ Mich Dearborn MI 48128-1491

LIN, PI-ERH, MATHEMATICAL STATISTICS. *Current Pos:* asst prof, 68-74, assoc prof, 74-80, PROF STATIST, FLA STATE UNIV, 80- *Personal Data:* b Taiwan, China, Jan 8, 38; m 63; c 3. *Educ:* Taiwan Norm Univ, BSc, 61; Columbia Univ, PhD(math statist), 68. *Prof Exp:* Consult med ctr, Columbia Univ, 67-68. *Concurrent Pos:* Fla State Univ fac res grant, 71-72. *Mem:* Inst Math Statist; Am Statist Asn; Bernoulli Soc. *Res:* Multivariate analysis; statistical inference. *Mailing Add:* Dept Statist Fla State Univ 600 College Ave W Tallahassee FL 32306-1096

LIN, PING-WHA, ENVIRONMENTAL ENGINEERING. *Current Pos:* prof, 66-79, prof & Dresser chair prof, 81-95, EMER PROF, ENVIRON ENG, TRI-STATE UNIV, 95-; PRES, LIN TECHNOLOGIES, INC, 88- *Personal Data:* b Canton, China, July 11, 25; m 60; c 2. *Educ:* Jiao Tung Univ, BS, 47; Purdue Univ, MS, 49, PhD(sanit eng), 51. *Honors & Awards:* Achievement Award, United Inventors & Scientists of Am, 74. *Prof Exp:* Engr, Amman & Whitney, NY, 51-54, Ebesco, 54-55, Parsons, Brinkerhoff, Hall & MacDonald, 55-57 & Lockwood Greene Engrs, 57-59; engr, World Health Orgn, 59-60, consult, 62-66; engr, John Graham & Co, NY, 60-61. *Concurrent Pos:* Fel, NSF workshop, Mass Inst Technol, 69; Dept Energy indiv grant, 82; proj mgr, WHO, 79-81, consult, 86. *Mem:* Fel Am Soc Civil Engrs; Am Water Works Asn; Sigma Xi; Am Chem Soc. *Res:* Acid neutralization; metal waste treatment; fly ash utilization; soil stabilization; quenching process; flue gas desulfurization; energy development; gas kinetics; Lin's theory of flux. *Mailing Add:* 506 S Darling St Angola IN 46703

LIN, RAY Y, COATING & THIN FILM TECHNOLOGY. *Current Pos:* PROF MAT SCI & ENG, UNIV CINCINNATI, 83- *Personal Data:* m 76, Alice T Su; c Andrew R. *Educ:* Nat Taiwan Univ, BS, 71; Univ Wis, MS, 76. *Hon Degrees:* DSc, Mas Inst Technol, 91. *Prof Exp:* Metall engr, Kennecott Lab, 79-80; mem tech staff, GTE Lab, 80-82; res scientist, Energy Lab, Mass Inst Technol, 82-83. *Concurrent Pos:* Chair, Process Fundamentals Comt, Minerals, Metals & Mat Soc, 83; vchair, Thermodyn Activity & Phase Equilibra Comt, Am Soc Metals Int, 83-; consult appl sci, 84-; vis prof, Tohoku Univ, 90-91 & 94-95; sr tech adv, UN World Develop Prog, 91. *Mem:* Minerals, Metals & Mat Soc; Am Soc Metals Int; Am Ceramic Soc; Mat Res Soc; Am Composite Soc; Iron & Steel Soc. *Res:* Coatings and thin film processing with sputter deposition; chemical vapor deposition and electroplating; infrared processing of materials; composite materials processing; metal matrix composites; composite interfaces; infrared joining of metals; superalloys and intermetallic compounds; engineering interlayer material development; functionally gradient materials. *Mailing Add:* Univ Cincinnati ML No 12 Cincinnati OH 45221-0012. *Fax:* 513-556-2569

LIN, RENEE C, LIPID METABOLISM, CULTURE HEPATOCYTES. *Current Pos:* ASST PROF MED, SCH MED, IND UNIV, 85- *Educ:* Univ Wis, Madison, PhD(biochem), 69. *Prof Exp:* ASSOC SCIENTIST MED RES, VET ADMIN MED CTR, 74- *Mailing Add:* Dept Med Ind Univ Sch Med 975 W Walnut St-1B 424 Indianapolis IN 46202-5121

LIN, REN-LANG, TOXICOLOGY, PSYCHOPHARMACOLOGY. *Current Pos:* CHIEF TOXICOLOGIST, NJ STATE MED EXAMR OFF, 83- *Personal Data:* b Hsin-Chu, Taiwan, Feb 28, 37; m 65; c 2. *Educ:* Nat Taiwan Univ, BS, 59, MS, 63; Okla State Univ, PhD(biochem), 69. *Prof Exp:* Fel, Univ Wis-Madison, 69-71; res scientist, Galesburg State Hosp, Ill, 71-75; res scientist, Ill State Psychiat Inst, 75-78; asst chief toxicologist, Off Med Examiner, Cook County, 78-83. *Mem:* Am Chem Soc; AAAS. *Res:* Forensic toxicology; biochemistry of mental illness; biosynthesis and metabolism of biogenic amines; biochemistry and pharmacology of psychoactive drugs. *Mailing Add:* Dept Molecular Biochem Beckman Res Inst 1450 E Duarte Rd Duarte CA 91010-3000

LIN, ROBERT I-SAN, SCIENCE ADMINISTRATION, NUTRITION & DEGENERATIVE DISEASES. *Current Pos:* EXEC VPRES, NUTRIT INT, 91- *Personal Data:* b Fukien, China, 42; m 71, Cecile V Fung; c Sylvia H, Alva H, Rose H & David H. *Educ:* Nat Taiwan Univ, BS, 61; Univ Calif, Los Angeles, MS, 65, PhD(biophy & nuclear med), 68. *Prof Exp:* Res fel chem, Calif Inst Technol, 68-70; clin trainee metab dis, Med Ctr, Univ Calif, 70-71; life sci mgr, Gen Tel & Electronic Corp, 71-73; dir enzyme prod, Worthington Biochem Corp, 73-74; vpres technol diag prod, RIA Inc, 74-75; chief scientist, Frito-Lay Inc, 75-82; vpres, Natural Prod Div, Richardson Vicks, 82-85; sr vpres, Makers of Kal, 86-87 & Weider Health & Fitness, 88-90. *Concurrent Pos:* Vis prof biochem & molecular biol, Pepperdine Univ, 69-70; trainee biotechnol & nutrit, Mass Inst Technol, 71; vis distinguished prof nutrit & food sci, Tex Woman's Univ, 81-; chmn, First World Cong on Health Significance Garlic, 90, Nutrit Sect, Seventh World Cong Food Sci & Technol; dir, Cert Bd Nutrit Specialists. *Mem:* NY Acad Sci; Sigma Xi; Am Photobiol Soc; Soc Appl Nutrit; Am Agr Econ Asn; Am Mgt Asn; Am Col Nutrit; Am Col Sport Med; Inst Food Technol; Am Chem Soc. *Res:* Diet, nutrition, aging and degenerative diseases; biotechnology and genetic engineering: recombinant DNA--hybridoma and subcellular organelle transfer; chemistry and rheology of natural and synthetic polymers; physical chemistry of surfactants and viscosity modifiers; sport nutrition, herbal sciences and pharmacognosy; management of technological development and industrialization; operation research and econometrics. *Mailing Add:* 6 Silverfern Irvine CA 92612-3707. *Fax:* 714-854-6170

LIN, ROBERT PEICHUNG, SOLAR & SPACE PLASMA PHYSICS, HIGH ENERGY ASTROPHYSICS. *Current Pos:* From asst res physicist to assoc res physicist, Univ Calif, 67-79, res physicist, 79-88, sr fel, 80-88, adj prof astron, 88-90, PROF PHYSICS, UNIV CALIF, 91-, ASSOC DIR, SPACE SCI LAB, 92- *Personal Data:* b China, Jan 24, 42; US citizen; m 83. *Educ:* Calif Inst Technol, BS, 62; Univ Calif, Berkeley, PhD(physics), 67. *Concurrent Pos:* Prin investr, NASA & ESA Giotto Mission, 79-, ISTP/GGS Wind, 81-, Mars Observer, 87-, Max 91 Balloon, 89- & Hiregs Antarctica, 94. *Mem:* Am Geophys Union; Am Astron Soc. *Res:* Solar flares, radio bursts and cosmic rays; interplanetary particles; magnetospheric processes; lunar magnetism; astrophysical x-ray and gamma ray spectroscopy; comets. *Mailing Add:* 80 Hill Rd Berkeley CA 94708

LIN, RUEY Y, CHEMISTRY. *Current Pos:* sr mat res engr, 84-87, prin res scientist, 87-90, ASST DIR, HOWMEDICA, INC, 90- *Educ:* Nat Taiwan Univ, BS, 55; WVa Univ, MS, 59, PhD(chem), 62. *Prof Exp:* Res fel, State Univ NY, Buffalo, 62-63; sr chemist, Res Br, Res & Develop Div, Carborundum Co, 63-67, res assoc, 67-69, sr res assoc, 70-71, proj mgr, 71-73, sr develop assoc, 74-77; proj mgr nonwoven prod develop, Am Kynol, Inc, 75-76; res assoc, Eastern Res Ctr, Stauffer Chem Co, 77-84. *Mem:* Am Chem Soc; Sigma Xi. *Res:* Development of composite materials for orthopaedic applications; engineering thermoplastics; reaction injection molding technology; flame retarding area; high performance composites; refractory fibers; author of 15 publications; granted 13 US patents. *Mailing Add:* Howmedica Inc 359 Veterans Blvd Rutherford NJ 07070-2584

LIN, SHAO-CHI, AEROSPACE ENGINEERING. *Current Pos:* PROF ENG PHYSICS, UNIV CALIF, SAN DIEGO, 64- *Personal Data:* b Canton, China, Jan 5, 25; nat US; m 55. *Educ:* Nat Cent Univ, China, BSc, 46; Cornell Univ, PhD(aeronaut eng), 52. *Honors & Awards:* Res Award, Am Inst Aeronaut & Astronaut, 66. *Prof Exp:* Engr, Bur Aircraft Indust, China, 47-48; asst, Cornell Univ, 48-51, actg instr, 52, res assoc, 52-54, actg asst prof, 54; prin res scientist, Avco-Everett Res Lab, Mass, 55-64. *Concurrent Pos:* Consult, Aerospace Corp, Avco-Everett Res Lab, Inst Defense Anal & Rand Corp; panel mem re-entry physics, Nat Acad Sci-Nat Res Coun. *Mem:* Am Inst Aeronaut & Astronaut; Am Phys Soc; Am Astronaut Soc; Am Geophys Union. *Res:* Physical gas dynamics; hypersonic flight; reentry physics; laser physics and interaction. *Mailing Add:* Univ Calif 9500 Gilman Dr La Jolla CA 92093-0411

LIN, SHENG HSIEN, CHEMICAL KINETICS, CHEMICAL PHYSICS. *Current Pos:* from asst to assoc prof, 65-72, PROF CHEM, 72, REGENT PROF, ARIZ STATE UNIV, 88- *Personal Data:* b Sept 17, 37; US citizen; m 70, Pearl H Pi. *Educ:* Nat Taiwan Univ, BS, 59, MS, 61; Univ Utah, PhD(chem), 64. *Prof Exp:* Fel chem, Columbia Univ, 64-65. *Concurrent Pos:* A P Sloan fel, 67-69; Guggenheim fel, 71-73; Humboldt Sr US scientist awardee, 79-80 & 88-89; Hon prof, Nanjing Univ, 88- *Mem:* Am Chem Soc; Acad Sinica. *Res:* Energy transfer; femtosecond processes; optical rotations and the Faraday effect; reaction kinetics; electron transfer; magnetic properties of molecules; multi-photon processes; molecular relaxation processes; theory of time-resolved x-ray diffraction. *Mailing Add:* Dept Chem Ariz State Univ Tempe AZ 85281. *Fax:* 602-965-2747; *E-Mail:* lin@asucps

LIN, SHENG-XIANG, ENZYMOLOGY, STRUCTURAL BIOLOGY. *Current Pos:* vis prof, Dept Biochem, 88-89, SR SCIENTIST & ASSOC PROF, DEPT PHYSIOL, LAVAL UNIV MED CTR, 89- *Personal Data:* b Shanghai, China, Aug 27, 45; m 85, Ming Zhou. *Educ:* Fudan Univ, Shanghai, BSc, 68; Shanghai Inst Biochem, MSc, 79; Nat Ctr Sci Res, France, Dr, 82; Univ Louis Pasteur, DSc, 84. *Honors & Awards:* Commemorative Medal, Gov-Gen Can, 93. *Prof Exp:* Asst prof, Shanghai Inst Biochem, Acad Sinica, 84-85, assoc prof, 85-87; vis assoc prof, Dept Biochem, Case Western Res Univ, 87-88. *Concurrent Pos:* Prin investr, Laval Univ Med Ctr, 90- *Mem:* Am Soc Exp Biol; Protein Soc; Can Physiol Soc; Chinese Asn Biochem; Fr-Chinese Asn Res Biol & Med. *Res:* Protein chemistry, enzymology and enzyme structure studies, especially for aminoacyl-tRNA synthetases and steroid dehydrogenases. *Mailing Add:* Lab Endocrinol CHUL 2705 Blvd Laurier Local T3-67 Ste-Foy PQ G1V 4G2 Can. *Fax:* 418-654-2761

LIN, SHIN, BIOCHEMISTRY, BIOPHYSICS. *Current Pos:* from asst prof to assoc prof, 74-82, PROF BIOPHYS, JOHNS HOPKINS UNIV, 82-, PROF BIOL, 85- *Personal Data:* b Hong Kong, Feb 14, 45; US citizen; m 69; c 2. *Educ:* Univ Calif, Davis, BS, 65; San Diego State Univ, MS, 67; Univ Calif, Los Angeles, PhD(biol chem), 71. *Prof Exp:* Fel, Univ Calif, San Francisco, 71-74. *Concurrent Pos:* NIH res career develop award, 76-81; chmn biophys, Johns Hopkins Univ, 83-96. *Mem:* AAAS; Am Soc Biol Chemists; Am Soc Cell Biol; Biophys Soc. *Res:* Biochemical and biophysical studies on cytoskeletal and motile functions of eukaryotic cells, with emphasis on drugs and cellular proteins affecting the assembly and interactions of actin filaments in vivo and in vitro. *Mailing Add:* Dept Biophys Johns Hopkins Univ 3400 Charles St Baltimore MD 21218-2684. *Fax:* 410-516-5170; *E-Mail:* shin.lin@jhu.edu

LIN, SHU, ELECTRICAL ENGINEERING, INFORMATION SCIENCES. *Current Pos:* PROF & CHMN, UNIV HAWAII, 88- *Personal Data:* b Nanking, China, May 20, 36; m 63; c 3. *Educ:* Nat Taiwan Univ, BS, 59; Rice Univ, MS, 64, PhD(elec eng), 65. *Prof Exp:* Res assoc, Univ Hawaii, 65-66, from asst prof to assoc prof elec eng, 66-73, prof, 73-81, prof elec eng, 86-88; prof elec eng, 82-88, Irma Runyon Chair Prof, Tex A&M Univ, 88- *Concurrent Pos:* NSF grants, 67-92; Air Force Cambridge Res Lab grant, 70-71, NASA grants, 83-91; vis scholar, Univ Utah, 71-72; vis scientist, IBM Watson Res Ctr, 78-79. *Mem:* Fel Inst Elec & Electronics Engrs; Sigma Xi. *Res:* Coding theory and error control in data transmission systems; coding theory and multi-access communications. *Mailing Add:* Elec Eng 0 2500 Campus Rd Honolulu HI 96822-2270

LIN, SHWU-YENG TZEN, TOPOLOGY. *Current Pos:* lectr, 64-65, asst prof, 65-71, ASSOC PROF MATH, UNIV SFLA, 71- *Personal Data:* b Tainan, Formosa, May 11, 34; m 60; c 3. *Educ:* Nat Taiwan Normal Univ, BSc, 58; Tulane Univ, MS, 62; Univ Fla, PhD(math), 65. *Prof Exp:* Asst math, Inst Math, Academia Sinica, 58-60; instr, Tulane Univ, 61-63. *Concurrent Pos:* Reviewer, Math Rev, Am Math Soc, 68-; Zentralblatt fur Mathmatik, 70- *Mem:* Math Asn Am. *Res:* Topology and relation-theory. *Mailing Add:* Dept Math Phy 114 Univ SFla 4202 E Fowler Ave Tampa FL 33620

LIN, SIN-SHONG, HIGH TEMPERATURE CHEMISTRY. *Current Pos:* RES CHEMIST, ARMY RES LAB MAT DIRECTURATE. *Personal Data:* b Taiwan, Oct 24, 33; m 64; c 3. *Educ:* Nat Taiwan Univ, BS, 56; Nat Tsing-Hua Univ, Taiwan, MS, 58; Univ Kans, PhD(chem), 66. *Prof Exp:* Fel, Northwestern Univ, Evanston, 66-67. *Mem:* Am Chem Soc; Am Vacuum Soc; Electrochem Soc; Am Carbon Soc; Soc Advancement Mat & Process Eng. *Res:* Thermodynamics of vaporization processes; material research and development; atmospheric sampling of gases; carbon fiber processing and characterization; electron spectroscopy for chemical analysis & auger electron spectroscopy. *Mailing Add:* 40 Lyons Rd Westwood MA 02090-2230. *Fax:* 617-923-5385

LIN, SPING, NEUROCHEMISTRY, PHYSIOLOGY. *Current Pos:* res fellow, Med Sch, Univ Minn, Minneapolis, 54-61, res assoc, 61-63, from asst prof to assoc prof, 63-86, EMER PROF NEUROL, MED SCH, UNIV MINN, MINNEAPOLIS, 86- *Personal Data:* b Canton, China, Sept 8, 18; nat US; m 46, Ying-hgsh; c James Tseuming & Judy Tse-mei. *Educ:* Sun Yat-Sen Univ, BA, 40; Univ Minn, MS, 50, PhD(entom), 52. *Prof Exp:* Asst entom, Sun Yat-Sen Univ, 40-44, instr, 44-47. *Mem:* Int Soc Neurochem; AAAS; Am Soc Neurochem; Sigma Xi. *Res:* Neurobiology; neurochemistry. *Mailing Add:* 1785 Fairview Ave N St Paul MN 55113. *E-Mail:* linxx024@maroon.tc.umn.edu

LIN, STEPHEN FANG-MAW, PHYSICAL CHEMISTRY. *Current Pos:* ASSOC PROF CHEM, NC CENT UNIV, 70- *Personal Data:* b Nantou, Taiwan, Aug 21, 37; m 66; c 1. *Educ:* Nat Taiwan Univ, BS, 60; Univ Ill, Urbana, MS, 68, PhD(phys chem), 70. *Mem:* AAAS; Sigma Xi; Am Chem Soc. *Res:* Conformation and stability of sulfur ring compounds; molecular spectroscopy. *Mailing Add:* 3116 Annandale Rd Durham NC 27705-5466

LIN, STEPHEN Y, LIGNIN CHEMISTRY, ORGANIC CHEMISTRY. *Current Pos:* RES MGR, LIGNOTECH US INC, 91- *Personal Data:* b Pingtung, Taiwan, Apr 23, 39; US citizen; m 72, Ilona K Szabo; c Stephen S & Eva M. *Educ:* Nat Taiwan Univ, Taipei, BS, 62; Univ Wash, Seattle, MS, 67; NC State Univ, Raleigh, PhD(chem), 70. *Honors & Awards:* George Olmsted Award, Am Paper Inst, 71. *Prof Exp:* Res chemist, Westvaco Corp, 72-76, sr res chemist, 76-79; res assoc, Lignin Chem Res, Am Can Co, 79-80, supvr res, 80-81, sr supv res, 81-82; res mgr, Reed Lignin Inc, 83-88 & Daishowa Chemicals Inc, 89-91. *Concurrent Pos:* Adj prof, NC State Univ. *Mem:* Tech Asn Pulp & Paper Indust; Am Chem Soc. *Res:* Lignin organic-physical chemistry; modification and application of industrial lignins, including kraft and sulfite lignins; dispersants. *Mailing Add:* 1816 Daffodil Lane Wausau WI 54401. *Fax:* 715-355-3648

LIN, SUE CHIN, mathematics, for more information see previous edition

LIN, SUI, HEAT & MASS TRANSFER, FLUID MECHANICS. *Current Pos:* asst prof thermodyn & fluid mech, 70-75, assoc prof, 75-81, PROF HEAT TRANSFER & FLUID MECHANICS, DEPT MECH ENG, CONCORDIA UNIV, MONTREAL, 81- *Personal Data:* b Wenlin, Zhejiang, China, 1929; Can citizen; c 2. *Educ:* Ord Eng Col, Taiwan, BS, 53; Univ Karlsruhe, WGer, Dipl-Ing 62, Dr-Ing(mech eng), 64. *Prof Exp:* Res assoc refrig, Inst Refrig Eng, Univ Karlsruhe, WGer, 62-65 & gas dynamics, Inst Fluid Mech & Fluid Mach, 65-69; fel sonic boom, Inst Aerospace studies, Univ Toronto, Ont, 69-70. *Concurrent Pos:* Sr vis scientist, QIT-Fer et Titane Inc, Sorel, Quebec, 84-85. *Mem:* Eng Inst Can; Can Soc Mech Eng; Am Soc Heating, Refrig & Air Conditioning Engrs; Deutsche Gesellschaft fuer Luft-und Raum-fahrt. *Res:* Heat and mass transfer with phase changes; confined vortex flows; heat pump systems for cold climates; freezing preservation of biological cells; similarity and modelling processes. *Mailing Add:* Dept Mech Eng Concordia Univ 1455 de Maisonneuve Blvd W Montreal PQ H3G 1M8 Can. *Fax:* 514-848-3175

LIN, SUNG P, FLUID MECHANICS, APPLIED MATHEMATICS. *Current Pos:* from asst prof to assoc prof mech eng, 66-74, chmn fluid & thermal sci group, 78-80, PROF MECH ENG, CLARKSON UNIV, 74-, CHMN APPL MECH PROG, 81-, CHMN, DEPT MECH & AERONAT ENG, 94- *Personal Data:* b Taipei, China, Apr 18, 37; US citizen; m 66; c 2. *Educ:* Taiwan Univ, BS, 58; Univ Utah, MS, 61; Univ Mich, PhD(eng mech), 65. *Prof Exp:* Engr, Ministry Econ, China, 58-60; lectr eng mech, Univ Mich, 65-66. *Concurrent Pos:* NSF initiation grant, 67-69, res grants, 70-72, 74-76, 78-80, 80-85 & 88-91; sr vis, Cambridge Univ, 73-74; Kodak grant, 74-76, consult, Eastman Kodak Co, 77-81; vis prof, Rochester Univ & Stanford Univ, 80-81; Bausch & Lomb grant, 80-81; NASA fel, 83 & 84; grantee, NASA, 84-86 & 93-, ARO, 85- *Mem:* Fel Am Phys Soc; Am Soc Mech Engrs; assoc fel Am Inst Aeronaut & Astronaut. *Res:* Theory and application of mechanics; fluid and biofluid mechanics; hydrodynamic stability; flow separation; heat transfer; transient phenomena; film coating technology; aerosol dynamics; atomization. *Mailing Add:* Dept Mech & Aeronaut Eng Clarkson Univ Potsdam NY 13676

LIN, TAI-SHUN, medicinal chemistry, organic chemistry; deceased, see previous edition for last biography

LIN, TIEN-SUNG TOM, PHYSICAL CHEMISTRY, SPECTROSCOPY. *Current Pos:* from asst prof to assoc prof, 76-86, PROF CHEM, WASHINGTON UNIV, 86- *Personal Data:* b Taiwan, China, Jan 9, 38; m 66, Loretta I-Hsing; c Robin, Irvin & Natatia. *Educ:* Tunghai Univ, BS, 60; Syracuse Univ, MS, 66; Univ Pa, PhD(phys chem), 69. *Prof Exp:* Res fel, Harvard Univ, 70. *Concurrent Pos:* Scientist-in-Res, Argonne Nat Lab, 80; vis prof, Leiden Univ, Neth 90 & Inst Atomic & Molecular Sci, Academia Sinica, Taiwan, 95. *Mem:* Am Chem Soc. *Res:* Molecular spectroscopy; photophysical and photochemical processes; structural aspects of organic free radicals; free radical pathology and anti-oxidants. *Mailing Add:* Dept Chem Washington Univ St Louis MO 63130. *Fax:* 314-935-4481; *E-Mail:* lin@wuchem.wustl.edu

LIN, TSAU-YEN, ENZYMOLOGY. *Current Pos:* MEM, LIN & ASSOCS, 92- *Personal Data:* b Taiwan, China, July 18, 32; m 67, Woan-Jung Chen. *Educ:* Nat Taiwan Univ, BS, 55, MS, 57; Univ Calif, Berkeley, PhD(biochem), 65. *Prof Exp:* Instr clin chem, Kaohsiung Med Col, Taiwan, 57-58; res chemist, China Chem & Pharmaceut Co, 58-59; res asst biochem, US Naval Med Res Unit Number 2, Taiwan, 59-61; res assoc, Univ Calif, Berkeley, 65-67, asst res biochemist, 67-68; biochemist, Merck Sharp & Dohme Res Labs, 69-91; scientist, Cal-Test Diagnostic, 91-92. *Mem:* AAAS; Am Chem Soc; Am Soc Biol Chemists; Sigma Xi. *Res:* Biosynthesis and function of complex carbohydrates; mechanism and active site structure of enzymes; biochemical characterization of complement. *Mailing Add:* Lin & Assocs 9365 Wickham Way Orlando FL 32836-5518. *E-Mail:* tsauyen@aol.com

LIN, TSUE-MING, IMMUNOLOGY, MICROBIOLOGY. *Current Pos:* dir res, 86-90, VPRES, RES & DEVELOP, DIAMEDIX CORP, 90- *Personal Data:* b Ping-tung, Taiwan, June 10, 35; US citizen; m 64; c 3. *Educ:* Nat Taiwan Univ, DVM, 58, dipl pub health, 60; Tulane Univ, MS, 64; Univ Tex Med Br, PhD(microbiol), 68. *Prof Exp:* Teaching asst & lab instr med parasitol, Col Med, Nat Taiwan Univ, 60-62; res assoc, 68-69, from instr to assoc prof pediat, 69-80, res assoc prof pediat, Med Sch, Univ Miami, 80-86. *Concurrent Pos:* Teaching asst & lab instr, Taipei Med Col, 61-62; consult, Cordis Labs, 72-74 & sr staff immunologist to asst dir res & develop, 77-86. *Mem:* AAAS; Am Soc Microbiol; Am Asn Immunol. *Res:* Host-parasite relationship; enzyme-linked immunoassays for infectious and immunological diseases; immunology; human heart autoimmune system; trichinosis; amebiasis; toxoplasmosis; human pregnancy-associated plasma proteins. *Mailing Add:* Hyperion Inc 14100 SW 136th St Miami FL 33186

LIN, TSUNG-MIN, PHYSIOLOGY, PHARMACOLOGY. *Current Pos:* CONSULT, MED RES METHODIST HOSP, INDIANAPOLIS, IND, 86- *Personal Data:* b Chefoo, China, Oct 8, 16; nat US; m 42, Hsia Lin; c 2. *Educ:* Nat Tsing Hua Univ, China, BS, 38; Univ Ill, MS, 52, PhD, 54. *Prof Exp:* Asst physiol, Nat Tsing Hua Univ, China, 39-40; asst, Nat Chung Cheng Med Col, 40-41, lectr physiol, 41-43; lectr, Nat Kweiyang Med Col, 43-46, asst prof, 46-48; sr instr, Peking Union Med Col, 48-51; asst prof clin sci, Col Med, Univ Ill, 54-56; pharmacologist, Res Labs, Eli Lilly & Co, 56-59, res scientist, 59-63, sr res scientist, 64-85. *Concurrent Pos:* Adj prof physiol, Ind Univ Sch Med, 87-88; consult med res, Methodist Hosp, Indianapolis, Ind. *Mem:* Am Physiol Soc; Am Soc Pharmacol & Exp Therapeut; Am Gastroenterol Asn; Am Pancreatic Asn. *Res:* Gastrointestinal physiology and pharmacology. *Mailing Add:* 15 Kingspark Ct Little Rock AR 72227-2931. *Fax:* 317-846-1250

LIN, TU, INTERNAL MEDICINE, ENDOCRINOLOGY & METABOLISM. *Current Pos:* CHIEF, ENDOCRINE SECT, WILLIAM JENNINGS BRYAN DORN VET HOSP, 74- *Personal Data:* b Fukien, China, Jan 18, 41; US citizen; m 67; c 3. *Educ:* Nat Taiwan Univ, Taipei, MD, 66. *Prof Exp:* Intern, Episcopal Hosp, Temple Univ, 67-68; resident med, Berkshire Med Ctr, Union Univ, 68-70; fel endocrinol, Lahey Clin, Boston, 70-71, Roger Williams Gen Hosp, Brown Univ, 71-73; staff physician, Vet Admin Hosp, Salisbury, 73-75; from asst prof to assoc prof, 76-84, PROF ENDOCRINOL, SCH MED, UNIV SC, 84- *Concurrent Pos:* Physician, Richland Mem Hosp, Columbia, SC, 77- *Mem:* Endocrine Soc; Am Fedn Clin Res; Am Soc Andrology; fel Am Col Physicians. *Res:* Male reproductive endocrinology; Leydig cell function including cell membrane receptors, cyclic AMP metabolism, steroid receptors, steroidogenesis, phospholipid turnover and long term cell culture; insulin receptors, insulin-like growth factors I and II receptors of Leydig cells. *Mailing Add:* Vet Admin Med Ctr Columbia SC 29201

LIN, TUNG HUA, MECHANICS. *Current Pos:* prof eng, 56-78, EMER PROF, UNIV CALIF, LOS ANGELES, 78- *Personal Data:* b Chungking, China, May 26, 11; nat US; m 39; c 3. *Educ:* Tangshan Col Eng, BS, 33; Mass Inst Technol, SM, 36; Univ Mich, DSc(eng mech), 53. *Honors & Awards:* Theodore Van Karman Award, Am Soc Civil Engrs, 88. *Prof Exp:* From assoc prof to prof aeronaut eng, Tsing Hua Univ, China, 37-39; from designer to chief engr & prod mgr, Chinese Aircraft Mfg Plant, 39-45; mem, Chinese Tech Mission in Eng, 45-49; from assoc prof to prof aeronaut eng, Univ Detroit, 49-56. *Concurrent Pos:* Consult, Continental Motor Corp, Mich, 54-55, Off Ord Res, 58, NAm Aviation Inc, 62-68 & ARA Inc, 66-94; prin investr res projs, Off Sci Res, USAF, 55-59, 88-, NSF, 61-78 & US Off Naval Res, 85-93. *Mem:* Nat Acad Eng; Soc Eng Sci; fel Am Acad Mech; Am Soc Civil Engrs; fel Am Soc Mech Engrs. *Res:* Micromechanics; multiaxial stress-strain relations based on microstress fields in polycrystals; fatigue crack initiation mechanism based microstresses; inelastic structures; el asto-plastic analysis of beams, columns and plates; creep analysis of columns and plates. *Mailing Add:* 906 Las Palgas Rd Pacific Palisades CA 90272. *Fax:* 310-206-2222

LIN, TUNG YEN, STRUCTURAL ENGINEERING. *Current Pos:* BD CHMN, LIN TUNG-YEN CHINA INC, 93- *Personal Data:* b Foochow, China, Nov 14, 11; Nat US; M 41, Margaret Kao; c Paul & Verna. *Educ:* Chiaotung Univ, BS, 31; Univ Calif, Berkeley, MS, 33. *Hon Degrees:* LLD, Chinese Univ Hong Kong, 72; Golden Gate Univ, San Francisco, 82, Jiaotung Univ, Taiwan & Tongji Univ, Shanghai, 87; Chiautung Univ, 87. *Honors & Awards:* Howard Gold Medal, Am Soc Civil Engrs; Nat Medal Sci, 86; Award of Merit, Am Consult Engrs Coun, 87; Roebling Medal, Bridge Eng, 90; Leadership Award, Am Segmental Bridge Inst, 92; Lifetime Achievement Award, Asian Am Archives & Eng Asn, 93; Medal of Honor, Prestressed Concrete Inst. *Prof Exp:* From engr to chief designer, Ministry of Rwy, China, 33-46; prof bridge eng, Tungchi Univ, 39-41; chief engr, Kung Sing Eng Corp, 41-45; comnr, Taiwan Sugar Rwy, 45-46; from asst prof to prof civil eng, Univ Calif, Berkeley, 46-76, chmn, Div Struct Eng & Mech & dir lab, 60-63; chmn bd, TY Lin Int, 53-87, hon chmn bd, 87-92. *Concurrent Pos:* Hon prof, Tsinghua Univ & Tongji Univ, Beijing, China, Jiaotung Univ, Shanghai & Omei; pres, Inte-Continental Peace Bridge, Inc, 68- *Mem:* Nat Acad Eng; fel Am Soc Civil Engrs; Int Asn Bridge & Struct Engrs; hon mem Am Concrete Inst; Am Soc Eng Educ; Int Fedn Prestressing; Prestressed Concrete Inst. *Res:* Bridge and structural engineering; design of prestressed concrete and steel structures; structural concepts and systems; author of numerous publications. *Mailing Add:* Lin Tung-Yen China Inc 315 Bay St San Francisco CA 94133-1923. *Fax:* 510-526-0842

LIN, TUNG-PO, MATHEMATICS. *Current Pos:* from asst prof to assoc prof math, 61-69, PROF MATH, CALIF STATE UNIV, NORTHRIDGE, 69- *Personal Data:* b Fukien, China, Dec 31, 26; nat US; m 56; c 4. *Educ:* Nat Cent Univ, China, BSc, 49; Mass Inst Technol, PhD(phys chem), 58. *Prof Exp:* Res chemist, E I du Pont de Nemours & Co, Del, 58-61. *Concurrent Pos:* Consult, IBM Corp, 61-68. *Mem:* Am Math Soc; Math Asn Am. *Res:* Functional analysis; applied mathematics. *Mailing Add:* Calif State Univ Northridge CA 91330-0001

LIN, TZ-HONG, ORGANIC CHEMISTRY, RADIOPHARMACEUTICAL RESEARCH. *Current Pos:* GUEST SCIENTIST, LAWRENCE BERKELEY LAB, BERKELEY, CALIF, 92- *Personal Data:* b Taiwan, Jan 30, 34; m 69, KY Y; c Alan & Brian. *Educ:* Nat Taiwan Univ, BS, 56; NMex Highlands Univ, MS, 64; Univ Calif, Berkeley, PhD, 69. *Prof Exp:* Teaching & res asst, Dept Chem, NMex Highlands Univ, 61-63; teaching asst, Dept Chem, Univ Calif, Berkeley, 63-64, res asst, Biodynamics Lab, Lawrence Radiation Lab, 64-69; vis asst prof, Dept Chem, La State Univ, 69-71; dir res chem, Medi-Physics, Inc, 71-74, res group leader, 74-78, proj mgr, 78-83, assoc dir, Res & Develop, 83-85; consult, Photon Diag Inc, 85-87; vpres, IMP Inc, 90-92. *Concurrent Pos:* Consult. *Mem:* Soc Nuclear Med; Am Chem Soc; AAAS. *Res:* Research and development of new radiopharmaceuticals; hot atom chemistry; free radical chemistry; antibody research. *Mailing Add:* THL Research 1765 Ondina Dr Fremont CA 94539-3784

LIN, WEI, WATER & WASTEWATER TREATMENT, HAZARDOUS WASTE MANAGEMENT. *Current Pos:* RES ASST PROF, DEP CIVIL & ENVIRON ENG, WVa UNIV, 96- *Personal Data:* m, Xing-guang Wang; c Jack & Patrick. *Educ:* Beijing Inst Civil Eng & Archit, BS, 82; State Univ NY, Buffalo, MS, 89, PhD(environ eng), 92. *Prof Exp:* Asst lectr, Beijing Inst Civil Eng & Archit, 82-85; sr engr, Ecol & Environ, Inc, 92-95. *Mem:* Water Environ Fedn. *Res:* Experimental studies and mathematical model analyses of physico-chemical and biological unit processes for water and wastewater treatment; kinetic studies of biological growth and organic pollutant degradation in natural environment and in wastewater treatment systems. *Mailing Add:* 102 Horizon Dr Morgantown WV 26505. *E-Mail:* lin@cemr.wvu.edu

LIN, WEI-CHING, SPACE PHYSICS. *Current Pos:* RETIRED. *Personal Data:* b Taipei, China, Dec 31, 30; m 59. *Educ:* Nat Taiwan Univ, BSc, 54; Univ Iowa, MSc, 61, PhD(physics), 65. *Prof Exp:* Res assoc space physics, Univ Iowa, 63-64; asst prof, Dalhousie Univ, 64-68; assoc prof space physics, Univ PEI, 68- *Mem:* Am Geophys Union; Am Asn Physics Teachers. *Res:* Galactic and solar cosmic rays. *Mailing Add:* 56 Maplewood Crescent Charlottetown PE C1A 2X5 Can

LIN, WEN-C(HUN), ELECTRICAL & COMPUTER ENGINEERING. *Current Pos:* PROF ELEC & COMPUT, UNIV CALIF, DAVIS, 78- *Personal Data:* b Kutien, China, Feb 22, 26; US citizen; m 56; c 3. *Educ:* Taiwan Univ, BS, 50; Purdue Univ, MS, 56, PhD(elec eng), 65. *Prof Exp:* Engr, elec lab, Taiwan Power Co, 50-54; engr high voltage lab, Gen Elec Co, 56-59; sr engr, electronic data processing div, Honeywell Inc, 59-61; instr, Purdue Univ, 61-65; from asst prof to prof syst eng, Case Western Reserve Univ, 65-78. *Concurrent Pos:* Autonomous Mobile Robot Syst. *Mem:* Inst Elec & Electronics Engrs. *Res:* Special electronic instrumentation; signal processing; pattern recognition; microcomputers; artificial neuron network. *Mailing Add:* Dept Elec & Comput Eng 2064 Eng R II Univ Calif Davis CA 95616-5294

LIN, WILLY, PLANT PHYSIOLOGY, PLANT MOLECULAR BIOLOGY. *Current Pos:* staff scientist, Cent Res & Develop Exp Sta, 77-86, STAFF SCIENTIST, AGR PROD DEPT, E I DU PONT DE NEMOURS & CO, INC, 87- *Personal Data:* b Taiwan, China, July 2, 44; m 71; c 2. *Educ:* Nat Taiwan Norm Univ, BS, 67; Ill State Univ, MS, 72; Univ Ill, Urbana, PhD(biol), 76. *Prof Exp:* Res assoc, Dept Biol, Brookhaven Nat Lab, 76-77. *Mem:* Am Soc Plant Physiologists; Am Inst Biol Sci; Sigma Xi; NY Acad Sci; Int Asn Plant Tissue Culture; AAAS. *Res:* Ion transport mechanism in plant tissues; plant tissue culture and genetic transformation. *Mailing Add:* 12 Anderson Lane Newark DE 19711

LIN, WUNAN, GEOPHYSICS, ROCK MECHANICS. *Current Pos:* GEOPHYSICIST, LAWRENCE LIVERMORE LAB, UNIV CALIF, 77-, TASK LEADER, YUCCA MOUNTAIN PROJ, 90- *Personal Data:* b Tainan, Taiwan, Aug 1, 42; US citizen; m 71, Doris Shieh. *Educ:* Cheng-Kung Univ, BSE, 64; Univ Calif, Berkeley, MS, 69, PhD(geophys), 77. *Prof Exp:* Prof asst mining eng, Cheng-Kung Univ, 65-67; res asst, Univ Calif, Berkeley, 67-68 & 71-77. *Concurrent Pos:* Chou Kai-Chi fel, 62-64; Jane Lewis fel, 68-70. *Mem:* Am Geophys Union; Int Soc Rock Mech; Inst Elec & Electronic Engrs. *Res:* Solid earth geophysics; physical properties of rocks at high pressure and high temperature. *Mailing Add:* Lawrence Livermore Nat Lab L-201 PO Box 808 Livermore CA 94551. *Fax:* 510-423-1057

LIN, XI-WEI, SUBMICRON INTEGRATED CIRCUIT PROCESS TECHNOLOGY, MULTI LEVEL INTERCONNECT INTEGRATION. *Current Pos:* STAFF ENGR, VLSI TECHNOL INC, 95- *Personal Data:* b Gejiu, China, Dec 18, 61; m 89, Jiawen Wang. *Educ:* Beijing Univ, BS, 82; Univ Paris, MS, 84, PhD(solid state physics), 87. *Prof Exp:* Res assoc, Northwestern Univ, 87-91; staff scientist, Lawrence Berkeley Lab, 91-95. *Concurrent Pos:* Vis scientist, Univ Quebec, 85; vis scholar, Univ Fed Rio Grande Do Sul, Brazil, 94. *Mem:* Mat Res Soc; Inst Elec & Electronics Engrs. *Res:* Interconnect, metallization, ion implantation, process integration, device engineering, materials defects; interfacial reactions, phase transformation, molecular beam epitaxy, metal hydrogenation, superconductivity and computer simulations; author of over 50 publications in field; patentee in field. *Mailing Add:* 38660 Lexington St No 585 Fremont CA 94536. *Fax:* 408-922-5393; *E-Mail:* xi-wei.lin@sanjose.vlsi.com, xwlin@aol.com

LIN, Y(U) K(WENG), STRUCTURAL ENGINEERING, APPLIED PROBABILITY. *Current Pos:* CHARLES E SCHMIDT EMINENT SCHOLAR ENG, FLA ATLANTIC UNIV, 83- *Personal Data:* b Foochow, China, Oct 30, 23; US citizen; m 52, Ying-yuh Wang; c Jane, Della, Lucia & Winifred. *Educ:* Amoy Univ, BS, 46; Stanford Univ, MS, 55, PhD(struct eng), 57. *Hon Degrees:* DEng, Univ Waterloo, Can, 94. *Honors & Awards:* Alfred M Freudenthal Medal, Am Soc Civil Engrs, 84; Stochastic Dynamics Res Award, Int Asn Struct Safety & Reliability. *Prof Exp:* Stress engr, Vertol Aircraft Corp, Pa, 56-57; prof eng, Imp Col Eng, Ethiopia, 57-58; res engr, Boeing Co, 58-60; asst prof aeronaut eng, Univ Ill, Urbana, 60-62, from assoc prof aeronaut & asstronaut eng to prof, 62-83. *Concurrent Pos:* Consult, transport div, Boeing Co, 61, Wichita Div, 62, Gen Dynamics/Convair, 67, US Army Weapons Command, Ill, 72-77, Res Labs, Gen Motors Corp, 75-,

TRW Defense & Space Systs, 78- & Brookhaven Nat Lab, 90-; vis prof, Mass Inst Technol, 67-68; sr vis fel, Inst Sound & Vibration Res, Univ Southampton, Eng, 76; NSF sr fel, 67-68. *Mem:* Am Inst Aeronaut & Astronaut; Acoust Soc Am; Am Acad Mech; Am Soc Civil Engrs; Int Asn Struct Safety & Reliability; Am Asn Wind Eng; Earthquake Eng Res Inst. *Res:* Structural dynamics; random vibrations; systems reliability. *Mailing Add:* Col Eng Fla Atlantic Univ Boca Raton FL 33431-0991. *Fax:* 561-367-2868

LIN, YEONG-JER, METEOROLOGY, ATMOSPHERIC SCIENCES. *Current Pos:* from asst prof to assoc prof, 69-76, PROF METEOROL, ST LOUIS UNIV, 76- *Personal Data:* b Taiwan, China, Nov 11, 36; m 66, Chiung-Chen Wang; c Kathleen & Diana. *Educ:* Nat Taiwan Univ, BS, 59; Univ Wis-Madison, MS, 64; NY Univ, PhD(meteorol), 69. *Prof Exp:* Res asst meteorol, Univ Wis-Madison, 62-64; asst res scientist, NY Univ, 65-69, assoc res scientist, 69. *Concurrent Pos:* NSF res grants, St Louis Univ, 70-93. *Mem:* Am Meteorol Soc; Am Geophys Union. *Res:* Dynamical and observational studies of severe local storms; numerical modelling of meso-scale circulation. *Mailing Add:* Dept Earth & Atmospheric Sci St Louis Univ St Louis MO 63103

LIN, YI-JONG, DRUG METABOLISM, TOXICOLOGY. *Current Pos:* sr res pharmacologist, 79-84, group leader, 84-90, SECT LEADER PHARMACOL, COLGATE-PALMOLIVE CO, 90- *Personal Data:* b Feng Yuan, Taiwan, June 19, 44; US citizen; c 2. *Educ:* Univ Tokyo, BS, 67, MS, 71, PhD(pharmaceut), 75. *Prof Exp:* Postdoctoral fel pharmacol, Univ Mich, 75-76; res assoc pharmaceut, State Univ NY, Buffalo, 76; res fel pharmacol, Univ Mo, Kansas City, 77-79. *Concurrent Pos:* Prin, CACA Mid-Jersey Chinese Sch, 87-88. *Mem:* Am Pharmaceut Soc; Am Soc Pharmacol & Exp Therapeut. *Res:* Plan and execute projects on pharmacokinetics, drug metabolism, drug delivery, bucal absorption and drug safety evaluation; plan and monitor acute, chronic toxicity, carcinogenicity, clinical pharmacokinetics, mutagenicity and reproductive toxicology studies. *Mailing Add:* Seven Argyle Way Robbinsville NJ 08691-9017

LIN, YONG YENG, bio-organic chemistry, for more information see previous edition

LIN, YOU-FENG, TOPOLOGY. *Current Pos:* from asst to assoc prof, 64-69, res asst prof, 65-66, PROF MATH, UNIV SFLA, 69- *Personal Data:* b Feng-Shan, Taiwan, July 31, 32; m 60; c 3. *Educ:* Nat Taiwan Normal Univ, BS, 57; Univ Fla, PhD(math), 64. *Prof Exp:* Asst math, Inst Math, Chinese Acad Sci, 56-59. *Concurrent Pos:* Reviewer, Math Rev, Am Math Soc, 65- *Mem:* Am Math Soc; Math Asn Am. *Res:* Topological algebra; structure of topological semigroups; semigroup of measures; topology and relation-theory. *Mailing Add:* Dept Math Phy 114 Univ SFla 4202 E Fowler Ave Tampa FL 33620

LIN, YU, SPACE PLASMA PHYSICS, MAGNETOSPHERIC PHYSICS. *Current Pos:* ASST PROF, AUBURN UNIV, 94- *Educ:* Peking Univ, BS, 85; Inst Geophys, MS, 88; Univ Alaska, PhD(space physics), 93. *Mem:* Am Geophys Union. *Res:* Theoretical and simulation studies of the magnetic reconnection processes in the Earth's magnetosphere; interaction of interplanetary discontinuities with the Earth's magnetosphere; structure and ion heating of collisionless shocks. *Mailing Add:* Physics Dept Auburn Univ Auburn AL 36849-5311. *E-Mail:* ylin@physics.auburn.edu

LIN, YU-CHONG, PHYSIOLOGY. *Current Pos:* from asst prof to assoc prof, 69-76, PROF PHYSIOL, SCH MED, UNIV HAWAII, MANOA, 76- *Personal Data:* b Taiwan, Repub China, Apr 24, 35; m 60, Dora Liaw; c Mimi & Betty. *Educ:* Taiwan Norm Univ, BS, 59; Univ NMex, MS, 64; Rutgers Univ, PhD(physiol), 68. *Prof Exp:* Teaching asst biol, Taiwan Norm Univ, 60-62; res assoc, Univ Calif, Santa Barbara, 68-69; sr res fel,Ames Res Ctr, Moffett Field, NASA, 75-76. *Concurrent Pos:* Physiologist consult, Tripler Army Med Ctr, 79-; vis prof, Nat Yang Ming Med Col, Taipei, Taiwan, 83-, Kosin Med Col, Basan, Korea, 83-, Nat Defense Med Col, Taipei, Taiwan, 89- *Mem:* AAAS; Am Physiol Soc; Fedn Am Socs Exp Biol; Undersea & Hyperbaric Med Soc. *Res:* Cardiovascular research in the area of diving, exercise, and effect of environmental factors. *Mailing Add:* Dept Physiol Sch Med Univ Hawaii 1906 East-West Rd Honolulu HI 96822. *Fax:* 808-956-9722; *E-Mail:* liny@jabsom.biomed.hawaii.edu

LIN, YUE JEE, CYTOGENETICS. *Current Pos:* asst prof, 76-82, ASSOC PROF GENETICS & CYTOGENETICS, ST JOHN'S UNIV, 82- *Personal Data:* b Canton, China, Oct 8, 45; US citizen; m 72, Chen; c 2. *Educ:* Nat Taiwan Univ, BS, 67; Ohio State Univ, MS, 72, PhD(genetics), 76. *Prof Exp:* Res asst, Nat Taiwan Univ, 68-69, Taiwan Agr Res Inst, 69-70; teaching assoc genetics & biol, Ohio State Univ, 70-76. *Concurrent Pos:* Mem bd dirs, Chinese Am Acad & Prof Soc, 87-92. *Mem:* Am Soc Cell Biol; Genetics Soc Am; Am Genetic Asn; Sigma Xi. *Res:* Cytogenetics of complex heterozygotes, Rhoeo spathacea; cytogenetics of polyploids; cytogenetic effects of mutagens and environmental chemicals. *Mailing Add:* Dept Biol St John's Univ Jamaica NY 11439

LINAM, JAY H, ENTOMOLOGY. *Current Pos:* from instr to assoc prof, 65-75, chmn dept life sci, 87-88, PROF BIOL, UNIV SOUTHERN COLO, 75- *Personal Data:* b Carey, Idaho, Mar 9, 31; m 65; c 2. *Educ:* Univ Idaho, BS, 53; Univ Utah, MS, 57, PhD(entom, zool), 65. *Prof Exp:* Asst entomologist, Ecol Res Lab, Univ Utah, 58-59; mgr, Magna Mosquito Abatement Dist, Utah, 60-62. *Mem:* Entom Soc Am; Am Mosquito Control Asn. *Res:* Taxonomy and biology of mosquitoes of Western United States. *Mailing Add:* 2791 Country Farm Rd Pueblo CO 81006

LINARES, OLGA F, AGRARIAN SYSTEMS, TROPICAL FOREST SOCIETIES. *Current Pos:* SR SCIENTIST, SMITHSONIAN TROP RES INST, 74- *Personal Data:* b Nov 10, 36; m, Martin H Moynihan. *Educ:* Vassar Col, BA, 58; Harvard Univ, PhD(anthrop), 64. *Prof Exp:* Lectr anthrop, Univ Pa, 66-71. *Concurrent Pos:* Vis prof anthrop, Univ Tex, Austin, 74, Stanford Univ, 82; res cur Cent Am archaeol, Peabody Mus, Harvard Univ, 74-; fel, Ctr Advan Study Behav Sci, Stanford Univ, Calif, 79-80; St John's overseas vis fel, Cambridge Univ, UK, 86-87. *Mem:* Nat Acad Sci; Am Anthrop Asn; African Studies Asn; Royal Anthrop Asn; Latin Am Studies Asn; fel AAAS. *Res:* Agrarian practices and political economy of West African and Central American rural populations. *Mailing Add:* Smithsonian Trop Res Inst Unit 948 APO AA 34002-0948

LINASK, KERSTI KATRIN, CELL ADHESION, SIGNAL TRANSDUCTION. *Current Pos:* ASST PROF PEDIAT, UNIV PA, 90- *Personal Data:* b Zittau, Ger, Feb 10, 45; US citizen; m 67, Juri; c 2. *Educ:* Russell Sage Col, BA, 67; Univ Calif, Los Angeles, MA, 68; Univ Pa, PhD(develop biol), 86. *Prof Exp:* Instr biol, Holy Family Col, 70-80; fel develop biol, Thomas Jefferson Univ, 86-89. *Concurrent Pos:* Asst prof, Children's Hosp Philadelphia, 90-; mem, Basic Sci Coun, Am Heart Asn Coun Cardiovasc Dis of the Young; mem, Tumor Cell Biol Sect, Pa Cancer Ctr. *Mem:* Soc Develop Biol; Am Soc Cell Biol; Int Soc Develop Biol; Am Heart Asn; AAAS. *Res:* Mechanisms underlying cell adhesion systems, growth factor signalling and signal transduction during early avian and mammalian heart development. *Mailing Add:* Dept Cell Biol Univ Med & Dent NJ 2 Medical Center Dr Stratford NJ 08084

LINAWEAVER, FRANK PIERCE, ENVIRONMENTAL ENGINEERING, CIVIL ENGINEERING. *Current Pos:* RETIRED. *Personal Data:* b Woodstock, Va, Aug 22, 34; m 68; c 2. *Educ:* Johns Hopkins Univ, BES, 55, PhD(water resources, sanit eng), 65; Am Acad Environ Engrs, dipl. *Prof Exp:* From jr civil engr to sr civil engr, Bur Water Supply, Baltimore, 55 & 58-61; res staff asst, Dept Sanit Eng & Water Resources, Johns Hopkins Univ, 61-65, res assoc, Dept Environ Eng Sci, 65-66, assoc prof environ sci, Dept Environ Eng & Geog, 67-68; res staff mem, water resources group, Resources for Future, Inc, DC, 66; White House fel, US Govt, 66-67; dep dir, Dept Pub Works, City of Baltimore, 68-69, dir, 69-74; consult environ & civil eng, 74-78; partner, Rummel, Klepper & Kahl, Consult Engrs, 78-86; pres, E A Eng Inc, 86-93. *Concurrent Pos:* Mem, President's Air Qual Adv Bd, 68-71; consult rev panel, URS, Inc, 70-72; vis comt, Sch Archit, Univ Md, 75-78; dir, T Rowe Price Mutual Funds, 79-; trustee, Johns Hopkins Univ, 80-86, 87- *Mem:* Fel Am Soc Civil Engrs; Am Acad Environ Eng; fel AAAS; Nat Soc Prof Engrs; Am Water Works Asn; Am Consult Engrs Coun. *Res:* Residential and commercial water use and their impact on urban water systems; urban water management and water resources; street cleaning relation to water pollution control; public works; sanitary environmental engineering; hydrology. *Mailing Add:* 224 Wendover Rd Baltimore MD 21218

LINBERG, STEVEN E, BIOLOGY. *Current Pos:* PRES & CONSULT, LINBERG RES, INC, 92- *Educ:* Univ Del, BA, 73; Pa State Univ, MS, 75, PhD(physiol), 78. *Prof Exp:* Asst prof path, Grad Fac, Univ Md, 80-84; proj leader & clin res scientist, Med Div, Burroughs Wellcome Co, 85-86; assoc dir clin res & proj leader, Boehringer Mannheim Pharmaceut, 86-92; dir clin res, Univax Biologics, Inc, 92. *Concurrent Pos:* Res assoc clin physiol, Inst Emergency Med Serv Syst, Univ Md, 78-84, vis res assoc, 85-91; founder, exec dir & mem bd dir, Shock Trauma Res Fund, 83-92; pres & founder, Res Fund Inc, 92- *Mem:* Am Physiol Soc; Am Soc Microbiol; Am Col Cardiol; Am Soc Nephrology; Am Heart Asn; Regulatory Affairs Prof Soc. *Res:* Physiology; biology. *Mailing Add:* Clin Prod Develop 22401 Rolling Hill Lane Gaithersburg MD 20882-2345

LIN-CHUNG, PAY-JUNE, SEMICOUNDUCTOR PHYSICS, THEORETICAL SOLID STATE PHYSICS. *Current Pos:* RES PHYSICIST, NAVAL RES LAB, 67- *Personal Data:* b Tienjin, China; Nat US; m 67; c 2. *Educ:* Nat Taiwan Univ, China, BS, 58; Univ Penn, MS, 61, PhD(physics), 65. *Prof Exp:* Res physicist, Inst Metals, Univ Chicago, 64-65; res physicist, Univ Calif, Berkeley, 65-66; asst prof physics, State Univ Northridge Calif, 66-67. *Concurrent Pos:* Vis scientist, Argonne Nat Lab, 71, Cambridge Univ, England, 78-79; vis lectr, Univ Durham, England, 73-74. *Mem:* Am Phys Soc; Mat Res Soc. *Res:* Theoretical investigations of the electronic and lattice vibrational structure and of electro-optical effects in solids; defects, surfaces and superlattices on semiconductors. *Mailing Add:* Naval Res Lab Code 6877 4555 Overlook Ave SW Washington DC 20375-5000

LINCICOME, DAVID RICHARD, PARASITOLOGY, PHYSIOLOGY. *Current Pos:* RETIRED. *Personal Data:* b Champaign, Ill, Jan 17, 14; m 41, 53, Margaret Stirewalt; c Judith A & David. *Educ:* Univ Ill, BS & MS, 37; Tulane Univ, PhD(parasitol), 41; Am Bd Med Microbiol, dipl, 65. *Honors & Awards:* Anniversary Award, Helminthological Soc, 76. *Prof Exp:* Asst zool, Univ Ill, 37; asst trop med, Sch Med, Tulane Univ, 34-41; from instr to asst prof zool, Univ Ky, 41-47; asst prof parasitol, Univ Wis, 47-49; sr res parasitologist, E I du Pont de Nemours & Co, 49-54; from asst prof to prof zool, Howard Univ, 55-70. *Concurrent Pos:* Ed & Founder Exp Parasitol, 49- & chmn ed bd, 50-76; guest scientist, Naval Med Res Inst, 55-61; USPHS res grants, 58-68; ed, Int Rev Trop Med, 60-; vis scientist, Lab Phys Biol, Nat Inst Arthritis & Metab Dis, 64-65; ed, Trans, Am Micros Soc, 70-71; chmn comt exam & cert, Am Bd Med Microbiol, 72-; dir, Am Dairy Goat Asn, 72-88 & Nat Pygmy Goat Asn; dir res, Am Dairy Goat Asn, mem bd dirs, 73-79; founder & ed, Int Goat & Sheep Res; guest scientist, USDA Exp Sta, Beltsville, Md, 78-; vis scholar, Nat Agr Libr, 90-92; dist dir, Natural Colored Wool Growers Asn, 90-; dir & registrar, Jacob Sheep Conservancy; dir, Am Goat Soc, 91- *Mem:* Fel AAAS; Am Soc Parasitol; Helminth Soc (secy, 60, vpres, 61, pres, 68); fel NY Acad Sci; Am Dairy Goat Asn; Nat Pygmy Goat Asn (pres, 79); Natural Colored Wool Growers Asn. *Res:* Diagnosis of protozoan and helminthic diseases; amebiasis; taxonomy and systematics of Acanthocephala, Nematoda and Cestoda; epidemiology of tropical diseases; molecular biology of parasitism; nutritional exchange between parasite and host. *Mailing Add:* 3032 Courtney School House Rd Midland VA 22728

LINCK, ALBERT JOHN, PLANT PHYSIOLOGY. *Current Pos:* RETIRED. *Personal Data:* b Portsmouth, Ohio, Aug 18, 26; m 57; c 2. *Educ:* Ohio State Univ, BSc, 50, MSc, 51, PhD(plant physiol), 55. *Prof Exp:* From instr to prof plant physiol, Univ Minn, St Paul, 55-84, asst dir, Minn Agr Exp Sta, 66-71, dean, Col Agr, 71-73, assoc vpres acad admin, 73-84; provost & acad vpres, Colo State Univ, 84-88. *Mem:* AAAS; Am Soc Plant Physiol; Bot Soc Am; Scand Soc Plant Physiol; Am Inst Biol Sci. *Res:* Translocation of inorganic and organic compounds; mechanism of action of growth regulators. *Mailing Add:* 1710 Grandview Ave Portsmouth OH 45662

LINCK, RICHARD WAYNE, BIOCHEMISTRY, CELL & MOLECULAR BIOLOGY. *Current Pos:* assoc prof, 84-87, PROF, DEPT CELL BIOL & NEUROANAT, UNIV MINN, 87- *Personal Data:* b Los Angeles, Calif, Apr 9, 45; m 72, Madeleine A Hecht; c Guthrie, Peter, Theodor & Anna. *Educ:* Stanford Univ, BA, 67; Brandeis Univ, PhD(biol), 72. *Prof Exp:* Fel, Lab Molecular Biol, Med Res Coun, Cambridge, Eng, 71-73; instr, Harvard Med Sch, 74-75, asst prof, 75-81, assoc prof, 81-84. *Mem:* Am Soc Cell Biol; Biophys Soc; AAAS. *Res:* Function of microtubule cystoskeleton in motility, development and morphogenesis, using biochemistry, molecular biology and structural studies; cytology. *Mailing Add:* Dept Cell Biol & Neuroanat Univ Minn 321 Church St Se 14-135 Jackson Minneapolis MN 55455

LINCK, ROBERT GEORGE, INORGANIC CHEMISTRY. *Current Pos:* from asst prof to assoc prof, 81-86, PROF CHEM, SMITH COL, 88- *Personal Data:* b St Louis, Mo, Nov 18, 38; m 62. *Educ:* Case Western Res Univ, BS, 60; Univ Chicago, PhD(chem), 63. *Honors & Awards:* Catalyst Award, Chem Mfrs Asn. *Prof Exp:* Asst prof chem, Univ Calif, 66-72, assoc prof, 72-81; assoc prof, US Naval Acad, 86-88. *Mem:* AAAS; Am Chem Soc. *Res:* Rates of inorganic reactions, especially electron-transfer reactions; electronic structure and photochemistry of complex ions. *Mailing Add:* Dept Chem Smith Col Northampton MA 01063-0048

LINCOLN, CHARLES ALBERT, THEORETICAL PHYSICS. *Current Pos:* RETIRED. *Personal Data:* b Rudyard, Mont, May 13, 39; m 63; c 3. *Educ:* Mont State Univ, BS, 62, MS, 64; Univ Va, DSc(eng physics), 69. *Prof Exp:* From instr to assoc prof physics, State Univ NY Col Fredonia, 64-79. *Concurrent Pos:* NDEA fel, Univ Va, 66-69; NSF assistantship, Theoret Inst Physics, Boulder, 68 & Inst Statist Mech & Theoret Thermodyn, Univ Tex, 70; Fulbright exchange prof, Newcastle upon Tyne Polytech, Newcastle/Tyne, Eng, 73-74; adj instr, Walla Walla Community Col, 81-; adj res assoc physics, Whitman Col, 84-; consult electro-acoust, noise control & archit acoust. *Mem:* Am Phys Soc; Am Asn Physics Teachers; Inst Elec & Electronic Eng; Am Sci Affil; Audio Eng Soc; Am Astron Soc; Astron Soc Pac; Int Soc Optical Eng. *Res:* Field theoretic methods in statistical mechanics and fluids; a generalized dynamical formalism of statistical mechanics; information theory and electroacoustics; astrophysics. *Mailing Add:* 2163 Granite Dr Walla Walla WA 99362

LINCOLN, DAVID ERWIN, CHEMICAL ECOLOGY. *Current Pos:* asst prof, 80-86, ASSOC PROF BIOL, UNIV SC, 87- *Personal Data:* b Detroit, Mich, Oct 8, 44; m 70. *Educ:* Kalamazoo Col, BA, 71; Univ Calif, Santa Cruz, PhD(biol), 78. *Prof Exp:* Fel, Stanford Univ, 78-80. *Mem:* Ecol Soc Am; Bot Soc Am; AAAS; Entom Soc Am; Int Soc Chem Ecol; Phytochem Soc NAm. *Res:* Environmental and genetic control of secondary chemical production by plants and the roles of these chemicals in plant-herbivore coevolution; effects of rising atmospheric carbon dioxide on plant-herbivore interactions. *Mailing Add:* Dept Biol Univ SC Columbia SC 92908-0001

LINCOLN, JEANNETTE VIRGINIA, GEOPHYSICS, SOLAR PHYSICS. *Current Pos:* RETIRED. *Personal Data:* b Ames, Iowa, Sept 7, 15. *Educ:* Wellesley Col, BA, 36; Iowa State Univ, MS, 38. *Honors & Awards:* Gold Medal, Dept of Com, 73. *Prof Exp:* Asst household equip, Iowa State Univ, 37-38, instr, 38-42; physicist, Nat Bur Stands, DC, 42-54, sect chief, Radio Warning Serv, Colo, 59-65, dep chief data serv, Inst Telecommun Sci & Aeronomy, Environ Sci Serv Admin, 65-66, dep chief data serv & chief, Upper Atmosphere Geophys, 66-70, chief data serv & dir, World Data Ctr A, Solar-Terrestrial Physics, Nat Geophys & Solar Terrestrial Data Ctr, Environ Data & Info Serv, Nat Oceanic & Atmospheric Admin, 70-81. *Concurrent Pos:* Mem US preparatory comt study group ionospheric propagation, Int Radio Consult Comt, 59-80; secy, Int Ursigram & World Days Serv, 61-81, mem, US Comn G, Int Sci Radio Union, 63-, secy, Ionospheric Network Adv Group, 69-72, vchmn, 72-81; forecasting reporter, Int Asn Geomagnetism & Aeronomy, 63-67, mem comns IV & V, 67-73; mem working groups 3 & 5, Inter-Union Comn on Solar-Terrestrial Physics, 69-72; Am Geophys Union mem, Am Geophys Union-Int Sci Radio Union Bd of Radio Sci, 69-74, US Nat Comt, Int Union Geodesy & Geophys, 76-79; chmn working group V6, Geophys Indices, 73-81; mem comn 40, Int Astron Union, 76- *Mem:* Fel AAAS; Sigma Xi; fel Am Geophys Union; Am Astron Soc; fel Soc Women Engrs. *Res:* Radio propagation disturbances and forecasts; solar-terrestrial relationships; publication of solar and geophysical data; prediction of solar indices; data center management. *Mailing Add:* 2005 Alpine Dr Boulder CO 80304-3607

LINCOLN, KENNETH ARNOLD, HIGH TEMPERATURE CHEMISTRY, MASS SPECTROMETRY. *Current Pos:* ELORET INST, PALO ALTO, CALIF, 86- *Personal Data:* b Oakland, Calif, Oct 1, 22; m 56, Shirley Simpson; c 4. *Educ:* Stanford Univ, AB, 44, MS, 48, PhD(phys chem), 57. *Prof Exp:* Phys chemist, US Naval Radio Defense Lab, 58-69; res scientist, NASA-Ames Res Ctr, 70-86. *Mem:* Am Chem Soc; Am Soc Mass Spectrometry; Am Sci Affil; Combustion Inst. *Res:* Thermochemistry of the vaporization of refractory materials; thermokinetics of pulsed energy deposition; development of instrumentation combining lasers and high-speed mass spectrometry for in-situ analyses of short-lived chemical species; space flight spectrometric instrumentation. *Mailing Add:* 2016 Stockbridge Ave Redwood City CA 94061-4131

LINCOLN, LEWIS LAUREN, PHOTOGRAPHIC CHEMISTRY. *Current Pos:* Lab technician, 46-60, res chemist, 60-65, sr res chemist, 65-70, RES ASSOC CHEM, RES LABS, EASTMAN KODAK, 70- *Personal Data:* b Canandaigua, NY, Oct 9, 26; m 49; c 6. *Mem:* Am Chem Soc. *Res:* The study and synthesis of photographic sensitizing dyes and addenda. *Mailing Add:* 426 Mount Airy Dr Rochester NY 14617-2164

LINCOLN, RICHARD CRIDDLE, APPLIED PHYSICS. *Current Pos:* TECH STAFF MEM APPL PHYSICS, SANDIA LABS, 71-, SUPVR, APPL TECHNOL DIV. *Personal Data:* b Boston, Mass, Nov 25, 42; c 2. *Educ:* Cornell Univ, BEP, 66, MS, 68, PhD(mat sci), 71. *Prof Exp:* Instr & res assoc mat sci, Cornell Univ, 70-71. *Res:* High pressure and high temperature experimental techniques; analysis of nuclear waste management systems. *Mailing Add:* 37 Sage Hill Dr Placitas NM 87043

LINCOLN, THOMAS M, MOLECULAR BIOLOGY, CELLULAR BIOLOGY. *Current Pos:* DIR GRAD PROG PATH, UNIV ALA, BIRMINGHAM, 92-, INTERIM DIR MOLECULAR & CELLULAR PATH, 92- *Personal Data:* b Orange, NJ, Sept 21, 48. *Educ:* Univ Tenn, PhD(zool), 74. *Res:* Molecular biology; cellular biology; signal transduction. *Mailing Add:* Dept Pathol Volker Hall G038 Univ Ala 1670 University Blvd Birmingham AL 35294-0019

LIND, ARTHUR CHARLES, NUCLEAR MAGNETIC RESONANCE, MATERIALS CHARACTERIZATION. *Current Pos:* assoc scientist, McDonnell Douglas Res Labs, 66-76, scientist, 76-79, sr scientist, 79-83, prin scientist, 83-88, chief scientist, 88-89, dir res, 89-93, chief tech specialist, 93-94, MDC FEL, MCDONNELL DOUGLAS RES LABS, 94- *Personal Data:* b Chicago, Ill, May 28, 32; m 57, Barbara Collins; c Julie (Northrip), Catherine (Lind-Kern) & Charles. *Educ:* Univ Ill, Urbana, BS, 55; Rensselaer Polytech Inst, PhD(physics), 66. *Prof Exp:* Physicist, Knolls Atomic Power Lab, 58-61 & Watervliet Arsenal, US Army, 63-66. *Mem:* Am Phys Soc; Am Chem Soc; Am Inst Aeronaut & Astronaut. *Res:* Invent, design and characterize materials having tailored electromagnetic properties; electromagnetic processing of composite materials; nuclear magnetic resonance studies of polymers; theoretical and experimental studies of electromagnetic scattering; propagation of electromagnetic waves in turbulent media. *Mailing Add:* 15450 Country Mill Ct Chesterfield MO 63017. *E-Mail:* lind@mdcgwy.mdc.com

LIND, CAROL JOHNSON, MINERAL IDENTIFICATION, CHEMICAL ANALYSIS. *Current Pos:* phys sci tech pollen identification, 63-66, phys sci tech chem res, 66-67, RES CHEMIST, US GEOL SURV, 67 - *Personal Data:* b Minneapolis, Minn, Dec 8, 26; div; c Karen & John. *Educ:* Univ Minn, BS, 49. *Prof Exp:* Anal chemist coal anal, Twin City Testing Co, 49-50; jr chemist org res, Julius Hyman Co, 50-52. *Mem:* Am Chem Soc; Am Geophys Union; Int Union Pure & Appl Chem. *Res:* Natural-water chemistry of aluminum, aluminum-silicon, trace metals and manganese and their corresponding natural-organic influences. *Mailing Add:* 3727 Hamilton Way Redwood City CA 94062

LIND, DAVID ARTHUR, NUCLEAR PHYSICS & PHYSICS OF SNOW & AVALANCHE PHENOMENA. *Current Pos:* from assoc prof to prof, 56-83, chmn dept physics & astrophys, 74-78, EMER PROF PHYSICS, UNIV COLO, BOULDER, 83- *Personal Data:* b Seattle, Wash, Sept 12, 18; m 48, Mary Duncan; c 4. *Educ:* Univ Wash, Seattle, BS, 40; Calif Inst Technol, MS, 43, PhD(physics), 48. *Prof Exp:* Jr aerodynamicist, Boeing Airplane Co, Wash, 42-43; physicist, Appl Physics Lab, Univ Wash, Seattle, 43-45; res fel physics, Calif Inst Technol, 48-50; Guggenheim fel, Nobel Inst Physics, Stockholm, 50-51; asst prof, Univ Wis, 51-56. *Concurrent Pos:* Consult off instnl prog, NSF, 63-66; physicist div res, US AEC, 69-70; mem prog adv comn, Los Alamos Meson Facil, 71-77, chmn users group, 75-76; consult, Los Alamos Nat Lab, 83- *Mem:* Fel Am Phys Soc; Sigma Xi. *Res:* X-rays; crystal diffraction; nuclear spectroscopy; sector focused cyclotron design; charged particle scattering; reaction studies; fast neutron spectroscopy; particle beam optics; physics of snow and avalanche phenomena; physics of skiing. *Mailing Add:* 920 Jasmine Circle Boulder CO 80304

LIND, DAVID MELVIN, SURFACE PHYSICS, MAGNETIC ORDERING IN OXIDE LAYERED & OTHER NOVEL MATERIALS. *Current Pos:* asst prof, 88-93, ASSOC PROF PHYSICS, FLA STATE UNIV, 93- *Personal Data:* m 81, Celeste Williams; c Christa, Eric, Jennifer, Kyle & Wesley. *Educ:* Brigham Young Univ, BS, 81; W M Rice Univ, MA, 85, PhD(physics), 87. *Prof Exp:* Off Naval Training/Am Soc Eng Educ fel, US Naval Res Lab, 86-88. *Concurrent Pos:* Prin investr, NSF, 92-, US Off Naval Res, 92- *Mem:* Am Vacuum Soc; Am Phys Soc; AAAS. *Res:* Structural and magnetic ordering in heteroepitaxial oxide and metallic single-crystalline thin-films;

superlattice and ultrathin-film synthesis by molecular beam epitaxy; spin-resolved electron spectroscopies, magnetometry and diffraction based probes of magnetocrystalline properties. *Mailing Add:* Dept Physics Fla State Univ Tallahassee FL 32306-3016. *Fax:* 850-644-6504; *E-Mail:* lind@magnet.fsu.edu

LIND, DOUGLAS A, MATHEMATICS. *Current Pos:* PROF MATH, UNIV WASH, 76- *Personal Data:* b Arlington, Va, Aug 11, 46. *Educ:* Univ Va, BS, 68; Stanford Univ, MA, 71, PhD(math), 73. *Mem:* Am Math Soc. *Res:* Researches the interplay between symbol dynamics; smooth dynamical systems and data storage and transmission. *Mailing Add:* Univ Wash GN-50 Seattle WA 98195-0001

LIND, MAURICE DAVID, PHYSICAL CHEMISTRY, X-RAY CRYSTALLOGRAPHY. *Current Pos:* MEM TECH STAFF, SCI CTR, ROCKWELL INT, 66- *Personal Data:* b Jamestown, NY, July 25, 34; m 62; c 1. *Educ:* Otterbein Col, BS, 57; Cornell Univ, PhD(phys chem), 62. *Prof Exp:* NSF fel, 62-63; res chemist phys chem, Union Oil Co, Calif, 63-66. *Concurrent Pos:* Vis prof appl physics, Tech Univ Denmark, 85. *Mem:* Am Phys Soc; Am Crystallog Asn; Sigma Xi; Am Asn Crystal Growth. *Res:* X-ray crystal mography; crystal growth. *Mailing Add:* 4501 Amberwood Rd Haw River NC 27258

LIND, NIELS CHRISTIAN, APPLIED MECHANICS, RISK ASSESSMENT. *Current Pos:* from assoc prof to prof, 60-91, dir, Inst Risk Res, 82-87, DISTINGUISHED EMER PROF CIVIL ENG, UNIV WATERLOO, 92- *Personal Data:* b Copenhagen, Denmark, Mar 10, 30; Can citizen; m 84; c Julie W (Robbins), Peter C, Adam C & Andreas M. *Educ:* Royal Tech Univ Denmark, MSc, 53; Univ Ill, PhD(theoret & appl mech), 59. *Honors & Awards:* A Ostenfeld Gold Metal. *Prof Exp:* Design engr, Dominia Ltd, Denmark, 53-54; engr, Bell Tel Co, Can, 54-55; field engr, Drake & Merritt Co, Labrador, 55-56; design engr, Fenco, Que, 56; asst stress anal, Univ Ill, 56-57, instr, 57-58, res assoc, 58-59, asst prof theoret & appl mech, 59-60. *Concurrent Pos:* Mem, Can Nat Study Group Math Higher Educ, Orgn Econ Coop & Develop, 63-65, Adv Comt Nuclear Safety, Atomic Energy Control Bd, 81-95; vis prof, Univ Laval, 69, Inst Eng, Nat Univ Mex, 75 & 81 & Tech Univ Denmark, 77-78; adj prof, Univ Victoria, 93-96. *Mem:* Fel Am Acad Mech (pres, 71-72); fel Royal Soc Can. *Res:* Structural mechanics; theory of design; structural reliability and optimization; risk assessment. *Mailing Add:* 504-640 Montreal St Univ Victoria Victoria BC V8V 1Z8 Can. *Fax:* 250-721-6051; *E-Mail:* nlind@hamilton.uvic.ca

LIND, OWEN THOMAS, LIMNOLOGY, WATER RESOURCES. *Current Pos:* from asst prof to assoc prof, 66-79, PROF BIOL, BAYLOR UNIV, 79- *Personal Data:* b Emporia, Kans, June 2, 34; m 54, 90, Laura Davalos; c Thomas & Richard. *Educ:* William Jewell Col, AB, 56; Univ Mich, MS, 60; Univ Mo, PhD(zool), 66. *Prof Exp:* Biologist, Parke, Davis & Co, Mich, 56-60; asst prof biol, William Jewell Col, 60-62; res assoc limnol, Univ Mo, 66. *Concurrent Pos:* Prin investr, Off Water Resource & Technol, 71, 73, 76, NSF, 83, 88; consult, US Nat Park Serv, 69, 74-76, Corps Engrs, 79, USAID, 81-83, State of Tex, 82; dir, Inst Environ Studies, 71-76; mem exec comt, Tyler Ecol Award, 74- *Mem:* Am Soc Limnol & Oceanog; Sigma Xi; Int Asn Theoret & Appl Limnol; Brit Freshwater Biol Asn; NAm Lake Mgt Soc. *Res:* Factors governing production of lakes and reservoirs; tropical limnology and water resources of third world countries. *Mailing Add:* Dept Biol Baylor Univ BU Box 97388 Waco TX 76798-7388. *Fax:* 254-755-2969; *E-Mail:* owen_lind@baylor.edu

LIND, ROBERT WAYNE, THEORETICAL PHYSICS, ENGINEERING PHYSICS. *Current Pos:* assoc prof, 78-83, PROF PHYSICS & ELECT ENG, UNIV WIS-PLATTEVILLE, 83- *Personal Data:* b Ishpeming, Mich, Aug 25, 39; m 64, Eugenia; c Ingrid & Erik. *Educ:* Mich Technol Univ, BS, 61; Univ Pittsburgh, PhD(physics), 70. *Prof Exp:* Engr, Ford Motor Co, 63-66; res assoc physics, Syracuse Univ, 70-72; sr res assoc, Temple Univ, 72-73; res assoc, Fla State Univ, 73-74; asst prof physics, WVa Inst Technol, 74-76, chmn dept & assoc prof, 76-78. *Concurrent Pos:* Res physicist, Naval Res Lab, 87-88. *Mem:* Am Asn Physics Teachers; Int Soc Gen Relativity & Gravitation; AAAS. *Res:* General relativity and electromagnetism; analysis of high frequency radio wave probing of the ionosphere; elementary and middle school science education. *Mailing Add:* Dept Physics Univ Wis-Platteville 1 University Plaza Platteville WI 53818-3099. *Fax:* 608-342-1561; *E-Mail:* lindr@uwplatt.edu

LIND, VANCE GORDON, PHYSICS, ASTROPHYSICS. *Current Pos:* from asst prof to assoc prof, 64-75, dept head, 81-88, PROF PHYSICS, UTAH STATE UNIV, 75-, CAZIER PROF, 95- *Personal Data:* b Brigham City, Utah, Feb 12, 35; m 64; c Bretton R, Mark G, Kimara S (Thompson), Cherise D, Justin A, Zachary L, Rixa E, Vanessa A, Marilyse L, Lisette C & Tyson F. *Educ:* Utah State Univ, BS, 59; Univ Wis, MS, 61, PhD(elem particles), 64. *Prof Exp:* Eng asst, Edgerton, Germeshausen & Grier, Inc, summer, 59, res asst, 60; res assoc, Univ Mich, 64. *Concurrent Pos:* Woodrow Wilson fel, 59-64; Utah State Univ Res Found grant, 64-66, 72-76 & 78-79; investr, NSF res grant, Utah State Univ, 66-71, 77-80, 80-85, Dept Energy res grant, 86- *Mem:* Am Asn Physics Teachers; Am Phys Soc; Sigma Xi; Am Solar Energy Soc; Int Solar Energy Soc. *Res:* Basic interactions; elementary particle interactions, meson and nucleon interactions with nuclei, nuclear mass measurements, astronomy and astrophysics; solar energy technology; beta delayed nuclear particle decay; physics education. *Mailing Add:* Dept Physics Utah State Univ Logan UT 84322-4415. *Fax:* 435-750-2492; *E-Mail:* glind@usu.edu

LIND, WILTON H(OWARD), CHEMICAL ENGINEERING. *Current Pos:* RETIRED. *Personal Data:* b Oakland, Calif, Feb 14, 27; m 51, Audrey Kilgour; c Howard & Barbara. *Educ:* Univ Calif, Berkeley, BS, 50, MS, 52; JD, Empire, Col, 77. *Prof Exp:* From asst res engr to sr res engr, Chevron Res Co, 51-78, analyst, 78-80, asst secy, Finance Dept, 80-85, mgr, Legal Process & Secy Dept, Chevron Corp, 85-86. *Mem:* Am Chem Soc; Am Inst Chem Engrs. *Res:* Petrochemical research and development; aromatics chemistry; pilot plant design and operation. *Mailing Add:* PO Box 30004 Walnut Creek CA 94598

LINDAHL, CHARLES BLIGHE, SYNTHETIC INORGANIC CHEMISTRY, FLUORINE. *Current Pos:* head new prod develop, 71-72, tech dir, 73-90, GEN MGR & TECH DIR, OZARK-MAHONING CO, 90- *Personal Data:* b N Platte, Nebr, Feb 4, 39; m 59, 91, Jeanne Moore; c David & Laura M. *Educ:* Iowa State Univ, BS, 60; Univ Calif, Berkeley, PhD(chem), 64. *Prof Exp:* Chemist, Ames Lab, 60; res asst, Lawrence Berkeley Lab, 61-64; sr chemist, Eastman Kodak, 64-65; mem tech staff, Rocketdyne Div, Rockwell Int, 65-70; sr chemist, Reheis Chem, 70-71. *Mem:* Am Chem Soc; Am Asn Dent Res; Int Asn Dent Res; Sigma Xi. *Res:* Inorganic synthesis; fluorides for dental applications; oxidizer chemistry; unusual oxidation states. *Mailing Add:* 2003 N Santa Fe Ave Tulsa OK 74127

LINDAHL, LASSE ALLAN, MOLECULAR GENETICS, RNA. *Current Pos:* PROF & CHAIR BIOL SCI, UNIV MD, BALTIMORE CO, 94- *Personal Data:* b Copenhagen, Denmark, Sept 9, 44; m 78; c 3. *Educ:* Univ Copenhagen, MSc, 69, PhD(microbiol), 73. *Prof Exp:* Fel molecular biol, Univ Wis-Madison, 73-76; asst prof, Univ Aarhus, Denmark, 76-78; from asst prof to prof biol, Univ Rochester, 78-94. *Mem:* Am Soc Microbiol; AAAS. *Res:* Molecular basis for the regulation of ribosome synthesis; ribosomal RNA processing; assembly of ribosomes. *Mailing Add:* Dept Biosci Univ Md 1000 Hilltop Circle Baltimore MD 21250. *Fax:* 410-455-3875; *E-Mail:* lindahl@umbc.edu

LINDAHL, RONALD GUNNAR, MOLECULAR BIOLOGY, BIOCHEMISTRY. *Current Pos:* PROF & CHAIR, DEPT BIOCHEM & MOLECULAR BIOL, SCH MED, UNIV SDAK, 89- *Personal Data:* b Detroit, Mich, Aug 11, 48; m 70, Diane; c Jared & Melissa. *Educ:* Wayne State Univ, BA, 70, PhD(biol), 73. *Prof Exp:* Fel, Argonne Nat Lab, 74-75; prof biol, Univ Ala, 75-89. *Concurrent Pos:* Prin investr, Nat Cancer Inst grant, 79-; univ res prof, Univ Ala, 84-89; reviewer, NSF, 87-90 & NIH, 89-90; co-prin investr, Nat Inst Alcohol Abuse & Alcoholism, 87- *Mem:* Am Soc Biochem & Molecular Biol; Am Asn Cancer Res; AAAS; Int Soc Biomed Res Alcoholism; Sigma Xi. *Res:* Molecular biology of gene expression; aldehyde dehydrogenases; genetic changes in carcinogenesis, transplacental and perinatal; Biochemical changes during neoplasia; Genetic regulation of enzyme activity. *Mailing Add:* Biochem & Molecular Biol Dept Univ SDak Sch Med 414 E Clark St 145 Lee Med Bldg Vermillion SD 57069. *Fax:* 605-677-5124

LINDAHL, ROY LAWRENCE, DENTISTRY. *Current Pos:* RETIRED. *Personal Data:* b Los Angeles, Calif, Aug 22, 25; m 48, 76; c 7. *Educ:* Univ Southern Calif, BS & DDS, 50; Univ Mich, MS, 52; Am Bd Pedodontics, dipl, 56. *Prof Exp:* From asst prof to prof, Sch Dent, Univ NC, Chapel Hill, 52-85, dir continuing educ & dent demonstr pract, 70-83, emer prof pediat dent, 85-; pres, Delta Dent Plan of NC, 85-97. *Concurrent Pos:* Mem bd trustees, NC Cerebral Palsy Hosp, 57-63; consult, Womack Army Hosp, Ft Bragg, NC, 60-78; examr, Am Bd Pedodontics, 60-67, chmn, 67. *Mem:* AAAS; Am Soc Dent Children (from secy to pres, 69-73); Am Dent Asn; Am Acad Pedodontics (vpres, 62-63, pres-elect, 63-64, pres, 64-65); Int Asn Dent Res. *Res:* Pedodontics; effective utilization of dental auxiliary personnel; problems of the handicapped patient; pre-payment dental care programs; health services research-quality assurance. *Mailing Add:* 305 Clayton Rd Chapel Hill NC 27514

LINDAMOOD, JOHN BENFORD, DAIRY TECHNOLOGY. *Current Pos:* RETIRED. *Personal Data:* b Galax, Va, Aug 6, 29; m 53; c 1. *Educ:* Va Polytech Inst & State Univ, BS, 53, MS, 55; Ohio State Univ, PhD(educ), 74. *Prof Exp:* Prod mgr, Evaporated Milk Div, Carnation Co, 56-61; from asst prof to assoc prof, Dept Food Sci & Nutrit, Ohio State Univ, 74-92. *Mem:* Inst Food Technologists; Am Dairy Sci Asn; Int Asn Milk, Food & Environ Sanitarians. *Res:* Milk and milk products. *Mailing Add:* Dept Food Sci & Technol Ohio State Univ Main Campus 2121 Fyffe Rd Columbus OH 43210

LINDAU, EVERT INGOLF, SOLID STATE PHYSICS. *Current Pos:* res assoc physics, 72-74, PROF PHYSICS, STANFORD UNIV, 74- *Personal Data:* b Vaxjo, Sweden, Oct 4, 42. *Educ:* Chalmers Univ Technol, Sweden, Civilingenjor, 68, Technol Licentiat, 70, PhD(physics), 71, DrTechnol, 72. *Prof Exp:* Res asst physics, Chalmers Univ Technol, Sweden, 68-71; res scientist, Varian Assocs, 71-72. *Mem:* Am Phys Soc; Am Vacuum Soc; Swed Soc Technol. *Res:* Optical and photoemission studies of the electronic structure of materials using synchrotron radiation with emphasis on surface properties; surface states, surface photoemission, physisorbtion, chemisorbtion, surface composition and catalytic activities. *Mailing Add:* Stanford Electronics Lab Stanford Univ Stanford CA 94305

LINDAUER, GEORGE CONRAD, NUCLEAR ENGINEERING, INFORMATION SCIENCE. *Current Pos:* PROF NUCLEAR SCI & LIBRN, SPEED SCI SCH, UNIV LOUISVILLE, 71-, PROF MECH ENG, 79- *Personal Data:* b Queens, NY, Nov 5, 35; m 59; c 3. *Educ:* Cooper Union, BS, 56; Mass Inst Technol, ScM, 57; Univ Pittsburgh, PhD(mech eng), 62; Long Island Univ, MS, 71. *Prof Exp:* From jr engr to sr engr, Bettis Atomic

Power Lab, Westinghouse Elec Corp, 57-64; from asst chem engr to chem engr, Brookhaven Nat Lab, 64-71. *Mem:* Am Soc Mech Engrs. *Res:* heat transfer; fluid dynamics. *Mailing Add:* Mech Eng Univ Louisville 2301 S 3rd St Louisville KY 40292

LINDAUER, IVO EUGENE, PLANT ECOLOGY, SCIENCE EDUCATION. *Current Pos:* from asst prof to assoc prof, 67-75, asst dean, Col Arts & Sci, 76-81, PROF BOT, UNIV NORTHERN COLO, 75-*Personal Data:* b Grand Valley, Colo, Apr 7, 31; m 57, Betty J Barstow; c Julia A & Sarah D. *Educ:* Colo State Univ, BS, 53, PhD(bot), 70; Univ Northern Colo, MA, 60. *Prof Exp:* Instr biol, Univ Northern Colo, 60-64, asst prof sci, 64-65; res assoc & teaching asst bot, Colo State Univ, 65-67. *Concurrent Pos:* Tri-Univ Proj grant, NY Univ, 70; US Bur Reclamation grant, proposed Narrows Dam site, 70-72 & 72-75; mem, vpres & pres bd trustees, Colo Nature Conserv; Northwest Colo Wildlife Consortium grant, 81-83, Colo Div Wildlife grant, 84-85; prog dir, NSF, 92-94. *Mem:* Nat Asn Res Sci Teaching; Nat Asn Biol Teacher (secy-treas, 69-70, pres, 93); Am Inst Biol Sci; Sigma Xi; Am Educr Teacher Sci. *Res:* Analysis of vegetational communities found along flood plains; ecological studies of river bottom ecosystems; ecosystem modeling and assessment of remote sensing vegetation data bases; use of analogies in teaching science and profiler of high school biology and junior high. *Mailing Add:* 1832 23rd Avenue Lane Greeley CO 80631. *Fax:* 970-351-2335; *E-Mail:* ivo38@aol.com

LINDAUER, MAURICE WILLIAM, ANALYTICAL CHEMISTRY, PHYSICAL CHEMISTRY. *Current Pos:* RETIRED. *Personal Data:* b Millstadt, Ill, Sept 25, 24; m 46, J Ruth Shiver; c Jane (Elder), Rosemary (Brannen) & Jack. *Educ:* Wash Univ, AB, 49, AM, 53; Harvard Univ, MEd, 62; Fla State Univ, PhD, 70. *Prof Exp:* Res chemist, Mallinckrodt Chem Works, 52-55 & Am Zinc, Ill, 55-56; res chemist, Nitrogen Div, Allied Chem & Dye Corp, 56-57; assoc prof anal & phys chem, Valdosta State Col, 57-71, prof chem, 71-84, head dept, 81-84. *Mem:* Am Chem Soc; Sigma Xi. *Res:* Mossbauer spectroscopy; history of chemistry; thermodynamics and chemical equilibrium. *Mailing Add:* 1401 Miramar St Valdosta GA 31601-3616

LINDBECK, WENDELL ARTHUR, ORGANIC CHEMISTRY. *Current Pos:* from assoc prof to prof phys sci & chem, 49-78, EMER PROF CHEM, NORTHERN ILL UNIV, 78- *Personal Data:* b Rockford, Ill, Sept 28, 12; m 38, Jane E Rounds; c Wendelyn (Hugstad), Joanne (Miller) & Richard. *Educ:* Beloit Col, BS, 36; Univ Wis, PhM, 37, PhD(chem), 40. *Prof Exp:* Teacher, Tenn Jr Col, 40-44; tech coord, Goodyear Synthetic Rubber Corp, Ohio, 44-47; assoc prof & chmn, Natural Sci Div, Univ Ill, 47-49. *Concurrent Pos:* NSF sci fac fel, Univ Calif, Berkeley, 60-61; US AEC grant, Argonne Nat Lab, 69-70. *Mem:* Am Chem Soc; Sigma Xi. *Res:* Synthesis of organic compounds. *Mailing Add:* 204 Windsor Dr De Kalb IL 60115

LINDBERG, CRAIG ROBERT, STATISTICS & SIGNAL PROCESSING, WAVE PROPAGATION. *Current Pos:* VIS RES SCIENTIST, PRINCETON UNIV, 91- *Personal Data:* b Edmonton, Alta. *Educ:* Univ Alta, BSc, 79; Univ Calif, San Diego, PhD(earth sci), 86. *Prof Exp:* Researcher geophys, Esso Resources Ltd, 79; res asst physics, Mass Inst Technol, 79-80; res asst geophys, Univ Calif, San Diego, 80-86, postgrad geophysicist, 86-88; postdoctoral mem tech staff, AT&T Bell Labs, 88-90, resident visitor, 91-92. *Concurrent Pos:* Assoc prin investr, Univ Calif, San Diego, 84-88; consult, AT&T Bell Labs, 87; assoc ed, Am Geophys Union, 90- *Mem:* Soc Indust & Appl Math; Am Statist Asn; Inst Elec & Electronic Engrs; Am Geophys Union. *Res:* Statistical signal processing and application to physical problems; robust regression methods; climate change; seismic and speech data analysis; group theory solution of pdes. *Mailing Add:* 1831 Crofton Pkwy Apt F Crofton MD 21119

LINDBERG, DAVID ROBERT, PALEOBIOLOGY, EVOLUTIONARY ECOLOGY. *Current Pos:* sr mus sci, 82-84, asst res paleontologist, 84-86, ASSOC RES PALEONTOLOGIST, MUS PALEONT, UNIV CALIF, BERKELEY, 84-, ADJ ASSOC PROF, DEPT INTEGRATIVE BIOL, 89-, ASST DIR, 91- *Personal Data:* b Elgin, Ill, Feb 7, 48; m 68, Dixie Scott; c Jason D. *Educ:* San Francisco State Univ, BA, 77; Univ Calif, Santa Cruz, PhD(biol), 83. *Honors & Awards:* Award for Excellence, Pac div, AAAS, 80. *Prof Exp:* Dir res, Farallon Res Group, Oceanic Soc, 73-77; res biologist, Dept Invert Zool, Calif Acad Sci, 75-77. *Concurrent Pos:* Res assoc, Dept Invert Zool, Calif Acad Sci, San Francisco, 77-; co-investr, res prog, US Fish & Wildlife Serv, Univ Calif, Santa Cruz, 79-91; res assoc, Dept Invert Paleont, Nat Hist Mus Los Angeles, Calif, 86-; fel, Calif Acad Sci, 85-, Willi Hennig Soc, Stockholm, 88. *Mem:* Am Soc Zoologists; Am Malacological Union; Paleont Res Inst; Paleont Soc; Soc of Systematic Zoologists. *Res:* The evolution and biology of patellacean limpets; the evolution of brooding and hermaphroditism in molluscs; rocky intertidal community structure; molluscan evolution. *Mailing Add:* Integrative Biol Univ Calif Berkeley 345 Mulford Hall Berkeley CA 94720-0001. *Fax:* 510-642-1822; *E-Mail:* davidl@ucmp1.berkeley.edu

LINDBERG, DONALD ALLAN BROR, PATHOLOGY, COMPUTER SCIENCE. *Current Pos:* DIR NAT LIBR MED, NIH, 84- *Personal Data:* b Brooklyn, NY, Sept 21, 33; m 57; c 3. *Educ:* Amherst Col, AB, 54; Columbia Univ, MD, 58; Am Bd Path, dipl, 63. *Hon Degrees:* ScD, Amherst Col, 79 & State Univ NY, Syracuse, 87; LLD, Univ Mo, 90. *Honors & Awards:* Silver Core Award, Int Fedn Info Processing, 86; Surgeon General's Medallion, USPHS, 89; Nathan Davis Award, AMA, 89; Presidential Sr Exec Rank Award, 90; Outstanding Service Medal, Uniformed Serv Univ Health Sci, 92; Computers in Healthcare Pioneer Award, Computers in Healthcare Publ, 93; Silver Award, US Nat Comn Libr & Info Sci, 96. *Prof Exp:* From instr to prof path, Sch Med, 62-84. *Concurrent Pos:* Markle scholar, 64-69; mem, Comput Res & Biomath Study Sect, NIH, 67-71 & Comput Sci & Eng Bd, Nat Acad Sci, 71-73; chmn, CBX Adv Comt, Nat Bd Med Examrs, 71-74, mem, Joint CBX Comt, Nat Bd Med Examrs & Am Bd Internal Med, 74-81; US rep, Comt Comput Med, Int Fedn Info Processing; mem, Biomed Rev Libr Comt, Nat Libr Med, 79-80; consult & mem, Peer Rev Group, TRIMIS, Dept Defense, 77-84; prof & chmn, Dept Info Sci, Sch Libr & Info Sci, 69-71, dir info sci group, Sch Med, 71-84, dir, Health Serv Res Ctr & Health Care Technol Ctr, Univ Mo, Columbia, 76-80; adj prof path, Sch Med, Univ Md, 84-; mem coun, Inst Med-Nat Acad Sci, 90-; dir, Nat Coord Off High Performance Comput & Commun, 92-95. *Mem:* Inst Med-Nat Acad Sci; Am Med Informatics Asn; Col Am Pathologists; Am Asn Artificial Intel; fel Am Inst Med & Biol Eng; fel Am Col Med Informatics; Sigma Xi; fel AAAS. *Res:* Information processing; computers in medicine; infectious diseases; author of 4 books and over 100 technical articles. *Mailing Add:* Nat Libr Med MLN Bldg 38 8600 Rockville Pike Rm 2E 17B Bethesda MD 20894

LINDBERG, EDWARD E, MECHANICAL ENGINEERING. *Current Pos:* asst prof mech eng, 63-67, ASSOC PROF MECH ENG, WESTERN NEW ENG COL, 67-, DIR COMPUT CTR, 68- *Personal Data:* b Boston, Mass, Aug 16, 38; m 58; c 2. *Educ:* Worcester Polytech Inst, BSME, 60, MSME, 63. *Prof Exp:* Test engr, Scintilla Div, Bendix Corp, 60-61; engr, Alden Res Labs, Worcester Polytech Inst, 61-63. *Mem:* Am Soc Mech Engrs; Am Soc Eng Educ; Instrument Soc Am; Sigma Xi. *Res:* Automatic controls; fluid mechanics; thermodynamics; computer sciences. *Mailing Add:* 76 Craiwell Ave West Springfield MA 01089-2916

LINDBERG, GEORGE DONALD, PLANT PATHOLOGY. *Current Pos:* RETIRED. *Personal Data:* b Salt Lake City, Utah, Feb 9, 25; m 55; c 3. *Educ:* Ariz State Univ, BS, 50; Okla State Univ, MS, 52; Univ Wis, PhD(plant path), 55. *Prof Exp:* From asst prof to prof plant path, La State Univ, Baton Rouge, 55-94. *Mem:* Am Phytopath Soc. *Res:* Plant virology; diseases of forage crops; abnormalities in the fungi. *Mailing Add:* 2074 Cambridge Circle Pensacola FL 32514

LINDBERG, JAMES GEORGE, ORGANIC CHEMISTRY. *Current Pos:* From asst prof to assoc prof, 67-78, PROF CHEM, DRAKE UNIV, 78- *Personal Data:* b Grand Rapids, Mich, Sept 19, 40; c 3. *Educ:* Kalamazoo Col, BA, 62; Baylor Univ, PhD, 69. *Concurrent Pos:* Vis scholar, Stanford Univ, 83-84. *Mem:* Am Chem Soc; Royal Soc Chem. *Res:* Nuclear magnetic resonance spectroscopic studies of steric effects; conformational analysis of cyclohexanones. *Mailing Add:* Dept Chem Drake Univ Des Moines IA 50311-4516

LINDBERG, JOHN ALBERT, JR, MATHEMATICAL ANALYSIS. *Current Pos:* from asst to assoc prof, 62-72, PROF MATH, SYRACUSE UNIV, 72- *Personal Data:* b New York, NY, Apr 19, 34; m 64; c 2. *Educ:* Wagner Col, BA, 54; Univ Minn, MA, 57, PhD(math), 60. *Prof Exp:* Instr math, Univ Minn, 58-59 & Yale Univ, 60-62. *Concurrent Pos:* Res fel math, Yale Univ, 68-69. *Mem:* AAAS; Am Math Soc; Math Asn Am; Sigma Xi. *Res:* Theory of algebraic extensions of Banach algebras and factorization of polynomials over such algebras; inverse producing normed extensions. *Mailing Add:* 215 Carnegie Syracuse Univ Syracuse NY 13244-1150

LINDBERG, LOIS HELEN, MEDICAL MICROBIOLOGY. *Current Pos:* asst prof bact, 58-65, assoc prof biol, 65-70, prof biol, 70-80, assoc dean fac, 78-79, PROF MICROBIOLOGY, SAN JOSE STATE UNIV, 80- *Personal Data:* b Air Force Base, Ill, Sept 1, 32. *Educ:* San Jose State Col, AB, 52; Univ Calif, MPH, 58; Stanford Univ, PhD, 67. *Prof Exp:* Jr microbiologist, State Dept Pub Health, Calif, 53-54; instr bact, San Jose State Col, 54-55; assoc pub health, Pub Health Lab, Univ Calif, 55-58. *Concurrent Pos:* NSF sci teachers fel, 62, fel, 66 & 67; res assoc, Stanford Univ Med Sch. *Mem:* AAAS; Am Pub Health Asn; Am Soc Microbiol. *Res:* Medical microbiology as related with the pathology and immunology of streptococcal infections. *Mailing Add:* 211 Santa Margarita Ave Menlo Park CA 94025-2726

LINDBERG, R(OBERT) G(ENE), zoology, for more information see previous edition

LINDBERG, STEVEN EDWARD, organic chemistry, polymer chemistry, for more information see previous edition

LINDBERG, STEVEN ERIC, GEOCHEMISTRY, ENVIRONMENTAL SCIENCES. *Current Pos:* res assoc, 74-78, res staff, 79-84, SR RES STAFF, ENVIRON SCI DIV, OAK RIDGE NAT LAB, 85- *Personal Data:* b Waukegan, Ill, May 9, 47; m 69, Kay Caulk; c Kristina. *Educ:* Duke Univ, BS, 69; Fla State Univ, MS, 73, PhD(oceanog), 79. *Honors & Awards:* Environ Sci Achievement Award, Oak Ridge Nat Lab, 84; Martin Marietta Tech Achievement Award, 87. *Prof Exp:* Teacher & adv, Antioch Upper Grade Ctr, 69-71; fel chem oceanog, Fla State Univ, 71-74. *Concurrent Pos:* Chmn, Nat Atmosphere Deposition Prog; chmn, Int Conf Heavy Metals Environ; Alexander von Humboldt fel, 87; vis prof, Inst Bioclimat, Univ Gottingen, Ger, 88; adj res prof, Sch Agr, Univ Tenn, 91-; adj prof, Univ Mich, 96- *Mem:* AAAS; Am Geophys Union. *Res:* Influence of fossil fuel utilization on geochemical cycles, especially the role of atmosphere/surface exchange in the biogeochemistry of forests. *Mailing Add:* Environ Sci Div Oak Ridge Nat Lab Bldg 1505 Box 2008 Oak Ridge TN 37831-6038. *E-Mail:* sll@ornlstc

LINDBERG, VERN WILTON, SOLID STATE PHYSICS, PHYSICAL VAPOR DEPOSITION. *Current Pos:* ASSOC PROF PHYSICS, ROCHESTER INST TECHNOL, 79- *Personal Data:* b Rimbey, Alta, May 5, 49; m 73, Joan Gray; c David & Daniel. *Educ:* Univ Alta, BSc, 69; Case Western Res Univ, MS, 72, PhD(physics), 76. *Prof Exp:* Asst prof physics, Hartwick Col, 76-79. *Concurrent Pos:* Vis researcher, Case Western Res Univ, 76 & 78; vis res scientist, Kodak Res Labs, 84-85; fac fel, Ctr Interfacial Eng, Univ Minn, 93-94. *Mem:* Am Asn Physics Teachers; Am Vacuum Soc. *Res:* Vacuum deposition of thin films by evaporation and sputtering; adhesion of thin films to polymers, surface morphology, resistivity of thin films; use of glow discharge and ion beam to modify substrate; optical thin films. *Mailing Add:* Dept Physics Rochester Inst Technol Rochester NY 14623-0887. *E-Mail:* vwlsps@isc.rit.edu

LINDBLAD, WILLIAM JOHN, WOUND HEALING, COLLAGEN BIOCHEMISTRY. *Current Pos:* ASSOC PROF, DEPT PHARMACEUT SCI, WAYNE STATE UNIV, 90- *Personal Data:* b Glen Head, NY, Oct 14, 54; m 85; c 2. *Educ:* Univ Maine, BS, 76; Cleveland State Univ, MS, 77; Univ RI, PhD(pharmacol), 80. *Prof Exp:* Postdoctoral fel, Dept Surg, Med Col Va, 80-81, res assoc, 81-83, from asst prof to assoc prof, 89-90. *Mem:* Am Asn Study Liver Dis; NY Acad Sci; Am Soc Pharmacol & Exp Therapeut; Wound Healing Soc. *Res:* Fibrogenic response to tissue injury; developing pharmacologic approaches to control fibrogenesis in pathologic conditions; determine the ability of extracellular matrices to control cellular phenotype. *Mailing Add:* Dept Pharmaceut Sci Wayne State Univ 721 Shapero Hall Detroit MI 48202

LINDBURG, DONALD GILSON, ANIMAL BEHAVIOR. *Current Pos:* RES BEHAVIORIST, SAN DIEGO ZOO, 79- *Personal Data:* b Wagner, SDak, Nov 6, 32; m 54; c 3. *Educ:* Houghton Col, BA, 56; Univ Chicago, MA, 62; Univ Calif, Berkeley, PhD(anthrop), 67. *Honors & Awards:* Nat Zoo Centennial Award for Excellence in Zoo Res, 90. *Prof Exp:* Res asst primatol, Nat Ctr Primate Biol, 64-66; res anthropologist, Sch Med, Univ Calif, Davis, 69-72, asst prof anthrop, Univ Calif, Davis, 67-73; chmn & assoc prof, Ga State Univ, 73-75; assoc prof anthrop, Univ Calif, Los Angeles, 75-79. *Concurrent Pos:* Res anthropologist, Nat Ctr Primate Biol, 66-69; NSF fel, Univ Calif, Davis, 72-75; vis lectr, Univ Calif, Berkeley, 72, Univ Calif, San Diego, 85; exec bd, Int Primatol Soc, 84-86; PI, Inst Mus Serv grant "Conserv lion-tailed macaque," 84-85; mem, Res Adv Bd, Int Soc Endangered Cats, 88-; ed, Zoo Biol, 88- *Mem:* Am Soc Primatology (pres, 84-86); Animal Behav Soc; Int Primatol Soc; Am Asn Phys Anthrop Int Primatol Soc. *Res:* Captive reproduction of exotic mammals; behavioral correlates of steroid hormone excretions during different phases of the reproductive cycle in primates and carnivores. *Mailing Add:* Zool Soc San Diego PO Box 551 San Diego CA 92112

LINDE, ALAN TREVOR, GEOPHYSICS. *Current Pos:* STAFF SCIENTIST, DEPT MAGNETISM, CARNEGIE INST, 72- *Personal Data:* b Lowood, Australia, Feb 13, 38; m 60; c 3. *Educ:* Univ Queensland, BSc, 59, PhD(physics), 72. *Prof Exp:* Lectr physics, Univ Queensland, 62-72. *Mem:* Am Geophys Union; Seismol Soc Am; fel Japan Soc Prom Sci. *Res:* Theoretical and observational studies of earthquake source mechanisms to determine properties of the earth's interior and hence to understand the earth's tectonic engine. *Mailing Add:* Carnegie Inst 5241 Broad Branch Rd NW Washington DC 20015

LINDE, ANDREI, COSMOLOGY, THEORY OF PHASE TRANSITIONS. *Current Pos:* PROF PHYSICS, STANFORD UNIV, 90- *Personal Data:* b Moscow, Russia, Mar 2, 48; m 75, Renata Kallosh; c Dmitri & Alexander. *Educ:* Lebedeu Phys Inst, Moscow, PhD(physics), 75. *Honors & Awards:* Lomonosov Award, Acad Sci, USSR, 78. *Prof Exp:* Prof physics, Lebedev Phys Inst, Moscow, 84-89; staff mem, Europ Org Nuclear Res, Switz, 89-90. *Res:* Co-author of theory of cosmological phase transitions and of inflationary cosmology; author of two books and 140 papers. *Mailing Add:* Dept Physics Stanford Univ Stanford CA 94305-4060. *Fax:* 650-725-6544; *E-Mail:* linde@physics.stanford.edu

LINDE, HARRY WIGHT, ANESTHESIOLOGY. *Current Pos:* RETIRED. *Personal Data:* b Woodbridge, NJ, Jan 1, 26; m 56; c 2. *Educ:* Tufts Col, BS, 50; Mass Inst Technol, PhD(chem), 53. *Prof Exp:* Sr chemist, Res Labs, Air Reduction Co, Inc, 53-56; res assoc anesthesia, Med Sch, Univ Pa, 56-63; group leader, Air Prod & Chem, Inc, 63-65; asst prof, Northwestern Univ, 65-70, asst dir, Anesthesia Res Ctr, 67-71, from assoc prof to prof, 70-91, coordr res res & sponsored progs, 71-76, assoc dean hons prog med educ, 76-91, vchmn res, 77-91, emer prof anesthesia, Med Sch, 91- *Concurrent Pos:* Res assoc, Col Med, Univ Ill, 55-56; mem, Comt Admis, Northwestern Univ, 67-72, human subj rev, 70-76 & res comt, 71-76, gen fac comt, 85-88, chair, 87-88; consult res anesthesia, Vet Admin Lakeside Med Ctr, Chicago, 68-91; assoc staff mem, Chicago Wesley Mem Hosp, 69-72 & Northwestern Mem Hosp, 72-; consult, US Naval Hosp, Great Lakes, 69-78; assoc ed, Yearbk Anesthesia, 70-81. *Mem:* Fel AAAS; Am Chem Soc; Int Anesthesia Res Soc; Am Soc Anesthesiol; Sigma Xi. *Res:* Pharmacology of anesthesia; gas analysis; bioanalytical chemistry. *Mailing Add:* 89 Metedeconk Rd Brick NJ 08723

LINDE, LEONARD M, CARDIOLOGY, PHYSIOLOGY. *Current Pos:* PROF PEDIAT CARDIOL, SCH MED, UNIV SOUTHERN CALIF, 76- *Personal Data:* b New York, NY, June 1, 28; m 51, Shirley Dann; c Bruce, Lauren, Brian & Peter. *Educ:* Univ Calif, BS, 47, MD, 51; Am Bd Pediat, dipl & cert cardiol, 61, dipl & cert pediat, 75. *Honors & Awards:* Ross Award for Pediat Res, 62. *Prof Exp:* Intern, Morrisania City Hosp, New York, 51-52; sr resident pediat, Children's Hosp, Los Angeles, 52-53 & 55-56; prof pediat & cardiol, Sch Med, Univ Calif, Los Angeles, 57-76, physiol, 59-76. *Concurrent Pos:* Fel pediat cardiol, Med Ctr, Univ Calif, Los Angeles, 56-57; consult, Child Cardiac Clin, Los Angeles City Health Dept, 57- & Surg Gen, USAF; vis prof, Univ Tokyo, 65-; chief pediat cardiol, St Vincent's Hosp, Los Angeles, 73-86. *Mem:* Soc Pediat Res; Am Pediat Soc; fel Am Acad Pediat. *Res:* Pediatric cardiology; cardiopulmonary physiology; clinical cardiology; psychological aspects of congenital heart disease; cholesterol problems in children. *Mailing Add:* Div Cardiol Children's Hosp-Los Angeles Los Angeles CA 90027. *Fax:* 213-669-7317; *E-Mail:* llinde@hsc.usc.edu

LINDE, PETER FRANZ, physical chemistry, electrochemistry, for more information see previous edition

LINDE, RONALD K(EITH), PHYSICS OF SOLIDS, ENVIRONMENTAL SCIENCE. *Current Pos:* CHMN BD, RONALD & MAXINE LINDE FOUND; CO-CHMN, TITAN FINANCIAL GROUP. *Personal Data:* b Los Angeles, Calif, Jan 31, 40; m 60, Maxine H Stern. *Educ:* Univ Calif, Los Angeles, BS, 61; Calif Inst Technol, MS, 62, PhD(mat sci), 64. *Prof Exp:* Engr, Litton Systs, Inc, 61; res asst, Calif Inst Technol, 61-64; mat scientist, SRI Int, 64-67, head solid state res, Poulter Labs, 65-67, chmn shock & high pressure physics dept & mgr tech serv, 67-68, chief exec, 68-69, dir phys sci, 68-69; chmn bd & chief exec officer, Envirodyne Industs Inc, 69-89. *Concurrent Pos:* Vchmn bd trustees, Harvey Mudd Col; trustee, Calif Inst Technol; mem deans adv coun & mem law & bus adv coun, Stanford Univ Law Sch. *Res:* Environmental engineering; pollution control; solid state physics; properties of materials; physical chemistry; crystallographic phase transformations; shock wave propagation in solids; physics of soilds. *Mailing Add:* 180 E Pearson St Chicago IL 60611

LINDEBERG, GEORGE KLINE, SOLID STATE PHYSICS. *Current Pos:* PHYSICIST, MINN MINING & MFG CO, 57- *Personal Data:* b Spencer, Iowa, June 6, 30; m 54; c 2. *Educ:* St Olaf Col, BA, 52; Princeton Univ, PhD(exp physics), 57. *Prof Exp:* Asst physics, Princeton Univ, 56-57. *Mem:* Am Phys Soc. *Res:* Non-equilibrium electronic processes in solids; thermodynamics; physics operations research. *Mailing Add:* 276 W Grove Rd Hudson WI 54016

LINDELL, ISMO VEIKKO, ELECTROMAGNETIC THEORY. *Current Pos:* From asst prof to assoc prof radio eng, 62-89, prof electromagnetics, 89-96, ACAD PROF ELECTROMAGNETICS ACAD FINLAND, HELSINKI UNIV TECHNOL, 96- *Personal Data:* b Viipuri, Finland, Nov 23, 39; m 64, Liisa Nopula; c Riina & Antti. *Educ:* Helsinki Univ Technol, dipl eng, 63, LicTech, 67, DrTech(radio eng), 71. *Honors & Awards:* SA Schelkunoff Prize, Inst Elec & Electronics Engrs, Antennas & Propagation Soc, 87. *Concurrent Pos:* Vis prof, Univ Ill, 72-73; vis scientist, Mass Inst Technol, 86-87. *Mem:* Fel Inst Elec & Electronics Engrs Antennas & Propagation Soc; Int Union Radio Sci. *Res:* Electromagnetic theory; author of 2 books. *Mailing Add:* Elec Eng Dept Helsinki Univ Technol Espoo 02150 Finland. *E-Mail:* ismo.lindell@hut.fi

LINDELL, THOMAS JAY, MOLECULAR & CELLULAR BIOLOGY. *Current Pos:* Assoc prof pharmacol, Health Sci Ctr, 70-83, ACTG HEAD MOLECULAR & CELLULAR BIOL, UNIV ARIZ, 83- *Personal Data:* b Red Wing, Minn, July 22, 41; div; c 2. *Educ:* Gustavus Adolphus Col, BS, 63; Univ Iowa, PhD(biochem), 69. *Concurrent Pos:* USPHS fel biochem, Univ Wash, 68-69 & biochem, biophys & develop biol, Univ Calif, San Francisco, 69-70; assoc ed, J Life Sci. *Mem:* AAAS; Sigma Xi; Am Soc Biol Chemists; Am Soc Microbiol. *Res:* Control of eukaryotic transcription. *Mailing Add:* Dept Molecular Cellular Biol Univ Ariz Life Sci 254 Tucson AZ 85721-0001

LINDEMAN, ROBERT D, INTERNAL MEDICINE, NEPHROLOGY. *Current Pos:* CHIEF, DIV GERONTOL, DEPT MED, UNIV NMEX, 88- *Personal Data:* b Ft Dodge, Iowa, July 19, 30; m 54, 82, E Lynn Lind; c William Douglas, Ann Denise (Hendrix), James Lawrence, Peter Verlus, David Matthew, Laurel (Lisinski), Lisa (Ringhoff), Kristine (Cannaday) & Robert M Lind. *Educ:* State Univ NY Col Forestry, Syracuse Univ, BS, 52; State Univ NY, MD, 56. *Prof Exp:* From asst resident to asst instr internal med, State Univ NY Upstate Med Ctr, 57-60; med officer, Okla State Dept Health, 60-62; med officer geront, Baltimore City Hosps, Md, 62-66; asst prof med & prev med, Med Ctr, Univ Okla, 66-68, assoc prof med & physiol, 68-71, assoc prof biostatist & epidemiol, 69-77, prof med & physiol, 71-77, chief renal sect, 67-77; assoc dean, Vet Admin Affairs & prof med, Sch Med Univ Louisville, 77-88; chief staff, Louisville Vet Admin Med Ctr, 77-88; prof med & assoc dean, George Washington HSC, 83-88; prof med, Georgetown Sch Med, 83-88; chief-of-staff, Washington Vet Admin Med Ctr, 83-88; chief geriat & extended care, Albuquerque Vet Admin Med Ctr, 88-91. *Concurrent Pos:* Clin asst med, Univ Okla, 60-62; instr, Sch Med, Johns Hopkins Univ, 62-66; asst chief res staff, Oklahoma City Vet Admin Hosp, 67-77; assoc ed, The Kidney, 74-77; mem, US Pharmacopeia Comt Rev & chmn, Subcomt Electrolytes, Large Volume Parenterals & Renal Drugs, 75-; prof, Univ NMex, 88- *Mem:* Cent Soc Clin Res; Int Soc Nephrology; Southern Soc Clin Invest; fel Am Col Physicians; Master Am Col Nutrition; fel Am Geriat Soc. *Res:* Renal and electrolyte problems; hypertension; renal and cardiovascular physiology; aging; trace metal metabolism and nutrition. *Mailing Add:* 2513 Myra Pl NE Albuquerque NM 87112-2509. *Fax:* 505-272-4628

LINDEMANN, CHARLES BENARD, CELL PHYSIOLOGY, BIOPHYSICS. *Current Pos:* PROF PHYSIOL, OAKLAND UNIV, 74- *Personal Data:* b Staten Island, NY, Dec 17, 46; m 75; c 3. *Educ:* State Univ NY Albany, BS, 68, PhD(biol), 72. *Prof Exp:* Res assoc cell physiol, Pac Biomed Res Ctr, Univ Hawaii, 72-73; res assoc biophys, State Univ NY

Albany, 73-74. *Mem:* Biophys Soc; Am Soc Cell Biol; Soc Study Reprod. *Res:* Flagellar motility: the mechanisms of force production and the factors which control motility onset are under investigation in mammalian sperm. *Mailing Add:* Dept Biol Sci Oakland Univ Rochester MI 48309-4401. *Fax:* 248-370-2286

LINDEMANN, MARTIN K, CHEMISTRY OF POLYVINYL ACETATE & POLYVINYL ALCOHOL, EMULSION POLYMERIZATION. *Current Pos:* CHEM CONSULT, SEQUA CHEM INC, CHESTER, SC, 81- *Educ:* Tech Univ Hanover, Ger, BS, 51; Polytech Inst NY, MS, 62. *Honors & Awards:* Olney Medal Achievements Polymer & Textile Chem, Am Asn Textile Chemists & Colorists, 88. *Prof Exp:* Res chemist, Onyx Oil & Chem Corp, Jersey City, NJ, 51-54; polymer develop supvr, Air Reduction Co, Inc, Bound Brook, NJ, 55-66; mgr resin res, Mobil Chem Corp, Edison, NJ, 66-68; vpres & tech dir, C S Tanner Co, Subsid Ciba-Geigy Corp, Greenville, SC, 68-80. *Mem:* Am Chem Soc; Tech Asn Pulp & Paper Indust; Fedn Paint Socs; Am Asn Textile Chemists & Colorists. *Res:* Polymer and organic chemistry; author of numerous publications and granted several patents. *Mailing Add:* 102 Independence Dr Hwy 72 Bypass PO Box 70 Greenville SC 29615-3210

LINDEMANN, WALLACE W(ALDO), ELECTRICAL ENGINEERING. *Current Pos:* RETIRED. *Personal Data:* b Bigelow, Minn, Aug 7, 25; m 50; c 6. *Educ:* Univ Minn, BEE, 50, MS & PhD(elec eng), 55. *Prof Exp:* Asst, Univ Minn, 50-51, res fel, 51-55; prin scientist, Gen Mills, Inc, 55-60; dir solid state res, Control Data Corp, 60-69, gen mgr, 69-79, vpres, Comput Components Div, 79-85; prof elec eng & dir ctr microelectronics & comput sci, Univ Minn, 85-90. *Mem:* Inst Elec & Electronics Engrs. *Res:* Solid state device development; microelectronics including thin film and semiconductor technologies. *Mailing Add:* 7979 Martindale Dr Prior Lake MN 55372

LINDEMANN, WILLIAM CONRAD, SOIL MICROBIOLOGY. *Current Pos:* ASST PROF SOIL MICROBIOL, NMEX STATE UNIV, 78- *Personal Data:* b East St Louis, Ill, Aug 31, 48; m 78. *Educ:* Southern Ill Univ, BS, 70; Univ Minn, MS, 74, PhD(soil sci), 78. *Prof Exp:* Res asst, Univ Minn, 72-74, 75-77; tech asst, Res Seeds Inc, 74-75. *Mem:* AAAS; Am Soc Microbiol; Am Soc Agron; Soil Sci Soc Am; Sigma Xi. *Res:* Soil nitrogen fixation; rhizobiology; legume innoculation; legume nutrition. *Mailing Add:* Crop & Soil Sci Box 3Q NMex State Univ Las Cruces NM 88003

LINDEMER, TERRENCE BRADFORD, HIGH TEMPERATURE CHEMISTRY, NUCLEAR CHEMISTRY. *Current Pos:* MEM RES STAFF, CHEM TECHNOL DIV, OAK RIDGE NAT LAB, 66- *Personal Data:* b Gary, Ind, Feb 17, 36; m 62; c 2. *Educ:* Purdue Univ, BS, 58; Univ Fla, PhD(metall eng), 66. *Prof Exp:* Mem res staff, Inland Steel Co, 58-61 & Solar Aircraft Co, 61-63. *Mem:* Fel Am Ceramic Soc; Mat Res Soc. *Res:* Thermodynamic and kinetic factors affecting reactor performance of nuclear fuels and fission products; ceramic superconductors; structural ceramics. *Mailing Add:* 10931 Sallings Rd Knoxville TN 37922

LINDEMEYER, ROCHELLE G, PEDIATRIC DENTISTRY. *Current Pos:* asst prof oper dent, 79-81, ASSOC PROF ORAL PEDIAT, SCH DENT, TEMPLE UNIV, 81- *Personal Data:* b Philadelphia, Pa. *Educ:* West Chester State Col, BA, 72; Univ Pittsburgh, DMD, 77. *Honors & Awards:* Am Acad Gen Dent Award, 77. *Prof Exp:* Residency pedodontics, Children's Hosp Philadelphia, 77-79. *Concurrent Pos:* Pvt pract pedodontics, 77-; clin affil, Children's Hosp Philadelphia, 79- & St Christopher's Hosp Children, 82-; dipl & fel, Am Bd Pediat Dent, 89- *Mem:* Int Asn Dent Res; Sigma Xi; Am Acad Pediat Dent; Am Dent Asn; Am Soc Dent Children; Int Col Dentists. *Res:* Hormone receptors; periodontitis in the pediatric dental patient. *Mailing Add:* Oper Dent Div Pediat Dent Temple Univ 3223 N Broad St Philadelphia PA 19140

LINDEN, CAROL D, CELL MEMBRANE, ENDOCYTOSIS. *Current Pos:* BIOLOGIST, US ARMY MED RES INST, 79- *Personal Data:* b Philadelphia, Pa, Oct 1, 49; c 2. *Educ:* Univ Calif, Los Angeles, PhD(molecular biol), 74. *Mem:* Am Soc Cell Biol; AAAS; Am Women in Sci. *Mailing Add:* Prog Anal Off US Army Med Res Inst Infectious Dis Ft Detrick Frederick MD 21701. *Fax:* 301-619-2893

LINDEN, DENNIS ROBERT, SOIL SCIENCE, HYDROLOGY. *Current Pos:* SOIL SCIENTIST, AGR RES, USDA, 70- *Personal Data:* b Greeley, Colo, June 22, 42; m 66; c 2. *Educ:* Colo State Univ, MS, 68, MS, 70; Univ Minn, PhD(soil), 79. *Honors & Awards:* Emil Truog Soil Sci Award. *Mem:* Am Soc Agron; Soil Sci Soc Am; Int Soil Sci; Int Soil & Tillage Res Org. *Res:* Soil physics and hydrology; water and energy transport within soil and exchange with the atmosphere at the soil-atmosphere interface; earthworm ecology and impact in agricultural systems. *Mailing Add:* Soil Sci 170 Borlaug Hall Univ Minn St Paul 1991 Upper Burford Cr St Paul MN 55108. *E-Mail:* dlinden@soils.umn.edu

LINDEN, DUANE B, PLANT GENETICS, CELL BIOLOGY. *Current Pos:* assoc prof biol, 65-69, PROF BIOL, KEAN COL NJ, 69-, CHMN DEPT, 73- *Personal Data:* b Toledo, Ohio, June 1, 30; m 67; c 3. *Educ:* Hiram Col, AB, 52; Univ Minn, PhD(plant genetics), 56. *Prof Exp:* Res assoc plant genetics, Univ Minn, 56-57; asst prof genetics, Univ Fla, 57-61; assoc scientist, PR Nuclear Ctr, 61-65. *Mem:* AAAS; Am Inst Biol Sci; Genetics Soc Am; Nat Asn Biol Teachers; Inst Soc Ethics & Life Sci. *Res:* Effects of radiation on biological systems; study of paramutagenic systems in maize. *Mailing Add:* 1238 Medinah Dr Ft Myers FL 33919

LINDEN, HENRY R(OBERT), RESEARCH ADMINISTRATION, ENERGY POLICY & ECONOMICS. *Current Pos:* Frank W Gunsaulus distinguished prof chem eng, Ill Inst Technol, 87-90, interim pres & chief exec officer, 89-90, MAX MCGRAW PROF ENERGY & POWER ENG & MGT, ILL INST TECHNOL, 90- *Personal Data:* b Vienna, Austria, Feb 21, 22; nat US; m 67, Natalie Goredavica; c Robert S & Debra J (Thomas). *Educ:* Ga Inst Technol, BS, 44; Polytech Inst Brooklyn, MChE, 47; Ill Inst Technol, PhD(chem eng), 52. *Honors & Awards:* Oper Sect Award, Am Gas Asn, 56; Coal Res Awards, Am Chem Soc, 59 & 62, Henry H Storch Award, 67; Walton Clark Medal, Franklin Inst, 72; Bunsen Pettenkofer Ehrentafel Award, Deut Ver des Gas und Wasserfaches, 78; Gas Indust Res Award, Am Gas Asn, 82; Nat Energy Resources Orgn Res Award, 86; Homer H Lowry Award, US Dept Energy, 91; US Energy Award, US Energy Asn, 93. *Prof Exp:* Chem engr, petrol fuel res, Socony-Vacuum Labs, 44-47; supvr oil gasification, Inst Gas Technol, 47-52, from asst res dir to dir, 52-69, exec vpres, 69-74, pres & trustee, 74-78, pres & mem bd dirs, 76-87. *Concurrent Pos:* From adj assoc prof to adj prof, Ill Inst Tech, 54-78, res prof chem eng, 78-87, prof gas eng, 78-85, dir, Energy & Power Ctr, 90-, actg dir, Ctr Excellence Polymer Sci & Eng, 95-; chmn, Gordon Res Conf Coal Sci, 65; chief operating officer, Gas Develop Corp, subsid Inst Gas Technol, 65-73, chief exec officer, 73-78, dir, 65-78; chmn, Div Fuel Chem, Am Chem Soc, 67; dep dir, Supply Tech Adv Task Force, Nat Power Survey, Fed Power Comn, 72-75; consult, Energy Res & Develop Off, Fed Energy Admin, 74-75; sr adv, Putnam, Hayes & Bartlett Inc, 96-; pres & mem bd dirs, Gas Res Inst, 76-87. *Mem:* Nat Acad Eng; Am Chem Soc; Am Gas Asn; fel Am Inst Chem Engrs; fel Brit Inst Fuel; Sigma Xi; fel Inst Energy. *Res:* Petroleum properties; petrochemicals; fossil fuel combustion and gasification; synthetic fuels; coal and petroleum pyrolysis and hydrogenolysis; energy economics; energy policy; hydrocarbon resource economics; sustainable energy systems; global climate change; author and co-author of over 200 publications; granted 27 patents. *Mailing Add:* Ill Inst Technol PH-135 10 W 33rd St Chicago IL 60616-3793. *Fax:* 312-567-3967

LINDEN, JAMES CARL, PLANT BIOCHEMISTRY, INDUSTRIAL MICROBIOLOGY. *Current Pos:* assoc prof, Dept Agr, Chem Eng & Microbiol, 78-97, PROF, DEPT CHEM, BIORESOURCE ENG & MICROBIOL, COLO STATE UNIV, 97- *Personal Data:* b Greeley, Colo, Sept 12, 42; m 68, Susan; c Diana & Christina. *Educ:* Colo State Univ, BS, 64; Iowa State Univ, PhD(biochem), 69. *Prof Exp:* Alexander von Humboldt stipend, Bot Inst, Univ Munich, 69, fel plant biochem, 71; fel mammalian cell cult, Dept Microbiol, St Louis Univ, 71-72; biochemist, Great Western Sugar Co, 72-76; sr chemist, Adolph Coors Co, 77-78. *Concurrent Pos:* Prin investr, Colo Res Develop Corp, 84-85; consult, Dept Biotechnol, Swiss Fed Inst Technol, 80; vis scientist, Univ Regensburg, 94. *Mem:* Am Chem Soc; Soc Indust Microbiol; Am Soc Plant Physiol. *Res:* Fuels from biomass, lignocellulose pretreatment, cellulase enzymology; membrane biochemistry; microbial fermentations acetone and butanol, ethanol and lactic acid; plant cell culture; plant signal transduction. *Mailing Add:* 109 Glover Bldg Colo State Univ Ft Collins CO 80523-1370. *Fax:* 970-491-1815; *E-Mail:* jlinden@vines.colostate.edu

LINDEN, JOEL MORRIS, PHARMACOLOGY, CARDIOLOGY. *Current Pos:* res assoc, Dept Pharmacol, 78-80, asst prof physiol, 86-89, RES ASST PROF PHYSIOL & PHARMACOL, UNIV VA, 80-, ASSOC PROF INTERNAL MED, 89- *Personal Data:* b Boston, Mass, May 30, 52. *Educ:* Brown Univ, BS, 74; Univ Va, PhD(pharmacol), 78. *Prof Exp:* Asst mem, Okla Med Res Found, 82-86. *Mem:* Am Soc Pharmacol & Exp Therapeut; Am Physiol Soc. *Res:* Molecular cloning and characterization of adenosine receptors. *Mailing Add:* PO Box 158 Health Sci Ctr Univ Va Charlottesville VA 22908-0001

LINDEN, KURT JOSEPH, OPTOELECTRONICS, SOLID STATE PHYSICS. *Current Pos:* mgr, 84-88, dir, Electronic Mat Div, 89-92, MGR, LASER PROF DEVELOP, SPIRE CORP, 93- *Personal Data:* b Berlin Ger, Dec 27, 36; US citizen; m 62, Alpert; c Judith, Philip & Benjamin. *Educ:* Univ Utah, BS, 59; Mass Inst Technol, MS, 61; Purdue Univ, PhD(elec eng), 66. *Prof Exp:* Engr physics, Air Force Cambridge Res Lab, 63; sr engr infrared, Raytheon Co, 66-76; mgr solid state device activ, laser anal, Div Spectra Physics, 76-84. *Concurrent Pos:* Res asst elec eng, Mass Inst Technol, 59-61, teaching asst, 61-63, guest lectr, 79-; instr, Purdue Univ, 63-66, NSF fel, 65; sr lectr, Northeastern Univ, Ctr Continuing Educ, 77- *Mem:* Sr mem Inst Elec & Electronic Engrs; Am Phys Soc; Int Soc Optical Engrs. *Res:* Optoelectronic semiconductor materials and devices; infrared detectors and emitters; low energy detectors and diode lasers of gallium arsenide, gallium aluminum arsenide and lead salts; management of research and development and manufacturing activities. *Mailing Add:* 17 Keith Rd Wayland MA 01778-4560. *Fax:* 781-275-7470

LINDENAUER, S MARTIN, SURGERY. *Current Pos:* From instr to assoc prof, 64-72, asst dean, Med Sch, 74-81, PROF SURG, UNIV MICH, ANN ARBOR, 72- *Personal Data:* b New York, NY, Dec 10, 32; m 56; c 4. *Educ:* Tufts Univ, MD, 57. *Concurrent Pos:* Chief surg serv, Vet Admin Hosp, 68-74, chief staff, 74-81. *Mem:* Am Col Surg; Asn Acad Surg; Soc Vascular Surg; Int Cardiovasc Soc; Soc Surg Alimentary Tract. *Res:* Vascular surgery; biliary tract surgery. *Mailing Add:* Dept Surg Rm 2922 G Univ Mich Med Ctr/Taubman Ctr Ann Arbor MI 48109-0329

LINDENBAUM, JOHN, SCIENCE EDUCATION. *Current Pos:* PROF, COLUMBIA UNIV. *Honors & Awards:* Corson Medal, Franklin Inst, 95. *Mailing Add:* Columbia Univ 116 St & Broadway New York NY 10027

LINDENBAUM, S(EYMOUR) J(OSEPH), physics, for more information see previous edition

LINDENBERG, KATJA, CHEMICAL PHYSICS, STATISTICAL MECHANICS. *Current Pos:* lectr chem & res chemist, Univ Calif, 69-72, asst prof chem residence, 72-73, from asst prof to assoc prof, 73-81, PROF CHEM, UNIV CALIF, SAN DIEGO, 81-; ASSOC DIR, INST NONLINEAR SCI, 86- *Personal Data:* b Quito, Ecuador, Nov 2, 41; US citizen; m 70, 90, Theodore Groves; c Misha & Dania. *Educ:* Alfred Univ, BA, 62; Cornell Univ, PhD(theoret chem), 67. *Prof Exp:* Res assoc & asst prof physics, Univ Rochester, 67-69. *Concurrent Pos:* Res physicist, Univ Calif, San Diego, 69-71; researcher, Oak Ridge Summer Inst Theoret Biophys, 69-75; consult, Chem Div, Oak Ridge Nat Lab, 75; assoc, La Jolla Inst, 79-88; chmn, Dept Chem,Inst Nonlinear Sci, 92-96. *Mem:* Fel Am Phys Soc; Am Chem Soc; Mat Res Soc; Am Women Sci. *Res:* Theory of stochastic processes with applications to physical and chemical systems; non-equilibrium statistical mechanics; condensed matter theory; nonlinear systems. *Mailing Add:* Chem 0340 Univ Calif San Diego La Jolla CA 92093-0340. *Fax:* 619-534-7244; *E-Mail:* klindenberg@ucsd.edu

LINDENBERG, RICHARD, neuropathology; deceased, see previous edition for last biography

LINDENBLAD, IRVING WERNER, ASTROMETRY, GEODETIC ASTRONOMY. *Personal Data:* b Port Jefferson, NY, July 31, 29; m 94, Joyce Waters; c Werner & Nils. *Educ:* Wesleyan Univ, BA, 50; Colgate Rochester Divinity Sch, MDiv, 56; George Washington Univ, MA, 63. *Prof Exp:* Astronr, US Naval Observ, 53, 58-60, 63-89; Chaplain intern, Washington Hosp Ctr, 90-92. *Mem:* Fel Royal Astron Soc; Am Astron Soc. *Res:* Photographic visual binary stars; motion and magnitude difference of the components of sirius; variation of latitude; rotation and polar motion of the earth; sunspots. *Mailing Add:* 4507 Macarthur Blvd NW Washington DC 20007-4201

LINDENFELD, PETER, LOW TEMPERATURE PHYSICS. *Current Pos:* from instr to assoc prof, 53-66, PROF PHYSICS, RUTGERS UNIV, 66- *Personal Data:* b Vienna, Austria, Mar 10, 25; nat US; m 53, Lore Kadden; c Thomas & Naomi. *Educ:* Univ BC, BASc, 46, MASc, 48; Columbia Univ, PhD(physics), 54. *Honors & Awards:* Robert A Millikan Medal, Am Asn Physics Teachers, 89. *Prof Exp:* Asst physics, Univ BC, 46-47; asst, Columbia Univ, 48-52, res scientist, 53; vis lectr, Drew Univ, 52-53. *Concurrent Pos:* Dir NSF in-serv insts for high sch teachers, 64-66; regional counr NJ, Am Inst Physics, 63-71; Rutgers Res Coun fel & guest scientist fac sci, Univ Paris-South, 70-71; guest scholar, Kyoto Univ, 82. *Mem:* Fel Am Phys Soc; Am Asn Physics Teachers; AAAS; Am Asn Univ Prof. *Res:* Metal-insulator transition and its relation to superconductivity; thin superconducting films; electric, magnetic, and thermal properties of materials. *Mailing Add:* Dept Physics Rutgers Univ Piscataway NJ 08855. *E-Mail:* lindenf@ruthep.rutgers.edu

LINDENLAUB, JOHN CHARLES, ELECTRICAL ENGINEERING, COMPUTER ENGINEERING. *Current Pos:* From asst prof to assoc prof, 61-72, dir, Ctr Instrnl Develop Eng, 77-81, PROF ELEC ENG, PURDUE UNIV, 72- *Personal Data:* b Milwaukee, Wis, Sept 10, 33; m 57, Deborah Hart; c Brian, Mark, Anne & David. *Educ:* Mass Inst Technol, BS, 55, MS, 57; Purdue Univ, PhD(elec eng), 61. *Honors & Awards:* Helen Plants Award, Frontiers in Educ Conf, 80, 87 & 93; Educ Soc Achievement Award, Inst Elec & Electronics Engrs, 84; Chester F Carlson Award, Am Soc Eng Educ, 88. *Concurrent Pos:* Danforth Assoc, Danforth Found, 66; mem tech staff, Bell Tel Labs, Inc, 68-69; prog leader technol transfer, Lab Appln Remote Sensing, Purdue Univ, 74-79, dir, Ctr Instrnl Develop Eng, 77-81, dir instrnl develop, Elec Eng Sch, 84- *Mem:* Fel Inst Elec & Electronics Engrs (sec/treas, 73-74, vpres, 75-76, pres, 77); fel Am Soc Eng Educ. *Res:* Computer engineering; engineering education; author of numerous publications. *Mailing Add:* 339 Fernleaf Dr West Lafayette IN 47906. *E-Mail:* linden@ecn.purdue.edu

LINDENMAYER, GEORGE EARL, BIOCHEMICAL PHARMACOLOGY. *Current Pos:* assoc prof pharmacol & med, 75-77, PROF PHARMACOL & ASSOC PROF MED, MED UNIV SC, 77- *Personal Data:* b Port Arthur, Tex, Aug 22, 40; m 63; c 2. *Educ:* Baylor Univ, BS, 62; Baylor Col Med, MD & MS, 67, PhD(pharmacol), 70. *Prof Exp:* Instr pharmacol, Baylor Col Med, 69-70; staff assoc cardiol, Nat Heart & Lung Inst, 70-72; asst prof pharmacol & med, Baylor Col Med, 72-74, assoc prof cell biophys & med, 74-75. *Concurrent Pos:* Estab investr, Am Heart Asn, 73-78. *Mem:* Am Soc Pharmacol & Exp Therapeut; Int Study Group Res Cardiac Metab; Am Chem Soc; Biophys Soc; Am Heart Asn; Sigma Xi. *Res:* Information transfer between extracellular and intracellular environments of myocardial cells. *Mailing Add:* Dept Pharmacol Med Univ SC 80 Barre St Charleston SC 29401-1106. *Fax:* 803-792-2475

LINDENMEIER, CHARLES WILLIAM, THEORETICAL PHYSICS, NUCLEAR PHYSICS. *Current Pos:* RETIRED. *Personal Data:* b Ft Collins, Colo, Dec 2, 30; m 58; c 2. *Educ:* Colo State Univ, BS, 52; Cornell Univ, PhD(theoret physics), 60. *Prof Exp:* Sr physicist, Hanford Labs, Gen Elec Co, 60-63, mgr theoret physics, 63-64; mgr, Pac Northwest Labs, Battelle Mem Inst, 65-70, mgr math & physics res, 70-73; mgr design anal, Laser Enrichment Dept, Advan Nuclear Fuels Corp, 74-81, mgr neutron develop, neutron & fuel mgt, 81-90, sr staff engr, 90-94. *Mem:* Am Phys Soc; Am Nuclear Soc. *Res:* Reactor physics; neutron thermalization; nuclear reactions; computer applications; laser isotope separation. *Mailing Add:* 1307 Canyon Ave Richland WA 99352

LINDER, ALLAN DAVID, VERTEBRATE ZOOLOGY. *Current Pos:* RETIRED. *Personal Data:* b Grand Island, Nebr, Sept 27, 25; m 49; c 1. *Educ:* Univ Nebr, BSc, 51; Okla State Univ, MSc, 52, PhD(zool), 56. *Prof Exp:* Asst prof zool, Univ Wichita, 56-59 & Southern Ill Univ, 59-60; chmn dept, Idaho State Univ, 60-75, assoc dean, Col Lib Arts, 66-69 & 76-78, prof zool, 60-87. *Mem:* Am Soc Ichthyologists & Herpetologists; Soc Study Amphibians & Reptiles; Sigma Xi; Soc Vert Paleont; Wilderness Soc. *Res:* Ichthyology, paleo-ichthyology and herpetology. *Mailing Add:* 14 Tower Bridge Ct Pueblo CO 81001-1360

LINDER, BRUNO, THEORETICAL CHEMISTRY, CHEMICAL PHYSICS. *Current Pos:* from asst prof to assoc prof, 57-65, assoc chmn dept, 80-83, PROF PHYS CHEM, FLA STATE UNIV, 65- *Personal Data:* b Sniatyn, Poland, Sept 3, 24; nat US; m 53, Cecelia Fahn; c William, Diane, Richard, Nancy & Carolyn. *Educ:* Upsala Col, BS, 48; Univ Ohio, MS, 50; Univ Calif, Los Angeles, PhD(chem), 55. *Prof Exp:* Asst chem, Univ Ohio, 48-49; asst chem, Univ Calif, Los Angeles, 50-55, asst res chemist, 55; proj assoc theoret chem, Naval Res Lab, Wis, 55-57. *Concurrent Pos:* Guggenheim fel, Inst Theoret Physics, Univ Amsterdam, 64-65; chmn chem physics prog, Fla State Univ, 71-73 & 75-; vis prof, Hebrew Univ, Jerusalem, 73. *Mem:* Am Phys Soc; Sigma Xi. *Res:* Intermolecular forces; van der Waals dipoles; liquid crystal theory; solvent effects on infrared and Raman intensities. *Mailing Add:* Dept Chem Fla State Univ Tallahassee FL 32306. *Fax:* 352-694-8281

LINDER, DONALD ERNST, LIQUID CHROMATOGRAPHY, GEL PERMEATION CHROMATOGRAPHY. *Current Pos:* ENVIRON PROJ COORDR, CONOCO, INC, 66- *Personal Data:* b Yoakum, Tex, Oct 4, 38; m 61; c 3. *Educ:* Sul Ross State Univ, BS, 61; Tex A&M Univ, 64, PhD(chem), 67. *Mem:* Am Chem Soc. *Res:* Liquid chromatography, adsorption, liquid-liquid, ion exchange and gel permeation; large scale preparative gas-liquid chromatography; analytical distillations; environmental sampling and testing; EPA protocol groundwater monitoring. *Mailing Add:* 2409 Cardinal Ponca City OK 74604-2806

LINDER, ERNEST G, MICROWAVE DEVELOPMENT, SOLAR CELLS. *Current Pos:* RETIRED. *Personal Data:* b Waltham, Mass, May 16, 02; m 44; c 2. *Educ:* State Univ Iowa, BA, 25, MS, 27; Cornell Univ, PhD(physics), 31. *Prof Exp:* Res assoc, Cornell Univ, 28-32; res physicist, Res Dept, RCA, 32-42 & RCA Labs, 42-55, spec proj mgr, 55-68. *Concurrent Pos:* Comt insulation, Nat Res Coon, 29; deleg, int Conf Peaceful Usage Atomic Energy, Geneva, Switz, 55; consult, Pub Broadcast Syst, 74-79. *Mem:* fel Am Phys Soc; fel Am Inst Elec Engrs; Union Concerned Scientists; Sigma Xi. *Res:* Electrical discharges in gases, microwaves, magnetrons, electron physics, nuclear and solar batteries, radar, microwave propagation. *Mailing Add:* 16 Colonial Club Dr Apt 205 Boynton Beach FL 33435-8304

LINDER, HARRIS JOSEPH, ZOOLOGY. *Current Pos:* asst prof, 58-63, ASSOC PROF ZOOL, UNIV MD, COLLEGE PARK, 63- *Personal Data:* b Brooklyn, NY, Jan 3, 28; m 52; c 4. *Educ:* Long Island Univ, BS, 51; Cornell Univ, MS, 55, PhD(zool), 58. *Prof Exp:* Asst zool, Cornell Univ, 52-57; resident res assoc, Div Biol & Med, Argonne Nat Lab, 57-58. *Concurrent Pos:* Contrib ed, Instrnl Media, J Col Sci Teaching, 76-79. *Mem:* AAAS; Am Soc Zool; Am Micros Soc; Am Inst Biol Sci; Soc Study Reproduction; Sigma Xi. *Res:* Comparative invertebrate endocrinology; neurosecretion; experimental studies on earthworm reproduction. *Mailing Add:* Dept Zool Univ Md College Park MD 20742-0001

LINDER, JAMES, PATHOLOGY, MICROBIOLOGY. *Current Pos:* from asst prof to assoc prof path, Univ Nebr, 83-89, dir path residency prog, 83-89, dir regional lab, 89-90, DIR CYTOPATH, DEPT PATH & LAB MED, MED CTR, UNIV NEBR, 83-, DIR SURG PATH, 85-, PROF PATH & MICROBIOL, 89- *Personal Data:* b Omaha, Nebr, Oct 21, 54. *Educ:* Iowa State Univ, BS, 76; Univ Nebr, MD, 80; Am Bd Path, cert anat & clin path, 83, cert cytopath, 89. *Prof Exp:* Teaching asst, Dept Biochem, Iowa State Univ, 75-76, Univ Minn, 76-77; clin path fel, Duke Univ/Caberras Hosp, 81-83. *Concurrent Pos:* Med examr, Durham, NC, 81-82; path resident, Med Ctr, Duke Univ, 80-82, Univ Nebr, 82-83; mem grad fac, Med Ctr, Univ Nebr, 84-87; consult. *Mem:* Am Fedn Clin Res; Am Soc Cytol; Am Asn Pathologists; fel Col Am Pathologists; Col Am Soc Clin Pathologists; AMA; Sigma Xi. *Res:* Immune disorders; hematologic disorders. *Mailing Add:* Dept Path & Microbiol Med Ctr Univ Nebr 600 S 42nd St Omaha NE 68198-3135

LINDER, JOHN SCOTT, MICROELECTRONICS, SOLID STATE PHYSICS. *Current Pos:* PROF ELEC ENG, TEX A&M UNIV, 79- *Personal Data:* b Baton Rouge, La, May 3, 35. *Educ:* La State Univ, BS, 56, MS, 60; Univ Ariz, PhD(elec eng), 67. *Prof Exp:* Tech investr chem processing, E I du Pont de Nemours & Co, 56-58; assoc elec eng, La State Univ, 58-60, instr, 62-63; sr engr, comput div, Bendix Corp & Control Data Corp, 60-62; instr elec eng, Univ Ariz, 63-67; asst prof elec eng, Tex A&M Univ, 67-68, assoc prof, 68-79. *Concurrent Pos:* Mem tech staff, Sandia Corp, 66; consult, Burr Brown Corp, 67-68, missiles & space div, LTV Aerospace Corp & Consoltec Inc, 69-, Teledyne 79- *Mem:* Inst Elec & Electronics Engrs; Am Soc Eng Educ; Am Phys Soc. *Res:* Solid state devices; semiconductor technology; solid state materials; active and distributed synthesis. *Mailing Add:* Dept Elec Eng & Comput Sci Tex A&M Univ Kingsville TX 78363

LINDER, LOUIS JACOB, ANALYTICAL CHEMISTRY & OPTICAL EMISSION SPECTROSCOPY. *Current Pos:* RETIRED. *Personal Data:* b East St Louis, Ill, May 10, 16; m 48, Elizabeth Schaeffer; c Harriett, Louis III & Mark. *Educ:* Wash Univ, AB, 41. *Prof Exp:* Chemist, Eagle-Picher Lead Co, 41-44 & US Army Chem Warfare Serv, 44-46; anal chemist, Alumina &

Chem Div, Res Labs, Aluminum Co Am, 46-50, res chemist, 50-72; lab mgr Sch Sci, Southern Ill Univ, Edwardsville, 72-86. *Mem:* Soc Appl Spectros. *Res:* Analytical procedures on aluminous materials; application of optical emission spectroscopy to analysis of alumina, aluminous ores and sodium aluminate liquors; spectrographic analysis of gallium oxide and metal. *Mailing Add:* 7907 W Washington St Belleville IL 62223-2317

LINDER, MARIA C, CHEMISTRY, GENERAL BIOCHEMISTRY. *Current Pos:* PROF BIOCHEM, CALIF STATE UNIV, 78- *Personal Data:* b New York, NY. *Mailing Add:* Chem & Biochem Dept Calif State Univ Fullerton CA 92634. *Fax:* 714-449-5316

LINDER, MAURINE E, BIOCHEMISTRY. *Current Pos:* ASST PROF CELL BIOL, WASHINGTON UNIV MED SCH, 93- *Personal Data:* b Dagget, Mich, Jan 18, 55. *Educ:* Mich State Univ, BS, 76; Univ Tex, Dallas, PhD(cell biol), 87. *Prof Exp:* Fel signal transduction, Univ Tex, 87-89, asst instr pharmacol, 89-91, instr, 91-93. *Mem:* Am Soc Biochem & Molecular Biol; AAAS; Am Soc Cell Biol. *Mailing Add:* Dept Cell Biol & Physiol Sch Med Box 8228 Washington Univ 660 S Euclid Ave St Louis MO 63110-1093

LINDER, REGINA, MICROBIOLOGY, BIOCHEMISTRY. *Current Pos:* asst prof, 82-87, ASSOC PROF HEALTH SCI, HUNTER COL, CITY UNIV NEW YORK, 87-, DIR MED LAB SCI PROG, 89- *Personal Data:* b New York, NY, June 21, 45. *Educ:* City Col New York, BS, 67; Univ Mass, MS, 69; NY Univ, PhD(microbiol), 75. *Prof Exp:* Asst res scientist, Sch Med, NY Univ, 75-78, asst prof microbiol, 78-82. *Concurrent Pos:* Adj assoc prof microbiol, Sch Med, NY Univ. *Mem:* Am Soc Microbiol; Sigma Xi. *Res:* Investigation of the mechanism of action of bacterial and animal toxins which specifically interact with membrane lipids; pathogenesis of rhodococcus equi. *Mailing Add:* Hunter Col Sch Health Sci 425 E 25th St New York NY 10010. *E-Mail:* rlinder@shiva.hunter.cuny.edu

LINDER, SEYMOUR MARTIN, ORGANIC ANALYTICAL CHEMISTRY, INDUSTRIAL ORGANIC CHEMISTRY. *Current Pos:* RETIRED. *Personal Data:* b New York, NY, Dec 17, 25; m 55, Elise Meyers; c Bonnie & Karen (Staubs). *Educ:* City Col New York, BS, 46; Polytech Inst Brooklyn, MS, 49, PhD(chem), 53. *Prof Exp:* Jr chemist, Hoffmann-La Roche, Inc, 46-51; proj leader, Becco Chem Div, FMC Corp, 53-58 & Org Chem Div, 58-72; dir synthesis res, Alcolac, Inc, 72-80; prin chemist & shift leader, Patapsco & Back River Wastewater Treatment Plants, Balto City, 81-90. *Mem:* Am Chem Soc; fel Am Inst Chemists. *Res:* Chemistry of hydrogen peroxide and peroxy acids; epoxidations; epoxyresins; process development; terpene and medicinal chemistry; insecticides; gas chromatography; specialty organic chemicals; functional monomers; (meth)acrylate esters; organometallic compounds; quaternary salts; copolymerizable surfactants; analysis of wastewater and sludge; determination of primary pollutants by GC and GC/MS; toxicity studies on wastewater treatment plant biomass. *Mailing Add:* 1902 Tadcaster Rd Baltimore MD 21228

LINDER, SOLOMON LEON, INFRARED SYSTEMS, LASER SYSTEMS. *Current Pos:* sr group engr, McDonnell Aircraft Corp, 62-67, SR GROUP ENGR & TECH SPECIALIST, McDONNELL DOUGLAS ASTRONAUT CO, 67- *Personal Data:* b Brooklyn, NY, Mar 13, 29; m 53; c 3. *Educ:* Rutgers Univ, BS, 50; Wash Univ, PhD(physics), 55. *Prof Exp:* Mem tech staff, Bell Tel Labs, Inc, 55-62. *Concurrent Pos:* Eve instr, Fairleigh Dickinson Univ, 59-62, Univ Col, Wash Univ, 63-67, Fla Technol Univ, 70-71, Southern Ill Univ, Edwardsville, 74-75 & Univ Col, Wash Univ, 75- *Mem:* Optical Soc Am; sr mem Inst Elec & Electronics Engrs. *Res:* Nuclear magnetic resonance; military systems; electrooptics. *Mailing Add:* 14571 Coeur Dalene Ct Chesterfield MO 63017

LINDERMAN, ROBERT G, PLANT PATHOLOGY. *Current Pos:* SUPVRY RES PLANT PATHOLOGIST, RES LEADER & COURTESY PROF BOT & PLANT PATH, ORE STATE UNIV, 73- *Personal Data:* b Crescent City, Calif, Feb 2, 39; m 61, Lynne; c Matthew, Stacey & Tami. *Educ:* Fresno State Col, BA, 60; Univ Calif, Berkeley, PhD(plant path), 67. *Prof Exp:* Lab technician plant path, Univ Calif, Berkeley, 64-67, asst res plant pathologist, 67; res plant pathologist, Agr Res Serv, USDA, 67-73. *Mem:* Am Phytopath Soc. *Res:* Ecology of soil-borne fungus plant pathogens; biological control; biological effects of plant residue decomposition in soil; ornamental plant diseases; mycorrhizal fungi. *Mailing Add:* USDA-ARS Hort Crops Res Lab 3420 NW Orchard Ave Corvallis OR 97330. *Fax:* 541-570-8764; *E-Mail:* lindermr@bcc.orst.edu

LINDERS, JAMES GUS, COMPUTER SCIENCE, MATHEMATICS. *Current Pos:* chmn, Dept Comput & Info Sci, 77-82, PROF, UNIV GUELPH, 77-, CHMN, DEPT COMPUT & INFO SCI, 95- *Personal Data:* b St Catharines, Ont, June 27, 36; m 65, Jean E Britton; c John, Donald & Heather. *Educ:* Univ Toronto, BASc, 60, MASc, 61; Univ London, DIC & PhD(comput sci), 69. *Prof Exp:* Teaching fel math, St Michael's Col, Univ Toronto, 61-63; lectr comput sci, Ryerson Polytech Inst, 62-65; lectr, Imp Col, Univ London, 65-69; asst prof, Univ Waterloo, 69-77. *Concurrent Pos:* Consult, Dept Energy, Mines & Resources, Can, 67- & Ministry Natural Resources, Ont, 77-; pres, Georef Systs Ltd, Waterloo, Can. *Mem:* Fel Brit Comput Soc; fel Royal Geog Soc; Asn Comput Mach; Inst Elec & Electronics Engrs; Am Asn Artificial Intel. *Res:* Computer-aided design; data base design; knowledge base engineering; remote sensing and data fusion; geo referenced data systems. *Mailing Add:* Dept Comput & Info Sci Univ Guelph Guelph ON N1G 2W1 Can. *Fax:* 519-885-4946; *E-Mail:* jgl@snowhite.cis.uoguelph.ca

LINDFORS, KARL RUSSELL, PHYSICAL CHEMISTRY. *Current Pos:* PROF CHEM, CENT MICH UNIV, 64-, CHMN DEPT, 78 - *Personal Data:* b Saginaw, Mich, July 10, 37; m 58; c 2. *Educ:* Univ Mich, BS, 59; Univ Wis, PhD(phys chem), 64. *Prof Exp:* Spectroscopist, Tracerlab, 63-64. *Mem:* Am Chem Soc. *Res:* Molecular spectroscopy; species in solution. *Mailing Add:* Dept Chem Cent Mich Univ Mt Pleasant MI 48859-0002

LINDGREN, ALICE MARILYN LINDELL, RADIATION BIOLOGY, IMMUNOLOGY. *Current Pos:* From instr to assoc prof, 63-81, PROF BIOL, BEMIDJI STATE UNIV, 81- *Personal Data:* b Minneapolis, Minn, Jan 31, 37; m 59, Gordon; c 3. *Educ:* Augsburg Col, BA, 58; Univ Minn, Minneapolis, MS, 61; Univ Iowa, PhD(radiation biol), 70. *Concurrent Pos:* Consult, Agassiz Nursing Educ Consortium, 72- & Itasca Nursing Educ Consortium, 81-; vis asst prof radiation biol, Univ Iowa, 75; vis prof radiol, Univ Iowa, 84-85. *Mem:* Sigma Xi; Radiation Res Soc; Cell Kinetics Soc. *Res:* Cell cycle kinetics; effect of radiation on the cell cycle; control of the cell cycle; response of rat lens epithelial cells to a wound stimulus; lymphocyte blast cell formation (perturbation by drugs and radiation). *Mailing Add:* Sci Div Bemidji State Univ Bemidji MN 56601. *Fax:* 218-755-4107

LINDGREN, BERNARD WILLIAM, MATHEMATICS. *Current Pos:* from instr to assoc prof, 53-69, chmn dept, 63-73, PROF STATIST, UNIV MINN, MINNEAPOLIS, 69- *Personal Data:* b Minneapolis, Minn, May 13, 24; m 45; c 3. *Educ:* Univ Minn, PhD(math), 49. *Prof Exp:* Instr math, Univ Minn, 43-44, 46-49 & Mass Inst Technol, 49-51; res mathematician, Minn-Honeywell Regulator Co, 51-53. *Mem:* Fel Am Statist Asn; Int Statist Inst; Sigma Xi. *Res:* Analysis; probability; statistics. *Mailing Add:* Statist 270 Vincent Hall Univ Minn 206 Church St SE Minneapolis MN 55455-0488

LINDGREN, BO STAFFAN, PEST MANAGEMENT, CHEMICAL ECOLOGY. *Current Pos:* RES DIR, PHERO TECH INC, 84-; ASST PROF, FORESTRY PROG, UNIV NORTHERN BC. *Personal Data:* b Norrkoping, Sweden, July 18, 50; Can citizen; m 85, Laurie M Frijkie; c Mitchell O & Jordan M. *Educ:* Uppsala Univ, Sweden, Filosofie Kandidat, 75; Simon Fraser Univ, MS, 80, PhD(biol), 82. *Prof Exp:* Fel, Univ BC, 82-84. *Concurrent Pos:* Indust fel, Phero Tech Inc, 84-86; lectr, Simon Fraser Univ; vis scientist, Swed Univ Agr Sci, 93. *Mem:* Entom Soc Can; Entom Soc Am. *Res:* Chemical ecology of bark beetles, particularly the application of sermiochemicals for pest management purposes; chemical ecology of other insect groups. *Mailing Add:* Forestry Prog Univ Northern BC 3333 University Way Prince George BC V2N 4Z9 Can. *Fax:* 604-940-9433

LINDGREN, CLARK ALLEN, synaptic physiology, neuromuscular physiology, for more information see previous edition

LINDGREN, DAVID LEONARD, ENTOMOLOGY. *Current Pos:* Jr entomologist, 35-41, from asst entomologist to entomologist, 41-74, EMER ENTOMOLOGIST & LECTR, CITRUS EXP STA, UNIV CALIF, RIVERSIDE, 74- *Personal Data:* b St Paul, Minn, Sept 17, 06; wid; c 3. *Educ:* Univ Minn, BS, 30, MS, 31, PhD(entom), 35. *Mem:* Fel AAAS; Entom Soc Am; Am Asn Cereal Chemists. *Res:* Insecticides; citrus insects; stored product insects. *Mailing Add:* 4738 Elmwood Ct Riverside CA 92506

LINDGREN, E(RIK) RUNE, THEORETICAL & EXPERIMENTAL FLUID MECHANICS. *Current Pos:* PROF ENG SCI, UNIV FLA, 65- *Personal Data:* b Sodertlje, Sweden, Aug 15, 19; m 63, Joan L Smith; c Jan E, Lisa L & Maja B. *Educ:* Tech Col Stockholm, BS, 43; Royal Inst Technol, Sweden, MS, 47, Tekn lic, 56, DSc, 57. *Prof Exp:* Resident assoc, Lumalampan Inc, Sweden, 45-47 & Aeronaut Lab, Royal Inst Technol, Sweden, 47-49; lectr physics & mech, Tech Col Stockholm, 49-51; res fel fluid mech, Royal Inst Technol, Sweden, 51-59, lectr, 59-61; vis asst prof mech, Johns Hopkins Univ, 61-63; assoc prof mech & fluid mech, Okla State Univ, 63-65. *Concurrent Pos:* Consult, Kockums Shipyard & Royal Swed Naval Bd, 51-59 & Res Lab, Presby Hosp, 62-63; res grants, Swed State Coun Tech Res, 53-56, Air Res & Develop Command, US Air Force, 56-59, Docent Fluid Dynamics, Royal Inst Technol, Sweden, 59-, David Taylor Model Basin, US Bur Ships, 62-65, NSF, 66-80 & Off Naval Res, 75-80; vis prof mech, Roy Inst Technol, Sweden, 72- *Mem:* Am Phys Soc; Swed Math Soc. *Res:* Experimental mechanics; cavitation; turbulent transition; structure of shear in flows of Newtonian and non-Newtonian systems, specifically liquid crystals; dynamics of immersed bodies; Theory of inviscid, imcompressible fluid dynamics; non-linear mechanics. *Mailing Add:* AeMES Dept Univ Fla Aero Bldg Gainesville FL 32611. *Fax:* 904-392-7303

LINDGREN, FRANK TYCKO, BIOPHYSICS. *Current Pos:* From res asst to res assoc biophysicist, 55-67, RES BIOPHYSICIST, DONNER LAB, UNIV CALIF, BERKELEY, 67- *Personal Data:* b San Francisco, Calif, Apr 14, 24; m 52, Univ Calif, Berkeley, BA, 47, PhD(biophys), 55. *Concurrent Pos:* Assoc ed, Lipids, Am Oil Chemists Soc, 66-76; fel, coun arteriosclerosis, Am Heart Asn; reviewer, NIH, NSF grants. *Mem:* Am Oil Chemists Soc; Sigma Xi; AAAS; Am Heart Asn. *Res:* Physical chemistry and biochemistry of blood lipids and lipo-proteins as they occur in states of health and diseases; instrumentation and engineering necessary to facilitate such investigations. *Mailing Add:* 2707 Rose St Berkeley CA 94708

LINDGREN, GORDON EDWARD, PHYSICS, MATH. *Current Pos:* from instr to assoc prof, 63-77, dean sci & math, 72-80, PROF PHYSICS, BEMIDJI STATE UNIV, 77- *Personal Data:* b Minneapolis, Minn, Apr 29, 36; m 59; c 3. *Educ:* Augsburg Col, BA, 59; Univ SDak, MA, 63; Univ Iowa, PhD(sci educ), 70. *Prof Exp:* Teacher physics/math, Minnetonk High Sch, Excelsior, Minn, 59-61. *Mem:* Am Asn Physics Teachers; Am Asn Univ Prof; Radiation Res Soc. *Res:* Electron spin resonance; radiation physics. *Mailing Add:* 143 S Lake Movil Rd NW Bemidji MN 56601

LINDGREN, RICHARD ARTHUR, NUCLEAR PHYSICS. *Current Pos:* ASSOC PROF, NUCLEAR PHYSICS GROUP, UNIV MASS, AMHERST, 77- *Personal Data:* b Providence, RI, June 2, 40; m 63; c 4. *Educ:* Univ RI, BA, 62; Wesleyan Univ, MA, 64; Yale Univ, PhD(nuclear physics), 69. *Prof Exp:* Res assoc nuclear physics, Univ Md, College Park, 69-70; res assoc, Nat Res Coun, Nat Acad Sci, 70-71 & Univ Rochester, 71-73; res physicist nuclear physics, Naval Res Lab, Washington, DC, 73-77. *Concurrent Pos:* Instr, George Mason Univ, 73-75; assoc prof, Cath Univ Am, 75-76; consult, Naval Res Lab, 77- & Lawrence Livermore Nat Lab, 81- *Mem:* Sigma Xi; Am Phys Soc. *Res:* Nuclear structure studies using inelastic electron scattering, particularly those nuclear states excited strongly via nuclear magnetization currents; comparison of inelastic proton and electron scattering for high spin stretched states. *Mailing Add:* Dept Physics Univ Va Charlottesville VA 22901

LINDGREN, WILLIAM FREDERICK, MATHEMATICS. *Current Pos:* assoc prof, 71-80, PROF MATH, SLIPPERY ROCK STATE COL, 80- *Personal Data:* b San Mateo, Calif, Dec 23, 42; c 1. *Educ:* SDak Sch Mines & Technol, BS, 64, MS, 66; Southern Ill Univ, PhD(math), 71. *Prof Exp:* Mathematician & analyst, Atomic Energy Div, Phillips Petrol Co, 66-67. *Concurrent Pos:* Vis prof math, Va Polytech Inst, 78-79. *Mem:* Am Math Soc; Sigma Xi. *Res:* General topology. *Mailing Add:* Slippery Rock Univ Pa Slippery Rock PA 16057-9989

LINDH, ALLAN GODDARD, SEISMOLOGY, EARTHQUAKE PREDICTION. *Current Pos:* GEOPHYSICIST, US GEOL SURV, 73- *Personal Data:* b Mason City, Wash, Mar 18, 43; m 71; c 2. *Educ:* Univ Calif, BA; Stanford Univ, MS, PhD(geophys). *Mem:* AAAS; Soc Explor Geophys; Am Geophys Union. *Res:* Earthquake prediction and estimation of probabilities of earthquake occurrence; quantification of earthquake characteristics. *Mailing Add:* US Geol Surv MS 977 345 Middlefield Rd Menlo Park CA 94025

LINDHEIMER, MARSHALL D, INTERNAL MEDICINE, NEPHROLOGY. *Current Pos:* from asst to assoc prof, 70-76, PROF MED, OBSTET & GYNEC, UNIV CHICAGO, 76- *Personal Data:* b Brooklyn, NY, June 28, 32; m 58, Jaqueline; c Daniele, Joel, Philippe, Robin & Claire. *Educ:* Cornell Univ, AB, 52; Univ Geneva, BSM, 57, MD, 61. *Honors & Awards:* Chesley Award, 88. *Prof Exp:* Intern, Rochester Gen Hosp, 61-62; resident, Brooklyn Vet Admin Hosp, 62-63; resident & chief resident, Brookdale Hosp, Brooklyn, 63-64; US Pub Health Serv fel, Boston Univ, 64-66; sr instr med, Case Western Res Univ, 66-69; asst prof, Northwestern Univ, 69-70. *Concurrent Pos:* Prin investr grants, NIH, 72-; fel, High Blood Pressure Res Coun, Am Heart Asn, 80, Asn Am Physicians, 85. *Mem:* Am Physiol Soc; Soc Gynec Invest; fel Am Col Physicians; Int Soc Study Hypertension Pregnancy (secy-treas, 81-87, pres elect, 88); Asn Am Physicians. *Res:* Salt and water physiology and renal disease; renal physiology and hypertension in pregnancy; volume homeostasis and vasopressin in gravid animal models. *Mailing Add:* 5841 S Maryland Ave Chicago Hosp & Clins MC 5100 Chicago IL 60637

LINDHOLM, FREDRIK ARTHUR, ELECTRICAL ENGINEERING. *Current Pos:* PROF ELEC ENG, UNIV FLA, 66- *Personal Data:* b Tacoma, Wash, Feb 26, 36; m 59, 69. *Educ:* Stanford Univ, BS, 58, MS, 60; Univ Ariz, PhD(elec eng), 63. *Honors & Awards:* Awards, Inst Elec & Electronics Engrs, 63 & 65. *Prof Exp:* From instr to assoc prof elec eng, Univ Ariz, 60-66. *Concurrent Pos:* Assoc scientist, Lockheed Corp, 60; sr engr, Motorola Semiconductor Prods, Phoenix, Ariz, 63-66; mem res adv comt electronics, NASA, 68-70; vis prof elec eng, Univ Leuven, Belg, 73-74; consult, Jet Propulsion Lab, Pasadena, Calif, 78-, Los Alamos Nat Lab, 81- & Motorola Bipolar Technol Ctr, Mesa, Ariz, 84- *Mem:* Fel Inst Elec & Electronics Engrs; Am Phys Soc; Am Asn Physics Teachers. *Res:* Semiconductor device physics, including transistors, diodes, integrated circuits, photovoltaics, photoconductivity and equivalent circuit representations; solar cells. *Mailing Add:* Dept Elec Eng Univ Fla Gainesville FL 32611

LINDHOLM, JOHN C, MACHINE DESIGN, DYNAMICS. *Current Pos:* RETIRED. *Personal Data:* b Wichita, Kans, Nov 3, 23; m 47, Mildred Socolofsky; c Martha (Milleson), Susan (Harrington), John C Jr & Barbara (Angell). *Educ:* Kans State Univ, BS(mech eng) & BS(bus admin), 49; Univ Kans, MS, 56; Purdue Univ, PhD(mach design), 61. *Prof Exp:* Design engr, Gen Elec Co, 49-52; sr engr, Midwest Res Inst, 52-54; instr mech eng, Univ Kans, 54-57 & Purdue Univ, 57-59; assoc prof, Kans State Univ, 60-74, prof mech eng, 74-80, prof eng tech & head dept, 80-87, prof mech eng, 87-89. *Concurrent Pos:* Vis prof, Univ Assiut, 64-66, Univ Assiut, Egypt, 92-93; Fulbright prof, Univ S Pac, 87-88 & Univ Assiut, Egypt, 92-93. *Mem:* Am Soc Mech Engrs; Am Soc Eng Educ; Soc Exp Mech. *Res:* Three-dimensional photoelastic stress analysis; mechanical properties materials at intermediate strain rates; kinematic synthesis of mechanisms. *Mailing Add:* 744 Elling Dr Manhattan KS 66502-3636. *Fax:* 785-532-7057; *E-Mail:* lindholm@ksume.me.ksu.edu

LINDHOLM, ROBERT D, physical chemistry, for more information see previous edition

LINDHOLM, ROY CHARLES, SEDIMENTOLOGY. *Current Pos:* from asst prof to assoc prof, 67-77, chmn geol, 86-89 PROF GEOL, GEORGE WASHINGTON UNIV, 77- *Personal Data:* b Washington, DC, Mar 8, 37; m 65; c 2. *Educ:* Univ Mich, BS, 59; Univ Tex, MA, 63; Johns Hopkins Univ, PhD(geol), 67. *Prof Exp:* Instr, Johns Hopkins Univ, 65-66. *Mem:* Nat Asn Geol Teachers; Soc Econ Paleont & Mineral. *Res:* Paleozoic carbonate rocks of eastern United States; sequences of carbonate cements; geology of Triassic-Jurassic rocks in Virginia; lacustrine deposits; sedimentology of Cretaceous sandstones in northern Virginia. *Mailing Add:* 97517 Franklin Ridge Chapel Hill NC 27514-8319

LINDHOLM, ULRIC S, MATERIALS SCIENCE, APPLIED MECHANICS. *Current Pos:* Sr res engr, Southwest Res Inst, 60-64, mgr eng mech, 64-71, asst dir, Dept Mech Sci, 71-73, dir, Dept Mat Sci, 73-85, VPRES DIV ENG & MAT SCI, SW RES INST, 85- *Personal Data:* b Washington, DC, Sept 11, 31; m 61; c 4. *Educ:* Mich State Univ, BS, 53, MS, 55, PhD(appl mech), 60. *Mem:* Fel Am Soc Mech Engrs; Sigma Xi; Am Soc Metals; fel AAAS. *Res:* Applied mechanics, structural dynamics and vibrations; wave propagation; material properties. *Mailing Add:* 110 Honey Bee Lane San Antonio TX 78231

LINDL, JOHN D, INERTIAL CONFINEMENT FUSION. *Current Pos:* physicist, Inertial Confinement Fusion, Lawrence Livermore Nat Lab, 72-78, group leader, 78-81, assoc div leader, 81-83, div leader, 83-90, dep prog leader, 90-94, ACT INERTIAL CONFINEMENT FUSION, LAWRENCE LIVERMORE NAT LAB, 94- *Personal Data:* b Toledo, Ohio, July 27, 46; m, Anne Miller; c 2. *Educ:* Cornell Univ, Bs, 68; Princeton Univ, MA, 70; PhD(astrophys), 72. *Concurrent Pos:* Assoc prog leader, Inertial Confinement Fusion, Lawrence Livermore Nat Lab, 83-89, dep prog leader, 89-90. *Mem:* Fel Am Phys Soc. *Res:* Theory and target design. *Mailing Add:* Rte 2 Del Valle Rd Livermore CA 94550

LINDLEY, BARRY DREW, PHYSIOLOGY, BIOPHYSICS. *Current Pos:* VCHANCELLOR ACAD AFFAIRS, UNIV ARK MED SCI, 93- *Personal Data:* b Orleans, Ind, Jan 25, 39; m 82, Elizabeth Price; c Theodore, Matthew & Sarah. *Educ:* DePauw Univ, BA, 60; Case Western Res Univ, PhD(physiol), 64. *Prof Exp:* From asst prof to prof, Sch Med, Case Western Res Univ, 65-93, assoc dean med educ, 85-93, prof & actg chmn anat. *Concurrent Pos:* NSF fel neurophysiol, Nobel Inst Neurophysiol, Karolinska Inst, Sweden, 64-65; Lederle med fac award, 67-70; USPHS res career develop award, 71-76; mem, Physiol Study Sect, NIH, 75-79; prof physiol & biophysics, Univ Ark Med Sci, 93-, dean, Grad Sch, 96- *Mem:* Am Physiol Soc; Soc Gen Physiologists; Biophys Soc. *Res:* Muscle biophysics; ion and water transport; membrane permeability; irreversible thermodynamics; electrophysiology of nerve, muscle and glandular tissue. *Mailing Add:* Univ Ark Med Sci 4301 W Markham MS-541 Little Rock AR 72205. *E-Mail:* lindleybarryd@exchange.uams.edu

LINDLEY, CHARLES A(LEXANDER), AEROSPACE SYSTEMS ENGINEERING, ALTERNATIVE ENERGY SYSTEMS. *Current Pos:* CONSULT. *Personal Data:* b Union City, Ind, May 12, 24; m 46; c 2. *Educ:* Ohio State Univ, BAeroEng & MS, 49; Calif Inst Technol, PhD(aeronaut), 56. *Prof Exp:* Instr, Ohio State Univ, 47-48; eng aid, Nat Adv Comt Aeronaut, 48; compressor design engr, Thompson Aircraft Prod, Inc, 49-52, consult, 52-55; eng specialist, Marquardt Corp, 55-57, mgr engine res, 57-59, res consult, 59-61, chief res consult, 61-63; sr staff engr, Appl Mech Div, Aerospace Corp, 63-65, dir vehicle design, Satellite Systs Div, 65-73; res assoc, Environ Qual Lab, Calif Inst Technol, 73-74; assoc dir advan systs off, Energy Systs Group, Aerospace Corp, 74-78, sr staff engr, Threat Anal off, 78-91. *Concurrent Pos:* Lectr & consult wind power & wind resources, Univ Calif, Santa Barbara. *Mem:* AAAS; assoc fel Am Inst Aeronaut & Astronaut; Sigma Xi. *Res:* Aeronautical and space propulsion; air breathing and recoverable boosters; physics and chemistry of the upper atmosphere; satellite systems engineering; wind and solar energy; manned and unmanned space vehicle systems engineering; energy conversion devices; meteorology. *Mailing Add:* 18900 Pasadero Dr Tarzana CA 91356

LINDLEY, KENNETH EUGENE, ELECTRICAL ENGINEERING, MATHEMATICS. *Current Pos:* RETIRED. *Personal Data:* b Stratton, Colo, Mar 16, 24; m 48; c 4. *Educ:* Univ Wis, BS, 48, MS, 49; State Univ Iowa, PhD(elec eng), 53. *Prof Exp:* From instr to prof elec eng, SDak State Col, 49-63; prof physics & math & chmn, Sci & Math Div, Houghton Col, 63-89. *Concurrent Pos:* Develop consult, Acme Elec Corp, 66- *Mem:* Am Sci Affil; Inst Elec & Electronics Engrs; Am Soc Eng Educ. *Res:* Electrical power supplies. *Mailing Add:* 7343 Park Dr Houghton NY 14744

LINDMAN, ERICK LEROY, JR, COMPUTATIONAL PLASMA PHYSICS, COMPUTATIONAL ELECTROMAGNETISM. *Current Pos:* SR SCIENTIST, MISSION RES CORP, 87- *Personal Data:* b Seattle, Wash, Mar 20, 38; m 63, Joy Langfur; c Barbara, Susan, Melissa, Jennifer & Allison. *Educ:* Calif Inst Technol, BS, 60; Univ Calif, Los Angeles, MS, 63, PhD(physics), 64. *Prof Exp:* Res scientist, Univ Tex, Austin, 64-65, asst prof physics, 65-68; physicist, Austin Res Assocs, 68-71; staff mem, Los Alamos Nat Lab, 71-78, assoc group leader laser fusion target design, 78-80, assoc group leader inertial fusion supporting physics, 80-82, group leader, advan concept & Plasma applns, 83-86, staff mem Inertia Fusion, 86-87. *Concurrent Pos:* Vis prof, sr vis fel, UK Sci & Eng Res Coun, Blackett Lab, Imp Col, London UK, 82-83; sr scientist, Mission Res Corp, 87-92; staff mem, Inertial Fusion, 92- *Mem:* Am Phys Soc. *Res:* Computational theoretical and experimental plasma physics including computer simulation code development with applications to plasma opening switches; particle beam sources; space plasmas and intense laser and particle beam interaction with matter. *Mailing Add:* Grp XTZ MS B220 Los Alamos Nat Lab Los Alamos NM 87545. *Fax:* 505-662-2227; *E-Mail:* ell@lanl.gov

LINDMAYER, JOSEPH, solid state physics; deceased, see previous edition for last biography

LINDNER, DUANE LEE, PHYSICAL CHEMISTRY, THERMODYNAMICS. *Current Pos:* Mem tech staff, 77-86, supvr, Chem Div, 86-89, mgr mat sci & technol, 89-92, MGR, ADVAN DESIGN & MFG PROG, SANDIA NAT LABS, 93- *Personal Data:* b Ft Dodge, Iowa, May 7, 50; m 77, Deborah Ford; c John, Nathaniel & Elizabeth. *Educ:* Mass Inst Tehnol, SB, 72; Univ Calif, Berkeley, PhD(chem), 77. *Mem:* Am Chem Soc; Mat Res Soc; Sigma Xi. *Res:* Chemical kinetics and reaction mechanisms of solid-solid and gas-solid systems, particularly metal-hydrogen reactions; materials engineering; advance product realization, systems development. *Mailing Add:* MS 9405 Sandia Nat Labs Livermore CA 94551-0969. *Fax:* 510-294-3410; *E-Mail:* dllindu@sandia.gov

LINDNER, ELEK, analytical biochemistry, marine biology, for more information see previous edition

LINDNER, LUTHER EDWARD, PATHOLOGY. *Current Pos:* ASSOC PROF PATH, LAB MED, TEX A&M UNIV, 82- *Personal Data:* b Toledo, Ohio, Aug 6, 42; m 69, Elizabeth Rosenberry; c 3. *Educ:* Univ Toledo, BS, 64; Western Res Univ, MD, 67, Case Western Res Univ, PhD(exp path), 74. *Prof Exp:* From intern to resident, Univ Hosp, Cleveland, 67-72; fel path, Case Western Res Univ, 69-72; staff pathologist, William Beaumont Army Med Ctr, 72-74, chief, Anatomic Path, 74-75; asst prof lab med, Univ Nev, 75-82; vpres, Pac Biotech Int Inc, Houston. *Concurrent Pos:* Consult path, Marlin Vet Admin Hosp, St Joseph's Hosp, Bryan, Tex Brazos Med Ctr, College Station; Tex; dir lab, Path Consult Serv, Tex A&M Univ. *Mem:* Am Soc Cytol; Am Soc Clin Path; Col Am Pathologists; US-Can Acad Path. *Res:* Studies of anatomic changes in disease with histochemical correlations and application to diagnosis; sexually transmitted diseases; other infectious diseases. *Mailing Add:* Dept Path & Lab Med Tex A&M Univ College Station TX 77843-1114. *Fax:* 409-862-1299; *E-Mail:* lindner@tamu.edu

LINDNER, MANFRED, NUCLEAR CHEMISTRY, RADIOCHEMISTRY. *Current Pos:* RETIRED. *Personal Data:* b Chicago, Ill, Oct 21, 19; m 46; c Mark J & Roger B. *Educ:* Northwestern Univ, Ill, BS, 40; Univ Calif, Berkeley, PhD(nuclear chem), 48. *Prof Exp:* Chemist, Hanford Eng Works, Wash, 44-46; res asst, Univ Calif, Berkeley, 46-48; asst prof chem, Wash State Col, 48-51; chemist, Calif Res & Develop Co, 51-53; sr chemist, Radiochem Div, Lawrence Livermore Lab, 53-88. *Concurrent Pos:* Rothschild fel, Weizmann Inst Sci, 62-63. *Mem:* AAAS; Am Phys Soc; Sigma Xi. *Res:* Neutron capture cross-sections; nuclear structure; fission yield distribution; half life determination. *Mailing Add:* 32 Corte Nogal Danville CA 94526

LINDORFF, DAVID EVERETT, HYDROGEOLOGY. *Current Pos:* hydrogeologist, 80-93, HYDROGEOLOGIST SUPVR, WIS DEPT NAT RESOURCES, 93- *Personal Data:* b Moline, Ill, Aug 25, 45; m 72, Ruth Kalweit; c Paul & Tim. *Educ:* Augustana Col, BA, 67; Univ Wis-Madison, MA, 69, MS, 71. *Prof Exp:* Geologist, Pa Dept Environ Resources, 71-75; asst geologist, Ill State Geol Surv, 75-80. *Concurrent Pos:* Coordr, Midwest Groundwater Conf, 87; treas, Am Water Resources Asn, Wis Chap, 94- *Mem:* Asn Ground Water Scientists & Engrs. *Res:* Ground-water contamination; hydrogeology of strip mines; siting of sanitary landfills; ground-water standards; ground-water sampling procedures. *Mailing Add:* Dept Natural Resources PO Box 7921 Madison WI 53707. *Fax:* 608-267-7650; *E-Mail:* lindod@dnr.state.wi.us

LINDOW, DONALD FRANK, AGRICULTURE & FINE CHEMICAL INTERMEDIATE SYTHESIS RESEARCH & DEVELOPMENT, QUALITY CONTROL & ASSURANCE. *Current Pos:* VPRES TECH OPERS, LOBECO PROD INC, 90- *Personal Data:* b Cleveland, Ohio, Nov 2, 38; c Erica L (Butler) & Susan E. *Educ:* Case Inst Technol, BS, 60, PhD(org chem), 68. *Prof Exp:* Asst prof chem, State Univ, NY, Buffalo, 65-68; asst prof, Ben May Lab Cancer Res, Univ Chicago, 68-73; res & develop mgr, Mobay Chem Corp, 74-86 & Rm Engineered Prod, 86-90. *Res:* Research, development and batch industrial custom organic synthesis of fine chemical intermediates for dyestuff, pigment, agricultural and pharmaceutical industries. *Mailing Add:* Lobeco Prod Inc PO Box 630 Lobeco SC 29931. *Fax:* 803-846-4777

LINDOWER, JOHN OLIVER, SCIENCE EDUCATION. *Current Pos:* prof & chmn pharmacol, 75-82, from asst dean to assoc dean Curric Affairs, 76-81, assoc dean Acad Affairs, 81-87, PROF PHARMACOL & TOXICOL, WRIGHT STATE UNIV, 82-, INTERIM DEAN, 87- *Personal Data:* b Ashland, Ohio, March 15, 29; m 51; c 3. *Educ:* Ashland Col, AB, 50; Ohio State Univ, MD, 55, PhD(pharmacol), 68. *Prof Exp:* Gen rotating internship, Miami Valley Hosp, Dayton, Ohio, 55-56, asst surg resident, 58-59; gen med officer, US Army, 56-58; gen med pract, Dayton, Ohio, 59-65; fel pharmacol, Col Med, Ohio State Univ, 65-68, from instr to assoc prof, 68-75. *Concurrent Pos:* Coordr curric affairs, Sch Med, Wright State Univ, 75-76; mem, Comn Accrediting, Asn Theol Schs US & Can, 78-80; mem, NCent Res Rev & Adv Comn, Am Heart Asn, 79-81; proj dir, Area Health Educ Ctr, Region IV, Ohio, 82-87; mem, Drug Info Adv Panel Geriat, US Pharmacopoieia, Inc, 85- *Mem:* AMA. *Res:* Clinical pharmacology; cardiovascular research; subcellular and ultrastructural pharmacology. *Mailing Add:* Dept Pharmacol Sch Med Wright State Univ PO Box 927 Dayton OH 45401-0927

LINDQUIST, ANDERS GUNNAR, SYSTEMS AND CONTROL. *Current Pos:* PROF OPTIMIZATION & SYSTS THEORY, ROYAL INST TECHNOL, 82- *Personal Data:* b Lund, Sweden, Nov 21, 42; m 66, 86, Galina Degtyareva; c Johan, Martin & Max. *Educ:* Royal Inst Technol, Sweden, MS, 67, TeknL, 68, TeknD(optimization & systs theory), 72. *Prof Exp:* Res assoc optimization, Royal Inst Technol, Sweden, 69-72, docent, 72; vis asst prof math, Univ Fla, 72-73; assoc prof, Brown Univ, 73; assoc prof, Univ Ky, 74-80, prof, 80-83. *Concurrent Pos:* Affil prof, Washington Univ, St Louis, 89- *Mem:* Soc Indust & Appl Math; fel Inst Elec & Electronics Engrs; Royal Swed Acad Eng Sci; Hungarian Oper Res Soc. *Res:* Stochastic systems theory, control theory and estimation. *Mailing Add:* Dept Math Royal Inst Technol Stockholm 10044 Sweden. *E-Mail:* alq@math.kth.se

LINDQUIST, DAVID GREGORY, ICHTHYOLOGY. *Current Pos:* From asst prof to assoc prof, 75-86, PROF BIOL, UNIV NC, WILMINGTON, 86- *Personal Data:* b Chicago, Ill, Feb 14, 46; m 73; c 2. *Educ:* Univ Calif, Los Angeles, BA, 68; Calif State Univ, Hayward, MA, 72; Univ Ariz, PhD(zool), 75. *Concurrent Pos:* Fulbright Fel, 88. *Mem:* Am Soc Ichthyologists & Herpetologists. *Res:* Behavioral ecology and early life history of reef fishes; natural history of Southeastern freshwater fishes. *Mailing Add:* Dept Biol Sci Univ NC Wilmington NC 28403-3297. *Fax:* 910-962-7276; *E-Mail:* lindquist@vxc.uncwil.edu

LINDQUIST, EVERT E, ACAROLOGY, SYSTEMATIC ENTOMOLOGY. *Current Pos:* res scientist, 62-75, sr res scientist, 75-93, PRIN RES SCIENTIST, BIOSYST RES CTR, AGR CAN, 94- *Personal Data:* b Susanville, Calif, June 26, 35; m 57, Maxine Russo; c Evert A, Catherine A, Adele M & Leah F. *Educ:* Univ Calif, Berkeley, BS, 57, MS, 59, PhD(entom), 63. *Honors & Awards:* Acarology Award, Ohio State Univ, 74, Agr Acarology Award, 88. *Concurrent Pos:* Adj prof, Carleton Univ, 71-83; vis lectr, Summer Acarology Prog, Ohio State Univ, 72-88; vis lectr, Univ Nat Auton Mex, 83 & 87, Col Postgrad Mex, 87, Inst Polytech Nat Mex, 87; mem, Exec Comt, Int Cong Acarology, 90- *Mem:* Fel Entom Soc Can; Acarological Soc Am; Sigma Xi; Europ Asn Acarologists. *Res:* Systematics, cladistics and classification of Acari diversi; symbiotic relationships between mites, insects, namatodes and fungi; homology of acarine external structures; biodiversity of targeted mite taxa in selected ecosystems; predatory mites as bio-indicators in environmental monitoring. *Mailing Add:* Biosyst Res Ctr Agr Can Ottawa ON K1A 0C6 Can. *Fax:* 613-759-1927; *E-Mail:* lindquiste@lm.agr.ca

LINDQUIST, H D ALAN, PARASITOLOGY, DIAGNOSTIC TESTS FOR WATER SUPPLY. *Current Pos:* MICROBIOLOGIST, BIOHAZARD ASSESSMENT BR, NAT EXPOSURE RES LAB, US ENVIRON PROTECTION AGENCY, 96- *Personal Data:* b New York, NY, Aug, 61; m 91, Wantana Anachai. *Educ:* Miami Univ, Ohio, BA, 83, MEn, 86; Uniformed Serv Univ, PhD(parasitol), 95. *Prof Exp:* Biologist, Environ Monitoring & Support Lab, US Environ Protection Agency, 86; vol malaria control, US Peace Corps, 86-89; postdoctoral asst parasitol, Uniformed Serv Univ Health Sci, 95; postgrad fel parasitol, Oak Ridge Inst Sci & Educ, 95-96. *Mem:* Am Soc Parasitologists; Am Soc Microbiologists; Sigma Xi; Maleria Asn Thailand. *Res:* Develop molecular and immunological protocols for use in water to detect and identify protozoan parasites of significance in causing human disease. *Mailing Add:* US Environ Protection Agency 26 W Martin Luther King Dr Cincinnati OH 45268-1320. *Fax:* 513-569-7117; *E-Mail:* lindquist.alan@epamail.epa.gov

LINDQUIST, RICHARD KENNETH, entomology, for more information see previous edition

LINDQUIST, RICHARD WALLACE, PHYSICS. *Current Pos:* assoc prof, 65-77, chair, 78-84 & 86-89, PROF PHYSICS, WESLEYAN UNIV, 77- *Personal Data:* b Worcester, Mass, May 6, 33; m 57, Jane Tandy; c Peter & David. *Educ:* Worcester Polytech Inst, BS, 54; Princeton Univ, AM, 57, PhD(physics), 62. *Prof Exp:* Instr physics, Princeton Univ, 58-60; asst prof, Adelphi Univ, 60-64; res assoc, Univ Tex, 64-65. *Concurrent Pos:* Chair, Math, Sci & Technol, Charter Oak State Col, 95-97. *Mem:* Am Phys Soc; Am Asn Physics Teachers. *Res:* General relativity; geometrodynamics; gravitational collapse. *Mailing Add:* Dept Physics Wesleyan Univ Middletown CT 06459. *Fax:* 860-685-2001; *E-Mail:* rlindquist@weleyan.edu

LINDQUIST, ROBERT HENRY, PHYSICAL CHEMISTRY. *Current Pos:* PRES, LINDQUIST CONSULTS, 88- *Personal Data:* b Minneapolis, Minn, Feb 27, 28; m 50; c 2. *Educ:* Univ Minn, BChem, 49, MS, 50; Univ Calif, PhD(chem), 55. *Prof Exp:* Res chemist, Chevron Res Co, 55-60, sr res chemist, 60-64, sr res assoc, 64-75, asst to pres, 75-78, mgr solar, 78-80; consult corp develop, Chevron Corp, 80-86, mgr corp res & planning dept, Chevron Res Co. 86-88. *Concurrent Pos:* Consult, high tech bus profitability. *Mem:* Am Chem Soc; Am Phys Soc. *Res:* Solid state physics; magnetic resonance; physics of ultra-fine particles; heterogeneous catalysis; reaction kinetics; synthetic fuels; alternate energy sources. *Mailing Add:* 225 Arlington Berkeley CA 94707-1401

LINDQUIST, ROBERT MARION, ORGANIC CHEMISTRY, PHOTOGRAPHIC CHEMISTRY. *Current Pos:* assoc chemist photog processes, IBM Corp, 56-57, staff chemist, 57-62, adv chemist, 62-63, develop chemist, 63-65, SR CHEMIST, IBM CORP, 65- *Personal Data:* b Cumberland, Wis, Dec 4, 23; c 3. *Educ:* Univ Wis, BS, 44; Univ Minn, PhD, 50. *Honors & Awards:* First Level Invention Award, IBM Corp, 62, Outstanding Contrib Award, 74. *Prof Exp:* Res chemist photog res, Gen Aniline & Film Corp, 50-56. *Mem:* Sr mem Am Chem Soc; Sigma Xi; fel Am Inst Chemists; sr mem Soc Photog Scientists & Engrs. *Res:* Electrophotographic processes. *Mailing Add:* 4788 Briar Ridge Trail Boulder CO 80301

LINDQUIST, ROBERT NELS, BIOCHEMISTRY, ORGANIC CHEMISTRY. *Current Pos:* from asst prof to assoc prof, 71-80, PROF CHEM, SAN FRANCISCO STATE UNIV, 80- *Personal Data:* b Bakersfield, Calif, Sept 29, 42; m 68. *Educ:* Occidental Col, BA, 65; Ind Univ, PhD(chem), 68. *Prof Exp:* Chemist, Shankman Labs, 65-66; res chemist, Shell Develop Co, 68-71. *Mem:* AAAS; Am Chem Soc. *Res:* Enzyme and enzyme model reaction kinetics and mechanisms. *Mailing Add:* Dept Chem San Francisco State Univ 1600 Holloway Ave San Francisco CA 94132-1722

LINDQUIST, SUSAN LEE, STRUCTURE & FUNCTION OF CHAPERONE PROTEINS, ABNORMAL PROTEINS & PRIONS. *Current Pos:* Am Cancer Soc postdoctoral fel, 76-78, from asst prof to assoc prof, 78-88, PROF, DEPT MOLECULAR GENETICS & EELL BIOL, UNIV CHICAGO, 88-; INVESTR, HOWARD HUGHES MED INST, 88- *Personal Data:* b Chicago, Ill, June 5, 49; m, Edward Buckbee; c Eleanora & Alana. *Educ:* Univ Ill, Champaign-Urbana, BA, 71; Harvard Univ, PhD(biol), 76. *Honors & Awards:* Berlin Lectr, Northwestern Univ, 95; Boyce Thompson Lectr, Cornell Univ, 95. *Concurrent Pos:* Mem, Genetic Basis Dis Study Sect, NIH, 82, Biomed Sci Study Sect, 88-90; consult, Mus Sci & Indust, Chicago, 83-87; vis scholar, Cambridge Univ, Eng, 83. *Mem:* Nat Acad Sci; Am Acad Arts & Sci; Molecular Med Soc; Am Soc Cellular biol; Genetics Soc Am; Am Soc Microbiol; Fedn Am Scientists Exp Biol. *Res:* Mechanisms that organisms employ to protect themselves from environmental stresses, such as high temperatures, ethanol and toxic metal ions; problems of protein folding related to human disease. *Mailing Add:* Howard Hughes Med Inst Univ Chicago 5841 S Maryland Ave Rm N339 MC 1028 Chicago IL 60637-1463. *Fax:* 773-702-7254; *E-Mail:* s_lindquist@uchicago.edu

LINDQUIST, WILLIAM BRENT, NUMERICAL SOLUTION OF PDES, RIEMANN PROBLEMS. *Current Pos:* ASSOC PROF APPL MATH, STATE UNIV NY, STONY BROOK, 89- *Personal Data:* b Ft Frances, Ont, June 23, 53; m 89, Carol F Shepherd; c Lars I. *Educ:* Univ Man, BS, 75; Cornell Univ, PhD(physics), 81. *Prof Exp:* Assoc res scientist, Courant Inst Math Sci, NY Univ, 81-85, from res asst prof to res assoc prof, 85-89. *Concurrent Pos:* Consult, Inst Energy Technol, Kjeller, Norway, 85-88. *Mem:* Am Phys Soc; Soc Indust & Appl Math; Am Math Soc; Soc Petrol Engrs; Am Geophys Union. *Res:* Hyperbolic equations; numerical methods for PDE's; flow in porous media; anomalous magnetic moment of the electron. *Mailing Add:* Dept Appl Math & Statist State Univ NY Stony Brook NY 11794-3600. *Fax:* 516-632-8490; *E-Mail:* lindquis@ams.sunysb.edu

LINDROOS, ARTHUR E(DWARD), CHEMICAL ENGINEERING. *Current Pos:* RETIRED. *Personal Data:* b Worcester, Mass, Aug 14, 22; m 44; c 4. *Educ:* Worcester Polytech Inst, BS, 43, MS, 44; Yale Univ, DEng, 49. *Prof Exp:* Chem engr res & develop, Kellex Corp, 49-53; chem engr process develop, Air Reduction Chem Co, NJ, 53-59, mgr develop, 59-61; tech mgr, Cumberland Chem Corp, 61-62; mgr process eng, Air Reduction Chem & Carbide Co, 62-67; mgr process eng, Airco Chem & Plastics Co, 67-69, eng mgr, 69-71; vpres, Techni-Chem Co, 71-76; div suprv, Unit CPC Int, Penick Corp, 76-79, assoc mgr eng, 79-85, mgr eng, 85-86, dir eng, 86-90. *Mem:* Am Chem Soc; Am Inst Chem Engrs; Sigma Xi. *Res:* Mass transfer; phase equilibria at elevated pressures; nuclear reactor fuel reprocessing; acetylenic chemistry; vinyl monomers; resins and emulsions; polyvinyl alcohol; calcium carbide; lime recovery; chlorinated hydrocarbons, narcotics; pharmaceuticals. *Mailing Add:* 40 Moon Compass Lane Sandwich MA 02563-2765

LINDROTH, RICHARD L, BIOLOGICAL SCIENCES, ECOLOGY. *Current Pos:* From asst prof to assoc prof, 88-96, PROF, DEPT ENTOM, UNIV WIS-MADISON, 96- *Personal Data:* b 1954; m 78, Nancy A Taylor; c Kristen L & Nicole R. *Educ:* Iowa State Univ, BS, 77; Univ Ill, Urbana, PhD(ecol), 84. *Concurrent Pos:* Fulbright sr scholar, AgRes Grassland Res Ctr, Palmerston, NZ, 97. *Mem:* Ecol Soc Am; Entom Soc Am; Int Soc Chem Ecol. *Res:* Chemical ecology of plant-insect interactions; ecological effects of global environmental change. *Mailing Add:* Dept Entom Univ Wis-Madison Madison WI 53706. *Fax:* 608-262-3322; *E-Mail:* lindroth@entomology.wisc.edu

LINDSAY, BRUCE GEORGE, MATHEMATICAL STATISTICS. *Current Pos:* From asst prof to prof, 79-91, DISTINGUISHED PROF STATIST, PA STATE UNIV, 91- *Personal Data:* b The Dalles, Ore, Mar 7, 47; div; c Dylan & Camden. *Educ:* Univ Ore, BA, 69; Univ Wash, PhD(biomath), 78. *Honors & Awards:* Humboldt Sr Scientist Award, Humboldt Found, Ger, 90; Landsdowne Lectr, Univ Victoria, Can, 97. *Concurrent Pos:* Prin investr, NSF, 79-; vis prof, Johns Hopkins Univ, 87, Cornell Univ, 88 & Yale Univ, 90; Guggenheim fel, 96-97. *Mem:* Fel Inst Math Statist; Am Statist Asn; fel Int Statist Inst. *Res:* Statistical methods in semiparametric models, with emphasis on maximum likelihood and minimum distance methods in mixture models and computation. *Mailing Add:* 422 Classroom Bldg University Park PA 16802. *Fax:* 814-863-7114; *E-Mail:* bgl@psu.edu

LINDSAY, CHARLES MCCOWN, MATHEMATICS. *Current Pos:* From instr to assoc prof, 57-71, interim dean, 75-76, CHMN DEPT, COE COL, 63-, PROF MATH, 71- *Personal Data:* b Fayetteville, Tenn, July 5, 32; m 55, Phyllis M Bullerman; c Christine, Sarah, Virginia & Roger. *Educ:* Univ of the South, BS, 54; Univ Iowa, MS, 57; George Peabody Col, PhD(math), 65. *Mem:* Math Asn Am; Nat Coun Teachers Math. *Res:* Mathematics education. *Mailing Add:* Coe Col 1220 First Ave NE Cedar Rapids IA 52402

LINDSAY, DAVID TAYLOR, DEVELOPMENTAL BIOLOGY. *Current Pos:* From asst prof to assoc prof zool, 62-77, MEM FAC, UNIV GA, 77- *Personal Data:* b Philadelphia, Pa, Mar 22, 35; m 59; c 1. *Educ:* Amherst Col, BA, 57; Johns Hopkins Univ, PhD(biol), 62. *Concurrent Pos:* Nat Sci Found res grant develop biol, 63-66. *Mem:* AAAS; Soc Develop Biol; Am Soc Zoologists; NY Acad Sci. *Res:* Mechanisms of cellular differentiation; regulation of protein systhesis in differentiation; biological role of histone proteins; bilateral symmetry. *Mailing Add:* Dept Zool Univ Ga 1180 E Broad St Athens GA 30601-3040

LINDSAY, DEREK MICHAEL, PHYSICAL CHEMISTRY, CHEMICAL PHYSICS. *Current Pos:* PROF CHEM, CITY COL NEW YORK, 78- *Personal Data:* b Belfast, Northern Ireland, Oct 3, 44; m 70. *Educ:* Trinity Col, Dublin, BA, 67; Harvard Univ, PhD(chem), 75. *Prof Exp:* Res asst, Mass Inst Technol, 75-76; res asst chem, Coop Inst Res Environ Sci & Univ Colo, Boulder, 76-78. *Mem:* Am Chem Soc; Am Phys Soc. *Res:* Laser fluorescence and electron spin resonance studies of small metal clusters; application of this research to catalysis, surface science and solid state physics; intramolecular perturbations and gas-phase energy transfer processes. *Mailing Add:* Dept Chem City Col NY 160 Convent Ave New York NY 10031-9101

LINDSAY, DWIGHT MARSEE, mammalogy; deceased, see previous edition for last biography

LINDSAY, EVERETT HAROLD, JR, VERTEBRATE PALEONTOLOGY. *Current Pos:* From asst prof to assoc prof, 67-80, PROF GEOL, UNIV ARIZ, 80- *Personal Data:* b La Junta, Colo, July 2, 31; div; c 3. *Educ:* Chico State Col, AB, 53, MA, 57; Cornell Univ, MST, 62; Univ Calif, Berkeley, PhD(paleont), 67. *Mem:* AAAS; Soc Vert Paleont; Geol Soc Am; Paleont Soc. *Res:* Biostratigraphy; magnetostratigraphy; taxonomy and evolution of small mammal fossils. *Mailing Add:* 2771 N Treat Ave Tucson AZ 85716-2159

LINDSAY, GEORGE EDMUND, PLANT TAXONOMY. *Current Pos:* RETIRED. *Personal Data:* b Pomona, Calif, Aug 17, 16. *Educ:* Stanford Univ, BA, 51, PhD, 56. *Prof Exp:* Dir, Desert Bot Garden, Ariz, 39-40; admin asst, Arctic Res Lab, Off Naval Res, 52-53; exec dir, San Diego Mus Natural Hist, 56-63; exec dir, Calif Acad Sci, 63-82; dir, Pepperwood Ranch Natural Preserve, 82-86. *Mem:* AAAS; Cactus & Succulent Soc Am; Int Orgn Succulent Plant Studies; Am Asn Mus; Asn Dirs Sci Mus. *Res:* Taxonomic botany; taxonomy and ecology of Cactaceae and xerophytic plants of Baja California and other parts of Mexico. *Mailing Add:* 87 Barbaree Way Tiburon CA 94920

LINDSAY, GLENN FRANK, INDUSTRIAL ENGINEERING, OPERATIONS RESEARCH. *Current Pos:* asst prof opers res, 65-69, ASSOC PROF OPERS RES, NAVAL POSTGRAD SCH, 69- *Personal Data:* b Portland, Ore, June 13, 35; m 65. *Educ:* Ore State Univ, BSc, 60; Ohio State Univ, MSc, 62, PhD(indust eng), 68. *Prof Exp:* Res assoc, Systs Res Group, Ohio State Univ, 61-65. *Mem:* Opers Res Soc Am; Inst Mgt Sci; Am Soc Eng Educ. *Res:* Counter-insurgency small-unit military operations; industrial inspection systems. *Mailing Add:* Dept Opers Naval Postgrad Sch Res Monterey CA 93943-5000

LINDSAY, HAGUE LELAND, JR, VERTEBRATE ZOOLOGY. *Current Pos:* PROF ZOOL, UNIV TULSA, 56- *Personal Data:* b Ft Worth, Tex, Jan 24, 29; m 56; c 4. *Educ:* Tex Christian Univ, BA, 49; Univ Tex, MA, 51, PhD(zool), 58. *Prof Exp:* Res scientist, Univ Tex, 54. *Mem:* AAAS; Am Fisheries Soc; Am Soc Ichthyol & Herpet. *Res:* Vertebrate speciation, especially with amphibians; fish distribution and ecology, especially with darters. *Mailing Add:* 8518 E 35th St Tulsa OK 74145

LINDSAY, HARRY LEE, virology; deceased, see previous edition for last biography

LINDSAY, HUGH ALEXANDER, PHYSIOLOGY. *Current Pos:* from asst prof to assoc prof, 55-70, PROF PHYSIOL, SCH MED, WVA UNIV, 70- *Personal Data:* b Moose Jaw, Sask, Mar 5, 26; m 56; c 3. *Educ:* Univ Western Ont, BSc, 49, MSc, 52; Univ Toronto, PhD(pharmacol), 55; WVa Univ, MD, 73. *Prof Exp:* Asst pharmacol, Univ Toronto, 52-55. *Mem:* AAAS; NY Acad Sci; Am Physiol Soc; Pharmacol Soc Can. *Res:* Growth in congenital cardiovascular disease; osteoporosis. *Mailing Add:* 1133 Van Voorhis Rd Morgantown WV 26505-3431

LINDSAY, JAMES EDWARD, JR, ELECTRICAL ENGINEERING. *Current Pos:* assoc prof, 76-80, PROF ELEC ENG, UNIV WYO, 80- *Personal Data:* b Denver, Colo, Feb 26, 28; m 49; c 5. *Educ:* Univ Denver, BS, 53; Univ Colo, Boulder, MS, 58, PhD(elec eng), 60. *Prof Exp:* Res engr, RCA Labs, 53-55; instr elec eng, Univ Denver, 55-56, res engr, Denver Res Inst, 57-58; from instr to assoc prof appl math & elec eng, Univ Colo, 58-62; from asst prof to assoc prof elec eng, Univ Denver, 62-65; res engr, Martin Marietta Co, 66-67; assoc prof geophys & basic eng, Colo Sch Mines, 67-70; res engr, Denver Res Inst, Univ Denver, 70-76. *Mem:* Soc Indust & Appl Math; Inst Elec & Electronics Engrs; Sigma Xi. *Res:* Electromagnetic field theory; antennas and propagation; teaching of graduate and undergraduate courses in electrical engineering, geophysics and applied mathematics. *Mailing Add:* 1938 Riverwood Trails Dr Florissant MO 63031-7438

LINDSAY, KENNETH LAWSON, ORGANIC CHEMISTRY. *Current Pos:* AUTOMATED PUBLISHING CONSULT, 85- *Personal Data:* b Springfield, Ill, Aug 26, 25; m 49; c 1. *Educ:* Univ Ill, BS, 48; Univ Minn, PhD(chem), 52. *Prof Exp:* Res chemist, Ethyl Corp, 52-55, develop chemist, 55-61, develop assoc, 61-63, process res supvr, 63-78, sr res assoc, 78-82. *Mem:* Am Chem Soc; Am Inst Chem. *Res:* Applied kinetics; organometallic chemistry; chlorine chemistry. *Mailing Add:* PO Box 148 Laie HI 96762-0148

LINDSAY, RAYMOND H, BIOCHEMISTRY, PHARMACOLOGY. *Current Pos:* RETIRED. *Personal Data:* b Perry, Ga, Dec 9, 28; m 85; c 5. *Educ:* Jacksonville State Col, BS, 48; Univ Ala, MS, 57, PhD(pharmacol), 61. *Prof Exp:* From asst prof to assoc prof pharmacol, Univ Ala, Birmingham, 63-71, from asst prof to assoc prof med, 63-72, prof med, Med Ctr, 72-90, prof pharmacol, 71-90; dir pharmacol res unit, Vet Admin Hosp, 71-90. *Concurrent Pos:* NIH fel physiol chem, Univ Wis, 60-62, univ fel, 62-63; dir metab res, Vet Admin Hosp, Birmingham, 65-67, asst chief radioisotope serv, 64-72. *Mem:* AAAS; Endocrine Soc; Am Thyroid Asn; Am Chem Soc; Am Physiol Soc; Am Soc Pharmacol & Exp Therapeut. *Res:* Biochemistry, pharmacology and physiology of thyroid function; antithyroid drugs; environmental goitrogens. *Mailing Add:* PO Box 5189 Navarre FL 32566

LINDSAY, RICHARD H, NUCLEAR PHYSICS. *Current Pos:* assoc prof, 61-66, PROF PHYSICS, WESTERN WASH UNIV 66- *Personal Data:* b Portland, Ore, Sept 24, 34; m 58; c 6. *Educ:* Univ Portland, BS, 56; Stanford Univ, MS, 58; Wash State Univ, PhD(nuclear physics), 61. *Prof Exp:* Teaching assoc physics, Wash State Univ, 60-61. *Mem:* Am Phys Soc; Am Asn Physics Teachers. *Res:* Nuclear reactions with 30 to 65 million electron volts alpha particles; reactions with 14 million electron volts neutrons; theoretical nuclear physics; instrument design. *Mailing Add:* 612 Ridgeway Dr Bellingham WA 98225

LINDSAY, ROBERT CLARENCE, FOOD SCIENCE, FOOD CHEMISTRY. *Current Pos:* assoc prof, 69-74, PROF FOOD SCI, UNIV WIS-MADISON, 74- *Personal Data:* b Montrose, Colo, Nov 30, 36; m 57, Glenda Boyd; c Alison & Kellie. *Educ:* Colo State Univ, BS, 58, MS, 60; Ore State Univ, PhD(food sci), 65. *Honors & Awards:* Dairy Res Found Award, 86; Elected Fel, Inst Food Technologists, 88. *Prof Exp:* Asst prof food sci, Ore State Univ, 64-69. *Mem:* Am Chem Soc; fel inst Food Technologists; Am Dairy Sci Asn; Am Soc Microbiol. *Res:* Flavor chemistry; sensory evaluation of food; enzymic generation of flavor chemicals and biotechnological applications. *Mailing Add:* Dept Food Sci Univ Wis-Madison Madison WI 53706

LINDSAY, ROBERT KENDALL, ARTIFICIAL INTELLIGENCE, COGNITIVE THEORY. *Current Pos:* RES SCIENTIST PSYCHOL, UNIV MICH, 65- *Personal Data:* b Cleveland, Ohio, Aug 13, 34; m 70; c 2. *Educ:* Carnegie-Mellon Univ, BS, 56, PhD(admin), 61; Columbia Univ, MA, 57. *Prof Exp:* From asst prof to assoc prof psychol, Univ Tex, Austin, 60-65. *Mem:* Am Asn Artificial Intel; AAAS. *Res:* Artificial intelligence and cognitive science, especially verbal and spatial reasoning and their interactions; expert systems; methodological and philosophical aspects of psychological theory and computation. *Mailing Add:* Psychol W Quad Annex Univ Mich Main Campus 580 Union Dr Ann Arbor MI 48109-1346. *Fax:* 313-747-4130; *E-Mail:* lindsay@umich.edu

LINDSAY, STUART, BIOPHYSICS. *Current Pos:* FAC MEM, DEPT PHYSICS, ARIZ STATE UNIV, 79- *Personal Data:* b London, Eng, July 3, 51. *Educ:* Univ Manchester, BS, 72, PhD(physics), 76. *Prof Exp:* Res scientist, Philips Industs, 77-79. *Mem:* Am Phys Soc. *Mailing Add:* Dept Physics Ariz State Univ 201 E Minton Dr Tempe AZ 85287

LINDSAY, WILLARD LYMAN, SOIL SCIENCE. *Current Pos:* asst prof agron, Colo State Univ, 60-62, from assoc prof to prof, 62-70, centennial prof, 70-78, PROF AGRON, COLO STATE UNIV, 74- *Personal Data:* b Dingle, Idaho, Apr 7, 26; m 51; c 4. *Educ:* Utah State Univ, BS, 52, MS, 53; Cornell Univ, PhD(soil sci), 56. *Prof Exp:* Res asst Utah State Univ, 52-53 & Cornell Univ, 53-56; soil chemist, Soils & Fertilizer Res Br, Tenn Valley Authority, 56-60. *Concurrent Pos:* Vis prof, State Agr Univ, Wageningen, Neth, 72. *Mem:* Soil Sci Soc Am; fel Am Soc Agron; Int Soc Soil Sci; Sigma Xi. *Res:* Chemical reactions of phosphate in soils; physicochemical equilibria of plant nutrients in soils; chemistry and availability of micronutrients to plants; equilibrium of metal chelates in soils; solubility of heavy metals in soils. *Mailing Add:* 129 Columbia Rd Ft Collins CO 80525

LINDSAY, WILLIAM GERMER, JR, PHYSIOLOGY. *Current Pos:* RETIRED. *Personal Data:* b Cleveland, Ohio, Nov 22, 28; m 56; c 3. *Educ:* Oberlin Col, AB, 51; Univ Pa, MS, 57, PhD(zool), 62. *Prof Exp:* Instr physiol, Albany Med Col, 62-66; asst prof biol, Elmira Col, 66-69, assoc prof, 69-75, prof biol, 75-96. *Mem:* AAAS; Soc Study Reproduction. *Res:* Spermatozoa metabolism; biological limnology. *Mailing Add:* 505 Euclid Ave Elmira NY 14915

LINDSAY, WILLIAM TENNEY, JR, CHEMICAL ENGINEERING. *Current Pos:* CONSULT, LINDSAY & ASSOC, 83- *Personal Data:* b Scranton, Pa, Apr 4, 24; m 51; c 2. *Educ:* Rensselaer Polytech Inst, BChE, 48; Mass Inst Technol, PhD(phys chem), 52. *Prof Exp:* Engr, Procter & Gamble Co, 48; asst, Mass Inst Technol, 49-51, res assoc, 52-53; sr scientist, Atomic Power Div, Westinghouse Elec Corp, 53-54, supv engr, 55-59, fel engr, Res Labs, 59-64, mgr phys chem dept, 64-73, mgr phys & inorg chem dept, Res Labs, 73-77, consult, Res & Develop Ctr, Westinghouse Elec Corp, 77-83,. *Mem:* Fel AAAS; Am Chem Soc; Am Phys Soc; Electrochem Soc; NY Acad Sci; Am Soc Testing & Mat; Am Inst Chem Engrs. *Res:* Electrolytic solutions; nuclear reactor coolant technology. *Mailing Add:* 47 E Main St Hopkinton MA 01748-1238

LINDSEY, ALTON ANTHONY, PLANT ECOLOGY. *Current Pos:* from asst prof to prof, 47-74, EMER PROF BIOL, PURDUE UNIV, 74- *Personal Data:* b Monaca, Pa, May 7, 07; m 39; c 2. *Educ:* Allegheny Col, BS, 29; Cornell Univ, PhD, 35. *Hon Degrees:* ScD, Allegheny Col, 88. *Honors & Awards:* Spec Cong Medal & Eminent Ecologist Award, Ecol Soc Am, 76. *Prof Exp:* Asst bot, Cornell Univ, 29-33; biologist, Byrd Antarctic Exped, 33-35; asst bot, Cornell Univ, 35-37; instr bot, Am Univ, 37-40; asst prof, Univ Redlands, 40-42 & Univ NMex, 42-47. *Concurrent Pos:* Botanist, Purdue Can-Arctic Permafrost Exped, 51, ecologist, Purdue Res Team, Sonoran Desert, 53-54; bot ed, Ecol, Ecol Soc Am, 57-61, managing ed, Ecol & Ecol Monogr, 72-74; dir, Ind Natural Areas Surv, 67-68; Lindsey fel, Goshen Col, 77; Lindsey grad res fel, Purdue Univ, 93. *Mem:* Fel AAAS; Ecol Soc Am; Sigma Xi. *Res:* Indiana vegetation; flood plain ecology; 8 technical and 2 popular books. *Mailing Add:* 6834 S Toledo Ave 334 Tulsa OK 74136

LINDSEY, BRUCE GILBERT, NEUROPHYSIOLOGY, NEUROANATOMY. *Current Pos:* FROM ASST PROF TO PROF PHYSIOL & BIOPHYS, UNIV SFLA MED CTR, 77-, CHAIR, 96- *Personal Data:* b Rockland, Maine, June 22, 49. *Educ:* Williams Col, BA, 71; Univ Pa, PhD(neuroanat), 74. *Prof Exp:* Fel neurophysiol, Univ Pa, 74-77. *Mem:* Soc Neurosci; AAAS; Am Physiol Soc. *Res:* Parallel information processing in the nervous system; sensory-motor intergration; brain stem control of breathing. *Mailing Add:* Dept Physiol Univ SFla Tampa FL 33612

LINDSEY, CASIMIR CHARLES, ICHTHYOLOGY. *Current Pos:* dir, Inst Animal Resource Ecol, 80-88, EMER PROF ZOOL, UNIV BC, VANCOUVER, 88- *Personal Data:* b Toronto, Ont, Mar 22, 23; m 48. *Educ:* Univ Toronto, BA, 48; Univ BC, MA, 50; Cambridge Univ, PhD(zool), 52. *Prof Exp:* Res biologist, BC Dept Game, 52-57; from asst prof to assoc prof zool, Univ BC, 57-66, cur fishes, Inst Fisheries, 52-66; prof zool, Univ Man, 66-79. *Concurrent Pos:* Vis prof, Univ Singapore, 62-63, Wallace mem lectr, 63; fisheries consult, Pakistan, 64; Univ S Pac, Can Int Develop Agency, 71-72, Can Deleg Pac Sci, Cong, Thailand, 57, Japan, 66, Australia, 71, Vancouver, 75, Khabarovsk USSR, 79. *Mem:* fel Royal Soc Can; Can Soc Zoologists (pres, 77-78). *Res:* Meristic variation; taxonomy; zoogeography of northern freshwater fishes; comparison of tropical and temperate fisheries. *Mailing Add:* 3757 W 36th Ave Vancouver BC V6N 2S3 Can

LINDSEY, DAVID ALLEN, GEOLOGY. *Current Pos:* Geologist, US Geol Surv, Colo, 67-74 & 76-86, staff geologist mineral resources, Va, 74-75, chief, Br Cent Mineral Resources, 87-91, GEOLOGIST, US GEOL SURV, COLO, 92- *Personal Data:* b Nebraska City, Nebr, May 26, 42; m 66, Barbara G; c 2. *Educ:* Univ Nebr, BS, 63; Johns Hopkins Univ, PhD(geol), 67. *Honors & Awards:* Meritorious Serv Award, Dept Interior. *Concurrent Pos:* Geol Soc Am res grant, 65-66. *Mem:* Geol Soc Am; Am Asn Petrol Geol. *Res:* Glacial deposits, alluvial conglomerates and sandstones; beryllium deposits and volcanic rocks in Utah; intrusive complexes in central Montana; copper in sedimentary rocks; laramide and tertiary tectonics; stream gravels for aggregate. *Mailing Add:* US Geol Surv MS 905 Fed Ctr Lakewood CO 80225

LINDSEY, DONALD L, PLANT PATHOLOGY. *Current Pos:* from asst prof to assoc prof, 69-81, PROF PLANT PATH, NMEX STATE UNIV, 81- *Personal Data:* b Stockton, Kans, May 25, 37; m 61; c 3. *Educ:* Ft Hays Kans State Col, BS, 59; Colo State Univ, MS, 62, PhD(plant path), 65. *Prof Exp:* Jr plant pathologist, Colo State Univ, 61-65, asst plant pathologist, 66-69; instr bot, Colo State Col, 66. *Mem:* Am Phytopath Soc; Sigma Xi; Soc Nematologist. *Res:* Biological control of plant pathogens; ecology of soil fungi; mine spoil revegetation. *Mailing Add:* PO Box 30003 3BE NMex State Univ/EPWS Las Cruces NM 88003

LINDSEY, DORTHA RUTH, THERAPEUTIC EXERCISE, GEROKINESIATRICS. *Current Pos:* RETIRED. *Personal Data:* b Kingfisher, Okla, Oct 26, 26. *Educ:* Okla State Univ, BS, 48; Univ Wis, MS, 56; Ind Univ, PED, 63. *Honors & Awards:* Julian Vogel Mem Award, Am Kinesiotherapy Asn, 88. *Prof Exp:* Instr health, phys educ & recreation, Okla State Univ, 48-50; instr, Monticello Col, 51-54, DePauw Univ, 54-56; prof health, phys educ & recreation, Okla State Univ, 56-75; vis prof, Univ Utah, 75-76; prof, Calif State Univ, Long Beach, 76-88. *Concurrent Pos:* Ed, Fencing Guide, Am Asn Health, Phys Educ & Recreation, 61-62; consult, Payne Co Guid Ctr, 66-71; author & lectr, phys fitness & wellness, 68-; vis prof, Utah Univ, 75-76; consult fitness & exercise, Ask the Profs, 82-; ed, Perspectives: J Western Soc, Phys Ed Col Women, 87-95; mem, Coun on Aging & Adult Develop. *Mem:* Am Alliance Health, Phys Ed, Recreation & Dance; Am Kinesiotherapy Asn; Nat Coun Against Health Fraud. *Res:* Physical education; kinesiotherapy; electromyographical and kinesiological analyses of muscle action; quackery in physical fitness and reducing; therapeutic exercise; gerokinesiatrics; proprioceptive neuromuscular facilitation exercise effect on range of neck motion; physical fitness and wellness. *Mailing Add:* 9332 Ambassador Dr Westminster CA 92683

LINDSEY, EDWARD STORMONT, MEDICINE. *Current Pos:* from instr to assoc prof, 63-76, CLIN ASSOC PROF SURG, TULANE UNIV, 76-, DIR TRANSPLANTATION RES UNIT, 66- *Personal Data:* b West Palm Beach, Fla, June 3, 30; m 53; c 2. *Educ:* Tulane Univ, BS, 51, MD, 58, MMedSci, 68. *Prof Exp:* Intern, Charity Hosp, La, 58-59, resident surg, 59-61

& thoracic surg, 63-64. *Concurrent Pos:* Resident surg, Southern Baptist Hosp, 61-62; Nat Heart Inst spec fel, Univ Edinburgh, 64-65; consult surg, Charity Hosp La & Keesler Air Force Hosp, 65-; mem adv comt, Nat Transplant Registry, 66-67. *Mem:* Transplantation Soc; Am Col Surg; NY Acad Sci; Asn Advan Med Instrumentation; Am Soc Artificial Internal Organs. *Res:* Thoracic and vascular surgery; transplantation biology. *Mailing Add:* 2820 Napolean Ave Suite 420 New Orleans LA 70115

LINDSEY, GEORGE ROY, MILITARY STRATEGIC ANALYSIS, SYSTEMS ANALYSIS. *Current Pos:* SR RES FEL, CAN INST STRATEGIC STUDIES, 87- *Personal Data:* b Toronto, Ont, June 2, 20; m 51, June M Broomhead; c Robin & Jane. *Educ:* Univ Toronto, BA, 42; Queen's Univ Ont, MA, 46; Cambridge Univ, PhD(physics), 50. *Honors & Awards:* Award of Merit, Can Opers Res Soc, 84; Officer of the Order of Can, 89. *Prof Exp:* Defense sci officer oper res, Can Defense Res Bd, 50-53; sr oper res officer, Air Defense Command, Royal Can Air Force, 54-59; dir, Defense Systs Anal Group, Can Dept Nat Defense, 59-61; oper res group leader, Antisubmarine Warfare Res Ctr, Supreme Allied Comdr, Atlantic, Italy, 61-64; sr oper res scientist, Dept Nat Defense, 64-67, chief oper res anal estab, 67-87. *Concurrent Pos:* Mem, Can Govt Bicult Develop Prog, 70-71 & Can Comt Int Inst Appl Systs Anal, 73-79; consult, Inst Res Pub Policy, 75-78; head, Can deleg NATO High Level Group Nuclear Planning, 77-87; chmn, TTCP Panel, Undersea Warfare, 81-86; vis fel, Can Inst Int Peace & Security, 90-92; mem bd dirs, Can Inst Strategic Studies, 92-; dir, Int Inst Strategic Studies, 92- *Mem:* Opers Res Soc Am; Can Inst Strategic Studies; Int Inst Strategic Studies; Can Oper Res Soc (pres, 61); Can Inst Int Affairs; Royal Can Astron Soc. *Res:* Arms control; advancing military technology and security analysis of strategic problems related to the attainment and preservation of a stable military balance. *Mailing Add:* 55 Westward Way Ottawa ON K1L 5A8 Can. Fax: 613-745-3161

LINDSEY, GERALD HERBERT, MECHANICAL & AERONAUTICAL ENGINEERING. *Current Pos:* prof aeronaut eng, Naval Postgrad Sch, 66-97, dean acad admin, 82-89, assoc dean eng, 90-93, CHMN, DEPT AERONAUT ENG, NAVAL POSTGRAD SCH, 97- *Personal Data:* b Marshall, Mo, Aug 3, 34; m 58, Beth Bryson; c Stuart P, Greg A, Kristine, Bryan S, Bradley P & Karen D. *Educ:* Brigham Young Univ, BES, 60, MS, 62; Calif Inst Technol, PhD(aeronaut eng), 66. *Concurrent Pos:* Consult, Chem Systs Div, United Technol, 66-72. *Mem:* Am Inst Aeronaut & Astronaut; Am Soc Eng Educ. *Res:* Fracture, aircraft fatigue and design; viscoelastic stress and fracture. *Mailing Add:* Dept Aeronaut Naval Postgrad Sch Monterey CA 94943

LINDSEY, JAMES RUSSELL, PATHOLOGY. *Current Pos:* chmn dept com med, 67-75, prof, 67-86, assoc prof path, 69-85, PROF PATH, UNIV ALA, BIRMINGHAM, 85-, PROF & CHMN COMP MED, SCH MED & DENT, 86- *Personal Data:* b Tifton, Ga, Dec 6, 33; m 58; c 4. *Educ:* Univ Ga, BS, 56, DVM, 57; Auburn Univ, MS, 61; Am Col Lab Animal Med, dipl, 67; Am Col Vet Pathologists, dipl, 67. *Honors & Awards:* Charles River Prize Lab Animal Med, Am Vet Med Asn, 79; T S Williams lectr, Tuskegee Inst, 82. *Prof Exp:* From instr to asst prof, Sch Vet Med, Auburn Univ, 57-61; from instr to asst prof, lab animal med & path, Johns Hopkins Univ Sch Med, 61-67. *Concurrent Pos:* Fel path, Johns Hopkins Univ, 61-63; chief, RILAMSAT, Birmingham Vet Admin Hosp, 68-; adj prof, Sch Vet Med, Auburn Univ, 80-; vis scientist & consult lab animal dis, Orgn Health Res, Inst Exp Gerontol & Radiobiol, Rijswijk, Neth & Cent Lab Animal Breeding Fac, Zeist, Neth, 78-79. *Mem:* Am Vet Med Asn; Sigma Xi; Int Acad Path; Am Asn Pathologists; Am Thoracic Soc; Am Soc Microbiol; Int Orgn Mycoplasmologists. *Res:* Comparative pathology; mycoplasmal respiratory disease; laboratory animal diseases complicating research. *Mailing Add:* Dept Comp Med Univ Ala Sch Med Birmingham AL 35294-0019

LINDSEY, JULIA PAGE, mycology, plant pathology, for more information see previous edition

LINDSEY, LEANN L, fertilization, for more information see previous edition

LINDSEY, MARVIN FREDERICK, PLANT BREEDING. *Current Pos:* RETIRED. *Personal Data:* b Stockville, Nebr. *Educ:* Univ Nebr, BSc, 53, MSc, 55; NC State Univ, PhD(genetics), 60. *Prof Exp:* Asst prof agron, Univ Nebr, 60-63; geneticist, Rockefeller Found, 64-66; asst prof agron, Univ Wis, 66-69; area dir, Dekalb-Pfizer Genetics, 70-90. *Mem:* Am Soc Agron; Crop Sci Soc Am. *Res:* Maize breeding and genetics. *Mailing Add:* 520 Q St Beaver City NE 68926

LINDSEY, NORMA JACK, CLINICAL MICROBIOLOGY. *Current Pos:* RETIRED. *Personal Data:* b Canton, Tex, June 16, 29. *Educ:* Tex Woman's Univ, BA & BS, 51; Univ Calif, MPH, 64; Colo State Univ, PhD(microbiol), 69. *Prof Exp:* Bacteriologist, Dallas Health Dept Lab, Tex, 51-54; microbiologist, Ariz Health Dept Labs, Tucson, 56-65; teaching asst microbiol, Colo State Univ, 66-67; chief, NMex Health Labs, 69-70; res microbiologist, HEW, 70-73; asst prof path & actg head, Microbiol Sect, Clin Labs, Univ Kans Med Ctr, 73-92. *Mem:* NY Acad Sci; Am Soc Microbiol; Am Pub Health Asn; AAAS; Sigma Xi. *Res:* Clinical and applied microbiology. *Mailing Add:* 9931 Cedar Dr Overland Park KS 66207

LINDSEY, ROLAND GRAY, CHEMICAL ENGINEERING. *Current Pos:* RETIRED. *Personal Data:* b Sylvatus, Va, June 26, 27; m 48; c 3. *Educ:* Univ Del, BChE, 51; Ohio State Univ, MSc, 54, PhD(chem eng), 59. *Prof Exp:* Chem engr, Polychem Div, Dow Chem Corp, 56-59, proj leader polymer res, 59-60; res engr, Fabrics & Finishes Dept, E I Du Pont de Nemours & Co, 60-66, staff engr, 66-85, res assoc, 85-87, sr res assoc, 87. *Concurrent Pos:* Consult, 87-91. *Mem:* Am Chem Soc; Am Inst Chem Engrs. *Res:* Computerized kinetic model description of free radical polymer processes using numerical and Monte Carlo methods. *Mailing Add:* 613 Sherman Rd Springfield PA 19064-3425

LINDSEY, WILLIAM C, ELECTRICAL ENGINEERING. *Current Pos:* PROF ELEC ENG, UNIV SOUTHERN CALIF, 68- *Educ:* Univ Ark, BS, 58; Purdue Univ, MS, 59, PhD(elec eng), 62. *Concurrent Pos:* First vchmn & second chmn, Commun Theory Comt; vpres tech affairs, Inst Elec & Electronics Engrs; mem, Commun C, Signals & Systs Int Sci Union & Commun Change Initiation Request Stands Comt. *Mem:* Nat Acad Eng; fel Inst Elec & Electronics Engrs. *Res:* Channel characterization, measurement, synchronization and communication techniques as applied to global mobile communication and navigation systems; satellite communications and personal communication networks. *Mailing Add:* Elec Eng Dept EEB510 Univ Southern Calif Los Angeles CA 90089

LINDSKOG, GUSTAF ELMER, SURGERY. *Current Pos:* from instr to prof, 33-71, EMER PROF SURG, SCH MED, YALE UNIV, 71- *Personal Data:* b Boston, Mass, Feb 7, 03; m 34; c 2. *Educ:* Mass Agr Col, BS, 23; Harvard Univ, MD, 28; Am Bd Surg, dipl & Am Bd Thoracic Surg, cert, 52. *Prof Exp:* Intern surg, Lakeside Hosp, 28-29; asst surg & path, Sch Med, Yale Univ, 29-30; asst res surgeon, obstetrician & gynecologist, New Haven Hosp, 30-32; Nat Res Coun fel, Mass Gen Hosp, 32-33. *Concurrent Pos:* Res surgeon, New Haven Hosp, 33-34; chmn, Am Bd Surg, 57-58. *Mem:* Soc Univ Surg; Soc Clin Surg; Am Asn Thoracic Surg; Am Surg Asn; fel Am Col Surg; Sigma Xi. *Res:* Thoracic surgery and physiology. *Mailing Add:* 15 Cow Path Lane Woodbridge CT 06525

LINDSLEY, DAN LESLIE, DROSOPHILA CYTOGENETICS. *Current Pos:* prof, 67-91, chmn dept, 77-79, EMER PROF BIOL, UNIV CALIF, SAN DIEGO, 91- *Personal Data:* b Evanston, Ill, Oct 13, 25; m 47; c 4. *Educ:* Univ Mo, AB, 47, MA, 49; Calif Inst Technol, PhD(genetics), 52. *Honors & Awards:* T H Morgan Medal, Genetics Soc Am, 89. *Prof Exp:* Nat Res Coun fel biol, Princeton Univ, 52-53; NSF fel, Univ Mo, 53-54; from assoc biologist to biologist, Oak Ridge Nat Lab, 54-67. *Concurrent Pos:* NSF sr fels, Univ Sao Paulo, 60-61 & Inst Genetics, Univ Rome, 65-66; USPHS spec fel, Dept Genetics, Div Plant Indust, Commonwealth Sci & Indust Res Orgn, Canberra, Australia, 72-73, Fogarty Int fel, Dept Develop Genetics, Ctr Molecular Biol, Autonomous Univ Madrid, Spain, 80-81; vis scientist, Inst Molecular Biol, Univ Rome, Italy, 92. *Mem:* Nat Acad Sci; Genetics Soc Am (treas, 75-78, vpres, 85, pres, 86); Am Acad Arts & Sci; Lepidopterists Soc. *Res:* Cytogenetics of Drosophila. *Mailing Add:* Dept Biol Univ Calif San Diego 9500 Gilman Dr La Jolla CA 92093-0322

LINDSLEY, DAVID FORD, NEUROPHYSIOLOGY. *Current Pos:* ASSOC PROF PHYSIOL, MED SCH, UNIV SOUTHERN CALIF, 67- *Personal Data:* b Cleveland, Ohio, May 18, 36; m 60, Elizabeth McBride; c Eric, Karen & Victoria. *Educ:* Stanford Univ, BA, 57; Univ Calif, Los Angeles, PhD(anat, neurophysiol), 61. *Prof Exp:* Asst prof physiol, Med Sch, Stanford Univ, 63-67. *Concurrent Pos:* USPHS fels, Moscow State Univ, 61-62 & Cambridge Univ, 62-63; Lederle med fac award, 64-67; visitor, Max Planck Inst Psychiat, Munich, 71 & 74-75; Guggenheim fel, 74-75. *Mem:* AAAS; Am Physiol Soc; Am Asn Anatomists; Soc Neurosci; Int Brain Res Orgn. *Res:* Central nervous system neurophysiology; behavioral neurophysiology; brain mechanics of attention and perception, using single neurons of central visual system of primates with particular interest in where in the brain and how incoming sensory stimuli become tagged as significant. *Mailing Add:* Dept Physiol USC Med Sch 1333 San Pablo St Los Angeles CA 90033-4526. Fax: 213-342-2283

LINDSLEY, DONALD B, PSYCHOPHYSIOLOGY, NEUROPSYCHOLOGY. *Current Pos:* prof, 51-77, chmn, DeptPsychol, 59-62, EMER PROF PSYCHOL & PHYSIOL, UNIV CALIF, LOS ANGELES, 77- *Personal Data:* b Brownhelm, Ohio, Dec 23, 07; m 33, Ellen Ford; c David F, Margaret, Robert K & Sara E. *Educ:* Wittenberg Univ, AB, 29; Univ Iowa, MA, 30, PhD, 32. *Hon Degrees:* DSc, Brown Univ, 58, Wittenberg Univ, 59, Trinity Col, Conn, 65 & Loyola Univ Chicago, 68; PhD, Johannes Gutenberg Univ, Mainz, WGer, 77. *Honors & Awards:* William James lectr, Harvard Univ, 58; Distinguished Sci Contrib Award, Am Psychol Asn, 59; Donald B Lindsley Prize, Soc Neurosci, 78; Distinguished Sci Contrib Award, Soc Psychophysiol Res, 84; Ralph Gerard Prize, Soc Neurosci, 88; Gold Medal Award for Life Achievement in Psychol Sci, Am Psychol Found, 89; Herbert Jasper Award & lectr, Am EEG Asn, 94; Wilder Penfield Award & lectr, Western EEG Soc, 96. *Prof Exp:* Instr psychol, Univ Ill, 32-33; Nat Res Coun fel physiol & neuropsychiat, Harvard Med Sch & Mass Gen Hosp, Boston, 33-35; res assoc anat, Sch Med, Western Res Univ, 35-38; asst prof psychol, Brown Univ, 38-46; prof, Northwestern Univ, 46-51. *Concurrent Pos:* Dir, Psychol & Neurophysiol Labs, Bradley Hosp, East Providence, RI, 38-46 & Nat Defense Res Comt Proj, Off Sci Res & Develop, Yale Univ Contract, Camp Murphy & Boca Raton AFB, Fla, 43-46; mem, Sci Adv Bd, USAF, 47-49, chmn, Human Resources Comt, 48-49; mem, Aviation Psychol Comt, Nat Res Coun, 47-49 & Undersea Warfare Comt, 51-64; consult, Study Sect USPHS, NIMH, 51-54, Nat Inst Neurol Dis & Blindness, 58-61, Nat Inst Gen Med Sci, 65-69, exp psychol comt, NSF, 52-54 & Guggenheim Found, 63-70; mem, Adv Comt Psychiat & Neurol, Vet Admin Ctr Washington, DC, 56-58; Guggenheim fel, 59; mem, Am Inst Biol Sci-NASA Behav Biol Panel, 65-70; mem, Space Sci Bd, Nat Acad Sci, 65-70, chmn, Long-duration Missions Space Comt, 67-71, mem, Space Med Comt, 67-; treas, Int Brain Res Orgn, 67-71; mem, Sci & Technol Adv Coun, Calif State Assembly, 69-71. *Mem:* Nat Acad Sci; Am Psychol Asn; AAAS; Soc Neurosci; Am Physiol Soc; hon fel Am Electroencephalog Soc (pres, 65); Soc

Psychophysiol Res; Soc Exp Psychol; Am Acad Arts & Sci; foreign mem Finnish Acad Sci; Am Psychol Soc. *Res:* Brain function; emotion; behavior disorders; electroencephalography; neurophysiology; vision and visual perception; brain organization and behavior. *Mailing Add:* Dept Psychol Univ Calif Los Angeles CA 90024-1563

LINDSLEY, DONALD HALE, PHASE EQUILIBRIA, GEOTHERMOMETRY. *Current Pos:* PROF PETROL, DEPT EARTH & SPACE SCI, STATE UNIV NY STONY BROOK, 70- *Personal Data:* b Princeton, NJ, May 22, 34; m 59, Carol Streib; c Glenn, Janet & Bruce. *Educ:* Princeton Univ, AB, 56; Johns Hopkins Univ, PhD(geol), 61. *Prof Exp:* Fel, Geophys Lab, Carnegie Inst, Washington, 60-62, petrologist, 62-70. *Concurrent Pos:* Vis assoc prof, Calif Inst Technol, 69; vis scientist, Univ BC, 76-77; adj prof, Univ Wyo, 90- *Mem:* Mineral Soc Am (vpres, 81, pres, 82); Geol Soc Am; Geochem Soc (vpres, 89-91, pres, 91-93); Am Geophys Union; AAAS; Mineralogical Asn Can. *Res:* High-pressure and high-temperature phase relations and thermodynamic solution models of mineral systems; redox reactions in earth; origin of anorthosites and related rocks; origin of lunar magmas. *Mailing Add:* Dept Earth Sci State Univ NY 100 Nicolls Rd Stony Brook NY 11794-0001

LINDSTEDT, P(AUL) M, CHEMICAL ENGINEERING. *Current Pos:* RETIRED. *Personal Data:* b Stromsburg, Nebr, Feb 28, 17; m 42, Olga M Misitigh; c Joan, Gary & David. *Educ:* Univ Nebr, BS, 39. *Prof Exp:* Trainee eng, Goodyear Tire & Rubber Co, 39-40, jr chem engr, 40-44, sect head, 44-49, asst mgr chem eng & pilot plants, 49-51, mgr, 51-80. *Concurrent Pos:* Pres, Akron Sect, Am Inst Chem Engrs, 54 & Akron Coun Sci Soc, 56. *Mem:* Am Inst Chem Engrs. *Res:* Synthetic rubber drying process; process development of elastomers, resins, antioxidants and rubber accelerators. *Mailing Add:* 2830 Hastings Rd Cuyahoga Falls OH 44224

LINDSTEDT-SIVA, K JUNE, BIOLOGY. *Current Pos:* sci adv, Atlantic Richfield Co, 73-77, sr sci adv, 77-81, mgr, environ sci, 81-86, MGR, ENVIRON PROTECTION, ATLANTIC RICHFIELD CO, 86- *Personal Data:* b Minneapolis, Minn, Sept 24, 41; m 69, Ernest H Siva. *Educ:* Univ Southern Calif, AB, 63, MS, 67, PhD(biol), 71. *Honors & Awards:* Trident Award Marine Sci, Int Rev Underwater Activities, Ustica, Italy, 70; Award of Merit, Am Soc Testing & Mat, 90. *Prof Exp:* Asst coordr sea grant progs, Univ Southern Calif, 71; environ specialist, Southern Calif Edison Co, 71-72; asst prof biol, Calif Lutheran Col, 72-73. *Concurrent Pos:* Consult, Jacques Cousteau, Metromedia Producers Co, 70 & Southern Calif Edison Co, 72; mem task force, Fate & Effects of Oil, Am Petrol Inst, 73-80, chmn biol res subcomt; chmn, Environ Subcomt, Marine Indust Group, 81-82; chmn, Spills Technol Comt, 83-85, Int Oil Spill Conf, 89; mem bd trustees, Bermuda Biol Sta Res, 79-, res subcomt, 86-; chmn, Dispersant Use Guidelines Task Force, Am Soc Testing & Mat, 82-; mem bd dir, Southern Calif Acad Sci, 84-93, pres, 90-92; mem, Nat Sci Bd, 84-90, Alaska OCS Panel, Nat Acad Sci, 92-, Polar Res Bd, 93-; mem adv bd, Cabrillo Marine Museum, 85-; biol adv coun, Calif State Univ, Long Beach, 81-; mem, Nat Acad Sci Ecol Panel, Outer Continental Shelf Environ Studies Prog Rev, 82-84, Nat Sci Bd Comt, Educ & Human Resources, 85-90, Int Sci, 88-, Polar Regions, 87-90, Sci Indications, 89 & Biodiversity, 89-90; mem, Univ Southern Calif; mem panel ecol risk reduction, Environ Protection Agency, 90; mem panel oil spill res & develop, Nat Acad Sci, 90- *Mem:* Soc Petrol Indust Biologists (pres); Marine Technol Soc; AAAS; Sigma Xi; Am Inst Biol Sci; fel Am Soc Testing & Mat. *Res:* Effects of oil on marine organisms; oil spill response planning; oil spill cleanup and control; environmental planning and management in industry; use of dispersants in oil spill response. *Mailing Add:* 9570 Mias Canyon Rd Banning CA 92220-1924. *Fax:* 213-486-2021; *E-Mail:* jsiva@isdis.net

LINDSTROM, DAVID JOHN, GEOCHEMISTRY. *Current Pos:* SCIENTIST, JOHNSON SPACE CTR. *Personal Data:* b Ashland, Wis, Mar 1, 45; m 71. *Educ:* Univ Wis-Madison, BS, 66; Univ Chicago, SM, 68; Univ Ore, PhD(chem), 76. *Prof Exp:* Res assoc lunar sci, Goddard Space Flight Ctr, NASA, 75-77; res scientist geochem, Dept Earth & Planetary Sci, Wash Univ, 71- *Res:* Experimental trace element geochemistry; experimental petrology; properties of silicate liquids; extraterrestrial materials processing. *Mailing Add:* SN4 NASA Johnson Space Ctr Houston TX 77058

LINDSTROM, DUAINE GERALD, MECHANICAL ENGINEERING. *Current Pos:* ASSOC PROF & PROG COORDR NUCLEAR & CHEM ENG, WASH STATE UNIV, RICHLAND, WASH, 82- *Personal Data:* b Raymond, Wash, Jan 18, 37; m 67, Vieno Ojala. *Educ:* Univ Wash, BS, 59, PhD(nuclear eng), 68; Univ Mich, MS, 60. *Prof Exp:* Physics specialist, Aerojet Nuclear Systs Co, Sacramento, 68-71; lectr nuclear technol, Imperial Col, London, 71-75; assoc prof nuclear eng, Univ Okla, 75-82. *Concurrent Pos:* Lectr, Calif State Univ, Sacramento, 69-70. *Mem:* Am Nuclear Soc; Brit Nuclear Energy Soc; Health Physics Soc; Sigma Xi; Am Inst Chem Engrs. *Res:* Radiation transport, radiation shielding and protection; nuclear fuel cycle; reactor operations; power systems and incineration. *Mailing Add:* Wash State Univ TC 100 Sprout Rd Richland WA 99352

LINDSTROM, ERIC JON, PHYSICAL OCEANOGRAPHY. *Current Pos:* dir, 88-89, PROG SCIENTIST, US WORLD OCEAN CIRCULATION EXP INTERAGENCY OFF, 89-; RES SCIENTIST, TEX A&M UNIV, 92- *Personal Data:* b Long Beach, Calif, June 22, 56. *Educ:* Mas Inst Technol, BS, 77; Univ Wash, MS, 79, PhD(oceanog), 83. *Prof Exp:* Sr res scientist, Commonwealth Sci & Indust Res Orgn, Australia, 83-90; assoc dir, Toga Coare Proj Off, 90-91. *Mem:* Am Meteorol Soc; Am Geophys Union; Oceanog Soc; Australian Marine Sci Asn; Australian Meteorol & Oceanog Soc. *Res:* General circulation of the oceans; western tropical Pacific circulation. *Mailing Add:* NASA 300 E St SW Washington DC 20546. *Fax:* 202-857-5219; *E-Mail:* woce@access.digex.net

LINDSTROM, EUGENE SHIPMAN, BACTERIOLOGY. *Current Pos:* RETIRED. *Personal Data:* b Ames, Iowa, Jan 12, 23; m 49; c 4. *Educ:* Univ Wis, BA, 47, MS, 48, PhD(bact), 51. *Prof Exp:* Asst bact, Univ Wis, 46-51, AEC fel enzyme chem, 51-52; from asst prof to assoc prof, Pa State Univ, 52-64, from asst dean to assoc dean col sci, 66-77, prof bact, 64-68, head Dept Biol, 77-88. *Concurrent Pos:* NSF fel, Univ Minn, 61. *Mem:* Am Soc Microbiol; Am Acad Microbiol; Am Soc Biol Chem & Molecular Biol. *Res:* Bacterial physiology; physiology of Athiorhodaceae; physiology and ecology of photosynthetic bacteria. *Mailing Add:* 236 Ellen Ave State College PA 16801

LINDSTROM, FREDRICK THOMAS, APPLIED MATHEMATICS. *Current Pos:* Res asst, 64-69, asst prof, 69-74, ASSOC PROF STATIST & MATH, ORE STATE UNIV, 74- *Personal Data:* b Astoria, Ore, July 30, 40; m 64; c 2. *Educ:* Ore State Univ, BS, 63, MS, 65, PhD(appl math), 69. *Mem:* Soc Indust & Appl Math; Am Math Soc; Am Statist Asn; Sigma Xi. *Res:* Mass transport phenomenon, especially in porous and permeable mediums; compartmental analysis and the mathematical modeling of drug distributions in mammalian tissue systems. *Mailing Add:* 6743 Dominion Ct Las Vegas NV 89103-4374

LINDSTROM, GARY J, SEMICONDUCTOR PROCESS ENGINEERING, PROCUREMENT ENGINEERING. *Current Pos:* FIELD APPLN ENGR, GASONICS INC, 96- *Personal Data:* b Beacon, NY, Aug 4, 39; m 63. *Educ:* Marist Col, BA, 69. *Prof Exp:* Adv engr, IBM Corp, 64-90; substitute teacher math & saci, Beacon City Sch Dist & Wappingers Cent Sch Dist, 90-93. *Res:* Science education; field applications engineering. *Mailing Add:* 52 Kent Rd Wappingers Falls NY 12590-3845

LINDSTROM, IVAR E, JR, PHYSICS. *Current Pos:* MEM STAFF PHYSICS, LOS ALAMOS NAT LAB, UNIV CALIF, 58- *Personal Data:* b Milligan, Nebr, Oct 15, 29; m 52; c 2. *Educ:* Nebr Wesleyan Univ, AB, 50; Univ Ore, MA, 52, PhD(physics), 59. *Mem:* Am Phys Soc; Sigma Xi. *Res:* Explosives, particularly initiation by shock waves; nuclear spectroscopy; solid state physics. *Mailing Add:* 327 Venado St Los Alamos NM 87544

LINDSTROM, JON MARTIN, AUTOIMMUNITY. *Current Pos:* TRUSTEE PROF NEUROL SCI & PHARMACOL, MED SCH, UNIV PA, 90- *Personal Data:* b Moline, Ill, Nov 9, 45; m 77, Suzanne Stevenson; c Laurel A, Kara M & Jon K. *Educ:* Univ Ill, BA, 67; Univ Calif, San Diego, PhD(biol), 71. *Honors & Awards:* McKnight Neurosci Develop Award; Jacob Javits Award. *Prof Exp:* Muscular Dystrophy Asn fel, Salk Inst Biol Studies, 71-73, from asst res prof to assoc res prof, 73-83, assoc prof neurosci & mem, 83-90. *Concurrent Pos:* Sloan fel; adj prof neurosci, Univ Calif, San Diego, 87-90; mem sci adv comt, MDA, Los Angeles & Calif chap MG Found. *Mem:* Soc Neurosci. *Res:* Acetylcholine receptor structure and function; pathological mechanisms in myasthenia gravis. *Mailing Add:* Dept Neurosci Univ Pa Med Sch 217 Stemmler Hall Philadelphia PA 19104-6074. *Fax:* 215-573-2015

LINDSTROM, MARILYN MARTIN, GEOCHEMISTRY & COSMOCHEMISTRY, IGNEOUS PETROLOGY. *Current Pos:* PLANETARY SCIENTIST, NASA JOHNSON SPACE CTR, 86- *Personal Data:* b Jacksonville, Fla, Nov 28, 46; m 71, David J; c Peter & Ingrid. *Educ:* Univ Calif, San Diego, BA, 69; Univ Ore, PhD(geochem), 76. *Prof Exp:* Technician geochem, Geol Dept, Univ Ore, 68-69; res assoc, Univ Md, 75-77; res scientist, 77-79, sr res scientist geochem, Dept Earth & Planetary Sci, Wash Univ, 79-86. *Concurrent Pos:* Prin investr, NSF & NASA grants; assoc ed, Proc Lunar & Planetary Sci Conf & Geochim Cosmochim Acta; GSA Penrose grants. *Mem:* Geochem Soc; Am Geophys Union; Meteoritical Soc; Asn Women Geoscientists; Am Asn Univ Women. *Res:* Geochemistry and petrology of igneous rocks and extraterrestrial materials; oceanic volcanic rocks, lunar samples and meteorites; trace element geochemistry; instrumental neutron activation analysis. *Mailing Add:* NASA Johnson Space Ctr Code SN2 Houston TX 77058. *Fax:* 713-483-5347; *E-Mail:* lindstrom@curate.nasa.jsc.gov

LINDSTROM, MERLIN RAY, COATINGS CHEMISTRY, POLYMER CHEMISTRY. *Current Pos:* CHEMIST, PHILLIPS PETROL CO, 78- *Personal Data:* b New Rockford, NDak, Oct 28, 51; m 72; c 3. *Educ:* NDak State Univ, BS, 73, PhD(chem), 78. *Mem:* Fedn Coatings Technol; Soc Mfg Engrs. *Res:* Coatings; sulfur chemicals; metal cleaners; adhesives; water soluble resins; electroplating; sealants. *Mailing Add:* 919 Kings Circle Bartlesville OK 74006

LINDSTROM, RICHARD EDWARD, PHYSICAL PHARMACY. *Current Pos:* PROF, NOVA SOUTHEASTERN UNIV. *Personal Data:* b Bristol, Conn, June 15, 32; m 52; c 3. *Educ:* Univ Conn, BS, 55; Syracuse Univ, MS, 62, PhD(phys chem), 67. *Prof Exp:* Asst prof chem, USFA, 62-66 & Salem State Col, 66-68; from assoc prof to prof pharmaceut, Univ Conn, 68- *Concurrent Pos:* Consult, Vick Chem Co, 74-, US, 80- & USAF, 81- *Mem:* Am Chem Soc; Am Pharmaceut Asn; Acad Pharmaceut Sci. *Res:* Thermodynamics of solution phenomena via molar volume and solubility data. *Mailing Add:* One Club Circle Tequesta FL 33469

LINDSTROM, RICHARD S, HORTICULTURE. *Current Pos:* PROF HORT, VA POLYTECH INST & STATE UNIV, 68- *Personal Data:* b Cleveland, Ohio, Mar 5, 27; m 53; c 3. *Educ:* Ohio State Univ, BS, 50, MS, 51, PhD(hort), 56. *Prof Exp:* Instr hort, Mich State Univ, 53-56, from asst prof to assoc prof, 56-68. *Mem:* Am Soc Hort Sci; Sigma Xi. *Res:* Physiology of floricultural plants including work with growth regulators, nutrition and photoperiodic control. *Mailing Add:* 18 Henzie St Reading MA 01867-1642

LINDSTROM, TERRY DONALD, DRUG METABOLISM, PHARMACOKINETICS. *Current Pos:* sr pharmacologist, Lilly Res Labs, 79-85, from res scientist to sr res scientist, 85-94, head CNS Res, 87-88, RES ADVISOR, LILLY RES LABS, 94-; ASST PROF, DEPT PHARMACOL, MED SCH, IND UNIV, 82- *Personal Data:* b Minneapolis, Minn, Sept 23, 51; m 76; c 2. *Educ:* Augsburg Col, BA, 73; Univ Minn, PhD(pharmacol), 77. *Prof Exp:* Fel biochem, Mich State Univ, 77-79. *Concurrent Pos:* Mem, Ind drug Utilization Rev Bd. *Mem:* Am Soc Pharmacol & Exp Therapeut; Int Soc Study Xenobiotics; Int Union Pharmacol; Soc Toxicol. *Res:* Oxidative and reductive metabolism of various drugs in subcellular, cellular and in vivo metabolism models; pharmacokinetics and toxicokinetic relationships with efficacy and toxicity. *Mailing Add:* Drug Metab & Disposition Lilly Res Labs Eli Lilly & Co Lilly Corp Ctr Indianapolis IN 46285-0001. *Fax:* 317-276-4218

LINDSTROM, WENDELL DON, MATHEMATICS. *Current Pos:* from assoc prof to prof, 58-88, EMER PROF MATH, KENYON COL, 88- *Personal Data:* b Kiron, Iowa, Feb 7, 27; m 50, Miriam Bratt; c Astrid & Greta (Cornell). *Educ:* Univ Iowa, AB, 49, MS, 51, PhD(math), 53. *Hon Degrees:* DSc, Kenyon Col, 88. *Prof Exp:* From instr to asst prof math, Iowa State Univ, 53-58. *Concurrent Pos:* NSF sci fac fel, Univ Calif, Berkeley, 62-63; vis prof, Robert Col, Istanbul, 68-69; Dana Early Retirement fel, 88-92. *Mem:* Am Math Soc; Math Asn Am. *Res:* Fields, rings, algebras, differential algebra; algebraic geometry. *Mailing Add:* Box 212 Gambier OH 43022

LINDT, JAN THOMAS, POLYMER ENGINEERING, CHEMICAL ENGINEERING. *Current Pos:* assoc prof, 78-85, PROF POLYMER ENG, UNIV PITTSBURGH, 85- *Personal Data:* b Amsterdam, Holland, July 8, 42; m 77; c 3. *Educ:* Delft Univ Technol, MSc, 64, PhD(chem eng), 71. *Prof Exp:* Asst prof chem eng, Delft Univ Technol, 69-71; scientist polymer eng, Shell Res Ltd, 72-77. *Concurrent Pos:* Fel, Nat Ctr Sci Res, 83 & 87. *Mem:* Soc Rheology; Soc Plastics Engrs; Polymer Proc Soc. *Res:* Plasticating extrusion; reaction injection molding; reactive extrusion of polymers; devolatilization of polymer solutions; polyurethane foaming processes; polymer composites; polymer blends. *Mailing Add:* Dept Chem Eng 1248 Benedam Hall Univ Pittsburgh Main Campus Pittsburgh PA 15260

LINDZEN, RICHARD SIEGMUND, DYNAMIC METEOROLOGY, APPLIED MATHEMATICS. *Current Pos:* DISTINGUISHED VIS SCIENTIST, JET PROPULSION LAB, 88- *Personal Data:* b Webster, Mass, Feb 8, 40; m 65, Nadine Kalouguine; c Eric & Nathaniel. *Educ:* Harvard Univ, AB, 60, SM, 61, PhD(appl math), 64. *Honors & Awards:* Meisinger Award, Am Meteorol Asn, 68, Charney Award, 85 & Bernhard Haurwitz Mem Lectr, 96; Macelwane Award, Am Geophys Union, 69; Landsdowne Lectr, Univ Victoria, 93. *Prof Exp:* Res fel meteorol, Univ Wash, 64 & Univ Oslo, 64-65; res scientist, Nat Ctr Atmospheric Res, 65-68; prof, Univ Chicago, 68-72; prof meteorol, Harvard Univ, 72-83, dir, Ctr Earth & Planetary Physics, 80-83. *Concurrent Pos:* Exec mem, Nat Acad Comt Global Atmospheric Res Prog, 68-79; Alfred P Sloan fel, 70-76; consult, Naval Res Lab, 72-83, Control Data Corp, 77 & NASA, 77-85; mem, Nat Acad Assembly Math & Phys Sci, 78-81, Nat Resource Coun Math Sci Educ Bd, 87-90, Space Studies Bd, 88- & NRS Bd Atmospheric Sci & Climate, 90-; fel, Japanese Soc Prom Sci, 86-87; mem staff, Woods Hole Oceanog Inst Corp, 87-; Sackler vis prof, Tel Aviv Univ, 92; vis scientist, Jet Propulsion Lab. *Mem:* Nat Acad Sci; fel Am Acad Arts & Sci; fel Am Meteorol Soc; fel Am Geophys Union; fel AAAS; Sigma Xi; Norweg Acad Sci & Lett. *Res:* Hydrodynamic stability; climatology; upper atmosphere dynamics; general atmospheric circulation; tides. *Mailing Add:* Bldg 54 Rm 1720 Mass Inst Technol Cambridge MA 02139. *Fax:* 617-964-3953; *E-Mail:* lindzen@wind.mit.edu

LINE, JOHN PAUL, MATHEMATICS, APPLIED MATHEMATICS. *Current Pos:* asst prof, 56-62, ASSOC PROF MATH, GA INST TECHNOL, 62- *Personal Data:* b Pontiac, Mich, Mar 2, 29; m 57, Frances Winn; c Paul, Carl, Mark & John. *Educ:* Univ Mich, BS, 50, MS, 51. *Prof Exp:* Instr math, Oberlin Col, 55 & Univ Rochester, 55-56. *Mem:* Am Math Soc; Math Asn Am. *Res:* Integral transformations as applied to solution of boundary value problems in partial differential equations. *Mailing Add:* Sch Math Ga Inst Technol 225 North Ave NW Atlanta GA 30332-0001

LINEBACK, DAVID R(AY), CARBOHYDRATE CHEMISTRY. *Current Pos:* PROF FOOD SCI & HEAD DEPT, NC STATE UNIV, 80- *Personal Data:* b Russellville, Ind, June 7, 34; m 56; c 3. *Educ:* Purdue Univ, BS, 56; Ohio State Univ, PhD(org chem), 62. *Honors & Awards:* Spec Award Merit, Japanese Soc Starch Sci, 85; William F Geddes Mem Lecturship, 88. *Prof Exp:* Res chemist, Monsanto Chem Co, 56-57; fel, Univ Alta, 62-64; from instr to asst prof biochem, Univ Nebr, Lincoln, 64-69; from assoc prof to prof grain sci & indust, Kans State Univ, 69-76; prof food sci & head dept, Pa State Univ, 76-80. *Concurrent Pos:* Regional adv, Wheat Indust Coun, 82-86; mem ed bd, Lebensmittel-Wissenschaft und Technologie, 82-; fel Inst Food Technologists, 82; mem Comt on Food Protection Bd, Nat Res Coun, Nat Acad Sci, 83-85; mem bd dir, League for Int Food Educ, 83-87; mem bd gov, Food Processing Inst, 86-, bd dir, 87-, prog chmn, 88- *Mem:* Am Asn Cereal Chem (pres-elect, 82-83, pres, 83-86); Inst Food Technol (exec comt, 88-); Am Chem Soc; Soc Nutrit Educ; Am Inst Nutrit; Japanese Soc Starch Sci. *Res:* Reaction and structure of carbohydrates; characterization of enzymes of starch hydrolysis and synthesis; cereal chemistry; structure of starch and functionality in food products. *Mailing Add:* Dept Food Sci NC State Univ Box 7624 Raleigh NC 27695-7624

LINEBACK, JERRY A(LVIN), REGIONAL GEOLOGY. *Current Pos:* RETIRED. *Personal Data:* b Ottawa, Kans, Oct 25, 38; m 69, Mary Price; c Nathan, Benjamin & Daniel. *Educ:* Univ Kans, BS, 60, MS, 61; Ind Univ, PhD(geol), 64. *Prof Exp:* From asst geologist to geologist, Stratig & Areal Geol Sect, Ill State Geol Surv, 64-81; sr geologist, Robertson Res, 81-86; asst state geologist & regulatory support prog mgr, Ga Geol Surv, 87-95. *Mem:* Fel Geol Soc Am. *Res:* Ground water quality and protection; ground water resource development and management; Mississippian stratigraphy; regional geology. *Mailing Add:* 22 W Third St Garnett KS 66032. *Fax:* 404-657-8379

LINEBERGER, ROBERT DANIEL, HORTICULTURE, PLANT PHYSIOLOGY. *Current Pos:* ASSOC PROF HORT, OHIO STATE UNIV, 77- *Personal Data:* b Dallas, NC, Nov 9, 48; m 71; c 3. *Educ:* NC State Univ, BS, 71; Cornell Univ, MS, 74, PhD(hort), 78. *Prof Exp:* L H Bailey res asst, Dept Floricult, Cornell Univ, 71-77. *Mem:* Tissue Cult Asn; Am Soc Hort Sci; Am Soc Plant Physiologists; Bot Soc Am. *Res:* Plant cell and tissue culture; freeze preservation of germ plasm; freezing injury to plant cells; plant cell ultrastructure. *Mailing Add:* Dept Hort Tex A&M Univ College Station TX 77843-0100

LINEBERGER, WILLIAM CARL, CHEMICAL PHYSICS. *Current Pos:* res assoc physics, Joint Inst Lab Astrophys, Univ Colo, 68-70, mem, 70- 71, from asst prof to prof, 70-85, chmn, 85-86, E U CONDON DISTINGUISHED PROF CHEM, UNIV COLO, BOULDER, 85-, FEL PHYSICS, JOINT INST LAB ASTROPHYS, 71- *Personal Data:* b Hamlet, NC, Dec 5, 39; m 79, Katherine Edwards. *Educ:* Ga Inst Technol, BEE, 61, MSEE, 63, PhD, 65. *Honors & Awards:* Hanon Rosenthal lectr, Yale & Columbia Univs, 77; Broida Prize, Am Phys Soc, 81, Earle K Plyler Prize, 92; Bomem Michaelson Prize, 87; Fred M Garland Mem lectr, Tex A&M Univ, 87; Meggers Prize, Optical Soc Am, 88; Jonathan Rohrig Distinguished lectr, Carleton Col, 88; Davidson lectr, Univ Kans, 90; George B Kistiakowsky lectr, Harvard Univ, 92; George C Pimentel lectr, Univ Calif, Berkeley, 93; Reilly lectr, Notre Dame Univ, 94; Ilangmair Prize, Am Chem Soc, 96. *Prof Exp:* Asst prof elec eng, Ga Inst Technol, 65; res physicist atmospheric physics, US Army Ballistic Res Lab, Aberdeen Proving Ground, Md, 65-68. *Concurrent Pos:* Assoc ed, Atomic Data & Nuclear Data Tables, 74-82 & Chem Physics Lett, 82-; mem, Comt Atomic & Molecular Sci, Nat Acad Sci, 79-82, chair, Sect Chem, 93-; distinguished vis prof, Univ Calif, Irvine, 80, Univ Rochester, 81, Univ Fla, 82 & 93, NDak State Univ, 85 & Northwestern Univ, 85; J S Guggenheim mem fel, 81-82; vchmn, Div Chem Physics, Am Phys Soc, 81-82, chmn, 82-83, vchmn, Div Atomic, Molecular & Optical Physics, 86, chmn, 87, vchair & chair elect, Topical Group Laser Sci, 92-95; vis prof, Stanford Univ & Univ Chicago, 82; mem, Bd Physics & Astron, Nat Res Coun, 83-88, Bd Chem Sci & Technol, 89-95; chair, comn phys sci, math, appns, Nat Res Coord; chair, Basic Energy Sci Adv Comt, Dept Energy, 90-95. *Mem:* Nat Acad Sci; fel AAAS; Am Chem Soc; fel Am Phys Soc; Optical Soc Am. *Res:* Negative ion structure; molecular fluorescence; ion molecule reactions; tunable lasers; ultrafort processes. *Mailing Add:* Dept Chem & Biochem Joint Inst Lab Astrophys Univ Colo PO Box 215 Boulder CO 80309-0440. *E-Mail:* wcl@sila.colorado.edu

LINEHAN, JOHN HENRY, MECHANICAL & BIOMEDICAL ENGINEERING. *Current Pos:* instr mech eng, 62-64, from asst prof mech & biomed eng to prof, 68-89, PROF & CHAIR, DEPT BIOMED ENG, MARQUETTE UNIV, 89-; PROF PHYSIOL, MED COL WIS, 79- *Personal Data:* b Chicago, Ill, July 8, 38; m 60; c 5. *Educ:* Marquette Univ, BSME, 60; Rensselaer Polytech Inst, MSME, 62; Univ Wis-Madison, PhD(mech eng), 68. *Prof Exp:* Engr, Knolls Atomic Power Lab, NY, 60-62. *Mem:* Am Soc Mech Engrs; Am Physiol Soc; Biomed Eng Soc; Am Soc Eng Educ; Microcirculatory Soc; Am Thoracic Soc. *Res:* Multiphase flow; heat and mass transfer; hemodynamics; lung physiology; fluid mechanics; biomedical instrumentation, medical imaging. *Mailing Add:* Dept Biomed Eng Marquette Univ PO Box 1881 Milwaukee WI 53201-1881. *E-Mail:* linehanj@vms.csd.mu.edu

LINEHAN, URBAN JOSEPH, PHYSICAL GEOGRAPHY, HISTORY & PHILOSPHY OF SCIENCE. *Current Pos:* RETIRED. *Personal Data:* b Brockton, Mass, Oct 13, 11; m 50, Mary Criste; c Mary A, Katherine A & Teresa M. *Educ:* Bridgewater State Col, BS, 33; Clark Univ, MA, 46, PhD(geog), 55. *Prof Exp:* Instr geog, Univ Cincinnati, 40-45; from instr to asst prof, Univ Pittsburgh, 45-48; asst prof, Cath Univ Am, 48-56; analyst, US Govt, 56-73. *Res:* Synoptic climatology of Pittsburgh, Pennsylvania; areal and temporal distribution of tornado deaths in the United States; landscapes and off-road recreation of southwestern United States. *Mailing Add:* 13921 Pinetree Dr Sun City West AZ 85375

LINEHAN, WILLIAM MARSTON, CANCER RESEARCH, MOLECULAR BIOLOGY. *Current Pos:* HEAD, UROL & ONCOL SECT, SURG BR, NAT CANCER INST, 82- *Personal Data:* b Tulsa, Okla, June 25, 47; m 79, Tracey Renault; c Erin L & Emily P. *Educ:* Brown Univ, BA, 69; Univ Okla, MD, 73. *Honors & Awards:* Gold Cysooscom Award, Am Urol Asn. *Concurrent Pos:* Sr investr, Nat Cancer Inst, NIH, 82- *Mem:* Am Urol Asn; Soc Univ Surgeons; Am Col Surgeons. *Res:* Co-discoverer of the gene for kidney cancer. *Mailing Add:* Nat Cancer Inst Bldg 10 2B47B Bethesda MD 20892. *Fax:* 301-402-0922; *E-Mail:* wml@helix.nih.gov

LINEMEYER, DAVID L, BIOCHEMISTRY REGULATION. *Current Pos:* res fel, Dept Biochem Genetics, Merck Sharp & Dohme Res Labs, Rahway, NJ, 81-85, Dept Biochem Fundamental & Exp Res, 85-86, Dept Molecular Pharmacol & Biochem, 86-89, ASSOC DIR, DEPT BIOCHEM, MERCK RES LABS, RAHWAY, NJ, 89- *Personal Data:* b Apr 19, 49. *Educ:* Colo State Univ, BS, 71; Univ Wash, MS, 73, PhD(microbiol), 77. *Prof Exp:* Staff fel, Lab Tumor Virus Genetics, Nat Cancer Inst, NIH, Bethesda, Md, 77-80, sr staff fel, 80-81. *Mem:* AAAS; Am Soc Biochem & Molecular Biol. *Res:* Author of numerous scientific publications. *Mailing Add:* Synaptic Pharmaceut Corp 215 College Rd Paramus NJ 07652-1431

LINES, MALCOLM ELLIS, THEORETICAL MATERIALS PHYSICS. *Current Pos:* mem tech staff, 63-65 & 66-85, DISTINGUISHED MEM TECH STAFF, AT&T BELL LABS, 85- *Personal Data:* b Banbury, Eng, Apr 26, 36; m 62, Kathleen Morse; c Richard & Stephen. *Educ:* Oxford Univ, BA, 59, MA & DPhil(physics), 62. *Prof Exp:* Fel physics, Magdalen Col, Oxford Univ, 61-63, 65-66. *Concurrent Pos:* Consult, Atomic Energy Res Estab, Harwell, Eng, 73. *Mem:* Fel Brit Inst Physics; Am Ceramic Soc; fel Phys Soc Gt Brit; Soc Photo-Optical Instrumentation Engrs. *Res:* Statistical mechanics; magnetism; ferroelectricity; structure of glasses; light scattering; author of four books on math and physics. *Mailing Add:* 10 E Rayborn Rd Millington NJ 07946

LINEVSKY, MILTON JOSHUA, PHYSICAL CHEMISTRY. *Current Pos:* PHYSICS CHEMIST, JOHNS HOPKINS APPL PHYSICS LAB, LAUREL, MD, 79-; STAFF MEM, NSF, WASHINGTON, 93- *Personal Data:* b Glen Cove, NY, Apr 20, 28; m 58, Barbara J Ruttenberg; c Joanne & Richard. *Educ:* Rensselaer Polytech Inst, BS, 49; Pa State Univ, MS, 50, PhD, 53. *Prof Exp:* Phys Chemist, US Army 55-57, Gen Elec, King Of Prussia, Pa, 57-79. *Mem:* Am Chem Soc. *Res:* Invention and development of technique for matrix isolation applied to high temperature materials; development of first flam laser using chemical pumping reactions. *Mailing Add:* 700 Hermleigh Rd Silver Spring MD 20902-1697

LINFIELD, WARNER MAX, SURFACE & SURFACTANT CHEMISTRY, LIPID CHEMISTRY. *Current Pos:* CONSULT, 84- *Personal Data:* b Hannover, Ger, Jan 8, 18; nat US; m 45, Shirley Evenstein; c Suzanne L (Spindler). *Educ:* George Washington Univ, BS, 40; Univ Mich, MS, 41, PhD(pharmaceut chem), 43. *Honors & Awards:* Alton E Bailey Medal, Am Oil Chem Soc. *Prof Exp:* Anna Fuller Fund res fel, Northwestern Univ, 43-44; res chemist, Emulsol Corp, Ill, 44-46; group leader, E F Houghton & Co, Pa, 46-52 & Quaker Chem Prod Co, 52-55; dir res, Soap Div, Armour & Co Ill, 55-58, tech dir grocery prod div, 58-63; vpres, Culver Chem Co, 63-65; mgr org chem res, IIT Res Inst, 65-71; res leader, Eastern Regional Res Ctr Div, 71-84. *Concurrent Pos:* Assoc ed, J Am Oil Chemists Soc, 74-84. *Mem:* Am Chem Soc; Am Oil Chemists Soc; Am Inst Chem; Sigma Xi. *Res:* Surface-active agents; soaps and detergents; synthesis of germicides; anti-malarial drugs; textile finishing agents; food technology; enzymatic fat splitting. *Mailing Add:* 8287 NW 70th St Tamarac FL 33321-2749

LINFOOT, JOHN ARDIS, MEDICINE, ENDOCRINOLOGY. *Current Pos:* CLIN PROF MED, UNIV CALIF, DAVIS, SACRAMENTO MED CTR, 81- *Personal Data:* b Grand Forks, NDak, May 16, 31; m 55; c 3. *Educ:* Univ NDak, BA, 53, BS & MS, 55; Harvard Univ, MD, 57; Am Bd Internal Med, dipl; Am Bd Endocrinol, dipl; Am Bd Nuclear Med, dipl. *Prof Exp:* Fel metab & endocrinol, Univ Utah Hosps, 59-60; sr staff scientist, Lawrence Berkeley Lab, 61-76; sr staff scientist, Donner Lab, Univ Calif, Berkeley, 61-81. *Concurrent Pos:* Consult, Martinez Vet Admin Hosp & Children's Hosp, East Bay; dir endocrine & metab servs, Alta Bates Hosp, 70; dir, Diabetes & Endocrine Inst, Providence Hosp. *Mem:* AAAS; Am Fedn Clin Res; fel Am Col Physicians; Endocrine Soc; Am Diabetes Asn. *Res:* Growth hormone; acromegaly; Cushing's syndrome; diabetic retinopathy; heavy particle pituitary irradiation. *Mailing Add:* Providence Hosp 350 30th St Suite 208 Oakland CA 94609-3425

LINFORD, GARY JOE, LASER PHYSICS, NONLINEAR OPTICS. *Current Pos:* RES DIR & SR SCIENTIST, PFEIFER SCI ASSOC, 94- *Personal Data:* b Laramie, Wyo, June 13, 40; m 63, 86; c 3. *Educ:* Mass Inst Technol, BS, 62; Univ Utah, PhD(physics), 71. *Prof Exp:* Res asst physics, Electronics Res Lab, Mass Inst Technol, 61-62; mem tech staff laser physics, Laser Technol Dept, Aerospace Group, Hughes Aircraft Co, 63-68, group head, Laser Div, 68-69; teaching asst physics & astron, Univ Utah, 69-71; sect head, Laser Div, Hughes Aircraft Co, 71-74; group head laser res, Laser Fusion Prog, Lawrence Livermore Nat Lab, Univ Calif, 74-82; physicist laser res, Max Planck Inst Quantum Optics, WGer, 82-83; sect head, Appl Tech Div, 83-84, mgr, Advan Technol Dept, TRW, 84-86; chief scientist, Optics & Directed Energy Lab, 86-90, area leader advan laser technol, 90-94; chief scientist, Odel TRW, 86-90. *Concurrent Pos:* Guest lectr, Dept Physics, Calif State Univ, 81-82; guest scientist, Max Planck Inst for Plasma Physics, 78-79. *Mem:* Am Phys Soc; Int Soc Optical Engr. *Res:* Inertial confinement laser fusion; harmonic conversion of infrared light to ultraviolet; design of laser amplifiers and high power propagation optics; target irradiation experiments and diagnostics; non-linear optics; excimer lasers; chemical lasers; free electron lasers; raman laser physics; phase conjugation; spacecraft telescopes; xenon lasers, xenon flashlamps; zeeman spectroscopy; remote sensing; long lasers; semi-conductor laser diodes. *Mailing Add:* 1308 Steele St Laramie WY 82070. *E-Mail:* lin4d@aol.com

LINFORD, RULON KESLER, MAGNETIC CONFINEMENT SYSTEMS FOR FUSION ENERGY. *Current Pos:* Staff mem, Los Alamos Nat Lab, 73-75, asst group leader, 75-77, group leader, 77-80, asst div leader, 80-81, assoc div leader, 81-86, prog dir, 86-89, div leader, 89-91, prog dir, 91-93, staff mem, 93-94, UNIV CALIF COORDR SCI & TECHNOL, LOS ALAMOS NAT LAB, 94- *Personal Data:* b Cambridge, Mass, Jan 31, 43; M 65, Cecile Tadje; c R Scott, Laura, Hilary & Philip L. *Educ:* Univ Utah, BS, 66; Mass Inst Technol, SM & EE, 69, PhD(elec eng), 73. *Honors & Awards:* E O Lawrence Award, Dept Energy, 92. *Concurrent Pos:* Mem, Magnetic Fusion Adv Comt, 82-86, Ignition Tech Oversight: CIT Steering Comt, 85-90, Int Thermonuclear Exp Reactor Steering Comt, 90; mem var comts, Am Phys Soc Div Plasma Physics, 87-91. *Mem:* Fel Am Phys Soc; Sigma Xi. *Res:* Fusion energy and accelerator transmution of radioactive waste. *Mailing Add:* 1166 Big Rock Loop Los Alamos NM 87544. *Fax:* 505-665-3199; *E-Mail:* rlinford@lanl.gov

LIN-FU, JANE S, GENETICS. *Current Pos:* dir, childhood Lead Poisoning Prev Prog & Pediat & consult, Bur Health Care Delivery & Assistance, 82-87, Bur Maternal & Child Health & Resources Develop, 87-90, CHIEF, GENETIC SERV BR, HEALTH RESOURCES & SERV ADMIN, DEPT HEALTH & HUMAN SERVS, 90- *Educ:* Univ Santo Thomas, Phillippines, MD, 55; Am Bd Pediat, dipl, 62. *Honors & Awards:* H John Heinz III Nat Leadership Award, USPHS, 93. *Prof Exp:* Pediat consult, Children's Bur, HEW, 63-69, Maternal & Child Health Servs, 69-73. *Concurrent Pos:* mem, Task Force Surgeon General's Statement Childhood Lead Poisoning Prev, 70, President's Comt Ment Retardation, 72, Task Force Opportunities Women Pediat, Dept Health & Human Serv, 82, Task Force Women's Health Issues, Pub Health Serv, 85; coordr, Comt Women's Health, Food & Drug Admin, 87. *Mem:* Fel Am Acad Pediat. *Res:* Authored numerous papers in professional journals. *Mailing Add:* HRSA DHHS Rm 18A-20 5600 Fishers Lane Rockville MD 20857. *Fax:* 301-443-1728; *E-Mail:* jlin-fu@hrsa.ssw.dhhs.gov

LING, ALAN CAMPBELL, radiochemistry; deceased, see previous edition for last biography

LING, ALFRED SOY CHOU, clinical research, development, for more information see previous edition

LING, CHUNG-MEI, BIOCHEMISTRY. *Current Pos:* chmn bd, 84-87, CHIEF SCI OFFICER, GEN BIOL CORP, TAIWAN, ROC, 88-; HON CHMN, 91- *Personal Data:* b Chekiang, China, May 5, 31; m 57, Amy Hsieh; c 2. *Educ:* Nat Taiwan Univ, BS, 58; Ill Inst Technol, MS, 62, PhD(biochem), 65. *Prof Exp:* Teaching asst biochem & physiol, Ill Inst Technol, 60-64; res assoc biochem res, Michael Reese Res Found, Chicago, 64-65; asst prof biochem, Ill Inst Technol, 65-68; molecular biologist, Abbott Labs, 68-71, assoc res fel virol, 71-74, res fel, Dept Biochem, 74-84, head, Molecular Biol Lab, 74-77, head, virol lab, 77-82, mgr, Res & Develop Diag Div, 82-84. *Concurrent Pos:* Adj asst prof, Ill Inst Technol, 68-69; chief sci consult, Kangling Biotech, 88-; adj prof, Nat Tsing Hua Univ, Taiwan, 91-93. *Mem:* AAAS; Sigma Xi; Am Soc Biol Chemists; Am Soc Clin Chem; fel Am Acad Microbiol. *Res:* Research in areas of molecular biology, immunodiagnostics, and biofunctional and health products; more than 50 scientific publications and numerous US and other patents. *Mailing Add:* Gen Biol Corp No Six Innovation First Rd Sci-Based Indust Pk HsinChu 30077 Taiwan. *Fax:* 886-35-783158

LING, DANIEL, AUDIOLOGY, COMMUNICATIONS. *Current Pos:* CONSULT, 91- *Personal Data:* b Wetherden, Eng, Mar 16, 26; Can citizen; m 58; c 2. *Educ:* St John's Col, Univ York, dipl, 50; Victoria Univ, Manchester, dipl, 51; McGill Univ, MS, 66, PhD(human commun dis), 68. *Prof Exp:* Organizer educ deaf, Reading Educ Comt, 55-63; prin, Montreal Oral Sch Deaf, 63-66; dir res deaf children, McGill Univ, 66-70, asst prof audiol, Sch Human Commun Dis, 68-70; dir, Speech & Hearing Div, Royal Victoria Hosp, 70-91; assoc prof & dir oral rehab, Sch Human Commun Dis, Univ Western Ont, 70-91, prof aural habilitation & educ, Dept Commun Dis, 74-91. *Concurrent Pos:* Can Fed Prov Health grants, McGill Univ, 66-; res assoc educ, Cambridge Univ, 55-58; hon dir, Coun Children's Audiol Rehab, Ctr Deaf Children, Mexico City, 66-; dir, Speech & Hearing Div, 70- *Mem:* Am Speech & Hearing Asn; Can Speech & Hearing Asn; Am Audiol Soc; Acoust Soc Am. *Res:* Communication development in deaf children; speech production among hearing impaired children; speech recognition using linear and coding amplifiers; diagnostic procedure relative to deafness. *Mailing Add:* 956 Cherry Point Rd RR 3 Cobble Hill BC V0R 7L0 Can

LING, DANIEL SETH, JR, THEORETICAL PHYSICS. *Current Pos:* RETIRED. *Personal Data:* b Chicago, Ill, Oct 22, 24; m 46; c 2. *Educ:* Univ Mich, BSE(physics) & BSE(math), 44, MS, 45, PhD(physics), 48. *Prof Exp:* From asst prof to assoc prof physics, Univ Kans, 48-87, assoc prof astron, 73-87. *Mem:* AAAS; Am Phys Soc. *Res:* Nuclear physics. *Mailing Add:* 5905 W Ridgecrest Dr Spokane WA 99208

LING, F(REDERICK) F(ONGSUN), TRIBOLOGY, MANUFACTURING. *Current Pos:* EARNEST F GLOYNA REGENTS CHAIR ENG, UNIV TEX, AUSTIN, 92-, ASSOC DIR ENG, MFG SYSTS CTR, 92- *Personal Data:* b Tsingtao, China, Jan 2, 27; m 54, Linda Kwok; c Erica H, Alfred F & Arthur T. *Educ:* St John's Univ, China, BS, 47; Bucknell Univ, BS, 49; Carnegie Inst Technol, MS, 51, DSc, 54. *Honors & Awards:* Nat Award, Soc Triboligists & Lubrication Engrs, 70; Mayo D Hersey Award, Am Soc Mech Engrs, 84; Charles Russ Richards Mem Award, Am Soc Mech Engrs, 91. *Prof Exp:* Proj mech engr, Carnegie Inst Technol, 52-54, asst prof math, 54-56; from asst prof to prof mech, Rensselaer Polytech Inst, 55-70, William Howard Hart prof rational & tech mech, 70-88, chmn, Dept Mech Eng, Aeronaut Eng & Mech, 74-86; prof mech eng, Columbia Univ, 87-90, dir, Columbia Eng Prod Ctr, 87-90; pres, Inst Productivity Res, 90-92. *Concurrent Pos:* Consult, Southwest Res Inst, 59-65, Gen Elec Co, 60-62, Mitre Corp, 61-63, Alco Prod, Inc, 61-62, Mech Tech, Inc, 62-70 & Wear Sci Corp, 71-; NSF sr fel, 70; vis prof, Univ Leeds, 70-71; Jacob Wallenburg Found grantee, Sweden, 87; hon mem Acad Romania, 94. *Mem:* Nat Acad Eng; fel Am Soc Mech Engrs; fel Am Acad Mech; fel AAAS; fel Soc Tribologists & Lubrication Engrs; fel Am Soc Mfg Engrs. *Res:* Gradual wear life prediction theory of lubricating surface films; questions of factories of the 21st century, including in-situ micro-sensors in the small scale and larger questions concerning the total systems. *Mailing Add:* Dept Mech Eng Univ Tex Austin TX 78712-1063. *Fax:* 512-471-9155

LING, GILBERT NING, PHYSIOLOGY. *Current Pos:* DIR DEPT MOLECULAR BIOL, PA HOSP, 62- *Personal Data:* b Nanking, China, Dec 26, 19; m 51; c 3. *Educ:* Nat Cent Univ, China, BSc, 43; Univ Chicago, PhD(physiol), 48. *Prof Exp:* Comen fel, Univ Chicago, 48-50; instr physiol optics, Sch Med, Johns Hopkins Univ, 50-53; from asst prof to assoc prof neurophysiol, Univ Ill, 53-57; sr staff scientist, Eastern Pa Psychiat Inst, 57-62. *Concurrent Pos:* Mem, Woods Hole Marine Biol Corp. *Mem:* Am Physiol Soc. *Res:* Molecular mechanisms in cell function. *Mailing Add:* 307 Berkeley Rd Merion PA 19066

LING, HAO, ELECTROMAGNETICS, ANTENNAS. *Current Pos:* Asst prof, 86-90, ASSOC PROF ELEC ENG, DEPT ELEC & COMPUT ENG, UNIV TEX, AUSTIN, 90- *Personal Data:* b Taichung, Taiwan, Sept 26, 59; US citizen; m 84, Wei-Na Lee; c Chloe. *Educ:* Mass Inst Technol, BS, 82; Univ Ill, Urbana-Champaign, MS, 83, PhD(elec eng), 86. *Concurrent Pos:* Engr, IBM Res Lab, 82; NSF presidential young investr award, 87; vis fac mem, Lawrence Livermore Nat Lab, 87; Air Force fel, Rome Air Develop Ctr, Hanscom AFB, 90. *Mem:* Inst Elec & Electronics Engrs; Int Union Radio Sci; Appl Comput Electromagnetics Soc. *Res:* Electromagnetic scattering; numerical methods; radar signature prediction; target identification. *Mailing Add:* Dept Elec & Comput Eng Univ Tex Eng Sci Bldg Austin TX 78712. *Fax:* 512-471-5445; *E-Mail:* ling@ling0.ece.utexas.edu

LING, HARRY WILSON, INORGANIC CHEMISTRY. *Current Pos:* Res chemist, Pigments Dept, Res Div, E I DuPont de Nemours & Co, Inc, 54-64, tech serv chemist, Sales Div, 64-67, sr res chemist, 67-69, supvr, 69-72, prod mgr, 72-74, MGR TECH SERV, E I DUPONT DE NEMOURS & CO, INC, 74- *Personal Data:* b Painesville, Ohio, Feb 14, 27; div. *Educ:* Bowling Green State Univ, AB, 50; Ohio State Univ, PhD(inorg chem), 54. *Mem:* Am Chem Soc; Fedn Soc Paint Technol; Sigma Xi. *Res:* Inorganic nitrogen chemistry; elemental silicon; anodic oxidation of metal substrates; electrolytic capacitors; titanium dioxide pigments; pigment colors. *Mailing Add:* 2410 Alister Dr Wilmington DE 19808

LING, HSIN YI, MICROPALEONTOLOGY. *Current Pos:* PROF, GEOL DEPT, NORTHERN ILL UNIV, 78- *Personal Data:* b Taiwan, Dec 5, 30; m 58; c 2. *Educ:* Nat Taiwan Univ, BS, 53; Tohoku Univ, MS, 58; Wash Univ, PhD(geol), 63. *Prof Exp:* Instr geol, Nat Taiwan Univ, 54-55; res engr, Res Ctr, Pan Am Petrol Corp, Okla, 60-63; res instr geol oceanog, Dept oceanog, Univ Wash, 63-64, from res asst prof to res assoc prof, 64-74, res prof, 74-78. *Mem:* Fel AAAS; Soc Econ Paleontologists & Mineralogists; Paleont Soc; Paleont Res Inst; Sigma Xi. *Res:* Marine micropaleontology and palynology. *Mailing Add:* Dept Biol Sci Northern Ill Univ W Lincoln Hwy De Kalb IL 60115-2825

LING, HUBERT, MICROBIAL GENETICS, PLANT TISSUE CULTURE. *Current Pos:* ASSOC PROF BIOL, CO COL MORRIS, 83- *Personal Data:* b Chungking, China, Apr 28, 42; US citizen; m 68, Mildred Leung; c Jonathan & Matthew. *Educ:* Queens Col, BS, 63; Brown Univ, MS, 66; Wayne State Univ, PhD(biol), 69; Co Col Morris, RN, 94. *Prof Exp:* Assoc prof biol, Univ Del, 69-77; res microbiologist, E I du Pont, 77-80; sterilization scientist, Johnson & Johnson, Ethicon, 80-81; plant scientist tissue cult, Samsen Lab, 81. *Concurrent Pos:* Consult, Morton Salt Co, 72-74 & Int Chem Co, 74-75. *Mem:* Torrey Bot Club; Am Orchid Soc. *Res:* Genetic control of asexual cell fusion in Myxomycetes; ultrastructure of Myxomycetes; control of sporulation in Myxomyetes; tissue culture propagation of North American terrestrial orchids: Platanthera, Cypripedium and Calopogon. *Mailing Add:* Biol Dept County Col Morris Rte 10 Randolph NJ 07869-2086. *E-Mail:* hling@ccm.edu

LING, HUEI, COMPUTER ARCHITECTURE & LOGIC DESIGN. *Current Pos:* res staff mem, San Jose Res Lab, 65-77, mgr logic design & exp eng, 77-80, DEPT MGR COMPUT ENG, IBM RES CTR, IBM CORP, 80- *Personal Data:* b Fukien, China, Feb 24, 34; m 64. *Educ:* Nat Taiwan Univ, BSc, 57; Univ NB, MSc, 61; Univ Okla, PhD(elec eng), 65. *Prof Exp:* Method supvr, Bell Tel Can, 61; electronic engr, Sundstrand Aviation, 62-63; asst prof, Fla State Univ, 65. *Concurrent Pos:* Adj assoc prof, Fairleigh-Dickinson Univ, Teaneck Campus, 67-68, adj prof, 68. *Mem:* Asn Comput Mach; Inst Elec & Electronics Engrs. *Res:* Computer design. *Mailing Add:* 5 Whippoorwill Rd Chappaqua NY 10514

LING, HUNG CHI, MATERIALS SCIENCE & ELECTRONIC CERAMICS, FIBER OPTICS. *Current Pos:* TECH MGR & DISTINGUISHED MEM TECH STAFF, AT&T BELL LABS ENG RES CTR, PRINCETON, NJ, 81- *Personal Data:* b Wenchow, China, 1950; US citizen; m 79, Gigi Hsu; c Maya, Alicia & Byron. *Educ:* Mass Inst Technol, BS, 72, ScD, 78; State Univ NY, Stony Brook, MA, 74. *Prof Exp:* Res assoc mat sci, Dept Mat Sci & Eng, Mass Inst Technol, 78-81. *Concurrent Pos:* Vis lectr, Shanghai Jiao Tong Univ, Peoples Repub China, 82. *Mem:* Metall Soc Am Inst Mech Engrs; Sigma Xi; Mat Res Soc; fel Am Ceramic Soc; sr mem Inst Elec & Electronics Engrs; Optical Soc Am. *Res:* Solid state phase transformations; thin film materials; electronics ceramics; dielectrics and varistors; superconducting oxides; metal-ceramic interaction; fiber optics; optoelectronics packaging. *Mailing Add:* Lucent Technol Bell Labs PO Box 900 Princeton NJ 08542-0900. *Fax:* 609-639-2343; *E-Mail:* hling@lucent.com

LING, JOSEPH TSO-TI, AIR & WATER POLLUTION & HAZARDOUS WASTE TECHNOLOGY. *Current Pos:* INDEPENDENT CONSULT, 84- *Personal Data:* b Peking, China, June 10, 19; US citizen; m 44, Rose S Hsu; c Lois, Rosa-mei, Louis & Lorraine. *Educ:* Hangchow Christian Col, Shanghai, BS, 44; Univ Minn, Minneapolis, MS, 50, PhD(sanit eng, pub health), 52. *Honors & Awards:* Edward Cleary Award, Am Acad Environ Engrs, 81; First Gold Medal Int Corp Environ Award, World Environ Ctr, 85; Queneau Palladium Medal, Nat Audubon Soc, 90; Leadership Award, Nat Asn Photog Mfrs, 90; Distinguished Award, Ministry Econ Affairs, Taiwan, 93. *Prof Exp:* Dist engr, Nanking-Shanghai RR Syst, 44-47; res asst sanit eng, Univ Minn, 48-52; sr staff engr, Gen Mills, Inc, 53-55; dir, Nat Res Inst Munic Eng, Peking, China, 56-57; prof civil eng, Baptist Univ, Hong Kong, 58-59; mgr, water & sanit eng, 3M Co, 60-65, mgr, sanit & civil eng, 66-69, dir, environ eng & pollution control, 70-74, vpres, environ eng & pollution control, 74-84; exec consult, Community Serv Exec Prog, 84-87. *Concurrent Pos:* Adv, Ohio River Water Sanit Comn, 62-70, Environ Pollution Panel, US Chamber of Com, 67-72 & Tech Contact, Nat Indust Pollution Control Coun, 71-84; President's adv bd air qual, 74-78; mem environ health comt, President's Domestic Policy Rev, 78-80; sci adv bd, US Environ Protection Agency, 84-88; mem, World Environ Ctr, 84-; mem, Am Inst Pollution Prevention, 88-; bd mem, Freshwater Found, 74- *Mem:* Nat Acad Eng; Am Soc Civil Engrs; Air Pollution Control Asn; Water Pollution Control Fedn; Am Water Works Asn; Am Acad Environ Engrs. *Res:* Water filtration and related purification processes; biological oxidation and advanced treatment technology for water pollution control; thermo-oxidation, control techniques in air pollution and solid and hazardous waste disposal; waste minimization technologies. *Mailing Add:* 2090 Arcade St St Paul MN 55109

LING, NICHOLAS CHI-KWAN, PEPTIDE CHEMISTRY, PEPTIDE HORMONES. *Current Pos:* dir peptide chem, 94-95, SR DIR PEPTIDE CHEM, NEUROCRINE BIOSCI, INC, 96- *Personal Data:* b Hong Kong, Aug 15, 40; m 71, Betty Lee; c Aaron. *Educ:* San Jose State Univ, BS, 64; Stanford Univ, PhD(org chem), 69. *Honors & Awards:* Sidney H Ingbar Distinguished Serv Award, Endocrine Soc, 94. *Prof Exp:* Res assoc crystallog, Stanford Univ, 69-70; res assoc biochem, Stalk Inst, 70-73, asst res prof, 74-78, assoc res prof, 79-88; sr mem, Whittier Inst, 89-93. *Concurrent Pos:* Mem, Endocrinol Study Sect, NIH, 90-93. *Mem:* Am Chem Soc; AAAS; Protein Soc; Endocrine Soc; Am Soc Biol Chem; Soc Neurosci. *Res:* Isolation and characterization of peptide hormones; synthesis of peptides by solid phase methodology; peptide sequence determination by mass spectrometry and Edman technique; biological function of peptide hormones. *Mailing Add:* Neurocrine Biosci Inc 3050 Sci Park Rd San Diego CA 92121

LING, ROBERT FRANCIS, STATISTICS. *Current Pos:* assoc prof, 75-76, PROF STATIST, CLEMSON UNIV, 77- *Personal Data:* b Hong Kong, Apr 21, 39; US citizen; m 63; c 1. *Educ:* Berea Col, BA, 61; Univ Tenn, MA, 63; Yale Univ, MPhil, 68, PhD(statist), 70. *Honors & Awards:* Frank Wilcoxon Prize, 84. *Prof Exp:* Asst prof math, E Tenn State Univ, 64-66; from instr to asst prof statist, Univ Chicago, 70-75. *Concurrent Pos:* Vis prof, Owen Grad Sch Bus, 82, Grad Sch Bus, Univ Chicago, 83, Mass Inst Technol, 89, Harvard, 90; assoc ed, J Am Statist Asn, 77-85; vis lectr, Comt Pres Statist Socs, 83-86; mem coun, Classification Soc NAm, 74-77, prog chmn, 82 & 89, bd dirs, 88-90. *Mem:* Fel Am Statist Asn; Classification Soc NAm. *Res:* Applied statistics; statistical computing; interactive data analysis; regression diagnostics. *Mailing Add:* Dept Math Sci Clemson Univ Clemson SC 29632-0001. *Fax:* 864-654-4755; *E-Mail:* rfling@clemson.clemson.edu

LING, RUNG TAI, COMPUTATIONAL ELECTROMAGNETICS, COMPUTATIONAL FLUID DYNAMICS. *Current Pos:* SR TECH SPECIALIST, NORTHROP GRUMMAN CORP, 84- *Personal Data:* b Taipei, Taiwan, July 28, 43; US citizen. *Educ:* Nat Taiwan Univ, BS, 65; Univ Mo, Columbia, MS, 68; Univ Calif, San Diego, PhD(physics), 72. *Prof Exp:* Lectr physics, San Diego State Univ, 72-73; res fel, Calif Inst Technol, 73-76; sr res scientist, STD Res Corp, 76-78 & R & D Assoc, 78-81; sr res specialist, Lockheed Corp, 81-84. *Concurrent Pos:* Mem, Electromagnetics Acad, 90. *Mem:* Am Phys Soc. *Res:* Computational physics including numerical solutions and modelling of atomic and molecular physics problems; electromagnetic and acoustic scattering phenomena; fluid dynamics including magnetohydrodynamics and radiation hydrodynamics. *Mailing Add:* 4715 Lasheart Dr La Canada CA 91011

LING, TA-YUNG, ELEMENTARY PARTICLE PHYSICS. *Current Pos:* from asst prof to assoc prof, 77-83, PROF PHYSICS, OHIO STATE UNIV, COLUMBUS, 83- *Personal Data:* b Shianghai, China, Feb 2, 43; US citizen; m 69; c 3. *Educ:* Tunghai Univ, Taiwan, BS, 64; Univ Waterloo, Ont, MS, 66; Univ Wis-Madison, PhD(physics), 71. *Honors & Awards:* Outstanding Jr Investr, Dept Energy, 77. *Prof Exp:* Teaching asst physics, Univ Waterloo, Can, 65-66; teaching asst physics, Univ Wis-Madison, 66-67, res asst, 67-71; res assoc physics, Univ Pa, 72-75, asst prof, 75-77. *Mem:* Am Phys Soc. *Res:* Experimental high energy physics: deep inelastic neutrino- nucleon scattering, neutrino masses and mixing, neutrino oscillations, deep inelastic electron-proton scattering, high energy proton-proton collisions. *Mailing Add:* Dept Physics Smith Lab Ohio State Univ 174 W 18th Ave Columbus OH 43210

LING, VICTOR, EXPERIMENTAL THERAPEUTICS. *Current Pos:* VPRES RES, BC CANCER RES CTR, 96-; PROF, DEPT PATH & BIOCHEM, UNIV BC, 96- *Personal Data:* b Mar 16, 43. *Educ:* Univ Toronto, BS, 66; Univ BC, PhD (biochem) 69. *Honors & Awards:* Cancer Res Award, Milken Family Med Found, 88; Kettering Prize, Gen Motors Cancer Res Found, 91; Int Award, Gairdner Found, 92; Bruce F Cain Mem Award, Am Asn Cancer Res, 93. *Prof Exp:* Staff scientist, Ont Cancer Inst, 71-96; prof med biophys, Univ Toronto, 83-96, head, Div Molecular & Struct Biol, 89-96. *Concurrent Pos:* Bd govs, Wellesly Hosp Res Inst, 88-90; mem, Coun Sch Grad Studies, Univ Toronto, 84, Fac Med Res Comt, 85-, vchmn, 88-; mem, Study Sect Exp Therapeut, NIH, 86-, bd sci coun, Dir Cancer Treatment, 90-;

Scholar Comt, Med Res Coun, Can, 88-; bd dirs, Hosp Sick Children Found, Am Asn Cancer Res & Can Cancer Soc, 92- *Mem:* Fel Royal Soc Can; Am Asn Cancer Res; Am Soc Cell Biol; Can Cancer Soc; Can Soc Cell Biol; Can Biochem Soc. *Res:* Cellular physiology; molecular pharmacology. *Mailing Add:* BC Cancer Res Ctr 601 W Tenth Ave Vancouver BC V5Z 1L3 Can

LINGAFELTER, EDWARD CLAY, JR, CHEMISTRY. *Current Pos:* Assoc phys chem, 39-41, from instr to prof, 41-84, assoc dean, Grad Sch, 60-68, EMER PROF CHEM, UNIV WASH, 84- *Personal Data:* b Toledo, Ohio, Mar 28, 14; m 38, Roberta C Kneedler; c Robert E, Thomas E, James E, Richard E & Daniel E. *Educ:* Univ Calif, BS, 35, PhD(chem), 39. *Mem:* AAAS; Am Chem Soc; Am Crystallog Asn (pres, 74); Sigma Xi. *Res:* Colloidal electrolytes; crystal structure of paraffin-chain compounds; structure of coordination compounds; hydrogen bond. *Mailing Add:* Dept Chem BG-10 Univ Wash Box 351700 Seattle WA 98195-0001

LINGANE, JAMES JOSEPH, analytical chemistry; deceased, see previous edition for last biography

LINGANE, PETER JAMES, ELECTROCHEMISTRY, HYDROMETALLURGY. *Current Pos:* SUPVR, STAND ALASKA PROD CO, 84- *Personal Data:* b Oakland, Calif, May 12, 40; m 67; c 2. *Educ:* Harvard Univ, AB, 62; Calif Inst Technol, PhD(chem), 66. *Prof Exp:* Asst prof chem, Univ Minn, Minneapolis, 66-70; sr chemist, Ledgemont Lab, Kennecott Copper Corp, 70-77; group leader, Prod Res Div, Conoco, 77-84. *Mem:* Am Chem Soc; Soc Petrol Engrs. *Res:* Chemistry related to the solution mining of nonferrous ore minerals and to enhanced oil recovery, specifically carbon dioxide flooding; kinetics and mechanisms of solution reactions with particular emphasis upon the reactions which surround electrode processes; phase behavior of hydro carbon systems. *Mailing Add:* 852 Acampo Dr Lafayette CA 94549-5040

LINGAPPA, BANADAKOPPA THIMMAPPA, MICROBIOLOGY. *Current Pos:* from asst prof to assoc prof, 62-68, PROF BIOL, COL HOLY CROSS, 68- *Personal Data:* b Mysore, India, Mar 19, 27; nat US; m 53; c 3. *Educ:* Benaras Hindu Univ, BSc, 50, MSc, 52; Purdue Univ, PhD, 57. *Prof Exp:* Lectr mycol, Benaras Hindu Univ, 52-53; res asst, Purdue Univ, 53-57; res assoc, Univ Mich, 57-59 & res assoc, Mich State Univ, 59-60, asst prof med mycol, 60; Nat Inst Sci India sr res fel, Bot Lab, Univ Madras, 61; asst prof, Mich State Univ, 61-62. *Concurrent Pos:* Vis scientist, Mass Inst Technol, 68-69; vis prof, Inst Gen Bot, Univ Geneva, 69-70; vis scientist, Worc Found Exp Biol, 76-77, Harvard Univ, 88; fac fel, Col Holy Cross, 70 & 88. *Mem:* Mycol Soc Am; Am Soc Microbiol; Sigma Xi; AAAS; Am Phytopath Soc. *Res:* Physiology of fungi, dormancy and germination of spores; methane production by anaerobic fermentation of solid waste; molecular biology. *Mailing Add:* 4 McGill St Worcester MA 01607

LINGAPPA, JAISRI RAO, INFECTIOUS DISEASES. *Current Pos:* Resident internal med, 87-90, INFECTIOUS DIS FEL, DEPT MED, UNIV CALIF, SAN FRANCISCO, 90- *Personal Data:* b Ann Arbor, Mich, June 11, 59. *Educ:* Swarthmore Col, BA, 79; Harvard Univ, PhD(cell biol), 85; Univ Mass, Worcester, MD, 87. *Honors & Awards:* Am Med Women's Asn Award, 87. *Mem:* Sigma Xi. *Mailing Add:* 49 Cragmont Ave San Francisco CA 94116-1309

LINGAPPA, YAMUNA, MICROBIOLOGY. *Current Pos:* RES ASSOC BIOL, COL HOLY CROSS, 63- *Personal Data:* b Mysore, India, Dec 6, 29; nat US; m 53; c 3. *Educ:* Mysore Univ, BSc, 49; Madras Univ, BT, 51; Purdue Univ, MS, 55, PhD, 58. *Prof Exp:* Res assoc, Univ Mich, 57-59 & Mich State Univ, 59-60; sci pool officer, Govt India, 61. *Concurrent Pos:* Vis scientist, Inst Bot, Univ Geneva, 69-70; instr human nutrit, Clark Univ & Worcester State Col, 74; res consult, Dept Pub Health, City Worcester; fac adv, Undergrad Res Partic Proj Methane Generation, Col Holy Cross, vis lectr nutrit & world hunger, 78; comnr, Gov's Comn on Status of Women, Mass, 77-79. *Mem:* Mycol Soc Am; Am Soc Microbiol; Sigma Xi; Am Inst Biol Sci. *Res:* Human nutrition; solid waste disposal; physiology of pathogenic fungi; microbial interactions. *Mailing Add:* Four McGill St Worcester MA 01607

LINGELBACH, D(ANIEL) D(EE), ELECTROMECHANICAL ENERGY CONVERSION. *Current Pos:* asst prof, 55-61, assoc prof, 61-79, prof elec eng, 79-86, EMER PROF ELEC & COMPUT ENG, OKLA STATE UNIV, 86- *Personal Data:* b Wilkinsburg, Pa, Oct 4, 25; m 49, Ruby E Dickey; c Jean M, Dickey L & David G. *Educ:* Kans State Col, BSEE, 47, MS, 48; Okla State Univ, PhD, 60. *Honors & Awards:* Charles Schneider Award, Nat Asn Relay Mfrs, 68. *Prof Exp:* From instr to asst prof elec eng, Univ Ark, 48-55. *Mem:* Am Soc Eng Educ; Nat Soc Prof Engrs; Inst Elec & Electronics Engrs; Sigma Xi. *Res:* Electric power system modeling and optimization; power systems analysis. *Mailing Add:* 1116 S Gray St Stillwater OK 74074. *Fax:* 405-744-7554

LINGENFELTER, RICHARD EMERY, ASTROPHYSICS, COSMIC RAY PHYSICS. *Current Pos:* RES PHYSICIST, CTR ASTROPHYS & SPACE SCI, UNIV CALIF, SAN DIEGO, 79- *Personal Data:* b Farmington, NMex, Apr 5, 34; m 57, Naomi Brefka; c Andrea & Kendale. *Educ:* Univ Calif, Los Angeles, AB, 56. *Prof Exp:* Physicist, Lawrence Radiation Lab, Univ Calif, 57-62; assoc res geophysicist, Univ Calif, Los Angeles, 62-66, res geophysicist, Inst Geophys & Planetary Physics, 66-69, prof in residence, Dept Geophys & Space Physics, 69-79 & Dept Astron, 74-79. *Concurrent Pos:* Fulbright res fel geophys & planetary physics, Tata Inst Fundamental Res, Bombay, India, 68-69. *Mem:* Fel Am Phys Soc; Int Astron Union; Am Astron Soc. *Res:* Cosmic ray origins and interactions; gamma ray astronomy; solar flare particle interactions; planetology; radiocarbon variations. *Mailing Add:* Ctr Astrophys & Space Sci Univ Calif San Diego La Jolla CA 92093-0424. *Fax:* 619-534-2294; *E-Mail:* rlingenfelter@ucsc.edu

LINGG, AL J, MICROBIOLOGY. *Current Pos:* PROF MICROBIOL, UNIV IDAHO, 69- *Personal Data:* b Mt Hope, Kans, Mar 26, 38; m 61; c 3. *Educ:* Kans State Univ, BS, 64, MS, 66, PhD(microbiol), 69. *Prof Exp:* Instr, Kans State Univ, 66-68. *Concurrent Pos:* Fulbright lectr, Nepal, 79-80. *Mem:* Sigma Xi; Am Soc Microbiol. *Res:* Environmental microbiology; water quality; fungal insect pathogens. *Mailing Add:* 839 Indian Hills Dr Moscow ID 83843

LINGLE, SARAH ELIZABETH, PHYSIOLOGY, BIOCHEMISTRY. *Current Pos:* res assoc, Fargo, ND, 82-84, actg res leader, Weslaco, 91-92, PLANT PHYSIOLOGIST, USDA, AGR RES SERV, WESLACO, TEX, 84- *Personal Data:* b Woodland, Calif, July 22, 55; m 89, Thomas P Washington IV. *Educ:* Univ Calif, Davis, BS, 77; Univ Nebr, MS, 78; Wash State Univ, PhD(agron), 82. *Prof Exp:* Res asst, Univ Nebr, 77-78; teaching asst plant breeding, Wash State Univ, 79-80, res asst, 79-82. *Mem:* Am Soc Agron; Crop Sci Soc Am; Am Soc Plant Physiologists; AAAS; Sigma Xi. *Res:* Physiology and biochemistry of sucrose accumulation in sugarcane, specifically the transport and metabolism of sucrose and how it relates to the balance between growth and storage in the stalk. *Mailing Add:* USDA Agr Res Serv Weslaco TX 78596

LINGREL, JERRY B, MOLECULAR GENETICS. *Current Pos:* From asst prof to prof biol chem, 62-81, PROF & CHMN MOLECULAR GENETICS, BIOCHEM & MICROBIOL, UNIV CINCINNATI, 81- *Personal Data:* b Byhalia, Ohio, July 13, 35; m 58; c 2. *Educ:* Otterbein Col, BS, 57; Ohio State Univ, PhD(biochem), 60. *Honors & Awards:* George Rieveschl Award. *Concurrent Pos:* Fel biol, Calif Inst Technol, 60-62. *Mem:* Am Soc Biol Chemists; Am Soc Cell Biol. *Res:* Regulation of gene expression in animal cells; hemoglobin biosynthesis; messenger RNA; gene structure. *Mailing Add:* Dept Micro & Molecular Genetics Univ Cincinnati Col Med PO Box 670524 Cincinnati OH 45267-0524

LINGREN, WESLEY EARL, PHYSICAL CHEMISTRY, OCEANOGRAPHY. *Current Pos:* from asst prof to assoc prof, 62-68, chmn dept, 68-73, PROF CHEM, SEATTLE PAC UNIV, 68-, DIR GEN HONORS, 70-, DEAN SCH SCI, 90- *Personal Data:* b Pasadena, Calif, Aug 27, 30; m 61; c 2. *Educ:* Seattle Pac Col, BS, 52; Univ Wash, MS, 54, PhD(electrochem), 62. *Prof Exp:* Instr phys sci, Pasadena Col, 56-58. *Concurrent Pos:* Res assoc, US Naval Radiol Defense Lab, 63-69; NSF fel, Yale Univ, 67-68, Solar Energy Res Inst, 84. *Mem:* Am Chem Soc; Sigma Xi. *Res:* Rates of electrode reactions; electroanalytical chemistry; oxidation states of elements in seawater oceanography. *Mailing Add:* 10628 NE 16th St Bellevue WA 98004

LINGWOOD, CLIFFORD ALAN, PROTEIN-GLYCOLIPID INTERACTIONS. *Current Pos:* res fel, Debt Biochem, Univ Toronto, 77-80, asst prof, Dept Clin Biochem, 83-89, asst prof, Dept Biochem, 84-89, ASSOC PROF, DEPT CLIN BIOCHEM, BIOCHEM & MICROBIOL, UNIV TORONTO, 89-, PROF, DEPT PATH & LAB MED & BIOCHEM, 97-; SR SCIENTIST, RES INST, DIV MICROBIOL, DEPT PEDIAT LAB MED & BIOCHEM, HOSP SICK CHILDREN, 89-, PROF, DEPT PEDIAT LAB MED, 97- *Personal Data:* b Dorset, Eng, Jan 2, 50; m 74; c 3. *Educ:* Univ Hull, BSc, 71; Univ London, PhD(cell biol), 75. *Prof Exp:* Res fel, Dept Pathobiol, Univ Wash, Seattle, 75-76; vis scientist, Dept Biochem Oncol, Fred Hutchinson Cancer Res Ctr, Seattle, Wash, 76-77; res fel, Dept Biochem, Hospital Sick Children, Toronto, 77-81, Med Res Coun scholar, 81-86, asst prof, 82-89, asst prof, Dept Microbiol, 87-89; res fel, 77-81, asst prof, dept biochem, Hosp Sick Children, Toronto, 81-, assoc prof, dept microbiol, 87- *Mem:* Am Soc Cell Biol; Soc Complex Carbohydrates; Am Soc Microbiol; Can Biochem Soc. *Res:* Metabolism and function of cell membrane sulfoglycolipids during spermatogenesis fertilization; glycolipid receptors for microorganisms; glycolipid binding by bacterial toxins. *Mailing Add:* Dept Pediat Lab Med Div Microbiol Hosp Sick Children 555 University Ave Toronto ON M5G 1X8 Can. *Fax:* 416-813-5993; *E-Mail:* cling@sickkids.on.ca

LINHARDT, ROBERT JOHN, BIOPOLYMER CARBOHYDRATE CHEMISTRY, APPLIED ENZYMOLOGY. *Current Pos:* from asst prof to assoc prof, 82-89, PROF MED CHEM & NATURAL PRODS CHEM, COL PHARM, UNIV IOWA, 89-, PROF CHEM & BIOCHEM ENG, 96- *Personal Data:* b Passaic, NJ, Oct 18, 53; m 75, Kathryn Burns; c Kelley & Barbara. *Educ:* Marquette Univ, BS, 75; Johns Hopkins Univ, MA, 77, PhD(org chem), 79. *Honors & Awards:* Horace S Isbell Award, Am Chem Soc, 94. *Prof Exp:* Res assoc, Dept Appl Biol, Biochem Eng Labs, Mass Inst Technol 79-81, Johnson & Johnson fel, Whitaker Col Health Sci, Technol & Mgt, 81-82. *Concurrent Pos:* F Wendell Miller distinguished prof, Univ Iowa, 96. *Mem:* Am Chem Soc; AAAS. *Res:* Bio-organic chemistry and applied enzymology in the study of the structure-activity-relationship of complex polysaccharides; biopolymeric drugs and carbohydrate chemistry. *Mailing Add:* Dept Med Chem & Natural Prods Univ Iowa Col Pharm Iowa City IA 52242. *Fax:* 319-335-6634; *E-Mail:* robert-linhardt@uiowa.edu

LINHART, YAN BOHUMIL, EVOLUTION, ECOLOGY. *Current Pos:* asst specialist, 65-66, from asst prof to assoc prof, 71-83, PROF BIOL, UNIV COLO, BOULDER, 83- *Personal Data:* b Prague, Czech, Oct 8, 39; US citizen. *Educ:* Rutgers Univ, New Brunswick, BS, 61; Yale Univ, MF, 63;

Univ Calif, Berkeley, PhD(genetics), 72. *Prof Exp:* Jr specialist forest genetics, Sch Forestry, Univ Calif, Berkeley, 63-65. *Concurrent Pos:* Res grant, Univ Colo, Boulder, 71-73; Colo Energy Res Inst grant, 75-76; NSF grants, 75-78, 78-80, 81-84 & 85-90; Nat Geog Soc grant, 84-85. *Mem:* AAAS; Am Inst Biol Sci; Brit Ecol Soc; Soc Study Evolution; Soc Am Foresters; Asn Trop Biol; Am Soc Naturalists; Bot Soc Am; Ecol Soc Am. *Res:* Adaptation; population biology; reproductive biology of plants; pollination biology; forest biology; plant biogeography. *Mailing Add:* EPO Biol Univ Colo Boulder PO Box 334 Boulder CO 80309-0334

LINHOLM, L W, ELECTRICAL ENGINEERING. *Current Pos:* GROUP LEADER INTEGRATED CIRCUITS TECHNOL GROUP, NAT INST STAND & TECHNOL, 78- *Personal Data:* b Nov 14, 45. *Educ:* Univ Md, MA, 73. *Mailing Add:* Nat Inst Stand & Technol Integrated Circuits Technol Group Gaithersburg MD 20899

LININGER, LLOYD LESLEY, MATHEMATICS, MATHEMATICAL STATISTICS. *Current Pos:* ASSOC PROF MATH, STATE UNIV NY, ALBANY, 70- *Personal Data:* b Iowa City, Iowa, Mar 13, 39; m 59; c 3. *Educ:* Univ Iowa, PhD(math), 64. *Prof Exp:* Asst prof math, Univ Mo, 64-65; asst to Prof Montgomery, Inst Advan Study, Princeton Univ, 65-67; res instr, Univ Mich, 67-70. *Concurrent Pos:* Statistician, Biometry Sect, NIH, Bethesda, 77-78; statistician, Environ Protection Agency, 85-88. *Mem:* Am Math Soc; Am Statist Asn; Am Pub Health Asn. *Res:* Applications of statistics; biostatistics. *Mailing Add:* Dept Math State Univ NY Albany 1400 Washington Ave Albany NY 12222-1000

LINK, BERNARD ALVIN, MEAT SCIENCE, FOOD SCIENCE. *Current Pos:* res biochemist, 73-77, MGR, PROTEIN RES, CARGILL INC, 77- *Personal Data:* b Columbus, Wis, Mar 23, 41. *Educ:* Univ Wis-Madison, BS, 62, MS, 64, PhD(meat & animal sci), 68. *Prof Exp:* Res asst meat sci, Univ Wis-Madison, 62-68; Welch Found fel, Tex A&M Univ, 68-72, res scientist meat chem, 70-72, res assoc biochem & biophys, 72-73. *Mem:* Am Meat Sci Asn; Sigma Xi; Am Asn Cereal Chemists; Inst Food Technol. *Res:* Soy protein products. *Mailing Add:* 108 Gibson Ave Wilmington DE 19803-4910

LINK, CONRAD BARNETT, HORTICULTURE. *Current Pos:* prof, 48-82, EMER PROF HORT, UNIV MD, COLLEGE PARK, 82- *Personal Data:* b Dunkirk, NY, Mar 5, 12; m 40, 49, Kathleen Barber; c Helen, Leora A & Conrad O. *Educ:* Ohio State Univ, BS, 33, MS, 34, PhD(hort), 40. *Honors & Awards:* Ware Award, Am Soc Hort Sci, L H Vaughan Award. *Prof Exp:* Hybridist, Good & Reese Co, Ohio, 34-35; asst hort, Ohio State Univ, 35-38, exten specialist, 39-40; from instr to asst prof floricult, Pa State Univ, 38-45; horticulturist, Brooklyn Bot Garden, 45-48. *Mem:* Fel AAAS; fel Am Soc Hort Sci; Bot Soc Am; Am Hort Soc (secy, 48-49); Int Soc Hort Sci; Soc Econ Bot. *Res:* Photoperiodism; plant anatomy, nutrition and plant propagation of greenhouse and nursery crops. *Mailing Add:* Dept Hort Plant Sci Bldg Univ Md College Park MD 20742-5611. *Fax:* 301-314-9308

LINK, GORDON LITTLEPAGE, PHYSICAL CHEMISTRY. *Current Pos:* RETIRED. *Personal Data:* b Charleston, WVa, Feb 9, 32; m 55; c 1. *Educ:* Col William & Mary, BS, 54; Univ Va, PhD(phys chem), 58. *Prof Exp:* mem tech staff, Bell Labs, Inc, 58-87. *Mem:* Sigma Xi. *Res:* Dielectrics. *Mailing Add:* Tingley Rd PO Box 87 Brookside NJ 07926

LINK, JOHN CLARENCE, ELECTROMAGNETIC REFLECTORS. *Current Pos:* RETIRED. *Personal Data:* b Iowa, Jan 5, 08; m 36, Melita Haardt; c Joseph (deceased), James & Melita. *Educ:* Creighton Univ, AB, 28; Cath Univ Am, MA, 29. *Prof Exp:* Electronic scientist, US Dept Navy, 29-64, consult, Naval Res Lab, 55-64; mgr missile projs, Aerospace Corp, 64-66; mem staff, Avco Missile Systs Div, 66-68; independent consult electromagnetic reflectors, 68-81. *Res:* Countermeasures; electromagnetic reflectors; energy conversion. *Mailing Add:* 6413 Halleck St District Heights MD 20747

LINK, PETER K, GEOLOGY, METEOROLOGY. *Current Pos:* CONSULT, 73- *Personal Data:* b Batavia, Java, Nov 7, 30; US citizen; m 90; c 2. *Educ:* Univ Wis, BS, 53, MS, 55, PhD(stratig geol), 61. *Prof Exp:* Geologist, Esso Stand Inc, Libya, 57-58, party chief, 58-59, subsurface geologist, 59-60, regional geologist, 60-61; regional geologist, Humble Oil & Refining Co, Okla, 62-63; res geologist, Atlantic Richfield Co, Dallas, 65-68, sr res geophysicist, 68-70; sr res scientist, Amoco Prod Co, 70-73. *Concurrent Pos:* Adj prof geol, Univ Tulsa, 74-77; found mem, Associated Resource Consult Inc, Tulsa, 79; staff instr, Oil & Gas Consult Int, Inc, Tulsa, 79- *Mem:* Am Asn Petrol Geologists; fel Geol Soc Am. *Res:* Stratigraphy; structure; tectonics; field, regional, well site, subsurface and petroleum geology; research operations; stratigraphic-seismic research exploration; exploration programs; sedimentation; photogeology; minerals and petroleum exploration; author one book. *Mailing Add:* 7637 S Centaur Dr Evergreen CO 80439

LINK, WILLIAM B, ANALYTICAL CHEMISTRY, ORGANIC CHEMISTRY. *Current Pos:* RETIRED. *Personal Data:* b Darke, WVa, Mar 25, 28; m 56, Ruby J Burton; c Wesley B, Gregory C & David G. *Educ:* Shepherd Col, BS, 53. *Prof Exp:* Med technician, Baker Vet Ctr, Martinsburg, WVa, 55; chemist, US Food & Drug Admin, 55-57, anal chemist, 57-62, supvy chemist, 62-63, supvy anal res chemist, 63-85. *Res:* Chemistry of all color additives used in foods, drugs and cosmetics. *Mailing Add:* 4113 LaMarre Dr Fairfax VA 22030

LINK, WILLIAM EDWARD, ANALYTICAL CHEMISTRY. *Current Pos:* DIR RES & DEVELOP, SHEREX CHEM CO, 79- *Personal Data:* b Ironwood, Mich, Jan 24, 21; m 47; c 2. *Educ:* Northland Col, BA, 42; Univ Wis, MS, 51, PhD, 54. *Prof Exp:* Asst prof chem, Northland Col, 47-52; group leader, Res Lab, ADM Chem, 54-69, group leader, Res Ctr, Ashland Chem Co, 69-71, mgr, Anal Chem Res & Develop Div, Ashland Oil & Refining Co Ohio, 71-76, res mgr, Chem Prod Div, 76-78. *Concurrent Pos:* Ed, Off & Tentative Methods, Am Oil Chemists Soc, 71- *Mem:* Am Chem Soc; Am Oil Chemists Soc (pres, 75-76). *Res:* Organic analytical research; fats and oils chemistry; industrial fatty derivatives; specialty chemicals; fatty nitrogen chemicals; industrial fatty derivatives analysis; resin analysis. *Mailing Add:* 6039 Sedgwick Rd Columbus OH 43235

LINKE, HARALD ARTHUR BRUNO, MICROBIOLOGY. *Current Pos:* from asst prof to assoc prof, 73-85, PROF, DEPT MICROBIOL, NY UNIV DENT CTR, 85- *Personal Data:* b Bautzen, Ger, Aug 18, 36; m 71; c 1. *Educ:* Univ Berlin, BSc, 61; Univ Gottingen, MSc, 63, PhD(biochem, microbiol), 67. *Prof Exp:* Res assoc enzym, Univ Gottingen, 66-67; fel biochem, Rutgers Univ New Brunswick, 67-69; res microbiologist, Allied Chem Corp, 69-72; res assoc, Inst Microbiol, Rutgers Univ, 72-73. *Concurrent Pos:* Referee, Zentralblatt Bakteriologie II. Abteilung, 66- *Mem:* NY Acad Sci; Am Soc Microbiol; Ger Chem Soc; Am Asn Dental Res; Europ Orgn Caries Res. *Res:* Isolation and characterization of enzymes; utilizing isotope techniques in the study of microorganisms; biosynthesis and biodegradation of chemical and natural compounds; taxonomy of streptococci; etiology of dental caries and periodontal disease; artificial sweeteners. *Mailing Add:* Dept Microbiol NY Univ Dent Ctr 421 First Ave New York NY 10010

LINKE, RICHARD ALAN, HARDWARE SYSTEMS. *Current Pos:* SR RES SCIENTIST, NEC RES INST, 89- *Personal Data:* b Plainfield, NJ, Feb 15, 46; m 67; c 2. *Educ:* Columbia Col, BA, 68, MS, 70, PhD(physics), 72. *Honors & Awards:* Traveling Lectr Award, Inst Elec & Electronic Engrs/Lazers & Electro-optics Soc. *Prof Exp:* Mem tech staff radio physics res, Bell Tel Labs, 72-86, head, Lightware Commun Res Dept, 86-89. *Mem:* Fel Optical Soc Am; fel Inst Elec & Electronics Engrs. *Res:* Application of optical communications techniques to computing; optical fiber communications systems; development of low noise millimeter wave receivers. *Mailing Add:* Eight Anderson St Princeton NJ 08611

LINKE, SIMPSON, ELECTRICAL ENGINEERING EDUCATION. *Current Pos:* From instr to prof, 46-86, asst dir lab plasma, 67-75, acting dir, 75-76, coordr Elec Eng Grad Studies, 81-84, EMER PROF ELEC ENG, CORNELL UNIV, 86- *Personal Data:* b Jellico, Tenn, Aug 10, 17; m 46; c 2. *Educ:* Univ Tenn, BS, 41; Cornell Univ, MEE, 49. *Concurrent Pos:* Consult, Philadelphia Elec Co, 56-57, Brookhaven Nat Labs, 76-80 & NMex Pub Serv Comn, 80-82; chief investr, NSF res grant, 61-64, prog mgr, NSF, 71-72; mem, US Nat Comt, Int Conf Large Elec Systs, 63-88; Attwood assoc, US Nat Comt, Int Conference Large Elec Systs, 88- *Mem:* Inst Elec & Electronics Engrs; Sigma Xi. *Res:* Transient stability of synchronous machines; energy conversion, electric energy systems; high voltage direct current transmission; electric power transmission. *Mailing Add:* 383 The Parkway Ithaca NY 14850-2275

LINKE, WILLIAM FINAN, PHYSICAL CHEMISTRY. *Current Pos:* group leader phys chem, Am Cyanamid Co, 57-59, group leader paper chem, 59-64, mgr res & develop paper & film chem, 65-67, tech dir paper chem dept, 67-70, dir res, Indust Chem & Plastics Div, 71, dir, Stamford Res Ctr, 72-79, dir, technol assessment & licensing, 80-85, DIR, CHEM RES DIV, AM CYANAMID CO, 86- *Personal Data:* b Ravena, NY, Aug 5, 24; m 49, Ruth A Renz; c William, Robert & Jennifer. *Educ:* City Col New York, BS, 45; NY Univ, MS, 46, PhD(chem), 48. *Prof Exp:* Asst chem, NY Univ, 45-48, from instr to asst prof, 48-57. *Concurrent Pos:* Adv comt, Univ Conn. *Mem:* AAAS; Am Chem Soc; Tech Asn Pulp & Paper Indust; Soc Chem Indust; Indust Res Inst. *Res:* Solubilities; phase equilibria; polyelectrolytes; stability of colloids; flocculation; adsorption; mining and paper chemicals; sizing; polymers; monomers; petrochemical processes; refinery catalysts; auto exhaust catalysts; research management and direction. *Mailing Add:* 75 Ridgecrest Rd Stamford CT 06903-3120

LINKER, ALFRED, BIOCHEMISTRY, CARBOHYDRATE CHEMISTRY. *Current Pos:* res prof biochem & path, 60-64, assoc res prof biochem, 64-72, ASSOC PROF PATH, COL MED, UNIV UTAH, 64-; RES PROF BIOCHEM, 72- *Personal Data:* b Vienna, Austria, Nov 23, 19; US citizen; m 54; c 2. *Educ:* City Col New York, BS, 49; Columbia Univ, PhD(biochem), 54. *Prof Exp:* Assoc biochem, Columbia Univ, 56-59. *Concurrent Pos:* Res biochemist, Vet Admin Hosp, Salt Lake City, 60- *Mem:* Am Soc Biol Chemists; AAAS. *Res:* Structure, function and metabolism of the glycosaminoglycans of connective tissue, including studies of heparin, heparitin sulfate, the chondroitin sulfates, hyaluronic acid, and a variety of degradative enzymes isolated from mammalian and bacterial sources. *Mailing Add:* Vet Admin Hosp Res Serv 151 E Salt Lake City UT 84148-0001

LINKER-ISRAELI, MARIANA, AUTOIMMUNE DISEASE, CYTOKINES. *Current Pos:* RES SCIENTIST, CEDARS SINAI MED CTR, 89-; ASSOC PROF MED, UNIV CALIF, LOS ANGELES, 95- *Personal Data:* b Bucharest, Romania, Sept 1, 39; US citizen; m 66, Leonard; c Dana & Sharon. *Educ:* Hebrew Univ, Jerusalem, Israel, BSc, 62, MSc, 65; Weizman Inst, Rehovot, Israel, PhD(immunol), 72. *Prof Exp:* From asst prof to assoc prof med, Univ Southern Calif, 81-89. *Mem:* Am Asn Immunologists. *Res:* Immune regulation; regulation of cytokine expression and other genes that contribute to dysregulated responses in autoimmune diseases. *Mailing Add:* Dept Med/Rheumatol Cedars-Sinai Med Ctr 8700 Beverly Pl D-5073 Los Angeles CA 90048. *Fax:* 310-652-8411; *E-Mail:* linker@csmc.edu

LINKINS, ARTHUR EDWARD, BIOLOGY. *Current Pos:* chmn, Dept Biol, 85-92, BAYARD D & VIRGINIA C CLARKSON PROF BIOL, CLARKSON UNIV, POTSDAM, NY, 85-, DEAN, SCH SCI, 89-, VPRES, ACAD AFFAIRS, 93-, ASSOC COL INDEPENDENT SCHOLAR. *Personal Data:* b Middletown, Ohio, Jan 13, 45; m 74; c 2. *Educ:* Dartmouth Col, AB, 67; Univ Mass, Amherst, PhD(bot), 73. *Prof Exp:* Fel plant physiol, Dept Plant Sci, Univ Calif, Riverside, 72-74; from asst prof to assoc prof, Dept Biol Va Polytech Inst & State Univ, Blacksburg, Va, 74-85. *Concurrent Pos:* Adj assoc prof, Inst Arctic Biol, Univ Alaska, 80-, sr res prof, 80-91. *Mem:* Am Soc Microbiol; Soil Sci Soc Am; Mycological Soc Am; AAAS; Am Inst Biol Sci. *Res:* Fungal physiological ecology: role of temperature in regulation of physiology and role of temperature, oxygen, and substrate quality in regulation of fungal associated decomposition of organic matter. *Mailing Add:* State Univ NY 44 Pierrepont 313 Carson Hall Potsdam NY 13676. *Fax:* 315-268-6670

LINMAN, JAMES WILLIAM, MEDICINE. *Current Pos:* PROF MED, JOHN A BURNS SCH MED, UNIV HAWAII, 79- *Personal Data:* b Monmouth, Ill, July 20, 24; m 46; c 4. *Educ:* Univ Ill, BS, 45, MD, 47; Am Bd Internal Med, dipl, 55, cert hemat, 74. *Prof Exp:* From intern to jr clin instr internal med, Univ Mich, 47-51, instr, 51-52 & 54-55, asst prof, 55-56; from asst prof to assoc prof med, Northwestern Univ, 56-65; from assoc prof to prof internal med, Mayo Grad Sch Med, Univ Minn, 65-72, consult, Div Hemat, Mayo Clin, 65-72; prof med & dir, Osgood Leukemia Ctr, Univ Ore Health Sci Ctr, 72-79, head Div Hemat, 74-78. *Mem:* Fel Am Col Physicians; Int Soc Hemat; Am Soc Clin Invest; Am Soc Hemat. *Res:* Hematology. *Mailing Add:* Univ Hawaii John A Burns Med Sch 1356 Lusitana St Honolulu HI 96813-2427

LINN, BRUCE OSCAR, MEDICINAL CHEMISTRY, BIOCHEMISTRY. *Current Pos:* RETIRED. *Personal Data:* b East Orange, NJ, Dec 12, 29; m 51; c 3. *Educ:* Duke Univ, BS, 52, PhD(org chem), 56. *Prof Exp:* Asst, Duke Univ, 52-54 & Off Naval Res, 53-54; sr chemist, Merck Sharp & Dohme Res Lab, 56-75, res fel 76-93. *Mem:* Am Chem Soc. *Res:* Medicinal and synthetic organic chemistry in human and animal health. *Mailing Add:* 743 Wingate Dr Bridgewater NJ 08807-1608

LINN, DEVON WAYNE, LIMNOLOGY. *Current Pos:* from asst prof to assoc prof, 64-73, chmn dept, 69-73, PROF BIOL, SOUTHERN ORE STATE COL, 73- *Personal Data:* b Estherville, Iowa, Oct 9, 29; m 53; c 3. *Educ:* Mankato State Col, BA, 52; Ore State Univ, MS, 55; Utah State Univ, PhD(fishery biol, statist), 62. *Prof Exp:* Chemist, Mayo Clin, Minn, 52-53; res biologist, Fisheries Res Inst, Univ Wash, 55-58; asst prof biol, Dakota Wesleyan Univ, 62-64. *Concurrent Pos:* Consult, Northwest Biol Consults, 62-; Peace Corps vol serving as Dep to Chief Fisheries Officer, Fisheries Dept Ministry Agr & Natural Resources, Lilongwe, Malawi, EAfrica, 73-75; vis prof biol, Univ Swaziland, Kwaluseni, Africa, 83-85. *Mem:* Am Sci Affil. *Res:* Physiological effects of radiation; water pollution and abatement; environmental quality and resource management. *Mailing Add:* 899 Hillview Dr Ashland OR 97520

LINN, JOHN CHARLES, COMPUTER SCIENCE, SYSTEMS THEORY. *Current Pos:* MEM TECH STAFF COMPUT SCI, TEX INSTRUMENTS INC, 73- *Personal Data:* b Bellingham, Wash. *Educ:* Univ Wash, BS, 68; Stanford Univ, MS, 69, PhD(elec eng), 73. *Prof Exp:* Res engr laser commun, Honeywell Inc, 68; instr comput sci, Stanford Univ, 72. *Mem:* Inst Elec & Electronics Engrs; Asn Comput Mach. *Res:* Computer architecture; algorithms, memory organization; human speech and language. *Mailing Add:* Tex Instruments Inc 305 Mail Sta 8373 PO Box 655303 Dallas TX 75265

LINN, STUART MICHAEL, BIOCHEMISTRY. *Current Pos:* CONSULT, 90- *Personal Data:* b Chicago, Ill, Dec 16, 40; m 67; c 3. *Educ:* Calif Inst Technol, BS, 62; Stanford Univ, PhD(biochem), 66. *Prof Exp:* Helen Hay Whitney fel, Univ Geneva, 66-68; from asst prof to prof biochem, 68-87, Univ Calif, Berkeley, head, div biochem & molecular biol, 87-90. *Concurrent Pos:* Res grants, USPHS, Univ Calif, Berkeley, 68- & Dept Energy, 70-; Guggenheim fel, 74-75. *Mem:* AAAS; Am Soc Microbiol; Am Soc Biol Chemists. *Res:* Biochemistry of nucleic acids; nucleic acid enzymes. *Mailing Add:* Div Biochem & Molecular Biol Barker Hall Univ Calif Barker Hall Berkeley CA 94720-3202

LINN, WILLIAM JOSEPH, ORGANIC CHEMISTRY. *Current Pos:* SR RES ASSOC, AGR PROD DEPT, E I DU PONT DE NEMOURS & CO, INC, 53- *Personal Data:* b Crawfordsville, Ind, July 14, 27; m 56; c 2. *Educ:* Wabash Col, AB, 50; Univ Rochester, PhD(chem), 53. *Concurrent Pos:* Res assoc, Northwestern Univ, 69-70. *Mem:* Am Chem Soc; AAAS; Catalysis Soc. *Res:* Organometallic compounds; heterogeneous and homogeneous catalysis; catalytic oxidation; process chemistry. *Mailing Add:* 1311 Circle Dr West Chester PA 19382-8241

LINNA, TIMO JUHANI, CANCER, IMMUNOLOGY. *Current Pos:* DIR RES, SYNTEX RES, 90- *Personal Data:* b Tavastkyro, Finland, Mar 16, 37; m 61; c 3. *Educ:* Univ Uppsala, BMed, 59, MD, 65, PhD(histol), 67. *Prof Exp:* Asst prof histol, Med Sch, Univ Uppsala, 67-71; from asst prof to assoc prof, 70-78, adv clin immunol, 72-80, prof, 78-80, res prof microbiol & immunol, Sch Med, Temple Univ, 80-; group leader, Immunol Control Res & Develop Dept, E I Dupont De Nemours & Co, Inc, Wilmington, 80-90. *Concurrent Pos:* USPHS int res fel, Univ Minn, Minneapolis, 68-70, Univ Minn spec res fel, 70; consult immunol, UN Develop Prog/World Bank/WHO spec prog for res & training in tropical dis, WHO, Geneva, Switz, 78-79. *Mem:* Am Soc Exp Path; NY Acad Sci; Reticuloendothelial Soc; Swed Royal Lymphatic Soc; Am Asn Immunologists; Am Asn Cancer Res. *Res:* Immunobiology; experimental pathology; tumor immunology; cell kinetics. *Mailing Add:* Roche Labs 3401 Hillview Ave A3-208 Palo Alto CA 94304-1397

LINNARTZ, NORWIN EUGENE, FOREST SOILS, SILVICULTURE. *Current Pos:* RETIRED. *Personal Data:* b Fischer, Tex, Apr 9, 26; m 57, Melba Robertson; c E Duane & Darren C. *Educ:* Tex A&M Univ, BS, 53; La State Univ, MF, 59, PhD(soils), 61. *Prof Exp:* Range mgt asst soil conserv serv, USDA, 53-54, range conservationist, 54-57; res asst, Sch Forestry & Agr Exp Sta, La State Univ, Baton Rouge, 57-60, from asst prof to emer prof Forestry, 61-92, asst dean, Grad Sch, 77-80. *Concurrent Pos:* Asst dir, Sch Forestry, Wildlife & Fisheries, 86-90. *Mem:* Fel Soc Am Foresters. *Res:* Hardwoods silviculture; forest soil-moisture-plant relationships; forest fertilization; forest range. *Mailing Add:* Sch Forestry Wildlife & Fisheries La State Univ Baton Rouge LA 70803-6202

LINNELL, ALBERT PAUL, ASTROPHYSICS. *Current Pos:* chmn, Astron Dept, 66-76, prof, 66-91, EMER PROF PHYSICS & ASTRON, MICH STATE UNIV, 91- *Personal Data:* b Canby, Minn, June 30, 22; m 44, 93, Ann Kremer; c Carol Anne, Paul Huston, John Andrew, Barbara Marie (Westerwick) & James Scott. *Educ:* Col Wooster, AB, 44; Harvard Univ, PhD(astron), 50; Amherst Col, MA, 62. *Hon Degrees:* MA, Amherst Col, 62. *Prof Exp:* From instr to prof astron, Amherst Col, 49-66. *Concurrent Pos:* Mem adv comt, Comput Ctr, Mass Inst Technol, 60-63; mem bd dirs, Asn Univs for Res Astron, 62-65. *Mem:* Int Astron Union; AAAS; Am Astron Soc; Sigma Xi. *Res:* Instrumentation for photoelectric photometry; photometry and theory of eclipsing binaries; computer modeling; binary stars including accretion disks; synthetic spectra. *Mailing Add:* 5323 NE 42nd St Seattle WA 98105

LINNELL, J ANDREW, STORAGE SUBSYSTEMS, VIRTUAL REALITY & THE HUMAN FUTURE. *Current Pos:* mgr, 86-90, ENG MGR, DIGITAL EQUIP CORP, 90- *Personal Data:* b Northampton, Mass, Jan 18, 50; div; c David, Nathan & Moriah. *Educ:* Univ Mich, BSE, 72, MSE, 73. *Prof Exp:* Proj leader & engr, IBM, 73-80; sect mgr II, Wang Labs, 80-86. *Concurrent Pos:* Pres, NH Citizens Choice in Educ, 92-94. *Mem:* Asn Comput Mach; Inst Elec & Electronics Engrs Comput Soc. *Res:* Network attached storage servers; effects of virtual reality on future culture, society. *Mailing Add:* 23 Blueberry Lane Peterborough NH 03458. *E-Mail:* linnell@mail.dec.com

LINNELL, RICHARD D(EAN), AERODYNAMICS. *Current Pos:* RETIRED. *Personal Data:* b Rapid River Twp, Mich, Sept 18, 20; m 58; c 1. *Educ:* Univ NH, BS, 46; Mass Inst Technol, SM, 48, ScD(aerodyn eng), 50. *Prof Exp:* Aerodyn engr, United Aircraft Corp, 48; aerodyn engr, Mass Inst Technol, 49, sr engr, 50-52; aerodyn engr, Convair Div, Gen Dynamics Corp, 52-55, staff scientist aerodyn, 56-60; actg mgr aerothermodyn, Gen Elec Co, 55-56; Chance Vought prof aeronaut eng, Sch Eng, Southern Methodist Univ, 60-62; analyst, Ctr Naval Anal, 62-79; engr, Tracor Inc, 81-85. *Mem:* Am Phys Soc; Am Inst Aeronaut & Astronaut. *Res:* Systems analysis; fluid mechanics; vehicle design. *Mailing Add:* 154 N Main St Apt 3A Concord NH 03301

LINNELL, ROBERT HARTLEY, ACADEMIC ADMINISTRATION, INSTITUTIONAL RESEARCH. *Current Pos:* dean, Col Lett, Arts & Sci, Univ Southern Calif, 69-70, prof chem, 69-85, dir, Off Instl Studies, 70-82, chmn, Dept Safety Sci, 82-85, EMER PROF CHEM, UNIV SOUTHERN CALIF, 85-; CONSULT, ENVIRON HEALTH & SAFETY. *Personal Data:* b Kalkaska, Mich, Aug 15, 22; m 50, Myrle Talbot; c Charlene, Lloyd, Randa & Dean. *Educ:* Univ NH, BS, 44, MS, 47; Univ Rochester, PhD(chem), 50. *Prof Exp:* Instr chem, Univ NH, 47; asst prof, Am Univ Beirut, 50-52, assoc prof & chmn dept, 52-55; vpres, Tizon Chem Co, 55-58, dir, 55-62; assoc prof chem, Univ Vt, 58-61; lab dir, Scott Res Labs, 61-62; prog dir phys chem, NSF, 62-65, staff assoc planning, 65-67, dep dir, Dept Develop Prog, 67-69. *Concurrent Pos:* Grants, Res Corp, 50-54 & 58-60, NSF, 59-61, USPHS, 61-62, Am Petrol Inst, 61-62, Exxon Educ Found, 74-76 & 78-80 & Carnegie Corp, 76-77 & 78-80; consult, Reheis Corp, 58-61, Tizon Chem Co, 58-62, Col Chem Consult Serv, Lake Erie Environ Studies Prog & Environ Protection Agency; consult environ health & safety, 85-; mem bd dirs, Cent Calif Chap, Am Lung Asn, 86-, pres, 91-92. *Mem:* AAAS; Am Chem Soc; Asn Instnl Res; Am Soc Safety Engrs. *Res:* Hydrogen bonds; air pollution energy planning; science and public policy; science manpower; faculty and staff personnel research (salaries, fringe benefits, policies for consulting, intellectual properties and adult education); student and faculty surveys; higher education evaluation and planning; indoor air pollution; asbestos; radon; environmental health and safety; drunk driving. *Mailing Add:* 255 Kings Hwy W White River Junction VT 05001-3200. *Fax:* 802-295-9575

LINNEMANN, ROGER E, RADIOLOGY, NUCLEAR MEDICINE. *Current Pos:* radiologist, Hosp, 68-69, asst prof, 69-74, ASSOC PROF CLIN RADIOL, UNIV PA, 74-; PRES, RADIATION MGT CORP, 69- *Personal Data:* b St Cloud, Minn, Jan 12, 31; m 51; c 5. *Educ:* Univ Minn, Minneapolis, BA, 52, BS & MD, 56; Am Bd Radiol, cert, 64; Am Bd Nuclear Med, cert, 72. *Prof Exp:* Intern, Walter Reed Army Hosp, 56-57; physician, US Army, Europe, 57-61; res assoc radiobiol, Walter Reed Army Hosp, 61-62, resident radiol, 62-65; cmndg officer, Nuclear Med Res Detachment, US Army, Europe, 65-68; asst prof radiol, Univ Minn, Minneapolis, 68. *Concurrent Pos:* US deleg radiation protection comt & panel experts med aspects nuclear biol & chem warfare, NATO, 65-68; Nat Res Coun James Picker Found res grant radiol, 68-69; nuclear med consult, Philadelphia Elec Co, 68-; mem ad hoc comt med aspects radiation accidents, AEC, 69-; vis assoc prof clin radiol, Northwestern Univ Sch Med, 77-; res scholar, Univ Minn. *Mem:* AMA; Am Col Radiol; Am Nuclear Soc; Am Pub Health Asn; Indust Med Asn. *Res:* Medical aspects of nuclear industry accidents; kidney function studies using isotopes; radiological health. *Mailing Add:* Radiation Mgt Consult 3021 Darnell Rd Philadelphia PA 19154-3201

LINNER, JOHN GUNNAR, electron microscopy, immunocytochemistry, for more information see previous edition

LINNERT, GEORGE EDWIN, metallurgy of welding; deceased, see previous edition for last biography

LINNERUD, ARDELL CHESTER, EXPERIMENTAL STATISTICS. *Current Pos:* fel biomath, 64-67, asst prof statist, 67-75, ASSOC PROF STATIST, NC STATE UNIV, 75- *Personal Data:* b Whitehall, Wis, Apr 9, 31; m 56. *Educ:* Wis State Univ River Falls, BS, 53; Univ Minn, MS, 62, PhD(dairy husb), 64. *Prof Exp:* Res asst dairy husb, Univ Minn, 57-63, consult biomet, 64. *Concurrent Pos:* Statist consult, Inst for Aerobics Res, 74- *Mem:* Am Dairy Sci Asn; Am Soc Animal Sci. *Res:* Design of experiments and mathematical model building; animal science and exercise physiology. *Mailing Add:* 1309 DeBoy St Raleigh NC 27606

LINNOILA, MARKKU, ALCOHOLISM. *Current Pos:* SCI DIR, NAT INST ALCOHOL ABUSE & ALCOHOLISM, NIH, 91- *Mailing Add:* NIH Nat Inst Alcohol Abuse & Alcoholism Sci Dir AAA Bldg 10 Rm 3C103 10 Center Dr MSC 1256 Bethesda MD 20892-1256

LINNSTAEDTER, JERRY LEROY, MATHEMATICS. *Current Pos:* assoc prof, 68-71, chmn, Dept Comput Sci, Math & Physics, 68-95, PROF MATH, ARK STATE UNIV, 71-; ASSOC DEAN ARTS & SCI, 95- *Personal Data:* b Lindale, Tex, July 25, 37; m 62, Julie McCulley; c Jean, Joan & Jane. *Educ:* Tex A&M Univ, BA, 59, MS, 61; Vanderbilt Univ, PhD(math), 70. *Prof Exp:* Instr math, Northeast La Univ, 61-63 & Vanderbilt Univ, 67-68. *Concurrent Pos:* Prin investr NASA res grant, Ark State Univ, 69-71; mem, Ark Comn Improving Pub Sch Basic Skill Opportunities. *Mem:* Am Math Soc; Math Asn Am; Sigma Xi. *Res:* Multistage calculus of variations; classical analysis; multi stage bolza problems and related control problems; trajectory analysis; Zermelo flow problems. *Mailing Add:* Ark State Univ Col Arts & Sci Box 1030 State University AR 72467. *Fax:* 870-972-3827; *E-Mail:* linnstoedter@caddo.astate.edu

LINOWSKI, JOHN WALTER, PHYSICAL CHEMISTRY, ANALYTICAL CHEMISTRY. *Current Pos:* sr res chemist, Dow Chem Co, 76-81, res leader, 81-82, group leader, 82-87, res mgr, 87-91, sr res mgr, 91, lab dir, 91-92, GLOBAL DIR CATALYSIS TECHNOL, DOW CHEM CO, 92- *Personal Data:* b Boston, Mass, July 7, 45; m 72, Rosemary Bodo. *Educ:* Boston Col, BS, 67; Canisius Col, MS, 70; Rutgers Univ, PhD(phys chem), 74. *Honors & Awards:* Rieman Award 1976. *Prof Exp:* Res assoc molecular dynamics, Univ Ill, 74-76. *Mem:* Am Chem Soc; Sci Res Soc NAm; Sigma Xi. *Res:* Dynamic nuclear polarization; molecular dynamics of liquids at high pressure and extreme temperatures; nuclear magnetic resonance; catalysis; process chemistry. *Mailing Add:* 702 Lake Rd Lake Jackson TX 77566

LINS, THOMAS WESLEY, marine geology, structural geology, for more information see previous edition

LINSAY, ERNEST CHARLES, ORGANIC CHEMISTRY. *Current Pos:* From res chemist to sr res chemist, Organics Dept, 68-83, tech supt, 83-86, res & develop supt, 86-87, RES SCIENTIST, COATINGS & ADDITIVES, HERCULES INC, 87- *Personal Data:* b Cleveland, Ohio, May 3, 42; m 66; c 3. *Educ:* Yale Univ, BS, 63; Univ Wis-Madison, PhD(org chem), 68. *Mem:* Am Chem Soc; Soc Automotive Engrs. *Res:* Physical organic chemistry; rosin and fatty acids; dispersions and emulsions; rosin-, terpene- and hydrocarbon-based resins; coatings; nitrocellulose; jet engine lucricants; wood preservatives. *Mailing Add:* 43 Slashpine Circle Hockessin DE 19707-9206

LINSCHEID, HAROLD WILBERT, MATHEMATICAL ANALYSIS. *Current Pos:* from assoc prof to prof, 58-77, EMER PROF MATH, WICHITA STATE UNIV, 77- *Personal Data:* b Goessel, Kans, Sept, 24, 06; m 33; c 3. *Educ:* Bethel Col, Kans, BA, 29; Phillips Univ, MEd, 36; Univ Okla, MA, 40, PhD, 55. *Prof Exp:* From high sch, Okla, 29-36; instr, Okla Jr Col, 36-38; instr math, Univ Okla, 38-41; instr math & physics, Bluffton Col, 41-43; army specialized training prog, Univ Nebr, 43-44; asst prof math & physics, Eastern NMex Col, 44-46; assoc prof, Col Emporia, 51-58. *Mem:* Am Math Soc; Math Asn Am. *Res:* Algebra; geometry; physics; electricity and magnetism. *Mailing Add:* 3701 E Funston Wichita KS 67218

LINSCHITZ, HENRY, PHYSICAL CHEMISTRY. *Current Pos:* assoc prof, 57-59, PROF CHEM, BRANDEIS UNIV, 59-, CHMN DEPT, 58- *Personal Data:* b New York, NY, Aug 18, 19; m 64; c 1. *Educ:* City Col New York, BS, 40; Duke Univ, MA, 41, PhD(chem), 46. *Prof Exp:* Mem staff, Explosives Res Lab, Nat Defense Res Comt, 43; sect leader, Los Alamos Sci Lab, 43-45; fel, Inst Nuclear Studies, Univ Chicago, 46-48; from asst prof to assoc prof chem, Syracuse Univ, 48-57. *Concurrent Pos:* Vis scientist, Brookhaven Nat Lab, 56-57; Fulbright vis prof, Hebrew Univ, Israel, 60; mem adv comt space biol, NASA, 60-61, study sect biophys & biophys chem, NIH, 62-66 & comt photobiol, Nat Res Coun, 64-69; Guggenheim fel, Weizmann Inst, 71-72. *Mem:* AAAS; Am Chem Soc; Am Acad Arts & Sci; Fedn Am Scientists. *Res:* Photochemistry; spectroscopy and luminescence of complex molecules; photobiology. *Mailing Add:* Dept Chem Brandeis Univ Waltham MA 02254

LINSCOTT, WILLIAM DEAN, IMMUNOLOGY. *Current Pos:* RETIRED. *Personal Data:* b Bakersfield, Calif, Apr 23, 30; m 55; c 3. *Educ:* Univ Calif, Los Angeles, BA, 51, PhD(infectious dis), 60. *Prof Exp:* From asst prof to prof microbiol, Med Ctr, Univ Calif, San Francisco, 64-85. *Concurrent Pos:* USPHS res fels, Labs Microbiol, Howard Hughes Med Inst, Fla, 60-62 & Div Exp Path, Scripps Clin & Res Found, Calif, 62-64; publ, Linscott's Dir Immunol & Biol Reagents. *Res:* Complement; immunologic unresponsiveness. *Mailing Add:* 4877 Grange Rd Santa Rosa CA 95404

LINSKY, CARY BRUCE, BIOLOGICAL CHEMISTRY. *Current Pos:* PROD DIR, ETHICON INC. *Personal Data:* b Chicago, Ill, June 9, 42; m 68; c 2. *Educ:* Univ Wis-Madison, BS, 64; Loyola Univ, PhD(biochem), 71. *Prof Exp:* Res assoc, Johnson & Johnson, 71-, asst mgr, 80- *Mem:* Am Chem Soc; Sigma Xi; Am Burn Asn. *Res:* Role of inflammatory response and local environment in cutaneous wound healing; cellular components of inflammation; scar formation in surgical wounds; collagen biochemistry; hemostasis; prevention of post surgical adhesions. *Mailing Add:* 25 Beacon Hill Dr East Brunswick NJ 08816

LINSKY, JEFFREY L, SPACE PHYSICS, SOLAR PHYSICS. *Current Pos:* Res assoc astrophys, 68-69, assoc prof adjoint, 74-79, LECTR, DEPT PHYSICS & ASTROPHYS, & DEPT ASTROGEOPHYS, UNIV COLO, 69-, PROF ADJOINT, DEPT ASTRON, PLANETARY & ATMOSPHERIC SCI, 79- *Personal Data:* b Buffalo, NY, June 27, 41; m 67, Lois Fleischer; c 2. *Educ:* Mass Inst Technol, BS, 63; Harvard Univ, AM, 65, PhD(astron), 68. *Honors & Awards:* Medal for Except Sci Achievement, NASA, 88. *Prof Exp:* Mem, Joint Inst Lab Astrophys, 68-71, fel, 71-; consult, NASA, 72-; astronomer, Lab Astrophys, Nat Inst Stand & Technol, 69- *Mem:* Am Astron Soc; Int Astron Union. *Res:* Radiative transfer; formation of spectral lines in the solar and stellar chromospheres; atmospheres of latetype stars; stellar coronae; ultraviolet and x-ray astronomy from space. *Mailing Add:* 1645 Bear Mountain Dr Boulder CO 80303. *Fax:* 303-492-5235; *E-Mail:* jlinsky@jila.colorado.edu

LINSLEY, JOHN, PHYSICS, ASTRONOMY. *Current Pos:* adj prof, 72-77, RES PROF PHYSICS, UNIV N MEX, 77- *Personal Data:* b Minneapolis, Minn, Mar 12, 25; m 66; c 3. *Educ:* Univ Minn, BPhys, 47, PhD(physics), 52. *Prof Exp:* Asst prof physics, Univ Va, 51-52; res fel, Univ Minn, 52-54; res assoc, Mass Inst Technol, 54-55, asst prof, 55-58, res assoc, 58-72. *Mem:* Fel Am Phys Soc; Sigma Xi; Am Astron Soc. *Res:* Origin and behavior of highest-energy cosmic rays by means of experimental and theoretical investigations of extensive air showers. *Mailing Add:* 1712 Old Town Rd NW Albuquerque NM 87104

LINSLEY, PETER SEAN, GENERAL BIOLOGY. *Current Pos:* SR SCIENTIST & SR RES FEL, BRISTOL-MYERS SQUIBB, 83- *Personal Data:* m, Leslie; c Jeremy & Drew. *Educ:* Univ Calif, Los Angeles, PhD(molecular biol), 80. *Mem:* AAAS; Am Asn Internists. *Res:* T lymphocyte costimulatory receptors. *Mailing Add:* Bristol-Myers Squibb 3005 First Ave Seattle WA 98121. *E-Mail:* tadpole1@haleyon.com

LINSLEY, ROBERT MARTIN, INVERTEBRATE PALEONTOLOGY. *Current Pos:* Ford intern Colgate Univ, Colgate Univ, 54-55, from instr to prof, 55-78, chmn dept, 64-71, dir natural sci course, 62-70, phys sci course, 59-64, Harold Orville Whitnall prof, 78-92, EMER HAROLD ORVILLE WHITNALL PROF GEOL, COLGATE UNIV, 92- *Personal Data:* b Chicago, Ill, Feb 19, 30; div, JoAnn Hoehler; c David, Barbara & Christopher. *Educ:* Univ Mich, BS, 52, MS, 53, PhD(geol), 60. *Concurrent Pos:* Trustee, Paleont Res Inst. *Mem:* AAAS; Geol Soc Am; Paleont Soc; Soc Study Evolution; Sigma Xi. *Res:* Evolution, functional morphology; behavior and taxonomy of Gastropoda. *Mailing Add:* 152 Bonney Rd No A Hamilton NY 13346

LINSTEDT, KERMIT DANIEL, SANITARY ENGINEERING. *Current Pos:* RETIRED. *Personal Data:* b Portland, Ore, Nov 6, 40; m 64, Cynthia Moir; c Jennifer E, Melissa L & Joseph P. *Educ:* Ore State Univ, BS, 62; Stanford Univ, MS, 63, PhD(sanit eng), 68. *Honors & Awards:* Dow Award, Am Soc Eng Educrs, 72; Bedell Award, Water Pollution Control Fedn, 73; Res Div Award, Am Water Works Asn, 78. *Prof Exp:* Sanit engr asst, Los Angeles Dept Water & Power, 61-62; from asst prof to prof sanit eng, Dept Civil & Environ Eng, Univ Colo, 67-81; proj mgr, Black & Veatch, Denver, 81-88, partner, 89-92, regional off mgr, 88-94, sr partner, 92-94. *Concurrent Pos:* Consult, Denver Metro Dist, 69-71 & Environ Protection Agency, 78-81. *Mem:* Water Environ Fedn; Am Water Works Asn; Am Acad Environ Engrs. *Res:* Treatment methods for water reuse; characterization and treatment of oil shale retort water. *Mailing Add:* 6647 Apache Ct Niwot CO 80503

LINSTONE, HAROLD A, CORPORATE PLANNING, FORECASTING. *Current Pos:* dir systs sci PhD prog, 70-77, prof systs sci, 77-86, EMER PROF, PORTLAND STATE UNIV, 86- *Personal Data:* b Hamburg, Ger, June 15, 24; m 46; c Fred & Clark. *Educ:* City Col NY, BS, 44; Columbia Univ, MA, 47; Univ Southern Calif, PhD(math), 54. *Prof Exp:* Sr scientist, Hughes Aircraft Co, 49-61 & Rand Corp, 61-63; assoc dir corp develop planning, Lockheed Aircraft Corp, 63-70. *Concurrent Pos:* Ed-in-chief, Technol Forecasting & Social Change, 69-; consult, IBM, Electric Power Resource Inst, Atlantic Richfield Co, Weyerhauser, Nero & Assocs, Inc, UN Asian-Pac Ctr Technol Transfer, 70-; pres, Systs Forecasting Inc, 70-; vis prof, Univ Rome, 74, Univ Wash, 77, Univ Calif, Riverside, 85-86, Univ Kiel, 89. *Mem:* Opers Res Soc Am; Inst Mgt Sci; Int Soc Systs Sci (pres, 93-94). *Res:* Multiple perspectives for decision making; technological forecasting; futures research; corporate planning; risk analysis; systems science; policy analysis. *Mailing Add:* 70 Wheatherstone Ct Lake Oswego OR 97035. *Fax:* 503-725-4882

LINSTROMBERG, WALTER WILLIAM, ORGANIC CHEMISTRY. *Current Pos:* RETIRED. *Personal Data:* b Beaufort, Mo, Oct 30, 12; m 43; c 2. *Educ:* Univ Mo, AB, 37, MA, 50, PhD(chem), 55. *Prof Exp:* Instr chem, Univ Mo, 52-55; from asst prof to prof org chem, Univ Nebr, Omaha, 55-78. *Concurrent Pos:* Vis prof, Utah State Univ, 57; vis prof & res assoc, Univ Nebr, 60. *Mem:* Am Chem Soc; Sigma Xi. *Res:* Pharmaceutical chemistry. *Mailing Add:* 630 S 90th St Omaha NE 68114-5114

LINT, THOMAS F, IMMUNOLOGY. *Current Pos:* Fel immunochem, Rush Univ Med Ctr, 73-75, from asst prof to assoc prof, 75-90, PROF IMMUNOL, RUSH UNIV MED CTR, 90- *Personal Data:* b Pittsburgh, Pa, Dec 22, 46. *Educ:* Univ Dayton, BS, 68; Tulane Univ, PhD(biochem), 73. *Mem:* Am Asn Immunologists; Am Fedn Clin Res; Clin Immunol Soc. *Mailing Add:* Dept Immunol & Microbiol, Rush Univ Med Ctr 1653 W Congress Pkwy Chicago IL 60612-3833

LINTNER, CARL JOHN, JR, PHARMACEUTICAL CHEMISTRY. *Current Pos:* CONSULT, 82- *Personal Data:* b Louisville, Ky, July 15, 17; m 48; c 2. *Educ:* Univ Ky, BS, 40; Univ Wis, PhD(pharmaceut chem), 50. *Honors & Awards:* W E Upjohn Award. *Prof Exp:* Res chemist, Upjohn Co, 50-55, sect head, 55-82. *Concurrent Pos:* Adj prof, Fla A&M Univ, Col Pharm, 75- *Mem:* AAAS; fel Acad Pharmaceut Sci; Am Pharmaceut Asn. *Res:* Organic synthesis; determination of functional groups; essential oil determination; kinetic studies; chromatography and ion exchange resins; phytochemistry; tablet coatings; ointment bases; chemistry of antibiotics; instrumentation tablet compression; pharmaceutical product stability. *Mailing Add:* 2125 Aberdeen Dr Kalamazoo MI 49008

LINTON, EVERETT PERCIVAL, PHYSICAL CHEMISTRY. *Current Pos:* RETIRED. *Personal Data:* b St John West, NB, Dec 30, 06; m 36, 80; c 3. *Educ:* Mt Allison Univ, BSc, 28; McGill Univ, MSc, 30, PhD(chem), 32. *Hon Degrees:* DSc, Acadia Univ, 78. *Prof Exp:* Instr chem, Mt Allison Univ, 28-29; Royal Soc Can fel, Univ Munich, 32-33; chemist, Biol Bd Can, Halifax, NS, 34-36; instr chem, Acadia Univ, 36-41; asst phys chemist, Fisheries Res Bd, Halifax, 41-44; prof chem, Acadia Univ, 44-75, head dept, 66-75. *Mem:* Am Chem Soc. *Res:* Preparation of hydrogen peroxide; measurement of dielectric constants; interaction of neutral molecules; air-drying solids; smokes; colloidal chemistry; dipole moments of amine oxides; drying and smoke curing of fish. *Mailing Add:* 39 Highland Ave Wolfville NS B0P 1X0 Can

LINTON, FRED E J, MATHEMATICS. *Current Pos:* From asst prof to assoc prof, 63-72, chmn dept, 75, PROF MATH, WESLEYAN UNIV, 72- *Personal Data:* b Italy, Apr 8, 38; US citizen; m 90, Barbara Mikolajewska. *Educ:* Yale Univ, BS, 58; Columbia Univ, MA, 59, PhD(math), 63. *Hon Degrees:* MA, Wesleyan Univ, 72. *Honors & Awards:* Hon Gold Medal, Polytech Univ Blagoevgrad, Bulgaria, 87. *Concurrent Pos:* Res assoc, Univ Chicago, 64-65; Nat Res Coun res fel, Swiss Fed Inst Technol, 66-67; Izaak Walton Killam sr res fel, Dalhousie Univ, 69-70. *Mem:* Am Math Soc; Math Asn Am. *Res:* Categorical algebra, a branch of positive speculative philosophy. *Mailing Add:* Wesleyan Univ Middletown CT 06459

LINTON, RICHARD WILLIAM, SURFACE SPECTROSCOPY, MICROBEAM ANALYSIS. *Current Pos:* From asst prof to assoc prof, 77-88, asst vpres res, 86-91, PROF CHEM, UNIV NC, CHAPEL HILL, 89-, ASSOC VPRES RES, 91- *Personal Data:* b Scranton, Pa, Apr 17, 51. *Educ:* Univ Del, BS, 73; Univ Ill, MS, 75, PhD(chem), 77. *Honors & Awards:* Outstanding Young Scientist Award, Microbeam Anal Soc, 80, Presidential Serv Award, 95. *Concurrent Pos:* Vis prof, Univ Antwerp, Belg, 86; consult, Glaxo Inc, 89-91, Monsanto, 92-; vis scholar, Chem Res Prom Ctr, Nat Sci Coun, Taiwan, 91; ed-in-chief, Microbeam Anal J, 91-96; current prin investr, ARO, Environ Protection Agency, USDA. *Mem:* Am Chem Soc; Microbeam Analysis Soc; Micros Soc Am; Am Soc Mass Spectrometry; Am Vacuum Soc; Nat Coun Univ Res Adminr. *Res:* Surface and microprobe techniques for chemical analysis (dynamic and static SIMS, XPS); biological microanalysis; ion beam-surface interactions; environmental analytical chemistry; chemistry and characterization of polymer surfaces. *Mailing Add:* Dept Chem CB#3290 Univ NC Chapel Hill NC 27599-3290. *Fax:* 919-962-2388; *E-Mail:* rwl@ga.unc.edu

LINTON, THOMAS LARUE, FISHERIES. *Current Pos:* AT DEPT WILDLIFE & FISHERIES SCI, TEX A&M UNIV. *Personal Data:* b Carlisle, Tex, July 25, 35; m 61; c 2. *Educ:* Lamar State Col, BS, 59; Univ Okla, MS, 61; Univ Mich, PhD(fisheries), 66. *Prof Exp:* Res asst zool, Univ Ga, 63-65, res assoc, 65-67, asst prof, 67-70; mem staff, Div Com Sports Fisheries, NC Dept Conserv & Develop, 70-73, mem staff, NC Dept Natural & Econ Resources, 73-80. *Concurrent Pos:* Res grants, Ga Game & Fish Comn, 65-68 & US Dept Interior, 66-; Ga rep biol comt, Atlantic State Marine Fisheries Comn, 64-66. *Mem:* AAAS; Am Fisheries Soc. *Res:* Physiology; commercial and sport fisheries; pollution ecology. *Mailing Add:* Dept Wildlife & Fisheries Sci Tex A&M Univ College Station TX 77843-0100

LINTVEDT, RICHARD LOWELL, PHYSICAL INORGANIC CHEMISTRY. *Current Pos:* asst prof inorg chem, 66-71, assoc prof, 71-76, PROF CHEM, WAYNE STATE UNIV, 76-, CHMN DEPT, 83- *Personal Data:* b Edgerton, Wis, June 23, 37; m 59; c 3. *Educ:* Lawrence Univ, BA, 59; Univ Nebr, PhD(inorg chem), 66. *Prof Exp:* Res chemist, Chem Div, Morton Int, 59-62. *Concurrent Pos:* Petrol Res Fund grant, 66-68, 70-73, 76-78 & 84-86; Res Corp grant, 69-71; NSF grant, 76-90; Dept of Energy grant, 78-83. *Mem:* Am Chem Soc; fel AAAS. *Res:* Electronic structure and bonding in inorganic coordination and chelate compounds; electrochemistry; physical inorganic chemistry; magnetochemistry of transition metal complexes. *Mailing Add:* 4047 Fac Admin Bldg Wayne State Univ Detroit MI 48202

LINTZ, JOSEPH, JR, geology, for more information see previous edition

LIN-VIEN, DAIMAY, INFRARED-SPECTROSCOPTIST, POLYMER SPECTROSCOPIST. *Current Pos:* Assoc res chemist, 88-97, SR RES CHEMIST ANALYSIS CHEM, SHELL DEVELOP CO, 97- *Personal Data:* Taiwan citizen; c 1. *Educ:* Kans State Univ, PhD(anal chem), 88. *Mem:* Soc Appl Spectros; Coblenz Soc. *Res:* Analytical applications of fourier transform infrared spectroscopy; fourier transform infrared microspectroscopy; raman spectroscopy; polymer characterization; polymer-polymer interaction; additive-polymer interaction. *Mailing Add:* 4415 Warwick Dr Sugar Land TX 77479

LINVILL, JOHN G(RIMES), ELECTRICAL ENGINEERING, SOLID-STATE ELECTRONICS. *Current Pos:* assoc prof elec eng, Stanford Univ, 55-57, chmn dept, 64-80, assoc dean, Sch Eng, 72-80, prof elec eng, 57-89, prof integrated systs & dir, Ctr Integrated Systs, 81-91, EMER PROF INTEGRATED SYSTS, STANFORD UNIV, 89- *Personal Data:* b Kansas City, Mo, Aug 8, 19; m 43, Marjorie Webber; c Gregory T & Candace (Berg). *Educ:* William Jewell Col, AB, 41; Mass Inst Technol, SB, 43, SM, 45, ScD(elec eng), 49. *Hon Degrees:* DAppSc, Cath Univ Louvain, 66; DSc, William Jewell Col, 92. *Honors & Awards:* Educ Medal, Inst Elec & Electronics Engrs, 76; John Scott Award, 80; Medal Achievement, Am Electronics Asn, 83; Louis Braille Prize, Deutscher Blindenverband, 84. *Prof Exp:* Asst prof elec eng, Mass Inst Technol, 49-51; mem tech staff, Bell Tel Labs, Inc, 51-55. *Concurrent Pos:* Co-founder & dir, Telesensory Systs, Inc, 71- *Mem:* Nat Acad Eng; fel Inst Elec & Electronics Engrs; fel AAAS; fel Am Acad Arts & Sci. *Res:* Custom integrated circuits and systems as sensory aids for the blind. *Mailing Add:* Dept Elec Eng Stanford Univ Stanford CA 94305-4070

LINZ, PETER, COMPUTER SCIENCE. *Current Pos:* from asst prof to assoc prof, 70-77, prof math, 77-83, PROF COMPUT SCI UNIV CALIF, DAVIS, 83- *Personal Data:* b Apatin, Yugoslavia, July 19, 36; US citizen; m 82; c 2. *Educ:* McGill Univ, BSc, 57; Univ Mich, MS, 60; Univ Wis, PhD(comput sci), 68. *Prof Exp:* Res engr, Dominion Eng Ltd, 57-59; assoc programmer, IBM Corp, 63-65; staff specialist numerical anal, Comput Ctr, Univ Wis, 65-68; asst prof comput sci, NY Univ, 68-70. *Res:* Numerical analysis; quadrature methods; solution and applications of integral equations; numerical software. *Mailing Add:* 830 Linden Lane Davis CA 95616

LINZER, MELVIN, ULTRASOUND, PHYSICAL CHEMISTRY. *Current Pos:* Nat Acad Sci-Nat Res Coun fel, 61-63, group leader signal processing & imaging, 78-81, PHYSICAL CHEMIST, NAT BUR STANDS, 63-, GROUP LEADER, FRACTURE & DEFORMATION DIV, 81- *Personal Data:* b New York, NY, Aug 5, 37; m 64; c 4. *Educ:* Brooklyn Col, BS, 57; Princeton Univ, MA, 59, PhD(chem), 62. *Honors & Awards:* Ross Coffin Purdy Award, Am Ceramic Soc, 75; US Dept Commerce Gold Medal Award, 77; Nat Bur Stands Appl Res Award, 78. *Prof Exp:* Res assoc chem, Princeton Univ, 61. *Concurrent Pos:* Ed-in-Chief, Ultrasonic Imaging, 79-; chmn, Int Symp Ultrasonic Imaging & Tissue Characterization, 75-, cochairperson, Ultrasonic Tissue Signature Working Group, 76-78,; chmn, Int Symp on Ultrasonic Mat Characterization, 78- *Mem:* Am Phys Soc; Am Inst Ultrasound in Med; Sigma Xi. *Res:* Nondestructive evaluation; ultrasound medical diagnosis; acoustic emission; laser spectroscopy; combustion diagnostics; magnetic resonance spectroscopy; measurement techniques for spectroscopic and materials applications; shock wave structure. *Mailing Add:* 2 Fulham Ct Silver Spring MD 20902

LINZEY, ALICIA VOGT, POPULATION & COMMUNITY ECOLOGY OF MAMMALS, CONSERVATION BIOLOGY. *Current Pos:* from asst prof to assoc prof, 82-88, PROF BIOL, IND UNIV, PA, 88- *Personal Data:* b Bloomingburg, NY, Jan 27, 43; m 85, Neil J Asting; c David W & Thomas A. *Educ:* Cornell Univ, BS, 64, MS, 65; Va Polytech Inst & State Univ, 81. *Prof Exp:* Asst prof biol, Roanoke Col, 81-82. *Concurrent Pos:* Fulbright fel, Sub-Saharan Africa Reg Res Prog, 92-93; bd dirs, Am Soc Mammalogists, 88-93, assoc ed, Mammalian Species, 93-95; managing ed, Mammalian Species, 95-96. *Mem:* Am Soc Mammalogists (2nd vpres, 93-94, 1st vpres, 94-96, pres, 96-98); Ecol Soc Am; Soc Conserv Biol; Am Inst Biol Sci; Zool Soc Southern Africa. *Res:* Population and community ecology of small mammals; related applied areas in conservation biology, including ecotoxicology, effects of large mammals on small mammal diversity, species of special concern. *Mailing Add:* Dept Biol Ind Univ Pa Indiana PA 15705. *Fax:* 412-357-5700; *E-Mail:* avlinzey@iup.edu

LIOI, ANTHONY PASQUALE, FLUID MECHANICS. *Personal Data:* b Pittsburgh, Pa, May 15, 49; m 75; c 5. *Educ:* Univ Pittsburgh, BS, 71; Drexel Univ, MS, 76, PhD(biomed eng), 79 INC, 86- *Prof Exp:* Co-prin investr, Univ Utah Artificial Heart Res Lab, 82-85, prin investr, 85-86; co-prin investr, res scientist & mgr, Med Devices, Nu-Tech Indust, Inc, 86- *Concurrent Pos:* Res instr surg, Univ Utah Artificial Heart Res Lab, 79-86. *Res:* Artificial heart research; development of automatic physiolosic control methods and the design and development of a miniature hydraulic pump drive system for the artificial heart; blood pump design. *Mailing Add:* 1305 Round Rock West Cove Austin TX 78681

LIONETTI, FABIAN JOSEPH, BIOCHEMISTRY. *Current Pos:* SR INVESTR, CTR BLOOD RES, 68- *Personal Data:* b Jersey City, NJ, Mar 3, 18; m 43; c Karen, Fabian Jr & Donald. *Educ:* NY Univ, AB, 43, MS, 45; Rensselaer Polytech Inst, PhD(phys chem), 48. *Honors & Awards:* Mathewson Medal, Am Inst Metals, 52. *Prof Exp:* From instr to assoc prof biochem, Sch Med, Boston Univ, 49-65; assoc mem, Inst Health Sci, Brown Univ, 65-68. *Mem:* Am Soc Biol Chemists; Am Chem Soc. *Res:* Metabolism and preservation of human blood cells. *Mailing Add:* 800 Huntington Ave Boston MA 02115-6399

LIONS, JACQUES LOUIS, PHYSICS. *Current Pos:* PROF MATH, COL FRANCE, PARIS, 73- *Personal Data:* b Grassee, France, May 2, 28; m 50, Andree Oliver; c Pierre L. *Educ:* Univ Paris, DSc, 54. *Hon Degrees:* Dr, Univ Liege, 73, Univ Madrid, 76, Univ Fudan, 81 Goteborg Univ, 84, Heriot Watt Univ, Edinburgh, 82, Polytech Univ, Madrid, 88, St Jacques de Compostella, 93-94, Univ Malaga, 97, Univ Santiago, Chile, 97. *Honors & Awards:* Japan Prize, 91; Harvey Prize, 91. *Prof Exp:* Fac mem, Univ Nancy, France, 54-62, Univ Paris, 62-73. *Concurrent Pos:* Prof, Ecole Polytech, Paris, 67-86; pres, Nat Inst Res Informatique & Automatique, 80-84, Nat Ctr Specialty Studies, 84-92; high sci adv, Dassault Indust, 93-; bd dir, St Gobain & Pechiney & Dassault Syst. *Mem:* Foreign assoc Nat Acad Sci; French Acad Sci (pres, 97-); Royal Acad Sci; Pontifical Acad Sci; Brasil Acad Sci; Royal Acad Belgium; Russ Acad Sci; Ukraine Acad Sci; Am Acad Arts & Sci; Int Acad Astronaut Chile Acad Sci. *Mailing Add:* Col France 3 rue d'Ulm Paris 75231 Cedex 05 France

LIONS, PIERRE LOUIS, MATHEMATICS. *Current Pos:* PROF, UNIV PARIS-DAUPHINE, FRANCE, 79-; PROF, POLYTECH SCH, PALAISEAU, FRANCE, 84- *Personal Data:* b Grasse, France, Aug 11, 56; m 79, Lila Laurenti; c Dorian C. *Educ:* Univ Paris VI, DSc, 79. *Hon Degrees:* Dr, Heriot & Watt Univ, Edinburgh, 95. *Honors & Awards:* Fields Medal, 94. *Concurrent Pos:* Consult, Cisi, Paris, 79-, Cea-Dam, Paris, 82-, Cognitech, Santa-Monica, 90-, CRS4, Cagliari, 94-, Ctr Dis Control, Paris, 95-, Pechiney, St-Jean de Maurienne, 95-, Aerospatiable, Space Defense, Mureaux, 96; dir, Ceremade, Paris, 91-96. *Mem:* Fr Acad Sci; Acad Europea. *Res:* Published articles in professional journals. *Mailing Add:* 42 rue du Hameau Paris 75015 France

LIOR, NOAM, ENERGY CONVERSION, WATER DESALINATION. *Current Pos:* from asst prof to assoc prof, 73-85, chmn, Mech Eng Grad Group, 86-90, PROF MECH ENG, DEPT MECH ENG & APPL MECH, UNIV PA, 85- *Personal Data:* b Mar 11, 40; US citizen; c 3. *Educ:* Technion, Israel, BS, 62, MS, 66; Univ Calif, Berkeley, PhD(mech eng), 73. *Hon Degrees:* MA, Univ PA, 78. *Honors & Awards:* Ralph Teetor Award, 86. *Prof Exp:* Instr, Dept Mech Eng, Technion, 65-66; res asst res eng water desalination, Seawater Conversion Lab, Univ Calif, Berkeley, 66-73. *Concurrent Pos:* Prin investr, NSF grants, Pa Sci & Eng Found grant, US HUD grant, 75- & US Dept Energy grant, 75-; mem, Solar Collector Stand Comt, Alm Soc Heating, Refrig & Air Conditioning Engr, 75; consult, Westinghouse Elec Corp, 77-78, Lawrence Livermore Labs & Solar Energy Res Inst, Argonne Nat Lab; sr fel, Japan Soc Prom Sci, 91; vis prof, Dept Mech Systs Eng, Tokyo Univ Agr & Technol, 91-92. *Mem:* Fel Am Soc Mech Engrs; Int Solar Energy Soc; Am Soc Heating, Refrig & Air Conditioning Engrs; Int Desalination Asn; Int Found Water Sci Technol. *Res:* Heat transfer, thermodynamics and fluid mechanics as related to solar energy applications, water desalination, combustion and crystal growth; thermo-fluid measurements. *Mailing Add:* Dept Mech Eng Univ Pa Philadelphia PA 19104-6315. *Fax:* 215-573-2065; *E-Mail:* lior@eniac.seas.upenn.edu

LIOTTA, DENNIS C, DRUG DESIGN. *Current Pos:* From asst prof to assoc prof, 76-88, PROF CHEM, EMORY UNIV, 88-, CHMN DEPT, 93- *Personal Data:* b Brooklyn, NY, Jan 31, 49; m, Helene M Saxton; c John & Matthew. *Educ:* Queens Col, City Univ New York, BA, 70, PhD, 74. *Concurrent Pos:* Fel, Alfred P Sloan Found, 80-84; Camille & Henry Dreyfus teacher scholar fel, 81-86; Alexander von Humboldt sr scientist fel, 94- *Mem:* Am Chem Soc; AAAS. *Res:* Drug design and drug development; new synthetic methodology; molecular modeling. *Mailing Add:* Off Res Emory Univ Rollins Bldg G65 1510 Clifton Rd Atlanta GA 30322

LIOTTA, LANCE, PATHOLOGY. *Current Pos:* Actg chief, 81-82, CHIEF, LAB PATH, NAT CANCER INST, NIH, 82- *Mailing Add:* Path Bldg 10 Rm 2A33 NCI NIH 10 Center Dr MSC 1500 Bethesda MD 20892-1500

LIOU, JUHN G, metamorphic petrology, geochemistry, for more information see previous edition

LIOU, KUO-NAN, ATMOSPHERIC PHYSICS, REMOTE SENSING. *Current Pos:* assoc prof, 75-80, PROF METEOROL, UNIV UTAH, 80-, DIR, CTR ATMOSPHERIC & REMOTE SOUNDING STUDIES, 87-, CHMN, DEPT METEOROL, 96- *Personal Data:* b Taipei, Taiwan, Nov 14, 44; US citizen; m 68; c Julia & Clifford. *Educ:* Nat Taiwan Univ, BS, 65; NY Univ, MS, 68, PhD(atmospheric physics), 70. *Honors & Awards:* Creativity Award, NSF, 96. *Prof Exp:* Res asst, NY Univ, 66-70; res assoc, Goddard Inst Space Studies, 70-72; asst prof atmospheric sci, Univ Wash, 72-74. *Concurrent Pos:* Vis scientist, Nat Ctr Atmospheric Res, 75; prin investr, NSF, NASA, Air Force, 80; vis prof, Univ Calif, Los Angeles, 81; mem adv panel, Int Satellite Cloud Climat Prog, Climate Res Comt, Nat Acad Sci, 84-87; consult, Ames Res Ctr, NASA, 84; vis scholar, Harvard Univ, 85; ed, Theoret & Appl Climat & Meterol & Atmosheric Physics, 85-; vis prof, Peking Univ, China, 89-; adj prof geophysics & res prof physics, Univ Utah, 92-; vis prof, Univ Ariz, 95. *Mem:* Fel Optical Soc Am; fel Am Meteorol Soc; fel Am Geophys Union; AAAS. *Res:* Cloud-radiation and radiative transfer in bonds; feedbacks in numerical models, remote sensing of cloud microphysics, light scattering by ice crystals; optics. *Mailing Add:* Dept Meteorol Univ Utah Salt Lake City UT 84112. *Fax:* 801-581-4065; *E-Mail:* knlion@climate.utah.edu

LIOU, MENG-SING, COMPUTATIONAL FLUID DYNAMICS, AEROPROPULSION. *Current Pos:* scientist, 86-88, br chief, 88-90, SR SCIENTIST, LEWIS RES CTR, NASA, 90- *Personal Data:* b Taichung, Taiwan, Nov 20, 47; US citizen; m, May Fun; c Victoria, Yu-Ming & Deng-Yuan. *Educ:* Nat Cheng Kung Univ, BS, 69; Nat Taiwan Univ, MS, 72; Univ Mich, MS, 75, PhD(aerospace eng), 77. *Prof Exp:* Res investr, Univ Mich, 77-78; res scientist, McDonnell Douglas Corp, 78-81; prof & chmn aerodynamics propulsion & combustion, Nat Cheng Kung Univ, 81-84; vis assoc prof computational fluid dynamics, Univ Mich, 84-86. *Concurrent Pos:* Consult, Aeronaut Indust Develop Ctr, 81-84; mem, Nat Aerospace Plane Prog, 90; vis prof, Nat Cheng Kung Univ, 97. *Mem:* Assoc fel Am Inst Aeronaut & Astronaut. *Res:* Advanced numerical methods for computational fluid dynamics; solving problems with complex physics in practical applications; author of over 100 publications. *Mailing Add:* MS 5-11 NASA Lewis Res Ctr Cleveland OH 44135. *Fax:* 216-433-5802; *E-Mail:* fsmsl@lerc.nasa.gov

LIOU, MING-LEI, ELECTRICAL ENGINEERING. *Current Pos:* PROF, HONG KONG UNIV SCI & TECHNOL, 92-; DIR, HONG KONG TELECOM INST INFO TECH, 93- *Personal Data:* b Tinghai, China, Jan 6, 35; US citizen; m, Pearl B Shen; c Michael, Christopher & Derek. *Educ:* Nat Taiwan Univ, BSEE, 56; Drexel Univ, MSEE, 61; Stanford Univ, PhD(elec eng), 64. *Prof Exp:* Commun engr, Chinese Govt Radio Admin, 57-58; instr, Dept Elec Eng, Drexel Univ, 58-61; res asst, Stanford Electronics Labs, Stanford Univ, 61-63; mem tech staff, Bell Labs, 63-66, supvr, AT&T Bell Labs, 66-84, dir, Bell Commun Res, 84-92. *Concurrent Pos:* Ed, Trans Circuits & Systs, Inst Elec & Electronics Engrs, 79-81, Trans Circuits & Systs Video Technol, 91-95. *Mem:* Fel Inst Elec & Electronics Engrs; fel Hong Kong Inst Engrs; Inst Elec & Electronics Engrs Circuits & Systs Soc; Sigma Xi. *Res:* Contributed chapters to engineering books. *Mailing Add:* Dept Elec & Electronics Eng Hong Kong Univ Sci & Technol Clearwater Bay Kowloon Hong Kong People's Republic of China

LIOU, SY-HWANG, MAGNETIC MATERIALS, SUPERCONDUCTING MATERIALS. *Current Pos:* asst prof, 88-93, ASSOC PROF DEPT PHYSICS & ASTRON, UNIV NEBR, 93- *Personal Data:* m 77, Mei-Lan Lin; c Jenny. *Educ:* Soochow Univ, Taiwan, BS, 74; Fla Inst Technol, MS, 79; Johns Hopkins Univ, PhD(physics), 85. *Prof Exp:* Inst modern physics lab, Soochow Univ, 76-77; fel, Johns Hopkins Univ, 85-86, AT&T Bell Labs, 86-88. *Concurrent Pos:* Co-ed, Appl Physics Commun, 90- *Mem:* Am Phys Soc; Mat Res Soc. *Res:* Nano composite films and high temperature superconductors; fundamental studies of interfaces and crystallite size effects; microstructural characterization. *Mailing Add:* Physics/Astron 260 Bel Univ NE Lincoln PO Box 88011 Lincoln NE 68588-0111. *Fax:* 402-472-2879; *E-Mail:* sliou@unlinfo.unl.edu

LIOY, FRANCO, PHYSIOLOGY. *Current Pos:* from asst prof to assoc prof, 67-75, PROF PHYSIOL, UNIV BC, 75- *Personal Data:* b Gorizia, Italy, May 24, 32; m 66; c 1. *Educ:* Univ Rome, MD, 56; Univ Minn, Minneapolis, PhD(physiol), 67. *Prof Exp:* Instr med, Univ Rome, 56-61; instr physiol, Univ Minn, Minneapolis, 66-67. *Concurrent Pos:* Mem, Sci Subcomt, Can Heart Found. *Mem:* Can Physiol Soc. *Res:* Cardiovascular physiology; coronary circulation; effect of hyperthermia on circulatory system; sympathetic control of circulation. *Mailing Add:* Dept Physiol Univ BC 2075 Westbrook Mall Vancouver BC V6T 1W5 Can

LIOY, PAUL JAMES, ENVIRONMENTAL HEALTH, HUMAN EXPOSURE ASSESSMENT & AEROSOLS. *Current Pos:* assoc prof environ & community med, 85-88, DIR, EXPOSURE, MEASUREMENT & ASSESSMENT DIV, UNIV MED & DENT NJ, 86-, PROF ENVIRON & COMMUNITY MED, 88-; DEP DIR ENVIRON & OCCUP HEALTH SCI INST. *Personal Data:* b Passaic, NJ, May 27, 47; m 71, Mary J Yonone; c Jason. *Educ:* Montclair State Col, BA, 69; Auburn Univ, MS, 71; Rutgers Univ, MS, 73, PhD(environ sci), 75. *Prof Exp:* Sr air pollution engr, Interstate Sanit Comn, NY, 75-78; from asst prof to assoc prof environ med, Inst Environ Med, NY Univ Med Ctr, 78-85. *Concurrent Pos:* Lectr, Dept Civil & Environ Eng, Polytech Inst NY, 76-78; consult, State NJ, 78-90, indust orgn, 80-, US Environ Protection Agency Off Res & Develop, 84-91; mem, NJ Clean Air Coun, 81-, chmn, 83-85; mem, Comt Air Pollution epidemiol, Nat Acad Sci, 84-85, chmn, 87-90, mem, Comn Air Pollution Exposure Assessment, 90, comt on Dept Energy Site Remediation, 93-94; dir human exposure, Environ & Occup Health Sci Inst, Univ Med & Dent NJ, Rutger Univ, 86-, co-dir, Joint Grad Prog Exposure Assessment, 90-94; mem, Sci Adv Bd Comt Indoor Air & Total Human Exposure, Environ Protection Agency, 89-; exed ed, Atmos Environ, 89-94; mem, US-Can Air Quality Bd, Int Joint Comn, 92-; assoc ed, Environ Res, 94- *Mem:* Air Pollution Control Asn; fel NY Acad Sci; Int Soc Environ Epidemiol; Am Asn Aerosol Res; Air & Waste Mgt Asn; Int Soc Exposure Anal (treas, 91-93, pres, 93-94); Am Conf Govt Indust Hygienists. *Res:* Atmospheric transport of pollutants; chemical characteristics of inorganic trace elements and organic species in multiple media; aerosol and gaseous monitoring equipment and techniques; industrial and occupational hygiene; environmental health; human exposure to toxic pollutants and epidemiology; hazardous wastes and multimedia pollution issues; modeling of human exposure and dose response relationships; strategies for measuring industrial and community exposures & toxic substances; author 150 peer reviewed publications, patentee in field. *Mailing Add:* Environ & Occup Health Sci Inst Univ Med & Dent NJ Rutgers 681 Frelinghuysen Rd Piscataway NJ 08855. *Fax:* 732-445-0116; *E-Mail:* plioy@eohsi.rutgers.edu

LIPARI, NUNZIO OTTAVIO, SOLID STATE PHYSICS, MOLECULAR PHYSICS. *Current Pos:* MEM RES STAFF, IBM THOMAS J WATSON RES CTR, 77- *Personal Data:* b Ali' Terme, Italy, Jan 1, 45. *Educ:* Univ Messina, Laurea Physics, 67; Lehigh Univ, PhD(physics), 70. *Prof Exp:* Res asst solid state physics, Lehigh Univ, 67-70; res assoc, Univ Ill, 70-72; from asst scientist to scientist sr physics, Webster Res Lab, Xerox Corp, 75-77. *Mem:* Fel Am Phys Soc. *Res:* Optical properties of solids; electron-phonon interaction in molecular systems; excitation and impurity states in semiconductors. *Mailing Add:* 8702 Carpenter Rd Baldwinsville NY 13027

LIPE, JOHN ARTHUR, horticulture, plant physiology; deceased, see previous edition for last biography

LIPELES, MARTIN, DIGITAL TYPE, COMPUT GRAPHICS. *Current Pos:* COMPUTER CONSULT, 88- *Personal Data:* b New York, NY, June 22, 38; m 68; c 2. *Educ:* Columbia Univ, AB, 60, MA, 62, PhD(physics), 66. *Prof Exp:* Part-time res physicist, Radiation Lab, Columbia Univ, 62-66; mem tech staff, Sci Ctr, Rockwell Int, 66-76; pres, Med Microcomputers Inc, 77-78; dir res & develop, Autologic Inc, 78-83; mgr systs eng, Alpharel Inc, 83-88. *Mem:* AAAS; Am Phys Soc; Am Chem Soc; Sigma Xi; Asn Comput Mach. *Res:* Design of large systems for engineering graphics; software for design of digital type and typesetter design; inelastic, ion-atom collisions at low energies; physics and chemistry of photochemical aerosol formation in the atmosphere. *Mailing Add:* 1476 Warwick Ave Thousand Oaks CA 91360-3549

LIPICKY, RAYMOND JOHN, INTERNAL MEDICINE, PHARMACOLOGY. *Current Pos:* med officer, Div Cardiorenal Drug Prods, 79-81, actg dir, 81-84, DIR, FOOD & DRUG ADMIN, 84- *Personal Data:* b Cleveland, Ohio, May 3, 33; m 83, Freda Jacobsen Sanders; c Laura Lee, Josh Wesley, Ronald Lowell, Robert Boardwell & Elizabeth Dorenda. *Educ:* Ohio Univ, AB, 55; Univ Cincinnati, MD, 60. *Prof Exp:* From intern to resident med, Barnes Hosp, St Louis, Mo, 60-62; resident, Strong Mem Hosp, Rochester, NY, 64-65; from asst prof to assoc prof pharmacol, Col Med, Univ Cincinnati, 66-72, from asst prof to assoc prof med, 66-73, prof pharmacol, 72-79, prof med & dir, Div Clin Pharmacol, 73-79. *Concurrent Pos:* Fel pharmacol, Univ Pa, 62-63 & Univ Cincinnati, 63-64; trainee cardiol, Strong Mem Hosp, Rochester, 65-66; mem corp, Marine Biol Lab, Woods Hole, Mass; guest worker, Lab Biophysics, NIH, 79-84. *Mem:* Soc Neurosci; Biophys Soc; Am Physiol Soc; Am Soc Pharmacol & Exp Therapeut; Am Soc Hypertension. *Res:* Ion transport; clinical pharmacology; membrane permeability; bioelectric potentials; hemodynamics. *Mailing Add:* 15201 Apricot Lane Gaithersburg MD 20878

LIPIN, BRUCE REED, PETROLOGY, ECONOMIC GEOLOGY. *Personal Data:* b New York, NY, Nov 27, 47; m 71, Cookie Marviglio; c Adam & Jonah. *Educ:* City Col New York, BS, 70; Pa State Univ, PhD(mineral, petrol), 75. *Prof Exp:* Fel, Geophys Lab, Carnegie Inst Wash, 73-74; Nat Res Coun res assoc fel, US Geol Surv, 74-75, geologist, 75-84 & 89-93, chief Eastern Mineral Resources, 84-89, assoc chief, Off Mineral Resources, 93-96. *Concurrent Pos:* Consult res, George Washington Univ, 93-95. *Mem:* Soc Econ Geol. *Res:* Economic geology of ultramafic rocks including chromite, platinum, asbestos and talc; petrology and origin of ultramafic rocks. *Mailing Add:* US Geol Surv MS 954 Nat Ctr Reston VA 22092. *Fax:* 703-648-6338

LIPINSKI, BOGUSLAW, BIOELECTRICITY. *Current Pos:* assoc dir, Vascular Lab, 76-81, DIR, BIOELEC LAB, ST ELIZABETH'S HOSP, TUFTS UNIV SCH MED, 81- *Personal Data:* b Sochaczew, Poland, July 21, 33; US citizen; m 57; c 1. *Educ:* Inst Nuclear Res, Warsaw, PhD(biochem), 62; Univ Lodz, Poland, DSc, 71. *Prof Exp:* Vis prof, Vascular Lab, Lemnel Shattuck Hosp, Sch Med, Tufts Univ, 71-76. *Concurrent Pos:* Asst ed, J Bioelec, 81- *Mem:* AAAS; Int Soc Thrombosis & Hemostosis; Fedn Am Scientists; Int Soc Bioelec (pres, 80-). *Res:* Mechanism of intravascular coagulation and fibrinolysis; effect of nutrition on thrombosis and atherosclerosis; effect of electricity on biological systems in relation to tissues regeneration and healing. *Mailing Add:* 97 Beaumont Ave Newton MA 02160

LIPINSKI, CHRISTOPHER ANDREW, ORGANIC CHEMISTRY. *Current Pos:* res sci, 70-74, sr res sci, 74-76, sr res investr, 76-81, prin res investr, 81-86, RES ADV, MED RES LABS, PFIZER CENT RES, 86- *Personal Data:* b Dundee, Scotland, Feb 1, 44; US citizen; m 69; c 2. *Educ:* San Francisco State Col, BS, 65; Univ Calif, Berkeley, PhD(org chem), 68. *Prof Exp:* Nat Inst Gen Med Sci fel, Calif Inst Technol, 69-70. *Mem:* Am Chem Soc. *Res:* Medicinal chemistry of gastrointestinal and antidiabetic agents; histamine M2-receptor antagonists; aldose reductase inhibitors; bioisosteusm. *Mailing Add:* Pfizer Cent Res Groton CT 06340-5196

LIPINSKI, JOSEPH FLOYD, PSYCHOTIC DISORDERS, MOVEMENT DISORDERS. *Current Pos:* ASSOC PROF PSYCHIAT, MED UNIV SC, 93-, DIR, AFFECTIVE DIS PROG. *Personal Data:* b New Kensington, Pa, Jan 22, 40; m 79, Edith; c Jed & Tom. *Educ:* Jefferson Med Col, MD, 66. *Prof Exp:* Internship med, Jefferson Med Hosp, 67; residency psychiat, Harvard Med Sch, Mass Gen Hosp, 71, fel, 72-73; residency psychiat, Harvard Med Sch-Mass Gen Hosp, 71, fel, 72-73, from asst prof to assoc prof, 73-93; dir, Clin Res Ctr Study Psychotic Disorder & chief, Psychopharmacol Lab, Maulman Res Ctr, McLean Hosp. *Mem:* Am Col Neuropsychopharmacol; Psychiat Res Soc; Cong Int Neuropsychopharmacol; AAAS. *Res:* Pathophysiology of the major psychiatric and neurological movement disorders. *Mailing Add:* Med Univ SC 171 Ashley Ave Charleston SC 29425. *Fax:* 803-792-4394

LIPINSKI, WALTER C(HARLES), ELECTRICAL ENGINEERING, NUCLEAR ENGINEERING. *Current Pos:* RETIRED. *Personal Data:* b Chicago, Ill, Jan 5, 27; m 51, Jo A Miller; c Marjorie. *Educ:* Univ Ill, BSc, 50; Ill Inst Technol, MSc, 63, PhD(elec eng), 69. *Prof Exp:* From asst elec engr to sr elec engr, Argonne Nat Lab, 50-96. *Concurrent Pos:* Consult, Adv Comt Reactor Safeguards, US Nuclear Regulatory Comn, 64-96. *Res:* Control engineering; instrumentation; nuclear reactor control and instrumentation; nuclear power plant development; nuclear reactor safety. *Mailing Add:* 9700 S Cass Ave Bldg 208 Argonne Nat Lab Argonne IL 60439

LIPINSKY, EDWARD SOLOMON, SYSTEMS ANALYSIS COMMERCIAL DEVELOPMENT. *Current Pos:* PRES, INNOVATIVE THINKING INC, 95- *Personal Data:* b Asheville, NC, Nov 15, 29; m 54, Sherry Dobrow; c Edward & Sarah. *Educ:* Mass Inst Technol, BS, 52; Harvard Univ, AM, 54. *Honors & Awards:* Tech Achievement Award, US Dept Energy, 94 & 95. *Prof Exp:* Res assoc, Ohio State Univ, 57-59; prin res scientist, Battelle Columbus Memorial Inst, 59-71, assoc div chief bus & tech planning, 71-74, res leader, 75-79, sr res leader res mgt, 79-85, res leader org & polymer chem, 85-95. *Mem:* Am Chem Soc; fel AAAS; Sigma Xi; Am Inst Chem Engrs; Commercial Develop Asn; Tech Asn Pulp & Paper Indust. *Res:* Chemicals from biomass; renewable resource technology; diffusion-controlled reactions; computer-aided idea generation; dynamic simulation modeling of chemical processes. *Mailing Add:* 6481 Bellbrook Pl Worthington OH 43085-2988. *E-Mail:* elipinsk@sprynet.com

LIPKA, BENJAMIN, ORGANIC CHEMISTRY. *Current Pos:* CONSULT TECHNOLO GROUP, STAMFORD, CT, 92- *Personal Data:* b New York, NY, Feb 5, 29; m 58; c 3. *Educ:* NY Univ, BA, 49, PhD(org chem), 58. *Prof Exp:* Chemist, Geigy Chem Corp, 59-60; sr chemist, Allied Chem Corp, 60-67; sr develop chemist, Upjohn Co, 67-92. *Mem:* Am Chem Soc. *Res:* Laboratory synthesis and chemical plant production of organic compounds. *Mailing Add:* 19 Northrop Rd Woodbridge CT 06525-1722

LIPKA, JAMES J, BIOINORGANIC CHEMISTRY. *Current Pos:* sr res biochemist, Dept Hepatitis Tech Prod Develop, 93-94, PATENT LIAISON, DEPT TECHNOL ASSESSMENT & ACQUISITIONS, ABBOTT LABS, ABBOTT PARK, ILL, 94- *Personal Data:* b Highland Park, Mich, Aug 1, 54; m 80. *Educ:* Univ Mich, BS, 76; Columbia Univ, MA, 77, PhD(chem), 82. *Prof Exp:* asst res chemist res serv, Vet Admin Med Ctr, San Francisco & Anesthesia Dept, Univ Calif, San Francisco, 55-87; res assoc, Dept Path, Stanford Univ Blood Bank, Stanford Univ Med Sch, Palo Alto, Calif, 87-92; mgr diag prod develop, Genelabs, Inc, Redwood City, Calif, 92-93. *Concurrent Pos:* Consult, Genelabs Asia Ltd, Singapore, 91-92. *Mem:* Am Chem Soc; Sigma Xi; AAAS; NY Acad Sci. *Res:* Methods for labelling biological polymers and assemblies with heavy atoms for the purpose of increasing contrast in high-resolution electron microscopy. *Mailing Add:* Dept 7CE Bldg Ap 32sw-3 Abbott Labs Blds 200 Abbott Park Rd Abbott Park IL 60064-3537

LIPKE, PETER NATHAN, CELL ADHESION, CELL SURFACE DEVELOPMENT. *Current Pos:* from asst prof to assoc prof, 76-89, PROF MOLECULAR CELL BIOL, DEPT BIOL SCI, HUNTER COL, 90- *Personal Data:* b San Francisco, Calif, June 18, 50; m 71, Anne Michael; c Jonathan, Maria, David, Nathan, Michael, Jermaine & Omar. *Educ:* Univ Chicago, BS, 71; Univ Calif, Berkeley, PhD(biochem), 76. *Prof Exp:* Fel, Dept Zool, Univ Wis-Madison, 76-78. *Concurrent Pos:* Lectr, Fed Am Soc Exp Biol. *Mem:* Am Soc Microbiol; fel AAAS; Am Soc Biochem & Molecular Biol. *Res:* Molecular basis for cell-cell adhesion in eukaryotes, using mating in Saccharomyces cerevisiae as a model; developmental changes in cell surface structure; architecture and biosynthesis of fungal cell walls; fungal cell wall structure. *Mailing Add:* Dept Biol Hunter Col 695 Park Ave New York NY 10021. *Fax:* 212-772-5227; *E-Mail:* lipke@genectr.hunter.cuny.edu

LIPKE, WILLIAM G, PLANT PHYSIOLOGY, PLANT BIOCHEMISTRY. *Current Pos:* From asst prof to assoc prof plant physiol, 65-74, ASSOC PROF BIOL, NORTHERN ARIZ UNIV, 74-, PLANT PHYSIOLOGIST, 65- *Personal Data:* b Chesterton, Ind, Dec 19, 36; m 57; c 4. *Educ:* Purdue Univ, BS, 59; Univ Nebr, MS, 62; Tex A&M Univ, PhD(plant physiol), 66. *Mem:* AAAS; Am Soc Plant Physiol. *Res:* Plant physiology, especially mineral nutrition; weed science, especially plant enzymes. *Mailing Add:* 452 W Spruce St Camp Verde AZ 86322

LIPKIN, DAVID, NUCLEIC ACID CHEMISTRY, PHOSPHORUS CHEMISTRY. *Current Pos:* from assoc prof to prof chem, Washington Univ, 46-69, chmn dept, 64-70, William Greenleaf Eliot prof chem, 69-81, EMER WILLIAM GREENLEAF ELIOT PROF CHEM, WASHINGTON UNIV, 81- *Personal Data:* b Philadelphia, Pa, Jan 30, 13; m 42, Silvia Stantic; c Jeffrey A & Edward W. *Educ:* Univ Pa, BS, 34; Univ Calif, PhD(chem), 39. *Honors & Awards:* St Louis Award, Am Chem Soc, 70. *Prof Exp:* Petrol res chemist, Res & Develop Dept, Atlantic Ref Co, Pa, 34-36; res fel chem, Univ Calif, 39-42, chemist, 42-43; chemist & group leader, Manhattan Dist, Los Alamos, NMex, 43-46. *Concurrent Pos:* Guggenheim fel, 55; trustee, Argonne Univs Asn, 69-71; vis res scientist, John Innes Inst, Norwich, England, 60 & 71, spec consult, 78. *Mem:* Am Chem Soc; Sigma Xi. *Res:* Free radicals; organic phosphorus compounds; nucleic acids; electrochemical synthesis; aromatic hydrocarbons. *Mailing Add:* Dept Chem Washington Univ St Louis MO 63130

LIPKIN, GEORGE, MEDICINE, DERMATOLOGY. *Current Pos:* From instr to assoc prof, 61-74, PROF DERMAT, MED SCH, NY UNIV, 74- *Personal Data:* b New York, NY, Dec 31, 30; m 57, Sari Berger; c Michael D & Lisa S. *Educ:* Columbia Univ, AB, 52; State Univ NY Downstate Med Ctr, MD, 55. *Concurrent Pos:* Prin investr, Nat Cancer Inst res grants, Dermat Found, Med Ctr, NY Univ, 61-97; vis scientist, Univ Zurich, 72-73; dir, Berger Found Cancer Res. *Mem:* Soc Invest Dermat; AAAS; Am Acad Dermat; Harvey Soc; Union Concerned Scientists. *Res:* Biology of malignant melanoma; biologic transformation of malignant cells; endogenous inhibitors of growth. *Mailing Add:* 61 Virginia Ave Clifton NJ 07012. *Fax:* 212-263-6649

LIPKIN, HARRY JEANNOT, nuclear physics, particle physics, for more information see previous edition

LIPKIN, LEWIS EDWARD, NEUROPATHOLOGY, COMPUTER SCIENCES. *Current Pos:* dir, Div Cancer Biol & Diagnosis, head, Image Processing Unit Off, 72-80, CHIEF IMAGE PROCESSING SECT, LAB MATH BIOL, NAT CANCER INST, NIH, 80- *Personal Data:* b New York, NY, Nov 2, 25; m 52; c 2. *Educ:* NY Univ, BA, 44; Long Island Col Med, MD, 49; Am Bd Path, dipl & cert anat path & neuropath, 52. *Prof Exp:* From intern med to resident path, Mt Sinai Hosp NY, 49-53; asst prof path & neuropath, State Univ NY Downstate Med Ctr, 56-62; head neuropath, Path Sect, Perinatal Res Br, Nat Inst Neurol Dis & Stroke, 62-72. *Concurrent Pos:* Asst pathologist, Kings County Hosp, 56-62; USPHS sr res fel neuropath, Mt Sinai Hosp NY, 55-56; USPHS res grant, 59-62; consult, Nat Inst Neurol Dis & Stroke, 61-62. *Mem:* Asn Res Nerv & Ment Dis; Int Acad Path; Am Asn Neuropath; Asn Comput Mach. *Res:* Computer analysis of microscopic images, especially neuropathologic material; automation of analysis of two dimensional gel electrophoresis; analysis and synthesis of nucleic acid secondary structure. *Mailing Add:* 9913 Belhaven Rd Bethesda MD 20817-1733

LIPKIN, MARTIN, GASTROENTEROLOGY, ONCOLOGY. *Current Pos:* PROF MED, MED COL & GRAD SCH MED SCI, CORNELL UNIV, 78-; MEM & ATTEND PHYSICIAN, MEMORIAL SLOAN-KETTERING CANCER CTR, 85-, HEAD, IRVING WEINSTEIN LAB GASTROINTESTINAL CANCER PREV, 90-; DIR CLIN RES, STRANG CANCER PREV CTR, ROCKEFELLER UNIV, 96- *Personal Data:* b New York, NY, Apr 30, 26; m 58, Joan Schulein; c Richard & Steven. *Educ:* NY Univ, AB, 46, MD, 50. *Prof Exp:* Instr physiol, Sch Med, Univ Pa, 53-54; from instr to assoc prof, Cornell Univ, 55-78. *Concurrent Pos:* Fel physiol, Med Col, Cornell Univ, 52-53, fel med, 55-58; USPHS res fel, 55-56; res collabr, Brookhaven Nat Lab, 58-72; dir gastroenterol res unit, Cornell Med Div, Bellevue Hosp, 58-68; guest investr, Rockefeller Inst, 59-60; NIH res career prog award, 61-71; assoc attend physician, New York Hosp, 70- & Mem Hosp, 71-; assoc prof, Grad Sch Med Sci, Cornell Univ, 71-78; award lectr, Med Soc State NY, 71, secy, Sect Gastroenterol & Colon & Rectal Surg, 71, vchmn, 72, chmn, Sci Prog Comt, 73; hon pres, Int Acad Pathol Conf colorectal cancer, 81; ann hon lectr, Israel Med Asn & Gastroenterol Soc, 82; vis physician, Rockefeller Univ Hosp. *Mem:* Fel Am Col Physicians; Am Soc Clin Invest; Am Physiol Soc; Am Gastroenterol Asn; Am Asn Cancer Res. *Res:* Cancer prevention, chemoprevention, natural compounds and pharmaceutical agents; proliferation and differentiation of premalignant and malignant gastrointestinal cells in man; application of intermediate biomarkers to human chemoprevention studies and analyses of chemopreventive properties of naturally occurring and pharmaceutical compounds. *Mailing Add:* Rockefeller Univ Strang Cancer Res Lab 1730 York Ave New York NY 10021

LIPKOWITZ, KENNY BARRY, COMPUTATIONAL CHEMISTRY, PHYSICAL ORGANIC CHEMISTRY. *Current Pos:* from asst prof to assoc prof, 77-90, PROF CHEM, PURDUE UNIV, 90- *Personal Data:* b Bronx, NY, Apr 1, 50; m 78; c 2. *Educ:* State Univ NY, Geneseo, BS, 72; Mont State Univ, PhD(chem), 75. *Prof Exp:* Asst chem, Ohio State Univ, 76-77. *Concurrent Pos:* Vis prof, Princeton Univ, 81-82, Univ Calif, San Francisco, 89-90. *Mem:* Am Chem Soc. *Res:* Theoretical studies of organic molecules using quantum mechanical and molecular mechanics methods. *Mailing Add:* Dept Chem IUPUI Purdue Univ 402 N Blackford St Indianapolis IN 46202-3274

LIPMAN, DAVID J, BIOTECHNOLOGY. *Current Pos:* DIR, NAT CTR BIOTECHNOL INFO, NAT LIBR MED, NIH, 88- *Mailing Add:* NIH Nat Libr Med Nat Ctr Biotechnol Info Bldg 38A Rm 8N803 8600 Rockville Pike Bethesda MD 20894

LIPMAN, JACK M, PATHOLOGY, CELLULAR TOXICOLOGY. *Current Pos:* ASSOC RES INVESTR, HOFFMAN-LA ROCHE, 93- *Personal Data:* b Huntington, NY, Oct 25, 54. *Educ:* State Univ NY, PhD(exp path), 86- *Res:* Alternatives to animal research. *Mailing Add:* Dept Toxicol & Pathol Invest Toxicol Hoffman-La Roche Inc 340 Kingsland St Bldg 100/1 Nutley NJ 07110-1199

LIPMAN, JOSEPH, MATHEMATICS. *Current Pos:* from asst prof to assoc prof, 68-72, HEAD, MATH DEPT, PURDUE UNIV, WEST LAFAYETTE, 87- *Personal Data:* b Toronto, Ont, Can, June 15, 38; m 62; c 2. *Educ:* Univ Toronto, BA, 60; Harvard Univ, MA, 61, PhD(math), 65. *Prof Exp:* Asst prof math, Queen's Univ, Ont, 65 & Purdue Univ, 66-67; vis asst prof, Columbia Univ, 67-68. *Mem:* Am Math Soc; Can Math Cong. *Res:* Algebraic geometry. *Mailing Add:* Purdue Univ West Lafayette IN 47907-1968

LIPMAN, MARC JOSEPH, GRAPH THEORY. *Current Pos:* CHMN, MATH SCI, OAKLAND UNIV, ROCHESTER, MI, 97- *Personal Data:* b Chicago, Ill, Mar 19, 50; m 81; c 2. *Educ:* Lake Forest Col, BA, 71; Dartmouth Col, AM, 73, PhD(math), 76. *Prof Exp:* Lectr math, Dartmouth Col, 73; from asst prof to assoc prof, Ind Univ/Purdue Univ, Ft Wayne, 76-89. *Concurrent Pos:* Assoc, Nat Res Coun, Naval Res Lab, 80. *Mem:* Math Asn Am; Soc Indust & Appl Mathematicians; Asn for Comput Mach; Sigma Xi. *Res:* Graph theory; intelligent systems. *Mailing Add:* Dept Math Sci Oakland Univ Rochester MI 48309

LIPMAN, PETER WALDMAN, GEOLOGY. *Current Pos:* GEOLOGIST, US GEOL SURV, 62- *Personal Data:* b New York, NY, Apr 21, 35; m 62, Beverly Showalter; c Ben & Tim. *Educ:* Yale Univ, BS, 58; Stanford Univ, MS, 59, PhD(geol), 62. *Honors & Awards:* Burwell Award, Geol Soc Am, 83. *Concurrent Pos:* NSF fel, Geol Inst, Tokyo, 64-65. *Mem:* Geol Soc Am; Mineral Soc Am; Am Geophys Union. *Res:* Petrology and structural geology; volcanology, especially geology of calderas and related ash flows. *Mailing Add:* US Geol Surv MS 910 345 Middlefield Rd Menlo Park CA 94025. *E-Mail:* plipman@mojave.wr.usgs.gov

LIPNER, HARRY JOEL, REPRODUCTIVE ENDOCRINOLOGY. *Current Pos:* RETIRED. *Personal Data:* b New York, NY, Aug 26, 22; m 49; c 4. *Educ:* Long Island Univ, BS, 42; Univ Chicago, MS, 47; Univ Iowa, PhD(physiol), 52. *Prof Exp:* Res assoc thyroid iodine trap, Univ Iowa, 52; Nat Cancer Inst res fel thyroid physiol, 52-54; instr clin path, Chicago Med Sch, 54-55; from asst prof to prof physiol, Fla State Univ, 55-90. *Concurrent Pos:* NIH fel & vis prof, Dept Anat, Harvard Med Sch, 69-70; Fulbright vis prof, Ctr Advan Biochem, Indian Inst Sci, Bangalore, India, 74-75; mem, Regulatory Biol Rev Panel, NSF, 84-87. *Mem:* AAAS; Endocrine Soc; Sigma Xi; Soc Study Reproduction; Am Physiol Soc. *Res:* Mechanism of ovulation; nonsteroidal gonadal feedback control of Gonadotropin secretion. *Mailing Add:* 1471 Live Oak Dr Tallahassee FL 32308

LIPNER, STEVEN BARNETT, SOFTWARE SYSTEMS, COMPUTER SECURITY. *Current Pos:* GROUP MGR, SECURE SYSTS, DIGITAL EQUIP CORP, 81- *Personal Data:* b Independence, Kans, Sept 30, 43; m 80. *Educ:* Mass Inst Technol, SB, 65, SM, 66. *Prof Exp:* Assoc dept head, Intel & Info Syst, MITRE Corp, 77-80 & Command & Control Systs, 80-81. *Concurrent Pos:* Chmn comt security & privacy, Inst Elec & Electronics Engrs Comput Soc, 83-84, mem, Nat Res Coun Comt Comput Security, Dept Energy, 87-88, Nat Computer Systs Security & Privacy Adv Bd, 89- *Mem:* Asn Comput Mach; Sigma Xi; Inst Elec & Electronics Engrs Comput Soc. *Res:* Security controls for computer systems; theoretical and practical advances in network security and secure operating systems. *Mailing Add:* 11711 Sumacs St Oakton VA 22124-2216

LIPNICK, ROBERT LOUIS, TOXICOLOGICAL MECHANISM, PREDICTIVE TOXICOLOGY. *Current Pos:* chemist, 79-80, leader structure activ group, 80-85, SR CHEMIST, US ENVIRON PROTECTION AGENCY, 85- *Personal Data:* b Baltimore, Md, Sept 9, 41; m 67, Anne R Goldberg; c Deborah E & David H. *Educ:* Univ Md, College Park, BS, 63; Brandeis Univ, PhD(org chem), 69. *Prof Exp:* Fel chem, Univ Minn, Minneapolis, 69-72; vis scientist, var African univs, 73-74; res assoc, Sloan-Kettering Inst, 74-79. *Concurrent Pos:* Vis scientist, Borstel Res Inst, Fed Repub Ger, 86 & Pharmacol Inst, Univ Lund, Sweden, 89; assoc ed, Soc Environ Toxicol, 89-; co-organizer workshop, Environ Protection Agency, 88; invited lectr, Comn Europ Communities, Ispra, Italy, 90; mem, Int Sci Comt, Fourth Int Workshop Quant Struct-Activ Relationship in Environ Toxicol & Chem, Veldhoven, Neth, 90. *Mem:* Am Chem Soc; Asn Gov Toxicologists; Soc Environ Toxicol & Chem; Int Group Correlation Anal Org Chem; Chemometrics Soc. *Res:* Development of quantitative structure-activity relationships for predictive toxicology; estimation of physicochemical, conformational and reactive properties of molecules from chemical structure; quantitative structure activity relationship; computational chemistry; molecular modeling. *Mailing Add:* 5308 Pender Ct Alexandria VA 22304-1937. *Fax:* 202-260-1236; *E-Mail:* lipnick.robert@epamail.epa.gov

LIPO, THOMAS ANTHONY, POWER ELECTRONICS, ELECTRICAL MACHINES. *Current Pos:* prof, 81-90, W W GRAINGER PROF POWER ELECTRONICS & ELECT MACH, UNIV WIS-MADISON, 90- *Personal Data:* b Milwaukee, Wis, Feb 1, 38; m 64; c 4. *Educ:* Marquette Univ, BEE, 62, MSEE, 64; Univ Wis-Madison, PhD, 68. *Honors & Awards:* Outstanding Achievement Award, Inst Elec & Electronic Engrs, Indust Applications Soc, 86; William E Newell Award, Inst Elec & Electronic Engrs, Power Electronics Soc, 90. *Prof Exp:* Grad trainee, Allis-Chalmers Mfg Co, Milwaukee, 62-64, eng analyst, 64; instr, Univ Wis-Milwaukee, 64-66; Nat Res Coun res fel, Univ Manchester Inst Sci & Technol, Eng, 68-69; elec engr, Gen Elec Co, Schenectady, 69-79; prof, Purdue Univ, 79-80. *Concurrent Pos:* Vis assoc prof, Purdue Univ, 73-74; co-dir, Wis Elec Mach & Power Electronics Consortium, 81-; ed, Inst Elec & Electronic Engrs, Power Electronics Soc Trans, 83-90; dir, Wis Power Electronics Res Ctr, 87-; vis prof, Univ Sydney, 89; chmn, Indust Power Conversion Systs, Inst Elec & Electronic Engrs, Indust Applications Soc, 89- *Mem:* Fel Inst Elec & Electronic Engrs; Inst Elec & Electronic Engrs Power Eng Soc; Inst Elec & Electronic Engrs Indust Applications Soc; Inst Elec & Electronic Engrs Power Electronics Soc. *Res:* New power electronic circuits, controls and electrical machines for alternating current adjustable speed drives for industrial, commercial and utility applications. *Mailing Add:* Dept Elec & Comput Eng Univ Wis 1415 Johnson Dr Madison WI 53706

LIPOVSKI, GERALD JOHN (JACK), COMPUTER ENGINEERING, ELECTRICAL ENGINEERING. *Current Pos:* assoc prof, 76-82, PROF ELEC ENG & COMPUT SCI, UNIV TEX, AUSTIN, 82- *Personal Data:* b Coleman, Alta, Jan 28, 44; m 68; c 3. *Educ:* Univ Notre Dame, AB & BSEE, 66; Univ Ill, Urbana, MS, 67, PhD(elec eng), 69. *Prof Exp:* Res fel automata theory, Coordinated Sci Lab, Univ Ill, Urbana, 66-68, asst electronics, 67-68, asst comput archit, 68-69; asst prof elec eng, Univ Fla, 69-76. *Concurrent Pos:* Consult, Harris Semiconductor, 73-74 & Sycor, 76-77. *Mem:* Asn Comput Mach; Comput Soc of Inst Elec & Electronics Engrs. *Res:* Computer architecture; parallel and distributed computer architectures; data base processor architectures; microcomputer architectures and applications; hardware design languages. *Mailing Add:* Dept Elec Eng & Comput Sci Univ Tex Austin TX 78712

LIPOWITZ, JONATHAN, ORGANOMETALLIC CHEMISTRY, MATERIALS SCIENCE & CERAMICS ENGINEERING. *Current Pos:* res chemist, Dow Corning Corp, 65-74, res specialist, 74-75, sr res specialist, 75-79, assoc scientist, 79-87, SCIENTIST, RES DEPT, DOW CORNING CORP, 87- *Personal Data:* b Paterson, NJ, Apr 25, 37; m 60, Evelyn Jacobs; c Robert A & Suzanne J. *Educ:* Rutgers Univ, Newark, BS, 58; Univ Pittsburgh, PhD(chem), 64. *Prof Exp:* Fel, Pa State Univ, University Park, 64-65. *Mem:* Am Chem Soc; Sigma Xi; Am Ceramic Soc; Mat Res Soc; AAAS; NY Acad Sci. *Res:* Silicone flammability, mechanisms of effects of silicones on flammability of organic polymers; silicone chemistry and physical properties; characterization of advanced ceramics; preparation of ceramic fibers from polymers. *Mailing Add:* Dow Corning Corp 3901 S Saginaw Rd Midland MI 48686-0995

LIPOWSKI, ZBIGNIEW J, psychiatry, for more information see previous edition

LIPP, STEVEN ALAN, INORGANIC CHEMISTRY. *Current Pos:* MEM TECH STAFF, SARNOFF CORP, 70- *Personal Data:* b Brooklyn, NY, Jan 25, 44; c 2. *Educ:* Brooklyn Col, BS, 65; Univ Calif, Berkeley, PhD(inorg chem), 70. *Honors & Awards:* Achievement Award, RCA Labs, 74, David Sarnoff Award, RCA Corp, 75. *Mem:* Electrochem Soc; Soc Info Display. *Res:* Preparation and evaluation of new cathodoluminescent materials, as well as the design and testing of enhancements for chemical milling; fabrication of active liquid crystal display substrate involving all photolithography and processing. *Mailing Add:* Sarnoff Corp C N 5300 Washington Rd Princeton NJ 08543-4300

LIPPA, ERIK ALEXANDER, OPHTHALMOLOGY, CLINICAL RESEARCH. *Current Pos:* DIR, MED AFFAIRS, ALLERGAN, INC, IRVINE, CA, 93- *Personal Data:* b Minneapolis, Minn, Nov 7, 45; m 80, Linda S Mottow; c 2. *Educ:* Calif Inst Technol, BS, 67; Univ Mich, MS, 68, PhD(math), 71; Albert Einstein Col Med, MD, 80. *Prof Exp:* NATO fel math, Oxford Univ, 71-72; asst prof math, Purdue Univ, West Lafayette, 72-78; med intern, NY Univ & Manhattan Vet Admin Hosp, 80-81; ophthal resident, Ill Eye & Ear Infirmary, Chicago, Ill, 81-84, ophthalmologist, St Paul, Minn, 84-85; from assoc dir to dir clin res, Merck Res Lab, Blue Bell, Pa, 85-93. *Concurrent Pos:* Adj clin asst prof, Jefferson Med Col, Philadelphia, Pa, 86-89, 91-96; clin lectr, Dept Ophthal, Univ Pa, Philadelphia, 87-93; instr, Wills Eye Hosp, Philadelphia, 86-91, asst surgeon, 91-93. *Mem:* Am Acad Ophthal; Asn Res Vision & Ophthal; Int Soc Eye Res; Sigma Xi; Europ Glaucoma Soc; Am Glaucoma Soc. *Res:* Ophthalmology; clinical pharmacology and clinical research; drug development; applications of mathematics to medicine and pharmaceutical sciences; analytic number theory. *Mailing Add:* PO Box 16517 Irvine CA 92623-6517. *Fax:* 714-246-6756; *E-Mail:* lippa__erik@allergan.com

LIPPA, LINDA SUSAN MOTTOW, OCULAR PATHOLOGY, MEDICAL OPHTHALMOLOGY. *Current Pos:* ASSOC CLIN PROF, UNIV CALIF, IRVINE, 94- *Personal Data:* b Boston, Mass, Apr 9, 51; m 80; c 2. *Educ:* Harvard Univ, AB, 73; Columbia Univ, MD, 77. *Prof Exp:* Intern internal med, St Luke's Hosp & Med Ctr, New York, NY, 77-78; resident ophthal, Montefiore Hosp & Med Ctr & Albert Einstein Col Med, Bronx, NY, 78-80, chief resident, 80-81; fel ophthalmic path, Eye & Ear Infirmary, Univ Ill, Chicago, 81-82; clin instr ophthal, Loyola Univ Med Ctr, Chicago, Ill & Hines Vet Admin Hosp, 82-83, clin asst prof, 83-84; clin asst prof ophthalmologist, Univ Minn & attend opthalmologist & ocular pathologist, St Paul Ramsey Med Ctr, 84-85; clin asst prof, Jefferson Med Col, Philadelphia, Pa, 86-93. *Concurrent Pos:* Josephine Murray traveling fel, Radcliffe Col Res London, 72; org chem, Harvard Bur Study Coun, 73; lab teaching asst, Harkness Eye Inst, 74 & Albert Einstein Col Med, 78; mem, Path Curric Comt, Dept Ophthal, Montefiore Hosp & Med Ctr, Albert Einstein Col Med; rep, Ophthalmologists in Training Comt, Am Acad Ophthal, 78- 81, adv fac, Continuing Educ Comt, 78-81, chmn, Ophthalmologists in Training Comt & Continuing Educ Comt, 80-81; clin attend & ocular pathologist, Hines, VA, 81-84; attend ophthalmologist & ocular pathologist, Cook Co Hosp, Chicago, Ill, 82-84; vis lectr, Dept Ophthal, Univ Md, 85; attend ophthalmologist, Wills Eye Hosp, 85, ocular path, 85-86, asst surgeon opthal, 85-93. *Mem:* Am Acad Ophthal; AMA. *Res:* Retinal embryonal development; inflammatory and neoplastic ocular and adnexal disease; glaucoma; development of pharmacologic models for new compound and vehicle assessment; ophthalmology. *Mailing Add:* PO Box 16517 Irvine CA 92713-6517

LIPPARD, STEPHEN J, INORGANIC CHEMISTRY, BIOCHEMISTRY. *Current Pos:* prof, 82-88, ARTHUR AMOS NOYES PROF CHEM, MASS INST TECHNOL, 88-, HEAD, CHEM DEPT, 95- *Personal Data:* b Pittsburgh, Pa, Oct 12, 40; m 64, Judith Drezner; c Joshua & Alexander. *Educ:* Haverford Col, BA, 62; Mass Inst Technol, PhD(chem), 65. *Hon Degrees:* DSc, Tex A&M Univ, 95. *Honors & Awards:* Camille & Henry Dreyfus Teacher-Scholar Award, 72; Henry J Albert Award, Int Precious Metals Inst, Eng, 85; Inorg Chem Award, Am Chem Soc, 87, Remson Award, 88, Inorg Chem Award, 94; Alexander von Humboldt Award, 88; Bailar Medal, 93; Nichols Medal, 95. *Prof Exp:* NSF fel, Mass Inst Technol, 65-66; from asst prof to prof chem, Columbia Univ, 66-82. *Concurrent Pos:* Consult, Esso Res & Eng Co, 67-73 & John Wiley & Sons, Inc, 81-; Alfred P Sloan Found fel, 68-70; John Simon Guggenheim mem fel, Sweden, 72; ed, Progress in Inorganic Chem, John E Fogarty Sr Int fel, 78-79; consult, Engelhard Indust, 82, Sun Oil Co, 82, chair, 87-, Procept, 95-, NextCell, 96-, Johnson Matthey, 89-93; Exxon Corp, Smith Kline & Beckman; assoc ed, J Am Chem Soc; chmn, Gordon Res Conf, Inorg Chem, 85; chair, Metals Biol Gordon Conf, 96. *Mem:* Nat Acad Sci; Inst Med-Nat Acad Sci; Am Crystallog Asn; hon mem Ital Chem Soc; Am Acad Arts & Sci; fel AAAS; Am Chem Soc. *Res:* Inorganic, bioinorganic and organometallic chemistry, especially preparation, structural properties and reactions of transition metal complexes; ligand bridged bimetallic complexes and proteins; metal binding to nucleic acids; platinum antitumor drugs; methane monooxygenase; neurochemistry. *Mailing Add:* Mass Inst Technol Rm 18-590 Cambridge MA 02139. *Fax:* 617-258-8150

LIPPEL, KENNETH, ATHEROSCLEROSIS LIPID METABOLISM. *Current Pos:* RETIRED. *Personal Data:* b New York, NY, Feb 21, 29; m 61; c 1. *Educ:* City Col NY, BS, 49, MBA, 60; Univ Fla, PhD(biochem), 66. *Prof Exp:* NIH fel biochem, Univ Calif, Los Angeles, 66-68; asst prof dermat & biochem, Sch Med, Univ Miami, 68-70; res biochemist, Lipids Br, Human Nutrit Res Div, Agr Res Serv, USDA, 70-72; health sci adminr, Lipid Metab Br, Div Heart & Vascular Dis, Nat Heart, Lung & Blood Inst, NIH, 72-93. *Concurrent Pos:* Fel, Coun Arteriosclerosis, Am Heart Asn, 75- *Mem:* AAAS; Am Soc Biol Chem; Am Heart Asn; Am Chem Soc; Fedn Am Socs Exp Biol; Sigma Xi; Am Asn Clin Chem. *Res:* Regulation of fatty acid and lipid metabolism; relationship of lipoprotein metabolism to atherosclerosis; vitamin A metabolism. *Mailing Add:* 4400 East-West Hwy Apt 715 Bethesda MD 20814

LIPPERT, BRUCE J, enzyme chemicals, for more information see previous edition

LIPPERT, BYRON E, phycology, for more information see previous edition

LIPPERT, LAVERNE FRANCIS, PLANT PATHOLOGY. *Current Pos:* RETIRED. *Personal Data:* b Deerlodge, Mont, Sept 21, 28; m 50; c 5. *Educ:* State Col Wash, BS, 50; Univ Calif, Davis, PhD(plant path), 59. *Prof Exp:* Asst plant path, Univ Calif, Davis, 55-58; from asst olericulturist to assoc olericulturist, Univ Calif, Riverside, 58-72, prof veg crops & olericulturist, 72-88, vchmn, Dept Plant Sci, 75-88. *Mem:* Am Genetic Soc; Am Hort Soc. *Res:* Vegetable crops breeding, especially peppers and melons. *Mailing Add:* 2308 Forest View Lane Anacortes WA 98221

LIPPERT, LLOYD EDWARD, TRANSFUSION MEDICINE, IMMUNOGENETICS. *Current Pos:* PROJ MGR, BIONETICS CORP, 95- *Personal Data:* b Hoven, SDak, Mar 31, 44. *Educ:* SDak State Univ, MS, 70; Bowling Green State Univ, SAB, 75, MS, 75; Med Col Va, PhD(path), 87. *Prof Exp:* Lab mgr & chief blood bank, Tripler Army Med Ctr, 80-83; chief res opers, Walter Reed Army Med Ctr, 87-92, lab mgr, 93-95; prof mgr, Off Asst Secy Health Affairs, Dept Defense, 92-93. *Res:* Extending the shelflife of liquid stored red blood cells beyond 42 days to 8 weeks and possibly longer; manufacture precision grade hemoglobin-based blood substitute for research. *Mailing Add:* Bionetics Corp 11113 Pinion Ct Gaithersburg MD 20878

LIPPES, JACK, OBSTETRICS & GYNECOLOGY, REPRODUCTION. *Current Pos:* Clin instr, State Univ NY, Buffalo, 52-60, clin assoc, 60-66, assoc prof, 66-75, PROF OBSTET & GYNEC, SCH MED, STATE UNIV NY BUFFALO, 75- *Personal Data:* b Buffalo, NY, Feb 19, 24; m 47; c Howard, B Fredda & Harold. *Educ:* Univ Buffalo, MD, 47. *Concurrent Pos:* Consult, Rockefeller Univ, 59-75, Birth Control Ministries Health, SKorea, Taiwan, Pakistan, India, Turkey & Tunisia, 64-66, Pop Coun, 66-70, World Neighbors Found, Okla, 66-78, Ortho Pharmaceut Corp, 66-78, Syntex Res, 78-79, WHO Comt Studying Human Reprod, 74-78 & Sterling-Winthrop Pharmaceut Corp grant, 77-78; investr, Upjohn Pharmaceut Co, 75-78 & Prog Appl Res Fertil Regulation, 75-78; chmn, Dept Obstet & Gynec, Deaconess Hosp, Buffalo, 75-81; vis prof obstet & gynec, Charing Cross Hosp, Med Sch, London, 81; clin chief, Erie Co Med Ctr, Buffalo, NY, 81-94. *Mem:* Asn Planned Parenthood Physicians; Planned Parenthood Fedn; Am Fertil Soc; Am Col Obstet & Gynec; Asn Health Reproductive Professionals. *Res:* Human oviductal fluid; contraception, especially intrauterine contraception; inventor and researcher of intrauterine contraceptive device known as the Loop; immunology of the genital tract; immunosuppresive proteins in the female genital tract. *Mailing Add:* Dept Gynec/Obstet Erie Co Med Ctr 462 Grider St Buffalo NY 14215. *Fax:* 716-898-4425; *E-Mail:* jlip@acu.buffalo.edu

LIPPINCOTT, BARBARA BARNES, MICROBIOLOGY, PLANT PHYSIOLOGY. *Current Pos:* Res assoc biol sci, 60-80, sr res assoc biochem, molecular biol & cell biol, 80-, PROF, NORTHWESTERN UNIV. *Personal Data:* b Raleigh, Ill, Oct 27, 34; m 56, James A; c Jeanne M, Thomas R & John J. *Educ:* Washington Univ, St Louis, AB, 55, MA, 57, PhD(zool & molecular biol), 59. *Prof Exp:* Jane Coffin Childs Mem Fund Med Res fel physiol genetics, Lab Physiol Genetics, Nat Ctr Sci Res, France, 59-60. *Concurrent Pos:* Vis scholar, Univ Calif, Berkeley, 70-71; lectr, Northwestern Univ, 72-73 & 81-; vis scientist, Inst Bot, Univ Heidelberg, 74. *Mem:* Am Soc Microbiol; Sigma Xi. *Res:* Electron spin resonance in biological systems; crown-gall tumor formation; control mechanisms in replication, growth and development. *Mailing Add:* 2815 Harrison St Northwestern Univ Evanston IL 60201

LIPPINCOTT, EZRA PARVIN, NUCLEAR PHYSICS, SHIELDING. *Current Pos:* SR SCIENTIST, NUCLEAR ENG, WESTINGHOUSE ELEC CORP, 72- *Personal Data:* b Philadelphia, Pa, Sept 7, 39; m 63, Sharon Melton; c George, John & Susan. *Educ:* Mass Inst Technol, BS, 61, PhD(nuclear physics), 66. *Prof Exp:* Sr scientist, Battelle-Northwest Labs, 66-72. *Mem:* Am Nuclear Soc; Am Phys Soc; Am Soc Testing & Mat. *Res:* Experimental and theoretical reactor physics; passive and active neutron and gamma-ray dosimetry; data analysis; methods development; nuclear cross section measurement and data file evaluation; standards preparation. *Mailing Add:* 1776 McClure Rd Monroeville PA 15146

LIPPINCOTT, JAMES ANDREW, PLANT PHYSIOLOGY. *Current Pos:* from asst prof to prof biol sci, 60-81, assoc dean biol sci, 80-83, prof, 81-95, EMER PROF BIOCHEM, MOLECULAR & CELL BIOL, NORTHWESTERN UNIV, 95- *Personal Data:* b Cumberland Co, Ill, Sept 13, 30; m 56, Barbara Barnes; c Jeanne M, Thomas R & John J. *Educ:* Earlham Col, AB, 54; Wash Univ, AM, 56, PhD, 58. *Honors & Awards:* Centennial lectr, Mich State Univ Agr Exp Sta, 75; Tanner-Shaughnessy Merit Award, Ill Soc Microbiol, 81. *Prof Exp:* Res assoc plant physiol & lectr bot, Wash Univ, 58-59; Jane Coffin Childs Mem Fund Med Res fel, Lab Phytotron, Nat Ctr Sci Res, France, 59-60. *Concurrent Pos:* Vis assoc prof, Univ Calif, Berkeley, 70-71; vis prof, Univ Heidelberg, 74. *Mem:* AAAS; Am Soc Plant Physiol; Bot Soc Am; Am Soc Microbiol; Am Phytopath Soc; Sigma Xi; Am Soc Biol Chemists. *Res:* Crown-gall tumor formation; control mechanisms in replication, growth and development; tumor induction in plants by Agrobacterium tumefaciens. *Mailing Add:* 2815 Harrison St Evanston IL 60201

LIPPINCOTT-SCHWARTZ, JENNIFER, MOLECULAR MEMBRANE BIOLOGY, INTRACELLULAR MEMBRANE TRAFFICKING. *Current Pos:* SR STAFF SCIENTIST, NAT INST CHILD HEALTH & HUMAN DEVELOP, NIH, 90- *Personal Data:* b Kans, Oct 19, 52; m 75; c 2. *Educ:* Swarthmore Col, BA, 74; Stanford Univ, MS, 79; Johns Hopkins Univ, PhD(biol), 86. *Prof Exp:* Fel, Pharmacol Res Assoc, Nat Inst Gen Med Sci, 86-88; fel, Nat Res Serv Award Prog, 88-90. *Mem:* Am Soc Cell Biologists; AAAS. *Res:* Intracellular membrane transport pathways and the molecular basis for intracellular membrane sorting and the biogenesis of organelles. *Mailing Add:* Cell Biol & Metab Br Nat Inst Child Health & Human Develop NIH 9000 Rockville Pike Bldg 18T Bethesda MD 20892

LIPPITT, LOUIS, GEOPHYSICS. *Current Pos:* RETIRED. *Personal Data:* b New York, NY, Mar 19, 24; m 48, Adele D Wissmann; c Laurie, Craig, Bonnie & Nancie. *Educ:* City Col New York, BS, 47; Columbia Univ, MA, 53, PhD(geol), 59. *Prof Exp:* Physicist, Columbia Univ, 47-50 & NY Univ, 51-53; geologist, Stand Oil Co, Calif, 54-58; staff engr, Lockheed Missles & Space Co, 58-87. *Concurrent Pos:* Instr earth scis, Allan Hancock Col, 69- & Chapman Col, 85-86. *Mem:* Sr fel Geol Soc Am; Am Geophys Union; Sigma Xi. *Res:* Satellite systems; geophysical exploration. *Mailing Add:* 696 Raymond Ave Santa Maria CA 93455-2760

LIPPKE, HAGEN, ANIMAL NUTRITION. *Current Pos:* From asst prof to assoc prof ruminant nutrit, 66-74, ASSOC PROF ANIMAL SCI, TEX A&M UNIV, 74- *Personal Data:* b Yorktown, Tex, Nov 4, 36; m 58; c 3. *Educ:* Tex A&M Univ, BS, 59, MS, 61; Iowa State Univ, PhD(animal nutrit), 66. *Mem:* Am Dairy Sci Asn; Am Soc Animal Sci; AAAS. *Res:* Ruminant nutrition; forage utilization by cattle; forage characteristics influencing intake and digestibility. *Mailing Add:* 617 Cenizo Blvd Uvalde TX 78801

LIPPMAN, ABBY, WOMENS HEALTH, GENETIC SCREENING & TESTING. *Current Pos:* PROF EPIDEMIOL, MCGILL UNIV, 80-, PROF, DEPT HUMAN GENETICS, 92- *Personal Data:* b Brooklyn, NY; c 2. *Educ:* Cornell Univ, BA, 60; McGill Univ, PhD(human genetics), 79. *Honors & Awards:* Marion Porter Prize, Can Res Inst Advan Women. *Concurrent Pos:* Nat health res scholar, Health & Welfare Can, 81-86 & 86-92; mem, McGill Ctr Res & Teaching Women, McGill Univ, 88-, res assoc social studies med, 90-; adj prof, Dept Prev Social Med, Univ Montreal, 89-; assoc mem, Univ Que, Montreal, 91- *Mem:* Fel Can Col Med Geneticists; fel Am Col Epidemiol; Am Public Health Asn; Am Soc Human Genetics; fel AAAS; fel Can Soc Obstet & Gynecol. *Res:* Women's health; social, ethical and political implications of genetic screening and testing; feminist critique of biomedicine. *Mailing Add:* Dept Epidemiol McGill Univ 1020 Pine Ave W Montreal PQ H3A 1A2 Can. *Fax:* 514-398-4503; *E-Mail:* abbyl@epid.lan.mcgill.ca

LIPPMAN, ALFRED, chemical engineering; deceased, see previous edition for last biography

LIPPMAN, GARY EDWIN, MATHEMATICAL ANALYSIS, COMPUTER SCIENCE. *Current Pos:* PROF MATH, CALIF STATE UNIV, HAYWARD, 71- *Personal Data:* b Little Rock, Ark; c 2. *Educ:* San Jose State Col, BA, 63; Univ Calif, Riverside, MA, 65, PhD(math), 70; Univ San Francisco, JD, 78. *Prof Exp:* Asst prof math, Kenyon Col, 70-71. *Concurrent Pos:* Vis asst prof math, Univ Tenn, vis assoc prof comput sci & statist, Univ RI, 78-79; vis prof elec eng & computer sci, Univ Calif, Berkeley, 83-88. *Mem:* Am Math Soc; Math Asn Am; Comput Law Soc. *Res:* Fourier analysis; patent law. *Mailing Add:* Dept Math & Comput Sci Calif State Univ 25800 Carlos Bee Blvd Hayward CA 94542-3000

LIPPMAN, MARC ESTES, BREAST CANCER. *Current Pos:* DIR, VINCENT T LOMBARDI CANCER CTR, WASHINGTON, DC & PROF MED & PHARMACOL, GEORGETOWN UNIV SCH MED, 88- *Personal Data:* b Brooklyn, NY, Jan 15, 45. *Educ:* Cornell Univ, BA, 64; Yale Med Sch, MD, 68. *Honors & Awards:* Mallinckrodt Award, Clin Radioassay Soc, 78; Sidney Sachs Mem Lectr, Case Western Res, 85; D R Edwards Lect & Medal, Tenovus Inst, Wales, 85; Gosse Lectr, Dalhousie Univ, Halifax, NS, 87; Transatlantic Medal & Lect, Brit Endocrine Socs, 89; Tiffany Award of Distinction, Komen Found, 89; Barofsky Lectr, Howard Univ, 90; Rose Kushner Mem Lectr, Long Beach Mem Med Ctr, 90; Henrietta Banting Mem Lectr, Long Beach Mem Med Ctr, 90; Edward B Astwood Lect Award, Endocrine Soc, 91; Constance Wood Mem Lectr, Hammersmith Hosp, Eng, 91. *Prof Exp:* Intern, Osler Med Serv, Johns Hopkins Hosp, Baltimore, Md, 68-69; asst resident, 69-70; clin assoc, Leukemia Serv, Nat Cancer Inst, NIH, 70-71; clin assoc, Lab Biochem, 71-73; sr investr, Med Br, 74-88; head, Med Breast Cancer Sect, 76-88; clin prof med & pharmacol, Uniformed Serv, Univ Health Sci, 78- *Concurrent Pos:* Fel endocrinol, Yale Med Sch, New Haven, Conn, 73-74; mem, Merit Rev Bd Oncol, Vet Admin Med Res Serv, 77-81, Endocrine Treatment Comt, Nat Surg Adjuvant Breast Proj, 77-86 & pub affairs comt, Endocrine Soc, 80-81; consult, Dept Pharmacol, George Wash Sch Med, 78-89; co-chmn, Gordon Res Conf on Hormone Action, 84, chmn, 85; treas, Int Cong Hormones & Cancer, 84-; mem, med adv bd, Nat Alliance Breast Cancer Orgn, 86-; mem prog comt, Am Asn Cancer Res, 86, Am Soc Clin Oncol, 87-89 & Am Soc Clin Invest, 88; mem, Stage III Monitoring Comt, Nat Surg Adjuvant Proj Breast & Bowel Cancers, 87-89; chmn, local organizing comt, Am Soc Clin Oncol, 89-90; bd trustees, Am Cancer Soc, Dist of Columbia, 89-92; sci adv bd, Coord Coun Cancer Res, 89-; hon dir, Y-ME, Nat Orgn Breast Cancer Info & Support, 90-; Woodward vis prof, mem Sloan-Kettering, 90. *Mem:* Asn Am Physicians; Am Soc Clin Invest; Am Soc Biol Chemists; fel Am Col Physicians; Am Fedn Clin Res; Endocrine Soc; Am Soc Cell Biol; Am Asn Cancer Res; Am Soc Clin Oncol; Metastasis Res Soc. *Res:* Growth regulation of cancer; breast cancer; cancer endocrinology; growth factor receptors. *Mailing Add:* Vincent T Lombardi Cancer Res Ctr Georgetown Univ Res Bldg 5th Floor Rm E501 Washington DC 20007

LIPPMANN, DAVID ZANGWILL, CHEMICAL KINETICS, STATISTICAL MECHANICS. *Current Pos:* asst prof, 63-69, ASSOC PROF CHEM, SW TEX STATE UNIV, 69- *Personal Data:* b Houston, Tex, July 6, 25; m 69, Jane Neustein. *Educ:* Univ Tex, BSc, 47, MA, 49; Univ Calif, Berkeley, PhD(phys chem), 53. *Prof Exp:* Chemist, Reaction Motors, Inc, 54-57, Fulton-Irgon Div, Lithium Corp Am, 57-61 & Proteus, Inc, 61-63. *Concurrent Pos:* Vis scholar, Univ Tex, Austin, 80- *Mem:* Am Chem Soc; Sigma Xi; AAAS. *Res:* Theoretical physical chemistry, especially thermodynamics and statistical mechanics; rocketry and ballistics; properties of gems. *Mailing Add:* Dept Chem Southwest Tex State Univ San Marcos TX 78666. *Fax:* 512-245-2374; *E-Mail:* lippmann@physics.utexas.edu

LIPPMANN, HEINZ ISRAEL, MEDICINE, REHABILITATION MEDICINE. *Current Pos:* From asst prof to prof, 55-76, EMER PROF REHAB MED, ALBERT EINSTEIN COL MED, 76- *Personal Data:* b Breslau, Ger, May 21, 08; nat US; m 36, Alisa Moscato; c Ruth C, Robert, & Lawrence. *Educ:* Univ Freiburg, BA, 26; Univ Berlin, MD, 31; Univ Genoa, MD, 33. *Honors & Awards:* NAm Roentgen Soc Award, 58; Gold Medal Sci Exhibit, Am Cong Rehab Med, 59; Distinguished Clinician's Award, Am Acad Phys Med & Rehab, 86. *Concurrent Pos:* Assoc attend physician, Montefiore Hosp, Bronx, 44-86; lectr, Columbia Univ, 46-62; chief, Peripheral Vascular Clin, Sydney Hillman Health Ctr, 51-67; chief phys med, Workman's Circle Home for Aged, 51-87; chief, Peripheral Vascular Clin & vis physician, Bronx Munic Hosp Ctr, 56-; chief attend physician, Prosthetic & Brace Clin, 57-67, chief, Peripheral Vascular Clin, 57-, dir, Amputee Ctr, 61-76; consult peripheral vascular dis, Englewood Hosp, NJ & Vet Admin Hosp, East Orange, NJ, 67-93; dir rehab med, Jewish Hosp & Rehab Ctr, Jersey City, 74-85; attend physician & chief, Rehab Med Dept, Barnert Mem Hosp, Paterson, NJ, 75-85; consult rehab med, NJ & Vet Admin Hosp, East Orange & St Joseph's Hosp, Paterson NJ, 75-93. *Mem:* NY Acad Med; fel Am Col Physicians; Am Cong Rehab Med; NY Acad Sci; Am Acad Phys Med & Rehab. *Res:* Vascular physiology; peripheral vascular diseases; prosthetics; rheumatology; geriatrics; musicians disabilities; disabling venous diseases as health problems (in USA); disabled performing artists, pathophysiology and management. *Mailing Add:* Dept Rehab Med Albert Einstein Col Med New York NY 10461. *Fax:* 718-904-2846

LIPPMANN, MARCELO JULIO, GEOTHERMICS, GROUNDWATER HYDROLOGY. *Current Pos:* STAFF SCIENTIST, EARTH SCI DIV, LAWRENCE BERKELEY LAB, 76-, LEADER GEOTHERMAL GROUP, 83- *Personal Data:* b Buenos Aires, Arg, May 27, 39; m 65, Martha Costas; c 1. *Educ:* Univ Buenos Aires, MS, 66; Univ Calif, Berkeley, MS, 69, PhD(eng sci), 74. *Prof Exp:* Asst geologist, Arg Geol Serv, 63-66, sedimentologist, 66-67; asst res eng, Dept Civil Eng, Univ Calif, Berkeley, 74-76. *Concurrent Pos:* Consult hydrogeologist, Hidrosud SA, Buenos Aires, 67; Jane Lewis fel, Univ Calif, Berkeley, 69-71; US tech coordr, Dept Energy, Comn Federal de Electricidad, 77-; assoc ed, Geothermics, 91-95; pvt consult Hydrogeol-Geothermal Energy. *Mem:* Am Geophys Union; Soc Petrol Engrs. *Res:* Geothermal and groundwater resources; physics and numerical modeling of processes in porous media. *Mailing Add:* Earth Sci Div Lawrence Berkeley Nat Lab Bldg 90 Berkeley CA 94720. *Fax:* 510-486-5686; *E-Mail:* mjlippmann@lbl.gov

LIPPMANN, MORTON, ENVIRONMENTAL SCIENCES. *Current Pos:* assoc res scientist aerosol physiol, 64-67, from asst prof to assoc prof, 67-77, PROF ENVIRON MED & DIR, HUMAN EXPOSURE & HEALTH EFFECTS PROG, INST ENVIRON MED, NY UNIV, 77- *Personal Data:* b Brooklyn, NY, Sept 21, 32; m 56, Janet Gurian; c Amy, Stanley & David. *Educ:* Cooper Union, BChE, 54; Harvard Univ, SM, 55; NY Univ, PhD(indust hyg), 67. *Honors & Awards:* David Sinclair Award, Am Asn Aerosol Res; Donald E Cummings Award, Am Indust Hyg Asn; Herbert E Stokinger Award, Am Conf Govt Indust Hygienists; Henry F Smyth Jr Award, Am Acad Indust Hyg. *Prof Exp:* Indust hygienist, USPHS, Ohio, 55-57, US AEC, NY, 57-62; sr res engr, Del Electronics Corp, 62-64. *Concurrent Pos:* Chmn, Environ Protection Agency Clean Air Sci Adv Comn, 83-87, Environ Protection Agency Indoor Air & Total Human Exposure Adv Comt, 87-93; mem & chmn, bd sci counr, Nat Inst Occup Safety & Health, 88-93. *Mem:* Am Conf Govt Indust Hygienists; Am Indust Hyg Asn; Int Soc Environ Epidemiol; Am Asn Aerosol Res; Int Soc Exposure Anal. *Res:* Environmental hygiene; regional deposition and clearance of inhaled particles; sampling and analysis of atmospheric particles; aerodynamic behavior of respirable aerosols; field and laboratory studies of health effects of airborne toxicants. *Mailing Add:* NY Univ Nelson Inst Environ Med Tuxedo NY 10987

LIPPMANN, SEYMOUR A, APPLIED PHYSICS. *Current Pos:* RETIRED. *Personal Data:* b Brooklyn, NY, Nov 23, 19; m 45; c 3. *Educ:* Cooper Union, BChE, 42. *Prof Exp:* Group leader appl physics, Res Dept, US Rubber Co, 47-60, dept mgr phys res, 60-71, res assoc, 71-75; mgr Tire-Vehicle Systs Labs, Uniroyal Tire Co, Uniroyal, Inc, 75-85. *Concurrent Pos:* Sci consult; sem instr, Tire & Vehicle Dynamics, Soc Automotive Engrs. *Mem:* Am Phys Soc; Fel Soc Automotive Eng; Inst Elec & Electronics Eng; Am Soc Testing & Mat; Sigma Xi. *Res:* Physics of polymeric materials; transmission of noise and vibrations; design of electronic instrumentation for the study of dynamic systems and properties; perception of sound in the presence of background noise; dynamics of the human as a link in control systems; mechanics of laminates and tires. *Mailing Add:* 12767 Lincoln Huntington Woods MI 48070

LIPPMANN, WILBUR, BIOCHEMICAL PHARMACOLOGY. *Current Pos:* RETIRED. *Personal Data:* b Galveston, Tex, Sept 6, 30. *Educ:* Tex A&M Col, BS, 51; Univ Tex, MA, 56, PhD(biochem), 61. *Prof Exp:* Res biochemist, Biochem Inst, Univ Tex, 54-56, 58-62; res biochemist, Virus Inst, Univ Calif, Berkeley, 56-58; res biochemist, Univ Tex, M D Anderson Hosp & Tumor Inst, 58; res biochemist, Lederle Labs, Am Cyanamid Co, NY, 62-66; head biogenic amine lab, Ayerst Labs, Can, 66-69, dir, Dept Biochem Pharmacol, 69-80. *Concurrent Pos:* Fel, Univ Tex, 61-62. *Mem:* AAAS; Am Chem Soc; Am Soc Pharmacol & Exp Therapeut; Pharmacol Soc Can; NY Acad Sci. *Res:* Biosynthesis and mode of action of the biogenic amines; biochemical mechanisms of action of drugs with respect to cardiovascular, central nervous and gastrointestinal systems; biochemical mechanisms involved with gonadotrophin secretion. *Mailing Add:* 2334 W Coventry Circle Fullerton CA 92633-1267

LIPPS, FREDERICK WIESSNER, THEORETICAL PHYSICS, MATHEMATICS. *Current Pos:* RETIRED. *Personal Data:* b Baltimore, Md, Feb 18, 29; m 69; c 3. *Educ:* Johns Hopkins Univ, AB, 50, PhD(theoret physics), 56. *Prof Exp:* Meson physics, Lorentz Inst, Holland, 56-57; physicist, cesium-clock, Nat Co, Mass, 57-59, cesium-rocket, Electro- Optical Systs, Calif, 60-63, fusion, Hughes Aircraft Co, DC, 63-64 & Apollo, TRW Syst Inc, 66-69; asst prof math, Tex Southern Univ, 71-73; res scientist solar energy, Energy Lab, Univ Houston, 73-84, res scientist, Appl Geophysics Lab, Elastic Layer Seismograms, 85- *Concurrent Pos:* Co-founder, Ophidra Prod (Biotech Co). *Mem:* Am Phys Soc; Am Math Soc; Sigma Xi. *Res:* Research concerning the possibilities of strong artificial intelligence underlying mathematics. *Mailing Add:* 4509 Mimosa St Bellaire TX 77401. *Fax:* 713-667-4027; *E-Mail:* bdcw03a@prodigy.com

LIPPS, JERE HENRY, GEOLOGY, INVERTEBRATE PALEONTOLOGY. *Current Pos:* prof paleont, 88-89, PROF INTEGRATIVE BIOL & DIR MUS PALEONT, UNIV CALIF, BERKELEY, 89- *Personal Data:* b Los Angeles, Calif, Aug 28, 39; m 73, Susanna L; c Jeremy C & Jamison W. *Educ:* Univ Calif, Los Angeles, AB, 62, PhD(geol), 66. *Honors & Awards:* Lipps Island, Antarctica named in honor. *Prof Exp:* Asst res geologist invert paleont, Calif Res Corp, 63-65; res geologist, Univ Calif, Los Angeles, 65-67; from asst prof to prof geol, Univ Calif, Davis & Bodega Marine Lab, 67-88. *Concurrent Pos:* Res assoc, Los Angeles Co Mus, 63-; guest prof, Aarhus Univ, Denmark, 77; prin investr grants, NSF, 68-88 & Nat Park Serv, 70-73; dir, Cushman Found Foraminiferal Res. *Mem:* Fel AAAS; fel Geol Soc Am; Paleont Soc (pres, 96-97); Soc Econ Paleont & Mineral; Brit Micropaleont Soc; Cushmann Found. *Res:* Ecology of Foraminifera; evolutionary biology of protists; marine ecology and evolution; geology; Antarctica. *Mailing Add:* Dept Integrative Biol Univ Calif Berkeley CA 94720

LIPSCHULTZ, FREDERICK PHILLIP, PHYSICS. *Current Pos:* asst prof, 67-72, ASSOC PROF PHYSICS, UNIV CONN, 72- *Personal Data:* b Los Angeles, Calif, Aug 27, 37. *Educ:* Stanford Univ, BS, 59; Cornell Univ, PhD(physics), 66. *Prof Exp:* Res assoc physics, Cornell Univ, 62-65; fel, Brookhaven Nat Lab, 65-67. *Concurrent Pos:* Vis fel physics, Univ Nottingham, 76-77. *Mem:* AAAS; Am Phys Soc; Inst Elec & Electronic Engrs. *Res:* Thermal conductivity; low temperature physics; ultrasonics; use of thermal and acoustic properties of materials to investigate microscopic defects in solids; laboratory computer interfacing for research and teaching. *Mailing Add:* 72 Marsh Rd Willington CT 06279

LIPSCHUTZ, MICHAEL ELAZAR, RADIOCHEMISTRY CHEMISTRY, COSMOCHEMISTRY. *Current Pos:* asst prof chem, Purdue Univ, 65-68, asst prof geosci, 67-68, assoc prof, 68-73, prof chem & geosci, 73-78, PROF CHEM, PURDUE UNIV, 73-, DIR CHEM OPERS, PRIMELAB, 90-, ASSOC HEAD CHEM, 93- *Personal Data:* b Philadelphia, Pa, May 24, 37; m 59, Linda Lowenthal; c Joshua H, Mark D & Jonathan M. *Educ:* Pa State Univ, BS, 58; Univ Chicago, SM, 60, PhD(phys chem), 62. *Honors & Awards:* NASA Group Achievement Award, 83; Nininger Meteorite Res Award, 62; Cert of Recognition for Creative Develop Technol, Cert of Spec Recognition, NASA, 79; Cert of Appreciation, Nat Comn Space, 86; minor planet 2641 Lipschutz named by Int Astron Union. *Prof Exp:* NSF and NATO fel, Physics Inst, Berne, 64-65. *Concurrent Pos:* Fulbright-Hays scholar, Tel Aviv Univ, 71-72; consult, NASA, 73- & Lunar Planetary Inst, 81-; vis prof chem, Max-Planck Inst Chem, Mainz, Ger, 87; COSPAR/SAFISY Panel Space Sci Experts, 90- *Mem:* AAAS; Am Geophys Union; fel Meteoritical Soc; Am Chem Soc; Planetary Soc; Sigma Xi; Int Astron Union. *Res:* Neutron activation, atomic absorption and accelerator mass spectrometric methods for trace and ultratrace analysis; geochemistry; stable isotopes in lunar samples and meteorites; cosmogenic nuclear reactions; high pressure and temperature reactions; author or co-author of over 160 scientific papers. *Mailing Add:* Dept Chem Purdue Univ West Lafayette IN 47907. *Fax:* 765-494-0239; *E-Mail:* rnaapuml@vm.cc.purdue.edu

LIPSCOMB, DAVID M, FORENSIC AUDIOLOGY, HEARING CONSERVATION. *Current Pos:* PRES, CORRECT SERV, INC, 86- *Personal Data:* b Morrill, Nebr, Aug 4, 35; m 95, JoAnn M Hoogstad; c Scott, Steven, Doris, Anthony, Shari, Clinton & Julia. *Educ:* Univ Redlands, BA, 57, MA, 59; Univ Wash, PhD(audiol), 66. *Prof Exp:* Asst prof audiol, WTex State Univ, 60-62; asst prof, Univ Tenn, Knoxville, 62-64 & 66-69, assoc prof, 69-72, prof audiol & speech path, 72-87, dir, Noise Res Lab, 71-87. *Concurrent Pos:* Consult, various industs & attorneys. *Mem:* Fel Am Speech & Hearing Asn; Acoust Soc Am; Am Auditory Soc; Nat Hearing Conserv Asn; Am Acad Audiol. *Res:* Effect of high intensity noise upon the peripheral auditory mechanism. *Mailing Add:* PO Box 1680 Stanwood WA 98292-1680. *Fax:* 360-629-3755; *E-Mail:* corrserv@whidbey.net

LIPSCOMB, ELIZABETH LOIS, biochemistry, for more information see previous edition

LIPSCOMB, JOHN DEWALD, SPECTROSCOPY ENZYMOLOGY. *Current Pos:* Fel, Freshwater Biol Inst, 75-77, from asst to assoc prof, 77-87, PROF BIOCHEM, DEPT BIOCHEM, UNIV MINN, 87- *Personal Data:* b Wilmington, Del, Apr 16, 47; m 72; c 1. *Educ:* Amherst Col, BA, 69; Univ Ill, MS, 71, PhD(biochem), 74. *Concurrent Pos:* Prin investr, NIH res grant, 78- *Mem:* Am Chem Soc; Sigma Xi; Am Soc Biol Chemists. *Res:* Enzyme mechanisms, in particular metalloenzymes such as dioxygenases, monooxygenases iron-sulfur proteins; resonance spectroscopy; chemical modification reactions; transient kinetics. *Mailing Add:* 4-225 Millard Hall Biochem Med Univ Minn 435 Delware Minneapolis MN 55455-0347

LIPSCOMB, NATHAN THORNTON, POLYMER CHEMISTRY. *Current Pos:* From asst prof to assoc prof, 60-75, PROF CHEM, UNIV LOUISVILLE, 75- *Personal Data:* b Jan 16, 34; US citizen; m 62; c 2. *Educ:* Eastern Ky State Col, BS, 56; Univ Louisville, PhD(phys chem), 60. *Concurrent Pos:* Consult, ORGI, 88- *Mem:* Am Chem Soc; Sigma Xi. *Res:* Kinetics of polymerization; radiation induced polymerization; polymer characterization; polymer properties. *Mailing Add:* Dept Chem Univ Louisville Bel Knap Campus Louisville KY 40292

LIPSCOMB, PAUL ROGERS, ORTHOPEDIC SURGERY. *Current Pos:* CONSULT. *Personal Data:* b Clio, SC, Mar 23, 14; m 40; c 2. *Educ:* Univ SC, BS, 35; Med Col, SC, MD, 38; Univ Minn, MS, 42; Am Bd Orthop Surg, dipl. *Prof Exp:* Intern, Cooper Hosp, NJ, 38-39; resident orthop surg, Mayo Found, Univ Minn, 39-42, from asst prof to prof, 49-69; prof orthop, Surg & Chmn Dept, Sch Med, Univ Calif, Davis, 69-81, chmn, Leadership Fund, 84. *Concurrent Pos:* Consult, Mayo Clin, Minn, St Mary's Hosp Methodist Hosp, 42-69, David Grant US Air Force Med Ctr, Travis AFB, Calif, 70-81, Letterman Gen Hosp, Presidio, San Francisco, 72- & Woodland Clin, Woodland, Calif, 81-86; secy, Am Bd Orthop Surg, 68, pres, 71-73; trustee, Sterling Bunnell Found, 84-; pres, Woodland Clin Res & Educ Found, 84-85. *Mem:* Clin Orthop Soc; AMA; Am Col Surg; Am Acad Orthop Surg; Am Orthop Asn (pres, 74-75). *Res:* Surgery of the hand. *Mailing Add:* 749 Sycamore Lane Davis CA 95616

LIPSCOMB, ROBERT DEWALD, ORGANIC CHEMISTRY, POLYMER CHEMISTRY. *Current Pos:* RETIRED. *Personal Data:* b Tulia, Tex, Dec 29, 17; m 43, Ruth Thygeson; c John & Thomas. *Educ:* Univ Nebr, BS, 40, MS, 41; Univ Ill, PhD(org chem), 44. *Prof Exp:* Tech asst chem, Univ Nebr, 40-41; spec asst, Univ Ill, 41-42, investr, Off Sci Res & Develop & Nat Defense Res Comt, 42-44 & Univ Nebr, 44-45; res chemist, E I du Pont de Nemours & Co, 45-81. *Concurrent Pos:* Consult polymer chem & sci educ, 82- *Mem:* Am Chem Soc; Sigma Xi. *Res:* Chemistry of quinoline and benzoquinoline derivatives; amine bisulfites; organic polysulfides; free radicals; high temperature chemistry; polymerization. *Mailing Add:* 300 Jackson Blvd Wilmington DE 19803

LIPSCOMB, STEPHEN LEON, SYMMETRIC INVERSE SEMIGROUP, IMBEDDING FINITE DIMENSIONAL METRIC SPACES. *Current Pos:* assoc prof math, Mary Washington Col, 83-89, chmn, Dept Math Sci, 84-87, chmn, Dept Math, 90-96, PROF MATH, MARY WASHINGTON COL, 90- *Personal Data:* b Junior, WVa, Jan 31, 44; m 62, Patrecia Skidmore; c Stephen II & Darrin Joel. *Educ:* Fairmont State Col, BA, 65; WVa Univ, MA, 67; Univ Va, PhD(math), 73. *Prof Exp:* Sr mathematician, Naval Surface Warfare Ctr, 67-83. *Concurrent Pos:* Adj prof math, Va Inst Technol, 76-92; sr fel, USN-Am Soc Eng Educ, 94 & 95. *Mem:* Am Math Soc. *Res:* Topology; dimension theory; semigroups; path notation; author of numerous research articles. *Mailing Add:* 10406 Amherst Ct Fredericksburg VA 22408. *E-Mail:* slipscomb@mwcgw.mwc.edu

LIPSCOMB, WILLIAM NUNN, JR, PHYSICAL CHEMISTRY. *Current Pos:* prof chem, Harvard Univ, 59-71, chmn dept, 62-65, Abbott & James Lawrence prof, 71-90, EMER ABBOTT & JAMES LAWRENCE PROF CHEM, HARVARD UNIV, 90- *Personal Data:* b Cleveland, Ohio, Dec 9, 19; m 44, 83; c 3. *Educ:* Univ Ky, BS, 41; Harvard Univ, MA, 59 Calif Inst Technol, PhD(phys chem), 46. *Hon Degrees:* DSc, Univ Ky, 63, Long Island Univ, 77, Rutgers Univ, 79, Gustavus Adolphus Col, 80, Marietta Col, 81, Miami Univ, 83, Univ Denver, 85 & Ohio State Univ, 91; Dr, Univ Munich, 76. *Honors & Awards:* Nobel Prize in Chem, 76; Howe Award, Am Chem Soc, 58, Peter Debye Award, 73, Remsen Award, 76; Welch Found lectr, Univ Tex, 66; Phillips lectr, Univ Okla & Priestly lectr, Pa State Univ, 67; William Pyle Phillips lectr, Haverford Col, 68; Baker lectr, Cornell Univ & Coover lectr, Iowa State Univ, 69; Weizmann Lectr, Rehovoth, Israel, 74; VantHoff centenary commemoration lectr, Univ Leiden & Gilbert Newton Lewis mem lectr, Berkeley, 74; Renaud lectr, Mich State Univ, 75; Dreyfus distinguished scholar-lectr & John Strauffer Mem lectr, Univ Southern Calif, Los Angeles, 80; Centenary lectr, Chem Soc, 72; Probst lectr, Souther Ill Univ-Edwardville, 80. *Prof Exp:* From asst prof to prof phys chem, Univ Minn, 46-59, actg chief div, 52-54, chief, 54-59. *Concurrent Pos:* Guggenheim fel, Oxford, 54-55 & Cambridge, 72-73; NSF sr fel, 65-66; Mem nat comt crystallog, Nat Res Coun, 54-58, 60-63 & 65-67; mem rev comt, Chem Div, Argonne Nat Lab, 56-65; grants, Off Naval Res, 58-77, Off Ord Res, 54-56, NSF, 56-65 & 77-78, Air Force Off Sci Res, 58-64, NIH, 58-, Upjohn Co, 58 & Adv Res Projs Agency, 61-73; distinguished lectr, Howard Univ, 66; Mem nat comt crystallog, Nat Res Coun, 54-58, 60-63, 65-67; mem, adv comt, Ctr Struct Biochem, Brookhaven Nat Labs, 70, bd assocs, Linus Pauling Inst Sci & Med, 77, bd dirs, Dow Chem Co, 82-89 & adv comt, Inst Amorphous Studies, 83-; mem sci adv bd, Robert A Welch Found, 82-, Daltex Med Sci, Inc, 84-, Nova Pharmaceut Corp, 85- & Gensia Pharmaceut, Inc, 91-; Harvard lectr, Yale, 72; Centenary lect, Chem Soc, 72; Dreyfus distinguished scholar, Univ Chicago, 80, Probst lectr, Southern Ill Univ at Edwardsville, 80, speaker/session chmn, Conf Quantum Chem in Biomed Sci, NY Acad Sci, 80, invited lectr and speaker at many univs throughout the world. *Mem:* Nat Acad Sci; fel Am Phys Soc; Am Chem Soc; Am Crystallog Asn (pres, 55); fel Am Acad Arts & Sci; Sigma Xi; hon mem Chem Soc London; hon fel Royal Soc Chem; Int Acad Quantum Mech Sci; Mineral Soc Am; hon mem Int Asn Bioinorg Scientists; foreign mem Neth Acad Arts & Sci. *Res:* Diffraction studies of crystals and molecules of biochemical interest; relationship between structure and function, including the relationship of three-dimensional structure and mechanisms of enzymes and other proteins; relationship of geometric and electronic structures in theoretical inorganic and organic chemistry. *Mailing Add:* Dept Chem Harvard Univ 12 Oxford St Cambridge MA 02138

LIPSETT, FREDERICK ROY, FLUORESCENCE MEASUREMENTS, CRYSTAL GROWTH & MICROGRAVITY. *Current Pos:* CONSULT, 87- *Personal Data:* b Vancouver, BC, Can, Sept 26, 25; m 57; c 2. *Educ:* Univ BC, BApSc, 48, MApSc, 51; Univ London, PhD(physics), 54. *Prof Exp:* Sr res officer elec eng div, Nat Res Coun, 54-87. *Concurrent Pos:* Part time lectr, Carleton Univ, Can, 62-64. *Mem:* Catgut Acoustical Soc; Am Asn Crystal Growth; AAAS; Acoust Soc Am; World Forum Acoust Ecol. *Res:* Luminescence; analysis and computer simulation of police patrol operations; floating zone crystal growth; science and music. *Mailing Add:* 37 Oriole Dr Gloucester ON K1J 7E8 Can

LIPSEY, SALLY IRENE, MATHEMATICS EDUCATION. *Current Pos:* RETIRED. *Personal Data:* b Dec 31, 26; US citizen; m 48, Robert; c Marion, Carol & Eleanor. *Educ:* Hunter Col, AB, 47; Univ Wis, AM, 48; Columbia Univ, DEduc, 65. *Prof Exp:* Asst, Dept Math, Univ Wis, 47-48; high sch teacher, Bd Educ, New York, 48-49; lectr, Hunter Col, 49-53 & Barnard Col, 53-59; asst prof, Bronx Community Col, 59-65; asst prof educ, Brooklyn Col, 65-70, from asst prof to assoc prof Math, 70-85. *Mem:* Nat Coun Teachers Math; Math Asn Am; Am Math Soc; Asn Women Math; NY Acad Sci. *Res:* Writer on the following subjects: the teaching of mathematics, mathematics in nursing science; women in mathematics; editor of articles on mathematics education. *Mailing Add:* 70 E Tenth St New York NY 10003-5106

LIPSHITZ, HOWARD DAVID, DEVELOPMENTAL GENETICS, DEVELOPMENTAL BIOLOGY. *Current Pos:* asst prof, Div Biol, 86-92, ASSOC PROF, CALIF INST TECHNOL, PASADENA, 92- *Personal Data:* b Durban, SAfrica, Oct 30, 55; US citizen; m 86, Susanna M Lewis; c Sarash S. *Educ:* Univ Natal, Durban, SAfrica, BSc, 75, BSc Hons, 76; Yale Univ, New Haven, Conn, MPhil, 80, PhD(biol), 83. *Prof Exp:* Res fel, Dept Biochem, Stanford Univ, 83-86. *Concurrent Pos:* Prin investr, NIH, 87-93, March of Dimes Birth Defects Found, 90-92, Am Cancer Soc, 92; Searle scholar, 88-91; mem, Eukaryotic Genetics Panel, NSF, 93- *Mem:* Fel AAAS; Genetics Soc Am; Am Soc Cell Biol; Soc Develop Biol. *Res:* Molecular genetics of embryonic pattern formation and morphogenesis in Drosophila Melanogaster; localization of RNA in the egg; specification of germ line. *Mailing Add:* Div Biol 156-29 Calif Inst Technol Pasadena CA 91125. *Fax:* 626-564-8709; *E-Mail:* lipshitzh@starbase1.caltech.edu

LIPSHITZ, STANLEY PAUL, ELECTROACOUSTICS, SOUND RECORDING & REPRODUCTION. *Current Pos:* from asst prof to assoc prof, 70-88, PROF APPL MATH & PHYSICS, UNIV WATERLOO, 88- *Personal Data:* b Cape Town, SAfrica, Nov 25, 43; Can citizen. *Educ:* Univ Natal, BSc, 64; Univ SAfrica, MSc, 65; Univ Witwatersrand, PhD(math), 70. *Prof Exp:* Vis lectr math, Univ Ariz, 67-68. *Mem:* Fel Audio Eng Soc (pres, 88-89); Acoust Soc Am; Inst Elec & Electronics Engrs. *Res:* Mathematical, physical, and engineering problems of audio and electroacoustics; transducer design and measurement; digital audio signal processing; stereo and surround sound recording and reproduction. *Mailing Add:* Dept Appl Math Univ Waterloo Waterloo ON N2L 3G1 Can

LIPSHULTZ, LARRY I, UROLOGY. *Current Pos:* ADJ ASST PROF UROL, BAYLOR COL MED 76- *Personal Data:* b Philadelphia, Pa, Apr 24, 42; m 66; c 2. *Educ:* Franklin & Marshall Col, BS, 60; Univ Pa, MD, 68. *Prof Exp:* Asst instr urol, Univ Pa, 73-74, instr, 74-75; asst prof & clin fel reprod med, Med Br, Univ Tex, Houston, 75-77, assoc prof, 77-80, prof urol, 80- *Concurrent Pos:* Res scholar, Am Urol Asn, 75-77. *Mem:* Am Fertil Soc; Am Soc Andrology; Am Urol Asn; Soc Univ Urol. *Res:* The evaluation and diagnosis of reproductive disorders in the male, especially in the field of infertility; androgen binding protein in the human testis and epididymis and evaluation of androgen binding protein as a possible marker of sertoli cell function. *Mailing Add:* Dept Urol Baylor Col Med 6560 Fannin Houston TX 77030-2706

LIPSHUTZ, NELSON RICHARD, ECONOMICS. *Current Pos:* PRES, REGULATORY RES CORP, 77- *Personal Data:* b Philadelphia, Pa, July 14, 42; m 64; c 3. *Educ:* Univ Pa, AB, 62, MBA, 72; Univ Chicago, SM, 63, PhD(physics), 67. *Prof Exp:* Res assoc physics, Univ Chicago, 67; from instr to asst prof, Duke Univ, 67-70; mgt res analyst, Mgt & Behav Sci Ctr, Wharton Sch Finance & Commerce, Univ Pa, 70-72; mgr consult, Arthur D Little, Inc, 72-77. *Concurrent Pos:* Instr, Sch Bus, Northeastern Univ, 86. *Mem:* Am Phys Soc; Inst Mgt Sci; AAAS; NY Acad Sci; Nat Asn Forensic Econs. *Res:* Theory of elementary particles; mathematical analysis of management decision problems; economic analysis of regulated industries; anti-trust economics; business valuation. *Mailing Add:* 24 Radcliff Rd Regulatory Res Corp Waban MA 02168

LIPSICH, H DAVID, MATHEMATICS. *Current Pos:* From instr to assoc prof, 46-61, vprovost, 67, head dept, 61-77, provost undergrad studies, 67-77, PROF MATH, UNIV CINCINNATI, 61-, DEAN, MCMICKEN COL ARTS & SCI, 77- *Personal Data:* b Pittsburgh, Pa, Feb 20, 20; m 46; c 2. *Educ:* Univ Cincinnati, MA, 45, PhD(math), 49; Princeton Univ, MA, 46. *Concurrent Pos:* NSF fac fel, 59-60. *Mem:* Am Math Soc; Math Asn Am; Asn Symbolic Logic. *Res:* Mathematical logic; set theory. *Mailing Add:* 427 W Galbraith Rd Cincinnati OH 45215-5005

LIPSICK, JOSEPH STEVEN, MOLECULAR ONCOLOGY. *Current Pos:* ASSOC PROF, DEPT PATH, STANFORD UNIV, 93- *Personal Data:* b Sharon, Pa, Jan 6, 55; m 78; c 2. *Educ:* Oberlin Col, BA, 74; Univ Calif, San Diego, PhD(physiol, pharmacol), 81, MD, 82. *Prof Exp:* Asst prof residence molecular path, Univ Calif, San Diego, 86-89; assoc prof, dept microbiol, State Univ NY, Stony Brook, 89-93. *Mem:* Am Soc Microbiol; AAAS. *Res:* To understand the molecular mechanisms by which nuclear protein products of oncogenes cause leukemia, particulary the myb oncogene, which is highly conserved in evolution. *Mailing Add:* Dept Path Stanford Univ Sch Med Stanford CA 94305-9991

LIPSIG, JOSEPH, PHYSICAL CHEMISTRY. *Current Pos:* asst prof, 66-68, ASSOC PROF CHEM, STATE UNIV NY COL OSWEGO, 68- *Personal Data:* b Brooklyn, NY, Dec 13, 30; m 60; c 1. *Educ:* Brooklyn Col, BA, 50; Polytech Inst Brooklyn, PhD(phys chem), 61. *Prof Exp:* Res assoc, Cornell Univ, 60-62; sr res chemist, Atlantic Ref Co, 62-66. *Mem:* Am Chem Soc. *Res:* Catalysis; geochemistry. *Mailing Add:* Dept Chem Oswego State Col Oswego NY 13126

LIPSITT, DON RICHARD, PSYCHIATRY, PSYCHOANALYSIS. *Current Pos:* Asst, 62-65, from instr to assoc prof psychiat, 74-90, CLIN PROF, HARVARD MED SCH, 90- *Personal Data:* b Boston, Mass, Nov 24, 27; m 53, Merna Pilot; c Eric D & Steven D. *Educ:* NY Univ, BA, 49; Boston Univ, MA, 50; Univ Vt, MD, 56; Boston Psychoanal Soc & Inst, cert. 69. *Hon Degrees:* MA, Harvard Univ, 90. *Honors & Awards:* Soc Liaison Psychiat Award, 94. *Concurrent Pos:* Teaching fel psychiat, Harvard Med Sch, 60-62; Dept Health, Educ & Welfare res grant, 66-68; head integration clin, Beth Israel Hosp, Boston, 62-69, asst psychiat, 62-64, assoc, 64-66, dir med psychol liaison serv, 66-69; consult behav sci, Lincoln Lab, Mass Inst Technol, 69-73; mem fac, Boston Psychoanal Soc & Inst, Simmons Col, 71-72 & 81, adj prof, Sch Social Work, 71-80; consult, Dept Psychiat, Cambridge Hosp, 71- & NIMH, 74-80; consult psychiatrist, McLean Hosp, 71-; ed, Int J Psychiat Med, 70-79, Gen Hosp Psychiat, 79-; fac div primary care & family med, Harvard Med Sch, 77-; pres, Mass Psychiat Soc, 96-97. *Mem:* Am Psychiat Asn; Am Psychosom Soc; Asn Acad Psychiat; fel Am Col Psychiat; Am Asn Gen Hosp Psychiat; Acad Psychosom Med; Int Col Psychosom Med (pres elect). *Res:* Application of medical psychology to health problems in hospital and community; relationship of varieties of doctor-patient interaction to invalidism and chronicity; psychiatry and primary care; hypochondriasis; factitious illness. *Mailing Add:* Dept Psychiat Mt Auburn Hosp 330 Mt Auburn St Cambridge MA 02138-5597. *Fax:* 617-499-5498; *E-Mail:* dlipsitt@warren.med.harvard.edu

LIPSITT, LEWIS PAEFF, INFANT BEHAVIOR & DEVELOPMENT. *Current Pos:* from instr to prof med sci, Brown Univ, 57-96, dir child training, 60-80, dir, Child Study Ctr, 67-91, emer prof psychol, med sci & human develop, 96, RES PROF PSYCHOL, BROWN UNIV, 96- *Personal Data:* b New Bedford, Mass, June 28, 29; m 52, Edna Duchin; c Mark S & Ann D. *Educ:* Univ Chicago, BA, 50; Univ Mass, MS, 52; Univ Iowa, PhD(child psychol), 57. *Hon Degrees:* MS, Brown Univ, 66. *Honors & Awards:* Sauer Lectr, Northwestern Univ, 80. *Prof Exp:* Clin psychologist, USAF, 52-54. *Concurrent Pos:* USPHS fel, 71; Guggenheim fel behav develop, Res Unit, St Mary's Hops, London 72-73; fel, Ctr Advan Study Behav Sci, Stanford Univ, 79-80; mem bd sci counr, Nat Inst Child Health & Human Develop, 84-88; mem bd adv, Archives Hist Am Psychol, 86-; consult, Behav Sci Panel, NIMH, 87-88; mem, Int Conf Infant Studies. *Mem:* Am Psychol Asn; AAAS; Soc Res Child Develop; Am Asn Univ Prof; Am Psychol Soc; Psychonomic Soc. *Res:* Infant behavior and development, particularly sensory and learning processes of babies; crib death; adolescent suicide; study of behavioral misadventures or hazards; lifespan consequences of early experience. *Mailing Add:* Dept Psychol Brown Univ Providence RI 02912. *Fax:* 401-863-1300; *E-Mail:* llipsitt@brownvm.brown.edu

LIPSITZ, PAUL, ORGANIC CHEMISTRY. *Current Pos:* RETIRED. *Personal Data:* b York, Pa, Apr 23, 23; m 48; c 4. *Educ:* Lebanon Valley Col, BS, 44; Univ Cincinnati, MS, 48, PhD(chem), 50. *Prof Exp:* Chemist, E I du Pont de Nemours & Co, 50-59; sr patent agent, Pennsalt Chems Corp, 59-69, Patent & Licences Dept, Sun Ventures, Inc, 69-83. *Mem:* Am Chem Soc; Am Inst Chem. *Mailing Add:* 1001 Easton Rd M-815 Willow Grove PA 19090-2028

LIPSITZ, PHILIP JOSEPH, PEDIATRICS, NEONATAL-PERINATAL. *Current Pos:* dir pediat, South Shore Div, Long Island Jewish-Hillside Med Ctr, Far Rockaway, 73-74, CHIEF NEONATAL-PERINATAL MED, SCHNEIDER CHILDREN'S HOSP, LONG ISLAND JEWISH-HILLSIDE MED CTR, NEW HYDE PARK, 74-; PROF PEDIAT, ALBERT EINSTEIN COL MED, 90- *Personal Data:* b Piketberg, SAfrica, May 17, 28; m 58, Shar V Lenore; c Keith, David & Lee. *Educ:* Univ Cape Town, MB, ChB, 52; Royal Col Physicians & Surgeons, dipl child health, 56; Am Bd Pediat, dipl, neonatal-perinatal med, cert. *Prof Exp:* House surgeon, Univ Cape Town, 52; house physician, Somerset Hosp, Cape Town, SAfrica, 53; resident surg house officer, Gen Hosp, Salisbury, SRhodesia, 53; Charles' house physician, St Hosp, London, Eng, 55; resident med officer, Banstead Br, Queen Elizabeth Hosp for Children, 56; house physician, Royal Hosp Sick Children, Edinburgh, Scotland, 56; registr, Prof Unit, Children's Hosp, Sheffield, Eng, 57-58; resident med officer, Red Cross War Mem Children's Hosp, Univ Cape Town, 58; with hosp appointments, Southwest Africa, 62-65; asst prof pediat, Med Col Ga, 65-67, assoc prof, 67-68; assoc prof, Beth Israel Med Ctr & Mt Sinai Sch Med, 68-73; prof pediat, Health Sci Ctr, State Univ NY, Stony Brook, 73-90. *Concurrent Pos:* Fel pediat, Sch Med, Western Reserve Univ, 58-60; clin & res fel pediat & med, Children's Hosp Med Ctr, Harvard Med Sch, 60-61. *Mem:* Royal Col Physicians & Surgeons; Soc Pediat Res; NY Acad Sci; Am Acad Pediat. *Res:* Physiology of the newborn. *Mailing Add:* Schneider Children's Hosp LI Jewish-Hillside Med Ctr 270-05 76th Ave New Hyde Park NY 11040

LIPSIUS, STEPHEN LLOYD, PHYSIOLOGY. *Current Pos:* ASST PROF, DEPT PHYSIOL, LOYOLA UNIV, 78- *Personal Data:* b New York, NY, Sept 25, 47. *Educ:* State Univ NY, BA, 69, PhD(physiol), 75. *Prof Exp:* Teaching asst, Downstate Med Ctr, 70-75; res fel, 75-78. *Concurrent Pos:* NIH fel, Univ Vt, 76-78. *Mem:* Int Study Group Res Cardiac Metab; Cardiac Electrophysiolic Soc. *Mailing Add:* Dept Physiol Loyola Univ Stritch Sch Med 2160 S First Ave Maywood IL 60153-5589

LIPSKY, JOSEPH ALBIN, PHYSIOLOGY. *Current Pos:* From asst prof to assoc prof, 61-77, PROF PHYSIOL, COL MED, OHIO STATE UNIV, 77- *Personal Data:* b Glen Lyon, Pa, Mar 31, 30; m 57; c 2. *Educ:* Pa State Univ, BSc, 51; Ohio State Univ, MSc, 59, PhD(physiol), 61. *Concurrent Pos:* Consult to coun, Nat Bd Dent Exam, 67- *Mem:* AAAS; Fedn Am Socs Exp Biol; Am Physiol Soc; Sigma Xi. *Res:* Carbon dioxide transients and stores; hyperventilation. *Mailing Add:* Dept Physiol Ohio State Univ Col Med 219 Hamilton Hall 1645 Columbus OH 43210

LIPSKY, ROBERT H, MOLECULAR BIOLOGY. *Current Pos:* SCIENTIST I, AM RED CROSS, 88- *Personal Data:* b Washington, DC, Oct 27, 55. *Educ:* Va Polytech Inst & State Univ, BS, 77; Med Col Va, MS, 79; Cornell Univ, PhD(genetics), 83. *Prof Exp:* NIH sr staff fel develop neurol biol, Molecular Biol Lab, Nat Inst Neurol Dis & Stroke, 83-87. *Mem:* Am Soc Cell Biol; Am Soc Biochem & Molecular Biol. *Mailing Add:* Am Red Cross 15601 Crabbs Branch Way Rockville MD 20855-2743

LIPSKY, STEPHEN E, SIGNAL PROCESSING, ARTIFICAL INTELLIGENCE. *Current Pos:* SR VPRES ENG & CHIEF TECH OFFICER, AEL DEFENSE CORP, 79- *Personal Data:* b New York, NY, Jan 18, 32; m 79; c 3. *Educ:* NY Univ, Col Eng, BEE, 53, MEE, 62. *Honors & Awards:* Bronze Medal, Armed Forces Commun & Electronics Asn, 53. *Prof Exp:* Eng Officer, TV eng, US Army Pictorial Ctr, 53-55; design eng microwaves, Prod Res Corp, 55-58; proj leader eng, Fisher Radio Corp, 58-63; corp vpres eng, Polarad Elec Corp, 63-70; dir adv systs, Govt Systs Div, Gen Instrument Corp. 70-79. *Concurrent Pos:* Eng consult, Electro Acoust Res Labs, 58-60 & Radiometric Div Polarad, 70-77; ed consult, 85-; mem, Comt 1989 Symp, IEEE Ant/Microwave Prop Soc, 85-87; adj univ prof microwaves, Drexel Univ Grad Sch, 87- *Mem:* Fel Inst Elec & Electronic Engrs; Armed Forces Commun & Electronics Asn; British Inst Elec Engrs. *Res:* Monopulse passive direction finding and receiving methods for detection and identification of radar and communications signals; microwave analytic design techniques for antenna systems and associated feed networks; author of publication on Microwave Passive Direction Finding. *Mailing Add:* 1254 Cox Rd Rydal PA 19046

LIPSON, EDWARD DAVID, PHOTOBIOLOGY, SENSORY TRANSDUCTION. *Current Pos:* from asst prof to assoc, 76-85, PROF PHYSICS, SYRACUSE UNIV, 85-, DIR GRAD BIOPHYSICS PROG, 83- *Personal Data:* b Winnipeg, Man, Oct 27, 44; m 66; c 2. *Educ:* Univ Man, BSc, 66; Calif Inst Technol, PhD(physics), 71. *Prof Exp:* Res fel biol, Calif Inst Technol, 71-74, sr res fel, 74-76. *Concurrent Pos:* Res fel, Alfred P Sloan Found, 79-83. *Mem:* Biophys Soc; AAAS; Am Soc Photobiol; Am Phys Soc. *Res:* Light-growth responses of the microorganism, Phycomyces, with approaches from genetics, biochemistry and nonlinear systems theory, to elucidate the cellular and molecular mechanisms of sensory transduction and adaptation. *Mailing Add:* Dept Physics Syracuse Univ Syracuse NY 13244-1130

LIPSON, HERBERT GEORGE, SOLID STATE PHYSICS. *Current Pos:* RETIRED. *Personal Data:* b Boston, Mass, July 4, 25; m 51, Gloria Freedman; c Neil, Jerold & Elayne. *Educ:* Mass Inst Technol, BS, 48; Northeastern Univ, MS, 64. *Prof Exp:* Jr physicist metall physics, Sylvania Elec Prods, Inc, 48-50; physicist, Brookhaven Nat Lab, 51, Naval Res Lab, 51-55, Lincoln Lab, Mass Inst Technol, 55-58, Dept Electronic Technol, Rome Air Develop Ctr, Hanscom AFB, 58-90. *Mem:* Am Phys Soc; Mat Res Soc. *Res:* Optical properties of solids; lattice vibrations, impurities and plasma effects in semiconductors; laser and laser window material properties; infrared optical properties of impurities in quartz, radiation effects on quartz for radiation hardened oscillators. *Mailing Add:* 68 Aldrich Rd Wakefield MA 01880

LIPSON, MELVIN ALAN, ORGANIC CHEMISTRY. *Current Pos:* PRES, LIPSON ASSOC, 92- *Personal Data:* b Providence, RI, June 1, 36; m 61, Jacqueline Barclay; c Donna, Robert, Michelle & Judith. *Educ:* Univ RI, BS, 57; Syracuse Univ, PhD(org chem), 63. *Prof Exp:* Res chemist, I C I (Organics) Inc, 63 & Eltex Res Corp, 63-64; res supvr org synthesis, Wayland Chem Div, Philip A Hunt Chem Corp, RI, 64-67, res mgr, 67-69; tech dir, Morton Thiokol Inc, 69-72, vpres, 72-82, sr vpres, Tech Opers, 82-85, exec vpres, 85-86, pres, Dynachem Div, 86-89; vpres, Morton Int, 89-92. *Concurrent Pos:* Chief exec officer, Avrelon, 94-, Pivotech, Inc, 96- *Mem:* AAAS; Am Chem Soc; The Chem Soc. *Res:* Amino acids and peptides; chelating agents; photographic chemicals; surface active compounds; polymers; dyestuffs; carbohydrates; photopolymers; photoresists; electroless plating; corrosion inhibitors; coatings; adhesives; inks. *Mailing Add:* 1715 Plaza Del Sur Newport Beach CA 92661-1417. *Fax:* 714-675-3621

LIPSON, STEVEN MARK, ENVIRONMENTAL MICROBIOLOGY & IMMUNOLOGY. *Current Pos:* DIR, DIAG VIROL LAB, DIV INFECTIOUS DIS, NORTH SHORE UNIV HOSP, CORNELL UNIV MED COL, 90-, ASST PROF MICROBIOL MED. *Personal Data:* b New York, NY, May 25, 45; m 71; c 2. *Educ:* Long Island Univ, BS, 67; C W Post Col, MS, 72; NY Univ, PhD(microbiol), 82. *Prof Exp:* Teacher biol, Erasmus Hall & Prospect Heights High Schs, 67-72; teaching fel biol, NY Univ, 74-75; technologist microbiol, Mem Hosp, 75-76; res assoc biol, NY Univ, 74-80; res assoc, Dept Neoplastic Dis, Mt Sinai Med Ctr, 81-83; supvr, Hemat/Oncol Lab, Brooklyn Hosp/Caledonian Hosp, 83-84; chief, Virol Lab, Nassau County Med Ctr, NY, 84-90. *Concurrent Pos:* Vis lectr microbiol, Adelphi Univ, 76; adj instr biol, Fordham Univ, 81-82; adj asst prof, Fiorello H LaGuardia Community Col & Manhattan Community Col, 83-85; adj prof, biol, C W Post Col, 87- *Mem:* Am Soc Microbiol. *Res:* Epidemiology and rapid identification medically relevant viruses; surface interactions between viruses, cells, polymers, and particulates; polymerase chain reaction in the identification of viruses; antiviral susceptibility; testing flow cytometry. *Mailing Add:* Infectious Dis Dept Med North Shore Univ Hosp Sch Med NY Univ 300 Community Dr Manhasset NY 11030. *Fax:* 516-562-2626

LIPTAY, ALBERT, HORTICULTURE, PLANT PHYSIOLOGY. *Current Pos:* RES SCIENTIST VEG MGT, AGR CAN, 74- *Personal Data:* b Hampton, Ont, Nov 9, 41; m 67; c 3. *Educ:* Univ Guelph, BSA, 66, MSc, 67; McMaster Univ, PhD(biol), 72. *Prof Exp:* Lectr life sci, Conestoga Col, 72-73; asst prof biol, Camrose Lutheran Col, 73-74. *Mem:* Am Soc Hort Sci; Int Soc Hort Sci; Can Soc Hort Sci; Agr Inst Can. *Res:* Vegetable management and physiology; seed germination; seed vigour; plant establishment; growth factors. *Mailing Add:* Res Ctr Agr & Agr Food Can Greenhouse & Process Crops 2585 Hwy 18E Harrow ON N0R 1G0 Can

LIPTON, ALLAN, INTERNAL MEDICINE, ONCOLOGY. *Current Pos:* from asst prof to assoc prof, 71-80, PROF, MED CTR, PA STATE UNIV, 80-, CHIEF, DIV ONCOL, DEPT MED, 74- *Personal Data:* b New York, NY, Dec 29, 38; m 65; c 3. *Educ:* Amherst Col, BA, 59; NY Univ, MD, 63; Am Bd Internal Med, dipl, 70. *Prof Exp:* Intern med, Bellevue Hosp, NY, 63-64, resident, 64-65. *Concurrent Pos:* Fel hemat, Mem Hosp, New York, 67-68, fel oncol, 68-69; Dernham fel, Salk Inst Biol Studies, 69-71. *Mem:* AAAS; Am Asn Cancer Res; Am Fedn Clin Res. *Res:* Control of growth of normal and malignant cells by serum factors. *Mailing Add:* Dept Med Hershey Med Ctr Pa State Univ Hershey PA 17033

LIPTON, JAMES MATTHEW, NEUROSCIENCES. *Current Pos:* PROF PHYSIOL, SOUTHWESTERN MED CTR, UNIV TEX, DALLAS. *Educ:* Univ Colo, PhD, 64. *Concurrent Pos:* USPHS fel, Neuropath Lab, Med Sch, Univ Mich, 64-66; USPHS sr fel, Inst Animal Physiol, UK, 70-71; consult neurol, Vet Admin Hosp, Dallas, 74-80; mem staff, Anesthesiol Dept, Southwestern Med Sch, Southwestern Med Ctr, Univ Tex, Dallas, 81-, mem, Neurol Study Sect, 86-90. *Mem:* AAAS; Soc Neurosci; Am Physiol Soc. *Res:* Inflammation and antiinflammatury peptides; central nervous system and peripheral modulation of inflammation. *Mailing Add:* Dept Physiol Southwester Med Ctr Univ Tex 5323 Harry Hines Blvd Dallas TX 75235-9040. *E-Mail:* lipton@utsw.swmed.edu

LIPTON, MICHAEL FORRESTER, PROCESS DEVELOPMENT. *Current Pos:* MEM STAFF, UPJOHN CO, 80- *Personal Data:* b Huntington, WVa, Oct 28, 50; m 85, Kathy O'Falvahee; c Grayson B & Logan M. *Educ:* Purdue Univ, BS, 72; Univ Colo, PhD(chem), 76. *Prof Exp:* Res assoc chem, Fordham Univ, 76-78; asst prof, Mich State Univ, 78-80. *Concurrent Pos:* Res assoc, Dept Entom, USDA, Mich State Univ, 79-80. *Mem:* Am Chem Soc. *Res:* Process development in the pharmaceutical industry; rapid scale-up and design of chemical routes of synthesis of biologically active molecules. *Mailing Add:* Pharmacia & Upjohn Inc 7171 Portage Rd Kalamazoo MI 49001-0199. *Fax:* 616-833-9282; *E-Mail:* mflipton@pwinet.upj.com

LIPTON, STUART ARTHUR, CELLULAR & MOLECULAR NEUROSCIENCE. *Current Pos:* asst prof neurol & neurosci, 83-87, ASSOC PROF NEUROL & NEUROSCI, HARVARD MED SCH, 87-; CHIEF, CENT NERVOUS SYST RES INST, BRIGHAM & WOMEN'S HOSP, 97- *Personal Data:* b Danbury, Conn, Jan 11, 50; m 80, Elisabeth Kay Ament; c Jennifer Ann & Jeffrey Harris. *Educ:* Cornell Univ, BA, 71; Univ Pa, MD, 77, PhD, 77; Am Bd Psychiat & Neurol, dipl, 82. *Honors & Awards:* Nobel Lectr, Karolinska Inst, 94. *Prof Exp:* Resident neurol, Beth Israel, Brigham Hosp, Women's Hosp, Boston & Children's Hosp, Boston, 78-80; chief neurol resident, Beth Israel, Brigham Hosp, Women's Hosp, Boston & Children's Hosp, Boston, 80-81; instr neurol, Harvard Med Sch, 81-83. *Concurrent Pos:* Res fel neurbiol, Harvard Med Sch, 80-83; dir cellular & molecular neurosci, Children's Hosp & Harvard Med Sch; neurologist, Mass Gen Hosp, Brigham

Hosp, Women's Hosp, Beth Israel Hosp & Children's Hosp; fel, Hartford Found, 81-84; NIH fel, 84-89; investr, Am Heart Asn, 88-93. Mem: AAAS; Am Acad Neurol; Am Neurol Asn; Soc Neurosci; Asn Res Vision & Ophthal; Biophys Soc. Res: Contributed articles to professional journals; patentee. Mailing Add: Children's Hosp 300 Longwood Ave Boston MA 02115-5737

LIPTON, WERNER JACOB, FOOD SCIENCE & TECHNOLOGY, PLANT PHYSIOLOGY. Current Pos: CONSULT, 87- Personal Data: b Ger, Oct 16, 28; nat US; m 52; c 4. Educ: Mich State Univ, BS, 51, MS, 53; Univ Calif, PhD(plant physiol), 57. Prof Exp: Asst, Univ Calif, 53-57; sr pant physiologist, Hort Field Sta, USDA, 57-87. Concurrent Pos: Assoc ed, Am Soc Hort Sci, 72-76, 78-, chmn postharvest hort sect, 76-77, vpres, W Sect, 81-82, sci ed, 88- Mem: AAAS; fel Am Soc Hort Sci; Sigma Xi. Res: Postharvest physiology of vegetables; emphasis on effects of modified atmospheres and preharvest environmental factors. Mailing Add: PO Box 5558 Fresno CA 93755-5558

LIRA, EMIL PATRICK, ORGANIC CHEMISTRY. Current Pos: RETIRED. Personal Data: b Chicago, Ill, Mar 17, 34; m 58; c 4. Educ: Elmhurst Col, BS, 56; Rutgers Univ, PhD(org chem), 63. Prof Exp: Chemist, Swift & Co, 56; chemist, Corn Prod Co, 58-59; res chemist, Int Mineral & Chem Corp, 63-69, supvr org synthesis, 69-73, mgr org chem, 73-74; dir res, Velsicol Chem Corp, 74-76; dir agr-chem res, Northwest Ind Inc, Chicago Lab, 76-86; dir process technol, Sandoz, 86-97. Mem: Am Chem Soc; Indust Res Inst. Res: Organic research and development with plasticizers, adhesives, polymer additives; plant growth regulators; pesticides; animal health products; synthetic sweeteners; organic processes. Mailing Add: 8129 Manchester Lane No 25 Lake Mills WI 53551-9733

LIS, ADAM W, BIOCHEMISTRY, OBSTETRICS-GYNECOLOGY & ONCOLOGY MEDICINE. Current Pos: PROF BIOCHEM, HUXLEY COL, WESTERN WASH UNIV, BELLINGHAM, WASH, 81- Personal Data: b Przemysl, Poland, Jan 5, 25; US citizen; c 4. Educ: Univ Ark, BS, 49; Univ Calif, Berkeley, PhD(biochem), 60. Honors & Awards: Copernican Medal Med, 73. Prof Exp: Res biochemist, Univ Calif, San Francisco, 60-62; res assoc, Univ Ore Health Sci Ctr, 63-65, asst prof, 65-67, assoc prof nucleic acids, 67-77, dir nucleic acids lab, 66-77; dir, Intermediary Metab Inst, 77- Concurrent Pos: Nat Cancer Inst fel, Univ Uppsala, 62-63; ed, Physiol Chem & Physics, 67-80. Mem: Brit Biochem Soc; Am Chem Soc; Am Soc Cell Biol; Radiation Res Soc Am; Biophys Soc. Res: Minor components in nucleic acids and their function; body fluids analysis in malignant and metabolic diseases; discovery and characterization of Minor Bases in Ribonucleic Acid; pseudouridine, 5-hydroxyuracil; 5-chloro-deuxyuridine and enzymes c-csynthetase; diagnoses of autism and mental deficiencies of metabolic origin; chemistry of stress and its pathology. Mailing Add: 1117 SE Umatilla St Portland OR 97202

LIS, ELAINE WALKER, nutrition, biochemistry, for more information see previous edition

LIS, JOHN THOMAS, MOLECULAR GENETICS. Current Pos: asst prof, 78-84, ASSOC PROF BIOCHEM, CORNELL UNIV, 84- Personal Data: b Willimantic, Conn, June 15, 48; c 1. Educ: Fairfield Univ, BS, 70; Brandeis Univ, PhD(biochem), 75. Prof Exp: Fel, Dept Biochem, Stanford Univ, 75-78. Res: Relationship between genome structure and gene regulation using the heat shock genes of Drosophila melanogaster and yeast as model systems. Mailing Add: Molecular Biol Cornell Univ Biotechnol Bldg Ithaca NY 14853-0001

LIS, STEVEN ANDREW, OPTICAL COMPUTING, MATERIALS RESEARCH. Current Pos: PRIN INVESTR, SPARTA INC, 88- Personal Data: b Dunkirk, NY, Oct 13, 50; m 76; c 2. Educ: Fredonia State Univ Col, NY, BS, 72; Princeton Univ, PhD(chem), 77. Prof Exp: Sr scientist, Radiation Monitoring Devices, 77-81 & GCA Corp, 81-88. Concurrent Pos: Sr prin develop engr, Honewell Electro-Optics Div, 88. Mem: Am Phys Soc; Electro-Chem Soc. Res: Optical computing systems; holography; materials and device; integrated circuit process development; advanced lithographic equipment. Mailing Add: 254 Marked Tree Rd Needham MA 02192

LISACK, JOHN, JR, SURVEYING & MAPPING. Current Pos: EXEC DIR, AM CONG SURV & MAPPING, 90- Personal Data: b May 22, 45; m 72; c 3. Educ: Univ Mass, BSCE, 68, MBA, 70. Prof Exp: Asst adminr, Prince William Co, 71-72; mgr land develop & planning, Foxvale Construct Co Inc, 72-73; exec dir property admin, Real Equity Investments Inc, 73-74; financial analyst, Co Fairfax, 74-75; dep dir, Am Soc Eng Educ, 75-86; exec vpres, Nat Asn Personnel Consult, 86-90. Concurrent Pos: Chmn, Coun Eng & Sci Soc Execs Comts. Mailing Add: Am Cong Surv 5410 Grosvenor Lane Bethesda MD 20814-2144

LISAK, ROBERT PHILIP, NEUROLOGY, IMMUNOLOGY. Current Pos: PROF NEUROL & CHMN DEPT, SCH MED, WAYNE STATE UNIV, 87-, PROF IMMUNOL & MICROBIOL. Personal Data: b Brooklyn, NY, Mar 17, 41; m 64; c Ilene & Michael. Educ: NY Univ, BA, 61; Columbia Univ, MD, 65. Honors & Awards: Physician's Award, Myasthenia Gravis Found, 91. Prof Exp: Intern med, Montefiore Hosp & Med Ctr, 65-66; res assoc immunol, Lab Clin Sci, NIMH, 66-68; jr resident med, Bronx Munic Med Ctr, Albert Einstein Col Med, 68-69; resident neurol, Hosp, Sch Med, Univ Pa, 69-72, trainee allergy & immunol, 71-72, from asst prof to prof neurol, 72-87, mem immunol grad group, 75-87. Concurrent Pos: Consult neurol, Vet Admin Hosp, Philadelphia, 72-82; spec consult, Nat Multiple Sclerosis Soc, 75 & Swiss Acad Med, 81; Fulbright-Hays sr res scholar, UK, 78-79; mem, Res Comt A, Nat Mult Sclerosis Soc & Med Adv Bd. Mem: Am Asn Immunologists; Am Fedn Clin Res; Am Acad Neurol; AAAS; NY Acad Sci; Soc Neurosci; Am Neurol Asn; Int Soc Neuroimmunol (secy, treas); Nat Soc Prev Blindness, 86-90. Res: Humoral and cell-mediated immunologic mechanisms involved in clinical and experimental diseases of the central and peripheral nervous system and muscle. Mailing Add: Dept Neurol Sch Med Wayne State Univ Health Ctr 6E 4201 St Antoine Detroit MI 48201

LISANO, MICHAEL EDWARD, REPRODUCTIVE PHYSIOLOGY, ENDOCRINOLOGY. Current Pos: asst prof, 70-77, ASSOC PROF PHYSIOL, AUBURN UNIV, 77- Personal Data: b Houston, Tex, Oct 6, 42; c 2. Educ: Sam Houston State Univ, BS, 64, MS, 66; Tex A&M Univ, PhD(physiol), 70. Prof Exp: Instr biol, Hardin-Simmons Univ, 66-67. Mem: Wildlife Soc; Southeastern Asn Fish & Wildlife Agencies. Res: Reproductive physiology and endocrinology of economically important game species. Mailing Add: Dept Zool Auburn Univ Auburn AL 36849-3501

LISCHER, LUDWIG F, ENGINEERING. Current Pos: RETIRED. Personal Data: b Mar 1, 15; US citizen. Educ: Purdue Univ, BSEE, 37. Hon Degrees: DEng, Purdue Univ, 76. Prof Exp: Mem staff, Commonwealth Edison Co, 37-64, vpres-in-chg eng & res, 64-80. Concurrent Pos: Dir, Chicago Eng & Sci Ctr, Proj Mgt Corp; chmn res adv comt, Elec Power Res Inst; mem var adv comts, NSF, Nat Acad Sci & Nat Acad Eng. Mem: Nat Acad Eng; fel Inst Elec & Electronics Engrs; Am Soc Mech Engrs; Am Nuclear Soc. Res: Electric utility systems for the development of government and industry energy policy. Mailing Add: 441 N Park Blvd Glen Ellyn IL 60137

LI-SCHOLZ, ANGELA, ATOMIC PHYSICS, NUCLEAR PHYSICS. Current Pos: RES PROF, DEPT PHYSICS, STATE UNIV NY, ALBANY, 78- Personal Data: b Hong Kong, Aug 15, 36; US citizen; m 66; c 2. Educ: Manhattanville Col, BA, 56; NY Univ, MS, 57, PhD(physics), 63. Prof Exp: Jr res assoc nuclear physics, Brookhaven Nat Lab, 60-63; res assoc high energy physics, NY Univ, 63; res assoc nuclear physics, Yale Univ, 63-65; asst prof physics, City Col New York, 65-66; res assoc solid state physics, Univ Pa, 67-70; res assoc nuclear chem, Rensselaer Polytech Inst, 70-72; assoc prof, 72-77, prof sci, State Univ NY, Empire State Col, 77- Concurrent Pos: Ed, Atomic Data & Nuclear Data Tables, 82- Mem: Am Phys Soc. Res: Atomic inner shell ionization; microbeam analysis; interaction of nuclei with electromagnetic fields in solids. Mailing Add: Dept Physics State Univ NY Albany NY 12222. Fax: 518-442-5260

LISCUM, LAURA, PHYSIOLOGY. Current Pos: ASST PROF, DEPT PHYSIOL, SCH MED, TUFTS UNIV, 85- Personal Data: b Boston, Mass, Sept 1, 54. Educ: Hunter Col, BA, 76; Columbia Univ, MA, 78, PhD, 82. Honors & Awards: John S Newberry Prize, 82. Prof Exp: Fac fel, Dept Biol Sci, Columbia Univ, 76-82; postdoctoral fel, Dept Molecular Genetics, Health Sci Ctr, Univ Tex, Dallas, 82-85. Concurrent Pos: Am Heart Asn estab investr, 87-92. Res: Author of numerous publications. Mailing Add: Dept Physiol Sch Med Tufts Univ 136 Harrison Ave Boston MA 02111-1800

LISELLA, FRANK SCOTT, PUBLIC HEALTH. Current Pos: DIR, ENVIRON HEALTH & SAFETY OFF, EMORY UNIV, 88- Personal Data: b Lancaster, Pa, Aug 11, 36; m 90, Lynn Williams; c Brad & Michael. Educ: Millersville State Univ, 57; Tulane Univ, MPH, 61; Univ Iowa, PhD(prev med), 70. Prof Exp: Sanitarian, Pa Dept Health, 57-64; coordr, Commun Dis Control Proj, USPHS, Fla, 64-66; chief training & consult, Pesticides Prog, Nat Commun Dis Ctr, 66-68; asst to dir, Div Community Studies, Food & Drug Admin, Ga, 69-70; asst dir, Div Pesticide Community Studies, Environ Protection Agency, 70-72; health sci adv, Nat Med Audiovisual Ctr, 72-73; chief, Prog Develop Br, Environ Health Servs Div, Ctr Dis Control, 73-81, asst dir, Chronic Dis Div, 81-84, dir, Off Biosafety, Ctr Dis Control, Ga, 84-87; head biosafety off & leader, Hazardous Mat Group, Ga Tech Res Inst, 87-88. Concurrent Pos: Adj prof, Dekalb Col, 70-75; adj clin assoc prof, Emory Sch Pub Health, 78- Mem: Nat Environ Health Asn; Am Pub Health Asn; Am Biol Safety Asn; Can Asn Biol Safety. Res: Epidemiology of acute intoxications involving chemical agents of various types; etiology of self-induced intoxications involving medicants, pesticides and other chemical compounds and measures for prevention of repetitive episodes; control/containment of hazardous chemicals & biologicals. Mailing Add: 64 Robin Hood Lane Hartwell GA 30643

LISENBEE, ALVIS LEE, STRUCTURAL GEOLOGY. Current Pos: dept head, 78-85, PROF GEOL, DEPT GEOL ENG, SDAK SCH MINES, 72- Personal Data: b Lamesa, Tex, Dec 3, 40; m 68; c 2. Educ: Univ NMex, BS, 64, MS, 67; Pa State Univ, PhD(geol), 72. Prof Exp: Asst geologist, Ark & La Gas Co, 64; chief geologist, Posora Mining Co, Esfahan, Iran, 73-76. Concurrent Pos: Consult, Armco Steel Corp, 79-81, Gulf Oil Corp, 81-82, Exxon Mineral Co, 82, SDak Geol Surv, 82 & Turkish Nat Petrol Co, 85-89; Fulbright prof, Turkey, 83 & Yates Petrol Co, 91-; Homestabe Mining Co, 94- Mem: Geol Soc Am; Sigma Xi. Res: The evolution of mountain systems, specifically the timing and types of geological features which evolved in the northern Rocky Mountains and the Basin and Range of the US. Mailing Add: Dept Geol Eng SDak Sch Mines Rapid City SD 57701. Fax: 605-394-6703; E-Mail: alisenbee@msmailgus.sdsmt.edu

LISK, DONALD J, OCCUPATIONAL EPIDEMIOLOGY, EFFECTS OF SOLID WASTES IN AGRICULTURE. Current Pos: PROF TOXICOL & DIR, TOXIC CHEMICALS LAB, NY STATE COL AGR, CORNELL UNIV, 56- Personal Data: b Buffalo, NY, May 12, 30; m 59; c 4. Educ: Univ Buffalo, BA, 52; Cornell Univ, MS, 54, PhD (soil chem), 56. Mem: Soc

Toxicol; Am Chem Soc. *Res:* Fate of toxicants in agriculture and environmental systems; heavy metals; pesticides; industrial toxicants. *Mailing Add:* Toxic Chemicals Lab NY State Col Agr Cornell Univ Tower Rd Ithaca NY 14853-7401

LISKA, BERNARD JOSEPH, FOOD TECHNOLOGY. *Current Pos:* from asst prof to assoc prof animal sci, Purdue Univ, 59-65, dir, Food Sci Inst, 68-75, assoc dir, Agr Exp Sta, 72-75, dir & assoc dean, 75-80, PROF FOOD SCI, PURDUE UNIV, 65-, DEAN AGR, 80- *Personal Data:* b Hillsboro, Wis, May 31, 31; m 52; c 2. *Educ:* Univ Wis, BS, 53, MS, 56, PhD(dairy & food technol), 57. *Honors & Awards:* Babcock Hart Award Jury, Inst Food Technologists, 69-73. *Prof Exp:* Asst prof, Univ Fla, 57-59. *Concurrent Pos:* Sci ed, J Food Sci, 70-80; vchmn, Expert Panel on Food Safety & Nutrit, 71-77. *Mem:* Fel Inst Food Technologists; Am Dairy Sci Asn; Am Chem Soc; Sigma Xi. *Res:* Food bacteriology; lactic cultures; bulk handling of milk; milk quality and enzymes; food chemistry; food microbiology; chemical residues in food; pesticide residue analysis. *Mailing Add:* Dept Food Sci Purdue Univ West Lafayette IN 47907-1968

LISKA, JOHN W, MECHANICAL PROPERTIES OF FIBERS. *Current Pos:* RETIRED. *Personal Data:* b Chicago, Ill, July 20, 04. *Educ:* Ripon Col, BS, 28; Univ Minn, PhD(physics), 34. *Prof Exp:* Res scientist, Firestone Tire & Rubber Co, 32-64. *Mem:* Am Phys Soc. *Mailing Add:* 2915 Parkwood Dr Cuyahoga Falls OH 44224

LISKA, KENNETH J, CHEMISTRY, PHARMACOLOGY. *Current Pos:* RETIRED. *Personal Data:* b Hinsdale, Ill, June 4, 29; m 57, Paula Hoenecke; c 3. *Educ:* Univ Ill, BS, 51, MS, 53, PhD(med chem), 56. *Prof Exp:* Assoc prof pharmaceut chem, Duquesne Univ, 56-61 & Univ Pittsburgh, 61-69; assoc prof chem, US Int Univ, 69-75; prof chem, Mesa Col, 75-93. *Concurrent Pos:* Chmn, San Diego Sect, Am Chem Soc 75-76. *Mem:* Am Chem Soc; AAAS. *Res:* Synthetic organic medicinal chemistry; author of seven books. *Mailing Add:* 2947 Honors Ct San Diego CA 92122

LISKAY, ROBERT MICHAEL, GENETIC RECOMBINATION, SOMATIC CELL GENETICS. *Current Pos:* asst prof, 80-84, ASSOC PROF THERAPEUT RADIOL & HUMAN GENETICS, SCH MED, YALE UNIV, 84- *Personal Data:* b Apr 16, 48; US citizen. *Educ:* Univ Calif, Irvine, BS, 70; Univ Wash, Seattle, PhD(genetics), 74. *Prof Exp:* Res assoc, Univ Colo, 77-80. *Concurrent Pos:* Scholar, Leukemia Soc Am, 84- *Mem:* Genetics Soc Am. *Res:* Homologous recombination in mammalian cells, its mode of action and cellular processes that it influences; X-chromosome inactivation in mammals. *Mailing Add:* Dept Genetics Ore Univ Scis Univ Sch Med 3181 SW Sam Jackson MC L-103 BSAC 4502 Portland OR 97201

LISKEY, NATHAN EUGENE, HEALTH SCIENCE. *Current Pos:* from asst prof to assoc prof, 65-75, PROF HEALTH SCI, CALIF STATE UNIV, FRESNO, 75- *Personal Data:* b Live Oak, Calif, Apr 26, 37; m 57; c 2. *Educ:* La Verne Col, BA, 59; Ind Univ, Bloomington, MS, 61, HSD(health safety), 69. *Prof Exp:* Teacher pub schs, Calif, 59-65. *Concurrent Pos:* USPHS grant, HEW, 68-69; sex therapist, Ctr Coun & Ther, 73- *Mem:* Soc Sci Study Sex; Am Asn Sex Educ & Coun; Nat Coun for Int Health. *Res:* Physical and emotional aspects of behavior relating to accident prevention; human sexuality; sexual behavior of the aged. *Mailing Add:* 27931 Calle Casal Mission Viejo CA 92692

LISKOV, BARBARA H, SOFTWARE SYSTEMS. *Current Pos:* PROF COMPUT SCI, MASS INST TECHNOL, 72- *Personal Data:* b Los Angeles, Calif, Nov 7, 39; m 70; c 1. *Educ:* Univ Calif, Berkeley, BA, 61; Stanford Univ, MS, 65, PhD(philos), 68. *Prof Exp:* Programmer, Mitre Corp, 61-62, Harvard Univ, 62-63; res asst, Stanford Univ, 63-68; tech staff, Mitre Corp, 68-72. *Concurrent Pos:* Consult, Digital Equip Co, Hewlett-Packard, NCR, Prime Comput & BBN. *Mem:* Nat Acad Eng; Asn Comput Mach; Inst Elec & Electronics Engrs; fel Am Acad Arts & Sci. *Res:* Programming methodology; distributed computing; programming languages; operating systems; numerous articles, papers and publications. *Mailing Add:* Lab Comput Sci 545 Technol Sq Rm 528 Cambridge MA 02139

LISMAN, FREDERICK LOUIS, NUCLEAR CHEMISTRY. *Current Pos:* RETIRED. *Personal Data:* b Wilkes-Barre, Pa, Jan 14, 39; m 62; c 3. *Educ:* Fairfield Univ, BS, 60; Purdue Univ, PhD(nuclear chem), 65. *Prof Exp:* Sr res radiochemist, Idaho Nuclear Corp, 65-70; asst prof, Fairfield Univ, 70-72, chmn dept, 75-79, assoc prof chem, 72-89. *Mem:* AAAS; Am Chem Soc. *Res:* Fission yield determination; radiochemical separations; mass spectrometric techniques; measurement of fissionable material; mass and charge distribution in low Z fission; chemical separation techniques; energy resources. *Mailing Add:* 201 Platt Lane Milford CT 06460-2063

LISMAN, HENRY, MATHEMATICS. *Current Pos:* RETIRED. *Personal Data:* b Boston, Mass, July 3, 13; m 38; c 2. *Educ:* Univ Boston, BS, 34, MS, 35, PhD(physics), 39. *Prof Exp:* Asst physics, Univ Boston, 34-35; instr, Northeastern Univ, 40-42; from assoc physicist to physicist, Sig Corps Eng Labs, NJ, 42-47; from instr to prof math, Yeshiva Univ, 47-78. *Concurrent Pos:* Consult physicist, US Army Electronics Labs, 49-68. *Res:* Electromagnetic wave propagation. *Mailing Add:* 3777 Independence Ave Bronx NY 10463

LISMAN, PERRY HALL, RESEARCH ADMINISTRATION, SYSTEMS DEVELOPMENT & ELECTRONICS SYSTEMS. *Current Pos:* RETIRED. *Personal Data:* b Sweetwater, Tex, July 21, 32. *Educ:* Univ Tex, BA, 61. *Prof Exp:* Res scientist, Defense Res Lab, Univ Tex, Austin, 61-67; sr staff mem, Appl Physics Lab, Johns Hopkins Univ, 67-74; dep dir, Systs Develop Div, SRI Int, 74-91. *Mem:* Sr mem Inst Elec & Electronics Engrs. *Res:* Foreign technology; electronics systems; countermeasures; research and development management; radar. *Mailing Add:* 6 Wood Lane Menlo Park CA 94025

LISONBEE, LORENZO KENNETH, BIOLOGY, SCIENCE EDUCATION. *Current Pos:* RETIRED. *Personal Data:* b Mesa, Ariz, Nov 25, 14; m 38; c 8. *Educ:* Ariz State Univ, BA, 37, MA, 40, EdD, 63. *Prof Exp:* Teacher sci & dept chmn high schs, Ariz, 40-58; sci supvr, Phoenix High Schs, 58-85; fac assoc, Ariz State Univ, 63-85. *Concurrent Pos:* Consult, Am Geol Inst & Am Inst Biol Sci & Biol Sci Curriculum Study; vis prof, San Jose State Univ, 56; pres, Ariz Sci Teachers Asn, 56, Ariz Acad Sci, 63-64; contribr, Encyclopedia Britannica, 62 & 74; chmn, Ariz Comt Corresp, 84-86; summer fac, San Jose State Univ. *Mem:* Fel AAAS; Nat Asn Res Sci Teaching; Nat Sci Teachers Asn; Nat Asn Biol Teachers. *Res:* Research in science teaching; desert biology. *Mailing Add:* 4844 W Commonwealth Pl Chandler AZ 85226

LISS, ALAN, MICROBIOLOGY, BIOPHARMACEUTICALS. *Current Pos:* DIR, WORLDWIDE QUAL SYSTS, CENTEON LLC, 96- *Personal Data:* b Pittsburgh, Pa, Sept 14, 47; m 71, Connie Jacobson; c Brian Z, Gordon D & Jonathan S. *Educ:* Univ Calif, Berkeley, BS, 69; Univ Rochester, PhD(microbiol), 73. *Honors & Awards:* Sigrid Juselius Found Award, 75. *Prof Exp:* Fel microbiol, York Univ, 73-74; Nat Cancer Inst fel, Scripps Clin & Res Found, 74-75; asst prof biol, Univ Conn, 75-77; sr staff fel, NIH, 77-79, expert-consult, Nat Inst Allergy & Infectious Dis, Rocky Mountain Labs, 79-82; asst prof biol, State Univ NY, Binghamton, 82-89; res dir, Ecol Eng Assocs, 89-91; dir, Qual Systs & Technol Develop, Adams Sci 91-93; dir qual assurance & control, Inst Molecular Biol, Inc, 94-96; gen mgr, Aeropharm, Inc, 96. *Concurrent Pos:* Pres, IOEA Consult. *Mem:* Am Soc Qual Control; Int Soc Pharmaceut Engrs. *Res:* Develop quality systems for continuous improvement of biotechnology and pharmaceuticals. *Mailing Add:* 102 Summit Lane Bala Cynwyd PA 19004. *Fax:* 610-668-0378; *E-Mail:* lissnest@aol.com

LISS, IVAN BARRY, COMPUTER SCIENCE EDUCATION, DATA STRUCTURES. *Current Pos:* prof comput sci, Radford Univ, 85-91, chair, 91-93, assoc dean, 93-96, INTERIM DEAN, COL ARTS & SCI, RADFORD UNIV, 96- *Personal Data:* b Lebanon, Ky, June 21, 38; m 77, Frances C Mitchell; c Barry & David. *Educ:* Georgetown Col, BA, 60; Univ Ky, MA, 63; Univ Louisville, PhD(chem), 73; Univ Ill, Springfield, MA, 85. *Prof Exp:* Teacher chem, Shelby Co High Sch, Ky, 60-65; chemist, Reliance Universal, Inc, 65-67; NDEA fel, Univ Louisville, 68-71, instr chem, 71-73; fel, Univ Mo, Columbia, 73-74; prof chem, Blackburn Col, Ill, 74-85. *Concurrent Pos:* Dir acad comput, Radford Univ, 88-91. *Mem:* Am Chem Soc; Sigma Xi. *Res:* Methods and approaches for computer science education at the university level. *Mailing Add:* Radford Univ PO Box 6940 Radford VA 24142. *Fax:* 540-831-5970; *E-Mail:* iliss@runet.edu

LISS, LEOPOLD, NEUROPATHOLOGY. *Current Pos:* assoc prof, 60-64, PROF NEUROPATH, OHIO STATE UNIV, 64-, CO-DIR OFF GERIAT MED, COL MED, 77- *Personal Data:* b Lwow, Poland, Nov 19, 23; nat US; m 48; c 2. *Educ:* Lwow Gramar Sch, Poland, BA, 41; Univ Heidelberg, MD, 50; Univ Mich, MS, 55. *Prof Exp:* From instr to asst prof neuropath, Univ Mich, 51-60. *Mem:* Am Asn Neuropath; Soc Neurosci; Int Acad Path; Am Geriat Soc; Asn Res Nerv & Ment Dis; Sigma Xi. *Res:* Clinical and experimental neuropathology; aging brain; Dementia; Alzheimer's disease; alcoholic encephalopathies; aluminum neurotoxicity. *Mailing Add:* 2124 Chardon Rd Columbus OH 43220-4461

LISS, MAURICE, BIOCHEMISTRY, BIOLOGY. *Current Pos:* assoc prof, 68-73, PROF BIOL, BOSTON COL, 73- *Personal Data:* b Boston, Mass, Dec 18, 26. *Educ:* Harvard Univ, AB, 49; Tufts Univ, PhD(biochem), 58. *Prof Exp:* Chemist, Peter Bent Brigham Hosp, 49-51; chemist, Mass Dept Pub Safety, 51-53; Am Cancer Soc res fel, enzymol, Brandeis Univ, 58-60; res assoc dermat, Sch Med, Tufts Univ, 61-63; from asst prof to assoc prof, 63-68. *Concurrent Pos:* Vis prof, Dept Immunol, Hadassah Med Sch, Jerusalem, 82. *Mem:* Am Chem Soc; Am Soc Biol Chem; AAAS; Am Soc Microbiol. *Res:* Proteins; amino acid metabolism. *Mailing Add:* 1550 Worcester Rd Framingham MA 01701

LISS, WILLIAM JOHN, FISHERIES ECOLOGY, LIMNOLOGY. *Current Pos:* Res assoc, 77-78, asst prof, 78-85, ASSOC PROF FISHERIES, ORE STATE UNIV, 85- *Personal Data:* b Pittsburgh, Pa, June 18, 47. *Educ:* Pa State Univ, BS, 69; Ore State Univ, MS, 74, PhD(fisheries), 77. *Mem:* Sigma Xi. *Res:* Population and community ecology of aquatic and terrestrial organisms; fisheries exploitation theory; effects of toxic substances on aquatic communities; watershed and stream classification. *Mailing Add:* Wildlife Mgt Ore State Univ 104 Nash Hall Corvallis OR 97331-3801

LISSAMAN, PETER BARRY STUART, AERODYNAMICS. *Current Pos:* ADJ PROF, AEROSPACE ENG, UNIV SOUTHERN CALIF, 91- *Personal Data:* b Durban, SAfrica, Apr 10, 31; US citizen; m 55, 80, Garbilla Hoeglund; c 4. *Educ:* Univ Natal, BS, 51; Cambridge Univ, MA, 54; Calif Inst Technol, MS, 55, PhD(aeronaut), 66. *Hon Degrees:* Dr, Natal Univ, 90. *Honors & Awards:* Longstreth Medal, Franklin Inst, 79; Kremer Medal, Royal Aeronaut Soc, 79. *Prof Exp:* Designer & struct analyst, Bristol Aircraft Co, Eng, 55-56; res aerodynamicist, Handley-Page Aircraft, Eng, 56-58; asst prof aeronaut, US Naval Postgrad Sch, 58-62, Calif Inst Technol, 62-69 & Jet Propulsion Lab, 68-69; dir continuum mech lab, Northrop Corp, 69-71; vpres, Aerovironment Inc, 72-91. *Concurrent Pos:* Consult, McDonnell Douglas Corp, 65-68; distinguished lectr, Am Inst Aeronaut & Astronaut, 72-79; prof, Art Ctr of Design, 76-, Southern Calif Inst Archit, 92-; nat lectr, Sigma Xi Soc, 86-89. *Mem:* Fel Am Inst Aeronaut & Astronaut; Soc Exp Test Pilots. *Res:* Aerodynamics, hydrodynamics, structure and dynamics of aircraft; marine and ground vehicles; wind and marine turbines; automotive aerodynamics; wing, rotor theory; turbulence, diffusion, plume modelling; energy systems; bird flight; engineering education. *Mailing Add:* Aerospace Dept Univ Southern Calif Los Angeles CA 90089-1191. *Fax:* 213-740-7774; *E-Mail:* tissaman@spock.usc.edu

LISSANT, ELLEN KERN, PHYCOLOGY, ENVIRONMENTAL SCIENCE. *Current Pos:* RETIRED. *Personal Data:* b St Louis, Mo, Nov 4, 22; m 47, Kenneth J; c Joyce E, Keith J & Nathan K. *Educ:* Washington Univ, St Louis, AB, 44, AM, 46, PhD(bot), 68C. *Prof Exp:* Lab instr bot, Wash Univ, St Louis, 43-45; teacher, Webster Groves High Sch, 45-46; asst bot, Wash Univ, St Louis, 46-47; asst herbarium, Stanford Univ, 47; from lectr to prof biol, Fontbonne Col, 60-78. *Concurrent Pos:* Bot artist, 45-; fac assoc, Wash Univ, 79-81; instr, St Louis Community Col, Meramec, 81-85. *Mem:* Bot Soc Am; Phycol Soc Am; Sigma Xi; Int Phycol Soc. *Res:* Palaeobotany; genetics; morphogenetic studies in the genus Erythrocladia Rosenvinge. *Mailing Add:* 851 Carob Rd Clever MO 65631

LISSANT, KENNETH JORDAN, COLLOID CHEMISTRY, EMULSIONS. *Current Pos:* RETIRED. *Personal Data:* b London, Eng, Aug 6, 20; nat US; m 47, Ellen M Kern; c Keith J, Joyce E & Nathan K. *Educ:* Ottawa Univ, Kans, AB, 41; Wash Univ, St Louis, MS, 43; Stanford Univ, PhD(chem), 47. *Prof Exp:* Asst chem, Ottawa Univ, Kans, 39-41; asst chem, Washington Univ, St Louis, 41-44, instr physics, 43-44; res chemist, Petrolite Corp, 44-65, advan res coordr, 65-68, dir advan res, 68-80. *Concurrent Pos:* Consult, 85- *Mem:* AAAS; Am Chem Soc. *Res:* Solubilization of liquids; polymerization of unsaturates; foams; surfactants; emulsions; information retrieval; pollution abatement; glyphs. *Mailing Add:* 851 Carob Rd Clever MO 65631. *E-Mail:* KLissant@aol.com

LISSAUER, DAVID ARIE, ELEMENTARY PARTICLE PHYSICS. *Current Pos:* PHYSICIST, BROOKHAVEN NAT LAB, 85- *Personal Data:* b Haifa, Israel, Mar 23, 45; m 68, Elaine Heller; c Ariella, Michal & Jonathan. *Educ:* Univ Calif, Berkeley, BA, 66, MA, 68, PhD(physics), 71. *Prof Exp:* Lectr physics, Tel Aviv Univ, 72-74, sr lectr, 75-77, assoc prof, 79-81; res assoc, Argonne Nat Lab, 74-75, European Nuclear Res Orgn (CERN), 77-78 & 81-82. *Concurrent Pos:* Prof, Tel-Aviv Univ, 87-93. *Mem:* Am Phys Soc. *Res:* Lepton production in high energy interactions; relativistic heavy ion collisions. *Mailing Add:* Brookhaven Nat Lab 510 A Upton NY 11973. *Fax:* 516-282-5568; *E-Mail:* lissauer@bnl.gov

LISSAUER, JACK JONATHAN, PLANETARY SCIENCE, PLANET FORMATION. *Current Pos:* SPACE SCIENTIST, AMES RES CTR, NASA, 96- *Personal Data:* b San Francisco, Calif, Mar 25, 57. *Educ:* Mass Inst Technol, SB, 78; Univ Calif, Berkeley, PhD(appl math), 82. *Honors & Awards:* Harold C Urey Prize, Div Planetary Sci, Am Astron Soc, 92. *Prof Exp:* Nat Acad Sci-Nat Res Coun, resident res assoc, Ames Res Ctr, NASA, Calif, 83-85; asst res astronr, Univ Calif, Berkeley, 85; vis researcher, Univ Calif, Santa Barbara, 85-87; Alfred P Sloan Found fel, 87-91. *Concurrent Pos:* Vis scholar, Dept Planetary Sci & Lunar & Planetary Lab, Univ Ariz, Tucson, 90, Astron Dept, Univ Calif, Berkeley, 94-95; invited prof, Dept Physics, Paris Observ, Univ Paris VII, 90; vis asst res physicist, Inst Theoret Physics, Univ Calif, Santa Barbara, 92; assoc researcher, Inst Astrophys, Paris, 93; adj assoc prof, Astron Group, State Univ NY, Stony Brook, 96- *Mem:* Am Astron Soc; Int Astron Union. *Res:* Modelling the formation of the solar system and of planetary systems in general, with particular emphasis on the dynamical processes involved in the final stages of planetary growth and the consequences for time scales of planetary growth and the origin of planetary rotation. *Mailing Add:* Space Sci 245-3 Ames Res Ctr NASA Moffett Field CA 94035. *Fax:* 650-604-6779; *E-Mail:* jlissauer@ringside.arc.nasa.gov

LISSNER, DAVID, MATHEMATICS. *Current Pos:* from asst prof to assoc prof, 62-77, PROF MATH, SYRACUSE UNIV, 77- *Personal Data:* b Rochester, NY, July 25, 31. *Educ:* Mass Inst Technol, BS, 53; Cornell Univ, PhD(math), 59. *Prof Exp:* Design engr, NAm Aviation, Inc, 53-55; Off Naval Res fel math, Northwestern Univ, 59-60; instr, Yale Univ, 60-62. *Mem:* Am Math Soc. *Res:* Ring theory; linear, commutative and homological algebra; algebraic geometry. *Mailing Add:* Dept Math Syracuse Univ 100 University Pl Syracuse NY 13244-0001

LIST, ALBERT, JR, PLANT PHYSIOLOGY. *Current Pos:* assoc prof biol, 67-74, ASSOC PROF BIOL SCI, DREXEL UNIV, 74- *Personal Data:* b East Orange, NJ, Nov 5, 28; m 53; c 2. *Educ:* Univ Mass, BS, 53; Cornell Univ, MS, 58, PhD(plant physiol), 61. *Prof Exp:* Instr bot, Douglass Col, Rutgers Univ, 61-62, asst prof bot & biol, 62-65; fel, Univ Pa, 65-66, lectr biomet & bot, 66-67. *Concurrent Pos:* NSF res grants, 63-65, 66-67 & 70-72; USPHS grant, 70-73. *Mem:* AAAS; Bot Soc Am; Am Soc Plant Physiol; Am Inst Biol Sci; Soc Develop Biol. *Res:* Developmental botany; control theory for plant root growth; relationships of relative elemental growth rates to bioelectric and membrane properties in roots; air pollution effects on growth. *Mailing Add:* Dept Biol Sci Drexel Univ 3141 Chestnut St Philadelphia PA 19104-2816

LIST, HARVEY L(AWRENCE), PROCESS HAZARDS ANALYSIS, INCIDENT INVESTIGATION. *Current Pos:* from assoc prof to prof, 55-80, EMER PROF CHEM ENG, CITY COL NEW YORK, 80-; PRES, LIST ASSOCS, INC, 69- *Personal Data:* b Brooklyn, NY, Sept 5, 24; m 46, Anita R; c Eric & Ian. *Educ:* Polytech Inst Brooklyn, BChE, 50, DChE, 58; Univ Rochester, MS, 50. *Prof Exp:* Process engr chem eng, Esso Res & Eng Co, 50-55. *Concurrent Pos:* Private consult, 55-; Fulbright prof, Tunghai Univ, 63-64; tech coordr, Adhesive & Sealant Coun, Ill; ed, Int Petrochem Develop 80-89; pres, Rickian Inc, Forensic Chem Engrs, 82-94. *Mem:* Am Chem Soc; Am Soc Eng Educ; Am Inst Chem Engrs. *Res:* Fluidization of solids; petroleum refining; chemical process economics; international relations; risk analysis; hazard and operability studies; accident investigation. *Mailing Add:* 3501 S Ocean Blvd No 103 Palm Beach FL 33480-5951. *Fax:* 561-585-8593

LIST, JAMES CARL, HERPETOLOGY. *Current Pos:* from instr to prof biol, 57-88, EMER PROF BIOL, BALL STATE UNIV, 88- *Personal Data:* b Paducah, Ky, July 6, 26; m 47; c 2. *Educ:* Notre Dame Univ, BS, 48, MS, 49; Univ Ill, PhD(zool), 56. *Prof Exp:* From instr to asst prof biol, Loyola Univ, Ill, 52-57. *Mem:* Am Soc Ichthyol & Herpet; Herpetologists League; Soc Study Amphibians & Reptiles; Sigma Xi. *Res:* Anatomy and ecology of amphibians and reptiles. *Mailing Add:* 7522 W Bethel Ave Muncie IN 47304

LIST, ROLAND, ATMOSPHERIC PHYSICS. *Current Pos:* prof, 84-95, EMER PROF PHYSICS, UNIV TORONTO, 95- *Personal Data:* b Frauenfeld, Switz, Feb 21, 29; m 56, 96, Gertrud K Egli; c Beat R & Claudia G. *Educ:* Swiss Fed Inst Technol, Dipl phys; Nat Swiss Fed Inst Technol, DSc, 60. *Honors & Awards:* Medal, Univ Leningrad, 70; Patterson Medal, 79. *Prof Exp:* Sect head atmospheric ice formation, Swiss Fed Inst Snow & Avalanche Res, 52-63; prof physics, Univ Toronto, 63-82, assoc chmn, Dept Physics, 69-73; dep secy-gen, World Meteorol Orgn, Geneva, Switz, 82-84. *Concurrent Pos:* Chmn working groups cloud physics & weather modifications, World Meteorol Orgn, 69-82; chmn, Comt Meteorol & Atmospheric Sci, Nat Res Coun; vis prof, Swiss Fed Inst Technol, 74; bd dir, US Nat Ctr Atmospheric Res, Univ Corp Atmospheric Res, 75-78; mem, Shuttle Sci Coun, Univ Space Res Asn, 78-81; chmn, Ital Sci Comt Rain Enhancement, Techagro, Rome, 90-; rep, Int Union Geol & Geophys, World Meteorol Orgn, 95- *Mem:* Fel Am Meteorol Soc; Am Geophys Union; fel Royal Meteorol Soc; Can Meteorol Soc; Swiss Acad Natural Sci; Can Acad Sci; fel Royal Soc Can; Int Asn Meteorol & Atmospheric Sci (secy-gen, 95-). *Res:* Precipitation physics; cloud dynamics; weather modification; heat and mass transfer; aerodynamics; all activities experimental, theoretical numerical and field. *Mailing Add:* Dept Physics Univ Toronto Toronto ON M5S 1A7 Can. *Fax:* 416-978-8906; *E-Mail:* list@atmosp.physics.utoronto.ca

LISTER, CHARLES ALLAN, ELECTRICAL ENGINEERING, ELECTRONICS ENGINEERING. *Current Pos:* CONSULT ENGR, 84- *Personal Data:* b Trenton, NJ, Nov 15, 18; m 46, Janet A Dressler; c Joan, Judith & Robert. *Educ:* Tufts Univ, BS, 40; Case Western Reserve Univ, MS, 51. *Prof Exp:* Test engr, Gen Elec Co, NY, 40-41, design engr, 41-43, appln engr, 46-47; asst prof elec eng, Swarthmore Col, 47-49; develop engr, Elec Controller & Mfg Div, Square D Co, Cleveland, 49-54, asst supvr, 54-56, supvr new prod develop, 56-62; design specialist, Lockheed Missiles & Space Co, Calif, 62-63, mgr test equip eng, 63-64; mgr spec devices eng, Lockheed Aircraft Serv Co, 64-65; dept head, Res & Develop, Otis Elevator Co, 65-67, mgr prod eng, 67-72, asst to vpres, 72-74, mgr proj admin, 74-75; mgr eng serv, 76-83, sr staff engr, Square D Co, Columbia, SC, 83-84. *Mem:* Inst Elec & Electronics Engrs; Sigma Xi. *Res:* Electromechanical and electronic systems and devices; high-voltage contactors; electric brakes; lifting magnets; elevator dispatching computer systems; elevator control systems; arc interruption; standards for industrial controls. *Mailing Add:* 3215 Gulf Shore Blvd N Apt 511 Naples FL 34103-3915. *Fax:* 941-262-3575

LISTER, CLIVE R B, heat flow, geodynamics; deceased, see previous edition for last biography

LISTER, EARL EDWARD, ruminant nutrition, for more information see previous edition

LISTER, FREDERICK MONIE, MATHEMATICS. *Current Pos:* RETIRED. *Personal Data:* b Trenton, NJ, May 9, 23; m 54; c 3. *Educ:* Tufts Univ, BS, 47; Univ Mich, MA, 51; Univ Utah, PhD(math), 66. *Prof Exp:* Instr math, Phillips Acad, Mass, 47-49; instr, Western Wash Col Educ, 54-56, from asst prof to assoc prof, 58-67; asst prof, Chico State Col, 57-58; prof, Southern Ore Col, 67-68; assoc prof math, Cent Wash State Col, 68-69, prof, 69-88. *Mem:* Am Math Soc; Math Asn Am. *Res:* Geometric topology; embeddings of 2-spheres in Euclidean 3-space. *Mailing Add:* Cent Wash Univ Ellensburg WA 98926

LISTER, MARK DAVID, EXPERIMENTAL BIOLOGY. *Current Pos:* scientist I, 89-92, SCIENTIST II, SPHINX PHARMACEUT CO, 92- *Personal Data:* b Kansas City, Mo, Aug 12, 53; m, Deborah Adams; c Hannah. *Educ:* William Jewell Col, BA, 75; Univ Mo, PhD(chem), 85. *Prof Exp:* Fel lipid enzymol, Univ Calif, San Diego, 85-89. *Mem:* Am Chem Soc; AAAS; Am Soc Biochem & Molecular Biol. *Res:* Protein purification; enzymatic characterization; kinetics; inhibitor studies; chemical and enzymatic synthesis; study of second messengers in cell signal transduction; development of high through-put assays for drug screening programs. *Mailing Add:* Sphinx Pharmaceut Co Div Eli Lilly 4615 University Dr Durham NC 27707-3458. *Fax:* 919-489-1308

LISTER, MAURICE WOLFENDEN, inorganic chemistry, for more information see previous edition

LISTER, RICHARD MALCOLM, PLANT VIROLOGY. *Current Pos:* assoc prof, 66-72, PROF PLANT VIROL, PURDUE UNIV, WEST LAFAYETTE, 72- *Personal Data:* b Sheffield, Eng, Nov 14, 28; m 53, Jean I Mills; c Susan, Christina, Rosalind & John. *Educ:* Sheffield Univ, BSc, 49, dipl ed, 50; Cambridge Univ, dipl agr sci, 51; Imp Col Trop Agr, Trinidad, dipl, 52; St Andrews Univ, PhD, 63. *Honors & Awards:* Ruth Allen Award, Am Phytopath Soc, 86. *Prof Exp:* Plant pathologist, WAfrican Cocoa Res Inst, 52-56 & Scottish Hort Res Inst, 56-66. *Concurrent Pos:* Fel bot & plant path, Purdue Univ, 63-64; res grants, NSF & USDA. *Mem:* Fel Am Phytopath Soc; Brit Asn Appl Biol. *Res:* Methods in plant virology; properties and interactions of virus-specific products of virus infections; serological techniques; transmission, purification, properties, and relationships of selected plant viruses, especially of cereals, soybeans and fruit plants. *Mailing Add:* Dept Bot & Plant Path Life Sci Bldg Purdue Univ West Lafayette IN 47907

LISTERMAN, THOMAS WALTER, SOLID STATE SCIENCE. *Current Pos:* asst prof, Wright State Univ, 67-72, asst provost, 71-73, asst dean sci & eng, 70-71, ASSOC PROF PHYSICS, WRIGHT STATE UNIV, 72- *Personal Data:* b Cincinnati, Ohio, Dec 21, 38; m 69; c 2. *Educ:* Xavier Univ, BS, 59; Ohio Univ, PhD(solid state physics), 65. *Prof Exp:* Sr res physicist, Mound Lab, Monsanto Res Corp, 65-67. *Concurrent Pos:* Vis res assoc prof elec eng, Univ Cincinnati, 87-88. *Mem:* Inst Elec & Electronics Engrs; Mat Res Soc. *Res:* Electronic properties of materials; cryogenics; semiconductor device physics. *Mailing Add:* Eng Physics Prog & Dept Physics Wright State Univ 3640 Colonel Glenn Dayton OH 45435. *E-Mail:* tlisterman@wright.edu

LISTGARTEN, MAX, DENTISTRY, PERIODONTOLOGY. *Current Pos:* assoc prof, 68-71, dept chmn, 84-92, PROF PERIODONT & DIR PERIODONT RES, UNIV PA, 71- *Personal Data:* b Paris, France, May 14, 35; Can citizen; m 63, Eileen Gregory; c Karen, Sheralyn & Michael. *Educ:* Univ Toronto, DDS, 59; FRCD(C), 69. *Hon Degrees:* MA, Univ Pa, 71; PhD, Univ Athens, Greece, 93. *Honors & Awards:* Award Basic Res Periodont Dis, Int Asn Dent Res, 73; William J Gies Periodont Award, Am Acad Periodont, 81, Clin Res Award, 87. *Prof Exp:* Intern dent, Hosp for Sick Children, Toronto, 59-60; res assoc periodont, Harvard Med Sch, 63-64; from asst prof to assoc prof, Fac Dent, Univ Toronto, 64-68. *Concurrent Pos:* Nat Res Coun Can fel periodont, Harvard Med Sch, 60-63; US ed, J Biol Buccale, 72-92; oral biol & med study sect, NIH, 80-84; pres, Am Asn Dent Res, 91-92. *Mem:* Fel AAAS; Am Dent Asn; fel Am Acad Periodont; Int Asn Dent Res; Am Asn Dent Res. *Res:* Ultrastructural investigations of the supporting structures of teeth and associated microbial flora in health and disease; microbiological diagnosis in the treatment of periodontal diseases. *Mailing Add:* Dept Periodont Sch Dent Med Univ Pa 4001 Spruce St Philadelphia PA 19104. *Fax:* 215-573-2117; *E-Mail:* maxl@biochem.dental.upenn.edu

LISTON, AARON IRVING, BOTANY. *Current Pos:* ASST PROF & DIR HERBARIUM, DEPT BOT & PLANT PATH, ORE STATE UNIV, CORVALLIS, 91- *Personal Data:* b Cleveland, Ohio, Dec 2, 59; m 90, Sara N Meury. *Educ:* Hebrew Univ, BSc, 82, MSc, 84; Claremont Grad Sch, PhD(bot), 90. *Prof Exp:* Herbarium asst, Hebrew Univ, 82-86; res asst, Rancho Santa Ana Bot Garden, Calif, 87-89; fel researcher, Dept Genetics, Univ Calif, Davis, 90. *Concurrent Pos:* Prin investr, Claremont Grad Sch, 86, 87 & 89, Sigma Xi, 88, NSF, 88, 93, 94, Ore Dept Agr, 91, M J Murdock Charitable Trust, 91-92, Hardman Found & Hoover Trust, 93 & 94, Nat Acad Sci/Nat Res Coun, 93 & The Nature Conservancy, 94. *Mem:* AAAS; Am Soc Plant Taxonomists; Asn Systs Collections; Bot Soc Am; Soc Molecular & Biol Evolution; Soc Syst Biologists. *Res:* Botany; plant conservation genetics; molecular systematics. *Mailing Add:* Ore State Univ 2082 Cordley Hall Corvallis OR 97331-2902. *E-Mail:* listona@bcc.orst.edu

LISTON, RONALD ARGYLE, MECHANICAL ENGINEERING, ENGINEERING MECHANICS. *Current Pos:* SUPVR RES GEN ENGR, US ARMY COLD REGIONS RES & ENG LAB, 75- *Personal Data:* b Buffalo, NY, Apr 11, 26; m 81, Nancy Cummings; c 9. *Educ:* Univ Vt, BS, 49; Univ Mich, MS(mech eng), 58, MS(eng mech), 61; Mich Technol Univ, PhD(eng mech), 73. *Prof Exp:* Proof officer ballistics & automotive, US Army, 50-56, supvr automotive res engr, Tank-Automotive Command, 58-70, res mech engr, Cold Regions Res & Eng Lab, 70-74; res ctr dir, Mich Technol Univ, 74-75. *Concurrent Pos:* Secy, Army Res & Study fel. *Mem:* Fel Int Soc Terrain-Vehicle Systs (gen secy); Sigma Xi; Am Soc Mech Engrs. *Res:* Off road vehicles; over snow vehicles; simulation of engineer activities in combat operations; rapid stabilization of soils. *Mailing Add:* US Army Cold Regions 72 Lyme Rd Hanover NH 03775

LISTOWSKY, IRVING, BIOCHEMISTRY. *Current Pos:* From instr to assoc prof, 65-78, PROF BIOCHEM, ALBERT EINSTEIN COL MED, 79- *Personal Data:* b Vilna, Poland, Dec 21, 35; US citizen; m 63; c 3. *Educ:* Yeshiva Univ, BA, 57; Polytech Inst Brooklyn, PhD(org chem), 63. *Concurrent Pos:* NIH career develop award, 71-76; sr investr, NY Heart Asn, 67-70. *Mem:* Am Soc Biol Chemists. *Res:* Structure-function relationships of biological substances; iron metabolism, intracellular transport and detoxification mechanisms. *Mailing Add:* Albert Einstein Col Med 1300 Morris Park Ave Bronx NY 10461

LISY, JAMES MICHAEL, SPECTROSCOPY, MOLECULAR BEAMS. *Current Pos:* asst prof, 81-87, ASSOC PROF CHEM, UNIV ILL, 87- *Personal Data:* b Cleveland, Ohio, Aug 5, 52; m 76; c 2. *Educ:* Iowa State Univ, BS, 74; Harvard Univ, MA, 77, PhD(chem physics), 79. *Prof Exp:* Res assoc, Lawrence Berkeley Lab, 79-81. *Concurrent Pos:* Alfred P Sloan Res fel, 87-91. *Mem:* Am Chem Soc; Am Phys Soc. *Res:* Structure, bonding and intramolecular energy transfer of small molecular and ion clusters are studied using molecular beam techniques and laser spectroscopy. *Mailing Add:* Sch Chem Sci Univ Ill 600 S Mathews Ave Urbana IL 61801-3617

LISZT, HARVEY STEVEN, RADIO ASTRONOMY, MICROCOMPUTER APPLICATIONS IN DATA PROCESSING. *Current Pos:* res assoc, 73-75, assoc scientist, 76-79, SCIENTIST ASTRON, NAT RADIO ASTRON OBSERV, 79- *Personal Data:* b Newark, NJ, Dec 5, 45; m 73, Mehrak Birjandi; c Jeffrey B & Gregory B. *Educ:* Univ Mass, BS, 67; Princeton Univ, AM, 69, PhD(astron), 74. *Prof Exp:* Res assoc spectros, Princeton Univ Observ, 69-71; asst prof physics, Univ Pittsburgh, 75-76. *Concurrent Pos:* Res prof, Univ Va, 81-, proj scientist, 95- *Mem:* Sigma Xi; Int Astron Union. *Res:* Structure and evolution of interstellar clouds; radiation transport in simple interstellar molecules; structure of the galactic nucleus, interstellar chemistry. *Mailing Add:* Nat Radio Astron Observ Edgemont Rd Charlottesville VA 22903-2475

LIT, ALFRED, VISION, EXPERIMENTAL PSYCHOLOGY. *Current Pos:* prof psychol, 61-85, EMER PROF PSYCHOL & MEM ADV BD, EMER COL, SOUTHERN ILL UNIV, 85- *Personal Data:* b New York, NY, Nov 24, 14; m 47, Imogene Speegle. *Educ:* Columbia Univ, BS, 38, AM, 43, PhD, 48. *Honors & Awards:* Sigma Xi-Kaplan Res Award. *Prof Exp:* Lectr optom, Columbia Univ, 46-48, assoc, 48-49, asst psychol, 49, from asst prof to assoc prof optom, 49-56; res psychologist, Univ Mich, 56-59; head, Human Factors Staff, Systs Div, Bendix Corp, 59-61; res prof, Schnurmacher Inst Vision Resm Col Optom, State Univ NY, 85-86. *Concurrent Pos:* Res grant, Am Acad Optom, Columbia Univ, 49, mem psychol staff, Off Naval Res Contract, 49-56; lectr, Univ Mich, 57-58; res grants, Eye Inst, USPHS & NSF, 62; mem, Armed Forces-Nat Res Coun Comt Vision; consult, Goodyear Aerospace Corp, Nat Res Coun Comt on Vision, Nat Acad Sci & Spec Study Sect, USPHS; sci referee, Am J Optom, 73. *Mem:* Fel AAAS; fel Optical Soc Am; fel Am Psychol Asn; hon fel NY Acad Optom; fel Am Acad Optom; fel Soc Eng Psychologists; fel Psychonomic Soc Am; Human Factors Soc; Am Asn Univ Prof; Asn Res Vision & Ophthal. *Res:* Perception; applications of visual psychophysics to ophthalmic clinical practice; spatio-temporal factors influencing visual latency and persistence. *Mailing Add:* Dept Psychol Southern Ill Univ Carbondale IL 62901-6502. *E-Mail:* gaiizo@siucvmb.bitnet

LIT, JOHN WAI-YU, OPTICS. *Current Pos:* assoc prof, 77-80, PROF PHYSICS, WILFRID LAURIER UNIV, 80-, CHMN PHYSICS DEPT, 80-86 & 92- *Personal Data:* b Canton, China, Aug 31, 37; Can citizen; m, Chi M Lee; c Wilson & Eugene. *Educ:* Univ Hong Kong, BSc, 58, dipl Ed, 61; Univ Laval, PhD (optics), 69. *Prof Exp:* Head physics, Diocesan Boys Sch, 61-64; teacher sci, Quebec High Sch, 64-65; fel optics, Univ Western Ont, 68-69; res assoc, 69-71, from asst prof to assoc prof optics, Univ Laval, 71-77. *Concurrent Pos:* Consult, various indust & govt labs; assoc ed, Optical Soc Am, 74-79; chmn, Div Optical Physics, Can Asn Physicists, 77-78 & 88-89; adj prof elec eng & elec comput eng, Univ Waterloo, 87-93, adj prof physics, 80-; mem exec comt, bd dirs, Nat Optics Inst, 88-91; chair gen physics, Grants Selection Comt, Natural Scis & Eng Res Coun Can; founding pres, Southwestern Ont Sect, Opt Soc Am, 94-95. *Mem:* Can Asn Physicists; fel Optical Soc Am; Inst Elec & Electronics Engrs. *Res:* Fiber and integrated optics; optical sensing; optical instrumentation. *Mailing Add:* Dept Physics & Comput Wilfrid Laurier Univ Waterloo ON N2L 3C5 Can

LITCHFIELD, CARTER, BIOCHEMISTRY. *Current Pos:* WRITER & PUBL, OLEARIUS ED, 79- *Personal Data:* b Pasadena, Calif, Feb 18, 32; m 60. *Educ:* Rensselaer Polytech Inst, BS, 53; Am Inst Foreign Trade, BFT, 57; Tex A&M Univ, PhD(chem), 66. *Honors & Awards:* Bond Award, Am Oil Chem Soc, 63, 66 & 78. *Prof Exp:* Chemist, Procter & Gamble Co, 53-60; from asst prof to assoc prof lipid biochem, Tex A&M Univ, 60-69; assoc prof lipid biochem, Rutgers Univ, 69-73, from assoc prof to prof biochem, 73-79. *Concurrent Pos:* Vis scientist, Fisheries Res Bd Can, 67 & Univ Trondheim, 75 & 79. *Mem:* Soc Hist Technol; Am Oil Chem Soc; Soc Indust Archeol. *Res:* Biochemistry of lipids of marine organisms; analysis of natural fat triglyceride mixtures; gas liquid chromatography of lipids; biochemical systematics of lipids; history of lipid biochemistry; history of fats & oils technology. *Mailing Add:* 28 White Oak Rd Kemblesville PA 19347

LITCHFIELD, JOHN HYLAND, FOOD SCIENCE, INDUSTRIAL MICROBIOLOGY. *Current Pos:* sr food technologist, Battelle Mem Inst, 60-61, proj leader biosci, 61-62, asst chief biosci res, 62-64, chief biochem & microbiol res, 64-67 & microbiol & environ biol res, 67-68, assoc mgr life sci, Dept Chem Eng, 68-70, mgr biol & med sci sect, Columbus Labs, 70-72, sr tech adv, 73-76, mgr Bioeng & Health Sci Sect, 76-80, prog mgr biol sci, 80-81, RES LEADER BIOTECHNOL, COLUMBUS LABS, BATTELLE MEM INST, 81-; ADJ PROF, DEPT FOOD SCI & TECHNOL, OHIO STATE UNIV, COLUMBUS, OHIO, 90- *Personal Data:* b Scituate, Mass, Feb 13, 29; wid; c Robert. *Educ:* Mass Inst Technol, SB, 50; Univ Ill, MS, 54, PhD(food technol), 56. *Honors & Awards:* Charles Porter Award, Soc Indust Microbiol, 77; Carl R Fellers Award, Inst Food Technol, 94. *Prof Exp:* Chief chemist, Searle Food Corp, Fla, 50-51; res food technologist, Swift & Co, Ill, 56-57; asst prof food eng, Ill Inst Technol, 57-60. *Concurrent Pos:* Consult to food indust, 57-60; adj assoc prof human nutrit & food mgt, Ohio State Univ, Columbus, Ohio, 77-78. *Mem:* Fel AAAS; fel Am Inst Chemists; fel Am Acad Microbiol; fel Soc Indust Microbiol (pres, 70-71); fel Am Pub Health Asn; fel Inst Food Technologists (pres, 91-92). *Res:* Food processing and preservation; fermentation technology, food, industrial, sanitary and public health microbiology; microbial biochemistry; mass cultivation of microorganisms. *Mailing Add:* Battelle Mem Inst 505 King Ave Columbus OH 43201

LITCHFIELD, WILLIAM JOHN, BIOCHEMISTRY, CLINICAL CHEMISTRY. *Current Pos:* res biochemist, Instrument Prod Div, E I DuPont De Nemours & Co, Inc, 76-78, new bus develop mgr, 78-90, prod & res mgr, 90-93, QUAL ASSURANCE MGR, E I DUPONT DE NEMOURS & CO, INC, 93-, METHODS MGR, 96- *Personal Data:* b Waukegan, Ill, Feb 28, 50; m 72, Marilyn Kommade; c 2. *Educ:* Univ Ill, BS, 72, MS, 73; Mich

State Univ, PhD(biochem), 76. *Prof Exp:* Fel biophys, Johnson Res Found, Sch Med, Univ Pa, 76-77. *Concurrent Pos:* NIH fel, 76-77. *Mem:* Am Chem Soc; Am Asn Clin Chem; Biophys Soc; Am Asn Immunologists; Soc Qual Assurance. *Res:* Biophysics; solid state biochemical reactions; free-radical reactions in leukocytes, mitochondria and photosystems; immunology, enzymology, lipid chemistry; immunochemistry; immunodiagnostics. *Mailing Add:* 23 Covered Bridge Lane Newark DE 19711-2062. *E-Mail:* litchfwj@esvax.dnet.dupont.com

LITCHFORD, GEORGE B, ELECTRONICS. *Current Pos:* asst supvr Navig Dept, 51-55, head, Dept Aviation Systs Res, 57-65, PRES & HEAD DEPT AVIATION SYSTS CONSULT BUS, LITCHFORD SYSTS, 65-; GEN PARTNER, LITCHSTREET CO. *Personal Data:* b Long Beach, Calif, Aug 12, 18; m 42; c 2. *Educ:* Reed Col, BA, 41. *Honors & Awards:* Wright Bros Lect Medal & Citation, Am Inst Aeronaut & Astronaut, 78; Lamme Medal, Inst Elec & Electronics Engrs, 81. *Prof Exp:* Head eng sect, Aircraft Radio Dept, Sperry Gyroscope Co, 41-51. *Concurrent Pos:* Consult, Dept Transp, Dept Defense, NASA & indust, mem, Radio Tech Comn Aeronaut. *Mem:* Fel Inst Elec & Electronics Engrs; fel Am Inst Aeronaut & Astronaut. *Res:* Inventor of many systems including precision omniranges, navy and shuttle landing systems, secondary radar systems; developed collision avoidance systems, now in production; holder of over 70 patents; development of Passur, passive ground range. *Mailing Add:* Litchstreet Co 32 Cherry Lawn Lane Northport NY 11768

LITHERLAND, ALBERT EDWARD, PHYSICS, ACCELERATOR MASS SPECTROMETRY RADIOCARBON DATING. *Current Pos:* from prof to univ prof, 66-93, EMER UNIV PROF PHYSICS, UNIV TORONTO, 93- *Personal Data:* b Wallasey, Eng, Mar 12, 28; nat Can; m 56, Anne Allen; c Jane E & Rosamund M. *Educ:* Univ Liverpool, BSc, 49, PhD, 55. *Honors & Awards:* Gold Medal Physics, Can Asn Physicists, 71; Rutherford Medal, Inst Physics, London, 74; Henry Marshall Tory Medal, Royal Soc Can, 93. *Prof Exp:* Rutherford scholar, Atomic Energy Can, 53-55, sci officer, 55-66. *Concurrent Pos:* Killam fel, 80-81; Guggenheim fel, 86-87. *Mem:* Fel Royal Soc Can; Can Asn Physicists; fel AAAS; fel Am Phys Soc. *Res:* Radiocarbon dating for art/archaeology/geophysics using accelerator mass spectrometry; iodine-129 tracing for oceanography; fundamentals of accelerator mass spectrometry. *Mailing Add:* 3 Hawthorn Gardens Toronto ON M4W 1P4 Can

LITKE, JOHN DAVID, COMPUTER SCIENCE, PHYSICS. *Current Pos:* DIR FUTURE TECHNOL, ABC BROADCASTING, 96- *Personal Data:* b Winchester, Mass, May 30, 44; m 66. *Educ:* Mass Inst Technol, BS, 65; Johns Hopkins Univ, PhD(physics), 76. *Prof Exp:* Instr physics, Johns Hopkins Univ, 67-75; Bell Lab, 76-80, prin scientist photociruits, 80-84; dir res, Northrop Grumman, 85-96. *Concurrent Pos:* Consult, Off Automation Technol, 86- *Mem:* Sigma Xi; Am Phys Soc; Inst Elec & Electronics Engrs; Asn Comput Mach; Soc Motion Picture & Television Engrs. *Res:* Sofware engineering; distributed and fault tolerant systems; real time multi-media systems. *Mailing Add:* 645 Park Ave Huntington NY 11743. *Fax:* 212-456-2251; *E-Mail:* litkej@abc.com

LITMAN, BERNARD, ELECTRICAL ENGINEERING. *Current Pos:* RETIRED. *Personal Data:* b New York, NY, Oct 26, 20; m 49, Ellen Kaufman; c Barbara & Richard. *Educ:* Columbia Univ, BS, 41, PhD(elec eng), 49; Univ Pittsburgh, MS, 43. *Prof Exp:* Engr mach design, Westinghouse Elec Corp, 41-47; instr elec eng, Univ Pittsburgh, 47; engr fire control & guid, Ambac Industs, Div United Technologies Corp, 48-53, mgr airborne equip, 56-58, res, 59-61, chief engr, 63-83; prin scientist, Avionics Systs, Cull Inc, 83-93; sci consult, 93-95. *Mem:* Sr mem Inst Elec & Electronics Engrs; assoc fel Am Inst Aeronaut & Astronaut. *Res:* Electromechanical control and computing equipment; weapon control and navigation; inertial guidance; data management systems for aircraft and scientific instruments. *Mailing Add:* 228 Wagon Wheel Lane Columbus NJ 08022

LITMAN, BURTON JOSEPH, BIOCHEMISTRY, BIOPHYSICS. *Current Pos:* SECT CHIEF, SECT FLUORESCENCE STUDIES, LAB MEMBRANE BIOCHEM & BIOPHYSICS, NAT INST ALCOHOL ABUSE & ALCOHOLISM, NIH, 93- *Personal Data:* b Boston, Mass, May 8, 35; m 58, Elaine Freeman; c Deborah & Daniel. *Educ:* Boston Univ, BA, 58; Univ Ore, PhD(biophys chem), 66. *Prof Exp:* Fel, NIH, Dept Biochem, Univ Va, 66-68, from asst prof to prof biochem, 68-93, asst dean, Sch Med, 81-83, chmn, Dept Biochem, 84-93. *Concurrent Pos:* Vis prof, Dept Biochem, Univ Va, 93-94. *Mem:* Biophys Soc; Am Soc Biochem & Molecular Biol; Res Soc Alcoholism. *Res:* Structure-function relationships in biological membranes with particular emphasis on the molecular mechanism of vision; signal transduction in vision; role of lipid composition in modulating membrane protein function; mechanism of action of ethanol and general anesthetics. *Mailing Add:* NIH Lab Membrane Biochem & Biophys 12501 Washington Ave Rm 2 Rockville MD 20852. *Fax:* 301-594-0035; *E-Mail:* litman@helix.nih.gov

LITMAN, DIANE JUDITH, COMPUTATIONAL LINGUISTICS, KNOWLEDGE REPRESENTATION & REASONING. *Current Pos:* PRIN TECH STAFF MEM, AT&T LABS RES, 85- *Personal Data:* b New York, NY, Mar 5, 58. *Educ:* Col William & Mary, BA, 80; Univ Rochester, MS, 82, PhD(comput sci), 86. *Concurrent Pos:* Asst prof comput sci, Columbia Univ, 90-92. *Mem:* Asn Computational Ling; Am Asn Artificial Intel. *Res:* Artificial intelligence, particularly computational linguistics, knowledge representation and reasoning, plan recognition, spoken dialogue agents, user modeling and applications of machine learning. *Mailing Add:* AT&T Labs Res Rm A211 180 Park Ave Florham Park NJ 07932-0971

LITMAN, GARY WILLIAM, IMMUNOLOGY, BIOCHEMISTRY. *Current Pos:* CHMN, DEPT MOLECULAR GENETICS, RES INST, SHOWA UNIV. *Personal Data:* b Shoemaker, Calif, June 26, 45; m 70. *Educ:* Univ Minn, BA, 67, PhD(microbiol), 72. *Prof Exp:* Res asst microbiol, Univ Minn, 67-68, teaching specialist microbiol & pediat, 68-70, instr pediat & path, 70-72, asst prof path, 72; assoc mem, Dept Macromolecular Biochem, Sloan-Kettering Inst, 72-; assoc prof biol, Sloan-Kettering Div, Grad Sch Med Sci, Cornell Univ, 73- *Concurrent Pos:* Assoc prof genetics, Sloan-Kettering Div, Grad Sch Med Sci, Cornell Univ, 76-, chmn biol unit, 78-80, assoc prof immunol, 80. *Mem:* AAAS; Am Asn Immunologists; Am Asn Biol Chemists; Am Soc Zoologists; Biophys Soc. *Res:* Evolution of immunoglobulin structure; a typical solubility characteristics of proteins; chemical carcinogenesis; chromosomal proteins. *Mailing Add:* Dept Pediat Univ SFla All Childrens' Hosp 801 Sixth Ave S PO Box 707 St Petersburg FL 33701-4899

LITMAN, IRVING IRA, FOOD TECHNOLOGY. *Current Pos:* RES DIR, STEPAN FLAVORS & FRAGRANCES, INC, 66-; PRES, LITMAN TECHNOL CORP, 87- *Personal Data:* b Chelsea, Mass, Nov 16, 25; c 6. *Educ:* Univ Mass, BA, 49, MS, 51; Wash State Univ, PhD(food technol), 56. *Prof Exp:* Processed food inspector, Prod & Mkt Admin, USDA, 50-51; food technologist, Gen Prod Div, Qm Food & Container Inst, US Armed Forces, 51-53; asst dairy technologist, Wash State Univ, 53-55; jr res chemist, Univ Calif, 55-56; proj leader, Res Ctr, Gen Foods Corp, 56-62; flavor chemist, Givaudan Corp, 62-64; sect head, Durkee Famous Foods, 64-65; dir res, Stepan Chem Corp, 66-81, Globe Fla Corp, 81-83 & Manheimer Corp, 84-86. *Mem:* Royal Soc Chem; Inst Food Technologists; AAAS; Sigma Xi; Flavor Chemists Soc. *Res:* Development of synthetic and natural flavorings for food, tobacco and pharmaceuticals. *Mailing Add:* 447-B New Haven Way Jamesburg NJ 08831-1824

LITMAN, NATHAN, PEDIATRICS, INFECTIOUS DISEASES. *Current Pos:* ATTEND PEDIAT & INFECTIOUS DIS, MONTEFIORE HOSP & MED CTR, 78- *Personal Data:* b New York, NY, Nov 22, 46; m 69; c 3. *Educ:* Brooklyn Col, BS, 67; Albert Einstein Col Med, MD, 71. *Prof Exp:* Intern, resident & chief resident pediat, Montefiore Hosp & Med Ctr, 71-74; lieutenant comdr pediat, USPHS, 74-76; fel infectious dis, Albert Einstein Col Med, 76-78. *Mem:* Fel Am Acad Pediat; Infectious Dis Soc Am. *Res:* Infectious etiologies of pediatric diarrhea. *Mailing Add:* Dept Pediat NCent Bronx Hosp Bronx NY 10467

LITOSCH, IRENE, PHYSIOLOGICAL CHEMISTRY. *Current Pos:* FEL RES, SECT PHYSIOL CHEM, BROWN UNIV, 79- *Personal Data:* b New York, NY, June 7, 52. *Educ:* New York Univ, Univ Arts & Sci, BA, 74; State Univ NY, Downstate Med Ctr, PhD(pharmacol), 79. *Mem:* NY Acad Sci. *Res:* Mechanism of regulation of intiacularlur calcium. *Mailing Add:* Dept Pharmacol Univ Miami Med Sch PO Box 016189 Miami FL 33101-6189

LITOV, RICHARD EMIL, CLINICAL NUTRITION. *Current Pos:* DIR RES & DEVELOP, NUTRATEC, 93- *Personal Data:* b New York, NY, 53; m, Davis S Wagner. *Educ:* Univ Calif, Davis, BS, 75, PhD(nutrit), 80. *Prof Exp:* Staff res assoc, Univ Calif, Med Sch & Primate Res Ctr, Davis, 75-76, res asst, 76-80; scientist, Bristol-Myers Squibb, 81-85, sr scientist res, 85-93. *Concurrent Pos:* Reviewer, Am J Clin Nutrit, 86-, Pediat, 90- & USDA Competitive Grants Prog, 90-; bd trustees, Evansville Mus Arts & Sci, 87- *Mem:* Inst Food Technologists; Am Soc Clin Nutrit; Am Inst Nutrit. *Res:* Functional foods; infant and enteral formulas; therapeutic biologics; oral rehydration solutions; antiinfections; mineral bioavailability; burn injury; selenium bioavailability and aluminum status. *Mailing Add:* 3210 Arrowhead Dr Evansville IN 47720. *Fax:* 812-422-9440; *E-Mail:* nutratec@aol.com

LITOVITZ, THEODORE AARON, PHYSICS. *Current Pos:* From asst prof to assoc prof, 50-59, PROF PHYSICS, CATH UNIV AM, 59-, CO-DIR, VITREOUS STATE LAB, 68- *Personal Data:* b New York, NY, Oct 14, 23; m 46; c 2. *Educ:* Cath Univ, AB, 46, PhD, 50. *Concurrent Pos:* Consult, Univ Hosp, Georgetown, 50-57. *Mem:* Fel Am Phys Soc; fel Acoust Soc Am; Am Philos Soc. *Res:* Ultrasonic propagation and light scattering in studies of molecular motions in liquids and glasses; development of glasses with unique technical applications. *Mailing Add:* Dept Physics Cath Univ Washington DC 20064

LITSEY, LINUS R, GEOLOGY. *Current Pos:* RETIRED. *Educ:* Univ Mich, BS, 47; Univ Colo, PhD(geol), 55. *Prof Exp:* Uranium geologist, US Geol Surv, 54-57; geologist, Chevron Oil Co, New Orleans, La, 57-63, dipmeter res, Chevron Res Co, La Habra, Calif, 63-65, dipmeter analyst, Chevron Oil Co, New Orleans, 65-69, digital well log processing, Houston, Tex, 69-72; well log analyst, 72-74, supvr reservoir description unit, Aramco, Arabia, 74-76; formation eval geologist, Chevron Oil Co, Denver, Colo, 76-80; sr consult, Sci Software-Intercomp, 80-96. *Mem:* Am Asn Petrol Geologists; Geol Soc Am; Soc Prof Well Log Analysts; Sigma Xi. *Mailing Add:* 14 Aspen Way Parachute CO 81635

LITSKY, BERTHA YANIS, MICROBIOLOGY, HOSPITAL ADMINISTRATION. *Current Pos:* NURSE CONSULT, BINGHAM ASSOCS FUND, NEW ENG MED CTR HOSP, 74- *Personal Data:* b Chester, Pa, Jan 2, 20; m 65; c 2. *Educ:* Philadelphia Col Pharm, BSc, 42; NY Univ, MPA, 64; Walden Univ, PhD(educ), 76. *Prof Exp:* Head dept bact, Assoc Labs of Philadelphia, 42-44; asst supvr prod, Nat Drug Co, 44-45; res bacteriologist, Univ Pa, 45-50; self-employed, Pa & NY, 50-56; head dept bact, Staten Island Hosp, NY, 56-64; environ microbiol consult, 64-74. *Concurrent Pos:* Mem, Standards Comt, Asn Operating Room Nurses, 75-

Mem: Am Hosp Asn; Am Soc Microbiol; Am Pub Health Asn; Inst Sanit Mgt; Royal Soc Health. *Res:* Environmental and clinical microbiology; control of cross-infection in hospitals; hospital sanitation, environmental microbiology and administration; antimicrobial agents, antiseptics, disinfectants and germicides; disinfection and sterilization; aseptic practices in the operating room. *Mailing Add:* 9 Kettle Pond Rd Amherst MA 01002

LITSKY, WARREN, bacteriology; deceased, see previous edition for last biography

LITSTER, JAMES DAVID, SOLID STATE PHYSICS, SCATTERING SPECTROSCOPY. *Current Pos:* From instr to assoc prof, Mass Inst Technol, 65-75, head, Div Atomic, Condensed Matter & Plasma Physics, Dept Physics, 79-83, dir, Francis Bitter Nat Magnet Lab, 88-91, dean & vpres res, 91-95, PROF PHYSICS, MASS INST TECHNOL, 75-, VPRES RES & DEAN GRAD EDUC, 96- *Personal Data:* b Toronto, Ont, Can, June, 19, 38; m 65, Cheryl Schmidt; c Robin & Heather. *Educ:* McMaster Univ, BEng, 61; Mass Inst Tech, PhD(physics), 65. *Hon Degrees:* DSc, McMaster Univ, 92. *Honors & Awards:* Irving Langmuir Prize, Chem Physics, 93. *Concurrent Pos:* Fel, John Simon Guggenheim Mem Found, 71-72; vis prof, Univ Paris, Orsay, 71-72; lectr physics, Harvard Med Sch, 74-85; vis scientist, Riso Nat Lab, Denmark, 78; mem Mat Res Adv Comt, NSF, 78-81, chmn, Condensed Matter Sci Subcomt, 80-81; dir, Ctr Mat Sci & Eng, Mass Inst Technol, 83-88; regional ed, Molecular Crystals & Liquid Crystals, 86-; mem, Solid State Sci Panel, Nat Res Coun, 86- *Mem:* Fel AAAS; fel Am Phys Soc; fel Am Acad Arts & Sci. *Res:* Magnetism; light scattering; liquid crystals; x-ray scattering using synchrotron radiation. *Mailing Add:* Dept Physics Mass Inst Technol Cambridge MA 02139. *E-Mail:* litster@mit.edu

LITT, IRIS F, MEDICINE. *Current Pos:* assoc prof pediat, Stanford Univ Sch Med, 76-82, prof, 82-87, DIR, DIV ADOLESCENT MED, STANFORD UNIV SCH MED, 76-; PROF PEDIAT, 87-, DIR, INST RES WOMEN & GENDER, 90- *Personal Data:* b Dec 25, 40. *Educ:* Cornell Univ, BA, 61; State Univ NY, MD, 65, Am Bd Pediat, cert, 93. *Honors & Awards:* Sect Adolescent Health Award, Am Acad Pediat, 82; Eli & Edith Friedman Mem Lectr, Boston Univ Sch Med, 88; Ellen Soefer Lectr, Temple Univ Sch Med, 92; Outstanding Achievement Award Adolescent Med, Soc Adolescent Med, 92. *Prof Exp:* Intern, NY Hosp, 65-66, jr resident, 66-67, asst chief resident, 67-68; instr pediat, Albert Einstein Col Med, NY, 68-70, asst prof, 70-76, assoc prof, 76; dir, Juv Ctr Serv Div Adolescent Med, Montefiore Hosp & Med Ctr NY, 68-73, asst dir adolescent med, 68-76, med dir, Adolescent Reception & Detention Ctr, Rikers Island Prison Health Serv, 74-76. *Concurrent Pos:* Teaching fel, Cornell Univ Med Col, New York, 67-68; fel, Stanford Ctr Study Youth Develop, Stanford Univ, 76-95; mem, Comt Toxic Shock Syndrome, Inst Med-Nat Acad Sci, 81-82, Comt Youth Develop, 95-96; J Pediat vis prof, State Univ NY Downstate Med Ctr, 82 & Tulane Univ Sch Med, 83; fel, Ctr Adv Study Behav Scis, Stanford, 84-85; Wyeth vis prof, Soc Adolescent Med, 90; ed-in-chief, J Adolescent Med, 90- *Mem:* Inst Med-Nat Acad Sci; Soc Adolescent Med (pres, 81-82); Ambulatory Pediatric Asn; Am Acad Pediat; Soc Pediat Res; Am Pediat Soc; Soc Res Child Develop. *Mailing Add:* Dept Pediat Div Adolescent Med Stanford Univ Sch Med 750 Welch Rd Suite 325 Palo Alto CA 94304

LITT, LAWRENCE, MEDICAL PHYSICS, NEUROSCIENCES. *Current Pos:* from asst prof to assoc prof, 83-92, PROF ANESTHESIA & RADIOL, UNIV CALIF, SAN FRANCISCO, 92- *Personal Data:* b Brooklyn, NY, Oct 31, 41; m 67; c Natayla E & Jonathan E. *Educ:* Columbia Univ, AB, 63; Harvard Univ, AM, 64, PhD(physics), 71; Univ Miami, MD, 79. *Prof Exp:* Fel, Rockefeller Univ, 71-74; asst prof physics, Mich State Univ, 74-77; asst prof anesthesia, Stanford Univ, 82-83. *Concurrent Pos:* Vis res physicist, CERN, Geneva, Switz, 71-74; prin investr, NIH, 85-88 & 89-; mem, Neurol A Study Sect, NIH, 91- *Mem:* Fel Am Phys Soc; fel Am Col Physicians; Int Soc Cerebral Blood Flow & Metab; Soc Magnetic Resonance Med; Int Soc Magnetic Resonance. *Res:* Studies of cerebral metabolic protection during oxygen deprivation; provide new insights for stroke protection and treatment. *Mailing Add:* Anesthesia Dept Rm C-450 Univ Calif PO Box 0648 San Francisco CA 94143

LITT, MICHAEL, GENETICS. *Current Pos:* assoc prof biochem, 67-71, PROF BIOCHEM & MED GENETICS, MED SCH, UNIV ORE, 71-, PROF MOLECULAR & MED GENETICS, 96- *Personal Data:* b New York, NY, Apr 17, 33; m 56, 70, Ruth Howell; c Barbara & David. *Educ:* Oberlin Col, BA, 54; Harvard Univ, PhD(chem), 58. *Prof Exp:* Instr chem, Reed Col, 58-62, assoc prof, 64-67. *Concurrent Pos:* NIH spec fel, Mass Inst Technol, 62-63; NSF fel, Auckland Univ, 66-67; vis prof cellular, viral & molecular biol, Univ Utah Med Sch, 81-82. *Mem:* Am Soc Human Genetics. *Res:* Human gene mapping with DNA polymorphisms. *Mailing Add:* Dept Molecular & Med Genetics Ore Health Sci Univ 3181 SW Sam Jackson Park Rd Portland OR 97201-3098

LITT, MITCHELL, BIOENGINEERING, CHEMICAL ENGINEERING. *Current Pos:* from asst prof to assoc prof, 61-71, chmn, Dept Bioeng, 81-90, PROF CHEM ENG, UNIV PA, 71-, PROF BIOENG, 73- *Personal Data:* b Brooklyn, NY, Oct 11, 32; m 55, Zelda S Levine; c Ellen Beth & Steven Eric. *Educ:* Columbia Univ, AB, 53, BS, 54, MS, 56, DEngSc(chem eng), 61. *Prof Exp:* Res engr, Esso Res & Eng Co, NJ, 58-61. *Concurrent Pos:* Vis prof, Weizmann Inst, 79. *Mem:* Am Inst Chem Engrs; Am Soc Eng Educ; Biomed Eng Soc; Am Chem Soc; Int Soc Biorheology; Eng Med Biol Soc; Soc Rheology. *Res:* Application of chemical engineering techniques to biomedical problems; biorheology, with applications to blood and epithelial secretions. *Mailing Add:* Dept Bioeng Univ Pa Philadelphia PA 19104. *E-Mail:* litt@eniac.seas.upenn.edu

LITT, MORTIMER, IMMUNOLOGY. *Current Pos:* instr, Harvard Med Sch, 56-59, assoc, 60-65, asst prof, 65-71, asst dean teaching resources, 73-78, ASSOC PROF MICROBIOL & MOLECULAR GENETICS, HARVARD MED SCH, 71-, ASSOC DEAN EDUC PROGS, 79- *Personal Data:* b Brooklyn, NY, Sept 28, 25; m 54; c 3. *Educ:* Columbia Univ, BA, 47; Univ Rochester, MD, 52. *Prof Exp:* Med house officer & asst resident physician, Peter Bent Brigham Hosp, 52-54. *Concurrent Pos:* Res fel, Harvard Med Sch, 54-56 & 56-59; Helen Hay Whitney Found fel, 59-63; estab investr, Am Heart Asn, 63-68; asst dir, Dept Bact, Boston City Hosp, 69-77. *Res:* Eosinophil leukocyte. *Mailing Add:* Harvard Med Sch 25 Shattuck St Boston MA 02115

LITT, MORTON HERBERT, POLYMER CHEMISTRY. *Current Pos:* assoc prof, 67-76, PROF POLYMER SCI, CASE WESTERN RESERVE UNIV, 76- *Personal Data:* b Brooklyn, NY, Apr 10, 26; m 57, Lola Abrahamson; c Jonathon & Jennifer. *Educ:* City Col New York, BS, 47; Polytech Inst Brooklyn, MS, 53, PhD(polymer chem), 56. *Prof Exp:* Turner & Newall res fel, Manchester Univ, 56-57; res assoc, State Univ NY Col Forestry, Syracuse, 58-60; sr scientist, Cent Res Lab, Allied Chem Corp, 60-64, assoc dir res, 65-67. *Mem:* Fel AAAS; Am Chem Soc; NY Acad Sci; fel Am Phys Soc; The Chem Soc. *Res:* Ionic and free radical polymerization mechanisms; organo-fluorine chemistry; polymer mechanical properties; polymer electrical properties; emulsion polymerization; solid polymer electrolytes. *Mailing Add:* K H Smith Bldg Case Western Res Univ Cleveland OH 44106-7202. *Fax:* 216-368-4202; *E-Mail:* mhl2@po.cwru.edu

LITTAUER, ERNEST LUCIUS, ELECTROCHEMISTRY, METALLURGY. *Current Pos:* CONSULT, RES & DEVELOP/TECHNOL MGT, 97- *Personal Data:* b London, Eng, Mar 8, 36; US citizen; m 69, Deveda McDonough. *Educ:* Univ London, BSc, 58, PhD(electrometall), 61. *Honors & Awards:* Silver Knight Award, Nat Mgt Asn. *Prof Exp:* Res scientist, Derby Luminescents Div, Derby Metals, London, 62-63; sr scientist, Lockheed Aircraft Serv Co, 63-67, mgr, Electrochem Dept, 67-72, mgr, Chem Dept, 72-84, dir mat sci, Res & Develop Div, 84-90, vpres & asst gen mgr, Lockheed Missile & Space Co, 90-95, vpres, Adv Technol Ctr, Lockheed Martin Missiles & Space, 95-96. *Concurrent Pos:* Fel corrosion, Battersea Col Technol, 61-62; lectr, Sir John Cass Col & Enfield Col, London, 62-63; chmn, Res Coun Corrosion Comt, Lockheed Aircraft Corp, 66-; lectr electrochem, Univ Santa Clara, 74-76; bd mem, Planning Systs Inc, McClean, Va, 91- *Mem:* Electrochem Soc; assoc fel Am Inst Aeronaut & Astronaut; Mat Res Soc. *Res:* Electrochemistry; energy conversion; process chemistry; analytical, inorganic and plasma chemistry; materials evaluation; chemical and chemical engineering development and design; metallurgy; materials science engineering; nondestructive test technology. *Mailing Add:* 27305 Deer Springs Way Los Altos Hills CA 94022. *E-Mail:* ellittauer@aol.com

LITTAUER, RAPHAEL MAX, HIGH ENERGY PHYSICS, ELECTRONICS. *Current Pos:* res assoc prof physics, Cornell Univ, 55-63, res prof, 63-65, chmn dept, 74-77, PROF PHYSICS & NUCLEAR STUDIES, CORNELL UNIV, 65- *Personal Data:* b Leipzig, Ger, Nov 28, 25; US citizen; m 50; c 2. *Educ:* Cambridge Univ, MA & PhD(physics), 50. *Prof Exp:* Asst physics, Cambridge Univ, 47-50; res assoc nuclear physics, Cornell Univ, 50-54 & Synchrotron Lab, Gen Elec Co, 54-55. *Mem:* Am Phys Soc. *Mailing Add:* Newman Lab Cornell Univ Ithaca NY 14853

LITTELL, RAMON CLARENCE, AGRICULTURAL STATISTICS, MATHEMATICAL STATISTICS. *Current Pos:* PROF STATIST, UNIV FLA, GAINESVILLE. *Personal Data:* b Rolla, Kans, Nov 18, 42; m 66; c 2. *Educ:* Kans State Teachers Col, BS, 64; Okla State Univ, MS, 66, PhD(statist), 70. *Concurrent Pos:* Consult. *Mem:* Am Statist Asn; Biomet Soc; fel Am Statist Asn. *Res:* Combining tests of significance; lineas models; experimental design. *Mailing Add:* 3840 NW 35th Pl Gainesville FL 32606

LITTEN, RAYE Z, III, PHYSIOLOGY. *Current Pos:* PHYSIOLOGIST & PROG OFFICER, TREAT RES BR, DIV CLIN & PREVENTION RES, NAT INST ALCOHOL ABUSE & ALCOHOLISM, ROCKVILLE, MD, 89- *Educ:* Bridgewater Col, BA, 69; Med Col Va, MS, 72, PhD(physiol), 76. *Prof Exp:* Instr, Dept Physiol, Med Col Va, 76, postdoctoral fel, 76-78; res asst prof, Dept Physiol & Biophys, Univ Vt, 78-85; res physiologist, Armed Forces Radiobiol Res Inst, Bethesda, Md, 85-89. *Concurrent Pos:* Numerous grants, univs & asns, 76-90; vis res assoc, Dept Surg Res, Naval Med Res Inst, Bethesda, 85-87; instr, Washington Area Coun Alcoholism & Drug Abuse, 91- *Mem:* Am Physiol Soc; Sigma Xi. *Res:* Biochemistry of contractile proteins from vascular smooth muscle; biochemistry of contractile proteins from hypertrophied hearts; cardiovascular alterations from whole-body irradiation, myosin isoenzymes and pituitary-thyroid function; biochemical markers of alcoholism, nutrition and alcohol-induced pathophysiology; numerous scientific publications. *Mailing Add:* Div Clin & Prev Res NIAAA Willco Bldg Suite 505 6000 Exec Blvd MSC-7003 Bethesda MD 20892-7003

LITTENBERG, LAURENCE STEPHEN, EXPERIMENTAL K DECAY. *Current Pos:* from assoc physicist to physicist, 74-89, SR PHYSICIST, BROOKHAVEN NAT LAB, 89- *Personal Data:* b Brooklyn, NY, Oct 30, 41; m 70, Marcia Brazina; c Jeffrey. *Educ:* Cornell Univ, AB, 63; Univ Calif, San Diego, PhD(physics), 69. *Prof Exp:* Sr res assoc, Davesbury Lab, 70-74. *Concurrent Pos:* Prin investr high energy physics, Physics Dept, Brookhaven Nat Lab, 89-; mem, High Energy Physics Adv Panel, Dept Energy, 90-93. *Mem:* Fel Am Phys Soc. *Res:* Rare decays of charged and neutral kaons; new interactions and new forms of hadronic matter. *Mailing Add:* Physics S10A Brookhaven Nat Lab Upton NY 11973. *Fax:* 516-344-5568; *E-Mail:* littenbe@bnl.gov

LITTERIA, MARILYN, neuroendocrinology, for more information see previous edition

LITTERST, CHARLES LAWRENCE, PHARMACOLOGY. *Current Pos:* toxicologist, Nat Cancer Inst, 72-87, TOXICOLOGIST, NIAID, BETHESDA, MD, 87- *Personal Data:* b Cleveland, Ohio, 1944; c 2. *Educ:* Purdue Univ, BS, 66; Univ Wis, MS, 68, PhD(toxicol), 70. *Prof Exp:* Pharmacologist, Food & Drug Admin, Washington, DC, 70-72. *Concurrent Pos:* Mem, Toxicol Info subcomt HEW comt to coord toxicol & related progs, 74-79; faculty FAES-NIH (Toxicology), 74-; mem, Occup Safety Health Comt, NIH, 96- *Mem:* Am Soc Pharmacol & Exp Therapeut; Soc Toxicol; Sigma Xi; Am Asn Cancer Res. *Res:* Factors altering hepatic microsomal drug metabolism; toxicology and pharmacology of platinum; toxicology of antineoplastic and antiviral drugs. *Mailing Add:* Drug Develop & Clin Sci Br AIDS Div NIAID 6003 Executive Blvd Bethesda MD 20892. *E-Mail:* cl30x@nih.gov

LITTLE, A BRIAN, OBSTETRICS & GYNECOLOGY. *Current Pos:* prof & chmn, 83-94, PROF OBSTET & GYNEC, MCGILL UNIV, 83- *Personal Data:* b Montreal, Que, Mar 11, 25; US citizen; m 49, 84, Bitten Stripp; c Michael (deceased), Deborah, Susan, Catherine, Jane & Lucinda. *Educ:* McGill Univ, BA, 48, MD, CM, 50; Royal Col Physicians & Surgeons, Can, cert obstet & gynec, 55, FRCS(C), 57; Am Bd Obstet & Gynec, dipl, 59. *Prof Exp:* Intern, Montreal Gen Hosp, 50-51; asst resident & resident, Boston Lying-in-Hosp & Free Hosp Women, Boston, 51-54; asst obstet, Harvard Med Sch, 55-56, instr obstet & gynec, 56-58, tutor med sci, 57-65, assoc obstet & gynec, 58-63, asst prof, 63-65; prof obstet & gynec, Sch Med, Case Western Res Univ, 66-72, Arthur H Bill prof & dir, Dept Reproductive Biol, 72-83. *Concurrent Pos:* Teaching fel obstet & gynec, Harvard Med Sch, 52-54; instr, Sch Nursing, Boston Univ, 51 & 55-57; asst obstetrician outpatients, Boston Lying-in-Hosp, 55-56, asst obstetrician, 56-58, assoc, 58-59, obstetrician & gynecologist, 59-65; sr obstetrician prenatal metab div, USPHS, 55-56; assoc vis surgeon, Boston City Hosp, 55-64, assoc dir dept obstet & gynec, 58-63, dir, 63-65, vis surgeon, 65; asst surgeon, Free Hosp Women, 58-64, mem courtesy staff, 64-65; mem consult staff, Sturdy Mem Hosp, Attleboro, 61-65; chief consult, Hunt Mem Hosp, Danvers, 62-65; mem consult staff, Elliott Community Hosp, Keene, NH, 63-65; dir, Dept Obstet & Gynec, Cleveland Metrop Hosp, Ohio, 66-72; assoc obstetrician & gynecologist, Univ Hosps, Cleveland, 66-72; dir Dept Obstet & Gynec, 72-82; chief obstet & gynec, Royal Victoria Hosp, Montreal, 83-94; clin prof obstet & gynec, NJ Med Sch, 94- *Mem:* Fel Am Col Obstet & Gynec; Am Gynec & Obstet Soc; Soc Gynec Invest; fel Am Col Surgeons; Endocrine Soc. *Res:* Steroid mechanism in vivo, in vitro, primarily in reproduction. *Mailing Add:* Dept Obstet & Gynec Royal Victoria Hosp McGill Univ Sch Med 687 Pine Ave W Montreal PQ H3A 1A1 Can

LITTLE, ALEX G, THORACIC SURGERY. *Current Pos:* PROF & CHMN SURG, UNIV NEV, 88- *Personal Data:* b Atlanta, Ga, Aug 24, 43; m 75; c 2. *Educ:* Univ NC, BA, 65; Johns Hopkins Univ, MD, 74. *Prof Exp:* From asst prof to assoc prof surg, Univ Chicago, 81-88. *Mem:* Am Col Surgeons; Am Assoc Thoracic Surg; Soc Thoracic Surgeons; Soc Univ Surgeons; Am Surg Asn. *Res:* Pathophysiology of benign esophageal diseases; research in basic mechanisms of esophageal and lung cancer. *Mailing Add:* Dept Surg Univ Nev 2040 W Charleston Bld Suite 601 Las Vegas NV 89102-2227

LITTLE, ANGELA C, HISTORY OF MEDICINE & HEALTH REGIMENS. *Current Pos:* Res asst food sci, Univ Calif, Berkeley, 53-56, jr specialist, 56-58, from asst specialist to assoc specialist, 58-69, asst food scientist, 69-71, assoc food scientist, 71-79, lectr food sci, 69-79, from assoc prof to prof, 79-82, EMER PROF, UNIV CALIF, BERKELEY, 85- *Personal Data:* b San Francisco, Calif, Jan 12, 20; m 47; c 1. *Educ:* Univ Calif, AB, 40, MS, 54, PhD(agr chem), 69. *Concurrent Pos:* Vis scholar, Univ Wash, Seattle, 76-77; fac, Fromm Inst, Univ San Francisco, 93- *Mem:* NY Acad Sci; Sigma Xi. *Res:* Taste perception related to changes in physiological state; determinants of human food practices-historical, cultural, ecological, religious, etc; history of medical systems. *Mailing Add:* 85 Cleary Ct No 3 San Francisco CA 94109

LITTLE, BRENDA JOYCE, MICROBIOLOGICALLY INFLUENCED CORROSION, COLLOID & INTERFACE CHEMISTRY. *Current Pos:* br head, Naval Ocean Res & Develop Activ, 85-86, RES CHEMIST, NAVAL RES LAB, 76- *Personal Data:* b Akron, Ohio. *Educ:* Baylor Univ, BS, 67; Tulane Univ, PhD(chem), 83. *Prof Exp:* Microbiologist, Nat Park Serv, 74-76. *Mem:* Am Chem Soc; Int Humic Substances Soc; Nat Asn Corrosion Engrs; Adhesion Soc; Sigma Xi. *Res:* Factors influencing the absorption of dissolved organic material from natural waters and their impact on adhesion of microorganisms; elucidation of mechanisms for biodeterioration of metals in marine environments. *Mailing Add:* 6528 Alakoko Dr Diamondhead MS 39525-3421. *Fax:* 228-688-5379

LITTLE, BRIAN WOODS, NEUROPATHOLOGY & NEUROMUSCULAR PATHOLOGY. *Current Pos:* ATTEND PATHOLOGIST, LEHIGH VALLEY HOSP CTR, 87- *Personal Data:* b Boston, Mass, Dec 15, 45. *Educ:* Cornell Univ, BA, 67; Univ Vt, MD, 73, PhD(biochem), 77. *Prof Exp:* Resident pathologist, Med Ctr Hosp Vt, 73-76, attend pathologist, 76-84; asst prof path, Univ Vt, 76-84, asst prof biochem, 80-84; Vet Admin Med Ctr, Northport, NY; asst prof path, State Univ NY, Stony Brook, 84-87. *Mem:* Am Soc Clin Pathologists; Col Am Pathologists. *Res:* Mammalian nucleic acid metabolism; muscle disease; histochemistry; epidemiology of CNS disorders; pediatric, anatomic and clinical pathology. *Mailing Add:* Pathol Dept Med Col Hahnemann Univ MS 435 Broad & Vine Sts Philadelphia PA 19102

LITTLE, CHARLES DURWOOD, JR, ANATOMY, CELL BIOLOGY. *Current Pos:* asst prof, 81-87, ASSOC PROF ANAT, UNIV VA, 87- *Personal Data:* b Denver, Colo, Dec 28, 46. *Educ:* Calif State Polytech Univ, Pomona, BS, 73; Univ Pittsburgh, PhD(anat & cell biol), 77. *Prof Exp:* Res fel, Develop Biol Lab, Mass Gen Hosp, Harvard Med Sch, 77-79; fel, Biol Dept, Univ Calif, San Diego, 79-81. *Concurrent Pos:* Adv panel develop biol, NSF; mem, PBC Study Sect, NIH; bd trustees, Soc Develop Biol. *Mem:* Develop Biol Soc; Am Soc Cell Biol. *Res:* Developmental biology of the extracellular matrix; cell surface matrix interactions; double immunolabeling techniques for use in fluorescence and electron microscopy. *Mailing Add:* Dept Cell Biol Med Univ SC 171 Ashley Ave Charleston SC 29425-2204

LITTLE, CHARLES EDWARD, mathematics, for more information see previous edition

LITTLE, CHARLES GORDON, ATMOSPHERIC PHYSICS, REMOTE SENSING. *Current Pos:* RETIRED. *Personal Data:* b Hunan, China, Nov 4, 24; m 54, Mary Zughaib; c Deane, Joan, Katherine, Margaret & Patricia. *Educ:* Univ Manchester, BSc, 48, PhD(radio astron), 52. *Honors & Awards:* Cleveland Abbe Award, Am Meteorol Soc, 84; R M Losey Amos Sci Award, Am Inst Aeronaut & Astronaut, 92. *Prof Exp:* Jr engr, Cosmos Mfg Co, Eng, 44-46; jr physicist, Ferranti, Ltd, 46-47; asst lectr physics, Univ Manchester, 52-53; prof geophys res & dep dir, Geophys Inst, Univ Alaska, 54-58; chief, Radio Astron & Arctic Propagation Sect, Nat Bur Stand, 58-60, Upper Atmosphere & Space Physics Div, Boulder Labs, 60-62, dir, Cent Radio Propagation Lab, 62-65; dir, Inst Telecommun Sci & Aeronomy, Environ Sci Serv Admin, Nat Oceanic & Atmospheric Admin, 65-67 & Wave Propagation Lab, 67-86; sr fel, Univ Corp Atmospheric Res, Naval Environ Res Prediction Facil, 87-89; George Haltiner res prof, Naval Postgrad Sch, 89-90. *Concurrent Pos:* Consult, US Nat Comt Int Geophys Yr, 57-59. *Mem:* Nat Acad Eng; AAAS; Inst Elec & Electronics Engrs; Am Meterol Soc. *Res:* Remote measurement of atmosphere and ocean, using electromagnetic and acoustic waves. *Mailing Add:* 4907 Country Club Way Boulder CO 80301

LITTLE, CHARLES ORAN, ANIMAL NUTRITION, AGRICULTURE. *Current Pos:* vchancellor for res & dir, Exp Sta, 85-88, DIR AGR EXP STATION & DIR COOP EXTEN, LA STATE UNIV, 88- *Personal Data:* b Schulenburg, Tex, July 21, 35; m 55; c 3. *Educ:* Univ Houston, BS, 57; Iowa State Univ, MS, 59, PhD(animal nutrit), 60. *Honors & Awards:* Distinguished Nutritionist Award, Nat Distillers Feed Res Coun, 64; Outstanding Res Awards, Thomas Poe Cooper & Ky Res Founds, 67. *Prof Exp:* Res asst animal nutrit, Iowa State Univ, 57-60; from asst prof to assoc prof, Col Agr, Univ Ky, 60-67, indust res grants, 61-72, Agr Res Serv grant, 64-67, prof animal sci, 67-85, assoc dean res, 69-85, dean, 88- *Concurrent Pos:* Assoc dir, Ky Agr Exp Sta, 69-; mem & chmn, Southern Regional Res Comt, 72-75; mem, Southern Res Planning Comt, 73-75, chmn, Southern Asn Agr Exp Sta Dirs, 76-77, mem, Exp Sta Comt on Policy, 78- *Mem:* AAAS; Am Soc Animal Sci; Am Inst Nutrit. *Mailing Add:* 2357 The Woods Lane Lexington KY 40502

LITTLE, EDWIN DEMETRIUS, ORGANIC CHEMISTRY. *Current Pos:* RETIRED. *Personal Data:* b Orlando, Fla, July 2, 26. *Educ:* Rollins Col, BS, 48; Duke Univ, AM, 53. *Prof Exp:* Sr res chemist, Nitrogen Div, Allied Chem Corp, 53-63, supvry res chemist, 63-66, res assoc, Plastics Div, 66-74, group leader, Specialty Chem Div, 74-79; res assoc, Va Chem Inc, 79-85; res chemist, Merck Sharp & Dohme Res Lab, Merck & Co, Inc, 85-93. *Mem:* Fel Am Inst Chem; Am Chem Soc; NY Acad Sci. *Res:* Heterocyclic nitrogen compounds; epoxide reactions; monomer synthesis. *Mailing Add:* 3213 W Broadway Ave Hopewell VA 23860-1811

LITTLE, ELBERT L(UTHER), JR, BOTANY, DENDROLOGY. *Current Pos:* collabr, 65-76, RES ASSOC, DEPT BOT, US NAT MUS NATURAL HIST, SMITHSONIAN INST, WASHINGTON, DC, 76- *Personal Data:* b Ft Smith, Ark, Oct 15, 07; m 43, Ruby R Rice; c Gordon R, Melvin W & Alice (Conner). *Educ:* Univ Okla, AB, 27, BS, 32; Univ Chicago, MS & PhD(bot), 29. *Honors & Awards:* Barrington Moore Award, Soc Am Foresters, 86. *Prof Exp:* Asst prof biol, Southwestern Okla State Univ, 30-33; from asst forest ecologist to assoc forest ecologist, Ariz, 34-42; dendrologist, US Forest Serv, Washington, DC, 42-76. *Concurrent Pos:* Botanist, Econ Admin, Bogota, 43-45; prod specialist, US Com Co, Mexico City, 45; vis prof, Univ Andes, Venzuela, 53-54 & 60; botanist from Univ Md, Guyana, 55; consult, UN mission, Costa Rica, 64-65 & 67, Ecuador, 65 & 75, Nicaragua, 71 & Okla Forestry Div 30, 77-78; vis prof, Va Polytech Inst & State Univ, 66-67 & Univ DC, 79. *Mem:* Fel Explorers Club; fel Soc Am Foresters; Bot Soc Am; Am Soc Plant Taxon; Am Inst Biol Sci; Ecol Soc Am. *Res:* Trees of United States and tropical America, their identification, classification, nomenclature, and distribution; pinyons; conifers; ecology; author of tree identification books. *Mailing Add:* 924 20th St S Arlington VA 22202-2616

LITTLE, GWYNNE H, BIOCHEMISTRY OF DEVELOPMENT, PROGRAMMED CELL DEATH. *Current Pos:* ASSOC PROF BIOCHEM, HEALTH SCI CTR, TEX TECH UNIV, 80- *Personal Data:* Birmingham, Ala, June 25, 41; m 66, Donnie T; c Mary E (Carol) & Sally L (Ball). *Educ:* Med Col Ga, PhD(biochem), 70. *Mem:* Am Soc Biol Chem. *Mailing Add:* Dept Biochem Sch Med Tex Tech Univ Health Sci Ctr Lubbock TX 79430-0001

LITTLE, HAROLD FRANKLIN, ENTOMOLOGY, FUNCTIONAL MORPHOLOGY. *Current Pos:* from asst prof to assoc prof, 63-71, chmn, Div Nat Sci, 68-71 & 73-79, chmn, Biol Dept, 73-78, PROF BIOL, UNIV HAWAII, HILO, 71-, CHMN DEPT, 86- *Personal Data:* b Williamsport, Pa, June 18, 32; m 59; c 1. *Educ:* Lycoming Col, AB, 54; Pa State Univ, MS, 56,

PhD(zool), 59. *Prof Exp:* Asst prof biol, WVa Wesleyan Col, 59-63. *Mem:* Entom Soc Am. *Res:* Damage to Medfly pupal flight mucles; histology and ultrastructure of tephritid fruit fly pheromone glands. *Mailing Add:* Div Nat Sci Univ Hawaii Hilo 200 W Kawili St Hilo HI 96720-4075. *Fax:* 808-933-3693

LITTLE, JACK EDWARD, PETROLEUM ENGINEERING. *Current Pos:* div prod mgr, Onshore Div, SRegion Shell Oil Co, New Orleans, 78-79, gen mgr prod, Western Explor & Prod Region, Houston, 79-80, gen mgr, Pac Div, 80-81, vpres corp planning, 81-82, sr vpres admin, 85-86, exec vpres explor & prod, Shell Oil Co, Houston, 86-95, PRES & CHIEF EXEC OFFICER, SHELL EXPLOR & PROD CO, 95- *Personal Data:* b Dallas, Tex, Sept 9, 38. *Educ:* Tex A&M Univ, BS, 60, MS, 61, PhD, 66. *Prof Exp:* Dir prod res & explor res, Bellaire Res Ctr, Shell Develop Co, Houston, 77. *Concurrent Pos:* Chmn nat comts career guid, investments & mgt, Soc Petrol Engrs, 67-81, bd dirs, Houston Sect, 69, Bakersfield Sect, 70, nat bd dirs, 77-78; head, SE Asia Div, Shell Int Petrol Co, London, 82-85; dir, Nat Ocean Indust Asn; vchmn & dir, Gas Res Inst. *Mem:* Nat Acad Eng; Soc Petrol Engrs; Mid-Continent Oil & Gas Asn; Nat Ocean Indust Asn. *Res:* Petroleum engineering; exploration and production. *Mailing Add:* Shell Explor & Prod Co 900 Louisiana St Houston TX 77002

LITTLE, JAMES ALEXANDER, METABOLISM, LIPIDS & DIABETES. *Current Pos:* Res assoc med, St Michael's Hosp, Univ Toronto, 52-67, clin teacher, 54-63, dir, Diabetic Clin, 54-70, assoc, 63-66, dir, Clin Invest Unit, 64-72, res coordr & secy, Res Soc, 64-92, from asst prof to assoc prof, 66-74, dir, Lipid Clin, 66-90, PROF MED, ST MICHAEL'S HOSP, UNIV TORONTO, 74- *Personal Data:* b Detroit, Mich, Dec 8, 22; Can citizen; m 53, 85, Barbara Bradt; c Ann & Roger. *Educ:* Univ Toronto, MD, 46, MA, 50; FRCP(C), 52. *Prof Exp:* Res & dir, Atherosclerosis Proj, 52-67. *Concurrent Pos:* Nat Res Coun Can fel biochem, Univ Toronto, 47-49; Can Red Cross fel arthritis, Sunnybrook Dept Vet Affairs Hosp, 51-52, res & assoc dir, Arteriosclerosis Proj, 52-67; dir, Div Endocrinol, Metab & Nephrol, Lipid Clin, St Michael's Hosp, 70-73; mem, Can Nat Comn, Int Union Nutrit Sci, 71-75; mem, Comt Nutrit & Cardiovasc Dis, Health Protection Br, Govt Can, 74-76 & Med Comt; proj dir, McMaster Lipid Res Ctr, Univ Toronto, 72-93; mem, Exec Comt, Coun Atherosclerosis, Am Heart Asn, 74-77; Pfizer Travelling fel, Clin Res Inst Montreal, 84; pres, Can Lipoprotein Conf, 89-90. *Mem:* Am Heart Asn; Can Cardiovasc Soc; Am Diabetes Asn; Nutrit Soc Can; Can Soc Clin Invest; Can Atherosclerosis Soc (pres, 87-88). *Res:* Relation between human atherosclerosis, plasma lipoproteins, nutrition and genetic factors; effect of insulin antibodies on diabetic complications. *Mailing Add:* RR No 1 Nobel ON P0G 1G0 Can. *E-Mail:* alick@zeuter.com

LITTLE, JAMES NOEL, ANALYTICAL CHEMISTRY. *Current Pos:* vpres, 81-82, SR VPRES, ZYMARK CORP, 83- *Personal Data:* b Kansas City, Mo, July 3, 40; m 91, Barbara Killeen; c David, Matthew & Sarah. *Educ:* Univ Kans, BS, 62, Mass Inst Technol, PhD(anal chem), 66. *Prof Exp:* Res chemist, Hercules, Inc, Del, 66-67; sr res chemist, Waters Assocs, Inc, 68-69, mgr chromatography res, 69-71, vpres, 71-81. *Concurrent Pos:* Dir, Rhenometrics, 82-85, Cyborg Corp, 82-87 & Microfluidics Corp. *Mem:* Am Chem Soc. *Res:* Separations; chromatography; polymer characterization; analytical methods development; spectroscopy; robotics. *Mailing Add:* Zymark Corp Zymark Ctr Hopkinton MA 01748

LITTLE, JOHN BERTRAM, CANCER BIOLOGY, RADIATION BIOLOGY. *Current Pos:* USPHS res fel, Harvard Sch Pub Health, 61-63, instr physiol, 63-65, from asst prof to assoc prof, 65-75, chmn dept, 80-83, PROF RADIOBIOL, 75-, JAMES STEVENS SIMMONS PROF, HARVARD SCH PUB HEALTH, 88- *Personal Data:* b Boston, Mass, Oct 5, 29; m 60, Francoise Cottereau; c Jean B & Frederic. *Educ:* Harvard Univ, AB, 51; Boston Univ, MD, 55; Am Bd Radiol, dipl, 61, cert nuclear med, 61. *Honors & Awards:* Failla Award, Radiation Res Soc NAm, 94. *Prof Exp:* Intern med, Johns Hopkins Hosp, 55-56; resident radiol, Mass Gen Hosp, 58-61. *Concurrent Pos:* Consult, Mass Gen Hosp, 65-; Peter Bent Brigham Hosp, 68-; Nat Cancer Inst & Am Cancer Soc fels, Sch Pub Health, Harvard, 68-78, lectr, Med Sch, 68-; chmn, Bd Sci Counr, Nat Inst Environ Health Sci, 82-84; dir, Kresge Ctr Environ Health, 81-; bd sci counselors, Nat Toxicol Prog, Nat Cancer Inst, 87-91, Outstanding Investr grant, 88-; coun deleg med sci, AAAS, 88-90, Coun Affairs Comt, 89-91; chmn, Bd Radiation Effects Res, Nat Acad Sci, 92-; mem coun, Nat Coun Radiation Protection, 92-; sci coun, Radiation Effects Res Found, Hiroshima, Japan, 93-; mem coun, Int Asn Radiation Res, 95- *Mem:* AAAS; Am Physiol Soc; Health Physics Soc; Am Asn Cancer Res; Radiation Res Soc (pres-elect, 85, pres, 86-87); Am Soc Photobiol. *Res:* Cellular and molecular radiation biology with emphasis on mutagenesis; experimental carcinogenesis. *Mailing Add:* Dept Cancer Biol Sch Pub Health Harvard Univ Boston MA 02115. *Fax:* 617-432-0107

LITTLE, JOHN C, ENVIRONMENTAL ENGINEERING. *Current Pos:* ASST PROF ENVIRON ENG, VA POLYTECH INST & STATE UNIV, 93- *Personal Data:* b Capetown, SAfrica, Aug 11, 56. *Educ:* Univ Capetown, MSc, 84, BSc, 85; Univ Calif, Berkeley, MS, 88, PhD(environ eng), 90. *Honors & Awards:* NSF Career Award, 96. *Prof Exp:* Postdoctoral fel, Lawrence Berkeley Nat Labs, Calif, 90-93. *Mailing Add:* Environ Eng Va Polytech Inst & State Univ Blacksburg VA 24061. *Fax:* 440-231-7532

LITTLE, JOHN CLAYTON, ORGANIC CHEMISTRY, PROCESS DEVELOPMENT. *Current Pos:* RETIRED. *Personal Data:* b Battle Creek, Mich, Jan 1, 33; m 87; c 4. *Educ:* Univ Calif, BS, 54; Univ Ill, PhD(org chem), 57. *Prof Exp:* Res chemist, Dow Chem USA, 57-62, proj leader, 62-64, group leader, 64-71, res mgr, 71-81, mgr chem technol, Agr Prod Dept, 81-89, facil prog mgr, Western Div Res & Develop, 89-93. *Concurrent Pos:* Mem, Mich Found Advan Res; sect ed, Chem Abstracts, 64-68. *Mem:* Am Chem Soc; Sigma Xi; The Chem Soc. *Res:* Pilot plant and process development studies; organic syntheses and structure-biological activity relationships; chemical manufacturing, environmental studies; petrochemical processing; chlorination; catalytic oxidation and reduction; Diels-Alder reactions and synthetic methods; fluorination processes; research facilities design and management. *Mailing Add:* 2524 Pebble Beach Loop Lafayette CA 94549

LITTLE, JOHN DUTTON CONANT, OPERATIONS RESEARCH, MANAGEMENT SCIENCE. *Current Pos:* assoc prof opers res, Mass Inst Technol, 62-67, dir opers res ctr, 69-75, prof opers res & mgt, 67-68, head Mgt Sci Group, 72-82, head behav & policy scis area, 82-88, George M Bunker prof mgt sci, Sloan Sch, 78-89, INST PROF, MASS INST TECHNOL, 89- *Personal Data:* b Boston, Mass, Feb 1, 28; m 53, Elizabeth D Alden; c John N, Sarah A, Thomas D C & Ruel D. *Educ:* Mass Inst Technol, SB, 48, PhD(physics), 55. *Hon Degrees:* Dr, Univ Liege, Belg, 92. *Honors & Awards:* Charles Coolidge Parlin Award, 78; Kimball Medal, Opers Res Soc Am, 87; Converse Award, Am Mkt Asn, 92. *Prof Exp:* Engr tube develop, Gen Elec Co, 49-50; asst physics, Mass Inst Technol, 51-54; from asst prof to assoc prof opers res, Case Inst Technol, 57-62. *Concurrent Pos:* Pres, Mgt Decision Systs, Inc, 67-80, chmn, 67-85; dir Info Resources Inc, 85-; adv panel of Decision, Risk & Mgt Sci Prog, Nat Sci Found, 86-89; vis prof, Europ Inst Bus Admin, Fontainebleau, France, 89; Philip McCord Morse lectr, Opers Res Soc Am, 89-90. *Mem:* Nat Acad Eng; fel AAAS; Opers Res Soc Am (pres, 79-80); Inst Mgt Sci (vpres, 76-79, pres, 84-85); Am Mkt Asn; Inst Opers Res & Mgt Sci (pres, 95). *Res:* Research on mathematical programming; queueing theory; marketing; traffic control; decision support systems. *Mailing Add:* 37 Conant Rd RR 3 Lincoln MA 01773-3912

LITTLE, JOHN LLEWELLYN, computer standards, physics; deceased, see previous edition for last biography

LITTLE, JOHN RUSSELL, JR, IMMUNOLOGY. *Current Pos:* Fel microbiol, 62-64, from asst prof to assoc prof med & microbiol, 69-73, PROF MED & MICROBIOL, SCH MED, WASHINGTON UNIV, 73- *Personal Data:* b Cheyenne, Wyo, Oct 23, 30; m 55; c 3. *Educ:* Cornell Univ, AB, 52; Univ Rochester, MD, 56. *Res:* Medicine and lymphocyte membrane structure and function. *Mailing Add:* Barnes-Jewish Hosp Wash Univ Sch Med 216 S Kingsway St Louis MO 63110-1092

LITTLE, JOHN STANLEY, organic chemistry, for more information see previous edition

LITTLE, JOHN WESLEY, BIOCHEMISTRY. *Current Pos:* adj asst prof microbiol, Univ Ariz, 78-80, adj assoc prof molecular & med microbiol, 80-81, asst prof biochem, 82-85, assoc prof, 85-91, PROF, BIOCHEM & MOLECULAR & CELLULAR BIOL, UNIV ARIZ, 91- *Personal Data:* b Washington, DC, June 24, 41; m 69, Meredith; c Christopher & Bernice. *Educ:* Stanford Univ, BS, 62, PhD(biochem), 67. *Prof Exp:* Sr asst scientist, NIH, 67-69, sr staff fel, 69-72; res fel, Stanford Univ, 73-76; res assoc, Univ Ariz, 77-78. *Mem:* AAAS; Am Soc Biol Chemists; Am Soc Microbiol. *Res:* Regulatory system which controls how E coli responds to conditions which damage DNA including the biochemistry of the proteins which control this response. *Mailing Add:* Dept Biochem Univ Ariz Life Sci S Bldg Tucson AZ 85721. *E-Mail:* jlittle@biosci.arizona.edu

LITTLE, JOSEPH ALEXANDER, MEDICINE. *Current Pos:* PROF PEDIAT & HEAD DEPT, SCH MED, LA STATE UNIV, SHREVEPORT, 70- *Personal Data:* b Bessemer, Ala, Mar 16, 18; m 41; c 3. *Educ:* Vanderbilt Univ, BA, 40, MD, 43. *Prof Exp:* Intern, Vanderbilt Univ Hosp, 43 & 46-47; resident, Childrens Hosp, Univ Cincinnati, 47-48, instr pediat, Col Med, Univ, 48-49; from asst prof to prof, Sch Med, Univ Louisville, 49-62; assoc prof, Sch Med, Vanderbilt Univ, 62-70. *Concurrent Pos:* Dir outpatient dept, Childrens Hosp, 48-49, physician in chief, 56-; med dir, State Crippled Children Comn, Ky, 51-54; consult, State Dept Health, Ky, 49-51. *Mem:* AAAS; Am Pediat Soc; Am Acad Pediat; NY Acad Sci. *Res:* Pediatric cardiology. *Mailing Add:* 185 Turning Point Lane Sewanee TN 27275-9706

LITTLE, JOYCE CURRIE, COMPUTER ETHICS, SOFTWARE ENGINEERING. *Current Pos:* CHAIR, DEPT COMPUT & INFO SCI, TOWSON STATE UNIV, 84-, PROF, 91- *Personal Data:* b Pioneer, La, 1934. *Educ:* Northeast La State Col, BS, 57; San Diego State Col, MS, 63; Univ Md, College Park, PhD(educ admin & computer science), 84. *Concurrent Pos:* Consult, Univ Md, College Park, 86- *Mem:* Asn Comput Mach; Inst Elec & Electronics Engrs Computer Soc; Am Asn Univ Professors; Sigma Xi. *Res:* Computer personnel research. *Mailing Add:* Dept Comput & Info Sci Towson State Univ Baltimore MD 21204-7097

LITTLE, MAURICE DALE, MEDICAL PARASITOLOGY. *Current Pos:* from instr to asst prof, Sch Med, 63-68, assoc prof, 68-76, PROF PARASITOL, SCH PUB HEALTH & TROP MED, TULANE UNIV, 76- *Personal Data:* b North Grove, Ind, Apr 13, 28; m 55, Marcella West; c Julie, Randall & Linda. *Educ:* Purdue Univ, BS, 50; Tulane Univ, MS, 58, PhD(parasitol), 61. *Prof Exp:* Microbiologist, Ind State Bd Health, 53-56. *Concurrent Pos:* NIH fel, Tulane Univ, 61-63; assoc ed, Am Soc Trop Med & Hyg, 75-84. *Mem:* AAAS; Am Micros Soc; Am Soc Parasitologists (secy-treas, 80-81); Am Soc Trop Med & Hyg; Wildlife Dis Asn. *Res:* Morphology, biology and epidemiology of Strongyloides species; zoonotic helminthiases; soil-transmitted helminths; parasites in sewage sludges. *Mailing Add:* Pub Health Tulane Univ Sch Pub Health 1430 Tulane Ave New Orleans LA 70112-2699

LITTLE, MICHAEL ALAN, PHYSICAL ANTHROPOLOGY. *Current Pos:* from asst prof to assoc prof, 71-81, PROF ANTHROP, STATE UNIV NY, BINGHAMTON, 81- *Personal Data:* b Abington, Pa, Mar 24, 37; m 65, Adrienne B Veeson; c Jason P & Diana A. *Educ:* Pa State Univ, BA, 62, MA, 65, PhD(anthrop), 68. *Prof Exp:* Asst prof anthrop, Ohio State Univ, 67-70. *Concurrent Pos:* Ohio State Univ res fel, Nunoa, Peru, 68; State Univ NY Binghamton res fel & grant, Nunoa, 72; vis assoc prof anthrop & sci coordr, US Int Biol Prog, Human Adaptability Component, Pa State Univ, 72-73; NSF sci equip grants, 74 & 80 & res grant, 78, 80, 82, 85, 87, 88-90; mem, US Nat Comn Man & the Biosphere Prog, 83-94, vchair 89-94; mem, US Nat Comn, Int Union Biol Sci 88-94; Nat Geog Soc grant, 93-94. *Mem:* Fel AAAS; Am Asn Phys Anthrop (vpres, 88-90, pres 91-93); Soc Study Human Biol; Human Biol Asn (secy-treas, 73-75, exec comt, 87-91); Am Anthrop Asn (pres, 96-98). *Res:* Biocultural adaptations; human biology; environmental stress; heat and cold adaptation; circadian rhythms; human populations at high altitude; child growth and development; ecology of savanna pastoralists. *Mailing Add:* Dept Anthrop State Univ NY Binghamton NY 13902-6000. *Fax:* 607-777-2477; *E-Mail:* mlittle@bingvmb

LITTLE, PATRICK JOSEPH, PSYCHIATRY. *Current Pos:* POSTDOCTORAL FEL, DEPT PHARMACOL, MED CTR, DUKE UNIV, 90- *Personal Data:* b Washington, DC, Oct 6, 58. *Educ:* Col William & Mary, BS, 81; Va Commonwealth Univ, PhD(pharmacol & toxicol), 89. *Prof Exp:* Lab specialist, Dept Pharmacol & Toxicol, Med Col Va, 81-85; postdoctoral fel, Dept Psychiat, Sch Med, Wash Univ, St Louis, 89-90. *Mem:* Am Soc Pharmacol & Exp Therapeut; Soc Neurosci. *Res:* Drug dependence. *Mailing Add:* Dept Pharmacol Med Ctr Duke Univ Box 3813 Durham NC 27710

LITTLE, PERRY L, NUTRITION, PHYSIOLOGY. *Current Pos:* assoc prof, 62-80, PROF POULTRY SCI, SAM HOUSTON STATE UNIV, 80- *Personal Data:* b Ball Ground, Ga, Aug 3, 28; m 51; c 1. *Educ:* Berry Col, BS, 50; Auburn Univ, MS, 57, PhD(path, nutrit, physiol), 66. *Prof Exp:* High sch teacher, Ala, 50-52 & 53-55; res asst poultry sci, Auburn Univ, 55-62. *Mem:* Poultry Sci Asn; World Poultry Sci Asn. *Res:* Nutrition of parasites which involve poultry, currently doing alligator nutrition. *Mailing Add:* Dept Agr Sam Houston State Univ Huntsville TX 77341-1001

LITTLE, RANDEL QUINCY, JR, ORGANIC CHEMISTRY. *Current Pos:* RETIRED. *Personal Data:* b Richmond, Va, Aug 14, 27; m 49, Ann Clark; c 3. *Educ:* Univ Richmond, BS, 48; Univ Mich, MS, 49, PhD(org chem), 54. *Prof Exp:* Res chemist, Am Oil Co, Stand Oil Co, Ind, 53-60, group leader motor oil additives, 60-62, res supvr, 62-68, asst dir lubricants res, 68-74, dir lubricants & agr prod res, 74-83, dir fuels res, Amoco Oil Co, 83-87. *Mem:* Am Chem Soc; Sigma Xi; Soc Automotive Engrs. *Res:* Organic reactions; motor oil additives; lubricants; fuels. *Mailing Add:* 860 W Driveway Glen Ellyn IL 60137-6155

LITTLE, RAYMOND DANIEL, ORGANIC CHEMISTRY. *Current Pos:* from asst prof to assoc prof, 75-86, PROF ORG CHEM, UNIV CALIF, SANTA BARBARA, 86- *Personal Data:* b Superior, Wis, Sept 12, 47; m 72; c 3. *Educ:* Univ Wis-Superior, BS, 69; Univ Wis-Madison, PhD(org chem), 74. *Honors & Awards:* Plous Award, Univ Calif, Santa Barbara, 81. *Prof Exp:* Postdoctoral fel, Yale Univ, 74-75. *Concurrent Pos:* Vis prof, Univ British Columbia, Vancouver, Can, 87. *Mem:* Am Chem Soc; Sigma Xi. *Res:* Development of new synthetic methods, especially diyl trapping and electroreductive cyclization; total synthesis of pharmacologically active molecules; mechanistic organic chemistry of thermal, electro and photochemical reactions. *Mailing Add:* Dept Chem Univ Calif Santa Barbara CA 93106

LITTLE, RICHARD ALLEN, GENERAL MATHEMATICS, GENERAL COMPUTER SCIENCES. *Current Pos:* chmn, Math Dept, 78-83, PROF MATH & COMPUT SCI, BALDWIN-WALLACE CO, OHIO, 75- *Personal Data:* b Coshocton, Ohio, Jan 12, 39; m 60, 91, Laura Novosel; c Eric, Alice & Stephanie. *Educ:* Wittenburg Univ, BSc, 60; Johns Hopkins Univ, MA, 61; Harvard Univ, EdM, 65; Kent State Univ, PhD(math educ), 71. *Honors & Awards:* Christofferson-Fawcett Award, Long & Dedicated Serv Maths & Maths Teaching Ohio, Ohio Coun Teachers Maths, 90. *Prof Exp:* Teacher & coach math, Culver Acad, Ind, 61-65; instr & curric consult math, Nigerian Proj, Harvard Univ, 65-67; from instr to assoc prof math, Kent State Univ, Stark, 67-75. *Concurrent Pos:* Scholarship, Gen Motors Corp, Wittenburg, 57-60, Ford Found, Johns Hopkins Univ, 60-61 & NSF, Harvard Univ, 63-64; curric consult math, India Inst Proj, NSF, 67; vis prof math, Ohio State Univ, Columbus, 87-88; mathematician educr, Initiative Proj Discovery, Ohio State Univ, NSF, 92-96; vis prof maths & maths educr, Ohio State Univ, 92-96. *Mem:* Asn Comput Mach; Math Asn Am; Nat Coun Teachers Math. *Res:* Mathematics and computer science education; computer applications in small to medium size businesses. *Mailing Add:* Baldwin-Wallace Col Berea OH 44017. *Fax:* 440-826-6973; *E-Mail:* rlittle@baldwinw.edu

LITTLE, ROBERT, plasma physics, for more information see previous edition

LITTLE, ROBERT COLBY, PHYSIOLOGY, MEDICINE. *Current Pos:* chmn, Dept Physiol, 73-86, prof physiol & med, 73-89, EMER PROF PHYSIOL & MED, MED COL GA, 89- *Personal Data:* b Norwalk, Ohio, June 2, 20; m 45; c 2. *Educ:* Denison Univ, AB, 42; Western Res Univ, MD, 44, MS, 48. *Prof Exp:* Intern, Grace Hosp, Detroit, Mich, 44-45; resident med, Crile Vet Hosp, Cleveland, 49-50; from asst prof to assoc prof physiol, Univ Tenn, 50-54, assoc prof med, 53-54; dir clin res, Mead Johnson & Co, 54-57; dir, Cardio-Pulmonary Labs, Scott & White Clin, Tex, 57-58; prof physiol, Seton Hall Col Med, 58-64, asst prof med, 59-64; prof physiol, chmn dept & asst prof med, Col Med, Ohio State Univ, 64-73. *Concurrent Pos:* USPHS res fel, Western Res Univ, 48-49. *Mem:* Am Physiol Soc; Soc Exp Biol & Med; Am Heart Asn; Am Fedn Clin Res; AMA; Sigma Xi. *Res:* Cardiovascular dynamics; heart sounds; clinical physiology; muscle dynamics. *Mailing Add:* 44 Plantation Hills Dr Evans GA 30809

LITTLE, ROBERT E(UGENE), MECHANICAL DESIGN, MECHANICAL METALLURGY. *Current Pos:* assoc prof, 65-68, PROF MECH ENG, UNIV MICH, DEARBORN, 68- *Personal Data:* b Enfield, Ill, May 24, 33; m 61, Barbara Farrell; c Susan, James, Richard & John. *Educ:* Ohio State Univ, MSME, 60; Univ Mich, PhD(mech eng), 63. *Prof Exp:* Asst prof mech eng, Okla State Univ, 63-65. *Mem:* Am Soc Testing & Mat. *Res:* Modes of failure; fatigue; reliability; planned experiments; composites. *Mailing Add:* Dept Mech Eng Univ Mich 4901 Evergreen Rd Dearborn MI 48128-1491. *Fax:* 313-593-9967

LITTLE, ROBERT LEWIS, GEOLOGY. *Current Pos:* RETIRED. *Personal Data:* b Monticello, Miss, July 1, 29; m 53; c 2. *Educ:* Univ Miss, BA, 51, MS, 59; Univ Tenn, Knoxville, PhD(geol), 69. *Prof Exp:* Instr geol, Univ Miss, 58-59 & Univ Tenn, Knoxville, 59-69; from asst prof to assoc prof, Valdosta State Col, 69-81, head dept, 69-81, prof geol & dept head physics, astron & geol, 81-85. *Mem:* Geol Soc Am; Am Asn Univ Prof; Nat Asn Geol Teachers. *Res:* Areal geology; stratigraphy and structural geology. *Mailing Add:* 711 Northside Dr Valdosta GA 31602

LITTLE, SARAH ALDEN, EXPERIMENTAL JET FLOW, CONVECTION. *Current Pos:* FINANCE ENGR, LEWTON TECHOL, 95- *Personal Data:* b Cleveland, Ohio, Apr 27, 59. *Educ:* Stanford Univ, BS, 81; Mass Inst Technol, PhD(marine geophys), 88. *Prof Exp:* Postdoctoral fel, Ctr Water Res, Univ Western Australia, 88-89; consult, Mackie Martin & Assoc, 89-90; vis investr, Woods Hole Oceanog Inst, 90-95. *Concurrent Pos:* Hon postdoctoral, Dept Math, Univ Western Australia, 89-90. *Mem:* Am Geophys Union; Am Women Sci. *Res:* Developing techniques and applications of dynamical systems analysis to natural systems such as fluid flow, ecology and earthquakes. *Mailing Add:* 14 Montvale Rd Wellesley MA 02181

LITTLE, STEPHEN JAMES, ASTRONOMY, ASTROPHYSICS. *Current Pos:* RES ASSOC, CASA, UNIV COLO, 90- *Personal Data:* b Akron, Ohio, July 5, 39; m 73, Irene R Marenin; c Erika & Kevin. *Educ:* Univ Kans, BA, 61, MA, 63; Univ Calif, Los Angeles, PhD(astron), 71. *Prof Exp:* Fac assoc astron, Univ Tex, Austin, 68-70; asst prof, Ferris State Col, Big Rapids, Mich, 70-75; asst prof astron, Wellesley Col, 75-83; sr post doctoral, Nat Res Coun, 83-85; asst prof, Bentley Col, 85-90. *Concurrent Pos:* Consult scientist, Solar Physics Div, Am Sci & Eng, Cambridge, 76-77; sci tech staff, Gen Res Co, 86-90. *Mem:* Am Astron Soc; Sigma Xi. *Res:* Astronomical spectroscopy and photometry of red giant stars, Ap stars, and planets; solar x-ray physics. *Mailing Add:* CASA Univ Colo PO Box 389 Boulder CO 80309

LITTLE, WILLIAM ARTHUR, PHYSICS. *Current Pos:* from asst prof to assoc prof, 58-65, PROF PHYSICS, STANFORD UNIV, 65- *Personal Data:* b Adelaide, SAfrica, Nov 17, 30; nat US; m 55; c 3. *Educ:* Univ SAfrica, BSc, 50; Rhodes Univ, SAfrica, PhD, 55; Univ Glasgow, PhD, 57. *Prof Exp:* Nat Res Coun Can fel, Univ BC, 56-58. *Concurrent Pos:* Alfred P Sloan fel, 59-62; Guggenheim fel, 64-65; invited prof, Univ Geneva, 64-65; NSF sr fel, 71-72; chmn, MMR Technol Inc. *Mem:* Fel Am Phys Soc. *Res:* Organic fluorescence; magnetic resonance; low temperature physics; superconductivity; phase transition; chemical physics; neural network theory. *Mailing Add:* Dept Physics Stanford Univ Stanford CA 94305

LITTLE, WILLIAM ASA, obstetrics & gynecology; deceased, see previous edition for last biography

LITTLE, WILLIAM C, CARDIOLOGY, CARDIAC PHYSIOLOGY. *Current Pos:* assoc prof, 86-89, PROF MED, BOWMAN GRAY SCH MED, 89-, CHIEF, CARDIOL SECT, 90- *Personal Data:* b Cleveland, Ohio, May 1, 50; m 75; c 2. *Educ:* Oberlin Col, Ohio, BA, 72; Ohio State Univ, MD, 75. *Honors & Awards:* Harrison Award, Southern Soc Clin Invest, 93. *Prof Exp:* Instr, Univ Ala Sch Med, 80-81; from asst prof to assoc prof med, Univ Tex Health Sci Ctr, 81-86. *Concurrent Pos:* Prin investr, NIH, 86-92 & 89-94, mem, Study Sect, 89-90; Am Heart Asn estab investr award, 86; Am Fedn Clin Res young investr award, 91. *Mem:* Am Soc Clin Invest; Am Physiol Soc; Cardiac Syst Dynamics Soc; Asn Univ Cardiologists; Asn Professors Cardiol. *Res:* Cardiac dynamics and pathophysiology of myocardial infarction. *Mailing Add:* Sect Cardiol Bowman Gray Sch Med Medical Center Blvd Winston-Salem NC 27157-1045

LITTLE, WILLIAM FREDERICK, ORGANIC CHEMISTRY, INORGANIC CHEMISTRY. *Current Pos:* RETIRED. *Personal Data:* b Morganton, NC, Nov 11, 29; m 58, Dell Hoyle; c 1. *Educ:* Lenoir Rhyne Col, BS, 50; Univ NC, MA, 52, PhD(org chem), 55. *Hon Degrees:* DSc, Lenoir Rhyne Col, 84. *Honors & Awards:* Thomas Jefferson Award, 80. *Prof Exp:* Instr chem, Reed Col, 55-56; from instr to assoc prof, Univ NC, Chapel Hill, 56-65, prof chem & chmn dept, 65-70, vchancellor develop & pub serv, 73-73, univ distinguished prof, 77-96, interim provost, 91-92, vpres acad affairs & vpres, Univ NC Syst. *Concurrent Pos:* Consult, Res Triangle Inst, 56-69; asst to dean, Grad Sch Res Admin, Univ NC, Chapel Hill, 59-62; pres, Triangle Univ Ctr Adv Studies, Inc, 82-86; corp secy & chmn exec comt, Res Triangle Found, 86- *Mem:* Am Chem Soc; Sigma Xi. *Res:* Organometallic compounds, especially metallocenes, and group VIII metals. *Mailing Add:* 201 Markham Dr Chapel Hill NC 27514

LITTLE, WINSTON WOODARD, JR, NUCLEAR ENGINEERING. *Current Pos:* STAFF SCIENTIST, BATTELLE NW LABS, 82- *Personal Data:* b Gainesville, Fla, Sept 4, 38. *Educ:* Mass Inst Technol, BS, 60, MS, 62, ScD(nuclear eng), 64. *Prof Exp:* Mgr Fast Flux Test Facil, Nuclear Design & Analysis Unit, Pac NW Labs, Battlelle Mem Inst, 66-77; consult scientist, Westinghouse Hanford Co, 77-82. *Mem:* Am Nuclear Soc. *Res:* Nuclear design of the fast flux test facility. *Mailing Add:* Battelle 3230 Q Ave Richland WA 99352

LITTLEDIKE, ERNEST TRAVIS, ENDOCRINOLOGY, MINERAL METABOLISM. *Current Pos:* res leader, USDA, 65-85, nat prog leader, 85-88, res leader, Agr Res Serv, 89-94, DIR, VET TECH PROG, USDA, 94- *Personal Data:* b Logan, Utah, Feb 25, 35; m 60; c 4. *Educ:* Utah State Univ, BS, 58; Wash State Univ, DVM, 60; Univ Ill, PhD(physiol), 65. *Prof Exp:* Instr anat, Univ Ill, 60-62, NIH fel physiol, 62-64; fel endocrinol, Univ Wis, 64-65; vet med officer physiol, Nat Animal Dis Ctr, 65-85. *Concurrent Pos:* Vis scientist endocrinol, Mayo Clinic, 75-76; adj prof, Col Vet Med, Iowa State Univ, 70-85, Vet Sci, Univ Nebr, 89-96; Cong Res Workers Am Dis. *Mem:* Endocrine Soc; Am Soc Bone & Marine Res; World Vet Anatomists Asn; World Vet Physiologists & Pharmacologists Asn; Animal Sci Asn. *Res:* Mineral metabolism in domestic amimals and the diseases that result from mineral imbalances; factors that effect mineral metabolism and the pathogenesis of diseases of mineral metabolism in domestic animals; respiratory diseases of cattle and sheep and food safety research in cattle and sheep; copper metabolism in cattle & sheep. *Mailing Add:* Omaha Col Health Careers 10845 Harney St Omaha NE 68154

LITTLEFIELD, JOHN WALLEY, GENETICS, PEDIATRICS. *Current Pos:* prof pediat & chmn dept, 74-85, prof physiol & chmn dept, 85-92, EMER PROF PHYSIOL & PEDIAT, JOHNS HOPKINS UNIV, 92- *Personal Data:* b Providence, RI, Dec 3, 25; m 50, Elizabeth L Legge; c Peter, John Jr & Elizabeth. *Educ:* Harvard Med Sch, MD, 47; Johns Hopkins Univ, Sch Hyg & Pub Health, 92. *Prof Exp:* From intern to resident med, Mass Gen Hosp, 47-50; from clin & res fel to asst prof med, Harvard Med Sch, 54-66, tutor, 59-65, asst prof pediat, 66-69, prof, 70-73. *Concurrent Pos:* USPHS fel, Inst Enzyme Res, Univ Wis, 51; Am Cancer Soc scholar, 56-59; tutor, Harvard Univ, 59-65; Guggenheim fel, 65-66; Josiah Macy scholar, 79. *Mem:* Nat Acad Sci; Am Soc Human Genetics; Am Soc Clin Invest; Am Pediat Soc; Am Soc Biol Chemists; Soc Pediat Res; Asn Am Physicians. *Res:* Human, somatic cell and molecular genetics; developmental biology. *Mailing Add:* Johns Hopkins Univ Sch Med 1830 E Monument St Rm 7300 Baltimore MD 21205. *Fax:* 410-955-1561

LITTLEFIELD, LARRY JAMES, PLANT PATHOLOGY. *Current Pos:* PROF & HEAD, DEPT PLANT PATH, OKLA STATE UNIV, 85- *Personal Data:* b Ft Smith, Ark, Feb 7, 38; m 63. *Educ:* Cornell Univ, BS, 60; Univ Minn, MS, 62, PhD(plant path), 64. *Prof Exp:* NSF res fel, Uppsala, 64-65; from asst prof to prof plant path, NDak State Univ, 65-85. *Concurrent Pos:* NIH fel, Purdue Univ, 69-70; res fel, Oxford Univ, 73-74. *Mem:* Mycol Soc Am; Brit Mycol Soc; Am Phytopath Soc. *Res:* Histology of host-parasite relations; fungus physiology; electron microscopy of fungi and diseased plants. *Mailing Add:* Plant Path Dept Okla State Univ Stillwater OK 74078. *Fax:* 405-744-7373; *E-Mail:* ljlplpa@okway.okstate.edu

LITTLEFIELD, NEIL ADAIR, TOXICOLOGY. *Current Pos:* toxicologist, 72-79, DIR, DIV CHEM TOXICOL, NAT CTR TOXICOL RES, FOOD & DRUG ADMIN, 79- *Personal Data:* b Santa Fe, NMex, Apr 25, 35; m 60; c 5. *Educ:* Brigham Young Univ, BS, 61; Utah State Univ, MS, 64, PhD(toxicol), 68. *Prof Exp:* Res assoc air pollution, Univ Utah, 66-67; staff scientist inhalation toxicol, Hazleton Lab, Inc, 67-70; pharmacologist pesticide regulation, Environ Protection Agency, 71-72. *Concurrent Pos:* Chmn, Interagency Task Force Inhalation Chronic Toxicity & Carcinogenesis, 74-75; mem, Food & Drug Admin Task Force Aerosol Prod, 75- *Mem:* Sigma Xi. *Res:* Investigations in concepts of long-term, low-dose exposures; extrapolation of animal toxicology data to risk-benefit in man; carcinogenesis. *Mailing Add:* 3404 Millbrook Rd Little Rock AR 72227

LITTLEJOHN, OLIVER MARSILIUS, PHARMACY. *Current Pos:* RETIRED. *Personal Data:* b Cowpens, SC, Sept 29, 24; m 48; c 2. *Educ:* Univ SC, BS, 48 & 49; Univ Fla, MS, 51, PhD(pharm), 53. *Prof Exp:* Asst prof pharm & head dept, Southern Col Pharm, 53-56; prof & head dept, Univ Ky, 56-57; dean, Southern Sch Pharm, Mercer Univ, 57-87. *Mem:* Fel Am Found Pharmaceut Educ; Sigma Xi. *Res:* Pharmaceutical preservatives. *Mailing Add:* 6485 Bridgewood Valley Rd NW Atlanta GA 30328

LITTLE-MARENIN, IRENE RENATE, ASTROPHYSICS. *Current Pos:* asst prof, 77-89, ASSOC PROF ASTRON, WELLESLEY COL, 89- *Personal Data:* b Pilsen, Czech, May 4, 41; US citizen; m 73, Stephen J Little; c Erika & Kevin. *Educ:* Vassar Col, AB, 64; Ind Univ, MA, 66, PhD(astrophys), 70. *Prof Exp:* Fel astron, Ohio State Univ, 70-72; asst prof, Univ Western Ont, 72-73; teaching fel, Ferris State Col, 74; res asst soft x-rays, Am Sci & Eng, 76-77. *Concurrent Pos:* Vis asst prof, Dennison Univ & Ohio State, 80-81; vis scientist, Univ Colo, 80-81; res fel, JILA, 83-84, Univ resident res fel, AFGL, 86-88; NSF vis prof women, Univ Colo, 90-91. *Mem:* Am Astron Soc; Sigma Xi. *Res:* A search for the radioactive element technetium in long-period variable stars; analysis of infrared absorption spectroscopy; low resolution spectra of circumstellar dust in evolved stars; correlation of water maser emission and optical light curves for long period variable stars. *Mailing Add:* Whitin Observ Wellesley Col Wellesley MA 02181. *E-Mail:* ilittle@wellesley.edu

LITTLEPAGE, JACK LEROY, BIOLOGICAL OCEANOGRAPHY. *Current Pos:* Asst prof, 65-71, ASSOC PROF BIOL, UNIV VICTORIA, 71- *Personal Data:* b San Diego, Calif, Apr 14, 35; m 60. *Educ:* San Diego State Col, BA, 57; Stanford Univ, PhD(biol), 66. *Concurrent Pos:* Oceanog consult to mining industs, 71- *Mem:* AAAS; Am Soc Limnol & Oceanog. *Res:* Physiology and ecology of marine zooplankton, especially copepods and euphausids; pollution monitoring; salmonid IHN virus; geothermal aguaculture. *Mailing Add:* Dept Biol Univ Victoria PO Box 1700 Victoria BC V8W 2Y2 Can

LITTLER, DIANE SCULLION, EXPERIMENTAL TAXONOMY, NATURAL HISTORY OF MARINE PLANTS. *Current Pos:* RES ASSOC, SMITHSONIAN INST, 82-; SR SCIENTIST, HARBOR BR OCEANOG INST, 94- *Personal Data:* b Salem Ohio, Aug 26, 45; m 66, Mark M. *Educ:* Univ Hawaii, BS, 68; Pac Western Univ, PhD(marine bot), 85. *Prof Exp:* Res assoc, Univ Hawaii, 69-70, Univ Calif, Irvine, 70-82. *Mem:* Phycol Soc Am; Int Phycol Soc; Int Soc Reef Studies; Europ Phycol Soc; Soc Women Geogrs. *Res:* Experimental taxonoy, functional morphology biodiversity and natural history of marine plants; effects of disturbance on the structure and function of marine ecosystems. *Mailing Add:* Dept Bot No 166 Smithsonian Inst Washington DC 20560

LITTLER, MARK MASTERTON, TAXONOMY, FUNCTIONAL MORPHOLOGY. *Current Pos:* chmn cur bot res, 82-87, SR SCIENTIST, SMITHSONIAN INST, 85- *Personal Data:* b Athens, Ohio, Sept 24, 39; m 66. *Educ:* Ohio Univ, BS, 61, MS, 66; Univ Hawaii, PhD(marine bot), 71. *Honors & Awards:* Earle C Anthony Innovative Res Award, 73; Durbaker Prize, Bot Soc Am, 84. *Prof Exp:* Chemist, Testing Lab, Ohio State Hwy Dept, 61-64; from asst prof to prof biol res, Univ Calif, Irvine, 70-82. *Concurrent Pos:* Vis prof, Stanford Univ, 73 & 74, Univ SCalif, 73 & 75; mem bd, SCalif Acad Sci, 80-82; distinguished vis scientist, Univ Nebr, Lincoln, 81, Northwestern Univ, 81; assoc ed, Aquatic Bd, 82-85, J Psycol 82-86, ed, Smithsonian Contrib to Bot, 82-87; assoc ed, Phycolog Soc Am, 82-86; adj prof, George Mason Univ, 84-; mem bd vis, Ohio Univ Col Arts & Sci, 85-88; rep, Int Univ Biol Sci, Biol Monitoring Proj, Int Phycol Soc, 85- *Mem:* Ecol Soc Am; Int Phycol Soc; Phycol Soc Am; Int Soc Reef Studies; Am Soc Limnol & Oceanog. *Res:* Man's effect on marine ecosystems; taxonomy, developmental morphology and seasonal cycles of marine benthos and phytoplankton; standing stock, productivity and the physiological ecology of temperate and reef-building benthic organisms. *Mailing Add:* Dept Bot NHB 166 Nat Mus Natural Hist Smithsonian Inst MRC-166 Washington DC 20560

LITTLETON, H(AROLD) T(HOMAS) J(ACKSON), CHEMICAL ENGINEERING. *Current Pos:* RETIRED. *Personal Data:* b Parksley, Va, June 28, 21; m 48, Marian Mote; c Thomas J. *Educ:* Univ Va, BChE, 43. *Prof Exp:* Chem engr, Naval Res Lab, 43-46; chem engr, Res Div, Polychem Dept, Exp Sta, E I Du Pont de Nemour Co, Inc, 46-53, res supvr, 53-62, sr res engr, Plastic Dept, 62-69, res assoc, 69-73, lab adminr, Platics Prod & Resins Dept, 74-82. *Mem:* Am Chem Soc. *Res:* Process development on nylon intermediates; high pressure processes; new plastics and plastics processing methods. *Mailing Add:* 320 Walden Rd Sharpley Wilmington DE 19803

LITTLETON, JOHN EDWARD, STELLAR EVOLUTION, MOLECULAR SPECTROSCOPY. *Current Pos:* from asst prof to assoc prof, 75-88, PROF PHYSICS, WVA UNIV, 88- *Personal Data:* b Ballston Spa, NY, July 28, 43; m 88, Rebecca A Lawson. *Educ:* Cornell Univ, BS, 65; Univ Rochester, PhD(astrophys), 72. *Prof Exp:* Res assoc astrophys, Belfer Grad Sch Sci, Yeshiva Univ, 72-73; res fel, Harvard Col Observ, 73-74, res assoc, 74-75. *Concurrent Pos:* Vis assoc prof, Univ Ill, 82; vis assoc res astron, Univ Calif Berkeley, 84, 85, 86 & 93-94; vis scientist, Ind Univ, 84. *Mem:* Am Astron Soc; Am Asn Physics Teachers; Astron Soc Pac. *Res:* Plasma fluctuations in astrophysical media; structure of detonation waves in degenerate stellar cores; hydrodynamic properties of stellar atmospheres; molecular bands in cool, stellar atmospheres. *Mailing Add:* WVa Univ Physics Dept PO Box 6315 Morgantown WV 26506-6415. *E-Mail:* jel@wvnvms.wvnet.edu

LITTLETON, PRESTON A, JR, dental research, for more information see previous edition

LITTLETON, ROBERT T, ENGINEERING GEOLOGY. *Current Pos:* RETIRED. *Personal Data:* b Sheridan, Wyo, Jan 14, 16. *Educ:* Ore State Univ, BS, 41. *Prof Exp:* Regional geologist, US Bur Reclanation, 61-80. *Mem:* Geol Soc Am. *Mailing Add:* 624 Don Vincente Dr Boulder City NV 89005

LITTLEWOOD, BARBARA SHAFFER, BIOCHEMISTRY, GENETICS. *Current Pos:* res assoc biochem, 70-73, res assoc physiol chem, 73-76; RES ASSOC BIOCHEM, UNIV WIS-MADISON, 76- *Personal Data:* b Buffalo, NY, Oct 8, 41; m 70. *Educ:* Univ Rochester, BA, 63; Univ Pa, PhD(biochem), 68. *Prof Exp:* NIH trainee, Cornell Univ, 68-70. *Concurrent Pos:* Lectr, Dept Genetics, Cornell Univ, 70 & Dept Biochem, Univ Wis-Madison, 72. *Mem:* Genetics Soc Am; Am Soc Microbiol. *Res:* Yeast genetics and biochemistry. *Mailing Add:* 5109 Coney Weston Pl Madison WI 53711

LITTLEWOOD, PETER B, CONDENSED MATTER PHYSICS. *Current Pos:* mem tech staff, 80-81 & 82-91, HEAD, THEORET PHYSICS DEPT, AT&T BELL LABS, 91- *Personal Data:* b May 18, 55. *Educ:* Univ Cambridge, Eng, BA, 76, PhD(physics), 80. *Prof Exp:* Kennedy scholar, Mass Inst Technol, 76-77. *Mem:* Fel Am Phys Soc. *Res:* Dynamics of sliding charge density; nucleation at a first order phase transition; electron gas in high magnetic fields; high temperature superconductivity; flux lattice in type II superconductors. *Mailing Add:* AT&T Bell Labs ID 426 600 Mountain Ave Murray Hill NJ 07974

LITTLEWOOD, ROLAND KAY, COMPUTER SCIENCE, MOLECULAR BIOLOGY. *Current Pos:* NIH fel, Lab Molecular Biol, Univ Wis-Madison, 70-72, res assoc, 72-78, asst scientist, 78-86, sr info processing consult, Biophys Lab, 86-93, DISTINGUISHED INFO PROCESSING CONSULT, INST MOLECULAR VIROL, UNIV WIS-MADISON, 93- *Personal Data:* b Mendota, Ill, Nov 26, 42; m 70, Barbara Shaffer; c David & Peter. *Educ:* Univ Ill, Urbana, BS, 64; Cornell Univ, PhD(genetics), 70. *Concurrent Pos:* Proprietor, Digital Comput Appl, 74- *Mem:* Asn Comput Mach. *Res:* Application of computers in the biological sciences. *Mailing Add:* Inst Molecular Virol 1525 Linden Dr Univ Wis Madison WI 53706. *E-Mail:* rklittle@facstaff.wisc.edu

LITTMAN, ARMAND, MEDICINE. *Current Pos:* from clin asst to assoc prof, 46-64, PROF MED, COL MED, UNIV ILL, 64-; CHIEF MED SERV, HINES VET ADMIN HOSP, 59- *Personal Data:* b Chicago, Ill, Apr 4, 21; m 52; c 3. *Educ:* Univ Ill, Chicago, BS, 42, MD, 43, MS, 48, PhD(physiol), 51. *Prof Exp:* Intern, Cook Co Hosp, Chicago, 44. *Concurrent Pos:* Raymond B Allen instructorship award, Univ Ill, 57; US AEC travel award, 58; resident, Cook County Hosp, Chicago, 48-50; pvt pract, 52-59; attend physician, Res & Educ Hosps, 55-; prof, Cook County Grad Sch Med, 58- *Mem:* AMA; Am Col Physicians; Am Fedn Clin Res; Am Gastroenterol Asn; Sigma Xi. *Res:* Gastroenterology; physiology. *Mailing Add:* Vet Admin Hosp Hines IL 60141

LITTMAN, BRUCE H, EXPERIMENTAL MEDICINE. *Current Pos:* SR ASSOC DIR EXP MED, PFIZER CENTRES, PFIZER INC, GROTON, CONN, 89- *Personal Data:* b New York, NY, Nov 18, 44; m; c 1. *Educ:* Univ Wis, BS, 66; State Univ NY, MD, 70; Am Bd Internal Med, dipl, 75, dipl rheumatology, 78. *Prof Exp:* Intern med, Tufts New Eng Med Ctr, Boston, 70-71; staff assoc tumor & immunol res, Nat Cancer Inst, NIH, Bethesda, Md, 71-73; resident, Tufts New Eng Med Ctr, 73-74; res fel, Robert B Brigham Hosp, Harvard Med Sch, 74-76, asst med, Peter Bent Brigham Hosp, 74-76; postdoctoral fel, Am Cancer Soc, Mass Div, Boston, 74-76; from asst prof to assoc prof med & microbiol, Med Col Va, 76-89. *Concurrent Pos:* Vis scientist, Metab Br, Nat Cancer Inst, Bethesda, Md, 81-82; chief, Rheumatology Sect, Med Serv, McGuire Vet Admin Med Ctr, Richmond, 82-89; mem, Immunol Sci Study Sect, Div Res Grants, NIH, 83-87. *Mem:* Fel Am Col Rheumatology; Am Fedn Clin Res; Am Asn Immunologists; fel Am Col Physicians; Sigma Xi. *Res:* Transplantation immunity in dogs; cellular immunology; immunogenetics; nucleotide biochemistry; author of numerous articles, chapters and books. *Mailing Add:* Pfizer Cent Res Pfizer Inc Eastern Point Rd Groton CT 06340-5196

LITTMAN, HOWARD, FLUID-PARTICLE SYSTEMS. *Current Pos:* assoc prof, 65-67, PROF CHEM ENG, RENSSELAER POLYTECH INST, 67- *Personal Data:* b Brooklyn, NY, Apr 22, 27; m 55, Arline C Caruso; c Susan J, Vicki K & Paul W. *Educ:* Cornell Univ, BChE, 51; Yale Univ, PhD(chem eng), 56. *Prof Exp:* From asst prof to assoc prof chem eng, Syracuse Univ, 56-65. *Concurrent Pos:* Resident res assoc, Argonne Nat Lab, 57-59; res asst chem eng, Brookhaven Nat Lab, NY, 57; vis prof, Imperial Col, London, 71-72; Fulbright-Hays lectr, Univ Belgrade, 72; vis prof, Chonnam Nat Univ, Kwangju, Korea; Irex grantee, Univ Belgrade, 73. *Mem:* Am Chem Soc; Am Inst Chem Engrs. *Res:* Fluidization and fluid-particle systems. *Mailing Add:* Dept Chem Eng Rensselaer Polytech Inst 110 Eighth St Troy NY 12180-3590. *Fax:* 518-276-4030; *E-Mail:* littmh@rpi.edu

LITTMAN, MICHAEL GEIST, TUNABLE LASER DESIGN, ARTIFICIAL MOTOR CONTROL OF BIOLOGICALLY-INSPIRED ROBOTIC SYSTEMS. *Current Pos:* Asst prof, 79-85, ASSOC PROF MECH & AEROSPACE ENG, PRINCETON UNIV, 85- *Personal Data:* b Washington, DC, Mar 29, 50; m 71, L Marion Katz; c Emily & Eric. *Educ:* Brandeis Univ, AB, 72; Mass Inst Technol, PhD(physics), 77. *Concurrent Pos:* Vis scientist, TJ Watson Lab, IBM, 79; mem, Comt Line Spectra Elements, Nat Res Coun, 79-83; founding topical ed, J Optical Soc Am, 80-83; vis prof, Bar-Ilan Univ, Israel, 82. *Mem:* Optical Soc Am; Sigma Xi. *Res:* Design of tunable laser cavities; learning control and its application to control of wave and quantum phenomena; artificial neural networks for the control of anthropomorphic robots. *Mailing Add:* Princeton Univ D202 Eng Quadrangle Princeton NJ 08544. *E-Mail:* mlittman@princeton.edu

LITTMAN, WALTER, MATHEMATICAL ANALYSIS. *Current Pos:* from asst prof to assoc prof, 60-66, PROF MATH, UNIV MINN, MINNEAPOLIS, 66- *Personal Data:* b Vienna, Austria, Sept 17, 29; US citizen; m 60; c 3. *Educ:* Univ NY, BA, 52, PhD(math), 56. *Prof Exp:* Instr math, Univ Calif, Berkeley, 56-58, lectr, 58-59; asst prof, Univ Wis, 59-60. *Concurrent Pos:* Vis mem, Courant Inst Math Sci, NY Univ, 67-68; vis prof, Mittag-Leffler Inst, Djursholm, Sweden, 74, Chalmers Technol Univ, Gothenburg, Sweden, 75, Hebrew Univ, Jerusalem, Israel, 81-82 & 89. *Mem:* Am Math Soc. *Res:* Partial differential equations; functional analysis; mathematical physics. *Mailing Add:* 127 Vincent Hall Univ Minn 206 Church SE Minneapolis MN 55455-0100

LITTMANN, MARTIN F(REDERICK), METALLURGY & PHYSICAL METALLURGICAL ENGINEERING. *Current Pos:* RETIRED. *Personal Data:* b Brazil, Ind, Feb 9, 19; m 44, Anne Aker; c Carol & Daniel. *Educ:* Univ Cincinnati, ChemE, 41, MS, 43. *Prof Exp:* From jr res engr to sr res engr, Armco Inc, 43-68, prin res assoc, 68-75, prin res engr, 68-75, prin res engr, 75-83. *Concurrent Pos:* Consult, 83-94. *Mem:* Inst Elec & Electronics Engrs; Am Inst Mining, Metall & Petrol Engrs; Sigma Xi; Am Soc Affil. *Res:* Deformation and recrystallization orientations in soft magnetic materials; studies of magnetic properties in relation to metallurgy of soft magnetic materials. *Mailing Add:* 2104 Tullis Dr Middletown OH 45042-2965

LITVAK, AUSTIN S, UROLOGY. *Current Pos:* MED DIR, 94- *Personal Data:* b Staten Island, NY, Dec 1, 33. *Educ:* Wagner Col, BS, 54; Univ Va, MD, 58; Am Bd Urol, dipl. *Honors & Awards:* First Prize, Nat Clin Soc, 68. *Prof Exp:* Intern surg, Univ Va Hosp, 58-59; NIH fel, Surg Br, Nat Cancer Inst, 59-60; USPHS surgeon, Claremore Indian Hosp, Okla, 60-61; resident urol, Hosp Univ Pa, Jefferson Med Col Serv & Philadelphia Gen Hosp, 61-63; pvt pract, 63-73; asst in surg, Div Urol, Hahnemann Med Col, 70-73; from asst prof to assoc prof surg, Div Urol, Univ Ky Med Ctr, 76-83; pvt pract, 83-88. *Concurrent Pos:* Asst attend urol, Monmouth Med Ctr & Riverview Hosp; assoc attend & div rep, Bayshore Hosp; courtesy staff, Jersey Shore Med Ctr; asst urol staff, Hahnemann Med Col; mem urol staff, Univ Ky Med Ctr 73-78; consult urol, Vet Admin Hosp, 73-75; active staff, St Josephs Hosp, Central Baptist Hosp & Claril County Hosp. *Mem:* Am Urol Asn; Am Fertil Soc; AMA; fel Am Col Surgeons; fel Int Col Surgeons. *Res:* Embryology of the kidney; acute and chronic prostatitis; lower urinary tract infections in children and adults; diseases of the kidney, urethra and bladder in children. *Mailing Add:* 75 Raisen Tree Circle Baltimore MD 21208

LITVAK, MARVIN MARK, QUANTUM ELECTRONICS, DIGITAL IMAGE PROCESSING. *Current Pos:* CHIEF SCIENTIST, TECHNOL RES ASSOCS, 92- *Personal Data:* b Newark, NJ, Oct 20, 33; m 63, Marilyn Canney; c Stephanie & David. *Educ:* Cornell Univ, BEngPhys, 55, PhD(theoret physics), 60. *Prof Exp:* Consult, Avco Corp, 55-60, sr staff mem, Avco Res Lab, 60-63; group leader, Lincoln Lab, Mass Inst Technol, 63-70; sr radio astronomer, Smithsonian Astrophys Observ, 70-78; mem tech staff, Jet Propulsion Lab, Calif Inst Technol, 78-85; sr staff scientist, TRW, 85-92. *Concurrent Pos:* Lectr, Harvard Col Observ, 70-78; consult, Lincoln Lab, Mass Inst Technol, 77-92 & Jet Propulsion Lab, Calif Inst Technol, 93- *Mem:* Int Astron Union; Am Phys Soc; Am Astron Soc. *Res:* Non-linear propagation effects of lasers, interstellar molecules and masers; millimeter-wave radio astronomy and aeronomy; digital image correction. *Mailing Add:* 1525 Espinsoa Circle Palos Verdes Estates CA 90274

LITVAN, GERARD GABRIEL, SURFACE CHEMISTRY. *Current Pos:* prin res officer, 62-93, CONSULT, INST RES CONSTRUCT, NAT RES COUN CAN, 93- *Personal Data:* b Vienna, Austria, May 17, 27; Can citizen; m 64; c 1. *Educ:* Eotovos Univ, Budapest, Dipl, 52; Univ Toronto, PhD(surface chem), 62. *Prof Exp:* Asst prof phys chem, Inst Phys Chem, Eotovos Univ, 52-55; assoc phys chem, Cent Chem Res Inst, Hungarian Acad Sci, 55-56; res chemist phys polymer chem, Can Industs Ltd, 57-59. *Concurrent Pos:* Lectr, Chem Dept, Carleton Univ, 66-67; First Int Conf Durability of Bldg Mat & Components; Can Stand Asn Subcomt chmn, 78. *Mem:* Fel Am Ceramic Soc; Am Concrete Inst; Am Chem Soc; fel Chem Inst Can; Am Soc Testing & Mat; Can Stand Asn. *Res:* Phase transitions of substances adsorbed in porous solids; mechanism of cyroinjury and cyroprotection in plant and animal tissue; mechanism of frost action in porous building materials; materials science engineering; corrosion of reinforcing steel in concrete,; rehabilitation of concrete structures. *Mailing Add:* 248 Range Rd Ottawa ON K1N 8J8 Can. *Fax:* 613-565-6189

LITVIN, FAYDOR L, ANALYSIS & KINEMATICS OF MECHANISMS, COMPUTERIZED GENERATION. *Current Pos:* prof, 79-93, EMER RES PROF, UNIV ILL, CHICAGO, 93- *Personal Data:* US citizen; m 38, Shifra Gershenovich; c Boris & Julia. *Educ:* Leningrad Polytech Inst, BSc, 37, Dr of Tech Sc, 54; Tomsk Polytech Inst, PhD(mech eng), 44. *Honors & Awards:* Tech-Brief Awards, NASA, 87, 88, 90, 91 & 93. *Prof Exp:* Prof theory mech, Leningrad Polytech Inst, 49-64; prof & dept head, Leningrad Inst Precision Mechs & Optics, 64-78. *Concurrent Pos:* Consult, Clow Corp, 80-81, Ingersol Milling Mach, 81-82, Dana Corp, 83-93, Braun Eng Co, 88-90, Cone Drive, 89-90, Gleason Works, 91-94, Nissan, Japan, 91-, Ford Motor Co, 92- *Mem:* Fel Am Soc Mech Engrs; mem Am Gear Mfrs Asn. *Res:* Theory of gearing and application; analysis and synthesis of mechanisms; meshing and contact of gears. *Mailing Add:* 8637 N Avers Ave Skokie IL 60076. *Fax:* 312-413-0447

LITWACK, GERALD, BIOCHEMISTRY & ENDOCRINOLOGY, CELL BIOLOGY & MOLECULAR BIOLOGY. *Current Pos:* chmn, Dept Pharmacol & dep dir, Jefferson Cancer Inst, Thomas Jefferson Univ, 91-97, assoc dir basic sci, 93-97, CHMN, DEPT BIOCHEM & MOLECULAR PHARMACOL, JEFFERSON CANCER CTR, 96-, ASSOC DEAN SCI AFFAIRS, 96- *Personal Data:* b Boston, Mass, Jan 11, 29; m 56, 73, Ellen J Schatz; c Katherine V, Geoffrey S & Claudia. *Educ:* Hobart Col, BA, 49; Univ Wis, MS, 51, PhD(biochem), 53. *Honors & Awards:* Lalor Found Award, 56; Fac Res Award, Temple Univ, 87. *Prof Exp:* from asst prof to prof biochem, Rutgers Univ, 54-64; prof biochem, Sch Med, Temple Univ, 64-91, fels res inst, 64-91, dep dir, 78-91, Laura H Carnell prof biochem, 88-91. *Concurrent Pos:* Nat Found Infantile Paralysis fel, Biochem Lab, Univ Sorbonne, 53-54; trainee, Oak Ridge Inst Nuclear Studies, 55; vis prof, Univ Calif, 56; res assoc prof, Grad Sch Med, Univ Pa & dir biochem, Div Cardiol, Philadelphia Gen Hosp, 60-64; hon prof, Rutgers Univ, 60-64; Nat Inst Arthritis & Metab Dis res career develop award, 63-69; vis scientist, Univ London, 71 & Univ Calif, 72; mem adv bd, Biochem & Chem Carcinogenesis, Am Cancer Soc, 77-80, chmn, 79, Endocrinol, 80-83, Anticancer Res, 82-, Oncol Res, 92-, Oncol Reports, 93-; mem, Cell Physiol Panel, NSF, 80-83; counc, Soc Exp Biol & Med, 84-; spec study, Reproductive Endocrine Sect, NIH, 85, Israel Cancer Res Fund, Study Sect, 92-93, US Army Breast Cancer Study Sect, 94; ed-in-chief, Receptor, 91-, Vitamins & Hormones, 93- *Mem:* Am Soc Biochem & Molecular Biol; Am Asn Cancer Res; Endocrine Soc; Am Chem Soc. *Res:* Ligandin; hormonal control of enzyme formation and activity; glucocorticoid receptor; mineralocorticoid receptor; immunophilins apoptosis modulator. *Mailing Add:* Dept Biochem & Molecular Pharmacol Jefferson Med Col Thomas Jefferson Univ Tenth & Locust Sts Philadelphia PA 19107. *Fax:* 215-503-5393; *E-Mail:* litwack@hendrix.jci.tju.edu

LITWAK, ROBERT SEYMOUR, SURGERY. *Current Pos:* PROF SURG, MT SINAI SCH MED, 71- *Personal Data:* b New York, NY, Nov 25, 24; c 3. *Educ:* Ursinus Col, BS, 45; Hahnemann Med Col, MD, 49; Am Bd Surg, dipl, 56; Am Bd Thoracic Surg, dipl, 58. *Prof Exp:* Asst surg, Sch Med, Boston Univ, 52; from instr to assoc prof surg, Med Sch, Univ Miami, 56-62; attend surgeon & chief div cardiothoracic surg, Mt Sinai Hosp, 62- *Concurrent Pos:* Consult, Vet Admin Hosp, Coral Gables, Fla, 57- & Variety Children's Hosp, 59-; chief div thoracic & cardiovascular surg, Jackson Mem Hosp, 59-62. *Mem:* Fel Am Col Surg; fel Am Col Chest Physicians; fel Am Col Cardiol; fel NY Acad Sci. *Res:* Cardiovascular physiology; cardiac surgery. *Mailing Add:* CUNY Mt Sinai Sch Med One Gustave L Levy Pl New York NY 10029-6504

LITWHILER, DANIEL W, OPERATIONS RESEARCH. *Current Pos:* assoc prof, USAF Acad, 72-74 & 77-81, tenure prof, 83-85, prof math & head, Dept Math Sci, 86-91, vdean fac, 92-94, CHMN, DIV BASIC SCI, USAF ACAD, 94- *Personal Data:* b Ringtown, Pa, Feb, 28, 42; m 66, Peggy Pendergast; c Daniel, Christopher, Kevin & Heather. *Educ:* Fla State Univ, BS, 63, MS, 65; Univ Okla, PhD(indust eng), 77. *Prof Exp:* Opers officer, mgt analyst, comptroller & progs officer, US Air Force, 65-72; plans & issue analyst, staff group, Off Secy Air Force, 82. *Mem:* Opers Res Soc Am. *Res:* Location theory, particularly large regions; military applications of operations research. *Mailing Add:* Prof & Head Dept Math Sci US Air Force Acad Colorado Springs CO 80840. *E-Mail:* lithwhilerdw.dfms@usafa.af.mil

LITWIN, MARTIN STANLEY, SURGERY. *Current Pos:* from asst prof to prof, 66-77, ASSOC DEAN MED DIR FAC PRACT, ROBERT & VIOLA LOBRANO PROF SURG, SCH MED, TULANE UNIV, 77- *Personal Data:* b Florence, Ala, Jan 8, 30; m 85, Cheryl Mason; c Anna M, Rebecca, Benjamin & Martin. *Educ:* Univ Ala, BS, 51, MD, 55; Am Bd Surg, dipl, 63. *Honors & Awards:* Ralph McBurney Outstanding Med Serv Award. *Prof Exp:* Instr med physiol, Sch Med, Univ Ala, 53; intern surg, Michael Reese Hosp, Chicago, 55-56; asst, Peter Bent Brigham Hosp, Boston, 56-58, jr asst resident, 57 & 58-59, sr asst resident, 60-61, sr resident, 61-62; instr, Harvard Med Sch, 66. *Concurrent Pos:* Surg res fel, Harvard Med Sch, 56-58; surg registr, St Mary's Hosp & Med Sch, London, 59-60; George Gorham Peters fel, Peter Bent Brigham Hosp, Boston, 59-60, chief surg res, 65, jr assoc surg, 65-66; Am Cancer Soc clin fel, 61-62; regr to prof teaching unit, St Mary's Hosp, London, 59-60; clin invetr, Vet Admin Hosp, W Roxbury, 64-66, consult, 66-; adj prof biomed eng, Northeastern Univ, 64-67; mem, Surgeon-Gen Adv Comt Optical Lasers, Working Group Safety Stand Use Lasers, Armed Forces Nat Res Coun Comt Vision, Ad Hoc Initial Rev Group, Nat Ctr Radiol Health & Spec Study Sect Laser & NIH session chmn, Gordon Conf Lasers Biol Med, 65-67; sr vis surgeon, Charity Hosp of La, mem active staff, Tulane Hosp; Nat Heart Inst investr career develop award, 68-72. *Mem:* Fel Am Col Surgeons; Am Surg Asn; Am Asn Surg Trauma; Soc Univ Surgeons; Soc Surg Alimentary Tract; Int Surg Soc. *Res:* Blood rheology; vascular and gastrointestinal surgery; surgical metabolism; blood transfusion and treatment of skin cancer. *Mailing Add:* Tulane Univ Med Sch 1415 Tulane Ave New Orleans LA 70112

LITYNSKI, DANIEL MITCHELL, OPTICAL SIGNAL PROCESSING. *Current Pos:* Exec officer B, 2/34 Armor Battalion, Vietnam, US Army, 66-67, commanding officer, 551st Lt Maint Co, Vietnam and H0 Co, US Ord Ctr, 67-68, res physicist, Ballistics Res Labs, 72-73, asst prof physics, US Mil Acad, 74-78, exec officer, 19th Maintenance Battalion, WGer, 78-80, assoc prof, 80-86, prof, dep & actg head, Elec Engr, 86-89, US ARMY, 91, PROF & HEAD ELEC ENG & COMPUT SCI, US MIL ACAD, WEST POINT, NY, 90- *Personal Data:* b Amsterdam, NY, Mar 13, 43; m 63; c 3. *Educ:* Rensselaer Polytech Inst, BS, 65, PhD(physics), 78; Univ Rochester, MS, 71. *Concurrent Pos:* Vis researcher, Harry Diamond Labs, 74 & 75; lectr, Europ Div, Univ Md, 80; prin investr, US Army Res Off, 81-; adj res prof, Elec Comput & Syst Engr Dept, Rensselaer Polytech Inst, 87-; USMA fel, Indust Col Armed Forces, 88-89. *Mem:* Sigma Xi; Inst Elec & Electronics Engrs; Optical Soc Am; Soc Photo-Optical Instrumentation Engrs; Am Soc Eng Educ; NY Acad Sci; Armed Forces Commun & Electronics Asn. *Res:* Optical signal processing using surface acoustic wave devices; optical matrix processing; optical computing. *Mailing Add:* Dept Elec Eng & Comput Sci US Mil Acad 600 Thayer Rd West Point NY 10996-1787

LITZ, CHARLES J, JR, MATHEMATICAL PHYSICS, SPACE ENVIRONMENT SIMULATION. *Current Pos:* SR ENG SCIENTIST, MCDONNELL DOUGLAS AEROSPACE, 86- *Personal Data:* m 71, Ronalda C Kapczynski; c Stacey A & Mark C. *Educ:* Univ Del, BME, 51; Tex Western Univ, BS, 55; LaSall Col, MS, 59. *Prof Exp:* Mech engr, US Navy, Pa, 51-54; lectr electronic physics, US Army, Ft Bliss, 54-56, sr med engr, Frankfort Arsenal, 58-77; electro-mech engr, Honeywell, 56-58; sr design engr, Ford Motor & Aerospace, 77-86. *Concurrent Pos:* Lectr Nike missile systs, US Army, 54-56, ord prin investr, Duke Univ, 61-67; Minute Man Mark X & XII consult, USAF, 59-61; air bag prin investr, Ford Motor Co, 77-81; prin investr, US Army Soc Mech Engrs, 96. *Mem:* Am Soc Mech Engrs; Prof Engrs Asn. *Res:* Design test electromechanical ordnance devices; aircraft life support and guided missile systems; design of experiments in statistical analysis of test data; aerospace simulation and testing of space station system; granted 11 patents. *Mailing Add:* 29221 Tieree St Laguna Niguel CA 92677. *Fax:* 714-896-2439

LITZ, LAWRENCE MARVIN, GAS LIQUID SOLID MIXING, MEMBRANE APPLICATIONS & ENGINEERING. *Current Pos:* PRES, LITZ GLOBAL CONSULT, 92- *Personal Data:* b Chicago, Ill, Oct 22, 21; m 42; c Barbara, Heidi, Michelle & Lisa. *Educ:* Univ Chicago, BS, 42; Ohio State Univ, PhD(phys chem), 48. *Honors & Awards:* Kirkpatrick Award, Chem Eng J, 75. *Prof Exp:* Res chemist, Tenn Valley Auth, 42-43; res metallurgist, Manhattan Proj, Los Alamos, 43-45; res chemist catalysis, Allied Chem Corp, 47-51; group leader chem metal, Standard Oil Calif, 51-53; group leader high temperature mat, Carbon Div, Union Carbide Co, 53-62, develop mgr fuel cells, Advan Develop Dept, 62-66, sr group leader membrane technol, Corp Develop, 66-72, gen mgr, Membrane Systs, 72-77, sr develop assoc, 77-86, mgr process chem, Linde Div, 86-90, corp fel, Union Carbide Indust Gases, Inc, 86-92. *Mem:* Am Inst Chem Engrs; Am Chem Soc; Electrochem Soc; Soc Mining & Metall Engrs; Sigma Xi. *Res:* Membrane technology; high temperature materials and processes; electrochemical and process engineering; fuel cells, nuclear chemistry; chemical and physical metallurgy; gas-liquid chemical processing; bioengineering. *Mailing Add:* 16 Briarwood Lane Pleasantville NY 10570

LITZ, RICHARD EARLE, PLANT PATHOLOGY, HORTICULTURE. *Current Pos:* fel, 76-77, res assoc plant path, 77-78, asst prof, 79-84, ASSOC PROF, FRUIT CROPS DEPT, UNIV FLA, 84- *Personal Data:* b Presque Isle, Maine, July 3, 44; m 69; c 2. *Educ:* Dalhousie Univ, BA, 66, MSc, 68; Univ Nottingham, PhD(plant virol), 71. *Prof Exp:* Fel mycol, Univ Durham, 71-73; res officer plant path, Twyford Labs Ltd, 73-76. *Concurrent Pos:* Rare Fruits Coun Int grant, 78-; USDA grant, 79-84; Rockefeller Found grants, 79-81 & 81-85. *Mem:* Int Asn Plant Tissue Cult; Sigma Xi; Am Soc Hort Sci; Int Soc Plant Molecular Biol. *Res:* Tissue culture of tropical fruits; disease resistance in tropical fruits. *Mailing Add:* 29500 SW 205th Ave Homestead FL 33030

LITZENBERGER, LEONARD NELSON, lasers; deceased, see previous edition for last biography

LITZENBERGER, SAMUEL CAMERON, agronomy, field crops; deceased, see previous edition for last biography

LIU, ALICE YEE-CHANG, HEAT SHOCK GENES, CELL AGING. *Current Pos:* assoc prof, 84-89, PROF, DEPT BIOL SCI, RUTGERS STATE UNIV, 89-, DIR GRAD PROG, CELL & DEVELOP BIOL. *Personal Data:* b Hunan, China, July 12, 48; US citizen; m 78, Kuang Y Chen; c Andrew & Winston. *Educ:* Chinese Univ Hong Kong, BSc Hons, 69; City Univ New York, PhD(pharmacol), 74. *Prof Exp:* Instr pharmacol, Mt Sinai Sch Med, 73; fel, Sch Med, Yale Univ, 73-77; asst prof pharmacol, Med Sch, Harvard Univ, 77-84. *Concurrent Pos:* Mem, Pharm Sci Rev Comt, NIQMS, NIH, 84-88; mem, Cell Biol Panel, NSF, 89-93; Am Cancer Soc scholar award, 82-85; chmn, Educ Policy Comt, Rutgers State Univ. *Mem:* Am Soc Biochem & Molecular Biol; Am Soc Pharmacol Exp Therapeut. *Res:* Signal transduction and gene expression; transcriptional regulation of heat shock genes in cell aging and differentiation. *Mailing Add:* Dept Biol Sci Nelson Biol Bldg Rutgers State Univ Piscataway NJ 08854-1059. *Fax:* 732-445-3694; *E-Mail:* liu@biology.rutgers.edu

LIU, ANDREW TZE-CHIU, INTERNATIONAL BUSINESS DEVELOPMENT & PETROLEUM ACREAGE ACQUISITION, DENTAL MATERIALS RESEARCH & DEVELOPMENT. *Current Pos:* SPEC PROJ MGR, BISCO INC, 93- *Personal Data:* b Hong Kong, July 20, 29; US citizen; m 55, Helena L Chang; c Genevia K & Andrea K. *Educ:* Ind Univ, Bloomington, BS, 51; Univ Mass, Lowell, MS, 53; London Univ, PhD(org chem), 61; Imp Col London, Eng, DIC, 62. *Prof Exp:* Chemist, A C Lawrence Leather Co, Div Swift Co, 53-55; engr, Textile Res Inst, Beijing, China, 56-58; tech officer, ICI, Ltd, Manchester, Eng, 61-67; res chemist, E I du Pont de Nemours & Co, 67-71; chief exec officer & founder, Marble Industs, Liu Indust Corp, 71-77; prof polymer chem, Ling Nam Univ, 73-74; proj coordr, Conoco, Inc, 77-80, vpres, Continental Overseas Oil, 80-85; chief exec officer, China Ctr Technol Develop, 85-88; dir polymer res & develop & sr res scientist, Dentsply Int, 88-93. *Concurrent Pos:* Lectr polymer chem, Georgetown Univ, 75-76, mgt technol, 91. *Mem:* Am Chem Soc; Int Asn Dent Res; Soc Plastic Engrs; Am Dent Soc; Adhesion Soc. *Res:* Biocompatible polymer process synthesis of monomers; photo initiator synthesis; strategic planning of research and development; management of scientific research and technology development; entrepreneurship in chemical products; granted thirteen patents; inventor of self-lubricating denture teeth material, and computer aided design and manufacturing of denture teeth mold process now used by world largest dental material manufacturer. *Mailing Add:* 1045 Wetherburn Dr York PA 17404. *Fax:* 717-764-8112

LIU, ANTONY A K, REMOTE SENSING, IMAGE PROCESSING. *Current Pos:* oceanogr, 86-92, SR SCIENTIST, GODDARD SPACE FLIGHT CTR/NASA, 93- *Personal Data:* b Taipei, Taiwan, Sept 7, 47; US citizen; m, Linda Chi; c Eileen & Eric. *Educ:* Nat Chung-Hsiing Univ, BS, 70; Johns Hopkins Univ, PhD(mech), 76. *Honors & Awards:* Distinguished Authorship Award, Nat Oceanic & Atmospheric Admin, 86; Award of Excellence, Fed Asian Pac Am Coun, 95. *Prof Exp:* Res scientist, Dynamics Technol Inc, 76-81, sect head ocean technol, 81-86. *Concurrent Pos:* Sci officer, Off Naval Res, 88-89; prin investr, Earth Resources Satellite Proj, Europ Space Agency, 91-, Satellite Verification Proj, Japan Earth Remote Sensing Satellite, 93-95, Const Watch Prog, Nat Oceanic & Atmospheric Admin, 96- & Can Radar Sat Res Prog, 96; vis prof, Ocean Univ Qingdao, China, 94-96 & Nat Taiwan Ocean Univ, 96; consult, Taiwan Cent Weather Bur, 95-97. *Mem:* Am Phys Soc; Am Geophys Union; Sigma Xi; Oceanog Soc. *Res:* Remote sensing research in air-sea-ice interaction, ship wakes, ocean waves and data analysis with applications to climate study, fisheries, oceanography and ocean coastal monitoring using satellite data. *Mailing Add:* Goddard Space Flight Ctr NASA Code 971 Greenbelt MD 20771. *Fax:* 301-286-0240; *E-Mail:* liu@neptune.gsfc.nasa.gov

LIU, BEDE, ELECTRICAL ENGINEERING. *Current Pos:* from asst prof to assoc prof, 62-69, PROF ELEC ENG & DEPT CHMN, PRINCETON UNIV, 69- *Personal Data:* b Shanghai, China, Sept 25, 34; US citizen; m 59; c 1. *Educ:* Nat Taiwan Univ, BSEE, 54; Polytech Inst Brooklyn, MEE, 56, DEE, 60. *Honors & Awards:* Centennial Medal, Inst Elec & Electronic Engrs, 85, Tech Achievement Award, Signal Processing Soc, 85, Educ Award, Circuits Systs Soc, 88. *Prof Exp:* Equipment engr, Western Elec Co, 54-56; mem tech staff commun systs, Bell Tel Labs, 59-62. *Concurrent Pos:* Mem bd dirs, Inst Elec & Electronic Engrs, 84-85. *Mem:* Fel Inst Elec & Electronic Engrs; Inst Elec & Electronic Engrs Circuit Systs Soc (pres, 82). *Res:* Signal and image processing. *Mailing Add:* Dept Elec Eng Princeton Univ Princeton NJ 08544-1099. *E-Mail:* liu@ee.princeton.edu

LIU, BENJAMIN Y H, MECHANICAL ENGINEERING. *Current Pos:* from asst prof to assoc prof, 60-69, PROF MECH ENG, UNIV MINN, MINNEAPOLIS, 69- *Personal Data:* b Shanghai, China, Aug 15, 34; m 58; c 1. *Educ:* Univ Nebr, BSME, 56; Univ Minn, Minneapolis, PhD(mech eng), 60. *Hon Degrees:* Dr, Univ Kupio, Finland, 91. *Honors & Awards:* Fuchs' Prize, Aerosal Soc US, Japan & Ger, 94. *Concurrent Pos:* Guggenheim fel, 68-69, dir, Particle Technol Lab, 73-; sr US scientist award, Alexander von Humboldt Found, WGer. *Mem:* Nat Acad Eng; Solar Energy Soc; Am Soc Heat, Refrig & Air-Conditioning Engrs; Air Pollution Control Asn; fel AAAS. *Res:* Terrestrial and space application of solar energy; aerosol science and technology; instrumentation and measurement. *Mailing Add:* Dept Mech Eng Univ Minn Minneapolis MN 55455

LIU, BING, COATINGS, INKS. *Current Pos:* DIR TECHNOL, ELECTROCAL INC, 96- *Personal Data:* b Linzhon, China, Jan 31, 57; m 85, Yubin Shao; c Ronald & William. *Educ:* SChina Univ Technol, BS, 82; NY Univ, PhD(chem), 96. *Prof Exp:* Chemist, Polytex Environ Inks, 92-94; sr chemist, Pa Color Inc, 94-96. *Mem:* Am Chem Soc; Soc Plastics Engrs. *Mailing Add:* 78 Edwin Rd Electrocal Inc South Windsor CT 06074. *Fax:* 860-289-7847

LIU, C(HANG) K(ENG), MECHANICAL ENGINEERING. *Current Pos:* RETIRED. *Personal Data:* b Soochow, China, Mar 28, 21; nat US; m 51; c 2. *Educ:* Nat Chiao-Tung Univ, China, BS, 43; Univ Ill, MS, 46, PhD(theoret & appl mech), 50. *Prof Exp:* Res assoc theoret & appl mech, Univ Ill, 50-52; ammunition design engr, Picatinny Arsenal, 52; res assoc appl math, Brown Univ, 52-54; from asst prof to prof mech eng, Univ Ala, Tuscaloosa, 63-86. *Concurrent Pos:* Consult, Marshall Space Flight Ctr, NASA, 60-68; fallout shelter analyst, 66- *Mem:* Am Soc Mech Engrs; Am Soc Eng Educ; Soc Eng Sci; Am Inst Aeronaut & Astronaut. *Res:* Radiation safety; fluid mechanics; viscous fluid flow; stability of social and human behavior; heat conduction in solids. *Mailing Add:* 2236 Woodland Rd Tuscaloosa AL 35404-5086

LIU, CHAIN T, CERAMICS ENGINEERING. *Current Pos:* CORP FEL, MARTIN MARIETTA ENERGY SYSTS, INC, 85- *Educ:* Nat Taiwan Univ, BS, 60; Brown Univ, MS, 64, PhD(Mat Sci & Eng), 67. *Honors & Awards:* Pioneer/Jupiter Award, NASA, 74, Pioneer II Saturn Mission Team Award, 77, Spacecrafts Voyage I & II Team Award, 84; IR 100 Award, 79 & 83; Henry J Albert Award, Int Precious Metals Inst, 80; E O Lawrence Award, US Dept Energy, 88; RD 100 Award, 90; Outstanding Achievement Award to Galileo RTG Team, Dept Energy, 90. *Prof Exp:* Teaching asst, Brown Univ, 62-96; sr res staff mem, Oak Ridge Nat Lab, 67-82, group leader, alloying behav & design group, metals & ceramics div, 83- *Concurrent Pos:* Prin ed, J Mat Res, 90-; mem, Adv Tech Awareness Coun, Am Soc Metals, 84. *Mem:* Fel Am Soc Metals; hon platinum mem Int Precious Metals Inst. *Res:* Mechanical behavior of metals, alloys and intermetallic compounds; phase transformation; gas-metal interactions; alloy design of high-temperature materials; metal-matrix composites; environmental effects on ductability and fracture in metals and alloys; 14 patents; numerous technical publications. *Mailing Add:* 122 Newell Lane Oak Ridge TN 37830

LIU, CHAMOND, PERFORMANCE OF OPERATING SYSTEMS. *Current Pos:* AT CLEARITY COMPUT, 94- *Personal Data:* b Waltham, Mass, Sept 28, 48. *Educ:* Univ Calif, Berkeley, AB, 68; Cornell Univ, MS, 71, PhD(math), 73. *Prof Exp:* Asst prof math, Fordham Univ, 73-79; sr assoc programmer, IBM Corp, 79-81, staff programmer, 81-94. *Concurrent Pos:* NSF grant, 75-76. *Mem:* Am Math Soc; Math Asn Am; Asn Comput Mach. *Res:* Performance and performance methodology of large operating systems including automatic work load characterization, automatic work load generation and architectural design. *Mailing Add:* Clearity Comput 4 Elderado Poughkeepsie NY 12603

LIU, CHAO-HAN, PHYSICS, ELECTRICAL ENGINEERING. *Current Pos:* PROF & PRES, NAT CENT UNIV, CHUNG-LI, TAIWAN, 90- *Personal Data:* b Kwangsi, China, Jan 3, 39; m 63, Tsuei-ChuMong; c Alice & Robert. *Educ:* Nat Taiwan Univ, BS, 60; Brown Univ, PhD(elec sci), 65. *Prof Exp:* Res assoc, Univ Ill, Urbana-Champaign, 65-66; from asst prof to prof elec eng, 66-94. *Concurrent Pos:* Chair prof, Nat Taiwan Univ, 81; distinguished lectr, Nat Sci Coun, Taiwan, 88. *Mem:* Am Phys Soc; Am Geophys Union; fel Inst Elec & Electronics Engrs. *Res:* Ionosphere, plasma and atmospheric physics; wave propagation in plasma and random media; radar remote sensing. *Mailing Add:* Nat Cent Univ Chungli Taiwan. *E-Mail:* t341426@ncu865.ncu.edu.tw

LIU, CHEN YA, MECHANICAL ENGINEERING, APPLIED MATHEMATICS. *Current Pos:* CONSULT, 87- *Personal Data:* b Shanghsien, China, Sept 21, 24; US citizen; m 56, Anita Go; c Leo, Isabel & Ursula. *Educ:* Cent Univ, China, BS, 48; NY Univ, MME, 55, EngScD, 59. *Honors & Awards:* Tech Award, NASA. *Prof Exp:* Res engr, Ord Serv, China, 48-52, proj engr, 52-54; instr mech eng, NY Univ, 55-59; asst prof, Carnegie Inst Technol, 59-61; sr res engr, Res Ctr, B F Goodrich Co, 61-64; sr res engr, Columbus Labs, Battelle Mem Inst, 65-69, assoc fel, 69-72, fel, 72-87. *Concurrent Pos:* Consult, Budd Electronics, Inc, 61; lectr, Univ Akron, 62-64. *Mem:* Am Inst Aeronaut & Astronaut; Am Soc Mech Engrs. *Res:* Fluid mechanics and heat transfer; elasticity of orthotropic materials. *Mailing Add:* 3139 Alameda Menlo Park CA 94025

LIU, CHEN-CHING, ELECTRICAL ENGINEERING. *Current Pos:* from asst prof to assoc prof, 83-91, PROF ELEC ENG, UNIV WASH, 91- *Personal Data:* b Taiwan, Dec 30, 54. *Educ:* Nat Taiwan Univ, BS, 76, MS, 78; Univ Calif, Berkeley, PhD(comput sci & elec eng), 83. *Honors & Awards:* Presidential Young Investr Award. *Prof Exp:* Instr elec, Army Signals & Electronic Sch, Taiwan, 78-80. *Concurrent Pos:* Chmn, Expert Syst Task Force, Inst Elec & Electronics Engrs, 87, Seattle Sec, 87-88, Tech Comt on Power Syst, 89; mem exec bd, Power Eng Soc, Inst Elec & Electronics Engrs, 92- *Mem:* Fel Inst Elec & Electronics Engrs; Int Conf Large High Voltage Elec Systs. *Res:* Application of expert systems to electric power systems; develop analytical and computer methods for power systems planning and operation; power electronic circuits analysis. *Mailing Add:* Dept Elec Eng FT-10 Univ Wash Seattle WA 98195. *Fax:* 206-543-3842; *E-Mail:* liu@ee.washington.edu

LIU, CHIEN, INFECTIOUS DISEASES, VIROLOGY. *Current Pos:* assoc prof pediat, 58-63, PROF MED & PEDIAT, SCH MED, UNIV KANS, 63- *Personal Data:* b Canton, China, Mar 6, 21; m 47; c 4. *Educ:* Yenching Univ, BS, 42; WChina Union Univ, MD, 47; Am Bd Pediat, dipl, 64. *Prof Exp:* Intern, Ill Masonic Hosp, 46-47; med intern, Garfield Mem Hosp, Washington, DC, 47-48; asst med, Johns Hopkins Univ, 51-52, asst physician, Johns Hopkins Hosp, 49-52; res assoc bact & immunol, Harvard Med Sch, 52-55, assoc, 55-58, asst prof, 58. *Concurrent Pos:* Res fel med, Sch Med, Johns Hopkins Univ, 49-51; USPHS res career award & Res Career Award, Nat Inst Allergy & Infectious Dis, 63-; vis prof, Nat Defense Med Ctr, Taiwan, 66-67; med consult, US Naval Med Res Unit 2, 66-67. *Mem:* Soc Pediat Res; Am Soc Microbiol; Am Asn Immunologists; Am Acad Microbiol; Infectious Dis Soc Am. *Mailing Add:* Dept Med Univ Kans Sch Med 39th & Rainbow Blvd Kansas City KS 66103-3337

LIU, CHI-LI, bacteriology, biochemistry, for more information see previous edition

LIU, CHING SHI, AERONAUTICS, FLUID DYNAMICS. *Current Pos:* ASSOC PROF ENG SCI, STATE UNIV NY, BUFFALO, 68- *Personal Data:* b Shanghai, China, July 23, 35. *Educ:* SDak Sch Mines & Technol, BS, 57; Kans State Univ, MS, 58; Northwestern Univ, PhD(mech eng), 61. *Prof Exp:* Design engr, Int Harvester Co, 56-57; res engr, Bendix Corp, 59-60; asst prof gas dynamics, Northwestern Technol Inst, 61-68. *Concurrent Pos:* Consult, Cook Res Lab, Ill, 61-62; res assoc, Argonne Nat Lab, 63-64; sr res fel, Calif Inst Technol, 65- *Mem:* Am Inst Aeronaut & Astronaut; Am Soc Mech Engrs; Am Soc Eng Educ; Inst Elec & Electronics Engrs. *Res:* Gas dynamics; magneto gas dynamics; plasma physics. *Mailing Add:* Dept Mech Eng 3435 Main St 316 State Univ NY Buffalo Jarvis Hall Buffalo NY 14260

LIU, CHING-TONG, PHYSIOLOGY, PHARMACOLOGY. *Current Pos:* chief, Dept Clin & Exp Physiol, 84-92, RES PHYSIOLOGIST, US ARMY MED RES INST INFECTIOUS DIS, 73-, ASST CHIEF, DEPT PHYSIOL PHARMACOL, 92- *Personal Data:* b Tai-Shin, Kiangsu, China, Oct 19, 31; US citizen; m 70, In-May Hsin; c Rex, Grace, Jeannette & Christine. *Educ:* Nat Taiwan Univ, BS, 56; Univ Tenn, MS, 59, PhD(physiol), 63. *Prof Exp:* Assoc res biologist pharmacol, Sterling-Winthrop Res Inst, 65-66; asst prof physiol, Baylor Col Med, 66-73. *Concurrent Pos:* USPHS trainee, 63-65; adj prof physiol, Baylor Col Med, 80- *Mem:* Am Soc Pharmacol & Exp Therapeut; Am Physiol Soc; Soc Exp Biol & Med. *Res:* Cardiovascular and renal physiology; water, electrolyte and lipid metabolism; mechanisms of infectious diseases and toxemias; effect of muscle trauma; dynamic functional changes and systematically integrated responses to certain viral infections and toxemias in animals. *Mailing Add:* US Army Med Res Inst Infect Dis SGRD-UIT-P Fort Detrick Frederick MD 21702-5011. *Fax:* 301-619-2348

LIU, CHI-SHENG, PHYSICAL ELECTRONICS, MATHEMATICS. *Current Pos:* SR RES SCIENTIST GASEOUS DISCHARGE, WESTINGHOUSE RES LABS, 69- *Personal Data:* b Chinan, China, Nov 1, 34; US citizen; m 60; c 3. *Educ:* Nat Taiwan Univ, BSEE, 57; WVa Univ, MSEE, 62; Univ Ill, Urbana, PhD(elec eng), 68. *Prof Exp:* Elec engr radio, Philco Corp, 60-61; mem eng staff TV, RCA Consumer Electronics Div, 62-69. *Concurrent Pos:* David Sarnoff fel, RCA, 65-68. *Mem:* Am Phys Soc. *Res:* Study of high pressure gas discharges; high efficiency arc lamps and gas lasers. *Mailing Add:* 11625 Caminito Magnifica San Diego CA 92131

LIU, CHONG TAN, INORGANIC CHEMISTRY. *Current Pos:* sr res chemist, 72-78, GROUP SUPVR, STAUFFER CHEM CO, 79- *Personal Data:* b Shanghai, China, May 11, 36; US citizen; m 63; c 3. *Educ:* Nat Taiwan Univ, BSc, 56; Univ Pittsburgh, PhD(inorg chem), 64. *Prof Exp:* Sr res chemist, Hooker Chem Corp, 64-71. *Mem:* Am Chem Soc. *Res:* Water treatment; industrial chemical processes; metal finishing; plating on plastics; corrosion controls; high temperature chemistry; coordination chemistry. *Mailing Add:* 3 Demarest Mill Ct West Nyack NY 10994-1502

LIU, CHUAN SHENG, THEORETICAL SPACE PHYSICS, PLASMA PHYSICS. *Current Pos:* chmn, Dept Physics & Astron, 85-90, PROF PHYSICS, UNIV MD, 90- *Personal Data:* b Kwanhsi, China, Jan 9, 39; m 65, Jing Y Hong; c Albert, Benjamine, Jennifer & Anna. *Educ:* Tunghai Univ, BS, 60; Univ Calif, Berkeley, MA, 64, PhD(physics), 68. *Prof Exp:* Asst prof in residence physics, Univ Calif, Los Angeles, 68-70; vis scientist, Gulf Gen Atomic, Inc, 70-71; mem, Inst Advan Study, 71-74. *Concurrent Pos:* Dir, Theoret Sci Div, GA Technolofgies, 81-84; chmn, Div Plasma Physics, Am Phys Soc. *Mem:* Fel Am Phys Soc; AAAS. *Res:* Fusion and plasma physics; space plasma physics. *Mailing Add:* Dept Physics Univ Md College Park MD 20742

LIU, CHUI HSUN, ANALYTICAL CHEMISTRY, INORGANIC CHEMISTRY. *Current Pos:* prof, 65-95, EMER PROF CHEM, ARIZ STATE UNIV, 95- *Personal Data:* b China, Nov 5, 31; US citizen; m 62. *Educ:* Univ Ill, BA, 52, PhD(chem), 57. *Prof Exp:* From asst prof to assoc prof chem, Polytech Inst Brooklyn, 57-65. *Mem:* Am Chem Soc. *Res:* Chemistry, electrochemistry and spectroscopy in molten salts and other nonaqueous solvents; chemistry of coordination compounds; chelating agents in chemical separations and analyses. *Mailing Add:* Dept Chem & Biochem Ariz State Univ PO Box 871604 Tempe AZ 85287-1604

LIU, CHUNG LAUNG, COMPUTER SCIENCE. *Current Pos:* PROF COMPUT SCI, UNIV ILL, URBANA, 73- *Personal Data:* b Canton, China, Oct 25, 34; US citizen; m 60; c 1. *Educ:* Cheng Kung Univ, Taiwan, BSc, 56; Mass Inst Technol, SM, 60, ScD(elec eng), 62. *Honors & Awards:* Karl V Karlstron Outstanding Educr Award, Asn Comput Mach, 90. *Prof Exp:* From asst prof to assoc prof elec eng, Mass Inst Technol, 62-72. *Mem:* Inst Elec & Electronics Engrs; Asn Comput Mach. *Res:* Theory of computation; combinatorial mathematics. *Mailing Add:* Dept Comput Sci Univ Ill 1304 W Springfield Urbana IL 61801-2910

LIU, CHUNG-CHIUN, CHEMICAL ENGINEERING. *Current Pos:* PROF CHEM ENG, CASE WESTERN RESERVE UNIV, 78- *Personal Data:* b Canton, China, Oct 8, 36; m 67; c Peter. *Educ:* Cheng Kung Univ, Taiwan, BS, 59; Calif Inst Technol, MS, 62; Case Western Reserve Univ, PhD(chem eng), 68. *Prof Exp:* Res assoc, Eng Design Ctr, Case Western Reserve Univ, 68; prof chem eng, Univ Pittsburgh, 68-78. *Concurrent Pos:* Wallace R Persons Prof sensor technol & control. *Mem:* Am Inst Chem Engrs; Electrochem Soc. *Res:* Electrochemistry; biomedical engineering; material science. *Mailing Add:* 2917 E Overlook Rd Cleveland OH 44118. *Fax:* 216-368-8738; *E-Mail:* cxl9@po.cwru.edu

LIU, CHUNG-YEN, AERONAUTICAL ENGINEERING. *Current Pos:* From asst prof to prof eng, 62-, EMER PROF, UNIV CALIF, LOS ANGELES. *Personal Data:* b Canton, China. *Educ:* Nat Cheng-Kung Univ, BS, 56; Brown Univ, MS, 58; Calif Inst Technol, PhD(aeronaut), 62. *Mem:* Am Phys Soc; Am Inst Aeronaut & Astronaut. *Res:* Fluid mechanics. *Mailing Add:* 860 Gregna Greenway Los Angeles CA 90049. *Fax:* 310-838-5654

LIU, DARRELL T, BIOCHEMISTRY. *Current Pos:* dep dir, Div Bact Prod Chief, Biochem Br, Bur Biol, 75-80, DIR, DIV BIOCHEM & BIOPHYS, OFF BIOL RES, CTR BIOL, EVAL RES, FOOD & DRUG ADMIN, 80- *Personal Data:* b Taiwan, Repub China, May 24, 32; US citizen; c 3. *Educ:* Nat Taiwan Univ, BS, 55; Univ Pittsburgh, PhD, 61. *Prof Exp:* Res assoc, Rockefeller Univ, 61-65, asst prof, 65-67; biochemist, Brookhaven Nat Lab, 67-69, sr biochemist, 69-73; res chemist, Develop Immunol Br, Nat Inst Child Health Develop, NIH, 73, sr chief biochem microbial struct, 74. *Concurrent Pos:* Mem, Regulatory Sci Prom Comt, Food & Drug Admin, 79-80, Recombinant DNA Rev Comt, 81-89. *Mem:* Sigma Xi; Am Soc Biol Chemists. *Res:* Human C-reactive protein; prototypic acute phase reactant; employing molecular cloning techniques to explore the mechanism of induction and control of the biosynthesis of this protein at the chromosomal level; technique of homologous gene transfection is being pursued to investigate the possible physiological function of CRP in xenopus; isolation and cloning of the genes coding for the enzymes and substrate proteins associated with a unique coagulation cascade system form Limulus. *Mailing Add:* Academia Sinica Nankang Taipei Taipei 115 Taiwan

LIU, DAVID H(O-FENG), CHEMICAL ENGINEERING. *Current Pos:* MGR NEW PROD DEVELOP, J T BAKER, INC, 82- *Personal Data:* b Chekiang, China, Feb 24, 28; m 56; c 2. *Educ:* Jadavpur Univ, BSc, 51; Univ Pa, MSc, 54, PhD(chem eng), 56. *Prof Exp:* Sr chem engr, Monsanto Chem Co, 55-62; supvr chem eng res, Mobil Chem Co, Tex, 64-66; sr res chemist, Uniroyal Inc, 66-74; mgr process develop, Rhone-Poulenc Inc, 74-82. *Mem:* Am Chem Soc; Am Inst Chem Engrs. *Res:* Chemical thermodynamics; reaction kinetics; unit operations, engineering and economic analysis; pollution abatement; petrochemical processes; aroma chemicals; polymers; rubber and specialty chemicals; research specialty chemical, and electronic chemicals. *Mailing Add:* 829 Cherry Hill Rd Princeton NJ 08540-7712

LIU, DAVID SHIAO-KUNG, FLUID MECHANICS, NUMERICAL METHODS. *Current Pos:* Phys scientist fluid mech, 72-76, SR PHYS SCIENTIST, RAND CORP, 76-; PROF HYDRAUL, NAT CHENG-KUNG UNIV, 77- *Personal Data:* b Chung-King, China, Aug 27, 40; US citizen; m 66; c 3. *Educ:* Cheng-Kung Univ, Taiwan, BS, 62; Univ Calif, Berkeley, MS, 65; New York Univ, PhD(appl math & hydraul), 73. *Concurrent Pos:* Sr consult, Va Inst Marine Sci, 77-; adv, Sci & Technol adv Group, Taiwan. *Mem:* Am Soc Civil Eng; Int Asn Water Resources. *Res:* Numerical modeling of three-dimensional non-homogeneous geophysical fluid systems; stochastic analysis and control theory of physical systems. *Mailing Add:* 3706 Oceanhill Way Malibu CA 90265

LIU, DENNIS DONG, THIN FILM TECHNOLOGIES, SEMICONDUCTOR TECHNOLOGIES. *Current Pos:* SR ENGR, SILTEC SILICON, 94- *Personal Data:* m 86, Shauna H Wang. *Educ:* Xian Jiantong Univ, BSc, 82; Univ Man, MSc, 85, PhD(mat & devices), 92. *Prof Exp:* Res assoc, Dept Elec Eng, Univ Alta, 92-94. *Mem:* Mat Res Soc. *Res:* Thin film technologies for the deposition and characterization of films; application of plasma technologies; semiconductor processes for electronic devices; vacuum and gas flow systems. *Mailing Add:* Siltec Silicon 1351 Tandem Ave Salem OR 97302-0139. *Fax:* 541-540-2600

LIU, DICKSON LEE SHEN, MICROBIOLOGY, WATER POLLUTION. *Current Pos:* assoc prof, 81-89, PROF, DEPT ENVIRON HEALTH SCI, TULANE MED CTR, NEW ORLEANS, LA, 90-; RES SCIENTIST TOXIC SUBSTANCES, NAT WATER RES INST, 75- *Personal Data:* b Shantung, China, Apr 6, 35; Can citizen; m 67, Alice; c Stanley K. *Educ:* Nat Taiwan Chung Hsin Univ, BSc, 62; Univ BC, MSc, 66, PhD(microbiol), 71. *Prof Exp:* Res scientist marine biochem, BC Res Coun, 66-68; res scientist eutrophication, Can Ctr Inland Waters, 71-72; res scientist wastewaters, Can Wastewater Technol Ctr, 72-75. *Concurrent Pos:* Expert, Food Agr Orgn, UN, 68-; adv, Wastewater Technol Ctr, 75-; tech ed, Can Res, 77-83; mem, Assoc Comt Sci Criteria Environ Qual, Nat Res Coun Can, 77-80; expert biodegradation, Can Nat Comt, Int Orgn Stand, 77-; co-chmn, Int Symposia on Toxicity Assessment using Microbial Systs, 83-; co-ed, Toxicity Assessment: An Int J, 86-90, Environ Toxicol Water Qual, Int J, 91-; vis prof, Okayama Univ, Japan, 93. *Res:* Biodegradation of toxic substances; development of standard procedure for assessing the persistence of new substances in the natural environments; lake and river eutrophication; biological treatment of toxic industrial wastewaters; environmental toxicology; biotechnology. *Mailing Add:* Nat Water Res Inst PO Box 5050 Burlington ON L7R 4A6 Can. *Fax:* 905-336-4989; *E-Mail:* dickson.liu@cciw.ca

LIU, FOOK FAH, high energy physics; deceased, see previous edition for last biography

LIU, FRED WEI JUI, PHYSICAL CHEMISTRY. *Current Pos:* DIR, CONTINENTAL CONSULTS, INC, 64-; PRES, CONTINENTAL TRADING CO, 65- *Personal Data:* b Canton, China, Jan 29, 26; nat US; m 61. *Educ:* St John's Univ, China, BS, 48; Temple Univ, MA, 50; Lehigh Univ, PhD(chem), 52. *Prof Exp:* Res assoc, Lehigh Leather Inst, Pa, 52-53; chief chemist, Lester Labs, Inc, 53-64. *Mem:* Am Chem Soc; Nat Asn Corrosion Engrs. *Res:* Colloid or surface chemistry; detergents; cleaning and maintenance chemicals formulation; corrosion; water treatment; foreign trade; industrial chemicals. *Mailing Add:* 157 Lake Forest Lane NE Atlanta GA 30342-3209

LIU, FREDERICK F, SYSTEMS DESIGN & SYSTEMS SCIENCE. *Current Pos:* PRES & SCI DIR, QUANTUM DYNAMICS, INC, 59- *Personal Data:* b Chefoo, China, Apr 19, 19; US citizen; m 46; c 2. *Educ:* Technische Hochschule, Berlin, dipl, 39; Carnegie Inst Technol, BS, 46; Princeton Univ, PhD(sci admin), 51. *Hon Degrees:* DSc, Polytech Univ Inst, China, various univ & insts, 54. *Prof Exp:* Res asst, Princeton Univ, 50-52, res assoc, 52-55; res eng specialist, Rockethyne & Atomics Int, NAm Aviation, Inc, 55-57; dir res, Dresser Dynamics, Inc, 57, exec vpres, 57-59. *Concurrent Pos:* Vis lectr, Mass Inst Technol, 56 & Cambridge Univ, Eng, 64; vis scientist, Kyoto Univ, Japan, 67-; guest lectr, Technische Univ, Berlin, 70-; vis scientist & prof, Inst Mech, Chinese Acad Sci, 79- *Mem:* Sigma Xi; Am Phys Soc; Am Inst Aeronaut & Astronaut; assoc fel Int Inst Refrigeration; fel Am Inst Elec Eng. *Res:* Extremely fast, dynamic and transient phenomena relating to propulsion, weapon, nuclear and space; low temperature physical phenomena, trans-regine viscosity effects on fluid flow theory, together with the development of a range of modern instrumentation and computing technologies. *Mailing Add:* 17812 Community St Northridge CA 91325-3928

LIU, FU-WEN (FRANK), pomology, postharvest horticulture, for more information see previous edition

LIU, GANG-YU, CHEMISTRY. *Current Pos:* ASST PROF CHEM, WAYNE STATE UNIV, 94- *Personal Data:* b Zhengzhou, China, Apr 19, 64; m 87, Xiaoyuan Li. *Educ:* Peking Univ, China, BS, 88; Princeton Univ, MS, 90, PhD, 92. *Prof Exp:* Postdoctoral assoc, Univ Calif, Berkeley, 92-94. *Concurrent Pos:* Miller res fel, Miller Res Inst Basic Res Sci, 92-94; Camille & Henry Dreyfus fel, 94- *Mem:* AAAS; Am Chem Soc; Am Phys Soc; Am Vacuum Soc. *Mailing Add:* Dept Chem Wayne State Univ Detroit MI 48202

LIU, HAIYING, MAGNETIC RESONANCE IMAGING, BIOMEDICAL ENGINEERING. *Current Pos:* ASST PROF RADIOL, UNIV MINN, 96- *Personal Data:* b Shanghai, China, 63. *Educ:* Jilin Univ, BS, 85; Univ Minn, PhD(solid state physics), 91. *Prof Exp:* Staff scientist, Picker Int Inc, 90-96. *Mem:* Am Phys Soc. *Res:* Develop a better magnetic resonance imaging system for clinical diagnosis and interventional procedure; reserch and develop new medical devices for minimally invasive surgical procedures; solid state device physics; fabrication and application in medicine. *Mailing Add:* Mayo Bldg Box 292 420 Delaware St SE Minneapolis MN 55455. *E-Mail:* liu@spaarky.drad.umn.edu

LIU, HAN-SHOU, EARTH PHYSICS, SPACE PHYSICS. *Current Pos:* SCIENTIST, GODDARD SPACE FLIGHT CTR, NASA, 65- *Personal Data:* b Hunan, China, Mar 9, 30; US citizen; m 57; c 2. *Educ:* Cornell Univ, MS, 62, PhD, 63. *Honors & Awards:* Apollo Achievement Award, NASA,

69. *Prof Exp:* Res assoc, Nat Acad Sci, 63-64. *Mem:* Fel AAAS; Am Astron Soc; Am Geophys Union; Am Inst Aeronaut & Astronaut; Planetary Soc. *Res:* Physics of the earth; planetary interiors. *Mailing Add:* Goddard Space Flight Ctr Code 921 NASA Greenbelt MD 20771

LIU, HAO-WEN, MECHANICS, MATERIALS SCIENCE. *Current Pos:* RETIRED. *Personal Data:* b China, Aug 20, 26; nat US; m 55; c 5. *Educ:* Univ Ill, BS, 54, MS, 56, PhD(appl mech), 59. *Prof Exp:* Asst prof appl mech, Univ Ill, 59-61; sr res fel, Calif Inst Technol, 61-63; assoc prof metall, Syracuse Univ, 63-68, prof mat sci, 68-84, prof mech & aeronaut eng, 84-93. *Mem:* Am Soc Mech Engrs; Am Inst Mech Engrs; Am Soc Testing & Mat; Sigma Xi. *Res:* Mechanical behavior and properties of materials and applied mechanics. *Mailing Add:* 1040 Continentals Way Belmont CA 94002

LIU, HENRY, FLUID MECHANICS. *Current Pos:* From asst prof to assoc prof, 65-77, PROF CIVIL ENG, UNIV MO-COLUMBIA, 77- *Personal Data:* b Peking, China, June 3, 36; m 64. *Educ:* Nat Taiwan Univ, BS, 59; Colo State Univ, MS, 63, PhD(fluid mech), 66. *Honors & Awards:* Aerospace Div Award, Am Soc Civil Engrs; Distinguished Lectr Award, Int Freight Pipeline Soc. *Concurrent Pos:* Prin investr water resources res grants, Dept Interior, 66-68, Capsule Pipeline res grants, US Dept Energy, 78-81 & NSF grants, 80-86; vis prof, Univ Melbourne, Australia, 80; prof, Natural Gas Pipeline Co, 83-87, endowed chair, James C Dowell, 88-; bd dirs, US Wind Eng Res Coun, 85-89; chmn, Exec Comt, Aerospace Div, Am Soc Civil Engrs, 89-90. *Mem:* Am Soc Civil Engrs; Am Wind Energy Asn; Sigma Xi; US Wind Eng Res Coun; Int Freight Pipeline Soc (pres, 89-93). *Res:* Electrokinetics; exploration of the physics of streaming potential fluctuations and the utilization of this phenomenon to study turbulence characteristics in liquid flows; dispersion of pollutants in river; hydraulic capsule pipeline; wind pressure inside buildings; flow measurement; cherepnov water lifter; hydropower; wind damage mitigation; wind energy utilization. *Mailing Add:* Dept Civil Eng Univ Mo E2509 Eng Bldg Columbia MO 65211

LIU, HOUNG-ZUNG, BIOCHEMICAL & PLANT PROTOPLAST GENETICS. *Current Pos:* assoc prof genetics, 64-69, actg dean, Fac Arts & Sci, 81-82, prof genetics & chmn, Dept Biol Sci, 69-81, DEAN, FAC ARTS & SCI, STATE UNIV NY COL, PLATTSBURGH, 83- *Personal Data:* b China, Jan 23, 31; m 69; c 2. *Educ:* Taiwan Prov Col, BS, 53; NDak State Col, MS, 59; Cornell Univ, PhD(genetics, biochem, plant physiol), 64. *Prof Exp:* Asst cytol, Taiwan Agr Res Inst, Taipei, 54-56; asst gen genetics, Cornell Univ, 59-64. *Concurrent Pos:* NIH spec res fel, Marquette Univ, 67-68; res collabr, Brookhaven Nat Lab, 73-74. *Mem:* AAAS; Am Chem Soc; Genetics Soc Am; Int Plant Tissue Asn. *Res:* Tryptophan operon mutants of Escherichia coli and indoleglycerol-phosphate synthetase; plant protoplast fusion and culture; plantlet regeneration. *Mailing Add:* Dean Arts & Sci State Univ NY Col Plattsburgh 95 Broad St Plattsburgh NY 12901-2601

LIU, HSING-JANG, SYNTHETIC METHODS NATURAL PRODUCTS SYNTHESIS. *Current Pos:* from asst prof to assoc prof, 71-83, PROF CHEM, UNIV ALTA, 83- *Personal Data:* b Kiang-Su, China, Dec 2, 42; m 66, Hsiao-Ku Liao; c Richard, Jonathan & Mimi. *Educ:* Nat Taiwan Norm Univ, BSc, 64; Univ NB, Fredericton, PhD(chem), 68. *Honors & Awards:* Int Union Pure & Appl Chem Award, Can Nat Comt, 84. *Prof Exp:* Fel chem, Univ NB, Fredericton, 68-69; res assoc, Columbia Univ, 69-70; teaching & res assoc, Univ NB, Fredericton, 70-71. *Concurrent Pos:* Sci consult, Torcan Chem Ltd, Aurora, Can, 84-; vis examr chem, Chinese Univ Hong Kong, 91-94; natural prod ed, Can J Chem, 95- *Mem:* Am Chem Soc; fel Chem Inst Can. *Res:* Natural products, isolation, identification and synthesis; development of novel synthetic methods. *Mailing Add:* Dept Chem Univ Alta Edmonton AB T6G 2G2 Can. *Fax:* 403-492-8231

LIU, HUA-KUANG, LASER OPTICS, ELECTROOPTICS. *Current Pos:* PROF, UNIV SALA, 95- *Personal Data:* b Kueilin, China, Sept 2, 39; m 65; c 2. *Educ:* Nat Taiwan Univ, BS, 62; Univ Iowa, MS, 65; Johns Hopkins Univ, PhD(elec eng), 69. *Prof Exp:* Res asst, Univ Iowa, 63-64; instr elec eng, Va Mil Inst, 64-65; res asst, Johns Hopkins Univ & jr instr, Eve Col, 65-69; from asst prof to prof elec eng, Univ Ala, 69-84; sr res eng, Jet Propulsion Lab, Calif Inst Technol, 84-95. *Concurrent Pos:* Consult, Optimal Data Corp, Ala, 69-, NASA Marshall Space Flight Ctr, US Army Missile Command, 73 & Newport Res Corp, Rockwell Int; res grants, Univ Ala, Tuscaloosa, 70-71, NSF, 71-73 & 75-77 & NASA, 73-78; pres, Lumin, Inc, 75; vis assoc prof elec eng, Stanford Univ, 75-76; vis prof, Nat Taiwan Univ & Univ Wis-Madison, 82-83. *Mem:* Sr mem Inst Elec & Electronics Engrs; fel Optical Soc Am; fel Soc Photo-Instrumentation Engrs. *Res:* Solid-state electronics; nonlinear optical image processing; optical pattern recognition, holography and holographic nondestructive testing; halftone contact screens for printing. *Mailing Add:* 1240 Blair Ave South Pasadena CA 91030

LIU, HUNG-WEN, BIO-ORGANIC CHEMISTRY, MECHANISTIC ENZYMOLOGY. *Current Pos:* Fel enzym, 81-84, from asst prof to assoc prof, 84-94, PROF BIO-ORG CHEM, UNIV MINN, 94- *Personal Data:* b Taipei, Taiwan, Aug 28, 52. *Educ:* Tang-hai Univ, Taiwan, BS, 74; Columbia Univ, PhD(chem), 81. *Honors & Awards:* Distinguished New Fac Chem, Dryfuss Found, 84; Res Career Develop Award, NIH, 90; Jr Fac Award, Am Chem Soc, 85, Horace Isabelle Award, 93. *Mem:* Am Chem Soc; AAAS; Am Soc Biochem & Molecular Biol; Chinese Am Chem Soc. *Res:* Bio-organic chemistry; mechanistic enzymology. *Mailing Add:* Dept Chem Univ Minn Minneapolis MN 55455

LIU, J(OSEPH) T(SU) C(HIEH), FLUID MECHANICS. *Current Pos:* from asst prof to assoc prof, 66-73, PROF ENG, BROWN UNIV, 73- *Personal Data:* b Shanghai, China, Nov 9, 34; US citizen; m 64; c 3. *Educ:* Univ Mich, BSE, 57, MSE, 58; Calif Inst Technol, PhD(aeronaut), 64. *Honors & Awards:* Nat Award, Inst Aeronaut Sci, 58. *Prof Exp:* Propulsion engr aerothermodyn group, Gen Dynamics & Convair, 58-59; res assoc aerospace & mech sci, Gas Dynamics Lab, Princeton Univ, 64-66. *Concurrent Pos:* Consult, Space Systs Div, Avco Corp, Mass, 66-67, Systs Div, 69-70; vis, Dept Math, Imperial Col, Univ London, 72-73 & 79-80. *Mem:* Am Soc Mech Engrs; Am Phys Soc; Am Meteorol Soc; Am Inst Aeronaut & Astronaut. *Res:* Coherent structures in turbulent shear flows, nonlinear hydrodynamic stability and transition; aeroacoustics; fluidized bed instabilities. *Mailing Add:* Div Eng Brown Univ Providence RI 02912-9127

LIU, JIA-MING, OPTICS, ELECTRICAL ENGINEERING. *Current Pos:* assoc prof, 86-93, PROF ELEC ENG, UNIV CALIF, LOS ANGELES, 93- *Personal Data:* b Taichung, Taiwan, July, 13, 53; US citizen; m 90, Vida Chang; c Janelle J. *Educ:* Nat Chiao Tung Univ, BS, 75; Harvard Univ, SM, 79, PhD(appl physics), 82. *Prof Exp:* Asst prof elec eng, State Univ NY, Buffalo, 82-84; sr mem tech staff, Gen Tel & Electronics Corp Labs, Inc, 83-86. *Concurrent Pos:* Consult, Jaycor, 87-; Battelle Columbus Div, US Army, 89-90; Gen Tel & Electronics Corp, Patent Award, 86, 87, 88, 89. *Mem:* Fel Optical Soc Am; sr mem Inst Elec & Electronics Engrs Laser & Electro-Optics Soc; Am Phys Soc; Sigma Xi. *Res:* Ultrashort laser pulses and applications; nonlinear optics; optical wave propagation; semiconductor lasers optoelectronics; fiber optics. *Mailing Add:* Elec Eng Dept Univ Calif 56-147C Eng IV Los Angeles CA 90024. *Fax:* 310-206-8495; *E-Mail:* liu@ee.ucla.edu

LIU, JIN-ZHOU, INFANT NUTRITION, PREVENTIVE MEDICINE. *Current Pos:* PROJ LEADER RES & DEVELOP, ABBOTT LABS, 94- *Personal Data:* b Teng-Zhou, China, Oct 20, 55; m 84, Shen Pan; c Fang Yuan & Devin R. *Educ:* Shandong Med Univ, China, MD, 82, MS, 85; Pa State Univ, PhD(nutrit), 93. *Honors & Awards:* Nat Med Res Award, Chinese Ministry Pub Health, 86; Young Outstanding Scientist Award, Chinese Nutrit Soc, 88; Med Discoverer in 20th Century, Chinese Acad Med Sci, 89. *Prof Exp:* Asst prof nutrit, Shandong Med Univ, 86-87; res asst prof, Pa State Univ, 93-94. *Concurrent Pos:* Adj asst prof & prin investr, Pa State Univ, 95-96. *Mem:* Am Soc Nutrit Sci; Am Soc Clin Nutrit; Asn Gnotobiotics; Chinese Nutrit Soc. *Res:* Dietary factors for preventing cancer; nutritional factors for preventing infant diseases; novel approaches for preventing infectious diseases. *Mailing Add:* Ross Prod Div Abbott Labs 625 Cleveland Ave Columbus OH 43215. *Fax:* 614-624-3453; *E-Mail:* t75jil1@ov.rossnutrition.com

LIU, JOHN, OPHTHALMIC PHARMACOLOGY. *Current Pos:* ASSOC PROF, DEPT OPHTHAL, UNIV CALIF LOS ANGELES, 91- *Personal Data:* b Taiwan. *Prof Exp:* Assoc scientist, Eye Res Inst, 88-91. *Mailing Add:* Dept Ophthal Univ Calif Los Angeles San Diego 9500 Gilman Dr La Jolla CA 92093-0946

LIU, JOHN K(UNGFU), MECHANICS. *Current Pos:* VPRES, CLUTCH DIV, PHILADELPHIA GEAR CORP, 68- *Personal Data:* b Hankow, China, Aug 22, 30; nat US; m 57. *Educ:* Univ Pa, BSME, 52; Ill Inst Technol, MS, 57. *Prof Exp:* Struct engr, Shih & Assoc, 48-52; from design engr to proj engr, Int Harvester Co, 52-57; from sr proj engr to actg dir res & develop, Clearing Div, US Industs, 57-60, dir marine tech dept, Tech Ctr, 59-60; mgr marine tech lab, Stromberg Carlson Co Div, Gen Dynamics Co, 60-62; vpres, Force Control, Inc, 62-68. *Mem:* Am Soc Mech Engrs; Sigma Xi; Am Soc Inventors. *Res:* Oceanographic instruments and devices; solid and fluid mechanics; marine propulsion equipment; pressure vessel design and development; fluid shear power transmission devices; industrial electronics and transducers. *Mailing Add:* 2749 Paige St Lower Burrell PA 15068-3111

LIU, JOSEPH JENG-FU, CELESTIAL & THEORETICAL MECHANICS, APPLIED MATHEMATICS. *Current Pos:* CHIEF, ASTRODYNAMICS DIVISION, HQ A F SPACE COMMAND, 86- *Personal Data:* b Chiangsi, China, Oct 24, 40; m 71; c 3. *Educ:* Cheng Kung Univ, Taiwan, BS, 62; Auburn Univ, MS, 66, PhD(celestial mech), 71. *Honors & Awards:* P V H Weems Award, Inst Navig, 88. *Prof Exp:* Teaching asst appl mech, Cheng Kung Univ, 63-64 & Auburn Univ, 66-71; mem res staff astrodyn, Northrop Serv, Inc, Huntsville, Ala, 71-77; mem tech staff Astrodyn Aerospace Defense Command, 77-86. *Concurrent Pos:* Adj, asst prof appl math, Univ Colo, Colorado Springs, 87- *Mem:* Assoc fel Am Inst Aeronaut & Astronaut; Am Astronaut Soc; Am Astron Soc. *Res:* General, special perturbation and semi-analytic theories, their applications for the orbital and attitude motions of an artificial satellite perturbed by conservative and nonconservative forces. *Mailing Add:* HQ AFSPACECOM/DOJY Stop 7 Peterson AFB CO 80914-4110

LIU, JUN S, MATHEMATICAL STATISTICS. *Current Pos:* ASST PROF STATIST, HARVARD UNIV, 91- *Personal Data:* b Beijing, China, Apr 26, 65. *Educ:* Beijiung Univ, BS, 86; Univ Chicago, PhD(statist), 91. *Concurrent Pos:* Vis fac, Nat Ctr Biotechnol Info, NIH, 93. *Mem:* Am Statist Asn; Inst Math Statist. *Res:* Bayesian methodology in statistical analysis, including theory, applications and computing, especially applications in molecular biology and genetics; Markov chain theory and missing data problems. *Mailing Add:* Dept Statist Stanford Univ Stanford CA 94305. *E-Mail:* jliu@stat.harvard.edu

LIU, K J RAY, SIGNAL PROCESSING, COMMUNICATIONS. *Current Pos:* Asst prof, 90-95, ASSOC PROF, UNIV MD, 95- *Personal Data:* b Taiwan, Feb 11, 61; US citizen. *Educ:* Nat Taiwan Univ, BS, 83; Univ Calif, Los Angeles, PhD(elec eng), 90. *Honors & Awards:* Young Investr Award, NSF, 94. *Concurrent Pos:* Vis assoc prof, Stanford Univ, 96-97; chief scientist, Neo Paradigm Lab, 96-97. *Res:* Signal processing with application to image video, wireless communication, networking and medical technology. *Mailing Add:* Elec Eng Dept Univ Md College Park MD 20742

LIU, KAI, CONTROL & SYSTEMS, MODELING & SIMULATION. *Current Res Pos:* SR RES ENGR, AUTOMATION & ROBOTICS RES INST, UNIV TEX, ARLINGTON, 90- *Personal Data:* b Beijing, China, June 20, 48; m, Hong Xu; c Julie. *Educ:* Beijing Normal Univ, China, BS, 80; Beijing Polytech Univ, China, MS, 82; Ga Inst Technol, PhD(elec eng), 90. *Prof Exp:* Lectr, Elec Eng Dept, Beijing Polytech Univ, 82-86. *Concurrent Pos:* Specialist, Elec Eng Dept, Univ Tex Arlington, 91- *Mem:* Sigma Xi; Inst Elec & Electronics Engrs; Inst Elect & Electronics Engrs Robotics & Automation Soc; Inst Elec & Electronics Engrs Control Systs Soc; Inst Elec & Electronics Engrs Neural Networks Coun. *Res:* Theoretical issues about fuzzy logic control and neural nets and their applications in automatic control, material handling, system identification and signal processing; continuous robust techniques to various industrial applications. *Mailing Add:* 2101 Oak Bluff Dr Arlington TX 76006-5758. *Fax:* 817-794-5952; *E-Mail:* kliu@arri.uta.edu

LIU, LEROY FONG, DNA TOPOISOMERASES, CANCER PHARMACOLOGY. *Current Pos:* from asst prof to assoc prof, 80-88, PROF BIOCHEM, JOHNS HOPKINS UNIV, 88- *Personal Data:* b Tao-yuan, Taiwan, July 28, 49; US citizen; m; c 2. *Educ:* Nat Taiwan Univ, Taiwan, BS, 71; Univ Calif, Berkeley, PhD(biophys chem), 77. *Prof Exp:* Fel molecular biol, Harvard Univ, 77-78 & Univ Calif, San Francisco, 78-80. *Concurrent Pos:* Vis prof, Inst Molecular Biol, Academia Sinica, Taiwan, 86-87. *Mem:* Am Soc Biochem & Molecular Biol; Am Asn Cancer Res; Am Math Soc. *Res:* Biological functions of multiple DNA topoisomerases; DNA topoisomerases as therapeutic targets. *Mailing Add:* Dept Pharmacol UMDNJ-Robert Wood Johnson Med Sch 675 Hoes Lane Piscataway NJ 08854

LIU, LIU, THEORY OF ELECTRONIC PROPERTIES OF SOLIDS. *Current Pos:* From asst prof to assoc prof, 61-74, PROF PHYSICS, NORTHWESTERN UNIV, ILL, 74- *Personal Data:* b Shanghai, China, Aug 12, 30; m 56; c 3. *Educ:* Univ Taiwan, BS, 54; Univ Chicago, MS, 57, PhD(physics), 61. *Concurrent Pos:* Consult, Argonne Nat Lab, 61-64; Fulbright sr res scholar, France, 75-76. *Mem:* Fel Am Phys Soc. *Res:* Theory of narrow-gap and zero-gap semiconductors and magnetic semiconductors. *Mailing Add:* Dept Physics Northwestern Univ 633 Clark St Evanston IL 60201

LIU, LON-CHANG, PHYSICS, NUCLEAR STRUCTURE. *Current Pos:* STAFF MEM, LOS ALAMOS NAT LAB, 79- *Personal Data:* b China; US citizen. *Educ:* Univ Neuchatel, PhD(physics), 73. *Prof Exp:* Instr, City Univ New York, 73-75, asst prof physics, 75-79. *Mem:* Am Phys Soc; Sigma Xi. *Res:* Theoretical intermediate energy nuclear physics; meson nucleus interaction; neural network. *Mailing Add:* Group T-2 MS B243 Los Alamos Nat Lab Los Alamos NM 87545. *E-Mail:* liu@lanl.gov

LIU, MAO-ZU, MATHEMATICAL MODELING OF PHYSIOLOGICAL SYSTEM & BIOMEDICAL ENGINEERING, TECHNICAL MANAGEMENT. *Current Pos:* DIR DEPT BIOMED ENG, BRONX-LEBANON HOSP CTR, 92- *Personal Data:* b Sichuan, China, June 27, 46; m 89, Jane X Ding; c Rose D & Thomas Y. *Educ:* Univ Sci & Technol China, BS, 65; Temple Univ, MA, 84; Drexel Univ, PhD(biomed eng), 89. *Honors & Awards:* Award First Sci Convocation of Anhui Prov, State Coun Anhui Prov, China & State Coun, People's Repub China, 78. *Prof Exp:* Researcher & mgr, Anhui Inst Seismol, Anhui, China, 72-79; lectr physics, Univ Sci & Technol, Shanghai, China, 79-80; researcher, Seismic Telecommun Network, Shanghai, China, 80-81; asst prof, Univ Tenn, 89-92; res biomed engr, Westchester County Med Ctr, 91-92. *Mem:* Inst Elec & Electronics Engrs; Biomed Eng Soc. *Res:* Mathematical modeling of the cardiovascular system and the application of computer techniques to cardiovascular dynamics and pharmacokinetics; the design and optimization of devices used in cardiovascular treatment and biomedical instrumentation. *Mailing Add:* 7 Belmont St White Plains NY 10605

LIU, MATTHEW J P, MATHEMATICS. *Current Pos:* From instr to assoc prof, 61-76, PROF MATH, UNIV WIS, STEVENS POINT, 76- *Personal Data:* b Peking, China, July 19, 35; US citizen; m 61; c 2. *Educ:* Lafayette Col, BS & BA, 58; Ill Inst Technol, MS, 61; Ind Univ, PhD(math), 75. *Concurrent Pos:* NSF fel, Ind Univ, 67-68. *Mem:* Math Asn Am; Am Math Soc; Nat Coun Teachers Math. *Res:* Mathematics, summability. *Mailing Add:* Dept Math Univ Wis Stevens Point 2100 Main St Stevens Point WI 54481-3871

LIU, MAW-SHUNG, MEDICAL PHYSIOLOGY, SURGERY. *Current Pos:* PROF PHYSIOL, SCH MED, ST LOUIS UNIV, 82- *Personal Data:* b Taiwan, Feb 2, 40; m 66, Min-chan Chang; c Chien-Ye. *Educ:* Kaohsiung Med Col, Taiwan, DDS, 64; Univ Ky, MSc, 70; Univ Ottawa, PhD(physiol), 76. *Prof Exp:* Staff dent & lectr oral surg, Chinese Army Hosp, Kaohsiung Med Col Hosp, Taiwan, 64-68; intern path, Med Ctr, Univ Ky, 68-69; Med Res Coun Can fel, 70-73; Alcoholism & Drug Addiction Res Found Ont res scholar, 73-74; vis prof physiol, 74-76, asst prof physiol, Sch Med, La State Univ Med Ctr, New Orleans, 76-78; assoc prof physiol, Bowman Gray Sch Med, Wake Forest Univ, Winston-Salem, NC, 78-82. *Concurrent Pos:* Hon prof, Nanjing Med Col, China, 84, Hunan Med Univ, China, 88; vis prof, Beijing Med Univ, 84, 86, 92, Zhejiang Med Univ China, 86, 88, Kaohaiung Med Col & Chang Gung Med Col, 89-; mem, Surg, Anesthesiol & Trauma Study Sect, NIH, 88-92. *Mem:* Int Soc Heart Res; Shock Soc; Am Physiol Soc. *Res:* Myocardial and hepatic intermediary metabolism in endotoxic and septic shock; published over 60 full-length papers and 60 abstracts. *Mailing Add:* Dept Pharmacol & Physiol Sci St Louis Univ Sch Med 1402 S Grand Blvd St Louis MO 63104-1080. *Fax:* 314-577-8233

LIU, MIAN, tectono physics, numerical modelling, for more information see previous edition

LIU, MICHAEL T H, PHYSICAL CHEMISTRY, PHYSICAL ORGANIC CHEMISTRY. *Current Pos:* from asst prof to assoc prof, 68-80, PROF CHEM, UNIV PRINCE EDWARD ISLAND, 80- *Personal Data:* b Hong Kong, China, Mar 1, 39; Can citizen; m 75, Betty; c David, Stephen & Peter. *Educ:* St Dunstan's Univ, BSc, 61; St Francis Xavier, MA, 64; Univ Ottawa, PhD(phys chem), 67. *Honors & Awards:* Haut Niveau Award, Ministry Educ, Paris, 89; Int Collabr Award, Nat Sci & Eng Res Coun Can, 91 & 93. *Prof Exp:* Technician, Can Celanese Ltd, 61-62; group leader qual control, Chemcell Ltd, 64; Nat Res Coun fel, Univ Reading, 67-68. *Concurrent Pos:* Nat Sci & Eng Res Coun Can grant-in-aid, 68-; Def Res Bd of Can grant-in-aid, 74-76; sabbatical leave, Univ BC, 75 & Univ Geneva, 82; adj prof, Dalhousie Univ, 79-85, Univ Bordeaux, 88-89; ed, CRC Press, Boca Raton, Fla, 87; vis prof, Univ Bordeaux 1, 93 & 95; res chair, Kyushu Univ, Japan, 97-98. *Mem:* Fel Chem Inst Can; Inter-Am Photochem Soc. *Res:* Carbene chemistry; synthesis of new diazirines and 1,2-hydrogen migration; cyclopropanation of electrophilic and ambiphilic carbenes; thermolysis, photolysis and laser photolysis of diazirines; 1,2-H shift in ammonium ylide; 1,5 cyclization of pyridinium ylide; cycloaddition of carbenes to carbon 60. *Mailing Add:* Dept Chem Univ Prince Edward Island Charlottetown PE C1A 4P3 Can. *Fax:* 902-566-0632; *E-Mail:* liu@upe1.ca

LIU, MING-BIANN, PHYSICAL CHEMISTRY, CHEMICAL ENGINEERING. *Current Pos:* ASST CHEMIST, DOW CHEM CO, 81- *Personal Data:* b Chang-Hua, Taiwan, June 22, 42; m 75; c 2. *Educ:* Cheng-Kung Univ, Taiwan, BS, 68; Ill Inst Technol, PhD(chem), 74, MS, 80. *Prof Exp:* Res & teaching, Univ Kans, 74-75; res, Chem Div, Argonne Nat Lab, 76-78, asst chemist, Chem Eng Div, 78-81. *Mem:* Am Chem Soc; Electrochem Soc. *Res:* High temperature materials and technology; plasma surface interaction; gas surface interaction; electrochemical processes and technology; flame retardants. *Mailing Add:* 386 Mount Sequoia Pl Clayton CA 94517

LIU, MING-TSAN, COMPUTER SCIENCE, COMPUTER ENGINEERING. *Current Pos:* assoc prof, 69-78, PROF COMPUT & INFO SCI, OHIO STATE UNIV, 78- *Personal Data:* b Taiwan, China, Aug 30, 34; US citizen; m 66; c 3. *Educ:* Cheng Kung Univ, BS, 57; Univ Pa, MS, 61, PhD(elec eng), 64. *Prof Exp:* Asst elec eng, Cheng Kung Univ, 59-60; instr, Moore Sch Elec Eng, Univ Pa, 62-65, asst prof, 65-69. *Concurrent Pos:* Consult, Comput Command & Control Co, Philadelphia, Pa, 64-65, Burroughs Corp, Paoli, Pa, 77 & AT&T Bell Labs, Columbus, Ohio, 82-84; distinguished vis, Comput Soc, Inst Elec & Electronics Engrs, 81-84; ed, Inst Elec & Electronics Engrs Trans Comput, 82-86 & ed-in-chief, 86- *Mem:* Fel Inst Elec & Electronics Engrs; Asn Comput Mach; Sigma Xi. *Res:* Computer architecture; computer networks; distributed processing; microcomputer systems; computer communication. *Mailing Add:* CIS Dept 2015 Neil Ave Ohio State Univ Columbus OH 43210-1277

LIU, PAN-TAI, APPLIED MATHEMATICS. *Current Pos:* Asst prof, 68-74, assoc prof, 74-80, PROF MATH, UNIV RI, KINGSTON, 80- *Personal Data:* b Taipei, Taiwan, Sept 22, 41; m 66; c 1. *Educ:* Nat Taiwan Univ, BS, 63; State Univ NY, Stony Brook, PhD(appl math), 68. *Concurrent Pos:* Vis prof, Dept Elec Eng, Nat Taiwan Univ, Taipei, Taiwan, 74-75. *Mem:* Am Math Soc. *Res:* Optimal controls; differential games; stochastic processes. *Mailing Add:* Dept Math Univ RI Kingston RI 02881

LIU, PAUL CHI, PHYSICAL OCEANOGRAPHY, COASTAL ENGINEERING. *Current Pos:* res phys scientist, Lake Surv Ctr, Nat Ocean Surv, 71-74, OCEANOGR, GREAT LAKES ENVIRON RES LAB, NAT OCEANIC & ATMOSPHERIC ADMIN, 74- *Personal Data:* b Chefoo, China, June 18, 35; m 65, Teresa S Wang; c Christina. *Educ:* Nat Taiwan Univ, BS, 56; Virginia Polytech Inst, MS, 61; Univ Mich, PhD(oceanic sci), 77. *Prof Exp:* Res phys scientist, US Lake Surv, Army CEngr, 65-71. *Concurrent Pos:* Vis scholar, Univ Mich, 78-; fel, Coop Inst Limnol & Ecosyst Res, 90- *Mem:* Am Geophys Union; Am Meterol Soc; Am Soc Civil Engrs; Int Asn Great Lakes Res; Soc Indust & Appl Math; Sigma Xi. *Res:* Nearshore hydrodynamics; evolution of wind wave spectra; wavelet analysis; nonlinear and chaotic dynamics. *Mailing Add:* 48328 Castleside Dr Canton MI 48187. *E-Mail:* liu@glerl.noaa.gov

LIU, PAUL ISHEN, CLINICAL PATHOLOGY. *Current Pos:* CHIEF PATH, OLIVEVIEW MED CTR, 92- *Personal Data:* b Taiwan, Nov 23, 32; US citizen. *Educ:* Nat Taiwan Univ, MD, 60; St Louis Univ, PhD(path), 69. *Prof Exp:* Assoc prof path, Med Ctr, Univ Kans, 73-74; assoc dir lab med, Med Col Ga, 74-76; prof & vchmn, Med Univ SC, 76-80; prof path & vchmn dept, Univ SAla, 81-92. *Mem:* AMA; Col Am Path; Am Soc Clin Path; Asn Clin Sci; Am Soc Microbiol. *Res:* Leukemia; immunology. *Mailing Add:* Dept Path/A116 Oliveview Med Ctr 14445 Oliveview Dr Sylmar CA 91342

LIU, PHILIP L-F, HYDRODYNAMICS, COASTAL ENGINEERING. *Current Pos:* from asst prof to assoc prof environ eng, Cornell Univ, 74-83, assoc dir, Sch Civil & Environ Eng, 85-86, assoc dean, Col Eng, 86-87, PROF ENVIRON ENG, CORNELL UNIV, 83- *Personal Data:* b Fu-Chu, China, Dec 11, 46; c 2. *Educ:* Nat Taiwan Univ, BS, 68; Mass Inst Technol, SM, 71, ScD(hydrodyn), 74. *Honors & Awards:* Walter L Huber Prize, Am Soc Civil Engrs, 78. *Prof Exp:* Res asst civil eng, Mass Inst Technol, 69-74. *Concurrent Pos:* Justice asst prof, Justice Found, 78-79; Eng Found fel, 79; J S Guggenheim fel, 80; vis assoc, Calif Tech, 80-81; vis scientist, Delft Hydraulics, 87; vis prof, Tech Univ Denmark, 88 & Nat Taiwan Univ, 94. *Mem:* Am Soc Civil Engrs; Am Geophys Union; Soc Indust & Appl Math; Am Phys Soc. *Res:* Wave hydrodynamics in coastal engineering; coastal currents and shoreline processes; numerical methods for nonlinear free surface problems; groundwater flow modeling. *Mailing Add:* Sch Civil & Environ Eng Cornell Univ Ithaca NY 14853

LIU, PINGHUI VICTOR, MEDICAL MICROBIOLOGY. *Current Pos:* from instr to assoc prof, 57-69, prof microbiol, 69-81, PROF MICROBIOL & IMMUNOL, SCH MED, UNIV LOUISVILLE, 81- *Personal Data:* b Formosa, China, Feb 9, 24; nat US; m 59; c 2. *Educ:* Tokyo Jikei-kai Sch Med, MD, 47; Tokyo Med Sch, PhD(microbiol), 57; Am Bd Med Microbiol, dipl, 62. *Prof Exp:* Intern, Mercy Hosp, Cedar Rapids, Iowa, 54-55; intern internal med, Louisville Gen Hosp, 55-56. *Concurrent Pos:* Res fel microbiol, Sch Med, Univ Louisville, 56-57; USPHS sr res fel, 59-, res career develop award, 62-; mem, Subcomt Pseudomonas & Related Organisms, Int Comt Bact Nomenclature, 63- *Mem:* AAAS; Am Soc Microbiol; Infectious Dis Soc Am; NY Acad Sci. *Res:* Pathogenesis and taxonomy of pseudomonads and related organisms, such as aeromonads and vibrios; extracellular toxins, such as hemolysin, lecithinase and protease; immunities to infections. *Mailing Add:* Microbiol & Immunol Univ Louisville Sch Med 2301 S Third St Louisville KY 40292-0001

LIU, PU, HUMAN GENETICS, CANCER GENETICS. *Current Pos:* SR STAFF FEL & INVESTR HUMAN GENOME RES, NAT CTR HUMAN GENOME RES, NIH, 93- *Personal Data:* b Beijing, China, June 22, 57; m 85, Yao-yao Zhu. *Educ:* Beijing Second Med Col, China, MD, 82; Univ Tex, Houston, PhD(genetics), 91. *Prof Exp:* Resident internal med, Peking Union Med Col, China, 83-85; proj investr, M D Anderson Cancer Ctr, Univ Tex, 91-92; res assoc, Howard Hughes Med Inst, Univ Mich, 92-93. *Mem:* Am Soc Human Genetics. *Res:* Identification and studying of genes responsible for human inherited diseases and cancers; development of reagents and tools for human gene therapy. *Mailing Add:* 49 Convent Dr Rm 3A18 Bethesda MD 20892. *Fax:* 301-402-4929; *E-Mail:* pliu@helix.nih.gov

LIU, QING-HUO, wave propagation, numerical analysis, for more information see previous edition

LIU, RAY HO, FORENSIC DRUG URINALYSIS, CRIMINALISTICS. *Current Pos:* assoc prof, 84-89, PROF FORENSIC SCI, UNIV ALA, BIRMINGHAM, 89- *Personal Data:* b Taiwan, Apr 3, 42; US citizen; m 65; c 3. *Educ:* Cent Police Col, Taiwan, LLB, 65; Southern Ill Univ, PhD(chem), 76. *Prof Exp:* Asst prof forensic sci, Univ Ill, Chicago, 77-80; mass spectrometrist, US Environ Protection Agency, 80-82; ctr mass spectrometrist, USDA, 82-83. *Concurrent Pos:* Vis prof, Taiwanese Nat Sci Coun, 81, 94 & 96; tech dir, Environ Health Res & Testing, Inc, 87-91; drug urinalysis expert witness & resource person, USCG, 88-93; lab inspector, Nat Inst Drug Abuses Nat Lab Cert Prog, 88-; ed-in-chief, Forensic Sci Rev J, 89-; dir, Forensic Sci Grad Prog, Univ Ala, Birmingham, 91- *Mem:* Fel Am Acad Forensic Sci; Am Chem Soc; Am Soc Mass Spectrometry. *Res:* Application and development of new approaches for solving existing and emerging problems in forensic sciences, with special emphasis on analytical approaches that may be used for sample differentiation purposes. *Mailing Add:* Dept Justice Sci Univ Ala Birmingham AL 35294

LIU, ROBERT SHING-HEI, ORGANIC CHEMISTRY. *Current Pos:* assoc prof, 68-72, PROF CHEM, UNIV HAWAII, 72- *Personal Data:* b Shanghai, China, Aug 1, 38; m 67, Regina S Ro; c 2. *Educ:* Howard Payne Col, BS, 61; Calif Inst Technol, PhD(chem), 65. *Honors & Awards:* Creativity Award, NSF, 87; Merit Award, NIH, 89. *Prof Exp:* Res chemist, E I du Pont de Nemours & Co, Inc, 64-68. *Concurrent Pos:* Alfred P Sloan fel, 70-72; John Simon Guggenheim Found fel, 74-75; UH Fujio Matsuda Scholar, 84-85. *Mem:* Inter-Am Photochem Soc; Am Chem Soc; Am Soc Photobiol. *Res:* Photochemistry of polyenes; energy transfer processes in solutions; bioorganic reaction mechanisms; new geometric isomers of vitamin A and carotenoids; visual pigments: primary processes, analogs and binding sites; bacteriorhodopsin analogs; nuclear magnetic resonance of retinoid and carotenoid binding proteins. *Mailing Add:* Dept Chem Univ Hawaii Honolulu HI 96822. *Fax:* 808-956-5908; *E-Mail:* rliu@gold.chem.hawaii.edu

LIU, RUEY-WEN, ELECTRICAL ENGINEERING. *Current Pos:* From asst prof to assoc prof, 60-66, PROF ELEC ENG, UNIV NOTRE DAME, 66- *Personal Data:* b Kiangsu, China, Mar 18, 30; US citizen; m 57; c 2. *Educ:* Univ Ill, BS, 54, MS, 55, PhD(elec eng), 60. *Concurrent Pos:* NSF grants 62-63, 64-66 & 71-73; vis assoc prof, Univ Calif, Berkeley, 65-66; vis prof, Nat Taiwan Univ, 69 & Univ Calif, Berkeley, 77-78. *Mem:* Am Math Soc; fel Inst Elec & Electronics Engrs. *Res:* System and network theory; large-scale dynamical systems. *Mailing Add:* Dept Elec Eng Univ Notre Dame Notre Dame IN 46556

LIU, S(HING) G(ONG), ELECTRICAL ENGINEERING, APPLIED PHYSICS. *Current Pos:* RES SCIENTIST, RCA LABS, 63- *Personal Data:* b Soochow, China, Oct 24, 33; m 60; c 3. *Educ:* Univ Taiwan, BS, 54; NC State Col, MS 58; Stanford Univ, PhD(elec eng), 63. *Prof Exp:* Jr engr, IBM Corp, 58-59, assoc engr, 59; asst microwave ferrites, Stanford Univ, 59-63. *Mem:* Am Phys Soc; Inst Elec & Electronics Engrs. *Res:* Spin waves in ferrites; microwave and optical frequency devices using semiconductors; ion implantation in gallium arsenide and related III-V compound semiconductors. *Mailing Add:* MMTC Inc Princeton NJ 08540

LIU, SAMUEL HSI-PEH, THEORETICAL SOLID STATE PHYSICS. *Current Pos:* RETIRED. *Personal Data:* b Taiyuan, China, Apr 17, 34; m 61; c 2. *Educ:* Taiwan Univ, BS, 54; Iowa State Univ, 58, PhD(physics), 60. *Prof Exp:* Assoc res mem, Res Lab, IBM Corp, 60-61, res staff mem, 61-64; from assoc prof to prof physics, Iowa State Univ, 64-81; sr res staff mem, Oak Ridge Nat Lab, 81-89, corp fel, 89-94. *Concurrent Pos:* Vis prof, Ruhr Univ Bochum, WGer, 70, H C Oersted Inst, Copenhagen Univ, 71-72, Univ Calif, Berkeley, 75-76 & 86, Free Univ, Berlin, WGer, 80. *Mem:* Fel Am Phys Soc; AAAS; Sigma Xi. *Res:* Solid state theory; electronic and magnetic properties of metals and metallic compounds; solid surfaces and disordered solids. *Mailing Add:* 7240 D Calabria Ct San Diego CA 92122

LIU, SHIH-CHUN, HEMATOLOGY RESEARCH IN BIO-MEMBRANE. *Current Pos:* asst res prof, 78-92, ASSOC RES PROF, TUFTS UNIV, ST ELIZABETH HOSP, 92- *Personal Data:* b Taipei, Taiwan, Jan 2, 46. *Educ:* Fu-Jen Catholic Univ, Taiwan, BS, 69; Carnegie-Mellon Univ, PhD(biochem), 75. *Prof Exp:* Fel, Univ Mass Med Sch, St Vincent Hosp, 75-78. *Concurrent Pos:* Prin investr, NIH, 92- *Mem:* Am Soc Cell Biol; Am Hemat Soc. *Res:* Hematology in bio-membrane. *Mailing Add:* Dept Biomed Res Tufts Univ St Elizabeth Hosp 736 Cambridge St Boston MA 02135-2997

LIU, SHU QIAN, MECHANICAL ENGINEERING. *Current Pos:* ASST PROF BIOMED ENG DEPT, NORTHWESTERN UNIV, 95- *Personal Data:* b Lian-cheng, China, Dec 22, 56; m 83, Wu Yu-Hua; c Diana & Charley. *Educ:* Med Sch NeiMongu, China, BS, 80, MS, 83; Univ Calif, San Diego, PhD, 90. *Honors & Awards:* Melville Medal, Am Soc Mech Engrs, 94. *Prof Exp:* Postdoctoral fel, Univ Calif, San Diego, 90-92, asst res bioengr, 92-95. *Concurrent Pos:* Whitaker Res Award, Whitaker Found, 93-96. *Mem:* Am Soc Mech Engrs; AAAS; Biomed Eng Soc. *Mailing Add:* Biomed Eng Dept Northwestern Univ 2145 Sheldon Rd Evanston IL 60208-3107. *Fax:* 847-491-4928; *E-Mail:* sliu@nwu.edu

LIU, SI-KWANG, VETERINARY PATHOLOGY. *Current Pos:* assoc pathologist, Animal Med Ctr, 64-66, cardiopulmonary pathologist, 66-69, asst head, Dept Path, 69-73, SR STAFF MEM, ANIMAL MED CTR, 73- *Personal Data:* b Kwangsi, China, Dec 1, 25; m 60; c David, Ernie, Diana & Phillip. *Educ:* Vet Col Chinese Army, DVM, 49; Univ Calif, Davis, PhD(vet path), 64. *Honors & Awards:* Ralston Purina Res Award Cardiovasc Path, 82; Carnation Res Awards Feline Dis & Nutrit, 84; Beecham Award Res Excellence, 86; ROC Award Comp Path, Chinese Histopath Soc, 89; Chinese Vet Med Asn Res Awards, 93 & 95. *Prof Exp:* Sr vet res & diag, Provincial Taitung Agr Sta, China, 50-55; lectr vet path, Col Agr, Taiwan Univ, 56-59, chief, Path Lab, Univ Vet Hosp, 56-59; res asst path & parasitol, Sch Vet Med, Univ Calif, Davis, 59-64. *Concurrent Pos:* Vis prof vet path, Nat Taiwan Univ & vis expert, Chinese Sci Coun, 76-77 & 85-86; sci fel, NY Zool Soc, Bronx Zoo, 79-; clin prof comp path, NY Med Col; consult, Pig Res Inst, Taiwan, Repub China, 85. *Mem:* hon mem Am Vet Med Asn; Am Soc Parasitol; Sigma Xi; NY Acad Sci; Int Acad Path; Int Skeletal Soc; Int Cardiovasc Path Soc. *Res:* Cardiovascular pathology in domestic animals as well as zoo animals; comparative pathology in cardiovascular and orthopaedic diseases. *Mailing Add:* Animal Med Ctr 510 E 62nd St New York NY 10021

LIU, STEPHEN C Y, MICROBIOLOGY, IMMUNOLOGY. *Current Pos:* from asst prof to assoc prof, 65-74, PROF MICROBIOL, EASTERN MICH UNIV, 74- *Personal Data:* b Hunan, China, Feb 24, 27; m 54; c 4. *Educ:* Taiwan Univ, BSc, 51, MSc, 54; Univ Minn, PhD, 57. *Prof Exp:* Instr plant path, Taiwan Univ, 51-54; from res asst to res assoc, Univ Minn, 54-58; res plant virologist, Nat Res Coun, 58-62, asst mgr Chas Pfizer & Co, Inc, 62-65. *Concurrent Pos:* Tech consult, People's Republic China, UN, 80-81. *Mem:* AAAS; Am Phytopath Soc; Am Soc Microbiol; NY Acad Sci; Sigma Xi. *Res:* Genetics of bacteria; immunology; virology; hydrobiology. *Mailing Add:* 2901 Pebble Creek Rd Ann Arbor MI 48108-1729

LIU, TAI-PING, MATHEMATICAL ANALYSIS. *Current Pos:* From asst prof to assoc prof, 73-81, PROF, UNIV MD, COLLEGE PARK, 81- *Personal Data:* b Taiwan, Repub of China, Nov 18, 45; m 73. *Educ:* Nat Taiwan Univ, BS, 68; Ore State Univ, MS, 70; Univ Mich, PhD(math), 73. *Concurrent Pos:* Sloan fel; Guggenheim fel. *Mem:* Am Math Soc. *Res:* Nonlinear partial differential equations and mechanics; qualitative behavior of solutions to physical systems such as compressible flow and elastic models; gas dynamics. *Mailing Add:* Bldg 380 Rm 2125 Stanford Univ Stanford CA 94305-2060

LIU, TEH-YUNG, biochemistry, for more information see previous edition

LIU, TING-TING Y, starch biosynthesis, for more information see previous edition

LIU, TONY CHEN-YEH, STRUCTURAL ENGINEERING, CIVIL ENGINEERING. *Current Pos:* res engr, Waterways Exp Sta, 76-81, CHIEF MAT ENG, US ARMY CORPS ENGRS, 81- *Personal Data:* b Fu-Chien, China, July 27, 43; US citizen; m 69; c 2. *Educ:* Nat Chung-Hsing Univ, Taiwan, BS, 65; SDak Sch Mines & Technol, MS, 68; Cornell Univ, PhD(civil eng), 71. *Honors & Awards:* Wason Res Medal, Am Concrete Inst, 74 & 83. *Prof Exp:* Struct engr civil eng, Ammann & Whitney Inc, 71; group leader nuclear eng, Gen Atomic Co, 72-76. *Concurrent Pos:* Guide prof, World Open Univ, 75. *Mem:* Fel Am Concrete Inst; Am Soc Civil Engrs; Sigma Xi; Am Soc Testing & Mat. *Res:* Design of concrete hydraulic structures, precast concrete structures, repair and rehabilitation of deteriorated concrete structures and thermal stress analysis for mass concrete structures. *Mailing Add:* 1284 Towlston Rd Great Falls VA 22066

LIU, TUNG, CHEMICAL ENGINEERING. *Current Pos:* RETIRED. *Personal Data:* b Peking, China, Mar 12, 26; nat US; m 58; c 3. *Educ:* Nankai Univ, Tientsin, BS, 47; Univ Ill, MSc, 51, PhD(chem eng), 53. *Prof Exp:* Chem engr, Pittsburgh Consol Coal Co, 53-55; res chem engr, Monsanto Chem Co, 56-60; res mat engr, Air Force Mat Lab, 60-68; sr res engr, Occidental Petrol Corp, 68-77; res engr, Bendix Res Labs, 77-91. *Concurrent Pos:* Chem engr, Garrett Corp, 70-77. *Mem:* Am Chem Soc; Am Inst Chem Engrs; Sigma Xi. *Res:* Friction, lubrication and wear. *Mailing Add:* 16734 Hapton Dr Granger IN 46530-9176

LIU, VI-CHENG, AEROSPACE ENGINEERING. *Current Pos:* res assoc eng, Res Inst, Univ Mich, Ann Arbor, 48-50, res engr, 50-59, prof, 59-89, EMER PROF AEROSPACE ENG, UNIV MICH, ANN ARBOR, 89- *Personal Data:* b China, Sept 1, 17; nat US; m 47, Hsi-Yen Wang. *Educ:* Chiao Tung Univ, BS, 40; Univ Mich, MS, 47, PhD(aeronaut eng), 51. *Prof Exp:* Res asst aerodyn, Aeronaut Res Inst, Tsing Hua Univ, China, 40-44, res instr, 44-46; res fel, Ministry Educ, 46-48. *Concurrent Pos:* Vis prof, Inst Mech, Chinese Acad Sci, Beijing, 80; vis chair prof, Nanjing Aeronaut Inst, China, 90, hon prof, 91. *Mem:* Am Phys Soc; assoc fel Am Inst Aeronaut & Astronaut. *Res:* Upper atmosphere; rocket flight, rarefied gas and ionospheric gas dynamics; thermal diffusion; boundary layer flow; turbulent dispersion; plasma interaction; magnetospheric physics; geophysical Fluid Dynamics; ionospheric aerodynamics. *Mailing Add:* 2104 Vinewood Ann Arbor MI 48104

LIU, WEI, modeling of short-rotation intensive suture woody biomass production, harvesting processing & transportation systems, for more information see previous edition

LIU, WING KAM, WAVELETS, FINITE ELEMENTS. *Current Pos:* from asst prof to assoc prof, 80-88, PROF MECH & CIVIL ENG, NORTHWESTERN UNIV, 88- *Personal Data:* b Hong Kong, May 19, 52; US citizen; m 86, Betty Hsia; c Melissa & Michael. *Educ:* Univ Ill, Chicago, BSc, 76; Calif Inst Technol, MSc, 77, PhD(civil eng), 81. *Honors & Awards:* Melville Medal, Am Soc Mech Engrs, 79; Pi Tau Sigma, Gold Medal, 85; Ralph Teetor's Award, Soc Automotive Engrs, 83; Thomas J Jaeger Prize, Int Asn Struct Mech Reactor Technol, 89; Gustus L Larson Mem Award, Am Soc Mech Engrs, 95. *Prof Exp:* Res asst, Univ Ill, Chicago, 74-76 & Calif Inst Technol, 76-80. *Concurrent Pos:* Consult, Reactor Anal & Safety Div, Argonne Nat Lab, 81-; grants, NSF, Army Res Off, NASA, ONR & Air Force Off Sci Res. *Mem:* Fel Am Soc Mech Engrs; fel Am Soc Civil Engrs; Am Acad Mech. *Res:* Finite elements; computer simulations; fluid-structure interactions; non-linear and inelastic analysis; computer-aided engineering; liquid storage tanks; wavelets and reproducing kernel methods; virtual manufacturing prototyping. *Mailing Add:* Dept Mech Eng Northwestern Univ Evanston IL 60208. *Fax:* 847-491-3915

LIU, WING-KI, SURFACE SCIENCE. *Current Pos:* ASSOC PROF, DEPT PHYSICS, UNIV WATERLOO, 86- *Personal Data:* b Hong Kong, Feb 24, 50. *Educ:* Univ Ill, Urbana, BS, 71, MS, 72 & PhD(physics), 75. *Prof Exp:* Fel, Calif Inst Technol, 75-76, res assoc, 76-79, vis assoc, 79-80, vis asst prof, 80-81, res asst prof, 81-85, res assoc prof, 85-86. *Mem:* Am Phys Soc; Can Assoc Physicists. *Res:* Classical and quantum chemical dynamics; theory of chemical physics of solid surfaces. *Mailing Add:* Dept Physics Univ Waterloo Waterloo ON N2L 3G1 Can

LIU, WINGYUEN TIMOTHY, REMOTE SENSING, AIR-SEA INTERACTION. *Current Pos:* SR RES SCIENTIST SATELLITE OCEANOG, JET PROPULSION LAB, CALIF INST TECHNOL, 79- *Personal Data:* US citizen. *Educ:* Ohio Univ, BS, 71; Univ Wash, MS, 74, PhD(atmospheric sci), 78. *Honors & Awards:* Medal for Except Sci Achievement, NASA. *Prof Exp:* Res assoc atmospheric sci, Univ Wash, 78-79. *Mem:* Am Meteorol Soc; Am Geophys Union. *Res:* Study of the boundary layers, the energy exchanges across the atmosphere-ocean interface and their effects on climate variability. *Mailing Add:* Jet Propulsion Lab MS 300-323 4800 Oak Grove Dr Pasadena CA 91109

LIU, XIAOHUA, LIGHT SCATTERING, ELECTRICAL TESTING & MEASUREMENT. *Current Pos:* MEM TECH STAFF, LUCENT TECHNOL, 96- *Personal Data:* m, Ying Qian; c Jennifer. *Educ:* Nanjing Univ, China, BS, 86; Ohio State Univ, MS, 95, PhD(physics), 96. *Prof Exp:* Res asst, Narjing Univ, China, 86-90. *Res:* Light scattering technique to study sound and magnetic waves in magnetic thin films. *Mailing Add:* Lucent Technol 6200 E Broad St Columbus OH 43213

LIU, XICHUN, semiconductor physics, magnetospectroscopy, for more information see previous edition

LIU, XUAN, TRANSCRIPTION, CANCER RESEARCH. *Current Pos:* DAMON RUNYON-WALTER WINCHELL FEL, UNIV CALIF, LOS ANGELES, 90- *Personal Data:* b Beijing, China, Apr 8, 59. *Educ:* Beijing Med Univ, MD, 83; WVa Univ, PhD(biochem), 90. *Mem:* Am Soc Cell Biologists; AAAS. *Res:* Study tumor suppressor transcriptional regulation during cell cycle control. *Mailing Add:* 600 Central Ave Apt 138 Riverside CA 92507

LIU, YI, LASER MATERIAL INTERACTION, MACHINE VISION. *Current Pos:* DIR RES & DEVELOP & QUAL MGR, UTILASE INC, 93- *Personal Data:* b Zhengjiang, Jiangsu, China, Oct 8, 63; m 91, Liqun Fu. *Educ:* Beijing Univ, China, BS, 84; Ohio State Univ, MS, 86, PhD(physics), 91. *Prof Exp:* Teaching asst gen physics, Ohio State Univ, 84-86, res assoc, 86-91; res scientist, Argonne Nat Lab, 91-93. *Mem:* Soc Mfg Engrs; Am Welding Soc; Int Soc Optical Eng; Soc Appl Spectros; Am Soc Qual Control. *Res:* Laser material interaction; laser application; develop on-line real time process monitoring systems; develop machine vision systems for quality control. *Mailing Add:* 39394 Carrie Dr Sterling Heights MI 48313. *Fax:* 313-839-0062

LIU, YONG-BIAO, PESTICIDE RESISTANCE, CHEMICAL ECOLOGY. *Current Pos:* ASST RES SCIENTIST, UNIV ARIZ, 97- *Personal Data:* b Ningxia, China May 15, 60; m 92, Min Hu; c Yang. *Educ:* Beijing Forestry Univ, BA, 82; Univ BC, MS, 87; Univ Maine, PhD(biol sci), 90. *Honors & Awards:* Fred Griffee Mem Award, Maine Agr Exp Sta, 90, George F Dow Award, 90. *Prof Exp:* Scholar, Univ Ky, 90-93; fel, Univ Hawaii, 93-97. *Mem:* Entom Soc Am; Sigma Xi. *Res:* Toxicology of limonoid insect antifeedants; sex pheromone-mediated insect behavior; pesticide resistance; granted 1 US patent. *Mailing Add:* Dept Entom Univ Ariz Tucson AZ 85721. *Fax:* 520-621-1150

LIU, YOUNG KING, BIOMECHANICS, BIOMEDICAL ENGINEERING. *Current Pos:* PRES, UNIV NORTHERN CALIF, 94- *Personal Data:* b Nanking, China, May 3, 34; US citizen; div; c 2. *Educ:* Bradley Univ, BS, 55; Univ Wis-Madison, MS, 59; Wayne State Univ, PhD(mech), 63. *Prof Exp:* Instr mech, Wayne State Univ, 60-63; lectr, Univ Mich, Ann Arbor, 63-64, asst prof, 64-68; vis asst prof aeronaut & astronaut, Stanford Univ, 68-69; assoc prof, Tulane Univ, 69-72, prof biomech, 72-78; prof & dir, Ctr Mat Res, Univ Iowa, Iowa City, 78-90; prof & dir, Biomech Lab, 90-94. *Concurrent Pos:* NIH spec res fel, Stanford Univ, 68-69; biophys consult, US Army Aeromed Res Lab, 72-; NIH res career develop award, 71-76; adv at large, Nat Res Coun, Comt Hearing, Bioacoust & Biomech, NAS, 79- *Mem:* Am Soc Eng Educ; Orthop Res Soc; Am Soc Eng Educ; Sigma Xi; Am Acad Mech; Int Soc Study Lumbar Spine; Int Soc Study Pain. *Res:* Biomechanics, biomaterials and physiologic basis of acupuncture. *Mailing Add:* Pres Off Univ Northern Calif 101 S San Antonio Rd Petaluma CA 94952

LIU, YU, optics, lasers, for more information see previous edition

LIU, YUNG SHENG, PHYSICS, LASERS. *Current Pos:* PHYSICIST, GEN ELEC RES CTR, 72-; ADJ PROF PHYSICS, STATE UNIV NY, ALBANY, 86- *Personal Data:* b China, Sept 23, 44; m 79, Ming Lee; c Alan & Jenny. *Educ:* Nat Taiwan Univ, BS, 66; Cornell Univ, PhD(appl physics), 72. *Prof Exp:* Teaching asst physics, Cornell Univ, 68-69, res asst, 70-73; prin investr & proj leader, GE Res & Develop Ctr, 72-86, prin scientist, 87-92, prin scientist, GE Med Systs, 90-92, prin investr, Res & Develop Consortium, 92-95, prog mgr, 92-96, Darpa Prog Mgr, Gen Electric Res Ctr, 72-94. *Concurrent Pos:* Vis scientist physics, Univ Calif, Los Angeles, 68-; fel, Cornell Univ, 69, Avco fel, 70; consult, UN Develop Prog, China, 86; prin investr & major grantee, USAF, Off Naval Res, Advan Res Projs Agency; adj prof, Dept Physics, State Univ NY, Albany, 86-92; mem, Comt Applns Physics, Am Phys Soc, 88-91; lectr, Max Planck Soc, Ger, 89 & 92; res prof, Physics Dept, Rensselaer Polytech Inst, 95-97. *Mem:* Optical Soc Am; Am Phys Soc; Sigma Xi; AAAS; Inst Elec & Electronics Engrs; Am Vacuum Soc; Mat Res Soc. *Res:* Laser physics; quantum electronics and optics; laser-matter interactions; semiconductor electronics; author or coauthor of over 60 publications; 20 patents. *Mailing Add:* GE Res & Dev Ctr PO Box 8 1 River Rd KW-B1307 Schenectady NY 12309. *Fax:* 518-387-5299; *E-Mail:* liuys@crd.ge.com

LIU, YUNG YUAN, CORROSION-EROSION, HOT CELL EXPERIMENTATION. *Current Pos:* assoc staff engr fast reactor fuel performance, Argonne Nat Lab, 78-82, staff engr & theorist radiation effects & nuclear mat-casting-solidification, Mat Sci & Technol Div, 82-85, staff engr high temperature corrosion-erosion, tribology, 86-88, staff engr irradiation performance, Mat & Components Technol Div, 89-93, STAFF ENGR TRANSP HAZARDOUS WASTE, ENERGY TECHNOL DIV, ARGONNE NAT LAB, 93- *Personal Data:* b Taipei, Taiwan, Mar 20, 50; US citizen; m 75, Teresa L Ngai; c Sharon & Alvin. *Educ:* Nat Tsing-Hua Univ, Taiwan, BS, 71; Mass Inst Technol, MS, 76, ScD(nuclear eng), 78. *Honors & Awards:* Significant Contrib Award, Mat Sci & Technol Div, Am Nuclear Soc, 92. *Prof Exp:* Res asst cogeneration, Dept Nuclear Eng, Mass Inst Technol, 74, teaching asst phys metall, 74-75, struct mech, 75 & radiation effects, 75-76, res asst light water reactor fuel performance, 76-78. *Concurrent Pos:* Staff engr light water reactor fuel performance, Entropy Ltd, Lincoln, Mass, 77-78; mem, fast reactor fuel performance code comt, US Dept Energy & Fuel Performance Eval Task Force, 78-81; prin investr, Argonne Nat Lab, Mat Sci & Technol Div, 78-; consult, Los Alamos Nat Lab, 82-83; staff reviewer, Nuclear Technol, 82-, Am Soc Mech Engrs, 83-; consult, Nordion Int, 96-97. *Mem:* Am Soc Metals; AAAS; Am Nuclear Soc. *Res:* Radiation effects on materials & development of nuclear fuel and breeder materials for fission and fusion reactors; packaging and transportation of radioactive materials; foam explosives. *Mailing Add:* Argonne Nat Lab 9700 S Cass Ave Bldg 308 Argonne IL 60439. *Fax:* 630-252-3250; *E-Mail:* yyliu@anl.gov

LIU, YUNG-PIN, CARCINOGENESIS MECHANISMS. *Current Pos:* PROG DIR CARCINOGENESIS MECHANISMS, NAT CANCER INST, 84- *Educ:* Baylor Univ, PhD(biochem), 69. *Res:* Biochemical pharmacology. *Mailing Add:* Div Cancer Etiol NIH Nat Cancer Inst EPN 700 6130 Executive Blvd Bethesda MD 20892-0001

LIU, YU-YING, SYNTHESIS OF LABELLED COMPOUND. *Current Pos:* sr scientist, 74-85, RES INVESTR, HOFFMANN LAROCHE, INC, 86- *Personal Data:* b China, May 16, 44. *Educ:* Taiwan Normal Univ, BS, 67; Univ Minn, PhD(chem), 72. *Prof Exp:* Fel, Am Health Found, 71-73. *Mem:* Am Chem Soc. *Res:* Natural product isolation; metabolism; quantitative analysis; synthesis of labelled compound of pharmaceutical interest. *Mailing Add:* Hoffmann LaRoche Inc Kingsland St Nutley NJ 07110-1199

LIU, ZHENGYU, PHYSICAL OCEANOGRAPHY, CLIMATE DYNAMICS. *Current Pos:* ASST PROF PHYS OCEANOG, UNIV WIS-MADISON, 93- *Personal Data:* m 87, Huixia Wu; c Neil & Diana. *Educ:* Nanjing Inst Meterol, BA, 82; Acad Sinica, MA, 85; Mass Inst Technol, PhD(phys oceanog). *Prof Exp:* Fel, Princeton Univ, 91-93. *Mailing Add:* 1225 W Dayton St Madison WI 53706. *E-Mail:* znl@meteor.wisc.edu

LIU, ZHUANGYI, CONTROL OF DISTRIBUTED PARAMETER SYSTEMS, PARTIAL DIFFERENTIAL EQUATIONS. *Current Pos:* Asst prof, 89-95, ASSOC PROF MATH, UNIV MINN, DULUTH, 95- *Personal Data:* b Shanghai, China, May 2, 54; US citizen; m 91, Junyi Tu; c Jieming & Yiming. *Educ:* Fudan Univ, BS, 82; Va Polytech Inst, MS, 86, PhD(math), 89. *Mem:* Soc Indust & Appl Math; Am Math Soc. *Res:* Published approximately 20 referred papers in professional journals on the topics of analysis, computation and control of elastic systems with various kinds of dampings. *Mailing Add:* Dept Math Statist Univ Minn CCTR140 10 University Dr Duluth MN 55812. *Fax:* 218-726-8399; *E-Mail:* zliv@d.umn.edu

LIU-GER, TSU-HUEI, THEORETICAL PHYSICS, SOFTWARE DEVELOPMENT. *Current Pos:* physicist, 75-82, SUPVRY ENGR, BONNEVILLE POWER ADMIN, US DEPT ENERGY, 82- *Personal Data:* b Kwei-yang, Kwei-chow, Repub China, Mar 10, 43; US citizen; m 71, Kai-Hwa; c Kwang-yi & Kwang-chien. *Educ:* Nat Taiwan Univ, BS, 64; Univ Ore, PhD(physics), 69. *Prof Exp:* Asst prof physics, Portland State Univ, 69-75. *Res:* Development of electromagnetic transient program of the power systems. *Mailing Add:* 3179 Oak Tree Ct West Linn OR 97068. *Fax:* 503-230-3212; *E-Mail:* 71203.736@compuserve.com

LIUIMA, FRANCIS ALOYSIUS, PHYSICS. *Current Pos:* RETIRED. *Personal Data:* b Utena, Lithuania, Mar 8, 19; nat US. *Educ:* Boston Col, MS, 50; St Louis Univ, PhD(physics), 54. *Prof Exp:* Asst prof physics, Boston Col, 54- *Mem:* Am Phys Soc; Am Asn Physics Teachers. *Res:* Microwave spectroscopy. *Mailing Add:* Dept Physics Boston Col Chestnut Hill MA 02167

LIUKKONEN, JOHN ROBIE, MATHEMATICAL ANALYSIS. *Current Pos:* Asst prof, 70-75, ASSOC PROF MATH, TULANE UNIV, 75- *Personal Data:* b Oakland, Calif, Oct 23, 42. *Educ:* Harvard Univ, BA, 65; Columbia Univ, PhD(math), 70. *Res:* Representations of locally compact groups; harmonic analysis on locally compact groups. *Mailing Add:* Dept Math Tulane Univ 6823 St Charles Ave New Orleans LA 70118-5665

LIUZZI, MICHEL, VIROLOGY & RIBONUCLEOTIDE REDUCTASE, HELICASE-PRIMASE & DNA METABOLISM. *Current Pos:* GROUP LEADER, BIO MEGA/BOEHRINGER INGELHEIM RES INC, 89- *Personal Data:* b Noci, Italy, May 13, 57; m 87, Natalie Rousseau; c Gabrielle A. *Educ:* Univ Liege, Belg, BSc, 80, PhD(chem), 84. *Prof Exp:* Fel, Cross Cancer Inst, Alta, 84-89. *Mem:* Antiviral Res Soc; Am Asn Cancer Res; Am Soc Biochem & Molecular Biol; AAAS. *Res:* Investigate mechanism of inhibition of herpes simplex virus replication by helicase-primase inhibitiors and ribonucleotide reductase subunit association inhibitions for the development of novel antiherpetic agents; DNA repair; enzymology; DNA replication. *Mailing Add:* Bio-Mega/Boehringer Ingelheim Res Inc 2100 Cunard St Laval PQ H7S 2G5 Can. *Fax:* 514-689-8434

LIUZZO, JOSEPH ANTHONY, FOOD SCIENCE. *Current Pos:* asst prof biochem, 58-62, assoc prof food sci & technol, 62-69, PROF FOOD SCI, LA STATE UNIV, BATON ROUGE, 69- *Personal Data:* b Tampa, Fla, Dec 16, 26; m 51, Elaine Grammer; c Paul A, Patricia J & Jolaine M. *Educ:* Univ Fla, BS, 50, MSA, 55; Mich State Univ, PhD(nutrit, biochem), 58. *Honors & Awards:* Prof Scientist Award, Southern Asn Agr Scientists, 85. *Prof Exp:* Res microbiologist, Univ Fla, 50-51, asst, 54-55; dir microbiol, Nutrilite Prod, Inc, Calif, 51-53, asst to dir biol res, 53-54; asst, Mich State Univ, 55-58. *Mem:* Sigma Xi; Am Inst Nutrit; fel Inst Food Technologists; Am Chem Soc. *Res:* Improved utilization of brown ad milled rice; radiation preservation of foods; utilization of by-products from agricultural commodities. *Mailing Add:* Dept Food Sci La State Univ Baton Rouge LA 70803-0001. *Fax:* 504-388-5300

LIV, PENG TU, BIOMETRICS. *Current Pos:* BR CHIEF, BIOMETRICS & RISK ASSESSMENT BR, CTR FOOD SAFETY & APPL NUTRIT, 81- *Personal Data:* b Taipei, Taiwan, Dec 23, 39. *Educ:* Nat Taiwan Univ, BS, 62; Univ Philippines, MS, 67; Johns Hopkins Univ, ScD, 71. *Prof Exp:* Asst prof, Johns Hopkins Sch Pub Health, 71-76; math statistician, Food & Drug Admin, 77-81. *Mem:* Am Statist Asn. *Mailing Add:* Biomet & Risk Assessment Ctr Food Safety & Appl Nutrit 200 C St SW Washington DC 20204. *Fax:* 202-205-5069

LIVANT, PETER DAVID, PHYSICAL ORGANIC CHEMISTRY. *Current Pos:* ASST PROF CHEM, AUBURN UNIV, 77- *Personal Data:* b New York, NY, Sept 18, 48. *Educ:* City Col New York, BS, 69; Brown Univ, PhD(chem), 75. *Prof Exp:* Vis asst prof chem, Univ Ill, Urbana-Champaign, 74-75, res assoc, 75-76; res assoc, Univ Guelph, 76-77. *Mem:* Am Chem Soc. *Res:* Mechanisms of radical reactions; chemistry of hypervalent species; tetracoordinate tetracovalent sulfur compounds; chemically induced dynamic nuclear polarization dependence on magnetic field strength. *Mailing Add:* Dept Chem Auburn Univ Auburn AL 36849-5312

LIVDAHL, PHILIP V, physics, for more information see previous edition

LIVE, DAVID H, BIOPHYSICS, PHYSICAL CHEMISTRY. *Current Pos:* SR RES ASSOC, DEPT BIOCHEM, MED SCH, UNIV MINN. *Personal Data:* b Philadelphia, Pa, Apr 3, 46. *Educ:* Univ Pa, BA, 67; Calif Inst Technol, PhD(chem), 74. *Prof Exp:* Res assoc biophys, Rockefeller Univ, 74-78, asst prof phys biochem, 78-85; assoc prof chem, Emory Univ, 86-91; mem prof staff, Calif Inst Technol 91-92; assoc lab mem, Mem Sloan Ketttering Cancer Ctr. *Concurrent Pos:* Consult, Jet Propulsion Lab, Calif Inst Technol, 75- *Mem:* Am Chem Soc; AAAS; NY Acad Sci. *Res:* Biophysical applications of magnetic resonance to studying molecular conformation, particularly in peptides and proteins; geochemical investigations by magnetic resonance of terrestrial and lunar samples. *Mailing Add:* Dept Biochem Univ Minn Med Sch 435 Delaware St SE Minneapolis MN 55455

LIVE, ISRAEL, VETERINARY SCIENCE. *Current Pos:* Asst histopath & clin path, Univ Pa, 34-37, from instr path to asst prof, 37-46, bact, 46-49, assoc prof, 49-53, PROF MICROBIOL, SCH VET MED, UNIV PA, 53- *Personal Data:* b Austria, Apr 26, 07; nat US; m 36; c 2. *Educ:* Univ Penn, VMD, 34, AM, 36, PhD(path), 40; Am Bd Microbiol, dipl. *Concurrent Pos:* Mem, Expert Comt Brucellosis, WHO; mem, Comt Brucellosis Res, Nat Acad Sci. *Mem:* Fel AAAS; fel Am Acad Microbiol; Am Vet Med Asn; Am Soc Microbiol; Asn; Am Col Vet Microbiol. *Res:* Diagnosis of filariasis in dogs; nature of Clostridium chauvoei aggressin; diagnosis, therapy and immunization in brucellosis; staphylococci in animals and man; serological characterization of staphylococci. *Mailing Add:* 3900 Ford Rd Apt E10 Philadelphia PA 19131-2039

LIVENGOOD, DAVID ROBERT, BIOPHYSICS, ELECTROPHYSIOLOGY. *Current Pos:* res physiologist, Dept Neurobiol, Armed Forces Radiobiol Res Inst, 73-79, chief, Radiation Biophysics Div, 79-80, chmn, Dept Physiol, 80-95, CHMN, DEPT CELLULAR RADIOBIOL, ARMED FORCES RADIOBIOL RES INST, 95- *Personal Data:* b LaJunta, Colo, Mar 18, 37; c 4. *Educ:* Butler Univ, BS, 60; Ind Univ, PhD(physiol), 70. *Prof Exp:* Res assoc, Dept Biophysics, Sch Med, Univ Md, 71-73. *Concurrent Pos:* Grass Found fel, Woods Hole Marine Biol Lab, 71; fel, Marine Biol Lab, STI, 76; res consult, Dept Physiol, George Washington Univ, 78-84; adj staff, Dept Physiol, Uniformed Serv Univ Health Sci, 80-90 & Dept Physiol & Biophys, Georgetown Univ Sch Med, 84- *Mem:* Biophys Soc; Soc Neurosci; Soc Gen Physiologists; Oxygen Soc. *Res:* Biophysical properties of the membranes of nerve and muscle cells; free radical damage; toxicology of depleated uranium. *Mailing Add:* Dept Cellular Radiobiol Armed Forces Radiobiol Res Inst 8901 Wisconsin Ave Bethesda MD 20889-5603. *Fax:* 301-295-0313; *E-Mail:* livengood@usuhsb.vsons.mil

LIVENGOOD, JOHN R, PREVENTATIVE MEDICINE. *Current Pos:* Assoc dir sci, Div Chronic Dis Control & Community Intervention, 91-96, DEP DIR, EPIDEMIOL & SURVEILLANCE DIV, NAT IMMUNIZATION & SURVEILLANCE DIV, CTR DIS CONTROL & PREV, 96- *Personal Data:* b Cumberland, Md, Mar 25, 54. *Educ:* Columbia Univ, MPhil, 90; Univ Md, MD, 80. *Mem:* Am Pub Health Asn. *Mailing Add:* Nat Immunization Prog Ctr Dis Control & Prev MSC E61 Atlanta GA 30333. *Fax:* 404-639-8616; *E-Mail:* jr1@nip1.em.cdc.gov

LIVENGOOD, SAMUEL MILLER, ORGANIC CHEMISTRY. *Current Pos:* RETIRED. *Personal Data:* b Salisbury Pa, Nov 1, 17; m 41, Ollie Meyers; c Judith (Maxwell), Nancy (Sampson) & Samuel M Jr. *Educ:* Juniata Col, BS, 38; Rutgers Univ, MS, 41, PhD(org chem), 43. *Prof Exp:* Instr chem, Rutgers Univ, 40-43; fel, Mellon Inst, 43-55, sr fel, 55-59; asst dir, Res & Develop Dept, Chem Div, Union Carbide Corp, 59-75, assoc dir, 59-79, dir res & develop, Ethylene Oxide Derivatives Div, 79-83. *Mem:* Am Chem Soc; Soc Chem Indust; Sigma Xi. *Res:* Detergents and cosmetics; textile intermediates; humectants; water soluble resins; hydraulic fluids; heat transfer fluids; metalworking fluids. *Mailing Add:* 11769 Woodlea Dr Waynesboro PA 17268

LIVERMAN, JAMES LESLIE, PLANT PHYSIOLOGY, BIOCHEMISTRY. *Current Pos:* EXPERT, ENVIRON & RADIOL SAFETY, DEFENSE NUCLEAR FACIL SAFETY BD, 92- *Personal Data:* b Brady, Tex, Aug 17, 21; m 43, 59, Mary J Creech; c Carol J, Barbara J, Robert J, James L Jr & Jean L. *Educ:* Tex A&M Univ, BS, 49; Calif Inst Technol, PhD(plant physiol, bio-org chem). *Prof Exp:* Fel plant physiol, Calif Inst Technol, 52-53; from asst prof to prof biochem, Agr & Mech Col, Univ Tex, 53-60; biochemist, AEC, 58-59, asst chief, Biol Br, 59-60, chief, 60-64; assoc dir, Biol Div, Oak Ridge Nat Lab, 64-67, asst dir life sci, 67-69, assoc dir biomed environ sci, 69-72; dir, Div Biomed & Environ Res, US AEC, 72-75, asst gen mgr biomed & environ res & safety, 73-75, dir, Div Biomed & Environ Res & asst adminr environ & safety, US Energy Res & Develop Admin, 77-77; actg asst secy, Dept Energy, 77-78, dep asst secy, 78-79; sr vpres & gen mgr, Appl Sci Div, Litton Bionetics Inc, 79-85, vpres bionetics res, 85-87; vpres prod develop, Organon Teknika Corp, 85-87;

consult, Maxwell Commun Biomed Res & Develop Planning, 87-88; consult & dir tech trf database, Univ Sci Eng & Tech, Inc, 88-90. *Concurrent Pos:* Consult agr chemist, 56-58; chmn, Gordon Conf Biochem & Agr, 61; interim dir, Univ Tenn-Oak Ridge Grad Sch Biomed Sci, 65-66. *Mem:* Fel AAAS; Am Soc Plant Physiol; Am Chem Soc; Radiation Res Soc; Ecol Soc Am; Am Mgt Asn. *Res:* Cell physiology; photoperiodism; radiation in biological systems; immunology; bioengineering; policy science. *Mailing Add:* 5308 Manor Lake Ct Rockville MD 20853. *Fax:* 301-460-3695

LIVERMAN, THOMAS PHILLIP GEORGE, MATHEMATICS. *Current Pos:* assoc prof, George Washington Univ, 58-60, chmn, Dept Math, 71-74 & 76-85, prof, 71-91, EMER PROF MATH & ADJ PROF ENG & APPL SCI, GEORGE WASHINGTON UNIV, 91- *Personal Data:* b Salzburg, Austria, June 18, 23; US citizen; m 85, Wivi B Jensen; c Thierry J. *Educ:* Univ Pa, MA, 48, PhD(math), 56. *Prof Exp:* Instr math, Univ Del, 46-48; engr, CNR Co, France, 48-49; interpreter, US Dept State, 50-51; mathematician, Appl Physics Lab, Johns Hopkins Univ, 51-58. *Mem:* Math Asn Am; Soc Indust & Appl Math. *Res:* Functional analysis and applied mathematics; function theory; operational calculus. *Mailing Add:* 10 Sundale Farm Lane Amissville VA 20106-4342

LIVERMORE, JOHN S, METALLURGY. *Honors & Awards:* Daniel C Jackling Award, Soc Mining Metall Explor, 95. *Mailing Add:* 1755 E Plumb St Suite 170 Reno NV 89502

LIVERSAGE, RICHARD ALBERT, DEVELOPMENTAL BIOLOGY, REGENERATION. *Current Pos:* from asst prof to assoc prof, Univ Toronto, 60-69, grad secy dept, 75-77, assoc chmn grad affairs, 78-84, actg chmn, 80-81, PROF ZOOL, UNIV TORONTO, 69- *Personal Data:* b Fitchburg, Mass, July 8, 25; m 54, June P Krebs; c John W, Robert R, James K & Ross A. *Educ:* Marlboro Col, BA, 51; Amherst Col, AM, 53; Princeton Univ, AM, 57, PhD(biol), 58. *Prof Exp:* Lab instr biol, Bowdoin Col, 53-54, Amherst Col, 54-55; instr biol, Princeton Univ, 58-60. *Concurrent Pos:* Vis investr, Huntsman Marine Lab, NB, Can, 68-71; vis prof, Dept Biophys, Strangeways Res Lab, Cambridge, Eng, 72. *Mem:* Can Soc Zool; Soc Develop Biol; Royal Can Inst; Sigma Xi. *Res:* Regulation of appendage regeneration in amphibians: role of hormones and nerves; determination and fate of the progenitor cell source(s) via gene expression; author of 87 publications. *Mailing Add:* Ramsay Wright Zool Labs Univ Toronto Toronto ON M5S 3G5 Can. *Fax:* 416-978-8532; *E-Mail:* liversag@zoo.utoronto.ca

LIVESAY, GEORGE ROGER, MATHEMATICS. *Current Pos:* res assoc, 56-58, from asst prof to assoc prof, 58-69, PROF MATH, CORNELL UNIV, 69- *Personal Data:* b Ashley, Ill, Dec 9, 24. *Educ:* Univ Ill, BS & MS, 48, PhD, 52. *Prof Exp:* Instr math, Univ Mich, 50-56. *Res:* Topology. *Mailing Add:* White Hall Rm 7901 Cornell Univ Ithaca NY 14853

LIVETT, BRUCE G, NEUROSCIENCES, BIOCHEMICAL PHARMACOLOGY. *Current Pos:* READER & DEP HEAD, DEPT BIOCHEM, UNIV MELBOURNE, AUSTRALIA, 83- *Personal Data:* b Melbourne, Australia, Aug 27, 43; m 76, Dianne Whelan; c Andrew & Erica. *Educ:* Monash Univ, BSc, 65, PhD(biochem), 68. *Prof Exp:* Nuffield Dominions demonstr pharmacol, Oxford Univ, 69-71, jr res fel, Wolfson Col, 70-71; Queen Elizabeth II res fel biochem, Monash Univ, 71-73, asst prof, 73-77; from assoc prof to prof med & biochem, Montreal Gen Hosp, McGill Univ, 77-83. *Concurrent Pos:* Med Res Coun fel neurosci, McMaster Univ, 75-76, prin investr, 77-; prin investr & mem adv bd, Muscular Dystrophy Asn Can, 78-82; coun mem, Int Soc Neurochem, 87-92 & Australian Neurosci Soc, 87-94. *Mem:* Int Brain Res Orgn; Int Soc Neurochem; Soc Neurosci; Australian Neurosci Soc; Australian Soc Biochem Molecular Biol; Australian Physiol & Pharmacol Soc; Australian Soc Comput Learning Tertiary Educ. *Res:* Investigation into the role of neuropeptides as neuromodulators of catecholamine secretion in the endocrine adrenal medulla and nervous system; structure-function studies of marine neurotoxins. *Mailing Add:* Dept Biochem Univ Melbourne Parkville Victoria 3052 Australia. *Fax:* 61-3-9-3477730; *E-Mail:* b.livett@biochemistry.unimelb.edu.au

LIVIGNI, RUSSELL ANTHONY, POLYMER CHEMISTRY. *Current Pos:* VPRES & DIR RES, GENCORP, 88- *Personal Data:* b Akron, Ohio, July 20, 34. *Educ:* Univ Akron, BS, 56, PhD(polymer chem), 60. *Prof Exp:* Res scientist polymer chem, Ford Sci Lab, Gen Tire & Rubber Co, 60-61, sr res chemist, 61-62, group leader, 62-63, sec head, 63-75, mgr, 75-80, assoc dir, 80-87. *Concurrent Pos:* chmn, Gordon Res Conf Elastomers, 78; trustee & mem bd dirs, Edison Polymer Innovation Corp, 86-; mem, NSF Indust Panel Sci & Technol, 90- *Mem:* Am Chem Soc; AAAS. *Res:* Technical programs resulting in advanced and improved products and processes, especially related to polymer based technology; granted 32 patents; author of several publications. *Mailing Add:* 2291 Manchester Rd Akron OH 44314-3602

LIVINGOOD, CLARENCE SWINEHART, DERMATOLOGY. *Current Pos:* RETIRED. *Personal Data:* b Elverson, Pa, Aug 7, 11; wid; c 5. *Educ:* Ursinus Col, BS, 32; Univ Pa, MD, 36; Am Bd Dermat, dipl, 41. *Hon Degrees:* DSc, Ursinus Col, 82. *Honors & Awards:* Gold Medal, Am Acad Dermatol, 75, Presidental Citation, 87; Cert Meritorious Achievement, Dermatol Found, 75; Stephen Rothman Award, Soc Invest Dermatol, 80; Distinguished Serv Award, AMA, 90. *Prof Exp:* Asst prof dermat & syphil, Med Sch, Univ Pa, 46-49; prof dermat, Jefferson Med Col, 48-49; prof dermat & syphil, Sch Med, Univ Tex, 49-53; chmn, Dept Dermat, Henry Hosp, 53-76. *Concurrent Pos:* Consult, Vet Admin & Surg Gen, US Army; mem, Comn Cutaneous Dis, Armed Forces Epidemiol Bd; adv, Panel Med Sch, Dept Defense, 55-60; secy gen, Int Cong Dermat, 62; secy, Am Bd Dermat, 63-92. *Mem:* AAAS; Soc Invest Dermat (pres, 55); hon mem Am Dermatol Asn (pres, 64-68); AMA; NY Acad Sci; Am Acad Dermatol (pres, 67). *Res:* Epidemiology and treatment of cutaneous bacterial infections; topical corticosteroid therapy of cutaneous disease. *Mailing Add:* Dept Dermatol Henry Ford Hosp 2799 W Grand Blvd Detroit MI 48202-2608. *Fax:* 313-886-0124

LIVINGOOD, JOHN N B, MATHEMATICS. *Current Pos:* RETIRED. *Personal Data:* b Birdsboro, Pa, June 8, 13; m 40, Lillian Millard; c Jeanne, Susan & Mary A. *Educ:* Gettysburg Col, AB, 34; Univ Pa, AM, 36, PhD(math), 44. *Prof Exp:* Teacher high sch, 36-38; instr math, Gettysburg Col, 38-42; Rutgers Univ, 42-44; mathematician, Nat Adv Comt Aeronaut, 44-47; asst prof math, Rutgers Univ, 47-48; aeronaut res scientist, Nat Adv Comt Aeronaut 48-58 & NASA, 58-73; lectr math, Col Boca Raton, Fla, 73-81. *Mem:* Am Math Soc. *Res:* Theory of numbers; aeronautical research; turbine cooling; nuclear engineering. *Mailing Add:* 20 NW 24th St Delray Beach FL 33444

LIVINGOOD, MARVIN D(UANE), CHEMICAL ENGINEERING. *Current Pos:* PARTNER, RCI LTD SYST CONSULTS, 83- *Personal Data:* b Corning, Kans, Aug 15, 18; m 47, Agnes Dyer; c Chris, Winifred, Matthew & Abigail. *Educ:* Okla State Univ, BS, 38, MS, 40; Mich State Univ, PhD(chem eng), 52. *Prof Exp:* Chem engr, Arzone Prod Co, 41; instr chem eng, Mo Sch Mines, 41-46; asst prof, Mich State Univ, 46-49, res asst prof, Eng Exp Sta, 49-52; res chem engr, E I Dupont de Nemours & Co Inc, 52-74, environ control supvr, 74-79, sr engr, 79-83. *Concurrent Pos:* Chmn, Prof Develop Comt, Am Inst Chem Engrs, 80-82, Steering Comt, 80-88, chmn fels, 82-86; secy, Mgt Div, Am Inst Chem Engrs, 83-86; consult, 83-; adj prof chem eng, Univ La, 85- *Mem:* Fel Am Inst Chem Engrs. *Res:* Chemical engineering design; economics; small scale pilot plant; safety in handling unstable materials; environmental compliance; accident investigation. *Mailing Add:* 2603 Landor Ave Louisville KY 40205-2333. *Fax:* 502-459-8888; *E-Mail:* mlgood@elephant1.wiu.net

LIVINGSTON, ALBERT EDWARD, MATHEMATICAL ANALYSIS. *Current Pos:* from asst prof to assoc prof, 67-75, PROF MATH, UNIV DEL, 75- *Personal Data:* b Hartford, Conn, Feb 28, 36. *Educ:* Boston Col, BA, 58, MA, 60; Rutgers Univ, MS, 62, PhD(math), 63. *Prof Exp:* Asst prof math, Lafayette Col, 63-67. *Mem:* Math Asn Am; Am Math Soc; Sigma Xi. *Res:* Univalent and multivalent functions, particularly the application of methods of extreme point theory and subordination chains to extremal problems in multivalent function theory. *Mailing Add:* Univ Del Newark DE 19716-0001

LIVINGSTON, CLARK HOLCOMB, PLANT PATHOLOGY. *Current Pos:* RETIRED. *Personal Data:* b Eau Claire, Wis, Nov 25, 20; m 47; c 2. *Educ:* Colo Agr & Mech Col, BS, 51, MS, 53; Univ Minn, PhD, 66. *Prof Exp:* Assoc prof bot & plant path, Colo State Univ, 55-85. *Mem:* Am Phytopath Soc; Potato Asn Am. *Res:* Potato diseases, particularly physiology of disease and viruses. *Mailing Add:* 3008 Shore Rd Ft Collins CO 80524

LIVINGSTON, DANIEL ISADORE, POLYMER PHYSICS, RUBBER TECHNOLOGY. *Current Pos:* PRES LIVINGSTON ASSOC CONSULTS, 86- *Personal Data:* b New York City, NY, Oct 15, 19; m 56, Helen Porritt; c 2. *Educ:* City Col New York, BS, 41; Polytech Inst Brooklyn, PhD(phys chem), 50. *Prof Exp:* Dir polymer chem, Gen Latex & Chem Corp, 50-51; scientist, Polaroid Corp, 51-55; sr res engr, Ford Motor Co, 55-57; sr res chemist, Continental Can Co, III, 57-59; head, Polymer Physics Sect, Goodyear Tire & Rubber Co, 59-84, res & develop assoc, 85-86. *Concurrent Pos:* Assoc ed, Rubber Chem & Technol, 69-72; ed, Tire Sci & Technol, 73-82. *Mem:* Am Chem Soc; Am Phys Soc; Tire Soc (pres, 86-88); Am Soc Testing & Mat. *Res:* Physical chemistry of polymers; high polymer synthesis, research and development; radiation effects in polymer systems; polymer physics; tire physics; materials science; rubber technology. *Mailing Add:* 731 Frank Blvd Akron OH 44320-1021

LIVINGSTON, DAVID M, MEDICINE. *Current Pos:* PROF MED, HARVARD MED SCH, BOSTON, MASS, 82-; CHMN, EXEC RES, DANA FARBER CANCER INST, 91- *Personal Data:* b Cambridge, Mass, Mar 29, 41; m 86, Emily Rabb; c Catherine & Julie. *Educ:* Harvard Univ, AB, 61; Tufts Univ, MD, 65; Am Bd Internal Med, cert, 71. *Prof Exp:* Intern med, Peter Bent Brigham Hosp, Boston, Mass, 65-66, jr resident, 66-67; res assoc, Lab Biochem, Nat Cancer Inst, NIH, 67-69, sr staff fel, 71-72; res fel biol chem, Harvard Med Sch, Boston, Mass, 69-71; assoc med, Brigham & Women's Hosp, Boston, Mass, 73-77, sr assoc med, 76-82. *Concurrent Pos:* Sr investr, Nat Cancer Inst, NIH, 72-73; from asst prof to assoc prof med, Harvard Med Sch, 73-82; sr clin assoc, Dana-Farber Cancer Inst, 73-77, assoc physician, 77-83, vpres, 89-91, dir & physician-in-chief, Dana-Farber Cancer Inst, Boston, Mass, 91-; vis physician med serv, Brigham & Women's Hosp, 74-85, mem, Med Internship Selection Comt, 75-, physician, 82-; mem, Virol Study Sect, Div Res Grants, NIH, 79-83 & 86-88. *Mem:* Nat Acad Sci; Inst Med-Nat Acad Sci; Am Soc Microbiol; Am Soc Clin Invest; Am Soc Biol Chem & Molecular Biol; Asn Am Physicians; Am Soc Virol; Am Fedn Clin Res. *Res:* Molecular biology of virus-induced neoplastic transformation; control of eukaryotic gene expression and DNA replication; author or co-author of over 90 publications. *Mailing Add:* Dana-Farber Cancer Inst 44 Binney St Boston MA 02115-6013

LIVINGSTON, DOUGLAS ALAN, PROCESS RESEARCH FOR ORGANIC SYNTHESES, MEDICINAL CHEMISTRY. *Current Pos:* ASSOC DIR CHEM OPERS, LAJOLLA PHARMACEUT CO, 92- *Personal Data:* b Nagoya, Japan, Dec 29, 54; US citizen; m 77, Elizabeth A Acorn; c Andrew S. *Educ:* Univ Wash, BS, 77; Columbia Univ, MA, 81,

MPhil, 82, PhD(org chem), 82. *Prof Exp:* Swiss NSF researcher, ETH-Zurich, 82-83; res scientist, Upjohn Co, 83-90, Burroughs-Wellcome Co, 90-92. *Res:* Design and synthesis of potential new pharmaceutical entities; development of new methodology for existing drugs including steroids, aminothioglycosides, alkaloids, nucleosides and oligonucleosides. *Mailing Add:* LaJola Pharm Co 6455 Nancy Ridge Dr San Diego CA 92121-2249

LIVINGSTON, G E, FOOD SCIENCE & NUTRITION. *Current Pos:* PRES FOOD SCI ASSOCS INC, 56-; CHMN, SIERRA SUNSET INC, 88- *Personal Data:* b Rotterdam, Neth, Feb 1, 27; m 91, Joan Bendel; c David J, Gary M & Nina J. *Educ:* NY Univ, BA, 48; Univ Mass, MS, 51, PhD(food technol), 52. *Honors & Awards:* Sigma Xi Res Award, 57; Carl R Fellers Award, Inst Food Technol, 93 & Food Serv Distinguished Achievement Award, 96. *Prof Exp:* Chemist, Bur Chem, NY Produce Exchange, 49; from asst prof to assoc prof food technol, Univ Mass, 51-59; dir, Food Sci Prog, Columbia Univ, 66-72; vpres, Mithcell Lane Kitchens Inc, 92-93. *Concurrent Pos:* Vis prof, Laval Univ, 54; vis lectr, City Col New York, 59-60; res supvr, Continental Baking Co, 59-62; mem, Adv Bd Mil Personnel Supplies, Nat Acad Sci-Nat Res Coun, 61-64, chmn, Comt Food Serv Systs, 68-71; mgr, Instnl Prod Dept, Morton Frozen Foods Co, 62-65; adj prof, Columbia Univ, 66-72; invitee, White House Conf Food, Nutrit & Health, 69; chmn, Food & Nutrit Coun, Am Health Found, 69-91, mem bd sci consults, 69-80; chmn, Panel VII, Nat Conf Food Protection, 71; consult, US Army Natick Labs, 71-83 & numerous others; mem, Bd Govs, Food Update, Food & Drug Law Inst, 71-75; adj prof, Pratt Inst, 73-78, 91 75-; mem, Food Stability Comn; co-ed, J Food Serv Systs, 80-83; ed-in-chief, Pioneers Food Sci, 92- *Mem:* Am Chem Soc; Soc Food Serv Systs (pres, 81-83); Fel Inst Food Technologists; Res & Develop Assocs Mil Food & Packaging Systs; fel Am Col Nutrit; fel AAAS; NY Acad Sci. *Res:* Food colorimetry; prepared foods; food service systems; nutritive value; fresh food safety; author of one hundred publications; granted two US patents. *Mailing Add:* Food Sci Assocs Inc PO Box 330 Dobbs Ferry NY 10522-0330. *Fax:* 914-693-1869; *E-Mail:* dr.guy@happy_francophile.com

LIVINGSTON, HUGH DUNCAN, RADIOCHEMISTRY, OCEANOGRAPHY. *Current Pos:* res assoc, 71-73, res specialist, 73-79, SR RES SPECIALIST CHEM, WOODS HOLE OCEANOG INST, 79- *Personal Data:* b Glasgow, Scotland, Nov 12, 40; US citizen; m 65. *Educ:* Glasgow Univ, BSc, 62, PhD(chem), 66. *Prof Exp:* Res assoc chem, Woods Hole Oceanog Inst, 67-69; res fel, Bowman Gray Sch Med, 69-71. *Res:* Studies of artificial radioisotopes in the marine environment. *Mailing Add:* 20 Wing Rd North Falmouth MA 02556

LIVINGSTON, JAMES DUANE, SUPERCONDUCTIVITY, FERROMAGNETISM. *Current Pos:* SR LECTR MAT SCI, DEPT MAT SCI & ENG, MASS INST TECHNOL, CAMBRIDGE, 89- *Personal Data:* b Brooklyn, NY, June 23, 30; m 53, 85, Sherry Penney; c Joan, Susan & Barbara. *Educ:* Cornell Univ, BEP, 52; Harvard Univ, MA, 53, PhD(appl physics), 56. *Prof Exp:* Physicist, Gen Elec Corp, Schenectady, NY, 56-89. *Concurrent Pos:* Guest prof, Univ Gottingen, 70; vis prof, Rensselaer Polytech Inst, 87-88; Gen Elec Coolidge fel, distinguished career award, Am Inst Metall Eng. *Mem:* Nat Acad Eng; fel Am Phys Soc; fel Am Soc Metals Int; AAAS; Metall Soc; Inst Elec & Electronics Engrs. *Res:* Superconducting, ferromagnetic and mechanical properties of materials and their relation to microstructure and processing. *Mailing Add:* Mass Inst Technol 13-4066 Cambridge MA 02139. *E-Mail:* jdliv@mat.edu

LIVINGSTON, KNOX W, FORESTRY. *Current Pos:* RETIRED. *Personal Data:* b Atlanta, Ga, Apr 24, 19; m 48; c 1. *Educ:* Univ SC, BS, 40; Duke Univ, MF, 48. *Prof Exp:* Asst forestry, Auburn Univ, 48-49, asst forester, 49-63, from asst prof to assoc prof, 63-78, emer assoc prof forestry, 78-85. *Mem:* Soc Am Foresters. *Res:* Density, site, growth relations, especially planted southern pine; soil, site relations. *Mailing Add:* 856 Cary Dr Auburn AL 36830

LIVINGSTON, MARILYN LAURENE, NUMBER THEORY. *Current Pos:* from asst prof to assoc prof, 69-78, PROF MATH, SOUTHERN ILL UNIV, 78- *Personal Data:* b High Prarie, Alta, Mar 3, 40; wid. *Educ:* Univ Alta, BSc, 61, MSc, 63, PhD(math), 66. *Prof Exp:* Asst prof, Western Wash State Col, 66-67; vis asst prof, Ore State Univ, 67-69. *Concurrent Pos:* Mem, Sch Math, Inst Advan Study, Princeton, NJ, 74-75; vis scholar, Univ Mich, Ann Arbor, 86-87. *Mem:* Asn Comput Mach; Soc Indust & Appl Math; Inst Elec & Electronic Engrs. *Res:* Combinatorics; design and analysis of algorithms; parallel algorithms for distributed memory machines. *Mailing Add:* Dept Comput Sci Southern Ill Univ Edwardsville 6 Hairpin Dr Edwardsville IL 62026-0001

LIVINGSTON, RALPH, CHEMICAL PHYSICS, MAGNETIC RESONANCE. *Current Pos:* RETIRED. *Personal Data:* b Keene, NH, May 16, 19; div; c Beverly, Sally, Donna & Stuart. *Educ:* Univ NH, BS, 40, MS, 41; Univ Cincinnati, DSc, 43. *Prof Exp:* Chemist, Metall Lab, Univ Chicago, 43-45, Gaseous Diffusion Proj, 45, chem Div, Oak Ridge Nat Lab, 45-84, group leader, 75-84. *Concurrent Pos:* Guggenheim & Fulbright fel, France, 60-61; vis prof chem, Cornell Univ, 61-62; prof, Univ Tenn, 64-76; res fel, Union Carbide Corp, 79; consult, 84- *Mem:* Am Chem Soc; Am Phys Soc. *Res:* Radiation chemistry; chemical physics; nuclear quadrupole spectroscopy and electron spin resonance. *Mailing Add:* 144 Westlook Circle Oak Ridge TN 37830

LIVINGSTON, ROBERT BURR, NEUROSCIENCES. *Current Pos:* chmn, Dept Neurosci, 65-71, PROF NEUROSCI, SCH MED, UNIV CALIF, SAN DIEGO, 65- *Personal Data:* b Boston, Mass, Oct 9, 18; m 54; c 3. *Educ:* Stanford Univ, AB, 40, MD, 44. *Honors & Awards:* Matrix Midland Award, 81; Sachs Mem Lectr, Dartmouth Med Sch, 81. *Prof Exp:* Intern, Stanford Hosp, 43, asst resident, 44; instr physiol, Sch Med, Yale Univ, 46-48; asst prof physiol, Sch Med & dir aeromed res unit, Yale Univ, 50-52; from assoc prof to prof physiol & anat, Univ Calif, Los Angeles, 52-56; dir basic res & sci dir, NIMH & Nat Inst Neurol Dis & Blindness, NIH, 56-60, chief lab neurobiol, NIMH, 60-63, chief gen res support br & assoc chief prog planning, Div Res Facil & Resources, 63-65. *Concurrent Pos:* Nat Res Coun sr fel neurol, Inst Physiol, Switz, 48-49; Gruber fel neurophysiol, Switz, France & Eng, 49-50; NIMH sr fel, Gothenburg Univ, 56; res asst, Harvard Med Sch, 47-48; asst to pres, Nat Acad Sci, 51-52; prof lectr, Univ Calif, Los Angeles, 56-59; assoc, Neurosci Res Prog, 63-76, hon assoc, 76-; guest prof, Univ Zurich, 71-72. *Mem:* Am Physiol Soc; Am Asn Neurol Surg; Am Neurol Asn; Am Asn Anatomists; Soc Neurosci; Int Physicians Prev Nuclear War. *Res:* Mechanisms relating to higher nervous processes, perception, learning and memory; plasticity of nervous system; three-dimensional analysis and display of neuroanatomical structures; mapping human brains in 3-D at microscopic levels of detail; individual differences in human brain structure-function relations. *Mailing Add:* Dept Neurosci M-024 Univ Calif at San Diego La Jolla CA 92093

LIVINGSTON, ROBERT SIMPSON, PHYSICS, RESEARCH ADMINISTRATION. *Current Pos:* CONSULT, 81- *Personal Data:* b Summerland, Calif, Sept 20, 14; m 55; c 5. *Educ:* Pomona Col, BA, 35; Univ Calif, MA, 41, PhD(physics), 41. *Prof Exp:* Asst physics, Pomona Col, 35-36; asst, Univ Calif, 36-39, res fel, Lawrence Radiation Lab, 39-43; physicist, Tenn Eastman Corp, 43-47; res supt, Carbide & Carbon Corp, 47-50; dir, Electronuclear Div, Oak Ridge Nat Lab, 50-71, dir prog planning & anal, 71-81. *Concurrent Pos:* Consult, Nuclear Physics Panel, Physics Surv Comt, Nat Acad Sci, 69-72; chmn, Ad Hoc Comt Heavy Ion Sources, Nuclear Sci Div, Nat Acad Sci, 72-74; chmn, NSF/Dept Energy study group on the role of electron accelerators in US medium energy nuclear sci, 77-78. *Mem:* Fel Inst Elec & Electronics Engrs; fel Am Phys Soc; fel AAAS; Am Nuclear Soc; Sigma Xi. *Res:* Long range planning of scientific research and development in energy; design of isochronous cyclotrons; heavy particle accelerators; new particle accelerator methods; high intensity ion sources. *Mailing Add:* 7204 Fairlane Dr Powell TN 37849-4441

LIVINGSTON, WILLIAM CHARLES, ASTRONOMY. *Current Pos:* from jr astronr to astronr, 59-93, EMER ASTRONOMER, KITT PEAK NAT OBSERV, 94-; ASTRONR, NAT OPTICAL ASTRON OBSERV, 84- *Personal Data:* b Santa Ana, Calif, Sept 13, 27; m 57, Dorothy Newell; c Peter & Ann. *Educ:* Univ Calif, Los Angeles, AB, 53; Univ Calif, PhD(astron), 59. *Prof Exp:* Observer, Mt Wilson Observ, Carnegie Inst, 51-53. *Mem:* Am Astron Soc; Int Astron Union; Astron Soc India; foreign mem Norweg Acad Sci. *Res:* Solar spectroscopy; solar magnetism; solar cycle studies. *Mailing Add:* PO Box 26732 Tucson AZ 85726

LIVINGSTONE, DANIEL ARCHIBALD, LIMNOLOGY, PALEOECOLOGY. *Current Pos:* from asst prof to assoc prof, 56-66, J B Duke prof zool, 83, geol, 89, PROF ZOOL, DUKE UNIV, 66- *Personal Data:* b Detroit, Mich, Aug 3, 27; m 89, Patricia Greene; c 5. *Educ:* Dalhousie Univ, BSc, 48, MSc, 50; Yale Univ, PhD(zool), 53. *Honors & Awards:* Hutchinson Medal, Am Soc Limnol & Oceanog. *Prof Exp:* Field collector, NS Mus Sci, summers & demonstr biol, Dalhousie Univ, winters, 47-50; asst zool, Yale Univ, 50-53; Nat Res Coun Can fels, Cambridge Univ, 53-54 & Dalhousie Univ, 54-55; asst prof zool, Univ Md, 55-56. *Concurrent Pos:* Spec lectr biogeog, Dalhousie Univ, 54-55; limnologist, US Geol Surv, 56-63; Guggenheim fel, 60-61; mem environ biol panel, NSF, 64-, consult NSF Polar Prog, 74-76. *Mem:* Ecol Soc Am (ed, Ecol Monogr, 62-66); Am Soc Limnol & Oceanog; Am Geophys Union; Am Quaternary Asn; Sigma Xi; Am Soc Ichthyol & Herpet. *Res:* Pollen analysis; history of lakes; Pleistocene geology of Alaska, Nova Scotia, West, East and Central Africa; geochemistry of hydrosphere; sodium cycle; coring technology; paleoecology; limnology; biogeography of African fishes; distribution of grasses and sedges. *Mailing Add:* Dept Zool Duke Univ Durham NC 27706. *Fax:* 919-684-6168; *E-Mail:* livingst@raphael.acpub.duke.edu

LIVINGSTONE, FRANK BROWN, PHYSICAL ANTHROPOLOGY. *Current Pos:* from asst prof to assoc prof, 59-68, PROF ANTHROP, UNIV MICH, ANN ARBOR, 68- *Personal Data:* b Winchester, Mass, Dec 8, 28; m 60; c 1. *Educ:* Harvard Univ, AB, 50; Univ Mich, MA, 53, PhD(anthrop), 57. *Prof Exp:* Nat Sci Found fel, 57-59. *Mem:* Am Asn Phys Anthropologists; Am Anthropol Asn. *Res:* Human and population genetics; abnormal hemoglobin; cultural determinants of human evolution. *Mailing Add:* Dept Anthrop 1054 LSA Univ Mich Main Campus 500 S State St Ann Arbor MI 48109-1382

LIVOLSI, VIRGINIA ANNE, ENDOCRINE PATHOLOGY, GYNECOLOGIC PATHOLOGY. *Current Pos:* PROF PATH & LAB MED & DIR SURG PATH, UNIV PA MED CTR, 83- *Personal Data:* b New York, NY, July 29, 43. *Educ:* Col Mt St Vincent, NY, BS, 65; Columbia Univ, MD, 69. *Hon Degrees:* MA, Univ Pa, Philadelphia, 83. *Honors & Awards:* Medal of Honor, Tokyo Univ, 92. *Prof Exp:* Instr path, Columbia Univ, 73-74; from asst prof to assoc prof path, Yale Univ Sch Med, 74-83. *Concurrent Pos:* Attend pathologist, Yale-New Haven Hosp, Conn, 74-83, dir, Lab Cytol, 75-77; consult path, Chester Co Hosp, Pa, 85- & Vet Admin Med Ctr, Philadelphia, 88-90. *Mem:* Am Acad Path; Can Acad Path; Am Thyroid Asn; Am Soc Clin Pathologists; Asn Dir Anat & Surg Path. *Res:* Evaluation of thyroid nodules, benign and malignant; clinical behavior. *Mailing Add:* Lab Med Box 4120 Hosp Univ PA 3400 Spruce St Founders 6042 Philadelphia PA 19104-4283. *Fax:* 215-349-5910

LJUNGDAHL, LARS GERHARD, BIOCHEMISTRY, MICROBIOLOGY. *Current Pos:* from mem fac to assoc prof, 67-75, PROF BIOCHEM, UNIV GA, 75- *Personal Data:* b Stockholm, Sweden, Aug 5, 26; m 49; c 2. *Educ:* Stockholm Tech Inst, BS, 45; Western Reserve Univ, PhD(biochem), 64. *Prof Exp:* Technician med chem, Karolinska Inst, Univ Sweden, 43-46; res chemist, Stockholm Brewery Co, 47-58; technician biochem, Case Western Reserve Univ, 58-59, sr instr, 64-66, asst prof, 66-67. *Concurrent Pos:* Alexander Von Humboldt Sr Scientist Award, 74- *Mem:* Am Soc Microbiol; Am Chem Soc; Brit Biochem Soc; Swed Chem Soc; Am Soc Biochem; Sigma Xi. *Res:* Carbohydrate metabolism, carbon dioxide fixation, and one carbon metabolism inanaerobic microorganism; role of corrinoids, tetrahydrofolate derivatives and properties of enzymes in these processes. *Mailing Add:* Dept Biochem Univ Ga A214 Life Sci Bldg Athens GA 30602

LLAURADO, JOSEP G, NUCLEAR MEDICINE, BIOMEDICAL ENGINEERING. *Current Pos:* CHIEF NUCLEAR MED SERV, VET ADMIN HOSP, LOMA LINDA, CALIF, 83-; PROF RADIATION SCI, UNIV LOMA LINDA SCH MED, 83- *Personal Data:* b Barcelona, Catalonia, Spain, Feb 6, 27; m 58, 66, Deirdre Mooney; c Thadd, Oleg, Montserrat, Raymund, Wilfred & Mireya. *Educ:* Balmes Inst, Barcelona, BA & BS, 44; Univ Barcelona, MD, 50, PhD, 60; Drexel Univ, MS, 63. *Honors & Awards:* Catalan Jocs Florals Prize, Amsterdam, 74 & Caracas, 75. *Prof Exp:* Inst med, Sch Med, Univ Barcelona, 50-52; asst med res, Postgrad Med Sch, Univ London, 52-54; asst prof exp surg, Med Sch, Univ Otago, NZ, 54-57; USPHS Found fel steroid biochem, Col Med Univ Utah, 58-59; assoc prof physiol, Sch Med, Univ Pa, 63-67; prof biomed eng & physiol, Marquette Univ & Med Col, Wis, 67-82. *Concurrent Pos:* Brit Coun scholar, Postgrad Med Sch, Univ London, 52-54; Hite Found fel exp med, Univ Tex M D Anderson Hosp & Tumor Inst, 57-58; fel, Coun Adv Sci Invests, Spain, 50-52; Rockefeller vis prof, Univ Valle, Colombia, 58; partic, Nat Colloquim Theoret Biol, NASA, Colo, 65; physician, Vet Admin Hosp, Wood, Wis, 67-; US rep, Int Atomic Energy Agency Symp Dynamic Studies Radioisotopes Med, Rotterdam, 70 & Knoxville, Tenn, 74; vis prof, Polytech Univ, Barcelona, Spain, 73 & 75; vis prof, Univ Zulia, Venezuela, 74 & 75 & Univ Padua, Italy, 75; ed, Int J Biomed Comput; consult, Good Samaritan Hosp, Milwaukee, Wis & St Joseph Mem Hosp, West Bend, 79-82; chief ed, Intl J Biomed Comput; consult, Kaiser Permanente, Riverside, Calif; dep ed, Environ Mgt & Health. *Mem:* Soc Nuclear Med; Am Soc Pharmacol & Exp Therapeut; Catalan Soc Biol; Biomed Eng Soc; sr mem Inst Elec & Electronics Engrs; Am Physiol Soc. *Res:* Radionuclides in cardiology (thallium-201 and analogs); radionuclide (P-32) treatment of pulmonary cancer; computers in nuclear medicine; biomathematics; compartmental analysis of electrolytes. *Mailing Add:* Loma Linda Univ Sch Med VA Hosp 115 Loma Linda CA 92357-0001. *Fax:* 909-422-3106

LLENADOL, RAMON, CHEMISTRY. *Current Pos:* GROUP VPRES, CLOROX CO, 91- *Educ:* Univ Santo Tomas, Philippines, BS; State Univ NY, PhD(chem). *Prof Exp:* Staff mem, Procter & Gamble Co, 72-83; div vpres household prod res, dir prod develop & vpres res & develop, L&F Prod Inc, 83-91. *Concurrent Pos:* Bd dirs, Soap & Detergent Asn & Chem Specialties Mfg Asn. *Res:* Chemistry; household products. *Mailing Add:* RAL Enterprises 150 Post St San Francisco CA 94108

LLEWELLYN, CHARLES ELROY, JR, PSYCHIATRY. *Current Pos:* PVT PRACT, 87- *Personal Data:* b Richmond, Va, Jan 16, 22; m 48, Grace Eldridge; c Charles III & Richard S. *Educ:* Hampden-Sydney Col, BS, 43; Med Col Va, MD, 46; Univ Colo, MSc, 53; Am Bd Psychiat & Neurol, dipl, 56. *Prof Exp:* Instr psychiat, Med Col Va, 46-47; assoc, Duke Univ, 55-56, asst prof, 56-63, asst dir, Psychiat Outpatient Div, 55-56, head, Psychiat Outpatient Div, 56-76, chief training, Community & Social Psychiat Div, 81-85, assoc prof psychiat, Sch Med, 63-87, head, Div Community & Social Psychiat Div, 76-81 & 85-87. *Concurrent Pos:* Partic, NIMH vis fac sem community psychiat, Lab Community Psychiat, Harvard Med Sch, 65-67; prog dir, Duke Study Group, Interuniv Forum Educr Community Psychiat, 67-71; consult, State Dept Social Serv, NC, 55-79; med consult, Substance Abuse Treatment Ctr, Durham Mental Health Prog, 70-90; chief psychiat consult for Peer Rev & Qual Assurance, NC Div Ment Health Serv, 75-78; psychiat consult, NC Med Peer Rev Found, 75-79. *Mem:* Pan-Am Med Asn; Am Med Asn; Am Psychiat Asn. *Res:* Community mental health; individual and group psychotherapy; marital and family therapy. *Mailing Add:* 3308 Durham-Chapel Hill Blvd No 110 Durham NC 27707. *Fax:* 919-490-3099; *E-Mail:* ellewellyn@juno.com

LLEWELLYN, GERALD CECIL, BIONUCLEONICS. *Current Pos:* from asst prof to assoc prof, 69-77, ASSOC BIOL EDUC, VA COMMONWEALTH UNIV, 77-, DIR, BUR TOXIC SUBSTANCES. *Personal Data:* b Lonaconing, Md, Feb 8, 40; m 62; c 3. *Educ:* Frostburg State Col, BS, 62; Purdue Univ, MS, 66, PhD(bionucleonics), 70. *Prof Exp:* Instr biol chem, Frederick County Bd Educ, Md, 62-66; lectr biol & microbiol, Frederick Community Col, 66-67. *Mem:* Nat Sci Teachers Asn; Sigma Xi. *Res:* Toxicological responses of hamsters to aflatoxin B. *Mailing Add:* Dept Toxicol & Pharmacol Va Commonwealth Univ PO Box 980613 12th & Clay Richmond VA 23298

LLEWELLYN, J(OHN) ANTHONY, ENGINEERING SCIENCE, CHEMICAL PHYSICS. *Current Pos:* PROF DEPT CHEM & MECH ENG, UNIV S FLA, 72-, ASSOC DEAN & DIR ENG COMPUT. *Personal Data:* b Cardiff, Wales, Apr 22, 33; m 57; c 3. *Educ:* Univ Wales, BSc, 55, PhD(chem), 58. *Prof Exp:* Nat Res Coun Can fel, 58-60; res assoc chem, Fla State Univ, 60-61, res assoc chem, Inst Molecular Biophys, 61-62, asst prof chem, 62-64, assoc prof eng sci, Sch Eng Sci, 64-72. *Concurrent Pos:* Scientist astronaut, NASA, 67-68. *Mem:* Am Chem Soc; Am Inst Aeronaut & Astronaut; Royal Inst Chemists; Am Soc Mass Spectrometry; Am Vacuum Soc. *Res:* Computing applications in medical imaging; theories of reaction rates; computer applications in chemical engineering. *Mailing Add:* Eng Comput Eng 118 Univ S Fla 4202 Fowler Ave Tampa FL 33620-9951

LLEWELLYN, RALPH A, NUCLEAR PHYSICS, ENVIRONMENTAL PHYSICS. *Current Pos:* dean, Col Arts & Sci, 80-84, PROF PHYSICS, UNIV CENT FLA, 80- *Personal Data:* b Detroit, Mich, June 27, 33; m 55, Laura D Alsop; c Mark, Rita, Lisa & Eric. *Educ:* Rose-Hulman Inst Technol, BS, 55; Purdue Univ, PhD(physics), 62. *Prof Exp:* Asst prof physics, Rose-Hulman Inst Technol, 61-64, assoc prof, 64-68, prof, 68-70, chmn dept, 69-70; prof & chmn dept, Ind State Univ, Terre Haute, 70-73; exec secy, Bd on Energy Studies, Nat Acad Sci, Nat Res Coun, 73-74; prof physics & chmn dept, Ind State Univ, Terre Haute, 74-80. *Concurrent Pos:* Mem, NSF Apparatus Develop Workshop, Rensselaer Polytech Inst, 64-65; prof physics & acting chmn dept, St Mary-of-the-Woods Col, 69-70. *Mem:* AAAS; Am Phys Soc; Am Asn Physics Teachers; NY Acad Sci; Sigma Xi; Nat Geog Soc. *Res:* Environmental physics, particularly beta and gamma decay; low level radiation in the environment; energy resources, energy and public policy; world energy resources; aluminum-26 in meteorites and lunar materials. *Mailing Add:* Dept Physics Univ Cent Fla Orlando FL 32816-2385. *Fax:* 407-823-5112; *E-Mail:* ralphl@pegasus.cc.ucf.edu

LLINAS, MIGUEL, NUCLEAR MAGNETIC RESONANCE SPECTROSCOPY, MOLECULAR BIOPHYSICS. *Current Pos:* assoc prof, Carnegie-Mellon Univ, 76-88, chmn grad prog biophys & biochem, 87-88, dir grad studies, Dept Chem, 87-91, PROF CHEM, CARNEGIE-MELLON UNIV, 88- *Personal Data:* b Cordoba, Arg, Oct 16, 38; div; c Laura D, Miguel Jr, Gabriel & Manuel. *Educ:* Cordoba Nat Univ, Argentina, Licentiate, 63; Univ Calif, Berkeley, PhD(biophys), 71. *Prof Exp:* Fel assoc, Univ Calif, Berkeley, 71-74; asst, Swiss Fed Inst Technol, Zurich, 74-76. *Concurrent Pos:* Vis prof, Univ Utrecht, 89, Catalonia Polytech Univ, 90. *Mem:* Biophys Soc; Am Chem Soc; AAAS; Protein Soc; Am Heart Asn. *Res:* Applications of nuclear magnetic resonance spectroscopy to the study of biological polypeptides; structure and function of antithrombotics; protein structure and dynamics; conformation of human plasminogen and its interaction with antifibrinolytics; domain structures in mosaic proteins. *Mailing Add:* Dept Chem Carnegie-Mellon Univ 4400 Fifth Ave Pittsburgh PA 15213-3890. *Fax:* 412-268-1061

LLINAS, RODOLFO R, NEUROBIOLOGY, ELECTROPHYSIOLOGY. *Current Pos:* PROF & CHMN, DEPT PHYSIOL & NEUROSCI, SCH MED, NY UNIV, 76-, THOMAS & SUZANNE MURPHY PROF NEUROSCI, 85- *Personal Data:* b Bogota, Colombia, Dec 16, 34; US citizen; m 65, Gillian Kimber; c Raphael & Alexander. *Educ:* Pontificial Univ Javeriana, Colombia, MD, 59; Australian Nat Univ, PhD(neurophysiol), 65. *Hon Degrees:* Dr, Univ Salamanca, 85, Univ Barcelona, 93 & Univ Nacional, Colombia, 94. *Honors & Awards:* Bowditch Lectr, Am Physiol Soc, 73; Lang Lectr, Marine Biol Lab, Woods Hole, 82; McDowall Lectr, King's Col, London, 84; Ulf von Euler Lectr, Karolinska Inst, 87; Ralph Gerard Lectr, Univ Calif, Irvine, 87; Craythorne Lectr, Univ Miami, 88; Luigi Galvani Lectr & Award, Georgetown Univ, 88; F O Schmitt Lectr & Award, Rockefeller Univ, 89; Albert Einstein Gold Medal Award in Sci, UNESCO, 91. *Prof Exp:* Instr neurophysiol, Nat Univ Colombia, 59; assoc prof, Univ Minn, 65-66; mem, Inst Biomed Res, AMA Educ & Res Found, 66-67, head, Dept Neurobiol, 68-70; prof physiol & biophys & head, Div Neurobiol, Univ Iowa, 70-76. *Concurrent Pos:* Res fel psychiat & neurosurg, Mass Gen Hosp, 59-61; fel physiol, Univ Minn, 61-63; res scholar, Australian Nat Univ, 63-65; prof lectr, Col Med, Univ Ill, 67-68, clin prof, 68-72; guest prof, Wayne State Univ, 67-74; assoc prof, Med Sch, Northwestern Univ, 67-71; mem, Neurol Sci Res Training A Comt, NIH, 71-74 & Neurol A Study Sect, 74-78, panel mem, Task Force Basic Sci, 78; consult, Sch Aerospace Med, USAF, 72-75; assoc, Neurosci Res Prog, Mass Inst Technol, 74-84; chief ed, Neurosci, 74-; mem, USA Nat Comt for IBRO, Nat Res Coun, 78-81, actg chmn, 82, chmn, 83-88. *Mem:* Nat Acad Sci; Am Soc Cell Biol; Soc Neurosci; Int Brain Res Orgn; Biophys Soc; Am Physiol Asn; Am Acad Arts & Sci; Am Philos Soc. *Res:* Structural and functional studies of neuronal systems; synaptic transmission in vertebrate and invertebrate forms; evolution and development of the central nervous system; author of 8 publications. *Mailing Add:* Dept Physiol & Biophys NY Univ Med Ctr New York NY 10016

LLOYD, DOUGLAS ROY, MEMBRANE SCIENCE, POLYMER SCIENCE. *Current Pos:* asst prof, 80-83, ASSOC PROF CHEM ENG, UNIV TEX, 83- *Personal Data:* b Kitchener, Ont, Sept 15, 48; m 74. *Educ:* Univ Waterloo, BASc, 73, MASc, 74, PhD(chem eng), 77. *Prof Exp:* Asst prof chem eng, Va Polytech Inst & State Univ, 78-80. *Concurrent Pos:* Res engr, Union Carbide Can, 69-70, Crane Can Ltd, 70-71; res assoc, Angelstone Ltd, 73; res assoc, Dept Chem Eng, Univ Waterloo, 72, fel, 77-78. *Mem:* Am Chem Soc; Am Inst Chem Engrs; NAm Membrane Soc. *Res:* Synthetic polymeric membranes; membrane separation processes; polymer physics; enzyme engineering. *Mailing Add:* Dept Chem Eng Univ Tex Austin TX 78712-1104

LLOYD, DOUGLAS SEWARD, PUBLIC HEALTH. *Current Pos:* COMNR, CONN STATE DEPT HEALTH SERV, 73- *Personal Data:* b Brooklyn, NY, Oct 16, 39. *Educ:* Duke Univ, AB, 61, MD, 71; Univ NC, MPH, 71. *Concurrent Pos:* Mem courtesy staff, Hartford Hosp, 73-; lectr, Sch Med, Yale Univ, 73- & Univ Conn Health Ctr, 73-; chmn, Asn State & Territorial Health Off Found, McLean, Va; comdr & spec consult to Naval Med Command, US Naval Res; health commentator, WFSB-TV, "House-Call" prog. *Mem:* Asn State & Territorial Health Off (past pres); US Interagency Comt Smoking & Health. *Mailing Add:* USHHS 5600 Fishers Lane Rm 14-15 Rockville MD 20857-0001

LLOYD, EDWARD C(HARLES), engineering, for more information see previous edition

LLOYD, EDWIN PHILLIPS, ENTOMOLOGY. *Current Pos:* RETIRED. *Personal Data:* b San Antonio, Tex, Sept 18, 29; m 54; c 1. *Educ:* Tex A&M Univ, BS, 51, MS, 52, PhD(entom), 58. *Honors & Awards:* Superior Serv Award, USDA, 74; Res Award, Miss Entom Asn, 74. *Prof Exp:* Res entomologist, Boll Weevil Res Lab, Agr Res Serv, USDA, 56-86, dir, 82-86. *Concurrent Pos:* Sci adv, pilot boll weevil eradication exp, 71-73; adj prof, Miss State Univ, 71-86. *Mem:* Entom Soc Am. *Res:* Cotton insects, specifically the boll weevil. *Mailing Add:* PO Box 1143 Starkville MS 39759

LLOYD, HARRIS HORTON, CANCER, CHEMOTHERAPY. *Current Pos:* CHIEF, INFO RESOURCES MGT, VA MED CTR, NORTH LITTLE ROCK, ARK, 83-; ADJ PROF COMPUT SCI, UNIV ARK, LITTLE ROCK, 87- *Personal Data:* b Conway, Ark, Nov 14, 37; m 60, Emily Balcom; c Beth, Dwight, Mark & John. *Educ:* Ouachita Baptist Univ, BA & BS, 59; Purdue Univ, PhD(phys chem), 68. *Prof Exp:* Chief, Dept Chem, 406th Med Lab, US Army Med Command, Japan, 64-67; res chemist, 68-72, head, Math Biol & Data Analysis Sect, Southern Res Inst, 72-83. *Mem:* Cell Kinetics Soc; Am Sci Affil. *Res:* Chemical kinetics; data analysis and mathematical simulation; pharmacokinetics; kinetics of tumor growth and cell killing; design of computer-based information management systems. *Mailing Add:* Vet Admin Med Ctr 2200 Ft Roots Dr North Little Rock AR 72114

LLOYD, JAMES EDWARD, INSECT BEHAVIORAL ECOLOGY. *Current Pos:* from asst prof biol sci & entom to assoc prof entom & nematol, 66-74, PROF ENTOM & NEMATOL, UNIV FLA, 74- *Personal Data:* b Oneida, NY, Jan 17, 33; m 58, Dorothy J Pafka; c 2. *Educ:* State Univ NY Col Fredonia, BS, 60; Univ Mich, MA, 62; Cornell Univ, PhD(entom), 66. *Honors & Awards:* Res Award, Sigma Xi, 74. *Prof Exp:* Teacher high sch, 60; NSF res assoc syst & evolutionary biol, 66. *Concurrent Pos:* NSF res grant 68, 80; Nat Geog Soc res grant, 80. *Mem:* Coleopterist's Soc. *Res:* Function of luminescence in insects; systematics, behavior and ecology of Lampyridae. *Mailing Add:* Dept Entom Univ Fla PO Box 110620 Gainesville FL 32611-0620

LLOYD, JAMES NEWELL, PHYSICS. *Current Pos:* From instr to assoc prof physics, 61-79, chmn, Dept Physics & Astron, 73-76, PROF PHYSICS, COLGATE UNIV, 79- *Personal Data:* b Orange, NJ, Oct 20, 32; m 59; c 2. *Educ:* Colgate Univ, BA, 54; Cornell Univ, PhD(physics), 63. *Mem:* Am Phys Soc; Am Asn Physics Teachers. *Res:* Ferromagnetic resonance and transport properties in metals. *Mailing Add:* Dept Physics & Astron Colgate Univ Hamilton NY 13346

LLOYD, JOHN EDWARD, VETERINARY & MEDICAL ENTOMOLOGY, ENTOMOLOGY EDUCATION. *Current Pos:* from asst prof to assoc prof, 68-76, actg head, Plant Sci Dept, 85-86, PROF ENTOM, UNIV WYO, 76- *Personal Data:* b Munhall, Pa, Sept 28, 40; m 62, Deanna J Dressler; c Gwendolyn J (Johnson) & John E Jr. *Educ:* Pa State Univ, BS, 62; Cornell Univ, PhD(entom), 67. *Prof Exp:* Asst prof entom, Pa State Univ, 67-68. *Mem:* Entom Soc Am; Am Mosquito Control Asn; World Asn Adv Vet Parasitol. *Res:* Economic entomology; insects affecting livestock; insects affecting man; veterinary parasitology. *Mailing Add:* Entom Sect Box 3354 Univ Wyo Laramie WY 82071. *Fax:* 307-766-5549; *E-Mail:* lloyd@uwyo.edu

LLOYD, JOHN RAYMOND, MECHANICAL ENGINEERING. *Current Pos:* univ distinguished prof, 83-92, chmn, Dept Mech Eng, 83-91, DISTINGUISHED PROF, MICH STATE UNIV, 91- *Personal Data:* b Minneapolis, Minn, Aug 1, 42; m 63, Mary Jane Whiteside; c Jay William & Stephanie Christine. *Educ:* Univ Minn, BS, 64, MSME, 66, PhD(mech eng), 71. *Honors & Awards:* Melville Medal, Am Soc Mfg Engrs, 78; Ralph E Teetor Educ Award, Soc Automotive Engrs, 86; Heat Transfer Mem Award, Am Soc Mfg Engrs, 95. *Prof Exp:* Develop engr, Proctor & Gamble Co, 66-67; prof mech eng, Univ Notre Dame, 70-83. *Concurrent Pos:* Consult, LeRoy Troyer & Assoc, Mishawaka, Ind, 80-90; Azdel Inc, Shelby, NC, 87-90; mem, Sci Coun, Int Ctr Heat & Mass Transfer, Yugoslavia, 86-; adv, NSF, 87-90; mem, Nat Bur Stand Assessment Panel, Nat Res Coun, 87-93; chmn, Midwest Energy Consortium, 93- *Mem:* Fel Am Soc Mech Engrs. *Res:* Contributed over 90 articles to professional journals; contributed chapters to books. *Mailing Add:* Dept Mech Eng Mich State Univ East Lansing MI 48824

LLOYD, JOHN WILLIE, III, ENDOCRINOLOGY, PHARMACOLOGY. *Current Pos:* ASSOC PROF ENDOCRINOL, HOWARD UNIV, 78- *Personal Data:* b Winchester, Va, May 25, 43; m 65; c 2. *Educ:* Shepherd Col, BS, 66; WVa Univ, MS, 69, PhD(endocrinol), 73. *Prof Exp:* Asst prof pharmacol, WVa Univ, 73-74; asst prof endocrinol, Eastern Va Med Sch, 74-78. *Concurrent Pos:* Dir, Endocrine Serv, Eastern Va Med Sch, 76-78. *Mem:* Sigma Xi; Soc Exp Biol & Med; Endocrine Soc; Am Physiol Soc. *Res:* Endocrinology; Reproductive physiology; hormonal regulation of the adrenal gland and accessory sex organs; prostatic cancer. *Mailing Add:* 503 S Stewart St Winchester VA 22601

LLOYD, KENNETH OLIVER, BIOCHEMISTRY, IMMUNOCHEMISTRY. *Current Pos:* assoc, 75-78, assoc mem, 78-87, MEM, SLOAN-KETTERING CANCER CTR, 87-, CHMN, IMMUNOL PROG, 89- *Personal Data:* b Denbigh, Wales, May 17, 36; US citizen; m 62; c 2. *Educ:* Univ Wales, BSc, 57, PhD(chem), 60. *Honors & Awards:* Philip Levine Award, Am Asn Clin Pathologists, 86. *Prof Exp:* Res assoc microbiol, Columbia Univ, 63-68, asst prof biochem, 68-74; assoc prof, Sch Med, Tex Tech Univ, 74-75. *Concurrent Pos:* Fel, Wash Univ, 60-61; USPHS res career develop award, 68-73; mem, Allergy & Immunol Study Sect, NIH, 84-88. *Mem:* AAAS; Am Chem Soc; Am Asn Immunologists; Soc Complex Carbohydrates; Am Asn Cancer Res. *Res:* Biochemistry, structure and immunochemistry of glycoproteins and glycolipids, particularly tumor antigens. *Mailing Add:* Mem Sloan Kettering Cancer Ctr 1275 York Ave New York NY 10021-6094. *Fax:* 212-717-3379; *E-Mail:* klloyd@mskcc.org

LLOYD, L KEITH, UROLOGY. *Current Pos:* from asst prof to assoc prof, 74-81, PROF UROL, DEPT SURG, UNIV ALA MED CTR, 81-; DIR UROL REHAB & RES CTR, SPAIN REHAB CTR, BIRMINGHAM, 77-, DIR, DIV UROL, 96- *Personal Data:* b 1941; m, Karen Hansen; c Kristen, Keith & Kevin. *Educ:* Centenary Col, BS, 62; Tulane Univ Sch Med, MD, 66. *Prof Exp:* Intern, US Pub Health Serv Hosp, Norfolk, Va, 66-67, med officer, 68-70, jr asst resident, Gen Practice Prog, 67-68; asst resident urol, Tulane Univ Sch Med, 70-71, asst resident instr, 70-72, res fel urol, 71-72, resident urol, 72-73, resident instr, 72-74, sr resident urol, 72-74. *Concurrent Pos:* Bd dirs & comt educ, Am Spinal Injury Asn, 86. *Mem:* Am Urol Asn; Am Med Asn; Am Col Surgeons; Am Spinal Injury Asn. *Res:* Urodynamics and neurogenic bladder; urologic care in spinal cord injury; male sexual dysfunction; over 60 publications on urology, nuclear and physical medicine and rehabilitation; author of 6 books in urology. *Mailing Add:* Div Urol Univ Ala Med Ctr 606 MEB Birmingham AL 35294. *Fax:* 205-934-4933; *E-Mail:* klloyd@mail.urology.uab.edu

LLOYD, LAURANCE H(ENRY), OPERATIONS RESEARCH, ELECTRICAL ENGINEERING. *Current Pos:* PRES, L-TECH SYSTS, 76- *Personal Data:* b Salem, Ore, Apr 24, 15; wid; c Margaret A. *Educ:* Ore State Univ, BS, 37; Ohio State Univ, MS, 51. *Prof Exp:* Engr, Idaho Power Co, 37-42; proj engr, Control Equip Br, Eng Div, Air Mat Command, Wright-Patterson AFB, 46-47, proj engr, Guided Missiles Br, Intel Dept, 48, chief, Nuclear Energy Br, 48, chief, Sci Br, 50, actg chief & chief engr, Signal Anal Sect, Air Technol Intel Ctr, 53; staff engr, Systs Eng Sect, Missile Test Proj, Radio Corp Am, Patrick AFB, 54; chief eval div, Dept Electronics Intel, Aerospace Technol Intel Ctr, Wright-Patterson AFB, 55-61, actg tech dir, 59-60, aerospace engr, Directorate of Synthesis, Systs Eng Group, 61-69 & Directorate of Opers Res, 69, opers res analyst, Simulation & Anal Div, 69-76; pres, Trident Marine Servs, 72-76. *Mem:* Fel AAAS; sr mem Inst Elec & Electronics Engrs. *Res:* System effectiveness evaluation; computer simulation; electrical waveform analysis; electrical measurement theory. *Mailing Add:* 180 Inlets Blvd Nokomis FL 34275

LLOYD, MILTON HAROLD, INORGANIC CHEMISTRY. *Current Pos:* RETIRED. *Personal Data:* b Des Moines, Iowa, Mar 27, 25; m 44; c 3. *Educ:* Creighton Univ, BS, 50, MS, 54. *Prof Exp:* Chemist prod develop, Tidy House Prod Co, 50-56; sect mgr process res & develop, Oak Ridge Nat Lab, 56-86. *Mem:* Am Chem Soc; AAAS. *Res:* Transuranium element isolation and purification; plutonia sol-gel processes for preparation of advanced reactor fuels; chemical studies of plutonium behavior in reactor fuel reprocessing and waste solutions. *Mailing Add:* 111 Locust Lane Oak Ridge TN 37830

LLOYD, MONTE, ANIMAL ECOLOGY, TROPICAL FOREST CONSERVATION. *Current Pos:* RETIRED. *Personal Data:* b Omaha, Nebr, July 6, 27; m 46, 69; c 4. *Educ:* Univ Calif, Los Angeles, AB, 52; Univ Chicago, PhD(zool), 57. *Prof Exp:* NSF fel, Bur Animal Pop, Oxford Univ, 57-59, Brit Nature Conserv res grant, 59-62; asst prof zool, Univ Calif, Los Angeles, 62-67; prof biol, Univ Chicago, 67- *Concurrent Pos:* Ed, Ecol, 68-72. *Mem:* Soc Study Evolution; Am Soc Nat; Ecol Soc Am. *Res:* Dynamics of animal populations and community ecology. *Mailing Add:* 8224 Pritchard Pl New Orleans LA 70118

LLOYD, NELSON ALBERT, ANALYTICAL CHEMISTRY. *Current Pos:* RETIRED. *Personal Data:* b Lorain, Ohio, Oct 12, 26; m 45; c 5. *Educ:* Southern Methodist Univ, BS, 50, MS, 51; Okla State Univ, PhD(analytical chem), 55. *Prof Exp:* Res chemist, Goodyear Atomic Corp, 54-56; assoc prof analytical chem, Northeastern La State Col, 56-61 & Univ Ala, Tuscaloosa, 61-67; chmn, Div Natural Sci, Mobile Col, 67-70; chief, Geochem Div, Geol Surv Ala, Tuscaloosa, 70-92. *Concurrent Pos:* Consult, Tuscaloosa Metall Res Ctr, US Bur Mines, 63-67 & State Oil & Gas Bd, Ala, 66-67. *Mem:* Am Chem Soc. *Res:* Rock analysis, whole rock and trace metals in rock; trace substances in water, heavy metals, pesticides herbicides and various nitrogen species. *Mailing Add:* 209 32nd Ave E Tuscaloosa AL 35404

LLOYD, NORMAN EDWARD, BIOCHEMISTRY, BIOTECHNOLOGY. *Current Pos:* RETIRED. *Personal Data:* b Oak Park, Ill, Feb 20, 29; m 51; c 8. *Educ:* Rockjurst Col, BS, 52; Kans State Col, MS, 53; Purdue Univ, PhD(biochem), 56. *Prof Exp:* Assoc chemist, Corn Prods Co, 56-58; cereal chemist, Int Milling Co, 58-59; supvr starch chem res, Clinton Corn Processing Co, 60-64, dir sci develop, 64-69, asst res dir, 69-70, supvr chem res, 70-78, dir res & develop, 78-79, vpres tech, 79-82, group dir biotechnol, 83-89. *Mem:* Am Chem Soc; Am Asn Cereal Chem. *Res:* Production and characterization of starches, sweeteners and enzymes; enzyme kinetics and immobilization; food biotechnology. *Mailing Add:* 4 Lincolnshire Ct Durham NC 27712-9456

LLOYD, RAY DIX, RADIATION PHYSICS, RADIOBIOLOGY. *Current Pos:* res assoc prof, 79-84, RES PROF, RADIOBIOL DIV, SCH MED, UNIV UTAH, 84- *Personal Data:* b Mar 10, 30; m 54, Louise Mortensen; c 5. *Educ:* Univ Utah, PhD(biol), 74; Am Bd Health Physics, cert, 68. *Prof Exp:* Res asst prof anat, Radiobiol Div, Dept Anat, Col Med, Univ Utah, 61-79. *Concurrent Pos:* Adj prof, Dept Mech Environ & Civil Eng; coun mem, Nat Coun Radiation Protection & Measurements, 80-92; lab dir, BioTrace Inc, Salt Lake City, Utah. *Mem:* Radiation Res Soc; fel Health Physics Soc; Int Radiation Protection Asn; Am Acad Health Physics. *Res:* Biological effects of ionizing radiation; internal emitters; dose-response models; risk assessment; risk modification by chelation therapy; application of radioactivity to biomedical studies; health physics; reconstruction of radiation dose from Nevada nuclear testing. *Mailing Add:* Radiobiol Div Bldg 586 Univ Utah Salt Lake City UT 84112

LLOYD, RAYMOND CLARE, NUCLEAR REACTORS, CRITICALITY ANALYSIS. *Current Pos:* STAFF SCIENTIST, BATTELLE PAC NORTHWEST LAB, 65- *Personal Data:* b Sioux Falls, SDak, July 22, 27; m 49; c 3. *Educ:* Augustana Col, BA, 49; SDak State Univ, MS, 51. *Prof Exp:* Scientist, Hanford Atomic Plant, Gen Elec Co, 51-65. *Mem:* Am Nuclear Soc. *Res:* Reactor physics and criticality analysis. *Mailing Add:* 2068 Hudson Ave Richland WA 99352

LLOYD, ROBERT, CHEMICAL ENGINEERING. *Current Pos:* RETIRED. *Personal Data:* b Jackson, Miss, Mar 1, 16; m 49; c 1. *Educ:* Purdue Univ, BS, 38; Temple Univ, MA, 46, PhD(phys chem), 54, Carnegie Mellon Univ, MS, 78. *Prof Exp:* Asst city engr, Gary, Ind, 38-41; chemist, Kingsbury Ord Plant, Ind, 41-42; chem engr, Graham Savage & Assocs, Inc, 45-55; chem engr, Bettis Atomic Power Lab, Westinghouse Elec Corp, 55-86. *Mem:* Am Chem Soc; Am Inst Chem Engrs. *Res:* Metal complexes; electrochemistry; electroplating procedures; engineering design; nuclear atomic power engineering. *Mailing Add:* 4004 Jane St West Mifflin PA 15122-1640

LLOYD, ROBERT MICHAEL, systematic botany; deceased, see previous edition for last biography

LLOYD, THOMAS A, OBSTETRICS & GYNECOLOGY, PHARMACOLOGY. *Current Pos:* from asst prof to assoc prof, 75-93, PROF, DEPT OBSTET & GYNEC & PHARMACOL, COL MED, PA STATE UNIV, HERSHEY, 93- *Personal Data:* b Olney, Ill, Sept 4, 42. *Educ:* Antioch Col, BA, 64; Harvard Univ, PhD(pharmacol), 70. *Prof Exp:* Res fel, Lab Neurochem, NIMH, 70-72, staff fel, 72-74, sr staff fel, 74-75. *Concurrent Pos:* Numerous res grants, 76-; estab investr, Am Heart Asn, 78-83. *Mem:* Am Soc Pharmacol & Exp Therapeut; Am Inst Nutrit; Am Soc Clin Nutrit; Am Soc Bone & Mineral Res. *Res:* Obstetrics and gynecology; pharmacology. *Mailing Add:* Dept Obstet & Gynec & Pharmacol Col Med Pa State Univ Hershey PA 17033-0850

LLOYD, THOMAS BLAIR, INDUSTRIAL CHEMISTRY, COLLOID CHEMISTRY. *Current Pos:* RES SCIENTIST, LEHIGH UNIV, 83- *Personal Data:* b Reedsville, WVa, Aug 29, 21; m 44, Barbara Sprintall; c Thomas B Jr, Judith & Althea. *Educ:* Washington & Jefferson Col, BS, 42; Western Res Univ, MS, 46, PhD(phys chem), 48. *Prof Exp:* Asst prof chem, Muhlenberg Co, 48-54; investr, 54-66, res supvr, NJ Zinc Co, 66-83. *Concurrent Pos:* Consult surface sci. *Mem:* Am Chem Soc; Sigma Xi. *Res:* Industrial process research, particularly pigments, hydrometallurgy and pollution control; particle dispersion in various media; surface science; PTFE etching; coal; adhesives. *Mailing Add:* 127 Bridle Path Rd Bethlehem PA 18017-3870. *Fax:* 610-758-6536; *E-Mail:* tbl0@lehigh.edu

LLOYD, WALLIS A(LLEN), CHEMICAL ENGINEERING. *Current Pos:* RES DIR, CANNON INSTRUMENT CO, 64- *Personal Data:* b Harrisburg, Pa, July 24, 26; m 55; c 4. *Educ:* Pa State Univ, BS, 49; Univ Minn, PhD(chem eng), 54. *Prof Exp:* Res assoc chem eng, Univ Minn, 54-55; design engr, Calif Res Corp Div, Standard Oil Co Calif, 55-56; asst prof chem eng, Pa State Univ, 56-64. *Mem:* Assoc mem Am Inst Chem Engrs; Am Nuclear Soc; Am Soc Testing & Mat; Sigma Xi. *Res:* Heat transfer; chemonuclear research; separation processes; viscometry. *Mailing Add:* 490 Orlando Ave State College PA 16803

LLOYD, WELDON S, CALCIUM & BONE METABOLISM. *Current Pos:* instr oral pharmacol, 68-71, assoc pharmacol res, 71-78, ASSOC PROF NUTRIT, BOSTON UNIV, 78- *Personal Data:* b Miami, Fla, July 26, 39; m 60; c 2. *Educ:* Boston Univ, BA, 66; Northeastern Univ, MS, 71. *Hon Degrees:* DSc, Boston Univ, 78. *Prof Exp:* Assoc, Harvard Univ, 63-68. *Concurrent Pos:* Sr lectr, Roxbury Community Col, 80. *Mem:* AAAS. *Res:* Bone disease and hormone related studies; calcium and bone metabolism related studies in health and disease. *Mailing Add:* Admissions 305 Boston Univ 100 E Newton St Boston MA 02118

LLOYD, WILLIAM GILBERT, ORGANIC CHEMISTRY, COAL SCIENCE. *Current Pos:* dean, Ogden Col Sci, Technol & Health, 80-85, prof, 80-88, EMER PROF CHEM, WESTERN KY UNIV, 88- *Personal Data:* b New York, NY, July 10, 23; m 50, Anne Henderson; c Susan (Schulz), David G & Peter H. *Educ:* Kalamazoo Col, AB, 47; Brown Univ, ScM, 50; Mich State Univ, PhD(org chem), 57. *Prof Exp:* Chemist, Dow Chem Co, 50-60, assoc scientist, 60-62; sr process res specialist, Lummus Co, NJ, 62-67; prof chem, Western Ky Univ, 67-74; sr res scientist, Inst Mining & Minerals Res, Univ Ky, 74-75, chief chemist, 75-77, assoc dir & mgr, Mat Div, 77-80. *Concurrent Pos:* Dir, Larox Res Corp, 72-92. *Mem:* Am Chem Soc. *Res:* Chemistry of coal and coal-derived products; catalysis of organic reactions. *Mailing Add:* Dept Chem Western Ky Univ Bowling Green KY 42101. *E-Mail:* wglloyd@mindspring.com

LLOYD, WINSTON DALE, ORGANIC CHEMISTRY. *Current Pos:* RETIRED. *Personal Data:* b Pensacola, Fla, Sept 9, 29; m 58, Luella Rote; c Pamela D, Donald G & Craig W. *Educ:* Fla State Univ, BS, 51; Univ Washington, PhD(org chem), 56. *Prof Exp:* Org chemist, Dow Chem Co, 56-58 & USDA, 59-62, Naval Stores Res Lab, USDA, 59-62; res prof, 65-66, Univ Tex, El Paso, assoc prof chem, 62-96. *Mem:* Am Chem Soc; Sigma Xi. *Res:* Stereochemistry of cyclic dienes; mechanisms of organic chemical reactions; natural products; synthesis. *Mailing Add:* Dept Chem Univ Tex El Paso TX 79968. *Fax:* 915-747-5748; *E-Mail:* lloyd@utep.edu

LLUBERES, ROSA P, BIOCHEMISTRY, IMMUNOLOGY. *Current Pos:* CHEMIST RES, DEPT VET AFFAIRS, 67- *Personal Data:* b Dominican Repub, Aug, 19, 34; US citizen; m, Edmundo; c Maribel & Ed. *Educ:* Univ Santo Domingo, Dominican Repub, Doctor, 55; Univ PR, Sch Med, MT, 56. *Prof Exp:* Chemist, Health Dept Dominican Repub, 56-61; res asst chem, Vet Admin Med Ctr, PR, 61-65, biochem, Univ PR, Sch Med, 65-67. *Concurrent Pos:* Lectr sch med technol, Univ PR, Sch Med, 72-78, Dept Microbiol, Sch Med Del Caribe, 84-86, Sagrado Corazon Univ, 86-87. *Mem:* Am Soc Microbiol; PR Soc Microbiol (pres, 78-79, 88-89 & 91-); Asn Women Sci; NY Acad Sci; Am Soc Chemists. *Res:* Immunology; principal objective is immunodefficiency reacted to rheumatology and gastroenterology. *Mailing Add:* Rio Predras Heights 1677 Sungari St Rio Piedras PR 00926

LLUCH, JOSE FRANCISCO, CONSTRUCTION MANAGEMENT, ENGINEERING EDUCATION. *Current Pos:* Instr civil eng, Univ PR, Mayaguez, 77-79, from asst prof to assoc prof, 81-89, actg dir grad studies, 85-86, asst dean eng, 86-88, DEAN ENG, UNIV PR, MAYAGUEZ, 88-, PROF CIVIL ENG, 89- *Personal Data:* b San German, PR, Jan 30, 54; m 79, Maria N Mercad; c 2. *Educ:* Univ PR, Mayaguez, BSCE, 75; Ga Inst Technol, MSCE, 76, PhD(construct mgt), 81. *Concurrent Pos:* Construct mgt consult, var construct contractors, 81-88; prin investr & co-prin investr, var externally funded res projs, NSF & others, 81-88. *Mem:* Am Soc Civil Engrs. *Res:* Construction project planning and control; computer applications in construction management. *Mailing Add:* Dean Eng Univ PR Mayaguez PR 00681-5000

LNENICKA, GREGORY ALLEN, ELECTROPHYSIOLOGY. *Current Pos:* asst prof, 87-93, ASSOC PROF, DEPT BIOL SCI, STATE UNIV NY, ALBANY, 94- *Personal Data:* b Cedar Rapids, Iowa, Dec 4, 52; m 83, Linda Stanhope; c Emily & Katherine. *Educ:* Univ Iowa, BA, 76; Univ Va, PhD(biol), 82. *Prof Exp:* Fel, Univ Toronto, 82-87. *Mem:* Soc Neurosci; AAAS; NY Acad Sci. *Res:* Physiology and plasticity of neurons and synapses. *Mailing Add:* Biol Dept State Univ NY 1400 Washington Ave Albany NY 12222. *Fax:* 418-442-4767; *E-Mail:* galsb@cnsibm.albany.edu

LNENICKA, WILLIAM J(OSEPH), STRUCTURAL ENGINEERING. *Current Pos:* RETIRED. *Personal Data:* b Hay Springs, Nebr, Oct 16, 22; m 47; c 2. *Educ:* Univ Nebr, BS, 49; Kans State Univ, MS; Ga Inst Technol, PhD, 61. *Prof Exp:* Instr civil eng, Univ Nebr, 49-51 & Kans State Univ, 52-54; asst prof eng mech, Univ Okla, 54-57 & La State Univ, 57-58; from asst prof to prof eng mech, Ga Inst Technol, 58-87, assoc vpres acad affairs, 78-87. *Concurrent Pos:* Consult, Aerial Tower Mfg Co, 54-59; mem bd dir, Vinings Chem Co, 64-73, Vinings Leasing Co, 68-73 & Wilroy & Assoc Consult Engrs, 70-78. *Mem:* Am Soc Eng Educ; Soc Am Mil Engrs; Soc Prof Engrs. *Res:* Chief field strength of materials. *Mailing Add:* 3235 Laramie Dr SE Atlanta GA 30339

LO, ANDREW W, FINANCIAL ECONOMICS. *Current Pos:* assoc prof, 88-91, PROF FINANCE, SLOAN SCH MGT, MASS INST TECHNOL, 91- *Personal Data:* US citizen. *Educ:* Yale Univ, BA, 80; Harvard Univ, MA & PhD(econ), 84. *Prof Exp:* Asst prof finance, Wharton Sch, Univ Pa, 84-87, assoc prof, 87-88. *Concurrent Pos:* Res assoc, Nat Bur Econ Res, 88-, Olin fel, 88; Batterymarch fel, Batterymarch Financial Mgt, 89. *Mem:* Am Finance Asn; Am Statist Asn; Am Econ Asn; Inst Math Statist; Econometric Soc; Soc Indust & Appl Math. *Res:* Statistical analysis of financial asset pricing models for equities, fixed income securities and derivative products; numerical computation of economic systems for financial forecasting. *Mailing Add:* Sloan Sch Mgt MIT 50 Memorial Dr E52-437 Cambridge MA 02142-1347

LO, ARTHUR W(UNIEN), COMPUTER SCIENCE. *Current Pos:* prof, 64-86, EMER PROF ELEC ENG & COMPUT SCI, PRINCETON UNIV, 86- *Personal Data:* b Shanghai, China, May 21, 16; nat US; m 50, Elizabeth Shen; c Katherine E & James A. *Educ:* Yenching Univ, China, BS, 38; Oberlin Col, MA, 46; Univ Ill, PhD(elec eng), 49. *Prof Exp:* Asst prof elec eng, Mich Col Mining & Technol, 49-50; lectr, City Col New York, 50-51; res & develop engr, Victor Div, Radio Corp Am, 51-52, sr mem tech staff, RCA Labs, 52-60; mgr adv tech develop, Data Systs Div, Int Bus Mach Corp, 60-64. *Mem:* Fel Inst Elec & Electronics Engrs. *Res:* Digital electronics and computer organization. *Mailing Add:* 102 Maclean Circle Princeton NJ 08540

LO, BERNARD, MEDICAL ETHICS. *Current Pos:* from asst prof to assoc prof, 80-93, actg chief, Div Med Ethics, 87-89, DIR PROG MED ETHICS, UNIV CALIF, SAN FRANCISCO, 89-, PROF MED, 93- *Educ:* Harvard Univ, AB, 66, AM, 70; Univ Sussex, MA, 68; Stanford Univ, MD, 75; Am Bd Internal Med, dipl, 78. *Honors & Awards:* Walter Zuckerman Lectr, Harvard Univ, 93; Robert S Boas Vis Lectr, Cornell Univ & N Shorte Univ Hosp, 93. *Prof Exp:* Intern & residency internal med, Univ Calif, Los Angeles, 75-77; residency internal med, Stanford Univ, 77-78, Robert Wood Johnson clin scholar, 78-80. *Concurrent Pos:* Mem, Data Safety Monitoring Bd, Genentech, 93-, Chiron, 94-, Div AIDS, Nat Inst Allergy & Infectious Dis, 95-; mem bd dirs, Am Soc Law, Med & Ethics, 94-, Bd Health Sci Pol, Inst Med, 94-; vis prof, Sch Med, Yale Univ, 93, Univ Rochester, 95 & Wash Univ, 96; William Chambers vis prof, Dartmouth Med Sch, 93; prog dir, Robert Wood Johnson Found Initiative on the Patient-Provider Relationship Changing Health Care Environ, 96- *Mem:* Inst Med-Nat Acad Sci; fel Am Col Physicians; Western Soc Clin Invest; Western Asn Physicians. *Mailing Add:* Univ Calif Rm C126 521 Parnassus Ave San Francisco CA 94143-0903

LO, CHENG FAN, WOOD CHEMISTRY. *Current Pos:* RES CHEMIST, BOISE CASCADE CHEM RES LAB, 69- *Personal Data:* b Taichung, Taiwan, Dec 14, 37; m 66; c 3. *Educ:* Nat Taiwan Univ, BS, 62; Auburn Univ, MS, 66; Ore State Univ, PhD(wood chem), 70. *Prof Exp:* Res asst, Dept Forestry, Auburn Univ, 64-66; wood chemist, Forest Res Lab, Ore State Univ, 66-69. *Mem:* Am Chem Soc; Tech Asn Pulp & Paper Indust; Forest Prod Res Soc. *Res:* By-products development in wood cellulose and lignin material; technical assistance to paper production. *Mailing Add:* 3817 SE 153rd St Vancouver WA 98683

LO, CHU SHEK, ENDOCRINOLOGY, BIOCHEMISTRY & PHYSIOLOGY. *Current Pos:* asst prof, 77-81, ASSOC PROF, DEPT PHYSIOL, UNIFORMED SERV UNIV HEALTH SCI, BETHESDA, MD, 81- *Personal Data:* b Hong Kong; US citizen; m 69; c 1. *Educ:* Nat Taiwan Univ, Taipei, Repub China, BS, 62; Univ Notre Dame, Ind, MS, 65; Ind Univ Med Sch, Indianapolis, PhD(physiol), 72. *Honors & Awards:* Sidney C Wener lectr, Dept Med, Col Physicians & Surgeon, Columbia Univ, 80. *Prof Exp:* Sr lab technician Dept Physiol, Sch Med, Univ Miami, 65-66 & Ind Univ, 67-68; fel, Cardiovasc Res Inst, Sch Med, Univ Calif, San Francisco, 72-75; asst prof Dept Physiol, Sch Med, Univ Md, Baltimore, 75-77. *Concurrent Pos:* Collaborator, Roche Res Found, Sci Exchange & Biomed, Switz, 76; guest worker, Metab Dis Br, NIH, 76-78; mem Grad Affairs Comt, Dept Physiol, Uniformed Servs Univ Health Sci, 85-, Grad Educ Comt, 88-90; mem res comt & peer rev subcomt, Md Affil, Inc, Am Heart Asn, 90-92. *Mem:* Am Physiol Soc; Am Soc Cell Biol; Soc Chinese Bioscientists Am. *Res:* Germ-free animal research; cellular aging including whole body electrolytes in young and old rats; effects of mucosal anaerobiosis on galactose transport across the apical membrane of the hamster small intestine; mode of action of thyroid hormone and corticosterone on sodium transport in rat kindney and small intestine; mechanism of action of catecholamine on sodium and potassium transport; molecular biological approaches to study the mechanisms of action of hormone(thyroid and gluocorticoid) on membrane transport and membrane biochemistry; mechanisms of action of growth factors on phosphatidylinositol metabolism in smooth muscle cell; signal transduction in diabetics glomerulus. *Mailing Add:* 5304 Elsmere Ave Bethesda MD 20814-4799

LO, CLIFFORD W, PEDIATRICS. *Current Pos:* CLIN ASSOC & INSTR PEDIAT, HARVARD MED SCH, MASS GEN HOSP, 84-; ASST MED, CHILDREN'S HOSP, BOSTON, 85-, DIR, HOME TPN PROG, 86-, ASSOC DIR, NUTRIT SUPPORT SERV, 90- *Personal Data:* b Hempstead, NY, Sept 9, 51; m 84; c 1. *Educ:* Stanford Univ, AB, 72; Univ Hawaii, MD, 77; Univ Calif, Los Angeles, MPH, 81; Mass Inst Technol, ScD(nutrit biochem), 86. *Honors & Awards:* Nat Osteoporosis Found Prize, 90. *Concurrent Pos:* Fulbright scholar, Univ Cambridge, Eng, 89; Royal Soc guest fel, MRC Dunn Nutrit Unit, Cambridge, Eng, 89; lectr nutrit, Inst Health Prof, Mass Gen Hosp, 89-90, adj assoc prof nutrit, 90- *Mem:* Am Gastroenterol Asn; NY Acad Sci; Hist Sci Soc; Am Soc Bone & Mineral Res. *Res:* Vitamin D, parathyroid hormone and calcium metabolism; calcium nutrition and bone density in adolescents; total parenteral nutrition in pediatrics; international nutrition. *Mailing Add:* 28 Litchfield Rd Cambridge England

LO, DAVID S(HIH-FANG), COMPUTER MEMORY TECHNOLOGY, SWITCH-MODE POWER CONVERSION. *Current Pos:* RETIRED. *Personal Data:* b China, Aug 27, 32; US citizen; m 59; c 2. *Educ:* Nat Taiwan Univ, BS, 54; Univ Minn, MS, 58, PhD(elec eng), 62. *Prof Exp:* Sr res scientist, Honeywell Res Ctr, 62-64; prin physicist, Unisys Corp, 64-71, staff physicist, 72-79, sr staff scientist, Electronic & Info Systs Group, 80-90. *Concurrent Pos:* Lectr, Univ Minn, 62- & adj prof, 82- *Mem:* Inst Elec & Electronics Engrs. *Res:* Electrical properties of ferric oxide semiconductors; ferromagnetic films; magnetic and optical memories; electroluminescent displays; optoelectronics; switch-mode power conversion. *Mailing Add:* 2313 Explorer Ct Burnsville MN 55337

LO, ELIZABETH SHEN, ORGANIC CHEMISTRY, POLYMER CHEMISTRY. *Current Pos:* RETIRED. *Personal Data:* b Shanghai, China, Feb 24, 26; m 50, Arthur; c Katherine & James. *Educ:* St John's Univ, Shanghai, BS, 45; Univ Ill, MS, 47, PhD(chem), 49. *Prof Exp:* Fel, Univ Ill, 49-50; res chemist, Metalsalsts Corp, 51; J T Baker Chem Co Div, Vick Chem Co, 51-52; M W Kellogg Co, 53-57; Permacel Div, Johnson & Johnson, 57-60; staff chemist, IBM Corp, 60-63; sr res chemist, Thiokol Chem Corp, 65-70; vis fel, Princeton Univ, 71-73; mgr adv chem process, Fairchild-PMS Prod, 74-75; mem tech staff, David Sarnoff Res Ctr, RCA, 76-77; chief chemist, Optel Div, Reflac Electronics Corp, 79-81; mgr polymer mat, Electro-Sci Labs, Inc, Pa, 82-90. *Mem:* Am Chem Soc; Int Soc Hybrid Microelectronics. *Res:* Polymer, rubber and resin chemistry; fluorocarbon polymers; liquid crystals; polymer thick film for electronic industry. *Mailing Add:* 102 Maclean Circle Princeton NJ 08540

LO, GEORGE ALBERT, CHEMICAL PROPULSION, TECHNICAL MANAGEMENT. *Current Pos:* sr staff scientist, 77-87, MGR, CHEM DEPT, LOCKHEED PALO ALTO RES LAB, 87- *Personal Data:* b Hong Kong, June 26, 34; US citizen; m 57, Jean Savola; c Deborah, Jeffrey & Laura. *Educ:* Univ Ore, BA, 57, MA, 60; Wash State Univ, PhD(chem), 63. *Prof Exp:* Mem tech staff, Rocketdyne Div, Rockwell Int Corp, 63-77. *Mem:* Am Chem Soc; Sigma Xi. *Res:* Chemical kinetics and propulsion; chemistry of inorganic complexes; environment monitor and remediation; polymers and composites. *Mailing Add:* Lockheed-Martin Palo Alto Dept H1-32 Bldg 204 3251 Hanover St Palo Alto CA 94304-1191

LO, GRACE S, FIBER RESEARCH. *Current Pos:* DIR FIBER RES, RALSTON PURINA CO, CHECKERBOARD SQ, 76- *Mailing Add:* Dept Fiber Res Ralston Purina Co HRN Checkerboard Sq St Louis MO 63164-0001

LO, HILDA K, SURGERY. *Current Pos:* postdoctoral fel, Div Endocrinol & Metab, Univ Miami, Sch Med, 74-77, instr med, 77-80, res instr, 81-89, RES ASST PROF, DEPT SURG, UNIV MIAMI, 89- & DEPT ORTHOP & REHAB, 90- *Educ:* Nat Taiwan Univ, BS, 64; Ill Inst Technol, MS, 68, PhD(biol), 74. *Prof Exp:* Res asst genetics, Dept Biol, Ill Inst Technol, 64-66, microbiol & virol, 66-68; res assoc, Dept Microbiol, Chicago Med Sch, 68-70; fel lipid biochem & microbiol, Ill Inst Technol, 70-74. *Res:* Author of numerous scientific articles, books and chapters. *Mailing Add:* Univ Miami 1600 NW Tenth Ave R-2 Miami FL 33136-1015

LO, HOWARD H, GEOCHEMISTRY, PETROLOGY & ENVIRONMENTAL SCIENCES. *Current Pos:* from asst prof to assoc prof, 70-92, PROF GEOL SCI, CLEVELAND STATE UNIV, 92- *Personal Data:* b Hsinchu, Taiwan, Sept 3, 37; US citizen; m 65, Polly B; c Wilbur & Gilbert. *Educ:* Nat Taiwan Univ, BS, 60; Univ Minn, MSc, 64; Wash Univ, PhD(geochem), 70. *Prof Exp:* Jr geologist, Geol Surv Taiwan, 60-62; res & teaching asst, Univ Minn, 62-64; mine geologist, Opemiska Copper Mines, Ltd, Que, 64-65; instr sci & math, Ottawa Col Inst, Can, 65-67; res asst, Washington Univ, St Louis, 67-70. *Concurrent Pos:* Vis res prof, Ctr Volcanology, Univ Ore, 74, Purdue Univ, 78; vis prof, Nat Taiwan Univ, 90. *Mem:* Am Geophys Union; Geol Soc Am; Geol Soc China; Chinese Earth Sci Asn NAm; Overseas Chinese Environ Engrs & Sci Asn. *Res:* Geochemical and petrological study of the volcanic rocks, igneous rocks and some metamorphic rocks, especially in the modern island arcs and Canadian shield; geochemical study of lake and river waters; environmental quality study including treatment of municipal and industrial wastewater. *Mailing Add:* Dept Geol Sci Cleveland State Univ Cleveland OH 44115. *Fax:* 216-687-9366; *E-Mail:* h.lo@bones.asic.csuohio.edu

LO, KWOK-YUNG, RADIO ASTRONOMY, ASTROPHYSICS. *Current Pos:* chair, Astron Dept, 95-97, PROF ASTRON, UNIV ILL, 86- *Personal Data:* b Nanking, China, Oct 19, 47; US citizen; m 73, Helen Chen; c Jan Hsin & Derek P Hsin. *Educ:* Mass Inst Technol, SB, 69, PhD(physics), 74. *Prof Exp:* Res fel radio astron, Owens Valley Radio Observ, Calif Inst Technol, 74-76; Miller fel basic res sci, Univ Calif, Berkeley, 76-78, asst res astronr, Radio Astron Lab, 78; sr res fel, Calif Inst Technol, 78-80, asst prof radio astron, 80-86. *Concurrent Pos:* Miller fel basic res sci, Univ Calif, Berkeley, 76-78; Assoc, Ctr Advan Study, Univ Ill, 91-92; Alexander von Humboldt Award, 94-; dir, Inst Astron & Astrophys Acad Sinica, Taipei, Taiwan, Repub China, 97- *Mem:* Am Astron Soc; Int Astron Union; Int Union Radio Sci. *Res:* Microwave spectroscopy studies of phenomena associated with star formation; studies of the intergalactic medium in nearby groups of galaxies; high angular resolution studies of galactic and extragalactic radio sources by interferometry and very long baseline interferometry techniques; millimeter-wave interferometry; galactic center; dwarf galaxies. *Mailing Add:* Univ Ill 1002 W Green St Urbana IL 61801. *Fax:* 217-244-7638; *E-Mail:* kyl@astro.uiuc.edu

LO, MIKE MEI-KUO, PHYSICAL CHEMISTRY. *Current Pos:* SR RES CHEMIST, S C JOHNSON & SON, INC, 67- *Personal Data:* b Formosa, China, Sept 21, 36; m 67. *Educ:* Nat Taiwan Univ, BS, 59; Univ Ill, MS, 65, PhD(chem), 67. *Concurrent Pos:* Res fel, Univ Ill. *Mem:* Am Chem Soc; Fine Particle Soc; Am Indust Hyg Asn; Am Soc Testing & Mat. *Res:* Microwave spectroscopy; ultrasonic impedometry; gas chromatography and mass spectroscopy; aerosol science and technology. *Mailing Add:* 3721 Spring Lake Dr Racine WI 53405

LO, THEODORE CHING-YANG, MEMBRANE FUNCTIONS, SOMATIC CELL GENETICS. *Current Pos:* from asst prof to assoc prof, 75-87, PROF BIOCHEM, UNIV WESTERN ONT, 87- *Personal Data:* b Shanghai, China, Dec 22, 43; Can citizen; m 74; c 2. *Educ:* Univ Man, BSc, 69; Univ Toronto, PhD(med biophys), 73. *Prof Exp:* Res fel biochem, Harvard Univ, 73-75. *Mem:* Am Soc Biol Chemists; Can Biochem Soc. *Res:* Molecular mechanisms for hexose transport in rat myoblasts; human muscle cells. *Mailing Add:* Dept Biochem Univ Western Ont London ON N6A 5C1 Can

LO, THERESA NONG, BIOCHEMISTRY. *Current Pos:* vis fel, Pulmonary Br, NIH, 75-77, vis fel, Lab Immunobiol, Nat Cancer Inst, 77-78, res chemist, Lab Cellular Metab, Nat Heart, Lung & Blood Inst, 79-82, res chemist, Lab Chem Pharmacol, 82-88, health sci adminr, Div Blood Dis & Resources, 88-89, health sci adminr, Div Extramural Activ, Nat Cancer Inst, 89-91, HEALTH SCI ADMINR, NAT INST ARTHRITIS & MUSCULOSKELETAL & SKIN DIS, NIH, 91- *Personal Data:* b Hai Pong, NViet Nam, Mar 16, 45; US citizen; m 69, Chu Shek; c Francesca C. *Educ:* Clarke Col, Dubuque, Iowa, BA, 68; Ind Univ, PhD(biochem), 74. *Prof Exp:* Lab asst dept chem, Clarke Col, 66-68; res asst dept biochem, Ind Univ, 68-73; USPHS trainee, Cardiovasc Res Inst, Univ Calif, San Francisco, 73-75. *Mem:* Am Soc Pharmacol & Exp Therapeut; Inflammation Res Asn; Am Soc Biochem & Molecular Biol; Sigma Xi. *Res:* Enzymology of blood constituents; mechanisms of action peptide cytotoxins; proteases and proteases inhibitors; mechanisms of action of nonsteroidal anti inflammatory drugs; chemotaxis; energy-linked transport processes; author and co-author of numerous articles. *Mailing Add:* 5304 Elsmere Ave Bethesda MD 20814-4799

LO, W(ING) C(HEUK), CERAMICS, METALLURGY. *Current Pos:* RETIRED. *Personal Data:* b Macao, May 20, 24; US citizen; m 57, Mary S Huang; c David D, Cynthia S & Alan Y. *Educ:* Lingnan Univ, BS, 47; Mo Sch Mines, BS, 54; Rutgers Univ, PhD(ceramic eng), 60. *Prof Exp:* Assoc ceramic engr, Crane Co, Ill, 54-55; res asst ceramics, Rutgers Univ, 55-59; mem tech staff, Bell Tel Labs, 59-86. *Mem:* Am Ceramic Soc; Nat Inst Ceramic Engrs. *Res:* Evaluation and development of material and process for the fabrication of components for light wave communication. *Mailing Add:* 1466 Locksley Dr Bethlehem PA 18018

LO, WOO-KUEN, LENS RESEARCH. *Current Pos:* assoc prof, 87-92, PROF ANAT, MOREHOUSE SCH MED, 92- *Personal Data:* b Hualien, Taiwan, Dec 20, 45; m 72, Ji-Hua Tsay; c Wayne, Cindy & Kevin. *Educ:* Wayne State Univ, PhD(anat), 78. *Concurrent Pos:* Dir, Electron Micros Facil. *Mem:* Am Soc Cell Biol; Am Asn Anatomists; Asn Res Vision & Ophthal. *Res:* Cell biology of the ocular lens; focusing on structures and functions of intercellular junctions, cell membranes and cytoskeleton, as well as their changes during cataractogenesis. *Mailing Add:* Dept Anat Morehouse Sch Med 720 Westview Dr SW Atlanta GA 30310-1495. *Fax:* 404-752-0693

LO, Y(UEN) T(ZE), ELECTRICAL ENGINEERING. *Current Pos:* from asst prof to prof, 56-90, dir, Electromagnetics Lab, 82-90, EMER PROF ELEC ENG, UNIV ILL, URBANA, 90- *Personal Data:* b China, Jan 31, 20; US citizen; m 53; c 2. *Educ:* Nat Southwest Assoc Univ, BS, 42; Univ Ill, MS, 49, PhD(elec eng), 52. *Honors & Awards:* John T Bolljahn Mem Award, Inst Elec & Electronics Engrs, 64, Centennial Medal, 84, Distinguished Achievement Award, 96; Halli Burt Eng, Educ & Leadership Award, 86. *Prof Exp:* Asst, Radio Res Inst, Tsinghua Univ, Peking, 42-46, instr, Tsinghua & Yenching Univs, 46-48; proj engr, Channel Master Corp, 52-56. *Concurrent Pos:* Consult, Westinghouse Elec Corp, 57-58, Andrew Corp, 63, Am Electronics Lab, 66, Emerson Elec, 68-69, IBM Corp, 69, Raytheon, 69-73, Jet Propulsion Lab, 81-85, TRW, 85-86, Ford Aerospace, 86 & Lockheed; hon prof, Northwest Telecommunications Eng Inst & Northwest Polytech Univ, People's Repub of China. *Mem:* Nat Acad Engr; Int Union Radio Sci; Sigma Xi. *Res:* Antenna; electromagnetic theory; waves in plasma; radio astronomy. *Mailing Add:* 704 Silver St Urbana IL 61801

LOACH, KENNETH WILLIAM, DATA ANALYSIS, TEACHING. *Current Pos:* asst prof, 63-73, ASSOC PROF ANALYTICAL CHEM, STATE UNIV NY COL PLATTSBURGH, 73- *Personal Data:* b Portsmouth, Eng, Sept 5, 34; m 66; c 2. *Educ:* Univ Auckland, BSc, 56, MSc, 58; Univ Wash, PhD(chem), 69. *Prof Exp:* Chemist, Ruakura Animal Res Sta, NZ, 58-60; div plant indust, Commonwealth Sci & Indust Res Orgn, Australia, 60-63. *Concurrent Pos:* NSF grants, Tufts Univ, 71, State Univ NY Col Plattsburgh, 72-73, State Univ NY Res Found fel & grant, 72-73 & 77-78; sr vis fel, Univ Leeds, 77-78; vis assoc prof, Univ Del, 85-86. *Mem:* AAAS; Am Chem Soc; Chemometrics Soc; United Univ Professions. *Res:* Principles of analytical chemistry; chemical computing. *Mailing Add:* Dept Chem State Univ NY Col Plattsburgh NY 12901-2681. *Fax:* 518-564-3152; *E-Mail:* loachkw@splava.cc.plattsburgh.edu

LOACH, PAUL A, BIOCHEMISTRY, PHYSICAL BIOCHEMISTRY. *Current Pos:* from asst prof to assoc prof, 63-73, PROF CHEM, NORTHWESTERN UNIV, 73-, PROF BIOCHEM & MOLECULAR BIOL, 74- *Personal Data:* b Findlay, Ohio, July 18, 34; m 57; c 4. *Educ:* Univ Akron, BS, 57; Yale Univ, PhD(biochem), 61. *Prof Exp:* Nat Acad Sci-Nat Res Coun fel photosynthesis, Univ Calif, Berkeley, 61-63. *Concurrent Pos:* Res career develop award, NIH, 71-76. *Mem:* AAAS; Am Chem Soc; Am Soc Biol Chem; Biophys Soc; Am Soc for Photobiology. *Res:* Primary photochemistry of photosynthesis; chemistry of porphyrins and metalloporphyrins; biological oxidation and reduction; structure and function in bioenergetic membranes; photochemical models of photosynthesis. *Mailing Add:* Dept Biochem & Molecular Biol Northwestern Univ Evanston IL 60208-3500

LOADER, CLIVE ROLAND, MATHEMATICAL STATISTICS. *Current Pos:* MEM TECH STAFF, AT&T BELL LABS, 90- *Personal Data:* b Saffron Walden, Eng, Mar 11, 65; NZ citizen. *Educ:* Univ Canterbury, NZ, BSc, 86; Stanford Univ, PhD(statist), 90. *Prof Exp:* Biometrician, Ministry Agr & Fisheries, 86. *Mem:* Inst Math Statist; Am Statist Asn. *Res:* Statistical applications of stochastic processes; boundary crossing problems; change points; sequential analysis; scan statistics; goodness of fit tests; confidence bands. *Mailing Add:* 390 Morris Ave Summit NJ 07901

LOADHOLT, CLAUDE BOYD, BIOSTATISTICS. *Current Pos:* ASSOC PROF BIOMET, MED UNIV SC, 70- *Personal Data:* b Fairfax, SC, Mar 26, 40; m 63; c 2. *Educ:* Clemson Univ, BS, 62, MS, 65; Va Polytech Inst, PhD(statist), 69. *Prof Exp:* Asst exp sta statistician, Clemson Univ, 65-66, asst prof exp statist, 68-70. *Mem:* Biomet Soc. *Res:* Statistical consultation in biological and medical research; design of experiments; statistical data processing. *Mailing Add:* 1341 Venning Rd Mt Pleasant SC 29464

LOAN, LEONARD DONALD, POLYMER CHEMISTRY. *Current Pos:* mem tech staff polymer chem, 66-74, HEAD PLASTICS CHEM, RES & ENG, AT&T BELL LABS, 74- *Personal Data:* b London, Eng, Oct 6, 30; m 55; c 3. *Educ:* Univ Birmingham, BSc, 51, PhD(polymer chem), 54. *Prof Exp:* Sci off combustion chem, Royal Aircraft Estab, 54-57; chemist, Arthur D Little Res Inst, 57-59; prin sci off rubber chem, Rubber & Plastics Res Asn, 59-66. *Mem:* Am Chem Soc. *Res:* Polymer crosslinking and aging. *Mailing Add:* 107 Central Ave New Providence NJ 07974

LOAN, RAYMOND WALLACE, IMMUNOBIOLOGY. *Current Pos:* ASSOC DEAN RES & GRAD INSTR, COL VET MED & PROF VET MICROBIOL & PARASITOL, TEX A&M UNIV, 78- *Personal Data:* b Ephrata, Wash, Apr 24, 31; m 52; c 4. *Educ:* Wash State Univ, BS, 52, DVM, 58; Purdue Univ, MS, 60, PhD(animal path), 61. *Prof Exp:* Instr vet microbiol, Purdue Univ, 58-61; from asst prof to prof vet microbiol, Univ Mo-Columbia, 61-78, chmn dept, 69-78. *Mem:* Am Vet Med Asn; Am Soc Immunol; Am Col Vet Microbiol; Am Soc Microbiol; Conf Res Workers Animal Dis. *Res:* Cell mediated immunity; immunologic aspects of avian leukosis; Bovine Respiratory Disease. *Mailing Add:* Dept Vet Microbiol & Parasitol Tex A&M Univ Col Vet Med Sci Bldg Rm 119 College Station TX 77843-4467

LOAR, JAMES M, AQUATIC ECOLOGY, FISHERIES BIOLOGY. *Current Pos:* RES ASSOC, ENVIRON SCI DIV, OAK RIDGE NAT LAB, 75- *Personal Data:* b Lancaster, Pa, Sept 10, 44. *Educ:* Gettysburg Col, BA, 66; Temple Univ, MEd, 69; Univ Wyo, PhD(zool), 75. *Prof Exp:* Teacher biol, Cherry Hill High Sch W, NJ, 66-70. *Concurrent Pos:* Prin investr, Oak Ridge Nat Lab, 75- *Mem:* AAAS; Am Fisheries Soc; Ecol Soc Am; Sigma Xi. *Res:* Assessment of impact of nuclear, fossil and hydroelectric energy technologies; responses of aquatic biota to altered flow regimes below hydroelectric projects. *Mailing Add:* 1712 Nighbert Lane Knoxville TN 37922-5427

LOATMAN, ROBERT BRUCE, COMPUTATIONAL LINGUISTICS, KNOWLEDGE-BASED SYSTEMS. *Current Pos:* comput scientist, 80-84, dir artificial intel develop, 84-93, CHIEF SCIENTIST, PRC INC, 90- *Personal Data:* b Washington, DC, Aug 23, 45; m 69, 96, Konthip Prabhailakshana; c Thomas, Cynthia, Ryan & Michael. *Educ:* Fordham Col, BA, 67; Fordham Univ, MA, 71, PhD(math), 76. *Honors & Awards:* Parallax Prize, Emhart Corp, 88; Advan Technol Achievement Award, Litton Indust, 96. *Prof Exp:* Programmer, Gen Elec Co, 68-69; instr math, Georgetown Univ, 73-76; tech dir, Killalea Assocs Inc, 76-80. *Concurrent Pos:* Mem tech staff, Mitre Corp, 78; consult, Phonic Ear Inc, 80. *Mem:* Am Asn Artificial Intel; Asn Computational Ling; AAAS; Am Math Soc. *Res:* Computational linguistics research and development; natural language text understanding systems; knowledge-based systems; intelligent visual interface. *Mailing Add:* 1117 Northwind Dr Reston VA 20194-1009. *Fax:* 703-556-1174; *E-Mail:* loatman_bruce@prc.com

LOBAUGH, BRUCE, BONE & MINERAL METABOLISM, VITAMIN D METABOLISM. *Current Pos:* Res assoc, Duke Univ Med Ctr, 80-83, asst res prof physiol & surg, 83-90, supvr, Surg Endocrinol-Oncol Lab, 83-90, asst res prof, Div Physiol, 90-93, dir, Lipid Lab & Supvr, Bone & Mineral Lab, 90-92, DIR, ENDOCRINOL METAB LAB, DUKE UNIV MED CTR, 92-, ASSOC RES PROF MED & CELL BIOL, DIVS ENDOCRINOL & PHYSIOL, 93- *Personal Data:* b Charleroi, Pa, Nov 4, 53; m 83, Leslie Anderson; c Trevor R & Stephanie M. *Educ:* Clarion Univ Pa, BS, 75, Pa State Univ, MS, 78, PhD, 81. *Concurrent Pos:* Prin investr, NIH res grants, 82-85 & 87-90; chairperson, Dept Labs QA1Q1 Comt, Duke Univ Med Ctr, 93- *Mem:* Am Physiol Soc; Am Soc Bone & Mineral Res; Am Fed Clin Res; Adv Mineral Metabolism; AAAS; Am Asn Clin Chem; Clin Lab Mgt Asn. *Res:* Characterization of the mechanisms underlying regulation of vitamin D metabolism in normal and disease states; changes in vitamin D metabolism which are attendant on the natural aging process. *Mailing Add:* Duke Univ Med Ctr PO Box 3208 Durham NC 27710. *E-Mail:* lobau003@mc.duke.edu

LOBB, BARRY LEE, COMPUTER SCIENCE, TOPOLOGY. *Current Pos:* PROF COMPUT SCI, LYNCHBURG COL, 85- *Personal Data:* b Easton, Pa, Nov 25, 43; c Angela (Marie) & Steven L. *Educ:* Lafayette Col, BS, 65; Duke Univ, MA, 68, PhD(math), 69; Ind Univ-Purdue Univ, MS, 85. *Prof Exp:* Prof math, Butler Univ, 69-85. *Mem:* Asn Comput Mach. *Res:* Computer science. *Mailing Add:* 3824 Faculty Dr Lynchburg VA 24501. *E-Mail:* lobb@acavax.lynchburg.edu

LOBB, CRAIG J, IMMUNOLOGY. *Current Pos:* instr, 80-82, asst prof, 82-89, ASSOC PROF, DEPT MICROBIOL, MED CTR, UNIV MISS, 89- *Personal Data:* b Salt Lake City, Utah, Apr 15, 49; m; c 3. *Educ:* Lewis & Clark Col, BS, 71; Utah State Univ, MS, 76, PhD(immunol), 80. *Prof Exp:* Adj asst, Dept Immunol & Med Microbiol, Sch Med, Univ Fla, 78-80. *Concurrent Pos:* Co-prin investr, USDA, 82-87, prin investr, Nat Inst Allergy & Infectious Dis, NIH, 82- *Mem:* Am Asn Immunologists; Int Soc Develop & Comp Immunol; Am Soc Microbiol; Am Fisheries Soc. *Res:* Antibody structure and function in ectothermic vertebrates; organization and phylogeny of immunoglobulin genes; immunity to gram-negative bacterial infections, especially as applied to aquaculturally important teleost fish; co-author of numerous scientific publications. *Mailing Add:* Dept Microbiol Univ Miss Med Ctr 2500 N State St Jackson MS 39216-4505

LOBB, DONALD EDWARD, PHYSICS. *Current Pos:* asst prof, 67-71, assoc prof, 71-87, PROF PHYSICS, UNIV VICTORIA, BC, 87- *Personal Data:* b Saskatoon, Sask, Apr 25, 40. *Educ:* Univ Sask, BE, 61, MSc, 63, PhD(physics), 66. *Prof Exp:* Nat Res Coun Can overseas fel, 66-67. *Mem:* Inst Elec & Electronics Engrs; Can Asn Physicists. *Res:* Beam optics. *Mailing Add:* Dept Physics Univ Victoria Victoria BC V8W 3P6 Can

LOBDELL, DAVID HILL, PATHOLOGY. *Current Pos:* assoc pathologist, 60-63, DIR LABS, ST VINCENTS MED CTR, 63-, DIR SCH MED TECHNOL, 63- *Personal Data:* b Erie, Pa, July 9, 30. *Educ:* Kenyon Col, AB, 52; Univ Mich, MD, 56. *Prof Exp:* From intern to resident path, Bellevue Hosp, New York, 56-59, asst pathologist, 59-60. *Concurrent Pos:* Instr, Sch Med, NY Univ, 59-61, asst clin prof path, 61-69; lectr histol, Fairfield Univ, 64-73. *Mem:* AMA; fel Col Am Path; fel Am Soc Clin Path. *Res:* Osmometry; myeloproliferative disorders. *Mailing Add:* 2800 Main St Bridgeport CT 06606-4292

LOBECK, CHARLES CHAMPLIN, PEDIATRICS. *Current Pos:* AT SCI CTR, MED SCH, UNIV WIS-MADISON. *Personal Data:* b New Rochelle, NY, May 20, 26; m 54; c 4. *Educ:* Hobart Col, AB, 48; Univ Rochester, MD, 52. *Prof Exp:* From instr to sr instr pediat, Sch Med & Dent, Univ Rochester, 55-58; from asst prof to prof, Sch Med, Univ Wis-Madison, 58-75, chmn dept, 64-74, assoc dean clin affairs, 74-75; dean, Sch Med, Univ Mo, Columbia, 75- *Mem:* Sigma Xi. *Res:* Metabolic disease; membrane transport; cystic fibrosis. *Mailing Add:* 3420 Valley Creek Circle Middleton WI 53562-1990

LOBEL, STEVEN A, CLINICAL IMMUNOLOGY DIRECTOR, IMMUNOPATHOLOGY. *Current Pos:* STAFF, SMITH, KLINE BEECHAM, MD, 93- *Personal Data:* b Brooklyn, NY, Feb 8, 52; m 78; c 3. *Educ:* Univ Tex, Austin, BA, 73; State Univ NY, Buffalo, MA, 75, PhD(immunol), 77; Am Bd Med Lab Immunol, dipl, 87. *Prof Exp:* Fel, immunol, HHH Ctr Cancer Res, Hadassah, Jerusalem, 77-78, Dept Pathol, Univ Pittsburgh, 78-80; asst prof immunol, Dept Pediat & Microbiol, Univ Ill, Chicago, 80-83, Dept Pathol, Med Col Ga, 83-88; lab dir, Immunol, Dept Clin Path, Am Med Labs, 88-93. *Concurrent Pos:* Fel, Lady Davis Found, 77. *Mem:* Am Asn Immunol; Am Asn Path; Am Soc Clin Path; Am Soc Microbiol; Am Asn Clin Chem; Clin Immunol Soc. *Res:* Cellular immunology of human immunodeficiency virus infection. *Mailing Add:* SmithKline Beecham Clin Labs 11425 Cronhill Dr Owings Mills MD 21117

LOBENE, RALPH RUFINO, DENTISTRY, PERIODONTOLOGY. *Current Pos:* assoc prof & acad adminr, Dent Asst Training Prog, Forsyth Dent Ctr, 63-73, dean, Forsyth Sch Dent Hygienists, 75-85, dir advan educ & sr mem staff, 70-91, EMER, FORSYTH DENT CTR, 91-; CONSULT, 91- *Personal Data:* b Rochester, NY, Mar 30, 24; m 50, Lucille Tubeolo. *Educ:* Univ Rochester, BS, 44; Univ Buffalo, DDS, 49; Tufts Univ, MS, 62; Am Bd Periodont, dipl, 65. *Honors & Awards:* Colgate Palmolive Co Award, Am Dent Asn, 88. *Prof Exp:* Res chemist, Manhattan Proj, Univ Rochester, 44-45; res chemist, Merck & Co, NJ, 45-46; intern periodont, Eastman Dent Dispensary, Rochester, NY, 49-50; resident oral surg, Strong Mem Hosp, Rochester, 50-51, asst dent surgeon, 53-62, instr dent & clin dent res, Sch Med & Dent, Univ Rochester, 53-62; asst prof periodont, Sch Dent, Univ Pac, 62-63. *Concurrent Pos:* Res grants, Colgate Palmolive Co, 54-55, 58-59 & 84-88; res grant, Sch Dent, Univ Pac, 62-63; res grant, Gen Elec Co, 62-65; staff dentist, Eastman Dent Dispensary, 53-54, res assoc, 58-62; pvt pract, 53-60; chief dent serv, State Indust & Agr Sch Boys, NY, 54-57; clin asst, Sch Dent Med, Tufts Univ, 61-62, lectr, 63-; asst mem staff, Forsyth Dent Ctr, Northeastern Univ, 63-66, lectr, 63-, head, Dept Clin Exp, Inst Res & Advan Study Dent, 66-80, sr mem staff, 70-91, emer sr mem staff, 91; consult, Dent Res Panel, Gen Elec Co, 63-; vis surgeon, Dept Dent, Boston City Hosp, 64-90; grants, Robert Wood Johnson Found, 73-74 & 76-77, Nat Inst Dent Res, Off Collab Res, 73-75, Merril Richardson Co, 75-77 & Johnson & Johnson Co, 78; mem, Am Dent Asn Clin Cleansing Comt, 74-84; mem, Mass Bd Dent Adv Comt, 78-; lectr periodont, Harvard Sch Dent Med, 80. *Mem:* Fel AAAS; fel Am Col Dent; Am Dent Asn; Am Acad Oral Med; Am Acad Periodont; fel Int Col Dentists; fel Am Acad Dent Sci. *Res:* Assessment of periodontal disease and evaluation of the effectiveness of therapeutic methods of treatment of periodontal disease; analytical methods for chemical analysis. *Mailing Add:* 1303 Primavera Dr W Palm Springs CA 92264-8447

LOBKOWICZ, FREDERICK, ELEMENTARY PARTICLE PHYSICS. *Current Pos:* Res assoc, 60-64, from asst prof to assoc prof, 64-73, PROF PHYSICS, UNIV ROCHESTER, 73- *Personal Data:* b Prague, Czech, Nov 17, 32; US citizen; m 60; c 2. *Educ:* Swiss Fed Inst Technol, 55, PhD(physics), 60. *Concurrent Pos:* Humboldt Found sr fel, 73-74; vis prof, Univ Munich, Ger, 73-74. *Mem:* Fel Am Phys Soc; Swiss Phys Soc. *Res:* Muon and photon interactions. *Mailing Add:* Dept Physics & Astron Univ Rochester Rochester NY 14627

LOBL, THOMAS JAY, PHARMACEUTICAL CHEMISTRY, REPRODUCTIVE PHYSIOLOGY. *Current Pos:* DIR, CHEM SCI DEPT, TANABE RES LABS USA, 90- *Personal Data:* b Danville, Va, Oct 20, 44; m 68; c 2. *Educ:* Univ NC, Chapel Hill, BS, 66; Johns Hopkins Univ, PhD(org chem), 70. *Honors & Awards:* President's Award, Am Soc Andrology. *Prof Exp:* Res fel biochem, Calif Inst Technol, 70-73; Sr res scientist chem & biochem, UpJohn Co, 73-88; Dir, Peptide Res Lab, Immunetech Pharmaceut, 88-90. *Concurrent Pos:* chair, Kalamazoo Sect, Am Chem Soc, 79, San Diego Sect, 92; Assoc ed, J Andrology & Arch Andrology, 80-84. *Mem:* Am Chem Soc; AAAS; Sigma Xi; Am Soc Andrology (treas, 81-84); NY Acad Sci; Am Peptide Soc. *Res:* Regulation of male reproduction; spermatogenesis; epididymal function; hormone transport and receptor proteins; male contraception; chemical and biological deaminations; heterocyclic and steroid synthesis; reproductive physiology; peptide synthesis and chemistry; peptide/protein chemistry and biochemistry; signal peptides; peptide secondary structure activity relationships; peptide transport and targeting; peptide membrane interaction, autoimmune diseases, immunology, rheumatoid arthritis, allergy, type I diabetes. *Mailing Add:* 415 Recluse Lane Encinitas CA 92024

LOBO, ANGELO PETER, BIO-ORGANIC CHEMISTRY. *Current Pos:* SR RES SCIENTIST, WADSWORTH CTR LABS & RES, NY STATE DEPT HEALTH, 70- *Personal Data:* b Masindi, Uganda, May 19, 39; m 67, Victoria K Leong; c Stephen & Michael. *Educ:* Univ Bombay, BSc, 58; Ind Univ, Bloomington, PhD(org chem), 66. *Prof Exp:* Rockefeller Found spec lectr org chem, Makerere Univ Col, Kampala, Uganda, 66-68; res asst chem, Rensselaer Polytech Inst, 68-70. *Mem:* Am Chem Soc. *Res:* Synthesis of nucleotide/nucleoside substrates and inhibitors, oligonucleotide synthesis. *Mailing Add:* Wadsworth Ctr Labs & Res NY State Dept Health Albany NY 12201

LOBO, CECIL T(HOMAS), ENGINEERING MECHANICS. *Current Pos:* from instr to assoc prof, 63-71, actg chmn dept, 71-72, PROF CIVIL ENG, ROSE-HULMAN INST TECHNOL, 71 - *Personal Data:* b Mangalore, India, Sept 22, 34; c 2. *Educ:* Gujarat Univ, India, BE, 55; Univ Notre Dame, MS, 60; Purdue Univ, PhD(civil eng), 66. *Prof Exp:* Asst engr, Shah Construct Co, Ltd, India, 56-57. *Concurrent Pos:* Consult, Universal Tank & Iron Works, Inc, Ind. *Mem:* Mem Am Soc Civil Engrs; Am Soc Eng Educ; Sigma Xi; Am Concrete Inst; Prestressed Concrete Inst. *Res:* Structural and soil mechanics. *Mailing Add:* 3561 N Limberlost Lane Terre Haute IN 47803-3999

LOBO, FRANCIS X, MICROBIOLOGY. *Current Pos:* assoc prof sci, 60-70, chmn Dept Biol, 70-74, PROF BIOL SCI, MARYWOOD COL, 70- *Personal Data:* b Aden, UAR, Oct 8, 25; US citizen; m 60; c 3. *Educ:* Univ Bombay, BS, 47, MS, 50; Inst Divi Thomae, PhD(exp med, biol), 59; Nat Registry Microbiol, cert. *Prof Exp:* Technician, Path Dept, Worli Gen Hosp, India, 50; control & res microbiologist-chemist, Chemo Pharma Labs Ltd, Worli, Bombay, 50-57. *Concurrent Pos:* Consult, Radio Corp Am, 65-; NSF grant, Argonne Nat Lab, 66, resident res assoc, 68-69; fac res partic, Argonne Nat Lab, 67 & St Jude Children Res Hosp, Memphis, Tenn, 70; mem eval team, Pa Dept Educ, 71. *Mem:* Am Soc Microbiol; NY Acad Sci. *Res:* Intestinal microorganisms by enrichment culture techniques; citric acid from a cane-sugar molasses; beef brain extract in controlling staphylococcus infections; etiology of sludge formation in industrial wastes. *Mailing Add:* Dept Sci Marywood Col 2300 Adams Ave Scranton PA 18509-1514

LOBO, PAUL A(LLAN), CHEMICAL ENGINEERING, MERGER & ACQUISITION IN THE CHEMICAL INDUSTRY. *Current Pos:* RETIRED. *Personal Data:* b La Cumbre, Colombia, Oct 10, 28. *Educ:* Mass Inst Technol, SB, 50, SM, 51; Univ Mich, PhD(chem eng), 55. *Prof Exp:* Supvr process develop sect, Petrochem Res Div, Continental Oil Co, Okla, 55-63, Europ rep, Res Dept, Holland, 63-64, petrolchem coord, Continental Oil Co, Ltd, Eng, 64-65, exec asst to pres, NY, 65-67, mgr develop, Petrochem Dept, 67-68; vpres & gen mgr, Pitt-Consol Chem Co, 68-70; dir bus develop & planning, Tenneco Chem Inc, Piscataway, 71-73, dir, Tech Group, 73-75, dir corp planning, Saddle Brook, NJ, 75-80, vpres planning, 80-83; vpres int, Nuodex, Inc, 83-88; sr vpres eng, Huls Am Inc, 89-93; prin, Lobo & Assocs, Inc, 93-94. *Concurrent Pos:* Lectr, Univ Okla, 56-63. *Mem:* Am Chem Soc; Am Inst Chem Engrs. *Res:* High pressure; petrochemical process development; reaction kinetics. *Mailing Add:* Lobo & Assocs Inc 155 Nantwich Ct Somerset NJ 08873

LOBO, WALTER E(DER), chemical engineering; deceased, see previous edition for last biography

LOBODZINSKI, SLAWOMIR M, BIOENGINEERING, BIOMEDICAL ENGINEERING. *Current Pos:* PROF ELEC ENG, CALIF STATE UNIV, 86- *Personal Data:* b Lublin, Poland, Apr 26, 48. *Educ:* Tech Univ Warsaw, BS, 71, MS, 72; Tech Univ Vienna, Austria, PhD(biomed eng), 78. *Prof Exp:* Res engr, Sch Med, Univ Vienna, 75 & 78; assoc prof elec eng, Calif State Polytech Univ, 79-83. *Concurrent Pos:* Fulbright scholar, Univ Auckland, NZ, 95-96. *Mem:* Inst Elec & Electronics Engrs; Am Soc Echocardiography; Int Soc Optical Eng; Asn Comput Mach. *Mailing Add:* Dept Elec Eng Calif State Univ 1250 Bellflower Blvd Long Beach CA 90840. *Fax:* 562-985-7561; *E-Mail:* slobol@csuib.edu

LOBSTEIN, OTTO ERVIN, CLINICAL BIOCHEMISTRY. *Current Pos:* RETIRED. *Personal Data:* b Czech, Apr 12, 22; nat US; m 52, Miriam T Goldberg; c Dennis D, Harvey R & Heidi M. *Educ:* Univ London, BSc, 45; Smae Inst, Eng, MSF, 45; Northwestern Univ, PhD(biochem), 52; Am Bd Clin Chem, dipl, 55. *Honors & Awards:* Sci Award, Cancer Fedn, 79. *Prof Exp:* Asst res chemist, Howards & Sons, Ltd, Eng, 42-46; biochemist, Elgin State Hosp, Ill, 47-48; instr chem, Wesley & Passavant Mem Hosps, Ill, 49-51; res assoc zool, Univ Southern Calif, 52-53; med dir res, Chemtech Labs, 52-62; biochemist-owner, Lobstein Biochem Lab, Calif, 62-64; asst prof chem, Loyola Univ, Calif, 64-65; head, Biochem Dept, St Elizabeth Hosp Med Ctr, 65-76; dir clin chem, Mt Sinai Hosp Med Ctr, Cook Co Hosp, 76-82; biochemist, 82-93. *Concurrent Pos:* Vis res prof, Univ Redlands, 59-65; secy-treas, Res Found Dis Eye, 59-65; vis assoc prof, Purdue Univ, 68-73, adj prof, 65-76; prof biochem & path, Rush Presby St Lukes Med Ctr, Chicago, 76-93, emer prof, 93. *Mem:* Fel AAAS; Am Soc Microbiol; sr mem Am Chem Soc; fel Am Asn Clin Chem (secy, 81-83); Am Chem Soc; fel Nat Acad Clin Biochem. *Res:* Biochemical investigation of the crystalline lens of the eye, protein structure and constitution in normal and in cataract lenses of the human and other species; changes in protein with a changed electrolyte environment; clinical investigation of lysozyme in carcinomatosis. *Mailing Add:* 2006 Maple Ave Northbrook IL 60062-5266

LOBUE, JOSEPH, PHYSIOLOGY, HEMATOLOGY. *Current Pos:* From asst prof to assoc prof, 62-71, PROF BIOL, NY UNIV, 71-, CO-DIR, A S GORDON LAB EXP HEMAT, 67- *Personal Data:* b Union City, NJ, Apr 19, 34; m 59, Catherine E Scully; c Philip, Joseph & Ellen. *Educ:* St Peter's Col, NJ, BS, 55; Marquette Univ, MS, 57; NY Univ, PhD(physiol), 62. *Honors & Awards:* Christian R & Mary F Lindback Found Award, NY Univ, 65. *Concurrent Pos:* NIH fel, 62; Sigma Xi grant-in-aid, 64-65; Am Cancer Soc grant, 65-66; Nat Cancer Inst grant, 71-73, 75-78 & 79-81; Nat Leukemia Asn grant, 74-76; assoc, Danforth Found, 68-; co-dir, Hemat Training Prog, NIH, 65-75. *Mem:* Int Soc Exp Hemat. *Res:* Mechanisms controlling leukocyte and erythrocyte production and release; pathophysiology and cytokinetics of rodent and avian leukemias. *Mailing Add:* Dept Biol New York Univ 100 Washington Sq E New York NY 10003-6688

LOBUGLIO, ALBERT FRANCIS, HEMATOLOGY, IMMUNOLOGY. *Current Pos:* DIR, COMPREHENSIVE CANCER CTR, UNIV ALA, BIRMINGHAM. *Personal Data:* b Buffalo, NY, Feb 1, 38; m 62; c 5. *Educ:* Georgetown Univ, MD, 62. *Prof Exp:* Intern med, Presby Univ Hosp, Pittsburgh, 62-63, resident, 63-65; instr, State Univ NY Buffalo, 67-68, asst prof, 68-69; assoc prof med, Ohio State Univ, 69-73, prof, 73-78; prof med, Univ Mich, 78- *Concurrent Pos:* Hemat fel, Thorndike Mem Lab, Boston City Hosp, 65-67; hemat consult, Vet Admin Hosp, Buffalo, 67-69, Dayton, Ohio, 69- *Mem:* Am Fedn Clin Res; Am Soc Hemat; Am Soc Clin Invest. *Res:* Tumor immunology; transplant immunology; human macrophage and lymphocyte functions. *Mailing Add:* Cancer Ctr & Div Hematol-Oncol Univ Al University Sta 1824 Sixth Ave S Rm 237 Birmingham AL 35294-3300

LOBUNEZ, WALTER, INDUSTRIAL CHEMISTRY. *Current Pos:* RETIRED. *Personal Data:* b Ukraine, Nov 22, 20; nat US; m 45; c 1. *Educ:* Univ Pa, MS, 52, PhD(chem), 54. *Prof Exp:* Res assoc immunol, Jefferson Med Col, 54-55; protein chem, Children's Hosp, Univ Penn, 55-59; sr scientist chem, Textile Res Inst, 59-60; res chemist, FMC Corp, 60-67, sr res chemist 67-80, res assoc, 80-83. *Res:* Chemistry of hydrocarbons; protein chemistry; chemistry of cellulose; soda ash processes; bromine and strontium processes. *Mailing Add:* 562 Ewing St Princeton NJ 08540

LOCALIO, S ARTHUR, SURGERY. *Current Pos:* From instr to assoc prof surg, 45-53, prof clin surg, 53-71, PROF SURG, MED SCH, NY UNIV, 71- *Personal Data:* b New York, NY, Oct 4, 11; m 45; c 4. *Educ:* Cornell Univ, AB, 33; Univ Rochester, MD, 36; Am Bd Surg, dipl, 45. *Hon Degrees:* DSc, Columbia Univ, 42. *Concurrent Pos:* Asst surgeon, Univ Hosp, 45-47, asst attend surgeon, 47-49, assoc attend surgeon, 49-52, attend surgeon, 52-, clin asst vis surgeon, 49-52, vis surgeon, 52-; Johnson & Johnson distinguished prof surg, NY Univ, 72. *Mem:* Am Asn Surg of Trauma; Am Gastroenterol Asn; Am Col Surg; Am Surg Asn; Sigma Xi. *Res:* Wound healing; surgery of gastro-intestinal disease. *Mailing Add:* Mill Village Rd Deerfield MA 01342

LOCASCIO, SALVADORE J, HORTICULTURE. *Current Pos:* Asst prof, 59-65, assoc horticulturist, 65-69, ASSOC PROF HORT, DEPT VEG CROPS, UNIV FLA, 65-, HORTICULTURIST, 69- *Personal Data:* b Hammond, La, Oct 29, 33; m 54; c 3. *Educ:* Southeastern La Col, BS, 55; La State Univ, MS, 56; Purdue Univ, PhD(plant physiol), 59. *Honors & Awards:* Pres Gold Medal Award, 78. *Mem:* Weed Sci Soc Am; Sigma Xi; fel Am Soc Hort Sci. *Res:* Fertilizer and water requirements of vegetables; strawberry culture; chemical weed control for vegetables; teaching of commercial vegetable crops and nutrition of horticultural crops. *Mailing Add:* 406 NW 32nd St Univ Fla Gainesville FL 32607

LOCHHEAD, JOHN HUTCHISON, INVERTEBRATE ZOOLOGY. *Current Pos:* from instr to prof, 42-75, EMER PROF ZOOL, UNIV VT, 75- *Personal Data:* b Montreal, Que, Aug 7, 09; nat US; m 38; c 2. *Educ:* Univ St Andrew's, MA, 30; Cambridge Univ, BA, 32, Bachelor schule, 33, PhD(zool), 37. *Prof Exp:* With Cambridge Univ Table, Marine Zool Sta, Naples, 34-35; sr cur, Mus Zool, Cambridge Univ, 35-38, instr zool, 36-38; fel by courtesy, Johns Hopkins Univ, 40; asst biologist, Va Fisheries Lab, 41-42. *Concurrent Pos:* Lectr, Col William & Mary, 41-42; instr, Woods Hole Marine Biol Lab, 43-55, mem corp, 44- *Mem:* Am Soc Zool; Crustacean Soc. *Res:* Anatomy and physiology of Crustacea including their feeding mechanisms, locomotion, factors controlling swimming positions, responses to light, functions for the blood and related tissues, molting and reproduction. *Mailing Add:* 49 Woodlawn Rd London SW6 6PS England

LOCHMULLER, CHARLES HOWARD, ANALYTICAL CHEMISTRY. *Current Pos:* From asst prof to assoc prof, 69-78, chmn dept, 82-87, PROF CHEM, DUKE UNIV, 78-, PROF BIOCHEM ENG, 87- *Personal Data:* b New York, NY, May 4, 40; m 63, Patricia Maracsov; c 3. *Educ:* Manhattan Col, BS, 62; Fordham Univ, MS, 64, PhD(analytical chem), 68. *Honors & Awards:* Chromatography Award, Am Chem Soc, 87. *Concurrent Pos:* Assoc, Purdue Univ, 67-69; chair, Analytical Div, Am Chem Soc, 83-84. *Mem:* Am Chem Soc; fel Royal Soc Chem; fel Am Inst Chemists. *Res:* Factors effecting separation processes; spectroscopy. *Mailing Add:* Dept Chem Duke Univ Durham NC 27708. Fax: 919-660-1599

LOCHNER, JANIS ELIZABETH, MEMBRANE BIOCHEMISTRY, CELLULAR COMMUNICATION. *Current Pos:* ASST PROF CHEM, LEWIS & CLARK COL, 81- *Personal Data:* b Bethesda, Md, Nov 27, 54. *Educ:* Allegheny Col, BS, 76; Univ Ore, PhD(biochem), 81. *Concurrent Pos:* Res fel biochem, Ore Health Sci Univ, 81- *Mem:* AAAS. *Res:* Role of the plasma membrane in cellular communication; mechanisms of membrane transduction. *Mailing Add:* Dept Chem Lewis & Clark Col 0615 SW Palatine Hill Rd Portland OR 97219-7899

LOCHNER, ROBERT HERMAN, STATISTICS. *Current Pos:* QUAL MEASUREMENT SPECIALIST, JOINT COMN ACCREDITATION HEALTH CARE ORGN, 93- *Personal Data:* b Madison, Wis, Apr 17, 39; m 62, Sarajane Gille; c Ann, Susan, Mary K & Daniel. *Educ:* Univ Wis-Madison, BS, 61, MS, 62 & 66, PhD(statist), 69. *Prof Exp:* Math analyst, A C Electronics Div, Gen Motors Corp, 62-65; from asst prof to assoc prof statist & math, Marquette Univ, 68-85; consult statist, & qual mgt, 85-93. *Concurrent Pos:* Lectr bus admin, Marquette Univ, 91-93. *Mem:* Am Statist Asn. *Res:* Statistical methods in reliability, life testing and quality improvement. *Mailing Add:* 2840 S Root River Pkwy Milwaukee WI 53227

LOCHSTET, WILLIAM A, PHYSICS. *Current Pos:* ASST PROF PHYSICS, UNIV PITTSBURGH, 86- *Personal Data:* b Port Jefferson, NY, Dec 5, 36; m 82; c 2. *Educ:* Univ Rochester, BS, 57, MA, 60; Univ Pa, PhD(physics), 65. *Prof Exp:* Instr, 65-66, asst prof physics, Pa State Univ, 66-86. *Mem:* Am Phys Soc; AAAS; Sigma Xi; Am Asn Physics Teachers. *Mailing Add:* Dept Physics Univ Pittsburgh Johnstown PA 15904

LOCICERO, JOSEPH CASTELLI, ORGANIC CHEMISTRY. *Current Pos:* RETIRED. *Personal Data:* b Ontario Center, NY, 14; m 37; c 2. *Educ:* Univ Rochester, AB, 34; Pa State Univ, MS, 47, PhD(biochem), 48. *Prof Exp:* Chemist, Hooker Electrochem Co, NY, 37-43; sr res chemist, Nuodex Prods Co, NJ, 43-45; res chemist, Rohm and Haas Co, 48-52, sr scientist, 52-71; from asst prof to prof chem, Camden County Col, 71-84. *Mem:* AAAS; Am Chem Soc. *Res:* Plasticizers, fungicides and insecticides; high pressure reactions; detergents; process development; ion exchange; sugar technology; halogenation; plastics. *Mailing Add:* 2113 Fleet Landing Blvd Atlantic Beach FL 32233-7501

LOCK, BRIAN EDWARD, SEDIMENTOLOGY. *Current Pos:* assoc prof, 77-80, PROF GEOL, UNIV SOUTHWESTERN LA, 80- *Personal Data:* b Yeovil, Eng, Mar 21, 44; m 68; c 3. *Educ:* Cambridge Univ, BA, 66, PhD(geol), 69, MA, 70. *Hon Degrees:* MA, Cambridge Univ, 70. *Prof Exp:* Consult, Fina Petrol Co, Belg, 69-70; lectr, Rhodes Univ, SAfrica, 70-74, sr lectr, 75-77. *Concurrent Pos:* Sr res assoc, Exeter Univ, Eng, 75-76; overseas res burser, Coun Sci & Indust Res, Pretoria, 75-76; consult basic appl geol, Superior Oil Co. *Mem:* Am Asn Petrol Geologists; Soc Econ Paleontologists & Mineralogists; Geol Soc Am; Int Asn Volcanology & Chemistry of the Earth's Interior; Int Asn Sedimentologists. *Res:* Sedimentology of carbonate rocks; other aspects of sedimentology and stratigraphy; field work in South Africa, Ireland, Spitsbergen, Reunion Island, Canada and United States. *Mailing Add:* Dept Geol Univ Southwestern La PO Box 44530 Lafayette LA 70504-9998

LOCK, COLIN JAMES LYNE, bioinorganic chemistry, crystallography; deceased, see previous edition for last biography

LOCK, G(ERALD) S(EYMOUR) H(UNTER), MECHANICAL ENGINEERING. *Current Pos:* From asst prof to assoc prof, 62-70, prof mech eng, 70-, EMER PROF MECH ENG, UNIV ALTA. *Personal Data:* b London, Eng, June 30, 35; m 59; c 3. *Educ:* Univ Durham, BSc, 59, PhD(mech eng), 62. *Honors & Awards:* Queen Elizabeth Silver Jubilee Medal, 79. *Concurrent Pos:* Chmn comt heat transfer, Nat Res Coun Can, 69-71; Sci Coun Can. *Mem:* Am Soc Mech Engrs; fel Eng Inst Can; fel Can Soc Mech Engrs (pres, 77-78). *Res:* Thermodynamics and heat transfer, especially ice engineering; technology assessment. *Mailing Add:* Dept Mech Eng Univ Alta Edmonton AB T6G 2M7 Can

LOCK, JAMES ALBERT, LIGHT SCATTERING. *Current Pos:* from asst prof to assoc prof, 78-90, PROF PHYSICS, CLEVELAND STATE UNIV, 90- *Personal Data:* b Cleveland, Ohio, Feb 12, 48; m 72. *Educ:* Case Western Reserve Univ, BS, 70, MS, 73, PhD(physics), 74. *Prof Exp:* Lectr, Case Western Reserve Univ, 70-74, res assoc physics, 74-78. *Mem:* Sigma Xi; Optical Soc Am. *Res:* Light scattering. *Mailing Add:* Dept Physics Cleveland State Univ Cleveland OH 44115

LOCK, KENNETH, ELECTRICAL ENGINEERING, COMPUTER SCIENCE. *Current Pos:* PRES, ZYBEX. *Personal Data:* b Wushi, China, Mar 15, 32; m 54; c 4. *Educ:* Battersea Polytech Inst, BSc, 55; Univ London, MSc, 57; Calif Inst Technol, PhD(elec eng, physics), 62. *Prof Exp:* From instr to asst prof elec eng, Calif Inst Technol, 59-65; advan programmer, Int Bus Mach Corp, 65-67, vis fel, 67-69; pres, Cyber Data Inc, Calif, 69-71; mgr design automation, Burroughs Corp, 71-77, dept mgr, MCO div, 77-80; pres, Cybertec, 80- *Concurrent Pos:* Consult, Jet Propulsion Lab, 62-65. *Mem:* Inst Elec & Electronics Engrs; Asn Comput Mach. *Res:* Physical systems on computers; network analysis; switching theory; programming system research; computer design; interactive use of computers in engineering, science and business. *Mailing Add:* 5425 Calumet Ave La Jolla CA 92037

LOCKARD, ISABEL, ANATOMY. *Current Pos:* from asst prof to prof, 52-85, EMER PROF ANAT, MED UNIV SC, 85- *Personal Data:* b Brandon, Man, June 27, 15. *Educ:* Northwestern Univ, BS, 38; Univ Mich, MA, 42, PhD(anat), 46. *Prof Exp:* Asst anat, Univ Mich, 42-44 & 47; instr, Univ Pittsburgh, 44-45; instr, Sch Med Georgetown Univ, 47-49, asst prof, 49-52. *Concurrent Pos:* Consult, Med Univ SC. *Mem:* Am Asn Anatomists; Sigma Xi. *Res:* Neuroanatomy; blood supply of central nervous system. *Mailing Add:* Dept Anat & Cell Biol Med Univ SC 171 Ashley Ave Charleston SC 29425

LOCKARD, J DAVID, BOTANY, SCIENCE EDUCATION. *Current Pos:* from asst prof to assoc prof, 61-70, PROF BOT & SCI EDUC, UNIV MD, COLLEGE PARK, 70-, DIR, SCI TEACHING CTR, 62- *Personal Data:* b Renovo, Pa, Dec 20, 29; m 51; c 4. *Educ:* Pa State Univ, BS, 51, MEd, 55; PhD(bot), 62. *Prof Exp:* Dept chmn sci dept high sch, Pa, 53-56; consult sci teaching improvement prog, AAAS, 56-58; asst bot, Pa State Univ, 58-61. *Concurrent Pos:* NSF-AAAS grant, Develop & Maintain Int Clearinghouse Sci & Math Curric Develops, 62-; dir off bio educ, Am Inst Biol Sci, 66-67; dir, NSF-AID Study Improvisation Sci Teaching Mat Worldwide, 68-72; NSF grants, acad year inst sci suprvs, 69-73; dir NSF Impact Study, 74-75; rep, US Nat Comn to UNESCO, 75- *Mem:* AAAS (vpres, 71); Am Soc Plant Physiol; Int Coun Asn Sci Educ (pres, 73-76); Nat Asn Res Sci Teaching (pres, 72-73); Nat Sci Teachers Asn; Sigma Xi; Nat Asn Biol Teachers. *Res:* Investigating medicinal and poisonous plants; improving science teaching techniques and equipment; studying science and math curriculum developments internationally; consulting in science education; science writing; studing use of computers in science instructions. *Mailing Add:* Dept Bot Univ Md College Park MD 20740

LOCKARD, RAYMOND G, HORTICULTURE. *Current Pos:* RETIRED. *Personal Data:* b Patricia, Alta, Jan 1, 25; m 51, Joyce M Powers; c Dianne, David & Kathleen. *Educ:* Univ BC, BSA, 49; Univ Idaho, MSc, 51; Univ London, PhD, 56. *Prof Exp:* Plant physiologist, Can For Aid, Malaysia, 54-59, Ghana, 59-64; tech expert, Food & Agr Orgn, Philippines, 64-67; from assoc prof to prof hort, Univ Ky, 67-81; prof crop sci & crop sci coordr, La State Univ, USAID Prog, Cent Agr Res Inst, Liberia, 81-84; horticulturist, Calif State Polytech Univ, Pomona, USAID Prog, Sanaa, Yemen Arab Repub, 85-88. *Mem:* Int Soc Hort Sci; Am Soc Hort Sci. *Res:* Chill requirements. *Mailing Add:* 2717 NE Knott Portland OR 97212

LOCKART, ROYCE ZENO, JR, MOLECULAR BIOLOGY. *Current Pos:* RETIRED. *Personal Data:* b Marshfield, Ore, Sept 7, 28; m 51; c 3. *Educ:* Whitman Col, AB, 50; Univ Wash, MS, 53, PhD(microbiol), 57. *Prof Exp:* Res fel, Nat Inst Allergy & Infectious Dis, 57-58, bacteriologist, Radiation Br, Nat Cancer Inst, 58-60; from asst prof to assoc prof microbiol, Univ Tex, 60-66; res supvr, E I du Pont de Nemours & Co, Inc, 66-80, biologist, 80-83, patent assoc, 83- *Res:* Virus cell interactions, particularly animal viruses and their control by natural means and by chemicals; image analysis of immunological cells; writing biotechnology patents. *Mailing Add:* 1418 Bucknell Rd Green Acres Wilmington DE 19803

LOCKE, BEN ZION, APPLIED STATISTICS, EPIDEMIOLOGY. *Current Pos:* from asst chief to chief, Ctr Epidemiol Studies, 67-85, CHIEF, EPIDEMIOL PSYCHOPATH BRANCH, NIMH, 85- *Personal Data:* b New York, NY, Sept 8, 21; m 47; c 4. *Educ:* Brooklyn Col, AB, 47; Columbia Univ, MS, 49. *Honors & Awards:* Rema Lapouse Award, Am Pub Health Asn, 90. *Prof Exp:* Statistician, NY State Health Dept, 47-56; chief consult sect, Biomet Br, NIMH, 56-66; assoc prof eval & dir res & eval, Community Ment Health Ctr, Temple Univ, 66-67. *Mem:* AAAS; fel Am Pub Health Asn; Am Statist Asn; Soc Epidemiol Res; fel Am Col Epidemiol. *Res:* Epidemiology of mental disorders; evaluation of programs designed to prevent and control mental disorders and promote mental health. *Mailing Add:* 11803 Saddlerock Rd Silver Spring MD 20902

LOCKE, CARL EDWIN, JR, CORROSION, POLYMER SCIENCE. *Current Pos:* DEAN ENG, UNIV KANS, 86- *Personal Data:* b Palo Pinto Co, Tex, Jan 11, 36; m 56, Sammie Batchelor; c Stephen & Carlene. *Educ:* Univ Tex, Austin, BS, 58, MS, 60, PhD(chem eng), 72. *Honors & Awards:* D Grant Mickle Award, Transp Res Bd, 88; Eben Junkin Award, Nat Asn Corrosion Engrs, 90. *Prof Exp:* Res engr, Continental Oil Co, 59-65; prod engr, R L Stone Co, 65-66; prog res engr, Tracor Inc, 66-68; instr & vis asst prof, Univ Tex, 71-73; from asst prof to assoc prof, Univ Okla, 73-80, prof & dir chem eng & mat sci, 80-86. *Concurrent Pos:* Proj dir, Okla Dept Transp, 75 & 76-79. *Mem:* Am Inst Chem Engrs; Nat Asn Corrosion Engrs; Am Soc Testing & Mat; Am Soc Eng Educ. *Res:* Corrosion; corrosion in concrete; electrochemistry of corrosion. *Mailing Add:* 4010 Learned Hall Univ Kans Lawrence KS 66045-0001. *Fax:* 785-864-5445; *E-Mail:* lok@kuhub.cc.ukans.edu

LOCKE, DAVID CREIGHTON, CHEMICAL SEPARATIONS. *Current Pos:* from asst prof to assoc prof, 68-76, PROF CHEM, QUEENS COL, NY, 76- *Personal Data:* b Garden City, NY, Mar 1, 39; m 62, Carol Anderson. *Educ:* Lafayette Col, BS, 61; Kans State Univ, PhD(chem), 65. *Prof Exp:* Res chemist, Esso Res & Eng Co, 65-67; NSF fel, Univ Col Swansea, Univ Wales, 67-68. *Mem:* AAAS; Am Chem Soc; Int Inst Conserv Hist & Artistic Works; NY Acad Sci. *Res:* Analytical chemistry; chemical separations; GC/MS; supercritical fluids; biosolids characterization. *Mailing Add:* Dept Chem Queens Col Flushing NY 11367-0904. *E-Mail:* dclqc@qcvaxa.acc.qu.edu

LOCKE, HAROLD OGDEN, PHYSICAL CHEMISTRY, ANALYTICAL CHEMISTRY. *Current Pos:* ANALYTICAL CHEMIST, GAF CORP, 65- *Personal Data:* b Camden, NJ, Sept 14, 31; m 59, Elizabeth Bellmer; c Bruce & David. *Educ:* Wesleyan Univ, BA, 53, MA, 56; Rutgers Univ, PhD(chem), 62. *Prof Exp:* Res chemist, Armstrong Cork Co, 61-65. *Mem:* Am Chem Soc. *Res:* X-ray crystallography; polymer characterization; surfactants. *Mailing Add:* 816 Prince St Palmer Twp Easton PA 18042-2435

LOCKE, JACK LAMBOURNE, PHYSICS. *Current Pos:* RETIRED. *Personal Data:* b Brantford, Ont, May 1, 21; m 46, Joyce Moxon; c John A & M Jane (Green). *Educ:* Univ Toronto, BA, 46, MA, 47, PhD(physics), 49. *Honors & Awards:* Rumford Medal, AAAS, 71. *Prof Exp:* Demonstr physics, Univ Toronto, 45-47; astrophysicist, Dom Observ, 49-59, chief, Stellar Physics Div, 59-66; radio astronr, Nat Res Coun Can, 66-70, assoc dir, Radio & Elec Eng Div & chief astrophys br, 70-75, dir, Herzberg Inst Astrophys, 75-85. *Concurrent Pos:* Officer-in-chg, Dom Radio Astrophys Observ, 59-62. *Mem:* Am Astron Soc; Can Astron Soc; Int Astron Union. *Res:* Astrophysics; radio astronomy; solar physics; molecular spectra; infrared spectrum of the atmosphere. *Mailing Add:* 2150 Braeside Ave Ottawa ON K1H 7J5 Can

LOCKE, JOHN LAUDERDALE, speech pathology, psycholingusitics, for more information see previous edition

LOCKE, KRYSTYNA KOPACZYK, BIOCHEMISTRY, ENZYMOLOGY. *Current Pos:* TOXICOLOGIST, TOXICOL BR, HAZARD EVAL DIV, OFF PESTICIDE PROGS, ENVIRON PROTECTION AGENCY, 77- *Personal Data:* b Warsaw, Poland, Dec 2, 26; m 70. *Educ:* Wayne State Univ, BS, 53; Western Reserve Univ, MS, 56; Univ Ill, Champaign-Urbana, PhD(lipid chem), 62. *Prof Exp:* Res nutritionist, Atherosclerosis Res Proj, Vet Admin Hosp, Downey, Ill, 56-58; Nat Inst Neurol Dis & Blindness fel biochem, Ment Health Res Inst, Univ Mich, Ann Arbor, 62-64; trainee, Inst Enzyme Res, Univ Wis-Madison, 64-66; proj assoc, 66-69; res biochemist, Biochem Toxicol Br, Div Toxicol, Food & Drug Admin, 69-77. *Mem:* NY Acad Sci; Am Chem Soc. *Res:* Effects of environmental agents on biochemistry and ultrastructure of mitochondria. *Mailing Add:* 6220 Garden Rd Springfield VA 22152

LOCKE, LOUIS NOAH, ANIMAL PATHOLOGY. *Current Pos:* RETIRED. *Personal Data:* b Stockton, Calif, Mar 14, 28; m 53, Frankie Shearer; c Jonathan M. *Educ:* Univ Calif, AB, 50, DVM, 56. *Honors & Awards:* Distinguished Serv Award, Wildlife Dis Asn, 84; Merton Rosen Mem Lectr, 85. *Prof Exp:* Vet, USPHS, 56-58; wildlife res biologist, Patuxent Wildlife Res Ctr, US Dept Interior, 58-60, histopathologist, 61-75; wildlife pathologist, Nat Wildlife Health Lab, US Fish & Wildlife Serv, 75-89. *Mem:* Wildlife Soc; Am Asn Avian Path; Am Vet Med Asn; emer mem Wildlife Disease Asn (secy, 88-91, pres, 91-93). *Res:* Wildlife diseases, especially diseases and parasites of the mourning doves, waterfowl; effects of pollutants upon wild birds; lead poisoning in migratory birds. *Mailing Add:* Nat Wildlife Health Res Ctr 6006 Schroeder Dr Madison WI 53711

LOCKE, MICHAEL, INSECT PHYSIOLOGY, INSECT STRUCTURE & CELL BIOLOGY. *Current Pos:* prof zool & chmn dept, 71-85, prof, 85-94, EMER PROF, DEPT ZOOL, UNIV WESTERN ONT, 94- *Personal Data:* b Nottingham, Eng, Feb 14, 29; m 53, 80, Janet V Collins; c John, Timothy, Marius & Vanessa. *Educ:* Cambridge Univ, BA, 52, MA, 55, PhD, 56, DSc, 76. *Honors & Awards:* Rockefeller Found Award, 60; Carnegie Award, 61; Gold Medal, Int Award Insect Morphol & Embryol. *Prof Exp:* Lectr zool, Univ WIndies, 56; from assoc prof to prof biol, Case Western Res Univ, 61-71. *Concurrent Pos:* Ed, Soc Develop Biol, 62-69; Raman prof, Univ Madras, 69; vis dir res, ICIPE, Nairobi, Kenya, 77-81; Killam res fel, 88. *Mem:* Fel AAAS; Am Soc Cell Biol; fel Royal Soc Can. *Res:* Coordination of growth in insects; insect cell development; insect morphogenesis; structure of the epidermis and fat body; cuticle secretion, ferritin and iron metabolism; author of over 200 papers. *Mailing Add:* Dept Zool Univ Western Ont London ON N6A 5B7 Can. *Fax:* 519-661-2014; *E-Mail:* mlocke@julian.uwo.ca

LOCKE, PHILIP M, MATHEMATICS. *Current Pos:* asst prof, 68-74, ASSOC PROF MATH, UNIV MAINE, ORONO, 74- *Personal Data:* b Rockford, Ill, July 12, 37; m 61; c 2. *Educ:* Bluffton Col, BS, 59; Univ NH, MS, 64, PhD(math), 67. *Prof Exp:* Asst prof math, Mont State Univ, 67-68. *Mem:* Math Asn Am. *Res:* Ordinary differential equations. *Mailing Add:* Univ Maine 236 E/M Orono ME 04469-0001

LOCKE, RAYMOND KENNETH, BIOCHEMISTRY, TOXICOLOGY. *Current Pos:* TOXICOLOGIST, OFF TOXIC SUBSTANCES, US ENVIRON PROTECTION AGENCY, 79- *Personal Data:* b Terre Haute, Ind, July 2, 40; m 70. *Educ:* Wash Univ, BS, 65. *Prof Exp:* Res asst biochem, Univ Tex, Dallas, 66-67; res chemist, Div Nutrit, Food & Drug Admin, 68-69; Biochem & Metab Sect, Div Pesticides, 69-71 & Metab Br, Div Toxicol, 71-73, res chemist, Biochem Toxicol Br, 73-77, chemist, Div Toxicol, Contaminants & Natural Toxicants Eval Br, 77-79. *Mem:* AAAS; Am Chem Soc; NY Acad Sci. *Res:* Biochemical studies of the comparative in vivo and in vitro metabolism of foreign compounds by animals, plants and man. *Mailing Add:* 6220 Garden Rd Springfield VA 22152-1504

LOCKE, STANLEY, MATHEMATICS, PHYSICS. *Personal Data:* b New York City, NY, June 18, 34; m 58, Jane L Hershkowitz; c 3. *Educ:* NY Univ, BME, 55, MS, 57, PhD(math), 60. *Prof Exp:* Res mathematician, Repub Aviation Corp, 59-60; mem sci staff, Schlumberger-Doll Res Ctr, 65-86; consult, Stanley Locke & Assoc, 87-88; consult engr, Teleco Oilfield Serv, 88-92. *Mem:* Sigma Xi; sr mem Inst Elec & Electronics Engrs. *Res:* Solution of mechanical, electro-magnetic, acoustic and nuclear problems arising in the development of new oil field services. *Mailing Add:* 17 Deerwood Ct Norwalk CT 06851

LOCKE, STEPHEN CHARLES, GRAPH THEORY & ALGORITHMS. *Current Pos:* From asst prof to assoc prof, 81-93, mem, Inst Comput Sci & Eng, 85-88, PROF, DEPT MATH, FLA ATLANTIC UNIV, 93- *Personal Data:* b London, Eng, May 30, 53; Brit & Can citizen; m 74, Katharine Joanne Thomson; c Geoffrey Charles & Daniel Richard. *Educ:* Univ Waterloo, BMath, 75, MMath, 76, PhD(combinatorics & optimization), 82. *Concurrent Pos:* Asst chmn, Dept Math, Fla Atlantic Univ, 92-, preprof chmn, 97- *Mem:* Am Math Soc; Math Asn Am; Can Math Soc. *Res:* Graph theory; cycle space; cycles in graphs; dirac-type conditions; independent sets in triangle-free graphs. *Mailing Add:* Dept Math Sci Fla Atlantic Univ Boca Raton FL 33431-0991. *E-Mail:* lockes@acc.fau.edu

LOCKE, STEVEN ELLIOT, BEHAVIORAL MEDICINE, MEDICAL INFORMATICS. *Current Pos:* Fel psychiat, Harvard Med Sch, 74-77, clin instr, 77-79, instr, 80-87, asst prof psychiat, 87-96, DIR PSYCHIAT INFORMATICS, CTR CLIN COMPUT, HARVARD MED SCH, 93-; CHIEF BEHAV MED, HARVARD PILGRIM HEALTH CARE, 95-; ASSOC PROF PSYCHIAT, MASS INST TECHNOL, 96- *Personal Data:* b Englewood, NJ, Dec 2, 45; m 84; c 2. *Educ:* Cornell Univ, AB, 68; Columbia Univ Col Physicians & Surgeons, MD, 72. *Honors & Awards:* First Prize, Sci Exhib, Am Col Emergency Physicians. *Prof Exp:* Intern, Mt Zion Hosp & Med Ctr, San Francisco, Calif, 72-73. *Concurrent Pos:* Intern, Mt Zion Hosp & Med Ctr, San Francisco, Calif, 72-73; resident, McLean Hosp, Belmont, MA, 74-77; fel, Boston Univ Sch Med, 77-79; assoc dir, Psychiat Consult Serv, Beth Israel Hosp, 80-87, dir, Comput in Psychiat, 87-, med student educ in psychiat, 89-; lectr, Beth Israel Hosp, 80-82; Assoc prof psychiat, Mass Inst Technol, 96- *Mem:* Biofeedback Soc Am; Am Med Informatics Asn; fel Am Psychiat Asn; Am Psychosom Soc; Soc Behav Med. *Res:* Interactive computing in psychiatry and medicine; behavioral medicine; co-author of five books, 30 papers and book chapters; disease & demand management; behavioral health-primary care integration, health promotion/disease prevention. *Mailing Add:* 185 Dartmouth St Boston MA 02116. *Fax:* 617-527-3343; *E-Mail:* steven_locke@hphc.org

LOCKE, WILLIAM, INTERNAL MEDICINE, ENDOCRINOLOGY. *Current Pos:* Pres staff, Alton Ochsner Med Found, 54-55, partner, Ochsner Clin, 57-81, mem staff, Ochsner Clin & Found Hosp, 50-86, emer head, Sect Endocrinol & Metab, 76-86, TRUSTEE, ALTON OCHSNER MED FOUND, 78- *Personal Data:* b Morden, Man, Mar 16, 16; m 45, Katherinee Acer. *Educ:* Univ Man, MD, 38; Univ Minn, MS, 47; McGill Univ, DTM, 45. *Concurrent Pos:* Nat Res Coun & Commonwealth Fund fel, Harvard Univ, 48-50; emer clin prof med, Sch Med, Tulane Univ, 87-; sr vis physician, Charity Hosp, New Orleans. *Mem:* AAAS; Am Diabetes Asn; fel Am Col Physicians; Endocrine Soc; Sigma Xi. *Res:* Metabolic diseases. *Mailing Add:* 4815 Dryades St New Orleans LA 70115-5533

LOCKER, JOHN L, MATHEMATICS. *Current Pos:* from assoc prof to prof, 60-92, EMER PROF MATH, UNIV NORTHERN ALA, 92- *Personal Data:* b Florence, Ala, Oct 11, 30; m 59; c 8. *Educ:* Auburn Univ, PhD(math), 60. *Prof Exp:* Instr, Auburn Univ, 56-59; mathematician, Redstone Arsenal, 54. *Concurrent Pos:* Lectr, NSF-Ala Acad Sci Vis Sci Prog, 61-65; consult math manipulative workshops. *Mem:* Math Asn Am; Nat Coun Teachers Math. *Res:* Statistics; geometry. *Mailing Add:* 338 Flurnoy Ave Florence AL 35633

LOCKETT, CLODOVIA, physiology, animal; deceased, see previous edition for last biography

LOCKEY, RICHARD FUNK, ALLERGY & IMMUNOLOGY, INTERNAL MEDICINE. *Current Pos:* from asst prof to assoc prof med, 73-83, asst dir, Div Allergy & Immunol, 79-82, PROF MED, PEDIAT & PUB HEALTH, COL MED, UNIV SFLA, TAMPA, 83-, DIR, DIV ALLERGY & IMMUNOL, 82-; CHIEF, SECT ALLERGY & IMMUNOL, VET ADMIN HOSP, TAMPA, FLA, 85- *Personal Data:* b Lancaster, Pa, Jan 15, 40; m, Carol L Madill; c Brian C & Keith E. *Educ:* Haverford Col, BS, 61; Univ Mich, Ann Arbor, MS, 72; Temple Univ, MD, 65. *Honors & Awards:* Claude P Brown Mem Lectr, Asn Clin Scientists Spring Meeting, 81. *Prof Exp:* Asst resident internal med, Univ Hosp, Univ Mich, 66-67, resident, 66-68 & fel allergy & immunol, 69-70; asst chief, Sect Allergy & Immunol, Vet Admin Hosp, Tampa, 73-82. *Concurrent Pos:* Chief, Allergy & Immunol Sect, Carswell AFB Hosp, USAF, Ft Worth, Tex, 71-73 & James A Haley Vet Admin Hosp, Tampa, Fla, 82-; co-ed, Allergol & Clin Immunol, 84-90, J Invest Allergol & Clin Immunol, 91-; dir, Am Bd Allergy & Immunol, 93-*Mem:* Fel Am Acad Allergy & Immunol (secy, 89-90, treas, 90-91, pres-elect, 91-92, pres, 92-93); fel Am Col Physicians; fel Am Col Chest Physicians; Am Asn Cert Allergists; AAAS; Int Asn Aerobiol; hon fel Can Soc Allergy & Clin Immunol; AMA; Clin Immunol Soc. *Res:* Hymenoptera hypersensitivity; imported fire ant; red tide toxin and its mechanism of action on tracheal smooth muscle; important aeroallergens of Florida; immunopharmacology and AIDS; immunity and the aged; asthma. *Mailing Add:* Vet Admin Hosp Div Allergy & Immunol 13000 Bruce B Downs Blvd Tampa FL 33612

LOCKHART, BENHAM EDWARD, PLANT PATHOLOGY, AGRICULTURE. *Current Pos:* asst prof, 76-80, ASSOC PROF PLANT PATH, UNIV MINN, ST PAUL, 80- *Personal Data:* b St Vincent, WI, Jan 18, 45; US citizen; m 70; c 2. *Educ:* Univ WI, Trinidad, BSc, 65; Univ Calif, Riverside, PhD(plant path), 69. *Prof Exp:* Res fels plant path, Univ Nebr, 69-70 & Univ Calif, Berkeley, 70-71; asst prof, Minn Proj, US AID, Rabat, Morocco, 71-76. *Mem:* Am Phytopath Soc; Am Soc Hort Sci; Int Soc Hort Sci. *Res:* Identification properties and control of viruses of vegetable and ornamental crops. *Mailing Add:* 495 Borlaugh Hall Univ Minn St Paul 1991 Upper Buford Circle St Paul MN 55108-6024

LOCKHART, BROOKS JAVINS, mathematics; deceased, see previous edition for last biography

LOCKHART, F(RANK) J(ONES), CHEMICAL ENGINEERING. *Current Pos:* head dept, 55-68, PROF CHEM ENG, UNIV SOUTHERN CALIF, 55- *Personal Data:* b Austin, Tex, Aug 10, 16; m 45; c 2. *Educ:* Univ Tex, BS, 36, MS, 38; Univ Mich, PhD(chem eng), 40. *Prof Exp:* Jr engr, Humble Oil & Refining Co, Tex, 38-39; from asst to instr chem eng, Univ Mich, 40-43; process engr, Union Oil Co Calif, 43-46; from asst prof to assoc prof chem eng, Southern Calif, 46-52, head dept, 50-52; mgr prod eng dept, Fluor Corp, Ltd, 52-55. *Concurrent Pos:* Consult, 46-; process engr, Fluor Corp, Ltd, 46. *Mem:* Am Chem Soc; Am Inst Chem Engrs. *Res:* Fluid dynamics; petroleum refining operations; distillation; gas absorption and stripping; design and operation of water cooling towers; liquid-liquid extraction; effect of time and concentration on overall mass transfer coefficients. *Mailing Add:* 648 33rd St Manhattan Beach CA 90266

LOCKHART, HAINES BOOTS, NUTRITION, BIOCHEMISTRY. *Current Pos:* RETIRED. *Personal Data:* b Crawfordsville, Ind, Oct 29, 20; m 44; c 2. *Educ:* Wabash Col, AB, 42; Univ Ill, PhD(biochem), 45. *Prof Exp:* Asst, Wabash Col, 41-42; chemist, Univ Ill, 42-45; from res chemist to head, Baby Foods Res Div, Swift & Co, 45-66, head, New Foods Div, 66-71; sect mgr nutrit res, Quaker Oats Co, 71-80, staff nutritionist, John Stuart Res Labs, 80-85. *Concurrent Pos:* Mem tech adv group, Comt on Nutrit, Am Acad Pediat. *Mem:* Am Chem Soc; Inst Food Technol. *Res:* Amino acids and proteins in nutrition; infant and geriatric nutrition. *Mailing Add:* 333 Sunset Dr Lakewood Crystal Lake IL 60014-5330

LOCKHART, HAINES BOOTS, JR, ENVIRONMENTAL CHEMISTRY, BIOCHEMISTRY. *Current Pos:* Sr res biochemist, Eastman Kodak Co, 72-81, tech assoc, Health & Safety Lab, 81-85, mgr, Health Regulations, 85-86, dir, Environmental Tech Serv, 86-88, dir, Occup Health Lab, 88-91, dir, corp environ, 91-94, DIR, HEALTH, SAFETY & ENVIRON PROGS, EASTMAN KODAK CO, 95- *Personal Data:* b Evergreen Park, Ill, Feb 4, 46; m 90; c 2. *Educ:* Wabash Col, AB, 67; Univ Nebr, Lincoln, MS, 69, PhD(chem), 73. *Mem:* Am Chem Soc; Soc Environ Toxicol & Chem. *Res:* Environmental impact of synthetic chemicals, their biodegradation, photodegradation and bioconcentration in aquatic organisms; risk assessment of chemical impacts on exposed populations. *Mailing Add:* Health, Safety & Environ Eastman Kodak Co Rochester NY 14652-6256

LOCKHART, JAMES MARCUS, LOW TEMPERATURE PHYSICS, SUPERCONDUCTING ELECTRONICS. *Current Pos:* assoc prof, 83-87, PROF PHYSICS, SAN FRANCISCO STATE UNIV, 87- *Personal Data:* b Portsmouth, Ohio, June 11, 48; m 81; c 2. *Educ:* Univ Mich, BS, 70; Stanford Univ, MS, 72, PhD(physics), 76. *Prof Exp:* Res affil, Stanford Univ, 76, actg instr physics, 76-77, actg asst prof, 77-80; asst prof physics, Colo Sch Mines, 80-81; sr res assoc, Stanford Univ, 82-83. *Concurrent Pos:* Fel, Dept Physics, Stanford Univ, 76-78; vis scholar, Stanford Univ, 83- *Mem:* Am Phys Soc; Am Asn Physics Teachers; Sigma Xi. *Res:* Low temperature electrical properties of solids; electron beams; superconductivity, superconducting detectors and electronics. Squids ultra-low; semiconductor device physics; musical acoustics; architectural acoustics; electroacoustics. *Mailing Add:* Physics & Astron Dept San Francisco State Univ 1600 Holloway Ave San Francisco CA 94132

LOCKHART, LILLIAN HOFFMAN, MEDICINE. *Current Pos:* From asst prof to assoc prof, 63-83, PROF PEDIAT & GENETICS, UNIV TEX MED BR, GALVESTON, 83- *Personal Data:* b Columbus, Tex, Oct, 23, 30; m 51; c 3. *Educ:* Rice Univ, BA, 51; Univ Tex Med Br, Galveston, MA, 55, MD, 57. *Concurrent Pos:* Fel hemat, Univ Tex Med Br, Galveston, 62-63. *Mem:* Am Acad Pediat. *Res:* Genetics; chromosome disorders. *Mailing Add:* 9 Perthuis Farms Rd La Marque TX 77568

LOCKHART, WILLIAM LAFAYETTE, INORGANIC CHEMISTRY. *Current Pos:* from asst prof to assoc prof, 67-77, chmn dept, 78-82, PROF CHEM, WEST GA COL, 77- *Personal Data:* b Nashville, Tenn, Oct 15, 36; m 60; c 2. *Educ:* Tenn Technol Univ, BS, 58; Univ Miss, MS, 61; Vanderbilt Univ, PhD(inorg chem), 67. *Prof Exp:* Res biochemist, US Food & Drug Admin, 60-63. *Res:* Kinetics and mechanisms of inorganic reactions. *Mailing Add:* 714 Frost Rd Bowdon GA 30108

LOCKHEAD, GREGORY ROGER, PSYCHOLOGY. *Current Pos:* from asst prof to prof psychol, 65-91, CHMN, DEPT EXP PSYCHOL, DUKE UNIV, DURHAM, 91- *Personal Data:* b Boston, Mass, Aug, 8, 31; m 57, Jeanne M Hutchinson; c Diane, Elaine & John. *Educ:* Tufts Univ, BS, 58; Johns Hopkins PhD, 65. *Prof Exp:* Psychologist res staff, IBM Res, NY, 58-61. *Concurrent Pos:* Prin investr, USPHS, 63-69, 70-79, NSF, 66-69, 79-84, Air Force Off Sci Res, 83-91; res assoc, Univ Calif, Berkeley, 71-72; vis prof, Stanford Univ, 71-72; fel, Wolfson Col, Oxford Univ, Eng, 80-81; consult human eng. *Mem:* Fel Am Psychol Asn; fel Am Psychol Soc; Psychonomic Soc; Int Soc Psychophys; Sigma Xi. *Res:* Psychology; human engineering. *Mailing Add:* Dept Exp Psychol Duke Univ Durham NC 27706

LOCKLEY, MARTIN GAUDIN, VERTEBRATE ICHNOLOGY, MUSEUM SCIENCE & CONSERVATION. *Current Pos:* Asst prof geol, 80-84, assoc prof, 84-93, PROF GEOL, UNIV COLO, DENVER, 93- *Personal Data:* b St Helier, Jersey, UK, Mar 17, 50; m, Linda-Dale Jennings; c Peter, Katie, Lois F Jennings & Linda F Jennings. *Educ:* Queens Univ, Northern Ireland, BS, 74; Birmingham Univ, Eng, PhD(geol), 77. *Prof Exp:* Res assoc, Glasgow Univ, 76-80. *Concurrent Pos:* Assoc cur, Mus Western Colo, 87-; prin investr, NSF, 87-; distinguished lectr, Am Asn Petrol Geologists, 91-92; assoc ed, Ichnos Int Trace Fossil J, 92- *Mem:* Paleont Soc; Paleont Asn; Soc Econ Paleontologists & Mineralogists; Am Asn Petrol Geologists. *Res:* Dinosaur tracks and other fossil footprints of North America, Europe and East Asia; author of numerous publications. *Mailing Add:* 31110 Robinson Hill Rd Golden CO 80403. *Fax:* 303-556-4822

LOCKRIDGE, OKSANA MASLIVEC, BIOCHEMICAL PHARMACOLOGY, BIOCHEMICAL GENETICS. *Current Pos:* ASSOC PROF, UNIV NEBR MED CTR, 90- *Personal Data:* b Czech, Sept 4, 41; US citizen; m, Lawrence Schopfer; c Katherine. *Educ:* Smith Col, BA, 63; Northwestern Univ, Ill, PhD(chem), 71. *Prof Exp:* Fel human genetics, Univ Mich, Ann Arbor, 72-74, res assoc pharmacol, 74-81, res scientist, 82-90. *Concurrent Pos:* Prin Investr, Univ Mich, Ann Arbor, 79-90. *Mem:* Am Chem Soc; Asn Women Sci; AAAS; Am Soc Biol Chemists; Am Soc Human Genetics. *Res:* Pharmacogenetics; biochemical and structural studies on genetic variants of human butyrylcholinesterase. *Mailing Add:* Univ Nebr Med Ctr Eppley Inst 600 S 42nd St Omaha NE 68198-6805. *Fax:* 402-559-4651; *E-Mail:* olockrid@unmc.edu

LOCKSHIN, MICHAEL DAN, RHEUMATOLOGY, IMMUNOLOGY. *Current Pos:* DIR EXTRAMURAL PROG, NAT INST ARTHRITIS & MUSCULOSKELETAL & SKIN DIS, NIH, 89- *Personal Data:* b Columbus, Ohio, Dec 9, 37; m 65; c 1. *Educ:* Harvard Col, AB, 59; Harvard Med Sch, MD, 63. *Prof Exp:* Intern, Second (Cornell) Div Med, Bellevue & Mem Hosp, New York, 63-64; epidemic intel serv officer, Epidemic Intel Serv, Commun Dis Ctr, 64-66; resident, Second (Cornell) Div Med, Bellevue & Mem Hosp, New York, 66-68; fel rheumatol, Columbia Presby Med Ctr, 68-70; from asst prof to prof med, Col Med, Cornell Univ, 82-89. *Concurrent Pos:* Adj asst prof epidemiol, Sch Pub Health, Univ Pittsburgh, 65-66; assoc scientist & assoc attend physician, Hosp Spec Surg, New York Hosp, 70-82, attending physician, 82-; consult rheumatol, Mem Hosp, New York, 70-; mem bd dirs, Arthritis Found, 75-89. *Mem:* Am Col Rheumatism; Am Col Physicians. *Res:* Cellular immunology; clinical rheumatology. *Mailing Add:* 535 E 70th St New York NY 10021-4872

LOCKSHIN, RICHARD ANSEL, PHYSIOLOGY, DEVELOPMENTAL BIOLOGY. *Current Pos:* from assoc prof to prof physiol, 75-83, CHMN, DEPT PHYSIOL, ST JOHN'S UNIV, NY, 83- *Personal Data:* b Columbus, Ohio, Dec 9, 37; m 63; c 2. *Educ:* Harvard Univ, AB, 59, AM, 61, PhD(biol), 63. *Prof Exp:* Asst prof physiol, Sch Med, Univ Rochester, 65-75. *Concurrent Pos:* NSF fel, Inst Animal Genetics, Univ Edinburgh, 63-64, NIH fel, 64-65. *Mem:* AAAS; Soc Cell Biol; Soc Develop Biol; Gerontol Soc; Am Soc Entom; fel Gerontol Soc Am. *Res:* Destruction of tissues during metamorphosis of insects; early developmental events in insect embryogenesis; cellular differentation. *Mailing Add:* Dept Biol Sci St John's Univ Grand Central/Utopia Pkwy Jamaica NY 11439-0001

LOCKWOOD, DAVID JOHN, SOLID STATE PHYSICS, RAMAN SPECTROSCOPY. *Current Pos:* sect head surface & interface physics, Nat Res Coun Can, 87-90, head, Phys Characterization Group, 90-92, Thin Films Group, 91-92, PRIN RES OFFICER PHYSICS, NAT RES COUN CAN, 78- *Personal Data:* b Christchurch, NZ, Jan 7, 42; m 79, Eugenia Dubovitskaya; c Alisa N, Ilana E & Lilia R. *Educ:* Univ Canterbury, BSc, 64, MSc, 66, PhD(physics), 69; Univ Edinburgh, DSc, 78. *Prof Exp:* Teaching fel physics, Univ Canterbury, NZ, 65-69; fel chem, Univ Waterloo, Can, 70-71; res fel physics, Univ Edinburgh, 72-78. *Concurrent Pos:* Univ bursaries, NZ Univ Grants Comt, 66-68; consult vis, Battelle Ctr de Res, Switz, 72-76; tutor, Open Univ, UK, 77-78; consult vis, Univ Paul Sabatier, Toulouse, France, 77-92; vis prof, Essex Univ, England, 81-83; prog consult & reviewer, Nat Sci & Eng Res Coun Can, 86-; distinguished vis prof, Ctr Nat Res France, 87-88; mem sci panel, NATO, 87-88, chmn, 89-90; mem Can adv group, NATO Sci Comt, 90-94; distinguished visitor, Chinese Acad Sci, Beijing, 92. *Mem:* Am Phys Soc; Royal Commonwealth Soc; World Fedn Scientists; Can Asn Physicists; Electrochem Soc; Mat Res Soc. *Res:* Light scattering studies of structural and magnetic phase transitions, electronic exitations, magnons and phonons in solids; optical properties of semiconductors and superlattices. *Mailing Add:* Microstruct Sci Nat Res Coun Ottawa ON K1A 0R6 Can. *Fax:* 613-993-6486; *E-Mail:* david.lockwood@nrc.ca

LOCKWOOD, DEAN H, BIOCHEMISTRY, MEDICINE. *Current Pos:* AT WARNER LAMBERT/PARKE-DAVIS, 91- *Personal Data:* b Milford, Conn, June 17, 37; m 58; c 3. *Educ:* Wesleyan Univ, AB, 59; Johns Hopkins Univ, MD, 63. *Prof Exp:* Intern & resident, Johns Hopkins Univ, 63-65, fel pharmacol, 67-69, asst & assoc prof med, 69-76; staff assoc, NIH, 65-67; prof med, Univ Rochester, 76-90. *Concurrent Pos:* NIH res develop award, 69-74 & res grant, 69-; mem endocrine merit rev bd, Vet Admin, 76-79; mem, NIH Metab Study Sect, 81-90. *Mem:* Am Soc Biol Chemists; Am Soc Clin Invest; Endocrine Soc; Am Fedn Clin Res; Am Diabetes Asn. *Res:* Mechanism of action of insulin and glucagon in normal and resistant states; plasma membrane receptors and biological responses emphasized. *Mailing Add:* 3431 Wagner Woods Ct Ann Arbor MI 48103-2167

LOCKWOOD, FRANCES ELLEN, LUBRICANT OXIDATION, TRIBOLOGICAL BEHAVIOR OF LIQUID CRYSTALS. *Current Pos:* VPRES TECHNOL PROD DEVELOP, VALVOLINE CO, 94- *Personal Data:* b Passaic, NJ; m 78; c 1. *Educ:* Rensselaer Polytech Inst, BS, 73, Pa State Univ, MS, 76, PhD(chem eng), 78. *Prof Exp:* Assoc sr res engr, Gen Motors Res Labs, 78-80; sr scientist, Martin Marietta Lab, 80-84; dir, Pennzoil Prod Co, 84-85, vpres phys sci, 85-94. *Mem:* Soc Tribologists & Lubrication Engrs; Am Inst Chem Engrs; Soc Automotive Engrs; Am Soc Testing & Mat. *Res:* Lubricant oxidation, tribological behavior of liquid crystals and lubrication of ceramic dry pressing; metal rolling and metal forging lubrication; the fluid state and hydrocarbon oxidation. *Mailing Add:* Valvoline Co PO Box 14000 Lexington KY 40512

LOCKWOOD, GEORGE WESLEY, ASTRONOMY, PLANETARY SCIENCES. *Current Pos:* ASTRONR, LOWELL OBSERV, 73- *Personal Data:* b Norfolk, Va, June 28, 41; m 92, Susan Bryant. *Educ:* Duke Univ, BS, 63; Univ Va, MA, 65, PhD(astron), 68. *Prof Exp:* Astronr, Kitt Peak Nat Observ, 68-73. *Mem:* Am Astron Soc; Int Astron Union; Astron Soc Pac; Am Geophys Union; Sigma Xi. *Res:* Planetary atmospheres; stellar/solar physics; solar-planetary relations; variable stars. *Mailing Add:* Lowell Observ 1400 W Mars Hill Rd Flagstaff AZ 86001-4499. *Fax:* 520-774-6296; *E-Mail:* gwl@lowell.edu

LOCKWOOD, GRANT JOHN, ELECTRON PHYSICS, RADIATION PHYSICS. *Current Pos:* DISTINGUISHED MEM TECH STAFF, SANDIA LABS, 63- *Personal Data:* b Byram, Conn, Oct 28, 31; m 56, Margaret Althaus; c Steven, Jeffrey, Dale & Nancy. *Educ:* Univ Conn, BA, 54, MS, 59, PhD(physics), 63. *Prof Exp:* Res asst physics, Univ Conn, 60-63. *Res:* Electronic, atomic and molecular interactions to include ion-atom, ion-molecule, atom-atom and atom-molecule; interaction with surface and solids of ion beams. *Mailing Add:* 7913 Hendrix Ave NE Albuquerque NM 87110

LOCKWOOD, HARRY F, SEMICONDUCTOR DEVICES. *Current Pos:* PRIN, LOCKWOOD GROUP, NEWTON, MASS, 92- *Personal Data:* b New York, NY, Jan 23, 35. *Educ:* St Johns Univ, BS, 57; New York Univ, PhD, 72. *Prof Exp:* Staff, GTE Inc, Waltham, Mass, 79-92, tech mgr, optoelectronic & high speed discrete & integrated devices, 79-82, dir, Advan Components Technol Ctr, 82-89, prog dir, 89-92. *Mem:* Fel Inst Elec & Electronics Engrs; Am Phys Soc. *Res:* Awarded 17 patents; published over 50 articles. *Mailing Add:* Lockwood Group PO Box 620132 Newton MA 02162

LOCKWOOD, JEFFREY ALAN, ECOLOGY & PEST MANAGEMENT, POPULATION BIOLOGY. *Current Pos:* from asst prof to assoc prof, 86-96, PROF ENTOM, UNIV WYO, 96- *Personal Data:* b Manchester, Conn, Mar 9, 60; m 82, Nancy Fosnaugh; c Erin K & Ethan J. *Educ:* NMex Tech, BS, 82; La State Univ, PhD(entom), 85. *Honors & Awards:* R T Gast Award, Entom Soc Am, 85; L D Newsom Award, La State Univ, 86. *Prof Exp:* Postdoctoral res entom, La State Univ, 85-86. *Concurrent Pos:* Vis fel, Div Bot & Zool, Australian Nat Univ, 93-94; vis scientist, CSIRO Div Entom, Australia, 93-94; adj prof natural sci, Univ Wyo, 96-; fel, Org Econ Coop & Develop, 97. *Mem:* Sigma Xi; Entom Soc Am; Orthopterists Soc. *Res:* Insect ecology; behavioral and population ecology of rangeland grasshoppers; nonlinear modeling of population dynamics; biological control and pest management. *Mailing Add:* Dept Plant Soil & Insect Sci Univ Wyo Univ Sta PO Box 3354 Laramie WY 82071. *Fax:* 307-766-5549; *E-Mail:* lockwood@uwyo.edu

LOCKWOOD, JOHN ALEXANDER, PHYSICS. *Current Pos:* RETIRED. *Personal Data:* b Easton, Pa, July 12, 19; m 42; c 3. *Educ:* Dartmouth Col, AB, 41, Lafayette Col, MS, 43; Yale Univ, PhD(physics), 48. *Honors & Awards:* Sci Award, NASA. *Prof Exp:* From asst to instr physics, Lafayette Col, 41-44; tech supvr, Tenn Eastman Corp, 44-45; asst physics, Yale Univ, 45-46, asst instr, 46-47, asst, 47-48; from asst prof to prof physics, Univ NH, 48-85. *Concurrent Pos:* Assoc dir res, Univ NH, 74-80, dir res, 80-82. *Mem:* AAAS; Am Phys Soc; Am Asn Physics Teachers. *Res:* Development of linear electron accelerators; cosmic ray; nuclear physics; gamma ray astronomy. *Mailing Add:* 49 Bucks Hill Rd Durham NH 03824

LOCKWOOD, JOHN LEBARON, PLANT PATHOLOGY. *Current Pos:* from assoc prof to prof, 55-90, EMER PROF BOT & PLANT PATH, MICH STATE UNIV, 90- *Personal Data:* b Ann Arbor, Mich, May 28, 24; m 59, Jean E Springborg; c James L & Laura A. *Educ:* Mich State Col, BA, 48, MS, 50; Univ Wis, PhD(plant path), 53. *Prof Exp:* Asst prof bot & plant path, Ohio Agr Exp Sta, 53-55. *Concurrent Pos:* NSF sr fel, Cambridge Univ, 70-71. *Mem:* Fel Am Phytopath Soc (pres, 84-85). *Res:* Ecology of root-infecting fungi; soybean diseases. *Mailing Add:* Dept Bot & Plant Path Mich State Univ East Lansing MI 48824. *Fax:* 517-353-1926

LOCKWOOD, JOHN PAUL, VOLCANOLOGY. *Current Pos:* PRES, GEOHAZARDS CONSULT INT, INC, 95- *Personal Data:* b Bridgeport, Conn, Oct 26, 39; m 63, Martha Bell; c Pamela & Glen. *Educ:* Univ Calif Riverside, AB, 61; Princeton Univ, PhD(geol), 66. *Prof Exp:* Geologist, US Geol Surv, 66-95. *Concurrent Pos:* Partic, Sci Exchange Prog, Nat Res Coun-Nat Acad Sci, USSR, res, Geol Inst Scad Sci, Moscow, 66, res Dir Volcanol, Bandung, Indonesia, 80-82; affil prof, Univ Hawaii. *Mem:* Geol Soc Am; Am Geophys Union; Int Asn Volcanology; Asn Am Inst Prof Geologists. *Res:* Petrology, mineralogy and structural features of serpentinites; general geology of the Sierra Nevada Mountains; circum-Pacific distribution of volcanic rocks; Caribbean geology; volcanic hazards; eruptive history and structure of Mauna Loa volcano, Hawaii; volcanic disaster assessments in Indonesia, Italy, Colombia, Cameroon, Northern Marianas Islands, Rwanda, Zaire and Philippines. *Mailing Add:* Geohazards Consult Int PO Box 479 Volcano HI 96785. *Fax:* 808-967-8525; *E-Mail:* geohaz@aloha.net

LOCKWOOD, LINDA GAIL, ENVIRONMENTAL BIOLOGY, SCIENCE EDUCATION. *Current Pos:* ASSOC PROF ENVIRON SCI, UNIV MASS, AMHERST, 73- *Personal Data:* b New York, NY, May 25, 36. *Educ:* Columbia Univ, BS, 60, MA, 61 & 65, PhD(bot), 69. *Prof Exp:* Asst prof bot & ecol, Teachers Col, Columbia Univ, 69-73. *Concurrent Pos:* Jessie Smith Noyes Found grant environ sci educ, Teachers Col, Columbia Univ, 71-73; prof plant & soil sci & Sch Educ, Univ Mass, Amherst, 73-; co-dir, US Off Educ grant, 74-75; Univ Mass fac res grant, 74-75 & Water Resources Res Ctr grant, 74-75; NSF grants, 75-79. *Mem:* Sigma Xi; AAAS; Scientist's Inst Pub Info; Nat Asn Biol Teachers; Audubon Soc. *Res:* Influence of photoperiod and exogenous nitrogen-containing compounds on the reproductive cycles of the liverwort Cephalozia media Lindb; experimental morphology and physiological ecology; environmental biology, especially physiological ecology, aquatic systems; environmental science education, especially teacher training, history and philosophy of science. *Mailing Add:* Plant & Sci Soil Univ Mass Amherst French Hall Amherst MA 01003-0002

LOCKWOOD, ROBERT GREENING, NATURAL & SYNTHETIC ELASTOMERS, SPECIAL ORGANIC COATINGS. *Current Pos:* RETIRED. *Personal Data:* b Faribault, Minn, Jan 12, 28; m 53; c 2. *Educ:* Carleton Col, BA, 49; Univ Minn, PhD(org chem), 53. *Prof Exp:* Lab instr inorg & org chem, Univ Minn, 49-53; res chemist, New Prod Develop Lab, Chem Div, Gen Elec Co, 53-54; sr chemist, 3M Co, 54-65, res specialist, 65-81, sr res specialist, 81-92. *Mem:* Am Chem Soc; Sigma Xi. *Res:* Organic synthesis; carboxylic acids and derivatives; condensation polymers; manufacture of alkylated aromatic hydrocarbons and polycarboxylic acids; pressure-sensitive adhesives; release agents. *Mailing Add:* 2 Hingham Circle St Paul MN 55118-1921

LOCKWOOD, WILLIAM RUTLEDGE, PHYSICS, GENERAL OPTICS. *Current Pos:* RETIRED. *Personal Data:* b Memphis, Tenn, Apr 10, 29; c 2. *Educ:* Univ Miss, BA, 49, MA, 50; Univ Tenn, Memphis, MD, 57. *Prof Exp:* Intern, Charity Hosp La, New Orleans, 57-58; resident med, Med Ctr, Univ Miss, 59-61, from instr to asst prof, 62-70, asst prof microbiol & path, 66-70, assoc prof med, 70-91. *Concurrent Pos:* USPHS fel, Med Ctr, Univ Miss, 61-64, grant, 64-67; vis instr, Wash Univ, 64; asst dean res & assoc chief staff res, Vet Admin Ctr, 69-73; attend physician, Univ Miss Hosp, 64- *Mem:* Fel Infectious Dis Soc Am; fel Am Col Chest Physicians; Am Soc Trop Med & Hyg; Am Soc Microbiol; fel Am Col Physicians. *Res:* Pathogenesis of acute inflammation; pharmacology of antimicrobial agents. *Mailing Add:* 13501 Bay View Circle Ocean Springs MS 39564

LOCKYER, NIGEL STUART, LIFETIME MEASUREMENT OF B-QUARKS, CHARGE-PARITY VIOLATION IN B-MESON DECAYS. *Current Pos:* asst prof, 84-90, ASSOC PROF PHYSICS, UNIV PA, 90- *Personal Data:* b Annan, Scotland, Nov 5, 52; m 76, Ellen; c Geoffrey, Martin & Sara. *Educ:* York Univ, BSc, 75; Ohio State Univ, PhD(physics), 80. *Prof Exp:* Postdoctoral fel, Stanford Linear Accelerator Ctr, 80-84. *Concurrent Pos:* Vis scientist, Fermilab, 87 & 88 & SSC Lab, 89-90. *Mem:* Am Phys soc. *Res:* Bottom quarks decay using collider detector; measured the branching ratio of several bottom decays and the bottom lifetime; charge-parity violation in B-decays. *Mailing Add:* 209 S 33rd Philadelphia PA 19104-6396. *Fax:* 215-898-8512; *E-Mail:* lockyer@lockyer.hep.upenn.edu

LOCOCK, ROBERT A, PHARMACEUTICAL CHEMISTRY, PHARMACOGNOSY. *Current Pos:* asst prof, 65-70, ASSOC PROF PHARM, UNIV ALTA, 70-, ASSOC PROF PHARMACEUT SCI, 74- *Personal Data:* b Toronto, Ont, Aug 14, 35; m 61. *Educ:* Univ Toronto, BSc, 59, MSc, 61; Ohio State Univ, PhD(pharm), 65. *Prof Exp:* Lectr pharmaceut chem, Univ BC, 61-62; asst pharm, Ohio State Univ, 64-65. *Mem:* AAAS; Am Chem Soc; Am Soc Pharmacog; Sigma Xi. *Res:* Chemistry of natural products; phytochemistry; chemotaxonomy; alkaloids and terpenoids. *Mailing Add:* Dept Pharm Univ Alta 13943 107A Ave Edmonton AB T5M 2A8 Can

LOCY, ROBERT DONALD, PLANT TISSUE CULTURE, PLANT CELL BIOLOGY. *Current Pos:* DIR, CELL SCI CTR, AUBURN UNIV, 91- *Personal Data:* b Defiance, Ohio, Jan 12, 47; m 69; c 3. *Educ:* Defiance Col, AB, 69; Purdue Univ, PhD(plant biochem), 74. *Prof Exp:* Res assoc biochem, McMaster Univ, 74-76; res fel, Dept Environ Res Lab, Mich State Univ, 76-78; asst prof hort, NC State Univ, 78-82; prof agr, Ind-Purdue, Ft Wayne, 82-83; sr res scientist, NPI, Salt Lake City, Utah, 83-88, mgr, floral prod res, 88-90. *Mem:* Am Soc Plant Physiol; Tissue Cult Asn Am; Sigma Xi; Gamma Sigma Delta. *Res:* Plant biochemistry as applied to crop plant improvement using tissue and cell culture; plant propagation in vitro using automated tissue culture systems. *Mailing Add:* Auburn Univ Auburn AL 36849

LODA, RICHARD THOMAS, SPECTROSCOPY. *Current Pos:* VPRES & CHIEF TECH OFFICER, EHS INC, 94- *Personal Data:* b Derby, Conn, May 19, 48. *Educ:* Waterburg State Tech Col, AAS, 68; Univ Bridgeport, BA, 71; Wesleyan Univ, PhD(phys chem), 80. *Prof Exp:* NIH fel, Chem Dept, Univ Ore, 80-81; chemist res dept, Instrumental Chem Analysis Br, Naval Weapons Ctr, 81-85; Naval Res Lab, 85-93. *Mem:* Am Chem Soc; Am Phys Soc. *Res:* Application of lasers and spectroscopy to problems of physical and chemical interest; photochemistry; site selection and linewidth phenomena in condensed phase systems; coherent antistokes Raman scattering. *Mailing Add:* 8 Larkfield Lane Laguna Niguel CA 92677-5323

LODATO, MICHAEL W, OPERATIONS RESEARCH. *Current Pos:* PRES, MWL INC, 80- *Personal Data:* b Rochester, NY, June 17, 32; m 59; c 4. *Educ:* Colgate Univ, AB, 54; Univ Rochester, MS, 59; Rutgers Univ, PhD(math), 62. *Prof Exp:* Scientist, LFE Monterey Lab, 62-63; mem tech staff, Appl Math Dept, Mitre Corp, Mass, 63-65, head opers anal sub dept, 65-66; sr exec adv, Douglas Aircraft Corp, 66-67, mgr, Info Technol Dept, McDonnell Douglas Corp, 67-68; pres, Macro Systs Assocs, Inc, 68-70; prin bus planner, Xerox Data Systs, 70-71; vpres indust systs, Informatics, Inc, 71-78; exec vpres, Spectrum Int, Inc, 78-80. *Mem:* Opers Res Soc Am; Asn Data Process Serv Orgn. *Res:* Topology; planning, scheduling and resource allocation; orbital mechanics; production and inventory control; strategic management; author of two books on computer sales and strategic management. *Mailing Add:* 32038 Watergate Ct Westlake Village CA 91361

LODEN, MICHAEL SIMPSON, OLIGOCHAETA, WATER QUALITY. *Current Pos:* DIR ENVIRON RESOURCES, GULF ENG & CONSULTS, INC, 90- *Personal Data:* b Fayette, Ala, Mar 30, 45; m 68, Karen Clark; c Jonathan M. *Educ:* Auburn Univ, BS, 67, MS, 73; La State Univ, PhD(zool), 78. *Prof Exp:* Aquatic biologist, Aquatic Control, Inc, 73-75; asst prof zool, La State Univ, 78-81; environ dir, Jefferson Parish, La, 81-90. *Mem:* Sigma Xi; NAm Benthol Soc; Am Micros Soc; Water Environ Fedn. *Res:* Systematics, life histories, ecology and distribution of aquatic Oligochaeta. *Mailing Add:* 13546 Shady Ridge Ave Baton Rouge LA 70817. *E-Mail:* loden@communique.net

LODER, EDWIN ROBERT, CHEMISTRY. *Current Pos:* RETIRED. *Personal Data:* b Irvington, NJ, Feb 24, 25; m 45; c 4. *Educ:* Syracuse Univ, BA, 52; Mass Inst Technol, PhD, 55. *Prof Exp:* Asst chem, Mass Inst Technol, 52-53, asst org microanal, 53-55; chemist, Eastman Kodak Co, 55-59, chief anal chemist, Maumee Chem, 59-62, dir res serv, 62-65, sect mgr & tech assoc, Gen Aniline & Film Co, NY, 65-66; from dep dir to dir res, Du Bois Chem Div, W R Grace & Co, 66-70, dir res & vpres, Du Bois Chem Div, Chemed Corp, 70-72, sr vpres corp affairs, 72-73, exec vpres, 73-74, group exec vpres, Du Bois Chem Div, Chemed Corp, 74-85; pres, Delray Chem Co, 85-90, GRL & Assoc, 90-97. *Concurrent Pos:* Instr, Univ Toledo, 61-62. *Mem:* Fel AAAS; fel Am Inst Chem; Am Chem Soc; Soc Photog Sci & Eng; Am Soc Qual Control; Sigma Xi. *Res:* Electrochemistry; spectroscopy; research management; statistics. *Mailing Add:* 12258 Eagles Landing Way Boynton Beach FL 33437

LODEWIJK, ERIC, SYNTHETIC ORGANIC CHEMISTRY. *Current Pos:* HEAD CHEM DEVELOP, F HOFFMANN & LA ROCHE LTD, 95- *Personal Data:* b Hague, Neth, Nov 15, 40. *Educ:* Univ Amsterdam, BSc, 65, PhD(org chem), 68. *Prof Exp:* Res chemist org chem, Syntex Chem, Inc, Bahamas, 69-70, group leader process develop, Chem Div, 70-73, sr res chemist, 73-77, group leader res org chem, 77-79, mgr process res, 79-86, dir res & develop, 86-91, group dir, Process Res & Develop, 91-95. *Mem:* Am Chem Soc. *Res:* Process development and process research on fine organic chemicals and drugs; synthesis of fluorocorticosteroids and IG steroids; antiflammatory analgesies, beta blockers. *Mailing Add:* F Hoffmann & La Roche Ltd Basel CH-4070 Switzerland

LODGE, ARTHUR SCOTT, PHYSICS. *Current Pos:* prof eng mech, 68-85, PROF RHEOLOGY, UNIV WIS-MADISON, 68-, CHMN DEPT, 69- *Personal Data:* b Liverpool, Eng, Nov 20, 22; m 45; c 3. *Educ:* Oxford Univ, BA, 45, MA, 48, DPhil(physics), 49. *Honors & Awards:* Bingham Medal, Soc Rheology, 71; Gold Medal, Brit Soc Rheology, 83. *Prof Exp:* Jr sci officer pile design, Atomic Energy, Montreal Anglo-Can Proj, 45-46 & rheology, Brit Rayon Res Asn, 49-60; lectr math, Inst Sci & Technol, Univ Manchester, 61-63, sr lectr rheology, 63-68. *Concurrent Pos:* Vis prof chem eng, Univ Wis-Madison, 65-66; vpres, Bannatek Co, Inc. *Mem:* Soc Rheology; Brit Soc Rheology; fel Brit Inst Physics & Phys Soc. *Res:* Rheological properties of concentrated polymer solutions; molecular theories of their constitutive equations and stress/optical properties; experimental methods. *Mailing Add:* 210 Durose Terr Madison WI 53705

LODGE, CHESTER RAY, electrical engineering, for more information see previous edition

LODGE, DAVID MICHAEL, LAKES, HERBIVORY. *Current Pos:* ASST PROF INVERT ZOOL & ECOL, DEPT BIOL SCI, UNIV NOTRE DAME, 85- *Personal Data:* b Athens, Tenn, Apr 1, 57; m 85, Andrea J Midgett; c 3. *Educ:* Univ South, BS, 79; Oxford Univ, DPhil(zool), 82. *Prof Exp:* Asst scientist, Ctr Limnol, Univ Wis, 82-85. *Concurrent Pos:* Exec comn, Am Midland Naturalist, 89-; assoc ed, J NAm Benthological Soc, 90-92; vis scientist, Inst Mar Sci, Univ NC, Chapel Hill, 92-93. *Mem:* Am Sci Affil; Am Soc Limnol & Oceanog; Ecol Soc Am; NAm Benthological Soc; Am Inst Biol Sci; Int Soc Limnol. *Res:* Determining the relative importance of biotic and abiotic factors in determining the distribution and abundance of freshwater benthic organisms; predation and herbivory; impact of exotic species on freshwater ecosystems; comparative ecology of plant-animal interactions in freshwater, marine and terrestrial ecosystems; interaction of benthic and pelagic habitats in lakes. *Mailing Add:* Dept Biol Sci Univ Notre Dame Notre Dame IN 46556. *Fax:* 219-631-7413; *E-Mail:* david.m.ledge.1@nd.edu

LODGE, JAMES PIATT, JR, ATMOSPHERIC CHEMISTRY, AIR POLLUTION. *Current Pos:* CONSULT ATMOSPHERIC CHEM, 74- *Personal Data:* b Decatur, Ill, Feb 4, 26; m 48, Nancy P Myers; c Martha (Newlon), Judith, Susan (Perry), Elizabeth (Anderson) & Eric. *Educ:* Univ Ill, BS, 47; Univ Rochester, PhD(chem), 51. *Honors & Awards:* Frank A Chambers Award, Air Pollution Control Asn, 74; Award of Appreciation, Am Soc Testing & Mat, 95. *Prof Exp:* Asst prof chem, Keuka Col, 50-52; chemist, Cloud Physics Lab, Univ Chicago, 52-55; chief chem res & develop sect, Robert A Taft Sanit Eng Ctr, USPHS, Cincinnati, Ohio, 55-61; prog scientist, Nat Ctr Atmospheric Res, 61-74. *Concurrent Pos:* Consult, Cook Res Labs, 51-53; affil prof, La State Univ, 66-69; mem, State Air Pollution Variance Bd, Colo, 66-70; chmn, State Air Pollution Control Comn, Colo, 70-76. *Mem:* Fel AAAS; Am Chem Soc; Am Geophys Union; Am Meteorol Soc; Air & Waste Mgt Asn; Am Soc Testing & Mat. *Res:* Air pollution and atmospheric chemistry; microchemical analysis; cloud physics; atmospheric electricity. *Mailing Add:* 801 Circle Dr Boulder CO 80302. *Fax:* 303-449-8577; *E-Mail:* jplodge@aol.com

LODGE, JAMES ROBERT, REPRODUCTIVE PHYSIOLOGY. *Current Pos:* res assoc dairy sci, 57-60, from asst prof to assoc prof, 60-69, PROF PHYSIOL, UNIV ILL, URBANA, 69- *Personal Data:* b Downey, Iowa, July 1, 25; m 47; c 2. *Educ:* Iowa State Univ, BS, 52, MS, 54; Mich State Univ, PhD(dairy), 57. *Prof Exp:* Asst dairy, Mich State Univ, 54-57. *Concurrent Pos:* Res fel, Nat Inst Child Health & Human Develop, 69-70. *Mem:* AAAS; Am Physiol Soc; Soc Study Reproduction; Am Soc Animal Sci; Am Dairy Sci Asn. *Res:* Physiology of reproduction and endocrinology. *Mailing Add:* 312 Animal Sci Lab Univ Ill 1207 W Gregory Dr Urbana IL 61801

LODGE, MALCOLM A, COMPUTER SCIENCE, ENGINEERING. *Current Pos:* PRES, ISLAND TECHNOL, INC, 86- *Personal Data:* b Borden, PEI, Can, Mar 16, 39; c 2. *Educ:* NS Tech Col, BEng, 62, MScEng, 69. *Prof Exp:* Sonar engr, Can Forces Dockyard, Halifax, 62-63; prod design engr, Can Westinghouse Co, Ltd, 64-69; prof elec eng, Holland Col, 69-77; res engr, Resource Ventures, Inc, 77-86. *Concurrent Pos:* Nat Res Coun fel, 64; tech progs officer, Inst Man & Resources, 77-86. *Mem:* Can Wind Energy Asn; Am Wind Energy Asn; Asn Prof Engrs. *Res:* Wind turbine systems; process x-ray applications; biomedical computer applications; energy conservation and supply systems. *Mailing Add:* 201 Water Charlottetown PE C1A 1B1 Can

LODGE, NICHOLAS JOHN, CARDIOVASCULAR PHYSIOLOGY, ELECTROPHYSIOLOGY. *Current Pos:* SR RES INVESTR II, BRYSTOL-MEYERS SQUIBB, 91- *Personal Data:* b Nottingham, Eng, Jan 31, 57. *Educ:* Univ Lancaster, BSc, 78, PhD(physiol), 82. *Prof Exp:* Res asst prof, Univ Miami, Fla Sch Med, 83-88; sr scientist, Wyeth Ayerst, 88-89, res scientist, 89-92. *Concurrent Pos:* Young investr award, Am Pediat Soc, 85. *Mem:* Biophys Soc; Physiol Soc. *Res:* Cardiovascular physiology; electrophysiology; cellular physiology. *Mailing Add:* Bristol Myers Squibb Res Inst PO Box 4000 Princeton NJ 08543-4000

LODGE, TIMOTHY PATRICK, POLYMER SOLUTION DYNAMICS. *Current Pos:* from asst prof to assoc prof, 82-91, PROF CHEM, UNIV MINN, 91- *Personal Data:* b Sale, Eng, Apr, 11, 54; m 88. *Educ:* Harvard Univ, BA, 75; Univ Wis, PhD(chem), 80. *Prof Exp:* Nat Res Coun assoc fel, Nat Bur Stand, 81-82. *Concurrent Pos:* US Regional ed, Macromolecular Chem & Physics, 94- *Mem:* Fel Am Chem Soc; Am Phys Soc; Soc Rheology; Sigma Xi. *Res:* Conformation and dynamics of macromolecules in solutions and melts studied by means of oscillatory flow birefringence, quasi-elastic light scattering, small angle neutron scattering, and forud rayleigh scattering. *Mailing Add:* Dept Chem Kolthoff & Smith Halls Univ Minn Minneapolis MN 55455-0431

LODHI, MOHAMMAD ARFIN KHAN, NUCLEAR PHYSICS, RENEWABLE SOURCES OF ENERGY. *Current Pos:* from asst prof to assoc prof, 63-73, PROF PHYSICS, TEX TECH UNIV, 73- *Personal Data:* b Agra, India, Sept 17, 33; m 65, Khalida; c 3. *Educ:* Univ Karachi, BSc, Hons, 52, MSc, 56; Univ London, DIC, 60, PhD(nuclear physics), 63. *Honors & Awards:* Alkhwarzmi Award. *Prof Exp:* Lectr math, S M Col, Karachi, 52-59. *Concurrent Pos:* Vis res scholar, Bohr Inst Theoret Physics, Copenhagen, Denmark, 62; vis asst prof, Univ Fla, Gainesville, 67 & Univ Wyo, Laramie, 68; res assoc, State Univ NY, Buffalo, 69; vis assoc prof, Univ Wash, 69-70 & Univ Calif, San Diego, 72; guest scientist, Pinstech, Pakistan, 73 & 76; UN expert & consult, var univs in Pakistan, 81 & 83; consult, Nat Inst Oceanog, Karachi, Pakistan, 84 & 85; vis prof, Bahauddin Zakariya Univ, Pakistan, 84-85; NSF coordr, deleg Int Nathiagali Summer Col, Pakistan; vis prof, Ctr Excellence Anal Chem, Sind Pakistan, 86; guest scientist, Ctr Solar Energy Hyderabad Sin Pakistan, 86-87; vis prof, Middle East Tech Univ, Ankara, Turkey, 87 & Univ Pertanian, Malaysia, 89-90; consult & expert, UN Nat Inst Oceanog, Karachi, Pakistan, 88. *Mem:* Brit Inst Physics; Pakistan Math Soc; fel Phys Soc UK; Sigma Xi; Am Phys Soc; Am Asn Univ Professors; Am Astronaut Soc; Pakistan Inst Physics; Solar Energy Soc Pakistan. *Res:* High energy electron scattering by nuclei and electromagnetics transitions in nuclei and their role in elucidating nuclear structure; nuclear shell, cluster and resonating group models and their relationship; nuclear nonlocal potential and nuclear systematics; short-range nucleon-nucleon correlations; solar-hydrogen system collection, transduction; extraction of energy from renewable sources, including ocean currents and tides. *Mailing Add:* Dept Physics Tex Tech Univ PO Box 41051 Lubbock TX 79409. *Fax:* 806-742-1182; *E-Mail:* b5mak@ttacs.ttu.edu

LODISH, HARVEY FRANKLIN, BIOCHEMISTRY, CELL BIOLOGY. *Current Pos:* from asst prof to assoc prof, 68-76, PROF BIOL, MASS INST TECHNOL, 76- *Personal Data:* b Cleveland, Ohio, Nov 16, 41; m 63, Pamela; c Heidi, Martin & Stephanie. *Educ:* Kenyon Col, AB, 62; Rockefeller Univ, PhD(genetics), 66. *Hon Degrees:* DSc, Kenyon Col, 82. *Honors & Awards:* Stadie Award, Am Diabetes Asn, 89; Berson Mem Lectr, Ninth Int Cong Endocrinol, 92; 16th Jim McGinnis Mem Lectr, Duke Univ, 94; Harry Eagle Mem Lectr, Albert Einstein Col Med, NY, 94. *Prof Exp:* Am Cancer Soc fel biol, Lab Molecular Biol, Med Res Coun, Eng, 66-68. *Concurrent Pos:* Res career develop award, Nat Inst Gen Med Sci, 71-75; mem panel develop biol, NSF, 72-; chmn, Gordon Conf on Animal Cells, 76, Red Blood Cells, 85 & Membrane Molecular Biol, 89; Guggenheim fel, 77-78; vis scientist, Imp Cancer Res Fund, 77-78; mem, Whitehead Inst Biomed Res, 82-; assoc mem, Europ Molecular Biol Orgn, 95- *Mem:* Nat Acad Sci; Am Soc Microbiol; Am Chem Soc; Am Soc Biol Chemists; Am Soc Cell Biol; fel AAAS; fel Am Acad Microbiol. *Res:* Structure, function and assembly of plasma membrane proteins; erythropoetin receptor; diabetes; endothelin receptor, TGF-B receptor. *Mailing Add:* Whitehead Inst Biomed Res 9 Cambridge Ctr Cambridge MA 02142. *Fax:* 617-258-9872; *E-Mail:* lodish@wi.mit.edu

LODMELL, DONALD LOUIS, VIROLOGY. *Current Pos:* sr scientist, 72-81, SCI DIR VIROL, ROCKY MOUNTAIN LAB, NIH, 81- *Personal Data:* b Polson, Mont, Aug 27, 39; m 63. *Educ:* Northwestern Univ, BA, 61; Univ Mont, MS, 63, PhD(microbiol), 67. *Prof Exp:* Scientist virol, Rocky Mountain Lab, NIH, 67-71; res assoc, Lab Oral Med, NIH, 71-72. *Concurrent Pos:* Fac affil, Dept Microbiol, Univ Mont, 78- *Mem:* Am Soc Microbiol; Am Asn Immunologists; Am Soc Virol. *Res:* Immunological mechanisms of host defense against viral infections of the central nervous system; rabies. *Mailing Add:* Rocky Mountain Lab 903 S Fourth St Hamilton MT 59840

LODOEN, GARY ARTHUR, POLYMER CHEMISTRY. *Current Pos:* res chemist, E I Du Pont de Nemours & Co, Inc, 70-73, sr res chemist, 73, res & develop supvr, 73-75, process supvr, 75-77, sr res chemist, 77-82, RES ASSOC, TEXTILE FIBERS DEPT, E I DU PONT DE NEMOURS & CO, INC, 83- *Personal Data:* b Camp Rucker, Ala, May 3, 43. *Educ:* Univ NDak, BS, 65; Cornell Univ, PhD(org chem), 69. *Prof Exp:* Fel, Univ Iowa, 69-70. *Mem:* Am Chem Soc. *Res:* Spandex chemistry and structure; polyester glycol synthesis and properties; development of new and novel raw materials for spandex yarns. *Mailing Add:* 2 Hickory Hill Lane Fishersville VA 22939

LODWICK, GWILYM SAVAGE, RADIOLOGY, BIOENGINEERING. *Current Pos:* actg dean, Sch Med, Univ Mo, Columbia, 59, assoc dean, 59-64, prof radiol & chmn dept, 56-78, interim chmn radiol, 80-81, chmn, Dept Radiol, 81-83, res prof, 78-83, EMER PROF, DEPT RADIOL, UNIV MO, COLUMBIA, 83- *Personal Data:* b Mystic, Iowa, Aug 30, 17; m 47, 70, Maria A Barata; c Gwilym S, Philip G, Malcolm K & Terry Ann. *Educ:* Univ Iowa, BA, 42, MD, 43. *Honors & Awards:* Founder's Gold Medal, Int Skeletal Soc, 90; Gold Medal, XIII Int Conf Radiol, Madrid, 73; Sakari Mustakallio Medal, Finland, 79; Med Tech Leadership Award, Nat Elec Mfrs Asn, 95. *Prof Exp:* Clin asst prof radiol, Univ Iowa, 52-55, assoc prof, Col Med, 55-56. *Concurrent Pos:* Fel, Armed Forces Inst Path, 51; Nat Inst Gen Med Sci spec fel, 67-68; chief radiol serv, Vet Admin Hosp, Iowa City, 52-55; consult, Ellis Fischel State Cancer Hosp, 59-; mem radiol training comt, Nat Inst Gen Med Sci, 66-70; consult, Jet Propulsion Lab, Calif Inst Technol, 69-73; mem, Comt Radiol, Nat Acad Sci; mem, Comt Radiol, Div Med Sci, Nat Res Coun, 70-75; Sigma Xi res Award, Univ Mo-Columbia, 72; dir, Mid-Am Bone Diag Ctr & Registry; vis prof, Sch Med, Keio Univ, Tokyo, 74 & Univ Turku, Finland, 79; mem, Radiation Study Sect, Div Res Grants, NIH, 76-79, Study Sect Diag Radiol & Nuclear Med, 79-82, chmn, 80-82; vis prof, Harvard Med Sch, 83-92; radiologist, Mass Gen Hosp, 83-92, hon radiologist, 92-; radiologist-in-chief, Spaulding Rehab Hosp, 86-92; chmn bd sci coun, Nat Libr Med, 87-89; distinguished practr, Nat Acad Pract Med, 84. *Mem:* Sr mem Inst Med-Nat Acad Sci; AAAS; AMA; Radiol Soc NAm (3rd vpres, 74-75); fel Am Col Radiol; fel Am Col Med Info. *Res:* Diagnostic radiology; diagnosis and prognosis of bone disease, computer-aided medical diagnosis; automated image analysis and pattern recognition; information systems. *Mailing Add:* 307 Playa del Mar 3900 Galt Ocean Dr Ft Lauderdale FL 33308-6631. *Fax:* 954-565-1804; *E-Mail:* lodwick@worldnet.att.net

LOE, HARALD, PERIODONTICS. *Current Pos:* RETIRED. *Personal Data:* b Steinkjer, Norway, July 19, 26; US citizen; c 2. *Educ:* Thirteen from US & foreign univs, 73-90. *Hon Degrees:* DSc, Univ Gothenburg, Sweden, 73, Cath Univ Leuven, Belg, Univ Athens, Greece & Royal Dental Col, Aarhus, Denmark, 80; Univ Lund, Malmo & Georgetown Univ Sch Dent, 83, Univ Bergen, 85, Univ Md, 86 & Univ Med & Dent NJ, 87. *Honors & Awards:* Peridont Award, William J Gies Found, 78; Int Asn Dent Res Award, 69; Ingv Stokke Prize, 65; Erik Berg Found Prize, 69; Aalborg Dent Soc Prize, 69; Am Soc Prev Dent Int Award, 72; Arthur Merritt Mem Lectr, Baylor Univ, 77; William J Gies Award, Am Acad Periodont, 78; Lister Hill Mem Lectr, Univ Ala, Birmingham, 83; Goldstein Lectr, Emory Univ, 86; Exemplary Serv Award, Surgeon Gen, 88; Swed Dent Soc Int Prize, 88; Award Distinction, Acad Dent Int, 90. *Prof Exp:* Instr oper dent, Sch Dent, Oslo, 52-55; res assoc, Norweg Inst Dent Res, 56-62; Fulbright res fel & res assoc oral path, Univ Ill, 57-58; univ res fel, Oslo Univ, 59-62; assoc prof periodont, Sch Dent, Oslo Univ, 60-61; vis prof, Hebrew Univ, Jerusalem, 66-67; prof & chmn periodont, Royal Dent Col, Aarhus, Denmark, 62-72, assoc dean & dean elect, 71-72; prof & dir, Dent Res Inst, Univ Mich, 72-74; dean & prof periodont, Sch Dent Med, Univ Conn, 74-82; dir, Nat Inst Dent Res, NIH, Bethesda, Md, 83-94. *Concurrent Pos:* Assoc ed, Scand J Dent Res Munksgaard, Copenhagen, Denmark, 62, bd dir, Scand Odontological Act, 65-72, ed, J Periodont Res, 65-85; vis prof periodont, Hebrew Univ, Jerusalem, 66-67; foreign expert mem, J Indian Dent Asn, 74-82; rapporteur, Conf Undergrad Dent Educ Europe, WHO, 68; mem & chmn, Comt Postgrad Educ, Oslo Dent Soc, 59-61; chmn, Scand Symp Periodont, Aarus, Denmark, 65; secy, World Workshop Periodont, Path Sect, Ann Arbor, 66; consult, Comt Foreign Rel, Am Asn Periodontologists, 67-71, Coun Dent Therapeut, Am Dent Asn, 77-82, Periodont Dis Clin Res Ctr, State Univ NY, Buffalo, 80-81, Coun Int Rel, Am Dent Asn, 83-88, J Am Dent Asn, 79-82, Procter & Gamble Co, 69-76, to the dir, Nat Inst Dent Res, 69-, Naval Dent Sch, Naval Med Command, 85-88, appraisals comt, Ont Coun Grad Studies & Lord Robens Appeal, Brit Soc Dent Res, 85, Med Res Coun, 87; co-chmn, Scan Symp Prosthetics & Periodont, Aarhos, Denmark & Int Conf Periodont Res, Rochester, NY, 69 & chmn, Aarhus Br, 72; chmn & mem, Basic Res Periodont Dis Award Comt, Int Asn Dent Res, 69-74, pres, Periodont Res Group, 70-71; mem, comt long range planning, Am Asn Periodontologist, 74-75, comt outreach activ, Univ Conn, dent sch res grant comt & periodont res prog comt, Int Asn Dent Res, 76, organizing comt, Int Conf Periodont Res, Gothenburg, Sweden, bd dirs, Int Asn Dent Res, 77-82, finance comt, 78-80, gen prog comt, 78-80, int rel comt, 79-82, hon mem comt, 81-84, comt res periodont, Am Asn Periodontologist, 74-79, comt Orban Prize competition, 76, foreign rel comt, 78- & chmn, 81-82, hom mem comt, 79-82, comt mission & goals, 84-87 & search comt ed J Periodont, 88 85 & chmn, 85-87; secy, Jury Int Prev Dent Award, Int Dent Fed, 76. *Mem:* Inst Med-Nat Acad Sci; Int Asn Dent Res (pres, 79-81); fel Int Col Dentists; fel Am Col Dentists; fel AAAS; corresp mem Swed Dent Asn; corresp mem Finnish Dent Soc; hon mem Scand Soc Periodont; hon mem Belg Periodont Soc; hon mem Norweg Dent Asn; Int Dent Fed; Int Col Dentists; Sigma Xi. *Res:* Epidemiology, experimental pathology and prevention of peridontal disease; author or coauthor of over 200 scientific articles; author of over 275 publications. *Mailing Add:* 1 Redwood Lane Farmington Hills Avon CT 06001

LOEB, ALEX LEWIS, CARDIOVASCULAR PHARMACOLOGY, ENDOTHELIUM DEPENDENT RESPONSES. *Current Pos:* lectr, Dept Anesthesia, 88-92, ASST PROF, DEPT ANESTHESIA & PHARMACOL, UNIV PA, 92- *Personal Data:* b Ithaca, NY, Aug 4, 55; m 83, Joan Saverino; c Orlando. *Educ:* Beloit Col, BS, 77; George Washington Univ, MS, 81, PhD(pharmacol), 84. *Prof Exp:* Chemist, Nat Bur Stand, 77; consult, Life Sci, Inc, 82-83; postdoctoral fel, Univ Va, 84-87, res asst prof, Dept Pharmacol, 87-88. *Concurrent Pos:* Teaching fel, George Washington Univ, 81-84. *Mem:* AAAS; Am Heart Asn; Am Soc Anesthesiologists; NAm Vascular Biol Asn; Microcirulatory Soc. *Res:* Characterization and properties of endothelium-derived relaxing factor from intact vessels and in cultured cells; interactions between endothelium, smooth muscle and platelets in microcirculation, in vivo; mechanisms of anesthetic action. *Mailing Add:* Dept Anesthesia Dulles 7 Univ Pa 3400 Spruce St Philadelphia PA 19104-4283. *E-Mail:* loeba@mail.med.upenn.edu

LOEB, ARTHUR LEE, CHEMICAL PHYSICS, DESIGN SCIENCE. *Current Pos:* SR LECTR VISUAL & ENVIRON STUDIES, CUR, CARPENTER CTR & MASTER, DUDLEY HOUSE, HARVARD UNIV, 70- *Personal Data:* b Amsterdam, Neth, July 13, 23; nat US; m 56, Charlotte I Aarts. *Educ:* Univ Pa, BSCh, 43; Harvard Univ, AM, 45, PhD(chem physics), 49. *Honors & Awards:* Golden Door Award, Int Inst Boston; Residency Rockefeller Found Villa Serbelloni Ctr, Scholars & Artists. *Prof Exp:* Mem staff, Bur Study Coun, Harvard Univ, 45-49; mem staff, Div Indust Coop & Lincoln Lab, Mass Inst Technol, 49-58, lectr, 56-58, from asst prof to assoc prof elec eng, 58-63; staff scientist, Ledgemont Lab, Kennecott Copper Corp, 63-73. *Concurrent Pos:* Actg head, Dept Chem, Barlaeus Gym, Neth, 46; consult, Mass Inst Technol, 49-, Godfrey Lowell Cabot, Inc, 58 & IBM Corp, NY, 59; mem guest res staff, Univ Utrecht, 54-55. *Mem:* Acad Mgt; Am Soc Eng Educ; fel Royal Soc Arts; Am Crystallog Asn; fel Am Inst Chem. *Res:* Mathematical crystallography; educational technology; design science; communication of two-dimensional and three-dimensional concepts and patterns. *Mailing Add:* Dept Visual & Environ Studies Harvard Univ Cambridge MA 02138

LOEB, GERALD ELI, NEUROPHYSIOLOGY, BIOMEDICAL ENGINEERING. *Current Pos:* DIR BIO-MED ENG & PROF PHYSIOL, QUEEN'S UNIV, 88- *Personal Data:* b New Brunswick, NJ, June 26, 48; m 68; c Jason. *Educ:* Johns Hopkins Univ, BA, 69, MD, 72. *Honors & Awards:* Commendation Medal, USPHS. *Prof Exp:* Resident surg, Univ Ariz, 72-73; med officer & sect chief, Nat Inst Neurol & Commun Dis & Stroke, 73-88. *Concurrent Pos:* Fel, Seeing Eye, 69-72; guest res assoc, Artificial Eye Proj, Univ Utah, 71 & adj assoc prof bioengineering, 85-88; vis scientist, Univ Calif, San Francisco, 79-83; pres, Biomed Concepts Inc, 81-88. *Mem:* Soc Neurosci; Can Physiol Soc; Can Med Biol Eng Soc. *Res:* Sensorimotor neurophysiology in mammals, neural prostheses. *Mailing Add:* Biomed Eng Queen's Univ Abramsky Hall Kingston ON K7L 3N6 Can. *Fax:* 613-545-6802; *E-Mail:* loeb@biomed.queensu.ca

LOEB, JEROD M, CARDIOVASCULAR PHYSIOLOGY. *Current Pos:* dir, Div Basic Sci, 87-88, Div Biomed Sci, 88-91, ASST VPRES SCI & TECHNOL & SECY COUN SCI AFFAIRS, AMA, 91- *Personal Data:* b Brooklyn, NY, Oct 21, 49; m 86, Sherri Topping; c Jennifer M & Rebecca E. *Educ:* City Univ New York, BS, 71; State Univ NY, PhD(physiol), 76. *Honors & Awards:* Established Investr Award, Am Heart Asn, 87. *Prof Exp:* Teaching asst physiol, State Univ NY Downstate Med Ctr, 72-76; res fel med, Harvard Med Sch, 76-77; res assoc physiol, Stritch Sch Med, Loyola Univ, Chicago, 77-79; from asst prof to assoc prof surg & physiol, Med Sch, Northwestern Univ, 79-87. *Concurrent Pos:* Mem Coun Basic Sci, Am Heart Asn; prin investr, Am Heart Asn Grant-in-Aid, 80-82; career develop award, Schweppe Found, Chicago, Ill, 80-83; prin investr, NIH Grant, 82-; adj prof physiol, Northwestern Univ, 87- *Mem:* Am Physiol Soc; Sigma Xi; NY Acad Sci; Soc Exp Biol & Med; Am Heart Asn; Am Pub Health Asn. *Res:* Electrophysiologic analysis of normal and abnormal cardiac pacemaker activity; autonomic control of cardiac pacemakers; electrophysiologic mapping of human cardiac arrhythmias. *Mailing Add:* Dept Res & Eval Joint Commission 1 Renaissance Blvd 515 N State St Oakbrook Terrace IL 60181. *Fax:* 312-464-5841

LOEB, JOHN NICHOLS, MECHANISMS OF HORMONE ACTION & CELLULAR TRANSPORT, ENERGY METABOLISM. *Current Pos:* instr med, Columbia Univ, 65-66, NIH trainee metab, 66-67 from asst prof to assoc prof, 67-79, PROF MED, COLUMBIA UNIV, 79- *Personal Data:* b New York, NY, Dec 17, 35. *Educ:* Harvard Col, AB, 57; Harvard Med Sch, MD, 61; Am Bd Internal Med, Cert, 68. *Prof Exp:* Intern Med, Mass Gen Hosp, 61-62; asst resident med, Presby Hosp, NY, 62-63, chief resident, 65-66; res assoc, Lab Molecular Biol, Nat Inst Arthritis & Metab Med Dis, NIH, 63-65. *Concurrent Pos:* Asst attend physician to assoc attend physician, Presby Hosp, NY, 67-79, attend physician, 79-; adj asst prof, Rockefeller Univ, 70-75, adj assoc prof, 75-81, adj prof, 81-83; vis prof, Dept Internal Med, Pahlavi Univ, Shiraz, Iran, 74 & 77; dir, Royal Soc Med Found, 84-95; merit award, NIH, 88-98. *Mem:* Fel Am Col Physicians; Am Soc Clin Invest; Asn Am Physicians; fel AAAS; Am Clin & Climat Soc; Asn Endocrin Soc. *Res:* Mechanisms of glucocorticoid and thyroid hormone action; mechanisms of glucose and sodium transport; physical chemistry of hormone-receptor interactions. *Mailing Add:* Dept Med Columbia Univ 630 W 168th St New York NY 10032

LOEB, LAWRENCE ARTHUR, CANCER, BIOCHEMISTRY. *Current Pos:* PROF DEPT PATH, SCH MED, UNIV WASH, 78-, DIR, GOTTSTEIN MEM CANCER RES LABS, 78-, ADJ PROF DEPT BIOCHEM, 78- *Personal Data:* b Poughkeepsie, NY, Dec 25, 36; m 58; c 3. *Educ:* City Col New York, BS, 57; NY Univ, MD, 61; Univ Calif, Berkeley, PhD(biochem), 67. *Prof Exp:* Intern, Med Ctr, Stanford Univ, 61-62; res assoc biochem, Nat Cancer Inst, 62-64; res assoc zool, Univ Calif, Berkeley, 64-67; asst mem biochem, Inst Cancer Res, 67-69, assoc mem 71-77, mem, 77-78. *Concurrent Pos:* Res grants, Am Cancer Soc, 67-69, Stanley C Dordick Found, 67, NIH & NSF, 69-75; assoc prof, Dept Path, Sch Med & mem biol & molecular biol grad groups, Univ Pa, 67-68. *Mem:* Am Asn Cancer Res (pres, 88-89); Fedn Am Socs Exp Biol; Am Soc Cell Biol; fel Am Col Physicians. *Res:* Fidelity of DNA replication; environmental carcinogenesis; human leukemia; mechanism of catalysis by DNA polymerases; zinc metalloenzymes; lymphocyte transformation. *Mailing Add:* Dept Path Univ Wash Sch Med Box 357705 Seattle WA 98195-7705. *Fax:* 206-543-3967

LOEB, MARCIA JOAN, INVERTEBRATE PHYSIOLOGY. *Current Pos:* PHYSIOLOGIST, USDA, 77- *Personal Data:* b New York, NY, Mar 26, 33; m 53, George; c 2. *Educ:* Brooklyn Col, BA, 53; Cornell Univ, MS, 57; Univ Md, PhD(physiol), 70. *Prof Exp:* Nat Res Coun res assoc physiol & endocrinol of coelenterate develop, Naval Res Lab, 70-72; instr biol & physiol, Northern Va Community Col, 73; res assoc marine biol, Marine Sci Lab, Univ Col NWales, 74; prof lectr physiol, Am Univ, 75-77. *Mem:* Am Soc Zoologists; Entom Soc Am; Int Soc Invert Reproduction; Sigma Xi; Soc Invitro Biol. *Res:* Environmental, physiological and endocrine control of strobilation in the Chesapeake Bay sea nettle, Chrysaora quinquecirrha; associated physiological phenomena in Chrysaora quinquecirrha; physiology of settlement in some marine bryozoan larvae; endocrinology and physiology of spermatogenesis in lepidoptera; hormones associated with the testis and reproductive tract of lepidoptera; insect midgut cell culture. *Mailing Add:* 6920 Fairfax Rd Bethesda MD 20014

LOEB, MARILYN ROSENTHAL, BIOCHEMISTRY OF BACTERIAL CELL SURFACE. *Current Pos:* from asst prof to assoc prof pediat, 78-89, SCIENTIST, MED SCH, UNIV ROCHESTER, 89- *Personal Data:* b New York, NY, Feb 26, 30; m 49; c 3. *Educ:* Barnard Col, Columbia Univ, BA, 51; Bryn Mawr Col, MA, 55; Univ Pa, PhD(biochem), 58. *Prof Exp:* Res assoc biochem, Univ Pa, 58-59; res assoc, Med Col Pa, 65-68; res assoc biochem, Inst Cancer Res, 68-75; asst res prof microbiol, Med Sch, George Washington Univ, 75-77; prog assoc cell biol prog, NSF, 77-78. *Mem:* AAAS; Am Soc Microbiol; Sigma Xi. *Res:* Role of outer membrane components in pathogenesis of gram negative bacteria. *Mailing Add:* Dept Pediat Univ Rochester Med Ctr 601 Elmwood Ave PO Box 690 Rochester NY 14642

LOEB, PETER ALBERT, MATHEMATICS. *Current Pos:* from asst prof to assoc prof, 68-75, PROF MATH, UNIV ILL, URBANA, 75- *Personal Data:* b Berkeley, Calif, July 3, 37; m 58; c 3. *Educ:* Harvey Mudd Col, BS, 59; Princeton Univ, MA, 61; Stanford Univ, PhD(math), 65. *Prof Exp:* Asst prof math, Univ Calif, Los Angeles, 64-68. *Concurrent Pos:* Grant, Ctr Advan Studies, 71. *Mem:* Am Math Soc. *Res:* Topology; potential theory; non-standard analysis. *Mailing Add:* Dept Math Urbana IL 61801-2917

LOEB, VIRGIL, JR, ONCOLOGY, HEMATOLOGY. *Current Pos:* from instr to asst prof med, 51-56, asst prof path, 55-78, from asst prof to assoc prof, 56-78, prof, 78-, EMER PROF CLIN MED, SCH MED, WASHINGTON UNIV. *Personal Data:* b St Louis, Mo, Sept 21, 21; m 50; c 4. *Educ:* Wash Univ, MD, 44. *Concurrent Pos:* Nat Cancer Inst trainee, Sch Med, Wash Univ, 49-50, Damon Runyan res fel hemat, 50-52; dir, Cent Diag Labs, Barnes Hosp, St Louis, 52-68; NIH grant prin investr, Southeastern Cancer Study Group, 56-77; chmn, Cancer Clin Invest Res Comt, Nat Cancer Inst, 66-69, consult, 66-, mem, Polycythemia Vera Study Group & Diag Res Adv Group; mem, Oncol Rev Group Vet Admin; mem bd sci counr, Div Cancer Prev & Control, Nat Cancer Inst, 83-; Am Joint Comt Cancer, 82-91. *Mem:* Int Med-Nat Acad Sci; fel Am Col Physicians; Am Asn Cancer Res; Am Soc Clin Oncol; Am Soc Hemat; Am Cancer Soc (pres, 86-87). *Res:* Medical oncology. *Mailing Add:* One Barnes Hosp Plaza Suite 16303 St Louis MO 63110

LOEBBAKA, DAVID S, X-RAY IMAGING IN FLUIDS. *Current Pos:* assoc prof, 72-77, PROF PHYSICS, UNIV TENN, 77- *Personal Data:* b Gary, Ind, Aug 18, 39; m 79; c 3. *Educ:* Calif Inst Technol, BS, 61; Univ Md, PhD(physics), 67. *Prof Exp:* Assoc res scientist, Univ Notre Dame, 66-68; asst prof high energy physics, Vanderbilt Univ, 68-72. *Concurrent Pos:* Fluids Div, Nat Bur Stand, 82-85. *Mem:* Sigma Xi; Am Asn Physics Teachers. *Res:* X-ray imaging in fluid flow. *Mailing Add:* Dept Geosci & Physics Univ Tenn Martin TN 38238-0001

LOEBENSTEIN, WILLIAM VAILLE, physical chemistry, dental research; deceased, see previous edition for last biography

LOEBER, JOHN FREDERICK, MECHANICAL ENGINEERING, ENGINEERING MECHANICS. *Current Pos:* Engr, Knolls Atomic Power Lab, 67-71, lead engr, 71-73, mgr methods develop, 75-81, mgr AFC reactor equip design, 81-84, resident engr, Develop Apparatus Rep, 84-89, MGR, NCSG MECH DESIGN, KNOLLS ATOMIC POWER LAB, 90- *Personal Data:* b White Plains, NY, Oct 5, 42; m 62, Linda Merritt; c Kenneth, Keith, Scott, Kimberly, Terrence, Russell & Victoria. *Educ:* Lehigh Univ, BS, 64, MS, 65, PhD(appl mech), 68; George Washington Univ, MEA, 86. *Concurrent Pos:* NASA fel, Lehigh Univ, 64-67. *Mem:* Am Soc Mech Engrs. *Res:* Finite element methods of structural analysis including computer program development and graphics; theoretical fracture mechanics. *Mailing Add:* 1659 Broadway Schenectady NY 12306

LOEBL, ERNEST MOSHE, CHEMICAL PHYSICS, QUANTUM CHEMISTRY. *Current Pos:* EMER PROF, POLYTECH UNIV, BROOKLYN, 90- *Personal Data:* b Vienna, Austria, July 30, 23; nat US; m 50; c 2. *Educ:* Hebrew Univ, MSc, 46; Columbia Univ, PhD(chem), 52. *Prof Exp:* Res chemist, Olamith Cement Co, 47; asst chemist, Columbia Univ, 48-50; instr, Rutgers Univ, 50-51; from instr to assoc prof, Polytech Univ, NY, 52-63, prof phys chem, 63-90, head div, 65-73, dep dept head chem, 88-90. *Concurrent Pos:* NSF fel, 63-64; lectr, Esso Res; vis prof, Uppsala Univ, Sweden, 63; Oxford Univ, Eng, 64; Sheffield Univ, Eng, 71 & Hebrew Univ, Jerusalem, 73; dean, Natural Sci & Math, Yeshiva Univ, Ny, 80. *Mem:* AAAS; Am Chem Soc; Am Phys Soc; Sigma Xi; Am Asn Univ Professors. *Res:* Theoretical chemistry; quantum theory; polyelectrolytes; solid state; catalysis. *Mailing Add:* 128 Willow St No 6A Brooklyn NY 11201

LOEBL, RICHARD IRA, MATHEMATICS. *Current Pos:* asst prof, 73-79, ASSOC PROF MATH, WAYNE STATE UNIV, 79- *Personal Data:* b Battle Creek, Mich, Oct 18, 45; m 76. *Educ:* Harvard Univ, AB, 67; Univ Calif, Berkeley, PhD(math), 73. *Prof Exp:* Teaching assoc, Univ Calif, Berkeley, 67-72; actg instr, Univ Calif, Santa Cruz, 72-73. *Concurrent Pos:* Res assoc, Univ Calif, Berkeley, 74; fac res award, Wayne State Univ, 75-76. *Mem:* Am Math Soc; Math Asn Am. *Res:* Functional analysis-operator theory. *Mailing Add:* 25319 Scotia Rd Huntington Woods MI 48070

LOEBLICH, ALFRED RICHARD, JR, micropaleontology, palynology; deceased, see previous edition for last biography

LOEBLICH, ALFRED RICHARD, III, PHYCOLOGY, MARINE BIOLOGY. *Current Pos:* ASSOC PROF BIOL, UNIV HOUSTON, 78- *Personal Data:* b New Orleans, La, Mar 2, 41; m 63; c 2. *Educ:* Univ Calif, Berkeley, AB, 63; Univ Calif, San Diego, PhD(marine biol), 71. *Honors & Awards:* Darbaker Prize, Bot Soc Am, 77. *Prof Exp:* Lab helper, Herbarium, Univ Calif, Berkeley, 62-63; teaching asst, Dept Bot, 63-64; lab technician marine biol, Univ Calif, San Diego, 70-71; asst prof & asst cur, Harvard Univ, 71-76, assoc prof & assoc cur, 76-78. *Concurrent Pos:* USPHS fel, Univ Calif, San Diego, 64-70; NIH grant, 72-78; NSF grant, 74-; Mass Sci & Technol Found grant, 75-77; mem, Nomenclature Comt Algae, Int Asn Plant Taxon, 75-; mem, Comt Systs & Evolution, Soc Protozoologists, 77-; mem, Darbaker Prize Comt, Bot Soc Am, 78- *Mem:* Phycol Soc Am; Soc Protozoologists; Int Phycological Soc; Am Soc Limnol Oceanog; Marine Biol Asn UK. *Res:* Dinoflagellate genetics; characterization of DNA of primitive algae; ultrastructure and physiology of unicellular algae; algal evolution. *Mailing Add:* Dept Biol Univ Houston Houston TX 77204-0001

LOEBLICH, HELEN NINA (TAPPAN), micropaleontology, paleoecology, for more information see previous edition

LOEBLICH, KAREN ELIZABETH, ANIMAL BEHAVIOR, ENTOMOLOGY. *Current Pos:* MEM STAFF, DEPT ENTOM, UNIV CALIF, DAVIS, 78-, FINE ARTS APPRAISER AND WRITER, 80- *Personal Data:* b Ft Sill, Okla, Oct 10, 44; m 75. *Educ:* Univ Calif, Los Angeles, AB, 66, MA, 67; Univ Calif, Davis, PhD(zool), 73. *Prof Exp:* Res assoc entomol, Univ Calif, Davis, 71-72; res assoc, Univ Calif, Riverside, 72-73; res assoc, Univ Hawaii, 74; lectr entomol & zool, San Francisco State Univ, 73-75; res scientist entomol, Agr Div, Upjohn Co, 75-76, mem staff, 75-80; lectr ecol & behav, San Diego State Univ, 77-78. *Mem:* Asn Study Animal Behav; Entomol Soc Am; Ecol Soc Am; Sigma Xi; AAAS. *Res:* Behavior and evolution of Diptera; Drosophilidae of Hawaii; insect grooming behavior; integrated pest management, especially of cotton. *Mailing Add:* PO Box 1164 Univ Calif Davis CA 95617

LOECHELT, CECIL P(AUL), CHEMICAL ENGINEERING. *Current Pos:* sr process design engr, 64-70, SR ECON EVAL ENGR, ETHYL CORP, 70- *Personal Data:* b Elfers, Fla, Nov 4, 35; m 56; c 3. *Educ:* Vanderbilt Univ, BE, 56; La State Univ, MS, 62, PhD(adsorption), 64. *Prof Exp:* Instr chem eng, La State Univ, 63-64. *Mem:* Am Inst Chem Engrs. *Res:* Mathematical simulation of physical processes; evaluation and design of chemical processes. *Mailing Add:* 1904 Stanford Ave Baton Rouge LA 70808

LOEFFLER, ALBERT L, JR, TURBULENCE. *Current Pos:* ADJ PROF, DOWLING COL, HOFSTRA UNIV, 90- *Personal Data:* b Mineola, NY, Oct 22, 27; m 57; c 3. *Educ:* Va Polytech Inst, BS, 49; Iowa State Univ, PhD(chem eng), 53. *Prof Exp:* Res engr, NASA, 54-59; res engr, Grumman Aerospace Corp, 59-60, group leader, 60-74, staff scientist, res dept, 74-90. *Mem:* Am Phys Soc; Am Inst Aeronaut & Astronaut; Sigma Xi. *Res:* Turbulence; boundary layers; magnetohydrodynamics; heat transfer; potential flow problems. *Mailing Add:* 125 Sixth St Hicksville NY 11801-5419

LOEFFLER, FRANK JOSEPH, PHYSICS. *Current Pos:* from asst prof to assoc prof, 58-67, PROF PHYSICS, PURDUE UNIV, 67- *Personal Data:* b Ballston Spa, NY, Sept 5, 28; m 51, Jane Chisholm; c Peter, James, Margaret & Anne Marie. *Educ:* Cornell Univ, BS, 51, PhD(physics), 57. *Prof Exp:* Mem staff, Princeton Univ, 57-58. *Concurrent Pos:* Vis prof, Univ Hamburg, 63-64, Univ Heidelberg, 71 & Univ Hawaii, 85-86. *Mem:* Fel Am Phys Soc; Sigma Xi. *Res:* Elementary particle physics; experimental study of elementary particle interactions at high energy using electronic detection systems; atmospheric physics; investigation of high energy gamma rays and muons from point sources in space; experimental astrophysics using the Haleakala Gamma Ray Observatory and the South Pole GASP facility. *Mailing Add:* Dept Physics Purdue Univ Lafayette IN 47907

LOEFFLER, LARRY JAMES, organic chemistry; deceased, see previous edition for last biography

LOEFFLER, ROBERT J, BOTANY. *Current Pos:* From asst prof to prof, 54-73, EMER PROF BOT, CONCORDIA COL, MOORHEAD, MINN, 73- *Personal Data:* b Worcester, Mass, Oct 20, 22; m 56; c 4. *Educ:* Syracuse Univ, BA, 48; Univ Wis, MS, 50, PhD(bot, zool), 54. *Mem:* Bot Soc Am; Am Inst Biol Sci. *Res:* Pollen analysis of Spiritwood Lake, North Dakota; phytoplankton; plant anatomy and morphology. *Mailing Add:* 704 Eighth St Moorhead MN 56560

LOEGERING, DANIEL JOHN, PHYSIOLOGY. *Current Pos:* from asst prof to assoc prof, 73-87, PROF PHYSIOL, ALBANY MED COL, 87- *Personal Data:* b Minn, Mar 11, 43; m 68; c 3. *Educ:* St John's Univ, Minn, BS, 65; Univ SDak, Vermillion, MA, 67; Univ Western Ont, PhD(physiol), 70. *Prof Exp:* Instr physiol, Med Col Wis, 69-73. *Concurrent Pos:* Wis Heart Asn fel, Med Col Wis, 70-72, NIH spec res fel, 72-73. *Mem:* Reticuloendothelial Soc; Am Physiol Soc. *Res:* Mononuclear phagocyte system function as related to systemic host defense following injury and the cell biology of macrophages. *Mailing Add:* Dept Physiol Albany Med Col Albany NY 12208

LOEHLE, CRAIG S, LIFE HISTORY THEORY, LANDSCAPE ECOLOGY. *Current Pos:* SCIENTIST, ARGONNE NAT LAB, 91- *Personal Data:* b Chicago, Ill, Oct 23, 52; m 80, Neda; c 3. *Educ:* Univ Ga, BS, 76; Univ Wash, MS, 78; Colo State Univ, PhD(math ecol), 82. *Prof Exp:* Sci programmer, SPSS, Inc, 82-84; postdoctoral ecol, Univ Ga, 84-87; res ecologist, Westinghouse Savannah River Co, 87-91. *Mem:* Ecol Soc Am; Int Soc Ecol Modeling. *Res:* Application of mathematics and statistics to ecology, including landscape ecology; simulation modeling; expert systems and artificial intelligence; plant morphology and reproductive strategies; stability theory; author of 80 publications, one book of philosophy and one book on creativity. *Mailing Add:* Argonne Nat Lab 9700 S Cass Ave Argonne IL 60439

LOEHLIN, JAMES HERBERT, PHYSICAL CHEMISTRY, CRYSTALLOGRAPHY. *Current Pos:* from asst prof to assoc prof, 66-77, chmn, 71-74, 81-83 & 86, PROF CHEM, WELLESLEY COL, 77- *Personal Data:* b Mussoorie, India, May 23, 34; US citizen; m 75, Alice Walker; c Robert C & David W. *Educ:* Col Wooster, BA, 56; Mass Inst Technol, PhD(phys chem), 60. *Prof Exp:* Instr chem, Swarthmore Col, 60-61; from instr to asst prof, Col Wooster, 61-64; asst prof, Swarthmore Col, 64-66. *Concurrent Pos:* Res assoc, Univ Chicago, 69-70; vis mem fac, Inst Chem, Univ Uppsala, 76-77; vis scholar, Brandeis Univ, 83-84, Cambridge Univ, 84; vis prof, Univ Minn, 90-91; vis scholar, Brandeis Univ, 97-. *Mem:* Am Crystallog Asn; Am Phys Soc; AAAS; Sigma Xi; Int Solar Energy Soc; Am Chem Soc. *Res:* Crystallography; molecular structure and solids; energy conversion; intermolecular hydrogen bonds in crystals. *Mailing Add:* Dept Chem Wellesley Col Wellesley MA 02181. *Fax:* 781-283-3642; *E-Mail:* jloehlin@lucy.wellesley.edu

LOEHMAN, RONALD ERNEST, CERAMICS, SOLID STATE CHEMISTRY. *Current Pos:* staff mem, 82-86, div supvr, 86-87, DEPT MGR, SANDIA NAT LABS, 87-; NAT LAB DISTINGUISHED PROF, UNIV NMEX, 91- *Personal Data:* b San Antonio, Tex, Feb 22, 43; m 65, 82, Ellen Griffith; c Rachel A & Matthew C. *Educ:* Rice Univ, BA, 64; Purdue Univ, PhD(chem), 69. *Honors & Awards:* Snow Award, Am Ceramic Soc, 84, Fulrath Award, 88. *Prof Exp:* Res fel mat res, Thermophys Properties Res Ctr, Purdue Univ, 69-70; from asst prof to assoc prof mat eng, Univ Fla, 70-78; staff mem, Sandia Labs, Albuquerque, 77-78; staff scientist, SRI Int, 78-82. *Concurrent Pos:* Vis scientist, Univ Rennes, France, 84, Nat Defense Acad, Japan, 88. *Mem:* Fel Am Ceramic Soc; AAAS; Nat Inst Ceramic Engrs; Sigma Xi. *Res:* Metal ceramic interfaces and ceramic joining; high temperature materials; electronic properties of materials; glass formation and crystallization; nitrogen ceramics. *Mailing Add:* Advan Mat Lab 1001 University Blvd SE Albuquerque NM 87106. *Fax:* 505-272-7304

LOEHR, RAYMOND CHARLES, ENVIRONMENTAL ENGINEERING. *Current Pos:* H M ALHARTHY CENTENNIAL CHAIR & PROF CIVIL ENG, UNIV TEX, AUSTIN, 85-, HEAD, ENVIRON SOLUTIONS PROG, 90- *Personal Data:* b Cleveland, Ohio, May 17, 31; m 53; c 8. *Educ:* Case Inst Technol, BS, 53, MS 56; Univ Wis, PhD(sanit eng), 61. *Honors & Awards:* Water Conserv Award, Nat Wildlife Fedn, 67; Rudolph Hering Medal, Am Soc Civil Engrs, 69, G Brooks Earnest Lectr award, 91, Thomas R Camp Lectr award, 92; Billy & Claude Hocott Distinguished Centennial Eng Res Award, Univ Tex, 91, Joe J King Prof Achievement Award, 92; T H Feng Distinguished Lectr, Univ Mass, 94; Rachel Carson Award, Soc Environ Toxicol & Chem, 95. *Prof Exp:* From instr civil eng to asst prof, Case Inst Technol, 54-61; from assoc prof civil & sanit eng to prof, Univ Kans, 61-68; prof agr eng & civil eng, Cornell Univ, 68-85, dir, Environ Studies Prog, 72-80, Liberty Hyde Bailey prof eng, 81-85. *Concurrent Pos:* USPHS & Environ Protection Agency res grants, 63-; chmn, Technol Assessment & Pollution Control Adv Comt, Sci Adv Bd, Environ Protection Agency, 78-80, & Environ Eng Comt, 82-88; sr Fulbright scholar, NZ, 79; consult, 94-; mem bd, Environ Sci Toxicol, Nat Acad Sci, 95-98. *Mem:* Nat Acad Eng; AAAS; Am Soc Civil Engrs; Water Pollution Control Fedn; Asn Environ Eng Professors. *Res:* Environmental health engineering; water and wastewater treatment; hazardous waste treatment; industrial waste management; land treatment of wastes; use of hazardous waste management technologies for contaminated liquids, slurries, solids and soils; transformations, transport and fate of constituents when wastes are treated by hazardous and industrial waste management processes; over 250 technical publications. *Mailing Add:* Dept Civil Eng ECJ 9-102B Univ Tex Austin TX 78712

LOEHR, THOMAS MICHAEL, INORGANIC CHEMISTRY, BIOCHEMISTRY. *Current Pos:* from asst prof to assoc prof, 68-78, PROF CHEM, ORE GRAD CTR, 78- *Personal Data:* b Munich, Ger, Oct 2, 39; US citizen; m 65, Joann Sanders. *Educ:* Univ Mich, Ann Arbor, BS, 63; Cornell Univ, PhD(chem), 67. *Prof Exp:* Asst prof chem, Cornell Univ, 67-68. *Concurrent Pos:* NIH res grant, Ore Grad Ctr, 71-; vis lectr, Portland State Univ, 71-72; res grant, NSF, 74-77; vis assoc chem, Calif Inst Technol, 78-79; mem, NIH Metallobiochem Study Sect, 78-82; actg dept chmn, Ore Grad Ctr, 80-81; chmn, Gordon Res Conf, 87; actg dept head, Ore Grad Inst, 92-93. *Mem:* Am Chem Soc; Soc Appl Spectros. *Res:* Structural inorganic chemistry; infrared and Raman spectroscopy; metal ion complexes; metallobiochemistry; molecular and electronic structure of metalloproteins; resonance Raman spectroscopy. *Mailing Add:* Ore Grad Inst Sci Tech PO Box 91000 Portland OR 97291-1000. *Fax:* 503-690-1464; *E-Mail:* loehr@admin.ogi.edu

LOEHRKE, RICHARD IRWIN, MECHANICAL ENGINEERING. *Current Pos:* asst prof, 71-76, ASSOC PROF MECH ENG, COLO STATE UNIV, 76- *Personal Data:* b Milwaukee, Wis, May 11, 35; m 57; c 2. *Educ:* Univ Wis, BS, 57; Univ Colo, MS, 65; Ill Inst Technol, PhD(mech eng), 70. *Prof Exp:* Tech engr aircraft nuclear propulsion dept, Gen Elec Co, 57-61; res engr, Sundstrand Corp, 61-65; asst prof mech eng, Ill Inst Technol, 70-71. *Mem:* Am Soc Mech Engrs; Am Inst Aeronaut & Astronaut; Sigma Xi. *Res:* Heat transfer; fluid mechanics. *Mailing Add:* 1901 Rangefield Dr Ft Collins CO 80524-1922

LOELIGER, DAVID A, COORDINATION CHEMISTRY, ARCHAEOLOGICAL SOILS. *Current Pos:* dir, Int Educ Exchange, 81-87, ASSOC PROF CHEM, INT CHRISTIAN UNIV, 72-, RES CONSULT, ARCHEOL RES CTR, 75- *Personal Data:* b Scranton, Pa, Mar 1, 39; m 60; c 4. *Educ:* Col Wooster, BA, 61; Univ Chicago, MS, 62, PhD(chem), 65. *Prof Exp:* Asst prof chem, Purdue Univ, 64-67; sr res chemist, Eastman Kodak Co, 67-72. *Concurrent Pos:* Missionary, Am Lutheran Church, 72- *Mem:* Am Chem Soc; Japan Soc Sci Study of Cult Properties. *Res:* Oxidation-reduction and subtitution reactions of transition metal ions and complexes; application of chemical techniques to problems of archaeological interest; chemical analysis of archaeological artifacts and soils. *Mailing Add:* 920 Rockefeller Dr Apt 5B Sunnyvale CA 94087-2139

LOENING, KURT L, PHYSICAL CHEMISTRY, ORGANIC CHEMISTRY. *Current Pos:* MANAGING DIR, TOPTERM, 90- *Personal Data:* b Berlin, Ger, Jan 18, 24; nat US; m 45; c 2. *Educ:* Ohio State Univ, BS, 44, PhD(chem), 51. *Honors & Awards:* Austin M Patterson-E J Crane Award, 87. *Prof Exp:* From asst ed to sr assoc ed, Chem Abstracts, 51-63, assoc dir, Nomenclature, 63-64, dir, Nomenclature, 64-89. *Concurrent Pos:* Chmn, Interdiv Comt, Nomenclature & Symbols, Int Union Pure & Appl Chem, 76-87, comt nomenclature, Am Chem Soc, 64-89. *Mem:* AAAS; Am Chem Soc; Am Soc Testing & Mat. *Res:* Acid-catalyzed esterification of organic acids; chemical nomenclature; literature. *Mailing Add:* 2064 Inchcliff Rd Columbus OH 43221-2736

LOEPPERT, RICHARD HENRY, ORGANIC CHEMISTRY. *Current Pos:* from instr to assoc prof, 40-59, prof, 59-79, EMER PROF CHEM, NC STATE UNIV, 79- *Personal Data:* b Chicago, Ill, Mar 13, 14; m 40, Adeline Radtke; c Richard. *Educ:* Northwestern Univ, BS, 35; Univ Minn, PhD(phys chem), 40. *Prof Exp:* Asst, Univ Minn, 35-39; res chemist, Richardson Co, Ill, 39-40. *Mem:* Am Chem Soc. *Mailing Add:* 1317 Rand Dr Raleigh NC 27608

LOEPPERT, RICHARD HENRY, JR, SOIL CHEMISTRY. *Current Pos:* from asst prof to assoc prof, 79-91, PROF SOIL CHEM, TEX A&M UNIV, 91- *Personal Data:* b Raleigh, NC, Sept 26, 44; m 89, Sara Vela; c 1. *Educ:* NC State Univ, BS, 66; Univ Fla, MS, 73, PhD(soil sci), 76. *Prof Exp:* Asst county agriculturalist, Agr Exten Serv, Univ Fla, 66-69. *Concurrent Pos:* Chmn, Soil Chem Div, Soil Sci Soc Am, 90-91; assoc ed, Soil Sci Soc Am J, 92- *Mem:* Soil Sci Soc Am; Am Soc Agron; Am Chem Soc; Clay Minerals Soc; AAAS; Sigma Xi (pres, 91-92). *Res:* Soil chemical factors influencing availability of plant nutrients under nutrient stress and environmental stress conditions; soil carbonate chemistry; chemistry of arid region soils; soil testing and analysis; trace metal chemistry. *Mailing Add:* Dept Soil & Crop Sci Tex A&M Univ College Station TX 77843. *Fax:* 409-845-0456

LOEPPKY, JACK ALBERT, RESPIRATORY & ENVIRONMENTAL PHYSIOLOGY. *Current Pos:* Res assoc, Physiol Dept, 70-75, assoc scientist, 75-90, SCIENTIST, LOVELACE MED FOUND, 90- *Personal Data:* b Saskatoon, Sask; m 74, Janet By; c Kris & Ninya. *Educ:* Univ Sask, BA, 66; Univ NMex, MS, 69, PhD(biol), 73. *Concurrent Pos:* Technologist, Physiol Dept, Wellington Hosp, NZ, 75; adj asst prof, Univ NMex, 82-; prin investr grants, Am Heart Asn, 82-84 & 88-89, NASA, 89-95 & US Army, 96-; vis scientist, Max Planck Inst Exp Med, Gottingen, Ger, 83-84. *Mem:* Int Soc Gravitational Physiol; Am Physiol Soc. *Res:* Normal and pathological pulmonary physiology and gas exchange; effects of low oxygen and high altitude and increased carbon dioxide on lung gas exchange and circulation; fluid balance, circulatory and respiratory affects of simulated zero gravity. *Mailing Add:* Lovelace Inst 2425 Ridgecrest Dr SE Albuquerque NM 87108. *Fax:* 505-262-7043; *E-Mail:* jackat@lucy.tli.org

LOEPPKY, RICHARD N, PHYSICAL ORGANIC CHEMISTRY, MECHANISTIC TOXICOLOGY. *Current Pos:* from asst prof to assoc prof, 64-80, PROF CHEM, UNIV MO-COLUMBIA, 80- *Personal Data:* b Lewiston, Idaho, Aug 2, 37; c 2. *Educ:* Univ Idaho, BS, 59; Univ Mich, MS, 61, PhD(chem), 63. *Honors & Awards:* Kasimir Fajans Award, 65; Merit Award, Nat Cancer Inst, 86. *Prof Exp:* Instr chem, Univ Mich, 63; NIH fel org chem, Univ Ill, 63-64. *Concurrent Pos:* Resident vis, Bell Labs, 71-72; guest prof, Univ Kaiserslautern, Ger, 93-94; Fogarty sr fel, 93-94. *Mem:* Am Chem Soc; fel AAAS; Am Asn Cancer Res; Sigma Xi. *Res:* Chemical carcinogenesis and physical organic chemistry; chemical and biochemical transformation of nitrosamines directed at understanding their environmental and biochemical formation, transformation and destruction. *Mailing Add:* 123 Chem Dept Univ Mo Columbia MO 65211-0001. *Fax:* 573-882-2754; *E-Mail:* chemrnl@mizzou1

LOESCH, HAROLD CARL, BIOLOGICAL OCEANOGRAPHY. *Current Pos:* RETIRED. *Personal Data:* b Tex, Oct 3, 26; m 45, Mabel Treichler; c Stephen, Gretchen, Jonathon & Frederick. *Educ:* Tex A&M Univ, BS, 51, MS, 54, PhD(biol oceanog), 62. *Prof Exp:* Prin marine biologist & actg lab dir, Dept Conservation, State Ala, 52-57; assoc res scientist, Tex A&M Res Found, 58-60; shrimp biologist, Food & Agr Orgn, UN, 60-62, fisheries biologist, 62-66, fisheries officer, 67-68, proj mgr & sr resource assessment surveyor, fisheries proj, Bangladesh, 81-85; prof, dept zool & physiol, La State Univ, Baton Rouge, 68-69, prof, dept marine sci & Off Sea Grant Develop, 70-75; expert marine biol, UN develop prog, 76-79; estuarine ecologist, UNESCO, Mexico, 76-79; proj mgr, UN Food & Agr Orgn, Bangladesh, 81-85. *Concurrent Pos:* Consult, Unesco, 79-80, Shrimp Growers Asn Ecuador, 85; vis prof, Org Am States Marine Sci prog, Ecuador, 72. *Mem:* Am Fisheries Soc; Am Soc Limnol & Oceanog; Am Soc Ichthyologists & Herpetologists; fel Int Acad Fishery Sci; Sigma Xi; AAAS; World Maricult Soc. *Res:* Estuarine hydrology and biology; shrimp, spiney lobster and inshore fishes ecology; fisheries statistics. *Mailing Add:* 2140 E Scott St Pensacola FL 32503

LOESCH, JOSEPH G, MARINE BIOLOGY. *Current Pos:* Res asst bluefish migrations, 65-66, asst proj leader, Conn River Hering Study, 66-69, SHELLFISH POP STUDIES, 69-, ANADROMOUS FISH STUDIES, VA, 76-; PROF MARINE SCI, COL WILLIAM & MARY, 69- *Personal Data:* b Middle Village, NY, May 5, 30; m, Marilyn Neff; c 3. *Educ:* Univ RI, BS, 65; Univ Conn, MS, 68, PhD, 69. *Concurrent Pos:* Sr marine scientist, Va Inst Marine Sci; State-Fed fishery mgt comts, 76- *Mem:* Am Fisheries Soc. *Res:* Marine fisheries; life history studies of anadromous fishes; biometrics and population dynamics of commercially important fishes. *Mailing Add:* Dept Fisheries Sci Sch Marine Sci Col William & Mary Gloucester Point VA 23062. *Fax:* 804-642-7327; *E-Mail:* solo@vims.edu

LOESCHE, WALTER J, DENTAL DECAY, PERIODONTAL DISEASE. *Current Pos:* assoc prof oral biol, Univ Mich, Sch Dent, 69-74, assoc prof microbiol, 71-74, dir res, 87-89, PROF DENT & ORAL BIOL, UNIV MICH SCH DENT, 74-, MARCUS WARD PROF, SCH DENT. *Personal Data:* b New Haven, Conn, March 28, 35; m 58; c 3. *Educ:* Yale Univ, BA, 57; Harvard Sch Dent Med, DMD, 61; Mass Inst Technol, PhD(biochem), 67. *Hon Degrees:* Dr, Univ Goteborg, Sweden, & Univ Ghent, Belg. *Honors & Awards:* Int Asn Dent Res Award, 94. *Prof Exp:* Res assoc microbiol, Harvard Sch Dent Med, 61 & 64; mem staff, Forsyth Dent Ctr, 67-69. *Concurrent Pos:* Assoc nutrit, Mass Inst Technol, 64-66; mem, Nat Affairs Comt, Am Asn Dent Res, 85-88, bd dirs, 85-88; mem, Educ Affairs Comt, Univ Mich Sch Dent, 83-86, mem Grad Studies Comt, Univ Mich Sch Med, 73-; Rosenstat vis prof, Univ Toronto, 90. *Mem:* Am Soc Microbiol; Int Asn Dent Res; Am Asn Dent Res (pres, 87-88); Am Dent Asn. *Res:* Research intends to demonstrate dental decay is a specific S mutans infection and that advanced periodontal disease is a treatable anaerobic infection; clinical studies are used to document the role of the above bacteria in human decay and periodontal disease; relationship between dental disease and medical disease in older individuals. *Mailing Add:* 2220 Washtenaw Ave Ann Arbor MI 48104

LOESCHER, WAYNE HAROLD, PLANT PHYSIOLOGY. *Current Pos:* DEPT CHAIR, MICH STATE UNIV, 89- *Personal Data:* b Lima, Ohio, Nov 6, 42; m 67; c 1. *Educ:* Miami Univ, BA, 64, MS, 66; Iowa State Univ, PhD(plant physiol), 72. *Prof Exp:* Res assoc plant physiol, Dept Agron, Iowa State Univ, 71-73; physicist, Math Sci Northwest, 75-80; asst prof plant physiol & asst horticulturist, Wash State Univ, 75-80, assoc prof & assoc horticulturist, 80-89. *Res:* Plant growth and development; plant tissue culture. *Mailing Add:* Hort 288 Plant & Soil Scis Bldg Mich State Univ East Lansing MI 48824-1325

LOESCH-FRIES, LORETTA SUE, PLANT VIROLOGY. *Current Pos:* ASST PROF, PURDUE UNIV, 91- *Personal Data:* b Ventura, Calif, Sept 5, 47; m 76, Robert; c Michael & Matthew. *Educ:* Wash State Univ, BS, 69; Univ Wis, PhD(plant path), 74. *Prof Exp:* Res assoc, Dept Plant Path, Univ Fla, 76-77; res assoc, Dept Hort, Univ Wis, 77-80, asst scientist, 80-81; sr res scientist & consult, Agrigenetics, 81-89; asst adj prof, Univ Wis, 87-91. *Concurrent Pos:* Grants Rev Panel, Coop State Res Serv, USDA, 85 & 86, Dept Energy, 88. *Mem:* Am Phytopath Soc; Sigma Xi; AAAS; Am Soc Virol; Int Soc Plant Molecular Biol; Am Soc Plant Physiologist. *Res:* Genome organization and replication of plant viruses; determination of the role of the virus gene products in infection; how plant viruses cause disease and reduce crop yield; control of plant viruses; granted US patents. *Mailing Add:* Dept Bot & Plant Path Purdue Univ Agr Res Bldg West Lafayette IN 47907-1057. *Fax:* 765-494-5896; *E-Mail:* loeschfries@btny.purdue.edu

LOESER, EUGENE WILLIAM, MEDICINE. *Current Pos:* RETIRED. *Personal Data:* b Buffalo, NY, Nov 5, 26; m 55; c 1. *Educ:* Univ Buffalo, MD, 52. *Prof Exp:* Asst neurol, Columbia Univ, 56-57; asst prof, Univ NC, 57-61; asst prof clin neurol, NY Univ, 64-71; clin assoc prof neurol, Rutgers Med Sch, 71-78; mem staff, Kirkwood Outpatient Ctr, formerly. *Mem:* AMA; Am Acad Neurol. *Res:* Medical neurology. *Mailing Add:* 133 Lighthouse Dr Jupiter FL 33469-3511

LOESER, JOHN DAVID, NEUROLOGICAL SURGERY, PAIN MANAGEMENT. *Current Pos:* from asst prof to assoc prof, 69-81, PROF NEUROSURG, UNIV WASH, 81- *Personal Data:* b Newark, NJ, Dec 14, 35; m 77, Karen Winslow; c Sarah A, Thomas E, Derek W & David W. *Educ:* Harvard Univ, BA, 57; New York Univ, MD, 61. *Honors & Awards:* Sunderland Lect, Australian Pain Soc, 88. *Prof Exp:* Asst prof neurosurg, Univ Calif, Irvine, 67-68; med corp, US Army, 68-69. *Concurrent Pos:* Asst dean curric, Univ Wash, 77-82, dir, Multidisciplinary Pain Ctr, 83-; vis prof, Univ NSW, 80; chief neurosurg, Children's Hosp, Seattle, 85-93; Fulbright sr scholar, Australia, 89-90. *Mem:* Am Pain Soc (treas, 80-85, pres, 86-87); Am Asn Neurol Surgeons; Int Asn Study Pain (secy, 84-90, pres, 93-96); AAAS; Soc Neurosci; Am Acad Pain Med. *Res:* Clinical and research aspects of chronic pain, pain associated with injuries to nervous system, epidemiology and etiology of low back pain, pediatric neurosurgery, especially congenital malformations. *Mailing Add:* Dept Neurol Surg Univ Wash RC-95 Seattle WA 98195. *Fax:* 206-548-4576; *E-Mail:* jdloeser@u.washington.edu

LOEV, BERNARD, ORGANIC CHEMISTRY, MEDICINAL CHEMISTRY. *Current Pos:* PRES, CHEM & PHARMACEUT CONSULT SERV INC, 86- *Personal Data:* b Philadelphia, Pa, Feb 26, 28; m 54; c 3. *Educ:* Univ Pa, BSc, 49; Columbia Univ, MA, 50, PhD(org chem), 52. *Honors & Awards:* Award Outstanding Contrib Med & Org Chem, Am Chem Soc, 74. *Prof Exp:* Instr inorg & org chem, Columbia Univ, 49-51; proj leader, Pennsalt Chem Co, 52-58; group leader, Smith Kline & French Labs, Pa, 58-66, sr investr, 66-67, from asst dir to assoc dir chem, 67-75; dir, Chem Res & Develop Div, USV Pharmaceut Corp, Revlon Health Care Group, 75-80, vpres chem res & develop, 80-83, vpres tech affairs, 83, vpres sci affairs,

83-86. *Concurrent Pos:* Mem adv bd, Index Chemicus & Intra-Sci Res Found; mem bd dirs, Int Heterocyclic Cong; exec vpres, Creative Licensing Int, 86- *Mem:* AAAS; Am Chem Soc; Am Inst Chem; NY Acad Sci. *Res:* Organic synthesis; organic sulfur compounds; medicinal chemistry; nitrogen and sulfur heterocycles; natural products; central nervous system, cardiovascular, asthma, anti-arthritic, anti-ulcer areas; dermatology; patent, strategies and licensing. *Mailing Add:* 19 Candlewood Terr Medford NJ 08055. *Fax:* 914-472-7936

LOEVINGER, ROBERT, DOSIMETRY. *Current Pos:* RETIRED. *Personal Data:* b St Paul, Minn, Jan 31, 16; m 52, Ruth Schimmel; c Nancy, David & Neal. *Educ:* Univ Minn, BA, 36; Harvard Col, MA, 38; Univ Calif, Berkeley, PhD, 47. *Honors & Awards:* William D Coolidge Award, Am Asn Physicists Med, 95. *Prof Exp:* Asst physicist, Mt Sinai Hosp, New York, 47-56; asst prof, Stanford Univ Med Sch, Palo Alto, Calif, 57-65; chief, Dosimetry Sect, Int Atomic Energy Agency, Vienna, Va, 65-68; dosimetry group leader, Nat Inst Stand & Technol, Washington, 68-88. *Mem:* Am Asn Physicists Med; Health Physics Soc. *Mailing Add:* 316 New Mark Esplanade Rockville MD 20850-2734

LOEW, ELLIS ROGER, VISUAL PHYSIOLOGY, SENSORY BIOPHYSICS. *Current Pos:* res fel, 75-77, asst prof, 77-83, ASSOC PROF PHYSIOL, CORNELL UNIV, 83- *Personal Data:* b Los Angeles, Calif, Jan 18, 47; c 2. *Educ:* Univ Calif, Los Angeles, BA, 68, MA, 72, PhD(biol), 73. *Prof Exp:* Fel, Vision Unit, Med Res Coun, 73-74; vis fel, 74-75. *Mem:* AAAS; Brit Photobiol Asn; Inst Elec & Electronic Engrs; Asn Res Vision & Ophthal. *Res:* Physiology and biochemistry of visual photoreceptors; biochemistry and biophysics of visual pigments; sensory ecology. *Mailing Add:* 63 Lake Rd Dryden NY 13053

LOEW, FRANKLIN MARTIN, NUTRITIONAL TOXICOLOGY. *Current Pos:* PRES & CHIEF EXEC OFFICER, MED FOODS, INC, 97- *Personal Data:* b Syracuse, NY, Sept 8, 39; c Timothy & Andrew. *Educ:* Cornell Univ, BS, 61, DVM, 65; Univ Sask, PhD(pharmacol, nutrit), 71. *Honors & Awards:* Gov-Gen's Medal, Can, 77; NB Lectr, Am Soc Microbiol, 84; Armistead lect, Asn Am Vet Med Cols, 87; Schofield lectr, Univ Guelph, 87; Smith lectr, Univ Sask, 87; Schalm lectr, Univ Calif, 89 & Inst Med Nat Acad Sci, 92. *Prof Exp:* Res scientist, R J Reynolds Tobacco Co, 65-66; res asst, Med Sch, Tulane Univ, 66-67; lectr vet med, Univ Sask, 67-69, MRC fel, 69-71, dir animal resources, 71-74, prof toxicol, 74-77; chief, Lab Animal Med, Johns Hopkins Univ, 77-82, dir, Div Comp Med, 79-82; dean, Sch Vet Med, Tufts Univ, 82-95; dean vet med, Cornell Univ, 95-97. *Concurrent Pos:* Consult, Am Asn Accreditation Lab Animal Care, 78-81, Human Nutrit Inst, USDA, 78-82, Div Res Resources, NIH & Nat Inst Aging, Howard Hughes Med Inst, 87, Columbia Univ & Univ Pa; chmn, Inst Lab Animal Resources, Nat Acad Sci, 81-87, mem bd trustees, Boston Zool Soc, 84-89, Foster prof comp med, 85-; mem, Comt Life Sci, Nat Acad Sci, 81-88, Nat Coun, Div Res Resources, NIH, 88-; bd dir, Ma Biotech Res Inst, 86- & Commonwealth Bioventures Inc, 88-95; Blue Ribbon Panel, Animal & Plant Health Inspection Serv, USDA, 87-89; mem, Pew Fedn, Nat Adv Comn Vet Med Educ, 87-93; Sci Adv Bd, Primate Ctr, Harvard Univ, 88-89; bd trustees, Mass Biotech Res Inst, 88-; mem, Mass Govt Adv Comn Sci & Technol, 89-; pres, Tufts Biotechnol Corp, Inc, 93-95; bd trustees, New Eng Aquarium, 91-94 & Marine Biol Lab, Woods Hole, 91-93. *Mem:* Soc Toxicol; Am Soc Nutrit Sci; Am Col Lab Animal Med; Am Asn Lab Animal Sci; Fedn Am Soc Exp Biol; AAAS; Asn Am Vet Med Cols (pres, 85-86). *Res:* Thiamin deficiency and metabolism; toxicology of long chain fatty acids; diseases of laboratory animals; animal nutrition, especially in the laboratory and altered physiologic states of laboratory animals, including humane care and use; public policy questions regarding animal-related issues of social contention; animal biotechnology; technology transfer of nutritional science. *Mailing Add:* Med Food Inc 201 Broadway Cambridge MA 02139. *Fax:* 617-508-1616; *E-Mail:* floew@medical-foods.com

LOEW, GILDA HARRIS, THEORETICAL BIOLOGY, BIOPHYSICS. *Current Pos:* PRES, MOLECULAR RES INST, PALO ALTO, CALIF, 79- *Personal Data:* b New York, NY; c 4. *Educ:* NY Univ, BA, 51; Columbia Univ, MA, 52; Univ Calif, Berkeley, PhD(chem physics), 57. *Prof Exp:* Res physicist, Lawrence Radiation Lab, Univ Calif, Berkeley, 57-62 & Lockheed Missiles & Space Co, 62-64; assoc quantum biophys, Biophys Lab, Stanford Univ, 64-66; from asst prof to assoc prof physics, Pomona Col, 66-69; res biophysicist & instr biophys, Med Sch, Stanford Univ, 69-79, adj prof genetics, Med Ctr, 74-79; prog dir molecular theory, Life Sci Div, Stanford Res Inst, 79- *Concurrent Pos:* Grants, NSF, 66-, NASA, 69- & NIH, 74-; adj prof, Rockefeller Univ, 79- *Mem:* Biophys Soc; fel Am Phys Soc; Int Soc Magnetic Resonance. *Res:* Molecular orbital and crystal field quantum chemical calculations; models for protein active sites; mechanisms and requirements for specific drug action; theoretical studies related to chemical evolution of life. *Mailing Add:* Molecular Res Inst 845 Page Mill Rd Palo Alto CA 94304

LOEW, LESLIE MAX, PHYSICAL ORGANIC CHEMISTRY, BIOPHYSICAL CHEMISTRY. *Current Pos:* assoc prof physiol, 84-87, PROF PHYSIOL, UNIV CONN, 87- *Personal Data:* b New York, NY, Sept 2, 47; m 70, Helen Jeremias; c Daniel, Rena & Aviva. *Educ:* City Col New York, BS, 69; Cornell Univ, MS, 72, PhD(chem), 74. *Prof Exp:* Res assoc chem, Harvard Univ, 73-74; from asst prof to assoc prof chem, State Univ NY, Binghamton, 74-84. *Concurrent Pos:* Career develop award, NIH, 81; vis scientist, Weizmann Inst Sci, 81-82; vis assoc prof, Cornell Univ, 84; adj prof physiol, Univ Mass, 91- *Mem:* Am Chem Soc; Biophys Soc; AAAS. *Res:* Organic dye chemistry; biomembranes; theoretical organic chemistry; electrical, adhesive and chemical properties of biomembranes using spectroscopic techniques; microscopy; image processing, cell physiology, cell biophysics. *Mailing Add:* Dept Physiol Univ Conn Farmington CT 06030

LOEWE, WILLIAM EDWARD, APPLIED PHYSICS. *Current Pos:* RETIRED. *Personal Data:* b Chicago, Ill, Apr 22, 32; m 53, Virginia Decker; c Nancy Jean, Mary Ellen & William Edward. *Educ:* Univ Chicago, AB, 52; Univ Ill, BS, 53; Ill Inst Technol, MS, 59, PhD(physics), 63. *Prof Exp:* Reactor physicist, Savannah River Lab, E I du Pont de Nemours & Co, 53-54, Savannah River Plant, 54-57; assoc physicist, IIT Res Inst, 57-59, res physicist, 59-62, res physicist group leader, 62-63, mgr nuclear physics, 63-66; adv scientist, Nerva, Astro-nuclear Lab, Westinghouse Elec Corp, 66-67; sr physicist, Lawrence Livermore Nat Lab, Univ Calif, 67-90. *Concurrent Pos:* Consult, 91- *Mem:* Am Phys Soc. *Res:* Physics of ionized media and radiation transport, applied hydrodynamics, and criticality safety. *Mailing Add:* 1072 Xavier Way Livermore CA 94550. *Fax:* 415-443-3949

LOEWEN, ERWIN G, OPTICS. *Current Pos:* RETIRED. *Personal Data:* b Frankfurt am Maine, Ger, Apr 12, 21; m 52, Joanna Wills; c Oliver F & Heidi R. *Educ:* NY Univ, BME, 41; Mass Inst Technol, SM, 49, ME, 50, ScD, 52. *Honors & Awards:* David Richardson Medal, Optical Soc Am, 84, Fraunhofer Medal, 93; F W Taylor Medal, Soc Mfg Engrs, 82. *Prof Exp:* Tech dir, Taft-Peirce Mfg Co, 55-60; head dept metrol, Bausch & Lomb Co, 60-67, dir, Grating & Metrol Labs, 67-84; vpres res, Develop & Eng, Milton Roy, 85-87; emer prof, Univ Rochester, 88-97. *Mem:* AAAS; Am Soc Mech Engrs; Soc Mfg Engrs; Optical Soc Am; Soc Photo Instr Engrs. *Res:* Precision Engineering; metrology; diffraction; co-author of one publication. *Mailing Add:* 34A Brook Hill Lane Rochester NY 14625

LOEWENFELD, IRENE ELIZABETH, PHYSIOLOGY. *Current Pos:* from asst prof to assoc prof, 68-81, PROF OPHTHAL, SCH MED, WAYNE STATE UNIV, 81- *Personal Data:* b Munich, Ger, June 2, 21; nat US. *Educ:* Univ Bonn, PhD(zool), 56. *Prof Exp:* Asst ophthal, Columbia Univ, 58-61, instr, 61-62, res assoc, 62-68. *Mem:* Asn Res Vision & Ophthal. *Res:* Neurophysiology; neuroophthalmology; autonomic nervous system; pupil; visual physiology. *Mailing Add:* Three Maker Lane Falmouth MA 02540

LOEWENSON, RUTH BRANDENBURGER, BIOMETRICS. *Current Pos:* CONSULT, 90- *Personal Data:* b Zurich, Switz; US citizen; c 2. *Educ:* Univ Minn, Minneapolis, BA, 59, MS, 61, PhD(biomet), 68. *Prof Exp:* From instr to asst prof, Sch Med, Univ Minn, Minneapolis, 65-72, assoc prof neurol & biomet, 72-90. *Concurrent Pos:* Consult statistician, Vet Admin Hosp, Minneapolis, 71-83, FDA Neurol Devices Panel, 83- *Mem:* Am Statist Asn; Biomet Soc; Soc Epidemiol Res; Soc Clin Trials. *Res:* Clinical studies in neurology; clinical trials in neurology. *Mailing Add:* 3320 Louisiana Ave S No 408 Minneapolis MN 55426

LOEWENSTEIN, ERNEST VICTOR, OPTICS, SPECTROSCOPY. *Current Pos:* ASSOC PROF, NEW ENG COL OPTOM, 78- *Personal Data:* b Offenbach am Main, Ger, Sept 3, 31; US citizen; m 61; c 2. *Educ:* Cornell Univ, AB, 53; Johns Hopkins Univ, PhD(physics), 60. *Prof Exp:* Physicist, Optical Physics Lab, Air Force Cambridge Res Labs, 62-75. *Concurrent Pos:* Pvt pract optometrist. *Mem:* Fel Optical Soc Am. *Res:* Optical properties of far infrared materials; optical properties of the atmosphere; Fourier spectroscopy. *Mailing Add:* 57 Hyde St Newton MA 02161

LOEWENSTEIN, HOWARD, FORESTRY. *Current Pos:* RETIRED. *Personal Data:* b New York, NY, Jan 1, 24; m 58; c 2. *Educ:* Colo State Univ, BS, 52; Univ Wis, PhD(soils), 55. *Prof Exp:* Instr soils, Univ Wis, 55-56; asst prof silvicult, Col Forestry, State univ NY, Syracuse, 57-58; from asst prof to prof forest soils, Univ Idaho, 58-89. *Mem:* Soil Sci Soc Am. *Res:* Forest soil-site relationships; forest fertilization; problems of tree seedling establishment; soil microbiology. *Mailing Add:* 1010 Valdal Rd Moscow ID 83843

LOEWENSTEIN, JOSEPH EDWARD, ENDOCRINOLOGY, INTERNAL MEDICINE. *Current Pos:* CHIEF, DIV ENDOCRINOL & METAB, MERIDIA HURON HOSP, 91-; ASSOC CLIN PROF MED, CASE WESTERN RES UNIV, 92- *Personal Data:* b Crockett, Tex, Nov 25, 37; m 58, Marjorie Thomson; c Sarah F & Edward B. *Educ:* Univ Tex, Austin, BA, 59; Wash Univ, MD, 63. *Prof Exp:* Intern internal med, Barnes Hosp, St Louis, 63-64, resident, 67-69; res assoc, Nat Cancer Inst, 64-66, mem staff, 66-67; instr med, Wash Univ, 70; from asst prof to prof med, La State Univ, Shreveport, 70-84, chief sect endocrinol, 70-84, clin prof med, 84-91. *Concurrent Pos:* Nat Inst Arthritis & Metab Dis fel metab, Wash Univ, 69-70; consult, US Vet Admin Hosp, Shreveport, 70-; mem, Endocrine & Metab Drugs Adv Comt, US Food & Drug Admin, 80-84, chmn, 82-84. *Mem:* Endocrine Soc; fel Am Col Physicians. *Res:* Physiology of prolactin in humans; kinetics of iodine metabolism in thyroid; metabolic acidosis in diabetes. *Mailing Add:* Meridia Huron Hosp Dept Med 13951 Terrance Rd Cleveland OH 44112-4308

LOEWENSTEIN, MATTHEW SAMUEL, GASTROENTEROLOGY, FOOD POISONING. *Current Pos:* SR RES ASSOC, MALLORY GASTROENTEROL RES LAB, BOSTON CITY HOSP, 76- *Personal Data:* b New York, NY, Dec 3, 41; m 65, Davida Gersten; c Andrew, Mara & Laura. *Educ:* Union Col, BS, 62; Harvard Med Sch, MD, 67. *Prof Exp:* Intern, Harvard Med Unit, Boston City Hosp, 67-68, jr asst resident, 68-69, dep chief, Salmonella Unit, Ctr Dis Control, 69-70, chief, Enteric Dis Sect, USPHS, 70-72; sr resident, Harvard Med Unit, Boston City Hosp, 72-73, clin fel, instr & clin res assoc, 73-75, asst vis physician, 75-80. *Concurrent Pos:* Asst prof med, Harvard Med Sch, 75-; courtesy staff, Mt Auburn Hosp, 75-77, active staff, 78- *Mem:* Am Gastroenterol Asn; Am Soc Gastrointestinal Endoscopy. *Res:* Clinical use of tumor markers, particularly carcinoembryonic antigen. *Mailing Add:* Mt Auburn Hosp 330 Mt Auburn St Cambridge MA 02138

LOEWENSTEIN, MORRISON, DAIRY CHEMISTRY, NUTRITION. *Current Pos:* prof, 66-81, EMER PROF DAIRY SCI, UNIV GA, 81- *Personal Data:* b Kearney, Nebr, Aug 21, 15; m 39, Genevieve Johnson; c Kentley A, Roger E & Douglas B. *Educ:* Univ Nebr, BS, 38; Kans State Univ, MS, 40; Ohio State Univ, PhD(dairy tech), 54. *Prof Exp:* Asst dairy, Kans State Col, 38-39; asst supt, Roberts Dairy Co, 39-40; instr dairy, NMex State Col, 40-41; from asst prof to assoc prof dairy, Okla State Univ, 47-55; res dir, Crest Foods Co, Inc. 55-66, chmn bd, Sutton Crest Proteins Ltd, Can, 64-66. *Mem:* Am Dairy Sci Asn; Inst Food Technol; AAAS; Sigma Xi. *Res:* Development, modification and compositional control of new and improved dairy products and milk protein concentrates and their application in special nutritional formulations. *Mailing Add:* Presbyterian Village 1957 Overbrooke Way Austell GA 30001-1130. *E-Mail:* 71203.417@compuserve.com

LOEWENSTEIN, WALTER B, RESEARCH ADMINISTRATION, SAFETY MANAGEMENT. *Current Pos:* CONSULT, 89- *Personal Data:* b Gensungen, Ger, Dec 23, 26; US citizen; m 59, Lenore C Pearlman; c Mark V & Marcia B. *Educ:* Univ Puget Sound, BS, 49; Ohio State Univ, PhD(physics), 54. *Prof Exp:* From asst physicist to sr physicist reactor physics, Argonne Nat Lab, 54-63, head, Fast Reactor Analysis Sect, Reactor Physics Div, 63-66, mgr physics sect, Liquid Metal Fast Breeder Reactor, prog off, 66-68, assoc dir, EBR-II Proj, 68-72, actg dir, 72, dir, 72-73; dir, Safety & Analysis Dept, Elec Power Res Inst, 73-81, dep dir, Nuclear Power Div, 81-89. *Concurrent Pos:* Tech adv, US deleg, Int Conf Peaceful Uses Atomic Energy, Geneva, 58; mem staff, UK Atomic Energy Authority, Dounreay, Scotland, 59; mem, Int Atomic Energy Agency Symp, Vienna, 61, Europ-Am adv comt reactor physics, Atomic Energy Comn, 66-73 & adv comt reactor physics, 66-73; secy-treas, Am Asn Eng Soc, 90. *Mem:* Nat Acad Eng; fel Am Nuclear Soc (vpres, 88-89, pres, 89-90); fel Am Phys Soc. *Res:* Fast reactor physics and related technology, including fast reactor design, analysis and planning of fast critical experiments, fast flux irradiation facilities and conceptual studies; reactor safety; research program development; space nuclear power; technology transfer; research management; safety management. *Mailing Add:* 515 Jefferson Dr Palo Alto CA 94303. *Fax:* 650-327-7128

LOEWENSTEIN, WERNER RANDOLPH, BIOPHYSICS, CELL BIOLOGY. *Current Pos:* PROF PHYSIOL & BIOPHYS & CHMN DEPT, SCH MED, UNIV MIAMI, 71- *Personal Data:* b Spangenberg, Ger, Feb 14, 26; m 52, 71; c 4. *Educ:* Univ Chile, BSc(physics) & BSc(biol), 45, PhD(physiol), 50. *Prof Exp:* From instr to assoc prof physiol, Univ Chile, 51-57; res zoologist, Univ Calif, Los Angeles, 54-55; from asst prof to prof physiol, Col Physicians & Surgeons, Columbia Univ, 57-71. *Concurrent Pos:* Fel neurophysiol, Sch Med & Hosp, Johns Hopkins Univ, 53-54, Kellogg Int fel physiol, 53-55; Block lectr, Univ Chicago, 60; lectr, Royal Swedish Acad Sci, 66; ed, Biochem & Biophys Acta, 67-73; Fulbright distinguished prof, 70; USSR Acad Sci lectr, Leningrad, 75; mem, Biochem, Molecular Genetics & Cell Biol Sect, President's Biomed Res Adv Panel, 77; USAF sci adv bd, 82-86; ed, Handbook Sensory Physiol, 12 vols, 71-77; ed-in-chief, J Membrane Biol, 69- *Mem:* AAAS; Biophys Soc; Am Physiol Soc; Harvey Soc; fel NY Acad Sci. *Res:* Mechanisms of nerve impulse production and energy conversion at sensory nerve endings; excitation of the nerve cells; biophysics of cellular membranes; intercellular communication. *Mailing Add:* Dept Physiol & Biophys R430 Univ Miami Sch Med PO Box 016430 Miami FL 33101-6430

LOEWENTHAL, LOIS ANNE, DEVELOPMENTAL BIOLOGY, HISTOLOGY. *Current Pos:* from instr to assoc prof zool, 57-74, prof, 74-82, EMER PROF EXP BIOL, UNIV MICH, ANN ARBOR, 82- *Personal Data:* b Middletown, Conn, Oct 31, 26. *Educ:* Mt Holyoke Col, AB, 48; Brown Univ, AM, 50, PhD, 54. *Prof Exp:* Asst biol, Brown Univ, 48-53; res assoc zool, Mt Holyoke Col, 50-51; instr animal genetics, Univ Conn, 54-56. *Res:* Histology and embryology; skin and hair growth. *Mailing Add:* 55 Miner Brook Rd Middletown CT 06457

LOEWUS, FRANK A, BIOCHEMISTRY, PLANT PHYSIOLOGY. *Current Pos:* agr chemist, Dept Agr Chem, Wash State Univ, 75-80, prof biochem, 75-89, fel, 80-90, EMER PROF, INST BIOL CHEM, WASH STATE UNIV, 90- *Personal Data:* b Duluth, Minn, Oct 22, 19; m 47, Mary Walz; c Rivkah R, David I & Daniel. *Educ:* Univ Minn, BSc, 42, MSc, 50, PhD(biochem), 52. *Honors & Awards:* Charles Reid Barnes Award, Am Soc Plant Physiologists, 93. *Prof Exp:* Asst agr biochem, Univ Minn, 47-51; res assoc biochem, Univ Chicago, 52-55; chemist, USDA, 55-64; prof cell & molecular biol, Dept Biol, State Univ NY, Buffalo, 64-75. *Concurrent Pos:* Ed, Phytochem Soc NAm, 76, 80-84; mem staff, Marine Biol Lab, Woods Hole, 69-74. *Mem:* Life mem Phytochem Soc NAm (pres, 75-76); AAAS; Am Chem Soc; Am Soc Biochem & Molecular Biol; Am Soc Plant Physiol; NY Acad Sci. *Res:* Intermediary metabolism in plants, mechanisms of enzyme action; biochemistry of natural products; pollen physiology and enzymology. *Mailing Add:* Inst Biol Chem Wash State Univ PO Box 646340 Pullman WA 99164-6340. *Fax:* 509-335-7643; *E-Mail:* loewus@wsu.edu

LOEWUS, MARY W, BIOCHEMISTRY, ENZYMOLOGY. *Current Pos:* RETIRED. *Personal Data:* b Duluth, Minn, Feb 15, 23; m, Frank A; c Rivkah R, David I & Daniel. *Educ:* Univ Minn, PhD(biochem), 53. *Prof Exp:* Assoc scientist, Inst Biol Chem, Wash State Univ, 76-88. *Mem:* Am Soc Biochem & Molecular Biol. *Mailing Add:* NE 1700 Upper Dr Pullman WA 99163-4624

LOEWY, ARIEL GIDEON, CELL BIOLOGY. *Current Pos:* from instr to assoc prof, 53-65, PROF BIOL, HAVERFORD COL, 65-, CHMN DEPT, 57- *Personal Data:* b Bucharest, Roumania, Mar 12, 25; US citizen; m 51; c Michael, Andreas, Eva, Daniel & Ridley. *Educ:* McGill Univ, BSc, 45, MSc, 47; Univ Pa, PhD, 51. *Honors & Awards:* James F Mitchell Found Award, 73; Glenn Found Award, 96. *Prof Exp:* Asst instr, Univ Pa, 47-49; NIH fel & univ res fel phys chem, Harvard Univ, 50-52; Nat Res Coun fel, Cambridge Univ, 52-53. *Mem:* Am Soc Biol Chem; Am Soc Cell Biol; Am Soc Hemat; Sigma Xi. *Res:* Photosynthesis; protoplasmic streaming and contract; fibrin formation; structural proteins in cellular physiology. *Mailing Add:* Dept Biol Haverford Col Haverford PA 19041. *Fax:* 610-896-4963; *E-Mail:* aloewy@haverford.edu

LOEWY, ARTHUR D(ECOSTA), NEUROANATOMY. *Current Pos:* from asst prof to assoc prof, 75-85, PROF ANAT & NEUROBIOL, SCH MED, WASHINGTON UNIV, 85- *Personal Data:* b Chicago, Ill, Jan 9, 43; m 71; c 1. *Educ:* Lawrence Univ, BA, 64; Univ Wis-Madison, PhD(anat), 69. *Honors & Awards:* Merit Award, Nat Heart, Lung & Blood Inst, 89. *Prof Exp:* Res assoc & instr neuroanat, Univ Chicago, 69-71; res assoc, 71-74, sr res fel neuroanat, Mayo Grad Sch Med, Univ Minn, 74-75. *Concurrent Pos:* Investr, Am Heart Asn. *Mem:* Soc Neurosci; Am Physiol Soc. *Res:* Organization of central autonomic pathways; neural control of cardiovascular system. *Mailing Add:* Dept Anat & Neurobiol Sch Med Wash Univ 660 S Euclid Ave St Louis MO 63110. *Fax:* 314-362-3446

LOEWY, ROBERT G(USTAV), AERONAUTICAL & MECHANICAL ENGINEERING. *Current Pos:* PROF & CHMN, SCH AEROSPACE ENG, GA INST TECHNOL, 93- *Personal Data:* b Philadelphia, Pa, Feb 12, 26; m 55, Lila Spinner; c Esther Elizabeth, Joanne Victoria & Raymond Matthew. *Educ:* Rensselaer Polytech Inst, BAE, 47; Mass Inst Technol, MS, 48; Univ Pa, PhD(eng mech), 62. *Honors & Awards:* Lawrence Sperry Award, Am Inst Aeronaut & Astronaut, 58; Except Civilian Serv Award, USAF, 66, 75 & 85; Nikolsky Mem Lectr, Am Helicopter Soc, 84; Spirit of St Louis Medal, Am Soc Mech Engrs, 96. *Prof Exp:* Res asst, Mass Inst Technol, 48; sr vibration engr, Martin Co, Md, 48-49; assoc res engr, Cornell Aero Lab, Buffalo, 49-52, prin engr, 53-55; staff stress engr, Piasecki Helicopter Corp, Pa, 52-53; chief dynamics engr, Vertol Aircraft Corp, Pa, 55-58, chief tech engr, 58-62; from assoc prof to prof mech & aerospace sci, Univ Rochester, 62-74, dean, Col Eng & Appl Sci, 67-74; vpres acad affairs & provost, Rensselaer Polytech Inst, 74-78, inst prof mech & aerospace sci, 78-93, dir, Rotorcraft Technol Ctr, 82-93. *Concurrent Pos:* Consult, 59-; chief scientist, Dept Air Force, 65-66, dir, Space Sci Ctr, Univ Rochester, 66-71; mem, Res & Eng Adv Coun, US Post Off Dept, 66-68 & Aviation Sci Adv Group, US Army Aviation Mat Command, 67-71; mem, Div Adv Group, Aeronaut Systs Div, USAF, 67-69, chmn, 78-84 Sci Adv Bd, 67-76 & 78-85, vchmn, 71-73, chmn, 73-76; mem, Mil Aircraft Panel, President's Sci Adv Coun, 68-72; mem, Aeronaut Comt, Res & Technol Adv Coun, NASA, 71-74, chmn, Aeronaut Adv Comt, 77-83. *Mem:* Nat Acad Eng; hon fel Am Inst Aeronaut & Astronaut; hon fel Am Helicopter Soc; Am Soc Eng Educ; fel AAAS. *Res:* Structural dynamics and aeroelasticity; unsteady aerodynamics; rotorcraft technology. *Mailing Add:* 3420 Wood Valley Rd Atlanta GA 30327. *Fax:* 404-894-2760

LOF, JOHN L(ARS) C(OLE), ELECTRICAL ENGINEERING. *Current Pos:* from asst prof to prof, 52-76, dir, Comput Ctr, 61-76, EMER PROF ELEC ENG, UNIV CONN, 76- *Personal Data:* b Denver, Colo, Dec 11, 15; m 48, Ruth Addison; c Richard. *Educ:* Univ Denver, BS, 38; Mass Inst Technol, SM, 41, EE, 51. *Honors & Awards:* Inst Elec Eng Prize, Inst Elec & Electronics Engrs, 58. *Prof Exp:* Asst elec eng, Mass Inst Technol, 38-45, res assoc, 45-49, instr, 49-52. *Mem:* Am Soc Eng Educ; Inst Elec & Electronics Engrs; Sigma Xi. *Res:* Electronic computing systems; analog and digital computers; digital differential analyzers. *Mailing Add:* 74 Willington Hill Rd Storrs CT 06268

LOFERSKI, JOSEPH J, SEMICONDUCTORS, PHOTOVOLTAIC ENERGY CONVERSION. *Current Pos:* assoc prof, Brown Univ, 61-66, chmn, Div Eng, 68-74, assoc dean, Grad Sch, 80-83, PROF ELEC ENG, BROWN UNIV, 66- *Personal Data:* b Hudson, Pa, Aug 7, 25; m 49; c 6. *Educ:* Univ Scranton, BS, 48; Univ Pa, MS, 49, PhD(physics), 53. *Honors & Awards:* Freeman Medal, Providence Eng Soc, 74; Wm E Cherry Award, Inst Elec & Electronics Engrs, 81. *Prof Exp:* Res assoc physics, Univ Pa, 52-53; res physicist, RCA Labs, 53-60. *Concurrent Pos:* Chmn exec comt, Div Eng, Brown Univ, 68-74; vis sr scientist Europ Space Res Orgn, Holland, 67-68; mem res & technol adv comt space power & elec propulsion, NASA, 69-71; mem solar energy panel, comt energy res & develop goals, US Off Sci & Technol, 71-72; consult, Exxon Labs, 73-80, Honeywell Inc, 77-79, & Jet Propulsion Labs, 78-85; exchange fel, US-Poland Acad of Sci, 74-75; pres, Solamat Inc, 77-82; mem, Organizing Comt II through XXII, Inst Elec & Electronics Engrs Photovoltaic Specialists Confs & Sixth Europ Photovolataic Conf, 84, First thru Fifth Int Photovoltaic Sci & Technol Confs, Japan, China & Australia, 84-90; sci counr, US Embassy, Warsaw, Poland, 85-87, co-dir, Ctr Thin Film Res, 87-; mem, US-Poland Joint Bd for Coop in Sci & Technol, 88-; chmn, Fifth Int Conf Solid Films & Surfaces, Brown Univ, 91. *Mem:* Fel AAAS; fel Inst Elec & Electronics Engrs; Am Phys Soc; Sigma Xi. *Res:* Semiconductor physics; photovoltaic effect; radiation effects in semiconductors and semiconductor devices; large scale utilization of solar energy; author or co-author of over 140 publications; thin film deposition and characterization. *Mailing Add:* 33 Slater Ave Providence RI 02906

LOFFELMAN, FRANK FRED, ORGANIC CHEMISTRY. *Current Pos:* Res chemist, 54-65, group leader, 65-76, proj leader, 76-81, MGR, PLASTICS ADDITIVES & FINE CHEM RES & DEVELOP, CHEM RES DIV, AM CYANAMID CO, 81- *Personal Data:* b St Louis, Mo, Nov 29, 25; m 45; c 1. *Educ:* Loyola Univ (Ill), BS, 49; Notre Dame Univ, PhD(chem), 54. *Mem:* Am Chem Soc; Sigma Xi; Soc Plastics Engrs; Sigma Xi. *Res:* Organic synthesis; dyestuffs; optical bleaches; light stabilizers for thermoplastics; medicinals; fine chemicals; antioxidants; flame retardants. *Mailing Add:* 1255 Cornell Rd Bridgewater NJ 08807-2301

LOFGREEN, GLEN PEHR, ANIMAL NUTRITION. *Current Pos:* RETIRED. *Personal Data:* b St David, Ariz, Sept 28, 19; m 45; c 7. *Educ:* Univ Ariz, BS, 44; Cornell Univ, MS, 46; PhD(animal nutrit), 48. *Honors & Awards:* Am Feed Mfrs Nutrit Award, 63. *Prof Exp:* Asst prof animal husb, Mont State Col, 48; from asst prof to assoc prof, Univ Calif, Davis, 48-61, prof, 68-81, emer prof animal husb, 81-; dept animal sci, NMex State Univ. *Concurrent Pos:* Grant, Univ Hawaii, 58-59; consult, USDA; mem subcomt beef cattle nutrit, Nat Res Coun. *Mem:* Am Soc Animal Sci (vpres, 60); Am Dairy Sci Asn. *Res:* Nutrient requirements and feed evaluation on large domestic animals; calcium and phosphorus metabolism. *Mailing Add:* 1624 Driftwood Dr El Centro CA 92243

LOFGREN, CLIFFORD SWANSON, ENTOMOLOGY. *Current Pos:* PROF ENTOM, INST FOOD & AGR SCI, UNIV FLA, 80- *Personal Data:* b St James, Minn, July 29, 25; m 54; c 3. *Educ:* Gustavus Adolphus Col, BA, 50; Univ Minn, MS, 54; Univ Fla, PhD(entom), 68. *Prof Exp:* Entomologist, Entom Res Div, Agr Res Serv, USDA, 55-57 & Plant Pest Control Div, 57-63, entomologist, Insects Affecting Man Res Lab, 63- *Concurrent Pos:* Asst prof entom & asst entomologist, Univ Fla, 74-80. *Mem:* Entom Soc Am; Am Mosquito Control Asn; Int Union Study Social Insects. *Res:* Methods of controlling mosquitoes, imported fire ants and other insects of medical importance, particularly insecticides and equipment evaluation; studies on resistance, chemosterilants, pheromones and biology. *Mailing Add:* 1321 NW 31st Dr Gainesville FL 32605

LOFGREN, EDWARD JOSEPH, PHYSICS, ACCELERATORS. *Current Pos:* physicist, Lawrence Berkeley Nat Lab, Univ Calif, 40-44 & 45-46, group leader, 48-73, assoc dir, 73-79, sr staff scientist, 79-81, EMER ASSOC DIR, LAWRENCE BERKELEY NAT LAB, UNIV CALIF, 82- *Personal Data:* b Chicago, Ill, Jan 18, 14; m 38, 68; c Helen, Laurel (Phillipson) & Claire. *Educ:* Univ Calif, AB, 38, PhD(physics), 46. *Prof Exp:* Asst, Univ Calif, 38-40; group leader, Los Alamos Sci Lab, 44-45; asst prof physics, Univ Minn, 46-48. *Concurrent Pos:* With Europ Orgn Nuclear Res, 59; mem, High Energy Physics Adv panel, 67-70. *Mem:* Fel AAAS; fel Am Phys Soc. *Res:* Elementary particle physics; accelerators for particle and heavy-ion physics and for biomedical applications; separation of uranium isotopes; discovery of heavy component of cosmic rays. *Mailing Add:* Lawrence Berkeley Nat Lab Univ Calif Bldg 47 Berkeley CA 94720. *Fax:* 510-486-5392

LOFGREN, GARY ERNEST, EXPERIMENTAL PETROLOGY, PLANETARY SCIENCES. *Current Pos:* SPACE GEOSCIENTIST, JOHNSON SPACE CTR, NASA, 68- *Personal Data:* b Los Angeles, Calif, Apr 17, 41. *Educ:* Stanford Univ, BS, 63, PhD(geol), 69; Dartmouth Col, MA, 65. *Honors & Awards:* Super Achievement Award, NASA, 78; Spec Commendation, Geol Soc Am, 73. *Prof Exp:* Res asst geol, Dartmouth Col, 63-65; res geologist, Cold Regions Res & Eng Lab, 65; teaching asst, Stanford Univ, 65-68. *Concurrent Pos:* Mem, Lunar Sample Preliminary Exam Team, 69-72; team leader, Basaltic Volcanism Study Proj, 76-81; convener, Penrose Conf, Geol Soc Am, 76; adj prof, Univ Houston, 76-87. *Mem:* Fel Geol Soc Am; fel Mineral Soc Am; Am Geophys Union; Sigma Xi; fel Meteoritical Soc. *Res:* Crystallization properties of silicate melts with emphasis on the kinetics of nucleation and crystal growth; textures of igneous rocks and rock genesis. *Mailing Add:* Johnson Space Ctr NASA SN4 Houston TX 77058. *Fax:* 281-483-2696; *E-Mail:* gary.e.lofgren@jsc.nasa.gov

LOFGREN, JAMES R, PLANT BREEDING, GENETICS. *Current Pos:* STA MGR & PLANT BREEDER, PIONEER HI-BRED INT, INC, 93- *Personal Data:* b West Point, Nebr, May 18, 31; m 62; c 3. *Educ:* Univ Nebr, BS, 60; NDak State Univ, MS, 62; Kans State Univ, PhD(plant breeding, genetics), 68. *Prof Exp:* Asst agron, NDak State Univ, 60-62; res asst, Kans State Univ, 62-67; asst prof, Northwest Exp Sta, Univ Minn, 67-71; agronomist-plant breeder, Dahlgren & Co, Inc, 71-93. *Mem:* Am Soc Agron; Crop Sci Soc Am. *Res:* Breeding and genetics of sunflowers to improve productivity and quality. *Mailing Add:* RR 4 Moorhead MN 56560

LOFGREN, KARL ADOLPH, SURGERY. *Current Pos:* EMER STAFF MEM, MAYO CLIN, 82- *Personal Data:* b Killeberg, Sweden, Apr 1, 15; US citizen; m 42, Jean Frances Taylor; c Karl Edward & Anne. *Educ:* Harvard Med Sch, MD, 41; Univ Minn, MS, 47; Am Bd Surg, dipl, 53. *Prof Exp:* Intern, Univ Minn Hosp, 41-42; resident surg, Mayo Grad Sch Med, Univ Minn, 42-44 & 46-48; resident, Royal Acad Hosp, Univ Uppsala, 49; asst to staff, Mayo Clin, 49-50, mem surg staff, 50-81; from instr to asst prof, Mayo Grad Sch Med, 51-74, from assoc prof to prof, 74-81, emer prof surg, Mayo Med Sch, 82- *Concurrent Pos:* Head sect peripheral vein surg, Mayo Clin, 66-79, sr consult, 79-81. *Mem:* Fel Am Col Surgeons; Int Cardiovasc Soc; Soc Vascular Surg; Swed Surg Soc; Sigma Xi; Midwestern Vascular Surg Soc. *Res:* Peripheral venous disorders. *Mailing Add:* 1001 Seventh Ave NE Rochester MN 55906-7074

LOFGREN, PHILIP ALLEN, NUTRITION, RESEARCH ADMINISTRATION. *Current Pos:* CONSULT NUTRIT RES, NAT LIVESTOCK & MEAT BD, 92- *Personal Data:* b Iowa, July 30, 44; m 77, Lousanne Halverson; c Kristofer A. *Educ:* Iowa State Univ, BS, 66; Cornell Univ, MS, 69, PhD(nutrit), 71. *Prof Exp:* Res asst animal nutrit, Cornell Univ, 66-71; fel nutrit, Univ Calif, Berkeley, 72-73; asst dir, 73-85, dir grant serv, Nutrit Res, Nat Dairy Coun, 85-92. *Mem:* Am Dairy Sci Asn; Inst Food Technologists; Am Oil Chemists Soc; Am Inst Nutrit. *Res:* Human and animal nutrition; unidentified growth factors; nutrient interactions; nutritional physiology of food intake regulation; research program management; food, nutrition and health issues; research interpretation; technical writing. *Mailing Add:* 922 N East Ave Oak Park IL 60302-1330

LOFQUIST, GEORGE W, MATHEMATICS, COMPUTER SCIENCES. *Current Pos:* from asst prof to prof, 67-93, EMER PROF MATH, ECKERD COL, 93- *Personal Data:* b Brookhaven, Miss, Oct 6, 30; m 55; c 2. *Educ:* Univ NC, BS, 52, MEd, 59; La State Univ, Baton Rouge, MS, 63, PhD(math), 67; Univ SFla, MS, 89. *Prof Exp:* Instr math, La State Univ, New Orleans, 59-64 & Baton Rouge, 66-67. *Mem:* Am Math Soc; Math Asn Am. *Res:* Algebra; number theory. *Mailing Add:* 118 College Circle Swannanoa NC 28778

LOFQUIST, MARVIN JOHN, INORGANIC CHEMISTRY. *Current Pos:* mem fac, 73-88, prof & dept head, Phys Sci Dept, 81-92, ADMIN, FERRIS STATE UNIV, 92- *Personal Data:* b Chicago, Ill, Oct 19, 43; m 65; c 2. *Educ:* Augustana Col, BA, 65; Northwestern Univ, PhD(inorg chem), 70. *Prof Exp:* Asst prof chem, Camrose Lutheran Col, 69-73. *Mem:* Am Chem Soc. *Res:* Kinetics and mechanisms of organometallic transition metal complexes. *Mailing Add:* 478 Sheridan Rd Evanston IL 60202

LOFSTROM, JOHN GUSTAVE, ANALYTICAL CHEMISTRY. *Current Pos:* RETIRED. *Personal Data:* b Mason, Wis, June 4, 27; m 52, Adeline K Poulsen; c John R, Susan M & Christine L. *Educ:* Northwestern Univ, BS, 50; Univ Wis, PhD(chem), 54. *Prof Exp:* Asst prof chem, Univ Wis, 50-52; res chemist, Photo Prod Dept, E I du Pont de Nemours & Co, Inc, 53-66, sr res chemist, 66-85. *Mem:* Sigma Xi. *Res:* Instrumental analyses; granted 1 US patent. *Mailing Add:* 58 McGuire St Metuchen NJ 08840

LOFT, JOHN T, CHEMISTRY. *Current Pos:* new bus coordr, Loctite Corp, 77-79, proj mgr mkt, 79-83, mgr com develop, 83-86, MGR COM DEVELOP, NEW BUS DEVELOP, LOCTITE CORP, 86- *Personal Data:* b Mankato, Minn, July 21, 32; m 53; c 2. *Educ:* Gustavus Adolphus Col, BA, 54; State Univ Iowa, MS, 56, PhD(chem), 58. *Prof Exp:* Sr res chemist, Sundry Dix Oil Co, 58-65 & Celanese Corp, 65-68; com develop, Celanese Plastics Co, 68-72; projs mgr, Microporus Div, Amerace Corp, 72-77. *Concurrent Pos:* Lectr, Chem Dept, Univ Tulsa, 60; chmn, Tulsa Sect, Am Chem Soc, 63-65. *Mailing Add:* 18 Holly Lane Avon CT 06001-3432

LOFTFIELD, ROBERT BERNER, ORGANIC CHEMISTRY, BIOCHEMISTRY. *Current Pos:* chmn dept, 64-71 & 78-90, prof, 64-90, EMER PROF BIOCHEM, MED SCH, UNIV NMEX, 90- *Personal Data:* b Detroit, Mich, Dec 15, 19; wid; c 10. *Educ:* Harvard Univ, BS, 41, MA, 42, PhD(org chem), 46. *Honors & Awards:* Warren Triennial Prize, 53. *Prof Exp:* Asst chem, Harvard Univ, 42-44; res assoc, 44-46; res assoc, Mass Inst Technol, 46-48; res assoc, Mass Gen Hosp, 48-56, assoc biochemist, 56-64; assoc, Harvard Med Sch, 56-60, asst prof org chem, 60-64. *Concurrent Pos:* Fel, Brookhaven Nat Lab, 50; Runyon fel, Medinska Nobel Inst, Stockholm, 52-53; Guggenheim fel, Med Res Coun, Cambridge, Eng, 61-62; USPHS sr res fel, Dunn Sch Path, Oxford Univ, 71-72; chief spec assistance div, Off Strategic Serv, 46-47; tutor, Harvard Univ, 48-64; instr, Marine Biol Lab, Woods Hole, 59-62; mem biochem study sect, USPHS, 64-68; mem adv comn pathogenesis of cancer, Am Cancer Soc, 64-67, mem adv comn proteins & nucleic acids, 71-74; Fulbright prof, Abo Akademi, Turku, Finland, 77; mem, Fulbright Adv Comn, 78-81; Fulbright & Heinemann Stiftung fel, Med Univ, Hannover, Ger, 83. *Mem:* Am Chem Soc; Am Soc Biol Chem; Am Asn Cancer Res; Biophys Soc; Am Pub Health Asn. *Res:* Radioactive carbon 14 techniques; organic synthesis; organic reaction mechanisms; protein biosynthesis; mechanism of enzymic catalysis. *Mailing Add:* Univ NMex Med Sch Albuquerque NM 87131. *Fax:* 505-272-9107

LOFTIN, KARIN CHRISTIANE, AEROSPACE BIOMEDICINE, KNOWLEDGE-BASED SYSTEM IN MEDICINE. *Current Pos:* SR SCIENTIST, KRUG, LIFE SCIS INC, 89- *Personal Data:* m 72, Richard B; c Elisabeth & Benjamin. *Educ:* Oakland Univ, Mich, BA, 70; Univ Tex, MS, 73, PhD(biomed sci), 79. *Prof Exp:* Vis instr gen biol, Univ Houston, Univ Park, 79-81; res asst, Dept Pediat, Univ Tex Med Br, 82, res assoc, Microbiol Dept, 82, Henry Holcomb fel, Dept Clin Immunol & Biol Ther, Univ Tex-M D Anderson Hosp, 83-84, instr microbiol prog infectious dis & clin microbiol, Univ Tex Med Sch, Houston, 84-86, sr res assoc dept obstet gynec, 86-89. *Mem:* Sigma Xi; Nat Mgt Asn; Am Soc Microbiol; Am Asn Artificial Intel. *Res:* Study man's immune response and host resistance to do adverse environmental conditions such as high altitude and microgravity and the application of new technology, such as artificial intelligence, to medical systems. *Mailing Add:* 1906 Silver Bank Ct Houston TX 77058-4229. *Fax:* 281-212-1316; *E-Mail:* kloftin@medics.jsc.nasa.gov

LOFTNESS, ROBERT L(ELAND), nuclear engineering; deceased, see previous edition for last biography

LOFTSGAARDEN, DON OWEN, MATHEMATICAL STATISTICS. *Current Pos:* from asst prof to assoc prof, Univ Mont, 67-75, chmn dept, 78-79, dept chair, 92-95, PROF MATH, UNIV MONT, 75-,. *Personal Data:* b Big Timber, Mont, July 7, 39; m 62, Nenette Blake; c Debra, Lisa & Meta. *Educ:* Mont State Univ, BS, 61, MS, 63, PhD(math statist), 64. *Prof Exp:* Res engr, Autonetics Div, NAm Aviation, Inc, 62; statistician, Battelle Mem Inst, 63; instr statist, Mont State Univ, 64-65; asst prof, Western Mich Univ, 65-67. *Mem:* Am Statist Asn; Inst Math Statist; Math Asn Am. *Res:* Statistical inference. *Mailing Add:* Dept Math Univ Mont Missoula MT 59812. *Fax:* 406-243-2674; *E-Mail:* ma_dol@selway.umt.edu

LOFTUS, JOSEPH P, JR, STATISTICS, PSYCHOLOGY. *Current Pos:* chief, Opers Integ Br, Syst Eng Div, NASA, 64-68, mgr, Prog Eng Off, 68-70, chief, Tech Planning Off, 70-83, ASST DIR PLANS, JOHNSON SPACE CTR, NASA, 83- *Personal Data:* b Chicago, Ill, Aug 31, 30; m 58; c 6. *Educ:* Cath Univ Am, Wash, DC, BA, 53; Fordham Univ, NY, MA, 56. *Honors & Awards:* Commendation Medal, USAF, 62. *Prof Exp:* Res psychologist, Aerospace Med Lab, Wright-Patterson AFB, 59-61. *Concurrent Pos:* Vchmn, Tech Houston Sect, 73-75, Econ Tech Comt, 72-75, 77-79; Sloan fel, Grad Sch Bus, Stanford Univ, 75-76; chmn, Space Systs Tech Comt, 81, 83, 85, Space Transp Tech Comt, 86-87; gen chmn, Space Technol, Progs Conf, Houston, 86; ed, Orbital Debris From Upper Stage Breakup, Am Inst Aeronaut & Astronaut, Progress in Aeronaut & Astronaut, Vol 121, 89; gen chmn, Am Inst Aeronaut & Astronaut/Dept Defense Orbital Debris Conf, Baltimore, MD, 89; mem, IAA Life Sci Comt, 85-89, secy, Space Policies & Plans Comt, 89-; prog comt, Human Factor Soc, 80. *Mem:* Int Acad Astronaut; Am Astronaut Soc. *Res:* Orbital debris; launch system technologies; manned spacecraft control and life support systems. *Mailing Add:* NASA Johnson Space Ctr Webster-Seabrook Rd Houston TX 77058. *Fax:* 713-483-6636

LOGAN, ALAN, PALEOECOLOGY. *Current Pos:* asst prof, 67-70, assoc prof, 70-76, PROF GEOL, UNIV NB, ST JOHN, 76- *Personal Data:* b Newcastle-on-Tyne, Eng, Sept 20, 37; m 62; c 2. *Educ:* Univ Durham, BSc, 59, PhD(paleont), 62. *Prof Exp:* Lectr paleont, Univ Leeds, 64-67. *Concurrent Pos:* Nat Res Coun fel, McMaster Univ, 62-64; vis fel, Univ Calgary. *Mem:* Int Soc Reef Studies. *Res:* Paleontology, paleoecology and ecology of Permian, Triassic and Holocene bivalves and brachiopods; ecology of Holocene coral reefs. *Mailing Add:* Dept Phys Sci Univ NB Tucker Park St John NB E2L 4L5 Can. *Fax:* 506-648-5650; *E-Mail:* logan@unbsj.ca

LOGAN, BRIAN ANTHONY, NUCLEAR PHYSICS. *Current Pos:* lectr, 65-66, from asst prof to assoc prof, 66-81, PROF PHYSICS, UNIV OTTAWA, 81- *Personal Data:* b Newcastle-upon-Tyne, Eng, Dec 22, 38; m 69; c 2. *Educ:* Univ Birmingham, BSc, 60, PhD(physics), 64. *Prof Exp:* Res assoc physics, Univ Birmingham, 64-65. *Mem:* Can Asn Physicists; Am Phys Soc. *Res:* Nuclear physics. *Mailing Add:* Dept Physics Univ Ottawa Ottawa ON K1N 6N5 Can

LOGAN, CHARLES DONALD, WOOD CHEMISTRY. *Current Pos:* RETIRED. *Personal Data:* b St John, NB, May 15, 24; wid; c 3. *Educ:* Mt Allison Univ, BSc, 45; McGill Univ, PhD(org chem), 49. *Prof Exp:* From res chemist to sr res chemist, Que & Ont Paper Co, Ltd, 49-65, asst dir, 65-74, dir chem res, 74-84. *Mem:* Am Chem Soc; Am Pulp & Paper Assoc; Brit Paper & Board Makers Asn; Can Res Mgt Asn; Chem Inst Can. *Res:* Vanillin and lignin chemistry; ion exchange chemical recovery; pulp and paper by-product utilization; chemimech pulping. *Mailing Add:* 9 Marlene Dr St Catharines ON L2T 3E7 Can

LOGAN, CHERYL ANN, ANIMAL BEHAVIOR, NEUROPSYCHOLOGY. *Current Pos:* Asst prof, 74-79, ASSOC PROF PSYCHOL, UNIV NC, GREENSBORO, 80- *Personal Data:* b Syracuse, NY, Apr 1, 45. *Educ:* Southern Methodist Univ, BA, 67; Univ Calif, San Diego, PhD, 74. *Mem:* Animal Behav Soc; Am Ornith Union; Sigma Xi. *Res:* Animal communication; ecology and evolution of learning; structure and function of birdsong; territorial and reproductive function of mockingbird song. *Mailing Add:* Dept Psychol Univ NC 272 Eberhart Greensboro NC 27412

LOGAN, DARYL LEE, STRESS ANALYSIS USING FINITE ELEMENT METHOD, MACHINE DESIGN & ANALYSIS. *Current Pos:* chair, Mech Eng Dept, 93-96, PROF, UNIV WIS-PLATTEVILLE, 93- *Personal Data:* b Goodman, Wis, Nov 12, 48; m, Diane M Laechelt; c Katherine, Daryl Jr & Paul. *Educ:* Univ Ill, Chicago, BS, 71, MS, 72, PhD(struct mech), 77. *Prof Exp:* Asst prof, Rose Hulman Inst Technol, 77-82, assoc prof, 82-93. *Concurrent Pos:* Vis lectr, Univ Ill, Chicago, 83. *Mem:* Am Soc Eng Educ; Am Soc Mech Engrs. *Res:* Mechanics of materials and finite element method; author of several technical papers. *Mailing Add:* Dept Mech Eng Univ Wis 1 University Plaza Platteville WI 53818. *Fax:* 608-342-1566; *E-Mail:* logan@uwplate.edu

LOGAN, DAVID ALEXANDER, MICROBIOLOGY. *Current Pos:* PROF BIOL, CLARK ATLANTA UNIV, 95- *Personal Data:* b Abingdon, Va, Dec 7, 52; m 76. *Educ:* Knoxville Col, BS, 75; Univ Tenn, MS, 77, PhD(microbiol), 81. *Prof Exp:* Teaching asst microbiol, Univ Tenn, 75-80; instr biol, Knoxville Col, 80-81; lab asst med microbiol, Univ Calif, Irvine, 82, 83 & 84; asst prof biol, cell biol & microbiol, Drexel Univ, 84-95. *Mem:* Am Soc Microbiol; Mycol Soc Am. *Res:* Biochemistry of proteinases in fungi. *Mailing Add:* Dept Biol Sci Sci Res Ctr Clark Atlanta Univ Rm 4040 James P Brawley Dr SW Atlanta GA 30314

LOGAN, DAVID MACKENZIE, MOLECULAR BIOLOGY, BIOCHEMISTRY. *Current Pos:* from asst prof to assoc prof, 68-88, PROF MOLECULAR BIOL, YORK UNIV, 89; ASSOC DEAN PURE & APPL SCI, 93- *Personal Data:* b Toronto, Ont, July 23, 37; m 60, Susan E Hanna; c Richard, Heather & Michael. *Educ:* Univ Toronto, BA, 60, MA, 63, PhD(med biophys), 65. *Prof Exp:* Res assoc biochem, NIH, 65-67; Nat Res Coun Can fel, McMaster Univ, 67-68. *Concurrent Pos:* Jane Coffin Childs Mem Fund fel med res, 65-67. *Mem:* AAAS; Biophys Soc; Can Biochem Soc; NY Acad Sci; Environ Mutagen Soc. *Res:* Biochemical and biophysical aspects of nerve-muscle interactions; short term essays of biohazardous chemicals, in particular para-amino-hippuric acid bioremediation of contaminated sites; toxicology. *Mailing Add:* Off Pure & Appl Sci 108 Steacie Sci Bldg York Univ 4700 Keele St North York ON M3J 1P3 Can

LOGAN, GEORGE BRYAN, PEDIATRICS. *Current Pos:* From instr to prof pediat, Univ Minn, Mayo Grad Sch Med, 40-73, prof pediat, Mayo Med Sch, 73-75, EMER STAFF, MAYO CLIN, 75- *Personal Data:* b Pittsburgh, Pa, Aug 1, 09; m 39; c 2. *Educ:* Washington & Jefferson Col, BS, 30; Harvard Univ, MD, 34; Univ Minn, MS, 40; Am Bd Pediat, dipl, 41; Am Bd Allergy & Immunol, dipl, 72. *Concurrent Pos:* Consult, Sect Pediat, Mayo Clin, 40-68, sr consult, 68-75; chmn sub-bd allergy, Am Bd Pediat, 63-66. *Mem:* AAAS; Am Pediat Soc; AMA; Am Acad Allergy & Immunol; Am Acad Pediat (pres, 67-68). *Res:* Allergic and liver diseases in children. *Mailing Add:* 211 Second St NW Apt 907 Rochester MN 55902

LOGAN, H(ENRY) L(EON), engineering; deceased, see previous edition for last biography

LOGAN, JAMES COLUMBUS, BATTERY RESEARCH & DEVELOPMENT, CORPORATE MANAGEMENT. *Current Pos:* VPRES, ALTUS CORP, 79- *Personal Data:* b Baltimore, Md. *Educ:* Johns Hopkins Univ, BES, 68; Harvard Univ, MS, 69, PhD(appl physics), 73. *Prof Exp:* Res fel, Calif Inst Technol, 73-75; br head, Naval Ocean Syts Ctr, 75-79. *Mem:* Am Phys Soc; Am Soc Metals; AAAS. *Res:* Research and development of new batteries; lithium batteries and primary lithium batteries. *Mailing Add:* 2055 Yale St Palo Alto CA 94306

LOGAN, JAMES EDWARD, CLINICAL CHEMISTRY, HEMATOLOGY. *Current Pos:* RETIRED. *Personal Data:* b Thorndale, Ont, Jan 14, 20; m 82; c 2. *Educ:* Univ Western Ontario, BSc, 49, PhD(biochem), 52. *Honors & Awards:* Ames Award, Can Soc Clin Chem, 81. *Prof Exp:* Sr res asst biochem, Univ Western Ont, 52-54; chemist, Biol Control Labs, Can Dept Nat Health & Welfare, 54-59, sr biochemist, Clin Labs, 59-73, chief clin chem, 73-77, actg dir, Bur Med Biochem, 77-79, chief clin chem, Lab Ctr Dis Control, 79-84. *Concurrent Pos:* Chmn, Int Fedn Clin Chem Expert Panel, Evaluation Diag Reagent Sets, 79- *Mem:* Fel Nat Acad Clin Biochem; Can Soc Clin Chem; Am Asn Clin Chem; Can Biochem Soc. *Res:* Chemistry of peripheral nervous system; radioisotope tracer studies; quality control and methodology; hemoglobin; evaluation of diagnostic kits and clinical laboratory instruments; radioimmunoassay; reference methods; trace element analyses. *Mailing Add:* 2005 Saville Row Ottawa ON K2A 1A3 Can

LOGAN, JESSE ALAN, population ecology, entomology, for more information see previous edition

LOGAN, JOHN MERLE, STRUCTURAL GEOLOGY, TECTONOPHYSICS. *Current Pos:* from asst prof to assoc prof geol & geophys, 67-78, dir, Ctr Tectonophys, 84-86, PROF EXP ROCK DEFORMATION, DEPT GEOPHYS & GEOL, TEX A&M UNIV, 78- *Personal Data:* b Pittsburgh, Pa, July 7, 34; m 82, Lorna. *Educ:* Mich State Univ, BS, 56; Univ Okla, MS, 62, PhD(geol), 65. *Prof Exp:* Geologist, Shell Develop Co, 65-67. *Concurrent Pos:* Advan Projs Res Agency, US Dept Defense res grant, 71-78, US Geol Surv grant, 71-85 & NSF grant, 71-86; consult, Amoco Prod Co, 67-86, Los Alamos Nat Lab, 78-86 & John M Logan & Assocs, Inc. *Mem:* Assoc Geol Soc Am; assoc Am Geophys Union; AAAS. *Res:* Experimental rock deformation as applied to structural geological problems and architectural and engineering of building exteriors. *Mailing Add:* Dept Geol Tex A&M Univ College Station TX 77843-0100

LOGAN, JOSEPH GRANVILLE, JR, PHYSICS. *Current Pos:* RETIRED. *Personal Data:* b Washington, DC, June 8, 20; m 44; c 2. *Educ:* DC Teachers Col, BS, 41; Univ Buffalo, PhD(physics), 55. *Prof Exp:* Physicist aerodyn, Nat Bur Stand, 43-47; physicist aerodyn propulsion, Cornell Aeronaut Lab, Inc, 47-57; head aerophys lab, Space Technol Labs, Inc, 57-59, mgr propulsion res dept, 59-60; dir aerodyn & propulsion lab, Aerospace Corp, 60-67; spec asst to dir res & develop, Western Div, McDonnell Douglas Astronaut Co, 67-69, mgr vulnerability & hardening develop eng, 69-72, chief engr nuclear weapons effects, Western Div, 72-74; pres, Appl Energy Sci, Inc, 74-78; dir physics dept, Calif Polytech Univ, Pomona, 78-79; dir, Urban Univ Ctr, Univ Southern Calif, 79-89. *Mem:* Am Phys Soc; NY Acad Sci. *Res:* New energy systems. *Mailing Add:* 3652 Olympiad Dr Los Angeles CA 90043

LOGAN, JOSEPH SKINNER, INSULATORS, ELECTROSTATIC CHUCKS. *Current Pos:* CONSULT. *Personal Data:* b New York, NY, June 4, 32; m 52, Nancy Allen; c Jennifer M, Joseph S Jr, Susan (Huber) & Annette. *Educ:* Cornell Univ, BEE, 55, MS, 56; Stanford Univ, PhD(elec eng), 61. *Prof Exp:* Adv engr, IBM Corp, 60-71, sr engr, E Fishkill Facil, 71-83, sr engr res, 84-92. *Mem:* Inst Elec & Electronics Engrs; Electrochem Soc; Am Vacuum Soc. *Res:* Semiconductor surface physics and device development; radio frequency sputtering of thin insulator films; resputtering; plasma processing. *Mailing Add:* 149 Seaside Dr Jamestown RI 02835. *E-Mail:* 73772.27@compuserve.com

LOGAN, KATHRYN VANCE, MATERIALS RESEARCH & DEVELOPMENT. *Current Pos:* From res engr I to sr res engr, Ga Inst Technol, 70-92, HEAD, CERAMIC BR, GA INST TECHNOL, 89-, PRIN RES ENGR, 92-, INTERM ASST VPRES, INTERDISCIPLINARY PROG, 92- *Personal Data:* b Atlanta, Ga, June 12, 46; m 67, William S Sr; c Stephanie & William Jr. *Educ:* Ga Inst Technol, BCerE, 70, MSCerE, 80, PhD(ceramic eng), 92. *Honors & Awards:* Monie A Ferst Award, 70; Soc Women Engrs Award, 80. *Concurrent Pos:* Consult, 81-; prin investr, 82-; res award, Ga Tech Res Inst, 90. *Mem:* Fel Am Ceramic Soc; Nat Inst Ceramic Engrs; Ceramic Educ Coun; Sigma Xi; Mat Res Soc; Nat Soc Prof Engrs. *Res:* Materials characterization via analytical instrumentation, advanced materials development, microwave ferrites, directionally solidified composites; crystal growth by directional solidification; clay mineralogy; thermite synthesis and forming of titanium diboride. *Mailing Add:* Sch Mat Sci & Eng Ga Inst Technol Atlanta GA 30332-0245. Fax: 404-894-7339; E-Mail: Kathryn.logan@oip.gatech.edu

LOGAN, LOWELL ALVIN, ECOLOGY, PLANT TAXONOMY. *Current Pos:* RETIRED. *Personal Data:* b Langley, Ark, Oct 29, 21; m 44, Cherry A Moore. *Educ:* Henderson State Col, BS, 43; Univ Ark, MS, 47; Univ Mo, PhD(bot), 59. *Prof Exp:* Instr biol, Ark Polytech Col, 46-49, head dept, 49-60; assoc prof bot, La Polytech Inst, 60-62 & La State Univ, 62-65; prof, Memphis State Univ, 65-67; vpres acad affairs, Southern Ark Univ, Ark, 67-87. *Mem:* Ecol Soc Am; Bot Soc Am; Sigma Xi. *Res:* Ecology and distribution of American Beech; local floras; ecological factors affecting vegetation in restricted habitats. *Mailing Add:* 504 Alice St Magnolia AR 71753

LOGAN, R(ICHARD) S(UTTON), CHEMICAL ENGINEERING, TECHNICAL MANAGEMENT. *Current Pos:* RETIRED. *Personal Data:* b Carthage, Mo, Oct 8, 18; wid; c 1. *Educ:* Univ Mo, BS, 47; Okla Agr & Mech Col, MS, 53. *Prof Exp:* Mem staff lubricant & lubricant additives group, Res & Develop Dept, 48-57, Phillips Petrol Co, group leader uranium milling processes, 57-58 & lubricant additives, 58-60, mgr process develop sect, 60-62, mgr catalytic reactions sect, 62-66, mgr refining & separation br, 66-80, dir petrol res, 80, mgr, Petrol & Petrochemical Processes Div, 80-84. *Mem:* Am Inst Chem Engrs; Nat Soc Prof Engrs. *Res:* Petroleum processing; uranium milling; lubricant oils and additives; sulfonation; halogenation; alkylation; catalytic cracking; research and development management. *Mailing Add:* 1808 Skyline Place Bartlesville OK 74006

LOGAN, RALPH ANDRE, MATERIALS SCIENCE ENGINEERING. *Current Pos:* RETIRED. *Personal Data:* b Cornwall, Ont, Sept 22, 26; nat US; m 50, Ann Garvey; c Howard, Mary, Marguerite, Anthony, Enid, Alisa, Ruth, Thomas & John. *Educ:* McGill Univ, BSc, 47, MSc, 48; Columbia Univ, PhD(physics), 52. *Prof Exp:* Asst physics, Columbia Univ, 49-52; mem tech staff, Bell Labs, 52-82, distinguished mem tech staff, 82-96. *Mem:* Nat Acad Eng; fel Inst Elec & Electronics Engrs; fel Am Phys Soc. *Res:* Semiconductor research. *Mailing Add:* 7 Cindy Dr Manahawkin NJ 08050

LOGAN, ROBERT KALMAN, PHYSICS, COMMUNICATIONS. *Current Pos:* res asst, 67-68, asst prof, 68-75, ASSOC PROF PHYSICS, DEPT PHYSICS, UNIV TORONTO, 75-, ASSOC PROF PHYSICS, DEPT MEASUREMENT, EVAL & COMPUT APPLNS, 84- *Personal Data:* b New York, NY, Aug 31, 39. *Educ:* Mass Inst Technol, BS, 61, PhD(physics), 65. *Prof Exp:* Res asst physics, Univ Ill, 65-67. *Res:* Computer applications in education; impact and effect of communication media on science and society. *Mailing Add:* Dept Educ Res & Statist Ont Inst Educ 252 N Bloor St W Toronto ON M5S 1V6 Can. E-Mail: logan@physics.utoronto.ca

LOGAN, ROWLAND ELIZABETH, PHYSIOLOGY. *Current Pos:* RETIRED. *Personal Data:* b Los Angeles, Calif, Aug 1, 23. *Educ:* Univ Calif, AB, 45; Northwestern Univ, MS, 51, PhD(physiol), 54. *Prof Exp:* Instr physiol, Sch Med Univ Wis, 54-55; instr biol, Bard Col, 56-58; asst prof biol, Gettysburg Col, 58-88. *Mem:* AAAS. *Res:* Cell metabolism; arthropod behavior. *Mailing Add:* 8C60 Box 302 Islesboro ME 04848

LOGAN, TED JOE, INDUSTRIAL CHEMISTRY, TECHNICAL RECRUITING. *Current Pos:* Res chemist, 58-63, sect head, 63-78, MGR RECRUITING, PROCTER & GAMBLE CO, 78-, ASSOC DIR & MGR TECH RECRUITING, 91- *Personal Data:* b Ft Wayne, Ind, June 22, 31; m 54, Ruthanne Pattison; c Thomas E & Patricia A. *Educ:* Ind Univ, AB, 53; Purdue Univ, MS, 56, PhD(chem), 58. *Mem:* Am Chem Soc. *Res:* Product development. *Mailing Add:* 8880 Livingston Rd Cincinnati OH 45251. Fax: 513-627-2266

LOGAN, TERRY JAMES, SOIL CHEMISTRY. *Current Pos:* from asst prof to assoc prof, 72-80, PROF SOIL CHEM, OHIO STATE UNIV, 80- *Personal Data:* b Georgetown, Guyana, Feb 6, 43; US citizen; m 73; c 2. *Educ:* Calif Polytech State Univ, BS, 66; Ohio State Univ, MS, 69, PhD(soil sci), 71. *Honors & Awards:* Vis Scientist Award, Am Soc Agron, 84. *Prof Exp:* Asst prof soil chem, Ohio Agr Res & Develop Ctr, 71-72. *Mem:* Fel Soil Sci Soc Am; fel Am Soc Agron; Int Soil Sci Soc; Soil Conserv Soc Am; Intl Asn Great Lakes Res. *Res:* Non-point sources of pollution; phosphate chemistry of soil and sediments; land disposal of sewage sludge; erosion and sedimentation of agricultural soils. *Mailing Add:* Sch Nat Resources Ohio State Univ 2021 Coffey Rd Columbus OH 43210-1044

LOGCHER, ROBERT DANIEL, CIVIL ENGINEERING, COMPUTER SCIENCE. *Current Pos:* From asst prof to prof, 62-96, EMER PROF CIVIL ENG, MASS INST TECHNOL, 96- *Personal Data:* b The Hague, Neth, Dec 27, 35; US citizen; m 63; c 3. *Educ:* Mass Inst Technol, SB, 58, SM, 60, ScD(civil eng), 62. *Concurrent Pos:* Ford Found fel, 62-64; dir & sr consult, Eng Comput Int, Inc, Mass. *Mem:* Am Soc Civil Engrs; Asn Comput Mach; Sigma Xi. *Res:* Application of digital computer to structural design; development of computer-aided design techniques; design process; management of constructed facility projects; information systems. *Mailing Add:* 12 Chestnut Lane Bedford MA 01730

LOGDBERG, LENNART ERIK, cellular biology, cell adhesion, for more information see previous edition

LOGEMANN, JERILYN ANN, SPEECH PATHOLOGY. *Current Pos:* NIH fel, Northwestern Univ, Chicago, 68-70, res assoc, 70-74, from asst prof to assoc prof, 74-83, PROF COMMUN SCI & DIS, NEUROL & OTOLARYNGOL, NORWESTERN UNIV, CHICAGO, 83- *Personal Data:* b Berwyn, Ill, May 21, 42. *Educ:* Northwestern Univ, Chicago, BA, 63, MS, 64, PhD(speech path), 68. *Concurrent Pos:* Consult, Downey Vet Admin Hosp, 73-76; assoc attend staff, Northwestern Mem Hosp, 73-; fel, Inst Med Chicago. *Mem:* Am Speech & Hearing Asn; Linguistic Soc Am; Sigma Xi; fel Am Speech Language & Hearing Asn. *Res:* Speech science; laryngeal physiology; voice disorders; swallowing physiology; dysphagia. *Mailing Add:* Commun Sci & Dis Dept Northwestern Univ 2299 N Sheridan Rd Evanston IL 60208. Fax: 847-491-5692

LOGGINS, DONALD ANTHONY, heavy metal dynamics, for more information see previous edition

LOGGINS, PHILLIP EDWARDS, ANIMAL NUTRITION. *Current Pos:* RETIRED. *Personal Data:* b Yorkville, Tenn, Feb 12, 21; m 42; c 2. *Educ:* Okla State Univ, BS, 52, MS, 53. *Prof Exp:* Instr animal husb, Univ Fla, 53-55, from asst prof to assoc prof, 55-74, Animal Husbandman, Agr Exp Sta, 55-90, prof animal husb, 74-90. *Mem:* Am Soc Animal Sci. *Res:* Animal nutrition; parasitic effect on nutritional requirements; feeding requirements of animals during reproduction. *Mailing Add:* 1625 NW 14th Ave Gainesville FL 32608

LOGIC, JOSEPH RICHARD, CARDIOVASCULAR PHYSIOLOGY, NUCLEAR MEDICINE. *Current Pos:* resident nuclear med, 74, PROF NUCLEAR MED & MED, UNIV ALA MED CTR, BIRMINGHAM, 74- *Personal Data:* b Iron Mountain, Mich, Apr 23, 35; m 64, Margo L Mikesell. *Educ:* Marquette Univ, MD, 60, MS, 63, PhD(physiol), 64. *Prof Exp:* Intern med, C T Miller Hosp, St Paul, Minn, 60-61; instr physiol, Sch Med, Marquette Univ, 61-64 & 65-66; resident med, Mayo Clin, Rochester, Minn, 64-65; asst prof med, Col Med, Univ Ky, 66-69; assoc prof med & physiol, Univ Tenn, Memphis, 69-73. *Mem:* Am Heart Asn; Am Physiol Soc; Soc Nuclear Med. *Res:* Peripheral circulatory failure; adrenergic blockade; electrolyte role in cardiac electrophysiology and contractility; myocardial nuclear medicine. *Mailing Add:* Div Nuclear Med Univ Ala Med Ctr UAB Sta Birmingham AL 35294-0001

LOGIN, ROBERT BERNARD, ORGANIC CHEMISTRY, POLYMER CHEMISTRY. *Current Pos:* VPRES TECHNOL, SYBRON/TANATEX, 96- *Personal Data:* b Brooklyn, NY, Nov 15, 42; m 71, Lisa Bronfeld; c Joshua & Jason. *Educ:* Brooklyn Col, BA, 66; Purdue Univ, PhD(org chem), 70. *Prof Exp:* Chemist paper specialties, Spring House Lab, Rohm & Haas Co, 70-73; sr chemist, BASF-Wyandotte Corp, 73-74, sect head, 74-75, supvr fiber specialities, 75-80; tech dir, Jordan Chem Co, 80-85; dir surfactants & specialties res & develop, Gaf Chem Corp, 85-88; dir polymer sci res & develop, 88-93; dir polymer sci & prin scientist, ISP Corp, 93-96. *Mem:* Am Chem Soc; Am Asn Textile Chemists & Colorists; Soc Cosmetic Chemists. *Res:* Synthesis and applications of polymers and specialties derived from acetylenic-based intermediates; specialty polymers and surfactants. *Mailing Add:* 116 Glenbriar Ct Simpsonville SC 29681-5108

LOGOTHETIS, ANESTIS LEONIDAS, POLYMER CHEMISTRY. *Current Pos:* Res chemist, Cent Res Dept, E I Du Pont de Nemours & Co, Inc, 58-66, Elastomers Dept, 66-72, supvr develop, 72-76, div head fluoroelastomer res, 76-83, RES FEL, E I DUPONT DE NEMOURS & CO, INC, 83- *Personal Data:* b Thessaloniki, Greece, June 29, 34; c 2. *Educ:* Grinnell Col, BA, 55; Mass Inst Technol, PhD(org chem), 58. *Mem:* Am Chem Soc. *Res:* Fluoropolymers; development of new products. *Mailing Add:* 2816 Kennedy Rd Wilmington DE 19810-3430

LOGOTHETIS, ELEFTHERIOS MILTIADIS, SOLID STATE DEVICES, ELECTRONIC PROPERTIES OF MATERIALS. *Current Pos:* Res scientist, Ford Motor Co, 67-72, prin res scientist assoc, 72-76, staff scientist, 76-81, prin res scientist, 81-92, SR STAFF SCIENTIST, FORD RES LAB, FORD MOTOR CO, 92- *Personal Data:* b Almyros, Greece; US citizen; m 66; c 2. *Educ:* Univ Athens, BS, 59; Cornell Univ, MS, 65, PhD(physics), 67. *Concurrent Pos:* Adj prof physics, Wayne State Univ, 82- *Mem:* Fel Am Phys Soc; Mat Res Soc. *Res:* Electrical and optical properties of semiconductors, metal oxides, layered compounds, ionic materials and high temperature superconductors; defect chemistry and gas/solid interactions; solid state devices such as gas, optical and general automotive sensors. *Mailing Add:* 110 Aspen Birmingham MI 48009. Fax: 313-322-7044; E-Mail: elogothe@pobox.srl.ford.com

LOGOTHETOPOULOS, J, MEDICINE, PHYSIOLOGY. *Current Pos:* From asst prof to prof, 59-88, EMER PROF, BANTING & BEST DEPT MED RES, UNIV TORONTO, 88- *Personal Data:* b Athens, Greece, Mar 12, 18; Can citizen; m 53; c 1. *Educ:* Nat Univ Athens, MD, 41; Univ Toronto, PhD(physiol), 62. *Concurrent Pos:* Res fel, Postgrad Med Sch, Univ London, 52-56; fel med res, Banting & Best Dept Med Res, Univ Toronto, 56-59. *Mem:* Am Diabetes Asn; Am Soc Exp Path; Can Physiol Soc. *Res:* Structure and function of the thyroid and the pituitary gland; experimental diabetes; structure and function of the islets of Langerhans. *Mailing Add:* Banting & Best Dept Med Res Univ Toronto C H Best Inst Rm 410 112 College St Toronto ON M5G 1L6 Can

LOGSDON, CHARLES ELDON, PLANT PATHOLOGY. *Current Pos:* Res prof plant path, Univ Alaska, 53-68, plant pathologist, 53-71, prof, 68-78, assoc dir, Inst Agr Sci, 71-78, EMER PROF PLANT PATH, UNIV ALASKA, 78- *Personal Data:* b Mo, May 8, 21; m 48, Arloine (Schmidt); c Charles L, Onnalie M & John C. *Educ:* Univ Kansas City, AB, 42; Univ Minn, PhD, 54. *Concurrent Pos:* Pres, Agresources Co, 78-85; consult, Pleasant Green North, 86-92. *Mem:* AAAS; Am Phytopath Soc. *Res:* Potato and vegetable diseases. *Mailing Add:* PO Box 387 Palmer AK 99645

LOGSDON, DONALD FRANCIS, JR, BIOLOGY, MEDICAL TECHNOLOGY. *Current Pos:* INSTR, ENG AS SECOND LANG, SACRAMENTO SCH DIST, 90- & BACH VIET ASN, 92- *Personal Data:* b Chicago, Ill, Mar 7, 40; m 63, Nancy Graham; c David, Christopher, Cynthia & Valory. *Educ:* Northwestern Univ, BA, 61; Trinity Univ, MS, 70; LaSalle Exten Univ, LLB, 72; Colo State Univ, PhD(zool), 75, Thomas A Edison Col, BS, 77, Chapman Col, MAEd, 82, BA, 83, MS, 85, MA, 87, MA, 90; Nat Univ, MS, 94. *Prof Exp:* Chief clin lab, 4510th USAF Hosp, Luke AFB, Ariz, 66-67; chief, Radioisotope Lab, USAF Sch Aerospace Med, 67-70; assoc prof, Dept Life Sci, USAF Acad, 70-75; from asst chief to chief & staff biomed scientist, USAF Occup Environ Health Lab, 75-78; health sci coordr & asst prof, Chapman Col, 78-81, mkt dir, educ prog coordr & prof, Sacramento Area Residence Educ Ctr, 81-90. *Concurrent Pos:* Instr life sci, Am River Col, Sacramento, Calif, 75-79 & Sierra Col, Rocklin, Calif, 77-78, Embry-Riddle Aeronaut Univ, 80, Cosumner River Col, 90, Nat Univ, 93-, Golden Gate Univ, 93-, Univ Phoenix, 94-; instr, English as Second Lang, Bach Viet Asn, 92-, Union Inst, 96- *Mem:* AAAS; Sigma Xi; Am Indust Hyg Asn; Asn Off Anal Chemists; Am Soc Radiol Technologists. *Res:* Effects of radiation on living methods for radiation detection; action of radioprotective drugs; comparison of routine plating versus fluorescent antibody methods for the detection of Beta Streptococcus; medical technology. *Mailing Add:* 7341 Spicer Dr Citrus Heights CA 95621

LOGSDON, JOHN MORTIMER, III, SPACE POLICY. *Current Pos:* PROF POLIT SCI & INT AFFAIRS, GEORGE WASHINGTON UNIV, 70-, DIR, SPACE POLICY INST, 87-, DIR, CTR INT SCI & TECHNOL POLICY, 89- *Personal Data:* b Cincinnati, Ohio, Oct 17, 37; m 62, Roslyn Leibson; c David & Michael. *Educ:* Xavier Univ, BS, 60; NY Univ, PhD, 70. *Mem:* AAAS; Am Inst Aeronaut & Astronaut; Int Acad Astronaut. *Res:* Evolution, current status and future prospects of the US civilian space program and its relationships with the space programs of other countries; issues of national science and technology policy. *Mailing Add:* Space Policy Inst George Washington Univ Washington DC 20052. *Fax:* 202-994-1639; *E-Mail:* logsdon@gwisz.circ.gwu.edu

LOGSDON, SALLY D, SOIL PHYSICS, SOIL MANAGEMENT. *Current Pos:* res assoc, Soil & Water Group, St Paul, 87-90, SOIL SCIENTIST, NAT SOIL TILTH LAB, AGR RES SERV, USDA, 90- *Personal Data:* b 1957. *Educ:* Cedarville Col, BA, 77; Mich State Univ, MS, 81; Va Tech Inst & State Univ, PhD(soil physics), 85. *Prof Exp:* Vis asst prof biol, Wilmington Col, 86-87. *Concurrent Pos:* Asst prof & collabr agron & water resources, Iowa State Univ, 90- *Mem:* Soil Sci Soc Am; Am Soc Agron. *Res:* Preserving soil quality and soil structure; soil water cycle and plant use. *Mailing Add:* 2150 Pammel Dr Ames IA 50011

LOGUE, J(OSEPH) C(ARL), TECHNICAL CONSULTING. *Current Pos:* CONSULT TO INDUST, 86- *Personal Data:* b Philadelphia, Pa, Dec 20, 20; m 43; c 3. *Educ:* Cornell Univ, BEE, 44, MEE, 49. *Prof Exp:* Instr elec eng, Cornell Univ, 44-49, asst prof spec assignment, Brookhaven Nat Lab, 49-51; tech engr, IBM, 51-53, proj engr, 53-55, develop engr, 55-56, mgr mach develop, 56-57, mgr solid state circuit develop, 57-58, mgr explor eng, 58-59, mgr tech develop, 59-63, mgr adv tech systs, 63-64, mgr adv logic tech develop, 64-67, dir, Corp Tech Comt, 67-77, mgr technol & design systs, 77-85, dir packaging technol & systs, 86. *Concurrent Pos:* Secy, Int Solid State Circuits Conf, 57; fel, Eval Comt, Inst Elec & Electronics Engrs, 84-86; mem, Eval Comt, Nat Acad Eng Electronics, 89-92. *Mem:* Nat Acad Eng; fel AAAS; fel Inst Elec & Electronics Engrs; Sigma Xi. *Res:* Development and application of new discoveries to advanced digital computers and systems; solid state devices and their applications; electronic aids to aircraft navigation. *Mailing Add:* 52 Boardman Rd Poughkeepsie NY 12603-4228

LOGUE, JAMES NICHOLAS, EPIDEMIOLOGY. *Current Pos:* DIR, DIV ENVIRON HEALTH ASSESSMENT, PA DEPT HEALTH, 82- *Personal Data:* b Pittston, Pa, June 18, 46; m 72, Mary F Carey; c Melissa, Jimmy & Jeffrey. *Educ:* King's Col, BS, 68; Univ Mich, MPH, 71; Columbia Univ, DrPH(epidemiol), 78. *Prof Exp:* Statistician pharmaceut res, Warner-Lambert Res Inst, 69-70, 71-73; sr med biostatistician, Ciba-Geigy Pharmaceut Co, 73-78; sr environ epidemiologist mgt consult, Geomet, Inc, 78-80; chief, Epidemiol Sect, Epidemiol Studies Br, US Food & Drug Admin Bur Radiol Health, 80-82. *Concurrent Pos:* Adj asst prof, Pa State Univ Col Med, Hershey & Univ Pittsburg Grad Sch Pub Health. *Mem:* Soc Epidemiol Res; fel Am Col Epidemiol; Am Pub Health Asn; AAAS. *Res:* Chronic disease; epidemiology; environmental and occupational epidemiology; clinical trials research; mental health research; disaster research. *Mailing Add:* 62 Little Run Rd Camp Hill PA 17011

LOGUE, MARSHALL WOFORD, CHEMICAL SYNTHESIS. *Current Pos:* ASSOC PROF CHEM, MICH TECH UNIV, 81- *Personal Data:* b Danville, Ky, June 4, 42; m 80, Joan Newell; c Timothy & Lauren. *Educ:* Centre Col Ky, AB, 64; Ohio State Univ, PhD(chem), 69. *Prof Exp:* Res assoc chem, Univ Ill, 69-71; asst prof chem, Univ Md, Baltimore Co, 71-77; asst prof chem, NDak State Univ, 77-81. *Concurrent Pos:* Mem, Org Exam Comt, ACS DIVCHED Exam Inst, 78-95, chair, 88-95; mem, Comt Nomenclature, Am Chem Soc, 97- *Mem:* NY Acad Sci; AAAS; Am Chem Soc; Royal Soc Chem; Sigma Xi. *Res:* Synthetic organic chemistry; bio-organic chemistry; pyrimidines; nucleosides; synthesis of carbohydrates and nucleosides. *Mailing Add:* Dept Chem Mich Tech Univ 1400 Townsend Dr Houghton MI 49931-1295. *Fax:* 906-487-2061; *E-Mail:* mwlogue@mtu.edu

LOGULLO, FRANCIS MARK, ORGANIC POLYMER CHEMISTRY. *Current Pos:* REGULATORY AFFAIRS CONSULT, 93- *Personal Data:* b Wilmington, Del, Dec 19, 39; m 62; c 3. *Educ:* Univ Del, BS, 61; Case Inst Technol, PhD(org chem), 65. *Prof Exp:* Res chemist, E I du Pont de Nemours & Co Inc, 65-70, sr res chemist, 70-77, res assoc, 77-90, regulatory affairs consult, 90-93. *Mem:* Am Chem Soc. *Res:* Polymer chemistry; synthetic fibers; chemistry of arynes; regulatory affairs. *Mailing Add:* 521 Wayland Dr Hockessin DE 19707-9724. *Fax:* 302-239-3172; *E-Mail:* frank.logullo@dol.net

LOH, EDWIN DIN, PHYSICS. *Current Pos:* ASSOC PROF, MICH STATE UNIV, 87- *Personal Data:* b Suchow, China, Jan 21, 48; US citizen; c 1. *Educ:* Calif Inst Technol, BS, 69; Princeton Univ, PhD(physics), 77. *Prof Exp:* Physicist, US Army Missile Command, 69-71; from instr to asst prof physics, Princeton Univ, 76-87. *Res:* Astrophysics. *Mailing Add:* Mich State Univ 207 Physics-Astron Bldg East Lansing MI 48824-1116

LOH, EUGENE C, COSMIC RAY, HIGH ENERGY. *Current Pos:* assoc prof, 75-77, PROF & CHMN, DEPT PHYSICS, UNIV UTAH, 77- *Personal Data:* b Soochow, China, Oct 1, 33; US citizen; c 3. *Educ:* Va Polytech Inst, BS, 55; Mass Inst Technol, PhD, 61. *Prof Exp:* Res assoc physics, Mass Inst Technol, 61-64, asst prof, 64-65; sr res assoc nuclear studies, Cornell Univ, 65-75. *Concurrent Pos:* Vis scientist, Stanford Linear Accelerator Ctr, 80-81. *Mem:* Am Phys Soc; Sigma Xi. *Mailing Add:* Dept Physics 201 Jfb Univ Utah Salt Lake City UT 84112

LOH, HORACE H, BIOCHEMISTRY, BIOCHEMICAL PHARMACOLOGY. *Current Pos:* PROF & HEAD, DEPT PHARMACOL, MED SCH, UNIV MINN, MINNEAPOLIS, 89-, FREDERICK & ALICE STARK CHAIR NEUROSCI, 90- *Personal Data:* b Canton, China, May 28, 36; m 62; c 2. *Educ:* Nat Taiwan Univ, BS, 58; Univ Iowa, PhD(biochem), 65. *Honors & Awards:* Humboldt Award for Sr US Scientists, 77; Hamilton Davis lectr in Neurosci, Sch Med, Univ Calif, Davis, 88; Pfizer lectr, Med Col Wis, Milwaukee, 88; Merit Award, Nat Inst Drug Abuse, 88. *Prof Exp:* Lectr biochem pharmacol, Univ Calif, San Francisco, 67, asst res pharmacologist, 67-68; assoc prof biochem pharmacol, Wayne State Univ, 68-70; chief, Drug Dependence Res Ctr, Mendocino State Hosp, Talmage, Calif, 71-72; res specialist, Langley Porte Neuropsychiat Inst, 70-72; from assoc prof to prof, Dept Psychiat & Dept Pharmacol, Sch Med, Univ Calif, San Francisco, 72-88. *Concurrent Pos:* Fel biochem, Univ Calif, San Francisco, 65-66; USPHS career develop award, 73-78 & 78-83, res scientist award, 83-88, 89-94; mem, Preclin Psychopharmacol Study Sect, NIMH, 77-79 & Basic Psychopharmacol & Neuropsychopharmacol Res Rev Comt, 80-81; consult, US Army Res & Develop, Dept Defense, 80-84; mem, Biomed Res Rev Comt, Nat Inst Drug Abuse, 84-88, chair, 86-88; Wellcome vis prof award pharmacol, Fedn Am Socs Exp Biol & Burroughs Wellcome Labs, 85; chmn, Biochem Subcomt, Biomed Res Rev Comt, Nat Inst Drug Abuse, 86-88, Spec Rev Comt Drug Develop, 89 & Drug Abuse AIDS Res Rev Comt, 89-93; assoc ed, CRC Critical Rev Pharmacol Sci, 87-88, Annual Rev Pharmacol & Toxicol, 90- *Mem:* Am Chem Soc; Am Soc Pharm Exp Therapeut; Am Col Neuropsychopharmacol; Am Soc Chinese Bioscientists Am; Western Pharmacol Soc. *Res:* Opiate receptors; mechanisms of drug tolerance. *Mailing Add:* Dept Pharmacol 3-249 Millard Hall Univ Minn Med Sch 435 Delaware St SE Minneapolis MN 55455-0347. *Fax:* 612-625-8408; *E-Mail:* lohxx001@maroon.tc.umn.edu

LOH, PHILIP CHOO-SENG, ANIMAL VIROLOGY. *Current Pos:* assoc prof, 61-66, chmn, 85-91, PROF VIROL, UNIV HAWAII, 66- *Personal Data:* b Singapore, Sept 14, 25; nat US; m 55, Susie S H Lau; c Valerie K H & Rhonda K H. *Educ:* Morningside Col, BS, 50; Univ Iowa, MS, 53; Univ Mich, MPH, 54, PhD, 58; Am Bd Microbiol, dipl, 63. *Prof Exp:* Res assoc, Virus Lab, Univ Mich, 58-60, asst prof, 61. *Concurrent Pos:* USPH spec res fel, NIH, 67-68; Eleanor Roosevelt int cancer fel, Int Union Against Cancer, Geneva, 67; vis prof, Dept Pathol, Sch Med, Univ Bristol, UK, 75; vis sr scientist, NIH, 82. *Mem:* fel AAAS; Am Asn Immunol; Am Soc Microbiol; Soc Exp Biol & Med; Am Soc Virol; fel Am Acad Microbiol; Soc In Vitro Biol. *Res:* Biosynthesis and pathobiology of animal viruses at the cellular level and environmental virology; viral diseases of marine animals and development of animal cell culture systems. *Mailing Add:* 2552 Peter St Honolulu HI 96816

LOH, ROLAND RU-LOONG, HIGH TEMPERATURE SUPERCONDUCTING MATERIALS, STRUCTURAL & ELECTRONIC CERAMICS. *Current Pos:* DIR RES & DEVELOP, ADVAN CERAMETRICS, INC, 88- *Personal Data:* b Shanghai, China, Aug 1, 42; m 73, Grace A; c Lucian X. *Educ:* Shanghai Iron & Steel Inst, BS, 63; Univ Calif, Berkeley, MS, 85. *Prof Exp:* Lectr math, Iron & Steel Col, Shanghai, 64-65; engr, Shanghai Iron & Steel Co, 66-75, dir res & develop, Dept Ceramics, 76-81; vis scholar, Univ Calif, Berkeley, 82-83, staff scientist, Lawrence Berkeley Nat Lab, 83-85; sr engr, Lambertville Ceramic Mfg Co, 86-88. *Concurrent Pos:* Consult, Shanghai Bao-Shan Iron & Steel Complex, 88-90; prin investr, Dept Energy, 89-90 & NASA, 91-; collabr, Los Alamos Nat Lab, 91-93. *Mem:* Am Ceramic Soc; Mat Res Soc. *Res:* Transfering scientific concept and result into production implementation; advanced ceramics and composite materials; author of more than 40 publications; technology transfer and joint venture between United States companies and Far East countries' companies. *Mailing Add:* 1226 Pemeroke Newark OH 43055. *Fax:* 609-265-1718

LOH, YOKE PENG, CELLULAR NEUROBIOL, MOLECULAR ENDOCRINOLOGY. *Current Pos:* Vis fel, NIH, 74-76, sr staff fel, 76-79, res chemist, 79-83, SECT CHIEF, NIH, 83- *Personal Data:* b Singapore, July 27, 47; US citizen; m 87; c 1. *Educ:* Univ Col Dublin, BSc, 69; Univ Penn, PhD(molecular biol), 73. *Honors & Awards:* Super Serv Award, Pub Health Serv. *Concurrent Pos:* Adj prof biochem, Uniform Serv Univ Health Sci, Bethesda, 90- *Mem:* Am Soc Cell Biol; Soc Neurosci; Endocrinol Soc; Soc Neurochem. *Res:* Mechanisms involved in the intracellular trafficking and sorting of pro-hormones and pro-neuropeptides into regulated secretory granules for processing by unique proteolytic enzymes. *Mailing Add:* NICHD NIH Bldg 49 Rm SA38 Bethesda MD 20892-4480. *Fax:* 301-496-9938

LOHER, WERNER J, ZOOLOGY. *Current Pos:* RETIRED. *Personal Data:* b Landshut, Ger, June 27, 29; m 61; c 1. *Educ:* Univ Munich, PhD(zool), 55; Univ London, PhD(entom) & DIC, 59. *Honors & Awards:* A V Humboldt Sr Distinguished Sci Award. *Prof Exp:* Asst prof zoophysiol, Univ Tubingen, 60-65, pvt docent, 65-67; assoc prof, Univ Calif, Berkeley, 67-70, prof entom, 70-, dir, Gump SPac Biol Res Sta, Moorea, French, Polynesia, 85- *Concurrent Pos:* Sr res award, Antilocust Res Ctr, Eng, 56-59; vis lectr, Glasgow Univ, 67; mem, Acad Sci & Lit, Mainz, 83. *Mem:* AAAS; Animal Behav Soc; Brit Soc Exp Biol; Ger Zool Soc. *Res:* Hormonal control of reproduction in insects. *Mailing Add:* Dept Entom Univ Calif Berkeley CA 94720-0001

LOHMAN, KENNETH ELMO, geology; deceased, see previous edition for last biography

LOHMAN, STANLEY WILLIAM, geology; deceased, see previous edition for last biography

LOHMAN, TIMOTHY GEORGE, BODY COMPOSITION. *Current Pos:* PROF, DEPT EXERCISE & SPORTS SCI, UNIV ARIZ, 84- *Personal Data:* b Park Ridge, NJ, Dec 10, 40; m 61; c 4. *Educ:* Univ Ill, Urbana, BS, 62, MS, 64, PhD(body compos), 67. *Prof Exp:* Res assoc whole-body counting, 67-69, asst prof body compos animals & man, Dept Animal Sci, 69-77, assoc prof phys educ, Univ Ill, Urbana, 77-83. *Mem:* AAAS; Am Col Sports Med; Soc Study Human Biol; Am Acad Phys Educ; Am Alliance Health, Phys Educ & Recreation. *Res:* Exercise physiology; human body composition; physical exercise and body compositional and nutrition. *Mailing Add:* Dept Health Phys Educ Univ Ariz 1600 E University Blvd Tucson AZ 85721-0001

LOHMAN, TIMOTHY MICHAEL, BIOPHYSICAL CHEMISTRY, PROTEIN DNA INTERACTIONS. *Current Pos:* PROF BIOCHEM & MOLECULAR BIOPHYS, WASHINGTON UNIV, 90- *Personal Data:* b Rockville Ctr, NY, June 2, 51; m 78; c 2. *Educ:* Cornell Univ, Ithaca, AB, 73; Univ Wis-Madison, PhD(phys chem), 77. *Honors & Awards:* Fac Res Award, Am Cancer Soc. *Prof Exp:* Res asst biophys chem, Univ Calif, San Diego, 77-79; NIH fel, Univ Ore, 79-81; asst prof biochem & biophys, Tex A&M Univ, 81-85, assoc prof biochem, biophys & chem, 85-90. *Mem:* Biophys Soc; Am Soc Biochem & Molecular Biol; AAAS. *Res:* Thermodynamics and kinetics of macromolecular interactions; mechanisms of DNA helicases (motor proteins); protein-nucleic acid interactions involved in DNA replication, recombination and control of gene expressions. *Mailing Add:* Dept Biochem & Molecular Biophys Sch Med Washington Univ Box 8231 St Louis MO 63110

LOHNER, DONALD J, ORGANIC CHEMISTRY. *Current Pos:* RETIRED. *Personal Data:* b Brooklyn, NY, Mar 10, 39. *Educ:* Queens Col, BS, 61; Adelphi Univ, PhD(org chem), 66. *Prof Exp:* Instr chem, Adelphi Univ, 64-66; res chemist, E I du Pont de Nemours & Co, Inc, 66-76, res assoc, 76-85, sr res assoc, 85-89, res fel, 89-92. *Mem:* Am Chem Soc. *Mailing Add:* 33 Willow Lane Englishtown NJ 07726

LOHNES, ROBERT ALAN, GEOTECHNICAL ENGINEERING, GEOLOGY. *Current Pos:* from asst prof to assoc prof, 65-74, PROF CIVIL ENG, IOWA STATE UNIV, 74- *Personal Data:* b Springfield, Ohio, Feb 5, 37; div; c 2. *Educ:* Ohio State Univ, BSc, 59; Iowa State Univ, MS, 61, PhD(soil eng, geol), 64. *Prof Exp:* Asst geol, Iowa State Univ, 59-62, instr, 62-64; asst prof, Wis State Univ, River Falls, 64-65. *Concurrent Pos:* Vis assoc prof civil eng, Middle East Tech Univ, Ankara, Turkey, 73-74. *Mem:* Am Soc Civil Engrs; Am Geophys Union; Geol Soc Am; Am Rwy Engr Asn; Int Soc Soil Mech & Found Engrs. *Res:* Applied geomorphology; soil creep and shear strength; engineering properties of tropical soils; quantitative geomorphology; mechanics of bulk solids loads on buried pipes. *Mailing Add:* Dept Civil Eng Iowa State Univ 394 Town Eng Ames IA 50011-9012. *Fax:* 515-294-8216; *E-Mail:* rlohnes@iastate.edu

LOHR, D(ELMAR) FREDERICK, POLYMER CHEMISTRY. *Current Pos:* RETIRED. *Personal Data:* b Madison Co, Va, Sept 9, 34. *Educ:* Va Polytech Inst, BS, 62; Duke Univ, MA, 63, PhD(chem), 65. *Prof Exp:* Res org chemist, Firestone Tire & Rubber Co, 65-70, sr res scientist, 70-77, assoc scientist, 78-83, res assoc, 84-88, res assoc, Bridgestone/Firestone, Inc, 88-94. *Mem:* Am Chem Soc; Sigma Xi. *Res:* Synthesis and reactions of aromatic heterocycles, particularly those containing both nitrogen and sulfur; polymer synthesis and characterization. *Mailing Add:* 200 Casterton Ave Akron OH 44303-1517

LOHR, DENNIS EVAN, PHYSICAL BIOCHEMISTRY, GENE EXPRESSION. *Current Pos:* from asst prof to assoc prof, 79-90, PROF BIOCHEM, ARIZ STATE UNIV, 91- *Personal Data:* b Waukegan, Ill, Jan 12, 44. *Educ:* Beloit Col, BA, 65; Univ NC, Chapel Hill, PhD(biochem), 69. *Prof Exp:* Teacher chem, Peace Corps, Kenya, EAfrica, 70-71; res assoc biochem, Ore State Univ, 72-79. *Res:* Enzymatic investigation of the subunit structure of yeast chromatin the chromatin structure of enkaryotic promoters. *Mailing Add:* Dept Chem/Biochem Ariz State Univ Tempe AZ 85287-1604

LOHR, JOHN MICHAEL, PLASMA PHYSICS. *Current Pos:* STAFF PHYSICIST, GEN ATOMICS CO, SAN DIEGO, 76- *Personal Data:* b Chicago, Ill, June 21, 44. *Educ:* Univ Tex, Austin, BS, 66; Univ Wis-Madison, MS, 67, PhD(nuclear physics), 72. *Prof Exp:* Res assoc plasma physics, Fusion Res Ctr, Univ Tex, Austin, 72-76. *Mem:* Am Phys Soc. *Res:* Tokamak and plasma physics research. *Mailing Add:* Gen Atomics PO Box 85608 San Diego CA 92186

LOHR, LAWRENCE LUTHER, JR, THEORETICAL CHEMISTRY. *Current Pos:* assoc prof, 68-73, PROF CHEM, UNIV MICH, ANN ARBOR, 73- *Personal Data:* b Charlotte, NC, May 29, 37; m 63; c 1. *Educ:* Univ NC, BS, 59; Harvard Univ, AM, 62, PhD(chem), 64. *Prof Exp:* Res assoc chem, Univ Chicago, 63-65; res scientist, Sci Lab, Ford Motor Co, 65-68. *Concurrent Pos:* Consult, Ford Motor Co, 68-71 & Bell Tel Labs, 69 & 72; res fel, Alfred P Sloan, 69-71; vis prof & scholar, Univ Calif, Berkeley, 74-75; vis scientist, Inst Molecular Sci, Okazaki, Japan, 81, Univ Helsinki, Finland, 84, 88 & 96 & Univ Nac Auto Mexico, Mex City, 89; prog officer, NSF, Washington, DC, 92-93. *Mem:* Am Phys Soc; Am Chem Soc; AAAS. *Res:* Theories of chemical bonding; interpretation of electronic spectra of molecules and solids; relativistic quantum chemistry; reaction mechanisms; rotational dynamics of molecules. *Mailing Add:* Dept Chem 1040 Chem Bldg Univ Mich Ann Arbor MI 48109-1055

LOHRENGEL, CARL FREDERICK, II, GEOLOGY. *Current Pos:* from asst prof to assoc prof, 69-81, PROF GEOL & MATH, SNOW COL, 81- *Personal Data:* b Kansas City, Mo, Nov 24, 39; m 71. *Educ:* Univ Kansas City, BS, 62; Univ Mo-Columbia, MA, 64; Brigham Young Univ, PhD(geol), 68. *Prof Exp:* Res assoc, Marine Inst, Univ Ga, 68-69. *Mem:* Am Asn Petrol Geol; Am Inst Prof Geologists; Nat Asn Geol Teachers. *Res:* Palynology of the Upper Cretaceous of Utah; Upper Cenozoic and modern dinoflagellates of the Georgia coastal plain; Cretaceous stratigraphy of Utah; Upper Cretaceous stratigraphy of Wyoming. *Mailing Add:* Dept Phys Sci Southern Utah Univ 351 W Center St Cedar City UT 84720-2498

LOHRMANN, ROLF, BIO-ORGANIC CHEMISTRY. *Current Pos:* sr res assoc, 65-74, ASSOC RES PROF, SALK INST BIOL STUDIES, 74- *Personal Data:* b Bissingen-Enz, Ger, Mar 2, 30; m 60. *Educ:* Stuttgart Tech Univ, dipl(chem), 58, Dr rer nat(chem), 60. *Prof Exp:* Proj assoc, Inst Enzyme Res, Univ Wis, 62-65. *Mem:* Ger Chem Soc; Am Chem Soc. *Res:* Prebiotic chemistry; molecular evolution. *Mailing Add:* Molecular Biosysts Inc 10030 Barnes Canyon Rd San Diego CA 92121-2789

LOHSE, DAVID JOHN, POLYMER PHYSICS, NEUTRON SCATTERING. *Current Pos:* sr engr, Exxon Chem Co, 80-87, STAFF ENGR, EXXON RES & ENG CO, 88- *Personal Data:* b New York, NY, Sept 14, 52; m 78; c 2. *Educ:* Mich State Univ, BS, 74; Univ Ill, PhD(polymer sci), 78. *Prof Exp:* Res asst, Univ Ill, 74-78; res assoc, Nat Bur Standards, 78-80. *Mem:* Am Phys Soc; Am Chem Soc; Sigma Xi. *Res:* Physics of polymer systems, especially the morphology and thermodynamics of polymer blends and solutions and their structure-property relations. *Mailing Add:* 556 Stony Brook Dr Bridgewater NJ 08807. *Fax:* 908-730-2536; *E-Mail:* djlohse@erenj.com

LOHUIS, DELMONT JOHN, CHEMISTRY. *Current Pos:* RETIRED. *Personal Data:* b Oostburg, Wis, Jan 24, 14; m 37, Charlotte; c Ardyth, Arden & Daryl A. *Educ:* Carroll Col, Wis, BA, 34; Univ Wis, MS, 36. *Prof Exp:* Res dept, Am Can Co, 35-78, asst to corp vpres res & develop, 60-61 & 64-70, dir & vpres res & develop, 61-64. dir corp res & develop staff, 70-75, asst to pres, Tech Air Corp, 75-78. *Mem:* Am Chem Soc; fel Am Inst Chem. *Res:* Container construction materials; pyrolysis and gasification of ligno cellulosic materials; resource recovery from solid wastes; paper based consumer products; specialty chemicals. *Mailing Add:* 9450 River Lake Dr Roswell GA 30075

LOIGMAN, HAROLD, CONSTRUCTION MANAGEMENT, GEOTECHNICAL ENGINEERING. *Current Pos:* SR CONSULT, DAY & ZIMMERMANN, INC, 90- *Personal Data:* b Philadelphia, Pa, Jan 25, 30; m 51; c 2. *Educ:* Univ Pittsburgh, BS, 51; Univ Pa, MS, 63. *Prof Exp:* Supvry engr, US Army CEngr, 55-68; vpres, Valley Forge Labs, Inc, 68-72; pres, Site Engrs, Inc, 72-90. *Concurrent Pos:* Active reserve officer, Naval Reserve Construct Forces, 51-82, chief staff, 8th Reserve Naval Construct Regt, 72-74, cmndg officer, 21st Reserve Construct Battalion, 74-76; adj prof eng, Villanova Univ, 68-70, Temple Univ, 75-76, Grad Sch, Villanova Univ, 88-89 & Pa State Univ, 90. *Mem:* Am Soc Civil Engrs; Soc Am Mil Engrs; Nat Soc Prof Engrs; Am Soc Hwy Engrs; Int Soc Soil Mech & Found Engrs. *Mailing Add:* Day & Zimmermann Inc 1818 Market St Philadelphia PA 19103

LOIRE, NORMAN PAUL, ORGANIC CHEMISTRY. *Current Pos:* SR RES CHEMIST, MORTON THIOKOL INC, WOODSTOCK, ILL, 77- *Personal Data:* b St Louis, Mo, May 7, 27; m 53; c 3. *Educ:* Shurtleff Col, BS, 51; NY Univ, PhD(chem), 60. *Prof Exp:* Chemist, Ciba Pharmaceut Prod Co, 52-54;

res chemist, Benger Res Lab, Textile Fibers Dept, E I du Pont de Nemours & Co, 58-62; sr res chemist, Narmco Res & Develop Div, Whittaker Corp, 62-67; sr res chemist, Chemplex Co, 67-71; lab mgr, Saber Labs, Wheeling, 71-77. *Mem:* Am Chem Soc. *Res:* Development of new products based on water-borne polymer systems. *Mailing Add:* 36113 Karcher Rd Burlington WI 53105

LOIZZI, ROBERT FRANCIS, MILK SECRETION, MICROTUBULES. *Current Pos:* from asst prof to assoc prof, 66-78, asst dir, Res Resources Ctr, 86-97, PROF PHYSIOL, UNIV ILL, 78-, DIR, RESOURCE CTR WEST FACIL, 97- *Personal Data:* b Oak Park, Ill, Oct 18, 35; m 60, Charlotte M Nichols; c Robert G, Mary-Frances T (Zimmerman), Christopher M & John F. *Educ:* Loyola Univ, Ill, BS, 57; Marquette Univ, MS, 60; Iowa State Univ, PhD(cell biol), 66. *Prof Exp:* Instr physiol, Iowa State Univ, 65-66. *Concurrent Pos:* Assoc dean, Sch Basic Med Sci, Col Med, 80-81. *Mem:* AAAS; Am Soc Cell Biol; Am Physiol Soc. *Res:* Regulation and cell biology of mammary gland; cytoskeleton and milk secretion; hormonal regulation of microtubules; cyclic nucleotides and lactose synthesis; mammary tumor growth; fine structure of secretory processes. *Mailing Add:* 135 E View Lombard IL 60148. *Fax:* 312-996-0539

LOK, ROGER, ORGANIC CHEMISTRY. *Current Pos:* RES CHEMIST, EASTMAN KODAK CO, 74- *Personal Data:* b Macao, Oct 19, 43; US citizen; m 70; c 2. *Educ:* Univ Calif, Berkeley, BS, 66; Univ Washington, PhD(org chem), 71. *Prof Exp:* Fel, Dept Pharmacol, Yale Univ, 71-74. *Mem:* Am Chem Soc; Sigma Xi. *Res:* Organic synthesis; preparation of dyes; enzyme immobilization; affinity chromatography; synthesis of photographically active compounds; study of photographically active compounds. *Mailing Add:* 204 Dorchester Rd Rochester NY 14610-1327

LOKAY, JOSEPH DONALD, CHEMICAL ENGINEERING. *Current Pos:* PROF, UNIV PITTSBURGH, 83- *Personal Data:* b Chicago, Ill, Dec 17, 29; m 54, LaVerne; c Joe, William, Barbara & James. *Educ:* Ill Inst Technol, BS, 52, MS, 53, PhD(chem eng), 55. *Prof Exp:* Engr, Westinghouse Elec Corp, 55-59 & Argonne Nat Lab, 59-62; mgr res & develop, Continental Can Co, 62-66; staff engr res & develop, Gulf Oil Corp, 66-83. *Mem:* Am Inst Chem Engrs. *Res:* Application of computers to teaching; research and development planning; the commercial evaluation of research and development projects related to petroleum processes and products including synthetic fuels and minerals. *Mailing Add:* Dept Natural Sci Univ Pittsburgh 1150 Mt Pleasant Rd Greensburg PA 15601-5860

LOKEMOEN, JOHN THEODORE, RESEARCH OF NESTING WATERFOWL, WATERFOWL PHILOPATRY. *Current Pos:* Wildlife Res Biologist, US Fish & Wildlife Serv, Minn, 62-65, WILDLIFE RES BIOLOGIST, NAT BIOL SURV NORTHERN PRAIRIE SCI CTR, 65- *Personal Data:* b Merrill, Wis, Dec 12, 36; m 61, Luella Brillhart; c Matthew, Anne & Daniel. *Educ:* Univ Wis, Stevens Point, BS, 59; Univ Mont, MS, 62. *Mem:* Wildlife Soc; Am Ornith Union. *Res:* Primarily studied breeding waterfowl populations in the Northern Great Plains in the Prairie Pothole Region; study raptors, neo-tropical migrants in agricultural environments and upland game birds; published over 45 articles. *Mailing Add:* 818 Seventh Ave SW Jamestown ND 58401. *Fax:* 701-252-4217; *E-Mail:* lokemoen@mail.fws.gov

LOKEN, HALVAR YOUNG, ORGANIC & POLYMER CHEMISTRY. *Current Pos:* res chemist, E I DuPont de Nemours & Co, 72-76, sr res chemist, 76-80, carpet tech supvr, 80-81, mkt rep, 82-84, bus strategist & res assoc, 84-92, NEW PROD DEVELOP MGR, E I DUPONT DE NEMOURS & CO, 92- *Personal Data:* b Oslo, Norway, June 18, 44; US citizen; m 81, Sarah C Bryant; c Kaia, Rolf, Erik & Trygue. *Educ:* Clark Univ, AB, 66; Brown Univ, PhD(chem), 71. *Prof Exp:* Fel trace org anal, Nat Inst Allergy & Infectious Dis, Baker Lab, Cornell Univ, 70-72. *Concurrent Pos:* Chmn, Honeycomb Core Task Force, Suppliers Advan Composites Mfrs Asn, 85-90. *Mem:* Am Chem Soc; Soc Advan Mat & Process Eng; Am Soc Testing & Mat; Am Helicopter Soc. *Res:* Chemistry and physics of composite materials. *Mailing Add:* 4802 Pennington Ct Linden Heath Wilmington DE 19808

LOKEN, KEITH I, VETERINARY MICROBIOLOGY. *Current Pos:* Res fel vet med, Univ Minn, St Paul, 55-58, from instr to assoc prof, 58-71, prof vet microbiol, 71-74, PROF VET BIOL, UNIV MINN, ST PAUL, 74- *Personal Data:* b Sandstone, Minn, Oct 3, 29; m 57; c 3. *Educ:* Univ Minn, St Paul, BS, 51 DVM, 53, PhD(vet med), 59. *Concurrent Pos:* Fulbright res fel, NZ Dept Agr, Ruakura Agr Res Ctr, 65-66. *Mem:* Am Vet Med Asn; Wildlife Dis Asn; Am Soc Microbiol. *Res:* Teaching veterinary microbiology; host-parasite relationships; epidemiology of infectious diseases of animals. *Mailing Add:* 1645 Garden Ave St Paul MN 55113

LOKEN, MERLE KENNETH, NUCLEAR MEDICINE, BIOPHYSICS. *Current Pos:* instr biophys, Univ Minn, 53-56, from asst prof to assoc prof, 56-68, dir, Div Nuclear Med, 64-87, PROF RADIOL, UNIV MINN, MINNEAPOLIS, 68- *Personal Data:* b Hudson, SDak, Jan 21, 24; m 47; c 5. *Educ:* Augustana Col, BA, 46; Mass Inst Technol, BS, 48, MS, 49; Univ Minn, PhD(biophys), 56, MD, 62; Am Bd Nuclear Med, cert, 72. *Prof Exp:* Asst physics, Mass Inst Technol, 48-49; asst prof, Augustana Col, 49-51. *Concurrent Pos:* AMA comt non-mil radiation emergencies. *Mem:* Fel Am Col Radiol; Soc Nuclear Med; Radiol Soc NAm; AMA; Am Col Nuclear Physicians; Sigma Xi. *Res:* Clinical uses of radioisotopes; radiation dosimetry and hazards; effects of radiation on biological systems; applications of radioisotopes as tracer elements in metabolic studies of normal and cancer cells. *Mailing Add:* Nuclear Med Clin Box 382 Univ Minn Hosp Minneapolis MN 55455

LOKEN, STEWART CHRISTIAN, EXPERIMENTAL HIGH ENERGY PHYSICS. *Current Pos:* PHYSICIST, LAWRENCE BERKELEY LAB, UNIV CALIF, 74-, DIR INFO & COMPUT SCI DIV, 88- *Personal Data:* b Montreal, Que, Feb 16, 43; m 70; c 2. *Educ:* McMaster Univ, BSc, 66; Calif Inst Technol, PhD(physics), 71. *Prof Exp:* Res assoc physics lab nuclear studies, Cornell Univ, 71-74. *Mem:* Fel Am Phys Soc. *Res:* Measurement of high energy muon-nucleon scattering and experimental studies of rare muon-induced processes at high energies; study of high energy electron-positron interactions. *Mailing Add:* Bldg 50B-2239 Lawrence Berkeley Lab Univ Calif Berkeley CA 94720

LOKENSGARD, JERROLD PAUL, ORGANIC CHEMISTRY. *Current Pos:* from asst prof to prof, 67-93, chmn dept, 76-79 & 87-90, ROBERT MCMILLEN PROF CHEM, LAWRENCE UNIV, 93-, CHMN DEPT, 92- *Personal Data:* b Saskatoon, Sask, July 30, 40; US citizen; m 65, Elizabeth Hopkins; c Michael & Ann-Marie. *Educ:* Luther Col, Iowa, BA, 62; Univ Wis, Madison, MA, 64, PhD(org chem), 67. *Prof Exp:* NIH fel, 67; res assoc chem, Iowa State Univ, 67. *Concurrent Pos:* Res assoc chem, Univ Toronto, 73-74; vis assoc prof chem, Cornell Univ, 80-81. *Mem:* Am Chem Soc. *Res:* Organic reaction mechanisms; applications of nuclear magnetic resonance spectroscopy; identification & synthesis of natural products; strain effects on organic reactions. *Mailing Add:* Dept Chem Lawrence Univ PO Box 599 Appleton WI 54912-0599. *Fax:* 920-832-6726; *E-Mail:* lokensgj@lawrence.edu

LOKKEN, DONALD ARTHUR, INORGANIC CHEMISTRY, SOLID STATE CHEMISTRY. *Current Pos:* ASSOC PROF CHEM, UNIV ALASKA, FAIRBANKS, 70- *Personal Data:* b Tomahawk, Wis, Sept 27, 37; c 2. *Educ:* Univ Wis-Madison, BA, 63; Iowa State Univ, PhD(inorg chem), 70. *Prof Exp:* Chemist, Enzyme Inst, Univ Wis-Madison, 57-59, pesticide chem, Wis Alumni Res Found, 59-63; teaching & res asst, Iowa State Univ, 63-70. *Mem:* Am Chem Soc; Am Crystallog Asn; Sigma Xi. *Res:* Inorganic and solid state chemistry; x-ray crystallography; unusual oxidation states. *Mailing Add:* Dept Chem Univ Alaska PO Box 756160 Fairbanks AK 99775

LOKKEN, STANLEY JEROME, PHYSICAL CHEMISTRY. *Current Pos:* ASST PROF CHEM, BRUNSWICK JR COL, 77- *Personal Data:* b Fargo, NDak, Sept 22, 31; m 65. *Educ:* NDak State Univ, BS, 53; Univ Calif, Berkeley, MS, 54; Iowa State Univ, PhD(phys chem), 62. *Prof Exp:* Res chemist, Glidden Co, 62-65 & Continental Oil Co, 65-68; asst prof chem, Univ Wis-Platteville, 68-75. *Concurrent Pos:* Vis asst prof chem, Ill Inst Technol, 75-77. *Mem:* Am Chem Soc. *Res:* Ion exchange theory and techniques; radiochemistry; solution kinetics and mechanisms of reactions; titanium chemistry; phosphate chemistry. *Mailing Add:* 141 Belle Point Pkwy Brunswick GA 31520-2102

LOLLAR, ROBERT MILLER, LEATHER CHEMISTRY, ENVIRONMENTAL CHEMISTRY. *Current Pos:* Prof, Dept Basic Sci, 75-85, EMER PROF, UNIV CINCINNATI, 85- *Personal Data:* b Lebanon, Ohio, May 17, 15; wid; c Janet (Schneider) & Katherine. *Educ:* Univ Cincinnati, ChE, 37, MS, 38, PhD(leather chem), 40. *Honors & Awards:* Alsop Medal, Am Leather Chemists Asn, 54; Fraser Muir Moffat Medal, Leather Indust Am, 86. *Prof Exp:* Develop chemist, Best Foods Corp, Ind, 40-41; assoc prof tanning res & assoc dir, Tanners' Coun Res Lab, 41-58; tech dir, Armour Leather Co Div, Armour & Co, 58-64, dir tech eval, 65-73; tech dir, Leather Indust Am, 75-86. *Concurrent Pos:* Pres, Lollar & Assocs, Consults, 73- *Mem:* Am Chem Soc; Am Soc Qual Control; Am Leather Chemists Asn (pres, 66-68); Inst Food Technol; World Mariculture Soc. *Res:* Research administration; statistical quality control; collagen chemistry; industrial biochemistry; marine biology. *Mailing Add:* 7300 Dearwester Dr Apt 341 Cincinnati OH 45236-6111

LOLLE, SUSAN JANNE, PLANT DEVELOPMENT. *Current Pos:* RES ASSOC HARVARD UNIV, 96- *Personal Data:* b Copenhagen, Denmark, Feb 14, 58; Can citizen. *Educ:* Queen's Univ, BSc, 81; McGill Univ, PhD(biol), 87. *Prof Exp:* Fel, Nat Sci & Eng Res Coun Can, 87-89; McKnight fel, 90-92; adj asst prof biol, Reed Col, 92-96. *Concurrent Pos:* Grantee, USDA, 92-94. *Res:* Study cell-cell interactions in plant development using molecular and genetic approaches. *Mailing Add:* Biol Labs Harvard Univ 16 Divinity Ave Cambridge MA 02138. *Fax:* 503-777-7773; *E-Mail:* slolle@reed.edu

LOLLEY, RICHARD NEWTON, PHYSIOLOGY, BIOCHEMISTRY. *Current Pos:* asst prof, Sch Med, Univ Calif, Los Angeles, 66-70, assoc prof, 70-76, assoc mem, Jules Stein Eye Inst, 78-81, chair, Dept Anat & Cell Biol, 92-94, PROF ANAT, SCH MED, UNIV CALIF, LOS ANGLELES, 76-, MEM, JULES STEIN EYE INST, 81- *Personal Data:* b Blaine, Kans, May 25, 33; m 59; c 3. *Educ:* Univ Kans, BS, 55, PhD(physiol), 61. *Honors & Awards:* Jules Stein Living Tribute Award, R P Int, 85; R D Dow Neurol Sci Award, 92; Proctor Medal, Am Res Vision & Opthal, 94. *Prof Exp:* Pharmacist, Hawk Pharm, Inc, 55-56. *Concurrent Pos:* USPHS res fel biochem, Maudsley Hosp, Univ London, 61-62; fel neuropath, McLean Hosp & Harvard Med Sch, 62-65; res pharmacologist, Vet Admin Hosp, 65-71, chief, Lab Develop Neurol, 71-, actg assoc chief staff res, 78-80; Vet Admin res career scientist, 79-; mem, Nat Adv Eye Coun, NIH, 79-84; trustee, Biochem & Molecular Biol Sect, Asn Res Vision & Ophthal, 87-92. *Mem:* Int Soc Neurochem; Am Soc Neurochem; Soc Neurosci; Am Asn Anat; Asn Res Vision & Ophthal (pres, 91-92); Int Soc Eye Res. *Res:* Chemical and physiological investigation of retina and regions of the developing brain; quantitative histochemical studies of normal tissues and of regions of the central nervous system afflicted by inherited diseases; animal models of human blindness; role of cyclic nucleotides in photoreceptor cell function and disease. *Mailing Add:* Univ S Calif Sch Med 1975 Zonal Ave KAM 300 Los Angeles CA 90033

LOLY, PETER DOUGLAS, THEORETICAL PHYSICS, SOLID STATE PHYSICS. *Current Pos:* from asst prof to assoc prof, 68-80, assoc head, 89-91, PROF PHYSICS, UNIV MAN, 80- *Personal Data:* b Edmonton, Eng, Mar 7, 41; Can citizen; div; c 2. *Educ:* Univ London, BSc, 63, PhD(physics) & DIC, 66. *Prof Exp:* Fel, Theoret Physics Inst, Alta, 66-68. *Concurrent Pos:* Travel fel, Nat Res Coun Can, 75; sabbatical leave, Lab Solid State Physics, Univ Paris-Sud, 75-76, Physique, Univ Sherbrooke, 81-82, Imp Col, 82. *Mem:* Am Phys Soc; Can Asn Physicists; Brit Inst Physics; Am Asn Physics Teachers. *Res:* Spin waves; density of states; Brillouin zone sums; lattice green functions; real space rescaling; many-body problems; band structure modelling; crystals; physics pedagogy; mathematics, maple. *Mailing Add:* Dept Physics Univ Man Winnipeg MB R3T 2N2 Can. *E-Mail:* loly@cc.umanitoba.ca

LOMAN, JAMES MARK, RADIATION EFFECTS. *Current Pos:* STAFF ENGR, GEN ELEC CO, 83- *Personal Data:* b Waterbury, Conn, Nov 14, 54; m 75; c 3. *Educ:* Villanova Univ, BS, 75; Univ Notre Dame, MS, 77; Univ Del, PhD(physics), 80. *Prof Exp:* Res assoc, Brookhaven Nat Lab, 80-81; eng specialist, Ford Aerospace & Commun Corp, 81-83. *Mem:* Am Phys Soc. *Res:* Experimental radiation effects in electronic devices and insulators; spacecraft charging; radiation effects in geological material for nuclear waste disposal applications. *Mailing Add:* 206 Regent St Saratoga Springs NY 12866

LOMAN, M LAVERNE, MATHEMATICS. *Current Pos:* from asst prof to prof, 61-93, EMER PROF MATH, UNIV CENT OKLA, 93- *Personal Data:* b Stratford, Okla, June 10, 28; m 44, Coy E; c S Leigh (Easton). *Educ:* Univ Okla, BS, 56, MA, 57, PhD(math educ), 61. *Prof Exp:* From asst to instr math, Univ Okla, 56-61. *Mem:* Math Asn Am; Nat Coun Teachers Math. *Res:* Mathematics education. *Mailing Add:* 2201 Tall Oaks Trail Edmond OK 73003

LOMANITZ, ROSS, theoretical physics, for more information see previous edition

LOMAS, CHARLES GARDNER, FLUID FLOW INSTRUMENTATION. *Current Pos:* FAC MEM, ORE INST TECHNOL, 92- *Personal Data:* b Ft Peck, Mont; c 1. *Educ:* Univ Md, BS, 57, BS, 64, MS, 75. *Prof Exp:* Engr, Miller Fluid Power, 70-71; asst instr mech engr, Univ Md, 71-77; engr, Dantec Electronics, 77-80; instr eng sci, Lafayette Col, 80-82; asst prof mech eng, Rochester Inst Technol, 85-86; assoc prof fluid power technol, Northampton Community Col, 86-88; assoc prof eng technol, Calif Polytech State Univ, 88-92. *Mem:* Am Soc Mech Engrs; Am Soc Eng Educ. *Mailing Add:* Ore Inst Technol Klamath Falls OR 97601. *Fax:* 541-885-1855; *E-Mail:* lomasc@oit.osshe.edu

LOMAS, LYLE WAYNE, BEEF CATTLE NUTRITION. *Current Pos:* From asst prof to assoc prof, 79-92, HEAD, KANS STATE UNIV, SE AGR RES CTR, 85-, PROF ANIMAL SCI, 92- *Personal Data:* b Monett, Mo, June 8, 53; m 76, Connie G Frey; c Amy L & Eric W. *Educ:* Univ Mo, BS, 75, MS, 76; Mich State Univ, PhD, 79. *Concurrent Pos:* Bd dirs, Parsons Rotary Club, 92-, Res Ctr Adminr Soc, 93- *Mem:* Am Soc Animal Sci; Am Registry Prof Animal Scientists; Am Forage & Grassland Coun; Res Ctr Adminr Soc. *Res:* Ruminant nutrition; forage utilization by grazing stocker cattle. *Mailing Add:* RR 1 Dennis KS 67341. *E-Mail:* llomas@oznet.ksu.edu

LOMAX, EDDIE, ORGANIC CHEMISTRY. *Current Pos:* Control chemist, Puritan Chem Co, 51-53, res chemist, 53-57, lab mgr, 57-71, asst tech dir, 71-73, TECH DIR, PURITAN CHEM CO, 73- *Personal Data:* b Atlanta, Ga, Aug 12, 23; m 48. *Educ:* Morehouse Col, BS, 48; Atlanta Univ, MS, 51. *Concurrent Pos:* Sci consult, Atlanta Bd Educ. *Mem:* Am Chem Soc. *Res:* Free radical mechanism in solutions; surfactants, insecticides and disinfectants; floor polishes; cyclobutadiene series. *Mailing Add:* 495 Harlan Rd SW Atlanta GA 30311-2005

LOMAX, HARVARD, ENGINEERING, IED MATHEMATICS. *Current Pos:* teacher, 50-95, EMER PROF, STANFORD UNIV, 95- *Personal Data:* b Broken Bow, Nebr, Apr 18, 22; m 43; c 3. *Educ:* Stanford Univ, BA, 43, MA, 47. *Honors & Awards:* Fluid & Plasma Dynamics Award, Am Inst Aeronaut & Astronaut, 77. *Concurrent Pos:* Res scientist, Ames Res Ctr, NACA-NASA, 44-94. *Mem:* Nat Acad Eng; fel Am Inst Aeronaut & Astronaut. *Res:* Subsonic and supersonic dynamics; the upper-atmosphere aerodynamics of hypersonic blunt bodies; the foundations of computational fluid dynamics. *Mailing Add:* 770 Seale Ave Palo Alto CA 94303

LOMAX, MARGARET IRENE, MOLECULAR GENETICS, GENOME ORGANIZATION OF NUCLEAR GENES FOR CYTOCHROME C OXIDASE. *Current Pos:* Res assoc biol chem, Univ Mich, Ann Arbor, 64-67, instr, 67-88, asst res sci, Div Biol Sci, 74-85 & Dept Microbiol & Immunol, 85-88, ASST RES SCI, DEPT ANAT & CELL BIOL, UNIV MICH, ANN ARBOR, 88-, DIR, DNA SEQUENCING FACIL, 90- *Personal Data:* b Roanoke, Va, Nov 13, 38; m 64; c 2. *Educ:* Case Western Reserve Univ, BA, 60; Univ Mich, PhD(biol chem), 64. *Concurrent Pos:* Am Cancer Soc fel, 64-66. *Mem:* AAAS; Am Soc Microbiol; Am Soc Biol Chemists; Asn Women Sci. *Res:* Genome organization and molecular evolution of cytochromec oxidase in primates; tissue-specific expression of cytochrome C oxidase nuclear genes. *Mailing Add:* Dept Anat & Cell Biol Univ Mich Med Sch 4769 Med Sci II PO Box 0616 Ann Arbor MI 48109-0616

LOMAX, PETER, pharmacology, for more information see previous edition

LOMAX, RONALD J(AMES), SOLID STATE DEVICES, COMPUTER SIMULATION. *Current Pos:* From vis asst prof to assoc prof, 61-73, PROF ELEC ENG & COMPUT SCI, UNIV MICH, ANN ARBOR, 73- *Personal Data:* b Stockport, Eng, July 18, 34; m 64, Margaret I Smith; c Catherine & Ian. *Educ:* Cambridge Univ, BA, 56, MA & PhD(appl math), 60. *Prof Exp:* Bye fel Peterhouse, Univ Cambridge, Eng, 59-61. *Concurrent Pos:* Vis prof, Stanford Univ, 77-78. *Mem:* Inst Elec & Electronics Engrs; Soc Indust & Appl Math; Cambridge Philos Soc. *Res:* Solid-state devices; electron device modeling; finite element method; very large scale integrated circuit design. *Mailing Add:* Dept Elec Eng & Comput Sci Univ Mich Ann Arbor MI 48109-2122

LOMBARD, DAVID BISHOP, EXPERIMENTAL PHYSICS. *Current Pos:* PRES, DBL CONSULTS, 97- *Personal Data:* b Lexington, Mass, June 10, 30; m 52, Josephine Cooper; c Suzanne, Jonathan, Robin, Patricia & Katherine. *Educ:* Northeastern Univ, BA, 53; Pa State Univ, MS, 55, PhD(physics), 59. *Prof Exp:* Sr physicist, Lawrence Livermore Lab, Univ Calif, 59-70; mgr, Atcor, Inc, 70-71; pres, Geo-Resource Assocs, 71-72; vpres, Subcom, Inc, 72-74; prog mgr, NSF, 74; br chief, geothermal energy div, Energy Res Develop Admin, 75-77; br chief, geothermal & biomass progs, Dept Energy, 77-83, asst dir, off renewable technol, 83-87, team leader, geothermal res, 87-97. *Mem:* Sigma Xi; Am Phys Soc; Soc Petrol Engrs. *Res:* Geopressured geothermal energy; neutron physics, fission-to-indium age of neutrons in water; strong shocks in solids; applications of nuclear explosions; oil shale; geothermal energy applications; geothermal drilling technology; geothermal energy conversion. *Mailing Add:* DBL Consults 6640 Hazel Lane McLean VA 22101-5113. *E-Mail:* dlombard@sprynet.com

LOMBARD, JULIAN H, PHYSIOLOGY, ZOOLOGY. *Current Pos:* From asst prof to assoc prof, 77-88, PROF PHYSIOL, MED COL WIS, 88- *Personal Data:* b El Paso, Tex, Oct 31, 47. *Educ:* Univ Tex, El Paso, BA, 69; Ariz State Univ, MS, 71; Med Col Wis, PhD(physiol), 75. *Concurrent Pos:* Nat Res Serv award, NIH, 75-77; Young Investr res grant, Nat Heart, Lung & Blood Inst, 78-81; estab investr, Am Heart Asn, 85-; mem, Coun High Blood Pressure Res, Am Heart Asn; mem coun, Microcirculatory Soc. *Mem:* Am Physiol Soc; Soc Exp Biol & Med; Sigma Xi; Microcirculatory Soc; Shock Soc. *Res:* Vascular smooth muscle physiology; physiology of the microcirculation; local regulation of blood flow and nervous control of small blood vessels during hemorrhage, low flow states, and hypertension. *Mailing Add:* Dept Physiol Med Col Wis 8701 Watertown Plank Rd Milwaukee WI 53226-1408

LOMBARD, LOUISE SCHERGER, PATHOLOGY. *Current Pos:* assoc path, 75-77, VET PATHOLOGIST, ARGONNE NAT LABS, ILL, 77- *Personal Data:* b Wichita, Kans, Nov 20, 21; m 48; c 4. *Educ:* Kans State Univ, DVM, 44; Univ Wis, MS, 47, PhD(path), 50. *Prof Exp:* Assoc vet, Morgan's Animal Hosp, 44-45; diagnostician, Corn States Serum Co, 45-46; instr path, Univ Wis, 46-50; instr, Woman's Med Col Pa, 50-51; res assoc virol, Univ Pa, 51-53, asst prof path, 53-55; biologist, Nat Cancer Inst, 55-57; assoc pathologist, Argonne Nat Labs, Ill, 57-64; assoc prof path, Stritch Sch Med, Loyola Univ Chicago, 64-69; res scientist, Univ Chicago, 69-70, assoc prof path & pharmacol, 70-73; sect head path, Abbott Labs, Abbott Park, Ill, 73-75. *Concurrent Pos:* Consult pathologist, Chicago Zool Park, 60- & Argonne Nat Lab, 64-75. *Mem:* AAAS; Am Soc Exp Path; Wildlife Dis Asn; Am Vet Med Asn; Sigma Xi. *Res:* Neoplasms in animals; chemical carcinogenesis; viral oncology; radiobiology. *Mailing Add:* 373 Borica Dr Danville CA 94526-5457

LOMBARD, PORTER BRONSON, HORTICULTURE. *Current Pos:* assoc prof, 63-70, PROF HORT, ORE STATE UNIV, 70-, SUPT, SOUTHERN ORE EXP STA, 63-, EMER PROF. *Personal Data:* b Yakima, Wash, Feb 6, 30; m 55; c 3. *Educ:* Pomona Col, BA, 52; Wash State Univ, MS, 55; Mich State Univ, PhD(hort), 58. *Prof Exp:* Asst horticulturist, Citrus Exp Sta, Calif, 58-63. *Mem:* AAAS; Am Soc Hort Sci. *Res:* Pear varieties; rootstocks; nutrition, pear fruit bud hardiness and water requirements. *Mailing Add:* 2425 E Main St Medford OR 97504

LOMBARD, RICHARD ERIC, MORPHOLOGY. *Current Pos:* asst prof, 72-78, ASSOC PROF ANAT & EVOLUTIONARY BIOL, UNIV CHICAGO, 78-; RES ASSOC, FIELD MUS NATURAL HIST, 81- *Personal Data:* b Brooklyn, NY, May 16, 43; m 67; c 2. *Educ:* Hanover Col, AB, 65; Univ Chicago, PhD(anat), 71. *Prof Exp:* Res assoc, Mus Vert Zool, Univ Calif, Berkeley, 71; res assoc, Univ Southern Calif, 71-72. *Mem:* AAAS; Am Soc Ichthyologists & Herpetologists; Am Soc Zoologists; Soc Study Amphibians & Reptiles; Soc Study Evolution. *Res:* The evolutionary and functional morphology of major adaptive features of lower vertebrates including auditory periphery in frogs, feeding apparatus of frogs and salamanders and the vestibular system in salamanders. *Mailing Add:* Dept Anat Univ Chicago Pritzker Sch Med 1025 E 57th St Chicago IL 60637-1508

LOMBARDI, GABRIEL GUSTAVO, LASERS, NON-LINEAR OPTICS. *Current Pos:* PHYSICIST, MISSION RES CORP, 92- *Personal Data:* b Buenos Aires, Arg, Sept 5, 54. *Educ:* Univ Chicago, BA, 75; Harvard Univ, PhD(physics), 80. *Prof Exp:* Res assoc, Nat Bur Stand, 80-82; mem tech staff, TRW Inc, 83-84; mem res tech staff, Northrop Res & Tech Ctr, 84-92. *Mem:* Optical Soc Am; Am Phys Soc. *Res:* Experimental research in optical phase conjugation; stimulated brillouin scattering; stimulated raman scattering; atomic spectroscopy; gas discharge lasers; laser remote sensing. *Mailing Add:* Mission Res Corp 3625 Del Amo Blvd Suite 215 Torrance CA 90503. *Fax:* 310-793-1633; *E-Mail:* glombardi@mrcla.com

LOMBARDI, JOHN ROCCO, PHYSICAL CHEMISTRY. *Current Pos:* ASSOC PROF CHEM, CITY COL, CITY UNIV NEW YORK, 75- *Personal Data:* b June 10, 41; US citizen; c 1. *Educ:* Cornell Univ, AB, 63; Harvard Univ, AM, 66, PhD(chem), 67. *Prof Exp:* Asst prof chem, Univ Ill, 67-72; vis scientist physics, Univ Leiden, Neth, 72-73; vis scientist chem, Mass Inst Technol, 73-75. *Mem:* Int Photochem Soc; Sigma Xi. *Res:* Laser spectroscopy; molecular structure; scattering. *Mailing Add:* Dept Chem City Col City Univ New York 160 Convent Ave New York NY 10031-9101

LOMBARDI, MAX H, RADIATION BIOLOGY, NUCLEAR MEDICINE. *Current Pos:* PROF NUCLEAR MED, HILLSBOROUGH COMMUNITY COL, 77- *Personal Data:* b Huanuco City, Peru, Apr 25, 32; m 61; c 3. *Educ:* Univ Lima, BSc & DVM, 58; Cornell Univ, MSc, 61, Am Bd Sci Nuclear Med, cert, 79. *Prof Exp:* From asst prof to assoc prof biochem & nutrit, Vet Col Peru, 60-64; scientist biomed appln & consult, lectr & overall coord progs Latin Am, Oak Ridge Assoc Univs, 64-68, sr scientist & coordr, Radiation Biol & Med Radioisotope Training Progs, Oak Ridge Assoc Univs, 68-77. *Concurrent Pos:* Asst dir in vitro div, Tampa Gen Hosp, 77-79. *Mem:* Soc Nuclear Med; Clin Ligand Assay Soc; World Fedn Nuclear Med & Biol. *Res:* author of 24 publications in three languages. *Mailing Add:* Allied Health Hillsborough County Col PO Bopx 30030 Tampa FL 33630-3030

LOMBARDI, PAUL SCHOENFELD, MICROBIOLOGY, PHYSICAL SCIENCE EDUCATION. *Current Pos:* TEACHER, DAVIS SCH DIST, 85- *Personal Data:* b Salt Lake City, Utah, Nov 13, 40; m 68; c 3. *Educ:* Univ Utah, BA, 63, MA, 65; Univ Rochester, PhD(microbiol), 69. *Prof Exp:* Instr, Col Med, Univ Utah, 71-73, asst prof microbiol, 73-78. *Concurrent Pos:* Damon Runyon Mem Fund fel, Swiss Inst Exp Cancer Res, 69-70; Am Cancer Soc fel, Univ Utah, 71-73; NIH grant, 74-76. *Mem:* Am Soc Microbiol; Nat Sci Teachers Asn. *Res:* Cell-virus interactions of polyoma virus in permissive cells; structural proteins of polyoma virions; mycoplasma viruses and their interactions with mammalian cells. *Mailing Add:* 1026 Oakridge Dr Centerville UT 84014

LOMBARDINI, JOHN BARRY, PHARMACOLOGY. *Current Pos:* asst prof, 73-77, ASSOC PROF PHARMACOL, TEX TECH UNIV, HEALTH SCI CTR, 77- *Personal Data:* b San Francisco, Calif, July 2, 41; m 68; c 2. *Educ:* St Mary's Col Calif, BS, 63; Univ Calif, San Francisco, PhD(biochem), 68. *Prof Exp:* Fel, Sch Med, Johns Hopkins Univ, 68-72, res assoc pharmacol, 72-73. *Mem:* Am Soc Pharmacol & Exp Therapeut. *Res:* Function of taurine as a possible neurotransmitter or modulator of nerve impulses; role of taurine in cardiac and retinal tissues; formation, function and regulatory properties of S-adenosylmethionine synthetase. *Mailing Add:* Dept Pharmacol Sch Med Tex Tech Health Sci Ctr PO Box 4569 Lubbock TX 79430-0001

LOMBARDINO, JOSEPH GEORGE, RESEARCH ADMINISTRATION. *Current Pos:* Sr res investr, Pfizer, Inc, 77-79, res adv, 79-86, dir develop planning, 86-94, SR DIR OPER PLANNING, PFIZER, INC, 94- *Personal Data:* b Brooklyn, NY, July 1, 33; m 60, Roberta; c Anna-Marie, George & Anthony. *Educ:* Brooklyn Col, BS, 54; Polytech Univ, PhD, 58. *Honors & Awards:* Eli Whitney Award, Conn Patent Law Asn, 89. *Mem:* Am Chem Soc; Int Soc Heterocyclic Chem; Inflammation Res Asn; fel Am Inst Chemists; Proj Mgt Inst. *Res:* Synthetic organic medicinals; nitrogen heterocycles; anti-inflammatory drugs; immunoregulatory drugs. *Mailing Add:* 13 Laurel Hill Dr Niantic CT 06357

LOMBARDO, ANTHONY, ORGANIC CHEMISTRY. *Current Pos:* from asst prof to assoc prof, 68-82, PROF CHEM, FLA ATLANTIC UNIV, 82- & CHMN, 83- *Personal Data:* b Brooklyn, NY, Jan 4, 39. *Educ:* Queens Col, NY, BS, 61; Syracuse Univ, PhD(org chem), 67. *Prof Exp:* Fel, Univ Calif, Santa Barbara, 67-68. *Mem:* Sigma Xi. *Res:* Coenzyme models, donor-acceptor complexes; kinetics; spectroscopy. *Mailing Add:* Off Pres PO Box 3091 Boca Raton FL 33431-0991

LOMBARDO, R(OSARIO) J(OSEPH), CHEMICAL ENGINEERING. *Current Pos:* chem engr, E I Du Pont de Nemours & Co Inc, 51-56, tech supvr, 56-59, tech supt, 59-60, asst plant mgr, 61, asst dir tech serv lab, 61-64, mgr plants tech sect, Pigments Dept, 65-68, prod mgr, Chem & Pigments Dept, 68-79, MGR MFT SERV, CHEM & PIGMENTS DEPT, E I DU PONT DE NEMOURS & CO, INC, 79- *Personal Data:* b Pawcatuck, Conn, Oct 17, 21; c 3. *Educ:* Univ RI, BS, 43, MS, 47; Pa State Univ, PhD(chem eng), 51. *Prof Exp:* Engr, Hamilton Stand Div, United Aircraft Corp, 43-46. *Mem:* Am Inst Chem Engrs; Sigma Xi. *Res:* Engineering administration; production administration. *Mailing Add:* 1307 Copley Dr Wilmington DE 19803

LOMBOS, BELA ANTHONY, materials science, microelectronics, for more information see previous edition

LOMEDICO, PETER T, MOLECULAR BIOLOGY. *Current Pos:* CHIEF SCI OFFICER, MORPHOGENESIS, INC, 94- *Personal Data:* b New York, NY, Dec 23, 48; m 74, Marcia; c Mark & Alexandra. *Educ:* Villanova Univ, BS, 70; Univ Tex, PhD(molecular biol), 77. *Prof Exp:* At Hoffmann-LaRoche Inc, 80-93. *Mailing Add:* Genet Genome Therapeut Corp 100 Beaver St Waltham MA 02154. *Fax:* 973-783-5741

LOMEN, DAVID ORLANDO, APPLIED MATHEMATICS. *Current Pos:* from asst prof to assoc prof, 69-74, PROF MATH, UNIV ARIZ, 74-, UNIV DISTINGUISHED PROF, 96- *Personal Data:* b Decorah, Iowa, May 11, 37; m 61, Constance Trecek; c Catherine (Hoerth). *Educ:* Luther Col, Iowa, BA, 59; Iowa State Univ, MS, 62, PhD, 64. *Prof Exp:* Design specialist, Gen Dynamics & Astronaut, 63-66. *Concurrent Pos:* Consult var industs; Marshall Fund Award, Norway-Am Found, 80, 83; vis sr scientist, Norway, 80. *Mem:* Soc Indust & Appl Math; Am Math Soc; Soil Sci Soc Am; Geophys Union; Europ Geophys Soc. *Res:* Modeling water and solute flow in soils; curriculum and software development in mathematics. *Mailing Add:* Dept Math Univ Ariz Tucson AZ 85721. *Fax:* 520-621-8322; *E-Mail:* lomen@math.arizona.edu

LOMMEL, J(AMES) M(YLES), TECHNICAL INFORMATION, METALLURGY. *Current Pos:* metallurgist, Gen Elec Res & Develop Ctr, 57-69, mgr personnel & tech admin, Electronics Sci & Eng, 69-77, mgr info res oper, 77-83, consult, Info Systs, 83-87, mgr, Info Ctr, 88-91, mgr support serv, 91-95, MGR TECH INFO & PUBL SERV, GEN ELEC RES & DEVELOP CTR, 96- *Personal Data:* b Evanston, Ill, Feb 7, 32; m 59; c 2. *Educ:* Ill Inst Technol, BS, 53, MS, 54; Harvard Univ, PhD(appl physics), 58. *Prof Exp:* Metallurgist, H M Harper Co, 54-56. *Concurrent Pos:* Teaching asst, Tufts Univ, 55 & Harvard Univ, 55-56. *Mem:* Inst Elec & Electronics Engrs; Am Inst Mining, Metall & Petrol Engrs. *Res:* Physical metallurgy; magnetic materials and recording; computer systems service; information retrieval; technical information. *Mailing Add:* Gen Elec Res & Develop Ctr PO Box 8 Schenectady NY 12301. *E-Mail:* lommel@crd.ge.com

LOMNITZ, CINNA, SEISMOLOGY. *Current Pos:* PROF SEISMOL, INST GEOPHYS, NAT UNIV MEX, 68- *Personal Data:* b Cologne, Ger, May 4, 25; m 51, 88; c 4. *Educ:* Univ Chile, CE, 48; Harvard Univ, MS, 50; Calif Inst Technol, PhD(geophys), 55. *Honors & Awards:* Nat Sci Prize, Mex, 95. *Prof Exp:* Res fel seismol, Calif Inst Technol, 55-57; prof geophys, Univ Chile, 57-64, dir inst geophys & seismol, 58-64; assoc res seismologist, Seismog Sta, Univ Calif, Berkeley, 64-68. *Concurrent Pos:* Consult, Geol Surv, Chile, 58-; vis assoc, Calif Inst Technol & Univ Calif, San Diego, 69- *Mem:* Seismol Soc Am; Am Geophys Union; Sigma Xi. *Res:* Earthquake hazard; creep properties of rocks; viscoelasticity and internal friction in solids; seismicity; structure of the Andes; origin of earthquakes and tsunamis. *Mailing Add:* Geophys Inst Nat Univ Mex Mexico 04510 DF Mexico. *Fax:* 525-550-2486; *E-Mail:* cinna@ollin.igeofcu.unam.mx

LOMON, EARLE LEONARD, PARTICLE & NUCLEAR THEORY. *Current Pos:* assoc prof, 60-70, PROF PHYSICS, MASS INST TECHNOL, 70- *Personal Data:* b Montreal, Que, Nov 15, 30; nat US; m 51, Ruth M Jones; c M Glynis, C Dylan & Deirdre N. *Educ:* McGill Univ, BSc, 51; Mass Inst Technol, PhD(theoret physics), 54. *Prof Exp:* Res physicist, Can Defence Res Bd, 50-51 & Baird Assocs, Mass, 52-53; Nat Res Coun Can overseas res fel, Inst Theoret Physics, Denmark, 54-55; fel, Weizmann Inst, 55-56; res assoc, Lab Nuclear Studies, Cornell Univ, 56-57; assoc prof theoret physics, McGill Univ, 57-60. *Concurrent Pos:* Guggenheim Mem Found fel, 65-66; vis scientist, Cern, Geneva, 65-66, KFA, Julich, WGER, 86-90; vis scientist, Los Alamos Nat Lab, 68-; proj dir, Unified Sci & Math Elem Sch, 71-77; vis prof, Univ Paris, 79-80, & 86-87, Univ Calif, Los Angeles, 83 & Univ Wash, Seattle, 85; adj prof, Louvain-la-Neuve, Belg, 80; res fel, Univ Col, London, 80; Lady Davis vis prof, Hebrew Univ, Jerusalem, 93-94. *Mem:* Am Phys Soc; Can Asn Physicists. *Res:* Nuclear and medium energy particle physics; field theory. *Mailing Add:* Dept Physics Mass Inst Technol Cambridge MA 02139. *Fax:* 617-253-8674; *E-Mail:* lomon@mitlns.mit.edu

LOMONACO, SAMUEL JAMES, JR, MATHEMATICS, COMPUTER SCIENCE. *Current Pos:* PROF, DEPT COMPUT SCI, UNIV MD, BALTIMORE COUNTY CAMPUS, 80- *Personal Data:* b Dallas, Tex, Sept 23, 39; m 68; c 1. *Educ:* St Louis Univ, BS, 61; Princeton Univ, PhD(math), 64. *Prof Exp:* Asst prof math, St Louis Univ, 64-65 & Fla State Univ, 65-69; res mathematician & comput scientist, Tex Instruments, Inc, 69-71; assoc prof comput sci & math, State Univ NY Albany, 71-80. *Concurrent Pos:* Indust prof, Southern Methodist Univ, 69-71; actg chmn, Dept Comput Sci, State Univ NY, Albany, 73-74; vis, Inst Defense Analysis, Princeton, NJ, 74-76; vis lectr, Dept Math, Princeton Univ, 75-76. *Mem:* Am Math Soc; Asn Comput Mach; Math Asn Am; Soc Indust & Appl Math; Sigma Xi. *Res:* Algebraic topology, higher dimensional knot theory; algebraic coding theory; complexity theory. *Mailing Add:* 10236 Little Brick House Ct Ellicott City MD 21042

LOMONT, JOHN S, MATHEMATICAL PHYSICS. *Current Pos:* PROF MATH, UNIV ARIZ, 65- *Personal Data:* b Ft Wayne, Ind, Aug 26, 24. *Educ:* Purdue Univ, MS, 47, PhD(physics), 51. *Prof Exp:* Physicist theoret solid state physics, NAm Aviation, Inc, 51-52; physicist, Res Dept, Michelson Lab, Naval Ord Test Sta, 52-54; physicist, NY Univ, 54-57 & Int Bus Mach Corp, 57-60; prof math, Polytech Inst Brooklyn, 62-65. *Concurrent Pos:* Sabbatical, Courant Inst Math Sci, NY Univ, 71-72. *Mem:* Am Phys Soc; Am Math Soc. *Res:* Applied group theory; quantum field theory; functional analysis. *Mailing Add:* Univ Ariz Bldg 89 Tucson AZ 85721-0001

LONADIER, FRANK DALTON, PHYSICAL CHEMISTRY, INORGANIC CHEMISTRY. *Current Pos:* sr res chemist, Monsanto Res Corp, 59-61, group leader inorg & nuclear chem, 61-64, sect mgr mat eval, 64-65, sect mgr nuclear develop, 65-67, mgr nuclear prod, 67-69, mgr explosive technol, 69-76, mgr advan devices prod, 76-86, MGR, MFG MOUND LAB, MONSANTO RES CORP, 87- *Personal Data:* b Clarence, La, May 6, 32; m 59; c 2. *Educ:* Northwestern State Col, La, BS, 54; Univ Tex, PhD(phys chem), 59. *Prof Exp:* Res asst, Los Alamos Sci Lab, Univ Calif, 57-58.

Concurrent Pos: Tech Safety Appraisals for Radioactive Mfg. *Mem:* Am Chem Soc; Am Soc Qual Control. *Res:* Actinide elements, particularly uranium and plutonium; inorganic chemistry of polonium; behavior of secondary explosives; environmental pollutant abatement. *Mailing Add:* 221 Estates Dr Dayton OH 45459-2837

LONARD, ROBERT (IRVIN), PLANT TAXONOMY. *Current Pos:* ASST PROF BIOL, PAN AM UNIV, 70- *Personal Data:* b Valley Falls, Kans, June 5, 42; m 65; c 1. *Educ:* Kans State Teachers Col, BSE, 64, MS, 66; Tex A&M Univ, PhD(plant taxon), 70. *Mem:* AAAS; Am Soc Plant Taxonomists; Int Asn Plant Taxonomists. *Res:* Flora of south Texas; grass systematics. *Mailing Add:* Dept Biol Univ Tex Pan Am 1201 W University Dr Edinburg TX 78539-2909

LONBERG-HOLM, KNUD KARL, BIOCHEMISTRY. *Current Pos:* CONSULT, 88- *Personal Data:* b New York, NY, Sept 22, 31; m 52, 61; c 3. *Educ:* Harvard Univ, BA, 53; Univ Calif, Berkeley, PhD(biochem), 62. *Prof Exp:* Chemist, Hyman Labs, Fundamental Res, Inc, 59-60; biochemist, Cent Res Dept, E I Du Pont de Nemours & Co, Inc, 62-85. *Concurrent Pos:* USPHS fel, Univ Uppsala, 67-69; assoc prof microbiol & immunol, Sch Med, Temple Univ, 76-77; vis prof microbiol & immunol, Hahnemann Univ, 85-88; adj prof, Hahnemann Univ, 88-92. *Res:* Biochemistry of plasma proteins; virus-cell interaction; biochemical virology. *Mailing Add:* PO Box 95 Lockwood NY 14859. *E-Mail:* klonbergh@aol.com

LONDERGAN, JOHN TIMOTHY, MEDIUM-ENERGY NUCLEAR THEORY. *Current Pos:* from asst prof to assoc prof, 73-82, PROF PHYSICS, IND UNIV, 83-, CHAIR, PHYSICS DEPT, 90- *Personal Data:* b Niagara Falls, NY, Mar 13, 43; m 86; c 3. *Educ:* Univ Rochester, BS, 65; Oxford Univ, DPhil, 69. *Prof Exp:* Res assoc physics, Case Western Res Univ, 69-71, Univ Wis, 71-73. *Concurrent Pos:* Assoc dean, Grad Sch, 84-88; dir, Nuclear Theory Ctr, 85-87; vis prof, Swiss Inst Nuclear Res, 82-83; vis prof, Univ Adelaide, Australia, 89; consult, Los Alamos Nat Lab, 88- *Mem:* Am Phys Soc; Am Asn Univ Professors. *Res:* Intermediate-energy nuclear theory; photonuclear reactions; scattering theory at medium energies; structure of the nucleon. *Mailing Add:* Dept Physics Ind Univ Swain Hall W Rm 117 Bloomington IN 47405

LONDON, A(LEXANDER) L(OUIS), MECHANICAL ENGINEERING. *Current Pos:* from instr to prof, 38-78, EMER PROF MECH ENG, STANFORD UNIV, 78- *Personal Data:* b Nairobi, Kenya, Aug 31, 13; US citizen; m 38; c 3. *Educ:* Univ Calif, BS, 35, MS, 38. *Prof Exp:* Engr, Stand Oil Co Calif, 36-37; instr, Univ Santa Clara, 37-38. *Concurrent Pos:* Res assoc, Argonne Nat Lab, 55-56. *Mem:* Nat Acad Eng; Am Soc Mech Engrs; Am Soc Eng Educ; Soc Naval Eng. *Res:* Heat transfer; thermodynamics; fluid mechanics. *Mailing Add:* 4020 Amaranta Ave Palo Alto CA 94306

LONDON, DAVID, METAMORPHIC PETROLOGY, FLUID INCLUSION ANALYSIS. *Current Pos:* ASST PROF GEOL, UNIV OKLA, 83- *Personal Data:* b Ardmore, Okla, Feb 27, 53. *Educ:* Wesleyan Univ, BA, 75; Ariz State Univ, Tempe, MS, 79, PhD, 81. *Prof Exp:* Fel geol, Geophys Lab, Carnegie Inst, 81-83. *Concurrent Pos:* Consult exploration, Cabot Mineral Resources, 81-83; prin investr, res grant, US Bur Mines, 83- & NSF, 86- *Mem:* Am Geophys Union; Mineral Asn Can; Mineral Soc Am. *Res:* Internal evolution of fractionated granite-pegmatite systems; emphasis on crystallization sequences, melt-vapor equilibrium and trace element partitioning and formation of rare-element deposits. *Mailing Add:* Sch Geol Univ Okla 900 Asp Ave Norman OK 73019-4050

LONDON, EDYTHE D, NEUROCHEMISTRY, NEUROPHARMACOLOGY. *Current Pos:* pharmacologist, 84-85, chief, Neuropharmacol Lab, 85-92, CHIEF, BRAIN IMAGING SECT, NAT INST DRUG ABUSE, 92-, ACTG CHIEF, NEUROSCI BR, 95-, DIR, BRAIN IMAGING CTR, 96- *Personal Data:* b Rome, Italy, Sept 14, 48; US citizen; c 2. *Educ:* George Washington Univ, BS, 69; Towson State Univ, MS, 73; Univ Md, PhD(pharmacol), 76. *Honors & Awards:* Mathilde Salowey Award, 87. *Prof Exp:* Fel psychopharmacology, Sch Med, Johns Hopkins Univ, 76-78; staff fel, Nat Inst on Aging, 79-81, pharmacologist, 81-82. *Concurrent Pos:* Adj prof pharmacol & exp therapeut, Univ Md Sch Med; assoc prof radiol, Johns Hopkins Sch Med. *Mem:* Soc Neurosci; Am Soc Pharmacol Exp Therapeut; Am Soc Neurochem; Int Soc Cerebral Blood Flow & Metab; Am Col Neuropsychopharmacol; Col Probs Drug Dependence. *Res:* Regional cerebral metabolism and changes in neurotransmitter balance in the aging brain; localization of the actions of psychoactive drugs; developing methods for noninvasive imaging of brain function; positron emission tomography; studies on mechanisms of addiction and development of treatment. *Mailing Add:* NIDA Addiction Res Ctr 5500 Nathan Shock Dr Baltimore MD 21224-0180. *Fax:* 410-550-1441; *E-Mail:* elondon@irp.nida.nih.gov

LONDON, GILBERT J(ULIUS), MATERIALS SCIENCE, BERYLLIUM TECHNOLOGY. *Current Pos:* BR HEAD STRUCT MAT, NAVAL AIR DEVELOP CTR, 75- *Personal Data:* b Philadelphia, Pa, May 30, 31; m 76; c 4. *Educ:* Drexel Inst Technol, BS, 53; Univ Pa, MS, 55, PhD(metall eng), 59. *Prof Exp:* Metallurgist, Aerosci Lab, Gen Elec Co, 56-59; sr res metallurgist & mgr, Mech Metall Lab, Franklin Inst, Pa, 59-70; mgr metall res & develop, Kawecki Berylco Industs, 70-75. *Concurrent Pos:* Adj prof, Drexel Univ. *Mem:* Am Inst Mining, Metall & Petrol Engrs; Sigma Xi. *Res:* Flow and fracture of iron; dispersed hard particle strengthening of metals; beryllium; purification; high purity alloys; micro-strain properties; slip analysis; coextruded composites; beryllium alloys. *Mailing Add:* Naval Air Warfare Ctr Code 434P Patuxent River MD 20670

LONDON, IRVING M, MEDICINE. *Current Pos:* prof biol, Mass Inst Technol, 69-89, prof med, 72-89, Grover M Hermann prof health sci & technol, 77-89, EMER PROF BIOL & MED, MASS INST TECHNOL, 89-; EMER PROF MED, HARVARD MED SCH, 89- *Personal Data:* b Malden, Mass, July 24, 18; m 55; c 2. *Educ:* Harvard Univ, AB, 39, MD, 43. *Hon Degrees:* ScD, Univ Chicago, 66. *Honors & Awards:* Theobald Smith Award in Med Sci, AAAS, 53; Jean Oliver Lectr, State Univ NY, 57; Roger Morris Lectr, Univ Cincinnati, 58; Stuart McGuire Lectr, Med Col Va, 60; Eugene A Stead Jr Vis Lectr, Duke Univ Med Ctr, 70; E Stanley Emery Jr Mem Staff Lectr, Peter Bent Brigham Hosp, 71; Bloomfield Lectr & Bloomfield Medalist, Lady Davis Inst, Montreal, 86. *Prof Exp:* asst resident med serv, Presby Hosp NY, 46-47; from instr to assoc prof med, Columbia Univ, 47-55; prof & chmn dept, Albert Einstein Col Med, 55-70; prof, Harvard Med Sch, 72-89. *Concurrent Pos:* Asst physician, Presby Hosp, NY, 47-52, from asst attend physician to assoc attend physician, 52-54; mem, Med Fel Bd & Subcomt Blood & Related Probs, Nat Acad Sci-Nat Res Coun, 55-63; res coun mem, Pub Health Res Inst, NY, 58-63; bd sci consult, Sloan-Kettering Inst Cancer Res, 60-72; metab study sect mem, USPHS, 60-63, chmn, 61-63, mem bd sci coun, Nat Heart Inst, 64-68; dir, Harvard-Mass Inst Technol Prog Health Sci & Technol, 69-77, dir, Div Health Sci & Technol, 77-85, dir, Whitaker Col Health Sci Technol & Mgt, 78-82; vis prof med, Harvard Med Sch, 69-72; Albert Einstein Col Med, NY, 70-, Rockefeller Univ Hosp, 75 & Univ Rotterdam, Neth, 75; physician, Peter Bent Brigham Hosp; mem, Panel Biol Sci & Advan Med, Nat Acad Sci, 66-67; bd med, 67-70; mem adv comt to dir, NIH, 66-70; mem, Nat Cancer Adv Bd, 72-76; mem, Bd Sci Coun, Nat Inst Arthritis, Metab & Digestive Dis, 79-83; mem bd dirs, Johnson & Johnson, 82-89; sr consult med, Brigham & Women's Hosp, Boston, 87- *Mem:* Nat Acad Sci; Am Acad Arts & Sci; Am Asn Physicians; Am Soc Clin Invest (pres, 63-64); Am Soc Biol Chemists; fel AAAS; Int Soc Hemat; Soc Develop Biol; Harvey Soc. *Res:* Hemoglobin metabolism; metabolism of erythrocytes; eukaryotic protein synthesis; author of numerous publications. *Mailing Add:* Mass Inst Technol Harvard-MIT Div Health Sci & Technol Bldg E25 Rm 551 77 Massachusetts Ave Cambridge MA 02139

LONDON, J PHILLIP, BUSINESS ADMINISTRATION. *Current Pos:* mgr, CACI Int Inc, Arlington, Va, 72-76, vpres, 76-77, sr vpres, 77-79, exec vpres, 79-82, pres operating div, 82-84, pres & chief exec officer, 84-90, CHMN BD, CACI INT INC, 90- *Personal Data:* b Oklahoma City, Okla, Apr 30, 37; c J Phillip Jr & Laura (McLain). *Educ:* US Naval Acad, BSc, 59; US Naval Postgrad Sch, MSc, 67; George Washington Univ, Doctorate(bus admin), 71. *Prof Exp:* Prog mgr, Challenger Res Inc, 71-72. *Mem:* High Tech Entrepreneur Award, KPMG Peat Marwick, 95. *Mailing Add:* CACI Int Inc 1100 N Glebe Rd Arlington VA 22201-4798

LONDON, JULIUS, METEOROLOGY. *Current Pos:* prof astro-geophys, 61-87, chmn dept, 66-69, EMER PROF ASTROPHYS, PLANETARY & ATMOSPHERIC SCI, UNIV COLO, BOULDER, 87- *Personal Data:* b Newark, NJ, Mar 26, 17; m 46, Dorothy Sibulsky; c Richard A. *Educ:* Brooklyn Col, BA, 41; NY Univ, MS, 48, PhD, 51. *Hon Degrees:* DSc, Fed Inst Technol, Zurich, Switz, 91. *Prof Exp:* Meteorologist, US Weather Bur, 42; instr meteorol, USAF, 42-47; res assoc meteorol, NY Univ, 48-52, asst prof, 52-56, res assoc prof, 56-59, assoc prof, 59-61. *Concurrent Pos:* Lectr, Columbia Univ, 54-55; vis prof, Pa State Univ, 55; Max Planck Inst Physics, Gottingen, 58; mem, Int Ozone Comn, Int Asn Meteorol & Atmospheric Physics, 60-; vis res scientist, Nat Ctr Atmospheric Res, 61-66; chmn panel ozone, Nat Res Coun, Nat Acad Sci, 64-65, mem, Comt Human Resources, 78-81; vis prof, Swiss Fed Inst Technol, 67, 74-76; chief US deleg, XVII Gen Assembly, Int Asn Meteorol & Atmospheric Physics, 79; lectr, Chinese Acad Sci, Inst Atmospheric Physics, 80. *Mem:* AAAS; Int Asn Metorol & Atmospheric physics; Sigma Xi; Am Geophys Union; Int Radiation Comn (secy, 63-71, pres, 71-79). *Res:* Atmospheric radiation; physics of the atmosphere; ozone; observed and theoretical variations of atmospheric ozone; radiative, photochemical, and dynamical processes and their effect on responses of the stratosphere and mesosphere to solar perturbations or anthropogenic processes; Earth's radiation budget, its interaction with the large-scale motions of the atmosphere, and relation to climatic change. *Mailing Add:* Astrophys Planetary & Atmospheric Sci Dept Univ Colo Campus Box 391 Boulder CO 80309-0391. *Fax:* 303-492-6946; *E-Mail:* london@zodiac.colorado.edu

LONDON, MARK DAVID, IMPACT ASSESSMENT, MANAGEMENT. *Current Pos:* asst vpres, VPRES, ENVIRO-SCI INC. *Personal Data:* b Brooklyn, NY, May 24, 47; m 70; c 2. *Educ:* C W Post Col, Long Island Univ, BS, 70, MS, 74. *Prof Exp:* Biologist, Eng Sci, Inc, 69-72; environ scientist, Woodward-Clyde Consult, 72-76; biologist, Pub Serv Elec & Gas Co, 76-77, lead biologist, 77-79, sr staff biologist, 79-80, sr biologists, 80, environ studies mgr, 82-88; dir, Environ Rev Div, NY Dept City Planning, 88-91. *Concurrent Pos:* Mem, Twp Denville, NJ Environ Comn, 80-81, chmn, 81-87. *Mem:* Am Soc Testing & Mat; Soc Power Indust Biologists; Am Soc Limnol & Oceanog; Edison Elec Inst Biologist; Am Inst Biol Sci. *Res:* Director and chief reviewer of New York City's City Environmental Quality Review Process reviewing all non-as-of-right-construction in New York City. *Mailing Add:* Enviro-Sci Inc 111 Howard Blvd Suite 108 Mt Arlington NJ 07856

LONDON, MORRIS, BIOCHEMISTRY, ENZYMOLOGY. *Current Pos:* CHIEF CLIN CHEM, BROOKDALE MED CTR, 71- *Educ:* Ohio State Univ, PhD(physiol), 50. *Res:* Clinical chemistry. *Mailing Add:* 141-36 73rd Terr Flushing NY 11367-2307

LONDON, RAY WILLIAM, STRESS-CRISIS MANAGEMENT, BEHAVIORAL MEDICINE. *Current Pos:* CONSULT & PVT PRACT, ST JOSEPH HOSP, 73- *Personal Data:* b Burley, Idaho, May 29, 43. *Educ:* Weber State Col, BS, 67; Univ Southern Calif, MSW, 73, PhD(psychol), 76,

MBA, 89. *Prof Exp:* Clin trainee & fel, Vet Admin & Children's Hosp,71-74. *Concurrent Pos:* Res affil, Ctr Crisis Mgt, Univ Southern Calif, 87-; adv ed, Int J Clin & Exp Hypn, 81-; clin fac, Univ Calif Irvine Col Med, 78-; fel, Inst Social Scientist Neurobiology & Mental Illness, 78; mem fac, Univ Calif, Los Angeles, Univ Southern Calif, Calif State Univ, 76-86; res assoc, Nat Comt Protection Human Subjects Biomed & Behav Res, 76; res assoc, Bus Adv, Inc, 65-67; dir, Meaning Found, 66-69; mental health liasion, San Bernardino County Social Serv, 68-72; pres, Human Factors Prog, 76-; dir, Human Studies Ctr, 87-; chief exec officer, London Assoc Int, 76-; Erickson Scholar Dipl, Neuropsychology, Med Psychol, Family Psychol, Admin Psychol, Clin Hypn. *Mem:* Int Acad Med & Psychol (pres, 80-); Soc Clin & Exp Hypn (treas, 87-89); Int Psychosomatic Inst; Am Bd Psychol Hypn (pres, 89-); Am Bd Clin Hypn (pres, 90-); Int Consults Found. *Res:* Scientific investigation, integration and application of medical psychology, behavioral medicine, psychophysiology, hypnosis, cognitive, behavioral, organizational and psychosocial data to stress, crisis and human performance issues, problems and policy concerns. *Mailing Add:* 18062 Irvine Blvd Tustin CA 92681

LONDON, ROBERT ELLIOT, BIOPHYSICAL CHEMISTRY, NUCLEAR MAGNETIC RESONANCE. *Current Pos:* NUCLEAR MAGNETIC RESONANCE GROUP LEADER, LAB STRUCT BIOL, NAT INST ENVIRON HEALTH SCI, 84- *Personal Data:* b Brooklyn, NY, Oct 25, 46; m 69, Phyllis; c Stephen, Jeffrey & Elise. *Educ:* Brooklyn Col, BS, 67; Univ Ill, MS, 69, PhD(physics), 73. *Prof Exp:* Fel, Los Alamos Nat Lab, 73-75, staff mem biophys chem, 75-83. *Mem:* Am Soc Biochem & Molecular Biol; Biophys Soc. *Res:* Nuclear magnetic resonance studies of biologically important molecules. *Mailing Add:* MD MR-01 Nat Inst Environ Health Sci Box 12233 Research Triangle Park NC 27709. *Fax:* 919-541-5707; *E-Mail:* london@niehs.nih.gov

LONDON, WILLIAM THOMAS, INTERNAL MEDICINE, EPIDEMIOLOGY. *Current Pos:* assoc, 66-71, from asst prof to assoc prof, 71-78, ADJ PROF MED, SCH MED, UNIV PA, 78-; SR MEM, FOX CHASE CANCER CTR, 89- *Personal Data:* b New York, NY, Mar 11, 32; m 57, Linda Greenman; c Barbara, Katharine, Emily & Nancy. *Educ:* Oberlin Col, BA, 53; Cornell Univ, MD, 57. *Honors & Awards:* Med Excellente Award, Del Valley Cha, Am Liver Found, 91. *Prof Exp:* Intern med, Bellevue Hosp, 57-58, resident, Med Ctr, 58-60; res epidemiologist, Nat Inst Arthritis & Metab Dis, 62-66; res physician, Inst Cancer Res, 66-78. *Concurrent Pos:* Fel endocrinol, Sloan-Kettering Inst, NY, 60-62; asst, Med Col, Cornell Univ, 60-62; instr, Sch Med, George Washington Univ, 64-; sr res physician, Int Cancer Res, 78-89. *Mem:* Am Thyroid Asn; Am Asn Cancer Res; Am Soc Prev Oncol; Am Soc Virol; Soc Epidemiol Res; Am Col Physicians. *Res:* Susceptibility factors to cancer; variations in host response to hepatitis B infection; molecular epidemiology of hepatocellular carcinoma. *Mailing Add:* Fox Chase Cancer Ctr 7701 Burholme Ave Philadelphia PA 19111

LONE, M(UHAMMAD) ASLAM, EXPERIMENTAL NUCLEAR PHYSICS. *Current Pos:* Nat Res Coun Can fel, 68-70, from res officer physics to assoc res officer, 70-83, SR RES SCIENTIST PHYSICS, CHALK RIVER LABS, ATOMIC ENERGY CAN LTD, 83- *Personal Data:* b East Punjab, India, Jan 28, 37; m 70; c 3. *Educ:* Punjab Univ, West Pakistan, BSc, 58, MSc, 60; State Univ NY Stony Brook, PhD(physics), 67. *Prof Exp:* Lectr physics, Govt Col, Lahore, Pakistan, 60-62; fel, Ind Univ, Bloomington, 67-68. *Concurrent Pos:* Mem, Int Atomic Energy Agency, Nuclear Data Comt. *Mem:* Can Asn Physicists; Am Phys Soc; Can Radiol Prof Asn; Can Nuclear Soc. *Res:* Nuclear spectroscopy by gamma ray, neutron, and charged particle induced reactions; investigation of nuclear reaction mechanism; radiation physics, utilization of nuclear radiation for industrial processing; industrial neutron sources. *Mailing Add:* Chalk River Labs Atomic Energy Can Ltd Chalk River ON K0J 1J0 Can. *Fax:* 613-584-1849; *E-Mail:* lonea@crlc.crl.aecl.ca

LONERGAN, DENNIS ARTHUR, FOOD SCIENCE, FOOD TECHNOLOGY. *Current Pos:* GOLDEN VALLEY MICRO, WARE FOOD INC, 90- *Personal Data:* b West Bend, Ind, May 30, 49; m 80. *Educ:* Univ Wis-Madison, BS, 71, MS, 75, PhD(food sci), 78. *Prof Exp:* Scientist res, Pillsbury Co, 78-80; asst prof food analysis, Purdue Univ, 80-83; scientist res, Pillsbury Co, 83-90. *Mem:* Inst Food Technologists. *Res:* Functionality of casein as a food ingredient; methods of determining water mobility in food; membrane processing of foods. *Mailing Add:* 1825 County Rd 24 Long Lake MN 55356

LONERGAN, THOMAS A, BIOLOGICAL SCIENCE. *Current Pos:* PROF BIOL, UNIV NEW ORLEANS, 88- *Personal Data:* b Syracuse, NY. *Mailing Add:* Biol Sci Dept Univ New Orleans 2000 Lakeshore Dr New Orleans LA 70148-0001

LONEY, ROBERT AHLBERG, STRUCTURAL GEOLOGY, PETROLOGY. *Current Pos:* GEOLOGIST, US GEOL SURV, 56- *Personal Data:* b Odebolt, Iowa, June 16, 22; wid; c 3. *Educ:* Univ Wash, BS, 49, MS, 51; Univ Calif, Berkeley, PhD(geol), 61. *Prof Exp:* Geologist, Superior Oil Co, Tex, 51-52 & Wyo, 52-54. *Mem:* Am Geophys Union; Geol Soc Am; Mineral Soc Am; Ger Geol Asn. *Res:* Structural petrology and petrology of mafic-ultramafic complexes and associated terranes; Pacific coastal region including Alaska. *Mailing Add:* 12112 Foothill Lane Los Altos CA 94022

LONG, ALAN JACK, FOREST ECOLOGY, FOREST GENETICS. *Current Pos:* ASST PROF FORESTRY, UNIV FLA, 87- *Personal Data:* b Baton Rouge, La, Oct 17, 44; m 66; c 2. *Educ:* Univ Calif, Berkeley, BS, 67, MS, 71; NC State Univ, PhD(forestry, genetics), 73. *Prof Exp:* Asst prof forest genetics, Pa State Univ, 73-74; res scientist regeneration ecol, Weyerhaeuser Co, 74-79, forestry res field sta mgr, 80-87. *Concurrent Pos:* Field sta mgr trop forestry res, Indonesia, 79-80. *Res:* Technology requisite for plantation establishment and early growth of western conifers; use of clonal material in tree improvement and regeneration programs; root growth of conifer seedlings. *Mailing Add:* 1120 NW 94th St Gainesville FL 32606

LONG, ALAN K, SYNTHETIC ORGANIC & NATURAL PRODUCTS CHEMISTRY. *Current Pos:* Res assoc, Dept Chem, 79-92, LAB DIR, DEPTS CHEM, EARTH & PLANETARY SCI, HARVARD UNIV, 92- *Personal Data:* b Burlington, Vt, June 19, 50; m 84; c 1. *Educ:* Yale Univ, BS, 71; Harvard Univ, MA, 76, PhD(chem), 79. *Mem:* Am Chem Soc. *Res:* Development of the LHASA computer program for computer-assisted analysis of problems in synthetic organic chemistry; coordination of database expansion for LHASA. *Mailing Add:* Dept Chem Harvard Univ 12 Oxford St Cambridge MA 02138-2902

LONG, ALEXANDER B, NUCLEAR ENGINEERING. *Current Pos:* CONSULT. *Personal Data:* b New York, NY, Jan 16, 43; m 66. *Educ:* Williams Col, BA, 64; Univ Ill, Urbana, MS, 66, PhD(nuclear eng), 69. *Prof Exp:* Asst nuclear engr, Argonne Nat Lab, 69-78; mem staff elec power res, Nuclear Safety Anal, 78-; prog mgr, Elec Power Res Inst, 74-83; pres, Expert Ease Systs, 83-90. *Mem:* Am Nuclear Soc; Inst Elec & Electronics Engrs. *Res:* Reactor physics, especially experimental techniques for on line determination of reactor physics parameters; fission physics. *Mailing Add:* Elec Software Prod Inc 419 S San Antonio Rd Los Altos CA 94022

LONG, ALEXIS BORIS, cloud physics, weather modification, for more information see previous edition

LONG, ALTON LOS, JR, ELECTRONICS, MATERIALS TECHNOLOGY. *Current Pos:* develop engr lab, Unisys Defense Systs, 60-61, supvr testing & eval sect, 61-65, staff engr, Adv Develop Dept, 65-70, prog mgr, Comput Microfilm Systs, 70-72, prog mgr, Illiac IV Syst, 72-73, dept mgr, Components Eval, 73-77, prog mgr advan technol, 77-81, dir opers, Spec Devices Div, Systs Develop Corp, Burroughs Corp, 82-87, Mgr, Infusec Prod & Technols, 87-90, PROG MKT MGR, GOV PROG, COMPUTER SYSTS PROD GROUP, UNISYS DEFENSE SYSTS, 90- *Personal Data:* b Liberty, Tex, Sept 25, 32; m 55; c 4. *Educ:* Carnegie Inst Technol, BS, 53, MS, 55; Univ Penn, MS cand, 88. *Prof Exp:* Jr res chemist radiochem, Carnegie Inst Technol, 53-54; unit chief radiation effects, US Army Signal Res & Develop Labs, Ft Monmouth, 57-60, nuclear scientist, 60. *Concurrent Pos:* Instr, Monmouth Col, 58-59. *Mem:* Armed Forces Commun & Electronics Asn; Inst Elec & Electronic Engrs; Sigma Xi; Nat Mgt Asn; Inst Cert Prof Mechs. *Res:* Microelectronics; information science; radiation effects on materials; electronic materials; environmental science; physics of failure; radiocarbon dating; applied radiation technology; interconnection and packaging technology. *Mailing Add:* 87 Bismark Ave Tiverton RI 02878

LONG, ANDREW FLEMING, JR, MATHEMATICS. *Current Pos:* asst prof, 67-75, ASSOC PROF MATH, UNIV NC, GREENSBORO, 75- *Personal Data:* b Amboy, WVa, Dec 20, 38. *Educ:* WVa Univ, BS, 60, MS, 61; Duke Univ, PhD(math), 65. *Prof Exp:* Asst prof math, St Andrews Presby Col, 65-67. *Mem:* Math Asn Am; Sigma Xi; Asn Comput Mach. *Res:* Irreducible factorable polynomials over a finite field; number theory; computer software. *Mailing Add:* Dept Math Univ NC Greensboro NC 27412. *E-Mail:* longaf@iris.uncg.edu

LONG, AUSTIN, GEOCHEMISTRY. *Current Pos:* assoc prof geosci, 68-87, PROF GEOSCI, HYDROL & WATER RESOURCES & CHIEF SCIENTIST, LAB OF ISOTOPE GEOCHEM, UNIV ARIZ, 87- *Personal Data:* b Olney, Tex, Dec 12, 36; m 61; c 2. *Educ:* Midwestern Univ, BS, 57; Columbia Univ, MA, 59; Univ Ariz, PhD(geochem), 66. *Prof Exp:* Res asst geochem, Geochronol Labs, Univ Ariz, 59-63; geochemist, Smithsonian Inst, 63-68. *Mem:* Geochemistry Soc. *Res:* Pleistocene paleoclimatology; radiocarbon dating; stable isotope geochemistry. *Mailing Add:* Dept Geosci Univ Ariz 1600 E Univ Blvd Tucson AZ 85721-0001

LONG, AUSTIN RICHARD, ANIMAL DRUGS, METHODS DEVELOPMENT & ANALYTICAL. *Current Pos:* DIR, ATLANTA CTR NUTRIENT ANALYSIS, 96- *Personal Data:* b Akron, Ohio, Sept 15, 49. *Educ:* Ohio State Univ, BS, 80, MS, 83, PhD(food sci), 87. *Prof Exp:* Teaching asst food sci, Ohio State Univ, 82-83, Burgwald Fel, 84, res assoc, 85-87; sr fel biochem, La State Univ, 87-90; dir, Animal Drugs Res Ctr, Food & Drug Admin, 90-96. *Mem:* Veterinary drug residue in animal feed, edible animal tissue and aquaculture species; develop analytical methods for regulatory use; author and inventor. *Mailing Add:* Atlanta Ctr Nutrient Anal Food & Drug Admin 60 Eight St NE Atlanta GA 30309. *Fax:* 303-236-3099

LONG, BILLY WAYNE, PHYSIOLOGY. *Current Pos:* ASST PROF MED, UNIV MISS, 81- *Personal Data:* b Tupelo, Miss, Apr 5, 48; m 72, Holmes; c Scott & David. *Educ:* David Lipscomb Col, Nashville, BA, 69; Univ Miss, MD, 73. *Prof Exp:* Intern & resident med, Univ Miss, 73-75; clin assoc digestive dis, NIH, 75-77; fel gastroenterol, Univ Pa, 77-79, asst prof med, 79-81. *Mem:* Fel Am Col Gastroenterol; fel Am Col Physicians; Am Soc Gastrointestinal Endoscopy; AMA. *Res:* Physiology of pancreatic exocrine secretion; physiology of gastrointestinal hormones. *Mailing Add:* Gastro Assocs PA 1421 N State St Suite 203 Jackson MS 39202-1658

LONG, CALVIN H, ANALYTICAL CHEMISTRY. *Current Pos:* RETIRED. *Personal Data:* b Myerstown, Pa, Feb 16, 27; m 54; c 2. *Educ:* Univ Miami, BS, 50; Franklin & Marshall Col, MS, 56; Stanford Univ, PhD(chem), 63. *Prof Exp:* Chemist, Armstrong Cork Co, 50-58; res chemist, Chevron Res Co, 63-64; res group leader analytical chem, Kerr-McGee Corp, 64-68, sect mgr, 69-78, mgr, 79-88. *Mem:* Am Chem Soc. *Res:* Chemical equilibria; mineral benefication. *Mailing Add:* 3900 S Lockwood Ridge Rd No 21 Sarasota FL 34231-7625

LONG, CALVIN LEE, BIOCHEMISTRY. *Current Pos:* ADJ PROF NUTRIT SCI, UNIV ALA, BIRMINGHAM, 84-, DIR RES, BAPTIST MED CTR, 84- *Personal Data:* b NC, Jan 27, 28; m 51; c 3. *Educ:* Wake Forest Col, BS, 48; NC State Col, MS, 51; Univ Ill, PhD, 54. *Prof Exp:* Assoc chemist biochem, Gen Food Corp, 54-57, proj leader, 57-62; res assoc, Harvard Univ, 63 & Col Physicians & Surgeons, Columbia Univ, 64-74; from assoc prof to prof Biochem & Surg, Med Col Ohio, 75-84. *Mem:* AAAS; Am Inst Nutrit; Am Chem Soc; NY Acad Sci; Am Soc Parenteral & Enteral Nutrit. *Res:* Intermediary metabolism and nutritional biochemistry. *Mailing Add:* Dept Res Carraway Methodist Med Ctr 1600 Carraway Blvd Birmingham AL 35234

LONG, CALVIN THOMAS, ELEMENTARY NUMBER THEORY, COMBINATORIAL NUMBER THEORY. *Current Pos:* from asst prof to assoc prof, 56-65, chmn dept, 70-78, PROF MATH, WASH STATE UNIV, 65- *Personal Data:* b Rupert, Idaho, Oct 10, 27; m 52; c 2. *Educ:* Univ Idaho, BS, 50; Univ Ore, MS, 52, PhD(math), 55. *Prof Exp:* Analyst, Nat Security Agency, 55-56. *Concurrent Pos:* Educ consult, Wash State Dept Educ, 61-67 & NSF, 63-83; vis prof, Univ Jabalpur, India, 65, Univ BC, 72, Clemson Univ, 78-79, Portland State Univ, 79; consult, Educ Comn States, Nat Assessment Educ Progress, 75; educ consult, Rand McNally & Co, 75-77, William Clare, Ltd, 73-77, Wash State Dept Educ, 83, 87-88, 89, NSF, 85-87, Prentice Hall Publ Co, 87-; chair, Comt Rev Guidelines for the Accreditation of Col Math Progs, 74-78, mem, 78-80, mem, Comt Adult Educ, 78-80, Ad Hoc Comt NCATE Guidelines, 79-80, Comt Employment of Math, 80-88, chair, 83 & 85, Comt Math Educ of Teachers, 83-88, mem Ad Hoc Comt Accreditation, 86-90; assoc ed, Math Mag, 86-90; mem, Coun Conf Bd Math Sci, 78-80; mem, Task Force on Post Baccalaureate Educ of Teachers, 86-88. *Mem:* Math Asn Am; Nat Coun Teachers Math; Asn Teachers Math; Fibonacci Asn; Am Math Soc. *Res:* Probabilistic and combinatorial number theory and other combinatorial problems. *Mailing Add:* 2120 N Timberline Rd Flagstaff AZ 86004-7548

LONG, CARL F(ERDINAND), REINFORCED CONCRETE DESIGN, MANAGEMENT OF WATER WORKS COMPANY. *Current Pos:* RETIRED. *Personal Data:* b New York, NY, Aug 6, 28; m 55, Joanna M Tavares; c Carl F Jr & Barbara A. *Educ:* Mass Inst Technol, SB, 50, SM, 52; Yale Univ, DEng, 64. *Hon Degrees:* MA, Dartmouth Col, 71. *Honors & Awards:* Robert Fletcher Award, Thayer Sch Eng, 85. *Prof Exp:* Asst civil eng, Mass Inst Technol, 52-54, res engr, 54; from instr civil eng to assoc prof, 54-70; from assoc dean to dean, Thayer Sch Eng, Dartmouth Col, 72-84, prof eng, 70-94, emer dean & dir, Cook Eng Design Ctr, 84-94. *Concurrent Pos:* Consult, NH State Water Pollution Comn, 58-93 & Small Arms Systs Agency, US Army; trustee, Mt Wash Observ, 75-; mem bd overseers, Mary Hitchcock Mem Hosp, 73-; dir, Controlled Environ Corp, Grantham, NH, 75-81, vpres opers, 76-81; pres & dir, OS-Oxygen Processes, Portland, Maine, 79-84; dir, Micro-Tool Co Inc, Fitchburg, MA, 84-92; mem, ad hoc vis comt, Eng Coun Prof Develop, 73-81; mem, vis comt, Mass Bd Regents Higher Educ, 84-93; pres & dir, Roan Thayer Inc, 87-93; dir, Micro-Weigh Systs, Inc, 87-93; pres & dir, Hanover Water Works, Inc, 90- *Mem:* AAAS; Am Soc Civil Engrs; Am Soc Eng Educ. *Res:* Analytical and experimental investigations of structures and structural elements; planning and decision making for small towns and cities with time-sharing computers; maintenance, planning and funding modest size water distribution systems. *Mailing Add:* Thayer Sch Eng Dartmouth Col 25 Resevoir Rd Hanover NH 03755-1311

LONG, CAROLE ANN, IMMUNOLOGY, PARASITOLOGY. *Current Pos:* PROF, ALLEGHENY UNIV, 96- *Personal Data:* b Baltimore, Md, Oct 2, 44; m 80, Walter Cuskey; c 5. *Educ:* Cornell Univ, AB, 65; Univ Pa, PhD(microbiol & immunol), 70. *Prof Exp:* Fel, Univ Pa Sch Med, 70-73; sr res scientist, Wyeth Labs, Radnor, Pa, 73-75; asst mem, Inst Med Res, 76-77; from asst prof to prof, Hahnemann Univ, 77-96. *Concurrent Pos:* Chair, Adv Comn Parasitol, Burroughs-Wellcome Found, 96-; res grants, NIH & WHO. *Mem:* Am Asn Immunologists; Tissue Cult Asn (treas, 76); AAAS; Asn Women Sci; Sigma Xi; Am Soc Trop Med & Hyg (pres, 94-95). *Res:* Host-parasite relationships in malaria parasites; vaccine developement for malaria. *Mailing Add:* 38 Wistar Rd Villanova PA 19085-1513. Fax: 215-848-2271; *E-Mail:* longc@allegheny.edu

LONG, CEDRIC WILLIAM, BIOCHEMISTRY, VIROLOGY. *Current Pos:* chief, Preclin Trials Sect, 80-86, actg chief, Biol Resources Br, 84-85, actg assoc dir, Biol Response Modifiers Prog, DCT, 85, GEN MGR PROJ OFFICER, FREDERICK CANCER RES & DEVELOP CTR, NAT CANCER INST, 86- *Personal Data:* b Minneapolis, Minn, Mar 4, 37. *Educ:* Univ Calif, Los Angeles, BA, 60, MA, 62; Princeton Univ, PhD(biochem), 66. *Prof Exp:* Am Cancer Soc fel biochem, Univ Calif, Berkeley, 66-68; Nat Cancer Inst fel path, Med Sch, NY Univ, 68-69; instr cell biol, 69-70; sr scientist, Flow Labs, Inc 70-72, head, Cell & Viral Biol Sect, 72-76; head, Biol Type C Viruses Sect, Litton Bionetics, Inc, Frederick Cancer Res Ctr, 76-80. *Mem:* AAAS; Am Soc Microbiol; Am Soc Biol Chem; Am Soc Molecular Biol. *Res:* Genetic and biochemical aspects of mammalian cell growth; expression of retroviruses; functional aspects of viral proteins; modification of host reponse to tumor cells. *Mailing Add:* 2 Basildon Circle Rockville MD 20850-2724

LONG, CHARLES ALAN, ZOOLOGY, GENETICS. *Current Pos:* from asst prof to prof, 66-96, EMER PROF BIOL, UNIV WIS-STEVENS POINT, 96- *Personal Data:* b Pittsburg, Kans, Jan 19, 36; m 60, Claudine Lowder; c Alan & John. *Educ:* Pittsburg State Univ, BS, 57, MS, 58; Univ Kans, PhD(zool), 63. *Honors & Awards:* Sigma Xi Res Award, 96. *Prof Exp:* Asst zool, Univ Kans, 59-63; instr, Univ Ill, Urbana, 63-65, asst prof zool & life sci, 65-66. *Concurrent Pos:* Fac fel, Univ Ill, 64; cur mammals, Mus Natural Hist, 66-, dir, 68-83; consult, Lake Mich Proj, Argonne Nat Lab, 74-80 & Ojibway Tribe, Lac de Flambeau, 83-85; Univ Adv Minor Mus Tech, 74-; Fulbright Scholar, 77; vis prof, St Olaf Col, 91; joint appt, Wildlife Mgmt, 94- *Mem:* Am Soc Mammal; Sigma Xi. *Res:* Vertebrate zoology, systematics and zoogeography of mammals; morphology and ecology; variability of mammals; Wyoming and Wisconsin mammals; badgers; fractal geometry, tree branching and morphology; genetical theory for periodical cicados. *Mailing Add:* Dept Biol Univ Wis Stevens Point WI 54481

LONG, CHARLES ANTHONY, CHEMICAL PHYSICS. *Current Pos:* INSTRUMENTATION SUPVR, JOHNS HOPKINS UNIV, 79- *Personal Data:* b San Antonio, Tex, Feb 22, 45. *Educ:* Carleton Col, BA, 67; Ind Univ, PhD(chem physics), 72; Johns Hopkins Univ, BEE, 82, MAS, 92. *Honors & Awards:* Roseman Award, 85. *Prof Exp:* Fel chem physics, Univ Calif, Riverside, 72-73; asst prof chem, Lake Forest Col, 73-77; res assoc, Brookhaven Nat Lab, 77-79. *Concurrent Pos:* NSF res grant, 74. *Mem:* Am Phys Soc; Am Chem Soc; Inst Elec & Electronics Engrs. *Res:* Applications of lasers to problems of the chemistry and physics of small molecules; chemical instrumentation of all forms. *Mailing Add:* Dept Chem Johns Hopkins Univ 34th & Charles Baltimore MD 21218. *E-Mail:* selrahc@purcell400.chm.jhu.edu

LONG, CHARLES JOSEPH, NEUROPSYCHOLOGY. *Current Pos:* PROF PSYCHOL, MEMPHIS STATE UNIV, 67- *Personal Data:* b Caruthersville, Mo, Dec 25, 35; m 58; c 8. *Educ:* Memphis State Univ, BS, 60, MA, 62; Vanderbilt Univ, PhD(psychol), 67. *Concurrent Pos:* Dir, Neuropsychol Training Prog, 72-, Universal Trainer, Memphis State Univ, 72-; pres, Am Bd Prof Neuropsychol, 93. *Mem:* Sigma Xi; Am Psychol Asn; Int Neuropsychol Asn; Nat Acad Neuropsychologists (treas, 86). *Res:* Neuropsychological assessment and cognitive retraining of head injured, learning and neurologically impaired; study of functional factors influencing chronic pain. *Mailing Add:* 1308 Hayne Memphis TN 38119

LONG, CLAUDINE FERN, CHEMISTRY. *Current Pos:* SR LECTR CHEM, UNIV WIS, STEVENS POINT, 85- *Personal Data:* b Nevada, Mo, Sept 10, 38; m 60; c 2. *Educ:* Pittsburg State Univ, BS, 60; Univ Ill-Urbana, MS, 64. *Prof Exp:* Instr biol, 69-70, univ coordr student teachers, Univ Wis, Stevens Point, 71-75; teacher math & sci, PJ Jacobs Jr High Sch, Stevens Point, Wis, 76-79; instr biol, Univ Wis, 79-82; leader group nat res, Malaysia, 82-83. *Concurrent Pos:* Teacher sci, W Jr High Sch, Lawrence, Kans, 60-63 & Ben Franklin Jr High Sch, Stevens Point, Wis, 68; prof, Univ Malaya, Kuala Lumpur, 83; earthwatch researcher, Isle Rhum, Hebrides, Scotland, 85; prin investr serol hyaluronidase, 84- *Mem:* Nat Wildlife Fedn. *Res:* Insecticide resistant houseflies; natural history of birds and mammals; serological properties of hyaluronidase (trematoda); resources of Malaysia (tin, palm oil, pewter, etc); ecology of shore birds; Isle of Rhum, Hebrides, Scotland. *Mailing Add:* 3531 Yvonne Stevens Point WI 54481

LONG, CLIFFORD A, MATHEMATICS. *Current Pos:* From instr to assoc prof, 59-71, PROF MATH, BOWLING GREEN STATE UNIV, 71- *Personal Data:* b Chicago, Ill, Apr 10, 31; m 57; c 4. *Educ:* Univ Ill, BS, 54, MS, 55, PhD(math), 60. *Mem:* Soc Indust & Appl Math; Math Asn Am; Nat Coun Teachers Math. *Res:* Computer graphics; numerical analysis. *Mailing Add:* 1005 Gustin Bowling Green OH 43402

LONG, DALE DONALD, PHYSICS INSTRUCTION, EXPERIMENTAL PHYSICS. *Current Pos:* from asst prof to assoc prof, 67-92, PROF PHYSICS, VA POLYTECH INST & STATE UNIV, 92- *Personal Data:* b Louisa, Va, Jan 30, 35; m 65, Lou Rich; c Donald & Douglas. *Educ:* Va Polytech Inst, BS, 58, MS, 62; Fla State Univ, PhD(physics), 66. *Prof Exp:* Instr physics, Va Polytech Inst, 60; instr, Samford Univ, 60-62. *Concurrent Pos:* Vis assoc prof, Davidson Col, 88-89. *Mem:* Am Phys Soc; Am Asn Physics Teachers. *Res:* Development of multimedia materials for physics instruction; enhancement of the effectiveness of physics instruction, author of introductory physics textbooks; experimental nuclear physics. *Mailing Add:* Dept Physics Va Polytech Inst & State Univ Blacksburg VA 24061-0435

LONG, DARREL GRAHAM FRANCIS, CLASTIC & CARBONATE SEDIMENTOLOGY, COAL GEOLOGY. *Current Pos:* from asst prof to assoc prof, 81-89, PROF SEDIMENTOL, LAURENTIAN UNIV, SUDBURY, 89- *Personal Data:* b Yorkshire, Eng, Sept 6, 47; m 73; c 2. *Educ:* Univ Leicester, Eng, BSc, 69; Univ Western Ont, MSc, 73, PhD(geol), 76. *Prof Exp:* Fel geol, Geol Surv Can, 76-77, res scientist coal geol, 77-81. *Mem:* Geol Asn Can; Geol Soc Am; Int Asn Sedimentologists; Soc Econ Paleontologists & Mineralogists; Can Soc Petrol Geologists; Geol Soc Australia. *Res:* Clastic sedimentology of Precambrian sequences in Ontario, Yukon and Northwest Territory Canada; sedimentology and coal bearing sequences in British Columbia, Yukon, Northwest Territory and Ontario; phanerozoic sedimentology and tectonics of the Arctic Islands and Quebec. *Mailing Add:* Dept Earth Sci Laurentian Univ Ramsey Lake Rd Sudbury ON P3E 2C6 Can

LONG, DARYL CLYDE, SOIL SCIENCE. *Current Pos:* from asst prof to assoc prof sci & math, 67-81, PROF SCI, PERU STATE COL, 81- *Personal Data:* b Mason City, Iowa, Aug 19, 39; m 60, Peggy E Pribbenou; c Keith, Eric & Christy. *Educ:* Iowa State Univ, BS, 62, MS, 64; Univ Nebr, Lincoln, PhD, 67. *Prof Exp:* Instr soils, Univ Nebr, Lincoln, 64-67. *Mem:* Am Soc Agron; Soil Sci Soc Am; Nat Coun Teachers Math; Sigma Xi. *Res:* Mechanics of soil erosion and plant removal of nutrients from soil aggregates. *Mailing Add:* Dept Sci & Math Peru State Col Peru NE 68421

LONG, DAVID G, SCATTEROMETRY, RADAR. *Current Pos:* ASST PROF ELEC ENG, BRIGHAM YOUNG UNIV, 90- *Educ:* Brigham Young Univ, BS, 82, MS, 83; Univ Southern Calif, PhD(elec eng), 89. *Prof Exp:* Group leader, Jet Propulsion Lab, 83-90. *Concurrent Pos:* Prin investr, NASA, 89- *Mem:* Inst Elec & Electronic Engrs; Am Geophys Union. *Res:* Spaceborne scatterometry; radar; microwave remote sensing; mesoscale atmospheric dynamics; speech and signal processing; estimation theory. *Mailing Add:* ECEN Dept 459 CB Brigham Young Univ Provo UT 84602-1021. *Fax:* 801-378-6586; *E-Mail:* long@ee.byu.edu

LONG, DAVID MICHAEL, CARDIOVASCULAR SURGERY, THORACIC SURGERY. *Current Pos:* PRES & CHMN, ABEL LABS, INC, 91- *Personal Data:* b Shamokin, Pa, Feb 26, 29; c 6. *Educ:* Muhlenberg Col, BS, 51; Hahnemann Med Col, MS, 54, MD, 56; Univ Minn, PhD(physiol), 65; Am Bd Surg, dipl, 66; Bd Thoracic Surg, dipl, 67. *Honors & Awards:* First Prize Res, Am Urol Asn, 66. *Prof Exp:* Instr surg, Univ Minn, 65; from asst prof to assoc prof, Chicago Med Sch, 65-67; from assoc prof to prof surg, Abraham Lincoln Sch Med, Univ Ill Med Ctr, 69-73, attend staff & head div cardiovasc & thoracic surg, Hosp, 67-73; clin assoc prof radiol, Univ Calif, San Diego, 73-92. *Concurrent Pos:* Assoc prof, Cook County Grad Sch Med, 65-73; assoc attend staff, Cook County Hosp, 65-73; asst dir dept surg res, Hektoen Inst Med Res, 65-68, dir, 68-73; attend staff, W Side Vet Admin Hosp, 66-73; consult, Chicago State Tuberc Sanitarium, 67-72; pvt pract, 73-85; pres & chmn, Fluoromed Pharmaceut Inc, 85-88; founder & chmn, Alliance Pharmaceut Corp, 89-91. *Mem:* AAAS; Am Asn Thoracic Surg; fel Am Col Cardiol; fel Am Col Chest Physicians; fel Am Col Surg. *Res:* Surgical research; physiology and morphology; cancer chemotherapy; development of the radiopaque compound perfluorocarbon; development of fluorocarbon emulsions as blood substitutes; electropotential differential diagnosis of breast cancer. *Mailing Add:* 2737 Via Orange Way Suite 108 Spring Valley CA 91978

LONG, DIANA E, HISTORY OF MEDICINE & WOMENS STUDIES. *Current Pos:* dir, Women's Studies, 92-93, PROF HIST, UNIV SOUTHERN MAINE, 95- *Personal Data:* b New Haven, Conn, May 11, 38; m 60, 89; c 3. *Educ:* Smith Col, BA, 59; Yale Univ, MA, 60, PhD(hist sci & med), 66. *Prof Exp:* Res assoc, Yale Univ, 67-70; lectr biol, Boston Univ, 70-73, asst prof biol & hist, 73-83; dir, F C Wood Inst Hist Med, Col Physicians, Philadelphia, 83-89. *Concurrent Pos:* Fel, Radcliffe Inst, 76-77; NSF & NIH res grants, 76-78; vis sr historian, Nat Libr Med, 89-90. *Mem:* AAAS (secy, Sect L, 77-81); Hist Sci Soc; Am Asn Hist Med. *Res:* Biomedical research in twentieth century; eighteenth century medical science; sex research-scientific and social aspects. *Mailing Add:* 94 Bedford St Portland ME 04103

LONG, DONLIN MARTIN, NEUROSURGERY, ELECTRON MICROSCOPY. *Current Pos:* PROF NEUROL SURG & DIR DEPT, SCH MED, JOHNS HOPKINS UNIV, 73- *Personal Data:* b Rolla, Mo, Apr 14, 34; m 59; c 3. *Educ:* Univ Mo, MD, 59; Univ Minn, PhD(anat), 64. *Prof Exp:* Clin assoc, Surg Neurol Bd, NIH, 65-67; assoc prof neurosurg, Univ Minn Hosps, 67-73. *Concurrent Pos:* Consult neurosurgeon, Vet Admin Hosp, Minneapolis, 67- *Mem:* AAAS; Am Asn Neurol Surg; Cong Neurol Surg; Am Asn Neuropath; Soc Neurosci. *Res:* Low back pain and brain edema. *Mailing Add:* Dept Neurol Surg Johns Hopkins Univ Sch Med Baltimore MD 21205

LONG, EARL ELLSWORTH, PUBLIC HEALTH LABORATORY ADMINISTRATION. *Current Pos:* RETIRED. *Personal Data:* b Akron, Ohio, Mar 27, 19; m 41, Eileen Hildreth; c Robert E, Dan C, Jack C & James W. *Educ:* Univ Akron, BSc, 42; Univ Pa, MSc, 47. *Prof Exp:* Asst instr med bact, Sch Med, Univ Pa, 45-48; asst prof bact, Univ Akron, 48-49; dir labs, Akron Health Dept, 49-61; dir labs, Ga Dept Pub Health, 61-82. *Mem:* Am Soc Microbiol; fel Am Pub Health Asn; Asn State & Territorial Pub Health Labs Dirs (pres, 80); Sigma Xi. *Res:* State public health laboratory administration with emphasis on implementation of rapidly changing concepts in service and research. *Mailing Add:* 25313 Plantation Dr Atlanta GA 30324-2946

LONG, EDWARD B, WETLANDS ECOLOGY. *Current Pos:* ENVIRON CONSULT, 81- *Personal Data:* b White Plains, NY, Dec 5, 27; m 52, 70; c 3. *Educ:* Hamilton Col, BA, 52; Kent State Univ, MS, 71, PhD(biol), 75. *Prof Exp:* Mem staff mkt, Carbon Prod Div, Union Carbide Corp, 52-64, proj mgr, New Prod Mkt Develop, 64-69; tech mgr, Environ Prog, Northeast Ohio Areawide Coord Agency, 75-81. *Mem:* Am Soc Limnol & Oceanog; AAAS. *Res:* Environmental quality of Northeast Ohio. *Mailing Add:* 3140 N Martadale Dr Akron OH 44333

LONG, EDWARD R, POLLUTANT-CAUSED BIOLOGICAL EFFECTS. *Current Pos:* MARINE BIOLOGIST, NAT OCEANIC & ATMOSPHERIC ADMIN, 75- *Personal Data:* b Washougal, Wash, 1942. *Educ:* Ore State Univ, BS, 65, MS, 67. *Prof Exp:* Biol oceanogr, Naval Oceanog Off, 67-73; res biologist, Wapora, Inc, 73-75. *Concurrent Pos:* Lectr, George Washington Univ, 70-75. *Mem:* Marine Technol Soc; Estuarine Res Fedn. *Res:* Administration of technical aspects of marine pollution research, focusing upon measures of biological effects among fish, benthos, birds and mammals; chemical measures with observed biological effects. *Mailing Add:* NOAA 7600 Sand Point MS N ORCA22 Seattle WA 98115

LONG, EDWARD RICHARDSON, JR, MOLECULAR PHYSICS, MATERIALS SCIENCE. *Current Pos:* Res scientist human factors, Aeronaut & Space Mech Div, Guid & Control Br, Langley Res Ctr, NASA, 63-67, res scientist solid state physics, Appl Math & Physics Div, Chem & Physics Br, 69-72, res scientist org pollution, Environ & Space Sci Div, Laser & Molecular Physics Br, 72-76, res scientist mat sci, Mat Div, Mat Res Br, 76-80, RES SCIENTIST MAT SCI, MAT DIV, ENVIRON EFFECTS BR, LANGLEY RES CTR, NASA, 80- *Personal Data:* b Annapolis, Md, Sept 1, 41; m 68. *Educ:* Col William & Mary, BS, 63, MS, 67; NC State Univ, PhD(molecular physics, nuclear magnetic resonance), 74. *Concurrent Pos:* Assoc prof, George Washington Univ, 76- *Mem:* Am Phys Soc. *Res:* Solid state physics and organic chemical physics as applied to pollution spectroscopy and materials science. *Mailing Add:* One Ray Circle Hampton VA 23669

LONG, ERIC CHARLES, DNA-DRUG INTERACTIONS, PEPTIDE CHEMISTRY. *Current Pos:* ASST PROF CHEM, IND UNIV-PURDUE UNIV, INDIANAPOLIS, 91. *Personal Data:* b Reading, Pa, Nov 20, 62. *Educ:* Albright Col, Bs, 84, Univ Va, PhD(chem), 89. *Prof Exp:* Jane Coffin Childs fel, Dept Chem, Calif Inst Technol & Columbia Univ, 89-91. *Concurrent Pos:* Mem, Molecular & Biophys Prog, Ind Univ Grad Sch, 91- *Mem:* Am Chem Soc; Am Peptide Soc. *Res:* Design, synthesis and testing of structured peptides and metallopeptides that target nucleic acids sequence-selectively. *Mailing Add:* Dept Chem Ind Univ-Purdue Univ 402 N Blackford St Indianapolis IN 46202. *Fax:* 317-274-4701; *E-Mail:* long@chem.iupui.edu

LONG, F(RANCIS) M(ARK), MICROCIRCUITS. *Current Pos:* dir bioeng, Univ Wyo, 65-74, head, Dept Elec Eng, 77-87, from asst prof to prof, 60-95, ELEC ENG, UNIV WYO, 95- *Personal Data:* b Iowa City, Iowa, Nov 10, 29; wid, Mary A Coyne; c Ann (Brett), Mary (Bronwyn), Thomas M & Caitlin F. *Educ:* Univ Iowa, BS, 53, MS, 56; Iowa State Univ, PhD(elec eng, biomed electronics), 61. *Prof Exp:* Asst elec eng, Univ Iowa, 55-56; instr, Univ Wyo, 56-58 & Iowa State Univ, 58-60. *Concurrent Pos:* Engr, Collins Radio Co, 55, US Naval Air Missile Testing Ctr, Calif, 56 & Good-All Elec Co, 57; NIH spec fel, 72-73; Globe Union Co, 75, cofounder, Wyo Biotelemetry Inc, 78, teaching & consult surface mount technol, 83-, Naval Res Lab, 88, 89 & 91; adj prof, Univ Denveer. *Mem:* Sr mem Inst Elec & Electronics Engrs; Am Soc Eng Educ (vpres, 77-79); Alliance for Eng in Med & Biol (pres, 83-84); Int Soc Hybrid Microelectronics. *Res:* Instrumentation and system design; system modelling; microcircuit technology; animal biotelemetry; polymer thick film circuits; concurrent engineering/TOM. *Mailing Add:* 1888 S Jackson St No 701 Denver CO 80210. *E-Mail:* flong@du.edu

LONG, FRANKLIN A, SCIENCE POLICY, ARMS CONTROL. *Current Pos:* from instr to assoc prof chem, Cornell Univ, 37-42, prof, 46-79, chmn dept, 50-60, dir prog sci, technol & soc, 69-73, Luce prof sci & soc, 69-79, dir, Peace Studies Prog, 76-79, EMER PROF CHEM, CORNELL UNIV, 79- *Personal Data:* b Great Falls, Mont, July 27, 10; m 37; c 2. *Educ:* Univ Mont, AB, 31, MA, 32; Univ Calif, PhD(phys chem), 35. *Honors & Awards:* Parson's Award, Am Chem Soc, 85; Abelson Prize, AAAS, 89. *Prof Exp:* Instr chem, Univ Calif, 35-36; instr, Univ Chicago, 36-37. *Concurrent Pos:* Res supvr, Explosives Res Lab, Nat Defense Res Comt, 42-45; consult, Ballistics Res Lab, Dept Army, 53-59; mem sci adv bd, Air Force Off Sci Res, 56-60; mem, Pres Sci Adv Comt, 61 & 64-67; asst dir, US Arms Control & Disarmament Agency, 62-63; mem bd, Alfred P Sloan Found, 70-83, Arms Control Asn, 71-77, Assoc Univs, Inc, Albert Einstein Peace Prize Found, Fund Peace; mem, Indo-US Comn Educ & Cult, 74-82, co-chmn, 77-82; mem, Bd Sci & Technol Int Develop, Nat Acad Sci, 74-77; mem, Adv Panel, Policy Res & Anal Div, NSF, 77-80; mem bd & consult, Carrier Corp, 78-79, Exxon Corp, 79-80; adj prof, Univ Calif, 88- *Mem:* Nat Acad Sci; AAAS; Am Chem Soc; Am Acad Arts & Sci; Coun Foreign Rel. *Res:* Kinetics of solution reactions; isotopic chemistry; arms control; science and public policy. *Mailing Add:* 311 N Mountain Ave Claremont CA 91711

LONG, GABRIELLE GIBBS, MICRO STRUCTURE CHARACTERIZATION, X-RAY OPTICS. *Current Pos:* GROUP LEADER, NAT INST STAND & TECHNOL, 90- *Personal Data:* m, Knox S; c Janet C (Cox) & Daniel. *Educ:* Polytech Inst Brooklyn, PhD(physics), 72. *Prof Exp:* Res assoc physics, Columbia Univ, 72-76; asst prof physics, Vassar Col, 76-78 & State Univ NY, Stony Brook, 79. *Concurrent Pos:* Coun, Mat Res Soc, 95-97, Am Phys Soc, 96. *Mem:* Fel Am Physics Soc; Am Ceramic Soc; Mat Res Soc; Am Crystallog Asn. *Res:* Microstructure of characterization of materials; x-ray optics; x-ray ihelastic scattering; anomalous x-ray scattering; multiple-small-angle neutron scattering; x-ray dynamical diffraction by imperfect crystalls; surface x-ray absorbtion spectroscopy of ultrathin films. *Mailing Add:* 223/A163 Nat Inst Stand & Technol Gaithersburg MD 20899. *Fax:* 301-990-8729; *E-Mail:* gabrielle.long@nist.gov

LONG, GARY JOHN, PHYSICAL INORGANIC CHEMISTRY, SOLID STATE CHEMISTRY. *Current Pos:* From asst prof to assoc prof, 68-82, PROF CHEM, UNIV MO, ROLLA, 82- *Personal Data:* b Binghamton, NY, Dec 3, 41; m 63; c 1. *Educ:* Carnegie-Mellon Univ, BS, 64; Syracuse Univ, PhD(chem), 68. *Concurrent Pos:* Res assoc, Inorg Chem Lab & St John's Col, Oxford Univ, 74-75; res assoc, Atomic Energy Res Estab, Harwell, 75-81; NATO vis prof chem, Univ Padova, Italy, 83; sci & eng res coun fel, Univ Liverpool, Eng, 83-84; vis prof chem, Univ Padova, Italy, 86-88, Univ Geneva, Switz, 88; vis prof physics, Univ Liege, 92-94; J William Fulbright scholar, 93-94. *Mem:* Am Chem Soc; fel Royal Soc Chem; Sigma Xi; Am Phys Soc; Am Geophys Union. *Res:* Transition metal inorganic coordination chemistry and solid state chemistry; Mossbauer and electronic spectroscopy; high-pressure optical and infrared spectroscopy; magnetic studies of coupled systems and permanent magnetic materials; x-ray and neutron diffraction studies. *Mailing Add:* Dept Chem Univ Mo Rolla MO 65409-0010

LONG, GEORGE, CHEMICAL ENGINEERING. *Current Pos:* CONSULT, NATURAL GAS INDUST, 87- *Personal Data:* b Greenville, Miss, Jan 17, 22; m 51; c 1. *Educ:* Univ Tulane, BE, 44. *Prof Exp:* Res chemist, Div 8, Nat Defense Res Comt, Ohio, 44-45; chief chemist, USAAF, 45-46; res engr, Aluminum Co Am, 46-62; gen coordr res & develop, 62-67, dir, 67-77, mgr dir res & develop, Northern Ill Gas Co, 77-87. *Mem:* Am Gas Asn; Sigma Xi; fel Am Inst Chem; Chem Mkt Res Asn; Am Chem Soc. *Res:* Process metallurgy of aluminum melting and smelting; aluminum-water explosions; high temperature refractory materials; natural gas utilization, materials and devices for distribution systems, substitute natural gas processes and natural gas combustion; synthetic fuel processes. *Mailing Add:* 24 Sylvia Lane Naperville IL 60540-8014

LONG, GEORGE GILBERT, INORGANIC CHEMISTRY. *Current Pos:* RETIRED. *Personal Data:* b Cincinnati, Ohio, July 12, 29; m 52; c 3. *Educ:* Ind Univ, AB, 51; NC State Univ, MS, 53; Univ Fla, PhD(chem), 57. *Prof Exp:* Chemist, Ethyl Corp, 57-58; from asst prof to assoc prof, NC State Univ, 58-70, chmn analytical inorg chem, 69-77, prof chem, 70. *Mem:* Am Chem Soc. *Res:* Chemistry of group V metalloids-organometalloid compounds; 121-Sb Mossbauer spectroscopy, structure and syntheses; vibrational spectroscopy. *Mailing Add:* 2701 Kilgore Ave Raleigh NC 27607

LONG, GEORGE LOUIS, BIOCHEMISTRY, MOLECULAR BIOLOGY. *Current Pos:* assoc prof, 86-91, PROF BIOCHEM, UNIV VERMONT, 91- *Personal Data:* b Atkin, Minn, Dec 20, 43; m 67; c 5. *Educ:* Pac Lutheran Univ, BA, 66; Brandeis Univ, PhD(biochem), 71. *Prof Exp:* NIH trainee molecular endocrinol sch med, Univ Calif, San Diego, 71-73; asst prof chem, Pomona Col, 73-80; NIH sr fel biochem, Univ Wash, 80-82; scientist, Lilly Res Labs, 82-86. *Mem:* Am Soc Molecular & Biol Chem; Sigma Xi; Am Chem Soc; AAAS. *Res:* Comparative enzymology of glycolytic enzymes; molecular biology of hemostasis; bone biochemistry. *Mailing Add:* Dept Biochem Univ Vermont Sch Med B418 Given Bldg Burlington VT 05405

LONG, H(UGH) M(ONTGOMERY), ENHANCED OIL RECOVERY, SUPERCONDUCTING SYSTEMS. *Current Pos:* STAFF EXEC, ENHANCED ENERGY SYSTS, INC, 81- *Personal Data:* b Montgomery, Ala, June 28, 24; m 49; c 2. *Educ:* Ala Polytech Inst, BS, 47, MS, 49; Oxford Univ, DPhil(physics), 53. *Prof Exp:* Instr math, Auburn Univ, 47-48, res asst, 47-49; res physicist, Linde Div, Oak Ridge Nat Lab, Union Carbide Corp, 54-61, cryogenics consult, 61-71, group leader eng sci, Thermonuclear Div, 71-76, mgr elec energy systs prog, Energy Div, 76-80; assoc prof elec eng, Univ Tenn, Knoxville, 71-80; vpres mkt develop, Vedette Energy Res Inc, 80-81. *Concurrent Pos:* Mem, Nat Acad Sci-Nat Res Coun adv panel to Nat Bur Standards Cryogenic Eng Lab, 61-65; US rep, Comt I, Int Inst Refrig, 64-; mem & chmn, US Delegation USSR Scientific & Technol Exchange Superconductivity Power Transmission, 73-79. *Mem:* AAAS; Am Phys Soc; sr mem Inst Elec & Electronics Engrs; NY Acad Sci; Soc Petrol Engrs. *Res:* Low temperature physics; cryogenic engineering; gas liquefaction; low temperature phase equilibria; mechanical properties of materials at low temperatures; superconductivity; power system engineering; energy management. *Mailing Add:* 3551 Lilac Ave Corona Del Mar CA 92625

LONG, HOWARD CHARLES, ACOUSTICS, ATOMIC & MOLECULAR PHYSICS. *Current Pos:* chmn dept, 63-74, prof, 59-81, EMER PROF PHYSICS, DICKINSON COL, 81- *Personal Data:* b Seizholtzville, Pa, Dec 12, 18; m 45, Frances Monroe Hoke; c Howard C, David W & Carol (Boll). *Educ:* Northwestern Univ, BS, 41; Ohio State Univ, PhD(physics), 48. *Prof Exp:* Physicist, Naval Ord Lab, 42-45; instr physics, Ohio State Univ, 47-48; asst prof, Washington & Jefferson Col, 48-51; physicist, Naval Ord Lab, 51-52; assoc prof physics & chmn dept, Am Univ, 52-53; prof & chmn dept, Gettysburg Col, 53-59. *Concurrent Pos:* Consult, Naval Ord Lab, 54-73; NSF sci fac fel, 67-68. *Mem:* Am Phys Soc; Am Asn Physics Teachers. *Res:* Low period fluctuations in earth's magnetism; environmental noise reduction; air pollution by solid particulates; molecular structure and infrared spectroscopy; electromagnetism. *Mailing Add:* 240 Belvedere St Carlisle PA 17013

LONG, JAMES ALVIN, EXPLORATION GEOPHYSICS INTERPRETATIONS & OPERATIONS. *Current Pos:* Retired. *Personal Data:* b Porto Alegre, Brazil, July 13, 17; US citizen; wid; c 4. *Educ:* Univ Okla, BA, 37. *Prof Exp:* Comput & party chief, Stanolind Oil & Gas Co, 37-46; party chief supvr, United Geophys Corp, area mgr & regional opers mgr, South & Cent Am, 46-62, special tech & res assignments under MB Dobrin & others, 62-67 regional mgr, Latin Am, 67-72; sr geophysicist, Tetra Tech, Inc, 73-74; int consult geophysicist, Peru, US, Australia, Colombia, 73-84; geophys adv, Yacimientos Petroliferos Fiscales Bolivianos, Santa Cruz, Bolivia, 74-77. *Mem:* Soc Explor Geophysicists; fel Explorers Club; Earthwatch. *Res:* Seismic surface sources; special seismic interpretation problems and supervision of operations particularly in South America and Australia. *Mailing Add:* 622 Binnacle Dr Naples FL 34103-2724

LONG, JAMES DELBERT, AGRONOMY, HERBICIDE RESEARCH. *Current Pos:* RETIRED. *Personal Data:* b Dover, Okla, Dec 18, 39; c 5. *Educ:* Okla State Univ, BS, 62; Univ Md, College Park, MS, 67, PhD(hort), 69. *Prof Exp:* Res asst weed control, Univ Md, College Park, 64-67, instr hort, 67-68; res biologist agr chem, E I DuPont de Nemours & Co Inc, Wilmington, Del, 68-79, prod develop mgr, 79-83, res assoc, Agr Chem Dept, 83-92. *Mem:* Southern Weed Sci Soc; Sigma Xi. *Res:* Control and modification of plant growth through the use of chemicals; new herbicide discovery and development. *Mailing Add:* 213 Blake Rd Elkton MD 21921

LONG, JAMES DUNCAN, ZOOLOGY. *Current Pos:* assoc prof, 59-63, dir dept, 63-72, PROF BIOL, SAM HOUSTON STATE UNIV, 63- *Personal Data:* b Rusk, Tex, Sept 23, 25. *Educ:* Sam Houston State Col, BS, 48, MA, 51; Univ Tex, PhD, 57. *Honors & Awards:* Pres Citation, Am Mosquito Control Asn. *Prof Exp:* Teacher, High Sch, Tex, 48-49 & Pub Schs, 51-52; instr biol, Lamar State Col Technol, 52-53; asst, Univ Tex, 53-56; assoc prof biol & head dept, Ill Col, 56-59. *Concurrent Pos:* Newsletter ed, Am Mosquito Control Asn. *Mem:* Am Mosquito Control Asn; Entom Soc Am. *Res:* Mosquito biology. *Mailing Add:* Dept Biol Sam Houston State Univ Huntsville TX 77341-1001. *Fax:* 409-294-1598; *E-Mail:* bio__jdl@shsu.edu

LONG, JAMES FRANTZ, physiology, for more information see previous edition

LONG, JAMES WILLIAM, BIOCHEMISTRY. *Current Pos:* SR INSTR CHEM, UNIV ORE, 78- *Personal Data:* b Boise, Idaho, Aug 26, 43; m 65, Judith I Caron; c Gregory P & Jeffrey W. *Educ:* Univ Wash, BS, 65; Univ Calif, Berkeley, PhD(biochem), 69. *Prof Exp:* Res assoc biochem, Purdue Univ, West Lafayette, 70-71; NIH res fel, 71-72, res assoc, 72-73; res assoc, Univ Ore, 73-74; from asst prof to assoc prof chem, Col Great Falls, 74-78. *Mem:* Am Chem Soc; AAAS. *Res:* Computers in chemical education; structure-function relationships in enzymes; mechanisms of enzyme action; enzyme model systems; role of metal ions in enzyme catalysis. *Mailing Add:* Dept Chem Univ Ore Eugene OR 97403-1253. *Fax:* 541-346-4643; *E-Mail:* jlong@oregon.uoregon.edu

LONG, JEROME R, MAGNETIC AND TRANSPORT PHENOMENA. *Current Pos:* asst prof physics, 67-71, ASSOC PROF PHYSICS, VA POLYTECH INST & STATE UNIV, 71- *Personal Data:* b Lafayette, La, May 17, 35; m 90, Peggy Poff; c Christopher & Jeremy. *Educ:* Univ Southwestern La, BS, 56; La State Univ, MS, 58, PhD(physics), 65. *Prof Exp:* Res engr, Gen Dynamics/Pomona, 58-59; fel metall, Univ Pa, 65-67. *Concurrent Pos:* Vis prof, Simon Fraser Univ, 78-79, Mont State Univ, 86, Naval Res Lab, 87. *Mem:* Am Phys Soc; Int Elec & Electronics Engrs. *Res:* Transport and magnetic properties of metallic materials; cryophysics; squid susceptometry on layered and or film magnetic and or superconducting materials. *Mailing Add:* Dept Physics Va Polytech Inst & State Univ Blacksburg VA 24061-0435. *Fax:* 540-231-7511; *E-Mail:* jlong@vtpcn.phys.vt.edu

LONG, JIM T(HOMAS), ELECTRICAL ENGINEERING. *Current Pos:* From instr to assoc prof, 43-67, PROF ELEC ENG & COORDR UNDERGRAD PROG, CLEMSON UNIV, 67- *Personal Data:* b Central, SC, Oct 5, 23; m 46; c 1. *Educ:* Clemson Col, BEE, 43; Ga Inst Technol, MSEE, 49; PhD(elec eng), 64. *Concurrent Pos:* Asst, Ga Inst Technol, 48-49, asst prof, 57-64. *Mem:* Am Soc Eng Educ; Inst Elec & Electronics Engrs; Sigma Xi. *Res:* Electronics; network theory; solid state electronics. *Mailing Add:* 108 Mitchell Ave Clemson SC 29631

LONG, JOHN A, AGRONOMY, RESOURCE MANAGEMENT. *Current Pos:* CONSULT AGRON/HORT, 96- *Personal Data:* b Lewistown, Mont, Sept 1, 27; m 49, Jean Kirk; c Tim, Mark, Deborah & Christine. *Educ:* Univ Idaho, BS, 52; Wash State Univ, MS, 54; Tex A&M Univ, PhD(agron), 61. *Prof Exp:* Asst in agron, NMex State Univ, 54-56; instr, Tex A&M Univ, 56-61; proj leader agron, O M Scott & Sons Co, 61-63, from dir biochem res to dir prod develop, 63-90, consult, 90-95. *Concurrent Pos:* Chmn student interest comt, Southern Weed Control Asn, 59-60, turf sect, Weed Sci Soc Am, 63-64; chmn mem comt, Agr Res Inst, 72-73, mem prog comt, 73-74; pres, Nat Coun Com Plant Breeders, 79-80; chmn, Turf & Garden Com Fertilizer Inst, 87-88. *Res:* Agronomy; horticulture. *Mailing Add:* 17 Scott Circle Marysville OH 43040. *Fax:* 937-642-2664

LONG, JOHN ARTHUR, cytology, anatomy; deceased, see previous edition for last biography

LONG, JOHN FREDERICK, VETERINARY NEUROPATHOLOGY, COMPARATIVE PATHOLOGY. *Current Pos:* res assoc comp neuropath, Ohio State Univ, 63-64; NIH res fel, 64-66, instr vet path, 66-67, NIH spec res fel comp neuropath, 67-68, asst prof vet path, 68-71, ASSOC PROF VET PATH, OHIO STATE UNIV, 71- *Personal Data:* b Napoleon, Ohio, May 30, 24; m 48, Sarah E Brackney; c George L, Helen L (Corcoran), Harold R, Clara A (Lawrence) & Nancy C (Sieber). *Educ:* Ohio State Univ, BA, 47, MSc, 48, DVM, 55, PhD(comp neuropath), 66. *Prof Exp:* Asst, Dept Zool, Ohio State Univ, 47-49; res asst animal sci, Ohio Agr Exp Sta, 49-50; diag vet pathologist, Vet Diag Lab, State of Ohio, 55-63. *Mem:* Am Vet Med Asn; Am Asn Avian Path; Geront Soc Am; Am Chem Soc. *Res:* Comparative neuropathology; use of brain explant culture and germ-free animals in the study of the effects of encephalitogenic agents; development of model to visualize reactive oxygen metabolice generation within living cells; aging. *Mailing Add:* Dept Vet Biosci 325 Goss Lab Ohio State Univ Columbus OH 43210-1358

LONG, JOHN KELLEY, NUCLEAR PHYSICS. *Current Pos:* RETIRED. *Personal Data:* b NY, Dec 12, 21; m 48; c 3. *Educ:* Columbia Univ, BS, 42; Ohio State Univ, PhD(physics), 53. *Prof Exp:* Chemist plastics, Hercules Powder Co, 42-45; engr, Wright Field, 47-50; physicist, Battelle Mem Inst, 52-55; physicist, Idaho Div, Argonne Nat Lab, 55-74; Reactor Engr, US Nuclear Regulatory Comm, 74-83. *Concurrent Pos:* Consult, NUS Corp, 91- *Res:* Fast reactor physics; critical experiments; reactor licensing; fast reactor safety test facilities; plutonium toxicity. *Mailing Add:* 227 S 35th West Idaho Falls ID 83402

LONG, JOHN PAUL, PHARMACOLOGY. *Current Pos:* from asst prof to assoc prof, 56-62, prof, 62-70 & 83-85, head dept, 70-83, CARVOR PROF PHARMACOL, COL MED, UNIV IOWA, 85- *Personal Data:* b Albia, Iowa, Oct 4, 26; m 50; c 3. *Educ:* Univ Iowa, BS, 50, MS, 52, PhD(pharmacol), 54. *Prof Exp:* From asst to instr pharmacol, Univ Iowa, 50-54; res assoc, Sterling-Winthrop Res Inst, 54-56. *Mem:* Am Soc Pharmacol & Exp Therapeut; Soc Exp Biol & Med. *Res:* Structure-activity relationships of autonomic and anesthetic agents. *Mailing Add:* Dept Pharmacol Col Med Univ Iowa Iowa City IA 52242-0001

LONG, JOHN REED, INDUSTRIAL ENGINEERING, MANUFACTURING ENGINEERING. *Current Pos:* RETIRED. *Personal Data:* b Chicago, Ill, Oct 2, 22; wid; c Stephen K & J Craig. *Educ:* Northwestern Univ, BS, 47; Iowa State Univ, MS, 48, PhD(chem eng), 51. *Prof Exp:* AEC asst, Ames Lab, Iowa State Univ, 48-51; sr engr, Hercules, Inc, 51-60, process engr, 61-66, sr process engr, 66-80, supvr process engr, 80-85. *Mem:* Am Chem Soc; Am Inst Chem Engrs; Sigma Xi. *Res:* Process design of chemical plants. *Mailing Add:* 5 Clyth Dr Perth Wilmington DE 19803

LONG, JOHN VINCENT, PHYSICS. *Current Pos:* RETIRED. *Personal Data:* b San Diego, Calif, Feb 18, 10; m 38; c 4. *Educ:* Univ Calif, Los Angeles, AB, 37. *Prof Exp:* Lab asst physics, San Diego State Col, 32-35; serv demonstr, Ford Motor Co, Calif, 35-36; res engr, Douglas Aircraft Co, 36-37; geophysicist, Continental Oil Co, Okla, 37-40; res engr, Int Harvester Co, 40, res physicist & asst dir res, 46-51, dir res, Solar Div, 51-80; mem staff, MGL Develop, 80-81. *Mem:* Soc Explor Geophys; Acoust Soc Am; Soc Exp Stress Analysis; assoc Inst Elec & Electronics Engrs. *Res:* Ceramics; metallurgy; vibration and sound; high altitude research; ceramic coatings for high temperature corrosion and oxidation protection of iron, stainless steel; super alloys and refractory metals. *Mailing Add:* 1756 E Lexington Ave El Cajon CA 92019

LONG, JOSEPH POTE, OBSTETRICS & GYNECOLOGY. *Current Pos:* RETIRED. *Personal Data:* b Baker Summit, Pa, Feb 26, 13; m 42; c 4. *Educ:* Juniata Col, BS, 34; Jefferson Med Col, MD, 39; Univ Pa, MS, 48. *Prof Exp:* From demonstr to assoc prof obstet & gynec, Jefferson Med Col, Thomas Jefferson Univ, 48-75, clin prof, 75-78, hon clin prof, 78-90. *Mem:* AMA; Am Col Surg; Am Col Obstet & Gynec; Am Fertil Soc; NY Acad Sci. *Mailing Add:* 16 Strawberry Dr Carlisle PA 17013-4438

LONG, KEITH ROYCE, ENVIRONMENTAL HEALTH. *Current Pos:* RETIRED. *Personal Data:* b Lincoln, Kans, Mar 17, 22; m 45; c 5. *Educ:* Univ Kans, AB, 51, MA, 53; Univ Iowa, PhD, 60. *Prof Exp:* Asst instr bact, Univ Kans, 52-53, instr bact res, Med Ctr, 53-56; sr bacteriologist & virologist, State Hyg Lab, Col Med, Univ Iowa, 56-57, instr, Inst Agr Med, 57-58, asst bact, 58-60, assoc prof hyg & prev med, 60-69, dir, 74-83, prof prev med, Inst Agr Med & Environ Health, Col Med, 69-86, prof civil eng, 70-86. *Mem:* Am Pub Health Asn; NY Acad Sci. *Res:* Environmental toxicology; epidemiology; pesticides. *Mailing Add:* 2717 Friendship St Iowa City IA 52245

LONG, KENNETH MAYNARD, INORGANIC CHEMISTRY, SPELEOLOGY. *Current Pos:* from instr to assoc prof, 62-79, asst dean, 71-75, PROF CHEM, WESTMINSTER COL, PA, 79-, CHAIR, 83- *Personal Data:* b Nappanee, Ind, July 10, 32; m 52, Nancy Yoder; c Gregory, Steven, Jeffrey, Kristen & Kevin. *Educ:* Goshen Col, BS, 54; Mich State Univ, MA, 60; Ohio State Univ, PhD(chem), 67. *Prof Exp:* Instr, Parochial Sch, Ark, 54-56; instr, High Sch, Mich, 56-61. *Concurrent Pos:* NIH fel, 65-67; fel, Kent State Univ, 79; scholar-in-residence, Northeast Univ, Shenyang, Liaoning, Peoples Repub China, 88-89. *Mem:* Am Chem Soc; Nat Asn Geosci Teachers; Nat Speleol Soc. *Res:* Macrocyclic complexes of transition metals; catalytic properties of transition metal complexes; kinetics; hydrology; geology and mapping of caves. *Mailing Add:* Dept Chem Westminster Col New Wilmington PA 16172. *Fax:* 412-946-7158; *E-Mail:* longkm@westminster.edu

LONG, LARRY L, THIN FILMS, SURFACE PHYSICS. *Current Pos:* asst prof, 88-93, ASSOC PROF PHYSICS, PITTSBURG STATE UNIV, 93- *Personal Data:* b St Joseph, Mo, Aug 18, 55; m 84, Suzanna Maupin. *Educ:* NW Mo State Univ, BS, 77; Univ Mo-Rolla, MS, 82 & PhD(physics), 85. *Prof Exp:* Teaching asst physics, Univ Mo, Rolla, 79-85; sr engr optics & thin films, McDonnell Douglas Corp, 85-88. *Mem:* Am Phys Soc; Optical Soc Am; Am Asn Physics Teachers; Sigma Xi; Int Soc Optical Eng. *Res:* Thin films; application of surface plasmons to environmental issues; optical constants; application of thin films to thermal batteries; author of various publications; nonlinear optics. *Mailing Add:* Physics Dept Pittsburg State Univ 3202 N Free Kings Hwy Pittsburg KS 66762-9137

LONG, LAWRENCE WILLIAM, POLLUTION PREVENTION. *Current Pos:* proj leader chem, 74-77, mgr allied prod, 78-93, DIR SAFETY & ENVIRON INITIATIVES, ANHEUSER BUSCH, INC, 93- *Personal Data:* b Akron, Ohio, Nov 6, 42; m 69, Catherine Lawlor; c Anna & Susan. *Educ:* Franklin & Marshall Col, AB, 65; Wash Univ, MBA; Villanova Univ, PhD(chem), 71. *Prof Exp:* Instr biochem, Thomas Jefferson Univ, 71-73; res scientist, Stevens Inst Technol, 73-74. *Res:* Process optimization to reduce waste. *Mailing Add:* One Bush Pl OSC-1 St Louis MO 63118. *Fax:* 314-577-3581

LONG, LELAND TIMOTHY, GEOPHYSICS, SEISMOLOGY. *Current Pos:* From asst prof to assoc prof, 68-80, PROF GEOPHYS, GA INST TECHNOL, 81- *Personal Data:* b Auburn, NY, Sept 6, 40; m 70; c 3. *Educ:* Univ Rochester, BS, 62; NMex Inst Mining & Technol, MS, 64; Ore State Univ, PhD(geophys), 68. *Concurrent Pos:* Consult seismol, 78- *Mem:* Am Geophys Union; Seismol Soc Am; Soc Explor Geophys; Sigma Xi. *Res:* Seismic and gravity data acquisition and analysis; earthquake seismology; tectonophysics, vibrations from highways, gravity data acquisition and analysis. *Mailing Add:* Sch Earth & Atmospheric Sci Ga Inst Technol Atlanta GA 30332. *Fax:* 404-853-0232; *E-Mail:* tim.long@eas.gatech.edu

LONG, LEON EUGENE, GEOCHEMISTRY. *Current Pos:* from asst prof to assoc prof, 62-75, PROF GEOL, UNIV TEX, AUSTIN, 75- *Personal Data:* b Wanatah, Ind, May 4, 33; m 56; c 2. *Educ:* Wheaton Col, BS, 54; Columbia Univ, MA, 58, PhD(geochem), 59. *Prof Exp:* Geochemist, Lamont Geol Observ, Columbia Univ, 59-60; NSF fel, Oxford Univ, 60-62. *Mem:* Fel Geol Soc Am; Geochem Soc; Sigma Xi. *Res:* Isotopic age methods. *Mailing Add:* Dept Geol Sci Univ Tex Austin TX 78712-1026

LONG, LYLE NORMAN, COMPUTATIONAL PHYSICS, PARALLEL PROCESSING. *Current Pos:* ASST PROF, PENN STATE UNIV, 89- *Personal Data:* b Fergus Fall, Minn, Apr 7, 54; m 81, Laura Greuel; c David A & Robert A. *Educ:* Univ Minn, BME, 76; Stanford Univ, MS, 78; George Washington Univ, DSc, 83. *Honors & Awards:* Gordon Bell Prize, Inst Elec & Electronics Engrs, 93. *Prof Exp:* Res asst, Stanford Univ, 77-78; res assoc, George Washington Univ, 78-83; sr aerospace engr, Lockheed-Calif Co, 83-85; sr res scientist, Lockheed Aero Systs Co, 85-89. *Concurrent Pos:* Mem, Aerocomput Comt, Am Inst Aeronaut & Astronaut; mem, Fluid Dynamics Comt, Am Inst Aeronaut & Astronaut. *Mem:* Am Inst Aeronaut & Astronaut; Am Soc Eng Educ; Inst Elec & Electronics Engrs; Soc Indust & Appl Math. *Res:* Computational physics; fluid dynamics; unsteady aerodynamics; hypersonic aerodynamics; electromagnetics; parallel processing. *Mailing Add:* 908 Bayberry Dr State College PA 16801. *Fax:* 814-865-1172; *E-Mail:* lnl@cac.psu.edu

LONG, MAURICE W(AYNE), ELECTRONICS, PHYSICS. *Current Pos:* CONSULT, 75- *Personal Data:* b Madisonville, Ky, Apr 20, 25; m 50, 63, Beverly Benson; c Douglas Downing, Patricia Downing, Anne (Key) & Elizabeth (Rice). *Educ:* Ga Inst Technol, BEE, 46, MS, 57, PhD(physics), 59; Univ Ky, MSEE, 48. *Prof Exp:* Asst, Eng Exp Sta, Ga Inst Technol, 46-47; instr elec eng, Univ Ky, 47-49; res engr, Eng Exp Sta, Ga Inst Technol, 50-51, asst prof, 51-53, spec res engr, 53-65, head, Radar Br, 55-60, chief, Electronics Div, 59-68, prin res physicist, 65-75, prof elec eng, 68-74, dir res, Eng Exp Sta, Ga Tech Res Inst, 68-75. *Concurrent Pos:* Liaison scientist, Off Naval Res, London, 66-67; bd trustees, Ga Tech Res Inst, 68-82; mem comt remote sensing prog for earth resources surv, Nat Acad Sci, 77; NASA Space Appln Adv Comt, 83-86. *Mem:* Fel Inst Elec & Electronics Engrs; Acad Electromagnetics. *Res:* Antennas and propagation; radar; electromagnetic scattering from rough surfaces. *Mailing Add:* 1036 Somerset Dr NW Atlanta GA 30327

LONG, MICHAEL EDGAR, physical chemistry, technical management, for more information see previous edition

LONG, NANCY CAROL, EFFECT OF EXPOSURE TO ENVIRONMENTAL AGENTS ON HOST DEFENSE MECHANISMS IN THE LUNG. *Current Pos:* RES FEL, PHYSIOL PROG, HARVARD SCH PUB HEALTH, 91- *Personal Data:* b Columbus, Ohio, Oct 12, 63. *Educ:* Oberlin Col, BA, 85; Univ Mich, PhD(physiol), 89. *Prof Exp:* Fel, Yamaguchi Med Sch, Japan, 90-91. *Concurrent Pos:* Sect leader, Harvard Univ Col Arts & Sci, 93; adj instr, Grad Nursing Prog, Simmons Col, 93- *Mem:* Assoc mem Sigma Xi; Am Soc Zoologists; Am Physiol Soc. *Res:* Physiology of host-defense systems; mechanisms of fever and stress-induced hyperthermia; mechanism of the inflammatory response in the lung. *Mailing Add:* Boston Univ Col Gen Studies 881 Commonwealth Ave Boston MA 02215. *Fax:* 617-432-3468

LONG, PAUL EASTWOOD, JR, meteorology, numerical analysis, for more information see previous edition

LONG, PHILIP LEE, INFORMATION SCIENCE. *Current Pos:* PRES, PHILIP LONG ASSOCS LTD, SOUTH ORANGE, NJ, 93- *Personal Data:* b Cleveland, Ohio, Jan 24, 43; m 82, LeAnn Boyack Edvalson; c Sarah J, Caitlin T, Philip Imants & Michael Oskar. *Educ:* Ohio State Univ, BEE, 68, MSc, 70. *Prof Exp:* Assoc dir, Ohio Col Libr Ctr, 69-73; assoc comput systs develop, State Univ NY, Albany, 74-75; pres, Philip Long Assocs Inc, Salt Lake City, 75-81; vpres, Novell Data Systs, 81-82, Telerate Systs Inc, 83-93. *Concurrent Pos:* Instr comp sci, Ohio State Univ, libr sci, State Univ NY & Cath Univ Am; consult, UNESCO, Bibliotheque Nat France, Lib Cong, Nat Commun Libr & Info Sci, Nat Res Coun & Nat Acad Sci. *Mem:* Am Soc Info Sci; Inst Elec & Electronics Engrs; Asn Comput Mach. *Res:* Contributed articles to professional journals. *Mailing Add:* 397 Thornden St South Orange NJ 07079-1423

LONG, R(OBERT) B(YRON), chemical engineering, separation processes, for more information see previous edition

LONG, RAYMOND CARL, AGRONOMY. *Current Pos:* From asst prof to assoc prof, 66-82, PROF, CROP SCI, NC STATE UNIV, 82- *Personal Data:* b Shattuck, Okla, June 17, 39; m 59, Marie; c 4. *Educ:* Kans State Univ, BS, 61, MS, 62; Univ Ill, Urbana, PhD(plant physiol), 66. *Concurrent Pos:* Vis prof, agron dept, Univ Wis, Madison, 75-76. *Mem:* Am Soc Plant Physiol; Am Soc Agron; Crop Sci Soc Am. *Res:* Biochemistry of growth and senescence of higher plants; nitrogen metabolism; environmental stress and plant growth; production and bioprocessing of tobacco for engineered proteins and pharmaceuticals; precision application of agrichemicals. *Mailing Add:* Dept Crop Sci NC State Univ Raleigh NC 27695-7620. *Fax:* 919-515-7959; *E-Mail:* ray_long@ncsu.edu

LONG, RICHARD PAUL, SUBSURFACE DRAINAGE, FIELD BEHAVIOR OF CLAYS. *Current Pos:* from asst prof to assoc prof, 67-78, dept head, 77-90, PROF CIVIL ENG, UNIV CONN, 78- *Personal Data:* b Allentown, Pa, Nov 29, 34; m 64; c Marybeth & Christopher. *Educ:* Univ Cincinnati, CE, 57; Rensselaer Polytech Inst, MSCE, 63, PhD(civil eng), 66. *Honors & Awards:* AT&T Award Excellence Eng Educ, Am Soc Eng Educ, 88. *Prof Exp:* Mgt trainee, Lehigh Struct Steel Co, 57-58; NSF fel res, Rensselaer Polytech Inst, 66-67. *Concurrent Pos:* Proj mgr, Storch Engrs, 74; vis assoc prof, Mass Inst Tech, 75; chmn, Tech Comt, Transp Res Bd, Nat Acad Sci-Nat Res Ctr, 87-94. *Mem:* Am Soc Civil Engrs; Am Soc Eng Educ; Transp Res Bd. *Res:* Geotechnical engineering; invention of prefabricated underdrain for soils; development of techniques for analyzing field data for settlement of clay; investigation of the process of capping dredged material deposited at shallow ocean sites; investigation of corrosion of steel piles. *Mailing Add:* Dept Civil Eng Univ Conn PO Box U-37 Storrs CT 06269-2037. *Fax:* 860-486-2298

LONG, ROBERT ALLEN, PHARMACEUTICAL CHEMISTRY, MEDICAL SCIENCES. *Current Pos:* ASSOC DIR CLIN RES, CARDIOVASC/CRITICAL CARE, GLAXO WELLCOME, 95- *Personal Data:* b Kingman, Ariz, Aug 17, 41; m 63; c 3. *Educ:* Portland State Univ, BA, 64; Univ Utah, PhD(org chem), 70. *Prof Exp:* Res chemist, ICN Pharmaceut Inc, Calif, 70-77; clin res scientist, Cardiovasc Sect, Burroughs Wellcome Co, 77-83, sr clin res scientist, Cardiovasc Sect, Med Div, 83-95. *Mem:* Am Pharmaceut Asn; Acad Pharmaceut Sci; Am Soc Clin Pharmacol & Therapeut; Drug Info Asn. *Res:* Heterocyclic chemistry; nucleic acid chemistry; antiviral and antitumor research; cardiovascular and respiratory research, clinical trials of new drugs; continued medical support for marketed products; project leader for new product development. *Mailing Add:* Glaxo Wellcome Inc Five Moore Dr Research Triangle Park NC 27709

LONG, ROBERT LEROY, TECHNICAL MANAGEMENT. *Current Pos:* RETIRED. *Personal Data:* b Renovo, Pa, Sept 9, 36; m 57, Ann E Gullborg; c Beth Ann, Jeffrey, Alan & Mark Andrew. *Educ:* Bucknell Univ, BS, 58; Purdue Univ, MSE, 59, PhD(nuclear eng), 62. *Prof Exp:* Res assoc exp reactor physics, Argonne Nat Lab, 60-62; reactor specialist nuclear effects br, White Sands Missile Range, NMex, 62-65; from asst prof to prof nuclear eng, Univ NMex, 65-78, asst dean, 72-74, chmn chem & nuclear eng dept, 74-78; mgr, Generation Productivity Dept, GPU Nuclear Corp, 78-79, dir Reliability Eng Dept, Gen Pub Utilities Serv Corp, 79-80, dir, training & educ, 80-82, vpres, Nuclear Asn Div, 82-87, vpres Planning & Nuclear Safety Div, 87-89, vpres, corp serv & TMI-Z, 89-94, vpres Servs Div, 94. *Concurrent Pos:* Res partic, Sandia Corp, 65-78; consult, White Sands Missile Range Fast Burst Reactor Facil, 65-78; res assoc nuclear res div, Atomic Weapons Res Estab, Eng, 66-67; reactor engr, Con Edison, NY, 70-71; proj mgr nuclear eng & opers, Elec Power Res Inst, 76-77; mem, US Nuclear Energy Coun. *Mem:* Fel Am Nuclear Soc (pres-elect, 91-92); Soc Risk Analysis; Am Soc Eng Educ; Nuclear Energy Inst. *Res:* Reliability engineering data and applications; experimental reactor physics; fast burst reactors; power reactor technology; engineering teaching methods. *Mailing Add:* 9615 Elena NE Albuquerque NM 87122

LONG, ROBERT RADCLIFFE, METEOROLOGY. *Current Pos:* RETIRED. *Personal Data:* b Glen Ridge, NJ, Oct 24, 19; m 63; c 2. *Educ:* Princeton Univ, AB, 41; Univ Chicago, MS, 49, PhD, 50. *Prof Exp:* Meteorologist, US Weather Bur, 46-47; sr investr, Hydrodyn Lab, Univ Chicago, 49-51; from asst prof to assoc prof meteorol, Johns Hopkins Univ, 51-59, prof fluid mech, 59- *Concurrent Pos:* Mem adv panel gen sci, US Secy Defense Res & Eng. *Mem:* Am Meteorol Soc. *Res:* Geophysical fluid mechanics; theoretical studies and laboratory models of geophysical phenomena; general circulation of the atmosphere; atmospheric and oceanic flow over barriers. *Mailing Add:* PO Box 10381 Sarasota FL 34278

LONG, RONALD K(ILLWORTH), ELECTRICAL ENGINEERING. *Current Pos:* RETIRED. *Personal Data:* b Steubenville, Ohio, Dec 5, 32; m 59. *Educ:* Ohio Wesleyan Univ, BA, 54; Harvard Univ, MS, 56; Ohio State Univ, PhD, 63. *Prof Exp:* Res engr labs, Radio Corp Am, 55; asst, Harvard Univ, 55-56; res engr, NAm Aviation, Inc, 56-57; asst supvr, Antenna Lab, Ohio State Univ, 58-63, from asst prof to assoc prof, 63-69, prof elec eng, 69-80. *Res:* Lasers; atmospheric propagation; infrared techniques; computer data acquisition. *Mailing Add:* 1516 Essex Rd Columbus OH 43221

LONG, SALLY YATES, EMBRYOLOGY, TERATOLOGY. *Current Pos:* asst prof, 71-76, asst dean student affairs, 78-81, ASSOC PROF ANAT, MED COL WIS, 76-, ASSOC DEAN STUDENT AFFAIRS, 81- *Personal Data:* b Moyock, NC, Nov 8, 41; m 73; c 2. *Educ:* Col William & Mary, BS, 63; Univ Fla, PhD(anat), 67. *Prof Exp:* Lectr genetics, McGill Univ, 68-70; res assoc teratology, Karolinska Inst, Sweden, 70-71. *Concurrent Pos:* NIH fel, McGill Univ, 68-70. *Mem:* Teratology Soc (secy, 77-); Am Asn Anat; Europ Teratology Soc. *Res:* Interactions of genetic and environmental factors in causing malformations, especially cleft palate and limb defects. *Mailing Add:* Univ Wis Milwaukee 6186 Washington Circle Milwaukee WI 53213

LONG, SHARON RUGEL, DEVELOPMENTAL BIOLOGY. *Current Pos:* from asst prof to assoc prof, 82-92, PROF, DEPT BIOL SCI, STANFORD UNIV, 92- *Personal Data:* b San Marcos, Tex, Mar 2, 51; m 79; c 2. *Educ:* Calif Inst Technol, BS, 73; Yale Univ PhD(biol), 79. *Honors & Awards:* MacArthur Prize, 92; Presidential Young Investr, 84; Shell Res Found Award, 89; Charles Skull Award, 89. *Prof Exp:* Res fel, Dept Biol, Harvard Univ, 78-81. *Concurrent Pos:* Investr, Howard Hughes Med Inst, 94- *Mem:* Nat Acad Sci; Genetics Soc Am; Soc Develop Biol; Soc Plant Molecular Biol; Am Soc Microbiol; Am Soc Plant Physiologists; Am Soc Cell Biol. *Res:* Genetics and developmental biology of symbiotic nitrogen fixation in legumes; role of plasmids in symbiosis; plant cell biology; plant molecular biology. *Mailing Add:* Dept Biol Sci Stanford Univ Stanford CA 94305-5020

LONG, STEPHEN INGALLS, INTEGRATED CIRCUIT DESIGN, HIGH SPEED SEMI-CONDUCTOR DEVICES. *Current Pos:* PROF ELEC & COMPUT ENG, UNIV CALIF, SANTA BARBARA, 81- *Personal Data:* b Alameda, Calif, Jan 11, 46; m 66, Molly S Hammer; c Christopher A & Betsy E. *Educ:* Univ Calif, Berkeley, BS, 67; Cornell Univ, MS, 69, PhD(elec eng), 74. *Honors & Awards:* Microwave Applns Award, Inst Elec & Electronics Engrs, 78. *Prof Exp:* Sr engr, Varian Assocs, 74-77; mem tech staff, Rockwell Int Sci Ctr, 78-81. *Concurrent Pos:* Vis researcher, Gen Elec Co/Hirst Res Ctr, 88; consult, Jet Propulsion Lab, 91-92; Superconductor Technol, 92-; Fulbright res scholar, Tampere Univ Technol, Signal Processing Lab, Tampere, Finland, 94; vis prof, Tech Univ Denmark, 94. *Mem:* Sr mem Inst Elec & Electronics Engrs; Am Sci Affil. *Res:* Fabrication and design of high performance integrated circuits using compound semiconductor devices. *Mailing Add:* 895 N Patterson Ave Santa Barbara CA 93111-1107. *Fax:* 805-893-3262; *E-Mail:* long@ece.ucsb.edu

LONG, STERLING K(RUEGER), bacteriology; deceased, see previous edition for last biography

LONG, STUART A, APPLIED ELECTROMAGNETICS, ANTENNAS, SUPERCONDUCTORS. *Current Pos:* From asst prof to assoc prof 74-84, PROF ELEC ENG, UNIV HOUSTON, 85-, CHMN DEPT, 81- *Personal Data:* b Philadelphia, Pa, Mar 6, 45; m 69, Judy Mixon; c Meredith, Garrett & Brittany. *Educ:* Rice Univ, BA, 67, MEE, 68; Harvard Univ, PhD(appl physics), 74. *Mem:* Fel Inst Elec & Electronic Engrs; Antennas & Propagation Soc; Int Union Radio Sci. *Res:* Applied electromagnetics; antennas; applications of high temperature superconductors; subsurface communications; millimeter waveguiding and radiating structures. *Mailing Add:* Dept Elec Eng Univ Houston Houston TX 77204. *Fax:* 713-743-4440; *E-Mail:* long@uh.edu

LONG, TERRILL JEWETT, BOTANY. *Current Pos:* from asst prof to assoc prof, 67-83, PROF BIOL, CAPITAL UNIV, 83- *Personal Data:* b Newark, Ohio, Mar 19, 32; m 55; c 4. *Educ:* Ohio Univ, BSAg, 56; Ohio State Univ, MSc, 59, PhD(bot), 61. *Prof Exp:* NIH fel, Oak Ridge Nat Lab, 61-63, res assoc bot, 63-64; asst prof biol, Vanderbilt Univ, 64-65; res assoc biochem, Ohio State Univ, 65-67. *Concurrent Pos:* Consult, C S Fred Mushroom Co, 66-70. *Mem:* AAAS; Bot Soc Am; Mycol Soc Am. *Res:* Physiology and biochemistry of irradiated wheat and mushrooms and related fungi. *Mailing Add:* Dept Biol Capital Univ 2199 E Main St Columbus OH 43209

LONG, WALTER K, HUMAN GENETICS. *Current Pos:* RES SCIENTIST HUMAN GENETICS, UNIV TEX, AUSTIN, 59-, LECTR ZOOL, 70- *Personal Data:* b Austin, Tex, Jan 26, 19; m 50; c 1. *Educ:* Univ Tex, BA, 40; Harvard Univ, MD, 43. *Prof Exp:* Res asst cardiol, Thorndike Mem Lab, Boston City Hosp, Mass, 45-48. *Concurrent Pos:* Life ins med res fel, 47-48; chief, Cardiovasc Sect, William Beaumont Army Hosp, Ft Bliss, Tex, 51-53. *Mem:* Am Soc Human Genetics; Sigma Xi. *Res:* Relation between sulfahydryl compounds and pharmacology of organic mercurial diuretics; pentose phosphate metabolic pathway in relation to certain human diseases. *Mailing Add:* Townhouse J 404 Dresher Rd Horsham PA 19044-2016

LONG, WALTER KYLE, JR, VIROLOGY. *Current Pos:* from asst prof to assoc prof, Sch Dent, 76-86, ASSOC PROF MICROBIOL, SCH MED, TEMPLE UNIV, 86- *Personal Data:* b Montgomery, Ala, Dec 5, 44. *Educ:* Univ Ga, BS, 66; Univ Ill, PhD(microbiol), 72. *Prof Exp:* Fel, Dept Microbiol & Pediat, Univ Ala, Birmingham, 72-75, res assoc, 75-76. *Mem:* AAAS; Am Soc Microbiol; Sigma Xi. *Res:* Effects of antiviral drugs on herpes viruses; oncogenicity of herpes viruses; latency and reactivation of herpes viruses; role of DNA methylation in gene expression. *Mailing Add:* 404 Dresher Rd Townhouse J Horsham PA 19044

LONG, WILLIAM ELLIS, HYDROLOGY, GEOMORPHOLOGY. *Current Pos:* CHIEF, WATER RESOURCES SECT, ALASKA STATE GEOL SURV, 78- *Personal Data:* b Minot, NDak, Aug 18, 30; m 55, 71; c 6. *Educ:* Univ Nev, BS, 57; Ohio State Univ, MSc, 61, PhD(geol), 64. *Honors & Awards:* Long Hills, Antarctica named in honor. *Prof Exp:* Instr geol, Ohio State Univ, 63-64; explor geologist, Tenneco Oil Co, La, 64-65; from asst prof to assoc prof, 65-72, prof geol, Alaska Methodist Univ, 72- *Concurrent Pos:* Mem, US Antarctic Res Prog, NSF Geol Invest, 63-64; mem discharge prediction glacial melt-water, Off Water Res, 68-70; consult, Shelf Explor Co, 71 & Forest Oil Co, 74-75; investr potential natural landmarks in Alaska, Nat Park Serv, 71; vis lectr, Univ Canterbury, 72. *Mem:* Am Groundwater Asn; Am Asn Petrol Geol; Am Inst Prof Geol; Geol Soc Am; Glaciol Soc; Sigma Xi. *Res:* Stratigraphic, geologic and glaciological exploration of Gondwana sequences of Antarctica during International Geophysical Year and following years; stratigraphic and glacial geology; water resources of Alaska. *Mailing Add:* PO Box 1831 Palmer AK 99645-1831

LONG, WILLIAM HENRY, AGRICULTURAL CROP & PEST MANAGEMENT. *Current Pos:* prof, 65-85, DISTINGUISHED SERV PROF BIOL SCI, NICHOLLS STATE UNIV, 85-94. *Personal Data:* b Decatur, Ala, Sept 20, 28; m 53, Janice Rogers; c Janice F, Nancy A & Daniel H. *Educ:* Univ Tenn, BA, 52; NC State Col, MS, 54; Iowa State Col, PhD, 57. *Prof Exp:* From asst entomologist to prof entom, La State Univ, 57-65; prof, Nicholls State Univ, 65-85, Distiguished Serv prof biol sci, 85-94. *Concurrent Pos:* Independent agr consult, 65-, UN Food & Agr Orgn, United Arab Repub, 73-74; consult entom, state expert, Int Atomic Energy Agency, 75-76. *Mem:* Entom Soc Am; Am Soc Sugarcane Technologists; Nat Alliance Independent Crop Consult. *Res:* Development and refinement of sugarcane pest management programs; study of insects and other factors which affect sugarcane. *Mailing Add:* PO Box 1193 Thibodaux LA 70302. *Fax:* 504-446-3520; *E-Mail:* long@cajunnet.com

LONG, WILLIS FRANKLIN, ELECTRICAL ENGINEERING, ELECTRIC POWER SYSTEMS. *Current Pos:* from asst prof to prof elec eng & exten eng, 73-83, chmn exten eng, 80-83, PROF ELEC ENG & ENG PROF DEVELOP, UNIV WIS-MADISON, 85- *Personal Data:* b Lima, Ohio, Jan 30, 34; m 59, Ginger Carol Miller; c Andrew, Kristin & David. *Educ:* Univ Toledo, BS, 57, MS, 62; Univ Wis-Madison, PhD(elec eng), 70. *Prof Exp:* Proj engr, Doehler Jarvis, Nat Lead Co, 57, 59-60; asst, Univ Toledo, 60-62, instr elec eng, 62-66; NSF fel, Univ Wis-Madison, 67-68, lectr, 69; mem tech staff, Hughes Res Labs, 69-73; dir, ASEA Power Systs Ctr, New Berlin, Wis, 83-85. *Concurrent Pos:* Consult, Hughes Aircraft Co, Los Angeles Dept Power & Water, 73-, ABB Power Syst, 85-; Spec Adv Comt, Wis Dept Indust, Labor & Human Rels, 76-77. *Mem:* Fel Inst Elec & Electronics Engrs; Int Conf Large High Voltage Elec Systs. *Res:* Analysis, simulation and testing of interconnected AC/DC electric power systems; power electronics switching techniques; continuing education, electric power systems. *Mailing Add:* Univ Wis-Madison 432 N Lake St Madison WI 53706-1498

LONG, WILMER NEWTON, JR, MEDICINE, OBSTETRICS & GYNECOLOGY. *Current Pos:* assoc prof, 65-67, PROF GYNEC & OBSTET, SCH MED, EMORY UNIV, 67- *Personal Data:* b Hagerstown, Md, Apr 24, 18; m 42; c 2. *Educ:* Juniata Col, BS, 40; Johns Hopkins Univ, MD, 43. *Prof Exp:* Instr gynec & obstet, Sch Med, Johns Hopkins Univ, 48-65. *Concurrent Pos:* Pvt pract obstet, 48-65; med officer in chg obstet & gynec, Navajo Med Ctr, Ft Defiance, Ariz, 53-55. *Mem:* Am Col Obstet & Gynec; AMA. *Res:* Diabetes in pregnancy. *Mailing Add:* 69 Bulter St SE Atlanta GA 30303-3056

LONGACRE, RONALD SHELLEY, PARTICLE PHYSICS. *Current Pos:* asst physicist, 78-80, PHYSICIST, BROOKHAVEN NAT LAB, 80- *Personal Data:* b Lindsay, Calif, Aug 15, 41; wid; c 4. *Educ:* Calif Polytech State Univ, BS, 64; Univ Calif, Berkeley, MA, 68, PhD(physics), 74. *Prof Exp:* Res asst, Dept Physics Elem Particles, Comn L'Etude des Nuages-SACLAY, 74-75; res asst, Northeastern Univ, Boston, 75-78. *Res:* Determine Hadronic particle spectrum using three particle decay models; chief tool is the use of partial wave analyses via the Isobar model; model hadronic production in heavy ion collisions. *Mailing Add:* Dept Physics Brookhaven Nat Lab Bldg 510A Upton NY 11973

LONGACRE, SUSAN ANN BURTON, STRATIGRAPHY, SEDIMENTARY PETROLOGY & PETROLEUM GEOLOGY. *Current Pos:* prof specialist, Texaco Houston Res Ctr, 80-84, sr res consult, 84-90, sr scientist, 90-91, HON FEL, TEXACO HOUSTON RES CTR, 91- *Personal Data:* b Los Angeles, Calif, May 26, 41; m 64; c 2. *Educ:* Univ Tex, Austin, BS, 64, PhD(geol), 68. *Honors & Awards:* Distinguished Serv Award, Am Asn Petrol Geologists, 94. *Prof Exp:* Res assoc III, Getty Oil Co, 69-72, res assoc IV, 72-75, res scientist I geol, Explor & Prod Res Lab, 75-76, geol specialist II, Offshore Dist, 76-78, res scientist III explor & prod res, 78-80. *Concurrent Pos:* Comnr, NAm Comm Stratig Nomenclature, 79-, vchmn, 85-86, chmn, 86-87; adv coun, Earth Scis, Nat Sci Found, 93- Geol Found, Univ Tex, Austin, 93- *Mem:* Am Asn Petrol Geologists; Geol Soc Am; Soc Econ Paleontologists & Mineralogists. *Res:* Petrology and petrography of carbonate and clastic sediments, particularly those Permian, Jurassic and Cretaceous sediments that accumulated in shallow marine to continental depositional environments. *Mailing Add:* 3901 Briarpark Houston TX 77042

LONGANBACH, JAMES ROBERT, PHYSICAL-ORGANIC CHEMISTRY, FUEL CHEMISTRY. *Current Pos:* PROJ MGR, MORGANTOWN ENERGY TECHNOL CTR, US ENERGY DEPT, 87- *Personal Data:* b Akron, Ohio, July 4, 42; m 66, Mary L Marrone; c Diane M & David M. *Educ:* Univ Akron, BS, 64; Yale Univ, MS, 66, MPh, 67, PhD(chem), 69. *Prof Exp:* Chemist, E I du Pont de Nemours & Co, Inc, 69-71; sr chemist, Res Div, Occidental Petrol Corp, 71-76; prin res chemist, Columbus Labs, Battelle Mem Inst, 76-87. *Concurrent Pos:* Fuel div prog chmn, Am Chem Soc, 93. *Mem:* Am Chem Soc. *Res:* Physical-organic, energy and process develop chemistry; coal gasification. *Mailing Add:* 939 Vandalia Rd Morgantown WV 26505. *Fax:* 304-291-4469

LONGCOPE, CHRISTOPHER, ENDOCRINOLOGY, REPRODUCTIVE BIOLOGY. *Current Pos:* PROF OBSTET, GYNEC & MED, MED SCH, UNIV MASS, 80- *Personal Data:* b Lee, Mass, Aug 5, 28; m 61; c 3. *Educ:* Harvard Univ, AB, 49; Johns Hopkins Univ, MD, 53. *Prof Exp:* Intern, Presby Hosp, NY, 53-54, asst resident, 54-55, fel endocrinol, 59-60; asst resident, Johns Hopkins Hosp, 55-56; fel endocrinol, Univ Wash, Seattle, 60-62 & Univ Calif, San Francisco, 62-63; steroid training prog, Worcester Found Exp Biol, 65-66, staff scientist, 66-70, sr scientist, 70-80. *Concurrent Pos:* Asst med, Johns Hopkins Univ, 63-64, instr med, 64-65; consult endocrinol, Perry Point Vet Admin Hosp, Md, 63-65; from asst prof med to assoc prof and dir, Endocrine Outpatients Clin, Boston Univ, 68-; mem, Aging Review Comt, Nat Inst Aging, NIH, 73-77 & Breast Cancer Task Force, 80-84. *Mem:* Endocrine Soc; Am Physiol Soc; Soc Exp Biol & Med. *Res:* Steroid dynamics, steroid production and metabolism. *Mailing Add:* Dept Obstet & Gynec Med Sch Univ Mass 55 Lake Ave N Worcester MA 01655

LONGENECKER, BRYAN MICHAEL, IMMUNOLOGY, CELL BIOLOGY. *Current Pos:* Med Res Coun Can fel, Univ Alta, 68-71, Nat Cancer Inst Can res grant, 71-73, Nat Cancer Inst Can res scholar immunol, 71-77, ASST PROF IMMUNOL & MEM, NAT CANCER INST, UNIV ALTA, 77- *Personal Data:* b Dover, Del, Sept 1, 42; m 63; c 2. *Educ:* Univ Mo, AB, 64, PhD(zool), 68. *Mem:* AAAS. *Res:* Genetic control of allo-immunocompetence and resistance to virally induced neoplasms. *Mailing Add:* Biomira Inc 2011 94th St Edmonton AB T6N 1H1 Can. *Fax:* 403-463-0871

LONGENECKER, HERBERT EUGENE, BIOLOGICAL CHEMISTRY. *Current Pos:* RETIRED. *Personal Data:* b Lititz, Pa, May 6, 12; m 36, Jane Segar; c Herbert E Jr, Marjorie (White), Geoffrey H & Stanton L. *Educ:* Pa State Col, BS, 33, MS, 34, PhD(agr biol chem), 36. *Hon Degrees:* ScD, Duquesne Univ, 51; LLD, Loyola Univ, 63; LittD, Univ Miami, 72; DSc, Loyola Univ & Univ Ill, 76. *Prof Exp:* Asst agr & biochem, Pa State Col, 33-35, instr, 35-36; Nat Res Coun fel, Univ Liverpool, 36-37, Univ Cologne, 37-38 & Queen's Univ, Ont, 38; fac mem, Univ Pittsburgh, 38-55, from asst prof to prof, 38-55, dean res natural scis, 44-55, dean grad sch, 46-55; vpres in charge, Univ Ill Med Ctr, 55-60; pres, 60-75, emer pres, Tulane Univ, 75-; mgr dir, Int Trade Mart, 76-79. *Concurrent Pos:* Mem food & nutrit bd, Nat Res Coun, 43-53, chmn comt food protection, 48-53; mem res coun, Chem Corps Adv Bd, 49-65; mem adv panel biol & chem warfare, Off Asst Secy Defense, 53-61; mem nat selection comn Fulbright student awards, 53-55, chmn, Western Europe Sect, 54-55; mem bd gov, Inst Med Chicago, 57-60; mem, Coun Financial Aid to Educ, 64-71; chmn acad bd adv, US Naval Acad, 66-72; dir, A G Bush Found, 69-85; mem panel sci & technol, US House of Rep Comt Sci & Astronaut, 70-73; dir, CPC Int, 66-85, Equitable Life Assurance Soc US, 68-84, United Student Aid Funds, 71-84 & Fed Home Loan Bank Little Rock, 76-79. *Mem:* Am Chem Soc; Inst Nutrit; fel Am Inst Chem; Sigma Xi. *Res:* Nutrition; fat metabolism; research administration. *Mailing Add:* 2717 Highland Ave Suite 1002 Birmingham AL 35205

LONGENECKER, JOHN BENDER, nutrition, biochemistry, for more information see previous edition

LONGENECKER, WILLIAM HILTON, ORGANIC CHEMISTRY. *Current Pos:* RETIRED. *Personal Data:* b Cambridge, Md, Mar 28, 18; m 44. *Educ:* Ohio State Univ, BA, 41; Georgetown Univ, MS, 49. *Prof Exp:* Chemist, Kankakee Ord Works, 42, Universal Oil Prod Co, 43, Armour & Co, 43-44, Toxicity Lab, Univ Chicago, 44, NIH, 46-49, Exp Sta, E I Du Pont de Nemours & Co, Inc, 49-62, Am Petrol Inst, 62-63 & Tech Info Div, Ft Detrick, 63-70; chemist, Nat Agr Libr, USDA, 70-89. *Mem:* AAAS; Am Chem Soc; Sigma Xi. *Res:* Systematic chemical nomenclature; chemical notation systems and machine methods of chemical documentation; bibliography compilations. *Mailing Add:* 11311 Cedar Lane Beltsville MD 20705

LONGERICH, HENRY PERRY, ANALYTICAL CHEMISTRY, COMPUTER SCIENCE. *Current Pos:* res assoc, Mem Univ Nfld, 74-75, res fel, 75-78, asst prof, 78-84, assoc prof, 84-93, PROF EARTH SCI, MEM UNIV NFLD, 93- *Personal Data:* b Du Quoin, Ill, June 20, 40; m 64, Linda L; c Lora L. *Educ:* Millikin Univ, BS, 63; Ind Univ, PhD(chem), 67. *Prof Exp:* Asst prof chem, Univ Alaska, 67-72; fel, Dalhousie Univ, 72-74. *Concurrent Pos:* Sessional comput sci, Mem Univ, 79-82. *Mem:* Am Chem Soc; Spectros Soc Can; Soc Appl Spectros. *Res:* Real-time on-line computer control and data acquisiton at analytical instrumentation, ICP-MS. *Mailing Add:* Earth Sci Dept Mem Univ St John's NF A1B 3X5 Can. *Fax:* 709-737-2589; *E-Mail:* henry@sparky2.esd.mun.ca

LONGEST, WILLIAM DOUGLAS, INVERTEBRATE ZOOLOGY. *Current Pos:* from asst prof to assoc prof, 66-73, PROF BIOL, UNIV MISS, 73- *Personal Data:* b Pontotoc, Miss, Jan 22, 29; m 60. *Educ:* Baylor Univ, BSc, 54, MSc, 56; La State Univ, PhD(invert zool, ecol), 66. *Prof Exp:* Teacher, Parma High Sch, 55-56; instr biol, Northwest Jr Col, 56-59; prof natural sci, Blue Mountain Col, 59-62; instr biol, Memphis State Univ, 62-63; teaching asst zool, La State Univ, 63-65, instr, 65-66. *Mem:* Bot Soc Am; Am Soc Zool. *Res:* Botanical research; foliar embryos of Kalanchoe studied in an explant medium; taxonomy of freshwater Tricladida; study of freshwater triclads in the Florida Parishes of Louisiana. *Mailing Add:* RR 3 Box 226 Oxford MS 38655-9803

LONGFELLOW, DAVID G(ODWIN), MOLECULAR CARCINOGENESIS, BIOCHEMISTRY. *Current Pos:* Damon Runyon res fel breast cancer, Biol Lab, Div Cancer Biol, Nat Cancer Inst, NIH, 72-74, res fel, 74-75, res staff, 75-76, sect head, Molecular Carcinogenesis Sect, 76-79, asst chief, Chem & Phys Br, Div Cancer Etiology, 79-84, CHIEF CHEM & PHYS CARCINOGENESIS BR, DIV CANCER ETIOLOGY, NAT CANCER INST, NIH, 84- *Personal Data:* b Akron, Ohio, Nov 16, 42; m 65, Bente F Christensen; c Robyn M & Daniel G. *Educ:* Lynchburg Col, BS, 64; Johns Hopkins Univ, PhD(biol), 72. *Mem:* Am Asn Cancer Res; Int Soc Polycyclic Aromatic Compounds (pres elect, 93). *Res:* Chief of an extramural program awarding contracts and grants for research and resource support in the cause and prevention of chemical and physical carcinogenesis. *Mailing Add:* 5102 Marlyn Dr Bethesda MD 20816. *Fax:* 301-496-1040

LONGFIELD, JAMES EDGAR, PHYSICAL CHEMISTRY. *Current Pos:* RETIRED. *Personal Data:* b Mt Brydges, Ont, Mar 12, 25; nat US; m 47; c 3. *Educ:* Univ Western Ont, BSc, 47, MSc, 48; Univ Rochester, PhD(phys chem), 51. *Prof Exp:* Asst, Univ Rochester, 48-50; res chemist, Res Div, Am Cyanamid Co, 51-57, group leader eng res, 57-62, mgr eng res, 62-72, dir, process eng dept, Chem Res Div, 72-74, dir, Bound Brook Labs, 74-87. *Mem:* Am Chem Soc; Am Inst Chem Eng. *Res:* Vapor phase reactions of organic compounds; reaction kinetics; catalysis; reactor design and mechanism studies. *Mailing Add:* 8 Honey Locust Circle Hilton Head Island SC 29926-2680

LONGHI, JOHN, IGNEOUS PETROLOGY, PHYSICAL CHEMISTRY. *Current Pos:* SR RES SCIENTIST, LAMONT-DOHERTY GEOL OBSERV, 88- *Personal Data:* b White Plains, NY, Oct 12, 46; m 70; c 1. *Educ:* Univ Notre Dame, BS, 68; Harvard Univ, PhD(geol), 76. *Prof Exp:* Res assoc, Mass Inst Technol, 76-77; res assoc lunar petrol, Univ Ore, 77-80; from asst prof to assoc prof, Yale Univ, 80-88. *Concurrent Pos:* Jr fac fel, Yale Univ, 83-84. *Mem:* Am Geophys Union; Mineral Soc Am; Sigma Xi. *Res:* Origin and evolution of the moon and planets; experimental petrology; physical chemistry of silicates. *Mailing Add:* Lamont-Doherty Earth Observ Palisades NY 10964

LONGHI, RAYMOND, INORGANIC CHEMISTRY, ORGANIC CHEMISTRY. *Current Pos:* Res chemist, E I Du Pont de Nemours & Co Inc, 62-64, sr res chemist, 64-65, res supvr, 65-69, sr supvr tech, 69-71, sr supvr res & develop, 71-74, tech supt, 74-78, res & deveop site mgr, 78-85, mgr, Int Technol Transfer, 85-87, res mgr, 87-89, SR RES FEL, E I DU PONT DE NEMOURS & CO INC, 89- *Personal Data:* b Plymouth, Mass, Nov 14, 35; m 61; Betty H Johnson; c 3. *Educ:* Univ Mass, BS, 57; Dartmouth Col, MA, 59; Univ Ill, PhD(inorg chem), 62. *Mem:* Am Asn Textile Chemists & Colorists; Am Chem Soc; Sigma Xi. *Res:* Structures of transition metal complexes; reactions of nitrogen oxide; characterization of organic compounds; textile fibers; polymer chemistry. *Mailing Add:* E I du Pont de Nemours & Co Inc 450 N Access Rd Chattanooga TN 37415

LONGHURST, ALAN R, BIOLOGICAL OCEANOGRAPHY, MARINE ECOLOGY. *Current Pos:* RETIRED. *Personal Data:* b Plymouth, Eng, May 3, 25; Can citizen; m 63; c 2. *Educ:* Univ London, BSc, 52, PhD(zool), 62, DSc, 69. *Prof Exp:* Sci officer, African Fisheries Res Inst, Sierra Leone, 54-57; marine biologist, Fisheries Lab, Wellington, NZ, 57-58; sr sci officer, Fishery Develop & Res Unit, Sierra Leone, 58-60; prin sci officer, Fed Fisheries Serv, Lagos, Nigeria, 60-63; assoc res biologist, Scripps Inst Oceanog, 63-67; dir, Fishery-Oceanog Ctr, Nat Oceanic & Atmospheric Admin, 67-71; dep dir, Inst Marine Environ Res, Nat Environ Res Coun, Eng, 71-77; dir, Marine Ecol Lab, Bedford Inst Oceanog, NS, 77-79, dir gen, Ocean Sci & Surv, Atlantic, Can Dept Fisheries & Oceans, 79-86, res scientist, 87-96. *Concurrent Pos:* Coordr, Eastern Trop Pac Oceanog Expeditions, 67-70; mem, Group Experts Ocean Variability Intergovt Oceanog Comn/Integrated Global Ocean Sta Syst, 69-71; Food & Agr Orgn Adv Comt Marine Res, 69-74, Dartmouth Nat Park Comt, Devon Co Coun, 74-76, UK Deleg UN Conf Law Sea, 74-77; chmn, Continuous Monitoring Biol Oceanog, Sci Comt Oceanic Res/Adv Comt Marine Resources Res, 69-72; secy, Sci Coun Oceanic Res, 79-86. *Res:* Ecology of tropical benthos; population dynamics of tropical demersal fish; descriptive tropical physical oceanography; response to climate changes of marine biota; production and grazing relation in zooplankton in tropical, temperate and arctic oceans; formulation of large scale numerical ecological models; ecology of microplankton and sub-micron particles. *Mailing Add:* Place d l'Eglise Cajarc France. *Fax:* 902-426-7827

LONGHURST, JOHN CHARLES, CARDIOVASCULAR PHYSIOLOGY, INTERNAL MEDICINE. *Current Pos:* ASSOC PROF, DEPT MED, UNIV CALIF, SAN DIEGO. *Personal Data:* b Napa, Calif, Mar 18, 47; m 69; c 3. *Educ:* Univ Calif, Davis, BS, 69, MD, 73, PhD(physiol), 74; Am Bd Internal Med, dipl, 77. *Prof Exp:* Fac assoc internal med, 78-79, instr internal med & physiol, 79-80, asst prof internal med, Health Sci Ctr, Univ Tex, Dallas, 80-, asst prof physiol, 81- *Concurrent Pos:* Estab investr, Am Heart Asn, 81-86; mem, Coun Clin Cardiol & Coun Circulation, Am Heart Asn. *Mem:* Am Fedn Clin Res; Am Physiol Soc; fel Am Col Cardiol. *Res:* Neural control of the circulation; exercise physiology; physiology of the coronary circulation. *Mailing Add:* Dept Cardiovasc Med Univ Calif TB No 172 Davis CA 95616

LONGINI, IRA MANN, JR, EPIDEMIOLOGY. *Current Pos:* ASSOC PROF, DEPT EPIDEMIOL & BIOSTATIST, EMORY UNIV, 84- *Personal Data:* b Cincinnati, Ohio, Oct 2, 48. *Educ:* Univ Fla, BS, 71, MS, 73; Univ Minn, PhD(biomet), 77. *Prof Exp:* Assoc fel biomath, Int Ctr Med Res, 77-79; scholar biomet & lectr epidemiol, Dept Epidemiol, Univ Mich, 80-84. *Concurrent Pos:* Vis prof biomath, Univ Del Valle, 77-79. *Mem:* Biomet Soc; Soc Math Biol. *Res:* Development of mathmatical and statistical methods in epidemiology; genetics and biology. *Mailing Add:* 1284 Oakdale Rd NE Atlanta GA 30307

LONGINI, RICHARD LEON, PHYSICS, BIOENGINEERING. *Current Pos:* prof solid state electronics, 62-75, prof elec eng & urban affairs, 76-78, SUPVR, SYSTS ENG LAB, CARNEGIE-MELLON UNIV, 64-, EMER PROF ELEC ENG & URBAN AFFAIRS, 78- *Personal Data:* b US, Mar 11, 13; m 37; c 2. *Educ:* Univ Chicago, BS, 40; Univ Pittsburgh, MS, 44, PhD(physics), 48. *Prof Exp:* Physicist, Westinghouse Elec Corp, 41-51, sect mgr solid state electronics, 51-56, adv physicist, 56-58, sect mgr semiconductors, 58-60, consult physicist, 60-62. *Mem:* Fel Am Phys Soc; fel Inst Elec & Electronics Engrs. *Res:* Solid state and medical electronics; data analysis and automated aids for diagnoses; application of engineering principles to solution of social problems. *Mailing Add:* 100 Norman Dr No 161 Cranberry Township PA 16066

LONGLEY, B JACK, SURGERY. *Current Pos:* Instr, 47-49, ASSOC PROF SURG, SCH MED & ASST DIR TUMOR CLIN UNIV WIS-MADISON, 49-; ASST CHIEF SURG SERV, VET ADMIN HOSP, 50- *Personal Data:* b Dousman, Wis, July 19, 13; m 48; c 3. *Educ:* Univ Wis, BS, 34, PhD(pharmacol), 40, MD, 42. *Res:* Cardiovascular research. *Mailing Add:* 13065 N 99th Dr Sun City AZ 85351

LONGLEY, GLENN, JR, LIMNOLOGY. *Current Pos:* Asst prof, 69-77, assoc prof, 77-80, PROF AQUATIC BIOL, SOUTHWEST TEX STATE UNIV, 80- *Personal Data:* b Del Rio, Tex, June 2, 42; m 61; c 4. *Educ:* Southwest Tex State Univ, BS, 64; Univ Utah, MS, 66, PhD(environ biol), 69. *Concurrent Pos:* Res grants, USFWS, US SCS; dir environ consult firm, 80- *Mem:* Nat Water Well Asn; Am Water Res Asn; NAm Benthological Soc; AAAS; Water Pollution Control Fedn; Sigma Xi. *Res:* Use of subterranean fauna as indicators of ground water quality; Edwards Aquifer study; water pollution; heavy metals; organic wastes; pesticides; population dynamics; plankton; groundwater studies. *Mailing Add:* 248 Freeman Bldg Southwest Tex State Univ San Marcos TX 78666-4616

LONGLEY, H(ERBERT) JERRY, MATHEMATICS. *Current Pos:* RETIRED. *Personal Data:* b Tahoka, Tex, Jan 3, 26; div; c Elizabeth, Bonnie, Jerry J, Lyn L & Lea L. *Educ:* Univ Tex, BS, 46, PhD(physics), 52; Tex Tech Col, BS, 48. *Prof Exp:* Asst prof & res assoc physics, NMex Inst Mining & Technol, 52-54; staff mem, Los Alamos Sci Lab, Univ Calif, 54-76; prin physicist, Mission Res Corp, 71-78, consult, 78-79; consult, Lawrence Livermore Lab, Calif, 78-82, Radiation Res Assocs, Inc, Ft Worth, 82-89, & Fraunhofer-Int, Euskirchen, WGer, 89-92. *Concurrent Pos:* Res assoc, Los Alamos Nuclear Corp, 70-71, consult, 71-88. *Mem:* Am Phys Soc. *Res:* Nuclear weapons and weapons testing; hydrodynamics, numerical solutions; radioactive waste storage; nuclear weapons effects; electromagnetic pulse; nuclear physics; linec design; fundamental particles; author of numerous publications. *Mailing Add:* 5808 Chaparral Circle Farmington NM 87402-4880

LONGLEY, JAMES BAIRD, HISTOCHEMISTRY. *Current Pos:* RETIRED. *Personal Data:* b Baltimore, Md, June 27, 20; m 44; c 4. *Educ:* Haverford Col, BSc, 41; Cambridge Univ, PhD(zool), 50. *Prof Exp:* From asst scientist to scientist, Nat Inst Arthritis & Metab Dis, 50-60; assoc prof anat, Sch Med, Georgetown Univ, 60-62; prof anat & chmn dept, Sch Med, Univ Louisville, 62-86. *Concurrent Pos:* USPHS sr res fel, 60-62; instr, Sch Med, Johns Hopkins Univ, 51-52; asst ed, J Histochem & Cytochem, Histochem Soc, 57-64, actg ed, 64-65; ed, Stain Technol, Biol Stain Comn, 73-87. *Mem:* Histochem Soc; Am Asn Anat; Am Soc Cell Biol; Biol Stain Comn. *Res:* Renal histochemistry, morphology and physiology. *Mailing Add:* Dept Anat Univ Louisville Health Sci Ctr Box 35260 Louisville KY 40292

LONGLEY, ROBERT W(ILLIAM), NUTRITION, BIOCHEMISTRY. *Current Pos:* RETIRED. *Personal Data:* b Baltimore, Md, July 7, 25; m 50, 86, Maureen Jerring; c 5. *Educ:* Loyola Col, Md, BS, 45; George Washington Univ, MS, 55, PhD(biochem), 57. *Prof Exp:* Res asst, Res Lab, Brady Urol Inst, 47-53; technician biochem, George Washington Univ, 53-55, instr biochem, 56; investr, Dorn Lab Med Res, 56-58; asst prof, Med Col Ala, 58-60; biochemist, Cent Res Labs, Gen Mills, Inc, 60-62, res assoc, James F Bell Res Ctr, 62-67; dir food res, Nutrit Div, Mead Johnson Subsidiary, Bristol Myers Co, Ind, 67-68 & Drackett Co, 68-70, dir food prod res, Mead Johnson Res Ctr, 70-71; consult food indust, 71-72; pres, Grist Mill Co, Minn, 72-73; dir res, Delmark Co, Minneapolis, 73-86; dir regulatory affairs, Sandoz Nutrit Corp, 82-86. *Concurrent Pos:* Mgr res & develop, Camargo Foods Div, Drackett Co, Bristol Myers Co, Ohio, 69-71; mgr spec proj corp res & develop, Joseph Schlitz Brewing Co, Wis, 71. *Mem:* Am Asn Cereal Chemists; Inst Food Technologists; Am Soc Parenteral & Enteral Nutrit; Enteral Nutrit Coun. *Res:* Carbohydrate metabolism; diabetes; clinical nutrition. *Mailing Add:* 100 Sweetwater Dr St Paul MN 55124

LONGLEY, ROSS E, IMMUNOLOGY. *Current Pos:* GROUP LEADER IMMUNOL, HARBOR BR, OCEANOG INST, 87- *Personal Data:* b Enid, Okla, July 17, 52. *Educ:* Univ Okla, BS, 75, MS, 77, PhD(immunol), 81. *Prof Exp:* Fel immunol, Univ Okla, 81-84; asst prof immunol & microbiol, Univ Cent Fla, 84-87. *Res:* Immunology; microbiology. *Mailing Add:* Harbor Br Oceanog Inst DBMR 5600 US No 1N Ft Pierce FL 34946-7303

LONGLEY, W(ILLIAM) WARREN, GEOLOGY. *Current Pos:* from asst prof to assoc prof geol & geophys, 40-52, prof, 52-77, EMER PROF GEOL, UNIV COLO, BOULDER, 77- *Personal Data:* b Paradise, NS, Apr 8, 09; US citizen; m 35, 57; c 3. *Educ:* Acadia Univ, BS, 31; Univ Minn, MS & PhD(geol), 37. *Prof Exp:* Instr geol, Dartmouth Col, 35-40. *Concurrent Pos:* Consult, Que Dept Mines, 36-50, Kennecott Copper Corp, 45- & Kennco Explor Ltd, 46- *Mem:* Fel Geol Asn Can; fel Geol Soc Am; Soc Econ Geol; Am Asn Petrol Geol; Soc Explor Geophys. *Res:* Photogeology; mineral deposits in pre-Cambrian shield of Canada. *Mailing Add:* 821 Spring Dr Boulder CO 80303

LONGLEY, WILLIAM JOSEPH, REPRODUCTIVE PHYSIOLOGY, ENDOCRINOLOGY. *Current Pos:* CHEMIST, MARION LABS, 84- *Personal Data:* b Middleton, NS, May 25, 38; m 63; c 2. *Educ:* Univ Toronto, BSA, 61, MSA, 63; Univ Mass, PhD(vet animal sci), 67. *Prof Exp:* Lectr physiol, Med Sch, Dalhousie Univ, 67-68, asst prof, 68-73, asst prof path, 73-80; qual control tech prod mgr, Corning Glass Works, 80-81, prod develop mgr, Corning Med & Sci, 81-84. *Concurrent Pos:* Endocrinologist, NS Dept Pub Health, 73-80. *Mem:* Can Soc Clin Chem; Soc Study Reproduction; Sigma Xi. *Res:* Endocrinology of the female, particularly fetal-placental function as related to steroid synthesis; clinical chemistry of various hormones including thyroid and adrenal. *Mailing Add:* 8935 Outlook Dr Overland Park KS 66207-2112

LONGLEY, WILLIAM WARREN, JR, COMPUTER SCIENCES, PHYSICS. *Current Pos:* assoc prof, 83-93, ANALYST, PERU STATE COL, 93- *Personal Data:* b Hanover, NH, Aug 30, 37; m 60, Patricia Sweetman; c Elizabeth A (Schreiber) & Harold W. *Educ:* Univ Colo, BA, 58, PhD(physics), 63. *Prof Exp:* Physicist, Boulder Labs, Nat Bur Stand, 56-59; engr, Denver Div, Martin Co, 59-60, sr engr, 60-63; assoc physicist, Midwest Res Inst, 64-68; asst prof, Upper Iowa Col, Fayette, 68-70, assoc prof physics, 70-81, dir, Comput-Data Processing Ctr, 73-81; assoc prof math & comput sci, St Cloud State Univ, 81-83. *Concurrent Pos:* Fel, Theoret Physics Inst, Univ Alta, 63-64. *Mem:* Fel AAAS; Am Phys Soc; Sigma Xi; Am Econ Asn. *Res:* Computer applications; economic statistics. *Mailing Add:* Peru State Col PO Box 10 Peru NE 68421. *E-Mail:* longley@us.peru.edu

LONGMAN, RICHARD WINSTON, CONTROL THEORY, ANALYTICAL DYNAMICS. *Current Pos:* from asst prof to assoc prof, 70-79, PROF MECH ENG, COLUMBIA UNIV, 79- *Personal Data:* b Iowa City, Iowa, Sept 2, 43. *Educ:* Univ Calif, Riverside, BA, 65; Univ Calif, San Diego, MS, 67, MA & PhD(aerospace eng), 69. *Honors & Awards:* Dirk Brouwer Award, Am Astronaut Soc, 89. *Prof Exp:* Consult, Rand Corp, 66-69; mem tech staff, Control Systs Res Dept, Bell Tel Labs, NJ, 69-70. *Concurrent Pos:* Managing ed, J Astronaut Sci, 76-84; vis fac, Mass Inst Technol, Univ Bonn & Polytech Darmstadt, Univ Augsburg, Univ Heidelberg, Ger, Univ Newcastle, Australia, Nat Cheng Kung Univ & Taiwan Nanjing Aeronaut Inst, China; consult, Langley Res Ctr & Goddard Space Flight Ctr, NASA, Europ Space Opers Ctr, Lockheed Missiles & Space Co, Aerospace Systs Div, Naval Res Lab, Martin Marietta Corp, Gen Elec Co, Xerox Res Lab, Marine Environ Corp, Designatronics, Inc & Syst Develop Corp; Alexander von Humboldt res fel, Polytech Darmstadt, WGer, 77 & 80; sr fel, Nat Res Coun, 90-91. *Mem:* Fel Am Astronaut Soc (vpres, 78-84); fel Am Inst Aeronaut & Astronaut; fel Brit Interplanetary Soc; Am Soc Mech Engrs. *Res:* System dynamics and control: learning and repetitive control, system identification, robot optimal path planning, robotics in space, satelite dynamics, shape control of large flexible spacecraft, vibration control. *Mailing Add:* Dept Mech Eng Columbia Univ New York NY 10027. *Fax:* 212-854-3304; *E-Mail:* rwl4@columbia.edu

LONGMIRE, MARTIN SHELLING, ENGINEERING PHYSICS, GENERAL PHYSICS. *Current Pos:* RETIRED. *Personal Data:* b Morristown, Tenn, Mar 6, 31. *Educ:* Univ Cincinnati, BS, 53; Mass Inst Technol, PhD(phys chem), 61. *Prof Exp:* Res assoc phys chem, Ohio State Univ, 61-62; res fel, Mellon Inst, 62-64; res assoc, Mass Inst Technol, 64-65, physicist, Electronics Res Ctr, NASA, Cambridge, Mass, 65-70; assoc prof physics, Western Ky Univ, 70-88. *Concurrent Pos:* Res physicist, Nat Oceanic & Atmospheric Admin, 72 & Naval Res Lab, 71 & 73-88. *Mem:* AAAS; Am Phys Soc; emer fel Am Inst Chem; Sigma Xi. *Res:* Processing of signals from infrared sensors; development of infrared surveillance systems; absorption of solar ultraviolet light by atmospheric contaminants and minor constituents. *Mailing Add:* PO Box 105 Whitesburg TN 37891-0105

LONGMORE, WILLIAM JOSEPH, BIOCHEMISTRY. *Current Pos:* from asst prof to assoc prof, 66-73, PROF BIOCHEM, SCH MED, ST LOUIS UNIV, 73- *Personal Data:* b La Jolla, Calif, Oct 7, 31; m 53, Martha Baxter; c David J, William B, Timothy S & Christopher D. *Educ:* Univ Calif, Berkeley, AB, 57; Univ Kans, PhD(biochem), 61. *Prof Exp:* Nat Heart Inst fel metab res, Scripps Clin & Res Found, 61-63, res assoc biochem, 63-66. *Concurrent Pos:* USPHS res career develop award, 66-76; Fogarty int sr fel, State Univ Utrecht, Neth, 77-78. *Mem:* AAAS; Am Chem Soc; Am Soc Biol Chemists; Sigma Xi. *Res:* Phospholipid metabolism; control mechanisms for lipid metabolism, phospholipid trafficking, especially in lung tissue; pulmonary surtactant. *Mailing Add:* 517 Beaucaire Dr Warson Woods MO 63122

LONGMUIR, ALAN GORDON, CONTROL ENGINEERING. *Current Pos:* Control engr, Kaiser Aluminum & Chem Corp 68-78, mgr metals automation, 78-84, dir mfg systs, 84-88, VPRES RES DEVELOP, KAISER ALUMINUM & CHEM CORP, 88- *Personal Data:* b Vancouver, BC, Mar 1, 41; c 2. *Educ:* Univ BC, BASc, 64, PhD(elec eng), 68. *Concurrent Pos:* Assoc ed, Automatica, 76-83. *Mem:* Indust Res Inst. *Res:* Development of products and processes related to aluminum and its alloys. *Mailing Add:* Kaiser Aluminum & Chem Corp 6177 Sunol Blvd Pleasanton CA 94566. *Fax:* 510-847-4400; *E-Mail:* alan_longmuir@kacc.com

LONGMUIR, IAN STEWART, BIOCHEMISTRY, PHYSIOLOGY. *Current Pos:* PROF CHEM & BIOCHEM, NC STATE UNIV, 65- *Personal Data:* b Glasgow, Scotland, Mar 12, 22; m 49; c 4. *Educ:* Cambridge Univ, BA, 43, MA & MB, BChir, 48. *Prof Exp:* Res assoc colloid sci, Cambridge Univ, 48-51; prin sci officer, Ministry Supply, Eng, 51-54; sr lectr biochem, Univ London, 54-65. *Concurrent Pos:* Ed jour, Brit Polarographic Soc, 57-62; Isaac Ott fel, Univ Pa, 62-63. *Mem:* AAAS; Am Physiol Soc; Int Soc Oxygen Transport to Tissue; Am Soc Biol Chem; Aerospace Med Asn. *Res:* Oxygen transport in blood and tissue; inert gas metabolism. *Mailing Add:* Dept Biochem NC State Univ 2408 Tyson St Raleigh NC 27612-4729

LONGNECKER, DANIEL SIDNEY, ANATOMIC PATHOLOGY. *Current Pos:* PROF PATH, DARTMOUTH MED SCH, 72- *Personal Data:* b Omaha, Nebr, June 8, 31; m 52, Louise Miller; c Matthew, Daniel, Jane & Thomas. *Educ:* Univ Iowa, AB, 54, MD, 56, MS, 62. *Hon Degrees:* MA, Dartmouth Col, 74. *Prof Exp:* From asst to assoc prof path, Univ Iowa, 61-69; assoc prof, Sch Med, St Louis Univ, 69-72. *Concurrent Pos:* NIH spec fel & vis asst prof, Dept Path, Univ Pittsburgh, 65-67; USPHS res grants, Univ Iowa, 67-69, St Louis Univ, 69-71 & Dartmouth Col, 75-96. *Mem:* Am Soc Clin Path; Int Acad Path; Am Pancreatic Asn; Am Asn Investigative Path; Am Asn Cancer Res; Int Asn Pancreatology. *Res:* Biochemical mechanisms of cell injury; pancreatic carcinogenesis; pathology of pancreatic disease and experimental carcinogenesis in the pancreas; morphologic and molecular comparison of human and animal pancreatic carcinomas. *Mailing Add:* Dept Path Dartmouth Med Sch Lebanon NH 03756. *Fax:* 603-650-6120

LONGNECKER, DAVID EUGENE, ANESTHESIOLOGY. *Current Pos:* R D DRIPPS PROF & CHAIR, DEPT ANESTHESIA, UNIV PA, 88- *Personal Data:* b Kendallville, Ind, May 29, 39; m 63, Charlene Simmons; c Ann, Mary & Andrew. *Educ:* Ind Univ, AB, 61, MD, 64; Am Bd Anesthesiol, dipl, 69. *Honors & Awards:* Van Bergen Lectr, Univ Minn, 81; E M Papper Lectr, Univ Calif, Los Angeles, 84; Evan L Frederickson Res Lectr, Emory Univ, 93; Louis R Orkin Lectr, NY Acad Med, 93; E A Rovenstine Mem Lectr, Am Soc Anesthesiologists, 96. *Prof Exp:* Intern, Blodgett Mem Hosp, Grand Rapids, 64-65; resident anesthesiol, Ind Univ, Indianapolis, 65-68; clin assoc, NIH, 68-70; asst prof, Univ Mo, Columbia, 70-73; from assoc prof to prof, Univ Va, 74-88. *Concurrent Pos:* NIH spec res fel, Ind Univ, 67-68; res career develop award, Nat Heart & Lung Inst, 75; ed, Int J Microcirculation, 86-; pres, Am Bd Anesthesiol, 94- *Mem:* Inst Med-Nat Acad Sci; Inst Anesthesia Res Soc; Am Physiol Soc; Asn Univ Anesthetists (pres, 92-94); Am Soc Anesthesiologists; AMA; Microcirculatory Soc; Sigma Xi; Am Soc Critical Care Anesthesiologists; Europ Microcirculatory Soc; Int Soc Oxygen Transport to Tissue. *Res:* Microcirculatory mechanisms during hemorrhagic shock; effect of anesthetics on the microcirculation during normovolemia and hypovolemia. *Mailing Add:* Dept Anesthesia HUP 3400 Spruce St 4N Dulles Philadelphia PA 19104-4283. *Fax:* 215-349-5341

LONGO, DAN L, IMMUNOLOGY, MEDICAL ONCOLOGY. *Current Pos:* sr investr, 80-85, DIR, BIOL RESPONSE MODIFIERS PROG, MED BR, NAT CANCER INST, 85- *Personal Data:* b St Louis, Mo, Apr 25, 49; m 71, Nancy Schiffman; c Jennifer A, Adam D & Paul A. *Educ:* Wash Univ, AB, 70; Univ Mo, Columbia, MD, 75. *Honors & Awards:* Tovi Comet-Wallerstein Award, 92. *Prof Exp:* Resident internal med, Peter Bent Brigham Hosp, 75-77; fel med, Harvard Med Sch, 75-77; clin assoc med oncol, Med Br, Nat Cancer Inst, 77-78; clin assoc immunol, Lab Immunol, Nat Inst Allergy & Infectious Dis, 78-80. *Concurrent Pos:* Asst ed, Am J Clin Nutrit, 81-91; ed, Clin Oncol Alert, 85-; assoc ed, Cancer Res & J Nat Cancer Inst, 87-, Yr Bk Oncol & J Immunol, 88-, J Immunotherapy, 89- *Mem:* Am Asn Immunologists; Am Soc Clin Oncol; Am Fedn Clin Res; Am Asn Cancer Res; Am Soc Hemat; Am Soc Clin Invest. *Res:* Thymus function and control of lymphocyte proliferation and gene expression; treatment of lymphorproliferative diseases; biological therapy of human neoplastic infectious and immunological diseases. *Mailing Add:* 9610 Barroll Lane Kensington MD 20895-3503

LONGO, FRANK JOSEPH, DEVELOPMENTAL BIOLOGY. *Current Pos:* Asst prof, 70-75, ASSOC PROF ANAT, COL MED, UNIV IOWA, 75- *Personal Data:* b Cleveland, Ohio, Nov 16, 39; m 62; c 6. *Educ:* Loyola Univ, BS, 62; Ore State Univ, MS, 65, PhD(cell biol), 67. *Mem:* AAAS; Am Soc Cell Biol; Am Asn Anat; Soc Study Reproduction. *Res:* Cellular and developmental biology at the fine structural and biochemical levels; comparative pronuclear development and fusion; gametogenesis and fertilization; cell division and differentiation. *Mailing Add:* Dept Anat Univ Iowa Iowa City IA 52442-0001. *Fax:* 319-335-7198

LONGO, FREDERICK R, PHYSICAL CHEMISTRY. *Current Pos:* assoc prof, 57-68, head, Dept Chem & Chem Eng, Evening Col, 73-76, PROF CHEM, DREXEL UNIV, 68- *Personal Data:* b Trenton, NJ, May 4, 30; m; c 6. *Educ:* Villanova Col, BA, 53; Drexel Inst, MS, 58; Univ Pa, PhD(phys chem), 62. *Prof Exp:* Chemist, Am Biltrite Rubber Co, 55-57. *Concurrent Pos:* Sr res assoc, Nat Res Coun, 85-86. *Mem:* Am Chem Soc; Sigma Xi; NY Acad Sci. *Res:* Synthesis and spectral properties of porphyrins; investigation of microemulsions as media for controlled chemical reactions. *Mailing Add:* 2814 Midvale Ave Apt B Philadelphia PA 19129

LONGO, JOHN M, SOLID STATE CHEMISTRY, MINERAL REACTIONS. *Current Pos:* chemist, Corp Res Labs, 70-81, LONG RANGE RES, EXXON PROD RES, 81- *Personal Data:* b Hartford, Conn, Nov 6, 39; m 64, Ligita H Strele; c 3. *Educ:* Univ Conn, BA, 61, PhD(inorg chem), 64. *Prof Exp:* Fel, Univ Stockholm, 64-65; chemist, Lincoln Lab, Mass Inst Technol, 65-70. *Mem:* Am Chem Soc. *Res:* Preparation and characterization of solid state inorganic materials. *Mailing Add:* 13819 Taylorcrest Houston TX 77079-5814. *Fax:* 713-965-7369; *E-Mail:* john.m.longo@exxon.sprint.com

LONGO, JOSEPH THOMAS, SOLID STATE PHYSICS. *Current Pos:* fel, North Am Rockwell Sci Ctr, 68-69, mem tech staff, 69-72, mgr, 72-77, asst dir, 77-78, DIR, NORTH AM ROCKWELL SCI CTR, 78- *Personal Data:* b Ferndale, Mich, Jan 13, 42; m 64; c 2. *Educ:* Univ Detroit, BS, 64; Mich State Univ, MS, 66, PhD(solid state physics), 68. *Prof Exp:* Asst, Mich State Univ, 64-68. *Mem:* Am Phys Soc. *Res:* High field magnetoresistance and Hall effect in intermetallic compounds; crystal growth, optical and device properties of narrow gap semiconductors. *Mailing Add:* 712 Kenwood Ct Thousand Oaks CA 91360

LONGO, LAWRENCE DANIEL, DEVELOPMENTAL NEUROBIOLOGY, FETAL PHYSIOLOGY. *Current Pos:* PROF PHYSIOL, OBSTET & GYNEC, LOMA LINDA UNIV, 68-, HEAD, CTR PERINATAL BIOL, 70- *Personal Data:* b Los Angeles, Calif, Oct 11, 26; m 48, Betty Jeanne Mundall; c April Celeste, Lawrence Anthony, Elisabeth Lynn & Camilla Giselle. *Educ:* Pac Union Col, BA, 49; Loma Linda Univ,

MD, 54. *Prof Exp:* Asst prof obstet & gynec, Univ Ibadan, 59-62; asst prof, Univ Calif, Los Angeles, 62-64; lectr physiol, Univ Pa, 64-66, asst prof physiol, 66-68. *Concurrent Pos:* USPHS fel obstet & gynec, Univ Calif, Los Angeles, 59, spec fel physiol, Univ Pa, 64-66 & res career develop award, 66-68, res career develop award, Loma Linda Univ, 68- & grant, 69-; consult, Nat Inst Child Health & Human Develop, 71; ed, Classic Pages in Obstet & Gynec in Am, J Obstet & Gynec. *Mem:* AAAS; NY Acad Sci; Am Physiol Soc; Soc Gynec Invest (secy-treas, pres); Perinatal Res Soc; Am Col Obstet & Gynec; Soc Neurosci; fel Royal Col Obstet & Gynec. *Res:* Regulation of fetal growth and development; fetal and placental physiology; kinetics of placental transfer of respiratory gases; fetal oxygenation; developmental neurobiology. *Mailing Add:* Ctr Perinatal Biol Loma Linda Univ Loma Linda CA 92350

LONGO, MICHAEL JOSEPH, HIGH ENERGY PHYSICS, SCIENCE EDUCATION. *Current Pos:* from asst prof to assoc prof, 62-68, PROF PHYSICS, UNIV MICH, ANN ARBOR, 68- *Personal Data:* b Philadelphia, Pa, Apr 7, 35; m 58; c 3. *Educ:* La Salle Col, BA, 56; Univ Calif, Berkeley, PhD(physics), 61. *Prof Exp:* NSF fel physics, Saclay Nuclear Res Ctr, France, 61-62. *Mem:* Am Phys Soc; Sigma Xi. *Res:* Nucleon-nucleon interaction at high energies; proportional chambers and scintillation counters; neutrino interactions; magnetic monopoles; science communications; software systems; medical imaging. *Mailing Add:* Dept Physics Univ Mich Ann Arbor MI 48109. *E-Mail:* longo@mail.physics.lsa.umich.edu

LONGOBARDO, ANNA KAZANJIAN, TECHNICAL MANAGEMENT. *Current Pos:* RETIRED. *Personal Data:* b New York, NY; m 52, Guy; c Guy & Alicia. *Educ:* Columbia Univ, BS, 49, MS, 52. *Prof Exp:* Sr systs engr, Am Bosch Arma Corp, 50-65; res sect head, Sperry Rand Corp, 65-73, mgr eng personnel utilization, 73-77, mgr prog planning, 77-81, mgr planning, 81-82, dir tech serv, Unisys Corp, 82-89, dir field eng, 89-93, dir strategic initiatives, 93-96. *Concurrent Pos:* Mem bd dirs, Woodward-Clyde Group, Inc, 89- *Mem:* Sr mem Am Soc Mech Engrs; sr mem Am Inst Aeronaut & Astronaut; fel Soc Women Engrs. *Res:* Supervised the Independent Research and Development program and was the strategic planner of a large unit of the Sperry Corporation; supervised the activities of approximately 400 field engineers in sixty locations worldwide who are giving life cycle support to diverse equipments including weather radar systems, radar landing systems, sonar systems and combat systems. *Mailing Add:* 15 Crows Nest Rd Bronxville NY 10708. *Fax:* 914-779-2448

LONGOBARDO, GUY S, MECHANICAL ENGINEERING, BIOENGINEERING. *Current Pos:* CONSULT, CASE WESTERN UNIV, 88- *Personal Data:* b New York, NY, Oct 23, 28; m 52; c 2. *Educ:* Columbia Univ, BS, 49, MS, 50, EngScD, 61. *Prof Exp:* Develop engr, E I Du Pont de Nemours & Co, 50-52; instr mech eng, Sch Eng, Columbia Univ, 52-61, asst prof mech eng & bioeng, 61-65, dir, Fluid Mech Lab, 63-65; adv engr, Med Info Systs, IBM Corp, 65-77, mem corp staff, 77-81; sr forecaster, World Trade Corp, 81-88. *Concurrent Pos:* Consult, Am Mach & Foundry Co, 61-65 & Case Western Dept Med, 75- *Mem:* Assoc Am Soc Mech Engrs. *Res:* Medical information systems, clinical application of computer technology, operation of the respiratory control system and its unstable modes; medical information systems. *Mailing Add:* 15 Crows Nest Rd Bronxville NY 10708

LONGONE, DANIEL THOMAS, ORGANIC CHEMISTRY. *Current Pos:* from instr to assoc prof, 59-71, PROF ORG CHEM, UNIV MICH, ANN ARBOR, 71- *Personal Data:* b Worcester, Mass, Sept 16, 32; m 54. *Educ:* Worcester Polytech Inst, BS, 54; Cornell Univ, PhD(org chem), 58. *Prof Exp:* Res assoc org chem, Univ Ill, 58-59. *Concurrent Pos:* Am Chem Soc-Petrol Res Fund int fel, 67-68; Fulbright scholar, 70-71; vis prof, Univ Cologne, 70-71, Univ Calif, Los Angeles, 76. *Mem:* Am Chem Soc. *Res:* Synthetic and mechanistic organic chemistry; bridged aromatic compounds; cyclophane chemistry; monomer synthesis and polymerization. *Mailing Add:* 3537 Chem Bldg Univ Mich Ann Arbor MI 48109-1055

LONGPRE, EDWIN KEITH, SYSTEMATIC BOTANY. *Current Pos:* assoc prof bot & biol, 65-80, prof bot, 80-97, EMER PROF CONSULT, WESTERN STATE COL COLO, 97- *Personal Data:* b Detroit, Mich, Mar 7, 33; m 65; c 1. *Educ:* Univ Mich, BS, 55, MS, 56; Mich State Univ, PhD(bot), 67. *Prof Exp:* Instr bot, Tex Tech Col, 56-57. *Concurrent Pos:* Pres-elect, Colo-Wyo Acad Sci, 85-86. *Mem:* Am Soc Plant Taxon; AAAS; Sigma Xi. *Res:* Systematical studies in the tribe Heliantheae of the family Compositae; general cytotaxonomical and floristic studies. *Mailing Add:* 1200 US Hwy 50 C-5 Gunnison CO 81230

LONGROY, ALLAN LEROY, ORGANIC CHEMISTRY. *Current Pos:* asst prof, 67-69, ASSOC PROF CHEM, PURDUE UNIV, 69- *Personal Data:* b Flint, Mich, May 28, 36; m 55; c 3. *Educ:* Univ Mich, AB, 58, MS, 61, PhD(chem), 63. *Prof Exp:* Res fel chem, Brandeis Univ, 62-64; asst prof, Ind Univ, 64-67. *Mem:* Am Chem Soc. *Res:* Organic reaction mechanisms and kinetics; demonstrations in chemistry. *Mailing Add:* Dept Chem Ind Univ-Purdue Univ 2101 Coliseum Blvd E Ft Wayne IN 46805-1445

LONGSHORE, JOHN DAVID, PETROLOGY. *Current Pos:* PROF GEOL, HUMBOLDT STATE UNIV, 65- *Personal Data:* b Birmingham, Ala, Mar 8, 36; m 64; c 2. *Educ:* Emory Univ, BA, 57; Rice Univ, MA, 59, PhD(geol), 65. *Prof Exp:* Teacher, Westminster Sch, Ga, 60-62. *Concurrent Pos:* NASA res grant chem invest Medicine Lake Area, 67-69. *Res:* Chemistry and petrology of igneous rocks. *Mailing Add:* Dept Geol Humboldt State Univ 1 Harps St Arcata CA 95521-8299

LONGSTRETH, DAVID J, PLANT ECOPHYSIOLOGY. *Current Pos:* asst prof, 79-85, ASSOC PROF BOT, LA STATE UNIV, 85- *Personal Data:* b Phoenix, Ariz, Mar 22, 48. *Educ:* Ariz State Univ, BS 70, MS, 72; Duke Univ, PhD(bot), 76. *Prof Exp:* Fel, Duke Univ & Univ Calif, Los Angeles, 77-79. *Mem:* Am Soc Plant Physiologists; Ecol Soc Am; Sigma Xi; AAAS. *Res:* Plant carbon balance in aquatic and semiaquatic environments; salinity effects on plant water relations and photosynthetic response. *Mailing Add:* Dept Bot La State Univ Baton Rouge Baton Rouge LA 70803-0001

LONGSWORTH, RALPH C, MECHANICAL ENGINEERING. *Current Pos:* sr res engr, 68-80, sr res assoc, 80-92, CHIEF SCIENTIST, APD CRYOG, 92- *Personal Data:* b New York, NY, Jun 17, 34; m 58, Roberta; c Gordon & Margaret. *Educ:* Columbia Univ, AB, 56, BS, 57; Syracuse Univ, MS, 60, PhD(mech eng), 66. *Prof Exp:* Gen mgr, Cryomech Inc, 65-67. *Concurrent Pos:* Mem bd, Cryog Eng Conf, 76-87; prin investr, NASA & APD Cryo, 92-96. *Mem:* Am Soc Mech Engrs; Am Vacuum Soc. *Res:* Small cryogenic refrigeration; Gifford McMahon refrigeration; pulse tube refrigeration; cryopumps; small helium liquifiers; fast cooldown; Joule Thomson; commercialized refrigerant technology in small 80K refrigerators. *Mailing Add:* 1833 Vultee St Allentown PA 18103. *Fax:* 610-791-4494

LONGTIN, BRUCE, THERMODYNAMICS, NUCLEAR & RADIOCHEMISTRY. *Current Pos:* RETIRED. *Personal Data:* b North Fork, Calif, Aug 23, 13; m 53, Cecilia A Cotter; c 6. *Educ:* Univ Calif, BS, 35, MS, 37, PhD(chem), 38. *Prof Exp:* Asst chem, Shell Oil Co fel, 38-39; from instr to assoc prof, Ill Inst Technol, 39-51; from chemist to staff chemist, E I du Pont de Nemours & Co, Inc, 51-78; teaching assoc, Univ SC, Salkehatchie, 78-81 & 83-84. *Concurrent Pos:* Assoc chemist, Argonne Nat Labs, 48-49. *Mem:* Am Chem Soc. *Res:* Thermodynamics of industrial processes; thermodynamic properties of solutions; reactor water and water wastes; chemistry, radiolysis and control of impurities in water coolant and moderator of nuclear reactors; rheology and mechanical properties of polymers. *Mailing Add:* 1209 Summerhill Rd North Augusta SC 29841

LONGUEMARE, R NOEL, ENGINEERING. *Current Pos:* PRIN DEP UNDER SECY DEFENSE ACQUISITION & TECHNOL, DEPT DEFENSE, 93- *Personal Data:* b Mar 26, 32. *Educ:* Johns Hopkins Univ, MS, 58. *Mailing Add:* Dept Defense 3015 Defense Pentagon Washington DC 20301

LONGUET-HIGGINS, MICHAEL SELWYN, OCEAN PHYSICS, PROJECTIVE GEOMETRY. *Current Pos:* SR RES PHYSICIST, INST NON-LINEAR SCI, UNIV CALIF, SAN DIEGO, 86- *Personal Data:* b Lenhan, Eng, Dec 8, 25. *Educ:* Univ Cambridge, BA, 45, MA, 46, PhD(geophysics), 51. *Honors & Awards:* Sberdrup Gold Medal, Am Meteorol Soc, 83; Int Coastal Eng Award, Am Soc Civil Engrs, 84; Oceanog Award, Soc Underwater Technol, 90. *Prof Exp:* Res prof, Royal Soc, Univ Cambridge, 69-89; res emer fel, Trinity Col, 69-89. *Concurrent Pos:* Adj prof, Scripps Inst Oceanog, 88- *Mem:* Foreign assoc Nat Acad Sci; fel Am Geophys Union; fel Royal Soc London. *Mailing Add:* Inst Non-Linear Sci Univ Calif San Diego La Jolla CA 92093. *Fax:* 619-534-7664

LONGWELL, ARLENE CROSBY (MAZZONE), GENETICS & CYTOGENETICS, ANIMAL BREEDING. *Current Pos:* RES GENETICIST, LAB EXP BIOL, N ATLANTIC COASTAL FISHERIES RES CTR, NAT MARINE FISHERIES SERV, 65- *Personal Data:* b Buffalo, NY, Nov 26, 30; m 57, 62, Horace M; c Anne. *Educ:* SW Mo State Col, AB, 53; Univ Mo, PhD(genetics), 57. *Prof Exp:* Res assoc, Div Biol & Med Res, Argonne Nat Lab, 57-59 & Genetics Inst, Univ Lund, 59-60; res assoc path, Children's Cancer Res Found & Harvard Med Sch, 60-65. *Concurrent Pos:* Mem, Aquacult Comt, US/Japan Natural Resources Coun, 69-74, Maricult Comt, 78-87, Genetics Working Group, 81 & Int Coun Explor Sea, Copenhagen. *Mem:* Bot Soc Am; Am Genetic Asn; Sigma Xi. *Res:* Cytogenetics, genetics and breeding of commercial marine species; reproductive and mutagenic effects of marine pollutants and oil on marine species. *Mailing Add:* US Dept Com Nat Oceanic Atmospheric Admin Nat Marine Fish Serv NE Fisheries Ctr Milford Lab Milford CT 06460. *Fax:* 203-783-4217

LONGWELL, JOHN PLOEGER, CHEMICAL ENGINEERING, COMBUSTION. *Current Pos:* E R Gilliland prof chem eng, 77-88, EMER PROF CHEM ENG MASS INST TECHNOL, 88- *Personal Data:* b Denver, Colo, Apr 27, 18; m 45, Marion Valleau; c Martha (Meyer), Ann (Feresse) & John. *Educ:* Univ Calif, Berkeley, BS, 40; Mass Inst Technol, ScD(chem eng), 43. *Honors & Awards:* Sir Alfred Egerton Medal, Combustion Inst, 74; Chem Eng Pract Award, Am Inst Chem Engrs, 79. *Prof Exp:* Asst, Nat Defense Res Comt, Mass Inst Technol, 42-43; chem engr, Exxon Res & Eng Co, 43-55, asst dir, 55-58, head, Spec Proj Unit, 58-73, dir, Cent Basic Res Lab, 59-68, mgr, Corp Res Staff, 68-73, sr sci adv, 73-77. *Concurrent Pos:* Mem subcomt combustion, Nat Adv Comt Aeronaut; res adv, Comt Aeronaut Propulsion, NASA; tech adv panel ord, Asst Secy Defense Res & Eng; mem, Aeronaut Adv Comt, NASA, 78-84; chmn, Comt Advan Energy Storage, Nat Res Coun, 78-80, Comt Prod Technologies for Liquid Transp Fuels, Nat Res Coun, 89-90. *Mem:* Nat Acad Eng; Am Inst Chem Engrs; Am Chem Soc; Combustion Inst (pres); Sigma Xi. *Res:* Combustion; chemistry; propulsion and propellants; energy technology; coal conversion processes. *Mailing Add:* Mass Inst Technol 77 Massachusetts Ave Cambridge MA 02139

LONGWELL, P(AUL) A(LAN), CHEMICAL ENGINEERING. *Current Pos:* sr staff scientist, Aerojet-Gen Corp, 64-70, CHIEF SCIENTIST, ENVIROGENICS CO, AEROJET-GEN CORP, 70- *Personal Data:* b Santa Maria, Calif, Aug 4, 19; m 40; c 2. *Educ:* Calif Inst Technol, BS, 40, MS, 41, PhD(chem eng), 57. *Prof Exp:* Chemist, Shell Oil Co, Calif, 41; instr chem eng, Calif Inst Technol, 41-45; chem engr, US Naval Ord Test Sta, 45-50, head ord processing, 50-51, head, Explosives Dept, 51-54; from instr to assoc prof chem eng, Calif Inst Technol, 55-64. *Concurrent Pos:* Consult, Aerojet-Gen Corp, 61-64. *Mem:* Am Chem Soc; Am Inst Chem Engrs. *Res:* Applied mathematics in engineering problems; heat, mass and momentum transfer; cryogenic plant processes; desalting plant processes. *Mailing Add:* 1000 Crest Dr Encinitas CA 92024-4042

LONGWORTH, JAMES W, BIOPHYSICS, CHEMICAL PHYSICS. *Current Pos:* MEM STAFF, BIOL DIV, OAK RIDGE NAT LAB, 65- *Personal Data:* b Stockton Heath, Eng, Sept 16, 38; m 65; c 2. *Educ:* Univ Sheffield, BSc, 59, PhD(biochem), 62. *Prof Exp:* USPHS fel phys chem, Univ Minn, 62-63; mem staff, Bell Tel Labs, 63-65. *Concurrent Pos:* Mem, US Nat Comt Photobiol, 72-76, chmn, 76-78; prog comt, Int Congr Photobiol, 80; assoc ed, Biophysical J, 79-81, ed, Comments Molecular & Cellular Biophysics, 80- *Mem:* Am Soc Photobiol (pres, 78-79); Biophys Soc; Brit Biochem Soc; Brit Biophys Soc; Am Soc Biol Chem. *Res:* Photophysics and excited state chemistry of proteins, nucleic acids and their synthetic analogues, particularly their luminescent behavior; use of optical methods to study conformation and function of proteins and nucleic acids and their complexes. *Mailing Add:* Dept Physics Ill Inst Tech 3301 S Dearborn St Chicago IL 60616-3793

LONGWORTH, RUSKIN, POLYMER CHEMISTRY, POLYMER PHYSICS. *Current Pos:* RETIRED. *Personal Data:* b Oldham, Eng, Aug 13, 27; m 57, Joyce Kettaneh; c Monica, Kim, Jennifer & Alys. *Educ:* Univ London, BSc, 50, PhD(chem), 56. *Prof Exp:* Asst, Polytech Inst Brooklyn, 52-55; res fel, Univ Leiden, Holland, 55-56; chemist, Vauxhall Motors Ltd, Eng, 56-57; sr res chemist, Polymer Prod Dept, Exp Sta, E I Du Pont de Nemours & Co, Inc, 57-85. *Mem:* Am Chem Soc; fel Royal Soc Chem; AAAS. *Res:* Physical chemistry of polymers, especially rheology, solution properties, ionicpolymers, polyimides and polyolefines. *Mailing Add:* 10 Walnut Ridge Rd Greenville DE 19807

LONGYEAR, JUDITH QUERIDA, pure mathematics; deceased, see previous edition for last biography

LONIGRO, ANDREW JOSEPH, INTERNAL MEDICINE, PHARMACOLOGY. *Current Pos:* assoc prof, 76-84, PROF INTERNAL MED & PHARMACOL, ST LOUIS UNIV, 84- *Personal Data:* b St Louis, Mo, July 22, 36; m 68; c 3. *Educ:* St Louis Univ, BS, 58, MD, 66. *Prof Exp:* Intern-resident, St Louis Univ Hosps, 66-69, fel cardiol, 69-71; from instr to asst prof pharmacol & internal med, Med Col Wis, 71-76. *Concurrent Pos:* Spec res fel, USPHS, 69-71; res & educ assoc, Vet Admin, 72-74, clin investr, 74-76, prog specialist clin pharmacol, 76-; dir div clin pharmacol, Sch Med, St Louis Univ, 76-; chief clin pharmacol, Vet Admin Hosp, St Louis, 76-87. *Mem:* Am Fedn Clin Res; Am Soc Nephrology; Am Physiol Soc; Am Soc Pharmacol & Exp Therapeut. *Res:* Circulatory control mechanisms; protaglandins, hypertension; renal function. *Mailing Add:* 96 Lake Forest St Louis MO 63117-1361

LONKY, MARTIN LEONARD, electronic physics, solid state physics, for more information see previous edition

LNNERDAL, BO L, INFANT NUTRITION. *Current Pos:* vis asst res nutritionist, Univ Calif, Davis, 78-80, asst res nutritionist, 80-81, from asst prof to assoc prof, 81-85, PROF NUTRIT, UNIV CALIF, DAVIS, 85- *Personal Data:* b Linkoping, Sweden, Mar 5, 48; m 74; c 4. *Educ:* Univ Uppsala, BSc, 69, MSc, 71, PhD(biochem), 73. *Honors & Awards:* Henning Throne-Holst's Award, 77. *Prof Exp:* Res asst, Dept Biochem, Univ Uppsula, 69-74, res assoc, Inst Nutrit, 74-76. *Concurrent Pos:* Asst prof nutrit, Inst Nutrit, Univ Uppsula, 76- *Mem:* Am Inst Nutrit; Am Soc Clin Nutrit; Soc Exp Biol & Med. *Res:* Composition of breast milk, cow's milk and formulas; trace element metabolism in the perinatal period. *Mailing Add:* Dept Nutrit Univ Calif Davis CA 95616

LONNES, PERRY BERT, ENVIRONMENTAL SCIENCE, ANALYTICAL CHEMISTRY. *Current Pos:* MGR & CHIEF EXEC OFFICER, ENVIRON MEASUREMENTS, INTERPOLL, INC, 73- *Personal Data:* b St Paul, Minn, Feb 22, 40; m 65; c 1. *Educ:* Univ Minn, St Paul, BS, 63, MS, 65, PhD(environ sci), 72. *Prof Exp:* Instr air analysis, Univ Minn, St Paul, 68-70; mgr anal serv & contract res, Environ Res Corp, 70-73. *Mem:* Am Chem Soc; Air Pollution Control Asn. *Res:* Characterization of adsorbents to predict gas sampling potentials; gas sampling methodology; gas chromatography; air pollution analytical instrumentation. *Mailing Add:* 4500 Ball Rd NE Circle Pines MN 55014

LONNGREN, KARL E(RIK), PLASMA PHYSICS, ELECTRICAL ENGINEERING. *Current Pos:* from asst prof to assoc prof, 65-72, PROF ELEC ENG, UNIV IOWA, 72- *Personal Data:* b Milwaukee, Wis, Aug 8, 38; m 63; c 2. *Educ:* Univ Wis-Madison, BS, 60, MS, 62, PhD(elec eng), 64. *Prof Exp:* Alumni Res Found res asst, Univ Wis, 64; grant, Royal Inst Technol, Sweden, 64-65. *Concurrent Pos:* Vis scientist, Oak Ridge Nat Lab, 67 & 69, Univ Sask, 71, Inst Plasma Physics, Japan, 72, Math Res Ctr, Univ Wis-Madison, 76-77, Los Alamos Nat Labs, 79 & 80, Inst Space & Astronaut Sci, Japan, 81 & Danish Atomic Energy Comn, 82. *Mem:* Fel Am Phys Soc; fel Inst Elec & Electronics Engrs. *Res:* Nonlinear plasma physics. *Mailing Add:* Dept Elec Eng Univ Iowa 4400 Eng Blvd Iowa City IA 52242

LONSDALE, CAROL JEAN, INFRARED ASTRONOMY, GALAXY EVOLUTION. *Current Pos:* staff scientist, 85-90, GROUP SUPVR, CALIF INST TECHNOL, 90- *Personal Data:* b Stockport, Eng, Mar 9, 55; US citizen; m 89, Harding E Smith; c Kimberley J (Persson) & Tamsyn E (Lonsdale-Smith). *Educ:* Univ St Andrews, BSc, 76; Univ Edinburgh, PhD(astron), 80. *Prof Exp:* NATO res fel, Univ Hawaii, 80-81; asst prof astron, Univ Calif, Los Angeles, 81-83, fel, Jet Propulsion Lab, 83-85. *Concurrent Pos:* Organizer, Astrophys Data Prof, NASA, 85-92, mem user's comt, High Energy Astrophys Res Ctr, 92-93; ed, conf proc, Calif Inst Technol, 87. *Mem:* Int Astrophys Union; Am Astron Soc. *Res:* Study of the connection between active galactic nuclei and starbursts using infrared and radio interferometry techniques and the evolution of galaxies since their origin to the present. *Mailing Add:* 542 W Montecito Ave Sierra Madre CA 91024

LONSDALE, EDWARD MIDDLEBROOK, ELECTRICAL ENGINEERING. *Current Pos:* clin engr, 72-80, HEAD BIOMED ENG, ST JOSEPH'S HOSP, 80-, CONSULT CLIN ENG. *Personal Data:* b Kansas City, Mo, July 21, 15; m 41; c 2. *Educ:* Univ Kans, BS, 36; Univ Iowa, MS, 41, PhD, 52. *Prof Exp:* Dial telephone engr, Southwest Bell Telephone Co, 36-38; TV engr, Midland TV Co, 39-40; radar countermeasures engr, Naval Res Lab, 42-46; prof elec eng, Univ Iowa, 46-56; prof elec eng, Univ Wyo, 56-72. *Concurrent Pos:* Adj prof elec & comp eng, 82- *Mem:* Am Soc Eng Educ; Am Inst Elec & Electronics Engrs; Asn Advan Med Instrumentation. *Res:* Biomedical instrumentation; radio telemetry from fresh water fish. *Mailing Add:* Elec & Comput Eng Dept Univ Ariz Tucson AZ 85721

LONSDALE, HAROLD KENNETH, PHYSICAL CHEMISTRY, MEMBRANE SCIENCE & TECHNOLOGY. *Current Pos:* RETIRED. *Personal Data:* b Westfield, NJ, Jan 19, 32; m 53, 93, Bryn Hazell; c Karen (Trachsel) & Harold K Jr. *Educ:* Rutgers Univ, BS, 53; Pa State Univ, PhD(chem), 57. *Prof Exp:* Staff mem, Gen Atomic Co, 59-70; prin scientist, Alza Corp, 70-72; vis scientist, Max Planck Inst Biophys, 73; vis prof, Weizmann Inst, 74; pres, Bend Res, Inc, 75-87, chmn 87-90. *Concurrent Pos:* Ed, J Membrane Sci, 75-90. *Mem:* Am Chem Soc. *Res:* Transport in synthetic membranes, desalination by reverse osmosis; controlled release of biologically active agents. *Mailing Add:* 1420 NE Sharkey Terr Bend OR 97701

LONSDALE-ECCLES, JOHN DAVID, PROTEIN BIOCHEMISTRY, CELL BIOLOGY. *Current Pos:* SCIENTIST BIOCHEM, INT LAB RES ANIMAL DIS, NAIROBI, 83-, LAB COORDR, 91- *Personal Data:* b Cheshire, Eng, Jan 14, 46; m 73; c 4. *Educ:* Queen's Univ Belfast, BSc Hons, 70, PhD(biochem), 74. *Prof Exp:* Res fel biochem, Queen's Univ Belfast, 74-75; sr fel biochem, Univ Wash, Seattle, 75-78, res assoc, Dept Periodont, 78-82. *Concurrent Pos:* Lectr, Ctr Res Oral Biol, Seattle, 78-82; external examr, Univ Nairobi, 87-; consult, WHO, 90- *Mem:* Royal Soc Chem; Biochem Soc; NY Acad Sci; Am Soc Cell Biol; Protein Soc; Biochem Soc Kenya. *Res:* Disecting the biochemical aspects of endocytosis by African tryparosomes and their mechanisms of differentiation from one life cycle stage into another; protenses, protein binases and protein phosphates of the parasites. *Mailing Add:* Vestavia Hills 1309 Panorama Dr Birmingham AL 35216-0001

LONSKI, JOSEPH, developmental biology, for more information see previous edition

LONTZ, ROBERT JAN, PHYSICS. *Current Pos:* CO-FOUNDER, MAGNETIC IMAGING TECHNOL INC, 93-; PRES, R&D ANALYSIS INC, 93- *Personal Data:* b Wilmington, Del, Oct 19, 36; m 62; c 2. *Educ:* Yale Univ, BSc, 58; Duke Univ, PhD(physics), 62. *Prof Exp:* Asst, Physics Div, US Army Res Off, 62-64, chief, Gen Physics Br, 64-67, assoc dir, 67-73, dir, 73-88; consult, res funding, Res Definition & Mgt, Tech Writing, 88-93. *Concurrent Pos:* Dep asst res, Off Undersecy Defense Res & Eng, 78-79. *Res:* Paramagnetic resonance spectroscopy; lasers. *Mailing Add:* 3122 Surrey Rd Durham NC 27707

LONZETTA, CHARLES MICHAEL, ORGANIC CHEMISTRY, PHYSICAL-ORGANIC CHEMISTRY. *Current Pos:* RES CHEMIST, ROHM & HAAS CO, 78- *Personal Data:* b Hazleton, Pa, Jan 28, 50; m 71; c 3. *Educ:* Pa State Univ, BS, 71; Harvard Univ, AM, 74, PhD(org chem), 77. *Prof Exp:* Fel phys-org chem, Brandeis Univ, 76-78. *Concurrent Pos:* Head teaching fel, Harvard Exten Sch, 74-78. *Mem:* Am Chem Soc. *Res:* Mechanistic organic chemistry: singlet oxygen formation and reactions; organophosphorus reaction kinetics; free radical reactions; pulsed megawatt infrared laser reaction kinetics; monomer process technology. *Mailing Add:* Rohm & Haas Tex Inc PO Box 672 Tidal Rd Deer Park TX 77536-0672

LOO, BILLY WEI-YU, INSTRUMENT SCIENCE, X-RAY DETECTORS. *Current Pos:* SR ENG PHYSICIST, LAWRENCE BERKELEY LAB, UNIV CALIF, 72- *Personal Data:* b Chungking, China, Oct 26, 39; US citizen; m 65; c 2. *Educ:* Univ Mich, Ann Arbor, BSE, 63, MS, 65, PhD(physics & nuclear eng), 72. *Prof Exp:* Asst res physicist high energy physics, Univ Mich, 65-69. *Mem:* Am Phys Soc; AAAS. *Res:* Research and development in medical instrumentation, lung and bone density measurements, and special Si(Li) x-ray detectors for space and nuclear science applications; sampling and analysis of atmospheric aerosols. *Mailing Add:* Lawrence Berkeley Lab 1 Cyclotron Rd Mail Stop 7-222 Berkeley CA 94720

LOO, MELANIE WAI SUE, GENETICS. *Current Pos:* ASST PROF BIOL & GENETICS, DEPT BIOL SCI, CALIF STATE UNIV, SACRAMENTO, 77- *Personal Data:* b Honolulu, Hawaii, Nov 24, 48. *Educ:* Univ Calif, BA, BS, 70; Univ Wash, PhD(genetics), 74. *Prof Exp:* Proj res assoc genetics, Dept Physiol Chem, Univ Wis, 75-77. *Mem:* AAAS. *Res:* Genetic regulation. *Mailing Add:* Calif State Univ Sacramento 6000 J St Calif State Univ 6000 J St Sacramento CA 95819-2605

LOO, TI LI, CLINICAL PHARMACOLOGY, CANCER & AIDS CHEMOTHERAPY. *Current Pos:* RES PROF PHARMACOL, MED CTR, GEORGE WASHINGTON UNIV, 85- *Personal Data:* b Changsha, China, Jan 7, 18; nat US; m 51, Marie Lee; c Michael, Agnes & Jonathan. *Educ:* Tsing Hua Univ, China, BSc, 40; Oxford Univ, DPhil, 47 & DSc, 85. *Honors & Awards:* Gottlieb Award, Univ Tex M D Anderson Cancer Ctr, 87. *Prof Exp:* Asst pharmacol, Oxford Univ, 46-47; fel org chem, Univ Md, 47-51; res assoc, Christ Hosp Inst Med Res, 51-54; supvry chemist, NIH, 55-65; pharmacologist & prof, Dept Develop Therapeut, Univ Tex M D Anderson Hosp & Tumor Inst & prof pharmacol, Univ Tex Med Sch & Grad Biomed Sci, 65-85, Ashbel Smith prof ther, 81-85. *Concurrent Pos:* Adj prof pharmacol, Univ Houston, 77-85; spec lectr, Japan Soc Clin Pharmacol, 85. *Mem:* Am Chem Soc; Am Asn Cancer Res; Royal Soc Chem; Am Soc Clin Oncol; Am Soc Clin Pharmacol & Therapeut; Sigma Xi; Am Soc Pharmacol Exp Therapeut. *Res:* Pharmacology of anticancer and anti-AIDS drugs; cancer chemotherapy; metabolism of drugs; chemical structure and biological activities; pharmacokinetics; anti-AIDS chemotherapy. *Mailing Add:* Pharmacol Dept George Wash Univ Med Ctr 2300 Eye St NW Washington DC 20037-2337. *Fax:* 202-994-2870

LOO, YEN-HOONG, biochemistry; deceased, see previous edition for last biography

LOOK, DAVID C, SOLID STATE PHYSICS. *Current Pos:* SR RES PHYSICIST, WRIGHT STATE UNIV, 80- *Personal Data:* b St Paul, Minn, Dec 19, 38; m 68, Rita Beatty; c James & Christine. *Educ:* Univ Minn, BPhys, 60, MS, 62; Univ Pittsburgh, PhD(physics), 65. *Honors & Awards:* Outstanding Scientist Award, Eng Coun, Dayton. *Prof Exp:* Res physicist, Aerospace Res Labs, 66-69; sr res physicist, Univ Dayton, 69-80. *Mem:* Fel Am Phys Soc; Am Sci Affil; Inst Elec & Electronics Engrs; Electrochem Soc. *Res:* Transport properties in semiconductor materials and devices; nuclear magnetic resonance; ion implantation; radiation damage. *Mailing Add:* Univ Res Ctr Wright State Univ Dayton OH 45435. *Fax:* 937-255-3374; *E-Mail:* lookd@el.wpafb.uf.mil

LOOK, DWIGHT CHESTER, JR, THERMAL RADIATIVE HEAT TRANSFER, THERMOPHYSICAL PROPERTIES. *Current Pos:* from asst prof to assoc prof, 69-78, PROF MECH ENG, UNIV MO-ROLLO, 78- *Personal Data:* b Smith Center, Kans, Aug 25, 38; m 60, Wellbaum; c Dwight III & Douglas. *Educ:* Cent Col, Fayette, Mo, BA, 60; Univ Nebr, MS, 62, Univ Okla, PhD(mech & aerosysts), 69. *Honors & Awards:* R R Testor Award, Soc Automotive Engrs, 78. *Prof Exp:* Teaching asst eng physics, Univ Nebr, 60-63; aerosysts engr, Ft Worth Div, Gen Dynamics, 63-67. *Concurrent Pos:* Adj instr ele maths, Tex Christian Univ, 67; spec instr thermodyn, Univ Okla, 69; co-prin investr, NSF grants, 75- *Mem:* Am Soc Mech Engrs; Am Inst Aeronaut & Astronaut; Am Soc Eng Educ; Int Soc Optical Eng. *Res:* Experimental investigation of thermophysical properties, particularly the reflectance of light from solids and the electromagnetic scattering from small particles; thermodynamics. *Mailing Add:* 203 Mech Eng Bldg Univ Mo Rolla MO 65401. *Fax:* 573-341-4607; *E-Mail:* look@shuttle.cc.umr.edu

LOOKER, JAMES HOWARD, organic chemistry; deceased, see previous edition for last biography

LOOKER, JEROME J, ORGANIC CHEMISTRY. *Current Pos:* RES CHEMIST, EASTMAN KODAK CO, 62- *Personal Data:* b Columbus, Ohio, July 7, 35; m 57; c 3. *Educ:* Kenyon Col, AB, 58; Univ Ill, MS, 60, PhD(org chem), 61. *Prof Exp:* Nat Sci Found fel, Cornell Univ, 61-62. *Mem:* Am Chem Soc. *Res:* Synthetic organic chemistry. *Mailing Add:* 333 Panorama Terr Rochester NY 14625-2315

LOOKHART, GEORGE LEROY, ANALYTICAL CHEMISTRY & PHYSICAL BIOCHEMISTRY OF CEREAL PROTEINS. *Current Pos:* SR RES CHEMIST & PROG LEAD SCIENTIST, USDA, US GRAIN MKT RES LAB, 76- *Personal Data:* b North Platte, Nebr, Aug 25, 43; m 63, Judy Alexander; c Jeff, Jodii & Jill. *Educ:* Kearney State Col, BS, 68; Univ Wyo, PhD(phys chem), 73. *Concurrent Pos:* Teaching internship fel, Chem Dept, Univ Ky, 73-74; fel biochem dept, Univ Mo, Columbia, 74-76; adj asst prof, Grain Sci Dept, Kans State Univ, 80-85, adj prof, 85-; group leader, Baking Sci & Grain Qual Groups, 90- *Mem:* Am Chem Soc; Am Asn Cereal Chemists. *Res:* Develop high pressure liquid chromatographic methods of analysis for protein, estrogens, amino acids and vitamins; develop new electrophoretic methods to cereal proteins for identifying cultivars and characterizing individual proteins; relationships of protein groups or individuals with quality. *Mailing Add:* US Grain Mkt Res Lab 1515 College Ave Manhattan KS 66502. *Fax:* 785-776-2792; *E-Mail:* george@usgmrl.ksu.edu

LOOMANS, MAURICE EDWARD, DERMATOLOGY. *Current Pos:* RETIRED. *Personal Data:* b Wisconsin Rapids, Wis, Aug 10, 33; m 57; c 3. *Educ:* Hope Col, BA, 57; Univ Wis, MS, 59, PhD(biochem), 62. *Prof Exp:* Res chemist, Miami Valley Labs, Procter & Gamble Co, 62-93. *Mem:* Soc Invest Dermat. *Res:* Keratinization; epidermal cellular control; acne; percutaneous absorption; mediators of inflammation; animal models; rheumatology; arthritis. *Mailing Add:* 5231 Jessup Rd Cincinnati OH 45247

LOOMIS, ALDEN ALBERT, ENGINEERING GEOLOGY, MULTISPECTRAL REMOTE SENSING. *Current Pos:* AT ALDEN LOOMIS ASSOC, 94- *Personal Data:* b Pittsburgh, Pa, July 22, 34; m 74, Margi Mostue; c Tom & Sarah. *Educ:* Stanford Univ, AB, 56, PhD(petrol, geol), 61. *Prof Exp:* Asst prof geol, San Jose State Univ, 60-61; sr scientist, Jet Propulsion Lab, Calif Inst Technol, 61-94. *Concurrent Pos:* Assoc prof, Calif State Univ, Los Angeles, 65-66; consult geoscientist, 69-; eng geologist, State of Calif, 72- *Mem:* Sigma Xi; fel Geol Soc Am; Am Asn Petrol Geologists. *Res:* Space applications to oceanography and geology; igneous petrology, volcanology; metamorphic petrology; gravity and crustal structure; geology of moon and Mars; development of experiments for lunar and planetary exploration; engineering and environmental geology; mineral exploration; hazardous waste disposal. *Mailing Add:* 1262 E Rubio St Altadena CA 91001. *Fax:* 626-449-9573

LOOMIS, CARSON ROBERT, PROTEIN CHEMISTRY, DRUG DISCOVERY. *Current Pos:* VPRES RES, SPHINX PHARMACEUT, 91- *Personal Data:* b Syracuse, NY, Feb 17, 45; m 80, Mayre Mercer; c Nathan, Dawn & Duncan. *Educ:* Univ Vt, BA, 69; Boston Univ, PhD(chem), 76. *Prof Exp:* Res assoc, Duke Univ Med Ctr, 76-84, dep dir, Signal Transduction Div, Duke Univ Cancer Ctr, 85-87. *Mem:* Am Soc Biol Chemists. *Res:* Signal transduction mechanisms and protein kinases and phosphatases. *Mailing Add:* Sphinx Pharmceut Corp 4 University Pl Box 52330 Durham NC 27717. *Fax:* 919-489-9093

LOOMIS, EARL ALFRED, JR, CHILD DEVELOPMENT, SUBSTANCE DEPENDENCE. *Current Pos:* RETIRED. *Personal Data:* b Minneapolis, Minn, May 21, 21; m 69, Anita M; c Rebecca, Kathleen, Jennifer & Amy. *Educ:* Univ Minn, BA, 42, MD, 45; Am Bd Psychiat & Neurol, cert, 51 & 58. *Prof Exp:* Intern internal med & pediat, Evans Mem & Mass Mem Hosp, 45-46; resident psychiat, Western Psychiat Inst, Pittsburgh, 46-48; fel psychiat & child psychiat, Hosp Univ Pa & Inst Pa Hosp, 48-50; instr psychiat, Univ Pa, 49-52; assoc prof, Univ Pittsburgh, 52-56; chief, Div Child Psychiat, St Luke's Hosp, NY, 55-62; prof psychiat & relig, Union Theol Sem, NY, 56-63; psychiat dir child & adolescent psychiat, Blueberry Treatment Ctr Seriously Disturbed Children, 63-81; prof psychiat, Dept Psychiat & Health Behav, Med Col Ga, 81-90. *Concurrent Pos:* Consult child psychiat, Gov Bacon Health Ctr, Del, 49-57; res fel in residence child develop, Univ Geneva, Switz, 62-63; lectr, Herbert Holt Inst, 63-73; attend psychiatrist, Eastern Long Island Hosp, 73-81; psychiat dir, Child Adolescent Prog, Ga Regional Hosp, Augusta, 81-82 & Eugene Talmadge Hosp, 82-84. *Mem:* Am Psychiat Asn; Am Psychoanal Asn; Am Acad Child Psychiat; Am Soc Addiction Med. *Res:* Play patterns of non-verbal children as indices of ego function and dysfunction; conscience of condoners, abusers and abused in physical and sexual abuse; consequences of parallel and out of phase development of conscience and cognition. *Mailing Add:* 1002 Katherine St No 6 Augusta GA 30904-4481. *E-Mail:* amploomis@aol.com

LOOMIS, FREDERICK B, PETROLEUM & MINE GEOLOGY. *Current Pos:* CONSULT GEOLOGIST, 75- *Personal Data:* b Amherst, Mass, Feb 10, 15. *Educ:* Amherst Univ, BA, 37. *Prof Exp:* Direct mgr, Clark Oil Refining, Milwaukee, Wis, 39-59, geologist & mgr foreign oper, 60-70; mgr Can oper, Petro-Consult, Alta, Can, 70-75. *Mem:* Fel Geol Soc Am; Am Asn Petrol Geologists. *Mailing Add:* 2738 S Via Del Bac Green Valley AZ 85614

LOOMIS, HAROLD GEORGE, NUMERICAL WAVE THEORIES. *Current Pos:* asst prof math, 63-66, PROF OCEAN ENG, UNIV HAWAII, 82- *Personal Data:* b Erie, Pa, Aug 22, 25; m 47; c 4. *Educ:* Stanford Univ, BS, 50; Pa State Univ, MS, 52, PhD(math & physics), 57. *Prof Exp:* Scientist, HRB Singer, 52-55; instr math, Pa State Univ, 55-57; asst prof math, Amherst Col, 57-62; scientist, Nat Oceanic & Atmospheric Admin, 66-82. *Concurrent Pos:* Secy, Tsunami Comn, Int Union Geod & Geophys, 76-82. *Mem:* Soc Indust & Appl Math. *Res:* Numerical hydrodynamics; long and short water wave theories; time series analysis; statistics. *Mailing Add:* 9218 NE Bluefin Bainbridge Island WA 98110

LOOMIS, HERSCHEL HARE, JR, ELECTRICAL ENGINEERING, COMPUTER ENGINEERING. *Current Pos:* PROF ELEC & COMPUT ENG, NAVAL POSTGRAD SCH, MONTEREY, CALIF, 83- *Personal Data:* b Wilmington, Del, May 31, 34; m 57; c 2. *Educ:* Cornell Univ, BEE, 57; Univ Md, MS, 59; Mass Inst Technol, PhD(elec eng), 63. *Prof Exp:* Staff engr, Lincoln Lab, Mass Inst Technol, 60-61; from asst prof to assoc prof elec eng, Univ Calif, Davis, 62-74, chmn dept, 70-75, prof elec eng, 74-83; chair prof Navelex, 81-83. *Concurrent Pos:* Consult, Lawrence Livermore Lab, Univ Calif, 63-88; NSF grants, 64 & 67-69; consult, Signal Sci, Inc, Santa Clara, CA, 81- *Mem:* Inst Elec & Electronics Engrs; Asn Comput Mach. *Res:* Theory, design and applications of digital computers; digital design automation; digital signal processing systems. *Mailing Add:* 4086 Pine Meadows Way Pebble Beach CA 93953-3019

LOOMIS, ROBERT HENRY, ZOOLOGY, LIMNOLOGY. *Current Pos:* RETIRED. *Personal Data:* b Atlanta, Ga, Nov 9, 23; m 45; c 4. *Educ:* Univ Ga, BS, 47; Okla State Univ, MS, 51, PhD(zool), 56. *Prof Exp:* Instr biol, Piedmont Col, 48, Cent State Col, Okla, 51-52 & Jimma Agr Sch, Ethiopia, 52-54; asst prof, Cent State Col, Okla, 54-55; from asst prof to prof, Northeastern State Col, 55-63; prof, Parsons Col, 63-68; prof & chmn div sci, Pikeville Col, 68-75; prof life sci, Sacramento City Col, 75-78; mem fac dept biol, Calif State Univ, 78-89; dept life sci, Consumnes River Col. *Mem:* AAAS; Am Inst Biol Sci. *Res:* Watershed conditions on fish populations; food habits of mesopelagic fishes; identification of photosynthetic active components of phytoplankton communities; temperature acclimation in crayfish populations. *Mailing Add:* 7056 Pine Cone Dr Pollock Pines CA 95726

LOOMIS, ROBERT MORGAN, FORESTRY. *Current Pos:* RETIRED. *Personal Data:* b Mauston, Wis, Aug 31, 22; m 48; c 6. *Educ:* Univ Mich, BS, Univ Mo, MS, 65. *Prof Exp:* Forester, Ochoco Nat Forest, Ore, 48-51; adminr, Ottawa Nat Forest, Mich, 51-56 & Mo Nat Forests, 56-57; res forester, Cent States Forest Exp Sta, Columbia, Mo, 57-66, NCent Forest Exp Sta, Columbia, Mo, 66-71 & E Lansing, Mich, 71-80. *Mem:* Soc Am Foresters. *Res:* Forest fire effects, fuels and danger rating. *Mailing Add:* 104 Redwood Ct Atlantic Beach NC 28512

LOOMIS, ROBERT SIMPSON, PLANT PHYSIOLOGY. *Current Pos:* Instr agron & jr agronomist, Univ Calif, Davis, 56-58, from asst prof & asst agronomist to assoc prof & assoc agronomist, 58-68, dir, Inst Ecol, 69-72, assoc dean environ studies, 70-72, PROF AGRON & AGRONOMIST, UNIV CALIF, DAVIS, 68- *Personal Data:* b Ames, Iowa, Oct 11, 28; m 51; c 3. *Educ:* Iowa State Univ, BS, 49; Univ Wis, MS, 51, PhD(bot), 56. *Concurrent Pos:* NIH spec fel, Harvard Univ, 63-64; NZ Nat Res Adv Coun res fel, 71; vis scientist, Agr Univ, Wagenigen, 79; vis prof, Melbourne Univ, 85. *Mem:* Fel AAAS; Am Soc Plant Physiol (secy, 65-67); Am Soc Sugar Beet Technol; fel Am Soc Agron; Agr Hist Soc. *Res:* Physiology and ecology of field crops including growth and development; integrative physiology with emphasis on system simulation. *Mailing Add:* 708 Elmwood Dr Davis CA 95616

LOOMIS, STEPHEN HENRY, COMPARATIVE PHYSIOLOGY. *Current Pos:* asst prof, 80-86, ASSOC PROF COMPARATIVE PHYSIOL & INVERTEBRATE ZOOL, CONN COL, 86- *Personal Data:* b Flint, Mich, Oct 3, 52; m 80; c 2. *Educ:* Univ Calif, Davis, BS, 74, PhD(zool), 79. *Prof Exp:* Res asst prof, Rice Univ, 79-80. *Mem:* Am Soc Zoologists; AAAS; Soc Cryobiol; Sigma Xi. *Res:* Freezing tolerance of intertidal invertebrates. *Mailing Add:* Dept Zool Conn Col 270 Mohegan Ave New London CT 06320

LOOMIS, TED ALBERT, PHARMACOLOGY, TOXICOLOGY. *Current Pos:* assoc prof, 47-59, PROF PHARMACOL & TOXICOL, SCH MED, UNIV WASH, 59- *Personal Data:* b Spokane, Wash, Apr 24, 17; m; c 2. *Educ:* Univ Wash, BS, 39; Univ Buffalo, MS, 41, PhD(pharmacol), 43; Yale Univ, MD, 46. *Prof Exp:* Intern, US Marine Hosp, 46-47. *Concurrent Pos:* State toxicologist, Wash, 55-77. *Res:* Pesticide and insecticide toxicology; anticoagulant agents; alcohol research; toxicological methods; mechanisms of drug action and action of toxic chemicals. *Mailing Add:* 2707 E Becker Rd Clinton WA 98236-9003

LOOMIS, TIMOTHY PATRICK, PETROLOGY, REACTION KINETICS. *Current Pos:* asst prof, 74-76, ASSOC PROF GEOL, UNIV ARIZ, 76- *Personal Data:* b Alhambra, Calif, May 25, 46. *Educ:* Univ Calif, Davis, BS, 67; Princeton Univ, PhD(geol), 71. *Prof Exp:* J W Gibbs instr geol, Yale Univ, 71-73; adj asst prof, Univ Calif, Los Angeles, 73-74. *Mem:* Geol Soc Am; Am Geophys Union. *Res:* Heat and mass transfer and reaction kinetics in chemical processes. *Mailing Add:* 1605 Alison Ave Mountain View CA 94040

LOOMIS, WALTER DAVID, BIOCHEMISTRY. *Current Pos:* Instr biochem, 53-54, from asst prof to assoc prof, 54-68, PROF BIOCHEM, ORE STATE UNIV, 68- *Personal Data:* b Fayetteville, Ark, Mar 2, 26; m 52. *Educ:* Iowa State Univ, BS, 48; Univ Calif, PhD(comp biochem), 53. *Concurrent Pos:* USPHS res career develop award, 61-67; vis researcher, Univ Col Wales, 65-66. *Mem:* Am Chem Soc; Am Soc Plant Physiol; Am Soc Biol Chem; Phytochem Soc NAm; Can Soc Plant Physiol. *Res:* Plant enzymes and proteins; terpene metabolism. *Mailing Add:* Dept Biochem & Biophysics Ore State Univ Life Sci 2011 Corvallis OR 97331-7305

LOOMIS, WILLIAM FARNSWORTH, JR, DEVELOPMENTAL BIOLOGY. *Current Pos:* from asst prof to assoc prof, 66-79, PROF BIOL, UNIV CALIF, SAN DIEGO, 79- *Personal Data:* b Boston, Mass, Sept 17, 40; m 81, Patricia Hasegawa; c Catherine & Emily. *Educ:* Harvard Univ, BS, 62; Mass Inst Technol, PhD(microbiol), 65. *Prof Exp:* NIH fel, Brandeis Univ, 65-66. *Mem:* Soc Develop Biol (pres); Am Soc Biol Chemists. *Res:* Cellular interactions involved in the biochemical differentiation in Dictyostelium discoideum; genetics of slime molds; complex processes of cellular interaction can be dissected by molecular genetics; concepts generated in one system can often be applied to others. *Mailing Add:* Dept Biol Univ Calif San Diego La Jolla CA 92093-0322

LOONEY, NORMAN E, POMOLOGY, PLANT GROWTH REGULATION. *Current Pos:* POMOLOGIST & PLANT PHYSIOLOGIST, PAC AGR FOOD & AGR RES STA, 66-, HEAD HORT & BASIC STUDIES, 87- *Personal Data:* b Adrian, Ore, May 31, 38; m 57, 83, Norah Keating; c Pamela (Licopautis), Patricia (Braidwood) & Steven. *Educ:* Wash State Univ, BS, 60, PhD(hort), 66. *Prof Exp:* Sr exp aid hort, Wash State Univ, 60-62, res asst post-harvest hort, 62-66. *Concurrent Pos:* Vis scientist, CSIRO, Sydney, Australia, 71-72, East Malling Res Sta, Maidstone, Eng, 81-82 & Lincoln Univ, NZ, 90-91. *Mem:* Fel Am Soc Hort Sci; Can Soc Hort Sci; Int Soc Hort Sci. *Res:* Physiology of growth, development and ripening of temperate zone fruits; investigations of flowering physiology and plant growth regulator effects. *Mailing Add:* Head Hort & Basic Studies Group Pac Agr Food & Agr Res Sta Summerland BC V0H 1Z0 Can. *Fax:* 250-494-0755; *E-Mail:* looney@bcrssu.agr.ca

LOONEY, RALPH WILLIAM, physical chemistry, polymer chemistry; deceased, see previous edition for last biography

LOONEY, STEPHEN WARWICK, MULTIVARIATE ANALYSIS, QUALITY CONTROL. *Current Pos:* ASSOC PROF, SCH MED, UNIV LOUISVILLE, 91- *Personal Data:* b Atlanta, Ga, Sept 6, 52; m 80. *Educ:* Univ Ga, BS, 74, MS, 76, PhD(statist), 80. *Prof Exp:* Chief statist analyst, Northeast Ga Health Dist, 79-80; vis fel, Health & Welfare Can, 80-81; vis biostatist, Upjohn Co, 87-88; asst prof, La State Univ, 81-86, assoc prof quant bus analysis, 86-91, MBA dir, 89-91. *Mem:* Am Statist Asn; Am Soc Qual Control; Int Asn Statist Comput. *Res:* Research activity in applied statistics and how it can be applied in business research; quality control. *Mailing Add:* Dept Family & Commun Med 530 S Jackson St Rm A1 HOS/ACB Louisville KY 40292

LOONEY, WILLIAM BOYD, RADIOBIOLOGY, BIOPHYSICS. *Current Pos:* from asst prof to assoc prof, 61-68, PROF RADIOBIOL & BIOPHYS & DIR DIV, UNIV VA, 68- *Personal Data:* b South Clinchfield, Va, Mar 18, 22; m 55; c 2. *Educ:* Emory & Henry Col, BS, 44; Med Col Va, MD, 48; Cambridge Univ, PhD(radiobiol, biophys), 60. *Hon Degrees:* DSc, Emory & Henry Col, 78. *Prof Exp:* Intern, Presby Hosp, Chicago, 48-49, asst resident, 49-50; asst prof radiol, Johns Hopkins Univ, 59-60. *Concurrent Pos:* Mem interdisciplinary prog biophys, Univ Va, 66-; vis fel med oncol, Mem Sloan-Kettering Cancer Ctr, 78. *Mem:* AAAS; Am Asn Cancer Res; Am Soc Cell Biol; Biophys Soc; Radiation Res Soc; Sigma Xi. *Res:* Cancer; mathematical evaluation of tumor growth curves; cell cycle and cell kinetics studies in experimental tumors; modification of tumor growth rates and cell kinetics by radiation, alone or in combination with different chemotherapeutic agents; host-tumor interaction. *Mailing Add:* 2300 Suffolk Rd Charlottesville VA 22901

LOOP, MICHAEL STUART, VISION, HERPETOLOGY. *Current Pos:* asst prof, 78-81, ASSOC PROF PHYSIOL OPTICS, UNIV ALA, BIRMINGHAM, 81- *Personal Data:* b Pittsburgh, Pa, Feb 28, 46; c 4. *Educ:* Fla State Univ, BS, 68, MS, 71, PhD(psychobiol), 72. *Prof Exp:* NIH fel neurol surg, Univ Va, 72-74, Sloane Found fel physiol, 74-75; vis asst prof physiol & biophys, Univ Ill, 75-78. *Mem:* Soc Neurosci. *Res:* Vertebrate visual system psychophysics; comparative animal behavior. *Mailing Add:* Dept Psych Univ Ala Birmingham 1717 Seventh Ave S Birmingham AL 35294-0001

LOOP, ROSE-ANN, NUTRITION. *Current Pos:* PROF NUTRIT, UNIV TEX, AUSTIN, 81- *Personal Data:* b Cherokee, Okla, July 13, 43; c Jeffrey & Jamie. *Educ:* Emporia State Univ, BS, 64; Univ Tex, Austin, PhD(chem), 68. *Concurrent Pos:* Res grantee, USDA & FDA. *Mem:* Am Inst Nuritit; Am Soc Clin Nutrit; Am Dietetic Asn; Res Soc Alcoholism. *Res:* Role of nutrients on cholesterol homeostasis in humans; animal models of alcoholism. *Mailing Add:* Dept Grad Nutrit Univ Tex GEA 117 Austin TX 78712. *Fax:* 512-471-5844; *E-Mail:* zann@mail.utexas.edu

LOOS, HENDRICUS G, ENVIRONMENTAL PHYSICS, NEURAL NETWORKS. *Current Pos:* DIR, LAGUNA RES LAB, 74- *Personal Data:* b Amsterdam, Neth, Dec 18, 25; nat US; m 52; c 2. *Educ:* Univ Amsterdam, Drs(math), 51; Univ Delft, ScD, 52. *Prof Exp:* Res fel, Calif Inst Technol, 52-55; sr engr, Propulsion Res Corp, 55-57; sr physicist, Giannini Sci Corp, 57-66; mem staff, Douglas Advan Res Lab, 66-70, sr staff scientist, McDonnell-Douglas Astronaut Co, 70-71; prof math, Cleveland State Univ, 71-74. *Concurrent Pos:* Lectr, Univ Calif, Riverside, 63-64, assoc prof in residence, 64-70, adj prof, 70-76. *Mem:* Am Phys Soc; Am Optical Soc; Int Neural Network Soc. *Res:* Gauge theory; atmospheric physics; fluid mechanics; general relativity; neural networks. *Mailing Add:* 3015 Rainbow Glen Fallbrook CA 92028-9765

LOOS, JAMES STAVERT, HIGH-SPEED DIGITAL ELECTRONICS & ELECTRONIC PACKAGING. *Current Pos:* PHYSICS & ENG RES & DEVELOP, AT&T BELL LABS, 86- *Personal Data:* b Grafton, NDak, May 24, 40; m 61, Janet Grimson; c Rebecca (Palacios) & Michael W. *Educ:* Univ NDak, BS, 62; Univ Ill, MS, 63, PhD(physics), 68. *Prof Exp:* Res assoc high energy physics, Stanford Linear Accelerator Ctr, 68-72; asst prof physics, Duke Univ, 72-77; res physicist high energy physics, Argonne Nat Lab, 77-86. *Mem:* Am Phys Soc; Inst Elec & Electronics Engrs. *Res:* Experimental high energy physics; high energy particle detectors and techniques; high-speed electronics; electronic packaging; system interconnect. *Mailing Add:* Lucent Technol 2000 N Naperville Rd Rm 4F128 Naperville IL 60563

LOOS, KARL RUDOLF, physical chemistry, environmental analysis, for more information see previous edition

LOOSE, LELAND DAVID, PHYSIOLOGY, IMMUNOLOGY. *Current Pos:* proj leader immunother, 80-85, asst dir clin res, 85-88, ASSOC DIR CLIN RES, PFIZER INC, 88- *Personal Data:* b Reading, Pa, Jan 25, 40; m 71; c 3. *Educ:* Tenn Wesleyan Col, BS, 63; ETenn State Univ, MA, 65; Univ Mo, Columbia, PhD(physiol), 70. *Prof Exp:* Instr physiol, Lees-McRae Col, 65-67; asst prof, Sch Med, Tulane Univ, 70-74; asst prof physiol, Dept Physiol & Inst Exp Path & Toxicol, Albany Med Col, 74-75, assoc prof, 75-80. *Mem:* Am Physiol Soc; Am Soc Trop Med & Hyg; NY Acad Sci; Am Soc Zool; Sigma Xi; Am Rheumatic Assoc; Am Soc Microbiol; Am Asn Immunol. *Res:* Physiological control mechanisms of immune responses; influence of environmental chemicals on immune responses; differentiation of lymphoid tissue with special reference to hormonal effects; macrophage antigen processing; calcium alterations in shock; pharmacological control of inflammation. *Mailing Add:* Pfizer Inc Eastern Point Rd Groton CT 06340-5197

LOOSLI, JOHN KASPER, ANIMAL NUTRITION. *Current Pos:* from asst prof to prof, 39-74, head, Dept Animal Sci, 63-71, EMER PROF ANIMAL NUTRIT, CORNELL UNIV, 74- *Personal Data:* b Clarkston, Utah, May 16, 09; m 36; c 3. *Educ:* Utah State Univ, BS, 31; Colo State Univ, MS, 32; Cornell Univ, PhD(animal nutrit), 38. *Honors & Awards:* Am Feed Mfrs Award Nutrit, 50; Borden Award Dairy Prod, 51; Morrison Award, 56; Award of Honor, Am Dairy Sci Asn, 83. *Prof Exp:* Instr agr, Col Southern Utah, 33-35; asst animal nutrit, Cornell Univ, 35-38; agent, Bur Biol Surv, USDA, 38-39. *Concurrent Pos:* Collabr, US Fish & Wildlife Serv, 39-56; vis prof, Univ Philippines, 53-54 & 66 & Univ Ibadan, 72-74; consult, US Army Vet Grad Sch, 54 & USAID, Nigeria, 61; ed, J Animal Sci, 55-58; Fulbright lectr, Univ Queensland, 60; mem, Comt Animal Nutrit, Agr Bd, Nat Res Coun; vis prof, Univ Fla, 74-80, actg chmn, Dept Animal Sci, 75-76, actg dean res, 77, adj prof, 80-85. *Mem:* Fel Am Soc Animal Sci (vpres, 59, pres, 60); Am Dairy Sci Asn (pres, 70-71); fel Am Inst Nutrit; Brit Soc Animal Prod. *Res:* Fat metabolism and requirements; vitamin requirements; lactation; mineral requirements; feed composition. *Mailing Add:* 406 SW 40th St Gainesville FL 32607-2749

LOOV, ROBERT EDMUND, STRUCTURAL ENGINEERING. *Current Pos:* from asst prof to assoc prof, Univ Calgary, 63-74, asst to vpres, 70-73, actg head civil eng, 80-81, head, 84-89, PROF CIVIL ENG, UNIV CALGARY, 74- *Personal Data:* b Wetaskiwin, Alta, Oct 29, 33; m 79, Carrol J Hooper; c 2. *Educ:* Univ Alta, BSc, 58; Stanford Univ, MS, 59; Univ Cambridge, DPhil, 73. *Honors & Awards:* Award Merit, Can Stand Asn. *Prof Exp:* Sales engr, Con-Force Prod Ltd, 59-61, chief engr, 61-63. *Concurrent Pos:* Nat Res Coun Can res grants, 64-67 & 69-; on leave, Churchill Col, Eng, 67-69; vis prof, Univ NSW, Australia, 83; comt mem, Can Stand Asn, comt chmn, 90-te Design & Construct; prin investr concrete Can, Network Ctr Excellence High Performance Concrete, 96- *Mem:* Am Concrete Inst; fel Can Soc Civil Engrs; Prestressed Concrete Inst; Am Soc Testing & Mat. *Res:* Strength and behavior of precast connections; optimum design of reinforced and prestressed concrete; bond strength of reinforced and prestressed concrete; high strength concrete; generalized concrete stress-strain curves; shear of concrete. *Mailing Add:* Dept Civil Eng Univ Calgary Calgary AB T2N 1N4 Can. *Fax:* 403-282-7026

LOOYENGA, ROBERT WILLIAM, ANALYTICAL CHEMISTRY. *Current Pos:* from asst prof to assoc prof, 72-87, PROF CHEM, SDAK SCH MINES & TECHNOL, 87- *Personal Data:* b NDak, Oct 21, 39; m 63; c 4. *Educ:* Hope Col, AB, 61; Wayne State Univ, PhD(analytical chem), 69. *Prof Exp:* Fel chem, Univ Wis, Milwaukee, 70; res chemist, Printing Develop Inc, 70-72. *Concurrent Pos:* Chemist, SDak Racing Comn, 75-78; consult, SDak Law Enforcement Agencies; expert witness, Penn Co States Atty. *Mem:* Am Chem Soc; Sigma Xi. *Res:* Analytical research and analysis of trace metals and organics in municipal and natural waters, of new chemical deicers and of abused drugs; analytical separations and methods development. *Mailing Add:* Dept Chem & Eng SDak Sch Mines & Technol 501 E St Joseph St Rapid City SD 57701-3901

LOPARDO, VINCENT JOSEPH, MECHANICAL ENGINEERING. *Current Pos:* from assoc prof to prof, 60-94, chmn dept, 76-80, EMER PROF MECH ENG, US NAVAL ACAD, 94- *Personal Data:* b Pittsburgh, Pa, Dec 1, 25; m 50, Mary Leopardi; c 4. *Educ:* Univ Pittsburgh, BSME, 48, MSME, 51; Cath Univ Am, PhD(mech eng), 68. *Prof Exp:* Design engr, Peth & Reed Engrs, 48-49 & Hunting, Larsen & Dunnells Engrs, 51; from instr to asst prof mech eng, Univ Pittsburgh, 51-60. *Concurrent Pos:* Design engr, Hunting, Larsen & Dunnells Engrs, 51-55; res prof eng res div, Univ Pittsburgh, 51-53; consult, Charles M Wellons Consult Engrs, 55-60; sr assoc, Trident Eng Assocs, 61-; fac fel, NSF, 66; Naval Acad Res Coun grant, US Naval Acad, 68-69; Nat Bur Stand grant, Naval Ship Res & Develop Ctr, 81. *Mem:* Soc Exp Stress Analysis; Am Soc Eng Educ; Am Soc Mech Engr. *Res:* Stress analysis; stress and strains in large deformations of polyurethanes using photoelasticity and moire; exergy and the second law analyses of power systems; computer simulation of gas turbine engines. *Mailing Add:* Dept Mech Eng Rickover Hall US Naval Acad Annapolis MD 21402-5042

LOPATIN, DENNIS EDWARD, MICROBIOLOGY. *Current Pos:* From asst prof to assoc prof dent, 78-90, res scientist, 86-90, PROF DENT, UNIV MICH, 90- *Personal Data:* b Chicago, Ill, Oct 26, 48. *Educ:* Univ Ill, PhD(microbiol), 74. *Mem:* Am Asn Immunologists; Am Asn Dent Res; Am Asn Microbiol. *Res:* Studies host immunological response to members of the oral flora; primary interest in immunology of periodontal diseases. *Mailing Add:* Univ Mich Sch Dent 1011 N University Ave Box 1078 Ann Arbor MI 48109-1078

LOPATIN, WILLIAM, BIOCHEMISTRY, BIO-ORGANIC CHEMISTRY. *Current Pos:* dir sci info systs, 80-90, DIR SCI & OFF SYST, BAYER CORP, 90- *Personal Data:* b Brooklyn, NY, July 20, 46; m 67; c 2. *Educ:* Univ Fla, BS, 67; Univ SFla, MA, 71, PhD(chem), 77. *Prof Exp:* Teacher chem, Hillsborough Co, Fla Bd Pub Instr, 69-73; res assoc biochem, Univ Tex, 77-80. *Concurrent Pos:* Chmn sci dept, Blake High Sch, Tampa, 70-71. *Mem:* Sigma Xi; AAAS; Am Chem Soc. *Res:* Application of physical organic techniques to the study of enzyme reaction mechanisms. *Mailing Add:* 50900 Mercury Dr Granger IL 46530-9795

LOPER, CARL R(ICHARD), JR, METALLURGICAL ENGINEERING, ENVIRONMENTAL SCIENCE. *Current Pos:* instr metall eng, Univ Wis-Madison, 56-58, res proj asst, 58-60, from asst prof to assoc prof, 61-69, assoc dir, Univ-Indust Res Prog & assoc chmn, Dept Metall & Mineral Eng, 79-81, PROF METALL ENG & ENVIRON STUDIES, UNIV WIS-MADISON, 69- *Personal Data:* b Wauwatosa, Wis, July 3, 32; m 56, Jane L Loehning; c Cynthia L (Koch) & Anne E. *Educ:* Univ Wis, BS, 55, MS, 58, PhD(metall eng), 61. *Honors & Awards:* Adams Mem Award, Am Welding Soc, 64; H F Taylor Award, Am Foundrymen's Soc, 67, John A Penton Gold Medal, 72; EG Hoyt Lectr, 92; Medal, Chinese Foundrymen's Soc, 89. *Prof Exp:* Metall engr, Pelton Steel Castings Co, 55-56; res metallurgist, Allis Chalmers, 61. *Concurrent Pos:* Consult, Gray & Ductile Iron Founders Soc, 62-, Gen Motors Corp & Brillion Iron Works, 66-, Oil City Iron Works, 73- & Sperry-New Holland, 74-; res metallurgist, Allis Chalmers Mfg Co, 61-; invited lectr, Korea Foundry Soc & Korea Inst Sci & Technol, Seoul, 68, Disamatic Conv, Copenhagen, Denmark, 69, Korea Inst Sci & Technol & Korea Inst Advan Series, 74, Kyushu Univ, Japan, 74, Waseda Univ, Japan, 81, Zhejiang Univ, China, 81 & Brazilian Soc Metals, Santa Catarina, 81, Nat Sci Coun, Rep China, 89; pres, Int Comn Compacted Graphite Cast Iron, 77-; hon lectr, Antioquia Univ, Medellin, Colombia, 83 & Univ Nacional de Colombia, 84. *Mem:* Am Foundrymen's Soc; Am Welding Soc; fel Am Soc Metals; Sigma Xi; Am Inst Metall Eng; Foundry Educ Found. *Res:* Solidification and process control of cast irons; solidification and property relationships in aluminum and copper base alloys; fracture toughness of cast components; welding metallurgy; failure analysis; recycling of metallic solid wastes. *Mailing Add:* Dept Mat Sci & Eng 1509 University Ave Madison WI 53706. *Fax:* 608-262-8353; *E-Mail:* loper@engr.wisc.edu

LOPER, DAVID ERIC, MAGNETOHYDRODYNAMICS, APPLIED MATHEMATICS & MATHEMATICAL GEOPHYSICS. *Current Pos:* from asst prof to assoc prof, 68-77, PROF MATH, FLA STATE UNIV, 77- *Personal Data:* b Oswego, NY, Feb 14, 40; m 66; c 4. *Educ:* Carnegie Inst Technol, BS, 61; Case Inst Technol, MS, 64, PhD(mech eng), 65. *Prof Exp:* Sr scientist, Douglas Aircraft Corp, 65-68. *Concurrent Pos:* Nat Ctr Atmospheric Res fel, 67-68; sr vis fel, Univ Newcastle-upon-Tyne, Eng, 74-75; vis fel, Univ Cambridge, 90. *Mem:* Am Phys Soc; Am Geophys Union; Soc Indust & Appl Math; Sigma Xi. *Res:* Boundary layers in rotating, stably stratified, electrically conducting fluids; evolution of the earth's core including stratification, heat transfer, solidification and particle precipitation. *Mailing Add:* GFDI-3017 Fla State Univ Tallahassee FL 32306

LOPER, GERALD D, NUCLEAR PHYSICS. *Current Pos:* Asst prof, Wichita State Univ, 64-67, chmn dept, 66-78, asst dean grad studies, 86-87, assoc dean liberal arts & sci, 87-92, actg dean liberal arts & sci, 92-94, ASSOC PROF PHYSICS, WICHITA STATE UNIV, 67-, ASSOC VPRES RES & DIR OFFICE RES ADMIN, 94- *Personal Data:* b Brooklyn, NY, May 4, 37; m 60; c 1. *Educ:* Univ Wichita, AB, 59; Okla State Univ, MS, 62, PhD(physics), 64. *Mem:* Am Phys Soc; Sigma Xi. *Res:* Measurement of positron lifetimes in solids; nuclear spectroscopy; internal conversion. *Mailing Add:* Off Res Admin Wichita State Univ Wichita KS 67260-0007. *Fax:* 316-978-3750; *E-Mail:* loper@twsuvm.uc.twsu.edu

LOPER, GERALD MILTON, AGRONOMY, BIOCHEMISTRY. *Current Pos:* RETIRED. *Personal Data:* b Sykesville, Md, Jan 7, 36; m 62, Peiffer; c David Milton & Timothy Paul. *Educ:* Univ Md, Bsc, 58; Univ Wis, MSc, 60, PhD(agron), 61. *Prof Exp:* Res agronomist, USDA, SDak, 62-67; from assoc prof to prof agron & plant genetics, Univ Ariz, 74-97; res plant physiologist, Fed Honeybee Lab, 67-96. *Mem:* Bot Soc Am; Am Soc Agron; Entom Soc Am. *Res:* Effect of environment and infective organisms on the chemical composition of forages in relation to animal nutrition; attractiveness of forage legumes to honey bees; pollination physiology; seed production and crop physiology investigations of the genetics and mating biology of feral and Africanized honey bees. *Mailing Add:* Fed Honeybee Lab Agr Res Serv US Dept Agr 2000 E Allen Rd Tucson AZ 85719

LOPER, JOHN C, ENVIRONMENTAL TOXICOLOGY, BIODEGRADATION. *Current Pos:* from asst prof to assoc prof, 63-74, PROF MICROBIOL, COL MED, UNIV CINCINNATI, 74-, PROF ENVIRON HEALTH, 79- *Personal Data:* b Hadley, Pa, June 21, 31; m 56; c 3. *Educ:* Western Md Col, BA, 52; Emory Univ, MS, 53; Johns Hopkins Univ, PhD(biol), 60. *Prof Exp:* From instr to asst prof pharmacol, Sch Med, St Louis Univ, 60-63. *Concurrent Pos:* NIH res grants, 62-78; NIH spec vis fel genetics, Res Sch Biol Sci, Australian Nat Univ, 70-71; Environ Protection Agency grants, 76-86; mem biol comt, Argonne Nat Lab-Argonne Univ Asn, 70-73; mem subcomt toxicol, Safe Drinking Water Comt, Nat Res Coun, 78-79; assoc dir, Dept Molecular Genetics, Univ Cincinnati, 88-; co-investr, Nat Inst Environ Health Sci Superfund basic res prog grant, 88-91, prin investr, 91- *Mem:* Am Soc Microbiol; Genetics Soc Am; Am Chem Soc; Am Soc Biochem Molecular Biol. *Res:* Molecular genetics of cytochrome PHSO systems in yeasts; microbial pathways of detoxication and degradation of xenobiotic compounds; genetics of antifungal resistance. *Mailing Add:* Dept Molecular Genetics Biochem & Microbiol Univ Cincinnati Col Med Cincinnati OH 45267-0524. *E-Mail:* john.loper@uc.edu

LOPER, JOYCE E, PHYTOPATHOLOGY. *Current Pos:* from asst prof to assoc prof, 88-97, PROF, DEPT BOT & PLANT PATH, ORE STATE UNIV, 97-; RES PLANT PATHOLOGIST, AGR RES SERV, USDA, CORVALLIS, 87- *Educ:* Univ Calif, Davis, BS, 74, MS 78; Univ Calif, Berkeley, PhD(plant path), 83. *Honors & Awards:* Ciba-Geigy Award, Am Phytopath Soc, 95. *Prof Exp:* Res scientist, Biol Control Prog, Biotechnol Group, Chevron Chem Co, 83-85; res plant pathologist, Agr Res Serv, USDA, Beltsville, 85-86. *Concurrent Pos:* Sr ed, Am Phytopath Soc Press, 90-93; mem sci adv panel, NSF Ctr Microbial Ecol, Mich State Univ, 92-96; mem, Nat Res Coun Bd Agr, Nat Acad Sci, 92-95; assoc ed, Molecular Plant-Microbe Interactions, 96-; counr, Am Phytopath Soc, 97- *Mem:* Am Phytopath Soc; Am Soc Microbiol; Int Soc Molecular Plant-Microbe Interactions. *Mailing Add:* USDA Agr Res Serv Hort Crops Lab 3420 NW Orchard Ave Corvallis OR 97330

LOPER, WILLARD H(EWITT), AGRICULTURAL ENGINEERING. *Current Pos:* asst prof, 55-63, ASSOC PROF AGR ENG, CALIF POLYTECH STATE UNIV, SAN LUIS OBISPO, 63- *Personal Data:* b Alden, NY, Apr 30, 26; m 50; c 4. *Educ:* Cornell Univ, BA, 53. *Prof Exp:* Sales & serv rep, Holz Col, 53-54; design & prod engr, Cochran Equip Co, 54-55. *Concurrent Pos:* Civil engr, Bur Reclamation, US Dept Interior & State Div Hwys, 57 & 58; tech leader, Foreign Agr Serv, USDA, 59. *Mem:* Am Soc Agr Engrs. *Res:* Agricultural crop harvest mechanization. *Mailing Add:* 266 Luneta Dr San Luis Obispo CA 93405

LOPES, ANIBAL, PESTICIDE, RESIDUE CHEMISTRY, ANALYTICAL METHOD DEVELOPMENT. *Current Pos:* scientist, 81-92, SR RES SCIENTIST, RHONE-POULENC AGR CO, 92- *Personal Data:* b Sao Paulo, Brazil, Oct 30, 55; US citizen; m 88, Theresa Trimble. *Educ:* Fordham Univ, BS, 76; Columbia Univ, MA, 77, Univ Rochester, MS, 79, PhD(org chem), 81. *Mem:* Am Chem Soc. *Res:* Analytical methods for pesticides in soil, water, crops and animal tissues using solid phase extraction, liquid chromatography, gas chromatography and mass spectrometry. *Mailing Add:* 3500 E Jameston Rd Raleigh NC 27604-3969. *Fax:* 919-549-7420; *E-Mail:* anibal.lopes@rp.fr

LOPES, JOHN MANUEL, GENE EXPRESSION, TRANSCRIPTIONAL CONTROL. *Current Pos:* ASST PROF BIOCHEM, LOYOLA UNIV, CHICAGO, 91- *Personal Data:* b Coimbra, Portugal, June 24, 61; US citizen; m 85, Teresa D Parton; c Sean V. *Educ:* Univ RI, BS, 82; Univ SC, PhD(biol), 87. *Prof Exp:* Fel, Carnegie Mellon Univ, 87-91. *Mem:* Fel Genetics Soc Am; fel Am Soc Biochem & Molecular Biol; fel Am Soc Microbiol. *Res:* Study how cellular membranes are synthesized in yeast in particular how transcription affects gene expression of phospholipid biosynthetic genes. *Mailing Add:* 2160 S First Ave Maywood IL 60153

LOPES-GAUTIER, ROSALY, VOLCANOLOGY, PLANETARY SCIENCE. *Current Pos:* Nat Res Coun res assoc, 89-91, SCI COORDR, GALILEO PROJ, JET PROPULSION LAB, 91- *Personal Data:* b Rio de Janeiro, Brazil, Jan 8, 57; Brit citizen; m 90, Thomas N III; c Thomas N IV. *Educ:* Univ London, BSc, 78, PhD(planetary sci), 86. *Prof Exp:* Cur astron, Old Royal Observ, Greenwich, UK, 85-89; res assoc, Observ Vesuviano, Italy, 89 & Nat Res Coun 89-91. *Mem:* Int Astron Union; Am Geophys Soc; Am Astron Soc; Royal Astron Soc; Int Asn Volcanology & Chem Earth's Interior; Soc Hisp Prof Engrs. *Res:* Planetary and terrestrial surface processes, with emphasis on volcanology; volcanism on IO using infra-red and other spacecraft data; volcanic hazards on earth. *Mailing Add:* MS 183-601 Jet Propulsion Lab Pasadena CA 91109. *Fax:* 818-393-4530; *E-Mail:* rlopes@issac.jpl.nasa.gov

LOPES-VIRELLA, MARIA FERNANDA LEAL, IMMUNE MECHANISMS OF ATHEROSCLEROSIS, LIPOPROTEIN METABOLISM & CORONARY HEART DISEASE. *Current Pos:* From asst prof to assoc prof, 79-89, PROF MED & PATH, MED UNIV SC, 89- *Personal Data:* b Vila Nova De Foz Coa, Portugal, Dec 25, 42; US citizen; m, Gabriel Virella; c Sara & Isabel. *Educ:* Univ Lisbon, Portugal, MD, 67, ECFMG, 75, FLEX, 79, PhD(int med & biochem), 90. *Concurrent Pos:* Spec Emphasis Res Career Award, Nat Heart Lung Blood Inst, Nat Inst Arthritis Metab & Digestive Dis, 78-83; clin investr, Vet Admin Med Ctr, Charleston, SC, 84-86; Staff physician & chief, Nutrit Support Team, 87-; prin investr, Vet Admin Res Prog, 85-, Nat Heart Lung Blood Inst & NIH, 87-93; course dir & lectr, Clin Nutrit Med Students, Med Univ SC, 85-; mem, Coun Atherosclerosis, Am Heart Asn; Nutrit Study Sect, NIH, 91-95. *Mem:* Fel Am Heart Asn; fel Am Col Nutrit; Am Diabetes Asn; Am Fedn Clin Res. *Res:* Mechanisms leading to accelerated atherosclerosis in diabetes. *Mailing Add:* Med Univ SC 171 Ashley Ave Charleston SC 29425. *Fax:* 843-577-5011, ext 7682 (VAMC), 843-792-4114 (MUSC)

LOPEZ, ANTHONY, FOOD SCIENCE. *Current Pos:* RETIRED. *Personal Data:* b Chile, SAm, May 13, 19; US citizen; m 47; c Martita, Anthony & Michael. *Educ:* Catholic Univ, Chile, BS, 42; Univ Mass, PhD(food tech), 47. *Prof Exp:* Chemist, SA Organa, Chile, 42-45; tech dir, Indust de Productos Alimenticios, 48-52; assoc res prof food technol, Univ Mass, 52-53; assoc prof, Univ Ga, 53-54; prof food sci & technol, Va Polytech Inst & State Univ, 54-88. *Concurrent Pos:* Instr, UN Latin Am Fisheries Training Ctr, Chile, 52; lectr, Ministry Commerce, Spain, 60; consult food processing, Govt Spain, 62, 63; consult food technol, UN Food & Agr Orgn, Chile, 66 & Brazil, 69, 72, 75 & 79; Orgn Am States in Mex, 70-74; tech ed, Food Prod Mgt, 71-87; UN Food & Agr Orgn, Arg, 80, Chile, 84, Mex 89-90 & PR, 90-91. *Mem:* Am Chem Soc; fel Inst Food Technologists; Chilean Soc Nutrit. *Res:* Processing and nutritive value of fish; composition of fresh fruits and vegetables; processing of fruits and vegetables; chemical changes in processed foods during storage; food packaging; microwave irradiation of foods; effect of processing on nutritive value of foods. *Mailing Add:* 721 Hutcheson Dr Blacksburg VA 24060-3209

LOPEZ, ANTONIO VINCENT, pharmaceutical chemistry, pharmacognosy, for more information see previous edition

LOPEZ, CARLOS, IMMUNOLOGY, VIROLOGY. *Current Pos:* dir biol res, 87-93, exec dir infectious dis, 93-96, RES FEL, INFECTIOUS DIS, ELI LILLY, 96- *Personal Data:* b Ponce, PR, Jan 15, 42; m 70; c 1. *Educ:* Univ Minn, BS, 65, MS, 66, PhD(pub health), 70. *Prof Exp:* Res fel, Univ Minn, 70-72; asst prof path, 72-73; assoc mem, Sloan- Kettering Cancer Ctr & asst prof biol, Sloan-Kettering Div, Cornell Univ Sch med, 73-87. *Concurrent Pos:* NIH fel, 70-71; fel, Nat Thoracic & Respiratory Dis Asn, 71-73. *Mem:* Am Asn Immunologists; Am Asn Exp Pathologists; Am Soc Microbiol; AAAS. *Res:* Immunological resistance to virus infections; immunologic response to virus induced tumors. *Mailing Add:* Eli Lilly Lilly Corp Ctr Indianapolis IN 46285-0438

LOPEZ, DIANA MONTES DE OCA, MICROBIOLOGY, IMMUNOLOGY. *Current Pos:* Res assoc, 70-71, from instr to assoc prof, 71-83, PROF MICROBIOL, SCH MED, UNIV MIAMI, 83- *Personal Data:* b Havana, Cuba, Aug 26, 37; US citizen; m 58; c 3. *Educ:* Univ Havana, BS, 60; Univ Miami, MS, 68, PhD(microbiol), 70. *Concurrent Pos:* Sect leader tumor immunol, Sylvester Comprehensive Cancer Ctr, State Fla, 80- *Mem:* Am Soc Microbiol; Tissue Cult Asn; Sigma Xi; Am Asn Immunologists; NY Acad Sci; Int Asn Breast Cancer Res (pres-elect, 85, pres, 87-89). *Res:* Tumor immunology; viral oncogenesis; cell kinetics. *Mailing Add:* Dept Microbiol & Immunol Sch Med R-138 Univ Miami PO Box 016960 Miami FL 33101-6960

LOPEZ, GENARO, ECONOMIC ENTOMOLOGY. *Current Pos:* ASST PROF BIOL, TEX SOUTHMOST COL, 76-; PROF BIOL, UNIV TEX, BROWNSVILLE, 95- *Personal Data:* b Brownsville, Tex, Jan 24, 47; m 72, Lee Tole; c G Daniel & Adriana. *Educ:* Tex Tech Univ, BS, 70; Cornell Univ, PhD(econ entom), 75. *Prof Exp:* Res asst entom, Cornell Univ, 70-75; entomologist, Tex Agr Exten Serv, Tex A&M Univ, 75-76. *Mem:* Entom Soc Am; Acaralogical Soc Am. *Res:* Bionomics, ecology and control of insects affecting man's home environment; teaching biology to the bicultural/bilingual student at the college level; methylmercury levels in fish at Port of Brownsville. *Mailing Add:* Dept Biol Univ Tex Brownsville Brownsville TX 78520. *Fax:* 956-983-7115

LOPEZ, GUIDO WILFRED, THERMOFLUIDS, COMPUTER SIMULATION OF ENGINEERING SYSTEMS. *Current Pos:* CHMN, ENG & SCI DIV, DANIEL WEBSTER COL, 93- *Personal Data:* b Ibarra, Ecuador, July 31, 54. *Educ:* Nat Polytech Sch, ME, 78; Northeastern Univ, MS, 81 PhD(thermofluids), 93. *Prof Exp:* Asst prof thermodyn, Nat Polytech Sch, 81-86; lectr thermodyn, heat transfer & instrumentation, Northeastern Univ, 86-93. *Concurrent Pos:* Consult thermal systs, installation design & mfg, 81-86. *Mem:* Planetary Soc. *Res:* Energy generation for aerospace propulsion, nuclear fusion and electromagnetic space drive. *Mailing Add:* Daniel Webster Col Dept Math & Eng 20 Univ Dr Nashua NH 03063-1323

LOPEZ, JORGE ALBERTO, HEAVY ION REACTIONS, COMPUTATIONAL PHYSICS. *Current Pos:* ASSOC PROF PHYSICS, UNIV TEX, EL PASO, 90- *Personal Data:* b Monterrey, Mex, Jan 23, 55; m 79; c 2. *Educ:* Tex A&M Univ, PhD(physics), 86. *Prof Exp:* Postdoctoral researcher, Niels Bohr Inst, Denmark, 85-87 & Lawrence Berkeley Lab, 87-89; assoc prof, Calpoly State Univ, San Luis Obispo, 89-90. *Mem:* Am Phys Soc. *Res:* Nuclear physics; heavy ion physics; computational physics. *Mailing Add:* Physics Dept Univ Tex El Paso TX 79968-0515. *Fax:* 915-747-5447; *E-Mail:* gc00@utep.edu

LOPEZ, JOSE MANUEL, ENVIRONMENTAL CHEMISTRY, CHEMICAL OCEANOGRAPHY. *Current Pos:* ASSOC PROF, DEPT MARINE SCI, UNIV PR. *Personal Data:* b San Juan, PR, Jan 7, 50; m 73; c Sara, Christina, Yania & Kiani. *Educ:* Univ PR, BS, 71; Univ Wis, Madison, MS, 73; Univ Tex, PhD(environ chem), 76. *Prof Exp:* Res scientist marine chem, Res & Develop Ctr, Ctr Energy & Environ Res, 78-81, head, Marine Ecol Div, 81-85, sr scientist, 85. *Concurrent Pos:* Pres Sci Teachers Asn, 79-80; consult, indust & govt. *Mem:* AAAS; Am Chem Soc; Am Soc Limnol & Oceanog; Am Bot Soc; Water Pollution Control Fedn. *Res:* Sources, fate and significance of chemicals in aquatic ecosystems; biological availability of contaminants to aquatic organisms; nutrient dynamics; mangroves ecology; remote sensing of ocean color; biogeochemistry and primary production. *Mailing Add:* Univ PR Dept Marine Sci PO Box 5000 Mayaguez PR 00681. *Fax:* 787-834-8025; *E-Mail:* jo_lopez@rumac.upr.lcu.edu

LOPEZ, LEONARD ANTHONY, ENGINEERING SOFTWARE SYSTEMS. *Current Pos:* PROF CIVIL ENG, UNIV ILL, URBANA, 67- *Personal Data:* b Waltham, Mass, Dec 27, 40; m 61, Ruth-Linda; c Marianne, Christopher & Michael. *Educ:* Tufts Univ, BS, 62; Univ Ill, MS, 63, PhD(civil eng), 66. *Prof Exp:* Asst prof civil eng, Lehigh Univ, 66-67. *Concurrent Pos:* Von Humboldt res fel, 79-80. *Mem:* Am Soc Civil Engrs; Inst Elec & Electronics Engrs; Asn Comput Mach. *Res:* Digital simulation; numerical methods; mechanics of nonlinear solids; computer system and parallel processing. *Mailing Add:* Dept Civil Eng Univ Ill 205 N Mathews St Urbana IL 61801-2374

LOPEZ, R C GERALD, AGRICULTURAL FORMULATIONS RESEARCH. *Current Pos:* Sr scientist, 82-88, MGR AGR FORMULATIONS RES, ROHM & HAAS CO, 88-, MGR AGR CHEM OPERS. *Personal Data:* b London, Eng, Mar 12, 57; m 80; c 3. *Educ:* Oxford

Univ, BA, 80, PhD(org chem), 82. *Res:* Discovery and optimization of formulations for new and existing agricultural chemicals, including fungicides, herbicides and insecticides. *Mailing Add:* Rohm & Haas Co 2600 Douglas Rd Suite 1100 Coral Gables FL 33134

LOPEZ, RAFAEL, PEDIATRICS, HEMATOLOGY. *Current Pos:* RETIRED. *Personal Data:* b Dominican Repub, Dec 15, 29; m 56; c 2. *Educ:* Seton Hall Univ, BSc, 52; Univ PR, MD, 56. *Prof Exp:* Assoc prof pediat, Flower & Fifth Ave Hosp, 65-80; assoc prof pediat, NY Med Col, Our Lady Mercy Med Ctr, 80-96, dir pediat, 85-93, spec asst to pres & chief exec officer, 94-96. *Mem:* Soc Study Blood; Int Soc Hemat; Am Soc Hemat; NY Acad Sci; Am Acad Pediat; Am Col Qual Assurance. *Res:* Glutathione reductase as a tool for diagnosis of riboflavin deficiency in infants, children, adolescents; malabsorption syndromes and the effect of phototherapy upon this vitamin in the newborn. *Mailing Add:* 140 Cabrini Blvd New York NY 10033

LOPEZ-BERESTEIN, GABRIEL, ONCOLOGY, IMMUNOLOGY. *Current Pos:* Asst internist, 81-84, from asst prof to assoc prof, 81-91, PROF MED & INTERNIST, M D ANDERSON CANCER CTR, UNIV TEX, 91-, ASSOC PROF PHARM, MED SCH, 84- *Personal Data:* b La Habana, Cuba, Aug 13, 47; US citizen; c 1. *Educ:* Univ PR, San Juan, BA, 70; Univ Navarre, Spain, MD, 76. *Honors & Awards:* Stohlman Award, 90. *Concurrent Pos:* Assoc prof biomed sci, Health Sci Ctr, Univ Tex, 84-; mem, Biomed Sci Study Sect, NIH, 88- *Mem:* Am Asn Cancer Res; AMA; Am Soc Clin Oncol; AAAS; Am Soc Immunologists. *Res:* Oncology; immunology; tumor immunology; therapeutic drug targetting; macrophage biology. *Mailing Add:* M D Anderson Cancer Ctr Sect Immunobiol & Drug Carriers Univ Tex Box 60 1515 Holcombe Blvd Houston TX 77030. *Fax:* 713-796-7731

LOPEZ-ESCOBAR, EDGAR GEORGE KENNETH, MATHEMATICS. *Current Pos:* PROF MATH, UNIV MED, 66- *Personal Data:* b Buenos Aires, Arg, Jan 7, 37. *Educ:* Cambridge Univ, BS, 58, MA, 71; Univ Calif, Berkeley, MA, 61, PhD(math), 65. *Mem:* Asn Symbolic Logic; Soc Exact Philos; Am Math Soc. *Res:* Computer application as applied to mathematical logic. *Mailing Add:* 2703 Ogleton Rd Annapolis MD 21403-4216

LOPEZ-MAJANO, VINCENT, NUCLEAR MEDICINE, PULMONARY MEDICINE. *Current Pos:* CHMN NUCLEAR MED, COOK COUNTY HOSP, CHICAGO, 77- *Personal Data:* b Madrid, Spain, Apr 3, 21; US citizen; m 52; c 2. *Educ:* Inst Cardenal Cisneros, BA & BS, 39; Univ Madrid, MD, 45, PhD, 51. *Prof Exp:* Resident, Gen Hosp, Madrid, 45-51; physician, Sanatorium Carlos Duran, Costa Rica, 51-56 & Tuberc Sanatorium, Md, 55-60; chief, Pulmonary Function Lab, Vet Admin Hosp, Baltimore, 60-70; asst prof environ med, Johns Hopkins Inst, Baltimore, 68-70; clin assoc prof med, Loyola Stritch Sch Med, 70-73; dir nuclear med, Gottlieb Mem Hosp, 73-77; assoc prof med, Chicago Med Sch, 80-87. *Concurrent Pos:* Ed, Respiration, 70-71 & J Nuclear Med & Allied Sci, 82; chief training sect nuclear med, Vet Admin Hosp, Hine, Ill, 70-74; vis prof, Nat Univ Mex, 73; vis scientist, Nat Acad Sci, 81-84; vis scholar, Nat Cancer Inst, 85. *Mem:* Nuclear Med Soc; Physiol Soc; Mex Nuclear Med Soc; Am Fed Clin Res. *Res:* Inflammatory diseases of the lungs; regional lung function; staging of neoplasms; studies of cardiac function with radionuclides. *Mailing Add:* 3100 N Sheridan Rd Chicago IL 60657

LOPEZ-SANTOLINO, ALFREDO, MEDICINE, BIOCHEMISTRY. *Current Pos:* assoc prof, 67-74, PROF INTERNAL MED, MED SCH, LA STATE UNIV MED CTR, NEW ORLEANS, 74- *Personal Data:* b Salamanca, Spain, July 23, 31; m 62; c 2. *Educ:* Inst Ensenanza Media, Salamanca, BS, 49; Lit Univ Salamanca, MD, 55, PhD(med sci), 58; Tulane Univ, PhD(biochem), 63. *Prof Exp:* Asst prof physiol med, Sch Med, Lit Univ Salamanca, 56-58; instr biochem, Cali Univ Sch Med, 58-59; asst prof internal med, Col Med & biochemist, Clin Res Ctr, Univ Iowa, 64-67. *Concurrent Pos:* Mem coun atherosclerosis, Am Heart Asn. *Mem:* AAAS; Am Oil Chem Soc; Soc Nutrit Educ; Am Inst Nutrit; Am Soc Clin Nutrit. *Res:* Nutrition and metabolic diseases; metabolism of lipids and steroid hormones. *Mailing Add:* Dept Med La State Univ Sch Med New Orleans LA 70112

LOPINA, ROBERT F(ERGUSON), AERONAUTICAL ENGINEERING, AVIONICS. *Current Pos:* VPRES, ADVAN PROGS OFF, FORD AEROSPACE/LORAL AERONUTRONIC DIV, NEWPORT BEACH, CALIF, 88- *Personal Data:* b Jamestown, NY, May 13, 36; m 58; c 3. *Educ:* Purdue Univ, Lafayette, BS, 57; Mass Inst Technol, MSc, 65, ME, 66, PhD(mech eng), 67. *Prof Exp:* US Air Force, 57-83, assoc prof aeronaut, US Air Force Acad, 67-74, chief scientist, Europ Off Aerospace Res & Develop, 74-76, chief, Flight Control Div, Air Force Flight Dynamics Lab, 77-78, comdr & dir, Air Force Avionics Lab, 78-80, dep eng, Aeronaut Systs Div, 80-82, dep reconnaissance strike & extreme width, 82-83, dep Aeronaut Systs Div, 83-87; vpres eng & prog dir T-46, Fairchild Repub Co, Farmingdale, NY, 83-87; dir, Advan Develop, Ford Aerospace Corp, Detroit, Mich, 87- 88. *Mem:* Am Inst Aeronaut & Astronaut; Am Soc Mech Engrs; Sigma Xi; Air Force Asn; Nat Mgt Asn; Asn Old Crows. *Res:* Swirl flow heat transfer; computer applications in aeronautical education; night attack systems development; trainer aircraft development and production; integrated circuits for radio frequency applications. *Mailing Add:* Loral 29947 Avenida de los Bard Rancho Santa Margarita CA 92688. *Fax:* 714-459-4425

LO PINTO, RICHARD WILLIAM, MARINE BIOLOGY, BIOMONITORING & AQUATIC TOXICOLOGY. *Current Pos:* PROF BIOL, FAIRLEIGH DICKINSON UNIV, TEANECK, 70- *Personal Data:* b New York, NY, Nov 7, 42; m 70; c 2. *Educ:* Iona Col, BS, 63; Fordham Univ, MS, 65, PhD(physiol ecol), 72. *Prof Exp:* Res asst water pollution, Osborne Lab Marine Sci, 67-68, head biol testing, Org Econ Coop Develop, 84-85. *Concurrent Pos:* Cosult, Hackensack Meadowlands Develop Comn, 71-, Hart Mountain Indust Inc, 76-77; dir, Marine Biol Prog, Fairleigh Dickinson Univ, Rutherford, NJ, 72-; asst dir, Meadowlands Regional Study Ctr, 74-75; assoc, Seminar Pollution & Water Resources, Columbia Univ, 75; chmn tech adv comt, N NJ Water Quality Prog, 77-; assoc ed, Bulletin of the NJ Acad Sci, 78; consult, US Environ Protection Agency, 84; consult, Orgn Econ Coop & Develop, Paris, 84-85. *Mem:* Sigma Xi. *Res:* Bioassay development for marine and fresh water organisms; aquatic toxicology; phytoplankton physiology; microbial ecology. *Mailing Add:* Dept Biol Sci Fairleigh Dickinson Univ Teaneck NJ 07666-1996

LOPO, ALINA C, medical education, development of expertise, for more information see previous edition

LOPPNOW, HARALD, CELLULAR IMMUNOLOGY, VASCULAR CYTOKINES. *Current Pos:* lab instr microbiol, 81-83, RES ASSOC IMMUNOL, 83-88 & 90- *Personal Data:* Ger citizen. *Educ:* Kiel Univ, dipl microbiol, 83, PhD(immunol), 86. *Prof Exp:* Res assoc immunol, Sclavo Res Ctr, Siena I, 87 & Tufts Univ, Boston, 88-90. *Concurrent Pos:* Travel award, IV Int Conf Immunopharmacol, 88; lectr, Kiel Univ, 90. *Mem:* Ger Soc Immunol; Am Asn Immunologists. *Res:* Vascular and immune cell responses to pathophysiologically relevant stimuli such as bacterial lipopolysaccharide or cytokines; determine proliferation, cytokine production, or adhesion of cells; biochemical, cell biological, immunological and molecular biological methods. *Mailing Add:* Dept Biochem Forschungsinst Borstel Parkallee 22 23845 Borstel Germany

LOPREST, FRANK JAMES, PHYSICAL CHEMISTRY. *Current Pos:* ASSOC DIR BASIC RES, COLGATE-PALMOLIVE CO, 83- *Personal Data:* b New York, NY, Jan 8, 29; m 60; c 5. *Educ:* St John's Univ, NY, BS, 50; NY Univ, MS, 52, PhD, 54. *Prof Exp:* Res chemist, Oak Ridge Nat Lab, 54-56; sr res chemist & supvr adv res, Reaction Motors Div, Thiokol Chem Corp, 56-65; tech assoc, Res & Develop Div, GAF Corp, 65-67, sect mgr new imaging processes res, 67-69, mgr appl chem, Res & Develop & Res Serv, Indust Photo Div, 69-77; dir basic sci, Princeton Res Ctr, Am Can Co, 77-83. *Mem:* AAAS; Am Chem Soc; Sigma Xi; Licensing Execs Soc. *Res:* Heterogeneous equilibria; kinetics of liquid solid reactions; high temperature materials; physical chemistry of liquid and solid propellants; adhesion phenomena; cellulose and paper science; surface and colloid chemistry, detergency. *Mailing Add:* 590 Beverly Rd Holland PA 18966-2185

LOPRESTI, PHILIP V(INCENT), ELECTRICAL ENGINEERING. *Current Pos:* CONSULT MEM RES STAFF, ENG RES CTR, AT&T, 70- *Personal Data:* b Johnstown, Pa, Sept 27, 32; m 59, Patricia Litzinger; c Daniel P, David B & Amy P. *Educ:* Univ Notre Dame, BSEE, 54, MSEE, 58; Purdue Univ, Lafayette, PhD(elec eng), 63. *Honors & Awards:* Darlington Prize, Inst Elec & Electronics Engrs, Circuits & Systs Soc, 78. *Prof Exp:* Asst prof elec eng, Ill Inst Technol, 64-67 & Northwestern Univ, 67-70. *Concurrent Pos:* Instr, Univ Notre Dame, 58-60 & Purdue Univ, Lafayette, 60-63; consult, Ill Inst Technol, 64-70. *Mem:* Inst Elec & Electronics Engrs; Sigma Xi. *Res:* Automatic control theory; digital signal processing; analog integrated circuits; hybrid integrated circuits. *Mailing Add:* 327 Sked St Pennington NJ 08534

LOPUSHINSKY, THEODORE, GENERAL BIOLOGY, ECOLOGY. *Current Pos:* asst prof proj develop, Col Human Med, 73-75, from asst prof to assoc prof, Ctr Integrative Studies Sci, 75-95, PROF, CTR INTEGRATIVE STUDIES SCI, MICH STATE UNIV, 95- *Personal Data:* b Brooklyn, NY, Oct 25, 37; c Andrew & John. *Educ:* Pa State Univ, BS, 59; Univ Tenn, Knoxville, MS, 61; Mich State Univ, PhD(ecol, path), 69. *Honors & Awards:* Ohaus Award, Innovations Sci Teaching, Nat Sci Teachers Asn, 82. *Prof Exp:* Asst prof natural sci, Mich State Univ, 69-70; prog rep, Mich Asn Regional Med Progs, 70-71; actg dir, 72, dir prog develop, 72-73. *Concurrent Pos:* Archivist, Soc Col Sci Teachers, 81-86; nat mem chmn, Soc Col Sci Teachers, 84-87. *Mem:* Sigma Xi; Nat Sci Teachers Asn; Soc Col Sci Teachers (pres-elect, 87-89, pres, 89-91). *Res:* Parasitism and disease pathologies in wildlife populations; general education science; science-humanities relationships. *Mailing Add:* Rm 100 N Kedzie Lab Mich State Univ East Lansing MI 48824

LOPUSHINSKY, WILLIAM, PLANT PHYSIOLOGY. *Current Pos:* PLANT PHYSIOLOGIST, FORESTRY SCI LAB, USDA, 62- *Personal Data:* b Rome, NY, July 25, 30; m 60; c 3. *Educ:* State Univ NY, BS, 53, MS, 54; Duke Univ, PhD(plant physiol), 60. *Prof Exp:* Asst plant physiol, Duke Univ, 57-60, res assoc bot, 60-61. *Mem:* Am Soc Plant Physiol. *Res:* Plant water relations. *Mailing Add:* 322 Sunnyslope Heights Rd Wenatchee WA 98801

LORANCE, ELMER DONALD, SCIENCE EDUCATION. *Current Pos:* From asst prof to assoc prof, 70-80, chmn, Div Natural Sci & Math, 85-89, PROF CHEM, SOUTHERN CALIF COL, 80-, CHMN, DIV NATURAL SCI & MATH, 93- *Personal Data:* b Tupelo, Okla, Jan 18, 40; m 69, Phyllis I Miller; c Edward D & Jonathan A. *Educ:* Okla State Univ, BA, 62; Kans State Univ, MS, 67; Univ Okla, PhD(bioorg chem), 77. *Concurrent Pos:* Adj prof, Calif State Univ, Fullerton, 77. *Mem:* Am Chem Soc; AAAS; Am Sci Affil. *Res:* Isolation and structure elucidation of compounds from marine organisms; organic synthesis; chemical taxonomy of desert plants. *Mailing Add:* Div Natural Sci & Math Southern Calif Col 55 Fair Dr Costa Mesa CA 92626

LORAND, JOHN PETER, PHYSICAL ORGANIC CHEMISTRY. *Current Pos:* from asst prof to assoc prof, 71-77, PROF ORG CHEM, CENT MICH UNIV, 77- *Personal Data:* b Wilmington, Del, Dec 6, 36; m 64, Priscilla MacDuffie; c Susan, Katherine & David. *Educ:* Brown Univ, ScB, 58; Harvard Univ, PhD(org chem), 64. *Prof Exp:* NSF scientist, Univ Calif, Los Angeles, 64-65; asst prof org chem, Boston Univ, 65-71. *Concurrent Pos:* Vis prof, Univ Groningen, Neth, 77-78; vis assoc prof, Rutgers State Univ NJ, 86-88. *Mem:* Am Chem Soc; Sigma Xi. *Res:* C-H & N-H hydrogen bonding; amine N-oxides. *Mailing Add:* Dept Chem Cent Mich Univ Mt Pleasant MI 48859

LORAND, LASZLO, BIOCHEMISTRY, PHYSIOLOGY. *Current Pos:* from asst prof to prof chem, Northwestern Univ, Evanston, 55-74, prof biochem & molecular biol, 74-81, prof biochem, molecular & cell biol, 81-93, RES PROF, DEPT CELL & MOLECULAR BIOL & DISTINGUISHED INVESTR, FEINBERG CARDIOVASC INST, MED SCH, NORTHWESTERN UNIV, CHICAGO, ILL, 93- *Personal Data:* b Gyor, Hungary, Mar 23, 23; nat US; m 53; c 1. *Educ:* Budapest Univ, absolutorium med, 48; Leeds Univ, PhD(biomolecular struct), 51. *Hon Degrees:* DSc, Univ Ill. *Honors & Awards:* James F Mitchell Found Int Award Heart & Vascular Res, 73. *Prof Exp:* Demonstr biochem, Budapest Univ, 46-48; asst biomolecular struct, Leeds Univ, 48-52; res assoc physiol & pharmacol, Wayne State Univ, 52-53, asst prof, 53-55. *Concurrent Pos:* Beit mem fel, Eng, 52; Lalor fac award, 57; dir, Biochem Training Prog, Northwestern Univ, 61-66, dep dir basic sci, Cancer Ctr, 90-91; USPHS career award, 62-93; mem corp, Marine Biol Lab, Woods Hole, Mass; lectr, Japan Soc Prom Sci, 90- *Mem:* Nat Acad Sci; AAAS; Am Soc Biol Chem; Soc Exp Biol & Med; Am Physiol Soc; Brit Biochem Soc; Am Chem Soc; foreign mem Hungarian Acad Sci; fel Int Soc Hemat; Biophys Soc; fel Japan Soc Prom Sci; Am Soc Biochem & Molecular Biol; Am Heart Asn; Am Soc Cell Biol; Int Soc Thrombosis & Haemostasis; Asn Res Vision & Ophthal. *Res:* Blood proteins; coagulation of blood; muscle chemistry; protein and enzyme chemistry; author of numerous publications. *Mailing Add:* Dept Biochem & Molecular Biol Northwestern Univ Evanston IL 60611-3008

LORANGER, WILLIAM FARRAND, XERORADIOGRAPHY. *Current Pos:* RETIRED. *Personal Data:* b Detroit, Mich, Nov 6, 25. *Educ:* Denison Univ, BA, 47; Univ Ill, MS, 50, PhD(chem & x-ray diffraction), 52. *Prof Exp:* Asst, Anal Div, Ill State Geol Surv, 47-49; proj scientist, Wright Air Develop Div, USAF, Ohio, 51-54; instr physics & chem, US Mil Acad, 54-56; sales engr, X-Ray Dept, Gen Elec Co, 56-57; asst prof, Univ Fla, 57-58; tech adv indust sales, X-Ray Dept, Gen Elec Co, 58-61; prod mgr x-ray & electron optics, Picker X-Ray Corp, NY, 62-70, mkt mgr, Indust Div, Picker Corp, 70-72; new mkt res mgr, Xerox Corp, 72-73, dir educ, xeroradiography, 73-80, consult, xeroxmed systs, 80-84. *Mem:* AAAS; Am Chem Soc; Sigma Xi; Am Crystallog Asn. *Res:* X-ray diffraction and emission; optical methods of instrumental analysis; instrumental chemical analysis; radiography; diseases of the breast; diagnostic ultrasound; applied x-rays. *Mailing Add:* 1240 Mapleview Dr Charlottesville VA 22902

LORBEER, JAMES W, PLANT PATHOLOGY, MYCOLOGY. *Current Pos:* from asst prof to assoc prof, 60-72, PROF PLANT PATH, CORNELL UNIV, 72- *Personal Data:* b Oxnard, Calif, Oct 30, 31; m 64. *Educ:* Pomona Col, BA, 53; Univ Wash, MS, 55; Univ Calif, Berkeley, PhD(plant path), 60. *Prof Exp:* Asst bot, Univ Wash, 53-55; asst plant path, Univ Calif, Berkeley, 55-60. *Mem:* Mycol Soc Am; Am Phytopath Soc; NY Acad Sci; Brit Mycol Soc. *Res:* Diseases of vegetable crops; epidemiology; plant disease control; biology of Botrytis; fungal genetics. *Mailing Add:* Dept Plant Path Cornell Univ 334 Plant Sci Bldg Ithaca NY 14853-0001

LORBER, BENNETT, INFECTIOUS DISEASES. *Current Pos:* THOMAS M DURANT PROF MED & CHIEF INFECTIOUS DIS, TEMPLE UNIV HEALTH SCI CTR, 83- *Personal Data:* b Philadelphia, Pa, Apr 1, 43; m 64, Carole Finneburgh; c Samuel & Joshua Edward. *Educ:* Swarthmore Col, BA, 64; Univ Pa, MD, 68. *Hon Degrees:* DSc, Swarthmore Col, 96. *Prof Exp:* From asst prof to assoc prof med, Med Sch, Temple Univ, 74-83. *Mem:* Infectious Dis Soc Am; Am Col Physicians; Am Soc Microbiol; Am Fedn Clin Res; Physicians for Human Rights; Anerobe Soc Am. *Res:* Listeriosis, anaerobic infections, impact of societal change on disease patterns. *Mailing Add:* Infectious Dis Temple Hosp Philadelphia PA 19140

LORBER, HERBERT WILLIAM, ELECTRONIC WARFARE, DECISION ANALYSIS. *Current Pos:* SR STAFF SPECIALIST, LOCKHEED AERONAUT SYSTS CO, 82- *Personal Data:* b Indianapolis, Ind, July 12, 29; m 62; c 2. *Educ:* Purdue Univ, BS, 51; Rutgers Univ, MSc, 55; Univ Pa, PhD(elec eng), 62. *Prof Exp:* Engr, Signal Corp Eng Labs, 51 & 53-54; mem tech staff, RCA Labs, 55-62; sr sci specialist, Edgerton Germeshausen & Grier, Inc, 62-71; electron res specialist, Teledyne Ryan Aeronaut, 72-76; mem staff, Los Alamos Nat Lab, 76-82. *Concurrent Pos:* Consult, N J Damaskos, Inc, Los Alamos Tech Assocs, Inc & Convair Div Gen Dynamics, 82. *Mem:* Inst Elec & Electronic Engrs; Oper Res Soc Am; AAAS; Sigma Xi. *Res:* Interaction of spacecraft and military vehicles with radar systems; quantitative space-system concept assessment; applications of utility theory to management decision-making; analysis of military and business operations. *Mailing Add:* 3205 Deer Creek Dr Canton GA 30114-8978

LORBER, MORTIMER, PHYSIOLOGY, HEMATOLOGY. *Current Pos:* sr asst resident med, Univ Hosp, 58, from instr to asst prof, 59-68, ASSOC PROF PHYSIOL, SCH MED, GEORGETOWN UNIV, 68- *Personal Data:* b New York, NY, Aug 30, 26; m 56, Eileen Segal; c Kenneth & Stephanie. *Educ:* NY Univ, BS, 45; Harvard Univ, DMD, 50, MD, 52. *Prof Exp:* Rotating intern, Univ Chicago Clins, 52-53; resident hemat, Mt Sinai Hosp, NY, 53-54, asst resident med, 57; med officer hemat res, USN Med Corps, 54-55, Naval Med Res Inst, 55-56. *Concurrent Pos:* Lederle Med Fac Award, Georgetown Univ, 60-63, USPHS res career develop award, 63-70. *Mem:* Am Soc Hemat; Int Soc Hemat; Am Soc Cell Biol; Int Asn Dent Res; Am Physiol Soc; Asn Res Vision Ophthal. *Res:* Splenic function; iron metabolism in Gaucher's disease; organ regeneration, particularly of mammalian submandibular salivary glands following removal of parenchyma; exocrine gland structure and tension; mastication reflexly increases gastroduodenal motility. *Mailing Add:* 5823 Osceola Rd Bethesda MD 20816-2032. *Fax:* 202-687-7407

LORBER, VICTOR, physiology; deceased, see previous edition for last biography

LORCH, EDGAR RAYMOND, mathematics; deceased, see previous edition for last biography

LORCH, JOAN, CELL BIOLOGY, PROTOZOOLOGY. *Current Pos:* lectr, Canisius Col, 71-72, from asst prof to assoc prof, 72-84, chair, Biol Dept, 81-84, PROF BIOL, CANISIUS COL, 84- *Personal Data:* b Offenbach, Ger, June 13, 23; m 52; c 2. *Educ:* Univ Birmingham, BSc, 45; Univ London, PhD(physiol), 48. *Prof Exp:* Nuffield fel, King's Col, Univ London, 49-52; res assoc cell biol, Ctr Theoret Biol, State Univ NY Buffalo, 63-68, res asst prof, 68-72. *Concurrent Pos:* Vis prof for women, NSF, 84-85. *Res:* Nuclear-cytoplasmic relationships; species specificity; protozoa; bio-ethics; symbiosis. *Mailing Add:* Dept Biol Canisius Col 2001 Main St Buffalo NY 14208-1098

LORCH, LEE (ALEXANDER), MATHEMATICS. *Current Pos:* prof, 68-85, EMER PROF MATH, YORK UNIV, 85- *Personal Data:* b New York, NY, Sept 20, 15; wid; c Alice (Bartels). *Educ:* Cornell Univ, BA, 35; Univ Cincinnati, MA, 36, PhD(math), 41. *Hon Degrees:* LHD, City Univ NY, 90; LLD, York Univ, 93, Fisk Univ, 96. *Honors & Awards:* Lifetime Achievement Award, Nat Asn Mathematicians, 95. *Prof Exp:* Asst mathematician, Nat Adv Comt Aeronaut, 42-43; instr math, City Col New York, 46-49; asst prof, Pa State Univ, 49-50; assoc prof & chmn dept, Fisk Univ, 50-53, prof & chmn dept, 53-55; prof & chmn dept, Philander Smith Col, 55-58; from assoc prof to prof, Univ Alta, 59-68. *Concurrent Pos:* Vis lectr, Wesleyan Univ, 58-69. *Mem:* Am Math Soc; Can Math Soc; Asn Women Math; Nat Asn Mathematicians; fel Royal Soc Can; Math Asn Am; fel AAAS. *Res:* Fourier series; special functions; summability; ordinary differential equations. *Mailing Add:* Math Dept York Univ North York ON M3J 1P3 Can. *Fax:* 416-736-5757; *E-Mail:* lorch@mathstat.yorku.ca

LORCH, STEVEN KALMAN, FORENSIC SCIENCE, MANAGEMENT. *Current Pos:* supvr, Narcotics & Dangerous Drug Unit, East Lansing Sci Lab, 77-78, Madison Heights Sci Lab, 78-82, ASST LAB DIR, NORTHVILLE SCI LAB, FORENSIC SCI DIV, MICH STATE POLICE, 82- *Personal Data:* b New York, NY, Aug 21, 44; m 67, Harriet R Blum; c Jacob R, Elisar R & David P. *Educ:* City Col New York, BS, 66; State Univ NY Binghamton, MA, 70; Univ Md, PhD(plant physiol), 72. *Prof Exp:* Res assoc, Mich State Univ-AEC Plant Res Lab, 72-73; crime lab scientist, 73-75, chief drug identification unit, 75-77, Div Crime Detection, Mich Dept Pub Health. *Concurrent Pos:* Mich State Police rep, Sci Adv Comn, Mich Bd Pharm, 83-; team leader, Disaster Asst Recovery Team, 88-; guest lectr, Univ Detroit Mercy, 94- *Mem:* Am Chem Soc; Am Acad Forensic Sci. *Res:* Identification of controlled and prescription drugs; gas chromatographic-mass spectrometry; forensic plant identification; crime scene investigation, clandestine laboratories; development of latent fingerprints; automated fingerprint identification systems; major disaster victim identification. *Mailing Add:* Northville Forensic Sci Lab Mich State Police 6296 Dixie Hwy Bridgeport MI 48722-0608. *Fax:* 248-380-1005, 313-473-1005; *E-Mail:* aeo51@leo.nmc.edu

LORD, ARTHUR E, JR, PHYSICS, GEOSYNTHETICS. *Current Pos:* assoc prof, 68-75, PROF PHYSICS, DREXEL UNIV, 75- *Personal Data:* b Buffalo, NY, Apr 7, 35; m 62, Rose M DiGione; c Susan & Katherine. *Educ:* Purdue Univ, BSc, 57, MSc, 59; PhD(metall), Columbia Univ, 64. *Honors & Awards:* IR-100 Award, Indust Res & Develop Mag, 77. *Prof Exp:* Res assoc appl math, Brown Univ, 64-66, asst res prof physics, 66-68. *Concurrent Pos:* Fel, Columbia Univ, 64; mem, NASA Electromagnetic Containerless Processing Task Team, 77; consult, acoust, House Comt Kennedy & King Assasinations, 78. *Mem:* Am Phys Soc; Acoustic Emission Working Group; Int Geotextile Soc. *Res:* Nondestructive testing techniques in geotechnical problems; geomembranes and geotextiles; centrifuge modelling in geotechnical areas; removal of pollutants from soil by steam stripping techniques. *Mailing Add:* Dept Physics Drexel Univ 32nd & Chestnut St Philadelphia PA 19104. *Fax:* 215-895-1437

LORD, ARTHUR N(ELSON), PHYSICAL METALLURGY. *Current Pos:* Physical metallurgist, Adv Tech Labs, 58-65, METALLURGIST, KNOLLS ATOMIC POWER LAB, GEN ELEC CO, 65- *Personal Data:* b Los Angeles, Calif, May 7, 32; m 61; c 2. *Educ:* Stanford Univ, BS, 53, MS, 55, PhD(creep of aluminum), 60. *Mem:* Am Inst Mining, Metall & Petrol Engrs; Am Phys Soc; Am Soc Metals. *Res:* Transport properties of solids; effects of radiation damage in metals. *Mailing Add:* Seven Spring Rd Scotia NY 12302-2614

LORD, EDITH M, IMMUNOLOGY. *Current Pos:* sr instr, 76-77, ASST PROF ONCOL, UNIV ROCHESTER, 77- *Personal Data:* b Kingman, Kans. *Educ:* Univ Kans, BA, 70; Univ Calif, PhD(biol), 75. *Prof Exp:* Res immunologist, Univ Calif, San Francisco, 75-76. *Mem:* Am Asn Immunologists; Radiation Res Soc. *Res:* Interaction between host immune cells and tumor cells; modulation of these interactions for therapeutic advantage. *Mailing Add:* Dept Microbiol & Cancer Ctr Univ Rochester 601 Elmwood Ave Box 704 Rochester NY 14642-0001

LORD, ELIZABETH MARY, BOTANY. *Current Pos:* From asst prof to assoc prof, 78-89, PROF BOT, UNIV CALIF, RIVERSIDE, 89- *Personal Data:* b Baltimore, Md, July 2, 49; m 84, Barkin; c Matthew Larkin. *Educ:* Univ Mass, BA, 72; Univ Calif, Berkeley, PhD(bot), 78. *Honors & Awards:* Pelton Award, Bot Soc Am. *Concurrent Pos:* Mem, develop biol panel, NSF, 83-86. *Mem:* Am Soc Plant Physiologists; Sigma Xi; Asn Women Sci; Bot Soc Am. *Res:* Use of comparative development data as a tool to elucidate sequence of events leading to a mature floral form; pollination processes in flowering plants. *Mailing Add:* Dept Bot & Plant Sci Univ Calif Riveside 900 University Ave Riverside CA 92521-0101

LORD, HAROLD WILBUR, MEASUREMENT OF VOLTAGE TRANSIENTS. *Current Pos:* CONSULT ELEC ENGR, 66- *Personal Data:* b Eureka, Calif, Aug 20, 05; m 28; c 4. *Educ:* Calif Inst Technol, BS, 26. *Honors & Awards:* Centennial Award, Inst Elec & Electronics Engrs, 84. *Prof Exp:* Gen engr, Gen Elec Co, 26-66. *Concurrent Pos:* Chmn, sci & electronic comt, Inst Elec & Electronics Engrs, 62-63. *Mem:* Inst Elec & Electronics Engrs (tech vpres, 62). *Res:* Development of and design procedures for electromagnetic devices in electronics circuits; voltage transients due to switching. *Mailing Add:* 1565 Golf Course Dr Rohnert Park CA 94928

LORD, HARRY CHESTER, III, PHYSICAL CHEMISTRY, ANALYTICAL CHEMISTRY. *Current Pos:* PRES, AIR INSTRUMENTS & MEASUREMENTS, INC, 88- *Personal Data:* b Utica, NY, May 28, 39; m 61, 72, 89, Jessica; c 5. *Educ:* Tufts Univ, BS, 61; Univ Calif, San Diego, PhD(chem), 67. *Honors & Awards:* Gold Medal, Am Inst Chemists, 61. *Prof Exp:* Sr scientist, Jet Propulsion Lab, 67-69, vpres, 69-77; pres, Environ Data Corp, 77-81; pres, Syconex Corp, 80-88. *Concurrent Pos:* Chmn, Energy Technol & Control Ltd, 86-88; dir, Dosibi Environ Corp, 89-90. *Mem:* Am Chem Soc; Air Pollution Control Asn; Combustion Inst; Sigma Xi; Instrument Soc Am. *Res:* Modification of combustion, improved control techniques; hardware to increase efficiency and to reduce pollutant emissions; development of state-of-the-art sensors to monitor environmental emissions of toxic and reactive gases. *Mailing Add:* 1400 Edge Cliff Lane Pasadena CA 91107-1509. *Fax:* 626-338-2585

LORD, JERE JOHNS, PHYSICS, HIGH ENERGY PHYSICS & COSMIC RAYS. *Current Pos:* instr, 52-62, prof, 62-92, EMER PROF PHYSICS, UNIV WASH, 92- *Personal Data:* b Portland, Ore, Jan 3, 22; m 47; c 3. *Educ:* Reed Col, AB, 43; Univ Chicago, MS, 48, PhD(physics), 50. *Prof Exp:* Res assoc physics, Univ Chicago, 50-52. *Mem:* Fel Am Phys Soc; Am Asn Phys Teachers; fel AAAS; Marine Technol Soc. *Res:* Cosmic ray and high energy physics. *Mailing Add:* Dept Physics FM-15 Univ Wash PO Box 351560 Seattle WA 98195. *Fax:* 206-685-0635; *E-Mail:* lord@phys.washington.edu

LORD, JERE WILLIAMS, JR, SURGERY. *Current Pos:* RETIRED. *Personal Data:* b Baltimore, Md, Oct 12, 10; m 41, 71; c 3. *Educ:* Princeton Univ, AB, 33; Johns Hopkins Univ, MD, 37; Am Bd Surg, dipl. *Prof Exp:* From intern to resident surgeon, NY Hosp, 37-44; prof clin surg, Postgrad Sch Med, Med Ctr, NY Univ, 53-83. *Concurrent Pos:* Consult surgeon, Univ Hosp, Bellevue Hosp, Fourth Div Med Bd & Doctors Hosp & Hackensack Hosp, NJ, St Luke's Hosp, Newburgh, NY, Norwalk Hosp, Conn, 50-, Cent Suffolk Hosp, Riverhead, NY, 51-, Elizabeth Horton Mem Hosp, Middletown, NY, 54-, St Agnes Hosp, White Plains, NY, 55-, Paterson Gen Hosp, NJ, 58 & Univ Hosp; chief, Vascular Surg, Columbus Hosp, NY, 66-83. *Mem:* Am Col Surg; Am Surg Asn; James IV Asn Surg (secy, 67-75); Am Heart Asn (secy, 53-55); Int Cardiovasc Soc (treas, 53-60, vpres, 61-63). *Res:* Cardiovascular surgery, especially atherosclerosis; gastrointestinal surgery, particularly portal hypertension and intestinal obstruction. *Mailing Add:* 179 Greenwich Rd Bedford NY 10506

LORD, PETER REEVES, TEXTILE ENGINEERING, TEXTILE TECHNOLOGY. *Current Pos:* from assoc prof to prof, 69-75, Abel C Lineberger prof textiles, 75-90, EMER PROF, ABEL C LINEBERGER, NC STATE UNIV, 90-; PRES, RALTEX INC, 90- *Personal Data:* b Ruckinge, Eng, Feb 10, 23; m 47; Mavis Hatt; c 3. *Educ:* Battersea Polytech, Eng, BSc, 50; Univ London, PhD(eng), 66, DSc(eng), 76. *Honors & Awards:* Harold DeWitt Smith Award, Am Soc Testing & Mat, 79; Alexander von Humboldt US sr scientist award, 80; Warner Medal Textile Inst 91. *Prof Exp:* Res asst heat transfer, Delaney-Gallay Ltd, Eng, 45-46; draughtsman, Fairey Aviation Co Ltd, 46-47; sect leader eng, Vacuum Oil Co Ltd, 47-51; sr test engr, Vickers Armstrongs Ltd, 51-58; lectr textile technol, Univ Manchester, 58-69. *Mem:* Fel Brit Inst Mech Eng; fel Brit Textile Inst; Am Fiber Soc; Sigma Xi. *Res:* Modern methods of yarn formation; open-end spinning; fabric forming systems; sliver and yarn monitoring systems; design of textile machinery; physics of fibrous assemblies. *Mailing Add:* 3116 Monticello Dr Raleigh NC 27612. *Fax:* 919-787-5720

LORD, SAMUEL SMITH, JR, ANALYTICAL CHEMISTRY, POLYMER CHEMISTRY. *Current Pos:* RETIRED. *Personal Data:* b Rockland, Maine, Apr 10, 27; m 48, Evelyn Marlin; c 5. *Educ:* Tufts Col, BS, 47; Mass Inst Technol, PhD(analytical chem), 52. *Prof Exp:* Res chemist, Fabrics & Finishes Dept, E I du Pont de Nemours & Co, Inc, 47-49, res chemist, Org Chem Dept, 52-57, res supvr, Elastomer Chem Dept, 57-59, div head, 59-65, supt qual control, 65-67, supt monomer area, 67-70, gen prod supt, 70-71, asst works dir, Maydown Works, Du Pont Co (UK) Ltd, 71-75, works mgr, Beaumont Works, 75-84, works dir, Maydown Works, Du Pont, Eng, (UK), 84-88, managing dir, 86-88,. *Mem:* AAAS; Am Chem Soc. *Res:* Polarography; coulometry; infrared and ultraviolet spectrophotometry; urethane chemistry. *Mailing Add:* 1240 Nottingham Lane Beaumont TX 77706-4316

LORD, WILLIAM B, policy analysis, institutional analysis, for more information see previous edition

LORD, WILLIAM JOHN, POMOLOGY. *Current Pos:* RETIRED. *Personal Data:* b Farmington, NH, Nov 3, 21; m 47; c 1. *Educ:* Univ NH, BS, 43, MS, 53; Pa State Univ, PhD(hort), 55. *Prof Exp:* Exten prof pomol, Agr Exten Serv, Univ Mass, Amherst, 55-85. *Mem:* Am Soc Hort Sci. *Res:* Weed control; nutrition; growth regulators. *Mailing Add:* 73 N Silver Lane Sunderland MA 01375

LORDI, NICHOLAS GEORGE, PHARMACEUTICS. *Current Pos:* From asst prof to assoc prof, Rutgers Univ, 57-64, chmn dept, 77-82, asst dean, 81-96, PROF PHARM, RUTGERS UNIV, 64- *Personal Data:* b Orange, NJ, Mar 25, 30; m 61, Bertha Taylor; c Keith, Scott & Nicole. *Educ:* Rutgers Univ, BSc, 52 & MSc, 53; Purdue Univ, PhD(pharmaceut chem), 55. *Mem:* Am Chem Soc; AAAS; fel Am Asn Pharmaceut Sci. *Res:* Physical stability pharmaceutical systems; pharmaceutical technology; compaction thermal analysis. *Mailing Add:* Col Pharm Rutgers Univ PO Box 789 New Brunswick NJ 08855-0789. *Fax:* 732-445-5767

LORDS, JAMES LAFAYETTE, PHYSIOLOGY. *Current Pos:* from asst prof to assoc prof, 62-75, PROF MOLECULAR & GENETIC BIOL, UNIV UTAH, 75-, PROF BIOL, 75- *Personal Data:* b Salt Lake City, Utah, Apr 5, 28; m 55, Katherine Reeves; c Kevin & John. *Educ:* Univ Utah, BS, 50, MS, 51, PhD(plant physiol), 60. *Prof Exp:* Asst bot, Univ Utah, 56-58, instr biol, 58-59; proj assoc plant path, Univ Wis, 60-62. *Mem:* Am Physiol Soc. *Res:* Microwave interactions with biological systems. *Mailing Add:* Dept Biol Univ Utah 200 S University St Salt Lake City UT 84112. *E-Mail:* lords@bioscience.utah.edu

LORE, JAMES A, AGRICULTURAL ENVIRONMENTAL ISSUES. *Current Pos:* EXEC DIR, OLD COL FOUND. *Educ:* Univ Alta, BSc, 54. *Concurrent Pos:* Consult, Jim Lore & Assoc Ltd, 84- *Mem:* Fel Agr Inst Can; Int Right Way Asn; fel Can Consult Agrologists Asn; Can Soc Animal Sci; Can Range Mgt; Can Soc Agr Econs & Farm Mgrs; Can Soc Agron. *Mailing Add:* Old Col Found 4500 50th St Olds AB T4H 1R6 CAN

LORE, JOHN M, JR, OTOLARYNGOLOGY, SURGERY. *Current Pos:* PVT PRACT SISTERS HOSP, BUFFALO. *Personal Data:* b New York, NY, July 26, 21; m; c 4. *Educ:* Col Holy Cross, BS, 44; NY Univ, MD, 45; Am Bd Otolaryngol, dipl, 54; Am Bd Surg, dipl, 56. *Honors & Awards:* Hektoen Gold Medal, AMA, 52. *Prof Exp:* Intern, St Vincent's Hosp, New York, 45-46, resident otolaryngol & head & neck surg, 48-50; asst resident gen surg, St Clare's Hosp, 50-52, sr resident, 54-55; asst resident surg & radiation, Mem Cancer Ctr, 52-53; asst clin prof surg & asst attend surgeon, NY Med Col, Flower & Fifth Ave Hosps, 64-66; prof otolaryngol & chmn dept, Sch Med, State Univ NY, Buffalo, 66-90. *Concurrent Pos:* Fel exp surg, St Clare's Hosp, 53-54; asst vis surgeon, Metrop Hosp Ctr, New York, 64-66; dir surg, Good Samaritan Hosp, Suffern, attend surgeon, St Clare's Hosp, New York & consult surgeon, Tuxedo Mem Hosp, 65-66; head dept otolaryngol & chief combined head & neck serv, Buffalo Gen Hosp & Buffalo Children's Hosp, 66-; head dept otolaryngol & chief combined head & neck serv, Eric Co Med Ctr, 66-; consult, Buffalo Vet Admin Hosp, 66-; chmn dept otolaryngol, Sisters of Charity Hosp, 75-90; vis prof, Col Med, Baylor Univ, 67; consult, Roswell Park Mem Inst, 68-; clin consult, NY State Dept Health, 68-; vis prof, Denver Med Ctr, 69 & Dept Otolaryngol, Bethesda Naval Med Ctr, Md, 71; consult, Deaconess Hosp, Buffalo, NY & Buffalo Hearing & Speech. *Mem:* Fel Am Col Surg; Am Cancer Soc; fel Am Acad Ophthal & Otolaryngol; AMA; James Ewing Soc. *Res:* General surgery, including maxillofacial surgery and plastic surgery of the head and neck. *Mailing Add:* 2157 Main St Buffalo NY 14214-2648

LORENCE, MATTHEW C, EXPERIMENTAL BIOLOGY. *Current Pos:* ASSOC PROD LINE MGR, BIO-RAD LABS, 90- *Mailing Add:* Bio-Rad Labs 2000 Alfred Nobel Dr Hercules CA 94547. *Fax:* 510-741-1051

LORENS, STANLEY A, NEUROPHARMACOLOGY. *Current Pos:* assoc prof, 77-84, PROF PHARMACOL, LOYOLA UNIV MED CTR, 84- *Personal Data:* b Galion, Ohio, July 19, 36. *Educ:* Univ Notre Dame, BA, 65; Univ Chicago, PhD(biopsychol), 68. *Prof Exp:* Fel psychopharmacol, Univ Ill, 65-68; asst prof psychiat, Iowa Univ, 68-72; first lectr pharmacol, Univ Bergen Norway. *Mem:* Soc Neurosci; Am Soc Pharmacol & Exp Therapeut. *Res:* Neuropharmacology. *Mailing Add:* Lab Behav Pharmacol Bldg 135 Loyola Univ Med Ctr 2160 S First Ave Maywood IL 60153-5589

LORENSEN, LYMAN EDWARD, ORGANIC POLYMER CHEMISTRY. *Current Pos:* CONSULT, 88- *Personal Data:* b Lincoln, Nebr, Sept, 26, 23; m 50; c 3. *Educ:* Univ Nebr, BS, 47; Cornell Univ, PhD(chem), 52. *Prof Exp:* Jr chemist, Bristol Labs, 47-48; asst org chem, Cornell Univ, 50-52; chemist,

Shell Develop Co, 52-58 & 60-64, mem staff, Mfg Res Dept, Shell Oil Co, 58-60; mem staff, composites & polymer technol & actg technol leader, Lawrence Livermore Nat Lab, Univ Calif, 64-88. *Mem:* Am Chem Soc; Sigma Xi. *Res:* High temperature polymers; polymers for geothermal applications; unsaturated glycols; possible precursors in biosynthesis of rubber; lubricating oil additives; silicone and epoxy polymers; filled polymers; foams; coatings. *Mailing Add:* 9 Broadview Terr Orinda CA 94563

LORENTS, ALDEN C, DATABASE, COMPUTER AIDED SOFTWARE ENGINEERING. *Current Pos:* PROF COMPUT INFO SYSTS, NORTHERN ARIZ UNIV, 71- *Personal Data:* b Bagley, Minn, Apr 29, 37; m 60; c Heidi & Troy. *Educ:* Concordia Col Minn, BSBA, 60; Univ Minn, MBA, 62, PhD(acct), 71. *Prof Exp:* Programmer & analyst, Honeywell, 60-66; dir comput, Bemidji State Univ, 66-71. *Concurrent Pos:* Consult, Ariz Guid Ctr, 73-83 & Univ Kuwait, 83; internship, Lawrence Livermore Labs, 81, Sandia Labs, 83 & Ariz Pub Serv, 87-89 & 94-95. *Mem:* Soc Info Mgt; Data Processing Mgt Asn; Decision Sci Inst. *Res:* Software engineering; re-engineering; repository development; database development; computer aided software engineering. *Mailing Add:* Northern Ariz Univ Box 15066 Flagstaff AZ 86011. *E-Mail:* alden.lorents@nau.edu

LORENTS, DONALD C, LASER PHYSICS, ATOMIC CLUSTER PHYSICS. *Current Pos:* RETIRED. *Personal Data:* b Minn, Mar 26, 29; m 52, Doris M Bry; c Christine & Nancy. *Educ:* Concordia Col, Moorhead, Minn, BA, 51; Univ Nebr, MA, 54, PhD(physics), 58. *Prof Exp:* Res physicist, Westinghouse Res Labs, 58-59; physicist, SRI Int, 59-63, chmn, Dept Molecular Physics, 63-67, head, Atomic & Molecular Collisions Sect, 67-68, physicist, 69-70, sr physicist, 70-75, assoc dir, 75-79, dir, Molecular Physics Lab, 80-84, dir, Chem Physics Lab, 84-90, sci dir, Molecular Physics Lab, 90-94. *Concurrent Pos:* Vis res physicist, Inst Physics, Aarhus Univ, 68-69, 70, 87. *Mem:* AAAS; fel Am Phys Soc. *Res:* Atomic and molecular collision processes with emphasis on scattering, charge transfer and excitation in ion-atom or ion-molecule collisions; kinetic processes in electronically excited dense gases; molecular spectroscopy; cluster physics; fullerenes. *Mailing Add:* SRI Int 333 Ravenswood Menlo Park CA 94025

LORENTZ, GEORGE G, MATHEMATICAL ANALYSIS. *Current Pos:* prof, 69-80, EMER PROF MATH, UNIV TEX, AUSTIN, 80- *Personal Data:* b St Petersburg, Russia, Feb 25, 10; m 42; c 5. *Educ:* Univ Leningrad, Cand, 35; Univ Tuebingen, Dr rer nat(math), 44. *Hon Degrees:* Dr, Univ Tuebingen. *Honors & Awards:* Humboldt Prize, A von Humboldt Stiftung, 73. *Prof Exp:* Lectr math, Univ Leningrad, 36-42 & Univ Frankfurt, 46-48; prof, Univ Tubingen, 48-49; from asst to asst prof, Univ Toronto, 49-53; prof, Wayne State Univ, 53-58; prof, Syracuse Univ, 58-69. *Concurrent Pos:* Res grants, NSF & Off Sci Res. *Mem:* Am Math Soc; Math Asn Am; Ger Math Soc. *Res:* Mathematical analysis, especially approximations and expansions; summability; Birkhoff interpolation; functional analysis, especially Banach function spaces; interpolation theorems for operators; published several monographs on Approximation and Interpolation. *Mailing Add:* 2750 Sierra Sunrise Terr Apt 404 Chico CA 95928

LORENTZEN, KEITH EDEN, PHYSICAL ORGANIC CHEMISTRY. *Current Pos:* RETIRED. *Personal Data:* b Heber City, Utah, Apr 13, 21; m 47, 80, Evelyn McNees; c Rebecca A, Frank M, Heidi J, Wendy S, John K & Mitzi K. *Educ:* Univ Utah, BA, 42, MS, 47; Pa State Univ, PhD(chem), 51. *Prof Exp:* Chemist, Stand Oil Co, Ind, 51-62; from asst prof to assoc prof chem, Ind Univ NW, 63-88, from asst chmn to chmn dept, 66-88, chmn, Dept Physics & Astron, 77-88. *Mem:* Am Chem Soc; fel Am Inst Chemists; Am Asn Univ Professors. *Res:* Conductivity measurements; chemistry of lubricating oils and additives; organic analytical chemistry; chromatography; polarography; Friedel-Crafts methylation of xylenes; aromatic deuteration of methylbenzenes. *Mailing Add:* 1505 Melbrook Dr Munster IN 46321

LORENZ, CARL EDWARD, ORGANIC CHEMISTRY. *Current Pos:* RETIRED. *Personal Data:* b New York, NY, Aug 22, 33; m 56; c 3. *Educ:* NY Univ, BA, 53, PhD(chem), 57. *Honors & Awards:* Award, Am Inst Chem, 53. *Prof Exp:* Asst chem, NY Univ, 53-57; from chemist to sr res chemist, Plastics Dept, Exp Sta, E I Du Pont de Nemours & Co, Inc, 57-68, from supvr to sr supvr, 68-69, lab supt, 69-70, res lab mgr, Sabine River Works, 70-72, res mgr, Wilmington, 72-74, asst dir, Int Dept, 74-76, prod mgr, 76-78, dir, Feedstocks Div, 78-79, dir Res Div, Cent Res & Develop, 79-81, dir res & develop, Polymer Prod Dept, 81-83, dir, Ethylene Polymers Div, 83-85, dir, Chemicals & Pigments Dept, 85-90, vpres res & develop, Du Pont Chemicals, 90-93. *Mem:* Am Chem Soc; Am Inst Chem; The Chem Soc; NY Acad Sci. *Res:* Fluorocarbon monomer syntheses and polymerizations; high pressure hydrocarbon syntheses; heterogeneous catalysis; chemistry of anionic and radical polymerizations. *Mailing Add:* 103 Bellant Circle Wilmington DE 19807-2219. *E-Mail:* celorenz@aol.com

LORENZ, DONALD H, ORGANIC CHEMISTRY, POLYMER CHEMISTRY. *Current Pos:* PRES, RIDGE SCI ENTPRISES INC, 91- *Personal Data:* b Brooklyn, NY, Oct 18, 36; m 62, Patricia Marshall; c Peter M & Jeanne C. *Educ:* Polytech Inst Brooklyn, BS, 58, PhD(org chem), 63. *Prof Exp:* Asst org chem, Polytech Inst Brooklyn, 58-59, organometallics, 59-62; asst scientist chem eng res div, NY Univ, 62-63; sr polymer chemist, Tex-US Chem Co, 63-65; explor polymer chemist, Gen Aniline & Film Co, 65-70, group leader polymer synthesis, GAF Corp, 70-74, mgr vinyl polymer res, 74-80; dir res & develop, Hydromer Inc, 80-89, exec vpres, 89-91. *Mem:* Am Chem Soc; Asn Consult Chemists & Chem Engrs. *Res:* Organometallic chemistry; elastomers; resins; adhesives; polymers of vinyl ethers and vinyl amides; polyurethanes; fire retardants; ultraviolet and electron beam curable resins; coatings for medical devices; drug delivery systems; wound dressings; hydrogels; conductive adhesives. *Mailing Add:* 12 Radel Pl Basking Ridge NJ 07920. *Fax:* 908-534-9034

LORENZ, EDWARD NORTON, METEOROLOGY. *Current Pos:* res staff, Mass Inst Technol, 48-54, from asst prof to prof, 55-87, head, Dept Meteorol & Phys Oceanog, 77-81, EMER PROF METEOROL, MASS INST TECHNOL, 87- *Personal Data:* b West Hartford, Conn, May 23, 17; m 48, Jane Loban; c 3. *Educ:* Dartmouth Col, AB, 38; Harvard Univ, AM, 40; Mass Inst Technol, SM, 43, ScD, 48. *Hon Degrees:* DSc, McGill Univ, 83, Univ Ariz, 89, Rutgers Univ, 90, Dartmouth Col, 92. *Honors & Awards:* Clarence Leroy Meisinger Award, Am Meteorol Soc, 63, Carl Gustaf Rossby Res Med, 69; Symons Mem Gold Medal, Royal Meteorol Soc, 73; Holger & Anna-Greta Crafoord Prize, Royal Swed Acad Sci, 83; Elliott Creson Medal, Franklin Inst, 89; Roger Revelle Medal, Am Geophys Union, 92. *Prof Exp:* Asst meteorol, Mass Inst Technol, 46-48, mem staff, 48-54; vis assoc prof, Univ Calif, Los Angeles, 54-55. *Concurrent Pos:* Vis scientist, Lowell Observ, 51, Norweg Meteorol Inst, 62 & Europ Ctr Medium Range Weather Forecasts, 81-82; sr assoc, Nat Ctr Atmospheric Res, 73-74; vis sr scientist, Univ Oslo, 82. *Mem:* Fel Nat Acad Sci; fel Am Acad Arts & Sci; hon mem Am Meteorol Soc; hon mem Royal Meteorol Soc; hon fel Indian Acad Sci; Norweg Acad Sci & Lett; foreign mem USSR Acad Sci; foreign mem Royal Soc London. *Res:* General circulation of the atmosphere; dynamical and statistical weather prediction; chaotic dynamical systems; author of numerous publications. *Mailing Add:* Dept Earth Atmospheric & Planetary Sci Mass Inst Technol Cambridge MA 02139

LORENZ, JOHN DOUGLAS, MANUFACTURING SYSTEMS DESIGN, ASSEMBLY SYSTEMS DESIGN. *Current Pos:* From asst prof to assoc prof, GMI Eng & Mgt Inst, 73-78, dept head indust eng, 84-87, asst dean res & grad studies, 87-88, PROF INDUST ENG, GMI ENG & MGT INST, 78-, VPRES ACAD AFFAIRS & PROVOST, 88- *Personal Data:* b Talmage, Nebr, July 2, 42; m 67, Alice Heutzen; c Christian. *Educ:* Univ Nebr, Lincoln, BS, 65, MS, 67, PhD(indust eng), 73. *Concurrent Pos:* Richard L Terrell prof acad leadership, GMI Eng & Mgt Inst, 90-; dir, Jr Eng Tech Soc, 91- *Mem:* Soc Mfg Engrs; Soc Automotive Engrs; Nat Soc Prof Engrs; Am Soc Eng Educr. *Res:* Manufacturing systems design; assembly systems design; computer assisted assembly line balancing. *Mailing Add:* 3122 Beech Tree Lane Flushing MI 48433. *Fax:* 810-762-9836; *E-Mail:* jlorenz@nova.gmi.edu

LORENZ, KLAUS J, CEREAL CHEMISTRY. *Current Pos:* asst prof, 70-74, assoc prof, 74-78, PROF FOOD SCI & NUTRIT, COLO STATE UNIV, 78- *Personal Data:* b Berlin, Ger, June 22, 36; US citizen; m 60; c 3. *Educ:* Northwestern Univ, Ill, PhB, 68; Kans State Univ, MS, 69, PhD(food sci), 70. *Prof Exp:* Baking technologist, Am Inst Baking, 61-65; food technologist, Nat Dairy Prod Corp, 65-68. *Mem:* Am Asn Cereal Chem; Inst Food Technologists; Swiss Soc Food Sci & Technol. *Res:* Cereal chemistry and technology; carbohydrate chemistry. *Mailing Add:* Dept Food Sci Colo State Univ Ft Collins CO 80523-0001

LORENZ, OSCAR ANTHONY, VEGETABLE CROPS, PLANT NUTRITION. *Current Pos:* from instr to assoc prof, 41-55, vchmn dept, 55-64, chmn dept, 64-70, PROF VEG CROPS, COL AGR, UNIV CALIF, DAVIS, 55- *Personal Data:* b Colorado Springs, Colo, Dec 5, 14; m 47. *Educ:* Colo State Col, BS, 36; Cornell Univ, PhD(veg crops), 41. *Honors & Awards:* Vaughn Award, 42. *Prof Exp:* Asst hort, Colo State Col, 36-37; asst veg crops, Cornell Univ, 37-41. *Concurrent Pos:* Mem, Agr Comn to Bermuda, 39. *Mem:* Fel Am Soc Hort Sci; fel Am Soc Plant Physiol; fel Am Soc Agron; fel Am Potato Asn. *Res:* Mineral nutrition of vegetable crops; boron deficiency in table beets; soils and plant nutrient relationships; environmental factors affecting vegetable production. *Mailing Add:* 44163 Lakeview Dr El Macero CA 95618

LORENZ, PATRICIA ANN, INFORMATION SCIENCE, ANALYTICAL CHEMISTRY. *Current Pos:* info chemist, Exxon Res & Eng Co, 65-67 group head, Anal & Info Div, 78-83, sect head, Comput & Info Support Div, 83-87, res assoc, 87-92, sect head, info res analysis, 92-96, RES ASSOC CORP RES, INFO RES & ANALYSIS, EXXON RES & ENG CO, 96- *Personal Data:* b New York, NY, Jan 31, 38; m 62, Donald H; c Peter & Jeanne. *Educ:* Marymount Manhattan Col, BS, 59; Polytech Inst Brooklyn, PhD(anal chem), 65. *Prof Exp:* Consult info sci, 67-77. *Mem:* Am Chem Soc; Am Petrol Inst. *Res:* Mechanism of acid-base reactions in benzene. *Mailing Add:* Exxon Res & Eng Co Rte 22 E Annandale NJ 08801. *Fax:* 732-730-3516; *E-Mail:* paloren@erenj.com

LORENZ, PHILIP BOALT, PHYSICAL CHEMISTRY, PETROLEUM PRODUCTION. *Current Pos:* RETIRED. *Personal Data:* b Dayton, Ohio, Aug 14, 20; m 46, Irene McNeil; c Douglas, Eugene & David. *Educ:* Swarthmore Col, AB, 41; Harvard Univ, MA, 46, PhD(chem), 49. *Prof Exp:* Asst biol, Princeton Univ, 42-43; asst phys chem, SAM Labs, Columbia Univ, 44-45; phys chemist surface chem, Petrol Res Ctr, US Bur Mines, 49-71, res chemist, Petrol Prod & Environ Res, 71-75, res chemist, Bartlesville Energy Technol Ctr, US Dept Energy, 75-83; sci adv, Nat Inst Petrol & Energy Res, 83-85; consult, 85-93. *Mem:* Am Chem Soc; Soc Petrol Engrs. *Res:* Surface chemistry; electrochemistry; petroleum engineering. *Mailing Add:* 1541 Keeler Ave Bartlesville OK 74003-5723

LORENZ, PHILIP JACK, JR, ATMOSPHERIC PHYSICS. *Current Pos:* chmn dept, 66-74, assoc prof, 66-82, PROF PHYSICS, UNIV OF THE SOUTH, 82-, DIR OBSERV, 87- *Personal Data:* b Atlanta, Ga, Apr 15, 24; m 70; c 2. *Educ:* Oglethorpe Univ, BS, 49; Vanderbilt Univ, MS, 52. *Prof Exp:* Lab asst, Oglethorpe Univ, 48; qual control tech, Transparent Package Co, 50-51; asst prof physics, Lemoyne Col, 52-54, Ky Wesleyan Col, 54-56 & Upper Iowa Univ, 56-61; res assoc, Syracuse Univ, 63-65, vis instr, 65-66. *Concurrent Pos:* Lab asst, Vanderbilt Univ, 52; consult physicist, Empirical Explor Co, Ky, 56; univ fel, Syracuse Univ, 58-59, Nat Sci Found fac fel,

61-63; textbook consult, J B Lippincott Co, 71-72. *Mem:* Sigma Xi; Am Phys Soc; Am Asn Physics Teachers; Hist Sci Soc. *Res:* Atmospheric electricity in fair and foggy weather; geophysics of environmental radioactivity at sandstone sinkhole sites; history of medieval Persian and Arabic science; history of astronomy; designing laboratory experiments for premedical physics, optics and introductory astronomy; history of science in the post-bellum south. *Mailing Add:* Cordell-Lorenz Observatory Univ of the South Sewanee TN 37383

LORENZ, RALPH WILLIAM, forestry; deceased, see previous edition for last biography

LORENZ, ROMAN R, ORGANIC CHEMISTRY, MEDICINAL CHEMISTRY. *Current Pos:* Res org chemist, Sterling-Winthrop Res Inst, 62-69, sr res chemist & sect head, 69-74, sr res assoc & sect head, 74-76, dir chem develop, 77-90, EXEC DIR CHEM DEVELOP, STERLING RES GROUP, 90-; DIR, NIKOMET, 90- *Personal Data:* b Breslau, Ger, July 15, 35; US citizen; m 60, Dana Rebmann; c Peter, Robert & Stephen. *Educ:* Rensselaer Polytech Inst, BS, 58; Univ Mich, MS, 60, PhD(med chem), 62. *Mem:* Am Chem Soc. *Res:* Synthesis of organic and medicinal compounds. *Mailing Add:* 941 Evergreen Lane Chester Springs PA 19425

LORENZEN, COBY, ENGINEERING DESIGN, AGRICULTURAL MECHANIZATION. *Current Pos:* RETIRED. *Personal Data:* m 37, Ina; c Robert, Jacklyn, Donald & Kenneth. *Educ:* Univ Calif, BS, 29, MS, 34. *Honors & Awards:* Cyrus McCormick Gold Medal, Am Soc Agr Eng, 71. *Prof Exp:* Prof agr eng, Agr Eng Exp Sta, Univ Calif, 37-69. *Mem:* Am Soc Agr Engrs. *Res:* Developed mechanization for cutting apricots for drying; developed first commercially successful mechanical harvester for canning tomatoes. *Mailing Add:* 344 Country Club Dr Carmel Valley CA 93924

LORENZEN, HOWARD O(TTO), ELECTRONICS. *Current Pos:* RETIRED. *Personal Data:* b Atlantic, Iowa, June 24, 12; m 36; c 1. *Educ:* Iowa State Col, BSEE, 35. *Honors & Awards:* Dexter Conrad Award, 72; Space Pioneer Award, USN, 85. *Prof Exp:* Develop engr electronics, Colonial Radio Corp, 35-39 & Zenith Radio Corp, 39-40; head, Electronic Countermeasures Br, Naval Res Lab, 40-66, supt, Electronic Warfare Div, 66-70, supt, Space Systs Div, 70-73. *Concurrent Pos:* Tech adv, Chief Naval Opers Off, Off Secy Defense, Joint Chiefs Staff, dir, Naval Intel & dir, Naval Labs. *Mem:* Fel Inst Elec & Electronics Engrs. *Res:* Signal indication and analysis; direction finding; propagation; electronic countermeasures; satellite design; space data reduction. *Mailing Add:* 10905 176 Circle NE Redmond WA 98052

LORENZEN, JANICE R, ENDOCRINOLOGY. *Current Pos:* ENDOCRINOLOGIST, ENDOCRINE CLIN SE TEX, 97- *Personal Data:* b Chicago, Ill, May 29, 50. *Educ:* Valparaiso Univ, BS, 72; Albany Med Col, PhD(physiol), 76; Univ Ill, MD, 86. *Prof Exp:* Asst prof, Dept Biol Sci, Western Mich Univ, 81-82; physician, Rockford Clin, Col Med, Univ Ill, 86-97. *Mem:* Endocrine Soc; Am Col Physicians. *Mailing Add:* Endocrine Clin SE Tex 3070 Col Suite 403 Beaumont TX 77701

LORENZEN, JERRY ALAN, QUALITY IMPROVEMENT, APPLIED STATISTICS. *Current Pos:* DIR QUAL, FAIR-RITE PROD CORP, 96- *Personal Data:* b Grand Island, Nebr, Oct 3, 44; m 67, Barbara Callahan; c Jeffrey & Marc. *Educ:* Midland Lutheran Col, BS, 66; Okla State Univ, PhD(chem), 70. *Prof Exp:* Instr chem, Okla State Univ, 69-70; sr engr, IBM Corp, 70-92; prin, Lorenzen Consult, 92-96. *Mem:* Am Chem Soc; Am Soc Qual Control; Am Productivity & Inventory Control Soc; Am Statist Asn. *Res:* Environmental chemistry; quality improvement; engineering statistics; design of experiments. *Mailing Add:* 52 Spruce Valley Rd Stone Ridge NY 12484-9802

LORENZETTI, OLE JOHN, PHARMACOLOGY, BIOCHEMISTRY. *Current Pos:* scientist res & develop, Alcon Labs, Ft Worth, 69-72, mgr, Res & Develop Div, preclin sci, 72-75, assoc dir dermatol, 75-80, dir ophthal, 80-83, sr dir surg, 83-92, SR DIR THERAPEUT RES/LICENSING, ALCON LABS, FT WORTH, 92-, PRES THERAPEUT RES, 93- *Personal Data:* b Chicago, Ill, Oct 25, 36; m 61, Lorna Joyce Bailey; c Elizabeth A & Maria A & Darion. *Educ:* Univ Ill, Chicago, BS, 58; Ohio State Univ, MS, 63, PhD(pharmacol & toxicol), 65; Mass Inst Technol, MBA, 89. *Prof Exp:* Asst chief pharmacist, West Suburban Hosp, 58; instr pharm, Univ Ill, Chicago, 58-59; asst instr pharmacol, Ohio State Univ, 59-62; res fel, Ohio State Univ, Columbus, 64-65; scientist, Miles Lab, Elkhardt, Ind, 65-67; sr scientist, Dome Labs Div, Miles Labs, 67-69. *Concurrent Pos:* JJ Able lectr pharmacol, Ohio N Univ, 65, 69; Kaufman-Lattimer lectr, Ohio State Univ, 67, 70, 73, 78; toxicologist consult, South Bend, Ind, municipality, 67-69, Tarrant County Tex, 70-73; assoc prof pharmacol, Univ Tex Health Sci Ctr, Dallas, 70-90, clin prof dermatol, 74-80; adj prof, Tex Christian Univ, 72-82; vis lectr, therapeutic & drug res, Univ Ill, 73-80, Univ Tex Med Schs, 90-96. *Mem:* AAAS; Am Chem Soc; Soc Cosmetic Chem; Am Acad Clin Toxicol; Am Soc Pharmacol & Except Ther; Am Acad Ophthal; Am Intraocular Implant Soc; Am Pharmacol Asn; NY Acad Sci; Soc Investigative Dermatol; Am Col Toxicol; Inflamation Res Asn; Am Soc Clin Pharmacol; Asn Res & Vision & Opthal; Drug Info Asn; Sigma Xi. *Res:* Pharmacodynamics; evaluations of analgesic, anti-inflammatory agents and antiglaucoma agents; development of drug screening programs; autonomic and biochemical pharmacology; topical pharmacology and toxicology of eye and skin; ophthalmology; ophthalmic surgical devices; toxicology; immunology; drug metabolism; pharmacokinetics. *Mailing Add:* Alcon Labs Inc 6201 S Freeway Ft Worth TX 76134-2099. *Fax:* 817-551-4584; *E-Mail:* alconftw!rndvmail2!!lorenzetoj@alconatt.attmail.com

LORENZO, ANTONIO V, neuropharmacology, neurochemistry, for more information see previous edition

LORENZO, MICHAEL, ENGINEERING. *Current Pos:* FOUNDER & PRES, TECH PROTECTION ENG CO, 82- *Personal Data:* b Newton, NJ, 1920; m, Anastasia Hacket; c 5. *Educ:* Pa State Univ, BS, 47, George Washington Univ, MEA, 56. *Prof Exp:* Field instrumentation engr, Fischer & Porter Co, Pa, 47-52; Aerospace engr, Dept Defense, 52-65; staff, Westinghouse Elec Corp, 65-81, mgr air resources, Westinghouse Mgt Serv Inc, 66-70, dir environ qual control, 70-73; dep under-secy def, Washington, 81-82. *Res:* Patented stall surge sonic sensors; contributed articles to professional journals. *Mailing Add:* First Lady Realty Corp 3126 Shadeland Dr Falls Church VA 22044-1726

LORETZ, CHRISTOPHER ALAN, ENDOCRINOLOGY. *Current Pos:* asst prof, 81-87, ASSOC PROF, DEPT BIOL SCI, STATE UNIV NY BUFFALO, 87- *Personal Data:* b Santa Monica, Calif, Apr 28, 51. *Educ:* Univ Wash, BS, 72; Univ Calif, Los Angeles, MA, 74, PhD(comp physiol), 78. *Prof Exp:* Fel, Dept Zool & Cancer Res Lab, Univ Calif, Berkeley, 78-81. *Mem:* Am Soc Zoologists; NY Acad Sci; AAAS. *Res:* Osmoregulation in aquatic vertebrates; hormonal control of epithelial ion transport. *Mailing Add:* Dept Biol Sci State Univ NY Box 601300 Buffalo NY 14260-1300

LORETZ, THOMAS J, FIBEROPTIC IMAGING & COMMUNICATION, COMPUTER AIDED MANUFACTURING. *Current Pos:* PRES, COMPUT ENG SERV, 93- *Personal Data:* b Oceanside, NY, Mar 19, 51; m 83; c 2. *Educ:* State Univ NY, BS, 73, MS, 78. *Honors & Awards:* IR 100 Award, Res & Develop Mag, 80. *Prof Exp:* Proj engr glass res & develop, Schott Optical Glass, Duryea, Pa, 74-78; dir res & develop mat & electro-optics, Galileo Electro-Optics, Sturbridge Mass, 78-82; sr scientist fiberoptic med develop, Johnson & Johnson, Southbridge, Mass, 82-85; dir res & develop electro-optic glasses, Detector Technol, Brookfield, Mass, 85-93. *Concurrent Pos:* Consult & inventor, Buffalo Med Specialties, Fla, 76-90; prin investr, NASA, SBIR Progs Advan Space Telescopy, 85-; consult, NIH Spec Comt Fiberoptics Med, 86-87; secy bd, Bd Dirs, Charlton Credit Union, Mass, 90- *Mem:* Am Ceramic Soc; Nat Inst Ceramic Engrs; Soc Photog Instrumentation Engrs. *Res:* solid state, electron multiplication; glasses and geometries to enhance lifetime and characteristics of continuous dynode single channel and microchannel plate devices. *Mailing Add:* 33 Oak Ridge Dr Charlton MA 01507

LOREY, FRANK WILLIAM, PAPER CHEMISTRY. *Current Pos:* asst to gen mgr, 66-67, corp tech dir, 67-75, vpres res, 75-86, SR VPRES, GARDEN STATE PAPER CO, GARFIELD, 86- *Personal Data:* b Staten Island, NY, May 7, 29; m 51; c 3. *Educ:* State Univ New York Col Forestry, Syracuse, BS, 51, MS, 52. *Prof Exp:* Res engr, Mead Corp, Ohio, 52-54; assoc prof pulp & paper chem & pilot plant group leader, State Univ New York Col Forestry, Syracuse, 54-66. *Concurrent Pos:* Develop consult, AB Kamyr, Sweden, 65. *Mem:* Fel Tech Asn Pulp & Paper Indust; Int Asn Sci Papermakers. *Res:* Improved methods in pulping of wood and use of chemicals for influencing paper properties; development of processes and design of systems for deinking of waste papers. *Mailing Add:* 82 Dogwood Terr Ramsey NJ 07446

LORIA, EDWARD ALBERT, METALLURGY & PHYSICAL METALLURGICAL ENGINEERING. *Current Pos:* RETIRED. *Personal Data:* b Pittsburgh, Pa, Apr 29, 17; m 54, Helen Kerdys; c Elene, Diane & Corinne (Brody). *Educ:* Carnegie Inst Technol, BS, 44, MS, 46. *Honors & Awards:* Charles H Herty Award, Am Inst Mining & Metall Engrs, 67; Edgar C Bain Award, Am Soc Metals, 82, Andrew Carnegie Lectr, 84, William Hunt Eisenman Award, 91. *Prof Exp:* Asst metallurgist, Res Lab, Carnegie-Ill Steel Div, US Steel Corp, Pittsburgh, Pa, 44-46; fel, Mellon Inst Indust Res, Pittsburgh, Pa, 46-48, sr fel, 48-50; sr engr metall, Res & Eng Ctr, Carborundum Co, Niagara Falls, NY, 50-52; staff metall engr alloy & stainless steels, Cent Metall Dept, Crucible Steel Co Am, Pittsburgh, Pa, 53-59, prod metall engr titanium & superalloys, 57-59; mgr alloy & stainless steels & superalloys develop, Climax Molybdenum Co, Div Am Metal Climax, Inc, NY, 59-63; supv res metallurgist, Reno Metall Res Ctr, US Dept Interior, Bur Mines, 63-64; supvr mat & processes, Res & Develop Eng Div, Nat Steel Corp, Weirton, WVa, 64-75; tech dir, Roll Mfrs Inst, Pittsburgh, Pa, 75-77; div prod metallurgist, Universal-Cyclops Specialty Steel Div, Cyclops Corp, Pittsburgh, Pa, 77-84, consult, 84-86; consult, Niobium Prod Co, Subsid CBMM, Pittsburgh, Pa, 84-92. *Concurrent Pos:* Mem, Advan Res Medal Comt, Am Soc Metals, 75-77, Subcomt Roll Res, Asn Iron & Steel Engrs-RMI, 75-77 & Comt Gen Res, Am Iron & Steel Inst, 81-84. *Mem:* Minerals, Metals & Mat Soc; fel Am Soc Metals. *Res:* Practical application of metallurgy for an unusually wide range of metals and alloys and transferred significant research results into commercial practice; author of over 150 publications. *Mailing Add:* 1828 Taper Dr Pittsburgh PA 15241

LORIA, ROGER MOSHE, VIROLOGY, IMMUNOLOGY. *Current Pos:* from asst prof to assoc prof, 74-91, PROF MICROBIOL & PATH, MED COL VA, 91- *Personal Data:* b Antwerp, Belg, Apr 19, 40; US citizen; m 78; c 3. *Educ:* Bar-Ilan Univ, Israel, BS, 65; State Univ NY, Buffalo, MS, 68; Boston Univ, PhD(microvirol), 72. *Prof Exp:* Asst prof biochem, Mass Col Optom, 69-70; asst virol, Sch Med, Boston Univ, 68-72, instr microbiol, 72-74. *Concurrent Pos:* Mass Heart Asn fel, 72-74; res assoc, Sch Med, Boston Univ, 74; NIH res grants, Arthritis & Metab Dis, 74, 78 & 79, Heart & Lung Div, 75; young investr develop award, Am Diabetes Asn, 75-77; asst prof acad path, Sch Med, Harvard Univ, 80-82; instr pediat, Childrens Hosp, Boston, Mass, 80-81; adv, Consol Labs Commonwealth Va, 82-86; pres, Va Commonwealth Chap, Am Asn Univ Prof, 89, pres, 90. *Mem:* Am Soc Microbiol; AAAS; Am Fedn Clin Res; Reticuloendothelial Syst Soc; Am Diabetes Asn; Am Soc Virol; Am Asn Univ Professors; Int Soc for Anti-viral Res; Am Inst Nutrit; Am Soc Clin Nutrit; fel Am Acad Biol. *Res:* Investigation on the role of group B coxsackieviruses in diabetes, atherosclerosis and cardiovascular disease in experimental animal models;

general aspects of host-virus interaction; viral infection by the oral route; nutritional hypercholesteremia; effects on host resistance; rapid viral diagnosis; immune-up regulations; publication of 51 manuscripts and 64 abstracts, 2 US patents; pathogenic and immunological responses following virus infections; hormonal regulation of immune response to protect against infections, lethal infection by viruses or bacteria; viruses in diabetes; nutrition and lipids in infection. *Mailing Add:* Dept Microbiol & Immunol Med Col Va Box 678 MCV Sta Richmond VA 23298-0678

LORIAUX, D LYNN, growth & development, for more information see previous edition

LORIMER, GEORGE HUNTLY, CARBON METABOLISM, ENZYMOLOGY. *Current Pos:* RES LEADER, CENT RES & DEVELOP DEPT, EI DU PONT DE NEMOURS & CO, 78- *Personal Data:* b Eng, Oct 14, 42; m 70; c 2. *Educ:* Mich State Univ, PhD(biochem), 72. *Mem:* Nat Acad Sci; Am Soc Biol Chemists; Royal Soc. *Mailing Add:* E I du Pont de Nemours & Co Exp Sta E402 Cent Res & Develop Wilmington DE 19880-0402

LORIMER, JOHN WILLIAM, PHYSICAL CHEMISTRY. *Current Pos:* from asst prof to prof, 61-94, EMER PROF PHYS CHEM, UNIV WESTERN ONT, 94- *Personal Data:* b Oshawa, Ont, Apr 16, 29; m 54, Shirley E; c Charles CJ (deceased), Ian AJ & Nancy E. *Educ:* Univ Toronto, BA, 51, MA, 52, PhD(phys chem), 54. *Prof Exp:* Asst phys chem, Univ Leiden, Netherlands, 54-56; asst res officer, Atlantic Regional Lab, Nat Res Coun Can, 56-61, assoc res officer, 61. *Concurrent Pos:* Vis prof, Univ Southampton, 70-71, Murdoch Univ, Perth, Australia, 83 & Glasgow Univ, 83-84; mem, Comn V-8, Int Union Pure & Appl Chem, 79-, chmn, 87-91, mem bur, 94- *Mem:* Fel Chem Inst Can; Electrochem Soc. *Res:* Thermodynamics of liquids; transport in membranes; irreversible thermodynamics; electrochemistry. *Mailing Add:* Dept Chem Univ Western Ont London ON N6A 5B7 Can. *E-Mail:* lorimer@julian.uwo.ca

LORIMER, NANCY L, INSECT GENETICS. *Current Pos:* PROG COORDR, EASTERN FOREST HILLS. *Personal Data:* b Mishawaka, Ind, Feb 8, 47; m 72; c 3. *Educ:* Ind Univ, AB, 69; Univ Notre Dame, PhD(biol), 75. *Prof Exp:* Fel genetic control, Int Centre Insect Ecol & Physiol, 74-75; res entomologist, NCent Forest Exp Sta, Forest Serv, USDA, 75-; adj asst prof, Dept Entom, Fish Wildlife, Univ Minn, 79-92; staff entom, USDA FPM, 92- *Concurrent Pos:* Consult, WHO, 73; assoc ed, Am Midland Nat, 80- *Mem:* Entom Soc Am; Asn Women Sci; AAAS; Genetics Soc Am; Sigma Xi. *Res:* Assessment of genetic variation in forest insect populations and how these variations interact with other factors to influence population dynamics. *Mailing Add:* 1992 Folwell Ave St Paul MN 55108

LORINCZ, ALLAN LEVENTE, DERMATOLOGY. *Current Pos:* Res fel dermat, Cancer Clin, 50-51, from instr to assoc prof, 51-67, PROF DERMAT, UNIV CHICAGO, 67- *Personal Data:* b Chicago, Ill, Oct 31, 24; m 52, Lillian Tatter; c 3. *Educ:* Univ Chicago, SB, 45, MD, 47. *Concurrent Pos:* Mem dermat training grants comt, USPHS, 61-64; mem comt cutaneous syst, Div Med Sci, Nat Res Coun, 62-65; nat consult to Surgeon Gen, USAF, 62-; mem dermat adv comt, Food & Drug Admin, 71-72. *Mem:* Soc Invest Dermat; Soc Exp Biol & Med; Am Soc Dermatopath; Am Dermat Asn; Am Fedn Clin Res; Sigma Xi. *Res:* Psoriasis; cutaneous fungus infections; biochemistry and physiology of the skin, especially melanin chemistry and sebaceous gland control by endocrine factors; immunology. *Mailing Add:* 9905 S Kilbourn Ave Oak Lawn IL 60453-3539

LORINCZ, ANDREW ENDRE, PEDIATRICS, BIOCHEMISTRY. *Current Pos:* assoc prof biochem & dir Child Develop & Learning Disorders, Med Ctr, 68-80, PROF PEDIAT, MED CTR, UNIV ALA, BIRMINGHAM, 68-, PROF, SCH PUB HEALTH, 84- *Personal Data:* b Chicago, Ill, May 17, 26; m 65, Diane D. *Educ:* Univ Chicago, PhB, 48, BS, 50, MD, 52. *Prof Exp:* From intern to jr asst resident pediat, Univ Chicago Clin, 52-54, jr asst resident fel, Rosenthal Clin, 54-55, instr, Sch Med, 56-59; from asst prof to assoc prof, Sch Med, Univ Fla, 59-68. *Concurrent Pos:* Res fel, Univ Chicago, 54-55 & Arthritis & Rheumatism Found res fel, 55-58; instr, La Rabida Inst, 57-59; sci adv comt, Nat Tay-Sachs & Allied Dis Asn, 79-; mem, Nat Coalition on Prev Mental Retardation, 85- *Mem:* Am Chem Soc; Soc Pediat Res; fel Am Acad Pediat; Soc Invest Dermat; fel Am Acad Cerebral Palsy & Develop Med; Asn Clin Scientists. *Res:* Heritable disorders of connective tissue acid mucopolysaccharides; inborn errors of metabolism; mental retardation; biophysical cytochemistry; fluorescence microscopy. *Mailing Add:* Univ Ala Birmingham Univ Sta MJH Birmingham AL 35294-2010

LORING, ARTHUR PAUL, GEOLOGY, ENVIRONMENTAL GEOLOGY. *Current Pos:* from asst prof to assoc prof, 67-95, COORDR GEOL, YORK COL, NY, 73-, PROF, 95- *Personal Data:* b New York, NY, May 22, 36; m 63, Carol Lofterer; c Wendy (Slater), Karen S (Gemery) & David P. *Educ:* Columbia Univ, AB, 58; Pa State Univ, MS, 61; NY Univ, PhD(geol), 66. *Prof Exp:* Lectr geol, Brooklyn Col, 62-65; instr, 66-67; asst prof, Upsala Col, 67. *Concurrent Pos:* Consult geol & environ, Rock Soil Water Int, Inc, 85-92. *Mem:* Fel Geol Soc Am; Asn Eng Geol; Sigma Xi. *Res:* General geologic field mapping in areas of folded and faulted sediments; environmental geology & ground water hydrology. *Mailing Add:* Dept Geol York Col Jamaica NY 11451

LORING, BLAKE M(ARSHALL), physical metallurgy, for more information see previous edition

LORING, DAVID WILLIAM, NEUROPSYCHOLOGY. *Current Pos:* asst prof, 85-89, ASSOC PROF, DEPT NEUROL, MED COL GA, 89- *Personal Data:* b Richmond, Ind, July 13, 56; m 88; c 1. *Educ:* Wittenberg Univ, BA, 78; Univ Houston, MA, 80, PhD(clin neuropsychol), 82. *Prof Exp:* Fel, Baylor Col Med, 82-83; res assoc, Univ Tex Med Br, 83-84, instr, 84-85. *Mem:* AAAS; NY Acad Sci; Int Neuropsychol Soc; Am Psychol Asn; Soc Psychol Res; Soc Philos & Psychol. *Res:* Electrophysiological measures of human hippocampus; neurochemical manipulation of human hippocampal responses; memory function in patients with mesial temporal lobe damage. *Mailing Add:* Med Col Ga Sch Med 1120 15th St Augusta GA 30912-1003

LORING, DOUGLAS HOWARD, MARINE GEOCHEMISTRY. *Current Pos:* RES SCIENTIST, BEDFORD INST, 60- *Personal Data:* b Concord, NH, July 25, 34; Can citizen; m 61; c 3. *Educ:* Acadia Univ, BSc, 54, MSc, 56; Univ Manchester, PhD(geochem), 60. *Prof Exp:* Tech officer, Geol Surv Can, 54-55; res fel geochem, Univ Manchester, 57-60. *Concurrent Pos:* Spec lectr, Dalhousie Univ, 62-68. *Mem:* Mineral Asn Can; fel Geol Asn Can; Geochem Soc. *Res:* Geochemistry of ancient and modern marine sediments; development of analytical methods for the determination of trace metals in sediments and SPM. *Mailing Add:* Atlantic Oceanog Lab Bedford Inst Box 1006 Dartmouth NS B2Y 4A2 Can

LORING, ROGER FREDERIC, NONEQUILIBRIUM STATISTICAL MECHANICS, THEORY OF MOLECULAR SPECTROSCOPY. *Current Pos:* asst prof, 87-93, ASSOC PROF CHEM, CORNELL UNIV, 93- *Personal Data:* b Berkeley, Calif, Sept 14, 58; m 90. *Educ:* Univ Calif, Davis, BS, 80; Stanford Univ, PhD(phys chem), 84. *Prof Exp:* Res assoc chem, Univ Rochester, 84-87. *Concurrent Pos:* Fel Alfred P Sloan Found. *Res:* Dynamics of molecular electronic and vibrational excited states in condensed phases; solvation effects in electronic spectroscopy; theory of nonlinear spectroscopy; structure and dynamics of polymer fluids. *Mailing Add:* Baker Lab Dept Chem Cornell Univ Ithaca NY 14853-0001

LORING, STEPHEN H, PHYSIOLOGY. *Current Pos:* asst prof, 74-85, ASSOC PROF PHYSIOL, DEPT ENVIRON HEALTH, HARVARD SCH PUB HEALTH, 85- *Personal Data:* b Boston, Mass, July 9, 46. *Educ:* Amherst Col, BS, 68; Dartmouth Med Sch, BMS, 70; Harvard Med Sch, MD, 73. *Prof Exp:* Intern med, Univ Hosp, Boston, 73-74. *Mem:* Am Phys Soc; Am Thoracic Soc. *Mailing Add:* Dept Anesthesia Beth Israel Hosp 330 Brookline Ave DA-717 Boston MA 02115-6021. *Fax:* 617-432-3468

LORING, WILLIAM BACHELLER, ECONOMIC GEOLOGY. *Current Pos:* RETIRED. *Personal Data:* b Haileybury, Ont, Mar 4, 15; m 45; c 2. *Educ:* Mich Col Min, BS, 40; Univ Ariz, MS, 47, PhD, 59. *Prof Exp:* Field geologist, Noranda Mines Co, Can, 41-42; inspector, US Dept Eng, 42-43; field engr, US Bur Mines, Mich, 43-44; party chief, Nfld Geol Surv, 44; party chief, Mining Geophys Co, Can, 44-45; mine mgr, Discovery Yellowknife Gold Mine, 46; geologist, Great Northern Explor Co, Ariz, 46-48; geologist, Eagle-Picher Mining & Smelting Co, 49-55; chief geologist, Big Indian Dist, Hidden Splendor Mining Co, 55-62; staff geologist, Atlas Minerals, 62-66; mine geologist, US Smelting, Ref & Mining Co, NMex, 66-67; dist geologist, Cities Serv Minerals Corp, Wyo, 67-71, staff geologist, 71-78; consult, 78-82. *Mem:* Am Inst Mining, Metall & Petrol Eng; Soc Econ Geol; Can Inst Mining & Metall; Int Asn Genesis Ore Deposits. *Res:* Ore deposits, especially controlling structures and surface indications. *Mailing Add:* 611 E Bingham Lane Benson AZ 85602

LORIO, PETER LEONCE, JR, FOREST SOILS, TREE PHYSIOLOGY. *Current Pos:* soil scientist, 62-68, prin soil scientist, 68-76, SUPVRY SOIL SCIENTIST, FOREST INSECT RES PROJ, SOUTHERN FOREST EXP STA, US FOREST SERV, 76- *Personal Data:* b New Orleans, La, Apr 10, 27; m 57; c 6. *Educ:* La State Univ, BS, 53; Duke Univ, MF, 54; Iowa State Univ, PhD(forestry-soils), 62. *Honors & Awards:* Superior Serv Award, USDA, 84. *Prof Exp:* Soil scientist, Stand Fruit & Steamship Co, 54-58, chief soil scientist, 58-59. *Mem:* Am Soc Agron; Int Soc Trop Foresters; Sigma Xi; Soil Sci Soc Am; Int Soc Soil Sci; Soc Am Foresters. *Res:* Soil, tree, and stand factors affecting pine susceptibility to bark beetles; tree physiology; soil water; tree rooting; stand composition, age, density. *Mailing Add:* US Dept Agr Southern Forest Exp Sta 2500 Shreveport Hwy Pineville LA 71360

LOROS, JENNIFER JANE, CIRCADIAN CLOCK BIOLOGY, CLASSICAL & MOLECULAR GENETICS OF FUNGAL DEVELOPMENT. *Current Pos:* Res assoc, Dartmouth Med Sch, 84-88, res asst prof, 88-94, res assoc prof, 94-96, ASSOC PROF BIOCHEM, DARTMOUTH MED SCH, 96- *Personal Data:* b San Mateo, Calif, Apr 15, 50; m 84, Jay Clark Dunlap; c Marjorie E & Hayes M. *Educ:* Univ Calif, Santa Cruz, BA, 79, PhD(biol), 84. *Concurrent Pos:* Prin investr, NSF, 88-; ad hoc reviewer, NSF, 90-93, NIMH, 94; sci prog reviewer, USAF Off Sci Res, 92-93; mem, Neurospora Policy Comt, 93-97; assoc ed, Genetics. *Mem:* Genetics Soc Am; Soc Res Biol Rhythms; AAAS; Am Phys Soc. *Res:* Isolation and dissection of genes involved in photo-entrainment of the clock and genes under control of the biological clock in order to understand how the circadian clock is reset by light information; how the clock transfers temporal information out into the cell organism to control metabolism and development. *Mailing Add:* Dept Biochem Dartmouth Med Sch Hanover NH 03755. *Fax:* 603-650-1128; *E-Mail:* jennifer.lorus@dartmouth.edu

LORRAIN, PAUL, MAGNETOHYDRODYNAMICS OF NATURAL PHENOMENA. *Current Pos:* VIS PROF EARTH & PLANETARY SCI, MCGILL UNIV, 83- *Personal Data:* b Montreal, Que, Sept 8, 16; m 44, Dorothee Sainte-Marie; c Francois, Denis, Claire & Louis. *Educ:* Univ

Ottawa, BA, 37; McGill Univ, BSc, 40, MSc, 41, PhD(physics), 47. *Prof Exp:* Lectr physics, Sir George Williams Col, 42-43, Univ Laval, 43-46 & Inst Physics, Univ Montreal, 46; res assoc, Lab Nuclear Studies, Cornell Univ, 47-49; prof physics, Univ Montreal, 49-82, head dept, 57-66. *Concurrent Pos:* Mem, Nat Res Coun, 60-66; vis prof fac sci, Univ Grenoble, France, 61-62 & Univ Madrid, 68-69; vis fel, Oxford Univ, 81; vis prof, six Chinese univs, 85, Univ Murcia, 86-88; visitor, Inst Physics, Globe Paris, 89 & 90, Institut d'Astrophysiquve de Paris, 91-96. *Mem:* Royal Soc Can; Am Phys Soc; Can Asn Physicists (pres, 64-65). *Res:* Magnetohydrodynamics of natural phenomena. *Mailing Add:* Dept Earth Sci McGill Univ 3450 University Montreal PQ H3A 2A7 Can. *Fax:* 514-398-4680; *E-Mail:* paul_l@geosci.lan.mcgill.ca

LORSCH, HAROLD G, AIR CONDITIONING. *Current Pos:* RES PROF, DREXEL UNIV, 92- *Personal Data:* b Frankfurt, Ger, Aug 25, 19. *Educ:* Mass Inst Technol, SM 42, Columbia Univ, PhD(applied mech), 53. *Prof Exp:* Instr, Civil Eng, NY Univ, 48-50; asst prof, City Col New York, 50-57; head, stress anal, Curtiss-Wright Corp, 57-60; mgr, aerospace, Gen Elec Co, 60-70; res assoc, solar energy, Univ Pa, 71-73; mgr energy, Franklin Res Ctr, 74-83; lectr Mech eng, Drexel Univ, 83-92. *Mem:* Am Soc Heating, Refrigerating & Air Conditioning Engrs; Int Solar Energy Soc; Am Solar Energy Soc; Am Soc Civil Eng. *Res:* Primary research in area of energy, energy conservation in buildings through improved insulation and the use of renewable energy sources. *Mailing Add:* Dept Mech Eng Mech Drexel Univ 32 & Chestnut St Philadelphia PA 19104

LORSCHEIDER, FRITZ LOUIS, MEDICAL PHYSIOLOGY, ENDOCRINOLOGY. *Current Pos:* from asst prof to assoc prof, 70-80, PROF MED PHYSIOL, FAC MED, UNIV CALGARY, 80- *Personal Data:* b Rochester, NY, Aug 27, 39; m 67; c 4. *Educ:* Univ Wis, BS, 63; Mich State Univ, MS, 67, PhD(physiol, endocrinol), 70. *Prof Exp:* Res asst endocrinol, Radioisotope Unit, Med Col Wis, 63-64. *Concurrent Pos:* NIH fel, Mich State Univ, 70. *Mem:* Am Physiol Soc; Am Soc Biochem & Molecular Biol; Can Physiol Soc; Can Soc Clin Invest; AAAS; NY Acad Sci. *Res:* Reproductive and fetal physiology; chemistry and physiology of onco-fetal proteins; fetal macroglobulin and steroid metabolism; mercury released from dental amalgam fillings. *Mailing Add:* Dept Physiol & Biophys Univ Calgary Fac Med Calgary AB T2N 4N1 Can. *Fax:* 403-283-4740

LORTON, STEVEN PAUL, REPRODUCTIVE PHYSIOLOGY. *Current Pos:* VPRES SCI PROG & TECH SERV, MINITUBE INT INC, VERONA WIS, 94- *Personal Data:* b Brookline, Mass, Oct 9, 50; m 79, Lynn Conder. *Educ:* Clark Univ, BA, 72; Univ Wis-Madison, MS, 75, PhD(endocrinol & reproductive physiol), 78. *Prof Exp:* Res assoc, Animal Sci Dept, Cornell Univ, 78-80; res assoc, Am Breeders Serv, 80-84, res scientist, 84-89, mgr biol res, 89-93, mgr physiol & animal prod res, 93-94. *Concurrent Pos:* Adj assoc prof, Dept Meat & Animal Sci, Univ Wis-Madison, 84- *Mem:* Soc Study Reproduction; Sigma Xi; Int Embryo Transfer Soc; Am Soc Androl. *Res:* Physiology and cryopreservation of spermatozoa for use in artifical insemination, with emphasis on the domestic species; development of improved techniques of cryopreservation and characteristics of semen quality versus fertility. *Mailing Add:* 913 Sauk Ridge Trail Madison WI 53717. *E-Mail:* splorton@facstaff.wisc.edu

LORY, HENRY JAMES, ELECTRICAL ENGINEERING. *Current Pos:* MEM TECH STAFF, BELL TEL LABS, 63- *Personal Data:* b Baltimore, Md, Mar 3, 36; m 60; c 3. *Educ:* Johns Hopkins Univ, BES, 58, PhD(elec eng), 63. *Prof Exp:* Asst, Air Res & Develop Command Contract Proj, Johns Hopkins Univ, 57-58, mem res staff, Radiation Lab, 61-63. *Mem:* Sigma Xi. *Res:* Development of Schottky barrier devices, especially analysis of high temperature failure mechanisms; design of linear integrated circuits. *Mailing Add:* 3221 Stoudts Ferry Bridge Rd Reading PA 19605-1430

LOS, MARINUS, CHEMISTRY, HERBICIDES & SCREENING FOR HERBICIDES. *Current Pos:* RETIRED. *Personal Data:* b Ridderkerk, Neth, Sept 18, 33; m 57, Lorraine B Lowe; c Simon, Sija & Michael. *Educ:* Univ Edinburgh, BSc, 55, PhD(chem), 57. *Honors & Awards:* Nat Medal Technol, 93; Perkin Medal, 94; Achievement Award, Indust Res Inst, 94; Award for Creative Invention, Am Chem Soc, 95. *Prof Exp:* Res fel, Nat Res Coun Can, 58-60; res chemist, Am Cynamid Co, 60-71, group leader organic synthesis, 71-84, Herbicide Discovery, 84-86, mgr, Crop Protection Chem Discovery, 86-88, assoc dir, Crop Sci, 88-92, res dir, 92-96. *Concurrent Pos:* Sr res fel, Dept Pharmacol, Univ Edinburgh, 69-70. *Mem:* Am Chem Soc; Plant Growth Regulator Soc Am; AAAS. *Res:* Aliphatic and aromatic chemistry, especially nitrogen heterocycles; natural products, especially alkaloids and terpenes; screening for mode of action of and field testing of herbicides; synthesis of herbicides. *Mailing Add:* 107 Drummond Dr Pennington NJ 08534. *E-Mail:* losmar@aol.com

LOSCALZO, ANNE GRACE, MICROCHEMISTRY, ANALYTICAL CHEMISTRY. *Current Pos:* RETIRED. *Personal Data:* b New York, NY, Sept 2, 17; m 40; c 1. *Educ:* NY Univ, BA, 37, MS, 41, PhD(chem), 43. *Prof Exp:* Asst instr chem, Wash Square Col, NY Univ, 41-43, instr, 43-46; lectr, City Col New York, 53-58; from asst prof to assoc prof, Long Island Univ, 58-71, prof chem, 71. *Mem:* Am Chem Soc. *Res:* Educational projects to improve learning abilities of students in chemistry. *Mailing Add:* 3078 38th St Apt 4A Long Island City NY 11103

LOSCALZO, JOSEPH, THROMBOSIS, ATHEROSCLEROSIS. *Current Pos:* distinguished prof, 93-96, PROF BIOCHEM, BOSTON UNIV, 93-, WADE PROF MED, 97-, DIR, WHITAKER CARDIOVASC INST, 93- *Personal Data:* b Camden, NJ, Oct 26, 51; m 74, Anita Sendrow; c Julia & Alexander. *Educ:* Univ Pa, AB, 72, PhD(biochem), 77, MD, 77. *Honors & Awards:* Clin Scientist Award, Am Heart Asn, 83. *Prof Exp:* Res fel biochem, Univ Pa, 78; clin fel med, Harvard Univ, 78-81, clin fel cardiol, 81-83, instr med, 83-85, from asst prof to assoc prof med, 85-93. *Concurrent Pos:* Resident physician, Brigham & Women's Hosp, 78-81, chief resident physician, 83-84, assoc physician, 83- & dir, Ctr Res Thrombolysis, 87-; res fel med, Harvard Univ, 81-83; Sandoz med scholar, 84-90; consult, Cardiol Dept, Children's Hosp, Boston, 87-; chief, Cardiol Sect, Va Med Ctr, W Roxbury, 87-; prin investr, NIH grants & Nat Heart, Lung, Blood Inst grants, 88-93; asst ed, J Vascular Med & Biol; Glaxo cardiovasc res award, 89-94; dir, Nat Heart Lung & Blood Inst Spec Ctr Res, Boston Univ, 95-; assoc ed, NEng J Med, 95- *Mem:* Fel Am Col Cardiol; fel Am Col Physicians; AAAS; Am Heart Asn; Biophys Soc; Am Soc Biol Chemists; Am Soc Hemat; Am Soc Clin Invest. *Res:* The relationship of thrombosis to cardiovascular disease; the role of platelets and the fibrinolytic system in thrombotic events; the interactions between thrombosis and otherosclerosis; role of nitric oxide in the cardiovascular system. *Mailing Add:* Dept Med Boston Univ Boston MA 02118

LOSCHER, ROBERT A, COMPUTERIZED MANAGEMENT OF INFORMATION, COMPUTER NETWORKING. *Current Pos:* RETIRED. *Personal Data:* b Philadelphia, Pa, May 2, 30. *Educ:* Univ Pa, BS, 58, MS, 60. *Prof Exp:* Asst prof chem eng, Univ Pa, 59-60; res & develop engr, Selas Corp Am, 60-63 & Dupont Co, Chambers Works, 63-71; dir data processing, Glassboro State Col, 71-75, dir MIS, 75-87, dir telecommun, 87-92. *Concurrent Pos:* Adj prof, Glassboro State Col & Del Co Community Col. *Mem:* Am Inst Chem Engrs; AAAS; Asn Comput Mach; NY Acad Sci. *Res:* Computerization of gas chromatography and IR spectrometry; computer control of chemical manufacturing plants; digital process control; combustion control of lehrs and furnaces; computerization of information management; conversion from batch computer shops to on-line multi-station telecommunication systems. *Mailing Add:* 2607 SW 41st St Cape Coral FL 33914-5421

LOSCHIAVO, SAMUEL RALPH, INSECT PHYSIOLOGY, NUTRITION. *Current Pos:* RETIRED. *Personal Data:* b Transcona, Man, June 28, 24; m 50, Hilda Pankhurst; c Larry (deceased) & Ken. *Educ:* Univ Man, BSc, 46, MSc, 50, PhD, 64. *Prof Exp:* Chemist, Man Sugar Co, 48; res scientist, Can Dept Agr, 49-87. *Concurrent Pos:* Hon prof, Univ Man; res assoc, Univ Wisc, 61; vis prof, Univ Hawaii, 76. *Mem:* Fel Entom Soc Can; hon mem Entom Soc Can. *Res:* Biology, behavior and control of insects associated with stored grain and milled cereal products; Canadian and US patents. *Mailing Add:* 112 Linacre Rd Winnipeg MB R3T 3G6 Can

LOSECCO, JOHN M, WEAK INTERACTIONS, COLLIDER PHYSICS. *Current Pos:* PROF PHYSICS, UNIV NOTRE DAME DU LAC, 85- *Personal Data:* b New York, NY, Oct 21, 50; m 86, Lynne Sterkin; c Anna & Daniel. *Educ:* Cooper Union, BS, 72; Harvard, AM, 73, PhD(physics), 76. *Honors & Awards:* Bruno Rossi Prize, Am Astron Soc, 89. *Prof Exp:* Res assoc physics, Harvard Univ, 76-79; asst res scientist physics, Univ Mich, 79-81; asst prof physics, Calif Inst Technol, 81-85. *Concurrent Pos:* Outstanding jr investr, Dept Energy, 82-85. *Mem:* Am Phys Soc. *Res:* Studying extensions to the standard model of elementary particle; applications of particle physics to astrophysics and cosmology. *Mailing Add:* Physics Dept Univ Notre Dame Notre Dame IN 46556. *Fax:* 219-631-5952; *E-Mail:* losecco@nd.edu

LOSEE, DAVID LAWRENCE, SOLID STATE PHYSICS, SEMICONDUCTORS. *Current Pos:* RES ASSOC, EASTMAN KODAK CO, 67- *Personal Data:* b Mineola, NY, July 19, 39; m 63; c 2. *Educ:* Cornell Univ, BEng, 62, MS, 63; Univ Ill, PhD(solid state physics), 67. *Mem:* Am Phys Soc; Electrochem Soc; Sigma Xi. *Res:* Physics of the noble gas solids; physics of semiconductors and semiconductor devices. *Mailing Add:* 100 W Church St Fairport NY 14450

LOSEE, FERRIL A, ELECTRICAL ENGINEERING. *Current Pos:* RETIRED. *Personal Data:* b Lehi, Utah, June 5, 28; m 53; c 9. *Educ:* Univ Utah, BSEE, 53; Univ Southern Calif, MSEE, 57. *Prof Exp:* Elec engr, Hughes Aircraft Co, 53-59 & Aeronutronic Div, Philco Corp, 59-65; prof elec eng & chmn dept, Brigham Young Univ, 65-83; engr, SRS Technologies, 84-89; engr, EG&G SP, 89-93. *Res:* Communication; electronic countermeasures; systems engineering; radar engineering. *Mailing Add:* 3145 Bannock Dr Provo UT 84604

LOSEKAMP, BERNARD FRANCIS, POLYMER & ORGANIC CHEMISTRY, INFORMATION SCIENCE. *Current Pos:* from asst ed to assoc ed, Chem Abstr Serv, 64-69, sr indexer, 69-71, group leader, 71-72, SR ED, CHEM ABSTR SERV, COLUMBUS, OHIO, 72- *Personal Data:* b Cincinnati, Ohio, July 16, 36; wid; c 4. *Educ:* Xavier Univ, Ohio, BS, 58, MS, 61; Univ Akron, PhD(polymer chem), 66. *Hon Degrees:* LLD, Univ Akron, 90. *Prof Exp:* Res asst, Wm S Merrell Co, Ohio, 61; res chemist, Inst Polymer Sci, Univ Akron, 61-64. *Mem:* Am Chem Soc. *Res:* Acenaphthene arsenicals; synthesis and characterization of polymers; polymer nomenclature; thermal polymerization; information science. *Mailing Add:* 2011 Chelsea Rd Columbus OH 43212-1945

LOSEY, GEORGE SPAHR, JR, MARINE ZOOLOGY, ETHOLOGY. *Current Pos:* from asst prof to assoc prof zool, Univ Hawaii, 70-80, assoc dir, 80-90, chair, 90-93, PROF ZOOL, HAWAII INST MARINE BIOL, UNIV HAWAII, 80- *Personal Data:* b Louisville, Ky, June 30, 42; m 67; c 2. *Educ:* Univ Miami, BS, 64; Scripps Inst Oceanog, Univ Calif, PhD(marine biol), 68. *Honors & Awards:* Stoye Award, Am Soc Ichthyol & Herpet, 67. *Prof Exp:* NIH res fel fish behav, Hawaii Inst Marine Biol, 68-70. *Concurrent Pos:* Res fel, Univ Calif, Berkeley, 78; vis researcher, Univ Leiden, 87-88. *Mem:* Fel Animal Behav Soc; Am Soc Ichthyol & Herpet. *Res:* Ethology and ecology of fish; symbiotic cleaner fish; behavioral ecology of herbivorous fish; development of aggression; computerized data acquisition; learning and modification of species-typical behavior; ultraviolet coloration in fishes. *Mailing Add:* Dept Zool Univ Hawaii 2500 Campus Rd Honolulu HI 96822. *Fax:* 808-956-9812; *E-Mail:* losey@hawaii.edu

LOSEY, GERALD OTIS, ALGEBRA. *Current Pos:* RETIRED. *Personal Data:* b Detroit, Mich, Nov 13, 30; m 63. *Educ:* Univ Mich, BS, 52, MS, 53, PhD(math), 58. *Prof Exp:* Res instr math, Princeton Univ, 57-58; instr, Univ Wis, 58-61, asst prof, 61-64; from assoc prof to prof math, Univ Man, 64-84, prof comput sci, 84- *Mem:* Asn Comput Mach. *Res:* Group theory; ring theory. *Mailing Add:* 50 Sandra Bay Winnipeg MB R3T 0K1 Can

LOSICK, RICHARD MARC, MOLECULAR BIOLOGY. *Current Pos:* Harvard Soc fels jr fel biochem, Harvard Univ, 68-71, asst prof, 71-74, assoc prof, 74-77, PROF BIOL, HARVARD UNIV, 77- *Personal Data:* b Jersey City, NJ, July 27, 43; m 70. *Educ:* Princeton Univ, AB, 65; Mass Inst Technol, PhD(biochem), 69. *Honors & Awards:* Camille & Henry Dreyfus Award, Camille & Henry Dreyfus Found, 73. *Mem:* Nat Acad Sci; Am Soc Microbiol; Am Soc Biol Chemists. *Res:* Bacterial sporulation; regulatory subunits of RNA polymers. *Mailing Add:* Molecular & Cellular Biol Labs Harvard Univ Cambridge MA 02138

LOSIN, EDWARD THOMAS, PHYSICAL ORGANIC CHEMISTRY, ENERGY CONVERSION. *Current Pos:* CHEM CONSULT, 88- *Personal Data:* b Racine, Wis, July 9, 23; m 50; c 2. *Educ:* Univ Ill, BS, 48; Columbia Univ, AM, 50, PhD(chem), 54. *Prof Exp:* Res assoc, Eng Res Inst, Univ Mich, 54-57; res chemist, Union Carbide Corp, 57-61; chem dept mgr, Isomet Corp, 61-63; sr res scientist, Allis-Chalmers Corp, 63-71, mgr non-metallic mat, 71-73, sr res scientist, 73-88. *Mem:* Am Chem Soc; The Chem Soc; NY Acad Sci; AAAS; Sigma Xi. *Res:* Reaction mechanisms of organic, stereospecific and free radical gas-phase reactions; electrical insulation materials and systems for various applications; epoxy technology; high temperature fuel gas cleanup; coal combustion of pulverized fuel in entrained-bed combustors; coal-fired cement and iron ore pelletizing systems; coal water slurry fuels technology. *Mailing Add:* 100000 N Sheridan Rd Mequon WI 53092-6118

LOSOS, JONATHAN B, EVOLUTIONARY DIVERSIFICATION. *Current Pos:* ASST PROF BIOL, WASHINGTON UNIV, 92- *Personal Data:* b Dec 7, 61. *Educ:* Harvard Univ, AB, 84; Univ Calif, Berkeley, PhD(zool), 89. *Honors & Awards:* Dobzhansky Prize, Soc Study Evolution, 91. *Prof Exp:* Fel, Ctr Pop Biol, Univ Calif, Davis, 90-92. *Mem:* Soc Study Evolution; Soc Study Amphibians & Reptiles; Am Soc Naturalists; Soc Conserv Biologists; Am Soc Ichthyologists & Herpetologists. *Res:* Studies of evolutionary diversification, combining functional, behavioral, ecological, and evolutionary approaches (lizards of the genus Anolis used as a model system). *Mailing Add:* Dept Biol Washington Univ Campus Box 1137 St Louis MO 63130. *Fax:* 314-935-4432; *E-Mail:* losos@biodec.wustl.edu

LOSPALLUTO, JOSEPH JOHN, biochemistry; deceased, see previous edition for last biography

LOSS, FRANK J, FRACTURE MECHANICS, FAILURE ANALYSIS. *Current Pos:* EXEC VPRES, MAT ENG ASSOCS, LANHAM, MD, 82- *Personal Data:* b Homestead, Pa, May 14, 36; m 66; c 2. *Educ:* Carnegie Mellon Univ, BS, 58, MS, 59, PhD(mech eng), 61. *Prof Exp:* Engr, Westinghouse Bettis Atomic Power Lab, Pittsburgh, Pa, 61-62; first lt, US Army Corps Engrs, 62-64; head, Mech of Mat Br, US Naval Res Lab, Wash, DC, 64-82. *Mem:* Am Nuclear Soc; Am Soc Mech Engrs; Am Soc Testing & Mat. *Res:* Structural technology development; fracture mechanics of structural steels; corrosion fatigue; failure analysis; radiation embrittlement of nuclear materials; materials characterization in hostile environments; nuclear power plant structural reliability; consulting in materials analysis. *Mailing Add:* 9923 Kendale Rd Potomac MD 20854. *Fax:* 301-577-4936

LOSSING, FREDERICK PETTIT, CHEMICAL PHYSICS, ION CHEMISTRY. *Current Pos:* RETIRED. *Personal Data:* b Norwich, Ont, Aug 4, 15; m 38; c 3. *Educ:* Univ Western Ont, BA, 38, MA, 40; McGill Univ, PhD(phys chem), 42. *Prof Exp:* Res chemist, Shawinigan Chem, Ltd, 42-46; prin res officer, Div Chem, Nat Res Coun Can, 46-49 & 77-80, asst dir, 69-77; hon sr res prof, Dept Chem, Univ Ottawa, 80-94. *Mem:* Fel Royal Soc Can; Royal Astron Soc Can; Am Soc Mass Spectrometry. *Res:* Mass spectrometry; chemical kinetics; photochemistry; heats of formation of organic cations and free radicals; ionization processes. *Mailing Add:* 95 Dorothea Dr Univ Ottawa Ottawa ON K1Z 7C6 Can

LOSSINSKY, ALBERT S, EXPERIMENTAL NEUROPATHOLOGY, MICRO BLOOD VESSEL PATHOLOGY. *Current Pos:* res scientist path, 79-81, res scientist second neurobiol, 81-85, RES SCIENTIST NEUROBIOL, INST BASIC RES DEVELOP DISABILITIES, 85- *Personal Data:* b Passaic, NJ, May 17, 46; m 81; c 4. *Educ:* Kans Wesleyan Univ, BA, 69; Empire State Univ, MS, 74. *Prof Exp:* Chief res immunopath, Johns Hopkins Univ, 73-76; assoc res neuropath, Univ Md Sch Med, 76-79. *Concurrent Pos:* Asst supvr, Clin Electron Microscopy Lab, Inst Basic Res Develop Disabilities, 83- *Mem:* Am Soc Cell Biol; Soc Neuroscience; Am Asn Neuropathologists; NY Acad Sci. *Res:* Investigation using animal modes of mechanisms of macromolecular and inflammatory cell transport across the altered blood-brain barrier of mammals; electron microscopic analysis of human tissue biopsy material for clinical diagnosis. *Mailing Add:* Dept Fathol Neurobiol NYS Inst Basic Res Develop Disabilities 1050 Forest Hill Rd Staten Island NY 10314-6330

LOSURDO, ANTONIO, PHYSICAL CHEMISTRY. *Current Pos:* sect chief, Anal Sect, 88-91, SR TECH MGR, ROY F WESTON INC, 88-, SPEC PROJ GROUP LEADER/CHIEF CHEMIST, 91- *Personal Data:* b Spadafora, Italy, Jan 1, 43; US citizen; m, Claudia G Piva. *Educ:* Syracuse Univ, BA, 65, PhD(chem), 70. *Prof Exp:* Res asst chem, Syracuse Univ, 65-69; NIH fel, Rutgers Univ, New Brunswick, 69-70, instr, 70-71; mem vis fac chem, Syracuse Univ, 71-72; res assoc, Ohio State Univ, 72-73, lectr chem, 73-74; res assoc chem, Clark Univ, 74-75; chief chemist, Cambridge Instrument Co, 75-76; res asst prof chem oceanog, Univ Miami, 77-79, res assoc prof, 79-81; chief chemist & gas chromatography/mass spectrometry & qual assurance/qual control group leader, O'Brien & Gere Engrs, Inc, 82-87. *Mem:* Am Chem Soc; NY Acad Sci; Sigma Xi; AAAS. *Res:* Physical chemistry of multicomponent electrolyte solutions and seawater; thermochemistry and thermodynamics of solutions; solute-solvent and solute-solute interactions; transport properties of hydrophobic electrolytes; electroanalytical chemistry; trace organics analyses; gas chromatography and mass spectrometry of priority pollutants, polychlorinated dibenzo-p-dioxins and dibenzofurans; polynuclear aromatic hydrocarbons in several matrices of environmental concern. *Mailing Add:* 6 Chestnut Hill Rd Howell NJ 07731-1708

LOTAN, JAMES E, SILVICULTURE, FIRE ECOLOGY. *Current Pos:* PROPRIETOR, LUTAN HORSE LOGGING, 91- *Personal Data:* b Mich, Mar 20, 31; m 51; c Gloria (Stablein), Ellen (Hafner), Eric, Lei & Kari M. *Educ:* La State Univ, BSF, 59; Univ Mich, MF, 61, PhD, 70. *Prof Exp:* Forestry technician, Southern Forest Exp Sta, US Forest Serv, La, 57-59, fire control, Deerlodge Nat Forest, Mont, 59; asst forest res, Univ Mich, 60; res forester, Forest Serv, USDA, 61-65, proj leader forest sci res, 65-74, prog mgr, Fire Mgt Res & Develop Prog, 74-79, Northern Forest Fire Lab, 79-84, res forester, Forestry Sci Lab, 84-87; adj prof, Dept Forest Resources, Univ Idaho, Moscow, 87-91. *Mem:* Am Forestry Asn; Soc Am Foresters; NAm Horse & MuLe Loggers Asn (vpres, 92-). *Res:* Silviculture and ecology of Pinus contorta, Pinus ponderosa & Pseudotsuga menziesli; effects of fire on forests and rangelands of the northern Rocky Mountains; fire management RD & A program; fire effects research and development program; horse logging. *Mailing Add:* 1550 Mid Burnt Fork Rd Stevensville MT 59870. *E-Mail:* jimlotan@cyberhet1.com

LOTAN, REUBEN, BIOCHEMISTRY. *Current Pos:* PROF & CHMN, DEPT TUMOR BIOL, UNIV TEX, M D ANDERSON CANCER CTR, 84- *Personal Data:* b Sumarkand, USSR, Mar 19, 46. *Educ:* Tel Aviv Univ, MD, 71; Weizmann Inst, PhD(physics), 76. *Prof Exp:* Assoc prof biophys, Weizmann Inst, 80-84. *Concurrent Pos:* Vis asst prof develop biol, Univ Calif, Irvine, 78-80. *Mem:* Am Asn Cancer Res; Am Soc Cell Biol; Soc Complex Carbohydrates. *Mailing Add:* Tumor Biol Dept PO Box 108 Univ Tex M D Anderson Cancer Ctr 1515 Holcombe Blvd Houston TX 77030-4095. *Fax:* 713-794-0209

LOTH, JOHN LODEWYK, AERODYNAMICS. *Current Pos:* assoc prof, 67-71, PROF AEROSPACE ENG, WVA UNIV, 71- *Personal Data:* b Hague, Neth, Sept 14, 33; c 3. *Educ:* Univ Toronto, BASc, 57, MASc, 58, PhD(mech eng), 62. *Prof Exp:* French Govt fel aeronaut eng, Nat Ctr Sci Res, Ministry Ed, France, 58-59; lectr mech eng, Univ Toronto, 60-62; asst prof aeronaut eng, Univ Ill, Urbana, 62-67. *Concurrent Pos:* Consult, Ellard Wilson Assocs, Ont, 57-61; Air Force & ARO Inc, 63-66, Off Naval Res, 68-72 & Dept Energy, 73-; pres, Dynamic Flow Inc, 72-; prin investr, Lockheed Ga & US Dept Energy, chmn, Allegheney Sect, Am Inst Aeronaut & Astronaut. *Mem:* Assoc fel Am Inst Aeronaut & Astronaut; Sigma Xi; Am Soc Engr Educ. *Res:* Low speed aerodynamics; aerodynamic mixing and supersonics; combustion; aircraft design; propulsion. *Mailing Add:* Dept Aerospace Eng Eng Sci Bldg WVa Univ Morgantown WV 26506. *Fax:* 304-293-6689; *E-Mail:* jloth@wvu.edu

LOTHSTEIN, LEONARD, ANTI-CANCER DRUG RESISTANCE. *Current Pos:* asst prof, 88-93, MEM, CANCER CTR, UNIV TENN, 91-, ASSOC PROF, DEPT PHARMACOL, 93- *Personal Data:* b Newark, NJ, Aug 21, 54; m 82, Judith Soberman; c Katherine & Alexander. *Educ:* Bowdin Col, BA, 76; Vanderbilt Univ, PhD(molecular biol), 83. *Prof Exp:* Res assoc, Sloan Kettering Cancer Inst, 82-83; res assoc & fel, Albert Einstein Col Med, 83-88. *Mem:* Am Asn Cancer Res; NY Acad Sci; Sigma Xi; Am Soc Cell Biol. *Res:* Structure and activity analyses of novel anthracyclines; anthracycline resistance in tumor cells. *Mailing Add:* Dept Pharmacol Col Med Univ Tenn Memphis TN 38163. *E-Mail:* llothstein@utmemi.edu

LOTLIKAR, PRABHAKAR DATTARAM, BIOCHEMISTRY, PHARMACOLOGY. *Current Pos:* res instr, 67-68, from asst prof to assoc prof, 68-93, PROF BIOCHEM, FELS RES INST, SCH MED, TEMPLE UNIV, 93- *Personal Data:* b Shirali, India, May 21, 28; US citizen; m 60, Faye L Chin; c Jeffrey. *Educ:* Univ Bombay, BS, 50, MS, 54; Ore State Univ, PhD(biochem, pharmacol, bact), 60. *Prof Exp:* Asst chemist, Raptakos Brett & Co, Ltd, India, 50-55; proj assoc, McArdle Lab Cancer Res, Univ Wis, 63-65, instr, 65-66. *Concurrent Pos:* Res fel oncol, McArdle Lab Cancer Res,

Univ Wis, 60-63; res career develop award, USPHS, Nat Cancer Inst, 69-73. *Mem:* AAAS; Am Chem Soc; Am Asn Cancer Res; Am Soc Biol Chem; NY Acad Sci; Sigma Xi; Soc Exp Biol & Med; Biochem Soc (London). *Res:* Mechanisms of chemical carcinogenesis and cancer prevention. *Mailing Add:* Fels Res Inst Temple Univ Sch Med 3420 N Broad St Philadelphia PA 19140

LOTRICH, VICTOR ARTHUR, POPULATION ECOLOGY. *Current Pos:* ASSOC PROF ECOL, UNIV DEL, 69- *Personal Data:* b Pueblo, Colo, July 10, 34; m 55; c 3. *Educ:* Northern Colo Univ, BA, 56, MA, 60; Univ Ky, PhD(biol), 69. *Res:* Population dynamics of tide marsh fish and tide marsh estuarine interactions. *Mailing Add:* 19 Aldershot Dr Newark DE 19713

LOTSPEICH, FREDERICK BENJAMIN, ENVIRONMENTAL LAND CLASSIFICATION, GEOCHEMISTRY OF BIOTIC SYSTEMS. *Current Pos:* VOL RES PHYS SCIENTIST, NORTHWEST FOREST & RANGE EXP LAB, US FOREST SERV, 79- *Personal Data:* b Konawa, Okla, Jan 10, 14; m 48, Mildred A Snow; c Claire, Kurt, Richard & Paula. *Educ:* Wash State Univ, BS, 50, MS, 52, PhD(soil sci), 56. *Honors & Awards:* Boggess Award, Am Water Resources Asn, 80. *Prof Exp:* Soil scientist, US Geol Surv, 54-57, Agr Res Serv, USDA, 57-66 & Environ Protection Agency, 66-79. *Mem:* AAAS; Ecol Soc Am. *Res:* Geochemistry of soils and mineral exploration; physical properties of soils and soil compaction; geohydrology of groundwater, sediments and water quality; environmental land systems classification; geochemistry of nutrient supply and productivity of fresh water fishery; conservation biology; ecological economics. *Mailing Add:* 2006 Sterling Creek Rd Jacksonville OR 97530

LOTSPEICH, FREDERICK JACKSON, BIO-ORGANIC CHEMISTRY. *Current Pos:* PROF BIOCHEM, MED SCH, MARSHALL UNIV, 78- *Personal Data:* b Keyser, WVa, Mar 12, 25; m 48; c 1. *Educ:* WVa Univ, BS, 48, MS, 51; Purdue Univ, PhD(chem), 55. *Prof Exp:* Res chemist, E I du Pont de Nemours & Co, 48-50; asst org chem, WVa Univ, 50-52; asst, Purdue Univ, 52-53; asst prof chem, Simpson Col, 54-56; from asst prof to prof biochem, Med Ctr, WVa Univ, 66-78. *Mem:* Am Chem Soc; Sigma Xi; Am Asn Cancer Res; Am Soc Biochem & Molecular Biol. *Res:* The effect of B-carotene & vitamin A on carcinogenesis. *Mailing Add:* 2139 Enslow Blvd Huntington WV 25701

LOTSPEICH, JAMES FULTON, OPTICS. *Current Pos:* RETIRED. *Personal Data:* b Cincinnati, Ohio, Oct 22, 22; m 60, Helen Nelson. *Educ:* Princeton Univ, BA, 43; Univ Cincinnati, MS, 49; Columbia Univ, PhD(physics), 58. *Prof Exp:* Lab instr gen physics, Univ Cincinnati, 47-48; asst, Columbia Univ, 51-56; res physicist, Labs, Hughes Aricraft Co, 56-88. *Mem:* AAAS; Am Phys Soc; Sigma Xi; fel Optical Soc Am. *Res:* Microwave spectroscopy and molecular structure; electrooptic techniques; applied laser technology; photodetection techniques; integrated optics. *Mailing Add:* 25346 Malibu Rd Malibu CA 90265

LOTT, FRED WILBUR, JR, mathematics, mathematical statistics, for more information see previous edition

LOTT, FRED WILBUR, III, elementary particle physics; deceased, see previous edition for last biography

LOTT, JAMES ANTHONY, COMPOUND SEMICONDUCTORS. *Current Pos:* PROF ELEC ENG, AIR FORCE INST TECHNOL, 93- *Personal Data:* b San Jose, Calif, July 4, 61. *Educ:* Univ NMex, Albuquerque, PhD(elec eng), 93. *Prof Exp:* Mem tech staff, Sandia Nat Labs, 88-93. *Res:* Visible photonic devices and gallium arsenide integrated circuits. *Mailing Add:* Air Force Inst Technol Eng Bldg 640 2950 P St Wright-Patterson AFB OH 45433. *Fax:* 937-476-4055; *E-Mail:* jlott@afit.af.mil

LOTT, JAMES ROBERT, PHYSIOLOGY, BIOPHYSICS. *Current Pos:* from asst prof to assoc prof, 57-64, PROF BIOL, NTEX STATE UNIV, 64- *Personal Data:* b Houston, Tex, Jan 16, 24; m 42; c Jim, Linda, Lori & John. *Educ:* Univ Tex, BA, 49, MA, 51, PhD(physiol, bact), 56. *Prof Exp:* Med bacteriologist, Brackenridge Hosp, Austin, Tex, 55; lectr zool, Univ Tex, 55-56, res scientist, Radiobiol Lab, Balcones Res Inst, 56; instr physiol, Sch Med, Emory Univ, 56-57. *Concurrent Pos:* Sr res investr, AEC, 58-; NSF grant, 63-64. *Mem:* Am Physiol Soc; Alcohol Res Soc; Radiation Res Soc; Int Soc Biometeorol; Int Soc Bioelec; Am Coun Alcohol Res. *Res:* Neurophysiology; effects of electric fields on the nervous system; effects of electric fields on cancer growth; endocrinology; effects of alcohol on the nervous system. *Mailing Add:* Biol Sci Univ N Tex Box 5218 Denton TX 76203-0218

LOTT, JAMES STEWART, medicine, radiology; deceased, see previous edition for last biography

LOTT, JOHN ALFRED, CLINICAL CHEMISTRY. *Current Pos:* from asst prof to assoc prof, 68-79, PROF PATH, OHIO STATE UNIV, 79- & DIR, CLINIC CHEM LAB, OHIO STATE UNIV HOSP, 79- *Personal Data:* b Ger, Oct 30, 36; US citizen; m 63; c 1. *Educ:* Rutgers Univ, BS, 59, MS, 61, PhD(anal chem), 65. *Honors & Awards:* Katchman Award, Am Asn Clin Chem, 79, Outstanding Contrib Educ Award, 87; Presidential Award, Nat Acad Biochemist, 83. *Prof Exp:* Instr chem, Rutgers Univ, 64-65; asst prof, Flint Col, Univ Mich, 65-68. *Concurrent Pos:* Expert witness, clin chem. *Mem:* Am Assoc Clin Chem; Nat Acad Clin Biochemists, (treas, 78-79, pres, 81-82); Am Chem Soc; Asn Clin Scientists; Am Asn Univ Profs. *Res:* Instrumentation; methodology development; enzymology; specific-ion electrodes. *Mailing Add:* Starling Loving M-368 Ohio State Univ Med Ctr Columbus OH 43210-1240. *E-Mail:* jlott@magnus.acs.ohio-state.edu

LOTT, JOHN NORMAN ARTHUR, SEED PHYSIOLOGY, SEED ULTRASTRUCTURE. *Current Pos:* from asst prof to assoc prof, 69-81, PROF BIOL, MCMASTER UNIV, 81- *Personal Data:* b Summerland, BC, Jan 20, 43; m 66, Daphne; c Steven & Alison. *Educ:* Univ BC, BSc, 65; Univ Calif, Davis, MSc, 67, PhD(bot), 69. *Prof Exp:* Res asst bot, Univ Calif, Davis, 65-69. *Mem:* Can Bot Asn; Am Soc Plant Physiol; Bot Soc Am; Micros Soc Can; Micros Soc Am. *Res:* Ultrastructure and physiological studies of developing and germinating seeds, with special emphasis on protein bodies; mineral nutrient storage in seeds. *Mailing Add:* Dept Biol McMaster Univ Hamilton ON L8S 4K1 Can. *Fax:* 905-522-6066; *E-Mail:* lott@mcmaster.ca

LOTT, JOHNNY WARREN, MATHEMATICS EDUCATION, CURRICULUM DEVELOPMENT. *Current Pos:* PROF & SIMMS CO-DIR, UNIV MONT, 74- *Personal Data:* b July 2, 44; m 66, Carolyn Jernigan; c John J. *Educ:* Union Univ, BS, 65; Emory Univ, MAT, 69; Ga State Univ, PhD(math educ),73. *Prof Exp:* Teacher math, DeKalb Co Pub Schs, 65-69, Westminister Schs, 69-70; from instr to asst prof, Ga State Univ, 70-74. *Concurrent Pos:* Teacher math, Pelican Schs, 80-81. *Mem:* Math Asn Am; Nat Coun Teachers Math. *Res:* Curriculum development including geometry, logo, integrated math and math for elementary teachers. *Mailing Add:* Simms Proj Dept Math Sci Univ Mont Missoula MT 59812

LOTT, LAYMAN AUSTIN, PHYSICS. *Current Pos:* SR ENG SPECIALIST, IDAHO NAT ENG LAB, 73- *Personal Data:* b Ft Collins, Colo, Sept 21, 37; m 58; c 4. *Educ:* Colo State Univ, BS, 59, MS, 61; Iowa State Univ, PhD(physics), 65. *Prof Exp:* Res physicist, Rocky Flats Div, Dow Chem USA, 65-71, sr res physicist, 71-73. *Mem:* Am Phys Soc; Am Soc Nondestructive Test; Sigma Xi. *Res:* Solid state physics; physical properties of materials; nondestructive testing; development of advanced nondestructive testing methods. *Mailing Add:* 701 Ninth St Idaho Falls ID 83404

LOTT, PETER F, PHYSICAL CHEMISTRY, ANALYTICAL CHEMISTRY. *Current Pos:* LAB DIR, SPECIALIZED SCI SERV, LLC, 93- *Personal Data:* b Berlin, Ger, Mar 26, 27; nat US; m 56; c 2. *Educ:* St Lawrence Univ, BS, 49, MS, 50; Univ Conn, PhD(chem), 56. *Honors & Awards:* Benedetti-Pichler Award, Am Microchem Soc. *Prof Exp:* Asst instr chem, Univ Conn, 54-56; res chemist, E I du Pont de Nemours & Co, 56; assoc prof, Univ Mo, 56-59; chemist, Pure Carbon Co, 59-60; assoc prof, St John's Univ, NY, 60-64; emer prof, Univ Mo, Kansas City, 64-93. *Mem:* Am Chem Soc; Am Microchem Soc; Am Indust Hyg Asn. *Res:* Analytical methods development; trace and instrumental analysis; chemical kinetics; chemical microscopy; physical measurements; organic reagents; forensic chemistry; asbestos analysis. *Mailing Add:* Specialized Sci Serv LLC Twin Oaks N Lobby Box 151 500 Oak St Kansas City MO 64112. *Fax:* 816-756-2810

LOTT, SAM HOUSTON, JR, physics, health physics, for more information see previous edition

LOTTES, P(AUL) A(LBERT), MECHANICAL ENGINEERING. *Current Pos:* RETIRED. *Personal Data:* b Wilkinsburg, Pa, Aug 2, 26; m 47; c 3. *Educ:* Purdue Univ, PhD(mech eng), 50. *Prof Exp:* Assoc mech engr, Argonne Nat Lab, 50-60, sr mech engr, 60-91. *Mem:* Fel Am Soc Mech Engrs; fel Am Nuclear Soc. *Res:* Heat transfer and pressure drop in boiling; nuclear reactor safety. *Mailing Add:* 101 Green Valley Dr 9700 S Cass Ave Naperville IL 60540

LOTTI, VICTOR J, NEUROPHARMACOLOGY. *Current Pos:* RETIRED. *Personal Data:* b Trenton, NJ, Jan 6, 38. *Educ:* Univ Conn, BS, 59; Univ Mo, MS, 61; Univ Calif, Los Angeles, PhD(pharmacol), 65. *Prof Exp:* Sr res pharmacologist, Dept Pharmacol, Merck, Sharp & Dohme Res Labs, 67-69, res fel neuropharmacol, 69-73, dir neuropsychopharmacol, 73-75, sr dir res coordr, 75-77, sr dir, Dept Pharmacol, Chibret, France, 77-79, sr scientist, Dept Pharmacol, 79-93. *Mem:* Am Soc Pharmacol & Exp Therapeut; Am Chem Soc. *Mailing Add:* 214 Brookside Circle Harleysville PA 19438

LOTTMAN, ROBERT P(OWELL), CIVIL ENGINEERING. *Current Pos:* RETIRED. *Personal Data:* b Brooklyn, NY, Sept 24, 33; m 56. *Educ:* Polytech Inst Brooklyn, BCE, 54; Purdue Univ, MSCE, 56; Ohio State Univ, PhD, 65. *Prof Exp:* Proj engr, Struct Appln Sect, Grumman Aircraft Eng Corp, 56-57; supvr, Asphalt Tech Serv Lab, Stand Oil Co, Ohio, 57-59; res supvr hwy mat, Transp Eng Ctr, Ohio State Univ, 59-65, asst prof civil eng, 65-66; prof civil eng, Univ Idaho, 66- *Concurrent Pos:* Instnl & comt mem, Hwy Res Bd, Nat Acad Sci-Nat Res Coun, 60- *Mem:* Asn Asphalt Paving Technol; Am Soc Testing & Mat. *Res:* Study and evaluation of physical and chemical properties of construction materials to determine mechanical behavior under various loading and environmental conditions. *Mailing Add:* 3728 S Gandy St Spokane WA 99203-2709

LOTTS, ADOLPHUS LLOYD, NUCLEAR SAFETY, ISOTOPE SEPARATION. *Current Pos:* CONSULT, 89- *Personal Data:* b Buchanan, Va, June 10, 34; m 54; c 4. *Educ:* Va Polytech Inst, BS, 55, MS, 57. *Honors & Awards:* E O Lawrence Mem Award, US Dept Energy, 76. *Prof Exp:* Instr metall eng, Va Polytech Inst, 56-57; assoc mat scientist, Atomic Energy Div,

Babcock & Wilcox Co, 58-59; assoc metallurgist, Metals & Ceramics Div, Oak Ridge Nat Lab, 59-61, group leader Fuel Cycle Technol, 61-66, head Fuel Cycle Technol Oper, Metals & Ceramics Div, 66-70, assoc dir Gas-cooled Reactor & Thorium Utilization Progs, 70-78, dir Nuclear Waste Prog, 78-81, dir, Nuclear Regulatory Comn Prog, 81-83, chmn long range planning group, 69-83; dir, Atomic Vapor Laser Isotope Separation Div, Martin Marietta Energy Systs, Inc, 83-90; div dir res reactors, Oak Ridge Nat Lab. *Mem:* Fel Am Nuclear Soc; Am Soc Metals. *Res:* Nuclear fuel processing technology; economics and properties of nuclear fuel; materials for reactor systems; radioactive and toxic waste management; nuclear reactor and safety technology; laser isotope separation technology. *Mailing Add:* 157 Saligugi Way Loudon TN 37774

LOTZ, MARGARET M, CELL BIOLOGY. *Current Pos:* NRSA fel cell biol, 89-93, INSTR CELL BIOL, HARVARD MED SCH, NEW ENG DEACONESS HOSP, 93- *Personal Data:* b New York City, NY, Oct 29, 58. *Educ:* State Univ NY, BS, 82; Duke Univ, PhD(biol), 89. *Mem:* Am Soc Cell Biol. *Res:* Cell biology. *Mailing Add:* New Eng Deaconess Hosp 50 Binney St Boston MA 02115-6013

LOTZ, W GREGORY, ENDOCRINOLOGY, THERMAL PHYSIOLOGY. *Current Pos:* chief, Radiation Sect, 92-94, CHIEF, PHYS AGENTS EFFECTS BR, NIOSH, 94- *Personal Data:* m 72, Vicki Eley; c 3. *Educ:* Heidelberg Col, BS, 72; Univ Rochester, MS, 75, PhD(biophys), 77. *Prof Exp:* Chief, Environ Physiol Div, Naval Aerospace Med Res Lab, 76-92. *Mem:* Am Physiol Soc; Bioelectromagnetics Soc; AAAS. *Res:* Physiological affects of nonionizing radiation. *Mailing Add:* NIOSH DBBS PAEB MS C-27 4676 Columbia Pkwy Cincinnati OH 45226-1998. *Fax:* 513-533-8510; *E-Mail:* wgl0@cdc.gov

LOTZE, MICHAEL T, LYMPHOKINE RESEARCH, T-CELL IMMUNOBIOLOGY. *Current Pos:* SR INVESTR SURG, NAT CANCER INST, 82-; ASST PROF SURG, UNIFORMED SERV UNIV HEALTH SCI, 83- *Personal Data:* b Pasadena, Calif, July 11, 52; m 77; c 4. *Educ:* Northwestern Univ, BS, 73, MD 74. *Prof Exp:* Jr med fel surg, Md Anderson Tumor Inst, 75; Intern surg, Univ Rochester, 75-82; med officer, Nat Health Serv Corp, 77-78. *Mem:* Am Col Surgeons; Am Asn Immunol; Am Soc Clin Oncol; Am Asn Cancer Res; Soc Surg Oncol; Soc Univ Surgeons. *Res:* Tumor immunology and developmental therapeutics; lymphokine function and T-cell immunobiology; surgical treatment of primary and metastatic liver tumors and melanoma. *Mailing Add:* Dept Surg & Pittsburgh Cancer Inst Univ Pittsburgh 200 Lothrop St W1543 Pittsburgh PA 15224. *Fax:* 412-648-9551

LOU, ALEX YIH-CHUNG, ENGINEERING MATERIALS, MECHANICS. *Current Pos:* PHILLIPS PETROL, 81- *Personal Data:* b Chungking, China, Nov 10, 38; US citizen; m 69; c 2. *Educ:* Nat Taiwan Univ, BS, 60; Purdue Univ MS, 65, PhD(solid mech), 69. *Prof Exp:* Sr engr composites, The Boeing Co, 69-70; res scientist, 70-76, sr res scientist mat, Firestone Tire & Rubber Co, 76-81. *Mem:* Am Soc Mech Engr. *Res:* Characterization and evolution of composite; polymer materials for engineering applications; tire mechanics such as rolling resistance. *Mailing Add:* 2564 Georgetown Dr Bartlesville OK 74006

LOU, DAVID YEONG-SUEI, MECHANICAL ENGINEERING. *Current Pos:* PROF MECH ENG & CHMN DEPT, UNIV NEBR, LINCOLN, 93- *Personal Data:* b Yuncom, China, Nov 12, 37; m 64, Marjorie Feng; c Eugene & Derek. *Educ:* Taiwan Univ, BS, 59; Mass Inst Technol, MS, 63, MechE, 66, ScD(mech eng), 67. *Prof Exp:* Res asst mech eng, Mass Inst Technol, 61-63, asst thermionic energy conversion, 63-64, asst mech eng, 64-65, asst molecular beams, 65-67; thermodyn engr, Jackson & Moreland Consult Co, 63; from asst prof to prof mech eng, Univ Del, 67-79; prof & chmn mech eng, Univ Tex, Arlington, 79-90; prof & chmn mech & aerospace eng, Syracuse Univ, Syracuse, NY, 90-92. *Concurrent Pos:* Assoc ed, Am Soc Mech Engrs J Eng Gas Turbines & Power, 95-. *Mem:* Am Phys Soc; Am Inst Aeronaut & Astronaut; Am Soc Mech Engrs; Am Soc Elec Engrs. *Res:* Solar energy; kinetic theory of gases; molecular beams; thermodynamics; fluid mechanics; heat transfer; biomedical engineering. *Mailing Add:* Dept Mech Eng Univ Nebr Lincoln NE 68588. *Fax:* 402-472-1465; *E-Mail:* merdlou@engvms.unl.edu

LOU, JACK Y K, OFFSHORE STRUCTURES, FLUID-STRUCTURE INTERACTIONS. *Current Pos:* from assoc prof to prof, 74-95, EMER PROF CIVIL & OCEAN ENG, TEX A&M UNIV, 96- *Educ:* Mass Inst Technol, SM, 62; Polytech Inst, Brooklyn, PhD(appl mech), 69. *Honors & Awards:* Golden Cert Award, Am Soc Mech Engrs, 81, Bd Gov Award, 82. *Prof Exp:* Engr, Ingalls-Taiwan Shipbuilding & Dry Dock Co, 58-60; naval architect, George Sharp Co, 62-63; prin dynamics engr, Hydrospace Div, Repub Aviation Corp, 63-65, Marine div, Litton Industs, 65-66; staff engr, Hydrosysts Inc, 66-68; from asst prof to assoc prof ocean eng, Columbia Univ, 68-74. *Mem:* Fel Am Soc Mech Engrs; Am Soc Civil Engrs; Soc Naval Architects & Marine Engrs. *Res:* Dynamic analysis of offshore structures and fluid-structure interactions. *Mailing Add:* 3806 Walden Estates Dr Montgomery TX 77356

LOU, KINGDON, MICROBIOLOGY. *Current Pos:* RETIRED. *Personal Data:* b Stockton, Calif, Aug 3, 22; m 45; c 2. *Educ:* Stanford Univ, AB, 52, AM, 56; Am Bd Bioanal, dipl. *Prof Exp:* Dir, Immunol Dept, Res Div, Hyland Labs, Baxter, 57-67; sr immunochemist, Res Div, Hoffmann-La Roche, 67-68; dir immunol, Kallestad Labs, 68-69; vpres & dir immunol res, ICL Sci, 70-81; consult, Immunoassay Technol, Inc, 81-92. *Mem:* Am Soc Microbiol; Am Asn Clin Chemists; NY Acad Sci; AAAS. *Res:* Immunochemical diagnostic reagents; hybridoria and monoclonal antibodies; immunoassays. *Mailing Add:* PO Box 1849 Tustin CA 92681-1849

LOU, PETER LOUIS, MOLECULAR BIOLOGY, OPHTHALMOLOGY. *Current Pos:* INSTR OPHTHAL, HARVARD MED SCH, 79- *Personal Data:* b Shanghai, China, Dec 9, 45; US citizen; m 80, Vibeke E Pedersen; c Jared, Kristina & Elizabeth. *Educ:* Univ Ottawa, BSc, 67, MD, 74; McMaster Univ, Can, MSc, 70, Univ Toronto, dipl ophthal, 77. *Prof Exp:* Instr biol, McMaster Univ, 67-70; resident ophthal, Univ Toronto, 74-77; vitreo-retinal fel, Boston, 78. *Concurrent Pos:* Consult vitreo-retinal dis, 82-; surgeon, Mass Eye & Ear Infirmary, Boston, 95- *Mem:* Asn Res Vision & Ophthal; fel Am Acad Ophthal; Vitreous Soc; AMA. *Res:* Effect of near ultraviolet light on aphakic retina metabolism; diabetic retinopathy; pathophysiology of vitreous and retina; vitreo-retinal disorders. *Mailing Add:* 75 Blossom Ct Boston MA 02114

LOUBSER, PAUL GERHARD, SPINAL CORD INJURY, CARDIOVASCULAR ANESTHESIOLOGY. *Current Pos:* from clin instr to clin asst prof, 85-92, ASST PROF ANESTHESIOL, BAYLOR COL MED, 93- *Personal Data:* b Cape Town, SAfrica, July 19, 53. *Educ:* Univ Cape Town Sch Med, MB & ChB, 77; Am Bol Anesthesiol, dipl, 91. *Prof Exp:* Fel res, Tex Heart Inst, 84-85. *Concurrent Pos:* Res assoc, Heart Dis Res Found, 83-84; dir anesthesiol serv & prin investr, Inst Rehab & Res, 85-92. *Mem:* Am Soc Anesthesiol; Asn Appl Psychol Physiol & Bioffed Pain; Soc Cardiovasc Anesthesia; Int Soc Study Pain; Am Spinal Injury Asn. *Res:* Spinal cord injury-management of chronic spasticity and pain using regional anesthetic and intrathecal pharmaco therapy; cardiopulmanary bypass-cellular, humoral and immune chances considered detrimental. *Mailing Add:* 6550 Fannin Suite 1003 Houston TX 77030. *Fax:* 713-798-7345; *E-Mail:* ploubser@tmc.edu

LOUCK, JAMES DONALD, MATHEMATICAL PHYSICS. *Current Pos:* STAFF MEM, LOS ALAMOS NAT LAB, UNIV CALIF, 63- *Personal Data:* b Grand Rapids, Mich, Dec 13, 28; m 60; c 3. *Educ:* Ala Polytech Inst, BS, 50; Ohio State Univ, MS, 52, PhD(physics), 58. *Prof Exp:* Staff mem, Los Alamos Nat Lab, 58-60; assoc res prof physics, Auburn Univ, 60-63. *Mem:* Am Phys Soc; AAAS; Int Asn Math Physicists. *Res:* Application and development of group theoretical methods in physics. *Mailing Add:* 54 Wildflower Way Santa Fe NM 87501. *Fax:* 505-665-4055

LOUCKS, DANIEL PETER, SYSTEMS ANALYSIS. *Current Pos:* CONSULT, 81- *Personal Data:* b Chambersburg, Pa, June 4, 32; m 67, Marjorie A Grant; c Jennifer L & Susan L. *Educ:* Pa State Univ, BS, 54; Yale Univ, MS, 55; Cornell Univ, PhD(systs eng, econ), 65. *Honors & Awards:* Res Award, Am Soc Civil Engrs, 70 & 86; Alexander Von Humboldt Sr Scientist Award, 92. *Prof Exp:* Asst prof water resources eng, Col Eng, Cornell Univ, 65-70, assoc prof environ eng, 70-75, prof environ eng & chmn dept, 76-80, assoc dean res & grad study, 80-81. *Concurrent Pos:* Prin investr, NSF, Environ Protection Agency, Nato, Ford Found, Resources for the Future & US Dept Interior Res Grants, 67-; sem assoc, Columbia Univ, 67-80; res fel, Harvard Univ, 68; consult, UN Develop Prog, WHO, Food & Agr Orgn, NATO, UN & IRBD; economist, World Bank, 72-73; vis prof, Mass Inst Technol, 77-78; res scholar, Int Inst Appl Systs Anal, Austria, 81-82; distinguished vis prof, Univ Colo, 92, Univ Adelaide, 92, Aachen Univ Technol, 93 & Delft Univ Technol, 95. *Mem:* Nat Acad Eng; AAAS; Opers Res Soc Am; Int Mgt Sci; Am Geophys Union; fel Am Soc Civil Engrs; Asn Comput Mach; Int Hydraul Res Asn. *Res:* Applications of operations research to problems in environmental and water resources engineering; public policy analysis; interactive modelling and computer based decision support systems. *Mailing Add:* Hollister Hall Cornell Univ Ithaca NY 14853. *Fax:* 607-255-9004; *E-Mail:* dpl3@cornell.edu

LOUCKS, ORIE LIPTON, BIOLOGY, ECOLOGY. *Current Pos:* OHIO EMINENT SCHOLAR & PROF ZOOL, MIAMI UNIV, 89- *Personal Data:* b Minden, Ont, Oct 2, 31; m 55, Elinor Bernstein; c Eric D, Kimberly A & Edward R. *Educ:* Univ Toronto, BSc, 53, MSc, 55; Univ Wis, PhD(bot), 60. *Honors & Awards:* George Mercer Award, Ecol Soc Am, 64. *Prof Exp:* Forest ecologist, Dept Forestry, Can Govt, 55-62; from asst prof to prof bot, Univ Wis, Madison, 62-78; sci dir, Inst Ecol, 78-82; dir, Holcomb Res Inst, 83-89. *Concurrent Pos:* Univ Wis rep, State Bd Preserv Sci Areas, 64-78; coordr environ mgt progs, US/Int Biol Prog, Univ Tex, 73; co-chmn, Nat Res Coun/RSC comt Great Lakes Water Qual Agreement, 84-85; chmn, Nature Conservancy Bd Gov Sect, 90-; pres, Asn Ecosyst Res Ctrs, 90-92; chmn, Lucy Brown Asn Mixed Mesophytic Forest, 93- *Mem:* Fel AAAS; Soc Am Foresters; Ecol Soc Am; Am Inst Biol Sci; Am Soc Limnol Oceanog; Int Ecol Asn. *Res:* Forest ecology and ecosystem dynamics; lake ecosystem modeling and analysis; wetland systems studies; air pollution effects on forests and ecosystems; dynamics and trends in biological divesity; US/China research on environmental change. *Mailing Add:* Zool Dept Miami Univ Oxford OH 45056. *Fax:* 513-529-6900; *E-Mail:* loucks@msmail.muohio.edu

LOUCKS, VERNON R, JR, RESEARCH ADMINISTRATION. *Current Pos:* staff, Baxter Travenol Labs Inc, 66-76, exec vpres & bd dirs, 76-80, pres & chief oper officer, 80-87, CHIEF EXEC OFFICER & CHMN, BAXTER INT INC, 87- *Personal Data:* b Evanston, Ill, Oct 24, 34; m 72, Linda Kay Olson; c 6. *Educ:* Yale Univ, BA, 57; Harvard Univ, MBA, 63. *Prof Exp:* Sr mgt consult, George Fry & Assocs, Chicago, 63-65. *Concurrent Pos:* Bd dirs, Dun & Bradstreet Corp, Emerson Elec Co, Quaker Oats Co & Anheuser-Busch Co; bd adv, Nestle USA; trustee, Rush-Presby-St Luke's Med Ctr; assoc, Northwestern Univ. *Mem:* Health Indust Mfr Asn. *Mailing Add:* Baxter Healthcare Corp One Baxter Pkwy Deerfield IL 60015

LOUD, ALDEN VICKERY, CELL BIOLOGY, BIOPHYSICS. *Current Pos:* from assoc prof to prof, 68-90, EMER PROF PATH, NY MED COL, 90- *Personal Data:* b Boston, Mass, Apr 6, 25; m 50, Ruth Moody; c Kenneth R, Jane A, Thomas W & Peter A. *Educ:* Mass Inst Technol, BS & MS, 51, PhD(biophys), 55. *Prof Exp:* Res assoc, Detroit Inst Cancer Res & asst prof biophys, Col Med, Wayne State Univ, 57-65; asst prof path, Col Physicians & Surgeons, Columbia Univ, 65-68. *Concurrent Pos:* Res fel med, Mass Gen Hosp, 51-57. *Mem:* Electron Micros Soc Am; Am Soc Cell Biol; Int Soc Stereology; Royal Micros Soc; Am Heart Asn. *Res:* Stereologic morphometry; quantitative electron microscopy and methods of ultrastructure research; correlation of cellular ultrastructure with metabolic function. *Mailing Add:* 205 Washington Ave Tappan NY 10983

LOUD, OLIVER SCHULE, HISTORY & PHILOSOPHY OF SCIENCE. *Current Pos:* CONSULT, 81- *Personal Data:* b Vernal, Utah, Jan 16, 11; m 35; c 2. *Educ:* Harvard Univ, AB, 29; Columbia Univ, AM, 40, EdD, 43. *Prof Exp:* Master, Nichols Sch, NY, 29-32; instr high sch, Ohio, 32-36; teacher gen sci, Sarah Lawrence Col, 36-40; res assoc, Bur Educ Res Sci, Columbia, 39-43; asst prof physics, Antioch Col, 43-44; instr, Ohio State Univ, 44; tech supvr, Tenn Eastman Corp, Tenn, 44-45; from assoc prof to prof phys sci, Antioch Col, 45-78, distinguished univ prof, 78-81. *Concurrent Pos:* Ford Found fel, Harvard Univ, 52-53; mem staff fac develop prog, Great Lakes Cols Asn, Ann Arbor, Mich; mem staff, Wilmington Col, Ohio & Proj Talents, Lebanon Correctional Inst, Lebanon, Ohio. *Res:* Science in general education; suggestions for teaching problems of good land use. *Mailing Add:* 1430 Meadow Lane Yellow Springs OH 45387

LOUD, WARREN SIMMS, MATHEMATICS. *Current Pos:* from asst prof to prof, 47-92, EMER PROF MATH, UNIV MINN, MINNEAPOLIS, 92- *Personal Data:* b Boston, Mass, Sept 13, 21; m 47, Mary L Strasburg; c Margaret (McCamant), Elizabeth (Liebman) & John. *Educ:* Mass Inst Technol, SB, 42, PhD(math), 46. *Prof Exp:* Instr math, Mass Inst Technol, 43-47. *Concurrent Pos:* Res engr, Mass Inst Technol, 45-47, vis fel, 55-56; guest prof, Darmstadt Tech Univ, 64-65; vis prof, Kyoto Univ, Japan, 74-75 & Univ Florence & Univ Trento, Italy, 81-82. *Mem:* AAAS; Am Math Soc; Soc Indust & Appl Math; Math Asn Am. *Res:* Theory of differential equations; numerical methods of solution of differential equations; stationary solutions of Van der Pol's equation with a forcing term; nonlinear mechanics. *Mailing Add:* Sch Math Univ Minn 206 Church St SE Minneapolis MN 55455. *Fax:* 612-359-9858; *E-Mail:* loud@math.umn.edu

LOUDA, SVATA M, PLANT-INSECT INTERACTIONS, PLANT DEMOGRAPHY. *Current Pos:* from asst prof to assoc prof, 83-92, PROF BIOL, UNIV NEBR, LINCOLN, 92- *Personal Data:* b Prague, Czech; US citizen; m, Rodney W Otley; c Dan & Griffigh. *Educ:* Pomona Col, BA, 65; Univ Wash, Seattle, BS, 68; Univ Calif, Santa Barbara, MS, 72; Univ Calif, Riverside & San Diego State Univ, PhD(ecol), 78. *Honors & Awards:* George Mercer Award, Ecol Soc Am, 82. *Prof Exp:* Asst economist, Pac Northwest Bell Tel, 65-66 & Syst Develop Corp, 68-69; postdoctoral fel bot, Yale Univ, 79-81; res asst prof, Marine Lab, Beaufort & res scientist, Bot Dept, Durham, Duke Univ, 81-83. *Concurrent Pos:* Sr scientist, Rocky Mountain Biol Lab, 79-90; researcher & prin investr, Cedar Pt Biol Sta, 83-; assoc ed, Oecologia, 90-92; coun mem, Am Inst Biol Sci, 91-93; assoc ed ecol & ecol monogaphs, 92-94; panel mem ecol, NSF, 93-97. *Mem:* Ecol Soc Am; Am Inst Biol Sci; Entom Soc Am; Bot Soc Am; fel AAAS; Sigma Xi; Soc Conserv Biol. *Res:* Plant population dynamics; community ecology; interaction of plants with insects; biological control of weeds; insect herbivory; nontarget host plant use; prairie ecology; insect seed predation. *Mailing Add:* Sch Biol Sci 410A Manter Hall Univ Nebr Lincoln NE 68588-0118. *Fax:* 402-472-2080; *E-Mail:* slouda@unl.edu

LOUDEN, L RICHARD, GEOCHEMISTRY, SATELLITE COMMUNICATIONS. *Current Pos:* PRES, L-R RESOURCE DEVELOP CORP, 80- *Personal Data:* b Monroe, Wash, July 8, 33; m 63. *Educ:* Univ Wurzburg, PhD(geochem), 63. *Prof Exp:* Assoc prof geochem, Univ Houston, 63-64; geologist, Magnet Cove Barium Corp, 64-65; supvr, X-ray Dept, 65-67, mgr anal sect, 67-69, tech adv, 69-71, spec proj engr, 71-72, develop mgr, Dresser Pollution, Dresser Oilfield Prod Div, 72-73, prod mgr, 73-76, mkt mgr, Dresser-Swaco, 76-78; exec vpres res, eng, construct & mfg, The Analysts Inc, 78-80; vpres, satellite commun, Drilling Info Serv Co, 81-82. *Concurrent Pos:* Co-worker, NASA grant, Univ Houston, 63-64; vpres environ, Ecco Inc, Anchorage, 90- *Mem:* AAAS; Marine Tech Soc; Clay Minerals Soc; Ger Geol Asn; Nat Oilfield Equip Mfrs & Distribr Soc. *Res:* Organic geochemistry, oceanography, clay mineralogy, and x-ray analysis; new and novel equipment and chemicals for oilwell and other drilling practices; geotechnical services; project management; geophysical analysis; glycol recycling; oil/water seperation. *Mailing Add:* 8011 Highmeadow Dr Houston TX 77063

LOUDON, CATHERINE, PHYSIOLOGICAL ECOLOGY, INVERTEBRATE BIOMECHANICS. *Current Pos:* ASST PROF, KANS STATE UNIV, 93- *Personal Data:* b Chanute, Kans, Nov 1, 58; m 84, Andrew S Borovik; c Jedidiah E (Borovik). *Educ:* Brown Univ, ScB, 80; Duke Univ, PhD(zool), 86. *Prof Exp:* Res asst, Univ Minn, 86-88; NSF fel, Cornell Univ, 89-90; asst prof, Ithaca Col, 88-90; res asst, Univ Calif, Berkeley, 90-92. *Mem:* AAAS; Entom Soc Am; Am Soc Zoologists; Sigma Xi. *Res:* Physiology; physiological ecology; invertebrate biomechanics. *Mailing Add:* 1509 Indian Wells Ct Lawrence KS 66047-1615

LOUDON, GORDON MARCUS, BIOCHEMISTRY, ORGANIC CHEMISTRY. *Current Pos:* assoc prof, 77-83, PROF MED CHEM, PURDUE UNIV, 83-, ASSOC DEAN SCH PHARM, 87- *Personal Data:* b Baton Rouge, La, Oct 10, 42; m 64, Judy Blanchard; c Kyle & Christopher. *Educ:* La State Univ, Baton Rouge, BS, 64; Univ Calif, Berkeley, PhD(org chem), 68. *Prof Exp:* USPHS fel, Univ Calif, Berkeley, 69-70, lectr biochem, 70; from asst prof to assoc prof chem, Cornell Univ, 70-77. *Mem:* Am Soc Biol Chemists; Am Chem Soc; AAAS; Am Asn Cols Pharm. *Res:* Peptide chemistry; enzyme model systems; bioanalytical methods; textbook author. *Mailing Add:* Dept Med Chem & Pharmacog 1330 RHPH West Lafayette IN 47907-1330. *E-Mail:* marc.loudon.1@purdue.edu

LOUDON, ROBERT G, INTERNAL MEDICINE. *Current Pos:* PROF INTERNAL MED, MED CTR & DIR PULMONARY DIS DIV, COL MED, UNIV CINCINNATI, 71- *Personal Data:* b Edinburgh, Scotland, June 27, 25; US citizen; m 55; c 3. *Educ:* Univ Edinburgh, MB & ChB, 47. *Prof Exp:* House physician gen med, Western Gen Hosp, Edinburgh, Scotland, 47-48; sr house physician tuberc wards, City Hosp, 49-50; asst med officer, Tor-na-Dee Sanatorium, Aberdeen, 50-51; house physician, Chest Hosp, Brompton Hosp, London, Eng, 51-52; clin tutor gen med, Royal Infirmary, Edinburgh, 53-54; staff physician, South-East Kans Tuberc Hosp, Chanute, 56-60, supt, 60-61; from asst prof to assoc prof internal med, Univ Tex Southwestern Univ Med Sch Dallas, 61-69; assoc prof med, Sch Med, George Washington Univ, 69-71. *Concurrent Pos:* Assoc med, Univ Kans, 57-61; staff physician, Woodlawn Hosp, Dallas, 61-69; chief res in respiratory dis, Vet Admin Cent Off, Washington, DC, 69-71. *Mem:* Am Thoracic Soc; AMA. *Res:* Chest diseases; tuberculosis; aerobiology. *Mailing Add:* Dept Med Pulmonary Dis Univ Cincinnati Col Med 231 Bethesda Ave Cincinnati OH 45267-0001

LOUDON, RODNEY, QUANTUM OPTICS. *Current Pos:* prof, 84, PROF PHYSICS, ESSEX UNIV, 89- *Personal Data:* b Manchester, Eng, July 25, 34; m 60, Mary A Philips; c Anne Elizabeth & Peter Thomas. *Educ:* Oxford Univ, MA, DPhil, 59. *Honors & Awards:* Thomas Young Medal, Inst Physics, 87; Max Born Award Optical Soc Am, 92. *Prof Exp:* Sci civil servant, Radar Res Estab, 60-65; mem tech staff, Bell Labs, 65-66 & 70, RCA, 75 & Brit Telecommun Res Labs, 84 & 89-95. *Concurrent Pos:* Vis prof, Yale Univ, 75, Univ Calif, Irvine, 80, Sch Polytech, Lausanne, 85 & Univ Rome, 87 & 96. *Mem:* Fel Royal Soc; Optical Soc Am; Inst Physics UK. *Res:* Authored four books. *Mailing Add:* Physics Dept Univ Essex Wivenhoe Pk Colchester C04 3SQ England. *E-Mail:* loudr@essex.ac.uk

LOUGEAY, RAY LEONARD, PHYSICAL GEOGRAPHY, REMOTE SENSING. *Current Pos:* asst prof, 71-79, ASSOC PROF GEOG & DIR ENVIRON STUDIES, STATE UNIV NY COL GENESEO, 79- *Personal Data:* b Medford, Ore, Feb 9, 44; m 68. *Educ:* Rutgers Univ, AB, 66; Univ Mich, MS, 69, PhD(phys geog), 71. *Prof Exp:* Lectr phys geog, Univ Mich, 69-70. *Mem:* Asn Am Geogr; AAAS; Am Meteorol Soc; Am Soc Photogram. *Res:* Remote sensing; applied climatology and environmental modification as a function of radiative energy balances and hydrologic water balances; Alpine periglacial environments. *Mailing Add:* 11 Westview Cres Geneseo NY 14454

LOUGH, JOHN WILLIAM, JR, ANATOMY, CELL BIOLOGY. *Current Pos:* asst prof anat, 77-83, assoc prof 83-, PROF ANAT & CELLULAR BIOL, MED COL WIS. *Personal Data:* b St Louis, Mo, Apr 2, 43; m 68; c 3. *Educ:* St Louis Univ, BS, 65, MS, 68; Washington Univ, St Louis, PhD(cell biol & anat), 75. *Prof Exp:* Res assoc biol, Mass Inst Technol, 75-77. *Mem:* Am Soc Cell Biol; Am Asn Anatomists; Am Heart Asn. *Res:* Muscle differentiation in cell culture; changes in chromosomal proteins during myoblast differentiation. *Mailing Add:* Dept Anat Med Col Wis 8701 Watertown Plank Rd Milwaukee WI 53226

LOUGHEED, EVERETT CHARLES, HORTICULTURE. *Current Pos:* from asst prof to prof, 64-92, ASSOC GRAD FAC, UNIV GUELPH, ONT, 92- *Personal Data:* b Thornbury, Ont, July 16, 27; m 59, Leslie R Burness; c Stephen, Katherine & Robert. *Educ:* Ont Agr Col, BSc, 58; Univ Toronto, MSc, 60; Mich State Univ, PhD, 64. *Prof Exp:* Lectr, Ont Agr Col, 60-62. *Concurrent Pos:* Consult, Food & Agr Orgn, 85; mgr aid proj, Can Int Develop Agency, Arg, 89-92. *Mem:* Fel Am Soc Hort Sci; Agr Inst Can; Can Soc Hort Sci (pres, 73-74); Int Soc Hort Sci; Int Stands Orgn; Sigma Xi. *Res:* Horticulture; agriculture. *Mailing Add:* Dept Hort Univ Guelph Guelph ON N1G 2W1 Can

LOUGHLIN, KEVIN RAYMOND, UROLOGIC ONCOLOGY & RESEARCH, MALE INFERTILITY. *Current Pos:* DIR UROL RES, BRIGHAM & WOMEN'S HOSP, 87-; ASSOC PROF SURG, HARVARD MED SCH, 90- *Personal Data:* b 1949. *Educ:* Princeton Univ, AB, 71; NY Med Col, MD, 75; Am Bd Urol, cert. *Concurrent Pos:* Staff urologist, Brigham & Women's Hosp & Dana Farber Cancer Inst, Boston, 91- *Mem:* Soc Univ Urologists; fel Am Col Surgeons; Am Urol Asn; Soc Basic Urol Res. *Res:* New and novel therapies for superficial and invasive bladder cancer. *Mailing Add:* Brigham & Womens Hosp 75 Francis St Boston MA 02115-6195. *Fax:* 617-566-3475

LOUGHLIN, THOMAS RICHARD, MARINE MAMMALOGY, BEHAVIORAL ECOLOGY. *Current Pos:* MARINE MAMMAL RES SPECIALIST, NAT MARINE FISHERIES SERV, 77- *Personal Data:* b Santa Monica, Calif, July 19, 43; m 71; c 2. *Educ:* Univ Calif, Santa Barbara, BA, 72; Humboldt State Univ, MA, 74; Univ Calif, Los Angeles, PhD(biol), 77. *Concurrent Pos:* Biol consult, TerraScan, Inc, Environ Consults, 72-74;

recipient res funds, Univ Calif, 75 & US Marine Mammal Comn, 75-77; vis scientist, Smithsonian Inst & US Dept Com alt mem, US Endangered Species Sci Authority, 77-80; assoc prof, Ore State Univ, 85- *Mem:* AAAS; Am Asn Biol Sci; Am Soc Mammalogists; Animal Behav Soc; Soc Marine Mammalogists. *Res:* Natural history, including physiological and behavioral ecology of marine mammals and the impact of man caused perturbations on them; recovery of endangered species; phylogenetic relationship between marine mammals; general oceanography. *Mailing Add:* Nat Marine Fisheries Serv Nat Marine Mammal Lab 7600 Sand Point Way NE Seattle WA 98115-0070

LOUGHLIN, TIMOTHY ARTHUR, APPLIED MATHEMATICS. *Current Pos:* assoc prof, 76-91, PROF MATH, NEW YORK INST TECHNOL, 91-, CHMN DEPT MATH, 90- *Personal Data:* b Bay Shore, NY, Nov 16, 42; m 65, Carol E Olsen; c Shelley, Shannon, Sheryl & Scott. *Educ:* State Univ NY Stony Brook, BS, 64; Rensselaer Polytech Inst, MS, 66, PhD(math), 69. *Prof Exp:* Asst prof math, Union Col, NY, 69-76. *Mem:* Math Asn Am. *Res:* Network theory; realization of matrices as impedance and admittance matrices. *Mailing Add:* Dept Math New York Inst Technol PO Box 9029 Central Islip NY 11722. *Fax:* 516-348-0912

LOUGHMAN, BARBARA ELLEN EVERS, IMMUNOBIOLOGY. *Current Pos:* VPRES, DEVELOP SERVS, IMTCI-PRA, 95- *Personal Data:* b Frankford, Ind, Oct 26, 40; m 62; c 2. *Educ:* Univ Ill, BS, 62; Univ Notre Dame, PhD(microbiol & immunol), 72. *Prof Exp:* From asst res microbiologist to assoc res microbiologist, Ames Res Lab, Miles Labs Inc, 62-71, res scientist immunol, 71-72; staff fel immunol, Nat Inst Child Health & Human Develop, 72-74; res scientist, Hypersensitivity Dis Res, Upjohn Co, 74-79, res head immunol, 79-84, res mgr, 84-85; dir immunol res, Monsanto Co, 85-88; dir & consult proj mgt, Rorer Cent Res, 88-91; dir global regulatory affairs, Marion Merrell Dow, 91-95. *Mem:* AAAS; Asn Women Sci; Am Asn Immunologists. *Res:* Cellular immunology; regulatory mechanisms in cells using controlled in vitro and in vivo systems as models for specific intervention in an immume response; clinical research immunobiology of transplantation and blood dyscrasia; management; strategic planning; project and portfolio management. *Mailing Add:* Develop Servs IMTCI-PRA 16400 College Blvd Lenexa KS 66219

LOUGHMAN, WILLIAM D, CLINICAL CYTOGENETICS ESPECIALLY PRE-NATAL DIAGNOSIS & CANCER CYTOGENETICS. *Current Pos:* spec cytogeneticist, 82-89, DIR CYTOGENETICS LAB, CHILDRENS HOSP, OAKLAND, 89- *Personal Data:* b Oklahoma City, Okla, July 10, 32; m 67, Katherine Hershey; c Paul O, Elizabeth L & Donald E. *Educ:* Univ Calif, Berkeley, BS, 60, MS, 64, PhD(genetics),73; Am Bd Med Genetics, dipl, 82. *Prof Exp:* Biophysicist, Lawrence Berkeley Lab, 65-74; from asst res geneticist to assoc res geneticist, Univ Calif, San Francisco, 75-80, dir, Cytogenetics Lab, 75-82, assoc prof pediat, 80-82. *Concurrent Pos:* Lectr, Univ Calif, Berkeley, 74-77; adj assoc prof, Univ Calif, San Francisco, 80-82. *Mem:* AAAS; Sigma Xi; Am Soc Human Genetics; fel Am Col Med Genetics. *Res:* Cytogenetics; pre-natal diagnosis and cancer cytogenetics. *Mailing Add:* 393 Gravatt Dr Berkeley CA 94705-1503. *Fax:* 510-450-5874

LOUGHRAN, EDWARD DAN, ANALYTICAL CHEMISTRY. *Current Pos:* RETIRED. *Personal Data:* b Canton, Ohio, June 2, 28; wid; c Nancy (Wathen), Steven & Glenn. *Educ:* Ohio State Univ, BS, 50; MS, 53, PhD(chem), 55. *Prof Exp:* Asst chem, Res Found, Ohio State Univ, 53-55; mem staff, Los Alamos Nat Lab, 55-90, assoc group leader, 81-86, sect leader, 86-90. *Concurrent Pos:* Lab assoc, Los Alamos Nat Lab, 91- *Mem:* Am Soc Mass Spectrometry. *Res:* Analytical mass spectrometry; surveillance and compatibility studies of plastic-bonded explosives; physical properties, modes of decomposition and radiation chemistry of organic explosives. *Mailing Add:* 5116 Timan Ave NW Albuquerque NM 87114

LOUGHRAN, GERARD ANDREW, SR, ORGANIC CHEMISTRY, POLYMER CHEMISTRY. *Current Pos:* chemist, 60-86, PROJ SCIENTIST, MAT LAB, WRIGHT AERONAUT LABS, USAF, 86-; CONSULT, 86- *Personal Data:* b Mt Vernon, NY, Sept 10, 18; m 45, Kathleen O'Connor; c Maura, Kathleen, Gerard Jr & Judy. *Educ:* Fordham Univ, BS, 41; NY Univ, MS, 48. *Prof Exp:* Analytical chemist, NY Quinine & Chem Works, 41-43; asst chem, Fordham Univ, 43-44; chemist, Am Cyanamid Co, 46-56 & R T Vanderbilt Co, 56-59. *Concurrent Pos:* Mem, Rubber Div, Polymer Div & Polymer Sci & Eng Div, Am Chem Soc. *Mem:* Fel Am Inst Chem; emer mem Am Chem Soc; AAAS; NY Acad Sci. *Res:* Petroleum and rubber chemicals; polymer chemistry; high temperature materials; elastomers; organic synthesis. *Mailing Add:* 4575 Irelan St Kettering OH 45440

LOUGHRIDGE, MICHAEL SAMUEL, MARINE GEOLOGY. *Current Pos:* SUPVRY OCEANOGR, NAT GEOPHYS & SOLAR TERRESTRIAL DATA CTR, 78- *Personal Data:* b Jacksonville, Tex, Aug 27, 36; m 61; c 1. *Educ:* Rice Univ, BA, 58; Harvard Univ, MA, 61, PhD(geol), 67. *Prof Exp:* Grad res geologist II, Marine Phys Lab, Scripps Inst, Calif, 61-63, postgrad res geologist II, 63-64, postgrad res geologist III, 64-67, asst res geologist, 67-68; sci staff asst, Oceanog Surv Dept, US Naval Oceanog Off, 68-78. *Mem:* AAAS; Geol Soc Am; Am Geophys Union; assoc mem Soc Explor Geophys. *Res:* Studies of specialized techniques of echo sounding and the micro-topography of the sea floor; studies of fine scale magnetics of the sea floor; instrumentation for marine geology; seismic profiling; quantitative geomorphology; stream hydraulics; relationships between archaeology and geology. *Mailing Add:* 2630 Iliff St Boulder CO 80303

LOUGHRIN, JOHN HUDSON, PLANT-INSECT INTERACTIONS, NATURAL PRODUCTS CHEMISTRY. *Current Pos:* POSTDOCTORAL SCHOLAR, COMMUNITY RES SERV, KY STATE UNIV, 97- *Personal Data:* m 85, Linda Gilbert; c John James. *Educ:* Univ Ky, BS, 81, MS, 89, PhD(plant physiol), 91. *Prof Exp:* Prin lab technician, Dept Hort, Univ Ky, 84-97, postdoctoral scholar, Dept Entom, 95-97; res chemist, Insect Attractants, Behavior & Basic Biol Res Lab, 92-95. *Mem:* Entom Soc Am. *Res:* Feeding-induced odors in insect aggregation; biochemistry of host plant resistance, especially as regards biochemical changes induced in plants by insect feeding; circadian and diurnal rhythms. *Mailing Add:* Ky State Univ Frankfort KY 40601. *Fax:* 502-227-6381; *E-Mail:* jloughrin@uky.campus.mci.net

LOUGHRY, FRANK GLADE, SOIL CONSERVATION. *Current Pos:* RETIRED. *Personal Data:* b Marion Center, Pa, Apr 16, 10; m 44. *Educ:* Pa State Univ, BS, 31, PhD(agron, soils), 60; Ohio State Univ, MS, 34. *Prof Exp:* Asst agron, Ohio Agr Exp Sta, 31-33; soil scientist, USDA Soil Conserv Serv, 34-35, asst regional soil scientist, Northeastern US, 36-45, state soil scientist, Pa, 45-66; soil scientist, Pa Dept Health, 66-70; chief, Soil Sci Unit, Pa Dept Environ Resources, 71-77, consult soil scientist, 77-84. *Mem:* Fel AAAS; Am Soc Agron; Int Soc Soil Sci; fel Soil Conserv Soc Am. *Res:* Relation of soil morphology to aeration; soil factors affecting renovation of waste; interpretation of soil data for environmental protection; use of soil surveys in environmental programs. *Mailing Add:* Brethern Village Box 5093 Lancaster PA 17606-5093

LOUGHTON, ARTHUR, HORTICULTURE. *Current Pos:* RETIRED. *Personal Data:* b Wisbech, Eng, May 25, 31; Can citizen; m 55, Ruth Bullivant; c Martin & Graham. *Educ:* Univ Nottingham, Eng, BSc, 54, MSc, 60. *Prof Exp:* Hort officer res, Stockbridge House Exp Hort Sta, Ministry Agr, Fisheries & Food, Yorkshire, Eng, 54-62, dep dir, 62-67; res scientist veg res, Hort Res Inst Ont, Vineland Sta, 67-75; mgr transition crop team, Ont Ministry Agr & Food, Simcoe, 86-91, dir hort res, Hort Res Inst, 75-96. *Mem:* Can Soc Hort Sci; Agr Inst Can. *Res:* Production of field vegetables, including integrated pest management, specialising cole crops, management of total station research programs in fruit and vegetables. *Mailing Add:* RR 1 Vittoria ON N0E 1W0 Can

LOUI, MICHAEL CONRAD, THEORETICAL COMPUTER SCIENCE. *Current Pos:* Res asst prof, 82-86, res assoc prof, Coord Sci Lab & assoc prof elec & comput eng, 86-91, RES PROF, COORD SCI LAB & PROF ELEC & COMPUT ENG, UNIV ILL, URBANA, 91-, ASSOC DEAN, GRAD COL, 96- *Personal Data:* b Philadelphia, Pa, June 1, 55; m 83, Cynthia M Wood; c Eric & Jeremy. *Educ:* Yale Univ, BS, 75; Mass Inst Technol, MS, 77, PhD(comput sci), 80. *Concurrent Pos:* Vis res asst prof & vis assoc prof elec eng, Univ Ill, Urbana, 81-82; category ed, Comput Reviews, 87-; prog dir, NSF, Washington, DC, 90-91. *Mem:* Asn Comput Mach; Am Soc Eng Educ; Soc Indust & Appl Math; Inst Elec & Electronics Engrs. *Res:* Computational complexity theory; parallel and distributed computation. *Mailing Add:* Coord Sci Lab Univ Ill 1308 W Main St Urbana IL 61801. *E-Mail:* m-loui@uiuc.edu

LOUIE, DEXTER STEPHEN, GASTROENTEROLOGY. *Current Pos:* ASST PROF NUTRIT, UNIV NC, CHAPEL HILL, 91- *Personal Data:* b San Francisco, Calif. *Educ:* Univ Calif, Berkeley, AB, 74, BS, 76, PhD(nutrit), 82. *Prof Exp:* Res fel gastroenterol, Univ Mich, Ann Arbor, 85-87, res investr, 87-90, asst res scientist, 90-91. *Concurrent Pos:* Investr, Ctr Gastrointestinal Biol & Dis, 91- *Mem:* Am Gastroenterol Asn; Am Inst Nutrit; Am Pancreatic Asn; Am Physiol Soc. *Res:* Neurohormonal control of exocrine pancreatic secretion; intracellular messenger mechanisms. *Mailing Add:* Dept Nutrit CB 2202 McGarran-Greenberg Hall No 7400 Univ NC Chapel Hill NC 27599-7400. *Fax:* 919-966-7216; *E-Mail:* dlouie@sphvax.sph.unc.edu

LOUIE, MING, polymer in electronic application, electrochemistry, for more information see previous edition

LOUIE, RAYMOND, PLANT PATHOLOGY. *Current Pos:* ASSOC PROF VIROL, OHIO STATE UNIV & RES PLANT PATHOLOGIST, OHIO AGR RES & DEVELOP CTR, USDA, 67- *Personal Data:* b Canton, China, June 22, 36; US citizen; m 62; c 1. *Educ:* Univ Calif, Berkeley, BS, 59; Cornell Univ, MS, 65, PhD(plant path), 68. *Mem:* Am Phytopath Soc. *Res:* Epiphytology of plant viruses; virus vector relationships; mechanical transmission of plant viruses. *Mailing Add:* Dept Plant Path USDA/OARDC 1680 Madison Ave Wooster OH 44691-4096

LOUIE, ROBERT EUGENE, VIROLOGY. *Current Pos:* res microbiologist virol, 61-77, MGR VIROL RES DEPT, CUTTER LABS, 77- *Personal Data:* b Oakland, Calif, Aug 2, 29; m 62; c 1. *Educ:* Univ Calif, Berkeley, BA, 51, MA, 53, PhD(bacteriol), 63. *Prof Exp:* Res asst virol, Ft Detrick, Md, 54-55. *Mem:* Am Soc Microbiol; Sigma Xi. *Res:* Development of viral vaccines for human use; viral chemotherapy; virus-cell relationships. *Mailing Add:* 1026 Cragmont Ave Berkeley CA 94708

LOUIE, STEVEN GWON SHENG, THEORETICAL SOLID STATE PHYSICS. *Current Pos:* assoc prof, 80-84, PROF PHYSICS, UNIV CALIF, BERKELEY, 84- *Personal Data:* b Canton, China, Mar 26, 49; US citizen; m 75, Jane Wong; c Jonathan, Jennifer & Sarah. *Educ:* Univ Calif, AB, 72, PhD(physics), 76. *Honors & Awards:* US Dept Energy Award, 93; Rahman Prize, Am Phys Soc, 96. *Prof Exp:* NSF fel, Dept Physics, Univ Calif, Berkeley, 76-77; fel theoret solid state physics, T J Watson Res Ctr, IBM Corp, 77-79; asst prof physics, Univ Penn, 79-80. *Concurrent Pos:* A P Sloan fel, 80-82; prof, Miller Inst Basic Res Sci, 86-87; vis scholar, Univ Tokyo, 89; J S Guggenheim fel, 89-90; vis prof, Fourier Univ, Grenoble, France, 90; Sr fac scientist, Lawrence Berkeley Lab, 93-; prof, Miller Inst Basic Res, 95. *Mem:* Fel Am Phys Soc; Mat Res Soc. *Res:* Theoretical solid state physics; electronic properties of solids and of solid surfaces and interfaces; many-body effects in solids. *Mailing Add:* Dept Physics Univ Calif Berkeley CA 94720. *Fax:* 510-643-9473

LOUIS, JOHN, HEMATOLOGY, CLINICAL PHARMACOLOGY. *Current Pos:* CONSULT HEMAT & ONCOL, 70- *Personal Data:* b Chicago, Ill, June 21, 24; div. *Educ:* Univ Ill, BS, 48, MS & MD, 50. *Prof Exp:* Instr med, Col Med, Univ Ill, 51-65; chmn, Midwest Coop Chemother Group, 59-69; asst prof, Stritch Sch Med, Loyola Univ, Chicago, 65-70; Prof med, Chicago Med Sch, 75; chief hematol sect, Vet Admin Hosp, Downey, Ill, 75; assoc dir, Div Hematol & Oncol, Chicago Med Sch, 75. *Concurrent Pos:* Consult to various hosps & Chicago State TB Sanatorium, 58-; chmn, Leukemia Criteria Comt, NIH, 61-65; Leukemia Task Force, 62-65; US deleg, Eighth Int Cancer Cong, 62; prin investr, Leukemia A Group, MCCG, Eastern Coop Oncol Group. *Mem:* Am Soc Hemat; Am Soc Clin Oncol; Am Col Physicians; Am Soc Clin Path; emer mem Cent Soc Clin Res; Int Soc Hemat. *Res:* Clinical pharmacology of drugs relating to hematology and cancer. *Mailing Add:* 347 Circle Lane Lake Forest IL 60045

LOUIS, KWOK TOY, TEXTILE CHEMISTRY. *Current Pos:* tech dir, 76-77, VPRES, APEX CHEM CO, INC, 78- *Personal Data:* b Shanghai, China, Jan 22, 27; m 54, Harriet Poon; c Arthur, Mark & Jeffrey. *Educ:* Tex Tech Univ, BS, 51. *Prof Exp:* Lab dir, Otto Goedecke, Inc, Tex, 53-54; develop chemist, Burlington Indust, Inc, NC, 55-56; chief chemist, United Piece Dye Works, SC, 57-61; applns chems, Ciba Chem & Dye Co, 61-62, group leader appln res & qual control, 63-64, admin mgr res & appln, Tech Appln Prod, 64-68, mgr cent lab, 68-71; dir tech dept, Dyes & Chem Div, Crompton & Knowles Corp, NJ, 71-76. *Mem:* Am Asn Textile Chemists & Colorists; Nat Flaxseed Processors Asn. *Mailing Add:* 442 Ellis Place Wyckoff NJ 07481

LOUIS, LAWRENCE HUA-HSIEN, BIOCHEMISTRY. *Current Pos:* RETIRED. *Personal Data:* b Canton, China, Apr 23, 08; nat US; m 42; c 4. *Educ:* Univ Mich, BS, 32, MS, 33, ScD, 37. *Prof Exp:* Res org chem, Univ Berlin, Ger, 37-39; fel physiol, Univ Pa, 40-41; asst internal med, Univ Mich, Ann Arbor, 41-46, instr biochem, 46-48, from asst prof to assoc prof, 48-69, prof, 70-78. *Mem:* AAAS; Am Chem Soc; Am Soc Biol Chem. *Res:* Endocrinology and metabolism. *Mailing Add:* 2302 Manchester Rd Ann Arbor MI 48104-6566

LOUIS, THOMAS MICHAEL, REPRODUCTIVE ENDOCRINOLOGY. *Current Pos:* from asst prof to assoc prof, 76-85, PROF ANAT, SCH MED, EAST CAROLINA UNIV, 85- *Personal Data:* b Pensacola, Fla, Dec 27, 44; m 69; c 2. *Educ:* Va Polytech Inst & State Univ, BS, 68, MS, 71; Mich State Univ, PhD(sci), 75. *Honors & Awards:* Richard Hoyte Res Prize, Am Dairy Sci Asn, 75. *Prof Exp:* Lalor res fel reproductive endocrinol, Univ Oxford, 75-76. *Mem:* AAAS; Soc Gynec Invest; Sigma Xi; Soc Study Endocrinol; Am Asn Anatomists. *Res:* Chronic effects of alcohol, nicotine, and the nervous system on pregnancy and parturition; studies include endocrinology of parturition, fetal endocrinology, effects of fetal asphyxia on the neonate and endocrine control of the hypothalamus and pituitary. *Mailing Add:* Dept Anat Sch Med East Carolina Univ Greenville NC 27858-4353

LOUIS-FERDINAND, ROBERT T, PHARMACOLOGY. *Current Pos:* PROF, DEPT PHARMACOL, WAYNE STATE UNIV, 76- *Mailing Add:* Pharmaceut Sci Wayne State Univ Shapero Hall Detroit MI 48202. *Fax:* 313-577-2033

LOULLIS, COSTAS CHRISTOU, neurobiology, neurochemistry, for more information see previous edition

LOULOU, RICHARD JACQUES, OPERATIONS RESEARCH, PROBABILITY. *Current Pos:* From asst prof to assoc prof, 70-83, PROF OPERS RES, MCGILL UNIV, 83- *Personal Data:* b Relizane, Algeria, Apr 19, 44; Can citizen; m 67; c 2. *Educ:* Sch Polytech, Paris, BSc, 66; Univ Calif, Berkeley, MSc, 68, PhD(opers res), 71. *Hon Degrees:* DSc, Univ Grenoble, France, 78. *Concurrent Pos:* Consult, Archer, Seaden & Assocs, 72-73, Children's Hosp, Can Ministry Energy, Mines & Resources, 84-85. *Mem:* Inst Mgt Sci; Opers Res Soc Am; Can Opers Res Soc; Soc Indust & Appl Math. *Res:* Queueing theory; congested service systems; stochastic processes simulation; heuristics in optimization. *Mailing Add:* Dept Mgt McGill Univ Sherbrooke St W Montreal PQ H3A 2M5 Can

LOUNIBOS, LEON PHILIP, INSECT ECOLOGY, INSECT BEHAVIOR. *Current Pos:* PROF ENTOM, UNIV FLA, 93- *Personal Data:* b Petaluma, Calif, Aug 19, 47; div; c Andrea Lounibos & Andrew Pragnell. *Educ:* Univ Notre Dame, BS, 69; Harvard Univ MS, 70, PhD(biol), 74. *Prof Exp:* Res scientist & head, Int Ctr Insect Physiol & Ecol, Coastal Res Sta, 74-77; entomologist III, Fla Med Entom Lab, 77-83, assoc prof, 83-93. *Concurrent Pos:* NIH fel, 69-77, 88-89; prin investr, Nat Inst Allergy & Infectious Dis, NIH, 91-97 & 94-97. *Mem:* AAAS; Sigma Xi; Entom Soc Am; Animal Behav Soc; Ecol Soc Am; Am Soc Trop Med & Hyg. *Res:* Insect ecology: seasonality, diapause strategies, predator-prey relationships, community organization; insect behavior: building, predatory, oviposition behaviors; biosystematics. *Mailing Add:* Fla Med Entom Lab 200 Ninth St SE Vero Beach FL 32962. *Fax:* 561-778-7205

LOUNSBURY, JOHN BALDWIN, PHOTOLITHOGRAPHIC TECHNOLOGY, HIGH BANDWIDTH COMMUNICATION SYSTEMS. *Current Pos:* SR ENGR & MGR, IBM CORP, ARMONK, NY, 58- *Personal Data:* b Urbana, Ill, Jan 30, 36; m 63; c 3. *Educ:* Univ Vt, BA, 57; Columbia Univ, MA, 58; Ill Inst Technol, PhD(phys chem), 66. *Concurrent Pos:* Res assoc physics, Armour Res Found, Chicago, Ill, 59-62. *Res:* Career research activities include quantum chemistry of molecular structure, plasma chemistry, physics and materials/processes of photolithography for semiconductor fabrication; one patent and 20 publications. *Mailing Add:* Sunset Hill Rd Millbrook NY 12569

LOURENCO, RUY VALENTIM, MEDICINE, PHYSIOLOGY. *Current Pos:* assoc prof, 67-69, dir pulmonary sect, Dept Med, 70-77, PROF MED & PHYSIOL, ABRAHAM LINCOLN SCH MED, UNIV ILL COL MED, 69-, CHMN DEPT MED, 77-, FOLEY PROF MED, 78- *Personal Data:* b Lisbon, Portugal, Mar 25, 29; US citizen; m 60; c 2. *Educ:* Univ Lisbon, BSc, 46, MD, 51. *Prof Exp:* Intern, Lisbon City Hosps, 52, resident internal med, 53-55; instr med, Sch Med, Lisbon, 56-59; from asst prof to assoc prof, NJ Col Med, 63-67. *Concurrent Pos:* Attend physician, Nat Cancer Inst, Lisbon, Portugal, 55-61, Lisbon Univ Hosp, 56-61, Jersey City Med Ctr & VA Hosp, NJ & Newark City Hosp, 63-67; Univ Ill Hosp, Cook County Hosp & W Side VA Hosp, 67-; fel med, Cologne Univ, 57 & Columbia-Presby Med Ctr, 59-63; dir, Respiratory Physiol Lab, Univ Lisbon Med Sch, Portugal, 57-61, Respiratory Physiol, dept med, NJ Col Med, 63-67, Respiratory Res, Hektoen Inst Med Res, Chicago, 67-71, Respiratory Physiol Lab, Cook County Hosp, 67-69, dept pulmonary med, 69-70 & Pulmonary Sect & Labs, Univ Ill Med Ctr, 70-77; Lederle int fel, 59-60; Polachek Found fel, 61-63; consult physician, Vet Admin Hosps, 65-; mem cardio-pulmonary coun, Am Heart Asn; mem task force sci basis respiratory therapeut, Nat Heart & Lung Inst, 71-72; mem study sect, NIH, 72-76; consult, Career Develop Prog, Vet Admin, 72-; chmn sci assembly, Am Thoracic Soc, 74-75; vis prof, Cardiothoracic Inst, Brompton Hosp, Univ London, 75-76; physician-in-chief, Univ Ill Hosps, 77-; mem, inhalation toxicol comt, Nat Ctr Toxicol Res, 77-, Asn Prog Dirs Internal Med, 77-, comt smoking & health, Am Lung Asn, 81- & comt int affairs, Am Col Chest Physicians, 84-; reviewer, var physiol, respiratory & clin journals; lectr, var univs in US, Brazil, Portugal & Spain. *Mem:* Am Physiol Soc; Am Fedn Clin Res; Am Thoracic Soc; Am Soc Clin Invest; Soc Exp Biol & Med; Int Soc Aerosols Med; Asn Profs Med. *Res:* Internal medicine; chest diseases; respiratory physiology and biochemistry; regulation of ventilation; muscles of breathing; pulmonary defense mechanisms. *Mailing Add:* UMDNJ NJ Med Sch 185 S Orange Ave Newark NJ 07103-2714. *Fax:* 973-982-7104, 456-7104

LOURIA, DONALD BRUCE, INTERNAL MEDICINE, MICROBIOLOGY. *Current Pos:* PROF PREV MED & COMMUNITY HEALTH & CHMN DEPT, NJ MED SCH, COL MED & DENT NJ, 69- *Personal Data:* b New York, NY, July 11, 28; m 55; c 3. *Educ:* Harvard Univ, BS, 49, MD, 53. *Prof Exp:* From instr to assoc prof med, Col Med, Cornell Univ, 58-69. *Concurrent Pos:* Pres, NY State Coun Drug Addiction, 65-73. *Mem:* Am Soc Clin Invest; Am Fedn Clin Res; Am Soc Microbiol; Am Col Physicians. *Res:* Mycology, especially fungal toxins and the pathogenesis of Candida infections; prevention programs for adults; health education; health manpower; cancer epidemiology; health problems of the aging. *Mailing Add:* 100 Bergen Newark NJ 07103-2407

LOURIE, ALAN DAVID, ORGANIC CHEMISTRY. *Current Pos:* JUDGE, COURT APPEALS, FED CIRCUIT. *Personal Data:* b Boston, Mass, Jan 13, 35; m 59, Elizabeth S; c 2. *Educ:* Harvard Univ, AB, 56; Univ Wis, MS, 58; Univ Pa, PhD(org chem), 65; Temple Univ, JD, 70. *Prof Exp:* Res chemist, Monsanto Co, 57-59; res chemist, Wyeth Labs, 59-60, lit chemist, 60-62, patent chemist, 62-64; patent agent chem, Smith Kline & French Labs, 64-70, patent atty, 70-71, assoc patent coun, 71-74, asst dir, patent dept, 74-76, vpres corp patents, Smithkline Corp, 76-90. *Mem:* Am Chem Soc. *Res:* Synthesis of heterocyclic compounds; medicinal chemistry. *Mailing Add:* Court Appeals Fed Circuit 717 Madison Pl NW Nat Court Bldg Washington DC 20439

LOUSTAUNAU, JOAQUIN, MATHEMATICS. *Current Pos:* ASST PROF MATH, NMEX STATE UNIV, 65- *Personal Data:* b San Luis Potosi, Mex, Sept 17, 36; m 66. *Educ:* Okla State Univ, BS, 58, MS, 60; Univ Ill, PhD(math), 65. *Prof Exp:* Instr math, Inst Tech & Higher Educ, Monterrey, Mex, 60-61. *Mem:* Math Asn Am; Am Math Soc. *Res:* Functional analysis. *Mailing Add:* NMex State Univ Las Cruces NM 88003-0105

LOUTFY, RAFIK OMAR, PHOTOCHEMISTRY, PHYSICAL CHEMISTRY. *Current Pos:* mem sci staff, 74-80, AREA MGR, XEROX RES CTR CAN, 80- *Personal Data:* b Cairo, Egypt, Nov, 43; Can citizen; m 65; c 2. *Educ:* Ain Shams Univ, Cairo, BSc, 64, MSc, 67; Univ Western Ont, PhD(photochem), 72; Univ Toronto, MBA, 85. *Prof Exp:* Fel laser flash photolysis, Nat Res Coun Can, 72-74; fel photochem, Univ Toronto, 74. *Concurrent Pos:* Adj prof, Univ Western Ont, 79- *Mem:* Am Chem Soc; Chem Inst Can; Inter-Am Photochem Soc; Europ Photochem Soc; Soc Photog Scientists & Engrs. *Res:* Photophysics of small molecules and polymers; solar energy conversion using organic semiconductors; dye sensitization of semiconductors; electrochemistry and spectroscopy of organic molecules and dyes; photo conductors. *Mailing Add:* Xerox Res Ctr Can 2660 Speakman Dr Mississauga ON L5K 2L1 Can

LOUTTIT, RICHARD TALCOTT, BEHAVIORAL SCIENCES, NEUROSCIENCE. *Current Pos:* RETIRED. *Personal Data:* b Bloomington, Ind, Dec 5, 32; wid; c Robert & Cathy. *Educ:* DePauw Univ, AB, 54; Univ Mich, MA, 59, PhD(psychol), 61. *Prof Exp:* Asst prof psychol, Univ Pac,

61-64; health sci adminr, NIH, 64-70; prof & head, Dept Psychol, Univ Mass, Amherst, 70-75; div dir, Div Behav & Neural Sci, NSF, 75-93. *Concurrent Pos:* Staff dir, President's Biomed Res Panel, 75. *Mem:* Fel AAAS; Am Psychol Soc. *Mailing Add:* 225 Three Oaks Dr Gore VA 22637

LOUTTIT, ROBERT IRVING, EXPERIMENTAL HIGH ENERGY PHYSICS. *Current Pos:* RETIRED. *Personal Data:* b Honolulu, Hawaii, July 23, 29; m 54, 86, Anne Fincke; c Eric, Laura & Kimberly. *Educ:* Univ NH, BS, 52; Wash Univ, PhD(physics), 58. *Prof Exp:* From asst physicist to physicist, Brookhaven Nat Lab, 58-84, head, Accelerator Develop Br, 84-86, sr physicist, 84-86. *Concurrent Pos:* Physicist, Nuclear Res Ctr, Saclay, France, 63-64. *Mem:* AAAS; Am Phys Soc; Sigma Xi. *Res:* Bubble chamber development; neutrino interactions. *Mailing Add:* 205 McTeer Dr St Helena Island SC 29920

LOVAGLIA, ANTHONY RICHARD, MATHEMATICS. *Current Pos:* From asst prof to assoc prof, 51-60, PROF MATH, SAN JOSE STATE UNIV, 60- *Personal Data:* b San Jose, Calif, Jan 25, 23; m 44; c 3. *Educ:* Univ Calif, Los Angeles, AB, 45, PhD(math), 51; Stanford Univ, MS, 48; Univ Calif, Berkeley, MA(math), 51. *Mem:* Math Asn Am. *Res:* Analysis. *Mailing Add:* 278 Anchor Ct Boulder Creek CA 95006

LOVALD, ROGER ALLEN, ORGANIC POLYMER CHEMISTRY. *Current Pos:* RETIRED. *Personal Data:* b Marshall, Minn, Aug 8, 38; m 57; c 2. *Educ:* Univ Minn, BChem, 60; Univ Wis, PhD(org chem), 65. *Prof Exp:* Chemist, Spring Res Lab, Rohm & Haas Co, 65-67; cent res, Gen Mills Chem Inc, 67-71, sect leader resin develop, 71-75, tech dir resins, 75-97. *Mem:* Am Chem Soc. *Res:* Heteroaliphatic and organic chemistry; addition and condensation polymerization; acrylics; polyamides; polyesters; polyurethanes. *Mailing Add:* 340 Golfview Lane Amery WI 54001-1413

LOVALLO, WILLIAM ROBERT, BEHAVIORAL MEDICINE, PSYCHOPHARMACOLOGY. *Current Pos:* Asst prof, 80-85, ASSOC PROF, PSYCHIAT & BEHAV SCI, UNIV OKLA HEALTH SCI CTR, 85- *Personal Data:* b Newark, NJ, Nov 16, 46. *Educ:* Univ Calif, Los Angeles, BA, 68; Univ Colo, MA, 70; Univ Okla Health Sci Ctr, PhD(biol & psychol), 78. *Concurrent Pos:* NIH grant, Caffeine Effects, 85-; dir, Behav Sci Labs, Okla City Vet Admin Med Ctr, 86-; asst dir, Mind-Body Interactions, John D & Catherine T MacArthur Found Network. *Mem:* AAAS; Am Psychol Asn; Soc Psychophysiol Res; Soc Behav Med; Psychosomatic Soc. *Res:* Psychological and behavioral stress; the role of stress on the development of cardiovascular diseases. *Mailing Add:* Vet Admin Med Ctr 151A 921 NE 13th St Oklahoma City OK 73104

LOVAS, FRANCIS JOHN, MOLECULAR SPECTROSCOPY, RADIO ASTRONOMY & THERMAL RADIOMETRY. *Current Pos:* Assoc, Nat Res Coun-Nat Bur Stand, 70-72, DIR, MOLECULAR SPECTRA DATA CTR, NAT INST STAND & TECHNOL, 72- *Personal Data:* b Cleveland, Ohio, July 29, 41; m 70; c 1. *Educ:* Univ Detroit, BS, 63; Univ Calif, Berkeley, PhD(phys chem), 67. *Honors & Awards:* Gold Medal, Dept Com, 77. *Prof Exp:* Res grant, Lawrence Radiation Lab, Univ Calif, Berkeley, 67-68; NATO fel, Phys Inst, Free Univ Berlin, 68-70. *Mem:* Am Phys Soc; Am Chem Soc. *Res:* Properties of diatomic molecules by high temperature microwave adsorption and molecular beam electric resonance techniques; microwave spectroscopy of transient molecules and molecular radio astronomy; critical evaluation of microwave spectroscopic data. *Mailing Add:* Optical Technol Div 545 Nat Inst Stand & Technol Gaithersburg MD 20899. *Fax:* 301-975-2385; *E-Mail:* lovas@tiber.nist.gov

LOVASS-NAGY, VICTOR, APPLIED MATHEMATICS, ELECTRICAL ENGINEERING & CONTROL THEORY. *Current Pos:* prof math, 66-82, PROF ELEC ENG & MATH, CLARKSON UNIV, 82- *Personal Data:* b Debrecen, Hungary, Apr 25, 23; m 51, Klara Wolf; c Steven & Christine. *Educ:* Budapest Tech Univ, dipl, 47, PhD(math), 49. *Prof Exp:* Instr math, Budapest Tech Univ, 47-49, from asst prof to assoc prof, 49-58; consult engr, Ganz Elec Works, Hungary, 60-64; reader eng math, Univ Khartoum, 64-66. *Mem:* Sr mem Inst Elec & Electronics Engrs. *Res:* Matrix theory; numerical analysis; control theory. *Mailing Add:* Clarkson Univ Box 5720 Potsdam NY 13699-5820

LOVATT, CAROL JEAN, METABOLIC REGULATION. *Current Pos:* Res assoc, 80, asst prof plant physiol & asst plant physiologist, 80-87, ASSOC PROF PLANT PHYSIOL & ASSOC PLANT PHYSIOLOGIST, DEPT BOT & PLANT SCI, UNIV CALIF, RIVERSIDE, 87- *Personal Data:* b Kansas City, Mo, May 14, 47; div; c 2. *Educ:* Univ Mass, BA, 73; Univ RI, MS, 76, PhD(bot), 80. *Honors & Awards:* Fruit Publ Award, Am Soc Hort Sci, 87, Cross-Commodity Publ Award, 88. *Mem:* Am Soc Plant Physiologists; AAAS; Am Women Sci; Sigma Xi; Am Soc Hort Sci. *Res:* Metabolic regulation of nucleotide metabolism and arginine biosynthesis/urea cycle; citrus and avocado physiology: regulation of flowering, fruit set, and fruit growth; role of essential nutrient elements in plant metabolism. *Mailing Add:* Dept Bot & Plant Sci Univ Calif Riverside CA 92521

LOVE, ALLAN WALTER, ELECTROMAGNETISM, ANTENNAS & MICROWAVES. *Current Pos:* RETIRED. *Personal Data:* b Toronto, Ont, May 28, 16; US citizen; m 46, Shirley D Corrigan; c Karen M, Peter J & Elizabeth M. *Educ:* Univ Toronto, BA, 38, MA, 39, PhD(microwave physics), 51. *Prof Exp:* Res officer, Radiophysics Lab, Commonwealth Sci & Indust Res Orgn, Australia, 46-48; demonstr asst, Physics Lab, Univ Toronto, 48-51; chief instrumentation, Newmont Explor Ltd, Conn & Ariz, 51-57; staff scientist, Giannini Res Lab, Wiley Electronics Co, Ariz, 57-62, mgr, Physics Lab, Calif, 62-63; area mgr, Nat Eng Sci Co, 63-65; group scientist, Antenna Lab, Autonetics Div, NAm Aviation Inc, 63, group scientist theoret analysis, 65-71, mem tech staff, Space Div, NAm Rockwell Corp, 71-73, prog mgr, 73-76, prin scientist, Satellite Systs Div, Rockwell Int, 76-90. *Mem:* Fel Inst Elec & Electronics Engrs. *Res:* Microwave and millimeter wave physics; antenna theory and design; development of spacecraft antenna systems. *Mailing Add:* 518 Rockford Pl Corona Del Mar CA 92625-2721

LOVE, CALVIN MILES, PYROTECHNICS, EXPLOSIVES. *Current Pos:* Res specialist, 64-80, SR RES SPECIALIST, EG&G MOUND APPL TECHNOLOGIES, INC, 80- *Personal Data:* b Chicago, Ill, Mar 2, 37; m 60, Sue Ungerleider; c Peggy (High), David M & Andrew I. *Educ:* Ill Inst Technol, BS, 59; Mich State Univ, PhD(inorg chem), 64. *Mem:* AAAS; Am Chem Soc; NAm Thermal Analysis Soc. *Res:* Kinetics and mechanisms of inorganic oxidation-reduction reactions; plutonium separation and recovery; polonium process development; metal hydrides; radiation damage; thermal analysis; hydrides for hydrogen storage; chemistry of pyrotechnics; chemistry of explosives; calorimetry. *Mailing Add:* 7601 Eagle Creek Dr Dayton OH 45459. *Fax:* 513-865-3680

LOVE, CARL G(EORGE), SYSTEMS ANALYSIS. *Current Pos:* sr engr, Westinghouse Res & Develop Ctr, 67-71, fel engr, 72, mgr syst planning & tech assessment, 72-91, dir corp venture progs, Corp Planning, 84-91, SR SYSTS SCIENTIST, WESTINGHOUSE RES & DEVELOP CTR, 91- *Personal Data:* b Warsaw, NY, Sept 20, 40; m 71; c 2. *Educ:* Rochester Inst Technol, BS, 63; Carnegie Inst Technol, MS, 65, PhD(elec eng), 67. *Prof Exp:* Coop student, Rochester Gas & Elec Corp, 58-60; coop student, Delco Appl Div, Gen Motors Corp, 60-63, proj engr, 63. *Concurrent Pos:* Sr consult corp planning, Westinghouse Elec Corp, 82-84. *Mem:* Inst Elec & Electronics Engrs; Inst Mgt Sci; Opers Res Soc Am. *Res:* Technology forecasting; business analysis; energy analysis. *Mailing Add:* Carnegie-Mellon Univ Sch Comput Sci 500 Forbes Ave Pittsburgh PA 15213

LOVE, DANIEL JOSEPH, ELECTRICAL POWER GENERATION & DISTRIBUTION, ELECTRICAL & FIRE PROTECTION. *Current Pos:* CONSULT ENGR, CALIF, 87- *Personal Data:* b Fall River, Mass, Sept 27, 26; m 89, Adeline Aponte Esquivel; c Amy, Timothy, Terence, Kevin, Eric, Brian & Jason. *Educ:* Ill Inst Technol, BSEE, 51, MSEE, 56; Calif State Univ, MBA, 73. *Honors & Awards:* Outstanding Engr Award, Inst Adv Eng, 86; Richard Harold Kaufmann Award, Inst Elec & Electronics Engrs, 94. *Prof Exp:* Test engr, Int Harvester Co, 51-52; designer, Pioneer Serv & Eng Co, 52-53; proj engr & opers mgr, Panellit Co, 53-60; mkt mgr, Control Data Co, 61-62; mkt mgr & asst to pres, Emerson Elec Co, 63-65; pres & gen mgr, McKee Automation Co, 65-68; eng specialist, Bechtel Co, Calif, 68-80, chief elec engr, Madrid, 80-83, eng specialist, Norwalk, Calif, 83-87. *Concurrent Pos:* Chmn, Power Systs Comt, Indust Appln Soc, Inst Elec & Electronics Engrs, 90-91. *Mem:* Fel Inst Elec & Electronics Engrs; Soc Fire Protection Engrs; Nat Acad Forensic Engrs; Nat Soc Prof Engrs; Instrument Soc Am. *Res:* Contributed articles to professional journals. *Mailing Add:* 16300 E Soriano Dr Hacienda Heights CA 91745. *Fax:* 626-918-5205; *E-Mail:* donlove@compuserve.com

LOVE, DAVID VAUGHAN, FOREST MANAGEMENT. *Current Pos:* RETIRED. *Personal Data:* b St John, NB, Aug 25, 19; m 43; c 3. *Educ:* Univ NB, BSc, 41; Univ Mich, MF, 46. *Prof Exp:* From lectr to prof, Univ Toronto, 46-72, asst dean, 72-76, assoc dean, 77-83, dean, 84-85. *Concurrent Pos:* Vpres, Conserv Coun Ont, 59-64, pres, 74-75; vchmn, Can Coun on Rural Develop, 75-79; rep, Can Forestry Asn, 73. *Mem:* Soc Am Foresters; Can Pulp & Paper Asn; Can Inst Forestry (secy-mgr, 48-54, pres, 65-66); Ont Forestry Asn (vpres, 70-71, pres, 72-73); Can Forestry Asn (vpres, 74 & 75, pres, 75). *Res:* Land use; forests; acid precipitation. *Mailing Add:* 16 Marchwood Dr North York ON M3H 1J8 Can

LOVE, DAVID WAXHAM, QUATERNARY STRATIGRAPHY. *Current Pos:* ENVIRON GEOLOGIST, NMEX BUR MINES & MINERAL RESOURCES, 80- *Personal Data:* b Laramie, Wyo, Nov 1, 46; m. *Educ:* Beloit Col, BA, 69; Univ NMex, MS, 71, PhD(geol), 80. *Prof Exp:* Asst prof geol, Wash State Univ, 76-78. *Mem:* Geol Soc Am; Sigma Xi; Soc Archeol Sci. *Res:* Geomorphic processes and stratigraphy of surficial deposits in New Mexico and adjacent areas for assessing natural hazards and for determining stability of land forms for siting industrial plants or for storing hazardous materials. *Mailing Add:* NMex Bur Mines & Mineral Resources Campus Station Socorro NM 87801

LOVE, GEORGE M, ORGANIC CHEMISTRY. *Current Pos:* ASSOC DIR CHEM PROCESS DEVELOP, SCHERING-PLOUGH, 80- *Personal Data:* b Lima, Ohio, Oct 5, 44; m 72. *Educ:* DePauw Univ, BA, 66; Wake Forest Univ, MA, 68; Mich State Univ, PhD(org chem), 72. *Prof Exp:* Fel org chem, Rutgers Univ, 72-73; sr res chemist, Merck Inc, 73-80, res fel, 80. *Mem:* Sigma Xi; Am Chem Soc. *Res:* Process research in organic chemistry. *Mailing Add:* Schering Plough Res U-1-1 1011 Morris Ave Union NJ 07083

LOVE, GORDON ROSS, MATERIALS SCIENCE. *Current Pos:* TECH DIR CERAMICS, ALCOA TECH CTR, ALCOA, 80- *Personal Data:* b Cleveland, Ohio, July 31, 37; m 62; c 1. *Educ:* Case Inst Technol, BS, 58; Carnegie Inst Technol, MS, 61, PhD(metall), 63. *Prof Exp:* Metallurgist, Oak Ridge Nat Lab, 62-64, group leader superconducting mat, 64-70; asst mgr technol, Mat Syst Div, Union Carbide Corp, 70-78; staff mem, Sprague Elec, 78-87. *Concurrent Pos:* Lectr, Univ Tenn, 66-67; ed, Trans Comp Hyb Mfrs Tech, Inst Elec Electronics Engrs, 81-85. *Mem:* Sigma Xi; Inst Elec &

Electronics Engrs. *Res:* Diffusion; superconductivity; statistical process control; powder technology; surface and interface properties; ceramic dielectric materials. *Mailing Add:* 3901 Ash Dr Alcoa Tech Ctr 100 Technical Dr Allison Park PA 15101-3144

LOVE, HARRY SCHROEDER, JR, BOTANY, ECOLOGY. *Current Pos:* assoc prof, 67-80, PROF BIOL, EAST CENT OKLA STATE UNIV, 80- *Personal Data:* b Idabel, Okla, Aug 20, 27; m 52; c 2. *Educ:* Okla State Univ, BS, 52, MS, 58, PhD(bot), 71. *Mem:* AAAS; Am Inst Biol Sci; Nat Asn Biol Teachers. *Res:* Terrestrial plant ecology, especially clonal and root-graft relationships. *Mailing Add:* 1229 Scenic Dr Ada OK 74820

LOVE, HUGH MORRISON, PHYSICS. *Current Pos:* from asst prof to prof, 52-92, vprin, 76-92, EMER PROF PHYSICS, QUEEN'S UNIV, ONT, 92- *Personal Data:* b Northern Ireland, Aug 21, 26. *Educ:* Queen's Univ, Belfast, BSc & PhD(physics), 50. *Prof Exp:* Asst lectr, Queen's Univ, Belfast, 46-50; lectr, Univ Toronto, 50-52. *Mem:* Am Phys Soc. *Res:* Solid state physics; surface physics. *Mailing Add:* Dept Physics Queen's Univ Stirling Hall Kingston ON K7I 3N6 Can

LOVE, JIM, ORGANIC CHEMISTRY. *Current Pos:* res chemist, Dow Chem Co Mich, 65-67, Western Div, 67-74, res specialist, 74-77, group leader, 77-79, res mgr, 79-83, lab dir, Pittsburg, Calif, 83-88, lab dir, Midland, Mich, 88-95, GLOBAL DIR PROCESS RES, DOW ELAN CO IND, 95- *Personal Data:* b Bathgate, Scotland, Oct 21, 38; m 62; c 2. *Educ:* Univ Edinburgh, BSc, 60, PhD(carbohydrate chem), 63. *Prof Exp:* Fel, Scripps Inst, Univ Calif, 63-64 & Ohio State Univ, 64-65. *Mem:* Am Chem Soc; The Chem Soc. *Res:* Carbohydrate chemistry, particularly polysaccharide and mucopolysaccharide structural determination and biological activity; synthesis and biological activity of heterocyclic compounds. *Mailing Add:* Dow Elanco 9330 Zionsville Rd Bldg 306 Indianapolis IN 46268

LOVE, JIMMY DWANE, ANALYTICAL CHEMISTRY, THERMODYNAMICS & MATERIAL PROPERTIES. *Current Pos:* COM DEVELOP MGR, GA-PAC CORP, 88- *Personal Data:* b Plainview, Tex, Feb 2, 46; m 67; c 2. *Educ:* Stephen F Austin State Univ, Nacogdoches, Tex, BS, 69, MS, 76. *Prof Exp:* Bench chemist, Moore Bus Forms, 70-74, sr chemist, 74-78, lab mgr, 78-83, tech serv mgr, 80-83, qual assurance mgr, 83-85, carbonless paper prod mgr, Moore Bus Forms, 85-88. *Mem:* Am Chem Soc; Am Soc Qual Control; Am Soc Testing & Mat; Tech Asn Pulp & Paper Indust; Paper Indust Mgt Asn. *Res:* Micro encapsulation chemistry and techniques; coatings technology; papermaking chemistry; applied technology. *Mailing Add:* Ga Pac Corp 55 Park Pl Atlanta GA 30374

LOVE, JOHN DAVID, GEOLOGY. *Current Pos:* field asst, US Geol Surv, 38, asst geologist, 42-43, from assoc geologist to prin geologist, 43-56, supvr heavy metals, Jackson Proj, 66-68, Northern Rocky Mts Br, 64-66, 67-69, in charge Wyo basins fuels proj, 43-56, supvr, Laramie Off, Regional Geol Br, 69-87, STAFF GEOLOGIST, US GEOL SURV, 56-, EMER SCIENTIST, 87- *Personal Data:* b Riverton, Wyo, Apr 17, 13; m 40; c 4. *Educ:* Univ Wyo, BA, 33, MA, 34; Yale Univ, PhD(geol), 38. *Hon Degrees:* LLD, Univ Wyo, 61. *Honors & Awards:* Meritorious Serv Award, US Dept Interior, 77 & Distinguished Serv Award, 87; Nat Pub Serv Award, Am Asn Petrol Geologists, 91. *Prof Exp:* Asst geologist, Geol Surv Wyo, 33-37; from asst geologist to geologist, Shell Oil Co Inc, 38-42. *Concurrent Pos:* Distinguished lectr, Univ Wyo, 65, adj prof, 69-; instr & trustee, Teton Sci Sch, 65-85; affil prof geol, Univ Idaho, 74-; exten instr geol, Univ Calif, Davis, 77-; grad res adv, Univ Wash; affil, Univ Wash, 79-83 & Univ Minn, 81-83. *Mem:* AAAS; fel Geol Soc Am; Am Asn Petrol Geol; Sigma Xi. *Res:* Geology of fuels; uranium, vanadium and gold investigations; stratigraphic and structural geology; author and coauthor of about 220 scientific publications. *Mailing Add:* US Geol Surv PO Box 3007 Univ Sta Laramie WY 82071-3007

LOVE, JOSEPH E(UGENE), JR, CIVIL ENGINEERING. *Current Pos:* CONSULT, 85- *Personal Data:* b Chicago, Ill, Apr 9, 20; m 42, Barbara Duncan; c 2. *Educ:* Northwestern Univ, BS, 42, MS, 48, PhD(civil eng), 51. *Prof Exp:* Struct analyst, Curtiss-Wright Corp, 42-43; instr math & eng, Ripon Col, 43-45; from instr to asst prof civil eng, Northwestern Univ, 46-51; struct engr, Hanford Atomic Prod Oper, Gen Elec Co, 52-55, struct engr, Atomic Power Equip Dept, 55-66, mgr arrangements & structural design, 66-72, mgr advan eng, 72-75, mgr plant struct systs, nuclear energy div, 75-84. *Concurrent Pos:* Contribr, 1st Int Conf Peaceful Uses of Atomic Energy; chmn working group on containment, Int Orgn Standardization, Technol Comt 85, subcomt 3, 76-84, mem, working group on containment ISO, 84-88. *Mem:* Sigma Xi; Am Soc Civil Engrs. *Res:* Plasticity effects in flexure; nuclear power plant design. *Mailing Add:* 14799 Dove Rd Grass Valley CA 95949-7631. *E-Mail:* joslov@nccn.net

LOVE, L J CLINE, LUMINESCENCE, MICELLAR CHEMISTRY. *Current Pos:* from asst prof to assoc prof, 72-82, PROF ANALYTICAL CHEM, SETON HALL UNIV, 82-, DIR, CTR APPL SPECTROS, 85- *Personal Data:* b Richmond, Mo, Oct 1, 40; m 72; c 2. *Educ:* Univ Mo-Columbia, BS, 62, MA, 65; Univ Ill, Urbana, PhD(chem), 69. *Honors & Awards:* Spectros Medal, NY Soc Appl Spectros, 85. *Prof Exp:* Fel chem, Univ Fla, 69-70; asst prof analytical chem, Mich State Univ, 70-72. *Concurrent Pos:* Prin investr, NIH, 81-83, Environ Protection Agency, 82-84, NSF, 83-86; assoc ed, Appl Spectros 3, 83- *Mem:* Am Chem Soc; Soc Appl Spectros; Am Microchem Soc; Sigma Xi. *Res:* Development of new instrumentation and methodology in luminescence; analytical applications of micellar and cyclodextrin systems; fluorescence and phosphorescence spectroscopy; automation of chemical instrumentation; high performance liquid chromatography; computer factor analysis of data. *Mailing Add:* Dept Chem Seton Hall Univ 400 S Orange Ave South Orange NJ 07079

LOVE, LEON, RADIOLOGY. *Current Pos:* PROF RADIOL & CHMN DEPT, MED CTR, LOYOLA UNIV CHICAGO, 69- *Personal Data:* b New York, NY, Sept 7, 23; m 56; c 3. *Educ:* City Col New York, BS, 43; Chicago Med Sch, MD, 46; Am Bd Radiol, dipl, 51. *Prof Exp:* Radiologist, Cook Co Hosp, Chicago, 56-61; assoc prof radiol, Chicago Med Sch, 58-67, clin prof, 67-69. *Concurrent Pos:* Consult, Dwight Vet Admin Hosp, 56-62; dir diag radiol, Cook Co Hosp, Chicago, 61-69; consult, House of Correction, Chicago, 61- & WSide Vet Admin Hosp, 62- *Mem:* Am Col Radiol; Radiol Soc NAm. *Res:* Renal radiology; radiology of the gastro-intestinal tract. *Mailing Add:* Loyola Univ Stritch Sch Med 2160 S First Maywood IL 60153-5500

LOVE, NORMAN DUANE, LOW TEMPERATURE PHYSICS. *Current Pos:* software specialist, 77-82, commun consult, 82-94, NETWORK COMMUN CONSULT, DIGITAL EQUIP CORP, 94- *Personal Data:* b Howell, Mich, Jan 1, 39; m 62, Suzanne Keil; c Aaron M, Heather A (Constantino), Nathan D & Amber S. *Educ:* Albion Col, AB, 60; Western Mich Univ, MA, 62; Mich State Univ, PhD(physics), 67. *Prof Exp:* From asst prof to assoc prof, Maryville Col, 67-77, dir comput serv, 71-77. *Concurrent Pos:* Nat Sci Found comput grant, 68-73. *Mem:* Am Phys Soc; Am Asn Physics Teachers. *Res:* Effect of magnons on transport of phonons; phase boundaries in an antiferro magnetic material using calorimetric techniques. *Mailing Add:* Equip Corp 430 Blockhouse Rd Maryville TN 37803. *E-Mail:* loven@mail.dec.com

LOVE, RAYMOND CHARLES, CLINICAL PHARMACY. *Current Pos:* Dir, Area Health Educ Ctr, Cumberland, 77-78, ASST PROF CLIN PHARM, SCH PHARM, UNIV MD, 77- *Personal Data:* b Washington, DC, July 30, 53; m 76. *Educ:* Univ Md, Baltimore, DrPharm, 77. *Concurrent Pos:* Consult, Mem Hosp, Cumberland, Md, Sacred Heart Hosp, Thomas B Finan Ctr, & Memt Health Clin, Allegany Health Ctr, 77-; lectr, Squibb Pharmaceut, E R Squibb & Son, 78-; mem adv coun, Md High Blood Pressure Coord Coun, 78- *Mem:* Am Soc Hosp Pharmacists; Am Asn Cols Pharm. *Res:* Tardive dyskinesia; psychotherapeutic agents; hypertension; geriatric health care. *Mailing Add:* Dept Pharm Univ MD Sch Pharm 20 N Pine St Baltimore MD 21201-1180

LOVE, RICHARD HARRISON, UNDERWATER ACOUSTICS. *Current Pos:* OCEANOGR ACOUST, NAVAL RES LAB, 76- *Personal Data:* b Brooklyn, NY, Aug 23, 39; m 63; c 2. *Educ:* Univ Md, BS, 61, MS, 63; Cath Univ Am, PhD(mech eng), 76. *Prof Exp:* Res scientist fluid mech, Hydronautics, Inc, 63-65; mech engr, Naval Res Lab, 65-67; oceanogr acoust, Naval Oceanog Off, 67-76. *Mem:* Acoust Soc Am. *Res:* Scattering and reflection of underwater acoustic energy from marine organisms and ocean boundaries. *Mailing Add:* Naval Res Lab Stennis Space Ctr MS 39529

LOVE, ROBERT MERTON, range science, ecology; deceased, see previous edition for last biography

LOVE, RUSSELL JACQUES, SPEECH PATHOLOGY. *Current Pos:* from asst prof to assoc prof, 67-78, PROF HEARING & SPEECH SCI, SCH MED, VANDERBILT UNIV, 78- *Personal Data:* b Chicago, Ill, Jan 11, 31; m 61, Barbara Williams; c Steven & Gregory. *Educ:* Northwestern Univ, Ill, BS, 53, MA, 54, PhD(speech path), 62. *Prof Exp:* Speech & hearing therapist, Moody State Sch Cerebral Palsied Children, Tex, 54-56; staff clinician, Cerebral Palsy Speech Clin, Northwestern Univ, Ill, 58-61; audiologist, WSide Vet Admin Hosp, Chicago, Ill, 61-62; res speech pathologist, Vet Admin Hosp, Coral Gables, Fla, 62-64; assoc prof speech path, DePaul Univ, 64-67. *Concurrent Pos:* Consult speech pathologist, Michael Reese Hosp & Med Ctr, Chicago, Ill, 64-67; chief speech pathologist, Bill Wilkerson Hearing & Speech Ctr, Tenn, 67-71, consult & res speech pathologist, 71-; consult, Vet Admin Hosp, Murfreesboro, 70-89; mem, Nat Comt Accessible Environ, 74-78. *Mem:* Am Speech, Lang & Hearing Asn; Am Cleft Palate Asn; fel Am Speech Lang Hearing Asn. *Res:* Aphasia; Dyspraxia of speech; Dysarthria; childhood motor speech disability; rights of the handicapped; cerebral palsy; neurology of speech and language. *Mailing Add:* Hearing & Speech Sci Vanderbilt Univ 2201 W End Ave Nashville TN 37240-0001. *Fax:* 615-343-7705

LOVE, SYDNEY FRANCIS, MANAGEMENT SCIENCE, ELECTRONICS. *Current Pos:* RETIRED. *Personal Data:* b Winnipeg, Man, June 20, 23. *Educ:* Univ Toronto, BASc, 47, MA, 48; Univ Waterloo, MASc(systs design), 70. *Prof Exp:* Supvr appln, Can Gen Elec Co Ltd, 52-59; mgr TV & organ eng, Electrohome Ltd, 59-66; consult electronics, Sparton of Can, 66-68; pres mgt sci, Designectics Int Inc, 70-, pres, Advan Prof Develop Inst, 74- *Concurrent Pos:* Fel, Imp Oil Ltd, 67-68 & Cent Mortgage & Housing Corp, 68-70; consult, Xerox Corp, 72-74 & Govt of Can, 74-77. *Mem:* Sr mem Inst Elec & Electronics Engrs; Proj Mgt Inst. *Mailing Add:* 23022 Maraleste Rd Laguna Niguel CA 92677-2917

LOVE, TOM JAY, JR, HEAT TRANSFER, BIOMEDICAL ENGINEERING. *Current Pos:* from asst prof to assoc prof mech eng, Univ Okla, 56-65, dir sch, 63-72, prof aerospace & mech eng, 65-72, Halliburton Prof Eng, 72-88, George Lynn Gross Prof, 73-88, interim dean, Col Eng, 86-87, EMER GEORGE LYNN CROSS PROF, UNIV OKLA, 88- *Personal Data:* b Jonesboro, Ark, Oct 2, 23; m 45, Georgia Mathis; c Tom III, Deborah & Nancy. *Educ:* Univ Okla, BS, 48; Univ Kans, MS, 56; Purdue Univ, PhD(mech eng), 63. *Honors & Awards:* Thermophysics Award, Am Inst Aeronaut & Astronaut, 84; Heat Transfer Mem Award, Am Soc Mech Engrs. *Prof Exp:* Proj engr, Colgate Palmolive Co, 47-52; sr res engr, Midwest Res Inst, 52-56. *Concurrent Pos:* Mem bd dirs, Sverdrup-ARO, Inc, 77-81 & mem, adv coun, Sverdrup Technol, Inc, 77- Mem: Fel Am Inst Aeronaut & Astronaut; fel Am Soc Mech Engrs; Am Soc Eng Educ; Am Soc Testing & Mat; Am Acad Thermology. Res: Physiological heat transfer; radiative heat transfer; thermography. Mailing Add: 1600 Hawthorne Ct Norman OK 73072-6720

LOVE, WARNER EDWARDS, BIOPHYSICS. Current Pos: from asst prof to assoc prof, 57-65, chmn dept, 72-75 & 80-83, PROF BIOPHYS, JOHNS HOPKINS UNIV, 65- Personal Data: b Philadelphia, Pa, Dec 1, 22; m 45, Lois J Hosbach; c Rebecca (Burton) & Michael W. Educ: Swarthmore Col, BA, 46; Univ Pa, PhD(physiol), 51. Honors & Awards: Phillips Lectr, Haverford Col, 55. Prof Exp: Asst instr physiol, Univ Pa, 48-49, fel biophys, Johnson Found, 51-53, assoc, 53-55; res asst physics, Inst Cancer Res, 55-56, res assoc, 56-57. Mem: Protein Soc; Biophys Soc; Am Crystallog Asn; Am Soc Biol Chemists; Sigma Xi. Res: Biological ultrastructural basis of functions; x-ray crystallography of macromolecules, hemoglobins. Mailing Add: Johns Hopkins Univ 3400 N Charles St Baltimore MD 21218

LOVE, WILLIAM ALFRED, PHYSICS, ELEMENTARY PARTICLES. Current Pos: from asst physicist to assoc physicist, 60-66, PHYSICIST, BROOKHAVEN NAT LAB, 66- Personal Data: b Pittsburgh, Pa, Aug 4, 32; m 57; c 2. Educ: Carnegie Inst Technol, BS, 54, MS, 55, PhD(physics), 58. Prof Exp: Res physicist, Carnegie Inst Technol, 58-59; fel, Nat Sci Found, European Orgn Nuclear Res, Switzerland, 59-60. Mem: Fel Am Phys Soc. Res: Particle physics. Mailing Add: Dept Physics Brookhaven Nat Lab Upton NY 11973

LOVE, WILLIAM F, SOLID STATE PHYSICS. Current Pos: from asst prof to assoc prof, 54-63, PROF PHYSICS, UNIV COLO, BOULDER, 63- Personal Data: b Houston, Tex, July 3, 25; m 51; c 3. Educ: Rice Inst, BS, 45, MA, 47, PhD, 49. Prof Exp: Instr physics, Randal Morgan Lab, Univ Pa, 49-52, asst prof, 52-54. Mem: Am Phys Soc; Am Asn Physics Teachers; AAAS; Sigma Xi. Res: Symmetry properties of crystals; galvanomagnetic properties of metals and semiconductors in high magnetic fields; electrical noise in semiconductors. Mailing Add: 1250 Humboldt St Apt 905 Denver CO 80218

LOVE, WILLIAM GARY, NUCLEAR PHYSICS. Current Pos: from asst prof to assoc prof, 70-80, PROF PHYSICS, UNIV GA, 80- Personal Data: b Meridian, Miss, Aug 16, 41; m 66; c 2. Educ: Univ Tenn, BS, 63, PhD(physics), 68. Prof Exp: Res assoc physics, Fla State Univ, 68-70. Mem: Fel Am Phys Soc. Res: Study of the properties of the nucleon-nucleon interaction as they are manifested in many nucleon systems, for example, in scattering. Mailing Add: Dept Physics & Astron Univ Ga Athens GA 30602

LOVEALL, CLELLON LEWIS, CIVIL ENGINEERING. Current Pos: Bridge design engr, Tenn Dept Transp, 59-63, sr bridge design engr, 63-66, chief bridge design engr, 66-69, asst state bridge engr, 69-78, state bridge engr, 78-86, ASST DIR PLANNING & DEVELOP, TENN DEPT TRANSP, 86- Personal Data: b Carthage, Tenn, June 13, 38; m 60, Jane Ellen Johnson; c Lisa Renee, Sharon Kay & Angela Dawn. Educ: Vanderbilt Univ, BEng, 59. Honors & Awards: Govt Civil Engr Yr Award, Am Soc Civil Engrs, 84. Concurrent Pos: Mem, Transp Res Bd. Mem: Am Soc Civil Engrs; Am Soc Testing & Mat; Am Concrete Inst; Am Iron & Steel Inst; Am Asn State Hwy & Transp Officials; Prestressed Concrete Inst; Post Tensioning Inst; Segmental Bridge Inst. Mailing Add: Tenn Dept Transp Bur Planning & Develop James K Polk Bldg 505 Deaderick St Suite 700 Nashville TN 37243

LOVECCHIO, FRANK VITO, ANALYTICAL CHEMISTRY. Current Pos: RES CHEMIST, EASTMAN KODAK CO, 73- Personal Data: b Syracuse, NY, Apr 30, 43. Educ: Syracuse Univ, AB, 65, PhD(chem), 70. Prof Exp: Fel, Ohio State Univ, 70-73. Mem: Am Chem Soc; Am Photog Scientists & Engrs. Res: Reactions and mechanisms of coordination compounds, including electron transfer reactions. Mailing Add: 1185 Hidden Valley Trail Webster NY 14580-9133

LOVEJOY, DAVID ARNOLD, SOUTHERN NEW ENGLAND FLORA. Current Pos: From asst prof to assoc prof, 70-85, PROF BIOL, WESTFIELD STATE COL, 85- Personal Data: b Nashua, NH, Dec 12, 43; m 80, Maureen Fitzgerald; c Carolyn & Catherine. Educ: Univ Conn, BA, 65, PhD(zool, ecol), 70. Mem: Soc Protection Natural Hist Collections. Res: Flora of Massachusetts. Mailing Add: Dept Biol Westfield State Col Westfield MA 01086. Fax: 413-562-3613; E-Mail: dlovejoy@wisdom.wsc.mass.edu

LOVEJOY, DEREK R, ENERGY PHYSICS, SUSTAINABLE ENERGY PROGRAMS. Current Pos: RETIRED. Personal Data: b London, Eng, Jan 19, 28; Can citizen; m 53, Margot MacDonald; c Shaun, Kristin & Megan. Educ: Univ London, BS, 50; Univ Toronto, MA, 52, PhD(physics), 54. Prof Exp: Assoc res officer, Appl Physics Div, Nat Res Coun Can, 54-66; proj officer, Res Div, UN Develop Prog, 66-72, sr tech adv, Tech Adv Div, 72-78, sr tech adv new sources energy, 78-94. Concurrent Pos: Expert thermal metrol, Nat Phys Lab Metrol Proj, Cairo, United Arab Repub, UNESCO, 64-65. Mem: AAAS; US/Int Solar Energy Soc. Res: Liquid helium physics; temperature scales and measurements from very low to very high temperatures. Mailing Add: 166-04 81 Ave Jamaica NY 11432

LOVEJOY, DONALD WALKER, GENERAL EARTH SCIENCES. Current Pos: ASSOC PROF OCEANOG, PALM BEACH ATLANTIC COL, 79- Personal Data: b New York, NY, Mar 29, 31. Educ: Harvard Col, AB, 53; Columbia Univ, AM, 56 & PhD(geol), 58. Prof Exp: Asst prof geol, Univ Calif, Los Angeles, 57-58; dept chair geol, Rollins Col, Winter Park, 59-62; asst dean, Northeastern Univ, Boston, 62-69; fac dean, Mass Bay Community Col, 69-73; vpres, Nasson Col, Springvale, 73-75. Mem: Fel Geol Soc Am. Res: Florida pleistocene anastasia formation; karstification. Mailing Add: Palm Beach Atlantic Col PO Box 24708 West Palm Beach FL 33416-4708

LOVEJOY, JENNIFER CAROLE, DIABETES, OBESITY. Current Pos: asst prof, 91-97, ASSOC PROF, PENNINGTON BIOMED RES CTR, 97- Personal Data: b Seattle, Wash, Mar 30, 61; m 95, Robert M Straughn; c Teresa S. Educ: Duke Univ, BS, 82; Emory Univ, MA, 86, PhD(psychobiol), 88. Prof Exp: Postdoctoral fel, Dept Med, Emory Univ, 88-89, instr med, 89-91. Mem: Am Soc Clin Nutrit; Am Diabetes Asn; NAm Asn Study Obesity. Res: Role of diet and reproductive hormones in the etpology of obesity and type II diabetes in women; role of ethnic background in modulating risk for these chronic diseases. Mailing Add: Pennington Biomed Res Ctr 6400 Perkins Rd Baton Rouge LA 70808-4124

LOVEJOY, OWEN, HUMAN BIOLOGY, BIOMECHANICS. Current Pos: UNIV PROF, DEPT ANTHROP, KENT STATE UNIV, 68-; ASST CLIN PROF, DIV ORTHOP SURG, CASE WESTERN RES UNIV, SCH MED, 70- Personal Data: b Paducah, Ky, Feb 11, 43; m 69. Educ: Western Res Univ, BA, 65; Case Inst Technol, MA, 67; Univ Mass, Amherst, PhD(human biol), 70. Prof Exp: Assoc prof physics anthrop, 69-77, prof social & anthrop, Kent State Univ, 77- Mem: Brit Soc Study Human Biol; Am Asn Phys Anthrop; Am Eugenics Soc. Res: Primate anatomy, biomechanics and taxonomy; human palaeontology and palaeodemography; skeletal biology. Mailing Add: Dept Anthrop 239 Lowry Hall Kent State Univ Kent OH 44242-0001

LOVEJOY, SHAUN MACDONALD, NONLINEAR PHYSICS, MULTIMETALS. Current Pos: from asst prof to assoc prof, 85-97, PROF PHYSICS, MCGILL UNIV, 97- Personal Data: m 85, Helene Gaorsich; c Vanda & Igor. Educ: Trinity Col, BA, 76, MA, 81; McGill Univ, PhD(physics), 81. Prof Exp: Postdoctoral, Nat Meteorol, Paris, 81-85. Concurrent Pos: Univ res fel, Natural Sci & Eng Res Coun Can, 85-95; co-ed, Nonlinear Processes Geophys, 93-96. Mem: Europ Geophys Soc; Am Geophys Union. Res: All aspects of scale invariance; applications in turbulence, geophysics, hydrology and climate. Mailing Add: Physics Dept McGill Univ Montreal PQ H3A 2T8 Can. Fax: 514-398-8434; E-Mail: lovejoy@physics.mcgill.ca

LOVEJOY, THOMAS E, ECOLOGY. Current Pos: asst secy external affairs, 87-94, COUNR TO SECY BIODIVERSITY & ENVIRON AFFAIRS, SMITHSONIAN INST, 94- Personal Data: b New York, NY, Aug 22, 41; div; c Elizabeth & Katherine. Educ: Yale Col, BS, 64; Yale Univ, PhD(biol), 71. Hon Degrees: DSC, Colo State Univ, 89, Williams Col, 90; LHD, Lynn Univ, 91. Honors & Awards: Manley Lectr, Univ Calif, Santa Barbara, 81; Charles A Lindbergh Lectr, Woods Hole Marine Biol Lab, 81; David French Lectr, Claremont Col, 83; Ronneberg Lectr, Denison Univ, 87. Prof Exp: Res assoc biol, Univ Pa, 71-74; exec asst to sci dir & asst to vpres resources & planning, Acad Natural Sci, 72-73; prog dir, World Wildlife Fund-US, 73-78, vpres sci, 78-85, exec vpres, 85-87. Concurrent Pos: Res assoc ornithol, Acad Natural Sci, 71-74; treas, Int Coun Bird Preserv, 73-84; chmn, Wildlife Preserv Trust Int, 74-; vis lectr trop ecol, Ctr Environ Studies, Univ Wash, 81, Yale Sch Forestry & Environ Studies, 82; mem, Wildlife Panel, AAAS, 81; res assoc, Int Ctr African, Near Eastern & Asian Cult, 84-87; mem, Panel Microlivetock, Nat Res Coun, Comt Biodiversity, 87-91; mem, White House Sci Coun, Off Sci & Technol Policy, Exec Off Pres, 88-89; mem, Nat Policy Coun, Nat Inst Global Environ Change, 90-; mem, Nat Coun, Environ Defense Fund, 91-; rep, US Deleg, UN Conf Environ & Develop, 92. Mem: Fel AAAS; Am Inst Biol Sci; fel Am Ornithologists Union; Soc Conserv Biol (pres, 89-91). Res: Tropical ecology; ornithology; problems of ecology theory relating to conservation and natural resource management. Mailing Add: Smithsonian Inst Castle Bldg Rm 320 Washington DC 20560

LOVELACE, ALAN MATHIESON, CHEMISTRY. Current Pos: vpres sci & eng, Gen Dynamics Corp, 81-82, corp vpres prod & qual assurance, 82-85, corp vpres & gen mgr, Space Syst Div, 85-91, corp vpres, 91-93, CONSULT, GEN DYNAMICS CORP & EMER CHMN, COM LAUNCH SERV, INC, 93- Personal Data: b St Petersburg, Fla, Sept 4, 29; m 52, Kathryn Logan; c William M & Denise T. Educ: Univ Fla, BA, 51, MA, 52, PhD(chem), 54. Honors & Awards: Von Karman Medal, 84; Goddard Astronaut Award, Am Inst Aeronaut & Astronaut, 89; George Low Award, 91. Prof Exp: Mem staff, Air Force Mat Lab, Wright Patterson AFB, 54-72; dir sci & technol, Andrews AFB, Washington, DC, 72-73, prin dep asst secy, Air Force Res & Develop, 73-74; assoc admin, Aerospace Technol Off Aeronaut & Space Technol, 74-76; dep admin, NASA, 76-81. Concurrent Pos: Chmn, Adv Group Aerospace Res & Develop, NATO, 79-81. Mem: Nat Acad Eng; fel Am Inst Aeronaut & Astronaut; Am Astronaut Soc; Sigma Xi; Int Aeronaut Fedn. Res: High performance macromolecular materials; aliphatic fluorine chemistry; advance composite materials; space launch vehicles. Mailing Add: 1145 Inspiration Dr LaJolla CA 92703. Fax: 619-974-3717; E-Mail: lovelace@connectnet.com

LOVELACE, C JAMES, PLANT PHYSIOLOGY, BIOCHEMISTRY. Current Pos: PROF BOT, HUMBOLDT STATE UNIV, 65- Personal Data: b Holdenville, Okla, Sept 26, 34; div; c 3. Educ: Harding Col, BS, 61; Utah State Univ, MS, 64, PhD(plant physiol), 66. Concurrent Pos: Summer res assoc, Utah State Univ, Justus-Liebig Univ, Inst Plant Nutrit, Giessen, Ger,

87-88. *Mem:* Am Soc Plant Physiol; Int Soc Fluoride Res. *Res:* Plant mineral nutrition; fluoride research in relation to enzyme reactions within plants; heavy metal toxicants; iron metabolism in plants; chlorophyl biosynthesis. *Mailing Add:* Dept Biol Humboldt State Univ 1 Harps St Arcata CA 95521-8299

LOVELACE, CLAUD WILLIAM VENTON, THEORETICAL PHYSICS. *Current Pos:* PROF PHYSICS, RUTGERS UNIV, NEW BRUNSWICK, 70- *Personal Data:* b London, Eng, Jan 16, 34. *Educ:* Univ Capetown, BS, 54. *Prof Exp:* Dept Sci & Indust Res res fel, Imp Col, Univ London, 61-62, lectr physics, 62-65; sr physicist, Europ Orgn Nuclear Res, Geneva, 65-71. *Res:* Theoretical particle physics; strong interactions; high energy phenomenology. *Mailing Add:* Dept Physics & Astron Rutgers Univ New Brunswick NJ 08903

LOVELACE, RICHARD VAN EVERA, PLASMA PHYSICS, ASTROPHYSICS. *Current Pos:* FROM ASST PROF TO PROF APPL PHYSICS, CORNELL UNIV, 75- *Personal Data:* b St Louis, Mo, Oct 16, 41; c 2. *Educ:* Wash Univ, BS, 64; Cornell Univ, PhD(physics), 70. *Prof Exp:* Res assoc, Lab Plasma Studies, Cornell Univ, 70-73 & Plasma Physics Lab, Princeton Univ, 73-74. *Concurrent Pos:* Vis res assoc, US Naval Res Lab, 70-71; consult, Lawrence Livermore Lab, 71- & Plasma Physics Lab, Princeton Univ, 74-75; consult, Los Alamos Nat Lab, 86-; Guggenheim fel, 90; vis prof, Dept Physics, Univ Tex, Austin, 90; overseas fel, Churchill Col, Cambridge Univ, 94. *Mem:* Am Astron Soc; Am Phys Soc; Int Astron Union. *Res:* Plasma physics of large-orbit, high current controlled fusion systems; collective phenomena of galaxies and quasars; wave propagation through random media; relativistic magnetohydrodynamics of astrophysical jets, winds and accretion disks. *Mailing Add:* Dept Appl Physics Cornell Univ 237 Clark Hall Ithaca NY 14853. *Fax:* 607-255-7658; *E-Mail:* rvl1@cornell.edu

LOVELAND, DONALD WILLIAM, MATHEMATICS, COMPUTER SCIENCE. *Current Pos:* PROF COMPUT SCI, DUKE UNIV, 73- *Personal Data:* b Rochester, NY, Dec 26, 34; m 66, Amy S; c Robert & Douglas. *Educ:* Oberlin Col, AB, 56; Mass Inst Technol, SM, 58; NY Univ, PhD(math), 64. *Prof Exp:* Mathematician & programmer, Int Bus Mach Corp, 58-59; instr math, NY Univ, 63-64, asst prof, 64-67; from asst prof to assoc prof, Carnegie-Mellon Univ, 67-73. *Mem:* Asn Comput Mach; Asn Symbolic Logic; AAAS; fel Am Asn Artificial Intel. *Res:* Artificial intelligence; theorem proving by computer; logic programming; fast approximation algorithms for computationally hard problems. *Mailing Add:* 3417 Cambridge Rd Durham NC 27707-4507. *E-Mail:* dwl@cs.duke.edu

LOVELAND, ROBERT EDWARD, BIOLOGY. *Current Pos:* asst prof, 64-70, ASSOC PROF ZOOL, RUTGERS UNIV, NEW BRUNSWICK, 70- *Personal Data:* b Camden, NJ, May 3, 38; m 62; c 3. *Educ:* Rutgers Univ, Camden, AB, 59; Harvard Univ, MA, 61, PhD(biol), 63. *Prof Exp:* Asst prof biol, Long Beach State Col, 63-64. *Concurrent Pos:* NSF sci fac fel, Univ BC, 71-72. *Mem:* AAAS; Atlantic Estuarine Res Soc. *Res:* Distribution of marine invertebrates; behavioral modelling; population models of biological systems. *Mailing Add:* Dept Biol Sci Rutgers Univ New Brunswick NJ 08903

LOVELAND, WALTER (DAVID), NUCLEAR CHEMISTRY. *Current Pos:* res asst prof, 67-68, from asst prof to assoc prof, 68-81, PROF CHEM, ORE STATE UNIV, 81- *Personal Data:* b Chicago, Ill, Dec 23, 39; m 62, Patricia Rice. *Educ:* Mass Inst Technol, SB, 61; Univ Wash, PhD(chem), 66. *Prof Exp:* Res assoc chem, Argonne Nat Lab, 66-67. *Concurrent Pos:* US Dept Energy res grant, Ore State Univ, 68-; vis scientist, Lawrence Berkeley Lab, 76, 77 & 80; Tartar fel, Ore State Univ, 77. *Mem:* AAAS; Am Phys Soc; Am Chem Soc. *Res:* Nuclear reactions, especially heavy ion reactions and fission; activation analysis; use of computers for data acquisition; environmental chemistry. *Mailing Add:* Radiation Ctr Ore State Univ Corvallis OR 97331. *Fax:* 541-737-0480; *E-Mail:* loveland@loveland.chem.orst.edu

LOVELESS, SCOTT E, MACROPHAGE ACTIVATION, ADOPTIVE IMMUNOTHERAPY. *Current Pos:* RES IMMUNOTHERAPIST & PHARMACOLOGIST, E I DU PONT DE NEMOURS & CO, INC, 84- *Educ:* Va Commonwealth Univ, PhD(pharmacol), 80. *Mailing Add:* Immunotoxicol Cent Res Dept E I du Pont de Nemours & Co Inc Haskell Lab Elkton Rd PO Box 50 Newark DE 19714-0050. *Fax:* 302-366-5207

LOVELL, ASHLEY C, BUSINESS ANALYSIS & RISK MANAGEMENT, ACCOUNTING. *Current Pos:* assoc prof, 70-77, HEAD & PROF AGR ECON, TARLETON STATE UNIV, 93- *Personal Data:* b Texon, Tex, Nov 30, 44. *Educ:* Tarleton State Univ, BS, 67; Univ Mo, Columbia, MS, 70, PhD(agr econs), 71. *Prof Exp:* Exten specialist & prof, Tex Agr Exten Serv & Dept Agr Econs, Tex A&M Univ, 78-93. *Mem:* Am Agr Econ Asn. *Res:* Farm-level management and production economics, especially financial and managerial accounting; tax planning and management; business management and risk management computer applications and simulation, all within the context of public policy development and constraints. *Mailing Add:* Box T-0050 Stephenville TX 76402. *E-Mail:* lovell@tarleton.edu

LOVELL, BERNARD WENTZEL, COMPUTER SCIENCE, ELECTRICAL ENGINEERING. *Current Pos:* ASSOC PROF ELEC ENG, UNIV CONN, 69- *Personal Data:* b Greenfield, Mass. *Educ:* Mass Inst Technol, BS, 58, MS, 58, EE, 63; Univ Conn, PhD(comput sci), 69. *Prof Exp:* Electronic engr, US Naval Ord Lab, 54-59; instr elec eng, Mass Inst Technol, 59-63; asst prof, Univ Mass, 63-67. *Mem:* Inst Elec & Electronics Engrs; Am Phys Soc; Asn Comput Mach. *Res:* Automata theory; operating systems. *Mailing Add:* Dept Comput Sci & Eng Univ Conn U-155 260 Glennbrook Storrs Mansfield CT 06269-0002

LOVELL, CHARLES W(ILLIAM), JR, CIVIL ENGINEERING, SOIL MECHANICS. *Current Pos:* EMER PROF, CIVIL ENG, PURDUE UNIV, 93- *Personal Data:* b Louisville, Ky, Nov 16, 22; m 48; c 2. *Educ:* Univ Louisville, BCE, 44; Purdue Univ, MSCE, 51, PhD(civil eng), 57. *Prof Exp:* Instr civil eng, Univ Louisville, 46-48; from res asst to res engr & instr, Purdue Univ, 48-57, from asst prof to assoc prof, 57-76, prof civil eng, 76-93. *Concurrent Pos:* Vis assoc prof, Mass Inst Technol, 62-63; mem, Hwy Res Bd, Nat Acad Sci-Nat Res Coun. *Mem:* Nat Soc Prof Engrs; Am Soc Civil Engrs; Am Soc Eng Educ; Am Soc Testing & Mat. *Res:* Frost action; load-deformation characteristics of soils; subsurface exploration. *Mailing Add:* 3739 Capilano Dr West Lafayette IN 47906

LOVELL, EDWARD GEORGE, ENGINEERING, STRUCTURAL MECHANICS. *Current Pos:* prof eng mech, 68-95, chmn eng mech & astronaut, 92-95, PROF MECH ENG, UNIV WIS-MADISON, 95- *Personal Data:* b Windsor, Ont, May 25, 39; US citizen; c Elise & Ethan. *Educ:* Wayne State Univ, BSAE, 60, MSEM, 61; Univ Mich, Ann Arbor, PhD(eng mech), 67. *Prof Exp:* Instr eng mech, Univ Mich, Ann Arbor, 63-67; Nat Acad Sci-Nat Res Coun res associateship, Langley Res Ctr, NASA, 67-68. *Concurrent Pos:* Proj engr, Boeing Co, Wash, 62; design engr, Pratt & Whitney Aircraft, Conn, 70; NATO sr sci fel, Univ Manchester, Eng, 73, Fusion Technol Inst, Wis Ctr Appl Microelectronics, Univ Wis. *Mem:* Sigma Xi; Am Soc Mech Engrs; Am Soc Eng Educ. *Res:* Nonlinear vibrations of structures; structural instability; stress analysis; nuclear reactor structural mechanics; microelectromechanical systems. *Mailing Add:* Dept Mech Eng Univ Wis Madison WI 53706

LOVELL, HAROLD LEMUEL, FUEL SCIENCE, MINERAL ENGINEERING. *Current Pos:* asst chem micros, Pa State Univ, 73-44, microchem, 44-45, asst fuel technol, 47-51, res assoc spectros, 51-52, asst prof, 52-58, mineral prep, 58-64, assoc prof, 64-71, head, Dept Mineral Prep, 64-68, assoc prof, 71-76, prof mineral eng, 77-82, dir, Mine Drainage Res Sect, 68-82, EMER PROF MINERAL ENG, PA STATE UNIV, 82- *Personal Data:* b Bellwood, Pa, July 13, 22; m 44, Blanche M Wakefield; c Diann L (Walker) & Harold T. *Educ:* Pa State Univ, BS, 43, MS, 45, PhD(fuel tech), 52. *Prof Exp:* Res chemist, Manhatten Dist Proj, Mallinckrodt Chem Works, 45-47. *Concurrent Pos:* Consult, US Steel Corp, Appl Res Ctr, 60, US Dept Com-Com Tech Adv Bd, 74-75, Gov Sci Adv Comt, Dept Com, 79. *Mem:* Am Chem Soc; Am Inst Mining, Metall & Petrol Eng; Am Mining Cong; Soc Appl Spectros; Am Soc Testing & Mat. *Res:* Mineral preparation; analytical chemistry; absorption and emission; microchemistry; coal constitution chemistry; chemical utilization of coal; mine water pollution-treatment; coal preparation; physical processing of coal for synfuel feed stock management; science education. *Mailing Add:* 120 W Mitchell Ave State Col PA 16803-3544

LOVELL, JAMES A, ASTRONAUTICS. *Current Pos:* SR VPRES ADMIN, CENTEL CORP, 80- *Personal Data:* b Cleveland, Ohio, Mar 25, 28; m, Marilyn Gerlach; c Barbara L, James A, Susan K & Jeffrey C. *Educ:* US Naval Acad, BS, 52. *Honors & Awards:* Robert J Collier Trophy, 69. *Prof Exp:* Test pilot, Navy Air Test Ctr, 58-61, flight instr & safety officer, Fighter Sq adron 101, Naval Air Sta; astronaut, Manned Spacecraft Ctr, NASA, 62, dep dir sci & appln directorate, 71-73; pres, Fisk Tel Systs Inc, 77-81. *Concurrent Pos:* Astronaut, Gemini 7 flight, Gemini 6, 66, Gemini 12, 66, Apollo 8, 68 Apollo 13, 70. *Mem:* Fel Am Astronaut Soc. *Mailing Add:* Centel Corp 8725 W Higgins Rd Chicago IL 60631-2702

LOVELL, JAMES BYRON, ENTOMOLOGY. *Current Pos:* RETIRED. *Personal Data:* b Fallentimber, Pa, Mar 19, 27; c 2. *Educ:* Pa State Univ, BS, 50; Univ Ill, MS, 55, PhD(entom), 56. *Prof Exp:* Entomologist, US Army Chem Ctr, Md, 50-53; asst, Univ Ill, 53-56; prin scientist, Agr Res Div, Am Cyanamid Co, 56-91. *Mem:* AAAS; Entom Soc Am. *Res:* Insect physiology and toxicology; mode of action of insecticides; mechanism of resistance in insects. *Mailing Add:* 99 Woosamonsa Rd Pennington NJ 08534

LOVELL, RICHARD ARLINGTON, neurochemistry, for more information see previous edition

LOVELL, RICHARD THOMAS, FISHERIES, NUTRITION. *Current Pos:* assoc prof, 69-75, PROF FISHERIES & ALLIED AQUACULT, AUBURN UNIV, 75- *Personal Data:* b Lockesburg, Ark, Feb 21, 34; m 63; c 2. *Educ:* Okla State Univ, BS, 56, MS, 58; La State Univ, PhD(nutrit, biochem), 63. *Honors & Awards:* Prof Scientist Award, Southern Asn Agr Scientist, 78; Distinguished Serv Award, Catfish Farmers Am, 80; Cert Merit, Inst Food Technologists, 91. *Prof Exp:* From asst prof to assoc prof food sci, La State Univ, 63-69. *Concurrent Pos:* Consult fish cult, US AID, 72-74; columnist, Aquacult Mag, 74-; mem, Comt Animal Nutrit, Nat Res Coun-Nat Acad Sci, 74-; assoc ed, Trans Am Fisheries Soc, 75-; chmn, Comt Fish Nutrit, Nat Res Coun-Nat Acad Sci, 89-90. *Mem:* Fel Am Inst Chemists; Am Fisheries Soc; Inst Food Technologists; Am Inst Nutrit. *Res:* Fish nutrition, especially vitamin C requirements and energy metabolism of warm water fish cultured for food; environment-related off-flavors in intensively-cultured food fishes. *Mailing Add:* Dept Fisheries & Allied Aquacult Auburn Univ Auburn AL 36849-3501. *Fax:* 334-844-9208

LOVELL, ROBERT GIBSON, INTERNAL MEDICINE, ALLERGY. *Current Pos:* RETIRED. *Personal Data:* b Ann Arbor, Mich, May 13, 20; m 48; c 5. *Educ:* Univ Mich, MD, 44, AB, 57. *Prof Exp:* From instr to asst prof, Univ Mich, Ann Arbor, 50-73, fac secy, 54-56, asst dean sch med, 57-59, clin prof internal med, 73-90. *Concurrent Pos:* Consult physician, US Vet Admin Hosp, 54-55; consult, President's Comm Vet Pensions, USAF, 55 & Wayne

Co Gen Hosp, Mich, 59-; chmn med ed comt, St Joseph Mercy Hosp, 63- *Mem:* AMA; assoc Am Col Chest Physicians; fel Am Acad Allergy. *Res:* Use of medications and aerosol preparations in treatment of bronchial asthma. *Mailing Add:* 3000 Geddes Ave Ann Arbor MI 48104

LOVELL, ROBERT R(OLAND), SPACE TECHNOLOGY. *Current Pos:* CORP VPRES & PRES, SPACE SYSTS DIV, ORBITAL SCI CORP, 87- *Personal Data:* b Gladwin, Mich, Feb 22, 37. *Educ:* Univ Mich, BS & MS. *Honors & Awards:* Nat Medal Technol, 91; Yuri Gagarin Medal, USSR Acad Cosmonautics. *Prof Exp:* Var tech & tech mgt positions, Lewis Res Ctr, NASA, Cleveland, Ohio, 62-80, dir, Satellite Commun Advan Res & Develop Prog, NASA Hq, 80-87. *Concurrent Pos:* Mgr, Pegasus Prog, Orbital Sci Corp. *Mem:* Am Inst Aeronaut & Astronaut. *Res:* Development of unmanned spacecraft technology; communications systems; rocket propulsion; author of over 50 technical publications; holder of several patents. *Mailing Add:* Orbital Sci Corp 21700 Atlantic Blvd Dulles VA 20166

LOVELL, STUART ESTES, COMPUTER SCIENCE. *Current Pos:* RETIRED. *Personal Data:* b Seattle, Wash, Oct 8, 28; m 55; c 2. *Educ:* Univ Wash, BS, 53; Brown Univ, PhD(biochem), 58. *Prof Exp:* Proj assoc chem, Univ Wis, 58-63, asst prof comput sci, 63-67; mgr comput serv, Kitt Peak Observ, 65-75, System Analyst, 75-91. *Mem:* Asn Comput Mach. *Res:* Systems programming; computer based systems. *Mailing Add:* 5221 E Rosewoods Tucson AZ 85711

LOVELOCK, DAVID, MATHEMATICS, THEORETICAL PHYSICS. *Current Pos:* PROF MATH, UNIV ARIZ, 74- *Personal Data:* b Bromley, Eng. *Educ:* Univ Natal, BSc, 59, Hons, 60, PhD(math), 62, DSc, 74. *Prof Exp:* Res asst math, Univ Natal, 60-61; jr fel, Bristol Univ, 62-63, lectr, 63-69; assoc prof, 69-74, prof appl math, Univ Waterloo, Ont, 74. *Concurrent Pos:* Nat Res Coun Can grant, Univ Waterloo, 69-, adj prof appl math, 74- *Mem:* Am Math Soc; Tensor Soc. *Res:* General relativity; calculus of variations; differential geometry. *Mailing Add:* Dept Math Univ Ariz 1600 E University Blvd Tucson AZ 85721-0001

LOVELY, RICHARD HERBERT, NEUROBEHAVIORAL TOXICOLOGY, HEALTH PSYCHOLOGY. *Current Pos:* sr res scientist neurosci, Dept Biol, 79-89, epidemiol & biomet, 89-94, MOLECULAR BIOSCI, BATTELLE MEM INST, 95- *Personal Data:* b Santa Monica, Calif, Sept 20, 41; m 88, Anita Wong. *Educ:* Calif State Univ, Northridge, BA, 65; Cent Wash Univ, MS, 67; Univ Wash, Seattle, PhD(psychol), 74. *Prof Exp:* Instr psychol, Yakima Valley Col, 67-68; lectr psychol, Univ Wash, 70-72, psychol & rehab med, 73-75, asst prof, 75-79. *Concurrent Pos:* Vis prof, Calif State Univ, Chico, 72-73; consult & US-USSR exchange scientist, Nat Inst Environ Health Sci, 76-82, Nat Coun Radiation Protection & Measurements, 78-85; bd dirs, Bioelectromagnetic Soc, 85-88. *Mem:* Soc Neurosci; Psychonomic Soc; Neurobehav Teratol Soc; Bioelectromagnetics Soc. *Res:* Biopsychological effects of electromagnetic radiation exposure; AIDS in adolescents; in utero determinants of adult behavior; neurobehavioral toxicology; neural substrates of learning and memory, limbic system functions and constraints on animal behavior. *Mailing Add:* Molecular Biosci Battelle Mem Inst Seattle WA 98105. *Fax:* 206-528-3553

LOVENBERG, WALTER MCKAY, BIOCHEMISTRY. *Current Pos:* dir biochem sci, Merrel Dow Res Inst, 85-86, vpres Strasbourg, France, 86-89, PRES, MARION MERRELL DOW RES INST, 89- *Personal Data:* b Trenton, NJ, Aug 9, 34; m 58; c 2. *Educ:* Rutgers Univ, BS, 56, MS, 58; George Washington Univ, PhD(biochem), 62. *Prof Exp:* Biochemist, Nat Heart, Lung & Blood Inst, 59-72, trainee, 62-63, head sect biochem pharmacol, Hypertension-Endocrine Br, 72-85. *Concurrent Pos:* Exec ed, J Analytical Biochem; US ed, J Neurochem Int. *Mem:* Am Soc Biol Chem; Am Soc Pharmacol & Exp Therapeut; Biochem Soc; Am Soc Neurochem; Am Col Neuropsychopharmacol. *Res:* Enzymatic mechanisms and the chemistry of proteins involved in neurohumoral amine biosynthesis. *Mailing Add:* Lovenberg Assoc Inc 3008 Burning Tree Lane Cincinnati OH 45237

LO VERDE, PHILIP THOMAS, PARASITOLOGY, MEDICAL MALACOLOGY. *Current Pos:* ASST PROF PARASITOL, DEPT MICRO, SCH MED, STATE UNIV NY, BUFFALO, 81- *Personal Data:* b Benton Harbor, Mich, Oct 5, 46; m 65; c 3. *Educ:* Univ Mich, BS, 68, MS, 71, MS, PhD(epidemiol sci), 76. *Honors & Awards:* Chester A Herrick Award, Eli Lilly & Co, 74. *Prof Exp:* Mus asst, Zool Mus, Univ Mich, 68-69, NIH fel, 70-75, curatorial asst, 73-75, teaching fel, Dept Zool, 72-73; res assoc med malacol, Ain Shams Univ, Cairo, 74-75; asst prof parasitol, dept biol sci, Purdue Univ, 76-81. *Concurrent Pos:* Guest scientist, Naval Med Res Unit No 3, Cairo, Egypt, 74-75; Spec Study Sect, NIH, 83, Tropical Dis Unit Study Sect, 84, SBIR Study Sect, 86. *Mem:* Am Soc Parasitologists; AAAS; Am Soc Trop Med Hyg. *Res:* Host-parasite interrelationships; invertebrate defense mechanisms; parasite immunology and molecular biology; parasitology; malacology; schistosomiasis. *Mailing Add:* Microbiol 203 Sherman State Univ NY Buffalo Sch Med 3435 Main St Buffalo NY 14214-3001

LOVERING, EDWARD GILBERT, PHARMACEUTICAL CHEMISTRY. *Current Pos:* CONSULT, 93- *Personal Data:* b Winnipeg, Man, Oct 15, 34; m 58; c 3. *Educ:* Univ Man, BSc, 57, MSc, 58; Univ Ottawa, PhD(chem), 61. *Prof Exp:* Sci officer radiation chem, Defense Res Bd, 58-59; Nat Res Coun Can fel, Oxford Univ, 61-63; res chemist, Polymer Corp Ltd, 63-69, assoc scientist, Polymer Corp, 69-71; res scientist, Health & Welfare Can, 71-93. *Mem:* Am Chem Soc; Chem Inst Can; Sigma Xi. *Res:* Contaminants in drugs and cosmetics; drug raw material characterization; drug stability; pharmaceutical and cosmetic analysis. *Mailing Add:* 111 Beaver Ridge Nepean ON K2E 6E5 Can

LOVESTEDT, STANLEY ALMER, ORAL SURGERY. *Current Pos:* consult, 43-62, head sect, 55-62, SR CONSULT, DEPT DENT & ORAL SURG, MAYO CLIN, 62-; EMER PROF DENT, MAYO MED SCH, 78- *Personal Data:* b Iliff, Colo, June 7, 13; m 40; c Priscilla (Strand), Helen (Grant) & Robert A. *Educ:* Univ Southern Calif, BS & DDS, 38; Univ Minn, MS, 45; Am Bd Oral Surg, dipl. *Prof Exp:* Resident oral surg, Mayo Grad Sch Med, 38-43, mem fac, 46-60, from instr to assoc prof, 60-69, prof clin dent, 67-73, prof dent, 73-78. *Concurrent Pos:* Chief oral diag & roentgenology, US Army Dent Corps, Brooke Army Hosp, Ft Sam Houston, Tex, 53-55; mem, dent study sect, NIH, 64-68. *Mem:* Fel AAAS; Am Soc Oral Surgeons; Am Dent Asn; fel Am Acad Dent Radiol; fel Am Col Dent (vpres, 65-66, pres, 68-69); Sigma Xi; Am Asn Dent Schs; Am Acad Hist Dent; Am Acad Oral Path; Am Acad Hist Med; Am Cancer Soc; Am Acad Oral Med. *Res:* Radiology; oral medicine. *Mailing Add:* 211 Second St NW Apt 2102 Rochester MN 55901-3101

LOVETT, CHARLES MCVEY, DNA REPAIR, GENE REGULATION. *Current Pos:* From asst prof to assoc prof, 85-95, PROF CHEM, WILLIAMS COL, 95- *Personal Data:* b Oceanside, NY, Nov 23, 51; m, Jennifer Gordon; c 4. *Educ:* Calif State Polytech Univ, Pomona, BS, 79, MS, 80; Cornell Univ, PhD(biochem), 85. *Res:* Transcriptional regulation of inducible DNA repair in bacillus subtilis; regulation of competence development in bacillus subtilis. *Mailing Add:* Dept Chem Williams Col Williamstown MA 01267. *Fax:* 413-597-4116; *E-Mail:* charles.m.lovett@williams.edu

LOVETT, EDMUND J, III, EXPERIMENTAL BIOLOGY. *Current Pos:* DIR & CHIEF EXEC OFFICER, MAINE CYTOMETRY RES INST, 86- *Mailing Add:* Maine Med Res Inst 125 John Roberts Rd Suite 8 South Portland ME 04106-3295. *Fax:* 207-761-2130

LOVETT, EVA G, ORGANIC CHEMISTRY. *Current Pos:* INSTR CHEM, FOREST PARK COMMUNITY COL, 91- *Personal Data:* b Orange, NJ, Aug 17, 40; m 63. *Educ:* Douglass Col, Rutgers Univ, BA, 62; Univ Rochester, PhD(chem), 66. *Prof Exp:* Sr chemist, Merck, Sharp & Dohme Res Lab, 66-67; res assoc chem, Washington Univ, St Louis, 69-76; res chemist, Tretolite Div, Petrolite Corp, St Louis, 76-89; res assoc chem, Victoria Univ, Wellington, NZ, 89-90. *Mem:* AAAS; Am Chem Soc. *Res:* Synthesis, degradation and mass spectroscopy of natural products, particularly purines, pyrimidines and related heterocyclic compounds; polymer synthesis and characterization. *Mailing Add:* 6807 Pershing Ave St Louis MO 63130

LOVETT, GARY MARTIN, FOREST NUTRIENT CYCLING, ATMOSPHERE-FOREST INTERACTIONS. *Current Pos:* asst scientist, 85-89, assoc scientist, 89-95, SCIENTIST, INST ECOSYST STUDIES, 95- *Personal Data:* b Albany, NY, July 6, 53. *Educ:* Union Col, BS, 75; Dartmouth Col, PhD(biol), 81. *Prof Exp:* Res assoc, Oak Ridge Nat Lab, 81-85. *Concurrent Pos:* Assoc mem, Grad Prog Ecol, Rutgers Univ, 90- *Mem:* Ecol Soc Am; AAAS. *Res:* Forest nutrient cycling, in particular patterns and mechanisms of atmospheric deposition and atmosphere/canopy interactions; effects of air pollution insects and other stresses on forests. *Mailing Add:* Inst Ecosyst Studies Box AB Millbrook NY 12545

LOVETT, JAMES SATTERTHWAITE, botany, biochemistry; deceased, see previous edition for last biography

LOVETT, JOHN ROBERT, ORGANIC CHEMISTRY. *Current Pos:* PRES & MEM BD DIRS, AIR PROD EUROPE, INC, 81- *Personal Data:* b Norristown, Pa, June 17, 31; m 56; c 3. *Educ:* Ursinus Col, BS, 53; Univ Del, MS, 55, PhD(chem), 57. *Prof Exp:* Res chemist polymer processes, Esso Res & Eng Co, 57-59, res proj leader high energy propellants, 59-60, sr chemist, 60-61, sect head, 61-64, dir govt res lab, 65-68, dir petrol additives lab, 68-70, vpres paramins dept, Exxon Chem Co, 70-73, worldwide tech mgr, 73-76; vpres res, Air Prod & Chem Inc, 76-81, mem bd dir, 77-81. *Concurrent Pos:* Bd trustees, Cedar Crest Col, 77-81; adv bd, US Dept Energy, 78-81; dir, Amersham Int Plc & Am Chamber Com, UK, 82- *Mem:* Am Chem Soc; Indust Res Inst; Mfg Chemists Asn; AAAS. *Res:* Polymers; chemical additives; industrial gases; catalysts; fossil energy technology. *Mailing Add:* 2830 Liberty St Allentown PA 18104-4748

LOVETT, JOSEPH, ENVIRONMENTAL HEALTH, PUBLIC HEALTH. *Current Pos:* regional consult, Interstate Carrier Prog Environ Eng & Food Protection, USPHS, 60-64, chief mycol sect, Food Microbiol Br, 66-77, asst br chief, bact physiol br, Div Microbiol, Bur Foods, Food & Drug Admin, 77-87, CHIEF, MICROBIOL HAZARDS EVAL GROUP, LAB QUAL ASSURANCE BR, USPHS, 87- *Personal Data:* b Columbus Co, NC, Feb 24, 33; m 57; c 2. *Educ:* Wake Forest Univ, BS, 56; Univ NC, Chapel Hill, MSPH, 60; Univ Minn, Minneapolis, MS, 65, PhD(environ health, microbiol), 71. *Prof Exp:* Asst supt water treat, City of Raleigh, NC, 57-58. *Mem:* Int Asn Milk, Food & Environ Sanitarians; Am Soc Microbiol; Sigma Xi; Inst Food Technologists. *Res:* Toxic microbial metabolites in foods and the ecology of toxigenic and pathogenic microorganisms. *Mailing Add:* 1682 Vaquera Pl Cincinnati OH 45255

LOVETT, PAUL SCOTT, MICROBIOLOGY. *Current Pos:* from asst prof to assoc prof, 70-78, presidential res prof, 89-94, PROF BIOL SCI, UNIV MD, BALTIMORE CO, 78- *Personal Data:* b Philadelphia, Pa, Dec 14, 40. *Educ:* Delaware Valley Col, BS, 64; Temple Univ, PhD(microbiol), 68. *Honors & Awards:* Distinguished Young Scientist Award, Md Acad Sci, 75. *Prof Exp:* USPHS fel microbiol, Scripps Clin & Res Found, Calif, 68-70. *Concurrent Pos:* USPHS career develop award, 76-81; mem gen biol study sect, NSF, 78-81. *Mem:* Am Soc Microbiol; AAAS. *Res:* Microbial genetics; ribosomes; bacillus plasmids; regulation of inducible cat genes. *Mailing Add:* Dept Biol Sci Univ Md Baltimore Co Catonsville MD 21228. *Fax:* 410-455-3875

LOVETT-DOUST, JONATHAN NICOLAS, REPRODUCTIVE ECOLOGY, AQUATIC ECOLOGY & PLANT BIOMONITORING. *Current Pos:* PROF BIOL, UNIV WINDSOR, 88- *Personal Data:* b Croydon, Eng, Nov 5, 50; Can citizen; m, Lesley Clegg; c Henry, Leo & Jack. *Educ:* Queens Univ, Kingston, BSc, 73; Univ Wales, PhD(plant biol), 78. *Prof Exp:* Asst prof, Amherst Col, 81-87; assoc prof, Hartford Col, 87-88. *Concurrent Pos:* Assoc ed, Ecosci, 93- *Mem:* Brit Ecol Soc; AAAS; Bot Soc Am; Ecol Soc Am. *Res:* Population biology and reproductive ecology of plants; problems of sex allocation and the sex ratio; use of plants as biomonitors of organic contaminants in aquatic ecosystems. *Mailing Add:* Dept Biol Univ Windsor Windsor ON Can. *Fax:* 519-971-3609; *E-Mail:* jld@uwindsor.ca

LOVICH, JEFFREY EDWARD, morphometric analysis, evolutionary ecology, for more information see previous edition

LOVICK, ROBERT CLYDE, ENGINEERING, ELECTRONIC DEVELOPMENT. *Current Pos:* PRES, IDEAS FOR INDUST, 83- *Personal Data:* b Atchison, Kans, Aug 25, 21; m 45, Dorothy Ernst; c Barbara (Bradley). *Educ:* Univ Nebr, BSc, 44. *Prof Exp:* Sr tech assoc, Eastman Kodak Co, 44-83. *Concurrent Pos:* Soc Motion Picture & TV Eng fel, 63; lectr creativity & innovation. *Mem:* Fel Soc Motion Picture & TV Eng. *Res:* Development of proximity fuses for naval ordnance; systems for silver sound records on reversal color films; development of magnetic prestriping on removable backing color films; co-inventor multi-layer digital magnetic recording media; establishment of electronic-optical image evaluation center. *Mailing Add:* 2608 Kanuga Pines Dr Hendersonville NC 28739-7014

LOVINGER, ANDREW JOSEPH, POLYMER & MATERIALS SCIENCE. *Current Pos:* SR STAFF ASSOC & POLYMERS PROG DIR, DIV MAT RES, NSF, 95- *Personal Data:* b Athens, Greece, May 15, 48; US citizen; m 76; c Michael & Daniel. *Educ:* Columbia Univ, BS, 70, MS, 71, ScD, 77. *Honors & Awards:* Dillon Medal, Am Phys Soc, 85; Welch Found lectr, 87; Waldo Semon lectr, 96. *Prof Exp:* Mem tech staff, AT&T Bell Labs, 77-85, head, Polymer Chem Res Dept, 85-94. *Concurrent Pos:* Adj asst prof, Dept Chem Eng & Appl Chem, Columbia Univ, NY, 81-82, adj assoc prof, 82-83; assoc ed, MACROMOLECULES, Am Chem Soc, 88-; distinguished mem tech staff, Bell Labs, Lucent Technol, 85-; div counc, Am Phys Soc, 92- *Mem:* Fel Am Phys Soc; Am Chem Soc; fel AAAS; Mat Res Soc. *Res:* Structure and properties of polymeric and organic materials; morphology and phase transitions; high temperature and high strength polymers, electroactive polymers and organics. *Mailing Add:* NSF 4201 Wilson Blvd Arlington VA 22230

LOVINGOOD, JUDSON ALLISON, MATHEMATICS, ELECTRICAL ENGINEERING. *Current Pos:* RETIRED. *Personal Data:* b Birmingham, Ala, July 18, 36; m 55; c 4. *Educ:* Univ Ala, BSEE, 58, PhD(math), 68; Univ Minn, MS, 63. *Prof Exp:* Assoc engr, Martin Co, 58-59; res engr, Honeywell Inc, 59-62; aerospace engr, Marshall Space Flight Ctr, NASA, 62-64, dep chief astrodyn guid theory div, 64-69, chief dynamics & control div, Aero-Astrodyn Lab, 69-74, dir, Systs Dynamics Lab, 74-79, dept mgr, Space Shuttle Prog & Space Shuttle Main Engine, 79-87; dir eng & res, Thiokol Corp, 88-93. *Concurrent Pos:* Asst prof, Univ Ala, Huntsville, 68- *Mem:* Am Inst Aeronaut & Astronaut. *Res:* Optimal and adaptive control theory research applications to launch and space vehicles; mathematical research in guidance theory, control theory and celestial mechanics. *Mailing Add:* 108 Hickory Hill Rd Gurley AL 35748

LOVINS, AMORY B, RESOURCE & ENERGY EFFICIENCY, GLOBAL SECURITY. *Current Pos:* DIR RES, VPRES & CHIEF EXEC OFFICER, ROCKY MOUNTAIN INST, 82- *Personal Data:* b Nov 13, 47; m 79, L Hunter Sheldon. *Educ:* Oxford, MA. *Hon Degrees:* DSc, Bates Col, 79, Williams Col, 81, Kalamazoo Col, 83,d Univ Maine, 85; LLD, Ball State Univ, 83, Denver Sci Univ Col, 92. *Honors & Awards:* Right Livelihood Award, Onassis Prize; Nissan Prize; Mitchell Prize; Grauer lectr, Univ Boston Col, 79. *Prof Exp:* Res fel, Merton Col, Oxford, 69-71; vis scholar, IIASA, 77, distinguished vis scholar, Univ Okla, 79; Regents lectr, Univ Calif, 78 & 80; Luce vis pof, Dartmouth Col, 82; distinguished vis prof, Univ Colo, 82. *Concurrent Pos:* Prin tech consult, E Source Inc, 89-; prin, Lovins Group, 94. *Mem:* Fel AAAS; Am Inst Architects; Soc Automotive Engrs; Int Asn Energy Economists; Am Phys Soc; fel World Acad Arts Sci. *Res:* Advanced resources and energy efficiency; transforming car, real estate and electricity industries; links to environment, development and security; efficient and sustainable use of resources as a path to global security; author of 24 books. *Mailing Add:* Rocky Mountain Inst 1739 Snowmass Creek Rd Snowmass CO 81654-9199. *Fax:* 970-927-4178; *E-Mail:* ablovins@drmi.org

LOVRIEN, REX EUGENE, PHYSICAL BIOCHEMISTRY. *Current Pos:* from asst prof to assoc prof, 65-76, PROF BIOCHEM, UNIV MINN, 76- *Personal Data:* b Eagle Grove, Iowa, Jan 25, 28; m 56; c 3. *Educ:* Univ Minn, BS, 53; Univ Iowa, PhD, 58. *Prof Exp:* Res assoc phys chem, Yale Univ, 58-61. *Mem:* Am Chem Soc; Biophys Soc; Sigma Xi. *Res:* Macromolecular biochemistry; solution physical chemistry; light energy utilization; calorimetry enzymology; protein separation. *Mailing Add:* Dept Biochem 140 Gortner Lab Col Biol Sci Univ Minn 1479 Gortner Ave St Paul MN 55108

LOVSHIN, LEONARD LOUIS, JR, AQUACULTURE, HATCHERY MANAGEMENT. *Current Pos:* From asst prof to assoc prof, 72-85, PROF FISHERIES, AUBURN UNIV, 85- *Personal Data:* b Rochester, Minn, Mar 21, 42; m 73; c 2. *Educ:* Miami Univ, BA, 64; Univ Wis, MS, 66; Auburn Univ, PhD(fisheries), 72. *Concurrent Pos:* USAID-Auburn Univ proj coordr, Tech Assistance Prog Fisheries Develop, Ctr Ichthyol Res, Fortaleza, Brazil, 72-79, proj coordr to Govt of Panama, small farmer aquaculture develop, 81-84. *Mem:* Am Fisheries Soc; World Aquacult Soc. *Res:* Fish culture research dealing with Tilapias, all male hybrid tilapias, native species indigenous to Brazil, and the extension of research results to local fish farmers; integrated aquaculture development in rural, tropical Latin America, hatchery management. *Mailing Add:* Dept Fisheries Auburn Univ Auburn AL 36849-3501

LOW, BARBARA WHARTON, PROTEIN STRUCTURE & FUNCTION. *Current Pos:* from assoc prof to prof biochem, 56-85, prof biochem & molecular biophys, 85-90, EMER PROF & SPEC LECTR, COL PHYSICIANS & SURGEONS, COLUMBIA UNIV, 90- *Personal Data:* b Lancaster, Eng, Mar 23, 20; nat US; m 50, Melchie J E Bindka. *Educ:* Oxford Univ, BA, 42, MA, 46, DPhil(chem), 48. *Prof Exp:* Res assoc, Harvard Med Sch, 48, assoc phys chem, 48-50, asst prof, Harvard Univ, 50-56. *Concurrent Pos:* Spec Rockefeller Found fel, 47; assoc mem, Lab Phys Chem, Harvard Univ, 50-54; sr res fel, NIH, 59-63, career develop award, 63-68, mem, Biophy & Biophys Chem Study Sect, Div Res Grants, 66-69; consult, USPHS; vis prof, Univ Strasbourg, 65 & Tohoku Univ, 75; invited lectr, Chinese Acad Sci, 81, Acad Sci, USSR, 88. *Mem:* AAAS; Am Inst Physics; Am Soc Biol Chem; Am Crystallog Asn; Am Acad Arts & Sci; Biophys Soc; Int Soc Toxinology. *Res:* X-ray crystal structure of non-enzyme proteins and peptides, particularly snake venom post-synaptic neurotoxins; protein-protein interactions; prediction of protein conformation; curaremimetic toxins, interaction with acetylcholine receptors; water band to proteins in H2O. *Mailing Add:* Dept Biochem & Molecular Biophys Col Physicians & Surgeons Columbia Univ 630 W 168th St New York NY 10032. *Fax:* 212-305-5376

LOW, BOBBI STIERS, ECOLOGY. *Current Pos:* asst prof, 72-75, ASSOC PROF RESOURCE ECOL, SCH NATURAL RESOURCES, UNIV MICH, ANN ARBOR, 75- *Personal Data:* b Louisville, Ky, Dec 4, 42. *Educ:* Univ Louisville, BA, 62; Univ Tex, Austin, MA, 64, PhD(evolutionary zool), 67. *Prof Exp:* Demonst & Res Coun fel physiol, Univ BC, 67-69; Commonwealth Sci & Res Orgn res assoc ecol, Univ Melbourne & Univ SAustralia, 69-72. *Mem:* AAAS; Am Soc Naturalists; Sigma Xi; Soc Study Evolution. *Res:* Evolution of life history strategies; herbivorous competition; reproductive ecology in arid environments. *Mailing Add:* Sch Nat Res Dana Bldg Univ Mich Main Campus 430 E University Ave Ann Arbor MI 48109-1115

LOW, BOON-CHYE, PLASMA PHYSICS, FLUIDS. *Current Pos:* scientist, Nat Ctr Atmospheric Res, 81-87, head coronal interplanetary physics, 87-90, actg dir, High Altitude Observ, 89-90, SR SCIENTIST, HIGH ALTITUDE OBSERV, NAT CTR ATMOSPHERIC RES, 87- *Personal Data:* b Singapore, Feb 13, 46; m 71, Daphne N Yip; c Yi-Kai Liu. *Educ:* Univ London, UK, BSc, 68; Univ Chicago, MS, 69, PhD(physics), 72. *Prof Exp:* Res assoc, Enrico Fermi Inst, Univ Chicago, 72-73; vis scientist, High Altitude Observ, Nat Ctr Atmospheric Res, 73-74; Japan Soc Prom Sci fel, Tokyo Astron Observ, Tokyo Univ, 78-79; Nat Acad Sci-Nat Res Coun sr res assoc, NASA-Marshall Space Flight Ctr, 80-81. *Concurrent Pos:* Mem, Mission Oper Working Group Solar Physics, NASA, 92- *Mem:* Am Phys Soc; Am Astron Soc; Am Geophys Union. *Res:* Theoretical research in the fluid dynamics and magnetohydrodynamics of solar and astrophysical plasmas. *Mailing Add:* High Altitude Observ Nat Ctr Atmospheric Res PO Box 3000 Boulder CO 80307. *Fax:* 303-497-1589; *E-Mail:* low@hao.ucar.edu

LOW, CHOW-ENG, IMMUNOPATHOLOGY, ORGANIC ANALYTICAL CHEMISTRY. *Current Pos:* chmn dept chem, 86-89, PROF CHEM, NAT CHENG KUNG UNIV, TAINAN, TAIWAN, 84- *Personal Data:* b Perak, Malaysia, May 31, 38; m 66; c 3. *Educ:* Chung Chi Col, Chinese Univ, BS, 62; Tex Southern Univ, MS, 66; Univ Tex, Austin, PhD(org chem), 70. *Prof Exp:* Vis asst prof, Dept Chem, La State Univ, 70-71; res fel, Ind Univ, Bloomington, 72-75; res assoc, Dept Human Biol Chem & Genetics, Univ Tex Med Br, 76-78; asst prof biochem, George Washington Univ Med Ctr, 78-84. *Concurrent Pos:* Dir, Inst Chem, Nat Chen Kung Univ, Tainan, Taiwan, 86-89. *Mem:* Am Chem Soc; AAAS; Chem Soc London; Sigma Xi; Chinese Chem Soc. *Res:* Autoxidation of polyunsaturated fatty acids; lipoxygenase metabolites of polyunsaturated fatty acids; analysis of pollutants; Friedel-Crafts reaction mechanisms; catalytic transfer hydrogenation. *Mailing Add:* Dept Chem Nat Cheng Kung Univ One Ta-Hsieh Rd Tainan 70101 Taiwan

LOW, EMMET FRANCIS, JR, APPLIED MATHEMATICS. *Current Pos:* RETIRED. *Personal Data:* b Peoria, Ill, June 10, 22; m 74, Lana Wiles. *Educ:* Stetson Univ, BS, 48; Univ Fla, MS, 50, PhD(math), 53. *Prof Exp:* Instr phys sci, Univ Fla, 50-51, physics, 51-54; aeronaut res scientist, Nat Adv Comt Aeronaut, 54-55; asst prof math, Univ Miami, 55-59; vis res scientist, Courant Inst Math Sci, NY Univ, 59-60; assoc prof math & chmn dept, Univ Miami, 60-66, actg dean col arts & sci, 66-67, prof math & assoc dean faculties, 68-72; dean col & prof math, Clinch Valley Col, Univ Va, 72-86, chmn, Dept Math sci & prof math, 86-89. *Mem:* AAAS; Am Math Soc; Math Asn Am; Sigma Xi; Nat Coun Teachers Math. *Res:* Stress and functional analysis. *Mailing Add:* Box 3417 Wise VA 24293

LOW, FRANCIS EUGENE, THEORETICAL PHYSICS. *Current Pos:* prof, Mass Inst Technol, 57-68, Karl Compton prof, 68-85, dir, Ctr Theoret Physics, 74-83, dir, Lab Nuclear Sci, 79-85, provost, 80-85, inst prof, 85-92, EMER INST PROF & SR LECTR, MASS INST TECHNOL, 92- *Personal Data:* b New York, NY, Oct 27, 21; m 48, Natalie Sadigur; c Julie, Peter & Margaret. *Educ:* Harvard Univ, BS, 42; Columbia Univ, MS, 47, PhD(physics), 49. *Honors & Awards:* Loeb Lectr, Harvard Univ, 59 & 73. *Prof Exp:* Instr physics, Columbia Univ, 49-50; mem, Inst Advan Study, 50-52; from asst prof to assoc prof physics, Univ Ill, 52-56. *Concurrent Pos:*

Consult, AEC, 55-; Fulbright fel, 61-62; Guggenheim fel, 61-62; nat coun, Nat Acad Sci, 86-89; bd mem, Whitehead Inst, 87- *Mem:* Nat Acad Sci; Am Acad Arts & Sci (vpres, 86-87); fel Am Phys Soc; Fedn Am Scientists. *Res:* Theoretical, atomic and nuclear physics; field theory. *Mailing Add:* Rm 6-301 Ctr Theoret Physics Mass Inst Technol Cambridge MA 02139

LOW, FRANK JAMES, SOLID STATE PHYSICS. *Current Pos:* res prof, Lunar & Planetary Lab, Univ Ariz, 65-79, res prof, 71-93, Regents res prof, 88-93, REGENTS EMER PROF, STEWARD OBSERV, UNIV ARIZ, 93-; PRES, INFRARED LABS, INC, ARIZ, 67- *Personal Data:* b Mobile, Ala, Nov 23, 33; m 56; c 3. *Educ:* Yale Univ, BS, 55; Rice Univ, MA, 57, PhD(physics), 59. *Honors & Awards:* Helen B Warner Prize, Am Astron Soc, 68; Medal Except Sci Achievement, NASA, 84; Rumford Prize, Am Acad Arts & Sci, 86. *Prof Exp:* Mem tech staff, Tex Instruments, Inc, 59-62; assoc scientist, Nat Radio Astron Observ, WVa, 62-65. *Concurrent Pos:* Prof space sci, Rice Univ, 66-71, adj prof, 71-79. *Mem:* Nat Acad Sci; Am Phys Soc; Am Astron Soc; Sigma Xi; fel Am Acad Arts & Sci. *Res:* Infrared astronomy; solid state physics; low temperature physics. *Mailing Add:* Steward Observ Univ Ariz Tucson AZ 85721

LOW, FRANK NORMAN, ANATOMY. *Current Pos:* RETIRED. *Personal Data:* b Brooklyn, NY, Feb 9, 11. *Educ:* Cornell Univ, AB, 32, PhD(micros anat), 36. *Hon Degrees:* ScD, Univ NDak, 83. *Honors & Awards:* Henry Gray Award, Am Asn Anat, 88. *Prof Exp:* From instr to asst prof, Univ NC, 37-45; assoc, Sch Med, Univ Md, 45; assoc prof, Sch Med, WVa Univ, 46; asst prof, Sch Med, Johns Hopkins Univ, 46-49; from assoc prof to prof, Sch Med, La State Univ, 49-64; Hill res prof, Univ NDak, 64-73, Chester Fritz Distinguished prof, 75-77, res prof, 73-81. *Concurrent Pos:* Charlton fel anat, Med Sch, Tufts Univ, 36-37; mem, Great Plains Regional Res Rev & Adv Comt, Am Heart Asn, 72-74; assoc ed, Am J Anat, 75-; vis prof anat, Sch Med, La State Univ, New Orleans, 81- *Mem:* Electron Micros Soc Am; Am Asn Anat; Am Asn Hist Med; Am Soc Cell Biol; Sigma Xi. *Res:* Transmission and scanning electron microscopy; fine structure of lung; subarachnoid space; development of connective tissues; microdissection by ultrasonication; medical history. *Mailing Add:* 1100 Florida Ave La State Univ Med Ctr New Orleans LA 70112-2799

LOW, HANS, organic chemistry, for more information see previous edition

LOW, JAMES ALEXANDER, MEDICINE, OBSTETRICS & GYNECOLOGY. *Current Pos:* head dept, 65-85, PROF OBSTET & GYNEC, QUEEN'S UNIV, ONT, 85- *Personal Data:* b Toronto, Ont, Sept 22, 25; m 52, Margery; c Donald, Margaret & Norman. *Educ:* Univ Toronto, MD, 49; FRCS(C). *Prof Exp:* Clin teacher obstet & gynec, Univ Toronto, 55-65. *Mem:* Soc Gynec Invest; Can Soc Clin Invest; Soc Obstet & Gynec Can; Am Gynec & Obstet Soc; Am Acad Cerebral Palsy & Develop Med. *Res:* Perinatal medicine; fetal and newborn cardiorespiratory function mechanism leading to deficits in children; fetal and newborn asphyxia. *Mailing Add:* Dept Obstet & Gynec Queen's Univ Kingston ON K7L 3N6 Can

LOW, KENNETH BROOKS, JR, GENETICS, DNA RECOMBINATION. *Current Pos:* Asst prof radiobiol, Yale Univ, 68-71, asst prof radiobiol & microbiol, 71-73, assoc prof, 73-78, sr scientist radiobiol, 78-81, sr scientist radiobiol & biol, 81-84, PROF RES, YALE UNIV, 84- *Personal Data:* b New Rochelle, NY, Jan 19, 36; m 60, Elise Langworthy; c Kennan & David. *Educ:* Amherst Col, BA, 58; Univ Pa, MS, 60, PhD(molecular biol), 65. *Concurrent Pos:* USPHS fel, Med Ctr, NY Univ, 66-68; mem, Microbiol Genetics Study Sect, NIH, 78-82; consult, Comn Study Antibiotic Use in Animal Feeds, Nat Acad Sci, 79; mem, Prokaryotic Genetics Rev Panel, NSF, 86- *Mem:* Am Soc Microbiol. *Res:* Molecular genetics; genetic recombination and control. *Mailing Add:* 1211 W Lake Ave Guilard CT 06437

LOW, LAWRENCE J(ACOB), MECHANICAL ENGINEERING, OPERATIONS RESEARCH. *Current Pos:* RETIRED. *Personal Data:* b New York, NY, June 22, 21; m 51; c 1. *Educ:* Stevens Inst Technol, ME, 42. *Prof Exp:* Aerodynamicist, Curtiss Wright Airplane Div, WV, 42-43; res aerodynamicist, Cornell Aeronaut Lab, 46-50; sr res engr, Stanford Res Inst, 55-65; dir, Naval Weapons Res Ctr, SRI Int, 65-76, staff scientist, 76-83. *Concurrent Pos:* Mem US Marine air defense eval group, Off Naval Res, DC, 57-58; chmn opers anal sect, Advan Surface Missile Assessment Group, 65. *Mem:* AAAS; Sigma Xi; Am Inst Aeronaut & Astronaut; Opers Res Soc Am; Am Ord Asn. *Res:* Aerodynamics; fluid mechanics; weapon systems analysis and evaluation. *Mailing Add:* 60 Skywood Way Woodside CA 94062

LOW, LEONE YARBOROUGH, APPLIED STATISTICS, COMPONENTS OF VARIANCE. *Current Pos:* from asst prof to assoc prof, 64-88, EMER PROF MATH, WRIGHT STATE UNIV, 88- *Personal Data:* b Cushing, Okla, Aug 27, 35; div; c Corbey & David. *Educ:* Okla State Univ, BS, 56, MS, 58, PhD(math), 61. *Prof Exp:* Systs design engr, Chance Vought Aircraft, Dallas, Tex, 56-58; instr math, Univ Ill, 60-64. *Concurrent Pos:* Nat Res Coun res assoc, Wright-Patterson AFB, 67-68; Nat Acad Sci fel, 67-68; vis assoc prof, Iowa State Univ, 80-81; res scientist, Columbus Battelle Labs, 88- *Mem:* Inst Math Statist; Am Statist Asn; Sigma Xi; fel Royal Statist Soc; Biomet Soc; Am Daffodil Soc. *Res:* Variance component models in the analysis of variance; bootstrapping; experimental design; Taguchi design; inheritance of size and color in narcissus. *Mailing Add:* 381 N Enon Rd Yellow Springs OH 45387-9764

LOW, LOH-LEE, FISHERIES. *Current Pos:* FISHERY BIOLOGIST & OPERS RES ANALYST, NORTHWEST FISHERIES CTR, NAT MARINE FISHERIES SERV, 74- *Personal Data:* b Kuala Lumpur, Malaysia, Jan 15, 48; m 73; c 2. *Educ:* Univ Wash, BS, 70, MS, 72, PhD(fisheries), 74. *Prof Exp:* Fishery biologist, Univ Wash, 74. *Concurrent Pos:* Consult, Food & Agr Orgn, UN, 75; affil asst prof, Univ Wash, 78- *Res:* Fisheries population dynamics; computer modelling of fisheries systems; international fisheries management. *Mailing Add:* Alaska Fisheries Sci Ctr Nat Marine Fisheries Serv 7600 Sandpoint Way NE BINCI570 Seattle WA 98115-0070

LOW, MANFRED JOSEF DOMINIK, PHYSICAL CHEMISTRY. *Current Pos:* assoc prof, 67-72, PROF CHEM, NY UNIV, 72- *Personal Data:* b Karlsbad, Bohemia, June 18, 28; nat US; m 65. *Educ:* NY Univ, BA, 52, MS, 54, PhD(phys chem), 56. *Prof Exp:* Asst chem, NY Univ, 52-55; res chemist, Davison Chem Co Div, W R Grace & Co, 56-58; sr chemist, Texaco, Inc, 58-61; asst prof chem, Rutgers Univ, 61-67. *Mem:* Am Chem Soc; Soc Appl Spectros; NY Acad Sci. *Res:* Chemisorption; heterogeneous catalysis; infrared spectra of surfaces; infrared emission spectroscopy; surface chemistry and physics; Fourier transform spectroscopy; photoacoustic spectroscopy. *Mailing Add:* Dept Chem NY Univ 4 Washington Pl New York NY 10003-6621

LOW, MARC E, MATHEMATICS. *Current Pos:* Instr math, 64-65, asst prof, 65-71, ASSOC PROF MATH, WRIGHT STATE UNIV, 71-, ASST DEAN, COL SCI & ENG, 73- *Personal Data:* b Ada, Okla, Sept 25, 35; m 57; c 2. *Educ:* Okla State Univ, BS, 58, MS, 60; Univ Ill, PhD(math), 65. *Mem:* Math Asn Am; Am Math Soc. *Res:* Elementary and analytic number theory. *Mailing Add:* Dean Sci Wright State Univ 3640 Colonel Glenn Dayton OH 45435-0001

LOW, MARY ALICE, nutrition, for more information see previous edition

LOW, MORTON DAVID, NEUROPHYSIOLOGY. *Current Pos:* PRES, UNIV TEX HEALTH SCI CTR, HOUSTON, 89-, DIR, INST HEALTH POLICY RES & EDUC, 90- *Personal Data:* b Lethbridge, Alta, Mar 25, 35; m 59, 84, Barbara J McLeod; c Cecilia A, Sarah E, Peter J & Kelsey A. *Educ:* Queen's Univ, Ont, MD & CM, 60, MSc, 62; Baylor Univ, PhD(physiol), 66; FRCP(C), 73. *Prof Exp:* From instr to asst prof physiol, Baylor Col Med, 65-68; from assoc prof to prof, Div Neurol, Dept Med, Univ BC, 68-89, clin assoc dean, Fac Med, 74-76, actg assoc dean res & grad studies, 77-78, actg head, Div Neurol, 79-80, coordr health sci, 85-89. *Concurrent Pos:* Dir, Dept Diag Neurophysiol, Vancouver Gen Hosp, 68-87, serv staff consult, 87-89; consult med staff neurol, Univ Hosp, Univ BC Site, 70-89, attend staff, 89, dir, Evoked Potential Lab, 86-89; vis staff neurol EEG, Shaughnessy Hosp, Vancouver, 71-89; interim dir, Vancouver Gen Hosp Res Inst, 81-83, dir, 83-86; prof, Dept Neurol, Med Sch, Univ Tex Health Sci Ctr, Houston, 89-, prof mgt & policy sci, Sch Pub Health, 89-, prof neural sci, Grad Sch Biomed Sci, 89-; consult, Health Protection Br, Health & Welfare Can; mem, Coun Univ Teaching Hosps, 85-89, vchmn, 86-88, chmn, 89; mem bd dirs, Health Environ Inst, Univ Houston, 89-92; mem, Med Sci Adv Comt, US Info Agency, 91-93; vis prof & lectr, numerous univ, assocs & hosps; pres, Mickey Leland Nat Urban Air Toxics Res Ctr, 92-95. *Mem:* AMA; Am Coun Educ; Int Fedn Socs EEG & Clin Neurophysiol (secy, 81-85); fel Am EEG Soc; Can Soc Clin Neurophysiol (secy, 70-72, pres, 72-74); Can Soc Clin Invest; Can Asn Med Educ; Sigma Xi; AAAS; Can Soc EEG; Am Epilepsy Soc. *Res:* Electrophysiology of the central nervous system; cognitive neuroscience; sleep disorders; health policy research and development; health services research. *Mailing Add:* Univ Tex Health Sci Ctr PO Box 20036 Houston TX 77225-0036

LOW, NIELS LEO, MEDICINE. *Current Pos:* DIR PEDIAT, BLYTHEDALE CHILDREN'S HOSP, VALHALLA, NY, 67- *Personal Data:* b Copenhagen, Denmark, Dec 16, 16; nat US; m 43; c 2. *Educ:* Med Col SC, MD, 40. *Prof Exp:* Clin instr pediat, Marquette Univ, 46-53; res assoc neurol, Univ Ill, 54; assoc res prof pediat, Univ Utah, 56-58; asst prof neurol, 60-67, assoc prof clin neurol, 67-75, prof clin neurol & clin pediat, Col Physicians & Surgeons, Columbia Univ, 75- *Concurrent Pos:* Fel, Columbia Univ, 55 & 58-59; consult, NIH. *Mem:* Am EEG Soc; fel Am Acad Neurol; fel Am Acad Pediat; Am Epilepsy Soc; Int Child Neurol Asn (pres, 75-). *Res:* Pediatric neurology; metabolic disease affecting brain of children. *Mailing Add:* Blythedale Children's Hosp Valhalla NY 10595

LOW, PHILIP FUNK, colloid chemistry; deceased, see previous edition for last biography

LOW, PHILIP STEWART, BIOCHEMISTRY. *Current Pos:* from asst prof to assoc prof, 76-86, PROF BIOCHEM, DEPT CHEM, PURDUE UNIV, 86-, JOSEPH F FOSTER PROF CHEM, 95- *Personal Data:* b Ames, Iowa, Aug 8, 47; m 69; c 5. *Educ:* Brigham Young Univ, BS, 71; Univ Calif, San Diego, PhD(biochem), 75. *Honors & Awards:* Herbert Newby McCoy Award, 93. *Prof Exp:* Res assoc, Dept Chem, Univ Mass, 75-76. *Concurrent Pos:* Fel Int Union Against Cancer, 87. *Mem:* Am Soc Hemat; Controlled Release Soc; Am Soc Biochem & Molecular Biol; Am Soc Cell Biol. *Res:* Biochemistry and physical chemistry of biological membranes. *Mailing Add:* Dept Chem Purdue Univ 1393 Brwn Bldg West Lafayette IN 47907-1393

LOW, ROBERT BURNHAM, PHYSIOLOGY. *Current Pos:* asst prof physiol, 70-74, assoc prof, 74-79, PROF PHYSIOL & BIOPHYS & ASSOC DEAN RES, COL MED, UNIV VT, 79- *Personal Data:* b Greenfield, Mass, Sept 19, 40; m 67; c 2. *Educ:* Princeton Univ, AB, 63; Univ Chicago, PhD(physiol), 68. *Prof Exp:* NIH fel biol, Mass Inst Technol, 68-70. *Concurrent Pos:* NIH & Muscular Dystrophy res grants, Univ Vt; Sr Fogarty Int fel, 79, Univ scholar, 88. *Mem:* Am Soc Cell Biol; Am Thoraic Soc. *Res:* Mammalian protein turnover; physiology and biochemistry of muscle; cytoskeleton; tissue and cell remodeling; lung epithelial cells; smooth muscle. *Mailing Add:* Dept Physiol & Biophys 349 Waterman Bldg Burlington VT 05405-0068

LOW, TERESA LINGCHUN KAO, protein chemistry, thymic hormones, for more information see previous edition

LOW, WALTER CHENEY, NEUROPHYSIOLOGY, NERVE REGENERATION & TRANSPLATION. *Current Pos:* assoc prof, 90-93, PROF NEUROSURG, MED SCH, UNIV MINN, 93- *Personal Data:* b Madera, Calif, May 11, 50; m 83, Margaret Schwarz; c Matthew & Elizabeth. *Educ:* Univ Calif, Santa Barbara, BS, 72; Univ Mich, MS, 74, PhD(bioeng), 79. *Honors & Awards:* Nat Res Serv Award, NIH, 79-80 & 81-83. *Prof Exp:* NIH-Nat Inst Gen Med Sci fel bioeng, Univ Mich, 75-78, res assoc neurophysiol, 78-79; res fel neurophysiol, Cambridge Univ, 79-80 & Univ Vt, 80-83; from asst prof to assoc prof, Ind Med Sch, Ind Univ, 83-90, dir, Grad Prog Physiol, 85-88. *Concurrent Pos:* NIH-Nat Neurol & Commun Disorders & Stroke fel, Univ Mich, 79; NSF/NATO fel, Cambridge Univ, 79-80; fel, Univ Vt, 80-81, NIH-Nat Heart, Lung & Blood Inst, 81-82; prin investr, NIH, 84-85, NIA, 85-87; Alzheimer's Dis Asn, 88-89, Am Heart Asn, 87-; Nat Inst Neurol Cardiol Dis Soc, 87-91; Minn Med Found, 90-91; estab investr award, Am Heart Asn, 90- *Mem:* AAAS; Soc Neurosci; Am Physiol Soc; NY Acad Sci; Cell Transplant Soc; Am Heart Asn. *Res:* Central nervous system physiology; neural transplantation and the recovery of function; Parkinson's Disease; Alzheimer's Disease; stroke and cerebral ischemia; neural regeneration; brain tumors. *Mailing Add:* Dept Neurosurg Univ Minn Med Sch 2001 Sixth St SE Minneapolis MN 55455

LOW, WILLIAM, PHYSICS. *Current Pos:* assoc prof, Hebrew Univ, 59-60, prof, 61-70, chair & Sadie Danciger prof, 70-92, EMER PROF PHYSICS, HEBREW UNIV, ISRAEL, 92- *Personal Data:* b Vienna, Austria, Apr 25, 22; Can & Israeli citizen; m 48, 70, Sara Katzburg; c Esther, Nachuh, Abraham, Chava, Shimon, Zipporn, Ayala, Miriam & Rivea. *Educ:* Queen's Univ, Ont, BA, 46; Columbia Univ, MA, 47, PhD, 50. *Hon Degrees:* Dr, Yeshiva Univ, 89. *Honors & Awards:* Cressy Morrison Award, NY Acad Sci, 56; Israel Prize Exact Sci, 61; Rothschild Prize Physics, 64. *Prof Exp:* Tutor physics, Queen's Univ, Ont, 45-46; asst, Columbia Univ, 46-50; lectr, Hebrew Univ, Israel, 50-54, sr lectr, 55-58. *Concurrent Pos:* Vis scholar, Oxford Univ, 54; res assoc, Enrico Fermi Lab, Univ Chicago, 55-57; vis scientist, Argonne Nat Lab, 56, Univ Chicago, 59, Nat Magnet Lab, Mass Inst Technol, 59 & Nat Physics Lab, Ottawa, 63-67; vis prof, Inst Technol, Technion, Israel, 59-60, Inst Technol, 60-64, Weizmann Inst, Rehovot, 62-64, Mass Inst Technol, 64-65 & 82-83, Atomic Energy Lab, France, 74, Atomic Energy Estab, Venezuela, 77; consult scientist, AEC, Israel, 63-66; Guggenheim fel, 64-65; ed, Physics Letters; chmn, Israel Comt, Int Union Radio Sci; pres & rector, Jerusalem Col Technol, Israel, 69-81, chmn bd gov, 85; prof, Columbia Univ, 85-86, Tel Aviv, 88- & Univ Toronto, 90-92; consult to numerous indust firms. *Mem:* Am Phys Soc; NY Acad Sci; Phys Soc Israel (vpres, 58-60, pres, 60-61 & 70-72); Europ Phys Soc; Int Union Pure & Appl Physics. *Res:* Paramagnetic resonance in solids; microwave spectroscopy in gases; quantum electronics; electron density behind shock waves; light scattering from macromolecules. *Mailing Add:* Microwave Div Racah Inst Physics Hebrew Univ Jerusalem Israel. *E-Mail:* williaml@ce.huit.ac.il

LOWDEN, J ALEXANDER, BIOCHEMICAL GENETICS. *Current Pos:* VPRES & CHIEF MED DIR, CROWN LIFE, 89- *Personal Data:* b Toronto, Ont, Feb 21, 33; m 56, Anne Taylor; c John, Eleanor, Jane & Thomas. *Educ:* Univ Toronto, MD, 57; McGill Univ, PhD(biochem), 64; CCFMG, 83. *Prof Exp:* Resident pediat, Hosp Sick Children, 58-60; res assoc, Univ Toronto, 65-67, assoc pediat, 67-80; assoc scientist, Hosp Sick Children, 64-74, assoc dir, Res Inst, 75-89; Prof pediat & clin biochem, Univ Toronto, 80-89; pres, HSC Res & Develop Corp, 82-89. *Concurrent Pos:* Fel neurochem, Montreal Neurol Inst, 61-64; Helen Hay Whitney Found fel, 63-66. *Mem:* AAAS; Can Biochem Soc; Am Soc Pediat; Soc Pediat Res. *Res:* Inborn errors of metabolism, especially lysosomal storage disease. *Mailing Add:* 1901 Scarth St Regina SK S4P 3B1 Can. *Fax:* 306-751-6041

LOWDEN, RICHARD MAX, plant systematics, for more information see previous edition

LOWDER, J ELBERT, APPLIED PHYSICS. *Current Pos:* VPRES, SPARTA INC, 80- *Personal Data:* b Pinedale, Wyo, Mar 18, 40; m 64; c 3. *Educ:* Univ Calif, Berkeley, BS, 63, MS, 65; Univ Calif, San Diego, PhD(eng physics), 71. *Prof Exp:* Flight test engr, Northrop Aircraft Corp, 63-64; proj engr, Aeronutronic Div, Philco-Ford Corp, 65-68; mem staff, Lincoln Lab, Mass Inst Technol, 71-75, assoc group leader appl physics, 75-80. *Mem:* Optical Soc Am; Am Inst Aeronaut & Astronaut; Soc Photo-Optical Instrumentation Engrs. *Res:* Effects of atmospheric aerosols on propagation of laser radiation; interaction of high power laser radiation with solid surfaces; laser radar applications; passive infrared detection systems. *Mailing Add:* Sparta Inc 24 Hartwell Ave Lexington MA 02173

LOWDER, JAMES N, HEMATOLOGY, ONCOLOGY. *Current Pos:* assoc med dir, Immunocytometry Systs, 88-89, CORP MED DIR, ADVAN DIAGNOSTICS, BECTON DICKINSON, 89- *Personal Data:* b Cleveland, Ohio, Aug 26, 50. *Educ:* Case Western Res Univ, BS, 73, MD, 78. *Prof Exp:* Staff, Cleveland Clin Found, 86-88. *Mem:* Am Soc Hemat; AAAS; Am Soc Clin Chemists; Am Soc Clin Oncol; Am Soc Microbiol; Am Soc Immunol. *Mailing Add:* Dept Med Decton Dickinson Advan Diag 7 Loveton Circle PO Box 999 Sparks MD 21152-5555

LOWDER, WAYNE MORRIS, RADIATION PHYSICS, DOSIMETRY. *Current Pos:* RETIRED. *Personal Data:* b Chicago, Ill, Jan 6, 33; div; c 2. *Educ:* Harvard Univ, AB, 54; Int Sch Nuclear Sci & Eng, Argonne Nat Lab, cert, 55. *Prof Exp:* Physicist, Environ Measurements Lab, US Dept Energy, 55-94, prog mgr, Off Health & Environ Res, 77-86, dir, Radiation Physics Div, 87-94. *Concurrent Pos:* Co-organizer, Nat Rad Environ Symp, 63, 72, 78, 87, 91 & 95; mem, Sci Comt, Nat Coun Radiation Protection & Measurement, 73-; consult, UN Sci Comt, Effects Atomic Radiation, 77-; co-chmn, Radon Workgroup, Fed Comm Indoor Air Qual, 83-87; mem, Comt Hiroshima Nagaskai Dose Reassessment, Nat Acad Sci Nat Res Coun, 87. *Mem:* Am Phys Soc; Am Asn Variable Star Observers (pres, 94-96). *Res:* Measurement of ionizing radiation from natural and manmade environmental radionuclides and in the space environment and the assessment of dose to man from these sources. *Mailing Add:* 511 Grasslands Rd Valhalla NY 10595

LOWDIN, PER-OLOV, THEORETICAL PHYSICS, QUANTUM BIOLOGY. *Current Pos:* lectr math & physics, Univ Uppsala, 42-48, asst prof theoret physics, 48-55, assoc prof, Swed Nat Sci Res Coun, 55-60, prof & head, Dept Quantum Chem, 60-82, EMER PROF QUANTUM CHEM, UNIV UPPSALA, 83-; GRAD RES EMER PROF CHEM & PHYSICS, UNIV FLA, 93- *Personal Data:* b Uppsala, Sweden, Oct 28, 16; m 60, Karin Wilhelmina Hook; c Per Erik Assar & Anna Karin Charlotta. *Educ:* Univ Uppsala, Fil Kand, 37, Fil Mag, 39, Fil Lic, 42, Fil Dr(theoret physics), 48. *Hon Degrees:* Dr, Univ Gent, Belgium, 75, Univ Paris, 75, Turku Univ, Finland, 80. *Honors & Awards:* knight of the Swed Royal Order of North Star; Comdr Swed Royal Order Vasa; St Olaf's Medal, Norway, 75; Swed-Am Bicentennial Gold Medal, 79; Lavoisier Medal in Gold, Fr Acad Sci, 81; Chevalier of Legion of Honour, 82; Ultrastructure Award, Sanibel Prism, 85; Niels Bohr Medal, World Asn Theoret Org Chemists, 87; Oscar Carlson Gold Medal, Swed Chem Soc, 93. *Prof Exp:* Lectr mech & math physics, Univ Uppsala, 42-48, asst prof theoret physics, 48-55, assoc prof, 55-60, prof quantum chem & head dept, 60-82, emer prof quantum chem, 83-; grad res prof chem & physics, Univ Fla, 60-93. *Concurrent Pos:* Fel, Swiss Fed Inst Technol, 46; H H Wells Phys Lab, Univ Bristol, 49; vis prof & consult, Duke Univ, Univ Chicago, Mass Inst Technol & Calif Inst Technol, 50-59; founder & leader, Uppsala Quantum Chem Group, 55-82, Fla Quantum Theory Proj, 60-82; ed-in-chief, Int J Quantum Chem, 67-, Advan in Quantum Chem, 6-; mem Nobel Comt Physics, Swed Royal Acad Sci, 72-84; foreign mem Sci Coun Inst Molecular Sci, Okazaki, Japan, 83-86; founding dir, Fla Quantum Theory Proj, 83-; mem adv bd, Max Planck Soc, Carbon Res, Ruhr, WGer; sr investr, Nat Found Cancer Res, Washington, DC, 84-89; dir, Uppsala-Fla Exchange Proj, quantum sci, 60-, dir Fla- Latinamerican & Caribbean Basin Exchange Proj, 85- *Mem:* Swed Royal Soc Arts & Sci; Swed Royal Soc Sci; Norweg Acad Sci & Lett; Int Soc Quantum Biol (pres, 71-72, hon pres); Int Acad Quantum Molecular Sci (vpres, 68-79, pres, 79-85); Am Chem Soc; fel Am Phys Soc; hon mem Sigma Xi; Brit Phys Soc; Catalonian Quantum Chem Soc; World Asn Theoret Org Chemists (hon pres, 89-); foreign mem Korean Acad Sci & Technol. *Res:* Quantum Chem, Solid State Theory and quantum biology; foundations of quantum mechanics and quantum statistics and their reaction to classical mechanics, thermodynamics, etc; theory of chemical reactions, scattering states, and resonances; connection between quantum theory and the special and general theories of relativity; partitioning technique, wave and reaction operators, resolvent methods, rational approximations, etc; author of numerous publications. *Mailing Add:* Quantum Chem Group Box 518 S-75120 Uppsala Sweden

LOWE, A(RTHUR) L(EE), JR, METALLURGICAL & MATERIALS ENGINEERING. *Current Pos:* group supvr liquid metal fuel reactor exp mat, Babcock & Wilcox Co, 57-59, adv reactor concepts mat, 59-63, supvr metall eng group, Nuclear Develop Ctr, 63-65, staff specialist, Mat Processes Sect, 65-67, sr mat engr, Nuclear Power Generation Dept, 67-72, prin mat engr, 72-81, ADV ENGR MAT, NUCLEAR POWER GENERATION DIV, BABCOCK & WILCOX CO, 81- *Personal Data:* b Boyce, Va, Jan 25, 27; m 53; c 3. *Educ:* Va Polytech Inst, BS, 51; Lehigh Univ, MS, 55; Lynchburg Col, MBA, 73. *Prof Exp:* Proj engr, Richmond Eng Co, 51-53; res asst, Lehigh Univ, 53-54; welding engr, Metals Joining Div, Battelle Mem Inst, 54-57. *Concurrent Pos:* Pvt consult engr, 63- *Mem:* Am Soc Metals; Am Inst Mining, Metall & Petrol Engrs; Brit Inst Metals; Am Soc Testing & Mat. *Res:* Nuclear materials applications; metal corrosion and fabrication problems; general materials application problems; forensic engineering-failure analysis and accident reconstruction; technical problems. *Mailing Add:* 2708 Evergreen Rd Lynchburg VA 24503

LOWE, CARL CLIFFORD, PLANT BREEDING. *Current Pos:* From asst prof to prof plant breeding, 52-84, prof biomet, 70-84, EMER PROF, NY STATE COL AGR & LIFE SCI, CORNELL UNIV, 84- *Personal Data:* b West Salem, Ohio, Jan 1, 19; m 42; c 3. *Educ:* Colo Agr & Mech Col, BS, 48; Cornell Univ, MS, 50, PhD(plant breeding), 52. *Mem:* Am Soc Agron. *Res:* Forage crops breeding. *Mailing Add:* 1517 Slaterville Rd Ithaca NY 14850

LOWE, CHARLES HERBERT, JR, zoology, for more information see previous edition

LOWE, CHARLES UPTON, PEDIATRICS. *Current Pos:* actg assoc dir, med appln res, 80-82, SPEC ASST TO THE DIR, NAT INST CHILD HEALTH & DEVELOP, NIH, 83- *Personal Data:* b Pelham, NY, Aug 24, 21; m 55; c 4. *Educ:* Harvard Univ, BS, 42; Yale Univ, MD, 45. *Honors & Awards:* John F Kennedy Mem Lectr, 66; Clifford G Grulee Award, Am Acad Pediat, 71; Special Recognition Award, NIH, 88; Grover Powers Mem Lectr, 69. *Prof Exp:* From intern to asst resident pediat, Children's Hosp, Boston, 45-46; resident, Mass Gen Hosp, 47; assoc prof pediat, Sch Med, State Univ NY Buffalo, 51-55, res prof, 55-65; prof, Col Med, Univ Fla, 65-68, dir human develop ctr, 66-68; sci dir, Nat Inst Child Health & Human Develop, 68-74; exec dir, Nat Comn Protection Human Subjects Biomed & Behav Res, HEW, 74-77, spec asst child health affair, Off of Asst Secy Health, 74-79. *Concurrent Pos:* Nat Res Coun fel, Med Sch, Univ Minn, 48-51; Buswell fel, Sch Med, State Univ NY Buffalo, 55; ed-in-chief, Pediat Res, 66-74; exec dir, President's Biomed Res Panel, 74-76, mem, President's Reorgn Proj Food & Nutrit Study, 78. *Mem:* Soc Pediat Res; Soc Exp Biol & Med; Am Soc Exp Path; Am Pediat Soc; Am Soc Clin Invest; Sigma Xi. *Res:* Clinical and laboratory study of nutritional disease, including celiac and cystic fibrosis of the pancreas; relationship between adrenocortical steroids and nucleic acid metabolism; inborn errors of metabolism and parenteral fluid therapy. *Mailing Add:* 14 Hubbard Park Rd NICHD Bldg 31 Rm 2A20 Cambridge MA 02138

LOWE, DONALD RAY, SEDIMENTOLOGY, PRECAMBRIAN GEOLOGY. *Current Pos:* PROF GEOL, STANFORD UNIV, 88- *Personal Data:* b Sacramento, Calif, Sept 22, 42; m 64; c Nina & Deniz. *Educ:* Stanford Univ, BS, 64; Univ Ill, Urbana, PhD(geol), 67. *Prof Exp:* Instr geol, Univ Ill, Urbana, 67-68; res assoc, US Geol Surv, Calif, 68-70; from asst prof to prof geol, La State Univ, Baton Rouge, 70-88. *Concurrent Pos:* Prin investr, NSF, 77- *Mem:* Int Asn Sedimentologists; Geol Soc Am; Int Soc Study Origin Life; Soc Sedimentary Geol. *Res:* Archean sedimentology and the application of sedimentological principles to interpreting surface conditions on the early earth; composition of the early ocean and atmosphere; paleoecology of Archean life; deep-sea sedimentation and transport systems; Archean sedimentology. *Mailing Add:* Dept Geol & Environ Sci Stanford Univ Stanford CA 94305. *Fax:* 650-725-0979

LOWE, FORREST GILBERT, GENERAL MATHEMATICS, ELECTRICAL ENGINEERING. *Current Pos:* RETIRED. *Personal Data:* b Gilman City, Mo, Mar 27, 27; m 48, Joan B Blaine. *Educ:* NW Mo State Univ, BS(sec educ) & BS(physics & math), 51; Tex Christian Univ, MS, 62; Nova Univ, EdD, 89. *Prof Exp:* Teacher physics & math, Kansas City Sch Dist, 53-56; nuclear engr radiation effects, Convair Div, Gen Dynamics, Ft Worth, Tex, 56-59; instr physics, Kansas City Jr Col, 59-64 & Metrop Community Col Dist, 64-69; instr & chmn, Div Physics & Eng, Longview Community Col, 69-93. *Concurrent Pos:* Instr eng, Univ Mo, Kansas City, 83-, adj prof mech engr, 93- *Mem:* Am Asn Physics Teachers; Nat Soc Prof Engrs; Soc Mfg Engrs; Am Soc Eng Educ; Am Inst Physics; Comput & Automated Systs Asn; Robotics Int; Math Asn Am; Nat Asn Indust Technol. *Res:* Nuclear radiation effects; physics and engineering curriculum. *Mailing Add:* 8412 E 49th St Kansas City MO 64129. *Fax:* 816-235-1260

LOWE, HARRY J, ANESTHESIOLOGY. *Current Pos:* DIR, DEPT ANESTHESIOL, CITY OF HOPE MED CTR, 80-; EMER PROF, UNIV SOUTHERN CALIF. *Personal Data:* b Nogales, Ariz, Dec 21, 19; m 47; c 5. *Educ:* Univ Ariz, BS, 44; Johns Hopkins Univ, SM, 45, MD, 49. *Prof Exp:* Assoc prof biochem, Univ Tex, Southwest Med Sch, 53-56; prin res scientist, Roswell Park Mem Inst, NY, 58-62; resident anesthesiol & dir hyperbaric med, Millard Fillmore Buffalo, 62-66; prof anesthesiol & chmn dept, Pritzker Sch Med, Univ Chicago, 66-73; prof anesthesiol, Univ Southern Calif, 73-78; prof anesthesiol, Univ Ala, Birmingham, 79-80. *Concurrent Pos:* Am Cancer Soc fel, Johns Hopkins Univ, 49-52. *Mem:* AAAS; AMA; Am Chem Soc; Am Anesthesiol Soc; Sigma Xi. *Res:* Quantitative automated administration of volatile anesthetics in closed circuit systems; acid-base regulation of physiological ventilation during anesthesia. *Mailing Add:* 614 N Old Ranch Rd Arcadia CA 91007

LOWE, IRVING J, SOLID STATE PHYSICS, NUCLEAR MAGNETIC RESONANCE IMAGING. *Current Pos:* assoc prof, 62-66, PROF PHYSICS, UNIV PITTSBURGH, 66- *Personal Data:* b Woonsocket, RI, Jan 4, 29; m 53, 87, Irene Povlish; c Marc, Margo & Rachel. *Educ:* Cooper Union, BEE, 51; Washington Univ, St Louis, PhD(physics), 57. *Prof Exp:* Fel, Sloan Found & res assoc physics, Washington Univ, St Louis, 56-58; asst prof, Univ Minn, 58-62. *Concurrent Pos:* Anderson fel, Lovelace Inst, Albuquerque, NMex, 93-94. *Mem:* Fel Am Phys Soc; Soc Magnetic Resonance. *Res:* Experimental and theoretical studies of the structure and behavior of solids and biological systems using nuclear magnetic resonance techniques; nuclear magnetic resonance imaging; magnetic resonance in medicine. *Mailing Add:* Dept Physics Univ Pittsburgh Pittsburgh PA 15260

LOWE, JACK IRA, MARINE ECOLOGY, TOXICOLOGY. *Current Pos:* RETIRED. *Personal Data:* b Fairmount, Ga, Dec 8, 27; m 57. *Educ:* Berea Col, AB, 50; Univ Ga, MS, 55. *Prof Exp:* Biologist, US Fish & Wildlife Serv, 57-61 & US Bur Com Fisheries, 61-70; aquatic biologist, Environ Protection Agency, 70-71, dep lab dir, 71-75, assoc dir tech assistance, 75-76, chief exp environ br, Environ Res Lab, 76-85. *Mem:* Am Fisheries Soc; Nat Shellfisheries Asn; Gulf Estuarine Res Soc. *Res:* Estuarine and coastal ecology; effects of pollutants on marine organisms and their environment. *Mailing Add:* 4461 Sound Side Dr Gulf Breeze FL 32561

LOWE, JAMES, PARTICLE PHYSICS. *Current Pos:* RES PROF, UNIV NMEX, 89- *Personal Data:* b Birmingham, Eng, June 6, 35; m 59, Margaret Priest; c Gerald J. *Educ:* Univ Birmingham, BSc, 56, PhD(physics), 59. *Prof Exp:* Res assoc, Columbia Univ, 59-60, Brookhaven Nat Lab, 60-62. *Concurrent Pos:* Lectr physics, Univ Birmingham, 62- *Mem:* Inst Physics; Am Phys Soc. *Res:* Kaon physics, rare delays; strange particle physics including strange meson, hyperons, H-particles and strange nuclear matter. *Mailing Add:* Physics Dept Univ NMex Albuquerque NM 87131. *Fax:* 505-277-1520; *E-Mail:* lowe@baryon.phys.unm.edu

LOWE, JAMES EDWARD, CARDIAC SURGERY, ELECTROPHYSIOLOGY. *Current Pos:* From asst prof to assoc prof surg & path, 86-90, PROF SURG, DUKE UNIV, 91- *Personal Data:* b Brunswick, Ga, Dec 27, 46; m 69; c 2. *Educ:* Stanford Univ, BA, 69; Univ Calif, Los Angeles, MD, 73. *Concurrent Pos:* Investr, Am Heart Asn, 81-86; dir, Surg Electrophysiol Serv, 83- *Mem:* Am Col Surgeons; Am Col Cardiol; Am Col Chest Physicians; Am Heart Asn; Am Asn Thoracic Surg; Soc Thoracic Surgeons. *Res:* Etiology of cardiac arrhythmias; basic pathogenesis of global myocardial ischemic injury; non-blood contacting biventricular cardiac support devices. *Mailing Add:* Duke Hosp Box 3954 Durham NC 27710

LOWE, JAMES HARRY, JR, entomology, for more information see previous edition

LOWE, JAMES N, ORGANIC CHEMISTRY. *Current Pos:* from asst prof to assoc prof, 71-78, PROF CHEM, UNIV OF THE SOUTH, 78- *Personal Data:* b Grand Forks, NDak, May 3, 36; m 61; c 3. *Educ:* Antioch Col, BS, 59; Stanford Univ, PhD(chem), 64. *Prof Exp:* Asst prof chem, Smith Col, 63-65. *Concurrent Pos:* Am Chem Soc Petrol Res Fund grant, 64-66 & 67-69; fel, Univ Calif, Davis, 70-71; fel Univ Ill, 77-78; res corp grant, 80. *Mem:* Am Chem Soc; AAAS; Sigma Xi. *Res:* Coenzyme mechanisms. *Mailing Add:* Box 1995 Sewanee TN 37375

LOWE, JAMES URBAN, II, PHYSICAL ORGANIC CHEMISTRY. *Current Pos:* RETIRED. *Personal Data:* b Durham, NC, June 30, 21; m, Elizabeth Polk; c Joseph K Petway, Meredith Petway, Janet (Thompson) & James U III. *Educ:* Va State Col, BS, 42, MS, 46; Howard Univ, PhD, 63; Tenn State Univ, MPA, 82. *Prof Exp:* Asst prof chem, Tenn State Col, 47-52 & Ft Valley State Col, 52-56; fel, Howard Univ, 56-59, instr, 59-60; res chemist, US Govt, Md, 60-68; assoc prof biochem, Sch Med, Meharry Med Col, 68-87, from assoc dean to asst dean admin, 69-81, dir, Off Instnl Res, 81-84, Sch Med, Instnl Res, 84-87. *Concurrent Pos:* Co-founder & pres, Lophelps, Inc; consult, Info Serv; interim dir, Acad Develop & Support Serv Div, Grad Sch, Meharry Med Col, 89-94. *Mem:* Am Chem Soc; Sigma Xi. *Res:* Synthesis of 0-nitrobenzoates; aryloxyaliphatic acids; nitroguanidines; physical studies of beta diketones; nuclear magnetic resonance, ultraviolet, infrared spectroscopy of guanidines and perfluoroaromatics; longitudinal study of scholastic performance of Meharry medical students. *Mailing Add:* 4230 Eatons Creek Rd Nashville TN 37218. *Fax:* 615-299-0452

LOWE, JANET MARIE, MICROBIOLOGY, EMBRYOLOGY. *Current Pos:* RETIRED. *Personal Data:* b Ellensburg, Wash, Jan 13, 24. *Educ:* Univ Wash, BS, 45; Univ Chicago, SM, 47. *Prof Exp:* Res assoc bact, Univ Chicago, 47-49; instr biol, Cent Wash State Col, 49-54, from asst prof to assoc prof zool, 54-75, prof biol & dir, Allied Health Sci Prog, 74-90. *Concurrent Pos:* NSF res grant, 58-60. *Mem:* AAAS; Am Soc Microbiol; Am Inst Biol Sci. *Res:* Chick embryology; bacteriology. *Mailing Add:* 10901 176th Circle NE Redmond WA 98052

LOWE, JOHN, III, DAM ENGINEERING, GEOTECHNICAL ENGINEERING. *Current Pos:* INDEPENDENT CONSULT, DAM ENG & GEOTECH ENG, 84- *Personal Data:* b New York, NY, Mar 14, 16; m 43; c 3. *Educ:* City Col New York, BS, 36; Mass Inst Technol, MS, 37. *Honors & Awards:* Eighth Terzaghi Lect, Soc Soil Mech Mex, 71, Fourth Nabor Carrillo Lectr, 78; Second Ann Uscold Lectr, US Comt on Large Dams of Int Comn on Large Dams, 82; Townsend Harris Medal, City Col New York, 82; Martin Kapp Lectr, 86; Mueser-Rutledger Award, 97. *Prof Exp:* Instr civil eng, Univ Md & Mass Inst Technol, 37-44; physicist, David Taylor Model Basin, U S Navy, 45; head, Soil & Rock Eng Dept, Tippetts-Abbett-McCarthy-Stratton, 45-56, assoc partner, 56-62, partner, 62-83. *Mem:* Nat Acad Eng; fel Am Soc Civil Engrs; Int Soc Soil Mech & Found Eng; Int Soc Rock Mech; US Comn Large Dams. *Res:* Author of chapters in 4 engineering handbooks and of more than 30 technical papers; redam and geotechnical engineering. *Mailing Add:* 26 GrandView Blvd Yonkers NY 10710

LOWE, JOHN EDWARD, VETERINARY SURGERY. *Current Pos:* Intern vet surg, Cornell Univ, 59-60, resident, 60-61, instr vet path, 61-63, asst prof vet surg, 63-68, assoc prof vet surg, NY State Col Vet Med, 68-90, coord mgr, Equine Res Park, 74-88, EMER PROF VET SURG, CORNELL UNIV, 90- *Personal Data:* b Newark, NJ, May 20, 35; m 57, Audrey S; c William S & Stacy A. *Educ:* Cornell Univ, DVM, 59, MS, 63. *Mem:* Am Vet Med Asn; Am Asn Equine Practitioners. *Res:* Endocrine control of the equine skeletal system; effect of nutrition on equine bone and joint disease; equine gastrointestinal surgery. *Mailing Add:* NY State Col Vet Med 205 Diag Lab Cornell Univ Ithaca NY 14853. *Fax:* 607-253-3943

LOWE, JOHN PHILIP, QUANTUM CHEMISTRY. *Current Pos:* from asst prof to assoc prof, 66-86, PROF CHEM, PA STATE UNIV, UNIVERSITY PARK, 86- *Personal Data:* b Rochester, NY, Aug 28, 36; m 59; c 2. *Educ:* Univ Rochester, BS, 58; Johns Hopkins Univ, MAT, 59; Northwestern Univ, PhD(quantum chem), 64. *Prof Exp:* Teacher high sch, NJ, 59-60; NIH fel theoret chem, Johns Hopkins Univ, 64-66. *Concurrent Pos:* Petrol Res Fund starter grant, 66-68, type AC grant, 69-71. *Mem:* AAAS; Am Chem Soc; Am Phys Soc. *Res:* Chemical carcinogenicity; chemical reactivities; relations between Huckel and ab initio calculations; quantum chemistry of solids. *Mailing Add:* Dept Chem Pa State Univ University Park PA 16802

LOWE, JOSIAH L(INCOLN), taxonomy of flowering plants; deceased, see previous edition for last biography

LOWE, KURT EMIL, PETROLOGY. *Current Pos:* Lab asst & tutor geol, Eve Session, City Col New York, 33-42, tutor, 46-47, instr, 47-50, from asst prof to assoc prof, 50-64, chmn dept, 57-68, prof, 65-72, EMER PROF GEOL, CITY COL NEW YORK, 72- *Personal Data:* b Munich, Ger, Nov 21, 05; nat US; m 40; c 1. *Educ:* City Col New York, BS, 33; Columbia Univ, MA, 37, PhD(petrol), 47; Asn Prof Geol Scientists, cert. *Hon Degrees:* DSc, Jersey City State Col, 81. *Honors & Awards:* Neil Miner Award, Nat Asn Geol Teachers, 68. *Concurrent Pos:* Asst, Columbia Univ, 40-42; consult, NY, 36-42 & 47-; consult, NY Trap Rock Corp, 53-73. *Mem:* Fel AAAS; fel Am Geol Soc; fel Mineral Soc Am; fel NY Acad Sci; Nat Asn Geol Teachers (pres, 51-52). *Res:* Mineragraphy; optical mineralogy; structural petrology of granites; Storm King granite at Bear Mountain, New York; structure of the Palisades of Rockland County, New York. *Mailing Add:* 4901 Francis Lewis Blvd Flushing NY 11364

LOWE, LAWRENCE E, SOIL CHEMISTRY. *Current Pos:* from asst prof to assoc prof, 66-75, assoc dean agr sci, 85, PROF SOILS, UNIV BC, 75- *Personal Data:* b Toronto, Ont, Mar 29, 33; m 57; c 3. *Educ:* Oxford Univ, BA, 54, MA, 61; McGill Univ, MSc, 60, PhD(agr chem), 63. *Prof Exp:* Soil chemist, Res Coun Alta, 63-66. *Mem:* Can Soc Soil Sci; Int Soc Soil Sci; Soil Sci Soc Am. *Res:* Soil organic matter; sulphur in soil. *Mailing Add:* Dept Soil Sci Univ BC McMillian Bldg Rm 139 Vancouver BC V6T 1Z4 Can

LOWE, REX LOREN, PHYCOLOGY, LIMNOLOGY. *Current Pos:* asst prof, 70-74, PROF BIOL, BOWLING GREEN STATE UNIV, 80- *Personal Data:* b Marshalltown, Iowa, Dec 28, 43; m 64, Sheryn Stringer; c Terry & Christopher. *Educ:* Iowa State Univ, BS, 66, PhD(phycol), 70. *Prof Exp:* Asst bot, Iowa State Univ, 66-69. *Concurrent Pos:* Consult, Icthyol Assocs, 71-; vis prof, Univ Mich Biol Sta, 74- & Va Polytech Inst & State Univ, 82-83; collabr, US Nat Park Serv, 75-76; vis scientist, NZ CRI-NIWA, 92-93. *Mem:* Phycol Soc Am; Int Asn Great Lakes Res; NAm Benthological Soc. *Res:* Community ecology of aquatic ecosystems. *Mailing Add:* Dept Biol Bowling Green State Univ 1001 E Wooster St Bowling Green OH 43403-0001

LOWE, RICHIE HOWARD, PLANT PHYSIOLOGY, BIOCHEMISTRY. *Current Pos:* Res plant physiologist, 63-74, PLANT PHYSIOLOGIST, AGR RES SERV, USDA, 74- *Personal Data:* b Huff, Ky, Apr 9, 35; m 58; c 2. *Educ:* Univ Ky, BS, 58, MS, 59; Ore State Univ, PhD(plant physiol), 63. *Mem:* Am Soc Plant Physiol. *Res:* Enzymatic activity and biochemical changes associated with plant senescence and post harvest physiology; inorganic nitrogen and phosphorous metabolism. *Mailing Add:* 1077 Spurlock Lane Nicholasville KY 40356

LOWE, ROBERT FRANKLIN, JR, cardiovascular physiology, for more information see previous edition

LOWE, ROBERT PETER, AERONOMY, INFRARED ASTRONOMY. *Current Pos:* from asst prof to assoc prof, 68-80, PROF PHYSICS, UNIV WESTERN ONT, 80-, MEM, INST SPACE & TERRESTRIAL SCI, 87- *Personal Data:* b Cambridge, Eng, July 8, 35; Can citizen. *Educ:* Univ Western Ont, BSc, 57, PhD(atomic physics), 67. *Prof Exp:* Sci officer, Defense Res Bd, Can, 56-68. *Concurrent Pos:* Vis prof elect eng, Utah State Univ, 82. *Mem:* Am Geophys Union; Can Asn Physicists. *Res:* Infrared airglow; stratospheric composition; infrared spectroscopy of HII regions and planetary nebulae; electronic, vibrational and rotational excitation in ion-molecular collisions. *Mailing Add:* Dept Physics & Astron Univ Western Ont London ON N6A 3K7 Can

LOWE, RONALD EDSEL, rehabilitation counseling, mental health, for more information see previous edition

LOWE, SCOTT ARTHUR, WATER QUALITY MODELING, AIR QUALITY MODELING. *Current Pos:* PROF ENVIRON ENG, MANHATTAN COL, 94- *Personal Data:* b Wollongong, NSW, Mar 23, 65; m 96, Mary Erker. *Educ:* Univ Wollongong, BE, 86, PhD(civil eng), 90. *Prof Exp:* Res engr, Commonwealth Sci & Indust Res Orgn, 90-93. *Concurrent Pos:* Consult, Hydroqual Inc, 94- *Mem:* Am Soc Civil Engrs; Air & Waste Mgt Asn; Sigma Xi. *Res:* Modeling of water quality within natural and man-made systems from lakes, rivers and estuaries to reservoirs and dams. *Mailing Add:* Manhattan Col Riverdale NY 10471. *Fax:* 718-862-8018; *E-Mail:* slowe@manhattan.edu

LOWE, TERRY CURTIS, THEORETICAL MECHANICAL METALLURGY. *Current Pos:* MEM STAFF & GROUP LEADER, MAT RES PROCESSING SCI, LOS ALAMOS NAT LABS. *Personal Data:* b Spokane, Wash, Nov 10, 55; m 80. *Educ:* Univ Calif, Davis, BS, 78; Stanford Univ, MS, 79, PhD(mat sci), 83. *Prof Exp:* Mem tech staff, Sandia Nat Labs, Livermore, Calif, US Dept Energy, 82- *Concurrent Pos:* Lectr, Div Eng, San Francisco State Univ, 80-81; vis scholar, Dept Mat Sci, Stanford Univ, 83-86; chmn, Interagency Metal Forming Work Group, US Dept Energy, 85- *Mem:* Am Soc Metals; Am Inst Mining & Metall Engrs; Am Soc Mech Engrs; Sigma Xi. *Res:* Mathematical modeling of mechanical and physical processes of metals; crystal plasticity modeling of large strain plasticity; finite element analysis of metal forming processes. *Mailing Add:* MST-BO M/S G754 Los Alamos Nat Lab Los Alamos NM 87545

LOWE, WILLIAM WEBB, chemical engineering, for more information see previous edition

LOWE-KRENTZ, LINDA JEAN, BIOCHEMISTRY. *Current Pos:* ASST PROF CHEM, LEHIGH UNIV, 86- *Personal Data:* b Milwaukee, Wis, 1953; m 76; c 2. *Educ:* Northwestern Univ, PhD(biochem), 80. *Prof Exp:* Res asst prof biochem, Chicago Med Sch, Univ Health Sci, 85-86. *Mem:* AAAS; Am Soc Chem Biologists. *Res:* Endothelial heparan sulfate proteoglycans and their receptors. *Mailing Add:* Lehigh Univ 111 Res Dr Rm B217 Bethlehem PA 18015-4732

LOWELL, A(RTHUR) I(RWIN), POLYMER CHEMISTRY, EMULSION POLYMERS. *Current Pos:* RETIRED. *Personal Data:* b New York, NY, Nov 9, 25; m 54; c 3. *Educ:* Brooklyn Col, AB, 45; Univ Pa, MS, 48, PhD(chem), 51. *Prof Exp:* Res chemist, Air Reduction Co, Inc, 51-57, sect head, 57-58; res assoc, Lucidol Div, Wallace & Tiernan, Inc, 59-60, supvr appln res, 61-62; res assoc, Berkeley Chem Corp, 62 & Heyden Newport Chem Co, 63; sr res chemist, Mobil Chem Co, 64-66, group leader, 66-68, sect leader, 69-73; sci teacher pub schs, Edison, NJ, 73-76; group leader, Norton & Son, 77-78; sr res chemist, Sun Chem Corp, 78-91. *Mem:* Am Chem Soc. *Res:* Polymerization kinetics; organic peroxide initiators; polymer process and product development; emulsion polymerization; coatings; inks in offset printing. *Mailing Add:* 657C Nutley Dr Cranbury NJ 08512

LOWELL, GARY RICHARD, SKARN PETROLOGY, GREISEN GEOCHEMISTRY. *Current Pos:* From asst prof to assoc prof, 69-81, PROF GEOL, SE MO STATE UNIV, 81- *Personal Data:* b Modesto, Calif, Sept 26, 42; m 68; c 2. *Educ:* San Jose State Col, BS, 65; NMex Inst Mining & Technol, PhD(geol), 70. *Concurrent Pos:* Vis prof geol, Univ Fed do Para, Brazil, 78-80; consult, Houston Int Minerals Corp, Alaska, 80 & 81, Newmont Explor Ltd, 85 & 87. *Mem:* Mineral Asn Can. *Res:* Igneous and metamorphic petrology; tin and tungsten ore deposits. *Mailing Add:* Geol Sci SE Mo State Univ 1 University Plaza Cape Girardeau MO 63701-4710

LOWELL, JAMES DILLER, PETROLEUM GEOLOGY, STRUCTURAL GEOLOGY. *Current Pos:* PRES, COLEXCON, INC, 78- *Personal Data:* b Lincoln, Nebr, Aug 17, 33; m 57, Suzanne Hewitt; c Jennifer A (Marin), Carey E, Elizabeth S & Alexandra H. *Educ:* Univ Nebr, BSc, 55; Columbia Univ, MA, 57, PhD(geol), 58. *Prof Exp:* Geologist, Am Overseas Petrol Ltd, 58-65; asst prof geol, Washington & Lee Univ, 65-66; sr res specialist, Esso Prod Res Co, 66-73; explor geologist, Exxon Co, USA, 73-74; mgr geol, Northwest Explor Co, 74-76. *Concurrent Pos:* Assoc, Oil & Gas Consults Int Inc, 76-; consult geologist, 76- *Mem:* Fel Geol Soc Am; Am Asn Petrol Geologists; Explorer's Club. *Res:* Structural geology of sedimentary rocks. *Mailing Add:* 5836 S Colorow Dr Morrison CO 80465. *Fax:* 303-730-6549

LOWELL, PHILIP S(IVERLY), CHEMICAL ENGINEERING. *Current Pos:* prin engr, 88-91, CORP FEL, RADIAN CORP, 91- *Personal Data:* b Manila, Philippines, July 9, 31; US citizen; m 59, 74, 93, Elizabeth Runner; c 3. *Educ:* Univ Tex, BS, 54, MS, 63, PhD, 66. *Prof Exp:* Process engr, Jefferson Chem Co, Inc, 54-55; process engr, C F Braun & Co, 55-59, sr process engr, 59-60; sr engr, Tex Res Assocs, Inc, 60-64; asst dir chem res, Tracor, Inc, 64-69; vpres, Radian Corp, 69-77; pres, P S Lowell & Co, Inc, 77-87. *Concurrent Pos:* Adj prof, Univ Tex, Austin, 74 & 86; proj group mem, Environ Protection Coop Effort, US-USSR, 74-79. *Mem:* Am Inst Chem Engrs; Am Chem Soc. *Res:* Process engineering of chemical plants and refineries; application of thermodynamics to practical problems; research in air pollution control processes; granted 7 patents. *Mailing Add:* Radian Corp PO Box 201088 Austin TX 78720-1088

LOWELL, ROBERT PAUL, GEOPHYSICS, SEA FLOOR HYDROTHERMAL SYSTEMS. *Current Pos:* From asst prof to assoc prof, 71-90, PROF GEOPHYS, GA INST TECHNOL, 91- *Personal Data:* b Chicago, Ill, Apr 10, 43; m 81; c 5. *Educ:* Loyola Univ Chicago, BS, 65; Ore State Univ, MS, 67, PhD(geophys), 72. *Concurrent Pos:* Assoc prog dir marine geol & geophys, NSF, 87-89. *Mem:* Am Geophys Union. *Res:* Thermal geophysics; modeling of magmatic processes; geothermal energy; hydrothermal systems; fluid flow and chemical reactions in fractured and porous media. *Mailing Add:* Sch Earth & Atmosphere Sci Ga Inst Technol Atlanta GA 30332. *Fax:* 404-894-5638; *E-Mail:* bob@namazu.gatech.edu

LOWELL, SHERMAN CABOT, PHYSICS, THEORETICAL NUMERICAL ANALYSIS. *Current Pos:* RETIRED. *Personal Data:* b Olean, NY, Aug 15, 18; m 41; c 2. *Educ:* Univ Chicago, BS, 40; NY Univ, PhD(math), 49. *Prof Exp:* Sci liaison officer math sci, Office Naval Res, London, Eng, 49-51; from asst to assoc prof math, NY Univ, 51-57; prof math, head dept & dir grad progs math & appl sci, Adelphi Univ, 57-62; prof math & info sci, Wash State Univ, 62-66, mathematician, Comput Ctr, 62-95, prof physics & comput sci, 66-95. *Concurrent Pos:* Asst to sci dir, Inst Math Sci, NY Univ, 53-57; consult serv bur, Int Bus Mach Corp, 59-62 & Lawrence Livermore Lab, Univ Calif, 63-; vis scientist, Lab Physics of Solids, Paris, 68 & Nat Ctr Very Low Temp, Grenoble, France, 69. *Mem:* AAAS; Am Meteorol Soc; Soc Indust & Appl Math; Am Phys Soc. *Res:* Lattice dynamics; wave propagation; numerical analysis. *Mailing Add:* 622 Glenbrook Circle Florence OR 97439

LOWEN, GERARD G, MECHANICAL ENGINEERING. *Current Pos:* Prof mech eng, 54-87, dept head, 87-90, H KAYSER PROF MECH ENG, CITY COL NEW YORK, 87-, ASSOC DEAN GRAD STUDIES, 90-, EXEC OFFICER PHD PROG, GRAD SCH & UNIV CTR. *Personal Data:* b Munich, Ger, Oct 25, 21; US citizen; m 52, Doris Wolff; c Deborah, Nicole & Daniel. *Educ:* City Col New York, BME, 54; Columbia Univ, MSME, 58; Munich Tech Univ, Dr Ing, 63. *Honors & Awards:* Mechanism Comt Award, Am Soc Mech Engrs, 84, Mach Design Award, 87. *Concurrent Pos:* Consult, var indust, 63-; NSF grants, Army Res Off; expert witness, Army Armament Res & Develop Command res grants. *Mem:* AAAS; fel Am Soc Mech Engrs; Am Soc Eng Educ; NY Acad Sci; Soc Mfg Engrs; Verein Deutschor Engr. *Res:* Dynamics of high speed machinery; rigid and elastic body behavior of linkages and mechanisms; kinematic synthesis and analysis; stress and vibration analysis; safety and arming mechanisms. *Mailing Add:* Grad Eng Off Sch Eng City Col Rm T152 Convent Ave at 138th St New York NY 10031. *Fax:* 212-650-8029

LOWEN, W(ALTER), SYSTEMS SCIENCES, MECHANICAL ENGINEERING. *Current Pos:* dir sch advan technol, 67-68, dean, 68-77, prof systs sci, 67-90, EMER PROF, THOMAS J WATSON SCH, STATE UNIV NY, BINGHAMTON, 91- *Personal Data:* b Cologne, Ger, May 17, 21; nat US; m 43, Sylvia; c Robert G & John G. *Educ:* NC State Univ, BME, 43, MS, 47; Swiss Fed Inst Technol, DrSc(nuclear eng), 63. *Prof Exp:* Instr mech eng, NC State Col, 43-47; prof, Union Col, NY, 47-67, actg chmn dept, 59 & 67, chmn div eng, 56-59 & 66-67. *Concurrent Pos:* Consult, Alco Prod, Inc, 52-54, 56, Oak Ridge Nat Lab, 54-57 & Gen Elec Co, 60; consult inst appl technol, Nat Bur Stand, 65-66; vis prof, Swiss Fed Inst Technol, 65-66; dir, Vols for Int Tech Assistance, Inc, 66-69, mem charter bd, 69-; guest sabbaticant, IBM Systs Res Inst, 78 & 79; acad guest, Swiss Fed Inst Technol, Zurich, Switz, 82; auth, 82. *Mem:* Am Soc Mech Engrs; Am Nuclear Soc; Am Soc Eng Educ; NY Acad Sci; World Acad Arts & Sci; Asn Psychol Types; Int Soc Systs Sci; Sigma Xi. *Res:* Cognitive models and visual perception; human factors research. *Mailing Add:* 152 Moore Ave Binghamton NY 13903

LOWENGRUB, MORTON, MATHEMATICS. *Current Pos:* assoc prof, 67-72, chmn dept, 77-80, PROF MATH, IND UNIV, BLOOMINGTON, 72- *Personal Data:* b Newark, NJ, Mar 31, 35; m 61; c 1. *Educ:* NY Univ, BA, 56; Calif Inst Technol, MS, 58; Duke Univ, PhD(math), 61. *Prof Exp:* Instr math, Duke Univ, 60-61; asst prof, NC State Col, 61-62; Leverhulme res fel, Glasgow Univ, 62-63; asst prof, Wesleyan Univ, 63-66; NSF fel, Glasgow Univ, 66-67. *Concurrent Pos:* Sr res fel, Sci Res Coun, Gt Brit, 73-74; ed, Ind Math J, 77-81 & Math Reviews, 81- *Mem:* Math Asn Am; Am Math Soc; Soc Indust & Appl Math; Am Math Soc. *Res:* Mathematical theory of elasticity. *Mailing Add:* Ind Univ Col Arts & Sci Kirkwood Hall 104 Bloomington IN 47405

LOWENSOHN, HOWARD STANLEY, CORONARY PHYSIOLOGY, EXERCISE. *Current Pos:* ASSOC PROF PHYSIOL, UNIFORMED SERV UNIV HEALTH SCI, 80- *Personal Data:* b Columbus, Ohio, Jan 23, 31; m 53; c 1. *Educ:* Franklin & Marshall Col, BS, 56; Univ Southern Calif, MS, 62; Univ Md, PhD(physiol), 72. *Prof Exp:* Res physiologist, Walter Reed Army Inst Res, 63- *Concurrent Pos:* Consult, Johns Hopkins Univ, 77-85; res adv, Nat Res Coun, 80-; mem, ACE Comt & Grip Comt, Am Physiol Soc, 88-91. *Mem:* Am Physiol Soc; NY Acad Sci; AAAS; Am Heart Res Coun; Sigma Xi. *Res:* Hemodynamics of coronary blood flow in chronic conscious dogs at rest, during exercise and with varying degrees of ischemia; hypertrophied hearts, including the initial chronic studies of phasic coronary artery blood flow in the right heart in normal and hypertrophied and dilated hearts; cardiovascular and respiratory research director for pre- clinical drug development, including cooperative efforts with WHO. *Mailing Add:* 9105 Louis Ave Silver Spring MD 20910-2129. *Fax:* 301-427-6589

LOWENSTEIN, CARL DAVID, applied physics, for more information see previous edition

LOWENSTEIN, DEREK IRVING, HIGH ENERGY PHYSICS, ACCELERATOR OPERATIONS. *Current Pos:* asst physicist, Brookhaven Nat Lab, 73-75, assoc physicist, 75-77, physicist & head, exp planning & support div, 77-84, sr physicist, 83, dep chmn, Accelerator Dept, 81-84, CHMN, AGS DEPT, BROOKHAVEN NAT LAB, 84- *Personal Data:* b Hampton Court, Eng, Apr 26, 43; US citizen; m 68, Elaine Hartmann; c Jessica R & Peter D. *Educ:* City Col NY, BS, 64; Univ Pa, MS, 65, PhD(physics), 69. *Prof Exp:* Res assoc, Univ Pa, 69-70 & Univ Pittsburgh, 70-73. *Concurrent Pos:* Mem, US/USSR Joint Coord Comt Fundamental Properties Matter, Dept Energy, US/Japan Comt High Energy Physics, High Energy Physics Adv Panel, 93-96. *Mem:* Fel Am Phys Soc; AAAS; NY Acad Sci. *Res:* Experimental high energy physics; accelerator operations. *Mailing Add:* AGS Dept Brookhaven Nat Lab Upton NY 11973. *E-Mail:* lowenstein@bnldag.ags.bnl.gov

LOWENSTEIN, EDWARD, ANESTHESIOLOGY, CARDIOPULMONARY PHYSIOLOGY. *Current Pos:* Assoc anesthesia, 68-70, from asst prof to assoc prof, 70-81, PROF ANESTHESIA, HARVARD MED SCH, 81- *Personal Data:* b Duisburg, Ger, May 29, 34; US citizen; m 59; c 3. *Educ:* Univ Mich, MS, 59; Am Bd Anesthesiol, dipl, Harvard Univ, MA, 81. *Honors & Awards:* Distinguished Lectr Physiol, Am Col Chest Phys, 86. *Concurrent Pos:* Assoc anesthetist, Mass Gen Hosp, 68-71, anesthetist, 71- *Mem:* Am Soc Anesthesiol; Am Physiol Soc; Soc Critical Care Med. *Res:* Physiological effects of cardiac and pulmonary disease; cardiac anesthesia. *Mailing Add:* Anesthetist-in-Chief Beth Israel Hosp 330 Brookline Ave Boston MA 02215-5491. *Fax:* 617-735-5013

LOWENSTEIN, J(ACK) G(ERT), chemical engineering, technical management; deceased, see previous edition for last biography

LOWENSTEIN, JEROLD MARVIN, NUCLEAR MEDICINE. *Current Pos:* from asst clin prof to assoc clin prof, 63-81, CLIN PROF MED THYROID RES, MED CTR, UNIV CALIF, SAN FRANCISCO, 81- *Personal Data:* b Danville, Va, Feb 11, 26; m 81, Adrienne Zihlman; c 3. *Educ:* Columbia Univ, BS, 46, MD, 53. *Prof Exp:* Physicist, Los Alamos Sci Lab, 46-48; instr med & radiol, Sch Med, Stanford Univ, 57-58. *Concurrent Pos:* Nat Found fel radiobiol, 55-56; NIH res grant 60-66, 61-66 & 62-66; dir nuclear med, Presby Med Ctr, San Francisco, 59-; partic, Galapagos Int Sci Proj, 64. *Mem:* AMA; Soc Nuclear Med; fel AAAS. *Res:* Applications of physics to medicine, especially medical uses of radioactive isotopes; molecular evolution. *Mailing Add:* 2203 Scott San Francisco CA 94115

LOWENSTEIN, JOHN HOOD, QUANTUM FIELD THEORY, NONLINEAR DYNAMICS. *Current Pos:* res asst prof, 72-74, assoc prof, 74-81, chmn dept, 85-88, PROF PHYSICS, NY UNIV, 81- *Personal Data:* b Newark, NJ, Mar 15, 41; m 67, Marcia Greenberg; c Ethan & Alexander. *Educ:* Harvard Univ, AB, 62; Univ Ill, Urbana, MS, 63, PhD(physics), 66. *Prof Exp:* Res assoc physics, Univ Minn, 66-68; vis asst prof, Univ Sao Paulo, 68-70; res assoc, Univ Pittsburgh, 70-72. *Mem:* Am Phys Soc. *Res:* Quantum field theory, with emphasis on renormalized perturbation theory and soluble two-dimensional models; nonlinear dynamics. *Mailing Add:* Dept Physics NY Univ 4 Washington Pl New York NY 10003. *E-Mail:* lowenste@acfz. nyu.edu

LOWENSTEIN, JOHN MARTIN, BIOCHEMISTRY. *Current Pos:* prof, 59-77, HELENA RUBINSTEIN PROF BIOCHEM, BRANDEIS UNIV, 77- *Personal Data:* b Berlin, Ger, Oct 28, 26; m 54. *Educ:* Univ Edinburgh, BSc, 50; Univ London, PhD, 53. *Prof Exp:* Demonstr chem & biochem, Med Sch, St Thomas' Hosp, Eng, 50-53; res assoc biochem, Med Sch, Univ Wis, 53-55; Beit mem fel med res, Oxford Univ, 55-58. *Concurrent Pos:* Ed, Methods in Enzymol, Archives Biochem & Biophysics, 67-72, J Lipid Res, 79-, J Biol Chem, 79-; mem adv comt, Med Found Res Comt, 74-77, Biochem Study Sect, 77-81; lectr, Indian Dept Sci & Indust Res, 80. *Mem:* AAAS; Am Chem Soc; Am Soc Biol Chem; Brit Biochem Soc. *Res:* Regulated enzymes; integration and control of metabolism pathways. *Mailing Add:* Dept Biochem Brandeis Univ Waltham MA 02254-9110

LOWENSTEIN, MICHAEL ZIMMER, HARMONIC DISTORTION MITIGATION. *Current Pos:* PRES, HARMONICS LTD, 93- *Personal Data:* b Hornell, NY, Oct 4, 38; m 62; c 2. *Educ:* Oberlin Col, AB, 60; Ariz State Univ, MS, 62, PhD(x-ray crystallog), 65. *Prof Exp:* Asst prof chem, 64-71, prof chem, Adams State Col, 71-78; educ proj mgr, Joint US-Saudi Prog, Solar Energy Res Inst, 78-82, prog mgr, Biofuels Prog Off, 82-90; mgr, Power Qual Systs, Trans-Coil, Inc, 90-93. *Concurrent Pos:* AEC fac res assoc, Ariz State Univ, 70-71; consult, Citizen's Workshop, Energy Res & Develop Agency, 74-76, Dept Energy, 76-78; vis prof, Solar Energy Appln Lab, Colo State Univ, Ft Collins, 75-76; prof chem, Adams State Col, Alamosa, 71-77; dir, Solar Energy Div, Navarro Col, Tex, 77-78; lectr, Univ Wis, Milwaukee, 91- *Mem:* Inst Elec & Electronics Engrs Comput Soc; Power Eng Soc; Indust Appln Soc. *Res:* Power quality; mitigation of harmonic distortion. *Mailing Add:* 11036 N Westview Lane Mequon WI 53092

LOWENTHAL, DENNIS DAVID, PLASMA PHYSICS, ELEMENTARY PARTICLE PHYSICS. *Current Pos:* STAFF MEM, ACULIGHT CORP, 93- *Personal Data:* b Yakima, Wash, Nov 10, 42; m 66; c 2. *Educ:* Calif State Univ, Northridge, BS, 65; Univ Calif, Los Angeles, MS, 66; Univ Calif, Irvine, PhD(physics), 75. *Prof Exp:* Res & develop engr, Aeronutronic Div, Philco-Ford Corp, 66-75; physicist, Math Sci Northwest, 75-80. *Mem:* Am Phys Soc; Optical Soc Am; AAAS. *Res:* Experimental search for the double beta decay of selenium 82; geometrical and wave optics; plasma physics diagnostics. *Mailing Add:* 40 Lake Bellevue No 100 Bellevue WA 98005

LOWENTHAL, DOUGLAS H, RECEPTOR MODELLING, ANALYTIC CHEMISTRY. *Current Pos:* Teaching asst org chem, 74, res asst, 74-80, RES SPECIALIST, UNIV RI, 81- *Personal Data:* b New York, NY, Dec 19, 48; m 82. *Educ:* Tufts Univ, BA, 70; Univ RI, MS, 76, PhD(oceanog), 86. *Mem:* Air Pollution Control Asn. *Res:* Determination of regional sources of air pollution in the Arctic and eastern US; statistical source receptor modelling. *Mailing Add:* 399 Oregon Blvd Reno NV 89506-9484

LOWENTHAL, WERNER, EDUCATION, HEALTH CARE. *Personal Data:* b Krefeld, Ger, Dec 20, 30; US citizen; m 85, Hilda M Taylor; c John M & Julie D. *Educ:* Albany Col Pharm, Union Univ, NY, BS, 53; Univ Mich, PhD(pharmaceut chem), 58; Va Commonwealth Univ, MEd, 78. *Prof Exp:* Asst, Univ Mich, 53-55; res pharmacist, Abbott Labs, 57-61; asst prof pharm,

Med Col Va, Va Commonwealth Univ, 61-66, assoc prof, 66-71, prof pharm, Sch Pharm, 71-92, prof educ planning & develop, 74-92, dir continuing educ, 80-92. *Concurrent Pos:* Mem, US Pharmacopoeia Rev Comt, 75-80; chmn coun fac, Am Asn Cols Pharm, 80-81. *Mem:* Asn Psychol Types; Am Asn Cols Pharm. *Res:* Pharmaceutical product development; drug absorption; programmed instruction; continuing education; curriculum development; ethics; Myers Briggs personality preferences. *Mailing Add:* 51 Chantecler Ave Richmond VA 23226

LOWER, STEPHEN K, PHYSICAL CHEMISTRY. *Current Pos:* ASSOC PROF PHYS CHEM, SIMON FRASER UNIV, 65- *Personal Data:* b Oakland, Calif, Sept 8, 33; m 63. *Educ:* Univ Calif, Berkeley, BA, 55; Ore State Univ, MS, 58; Univ BC, MSc, 60, PhD(phys chem), 63. *Prof Exp:* Fel phys chem, Polytech Univ Brooklyn, 63-64 & Univ Calif, Los Angeles, 64-65. *Concurrent Pos:* Nat Res Coun Can grants, 65-71, mem panel on comput assisted instruction lang, 70- *Mem:* Am Chem Soc. *Res:* Instructional systems design; computer-assisted instruction and instructional technology applied to college science teaching. *Mailing Add:* Dept Chem Simon Fraser Univ Burnaby BC V5A 1S6 Can

LOWER, WILLIAM RUSSELL, genetics, environmental health, for more information see previous edition

LOWERY, BARBARA J, PSYCHIATRIC NURSING. *Current Pos:* instr, Sch Nursing, Univ Pa, 70-72, assoc, 72-73, from asst prof to assoc prof, 73-87, assoc dean res, 90-93, INDEPENDENCE FOUND, PROF, SCH NURSING, UNIV PA, 87-, ASSOC PROVOST, 95- *Educ:* Reading Hosp Sch, RN, 58; Villanova Univ, BSN, 66; Univ Pa, MSN, 68; Temple Univ, EdD, 73. *Prof Exp:* Staff & head nurse, Admis Serv, Danville State Hosp, Pa, 58-62; unit & hosp supvr, Norristown State Hosp, 60-63, instr nursing educ, 63-65, Nursing Dept, 61-65; dir, Eastern Pa Psychiat Inst, 68-69. *Concurrent Pos:* Prog dir, Psychiat Ment Health Nursing, 74-86, chair person, 78-84; assoc ed, Nursing Res, 78-83; ombudsman, Univ Pa, 84-86; dir, Robert Wood Johnson Clin Nurse Scholars Prog, 86-91; dir, Ctr Nursing Res, 86-94; consult numerous cols, univs & hosps. *Mem:* Inst Med-Nat Acad Sci; fel Am Acad Nursing. *Res:* Author or co-author of book chapters, articles and abstracts. *Mailing Add:* Sch Nursing Univ Pa 34th & Spruce Sts Philadelphia PA 19104

LOWERY, LEE LEON, JR, STRUCTURAL ENGINEERING, STRUCTURAL FAILURES. *Current Pos:* From asst prof to assoc prof, 61-71, PROF ENG, TEX A&M UNIV, 71- *Personal Data:* b Corpus Christi, Tex, Dec 26, 38; m 60; c 2. *Educ:* Tex A&M Univ, BS, 60, MS, 61, PhD(struct eng), 67. *Concurrent Pos:* Res engr, Albritton Eng Corp, 63-66, Tex Transp Inst, 67-; consult engr, Esso Prod Res Corp, 66-68, Shell Oil Corp, 76-78 & Marathon Oil Corp, 77-78; prof construct, Tex A&M Univ, Sch Archit, 65-69, prof struct, Dept Aerospace Eng, 67-70; failure analyst, Eng Consult, Inc, 70-76, prod failure analyst, 76-77. *Mem:* Am Soc Exp Stress Analysis; Am Soc Civil Engrs; Soc Marine Technol; Am Soc Eng Educ; Nat Soc Prof Engrs. *Res:* Basic research, engineering structures and products; applied research in areas of design and analysis of coastal, offshore structures; product failure analysis, consumer protection; engineering applications of computer analysis. *Mailing Add:* 2905 S College Ave Bryan TX 77801-2510

LOWERY, R(ICHARD) L, MECHANICAL ENGINEERING. *Current Pos:* from asst prof to prof, 61-72, HALLIBURTON PROF MECH ENG & DIR CTR TEACHING, OKLA STATE UNIV, 72- *Personal Data:* b Haven, Kans, July 25, 35; m 59; c 2. *Educ:* Tex Tech Col, BS, 56; Okla State Univ, MS, 57; Purdue Univ, PhD(mech eng), 61. *Prof Exp:* Instr mech eng, Tex Tech Col, 57-58. *Concurrent Pos:* Consult, Fed Aviation Agency, 64-65. *Mem:* Acoust Soc Am; Am Soc Eng Educ. *Res:* Acoustics; sonic boom research; ultrasonics; vibrations; instrumentation. *Mailing Add:* Sch Mech Eng Okla State Univ Main Campus Stillwater OK 74078-0001

LOWES, BRIAN EDWARD, GEOLOGY. *Current Pos:* from asst prof to assoc prof, 68-82, CHMN, EARTH SCI DEPT, PAC LUTHERAN UNIV, 77-, PROF, 82- *Personal Data:* b Harrow, Eng, Sept 21, 35; Can citizen; m 66; c 2. *Educ:* Imperial Col, London Univ, BSc, 57; Queen's Univ, Ont, MSc, 63; Univ Wash, Seattle, PhD(geol), 72. *Prof Exp:* Mine geologist asst, Opemiska Copper Ventures Ltd, 57-59; explor geologist, Hollinger Consol Gold Mines, 61-62; tech asst, Can Geol Surv, 63-64. *Mem:* Geol Soc Am; Geol Asn Can; Mineral Asn Can. *Res:* Structural geology and metamorphic petrology of crustal basement rocks in Pacific Northwest. *Mailing Add:* Dept Earth Sci Pac Lutheran Univ 12180 Park Ave S Tacoma WA 98447-0001

LOWEY, SUSAN, PROTEIN CHEMISTRY, PHYSICAL CHEMISTRY. *Current Pos:* assoc prof biochem, 72-74, PROF BIOCHEM, BRANDEIS UNIV, 74-, MEM STAFF, ROSENSTIEL BASIC MED SCI RES CTR, 72- *Personal Data:* b Vienna, Austria, Jan 22, 33; nat US. *Educ:* Columbia Univ, BA, 54; Yale Univ, PhD(chem), 58. *Prof Exp:* Res fel biol, Harvard Univ, 57-59. *Concurrent Pos:* Res assoc, Children's Cancer Res Found, 59-72. *Mem:* Am Chem Soc. *Res:* Physical chemistry of muscle proteins. *Mailing Add:* Rosenstiel Ctr Brandeis Univ 415 South St Waltham MA 02254-9110

LOWI, ALVIN, JR, THERMAL ENGINEERING & HEAT TRANSFER, ENGINE POWER & FUELS. *Current Pos:* VPRES, DAECO FUELS & ENG CO, INC, 76-; PRES, LION ENG, INC. *Personal Data:* b Gadsden, Ala, July 21, 29; m 53, Guillermina G Alverez; c David A, Rosamina, Edna V & Alvin III. *Educ:* Ga Inst Technol, BME, 51, MSME, 56; Univ Calif Los Angeles, PhD, 62. *Prof Exp:* Res asst eng exp pract, Ga Inst Technol, 54-56; design engr, Air Res Div, Garrett Corp, 56-58; mem tech staff eng, TRW Aerospace Corp, 58-66; pres, Terraqua, Inc, 59-76. *Concurrent Pos:* Lectr econ, Free Enterprise Inst, 60-70; prin, Alvin Louri & Assocs, Consult Engrs, 62-; fel, Inst Human Studies, 66-72; res assoc, Heather Found, 66-; vis lectr eng, Univ Pa, 72-74; dir, Southern Calif Tissue Bank, 83-; prin investr, Gas Res Inst, 86-; mem, Reactivity Adv Panel, Calif Air Resources Bd, 89- *Mem:* Am Soc Mech Engrs; Soc Automotive Engrs; Nat Soc Prof Engrs; Soc Am Inventors. *Res:* Simultaneous heat and mass transfer applied to novel cooling and distillation apparatus; supplementary fueling of diesel engines by fumigation of alternative volatile fuels; dissolution of natural gas in liquified petroleum materials for application to compact vehicular fuel storage; fire retardation of cellulose fibers for thermal insulation; facultative internal combustion processes; electrohydraulic fuel injection; multicolor pyrometry for particulate measurements; ozone formation of potential of hydrocarbons. *Mailing Add:* 2146 Toscanini Dr San Pedro CA 90731. *Fax:* 310-548-8457

LOWIG, HENRY FRANCIS JOSEPH, pure mathematics; deceased, see previous edition for last biography

LOWINGER, PAUL, PSYCHOTHERAPY & CLINICAL PHARMACOLOGY, PRISON & FORENSIC PSYCHIATRY. *Current Pos:* CLIN PROF, DEPT PSYCHIAT & DIV AMBULATORY & COMMUNITY MED, SCH MED, UNIV CALIF, SAN FRANCISCO, 85- *Personal Data:* b Chicago; m 48; c 3. *Educ:* Northwestern Univ, BS, 45; State Univ Iowa, MD, 49, MS, 53; Am Bd Psychiat & Neurol, dipl, 56. *Prof Exp:* Clin instr, psychiat, Tulane Univ Sch Med, 53-55, instr, 55-59, asst prof, 59-62, assoc prof, 62-71, adj assoc prof, 71-74, assoc clin prof, 74-85; med dir, Occupational Stress Clin, Inst Labor & Mental Health, Calif, 82- *Concurrent Pos:* Psychiat consult, San Francisco Co Jail, 80, Superior Court, Alameda Co, Oakland, 80-86, Prisoners Legal Serv, State Prison, Salem, Ore, 81-82, mental patients rights, dept mental health, San Francisco, 82 & 85, Fulton Co Jail, Legal Aid, Atlanta, 88, public defender, city & co of San Francisco, 83-; psychiat consult, Calif Dept Corrections, Brobeck, Phleger & Harrison & Prison Law Off, 85, 89-; numerous hosp staff mem & consultancies, 53-; res grants, NIMH, 57-62 & 80-82, teaching grant, 59-71, Demonstration Proj grant, Health Educ & Welfare, 74-79. *Mem:* NY Acad Sci; fel Am Psychiat Asn; Sigma Xi; Am Psychosomat Asn; fel Am Orthopsychiat Asn; Am Asn Advance Sci; Am Asn Univ Profs; Am Psychopath Asn; Nat Med Asn; Am Pub Health Asn; Acad Psychoanal. *Res:* Psychotherapy; psychosomatic medicine; psychosis; clinical pharmacology; legal medicine and social psychiatry. *Mailing Add:* 77 Belgrave Ave San Francisco CA 94117

LOWITZ, DAVID AARON, CHEMICAL PHYSICS. *Current Pos:* AFFIL PROF PHYSICS, VA COMMONWEALTH UNIV, 91- *Personal Data:* b Newark, NJ, Dec 18, 28; m 53, Doreen Jackson; c Mark A, Judith E, Ronna F (Meister) & Karen A. *Educ:* Rutgers Univ, BA, 50; Pa State Univ, MS, 53, PhD(physics), 55. *Honors & Awards:* IR 100 Award, 72; Philip Morris Jewel Award, 88 & 90. *Prof Exp:* Asst physics, Pa State Univ, 50-55, res assoc, 55-56; physicist, Gulf Res & Develop Co, 56-64; res assoc & head cent res physics sect, Lord Corp, 64-67; mgr, Physics Div, Philip Morris Res Ctr, 67-79, tech planning coordr appl res, 79-82, asst to dir appl res, 82-87, sr sci, 87- 92. *Concurrent Pos:* Am Petrol Inst fel, 52-56. *Mem:* Am Phys Soc; Int Soc Quantum Biol; Sigma Xi. *Res:* Microwave scattering; quantum mechanics; high pressure liquid viscosity; electromagnetic wave propagation; dielectrics; electron optics; electro-optic technology. *Mailing Add:* 4312 W Franklin St Richmond VA 23221. *Fax:* 804-353-4009, 367-8599; *E-Mail:* dlowitz@cabell.vcu.edu

LOWKE, GEORGE E, BIOTECHNOLOGY. *Current Pos:* DIR TECHNOL & FACIL DEVELOP, LIFE TECHS INC, 89- *Personal Data:* b Vernon, Tex, 1939. *Educ:* Tex A&M Univ, BS, 62; Northern Tex Univ, MS, 65; Univ Ariz, PhD, 69. *Prof Exp:* Staff mem, Pfizer, 70-79, Warner-Lambert, 79-85 & Johnson & Johnson, 83-87; dir res & develop diag prods, Igen Inc, 87-89. *Mem:* AAAS; Am Asn Clin Chemists; NY Acad Sci. *Res:* Diagnostic products. *Mailing Add:* Life Techs Inc 9800 Medical Center Dr PO Box 6482 Rockville MD 20849-6482

LOWMAN, BERTHA PAULINE, MATHEMATICS. *Current Pos:* asst prof, 62-78, PROF MATH, WESTERN KY UNIV, 78- *Personal Data:* b Newton, NC, Mar 17, 29. *Educ:* Lenoir-Rhyne Col, BS, 51; Univ Ala, MA, 52; George Peabody Col, PhD(math), 76. *Prof Exp:* Instr math, Campbell Col, 52-53; instr sci & math, Anderson Col, 53-54; asst, Univ NC, 55; asst prof math, Hardin-Simmons Univ, 55-59, ECarolina Col, 59-60 & Elon Col, 60-62. *Mem:* Math Asn Am; Nat Coun Teachers Math. *Res:* Number theory and algebra; geometry and history of mathematics; linear algebra. *Mailing Add:* 1025 Roselawn Way Bowling Green KY 42104-3158

LOWMAN, HENRY, CHEMISTRY, PROTEIN ENGINEERING. *Current Pos:* Researcher, 89-92, SCIENTIST, GENENTECH INC, 92- *Personal Data:* b Columbia, SC, June 14, 62. *Educ:* Johns Hopkins Univ, BA, 84; Univ Purdue, PhD(chem), 89. *Concurrent Pos:* NIH fel, 89. *Mem:* Am Chem Soc; AAAS. *Mailing Add:* Genentech Inc 205 Falcon Way Hercules CA 94547

LOWMAN, PAUL DANIEL, JR, ASTROGEOLOGY, PHOTOGEOLOGY. *Current Pos:* Staff, Goddard Space Ctr, 59-87, GEOPHYSICIST, GEOPHYS BR, LAB TERRESTRIAL PHYSICS, GODDARD SPACE FLIGHT CTR, NASA, 87- *Personal Data:* b Elizabeth, NJ, Sept 26, 31; m 58. *Educ:* Rutgers Univ, BS, 53; Univ Colo, PhD(geol), 63. *Honors & Awards:* John C Lindsay Mem Award, NASA, 74. *Concurrent Pos:* Vis lectr, US Air Force Inst Technol, 63-64; lectr, Cath Univ, 63-66 & Univ Calif, Santa Barbara, 70. *Mem:* Geol Soc Am; AAAS; Am Geophys Union. *Res:* Planetology; lunar geology; geologic application of orbital photography; remote sensing; comparative planetology. *Mailing Add:* Code 921 Goddard Space Flight Ctr Greenbelt MD 20771

LOWN, BERNARD, ARRHYTHMOLOGY. *Current Pos:* from asst prof to prof cardiol, Dept Nutrit & dir, Cardiovasc Res Lab, 61-91, EMER PROF CARDIOL, DEPT NUTRIT, HARVARD SCH PUB HEALTH, 91-; SR PHYSICIAN, BRIGHAM & WOMEN'S HOSP, 84- *Personal Data:* b Utena, Lithuania, June 7, 21; US citizen; m 46; c 3. *Educ:* Univ Maine, BS, 42; Johns Hopkins Univ, MD, 45. *Hon Degrees:* Numerous from US & foreign univs, 82-94. *Honors & Awards:* Nobel Peace Prize, 85; numerous named lect foreign & US univs, 62-92; Nickolay Burdenko Medal, Acad Med Sci USSR, 83; Andres Bello Medal, Ministry Educ & Ministry Sci, Venezuela, 86. *Prof Exp:* Dir, Samuel Levine Cardiovasc Res Lab, Peter Bent Brigham Hosp, 56-58. *Concurrent Pos:* From asst prof to assoc prof cardiol, Sch Pub Health, Harvard Univ, 61-74; sr assoc, Brigham & Womens Hosp, 63-70, physician, 70-84, sr physician, 84-; consult cardiol, Newton-Wellesley Hosp, 63-85, Beth Israel Hosp, 63-94, Childrens Hosp, 64-92, HCHP Hosp, 83-86; co-pres, Int Physicians Prev Nuclear War, 80-93; vis scientist, Mass Inst Technol, 87-; vis scientist, Clin Res Ctr, Mass Inst Technol, 87- *Mem:* Sr mem Inst Med-Nat Acad Sci; Nat Acad Sci Hungary; fel Am Acad Arts & Sci; fel Am Col Cardiol; Am Soc Clin Invest; Am Heart Asn; Asn Am Physicians; AAAS; corresp mem Brit Cardiac Soc; corresp mem Cardiac Soc Australia & NZ; corresp mem Swiss Soc Cardiol; corresp & hon foreign mem Belgian Royal Acad Med; fel Int Col Nutrit; corresp mem Croatia Acad Sci & Arts; foreign mem Russ Acad Med Sci. *Res:* Sudden cardiac death, identified potential victims and evolved programs for their protection; role of neural and psychologic factors provoking life threatening disturbances of heart rhythms. *Mailing Add:* 21 Longwood Ave Brookline MA 02146

LOWN, JAMES WILLIAM, BIOORGANIC CHEMISTRY. *Current Pos:* from asst prof to assoc prof, 64-75, PROF CHEM, UNIV ALTA, 74-; MEM, NAT CANCER INST CAN, 77- *Personal Data:* b Blyth, Eng, Dec 19, 34; m 62, Elizabeth Beatty; c Andrew James & Peter Wilslam. *Educ:* Univ London, BSc, 56, PhD(org chem) & dipl, Imp Col, 59. *Honors & Awards:* Hoffman-La-Roche Award Med Chem, 96. *Prof Exp:* Asst lectr chem, Imp Col, Univ London, 59-61; fel, Univ Alta, 61-62, asst prof, 62-63. *Concurrent Pos:* Res chemist, Walter Reed Army Inst Res, DC, 62-63; mem, UN Educ Sci & Cult Orgn Global Network Molecular & Cellular Biol, 89-; fel, Int Union Against Cancer, 92-; adj prof surg, Univ Alta, 94-; Killam res prof, 96- *Mem:* Am Chem Soc; The Chem Soc; Sigma Xi; Am Asn Cancer Res; Can Soc Chem. *Res:* Organic reaction mechanisms; heterocyclic synthesis; antibiotics; cancer and viral chemotherapy. *Mailing Add:* Dept Chem Univ Alta Edmonton AB T6G 2G2 Can. *Fax:* 403-492-8281

LOWNDES, DOUGLAS H, JR, SEMICONDUCTORS, PHOTOVOLTAIC CELL RESEARCH. *Current Pos:* SR RES STAFF MEM, SOLID STATE DIV, OAK RIDGE NAT LAB, 79- *Personal Data:* b Pasadena, Calif, Jan 3, 40; m 61; c 2. *Educ:* Stanford Univ, BS, 61; Univ Colo, PhD(physics), 69. *Prof Exp:* Res asst solid state physics, Hewlett-Packard Assocs, Calif, 62-63; NSF fel physics, Sch Math & Phys Sci, Univ Sussex, 68-70; from asst prof to prof physics, Univ Ore, 70-79. *Concurrent Pos:* Assoc, Solar Energy Ctr, 74-79; guest prof physics, Univ Nijemegen, 76-77; prof mat sci & eng, Univ Tenn, 86- *Mem:* Fel Am Phys Soc; Int Solar Energy Soc; sr mem Inst Elec & Electronics Engrs; Mat Res Soc. *Res:* Photochemical thin film growth; laser interactions with semiconductors; solar cells; nanosecond and piosecond laser measurements; pulsed laser annealing; superconductivity and magnetism; electronic materials. *Mailing Add:* 2720 Pine Hill Dr Knoxville TN 37932

LOWNDES, HERBERT EDWARD, NEUROTOXICOLOGY, NEUROPHARMACOLOGY. *Current Pos:* DISTINGUISHED PROF, COL PHARM, RUTGERS UNIV, 85- *Personal Data:* b Barrie, Ont, July 12, 43; m 66; c 3. *Educ:* Univ Sask, BA, 64, MSc, 70; Cornell Univ, PhD(pharmacol), 72. *Prof Exp:* Fel pharmacol, Univ Western Ont, 72-73; from asst prof to prof pharmacol, Col Med & Dent, NJ Med Sch, 73-81. *Concurrent Pos:* Vis prof, Univ Paul Sabatier, Toulouse, France, 66-; consult, Toxicol Data Bank, Nat Libr Med, 81-85, Health Res, Effects Grants Rev Panel, Environ Protection Agency, 84-, Toxicol Study Sect, 80-84, 89-93, Safety & Occup Health Study Sect, NIH, 85-88. *Mem:* Am Soc Pharmacol & Exp Therapeut; NY Acad Sci; Soc Toxicol; Soc Neurosci; Am Asn Neuropathologists. *Res:* Neurotoxicology and neuropharmacology of central and peripheral nervous system, particularly electrophysiological, histochemical and morphological correlates. *Mailing Add:* Dept Pharmacol & Toxicol Col Pharm Rutgers Univ PO Box 789 Piscataway NJ 08854. *Fax:* 732-445-6907; *E-Mail:* lowndes@eohsi.rutgers.edu

LOWNDES, JOSEPH M, BIOCHEMISTRY, MOLECULAR BIOLOGY. *Current Pos:* SR SCIENTIST, DEPT RES & DEVELOP, FIVE PRIME THREE PRIME, 91- *Personal Data:* b Duluth, Minn, Feb 28, 55. *Educ:* Univ Notre Dame, BS, 77; Univ Wis-Madison, MS, 83, PhD(biochem), 88. *Prof Exp:* Postdoctoral fel, Dept Pediat, Nat Jewish Ctr Immunol & Resp Med, 89-91. *Mem:* Am Soc Biochem & Molecular Biol; AAAS; Am Chem Soc; Sigma Xi. *Mailing Add:* Madison Area Tech Col 3550 Anderson St Madison WI 53704

LOWNDES, ROBERT P, physics, for more information see previous edition

LOWNEY, EDMUND DILLAHUNTY, DERMATOLOGY. *Current Pos:* PROF DERMAT, UNIV HOSP, COL MED, OHIO STATE UNIV, 69- *Personal Data:* b Port Arthur, Tex, Nov 8, 31; m 58; c 2. *Educ:* Univ Tex, BA, 53; Yale Univ, PhD(psychol), 57; Univ Pa, MD, 60. *Prof Exp:* From instr to asst prof dermat, Univ Mich, Ann Arbor, 64-67; assoc prof, Med Col Va, 67-69. *Mem:* Soc Invest Dermat; Am Dermatol Asn. *Res:* Immunology. *Mailing Add:* 907 Singing Hills Lane Worthington OH 43235-1250

LOWNEY, JEREMIAH RALPH, SEMICONDUCTOR ELECTRONICS, SEMICONDUCTOR PHYSICS. *Current Pos:* PHYSICIST, NAT INST STAND & TECHNOL, 79- *Personal Data:* b Fall River, Mass, Dec 16, 46; m 80, Anne Graham. *Educ:* Mass Inst Technol, Cambridge, BS, 67, MS, 68, PhD(elec eng), 75. *Prof Exp:* Physicist, Naval Ord Lab, 68-72 & Naval Surface Weapons Ctr, 75-79. *Mem:* Am Phys Soc; Inst Elec & Electronics Engrs; AAAS; Sigma Xi. *Res:* Electronic properties of semiconducting materials, such as band structure, mobility, lifetime, deep-level spectroscopy and impact ionization in silicon and compound semiconductors. *Mailing Add:* Bldg 225 Rm A-305 Nat Inst Standards & Technol Gaithersburg MD 20899. *Fax:* 301-948-4081; *E-Mail:* lowney@sed.eeel.nist.gov

LOWNIE, H(AROLD) W(ILLIAM), JR, metallurgy, engineering; deceased, see previous edition for last biography

LOWNSBERY, BENJAMIN FERRIS, PLANT NEMATOLOGY. *Current Pos:* from asst nematologist to nematologist, Exp Sta, Univ Calif, Davis, 54-83, lectr nematol, 60-70, prof, 70-83, EMER PROF NEMATOL, UNIV CALIF, DAVIS, 83- *Personal Data:* b Wilmington, Del, July 28, 20; m 50; c 1. *Educ:* Univ Del, BA, 42; Cornell Univ, PhD(plant path), 50. *Honors & Awards:* Stark Award, Am Soc Hort Sci, 70. *Prof Exp:* Chemist explosives div, E I du Pont de Nemours & Co, 42-45; asst plant path, Cornell Univ, 45-50; asst plant pathologist, Conn Agr Exp Sta, 51-53. *Concurrent Pos:* Mem subcomt nematodes, Agr Bd, Nat Acad Sci-Nat Res Coun, 66-68; sr ed, J Nematol, 77-78, ed-in-chief, 78-81. *Mem:* Soc Nematol; Am Phytopath Soc. *Res:* Forest and agricultural nematology. *Mailing Add:* Dept Nematol 824 Douglas Ave Davis CA 95616

LOWRANCE, EDWARD WALTON, ANATOMY. *Current Pos:* from assoc prof to prof, 50-78, EMER PROF ANAT, SCH MED, UNIV MO, COLUMBIA, 78- *Personal Data:* b Ogden, Utah, June 17, 08; m 35; c 2. *Educ:* Univ Utah, AB, 30, AM, 32; Stanford Univ, PhD(biol), 37. *Prof Exp:* Asst zool, Stanford Univ, 32-34, Rockefeller asst exp embryol, 34-36 & 37-38; from instr to assoc prof zool, Univ Nev, 38-49; asst prof anat, Sch Med, Univ SDak, 49-50. *Concurrent Pos:* Actg assoc prof, Sch Med, Univ Kans, 44-46; State secy, Mo State Anat Bd, 69-78. *Mem:* AAAS; Am Asn Anat; Am Micros Soc; NY Acad Sci. *Res:* Statistical treatment of weights and linear measurements of selected dimensions of bones of sub-adult and mature opossum and adult man; tendon growth and associated bone growth in postnatal rabbit. *Mailing Add:* 3300 New Haven Rd Columbia MO 65201

LOWRANCE, WILLIAM WILSON, JR, science policy, risk assessment, for more information see previous edition

LOWREY, CHARLES BOYCE, PHYSICAL ORGANIC CHEMISTRY. *Current Pos:* southern regional vpres sales, 82-92, southern serv region pres, 93-, SALES MGR, CHEM WASTE MGT, 93- *Personal Data:* b New Orleans, La, Mar 15, 41; m 61; c 3. *Educ:* Centenary Col, BS, 63; Univ Houston, PhD(heterocyclic chem), 68. *Prof Exp:* Teaching asst chem, Univ Houston, 63-66; from asst prof to assoc prof chem, Centenary Col La, 73-77, asst dean col, 74-77; gen mgr opers & prod, Petrol Assocs of Lafayette, Inc, 77-79; asst gen mgr & tech mgr, Port Arthur, Tex Facil, Chem Water Mgt, Inc, 79-81; consult hazardous waste disposal, Price-Curtis & Assoc Inc, 81-82. *Concurrent Pos:* Consult, Baifield Industs, La, 66-70; water pollution consult, Ford Battery Plant, Shreveport, 68-73 & Gould Battery Plant, Shreveport, 73-75. *Mem:* Am Chem Soc; Soc Petrol Engrs. *Res:* Synthesis and study of electronic effects in substituted benzo(b) furans and benzo(b) thiophenes. *Mailing Add:* 17047 Fenny Bridge Lane Spring TX 77379

LOWRIE, ALLEN, MARINE GEOLOGY, CONTINENTAL MARGINS. *Current Pos:* MEM STAFF, NAVAL OCEANOG OFF, 83- *Personal Data:* b Washington, DC, Dec 30, 37; div; c Tanya A. *Educ:* Columbia Univ, BA, 62. *Prof Exp:* Res asst marine geol, Lamont Geol Observ, 63-68; oceanogr marine geol, Naval Oceanog Off, 68-76 & 78-81 & Naval Ocean Res & Develop Act, 76-78; explorationist, Mobil Oil Corp, 81-83. *Concurrent Pos:* Consult geologist, Seagull Int Explor, Houston, Tex, Int Inc, Kenner, La & Bluebonnet Petrol New Orleans, La, 88-91; invited lectr, Cath Univ Am, Washington, DC, 72-73 & Universidad de Los Andes, Bogota, Colombia, 78-; guest lectr oceanog & ecol, Calverton Sch, Huntington, Md, 74-76; consult, St Stanislaus Sch, Bay St Louis, Miss, 76-79; instr, Tulane Univ, New Orleans, La, 82-85 & 92 & Univ Southern Miss, 84-88. *Mem:* Soc Econ Paleont & Mineral; Am Asn Petrol Geologists; NY Acad Sci; Am Inst Prof Geologists; Sigma Xi; Geol Soc Am. *Res:* Subduction zone interaction of North and South America; ocean basin sediment-type and thickness-acoustic response; evolution of passive margins and hydrocarbon traps; prospect developer, promoter and seismic response research; hydrogeology; petroleum exploration. *Mailing Add:* 230 FZ Goss Rd Picayune MS 39466-9423

LOWRIGHT, RICHARD HENRY, SEDIMENTOLOGY. *Current Pos:* asst prof, 71-78, ASSOC PROF GEOL, SUSQUEHANNA UNIV, 78- *Personal Data:* b Bethlehem, Pa, Aug 31, 40; m 66. *Educ:* Franklin & Marshall Col, AB, 62; Pa State Univ, PhD(geol), 71. *Prof Exp:* Teacher pub sch, NY, 64-66. *Concurrent Pos:* Consult geol, 73- *Mem:* Nat Water Well Asn. *Res:* Quantity and quality of ground water in Snyder County, Pennsylvania. *Mailing Add:* Dept Geol & Environ Sci Susquehanna Univ Selinsgrove PA 17870

LOWRY, BRIGHT ANDERSON, ASTRONOMY. *Current Pos:* PROF CHEM, ERSKINE COL, 74- *Personal Data:* b Newberry, SC, Apr 6, 36; m 65, Judith Smith; c Margaret R & Suzanne B. *Educ:* Mass Inst Technol, SB, 58; Univ Chicago, PhD(phys chem), 65. *Prof Exp:* Res assoc, Dartmouth Col,

63-64 & Univ NC, Chapel Hill, 64-66; from asst prof to assoc prof chem, Southern Methodist Univ, 66-74. *Mem:* Am Chem Soc; Am Phys Soc. *Res:* Physical properties of liquid crystals. *Mailing Add:* Dept Chem Erskine Col Box 535 Due West SC 29639

LOWRY, ERIC G, PHYSICAL CHEMISTRY. *Current Pos:* RETIRED. *Personal Data:* b Berlin, Ger, Nov 23, 16; US citizen; m 54; c 1. *Educ:* Univ Geneva, PhD(phys chem), 43. *Prof Exp:* Res chemist fluorochem, Gen Chem Div, Allied Chem Corp, 47-49; res chemist photog, Remington-Rand Div, Sperry Rand Corp, 51-58; res chemist lithography, Polychrome Corp, 59; res chemist, Addressograph-Multigraph Corp, 59-65, chief chemist reprography, 65-77, sect supvr, Charles Bruning Co Div, 77-81. *Mem:* AAAS; Am Chem Soc; Soc Photog Sci & Eng; Tech Asn Pulp & Paper Indust. *Res:* Reprography. *Mailing Add:* 73 Lewis St Middleton CT 06457-5226

LOWRY, GEORGE GORDON, PHYSICAL & POLYMER CHEMISTRY. *Current Pos:* RETIRED. *Personal Data:* b Chico, Calif, Jan 12, 29; m 53, Janet M Lucas; c 4. *Educ:* Chico State Col, AB, 50; Stanford Univ, MS, 52; Mich State Univ, PhD(phys chem), 63. *Prof Exp:* Res asst, Stanford Res Inst, 51; res chemist, Dow Chem Co, 51-62; NSF fel, 62-63; from asst prof to assoc prof chem, Claremont Men's Col, 63-68; from assoc prof to prof chem, Western Mich Univ, 68-93. *Concurrent Pos:* Independent consult, Environ Safety & Health. *Mem:* Am Chem Soc; Sigma Xi. *Res:* Polymerization kinetics and processes; copolymerization; statistical theory of kinetic chain processes; hazardous materials; safety and health. *Mailing Add:* 22 Fairwood Pl Palmyra VA 22963-2767

LOWRY, GERALD LAFAYETTE, FORESTRY, SOIL SCIENCE. *Current Pos:* assoc prof, 72-76, PROF FORESTRY, STEPHEN F AUSTIN STATE UNIV, 76- *Personal Data:* b Harrisburg, Pa, Sept 12, 28; m 49; c 3. *Educ:* Pa State Univ, BS, 53; Ore State Univ, MS, 55; Mich State Univ, PhD(forestry), 61. *Prof Exp:* Asst, Ore State Univ, 53-55; instr stripmine reclamation, Ohio Agr Exp Sta, Wooster, 55-61; res forester, Pulp & Paper Res Inst Can, 61-72. *Concurrent Pos:* Asst prof, Ohio State Univ, 57-58; spec res asst, Mich State Univ, 58-59; vchmn forestry comt, Coun Fertilizer Appln, 61-63, chmn, 63-65. *Mem:* Soc Am Foresters; Soil Sci Soc Am; Am Soc Agron; Am Soc Surface Mining & Reclamation. *Res:* Herbicide effectiveness and usage in the West Gulf region; success of seed-tree regeneration of Loblolly pine; pine site index on major soil types of East Texas; effectiveness of shearing in improving Christmas tree grade; author of numerous publications. *Mailing Add:* Col Forestry Stephen F Austin State Univ Nacogdoches TX 75962-6109

LOWRY, JAMES LEE, ELECTRICAL ENGINEERING. *Current Pos:* assoc prof, 63-65, PROF ELEC ENG, AUBURN UNIV, 65- *Personal Data:* b Birmingham, Ala, Feb 19, 31; m 56; c 3. *Educ:* Auburn Univ, BEE, 55, MS, 57; Univ Fla, PhD(elec eng), 63. *Prof Exp:* From instr to asst prof elec eng, Auburn Univ, 55-59; teaching assoc, Univ Fla, 62-63. *Concurrent Pos:* Consult, Ala Power Co. *Mem:* Sr mem Inst Elec & Electronics Engrs; Am Soc Eng Educ; Nat Soc Prof Engrs; Sigma Xi. *Res:* Circuit analysis and synthesis; power systems. *Mailing Add:* Dept Elec Eng Auburn Univ 200 Broun Hall Auburn AL 36849

LOWRY, JEAN, GEOLOGY. *Current Pos:* RETIRED. *Personal Data:* b Indianapolis, Ind, Feb 7, 21. *Educ:* Pa State Univ, BS, 42; Yale Univ, PhD(geol), 51. *Prof Exp:* Jr economist, Off Price Admin, 42-43; jr geologist, US Geol Surv, 43-46, asst geologist, 46-49; dist geologist, State Geol Surv, Va, 49-57; from asst prof to prof geol, E Carolina Univ, 58-83. *Concurrent Pos:* Vis prof, Concepcion Univ, Chile, 62-63. *Res:* Stratigraphy and structure of southern Appalachians; caves. *Mailing Add:* 211 S Eastern St Greenville NC 27858

LOWRY, JERALD FRANK, EXPERIMENTAL PHYSICS. *Current Pos:* sr engr appl physics, 63-80, SR RES SCIENTIST, WESTINGHOUSE SCI & TECHNOL CTR, 81- *Personal Data:* b Listie, Pa, Oct 22, 39; m 61, Patricia A Fitzgerald; c Jerald K, Jeffrey K, Brian C & Kristin A. *Educ:* Univ Pittsburgh, BS, 61; Cornell Univ, MS, 63. *Prof Exp:* Jr engr, Testing Reactor, Westinghouse Elec Corp, 61; teaching asst physics, Cornell Univ, 61-63. *Mem:* Am Phys Soc; AAAS. *Res:* Low pressure plasmas; fluorescent lamp discharges; generation of high power electron beams; measurement of power density distribution and beam radiance; gas discharge lasers, electron-beam sustained discharges; superconductivity. *Mailing Add:* 1730 Yorktown Pl Pittsburgh PA 15235

LOWRY, LEWIS ROY, JR, physics, electrical engineering; deceased, see previous edition for last biography

LOWRY, NANCY, PHYSICAL ORGANIC CHEMISTRY. *Current Pos:* from asst prof to assoc prof, 70-84, dean, nat sci, 89-92, PROF CHEM, HAMPSHIRE COL, 84- *Personal Data:* b Newburgh, NY, Sept 4, 38; m 61, Thomas H; c Kate, Sam & Alex. *Educ:* Smith Col, AB, 60; Mass Inst Technol, PhD(chem), 65. *Prof Exp:* Res assoc chem, Mass Inst Technol, 65-66 & Amherst Col, 66-67; lectr, Smith Col, 67-69, res assoc, 69-70. *Mem:* AAAS; Asn Women Sci; Am Chem Soc. *Res:* Women and science; science education; chemistry in herbs and medicines. *Mailing Add:* Sch Nat Sci & Math Hampshire Col Amherst MA 01002. *E-Mail:* nlowry@hamp.hampshire.edu

LOWRY, OLIVER HOWE, pharmacology, biochemistry; deceased, see previous edition for last biography

LOWRY, PHILIP HOLT, OPERATIONS RESEARCH. *Current Pos:* RETIRED. *Personal Data:* b New York, NY, Feb 20, 18; m 45; c 2. *Educ:* Princeton Univ, AB, 39; Yale Univ, MA, 42, PhD(int rels), 49. *Prof Exp:* Meteorologist, Brookhaven Nat Lab, 47-51; opers analyst, Opers Res Off, Johns Hopkins Univ, 51-61; opers analyst, Res Analysis Corp, 61-72; opers analyst, Gen Res Corp, 72-80; consult, 80-88. *Mem:* Opers Res Soc Am; Am Meteorol Soc; Am Astron Soc. *Res:* Military operations research; impact of technology on international relations; nuclear policy and strategy. *Mailing Add:* 8701 Georgetown Pike McLean VA 22102

LOWRY, RALPH A(DDISON), ENGINEERING, PHYSICS. *Current Pos:* Sr scientist, Res Labs Eng Sci, Univ Va, 55-62, from assoc prof to prof aerospace eng, 62-77, chmn, Dept Aerospace Eng & Eng Physics, 65-72, dean, Sch Eng & Appl Sci, 83-84, prof nuclear eng & eng physics, 77-91, John Lloyd Newcomb prof eng & appl sci, 78-91, assoc dean, Sch Eng & Appl Sci, 86-91, EMER PROF, UNIV VA, 91- *Personal Data:* b Clay County, Mo, Aug 9, 26; m 47, Jean Dunnell; c Stephen R, Margaret J, Cynthia A & John H. *Educ:* Iowa State Univ, BS, 49, PhD(physics), 55. *Mem:* Am Phys Soc; Am Soc Eng Educ; Sigma Xi; AAAS. *Res:* Atomic and molecular physics; isotope separation; gas centrifuges; fluid mechanics. *Mailing Add:* 507 Woodchuck Lane Charlottesville VA 22902. *E-Mail:* ral@virginia.edu

LOWRY, ROBERT JAMES, BOTANY. *Current Pos:* from asst prof to prof, 48-81, EMER PROF BOT, UNIV MICH, ANN ARBOR, 81- *Personal Data:* b Chelsea, Mich, Aug 26, 12; m 34; c 1. *Educ:* Univ Mich, BS, 40, MS, 41, PhD(bot), 47. *Prof Exp:* Res assoc, Univ Mich, 42-45; asst prof bot, Mich State Univ, 46-48. *Mem:* AAAS. *Res:* Cytotaxonomy; electron microscopy. *Mailing Add:* 630 Hampstead Lane Ann Arbor MI 48103

LOWRY, STEPHEN FREDERICK, SURGERY. *Current Pos:* Asst prof surg, 82-87, DIR HYPERALIMENTATION UNIT, NY HOSP-CORNELL MED CTR, 82-, ASSOC PROF SURG, 87- *Personal Data:* b Columbus, Ohio, Nov 1, 1947; c 3. *Educ:* Ohio, Wesleyan Univ, BA, 69; Univ Mich Sch Med, MD, 73. *Concurrent Pos:* Dir lab surg metab, NY Hosp Cornell Med Ctr, 82-; vis assoc physician, Rockefeller Univ, 82; asst attend surgeon, gastric & mixed tumor serv, 82 & nutrit, mem, Sloan-Kettering Cancer Ctr, 85-; traveling fel, James IV Asn Surgeons, 87. *Mem:* Am Col Surgeons; Asn Acad Surg; Soc Univ Surgeons; Fed Am Soc Exp Biol; Soc Surg Oncol; Int Soc Surg. *Res:* Identifications mechanisms inducing hypermetabolisms, protein regulation and tissue in trauma, sepsis and cancer; method for restoration of protein homeostasis by nutritional support. *Mailing Add:* Cornell Med Ctr Ny Hosp 525 E 68th St Rm F2016 New York NY 10021-4885

LOWRY, THOMAS HASTINGS, ORGANIC CHEMISTRY. *Current Pos:* from asst prof to assoc prof, 66-81, PROF CHEM, SMITH COL, 81- *Personal Data:* b New York, NY, June 16, 38; m 61; c 3. *Educ:* Princeton Univ, AB, 60; Harvard Univ, PhD(chem), 65. *Prof Exp:* NIH fel chem, Mass Inst Technol, 64-65, res assoc, 65-66. *Mem:* Am Chem Soc; AAAS. *Res:* Physical organic chemistry. *Mailing Add:* Dept Chem Smith Col Northampton MA 01063

LOWRY, WALLACE DEAN, GEOLOGY. *Current Pos:* assoc prof, 49-58, PROF GEOL, VA POLYTECH INST & STATE UNIV, 58- *Personal Data:* b Medford, Ore, Oct 5, 17; m 42, M Dorothea Wyckoff; c Robert E. *Educ:* Ore State Univ, BS, 39, MS, 40; Univ Rochester, PhD(geol), 43. *Prof Exp:* Geologist, Ore Dept Geol & Mineral Indust, 42-47, Texaco, Inc, 47-49. *Mem:* Fel Geol Soc Am; Am Asn Petrol Geol; Sigma Xi. *Res:* Late Cenozoic stratigraphy of the lower Columbia River basin; ferruginous bauxite deposits of Northwestern Oregon; silica sands of Western Virginia; porosity of sandstone reservoir rocks; role of Tertiary volcanism in tectonism; relation of silicification and dolomitization; geology of the Blue Mountains, Oregon; mechanics of Appalachian thrusting; North American geosynclines; exotic Cenozoic gravel deposits of Arizona and southern California. *Mailing Add:* 607 Rose Ave Blacksburg VA 24060-5741

LOWRY, WILLIAM THOMAS, OCCUPATIONAL SAFETY & HEALTH. *Current Pos:* from asst prof to assoc prof toxicol, Grad Sch Biomed Sci, Univ Tex Health Sci Ctr, 77-85. *Personal Data:* b Hobbs, NMex, Dec 11, 42; m 65; c 2. *Educ:* E Tex State Univ, BS, 65, MS, 67; Colo State Univ, PhD(natural prod chem), 71; Am Inst Chemists, cert, 75; Am Bd Forensic Toxicol, cert, 76. *Prof Exp:* Chemist, Fed Bur Invest, 65 & spec agent, 72-73; res assoc biochem, Va Polytech Inst & State Univ, 71-72; toxicologist, Southwestern Inst Forensic Sci, 73-85. *Concurrent Pos:* Assoc consult, attend staff toxicol, Parkland Mem Hosp, 73-; instr path, Univ Tex Southwestern Med Sch, 73-75, instr path & forensic sci, 75-77, asst prof path, 77-; adj asst prof chem, E Tex State Univ, 76-77, adj assoc prof, 77-80; adj asst prof civil eng, Univ Tex, Arlington, 82- *Mem:* Am Acad Clin Toxicol; Am Acad Forensic Sci; Am Chem Soc; Am Inst Chemists; Am Soc Pharmacog; Sigma Xi. *Res:* Environmental toxicology; biodegradation of toxic substances; utilizing bacteria; combustion and pulmonary toxicology. *Mailing Add:* Fielder Prof Pk 733 B N Fielder Rd Arlington TX 76012

LOWTHER, FRANK EUGENE, PETROLEUM ENGINEERING. *Current Pos:* CONSULT & TECH ADVISOR, 93-; ADV, ENERGY SCI, INC, CANADAIGUA, NY, 93-; CUSTOM TECH CREATIONS, INC, BUFFALO, NY, 93- *Personal Data:* b Orrville, Ohio, Feb 3, 29; m 51, Elizabeth E Koons; c 4. *Educ:* Ohio State Univ, BS, 52. *Prof Exp:* Sr engr, Raytheon Mfg Co, 52-57; consult, Gen Elec Co, 57-65; founder dir & vpres, Purification Sci, Inc, 65-75; sr eng assoc, Union Carbide, 75-79; sr res scientist, Atlantic Richfield Co, 80-82, chief scientist, Energy Conversion & Mat Lab, 82-83, prin scientist, 83-85, res adv, 85-93. *Mem:* Assoc fel Am Inst

Aeronaut & Astronaut; Inst Elec & Electronics Engrs; AAAS; NY Acad Sci. *Res:* Ozone technology; plasma generators; solid state power devices; internal combustion engines; thermoelectrics; virus and bacteria disinfection systems; oil field technology; electric power distribution; nuclear fusion; chemical and physical reactors; exploding bridge wires; weapons. *Mailing Add:* 817 Parkside Ave Buffalo NY 14216-2009

LOWTHER, GERALD EUGENE, CONTACT LENS RESEARCH. *Current Pos:* PROF OPTOM, IND UNIV, 94- *Personal Data:* b Sept 16, 43; m 66, Andrya G Huffman; c Karen & Daniel. *Educ:* Ohio State Univ, BSc, 66, OD, 67, MSc, 69, PhD(physiol optics), 72. *Honors & Awards:* John Neill Medal, Pa Col Optom, 85; Max Shapero Mem Lectr Award, Am Acad Optom, 94. *Prof Exp:* From asst prof to assoc prof optom, Ohio State Univ, 72-77; prof, Ferris State Univ, 77-89, Univ Ala, Birmingham, 89-94. *Concurrent Pos:* Ed, Int Contact Lens Clin J, 81-; vis prof optom, Univ NSW, 86; co dir, Borish Ctr Ophthal Res, 95- *Mem:* Fel Am Acad Optom (secy-treas, 93-94; pres-elect, 95-96, pres, 97-); Asn Optom Contact Lens Educrs (pres, 76-78); Am Optom Asn; Asn Res Vision & Ophthal; Int Soc Contact Lens Res (pres, 93-94); Int Asn Contact Lens Educrs. *Res:* Corneal physiology; tear chemistry; contact lens design and fitting; contact lens solutions; contact lens aftercare problems; contact lens deposits and coatings; dry eye and other ocular conditions. *Mailing Add:* Ind Univ Bloomington IN 47405. *Fax:* 812-855-8664; *E-Mail:* glowther@indiana.edu

LOWTHER, JAMES DAVID, MECHANICAL ENGINEERING. *Current Pos:* from asst prof to assoc prof, 63-73, univ distinguished prof, 88-93, PROF MECH ENG, LA TECH UNIV, 73- *Personal Data:* b Jackson, Miss, June 22, 39; m 61, Gayle Griffin; c 3. *Educ:* Miss State Univ, BS, 61, MS, 62; Univ Tex, Austin, PhD(mech eng), 68. *Prof Exp:* Mech engr, Baton Rouge refinery, Humble Oil & Refining Co, 62-63. *Concurrent Pos:* Prin investr, NSF res grant, 70-71, Naval Weapons Eng Suport Activ, 76-77, US Dept Energy, 80-81, Energy Anal & Diag Ctr, US Dept Energy, 84-85, La Dept Nat Resources, 86-89; consult, 73- *Mem:* Am Soc Mech Engrs; Am Soc Eng Educ; Sigma Xi. *Res:* Heat transfer; thermodynamics; energy conservation; computer-based measurement. *Mailing Add:* Dept Mech & Indust Eng La Tech Univ Ruston LA 71272-0046. *E-Mail:* lowther@engr.latech.edu

LOWTHER, JOHN LINCOLN, COMPUTER SCIENCE. *Current Pos:* from instr to asst prof, 74-77, ASSOC PROF COMPUT SCI, MICH TECHNOL UNIV, 77- *Personal Data:* b Burlington, Iowa, Sept 5, 43. *Educ:* Univ Iowa, BA, 65, MS, 67, PhD(comput sci), 75. *Prof Exp:* Instr math, Southwest State Univ, 67-71. *Mem:* Asn Comput Mach; Math Asn Am; Sigma Xi; Inst Elec & Electronics Engrs; Am Asn Artificial Intel. *Res:* Artificial intelligence; programming languages; computer graphics. *Mailing Add:* Dept Comput Sci Mich Technol Univ 1400 Townsend Dr Houghton MI 49931

LOWTHER, JOHN STEWART, PALEONTOLOGY, PALEOBOTANY. *Current Pos:* From instr to assoc prof, 56-80, PROF GEOL, UNIV PUGET SOUND, 80- *Personal Data:* b Cochrane, Ont, July 31, 25; m 53, 80. *Educ:* McGill Univ, BSc, 49, MSc, 50; Univ Mich, PhD(geol), 57. *Res:* Sedimentology; Mesozoic paleobotany and stratigraphy; pollen microstructure; palynology. *Mailing Add:* Dept Geol Univ Puget Sound 1500 N Warner St Tacoma WA 98416-0001

LOWY, DOUGLAS R, BIOMEDICAL RESEARCH. *Current Pos:* LAB CHIEF, CELLULAR ONCOL LAB, NAT CANCER INST, 83- *Personal Data:* b New York, NY, May 25, 42. *Educ:* Amherst Col, BA, 64; NY Univ, MD, 68. *Honors & Awards:* Sulzberger Award, Am Acad Dermat, 87; Wallace P Rowe Award Virol, Nat Inst Allergy & Infectious Dis, 93. *Concurrent Pos:* Ed, J Am Soc Microbiol. *Mem:* Am Soc Microbiol; Soc Invest Dermat. *Mailing Add:* Nat Cancer Inst Cellular Oncol Lab Bldg 36 Rm 1D32 Bethesda MD 20892. *Fax:* 301-480-5322; *E-Mail:* drl@helix.nih.gov

LOWY, PETER HERMAN, organic chemistry; deceased, see previous edition for last biography

LOWY, R JOEL, PHYSIOLOGY, CELL BIOLOGY. *Current Pos:* RES PHYSIOLOGIST, DEPT PHYSIOL, ARMED FORCES RADIOBIOL RES INST, 88- *Personal Data:* b Pittsburgh, Pa, Aug 24, 56. *Educ:* Col William & Mary, BS, 74; Va Inst Marine Sci, MA, 77; Ore State Univ, PhD(zool & biochem), 82. *Prof Exp:* Sr staff fel, NIH, 87-88. *Concurrent Pos:* Nat res serv award, NIH, 85-87. *Mem:* Sigma Xi; AAAS; Am Physiol Soc; Am Soc Cell Biol. *Mailing Add:* Dept Physiol Armed Forces Radiobiol Res Inst 8901 Wisconsin Ave Bethesda MD 20889-5603

LOWY, STANLEY H(OWARD), AEROSPACE ENGINEERING. *Current Pos:* RETIRED. *Personal Data:* b New York, NY, Mar 10, 22; m 45, Mildred A Wille; c Lauce K & Bret S (deceased). *Educ:* Purdue Univ, BS, 43; Univ Minn, MS, 47. *Prof Exp:* Test engr, Allison Div, Gen Motors Corp, 47; instr mech eng, Ore State Col, 47-50; struct design engr, Willamette Iron & Steel Co, 50-51; stand engr, Hughes Aircraft Co, 52; chief engr, Peters Co, 52-53; chief engr, A Young & Son Iron Works, 53-56; consult engr, Stan H Lowy & Assocs, 56-58; assoc prof aerospace eng, Univ Okla, 58-64; assoc prof, Tex A&M Univ, 64-77, assoc dir, Proj Themis, Res Found, 69-71, prof aerospace eng, 77-86, asst dean eng, 80-86, emer prof and dean Aerospace Eng, 86-91. *Concurrent Pos:* Proj dir space shuttle wind tunnel tests & analyses, Manned Spacecraft Ctr, NASA, 69-72. *Mem:* Am Soc Eng Educr; Am Inst Aeronaut & Astronaut; Am Helicopter Soc; Sigma Xi. *Res:* Aircraft design; aircraft power plants; orbital mechanics. *Mailing Add:* 1016 Walton Dr College Station TX 77840

LOXLEY, THOMAS EDWARD, EARTH-COUPLED BUILDING SYSTEMS, EDUCATION OUTREACH. *Current Pos:* FOUNDER, SR ENG SCIENTIST, INVERTED CAVE EDUC, 78- *Personal Data:* b Beaver, Pa, Jan 20, 40; div. *Educ:* Case Western Univ, Cleveland, BS, 61. *Prof Exp:* Mech engr, US Naval Weapons Lab, 61-65 & US Army Watervliet Arsenal, 65-68; syst engr, Int Hydrodyn, Ltd, 68-69; pres, Manned Submersible Syst Co, 69-71; mech engr, US Naval Surface Weapons Ctr, 71-75; asst prof tech resources, Va Polytech Inst & State Univ, 75-78. *Concurrent Pos:* Lectr, Nat Bur Stand, Denver, 80, Am Sol Energy Soc, Houston, 82, Royal Inst Tech, Stockholm, 87, N Sun Conf, Borlange, 88, Tech Univ, Vienna, 88, CSTB, Sophia Antipolis, 89, Fraunhofer Bauphysik, Heidenheim, 90, World Renewable Energy Cong, Reading, 90, SINTEF-NTH, Trondheim, 91, World Conf Innovative Housing, Vancouver, 93; writer, J Bldg Res & Pract, Paris, 85, J Bldg Res & Info, London, 92, Int Coun Bldg Res, World Cong, Wash, 86, Paris, 89. *Mem:* Int Coun Bldg Res Studies & Doc. *Res:* Developing practical low-rise buildings and equipment systems that are thermally coupled directly to the subsoil under them for ultra low-energy space heating and cooling. *Mailing Add:* 500 Beaver Rd No 601 Ambridge PA 15003

LOY, JAMES BRENT, PLANT BREEDING, DEVELOPMENTAL GENETICS. *Current Pos:* from asst prof to assoc prof, 67-81, PROF PLANT SCI, UNIV NH, 81- *Personal Data:* b Borger, Tex, Feb 28, 41; div, Sarah J Whitney; c Reed J, Laura M & James W. *Educ:* Okla State Univ, BS, 63; Colo State Univ, MS, 65, PhD(genetics), 67. *Concurrent Pos:* Vis scholar bot, Univ Calif, Berkeley, 74-75. *Mem:* Am Soc Hort Sci; Soc Econ Bot; Nat Agr Plastics Asn. *Res:* Cucurbit breeding; hormonal and genetic regulation of sex expression in Cucumis melo; morpho-physiological investigation of seed and fruit field in Cucurbito species. *Mailing Add:* Dept Plant Biol Univ NH 125 Technology Dr Durham NH 03824-4724. *Fax:* 603-862-4757

LOY, MICHAEL MING-TAK, PHYSICS TEACHING. *Current Pos:* PROF PHYSICS, HONG KONG UNIV SCI & TECHNOL, HONG KONG, 93-, ASSOC DEAN SCI, 95- *Personal Data:* b China, Jan 12, 45; US citizen; m 70, Ivy; c Michelle & Sharon. *Educ:* Univ Calif, Berkeley, BS, 66, PhD(physics), 71. *Prof Exp:* Res staff mem, Thomas Watson Res Ctr, IBM Corp, 71-77, mgr, 78-86, tech planning staff, 86-87, dept mgr, 87-93. *Concurrent Pos:* Prin investr, Off Naval Res, 78-89; mem steering comt, Laser Sci Topical Group, Am Phys Soc, 91-93; topical ed, J Optical Soc Am, 93- *Mem:* Fel Am Phys Soc; Optical Soc Am; Int Coun Optics. *Res:* Laser science; surface science; dynamic properties at or near surfaces; nonlinear optical spectroscopy techniques. *Mailing Add:* Physics Dept Hong Kong Univ Sci & Technol Clearwater Bay Kowloon Hong Kong People's Republic of China. *Fax:* 852-358-1652; *E-Mail:* phloy@usthk.ust.hk

LOY, REBEKAH, NEURAL ANATOMY, DEVELOPMENT & PLASTICITY. *Current Pos:* assoc prof, Dept Anat, 83-88, SCIENTIST, DEPT NEUROL & SURG, UNIV ROCHESTER, 88- *Personal Data:* b Berkeley, Calif, Dec 30, 47; m 78; c 4. *Educ:* Univ Calif, Irvine, BS, 66, PhD(psychobiol), 75. *Prof Exp:* Fel, Univ Calif, San Diego, 75-78, asst prof neurosci, 78-83. *Concurrent Pos:* Prin investr, Nat Inst Neurol & Commun Dis & Stroke, 78-; panel mem, Neurobiol Prog, Subpanel Integrative & Motor Processes, NSF, 82-84. *Mem:* AAAS; Soc Neurosci; Int Soc Develop Neurosci; Am Asn Anatomists. *Res:* Neuronal reorganization in response to brain injury; sex differences in brain function, development and repair; control of synaptic specificity and plasticity in development, after injury and in response to chronic drug treatment; Alzheimer's disease. *Mailing Add:* Dept Neurol Monroe Community Hosp 435 E Henrietta Rd Rochester NY 14620

LOY, ROBERT GRAVES, ANIMAL PHYSIOLOGY. *Current Pos:* from assoc prof to prof, 74-87, EMER PROF VET SCI, UNIV KY, 87- *Personal Data:* b Prescott, Ariz, Feb 7, 24; m 51; c 5. *Educ:* Ariz State Univ, BS, 55; Univ Wis, MS, 56, PhD(physiol of reprod) 59. *Prof Exp:* Instr genetics, Univ Wis, 56-59; asst prof animal husb, Univ Calif, Davis, 59-66; from asst to assoc prof vet sci, Univ Ky, 66-71; agr consult, 71-74. *Concurrent Pos:* Consult, Equine Reproduction, 87- *Mem:* Am Soc Animal Sci. *Res:* Physiology and endocrinology of reproduction in horses. *Mailing Add:* 1380 S Loy Rd Cornville AZ 86325

LOYALKA, SUDARSHAN KUMAR, NUCLEAR & MECHANICAL ENGINEERING. *Current Pos:* From asst prof to assoc prof, 67-77, PROF NUCLEAR ENG & CUR PROF, DEPT NUCLEAR ENG, UNIV MO-COLUMBIA, 89- *Personal Data:* b Pilani, India, Apr 11, 43; m, Nirja Awasthi; c Pranav, Prashant & Shashwat. *Educ:* Univ Rajasthan, BEMech, 64; Stanford Univ, MS, 65, PhD(nuclear eng), 67. *Concurrent Pos:* Vis scientist, Max Planck Inst Aerodyn, Gottingen, 69-71; Huber O Croft chair eng, Univ Mo-Columbia, 83- *Mem:* Sigma Xi; fel Am Nuclear Soc; fel Am Phys Soc; Am Chem Soc. *Res:* Kinetic theory of gases; neutron transport theory and reactor physics; nuclear reactor safety analysis; mechanics of aerosols. *Mailing Add:* Dept Nuclear Eng Univ Mo Columbia MO 65211

LOYD, DAVID HERON, ATOMIC PHYSICS, NUCLEAR PHYSICS. *Current Pos:* asst prof physics, 69-96, DEAN SCI, ANGELO STATE UNIV, 96- *Personal Data:* b Shreveport, La, July 3, 41; m 60; c 2. *Educ:* Univ Tex, Austin, BS, 63, MA, 64; Univ Wis-Madison, PhD(physics), 70. *Mem:* Am Phys Soc. *Res:* Atomic collisions. *Mailing Add:* Col Sci Angelo State Univ 2601 West Ave N San Angelo TX 76909. *Fax:* 915-942-2038

LOYNACHAN, THOMAS EUGENE, SOIL MICROBIOLOGY, SOIL FERTILITY. *Current Pos:* MEM TEACHING STAFF SOIL SCI, IOWA STATE UNIV, 78-, MEM RES STAFF FIXATION & SOIL ECOL, 78- *Personal Data:* b Oskaloosa, Iowa, Nov 18, 45; m 67, M Jean Henzel; c Mark, Timothy & Alan. *Educ:* Iowa State Univ, BS, 68, MS, 72; NC State Univ, PhD(soil sci), 75. *Prof Exp:* Asst prof agron, Univ Alaska, 75-78. *Mem:* AAAS; Soil Sci Soc Am; Am Soc Agron; Coun Agr Sci & Technol. *Res:* Nitrification inhibitors; oil degradation in Arctic soils; nitrogen fixation of legumes; mycorrhizae of soybean. *Mailing Add:* 1126 Agron Iowa State Univ Ames IA 50011. *Fax:* 515-294-8146; *E-Mail:* teloynac@iastate.edu

LOZANO, EDGARDO A, BACTERIOLOGY. *Current Pos:* asst prof bact, 65-68, ASSOC PROF BACT, VET RES LAB, MONT STATE UNIV, 68-, ASSOC PROF MICROBIOL, 80- *Personal Data:* b Tampico, Mex, Nov 20, 24; m 49; c 3. *Educ:* Univ Tex, BA, 48; Univ Wis, MS, 54; Mont State Univ, PhD(microbiol), 65. *Prof Exp:* Bacteriologist vaccine prod, Agr Res Serv, 48-50; res, Am Sci Labs, 54-55; dept head prod & develop, Corn States Labs, 55-59; dir bio-prod, Philips Roxane Inc, 63-64. *Res:* Bacteriological antigens and their purification; bacterial toxins; electrophoresis; telemetry of domestic animals. *Mailing Add:* 1924 Sourdough Rd Bozeman MT 59715

LOZERON, HOMER A, BIOCHEMISTRY. *Current Pos:* asst prof, 72-77, ASSOC PROF BIOCHEM, SCH MED, ST LOUIS UNIV, 77- *Personal Data:* b Grande Prairie, Alta, July 24, 34; m 67; c 2. *Educ:* Univ Alta, BSc, 56, MSc, 59; Univ Washington, PhD(biochem), 64. *Prof Exp:* Proj assoc, McArdle Lab Cancer Res, 65-67, instr, 67-72. *Mem:* Am Soc Biol Chemists; Am Soc Microbiol. *Res:* RNA processing pathways and regulation of gene expression in bacterial virus systems. *Mailing Add:* Dept Biochem St Louis Univ 1402 S Grand Blvd St Louis MO 63104-1080

LOZIER, DANIEL WILLIAM, NUMERICAL ANALYSIS, MATHEMATICAL SOFTWARE. *Current Pos:* MATHEMATICIAN, NAT BUR STAND, US DEPT COM, 69- *Personal Data:* b Portland, Ore, Apr 10, 41; m 66, Elaine Tolnitch; c Daniel W Jr. *Educ:* Ore State Univ, BA, 62; Am Univ, MA, 69; Univ Md, PhD(appl math), 79. *Prof Exp:* Mathematician, US Army Eng Res & Develop Lab, Ft Belvoir, Va, 63-69. *Concurrent Pos:* Adj prof, Inst Phys Sci & Technol, Univ Md, College Park. *Mem:* Soc Indust Appl Math; Math Asn Am; Asn Comput Mach; Sigma Xi. *Res:* Numerical analysis and mathematical software; computation of special functions; forward and backward recurrence methods; floating-point and level-index computer arithmetic; numerical aspects of programming languages; vector and parallel computing. *Mailing Add:* 5230 Sherrier Pl NW Washington DC 20016-3324. *Fax:* 301-990-4127; *E-Mail:* dlozier@nist.gov

LOZZIO, CARMEN BERTUCCI, MEDICAL GENETICS, CELL BIOLOGY. *Current Pos:* from res assoc to asst res prof, 65-72, assoc res prof med genetics, 72-78, DIR, BIRTH DEFECTS CTR, MEM RES CTR & HOSP, UNIV TENN, KNOXVILLE, 78-, PROF MED EXP, CTR HEALTH SCI, 78- *Personal Data:* b Buenos Aires, Arg, Dec 20, 31; US citizen; m 55; c 1. *Educ:* Univ Buenos Aires, physician, 55, MD, 60. *Honors & Awards:* Honor Cert, World Cong Obstet & Gynec & Int Cong Internal Med, 64. *Prof Exp:* Physician in chg cytol, Rivadavia Hosp, Buenos Aires, 56-60; instr genetics, Univ Buenos Aires, 60-65. *Concurrent Pos:* Arg Asn Prog Sci Millet fel & Arg Nat Res Coun fel radiation res, Rivadavia Hosp & Arg AEC, 57-60; grants, Arg Nat Res Coun, Univ Buenos Aires, 61-65, Pan Am Union, Biol Div, Oak Ridge Nat Lab, 64, Am Cancer Soc, Univ Tenn, Knoxville, 66-71, Nat Found-March of Dimes, 66-80, Physicians Med Educ & Res Found, 69-70, NIH, 69-71 & 75-81, US Dept Health, Educ & Welfare, 70-74, Tenn Dept Human Serv, 74-, Tenn Dept Ment Health, 74- & Tenn Dept Pub Health, 78- *Mem:* Genetics Soc Am; Genetics Soc Can; Am Asn Ment Deficiency; Am Soc Human Genetics; NY Acad Sci; Sigma Xi. *Res:* Studies on human genetics and cytogenetics; genetic counseling and prenatal diagnosis of hereditary disorders; experimental studies on cell culture of human diploid strains with genetic markers and the effect of antimetabolites on mammalian cell cultures. *Mailing Add:* 9709 Tunbridge Lane Knoxville TN 37922

LU, ADOLPH, HIGH ENERGY PHYSICS. *Current Pos:* RES PHYSICIST HIGH ENERGY PHYSICS, UNIV CALIF, SANTA BARBARA, 76- *Personal Data:* b Chengtu, China, Feb 19, 42; US citizen; 1993, Karen. *Educ:* Queen's Univ, BSc, 64; Univ Toronto, MA, 65; Univ Calif, Berkeley, PhD(physics), 73. *Prof Exp:* Researcher, Univ D'Orsay, Paris, 73-75. *Mem:* Am Phys Soc. *Res:* Bubble chamber physics; proton storage ring studies; photon cross sections; two-photon physics; Z physics; B-factory studies; dark matter physics. *Mailing Add:* Physics Dept Univ Calif Santa Barbara CA 93106. *E-Mail:* slacstanford.edu

LU, ANTHONY Y H, BIOCHEMISTRY. *Current Pos:* SR INVESTR, RES LABS, MERCK SHARP & DOHME LABS, 78- *Personal Data:* b Hupei, China, Jan 12, 37; m 65; c 1. *Educ:* Nat Taiwan Univ, BS, 58; Univ NC, Chapel Hill, PhD(biochem), 66. *Prof Exp:* Fel inst sci & technol, Univ Mich, Ann Arbor, 66-70; sr biochemist, Res Div, Hoffmann-La Roche Inc, 70-74, res fel, 74-78. *Mem:* AAAS; Am Chem Soc; Am Soc Pharmacol & Exp Therapeut; Am Soc Biol Chemists; NY Acad Sci. *Res:* Basic research in biochemistry and biochemical pharmacology. *Mailing Add:* Animal Drug Metab Merck Sharp & Dohme Res Lab PO Box 2000 R480-A2 PO Box 2000 NJ 07065-0900

LU, BENJAMIN C(HIH) Y(EU), CHEMICAL ENGINEERING. *Current Pos:* from asst prof to assoc prof, Univ Ottawa, 56-62, actg chmn dept, 60, chmn dept, 61-76, prof chem eng, 62-92, vdean eng, Fac Sci & Eng, 69-76, EMER PROF, UNIV OTTAWA, 92-, HON CHAIR CHEM ENG, 92- *Personal Data:* b Peking, China, Oct 20, 26; m 52, Katherine Sun; c Calvin, Joyce & John. *Educ:* Nat Cent Univ, China, BASc, 47; Univ Toronto, MASc, 51, PhD(chem eng), 54. *Hon Degrees:* DSc, Queens Univ, Kingston, Can, 93. *Honors & Awards:* R S Jane Mem lectr, Can Soc Chem Engrs, 90. *Prof Exp:* Asst engr, Chinese Petrol Corp, China, 47-50; res assoc, Ont Res Found, Can, 54-55; lectr, Univ Toronto, 55-56. *Concurrent Pos:* Mem, Grant Selection Comt, Nat Res Coun Can, 69-72 & Nat Comt Deans Eng & Appl Sci, 69-76; exchange scientist, Inst Chem Process Fundamentals, Czech Acad Sci, 75; vis prof, Univ Pittsburgh, 76, Nihon Univ, Japan, 90; exchange scientist, Japan Soc for Prom Sci, 77; UNESCO consult, Univ Zulia, Venezuela, 78; mem, Hazardous Prod Bd Rev, Can Govt, 80-82; hon prof, Beijing Inst Chem Technol, China, 82, Nanjing Inst Chem Technol, China, 85, Inner Mongolia Eng Col, China, 92; assoc ed, Can J Chem Eng, 90-96; hon prof, Beijing Inst Chem Technol, China, 82, Nanjing Inst Chem Technol, China, 85, Inner Mongolia Eng Col, China, 92. *Mem:* Fel Chem Inst Can; Can Soc Chem Engrs. *Res:* Phase equilibria; thermodynamic properties of solutions; cryogenic research; energy engineering; supercritical fluid extraction; equations of state. *Mailing Add:* Dept Chem Eng Univ Ottawa Ottawa ON K1N 6N5 Can. *Fax:* 613-562-5172; *E-Mail:* lu@eng.uottawa.ca

LU, BENJAMIN CHI-KO, GENETICS, CELL BIOLOGY. *Current Pos:* from asst prof to assoc prof, 67-79, PROF GENETICS, UNIV GUELPH, 79- *Personal Data:* b Changnow, China, Mar 9, 32; m 62, Jennie Huang; c Albert & Andrew. *Educ:* Taiwan Univ, BS, 55; Univ Alta, MS, 62, PhD(bot, genetics), 65. *Prof Exp:* Instr bot, Taiwan Univ, 58-60; fel fungal genetics, Cambridge Univ, 65-67; vis fel, Copenhagen Univ, 66. *Concurrent Pos:* Nat Res Coun Can overseas fel, 65-67, res grant, Rask-Orsted Found fel & Carlsberg Found grant, 66-67; Nat Res Coun grant, 68-78; res assoc, Univ Calif, Berkeley, 73-74; Univ NC, Chapel Hill, 83-84; Natural Sci & Eng Res Coun, Can grant, 79-; mem grant comt (cell biol & genetics), Nat Sci & Eng Res Coun Can, 85-88. *Mem:* Genetics Soc Can. *Res:* Meiosis-specific nucleases; cellular programs in meiosis; genetic recombination; synaptonemal complex; light/dark cycle and control of meiosis. *Mailing Add:* Dept Molecular Biol & Genetics Univ Guelph Guelph ON N1G 2W1 Can. *Fax:* 519-837-2075; *E-Mail:* blu@uoguelph.ca

LU, CHRISTOPHER D, RUMINANT NUTRITION, INTERNATIONAL AFFAIR. *Current Pos:* prof & dep dean, 92-93, DEAN, COL AGR, SULTON QABOOS UNIV, 93- *Personal Data:* b Taipei, Taiwan, Repub China, Aug 30, 51; US citizen; m; c 1. *Educ:* Nat Taiwan Univ, BS, 74; Univ Wis-Madison, MS, 78, PhD(dairy sci & biochem), 81. *Prof Exp:* From res asst to res assoc ruminant nutrit, Univ Wis-Madison, 78-82; scientist biochem & nutrit, Int Harvester Co, 82; res scientist ruminant nutrit, Prairie View A&M Univ, 82-85; prof & dir, Am Inst Goat Res, 85-89 & Int Prog, Langston Univ, 89-91. *Concurrent Pos:* Prin rep, Div Int Affairs, Nat Asn State Univs & Land Grant Cols, 88-91; trustee, Bd Southeast Consort Int Develop, 89-91; chairperson, Livestock Comt Goats, Am Soc Animal Sci, 89-90; mem, Mgt Award Comt, Am Soc Animal Sci, 90-91; ed-in-chief, Sultan Qaboos Univ, Sci Res Agr Sci; hon prof, Independent Univ Aztecas, Mex, Northwestern Agr Univ, China & Independent Univ Nuevo Leon, Mex. *Mem:* Am Dairy Sci Asn; Am Inst Nutrit; Nutrit Soc UK; Am Animal Sci; Qsn Dirs Int Progs; Int Good Asn (vpres, 96-). *Res:* Nutrient requirements for lactation, growth, pregnancy and fiber production in goats; energy and protein utilization; ruminant nutrition; metabolism and physiology. *Mailing Add:* Col Agr Sultan Qaboos Univ PO Box 34 Al-khod 123 Muscat Oman. *Fax:* 968-513366; *E-Mail:* chrislu@sou.edu

LU, FRANK CHAO, PHARMACOLOGY, SCIENCE COMMUNICATION. *Current Pos:* CONSULT TOXICOL, 79- *Personal Data:* b Hupeh, China, Mar 9, 15; nat US; m 39, Jean Wang; c Adolph Grant & Lilly. *Educ:* Cheeloo Univ, MD, 39. *Honors & Awards:* Int Achievement Award, Int Soc Regulatory Toxicol, 87. *Prof Exp:* Assoc ed, Coun Pub, Chinese Med Asn, 40-42; sr asst pharmacol, Cheeloo Univ, 42-44, lectr, 45-47; lectr, WChina Union Univ, 44-45; pharmacologist, Food & Drug Labs, Can Dept Nat Health & Welfare, 51-60, head, Pharmacol & Toxicol Sect, 60-65; chief food additives, WHO, 65-76; clin prof pharmacol, Sch Med, Univ Miami, 77-79. *Concurrent Pos:* Res fel exp surg, McGill Univ, 47-48, med res fel pharmacol, 48-51; spec lectr pharmacol, Univ Ottawa, 59-62; spec lectr toxicol, Univ Toronto, 59-62; lectr, Joint China-WHO Toxicol Course, 82; vis prof toxicol, Shanghai Med Univ, 85; managing ed, Biomed & Environ Sci, Acad Press, Inc; hon prof, Chinese Acad Med Sci, Chinese Acad Prev Med, Shanghai Med Univ, Peking Union Med Col. *Mem:* Am Col Toxicol; Am Soc Pharmacol & Exp Therapeut; Soc Toxicol; Europ Soc Toxicol; Can Pharmacol Soc; Int Acad Environ Safety; Int Soc Regulatory Toxicol. *Res:* physiology and pharmacology of coronary circulation; bioassay of drugs; cardiac glycosides; blood dyscrasias; toxicology of drugs, food additives, pesticides and contaminants; principles and procedures for toxicological evaluation of chemicals; assessment of the safety of chemicals, on the basis of toxicological data, by the use of the acceptable daily intake approach. *Mailing Add:* 7452 SW 143rd Ave Miami FL 33183-2919. *Fax:* 305-385-1350

LU, FRANK KERPING, AERODYNAMICS & GAS DYNAMICS, EXPERIMENTAL TECHNIQUES. *Current Pos:* asst prof, 87-93, ASSOC PROF AEROSPACE ENG, UNIV TEX, ARLINGTON, 93-, DIR, AERODYNAMICS RES CTR, 93- *Personal Data:* b Taipei, Taiwan, Oct 17, 54; US citizen; m 83, Jean Yang; c Richard. *Educ:* Cambridge Univ, BA, 76; Princeton Univ, MSE, 83; Pa State Univ, PHD(mech eng), 88. *Hon Degrees:* MA, Cambridge Univ, 80. *Prof Exp:* Eng Officer, Singapore Armed Forces, 76-79; admin asst, Singapore Civil Serv, 79; res asst, Princeton Univ, 79-82; proj engr, ICOS Corp of Am, 82-83; res asst, Pa State Univ, 84-87;

Concurrent Pos: Prin investr, NASA, 88-92, Tex Advan Res Prog, 94-96; co-prin investr, NASA, 93-; MSE, Inc, Butte, Montana, 95-; Office Naval Res, 97-; lectr, Launchspace, Inc, Falls Church, Va. Mem: Am Inst Aeronaut & Astronaut; Am Soc Mech Engrs; Am Phys Soc; Sigma Xi; Am Soc Eng Educ; Am Helicopter Soc. Res: Experimental supersonic and hypersonic aerodynamics; gas dynamics; turbomachinery and internal flows; unsteady flows and flow-induced vibrations; turbulence. Mailing Add: Mech & Aerospace Eng Dept Univ Tex Arlington TX 76019

LU, FREDERICK MING, MOLECULAR BIOLOGY, MEMBRANE SKELETON PROTEINS. Current Pos: RES ASSOC, DEPT HEMAT & ONCOL, CHILDRENS HOSP, BOSTON, 92- Personal Data: b Hing Sua, China, Mar 29, 60. Educ: Quingdao Univ, China, BA; Univ Calif, Santa Barbara, PhD(molecular biol), 90. Mem: Am Soc Cell Biol; AAAS. Res: Molecular biology; membrane skeleton proteins. Mailing Add: Dept Hemat & Oncol Childrens Hosp 300 Longwood Ave Boston MA 02115

LU, GRANT, DIAMOND FILM, OPTICAL FIBERS. Current Pos: sr res engr, 88-93, RES MGR, NORTON CO, NORTHBOROUGH, MASS, 94- Personal Data: b Ottawa, Ont, May 9, 56; US citizen. Educ: Univ Manchester, Eng, BSc, 76; Rutgers Univ, MS, 80, PhD(ceramic eng), 83. Honors & Awards: Mat News Res Award, 81. Prof Exp: Mat scientist, Naval Res Lab, Washington, DC, 83-88. Concurrent Pos: Ed, Am Ceramic Soc, 85-87. Mem: Am Ceramic Soc; Int Soc Optical Eng. Res: Thermal and optical applications of diamond film. Mailing Add: 237 South St Shrewsbury MA 01545

LU, GUANGQUAN, spectroscopic measurements of chemical reactions on solid surfaces, dynamics of surface processes during thermal & photo chemical vapor deposition of semiconductor materials, for more information see previous edition

LU, GUO-WEI, SPINAL PROJECTION NEURONS, PLASTICITY OF CENTRAL NERVOUS SYSTEM. Current Pos: asst prof physiol, 60-72, assoc prof neurophysiol & chmn dept, 72-80, PROF NEUROBIOL, CHMN DEPT & DIR, INST EXP MED, CAPITAL INST MED, 83- Personal Data: b Gaixian, China, Feb 10, 32; m 57; c 2. Educ: China Med Univ, MD, 55. Prof Exp: Asst prof pathophysiol, Beijing Med Univ, 55-60; int res fel neurosci, Fogarty Int Ctr, NIH, 80-82. Concurrent Pos: Vis prof neurol, Univ Wis-Madison, 87-88. Mem: Am Physiol Soc; Soc Neurosci; Int Asn Study Pain; Int Brain Res Orgn. Res: Pain physiology and antinociception; anatomico-physiological basis of acupuncture; singly and doubly projecting spinal systems; spinal injuries and stroke; developmental neurobiol of spinal cord and brain; adaptation to and plasticity of hypoxia and pain. Mailing Add: Dept Neurobiol Inst Exp Med Capital Inst Med You An Men St Beijing 100054 People's Republic of China

LU, HSIENG S, PROTEIN STRUCTURE. Current Pos: res scientist, Protein Develop & Microsequencing Group, 84-88, SR RES SCIENTIST PROTEIN STRUCT, AMGEN, 88- Personal Data: b Taiwan, China, July 28, 47. Educ: Nat Taiwan Univ, BS, 70, MS, 75; NTex State Univ, PhD(biochem), 81. Prof Exp: Res asst, Pharmacol & Microbiol Group, Panlabs, Inc, Taipei, 70-72; teaching asst biochem, Inst Biochem Sci, Nat Taiwan Univ, Taipei, 72-76, res asst prof, Dept Chem, 83-84. Concurrent Pos: Robert A Welch Found fel, 82-83. Mem: Am Soc Biochem & Molecular Biol; Protein Soc; AAAS. Res: Protein therapeutics; exploration and initial characterization of new therapeutic proteins; protein recovery process and structure-function studies; development of protein analytical methods, QC tests; extensive characterization of therapeutic proteins. Mailing Add: Dept Protein Struct Amgen Inc Amgen Ctr Thousand Oaks CA 91320-1789

LU, HUA, EXPERIMENTAL MECHANICS, PHOTO-MECHANICS. Current Pos: from asst prof to assoc prof, 89-94, PROF MECH ENG, RYERSON POLYTECH UNIV, 95- Personal Data: m 71, Guiping Yang; c Yisha. Educ: Tianjin Univ, BS, 68, MS, 82; State Univ NY, Stony Brook, PhD(mech eng), 89. Prof Exp: Engr, GCM Inc, China, 69-77; lectr, Tianjin Univ, China, 78-82. Concurrent Pos: Vis researcher, Res Div, Ont Hydro, 90-92. Mem: Soc Exp Mech; Soc Photo-Instrumentation Engrs. Res: Research and development of methods in experimental solid mechanics; applications of experimental methods in micro-mechanics; composite mechanics; interfacial mechanics; structure and stress analysis in mechanical engineering and electronic packaging engineering. Mailing Add: Dept Mech Eng Ryerson Polytech Univ 350 Victoria St Toronto ON M5B 2K3 Can. E-Mail: hlu@acs.ryerson.ca

LU, JOHN KUEW-HSIUNG, ENDOCRINOLOGY & NEUROENDOCRINOLOGY, REPRODUCTIVE PHYSIOLOGY. Current Pos: from asst prof to assoc prof, 77-88, PROF OBSTET, GYNEC & ANAT, CELL BIOL, UNIV CALIF, LOS ANGELES, 88- Personal Data: b Miaoli, Taiwan, China, Sept 16, 37; US citizen; m 69, Marianne M Wang; c Judith Maria & John Lawrence. Educ: Nat Taiwan Normal Univ, BSc, 61; Nat Taiwan Univ, MSc, 67; Mich State Univ, PhD(physiol), 72. Prof Exp: Teacher biol, Hsinchu Sr High Sch, Taiwan, 61-62; instr biol, Nat Taiwan Normal Univ, 63-65; res asst physiol, Nat Taiwan Univ, 65-67; res asst endocrinol, Purdue Univ, 67-68; teaching asst biol, Mich State Univ, 68-72; postdoctoral fel reproductive endocrinol, Univ Pittsburgh, 72-74; res assoc, Mich State Univ, 74-75; asst prof endocrinol, Univ Calif, San Diego, 75-77. Concurrent Pos: Prin investr res grants, Nat Inst Aging, 80-91 & 84-97. Method to Extend Res in Time Award, 87-92 & 92-97; mem biochem Endocrinol Study Sect, NIH, 89-94, health reviewers res, 94-98. Mem: Soc Gynec Invest; Am Physiol Soc; NY Acad Sci; Endocrine Soc; Soc Study Reproduction; Sigma Xi; Soc Exp Biol & Med. Res: Animal studies and laboratory investigations to reveal the interactions between ovarian and neuroendocrine functions during reproductive senescence & neuroendocrine aging. Mailing Add: Dept Obstet & Gynec Div Reprod Endocrinol Sch Med Univ Calif CHS-22-177 10833 Le Conte Ave Los Angeles CA 90095-1740. Fax: 310-206-6531; E-Mail: jlu@obgyn.medsch.ucla.edu

LU, KAU U, APPLIED MATHEMATICS, NUMBER THEORY. Current Pos: From asst prof to assoc prof, 68-79, PROF MATH, CALIF STATE UNIV, LONG BEACH, 79- Personal Data: b Canton, China, July 10, 39; US citizen; m 68; c 1. Educ: Nat Taiwan Univ, BS, 61; Calif Inst Technol, PhD(math), 68. Concurrent Pos: Consult, Tridea Electronics, 69-70; res assoc, Univ Calif, Berkeley, 81- Mem: Am Math Soc; Soc Indust & Appl Math; Planetary Soc. Res: Applied mathematics; theory of spiral galaxy; dynamics of earth, cyclone and pulsar; solar physics and sunspots; general relativistic bianary system; Riemann hypothesis. Mailing Add: Dept Math Calif State Univ Long Beach CA 90840

LU, KEWANG, BIOMATERIALS, DENTAL MATERIALS. Current Pos: res chemist, 89-93, SR RES CHEMIST, DENISPLY INT, 93- Personal Data: m, May Lu; c Zan Mei, David Luk & Dazhi Lu. Educ: WChina Univ Med Sci, MDent, 81. Prof Exp: Assoc prof, Kumming Med Col, 82-89. Mem: Int Asn Dental Res. Res: Develop new dental materials especially bicompatible resin reinforced glass ionomes materials and atraumatic restorative technique materials sponsored by World Health Organization. Mailing Add: 696 Independence Blvd Dover DE 19904

LU, KUO HWA, biostatistics, genetics; deceased, see previous edition for last biography

LU, LE-WU, STRUCTURAL ENGINEERING. Current Pos: Res asst civil eng, Lehigh Univ, 58-59, res assoc, 59-61, res asst prof, 61-65, res assoc prof, 65-67, assoc prof, 67-69, PROF CIVIL ENG, LEHIGH UNIV, 69- Personal Data: b Shanghai, China, June 5, 33; m 63; c 2. Educ: Nat Taiwan Univ, BS, 54; Iowa State Univ, MS, 56; Lehigh Univ, PhD(civil eng), 60. Honors & Awards: Leon Moisseiff Award, Am Soc Civil Engrs, 67. Concurrent Pos: USSR Fulbright-Hays lectureship, Int Coun Exchange Scholars, 75; hon prof, Harbin Civil Eng Inst, 80. Mem: Assoc Am Soc Civil Engrs; Am Concrete Inst; Int Asn Bridge & Struct Engrs; Am Soc Eng Educ; Earthquake Eng Res Inst; Int Asn Struct Safety & Reliability. Res: Behavior of building frames and their components in the elastic and inelastic range; planning and design of tall buildings; response of steel and reinforced concrete building structures to earthquake ground motion. Mailing Add: Dept Civil Eng Lehigh Univ 27 Memorial Dr W Bethlehem PA 18015-3044

LU, MARY KWANG-RUEY CHAO, ORGANIC CHEMISTRY, MATHEMATICS. Current Pos: PROF CHEM, WALTERS STATE COMMUNITY COL, MORRISTOWN, TENN, 78- Personal Data: b Liao-ning, China, Sept 6, 35; US citizen; m 61; c 2. Educ: Notre Dame Col, Ohio, BS, 59; Univ Detroit, MS, 61; Univ Tenn, Knoxville, PhD(org chem), 68. Prof Exp: Technician, Chem Lab, NY Hosp, New York, 59; chemist, US Testing Co, Inc, 61-63; asst prof chem, Morris Col, SC, 63-64; prof chem & math, Lincoln Mem Univ, 68-78. Concurrent Pos: US Dept Energy res grant. Mem: AAAS; Am Chem Soc. Res: Organometallic chemistry; silicon solar cells. Mailing Add: Div Natural Sci Walters State Comm Col 500 S Davey Crockett Morristown TN 37813

LU, MATTHIAS CHI-HWA, PHARMACY, MEDICINAL CHEMISTRY. Current Pos: asst prof med chem, Col Pharm, Univ Ill, Chicago, 73-78, assoc prof, 78-96, coordr curric affairs, 92-95, ASST HEAD CURRIC AFFAIRS, COL PHARM, UNIV ILL, CHICAGO, 95-, PROF MED CHEM, 96- Personal Data: b Fukien, China, Jan 3, 40; m; c 2. Educ: Kaohsiung Med Col, Taiwan, BSc, 63; Ohio State Univ, PhD(med chem), 69. Prof Exp: Res asst med chem, Univ Iowa, 64-67 & Ohio State Univ, 67-69; res assoc, Col Pharm, Univ Mich, Ann Arbor, 69-71, instr, 71-72, asst prof, 72-73. Concurrent Pos: Vis assoc prof, Grad Inst Pharmaceut Sci, Kaohsiung Col, Kaohsiung, Taiwan, 90, adj prof, Sch Pharm & Sch Chem, 90-; alt dir grad studies mem chem, Grad Col Univ Ill, Chicago, 94- Mem: Am Chem Soc; NAm Taiwanese Prof Asn; Am Asn Cols Pharm. Res: Steroidogenesis and metabolisms; drug design; site-directed, endocrine-selective design of antitumor agents; molecular structures as probes for cholinergic receptors; stereochemistry. Mailing Add: Dept Med Chem Col Pharm Univ Ill-Chicago 833 S Wood Chicago IL 60612-7231. Fax: 312-996-7107; E-Mail: mattlu@uic.edu

LU, NANCY CHAO, NUTRITION, NUTRITION METABOLISM. Current Pos: lectr nutrit & metab, 80-82, assoc prof, 82-87, PROF NEMATODE NUTRIT & NUTRIT METAB, DEPT NUTRIT & FOOD SCI, SAN JOSE STATE UNIV, CALIF, 87- Personal Data: b Sian, China, May 29, 41; US citizen; m 66, C K; c Richard. Educ: Nat Taiwan Univ, Taipei, Taiwan, BS, 63; Univ Wyoming, Laramie, MS, 65; Univ Calif, Berkeley, PhD(nutrit), 73. Honors & Awards: Ellsworth Dougherty Award, 76. Prof Exp: Res biochemist metab res, Highland Hosp, Oakland, Calif, 65-66; res biochemist cardiovasc res, Mt Zion Hosp, San Francisco, Calif, 66-68; NIH fel, Dept Nutrit Scis, Univ Calif, Berkeley, 73-75, fel, 75-76, res assoc, 76-78, res assoc & proj coordr NIH nematode grant, 78-80, teaching assoc, 79-80. Concurrent Pos: Dir Dietetic Prog Dietetics, 89- Mem: Am Inst Nutrit; Am Dietetic Asn; Inst Food Technologist; Soc Exp Biol & Med; Soc Nematol; Sigma Xi; Chinese Am Dietetic Asn. Res: Developing nematodes as a model for food and nutritional research; nutrient requirement and metabolism of vitamins, minerals and growth factors of nematodes; nematode as a screening organism for testing food additives; food toxins. Mailing Add: Dept Nutrit & Food Sci San Jose State Univ San Jose CA 95192

LU, PAU-CHANG, MECHANICAL ENGINEERING, AEROSPACE SCIENCE. *Current Pos:* assoc prof, 68-72, PROF MECH ENG, UNIV NEBR, LINCOLN, 72- *Personal Data:* b Kiangsu, China, Apr 11, 30; m 63. *Educ:* Nat Taiwan Univ, BS, 54; Kans State Univ, MS, 59; Case Western Res Univ, PhD, 63. *Prof Exp:* Mech engr, Taiwan Power Co, 54-56; asst eng, Cheng Kung Univ, Taiwan, 56-57, asst eng, Kans State Univ, 57-59 & Case Western Res Univ, 59-62, res assoc, 62-63, asst prof, 63-68. *Mem:* Am Soc Mech Engrs. *Res:* Viscous flow; magneto-fluid-mechanics; heat exchangers; free convection; integral transforms and other branches of applied mathematics. *Mailing Add:* Mech Eng 255 WSE Univ Nebr Lincoln PO Box 880656 Lincoln NE 68588-0656

LU, PHILLIP KEHWA, ASTRONOMY, PHYSICS. *Current Pos:* asst prof earth & space sci, Western Conn State Univ, 70-77, chem dept, 73-74, assoc prof astron, 77-81, DISTINGUISHED PROF ASTRON, WESTERN CONN STATE UNIV, 81- *Personal Data:* b Anhui, China, Oct 11, 32; m 59; c 3. *Educ:* Maritime Col, Taiwan, BS, 60; Welsleyan Univ, MA, 65; Columbia Univ, MPhil, PhD(astron & sci educ), 70. *Prof Exp:* Math analyst inst math, Chinese Acad Sci, 60-63; instr comput sci, Jefferson Prof Inst, 65-67; res assoc astron observ, Yale Univ, 67-70. *Concurrent Pos:* Consult, Bd Educ, NY, 74-75; sci educ scholar, NSF, 74-75; vis prof & consult, Nat Cent Univ, Taiwan; Carnegie-Mellon fel astron, Yale Univ, 83- *Mem:* Fel Royal Astron Soc; Am Astron Soc; Am Phys Soc; Sigma Xi. *Res:* Primodial helium and stellar chemical abundance of halo and high velocity stars using speckle interferometry; missing mass problem of Milky Way Galaxy using stellar kinematics of faint F-stars to one kiloparsec; photometry and spectroscopy. *Mailing Add:* Dept Physics & Astron Western Conn State Univ 181 White St Danbury CT 06810-6845

LU, PONZY, MOLECULAR BIOLOGY. *Current Pos:* PROF CHEM, UNIV PA, 73- *Personal Data:* b Shanghai, China, Oct 7, 42; US citizen. *Educ:* Calif Inst Technol, BS, 64; Mass Inst Technol, PhD(biophys), 70. *Prof Exp:* Arthritis Found fel biophys, Max Planck Inst Biophys Chem, 70-73; Europ Molecular Biol Orgn fel genetics, Univ Geneva, 73. *Concurrent Pos:* Biophys chem study sect, NIH, 82-86, med scis study sect, 92-96; Univ Space Res Asn, NASA biotechnol discipline working group, 86-91. *Mem:* AAAS; Biophys Soc; Sigma Xi; Am Soc Biol Chemists. *Res:* Molecular components involved in the regulation of gene expression. *Mailing Add:* Dept Chem Univ Pa Philadelphia PA 19104

LU, RENNE CHEN, PROTEIN STRUCTURE, CHEMICAL MODIFICATION. *Current Pos:* PRIN STAFF SCIENTIST, BOSTON BIOMED RES INST, 71- *Personal Data:* b China, Feb 13, 44; m 71; c 2. *Educ:* Univ Calif, San Diego, PhD(biochem), 70. *Mem:* Am Soc Biochem & Molecular Biol; Am Soc Cell Biol; Biophys Soc; Protein Soc. *Mailing Add:* Dept Muscle Res Boston Biomed Res Inst 20 Staniford St Boston MA 02114

LU, RUNDE, OPEN ARCHITECTED SOFTWARE DEVELOPMENT ENVIRONMENT DESIGN FOR INDUSTRIAL AUTOMATION, INDUSTRIAL AUTOMATION. *Current Pos:* CHIEF ARCHITECT & CHIEF ENG, INTELLUTION, INC, 93- *Personal Data:* m 79, Boqiu Guo; c Bo & Maxwell Ray. *Educ:* China Univ Mining & Technol, BS, 77; Bradford Univ, MS, 81, PhD(control eng), 83. *Honors & Awards:* Outstanding Young Scientist Award, Hedley Pac Mining Found, 89; Second Grade Sci & Technol Award, Chinese Govt, 90. *Prof Exp:* Prof automation, China Univ Mining & Technol, 85-90; asst prof res, WVa Univ, 90-91. *Res:* Pioneered soft logic in industrial automation; designed and fully implemented an open architectured software development system. *Mailing Add:* 6417 Woodsbriar Ct Lisle IL 60532. *Fax:* 630-357-9394; *E-Mail:* runde@wisdom.com

LU, SHIH-LAI, organic chemistry, polymer chemistry, for more information see previous edition

LU, TOH-MING, CONDENSED MATTER PHYSICS. *Current Pos:* asst prof, 82-86, ASSOC PROF, RENSSELAER POLYTECH INST, 86- *Personal Data:* b Sibu, Malaysia, June 28, 43. *Educ:* Cheng Kung Univ, BS, 68; Worcester Polytech Inst, 71; Univ Wis-Madison, PhD(physics), 76. *Prof Exp:* Guest scientist, US Nat Bur Stand, 79-80; res assoc, Univ Wis-Madison, 80-82. *Concurrent Pos:* Teacher, Cath High Sch, Malaysia, 77-79. *Mem:* Am Phys Soc; Am Vet Soc; Mat Res Soc. *Res:* Thin film, interfaces and surfaces. *Mailing Add:* Dept Physics Rensselaer Polytech Inst Troy NY 12180. *Fax:* 518-276-6680

LU, WEI-KAO, METALLURGY, PHYSICAL CHEMISTRY. *Current Pos:* from asst prof to assoc prof metall, 65-73, STELCO PROF METALL, MCMASTER UNIV, 73- *Personal Data:* b Kiangsu, China, Apr 6, 33; m 64. *Educ:* Cheng Kung Univ, Taiwan, BS, 57; Univ Minn, PhD(metall), 64. *Prof Exp:* Fel, Univ Minn, 64-65. *Mem:* Am Inst Mining, Metall & Petrol Engrs; Iron & Steel Inst Japan; Can Inst Mining & Metall. *Res:* Theoretical and experimental study of chemical kinetics of gas-solid and slag-metal reactions; heterogeneous kinetics of iron and steelmaking reactions; iron ore agglomeration; coke and carbonization. *Mailing Add:* Dept Metall & Mat McMaster Univ 1280 Main St W Hamilton ON L8S 4L8 Can

LU, WEI-YANG, PLASTICITY, EXPERIMENTAL STRESS ANALYSIS. *Current Pos:* Asst prof, 81-87, ASSOC PROF MECH, UNIV KY, 87- *Personal Data:* b Taiwan, Repub China, Mar 24, 50; US citizen; m 81. *Educ:* Nat Taiwan Univ, BS, 72; Univ NMex, MS, 76; Yale Univ, PhD(eng & appl sci), 81. *Concurrent Pos:* Consult, Sandia Nat Labs, 85-; prin investr, NSF, 86-; chmn ed comt, Soc Exp Mech, 88-; reviewer, NSF, Acta Mech, Exp Mech, J Eng Mat & Technol. *Mem:* Soc Exp Mech; Am Soc Mech Engrs; Sigma Xi. *Res:* The effects of inelastic deformation on materials, its application on manufacturing such as machining and forming, and on ultrasonic nondestructive material characterization. *Mailing Add:* 3512 Cheddington Lane Lexington KY 40502

LU, WU SHENG, DIGITAL SIGNAL PROCESSING. *Current Pos:* assoc prof, 87-91, PROF ELEC & COMPUT ENG, UNIV VICTORIA, 91- *Personal Data:* b Shanghai, China, Oct 5, 42; Can citizen; m 71, Catherine Chang; c Michael M. *Educ:* Fudan Univ, China, BS, 64; Univ Minn, MS, 83, PhD(control sci), 84. *Prof Exp:* Nat Sci & Eng Res Coun fel, 85; vis asst prof, Univ Minn, 86-87. *Mem:* Fel Eng Inst Can; sr mem Inst Elec & Electronic Engrs; Can Soc Elec & Comput Eng. *Res:* Robot motion and force control and kinematic control of redundant manipulators; multidimensional digital signal processing, especially one-dimensional and two-dimensional filter design, image restoration and compression; design of analysis-synthesis based filter banks. *Mailing Add:* Dept Elec & Comput Eng Univ Victoria PO Box 3055 Victoria BC V8W 3P6 Can

LU, YEH-PEI, MECHANICAL ENGINEERING. *Current Pos:* mech engr, 68-72, SR PROJ ENGR, DAVID W TAYLOR NAVAL SHIP RES & DEVELOP CTR, 72- *Personal Data:* US citizen. *Educ:* Nat Taiwan Univ, BS, 58; Univ Houston, MS, 64, PhD(mech eng), 67. *Prof Exp:* Second Lieutenant eng, Chinese Air Force, 58-60; customer engr, IBM Corp, Taiwan, 61; teaching & res fel, Univ Houston, 62-67. *Mem:* Am Soc Mech Engrs; Acoust Soc Am; Sigma Xi. *Res:* Vibration and acoustics; structural dynamics; fluid-structural interaction; numerical analyses. *Mailing Add:* 12713 Hoven Lane Bowie MD 20716

LUBAN, MARSHALL, PHYSICS. *Current Pos:* assoc prof, 67-74, PROF PHYSICS, IOWA STATE UNIV, 74- *Personal Data:* b Seattle, Wash, May 29, 36; m 82; c 2. *Educ:* Yeshiva Univ, AB, 57; Univ Chicago, SM, 58, PhD(theoret physics), 62. *Prof Exp:* Mem, Inst Advan Study, 62-63; asst prof physics, Univ Pa, 63-66; Guggenheim Mem Found fel, Bar-Ilan Univ, Israel, 66-67, chmn dept, 67-70, dean fac natural sci, 69-71. *Concurrent Pos:* Mem, Israel Coun Res & Develop, 70-73; mem bd trustees & exec coun, Bar-Ilan Univ, 71-74 & 79-81; mem bd trustees, Jerusalem Inst Technol, 79-81; vis prof, Washington Univ, Mo, 81-82. *Mem:* Israel Phys Soc (vpres, 78-79 & pres, 79-82); Am Phys Soc. *Res:* Theoretical condensed matter physics. *Mailing Add:* 2801 Torrey Pines Rd Ames IA 50014

LUBAR, JOEL F, NEUROSCIENCES, PSYCHOPHYSIOLOGY. *Current Pos:* assoc prof, 67-71, PROF PSYCHOL, UNIV TENN, 71- *Personal Data:* b Washington, DC, Nov 16, 38; m 61; c 2, Judith Ostrousky; c Sondra & Edward. *Educ:* Univ Chicago, BS, 60, PhD(biopsychol), 63. *Prof Exp:* Asst prof psychol, Univ Rochester, 63-67. *Concurrent Pos:* NIH grant, 65-73, prog dir, 70-75; vis lectr, Inst Physiol, Univ Bergen, Norway, 72; NSF fel, Sch Med, Univ Calif, Los Angeles, 75-76; regional ed, Physiol & Behav J, 70-; psychol consult, Vet Admin Hosp, 72-; co-dir, Southeastern Biofeedback Inst, 76-80, dir, 80-; assoc ed, Biofeedback & Self Regulation, 91- *Mem:* Am Psychol Asn; Sigma Xi; Soc Neurosci; Biofeedback Soc Am; fel NY Acad Sci; Asn Appl Psychophysiol & Biofeedback (pres, 96-97). *Res:* Operant control of electroencephalographic and electrophysiological responses with special emphasis on epilepsy, hyperkinesis, learning disabilities and psychophysiological disorders; neuroanatomical substrates of emotional and motivational behavior. *Mailing Add:* Dept Psychol Univ Tenn 310 AP Knoxville TN 37916

LUBAROFF, DAVID MARTIN, IMMUNOLOGY. *Current Pos:* from asst prof to assoc prof, 73-82, PROF UROL & MICROBIOL & DIR UROL RES, UNIV IOWA, 82- *Personal Data:* b Philadelphia, Pa, Feb 1, 38; m 61; c 3. *Educ:* Philadelphia Col Pharm & Sci, BS, 61; Georgetown Univ, MS, 64; Yale Univ, PhD(microbiol), 67. *Prof Exp:* Assoc, Univ Pa, 69-70, asst prof, 70-73. *Concurrent Pos:* USPHS fel, Univ Pa, 67-69; assoc res career scientist, Vet Admin, 85- *Mem:* Am Asn Immunologists; Transplant Soc; AAAS; Int Soc Prev Oncol; Am Asn Cancer Res; Am Urol Asn. *Res:* Delayed hypersensitivity reactions; transplantation immunology; tumor immunology; lymphocyte membrane antigens. *Mailing Add:* Dept Urol Univ Ia 200 Hawkins Dr Iowa City IA 52242-1089

LUBATTI, HENRY JOSEPH, PHYSICS. *Current Pos:* assoc prof, 69-74, SCI DIR VISUAL TECH LAB, UNIV WASH, 69-, PROF PHYSICS, 74- *Personal Data:* b Oakland, Calif, Mar 16, 37; m 68, Catherine Ledoux; c Karen, Henry Jr & Stephen. *Educ:* Univ Calif, Berkeley, AB, 60, PhD(physics), 66; Univ Ill, Urbana, MS, 63. *Prof Exp:* Physicist, Boeing Co, Wash, 60-61; res assoc physics, Linear Accelerator Lab, Univ Paris, 66-68; asst prof, Mass Inst Technol, 68-69. *Concurrent Pos:* Vis lectr, Int Sch Physics, Erice, Sicily, 68, Herceg-Novi Int Sch, Yugoslavia, 69 & XII Cracow Sch Theoret Physics, Zacopane, Poland, 72; vis scientist, Europ Orgn Nat Res, Geneva, Switz, 80-81; consult & collabr, Los Alamos Nat Lab, 82-86; mem ed adv comt, World Sci Publ Co, Ltd, 82-; guest scientist, SSC Lab, 91-93. *Mem:* Fel AAAS; fel Am Phys Soc. *Res:* Elementary particle physics, experimentalist; deep inelastic muon scattering and rare K-decay experiments; design of muon systems for high energy hadron colliders and development of drift cells. *Mailing Add:* Visual Tech Lab Dept Physics FM-15 Univ Wash Seattle WA 98195. *E-Mail:* lubatti@phys.washington.edu

LUBAWY, WILLIAM CHARLES, PHARMACOLOGY. *Current Pos:* Asst prof, 72-77, assoc prof pharmacol & Grad Ctr Toxicol, 77-82, PROF PHARMACOL & TOXICOL & ASSOC DEAN ACAD AFFAIRS, COL PHARM, UNIV KY, 83- *Personal Data:* b South Bend, Ind, Nov 30, 44; m

71; c 3. *Educ:* Butler Univ, BS, 67; Ohio State Univ, MS, 69, PhD(pharmacol), 72. *Mem:* Am Asn Col Pharm; Am Soc P-Col Exp Ther. *Res:* Factors influencing learning of basic science with the context of application to practice problems. *Mailing Add:* Col Pharm Univ Ky Lexington KY 40536-0082. *Fax:* 606-257-7297; *E-Mail:* lubawy@pop.uky.edu

LUBBERTS, GERRIT, SOLID STATE ELECTRONICS. *Current Pos:* ASSOC SCIENTIST, ROCHESTER INST TECHNOL, 95- *Personal Data:* b Oldemarkt, The Netherlands, Sept 15, 35; US citizen; m 59, Marcia Schumacher; c Emily & David. *Educ:* Univ Rochester, 62, MS, 67, PhD, 71. *Prof Exp:* Technician, Case-Hoyt Corp, 56-58; technician, Eastman Kodak Co, 58-62, res physicist, 62-71, sr res physicist, 71-78, res assoc, 78-92. *Mem:* Inst Elec & Electronics Engrs; Am Phys Soc. *Res:* Semiconductor physics; surface barrier photodetectors, charge coupled devices, high Tc superconducting thin films. *Mailing Add:* 17 Holley Brook Dr Penfield NY 14526

LUBCHENCO, JANE, MARINE ECOLOGY, CONSERVATION BIOLOGY. *Current Pos:* from asst prof to assoc prof, 78-88, chmn dept, 89-92, PROF ZOOL, ORE STATE UNIV, 88-, DISTINGUISHED PROF, 93-, VALLEY PROF MARINE BIOL, 95- *Personal Data:* b Denver, Colo, Dec 4, 47; m 71, Bruce A Menge; c Alexei & Duncan. *Educ:* Colo Col, BA, 69; Univ Wash, MS, 71; Harvard Univ, PhD(ecol), 75. *Hon Degrees:* DSc, Drexel Univ, 92, Colo Col, 93. *Honors & Awards:* George Mercer Award, Ecol Soc Am, 79. *Prof Exp:* Asst prof ecol, Harvard Univ, 75-77. *Concurrent Pos:* Prin investr, NSF, 76-; vis asst prof, Discovery Bay Marine Lab, 76; vis assoc prof, Univ Antofagasta, Chile, 85, Inst Oceanol, Qingdao, Peoples Repub China, 87; nat lectr, Phycological Soc Am, 87-89; prin investr grants, Andrew W Mellon Found, 89-91 & 93, Pew Charitable Trusts, 92-, John D & Catherine T MacArthur Found, 93-98; mem, Bd Environ Studies & Toxicol, Nat Res Coun, 89-92 & 92-95, chair, Natural Resources & Appl Ecol Working Group II, 90-92 & 92-95, comt Environ Res, 91-93; bd mem, Nat Mus Natural Hist, Smithsonian Inst, 92-94; sect coordr, Global Biodiversity Assessment, UN Environ Prog, 93-94; Int Coun Sci Union's SCA Comt problems Environ, SCOPE exec comt, 92-95, coordr sustainability cluster, 92-98, State of Oceans Comt, 96-99, Sustainable Biosphere Proj, adv comt, 92-; mem, US House Rep Comt Sci, Space & Tech, 92-93, UN Environ Prog Sci & Tech Adv Panel, 93-, Int Inst Appl Sys Anal US Adv Group, 94-, Environ Defense Fund Board Trustees & Sci Adv Comt, 95-, Monterey Bay Aquarium Bd Trustees & Prog Comt, 95-, Revelation & Environ, 95, Sci Steering Comt, 95-96, Pew fels Prog Conserv & Environ Adv Comt, 95-98, Pew Charitable Trusts Sea Web Spokesteam, 96-, Interrain Pac adv coun, 96-; adv ed, Ecol Studies, 93-, Conserv Ecol, 95-; chair, Nat Sci & Tech Coun Nat Forum Environ & Nat Resources Res & Develop, Biodiversity & Ecosystem Dynamics Group, 94; US deleg, Int Coun Sci Union, 96; bd dirs, World Resources Inst, 93-, Northwest Environ Watch, 97-97. *Mem:* Nat Acad Sci; Ecol Soc Am (vpres, 88-89, pres, 92-93) Phycol Soc Am; fel AAAS (pres, 96-97); fel Am Acad Arts & Sci; Soc Conserv Biol. *Res:* Evolutionary population and community ecology, biodiversity, conservation biology, ecological causes and consequences of global change; plant-herbivore and predator-prey interactions; competition; marine ecology; algal ecology; algal life histories; biogeography, chemical ecology; sustainable ecological systems. *Mailing Add:* Dept Zool Ore State Univ Corvallis OR 97331-2914. *Fax:* 541-737-3360; *E-Mail:* lubchenj@bcc.orst.edu

LUBECK, MICHAEL D, IMMUNOLOGY. *Current Pos:* ASSOC DIR, WYETH-AYERST LABS INC, 85- *Mailing Add:* Qual Biotech Inc 1667 Davis St Camden NJ 08103

LUBEGA, SETH GASUZA, EMBRYOLOGY, GENETICS. *Current Pos:* ASSOC PROF BIOL, OAKWOOD COL, 76- *Personal Data:* b Mubende, Uganda, Dec 24, 36; m 71; c 2. *Educ:* Oakwood Col, BA, 67; Howard Univ, MS, 69, PhD(zool), 75. *Prof Exp:* Instr biol, Oakwood Col, 71-72; asst prof, Ft Valley State Col, 75-76. *Mem:* Genetic Soc Am; Nat Inst Sci. *Res:* Isoenzymes of octanol dehydrogenase in populations of Drosophila species, developmental stages, and specific organs. *Mailing Add:* Dept Biol Oakwood Col Huntsville AL 35896-0001

LUBELL, DAVID, MATHEMATICS. *Current Pos:* assoc prof, 70-74, PROF MATH, ADELPHI UNIV, 75- *Personal Data:* b Brooklyn, NY, Apr 1, 32; m 60; c 3. *Educ:* Columbia Univ, BS, 56; NY Univ, PhD(math), 60. *Prof Exp:* Benjamin Peirce instr math, Harvard Univ, 60-61; res instr, NY Univ, 61-62; sr mathematician, Systs Res Group Inc, 62-66; asst prof math, NY Univ, 66-70. *Concurrent Pos:* Consult, Systs Res Group Inc, 66-67 & USAF, 67-68; math adv, Nassau Co Med Ctr, 69-72. *Mem:* Am Math Soc. *Res:* Combinatorics; biomathematics. *Mailing Add:* Dept Math Adelphi Univ 1 South Ave Garden City NY 11530-4213

LUBELL, JERRY IRA, ELECTRONICS, NUCLEAR ENGINEERING. *Current Pos:* from asst to pres, Systs Hardening, 80-87, VPRES, ELECTROMAGNETIC & RADIATION EFFECTS SECTOR, MISSION RES CORP, 87- *Personal Data:* b New York, NY, Oct 19, 43; m 66; c 2. *Educ:* Univ Wash, BS, 66, MS, 68. *Prof Exp:* Mem tech staff, TRW Systs Group, 69-73, head, Response Analysis Sect, 73-75, asst mgr, Electronic Syst & Technol Dept, 75-77; res scientist, Kaman Sci Corp, 77-78, mgr radiation & electromagnetics, 78-80. *Concurrent Pos:* Prof nuclear engr, State Calif, 77- *Mem:* Am Nuclear Soc. *Res:* Nuclear weapon effects on electronic systems, subsystems and piece parts; electromagnetic pulse, system generated electromagnetic pulse and transient radiation effects causing both temporary and permanent damage. *Mailing Add:* Mission Res Corp 102 S Tejon Colorado Springs CO 80903

LUBELL, MARTIN S, SUPERCONDUCTORS, TECHNICAL MANAGEMENT. *Current Pos:* res physicist, Oak Ridge Nat Lab, 67-73, asst dept mgr, 74-76, dep prog mgr, 81-88, SECT HEAD, OAK RIDGE NAT LAB, 76- *Personal Data:* b New York, NY, June 5, 32; m 62, Bernadean Frank; c Darrick A. *Educ:* Mass Inst Technol, SB, 54; Univ Calif, Berkeley, MA, 56. *Prof Exp:* Asst, Univ Calif, 55-56; res physicist, Res Labs, Westinghouse Elec Corp, 56-67. *Concurrent Pos:* Pres, Appl Superconductors Conf Inc, 80-83; mem, standing comt fusion-technol, Inst Elec & Electronics Engrs, Nuclear & Plasma Sci Soc, 77, chmn, 87-91; adv ed, Cryogenics, 85 & eng bd, 79-85; mem, Int Magnet Technol Comt, 83-88. *Mem:* Am Phys Soc; Inst Elec & Electronics Engrs; Sigma Xi. *Res:* Low temperature physics; superconductivity; fusion reactor technology; magnets; manage section activities in magnetics and superconductivity; develop superconductivity magnets for fusion machines and conduct research and development on high temperature superconductor magnets and applications. *Mailing Add:* 126 Wendover Circle Oak Ridge TN 37830. *Fax:* 423-574-0584; *E-Mail:* lubell@fedc06.fed.ornl.gov

LUBELL, MICHAEL S, ELECTRON & POSITRON INTERACTIONS, PHOTON-ATOM INTERACTIONS. *Current Pos:* assoc prof, 80-82, Sloan Found fel, 80-83, vis sci, Brookhaven Nat Lab, 86-87, PROF PHYSICS, CITY COL, CITY UNIV NEW YORK, 83- *Personal Data:* b New York, NY, Mar 25, 43; m 69, Ellen Bloom; c Karina. *Educ:* Columbia Univ, BA, 63; Yale Univ, MS, 65, PhD(physics), 69. *Prof Exp:* AEC fel physics, Yale Univ, 70-71, from instr to assoc prof, 71-80, Sloan Found fel, 79-80. *Concurrent Pos:* Prin investr, NSF, Dept Energy & Off Naval Res, 74-; sci & technol adv to US Sen Christopher J Dodd, Conn, 80-; steering comt, Nat Res Coun army res, 81-83, Nat Res Coun comt atomic molecular sci, 86, vchmn, 87-88, chmn, 88-90, past chmn, 90-91; mem panel pub affairs, Am Phys Soc, 84-85, chmn, subcomt studies, 84; prog comt, div electron atomic physics, Am Physics Soc, 78; org comt, div meeting dir electron, atomic physics, Am Physics Soc, 81; exec comt, Int Conf Physics Electronic Atomic Collisions, 83-, cochmn, org comt, 84-89; org comt, fifth topical Am Physics Soc Conf atomic process in high temperature plasmas, 84-85; mem comt pub info, Am Inst Physics, 88-92; vis lectr, Univ Tex, Austin, 90; chmn, Cong Liason Comt, Am Physics Soc, 91-, mem physics planning comt, 93- *Mem:* Fel AAAS; fel Am Phys Soc; NY Acad Sci; Sigma Xi. *Res:* Lepton-atom collisions; laser-atom interactions; polarized particle beams; electro-weak interactions at medium energy; high energy physics with Lepton beams; electron-electron correlation; synchrotron radiation. *Mailing Add:* Dept Physics City Col NY City Univ NY 138th St & Convent Ave New York NY 10031. *Fax:* 212-650-6940; *E-Mail:* lubell@sci.ceny.cuny.edu

LUBENSKY, TOM C, THEORETICAL CONDENSED MATTER PHYSICS. *Current Pos:* from asst prof to assoc prof, 71-80, PROF PHYSICS, UNIV PA, 80- *Personal Data:* b Kansas City, Mo, May 7, 43; m 68, Amy Waldstreicher; c David & Ellen. *Educ:* Calif Inst Technol, BS, 64; Harvard Univ, MA, 65, PhD(physics), 69. *Prof Exp:* NSF fel physics, Fac Sci, Orsay, France, 69-70; res asst, Brown Univ, 70-71. *Concurrent Pos:* Sloan Found fel, 75; Guggenheim fel, 81-82; prof, Univ de Paris VI, 81-82; consult, Exxon Res & Eng, 90-95. *Mem:* Am Phys Soc. *Res:* Liquid crystals, quasicrystals, phase transitions, complex fluids, cooperative phenomena in random systems and applications of the Wilson renormalization group. *Mailing Add:* Dept Physics Univ Pa Philadelphia PA 19104. *Fax:* 215-898-2010; *E-Mail:* tom@dept.physics.upenn.edu

LUBEROFF, BENJAMIN JOSEPH, INDUSTRIAL CHEMISTRY. *Current Pos:* RETIRED. *Personal Data:* b Philadelphia, Pa, Apr 17, 25; m 44, Renee Pines; c 3. *Educ:* Cooper Union, BChE, 49; Columbia Univ, AM, 50, PhD(phys org chem), 53. *Honors & Awards:* Cooper Medal, 49. *Prof Exp:* Statutory fel chem, Columbia Univ, 49-51; instr, Cooper Union, 51-53; chemist, high pressure lab, Am Cyanamid Co, 53-57; head gen chem res sect, Stauffer Chem Co, 57-62; mgr process res dept, Lummus Co, 62-70; ed, Chemtech, Am Chem Soc, 70-91. *Concurrent Pos:* Actg dir, Continuing Sci Educ, Rutgers Univ, 76-78. *Mem:* Am Chem Soc; Am Inst Chem; Am Inst Chem Eng; Am Soc Magazine Ed. *Res:* Research and development management; applied physical chemistry; high temperature and pressure processes; petrochemicals; catalysis; pesticides; analytical chemistry; technical journalism. *Mailing Add:* 19 Brantwood Dr Summit NJ 07901. *Fax:* 908-273-4923; *E-Mail:* bilphd@aol.com

LUBET, RONALD A, CANCER. *Current Pos:* NAT CANCER INST SPEC EXPERT, LAB COMP CARCINOGENESIS, NAT CANCER INST, FREDERICK CANCER RES & DEVELOP CTR, 87- *Personal Data:* b New York, NY, July 7, 46; m; c 3. *Educ:* Univ Tenn, Knoxville, BS, 69, MS, 73; Univ Tex Health Sci Ctr, PhD(radiation biol), 77. *Prof Exp:* Fel, Dept Biochem, Univ Tex Health Sci Ctr, 77-78; fel lab immunobiol, Nat Cancer Inst, 78-79; asst proj dir, Microbiol Assoc, 79-83, proj dir, 83-87. *Concurrent Pos:* Reviewer, Arch Environ Toxicol & Contamination, Arch Biochem & Biophys, Carcinogenesis, Biochem Pharm & J Nat Cancer Inst. *Mem:* Am Col Toxicol; Am Soc Pharm & Exp Therapeut; Am Asn Cancer Res. *Res:* Mechanisms of tumor promotion; induction of cytochrome P-450 by various xenobiotics; mechanisms of chemical carcinogenesis; mutagenicity of chemical carcinogens and chemotherapeutic compounds; metabolism of a variety of xenobiotics including carcinogens and chemotherapeutic agents; numerous publications. *Mailing Add:* 14221 Woodcrest Dr Rockville MD 20853

LUBIC, RUTH WATSON, NURSE-MIDWIFERY. *Current Pos:* instr clin nurse-midwifery, Downstate Med Ctr, Maternity Ctr Asn, 62, parent educ & consult, 63-67, gen dir, 70-95, DIR CLIN PROJ, MATERNITY CTR ASN, 95- *Personal Data:* b Bucks County, Pa, Jan 18, 27; m 55, William J; c Douglas W. *Educ:* Columbia Univ, BS, 59, MA, 61, EdD, 79. *Hon Degrees:* LLD, Univ

Pa, 85; DSc, Univ Med & Dent NJ, 86, State Univ NY, 93; DHL, Col New Rochelle, 92. *Honors & Awards:* Hattie Hemschemeyer Award, Am Col Nurse-Midwives, 83; MacArthur fel, John D & Catherine T MacArthur Found, 93. *Prof Exp:* Instr maternal nursing, Sch Nursing, Flower & Fifth Ave Hosp, 61. *Concurrent Pos:* Mem, First Off Am Med Deleg to People's Repub of China, 73; Kate Hanna Harvey prof, Community Health Nursing, Case Western Res Univ, 91; vis prof, King Edward Mem Hosp Women, Perth, Australia, 91; expert consult, Off Pub Health & Sci, Dept Health & Human Serv. *Mem:* Inst Med-Nat Acad Sci; fel AAAS; fel Am Acad Nurses; Am Col Nurse-Midwives; Am Pub Health Asn; fel Soc Appl Anthrop; Nat Asn Childbearing Ctrs. *Res:* Barriers and conflict in maternity care innovation. *Mailing Add:* 139 W 94th St New York NY 10025. *Fax:* 212-749-5286

LUBIN, ARTHUR RICHARD, MATHEMATICAL ANALYSIS. *Current Pos:* asst prof, 75-80, ASSOC PROF MATH, ILL INST TECHNOL, 81- *Personal Data:* b Newark, NJ, Mar 24, 47. *Educ:* Mich State Univ, BS, 67; Univ Wis, MA, 68, PhD(math), 72. *Prof Exp:* Asst prof math, Tulane Univ, 72-73 & Northwestern Univ, 73-75. *Mem:* Am Math Soc. *Res:* Operator theory; functional analysis; Hardy spaces. *Mailing Add:* Dept Math Ill Inst Technol 3300 Federal St Chicago IL 60616-3732

LUBIN, BERNARD, CLINICAL PSYCHOLOGY, UNIVERSITY TEACHING. *Current Pos:* prof, 76-88, CURATOR'S PROF PSYCHOL, UNIV MO, KANSAS CITY, 88- *Personal Data:* b Washington, DC, Oct 15, 23; m 58, Alice Weisbord. *Educ:* George Washington Univ, BA, 52, MA, 53; Pa State Univ, PhD(clin psychol), 58; Am Bd Prof Psychol, dipl, clin psychol, Am Bd Examr Psychol Hypnosis, dipl, exp hypnosis. *Honors & Awards:* NT Veatch Award, 81. *Prof Exp:* Fel psychother, Univ Wis Sch Med, 58; behav sci intern prog, NTL Inst, 60; assoc prof psychol, Ind Univ Med Ctr, 60-67; dir & psychologist, Greater Kansas City Ment Health Found, 67-74; dir clin prog, Dept Psychol, Univ Houston, 74-76. *Concurrent Pos:* Dir, Div Res & Training, Ind Dept Mental Health, 63-67; chairperson, Dept Psychol, Univ Mo, Kansas City, 76-83; bd dir, Nat Training Labs, 86-92; clin prof, Dept Psychiat, Univ Kans Med Ctr, 87-; chmn sponsor approval comt, Am Psychol Asn, 82-83, mem coun rep, 85-87; curators' prof, 88. *Mem:* Am Psychol Asn. *Res:* The measurement of affect or mood; the small group in treatment and training; psychological test development and validation. *Mailing Add:* 5305 Holmes St Kansas City MO 64110. *Fax:* 816-235-1062; *E-Mail:* lubin@cctr.umkc.edu

LUBIN, JONATHAN DARBY, NUMBER THEORY, ALGEBRAIC GEOMETRY. *Current Pos:* assoc prof, 67-70, PROF MATH, BROWN UNIV, 70- *Personal Data:* b Staten Island, NY, Aug 10, 36. *Educ:* Columbia Univ, AB, 57; Harvard Univ, AM, 58, PhD(math), 63. *Prof Exp:* Instr math, Bowdoin Col, 62-63, from asst to assoc prof, 63-67. *Concurrent Pos:* Assoc prof, Inst Henri Poincare, Univ Paris, 68-69; lectr, Math Inst, Copenhagen Inst, 74-75. *Mem:* Am Math Soc. *Res:* Algebraic geometry; number theory. *Mailing Add:* 386 Morris Ave Providence RI 02906

LUBIN, MARTIN, CELL BIOLOGY. *Current Pos:* prof, 68-93, EMER PROF MICROBIOL, DARTMOUTH MED SCH, 93- *Personal Data:* b NY, Mar 30, 23. *Educ:* Harvard Univ, AB, 42, MD, 45; Mass Inst Technol, PhD(biophys), 54. *Prof Exp:* Res assoc biol, Mass Inst Technol, 53-54; assoc pharmacol, Harvard Med Sch, 54-57, asst prof, 57-68. *Concurrent Pos:* USPHS sr res fel, 56-61; Lalor Found fel, 57-59; Guggenheim fel & Commonwealth Fund fel, Lab Molecular Biol, Cambridge Univ, 65-67. *Mem:* Am Soc Biol Chem; Biophys Soc; Am Soc Cell Biol; Soc Gen Physiol. *Res:* Regulation of cell proliferation. *Mailing Add:* Dept Microbiol Dartmouth Med Sch Hanover NH 03755. *Fax:* 603-643-1864; *E-Mail:* martin.lubin@dartmouth.edu

LUBINIECKI, ANTHONY STANLEY, PROCESS DEVELOPMENT FOR BIOTECHNOLOGY PRODUCTS, MAMMALIAN CELL CULTURE. *Current Pos:* VPRES BIOPHARM DEVELOP, SMITH KLINE BEECHAM, 88-; ADJ PROF CHEM & BIOCHEM ENG, UNIV MD, BALTIMORE CO CAMPUS, 91- *Personal Data:* b Greensburg, Pa, Oct 4, 46; m 68, Robin L Brudowsky; c Gregory M. *Educ:* Carnegie Inst Technol, BS, 68; Univ Pittsburgh, ScD, 72. *Honors & Awards:* Hyclone Award, Europ Soc Animal Cell Technol. *Prof Exp:* Res asst microbiol, Grad Sch Pub Health, Univ Pittsburgh, 71-72, asst res prof, 72-74; prin scientist immunol & virol, Meloy Labs Inc, 74-79, managing dir, 79-80; Tech Div Biol Prod, Flow Labs Inc, 80-82; mgr cell cult oper, Genentech Inc, 82-83, dir res & demonstration, 83-86, dir process transfers 86-88. *Concurrent Pos:* Mem, Dengue Task Force, US Army Med Res & Develop Command, 71-74, prin invest contract, 73-74; prin investr, Nat Inst Allergy & Infectious Dis grant, 73-74; prin investr contract, Nat Cancer Inst, 74-82, Nat Inst Child Health & Human Develop, 75-77; chmn, Process Technol Comt, 86-92, secy, 92-93, vchmn, 93-, Biol & Biotechnol Sect, Pharmaceut Mfrs Asn, Biotechnol Adv Comt, vchmn & chmn, 88-92, mem, 86-88, 92-; coun mem, Int Asn Biol Stand, 96- *Mem:* Am Soc Microbiol; AAAS; Soc Exp Biol & Med; NY Acad Sci; Europ Soc Animal Cell Technol; Int Asn Biol Stand. *Res:* Cell biology models of human genetic diseases and cancer; interferon; genetic mutants of mammalian cells and their viruses; infectious disease models; carcinogenesis; process development for recombinant; DNA pharmaceuticals and monoclonal antibodies. *Mailing Add:* 11681 Bennington Woods Rd Reston VA 22094

LUBINSKI, ARTHUR, mechanics; deceased, see previous edition for last biography

LUBITZ, CECIL ROBERT, NUCLEAR PHYSICS, NEUTRON CROSS SECTIONS. *Current Pos:* PHYSICIST, KNOLLS ATOMIC POWER LAB, LOCKHEED-MARTIN CORP, 60- *Personal Data:* b Brooklyn, NY, Mar 18, 25; m 46, 91, Lois New; c Faith, Martha & Benjamin. *Educ:* US Naval Acad, BS, 45; Univ Mich, MSEE, 49, PhD(physics), 60. *Prof Exp:* Res assoc elec eng, Res Inst, Univ Mich, 49-54. *Mem:* Am Nuclear Soc; Am Phys Soc. *Res:* Neutron cross sections for technological applications. *Mailing Add:* Knolls Atomic Power Lab Lockheed-Martin Corp Schenectady NY 12301. *Fax:* 518-395-7592; *E-Mail:* lubitz@kapl.gov

LUBKER, ROBERT A(LFRED), METALLURGICAL ENGINEERING. *Current Pos:* RETIRED. *Personal Data:* b Puyallup, Wash, May 19, 20; m 45, Virginia Hartmann; c Barbara L (Lunding) & Beverly L (Fantini). *Educ:* Univ Wash, BS, 42; Carnegie Mellon Univ, MS, 46. *Prof Exp:* Metall engr, Westinghouse Elec Corp, Pa, 42-46; supvr nonferrous metals, Metals Res Dept, Armour Res Found, Ill Inst Technol, 46-47, asst chmn, 47-51, assoc mgr, 51-53, mgr, 53-58; dir res & develop, Alan Wood Steel Co, 58-61, vpres res & develop, 61-67; dir res & develop, CF&I Steel Corp, 67-70 & Gen Cable Corp, 70-72; vpres technol, Assoc Metals & Minerals Corp, 72-74; vpres, AVA Steel Prod Int, Inc, 74-80, exec vpres, AVA-Toshin Corp, 76-80; pres, M&R Refractory Metals, Inc, Winslow, NJ, 80-83. *Mem:* Am Inst Mining, Metall & Petrol Engrs; Am Soc Metals; Am Iron & Steel Inst. *Res:* General physical metallurgy; welding; foundry; powder metallurgy; extractive metallurgy; mechanical metallurgy; copper, aluminum, titanium, molybdenum, tungsten and alloy steels; supervision and direction of research; engineering problems; wire and cable; steelmaking research and development. *Mailing Add:* 3150 Timberlake Point Ponte Vedra Beach FL 32082

LUBKIN, ELIHU, THEORETICAL PHYSICS. *Current Pos:* ASSOC PROF PHYSICS, UNIV WIS-MILWAUKEE, 66- *Personal Data:* b Brooklyn, NY, Oct 25, 33; m 62, Thelma R Silver; c Beta & Irene. *Educ:* Columbia Univ, AB, 54, AM, 57, PhD(physics), 60. *Prof Exp:* Asst theoret physics radiation lab, Univ Calif, Berkeley, 59-61; res assoc high energy group, Brown Univ, 61-63, res asst prof theoret physics, 63-66. *Mem:* Am Phys Soc. *Res:* Differential geometry used to interpret the old and for new constructions in physics; interpretation of quantum mechanics; quantum measurement theory; quantum psychology; thermodynamics. *Mailing Add:* Dept Physics Univ Wis PO Box 413 Milwaukee WI 53201. *E-Mail:* eli@csd4.csd.uwm.edu, eli@convex.csd.vwm.edu

LUBKIN, GLORIA BECKER, PHYSICS, SCIENCE POLICY. *Current Pos:* assoc ed, 63-69, sr ed, 70-84, ED, PHYSICS TODAY, AM INST PHYSICS, 85- *Personal Data:* b Philadelphia, Pa, May 16, 33; div; c David & Sharon. *Educ:* Temple Univ, AB, 53; Boston Univ, MA, 57. *Prof Exp:* Mathematician Aircraft Div, Fairchild Stratos Corp, 54 & Letterkenny Ord Depot, US Defense Dept, 55-56; physicist tech res group, Control Data Corp, 56-58; actg chmn, Dept Physics, Sarah Lawrence Col, 61-62; vpres, Lubkin Assocs, 62-63. *Concurrent Pos:* Consult, Ctr for Hist & Philos of Physics, Am Inst Physics, 66-67; Nieman fel, Harvard Univ, 74-75; mem exec comn, Forum Physics & Soc, Am Phys Soc, 77-78, exec comt, Hist Physics Div, 83-; mem, Nieman Adv Comt, Harvard Univ, 78-82; co-chair adv comn, Theoret Physics Inst, Univ Minn, 87-88, co-chair, Oversight Comt, 89- *Mem:* NY Acad Sci; fel Am Phys Soc; Nat Asn Sci Writers; fel AAAS. *Res:* Nuclear physics; science policy; physics reporting, writing and editing. *Mailing Add:* Am Inst Physics 1 Physics Ellipse College Park MO 20740

LUBKIN, JAMES LEIGH, STRUCTURAL ENGINEERING, ENGINEERING EDUCATION. *Current Pos:* PROF CIVIL & SANIT ENG, MICH STATE UNIV, 63- *Personal Data:* b New York, NY, Mar 5, 25; m 48; c 2. *Educ:* Columbia Univ, BA, 44, MS, 47, PhD(appl mech), 50. *Prof Exp:* Consult, Appl Mech & Eng Probs, Mergenthaler Linotype Co, 49-50; sr proj analyst, Appl Physics Div, Midwest Res Inst, 50-56; sr res engr & head theoret anal group, Cent Res Lab, Am Mach & Foundry Co, Conn, 56-63. *Concurrent Pos:* Fac fel, Ford Motor Co, 72-73. *Mem:* Am Soc Mech Engrs; Soc Exp Stress Analysis; Am Soc Eng Educ; Sigma Xi; Am Asn Univ Prof. *Res:* Computer-assisted testing and homework; individualized instruction; computer-aided design in engineering; computer applications in engineering education; vibration of vehicles; database management of traffic accident records. *Mailing Add:* Dept Civil Eng Mich State Univ East Lansing MI 48824

LUBLIN, FRED D, NEUROLOGY, BIOCHEMISTRY. *Current Pos:* from instr to assoc prof neurol, 76-86, res assoc biochem, 76-78, ASSOC PROF BIOCHEM & MOLECULAR BIOL, JEFFERSON MED COL, THOMAS JEFFERSON UNIV, 83-, PROF NEUROL, 86-, VCHMN, DEPT NEUROL, 89- *Personal Data:* b Philadelphia, Pa, Sept 28, 46; m 69. *Educ:* Temple Univ, Philadelphia, Pa, AB, 68; Jefferson Med Col, Philadelphia, Pa, MD, 72; Am Bd Med Examr, dipl, 73, Am Bd Psychiat & Neurol, 77. *Honors & Awards:* Roche Award, Jefferson Med Col, 70; Henry M Phillips Prize, 72; William Potter Mem Prize, 72. *Prof Exp:* Instr neurol, Cornell Med Col, 75-76. *Concurrent Pos:* Asst neurologist, NY Hosp, 73-75, neurologist, 75-76; attend neurologist, Thomas Jefferson Univ Hosp, 76-; prin investr, Basic Res Support Grant, NIH, 76-77, Nat Multiple Sclerosis Soc res grant, 81-93; adj asst prof biochem, Jefferson Med Col, Thomas Jefferson Univ, 78-83, dir, Div neuroimmunol, Dept Neurol, 87-; consult neurologist, Coatesville Vet Admin Hosp, Wilmington Vet Admin Hosp & Wills Eye Hosp; teacher investr develop award, Nat Inst Neurol & Commun Dis & Stroke, 78-83; mem, Comt Drug Develop, Nat Multiple Sclerosis Soc, 83-, chmn, Computer Database Comt, 86-; co-dir, Multiple Sclerosis Comprehensive Clin Ctr, 84-; examr neurol, Am Bd Psychiat & Neuro, 86; co-investr, Triton Biosci Inc, 86-90; mem, Neurol Dis Prog Proj B Comt, Nat Inst Neurol Dis & Stroke, 90- *Mem:* Am Neurol Asn; Am Acad Neurol; Soc Neurosci; Asn Res Nervous & Ment Dis; Sigma Xi; NY Acad Sci; AAAS; Alpers Soc Clin Neurol; Int Brain Res Orgn; Am Asn Immunologists. *Res:* Author of various publications. *Mailing Add:* Neurol Dept Jefferson Med Col 1025 Walnut St Philadelphia PA 19107-5083. *Fax:* 215-923-1959

LUBLIN, PAUL, PHYSICAL CHEMISTRY. *Current Pos:* RETIRED. *Personal Data:* b New York, NY, Sept 8, 24; m 52; c 3. *Educ:* NY Univ, BA, 48; Purdue Univ, MS, 49. *Prof Exp:* Res chemist, Pigment Div, Am Cyanamid Co, 51-53; asst res staff mem, Res Div, Raytheon Mfg Co, 53-54; appln engr, Instrument Div, Philips Electronics, 54-56; sr eng, Gen Tel & Electronics Labs, Inc, Waltham, 56-59, res engr, 59-61, adv res engr, 61-63, eng specialist, 63-67, mem tech staff, 67-78, mgr mat eval, 78-84. *Concurrent Pos:* Consult, 85- *Mem:* Am Crystallog Asn; Soc Appl Spectros; Sigma Xi; Microbeam Analysis Soc; fel Am Inst Chem. *Res:* Materials analysis, applications of x-ray diffraction and spectroscopy to structure and chemical identification of materials; electron probe and scanning electron microscopy as applied to electronic materials. *Mailing Add:* 16 Montgomery Dr Framingham MA 01701

LUBLINER, J(ACOB), MECHANICS, BIOPHYSICS. *Current Pos:* RETIRED. *Personal Data:* b Lodz, Poland, May 5, 35; US citizen; m 60; c 3. *Educ:* Calif Inst Technol, BS, 57; Columbia Univ, MS, 58, PhD(eng mech), 60. *Prof Exp:* Mem tech staff appl mech, Bell Tel Labs, 60; NSF fel, Polytech Sch, Paris, 60-61; preceptor civil eng, Columbia Univ, 61-62, asst prof, 62-63; from asst prof to assoc prof, Univ Calif, Berkeley, 63-68, from assoc prof to prof eng sci, 68-94. *Concurrent Pos:* NIH spec fel, Weizmann Inst Sci, Israel, 69-70; vis prof, Univ Andes, Bogota, Colombia, 77, Univ Costa Rica, San Jose, Costa Rica, 84, Univ Politec Catalunya, Barcelona, Spain, 86. *Mem:* Am Acad Mech. *Res:* Thermomechanics of viscoelastic, viscoplastic and plastic materials; wave propagation in solids; thermodynamics; mechanochemistry; wave propagation in biological systems; high frequency structural dynamics; segmented telescope design; modeling of concrete. *Mailing Add:* 2002 Yolo St Berkeley CA 94707. *E-Mail:* lubliner@ce.berkeley.edu

LUBMAN, DAVID, ACOUSTICS, ELECTRICAL ENGINEERING. *Current Pos:* staff engr underwater acoust, 60-67, SR STAFF ENGR, GROUND SYSTS GROUP, HUGHES AIRCRAFT CO, 76- *Personal Data:* b Chicago, Ill, Aug 3, 34; wid; c 1. *Educ:* Ill Inst Technol, BS, 60; Univ Southern Calif, MS, 62. *Prof Exp:* Sr scientist, LTV Corp Res Ctr, Anaheim, 67-68 & Bolt Beranek & Newman Inc, Van Nuys, 68-69. *Concurrent Pos:* Vis prof math, Chapman Col, Orange, 63-68; consult, D Lubman & Assocs, 69-; mem working group, Am Nat Standards Inst, 70-74; consult, Off Naval Res, Washington, DC, 69-76, Aircraft Engine Group, Gen Elec Co, 71-73, Nat Bur Standards, Washington, DC, 73-74 & Dept Archit & Construct, State of Calif, 76-; vis prof acoust, Calif State Univ, Los Angeles, 76-; vis lectr, Univ Calif, Santa Barbara, 76-; mem, Nat Coun Acoust Consult; chmn, Orange County Regional Chap, Acoust Soc Am, 89- *Mem:* Fel Acoust Soc Am; Inst Noise Control Eng; Am Soc Testing & Mat; Sigma Xi. *Res:* Architectural and underwater acoustics; characterization and measurement of the statistics of sound fields over space, time and frequency; reverberation chambers; measurement of sound power; noise quality; speech intelligibility. *Mailing Add:* 14301 Middletown Lane Westminster CA 92683-4514

LUBMAN, DAVID MITCHELL, LASER SPECTROSCOPY, MASS SPECTROMETRY. *Current Pos:* asst prof, 83-87, ASSOC PROF CHEM, UNIV MICH, 87- *Personal Data:* b Brooklyn, NY, Apr 23, 54; m 84; c 3. *Educ:* Cornell Univ, AB, 75; Columbia Univ, MA, 76; Stanford Univ, PhD(phys chem), 79. *Prof Exp:* Staff scientist chem, Quanta-Ray, Inc, 80-83. *Concurrent Pos:* Vis scientist chem, Weizmann Inst Sci, 82-83; Alfred P Sloan fel, 87-89, Eli Lilly teaching fel, 84. *Mem:* Optical Soc Am; Am Phys Soc; Am Chem Soc; Am Soc Mass Spectrometry; Soc Appl Spectros. *Res:* Laser-induced selective ionization of small biologicals and peptides for supersonic beam spectroscopy studies and mass spectrometry. *Mailing Add:* Dept Chem Univ Mich 930 N University Ann Arbor MI 48109. *Fax:* 313-747-4685

LUBORSKY, FRED EVERETT, PHYSICAL CHEMISTRY. *Current Pos:* PVT CONSULT, 92- *Personal Data:* b Philadelphia, Pa, May 14, 23; m 46; c 3. *Educ:* Univ Pa, BS, 47; Ill Inst Technol, PhD(phys chem), 52. *Honors & Awards:* Distinguished lectr, Inst Elec & Electronics Engrs, 79; Centennial Medal, Inst Elec & Electronics Engrs, 84. *Prof Exp:* Asst chemist, Ill Inst Technol, 47-51; res assoc res lab, Gen Elec Co, 51-52, phys chemist instrument dept, 52-55, physicist appl physics unit, 55-58, phys chemist, Res & Develop Ctr, 58-92. *Concurrent Pos:* Mem, Div Eng & Indust Res, Nat Acad Sci, 52-55; co-chmn, Tech Prog Comt, Int Conf Magnetism, 67; ed-in-chief, IEEE Trans Magnetics, 72-75; pres, Magnetics Soc, Inst Elec & Electronics Engrs, 75-77; gen chmn, Second Joint Int Conf Magnetics, Magnetism & Magnetic Mat Conf, 79; chmn adv comt, Conf Magnetism & Magnetic Mat, 80; Coolidge fel, Res & Develop, Gen Elec Co. *Mem:* Nat Acad Eng; Am Chem Soc; Am Phys Soc; fel Inst Elec & Electronics Engrs; NY Acad Sci; Am Inst Chemists; Res Soc; fel Brit Sci Res Coun; AAAS. *Res:* Nucleation and growth of sub-micron size particles; development of single domain particle permanent magnetic materials; electrochemistry; magnetism; magnetic thin films; amorphous magnetic materials; magnetic separation; magnetic-optic materials; preparation and properties of magnetic materials; superconducting materials. *Mailing Add:* 1162 Lowell Rd Schenectady NY 12308

LUBORSKY, JUDITH LEE, MEMBRANE RECEPTORS, CELL FUNCTIONS. *Current Pos:* ASSOC PROF DIR ENDOCRINOL, ROCHE MED CTR, 93- *Educ:* State Univ NY, Albany, PhD(biol), 75. *Prof Exp:* Asst prof obstet & gynec, Yale Univ, 76-93. *Res:* Cellular endocrinology. *Mailing Add:* 641 W Oakdale Ave Chicago IL 60657

LUBOWE, ANTHONY G(ARNER), CONNECTORS. *Current Pos:* mem tech staff, 61-73, TECH MGR, AT&T BELL LABS, 73- *Personal Data:* b New York, NY, Dec 21, 37; m 59, Joan Kramer; c David & Jennifer. *Educ:* Columbia Univ, AB, 57, BS, 58, MS, 59, EngScD(eng mech), 61. *Prof Exp:* Res asst, Sch Eng, Columbia Univ, 60-61. *Concurrent Pos:* Dir, Int Electronics Packaging Soc, 90-93; corp dir, Int Inst Connector & Interconnection Technol. *Mem:* Am Soc Mech Engrs; Int Electronics Packaging Soc; Int Inst Connectors Interconnection Technol. *Res:* Elasticity; orbit prediction; electronic assembly; electronic packaging. *Mailing Add:* Berg Electronics 67 Whippany Rd Rm 8C-027 Whippany NJ 07981. *Fax:* 973-386-2084; *E-Mail:* a.g.lubowe@att.com

LUBOWSKY, JACK, BIOMATHEMATICS. *Current Pos:* res assoc, State Univ NY Health Sci Ctr, 66-67, instr med comput sci, 67-70, assoc proc comput sci & biophys, 70-72, Dept Neurol, 72-73, DIR, SCI COMPUT CTR, STATE UNIV NY HEALTH SCI CTR, BROOKLYN, 73- *Personal Data:* b Brooklyn, NY, July 11, 40. *Educ:* City Col New York, BEE, 62; Polytech Inst Brooklyn, MSEE, 66, PhD(elec eng), 73. *Prof Exp:* Engr, Brookhaven Nat Labs, 61-62; proj engr, Airborne Instruments Lab, 62-66. *Concurrent Pos:* Co-investr, Spec Res Resources Div Biomath Comput Ctr, NIH, 72-73, prin investr, 73-75; asst prof, Dept Neurol, Down State Med Ctr, 73-78, assoc prof, Dept Neurol, 78-, Dept Biophys, 80-; congressional sci fel, AAAS & Inst Elec & Electronics Engrs, 83; sci adv, Sen Subcomt on Energy. *Mem:* Sr mem Inst Elec & Electronics Engrs; AAAS; Sigma Xi. *Res:* Application of computers to biomedical research; investigation of adaptive and optimal search techniques to the determination of recognition properties of visual system neurons. *Mailing Add:* 2064 Beverly Way Merrick NY 11566-5416

LUBY, ELLIOT DONALD, PSYCHIATRY, LAW. *Current Pos:* prof law, 62-76, PROF PSYCHIAT, WAYNE STATE UNIV, 65-; CHIEF PSYCHIAT, HARPER HOSP, 78- *Personal Data:* b Detroit, Mich, Apr 3, 24; m 50; c 3. *Educ:* Univ Mo-Columbia, BS, 47; Wash Univ, MD, 49; Am Bd Psychiat & Neurol, dipl, 57. *Honors & Awards:* Gold Medal Award, Am Acad Psychosom Med, 62; Nancy Roeske Med Stud Teaching Award, Am Psychiat Asn, 93. *Prof Exp:* Resident psychiat, Menninger Found, 50-51; sr asst surgeon, USPHS, 51-52; resident psychiat, Yale Univ, 52-54; chief adult inpatient sect, Lafayette Clin, Detroit, 57-62, assoc dir in chg clin serv, 62. *Concurrent Pos:* Prof law, Wayne State Univ, 80- *Mem:* NY Acad Sci; AMA; Am Psychiat Asn; Am Psychosom Soc; fel Am Col Psychiat. *Res:* Psychopharmacology; drug induced model psychoses and sleep deprivation; law and psychiatry; schizophrenia. *Mailing Add:* Dept Psychiat Wayne State Univ Detroit MI 48202

LUBY, PATRICK JOSEPH, AGRICULTURAL ECONOMICS. *Current Pos:* ADJ PROF, AGR & APPL ECON DEPT & ANIMAL SCI DEPT, UNIV WIS, 92-; ECON & MGT CONSULT, 92- *Personal Data:* b Zanesville, Ohio, May 20, 30; m 56, Margaret H Jauron; c James J, Julie M, Mary P & Robert J. *Educ:* Univ Dayton, BA, 52; Purdue Univ, MS, 54, PhD(agr econ), 56. *Prof Exp:* Instr agr econ, Purdue Univ, 54-56, asst prof, 56-58; economist, Oscar Mayer & Co, 58-66, gen mgr provisions, 66-71, gen mgr provisions & procurement, 71-74, vpres, 72-92, corp economist, 74-92. *Mem:* Am Agr Econ Asn. *Res:* Use of statistical methods to analyze and forecast meat and livestock supplies and prices; efficient marketing of livestock and meats. *Mailing Add:* 4506 Woods Ende Madison WI 53711

LUBY, ROBERT JAMES, OBSTETRICS & GYNECOLOGY. *Current Pos:* assoc dir obstet & gynec, Creighton Univ, 69-72, chmn dept, 72-77, prof, 69-96, EMER PROF OBSTET & GYNEC, CREIGHTON UNIV, 96- *Personal Data:* b Kansas City, Mo, Apr 13, 28; m 51; c 8. *Educ:* Rockhurst Col, BS, 48; Creighton Univ, MD, 52, MS, 59. *Prof Exp:* Intern obstet & gynec, Creighton Mem St Joseph Hosp, Omaha, 52-53, resident, 55-58; assoc prof, Col Med, Univ Nebr, 68-69. *Mem:* AMA; Am Col Obstet & Gynec; Am Col Surg. *Res:* Nutritional aspects of infectious perinatal morbidity and mortality. *Mailing Add:* 9230 Burt St Omaha NE 68114

LUBY, STEFAN, PHYSICS, SOLID STATE PHYSICS. *Current Pos:* Sci co-worker, Inst Elec Eng, Slovak Acad Sci, 69-83, dir, Inst Physics, 84-92, mem presidium, 92-93, first vpres, 93-94, actg pres, 94-95, PRES, SLOVAK ACAD SCI, 95- *Personal Data:* b Bratislava, Slovak Repub, May 6, 41; m 66, Zelmira Kosorinova; c Martina & Barbora. *Educ:* Slovak Tech Univ, dipl, 63, CSc, 69, PhD, 69; Slovak Acad Sci, DSc, 82. *Hon Degrees:* Doc Habil, Comenius Univ, 92; Dr(physics), Univ Lecce, Italy. *Honors & Awards:* Science Prize, Slovak Acad Sci, 83; Humboldt Medal, Ger; Socius Ordinarius, Acad Europaea Sci & Arts, 96. *Concurrent Pos:* Vis scientist, USSR Acad Sci, 69 & Tech Univ, Ger, 78; vis prof, Univ Lecce, 85-96, Univ Syracuse, 91 & Univ Chiba, Japan, 93; hon prof, Slovak Tech Univ, 96. *Mem:* Am Phys Soc; Slovak Acad Sci; Int Soc Optical Eng. *Res:* Unipolar integrated circuits; amorphous semiconductors; superconductors; metallic thin films and multilayers; electronics; ration in metallic films; multi-layered mirrors for x-ray optics; patentee in field. *Mailing Add:* Inst Physics-Slovak Acad Sci Dubravska 9 Bratislava 84228 Slovak Republic. *Fax:* 421-7-395689; *E-Mail:* luby@savba.sk

LUCANSKY, TERRY WAYNE, BOTANY, PLANT MORPHOLOGY. *Current Pos:* ASSOC PROF BOT, UNIV FLA, 71- *Personal Data:* b Massillon, Ohio, Aug 21, 42; m 66; c 1. *Educ:* Univ SC, BS, 64, MS, 67; Duke Univ, PhD(bot), 71. *Mem:* Bot Soc Am; Am Fern Soc; Am Inst Biol Sci; Sigma Xi; Torrey Bot Club. *Res:* Comparative anatomical and morphological studies of tropical pteridophytes; anatomical studies of aquatic plants and vines in relation to their habit and habitat; pteridology. *Mailing Add:* Dept Bot 220 Bartram Hall Univ Fla Gainesville FL 32611-2009

LUCANTONI, DAVID MICHAEL, COMPUTATIONAL PROBABILITY. *Current Pos:* MEM TECH STAFF, BELL LABS, 81- *Personal Data:* b Baltimore Md, Aug 31, 54. *Educ:* Towson State Univ, BS, 76; Univ Del, MS, 78, PhD(opers res), 82. *Mem:* Opers Res Soc Am; Math Asn Am; Am Math Soc. *Res:* Computationally stable algorithms for the solution of complex stochastic models such as those arising in the theory of queues. *Mailing Add:* Isoquantic Technologies 10 Oak Tree Lane Wayside NJ 07712

LUCAS, ALEXANDER RALPH, CHILD PSYCHIATRY. *Current Pos:* head, 71-81, CONSULT SECT CHILD & ADOLESCENT PSYCHIAT, MAYO CLIN, 71-; PROF PSYCHIAT, MAYO MED SCH, 76- *Personal Data:* b Vienna, Austria, July 30, 31; US citizen; m 56, Margaret A Thompson; c Thomas A, Nance E (Watson), Alexander E & Peter C. *Educ:* Mich State Univ, BS, 53; Univ Mich, MD, 57. *Prof Exp:* Rotating intern, Univ Mich Hosp, 57-58; resident child psychiat, Hawthorn Ctr, Northville, Mich, 58-59 & 61-62; from staff child psychiatrist to sr psychiatrist, 62-67; from asst prof to assoc prof psychiat, Wayne State Univ, 67-71; assoc prof, May Med Sch, 73-76. *Concurrent Pos:* Res child psychiatrist & res coordr, Lafayette Clin, Detroit, 67-71; consult, State of Minn Dept Pub Welfare, 72-80 & NIMH, 74-77. *Mem:* Am Orthop Asn; Am Psychiat Asn; Am Acad Child Psychiat; Soc Prof Child Psychiat; Soc Biol Psychiat. *Res:* Biologic aspects of child psychiatry; eating disorders. *Mailing Add:* Mayo Clin Rochester MN 55905. *Fax:* 507-284-4158

LUCAS, CAROL N, BIOMEDICAL MATHEMATICS. *Current Pos:* res asst biomed math & eng, Univ NC, Chapel Hill, 67-68, res assoc, Div Cardiothoracic Surg, 72, lectr biomed math & eng, 76-77, from asst prof to assoc prof, 77-89, actg chair biomed eng, 90-92, PROF SURG & BIOMED MATH & ENG, UNIV NC, CHAPEL HILL, 89-, CHAIR BIOMED ENG, 92- *Personal Data:* b Aberdeen, SDak, Feb 13, 40; m 61; c 2. *Educ:* Dakota Wesleyan Univ, BA, 61; Univ Ariz, MS, 67; Univ NC, Chapel Hill, PhD(biomed math, eng), 73. *Prof Exp:* Jr systs analyst, Cargill, Inc, Minneapolis, 62-65. *Concurrent Pos:* High sch teacher, US Army Educ Ctr, Furth, Ger, 61-62; teaching asst, Dept Math & Eng, Univ Ariz, 65-67, comput lab asst, 66-67; prof surg & prof applied sci. *Mem:* Am Heart Asn; Sigma Xi; Biomed Eng Soc; Inst Elec & Electronics Engrs; Cardiovasc Systs Dynamics Soc. *Res:* Mathematical modelling and computer simulation of physiological systems; digital processing of dynamic physiological data. *Mailing Add:* Dept Biomed & Eng Univ NC Chapel Hill NC 27599-7575. *E-Mail:* clucas@bme.unc.edu

LUCAS, COLIN ROBERT, COORDINATION CHEMISTRY. *Current Pos:* from asst prof to assoc prof, 74-93, PROF CHEM, MEM UNIV, NFLD, 93-, HEAD, DEPT CHEM, 97- *Personal Data:* b Toronto, Can, Oct 11, 43; m 69; c Neil, Stephen & Lesley. *Educ:* Acadia Univ, BSc, 68, MSc, 69; Oxford Univ, PhD(organometallic chem), 72. *Prof Exp:* Res fel, Univ Alta, 73-74. *Mem:* Fel Chem Inst Can. *Res:* Synthesis and properties of organometallic and coordination compounds containing sulphur; catalysis; liquid crystals. *Mailing Add:* Dept Chem Mem Univ St John's NF A1B 3X7 Can. *E-Mail:* rlucas@plato.ucs.mun.ca

LUCAS, DAVID OWEN, IMMUNOLOGY, BUSINESS DEVELOPMENT. *Current Pos:* PRES, PEDIAPHARM CORP, 94- *Personal Data:* b Orange, Calif, Oct 19, 42; m 84, Linda Workman; c Philip, Alan & Jason. *Educ:* Duke Univ, BA, 64, PhD(microbiol, immunol), 69. *Prof Exp:* From asst prof to assoc prof microbiol & immunol, Col Med, Univ Ariz, 70-86; vpres, Protein Technol, Petaluma, 86-90; vpres, Children's Hosp Oakland, 91-94. *Concurrent Pos:* Res fel immunol, Children's Hosp Med Ctr, Harvard Med Sch, 68-70, actg dept head, 77-79. *Mem:* AAAS; Am Asn Immunologists; Am Soc Microbiol; Licensing Exec Soc. *Res:* Cellular immunology; lymphocyte metabolism; interferon; hybridomas; nutritionals and pharmaceuticals development. *Mailing Add:* 686 Los Palos Dr Lafayette CA 94549-5357. *Fax:* 510-283-0919

LUCAS, DOUGLAS M, FORENSIC SCIENCE. *Current Pos:* RETIRED. *Personal Data:* b Windsor, Ont, May 5, 29; m 53, Marie Macdonald; c 5. *Educ:* Univ Toronto, BSc, 53, MSc, 57. *Honors & Awards:* Adelaide Medal, Int Asn Forensic Sci, 90; Gradwohl Medal, Am Acad Forensic Sci, 95; Derome Medal, Can Soc Forensic Sci, 96. *Prof Exp:* Dir, Ctr Forensic Sci, 67-94. *Concurrent Pos:* Chmn, Comt Alcohol & Drugs, Nat Safety Coun, 77-79; vpres, Int Comt Alcohol, Drugs & Traffic Safety, 84-86. *Mem:* Can Soc Forensic Sci (pres, 68-69); Am Acad Forensic Sci (pres, 72-73); Int Asn Forensic Sci (pres, 67-69); Am Soc Crime Lab Dirs (pres, 77-78). *Res:* Alcohol, drugs and traffic safety; investigation of fires and explosions; forensic science. *Mailing Add:* 5280 Lakeshore Rd No 1111 Burlington ON L7L 5R1 Can. *Fax:* 416-314-3225

LUCAS, EDGAR ARTHUR, ANATOMY, NEUROPHYSIOLOGY. *Current Pos:* DIR, SLEEP DISORDERS CTR, ALL SAINTS EPISCOPAL HOSP, 84- *Personal Data:* b Franklin, Ind, Oct 28, 33; m 60; c 2. *Educ:* Ball State Univ, BA, 61, MS, 65; Univ Calif, PhD(anat), 72. *Prof Exp:* Teacher, Sch, Town of Griffith, 61-62; planner admin, Rocketdyne Div, NAm Rockwell Corp, 62-63, assoc res engr, 64-65; from instr to assoc prof anat, Univ Ark Med Ctr, Little Rock, 72-84. *Concurrent Pos:* Mem comt Polysomnography Asn Sleep Disorder Ctrs, 76-87. *Mem:* Inc Soc Chronobiol; Asn Psychophysiol Study Sleep; Am Asn Anat; Sigma Xi; Clin Sleep Soc; Asn Prof Sleep Socs. *Res:* Biological rhythms; sleep; neurosciences. *Mailing Add:* Sleep Dis Ctr All Sts Episcopal Hosp PO Box 31 Ft Worth TX 76101-0031

LUCAS, FREDERICK VANCE, JR, BLOOD COAGULATION & THROMBOSIS, HEMATOLOGY. *Current Pos:* Res path, 75-79, staff physician, Lab Hemat, 79-88, CHMN DEPT PATH & LAB MED, CLEVELAND CLIN FLA, 88- *Personal Data:* b Rochester, NY, Nov 27, 49; m 75, Johna D; c William & Robert. *Educ:* Amherst Col, BA, 71; Univ Mo, MD, 75. *Concurrent Pos:* Dir Sch Med Technol, Cleveland Clin Found, 79-83; prin investr, Am Heart Asn, 83; coun hemat, Am Soc Clin Pathologist, 82-87; coagulation resource comt, Col Am Pathologist, 83-85; clin asst prof, Case Western Res Univ, Sch Med, 84-; co investr, NIH, 87- *Mem:* Am Heart Asn; Int Acad Path; Am Soc Hemat; AAAS. *Res:* Clinical coagulation and role of soluble fibrin in cardiovascular disease, specifically the contribution of tissue transglutamivase to crosslinking fibrin; fibrinogen in blood of patients with vascular occlusion; development of flowing whole blood model of clotlysis. *Mailing Add:* Cleveland Clin Fla 3000 W Cypress Creek Rd Ft Lauderdale FL 33309

LUCAS, GENE ALLAN, GENETICS. *Current Pos:* asst prof, 68-74, ASSOC PROF BIOL, DRAKE UNIV, 74- *Personal Data:* b Des Moines, Iowa, Oct 15, 28; m 48; c 3. *Educ:* Drake Univ, BA, 54, MA, 58; Iowa State Univ, PhD(genetics), 68. *Prof Exp:* Lab instr biol, Drake Univ, 54-59, instr, 60-67; asst genetics, Iowa State Univ, 61-66. *Mem:* AAAS; Genetics Soc Am; Int Oceanog Found. *Res:* Pigmentation, especially of aquarium fish; pigment genetics of Siamese fighting fish; application of biological principles to world problems; race and population problems; teaching; biology and behavior of Siamese fighting fish. *Mailing Add:* Dept Biol Drake Univ 2507 University Ave Des Moines IA 50311-4516

LUCAS, GEORGE BLANCHARD, plant pathology; deceased, see previous edition for last biography

LUCAS, GEORGE BOND, GEOCHEMISTRY. *Current Pos:* from asst prof to prof, 56-88, EMER PROF, COLO SCH MINES, 88- *Personal Data:* b New Orleans, La, Dec 21, 24; m 62; c 1. *Educ:* Tulane Univ, BS, 48; Iowa State Univ, PhD(chem), 52. *Prof Exp:* Postdoctoral fel, Northwestern Univ, 52-53; res chemist, Red Stong Arsenal Res Div, Rohm & Haas Co, 53-56. *Mem:* Am Chem Soc; Sigma Xi. *Res:* Reaction mechanisms organic particularly free radical mechanisms. *Mailing Add:* Dept Chem & Geochem Colo Sch Mines Golden CO 80401

LUCAS, GLENN E, MECHANICAL PROPERTIES OF MATERIALS. *Current Pos:* from asst prof to assoc prof, 78-87, PROF NUCLEAR ENG, UNIV CALIF, SANTA BARBARA, 87- *Personal Data:* b Los Angeles, Calif, Mar 8, 51; m 72; c 3. *Educ:* Univ Calif, Santa Barbara, BS, 73; Mass Inst Technol, MS, 75, ScD(nuclear eng), 77. *Honors & Awards:* Young Eng Achievement Award, Am Nuclear Soc, 91. *Prof Exp:* Engr, Exxon Nuclear, Inc, 78. *Concurrent Pos:* Prin investr, numerous res contracts, 78-; consult, govt & private bus, 78-; vis res prof, Tokyo Univ, 85, Hokkaido Univ, 85. *Mem:* Am Nuclear Soc; Am Soc Metals; AAAS; Sigma Xi; Mat Res Soc; Am Soc Testing & Mat. *Res:* Effects of environment on microstructural evolution; mechanical properties of structural steels and composite materials. *Mailing Add:* 529 Dorset Goleta CA 93117-1643. *Fax:* 805-893-4731; *E-Mail:* gene@squid.ucsb.edu

LUCAS, GLENNARD RALPH, ORGANIC POLYMER CHEMISTRY. *Current Pos:* RETIRED. *Personal Data:* b Marissa, Ill, Feb 22, 16; m 41; c 2. *Educ:* Monmouth Col, BS, 38; Columbia Univ, PhD(phys org chem), 42. *Prof Exp:* Asst chem, Monmouth Col, 36-38 & Columbia Univ, 38-41; res chemist, Gen Elec Co, Mass, 42-52, process engr, NY, 52-54, suprvr process eng, 54-56, mgr adv proj develop, Mass, 56-58; res dir, Signode Corp, 58-81. *Mem:* AAAS; Am Chem Soc; Am Mgt Asn; Soc Plastics Eng. *Res:* Mechanisms of organic reactions; polymer studies of styrene and silicone resins; plastic and steel strapping materials; high speed paint cure. *Mailing Add:* 1011 Hunter Rd Glenview IL 60025-3311

LUCAS, HENRY C, JR, INFORMATION TECHNOLOGY. *Current Pos:* assoc prof computer applications & info systs, Schs Bus, NY Univ, 74-78, prof & chmn, 78-84, prof info systs, Grad Sch Bus Admin, 84-88, RES PROF INFO SYSTS, LEONARD N STERN SCH BUS, NY UNIV, 88- *Personal Data:* b Omaha, Nebr, Sept 4, 44; m 68, Ellen Kuhbach; c Scott & Jonathan. *Educ:* Yale Univ, BS, 66; Mass Inst Technol, MS, 68, PhD, 70. *Prof Exp:* Consult, Arthur D Little, Inc, Cambridge, Mass, 66-70; asst prof computer & info systs, Grad Sch Bus, Stanford Univ, 70-74. *Concurrent Pos:* Ed, Sloan Mgt Rev, 67-68, Performance Eval Rev, 72-73; Chmn, Working Group Interaction of Info Systs & the Orgn, Int Fedn Info Processing, 75-80; assoc ed, Mis Quarterly, 78-83, Mgt Sci, 85-87, Asn Comput Mach Trans on Off, Info & Mgt; on leave, Europ Systs Res Inst, IBM, La Hulpe, Belgium, 81; vis prof, INSEAD, Fontainebleau, France, 85; vis researcher, Bell Commun Res, NJ, 91. *Mem:* Asn Comput Mach; Inst Mgt Sci; Inst Elec & Electronics Engrs; Asn Info Syst. *Res:* Information technology and organizations; information systems implementation; expert systems; value of technology; impact of technology; organization design. *Mailing Add:* 18 Portland Rd Summit NJ 07901. *Fax:* 212-995-4228; *E-Mail:* hlucas@stern.nyu.edu

LUCAS, J RICHARD, MINING & MINERAL ENGINEERING. *Current Pos:* RETIRED. *Personal Data:* b Scottdale, Pa, May 3, 29; m 52, Joan Hathaway; c Eric Scott & Jay Hathaway. *Educ:* Waynesburg Col, BS, 51; WVa Univ, BS, 52; Univ Pittsburgh, MS, 54; Columbia Univ, PhD(mining eng), 65. *Honors & Awards:* Donald S Kingery Award. *Prof Exp:* Miner, Crucible Steel Co Am, 48-52; field engr, Joy Mfg Co, 52-54; mem fac mining eng, Ohio State Univ, 54-56, head div, 57-61; head dept, Va Polytech Inst & State Univ, 61-71, head, Div Minerals Eng, 71-76, head, Dept Mining &

Minerals Eng, 76-87, Massey prof mining & minerals eng, 87-92. *Concurrent Pos:* Dir, US Off Coal Res Proj, Va Polytech Inst & State Univ, 62-; actg asst dir, Va Eng Exp Sta, 63-64; mem secy's res adv coun coal miner's health, HEW, 70-73; consult & reviewer, Prog Comn, Mining Safety & Health Admin, Dept Labor, 69-, NSF, 73-74, 76-77 & Ad-Hoc Panel Coal Mining Technol, Nat Res Coun, 75-78; mem, Joint Comt Coal Mining Health, Safety & Res, Mining Safety & Health Admin, US Dept Labor & Bur Mines, US Dept Interior, 70-, rev comt, Fel Prog Mining & Minerals Eng & Conserv, Off Educ, HEW, Wash DC, 79, prog comt, State Mine Recovery Competition, Div Mines, Va Mining Inst, 78-, ad hoc comt coal mine safety, Dept Indust & Resources, 79, Coal Conversion Fac, 79, exec comt, Va Mining & Mineral Resources Res Inst, 79-; coordr, Va Ctr Coal & Energy Res, Coal Inst, 77-; dir, Generic Mineral Technol Ctr, Mine Systs Design & Ground Control, 82- *Mem:* Am Inst Mining, Metall & Petrol Engrs; AAAS; Asn Advan Invention & Innovation. *Res:* Mining systems engineering; mineral property evaluation; mining design and layout; computer applications in underground coal mining systems; coal mining safety research; methane from coal seams; underground coal-mining research. *Mailing Add:* 408 E Hemlock Dr Blacksburg VA 24060

LUCAS, JAMES M, STATISTICAL METHODOLOGY. *Current Pos:* SR CONSULT STATIST, E I DU PONT DE NEMOURS & CO, INC, 65- *Personal Data:* b Philipsburg, Pa, July 21, 41. *Educ:* Pa State Univ, BS, 63; Yale Univ, MS, 65; Tex A&M Univ, PhD(statist), 72. *Honors & Awards:* Brumbaugh Award, Am Soc Qual Control, 76. *Concurrent Pos:* Adj prof, Univ Del, 72-; assoc ed, Technometrics, 81-, J Qual Technol, 83-, Chemometrics & Intelligent Lab Systs, 88; past pres, Del chap, Am Statist Asn. *Mem:* Fel Am Statist Asn; Am Soc Qual Control. *Res:* Methods for the control and improvement of industrial processes; cumulative sum techniques; experimental designs. *Mailing Add:* 5120 New Kent Rd Wilmington DE 19808

LUCAS, JAMES ROBERT, GEOLOGY. *Current Pos:* mgr, Spatial Analysis Lab, Lockheed Eng & Sci Co, Las Vegas, Nev, 90-94; DIR REMOTE SENSING, LOCKHEED STENNIS OPER, MISS, 94- *Personal Data:* b Mankato, Minn, Apr 26, 47. *Educ:* Mankato State Univ, BA, 69; Univ Iowa, MA, 73, PhD(geol), 77. *Prof Exp:* Instr earth sci, Providence Sch, South St Paul, Minn, 69-70; res geologist, Iowa Geol Surv, 75-76; appln scientist water resources, Earth Resources Observ Systs Data Ctr, SDak, 76-80, prin applns scientist geol, 80-81; vpres, Centaur Explor, Inc, Amarillo, Tex, 81-83; gen partner, Orion, Ltd, Midland, Tex, 83-87, owner, 87-90. *Concurrent Pos:* Adj instr geol, Univ Iowa, 75-76; prin investr, NASA contract, 75-76; adj fac, Univ Tex Permian Basin, 84-85 & Univ Nev, Las Vegas, 91- *Mem:* Am Soc Photogrammetry; Sigma Xi. *Res:* Remote sensing techniques applied to hydrocarbon, minerals and water resources exploration; Landsat digital image processing for natural resources analysis and interpretation; photographic enhancement of Landsat imagery for geological applications; land classification of Southeast Iowa from computer enhanced Landsat images; glacial geomorphology of Northwest Iowa; semi-quantitative analysis of clay minerals by x-ray diffraction. *Mailing Add:* Lockheed Stennis Oper Stennis Space Ctr MS 39529

LUCAS, JEFFREY ROBERT, OPTIMAL FORAGING THEORY, ENERGY REGULATION. *Current Pos:* asst prof, 87-94, ASSOC PROF, PURDUE UNIV, 94- *Personal Data:* b Rockville Center, NY, Jan, 53; m, Lynda Peterson; c Nicole. *Educ:* Fla Inst Technol, BS, 75; Univ Fla, MS, 78, PhD(zool), 83. *Prof Exp:* NATO fel, Oxford Univ, 83-84; vis asst prof, Col William & Mary, 84-86, Univ Redlands, 86-87. *Concurrent Pos:* Prin investr, NSF, 93. *Mem:* Animal Behav Soc; AAAS; Am Soc Naturalists; Ecol Soc Am; Sigma Xi; Int Soc Behav Ecol. *Res:* Ecological implications of energy regulation and food hoarding in birds and mammals; use of dynamic programming to study foraging behavior and life-history tactics. *Mailing Add:* Dept Biol Sci Purdue Univ West Lafayette IN 47907-1392. *E-Mail:* jlucas@bilbo.bio.purdue.edu

LUCAS, JOE NATHAN, CHROMOSOMAL FLOW CYTOMETRY. *Current Pos:* SR SCIENTIST, LAWRENCE LIVERMORE NAT LAB, UNIV CALIF, 78-; PROF, CALIF STATE UNIV, 96- *Personal Data:* b Lake Providence, La, Dec 18, 45; c 1. *Educ:* Univ Calif, Los Angeles, BS, 70, MS, 72, PhD(biophysics), 77. *Prof Exp:* Sci instr math & sci, Mill Col, 72-76; scientist & engr, Lawrence Berkeley Nat Lab, Univ Calif, 77-78; instr physics, Calif State Univ, 78-79. *Concurrent Pos:* Chmn bd, The Lucas Educ Found, Inc, 78-; Fulbright scholar, 77. *Mem:* Soc Analytical Cytometry; Radiation Res Soc. *Res:* Biological dosimetry: rapid image analysis to quantify chromosome aberrations (translocations) in man using chromosome specific probes; slit-scan and fringe-scan flow cytometers to measure the distribution of flourescent dye(s) along isolated chromosomes; flow cytometric devices and procedures for rapid, quantitative classification of chromosomes according to shape and/or flourescent band patterns. *Mailing Add:* Lawrence Livermore Nat Lab PO Box 808 L-4527 Livermore CA 94550

LUCAS, JOHN J, BIOCHEMISTRY, MOLECULAR BIOLOGY. *Current Pos:* PROF & DIR RES, HEALTH SCI CTR, STATE UNIV NY, 89- *Mailing Add:* Biochem & Molecular Biol Health Sci Ctr State Univ NY 766 Irving Ave Syracuse NY 13210-1605. *Fax:* 315-464-8750

LUCAS, JOHN PAUL, MICROBIOLOGY. *Current Pos:* MICROBIOLOGIST, FOOD & DRUG ADMIN, 74- *Personal Data:* b Youngstown, Ohio, Nov 16, 45; m 68. *Educ:* Univ Pittsburgh, BS, 67, MS, 69, ScD(microbiol), 73. *Prof Exp:* Res assoc virol, Grad Sch Pub Health, Univ Pittsburgh, 74. *Mem:* Am Soc Microbiol; Sigma Xi. *Res:* Develop growing area standards for shellfish. *Mailing Add:* Attn: Kathleen Carey Compensation Br Park Lawn Bldg Rm 4-50 5600 Fishers Lane Rockville MD 20857

LUCAS, JOHN W, MECHANICAL ENGINEERING, HEAT TRANSFER. *Current Pos:* RETIRED. *Personal Data:* b Pomona, Calif, Mar 14, 23; m 53, Genevieve Marie Blessent; c 3. *Educ:* Univ Calif, Berkeley, BS, 48; Univ Calif, Los Angeles, MS, 49, PhD(mech eng), 53. *Prof Exp:* NSF fel, Fritzhaber Inst, Berlin, Ger, 53-54; sr res engr, Jet Propulsion Lab, Calif Inst Technol, 54-59, group supvr, 59-65, res rep eng mech, 66-70, mgr res & planetary quarantine, 70-74, exec asst to dir, 74-76, mgr point focus distributed receiver solar energy technol proj, 76-85. *Mem:* Am Inst Aeronaut & Astronaut; Sigma Xi. *Res:* Ice nucleation in lemons; spacecraft advanced propulsion; radiation, conduction and convection heat transfer as related to spacecraft thermal control in space, on the moon and planets, and in solar thermal energy. *Mailing Add:* 865 Canterbury Rd San Marino CA 91108

LUCAS, KENNETH ROSS, ANALYTICAL CHEMISTRY, POLYMER PHYSICS. *Current Pos:* Res chemist, 66-71, sr res chemist, 71-81, ASSOC SCIENTIST, FIRESTONE TIRE & RUBBER CO, 81- *Personal Data:* b Bradford, Pa, June 4, 39; m 61; c 4. *Educ:* Univ Pittsburgh, BS, 61; Univ Ill, MS, 64, PhD(analytical chem), 66. *Mem:* Polymer Chem Div, Am Chem Soc, Rubber Div; Electron Micros Soc Am. *Res:* Molten salt and organic electrochemistry; x-ray diffraction; polymer physics; electro-organic synthesis; polymer morphology analysis; radiothermoluminescence; scanning electron microscopy; ESCA/Auger spectroscopy. *Mailing Add:* 314 Silver Ridge Akron OH 44321-1228

LUCAS, LEON THOMAS, PLANT PATHOLOGY, MICROBIOLOGY. *Current Pos:* from asst prof to assoc prof, 68-80, PROF PLANT PATH, NC STATE UNIV, 80- *Personal Data:* b Halifax, NC, July 30, 42; m 64; c 1. *Educ:* NC State Univ, BS, 64; Univ Calif, Davis, PhD(plant path), 68. *Prof Exp:* Res asst plant path, Univ Calif, Davis, 64-68. *Mem:* Am Phytopath Soc. *Res:* Diseases of turfgrasses and forage crops in North Carolina; bacterial diseases of plants. *Mailing Add:* Dept Plant Path NC State Univ Box 7616 Raleigh NC 27695-0001

LUCAS, LINDA C, BIOMEDICAL ENGINEERING, BIOMATERIALS. *Current Pos:* Orthop res asst, 78-82, PROF BIOMED ENG, UNIV ALA, BIRMINGHAM, 82- *Personal Data:* b Waltham, Mass, 1950. *Educ:* Univ Ala, BS, 71. *Mem:* Soc Biomat; Acad Dent Mat. *Mailing Add:* Sch Eng Univ Ala 1717 Seventh Ave S Birmingham AL 35294-0001

LUCAS, MARK ALAN, PHOTONUCLEAR REACTIONS, NUCLEON STRUCTURE. *Current Pos:* POSTDOCTORAL RES ASSOC, PHYSICS DEPT, UNIV SC, 94- *Personal Data:* b Santa Barbara, Calif, Apr 21, 64; m 91, Jodie Gordon; c Ryan. *Educ:* Purdue Univ, BS, 86; Univ Ill, Urbana-Champaign, PhD(physics), 94. *Concurrent Pos:* Guest scientist, Brookhaven Nat Lab, 94- *Mem:* Am Phys Soc. *Res:* Photopion production and nuclear compton scattering in the region of the delta resonance at the LEGS polarized photon source; studying nucleon structure. *Mailing Add:* Physics Lab Legs Group Brookhaven Nat Lab Upton NY 11973. *E-Mail:* lucas@bnl.gov

LUCAS, MYRON CRAN, BIOCHEMICAL GENETICS. *Current Pos:* from asst prof to assoc prof, 78-88, PROF BIOL, LA STATE UNIV, SHREVEPORT, 88- *Personal Data:* b Cincinnati, Ohio, Nov 15, 46. *Educ:* Lewis & Clark Col, BS, 69; Wash State Univ, PhD(genetics), 74. *Prof Exp:* Res assoc bot, Univ Ill, Urbana, 73-75; res assoc genetics, Univ Ga, 75-77; res assoc biochem, Univ Idaho, 77-78. *Concurrent Pos:* Adj asst prof biol, Fla State Univ, 77. *Mem:* Genetics Soc Am; Am Soc Microbiol; NY Acad Sci; AAAS. *Res:* Biochemical genetics of Neurospora crassa; structure and function of low molecular weight RNA; gene regulation and synthesis of messenger RNA; characterization of egg jelly glycoproteins in salamanders. *Mailing Add:* Dept Biol Sci La State Univ Shreveport One University Pl Shreveport LA 71115-2301

LUCAS, ROBERT ALAN, MECHANICAL ENGINEERING. *Current Pos:* asst prof, 58-69, ASSOC PROF MECH ENG, LEHIGH UNIV, 69-, ASSOC CHMN, DEPT MECH ENG & MECH, 96- *Personal Data:* b Allentown, Pa, June 13, 35; m 57, Joanne A Wetherhold; c Michael J, Elizabeth A, Leslie A & Marya C. *Educ:* Lehigh Univ, BS, 57, MS, 59, PhD(mech eng), 64. *Prof Exp:* Design engr, Air Prod & Chem, Inc, Pa, 57-58. *Concurrent Pos:* Resident res assoc, Nat Res Coun-Naval Res Lab, DC, 65-66. *Mem:* Am Soc Mech Engrs; Sigma Xi. *Res:* Machine system simulation and analysis; expert systems; optimization; applied mathematics; dynamics; computer aided design; computer aided instruction; vibrations. *Mailing Add:* Dept Mech Eng & Mech Packard Lab Bldg 19 Lehigh Univ Bethlehem PA 18015. *Fax:* 610-758-6224; *E-Mail:* ral1@lehigh.edu

LUCAS, ROBERT ELMER, AGRONOMY, HORTICULTURE. *Current Pos:* RETIRED. *Personal Data:* b Malolos, Philippines, June 27, 16; m 41, Norma Schultz; c Richard, Raymond, Milton, Keith & Charles. *Educ:* Purdue Univ, BSA, 39, MS, 41; Mich State Col, PhD(soil sci), 47. *Prof Exp:* Asst soils, Va Truck Exp Sta, 41-43 & Mich State Col, 45-46; agronomist, Wm Gehring, Inc, Ind, 46-51 & 77-78; from assoc prof to prof soil sci, Mich State Univ, 51-77, exten specialist, 53-77, emer prof, 77-81. *Concurrent Pos:* Vis prof, Agr Inst, Dublin 5, Ireland, 70 & Univ Fla, 79-80. *Mem:* Fel Soil Sci Soc Am; fel Am Soc Agron; Int Peat Soc. *Res:* Micronutrients in crop production; soil organic matter dynamics and models; physical and chemical properties of organic soils (histosols); comparison of four management systems in vegetable production; plant nutrient requirements. *Mailing Add:* 3827 Dobie Rd Okemos MI 48864

LUCAS, ROBERT EMERSON, JR, ECONOMICS. *Current Pos:* lectr, 62-63, from assoc prof to prof, 67-80, JOHN DEWEY DISTINGUISHED SERV PROF ECON, CHICAGO UNIV, 80- *Personal Data:* b Yakima, Wash, 1937. *Educ:* Univ Chicago, BA, 59, PhD, 64. *Honors & Awards:* Nobel Prize in Econs, 95. *Prof Exp:* Asst prof econs, Carnegie-Mellon Univ, 63-67. *Concurrent Pos:* Ford Found fac fel, Univ Chicago, 66-67, vis res prof, 74-75; assoc ed, J Econ Theory, 72-78, J Monetary Econ, 77; ed, J Polit Theory, 78-81; vis prof econs, Northwestern Univ, 81-82; Guggenheim Found fel, 81-82. *Mem:* Nat Acad Sci; fel AAAS; Economet Soc. *Res:* Author of several books. *Mailing Add:* Dept Econ Univ Chicago 1126 E 59th St Chicago IL 60637

LUCAS, RUSSELL VAIL, JR, PEDIATRIC CARDIOLOGY. *Current Pos:* assoc prof, 66-69, PROF PEDIAT, UNIV MINN, MINNEAPOLIS, 69- *Personal Data:* b Des Moines, Iowa, Nov 2, 28; m 51; c 4. *Educ:* Macalester Col, BA, 50; Wash Univ, MD, 54. *Honors & Awards:* Distinguished Achievement Award, Am Heart Asn, 66. *Prof Exp:* From intern to resident pediat, Univ Hosp, Univ Minn, Minneapolis, 54-58, resident, 58-59; from asst prof to assoc prof pediat, Med Ctr, WVa Univ, 61-66. *Concurrent Pos:* NIH fel pediat cardiol, Univ Hosps, Univ Minn, Minneapolis, 59-61; NIH res career develop award, WVa Univ, 63-66. *Mem:* Soc Pediat Res; Am Acad Pediat; Asn Am Med Cols; Am Fedn Clin Res; AMA. *Res:* Physiology of ventricular function; pathology, physiology and natural history of congenital cardiac defects. *Mailing Add:* Pediat 284 Vchh Univ Minn Minneapolis MN 55455

LUCAS, THOMAS RAMSEY, MATHEMATICS. *Current Pos:* from instr to assoc prof, 69-85, PROF MATH, UNIV NC, CHARLOTTE, 85- *Personal Data:* b Tampa, Fla, June 9, 39; m 70; c 2. *Educ:* Univ Fla, BS, 61; Univ Mich, Ann Arbor, MS, 62; Ga Inst Technol, PhD(math), 70. *Prof Exp:* Sr engr, Martin Co, 62-65. *Mem:* Am Math Soc; Soc Indust & Appl Math. *Res:* Numerical analysis; approximation theory; spline theory. *Mailing Add:* 9516 Glenwater Dr Charlotte NC 28262

LUCAS, WILLIAM FRANKLIN, OPERATIONS RESEARCH, APPLIED MATHEMATICS. *Current Pos:* PROF MATH, CLAREMONT GRAD SCH, 84- *Personal Data:* b Detroit, Mich, Apr 21, 33; m 57, Carolyn Donovan; c Robert, Thomas, Joan & Daniel. *Educ:* Univ Detroit, BS, 54, MA, 56, MS, 58; Univ Mich, PhD(math), 63. *Honors & Awards:* Chautaugua Lectr, AAAA, 75-79. *Prof Exp:* Instr math, Univ Detroit, 56-58 & 61-62, asst prof, 62-63; res instr, Princeton Univ, 63-65; Fulbright fel & vis assoc prof econ & statist, Mid East Tech Univ, Ankara, 65-66; vis assoc prof, Math Res Ctr, Univ Wis-Madison, 66-67; mathematician, Rand Corp, 67-69; assoc prof opers res & appl math, Cornell Univ, 69-70, dir ctr appl math, 71-74, prof opers res & appl math & math, 70-84. *Concurrent Pos:* Consult, Rand Corp, 69-72 & Educ Develop Ctr, 75-79; sci exchange with USSR, US Nat Acad Sci, 76 & 83. *Mem:* Am Math Soc; Math Asn Am; Soc Indust & Appl Math; Asn Women Math; AAAS; Inst Opers Res & Mgt Sci. *Res:* Elasticity; applied mathematics; game theory. *Mailing Add:* 1598 Beloit Claremont CA 91711-3108. *E-Mail:* lucasw@cgs.edu

LUCAS, WILLIAM JOHN, PLANT PHYSIOLOGY, PLANT BIOPHYSICS. *Current Pos:* from asst prof to assoc prof plant physiol, 77-83, PROF BOT, UNIV CALIF, DAVIS, 83- *Personal Data:* b Adelaide, SAustralia, Feb 23, 45; m 67; c 4. *Educ:* Univ Adelaide, BSc, 71, PhD(plant physiol), 75, DSc(plant physiol), 90. *Prof Exp:* Res assoc, Dept Bot, Univ Toronto, 75-77. *Concurrent Pos:* Guest prof, Univ Gottingen, WGer, 84-85; NSF grant, 78-94; mem, Int Comt for Phloem Physiol, 84- *Mem:* Am Soc Plant Physiologists; Australian Soc Plant Physiologists; Can Soc Plant Physiologists; Bot Soc Am; Soc Exp Biol. *Res:* Biophysical and physiological aspects of transport across plant membranes, in particular the plasmalemma; cell-to-cell communication via plasmodesmata; role of plasmodesmata in virus infection; plasmodesmal trafficking of macromolecules in regulation of developmental and physiological processes. *Mailing Add:* Sect Plant Biol Univ Calif Div Biol Scis Davis CA 95616. *Fax:* 530-752-5410

LUCAS, WILLIAM R(AY), INORGANIC CHEMISTRY, MATERIALS SCIENCE ENGINEERING. *Current Pos:* AEROSPACE CONSULT, 86- *Personal Data:* b Newbern, Tenn, Mar 1, 22; m 48, Polly Torti; c Donna (Watts), William R Jr & Michael L. *Educ:* Memphis State Univ, BS, 43; Vanderbilt Univ, MS, 50, PhD(chem, metall), 52. *Hon Degrees:* DHL, Mobile Col, 77; DSc, Southeastern Inst Technol, 80 & Univ Ala, Huntsville, 81. *Honors & Awards:* Except Sci Achievement Medal, NASA, 64; Oberth Award, Am Inst Aeronaut & Astronaut, 65, Holger N Toftoy Award, 76; Space Flight Award, Am Astronaut Soc, 82; Vet Foreign Wars Space Award, 83; Elmer A Speery Award, Am Instit Aeronaut & Astronautics, 86. *Prof Exp:* Instr chem, Memphis State Univ, 46-48; chemist, Guided Missile Develop Div, Redstone Arsenal, 52-54, chief, Chem Sect, 54-55; chief eng mat sect, Army Ballistic Missile Agency, 55-56, chief eng mat br, 56-60; chief Eng Mat Br, 60-63, chief Mat Div, 63-66, dir Propulsion & Vehicle Eng Lab, 66-68, dir prog develop, 68-71, dep dir, 71-74, dir, Marshall Space Flight Ctr, NASA, 74-86. *Mem:* Nat Acad Eng; fel Am Inst Aeronaut & Astronaut; fel Am Astronaut Soc; fel Am Soc Metals; Sigma Xi; Am Chem Soc. *Res:* Materials engineering, metallurgy and inorganic chemistry; environmental effects on materials, especially space; pioneering work in materials for liquid rockets. *Mailing Add:* 6805 Criner Rd Huntsville AL 35802

LUCAS-LENARD, JEAN MARIAN, MOLECULAR BIOLOGY. *Current Pos:* assoc prof biol, 70-76, prof, 76-95, EMER PROF BIOL, UNIV CONN, 95- *Personal Data:* b Bridgeport, Conn, July 17, 37; m 64, John Lenard. *Educ:* Bryn Mawr Col, AB, 59; Yale Univ, PhD(protein synthesis), 63. *Prof Exp:* USPHS fel enzymol, Inst Physiochem Biol, Paris, 63-64; guest investr protein synthesis, Rockefeller Univ, 64-65, res assoc, 65-68, asst prof, 68-70. *Concurrent Pos:* Estab investr, Am Heart Asn, 70-71; NIH career develop award, 71-76. *Mem:* AAAS; Am Soc Biochem & Molecular Biol; Am Soc Virol. *Res:* Mechanism of protein biosynthesis in eukaryotes; translational control mechanisms in virus infected cells. *Mailing Add:* Dept Molecular & Cell Biol Univ Conn U-125 Storrs CT 06268-3125. *E-Mail:* lucasl@uconnvm.uconn.edu

LUCAST, DONALD HURRELL, ORGANIC CHEMISTRY. *Current Pos:* RES CHEMIST, 3M, 83- *Personal Data:* b Minneapolis, Minn, July 11, 46; m 75; c 3. *Educ:* Univ Minn, BS, 68, PhD(org chem), 76. *Prof Exp:* Res chemist, Ethyl Corp, 77-83. *Concurrent Pos:* Fel, Univ Detroit, 75-76 & Wayne State Univ, 77. *Mem:* Am Chem Soc; Tech Asn Pulp & Paper Indust. *Res:* Organic synthesis; reaction mechanisms; polymer chemistry. *Mailing Add:* 2504 Skillman Ave E St Paul MN 55109-4052

LUCATORTO, THOMAS B, LASERS. *Current Pos:* RES PHYSICIST, NAT INST STAND & TECHNOL, 69- *Personal Data:* b New York, NY, May 9, 37; m 79; c 2. *Educ:* City Univ NY, BS, 60; Columbia Univ, MA, 64, PhD(physics), 68. *Honors & Awards:* IR-100 Award, 80 & 84; Silver Medal, Nat Bur Stand, 80. *Prof Exp:* Res assoc physics, Columbia Univ, 68-69. *Mem:* Fel Am Phys Soc; Am Optical Soc. *Res:* Multiphoton ionization; EUV optics; EUV microscopy. *Mailing Add:* 4015 52nd St NW Washington DC 20016-1927. *Fax:* 301-975-3038; *E-Mail:* toml@enh.nist.gov

LUCCA, JOHN J, dentistry, for more information see previous edition

LUCCHESI, BENEDICT ROBERT, CARDIAC ARRHYTHMIAS, MYOCARDIAL ISCHEMIA. *Current Pos:* PROF PHARMACOL, MED SCH, UNIV MICH, 68- *Educ:* Univ Mich, MD, 64. *Res:* Cardiovascular pharmacology. *Mailing Add:* Dept Pharmacol Univ Mich Med Sci Bldg 1301 C MSRB III Ann Arbor MI 48109-0632

LUCCHESI, CLAUDE A, ANALYTICAL CHEMISTRY, PHYSICAL CHEMISTRY. *Current Pos:* SR LECTR CHEM & DIR ANALYSIS SERV, NORTHWESTERN UNIV, 68-, CONSULT DIR, ANALYSIS SERV & SR EMER LECTR. *Personal Data:* b Chicago, Ill, Apr 20, 29; m 54; c 2. *Educ:* Univ Ill, BS, 50; Northwestern Univ, PhD, 54. *Prof Exp:* Asst, Northwestern Univ, 50-54; spectros group leader, Shell Develop Co, Tex, 54-56; dir anal res dept, Sherwin-Williams Co, 56-61; mgr anal & phys chem dept, Mobil Chem Co, 61-67, mgr cent coatings lab, 67-68. *Concurrent Pos:* Consult coatings, healthcare & instrument co; ed, Bull Anal Lab Mgr Asn, 84-87, Managing Modern Labs; contrib ed, Analy Chem, 74-80. *Mem:* Am Chem Soc; Soc Appl Spectros; Instrument Soc Am; Analyt Lab Mgr Asn. *Res:* General applied spectroscopy; nuclear magnetic resonance spectroscopy; chelate chemistry; plastics and coating characterization and analysis; laboratory management. *Mailing Add:* Dept Chem Northwestern Univ Evanston IL 60208. *Fax:* 847-491-7713; *E-Mail:* c_lucchesi@nwu.edu

LUCCHESI, JOHN CHARLES, GENETICS. *Current Pos:* from asst prof to prof zool & genetics, 65-80, PROF BIOL & GENETICS, UNIV NC, CHAPEL HILL, 80- *Personal Data:* b Cairo, Egypt, Sept 3, 34; US citizen; m 55; c 2. *Educ:* La Grange Col, AB, 55; Univ Ga, MS, 58; Univ Calif, Berkeley, PhD(zool), 63. *Prof Exp:* NIH res career develop award, 70-75; vis Kenan prof, Dept Genetics, Univ Calif, Berkeley, 78; adj prof genetics, Duke Univ, Durham, NC, 80-; Carry C Boshamer prof biol, 82-90; overseas fel, Churchill Col, Eng, 84-; chair, Genetics Study Sect, Div Res Grants, NIH, 87-90; Aza G Chandler prof biol, 90- *Mem:* Genetics Soc Am (vpres, 90, pres, 91); Am Soc Cell Biol; Soc Develop Biol. *Res:* Molecular genetics; biochemistry of development; sex differentiation and dosage compensation in Drosophila. *Mailing Add:* Dept Biol Emory Univ 1510 Clifton Rd OWR Res Ctr Atlanta GA 30322-1100

LUCCHESI, PETER J, PHYSICAL CHEMISTRY. *Current Pos:* RETIRED. *Personal Data:* b New York, NY, Sept 23, 26; m 49; c 2. *Educ:* NY Univ, AB, 49, MS, 53, PhD(chem), 54. *Prof Exp:* Instr chem, Adelphi Col, 52, NY Univ, 53-54 & Ill Inst Technol, 54-55; res chemist, Exxon Res & Eng Co, 55-68, dir, Corp Res Lab, 68-75, vpres corp res, 75-85. *Mem:* Am Chem Soc; AAAS. *Res:* Radiation chemistry; heterogeneous catalysis; crystal growth and dissolution. *Mailing Add:* 24 Brearly Rd Princeton NJ 08540-6766

LUCCHITTA, BAERBEL KOESTERS, PLANETARY GEOLOGY, GEOMORPHOLOGY. *Current Pos:* geologist, Br Astrogeol, 68-95, assoc chief, 86-91, EMER SCIENTIST, US GEOL SURV, 95- *Personal Data:* b Muenster, Ger, Oct 2, 38; US citizen; m 64, Ivo; c Maya. *Educ:* Kent State Univ, BS, 61; Pa State Univ, MS, 63, PhD(geol), 66. *Honors & Awards:* Spec Recognition Award, NASA, 79; G K Gilbert Award, Planetary Geol Div, Geol Soc Am, 95. *Concurrent Pos:* Prin investr, 3 lunar projs, NASA, 74-78, guest investr, Viking Lander Imaging Team, 76, prin investr, 4 martian projs, 78-, mem, Planetary Geol Rev Panel, 80-82, coordr, Galilean Satellite Geol Mapping Prog, 80-; assoc ed, J Geophys Res, 80-84; proj chief, Antarctica, 82-95; secy/treas, Planetary Geol Div, Geol Soc Am, 87-89, 2nd vchmn, 89-90, 1st vchmn, 90-91 & chmn, 91-92; planet cartog working group, 89; lectr, Sigma Xi, 90-91. *Mem:* Asn Women Geoscientists; Asn Women Sci; Geol Soc Am; Planetary Soc; Am Geophys Union; Int Glaciol Soc. *Res:* Dark mantles, secondary craters, basin formation, plains formation, scarps and ridges, northside and Apollo 17-site geological map of the moon; erosion, landform development, map of Ismenius Lacus, canyons and scarps, landslides, channels, glacial and periglacial features, Valles Marineris geology and structure of Mars; geomorphology and structural geology of earth; geologic map of Jupiter Satellite Europa; structure of Ganymede; Antarctic investigations with Landsat images, Antarctic coastal changes and glacier velocities. *Mailing Add:* Br Astrogeol US Geol Surv 2255 N Gemini Dr Flagstaff AZ 86001. *Fax:* 520-556-7014; *E-Mail:* blucchitta@flagmail.wr.usgs.gov

LUCCHITTA, IVO, GEOLOGY. *Current Pos:* Geologist, proj chief & coordr Apollo geol methods, US Geol Surv, 66-70, geologist & proj chief earth resources technol satellite appln & anal, 70-73, geologist nat landslide overview map, 73-74, dep asst chief geologist, 85-87, geologist & proj chief, Wariz Tectonics, 73-95, geologist, Shivwits-Grand Wash Wilderness Area, 80-95, proj chief Quaternary Grand Canyon, 90, EMER GEOLOGIST, US GEOL SURV, 95- *Personal Data:* b Budweis, Czech, June 17, 37; US citizen; m 64, Baerbel Koesters; c Mays. *Educ:* Calif Inst Technol, BSc, 61; Pa State Univ, PhD(geol), 67. *Honors & Awards:* Spec commendation, geol training astronauts, Geol Soc Am, 70; Group Achievement Award, Earth Resources Technol Satellite geol anal & image processing, NASA, 75; Super Serv Award, US Dept Int, 89. *Concurrent Pos:* Penrose Bequest grant, Geol Soc Am, 63; Museum NAriz grants, 63, 64; adj prof, Northern Ariz Univ, 74-; res fel, Univ Rome, Italy, 84; res grant, Nat Geog Soc, 84. *Mem:* Fel Geol Soc Am. *Res:* Tectonic history of southwestern Colorado plateau and of plateau basin and range transition; basement control of structure; tectonic heredity; history of Colorado River and Grand Canyon; Cenozoic continental rocks; quatenory chronology and processes; Quaternary of the Grand Canyon; structure and tectonics of Cordilleran core complexes. *Mailing Add:* US Geol Surv 2255 N Gemini Dr Flagstaff AZ 86001. *Fax:* 520-556-7149; *E-Mail:* ilucchitta@flagmail.w1.usgs.gov

LUCCI, ROBERT DOMINICK, ANALYTICAL CHEMISTRY. *Current Pos:* DIR, TECH DEVELOP, MOLECULAR BIO SYSTEMS INC, SAN DIEGO, 92- *Personal Data:* b Norwalk, Conn, July 11, 50; m 71; c 2. *Educ:* Univ Conn, BA, 72; Cornell Univ, PhD(org chem), 77. *Prof Exp:* Sr scientist, Hoffmann-Laroche, Inc, 77-87, Abbott Lab, 87-92. *Mem:* Am Chem Soc; Sigma Xi. *Res:* Safe, economic and environmentally sound industrial chemical processes from research synthesis. *Mailing Add:* 6364 St Therese Way San Diego CA 92120

LUCE, JAMES EDWARD, PAPER CHEMISTRY, PHYSICS. *Current Pos:* CONSULT, PAPER PERFORMANCE & PAPERMAKING, 95- *Personal Data:* b Toronto, Ont, Aug 24, 35. *Educ:* Univ Toronto, BASc, 56; McGill Univ, PhD(chem), 60; NY Inst Tech, MBA, 80. *Prof Exp:* Asst mgr basic res, CIP Res Ltd, 60-71; sci admin officer, Atomic Energy Can, Ltd, 71; sr mgr oper systs develop, Int Paper Co, 72-81, assoc dir advan develop, 81-84, mgr papermaking technol, 84-87, mgr paper sci & technol, 87-95. *Mem:* Fel Tech Asn Pulp & Paper Indust; Can Pulp & Paper Asn; Int Asn Sci Papermakers. *Res:* Application of modern instrumental techniques to control of pulp and paper processes; development of papermaking processes; paper structure and properties. *Mailing Add:* Paper Performance & Papermaking 29 Kings Ridge Rd Warwick NY 10990-2639. *Fax:* 914-987-2152; *E-Mail:* luce@warwick.net

LUCE, R(OBERT) DUNCAN, MATHEMATICAL PSYCHOLOGY, THEORY MEASUREMENT. *Current Pos:* Alfred North Whitehead prof psychol & math psychol, 76-81, Victor S Thomas prof psychol, 83-88, EMER VICTOR S THOMAS PROF, HARVARD UNIV, 88- *Personal Data:* b Scranton, Pa, May 16, 25; m 88, Carolyn A Scheer; c Aurora N (Luce). *Educ:* Mass Inst Technol, BS, 45, PhD(math), 50. *Hon Degrees:* MS, Harvard Univ, 76. *Honors & Awards:* Distinguished Sci Contrib Award, Am Psychol Asn, 70. *Prof Exp:* Mem staff, Res Lab Electronics, Mass Inst Technol, 50-53, asst prof sociol & math statist, Columbia Univ, 54-57; prof psychol, Univ Pa, 59-67, Benjamin Franklin prof, 67-68; vis prof social sci, Inst Advan Study, Princeton, 69-72; prof soc sci, Univ Calif, Irvine, 72-75; distinguished prof & dir, math behav sci, Univ Calif, Irvine, 88-92. *Concurrent Pos:* Lectr social rels, Harvard Univ, 57-59; vis prof psychol, Cath Univ Rio de Janeiro, 68-69; managing dir, Behav Models Proj, Columbia Univ, 53-57, fel, Ctr Advan Study Behav Sci, 54-55, 66-67 & 87-88; Guggenheim Found fel, 80-81; distinguished res prof cognitive sci & econ, Univ Calif, Irvine, 92- *Mem:* Nat Acad Sci; Am Acad Arts & Sci; Soc Math Psychol (pres, 79); Psychometric Soc (pres, 76-77); AAAS; Am Math Soc; fel Am Psychol Asn; Fedn Behav Psychol & Cognitive Sci (pres, 88-90); Am Philos Soc. *Res:* Theoretical work on measurement and structures, especially conjoint and utility ones; theoretical and experimental work in psychophysics, including absolute identification, detection and recognition, magnitude estimation and reaction time. *Mailing Add:* Social Sci Tower Univ Calif Irvine CA 92697-5100. *Fax:* 714-824-3733; *E-Mail:* rdluce@uci.edu

LUCE, ROBERT JAMES, ROCK MAGNETISM. *Current Pos:* ASSOC PROF PHYSICS & GEOL, WASHINGTON & JEFFERSON COL, 80- *Personal Data:* b Boston, Mass, Aug 7, 29; m 81. *Educ:* Drexel Univ, BS, 73; Univ Pittsburgh, MS, 75, PhD(geophysics), 80. *Mem:* Am Phys Soc; Am Asn Physics Teachers. *Res:* Theoretical models of hadronic atoms. *Mailing Add:* Dept Physics Washington & Jefferson Col Washington PA 15301

LUCE, WILLIAM GLENN, ANIMAL NUTRITION. *Current Pos:* PROF SWINE EXTEN, OKLA STATE UNIV, 68- *Personal Data:* b Beaver Dam, Ky, Mar 21, 36; m 70, Nancy Ebey Ballard; c William Glenn Jr & Bryan Ward. *Educ:* Univ Ky, BS, 58; Univ Nebr, MS, 64, PhD(animal nutrit), 65. *Honors & Awards:* Extension Award, Am Soc Animal Sci. *Prof Exp:* Mgt trainee grocery & meat merchandising, Kroger Co, Ky, 58-60, co-mgr grocery & meat merchandising, 60-62; asst nutrit res, Univ Nebr, 62-65; asst prof swine exten, Univ Ga, 65-68. *Mem:* Sigma Xi; Am Soc Animal Sci; Am Registry Prof Animal Scientists; Coun Agr Sci & Technol. *Res:* Swine nutrition; cereal grain utilization and amino acid requirements. *Mailing Add:* Dept Animal Sci Okla State Univ Stillwater OK 74078

LUCEY, CAROL ANN, THEORETICAL PHYSICS, PHILOSOPHY OF SCIENCE. *Current Pos:* Actg assoc dean instr, 76-78, PROF PHYSICS, JAMESTOWN COMMUNITY COL, 73- *Personal Data:* b Johnstown, NY, Sept 16, 43; m 64; c 1. *Educ:* Harpur Col, BA, 65; State Univ NY, Binghamton, MA, 68; Brown Univ, PhD(physics), 72. *Concurrent Pos:* Nat Endowment Humanities fel, 79-80. *Mem:* Am Phys Soc; Philos Sci Asn. *Res:* Study of cosmological implications for elementary particle physics; gauge theories and general relativity; scientific methodology. *Mailing Add:* 15 Clyde Ave Jamestown NY 14701

LUCEY, EDGAR C, PULMONARY. *Current Pos:* instr respiratory syst, Dept Physiol, 76-78, asst res prof med, 79-87, ASSOC RES PROF, SCH MED, BOSTON UNIV, 87-; RES PHYSIOLOGIST, BOSTON VET ADMIN MED CTR, 79- *Personal Data:* b Feb 27, 45; m 70, Lore Kniffler; c Mark & Jennifer. *Educ:* Morningside Col, Iowa, BS, 67; Idaho State Univ, Pocatello, MS, 71, PhD(physiol), 75. *Prof Exp:* Lectr physiol & instr human physiol & advan physiol, Humboldt State Univ, 74-76. *Concurrent Pos:* Mem, Animal Studies Subcomt, Vet Admin Med Ctr, 86- & chair, Res Safety Subcomt, 91-92. *Mem:* Am Physiol Soc; NY Acad Sci. *Res:* Pathogeneses of pulmonary emphysema, fibrosis and airway secretory cell metaplasia; author of various publications. *Mailing Add:* Res Serv Boston Vet Admin Med Ctr 150 S Huntington Ave Boston MA 02130

LUCEY, JEROLD FRANCIS, PEDIATRICS. *Current Pos:* from instr to assoc prof, 56-66, PROF PEDIAT, COL MED, UNIV VT, 66- *Personal Data:* b Holyoke, Mass, Mar 26, 26; m 50; c 3. *Educ:* Dartmouth Col, AB, 48; NY Univ, MD, 52. *Honors & Awards:* Goulee Award, Am Asn Pediatrics, 81; United Cerebral Palsy Prize, 84; McDonald Award, 90. *Prof Exp:* Intern pediat, Bellevue Hosp, New York, 52-53; asst resident, Columbia-Presby Med Ctr, 53-55. *Concurrent Pos:* Bowen Brooks scholar, NY Acad Med, Bellevue Hosp, New York, 54; Mead Johnson fel, Columbia-Presby Med Ctr, 54-55; Nat Found Infantile Paralysis res fel, Harvard Med Sch, 55-56; Markle scholar, 59-64; res fel biochem, Harvard Med Sch, 60-61; consult, Vt State Health Dept, 56-81; chmn, Nat Bd Med Exam, 68-72; mem, Am Bd Pediat Exam, 70; ed-in-chief, Pediatrics, 73-; Humboldt Found fel, 78; Litchfield lectr, Oxford Univ, 78. *Mem:* Soc Pediat Res; fel Am Acad Pediat; Am Pediat Soc; Am Soc Photobiol; Royal Soc Med; Sigma Xi. *Res:* Neonatal physiology; transcutaneous oxygen. bilirubin metabolism; surfactant. *Mailing Add:* Dept Pediat Fletcher Allen Health Care Burlington VT 05401

LUCEY, JOHN WILLIAM, NUCLEAR ENGINEERING, INDUSTRIAL ENERGY CONSERVATION. *Current Pos:* Asst prof, 65-68, ASSOC PROF NUCLEAR ENG, UNIV NOTRE DAME, 68- *Personal Data:* b Winthrop, Mass, Aug 21, 35; m 57, Nancy Brozovici; c Josephine, John M, Thomas & Christopher. *Educ:* Univ Notre Dame, BS, 57; Mass Inst Technol, SM, 63, PhD(nuclear eng), 65. *Concurrent Pos:* Dir, Ind Civil Defense Prof Adv Serv, 69-73; dir, Notre Dame Indust Assessment Ctr, 90- *Mem:* AAAS; Am Nuclear Soc; Am Soc Eng Educ; Health Physics Soc; Sigma Xi; Soc Radiol Protection; Am Soc Heating & Refrig Engrs. *Res:* Numerical methods for nuclear reactor calculations; radiation shielding; transport calculations; energy conservation for small and medium sized industry. *Mailing Add:* Dept Aerospace & Mech Eng Univ Notre Dame Notre Dame IN 46556. *Fax:* 219-631-8341; *E-Mail:* lucey.1@nd.edu

LUCEY, ROBERT FRANCIS, AGRONOMY. *Current Pos:* from asst to assoc prof field crops, 61-70, chmn, Dept Agron, 75-96, PROF FIELD CROPS, NY STATE COL AGR & LIFE SCI, CORNELL UNIV, ITHACA, 70-, EMER PROF AGRON, 96- *Personal Data:* b Worcester, Mass, Mar 13, 26; m 52; c 7. *Educ:* Univ Mass, BVA, 50; Univ Md, MS, 54; Mich State Univ, PhD(field crops), 59. *Prof Exp:* Asst prof agron, Univ NH, 57-61. *Mem:* Am Soc Agron. *Res:* Production of field crops, especially crop-climate relationships; adaptability; plant competition. *Mailing Add:* 9 Hunt Grove Rd Ithaca NY 14850

LUCHER, LYNNE ANNETTE, VIROLOGY, PROTEIN CHEMISTRY. *Personal Data:* b Houston, Tex, June 18, 54. *Educ:* Lindenwood Cols, St Charles, Mo, BA, 76; Rice Univ, Houston, PhD(biochem), 83. *Prof Exp:* Res assoc, Med Sch, St Louis Univ, 82-85; from asst prof to assoc prof virol & microbiol, Ill State Univ, Normal, 85-94. *Mem:* Am Soc Microbiol; Am Soc Virol; AAAS. *Res:* Biochemistry of adenovirus interaction with a host cell; reactions which determine whether a lytic infection or transformation occurs. *Mailing Add:* Dept Biol Sci Univ Alaska Sci Bldg Rm 128 3211 Providence Dr Anchorage AK 99508

LUCHINS, EDITH HIRSCH, MATHEMATICS. *Current Pos:* from assoc prof to prof, 62-73, EMER PROF MATH, RENSSELAER POLYTECHNIC INST, 73-, ADJ PROF, DEPT PHILOS, PSYCHOL & COGNITIVE SCI, 94- *Personal Data:* b Poland, Dec 21, 21; nat US; m 42; c 5. *Educ:* Brooklyn Col, BA, 42; NY Univ, MS, 44; Univ Ore, PhD(math), 57. *Prof Exp:* Govt inspector anti-aircraft dirs, Sperry Gyroscope Co, NY, 42-44; instr math, Brooklyn Col, 44-46 & 48-49; asst appl math lab, NY Univ, 46; Am Asn Univ Women res fel & res assoc math, Univ Ore, 57-58; from res assoc to assoc prof math, Univ Miami, 59-62. *Mem:* Math Asn Am; Am Math Soc; Soc Indust & Appl Math. *Res:* Banach algebras; functional analysis; mathematical psychology. *Mailing Add:* 53 Fordham Ct Albany NY 12209-1192

LUCHSINGER, WAYNE WESLEY, BIOCHEMISTRY. *Current Pos:* from assoc prof to prof, 66-84, EMER PROF CHEM, ARIZ STATE UNIV, 84- *Personal Data:* b Milaca, Minn, May 8, 24; m 43, Sadie L Johnson; c Sharon K, Jerry W, Susan W & David W. *Educ:* Univ Minn, BS, 51, MS, 54, PhD(biochem), 56. *Prof Exp:* Asst biochem, Univ Minn, 51-55; sr chemist, Kurth Malting Co, 56-58, asst dir res, 58-60; assoc prof biochem, WVa Univ, 60-66. *Mem:* AAAS; Am Chem Soc; Am Soc Brewing Chem; Am Asn Cereal Chem. *Res:* Enzymes; barley carbohydrates; chemistry and mechanism of action of enzymes; carbohydrate structure. *Mailing Add:* 3329 S Stanley Pl Tempe AZ 85282

LUCHTEL, DANIEL LEE, ELECTRON MICROSCOPY, CELL BIOLOGY. *Current Pos:* NIH fel, Univ Wash, 69-71, res assoc biol struct, 71-73, res assoc environ health, 73-75, asst prof, 75-82, ASSOC PROF ENVIRON HEALTH, UNIV WASH, 82- *Personal Data:* b Carroll, Iowa, Jan 13, 42. *Educ:* St Benedict's Col, Kans, BS, 63; Univ Wash, PhD(zool), 69. *Concurrent Pos:* Res fel, Hubrecht Lab, Utrecht, Neth, 72. *Mem:* AAAS; Sigma Xi; Am Soc Cell Biol; Am Inst Biol Sci; Electron Micros Soc Am. *Res:* Lung ultrastructure and effects of gaseous and particulate air pollutants; respiratory tract mucus and mechanisms of mucous cell secretion; lung development; mechanisms of pulmonary edema; tracheal organ cultures. *Mailing Add:* Environ Health S C034 Univ Wash 3900 Seventh Ave NE Seattle WA 98195-0001

LUCID, MICHAEL FRANCIS, INORGANIC CHEMISTRY. *Current Pos:* staff engr, Shell Mining Co, 78-80, mgr mining develop, 80-83, staff mining engr, 83-84, proj mgr, 85-87, SR STAFF MINING ENGR, SHELL MINING CO, 87- *Personal Data:* b Indianapolis, Ind, Feb 23, 37; m 67; c 3. *Educ:* Ind Univ, Bloomington, BS, 61; Purdue Univ, Lafayette, MS, 65. *Prof Exp:* Res chemist, Kerr McGee Corp, 65-67, sr res chemist, 67-75, res proj chemist, 75-78. *Mem:* Am Chem Soc. *Res:* Hydrometallurgy; solvent extraction; ion exchange; solution chemistry; geochemistry; solution mining, uranium, vanadium, copper, gold; oil shale. *Mailing Add:* 1622 Gunwale Houston TX 77062-4538

LUCID, SHANNON W, BIOCHEMISTRY, ASTRONAUTICS. *Current Pos:* ASTRONAUT, LYNDON B JOHNSON SPACE CTR, NASA, 79- *Personal Data:* b Shanghai, China, Jan 14, 43; m, Michael F; c Kawai D, Shandara M & Michael K. *Educ:* Univ Okla, BS, 6, MS, 70, PhD(biochem), 73. *Prof Exp:* Sr lab technician, Okla Med Res Found, 64-66; chemist, Kerr-McGee, 66-68. *Concurrent Pos:* Res assoc, Okla Med Res Found, 74- *Res:* Chemistry. *Mailing Add:* Astronaut Off Johnson Space Ctr NASA Houston TX 77058

LUCIER, GEORGE W, TOXICOLOGY. *Current Pos:* CHIEF, LAB BIOCHEM RISK ANALYSIS, NAT INST ENVIRON HEALTH SCI, NIH, 83-, ED, ENVIRON HEALTH PERSPECTIVES, 73-, DIR, ENVIRON TOXICOL PROGS. *Personal Data:* b Southbridge, Mass, June 23, 43. *Educ:* Univ Md, PhD(entom), 70. *Mem:* Am Soc Toxicol; Endocrine Soc; Teratology Soc. *Res:* Applications of biochemical data to human risk assessment. *Mailing Add:* Nat Inst Environ Health Sci NIH 111 Alexander Dr A3-02 Bldg 101 S Campus Research Triangle Park NC 27709. *Fax:* 919-541-2260

LUCIER, JOHN J, ORGANIC CHEMISTRY. *Current Pos:* Instr chem, Univ Dayton, 45-47 & 51-52, from asst prof to assoc prof, 52-63, chmn dept, 64-79, PROF CHEM, UNIV DAYTON, 63- *Personal Data:* b Detroit, Mich, Aug 10, 17. *Educ:* Univ Dayton, BS, 37; Western Res Univ, MS, 50, PhD(org chem), 51. *Concurrent Pos:* Distinguished serv prof, Univ Dayton, 88. *Mem:* AAAS; Am Chem Soc; Soc Appl Spectros; NY Acad Sci; Chem Soc. *Res:* Organic synthesis; infrared spectroscopy; history of science. *Mailing Add:* Dept Chem Univ Dayton Dayton OH 45469-2357

LUCIS, OJARS JANIS, ENDOCRINOLOGY, CLINICAL PHARMACOLOGY. *Current Pos:* MED PHARMACEUT REGULATORY CONSULT, 90- *Personal Data:* b Latvia, Apr 2, 24; Can citizen; m 49; c 2. *Educ:* Sir George Williams Univ, BSc, 54; McGill Univ, MSc, 57, PhD(invest med), 59, MD, CM, 61, cert clin chem, 74. *Prof Exp:* Res asst invest med, McGill Univ, 56-60; asst prof endocrinol, Dalhousie Univ, 65-71; med officer, Health & Welfare Can, 71-90, div chief endocrinol & Metab, 74-90. *Concurrent Pos:* Med Res Coun Can fel, McGill Univ, 62-63, res scholar, 63-65; Med Res Coun Can scholar steroid biochem, Dalhousie Univ, 65-68; asst pathologist, Prov NS Dept Pub Health, 66-68, assoc pathologist, 68-71; consult drug regulatory affairs, 90- *Res:* Biosynthesis and metabolism of hormones; immunochemical assays of hormones; interaction of trace elements with the cells and the mammalian organism; biosynthesis and isolation of cadmium binding proteins; pharmacology and toxicology of drugs; evaluation of pharmaceuticals. *Mailing Add:* 1512 Caverly Ottawa ON K1G 0Y1 Can

LUCIS, RUTA, COMPARATIVE ENDOCRINOLOGY. *Current Pos:* RETIRED. *Personal Data:* b Rujiena, Latvia, Apr 9, 25; Can citizen; m 49; c 2. *Educ:* Sir George Williams Univ, BSc, 57; McGill Univ, MS, 64, PhD(invest med), 66. *Prof Exp:* Res asst endocrinol, McGill Univ, 62-65; res asst, Path Inst, 66-71; clin chemist, Animal Res Inst, Ottawa, 72-90. *Mem:* NY Acad Sci. *Res:* Biochemistry of steroids; immunochemical assays and metabolism of hormones; environmental health. *Mailing Add:* 1512 Caverley St Ottawa ON K1G 0Y1 Can

LUCK, DAVID JONATHAN LEWIS, CYTOLOGY. *Current Pos:* res assoc, 62-64, from asst prof to assoc prof, 64-68, PROF CELL BIOL, ROCKEFELLER UNIV, 68-, VPRES, ACAD AFFAIRS, 94- *Personal Data:* b Milwaukee, Wis, Jan 7, 29. *Educ:* Univ Chicago, BS, 49; Harvard Med Sch, MD, 53; Rockefeller Univ, PhD, 62. *Concurrent Pos:* Intern Med, Mass Gen Hosp, 53-54, asst resident physician, 54-55, resident physician, 57-58; teaching fel, Harvard Med Sch, 57-59; fel, Rockefeller Univ, 58-62; res physician, Mass Gen Hosp, Boston, 57-59. *Mem:* Nat Acad Sci; Am Soc Cell Biol; Am Soc Biol Chemist; Am Soc Biochem & Molecular Biol; AAAS. *Res:* Biochemical cytology; cell structure; biochemical function; author of numerous publications. *Mailing Add:* Rockefeller Univ New York NY 10021-6399. *Fax:* 212-327-7444; *E-Mail:* luck@rockvotx.rockeller.edu

LUCK, DENNIS NOEL, MOLECULAR BIOLOGY. *Current Pos:* from asst prof to assoc prof, 72-82, PROF BIOL, OBERLIN COL, 82-, CHAIR BIOL, 95- *Personal Data:* b Durban, SAfrica, Dec 8, 39; m 69, Joan Burchall; c Roy B. *Educ:* Univ Natal, BSc, 61, MSc, 63; Oxford Univ, DPhil(molecular biol), 66. *Prof Exp:* Lectr biochem, Univ Natal, 66-68; vis asst prof pharmacol, Baylor Col Med, 69; asst prof zool, Univ Tex, Austin, 70-72. *Concurrent Pos:* Eleanor Roosevelt Int Cancer fel, Univ Oxford, 78-79; foreign expert, Shanxi Agr Univ, Taigu, Shanxi, People's Repub China, 82; consult biochemist, Gilford Instrument Lab, Oberlin, Ohio, 80-82; vis prof, Dept Biochem, Univ BC, Vancouver, Can, 84-85, 86-87 & 90-91. *Mem:* Brit Biochem Soc; Am Soc Biochem & Molecular Biol; Am Soc Cell Biol; Sigma Xi; Endocrine Soc; Am Soc Microbiol. *Res:* Structure-function studies on growth hormone and prolactin. *Mailing Add:* Dept Biol Oberlin Col Oberlin OH 44074-1413. *Fax:* 440-775-8960

LUCK, JOHN VIRGIL, MICROBIOLOGY. *Current Pos:* SR VPRES & TECH DIR, GEN MILLS, INC, MINNEAPOLIS, 70- *Personal Data:* b Chalmers, Ind, Jan 20, 26; m 45; c 3. *Educ:* Purdue Univ, BS, 49, MS, 51, PhD(microbiol, biochem), 54. *Prof Exp:* Dir beer fermentation res, Pabst Brewing Co, 53-55; proj leader chem res, Gen Foods Corp, NY, 55-58; head biol chem dept, Armour & Co, 58-60; dir res & develop, Durkee Famous Foods, Glidden Co, Ill, 60-70. *Concurrent Pos:* Mem, Res & Develop Assocs. *Mem:* AAAS; Am Chem Soc; Am Oil Chem Soc; Inst Food Technol; Soc Indust Microbiol; Int Life Sci Inst-Nutrit Fedn. *Res:* Food chemistry; fats; starch; proteins emulsifiers; enzymology. *Mailing Add:* 1 Marsh Bird Lane Savannah GA 31411-1602

LUCK, LEON D(AN), CIVIL ENGINEERING. *Current Pos:* from assoc prof to prof, 59-83, chmn dept civil & environ eng, 72-76, EMER PROF CIVIL ENG, WASH STATE UNIV, 83- *Personal Data:* b Spokane, Wash, Apr 25, 21; m 41; c 2. *Educ:* Wash State Univ, BS, 43; Univ Minn, MS, 51; Stanford Univ, CE, 60. *Honors & Awards:* Western Elec Educ Award, Am Soc Eng Educ, 82. *Prof Exp:* Mine engr, Pend Oreille Mines & Metals Co, 43 & 46-47; from instr to assoc prof civil eng, Wash State Univ, 47-57; lectr, Stanford Univ, 57-59. *Concurrent Pos:* Consult engr, Potlatch Forests, Inc, 56-60; Fulbright lectr, Chungbuk Nat Univ, Rep of Korea, 83-84. *Mem:* Am Soc Civil Engrs; Am Soc Eng Educ; Nat Soc Prof Engrs. *Res:* Shear characteristics of Palouse clay; seepage flow through porous soil media; rigid frame analysis by matrix methods with the aid of a digital computer. *Mailing Add:* 1507 SE Footloose Dr Pullman WA 99163

LUCK, MICHAEL S, BIOTECHNOLOGY, GASTROINTESTINAL PHARMACOLOGY & INFECTIOUS DISEASE. *Current Pos:* SR SCIENTIST, IMMUCEIL CORP, 96- *Personal Data:* b Milwaukee, Wis, May, 1954. *Educ:* Marquette Univ, BS, 76; Univ Wis, PhD(pharmacol), 94. *Prof Exp:* Med technologist, Milwaukee County Med Complex, 77-89; postdoctoral trainee toxicol, Univ Wis, 94-95. *Res:* Research and development of therapies for the treatment and/or prevention of gastrointestinal infectious disease; clinical development of vaccines and oral passive antibody treatment of gastrointestinal infectious disease; development of specific vaccines that produce high titer specific immunity against select antigens of infectious agents. *Mailing Add:* 56 Evergren Dr Portland ME 04103-1066. *E-Mail:* luckimcell@aol.com

LUCK, RICHARD EARLE, ASTROPHYSICS, ASTRONOMY. *Current Pos:* RES ASSOC, DEPT PHYSICS & ASTRON, LA STATE UNIV, 77-; WARNER PROF ASTRON, CHAIR, DEPT ASTRON & DIR, WARNER & SWAYZE OBSERV, 94- *Personal Data:* b Roanoke, Va, Mar 9, 50; m 78. *Educ:* Univ Va, BA, 72; Univ Tex, MA, 75, PhD(astron), 77. *Mem:* Am Astron Soc; Royal Astron Soc. *Res:* Chemical composition of late-type stars to determine the effects of stellar and galactic chemical evolution on such objects. *Mailing Add:* Dept Astron Case Western Reserve Univ University Circle Cleveland OH 44106

LUCK, RUSSELL M, POLYMER CHEMISTRY, ORGANIC CHEMISTRY. *Current Pos:* RETIRED. *Personal Data:* b Reading, Pa, May 11, 26; m 63; c 2. *Educ:* Albright Col, BSc, 47; Bucknell Univ, MSc, 48. *Prof Exp:* Asst chem, Bucknell Univ, 47-48; asst prod mgr, Wyomissing Glazed Papers, Inc, 48-51; engr, Mat Eng Dept, Westinghouse Elec Corp, 53-60, sr engr, Res & Develop Ctr, 60-71, fel scientist, 71-83, adv scientist, Res & Develop Ctr, 83-87. *Mem:* Am Chem Soc. *Res:* Organic and inorganic polymers for application as lubricants and electrical insulations with high temperature capabilities. *Mailing Add:* 1241 Harvest Dr Monroeville PA 15146

LUCK, STANLEY D, biophysical chemistry, for more information see previous edition

LUCKE, ROBERT LANCASTER, ATMOSPHERIC CHEMISTRY & PHYSICS. *Current Pos:* RES PHYSICIST, US NAVAL RES LAB, WASHINGTON, 82- *Personal Data:* b Norfolk, Va, July 22, 45. *Educ:* Johns Hopkins Univ, BA, 68, MA, 72, PhD(physics), 75. *Prof Exp:* Assoc res scientist physics, Johns Hopkins Univ, 75-76; Nat Res Coun fel, Goddard Space Flight Ctr, NASA, 76-78; asst prof physics & astron, Univ Toledo, Ohio, 79-81. *Mem:* Am Astron Soc. *Res:* Far ultraviolet albedo of the moon; coronal line emmission in supernova remnants; x-ray astronomy; astronomical instrumentation. *Mailing Add:* 10608 Ridge Rd Clinton MD 20735

LUCKE, WILLIAM E, ANALYTICAL CHEMISTRY. *Current Pos:* res assoc, Cincinnati Milling Mach Co, 69-71, supvr, Cimcool Customer Lab Serv, Cincinnati Milacron Inc, 71-74, SR ANALYTICAL CHEMIST, CIMCOOL DIV, CINCINNATI, MILACRON INC, 74- *Personal Data:* b Grand Island, Nebr, July 31, 36; m 59; c 5. *Educ:* Univ Nebr, BS, 58; Ohio State Univ, PhD(chem), 63. *Prof Exp:* Res chemist, Olympic Res Div, Rayonier Inc, 63-69. *Mem:* AAAS; Am Chem Soc. *Res:* Carbohydrate, cellulose and wood chemistry; analytical chemistry of industrial metal working products. *Mailing Add:* Milacron Inc PO Box 9013 Cincinnati OH 45209

LUCKENBACH, MARK WAYNE, MARINE BENTHIC ECOLOGY, SHELLFISH AQUACULTURE. *Current Pos:* Asst prof, 85-90, ASSOC PROF & DIR, OYSTER AQUACULT PROG & SCIENTIST-IN-CHARGE, EASTERN SHORE LAB, SCH MARINE SCI, VA INST MARINE SCI, COL WILLIAM & MARY, 90- *Personal Data:* b Houston, Tex, May 10, 55; m 79, Michelle R Hollinger; c Joshua D & Patrick J. *Educ:* Univ NC, BS, 77; Univ NC, PhD(biol), 85. *Mem:* AAAS; Estuarine Res Fedn; Nat Shellfisheries Asn. *Res:* Marine benthic ecology with emphasis on hydrodynamic effects on recruitment, feeding and growth of invertebrates; shellfish aquaculture. *Mailing Add:* 24235 Adelaide St Parksley VA 23421. *Fax:* 757-787-5831; *E-Mail:* luck@ches.vims.edu

LUCKENBILL-EDDS, LOUISE, DEVELOPMENTAL BIOLOGY, NEUROBIOLOGY. *Current Pos:* ASSOC PROF ZOOL & BIOMED SCI, OHIO UNIV, ATHENS, 77- *Personal Data:* b Lebanon, Pa, Nov 19, 36; m 71, 86. *Educ:* Oberlin Col, BA, 58; Brown Univ, PhD(biol), 64. *Prof Exp:* Arthritis Found res fel arthritis & connective tissue dis, Sch Med, Boston Univ, 65-66, instr res dermat, 66-68; sci fel, Hubrecht Lab, Royal Netherlands Acad Sci & Letters, 68-69; asst prof biol sect, Smith Col, 69-75; instr, Dept Neuropath, Harvard Med Sch, 75-77. *Concurrent Pos:* Guest scientist, Nat Inst Dent Res, NIH, Bethesda, Md, 85-86; sci fel, Max Planck Inst Biochem, Ger, 89-90; sr int fel, NIH, Fogarty Ctr, 89-90. *Mem:* AAAS; Am Soc Zool; Soc Develop Biol; Soc Neurosci; Sigma Xi. *Res:* Laminin-mediated neurite outgrowth; histogenesis of sympathetic neurons; migration and differentiation of neural crestcells. *Mailing Add:* Col Osteop Med Ohio Univ Irvine Hall Athens OH 45701-0001. *Fax:* 740-593-0300; *E-Mail:* luckenbill@cats.ohiou.edu

LUCKENS, MARK MANFRED, PHARMACOLOGY, TOXICOLOGY. *Current Pos:* RETIRED. *Personal Data:* b Kiev, Russia, Apr 7, 12; US citizen; m 43; c 2. *Educ:* Columbia Univ, BS, 35; NY Univ, MS, 50; Univ Conn, PhD(pharmacol, toxicol), 63; Polytech Inst New York, MSES, 72; Am Bd Indust Hyg, dipl. *Prof Exp:* Jr chemist, Wilkow Food Prod, 28-33, chemist, 33-36; chief chemist, Technichem Labs, 37-41; inspector, Chem Warfare Serv, 41-43; dir, Emmet Tech Assocs, 48-54; toxicologist, Conn State Dept Health, 54-61; from asst prof to assoc prof toxicol & pharmacol, Col Pharm, Univ Ky, 61-77, dir, Inst Environ Toxicol & Occup Hyg, 62-77, mem fac & co-dir interdisciplinary grad prog toxicol, 73-77. *Concurrent Pos:* Consult, Ky State Dept Human Resources, 61-, Lexington-Fayette County Dept Health, Ky Poison Info & Environ Health Control Prog, 61-, Lab Serv, Childrens's Hosp, Louisville, Ky, 63-, Spindletop Res Ctr, 65- & Nat Inst Occup Health & Safety, 77; Fulbright travel grant, 65-66; award, Partners-in-the-Americas, 65-66; mem, adv comt pesticides, Ky Dept Agr vis prof, Polytech Inst of Guayaquil; vis dir, Oceano vis prof, Polytech Inst of Guayaquil; dir, Hemispheric Prog Poison Info & Control; pvt pract, 77- *Mem:* Fel AAAS; fel Am Inst Chem; fel Am Acad Indust Hyg; fel Am Acad Forensic Sci; Am Chem Soc; Sigma Xi. *Res:* Toxicodynamics; comparative toxicology and pharmacology; environmental, occupational, clinical, analytical, food and forensic toxicology; chemical pathology; drug action in hibernation; biorhythms; effects of psychosocial parameters on toxicity and pharmacologic action. *Mailing Add:* 664 Sheridan Dr Lexington KY 40503

LUCKERT, H(ANS) J(OACHIM), AERODYNAMICS, APPLIED MATHEMATICS. *Current Pos:* RETIRED. *Personal Data:* b Ger, Aug 26, 05; nat Can; m 53, Ilse Schwabedissen; c Doris. *Educ:* Harvard Univ, AM, 29; Univ Berlin, Dr Phil, 33. *Prof Exp:* Asst to prof math, Mining Acad Freiberg, Ger, 29-34; aerodynamicist, Henschel Aircraft Co, 35-37; sr group leader aerodyn, Arado Aircraft Co, 37-45; scientist transl & aero res, Brit Ministry Supply, 45-47; consult aerodyn, Control Comn for Ger, 47-52; engr, Canadair, Ltd, 52-54, design specialist, 54-57, chief tech sect, Missiles & Systs Div, 57-63, sect chief missiles & space res, 63-64, staff scientist res & develop, 64-65; chief aerodynamicist, Space Res Inst, 65-68; chief aerodynamicist, Space Res Inst, Inc, 68-69, Space Res Corp, 69-80; consult, Potton Tech Indust, Inc, 80-81; Phoenix Eng, Inc, Newport, Vt, 82-83; Space Res Corp, 83-89. *Concurrent Pos:* Chmn, Nat Res Coun Res Coord Group, Upper Atmosphere Res Vehicles, 64-65; mem assoc comt aerodyn, 63-66; mem assoc comt space res, 64-67; hon res assoc, McGill Univ, 67-85. *Mem:* Assoc fel Am Inst Aeronaut & Astronaut; fel Can Aeronaut & Space Inst; Ger Soc Aeronaut & Astronaut. *Res:* Aerodynamics and physics; astronautics; aircraft and missiles. *Mailing Add:* 197 58th Ave Laval des Rapides PQ H7V 2A5 Can

LUCKETT, WINTER PATRICK, ANATOMY, EMBRYOLOGY. *Current Pos:* AT DEPT ANAT, UNIV PR, SAN JUAN. *Personal Data:* b Atlanta, Ga, Mar 23, 37. *Educ:* Univ Mo, AB, 61, MA, 63; Univ Wis-Madison, PhD(anat), 67. *Prof Exp:* Instr, Col Physicians & Surgeons, Columbia Univ, 68-69, asst prof anat, 69-75; assoc prof anat, Sch Med, Creighton Univ, 75- *Mem:* AAAS; Am Asn Anat; Soc Study Reproduction; Int Primatol Soc. *Res:* Comparative morphogenesis of the placenta and fetal membranes; comparative structure of the ovary; endocrinology of reproduction; evolution of primates. *Mailing Add:* Dept Anat Univ PR Med Sci Campus GPO Box 365067 San Juan PR 00936-0567

LUCKEY, GEORGE WILLIAM, PHYSICAL CHEMISTRY. *Current Pos:* RETIRED. *Personal Data:* b Dayton, Ohio, Apr 17, 25; m 58, Doris J Waring; c George R, Jana E & John A. *Educ:* Oberlin Col, BA, 47; Rochester Univ, PhD(chem), 50. *Prof Exp:* Mem staff, Photog Theory Dept, Eastman Kodak Co, 50-56, Appl Photog Div, 56-60 & Spec Res Dept, 61-77, res fel & lab head, Spec Res Lab, 77-86. *Mem:* Am Chem Soc; Am Phys Soc; Royal Soc Chem; Soc Photog Scientists & Engrs; Electrochem Soc; Sigma Xi. *Res:* Photochemistry; photographic theory; luminescence; photographic processing chemistry; photographic and radiographic systems. *Mailing Add:* 240 Weymouth Dr Rochester NY 14625-1917

LUCKEY, PAUL DAVID, JR, ELECTROMAGNETISM. *Current Pos:* mem sci res staff, 56-70, SR RES SCIENTIST PHYSICS, MASS INST TECHNOL, 70- *Personal Data:* b Pittsburgh, Pa, May 18, 28; wid; c 3. *Educ:* Carnegie Inst Technol, BS, 49; Cornell Univ, PhD(physics), 54. *Prof Exp:* Res assoc physics, Cornell Univ, 53-56. *Mem:* Am Phys Soc. *Res:* Meson physics; photoproduction of Pi mesons; electron synchrotrons. *Mailing Add:* CERN EP Div CH-1211 Geneva 23 Switzerland

LUCKEY, THOMAS DONNELL, BIOCHEMISTRY, NUTRITION. *Current Pos:* RETIRED. *Personal Data:* b Casper, Wyo, May 15, 19; m 43, Pauline; c Jane, Mary & Donna. *Educ:* Colo Agr Col, BS, 41; Univ Wis, MS, 44, PhD(biochem), 46. *Hon Degrees:* Hon prof, The Free Univ, Herborn, 82. *Honors & Awards:* Knighted, Greifenstein Castle, 84. *Prof Exp:* Asst, Agr & Mech Col, Tex, 41-42 & Univ Wis, 42-46; asst res prof biochem, Univ Notre Dame, 46-54; prof biochem, Sch Med, Univ Mo-Columbia, 54-84. *Concurrent Pos:* NSF traveling fel, Paris Nutrit Cong, 57; Univ Mo fel, Stockholm Microbiol Cong, 58; Commonwealth res fel, 61-62; Am Inst Nutrit traveling fel, Cong, 63; dir, WCent States Biochem Conf, 64-; moderator symp gnotobiol, Int Meeting Microbiol, Moscow, 66; mem, Subcomt Interaction of Infection & Nutrit, Nat Acad Sci, 72-74; nutrit consult, NASA Johnson Space Ctr, Houston; consult, McDonnell Aircraft Corp, Mygrodol Prod Inc & Gen Elec Co; Av Humboldt Sr Sci Award, 78-80; vis prof, Univ Qatar, 83; chief exec officer, Oralu Corp, 91-; bd dir, Radiation Sci & Health, Inc, 96- *Mem:* AAAS; Am Chem Soc; Soc Exp Biol & Med; Am Soc Microbiol; Am Inst Nutrit; Sigma Xi. *Res:* Nutrition and metabolism of germ-free vertebrates; folic acid and related compounds in chick nutrition; comparative nutrition; modes of action of antibiotics; gnotobiology; thymic hormones; hormesis; low level radiation effects; biochemistry and nutrition; author. *Mailing Add:* 1009 Sitka Ct Loveland CO 80538-4052. *Fax:* 970-669-0186

LUCKHAM, DAVID COMPTOM, COMPUTER SCIENCE. *Current Pos:* res comput scientist, 72-76, sr res assoc, 76-78, ADJ PROF ELEC ENG, STANFORD UNIV, 78- *Personal Data:* b Kingston, Jamaica, Sept 7, 36. *Educ:* Univ London, BSc, 56, MSc, 57; Mass Inst Technol, PhD(math logic), 63. *Prof Exp:* Res assoc comput sci, Mass Inst Technol, 63-65; lectr math, Univ Manchester, 65-68; res assoc comput sci, Stanford Univ, 68-70; from asst prof to assoc prof, Univ Calif, Los Angeles, 70-72. *Concurrent Pos:* Consult, Bolt, Beranek & Newman Inc, 63-65; Jet Propulsion Lab, 71- & Systs Control Inc, 78-; Sci Coun res grant, Univ Manchester, 65-68; lectr, Ctr Comput & Automation, Imp Col, Univ London, 67-68; Hayes sr fel, Harvard Univ, 76-77. *Mem:* Am Math Soc; Asn Comput Mach; Asn Symbolic Logic. *Res:* Theory of computation; automated proof procedures and applications to computer-aided programming; verification of programs; semantics of programming languages; parallel programs; microprocessor systems; artificial intelligence. *Mailing Add:* Comput Systs Lab Stanford Univ ERL 456 Palo Alto CA 94305

LUCKMANN, WILLIAM HENRY, ENTOMOLOGY. *Current Pos:* prof & head, 65-84, EMER PROF, OFF AGR ENTOM, COL AGR, UNIV ILL, 84- *Personal Data:* b Cape Girardeau, Mo, Jan 15, 26; m 49; c 5. *Educ:* Univ Mo, BS, 49; Univ Ill, MS, 51, PhD, 56. *Prof Exp:* Asst entomologist, State Natural Hist Surv, Ill, 51-53 & tech develop, Shell Chem Corp, Colo, 53-54; assoc entomologist, State Natural Hist Surv, Ill, 54-59, entomologist, 59-84, head sect econ entom, 65-84. *Mem:* Entom Soc Am. *Res:* Ecology; biology; applied control. *Mailing Add:* 2504 S Prospect Ave Champaign IL 61820

LUCKOCK, ARLENE SUZANNE, NEUROPHYSIOLOGY, ENDOCRINOLOGY. *Current Pos:* ASSOC PROF PHYSIOL, PALMER COL CHIROPRACTIC-W, 79- *Personal Data:* b Oakland, Calif, Nov 23, 48; m 76; c 2. *Educ:* Univ Calif, Berkeley, BA, 69, PhD(physiol), 74. *Prof Exp:* Fel, Dept Psychiat, Med Sch, Stanford Univ, 74-76 & Dept Genetics, 76-78; instr physiol, West Valley Col, Saratoga, Calif, 78-79. *Res:* Effects of thyroid hormones on mammalian brain development; genetic differences in testosterone synthesis in two strains of mice; genetic polymorphisms in testosterone-estradiol binding globulin in human populations. *Mailing Add:* Palmer Col Chiropractic W 1095 Dunford Way Sunnyvale CA 94087

LUCKRING, JAMES MICHAEL, AERODYNAMICS. *Current Pos:* SR RES ENGR, LANGLEY RES CTR, NASA, 74-; ASST PROF LECTR AERODYN, GEORGE WASHINGTON UNIV, 86- *Personal Data:* b Canton, Ohio, Aug 5, 51. *Educ:* Purdue Univ, BS, 73, MS, 74; NC State Univ, PhD(aerospace eng), 85. *Mem:* Assoc fel Am Inst Aeronaut & Astronaut. *Res:* Applied computational aerodynamics for advanced configurations. *Mailing Add:* Langley Res Ctr NASA MS 280 Hampton VA 23681

LUCKRING, R(ICHARD) M(ICHAEL), TECHNICAL MANAGEMENT. *Current Pos:* RETIRED. *Personal Data:* b Canton, Ohio, Feb 3, 17; m 54, Viola Link; c Mimi, Paula, Michael, Eve, Abby & Andrea. *Educ:* Heidelberg Col, BS, 40; Lehigh Univ, BSChE, 42. *Prof Exp:* Field engr, Eng Dept, E I Du Pont de Nemours & Co, 42-52, res engr, Pigments Dept, 52-53, res supvr, 53-55, res mgr, 55-71, tech mgr inorg fibers, 71-75, environ mgr, 75-78, planning assoc, Chem, Dyes & Pigments Dept, 78-81. *Mem:* Am Chem Soc; Am Inst Chem Engrs. *Res:* Process development; extractive metallurgy; refractory metals; titanate and titanium dioxide products and processes. *Mailing Add:* 108 Meriden Dr Hockessin DE 19707

LUCKY, GEORGE W(ILLIAM), ELECTRICAL ENGINEERING. *Current Pos:* from asst prof to assoc prof, 64-69, PROF ELEC ENG, NMEX STATE UNIV, 69- *Personal Data:* b Dallas, Tex, Nov 7, 23; m 48; c 1. *Educ:* Okla State Univ, BSEE, 44, MS, 60, PhD(eng), 65. *Prof Exp:* Asst engr, Southwestern Bell Tel Co, 46-52, sr engr, 52-56; asst prof, Okla State Univ, 56-64. *Concurrent Pos:* Consult, J B Payne Assocs, Inc, 60- *Mem:* Am Soc Eng Educ; Inst Elec & Electronics Engrs. *Res:* Computer characterization of electric networks; network synthesis. *Mailing Add:* Dept Elec Eng & Comput Eng Box 3-0 NMex State Univ Las Cruces NM 88003

LUCKY, ROBERT W, ELECTRICAL ENGINEERING. *Current Pos:* VPRES APPL RES, BELLCORE, 92- *Personal Data:* b Pittsburgh, Pa, Jan 9, 36; m 61, Joan; c 2. *Educ:* Purdue Univ, BSEE, 57, MSEE, 59, PhD(elec eng), 61. *Hon Degrees:* DEng, Purdue Univ, 88; DSc, NJ Inst Technol, 91. *Honors & Awards:* Edwin Armstrong Award, Inst Elec & Electronics Engrs Commun Soc, 75; Centennial Medal, Inst Elec & Electronics Engrs, 84, Edison Medal, 95; Marconi Int Prize, Marconi Found, 86. *Prof Exp:* Mem tech staff, Bell Labs, Holmdel, NJ, 61-64, supvr, Signal Theory Group, 64-65, head, Data Theory Dept, 65-76, dept head, Digital-Switching Processing Res Dept, 76-77, asst dir elec & comput systs, 78-82, exec dir, Res Commun Sci Div, 82-92. *Concurrent Pos:* Asst ed, Trans Commun, Inst Elec & Electronics Engrs, 70-73, assoc ed, Trans Info Theory, 71-74, ed, Proc Inst Elec & Electronics Engrs, 74-76, consult ed, J Telecommun Networks, 78-86; vpres, Inst Elec & Electronics Engrs, Commun Soc, 78; vchmn, Sci Adv Bd, USAF, 83-86, chmn, 86-89; mem, Strategic Defense Initiative Adv Comt, 86-89, Comput Sci & Technol Bd, Nat Res Coun, 86-, Off Sci & Technol Policy Nat Crit Technol Panel, 90- & Vis Comt Advan Technol, Nat Inst Stand & Technol, 91-92. *Mem:* Nat Acad Eng; fel Inst Elec & Electronics Engrs (vpres, 78-79 & 81-82). *Res:* Communication theory; information theory; data transmission; author of over 50 publications; awarded 11 patents. *Mailing Add:* Bellcore 331 Newman Springs Rd Red Bank NJ 07701-5699

LUCOVSKY, GERALD, SOLID STATE PHYSICS. *Current Pos:* UNIV PROF PHYSICS, NC STATE UNIV, RALEIGH, 80- *Personal Data:* b New York, NY, Feb 28, 35; m 57; c 5. *Educ:* Univ Rochester, BS, 56, MA, 58; Temple Univ, PhD(physics), 60. *Prof Exp:* Mem staff solid state physics, Philco Corp, Pa, 58-65; sr scientist, Xerox Corp, 65-67; assoc prof eng, Case Western Res Univ, 67-68; mgr, Photoconductor Res Br, Xerox Corp, 68-69, solid state res br, 69-70, solid state scientist, Palo Alto Res Ctr, 70-73, assoc lab mgr, Gen Sci Lab, 73-74, sr res fel, Gen Sci Lab, Palo Alto Res Ctr, 74-80. *Mem:* Fel Am Phys Soc. *Res:* Optical properties of solids; lattice dynamics; amorphous semiconductors. *Mailing Add:* Dept Physics NC State Univ Box 8202 Raleigh NC 27695

LUCZAK, RICHARD, PARALLEL PROGRAMMING, NUMERICAL GRID GENERATION. *Current Pos:* COMPUT MATHEMATICIAN, NUMERICAL ALGORITHMS GROUP INC, 91- *Personal Data:* b Lodz, Poland, Apr 8, 57; US citizen. *Educ:* Tech Univ Lodz, MS, 81, PhD(appl math), 88. *Prof Exp:* Appl mathematician, Tech Univ, Lodz, Poland, 81-88; res & develop engr, Unotech Corp, 89. *Mem:* Soc Indust & Appl Math; Asn Comput Mach. *Res:* Design, implementation, testing of algorithms for numerical solution of partial differential equations on parallel computers; design of a new computational technique applicable to finite element analysis resulting in a great speedup and better accuracy of coefficients of global stiffness matrix and load vector. *Mailing Add:* 18 W 086 Williamsburg Villa Park IL 60181. *E-Mail:* luczak@hotmail.com

LUDDEN, GERALD D, MATHEMATICS. *Current Pos:* from asst prof to assoc prof, 66-77, PROF MATH, MICH STATE UNIV, 77- *Personal Data:* b Quincy, Ill, Sept 6, 37; m 61; c 3. *Educ:* St Ambrose Col, BA, 59; Univ Notre Dame, MS, 61, PhD(math), 66. *Prof Exp:* Lectr math, Ind Univ, 65-66. *Mem:* Math Asn Am; Am Math Soc; Tensor Soc. *Res:* Hypersurfaces of manifolds with an f-structure; submanifolds of real and complex space forms. *Mailing Add:* Mich State Univ East Lansing MI 48824-0001

LUDDEN, PAUL W, BIOCHEMISTRY. *Current Pos:* asst prof, 81-85, ASSOC PROF BIOCHEM, UNIV WIS-MADISON, 85- *Personal Data:* b Omaha, Nebr, Nov 7, 50; m 74. *Educ:* Univ Nebr, Lincoln, BS, 72; Univ Wis-Madison, PhD(biochem), 77. *Prof Exp:* Res asst, Univ Wis-Madison, 72-77; res assoc, Mich State Univ, 77-78; asst prof biochem & asst biochemist, Univ Calif, Riverside, 78-81. *Concurrent Pos:* Fel, Rockefeller Found, 77-78. *Mem:* Am Soc Plant Physiol; Am Soc Microbiol. *Res:* Plant biochemistry; nitrogen metabolism in plants and bacteria; carbon monoxide oxidation. *Mailing Add:* Dept Biochem Univ Wis 420 Henry Mall Madison WI 53706-1569. *Fax:* 608-262-3453

LUDDEN, THOMAS MARCELLUS, biopharmaceutics, drug metabolism, for more information see previous edition

LUDEKE, CARL ARTHUR, PHYSICS, OCEANOGRAPHY. *Current Pos:* RETIRED. *Personal Data:* b Cincinnati, Ohio, Sept 26, 14. *Educ:* Univ Cincinnati, AB, 35, PhD(physics), 38. *Prof Exp:* Instr math, John Carroll Univ, 38-40; instr, Univ Cincinnati, 40-43, from asst prof to assoc prof mech, 42-54, prof physics, 54-72; prof, Phys Oceanog Lab, NY Inst Technol at Nova Univ, 72-75, sr scientist, 75-79. *Concurrent Pos:* Consult, Gen Elec Co, 56-70. *Mem:* Int Asn Analog Comput. *Res:* Nonlinear mechanics; vibration analysis; shock mounts; mathematical physics; energy from the sun, sea and atmosphere. *Mailing Add:* PO Box 21682 Ft Lauderdale FL 33335-1682

LUDEKE, RUDOLF, SOLID STATE PHYSICS, MATERIAL SCIENCE. *Current Pos:* RES STAFF MEM, T J WATSON RES CTR, IBM CORP, 68- *Personal Data:* b Hannover, Ger, May 6, 37; m 64; c 2. *Educ:* Univ Cincinnati, BS, 61; Harvard Univ, MA, 62, PhD(appl physics), 68. *Concurrent Pos:* Vis scientist, Max Planck Inst, Stuttgart, Ger, 77-78; Alexander Von Humboldt Found fel, 77; assoc ed, J Vacuum Sci & Tech, 82-84; vis scholar, Dept Physics, Univ Utah, 86-87; prog chmn & conf chmn, Conf on Physics & Chem Semi-conductor Interfaces, 87; comt mem, Elec Mat & Processing Div, Am Vacuum Soc, 86- *Mem:* Am Phys Soc; Sigma Xi; Mat Res Soc; Am Vacuum Soc. *Res:* Semiconductor physics; surface and interface physics; thin film technology; structure and electronic properties of semiconductor interfaces, growth and characterization of semiconductor thin films and structures by molecular beum epitary, co-investor of the man-made semiconductor super lattice, optial properties of solids. *Mailing Add:* IBM T J Watson Res Ctr PO Box 218 Yorktown Heights NY 10598

LUDEL, JACQUELINE, BIOPSYCHOLOGY, SENSORY SYSTEM. *Current Pos:* PROF BIOL & PSYCHOL, GUILFORD COL, 76- *Personal Data:* b Boston, Mass, Mar 17, 45. *Educ:* Queens Col, NY, BA, 66; Ind Univ, PhD(psychol), 71. *Prof Exp:* Asst prof psychol, Jacksonville Univ, 71-73 & Stockton State Col, 73-76. *Concurrent Pos:* Grad fel, NSF, 66-71; assoc instr, Ind Univ, 67-71; Danforth assoc, 79-85; trustee, Marine Mammal Stranding Ctr, 79-86; Kenan grant, Guilford Col, 77-78. *Mem:* Psychol Social Responsibility. *Res:* Sensory anatomy and physiology; stranded and beached cetaceans; science writing. *Mailing Add:* Depts Biol & Psychol Guilford Col 5800 W Friendly Ave Greensboro NC 27410-4108. *Fax:* 910-316-2951; *E-Mail:* ludelj@rascal.guilford.edu

LUDEMA, KENNETH C, MECHANICAL ENGINEERING, SURFACE PHYSICS. *Current Pos:* from asst prof to assoc prof, 64-72, PROF MECH ENG, UNIV MICH, ANN ARBOR, 72- *Personal Data:* b Dorr, Mich, Apr 30, 28; m 55; c 5. *Educ:* Calvin Col, BS, 55; Univ Mich, BS, 55, MS, 56, PhD(mech eng), 63; Cambridge Univ, PhD(physics), 65. *Prof Exp:* Instr mech eng, Univ Mich, 55-62; Ford Found & Univ Mich Inst Sci & Technol fac develop grant, Cambridge Univ, 62-64. *Mem:* Am Soc Mech Engrs; Am Soc Testing & Mat. *Res:* Sliding friction and wear behavior of solids, steels, plastics and rubbers; fundamental adhesion mechanisms between dissimilar materials; skid resistance properties of tires and roads. *Mailing Add:* Dept Mech Eng 2250GGB Univ Mich Main Campus 2351 Herbert Ave Ann Arbor MI 48109-2125

LUDEMANN, CARL ARNOLD, ACCELERATOR DESIGN & CONTROL. *Current Pos:* RETIRED. *Personal Data:* b Brooklyn, NY, June 21, 34; m 56; c 2. *Educ:* Brooklyn Col, BS, 56; Univ Md, PhD(nuclear physics, elec eng), 64. *Prof Exp:* Res assoc physics, Univ Md, 64-65; vis scientist, Oak Ridge Nat Lab, 64-65, physicist, Electronuclear Div, 65-71, physicist, 71-93. *Mem:* Am Phys Soc; Am Asn Physics Teachers. *Res:* Neutron threshold measurements; gamma ray spectroscopy; angular correlation and nuclear reaction mechanism; nuclear structure studies; accelerator control, accelerator design. *Mailing Add:* 130 Newhaven Rd Oak Ridge TN 37830

LUDERS, RICHARD CHRISTIAN, analytical chemistry, for more information see previous edition

LUDIN, ROGER LOUIS, NUCLEAR PHYSICS. *Current Pos:* LECTR PHYSICS, CALIF POLYTECH STATE UNIV, SAN LUIS OBISPO, 84- *Personal Data:* b Jersey City, NJ, June 13, 44; m 66, Dianne Wilson; c Stephen & Joyce. *Educ:* Brown Univ, ScB, 66; Worcester Polytech Inst, MS, 68, PhD(physics), 69. *Prof Exp:* Fel, Worcester Polytech Inst, 69-71; prof physics, Burlington Co Col, NJ, 71-86. *Mem:* AAAS; Am Phys Soc; Am Asn Physics Teachers. *Res:* Neutron-deuteron scattering. *Mailing Add:* Dept Physics Calif Polytech State Univ San Luis Obispo CA 93407. *E-Mail:* rludin@oboe.aix.calpoly.edu

LUDINGTON, MARTIN A, NUCLEAR PHYSICS. *Current Pos:* Chmn, Physics Dept, 80-83 & 89-92, PROF PHYSICS, ALBION COL, 69- *Personal Data:* b Detroit, Mich, Mar 7, 43; m 79, Kathryn; c Elizabeth & Andrew. *Educ:* Albion Col, AB, 64; Univ Mich, MS, 65, PhD(physics), 69. *Concurrent Pos:* Adj res scientist, Phoenix Mem Lab; mem, Coun Undergrad Res, Am Asn Physics Teachers & Am Phys Soc. *Mem:* Am Phys Soc; Am Asn Physics Teachers. *Res:* High accuracy efficiency calib of gamma detectors; low level counting. *Mailing Add:* Dept Physics Albion Col Albion MI 49224

LUDKE, JAMES LARRY, environmental biology, for more information see previous edition

LUDLAM, WILLIAM MYRTON, OPTOMETRY, PHYSIOLOGICAL OPTICS. *Current Pos:* assoc prof, 74-80, PROF PHYSIOL OPTICS & OPTOM, COL OPTOM, PAC UNIV, 80- *Personal Data:* b Teaneck, NJ, Mar 31, 31; m 54; c 4. *Educ:* Columbia Univ, BS, 53, MS, 54; Mass Col Optom, OD, 63. *Honors & Awards:* Skeffington Award, 77. *Prof Exp:* Dir, Vision Res Lab, Optom Ctr NY, 61-73; assoc prof physiol optics & optom, Col Optom, State Univ NY, 71-73. *Concurrent Pos:* Res grants, Am Optom Found, 55-56, NY Acad Optom, 57, Optom Ctr Res Fund, 60-61 & NIH, 63-74. *Mem:* Fel AAAS; fel Am Acad Optom; fel Optical Soc Am; fel NY Acad Sci. *Res:* Ocular dioptric components; pathophysiology of strabismus and its remediation; ametropia and its etiology; vision and learning. *Mailing Add:* PO Box 145 Forest Grove OR 97116

LUDLOW, CHRISTY L, NEUROPHYSIOLOGY, INTEGRATED SYSTEMS RESEARCH. *Current Pos:* RES SPEECH PATHOLOGIST, NAT INST DEAFNESS & OTHER COMMUN DIS, 74- *Personal Data:* b Montreal, Que, June 7, 44; m 68. *Educ:* McGill Univ, BSc, 65, MSc, 67; NY Univ, PhD(psycholing, speech path), 73. *Honors & Awards:* Dir Award, NIH, 77. *Prof Exp:* Res asst, McGill Univ, 66-67; res speech pathologist, Med Ctr, NY Univ, 67-70, W A Anderson fel, 70-72; vis lectr speech & hearing sci, Univ Md, 73-74. *Concurrent Pos:* Proj mgr, Am Speech & Hearing Asn, 73-74; liaison rep, AAAS, 77-81; ed consult, J Speech & Hearing Dis, 77- & J Speech & Hearing Res, 77-; chief, speech path unit intramural res prog, Nat Inst Neurol & Commun Dis & Stroke, NIH; consult, Vietnam Head Injury Study, Walter Reed Army Med Ctr, 81-85; adj prof, Med Sch, Georgetown Univ & Univ Md. *Mem:* Int Neuropsychol Soc; Acoust Soc Am; Soc Neurosci; AAAS; Asn Res Otolaryngol; fel Am Speech-Lang-Hearing Asn; Acad Aphasia; fel Am Laryngol Asn. *Res:* Speech science; neurolinguistics; aphasia; developmental language disorders; neuropharmacology; vocal pathologies; neurological disorders affecting speech and language functioning; neurophysiology of laryngeal movement control during speech in disorders of spasmodic dysphonia and stuttering. *Mailing Add:* Bldg 10 Rm 5D38 Voice & Speech Sect VSLB NIDCD 10 Center Dr MSC 1416 Bethesda MD 20892-1416. *Fax:* 301-480-0803; *E-Mail:* eludlow@pop.nidcd.nih.gov

LUDLOW, DOUGLAS KENT, CHARACTERIZATION OF SURFACE-SOLID PROPERTIES OF COAL CHAR & FLYASH, TRANSFORMATION & REMEDIATION OF INORGANIC AIR TOXIC METALS DURING COMBUSTION. *Current Pos:* PROF & CHAIR, UNIV MO, ROLLA, 96- *Personal Data:* b Spanish Fork, Utah, Mar 19, 57; m 79, Sherryl A Smith; c Chalise, Allison, Leslie, Katherine & Megan. *Educ:* Brigham Young Univ, BS, 82; Ariz State Univ, PhD(chem eng), 86. *Honors & Awards:* Res Initiation Award, Eng Found, 89. *Prof Exp:* Process engr, Monsanto Inorg Chem, 79-80; from asst prof to assoc prof chem eng, Univ NDak, 86-96, dept chair, 94-96. *Concurrent Pos:* Fulbright sr scholar, Coun Int Exchange Scholars, 92-93; vis prof chem, Hebrew Univ Jerusalem, Israel, 92-93, Fulbright sr scholar, 92-93. *Mem:* Am Inst Chem Engrs; Am Chem Soc; Am Soc Eng Educ; Sigma Xi. *Res:* Characterization of surfaces including coal, char and catalysts; application of fractal geometry to determine surface morphology from physisorption measurements; inorganic transformations during coal combustion; nitrous oxide selective catalytic reduction using fabric filters for simultaneous nitrous oxide and particulate removal. *Mailing Add:* Chem Eng 143 Schrenk Hall Rolla MO 65401. *Fax:* 573-341-4377; *E-Mail:* dludlow@umr.edu

LUDLUM, DAVID BLODGETT, ENVIRONMENTAL HEALTH. *Current Pos:* PROF PHARMACOL & MED, UNIV MASS SCH MED, 86-; AFFIL PROF CHEM, CLARK UNIV, WORCESTER, MASS, 96- *Personal Data:* b Brooklyn, NY, Sept 30, 29; m 52, Carlene L Dyke; c Valerie J (Wright) & Kenneth D. *Educ:* Cornell Univ, BA, 51; Univ Wis-Madison, PhD(chem), 54; NY Univ, MD, 62. *Prof Exp:* Res chemist, E I du Pont de Nemours & Co, Inc, Del, 54-58; intern, 3rd & 4th Med Divs, Bellevue Hosp, 62-63; asst prof pharmacol & Am Cancer Soc fac res assoc, Sch Med, Yale Univ, 63-68; from assoc prof to prof pharmacol, Sch Med, Univ Md, Baltimore City, 70-76; prof pharmacol, Albany Med Col, 76-86 chmn dept, 76-80, prof med, 80-86. *Concurrent Pos:* Markle scholar acad med, Yale Univ & Univ Md, 67-72; Nat Inst Gen Med Sci career develop award, Yale Univ, 68; vis prof oncol, Johns Hopkins Univ, Baltimore, Md, 73-76, Courtauld Inst, London, 70; adj prof chem, Rensselaer Poly Inst, Troy, NY, 77-80; assoc ed, Cancer Res, 80- *Mem:* Am Chem Soc; Am Soc Pharmacol & Exp Therapeut; Am Soc Biol Chem; Am Asn Cancer Res; Am Soc Clin Pharmacol & Therapeut. *Res:* Pharmacology of antineoplastic agents; cancer chemotherapy; mutagenesis and carcinogenesis; molecular and clinical pharmacology. *Mailing Add:* Dept Pharmacol Univ Mass Med Sch 55 Lake Ave N Worcester MA 01655. *Fax:* 508-856-5080

LUDLUM, JOHN CHARLES, GEOLOGY. *Current Pos:* from asst prof to prof, WVa Univ, 46-72, dir ctr resource develop, 62-63, dir off res & develop, Appalachian Ctr, 63-66, from asst dean to dean grad sch, 66-72, EMER PROF GEOL, WVA UNIV, 72- *Personal Data:* b Chevy Chase, Md, Feb 2, 13; m 40, Mildred Wells. *Educ:* Lafayette Col, BS, 35; Cornell Univ, MS, 39, PhD(struct geol), 42. *Prof Exp:* Mem staff, Socony Vacuum Oil Co, 35-37 & Amerada Petrol Corp, 37; from asst instr to instr geol, Cornell Univ, 37-42. *Concurrent Pos:* Consult, 46-62; coop econ geologist, State Geol Surv, 46-62. *Mem:* Fel Geol Soc Am; sr fel Soc Econ Geol; Am Asn Petrol Geol; Am Inst Mining Metall & Petrol Eng; Sigma Xi. *Res:* Structural and economic geology of West Virginia; natural and human resources research applied toward improvement of the economy and life in West Virginia and the Appalachian highlands. *Mailing Add:* 612 Callen Ave Morgantown WV 26505

LUDLUM, KENNETH HILLS, PHYSICAL CHEMISTRY. *Current Pos:* RETIRED. *Personal Data:* b Albany, NY, Nov 16, 29; m 53; c 4. *Educ:* Col Educ Albany, BA, 51, MA, 52; Rensselaer Polytech Inst, PhD(phys chem), 61. *Prof Exp:* Chemist, Beacon Res Lab, 61-62, Texaco Inc, 61-62, sr chemist, 62-65, res chemist, 65-73, sr res chemist, 73-80, res assoc, 80-92, coordr, Texaco BNV Cons & Toxicol, 87-92. *Mem:* Am Chem Soc; Catalysis Soc; Air Pollution Control Asn. *Res:* Reaction kinetics; air pollution studies and related environmental science; catalysis and surface chemistry. *Mailing Add:* 117 N Elm St Beacon NY 12508

LUDMAN, ALLAN, GEOLOGY, PETROLOGY. *Current Pos:* from asst to assoc prof, 75-82, PROF EARTH & ENVIRON SCI, QUEEN COL, NY, 82- *Personal Data:* b Brooklyn, NY, Mar 7, 43. *Educ:* Brooklyn Col, BS, 63; Ind Univ, Bloomington, AM, 65; Univ Pa, PhD(geol), 69. *Prof Exp:* Asst prof geol, Smith Col, 69-75. *Concurrent Pos:* Field geologist, Maine Geol Surv, 66- *Mem:* Geol Soc Am; Sigma Xi; AAAS; Geol Asn Can. *Res:* Regional geologic mapping in central and eastern Maine; low-temperature metamorphism of pelitic and calcareous rocks; tectonic evolution of northeastern New England. *Mailing Add:* Dept Geol Queens Col Flushing NY 11367-0904

LUDMAN, JACQUES ERNEST, SOLID STATE PHYSICS. *Current Pos:* PRES, NORTHEAST PHOTOSCI, INC, 90- *Personal Data:* b Chicago, Ill, Nov 26, 34; m 70; c 1. *Educ:* Middlebury Col, BA, 56; Northeastern Univ, PhD(solid state physics), 73. *Prof Exp:* Res physicist, Air Force Cambridge Res Lab, 59-75, chief, Optical Processing Sect, 75-89. *Mem:* Sigma Xi. *Res:* Injection laser development; radiation damage effects on semiconductor devices; infrared sensor physics. *Mailing Add:* 18 Flagg Rd Hollis NH 03049

LUDOVICI, PETER PAUL, MICROBIOLOGY. *Current Pos:* from instr to asst prof, Univ Ariz, 54-63, microbiol, obstet & gynec, 63-64, microbiol & cent tissue cult facil, 64-65, from assoc prof to prof, 65-87, EMER PROF MICROBIOL, UNIV ARIZ, 87- *Personal Data:* b Pittsburgh, Pa, Aug 9, 20; m 45, Lucy Carrozza; c Ralph, Joseph, Paul, JoAnn & Lisa. *Educ:* Washington & Jefferson Col, BS, 42; Univ Pittsburgh, MS, 49, PhD(bact), 51. *Prof Exp:* Res bacteriologist immunol, West Penn Hosp, 49-51; res assoc, Univ Pittsburgh, 51; res assoc obstet & gynec, Univ Mich, 51-54. *Mem:* AAAS; Am Soc Microbiol; Tissue Cult Asn; Soc Exp Biol & Med. *Res:* Tissue culture; cancer; virology; cell transformations. *Mailing Add:* 5425 E Rosewood Ave Tucson AZ 85711

LUDTKA, GERALD M, MATERIAL SCIENCE. *Current Pos:* STAFF MEM, METALS & CERAMICS DIV, MAT PROCESSING MODELING GROUP. *Honors & Awards:* E O Lawrence Mem Award, US Dept Energy, 94. *Mailing Add:* Metals & Ceramics Div Mat Processing Modeling Group Oak Ridge TN 37831-6056

LUDUENA, RICHARD FROILAN, BIOCHEMISTRY. *Current Pos:* from asst prof to assoc prof, 76-88, PROF BIOCHEM, UNIV TEX HEALTH SCI CTR, SAN ANTONIO, 88- *Personal Data:* b San Francisco, Calif, Feb 9, 46; m 81; c 1. *Educ:* Harvard Univ, BA, 67; Stanford Univ, PhD(biol), 73. *Prof Exp:* Fel pharmacol, Sch Med, Stanford Univ, 73-75, fel genetics, 75-76. *Concurrent Pos:* Jane Coffin Childs Mem Fund Med Res fel, 73-75. *Mem:* Am Soc Cell Biol; Int Soc Neurochem; Am Soc Biochem & Molecular Biol. *Res:* Regulation of microtubule assembly; structure and evolution of tubulin; pharmacology of microtubule proteins; tubulin isotypes. *Mailing Add:* Dept Biochem Univ Tex Health Sci Ctr 7703 Floyd Curl Dr San Antonio TX 78284-7760. *Fax:* 210-567-6595

LUDVIGSEN, CARL W, JR, PATHOLOGY. *Current Pos:* chief oper officer, 93-96, CHIEF MANAGING OFFICER, LAB ONE, 97-; CHIEF MANAGING OFFICER, EVP CORP, 97- *Personal Data:* b Palo Alto, Calif. *Educ:* Univ Colo, Boulder, BA, 74; Washington Univ, St Louis, Mo, MD & PhD, 80; Am Bd Path, cert, 85; Creighton Univ, JD, 88. *Prof Exp:* Teaching asst, Dept Anat, Sch Med, Washington Univ, St Louis, Mo, 76, tutor physiol, path & pharmacol, 76-77; clin path resident, Univ Minn, Minneapolis, 80-82, clin chem fel, 82-83; dir chem, spec chem & toxicol, Med Ctr, Univ Nebr, 83-86; emergency rm physician, Lutheran Hosp, Omaha, Nebr & Bryan Mem Hosp, Lincoln, Nebr, 86-88; dir, Emergency Rm & Labs, Sandstone Area Hosp, Minn, 88-89; chief pathologist & sr vpres, Home Off Res Lab, Lenexa, Kans, 89-90; clin assoc prof, Dept Path, Sch Med, Med Ctr, Univ Kans, Kansas City, 90-93. *Concurrent Pos:* Young investr award, Acad Clin Lab Physicians & Scientists, Seattle, Wash, 82; mem, Prod Eval & Stand Comt, 83-85; consult, Ariel Answer Prizes, 86-; assoc med dir, Bus Mens Assurance Co, Kansas City, Mo, 89- *Mem:* Fel Am Col Legal Med; Am Med Asn; fel Clin Asn Path; Am Soc Clin Pathologists; Am Soc Law & Med; AAAS; Am Asn Clin Chemists; Am Diabetes Asn; Acad Clin Lab Physicians & Scientists; Asn Clin Scientists. *Res:* Validation, verification and correlation of various toxicologic measurement modalities; aspects of lipid measurements as related to coronary artery dosage risk; general population studies; development of alcohol abuse markers suitable for population screening; author of various publications. *Mailing Add:* Dept Path Home Off Ref Lab PO Box 2035 Shawnee Mission KS 66201-1035. *Fax:* 913-894-0287

LUDVIGSEN, F J BERNHARD T, MEDICAL TECHNOLOGY, CLINICAL CHEMISTRY. *Current Pos:* ASSOC PROF MED TECHNOL, UNIV S ALA, 82-, ASSOC PROF ANESTHESIOL, 84- *Personal Data:* b Copenhagen, Denmark, Oct 3, 23; nat US; m 44, Ellon Krogh; c Lise-Lotte & Stig Michael. *Educ:* Copenhagen Univ, Denmark, PhD, 54. *Prof Exp:* Res chief clin chem, Med Lab, Copenhagen, 54-58; chief, Clin Serv Lab, Sask Cancer & Med Res Inst, 58-59; asst prof & head, Anethesia Res Lab, Univ Sask, 59; dir biochem, Muscular Dystrophy Res Lab, Univ Alta Hosp, 60-63;

head, Dept Chem, Greenville Hosp Syst, 63-76; pres, Blue Ridge Med Lab, 76-81. *Concurrent Pos:* Consult, Path Assoc, Greenville, SC, 67-76, Tech Corp, Tarrytown, NY, 69-71. *Mem:* Am Asn Clin Chemists. *Res:* Fibrogen and heavy metals; hypothermia; enzymes in muscle; tissue homogenization; lead poisoning; laboratory administration; automation and computers; blood loss monitoring; electrolyte monitoring; lactate monitoring, urea monitoring, instrumentation; several patents. *Mailing Add:* Univ S Ala 1504 Springhill Ave Mobile AL 36604. *Fax:* 334-434-3403; *E-Mail:* bludvigs@jaguar1.usouthal.edu

LUDWICK, ADRIANE GURAK, ORGANIC CHEMISTRY. *Current Pos:* from asst prof to assoc prof, 69-77, PROF CHEM, TUSKEGEE UNIV, 77- *Personal Data:* b Passaic, NJ, June 16, 41; m 68; c 2. *Educ:* Rutgers Univ, New Brunswick, AB, 63; Univ Ill, Urbana, MS, 65, PhD(chem), 67. *Prof Exp:* Asst prof chem, Tuskegee Univ, 67-68; vis asst prof & res assoc, Univ Ill, Urbana, 68-69. *Concurrent Pos:* Res assoc, Environ Sci Div, Oak Ridge Nat Lab, 74, Chem Div, Lawrence Livermore Lab, 78 & AT&T Bell Labs, 82-85; NIH fac fel, Macromolecular Res Ctr, Univ Mich, 78-79. *Mem:* NSF fac fel, Macromolecular Res Ctr, Univ Mich, 79-80. *Mem:* AAAS; Am Chem Soc; Sigma Xi. *Res:* Synthetic macromolecules and simpler organic molecules with potential biological activity; polycarbosilanes, fluoroepoxies. *Mailing Add:* Dept Chem Armstrong Hall Tuskegee Univ Tuskegee AL 36088

LUDWICK, LARRY MARTIN, INORGANIC CHEMISTRY. *Current Pos:* asst prof, 69-73, assoc prof, 74-76, PROF CHEM, TUSKEGEE UNIV, 76- *Personal Data:* b Jamestown, NY, Oct 15, 41; m 68, Adriane Gurak; c Michael & Douglas. *Educ:* Mt Union Col, BS, 63; Univ Melbourne, BSc, 65; Univ Ill, Urbana, MS, 67, PhD(inorg chem), 69; Univ Ala, MLS, 92. *Prof Exp:* Res chemist, PPG Industs, 65. *Concurrent Pos:* NIH fel, Biophys Res Div, Univ Mich, 78-80. *Mem:* AAAS; Am Chem Soc; Sigma Xi; Nat Sci Teachers Asn. *Res:* Metal binding studies; copper and zinc binding constants using superoxide dismutase. *Mailing Add:* Dept Chem Tuskegee Univ Tuskegee AL 36088. *E-Mail:* lludwick@acd.tusk.edu

LUDWICK, THOMAS MURRELL, ANIMAL PHYSIOLOGY. *Current Pos:* from assoc prof to prof, 48-83, EMER PROF DAIRY SCI, OHIO STATE UNIV, 83- *Personal Data:* b Cox's Creek, Ky, Aug 2, 14. *Educ:* Eastern Ky Teachers Col, BS, 36; Univ Ky, MS, 39; Univ Minn, PhD(dairy sci, animal genetics), 42; Univ Chicago, dipl, 42; Univ Va, dipl, 43. *Honors & Awards:* Am Dairy Sci Award, Ohio State Univ. *Prof Exp:* Dairy & tobacco farmer, Ky, 25-39; asst cattle breeding & physiol, Univ Minn, 39-42; asst prof dairy sci, Univ Ky, 46-48. *Concurrent Pos:* Teacher high sch, Ky, 37-38; dir, Ohio Regional Dairy Cattle Breeding Proj, 48-; instr meteorol & weather forecasting, USAF, 42-47. *Mem:* Am Soc Animal Sci; Am Dairy Sci Asn. *Res:* Physiology of reproduction and milk secretion; artificial insemination; animal breeding and biometeorology. *Mailing Add:* 7614 Stafford Rd SW Washington Court House OH 43160

LUDWIG, ALLEN CLARENCE, SR, ASPHALT-EMULSION TECHNOLOGY, PLASTICS TECHNIQUE. *Current Pos:* OWNER, ALLEN C LUDWIG, PE CONSULT, 86- *Personal Data:* b San Antonio, Tex, Nov 3, 38; m 60; c 4. *Educ:* Tex A&M Univ, BS, 60. *Honors & Awards:* IR 100 Award, 79. *Prof Exp:* Chem engr, Tech Serv Div, Monsanto Chem Co, 60; nuclear res chemist, ASAF, 60-63; res develop, Southwest Res Inst, 63-69, sr res engr, Systs Develop, Div Automotive Res, 69-74, Process Res & Eng Dept Vehicle & Traffic Safety, 74-82, Process Res & Eng, Dept Energy Conversion & Combustion Technol, Fuels & Lubricants Res Div, 82-86. *Res:* Sulfur product and process development have been principal areas of interest; numerous US and foreign patents; many technical publications. *Mailing Add:* 5914 Brenda Lane San Antonio TX 78240. *Fax:* 210-684-2747

LUDWIG, CHARLES HEBERLE, WOOD CHEMISTRY. *Current Pos:* RETIRED. *Personal Data:* b Minneapolis, Minn, May 1, 20; m 56; c 2. *Educ:* Macalester Col, BA, 42; Univ Wash, PhD(chem), 61. *Prof Exp:* Chemist, D A Dodd, Mfg Chemist, 47-55 & Univ Wash, 56-61; mem res staff, Ga Pac Corp, 61-82. *Mem:* Am Chem Soc; Sigma Xi. *Res:* Nuclear magnetic resonance spectroscopy of lignins and lignin models; chemistry of lignosulfonates and other lignins; nuclear magnetic resonance studies of lignin; model compounds and related materials; product development of lignosulfonates. *Mailing Add:* Waldron WA 98297

LUDWIG, CLAUS BERTHOLD, molecular spectroscopy, environmental physics, for more information see previous edition

LUDWIG, DONALD A, MATHEMATICS, APPLIED MATHEMATICS. *Current Pos:* PROF MATH, UNIV BC, 74- *Personal Data:* b New York, NY, Nov 14, 33; m 53; c 2. *Educ:* NY Univ, BA, 54, MS, 57, PhD(math), 59. *Prof Exp:* Res assoc math, Inst Math Sci, NY Univ, 59-60; Fine instr, Princeton Univ, 60-61; asst prof, Univ Calif, Berkeley, 61-64; from assoc prof to prof, NY Univ, 64-74. *Concurrent Pos:* Guggenheim fel, Tel Aviv, Rehovot, Dundee, 70-71. *Mem:* Am Math Soc; Soc Indust & Appl Math; fel Royal Soc Can. *Res:* Partial differential equations; mathematical methods for population biology. *Mailing Add:* Dept Math Univ BC 2204 Main Mall Vancouver BC V6T 1W5 Can

LUDWIG, EDWARD JAMES, NUCLEAR PHYSICS. *Current Pos:* from asst prof to assoc prof, 66-71, PROF PHYSICS, UNIV NC, CHAPEL HILL, 76- *Personal Data:* b New York, NY, Apr 13, 37; m 58, Helen Johnson; c Kenneth, Janet, Joanne & Carolyn. *Educ:* Fordham Univ, BS, 58; Ind Univ, MS, 60, PhD(physics), 63. *Prof Exp:* Res fel physics, Rutgers Univ, 63-66. *Concurrent Pos:* Prin investr, DOE res contract; vis prof, Univ Birmingham, 73, Lawrence Berkeley Lab, 80, Univ Munich, 89; assoc dir, Triangle Univ Nuclear Lab, 92- *Mem:* Am Phys Soc. *Res:* Nuclear reactions and scattering cross sections and polarization effects; reaction mechanisms; resonance studies; studies of few-nucleon systems. *Mailing Add:* Dept Physics Univ NC Chapel Hill NC 27599-3255. *Fax:* 919-962-0480; *E-Mail:* ludwig@tunl

LUDWIG, FRANK ARNO, ELECTROCHEMICAL OR THERMAL REGENERATIVE FUEL CELLS, ELECTROCHEMICAL SENSORS. *Current Pos:* CONSULT, 94- *Personal Data:* b West Reading, Pa, Jan 17, 31; m 73, Joann McGuire; c David, Annemarie, Heidi, Tom, Peter, Henry & Julianne. *Educ:* Calif Inst Technol, BS, 53; Case Western Reserve Univ, MS, 65, PhD(phys chem), 68. *Honors & Awards:* Hughes Electro-optical & Data Syst Group Pat Award. *Prof Exp:* Proj engr, Carter Labs, Inc, 53-56; res engr, Hughes Aircraft Co, 56-57; vpres, Tech Commun, Inc, 55-58; dept mgr fuel cells, thermogalvanics, Electro-Optical Systs, Inc, 58-62; dept mgr org electrolyte batteries, electrochem trace gas sensors, Whittaker Corp, 68-69; supvr, Res Lab, Ford Motor Co, 69-78; mgr, Near-Term Elec Vehicle Battery Contracts, Argonne Nat Lab, 78-79; prin engr corrosion, mat develop, Ford Aerospace & Commun Corp, 79-82; chief scientist, Mat Technol Lab, Hughes Aircraft Co, 82-94. *Res:* Materials, corrosion, chemical and electrochemical kinetics, ac impedance techniques; development of new batteries and fuel cells; electroanalytical device inventions; improvements in batteries for electric vehicles; energy storage and conservation device inventions; electrochemical sensors inventions; thermodynamics; electroplating and surface finishing innovations. *Mailing Add:* 29443 Whitley Collins Dr Ranch Palos Verdes CA 90275. *Fax:* 310-377-4989; *E-Mail:* joladwig@aol.com

LUDWIG, FREDERIC C, experimental pathology, for more information see previous edition

LUDWIG, FREDERICK JOHN, SR, ANALYTICAL CHEMISTRY, ORGANIC CHEMISTRY. *Current Pos:* group leader, 59-73, res scientist, Tretolite Div, 73-92, ANALYSIS RES SPECIALIST, PETROLITE CORP, 92- *Personal Data:* b St Louis, Mo, June 20, 28; m 56; c Frederick John Jr & Lawrence Charles. *Educ:* Washington Univ, AB, 50; St Louis Univ, PhD(chem), 53. *Prof Exp:* Lab asst chem, St Louis Univ, 50-53; res chemist, Uranium Div, Mallinckrodt Chem Corp, 55-59. *Mem:* Am Chem Soc; Sigma Xi. *Res:* Gas-liquid and liquid-solid chromatography; infrared spectroscopy; wax-polymers; water-treatment chemicals; nuclear magnetic resonance spectroscopy. *Mailing Add:* Res Lab Petrolite Corp 369 Marshall Ave St Louis MO 63119

LUDWIG, GARRY (GERHARD ADOLF), GENERAL RELATIVITY. *Current Pos:* From asst prof to assoc prof, 66-82, PROF MATH, UNIV ALTA, 82- *Personal Data:* b Mannheim, Ger, Sept 4, 40; Can & German citizen; m 68, Roberta. *Educ:* Univ Toronto, BSc, 62; Brown Univ, PhD(physics), 66. *Concurrent Pos:* Nat Res Coun grants, 67-97. *Mem:* Am Math Soc; Am Phys Soc; Can Math Soc; Int Soc Gen Relativity & Gravitation. *Res:* General relativity and gravitation; asymptotically flat spacetimes, H-space, exact solutions, spin-coefficient formalisms. *Mailing Add:* Dept Math Sci Univ Alta Edmonton AB T6G 2G1 Can. *Fax:* 403-492-6826; *E-Mail:* gludwig@vega.math.ualberta.ca

LUDWIG, GEORGE H, SPACE SYSTEMS DESIGN, SPACE SCIENCES. *Current Pos:* VIS SR SCIENTIST, CALIF INST TECHNOL, 89- *Personal Data:* b Johnson Co, Iowa, Nov 13, 27; m 50, Rosalie F Vickers; c Barbara R, George V, Sharon L & Kathy A (Ramsay). *Educ:* Univ Iowa, BA, 56, MS, 59, PhD(elec eng), 60. *Honors & Awards:* Golden Plate Award, Acad Achievement, 62; NOAA Prog & Mgt Award, Nat Oceanic & Atmospheric Admin, 77; Except Sci Achievement Medal, NASA, 84. *Prof Exp:* Res assoc space res, Univ Iowa, 60; head, Instrumentation Sect, Goddard Space Flight Ctr, NASA, 60-65, chief, Info Processing Div, 65-71, assoc dir data opers, 71-72; dir systs integration, Nat Environ Satellite Serv, Nat Oceanic & Atmospheric Admin, 72-75, dir opers, 75-80, tech dir, 80, sr scientist, Environ Res Labs, 80-81, dir, 81-83; asst chief scientist, NASA, 83-84; sr res assoc, Univ Colo, 85-91. *Concurrent Pos:* Consult data mgt & space sta, 84-92; vis sr scientist, Calif Inst Tech, NASA Hq, 89-91. *Mem:* Sigma Xi; sr mem Am Geophys Union; sr mem Inst Elec & Electronics Engrs. *Res:* Cosmic rays; development of space instrumentation; on board and ground data processing; co-discovery and investigation of Van Allen radiation belts; atmospheric, oceanic, hydrologic remote sensing and forecasting; direction of space, atmospheric and oceanic environmental research. *Mailing Add:* 215 Aspen Trail Winchester VA 22602. *E-Mail:* ludwiggh@visuallink.com

LUDWIG, GERALD W, POWER ELECTRONICS, SIMULATION. *Current Pos:* RETIRED. *Personal Data:* b New York, NY, Jan 7, 30; m 51; c 3. *Educ:* Harvard Univ, AB, 50, AM, 51, PhD(chem physics), 55; Rensselaer Polytech Inst, MA, 87. *Prof Exp:* Physicist, Res & Develop Ctr, Gen Elec Corp, 55-63, liaison scientist, 63-65, physicist, 65-71, mgr, Integrated Circuits Br, 71-74. *Mem:* Fel Am Phys Soc; sr mem Inst Elec & Electronics Engrs; Electrochem Soc. *Res:* Transport properties of semiconductors; electron paramagnetic resonance; Gunn effect; x-ray and cathode ray phosphors; semiconductor materials and processing; charge transfer devices; integrated circuits; modelling and simulation of power electronic circuits and systems. *Mailing Add:* 112 Glenhill Dr Scotia NY 12302

LUDWIG, HARVEY F, ENVIRONMENTAL & SANITARY ENGINEERING. *Current Pos:* PRES, SOUTHEAST ASIA TECHNOL, BANGKOK, THAILAND, 73- *Personal Data:* b Saskatoon, Sask, Can, Dec 4, 16. *Educ:* Univ Calif, Berkeley, BS, 38, MS, 42; Clemsen Univ, DEng, 65. *Prof Exp:* Sanit engr, USPHS, 43-45; assoc prof eng, Univ Calif, Berkeley, 49-51; chmn & pres, Eng Sci, Inc, 56-72. *Mem:* Nat Acad Eng; Sigma Xi. *Mailing Add:* 43 Alston Pl Santa Barbara CA 93108

LUDWIG, HOWARD C, CHEMICAL PHYSICS, PLASMA PHYSICS. *Current Pos:* RETIRED. *Personal Data:* b Beaver Falls, Pa, July 31, 16; m 41, Martha Summerfield; c Sandra K (Paradis). *Educ:* Geneva Col, BS, 41. *Honors & Awards:* IR 100 Award, 63; Lincoln Gold Medal, Am Welding Soc, 56. *Prof Exp:* Chem analyst, Armstrong Cork Co, 41-42; spectroscopist, Propeller Div, Curtiss-Wright Corp, 42-46; res engr, Res Labs, Westinghouse Elec Corp, 46-59; fel scientist, Res & Develop Ctr, 59-76; consult plasma physics, 76-80. *Concurrent Pos:* Musician. *Res:* Research and development of high and low pressure plasmas; range of gas pressures, microns to 40 atmospheres, welding arcs, illumination and circuit interruption. *Mailing Add:* 163 Curtis Dr Beaver Falls PA 15010-1056

LUDWIG, HUBERT JOSEPH, MATHEMATICS. *Current Pos:* from asst prof to assoc prof, 68-81, PROF MATH, BALL STATE UNIV, 81- *Personal Data:* b Lincoln, Ill, July 27, 34; m 65, Sharon L Clements; c Jonathan & Jennifer. *Educ:* Univ Ill, Urbana, BS, 56; St Louis Univ, MS, 64, PhD(math), 68. *Prof Exp:* Instr math, chem & eng mech, Springfield Col, Ill, 56-65; teaching asst math, St Louis Univ, 65-68. *Mem:* Math Asn Am; Nat Coun Teachers Math; Sigma Xi. *Res:* Chaotic dynamics; 2-metric spaces; logo and fractals; computers in secondary mathematics education. *Mailing Add:* 3209 W Twickingham Dr Muncie IN 47304. *E-Mail:* hjludwig@bsu.edu

LUDWIG, JOHN HOWARD, environmental sciences; deceased, see previous edition for last biography

LUDWIG, MARTHA LOUISE, BIOCHEMISTRY. *Current Pos:* from asst prof to assoc prof, 67-75, PROF BIOL CHEM & RES BIOPHYSICIST, BIOPHYS RES DIV, UNIV MICH, ANN ARBOR, 75- *Personal Data:* b Pittsburgh, Pa, Aug 16, 31; m 61. *Educ:* Cornell Univ, BA, 52, PhD(biochem), 56; Univ Calif, Berkeley, MA, 55. *Prof Exp:* Res fel biochem, Harvard Med Sch, 56-59; res assoc biol, Mass Inst Technol, 59-62; res fel chem, Harvard Univ, 62-67. *Mem:* Am Chem Soc; Am Soc Biol Chemists; Biophys Soc; Am Crystallog Asn. *Res:* Protein crystallography; protein structure and function. *Mailing Add:* Univ Mich 3038 Chem 930 N University Ave Ann Arbor MI 48109-1055

LUDWIG, MATTHIAS HEINZ, SEMICONDUCTOR TECHNOLOGY, POROUS SILICON. *Current Pos:* vis scientist, 92-94, ADJ PROF MAT SCI, UNIV FLA, 94- *Personal Data:* b Leipzig, Ger, July 13, 54; m 80, Angelika Glathe; c Kaj. *Educ:* Humboldt Univ, Berlin, Ger, BS, 80, MS, 81, PhD(physics), 87. *Prof Exp:* Prin investr infrared detectors, Werk fuer Fernsehelektronik, Ger, 87-89; res assoc semiconductor technol, Humboldt Univ, Ger, 89-92. *Concurrent Pos:* Vis scientist, Tech Univ Nowgorod/Univ Petersburg, Russia, 89; prin investr, Ger NSF, 91-94; consult, AME Laboremsanlagen Berlin, 93- *Mem:* Ger Asn Teachers; Mat Res Soc. *Res:* Luminescence of spark-processed porous silicon; infrared detectors made from III/V semiconductors; surface and interface properties of semiconductors. *Mailing Add:* Dept Mat Sci & Eng Univ Fla PO Box 116400 Rhines Hall Gainesville FL 32611. *Fax:* 352-846-0326; *E-Mail:* mludw@mail.mse.ufc.edu

LUDWIG, OLIVER GEORGE, PHYSICAL CHEMISTRY. *Current Pos:* ASSOC PROF CHEM, VILLANOVA UNIV, 68- *Personal Data:* b Philadelphia, Pa, Nov 15, 35. *Educ:* Villanova Univ, BS, 57; Carnegie Inst Technol, MS, 60, PhD(quantum chem), 61. *Prof Exp:* Mem math lab & sr res worker theoret chem, Cambridge Univ, 61-63; asst prof chem & fac assoc, Comput Ctr, Univ Notre Dame, 63-68. *Concurrent Pos:* NSF fel, 61-63; actg chmn, Dept Chem, Villanova Univ, 69-70. *Mem:* Am Chem Soc; Am Phys Soc; Asn Comput Mach. *Res:* Quantum chemistry; chemical applications of digital computers; development of methods for scientific computing. *Mailing Add:* Dept Chem Villanova Univ Villanova PA 19805. *E-Mail:* ludwig@rs6chem.vill.edu

LUDWIG, THEODORE FREDERICK, PROSTHODONTICS. *Current Pos:* RETIRED. *Personal Data:* b Castlewood, SDak, July 8, 24; m 45; c 1. *Educ:* Cent Col, Iowa, AB, 45; Ohio State DDS, 59, MSc, 63. *Prof Exp:* Asst prof dent, WVa Univ, 63-67; asst prof, Sch Dent, Univ Iowa, 67-69; assoc prof prosthodontics, Col Dent Med, Med Univ SC, 69-86. *Concurrent Pos:* NIH grant, 62-63; mem, Carl O Boucher Prosthodontic Conf, 66- *Mem:* Am Dent Asn. *Res:* Esthetics in complete dentures; design and metals in removable partial dentures. *Mailing Add:* 523 N Third Livingston MT 59047

LUDWIG, WILLIAM E, NUTRITION. *Current Pos:* ADMINR, FOOD & CONSUMER SERV, 93- *Educ:* La State Univ, BS; La Inst Technol, MBA. *Mailing Add:* 3101 Park Center Dr Alexandria VA 22302-1500

LUEBBE, RAY HENRY, JR, PHYSICAL CHEMISTRY. *Current Pos:* RETIRED. *Personal Data:* b Schenectady, NY, Mar 31, 31; m 59, Dorothy Gates; c Elizabeth, Karen & Melissa. *Educ:* Dartmouth Col, AB, 53; Univ Wis, PhD(phys chem), 58. *Prof Exp:* Asst phys chem, Univ Wis, 53-55; chemist, Photo Prod Dept, E I du Pont de Nemours & Co, 58-64; scientist, Xerox Corp, 64-79; unit mgr, Qwip Systs, Exxon Enterprises, 79-82; dir process technol, Environ Technol Inc, 82-85; sr process develop engr, Harris Graphics Co, 85-86; mgr electrophotog mat & process develop, Am Graphics, Am Int, 86-92. *Mem:* Am Chem Soc; Soc Photo Sci & Eng. *Res:* Hot atom and photo chemistry; photographic science; photopolymerization; electrophotography. *Mailing Add:* 305 Blackstone Dr Centerville OH 45459

LUEBBERS, RALPH H(ENRY), CHEMICAL ENGINEERING. *Current Pos:* RETIRED. *Personal Data:* b Burlington, Iowa, Mar 24, 06; m 35; c 3. *Educ:* Iowa State Col, BS, 27, MS, 32, PhD(chem eng, sanit bact), 35. *Prof Exp:* Plant chemist, Universal Gypsum Co, Iowa, 27; plant chemist & chem engr, Des Moines Water Works, 28; jr engr, Int Combustion Eng Corp, NY, 28-29; develop engr, Dorr Co, Inc, 29-31; chem & sanit engr, US Army Dept, Kans, 35-37; from instr to prof, Univ Mo, Columbia, 38-72; emer prof chem eng, 72-80. *Concurrent Pos:* Eng consult. *Mem:* Am Chem Soc; Am Soc Eng Educ; Am Water Works Asn; Am Inst Chem Eng; Nat Soc Prof Engrs; Sigma Xi. *Res:* Mixing of dry powders and liquids; heat transfer in packed columns; biological oxidation processes; fluid flow of suspensions. *Mailing Add:* 1408 Business Loop 70W Columbia MO 65202

LUEBKE, EMMETH AUGUST, PHYSICS, NUCLEAR SAFETY LAW. *Current Pos:* RETIRED. *Personal Data:* b Manitowoc, Wis, Aug 1, 15; m 37, Nora Weyer; c Dennis & Dorothy. *Educ:* Ripon Col, BA, 36; Univ Ill, PhD(physics), 41. *Honors & Awards:* Presidential Cert Merit. *Prof Exp:* Asst physics, Univ Ill, 36-41; group leader, Radiation Lab, Mass Inst Technol, 41-45; res assoc, Res Lab, Gen Elec Co, 45-50, mgr reactor eval, Knolls Atomic Power Lab, 50-55, gen physicist, Missile & Space Vehicle Dept, 55-58 & Gen Eng Lab, 58-63, physicist, Tempo, 63-72; admin judge, US Nuclear Regulatory Comn, 72-87. *Concurrent Pos:* Mem, Joint Liquid Metals Comt, US Navy AEC, 50-55; presiding tech mem, Atomic Safety & Licensing Bd. *Mem:* Fel Am Phys Soc; Am Nuclear Soc. *Res:* Linear accelerator; velocity spectrometer measurement of neutron cross section; microwave radar components; system design; liquid metal heat transfer; design and evaluation of reactor power plants; breeder; submarine propulsion; central station types; environmental controls. *Mailing Add:* 5500 Friendship Blvd Apt 1923 N Chevy Chase MD 20815

LUEBS, RALPH EDWARD, SOIL & WATER MANAGEMENT, SOIL FERTILITY. *Current Pos:* RETIRED. *Personal Data:* b Wood River, Nebr, Mar 21, 22; m 51; c 4. *Educ:* Univ Nebr, BS, 48, MS, 52; Iowa State Univ, PhD(soil fertil), 54. *Prof Exp:* Asst agron, Univ Nebr, 48-49; soil scientist, Agr Res Serv, Univ Nebr, USDA, 55-56, Ft Hays Exp Sta, Kans, 56-59 & Univ Calif, Riverside, 59-75; chief, agron div, Woodward-Clyde Consults, 75-81, sr proj scientist, Environ Systs Div, 81-82. *Concurrent Pos:* Int consult agronomist, 82- *Mem:* Am Soc Agron; Soil Sci Soc Am; Sigma Xi; Soil Conserv Soc Am. *Res:* Nitrogen availability and rainfall use efficiency for dryland crops; mined land reclamation; diagnosis of low crop production. *Mailing Add:* 13347 W Exposition Dr Lakewood CO 80228-3037

LUECK, CHARLES HENRY, ANALYTICAL CHEMISTRY. *Current Pos:* CHEM INSTR, BEAUFORT COMMUNITY COL, WASHINGTON, NC. *Personal Data:* b St Paul, Minn, Oct 1, 28; m 55; c 6. *Educ:* Col St Thomas, BS, 50; Univ Detroit, MS, 53; Wayne State Univ, PhD, 56. *Prof Exp:* Res assoc & anal res supvr, Textile Fibers Dept, E I du Pont de Nemours & Co, 56-85. *Mem:* Am Chem Soc; Am Soc Qual Control. *Res:* Spectrophotometric analysis; chemical degradation studies; quality systems; test method uniformity & control. *Mailing Add:* PO Box 789 Chocowinity NC 27817-0789

LUECKE, DONALD H, medical research, for more information see previous edition

LUECKE, FRANK, OPTICAL ENGINEERING. *Current Pos:* PRES, NEW FOCUS INC. *Honors & Awards:* Eng Excellence Award, Optical Soc Am, 95. *Mailing Add:* 2630 Walsh Ave Santa Clara CA 95051

LUECKE, GLENN RICHARD, MATHEMATICAL ANALYSIS. *Current Pos:* From asst prof to assoc prof, 69-80, PROF MATH, IOWA STATE UNIV, 80- *Personal Data:* b Bryan, Tex, May 19, 44; m 67; c 2. *Educ:* Mich State Univ, BS, 66; Calif Inst Technol, PhD(math), 70. *Mem:* Am Math Soc; Soc Indust & Appl Math; Asn Comput Mach. *Res:* Numerical solution of integral equations. *Mailing Add:* Dept Math & Comput Ctr Iowa State Univ 291 Durham Ctr Ames IA 50011-2551

LUECKE, GREG R, MECHANICAL ENGINEERING, ROBOTICS. *Current Pos:* ASST PROF MECH ENG, IOWA STATE UNIV, 92- *Personal Data:* b Orange, Tex, Dec 2, 56. *Educ:* Univ Mo, BSME, 79; Yale Univ, MS, 87; Pa State Univ, PhD, 92. *Honors & Awards:* Ralph R Teetor Educ Award, Soc Automotive Engrs, 96. *Prof Exp:* Assoc engr/scientist, McDonnell-Douglass Corp, Calif, 80-81; design engr, Mech Flight Controls, Sikorsky Aircraft, Conn, 81-88; VAX comput syst mgr, Dept Mech Eng, Pa State Univ, 88-92. *Concurrent Pos:* Mech design consult, Dept Mech Eng, Pa State Univ, 90; instr mech eng, Bridgeport Eng Inst, Conn; fac fel, Iowa Ctr Emerging Mfg & Technol, 92. *Mem:* Inst Elec & Electronics Engrs; Am Soc Mech Engrs; Soc Automotive Engrs; Am Helicopter Soc. *Res:* Dynamic system analysis and robot applications in virtual reality for interactive force feedback. *Mailing Add:* Iowa State Univ 2096 Black Eng Bldg Ames IA 50011. *Fax:* 515-299-3261; *E-Mail:* gluecke@iastate.edu

LUECKE, RICHARD H, CHEMICAL ENGINEERING, MATHEMATICAL & BIOLOGICAL MODELING. *Current Pos:* assoc prof, 67-80, PROF CHEM ENG, UNIV MO, COLUMBIA, 80-; CONSULT, DOT PROD CORP, 94- *Personal Data:* b Cincinnati, Ohio, Mar 27, 30; m 53; c Brad, Greg, Mark, Genise & Connie. *Educ:* Univ Cincinnati, BChE, 59; Univ Okla, MChE, 63, PhD(chem eng), 66. *Prof Exp:* Engr, E I du Pont de Nemours & Co, Inc, 53-62; res engr, Monsanto Co, 66-67. *Concurrent Pos:* Consult, Chemshare Corp, Okla, 69- & Dynamic Matrix Co, 88-90; fac res fel, Oak Ridge Assoc Univ, 90. *Mem:* Am Inst Chem Eng. *Res:* Process control; optimization; mathematical methods; bioengineering; biological modeling (200 publications including more than 50 refereed publications); authored 200 publications. *Mailing Add:* Chem Engr Univ Mo 1030 Engr Bldg Columbia MO 65211. *E-Mail:* luecke@ecvaxz.ecn.missouri.edu

LUECKE, RICHARD WILLIAM, BIOCHEMISTRY, NUTRITION. *Current Pos:* RETIRED. *Personal Data:* b St Paul, Minn, July 12, 17; m 41; c 3. *Educ:* Macalester Col, BA, 39; Univ Minn, MS, 41, PhD(biochem), 43. *Prof Exp:* Prof biochem, Mich State Univ, 45-87. *Concurrent Pos:* Assoc prof biochem, Tex A&M Univ, 43-45; consult, Armour Res Labs, Chicago, 55-66; mem comt on animal nutrit, Nat Res Coun, 55-65; mem food & nutrit bd, Food & Agr Orgn, UN, 60-65; consult, Merck Sharp & Dohme Res Labs, 62-69. *Mem:* Am Chem Soc; Am Inst Nutrit; Am Soc Biol Chemists. *Res:* Trace element metabolism in animals. *Mailing Add:* 1893 Birchwood Dr Okemos MI 48864-2766

LUEDECKE, LLOYD O, DAIRY BACTERIOLOGY. *Current Pos:* Asst prof dairy sci, Wash State Univ, 62-70, assoc prof & assoc dairy scientist, 70-73, assoc prof, 73-77, PROF FOOD SCI, WASH STATE UNIV, 77- *Personal Data:* b Hamilton, Mont, July 28, 34; m 57; c 2. *Educ:* Mont State Col, BS, 56; Mich State Univ, MS, 58, PhD(food sci), 62. *Mem:* Am Dairy Sci Asn; Inst Food Technol. *Res:* Heat resistance of psychrophiles; bacteriological aspects of mastitis. *Mailing Add:* Food Sci Wash State Univ 1 SE Stadium Way Pullman WA 99164-0001

LUEDEMAN, JOHN KEITH, ALGEBRA, MATHEMATICS EDUCATION. *Current Pos:* from asst prof to assoc prof, 68-80, PROF MATH, CLEMSON UNIV, 80-, PROF EDUC, 88- *Personal Data:* b Ft Wayne, Ind, Apr 27, 41; div; c Keith, Eric, Jody & Cathy. *Educ:* Valparaiso Univ, BA, 63; Southern Ill Univ, Carbondale, MA, 65; State Univ NY, Buffalo, PhD(math), 69. *Prof Exp:* Instr math, State Univ NY, Buffalo, 67-68. *Concurrent Pos:* Consult math, Oconee Co Sch Syst, SC, 74-; dir, Ctr Ex Math Sci Educ, Clemson Univ, 84- *Mem:* Am Math Soc; Math Asn Am; Sigma Xi; Nat Coun Teachers Math; Asn Math Teacher Educr. *Res:* Mathematics education; mathematical biology; semigroups; graph theory; computing on graphs. *Mailing Add:* Dept Math Clemson Univ Clemson SC 29634-1907. *Fax:* 864-656-5230; *E-Mail:* lued@clemson.clemson.edu

LUEDER, ERNST H, DIGITAL SIGNAL PROCESSING, OPTIMIZATION OF SYSTEMS. *Current Pos:* privat-dozent, 66-68, FULL PROF & DIR, INST NETWORK & SYSTS THEORY, UNIV STUTTGART, 71- *Personal Data:* b Schiltach, Ger, Feb 20, 32; m, Helen Abramson; c Tilmon & Christoph. *Educ:* Univ Stuttgart, Dipl Ing, 58, Dr Ing(elec commun), 62, Dr Ing habil, 66. *Honors & Awards:* Order of Merit 1st Class Fed Repub Ger, 91. *Prof Exp:* Mem tech staff, Bell Tel Labs, NJ, 68-71. *Concurrent Pos:* Consult, Fed Ministry Sci & Technol, Bonn; Heinrich-Hertz-Inst, Berlin. *Mem:* Fel Inst Elec & Electronics Engrs; Soc Info Display (vpres); Int Soc Hybrid Microelectronics; Int Soc Optical Eng; Soc Info Technol Ger; NY Acad Sci. *Res:* Design of passive, RC-active, switched capacitor, digital and saw filters; digital and optical signal processing; optimization of systems; realization of flat panel liquid crystal displays; thin film sensors. *Mailing Add:* Univ Stuttgart Pfaffenwaldring 47 70550 Stuttgart Germany

LUEG, RUSSELL E, ELECTRICAL ENGINEERING. *Current Pos:* assoc prof, 60-64, actg head dept, 66-68, PROF ELEC ENG, UNIV ALA, 64-, ASSOC DEAN ADMIN, 88- *Personal Data:* b Chicago, Ill, Nov 24, 29; m 56; c 5. *Educ:* Univ Ark, BS, 51; Univ Tex, MS, 56, PhD(elec eng), 61. *Prof Exp:* Prog engr, Gen Elec Co, NY, 53-54; radio engr & instr elec eng, Univ Tex, 54-60. *Concurrent Pos:* Consult, Army Missile Command, Ala, 64-65. *Mem:* Inst Elec & Electronics Engrs; Am Soc Eng Educ. *Res:* Nonlinear control systems. *Mailing Add:* 10688 Sexton Bend Rd Tuscaloosa AL 35406

LUE-HING, CECIL, CIVIL & ENVIRONMENTAL ENGINEERING. *Current Pos:* DIR RES & DEVELOP, METROP WATER RECLAMATION DIST, GREATER CHICAGO, 77- *Personal Data:* b Jamaica, WI, Nov 3, 30; m 52; c 2. *Educ:* Marquette Univ, BCE, 61; Case Inst Technol, MS, 63; Washington Univ, St Louis, DSc(sanit eng), 66. *Prof Exp:* Chief technician, Col Med, Univ Wis, 50-55; instr histol & cytol chem & lab supvr, Sch Med Technol, Mt Sinai Hosp, Wis, 55-61; res assoc clin biochem, Huron Rd Hosp, Ohio, 61-63; res assoc environ eng, Washington Univ, St Louis, 63-65, asst prof, 65-66; assoc, Ryckman, Edgerley, Tomlinson & Assocs, 66-68, sr engr, 68-77. *Concurrent Pos:* Fel, Washington Univ, Mo. *Mem:* AAAS; Am Soc Civil Engrs; Am Pub Health Asn; Water Pollution Control Fedn; Am Water Works Asn. *Res:* Pesticide pollution of water supplies; significance of enzyme response in pesticide detection in water supplies; phosphorus and nutrient removal from water supplies; industrial wastes detoxification and biodegradation. *Mailing Add:* Metrop Water Reclamation Dist Greater Chicago 100 E Erie St Chicago IL 60611

LUEHR, CHARLES POLING, APPLIED MATHEMATICS, MATHEMATICAL PHYSICS. *Current Pos:* RETIRED. *Personal Data:* b Plentywood, Mont, Sept 27, 30. *Educ:* Ore State Univ, BS, 53, MS, 56; Univ Calif, Berkeley, PhD(appl math), 62. *Prof Exp:* Mem prof staff, Tempo Ctr Adv Studies, Gen Elec Co, Calif, 62-68; fel, Univ Fla 68-70, from asst prof to assoc prof math, 70-82; sr res scientist, NMex Eng Res Inst, Univ NMex, 85-95. *Concurrent Pos:* Res visitor, Inst Nuclear Sci, Nat Univ Mex, 73-88; vis assoc prof math, Ore State Univ, 80-82; res scholar, Air Force Weapons Lab, Kirtland AFB, 83-84; intergovt personnel act, USAF Phillips Lab, Kirtland AFB, 90-93. *Mem:* Math Asn Am; Am Math Soc; Am Phys Soc; Soc Indust & Appl Math; Sigma Xi. *Res:* Methods of mathematical physics; tensor analysis; abstract theory of spinors with applications in quantum mechanics and relativity theory; modern differential geometry applied to physics; scientific computing. *Mailing Add:* 920 Continental Lp SE Apt 27 Albuquerque NM 87108

LUEHRMANN, ARTHUR WILLETT, JR, COMPUTER SCIENCE, SCIENCE EDUCATION. *Current Pos:* PARTNER, COMPUT LITERACY, 80- *Personal Data:* b New Orleans, La, Mar 8, 31; m 61, Martha Ramirez; c Mia & Nils. *Educ:* Univ Chicago, AB, 55, SB, 57, SM, 61, PhD(physics), 66. *Honors & Awards:* Fulbright lect, Fulbright Comn, Colombia, 69. *Prof Exp:* From instr to asst prof, Dartmouth Col, 55-70, adj assoc prof physics & dir, Off Acad Comput, 70-77; assoc dir, Lawrence Hall Sci, Univ Calif, Berkeley, 77-80. *Mem:* AAAS. *Res:* Solid state theory; band structure; computational physics; computer graphics; computer-based instruction; solid state physics. *Mailing Add:* 1466 Grizzly Peak Blvd Berkeley CA 94708

LUEHRS, DEAN C, INORGANIC CHEMISTRY. *Current Pos:* Asst prof, 65-69, ASSOC PROF CHEM, MICH STATE TECHNOL UNIV, 69- *Personal Data:* b Fremont, Nebr, Apr 20, 39; m 69; c 1. *Educ:* Mich State Univ, BS, 61; Univ Kans, PhD(chem), 65. *Mem:* Am Chem Soc. *Res:* Nonaqueous solvents; electrochemistry; QSAR. *Mailing Add:* Dept Chem Mich Technol Univ Houghton MI 49931

LUEKING, DONALD ROBERT, MICROBIAL BIOCHEMISTRY. *Current Pos:* ASSOC PROF, DEPT BIOL SCI, MICH TECHNOL UNIV. *Personal Data:* b Cincinnati, Ohio, Nov 24, 46; m 73. *Educ:* Ind Univ, Bloomington, BS, 69, PhD(microbiol), 73. *Prof Exp:* Trainee microbiol, Univ Pa, 73-74, fel, 74-75; fel, Univ Ill, Urbana, 75-78; asst prof, Tex A&M Univ, 78- *Mem:* Am Soc Microbiol; AAAS; Sigma Xi. *Res:* The use of the photosynthetic bacteria as a model system for the study of the factors involved in the regulation of membrane biosynthesis and differentiation. *Mailing Add:* Dept Biol Sci Mich Tech Univ Houghton MI 49931

LUENBERGER, DAVID GILBERT, SYSTEMS ENGINEERING, INVESTMENT SCIENCE. *Current Pos:* asst prof elec eng, 63-67, assoc prof eng-econ systs & elec eng, 67-71, PROF ENG-ECON SYSTS & ELEC ENG, STANFORD UNIV, 71-, CHMN, ENG-ECON SYSTS, 80- *Personal Data:* b Los Angeles, Calif, Sept 16, 37; m 62; c 4. *Educ:* Calif Inst Technol, BS, 59; Stanford Univ, MS, 61, PhD(elec eng), 63. *Honors & Awards:* Hendrik W Bode Lectr Prize, Control Systs Soc, Inst Elec & Electronics Engrs, 90. *Prof Exp:* Engr, Westinghouse Elec Corp, 61-63. *Concurrent Pos:* Consult, Stanford Res Inst, 66-, Intasa, Inc, 70-72, Systs Control Inc, 74-83, Time & Space Processing, 81 & Optimization Technol Inc, 83-; tech asst to dir, Off Sci & Technol, Exec Off of the Pres, 71-72; vis prof, Mass Inst Technol, 76 & Tech Univ Denmark, 86. *Mem:* Inst Mgt Sci; Am Asn Univ Prof; Inst Elec & Electronics Engrs; Economet Soc; Am Soc Eng Educ; Am Finance Asn; Soc Econ Dynamics & Control (pres, 87-); Soc Prom Econ Theory; Soc Advan Econ Theory. *Res:* Control systems, particularly multivariable systems; optimization, including control, operations research and estimation; economic systems; finance. *Mailing Add:* Eng-Econ Systs Dept Terman Ctr Mail Code 4023 Stanford Univ Palo Alto CA 94305

LUEPKER, RUSSELL VINCENT, EPIDEMIOLOGY, CARDIOLOGY. *Current Pos:* from asst prof to assoc prof, 76-87, assoc dir, Div Epidemiol, 86-91, PROF EPIDEMIOL & MED, UNIV MINN, MINNEAPOLIS, 87-, DIR, DIV EPIDEMIOL, 91- *Personal Data:* b Chicago, Ill, Oct 1, 42; m 66, Ellen L Thompson; c Ian & Carl. *Educ:* Grinnell Col, BA, 64; Univ Rochester, MD, 69; Harvard Univ, MS, 76. *Hon Degrees:* PhD, Univ Lund, Swed, 96. *Prof Exp:* Intern, Univ Hosp, San Diego Co & Univ Calif, San Diego, 69-70; from res asst to asst resident, Peter Bent Brigham Hosp/Med Ctr, 73-75, dir, Lipid Clin, 75-76. *Concurrent Pos:* Nat res serv award, Nat Heart, Lung & Blood Inst, 75-77; consult, NIH, 80-, Univ Southern Calif, Los Angeles, 85-; vis prof, Univ Goteborg, Sweden, 86; Bush leadership fel, 90; chmn, Coun Epidemiol, Am Heart Asn, 92- *Mem:* Fel Am Col Physicians; fel Am Col Cardiol; Am Heart Asn; fel Am Col Epidemiol; Am Epidemiol Soc. *Res:* Epidemiology and medicine; epidemiology and prevention of cardiovascular diseases at the individual and community levels. *Mailing Add:* Sch Pub Health Div Epidemiol Univ Minn 1300 S Second St Suite 300 Minneapolis MN 55454-1015. *Fax:* 612-624-0315

LUER, CARL A, BIOCHEMISTRY, IMMUNOLOGY. *Current Pos:* Staff scientist, 79-85, SR SCIENTIST, MOTE MARINE LAB, 85- *Personal Data:* b St Louis, Mo, Nov 9, 48. *Educ:* Duke Univ, BA, 70; Univ SFla, MS, 74; Univ Kans, PhD(biochem), 78. *Concurrent Pos:* Adj asst prof, Dept Med, Brown Univ, 91- *Mem:* Am Soc Biochem & Molecular Biol; Sigma Xi. *Mailing Add:* Mote Marine Lab 1600 Thompson Pkwy Sarasota FL 34236-1096. *Fax:* 941-388-4312

LUERSSEN, FRANK W, METALLURGY, PHYSICAL CHEMISTRY. *Current Pos:* RETIRED. *Personal Data:* b Reading, Pa, Aug 14, 27; m 50; c 5. *Educ:* Pa State Univ, BS, 50; Lehigh Univ, MS, 51; Xavier Univ, PhD, 56. *Hon Degrees:* LLD, Calumet Col; DPS, Xavier Univ, 92. *Honors & Awards:* Howe Mem Lectr, Am Inst Mining, Metall & Petrol Engrs, 84, Benjamin Fairless Award, 85. *Prof Exp:* Jr res engr, Bethlehem Steel Corp, 51-52; metallurgist, Inland Steel Co, 52-54, chief reduction & ref, 54-57, chief res engr, 57-61, asst mgr, Res Dept, 62-63, assoc mgr, 63-64, mgr, 64-68, vpres res, 68-77, vpres steel mfg, 77-78, exec vpres & pres, 78-82, pres & chief exec officer, 82-83, chmn & chief exec officer, 83- *Concurrent Pos:* Trustee, Northwestern Univ; chmn, Phys Chem Steelmaking Group, Am Iron & Steel

Inst, Gen Res Comt & Comt Mfg; mem, Indust Policy Adv Comt, US Dept Com, 88 & bd trustees, Mus Sci & Indust. *Mem:* Nat Acad Eng; hon mem Am Iron & Steel Inst; fel Am Soc Metals; Am Inst Mining, Metall & Petrol Engrs. *Res:* Physical chemistry of slag metal systems in steel refining; process research in ironmaking and steelmaking; physical metallurgy of iron base alloy systems. *Mailing Add:* 8226 Park View Ave Munster IN 46321

LUESCHEN, WILLIAM EVERETT, AGRONOMY. *Current Pos:* PROF AGRON & AGRONOMIST, SOUTHERN EXP STA, UNIV MINN, 68- *Personal Data:* b Springfield, Ill, Jan 29, 42; m 65; c 2. *Educ:* Southern Ill Univ, BS, 64; Univ Ill, MS, 66, PhD(agron), 68. *Mem:* Am Soc Agron; Crop Sci Soc Am; Weed Sci Soc Am; Coun Agr Sci & Tech; Am Reg Cert Prof Agron Crops & Soils; Am Forage & Grassland Coun. *Res:* Crop production, management and weed science. *Mailing Add:* Dept Agron/Plant Genetics Univ Minn 411 Borlaug HI 1991 Upper Buford Circle St Paul MN 55108

LUESSENHOP, ALFRED JOHN, MEDICINE, NEUROSURGERY. *Current Pos:* from instr to assoc prof neurosurg, 60-73, PROF SURG, SCH MED, GEORGETOWN UNIV, 73-, CHIEF DIV NEUROSURG, 65- *Personal Data:* b Chicago, Ill, Feb 6, 26; m 52; c 4. *Educ:* Yale Univ, BS, 49; Harvard Med Sch, MD, 52. *Prof Exp:* Intern surg, Univ Chicago, 52-53; resident neurosurg, Mass Gen Hosp, 53-58; vis scientist, Nat Inst Neurol Dis & Blindness, 59-60. *Concurrent Pos:* Teaching fel, Harvard Med Sch, 57-58; res fel neurosurg, Harvard Med Sch, 53-54; res consult, Nat Inst Neurol Dis & Stroke, 60-65; clin consult, 65-; clin consult, Vet Admin Hosp, 65-; consult, Fed Aviation Agency, 67 & Nat Naval Med Ctr, 67- *Mem:* Cong Neurol Surg; Am Asn Neurol Surg; Soc Neurol Surg; Am Acad Neurosurg. *Res:* Cerebrovascular disease. *Mailing Add:* Georgetown I-PHC 3800 Reservoir Rd NW Washington DC 20007

LUETZELSCHWAB, JOHN WILLIAM, HEALTH PHYSICS. *Current Pos:* From asst prof to assoc prof, 68-83, PROF PHYSICS, DICKINSON COL, 83- *Personal Data:* b Hammond, Ind, Sept 8, 40; m 63, Marcia Bonnemort; c Dana & Mark. *Educ:* Earlham Col, AB, 62; Wash Univ, MA & PhD(physics), 68; cert Am Bd Health Physics. *Mem:* Am Asn Physics Teachers; Health Physics Soc. *Res:* Environmental radioactivity; radon in the environment and in homes. *Mailing Add:* 1750 Valley Rd Etters PA 17319. *Fax:* 717-245-1642; *E-Mail:* luetzelj@dickinson.edu

LUFKIN, DANIEL HARLOW, SOLAR PHYSICS. *Current Pos:* RETIRED. *Personal Data:* b Philadelphia, Pa, Sept 26, 30; m 51; c 3. *Educ:* Mass Inst Technol, BS, 52, MS, 58; Univ Stockholm, Fil lic meteorol, 64. *Prof Exp:* Meteorol officer, Air Weather Serv, USAF, DC, 53-69, dir solar forecast facil, 69-73; asst prof astron, Hood Col, 75-87. *Concurrent Pos:* Dir, Off Systs & Advan Technol, Nat Oceanic & Atmospheric Admin, 76-86; consult, Solar Energy Sci Serv, 74-87. *Mem:* Am Meteorol Soc. *Res:* Optical instrumentation for satellite remote sensing. *Mailing Add:* 303 W College Terr Frederick MD 21701

LUFT, HAROLD STEPHEN, HEALTH ECONOMICS, HEALTH SERVICES RESEARCH. *Current Pos:* assoc prof, Univ Calif, San Francisco, 78-82, assoc dir, 86-93, actg dir, 93-95, PROF HEALTH ECON, INST HEALTH POLICY STUDIES, UNIV CALIF, SAN FRANCISCO, 82-, DIR, 96- *Personal Data:* b Newark, NJ, Jan 6, 47; m 70; c 2. *Educ:* Harvard Univ, AB, 68, MA, 70, PhD(econ), 73. *Honors & Awards:* Distinguished Article of the Year Award, Asn Health Servs Res, 88. *Prof Exp:* Instr, econ, Tufts Univ, 72-73; asst prof, health econ, Stanford Univ, 73-78. *Concurrent Pos:* Postdoctoral fel, Harvard Ctr Community Health & Med Care, Harvard Univ, 72-73; mem, Health Servs Study Sect, Nat Ctr Health Sci Res, 81-83; mem, Comt Design Strategy Qual Rev & Assurance Medicare, Inst Med, 88-90, Health Adv Comt, US Gen Acct Off, 88-96 & coun, Inst Med, 89-; res assoc, Nat Bur Econ Res, 82-; Flinn distinguished scholar healthcare mgt & policy, Univ Ariz & Ariz State Univ, 86; co-prin investr, Nat Ctr Health Serv Res, 86-91, prin investr, Agency Health Care Policy Res, 90-92 & 90-95; fel, Ctr Advan Study Behav Sci, 88-89; consult numerous orgns; sr assoc ed, J Health Serv Res, 96-; bd mem, Am Health Serv Res. *Mem:* Inst Med-Nat Acad Sci; Am Pub Health Asn; Asn Soc Sci Health; Am Econ Asn. *Res:* Topics in health economics: health maintenance organizations, biased selection in health insurance, hospital competition, relation between volume and outcome in hospital care, applicability of incentive systems in health care; author of numerous publications. *Mailing Add:* Inst Health Policy Studies Sch Med Univ Calif 1388 Sutter St 11th Floor San Francisco CA 94109

LUFT, JOHN HERMAN, histology, for more information see previous edition

LUFT, LUDWIG, PHYSICAL CHEMISTRY. *Current Pos:* RETIRED. *Personal Data:* b Lvov, Poland, Nov 9, 26; nat US; m 52, Anne D Franz; c Frederick J & Naomi M (Cameron). *Educ:* Univ Frankfurt, dipl, 51; Univ Kans, PhD(phys chem), 56. *Prof Exp:* Asst prof chem, Univ Miami, 55-57; res supvr, MSA Res Corp, 57-58; tech & managerial mem staff, Gen Elec Co, 58-62; sr scientist, Allied Res Assocs, 62-63; dir res, Instrumentation Lab Inc, 63; pres, Luft Instruments, Inc 63-97. *Concurrent Pos:* Lectr & adj prof chem eng, Tufts Univ, Medford, Mass, 82-85. *Mem:* AAAS; Am Chem Soc; Instrument Soc Am. *Res:* Chemical engineering; automatic controls; methods development; electrochemistry. *Mailing Add:* 3 Hillside Rd Lincoln MA 01773-0214

LUFT, STANLEY JEREMIE, GEOLOGY. *Current Pos:* RETIRED. *Personal Data:* b Turin, Italy, Sept 26, 27; US citizen; m 91, Eleanor J Shearer; c Andrew, Anthony, Stephen & Edmund. *Educ:* Syracuse Univ, AB, 49; Pa State Col, MS, 51. *Honors & Awards:* Gerard Gilbert Award. *Prof Exp:* Asst geol, Pa State Col, 49-51; explor geologist, NJ Zinc Co, 51-54; geologist mineral deposits, US Geol Surv, 54-56; geologist, Northern Pac Rwy Co, 56-58 & US Geol Surv, 61-88; prof geol & mineral & head dept, Oriente Univ, 59-60; proj geologist, Callahan Mining Corp, 61. *Mem:* Fel Geol Soc Am. *Res:* Petrography and petrology of volcanic rocks; drainage evolution of Kentucky; geology of uranium in Tertiary intermontane basins; basin analysis; Northern Powder River Basin; geologic hazards mitigation. *Mailing Add:* 16291 W 56th Pl Golden CO 80403

LUFTIG, RONALD BERNARD, MICROBIOLOGY, BIOPHYSICS. *Current Pos:* PROF MICROBIOL & HEAD DEPT, MED SCH, LA STATE UNIV, 83- *Personal Data:* b Brooklyn, NY, Dec 8, 39; m 61; c 4. *Educ:* City Col New York, BS, 60; NY Univ, MS, 62; Univ Chicago, PhD(biophys), 67. *Prof Exp:* Asst prof microbiol, Med Ctr, Duke Univ, 69-73; sr scientist, Worcester Found Exp Biol, 74-79; prof microbiol, Med Sch, Univ SC, 79-83. *Concurrent Pos:* NSF fel, Calif Inst Technol, 67-69; NIH res grant, Med Ctr, Duke Univ, 70-73; res grants, Worcester Found, 74-79, Univ SC Med Sch, 79-83 & La State Univ, 83- *Mem:* AAAS; Am Soc Biol Chem; Am Soc Microbiol; Am Soc Cell Biol; Sigma Xi; Am Soc Virol. *Res:* Leukemia virus morphogenesis; acquired immune deficiency syndrome (AIDS) virus proteinase inhibitors; enteric adenovirus structure. *Mailing Add:* Dept Microbiol La State Univ Med Ctr 1901 Perdido St New Orleans LA 70112-1393

LUGAR, RICHARD CHARLES, COMPUTERS IN CHEMISTRY. *Current Pos:* PROF ORG CHEM, DELAWARE VALLEY COL, 67- *Personal Data:* b Philadelphia, Pa, Apr 5, 40; div; c 1. *Educ:* Univ Pa, BS, 62, PhD(chem), 69. *Mem:* Am Chem Soc. *Res:* Conformational analysis of alicyclic systems. *Mailing Add:* Del Valley Col Doylestown PA 18901-2621

LUGASSY, ARMAND AMRAM, MATERIALS SCIENCE, PROSTHODONTICS. *Current Pos:* assoc prof, 71-77, PROF FIXED PROSTHODONT, SCH DENT, UNIV PAC, 77- *Personal Data:* b Kenitra, Morocco, July 23, 33; m 66; c 2. *Educ:* Toulouse Fac Med & Pharm, France, Chirurgien-Dentiste, 59; Univ Pa, DDS, 62, PhD(metall, mat sci), 68. *Prof Exp:* Monitor oper dent, Toulouse Fac Med & Pharm, France, 58-59; instr, Sch Dent Med, Univ Pa, 62-63; asst prof biol mat, Dent-Med Sch, Northwestern Univ, 68-71. *Concurrent Pos:* Nat Inst Dent Res traineeship, Sch Metall & Mat Sci, Univ Pa, 63-68; consult, USPHS Hosp, San Francisco, Calif, 71- & Vet Admin Hosp, Livermore, 80- *Mem:* Am Soc Metals; Int Asn Dent Res. *Res:* Physical properties of calcified tissues; behavior of materials and devices in clinical applications in living vertebrates. *Mailing Add:* Dept Fixed Prosthodont Univ Pac Sch Dent 2155 Webster St San Francisco CA 94115

LUGAY, JOAQUIN CASTRO, biochemistry, food science, for more information see previous edition

LUGER, GEORGE F, COMPUTER SCIENCE, INTELLIGENT SYSTEMS & COGNITIVE SCIENCE. *Current Pos:* PROF COMPUT SCI & PSYCHOL, DEPT COMPUT SCI, UNIV NMEX, ALBUQUERQUE, 79- *Personal Data:* b Spokane, Wash, Dec 1, 40; m 69, Kathleen Kelly; c Sara L, David & Peter. *Educ:* Gonzaga Univ, MS, 66; Univ Notre Dame, MS, 69; Univ Pa, PhD(artificial intel), 73. *Prof Exp:* Res fel, Dept Artificial Intel, Univ Edinburgh, Scotland, UK, 74-79. *Concurrent Pos:* Consult, Learning Tree Int, 84- *Mem:* Inst Elec & Electronics Engrs; Am Asn Artificial Intel; Asn Comput Mach; Cognitive Sci Soc. *Res:* Artificial intelligence, especially related to modelling human problem solving, machine learning and expert system design; cognitive science. *Mailing Add:* Dept Comput Sci Univ NMex Albuquerque NM 87106. *Fax:* 505-277-6927; *E-Mail:* luger@cs.unm.edu

LUGINBUHL, GERALDINE HOBSON, MICROBIOLOGY. *Current Pos:* asst prof, 74-80, ASSOC PROF MICROBIOL, NC STATE UNIV, 80- *Personal Data:* b Los Angeles, Calif, Feb 27, 44; m 65; c 1. *Educ:* Stanford Univ, BA, 65; Univ NC, Chapel Hill, PhD(bact, immunol), 71. *Prof Exp:* NIH fel bact, Duke Univ, 71-74. *Mem:* Am Soc Microbiol; Sigma Xi. *Res:* Genetics and physiology of virulence; alcaligenes. *Mailing Add:* Microbiol Box 7615 NC State Univ Raleigh NC 27695-0001

LUGINBUHL, WILLIAM HOSSFELD, PATHOLOGY. *Current Pos:* from asst prof to assoc prof, 60-67, assoc dean col, 67-70, PROF PATH, COL MED, UNIV VT, 67-, DEAN HEALTH SCI & COL, 70- *Personal Data:* b Des Moines, Iowa, Mar 11, 29; m 55; c 5. *Educ:* Iowa State Univ, BS, 49; Northwestern Univ, MD, 53. *Prof Exp:* Intern, Wesley Mem Hosp, Chicago, Ill, 53-54; resident path, Children's Mem Hosp, 54-55; resident, Univ Hosps Cleveland, Ohio, 55-57. *Concurrent Pos:* Fel, Col Med, Univ Vt, 59-60. *Mem:* Col Am Path; Am Soc Clin Path; Sigma Xi. *Res:* Gynecologic and obstetrical pathology; endometrial anatomy and physiology. *Mailing Add:* Dept Path Obstet-Gynec Col Med Alumni Bldg Univ Vt Burlington VT 05401

LUGMAIR, GUENTER WILHELM, COSMOCHEMISTRY, GEOCHRONOLOGY. *Current Pos:* chemist, Univ Calif, San Diego, 68-71, asst res chemist, 71-77, assoc res chem, 77-84, assoc res geochem, Scripps Inst Oceanog, 79-84, RES CHEMIST, UNIV CALIF, SAN DIEGO, 84-; DIR, MAX PLANCK INST CHEM & COSMOCHEM, MAINZ, GER. *Personal Data:* b Wels, Austria, Feb 5, 40; m 65, Rosemarie Roth; c Claus & Claudia.

Educ: Univ Vienna, Austria, PhD(physics), 68. *Honors & Awards:* G P Merrill Award, Nat Acad Sci, 87. *Prof Exp:* Fel nuclear physics, Max Planck Inst, Mainz, Ger, 65-68. *Concurrent Pos:* Consult, Jet Propulsion Lab, Calif Inst Technol, 69-71; co-investr, Lunar & Planetary Sci Prog, NASA, 69-81, mem-consult, Rev Panel, 78-80; assoc ed, J Geophys Res, 81-84; prin investr, NASA & NSF, 81-; lunar & planetary sci rev panel, NASA, 85-87. *Mem:* Am Geophys Union; fel Meteoritical Soc; AAAS; Max Planck Soc Ger. *Res:* Origin and history of the solar system; nucleosynthesis; extinct radioactivities; geo dating of terrestial and extraterrestial materials; cosmic ray effects. *Mailing Add:* SIO-GRD 0212 Univ Calif San Diego 9500 Gilman Dr La Jolla CA 92093-0212. *E-Mail:* glugmair@ucsd.edu

LUGO, ARIEL E, BOTANY, ECOLOGY. *Current Pos:* proj leader, Int Inst Trop Forestry, 80-92, dir, 86-92, actg dir & supvry res ecologist, Rio Piedras, PR, 92-94, DIR, INT INST TROP FORESTRY, USDA FOREST SERV, 94- *Personal Data:* b Mayaguez, PR, Apr 28, 43; m 84, Helen Nunci; c Ariel A & Alma V. *Educ:* Univ PR, BS, 63, MS, 65; Univ NC, Chapel Hill, PhD(ecol), 69. *Honors & Awards:* Distinguished Scientist Award, USDA Forest Serv, 90. *Prof Exp:* Asst prof, Dept Bot, Univ Fla, Gainesville, 69-73 & 75-76, assoc prof, 76-79, actg dir, Ctr Wetlands, 77-78; staff mem, Coun Environ Qual Exec Off Pres, Wash, 78-79. *Concurrent Pos:* Consult, Save Our Bays Asn, 70, Am Oil Co, HW Lochner, Inc, US Postal Serv & US Forest Serv, 72, US Dept Interior, 72, 73, 76 & 77, US EPA, 74, US Justice Dept 74 & 78, Unesco, 75-76, 78, 83 & 85-86, PR Dept Natural Resources, 75-76, SWFla Regional Planning Coun, 76-77, Environ Qual Bd, 76-77, Fla Dept Natural Resources, 76, Rockefeller Found, 76, Nat Audubon Soc & County Lee, Fla, 77, Nat Wildlife Fedn & World Bank, 78, Orgn Am States, 79-80, Collier Co Nature Conserv, 80; asst secy planning & resource anal, PR Dept Natural Resources, Puerta de Tierra, 73-74, sci & technol, 74-75; hon prof & lectr, Univ PR, 76-74 & 80-; co-chmn, Fed Comt Ecol Reserves, 77-79; head div, Ctr Energy & Environ Res, Univ PR, 80-88; pres, Sci Teachers Asn, PR, 81; coun, Asn Trop Biol, 85-87, pres, 90. *Mem:* Sigma Xi; Ecol Soc Am; Asn Trop Biol; Int Soc Trop Ecol; Int Asn Ecol; Nat Wetlands Tech Coun; Soc Restoration Ecol. *Res:* Subtropical wet forestry and dry forestry; mangrove forests; granite outcrops; hardwood forests; sandpine forest; farm ponds; fresh water praire; lab microcosms; assessment of the role of tropical forests in the carbon; cycle of the world; tropical tree plantations in Puerto Rico. *Mailing Add:* Int Inst Trop Forestry PO Box 2500 San Juan PR 00928-5000. *Fax:* 787-766-6263; *E-Mail:* a]lugo@upri.upr.clu.edu

LUGO, HERMINIO LUGO, plant physiology, for more information see previous edition

LUGO, TRACY GROSS, SOMATIC CELL GENETICS, GENE TRANSFER. *Current Pos:* FEL, NORRIS CANCER HOSP & RES INST, 82- *Educ:* Mass Inst Technol, PhD(biol), 82. *Mailing Add:* Univ Calif Riverside CA 92521-0001

LUGO-LOPEZ, MIGUEL ANGEL, SOIL SCIENCE. *Current Pos:* asst dir chg, Univ PR, Mayaguez, 60-61, asst dir, Agr Exp Sta, 61-64, actg dir, 64-66, assoc dir, 66-69, dir off progs & plans & assoc dean, Col Agr Sci, 69-72, dean students, 72-74, prof soil sci & soil scientist, 74-76, EMER PROF, UNIV PR, MAYAGUEZ, 89- *Personal Data:* b Mayaguez, PR, July 21, 21; m 45, Aurora de Menkinic; c Peter J & Miguel A. *Educ:* Univ PR, BSA, 41; Cornell Univ, MS, 45, PhD(soil sci), 50. *Prof Exp:* Asst, Fed Exp Sta, PR, 43-44; asst prof agron, Univ PR, 46-48; asst scientist & assoc soil scientist, Agr Exp Sta, 48-57, assoc soil scientist & soil scientist chg, Gurabo Substa, 57-60. *Concurrent Pos:* Consult, Cornell Univ-AID, 74-78, Tech Servs Caribbean, 80-85, Agr Exp Sta, Univ PR, 80-. Secy State Agr, Dominican Repub, Ministry Agr & Livestock, Costa Rica, Ministry Agr, Bolivia, Coop Agr, Norte, Uruguay, Haiti. *Mem:* Soil Sci Soc Am; Am Soc Agron; Am Soc Agr Sci; Int Soc Soils; Caribbean Food Crops Soc. *Res:* Tropical soils, fertility, management; physical properties of tropical soils. *Mailing Add:* Box 506 Isabela Agr Exp Sta Isabela PR 00662. *Fax:* 787-830-3721

LUGT, HANS JOSEF, FLUID DYNAMICS, VORTEX THEORY. *Current Pos:* RETIRED. *Personal Data:* b Bonn, Ger, Sept 12, 30; US citizen; m 57, Anneliese W Scheller; c Christian & Brigitte. *Educ:* Univ Bonn, Vordiplom, 52; Aachen Tech Univ, Diplom, 54; Stuttgart Tech Univ, PhD(eng), 60. *Honors & Awards:* David W Taylor Award 1974, US Navy, 75; Sigma Xi Award, 80; Alexander von Humboldt US Sr Scientist Award, Ger Govt, 81; Distinguished Civilian Serv Award, USN, 82. *Prof Exp:* Asst hydraul, Ruhrgas AG, Essen, Ger, 54-57, head, Physics Lab, 57-60; res physicist hydrodyn, US Naval Weapons Lab, Va, 60-66; scientist consult, Naval Surface Warfare Ctr, 67-74, head, Numerical Mech Div, 74-78, sr res scientist, 78-95. *Concurrent Pos:* Lectr, Am Univ, 62-66; prof lectr, 68-69, George Washington Univ, 88- *Mem:* Fel Am Phys Soc; Sigma Xi; Asn Appl Math & Mech Ger; Am Hist Soc Am. *Res:* Mathematical fluid dynamics; vortex motion; rotating fluids; numerical solution of Navier-Stokes equations. *Mailing Add:* 10317 Crown Point Ct Potomac MD 20854-3901. *Fax:* 301-983-3843

LUGTHART, GARRIT JOHN, JR, ENTOMOLOGY, GENETICS. *Current Pos:* assoc prof biol, 61-91, chmn dept, 79-91, EMER PROF BIOL, LE MOYNE COL, NY, 91- *Personal Data:* b Los Angeles, Calif, Feb 11, 23; m 55, Joan Waidele; c 3. *Educ:* Mich State Univ, BS, 50, MS, 51; Univ Wis, PhD(entom), 59. *Prof Exp:* Assoc prof biol, Adrian Col, 56-61. *Mem:* Entom Soc Am; Am Genetic Asn; Sigma Xi. *Res:* Biology and control of insects injurious to humans and human genetics. *Mailing Add:* Biol Dept Le Moyne Col Syracuse NY 13214

LUH, BOR SHIUN, MOLECULAR BIOLOGY, HORTICULTURE. *Current Pos:* res asst, Univ Calif, Berkeley, 48-52, jr specialist, Dept Food Technol, Davis, 52-56, from asst food technologist to food technologist, 57-86, EMER FOOD TECHNOLOGIST, UNIV CALIF, DAVIS, 86-; FOOD TECHNOL CONSULT, LUH ASSOCS, DAVIS, CALIF, 78- *Personal Data:* b Shanghai, China, Jan 13, 16; US citizen; m 40, Bai T Liu; c Janet S. *Educ:* Chiao Tung Univ, BS, 38; Univ Calif, MS, 48, PhD(agr chem), 52. *Honors & Awards:* Food Sci Achievement Award, Chinese Am Food Soc, 84; Achievement Award Inst Food Technol Albania, 94. *Prof Exp:* Instr, Chiao Tung Univ, 38-41; chemist, Far Eastern Chem Works, China, 41-43; chief chemist, Ma Ling Canned Foods Co, Ltd, 43-46. *Concurrent Pos:* Consult, Food Indust Res & Develop Inst, Hsinchu, Taiwan, 65-67 & 69-70, Food & Agr Orgn, UN, 68 & 87, UN Indust Develop Orgn, UN, Vienna, Austria, 72, 80 & 82; vis prof food sci, Shiraz Univ, Iran, 77-78, food technol, Shanghai Fisheries Univ, China, 86- *Mem:* Am Chem Soc; fel Inst Food Technologists; Am Oil Chemists Soc; Am Asn Cereal Chemists; Am Soc Hort Sci. *Res:* Food science and technology research; fruits, vegetables, rice & cereal processing; food chemistry; food packaging; food stability and food safety. *Mailing Add:* Div Food Technol Univ Calif Cruess Hall Davis CA 95616. *Fax:* 530-752-4759; *E-Mail:* bsluh@ucdavis.edu

LUH, JIANG, ALGEBRA. *Current Pos:* assoc prof, 68-71, PROF MATH, NC STATE UNIV, 71- *Personal Data:* b Haining, Chekiang, China, June 24, 32; m 56, Tsu-Yunn Ma; c Albert, Ellice & Michael. *Educ:* Taiwan Normal Univ, BS, 54; Univ Nebr, MS, 59; Univ Mich, PhD(math), 63. *Prof Exp:* Assoc prof math, Ind State Univ, 63-66 & Wright State Univ, 66-68. *Mem:* Am Math Soc; Math Asn Am. *Res:* Ring theory; semi-group theory; linear algebra. *Mailing Add:* 8908 Oodvine Ct Raleigh NC 27613

LUH, JOHNSON YANG-SENG, ELECTRICAL ENGINEERING, APPLIED MATHEMATICS. *Current Pos:* assoc prof, 65-71, PROF ELEC ENG, PURDUE UNIV, 71- *Personal Data:* b Shanghai, China, Apr 9, 25; US citizen; m 57; c 2. *Educ:* Utopia Univ, China, BS, 47; Harvard Univ, MS, 50; Univ Minn, PhD(elec eng), 63. *Prof Exp:* Teaching fel elec eng, Harvard Univ, 50-51; engr, Nat Pneumatic Co, 51-56 & Curtiss-Wright Corp, 56-57; assoc engr, Int Bus Mach Corp, 57-58, staff engr, 62-63; instr elec eng, Univ Minn, 58-60; sr res scientist, Honeywell, Inc, 63-65. *Concurrent Pos:* Lectr, Univ Minn, 63-65; prin investr, NASA res grant, Jet Propulsion Lab, 65- *Mem:* Soc Indust & Appl Math; sr mem Inst Elec & Electronics Engrs; sr mem Am Astronaut Soc; Sigma Xi. *Res:* Control and information systems and computer aided engineering design, especially bounded-state, stochastic control, learning and communication, and data reduction systems. *Mailing Add:* Dept Elec & Comput Eng Riggs Hall Clemson Univ Clemson SC 29634

LUH, YUHSHI, SPECIALTY CHEMICALS & MATERIALS, ADHESIVES. *Current Pos:* SR RES CHEMIST, AM CYANAMID CO, 84- *Personal Data:* b Kaohsiung, Taiwan, Feb 14, 49; c 2. *Educ:* Nat Taiwan Univ, BS, 71; Rice Univ, PhD(chem), 76. *Honors & Awards:* Welch Fund Award, 74. *Prof Exp:* Proj investr, M D Anderson Hosp & Tumor Inst, 77-78; NIH postdoctoral fel, Mass Inst Technol, 78-79; res chemist, Mobil Oil Corp, Mobil Res & Develop Co, 79-81; res scientist, Gulf Oil Co, Gulf Sci & Technol Co, 81-83; res chemist, Mine Safety & Appliances Co, 83-84. *Concurrent Pos:* Spec lectr, Univ New Haven, 89-90. *Mem:* Am Chem Soc. *Res:* Biomaterials; ultraviolet stabilizers; photochromics; adhesives; crosslinking chemistry; specialty chemicals; enhanced oil recovery; chemotherapy; pharmaceuticals; petrochemicals; process development; organic and polymer synthesis; product formulation and testing; product development; structure-property relationships. *Mailing Add:* 948 Red Fox Rd Orange CT 06477-1035

LUHBY, ADRIAN LEONARD, HEMATOLOGY, PEDIATRICS. *Current Pos:* from instr to assoc prof, 50-59, PROF PEDIAT, NEW YORK MED COL, 59- *Personal Data:* b New York, NY, Dec 21, 16; m 67; c 1. *Educ:* Columbia Univ, AB, 38; NY Univ, MD, 43. *Prof Exp:* Intern path & bact, Mt Sinai Hosp, New York, 44-45, intern med & surg, 45-46; res assoc immunol, Children's Hosp, Ohio State Univ, 48-49, asst resident pediat, Hosp & instr, Univ, 49-50. *Concurrent Pos:* Fel hemat, Children's Hosp, Boston, Mass, 46-48; pres, Am Bd Nutrit, 76- *Mem:* Am Asn Cancer Res; Am Physiol Soc; Am Inst Nutrit; Am Soc Clin Nutrit; Am Hemat Soc. *Res:* Morphologic hematology; oncology; nutrition; megaloblastic anemias; physiology, metabolism, biochemistry and nutrition of folic acid, vitamin B-12 and vitamin B-6. *Mailing Add:* Dept Pediat NY Med Col 2794 Webb Ave Bronx NY 10468-2547

LUI, YIU-KWAN, PHYSICAL CHEMISTRY. *Current Pos:* res chemist, 76-78, sr res chemist, 78-81, RES ASSOC, ENGELHARD INDUST DIV, ENGELHARD CORP, 81- *Personal Data:* b Hong Kong, Mar 24, 37; US citizen; m 67; c 1. *Educ:* Chung Chi Col, Hong Kong, BS, 59; Lehigh Univ, MS, 61, PhD(phys chem), 66. *Prof Exp:* Res chemist, Titanium Pigment Div, NL Indust, 65-74, Indust Chem Div, 75. *Mem:* Am Chem Soc. *Res:* Heterogeneous catalysis; preparation and characterization of precious metal catalysts; colloid and surface properties of silica and alumina; physical properties of rheological additives; dispersion stability; physical and surface properties of titanium dioxide pigments. *Mailing Add:* 3 Paprota Ct Parlin NJ 08859-2013

LUIBRAND, RICHARD THOMAS, ORGANIC CHEMISTRY. *Current Pos:* from asst prof to assoc prof, 72-81, PROF ORG CHEM, CALIF STATE UNIV, HAYWARD, 81- *Personal Data:* b Detroit, Mich, Apr 13, 45. *Educ:* Wayne State Univ, BS, 66; Univ Wis, PhD(org chem), 71. *Prof Exp:* Fel, Alexander von Humboldt Found, WGer, 71-72. *Concurrent Pos:* Cottrell res grant, Res Corp, 73. *Mem:* Am Chem Soc; AAAS. *Res:* Reaction mechanisms in organic chemistry; natural products chemistry; computational chemistry. *Mailing Add:* Dept Chem Calif State Univ Hayward CA 94542. *E-Mail:* rluibrand@csuhayward.edu

LUINE, VICTORIA NALL, NEUROCHEMISTRY. *Current Pos:* PROF, DEPT PSYCHOL, HUNTER COL & PROG BIOPSYCHOL & BIOL, CITY UNIV NEW YORK, 87- *Personal Data:* b Pine Bluff, Ark, Apr 22, 45; m 76, David Russell; c Richard. *Educ:* Allegheny Col, BS, 67; State Univ NY, Buffalo, PhD(pharmacol), 71. *Prof Exp:* Res assoc, Rockefeller Univ, 72-75, asst prof neurochem, 75-77, assoc prof, Dept Physiol, 77-87. *Concurrent Pos:* Adj prof, Rockefeller Univ, 87- *Mem:* AAAS; Soc Neurosci; Endocrine Soc; NY Acad Sci. *Res:* Steroid hormone regulation of central neurotransmitters and their role in behavior, memory and aging. *Mailing Add:* Dept Psychol Hunter Col City Univ New York 695 Park Ave New York NY 10021-5024

LUISKUTTY, C THOMAS, MOSSBAUER SPECTROSCOPY, HYDRAULIC FRACTURE MODELING. *Current Pos:* from asst prof to assoc prof, 80-89, PROF PHYSICS & ENG, ORAL ROBERTS UNIV, 89- *Personal Data:* b Kangazha, India, Oct 18, 44; m 66, Celia George; c Tom, Sara & George. *Educ:* Univ Kerala, India, BS, 65, MS, 69; Univ Louisville, PhD(physics), 74. *Prof Exp:* Sci asst, Bhabha Atomic Res Ctr, India, 65-67, sci officer trainee, 69; teacher & supt, Evangel Schs, Louisville, 74-80. *Concurrent Pos:* Consult, John Zink Co, 81, Amoco Res Ctr, 87-88; res fel & consult, Nat Inst Petrol & Energy Res, 85-86; res fel, Mech Eng Dept, Univ Tulsa, 86-87. *Mem:* Am Phys Soc; Am Soc Eng Educ. *Res:* Mossbauer spectroscopy and hydraulic fracture modeling; engineering and science education and the need for ethics and spirituality in society. *Mailing Add:* 2629 W Atlanta Pl Broken Arrow OK 74012. *Fax:* 918-495-6033; *E-Mail:* tluiskut@oru.edu

LUK, FRANKLIN T, PARALLEL COMPUTING, SIGNAL PROCESSING. *Current Pos:* PROF & CHAIR COMPUT SCI, RENSSELAER POLYTECH INST, 92- *Personal Data:* b Hong Kong, China, Mar 23, 50; US citizen; m 86, Vivian Lui; c Jessica & David. *Educ:* Calif Inst Technol, BS, 72; Stanford Univ, MS, 74 PhD(comput sci), 78. *Prof Exp:* Asst prof comput sci, Cornell Univ, 78-84, assoc prof elec eng, 84-88, prof, 88-91. *Concurrent Pos:* Vis prof, Chinese Univ, Hong Kong, 93-94. *Mem:* Am Comput Mech; Inst Elec & Electronics Engrs; Soc Indust & Appl Math. *Res:* Numerical Analysis; scientific computation; parallel processing; matrix algorithms. *Mailing Add:* Dept Comput Sci Amos Eton Bldg Rm 132 Rensselaer Polytech Inst Troy NY 12180-3590. *Fax:* 518-276-4033; *E-Mail:* luk@cs.rpi.edu

LUK, GORDON DAVID, POLYAMINES, GASTROENTEROLOGY. *Current Pos:* resident med, 75-77, fel gastroenterol, 77-79, PHYSICIAN, JOHNS HOPKINS HOSP, 79-; PROF, DALLAS VET ADMIN MED CTR, 91- *Personal Data:* b Shanghai, China, Nov 15, 50; US citizen; m 73; c 2. *Educ:* Univ Pa, BA, 71; Harvard Med Sch, MD, 75; Am Bd Internal Med, cert med, 78, cert gastroenterol, 79. *Prof Exp:* Asst prof med & oncol, Johns Hopkins Univ, 80-91. *Concurrent Pos:* Instr med, John Hopkins Univ, 79-80. *Mem:* Am Fedn Clin Res; Am Col Physician; Am Gastroenterol Asn; Am Soc Gastrointestinal Endoscopy; Am Asn Study Liver Dis. *Res:* Cell proliferation and differentiation with special emphasis on the potential regulatory role of polyamines; diseases of gastrointestinal epithelia and neoplastic diseases. *Mailing Add:* Gastroenterol Res Dallas Vet Admin Med Ctr 4500 S Lancaster Dallas TX 75216-7191

LUK, KIN-CHUN C, DESIGN & SYNTHESIS OF COMPOUNDS FOR USE AS DRUGS, CORPORATE CHEMICAL & BIOLOGICAL DATABASES. *Current Pos:* Sr scientist, 77-88, res investr, 88-96, RES LEADER, HOFFMANN-LA ROCHE INC, 96- *Personal Data:* b Hong Kong, Mar 11, 50. *Educ:* Univ Wis-Eau Claire, BS, 73; Mass Inst Technol, PhD(org chem), 77. *Mem:* Am Chem Soc; Sigma Xi; AAAS. *Res:* Design and synthesis of small organic molecules for use as drug, especially in the area of anti-bacterial, anti-viral and anti-inflammatory diseases; design and implementation of corporate chemical and biological databases. *Mailing Add:* Hoff-La Roche Inc 340 Kingsland St Nutley NJ 07110

LUK, KING SING, STRUCTURAL ENGINEERING. *Current Pos:* from asst prof to assoc prof, 60-65, from assoc chmn to chmn dept, 66-72, prof, 70-83, EMER PROF CIVIL ENG, CALIF STATE UNIV, LOS ANGELES, 82- *Personal Data:* b Canton, China, Sept 1, 32; US citizen; m 57, Kit Ming Wong; c Doris, Steven, Eric & Marcus. *Educ:* Calif State Univ, BS, 57; Univ Southern Calif, MSCE, 60; Univ Calif, Los Angeles, PhD(dynamics, soils & struct eng), 71. *Prof Exp:* Chief engr, R E Rule, Inc, Calif, 58-60. *Concurrent Pos:* Pres, King S Luk & Assoc, Calif, 60-; pres, Cathay Pac Inc, 74-; comnr, Calif Seismic Safety Comn, 79-83; dir, Mech Nat Bank, 82- *Mem:* Fel Am Soc Civil Engrs. *Res:* Engineering education; structural and earthquake engineering in design and practice of reinforced concrete and steel structures; foundations; time dependent soil and foundation engineering; reinforced concretes; author of numerous publications. *Mailing Add:* Luk & Luk Inc 55 S Raymond Ave Suite 302 Alhambra CA 91801-7106

LUKACH, CARL ANDREW, ORGANIC CHEMISTRY, POLYMER CHEMISTRY. *Current Pos:* RETIRED. *Personal Data:* b Wilkes-Barre, Pa, Dec 18, 30; m 53, Joan Wojcik; c Carl, Theodore, & Marianna. *Educ:* Lehigh Univ, BS, 52, MS, 53; Univ Notre Dame, PhD(org chem), 57. *Prof Exp:* Res chemist, Hercules Inc, 56-69, res supvr, 69-73, res mgr, Org Div, 73-78, mgr, Chem Sci Div, 78-79, proj mgr cellulose derivatives, 80-81, petrol recovery appln, 82-85, world-wide mgr, patrol appln, 87-89, res & develop mgr, France, 90-92; mgr, res & develop, Aqualon. *Mem:* Am Chem Soc; Sigma Xi; Soc Petrol Engrs; Am Petrol Inst. *Res:* Polymerization and copolymerization of olefins and olefin oxides; polymerization kinetics; conformational analysis; reverse osmosis; cross-linking agents; paper chemistry; cellulose chemistry; oil and gas drilling fluids, fracturing fluids and completion fluids; casing cement; cosmetics, toothpaste and shampoo; low fat substitutes in food. *Mailing Add:* 109 Downs Dr Limerick Wilmington DE 19807-2556. *Fax:* 302-654-6283

LUKACS, EUGENE, mathematics; deceased, see previous edition for last biography

LUKACSKO, ALISON B, PHARMACEUTICAL PRODUCT DEVELOPMENT. *Current Pos:* Mgr pharmacol/toxicol, 85-90, dir prod develop, 90-91, DIR RES & DEVELOP, BRISTOL MYERS PRODS, 91- *Personal Data:* b Utica, NY, Jan 30, 51; m 79, Peter; c Jeffrey & Michael. *Educ:* NY Med Col, MS, 78, PhD(pharmacol), 79. *Mem:* Fel Am Col Nutrit; Soc Toxicol; Prod Develop Mgt Asn. *Res:* Direct research and development and support activities associated with over the counter health care pharmaceutical development by integrating technology with consumer/ patient needs. *Mailing Add:* Res Personnel BMS Co Res Develop Lab 1350 Liberty Ave Hillside NJ 07205. *Fax:* 908-851-6149

LUKAS, GEORGE, INDUSTRIAL PHARMACY. *Current Pos:* res chemist, Ciba-Geigy Corp, 64-65, res biochemist, 65-67, group leader, Biochem Dept, 67-71, mgr drug metabol, 71-80, assoc dir, 80-81, dir pharmaceut & pharm technol, 81-90, EXEC DIR, PHARMACEUT & PHARM TECHNOL, CIBA-GEIGY CORP, 91- *Personal Data:* b Budapest, Hungary, Mar 16, 31; m 56; c 2. *Educ:* Univ Budapest, BS, 54; Polytech Inst Brooklyn, MS, 60; Mass Inst Technol, PhD(org chem), 63; NY Univ, MBA, 72. *Prof Exp:* Develop engr, United Pharmaceut Works, Hungary, 54-56; chemist, Avery Indusrts, Calif, 57; develop engr, Chas Pfizer & Co, 57-59; NIH fel, Inst Chem Natural Substances, Gif-Sur-Yvette, France, 63-64. *Concurrent Pos:* adj assoc prof, Dept Pharmacol, NY Med Col, 80-90, adj prof, Col Pharm, Univ RI, 89- *Mem:* Am Asn Pharmaceut Sci. *Res:* Chemistry of natural products; pharmacodynamics; absorption and disposition of drugs. *Mailing Add:* 91 Woodland Ave Summit NJ 07901

LUKAS, JOAN DONALDSON, LOGIC, PROGRAMMING LANGUAGES & COMPILERS. *Current Pos:* from asst prof to assoc prof, 67-93, PROF MATH, UNIV MASS, BOSTON, 93- *Personal Data:* b New Haven, Conn, June 19, 42; m 63, 90, Seamus Kearney; c David & Jon. *Educ:* Columbia Univ, AB, 63; Mass Inst Technol, PhD(math), 67. *Concurrent Pos:* Vis lectr, Brandeis Univ, 71 & 79, 94; consult, 81- *Mem:* Am Math Soc; Math Asn Am; Asn Symbolic Logic; Asn Comput Mach; Inst Elec & Electronics Engrs Comput Soc. *Res:* Mathematical logic; recursive function theory; compiler optimization for parallel architectures. *Mailing Add:* Dept Math & Comput Sci Univ Mass 100 Morrissey Blvd Boston MA 02125-3393. *Fax:* 617-265-7173; *E-Mail:* joan@cs.umb.edu

LUKAS, RONALD JOHN, NEUROCHEMISTRY. *Current Pos:* NEUROCHEMIST NEUROPHARMACOL, BARROW NEUROL INST, PHOENIX, ARIZ, 80-, VCHMN, DIV NEUROBIOL, 87-, SR STAFF SCIENTIST, 90- *Personal Data:* b Syracuse, NY, Aug 22, 49; m 72, Julie Southard; c Eric T. *Educ:* State Univ NY, Cortland, BS, 71; State Univ NY, Downstate Med Ctr, PhD(biophysics), 76. *Prof Exp:* Fel, Univ Calif, Berkeley, 76-78; res assoc, Lab Chem Biodynamics, 78-79; fel neurobiol, Stanford Univ, 79-80. *Concurrent Pos:* Res asst prof pharmacol, Univ Ariz, Tucson, 80-88, res assoc prof, 89-; adj prof chem, Ariz State Univ, Tempe, 88. *Mem:* Soc Neurosci; Am Soc Neurochem; Biophys Soc; Sigma Xi; Am Soc Pharmacol & Exp Therapeut; Int Soc Neurochem. *Res:* Neurotransmitters, neurotoxins and synaptic receptors, nervous system hormone, tropic factors and molecular aspects of developmental neurobiology. *Mailing Add:* Div Neurobiol Barrow Neurol Inst 350 W Thomas Rd Phoenix AZ 85013-4496

LUKASEWYCZ, OMELAN ALEXANDER, IMMUNOBIOLOGY, ACADEMIC ADMINISTRATION. *Current Pos:* asst prof, 75-78, ASST DEAN CURRICULAR AFFAIRS, SCH MED, UNIV MINN, DULUTH, 77-, ASSOC PROF MED MICROBIOL & IMMUNOL, 78- *Personal Data:* US citizen; m 68; c 2. *Educ:* St Joseph's Col, Pa, AB, 64; Villanova Univ, MS, 68; Bryn Mawr Col, PhD(microbiol), 72. *Prof Exp:* Res asst microbiol, Univ Tex, Austin, 70-72; lectr microbiol, Med Sch, Univ Mich, Ann Arbor, 73-75. *Concurrent Pos:* Res scholar tumor immunol, Med Sch, Univ Mich, Ann Arbor, 73-75; fel, Bush Found, Minn, 83. *Mem:* Am Soc Microbiol; AAAS; Am Asn Immunologists; Fedn Am Socs Exp Med; Sigma Xi. *Res:* Evaluation of immunocompetent cell populations in immune mechanisms of leukemia; contribution of B and T cell subsets; role of macrophage; role of histocompatibility antigens; role of copper in the immune response; effects of copper deficiency on tumor immunity. *Mailing Add:* Dept Curric Affairs Univ Minn Med Duluth MN 55812

LUKASIEWICZ, JULIUS, AEROSPACE ENGINEERING. *Current Pos:* PROF ENG, CARLETON UNIV, 71- *Personal Data:* b Warsaw, Poland, Nov 7, 19; US citizen; m 41; c 2. *Educ:* Univ London, BSc, 43, DIC, 45, DSc(eng), 66; Polish Tech Univ, Eng, dipl, 44. *Prof Exp:* Sr sci officer, Aerodyn Dept, Royal Aircraft Estab, Eng, 45- 48; head high speed aerodyn lab, Nat Res Coun Can, 49-57; chief Von Karman Gas Dynamics Facil, Arnold Eng Develop Ctr, ARO, Inc, Tenn, 58-68; prof aerospace eng & assoc dean grad studies & res, Col Eng, Va Polytech Inst & State Univ, 68-70, Whittemore prof eng, 70-71. *Concurrent Pos:* Chmn, Aeroballistic Range Asn, 61-62 & Supersonic Tunnel Asn, 61-62; mem, Adv Group Aeronaut Res & Develop, NATO, 62-68; consult adv comt, US Air Force Systs Command, Nat Acad Sci, 69-71; mgr transp study, Sci Coun Can, 77-78. *Mem:* Fel Am Inst Aeronaut & Astronaut; fel Can Aeronaut & Space Inst; fel Brit Inst Mech Engrs; NY Acad Sci. *Res:* High speed aerodynamics; test facilities; energy and transportation; technology-society interaction. *Mailing Add:* 46 Whippoorwill Dr Ottawa ON K1J 7H9 Can

LUKASIK, STEPHEN JOSEPH, PHYSICS. *Current Pos:* vpres & mgr, Northrop Res & Technol Ctr, 82-85, CORP VPRES TECHNOL, NORTHROP CORP, 85- *Personal Data:* b Staten Island, NY, Mar 19, 31; m 83; c 6. *Educ:* Rensselaer Polytech Inst, BS, 51; Mass Inst Technol, SM, 53, PhD(physics), 56. *Hon Degrees:* DEng, Stevens Inst Technol, 87. Honors

& Awards: Ottens Res Award, 63. Prof Exp: Asst physics, Mass Inst Technol, 51-55; scientist, Westinghouse Elec Corp, 55-57; chief, Fluid Physics Div, Davidson Lab, Stevens Inst Technol, 57-66, assoc res prof physics, 59-66; dir nuclear test detection, Advan Res Projs Agency, 66-68, dept dir, 68-71, dir, 71-74; vpres, Systs Develop Div, Xerox Corp, 75-76; vpres nat security res, Rand Corp, 77-78; chief scientist, 78-79; chief scientist, Fed Commun Comn, 79-82. Concurrent Pos: Acoust engr, Bolt, Beranek & Newman Co, 52-55; consult, Vitro labs, Vitro Corp Am, 59-66; mem, Bd Trustees, Stevens Inst Technol, 75-, Harvey Mudd Col, 87-; mem, Comput Sci Adv Comt, Stanford Univ, 76-82; ed, Info Soc, 78-; mem, bd dirs, Software Productivity Consortium, 85-; mem bd trustees, Nat Security Indust Asn, 86- Mem: AAAS; Am Phys Soc; Sigma Xi. Res: Relaxation processes in gases and liquids; viscous boundary layer phenomena; energy dissipation processes in water waves; interaction of explosives with magnetic fields. Mailing Add: 1714 Stone Canyon Rd Los Angeles CA 90077-1915

LUKASKI, HENRY CHARLES, TRACE ELEMENT METABOLISM, BODY COMPOSITION ASSESSMENT. Current Pos: USDA Agr Res Serv postdoctoral fel nutrit, Grand Forks Human Nutrit Ctr, Univ NDak, 79-80, biologist, 80-82, res physiologist, 83-90, INSTR MED, UNIV NDAK SCH MED, 88-; RES LEADER, GRAND FORKS HUMAN NUTRIT CTR, AGR RES SERV, USDA, 90- Personal Data: b Dearborn, Mich, Sept 28, 47; m 77; c 2. Educ: Eastern Mich Univ, BS, 73; Pa State Univ, MS, 76, PhD(physiol & nutrit), 79. Prof Exp: Res collabr, Brookhaven Nat Lab, 78-79. Concurrent Pos: Consult, NIH, 87- & Nat Sci & Eng Res Coun, Can, 89- Mem: Am Physiol Soc; Am Inst Nutrit; Am Soc Clin Nutrit; fel Am Col Sports Med; fel Human Biol Coun; NY Acad Sci. Res: Human nutritional requirements for trace minerals and the physiologic and functional effects of graded trace element deficiencies in humans; human body composition assessment. Mailing Add: Grand Forks Human Nutrit Res Ctr Agr Res Serv Univ Sta PO Box 9034 Grand Forks ND 58202-9034

LUKE, BRIAN, THEORETICAL CHEMISTRY. Current Pos: SR SCIENTIST, APPL ENRICHMENT CTR, IBM, KINGSTON, 87- Personal Data: b Montreal, Can, Oct 12, 53. Educ: Calif Inst Technol, BS, 75, NSF, 76; Univ Southern Calif, PhD(theoret chem), 80. Prof Exp: Fel, Carnegie-Mellon Univ, 81-83; staff scientist, Life Sci Div, SRI Int & The Molecular Res Inst, 83-87. Mem: Am Chem Soc; NY Acad Sci; AAAS; fel Am Inst Chemists. Res: Calibration and efficient usage of current theoretical methods; protein structure determination. Mailing Add: PO Box 1984 Kingston NY 12401

LUKE, HERBERT HODGES, PLANT PATHOLOGY. Current Pos: RETIRED. Personal Data: b Pavo, Ga, Feb 2, 23; m 46; c 2. Educ: Univ Ga, BS, 50; La State Univ, MS, 52, PhD, 54. Prof Exp: Plant pathologist, Delta Br Exp Sta, USDA, Miss, 54-55, Agr Exp Sta, 55-86; prof plant path, Univ Fla, 70-86. Mem: Am Phytopath Soc. Res: Chemical nature of disease resistance in plants, particularly isolation and identification of host metabolites that inhibit pathogenesis of pathogen; chemical and genetic control of small grain diseases. Mailing Add: 1401 NW 61st Terr Gainesville FL 32605

LUKE, JAMES LINDSAY, FORENSIC PATHOLOGY. Current Pos: FORENSIC PATH, FBI ACAD, 84-; DIR ENVIRON PATH, ARMED FORCES INST PATH, 93- Personal Data: b Cleveland, Ohio, Aug 29, 32; m 57; c 3. Educ: Columbia Univ, BS, 56; Western Res Univ, MD, 60. Prof Exp: Intern Path, Yale-New Haven Hosp, 60-61; chief resident, Inst Path, Western Res Univ, 61-63; staff researcher, Lab Exp Path, Nat Inst Arthritis & Metab Dis, 63-65; assoc med examr forensic path, Off Chief Med Examr, NY, 65-67; prof forensic path, Sch Med, Univ Okla & chief med examr, 71-83. Concurrent Pos: State med examr, Okla, 67-71; clin prof path, Georgetown Univ, George Washington Univ & Howard Univ, 71-83, 89-; chief med examr, Washington, DC, 71-83; dist scientist, Armed Forces Inst Path, 83-86; chief med examr, Univ Conn Health Ctr, 87-89. Mem: Fel Am Acad Forensic Sci; Nat Asn Med Examr. Res: Epidemiological research in legal medicine; pathology of asphyxia, strangulation, hanging and sudden natural death; aspects of forensic pathology as related to pediatrics; pathology of silicone implant capsular tissues. Mailing Add: Off Armed Forces Med Examr Armed Forces Inst Path Washington DC 20306. Fax: 301-319-0635

LUKE, JON CHRISTIAN, APPLIED MATHEMATICS. Current Pos: asst prof, 75-79, ASSOC PROF MATH SCI, IND UNIV-PURDUE UNIV, INDIANAPOLIS, 79- Personal Data: b Minneapolis, Minn, Aug 10, 40; m 83, Jeanne Z Kowalski; c Amanda K & Rosa E. Educ: Mass Inst Technol, SB, 62, SM, 63; Calif Inst Technol, PhD(appl math), 66. Prof Exp: NSF fel, 66-68; asst prof math, Univ Calif, San Diego, 68-73; postdoctoral assoc, Univ Minn, 73-74; vis assoc, Calif Inst Technol, 74-75. Mem: Sigma Xi; Soc Indust & Appl Math; NY Acad Sci. Res: Nonlinear methods in applied mathematics; applications in nonlinear wave problems, geomorphology, economics, biophysics and acoustics. Mailing Add: Dept Math Ind Univ-Purdue Univ Indianapolis 402 N Blackford St Indianapolis IN 46202

LUKE, ROBERT A, PARTICLE PHYSICS. Current Pos: From asst prof to assoc prof, 68-77, PROF PHYSICS, BOISE STATE UNIV, 77-, CHMN DEPT, 83- Personal Data: b Rigby, Idaho, Jan 5, 38; m 64; c 6. Educ: Utah State Univ, BS, 62, MS, 66, PhD(physics), 68. Mem: Am Asn Physics Teachers; Am Nuclear Soc. Res: X-ray investigation of clay mixtures; multi-pion production in pion proton interactions. Mailing Add: 9121 W Pattie Dr Boise ID 83704

LUKE, STANLEY D, MATHEMATICS. Current Pos: AT DEPT MATH, SEATTLE PAC COL, WASH. Personal Data: b Sialkot, WPakistan, Jan 1, 28; m 52; c 5. Educ: Univ Panjab, WPakistan, BA, 47, MA, 49; Carnegie-Mellon Univ, MS, 54; Univ Pittsburgh, PhD(math), 68. Prof Exp: Prof math, Gordon Col, WPakistan, 49-64; instr, Univ Pittsburgh, 67-68; prof math, Nebr Wesleyan Univ, 68- Mem: Math Asn Am. Res: Mathematical analysis with special interest in summability. Mailing Add: 2712 143rd Pl SE Mill Creek WA 98012

LUKEHART, CHARLES MARTIN, ORGANOMETALLIC CHEMISTRY, NANOCOMPOSITES. Current Pos: from asst prof to assoc prof, 73-82, PROF CHEM, VANDERBILT UNIV, 82- Personal Data: b DuBois, Pa, Dec 21, 46; m 73; c 3. Educ: Pa State Univ, BS, 68; Mass Inst Technol, PhD(inorg chem), 72. Prof Exp: Res assoc chem, Tex A&M Univ, 72-73. Concurrent Pos: Alfred P Sloan res fel, 79-83. Mem: Am Chem Soc; Mats Res Soc. Res: Synthesis, characterization and chemical reactivity of organometallic and coordination complexes containing transition metals; new synthetic routes to nanocomposite materials. Mailing Add: Dept Chem Vanderbilt Univ Nashville TN 37235. Fax: 615-322-4936; E-Mail: lukehacm@ctrvax.vandcerbilt.edu

LUKENS, HERBERT RICHARD, JR, CHEMISTRY, PSYCHOPHYSIOLOGY. Current Pos: CHEMIST, IRT CORP, 73- Personal Data: b Coquille, Ore, May 19, 21; m 45; c 2. Educ: Univ Calif, Berkeley, BA, 45; US Int Univ, San Diego, MA, 75, PhD(human behav), 78. Prof Exp: Chemist, Albers Milling Co, 45-46, Consumers Yeast Co, 46-48, Tracerlab Inc, 48-55, Shell Develop Co, 55-62 & Gen Atomic, 62-73. Concurrent Pos: Family counsr, San Diego Youth Serv, 75-77, consult, 77- Mem: Am Chem Soc. Res: Anxiety, its psychophysiology and existential aspects; biochemistry, immunochemical applications; nucleonics, nuclear fuel cycle. Mailing Add: 5616 Abalone Pl La Jolla CA 92037-7501

LUKENS, LEWIS NELSON, BIOCHEMISTRY. Current Pos: assoc prof, 66-73, chmn biol dept, 78-81, PROF BIOCHEM, WESLEYAN UNIV, 73- Personal Data: b Philadelphia, Pa, Jan 21, 27; m 64; c 4. Educ: Harvard Univ, AB, 49; Univ Pa, PhD(biochem), 58. Prof Exp: Instr biochem, Mass Inst Technol, 56-58; Nat Res Coun res fel chem, Columbia Univ, 58-59, USPHS res fel, 59-60; asst prof biochem, Yale Univ, 64-66. Mem: Am Soc Biol Chem. Res: Protein synthesis and its control in eukaryotes, especially collagen. Mailing Add: Dept Molecular Biol & Biochem Wesleyan Univ Middletown CT 06459-0175

LUKENS, PAUL W, JR, MAMMALOGY. Current Pos: RETIRED. Personal Data: b Hibbing, Minn, Apr 24, 28; m 60; c 2. Educ: Univ Minn, BS, 52, PhD(zool), 63; Tex A&M Univ, MS, 56. Prof Exp: From instr to assoc prof, Univ Wis-Superior, 61-70, prof zool, 70-91. Concurrent Pos: Bd regents res grant, Univ Wis, 65-66. Mem: Am Soc Mammal. Res: Identification, interpretation and paleoecology of vertebrate faunas from archaeological sites; paleozoology; environmental conservation. Mailing Add: 810 11th Ave Superior MN 55616

LUKENS, RAYMOND JAMES, PLANT PATHOLOGY. Current Pos: RETIRED. Personal Data: b Beverly, NJ, Feb 25, 30; m 54; c 5. Educ: Rutgers Univ, BS, 54, MS, 55; Univ Md, PhD(bot), 58. Prof Exp: Asst plant pathologist, Conn Agr Exp Sta, 57-60, assoc plant pathologist, 60-69, plant pathologist, 70-75; sr plant pathologist, Ortho Div, Chevron Chem Co, 75-86. Concurrent Pos: Lectr plant path, Univ Calif, Berkeley, 77-78. Mem: Soc Indust Microbiol; Am Phytopath Soc; Bot Soc Am; Sigma Xi. Res: Chemistry of fungicides; correlation between structure and activity of fungicides; fungicide screening and plant disease control. Mailing Add: 2009 Westview Ct Modesto CA 95350

LUKER, WILLIAM DEAN, analytical chemistry, chemical engineering; deceased, see previous edition for last biography

LUKERT, MICHAEL T, GEOLOGY, GEOCHEMISTRY. Current Pos: from asst prof to assoc prof, 67-74, PROF GEOL, EDINBORO UNIV PA, 74- Personal Data: b Kansas City, Mo, June 28, 37; m 61; c 3. Educ: Univ Ill, BS, 60; Northern Ill Univ, MS, 62; Case Western Reserve Univ, PhD(geol), 73. Prof Exp: Instr geol, Northern Ill Univ, 62-64. Concurrent Pos: Consult, Pa Geol Surv, 75; adj prof, Thiel Col, 75-76 & Mercyhurst Col, 79 & 81; geologist C, Va Div Mineral Resources, 76-77. Mem: Geol Soc Am. Res: Geochronology; igneous and metamorphic petrology; Precambrian geology; geostatistics. Mailing Add: Dept Geosci Edinboro Univ Pa Edinboro PA 16444

LUKERT, PHIL DEAN, MICROBIOLOGY. Current Pos: MEM FAC, COL VET MED, UNIV GA, 67- Personal Data: b Topeka, Kans, Nov 1, 31; m 56; c 4. Educ: Kans State Univ, BS, 53, DVM, 60, MS, 61; Iowa State Univ, PhD(microbiol), 67. Prof Exp: Res assoc microbiol, Kans State Univ, 60-61; res vet, Nat Animal Dis Lab, Agr Res Serv, USDA, Iowa, 61-67. Mem: Am Vet Med Asn; Am Soc Microbiol; Am Asn Avian Path. Res: Animal virology, particularly pathogenesis of viral infections, identification of new pathogenic viruses and the development of new diagnostic methods for viral diseases. Mailing Add: Dept Med Microbiol Col Vet Med Univ Ga Athens GA 30602

LUKES, ROBERT MICHAEL, ORGANIC CHEMISTRY. *Current Pos:* RETIRED. *Personal Data:* b San Francisco, Calif, Mar 27, 23; m 49, Mary Fragomeni; c 6. *Educ:* Univ San Francisco, BS, 43; Univ Calif, MS, 47; Univ Notre Dame, PhD(org chem), 49. *Prof Exp:* Res chemist, Merck & Co, Inc, 49-53; res assoc, Res Labs, Gen Elec Co, 54-58, supvr, Insulation Lab, Locomotive & Car Equip Dept, 58-64, mgr, Finish Systs Lab, Major Appliance Labs, 64-85. *Mem:* Am Chem Soc; fel Am Inst Chemists. *Res:* Hydrogenation; steroid synthesis; plastics; resins; electrical insulation; surface coatings; paint; surface chemistry; electroless plating. *Mailing Add:* 223 Bramton Rd Louisville KY 40207-3419

LUKES, THOMAS MARK, FOOD SCIENCE. *Current Pos:* assoc prof, 62-73, PROF FOOD PROCESSING & HEAD DEPT FOOD INDUST, CALIF POLYTECH STATE UNIV, SAN LUIS OBISPO, 73- *Personal Data:* b San Jose, Calif, Mar 28, 20; m 52; c 4. *Educ:* San Jose State Col, BS, 47; Univ Calif, Berkeley, MS, 49. *Prof Exp:* Microbiologist, Real Gold Citrus, Mutual Orange Distributor, 49-51; head lab qual control, Gentry Div, Consol Food Corp, 51-62. *Mem:* AAAS; Inst Food Technol; Am Chem Soc. *Res:* Application of evolutionary operations to the food processing industry; development of chemical methods of flavor evaluation and application of new developments in food dehydration to the industrial scale. *Mailing Add:* 176 Del Norte San Luis Obispo CA 93401-1508

LUKEZIC, FELIX LEE, PLANT PATHOLOGY. *Current Pos:* from asst prof to assoc prof, 65-75, PROF PLANT PATH, PA STATE UNIV, 75- *Personal Data:* b Florence, Colo, May 27, 33; m 55; c 2. *Educ:* Colo State Univ, BS, 56, MS, 58; Univ Calif, PhD(plant path), 63. *Prof Exp:* Asst plant path, Colo State Univ, 56-58; lab technician, Univ Calif, 58-63; plant pathologist, Div Trop Res, United Fruit Co, Honduras, 63-65. *Mem:* Am Phytopath Soc; Am Soc Microbiol. *Res:* Physiology of plant parasitism, especially bacterial caused diseases. *Mailing Add:* Dept Plant Path 121 Buckhout Lab Pa State Univ University Park PA 16802-4506

LUKIN, MARVIN, ORGANIC CHEMISTRY, BIOCHEMISTRY. *Current Pos:* from asst prof to prof, 75-96, EMER PROF CHEM, YOUNGSTOWN STATE UNIV, 96- *Personal Data:* b Cleveland, Ohio, Feb 12, 28; m 62, Judith; c Jonathan & Joshua. *Educ:* Ohio Univ, BS, 49; Case Western Res Univ, MS, 54, PhD(org chem), 56. *Prof Exp:* Fel org synthesis, Mellon Inst, 56-57; fel protein chem, Albert Einstein Col Med, 57-61; res assoc immunochem, St Lukes Hosp, 61-63; staff asst, Cleveland Clin, 63-65; fel antibiotics, Case Western Res Univ, 66-67. *Mem:* Am Chem Soc; Sigma Xi. *Res:* Organic synthesis; peptide synthesis. *Mailing Add:* 3411 Heritage Court Canfield OH 44406

LUKOW, ODEAN MICHELIN, CEREAL CHEMISTRY, CEREAL QUALITY. *Current Pos:* RES SCIENTIST CEREAL CHEM, AGR CAN, 82- *Personal Data:* b Winnipeg, Man. *Educ:* Univ Man, BSc, 74, MSC, 77, PhD(cereal chem), 82. *Prof Exp:* Lectr microbiol, Univ Man, 77-78. *Mem:* Am Asn Cereal Chemists; Inst Food Technologists; Sigma Xi. *Res:* Annual cereal quality evaluation of Western Canadian breeders' lines of wheat; the biochemical basis of cereal quality as related to the protein component. *Mailing Add:* Res Ctr Agr & Agri-Food Can 195 Dafoe Rd Winnipeg MB R3T 2M9 Can

LUKOWIAK, KENNETH DANIEL, NEUROPHYSIOLOGY, NEUROETHOLOGY. *Current Pos:* from asst prof to assoc prof, 78-85, PROF MED PHYSIOL, UNIV CALGARY, 85- *Personal Data:* b Newark, NJ, Jan 10, 47. *Educ:* Iona Col, BSc, 69; State Univ NY, Albany, PhD(neurophysiol), 73. *Prof Exp:* Fel neurophysiol, Univ Ky, 73-75; asst prof physiol, McGill Univ, 75-78. *Concurrent Pos:* NIH fel, 73-75; Med Res Coun Can grant, 75-78, 78-84 & 84-; vis prof med, Tribuhyan Univ, Kathmandu, Nepal, 81- *Mem:* Am Physiol Soc; Am Soc Zoologists; Can Physiol Soc; Sigma Xi; AAAS; Soc Neurosci. *Res:* Neural and peptidergic mechanisms of adaptive behavior including associative learning in invertebrates; interactions between the central and peripheral nervous systems in the mediation of habituation, sensitization and dishabituation; central pattern generations and behavior. *Mailing Add:* Dept Physiol FCC Fac Med Univ Calgary Calgary AB T2N 4N1 Can

LULL, DAVID B, CHEMICAL ENGINEERING. *Current Pos:* gen engr, US Naval Weapons Lab, 71-76, gen engr, 76-80, CHEM ENGR, NAVAL SURFACE WEAPONS CTR, 80- *Personal Data:* b Rochester, NY, Feb 21, 23; m 49; c 4. *Educ:* Mass Inst Technol, BS, 47, Univ Mich, MS, 49. *Prof Exp:* Res engr, Arthur D Little Inc, 49-62; prin scientist, Appl Sci Lab, GCA Tech Div, 62-71. *Res:* Generation and assessment of aerosols; propagation and suppression of dust explosions; fracture and propulsion of solids and liquids by high explosives; effectiveness of spaced armor. *Mailing Add:* 16621 Cashell Rd Rockville MD 20853

LULLA, JACK D, FLEXIBLE DIELECTRICS. *Current Pos:* SR VPRES, TECHNICAL TAPE, 86- *Educ:* City Col NY, BS, 50. *Mem:* Am Chem Soc. *Res:* Polymer coatings and adhesives. *Mailing Add:* 40 E 88th St New York NY 10128

LUM, BERT K B, PHARMACOLOGY. *Current Pos:* PROF PHARMACOL & CHMN DEPT, SCH MED, UNIV HAWAII, MANOA, 69- *Personal Data:* b Honolulu, Hawaii, May 9, 29; m 52, Annie P; c 4. *Educ:* Univ Mich, BS, 51, PhD(pharmacol), 56; Univ Kans, MD, 60. *Prof Exp:* From instr to asst prof pharmacol, Med Ctr, Univ Kans, 56-62; from asst prof to prof, Sch Med, Marquette Univ, 62-69, asst chmn dept, 64-69. *Mem:* Am Soc Pharmacol & Exp Therapeut; Cardiac Muscle Soc; Asn Med Sch Pharmacol. *Res:* Cardiovascular and autonomic pharmacology. *Mailing Add:* Dept Pharmacol Sch Med Univ Hawaii Honolulu HI 96822. *Fax:* 808-956-3165; *E-Mail:* bertl@hawaii.edu

LUM, KIN K, PHOTOGRAPHIC CHEMISTRY. *Current Pos:* sr res assoc, 68-94, RES FEL, EASTMAN KODAK CO RES LABS, 94- *Personal Data:* b Ipoh, Malaya, Sept 4, 40; US citizen; m 65; c 2. *Educ:* Hong Kong Baptist Col, BSc, 62; Baylor Univ, PhD(org chem), 66. *Prof Exp:* Res fel, Utah State Univ, 66-68. *Mem:* Am Chem Soc; Soc Photog Sci & Eng. *Res:* Application of novel imaging chemistry into color image transfer systems. *Mailing Add:* 633 Chatelaine Dr Webster NY 14580

LUM, LAWRENCE, experimental biology, for more information see previous edition

LUM, PATRICK TUNG MOON, ENTOMOLOGY. *Current Pos:* RETIRED. *Personal Data:* b Honolulu, Hawaii, Nov 6, 28; div; c 2. *Educ:* Earlham Col, BA, 50; Univ Ill, MS, 52, PhD(entom), 56. *Prof Exp:* Asst entom, Univ Ill, 54-56, res assoc, 56, USPHS res fel, 57; res biologist, Entom Res Ctr, Fla State Bd Health, 57-65; res entomologist, Stored Prod Insect Res & Develop, USDA, 65- *Mem:* Int Mgt Coun; Entom Soc Am. *Res:* Pathogenecity of micro-organisms to insects; photoperiodism and circadian rhythms in insects; physiology, behavior and morphology of reproduction in moths. *Mailing Add:* 1252 Silver Prospect Dr Las Vegas NV 89108

LUMB, ALAN M, WATER RESEARCH ENGINEERING, WATER SHED MODELING. *Current Pos:* CHIEF, NAT WATER INFO SYSTS, 95- *Personal Data:* b Kansas, Mo, Feb 42. *Educ:* Univ Kans, BS, 64, MS, 66; Stanford Univ, PhD(civil eng), 70. *Mem:* Am Soc Civil Engrs; Am Geophys Union; Am Water Resource Asn. *Mailing Add:* 437 Nat Ctr Reston VA 20192. *Fax:* 703-648-5295

LUMB, ETHEL SUE, biology; deceased, see previous edition for last biography

LUMB, GEORGE DENNETT, PATHOLOGY. *Current Pos:* prof path, 80-88, chmn, 86-88, EMER PROF PATH, HAHNE MANN UNIV, 88- *Personal Data:* b London, Eng, Jan 26, 17; nat US; m 45; c 1. *Educ:* Univ London, MB & BS, 39, MD, 46; MRCP, Eng, 54; FRC(path), 55; FCAP, 56. *Prof Exp:* Assoc prof path, Univ London, 53-57; prof, Univ Tenn, 57-59; dir clin labs & pathologist, James Walker Mem Hosp, 59-65; dir, Warner-Lambert Res Inst Can, 65-69, vpres & dir, Pharmaceut Co, Fla, 69-71; dir med serv & res & develop, 71-73; vpres med affairs, Synapse Commun Serv Inc, 73-77; vpres prod safety assessment, Searle Labs, 77-80. *Concurrent Pos:* Traveling res fel, Westminster Hosp, London, consult pathologist, 48-57; vis assoc prof health affairs, Sch Med, Univ NC, 60-; assoc prof, Univ Toronto, 66-71; scholar in residence, Dept Path, Med Ctr, Duke Univ, 86. *Mem:* Am Soc Exp Path; Am Asn Path & Bact; Col Am Path; Int Acad Path; Path Soc Gt Brit & Ireland. *Res:* Cardiac research; conduction of specialized muscle pathways in hogs; experimental production of infarcts in canine hearts. *Mailing Add:* 21 Sandy Pt Wilmington NC 28405

LUMB, JUDITH RAE M, IMMUNOLOGY. *Current Pos:* RETIRED. *Personal Data:* b Bridgeport, Conn, Mar 19, 43; m 64; c Timothy Alan & Jeffrey Thomas. *Educ:* Univ Kans, BA, 65, MA, 66; Stanford Univ, PhD(med microbiol), 69. *Prof Exp:* From asst prof to prof biol, Atlanta Univ, 69-87, actg chmn, 83-85. *Concurrent Pos:* NIH career develop award, 75-80. *Mem:* AAAS; Reticuloendothelial Soc; Am Soc Microbiol; Am Soc Cell Biol; Cellular Kinetics Soc. *Res:* Biochemistry of alkaline phosphatase of C57BL lymphomas; derepression of embryo functions in C57BL lymphomas; computer simulation of the development of the thymus; early lymphocyte differentiation. *Mailing Add:* Caye Caulker Belize

LUMB, RALPH F, PHYSICAL CHEMISTRY, NUCLEAR SCIENCES. *Current Pos:* PROP, RALPH LUMB ASSOCS, 86- *Personal Data:* b Worcester, Mass, May 27, 21; m 41; c 8. *Educ:* Clark Univ, AB, 47, PhD(phys chem), 51. *Prof Exp:* Instr chem, Assumption Col, 47-48 & Northeastern Univ, 49-51; chief, Chem-Physics Br, Div Nuclear Mat, US AEC, 51-56; proj leader, Quantum Inc, 56-59, vpres, 59-60; dir, Western NY Nuclear Res Ctr, Inc, 60-68; pres, Advan Technol Consult Corp, 68-71; pres, Nusac Inc, 71-84; sr consult, Nackenhut Advan Technol, 84-86. *Concurrent Pos:* Secy, adv comt uranium standards, AEC, 53-56; consult, Univ Buffalo Nuclear Reactor Proj, 56-60 & Safeguards Br, Int Atomic Energy Agency, 63- *Mem:* Fel AAAS; fel Am Inst Chemists; Am Nuclear Soc; fel Inst Nuclear Mat Mgt. *Res:* Applications of nuclear energy; nuclear research; reactor design, operation and utilization. *Mailing Add:* 8 Salem Dr Somers CT 06071

LUMB, ROGER H, BIOCHEMISTRY. *Current Pos:* from asst prof to assoc prof, 67-74, PROF BIOL, WESTERN CAROLINA UNIV, 74- *Personal Data:* b Union, NJ, June 29, 40; m 62; c 3. *Educ:* Alfred Univ, AB, 62; Univ SC, MS, 65, PhD(biol), 67. *Prof Exp:* Instr biol, Univ SC, 65-67. *Concurrent Pos:* Damon Runyon fel, 71-73; researcher, Utrecht, Neth, 75-76. *Mem:* Sigma Xi. *Res:* Lipid metabolism in lung; lipid metabolism in cancer cells; membrane biochemistry. *Mailing Add:* Dept Biol Western Carolina Univ Cullowhee NC 28723

LUMB, WILLIAM VALJEAN, VETERINARY SURGERY & ANESTHESIOLOGY. *Current Pos:* assoc prof med, Colo State Univ, 60-63, dir surg lab, 63-79, prof surg, 63-81, EMER PROF, COL VET MED, COLO STATE UNIV, 81- *Personal Data:* b Sioux City, Iowa, Nov 26, 21; m 49, Lilly Carlson; c John W. *Educ:* Kans State Univ, DVM, 43; Tex A&M Univ, MS, 53; Univ Minn, PhD(vet med), 57; Am Col Vet Anethesiologists, dipl; Am Col Vet Surgeons, dipl. *Honors & Awards:* Gaines Award, 65; Ralston-Purina Res Award, 80; Jakob Markowitz Award, Am Acad Surg Res, 87. *Prof Exp:* From intern to resident, Angell Mem Animal Hosp, Boston, 46-48; from instr to assoc prof med & surg, Tex A&M Univ, 49-52; assoc prof clin & surg, Colo State Univ, 54-58 & surg & med, Mich State Univ, 58-60. *Concurrent Pos:* Pres, Lubra Co. *Mem:* Nat Acad Sci; NY Acad Sci; Am Asn Vet Clinicians; Am Col Vet Surg; AAAS; Am Vet Med Asn; Am Col Vet Anesthesiologists. *Res:* Experimental surgery and anesthesiology; published 2 books and over 150 articles. *Mailing Add:* 1905 Mohawk Ft Collins CO 80525

LUMBERS, SYDNEY BLAKE, GEOLOGY, PETROLOGY. *Current Pos:* cur geol, 73-96, cur-in-chg, 80-96, EMER CUR GEOL, ROYAL ONTO MUS, 96- *Personal Data:* b Toronto, Ont, Aug 6, 33; m 82, Frances. *Educ:* McMaster Univ, BSc, 58; Univ BC, MSc, 60; Princeton Univ, PhD(geol), 67. *Prof Exp:* Geologist, Ont Div Mines, Ministry Natural Resources, 62-73. *Concurrent Pos:* Mem, Comt Study Solid Earth Sci Can, Sci Coun Can, 68-69; corresp, Subcomt Precambrian Stratig, Int Union Geol Sci, 72- *Mem:* Geol Soc Am; Mineral Asn Can; Geol Asn Can; Sigma Xi; Am Geophys Union; NY Acad Sci; Int Union Geol Sci. *Res:* Precambrian geology; evolution of Grenville Province of Canadian Precambrian Shield; metamorphism; petrogenesis of anorthosite suite rocks and alkalic rocks; geochronology; relationship of mineral deposits to stratigraphy, metamorphism and plutonism. *Mailing Add:* 7 Calle Alejandra Santa Fe NM 87505. *Fax:* 416-586-5814

LUMENG, LAWRENCE, MEDICINE, BIOCHEMISTRY. *Current Pos:* From asst prof to assoc prof, 71-79, PROF MED BIOCHEM, SCH MED, IND UNIV, INDIANAPOLIS, 79- *Personal Data:* b Manila, Philippines, Aug 10, 39; US citizen; m 66; c 2. *Educ:* Ind Univ, Bloomington, BS, 60; Ind Univ, Indianapolis, MD, 64, MS, 69; Am Bd Internal Med, dipl, 70. *Concurrent Pos:* Res & educ associateship, Vet Admin Hosp, Indianapolis, 71-73; clin investr, 73-76; chief in gastroenterol, 77-; dir gastroenterol & hepatol, Ind Univ Med Ctr, 84- *Mem:* Am Soc Clin Investr; Am Col Phys; Am Soc Biol Chemists; Am Gastroenterol Asn; Am Asn Study Liver Dis; Res Soc Alcoholism. *Res:* Regulation of metabolic pathways; ethanol metabolism; pyridoxine and thiamine metabolism; clinical liver diseases. *Mailing Add:* Med Res & Library Bldg Ind Univ Med Ctr 975 W Walnut Rm 424 Indianapolis IN 46202-5121

LUMLEY, JOHN L(EASK), FLUID MECHANICS, TURBULENCE. *Current Pos:* WILLIS H CARRIER PROF ENG, SIBLEY SCH MECH & AEROSPACE ENG, CORNELL UNIV, 77- *Personal Data:* b Detroit, Mich, Nov 4, 30; m 53, Jane French; c Katherine L, Jennifer F & John C. *Educ:* Harvard Univ, AB, 52; Johns Hopkins Univ, MSE, 54, PhD(aeronaut), 57. *Hon Degrees:* Haute Distinction Honoris Causa, Ecole Centrale Lyon, 87. *Honors & Awards:* Medallion, Univ Liege, 71; Fluid & Plasmadynamics Prize & Drydeh Lectr, Am Inst Aeronaut & Astronaut, 82; Fluid Dynamics Prize, Am Phys Soc, 90; Timoshenko Medal, Am Soc Mech Engrs, 93. *Prof Exp:* Asst & jr instr mech eng, Johns Hopkins Univ, 53-54, asst aeronaut, 54-57, res assoc mech eng, 57-59; from asst prof to assoc prof eng res, Pa State Univ, 59-61, from assoc prof to prof aerospace eng, 61-74, Evan Pugh prof, 74-77. *Concurrent Pos:* Instr, McCoy Col, 56-59; courtesy fel, Johns Hopkins Univ, 57-58, fel, 58-59; exchange prof, Univ Aix-Marseille, 66-67; vis prof, Univ Louvain-la-Neuve, Belg & Fulbright sr lectr, Univ Liege, 73-74; Guggenheim fel, Mech Fluids Lab, Sch Cent Lyon & Inst Mech Statist Turbulence, Univ d'Aix-Marseille II, France, 73-74; coordr, Grad Exchange Prog Cornell Univ/ Ecole Centrale de Lyon, 84-; mem adv comt, Stanford/NASA Ames Ctr Turbulence Res, 89, chmn, 90, 91, 95 & 97; chmn, peer rev comt, NASA Lewis Ctr Modeling Turbulence & Transition, 93. *Mem:* Nat Acad Eng; Soc Natural Philos; NY Acad Sci; fel Am Acad Mech; Am Inst Aeronaut & Astronaut; fel Am Acad Arts & Sci; fel Am Phys Soc. *Res:* Turbulence; stochastic processes; electronic instrumentation. *Mailing Add:* 256 Upson Hall Cornell Univ Ithaca NY 14853

LUMMA, WILLIAM CARL, JR, ORGANIC CHEMISTRY, MEDICINAL CHEMISTRY. *Current Pos:* sr res chemist process develop, Rahway, NJ, 70-72, res fel, 72-81, sr res fel med chem, 81-82, SR SCIENTIST, MERCK, SHARP & DOHME RES LABS, WEST POINT, PA, 90-; DIR MED CHEM, BERLEX LAB, CEDAR KNOLLS, NJ, 82- *Personal Data:* b Detroit, Mich, Apr 21, 41; m 75, Patricia A Kasinger; c Keith & Carl. *Educ:* Wayne State Univ, BS, 63; Mass Inst Technol, PhD(org chem), 66. *Prof Exp:* Asst prof chem, St Louis Univ, 66-70. *Mem:* Am Chem Soc; NY Acad Sci; AAAS. *Res:* Heterocyclic and organic synthetic chemistry. *Mailing Add:* 1447 Newman Rd Pennsburg PA 18073-1925. *E-Mail:* bill_lumma@merck.com

LUMPKIN, LEE ROY, DERMATOLOGY, PATHOLOGY. *Current Pos:* prof, 72-80, CLIN PROF DERMAT, ALBANY MED COL, 80- *Personal Data:* b Oklahoma City, Okla, Sept 6, 25; m 53; c 5. *Educ:* Univ Okla, BA, 49, MD, 53; Am Bd Dermat, dipl. *Honors & Awards:* Cert of Appreciation, Strategic Air Command, 64 & Surgeon Gen Air Force, 69; James Clarke White Award, 71. *Prof Exp:* Intern, Tripler Gen Hosp, USAF, Honolulu, Hawaii, 53-54, resident dermat, Walter Reed Gen Hosp, Washington, DC, 58-61, chief dermat serv & clins, 3070th Air Force Hosp, Torrejon AFB, Spain, 61-64, chief dermat & clins, Air Force Hosp, Carswell AFB, Tex, 65-67, chief dermat serv, Wilford Hall Air Force Med Ctr, Lackland AFB, 67-72, dir residency training, 69-72. *Concurrent Pos:* Fel dermal-path, Armed Forces Inst Path, 64-65; vis lectr, USAF Sch Aerospace Med; clin assoc prof, Univ Tex Med Sch, San Antonio; assoc mem comn of cutaneous dis, Armed Forces Epidemiol Bd; USAF rep, Nat Prog Dermat; pres, NY State Soc Dermat, 81-83. *Mem:* Fel Am Col Physicians; fel Am Acad Dermat; Soc Air Force Physician (pres-elect, 71). *Mailing Add:* 22 New Scotland Ave Albany NY 12208-3419

LUMPKIN, MICHAEL DIRKSEN, NEUROENDOCRINOLOGY, NEUROIMMUNOLOGY. *Current Pos:* from asst prof to assoc prof, 84-93, PROF & CHMN PHYSIOL, MED SCH, GEORGETOWN UNIV, 93- *Personal Data:* b Dallas, Tex, Feb 2, 53. *Educ:* Univ Tex, Austin, BA, 75; Univ Tex Health Sci Ctr, Dallas, PhD(physiol), 81. *Prof Exp:* Teaching asst physiol, Univ Tex Health Sci Ctr, Dallas, 75-76, NIH fel, 76-81, res assoc neuroendocrinol, 81-83. *Concurrent Pos:* Lectr, Univ Tex Health Sci Ctr, Dallas, 78-82; prin investr, NIH grants, 86-94; consult, Adamha, 88-, NSF, 88-, VA, 88- & March of Dimes, 88-, NIH, 89-; lectureship award, Univ Modena, Italy, 90. *Mem:* Endocrine Soc; Soc Neurosci; Soc Neuroimmunomodulation. *Res:* Neuropeptide control of anterior pituitary stress hormones; hypothalamic and pituitary hormone regulation of male and female gonadal function; cytokine regulation of neuroendocrine function and growth. *Mailing Add:* Dept Physiol Sch Med Georgetown Univ 3900 Reservoir Rd NW Washington DC 20007. *Fax:* 202-687-7407

LUMRY, RUFUS WORTH, II, BIOCHEMISTRY. *Current Pos:* assoc prof, 53-57, dir, Lab Biophys Chem, 63-86, PROF PHYS CHEM, UNIV MINN, MINNEAPOLIS, 57- *Personal Data:* b Bismarck, NDak, Nov 3, 20; div; c 3. *Educ:* Harvard Univ, AB, 42, AM, 48, PhD(chem physics), 48. *Prof Exp:* Res assoc, Div Eight, Nat Defense Res Comt, 42-45; Merck fel, Univ Utah, 48-50, asst prof phys chem, 50-53, asst res prof biochem, 51-53. *Concurrent Pos:* NSF sr fel & vis scientist, Lab Carlsberg, Copenhagen, 59-60; vis prof, Inst Protein Res, Osaka, Japan, 61; Inst Biol Chem Rome, 63; Univ Calif, San Diego, 77-78 & Univ Granada, Spain, 85. *Mem:* Am Chem Soc; Soc Biol Chem; Sigma Xi; Biophys Soc. *Res:* Biophysical chemistry; enzymes, proteins; fast reactions; water and water solutions. *Mailing Add:* Chem Dept Sch Chem Univ Minn 207 Pleasant St SE Minneapolis MN 55455-0431

LUMSDAINE, EDWARD, SOLAR ENERGY, PRODUCT QUALITY. *Current Pos:* DEAN & PROF MECH ENG, MICH TECHNOL UNIV. *Personal Data:* b Hong Kong, Sept 30, 37; US citizen; m 59, Monika Amsler; c Andrew, Anne J, Alfred & Arnold. *Educ:* NMex State Univ, BSME, 63, MSME, 64, ScD(eng), 66. *Prof Exp:* Res engr, Boeing Co, 66-67; from asst prof to assoc prof mech eng, SDak State Univ, 67-72; from assoc prof to prof fluid flow & aeroacoust, Univ Tenn, Knoxville, 72-77; sr res engr, Phys Sci Lab, NMex State Univ, 77-78, prof mech eng, 77-78; dir, NMex Solar Energy Inst, 78-81; dir & prof mech & aerospace eng, Univ Tenn, Knoxville, 81-83; dean & prof mech eng, Univ Mich, Dearborn, 82-88 & Univ Toledo, 88-93. *Concurrent Pos:* Vis prof, Cairo Univ, Egypt, 74; Tatung Inst Technol, Taipei, Repub of China, 78 & Qatar Univ, Doha, 83; UNESCO expert consult, Cairo Univ, 79-80; lectr, US Info Serv, 81; consult, Ford Motor Co, 84-; bd mem, Am Solar Energy Soc, 85-89; consult & bd mem, Am Supplies Inst, 86-; prin investr, NSF, Am Soc Heating, Refrig & Air Conditioning Engrs, NASA, Dept Energy, HEW and others. *Mem:* Fel Am Soc Mech Engrs; Am Soc Eng Educ; assoc fel Am Inst Aeronaut & Astronaut; Am Soc Testing & Mat; Am Solar Energy Soc; Nat Soc Prof Engrs. *Res:* Heat transfer; fluid mechanics; turbomachinery; aeroacoustics; solar energy applications in photovoltaics, desalineation & irrigation; energy conservation; teaching with microcomputers; product quality; noise-harshness vibrations; author on software in engineering mathematics and on creativity and problem solving. *Mailing Add:* 1300 Cedar St Hancock MI 49930-1018. *Fax:* 906-487-2782; *E-Mail:* lumsdain@mtu.edu

LUMSDEN, CHARLES JOHN, THEORETICAL PHYSICS. *Current Pos:* assoc prof, 83-90, PROF, DEPT MED, UNIV TORONTO, 81- *Personal Data:* b Hamilton, Ont, Can, Apr 9, 49. *Educ:* Univ Toronto, BSc, 72, MSc, 74, PhD(theoret physics), PhD, 78. *Honors & Awards:* Sir John Cunningham McLennan Award Physics, 72; E C Stevens Award Physics, 77. *Prof Exp:* Spec lectr biophys, Univ Toronto, 75-78; fel, Dept Biol, Harvard Univ, 79-82. *Concurrent Pos:* Scholar, Med Res Coun Can, 83-88, scientist, 88. *Mem:* Am Phys Soc; Soc Math Biol; Biophys Soc. *Res:* Published numerous articles on sociobiology, physiology, statistical mechanics & mathematical biology. *Mailing Add:* Inst Med Sci Univ Toronto Rm 7317 Med Sci Bldg Toronto ON M5S 1A8 Can

LUMSDEN, DAVID NORMAN, GEOLOGY. *Current Pos:* from asst prof to assoc prof, 67-77, PROF GEOL, MEMPHIS STATE UNIV, 77- *Personal Data:* b Buffalo, NY, Aug 29, 35; m 63; c 2. *Educ:* State Univ NY, Buffalo, BA, 58, MA, 60; Univ Ill, PhD(geol), 65. *Prof Exp:* Res engr, Carborundum Co, 60-62; sr geologist, Pan Am Petrol Corp, 65-67. *Mem:* Geol Soc Am; Am Asn Petrol Geol; Soc Econ Paleont & Mineral; Sigma Xi. *Res:* Study of carbonate and quartzose sedimentary rocks. *Mailing Add:* Dept Geol Memphis State Univ Memphis TN 38152

LUMSDEN, JESSIE B, SURFACE PHYSICS. *Current Pos:* SR SCIENTIST, ROCKWELL INT SCI CTR, 78- *Personal Data:* b Louisa, Va, Oct 29, 42. *Educ:* Univ Richmond, BS, 65; Ohio State Univ, PhD(physics), 70. *Prof Exp:* Staff mem, Dept Metall Eng, Ohio State Univ, 70-78. *Mem:* Am Phys Soc; Electrochem Soc. *Mailing Add:* Rockwell Int Sci Ctr PO Box 1085 Thousand Oaks CA 91360

LUMSDEN, RICHARD, cell biology, parasitology, for more information see previous edition

LUMSDEN, ROBERT DOUGLAS, PLANT PATHOLOGY. *Current Pos:* res plant pathologist, Agr Res Ctr W, 66-92, SUPVRY RES PLANT PATHOLOGIST, BIOCONTROL PLANT DIS LAB, PLANT SCI INST, BELTSVILLE AGR RES CTR, USDA, BELTSVILLE, MD, 92- *Personal Data:* b Washington, DC, June 21, 38; m 60, Valerie Brook; c 2. *Educ:* NC State Univ, BS, 61, MS, 63; Cornell Univ, PhD(plant path), 67. *Concurrent Pos:* Fel, USDA Agr Res Serv, 87. *Mem:* Fel Am Phytopath Soc. *Res:* Physiology of plant diseases, including the physiology of pathogenesis and disease resistance; pathology and biological control of plant pathogens, especially soilborne plant pathogens; soil ecology; mechanism of action of biological control agents. *Mailing Add:* 274 Biosci Bldg Agr Res Ctr W USDA Beltsville MD 20705. *Fax:* 301-504-5968

LUMSDEN, WILLIAM WATT, JR, GEOLOGY, PALEONTOLOGY. *Current Pos:* RETIRED. *Personal Data:* b Dallas, Tex, Dec 21, 20; m 45; c 2. *Educ:* Univ Calif, Los Angeles, AB, 55, PhD, 64. *Prof Exp:* Asst geol, Univ Calif, Los Angeles, 55-58; from asst prof to assoc prof, Calif State Univ, Long Beach, 58-70, chmn dept, 58-74, prof, 70-83. *Concurrent Pos:* Leverhulme fel for Gt Brit, Aberdeen Univ. *Mem:* AAAS; Paleont Soc; Soc Econ Paleont & Mineral; Am Asn Petrol Geol. *Res:* Invertebrate paleontology; field geology; stratigraphy. *Mailing Add:* PO Box 1556 Idyllwild CA 92549

LUNA, ELIZABETH J, CELL BIOLOGY, MEMBRANE BIOCHEMISTRY. *Current Pos:* sr scientist, 88-93, PRIN SCIENTIST, WORCESTER FOUND EXP BIOL, 93- *Personal Data:* b Poplar Bluff, Mo, Oct 18, 51; m 74, Alonzo H Ross. *Educ:* Southern Ill Univ-Carbondale, BA, 72; Stanford Univ, PhD(chem), 77. *Honors & Awards:* Robert A Bensley Award, Am Asn Anat, 93. *Prof Exp:* Res assoc, dept cell biol & develop biol, Harvard Univ, 77-81; asst prof biol, Princeton Univ, 81-88. *Mem:* AAAS; Am Chem Soc; Am Soc Cell Biol; Biophys Soc; Protein Soc; Am Asn Cancer Res. *Res:* Cytoskeleton membrane interaction and regulation. *Mailing Add:* Worcester Found Exp Biol 222 Maple Ave Shrewsbury MA 01545-2795. *Fax:* 508-842-3915; *E-Mail:* luna@sci.wfeb.edu

LUNARDINI, VIRGIL J(OSEPH), JR, MECHANICAL & ARCTIC ENGINEERING, HEAT TRANSFER. *Current Pos:* RES ENGR, US COLD REGIONS LAB, 79- *Personal Data:* b Holyoke, Mass, May 10, 35; m 60; c 3. *Educ:* Univ Notre Dame, BS, 57; Ohio State Univ, MS, 60, PhD(mech eng), 63. *Honors & Awards:* Eugene Jacob Award, Petroleum Div, Am Soc Mech Engrs, 81; Ralph James Award, 85; Am Soc Mech Engrs Award, 87. *Prof Exp:* Instr eng, Ohio State Univ, 58-63; asst prof, Clarkson Col Technol, 63-66; assoc prof, State Univ NY, Buffalo, 66-69; from assoc prof to prof mech eng, Univ Ottawa, 69-79. *Concurrent Pos:* Consult, NASA Lewis Labs, Ohio, 64, Pratt & Whitney Aircraft Div, United Aircraft Corp, 66-67, Chisolm-Ryder, NY, 68- & Govt Can, 78-79, Gulf Interstate, 83, Pace Consults, 83-85; State Univ NY Buffalo fac fel, 67; adj prof Thayer Sch, Dartmouth, 79- *Mem:* Am Soc Mech Engrs; Sigma Xi. *Res:* Permafrost heat transfer; cold regions engineering; energy conservation; global climate change. *Mailing Add:* US Cold Regions Lab 72 Lyme Rd Hanover NH 03755-1290

LUNCHICK, CURT, farm worker protection, human exposure to pesticides, for more information see previous edition

LUND, ANDERS EDWARD, WOOD SCIENCE & TECHNOLOGY. *Current Pos:* CONSULT, ANDERS E LUND, INC, 84- *Personal Data:* b Luverne, Minn, Sept 26, 28; m 93, Terry F Froehlin. *Educ:* Colo State Univ, BS, 55; Duke Univ, MF, 56, DF(wood sci, bus mgt), 64. *Prof Exp:* Forest prod technician, US Forest Prod Lab, 56-58; sr scientist, Koppers Co, Inc, 58-66; assoc prof wood sci, Clemson Univ, 66-67; head admin, Tex Forest Prod Lab, Tex A&M Univ, 67-73; dir, Inst Wood Res, Mich Technol Univ, 74-84. *Concurrent Pos:* Consult, Forest Prod Co, 66-; prof, Tex A&M Univ, 67-73; consult, Cent States Energy Res Comn, 77, Sci & Educ Admin, USDA, 78 & Mich Energy Admin, 78-84. *Mem:* Int Asn Wood Anatomists; Int Res Group Wood Preservation; Am Wood Preservers Asn; Forest Prod Soc; Soc Wood Sci & Technol; fel Inst Wood Sci; fel Am Soc Testing & Mat; Rwy Tie Asn. *Res:* Wood deterioration and prevention; composite wood products; research administration; wood preservation; fire behavior of wood; physical, mechanical and chemical properties of wood. *Mailing Add:* 21009 Green Hill Rd Farmington MI 48335. *Fax:* 248-477-4469

LUND, CHARLES EDWARD, STRUCTURAL & THERMAL ANALYSIS, FINITE ELEMENT METHODS. *Current Pos:* STRUCT METHODS SPECIALIST, PARKER ABEX NWL AEROSPACE, 77- *Personal Data:* b Fremont, Mich, Apr, 4, 46; m 94, Shirley Ganz; c Deanna. *Educ:* Univ Mich, BSE, 68, MSE, 70; Stanford Univ. *Prof Exp:* Assoc engr, McDonnell-Douglas Astro Co, 68-69; struct engr, Lockheed Missiles & Space Co, 70-77. *Concurrent Pos:* Lectr, Dept Mech Eng, Western Mich Univ, 84 & 85. *Mem:* Am Inst Aeronaut & Astronaut. *Res:* Carbon fiber-epoxy composite hydraulic actuaters; two patents. *Mailing Add:* 217 E Orleans St Otsego MI 49078-1126

LUND, DARYL B, FOOD ENGINEERING, FOOD PROCESSING. *Current Pos:* prof & chmn food sci & assoc dir, NJ Agr Exp Sta, 88-89, EXEC DEAN AGR & NAT RESOURCES, RUTGERS UNIV, 89- *Personal Data:* b San Bernardino, Calif, Nov 4, 41; m 63, Dawn Kreft; c Kristine & Eric. *Educ:* Univ Wis-Madison, BS, 63, MS, 65, PhD(food sci, chem eng), 68. *Honors & Awards:* Food Eng Award, Dairy & Food Industs Supply Asn/Am Soc Agr Eng, 87. *Prof Exp:* From instr to assoc prof food sci, Univ Wis-Madison, 67-77, prof food sci & agr eng, 77-87, chmn, Food Sci Dept, 84-87. *Concurrent Pos:* Vis expert, Bogor Agr Univ, Indonesia, 73, 90 & 92; invited vis prof, Agr Univ, Wageningen, Holland, 79. *Mem:* Fel Inst Food Technol; Am Soc Agr Eng; Am Inst Chem Engrs; Sigma Xi; Am Inst Nutrit. *Res:* Food engineering; fouling of heat exchangers; nutrient retention in processing; starch gelatinization; water movement in foods; microwave heat transfer. *Mailing Add:* 104 Martin Hall Rutgers Univ 104 Martin Hall PO Box 231 New Brunswick NJ 08903-0231. *Fax:* 732-932-6769; *E-Mail:* lund@aesop.rutgers.edu

LUND, DONALD S, physics; deceased, see previous edition for last biography

LUND, DOUGLAS E, GENETICS, EMBRYOLOGY. *Current Pos:* Asst prof zool, 62-68, PROF BIOL, KEARNEY STATE COL, 68- *Personal Data:* b Newcastle, Nebr, Dec 12, 33; m 58; c 2. *Educ:* Nebr Wesleyan Univ, BA, 58; Univ Nebr, MS, 60, PhD(zool), 62. *Mem:* AAAS; Sigma Xi. *Res:* Temperature effects on early developmental stages of mammalian embryos; carbon dioxide sensitivity in Drosophila. *Mailing Add:* Dept Biol Kearney State Col Kearney NE 68847

LUND, FREDERICK H(ENRY), AEROSPACE & ELECTRONICS ENGINEERING. *Current Pos:* RETIRED. *Personal Data:* b Seattle, Wash, June 2, 29; m 50, Joyce P Monpleasure; c Frederick B, Christopher H, Peter A & A Leslie. *Educ:* Univ Wash, BSEE, 51; Mass Inst Technol, SM, 57. *Prof Exp:* Combat engr, unit commander, US Army Corps Engrs, 51-53; sr res engr, Stanford Res Inst, 65-69; mem prof staff, Martin Marietta Corp, Orlando, 69-93; consult, 94-95. *Concurrent Pos:* Mem exec comt, Mil Opers Res Symp, Off Naval Res, 62-66; sect chmn, Inst Elec & Electronics Engrs, 62-63; mem, Missile Systs Tech Comt, Am Inst Aeronaut & Astronaut, 87-91. *Mem:* Inst Elec & Electronics Engrs; Sigma Xi; Asn Old Crows; Am Inst Aeronaut & Astronaut; Mil Opers Res Soc. *Res:* Conduct of system analyses; operations research studies; analysis of electronic and optical countermeasures systems; development, test and evaluation of missile weapon systems; development of electronic instrumentation for guided missile systems; military requirements analyses; ballistic missile defense studies; strategic defense initiative architecture studies; pershing II/intermediate range nuclear force (INF) studies. *Mailing Add:* 610 S Lake Sybelia Dr Maitland FL 32751

LUND, HARTVIG ROALD, AGRONOMY. *Current Pos:* assoc prof, 65-74, assoc dean, Col Agr & assoc dir, 74-79, PROF AGRON, NDAK STATE UNIV, 74-, DEAN, COL AGR & DIR, AGR EXP STA, 79- *Personal Data:* b Fargo, NDak, May 15, 33; m 57; c 4. *Educ:* NDak State Univ, BS, 55, MS, 58; Purdue Univ, PhD(agron, plant breeding), 65. *Prof Exp:* Res asst agron, NDak State Univ, 55-58, asst prof, 59-62; res asst, Purdue Univ, 62-65. *Concurrent Pos:* Asst dean, Col Agr & asst dir, Agr Exp Sta, NDak State Univ, 71-74. *Mem:* Am Soc Agron; Crop Sci Soc Am. *Res:* Rust genetics of durum wheat; chemical mutagenesis in corn; corn breeding and corn endosperm genetics. *Mailing Add:* 266 A Loftsgard Box 5051 Fargo ND 58105

LUND, J KENNETH, CHEMICAL ENGINEERING. *Current Pos:* SR VPRES, EXEC TECH RES, VARO CORP, 78- *Personal Data:* b Brooklyn, NY, Feb 11, 33; m 60; c 2. *Educ:* Polytech Inst Brooklyn, BChE, 55; Princeton Univ, MSE, 58, PhD(chem eng), 63. *Prof Exp:* Sr res engr, Plastics Div, Monsanto Co, Mass, 61-65, res group leader, Hydrocarbons & Polymers Div, Tex, 65-69, prod develop mgr, NJ, 69-71; dir res & develop, Polyester Div, Olin Corp, 71-73; asst to pres, Occidental Res Corp, 74-78. *Mem:* Am Chem Soc; Soc Plastics Engrs; Am Inst Chem Engrs. *Res:* Polymer melt rheology; shear degradation of polymer melts; polymer fatigue failure; high speed tensile studies; extrusion processing of polyolefins and foamed polystyrene polyolefins. *Mailing Add:* Lund & Assoc Inc 1300 Hollencrest Dr West Covina CA 91791-3711

LUND, JOHN EDWARD, VETERINARY PATHOLOGY. *Current Pos:* sr res scientist, Upjohn Co, 77-80, res head, 80-85, assoc dir, 85-90, dir, Tsukusa Lab, 90-92, DISTINGUISHED RES SCIENTIST, UPJOHN CO, 92- *Personal Data:* b Detroit, Mich, Mar 16, 39; m 59; c 2. *Educ:* Mich State Univ, BS, 62, MS & DVM, 64; Wash State Univ, PhD(vet sci), 69; Am Cl Vet Pathologists, dipl. *Prof Exp:* Instr path, Med Sch, Stanford Univ, 68-70; from asst prof to assoc prof, Sch Vet Sci & Med, Purdue Univ, 70-73; sr scientist, Battelle Northwest Labs, Wash, 73-74, mgr & res assoc, Exp Path Sect, Biol Dept, 74-77. *Concurrent Pos:* Consult & vet pathologist, Inst Chem Biol, Univ San Francisco, 69-72. *Mem:* Am Vet Med Asn; AAAS; Am Soc Vet Clin Path; Int Acad Path; Soc Toxicol Pathologists. *Res:* Hematologic diseases of animals; toxicologic pathology; chemical carcinogenesis. *Mailing Add:* Upjohn Co 301 Lienrietta St Kalamazoo MI 49007

LUND, JOHN TURNER, PHYSICAL CHEMISTRY, INTELLIGENT SYSTEMS. *Current Pos:* res chemist, 55-86, EXEC DIR EDUC AID, E I DU PONT DE NEMOURS & CO, INC, 86- *Personal Data:* b Brooklyn, NY, Nov 3, 29; m 55; c 2. *Educ:* Brown Univ, AB, 51; Univ Wash, PhD(phys chem), 54; Univ Del, MS, 85. *Prof Exp:* Fel, Univ Wash, 54-55. *Mem:* Am Chem Soc; Am Phys Soc. *Res:* Industrial research on textile fibers; intelligent computer systems for problem solving. *Mailing Add:* 901 Centre Rd Westover Hills Wilmington DE 19807-2801

LUND, LANNY JACK, SOIL MORPHOLOGY. *Current Pos:* Asst prof & asst soil scientist, Univ Calif, Riverside, 71-77, assoc prof & assoc soil scientist, 77-83, chmn, 85-90, assoc dean, Agr Exp Sta, 90-96, PROF SOIL SCI & SOIL SCIENTIST, UNIV CALIF, RIVERSIDE, 83- *Personal Data:* b Dalton, Nebr, May 1, 43; m 64; c 2. *Educ:* Univ Nebr, BS, 65, MS, 68; Purdue Univ, PhD, 71. *Mem:* Am Soc Agron; Soil Sci Soc Am. *Res:* Soil morphology, genesis and classification; soil and the environment. *Mailing Add:* Dept Soil & Environ Sci Univ Calif 900 University Ave Riverside CA 92521-0101

LUND, LOUIS HAROLD, CHEMICAL PHYSICS. *Current Pos:* instr math, 45-47, from asst prof to prof, 48-80, EMER PROF PHYSICS, UNIV MO-ROLLA, 80- *Personal Data:* b Jefferson City, Mo, Mar 17, 19; m 42; c 2. *Educ:* Kans Wesleyan Univ, AB, 40; Univ Mo, AM, 43, PhD(physics), 48. *Prof Exp:* Instr physics, Univ Mo, 43-44; physicist, Lucas-Harold Corp, 44-45. *Mem:* Am Phys Soc. *Mailing Add:* 36 McFarland Dr Rolla MO 65401

LUND, MARK WYLIE, LENS DESIGN, X-RAY OPTICS. *Current Pos:* DIR, MOXTEK, 90- *Personal Data:* b Santa Rosa, Calif, Sept 9, 52; m 77, Barbara Novakovich; c Ellen, Audrey, Andrea & Samuel. *Educ:* Brigham Young Univ, BS, 77; San Diego State Univ, MS, 79; Ariz State Univ, PhD(physics), 89. *Prof Exp:* Mem tech staff, Hughes Aircraft Co, 79-81; proj engr, Night Vision Div, Litton Industs, 81-83; sr electronic engr, Govt Electronics Div, Motorola, 83-86; prin engr, Optical Disk Div, Honeywell, 86-89. *Mem:* Optical Soc Am; Int Soc Optical Eng; Microbeam Anal Soc; Micros Soc Am; Mat Res Soc. *Res:* Developing products for the analytical x-ray market: energy dispersive detectors, ultra-low noise fets, x-ray multilayer optics, crystal growth of wide bandgap semiconductors; display systems; night vision; lens design; unconventional optical system design from far infrared through x-rays; x-ray spectrometry; coherent bremsstrahlung. *Mailing Add:* 969 E 200 N Orem UT 84057. *Fax:* 801-221-1121; *E-Mail:* lundm@xray.byu.edu

LUND, MELVIN ROBERT, DENTISTRY. *Current Pos:* prof oper dent & chmn dept, 71-91, EMER PROF DENT, IND UNIV, PURDUE UNIV, INDIANAPOLIS, 91- *Personal Data:* b Siren, Wis, Oct 17, 22; m 46; c 3. *Educ:* Univ Ore, DMD, 46; Univ Mich, MS, 54. *Prof Exp:* From instr to prof restorative dent, Loma Linda Univ, 53-71. *Concurrent Pos:* Fel, Claremont Grad Sch, 69-70. *Mem:* Int Asn Dent Res; Acad Oper Dent; Am Acad Gold Foil Opers (pres, 79-80). *Res:* Physical research in dental materials; biologic research in dental procedures. *Mailing Add:* 14706 Little Eagle Creek Ave Zionsville IN 46077

LUND, PAULINE KAY, GROWTH FACTORS, GASTROENTEROLOGY. *Current Pos:* asst prof physiol, Univ NC, 82-88, assoc prof physiol & pediat, 88-93, assoc dir, Ctr Gastrointestinal Biol & Dis, 89-92, PROF PHYSIOL, DEPT PHYSIOL & ASSOC PROF PEDIAT, DEPT PEDIAT, UNIV NC, 93-, DISTINGUISHED PROF UNIV TEACHING, 95- *Personal Data:* b Golborne, Lancashire, Apr 20, 55; m 80, Mark Smith; c Emma & Alice. *Educ:* Univ Newcastle, UK, BSc Hons, 75, PhD(gastrointestinal endocrinol), 79. *Prof Exp:* Demonstr physiol, Univ Newcastle, UK, 77-79; res fel, Lab Molecular Endocrinol, Harvard Med Sch, Mass Gen Hosp, 79-88. *Concurrent Pos:* Mem Endocrinol Study Sect, NIH, 89-93. *Mem:* Endocrine soc. *Res:* Insulin-like growth factors biosynthesis and action; role of growth factorsand peptide hormones in intestinal growth and development; molecular correlation of neuronal function; inflammatory bowel disease and fibrosis. *Mailing Add:* Dept Physiol Univ NC Chapel Hill NC 27514

LUND, RICHARD, VERTEBRATE PALEONTOLOGY. *Current Pos:* from asst prof to assoc prof, 74-81, PROF BIOL, ADELPHI UNIV, 81- *Personal Data:* b New York, NY, Sept 17, 39; m 65, 78; c 3. *Educ:* Univ Mich, Ann Arbor, BS, 61, MS, 63; Columbia Univ, PhD(zool), 68. *Prof Exp:* Asst cur fossil fish, Sect Vert Fossils, Carnegie Mus, 66-69; asst prof earth & plant sci, Univ Pittsburgh, 69-74. *Concurrent Pos:* Pittsburgh Found fel, Carnegie Mus, 67-69, res assoc, 69-; Pittsburgh Found fel, Univ Pittsburgh, 71-74; res assoc, WVa Geol Surv, 74; prin investr, NSF, Mississippian fishes from Montana, 74-85; res assoc Ichthyology, Am Mus Natural Hist, 82- *Mem:* AAAS; Soc Vert Paleont; Am Soc Icthyol & Herpet; Am Soc Zoologists; Ecol Soc Am; Am Elasmobranch Soc (secy, 84). *Res:* Fossil fish; late Paleozoic biostratigraphy; morphology and relationship of early osteichthyan and chondrichthyan fishes with emphasis on the fishes of the Mississippian Bear Gulch Limestone. *Mailing Add:* Dept Biol Adelphia Univ 1 South Ave Garden City NY 11530-4213

LUND, STEVE, AGRONOMY. *Current Pos:* EMER PROF, RUTGERS UNIV, 75- *Personal Data:* b Wis, Dec 3, 23; m 46; c 5. *Educ:* Clemson Col, BS, 49; Univ Wis, MS, 51, PhD(agron), 53. *Prof Exp:* Exten agronomist, Clemson Col, 53-54; from asst res specialist to assoc res specialist farm crops, Rutgers Univ, New Brunswick, 54-62, res prof, 62-75; supt & prof, Columbia Basin Agr Res Ctr, 75-85, EMER PROF, ORE STATE UNIV, 85- *Concurrent Pos:* Chmn dept soils & crops, Rutgers Univ, New Brunswick, 71-75. *Mem:* Am Soc Agron; Crop Sci Soc Am. *Res:* Cereal breeding. *Mailing Add:* 1201 SW 23rd St Pendleton OR 97801-4404

LUNDBERG, GEORGE DAVID, PATHOLOGY. *Current Pos:* CLIN PROF PATH, NORTHWESTERN & HARVARD UNIV, 82-, ADJ PROF HEALTH POLICY, HARVARD UNIV, 92- *Personal Data:* b Pensacola, Fla, Mar 21, 33; m 56, 83, Patricia Lorimer; c George, Charles, Carol, Christopher & Melinda. *Educ:* Univ Ala, BS, 52; Med Col Ala, MD, 57; Am Bd Path, dipl anat & clin path, 62; Baylor Univ, MS, 64. *Hon Degrees:* ScD, State Univ NY, Syracuse, 88, Eleanor Jefferson Univ, Phila, 93, Univ Ala, 94, Med Col Ohio, 95. *Honors & Awards:* Distinguished Serv Award, Asn Path Chairmen, 90, Am Soc Clin Path, 96, Col Am Path, 96. *Prof Exp:* Intern, Tripler Gen Hosp, Honolulu, Hawaii, 57-58; resident path, Brooke Gen Hosp, San Antonio, Tex, 58-62; chief anat path, Letterman Gen Hosp, San Francisco, Calif, 62-63, res officer, 63-64; chief path, William Beaumont Gen Hosp, El Paso, Tex, 64-67; from assoc prof to prof path, Sch Med, Univ Southern Calif, 67-77; from asst dir to assoc dir labs, Los Angeles Co/Univ Southern Calif Med Ctr, 67-77; prof & chair path, Sch Med, Univ Calif, Davis & dir path & labs, Med Ctr, Sacramento, 77-82. *Concurrent Pos:* US Army Med Res & Develop Command res grants, 63-64 & 65-67; vis prof forensic med, Lund Univ, Sweden, 76 & Univ London, 76-77; vpres sci info & ed-in-chief jour, AMA, 82-; mem bd dirs, Am Soc Clin Path; clin prof path, Georgetown & Northwestern, 82-92. *Mem:* Inst Med-Nat Acad Sci; Am Soc Clin Path (pres); Am Asn Path & Bact; Int Acad Path; Am Acad Forensic Sci; Col Am Path. *Res:* Laboratory computer applications; diseases produced by drugs; toxicology; drug abuse; laboratory management; boxing and brain damage; methods of education; strategic planning; biomedical communication; violence. *Mailing Add:* Am Med Asn 515 N State St Chicago IL 60610

LUNDBERG, JOHN L(AUREN), POLYMER SCIENCE, TEXTILE ENGINEERING. *Current Pos:* CALLAWAY PROF TEXTILE CHEM, GA INST TECHNOL, 72- *Personal Data:* b St Paul, Minn, Oct 8, 24; m 55; c 4. *Educ:* Univ Minn, BChE, 48; Univ Calif, PhD(chem), 52. *Prof Exp:* Mem tech staff, Bell Tel Labs, Inc, 52-68; assoc prof textile chem, Clemson Univ, 68-71, chmn dept, 70-71. *Concurrent Pos:* Vis assoc prof, Polytech Inst Brooklyn, 61-62, lectr, 63, adj prof, 64-68. *Mem:* AAAS; Am Asn Textile Chem & Colorists; Am Asn Textile Technol; Am Chem Soc; Am Inst Chem; Sigma Xi. *Res:* Physical chemistry and physics of polymers, fibers and textiles; solution chemistry, diffusion and physical properties of polymer solutions; light scattering by fibers, liquids and solutions. *Mailing Add:* Rte 1 Box H-609 Jasper GA 30143

LUNDBERG, ROBERT DEAN, POLYMER CHEMISTRY. *Current Pos:* RETIRED. *Personal Data:* b Valley City, NDak, May 30, 28; m 53, Patricia E Goeschel; c Michael & Barbara. *Educ:* Harvard Univ, BA, 52, MA & PhD(phys chem), 57. *Honors & Awards:* Chem Pioneer, Am Inst Chem, 86. *Prof Exp:* chemist, Eastman Kodak Co, 52-53; chemist, Union Carbide Corp, 57-62, group leader, Res & Develop Dept, Union Carbide Chem & Plastic Co, 62-69; vpres res, Inter-Polymer Res Corp, 69-70; res assoc, Exxon Chem Co, 70-71, sr res assoc, 71-76, sci adv, Exxon Res & Eng Res Lab, 76-84, chief scientist, 84-90. *Concurrent Pos:* Consult, Exxon Res & Eng Co, 90- *Mem:* Am Chem Soc; NY Acad Sci; Am Inst Chemists. *Res:* Synthesis of synthetic polypeptides; polymer interactions; ionic polymers; block copolymers; thermoplastic elastomers; polymer blends; dilute polymer solution behavior. *Mailing Add:* 3017 Travis Close Williamsburg VA 23185-7666. *Fax:* 908-730-2536

LUNDBLAD, ROGER LAUREN, BIOCHEMISTRY, BIOTECHNOLOGY. *Current Pos:* from asst prof to assoc prof, 68-77, PROF PATH & BIOCHEM, DENT RES CTR, UNIV NC, CHAPEL HILL, 77-; DIR SCI & TECH DEVELOP, BAXTER HEALTHCARE CORP, 92- *Personal Data:* b San Francisco, Calif, Oct 31, 39; div. *Educ:* Pac Lutheran Univ, BS, 61; Univ Wash, PhD(biochem), 65. *Prof Exp:* Res assoc biochem, Univ Wash, 65-66; res assoc, Rockefeller Univ, 66-68. *Concurrent Pos:* Mem, Coun Basic Sci & Coun Thrombosis, Am Heart Asn. *Mem:* AAAS; Am Chem Soc; Am Soc Biol Chem; Am Soc Microbiol. *Res:* Mechanism of blood coagulation; protein chemistry; salivary proteins; oral microbiology. *Mailing Add:* Hyland Div Baxter Healthcare Corp 1710 Flower Ave Duarte CA 91010-2923. *Fax:* 626-357-8348; *E-Mail:* 76770.237@compuserve.com

LUNDE, BARBARA KEGERREIS, (BK), electrical & radio engineering, health physics, for more information see previous edition

LUNDE, KENNETH E(VAN), chemical engineering; deceased, see previous edition for last biography

LUNDE, MILFORD NORMAN, PARASITOLOGY. *Current Pos:* RETIRED. *Personal Data:* b Dodgeville, Wis, Apr 17, 24; m 50; c 2. *Educ:* Luther Col, AB, 47; Univ NC, MPH, 48. *Prof Exp:* Bacteriologist, WVa State Hyg Lab, 48-51; parasitologist, Inst Trop Med, Bowman-Gray Sch Med, 51-52 & Am Found Trop Med, 52-53; bacteriologist, Army Med Ctr, Ft Detrick, Md, 53-55; res parasitologist, Lab Parasitic Dis, Nat Inst Allergy & Infectious Dis, NIH, 55-89. *Mem:* Am Soc Parasitologists; Am Soc Trop Med & Hyg. *Res:* Immunodiagnosis of parasitic diseases; application of enzyme immunoassay for detection of antigens and characterization of antibodies; toxoplasmosis; amebiasis and schistosomiasis. *Mailing Add:* North 985 Sarona WI 54870-9747

LUNDE, PETER J, CHEMICAL & SOLAR ENGINEERING. *Current Pos:* PRES, NEW ENERGY RESOURCES, INC, 81- *Personal Data:* b New York, NY, June 8, 31; m 57; c 3. *Educ:* Pa State Univ, BS, 53, MS, 60, PhD(chem eng), 62. *Prof Exp:* Instrument engr, Union Carbide Plastics Co, 56-57; chem engr process design, Chevron Res Corp, 61-63; sr chem engr, Res Div, Carrier Corp, 63-67; sr chem engr, Hamilton Standard Div, United Aircraft Corp, 67-69, head advan design & develop, Space Life Support Systs, 69-73, head chem process anal, 71-73; sr res scientist, Ctr Environ & Man, Inc, 73-77; solar eng consult, 77-81. *Concurrent Pos:* Vis prof, Univ Conn, 74-75, 77, 83-86; adj prof, Hartford Grad Ctr, 75-82. *Mem:* Am Inst Chem Engrs; Am Chem Soc; Am Soc Heating, Refrig & Air Conditioning Engrs; Int Solar Energy Soc; Sigma Xi. *Res:* Reaction kinetics, adsorption and catalysis; solar system performance prediction; solar air-conditioning. *Mailing Add:* 4 Daniel Lane West Simsbury CT 06092-2810

LUNDEEN, ALLAN JAY, ORGANIC CHEMISTRY. *Current Pos:* RETIRED. *Personal Data:* b New York, NY, Aug 24, 32; m 54; c 4. *Educ:* Southwestern Col, Kans, AB, 54; Rice Univ, PhD(chem), 57. *Prof Exp:* Res chemist org chem, Continental Oil Co, 57-60, sr res chemist, 60-62, res group leader, 62-70, dir explor res, 70-78, dir plastics res, 78-93. *Mem:* Am Chem Soc. *Res:* Chemistry of mustard oil glucosides; reactions of carbonium ions; heterogenous catalysis; chemistry of organoaluminum compounds; hydrocarbon oxidation; polymer chemistry. *Mailing Add:* 8501 Navidad Dr Austin TX 78735

LUNDEEN, CARL VICTOR, JR, BIOCHEMISTRY. *Current Pos:* asst prof chem, 72-74, asst prof biol, 74-77, ASSOC PROF BIOL, UNIV NC, WILMINGTON, 77- *Personal Data:* b Baltimore, Md, Jan 20, 43; m 65; c 3. *Educ:* Univ NC, Chapel Hill, AB, 65; Rockefeller Univ, PhD(life sci), 72. *Prof Exp:* Res assoc plant biol, Rockefeller Univ, 71-72. *Mem:* Sigma Xi. *Res:* Attempting to elucidate the mechanisms by which autonomous cells attain the capability for rapid growth. *Mailing Add:* Biol Sci Univ NC 601 S College Rd Wilmington NC 28403-3201

LUNDEGARD, ROBERT JAMES, SCIENCE POLICY, TECHNICAL MANAGEMENT. *Current Pos:* CHIEF, STATIST ENG DIV, NAT INST STANDARDS & TECHNOL, 87- *Personal Data:* b Youngstown, Ohio, Feb 22, 27; m 51; c 1. *Educ:* Ohio Univ, BS, 50; Purdue Univ, MS, 52, PhD(math), 56. *Honors & Awards:* Fleming award, US Govt, 67. *Prof Exp:* Dir, Math Sci Div, Dept Naval Reserve, 68-78, dep dir, 78-81, dir, naval cost analysis, Dept Navy, 81-87. *Mem:* Fel Am Statist Asn. *Res:* Develop statistical methods for engineering, with emphasis on achieving quality goals through the design of processes and products. *Mailing Add:* 950 Carya Ct Great Falls VA 22066

LUNDELIUS, ERNEST LUTHER, JR, VERTEBRATE PALEONTOLOGY. *Current Pos:* from asst prof to assoc prof, 57-69, PROF GEOL, UNIV TEX, AUSTIN, 69-, JOHN A WILSON PROF VERT PALEONT, 78- *Personal Data:* b Austin, Tex, Dec 2, 27; m 53, Judith Weiser; c Jennifer (Welch) & Rolf E. *Educ:* Univ Tex, BS, 50; Univ Chicago, PhD(paleozool), 54. *Prof Exp:* Fulbright scholar vert paleont, Univ Western Australia, 54-55, Fulbright sr scholar, 76; res fel paleoecol, Calif Inst Technol, 56-57. *Mem:* Soc Vert Paleont (secy-treas, 75-, pres, 81); Soc Study Evolution; Am Soc Mammalogists; Geol Soc Am; Am Soc Naturalists. *Res:* Pleistocene vertebrates; paleoecology; adaptive morphology; Australian marsupials. *Mailing Add:* 7310 Running Rope Austin TX 78731-2132

LUNDELL, ALBERT THOMAS, MATHEMATICS. *Current Pos:* assoc prof, 66-69, chmn dept, 70-72, PROF MATH, UNIV COLO, BOULDER, 70- *Personal Data:* b Riverside, Calif, Dec 23, 31; m 52, Virginia Owen; c John, Martha & David. *Educ:* Univ Utah, AB, 52, AM, 55; Brown Univ, PhD(math), 60. *Prof Exp:* Instr math, Brown Univ, 59-60; lectr, Univ Calif, Berkeley, 60-62; asst prof, Purdue Univ, 62-66. *Mem:* Am Math Soc. *Res:* Algebraic topology. *Mailing Add:* Dept Math Univ Colo Box 395 Boulder CO 80309. *E-Mail:* lundell@euclid.colorado.edu

LUNDELL, FREDERICK WALDEMAR, PSYCHIATRY, CHILD PSYCHIATRY. *Current Pos:* asst prof, 64-67, ASSOC PROF DEPT PSYCHIAT, MCGILL UNIV, 67- *Personal Data:* b Revelstoke, BC, Jan 31, 24; Can citizen; m 50; c 5. *Educ:* Univ BC, BA, 47; McGill Univ MDCM, 51. *Hon Degrees:* Dipl, McGill Univ, 56. *Honors & Awards:* Nobel Peace Prize. *Prof Exp:* Asst resident psychiat, Montreal Gen Hosp, 55, clin asst psychiat, 56, dir psychiat res, 63-67; asst psychiat, Montreal Children Hosp, 57, dir mental assessment & guidance clin, 61-64. *Concurrent Pos:* Consult psychiat, St Anne Mil Hosp, 56; lectr psychiat, Dept Psychiat, Sch Occup & Physiotherapy, McGill Univ, 59 & 61; coordr psychiat res, Queen Mary Vet & Ste Ann Mil Hosp, 63-76. *Mem:* Fel Royal Col Physicians & Surgeons Can; Am Psychiat Asn; Am Geriat Soc fel; fel Royal Soc Health; fel AAAS; NY Acad Sci; Can Gerontol Soc; Am Orthopsychiat Asn. *Res:* Active research and publications on substance abuse in adolescents; post-traumatic stress disorders in Canadian Vietnam veterans. *Mailing Add:* Suite 422 1538 W Sherbrooke Montreal PQ H3G 1L5 Can

LUNDELL, O ROBERT, PHYSICAL CHEMISTRY. *Current Pos:* from asst prof to assoc prof, York Univ, 61-71, actg chmn Dept Biol, 67-68, assoc dean, 68-74, PROF CHEM, YORK UNIV, 71-, DEAN, FAC SCI, 74- *Personal Data:* b Revelstoke, BC, Nov 7, 31; m 56; c 2. *Educ:* Queen's Univ, Ont, BA, 54; Mass Inst Technol, PhD(phys chem), 58. *Prof Exp:* Lectr chem, Royal Mil Col, Ont, 58-61. *Concurrent Pos:* Res assoc, Mass Inst Technol, 60-62. *Mem:* Chem Inst Can. *Res:* Calorimetry and kinetics of gas phase reactions. *Mailing Add:* Dept Chem York Univ 4700 Keele St Rm 124 CCB Downsview ON M3J 1P3 Can

LUNDEN, ALLYN OSCAR, PLANT BREEDING, PLANT GENETICS. *Current Pos:* RETIRED. *Personal Data:* b Toronto, SDak, Feb 5, 31; m 55; c 3. *Educ:* SDak State Col, BS, 52, MS, 56; Univ Fla, PhD(plant genetics), 60. *Prof Exp:* Asst agronomist, SDak State Col, 55-56; asst scientist plant genetics, Univ Tenn-AEC Agr Res Lab, 59-62, assoc prof agron, 62-64; assoc prof agron, SDak State Univ, 64-76, head, Seed Lab, 76-80, seed researcher, 81-86. *Mem:* Am Soc Agron; Asn Off Seed Anal. *Res:* Irradiation sensitivity of plant tissues; genetic effects of ionizing and ultraviolet irradiation of plant tissues; seed testing techniques; seed vigor testing; seed germination; seed technology; seed storage research. *Mailing Add:* 614 Seven Ave S Brookings SD 57006

LUNDERGAN, CHARLES DONALD, SYSTEMS RESEARCH, REMOTE SENSORS. *Current Pos:* RETIRED. *Personal Data:* b Washington, Ind, Sept 24, 23; m 72, Elaine M Prusha; c Michael, Timothy, Donal & Dan. *Educ:* Univ Notre Dame, BSc, 47, MSc, 51. *Prof Exp:* Instr math, St Louis Univ, 51-54, actg dir aeronaut eng, 52-54; instr physics, Agr & Mech Col, Tex, 54-56; physicist mat sci, Sandia Lab, 56-61, sect supvr, 61-62, div supvr, 62-67, mem staff mat res, 67-73, reactor safety res, 73-75 & mgt staff, 75-78, mem staff systs res, 78-89, consult, 89-95. *Concurrent Pos:* Res consult George Mallinckrodt Res, 53-54 & Ohio State, Wright-Patterson AFB, 62-63. *Res:* Equations of state of solids, propagation of shock waves in solids, dynamic stress-strain relations of metals; dynamic behavior of composites; effects of nuclear explosions; remote detection of nuclear effects. *Mailing Add:* 4409 Kellia Lane NE Albuquerque NM 87111

LUNDGREN, CLAES ERIK GUNNAR, PHYSIOLOGY. *Current Pos:* PROF PHYSIOL, SCH MED, STATE UNIV NY, BUFFALO, 77- *Personal Data:* b Stockholm, Sweden, Jan 21, 31. *Educ:* Univ Lund, MD, 59, PhD(physiol), 67. *Hon Degrees:* Docent Aviation & Navl Med, Univ Lund, 67. *Prof Exp:* Assoc prof physiol, Fac Med, Univ Lund, Sweden, 67-77. *Concurrent Pos:* Consult aviation med, Royal Swed Air Force, 59-77; vis assoc prof physiol, Univ Lund, Sweden, 74-77; dir, Ctr Res Spec Environ, State Univ NY, Buffalo, 85- *Mailing Add:* Ctr Res Spec Environ State Univ NY 124 Sherman Hall Buffalo NY 14214

LUNDGREN, DALE A(LLEN), AIR POLLUTION, INDUSTRIAL HYGIENE. *Current Pos:* PROF, ENVIRON ENG DEPT, UNIV FLA, 72- *Personal Data:* b Minn, Apr 26, 32; m 54; c 6. *Educ:* Univ Minn, BS, 58, MS, 62, PhD(environ health), 73. *Prof Exp:* Engr, Link-Belt Co, Minn, 55-58; asst mech eng, Univ Minn, 58-61; scientist, Electronics Div, Gen Mills, Inc, 61-63; prin scientist, Appl Sci Div, Litton Industs, Inc, 63-65; head air & particle anal lab, Ctr Air Environ Studies & instr mech eng & air pollution, Pa State Univ, 65-67; specialist & head aerosol lab, Statewide Air Pollution Res Ctr, Univ Calif, Riverside, 67-69; chief engr-dir, Air Pollution Control Equipment Sect, Environ Res Corp, St Paul, Minn, 69-72. *Concurrent Pos:* Consult, Dale A Lundgren Assoc, 72- & various indust. *Mem:* Air Pollution Control Asn; Am Indust Hyg Asn; Am Soc Mech Engrs; Am Asn Aerosol Res; Soc Aerosol Res Germany. *Res:* Aerosol physics; air pollution; industrial hygiene; air sampling instrumentation; air pollution control equipment. *Mailing Add:* 1411 NW 50th Terr Gainesville FL 32605

LUNDGREN, DAVID L(EE), RADIOBIOLOGY, INHALATION TOXICOLOGY. *Current Pos:* RADIOBIOLOGIST, LOVELACE INHALATION TOXICOL RES INST, 66- *Personal Data:* b Aberdeen, Wash, Sept 28, 31; wid; c 5. *Educ:* Ore State Univ, BS, 54; Univ Utah, MS, 61, PhD(microbiol), 68. *Prof Exp:* Bacteriologist, Univ Utah, 54-59, chief epizool diag lab, 59-62, chief infectious disease lab, 61-64, microbiologist, Biol Div, Dugway Proving Ground, 64-66. *Mem:* Radiation Res Soc; Am Soc Microbiol; Health Physics Soc; Soc Exp Biol & Med; Sigma Xi; AAAS; Am Pub Health Asn. *Res:* Toxicity of inhaled radionuclides from nuclear energy generation; biological effects of internally deposited radionuclides in experimental animals; extrapolation of data from laboratory animals to man. *Mailing Add:* ITRI PO Box 5890 Albuquerque NM 87115

LUNDGREN, HARRY RICHARD, STRUCTURAL ENGINEERING. *Current Pos:* from instr to prof, 62-89, EMER PROF STRUCT ENG, ARIZ STATE UNIV, 89- *Personal Data:* b Chicago, Ill, May 2, 28; m 55, Joyce E Boller. *Educ:* Purdue Univ, BSCE, 50; Ariz State Univ, MSE, 62; Okla State Univ, PhD(struct eng), 67. *Prof Exp:* Proj engr, Kawneer Co, Mich, 53-58; vpres eng, R B Feffer & Sons, Ariz, 58-59; sr civil engr, Salt River Proj, 59-61. *Concurrent Pos:* Pres, Comt Acad Sci & Eng. *Mem:* Am Soc Civil Engrs; Sigma Xi. *Res:* Finite element applications to structural engineering problems; structural stability; light gauge steel structures; wind engineering; software development. *Mailing Add:* 2837 N 76th Pl Scottsdale AZ 85257

LUNDGREN, J RICHARD, APPLICATIONS OF GRAPH THEORY. *Current Pos:* assoc prof, 81-86, chmn dept, 84-90, PROF MATH, UNIV COLO, DENVER, 86- *Personal Data:* b Springfield, Mass, Oct 1, 42; m 64; c 2. *Educ:* Worcester Polytech Inst, BS, 64; Ohio State Univ, MS, 69, PhD(math), 71. *Prof Exp:* Proj engr, New Eng Tel, 64-67; asst prof math, Allegheny Col, 71-77, assoc prof math, 77-81. *Mem:* Am Math Soc; Math Asn Am; Soc Indust & Appl Math; fel Inst Combinatorics & Its Appln. *Res:* Applications of graphs and matrices; mathematical modeling. *Mailing Add:* 2688 S Newcombe St Lakewood CO 80227-2764

LUNDGREN, LAWRENCE WILLIAM, JR, ENVIRONMENTAL GEOLOGY, RISK COMMUNICATION. *Current Pos:* From instr to assoc prof geol, 56-59, chmn, Dept Geol Sci, 71-74 & 76-86, PROF GEOL, UNIV ROCHESTER, 67- *Personal Data:* b Attleboro, Mass, Mar 17, 32; m 81, Ann Frodi; c Gary, Julie & Annika. *Educ:* Brown Univ, AB, 53; Yale Univ, PhD(geol), 58. *Concurrent Pos:* Fulbright lectr, Finland, 67-68; NSF fac fel geog & environ eng, Johns Hopkins Univ, 76; mem staff, US Geol Surv, Menlo Park, 77; vis researcher, Dept Water & Environ Studies, Univ Linkoping, Sweden, 91- *Mem:* AAAS; Geol Soc Am; Sigma Xi; Am Geophys Union. *Res:* Impact of Chernobyl on Sweden; geology and public policy. *Mailing Add:* Dept Geol Univ Rochester 500 Joseph C Wilson Rochester NY 14627-9000. *Fax:* 716-244-5689; *E-Mail:* lsqr@db1.cc.rochester.edu

LUNDHOLM, J(OSEPH) G(IDEON), JR, APPLIED PHYSICS, ENGINEERING PHYSICS. *Current Pos:* CONSULT, 86- *Personal Data:* b Emporia, Kans, Feb 19, 25; m 56; c 2. *Educ:* Kans State Univ, BS, 46, MS, 48; NC State Univ, PhD(eng physics), 56. *Prof Exp:* Instr math, Kans State Univ, 47-48; instrumentation develop engr, Oak Ridge Nat Lab, 48-52; res assoc physics, NC State Univ, 52-56, supvr, Raleigh Res Reactor, 52-57; staff res specialist, Reactor Develop Dept, Atomics Int Div, NAm Aviation, Inc, 57-59, supvr syst control & safety, Compact Power Plants, 59-60; mem tech staff, Res & Adv Develop Div, Avco Co, Mass, 60-62, proj mgr, Adv Space Systs, 62-64; dir adv res & tech, Space Systs Div, Fairchild-Hiller Corp, 64-65; mgr exp prog, Skylab Prog, Hq, 65-74, res prog mgr, Off Aeronaut & Space Technol Res Div, 74-81, adv technol mgr, adv land observations systs off, 81-83, study mgr, Adv Missions Anal Off, Goddard Space Flight Ctr, NASA, 83-86. *Concurrent Pos:* Mem, Comt on Radioactive Waste Mgt, Nat Acad Sci, 76-78; res assoc, Mat Sci Dept, Univ Md, 78-79. *Mem:* Assoc fel Am Inst Aeronaut & Astronaut; sr mem Am Astronaut Soc. *Res:* Space research and technology, especially space payloads, laser systems, advance energy conversion methods, ultra low temperature coolers; nuclear systems technology and safety; ultra high pressure research; instrumentation and control systems; earth remote sensing technology. *Mailing Add:* 8106 Postoak Rd Potomac MD 20854

LUNDIN, BRUCE T(HEODORE), mechanical engineering; deceased, see previous edition for last biography

LUNDIN, CARL D, PHYSICAL METALLURGY. *Current Pos:* MAGNOVOX PROF ENG, TENN TOMORROW PROF & DIR WELDING RES, UNIV TENN, KNOXVILLE, 77- *Personal Data:* b Yonkers, NY, Dec 16, 34; m 57; c 3. *Educ:* Rensselaer Polytech Inst, BMetEng, 57, PhD(mat sci), 66. *Honors & Awards:* Adams Mem Award, Am Welding Soc, 68 & 73, Sparager Award, 78; McKay-Helm Award, 81; Adams Mem lectr, Am Welding Soc, 81. *Prof Exp:* Res asst metall, Rensselaer Polytech Inst, 60-62, from instr to asst prof, 62-68; from assoc prof to prof metall & dir welding res, Univ Tenn, 68-75; welding sect mgr, Babcock & Wilcox Co, 75-77. *Concurrent Pos:* Supvr welding res mat div, Rensselaer Polytech Inst, 60-68; consult, Oak Ridge Nat Labs, 67-; NSF res initiation grant, 67-68; mem, Welding Res Coun & Pressure Vessel Res Comt. *Mem:* Am Welding Soc; Am Soc Metals. *Res:* Physical metallurgy associated with welding and joining--solid state transformations, solidification, diffusion, fissuring, arc physics; process development in welding industry. *Mailing Add:* Dept Mat Sci Univ Tenn 1345 Circle Park Knoxville TN 37996-0001

LUNDIN, FRANK E, JR, EPIDEMIOLOGY. *Current Pos:* RETIRED. *Personal Data:* b Chicago, Ill, Aug 25, 28; m 49, 79; c 4. *Educ:* Manchester Col, BA, 49; Ind Univ, MD, 53; Johns Hopkins Univ, MPH, 59, DrPH, 62. *Prof Exp:* USPHS, Norfolk, Va, 53-, intern, Hosp, 53-54; staff physician, Hosp, Carville, La, 54-56, epidemiologist, Cancer Invest, Nat Cancer Inst, Univ Tenn, 56-58, instr, Johns Hopkins Univ, 60-61, res assoc, 61-62, head special studies section, Epidemiol Br, Nat Cancer Inst, 62-67, sr epidemiologist, Occup Stuides, Nat Inst Environ Health Sci, NIH, 67-71, sr epidemiologist, Epidemiol Br, Epidemiol & Biomet Div, Nat Inst Child Health & Human Develop, 71-74, dep chief, 74-75, chief, 75- 80, sr epidemiologist, Epidemiol Stuides Br, Bur Radiol Health, Food & Drugs Admin, USPHS, 80-88, Consult, Food & Drugs Admin, 88-93. *Mem:* Soc Epidemiol Res; Am Pub Health Asn; Soc Occup & Environ Health; Am Med Asn. *Res:* Epidemiology of cancer, especially of the cervix; lung cancer; leukemia and lymphoma; occupational cancer, infant and fetal mortality and parental smoking; health effects of radiation. *Mailing Add:* 7212 Maple Ave Takoma Park MD 20912

LUNDIN, ROBERT ENOR, NUCLEAR MAGNETIC RESONANCE. *Current Pos:* res chemist, 58-81, res leader, 81-87, COLLAB, WESTERN REGIONAL RES CTR, USDA, 87- *Personal Data:* b Boston, Mass, Mar 19, 27; m 52, Jane Magee; c Rebecca & Susan. *Educ:* Harvard Univ, AB, 50; Univ Calif, Berkeley, PhD(chem), 55. *Prof Exp:* Res chemist, Res Ctr, Texaco, Inc, 55-58. *Mem:* AAAS; Am Chem Soc. *Res:* High resolution nuclear magnetic resonance spectroscopy; catalysis; radiation chemistry; gaseous thermodynamics. *Mailing Add:* Western Regional Res Ctr USDA Berkeley CA 94710. *Fax:* 510-559-5777; *E-Mail:* lundin@pw.usda.gov

LUNDIN, ROBERT FOLKE, GEOLOGY, PALEONTOLOGY. *Current Pos:* From asst prof to assoc prof, 62-74, res comt res grants, 66-67, 70-74 & 76, PROF GEOL, ARIZ STATE UNIV, 74-, ASSOC CHMN DEPT, 78- *Personal Data:* b Rockford, Ill, July 20, 36; m 58. *Educ:* Augustana Col, Ill, AB, 58; Univ Ill, MS, 61, PhD(geol), 62. *Concurrent Pos:* Petrol Res Fund res grants, 63-65, 66-68 & 70-72; Res Corp res grant, 70; guest scientist, Univ Uppsala, 70, distinguished vis prof, 73-74 & 81; Swed Natural Sci Res Coun res grant, 73-74 & 81; co-ed, J Paleont, 74-80. *Mem:* Soc Econ Paleont & Mineral; Am Asn Petrol Geol; Geol Soc Am; Paleont Soc; Int Paleont Asn. *Res:* Siluro, Devonian and Mississippi ostracodes, conodonts and stratigraphy; Cenozoic stratigraphy; freshwater ostracodes. *Mailing Add:* 2148 E Cairo Dr Tempe AZ 85282

LUNDQUIST, CHARLES ARTHUR, SPACE SCIENCES. *Current Pos:* dir res, 82-90, ASSOC VPRES RES, UNIV ALA, HUNTSVILLE, 90- *Personal Data:* b Webster, SDak, Mar 26, 28; m 51; c 5. *Educ:* SDak State Univ, BS, 49; Univ Kans, PhD(physics), 53. *Hon Degrees:* DSc, SDak State Univ, Brookings, 79. *Honors & Awards:* Herman Oberth Award, Am Inst Aeronaut & Astronaut, 78. *Prof Exp:* Asst prof eng res, Pa State Univ, 53-54; physicist, Tech Feasibility Study Off, Redstone Arsenal, 54-56, chief physics & astrophys sect, Army Ballistic Missile Agency, 56-60; chief, Physics & Astrophys Br, Marshall Space Flight Ctr, NASA, 60-62; asst dir sci, Smithsonian Astrophys Observ, 62-73; dir, Space Sci Lab, Marshall Space Flight Ctr, NASA, 73-82. *Concurrent Pos:* Assoc, Harvard Col Observ, 62-73; vis prof physics, Univ Ala, Huntsville, 73-81; dir, Consortium Mat Develop in Space, 85- *Mem:* AAAS; Int Astron Union; Am Astron Soc; Am Geophys Union; Am Phys Soc; NY Acad Sci; Nat Speleol Soc; Meteoritic Soc; Sigma Xi. *Res:* Spacecraft orbital mechanics and orbit determination; space technology; classical mechanics; radiative transfer. *Mailing Add:* 214 Jones Valley Dr SW Huntsville AL 35802-1724

LUNDRY, JERRY LEE, SUPERSONIC WING DESIGN, WAKE VORTICES. *Current Pos:* aerodyn engr, Boeing Com Airplanes, 70-77, supvr aerodyn, 77-94, chief engr, NWTC, 94-96, SUPVR AERODYN DESIGN PROCESSES & TECHNOL, BOEING COM AIRPLANES, 96- *Personal Data:* b Canton, Ill, Jan 18, 37. *Educ:* Univ Ill, BS, 58, MS, 59. *Honors & Awards:* Outstanding Performance Tech Mgt, Am Inst Aeronaut & Astronaut, 88. *Prof Exp:* Aerodynamicist, Douglas Aircraft Co, 59-70. *Mem:* Assoc fel Am Inst Aeronaut & Astronaut. *Res:* Induced drag; winglets; supersonic wing design; wake vertices. *Mailing Add:* 1000 Sunset Way Bellevue WA 98004-4023. *E-Mail:* jerry.1.lundry@boeing.com

LUNDSAGER, C(HRISTIAN) BENT, ENGINEERING, PLASTICS. *Current Pos:* CONSULT, 90- *Personal Data:* b Denmark, Feb 27, 25; nat US; m 47; c 4. *Educ:* Tech Univ Denmark, MSc, 50. *Prof Exp:* Engr, Tech Univ Denmark, 47-52 & E I du Pont de Nemours & Co, Inc, 52-62; res assoc, res div, W R Grace & Co, Columbia, Md, 62-90. *Mem:* Soc Plastics Engrs. *Res:* Thermoplastics processing; concept development of novel products and processes including ceramics. *Mailing Add:* 1308 Patuxent Dr Ashton MD 20861-9759

LUNDSTROM, LOUIS C, AUTOMOTIVE ENGINEERING, HIGHWAY SAFETY. *Current Pos:* RETIRED. *Personal Data:* b Tekamah, Nebr, June 7, 15; m 40; c 4. *Educ:* Univ Nebr, BS & MS, 39, PhD(eng), 62. *Prof Exp:* Dir proving ground, Gen Motors Corp, 56-65, dir auto safety, 65-73, exec dir environ activ, 73-80. *Concurrent Pos:* Chmn, Dept Transp Motor Vehicle Safety Adv Coun. *Mem:* Nat Acad Eng; fel Soc Automotive Engrs. *Res:* Vehicle and highway safety; vehicle and highway noise. *Mailing Add:* 18014 N 137th Dr Sun City West AZ 85375-5270

LUNDSTROM, MARK STEVEN, SEMICONDUCTOR DEVICES, COMPUTER SIMULATION. *Current Pos:* from asst prof to assoc prof, Purdue Univ, 80-88, dir, Opto Electronics Res Ctr, 89-93, asst dean eng, 91-93, PROF ELEC ENG, PURDUE UNIV, 88- *Personal Data:* b Alexandria, MN, June 8, 51; m 72, Mary; c Will & Nicholas. *Educ:* Univ Minn, BEE, 73, MSEE, 74; Purdue Univ, PhD(elec eng), 80. *Honors & Awards:* Frederick Emmons Termon Award, Am Soc Elec Engrs, 93. *Prof Exp:* Mem tech staff, Hewlett-Packard Corp, 74-77. *Mem:* Fel Inst Elec & Electronics Engrs; Am Inst Physics; Sigma Xi. *Res:* Physics of semiconductor devices, especially heterostructure and ultra small devices; theory, modeling and simulation as well as experimental work on device-related materials properties. *Mailing Add:* Sch Elec Eng Purdue Univ West Lafayette IN 47907. *Fax:* 765-494-6441; *E-Mail:* lundstro@purdue.edu

LUNDSTROM, RONALD CHARLES, BIOTECHNOLOGY, SEAFOOD TECHNOLOGY. *Current Pos:* RES FOOD TECHNOLOGIST, NAT MARINE FISHERIES SERV, 75- *Personal Data:* b Lynn, Mass, Mar 15, 52; m 77, Martha E MacKinnon; c Karin E & Kenneth C. *Educ:* Northeastern Univ, BA, 75. *Honors & Awards:* Silver Medal, US Dept Com, 89. *Concurrent Pos:* Assoc referee, Asn Anal Chemists, 78-93. *Mem:* Inst Food Technologists; Asn Anal Chemists; Electrophoresis Soc. *Res:* Seafood quality and safety; development of biochemical species identification methods; development of monoclonal antibody based immunoassay methods for fishery biology and technology based applications. *Mailing Add:* 591 Crowned Kinglet Retreat Charleston SC 29412. *Fax:* 803-762-8700; *E-Mail:* ron.lundstrom@noaa.gov

LUNDVALL, RICHARD, VETERINARY MEDICINE. *Current Pos:* RETIRED. *Personal Data:* b Boxholm, Iowa, Dec 10, 20; m 41; c 3. *Educ:* Iowa State Univ, DVM, 44, MS, 56. *Prof Exp:* From instr to assoc prof, Iowa State Univ, 44-71, prof vet med & surg, 71- *Res:* Large animal surgery; ophthalmology. *Mailing Add:* 1041 X Ave Boone IA 50036

LUNDY, JOHN KENT, FORENSIC ANTHROPOLOGY. *Current Pos:* FORENSIC ANTHROPOLOGIST, CENT INDENTIFICATION LAB, US ARMY, HAWAII, 86- *Personal Data:* b Vancouver, Wash, Jan 21, 46; m 68; c 1. *Educ:* Western Wash Univ, Bellingham, BA, 76, MA, 77; Univ Witwatersrand, Johannesburg, SAfrica, PhD(anat), 84; Am Bd Forensic Anthropol, dipl, 88. *Prof Exp:* Asst lectr anat, Univ Witwatersrand, 80; asst prof, Nat Col Naturopathic Med, 81-82; med examr & forensic anthropologist, Multnomah Co Med Examr, Portland, Ore, 82-86. *Concurrent Pos:* Consult forensic anthrop, 82-; adj asst prof, Dept Anthrop, Portland State Univ, 82-; adj asst prof & former dir, forensic studies, Dent Sch, Ore Health Sci Univ, 84-86; identification consult to USN, 87. *Mem:* Am Acad Forensic Sci; Am Asn Phys Anthropologists; Am Anthrop Asn; Sigma Xi. *Res:* Human variation and evolution; morphometric analysis; forensic anthropology; physical anthropology of Southern Africa; Pacific Northwest. *Mailing Add:* Dept Soc Sci Clark Col 1800 E McLoughlin Blvd Vancouver WA 98663-3598

LUNDY, RICHARD ALAN, HIGH ENERGY PHYSICS. *Current Pos:* RETIRED. *Personal Data:* b Sullivan, Ind, Aug 20, 34; m 60; c 2. *Educ:* Univ Chicago, PhD(physics), 62. *Honors & Awards:* Nat Medal Technol, US Govt, 89. *Prof Exp:* Assoc dir, Fermi Nat Accelerator Lab, 84-89. *Res:* High energy physics; large superconducting magnet systems. *Mailing Add:* PO Box 506 White Salmon WA 98672

LUNDY, TED SADLER, RESEARCH ADMINISTRATION, METALS & CERAMICS. *Current Pos:* assoc prof mech eng, 88-90, DIR, MFG CTR, TENN TECHNOL UNIV, 90- *Personal Data:* b Sumner Co, Tenn, Apr 24, 33; m 55; c Tina M. *Educ:* Univ Tenn, BS, 54, MS, 57, PhD(metall), 64; Oak Ridge Sch Reactor Technol, Dr Pile Eng, 58. *Prof Exp:* Instr eng drawing, Univ Tenn, 56-; metallurgist, Metals & Ceramics Div, Oak Ridge Nat Lab, 57-59, group leader diffusion studies, 59-71, supvr corrosion res, 71-72, group leader diffusion studies, 72-75, Prog Planning & Analysis, 75-76, nat prog mgr, Building Thermal Envelope Systs & Insulating Mats, 77-85, mgr, Energy Conversion & Utilization Technologies, 85-88. *Concurrent Pos:* Lectr, Univ Tenn, 66-; mem, Know Le Ct; mem bd dirs, Knoxville Urban League; consultative coun, Nat Inst Bldg Sci. *Mem:* Sigma Xi; Am Inst Mining, Metall & Petrol Engrs; Am Soc Metals; Am Soc Testing & Mat; Am Soc Heating Refrig & Air-Conditioning Engrs; Soc Mfg Engrs. *Res:* Solid state reactions; diffusion in metals and ceramics; building sciences; heat transfer and moisture flow; materials sciences. *Mailing Add:* 2875 Seven Springs Rd Cookeville TN 38501

LUNER, PHILIP, PHYSICAL CHEMISTRY. *Current Pos:* from res assoc to assoc prof, 57-64, PROF PULP & PAPER RES, STATE UNIV NY COL ENVIRON SCI & FORESTRY, 64-, SR RES ASSOC, EMPIRE STATE PAPER RES INST, 77- *Personal Data:* b Vilno, Poland, June 1, 25; US citizen; m 51; c 2. *Educ:* Loyola Col, BSc, 47; McGill Univ, PhD(phys chem), 51. *Prof Exp:* Res chemist, Pulp & Paper Res Inst Can, 51-54; group leader, Sulfite Pulp Mfrs League, 54-57. *Mem:* Am Chem Soc; Tech Asn Pulp & Paper Indust; Can Pulp & Paper Asn; Sigma Xi. *Res:* Diffusion and penetration studies of pulping; chromophores in model lignin compounds; mechanical properties of fibers and paper; surface chemical properties of wood polymers. *Mailing Add:* Col Environ Sci & Forestry State Univ NY Syracuse NY 13210

LUNER, STEPHEN JAY, IMMUNOCHEMISTRY, PATHOLOGY. *Current Pos:* asst prof, 77-91, ASSOC PROF PATH, DALHOUSIE UNIV, 91- *Personal Data:* b New York, NY, Oct 2, 40; m 65, Evelyn Goldin; c Sean, Beth & Susan. *Educ:* Calif Inst Technol, BS, 61; Univ Calif, Los Angeles, PhD(biophys), 69. *Prof Exp:* Res biophysicist, Univ Calif, Los Angeles, 68-71, asst res biophysicist, Biophys Lab, 71, asst prof in residence pediat, 72-77. *Concurrent Pos:* NIMH trainee, Univ Calif, Los Angeles, 69-71, vis assoc prof biol chem, 91-92. *Mem:* Am Soc Cell Biol. *Res:* Electrophoresis; cell surface antigens; effects of enzymes on cell interactions. *Mailing Add:* Dept Path Dalhousie Univ Tupper Bldg Halifax NS B3H 4H7 Can. *Fax:* 902-494-2519; *E-Mail:* sjluner@ac.dal.ca

LUNGSTROM, LEON, MEDICAL ENTOMOLOGY. *Current Pos:* biologist, 52-73, prof biol & head dept, 52-80, EMER PROF, BETHANY COL, KANS, 81- *Personal Data:* b Lindsborg, Kans, July 22, 15; m 65; c 2. *Educ:* Bethany Col, Kans, BS, 40; Kans State Univ, MS, 46, PhD(med entom), 50. *Prof Exp:* Entomologist, USPHS, Commun Dis Ctr, 49-52. *Concurrent Pos:* NSF fac fel, Stanford Univ, 59-60, Univ Okla, 65, Ariz State Univ, 62, Tulane Univ, 70 & Ft Hays Kans State Univ, 77; co dir, McPherson County Old Mill Mus & Park, 81-84; munic mosquito control, 89-91. *Mem:* Emer Mem Am Mosquito Control Asn; emer mem Sigma Xi. *Res:* Mosquitoes. *Mailing Add:* 518 E Lincoln Lindsborg KS 67456-2427

LUNIN, MARTIN, PATHOLOGY. *Current Pos:* RETIRED. *Personal Data:* b New York, NY, Aug 31, 17; m 47. *Educ:* Okla Agr & Mech Col, BS, 38; Wash Univ, DDS, 50; Columbia Univ, MPH, 52. *Prof Exp:* Assoc prof path, Univ Tex Dent Br, 59-64; asst dean curric affairs, Univ Md, Baltimore, 69-71, assoc dean acad affairs, 71-74, prof path & head, Sch Dent, 64-85, emer prof, Sch Dent, 85-94. *Concurrent Pos:* Sr consult, Univ Tex M D Anderson Hosp & Tumor Inst, 60-64; consult, Vet Admin Hosp, 62- & Children's & Lutheran Hosps, Baltimore, Md, 64- *Mem:* AAAS; Am Dent Asn; Am Acad Oral Path; Int Asn Dent Res. *Res:* Diseases of the soft and hard tissues of the head and neck. *Mailing Add:* Mountainville Rd Deer Isle ME 04627

LUNINE, JONATHAN IRVING, PLANETARY SCIENCES. *Current Pos:* Res assoc, 84-86, from asst prof to assoc prof, 86-95, PROF PLANETARY SCI, UNIV ARIZ, 95- *Personal Data:* b New York, NY, June 26, 59; m, Cynthia Ewing; c Joseph. *Educ:* Univ Rochester, BS, 80; Calif Inst Technol, MS, 83, PhD(planetary sci), 85. *Honors & Awards:* Harold C Urey Prize, Div Planetary Sci, Am Astron Soc, 88; Zeldovich Prize, Comt Space Res, Int Coun Sci Unions, 90; James Macelwane Medal, Am Geophys Union, 95. *Concurrent Pos:* Vis asst prof, Univ Calif, Los Angeles, 86; chmn, Solar Syst Explor Subcomt, NASA, 90- *Mem:* Sigma Xi; Am Astron Soc; fel Am Geophys Union. *Res:* Theoretical studies of outer solar system satellites, comets, their present nature and evolution, emphasizing physical chemistry of ices and volatiles; modeling of the evolution of substellar mass objects, brown dwarfs; terrestrial photochemical processes. *Mailing Add:* Lunar & Planetary Lab Univ Ariz Tucson AZ 85721. *Fax:* 520-621-4933; *E-Mail:* jlunine@lpl.arizona.edu

LUNK, WILLIAM ALLAN, ORNITHOLOGY. *Current Pos:* RETIRED. *Personal Data:* b Shamokin, Pa, May 6, 19; m 47; c 4. *Educ:* Univ WVa, AB, 41, MS, 46; Univ Mich, PhD(zool), 55. *Prof Exp:* Instr biol, Univ WVa, 46-47; preparator, Exhibit Mus, Univ Mich, Ann Arbor, 49-59, assoc cur exhibits & lectr zool, 59-85, actg dir, 85-88, cur exhibits, 64-89. *Concurrent Pos:* Consult, Kalamazoo Nature Ctr, Mich, 63-77. *Mem:* Cooper Ornith Soc; Wilson Ornith Soc; assoc Am Ornith Union. *Res:* Ornithological life history; taxonomy and distribution; fossil birds; exhibit techniques. *Mailing Add:* 865 N Wagner Rd Ann Arbor MI 48103-2146

LUNN, ANTHONY CROWTHER, BIOMATERIALS, POLYMER PHYSICS. *Current Pos:* sect mgr, Ethicon Inc, Johnson & Johnson Co, 81-90, MGR ADVAN TECHNOL, JOHNSON & JOHNSON INTERVENTIONAL SYSTS, 90- *Personal Data:* b Huddersfield, Eng, Sept 25, 46, US citizen; m 72, Phyllis Teitelbaum. *Educ:* Cambridge Univ, Eng, BA, 67; Harvard Univ, MS, 68; Mass Inst Technol, ScD, 72. *Prof Exp:* Res scientist, Pioneering Res Lab, Du Pont Co, 69; res assoc, Mass Inst Technol, 72-73; proj leader, Chem Res Div, Am Cyanamid Co, 73-81. *Mem:* Am Chem Soc; Fiber Soc; Int Soc Endovascular Surg; Sigma Xi; AAAS; Soc Biomat. *Res:* Development of novel products for use in angioplasty and minimally invasive surgery; implantable stents and other devices. *Mailing Add:* J&J Interventional Systs PO Box 4917 Warren NJ 07059-0917

LUNN, CHARLES ALBERT, PROTEIN ENGINEERING OF CYTOKINES-LYMPHOKINES, RATIONAL DRUG DESIGN. *Current Pos:* SR PRIN SCIENTIST, DEPT MOLECULAR BIOL, SCHERING-PLOUGH RES INST, 93- *Personal Data:* b Audubon, NJ, Dec 2, 53; m, Kathleen S Morgan; c Forrest H & K Danielle. *Educ:* Johns Hopkins Univ, BA, 76, PhD(biochem),84. *Honors & Awards:* President's Award, Schering-Plough Corp, 88. *Prof Exp:* Fel, Dept Biochem, State Univ NY, Stony Brook, 84-86. *Res:* Used protein mutagenesis and biochemical approaches to probe the importance of protein structure in biological function; results will be used to attempt to rationally design novel immunomodulatory drugs. *Mailing Add:* Schering-Plough Res Inst 2015 Galloping Hill Rd Kenilworth NJ 08817. *Fax:* 908-298-3083

LUNNEY, DAVID CLYDE, ANALYTICAL CHEMISTRY. *Current Pos:* from asst prof to assoc prof, 68-80, PROF CHEM, E CAROLINA UNIV, 80-, DIR, SCI INST DISABLED, 86- *Personal Data:* b Charleston, SC. *Educ:* Univ SC, BS, 59, PhD(phys chem), 65. *Prof Exp:* NIH fel, Duke Univ, 66-68. *Mem:* Audio Eng Soc; Am Chem Soc; AAAS; Found Sci & Disability. *Res:* Laboratory aids for disabled scientists, engineers and science students. *Mailing Add:* Dept Chem E Carolina Univ Greenville NC 27858-4353. *E-Mail:* chlunney@ecuvm1

LUNNEY, JOAN K, ANIMAL INFECTIOUS DISEASES, ANIMAL GENOME. *Current Pos:* RES IMMUNOLOGIST SWINE IMMUNOGENETICS, HELMINTHIC DIS LAB, AGR RES SERV, USDA, 83- *Personal Data:* b Philadelphia, Pa, July 19, 46; m 79. *Educ:* Chestnut Hill Col, Philadelphia, Pa, BS, 68; Johns Hopkins Univ, Baltimore, Md, PhD(biochem), 76. *Prof Exp:* Chemist cell surface receptors, Lab Biochem Pharmacol, Nat Inst Arthritis, Metab Digestive Dis, NIH, 73-76, postdoctoral fel swine immunogenetics & biochem, Immunol Br, Nat Cancer Inst, 76-79, sr staff fel, 79-83. *Concurrent Pos:* Panel mem, Cellular Physiol Panel, NSF, 83-87; adv coun mem, Portuguese NSF, 87-90; comt mem, Comt Res Animal Genome, US Exp Stas Comt Orgn & Policy, 90; chairperson, Swine CD Workshop, Int Union Immunol Sci, 90-92; mem, Vet Immunol Comt, Am Asn Immunologists, 90-93; comt mem, Nat Animal Genetic Resources Comt, USDA, 91-; secy, Swine Genome Comt, 93- *Mem:* Am Asn Immunologists; Transplantation Soc; Asn Women Sci; Int Soc Animal Genetics; Am Asn Vet Parisitologists; Am Asn Vet Immunologists. *Res:* Analyses of immunologic mechanisms and genetic control of swine responses to infectious diseases; understanding of basic swine immune responses and of complexity of swine genome. *Mailing Add:* LPSI Helminthic Dis Lab Bldg 1040 Rm 2 Agr Res Serv USDA Bldg 1040 Rm 104 Beltsville MD 20705

LUNSFORD, CARL DALTON, PHARMACEUTICAL CHEMISTRY. *Current Pos:* res chemist, A H Robins Co, Inc, 53-57, assoc dir chem res, 58, dir, 59-64, dir labs, 62-64, dir res, 64-66, asst vpres, 66-74, vpres, 73-80, SR VPRES, A H ROBINS CO, INC, 80- *Personal Data:* b Richmond, Va, Feb 11, 27; m 47; c 3. *Educ:* Univ Richmond, BS, 49, MS, 50; Univ Va, PhD(chem), 53. *Prof Exp:* Instr chem, Univ Va, 52-53. *Mem:* AAAS; Am Chem Soc; Am Inst Chemists. *Res:* Medicinal and organic chemistry and development. *Mailing Add:* 1807 Poplar Green Dr Richmond VA 23233-4171

LUNSFORD, JACK HORNER, HETEROGENEOUS CATALYSIS. *Current Pos:* from asst prof to assoc prof, 66-71, PROF CHEM, TEX A&M UNIV, 71- *Personal Data:* b Houston, Tex, Feb 6, 36; m 60; c 7. *Educ:* Tex A&M Univ, BS, 57; Rice Univ, PhD(chem eng), 62. *Honors & Awards:* Paul H Emmett Award, Catalysis Soc, 75; Catalysis Soc Metropolitan NY Award, Excellence Catalysis, 86. *Prof Exp:* Asst prof chem eng, Univ Idaho, 61-62; asst prof chem, Sam Houston State Col, 65-66. *Mem:* Am Chem Soc. *Res:* Surface chemistry and heterogeneous catalysis, using modern spectroscopic techniques. *Mailing Add:* 2000 Rockwood Dr Bryan TX 77801-2711

LUNSFORD, JESSE V(ERNON), CIVIL & SANITARY ENGINEERING. *Current Pos:* PROF CIVIL ENG, NMEX STATE UNIV, 58- *Personal Data:* b Ninnekah, Okla, Sept 4, 23; m 48; c 5. *Educ:* Univ NMex, BS, 53; Univ Calif, MS, 54. *Prof Exp:* Asst prof & asst res engr, Wash State Univ, 54-57; assoc prof, Rensselaer Polytech Inst, 57-58. *Mem:* Am Soc Civil Engrs; Nat Soc Prof Engrs; Am Soc Eng Educ; Am Pub Health Asn; Am Water Works Asn. *Res:* Anaerobic digestion; stream sanitation; algae production; water reclamation and utilization. *Mailing Add:* 2035 Corley Dr Las Cruces NM 88001

LUNSFORD, RALPH D, AUDIO-VIDEO EQUIPMENT & TAPES REGARDING CONSUMER PRODUCTS, LINEAR SOLID STATE APPLICATIONS ENGINEERING. *Current Pos:* RETIRED. *Personal Data:* b Ninety Six, SC, Jan 7, 34; m 57; c 1. *Educ:* Clemson Univ, BS, 56. *Prof Exp:* Elec engr audio electronics acoust, RCA Corp, 56-66; proj engr audio & acoust, CBS TV Network, 66-68; vpres eng, Audio Tape Duplication, Nat Tape Serv, Inc, 68-71; proj mgr, Audio & FM Receivers & Amplifiers, Brit Industs, Div Avnet, 71-73; sr proj engr, Audio Amplifiers Design, Dynaco, Inc, Div Tyco Labs, 73-76; sr engr audio for auto radios, Ford Motor Co, 76-79; mgr prod eng & qual or solid state appln engr, Thomson Consumer Electronics, Inc, 79-94. *Concurrent Pos:* Liaison officer UL/CSA matters, Thomson Consumer Electronics, Inc, 85-; mem, Camcorder Battery Stand Comt, Electronic Industs Asn, 90- *Mem:* Audio Eng Soc; Am Inst Physics. *Res:* Microphones used in space program; designer of audio electronic systems used in Ford auto radio; developed state of the art audio tape duplicating system; developed state of the art battery cycling equipment. *Mailing Add:* 3002 Raymond Ave Abington PA 19001

LUNT, HARRY EDWARD, FAILURE ANALYSIS, STANDARDS DEVELOPMENT. *Current Pos:* CORP CONSULT ENGR, BURNS & ROE ENTERPRISES, INC, 74- *Personal Data:* b New York, NY, Apr 30, 24; m 50; c 5. *Educ:* Syracuse Univ, AB, 48; Iowa State Univ, MS, 53. *Honors & Awards:* Award of Merit, Am Soc Testing & Mat, 81; Robert J Painter

Award, Standards Eng Soc, 89. *Prof Exp:* Res asst, Ames Lab, US Atomic Energy Comn, 50-53; develop metallurgist, US Steel Corp, 53-63; sr engr, Westinghouse Res Labs, 63-66; corp metallurgist, Worthington Corp, 67-74. *Concurrent Pos:* Chmn, Comt A-1 Steel, Am Soc Testing & Mat, 86-91, mem bd dirs, 91- *Mem:* Fel Am Soc Testing & Mat; fel Am Soc Metals; Nat Asn Corrosion Engrs; Am Welding Soc. *Res:* Development of standards for steel and liason among national and international standards organizations; metallurgy and failure analysis, particularly for power generation equipment. *Mailing Add:* 13 Brockden Dr Mendham NJ 07945

LUNT, OWEN RAYNAL, SOIL FERTILITY. *Current Pos:* from instr to assoc prof soil sci, Univ Calif, Los Angeles, 51-63, actg dir lab nuclear med & radiation biol, 65-68, actg chmn dept biophys, 65-70, PROF BIOL, UNIV CALIF, LOS ANGELES, 63-, DIR, LAB NUCLEAR MED & RADIATION BIOL, 68- *Personal Data:* b El Paso, Tex, Apr 8, 21; m 53; c 3. *Educ:* Brigham Young Univ, AB, 47; NC State Univ, PhD(agron), 51. *Prof Exp:* Lectr soil chem, NC State Univ, 50. *Concurrent Pos:* Tech Expert, Int Atomic Energy Agency, Columbia, 71, Kenya, 83, Malaysia, 85. *Mem:* Fel Soil Sci Soc Am; fel Am Soc Agron; Am Soc Hort Sci; Am Nuclear Soc. *Res:* Soil chemistry; environmental pollution. *Mailing Add:* 1200 Roberto Lane Los Angeles CA 90077-2334

LUNT, STEELE RAY, MEDICAL ENTOMOLOGY. *Current Pos:* From asst prof to assoc prof, 64-74, PROF BIOL, UNIV NEBR AT OMAHA, 74- *Personal Data:* b Mammoth, Utah, Jan 5, 35; m 59, Patricia Bills; c Nancy, David, Cathy, Susan & Kevin. *Educ:* Univ Utah, BS, 57, MS, 59, PhD(entom), 64. *Concurrent Pos:* Am Mosquito Control Asn, 75-76; ed bd, Mosquito Systs, 84-89. *Mem:* Soc Vector Ecol; Am Mosquito Control Asn; Entom Soc Am. *Res:* Control, systematics, ecology, and medical importance of mosquitoes; ecology. *Mailing Add:* 3853 N 100th Ave Omaha NE 68134. *Fax:* 402-554-3532

LUNTE, CRAIG EDWARD, BIOANALYTICAL CHEMISTRY. *Current Pos:* from asst to assoc prof, 87-97, PROF, DEPT CHEM, UNIV KANS, 97- *Personal Data:* b Aug 6, 57; m 83, Susan Hommel; c Alyson & Kathryn. *Educ:* Univ Mo, Rolla, BS, 79; Purdue Univ, PhD(analytical chem), 84. *Prof Exp:* Res scientist, Procter & Gamble, 84-86; res assoc, Univ Cincinnati, 86-87. *Concurrent Pos:* Adj prof, Dept Pharmaceut Chem, Univ Kans, 90- *Mem:* Am Chem Soc; Am Asn Pharmaceut Scientists; Soc Electroanal Chem; Int Soc Study Xenobiotics; Sigma Xi; AAAS. *Res:* Bioanalytical chemistry; development of microdialysis sampling for in vivo monitoring; developing microanalytical techniques such as capillary electrophoresis and microbore; liquid chromatography; detector development. *Mailing Add:* Univ Kans Dept Chem 2010 Malott Hall Lawrence KS 66045. *Fax:* 785-864-5396; *E-Mail:* clunte@kuhub.cc.ukans.edu

LUNTZ, MAURICE HAROLD, GLAUCOMA SURGERY, CATARACT SURGERY. *Current Pos:* CLIN PROF OPHTHAL, MT SINAI SCH MED, 78- *Personal Data:* b Cape Town, S Africa, July 27, 30; US citizen; m 57, Angela J Myerson; c Melvyn, Caryn & David. *Educ:* Univ Cape Town, MB ChB, 52; Univ Witwatersrand, MD, 74; FRCS Ed, 58, FACS, 78. *Honors & Awards:* Sam & Dora Cohen Medal, Univ Capetown, 84; Honor Award, Am Acad Ophthal, 86; Gold Medal, Univ Rome, 87. *Prof Exp:* Prof & chmn ophthal, Univ Witwatersrand, 64-78. *Concurrent Pos:* Academia, Ophthalmologica Int, 75-; consult, Corneal Disease Hip, NY, 78; dir ophthal, Beth Israel Med Ctr, 78-79, dir emer, 89-; chmn, Ophthal Sect, NY Acad Med, 89-90; pres bd surgeon dir, Manhattan Eye Ear & Throat Hosp, 91- *Mem:* Int Coun Ophthal; Int Glaucoma Cong. *Res:* Surgical procedures for glaucoma; new techniques for glaucoma surgery and evaluation of existing techniques. *Mailing Add:* 180 East End Ave New York NY 10128. *Fax:* 212-223-2561

LUNTZ, MYRON, RADIATION PHYSICS. *Current Pos:* from asst prof to assoc prof, 69-82, chmn dept, 78-84, PROF PHYSICS, STATE UNIV NY COL FREDONIA, 82- *Personal Data:* b New York, NY, Jan 16, 40; m 64, Susan Jassen; c Barbara & Jonathan. *Educ:* City Col New York, BS, 62; Univ Conn, MS, 64, PhD(physics), 68. *Prof Exp:* Res asst physics, Univ Conn, 64-68, fel, 68; vis scientist, Inst Physics, Univ Aarhus, 68-69. *Concurrent Pos:* Vis assoc prof physics, Univ Del, 75-76. *Mem:* Am Phys Soc; Am Asn Physics Teachers; Sigma Xi; Soc Physics Students. *Res:* Theoretical study of the penetration of matter by energetic charged particles, with emphasis on effects associated with the spatial distribution of energy desposition about particle tracks; experimental study of surface alteration of metal substrates by ion beam irradiation. *Mailing Add:* Dept Physics State Univ NY Col Fredonia NY 14063. *Fax:* 716-673-3347; *E-Mail:* luntzm@fredonia.edu

LUO, PEILIN, ELECTRONICS CIRCUIT & SYSTEM, MANUFACTURE METHODS. *Current Pos:* dep dir, Sci & Tech Admin, 93-82 & Sci & Tech Comt, Ministry Electronics Indust, 80-88, CONSULT, SCI & TECH ADV COMT, MINISTRY MACH & ELECTRONICS INDUST, 88- *Personal Data:* b Tianjin, China, Dec 30, 13; m 41; c 3. *Educ:* Nat Chiao-tung Univ, BS, 35; Calif Inst Technol, PhD(elec eng, physics & math), 52. *Honors & Awards:* Centennial Medal, Inst Elec & Electronics Engrs, 84. *Prof Exp:* Var tech positions, Chinese factories, 35-48; dept dir, Technol Dept, Admin Telecom Indust, 50-53; chief engr, NChina Combine Radio & Component Mfg, 53-56; dep chief engr, Admin Electronics Indust, 56-62. *Concurrent Pos:* Mem, Nat Natural Sci Award Comt, 65-90; guest prof, Peking Univ, Chinese Electronic Sci & Univ, Xi-Dian Electronics Sci & Tech Univ; hon prof, Beijing Inst Technol. *Mem:* Sigma Xi; fel Inst Elec & Electronics Engrs; fel Chinese Inst Electronics. *Res:* Electronic circuit, transmitters and receivers, radar system and decision theory; computer arithmatics; policy of science and especially electronics development; application of mathematics to national economics. *Mailing Add:* Sci & Tech Consult Comt Ministry Mach & Electronics Nanshagon 2 Entrance Bldg 11 Beijing Sarlihe 100823 People's Republic of China

LUO, STEVEN X L, CATALYSIS, POLYMERIZATION. *Current Pos:* RES SCIENTIST, BRIDGESTONE-FIRESTONE RES, 95- *Personal Data:* b Longchuan, China, Nov 27, 62. *Educ:* Sun Yatsen Univ, BS, 82; Yale Univ, MS, 86, MPhil, 87, PhD(chem), 90. *Prof Exp:* Res assoc, Leather Indust Res Inst, 82-84; postdoctoral res assoc, Yale Univ, 90-92; postdoctoral res fel, Los Alamos Nat Lab, 92-95. *Mem:* Am Chem Soc. *Res:* Transition metal organometallic chemistry and inorganic chemistry; coordination chemistry; Ziegler-Natta polymerization; homogeneous catalysis; polymer chemistry and design of new ligards for catalysis. *Mailing Add:* Bridgestone/Firestone Res 1200 Firestone Parwy Akron OH 44317. *Fax:* 330-379-7530; *E-Mail:* luo@bfs.e-mail.com

LUOMA, ERNIE VICTOR, INDUSTRIAL CHEMISTRY. *Current Pos:* chemist, Dow Chem Co, 57-62, group leader, 62-70, res mgr, 70-77, tech dir, 77-78, dir, Analytical Labs, 78-80, DIR ANALYTICAL SCI, CORP RES & DEVELOP, DOW CHEM CO, 80- *Personal Data:* b Sault Ste Marie, Mich, Sept 1, 32; m 54; c 5. *Educ:* Mich Technol Univ, BS, 54; Univ Calif, Berkeley, MS, 56; Mich State Univ, PhD(phys inorg chem), 66. *Prof Exp:* Instr chem, Mich Technol Univ, 56-57. *Mem:* Am Chem Soc; Am Inst Chem Engrs. *Res:* Industrial research. *Mailing Add:* 1030 Allen Ave Ashtabula OH 44092-2298

LUOMA, JOHN ROBERT VINCENT, PHYSICAL CHEMISTRY. *Current Pos:* asst prof, 69-74, ASSOC PROF CHEM, CLEVELAND STATE UNIV, 74- *Personal Data:* b Huntingdon, Pa, June 3, 38; m 61; c 3. *Educ:* Ohio Univ, BA & BS, 61; Purdue Univ, Lafayette, PhD(phys chem), 66. *Prof Exp:* Asst prof chem, NDak State Univ, 66-69. *Mem:* Am Chem Soc. *Res:* Chemical education; chemical demonstrations. *Mailing Add:* 4176 Tudor Ave Brunswick OH 44212-2932. *E-Mail:* j.iuoma@suohio.edu

LUONGO, CESAR AUGUSTO, SUPERCONDUCTING MAGNETS, THERMAL-FLUID SCIENCES. *Current Pos:* MGR, SMES TECHNOL, BECHTEL, 92- *Personal Data:* b Montevideo, Uruguay, Oct 5, 54; m 85, Maria Mena; c Francisco & Julia. *Educ:* Univ Uruguay, Montevideo, Ing, 79; Stanford Univ, Palo Alto, MS, 81, PhD(mech eng), 85. *Prof Exp:* Sr engr, Res & Develop Div, Bechtel, 86-88; mgr, Develop Gas Pipelines, Stoner Assocs Inc, 88-92. *Mem:* Inst Elec & Electronics Engrs. *Res:* Superconducting magnetic energy storage; magnet design; thermal and fluid dynamics analyses; electromagnetics; system studies. *Mailing Add:* 35 Delano Ave San Francisco CA 94112-2519. *E-Mail:* cluongo@bechtel.com

LUPAN, DAVID MARTIN, MEDICAL MYCOLOGY. *Current Pos:* From asst prof to assoc prof, 73-87, PROF MICROBIOL, SCH MED SCI, UNIV NEV, RENO, 87- *Personal Data:* b Cleveland, Ohio, Oct 23, 45; m 68, Joyce E Bricker; c Michael & Nicole. *Educ:* Univ Ariz, BS, 67; Univ Iowa, MS, 70, PhD(microbiol), 73. *Mem:* Sigma Xi; Am Soc Microbiol; Int Soc Human & Animal Mycol; Med Mycol Soc Am. *Res:* The mechanism of pathogenesis of fungi. *Mailing Add:* Sch Med Sci Univ Nev Reno NV 89557-0046. *Fax:* 702-784-1620; *E-Mail:* dmlupan@med.unr.edu

LUPASH, LAWRENCE O, KALMAN FILTER, NUMERICAL METHODS IN CONTROL THEORY. *Current Pos:* SR ANALYST, INTERMETRICS, INC, 80- *Personal Data:* b Bucharest, Romania, May 29, 42; US citizen; div. *Educ:* Polytech Inst Bucharest, Romania, MSc, 65, PhD(control & comput eng), 72. *Honors & Awards:* Medal, Albanian Acad Sci, 73. *Prof Exp:* Researcher-engr, control eng, Inst Automation, Bucharest, Romania, 65-68, sr researcher, 71-72; sr analyst & sr researcher control & comput appln, Univ Bucharest Comput Ctr, 72-79. *Concurrent Pos:* Asst prof, Fac Automation, Polytech Inst Bucharest, 66-68 & 71-72; lectr informatics & math, Univ Bucharest, Romania, 73-78; vis lectr, Univ Tirana, Albania, 73. *Mem:* Inst Elec & Electronics Engrs; Asn Comput Mach; Soc Indust & Appl Math. *Res:* Numerical techniques for software applications in technical-scientific problems; applied mathematics; optimization; numerical methods in control theory; estimation; stability and control of multivariable systems. *Mailing Add:* 2625 Monterey Place Fullerton CA 92833

LUPINSKI, JOHN HENRY, POLYMER CHEMISTRY. *Current Pos:* Res chemist, Res & Develop Ctr, 60-72, proj mgr, Corp Res & Develop Ctr, 72-79, UNIT MGR CORP RES & DEVELOP, GEN ELEC CO, 79- *Personal Data:* b Schenectady, NY, Feb 28, 27; m 54; c 3. *Educ:* State Univ Leyden, BS, 49, MS, 53, PhD(chem), 59. *Mem:* AAAS; Am Chem Soc; Fedn Am Scientist. *Res:* Organic conductors; polymer electro-chemistry; electrical insulation and polymer application processes; electrostatics. *Mailing Add:* PMSE 9318 Old Courthouse Vienna VA 22182

LUPLOW, WAYNE CHARLES, DEVELOPMENT OF HIGH DEFINITION TELEVISION FOR TERRESTRIAL BROADCAST, QUALITY & RELIABILITY OF SEMICONDUCTOR COMPONENTS. *Current Pos:* engr & leader television res, 64-74, eng dir components & reliability, 74-87, EXEC DIR RES & DEVELOP HDTV, ZENITH ELECTRONICS CORP, 87- *Personal Data:* b Milwaukee, Wis, Jan 16, 40; m 60; c 4. *Educ:* Univ Wis, BSEE, 62; Univ Pa, MSE, 64. *Prof Exp:* Engr television res, RCA, 62-64. *Concurrent Pos:* Publ chmn, Consumer Electronics Soc, Inst Elec & Electronics Engrs, 76-, Transactions ed, 80-; admin comt, Consumer Electronics Soc, 75- *Mem:* Sr mem Inst Elec & Electronics Engrs. *Res:* High definition television and other comunications systems relating to consumer electronics. *Mailing Add:* Zenith Electronics Corp 1000 Milwaukee Ave Glenview IL 60025

LUPO, ANTHONY ROCCO, SYNOPTIC SCALE DYNAMICS, CLIMATE DYNAMICS. *Current Pos:* POSTDOCTORAL RES ASSOC, STATE UNIV NY, ALBANY, 95- *Personal Data:* b Auburn, NY, Mar 13, 66; m, Allison A Wood; c Mary E & Grace A. *Educ:* State Univ NY, Oswego, BS, 88; Purdue Univ, MS, 91, PhD(atmospheric sci), 95. *Mem:* Am Meteorol Soc; Royal Meteorol Soc; Sigma Xi. *Res:* Large and synoptic-scale atmospheric dynamics; structure and maintenance of blocking anticyclones and transient cyclones. *Mailing Add:* 2404 Brandywine Pkwy Guilderland NY 12084-9352. *Fax:* 518-442-4494; *E-Mail:* tlupo@aspen.atmos.albany.edu

LUPSKI, JAMES RICHARD, HUMAN GENETICS, GENETIC ENGINEERING. *Current Pos:* res asst prof pediat, Baylor Col Med, 86-87, res asst prof, Inst Molecular Genetics, 87-92, assoc prof, Dept Molecular & Human Genetics & Dept Pediat, 92-95, DIR, MED SCIENTIST TRAINING PROG, BAYLOR COL MED, 93-, CULLEN PROF MOLECULAR & HUMAN GENETICS, 95-, PROF PEDIAT, 95- *Personal Data:* b Rockville Center, NY, Feb 22, 57; m 86, Gabriella R Geradi; c Alessandra M & Marcella D. *Educ:* NY Univ, BA, 79, MS, 83, PhD(molecular biol), 84; NY Univ Med Ctr, MD, 85. *Honors & Awards:* Young Investr Award, Abbott Labs, 89 & Southern Sect, Am Fedn Clin Res, 91. *Prof Exp:* Res asst prof biochem, Dept Biochem, NY Univ Med Ctr, 85-86. *Concurrent Pos:* Guest prof, Ctr Advan Molecular Biol, Punjab Univ, Lahore, Pakistan, 86; PEW scholar, Human Genetics, 90-94. *Mem:* AMA; fel AAAS; NY Acad Sci; Am Soc Microbiol; Genetics Soc Am; Am Soc Human Genetics; fel Am Acad Pediat; Soc Pediat Res; Am Fedn Clin Res; fel Am Col Med Genetics. *Res:* Regulation of complex gene systems in E coli and mechanisms of DNA rearrangements; mechanisms for disease causing mutations in humans; DNA fingerprinting of infectious disease agents. *Mailing Add:* 11102 Ashcroft Dr Houston TX 77096

LUPTON, CHARLES HAMILTON, JR, MEDICINE, PATHOLOGY. *Current Pos:* from assoc prof to prof, 55-83, chmn dept, 61-74, EMER PROF PATH, MED CTR, UNIV ALA, BIRMINGHAM, 83- *Personal Data:* b Norfolk, Va, July 17, 19; m 45, Mary E Rand; c Charles H III, W Kenan & Susan L. *Educ:* Univ Va, BA, 42, MD, 44; Am Bd Path, dipl, 51. *Prof Exp:* Asst prof path, Sch Med, Univ Va, 51-53. *Concurrent Pos:* Consult, Vet Admin, Birmingham, Tuskeegee. *Mem:* AAAS; Am Asn Path; Int Acad Path; AMA; Col Am Path. *Res:* Cardiovascular-renal diseases, especially the kidney as studied by simpler histochemical techniques. *Mailing Add:* Dept Path Univ Ala 587 LHRB UAB Sta Birmingham AL 35294-0001. *Fax:* 205-934-5499

LUPTON, JOHN EDWARD, CHEMICAL OCEANOGRAPHY, ISOTOPE GEOLOGY. *Current Pos:* assoc res oceanogr, 81-89, RES OCEANOGR, MARINE SCI INST, UNIV CALIF, SANTA BARBARA, 89- *Personal Data:* b Bakersfield, Calif, July 30, 44. *Educ:* Princeton Univ, BA, 66; Calif Inst Technol, PhD(physics), 72. *Prof Exp:* Asst res physicist, Scripps Inst Oceanog, 73-81. *Concurrent Pos:* Cruise coordr res vessel, Melville Vulcan Exped, Scripps Inst Oceanog, 80-81; adj assoc prof geol, Univ Calif, Santa Barbara, 81-89, adj prof, 89- *Mem:* Am Geophys Union. *Res:* Application of helium and rare gas isotopes to ocean circulation studies; geothermal and volcanic gases; outgassing of mantle volatiles; numerical modeling of ocean tracer distributions. *Mailing Add:* NOAA Pac Marine Environ Lab Marine Resources Res Div Hatfield Marine Sci Ctr 20300 S Marine Sci Dr Newport OR 97365

LUPTON, WILLIAM HAMILTON, PLASMA PHYSICS, ELECTRICAL ENGINEERING. *Current Pos:* RETIRED. *Personal Data:* b Charlottesville, Va, July 25, 30. *Educ:* Univ Va, BA, 50; Univ Md, PhD(physics), 60. *Prof Exp:* Physicist, Radio Div, Nat Bur Stand, 52-55 & Plasma Physics Div, US Naval Res Lab, 60-85; sr scientist, Jaycor, 85-92. *Mem:* Sigma Xi. *Res:* Plasma spectroscopy; high voltage and high current pulse technology; high power laser development. *Mailing Add:* 16509 Montecrest Lane Gaithersburg MD 20878-2163

LUQI, , RAPID PROTOTYPING, REAL-TIME SYSTEMS. *Current Pos:* from asst prof to assoc prof, 86-95, PROF, COMPUT SCI DEPT, NAVAL POSTGRAD SCH, 95- *Personal Data:* b Shanghai, China, May 4, 49; m 85; c 1. *Educ:* Jilin Univ, China, BS, 75; Univ Minn, MS, 84, PhD(computer sci), 86. *Honors & Awards:* Menneken Fac Award Excellence, 91. *Prof Exp:* Asst researcher, Sci Acad China, Peking, 75-80; Teaching res & proj asst, Comput Sci Dept, Univ Minn, 81-86. *Concurrent Pos:* Mem tech staff, Int Software Systs, Inc, 84-85; adj asst prof, Comput Sci Dept, Univ Minn, 86-90; assoc ed, J Systs Integration & Software Design & Process World, Honeywell Res & Electronics Engrs; mem, Prog Comt Syst Design & Network Conf, Inst Elec & Electronics Engrs, 89 & 90, first & second Int Conf Systs Integration, Inst Elec & Electronics Engrs/Asn Comput Mach; tech consult, Int Software Systs, Inc & Honeywell Res Ctr; prin investr, NSF, Dept Navy, Army & Air Force Off Scientific Res; NSF presidential young investr award, 90. *Mem:* Inst Elec & Electronics Engrs; Inst Elec & Electronics Engrs Comput Soc; Asn Comput Mach. *Res:* Computer aided software engineering; designs computer languages and computer support for software automation; rapid prototyping methodology and tools; author of numerous publications and books. *Mailing Add:* Dept Comput Sci Naval Postgrad Sch Monterey CA 93943. *Fax:* 408-656-2189; *E-Mail:* lugi@cs.nps.navy.mil

LURA, RICHARD DEAN, PHYSICAL ORGANIC CHEMISTRY. *Current Pos:* asst prof, 71-80, ASSOC PROF CHEM, MILLIGAN COL, 80- *Personal Data:* b Kenosha, Wis, Aug 21, 45; m 68. *Educ:* Univ Wis, BS, 67; Iowa State Univ, PhD(chem), 71. *Concurrent Pos:* Consult, R I Schattner Co, 72-79. *Res:* Research and devleopment of germicidal and sporicidal solutions for hospital and home use. *Mailing Add:* Dept Chem Milligan Col Milligan College TN 37682-4002

LURAIN, JOHN ROBERT, III, GYNECOLOGIC ONCOLOGY. *Current Pos:* from asst prof to assoc prof, 79-88, PROF OBSTET-GYNEC, SCH MED, NORTHWESTERN UNIV, 89- *Personal Data:* b Princeton, Ill, Oct 27, 46; m 69, Nell Snavely; c Alice & Kathryn. *Educ:* Oberlin Col, AB, 68; Univ NC, MD, 72. *Honors & Awards:* Purdue-Frederick Award, Am Col Obstet Gynec, 83. *Prof Exp:* Resident obstet-gynec, Magee Womens Hosp, Univ Pittsburgh, 72-75; lieutenant commander, med corps, USNR, Naval Regional Med Ctr, Portsmouth, Va, 75-77; fel gynec oncol, Roswell Park Cancer Inst, 77-79. *Concurrent Pos:* Galloway fel, Mem Sloan Kettering Cancer Ctr, 75; clin fel, Am Cancer Soc, 77-79, jr fac fel, 80-83; dir, div gynec oncol, Prentice Women's Hosp, Sch Med, Northwestern Univ, 85-; dir, John I Brewer Trophoblastic Dis Ctr, 79- *Mem:* Soc Gynec Oncologists; Am Soc Clin Oncol; Am Soc Colposcopy & Cervical Path; Am Col Obstetricians & Gynecologists. *Res:* Gestational trophoblastic disease; endometrial cancer; cervical cancer; laser therapy; hormone receptors; chemotherapy and surgery; ovarian cancer. *Mailing Add:* Prentice Women's Hosp 333 E Superior St Chicago IL 60611. *Fax:* 312-908-2188

LURCH, E(DWARD) NORMAN, ELECTRICAL ENGINEERING. *Current Pos:* assoc prof, 65-66, PROF ELECTRONICS, STATE UNIV NY AGR & TECH COL, FARMINGDALE, 66- *Personal Data:* b Morristown, NJ, Dec 23, 19; m 41; c 4. *Educ:* NY Univ, BEE, 40, MEE, 43. *Prof Exp:* Tutor elec eng, City Col New York, 41-43; instr, Manhattan Col, 43-47; asst prof, Univ Fla, 47; asst prof, Clarkson Col Technol, 48-49; assoc prof electronics, State Univ NY Agr & Tech Col, Farmingdale, 49-60; chief engr, Chemtronics, Inc, 60-61; aerospace technologist, Goddard Space Flight Ctr, NASA, 62-65. *Concurrent Pos:* Lectr grad div, State Univ NY Col, New Paltz, 58-61; consult engr, Oil Heat Inst, Long Island, 57-59. *Res:* Fundamentals of electronics; electric circuits. *Mailing Add:* 11 Black Duck Dr Stony Brook NY 11790

LURIA, S(AUL) M(ARTIN), PHYSIOLOGICAL PSYCHOLOGY. *Current Pos:* Res psychologist, 57-83, HEAD, VISION DEPT, US NAVAL SUBMARINE MED CTR, 83- *Personal Data:* b Athol, Mass, Dec 24, 29; m 63; c 2. *Educ:* Univ Richmond, BS, 49; Univ Pa, MA, 51, PhD(psychol), 55. *Concurrent Pos:* Lectr, Univ RI, 66-, Univ Conn, 68-70 & Univ New Haven, 71- 90. *Mem:* Fel AAAS; fel Am Psychol Asn; fel Optical Soc Am; Psychonomic Soc; fel NY Acad Sci. *Res:* Vision. *Mailing Add:* 35 Beacon Hill Dr Waterford CT 06385

LURIE, ALAN GORDON, RADIATION BIOLOGY, CARCINOGENESIS. *Current Pos:* Asst prof oral radiol, 73-77, asst prof oral diag, 77, ASSOC PROF ORAL DIAG, UNIV CONN HEALTH CTR, 77- *Personal Data:* b Los Angeles, Calif, Apr 23, 46; m 69; c 2. *Educ:* Univ Calif, Los Angeles, DDS, 70; Univ Rochester, PhD(radiation biol, biophys), 74. *Honors & Awards:* E H Hatton Award, Int Asn Dent Res, 69. *Concurrent Pos:* Consult oral radiol, Newington Vet Admin Hosp, 75-; HEW/NIH grants, Am Cancer Soc, 75- *Mem:* Am Asn Cancer Res; Radiation Res Soc; Int Asn Dent Res. *Res:* Radiation pathophysiology; radiation carcinogenesis and cocarcinogenesis at low doses; chemical carcinogenesis; mechanistic roles of vascular changes during carcinogenesis. *Mailing Add:* Dept Oral Radiol Univ Conn Health Ctr 263 Farmington Ave Farmington CT 06030-1605

LURIE, ARNOLD PAUL, ORGANIC CHEMISTRY. *Current Pos:* RETIRED. *Personal Data:* b Brooklyn, NY, July 22, 32; m 54; c 3. *Educ:* NY Univ, BA, 54; Purdue Univ, PhD(org chem), 58. *Prof Exp:* Lab asst org chem, Purdue Univ, 54-56, fel, 58; res chemist, Eastman Kodak Co, 58-61, sr res chemist, 61-66, info scientist, Res Lab, 65-89, res assoc, 66-89. *Mem:* Am Chem Soc. *Res:* Synthetic and theoretical organic chemistry related to photographic systems; computerized handling of information. *Mailing Add:* 4380 Camrose Lane West Palm Beach FL 33417

LURIE, FRED MARCUS, physics, for more information see previous edition

LURIE, HAROLD, ENGINEERING. *Current Pos:* EXEC DIR, PROG TECH WORKSHOPS WITH INDUST & EMER PROF ENG SCI, CALIF INST TECHNOL, 97- *Personal Data:* b Durban, SAfrica, Mar 28, 19; nat US; div; c 2. *Educ:* Univ Natal, BSc, 40, MSc, 46; Calif Inst Technol, PhD(aeronaut), 50; Northeastern Univ, JD, 89. *Prof Exp:* Lectr aeronaut, Calif Inst Technol, 48-50; head weapons effectiveness group, Rand Corp, 50-52; from asst prof appl mech to prof eng sci & assoc dean grad studies, Calif Inst Technol, 53-71; dir res & develop, New Eng Elec Syst, 71-79; dean eng, Polytech Inst NY, 79-81 & Northeastern Univ, Boston, 81-86; dean, Northeastern Univ, Boston, 81-86; assoc dir, Ctr Law, Sci & Technol, Univ Wash, 86-91, dir, Law Technol Ctr, Sch Law, 90-91; assoc dir, Calif Coun Sci & Technol, 92-96. *Concurrent Pos:* Sr develop engr, Oak Ridge Nat Lab, 56-57; consult, Yankee Atomic Elec Co, 70-71; actg dir, Advan Systs Dept, Elec Power Res Inst, 74-75; Nat Cong Lawyers & Scientists, 92-95. *Mem:* AAAS. *Res:* Energy conversion; nuclear and aerospace engineering; structural mechanics; law and technology. *Mailing Add:* Mail Code 1-90 Calif Inst Technol Pasadena CA 91125

LURIE, JOAN B, THEORETICAL SOLID STATE PHYSICS. *Current Pos:* ADVAN SYSTS MGR, TRW, 91- *Personal Data:* b New York, NY, Jan 21, 41; m 61; c 2. *Educ:* Brooklyn Col, BS, 61; Rutgers Univ, MS, 62, PhD(physics), 67. *Prof Exp:* Mem tech staff physics res, RCA Labs, 62-66; fel appl math, Univ Col, Univ London, 67-68; syst programmer comput sci, Appl Data Res, 69-70; fel solid state physics, Rutgers Univ, 70-72; from asst prof to assoc prof physics, Rider Col, 72-81; mem res staff, IDA, NJ, 81-84; dept mgr, Hughes, 84-89; prin scientist, Mitre Corp, 89-90. *Concurrent Pos:* Am Phys Soc indust fel, Colgate Palmolive Res Lab. *Mem:* Am Phys Soc; Inst

Elec & Electronics Engrs. *Res:* Theoretical research in lattice dynamics of solid state of rare gases; computer assisted instruction, particularly in physics and mathematics; image analysis. *Mailing Add:* 727 Ninth St Hermosa Beach CA 90254

LURIE, NORMAN A(LAN), NUCLEAR PHYSICS & ENGINEERING, ELECTROOPTICS. *Current Pos:* SR SCIENTIST, SCI APPLICATIONS INT CORP, 87-, DEPT DIR MGR, 89- *Personal Data:* b Detroit, Mich, Dec 2, 40; m 67; c 2. *Educ:* Univ Mich, BSE, 63, MSE, 65, PhD(nuclear eng), 69. *Prof Exp:* Fel physics, Univ Mo-Columbia, 69-71; sr res assoc, Brandeis Univ, 71-74; sr physicist, IRT Corp, 74-75; staff physicist, 75-76, prog mgr res, Nuclear Systs Div, 78-81, prin physicist, 79-86, mgr tech pers, 81-86. *Concurrent Pos:* Res collabr, Brookhaven Nat Lab, 71-74. *Mem:* Sigma Xi. *Res:* Applied nuclear physics; electrooptics. *Mailing Add:* 10436 El Comal Dr San Diego CA 92124-1005

LURIE, ROBERT M(ANDEL), CHEMICAL ENGINEERING, COLLOIDAL CHEMISTRY. *Current Pos:* RETIRED. *Personal Data:* b Boston, Mass, Feb 24, 31; m 53; c 3. *Educ:* Mass Inst Technol, SB, 52, ScD(chem eng), 55. *Prof Exp:* Chem engr & prod res mgr, Dewey & Almy Chem Co Div, W R Grace & Co, 55-60; sr chem engr, Ionics, Inc, 60-63; mgr mat develop, Res & Adv Develop Div, Avco Corp, 63-65, dir mats, Systs Div, 65-70; pres, Nyacol Prod Inc, 70-89. *Mem:* Am Chem Soc; Am Inst Chem Engrs; Sigma Xi; AAAS. *Res:* Polymer synthesis; adhesion of polymers; unit operations of polymer manufacture and polymer fabrications; electrochemistry; fuel cells; ablation phenomena; physics of reinforced plastics; reentry vehicle design; organic dyes; colloidal chemicals. *Mailing Add:* 4 Tufts Rd Lexington MA 02173

LURIX, PAUL LESLIE, JR, INFRARED SPECTROSCOPY, DATA BASE APPLICATIONS. *Current Pos:* PRES, LURIX CORP, 82- *Personal Data:* b Bridgeport, Conn, Apr 6, 49; m 70; c 3. *Educ:* Drew Univ, BA, 71; Purdue Univ, MS, 73. *Prof Exp:* Tech dir, Analysts Inc, 76-77; chief chemist, Caleb Brett USA, Inc, 77-80; vpres, Tex Labs, Inc, 80-82. *Concurrent Pos:* Consult, 77-82; Phillips 66, 86- & Conoco, Inc, 87-; vpres, Diesel King Corp, 80-82; Compaq Comput, 96- *Mem:* Fel Am Inst Chemists; Am Chem Soc; Am Soc Testing & Mat; Soc Appl Spectros; NY Acad Sci; AAAS. *Res:* Design and implementation of multi-user information systems; studies of liquid structure through infrared spectroscopy; granted one patent. *Mailing Add:* PO Box 148 Fulshear TX 77441. *Fax:* 281-346-1607; *E-Mail:* lurix@neosoft.com

LURKIS, ALEXANDER, ENGINEERING EXPERT IN POWER & LIGHTING. *Current Pos:* pres consult engrs, 64-90, CONSULT ENGR, ALEXANDER LURKIS, PE, 91- *Personal Data:* b New York, NY, Oct 1, 08; m 30; c 1. *Educ:* Cooper Union, BSEE, 30; NY Univ, BSEE, 34; Univ State NY, Tech Teacher Cert, 36. *Honors & Awards:* Design Excellence, Fifth Biennial Am Iron & Steel Inst, 72; Design Excellence, Fifth Biennial HUD Award, 72. *Prof Exp:* Jr elec engr, New York City Bd Transp & Transit Authority, 30-40, sr elec engr, 42-58; elec engr, F R Harris, Inc, consult engrs, 40-41; chief eng, Bur Gas & Elec, New York City Dept Water, Gas & Elec, 59-64, act comm, 61. *Concurrent Pos:* Vpres, Peak Tech Asn, 51-59; arbitrator, Am Arbitration Asn, 64-; chmn, Illuminating Eng Soc Energy Comt, 74-77; secy-treas, Glimmer Security Systs, 76-81; pres, Icare Press, 81-85. *Mem:* Fel Illuminating Eng Soc; sr mem Inst Elec & Electronics Engrs; fel NY Acad Sci. *Res:* Ten utility standard US patents; 1 Canadian standard patent; 1 traffic signal US patent; 1 US patent for museum security. *Mailing Add:* 193-12 Nero Ave Jamaica NY 11423

LURYI, SERGE, PHYSICS OF SEMICONDUCTOR DEVICES. *Current Pos:* PROF & CHAIR, DEPT ELEC ENG, STATE UNIV NY, STONY BROOK, 94- *Personal Data:* b Leningrad, USSR, Oct 9, 47; Can & US citizen; m 82, Nadia Lifshitz; c Helen, Nathan & Alex. *Educ:* Univ Leningrad, USSR, dipl physics, 71; Univ Toronto, Can, MSc, 75, PhD(physics), 78. *Prof Exp:* Res engr, VNIIG, Leningrad, 71-73; fel, Univ Toronto, 78-80; mem tech staff, AT&T Bell Labs, 80-85, supvr, 85-90, distinguished mem tech staff 90-94. *Concurrent Pos:* Ed, Inst Elec & Electronic Engrs Trans Elec Devices, 86-90. *Mem:* Fel Inst Elec & Electronic Engrs; fel Am Phys Soc; fel Inst Elec & Electronics Engrs. *Res:* Physics of exploratory semiconductor devices; Inventor of new semiconductor devices & technologies. *Mailing Add:* Dept Elec Eng St Univ NY Stony Brook NY 11794-2350. *E-Mail:* sluryi@sbee.sunysb.edu

LUSAS, EDMUND W, FOOD SCIENCE, FOOD TECHNOLOGY & FEEDS PROCESSING. *Current Pos:* dir, Food Protein Res & Develop Ctr, 78-93, HEAD, FATS, OILS & EXTRUSION PROGS, TEX A&M UNIV, 93- *Personal Data:* b Woodbury, Conn, Nov 25, 31; m 57; c 3. *Educ:* Univ Conn, BS, 54; Iowa State Univ, MS, 55; Univ Wis, PhD(food technol), 58; Univ Chicago, MBA, 72. *Prof Exp:* Proj leader, Res Labs, Quaker Oats Co, 58-64, mgr canned foods res, 64-66, mgr pet foods res, 66-72, mgr sci serv, 72-77. *Mem:* Sigma Xi; Inst Food Technol; Am Chem Soc; Am Oil Chemists Soc; Am Cereal Chem Asn; Am Soc Agr Engr. *Res:* Protein and oil utilization from cottonseed, peanuts, soy, sunflower and sesame; development of processes for converting crops into food, feed and industrial ingredients; human and pet food development; research and development administration; technical staff services management. *Mailing Add:* Food Protein Res & Develop Ctr FM 183 Tex A&M Univ College Station TX 77843-2476. *Fax:* 409-845-2744; *E-Mail:* ewlusas@tamu.edu

LUSCHER, ULRICH, ARCTIC ENGINEERING, HAZARDOUS WASTE ENGINEERING. *Current Pos:* mem staff, 67-74, PRIN MEM, WOODWARD-CLYDE CONSULTS, 75- *Personal Data:* b Oftringen, Switz, July 18, 32; m 62, 83, Joanne L; c Mark E & Dan R. *Educ:* Swiss Fed Inst Technol, BS, 56; Mass Inst Technol, SM, 59, ScD(civil eng & soil mech), 63. *Prof Exp:* Designer, Vevey Metal Works, Switz, 57 & Stone & Webster Eng Corp, 58-59; res eng, Mass Inst Technol, 59-60, asst prof civil eng, 63-67. *Mem:* Am Soc Civil Engrs; Int Soc Soil Mech & Found Eng; Am Consult Engrs; Soc Am Mil Engrs. *Res:* Soil mechanics and foundation engineering; research in soil mechanics; underground structures; permafrost and arctic engineering; remediation technologies. *Mailing Add:* Woodward-Clyde Consults 500 12th St Oakland CA 94607-4014

LUSCOMBE, HERBERT ALFRED, DERMATOLOGY. *Current Pos:* Prof, 59-, EMER PROF DERMAT, JEFFERSON MED COL. *Personal Data:* b Johnstown, Pa, Aug 9, 16; m 42, Sally T McHugh; c 3. *Educ:* St Vincent Col, BSc, 36; Jefferson Med Col, MD, 40. *Honors & Awards:* Fineraud Award, Dermatol Found, 81; Luscombe lectr, Jefferson Med Col, 84- *Mem:* Sigma Xi. *Mailing Add:* 111 S 11th St Suite G4480 Philadelphia PA 19107-4824

LUSHBAUGH, CLARENCE CHANCELUM, PATHOLOGY. *Current Pos:* RETIRED. *Personal Data:* b Covington, Ky, Mar 15, 16; m 42, 63, Dorothy B Hale; c William B, Robert & Nancy E (Forbes). *Educ:* Univ Chicago, BS, 38, PhD(path), 42, MD, 48. *Prof Exp:* Asst path, Univ Chicago, 39-42, from instr to asst prof, 42-49, pathologist, Toxicity Lab, 41-49; mem staff, Los Alamos Sci Lab, Univ Calif, 49-63; chief scientist appl radiobiol, Oak Ridge Assoc Univs, 63-75, NASA Total Body Irradiation Proj, 64-75, chmn, Med & Health Sci Div, 75-83, chief, Radiation Med, 84-90, pathologist, Radiation Assistance Ctr-Training Site, 74-90. *Concurrent Pos:* Pathologist, Los Alamos Med Ctr, NMex, 49-63; mem, Path Study Sect, NIH, 61-64; mem, Radiobiol Adv Panel, Space Sci Bd, Nat Acad Sci-Nat Res Coun, 66-72; mem, Adv Comt Space Radiation Effects Lab, Col William & Mary, 68-70. *Mem:* Am Soc Exp Path; Soc Exp Biol & Med; Health Physics Soc; Radiation Res Soc; AAAS. *Res:* Pathology of obstetric shock; chemotherapy of cancer; mitotic poisons; radiation damage; diagnostic radioisotopology; human radiobiology; electronic clinical pathology; primate pathology. *Mailing Add:* RR 2 Powell TN 37849

LUSHBOUGH, CHANNING HARDEN, NUTRITION, RESOURCE MANAGEMENT. *Current Pos:* DIR, MHJ TRUST, 97- *Personal Data:* b Watertown, SDak, Aug 11, 29; m 52, Eloise H Turner; c 4. *Educ:* Univ Chicago, AB, 48, AM, 52, PhD(nutrit, biochem), 56. *Prof Exp:* Res chemist, Res Lab, Carnation Co, Wis, 50-51; assoc biochemist & actg chief, Div Biochem & Nutrit, Am Meat Inst Found, Ill, 56-59; dir prod info, Res Ctr, Mead Johnson & Co, Ind, 59-67; vpres planning & develop, Blue Cross, NY, 67-71; assoc dir, Consumers Union US, 71-73; dir & exec secy, Citizens Comn on Science, Law & Food Supply, Rockefeller Univ, 73-75; vpres qual assurance, Kraft Inc, 75-81; mkt rep, Tweedy, Browne Inc, 81-84; mkt rep, Round Hill Asset Mgt Inc, 86-94. *Concurrent Pos:* Instr grad nutrit, Ill Inst Technol, 56; lectr, Univ Chicago, 57-59 & Northwestern Univ, 58-59. *Mem:* Am Inst Nutrit; AAAS; Gt Brit Nutrit Soc; Inst Food Technologists; NY Acad Sci; Sigma Xi. *Res:* Nutritional quality of natural proteins; effects of processing on vitamin retention; relations of dietary fat, protein and carbohydrate to atherosclerosis. *Mailing Add:* 420 Elm St Glenview IL 60025-4949

LUSHER, JEANNE MARIE, BLOOD COAGULATION, PLATELET DISORDERS. *Current Pos:* DIR, DIV HEMAT & ONCOL, CHILDREN'S HOSP MICH, 74-; PROF PEDIAT, WAYNE STATE UNIV SCH MED, 74-, MARION I BARNHART HEMOSTASIS RES PROF, 88- *Personal Data:* b Toledo, Ohio, June 9, 35. *Educ:* Univ Cincinnati, BS, 56, MD, 60. *Honors & Awards:* Lawrence Weiner Award, Wayne State Univ, Sch Med, 90; Kenneth Brinkhous Award, Nat Hemophilia Found, 93. *Prof Exp:* Internship, George Washington Univ Hosp, 60-61; residency pediat, Tulane Univ Charity Hosp La, 61-64; fel hemat-oncol, Child Res Ctr Mich & Wash Univ Sch Med, 64-66. *Concurrent Pos:* Mem hemat study sect, NIH, 81-86, mem res manpower comt, 87-91; med dir, Nat Hemophilia Found, 87-94; chmn, med sci adv coun, Nat Hemmophilia Found, 94-; chmn, Int Soc Thrombosis & Hemostasis Sci & Stand Comt, 96- *Mem:* Int Soc Thrombois Hemostasis; Am Soc Hemat; Soc Pediat Res; Am Soc Pediat Hemat-Oncol. *Res:* Hemostasis and in blood product safety; studying mechanism of inhibitor antibody development against clotting factors; alternatives to use of blood products for control of bleeding, role of DDAVP formulations. *Mailing Add:* Childrens Hosp Mich 3901 Beaubien Blvd Detroit MI 48201. *Fax:* 313-745-5237

LUSIGNAN, BRUCE BURR, ELECTRICAL ENGINEERING. *Current Pos:* Instr, Stanford Univ, 62-63, res asst, 62-64, actg asst prof, 63-65, asst prof, 65-68, assoc prof elec eng, 68-, dir, Commun Satellite Planning Ctr, 70-, DIR, CTR INT COOP IN SPACE, STANFORD UNIV. *Personal Data:* b San Francisco, Calif, Dec 22, 36; m 85, Eleanor Curtin; c Jeanne, Kerry, Anne (Hausch), Coleen Curtin, Noreen Curtin & Stephanie Curtin. *Educ:* Stanford Univ, BS, 58, MS, 59, PhD(elec eng), 63. *Res:* Applications of satellite, radio and digital technology to communications; transfer of planning and manufacturing knowledge to developing countries; Mars exploration; international space exploration policy. *Mailing Add:* Commun Satellite Planning Ctr Stanford Univ Elec Eng Dept Bldg 360 Rm 361 Stanford CA 94305-4053

LUSIS, ALDONS JEKABS, MOLECULAR BIOLOGY. *Current Pos:* AT DEPT MICROBIOL, UNIV CALIF, LOS ANGELES. *Personal Data:* b Esslingen, Ger, June 22, 47; US citizen. *Educ:* Wash State Univ, BS, 69; Ore State Univ, PhD(biochem), 73. *Prof Exp:* Res assoc molecular biol, Roswell Park Mem Inst, 73-80. *Concurrent Pos:* NIH fel, 74- *Mem:* Sigma Xi. *Res:* Mechanisms controlling developmental expression of enzymes in mammals; processing of mouse lysosomal enzymes. *Mailing Add:* Dept Med UCLA Sch Med 47-123 Ctr Health Sci Los Angeles CA 90095-1679

LUSK, JOAN EDITH, BIOCHEMISTRY. *Current Pos:* asst prof, 72-77, ASSOC PROF CHEM, BROWN UNIV, 77-, ASSOC DEAN GRAD STUDIES. *Personal Data:* b Teaneck, NJ, July 29, 42. *Educ:* Radcliffe Col, BA, 64; Harvard Univ, PhD(biol chem), 70. *Prof Exp:* Nat Cystic Fibrosis Res Found fel biol, Mass Inst Technol, 70-71, NIH fel biol, 71-72. *Concurrent Pos:* Prin investr, NIH res grant, 73- & NSF grant, 74-; NIH career develop award, 76. *Mem:* Am Soc Microbiol; AAAS. *Res:* Membrane structure and function; colicin action; transport. *Mailing Add:* Assoc Dean Grad Sch Box 1867 Brown Univ Providence RI 02912

LUSK, MARK THOMAS, PHASE TRANSITION KINETICS, EVOLVING MICROSTRUCTURES. *Current Pos:* asst prof eng, 94-97, PROF MECH & MAT, COLO SCH MINES, 97- *Educ:* US Naval Acad, BS, 82; Colo State Univ, MS, 87; Calif Inst Technol, PhD(appl mech), 92. *Prof Exp:* Asst prof elec eng, Iowa State Univ, 92-94. *Concurrent Pos:* Career award, NSF, 95. *Mailing Add:* Div Eng Colo Sch Mines Golden CO 80401-1887

LUSKIN, LEO SAMUEL, organic chemistry, polymer chemistry, for more information see previous edition

LUSKIN, MITCHELL B, NUMERICAL ANALYSIS, PARTIAL DIFFERENTIAL EQUATIONS. *Current Pos:* from asst prof to prof, 81-89, PROF MATH, UNIV MINN, 90- *Personal Data:* b Pasadena, Calif, Nov 13, 51; m 76, Barbara Roth; c Jonathan, Marlise & Benjamin. *Educ:* Yale Univ, BS, 73; Univ Chicago, MS, 74, PhD(math), 77. *Honors & Awards:* Presidential Young Investr Award, 84. *Prof Exp:* Hildebrandt asst prof math, Univ Mich, 77-79, asst prof, 79-81; prof appl math, Calif Inst Technol, 89-90. *Concurrent Pos:* Vis prof, Ecole Polytechnique Federale, Lausanne, Switz, 80; vis mem, Courant Inst, NY Univ, 80-81; ed, Soc Indust & Appl Math J Numerical Anal, 82-90, 96- ed-in-chief, 90-95; fel, Minn Supercomputer Inst, 85-, mem grad fac, Dept Aerospace Eng & Mech, 87-; ed, Dynamics & Differential Equations, 88-, J Comp Physics, 97- *Mem:* Am Math Soc; Soc Indust & Appl Math. *Res:* Scientific computing; numerical analysis; applied mathematics; partial differential equations; computational mechanics. *Mailing Add:* Sch Math Univ Minn 206 Church St SE Minneapolis MN 55455. *Fax:* 612-626-2017; *E-Mail:* luskin@math.umn.edu

LUSS, DAN, CHEMICAL REACTION ENGINEERING. *Current Pos:* from asst prof to assoc prof, 67-72, chmn dept, 75-85, PROF CHEM ENG, UNIV HOUSTON, 72- *Personal Data:* b Tel Aviv, Israel, May 5, 38; m 66, Amalia Rubin; c Noya & Limor. *Educ:* Israel Inst Technol, BSc, 60, MSc, 63; Univ Minn, Minneapolis, PhD(chem eng), 66. *Honors & Awards:* Honor Scroll, Indust & Eng Div, Am Chem Soc, 68; A P Colburn Award, 72; Prof Progress Award, Am Inst Chem Engrs, 78 & Wilhelm Award, 86. *Prof Exp:* Asst prof chem eng, Univ Minn, 66-67. *Concurrent Pos:* Dir, Am Inst Chem Engrs, 86-88. *Mem:* Nat Acad Eng; Am Chem Soc; fel Am Inst Chem Engrs. *Res:* Dynamics of chemical reactors; diffusional effects in catalysts; lumping of complex reactions networks; synthesis of superconducting ceramics. *Mailing Add:* Dept Chem Eng Univ Houston Houston TX 77204-4792

LUSSIER, ANDRE (JOSEPH ALFRED), INTERNAL MEDICINE, RHEUMATOLOGY. *Current Pos:* dir, Rheumatic Dis Unit, Univ Sherbrooke, 69-84, assoc prof med, 69-75, dir, Clin Res Ctr, 80-84, PROF MED, UNIV SHERBROOKE & UNIV HOSP CTR, 75- *Personal Data:* b Sherbrooke, Que, May 27, 33; m 61; c 3. *Educ:* Univ Montreal, BA, 54, MD, 59; Col Med, Que, cert internal med, 64 & cert rheumatology, 70; Royal Col Physicians & Surgeons, cert internal med, 65; FCRCP(C), 72. *Honors & Awards:* Basic Res Prize, Asn Fr Lang Physicians Can. *Prof Exp:* Assoc clin res, Can Arthritis Soc, 69-79. *Concurrent Pos:* Mem, Med Res Coun Can, 88- *Mem:* Am Rheumatism Asn; Royal Col Med; Can Rheumatism Asn (secy, 81-84 & vpres, 84-86, pres, 86-88); Pan Am League Against Rheumatism (vpres, 82-86); Can Soc Clin Invest; hon mem Fr Soc Rheumatology. *Res:* Etiopathogenesis and pathological ossification of the spine; mechanism of microcrystal arthritides; normalization of terminology used in semiology of musculoskeletal system; efficacy and toxicity of non steroidal antiinflammatory drugs, especially of the consecutive gastro-intestinal microbleeding; hyperostotic disease: basic and clin research (pathogenesis). *Mailing Add:* Dept Med Rheumatol Univ Sherbrooke Fac Med Sherbrooke PQ J1H 5N4 Can

LUSSIER, GILLES L, veterinary pathology, virology, for more information see previous edition

LUSSIER, ROGER JEAN, SYNTHETIC INORGANIC & ORGANOMETALLIC CHEMISTRY. *Current Pos:* res chemist, 70-80, sr res chemist, 80-82, res assoc, 81-84, ENG SPECIALIST, DAVISON DIV, W R GRACE & CO, 85- *Personal Data:* b Newport, RI, Apr 29, 43; m 66; c 2. *Educ:* Univ Mass, Amherst, BS, 65; Brown Univ, PhD(inorg chem), 69; Johns Hopkins Univ, MA, 75. *Prof Exp:* NSF grant, Cath Univ Am, 69-70. *Res:* Heterogeneous catalysis; reaction mechanisms; homogeneous catalysis; transition metal chemistry; surface chemistry; mineral synthesis and chemistry; zeolite synthesis and characterization. *Mailing Add:* 4018 Jay Em Circle Ellicott City MD 21042

LUSSKIN, ROBERT MILLER, ORGANIC CHEMISTRY. *Current Pos:* RETIRED. *Personal Data:* b Dec 14, 21; m 47; c 2. *Educ:* Harvard Univ, AB, 43; NY Univ, MS, 46, PhD(chem), 50. *Prof Exp:* Chemist, Spencer Kellogg & Sons, 43 & Grosvenor Labs, 45-46; with Trubek Labs, 47-55, res dir, 56-60; dir chem res, UOP Chem Co, Universal Oil Prod Co, 60-67; supt nonwoven lab, Kimberly-Clark Corp, Wis, 67-68, mgr basic & explor res, 68-72, mgr new concepts res, 72-75; tech dir, Resource Planning Assocs, 75-77; dir tech serv, Raltech Sci Serv, 77-82; dir, Cent Res & Develop, Ralston Purina Co, 82-86; adj prof chem, Univ Mo, St Louis, 87. *Mem:* AAAS; Am Chem Soc. *Res:* Business strategy development; consumer new products; polymer and fiber research; chemical intermediates; energy and materials management; analytical and environmental chemistry management. *Mailing Add:* 12856 Hawthicket Lane Des Peres MO 63131

LUSTBADER, EDWARD DAVID, biostatistics; deceased, see previous edition for last biography

LUSTED, LEE BROWNING, RADIOLOGY. *Current Pos:* RETIRED. *Personal Data:* b Mason City, Iowa, May 22, 22; m 43; c 2. *Educ:* Cornell Col, BA, 43; Harvard Med Sch, MD, 50; Am Bd Radiol, dipl. *Hon Degrees:* DSc, Cornell Col, 63. *Prof Exp:* Spec res assoc, Radio Res Lab, Harvard Univ, 43-46; from instr to asst prof radiol, Med Sch, Univ Calif, San Francisco, 55-57; asst radiologist, NIH, 57-58; from asst prof to assoc prof radiol, Sch Med, Univ Rochester, 58-60, prof biomed eng, 60-62; prof radiol, Med Sch, Univ Ore & sr scientist, Ore Primate Res Ctr, 62-68; prof radiol & chmn dept, Stritch Sch Med, Loyola Univ Chicago, 68-69; prof radiol & vchmn dept, Univ Chicago, 69-78; radiologist, Southern Calif Permanente Med Group, 78-89. *Concurrent Pos:* Chmn, Comt Comput Biol & Med, Nat Acad Sci-Nat Res Coun, 58-59; consult, Strong Mem Hosp, 58-62; chmn, Adv Comt Comput Res, NIH, 60-64; assoc dean prof affairs & chief of staff, Loyola Univ Hosp, Chicago, 68-69; clin prof radiol, Univ Calif, San Diego, 78-; ed-in-chief, Int J Med Decision Making, 78-85; adj distinguished clin mem, Scripps Clin & Res Found, La Jolla, 78- *Mem:* Fel AAAS; fel Am Col Radiol; fel Inst Elec & Electronics Engrs; Roentgen Ray Soc; Radiol Soc NAm; fel Am Col Med Informatics. *Res:* Study of medical decision making; application of signal detection theory to assess system and observer performance in radiographic diagnosis. *Mailing Add:* 323 Concord Dr Menlo Park CA 94025

LUSTER, MICHAEL I, IMMUNOTOXICOLOGY. *Current Pos:* GROUP LEADER, IMMUNOTOXICOL GROUP, NAT INST ENVIRON HEALTH, NIH, 76- *Personal Data:* b Malden, Mass, Sept 18, 47. *Educ:* Loyola Univ, PhD(microbiol & immunol), 74. *Mem:* Soc Toxicol; Am Asn Immunol; Int Soc Immunopharmacol. *Mailing Add:* NIOSH 1095 Willowdale Rd Morgantown WV 26505. *Fax:* 919-541-0870, 541-4704

LUSTGARTEN, RONALD KRISSES, SOLVOLYSIS, PATENTS. *Current Pos:* RES/STAFF SCIENTIST, UPJOHN CO, 72- *Personal Data:* b New York, NY, Feb 24, 42. *Educ:* Columbia Univ, AB, 62; Pa State Univ, PhD(chem), 66. *Prof Exp:* NIH fel, Univ Calif, Los Angeles, 66-68; res assoc & Mellon fel chem, Carnegie-Mellon Univ, 68-72. *Concurrent Pos:* NSF fel, 65; secy, Am Chem Soc, Kalamazoo Sect, 83-85. *Mem:* AAAS; Am Chem Soc; Fedn Am Scientists; Sigma Xi. *Res:* Organic mechanisms; reactive intermediates; kinetics. *Mailing Add:* 11 Kim Hunter Rd Englewood Cliffs NJ 07632

LUSTICK, SHELDON IRVING, ENVIRONMENTAL PHYSIOLOGY, VERTEBRATE ZOOLOGY. *Current Pos:* From asst prof to prof, 68-91, DIR, ENVIRON BIOL GRAD PROG, OHIO STATE UNIV, 77-, EMER PROF ZOOL, 91- *Personal Data:* b Syracuse, NY, Aug 16, 34; m 70; c Danielle & Erica. *Educ:* San Fernando Valley State Col, BA, 63; Syracuse Univ, MS, 65; Univ Calif, Los Angeles, PhD(zool), 68. *Concurrent Pos:* Dept Interior res grant, 69-72 & 73-75, NSF grant, 76-78 & 80-83 & Air Force Off Sci Res grant, 78-80. *Mem:* AAAS; Cooper Ornith Soc; Am Ornith Soc; Ecol Soc Am; Sigma Xi. *Res:* How animals adapt physiologically to environmental stress. *Mailing Add:* 6939 Riverside Dr Powell OH 43065

LUSTIG, BERNARD, BIOCHEMISTRY, BIOCHEMISTRY OF CANCER. *Current Pos:* RETIRED. *Personal Data:* b Kolomea, Austria, Dec 21, 02; nat US; m 38; c Naomi R (Wrong) & Dinah S. *Educ:* Univ Vienna, PhD(chem), 25. *Honors & Awards:* Prize, Asn Chocolate Mfrs, 30. *Prof Exp:* Chemist, Rudolf Hosp, Vienna, 26-32; chief biochemist, Pearson Cancer Found, 33-38 & West London Hosp, 38-40; biochemist, Lawrence R Bruce Inc, 40-44, dir res, 45-58; vpres in-chg res, Clairol Inc, 58-68, vpres & dir basic res, 68-70. *Mem:* Fel AAAS; Am Chem Soc; Soc Exp Biol & Med; fel Textile Inst Eng; fel NY Acad Sci; Biochem Soc Eng. *Res:* Chemistry and biochemistry of proteins and lipids; biochemistry of cancer; chemistry and technology of keratin fibers; author of over 100 publications & patents. *Mailing Add:* 38 Chester St Stamford CT 06905-3944

LUSTIG, HARRY, SOLAR ENERGY. *Current Pos:* RETIRED. *Personal Data:* b Vienna, Austria, Sept 23, 25; nat US; m 80, Rosalind Wells; c Lawrence J. *Educ:* City Col N Y, BS, 48; Univ Ill, MS, 49, PhD(physics), 53. *Prof Exp:* Asst physics, Univ Ill, 49-53; from instr to prof, City Col NY, 53-86, chmn dept, 65-70, exec officer PhD prog physics, 68-70, assoc dean sci, 72-75, dean, Col Lib Art, 73-74, dean sci, 75-82, provost & vpres acad affairs, 82-85, resident prof physics, 86-93. *Concurrent Pos:* Prin scientist, Nuclear Develop Corp Am, 56-61; vis res asst prof, Univ Ill, 59-60; fel, Colo Inst Theoret Physics, 60; Fulbright lectr, Univ Dublin, 64-65; vis prof, Univ Colo, 66 & Univ Wash, 67 & 69; sr officer, UNESCO, Paris, 70-72; consult, UNESCO, Paris, 72-75 & 79, US Int Commun Agency, 78, Univ SDak, 80, Univ SFla, 81, Univ Mass, 83, NJ State Dept Higher Educ, 83-; educ adv comt, NY Acad Sci, 82-84; mem, gov bd, NY Acad Sci, 82-84, Am Inst Physics, 85-97; mem, US Nat Comt, Int Union Pure & Appl Physics, 88-94. *Mem:* Fel Am Phys Soc (treas, 85-96); AAAS; fel NY Acad Sci (vpres, 84); Sigma Xi; Am Asn Physics Teachers; Am Asn Univ Prof. *Res:* Theoretical nuclear physics; Mossbauer effect; solar energy; science education; economics of scientific publishing. *Mailing Add:* 304 Chula Vista St Santa Fe NM 57801. *E-Mail:* eustig@earthlink.net

LUSTIG, HOWARD E(RIC), ELECTRONICS, SYSTEMS ENGINEERING. *Current Pos:* prog mgr, 76-80, VPRES, MGT INFO SYSTS TELEPHONICS CORP, 80- *Personal Data:* b Vienna, Austria, Oct 23, 25; US citizen; m 50; c 3. *Educ:* Columbia Univ, BS, 49, MSEE, 51, EE, 56. *Prof Exp:* Instr electronics, Sch Eng, Cooper Union, 49-51; proj supvr electronic eng, Ford Instrument Co, Sperry Rand Corp, 51-59; prod area mgr eng mgt, Radio Receptor Div, Gen Instrument Corp, 59-67; corp dir eng, Superior Mfg & Instrument Corp, 67-70; vpres eng, Am Comput Commun Co, Inc, 70-71 & Phonplex Corp, 71-74; asst vpres, Citibank, 74-76. *Mem:* Sr mem Inst Elec & Electronics Engrs; Am Soc Photogram; Marine Technol Soc. *Res:* Military reconnaissance systems; digital interface and processing systems; oceanographic sensors; engineering management. *Mailing Add:* 196-35 53rd Ave Flushing NY 11365

LUSTIG, MAX, INORGANIC CHEMISTRY, AIR POLLUTION. *Current Pos:* RETIRED. *Personal Data:* b Chicago, Ill, Apr 9, 32; m 54; c 1. *Educ:* Univ Calif, Los Angeles, BS, 57; Univ Wash, PhD(inorg chem), 62. *Prof Exp:* Chemist, Olin Mathieson Chem Corp, 57-58; res chemist, Redstone Arsenal Res Div, Rohm and Haas Co, Ala, 62-68; asst prof chem, Memphis State Univ, 68-73; res chemist, IIT Res Inst, 73-78, consult environ effects & chem hazards, 78-80; consult, 80-85. *Concurrent Pos:* Eve instr, Univ Ala, 63-68. *Mem:* Am Chem Soc; fel Am Inst Chemists. *Res:* Physical and chemical studies of boron hydrides; chemistry of non-metal compounds with oxygen and fluorine, especially peroxides and hypofluorites; free radical chemistry; organometallic compounds; air pollution studies; high vacuum techniques; reaction kinetics involving air pollutants in the troposphere and stratosphere. *Mailing Add:* 8303 Steven Lane West Hills CA 91304

LUSTIG, STANLEY, RESEARCH ADMINISTRATION, PLASTICS ENGINEERING. *Current Pos:* res & develop mgr, 86-90, DIR, RES & DEVELOP, VISKASE CORP, 90- *Personal Data:* b Brooklyn, NY, Feb 23, 33; m 60, Delores Goldberg; c Rochelle & Mark. *Educ:* Univ Toledo, BS, 58. *Prof Exp:* Chemist, Save Elec Corp, 58-59; res chemist, Union Carbide Corp 59-65, res proj leader, 65-70, group leader, 70-74, tech mgr, Films-Packaging Div, 74-86. *Mem:* Am Chem Soc; Soc Plastics Engrs; Inst Packaging. *Res:* Plastic packaging films design and development. *Mailing Add:* 561 Lakewood Blvd Park Forest IL 60466

LUSTMAN, BENJAMIN, METALLURGY, NUCLEAR MATERIALS. *Current Pos:* RETIRED. *Personal Data:* b Pittsburgh, Pa, Oct 31, 14; m 46; c 3. *Educ:* Carnegie-Mellon Univ, BS, 36, MS, 38, DSc(metall), 40. *Honors & Awards:* Order of Merit, Westinghouse Elec Corp, 56; Achievement Award, Am Nuclear Soc, 68; Kroll Mem Award, Colo Sch Mines, 78. *Prof Exp:* Metallurgist, Stand Steel Spring Co, 39-41, Metals Res Lab, 41-43 & Int Minerals & Chem Corp, 43-44; metallurgist res lab, Bettis Atomic Power Lab, Westinghouse Corp, 44-49, metallurgist, 49-79. *Mem:* Nat Acad Eng; Am Soc Metals; Am Nuclear Soc; Am Inst Mining Engrs. *Res:* Metallic corrosion; surface reactions; nuclear metallurgy; fuel element development. *Mailing Add:* 4601 Fifth Ave Apt 124 Pittsburgh PA 15213-3650

LUSTY, CAROL JEAN, MOLECULAR GENETICS. *Current Pos:* Assoc, Pub Health Res Inst, 68-78, assoc mem, Dept Biochem, 78-81, Dept Molecular Genetics, 81-86, MEM, DEPT MOLECULAR GENETICS, PUB HEALTH RES INST, 86- *Personal Data:* b Chicago, Ill, Sept 25, 36. *Educ:* Univ Mich, BS, 58; Wayne State Univ, PhD(biochem), 63. *Concurrent Pos:* Prin investr, PIR, 74-, mem, Nat Adv Comt, 85-88, mem, Phys Biochem Study Sect, 90-94. *Mem:* Am Chem Soc; Am Soc Biol Chemists; AAAS; NY Acad Sci; Harvey Soc. *Res:* Structure and evolution of carbamyl phosphate synthetases; regulatory mechanisms of mammalian arginine biosynthesis; protein structure and function. *Mailing Add:* Pub Health Res Inst 455 First Ave New York NY 10016-9102. *Fax:* 212-578-0804; *E-Mail:* lusty@phri.nyu.edu

LUSZTIG, GEORGE, THEORY OF GROUP REPRESENTATIONS. *Current Pos:* PROF MATH, MASS INST TECHNOL, 78- *Personal Data:* b May 20, 46; nat US citizen; m 72, Michal Abraham; c Irene & Tamar. *Educ:* Princeton Univ, MA, 71, PhD(math), 71. *Honors & Awards:* Cole Prize, Am Math Soc, 85. *Prof Exp:* From res fel to prof math, Univ Warwick, UK, 71-77. *Concurrent Pos:* Mem, Inst Advan Study, Princeton, NJ, 69-71. *Mem:* Nat Acad Sci; London Math Soc; Fel Royal Soc; Am Math Soc; fel Am Acad Arts & Sci. *Mailing Add:* Dept Math, MIT Rm 2-276 77 Massachusetts Ave Cambridge MA 02139

LUTCHEN, KENNETH R, BIOMEDICAL ENGINEERING. *Current Pos:* Asst prof, 85-91, ASSOC PROF BIOMED ENG, BOSTON UNIV, 91-, ASSOC CHMN DEPT, 93- *Personal Data:* b New York, NY, 1955. *Educ:* Univ Va, BS, 77; Case Western Res Univ, MS, 80, PhD(biomed eng), 83. *Mem:* Sr mem Biomed Eng Soc. *Mailing Add:* Biomed Eng Dept Boston Univ 44 Cummington St Boston MA 02215

LUTES, CHARLENE MCCLANAHAN, GENETICS, DEVELOPMENTAL BIOLOGY. *Current Pos:* From instr to prof, Radford Col, 64-80, chmn, Dept Biol, 81-87, dean, Col Arts & Sci, 87-91, PROF BIOL, RADFORD UNIV, 80- *Personal Data:* b Grundy, Va, Feb 4, 38; div. *Educ:* Radford Col, BS, 59; Ohio State Univ, MSc, 62, PhD(genetics), 68. *Mem:* Nat Asn Biol Teachers; Soc Col Sci Teaching; Am Inst Biol Sci. *Res:* Developmental genetics of wing venation patterns in Drosophila melanogaster. *Mailing Add:* Radford Univ Box 6931 Radford VA 24142-6931. *E-Mail:* clutes@qmail.biology.runet.edu

LUTES, DALLAS D, PLANT PATHOLOGY. *Current Pos:* RETIRED. *Personal Data:* b St Louis, Mo, July 12, 25; m 45; c 2. *Educ:* La Polytech Inst, BS, 49; Univ Mo, PhD(bot), 54. *Prof Exp:* Instr bot, ETex State Col, 54-55; from assoc prof to prof, La Tech Univ, 55-74, head dept, 63-73, prof bot & bact, 74-90. *Mem:* AAAS. *Res:* Disease resistance by breeding; virus transmission; seed germination affected by light; mistletoe seed germination; fern taxonomy and distribution. *Mailing Add:* Box 3052 Tech Sta Ruston LA 71272

LUTES, LOREN DANIEL, ENGINEERING MECHANICS. *Current Pos:* PROF CIVIL ENG, TEX A&M UNIV, 88- *Personal Data:* b Stapleton, Nebr, Dec 1, 39; m 82; c 4. *Educ:* Univ Nebr, BSc, 60, MSc, 61; Calif Inst Technol, PhD(appl mech), 67. *Honors & Awards:* Wason Res Medal, Am Concrete Inst, 64; State-of-the-Art Award, Am Soc Civil Engrs, 83. *Prof Exp:* Res engr, Jet Propulsion Lab, 67; from asst prof to prof & chair civil eng, Rice Univ, 67-87. *Concurrent Pos:* Vis prof, Univ Chile, 71; vis assoc prof civil eng, Univ Waterloo, 74-75; prof & head civil eng, Auburn Univ, 87 & 92-93. *Mem:* Am Soc Civil Engrs; Int Asn Struct Safety & Reliability; Soc Eng Sci; Am Asn Wind Eng. *Res:* Response of linear and nonlinear systems to random excitations; first-passage probabilities for stochastic processes; fatigue damage caused by stochastic loadings. *Mailing Add:* Dept Civil Eng Tex A&M Univ College Station TX 77843-3136

LUTEYN, JAMES LEONARD, SYSTEMATIC BOTANY. *Current Pos:* Assoc cur, 75-81, SR CUR BOT, NEW YORK BOT GARDENS, 81- *Personal Data:* b Kalamazoo, Mich, June 23, 48. *Educ:* Western Mich Univ, BA, 70; Duke Univ, MA, 72, PhD(bot), 75. *Concurrent Pos:* Assoc ed, BRITTONIA, 76-81; ed, Proceedings Int Rhododendron Conf, 78; assoc ed, Flora Neotropica 80-83, co-ed, 84- *Mem:* Am Soc Plant Taxonomists; Int Asn Plant Taxon; Bot Soc Am. *Res:* Evolution and systematics of the neotropical Ericaceae, Plumbaginaceae, and Companulaceae-Lobelioideae. *Mailing Add:* 777 N Macquesten Pkwy No 608 Mt Vernon NY 10552

LUTH, VERA G, ELEMENTARY PARTICLE PHYSICS. *Current Pos:* SCIENTIST, DEPT PHYSICS RES CTR, STANFORD UNIV, 74- *Personal Data:* b Ger, Dec 15, 43; m 77, Karl L Brown. *Educ:* Univ Heidelberg, MS, 69, PhD(physics), 74. *Concurrent Pos:* SSC Lab, 92-94. *Mem:* Am Phys Soc; Europ Phys Soc. *Res:* Experiments on CP violation in K and B decay weak interactions of heavy flavor particles; E plus E minus annihilation. *Mailing Add:* SLAC Stanford Univ PO Box 4349 Stanford CA 94305

LUTH, WILLIAM CLAIR, GEOLOGY, GEOCHEMISTRY. *Current Pos:* ADJ PROF, DEPT GEOL, ARIZ STATE UNIV, TEMPE, 96- *Personal Data:* b Winterset, Iowa, June 28, 34; m 53, Betty L Heubrock; c Linda D, Robert W & Sharon J. *Educ:* Univ Iowa, BA, 58, MS, 60; Pa State Univ, PhD(geochem), 63. *Prof Exp:* Res assoc geochem, Pa State Univ, 63-65; asst prof, Mass Inst Technol, 65-68; from assoc prof to prof geol, Stanford Univ, 68-79; supvr, Geophys Res Div, Sandia Nat Labs, 79-82, mgr, geosci dept, 82-89, mgr, environ technol dept, 89-90; mgr, Geosci Res Prog, US Dept Energy, 90-95, dir, Eng & Geosci Div, 95-96. *Concurrent Pos:* Alfred P Sloan Found res fel, Mass Inst Technol, 66-67; geoscientist, Off Basic Energy Sci, Dept Energy, Washington, DC, 76-78; vis staff mem, Los Alamos Nat Lab, 78. *Mem:* Am Geophys Union; Geol Soc Am; Mineral Soc Am; Geochem Soc; Sigma Xi. *Res:* Experimental petrology; physical chemistry of the igneous and metamorphic rocks; phase equilibria in silicate-volatile systems at high pressure and temperature; disposal radioactive wastes. *Mailing Add:* 3562 E June St Mesa AZ 85205. *E-Mail:* bluth@xroads.com

LUTHER, EDWARD TURNER, GEOLOGY. *Current Pos:* From geologist to chief geologist, 51-77, ASST STATE GEOLOGIST, TENN DIV GEOL, 67- *Personal Data:* b Nashville, Tenn, Feb 11, 28; m 55; c 2. *Educ:* Vanderbilt Univ, BA, 50, MS, 51. *Concurrent Pos:* Instr, Univ Tenn, Nashville, 55-57 & 76-78; fuels engr, Tenn Valley Authority, 57. *Mem:* Fel Geol Soc Am; Sigma Xi. *Res:* Areal and economic geology of various areas in Tennessee, particularly the stratigraphy and structural geology of the Cumberland Plateau; coal resources, particularly in Eastern United States. *Mailing Add:* 838 Summerly Dr Nashville TN 37209

LUTHER, GEORGE WILLIAM, III, INORGANIC & MARINE CHEMISTRY. *Current Pos:* assoc dean, Col Marine Studies, 86-88, PROF MARINE CHEM, UNIV DEL, 86- *Personal Data:* b Philadelphia, Pa, Feb 17, 47; m 71; c 2. *Educ:* LaSalle Col, BA, 68; Univ Pittsburgh, PhD(chem), 72. *Prof Exp:* From asst prof to prof chem, Kean Col, NJ, 72-86 & chmn, dept physics, 76-84. *Concurrent Pos:* Investr, Nat Oceanic & Atmospheric Admin grant, 76-80, Investr, NSF, 83-; chmn, North Jersey Am Chem Soc. *Mem:* Am Chem Soc; AAAS; Microbeam Analysis Soc; Sigma Xi; Am Geophys Union; Am Soc Limnol & Oceanog. *Res:* Sulphur, iodine, metal speriation in seawater and sediments; mineral dissolution and formation; x-ray microanalysis of particulates; chemical oceanography-ocean, estuaries and anoxic basins. *Mailing Add:* Col Marine Studies Univ Del Lewes DE 19958

LUTHER, HERBERT GEORGE, BIOENGINEERING & BIOMEDICAL ENGINEERING. *Current Pos:* PRES, LUTHER ASSOCS INC, 69-74 & 82- *Personal Data:* b Brooklyn, NY, Oct 1, 14; m 38; c 4. *Educ:* Cooper Union, New York, BChE, 40; NY Univ, MS, 44; Polytech Inst Brooklyn, DChE, 57. *Prof Exp:* Dir biochem labs, 41-44; asst dir tech serv, Chas Pfizer & Co, 45-52, dir agr res & develop, 52-59, sci dir agr, 59-69; dir animal health res, Hoffman-La-Roche Inc, Nutley, NJ, 74-82. *Concurrent Pos:* Expert, Comn Food Additives, WHO/Food Agr Orgn; consult res & develop. *Mem:* Am Chem Soc; Am Inst Chem Engrs; Am Asn Animal Sci; Poultry Sci Asn; Am Inst Chemists; Am Asn Agr Eng; Asn Consult Chemists & Chem Engrs; Am Asn Indust Vet; Inst Food Technol; NY Acad Sci; Math Asn Am; Animal Nutrit Res Coun; Sigma Xi; Int Union Pure & Appl Chem; AAAS. *Res:* Antibiotics; antibacterials; vitamins; steroids; tranquilizers; unidentified growth factors; enzymes; antioxidants; nutrition; animal health; pharmacokinetics; operations research; food and feed technology; bioengineering; biotechnology; agricultural engineering; clearance and approval of drugs through Food and Drug Administration and other regulatory agencies. *Mailing Add:* The Mill Head of the River Smithtown NY 11787-2699

LUTHER, HOLGER MARTIN, MASS SPECTROMETRY, ELECTRON OPTICS. *Current Pos:* staff mem, 80-87, CHIEF SCIENTIST, SENSOR SYSTS GROUP, C S DRAPER LABS, 87- *Personal Data:* b Gdynia, Poland, Feb 4, 40; US citizen; m 69. *Educ:* Marietta Col, BScL, 63; Pa State Univ, MS, 66, PhD(physics), 70. *Prof Exp:* Sr res physicist, CBS Labs, 69-75, EPSCO Labs, 75-76 & Electron Sci & Tech Ctr, Div Carson Alexiou Corp, 76-77; staff mem, Avco Everett Corp, 77-80. *Concurrent Pos:* Fac mem, Bridgeport Eng Inst, 71-77. *Mem:* Soc Photo-Optical Instumentation Engrs. *Res:* Electron-optical and elctro-optical instrumentation; compact radio frequency mass spectrometers; electron beam recorders and storage tubes; high speed tracking cameras for charged particle beams and ultra high resolution angle sensors. *Mailing Add:* 294 Perkins Row Topsfield MA 01983

LUTHER, LESTER CHARLES, INDUSTRIAL ENGINEERING. *Current Pos:* RETIRED. *Personal Data:* b Joliet, Ill, Apr 19, 31; m 54; c 4. *Educ:* Univ Ill, Urbana, BS, 53 & 58; Univ Nebr, Lincoln, MS, 60; Ariz State Univ, PhD(indust eng), 68. *Prof Exp:* Instr mech eng, Univ Nebr, 58-61; indust engr, Reynolds Metals Co, Ariz, 61-62; qual assurance engr, Motorola, Inc, 62-68; from assoc prof to prof, Calif State Univ, Sacramento, 68-86. *Concurrent Pos:* Indust engr, Cushman Motor Works, Nebr, 59-61 & McClellan AFB, Calif, 69-70; NSF fel, Sacramento State Col, 71-72. *Mem:* Am Inst Indust Engr; Am Soc Eng Educ. *Res:* Economic interactions between quality assurance and inventory control. *Mailing Add:* 3516 Chelsea Rd Shingle Springs CA 95682

LUTHER, LONNIE W, REGULATORY POLICY DEVELOPMENT FOR NEW ANIMAL DRUG PRODUCTS, QUALITY CONTROL OF NEW ANIMAL DRUG APPROVAL PROCESS. *Current Pos:* chief, Swine & Poultry Drugs Br, 86-89, CHIEF, GENETIC ANIMAL DRUG & QUAL CONTROL STAFF, CTR VET MED, 89- *Personal Data:* b Fayetteville, Ark, Apr 16, 45; m 70, Mina M Weyl; c Lonette W, Margaret A, Londell W & Marla W. *Educ:* Univ Ark, BS, MS; Tex A&M Univ, PhD(poultry nutrit). *Prof Exp:* Mgr, Turkey Exp Sta, Univ Ark, 69-71; grad res asst, Tex A&M Univ, 71-74; sci reviewer, Bur Vet Med, 74-76, chief, Poultry Drug Br, 76-86. *Mem:* Poultry Sci Asn; Am Registry Prof Animal Scientists. *Mailing Add:* 28711 Clarksburg Rd Demascus MD 20872. *Fax:* 301-594-2297

LUTHER, NORMAN Y, MATHEMATICAL DEMOGRAPHY. *Current Pos:* PROF MATH, HAWAII PAC COL, 87- *Personal Data:* b Palo Alto, Calif, June 3, 36; m 58, Rosalind Goforth; c Gregory, Gordon, Melissa & Marnie. *Educ:* Stanford Univ, BS, 58; Univ Iowa, MS, 60, PhD(math), 63. *Prof Exp:* Instr math, Univ Iowa, 63; NSF fel, 63-64; from asst prof to assoc prof math, Wash State Univ, 64-87. *Concurrent Pos:* Assoc prof, Albany State Col, Ga, 71-72; mem staff, East-West Ctr, 78-; vis assoc prof, Univ Hawaii, 82-83; Danforth Assoc, 72- *Mem:* Am Math Soc; Math Asn Am; Pop Asn Am. *Res:* Probability and statistics; measure theory; mathematical demography. *Mailing Add:* 1188 Fr St Mall Rm 242 Hawaii Pac Univ Honolulu HI 96813-2713. *Fax:* 808-944-7490

LUTHERER, LORENZ O, PHYSIOLOGY, INTERNAL MEDICINE. *Current Pos:* from asst prof to assoc prof, Dept Physiol, 72-86, asst prof, Dept Internal Med, 81-86, PROF, DEPT PHYSIOL & DEPT INTERNAL MED, HEALTH SCI CTR, SCH MED, TEX TECH UNIV, LUBBOCK, 86- *Personal Data:* b Cleveland, Ohio, Jan 20, 36; m. *Educ:* Haverford Col, AB, 58; Univ Iowa, MS, 64; Univ Fla, PhD(physiol), 69; Tex Tech Univ, MD, 77. *Prof Exp:* Grad res asst, Col Med, Univ Iowa, Iowa City, 61-62, grad teaching asst, 62-63; NIH trainee fel, 63-64; res physiologist, US Army Res Inst Environ Med, Natick, Mass, 64-65; NIH trainee fel, Col Med, Univ Fla, Gainesville, 66-69, postdoctoral fel, Dept Physiol, 69-71, Div Genetics, Endocrinol & Med, 71-72. *Concurrent Pos:* Res assoc, Arctic Inst NAm, Point Barrow, Alaska, 61; mem, bd dirs, Lubbock Chap, Tex Affil, Am Heart Asn, 75-79, 85-88, Prof Educ Comt, 75-76, Hypertension Screening Comt, 76-77, chmn, Prog Comt, 78 & 91, Hypertension Task Force, 85-87; coordr curric, Health Sci Ctr, Sch Med, Tex Tech Univ, Lubbock, 78-79, asst dean curric, 79-81, coordr, Grad Prog, Dept Physiol, 82-86, chmn, Instnl Animal Care & Use Comt, 85-89; mem, Radiation Safety Comt, Health Sci Ctr, Sch Med, Tex Tech Univ, 81-; secy & mem bd sci dirs, Tex Soc Biomed Res, 89- *Mem:* Am Physiol Soc; Shock Soc. *Res:* Author of various publications. *Mailing Add:* Physiol & Internal Med Dept-Sch Med Tex Tech Univ Health Sci Ctr Lubbock TX 79409

LUTHEY, JOE LEE, SPACE PHYSICS. *Current Pos:* resident res assoc space physics, Calif Inst Technol, 73-75, consult radiation physics, 75-77, mem tech staff, New Earth Probe, Jet Propulsion Lab, 77-93, MARKET ANALYSIS, COMPUT CONSULT, CALIF INST TECHNOL, 93- *Personal Data:* b Winslow, Ariz, Sept 21, 43. *Educ:* Univ Calif, Berkeley, AB, 65; Univ Kans, Lawrence, PhD(physics), 70. *Prof Exp:* Res assoc space physics, Univ Iowa, Iowa City, 70-73. *Concurrent Pos:* Consult, Physics Dept, Univ Iowa, 73-74; resident res assoc, Nat Res Coun, Jet Propulsion Lab, 73-75. *Mem:* Am Geophys Union; Am Phys Soc. *Res:* Test/create Jovian radiation belt models; determine x-ray and gamma-ray emission from natural and artificial satellites in the Jovian trapped electron proton belts. *Mailing Add:* 80 N Marion Ave 4 Victoria Sq Pasadena CA 91106-2034

LUTHRA, HARVINDER SINGH, RHEUMATOLOGY, IMMUNOLOGY. *Current Pos:* trainee rheumatology, Mayo Grad Sch, 72-74, assoc consult, 74-75, CONSULT RHEUMATOLOGY, MAYO CLIN, ROCHESTER, MINN, 75- *Personal Data:* b Amritsar, India, Mar 14, 45; m 75, Annu Duggal; c Payal, Guari & Sonaar. *Educ:* Christian Med Col, India, MB & BS, 67; Am Bd Internal Med, 73; Am Bd Internal Med & Rheumatology, 74. *Prof Exp:* Intern, Christian Med Col, India, 67, resident, 68; intern, Middlesex Gen Hosp, NB, 69; resident internal med, Mt Sinai Hosp, Chicago, Ill, 70-72. *Concurrent Pos:* Vchair res, Dept Med, Mayo Clin, Rochester, Minn, 93-96; prof med, John F Finn Minn Arthritis Found, 95-; chair, Div Rheumatology, Mayo Clin & Mayor Med Sch, Rochester, Minn, 96- *Mem:* Int Med Acad Sci; fel Am Rheumatism Asn; Sigma Xi; Am Fedn Clin Res; AAAS; fel Am Col Physicians; Am Asn Immunologists. *Res:* To understand genetic mechanisms involved in development of rheumatoid arthritis and potential new treatments; internal medicine. *Mailing Add:* Div Rheumatology & Internal Med Mayo Clin & Mayo Found 200 First St SW Rochester MN 55905-0002. *Fax:* 507-284-0564; *E-Mail:* luthra@mayo.edu

LUTHRA, KRISHAN LAL, HIGH TEMPERATURE & METALLURGICAL CHEMISTRY. *Current Pos:* Metallurgist, Corp Res & Develop, 76-89, MGR, COMPOSITES & STRUCT CERAMICS PROG, GEN ELEC CO, 89- *Personal Data:* b Jaipur, India, Sept 28, 49; m 81, Sudipti Pratap. *Educ:* Univ Rajasthan, BEng, 70; Indian Inst Technol, Kanpur, MTech, 72; Univ Pa, PhD(metall & mat sci), 76. *Concurrent Pos:* Sr res asst, Dept Metall Eng, Indian Inst Technol, Kanpur, 71-72; res fel, Dept Metall & Mat Sci, Univ Pa, 72-76. *Mem:* Electrochem Soc; Metall Soc; Am Ceramic Soc; Am Soc Metals. *Res:* Thermodynamic and kinetics of high temperature reactions; corrosion at elevated temperatures; gas-liquid-solid reactions; high temperature materials; ceramic composites. *Mailing Add:* 780 Red Oak Dr Schenectady NY 12309

LUTHY, JAKOB WILHELM, CHEMISTRY. *Current Pos:* RETIRED. *Personal Data:* b Staefa, Switz, Jan 31, 19; nat US; m 48, Margaret Marko; c Madeleine, Peter & Susan. *Educ:* Swiss Fed Inst Technol, MS, 44, DSc(org chem), 47. *Prof Exp:* Asst prof org technol, Swiss Fed Inst Technol, 46-47; chemist, Gen Aniline & Film Corp, NJ, 47-48; chemist, Sandoz Chem, 48-51; head appln lab, Chem Div, Sandoz, Inc, 51-54, dir appln & prom, 54-58, tech mgr, Dyestuff Div, 58-82, exec vpres, 64-82, pres, Colors & Chem Div & dir, 67-82. *Concurrent Pos:* Dir, Toms River Chem Corp, 58-81. *Mem:* Emer fel Am Chem Soc; fel Swiss Chem Soc. *Res:* Dyestuffs. *Mailing Add:* 643 Mountain Rd Kinnelon NJ 07405-2128

LUTHY, RICHARD GODFREY, ENVIRONMENTAL & CIVIL ENGINEERING. *Current Pos:* actg head, Carnegie Inst Technol, 85, from asst prof to assoc prof, 75-83, assoc dean, 86-89, PROF, DEPT CIVIL ENG, CARNEGIE INST TECHNOL, 83-, HEAD DEPT, 89- *Personal Data:* b June 11, 45; m 69, Mary F Sullivan; c Matthew, Mara & Jessica. *Educ:* Univ Calif, Berkeley, BS, 67, MS, 74, PhD(civil eng), 76; Univ Hawaii, MS, 69. *Honors & Awards:* G Tallman Ladd Award, Carnegie Inst Technol, 77; Nalco Award, Asn Environ Eng Prof, 78 & 82; Eddy Medal, Water Pollution Control Fedn, 80; Founders Award, US Nat Comn Int Asn Water Purification Res & Control, 86 & 93; Eng Sci Award, Asn Environ Eng Prof, 88. *Prof Exp:* Res asst, Dept Civil Eng, Univ Hawaii, 68-69; res proj officer, Naval Civil Eng Lab, Civil Eng Corps, US Navy, 70-71, asst officer-in-charge underwater construct team, 71-72; res asst, Div Sanit Eng, Univ Calif, Berkeley, 73-75. *Concurrent Pos:* Consult, Allied-Signal, Environ Res & Technol Inc, IT Corp, Baker Chem Co, Koppers Co, Inc, US Steel, Alcoa, SmithKline-Beckman, FMC Corp, Exxon, Aetna Casualty & Ins, Remediation Technol Inc, US Dept Energy & US Environ Protection Agency, Texaco, Baltimore Gas & Elec; chmn, Conf Fundamental Res Directions Environ Eng, NSF/Asn Environ Eng Prof, 88; deleg, Water Sci & Technol Bd, Nat Acad Eng, Wash, Beijing, 88. *Mem:* Water Environ Fedn; Am Soc Civil Engrs; Am Chem Soc; Int Asn Water Qual; Asn Environ Eng Prof (vpres, 86-87, pres, 87-88); Am Water Works Asn; Am Acad Environ Engrs. *Res:* Hazardous substances in wastewaters and ground waters; wastewater treatment and industrial wastewater treatment; chemistry of dilute aqueous systems; treatment of wastewaters from petroleum refining, chemical manufacturing, coal conversion, and iron and steel making. *Mailing Add:* Dept Civil Eng Carnegie Mellon Univ Pittsburgh PA 15213-3890. *Fax:* 412-268-7813; *E-Mail:* luthy@ce.cmu.edu

LUTON, EDGAR FRANK, INTERNAL MEDICINE. *Current Pos:* from asst to assoc prof, 61-74, PROF MED, CTR HEALTH SCI, UNIV TENN, MEMPHIS, 74- *Personal Data:* b Memphis, Tenn, Mar 3, 21; m 44; c 3. *Educ:* Univ Tenn, Memphis, MD, 44; Am Bd Internal Med, dipl & cert nephrol, 74. *Prof Exp:* Staff physician neuropsychiat serv med teaching group, Vet Admin Hosp, Memphis, 48-49, resident internal med, 49-51, staff physician med serv, 51-59, sect chief internal med & allergy, 59-67, sect chief allergy & nephrology, 67-77. *Mem:* Fel Am Col Physicians; Am Soc Nephrology; Int Soc Nephrology. *Res:* Nephrology. *Mailing Add:* 2242 Tidmington Dr Cordova TN 38018-4574

LUTRICK, MONROE CORNELIUS, AGRONOMY, SOIL CHEMISTRY. *Current Pos:* RETIRED. *Personal Data:* b Grayson, La, July 22, 27; m 52; c 4. *Educ:* La State Univ, BS, 51, MS, 53; Ohio State Univ, PhD(agron), 56. *Prof Exp:* Asst agron, La State Univ, 51-53; asst agronomist, Agr Res Educ Ctr, Univ Fla, 56-67, assoc soil chemist, 67-77, soil chemist, 77-91. *Mem:* Am Soc Agron; Soil Sci Soc Am. *Res:* Soil chemistry and maximum production of field crops; utilization of liquid digested sludge on agricultural lands; micronutrient status of field crops grown in North Florida. *Mailing Add:* 3880 Tom Lane Dr Pensacola FL 32504

LUTSCH, EDWARD F, ZOOLOGY. *Current Pos:* from asst prof to assoc prof, 68-74, PROF BIOL, NORTHEASTERN ILL UNIV, 74- *Personal Data:* b Chicago, Ill, Nov 23, 30; m 65; c 2. *Educ:* Northern Ill Univ, BS, 52; Northwestern Univ, MS, 57, PhD(biol), 62. *Prof Exp:* Asst prof zool, Univ Ill, Chicago, 62-68. *Concurrent Pos:* Lectr, Northwestern Univ, 69- *Mem:* AAAS; Am Inst Biol Sci; Am Soc Zoologists. *Res:* Biological rhythms and clocks; rhythmic response of animals to pharmacological drugs; comparative physiology; animal behavior. *Mailing Add:* Dept Biol Northeastern Ill Univ 5500 N St Louis Ave Chicago IL 60625-4625

LUTSKY, IRVING, laboratory animal medicine, for more information see previous edition

LUTT, CARL J, ANATOMY, PHYSIOLOGY. *Current Pos:* Dir, Student Health Serv, Calif State Univ, Hayward, 60-65, prof biol health & kinesiol, 60-87, asst dir student health serv, 73-85, dir sports med, 75-87, EMER PROF BIOL SCI, KINESIOL & PHYS EDUC, 87- *Personal Data:* b Guthrie Co, Iowa, Feb 10, 21; m 45; c 2. *Educ:* Creighton Univ, BSM, 42, MD, 45. *Mem:* Am Col Sports Med. *Mailing Add:* 20964 Woodside Way Groveland CA 95321

LUTTER, LEONARD C, MOLECULAR BIOLOGY. *Current Pos:* DIR, DEPT MOLECULAR BIOL, HENRY FORD HOSP, 88- *Mailing Add:* Dept Molecular Biol Henry Ford Hosp One Ford Pl Detroit MI 48202-3450

LUTTGES, MARVIN WAYNE, NEUROBIOLOGY, BIOENGINEERING. *Current Pos:* from asst prof to assoc prof, 69-79, PROF BIOENG, AEROSPACE ENG SCI, UNIV COLO, 80- *Personal Data:* b Chico, Calif, Feb 3, 41; m 69. *Educ:* Univ Ore, Eugene, BSc, 62; Univ Calif, Irvine, PhD(biol sci), 68. *Prof Exp:* Res asst dept psychol, Univ Ore, 62-64; teaching asst psychobiol, Univ Calif, Irvine, 64-68; USPHS fel neurochem, Med Sch, Northwestern Univ, 68-69. *Concurrent Pos:* Noise consult, City of Boulder, Colo, 76-78; Am Eng Soc res award, 79. *Mem:* Soc Neurosci; AAAS; Sigma Xi; Biophys Soc. *Res:* Neurobiological basis of learning and memory; nervous system degeneration and regeneration; biological and physical acoustics; comparative studies of brain structure and function. *Mailing Add:* 13500 Swaps Ct Grass Valley CA 95949

LUTTINGER, JOAQUIN MAZDAK, THEORETICAL PHYSICS. *Current Pos:* RETIRED. *Personal Data:* b New York, NY, Dec 2, 23. *Educ:* Mass Inst Technol, BS, 44, PhD(physics), 47. *Prof Exp:* Swiss-Am exchange fel, 47-48; Nat Res Coun fel, 48-49; Jewett fel, Inst Advan Study, 49-50; from asst prof to assoc prof physics, Univ Wis, 50-53; assoc prof, Univ Mich, 53-57 & Ecole Normale Superieure, Paris, 57-58; prof, Univ Pa, 58-60; prof, Columbia Univ, 60-93, chmn dept, 77-81. *Mem:* Nat Acad Sci; fel Am Phys Soc; Am Acad Arts & Sci. *Res:* Theoretical magnetism; quantum field theory; statistical mechanics; theory of solids; condensed matter physics. *Mailing Add:* Dept Physics Columbia Univ 826 Pupin Lab New York NY 10027

LUTTMANN, FREDERICK WILLIAM, MATHEMATICS. *Current Pos:* from asst prof to assoc prof, 70-81, PROF MATH, SONOMA STATE UNIV, 81- *Personal Data:* b New Brunswick, NJ, Aug 9, 40; div. *Educ:* Amherst Col, AB, 61; Stanford Univ, MS, 64; Univ Ariz, PhD(math), 67. *Prof Exp:* Assoc, Univ Ariz, 63-67; assoc prof math, Alaska Methodist Univ, 67-70. *Mem:* Math Asn Am. *Res:* Steiner symmetrization of convex bodies; polynomial interpolation. *Mailing Add:* Dept Math Sonoma State Univ Rohnert Park CA 94928

LUTTON, JOHN D, EXPERIMENTAL HEMATOLOGY. *Current Pos:* assoc prof med, 83-89, RES ASSOC PROF MED & ANAT, NY MED COL, 77-, PROF MED, 89-, ASSOC PROF MICROBIOL & IMMUNOL, 90-; SCIENTIST, ROCKEFELLER CTR, 90- *Personal Data:* b Sioux City, Iowa, Feb 3, 37; c 2. *Educ:* Univ Nebr, BS, 61, MS, 63; NY Univ, PhD(cell biol & physiol), 69. *Prof Exp:* Instr gen physiol, Dept Biol, NY Univ, 66-68, asst prof, 70-71, instr & res scientist, Dept Cell Biol, Med Sch, 71-76; asst prof physiol & hemat, Dept Physiol, Mt Sinai Sch Med, 76-77; asst prof hemat, Downstate Med Ctr, State Univ NY, 77. *Concurrent Pos:* Adj asst prof, Dept Biol, City Col, City Univ New York, 71-73; Baruch Col, 81-85. *Mem:* Am Soc Hemat; Int Soc Exp Hemat; Reticulo Endothelial Soc; AAAS. *Res:* Growth factors and the regulation of hematopoiesis: bone marrow growth and in vitro aspects on the regulation of erythropoiesis including regulatory aspects of hemebiosynthesis and degradation; in vitro characteristics of disorders such as anemia, polycythemins, neoplastic states and disorders of iron metabolism; granulopoiesis; differentiation of leukemic cells. *Mailing Add:* 42 Redwood Dr Highland Mills NY 10930

LUTTON, JOHN KAZUO, NEUROPHARMACOLOGY, ENZYMOLOGY. *Current Pos:* ASST PROF, CHEM DEPT, KENYON COL, 80- *Personal Data:* b Tokyo, Japan, July 11, 49; US citizen; m 71; c 1. *Educ:* Pac Lutheran Univ, BS, 71; Purdue Univ, PhD(biochem), 76. *Prof Exp:* Grad student, Dept Biochem, Purdue Univ, 71-76 & chem anal, Ind State Chem Off, 72-73; res assoc pharmacol, Med Sch, Univ Colo, 76-77 & Univ NC, 77-80. *Mem:* Am Chem Soc; AAAS; Sigma Xi. *Res:* Molecular mechanisms of hormone action especially the role of cyclic nucleotides in brain function and cell growth; enzymatic mechanisms of redox enzymes especially flavin-containing dehydrogenases. *Mailing Add:* 10758 Gaskin Ave Gambier OH 43022

LUTTON, LEWIS MONTFORT, CIRCADIAN RHYTHMS, EXERCISE PHYSIOLOGY. *Current Pos:* from asst prof to assoc prof, 80-93, PROF BIOL, MERCYHURST COL, 93- *Personal Data:* b Cincinnati, Ohio, July 14, 45; m 82, Marianne Hendow; c Wolf, Bram, Richard, Janine, Robert & Beth. *Educ:* Swarthmore Col, BA, 68; Cornell Univ, PhD(environ physiol), 76. *Prof Exp:* Inst, Allegheny Col, 74-76, asst prof, 76-80. *Concurrent Pos:* Pre med adv, Mercyhurst Col, 80-96, dir, Hon Prog, 83-90, dir, Biol Dept, 83-, pres, Col Senate, 85-86, chmn, Sci Div, 85-90. *Mem:* Am Soc Mammalogists; Nat Asn Biol Teachers; AAAS; Inst Religion & Sci; Soc Res Biol Rhythms. *Res:* Behavioral pharmacology of the Circadian rhythm of hamsters; elucidate the biochemical mechanisms underlying photic entrainment. *Mailing Add:* Mercyhurst Col Erie PA 16546. *Fax:* 814-824-2188; *E-Mail:* llutton@paradise.mercy.edu

LUTTRELL, ERIC MARTIN, PETROLEUM GEOLOGY. *Current Pos:* VPRES EXPLOR & NEW DEVELOP, BPX-ALASKA, 91- *Personal Data:* b Wheeling, WVa, May 12, 41; m 63, Janet Marie Quiss; c Dawn (Christilles) & Brooke (Calender). *Educ:* Univ Wis-Madison, BS, 62, MS, 65; Princeton Univ, PhD(geol), 68. *Prof Exp:* Geologist, Producing Dept, Texaco Inc, 68-69, sr geologist, 69-73, res geologist, Res & Tech Dept, 73-76, asst supvr geol res, 76-79, consult explor geologist, 79-80; regional geologist, Stand Oil Prof Co, 80-82, asst explor mgr, 82-84, proj mgr, Anadarko, 84-86, onshore explor mgr, 86-89; explor mgr, Latin Am, BP Explor, 89-90. *Mem:* Geol Soc Am; Soc Econ Paleontologists & Mineralogists; Am Asn Petrol Geologists. *Res:* Applications of seismic stratigraphy clastic sedimentology; organic geochemistry and geologic thermometry to petroleum exploration. *Mailing Add:* 4690 Southpark Bluff Dr Anchorage AK 99516

LUTTRELL, GEORGE HOWARD, ANALYTICAL CHEMISTRY. *Current Pos:* Res chemist anal, Alcon Labs, 69-72, Ctr Labs, 75-77, MEM STAFF, ALCON LABS PR, 77- *Personal Data:* b Glendale, Calif, Dec 23, 41; m 64. *Educ:* Univ Tex, BS, 65; Southern Methodist Univ, MS, 69; Univ Ga, PhD(chem), 75. *Mem:* Am Chem Soc; Sigma Xi. *Res:* Preconcentration of trace metal cations and oxyanions for analysis by x-ray fluorescence using immobilized complexing and chelating reagents. *Mailing Add:* Luttrell Consult Inc 3619 Lake Powell Dr Arlington TX 76016

LUTTS, JOHN A, COMPUTER SCIENCE. *Current Pos:* asst prof, 66-70, fac growth fel, 67, fac res grant, 70-71, ASSOC PROF MATH, UNIV MASS, HARBOR CAMPUS, 70- *Personal Data:* b Baltimore, Md, Feb 26, 32; m 67, Ruth M Hanson; c Judith, John, Eric, Irene, Claire, Paul & Laetitia. *Educ:* Spring Hill Col, BS, 57; Univ Pa, MA, 59, PhD(math), 61; Woodstock Col, Md, STL, 65. *Prof Exp:* From instr to asst prof math, Loyola Col, Md, 65-66. *Mem:* Math Asn Am. *Res:* Cultural history of mathematics; approximation theory; computer languages. *Mailing Add:* Dept Math/Comput Sci Univ Mass Harbor Campus Boston MA 02125-3393. *Fax:* 617-265-7173; *E-Mail:* lutts@cs.umb.edu

LUTWAK, ERWIN, MATHEMATICS. *Current Pos:* from asst prof to assoc prof, 75-86, PROF MATH, POLYTECH UNIV, 86- *Personal Data:* b USSR, Feb 9, 46; US citizen; m 68. *Educ:* Polytechn Inst Brooklyn, BS, 68, MS, 72; Polytech Inst NY, PhD(math), 74. *Prof Exp:* Asst prof math, Col Pharmaceut Sci, Columbia Univ, 70-75. *Concurrent Pos:* Chair, Math Sect NY Acad Sci, 88-90. *Mem:* Am Math Soc; London Math Soc; Math Asn Am; Sigma Xi; NY Acad Sci. *Res:* Convexity; integral geometry; analytic and geometric inequalities. *Mailing Add:* 333 Jay St Polytech Univ Brooklyn NY 11201-2990

LUTWAK, LEO, ENDOCRINOLOGY, NUTRITION. *Current Pos:* MED OFFICER, US FOOD & DRUG ADMIN, ROCKVILLE, MD, 92- *Personal Data:* b New York, NY, Mar 27, 28; m 50, 78, Victoria Jones; c Mark, Diane, Paul, Jean, Robert, David & Aviva. *Educ:* City Col New York, BS, 45; Univ Wis, MS, 46; Univ Mich, PhD(biochem), 50; Yale Univ, MD, 56. *Prof Exp:* Biochemist med, Brookhaven Nat Lab, 50-52; clin assoc metab, Metab Dis Br, Nat Inst Arthritis & Metab Dis, 57-59, sr investr, 60-63; Jameson prof clin nutrit, Grad Sch Nutrit, Cornell Univ, 63-72; prof med, Univ Calif, Los Angeles, 72-76, prof nutrit, Sch Pub Health, 73-76; sect chief metab, Vet Admin Hosp, Sepulveda, 72-76; prof med, Northeastern Ohio Univ, 76-84, prof nutrit & prog chief, 76-84; consult, 84-92. *Concurrent Pos:* NSF sr NASA fel, Ames Res Lab, Moffett Field, Calif, 70-71; prin investr, NASA, 63-80; consult, Div Res Grants, NIH, 64-69, NASA, 80-; consult, Tompkins Co Hosp, Ithaca, NY, 64-69; vis prof, Sch Med, Stanford Univ, 70-71; chmn, Dept Med, Akron City Hosp, Ohio, 76-78; mem, Am Bd Clin Nutrit, pres, 81-82; pvt pract, endocrinol, Huntsville, Ala, 85- *Mem:* AAAS; Endocrine Soc; Am Inst Nutrit; fel Am Col Physicians; fel Am Col Nutrit. *Res:* Isotope kinetics in metabolic bone disease; calcium, phosphorus and magnesium in human nutrition; effect of space flight on bone and muscle metabolism; obesity control; diabetes and electrolyte metabolism; hospital malnutrition. *Mailing Add:* 14504 Rich Branch Dr North Potomac MD 20878-2465. *Fax:* 301-443-9282; *E-Mail:* lutwakl@cder.fda.gov

LUTY, FRITZ, SOLID STATE PHYSICS. *Current Pos:* PROF PHYSICS, UNIV UTAH, 65- *Personal Data:* b Essen, Ger, Apr 12, 28; m 60; c 2. *Educ:* Univ Gottingen, dipl physics, 53; Stuttgart Univ, Dr rer nat(physics), 56. *Prof Exp:* Asst physics, Stuttgart Univ, 53-62, dozent, Physics Inst, 64-65; vis assoc prof, Univ Ill, Urbana, 63. *Concurrent Pos:* Vis prof, Soc Advan Sci, Japan, 73; distinguished res award, Univ Utah, 84. *Mem:* Fel Am Phys Soc; Ger Phys Soc. *Res:* Defects in ionic crystals; radiation damage; absorption and emission spectroscopy; field emission; magneto-optics, paraelectric and paraelastic effects; low temperature dielectric and electro-caloric studies; Raman-scattering; phase transitions; material development for tunable laser application. *Mailing Add:* Dept Physics Univ Utah Salt Lake City UT 84112

LUTZ, ALBERT WILLIAM, AGRICULTURAL CHEMISTRY. *Current Pos:* res chemist, Am Cyanamid Co, 57-59, sr res chemist, 59-69, group leaeer herbicides, 69-85, GROUP LEADER CHEM DISCOVERY, AGR DIV, AM CYANAMID CO, 85- *Personal Data:* b Baltimore, Md, Sept 26, 24; m 51; c 2. *Educ:* Johns Hopkins Univ, AB, 49, MA, 50, PhD(chem), 53. *Honors & Awards:* J Shelton Horsley Award. *Prof Exp:* Assoc prof chem, Col William & Mary, 53-56; res chemist, Chemagro Corp, 56-57. *Mem:* Am Chem Soc. *Res:* Pesticides, particularly growth regulants and herbicides. *Mailing Add:* 873 Cherry Hill Rd Princeton NJ 08540

LUTZ, ARTHUR LEROY, NUCLEAR PHYSICS. *Current Pos:* prof, 43-75, EMER PROF PHYSICS, WITTENBERG UNIV, 75- *Personal Data:* b Louisville, Ohio, Oct 22, 08; m 37, Martha Blohm; c Wendell R & Marcia A (Blust). *Educ:* Capital Univ, BS, 31; Ohio State Univ, MS, 36, PhD(physics), 43. *Prof Exp:* High sch teacher, Ohio, 31-40; asst physics, Ohio State Univ, 40-43. *Concurrent Pos:* Fac fel, NSF, 60-61. *Mem:* Sigma Xi; Am Phys Soc; Am Asn Physics Teachers. *Res:* Radioactive isotopes; internal conversion and K-capture in the radioactive isotopes of lead and bismuth. *Mailing Add:* 1500 Villa Rd No 105 Springfield OH 45503

LUTZ, BARRY LAFEAN, PLANETARY & COMETARY ATMOSPHERES, MOLECULAR SPECTROSCOPY. *Current Pos:* PROF PHYSICS & ASTRON, NORTHERN ARIZ UNIV, 91-, CHAIR DEPT, 92- *Personal Data:* b Windsor, Pa, Jan 2, 44; m 81, Mary S Maxwell. *Educ:* Lebanon Valley Col, BS, 65; Princeton Univ, AM, 67, PhD(astrophys sci), 68. *Prof Exp:* Fel physics, Nat Res Coun Can, 68-70; res astronr, Lick Observ, Univ Calif, 70-71; sr res assoc, State Univ NY Stony Brook, 71-78, from adj asst prof to adj assoc prof, 73-77; astronr, Lowell Observ, 77-91. *Concurrent Pos:* Vis astronr, Observ Paris, 79 & Univ Dijon, 80; adj assoc prof, Ariz State Univ, 81-83, adj prof, 83-86; adj prof, Northern Ariz Univ, 87-91; prin investr, NSF, 72-88, NASA, 75-; consult, Kitt Peak Nat Observ, 73, NASA Planetary Astron Mgt Oper Working Group, 85-; vis scholar, Dept Physics & Dept Astron, Univ Calif, Berkeley, 89. *Mem:* Int Astron Union; Am Astron Soc; Sigma Xi; Am Geophys Union. *Res:* High resolution spectroscopy of the interstellar medium, of comets and of stellar and planetary atmospheres; laboratory astrophysics; intensity measurements and long path length planetary atmospheres simulations; absolute spectrophotometry of planetary atmospheres and of comets and narrow band photopolarimetric imaging of planets. *Mailing Add:* Dept Physics & Astron Northern Ariz Univ Flagstaff AZ 86011-6010. *Fax:* 520-523-1371; *E-Mail:* barry.lutz@nau.edu

LUTZ, BRUCE CHARLES, PHYSICS. *Current Pos:* RETIRED. *Personal Data:* b London, Ont, May 16, 20; m 45; c 3. *Educ:* Western Ont Univ, BA, 42, MA, 44; Johns Hopkins Univ, PhD, 54. *Prof Exp:* Instr electronics & radio, Western Ont Univ, 41-44; lectr electronics & physics, Univ Man, 45-47; instr electronics, Univ Del, 47-57, assoc prof elec eng, 57-62, prof, 62-89, actg chmn dept, 73-89. *Mem:* Am Inst Aeronaut & Astronaut (treas, Rocket Soc, 59-60); Inst Elec & Electronics Eng. *Res:* Nuclear reactor physics and engineering; plasma-microwave interaction; signal analysis. *Mailing Add:* 101 Hullihen Ct Newark DE 19711

LUTZ, CHRIS P, PHYSICS. *Current Pos:* RES SCIENTIST, IBM ALMADEN RES CTR, SAN JOSE, CALIF. *Honors & Awards:* Newcomb Cleveland Prize, AAAS, 93 & 94. *Mailing Add:* IBM Almaden Res Ctr 650 Harry Rd San Jose CA 95120-6001

LUTZ, DONALD ALEXANDER, MATHEMATICS, DIFFERENTIAL EQUATIONS. *Current Pos:* PROF MATH, SAN DIEGO STATE UNIV, 86- *Personal Data:* b Syracuse, NY, Apr 2, 40; m 68, Margaret Weaver; c Catherine, Elizabeth & Christopher. *Educ:* Syracuse Univ, BS, 61, MS, 63, PhD(math), 65. *Prof Exp:* Instr math, Syracuse Univ, 65; from asst prof to prof math, Univ Wis-Milwaukee, 65-86. *Concurrent Pos:* Lectr, Univ Md, 67-69; vis asst prof, Math Res Ctr, Univ Wis-Madison, 69-70; vis assoc prof math, Univ Southern Calif, 73; Humboldt fel, Univ Ulm, WGer, 75-76. *Mem:* Am Math Soc; German Math Union. *Res:* Systems of linear ordinary differential equations with meromorphic coefficients; systems of linear difference equations. *Mailing Add:* Dept Math Sci San Diego State Univ San Diego CA 92182-0314. *E-Mail:* lutz@math.sdsu.edu

LUTZ, HARRY FRANK, NUCLEAR PHYSICS. *Current Pos:* RETIRED. *Personal Data:* b Philadelphia, Pa, Jan 30, 36; m 60; c 2. *Educ:* Univ Pa, AB, 57; Mass Inst Technol, PhD(physics), 61. *Prof Exp:* Physicist, Lawrence Livermore Lab, 61-96. *Mem:* Am Phys Soc. *Res:* Nuclear reactions and nuclear spectroscopy. *Mailing Add:* 4545 Entrada St Pleasanton CA 94566. *Fax:* 510-424-6889

LUTZ, JULIE HAYNES, ASTRONOMY. *Current Pos:* From asst prof to assoc prof, 72-84, PROF ASTRON, WASH STATE UNIV, 84- *Personal Data:* b Mt Vernon, Ohio, Dec 17, 44; wid; c Melissa & Clea. *Educ:* San Diego State Univ, BA, 65; Univ Ill, MS, 68, PhD(astron), 72. *Concurrent Pos:* Asst dean sci, Wash State Univ, 78-79, assoc provost, 81-82; dir, Div Astron Sci, NSF, 90-92; chair, Math & Astron, Wash State Univ, 92-96, dir, Prog Astron, 96-, Astron Sect, AAAS, 93-95, prog comm, 97- *Mem:* Int Astron Union; Royal Astron Soc; Am Astron Soc; Astron Soc Pac (pres, 90-92); AAAS. *Res:* Planetary nebulae; stellar evolution. *Mailing Add:* Prog Astron Wash State Univ Pullman WA 99164-3113. *E-Mail:* julielutz@wsu.edu

LUTZ, MICHAEL W, SCIENTIFIC COMPUTING, MATHEMATICAL MODELING OF BIOLOGICAL SYSTEMS. *Current Pos:* MGR RES DATA SYSTS, GLAXO INC, 88- *Personal Data:* b New York, NY, July 3, 60. *Educ:* Duke Univ, BS, 81, PhD(biomed eng), 86. *Mem:* Am Statist Asn; Biomed Eng Soc. *Mailing Add:* 12 Chimney Top Ct Durham NC 27705-5442

LUTZ, PAUL E, INVERTEBRATE ZOOLOGY, ECOLOGY & ENVIRONMENTAL SCIENCE. *Current Pos:* from instr to assoc prof, 61-70, PROF BIOL, UNIV NC, GREENSBORO, 70-, FAC MARSHAL, 92- *Personal Data:* b Hickory, NC, June 25, 34; c Carol S. *Educ:* Lenoir-Rhyne Col, AB, 56; Univ Miami, MS, 58; Univ NC, PhD(zool), 62. *Hon Degrees:* LHD, Lenoir-Rhyne Col, 83. *Prof Exp:* Grad asst zool, Univ Miami, 56-58 & Univ NC, 58-61. *Concurrent Pos:* Grantee, Am Philos Soc, 64 & NSF, 65-67 & 69-71; pres, NC Acad Sci, 93-94. *Mem:* AAAS; Ecol Soc Am; Sigma Xi; Am Inst Biol Sci. *Res:* Ecology and physiology of aquatic insects, especially effects of temperature and photoperiod as they affect seasonal regulation of developmental patterns in the Odonata. *Mailing Add:* Dept Biol Univ NC Greensboro NC 27412-5001. *Fax:* 910-334-5839; *E-Mail:* pelutz@goodall.uncq.edu

LUTZ, PETER LOUIS, RESPIRATION, OSMOREGULATION. *Current Pos:* MCGINTY CHAIR MARINE BIOL, FLA ATLANTIC UNIV, 90- *Personal Data:* b Glasgow, Scotland, Sept 29, 39. *Educ:* Glasgow Univ, Scotland, BSc, 64, PhD(zool), 70. *Prof Exp:* Lectr physiol, Univ Ife, Nigeria, 64-66, biol, Univ Glasgow, Scotland, 69-70; asst prof biol, Duke Univ, NC, 70-72; lectr biol, Bath Univ, Eng, 72-76; assoc prof, Miami Univ, Fla, 76-82, prof physiol & chmn, Marine Sch, 82-90. *Mem:* Soc Exp Biol; Am Soc Zoologists; Am Physiol Soc. *Res:* Animal physiology, particularly respiration and osmoregulation; anerobic brain metabolism; applied physiology of aquaculture of crustaceans; pollution; oil and plastics. *Mailing Add:* Fla Atlantic Univ Boca Raton FL 33431-0991

LUTZ, RAYMOND, INDUSTRIAL ENGINEERING, ENGINEERING ECONOMICS. *Current Pos:* dean, Sch Mgt, 73-78, exec dean grad studies & res, 79-91, PROF OPERS MGT, UNIV TEX, DALLAS, 73- *Personal Data:* b Oak Park, Ill, Feb 27, 35; m 58, Nancy Cole. *Educ:* Univ NMex, BS, 58, MBA, 62; Iowa State Univ, PhD(eng evaluation), 64. *Honors & Awards:* E L Grant Award, Am Soc Eng Educ, 72; Fred Crane Distinguished Serv Award, Inst Indust Engrs, 87. *Prof Exp:* Instr mech eng, Univ NMex, 58-61; asst indust eng, Iowa State Univ, 61-64; asst prof mech eng, NMex State Univ, 64-67; from assoc prof to prof indust eng, Univ Okla, 68-72. *Concurrent Pos:* Ed, Eng Economist, 72-77, Indust Mgt, 83-87; bd dirs, Sigma Xi. *Mem:* Fel AAAS; fel Am Inst Indust Engrs; Sigma Xi. *Res:* Operations management; industrial management; shipbuilding technology. *Mailing Add:* 10275 Hollow Way Dallas TX 75229. *Fax:* 214-369-2072; *E-Mail:* rplutz@utdallas.edu

LUTZ, RAYMOND PAUL, PHYSICAL ORGANIC CHEMISTRY. *Current Pos:* from asst prof to assoc prof, 68-83, PROF CHEM, PORTLAND STATE UNIV, 83- *Personal Data:* b Cleveland, Ohio, May 31, 32. *Educ:* Univ Fla, BS, 53, MS, 55; Calif Inst Technol, PhD(org chem), 62. *Prof Exp:* Res chemist, E I du Pont de Nemours & Co, Ky & Mich, 55-57; instr chem, Harvard Univ, 61-64, lectr, 64-65; asst prof, Univ Ill, Chicago, 65-68. *Mem:* Am Chem Soc. *Res:* Reaction mechanisms, including displacement reactions and thermal isomerizations. *Mailing Add:* Dept Chem Portland State Univ Portland OR 97207-0751

LUTZ, RICHARD ARTHUR, BIOLOGICAL OCEANOGRAPHY, MARINE ECOLOGY. *Current Pos:* asst prof, 79-84, PROF, DEPT MARINE & COASTAL SCI, RUTGERS UNIV, 87-, DIR, FISH & AQUACULT TEX CTR, 86- *Personal Data:* b New York, NY, June 8, 49; m 81; c 3. *Educ:* Univ Va, BA, 71; Univ Maine, PhD(oceanog), 75. *Honors & Awards:* Thurlow C Nelson Award, Nat Shellfisheries Asn, 73. *Prof Exp:* Res asst, dept oceanog, Univ Maine, 71-75, res assoc, Darling Ctr, 75-78; res assoc, dept geol & geophys, Yale Univ, 77-79. *Concurrent Pos:* Print investr, Nat Oceanic & Atmospheric Admin sea grants, 75-78; biol consult, Blue Gold Sea Farms, 76-; assoc investr, Nat Oceanic & Atmospheric Admin sea grant, Yale Univ, 78-; co-prin investr NSF grants, Univ Calif, Santa Barbara, 78-; prin investr NSF grant, Rutgers Univ, 81- *Mem:* World Mariculture Soc; Nat Shellfisheries Asn (vpres, 81-); Am Soc Zoologists; Estuarine Res Fedn; AAAS; Sigma Xi. *Res:* Shellfish biology; molluscan shell structure and mineralogy; shellfish aquaculture; bivalve larval ecology; marine ecology and paleoecology; malacology; waste heat, especially power plant effluent, utilization; paleoclimatology; deep-sea hydrothermal vents, ecology. *Mailing Add:* Inst Marine-Coastal Sci Rutgers Univ New Brunswick NJ 08903

LUTZ, ROBERT WILLIAM, CHEMICAL PHYSICS, COMPUTER SCIENCE. *Current Pos:* asst prof, Drake Univ, 69-73, dir comput serv, 74-86, dir comput & telecom, 86-93, ASSOC PROF PHYSICS, DRAKE UNIV, 73-, ASST PROVOST INFO TECHNOL, 93- *Personal Data:* b Mason City, Iowa, Sept 14, 37; m 56; c 4. *Educ:* Drake Univ, BA, 62; Univ NMex, MS,

66; Ill Inst Technol, PhD(physics), 69. *Prof Exp:* Res asst physics, Los Alamos Sci Lab, 62-64; staff mem, 64-66. *Concurrent Pos:* Chair, Am Comput Mach-Spec Int Group Univ Col Comput Serv, 83-85; mem, EDUCOM Bd Trustees, 89-. *Mem:* Combustion Inst; Sigma Xi; Asn Comput Mach. *Res:* Computer assisted instruction; computers in undergraduate curriculum. *Mailing Add:* Comput Ctr Drake Univ Des Moines IA 50311. *E-Mail:* rlutz@acad.drake.edu

LUTZ, THOMAS EDWARD, astronomy; deceased, see previous edition for last biography

LUTZ, WILSON BOYD, BIOCHEMISTRY, ORGANIC CHEMISTRY. *Current Pos:* from asst prof to assoc prof, 62-72, PROF CHEM, MANCHESTER COL, 72- *Personal Data:* b Mogadore, Ohio, May 12, 27; m 50; c 2. *Educ:* Manchester Col, BA, 50; Ohio State Univ, PhD(org chem), 55. *Prof Exp:* Fel biochem, Med Col, Cornell Univ, 55-57; scientist, Warner-Lambert Res Inst, 57-60, sr scientist, 60-62. *Concurrent Pos:* Consult, Warner-Lambert Res Inst, 63-66; guest worker, NIH, 71; res assoc & dir, Inst Biomed Res, Univ Tex, Austin, 81; consult, Miles Lab, Elkhart, Ind, 82. *Mem:* Am Chem Soc. *Res:* Synthesis of new derivatives of hydroxylamine and substances of biological interest including melanogenic indoles. *Mailing Add:* 806 E Second St Ext North Manchester IN 46962-9386

LUTZE, FREDERICK HENRY, JR, FLIGHT MECHANICS & CONTROL, OPTIMIZATION. *Current Pos:* from asst prof to assoc prof, 66-81, PROF AEROSPACE ENG, VA POLYTECH INST & STATE UNIV, 81- *Personal Data:* b Brooklyn, NY, Nov 27, 37; m 65, Jeanne Soults. *Educ:* Worcester Polytech Inst, BS, 59; Univ Ariz, MS, 64, PhD(aerospace eng), 67. *Prof Exp:* Mech engr, Eclipse Pioneer Div, Bendix Corp, 59-60; instr aerospace eng, Univ Ariz, 65-66. *Concurrent Pos:* Mem staff, Boeing Corp, 63 & NAm, 64, Adv Technol, Inc, 86-89; consult, EG&G, Inc, 81-89, Optimization Inc, 86-89 & Booz, Allen & Hamilton, 91-93. *Mem:* Assoc fel Inst Aeronaut & Astronaut; Am Astronaut Soc. *Res:* Trajectory optimization; flight mechanics; aircraft stability and control; orbital mechanics. *Mailing Add:* Dept Aerospace Eng Va Polytech Inst & State Univ Blacksburg VA 24061-0203. *Fax:* 540-231-9632; *E-Mail:* flime@vtvm1.cc.vt.edu

LUTZER, DAVID JOHN, MATHEMATICS. *Current Pos:* DEAN, DEPT MATH, COL WILLIAM & MARY, 87- *Personal Data:* b Sioux Falls, SDak, Mar 27, 43; m 82; c 4. *Educ:* Creighton Univ, Omaha, NE, BS, 64, Oxford Univ, Eng, dipl advan math, 66; Univ Wash, Seattle, PhD(math), 70. *Prof Exp:* From asst prof to assoc prof math, Univ Pittsburgh, 70-78; prof math, Tex Tech Univ, 76-82; prof & chair, Miami Univ, Oxford Ohio, 82-87. *Mem:* Am Math Soc; Math Asn Am; Soc Indust & Appl Math. *Res:* Self-theoretic topology in ordered spaces and function spaces. *Mailing Add:* Dean Arts & Sci Col William & Mary 188 Lewis Robert Lane Williamsburg VA 23185

LUU, JANE, COMETS, SMALL SOLAR SYSTEM OBJECTS. *Current Pos:* HUBBLE FEL, DEPT PHYSICS, STANFORD UNIV, 92- *Personal Data:* b Saigon, Vietnam, July 15, 63; US citizen. *Educ:* Stanford Univ, BS, 84; Mass Inst Technol, PhD(planetary astron), 90. *Honors & Awards:* Annie J Cannon Award, Am Asn Univ Women, 91. *Prof Exp:* Harvard-Smithsonian fel, Ctr Astrophys, Harvard Univ, 90-92. *Mem:* Am Astron Soc. *Res:* Origin of small bodies in the solar system and their interrelations; comet nuclei-their physical properties and their implications on the early solar system eg the origin and evolution of the Kuiper belt of comets. *Mailing Add:* Physics Dept Stanford Univ Stanford CA 94305-4060. *Fax:* 650-725-6544; *E-Mail:* luu@blinky.stanford.edu

LUUS, R(EIN), CHEMICAL ENGINEERING. *Current Pos:* from asst prof to assoc prof, 65-74, PROF CHEM ENG, UNIV TORONTO, 74- *Personal Data:* b Tartu, Estonia, Mar 8, 39; Can citizen; m 73; c Brian & Kristina. *Educ:* Univ Toronto, BASc, 61, MASc, 62; Princeton Univ, AM, 63, PhD(chem eng), 64. *Honors & Awards:* Steacie Prize, Nat Res Coun Can, 76; ERCO Award, Can Soc Chem Eng, 80. *Prof Exp:* Fel optimal control, Princeton Univ, 64-65. *Concurrent Pos:* Consult, Can Gen Elec Co, Ltd, 65-66, Shell Oil Co Can, 66-70 & P B 78-79, Milltronics Ltd, 67-71 & Imperial Oil Ltd, 74-77; dir, Chem Eng Res Consults Ltd, 66-; Nat Res Coun Can sr indust fel, 72-73; vis assoc, Calif Inst Technol, 79-80. *Mem:* Can Soc Chem Eng (secy, 67-68, vchmn, 68-69, chmn 69-70, past chmn, 70-71); fel Chem Inst Can; Am Inst Chem Eng. *Res:* Development of optimization procedures suitable for optimal and suboptimal control of nonlinear systems; nonlinear analysis; optimal control of time delay systems; parameter estimation; model reduction; dynamic programming. *Mailing Add:* Dept Chem Eng Univ Toronto Toronto ON M5S 1A4 Can

LUX, SAMUEL E, IV, ONCOLOGY. *Current Pos:* CHIEF, DIV HEMAT & ONCOL, CHILDREN'S HOSP, 85- *Mailing Add:* Div Hemat & Oncol Children's Hosp 300 Longwood Ave Boston MA 02115-5737. *Fax:* 617-735-7262

LUXEMBURG, WILHELMUS ANTHONIUS JOSEPHUS, MATHEMATICAL ANALYSIS. *Current Pos:* from asst prof to assoc prof, 58-62, exec officer, 70-85, PROF MATH, CALIF INST TECHNOL, 62- *Personal Data:* b Delft, Neth, Apr 11, 29; m 55; c 2. *Educ:* State Univ Leiden, BSc, 50, MSc, 53; Delft Univ Technol, PhD, 55. *Prof Exp:* Fel math, Queen's Univ, Can, 55-56; asst prof, Univ Toronto, 56-58. *Concurrent Pos:* Humboldt award, 80. *Mem:* Am Math Soc; Can Math Cong; Neth Math Soc; corresp mem Royal Acad Sci Amsterdam. *Res:* Functional analysis, particularly measure and integration theory, Banach function space theory and theory of locally convex spaces; Riesz spaces; nonstandard analysis. *Mailing Add:* 817 S El Molino Ave Pasadena CA 91106-4411

LUXENBERG, HAROLD RICHARD, COMPUTER VOICE INPUT & OUTPUT, COMPUTER GRAPHICS. *Current Pos:* PROF COMPUT SCI, CALIF STATE UNIV, CHICO, 70- *Personal Data:* b Chicago, Ill, Feb 2, 21; m 42, Jean Weisskopf; c Susan K, James R & Robert C. *Educ:* Univ Calif, Los Angeles, BA, 42, MA, 48, PhD(math), 50. *Honors & Awards:* Beatrice Winner Mem Award, Soc Info Display, 87. *Prof Exp:* Mathematician, Nat Bur Stand, 50-51; res physicist, Hughes Res & Develop Labs, 51-53; consult engr, Remington Rand, Inc, 53-55; proj consult, Litton Industs, 56-58; mgr, Display Dept, Thompson-Ramo-Wooldridge Corp, 59-60; vpres eng & asst gen mgr, Houston Fearless Corp, 61-63; consult, Lux Assocs, 64-70. *Concurrent Pos:* Lectr & instr, Univ Calif, Los Angeles, 52-69. *Mem:* Fel Soc Info Display (pres, 60-62); Sigma Xi. *Res:* Data display; document storage and retrieval; photo-optical systems; digital computers in command and control applications. *Mailing Add:* Comput Sci Calif State Univ 101 Orange St Chico CA 95929-0001. *Fax:* 530-898-5995; *E-Mail:* hluxenberg@oavax.csuchico.edu

LUXHOJ, JAMES THOMAS, LOGISTICS, DECISION SUPPORT SYSTEMS. *Current Pos:* Asst prof, 86-92, ASSOC PROF INDUST ENG, RUTGERS STATE UNIV NJ, 92- *Personal Data:* b Staten Island, NY, Jan 13, 56; m 82; c 2. *Educ:* Va Polytech Inst & State Univ, BS, 84, MS, 85, PhD(indust eng & opers res), 86. *Honors & Awards:* Ralph R Teetor Award Eng Educ Excellence, Soc Automotive Engrs, 89. *Concurrent Pos:* Co-investr, USDA, 87-89, Hackensack Water Co, 88 & NSF, 91-92; chief fac adv, Rutgers Univ Chap Inst Indust Engrs, 87-; prin investr, NASA Langley Res Ctr, 88; co-prin investr, Fed Aviation Admin, 89; assoc ed, Inst Indust Engrs Trans, 89-92; treas-secy, Eng Econ Div, Am Soc Eng Educ, 89, vchmn & prog chmn, 90-91, chmn, 91-92; dept ed, Inst Indust Engrs Trans, 93-; vis prof, Aalborg Univ, Denmark, 94-95; fel, Danish Res Acad, 94; prin investr, Fed Aviation Admin, 97-98. *Mem:* Sigma Xi; sr mem Inst Indust Engrs; sr mem Soc Logistics Engrs; Am Soc Eng Educ. *Res:* Production and operations management; logistics; decision support and expert systems. *Mailing Add:* Dept Indust Eng Rutgers Univ PO Box 909 Piscataway NJ 08855-0909

LUXMOORE, ROBERT JOHN, SOIL PHYSICS, WHOLE PLANT PHYSIOLOGY. *Current Pos:* SOIL & PLANT SCIENTIST, OAK RIDGE NAT LAB, 73- *Personal Data:* b Adelaide, Australia, Nov 7, 40; m 75, Annetta P Watson. *Educ:* Univ Adelaide, BAgSc, 62, BAgSc Hons, 63; Univ Calif, Riverside, PhD(soil physics), 69. *Prof Exp:* Agronomist, Dept Agr, SAustralia, 63-66; res asst, Univ Calif, Riverside, 66-69; res assoc, Univ Ill, 69-70; fel, Univ Calif, Riverside, 70-71; res assoc, Univ Wis-Madison, 71-72. *Concurrent Pos:* Vis scientist, Commonwealth Sci & Indust Res Orgn, Australia, 76; consult, Ctr Law & Social Policy, Washington, DC, 79; mem, Rural Abandoned Mines Prog, Tenn, 80-81; ed-chief, Soil Sci Soc Am, 91-93; adj prof, Univ Tenn, 92- *Mem:* Am Soc Agron; fel Soil Sci Soc Am; Crop Sci Soc Am; Am Geophys Union; fel AAAS; Int Soc Soil Sci. *Res:* Experimental and computer modeling research on the relationships between environmental variables and whole plant physiological processes including disruptions induced by pollutant stress and soil variability effects on hydrologic transport processes. *Mailing Add:* Environ Sci Div Oak Ridge Nat Lab PO Box 2008 Oak Ridge TN 37831-6038. *E-Mail:* rjl@ornl.gov

LUXON, BRUCE ARLIE, ANIMAL PHYSIOLOGY, MEDICINE. *Current Pos:* STAFF MEM, OUTPATIENT CLIN, UNIV ST LOUIS. *Personal Data:* b Ft Dodge, Iowa, Mar 8, 55; m 85. *Educ:* Univ Iowa, BS, 76; Univ Mo, Columbia, PhD(math), 83, MD, 85. *Prof Exp:* Asst prof, Dept Med, Univ Mo, 85-89; fel gastroenterol, Univ Calif, San Francisco, 89- *Mem:* Soc Indust & Appl Math; Soc Math Biol. *Res:* Biomathematics of hepatic transport; biophysics of bile formation; hepatic drug metabolism; removal of albumin-bound substances by liver cells. *Mailing Add:* 3660 Vista Ave St Louis MO 63110

LUXON, JAMES THOMAS, LASER SURFACE MODIFICATION, BEAM PROPAGATION. *Current Pos:* Analytical engr, New Departure Div, Gen Motors Corp, 59-61, instr physics, Gen Motors Inst, 61-67, assoc prof elec eng, 69-80, prof mat sci, 81-85, dept head sci math, 88-89, ALLIED DISTINGUISHED PROF & DIR LASER LAB, ENG & MGT INST, GEN MOTORS INST, 81-, DEAN, GRAD STUDIES, EXT SERVS & RES, 93- *Personal Data:* b Norwalk, Ohio, Nov 12, 34; m 61; c 2. *Educ:* Wabash Col, BA, 58; Mich State Univ, MS, 64, PhD(eng), 69. *Concurrent Pos:* Vis prof laser, Univ Lulea, Sweden, 81; Rhodes prof, Eng & Mgt Inst, Gen Motors Inst alumni grant, 83; laser mat processing consult. *Mem:* Optical Soc Am; Laser Inst Am (pres, 86); Soc Mfg Engrs. *Res:* Mathematical description of focusing and beam propagation for high-order mode laser beams; laser surface modification. *Mailing Add:* 11365 Grand Oak Dr Grand Blanc MI 48439

LUYBEN, WILLIAM LANDES, CHEMICAL ENGINEERING. *Current Pos:* assoc prof, 67-73, PROF CHEM ENG, LEHIGH UNIV, 73- *Personal Data:* b Omaha, Nebr, Oct 17, 33; m 62; c 2. *Educ:* Pa State Univ, BS, 55; Rutgers Univ, MBA, 58; Univ Del, MSChE, 62, PhD(chem eng), 63. *Prof Exp:* Process engr, Humble Oil & Refining Co, 55-58 & Iranian Oil & Refining Co, 58-60; tech serv engr, E I du Pont de Nemours & Co, Inc, 63-67. *Concurrent Pos:* Lectr, Univ Del, 63-66; consult, E I du Pont de Nemours & Co, Inc & Sun Oil Co, 67- *Mem:* Am Inst Chem Eng. *Res:* Process dynamics, control and simulation, particularly in distillation columns and chemical reactors. *Mailing Add:* Dept Chem Eng Lehigh Univ 27 Memorial Dr W Bethlehem PA 18015-3044

LUYENDYK, BRUCE PETER, MARINE GEOPHYSICS, MARINE SCIENCES. *Current Pos:* from asst prof to assoc prof, 73-81, PROF GEOL SCI, UNIV CALIF, SANTA BARBARA, 81- *Personal Data:* b Freeport, NY, Feb 23, 43; m 67, Taylor; c Loren T. *Educ:* San Diego State Col, BS, 65;

Scripps Inst Oceanog, Univ Calif, San Diego, PhD(oceanog), 69. *Honors & Awards:* Antarctic Serv Medal, NSG, 90. *Prof Exp:* Geophysicist, US Navy Electronics Lab, 65-66; res asst oceanog, Scripps Inst Oceanog, Univ Calif, San Diego, 65-69; fel, Woods Hole Oceanog Inst, 69-70, asst scientist, 70-73. *Concurrent Pos:* Mem working group marine geophys data, Comn Oceanog, Nat Acad Sci, 71; mem working group Mid-Atlantic Ridge, US Geodyn Comn, 71; ed adv, Geol Mag, 74-79, Marine Geophys Researchers, 76-92, J Geophys Res, 82-84, Tectonophysics, 88-92 & PAGEOPH, 88- *Mem:* AAAS; Am Geophys Union; fel Geol Soc Am. *Res:* Geotectonics; paleomagnetism; paleoceanography. *Mailing Add:* Dept Geol Sci Univ Calif Santa Barbara CA 93106

LUYKX, PETER (VAN OOSTERZEE), CYTOGENETICS, HUMAN GENETICS. *Current Pos:* from asst prof to assoc prof, 67-82, PROF BIOL, UNIV MIAMI, 82- *Personal Data:* b Detroit, Mich, Dec 14, 37; m 78; c 4. *Educ:* Harvard Univ, AB, 59; Univ Calif, Berkeley, PhD(zool), 64. *Prof Exp:* Asst prof zool, Univ Minn, Minneapolis, 64-67. *Concurrent Pos:* NIH res grants, 65-73; NSF res grants, 78-88. *Mem:* AAAS; Genetics Soc Am; Am Soc Cell Biol; Entom Soc Am; Am Soc Human Genetics. *Res:* Meiosis and mitosis; cytogenetics of termites; sex chromosome evolution. *Mailing Add:* Dept Biol Univ Miami PO Box 248106 Miami FL 33124-8106

LUYTEN, JAMES REINDERT, PHYSICAL OCEANOGRAPHY. *Current Pos:* asst scientist, 71-75, assoc scientist, 75-86, SR SCIENTIST, WOODS HOLE OCEANOG INST, 86-, DEPT CHMN, 89-, ASSOC DIR RES. *Personal Data:* b Minneapolis, Minn, Dec 26, 41; m 67, Meredith Fuller; c 3. *Educ:* Reed Col, AB, 63; Harvard Univ, AM, 65, PhD(chem physics), 69. *Prof Exp:* Res fel geophys fluid dynamics, Harvard Univ, 69-71. *Concurrent Pos:* Vis sci, NCAR, 83-84. *Mem:* Am Geophys Union. *Res:* Theoretical and observational study of the dynamics of low frequency variability of ocean circulation; moored current meter arrays; observations of the Gulf Stream system; equatorial current systems in Pacific and Indian Oceans. *Mailing Add:* Woods Hole Oceanog Inst Bell House Woods Hole MA 02543. *Fax:* 508-457-2189; *E-Mail:* jluyten@whoi.edu

LUYTEN, WILLEM JACOB, astronomy; deceased, see previous edition for last biography

LUZZI, THEODORE E, JR, ENGINEERING SCIENCE. *Current Pos:* RETIRED. *Personal Data:* b Floral Park, NY, June 15, 27; m 55; c 2. *Educ:* Stevens Inst Technol, ME, 51; Mass Inst Technol, MS, 53; Columbia Univ, Eng ScD, 63. *Prof Exp:* Engr, M W Kellogg Co, NY, 53-58; res engr, Grumman Aerospace Corp, 58-61; res scientist plasma physics, 63-73, staff scientist, 73-82, sr staff scientist, 82-90. *Mem:* Am Phys Soc; Am Inst Aeronaut & Astronaut; Am Soc Mech Eng; Sigma Xi. *Res:* Gas dynamics; plasma physics; heat transfer. *Mailing Add:* 4489 Terra Lane St Joseph MI 49085-9319

LUZZIO, ANTHONY JOSEPH, IMMUNOLOGY. *Current Pos:* RETIRED. *Personal Data:* b Lawrence, Mass, Oct 13, 24; m 52; c 4. *Educ:* Univ Mass, BS, 47; Kans State Col, MS, 50, PhD(microbiol), 55. *Prof Exp:* Bacteriologist, Wyo State Vet Lab, 47-49; asst, Univ Kans, 50-52; chemist, Hercules Powder Co, 52-54; chief, Immunol Br, US Army Med Res Lab, 55-71, res immunologist, Blood Transfusion Res Div, 71-74, immunologist, Letterman Army Inst Res, 74-80. *Concurrent Pos:* Lectr, Univ Louisville, 55-74; consult, 80- *Mem:* AAAS; Am Soc Microbiol; Am Asn Immunol; Radiation Res Soc. *Res:* Effects of ionizing radiation on immune mechanisms; effects of arctic climates on immunity; protein degradation and alterations in antigenic specificity by exposure to ionizing rays; immune mechanisms in leishmaniasis. *Mailing Add:* 2167 Bay St San Francisco CA 94123-1903

LUZZIO, FREDERICK ANTHONY, SYNTHETIC ORGANIC CHEMISTRY. *Current Pos:* asst prof, 88-95, ASSOC PROF, UNIV LOUISVILLE, 95- *Personal Data:* b Lawrence, Mass, Sept 17, 53. *Educ:* Vanderbilt Univ, BS, 76; Tufts Univ, MS, 79, PhD(chem), 82. *Prof Exp:* Res chemist, Arthur D Little, Inc, 76-78; fel, Harvard Univ, 82-85; sr develop chemist, E I du Pont de Nemours, 85-88. *Concurrent Pos:* Consult, Arthur D Little, Inc, 78-85. *Mem:* Am Chem Soc. *Res:* Synthetic organic chemistry; synthesis of natural products, nucleosides, carbohydrates; synthetic methods, chiral oxidation, ultrasound-promoted reactions; isolation and structural elucidation of marine natural products. *Mailing Add:* Dept Chem Univ Louisville Louisville KY 40292. *Fax:* 502-852-8149; *E-Mail:* faluzz01@ulkyvm.louisville.edu

LWOFF, ANDRE MICHEL, microbiology, virology; deceased, see previous edition for last biography

LWOWSKI, WALTER WILHELM GUSTAV, ORGANIC CHEMISTRY. *Current Pos:* RES PROF CHEM, NMEX STATE UNIV, 66- *Personal Data:* b Garmisch, Ger, Dec 28, 28; US citizen. *Educ:* Univ Heidelberg, dipl, 54, Dr rer nat, 55. *Prof Exp:* Fel, Univ Calif, Los Angeles, 55-57; asst, Univ Heidelberg, 57-59; fel res chem, Harvard Univ, 59-60; asst prof, Yale Univ, 60-66. *Concurrent Pos:* Mem bd dirs, Boehringer-Mannheim Corp, Indianapolis. *Mem:* Fel AAAS; Am Chem Soc; fel NY Acad Sci; Ger Chem Soc; Royal Soc Chem. *Res:* Reactions mechanisms; electron-deficient nitrogen intermediates; photochemistry; heterocyclic chemistry; heteroatom rearrangements. *Mailing Add:* 905 Conway Ave No 20 Las Cruces NM 88005-3773

LYBECK, A(LVIN) H(IGGINS), INDUSTRIAL CHEMISTRY. *Current Pos:* TECH MGR, CERRO WIRE & CABLE CO, 67- *Personal Data:* b Trenton, NJ, Feb 28, 19; m 45; c 1. *Educ:* Polytech Inst, Brooklyn, BS, 41. *Prof Exp:* Asst develop engr, US Rubber Co, 41-44; res chemist, Gen Cable Co, 44-47; sr res chemist, Congoleum-Nairn, Inc, 47-50; lab dir, William Brand & Co, Inc, 50-59; develop mgr, Brand-Rex Div, Am Enka Corp, Conn, 60-67. *Mem:* Am Chem Soc; Inst Elec & Electronics Eng; Am Inst Chem. *Res:* Development of electrical insulation systems for wire and cables. *Mailing Add:* 31 Surrey Lane Branford CT 06405

LYBRAND, TERRY PAUL, MOLECULAR BIOPHYSICS, MOLECULAR SIMULATION & MODELING. *Current Pos:* asst prof, 90-96, ASSOC PROF BIOENG & ADJ ASSOC PROF CHEM, UNIV WASH, 96- *Personal Data:* b Augusta, Ga, Oct 8, 57; m 84; c 2. *Educ:* Univ SC, BS, 80; Univ Calif, San Francisco, PhD(pharmaceut chem), 84. *Prof Exp:* Postdoctoral molecular biophys, Univ Houston, 85-87; asst prof med chem, Univ Minn, 88-90. *Concurrent Pos:* NSF presidential young investr, 87-92; McKnight-Land Grant Prof, Univ Minn, 88-90; Searle scholar, 88-92; affil staff scientist, Pac Northwest Nat Lab, Richland, Wash; Sci Med New Investr Lectr, 92. *Mem:* Am Chem Soc. *Res:* Computer simulation of biological molecules to gain an understanding of their properties and behavior in atomic detail; atomic motions in large biological molecules and the relationship of these motions to biological function. *Mailing Add:* Box 351750 Univ Wash Seattle WA 98195-1750. *Fax:* 206-616-4387

LYCETTE, R(ICHARD) (MILTON), PHYSIOLOGY, MICROBIOLOGY. *Current Pos:* LAB DIR & VPRES RES & DEVELOP, AFFIL MARINE PROD CO, BIOMED SYST CO, MAINE, 84- *Personal Data:* b Houlton, Maine, Sept 20, 26; m 52; c 5. *Educ:* Univ Maine, Orono, BS, 50; Ill Inst Technol, MS, 63, PhD(physiol), 68. *Prof Exp:* Food technologist bacteriol & foods chem, Gen Foods Corp, Albion, NY, 50-52; res scientist, Continental Can Co, Chicago, 52-62; res assoc blood physiol, Presby St Luke's Hosp & Med Sch, Univ Ill, Chicago, 62-69; dir blood prod res & develop, Parke-Davis Co, Detroit, 73-74; sr chemist polymers, Fuller/OBrien Corp, South Bend, Ind, 74-76; res assoc physiol, Med Sch, Wayne State Univ, 76-79; lab dir, World Wide Chem Corp, 80-82; lab dir & consult, SNP Chem Co, Saginaw, Mich, 82-84. *Concurrent Pos:* NIH fels, Nat Heart Inst & Off Surgeon Gen, US Army, 62-69; consult, Ind Biomed Systs Co, Mich, 69-; vis lectr & prof, Univ Maine, Augusta, 69-73; sci adv to gov, Off Res & Develop, Maine, 70-73; consult biochemist, Togus Vet Admin Hosp, Maine, 71-72; dir white cell res sect, Blood Res Ctr, Am Nat Red Cross, Bethesda, Md, 72-73; adj & res liaison, Detroit Polymer Inst & Indust Labs, 80-83; trustee, CCEE Soc, NY, 90. *Mem:* Am Soc Microbiol; Am Chem Soc; fel Royal Microbiol Soc. *Res:* Cell physiology and microbiology; influence of cell membranes and lipids on aggregation; bioenergetics in cancer; degradation polymers; blood coagulation process; immunology; Limulus substances for wide scale bacterial/viral diagnosis cures including AIDS, herpes, pioneering new device for study live membranes at angstrom levels. *Mailing Add:* 104 Worth St Houlton ME 04730

LYDA, STUART D, PLANT PATHOLOGY. *Current Pos:* from assoc prof to prof, 67-94, EMER PROF PLANT PATH, TEX A&M UNIV, 94- *Personal Data:* b Bridger, Mont, June 6, 30; m 53, JoAnne Koeneke; c Harriette A, Thomas D, Sonja J, Karen K & Timothy S. *Educ:* Mont State Col, BS, 56, MS, 58; Univ Calif, PhD(plant path), 63. *Prof Exp:* Lab technician, Univ Calif, 59-62; assoc prof plant path, Univ Nev, Reno, 62-67. *Mem:* AAAS; Mycol Soc Am; Am Phytopath Soc. *Res:* Fungus and plant physiology; mycology; ecology and physiology of plant pathogenic, soilborne fungi. *Mailing Add:* PO Box 3507 Tex A&M Univ Bryan TX 77805. *Fax:* 409-845-6483

LYDING, ARTHUR R, RHEOLOGICAL ADDITIVES, POLYURETHANES. *Current Pos:* SECT LEADER NL CHEM, NL INDUSTS, INC, HIGHTSTOWN, 75- *Personal Data:* b New York, NY, May 12, 25; m 57; c 1. *Educ:* Cornell Univ, BA, 45; Univ Pa, MS, 48, PhD(chem), 51. *Prof Exp:* Instr, Cornell Univ, 44-45; control chemist, Gen Baking Co, 46; res chemist, Heyden Chem Corp, 50-52; sr res chemist, Olin Industs, 52-56; group leader polymers div, Olin Mathieson Chem Corp, Conn, 57-64; tech asst to vpres res & develop, Pkg Div, 64-69; sr res scientist, FMC Corp, 69-75. *Concurrent Pos:* Asst prof, Southern Conn State Col, 64-69; sci Ger translr, 79- *Mem:* Am Chem Soc; Sigma Xi. *Res:* Agricultural chemicals; vinyl monomers and polymers; polyurethanes; oil additives; cellulose chemistry; textile stain repellents and flame retardants; fluorochemicals; emulsion polymerization; synthesis of polymers and plastics additives; coatings; rheological additives. *Mailing Add:* 24 Broadripple Dr Princeton NJ 08540-4012

LYDY, DAVID LEE, SKIN RESEARCH, DENTAL RESEARCH. *Current Pos:* Res chemist, 63-68, SECT HEAD, MIAMI VALLEY LABS, PROCTER & GAMBLE CO, 68- *Personal Data:* b Elwood, Ind, Apr 27, 36; m 59; c 3. *Educ:* Ind Univ, AB, 58; Univ Ill, PhD(inorg chem), 63. *Mem:* Am Chem Soc. *Res:* New opportunities research. *Mailing Add:* 3617 Pamajera Dr Oxford OH 45056

LYE, ROBERT J, GENETICS. *Current Pos:* POSTDOCTORAL RES FEL, HEALTH SCI CTR, UNIV VA, 95- *Personal Data:* b St Paul, Minn, May 30, 55. *Educ:* Johns Hopkins Univ, BA, 77; Univ Colo, Boulder, PhD(cell biol), 89. *Prof Exp:* Postdoctoral res fel, Sch Med, Wash Univ, 89-95. *Mem:* Genetics Soc Am; Am Soc Cell Biol. *Mailing Add:* Health Sci Ctr Dept Cell Biol Univ Va Box 439 Jordan Hall Charlottesville VA 22908

LYERLA, JO ANN HARDING, BIOLOGY, ECOLOGICAL GENETICS. *Current Pos:* ASSOC PROF BIOL, BECKER JR COL, LEICESTER, 76- *Personal Data:* b Long Beach, Calif, Sept 28, 40; m 64; c 1. *Educ:* Univ Calif, Davis, BS, 62; San Diego State Univ, MA, 67; Clark Univ, PhD(biol), 78. *Prof Exp:* Lab technician, Univ Calif, Davis, 62-63, Gen Atomics Div, Gen Dynamics Corp, 63-64, Rockefeller Univ, 66-67 & Pa State Univ, 67-70. *Mem:* Genetics Soc; Am Soc Zoologists. *Res:* Ecological genetics of terrestrial isopods; isozyme studies in animal population. *Mailing Add:* Dept Math & Sci Becker Col 61 Cever St Leicester MA 01609

LYERLA, TIMOTHY ARDEN, DEVELOPMENTAL GENETICS. *Current Pos:* from asst prof to assoc prof, 71-88, PROF, CLARK UNIV, 89-; ASSOC BIOCHEM, SHRIVER CTR MENT RETARDATION, WALTHAM, MASS, 80- *Personal Data:* b Long Beach, Calif, Mar 5, 40; m 64; Jo Ann Harding; c 1. *Educ:* Univ Calif, Davis, BA, 63; San Diego State Col, MA, 67; Pa State Univ, University Park, PhD(zool), 70. *Prof Exp:* NIH fel, Northwestern Univ, Ill, 70-71. *Concurrent Pos:* NSF sci fac fel, 78-79. *Mem:* Fel AAAS; Soc Integrative & Comp Biol; Soc Develop Biol; Sigma Xi; Am Soc Cell Biol; Soc In Vitro Biol. *Res:* Pigment genetics in vertebrates; cell differentiation in amphibian development; lysosomal storage diseases in humans. *Mailing Add:* Dept Biol Clark Univ 950 Main St Worcester MA 01610. *Fax:* 508-793-8861; *E-Mail:* tlyerlc@clarku.edu

LYERLY, HERBERT KIM, HIV ASSOCIATED MALIGNANCIES, GENE THERAPY. *Current Pos:* ASST PROF SURG, DUKE UNIV MED CTR, 90-, ASST PROF PATH, 91- *Personal Data:* b San Diego, Calif, Aug 26, 58. *Educ:* Univ Calif, Riverside, BA, 80; Univ Calif, Los Angeles, MD, 83. *Honors & Awards:* Achievement Award, Am Col Surgeons, 89. *Concurrent Pos:* Investr, Ctr AIDS Res & mem, Comprehensive Cancer Ctr, Duke Univ Med Ctr, 91-; mem, Sci Adv Comt, Am Found AIDS Res, 91- *Mem:* Sigma Xi. *Res:* Surgical oncology. *Mailing Add:* Dept Surgery Duke Univ Med Ctr Box 3551 Durham NC 27710

LYFORD, JOHN H, JR, ECOLOGY. *Current Pos:* from asst prof to assoc prof, 65-92, EMER PROF BIOL, ORE STATE UNIV, 92- *Personal Data:* b Chicago, Ill, July 10, 28; div; c 6. *Educ:* Carleton Col, BA, 50; Ore State Univ, MS, 62, PhD(bot), 66. *Prof Exp:* Pub sch teacher, Wash, 55-62; res biologist, Ore State Game Comn, 63-65. *Mem:* AAAS; Ecol Soc Am; Am Bryol Soc. *Res:* Trophic structure of aquatic communities; ecology and distribution of mosses. *Mailing Add:* 342 NW 21st St Corvallis OR 97330

LYFORD, SIDNEY JOHN, JR, ANIMAL NUTRITION, BIOCHEMISTRY. *Current Pos:* PROF ANIMAL NUTRIT, UNIV MASS, AMHERST, 63-, DIR, DEPARTMENTAL UNDERGRAD PROG, 92- *Personal Data:* b Exeter, NH, Jan 20, 37; m 61, Sheila English; c John N, Glenn S & Lisa K. *Educ:* Univ NH, BS, 58; NC State Univ, MS, 60, PhD(animal nutrit), 64. *Concurrent Pos:* Consult animal nutrit. *Mem:* Am Dairy Sci Asn; Am Soc Animal Sci; Sigma Xi. *Res:* Nutrition and feeding of dairy calves; nutritive evaluation of byproduct materials as animal feedstuffs. *Mailing Add:* Dept Vet & Animal Sci Stockbridge Hall Univ Mass Amherst MA 01003. *Fax:* 413-545-6326; *E-Mail:* lyford@vasci.umass.edu

LYGRE, DAVID GERALD, BIOCHEMISTRY. *Current Pos:* from asst prof to assoc prof, res corp grant, Cent Wash Univ, 70-79, asst dean, 80-83, assoc dean, 83-89, PROF CHEM, CENT WASH UNIV, 79- *Personal Data:* b Minot, NDak, Aug 10, 42; m 66, Laurae Johnson; c Jedd & Lindsay. *Educ:* Concordia Col, Moorhead, Minn, BA, 64; Univ NDak, PhD(biochem), 68. *Prof Exp:* Am Cancer Soc fel, Case Western Res Univ, 68-70. *Concurrent Pos:* Lectr, Am Inst Chem Engrs. *Mem:* Am Chem Soc; Sigma Xi; AAAS. *Res:* Enzymology of carbohydrate metabolism; biochemistry of aging; writing chemistry textbooks. *Mailing Add:* Dept Chem Cent Wash Univ Ellensburg WA 98926. *Fax:* 509-963-1050

LYJAK, ROBERT FRED, MATHEMATICS. *Current Pos:* assoc prof, Univ Mich, Dearborn, 66-69, chmn dept, 67-70, prof math, 69-84, EMER PROF MATH & COMPUTER SCI, UNIV MICH, DEARBORN, 84- *Personal Data:* b Detroit, Mich. *Educ:* Wayne State Univ, BS, 51; Univ Mich, Ann Arbor, MA, 53, PhD(math), 60. *Prof Exp:* Assoc mathematician, Res Inst, Univ Mich, 53-56, instr math, Univ, 56-58, mathematician, Res Inst, 59-62; res mathematician, Conduction Corp, 62-63 & Res Inst, Univ Mich, 63-66. *Mem:* Am Math Soc. *Res:* Transformation groups; mathematical models of stochastic systems. *Mailing Add:* 21410 Waterloo Rd Chelsea MI 48118

LYKE, EDWARD BONSTEEL, CYTOLOGY, INVERTEBRATE ZOOLOGY. *Current Pos:* From asst prof to assoc prof, 65-73, PROF BIOL SCI, CALIF STATE UNIV, HAYWARD, 73- *Personal Data:* b Boston, Mass, Nov 9, 37; m 62; c 2. *Educ:* Miami Univ, BA, 59; Univ Wis-Madison, MS, 62, PhD(zool), 65. *Mem:* AAAS; Am Soc Zoologists; Am Inst Biol Sci; Marine Biol Asn UK; Sigma Xi. *Res:* Invertebrate cytology and histology; spermatogenesis and oogenesis; ecology of estuarine invertebrates. *Mailing Add:* Dept Biol Sci Calif State Univ Hayward CA 94542

LYKKEN, DAVID THORESON, GENETICS, PSYCHIATRY. *Current Pos:* From asst prof to assoc prof, 57-65, PROF PSYCHOL, UNIV MINN, 65- *Personal Data:* b Minneapolis, Minn, June 18, 28; m 52; c 3. *Educ:* Univ Minn, BA, 49, MA, 52, PhD(psychol), 55. *Honors & Awards:* Distinguished Contrib to Psychol Award, Am Psychol Asn, 90. *Concurrent Pos:* Fel, Ctr Advan Study Behav Sci, 59-60. *Mem:* Fel Am Psychol Asn; fel AAAS; Soc Psychophysiol Res (pres, 80); Behav Genetics Soc. *Res:* Psychological studies of twins, reared together or apart, & their families; study of emergenic traits which are genetic but do not run in families; studies of polygraphic interogation (lie detection). *Mailing Add:* Dept Psychol N-218 Elliott Hall Univ Minn 75 E River Rd SE Minneapolis MN 55455-0280

LYKKEN, GLENN IRVEN, PHYSICS, NUTRITION. *Current Pos:* from asst prof to assoc prof, 65-76, PROF PHYSICS, UNIV NDAK, 76- *Personal Data:* b Grafton, NDak, Jan 27, 39; m 64, Dacon G McCorquodale; c Timothy, Mark, Christopher & Jennifer. *Educ:* Univ NDak, BSEE, 61; Univ NC, MS, 64, PhD(physics), 66. *Prof Exp:* Asst physics, Univ NDak, 61-62 & Univ NC, 62-65. *Concurrent Pos:* Vis prof, Univ NC, 69-70; res physicist, Grand Forks Human Nutrit Res Ctr, USDA, Grand Forks, NDak, 77-88, health physicist, 88- *Mem:* Sigma Xi; Am Phys Soc; Am Inst Nutrit. *Res:* Whole body counting of low level gamma emissions from humans; environmental radon uptake and distribution in the body; health effects in humans; bioavailability of essential trace elements; alpha particle spectroscopy-emissions from lead. *Mailing Add:* Human Nutr Res Ctr Univ Sta PO Box 7166 Grand Forks ND 58202

LYKOS, PETER GEORGE, PHYSICAL CHEMISTRY. *Current Pos:* from instr to assoc prof chem, 55-64, dir, Comput Ctr & Comput Sci Dept, 64-71, PROF CHEM, ILL INST TECHNOL, 64-, ASSOC DEAN PLANNING, 93- *Personal Data:* b Chicago, Ill, Jan 22, 27; m 50, Marie Shumicki; c George, Kristina & Andrew. *Educ:* Northwestern Univ, BS, 50; Carnegie Inst Technol, PhD(chem), 55. *Prof Exp:* Instr chem, Carnegie Inst Technol, 54-55. *Concurrent Pos:* Consult, Solid State Sci Div, Argonne Nat Lab, 58-67; consult, Dept Radiation Ther, Michael Reese Hosp, 66-70; pres, Four Pi, Inc, 66-; mem-at-large & chmn comt comput in chem, Nat Acad Sci-Nat Res Coun, 68-74; prog dir, Off Comput Activities, NSF, 71-73; originator series int conferences comput in chem res & educ, Ill, 71, Yugoslavia, 73, Venezuela, 76, USSR, 78, Japan, 80, Washington, DC, 82, WGer, Fed Repub Ger, 85, Beijing, 87 & Italy, 89; co-chmn, Nat Resource Comput in Chem Proposal Develop Team, Argonne Univs Asn-Argonne Nat Lab, 74-77; chmn, Comput in Chem Div, Am Chem Soc, 73-77, mem comt prof training, 77- & adv comt, Chem & Eng News, 77-80; dir, Interactive Instr TV Network, 76-78; mem bd, Asn Media-based Continuing Eng Educ, 76-78; sci consult, Video Satellite Delivery, Nat Tech Univ. *Mem:* Asn Comput Mach; Am Chem Soc; Sigma Xi. *Res:* Semi-empirical Quantum chemistry; computational chemistry; computers in chemical education. *Mailing Add:* Dept Chem Ill Inst Technol 3255 S Dearborn Chicago IL 60616. *Fax:* 312-567-8882; *E-Mail:* chemlykos@minna.acc.iit.edu

LYKOUDIS, PAUL S, AERONAUTICAL ENGINEERING. *Current Pos:* From asst prof to assoc prof, Purdue Univ, 56-60, dir aerospace sci lab, 68-73, head dept nuclear eng, 73-85, PROF AEROSPACE, ASTRONAUTICS & ENG SCI, PURDUE UNIV, 60-, PROF NUCLEAR ENG, 85- *Personal Data:* m 53; c 1. *Educ:* Nat Tech Univ, Greece, Mech & Elec Engr, 50; Purdue Univ, MS, 54, PhD, 56. *Honors & Awards:* Res Award, Sigma Xi, 87. *Concurrent Pos:* Consult, Rand Corp, 60-; NSF grant, 60- *Mem:* Assoc fel Am Inst Aeronaut & Astronaut; Am Phys Soc; Am Astron Soc; Am Nuclear Soc; Sigma Xi. *Res:* Contributor of numerous papers in field of fluid mechanics, magneto-fluid-mechanics, astrophysics, and fluid mechanics of physiological systems. *Mailing Add:* 116 Glenn Ct West Lafayette IN 47906

LYLE, BENJAMIN FRANKLIN, INDUSTRIAL ENGINEERING, SYSTEMS ANALYSIS. *Current Pos:* assoc prof, 70-76, PROF MATH, E TENN STATE UNIV, 76- *Personal Data:* b Johnson City, Tenn, Aug 14, 33; m 57; c 3. *Educ:* Univ Tenn, Knoxville, BS, 55, MS, 56; E Tenn State Univ, MA, 62; NMex State Univ, ScD(indust eng), 69. *Prof Exp:* Engr artist, Fisher Body Div, Gen Motors Corp, Mich, 55; pres, Lyle Furniture Co, Tenn, 55-61; instr math, E Tenn State Univ, 61-66; from instr to asst prof indust eng, NMex State Univ, 66-70. *Mem:* Am Inst Indust Eng; Am Soc Eng Educ; Nat Soc Prof Engrs. *Res:* Decision theory; economic evaluation; mathematical modeling. *Mailing Add:* Dept Technol E Tenn State Univ PO Box 10001 Johnson City TN 37614-0002

LYLE, EVERETT SAMUEL, JR, FORESTRY, SOIL SCIENCE. *Current Pos:* PVT CONSULT, 87- *Personal Data:* b Dyersburg, Tenn, Mar 17, 27; m 47; c 2. *Educ:* Univ Ga, BSF, 51; Duke Univ, MF, 52; Auburn Univ, PhD(soil sci), 69. *Prof Exp:* Staff asst, Union Camp Corp, 52-57; researcher, Auburn Univ, 57-86, land reclamation consult, 86-87. *Concurrent Pos:* Researcher, Ala Surface Mine Reclamation Coun, 73-77; state comnr, Ala Surface Mining Reclamation Comn, 76-80. *Mem:* Soc Am Foresters; Am Soc Agron; Soil Sci Soc Am; Can Land Reclamation Asn. *Res:* Coal surface mine reclamation; tree nutrition; forest soils. *Mailing Add:* 4201 Cliff Dr Jasper AL 35504

LYLE, GLORIA GILBERT, ORGANIC CHEMISTRY. *Current Pos:* ADJ PROF, UNIV TEX, SAN ANTONIO, 81-; PRES, GRL CONSULTS, 92- *Personal Data:* b Atlanta, Ga, Aug 7, 23; m 47, Robert E Jr. *Educ:* Vanderbilt Univ, BA, 45; Emory Univ, MS, 46; Univ NH, PhD, 58. *Honors & Awards:* Harry & Carol Mosher Nat Award, Am Chem Soc, 86. *Prof Exp:* Instr chem, Hollins Col, 46-47; res assoc, McArdle Lab Cancer Res, Univ Wis, 47-49; from instr to prof pharmacol, Univ NH, 51-77; asst prof pharmacol, Tex Col Osteop Med, 77-80. *Concurrent Pos:* USPHS res fel, 58-59; vis assoc prof, Univ Va, 73-74. *Mem:* Am Chem Soc; NY Acad Sci; Royal Soc Chem; Sigma Xi. *Res:* Organic synthesis; natural products; optical rotatory dispersion and circular dichroism; stereochemistry. *Mailing Add:* 12814 Kings Forest San Antonio TX 78230. *Fax:* 210-492-5330; *E-Mail:* geegeel@connecti.com

LYLE, LEON RICHARDS, TECHNICAL MANAGEMENT. *Current Pos:* chemist immunol, Mallinckrodt Med Inc, 73-75, group leader immunol, 75-80, asst dir, Hybridoma Lab, 80-85, assoc dir nuclear med, 85-89, assoc dir tech planning, 89-91, dir tech planning, 91-96, DIR TECH PLANNING, MALLINCKRODT INC, 96- *Personal Data:* b Ottumwa, Iowa, Nov 28, 41; m 72, Mary J Dueber; c Elizabeth & Daniel. *Educ:* Drake Univ, BA, 63, MA, 67; Mont State Univ, PhD(microbiol), 69. *Prof Exp:* Postdoctoral fel immunol, Sch Med, Washington Univ, 70-73. *Concurrent Pos:* Indust rep, Immunol Devices Adv Panel, Off Med Devices, Food & Drug Admin, 81-88;

sci prog chmn, Nat Meeting St Louis, Clin Ligand Assay Soc, 86-87. *Mem:* Am Asn Immunologists; AAAS. *Res:* Identification, implementation and administration of extramural research programs in medical and chemical divisions. *Mailing Add:* Mallinckrodt Inc 675 McDonnell Blvd PO Box 5840 St Louis MO 63134. *Fax:* 314-895-8992; *E-Mail:* lrlyle@mkg.com

LYLE, ROBERT EDWARD, JR, PHARMACEUTICAL CHEMISTRY, STRUCTURAL CHEMISTRY. *Current Pos:* VPRES & TREAS, GRL CONSULTS, 91- *Personal Data:* b Atlanta, Ga, Jan 26, 26; m 47, Gloria Gilbert. *Educ:* Emory Univ, BA, 45, MS, 46; Univ Wis-Madison, PhD(org chem), 49. *Honors & Awards:* Harry-Carol Mosher Award, Am Chem Soc, 87. *Prof Exp:* Asst prof chem, Oberlin Col, 49-51; prof chem, Univ NH, 51-76; prof & chair chem, Univ NTex, 76-79; vpres chem & chem eng, SW Res Inst, 79-91. *Concurrent Pos:* Adj prof, Univ Tex, San Antonio, 82-; vis prof, Univ Va. *Mem:* Am Chem Soc; Royal Soc Chem; AAAS; Am Asn Cancer Res. *Res:* Stereochemistry of nitrogen heterocycles; organic synthesis of heterocyclic compounds; microencapsulation and drug delivery systems. *Mailing Add:* 12814 Kings Forest San Antonio TX 78230. *Fax:* 210-492-5330; *E-Mail:* geegeel@connecti.com

LYLE, WILLIAM MONTGOMERY, OPTOMETRY. *Current Pos:* chief path sect, Univ Waterloo, 67-74, from assoc prof to prof optom, 67-84, dir clins, 74-77, adj prof, 84-89, EMER PROF OPTOM, UNIV WATERLOO, 89- *Personal Data:* b Summerside, PEI, Oct 4, 13; m 56; c 3. *Educ:* Col Optom Ont, dipl, 38, OD, 58; Ind Univ, Bloomington, MS, 63, PhD(physiol optics), 65. *Honors & Awards:* President's Award, Can Asn Optom. *Prof Exp:* Pvt pract optom, 38-60; res assoc physiol optics, Ind Univ, 60-62, lectr, 62-65; asst prof optom, Col Optom Ont, 65-67. *Concurrent Pos:* Pres, Asn Schs Optom Can, 71-73; ed, Am J Optom & Physiol Optics, 79-88; ed, Optom & Vision Sci, 89- *Mem:* Can Asn Optom (pres, 55-57); AAAS; Am Acad Optom; Am Soc Human Genetics; Am Optom Asn; Sigma Xi. *Res:* Side effects of drugs; inheritance of astigmatism; intraracial differences in refraction; lasers. *Mailing Add:* Sch Optom Univ Waterloo Waterloo ON N2L 3G1 Can. *Fax:* 519-746-7937; *E-Mail:* optjourn@sciborg.uwaterloo.ca

LYLES, LEON, AGRICULTURAL ENGINEERING, RESEARCH ADMINISTRATION. *Current Pos:* RETIRED. *Personal Data:* b Wetumka, Okla, Jan 18, 32; m 51; c 3. *Educ:* Okla State Univ, BS, 55; Kans State Univ, MS, 59, PhD(mech eng), 70. *Honors & Awards:* Distinguished Serv Award, USDA, 84. *Prof Exp:* Agr engr erosion res, Agr Res Serv, USDA, 57-60, water mgt res, 60-64, wind erosion res, 64-75, res leader, Wind Erosion Res Unit, 75-88. *Mem:* Am Soc Agr Engrs; Soil Sci Soc Am. *Res:* Wind erosion and water management (dryland) research. *Mailing Add:* 1801 Virginia Dr Manhattan KS 66502

LYLES, LESTER, AERONAUTICAL & ASTRONAUTICAL ENGINEERING. *Current Pos:* DIR, BALLISTIC MISSILE DEFENSE ORGN, DEPT DEFENSE. *Mailing Add:* Ballistic Missile Defense Orgn Dept Defense 7100 Defense Pentagon Washington DC 20301

LYLES, SANDERS TRUMAN, BACTERIOLOGY. *Current Pos:* EMER CONSULT ECOL & ENVIRON, 70- *Personal Data:* b Reeves, La, May 24, 07; m 46; c 4. *Educ:* Rice Univ, BA, 30, MA, 31; Southwestern Baptist Sem, ThM, 36, ThD, 49; Univ Tex, PhD(bact, biochem), 55. *Prof Exp:* From instr to prof biol, Tex Christian Univ, 46-77, res scientist, 52-54. *Mem:* Am Soc Microbiol; Sigma Xi. *Res:* Epidemiology and antibiotic resistance of staphylococcus; biochemical studies of blood serum. *Mailing Add:* 3901 Stadium Dr Ft Worth TX 76109

LYMAN, BEVERLY ANN, BIOCHEMISTRY, TOXICOLOGY. *Personal Data:* b Philadelphia, Pa, Aug 22, 56; m 81, Henry M Laboda; c Alex & Elizabeth. *Educ:* Thomas Jefferson Univ, BS, 78; Univ Pa, MS, 82; Hahnemann Med Col, PhD(biochem), 86. *Prof Exp:* Fel, Chem Indust Inst Toxicol, 87-88; assoc prof, Clin Lab Sci & Med Chem, Univ Tenn, Memphis, 89-93. *Mem:* Am Soc Biochem & Molecular Biol; AAAS; Sigma Xi; Am Soc Med Technol; Soc Toxicol. *Res:* Biochemical toxicology of anticancer drugs; biochemistry of surface-active antithrombotic agents for prostheses. *Mailing Add:* Wood Herron & Evans 2700 Carew Tower Cincinnati OH 45202

LYMAN, CHARLES PEIRSON, BIOLOGY. *Current Pos:* Asst physiol, Harvard Univ, 42, asst cur, Mus Comp Zool, 45-50, fel anat, Med Sch, 46-48, res assoc, 48-62, assoc cur, 50-57, res assoc, 58-68, from asst prof to assoc prof anat, 62-76, cur mammal, 68-81, prof, 76-81, EMER PROF BOIL, HARVARD UNIV, 81- *Personal Data:* b Brookline, Mass, Sept 23, 12; m 41; c 5. *Educ:* Harvard Univ, AB, 36, MA, 39, PhD(biol), 42. *Mem:* AAAS; Am Physiol Soc; Am Soc Zoologists; Am Acad Arts & Sci; Sigma Xi. *Res:* Hibernation and temperature regulation in mammals; physiological ecology. *Mailing Add:* 105 Elm St Canton MA 02021

LYMAN, DONALD JOSEPH, POLYMER CHEMISTRY, BIOMATERIALS. *Current Pos:* prof mat sci & res assoc prof surg, 69-89, prof bioeng, 74-89, EMER PROF MAT SCI & BIOENG, UNIV UTAH, 89- *Personal Data:* b Chicago, Ill, Nov 5, 26; m 78; c 2. *Educ:* Univ Nev, BS, 49; Univ Del, MS, 51, PhD(chem), 52. *Honors & Awards:* Am Soc Artificial Internal Organs Award, 69; Clemson Award Basic Res, Soc Biomaterials, 82; Distinguished Res Award, Univ Utah, 82. *Prof Exp:* Asst chem, Univ Del, 50-52; res chemist high polymers, E I du Pont de Nemours & Co, 52-61; sr polymer chemist, Stanford Res Int, 61-64, head biomed polymer res, 64-69, pres, Vascular Int Inc, 83-86. *Concurrent Pos:* Lectr, Dept Mat Sci, Stanford Univ, 64-68; chmn, Gordon Conf Sci & Technol Biomat; mem, comt surv mat sci & eng, Nat Acad Sci; mem, eval panel polymer div, Nat Bur Stand, 73-76; fel biomat sci & eng, World Biomat Cong, 94. *Mem:* AAAS; Am Chem Soc; Am Soc Artificial Internal Organs; Soc Biomat; Int Soc Artificial Organs. *Res:* Synthetic polymers and polymer intermediates; mechanisms of polymerization; structure-property relationships of polymers; biomedical polymers; implants for artificial organs and reconstruction surgery; applied spectroscopy. *Mailing Add:* PO Box 5314 Lacey WA 98509-5314

LYMAN, FRANK LEWIS, TOXICOLOGY. *Current Pos:* RETIRED. *Personal Data:* b Springfield, Ill, Nov 6, 21; m 47, Julia Kleinschmidt; c Patty, Frank III, Richard, Robert, Jon & Don. *Educ:* Swarthmore Col, AB, 43; Hahnemann Med Col, MD, 46; Bd Toxicol Sci, dipl. *Prof Exp:* Intern, WJersey Hosp, Camden, NJ, 47; physician, coach & instr biol, William Penn Col, 47-48; pvt pract, Iowa, 48-55; staff pediatrician, US Naval Hosp, Beaufort, SC, 55-57; assoc med dir, Mead Johnson & Co, 57-60; assoc dir, Med Dept, Geigy Chem Corp, 60-61; asst to med dir, 61-63; dir indust med, Ciba-Geigy Corp, 63-76; consult toxicol, 76-87. *Concurrent Pos:* Instr, Seton Hall Col, 60-62; mem var comts, Nat Acad Sci, 75-81; assoc prof, Sch Med, Temple Univ, 77- *Mem:* AMA; Am Col Toxicol; Soc Toxicol; fel Am Acad Clin Toxicol. *Res:* Dietary management of phenylketonuria; toxicology of fluorescent whitening agents; pesticide toxicology. *Mailing Add:* 1068-F Long Beach Blvd North Beach NJ 08008

LYMAN, FREDERIC A, MECHANICAL ENGINEERING. *Current Pos:* assoc prof, 70-78, PROF MECH & AEROSPACE ENG, SYRACUSE UNIV, 78- *Personal Data:* b Syracuse, NY, Sept 4, 34; m 54, Marilyn Mawson; c Ruth, Martha & Sarah. *Educ:* Syracuse Univ, BME, 55, MME, 57; Rensselaer Polytech Inst, PhD(eng mech), 61. *Prof Exp:* Preceptor eng mech, Columbia Univ, 61-62; aerospace res engr, Lewis Res Ctr, NASA, 62-66, head plasma flow sect, 66-67; assoc prof eng, Case Western Res Univ, 67-70. *Concurrent Pos:* Vis res engr, Princeton Univ, 77-78; prin res engr, Case Western Res Univ/NASA Lewis Inst Computational Mech Propulsion, 85-86. *Mem:* AAAS; Am Phys Soc; Am Soc Mech Engrs. *Res:* Fluid mechanics; heat transfer; plasma dynamics; acoustics; combustion. *Mailing Add:* 323 Scott Ave Syracuse NY 13224-1725

LYMAN, GARY HERBERT, PUBLIC HEALTH & EPIDEMIOLOGY, BIOMATHEMATICS. *Current Pos:* Chief med oncol, 79-83, chief med, H Lee Moffitt Cancer Ctr & Res Inst, 85-93, PROF MED & BIOSTATIST, UNIV SFLA, 77-, CHIEF EPIDEMIOL & BIOSTATIST, 93- *Personal Data:* b Buffalo, NY, Feb 24, 46; m 78, Carolyn Zalewski; c Stephen & Christopher. *Educ:* State Univ NY, BA, 68, MD, 72; Harvard, MPH, 82. *Mem:* AAAS; Am Soc Hemat; Am Soc Clin Oncol; Am Asn Cancer Res; Am Col Physicians. *Res:* Cancer epidemiology; clinical decision making; mathematical modeling; design and analysis of clncial trials; clinical pharmacology. *Mailing Add:* H Lee Moffitt Cancer Ctr & Res Inst 12902 Magnolia Dr Tampa FL 33612. *Fax:* 813-972-8468; *E-Mail:* lyman@aarlo.moffitt.usf.edu

LYMAN, HARVARD, PLANT PHYSIOLOGY, MOLECULAR BIOLOGY. *Current Pos:* ASSOC PROF BIOL, STATE UNIV NY, STONY BROOK, 68- *Personal Data:* b San Francisco, Calif, Sept 25, 31. *Educ:* Univ Calif, Berkeley, BA, 53; Univ Wash, MS, 57; Brandeis Univ, PhD(biol), 60. *Prof Exp:* Asst biol, Univ Wash, 55-57; instr, Brooklyn Col, 60-62; vis scientist biochem, Brookhaven Nat Lab, 62-63; asst prof biol, Brooklyn Col, 63-65; asst scientist microbiol, Brookhaven Nat Lab, NY, 65-67, assoc scientist, Med Dept, 67-68. *Concurrent Pos:* NIH res grant, 63-65; NSF travel grant, 64, grant, 70-72. *Mem:* AAAS; Am Soc Plant Physiologists; Soc Protozoologists; Am Soc Cell Biologists; Biophys Soc. *Res:* Biosynthesis and inheritance of cellular organelles; development, physiology and differentiation of algae and fleshy and unicellular fungi. *Mailing Add:* Dept Biol State Univ NY Stony Brook NY 11794-5215

LYMAN, JOHN (HENRY), SELF ORGANIZING SYSTEMS. *Current Pos:* PROF ENG & PSYCHOL, UNIV CALIF-LOS ANGELES, 51- *Personal Data:* b Santa Barbara, Calif, May 29, 21; wid; c 2. *Educ:* Univ Calif Los Angeles, BA, 43, MS, 50, PhD(exp psychol), 51. *Honors & Awards:* Paul M Fitts Award, Human Factors Soc, 71. *Prof Exp:* Res technician math, Lockheed Aircraft Corp, 40-44. *Concurrent Pos:* Managing ed, Human Factors Soc, 58-63, Ann Biomed Eng, Biomed Eng Soc, 71-76; head, Biotechnol Lab, Sch Eng & Appl Sci, Univ Calif-Los Angeles, 58-84; consult, Vet Admin, Los Angeles, 62 & 66-72, Human Factors Soc, 76-; vis prof bioeng, Technol Inst, Delft, Neth, 65; spec consult, Comt Prosthetics Res & Develop, Nat Acad Sci, 73. *Mem:* Human Factors Soc (pres, 67-68); Biomed Eng Soc (pres, 80-81); fel Am Psychol Asn; Systs Man & Cybernetics Soc; fel Am Psychol Soc; Inst Elec & Electronic Engrs Med & Biol Soc. *Res:* Functional optimization of human machine environment design interfaces; applications to neuromuscularly handicapped, teleoperations, robotic systems and human-computer shared functions in normal and stressful environments. *Mailing Add:* 3512 Beverly Ridge Dr Sherman Oaks CA 91423-4505

LYMAN, JOHN L, laser photochemistry, for more information see previous edition

LYMAN, JOHN TOMPKINS, BIOPHYSICS. *Current Pos:* Res asst, 59-65, biophysicist, 65-79, STAFF SR SCIENTIST, LAWRENCE BERKELEY LAB, 79- *Personal Data:* b Berkeley, Calif, May 25, 32; m 80; c 3. *Educ:* Univ Calif, AB, 54 & 58, PhD(biophys), 65. *Mem:* Am Asn Physicists in Med; AAAS; Sigma Xi. *Res:* Radiation physics; radiation therapy; radiobiology; heavy charged-particle radiation dosimetry; radiobiology and radiotherapy. *Mailing Add:* 10 Tanglewood Rd MS 55-121 Berkeley CA 94705-1421

LYMAN, ONA RUFUS, PHYSICS. *Current Pos:* RETIRED. *Personal Data:* b Jamaica, Vt, Nov 18, 30; m 54; c 3. *Educ:* Univ Vt, BA, 52. *Prof Exp:* Jr engr, Sprague Elec Co, 52-54; physicist, Terminal Ballistics Lab, Ballistics Res Lab, Aberdeen Proving Groun, 56-95. *Res:* Neutron shielding; combustion; interaction of laser beams with materials; blast and fragment protection for industrial workers; initiation mechanisms of explosives; explosive safety in storage and transport; vulnerability of gun propellants to hostile threats. *Mailing Add:* 303 Carter St Aberdeen MD 21001

LYMAN, W(ILKES) STUART, PHYSICAL METALLURGY. *Current Pos:* mgr tech serv & mkt res, 64-79, sr vpres, 79-81, sr vpres, 81-94, SR ADV, COPPER DEVELOP ASN INC, 94- *Personal Data:* b Mt Vernon, SDak, Apr 13, 24; m 48, Martha I Landon; c Mary C (Onkka), Richard F & Barbara L. *Educ:* Univ Notre Dame, BS, 44; Univ Calif, MS, 52. *Honors & Awards:* Prain Medal & Prize, Ins Mats, London, 96. *Prof Exp:* Jr metallurgist, Nat Adv Comt Aeronaut, Ohio, 44; head adv planning unit, Off Chief Engr, US Forces Frankfurt, Ger, 46-47, engr, Spec Assignment, Heidelberg, 48-49; asst, Univ Calif, 49-50, res engr, Inst Eng Res, 50-51; staff metallurgist, Mat Adv Bd, Nat Res Coun, 51-54; asst dept consult, Battelle Mem Inst, 55-57, div consult ferrous metall, 57-62, div chief, 62-64. *Mem:* Am Soc Metals Int; Metall Soc; Am Soc Mech Engrs; Am Soc Testing & Mat; Inst Mat. *Res:* Metal fabrication; materials application; alloy selection. *Mailing Add:* 15 N Bridge Terr Mt Kisco NY 10549. *Fax:* 212-251-7234; *E-Mail:* wsl@cds.copper.org

LYMAN, WILLIAM RAY, CHEMISTRY, RADIOISOTOPES IN RESEARCH. *Current Pos:* RETIRED. *Personal Data:* b Stratton, Vt, May 30, 20; m 44, Vera R Petersen; c 4. *Educ:* Univ Vt, BS, 41; Mass Inst Technol, PhD(org chem), 47; Columbia Univ, AM, 47. *Prof Exp:* Asst chem, Columbia Univ, 41-44; jr chemist, Tenn Eastman Corp Div, Eastman Kodak Co, 44-46; res chemist, Resinous Prod & Chem Co, 47-48; res chemist, Rohm & Haas Co, 48-66, lab head, 66-73, proj leader, 73-81, res sect mgr, 81-84, spec assignment, 84-85, consult, 85-87. *Mem:* Am Chem Soc. *Res:* Pesticide residue analysis; fate of pesticides in plant and animal systems and in the environment. *Mailing Add:* 728 Norristown Rd Apt G-209 Ambler PA 19002

LYMANGROVER, JOHN R, ENDOCRINOLOGY, ELECTROPHYISOLOGY. *Current Pos:* ASSOC PROF, DEPT PHYSIOL & PHARMACOL & DIR MED PHYSIOL TEACHING, BOWMAN-GRAY MED SCH, 80- *Personal Data:* b Ft Wayne, Ind, July 24, 44. *Educ:* Xavier Univ, BS, 66; Univ Ky, MS, 68; Univ Cincinnati, PhD(physiol), 72. *Prof Exp:* Fel res, Dept Biochem, Med Col Ohio, 72-75; asst prof, Dept Physiol, Tulane Univ, 75-80. *Concurrent Pos:* Adj assoc prof, Dept Elec Eng, Tulane Univ, 80-; consult, grants reviewer, NIH, 79-81; mem, Basic Sci & High Blood Pressure Coun, Am Heart Asn. *Mem:* AAAS; Sigma Xi; Bioelectromagnetics Soc; Endocrine Soc. *Res:* Neuroendocrinology; biological effects of electric fields; mechanism of peptide hormone action on adrenal cortical hormone release; role of endogenous opioids on adrenal steroid secretion and regulation of blood pressure. *Mailing Add:* 12909 Turkey Branch Pkwy Rockville MD 20853

LYMN, RICHARD WESLEY, BIOPHYSICS, BIOCHEMISTRY. *Current Pos:* sr staff fel biophys, Phys Biol Lab, Nat Inst Arthritis Metab & Digestive Dis, 74-78, grants assoc, Div Res Grants, 78-79, asst assoc dir, Arthritis, Musculoskeletal & Skin Dis, Nat Inst Arthritis, Diabetes, Digestive & Kidney Dis, 79-83, DIR MUSCLE BIOL PROG, NIH, 84- *Personal Data:* b Flushing, NY, July 26, 44; m 70; c 2. *Educ:* Johns Hopkins Univ, BA, 64; Univ Chicago, PhD(biophys), 70. *Prof Exp:* USPHS fel biophys, Univ Chicago, 70-71; Brit-Am fel, Am Heart Asn, MRC Lab Molecular Biol, Cambridge, Eng, 71-74. *Concurrent Pos:* Treas, Biophys Soc, 82-87, Publ Comt, 87-91, chair, 90-91. *Mem:* Biophys Soc; Am Soc Biol Chemists; AAAS. *Res:* Enzyme kinetics; cellular and morphological movement; mathematical modelling; molecular mechanism of muscle contraction and tension development; science administration. *Mailing Add:* Muscle Biol NIAMS NIH Natcher Bldg Rm 5AS49E MSC 6500 Bethesda MD 20892-6500

LYNCH, BENJAMIN LEO, ORAL SURGERY. *Current Pos:* From asst instr to assoc prof oral surg, Creighton Univ, 48-57, dean, Sch Dent, 54-61, dir, Oral Surg Dept, 54-67, coordr, Dent Sch Grad & Post-grad Prog, 67, PROF ORAL SURG, CREIGHTON UNIV, 57- *Personal Data:* b Omaha, Nebr, Dec 29, 23; m 56, Colleen Cook; c Kathleen, Mary Beth, Patrick, George, Martha & Estelle. *Educ:* Creighton Univ, BS, 45, DDS, 47, MA, 63; Northwestern Univ, MSD, 54; Am Bd Oral Surg, dipl. *Concurrent Pos:* Pres dent staff, Children's Mem Hosp, 52-53 & 59-60; fac mem, San Antonio Jr Col, 55, Med Field Sch, Ft Sam Houston, 55-56, Walter Reed Army Post-grad Sch Med, 56-57, guest lectr, 57-58; mem, Omaha-Douglas County Health Bd, 66-68, vpres, 67, pres, 68; mem, bd dir, Nebr Blue Cross-Blue Shield, 68-89, exec comt, 73-81; mem bd dirs, Nebr Dental Serv Corp, 72-78, pres, 74-78; treas, Children's Mem Hosp Med-Dent Staff, 79-81, staff mem, 50-88; consult, Vet Hosp & Strategic Air Command Hq, Omaha, Nebr & Jenny Edmundson Hosp, Council Bluffs, Iowa; staff mem & exec comt, Omaha Surg Ctr, 79-83, secy staff, 81-83. *Mem:* Am Soc Oral & Maxillofacial Surgeons; Am Dent Asn; fel Am Col Dent. *Res:* Dental education. *Mailing Add:* 509 S Happy Hollow Blvd Omaha NE 68106

LYNCH, BRIAN MAURICE, PHYSICAL ORGANIC CHEMISTRY, CHEMICAL INFORMATION. *Current Pos:* assoc prof, St Francis Xavier Univ, 62-68, prof org chem, 68-95, chmn dept, 72-79, & 80-86, SR RES PROF, CHEM MED UNIV, ST FRANCIS XAVIER UNIV, 95- *Personal Data:* b Melbourne, Australia, Jan 20, 30; m 56, Elizabeth Joan Wecton; c Alexandra Helen & Martin James. *Educ:* Univ Melbourne, BSc, 52, MSc, 54, PhD(chem), 56. *Prof Exp:* Fel & vis prof cancer chemother, NMex Highlands Univ, 56-57; asst prof org chem, St Francis Xavier Univ, Can, 57-58; res officer chem, Div Coal Res, Commonwealth Sci & Indust Res Orgn, Australia, 58-59; asst prof phys chem, Mem Univ Nfld, 59-62. *Concurrent Pos:* Nat Res Coun Can sr res fel, Australian Nat Univ, 68-69; Natural Sci & Eng Res Coun sr indust fel, NS Res Found, 81-82; proj Seraphim fel, Eastern Mich Univ, 88; mem, Educ Comt, Chem Info Div, Am Chem Soc, 96- *Mem:* Am Chem Soc; fel Can Soc Chem; fel Royal Soc Chem London; Soc Appl Spectros; fel Chem Inst Can. *Res:* Nuclear magnetic resonance; infrared spectra by Fourier transform techniques; internet resources for chemistry and health. *Mailing Add:* PO Box 5000 Chem Dept St Francis Xavier Univ Antigonish NS B2G 2W5 Can. *Fax:* 902-867-2414; *E-Mail:* blynch@juliet.stfsc.ca

LYNCH, CAROL BECKER, BEHAVIORAL GENETICS, EVOLUTIONARY GENETICS. *Current Pos:* DEAN GRAD SCH & ASSOC VCHANCELLOR RES, UNIV COLO, BOULDER, 92- *Personal Data:* b New York, NY, Dec 3, 42; m 67, G Robert. *Educ:* Mt Holyoke Col, AB, 64; Univ Mich, MA, 65; Univ Iowa, PhD(zool), 71. *Prof Exp:* NSF fel, Inst Behav Genetics, Univ Colo, 72-73; from asst prof to prof, Wesleyan Univ, 73-85, prof biol, 85-92, dean sci, 88-91. *Concurrent Pos:* Prog dir, Pop Biol & Physiol Ecol, NSF, 90-92. *Mem:* Behav Genetics Asn; AAAS; Soc Study Evolution; Am Soc Naturalists. *Res:* Genetic and environmental influences on behavioral and physiological thermoregulation in mice; empirical tests of quantitative; genetic theory; genetic influence on circadian rhythms. *Mailing Add:* Grad Sch Univ Colo EPOB CB334 Boulder CO 80309-0001. *Fax:* 303-492-5777; *E-Mail:* lynchcb@spot.colorado.edu

LYNCH, CHARLES ANDREW, SYNTHETIC FAT SUBSTITUTES, SYNTHETIC LUBRICANTS. *Current Pos:* tech dir, Dir Sales & Mkt/New Bus Develop, 81-90, VPRES TECHNOL, HATCO CORP, 91- *Personal Data:* b Brooklyn, NY, Jan 6, 35; m 60, Marilyn A Monaco; c Nancy & Cara. *Educ:* Manhattan Col, BS, 56; Univ Notre Dame, PhD(org chem), 60. *Prof Exp:* Res chemist, Esso Res & Eng Co, 60-65; mgr org appln res, FMC Corp, 65-74; exec vpres & tech dir, Am Oil & Supply Co, 74-80. *Mem:* Am Chem Soc; Am Oil Chemists Soc; Soc Tribologists & Lubrication Engrs; Soc Automotive Engrs; Chem Mgt & Resources Asn; Com Develop Asn. *Res:* Advanced high temperature liquid lubricant development; advanced dielectric fluids; fat substitutes; product and process research. *Mailing Add:* 19 Gordon Way Princeton NJ 08540-3925

LYNCH, DAN K, industrial chemistry, for more information see previous edition

LYNCH, DANIEL MATTHEW, PLANT ECOLOGY. *Current Pos:* from instr to assoc prof, 54-65, PROF BIOL, ST EDWARD'S UNIV, 65- *Personal Data:* b Detroit, Mich, June 28, 21. *Educ:* Univ Detroit, AB, 43; Mich State Univ, MS, 48; Wash State Univ, PhD(bot), 52. *Prof Exp:* Asst bot, Mich State Univ, 47-48 & Wash State Univ, 48-52. *Mem:* AAAS; Ecol Soc Am; Bot Soc Am. *Res:* Ecology of the southwestern grasslands and woodlands. *Mailing Add:* Dept Physics & Biol Sci St Edward's Univ 3001 S Congress Ave Austin TX 78704-6489

LYNCH, DANIEL ROGER, COMPUTATION, APPLIED MATHEMATICS. *Current Pos:* assoc dean eng, 85-89, prof, 89-93, MACLEAN PROF ENG, DARTMOUTH COL, 93- *Personal Data:* b Glens Falls, NY, 1950. *Educ:* Mass Inst Technol, BS & MS, 72; Princeton Univ, MS, 76, PhD(civil eng), 78. *Hon Degrees:* MA, Dartmouth Col, 93. *Honors & Awards:* B H Ketchum Award, Woods Hole Oceanog Inst, 90. *Prof Exp:* Engr, Stone & Webster, 72-73; qual assurance engr, C R Bard Inc, 73-75; hydrologist, US Geol Surv, 77-79; prin young investr, NSF, 84. *Concurrent Pos:* Exec dir, Regional Asn Res Gulf of Maine, 92-94. *Mem:* Am Geophys Union; Am Soc Civil Engrs. *Res:* Advanced computational methods for environmental simulation; coastal ocean. *Mailing Add:* Eng Dartmouth Col HB 8000 Hanover NH 03755-8000

LYNCH, DARREL LUVENE, ORGANIC CHEMISTRY, SOIL MICROBIOLOGY. *Current Pos:* from assoc prof to prof, 66-82, EMER PROF BIOL SCI, NORTHERN ILL UNIV, 82- *Personal Data:* b Dewey, Okla, Feb 6, 21; m 49, Dorothy Banner; c Alan, Francis, Alice & Margaret. *Educ:* Univ Ill, PhD(agron), 53; Univ Del, MS, 57. *Prof Exp:* Instr & asst soil biol, Univ Ill, 48-52; asst prof agron, Univ Del, 52-58; asst prof soil sci, Univ Alta, 58-60; assoc prof chem, Ga Southern Col, 60-62. *Mem:* Am Soc Microbiol. *Res:* Nitrogen fixation of Rhizobia and nodulation; soil organic matter; soil polysaccharides; morphology and nutrition studies with algae; ultrastructure studies with the Actinoplanaceae; pigment production in bacteria. *Mailing Add:* 306 Dresser Rd De Kalb IL 60115

LYNCH, DAVID DEXTER, THEORY OF INERTIAL INSTRUMENTS, MODELING & SIMULATION OF AUTOMOTIVE CRASH SENSORS. *Current Pos:* CHIEF SCIENTIST, GUIDANCE & CONTROL SYSTS DIV, LITTON SYSTS, INC, 95- *Personal Data:* b Brooklyn, NY, May 22, 34; m 54, M Lorene Perkins; c M Coleen (Barker), Christopher S, Kimberly A & Jonathan J. *Educ:* Tufts Univ, BS, 56; Harvard Univ, Am, 57, PhD(theoret physics), 67; Univ Calif, Santa Barbara, BA, 86. *Prof Exp:* Instr physics, Tufts Univ, 59-63; engr, Delco Systs Opers, Delco Electronics Corp, 63-67, head physics group, 67-69, head, Advan Instrument Technol Sect, 69-80, staff engr, 80-91, prin tech fel, 92-95. *Concurrent Pos:* Mem, Task Group on Design Marine Risers, Am Petrol Inst, 74-75, Tech Working Group 4-B (inertial) organized by Inst Defense Anal for Dept Defense, 87-89 & Gyro & Accelerometer Panel, Inst Elec & Electronics Engrs Aerospace & Electronic Systs Soc, 86-92. *Res:* Theory and design analysis of inertial instruments including the laser gyroscope, the fiber-optic gyroscope, and the hemispherical-resonator gyroscope; math modeling and simulation of crash sensors for automotive air-cushion restraint systems. *Mailing Add:* 5442 Berkeley Rd Santa Barbara CA 93111-1614. *Fax:* 805-961-6726; *E-Mail:* lynch@littongcs.com

LYNCH, DAVID H, IMMUNOLOGY. *Current Pos:* STAFF SCIENTIST IMMUNOL, IMMUNEX CORP, 88- *Personal Data:* b San Francisco, Calif, Aug 5, 50. *Educ:* Univ Calif, Santa Cruz, BS, 74; Univ Utah, PhD(exp path), 79. *Prof Exp:* Postdoctoral fel, Dept Path, Sch Med, Univ Utah, 79-81, res instr, Dept Obstet-Gynec, 81-82, res asst prof, 85-88; IPA investr, Immunol Br, Nat Cancer Inst, 82-85. *Mem:* Sigma Xi; Am Asn Immunologists. *Mailing Add:* Immunex Corp Dept Immunobiol 51 University St Seattle WA 98101-2977. *Fax:* 206-233-9733

LYNCH, DAVID WILLIAM, SOLID STATE PHYSICS. *Current Pos:* from asst prof to prof, 59-85, chmn dept, 85-90, DISTINGUISHED PROF PHYSICS, IOWA STATE UNIV, 85-, DIR, MICROELECTRONICS RES CTR, 95- *Personal Data:* b Rochester, NY, July 14, 32; m 54, 92, Glenys Bittick; c Jean, Richard & David. *Educ:* Rensselaer Polytech Inst, BS, 54; Univ Ill, MS, 55, PhD(physics), 58. *Prof Exp:* Fulbright fel, Pavia, Italy, 58-59. *Concurrent Pos:* Sr physicist, Ames Lab, US Dept Energy, 66-; vis prof, Univ Hamburg, 74; actg assoc dir, Synchrotron Radiation Lab, Stoughton, Wis, 84. *Mem:* AAAS; fel Am Phys Soc; Am Asn Physics Teachers. *Res:* Optical properties of solids, including use of synchrotron radiation and modulation-spectroscopy; photoelectron spectroscopy. *Mailing Add:* Dept Physics & Astron Iowa State Univ Ames IA 50011. *Fax:* 515-294-0689; *E-Mail:* dwl@ameslab.gov

LYNCH, DENIS PATRICK, ORAL PATHOLOGY, ORAL MEDICINE. *Current Pos:* PROF BIOLOGIC & DIAG SCI, UNIV TENN COL DENT, 93-, EXEC ASSOC DEAN, 93-, PROF MED, DIV DERMAT, COL MED, 94- *Personal Data:* b Kansas City, Kans, Oct 5, 51; m 73, Monica Colosimo; c Sydney A & Shannon M. *Educ:* Univ Calif, San Francisco, DDS, 76; Univ Ala, PhD, 86. *Honors & Awards:* Gabbs Award, Am Acad Oral Path Award, & Am Acad Oral Med Award, Univ Calif, San Francisco, 76; Golden Pen Award, Int Col Dent, 85; Award, Am Col Dent, 87; Award, Pierre Fauchard Acad, 87. *Prof Exp:* Asst prof path, Univ Tex Dent Br, 81-87, assoc dean acad affairs, 87-89, assoc prof, 88-93, exec assoc dean, 89-92. *Concurrent Pos:* Mem, Comn Accreditation, Am Dent Asn, 75-79; adj asst prof path & lab med, Col Med, Tex A&M Univ, 83-89, adj assoc prof, 89-93; adj assoc prof community med, Baylor Col Med, 89-93; chmn, Sect Path, Am Asn Dent Schs, 84-85; mem, Janssen Res Coun, Janssen Pharmaceut, 86-93; mem, Pres Task Force on AIDS, Univ Tex Health Sci Ctr, Houston, 86; vpres dent res & develop, Pearce Sci & Tech Assocs, 86-93; consult, Bering Clin, 87-93; curric consult, Comn Dent Accreditation, 90-96; pres, Exp Path Group, Int Asn Dent Res, 92-93; chair, Parameters Comt, Am Acad Oral Maxillofacial Path, 95- *Mem:* Am Asn Dent Schs; Int Asn Dent Res; Am Acad Oral Maxillofacial Path; Am Dent Asn; Sigma Xi. *Res:* Oral manifestations of Acquired Immune Deficiency Syndrome; opportunistic fungal infections; oral candidasis, mucocutaneous disease; recurrent oral ulcerations; infectious hazards in dentistry. *Mailing Add:* Col Dent Univ Tenn 875 Union Ave Memphis TN 38163. *Fax:* 901-448-1625; *E-Mail:* dlynch@dental.utmem.edu

LYNCH, DERMOT ROBORG, PLANT BREEDING, PLANT PHYSIOLOGY. *Current Pos:* asst prof potato & vegetable crops, NS Agr Col, RES SCIENTIST POTATO BREEDING, LETHBRIDGE RES STA, AGR CAN, 78- *Personal Data:* b Johannesburg, SAfrica, Feb 9, 40; Can citizen; m 65; c 2. *Educ:* Univ Natal, SAfrica, BSc, 63, MSc, 69; Univ Guelph, Can, PhD(plant physiol), 74. *Prof Exp:* Crop specialist, Tech Servs, Dept Agr, 65-66, res scientist potato mgt & physiol, 68-71; res scientist, McCain Foods Ltd, 74-75. *Mem:* Agr Inst Can; Potato Asn Am; Europ Asn Potato Res. *Res:* Potato breeding; physiology of the potato and development of superior management options. *Mailing Add:* Agr Can Res Sta Lethbridge AB T1J 4B1 Can

LYNCH, DON MURL, ORGANIC CHEMISTRY, MEDICAL DEVICES & DIAGNOSTICS. *Current Pos:* sr res chemist, Abbott Labs, 68-78, sr clin res assoc, 78-81, clin monitor, 81-84, CLIN PROJ MGR, ABBOTT LABS, 84- *Personal Data:* b Delano, Calif, Feb 19, 34. *Educ:* Fresno State Col, AB, 60; Univ Calif, Berkeley, PhD(org chem), 64. *Prof Exp:* Sr res chemist, Abbott Labs, 64-67; Cutter Labs, 67-68. *Res:* Synthesis of potential pharmaceuticals and agricultural chemicals; isolation, structure and synthesis of natural products; clinical investigation of IV nutritionals and diagnostic medical devices. *Mailing Add:* Abbott Labs D7B5 AP8B Abbott Park IL 60064

LYNCH, EDWARD CONOVER, INTERNAL MEDICINE, HEMATOLOGY. *Current Pos:* from instr to assoc prof, Baylor Col Med, 62-72, assoc dean, Med Sch, 71-74, dean student affairs, 74-76, PROF MED, BAYLOR COL MED, 72-, ASSOC CHMN DEPT, 77-, DISTINGUISHED SERV PROF, 95- *Personal Data:* b Fayette, Mo, Feb 24, 33; m 55, Nell R Robinson; c Edward D, David R, Deborah R & Stephen R. *Educ:* Wash Univ, BA, 53, MD, 56. *Prof Exp:* From intern to asst resident med, Barnes Hosp, St Louis, Mo, 56-58; from assoc resident to chief resident, Strong Mem Hosp, Rochester, NY, 58-60. *Concurrent Pos:* Adj assoc prof biomed eng, Rice Univ, 71-73, adj prof, 73- *Mem:* Am Col Physicians; Am Fedn Clin Res; Am Soc Hemat. *Res:* Effects of physical forces on erythrocytes and blood rheology; internal distribution of iron in various anemias. *Mailing Add:* 311 Wilchester Houston TX 77079

LYNCH, EUGENE DARREL, CERAMICS. *Current Pos:* RETIRED. *Personal Data:* b Danville, Ill, Sept 4, 21; m 43, Patricia J Grimes; c David A, Darrel R & Michael E. *Educ:* Univ Ill, BS, 43, MS, 45, PhD, 55. *Prof Exp:* Spec asst, Univ Ill, 43-45; ceramic engr & gen mgr, Kentuckiana Pottery Co, Ky, 45; asst develop mineral, Univ Tex, 45-46; asst high temperature ceramics, Air Materiel Command proj, Univ Ill, 46-47, from asst prof to prof ceramic eng, 47-58; assoc ceramist, Argonne Nat Lab, 58-66; mgr, Mat Lab, Lynchburg Res Ctr, Babcock & Wilcox Co, 66-72, mgr, Mat & Chem Lab, 72-84. *Mem:* Emer mem. & fel Am Ceramic Soc. *Res:* High temperature materials; ceramic nuclear fuels. *Mailing Add:* 2217 Oriole Pl Lynchburg VA 24503. *E-Mail:* exso50a@prodigy.com

LYNCH, FRANK W, ENGINEERING & ELECTRONICS, AERONAUTICS & AEROSPACE. *Current Pos:* RETIRED. *Personal Data:* b San Francisco, Calif, Nov 26, 21; m 50, Marilyn H; c Molly L & Kathryn L. *Educ:* Stanford Univ, AB, 43; Univ Calif, AB, 96. *Hon Degrees:* JD, Northrop Univ, 84. *Prof Exp:* Res lab analyst, Boeing Airplane Co, Seattle, 48-50; res engr, Northrop Aircraft Inc, 50, supvr dynamic anal, 50-51, gen supvr component develop, 51-52, asst chief guid & controls, 52-54 & 55-57, chief flight controls, 54-55; vpres eng, Hallamore Electronics, 57-59; vpres & mgr, Electro-Mech Div, 69-75; sr vpres opers, 76-79; sr vpres, Tactical & Electronic Systs Group, Northrop Corp, 79-80, pres & chief operating officer, 80-87, vchmn, 87-89. *Mem:* Aerospace Indust Asn Am; sr mem Inst Elec & Electronics Engrs; Am Ord Asn. *Res:* Analog computers and flight simulators; autopilots; guidance sensor systems; astroinertial guidance systems; aeronaptics & aerospace. *Mailing Add:* 1933 Altura Dr Corona Del Mar CA 92625

LYNCH, GEORGE ROBERT, PHYSIOLOGICAL ECOLOGY, COMPARATIVE PHYSIOLOGY. *Current Pos:* PROF ENVIRON POP & ORGANISMIC BIOL, UNIV COLO, 93- *Personal Data:* b Pittsburgh, Pa, Oct 5, 41; m 67, Carol Becker. *Educ:* Grove City Col, BS, 64; Univ Mich, MS, 66; Univ Iowa, PhD(zool), 73. *Prof Exp:* Instr zool, Ohio Wesleyan Univ, 66-67; instr biol, Augustana Col, Ill, 67-69; asst prof zool, Univ Maine, Orono, 74-75; from asst prof to prof biol, Wesleyan Univ, 75-92. *Concurrent Pos:* NIH fel, Inst Behav Genetics, Univ Colo, 72-73; Von Humbodlt fel, 84. *Mem:* Am Physiol Soc; Soc Neurosci; Soc Res Biol Rhythms. *Res:* Animal photoperiodism and the role that the neural clock plays in photoperiod time measurement. *Mailing Add:* Dept Environ Pop & Organismic Biol Univ Colo Boulder CO 80309-0334. *Fax:* 303-492-8699, 203-344-7952; *E-Mail:* lynchr@spot.colorado.edu

LYNCH, GERARD FRANCIS, PHYSICS, ENGINEERING PHYSICS. *Current Pos:* scientist, Atomic Energy Can Ltd, 73-81, head, Electronics Br, 81-84, exec asst, 84-85, gen mgr, local energy systs bus unit, chalk river nuclear labs, 85-91, VPRES MKT & SALES, ATOMIC ENERGY CAN LTD, 91- *Personal Data:* b Glascow, Scotland, Oct 10, 45; Can citizen; m 67; c 2. *Educ:* Glasgow Univ, BSc, 67; Queen's Univ, Can, PhD(physics), 71. *Prof Exp:* Lectr physics, Queen's Univ, 71-73. *Concurrent Pos:* Fel, Queen's Univ, 71, spec lectr, 79-; mem working group, Int Electrotech Comn, 76- *Mem:* Instrument Soc Am. *Res:* Instrumentation development for nuclear reactor applications; infrared spectroscopy; radiation detection and measurement, and analytical techniques. *Mailing Add:* 344 Slater St Atomic Energy Can Ltd Ottawa ON K1A 0S4 Can

LYNCH, HARRY JAMES, NEUROENDOCRINOLOGY. *Current Pos:* RETIRED. *Personal Data:* b Glenfield, Pa, Jan 18, 29; m 63. *Educ:* Geneva Col, BS, 57; Univ Pittsburgh, PhD(biol), 71. *Prof Exp:* Clin chemist, Western Pa Hosp, Pittsburgh, 55-66; sr tech fel res asst, Univ Pittsburgh, 66-71; NIH fel, Mass Inst Technol, 71-73, res assoc, Lab Richard Wurtman, 74-75, res scientist, Lab Neuroendocrine Regulation, Dept Appl Biol Sci, 81-92. *Concurrent Pos:* Res affil, Mass Inst Technol, 92- *Mem:* Endocrine Soc; Am Asn Clin Chemists; AAAS; Am Soc Zoologists. *Res:* Neuroendocrine regulation exemplified by the pineal gland of vertebrate animals; pineal gland function as evidenced by melatonin biosynthesis and excretion; physiological, pharmacological, and environmental factors that influence pineal function. *Mailing Add:* 42 Marivista Ave Waltham MA 02154-3059

LYNCH, HENRY T, MEDICAL GENETICS, MEDICAL ONCOLOGY. *Current Pos:* assoc prof, 67-71, PROF PREV MED & PUB HEALTH, SCH MED, CREIGHTON UNIV, 71-, CHMN DEPT, 67- *Personal Data:* b Lawrence, Mass, Jan 4, 28; m 51; c 3. *Educ:* Univ Okla, BS, 51; Univ Denver, MA, 52; Univ Tex, MD, 60. *Honors & Awards:* Billings Silver Medal, AMA, 66; Ungerman-Lubin lectr Cancer Res, 87. *Prof Exp:* Intern, St Mary's Hosp, Evansville, Ind, 60-61; resident internal med, Col Med, Univ Nebr, 61-64; asst prof biol & asst internist, M D Anderson Hosp & Tumor Inst, Tex, 66-67. *Concurrent Pos:* USPHS sr clin cancer trainee, Eppley Cancer Inst, Nebr, 64-66. *Mem:* Am Soc Clin Oncol; Am Asn Cancer Res. *Res:* Cancer genetics. *Mailing Add:* Dept Prev Med & Pub Health Creighton Univ Sch Med 2500 California Plaza Omaha NE 68178

LYNCH, JAMES CARLYLE, NEUROPHYSIOLOGY, NEUROANATOMY. *Current Pos:* asst prof anat, 81-82, assoc prof, 82-, ASST PROF RES OPHTHAL, UNIV MISS MED CTR, 87-, PROF ANAT. *Personal Data:* b Clifton Hill, Mo, Mar 1, 42; m 65; c 2. *Educ:* Univ Mo, AB, 64; Stanford Univ, MA & PhD(neurol sci), 71. *Prof Exp:* Instr physiol, Sch Med, Johns Hopkins Univ, 74-76; asst prof physiol, Mayo Med Sch, 76-81. *Concurrent Pos:* Nat Inst Neurol Dis & Stroke neurophysiol training grant, Dept Physiol, Sch Med, Johns Hopkins Univ, 71-73; assoc consult physiol, Mayo Found, 76-81; Andrew Mellon career develop award, 74. *Mem:* AAAS; Europ Neurosci Asn; Soc Neurosci; Asn Res Vision & Ophthal. *Res:* Central neural mechanisms of sensation, perception and motor control. *Mailing Add:* Dept Anat Univ Miss Sch Med 2500 N State St Jackson MS 39216-4505

LYNCH, JOHN AUGUST, ANALYTICAL CHEMISTRY. *Current Pos:* asst prof, 75-80, ASSOC PROF CHEM, UNIV TENN, CHATTANOOGA, 80- *Personal Data:* b Jan 29, 47; US citizen; m 71, 82. *Educ:* St Peter's Col, NJ, BS, 70; Pa State Univ, PhD(chem), 76. *Prof Exp:* NSF teaching asst chem, Pa State Univ, 70-71, PHS res fel, 71-75. *Concurrent Pos:* Univ Chattanooga Found grant, 76-78; Res Corp grant, 77-; NSF/URP grants, 80, 81; fel, Univ Chattanooga Found, 84 & 88. *Mem:* Am Chem Soc. *Res:* Thermometric methods of analysis used in conjunction with computer interpretation of data; automated titrations; development of instructional microcomputer software. *Mailing Add:* Dept Chem Univ Tenn Chattanooga TN 37403

LYNCH, JOHN BROWN, PLASTIC SURGERY. *Current Pos:* PROF PLASTIC SURG, VANDERBILT UNIV SCH MED, 73-, CHMN DEPT, 73- *Personal Data:* b Akron, Ohio, Feb 5, 29; m 50; c 2. *Educ:* Vanderbilt Univ, BS, 49; Univ Tenn, MD, 52; Am Bd Surg & Am Bd Plastic Surg, dipl. *Prof Exp:* Internship, John Gaston Hosp, Tenn, 53-54; resident surg, Univ Tex Med Br, Galveston, 56-59, res plastic surg, 59-62, from instr to assoc prof, 62-73. *Concurrent Pos:* Nat consult plastic surg to Surgeon Gen, USAF, 74-; mem, Food & Drug Admin Adv Panel, HHS, Gen Surg & Plastic Surg Devices, 74- *Mem:* AMA; Am Soc Plastic & Reconstructive Surgeons; Am Asn Plastic Surg; fel Am Col Surg; Plastic Surg Res Coun. *Res:* Pathophysiological aspects of burns and laboratory projects related to congenital anomalies. *Mailing Add:* Plastic Surg Med Ctr N Rm S-2221 Vanderbilt Univ Hosp Nashville TN 37232

LYNCH, JOHN DOUGLAS, ZOOLOGY, HERPETOLOGY. *Current Pos:* Asst prof zool, 69-73, assoc prof, 73-80, PROF LIFE SCI, UNIV NEBR, LINCOLN, 80- *Personal Data:* b Collins, Iowa, July 30, 42; c Jennifer (Anders) & Douglas. *Educ:* Univ Ill, Urbana, BA, 64, MS, 65; Univ Kans, PhD(zool), 69. *Concurrent Pos:* Vis prof, Nat Univ Colombia, Inst Natural Sci, 85, 92 & 96. *Mem:* Am Soc Ichthyol & Herpet; Soc Syst Biol; Soc Study Amphibians & Reptiles; Herpetologists' League; Willi Hennig Soc. *Res:* Systematics and zoogeography of leptodactyloid frogs especially of neotropical genus Eleutherodactylus; evolution in tropical ecosystems; conservation biology of cyprinodont fishes. *Mailing Add:* Sch Biol Sci Univ Nebr Lincoln NE 68588. *Fax:* 402-472-2083; *E-Mail:* jlynch@unlinfo.unl.edu

LYNCH, JOHN EDWARD, bacteriology, parasitology, for more information see previous edition

LYNCH, JOHN THOMAS, SPACE PLASMA PHYSICS. *Current Pos:* PROG DIR, NSF, 85- *Personal Data:* b Washington, DC, Mar 21, 38; m 59, 80, D Carol Rollins; c John T III & Michael G. *Educ:* Va Polytech Inst, BS, 63; Univ Wis, MS, 65, PhD(physics), 72. *Prof Exp:* Res assoc, Univ Wis-Madison, 72-75, asst scientist, 75-78, assoc scientist physics, 78-79; staff mem, Los Alamos Nat Lab, 79-81; prog scientist, NASA Hq, 81-85. *Concurrent Pos:* Lectr physics, Univ Wis-Madison, 72-78; vis staff mem, Los Alamos Nat Lab, 78-79; prog dir, Antarctic Aeronomy & Astrophys. *Mem:* Am Geophys Union; AAAS; Astron Soc Pac. *Res:* Aeronomy and astrophysics. *Mailing Add:* NSF Off Polar Progs Rm 755 4201 Wilson Blvd Arlington VA 22230. *Fax:* 703-306-0139; *E-Mail:* jlynch@nsf.gov

LYNCH, JOSEPH J, JR, CARDIOVASCULAR PHARMACOLOGY. *Current Pos:* Sr res pharmacologist, 88-91, ASSOC DIR, DEPT PHARMACOL, MERCK, SHARP & DOHME RES LABS, 91- *Personal Data:* b Baltimore, Md, Apr 18, 56. *Educ:* Loyola Col, BA, 78; Ohio State Univ, PhD(pharmacol), 82. *Mem:* Am Soc Therapeut. *Mailing Add:* Dept Pharmacol Merck Sharp & Dohme Res Labs WP 46-300 West Point PA 19486-0004

LYNCH, MAURICE PATRICK, BIOLOGICAL OCEANOGRAPHY, PHYSIOLOGICAL ECOLOGY. *Current Pos:* asst dir & head, Div Marine Resource Mgt, Col William & Mary, Univ Va, 81-86, assoc prof, 76-79, assoc grad dean, Sch Marine Sci, 87-89, PROF, SCH MARINE SCI & HEAD, OFF SPEC PROGS, SCH MARINE SCI, VA INST MARINE SCI, COL WILLIAM & MARY, VA UNIV, 75- *Personal Data:* b Boston, Mass, Feb 24, 36; m 65; c 2. *Educ:* Harvard Col, AB, 57; Col William & Mary, MA, 65, PhD(marine sci), 72. *Prof Exp:* Assoc marine scientist, Col William & Mary, 71-73, sr marine scientist & head, Dept Spec Progs, 73-75, asst dir & head, Div Biol Oceanogr, 75-77; asst dir & head, Div Spec Progs & Sci Serv, Va Inst Marine Sci, 77-82. *Concurrent Pos:* Adj prof earth sci, Va State Col, 74; USN, 57-88; vpres, Coastal Eviron Assoc, Inc, 74-; dir, Va Sea Grant Prog & Chesapeake Res Chesapeake Res Consortium, 84-88; chmn, Sci & Tech Adv Comt, Chesapeake Bay Prog, 85-89. *Mem:* Am Inst Biol Sci; Marine Technol Soc; Am Soc Zoologists; Am Fisheries Soc; Am Soc Limnol & Oceanog; Coastal Soc (pres-elect, 81-83, pres, 83-85); Atlantic Estuarine Res Soc; AAAS. *Res:* Management of marine and estuarine resources with special emphasis on management-research interactions and communications; physiology of marine and estuarine organisms with special emphasis on development of physiological condition indices. *Mailing Add:* PO Box 1346 William & Mary Sch Marine Sci Gloucester Point VA 23062

LYNCH, NANCY ANN, MATHEMATICS. *Current Pos:* assoc prof, 82-86, PROF COMPUT SCI, MASS INST TECHNOL, CAMBRIDGE, 86- *Personal Data:* b Brooklyn, NY, Jan 19, 48; m 69; Dennis C; c Patrick, Kathleen (deceased) & Mary. *Educ:* Brooklyn Col, BS, 68; Mass Inst Technol, PhD, 72. *Prof Exp:* Asst prof math, Tufts Univ, Medford, Mass, 72-73; Univ Southern Calif, Los Angeles, 73-76, Fla Int, Univ Miami, 76-77; assoc prof comput sci, Ga Tech Univ, Atlanta, 77-82. *Concurrent Pos:* Ellen Swallow Richards chair, Mass Inst Technol, 82-87; consult, Comput Corp Am, Cambridge, 84-86, Apollo Comp, Chelmsford & AT&T Bell Labs, Murray Hill, NJ, 86-89 & Digital Equip Corp, 90. *Mem:* Asn Comput Mach. *Res:* Computer science; mathematics; author of numerous articles. *Mailing Add:* Mass Inst Technol 545 Tech Sq Cambridge MA 02139

LYNCH, PETER JOHN, DERMATOLOGY. *Current Pos:* PROF DERMAT & CHAIR, DEPT DERMAT, UNIV CALIF, DAVIS, 95- *Personal Data:* b Minneapolis, Minn, Oct 22, 36; m 64; c 2. *Educ:* Univ Minn, Minneapolis, BS, 59, MD, 61. *Prof Exp:* Clin instr dermat, Univ Minn, Minneapolis, 65-66; from asst prof to assoc prof, Univ Mich, Ann Arbor, 70-73; assoc prof, Univ Ariz, 73-75, prof dermat & chief div, 75-95, assoc head, Dept Internal Med, 77-95. *Concurrent Pos:* Consult, Wayne Co Gen Hosp, Eloise, Mich, 68-73, Vet Admin Hosp, Ann Arbor, Mich, 71-73, Vet Admin Hosp, Tucson, Ariz & Kino Community Hosp, Tucson, Ariz, 74- *Mem:* AAAS; Am Acad Dermat; Soc Invest Dermat; Am Dermat Asn; Asn Am Med Cols. *Res:* Clinical subjects in diseases of the skin. *Mailing Add:* Dept Dermat Univ Calif 1605 Alhambra Blvd No 2300 Sacramento CA 95816

LYNCH, PETER ROBIN, PHYSIOLOGY. *Current Pos:* From instr to assoc prof physiol, 58-70, PROF PHYSIOL & RADIOL, TEMPLE UNIV SCH MED, 70-, PROF INTERNAL MED, 86-, CHMN, PHYSIOL DEPT, 87- *Personal Data:* b Philadelphia, Pa, July 18, 27; m 53; c 3. *Educ:* Univ Miami, BS, 50; Temple Univ, MS, 54, PhD(physiol), 58. *Concurrent Pos:* Adj prof, Druckkhammerlaboratorium, Kantonsppital, Zurich, Switz, 77-78. *Mem:* Am Physiol Soc; Sigma Xi; Am Heart Asn; AAAS; NAm Soc Cardiac Radiol. *Res:* Cardiovascular and radiologic physiology; rheology. *Mailing Add:* Dept Physiol Temple Univ Med Sch Philadelphia PA 19140

LYNCH, RICHARD G, PATHOLOGY. *Current Pos:* PROF & HEAD, DEPT PATH, COL MED, UNIV IOWA, IOWA CITY, 81-, PROF MICROBIOL, 82- *Personal Data:* b Apr 9, 34. *Educ:* Univ Mo, BA, 61; Univ Rochester, MD, 66. *Prof Exp:* Path resident, Washington Univ, St Louis, Mo, 66-69, postdoctoral immunol res fel, 69-72, from asst prof to assoc prof path, 72-80, dir, NIH Training Prog Membranes & Immunol, Sch Med, 80-81. *Concurrent Pos:* Chmn, Path B Study Sect, NIH, 83-86, mem, 82 & Bd Sci Counr, Div Cancer Biol & Diag, Nat Cancer Inst, 87-91; block chmn, Tumor Immunol Prog, 85 & Meetings, Am Asn Immunologists, 86. *Res:* Pathology; immunology. *Mailing Add:* Dept Path Col Med Univ Iowa 200 Hawkins Dr Rm 144ML Iowa City IA 52242-1101. *Fax:* 319-335-8348

LYNCH, RICHARD WALLACE, CHEMICAL PHYSICS, CHEMICAL ENGINEERING. *Current Pos:* Tech staff mem chem physics, Sandia Labs, 66 & 68-71, supvr, Appl Mat Sci Div, 71-73, supvr, Chem Technol Div, 73-76, mgr, Waste Mgt & Environ Progs, 76-83, dir nuclear waste mgt & transp, 83-90, dir environ safety & health, 90-92, DIR, GEOSCI & GEOTECHNOL, SANDIA LABS, 92- *Personal Data:* b Ft Leavenworth, Kans, June 17, 39; m 62, Myra Clark; c Susan, Sara & Andrew. *Educ:* Univ Calif, Berkeley, BS, 62; Univ Ill, MS, 64, PhD(chem eng), 66. *Mem:* AAAS; Am Inst Chem Engrs; Am Phys Soc; Sigma Xi. *Res:* Nuclear waste solidification; geologic isolation of nuclear wastes; exploration and production of gas, oil and geothermal resources. *Mailing Add:* 7500 Osuna Rd NE Albuquerque NM 87109

LYNCH, ROBERT EARL, ENTOMOLOGY. *Current Pos:* Agr res technician, USDA, 66-68, entomologist, 68-69, res entomologist, 69-83, SUPVRY RES ENTOMOLOGIST, USDA, 83- *Personal Data:* b Luxora, Ark, Oct 4, 43; m 61, Nita; c Robert Jr & Robin. *Educ:* Ark State Univ, BSE, 65; Iowa State Univ, MS, 69, PhD(entom), 74. *Mem:* Entom Soc Am; Am Peanut Res & Educ Asn. *Res:* Population distributions and economic thresholds of insects on forage grasses and peanuts; resistance in peanuts and forage grasses to insects. *Mailing Add:* Coastal Plain Exp Sta USDA ARS PO Box 748 Tifton GA 31793-0748. *Fax:* 912-387-2321

LYNCH, ROBERT EMMETT, NUMERICAL ANALYSIS. *Current Pos:* assoc prof, 67-84, PROF COMPUT SCI & MATH, PURDUE UNIV, 85- *Personal Data:* b Chicago, Ill, Feb 5, 32; m 55, Martha B Hacker; c Barbara A, William R & Pamela E. *Educ:* Cornell Univ, BEngPhys, 54; Harvard Univ, MA, 59, PhD(appl math), 63. *Prof Exp:* Sr res mathematician, Res Labs, Gen Motors Corp, 61-64; asst prof math & res mathematician, Univ Tex, Austin, 64-66, assoc prof, 66-67. *Mem:* Am Math Soc; Math Asn Am; Soc Indust & Appl Math; Sigma Xi. *Res:* Numerical analysis, particularly numerical solution of partial differential equations, applied mathematics and computational crystallography. *Mailing Add:* Dept Comput Sci Purdue Univ West Lafayette IN 47907. *Fax:* 765-494-0739; *E-Mail:* rel@cs.purdue.edu

LYNCH, ROBERT MICHAEL, STATISTICS, INFORMATION SYSTEMS. *Current Pos:* assoc dean, 84-94, PROF STATIST, UNIV NORTHERN COLO, 73-, DEAN, 94- *Personal Data:* b Brooklyn, NY, May 30, 44; m 69; c 2. *Educ:* State Univ NY, Brockport, BSc, 65; Univ Northern Colo, PhD(statist), 71. *Prof Exp:* Asst prof mgt, Eastern Ill Univ, 71-73. *Concurrent Pos:* Fel WIE, Inst Educ Leadership, George Washington Univ, 72-73; ed collabr & reviewer, Current Index to Statist, J Comput Reviews, 73-; consult ed, J Exp Educ, 78-82; Fulbright prof, Thammasat Univ, Bangkok, 78-79; vis prof, Col VI, 81-82; consult, Weiss & Assoc, Aurora Co, 82-89, Health Care Financing, State Wyo; labor & policies group, Oak Ridge Assoc Univs, Tenn, 82-; vis prof, Info Systs, Cowen Univ, Perth, Australia, 86-87; reviewer, Australian Computer J, 87-; ed, IBS Comput Quart, 89- *Mem:* Royal Statist Soc; Am Statist Asn; Asn Comput Mach; Inst Elec & Electronics Engrs. *Res:* Linear models; data base management systems. *Mailing Add:* Dean-COBA Univ Northern Colo Greeley CO 80639. *Fax:* 970-351-2500; *E-Mail:* rlynch@slinky.univnorthco.edu

LYNCH, STEVEN PAUL, SYSTEMATIC BOTANY, POLLINATION ECOLOGY. *Current Pos:* ASST PROF BIOL, LA STATE UNIV, 77- *Personal Data:* b Los Angeles, Calif, Aug 19, 46; m 67; c 1. *Educ:* Calif Polytech State Univ, San Luis Obispo, BS, 69, MA, 71; Univ Calif Davis, PhD(bot), 77. *Concurrent Pos:* Researcher, Univ Calif, Davis, 77; environ consult, Demopulos & Ferguson Inc Assoc Engrs, 78- *Mem:* Bot Soc Am; Am Soc Plant Taxonomists; Int Soc Plant Taxonomists; Sigma Xi. *Res:* Plant-animal coevolution; floral biology of Asclepias; Monarch Butterfly migratory and feeding behavior; systematics of the Asclepiadaceae and Euphorbiaceae; pollen morphology and Angiosperm Phylogeny; scanning electron microscopy techniques. *Mailing Add:* Dept Biol Sci La State Univ One University Pl Shreveport LA 71115-2399

LYNCH, T(HOMAS) E(LWIN), ENGINEERING. *Current Pos:* CHMN, CLEVELAND CRYSTALS INC, 72-; CHMN, DESIGN & MFG CO, 82- *Personal Data:* b Mexico, Maine, Aug 7, 14; m 44, Mary. *Educ:* Univ Maine, BS, 38. *Prof Exp:* Engr, Brush Develop Co, 39-43, head, Dept Electronics Eng, 43-52 & Clevite Corp, 52-57, gen mgt, Ord Prod Div, 57-59, vpres, 65-69; vpres, Gould Inc, 69-75. *Mem:* Audio Eng Soc; Am Defense Prep Asn; Nat Security Indust Asn; Inst Elec & Electronics Engrs. *Res:* Underwater sound; disc and magnetic recording; underwater ordnance; government contracting; energy technology. *Mailing Add:* Old Mill Rd Gates Mills OH 44040

LYNCH, THOMAS JOHN, POLYMER PROCESSING, APPLICATION OF ENGINEERING POLYMERS. *Current Pos:* dir, Environ Progs, 83-87, Prog Mgt, 87-90, DIR, POLYMER PROCESS TECHNOL, AMP INC, 90- *Personal Data:* b Quincy, Mass, Mar 3, 41; m 69. *Educ:* Boston Col, BS, 62; Mass Inst Tech, PhD(org chem), 66. *Prof Exp:* Res chemist, Gulf Res & Develop Co, 66-71, sr res chemist, 71-75 & Gulf Oil Chem Co, 75-78, res assoc, 78, mgr polystyrene prod res, 78-83. *Concurrent Pos:* Woodrow Wilson fel, 58-62; fel NSF, 62-66. *Mem:* AAAS; Am Chem Soc; The Chem Soc. *Res:* Application and modification of engineering polymer for electrical/electronic connectors; solid state polymerization and polymer recycling; program and production management. *Mailing Add:* Amp Inc MS 128-063 PO Box 3608 Harrisburg PA 17105-3608

LYNCH, WESLEY CLYDE, NEUROPSYCHOLOGY. *Current Pos:* ASST PROF PSYCHOL, MONT STATE UNIV, 80- *Personal Data:* b Vancouver, Wash, Feb 28, 44; m 65. *Educ:* Univ Hawaii, BA, 67; Hollins Col, MA, 68; Univ NMex, PhD(exp psychol), 72. *Prof Exp:* Fel physiol psychol, Rockefeller Univ, 71-73, asst prof, 73-75; vis asst fel physiol psychol, John B Pierce Found Lab, 75-80. *Concurrent Pos:* Adj asst prof, Rockefeller Univ, 75-; res assoc psychol, Yale Univ, 75- *Mem:* Am Psychol Asn; AAAS; Sigma Xi. *Res:* Psychological and physiological bases of motivation, reward and learning. *Mailing Add:* Dept Psychol Mont State Univ Bozeman MT 59717-0001

LYNCH, WILLIAM C, MATHEMATICS, COMPUTER SCIENCE. *Current Pos:* MEM RES STAFF, INTERVAL RES CORP, 93- *Personal Data:* b Cleveland, Ohio, Apr 27, 37; div; c John H, Michael W, Timothy P & Brian K. *Educ:* Case Western, BS, 59; Univ Wis, MS, 60, PhD(math), 63. *Prof Exp:* Actg instr numerical anal, Univ Wis, 62-63, asst prof, 63; from asst prof to prof comput eng, Case Western Res Univ, 63-76; prin scientist, Xerox Corp, 76-85, 86-93; Am Super Comput Inc, 85. *Concurrent Pos:* Vis prof, Comput Lab, Univ Newcastle, 70-71; vis prof, Univ Fed Rio de Janeiro, 75. *Mem:* AAAS; Asn Comput Mach; Am Math Soc; Sigma Xi. *Res:* Mathematical linguistics; design, construction, measurement and modelling of operating systems; signal processing. *Mailing Add:* 3331 Thomas Dr Palo Alto CA 94303. *Fax:* 650-354-0872; *E-Mail:* lynch@interral.com

LYNCH, WILLIAM GREGORY, NUCLEAR PHYSICS. *Current Pos:* RESEARCHER, CYCLOTRON LAB, MICH STATE UNIV, 80- *Educ:* Univ Colo, BS, 73; Univ Wash, MS, 75, PhD(physics), 80. *Honors & Awards:* Pres Young Investr Award, 85. *Mem:* Am Phys Soc. *Mailing Add:* Cyclotron Lab Mich State Univ East Lansing MI 48824

LYND, JULIAN QUENTIN, SOIL SCIENCE. *Current Pos:* assoc prof, 52-57, PROF AGRON, OKLA STATE UNIV, 57- *Personal Data:* b Joplin, Mo, Feb 11, 22; wid; c Donna & Joel. *Educ:* Univ Ark, BS, 43; Mich State Univ, MS, 47, PhD(soil sci), 48. *Prof Exp:* Asst prof soil sci, Mich State Univ, 48-51. *Mem:* Fel Am Soc Agron; fel Soil Sci Soc Am; Int Soc Soil Sci; Am Soc Microbiol; Mycol Soc Am. *Res:* Soil microbiology; induced antibiosis to carcinogenic mycotoxins and biopathway of biotoxin degradation; n-fixation. *Mailing Add:* Dept Agron Okla State Univ Stillwater OK 74078-0507. *Fax:* 405-744-5269; *E-Mail:* jql@gis.agr.okstate.edu

LYND, LANGTRY EMMETT, EXTRACTIVE METALLURGY, INORGANIC CHEMISTRY. *Current Pos:* RETIRED. *Personal Data:* b Can, Feb 8, 19; nat US; m 42, Violet Spence; c Robert & Catherine. *Educ:* Univ Man, BSc, 41; Rutgers Univ, MS, 55, PhD(geol), 57. *Prof Exp:* Res scientist & mgr, raw mat sect, res & develop dept, Titanium Pigment Div, Sayreville, NJ, N L Industs Inc, 48-72, sr res scientist, Cent Res Lab, Hightstown, NJ, 72-75; phys scientist & titanium specialist, Bur Mines, US Dept Interior, 77-91. *Mem:* Geol Soc Am; Am Inst Mining, Metall & Petrol Eng. *Res:* Preparation and evaluation of concentrates for titanium dioxide pigment processes; utilization of titaniferous magnetite; treatment of industrial plant wastes; titanium geology and mineralogy; petrography and mineragraphy. *Mailing Add:* 8800 Walther Blvd Apt 2001 Parkville MD 21234-9008

LYNDE, RICHARD ARTHUR, INORGANIC CHEMISTRY. *Current Pos:* Asst prof, Montclair State Col, 70-75, chmn, Dept Chem, 73-76, assoc prof, 75-80, actg dean, 76-80, PROF & DEAN, SCH MATH & NATURAL SCI, MONTCLAIR STATE COL, 80- *Personal Data:* b Orange, NJ, Apr 12, 42; m 61; c 2. *Educ:* Hamilton Col, AB, 64; Iowa State Univ, PhD(inorg chem), 70. *Mem:* Am Chem Soc; AAAS; Sigma Xi. *Res:* Elucidation of the stoichiometry, structure and bonding of compounds formed by the post-transition and transition metals in unusual oxidation states. *Mailing Add:* 138 Thackeray Dr Baskir.g Ridge NJ 07920-2634

LYNDEN-BELL, DONALD, ASTRONOMY. *Current Pos:* PROF ASTROPHYS, UNIV CAMBRIDGE & CLARE COL, 72- *Personal Data:* b Dover, Eng, Apr 5, 35; m 61, Ruth Marion Truscott; c Marion & Edward. *Educ:* Univ Cambridge, BA, 56, PhD, 60. *Hon Degrees:* DSc, Univ Sussex, 87. *Honors & Awards:* Schwarzsch Medal, Ger Astron Asn; Dirk Brouwer Prize, Am Astron Soc, 90; Eddington Medal, Royal Astron Soc, 84, Gold Medal, 93. *Prof Exp:* Harkness fel, Calif Inst Technol, 60-62; asst lectr math, Clare Col, Cambridge, 62-65; prin sci officer, Royal Greenwich Observ, 65-72; dir, Inst Astron, Univ Cambridge, 72-77, 82-87 & 92-94. *Concurrent Pos:* Res fel, Clare Col, 60-65; vis prof, Univ Sussex, 70-72; Einstein fel, Israeli Acad, 90; vis Oort prof, Leiden Univ, Neth, 92. *Mem:* Foreign assoc Nat Acad Sci; fel Royal Soc; fel Royal Astron Soc (pres). *Mailing Add:* Inst Astron Observ Madingley Rd Cambridge CB3 OHA England

LYNDS, BEVERLY T, ASTRONOMY. *Current Pos:* RETIRED. *Personal Data:* b Shreveport, La, Aug 19, 29; wid; c 1. *Educ:* Centenary Col, BS, 49; Univ Calif, PhD(astron), 55. *Prof Exp:* Res assoc astron, Nat Radio Astron Observ, Green Bank, WVa, 60-62; from asst prof & asst astronr to assoc prof astron & assoc astronr, Steward Observ, Univ Ariz, 62-71; asst dir, Kitt Peak Nat Observ, 71-78, astronr, 74-86. *Concurrent Pos:* Consult, Astron Adv Panel, NSF, 75-77 & NSF Sci & Technol Policy Off, Adv Group Sci Progs, 75-77, Asn Univ Res Astronomers,87 & Univ Hawaii, 88. *Mem:* Am Astron Soc; Int Astron Union. *Res:* Interstellar medium; galactic structure; composition of galaxies. *Mailing Add:* 3244 Sixth St Boulder CO 80304

LYNDS, CLARENCE ROGER, OBSERVATION COSMOLOGY. *Current Pos:* from asst to assoc astronr, 61-68, ASTRONR, KITT PEAK NAT OBSERV, 68- *Personal Data:* b Kirkwood, Mo, July 28, 28; m 54; c 1. *Educ:* Univ Calif, AB, 52, PhD(astron), 55. *Prof Exp:* Asst, Lick Observ, 52; astronr, Univ Calif, 53-54, jr res astronr & assoc astronr, 55-58; Nat Res Coun Can fel, Dom Astrophys Observ, Can, 58-59; asst astronr, Nat Radio Astron Observ, 59-61. *Mem:* Nat Acad Sci; Am Astron Soc; Royal Astron Soc; Int Astron Union. *Res:* Photometry and spectroscopy of quasi-stellar objects and galaxies; observational cosmology; optical interferometry. *Mailing Add:* Kitt Peak Nat Observ PO Box 26732 Tucson AZ 85726

LYNE, LEONARD MURRAY, SR, paper chemistry, for more information see previous edition

LYNK, EDGAR THOMAS, LASERS. *Current Pos:* STAFF PHYSICIST, RES & DEVELOP CTR, GEN ELEC CO, 74- *Personal Data:* b Kansas City, Mo, Aug 26, 41. *Educ:* Yale Univ, BS, 63, MS, 65, PhD(physics), 70. *Prof Exp:* Assoc prof physics, Southern Univ, 69-74. *Mem:* AAAS; Am Phys Soc; Inst Elec & Electronics Engrs. *Res:* Atomic excitation cross sections; computerized tomography; ultrasound for medical imaging. *Mailing Add:* 70 Park Terr Apt 2G New York NY 10034

LYNN, D JOANNE, ETHICS, GERIATRICS. *Current Pos:* from instr to prof, 76-92, assoc chmn, 90-92, PROF HEALTH CARE SCI & MED, GEORGE WASHINGTON MED CTR, 95-; DIR, CTR IMPROVE CARE DYING, GEORGE WASHINGTON UNIV, 95- *Personal Data:* b Oakland, Md, July 2, 51. *Educ:* Dickinson Col, BS, 70; Boston Univ, MD, 74; Am Bd Internal Med cert, 77; George Washington Univ, MA, 84; Dartmouth Col, MS, 95. *Hon Degrees:* MA, Dartmouth Col, 91. *Prof Exp:* Assoc med & humanities, Div Exp Prog, George Washington Univ, 78-81; staff physician, Washington Home, 79-92; assoc dir, Ctr Aging, Dartmouth-Hitchcock Med Ctr, 92-95; sr assoc, Ctr Evaluative Clin Sci, Dartmouth Med Sch, 92-95. *Concurrent Pos:* Resident, Geo Washington Univ Med Ctr, 74-77, Robert Wood Johnson clin scholar, 77-78; emergency room & triage physician, Wash Vet Admin Hosp, 77-78; private pract, Clinton, Md, 78-81; asst dir med studies, President's Comn Study Ethical Prob Med Biomed Behav Res, 81-83; mem, Comt Social & Ethical Impacts on Develop in Biomed, Inst Med-Nat Acad Sci, 92-94, Comt Eval NIH Women's Health Initiative, 93, Comt Care at End of Life, 96-; adj prof med community & family med, Dartmouth Med Sch, 95- *Mem:* Inst Med-Nat Acad Sci; fel Am Geriatrics Soc; Am Hosp Asn; fel Am Col Physicians. *Res:* Care of the dying; continuous quality improvement; geriatrics; managed care; measurement of quality; medical decision-making; medical ethics; outcomes research; palliative medicine; public policy; contributor of numerous publications. *Mailing Add:* Ctr Improve Care Dying George Washington Univ 1001 22nd St NW Suite 820 Washington DC 20037

LYNN, DENIS HEWARD, CILIATOLOGY, ELECTRON MICROSCOPY. *Current Pos:* from asst prof to assoc prof, Univ Guelph, 77-93, asst dean, 94-97, actg chair, 95-96, PROF ZOOL & PROTISTOL, UNIV GUELPH, 93- *Personal Data:* b Kingston, Ont, Apr 20, 47; m 73, Portia Holt; c Francis C & Robin P. *Educ:* Univ Guelph, BSc, 69; Univ Toronto, PhD(zool), 75. *Prof Exp:* Res assoc protozool, Dept Zool, Univ Md, College Park, 72-73; fel cell biol, Dept Zool, Univ St Andrews, Scotland, 75-77. *Mem:* Am Micros Soc; Soc Protozoologists; Can Soc Cell Biologists; Int Soc Evolutionary Protistology. *Res:* Form and function of ciliated protists as unicellular organisms using techniques of light and electron microscopy; ecology and systematics of protists, especially ciliates; using techniques of cytology, molecular biology (electrophoresis, DNA) and numerical taxonomy. *Mailing Add:* Dept Zool Univ Guelph Guelph ON N1G 2W1 Can

LYNN, HUGH BAILEY, SURGERY. *Current Pos:* PROF SURG, UNIV ALA, BIRMINGHAM, 78- *Personal Data:* b Verona, NJ, Aug 13, 14; m 40; c 3. *Educ:* Princeton Univ, AB, 36; Columbia Univ, MD, 40. *Prof Exp:* Assoc surg, Newark Babies Hosp, 52-53; assoc prof surg & chief sect pediat surg, Sch Med, Univ Louisville, 53-60; head sect pediat surg, Mayo Clin, 61-78, prof surg, Mayo Grad Sch Med, Univ Minn, 71-78. *Concurrent Pos:* Teaching fel, Harvard Univ, 51-52; surgeon-in-chief, Children's Hosp, Louisville, Ky, 53-60. *Mem:* Fel Am Col Surg; Am Acad Pediat. *Mailing Add:* Stonehedge Farm PO Box 1040 Middleburg VA 22117-1040

LYNN, JEFFREY WHIDDEN, SOLID STATE PHYSICS, SUPERCONDUCTIVITY. *Current Pos:* from asst prof to assoc prof, 76-86, actg dir, Ctr Superconductivity Res, 88-89, PROF PHYSICS, UNIV MD, 86-; STAFF SCIENTIST, NAT INST STAND & TECHNOL, 76- *Personal Data:* b Hackensack, NJ, Mar 2, 47; m 64; c 2. *Educ:* Ga Inst Technol, BS, 69, MS, 70, PhD(physics), 74. *Prof Exp:* Res asst physics, Oak Ridge Nat Lab, 72-74; res assoc, Brookhaven Nat Lab, 74-76. *Concurrent Pos:* Brookhaven Nat Lab fel, 74-76; NSF grant, 76-; Nat Inst Stands & Technol, 76-; Inst Laue Langevin, Grenoble, France, 83-84; Res Corp grant, 77-80. *Mem:* Fel Am Phys Soc; Am Inst Physics; AAAS; Mat Res Soc. *Res:* Neutron scattering-solid state research; magnetic properties of solids; spin dynamics; magnetic and structural phase transitions; structurally amorphous solids; magnetic superconductors; fundamental physics of neutrons. *Mailing Add:* Ctr Neutron Res Nat Inst Stand & Technol Gaithersburg MD 20899

LYNN, JOHN R, OPHTHALMOLOGY. *Current Pos:* from asst prof to assoc prof, 63-70, PROF SURG, UNIV TEX HEALTH SCI CTR DALLAS, 70-, CHMN, DEPT OPHTHAL, 63- *Personal Data:* b Dallas, Tex, Mar 8, 30; m 54; c 5. *Educ:* Rice Univ, BA, 51; Univ Tex, MD, 55. *Prof Exp:* Res assoc, Univ Iowa Hosps, 61-63. *Concurrent Pos:* Nat Inst Neurol Dis & Blindness spec fel, Univ Iowa Hosps, 61-63 & Eye Clin, Univ Tu bingen, 62-63. *Mem:* AMA; Am Acad Ophthal & Otolaryngol; Asn Res Vision & Ophthal. *Res:* Methods of clinical perimetry; acute visual function effects by raising the intraocular pressure; threshold, summation and visual acuity of accentric scotomatous areas during phototopic, mesopic and scotopic adaptations. *Mailing Add:* 7150 Greenville Ave Suite 300 Dallas TX 75231-5185

LYNN, JOHN WENDELL, ORGANIC CHEMISTRY. *Current Pos:* CONSULT, 85- *Personal Data:* b New York, NY, Mar 23, 25; m 46; c 3. *Educ:* Yale Univ, BS, 48, PhD(chem), 51. *Prof Exp:* Res chemist & proj leader, Org Chem Res Dept, Union Carbide Corp, 51-55, group leader, 55-60, res assoc, 60-61, asst dir res & develop, 61-69, mgr new mkt develop, 69-70, dir technol, Fibers & Fabrics, 69-72, new venture mgr chem & plastics, 72-73, assoc dir res & develop, 73-85. *Mem:* Am Chem Soc; Electrochem Soc; AAAS. *Res:* Nitrogenous substances; vinyl monomers; organic synthesis; synthetic fibers; vinyl fabrics; nonwovens; thermoplastic M & E resins; phenolic resins, water-soluble polymers. *Mailing Add:* 108 Rolling Hills Ct Seven Lakes, Box 646 West End NC 27376

LYNN, KELVIN G, SOLID STATE PHYSICS, MATERIALS SCIENCE. *Current Pos:* PHYSICIST, BROOKHAVEN NAT LAB, 74-, HEAD, MAT SCI DIV. *Personal Data:* b Rapid City, SDak, Feb 2, 48; m, Cindy Rice; c Molly & Adam. *Educ:* Univ Utah, BS, 71, BS, 72, PhD(mat sci), 74. *Honors & Awards:* Garner Doe Award, Solid State Physicists. *Prof Exp:* Res assoc, Dept Mat Sci, Univ Utah, 73-74. *Concurrent Pos:* Res vis, Bell Labs, 74-77; vis prof, State Univ NY, Stony Brook, 77-; adj prof, Univ Guelph, Ont; panel mem, Nat Acad Sci; mem adv bd, Int Positron Annihilation. *Mem:* Fel Am Phys Soc; Am Inst Metall Engrs; Am Soc Metals; Mat Res Soc. *Mailing Add:* Brookhaven Nat Lab 510B Upton NY 11973-5000

LYNN, LARRY, PHYSICS. *Current Pos:* Actg dir, 95, DIR DEFENSE ADVAN RES PROJ AGENCY, DEPT DEFENSE, 95- *Personal Data:* b Sept 5, 30. *Educ:* Tufts Univ, BS, 51. *Mailing Add:* Defense Advan Res Proj Agency Dept Defense 3701 N Fairfax Dr Arlington VA 22203

LYNN, MERRILL, POLYMER CHEMISTRY. *Current Pos:* CONSULT, 70- *Personal Data:* b New Columbia, Pa, Nov 20, 30; m 57, Lydia Tiemann; c Alexander & Katherine. *Educ:* Bucknell Univ, BS, 56; Univ Fla, PhD(chem), 61. *Prof Exp:* Res chemist, Esso Res & Eng Co, 61-69. *Concurrent Pos:* Sr develop assoc chem, Corning Inc, 70-95. *Mem:* Am Chem Soc; Am Inst Chem; Am Ceramic Soc. *Res:* Bonding to glass surfaces; glass reinforced plastics; polymer modifications; coating resins; immobilized enzymes; ceramic binders. *Mailing Add:* 16 Olcott Rd N Big Flats NY 14814

LYNN, R(ALPH) EMERSON, CHEMICAL ENGINEERING. *Current Pos:* RETIRED. *Personal Data:* b Elkhart, Ind, Mar 17, 20; m 46. *Educ:* Purdue Univ, BS, 42; Univ Tex, MS, 49, PhD(chem eng), 53. *Prof Exp:* Tech serv supvr, US Rubber Co, 43-46; sr res engr, B F Goodrich Co, 52-56, res scientist, 56, mgr chem eng res, 56-60, prog planning, B F Goodrich Chem Co Div, 60-66, mgr, E P Rubber Develop, B F Goodrich Chem Co, Ohio, 66-67; alcoa prof chem eng, Ohio State Univ, 67-82. *Mem:* AAAS; Am Chem Soc; fel Am Inst Chem Engrs; Soc Plastics Engrs; Am Soc Eng Educ. *Res:* Economics; thermodynamics; kinetics; polymerization and polymer processing. *Mailing Add:* 9221 W Broward Blvd No 2510 Ft Lauderdale FL 33324-2415

LYNN, RALPH BEVERLEY, CARDIOVASCULAR & THORACIC SURGERY. *Current Pos:* assoc prof, 58-62, PROF SURG, SCH MED, QUEEN'S UNIV, ONT, 62; HEAD CARDIOTHORACIC UNIT, KINGSTON GEN HOSP, 58-, EMER PROF, 80- *Personal Data:* b Penetanguishene, Ont, Aug 24, 21; m 44, Blanche Wellman; c 4. *Educ:* Queen's Univ, Ont, MD, CM, 45; FRCS(E), 48; FRCS, 49; Royal Col Physicians & Surgeons Can, cert, 57; FRCS, 58; FRCS(C), 65. *Prof Exp:* Jr intern, Kingston Gen Hosp, 44-46; sr intern surg, Royal Victoria Hosp, Montreal, Que, 46-47; sr registr, Post-Grad Med Sch, Univ London, 47-48; clin tutor, Royal Infirmary, Edinburgh, Scotland, 48-49; asst lectr surg, Post-Grad Med Sch, Univ London, 49-50 & 52-54; sr registr, Southampton Chest Hosp, Eng, 54-55; from asst prof to assoc prof surg, Univ Sask, 55-58. *Concurrent Pos:* Nat Res Coun Can scholar, Western Res Univ, 50-51; traveling fel, Post-Grad Med Fedn, Johns Hopkins Univ, 51-52; Markle scholar, Univ Sask, 55-57; surgeon, Cleveland City Hosp, Ohio, 50-51; consult, Hotel Dieu & Can Forces Hosp, 58- & Dept Vet Affairs, 58-; fel coun clin cardiol, Am Heart Asn, 65. *Mem:* Asn Thoracic Surg; fel Am Col Surg; fel Am Col Chest Physicians; Can Thoracic Soc; Royal Soc Med. *Res:* Thoracic, cardiovascular and peripheral vascular surgery. *Mailing Add:* Dept Surg Queen's Univ Sch Med Kingston ON K7L 3N6 Can

LYNN, RAYMOND J, MEDICAL MICROBIOLOGY, HOST-PARASITE INTERACTION. *Current Pos:* from asst prof to assoc prof, 61-70, PROF MICROBIOL, SCH MED, UNIV SDAK, VERMILLION, 70-, ASSOC DEAN, 83- *Personal Data:* b Bitner, Pa, Oct 23, 28; m 58; c 3. *Educ:* Univ Pittsburgh, BS, 52, MS, 53; Univ Pa, PhD(med microbiol), 56. *Prof Exp:* Asst biol, Univ Pittsburgh, 52-53; res investr microbiol, Univ Pa, 53-56, res microbiologist, 56-57; res assoc microbiol, Sch Med, Univ Pittsburgh, 58-60, instr, 60-61. *Concurrent Pos:* Secy-treas, SDak Bd Examr in Basic Sci, 71-79; rep Dak Affil, regional rev comt, Am Heart Asn, 75-78. *Mem:* AAAS; Am Pub Health Asn; Am Soc Microbiol; Soc Exp Biol & Med; NY Acad Sci. *Res:* Immunology of the Mycoplasmataceae; role of L-forms in sequelae disease states; immunochemistry of streptococcal L-forms and relation of such antigens to rheumatic fever and acute glomerular nephritis; cell-wall defective microorganisms as agents of immunoregulation. *Mailing Add:* Dept Microbiol Univ SDak Med Sch 414 E Clark Vermillion SD 57069-2307

LYNN, ROBERT K, DRUG METABOLISM. *Current Pos:* asst dir drug metab, Smith Kline & French Labs, Philadelphia, 82-86, dir, King of Prussia, Pa, 86-87, group dir drug metab & pharmacokinetics, Welwyn, Eng, 87-89, group dir drug metab, SmithKline Beecham Pharmaceuticals, King of Prussia, Pa, 89-90, DIR & VPRES DRUG METAB & PHARMACOKINETICS, SMITHKLINE BEECHAM PHARMACEUT, WELWYN, ENG, 91- *Personal Data:* b Ky, Oct 29, 47. *Educ:* Murray State Univ, BA, 69; Australian Nat Univ, PhD(chem), 74. *Prof Exp:* Res asst, Dept Pharmacol, Sch Med, Vanderbilt Univ, Nashville, 69-71; res scholar, Med Chem Group, Australian Nat Univ, Canberra, 71-74; res assoc, Dept Pharmacol, Sch Med, Ore Health Sci Univ, Portland, 74-77; res instr, Clin Pharmacol Div, 77-78, res asst prof, 78-82. *Concurrent Pos:* Prin investr, Nat Inst Environ Health Sci, 77-83, young environ health scientist award, 78-81. *Mem:* Am Soc Pharmacol & Exp Therapeut; Am Soc Mass Spectrometry; Am Chem Soc; AAAS. *Res:* Drug metabolism; pharmacokinetics; analytical chemistry; environmental chemical metabolism. *Mailing Add:* SmithKline Beecham Pharmaceut PO Box 1539 UW2730 King of Prussia PA 19406-0939. *Fax:* 215-270-5332

LYNN, ROBERT THOMAS, ANIMAL BEHAVIOR, ECOLOGY. *Current Pos:* PROF BIOL SCI, SOUTHWESTERN OKLA STATE UNIV, 67- *Personal Data:* b Coleman, Tex, Jan 15, 31; m 54; c 2. *Educ:* Fla State Univ, BA, 56, MA, 57; Univ Okla, PhD(zool), 63. *Prof Exp:* Instr biol, Austin Col, 57-59; asst prof, Emory & Henry Col, 63-64; assoc prof, Presby Col, SC, 64-67. *Mem:* AAAS; Ecol Soc Am; Am Inst Biol Sci; Am Ornith Union; Wilson Ornith Soc. *Res:* Ecology and behavior of birds and lizards. *Mailing Add:* 1208 N Indiana Weatherford OK 73096-2223

LYNN, ROGER YEN SHEN, COMPUTER SCIENCE, OPERATIONS RESEARCH. *Current Pos:* ASST & ASSOC PROF MATH, VILLANOVA UNIV, SC, 71- *Personal Data:* b Shanghai, China, Jan 18, 41; c 1. *Educ:* Cheng Kung Univ, Taiwan, BS, 61; Brown Univ, MS, 64; Courant, NY Univ, PhD(math), 68. *Prof Exp:* Lectr math, Univ Ind, Bloomington, 68-69, asst prof, 69-71. *Mem:* Am Math Soc; Soc Indust & Appl Math; NY Acad Sci; Asn Comput Mach. *Res:* Asymptotic solutions of differential equations; operations research; computer graphics. *Mailing Add:* Dept Math Sci Villanova Univ Villanova PA 19085-1672

LYNN, SCOTT, CHEMICAL ENGINEERING. *Current Pos:* actg prof, 67-69, PROF CHEM ENG, UNIV CALIF, BERKELEY, 69-, ASSOC DEAN, COL CHEM, 86- *Personal Data:* b Iola, Kans, June 18, 28; m 54; c 4. *Educ:* Calif Inst Technol, BS, 50, MS, 51, PhD(chem eng), 54. *Honors & Awards:* Fulbright lectr, Delft Tech Univ, Neth, 73. *Prof Exp:* Asst, Tech Hogesch, Holland, 53-54; res engr, Dow Chem Co, Calif, 54-67. *Concurrent Pos:* Ed, Indust Electrolytic Div, J Electrochem Soc, 60-90. *Mem:* Am Chem Soc; fel Am Inst Chem Engrs. *Res:* Separation processes; gas absorption; electrochemistry and electrochemical engineering; process synthesis and development. *Mailing Add:* 37 Janin Pl Pleasant Hill CA 94523-1115

LYNN, THOMAS NEIL, JR, MEDICINE, PREVENTIVE MEDICINE. *Current Pos:* RETIRED. *Personal Data:* b Ft Worth, Tex, Feb 14, 30; m 52; c 3. *Educ:* Univ Okla, BS, 51, MD, 55. *Prof Exp:* From intern to asst resident med, Barnes Hosp, St Louis, 55-57; clin assoc, Nat Heart Inst, 57-59; chief res, Med Ctr, Univ Okla, 59-61, instr, 61-63, asst prof prev med, 61-64, asst prof med, 63-69, assoc prof prev med & pub health, 64-69, vchmn dept, 63-69, prof family pract, community med & dent & chmn dept, 69-80, actg dean, Col Med, 74-76, dean, 76-80, vpres, Baptist Med Ctr, Oklahoma City, 80. *Mem:* AMA. *Res:* Epidemiology of coronary artery disease; psycho-social aspects of dependence and rehabilitation; ballistocardiography and electrocardiography. *Mailing Add:* 3300 Northwest Exp Oklahoma City OK 75112

LYNN, WALTER R(OYAL), CIVIL & ENVIRONMENTAL ENGINEERING. *Current Pos:* assoc prof, Cornell Univ, 61-67, dir, Ctr Environ Qual Mgt, 66-76, Sch Civil & Environ Eng, 70-78, Sci Tech & Soc Prog, 80-88, dean univ fac, 88-93, PROF CIVIL & ENVIRON ENG, CORNELL UNIV, 67- *Personal Data:* b New York, NY, Oct 1, 28; m 60; c 1. *Educ:* Univ Miami, Fla, BSCE, 50; Univ NC, MSSE, 54; Northwestern Univ, PhD, 63. *Prof Exp:* Asst prof civil eng, Univ Miami, 54-58, assoc prof, 58-61. *Concurrent Pos:* Dir res, Ralph B Carter Co, 55-57; consult, Reeder & Lynn, Consult Engrs, 57-61, Rockefeller Fdn, 76-80 & WHO, 69-; adj prof pub health, Med Col, Cornell Univ, 71-80, dir, Prog Sci, Tech & Soc, 80-; mem bd dir, Cornell Res Found, 78-, bd trustees, Cornell Univ, 80-85; assoc ed, J Oper Res, 68-76, J Environ Econs & Mgt, 78-; chmn, Water Sci & Technol bd, Nat Res Coun, 82-85, Comn Water Res, 87-91; chmn, NY State Water Res Planning Coun, 86-; chmn, Bd Nat Disaster, 92, US Nat Comt Nat Disaster Reduction, Nat Res Coun, 93- *Mem:* AAAS; Am Soc Civil Engrs; Sigma Xi. *Res:* Systems analysis and operations research applications in civil and environmental engineering and public health; environmental control; science, technology policy, science and technology for development. *Mailing Add:* Sch Civil & Environ Eng Cornell Univ 220 Hillister Hall Ithaca NY 14853-3501

LYNN, WARREN CLARK, SOIL SCIENCE. *Current Pos:* SOIL SCIENTIST, NAT SOIL SURV LAB, USDA, 63- *Personal Data:* b Satanta, Kans, Dec 4, 35; m 60; c 3. *Educ:* Kans State Univ, BS, 57, MS, 58; Univ Calif, PhD(soil sci), 64. *Mem:* Int Soc Soil Sci; Soil Sci Soc Am; Clay Minerals Soc; Int Peat Soc. *Res:* Properties of cat clays or acid sulfate soils; clay minerals in relation to soil properties; organic soils. *Mailing Add:* 2820 Leonard St Lincoln NE 68507-2849

LYNN, WILLIAM GARDNER, zoology; deceased, see previous edition for last biography

LYNN, WILLIAM SANFORD, medicine, for more information see previous edition

LYNN, YEN-MOW, APPLIED MATHEMATICS. *Current Pos:* assoc prof, 67-72, chmn dept, 76-82, PROF MATH, UNIV MD, BALTIMORE CO, 72- *Personal Data:* b Shanghai, China, Jan 17, 35; c Edward, Kirk & Genevieve. *Educ:* Nat Taiwan Univ, BS, 55; Calif Inst Technol, MS, 57, PhD, 61. *Prof Exp:* From asst res scientist to assoc res scientist, Courant Inst Math Sci, NY Univ, 60-64; assoc prof, Ill Inst Technol, 64-67. *Concurrent Pos:* Consult, Ames Res Ctr, NASA, 66 & Ballistic Res Lab, US Army, 69-75. *Mem:* Am Math Soc; Soc Indust & Appl Math; Am Phys Soc. *Res:* Magneto-gasdynamics; plasma physics; partial differential equations; rotating fluids. *Mailing Add:* Dept Math & Statist Univ Md Baltimore Co Baltimore MD 21250. *E-Mail:* lynn@math.umbc.edu

LYNNE-DAVIES, PATRICIA, RESPIRATORY PHYSIOLOGY. *Current Pos:* PROF, DEPT INTERNAL MED, WAYNE STATE UNIV, 80- *Personal Data:* b Swansa, Wales, July 4, 33. *Educ:* Conjoint Bd, London, MRCS-LRCP, 61; McGill Univ, PhD(physiol), 69. *Prof Exp:* Asst prof, Dept Med, Univ Alta, 69-74; assoc prof, Stanford Univ, 74-80. *Mem:* Am Fedn Clin Res; Am Physiol Soc. *Mailing Add:* 15801 Windmill Pointe Dr Grosse Pointe Park MI 48230-1841

LYNTON, ERNEST ALBERT, ACADEMIC ADMINISTRATION, LOW TEMPERATURE PHYSICS. *Current Pos:* RETIRED. *Personal Data:* b Berlin, Ger, July 17, 26; nat US; m 53, Carla Kaufmann; c David & Eric. *Educ:* Carnegie Inst Technol, BS, 47, MS, 48; Yale Univ, PhD(physics), 51. *Prof Exp:* Asst, Off Naval Res, Yale Univ, 47-50; AEC fel, Univ Leiden, 51-52; from asst prof to prof physics, Rutgers Univ, 52-74, dean Livingston Col, 65-74; sr vpres acad affairs, Univ Mass, 74-80, commonwealth prof physics, 74-94. *Concurrent Pos:* Vis prof, Univ Grenoble, 59-60; mem, Comn Higher Educ, Mid States Asn, 70-75. *Mem:* Fel Am Phys Soc; Sigma Xi; Am Asn Higher Educ. *Res:* Low temperature physics helium 3 and helium 4 mixtures; superconductors; dilute metallic alloys; thermal conductivity; policy in higher education emphasis on changing mission of universities and collaboration with industry; professional preparation and continuing education. *Mailing Add:* 14 Allerton St Brookline MA 02146. *Fax:* 617-566-4383; *E-Mail:* lynton@umbsky.cc.umb.edu

LYO, SUNGKWUN KENNETH, SEMICONDUCTOR PHYSICS, QUANTUM TRANSPORT & MANY-BODY THEORY. *Current Pos:* mem tech staff, 77-88, SR MEM TECH STAFF PHYSICS, SANDIA NAT LABS, 88- *Personal Data:* b Pyongnam, Korea, July 3, 41; m 71, Nahmyoung Lee; c John, Grace & Christopher. *Educ:* Seoul Nat Univ, Korea, BA, 64; Univ Calif, Los Angeles, PhD(physics), 72. *Honors & Awards:* Basic Energy Sci Award, US Dept Energy, 93. *Prof Exp:* Asst res physicist, Univ Calif, Los Angeles, 72-73; res assoc physics, Univ Chicago, 73-74; adj asst prof, Univ Calif, Los Angeles, 74-77. *Concurrent Pos:* Vis prof, Korea Advan Inst Sci, 80; vis scholar, Seoul Nat Univ, 91. *Mem:* Am Phys Soc; Mat Res Soc. *Res:* Ferromagnetic Hall effect; spin-lattice relaxation; hopping transport in disordered solids; quantum transport and many-body effects in metals, semiconductors and organic conductors; optical properties of quantum wells. *Mailing Add:* Sandia Nat Labs PO Box 5800 MS 1415 Albuquerque NM 87185-5800

LYON, CAMERON KIRBY, ORGANIC CHEMISTRY. *Current Pos:* RETIRED. *Personal Data:* b Islamgun, India, July 23, 23; US citizen; m 48; c 3. *Educ:* Col Wooster, BA, 47; Northwestern Univ, PhD(chem), 52. *Prof Exp:* Chemist, Jackson Lab, E I du Pont de Nemours & Co, 51-59; chemist, Western Regional Res Lab, USDA, Albany, 59-86. *Mem:* Am Chem Soc; Am Oil Chem Soc. *Res:* Polymers; urethanes; fats and oils; oilseed and leaf proteins. *Mailing Add:* Five North Lane Orinda CA 94563-2204

LYON, DAVID LOUIS, ECOLOGY, ORNITHOLOGY. *Current Pos:* asst prof, 65-73, ASSOC PROF BIOL, CORNELL COL, 73- *Personal Data:* b Oshkosh, Wis, Jan 20, 35; m 57; c 3. *Educ:* Beloit Col, BA, 56; Univ Mo, MA, 59; Iowa State Univ, PhD(wildlife ecol), 65. *Prof Exp:* Wildlife biologist, Nebr Game & Parks Comn, 59-61. *Mem:* AAAS; Ecol Soc Am; Am Ornithologists' Union. *Res:* Competition ecology, particularly territoriality and its relation to resource utilization; pollination ecology. *Mailing Add:* Dept Biol Cornell Col Mt Vernon IA 52314-1098

LYON, DAVID N, PHYSICAL CHEMISTRY. *Current Pos:* Res assoc, Univ Calif, Berkeley, 48-51, asst res chemist, 51-53, assoc res chemist, 53-59, res chem engr, 59-65, lectr chem eng, 57-65, asst dean, Col Chem, 69-72, PROF CHEM ENG, COL CHEM, UNIV CALIF, BERKELEY, 65- *Personal Data:* b Altoona, Kans, Apr 15, 19; m 42; c 2. *Educ:* Univ Mo, MA, 42; Univ Calif, PhD(chem), 48. *Mem:* NY Acad Sci; AAAS; Am Chem Soc; Am Inst Chem Eng; Sigma Xi. *Res:* Chemical thermodynamics; cryogenic engineering; chemical process design. *Mailing Add:* 266 Corliss Dr Moraga CA 94556-1313

LYON, DONALD WILKINSON, INORGANIC CHEMISTRY. *Current Pos:* RETIRED. *Personal Data:* b Manchester, Eng, Aug 6, 16; nat US; m 42, Martha Crane; c Richard, Evelyn (Brownlee) & David. *Educ:* Ohio Wesleyan Univ, BA, 37; Ohio State Univ, PhD(inorg chem), 41. *Honors & Awards:* Borman Award, Am Soc Eng Educ, 81, Freund Award, 93. *Prof Exp:* Res chemist, E I du Pont de Nemours & Co, Inc, 41-54, tech supvr, 54-62, admin supvr, Pigments Dept, 62-77, personnel coordr, Chem Dyes & Pigments Dept, 77-81. *Mem:* Am Chem Soc; Am Soc Eng Educ. *Res:* Titanium dioxide. *Mailing Add:* 110 Banbury Dr Windsor Hills Wilmington DE 19803-2602

LYON, DUANE EDGAR, FOREST PRODUCTS, WOOD SCIENCE. *Current Pos:* from asst prof to assoc prof, 73-85, PROF FOREST PROD, MISS FOREST PROD LAB, MISS STATE UNIV, 85- *Personal Data:* b Muskegon, Mich, Mar 12, 39; m 61, Diana Sibilsky; c Karla & Keith. *Educ:* Univ Mich, BS, 62, MS, 63; Univ Calif, Berkeley, PhD(forest prod), 75. *Prof Exp:* Asst technologist, Dept Wood Technol, Wash State Univ, 63-66; asst specialist, Forest Prod Lab, Univ Calif, 66-73. *Concurrent Pos:* Vis scientist, USDA Forest Prod Lab, 80; vis prof, MOI Univ, Kenya, 88; consult. *Mem:* Forest Prod Res Soc; Soc Wood Sci & Technol (pres, 96-97). *Res:* Development and characterization of composite engineering materials made wholly or in part from wood; wood performance; effect of adverse environments on wood performance; wood utility poles and furniture construction. *Mailing Add:* Miss State Univ PO Box 9820 Mississippi State MS 39762-9820. *Fax:* 601-325-8126

LYON, EDWARD SPAFFORD, GENITOURINARY SURGERY, ENDOUROLOGY. *Current Pos:* Intern, Univ Hosps, 53-54, resident surg, 54-56, resident urol, 56-59, from asst prof to prof, 59-96, EMER PROF UROL, UNIV CHICAGO, 96- *Personal Data:* b Chicago, Ill, Feb 26, 26; m 51, Valerie Traut; c Nancy, Susan, Ross, Janice, Roger, Alice, Paul, Steven, Sally, John, Valerie & Mark. *Educ:* Univ Chicago, PhB, 48, SB, 50, MD, 53. *Honors & Awards:* Pro Meritate Medal, Int Soc Urol Endoscopy. *Mem:* Am Urol Asn; Soc Univ Urologists; Int Soc Urol Endoscopy; Endourology Soc; Soc Urol & Eng. *Res:* Urolithiasis. *Mailing Add:* 11246 Longwood Dr Chicago IL 60643. *Fax:* 773-702-1001; *E-Mail:* e_lyon@uchicago.edu

LYON, GORDON EDWARD, PROGRAMMING TECHNIQUES. *Current Pos:* COMPUT SCIENTIST, NAT INST STAND & TECHNOL, 72-, MGR, PARALLEL PROCESSING GROUP, 92- *Personal Data:* b New London, Wis, June 8, 42; m 71, Carla Kaiser; c Merritt & Adrienne. *Educ:* Mich Technol Univ, BS, 64; Univ Mich, MS, 66 & 67, PhD(comput sci), 72. *Honors & Awards:* Silver Medal Award, US Dept Com, 78. *Prof Exp:* Mathematician, Comput Sci Dept, Gen Motors Res Labs, 67-68; res assoc, Dept Psychiat, Ment Health Res Inst, Univ Mich, 70-72. *Concurrent Pos:* Assoc prof lectr, Dept Elec Eng & Comput Sci, George Washington Univ, 78-79; adj prof lectr, Dept Decision Sci, George Mason Univ, 84-85. *Mem:* Asn Comput Mach; Soc Indust Appl Math; Comput Soc Inst Elec & Electronics Engrs. *Res:* Primarily interested in software programming techniques; have contributions in the areas of syntactic pattern recognition; scatter storage; programming language tools; performance measurement for parallel systems. *Mailing Add:* Nat Inst Stand & Technol 9216 Wooden Bridge Rd Rockville MD 20854-2416. *Fax:* 301-926-9675; *E-Mail:* lyon@nist.gov

LYON, GORDON FREDERICK, PHYSICS. *Current Pos:* RETIRED. *Personal Data:* b London, Eng, May 10, 22; Can citizen; m 43; c 1. *Educ:* Univ Sask, BA, 56, MA, 58, PhD(physics), 61. *Prof Exp:* Instr physics, Univ Sask, 56-62; from asst prof to assoc prof, Univ Western Ont, 62-69, prof physics, 69-88. *Concurrent Pos:* Mem comn 6, Int Union Geod & Geophys-Int Asn Geomag & Aeronomy, 63-; mem subcomt aeronomy, Nat Res Coun Can, 66- *Mem:* Am Geophys Union; Am Asn Physics Teachers; Can Asn Physicists. *Res:* Radio physics of the upper atmosphere; scattering of radio waves by ionospheric inhomogeneities; ionospheric absorption; travelling ionospheric disturbances; ionospheric electron content utilizing beacon satellites; associated geophysical phenomena; aurora. *Mailing Add:* Apt 114 Gainesborough Rd London ON N6G 1Z8 Can

LYON, IRVING, HEPATIC GLUTATHIONE HOMEOSTASIS. *Current Pos:* RETIRED. *Personal Data:* b Los Angeles, Calif, May 10, 21; m 48, Harriette Goodman; c David, Charles & Lawrence. *Educ:* Univ Calif, Los Angeles, AB, 42, MA, 49; Univ Calif, Berkeley, PhD(physiol), 52. *Prof Exp:* Lab & teaching asst mammalian anat & gen embryol, Univ Southern Calif, Los Angeles, 47-49, researcher & gen lab asst mammalian physiol, Univ Calif, Berkeley, 49-52; res biochemist physiol & biochem skin, med dept, Toni Co, Chicago, 54-58; res assoc physiol & biochem bone, orthop surg, Presby-St Luke's Hosp, Chicago, 58-62; asst prof biol chem, Univ Ill, Chicago, 58-62; assoc prof biochem, Chicago Med Sch, Ill, 62-67; prof biol, sci fac, Bennington Col, Vt, 67-72; sr visitor, Inst Biol Chem A, Univ Copenhagen, Denmark, 72-74; spec consult energy resources & conserv, Calif State Comn, Los Angeles, 75; res physiologist tumor-lipid biochem, Univ Calif, Los Angeles, 79-81; res biochemist hepatol, US Vet Admin Wadsworth Hosp Ctr, Los Angeles, 81-89. *Concurrent Pos:* Res & teaching fel, Rockefeller Found-Med Sci Dept Nutrit, Harvard Sch Pub Health, 52-54; lectr, Soc Gen Physiologists, Woods Hole, Mass, 63, Inst Med Res, Putnam Mem Hosp, Bennington, Vt, Dept Biochem, Physiol & Oncol, Univ Wis-Madison, Will Rogers Mem Hosp, Saranac Lake, NY & Lab Pharmacol, Baltimore Cancer Res Ctr, Nat Cancer Inst, 68; NSF res fel, dept physiol & biophys, Univ Ill, Urbana, 70; vis investr, Jackson Lab, Bar Harbor, Maine, 71; consult, environ health & nutrit, 75- *Mem:* Fel AAAS; fel Int Col Appl Nutrit; Am Physiol Soc; NY Acad Sci. *Res:* Liver transplantation studies; prevention of post-ischemic injury; hepatic enzymes and oxidant injury; consultant on EIR's for development projects proposed in environmentally-sensitive areas. *Mailing Add:* 708 Grant St Apt A Santa Monica CA 90405-1221

LYON, JAMES F, INTERNATIONAL PHYSICS. *Current Pos:* RES SCIENTIST, OAK RIDGE NAT LAB, 64- *Educ:* Mass Inst Technol, BS, 60, MS, 62; Univ Tenn, PhD(physics), 69. *Mem:* Am Phys Soc. *Mailing Add:* 984 W Outer Dr Oak Ridge TN 37830

LYON, JEFFREY A, IMMUNOLOGY. *Current Pos:* Res chemist, Div Biochem, 75-80, RES CHEMIST, DEPT IMMUNOL, WALTER REED ARMY INST RES, 80- *Personal Data:* c 2. *Educ:* Va Mil Inst, BS, 70; Univ SC, PhD(biochem), 74. *Mem:* Am Asn Immunologists; Am Soc Trop Med & Hyg; Sigma Xi. *Mailing Add:* Dept Immunol Walter Reed Army Inst Res Washington DC 20307-5100

LYON, JOHN B(ENNETT), CHEMICAL ENGINEERING. *Current Pos:* Res engr, Polychem Dept, E I du Pont de Nemours & Co Inc, 53-57, tech investr, Film Dept, 57-58, res engr, 58-59, engr res supvr, Yerkes Res Lab, 60-62, process develop supvr, Clinton Film Plant, Iowa, 62-65 & Spruance Film Plant, Richmond, Va, 65-76, sr engr, 76-80, staff engr, Sabine River Works, 80-85, SR TECH ASSOC, E I DU PONT DE NEMOURS & CO, INC, 86- *Personal Data:* b Washington, DC, Mar 13, 27; m 57; c 1. *Educ:* Catholic Univ, BChE, 50; Univ Del, PhD(chem eng), 53. *Mem:* Am Chem Soc; Am Inst Chem Engrs; Sigma Xi. *Res:* Heat and mass transfer; application of reaction kinetics. *Mailing Add:* 1824 Lindenwood Dr Orange TX 77630

LYON, JOHN BLAKESLEE, JR, BIOCHEMISTRY. *Current Pos:* RETIRED. *Personal Data:* b Auburn, NY, Mar 17, 25; m 48; c 2. *Educ:* Hamilton Col, AB, 50; Brown Univ, ScM, 52, PhD(biol), 54. *Prof Exp:* Asst biol, Brown Univ, 50-52; Life Inst Med Res Fund fel biochem, Emory Univ, 54-56, from instr to prof biochem, 56-92. *Concurrent Pos:* Lederle Med Fac award, Emory Univ, 56-59, USPHS sr res fel, 59. *Mem:* Am Soc Biol Chem. *Res:* Regulatory mechanisms of metabolism; glycogen metabolism; vitamin B-6. *Mailing Add:* PO Box 1269 Flowery Branch GA 30542. *Fax:* 404-727-2738

LYON, JOHN GRIMSON, REMOTE SENSOR & GLOBAL IONOSPHERIC STUDIES TECHNOLOGIES, ENVIRONMENTAL SCIENCE & ENGINEERING. *Current Pos:* ASSOC PROF CIVIL ENG, OHIO STATE UNIV, 81-, ASSOC PROF NATURAL RESOURCES, 82- *Personal Data:* b Berkeley, Calif, Feb, 54; m 86; c Sarah F. *Educ:* Reed Col, Portland, Ore, BA, 77; Univ Mich, Ann Arbor, MS, 79, PhD(natural resources), 81. *Prof Exp:* Res assoc, Sch Natural Resources, Univ Mich, 77-81; res assoc, NASA Ames Res Ctr, 76-77. *Concurrent Pos:* Civil engr, US Army Corps Engrs, Dist Detroit, 85-88; chair, Aerospace Div Remote Sensing Comt, Am Soc Civil Engrs, 87-89; assoc ed, Photogram Eng & Remote Sensing, 88-; vis scientist, US Environ Protection Agency, Environ Monitoring Systs Lab, 91-94; ed-in-chief, Lewis Publ. *Mem:* Am Soc Photogram & Remote Sensing; Am Soc Civil Engrs; Inst Elec & Electronics Engrs; Am Cong Surveying & Mapping; Am Soc Agr; Soil & Water Conserv Soc. *Res:* Application of remote sensor and geographic information system technologies to natural resource and engineering problems including wetlands, water quality, vegetation, soils, and landscape ecology; author of over 30 refereed journals. *Mailing Add:* Dept Civil Eng Ohio State Univ 2070 Neil Ave Columbus OH 43210-1226

LYON, K(ENNETH) C(ASSINGHAM), CERAMICS ENGINEERING, GLASS TECHNOLOGY. *Current Pos:* RETIRED. *Personal Data:* b La Harpe, Ill, Jan 22, 08; m 33; c 3. *Educ:* Univ Ill, BS, 31, MS, 33, PhD(ceramic eng), 36. *Prof Exp:* Asst, Eng Exp Sta, Univ Ill, 31-33; ceramic engr, Glass Tech Lab, Gen Elec Co, 35-40; asst chief chemist, Armstrong Cork Co, NJ, 40-42, chief chemist, 42-46, asst mgr glass res, 46-54; tech mgr, Ind Glass Co, 54-55; mgr glass res, Ball Bros Res Corp, 55-67, mgr glass process develop, Ball Bros Co, 67-71; res assoc & Glass Container Manufacturers Inst fel, Nat Bur Stand, Md, 72-73. *Concurrent Pos:* Chem & Chem Technol, Nat Res Coun, 50-53; mem, Div Chem & Technol, Nat Res Coun, 53-56. *Mem:* Fel Am Ceramic Soc (vpres, 55-56); fel Am Inst Chem; NY Acad Sci. *Res:* Quantitative relationship composition to physical and chemical properties of soda-lime glasses; surface tension of glass; electric melting of glass. *Mailing Add:* 500 S Main St No 415 Elkhart IN 46516-3207

LYON, LEONARD JACK, WILDLIFE ECOLOGY, FOREST ECOLOGY. *Current Pos:* WILDLIFE BIOLOGIST & PROJ LEADER FOREST WILDLIFE HABITAT, FORESTRY SCI LAB, INTERMOUNTAIN RES STA, US FOREST SERV, 62- *Personal Data:* b Sterling, Colo, Oct 31, 29; m 56; c 2. *Educ:* Colo State Univ, BS, 51, MS, 53; Univ Mich, PhD(wildlife mgt), 60. *Prof Exp:* Res biologist & proj leader pheasant habitat, Colo Game & Fish Dept, 55-62. *Concurrent Pos:* Res assoc, Univ Mont, 65-, Univ Idaho, 89- *Mem:* Wildlife Soc; Am Inst Biol Sci; Ecol Soc Am. *Res:* Forest seral ecology; wildlife habitat. *Mailing Add:* Forestry Sci Lab US Forest Serv Intermountain Res Sta Missoula MT 59807-8089

LYON, RICHARD H, MECHANICAL ENGINEERING, ACOUSTICS. *Current Pos:* prof 70-95, EMER PROF MECH ENG, MASS INST TECHNOL, 95-; PRES, R H LYON CORP, 76- *Personal Data:* b Evansville, Ind, Aug 24, 29; m, Jean Wheaton; c Katherine Ruth, Geoffrey Cleveland & Suzanne Marie. *Educ:* Evansville Col, AB, 52; Mass Inst Technol, PhD(physics), 55. *Hon Degrees:* DEng, Univ Evansville, 76. *Honors & Awards:* Rayleigh Medal, Inst Acoust, 95. *Prof Exp:* From asst prof to assoc prof, Elec Eng Dept, Univ Minn, 56-59; researcher, Bolt Beranek & Newman Inc, 60-64, dept head, 64-70, corp vpres & dir, Phys Sci Div, 67-70. *Concurrent Pos:* NSF post doctoral fel, Univ Manchester, 59; founder & prin, Cambridge Collaborative Inc, 70-90. *Mem:* Nat Acad Eng; fel Acoust Soc Am (pres, 93-94); fel AAAS; Sigma Xi; Inst Noise Control Eng. *Res:* Machine dynamics; random vibration; sound generation; interaction of sound and structures; application of statistics to engineering analysis; propogation of environmental noise. *Mailing Add:* R H Lyon Corp 691 Concord Ave Cambridge MA 02138. *Fax:* 617-864-0779; *E-Mail:* rhlyon@lyoncorp.com

LYON, RICHARD HALE, MICROBIOLOGY, BIOCHEMISTRY. *Current Pos:* DIR QUAL CONTROL, PABST MEAT SUPPLY INC, INVER GROVE HEIGHTS, MINN, 79- *Personal Data:* b Marquette, Mich, Nov 15, 20; c 3. *Educ:* Univ Minn, BA, 47, MS, 62, PhD(microbiol, biochem), 65. *Prof Exp:* City bacteriologist, Sioux City Dept Health, Iowa, 48-49; bacteriologist, Vet Admin Ctr, Sioux Falls, SDak, 49-54; res microbiologist, Bact Res Lab, Vet Admin Hosp, Minneapolis, 54-77; res microbiologist, Mastitis Res, Col Vet Med, Univ Minn, 77-79. *Mem:* Am Soc Microbiol; fel Am Inst Chem; Am Thoracic Soc; Inst Food Technologists; Sigma Xi. *Res:* Microbial physiology, specifically as it pertains to metabolic differences in the mycobacteria and to the relationship of these differences to drug susceptibility, taxonomy and virulence. *Mailing Add:* 8567 134th St W St Paul MN 55124

LYON, RICHARD KENNETH, PHYSICAL CHEMISTRY. *Current Pos:* Chemist, Exxon Res & Eng Co, 60-64, sr chemist, Cent Basic Res Lab, 64-67, res assoc, 67-75, sr res assoc, 75-80, sci adv, 80-86, SR SCIENTIST ENERGY & ENVIRON RES, EXXON RES & ENG CO, 86- *Personal Data:* b Cleveland, Ohio, Dec 22, 33; m 68; c John & David. *Educ:* Col William & Mary, BS, 55; Harvard Univ, PhD(phys chem), 60. *Honors & Awards:* Indust Res 100 Award; Chem Award, Am Chem Soc. *Mem:* Am Chem Soc; Combustion Inst. *Res:* Chemical reaction kinetics; combustion science; cage effect in solution and gas phase; gas phase detonations and shock waves; radiation and high pressure chemistry; laser isotope separation; nox control. *Mailing Add:* 20 Finn Rd Pittstown NJ 08867-9445

LYON, ROBERT LYNDON, FOREST ENTOMOLOGY, INSECT TOXICOLOGY. *Current Pos:* RETIRED. *Personal Data:* b Dolgeville, NY, Apr 17, 27; m 84; c 7. *Educ:* Syracuse Univ, BS, 53, MS, 54; Univ Calif, Berkeley, PhD(insect toxicol), 61. *Prof Exp:* Res entomologist, Pac Southwest Forest & Range Exp Sta, 53-72, supvry res entomologist & proj leader, Insecticide Eval Proj, 72-76, mem nat staff, Forest Insect & Dis Res, US Forest Serv, 76-, staff res forest entomologist, 76-92. *Mem:* Entom Soc Am. *Res:* Development of safe, selective, nonpersistent and effective chemical insecticides and techniques to manage forest insect populations and protect forest resource values with minimal adverse effects on the environment. *Mailing Add:* 1029 N Stuart St Apt 528 Arlington VA 22201

LYON, RONALD JAMES PEARSON, GEOLOGY, MINERALOGY. *Current Pos:* assoc prof, 65-71, prof mineral, EMER PROF APPL EARTH SCI, STANFORD UNIV. *Personal Data:* b Northam, WAustralia, Jan 15, 28; US citizen; m 61; c 4. *Educ:* Univ Western Australia, BS, 48, Hons, 49; Univ Calif, Berkeley, PhD(geol), 54. *Honors & Awards:* Photog Interpretation Award, Am Soc Photogram, 72. *Prof Exp:* Geologist, Lake George Mines, Captains Flat, NSW, 49-51; Goewey res fel geol, Univ Calif, Berkeley, 51-54; res off mining, Commonwealth Sci Res Orgn, Australia, 54-56; geochemist, Kennecott Res Ctr, Utah, 56-59; sr geochemist, Stanford Res Inst, 59-63; Nat Acad Sci sr fel geol, Ames Res Ctr, NASA, 63-65. *Concurrent Pos:* Fulbright travel grant, 51-54 & 78-79; chmn geol panel, Nat Acad Sci, Woods Hole, Mass, 67-69; consult planetary atmosphere, NASA, 68-70; consult & prin assoc, Earth Satellite Corp, 70-; mem remote sensing group, Int Hydrol Decade, Nat Acad Sci, 72- *Mem:* AAAS; Soc Econ Geol; Am Soc Photogram. *Res:* Use of airborne geophysical techniques and remote sensing in exploration for mineral deposits; recognition of rock and soil materials using land satellite and Skylab spectral data; airborne scanners. *Mailing Add:* Dept Earth Sci Stanford Univ Stanford CA 94305-2210

LYON, WALDO (KAMPMEIER), PHYSICS. *Current Pos:* chief scientist, Arctic Submarine Res, US Navy Electronics Lab, 41-66, dir, Arctic Submarine Lab, 66-84, CHIEF SCIENTIST, NAVAL OCEAN SYSTS CTR, 84- *Personal Data:* b Los Angeles, Calif, May 19, 14; m 37; c 2. *Educ:* Univ Calif, Los Angeles, AB, 36, MA, 37, PhD(physics), 41. *Honors & Awards:* Am Soc Naval Engrs Gold Medal Award, 59; Bronze Medal, Royal Inst Navigation, 85; Silver Medal, Geog Soc, Paris, 83. *Prof Exp:* Asst physics,

Univ Calif, Los Angeles, 40-41. *Concurrent Pos:* Sr scientist, Wave Measurement Group, Bikini atom bomb tests, 46; lectr, Univ Calif, Los Angeles, 48-49; physicist, Submarine Opers, US Navy-Byrd Antarctic exped, 46-47; chief scientist, US-Can Aleutian exped, 49, Beauford Sea expeds, 51-54; sr scientist, Transpolar Submarine Exped, 57-82. *Mem:* Fel AAAS; fel Am Phys Soc; fel Acoust Soc Am; fel Arctic Inst NAm; Am Soc Naval Eng; Am Geophys Union; Int Glaciological Soc. *Res:* Ocean-cryology and physics of sea ice; underice acoustics. *Mailing Add:* 1330 Alexandria Dr San Diego CA 92107

LYON, WILLIAM FRANCIS, ECONOMIC ENTOMOLOGY. *Current Pos:* asst & assoc, 74-76, PROF ENTOM, OHIO STATE UNIV, 82- *Personal Data:* b Mt Gilead, Ohio, Jan 24, 37; m 62, Marjorie; c Cynthia, Kara, Fred & Jim. *Educ:* Ohio State Univ, BSc, 59, MSc, 62, PhD(entom), 69. *Prof Exp:* County exten agent, Ohio Coop Exten Serv, 59-61, exten entomologist, 66-72; surv entomologist, Ohio Agr Res & Develop Ctr, 62-64; asst prof entom & plant protection entomologist, Makerere Univ, Uganda, 72-73; asst prof & pest mgt entomologist, Univ Nairobi, Kenya, 73-74; assoc prof, Afgoi Agr Res Sta, Mogdiscio, Somalia, 76-78. *Concurrent Pos:* USAID entom consult, Guinea Bissau, 88; res fel, Ohio State Univ Ctr African Studies; vols in Overseas Coop Assistance Entom consult, Egypt, 93. *Mem:* Entom Soc Am; Am Inst Biol Sci; E African Acad. *Res:* Identification and control of household/structural, livestock, poultry & pet pests, mosquito insects; 4-H youth projects. *Mailing Add:* Dept Entom Ohio State Univ 1991 Kenny Rd Columbus OH 43210-1090. *Fax:* 614-292-9783; *E-Mail:* lyon@agfax2.ag.ohio-state.edu

LYON, WILLIAM GRAHAM, PHYSICAL CHEMISTRY, ENVIRONMENTAL GEOCHEMISTRY. *Current Pos:* ENVIRON PHYS CHEMIST, MAN TECH ENVIRON TECHNOL INC, 88- *Personal Data:* b Chelsea, Mass, Apr 29, 44; m 65, Jean Kinder; c Laura & Steven. *Educ:* Univ Mich, BS, 66, MS, 68, PhD(chem), 73. *Prof Exp:* Fel phys chem, Univ Mich, 73-74; fel, Argonne Nat Lab, 74-76 & Phillips Petroleum Co, 76-88. *Mem:* Am Chem Soc; Sigma Xi; Soc Appl Spectros. *Res:* Environmental geochemistry; studies of the distribution and characterization of natural organic matter in the subsurface. *Mailing Add:* ManTech Environ Res Servs Corp PO Box 1198 Ada OK 74821-1198. *Fax:* 580-436-8501; *E-Mail:* lyon@ad3100.ada.epa.gov

LYON, WILLIAM SOUTHERN, JR, RADIOCHEMISTRY. *Current Pos:* CONSULT, 85- *Personal Data:* b Pulaski, Va, Jan 25, 22; m 46, Carey Greer; c 2. *Educ:* Univ Va, BS, 43; Univ Tenn, MS, 68. *Honors & Awards:* Radiation Indust Award, Am Nuclear Soc, 80; Hevesy Medal, 81. *Prof Exp:* Chemist, E I du Pont de Nemours & Co, WVa, 43-44 & Wash, 44-45; lab foreman, Tenn Eastman Corp, 45-47; chemist, Oak Ridge Nat Lab, 47-62, group leader radiochem, 62-77, head, analytical methodol, 77-85. *Concurrent Pos:* Consult, Thai Atomic Energy for Peace Lab, Bangkok, 66-; mem sci comt 25, Nat Coun Radiation Protection, 67-; assoc ed, Radiochem-Radioanal Lett, 70-; regional ed, J Radioanal Chem, 71- *Mem:* Am Chem Soc; Am Nuclear Soc. *Res:* Trace element analysis; new energy sources; nuclear decay schemes; specialized radioactivity measurements; scientometrics. *Mailing Add:* 638 Chapel Point Lane Knoxville TN 37922

LYONS, ANTHONY VINCENT, FLUID MECHANICS, PULP & PAPER TECHNOLOGY. *Current Pos:* LEADER PAPER TECHNOL, ECCI AM/PAC, 94- *Personal Data:* b Buffalo, NY, Feb 25, 55; m 87, Debra M Stillo; c Michael, Christine, Stephanie & John. *Educ:* Univ Buffalo, BS, 73, MS, 81; Lehigh Univ, PhD(chem eng), 85. *Prof Exp:* Dir coatings & finishings res, Repap Technol Inc, 89-94. *Mem:* Tech Asn Pulp & Paper Industs; Can Pulp & Paper Asn; Paper Indust Mgt Asn. *Res:* Kinetics of yeast fermentations and the hydrodynamics of bubble columns; mechanics of calendering; the fluid mechanics of coating; the rheology of coatings; the interactions of papermaking materials and their influence on paper properties. *Mailing Add:* 140 Saddle Run Ct Macon GA 31210. *Fax:* 912-552-7570; *E-Mail:* 75230.2510@compuserve.com

LYONS, CARL J(OHN), chemical engineering, for more information see previous edition

LYONS, DONALD HERBERT, PHYSICS. *Current Pos:* RETIRED. *Personal Data:* b Buffalo, NY, Feb 28, 29; m 51; c 3. *Educ:* Univ Buffalo, BA, 49; Univ Pa, MA, 51, PhD(physics), 54. *Prof Exp:* Staff scientist, Lincoln Lab, Mass Inst Technol, 56-61 & Sperry Rand Res Ctr, 61-63; res prof physics, Inst Solid State Physics, Univ Tokyo, 63-64; staff scientist, Sperry Rand Res Ctr, Mass, 64-66; from assoc prof to prof physics, Univ Mass, Boston, 66-94, chmn dept, 67-68 & 70-72. *Concurrent Pos:* Fulbright grant, 63-64. *Mem:* Am Phys Soc. *Res:* Theoretical magnetism; communication theory; theoretical nuclear physics. *Mailing Add:* 8 Gould Rd Lexington MA 02173

LYONS, EDWARD ARTHUR, RADIOLOGY, ULTRASOUND. *Current Pos:* ASSOC PROF ANAT & PROF RADIOL, OBSTET & GYNEC, UNIV MAN, 76- *Personal Data:* b Halifax, NS, Mar 15, 43; m 67; c 1. *Educ:* Univ Man, BSc, 63, MD, 68; FRCP(C), 73. *Hon Degrees:* FACR, 83. *Prof Exp:* Dir, Ultrasound Sect, Health Sci Ctr, Winnipeg, St Boniface Hosp, 73-86, head radiol, 90-96. *Mem:* Am Inst Ultrasound Med; Can Asn Radiologists; Soc Radiol Ultrasound; Am Col Radiol. *Res:* Long term effects of ultrasound; immunological effects of ultrasound; early pregnancy failure. *Mailing Add:* Sect Diag Ultrasound Health Sci Ctr 820 Sherbrook St Winnipeg MB R3A 1R9 Can. *Fax:* 204-787-3355; *E-Mail:* lyons@umanitoba.ca

LYONS, EUGENE T, PARASITOLOGY. *Current Pos:* Asst prof, 58-60 & 63-70, assoc prof, 70-77, PROF PARASITOL, UNIV KY, 77- *Personal Data:* b Yankton, SDak, May 6, 31. *Educ:* SDak State Univ, BS, 56; Kans State Univ, MS, 58; Colo State Univ, PhD(parasitol), 63. *Mem:* Am Soc Parasitol; Wildlife Dis Asn. *Res:* Parasites of jackrabbits, fur seals, horses, sheep and cattle. *Mailing Add:* 1149 E Cooper Dr Lexington KY 40502

LYONS, GEORGE D, OTOLARYNGOLOGY. *Current Pos:* From clin instr to clin assoc prof, 58-70, assoc prof, 70-71, PROF OTOLARYNGOL & HEAD DEPT, SCH MED, LA STATE UNIV, NEW ORLEANS, 71-, PROF BIOCOMMUN, 77- *Personal Data:* b New Orleans, La, Jan 19, 28; m 54; c 5. *Educ:* Southeastern La Col, BS, 50; La State Univ, New Orleans, MD, 54. *Honors & Awards:* Recognition Award, AMA. *Concurrent Pos:* Mem, Soc Acad Chmn Otolaryngol, 72- *Mem:* Fel Am Laryngol, Rhinol & Otol Soc; fel Am Acad Facial Plastic & Reconstruct Surg; fel Am Col Surg; fel Pan-Am Soc Otolaryngol. *Res:* Regional plastic surgery; otology. *Mailing Add:* La State Univ Med Ctr 2020 Gravier Suite A New Orleans LA 70112-2234

LYONS, HAROLD, ENVIRONMENTAL SCIENCE, MOLECULAR PATHOLOGY. *Current Pos:* assoc prof, 58-60, PROF CHEM, RHODES COL, 60- *Personal Data:* b New York, NY, Mar 27, 19; m 41, Helen G Panish; c Michael, William & Christopher. *Educ:* City Col New York, BS, 45; Okla State Univ, MS, 49, PhD(chem), 51. *Prof Exp:* Res chemist, Ruberoid Co, 45-48; sr res chemist, Gen Elec Co, 51-52 & Pa Salt Mfg Co, 52-55; lab mgr, Koppers Co, Inc, 55-58; prof path, Med Units Univ Tenn, Memphis, 63-85. *Mem:* AAAS; Am Chem Soc. *Res:* Instrumental analysis; forensic toxicology; analytical biochemistry; biochemistry. *Mailing Add:* 1656 Polar Estates Pkwy Germantown TN 38138

LYONS, JAMES EDWARD, ORGANIC CHEMISTRY, ORGANOMETALLIC CHEMISTRY. *Current Pos:* res chemist, 68-74, sr res chemist, 74-77, GROUP LEADER, SUN CO, 77- *Personal Data:* b Montpelier, Vt, Oct 20, 37; m 63; c 2. *Educ:* Boston Col, BS, 59; Purdue Univ, MS, 61; Univ Calif, Davis, PhD(org chem), 68. *Prof Exp:* Chemist, Res & Develop Ctr, Gen Elec Co, 62-64. *Mem:* AAAS; Am Chem Soc; NY Acad Sci. *Res:* Mechanisms and synthetic applications of transition metal catalyzed reactions in organic and organometallic systems. *Mailing Add:* 211 Cooper Dr Wallingford PA 19086-6827

LYONS, JAMES MARTIN, PLANT PHYSIOLOGY. *Current Pos:* chmn, Dept Veg Crops, Univ Calif, Davis, 70-73, assoc dean, Col Agr & Environ, 73-81, prof veg crops & plant physiologist, 70-91, asst dir, Exp Sta, EMER PROF VEG CROPS, UNIV CALIF, DAVIS, 91- *Personal Data:* b Livermore, Calif, Oct 9, 29; m 56; c 2. *Educ:* Univ Calif, Berkeley, BS, 51; Univ Calif, Davis, MS, 58, PhD(plant physiol), 62. *Honors & Awards:* Campbell Award, Am Inst Biol Sci, 71. *Prof Exp:* Asst plant physiologist, Univ Calif, Riverside, 62-66, vchmn, Dept Veg Crops, 64-66, asst prof, 65-66, assoc prof, chmn dept & assoc plant physiologist, 66-70. *Mem:* Am Soc Hort Sci; Am Soc Plant Physiol; Int Soc Hort Sci. *Res:* Biochemistry and physiology of fruit ripening; low temperature biology and chilling injury in vegetable crops. *Mailing Add:* Dept Vegetable Crops Univ Calif Davis CA 95616

LYONS, JERRY L, FLUID MECHANICS FOR COMPONENTS, SYSTEMS DESIGNS. *Current Pos:* PRES & CHIEF EXEC OFFICER, YANKEE INGENUITY INC, 74-; PRES & CHIEF EXEC OFFICER, INNOVATIVE CONTROLS INC, 91- *Personal Data:* b St Louis, Mo, Apr 2, 39; m; c Karen S (Andershock). *Educ:* Southwest Univ, MSME, 83, PhD(eng mgt), 84. *Honors & Awards:* Winston Churchhill Medal, 88; Dwight D Eisenhower Achievement Award, 90. *Prof Exp:* Proj engr, Harris Mfg Co, 65-70, Essex Cryogenics Indust, 70-73; mgr eng res, Chemetron Corp, 73-77; consult fluids control, Wis Univ, 77-90. *Concurrent Pos:* Vpres & gen mgr, Engr Res & Develop, Fluid Control Div, Essex Indust Inc, 77-90; pres, Lyons Pub Co, 83- *Mem:* Winston Churchhill Wisdom Soc; sr mem Soc Mfg Engrs; sr mem Instrument Soc Am; Comput & Automated Systs Asn; Nat Soc Prof Engrs; fel Am Soc Mech Engrs; Am Security Coun. *Res:* Control systems engineering; author of numerous publications. *Mailing Add:* 2607 Northgate Blvd Ft Wayne IN 46835

LYONS, JOHN BARTHOLOMEW, GEOLOGY. *Current Pos:* from asst prof to prof, 46-87, EMER PROF GEOL, DARTMOUTH COL, 87- *Personal Data:* b Quincy, Mass, Nov 22, 16; wid; c Rosemary, Lisa, John, Barbara & Diana. *Educ:* Harvard Univ, AB, 38, AM, 39, PhD(geol), 42. *Prof Exp:* Geologist, US Geol Surv, 41-45. *Mem:* Fel Geol Soc Am; Mineral Soc Am; Arctic Inst NAm. *Res:* Petrology; structural geology; glaciology. *Mailing Add:* Dept Earth Sci Dartmouth Col Hanover NH 03755

LYONS, JOHN WINSHIP, PHYSICAL CHEMISTRY. *Current Pos:* DIR, ARMY RES LAB, 93- *Personal Data:* b Reading, Mass, Nov 5, 30; m 53, Grace C Hanley; c Margaret, Maryann, John H & Louis M. *Educ:* Harvard Univ, AB, 52; Wash Univ, AM, 63, PhD(phys chem), 64. *Honors & Awards:* Gold Medal Award, US Dept Com, 77; Pres Mgt Improvement Award, White House, 77, Distinguished Exec Rank Award, 81. *Prof Exp:* Prof chemist, Monsanto Co, 55-73; dir, Ctr Fire Res, Nat Bur Stand, 73-77; dir, Nat Eng Lab, 77-90; dir, Nat Inst Stand & Technol, 90-93. *Concurrent Pos:* Chmn, Prod Res Comt, 74-79; mem adv comt eng, NSF & adv coun, Col Eng, Univ Md, 79-90; mem bd dir, Nat Fire Protection Agency, 78-84; mem, Comt Superconductivity, Fed Fed Adv Comm, Consol & Conversion Defense Res & Develop Labs & Blue Ribbon Comt, Res & Pub Serv, Univ Md. *Mem:* Nat Acad Eng; fel AAAS; Am Chem Soc; Am Inst Chem Engrs; Sigma Xi. *Res:*

Phosphorus compounds; rheology; fire and fire retardants; surface chemistry; polyelectrolytes; solution behavior of DNA. *Mailing Add:* Army Res Lab 2800 Powder Mill Rd Adelphia MD 20783. *Fax:* 301-394-5187; *E-Mail:* jlons@.army.mil

LYONS, JOSEPH F, RESEARCH ADMINISTRATION. *Current Pos:* RETIRED. *Personal Data:* b Wappingers Falls, NY, Nov 27, 20; m 46, Anna Hurst; c James, Teresa, Joanne, Mary, Joe & Michael. *Educ:* Fordham Univ, BS, 41; Purdue Univ, MS, 48, PhD(chem), 50. *Prof Exp:* Chemist, Texaco, Inc, 41-46 & 50-53, group leader, 53-60, res supvr, 60-73, asst mgr, 73-82. *Mem:* Am Chem Soc; Sigma Xi. *Res:* Synthesis of additives for lubricants and fuels and product development in these areas. *Mailing Add:* 17 Broadview Rd Poughkeepsie NY 12603

LYONS, JOSEPH PAUL, OPERATIONS RESEARCH, PUBLIC HEALTH. *Current Pos:* SCIENTIST ALCOHOLISM, RES INST ALCOHOLISM, 75- *Personal Data:* b Ardmore, Pa, Dec 9, 47; m 70; c 1. *Educ:* Bloomsburg State Col, BA, 70; Johns Hopkins Univ, ScD, 75. *Prof Exp:* Syst analyst ment health, Pa Off Ment Health, 70-71. *Concurrent Pos:* Nat Inst Ment Health trainee, Johns Hopkins Univ, 71-75; assoc consult, Elliott Assocs, 71-74; admin consult, Md Dept Ment Hyg, 73; asst clin prof, Dept Psychiat, Sch Med & adj asst prof, Dept Indust Eng, Sch Eng, State Univ NY Buffalo, 75- *Mem:* Oper Res Soc Am; AAAS; Asn Ment Health Admin. *Res:* Problem oriented record and its application to alcoholism service delivery; treatment planning in both in-patient and out-patient settings and systems design for delivery of alcoholism services. *Mailing Add:* Dept Indust Eng Bell Hall State Univ NY Buffalo Buffalo NY 14260-0001

LYONS, KENNETH BRENT, SOLID STATE PHYSICS. *Current Pos:* Mem res staff, 73-87, DISTINGUISHED MEM STAFF, AT&T BELL LABS, 87- *Personal Data:* b St Louis, Mo, Aug 31, 46; m 68; c 2. *Educ:* Univ Okla, BS, 68; Univ Colo, MS, 69, PhD(physics), 73. *Mem:* Am Phys Soc. *Res:* Raman and Brillouin light scattering in solids, with emphasis on non-equilibrium phenomena, phase transitions, and magnetic scattering in oxide superconductors; magnetooptics. *Mailing Add:* 1A126 Bell Labs 600 Mountain Ave Murray Hill NJ 07974

LYONS, MICHAEL JOSEPH, VIROLOGY, IMMUNOLOGY. *Current Pos:* PROF LIFE SCI, NY INST TECHNOL, 76- *Personal Data:* b Cork, Ireland, Sept 16, 30; US citizen; m 60, Yvonne Barnett; c Fiona, Conor, Patricia & Desmond. *Educ:* Nat Univ Ireland, BS, 53, MS, 54; Univ Glasgow, PhD(biochem), 59. *Prof Exp:* Res assoc, Rockefeller Univ, 61-66; asst prof microbiol, Univ Pa, 66-69, Cornell Univ Sch Med, 69-76. *Concurrent Pos:* Adj assoc prof, Rockefeller Univ, 78-92, adj prof, 92- *Mem:* Harvey Soc. *Res:* Virology and immunology; author of numerous publications. *Mailing Add:* 53 Eiler Lane Irvington NY 10533

LYONS, NANCY I, ECOLOGICAL STATISTICS. *Current Pos:* asst prof, 75-81, ASSOC PROF STATIST, UNIV GA, 81- *Personal Data:* b Akron, Ohio, Sept 17, 46. *Educ:* Kent State Univ, BS, 68, MA, 70; NC State Univ, PhD(statist), 75. *Prof Exp:* Statistician, Res Triangle Inst, 74-75. *Mem:* Am Statist Asn; Biomet Soc. *Res:* Statistical inference with applications to ecology; computer simulation techniques; sample surveys. *Mailing Add:* Dept Statist Univ Ga 1180 E Broad St Athens GA 30601-3040

LYONS, PAUL CHRISTOPHER, PALEOBOTANY, COAL GEOLOGY. *Current Pos:* RES GEOLOGIST, 91- *Personal Data:* b Cambridge, Mass, Oct 1, 38; m 63; c Sheryl, Russell, Crystal, Sandra & Jennifer. *Educ:* Boston Univ, AB, 63, AM, 64, PhD(geol), 69. *Prof Exp:* Pub sch teacher, Mass, 64-68; instr, Boston Univ, 68-69, asst prof phys sci, 69-75; adj prof chem, Univ Pittsburgh, 85-91. *Concurrent Pos:* Res grants, Boston Univ, 71-72 & Mineral Soc Gt Brit; lectr, Lowell Technol Inst, 72 & Boston Univ Metrop Col, 72-73. *Mem:* NY Acad Sci; fel Geol Soc Am; Am Asn Petrol Geologist; Bot Soc Am; Int Comn Coal Petrol. *Res:* Pennsylvanian stratigraphy, coal geology. *Mailing Add:* 11330 Dockside Circle Reston VA 20191-1834

LYONS, PETER BRUCE, plasma physics, for more information see previous edition

LYONS, PETER FRANCIS, PHYSICAL CHEMISTRY, POLYMER SCIENCE. *Current Pos:* Res chemist, E I Du Pont de Nemours & Co, Inc, 68-71, sr res chemist, 71-73, mkt rep, 73-78, mkt supvr, 78-80, bus strategist, 80-81, sr planning consult, 82-83, tech marketing mgr, 84, bus develop mgr, 84-86, int marketing mgr, 87-89, STRATEGIC PLANNING MGR, E I DU PONT DE NEMOURS & CO, INC, 89- *Personal Data:* b Philadelphia, Pa, Nov 29, 42; m 68; c 3. *Educ:* Villanova Univ, BS, 64; Princeton Univ, MA, 67, PhD(chem), 70. *Mem:* Am Chem Soc. *Res:* Physical chemistry of polymeric systems including work on degradation, strength mechanisms and viscosity theory. *Mailing Add:* Dupont NOW PO Box 80705 Wilmington DE 19880-0705

LYONS, PHILIP AUGUSTINE, PHYSICAL CHEMISTRY. *Current Pos:* from instr to prof, 48-87, chmn, 66-70, 78-79 & 83-84, EMER PROF CHEM, YALE UNIV, 87- *Personal Data:* b Lancaster, Eng, May 26, 16; US citizen; m 49, Margaret Morris; c Catherine, Ellen, Janet & William. *Educ:* La Salle Col, BA, 37; Univ Wis, PhD(chem), 48. *Prof Exp:* Spectroscopist, NAm Smelting Corp, 36-39; chemist, US Chem Warfare Serv, 40-45. *Concurrent Pos:* Vis prof, Univ Islamabad, WPakistan, 71; consult, Audiotape Corp, Robertshaw Fulton Corp, Bendin Aviation Corp, Pratt & Whitney Corp, TVA, Conn Comn Higher Educ, 73-76. *Mem:* Am Chem Soc; Sigma Xi. *Res:* Raman spectra; nonaqueous solutions; diffusion in liquids; Soret effect; reversible thermodynamics. *Mailing Add:* Ridgewood Terr North Haven CT 06473-1256

LYONS, RUSSELL DAVID, TREES, MEASURES. *Current Pos:* ASSOC PROF MATH, INDIANA UNIV, 90- *Personal Data:* b Stoneham, Mass, Sept 6, 57. *Educ:* Case Western Reserve Univ, BA, 79; Univ Mich, PhD(math), 83. *Prof Exp:* Asst prof math, Stanford Univ, 85-90. *Mem:* Am Math Soc; Math Asn Am. *Res:* Research combines harmonic analysis, functional analysis, erdotic theory and probability factors; random walks and percolation. *Mailing Add:* 912 E University St Bloomington IN 47401-5040

LYONS, RUSSETTE M, CELL BIOLOGY. *Current Pos:* CELL BIOL GROUP LEADER & RES SCIENTIST, GENETIC THER, INC, 90- *Personal Data:* b Smithtown, NY, Feb 13, 53. *Educ:* State Univ NY, BA, 75; Univ Nebr, MS, 78, PhD(life sci), 85. *Prof Exp:* Postdoctoral cancer biol, Vanderbilt Med Ctr, 85-88, asst res prof, Dept Cell Biol, 88-90. *Mem:* Am Asn Cancer Res; Am Soc Cell Biol. *Mailing Add:* Genetic Ther Inc 19 Firstfield Rd Gaithersburg MD 20878

LYONS, WILLIAM BERRY, GEOCHEMISTRY. *Current Pos:* Postdoctoral, geochem, Univ NH, 76-79, res scientist, 79-80, asst prof, 80-85, ASSOC PROF GEOCHEM, UNIV NH, 85- *Personal Data:* b Gainesville, Fla, Feb 8, 47. *Educ:* Brown Univ, BA, 69; Univ Conn, MSc, 72 & PhD(oceanog), 79. *Mem:* Am Geophys Union; Geochem Soc; Am Soc Immunol & Oceanog; Soc Econ Paleontologists & Mineralogists; Int Glaciol Soc; Int Asn Geochem & Cosmochem. *Res:* Chemistry of glacial ice and snow; geochemistry of lakes and lacustrine sediments as well as paleoclimatic studies. *Mailing Add:* Dept Geol Bevill Res Bldg Univ Ala Tuscaloosa AL 35487-0338

LYONS, WILLIAM GREGORY, MICROWAVE ENGINEERING, SUPERCONDUCTIVE ELECTRONICS. *Current Pos:* STAFF MEM, LINCOLN LAB, MASS INST TECHNOL, 89- *Personal Data:* b Amarillo, Tex, July 30, 60; m 93. *Educ:* Univ Ill, BS, 82, MS, 83, PhD(elec eng), 89. *Prof Exp:* Eng asst, Bryerton, Inc, 79; summer assoc, Circuit Packaging Div, IBM, Austin, Tex, 81; res asst, MBE Group, Univ Ill, 82-83, res asst, Electro-Physics Lab, 83-89. *Mem:* Inst Elec & Electronics Engrs; Am Phys Soc; Sigma Xi. *Res:* Fundamental properties of superconductors; development of superconducting microwave devices and system prototypes and rf circuits for communication, radar, remote sensing and instrumentation; built superconducting devices for two space experiments and microwave devices for the consortium for superconducting electronics; III-V microwave and optoelectronic devices and studies of collective quantum mechanical effects. *Mailing Add:* 244 Wood St Lexington MA 02173. *E-Mail:* lyons@ll.mit.edu

LYRENE, PAUL MAGNUS, PLANT BREEDING. *Current Pos:* Asst prof agron, 74-77, ASST PROF HORT, UNIV FLA EXP STA, 77- *Personal Data:* b Ala, Apr 16, 46. *Educ:* Auburn Univ, BS, 68; Univ Wis, MS, 70, PhD(plant breeding), 74. *Mem:* Am Soc Hort Sci. *Res:* Blueberry variety improvement; blueberry interspecific hybridization; blueberry cytogenetics and polyploidy; Zizyphus (Chinese date) investigations. *Mailing Add:* Dept Hort Univ Fla PO Box 110690 Gainesville FL 32611-0690

LYS, JEREMY EION ALLEYNE, high energy physics, for more information see previous edition

LYSAK, ROBERT LOUIS, SPACE PLASMA PHYSICS, MAGNETOSPHERIC PHYSICS. *Current Pos:* asst prof, 82-87, ASSOC PROF PHYSICS, UNIV MINN, 87- *Personal Data:* b Chicago, Ill, Jan 18, 55. *Educ:* Mich State Univ, BS, 75; Univ Calif, Berkeley, PhD(physics), 80. *Prof Exp:* Teaching asst physics, Univ Calif, 75-77, res asst, 76-80,asst researcher, 80-82. *Concurrent Pos:* Stipendiat, Max-Planch Inst fur Extraterrestrische Physik, 81. *Mem:* Am Geophys Union; Am Phys Soc. *Res:* Theoretical and numerical investigations of auroral current dynamics, particle accelerations, plasma instabilities, magnetic reconnection and MHD waves and turbulance. *Mailing Add:* 3314 E 26th St Minneapolis MN 55406

LYSEN, JOHN C, MECHANICAL ENGINEERING. *Current Pos:* assoc prof, Univ Mo, Columbia, 63-66, res coordr, Col Eng, 66-68, prof mech & aerospace eng, 68-76, DIR ENG EXP STA, UNIV MO, COLUMBIA, 76- *Personal Data:* b Benson, Minn, Sept 2, 31; m 58; c 2. *Educ:* St Olaf Col, BA, 53; Iowa State Univ, BS, 58, PhD(mech & aerospace eng), 62. *Prof Exp:* Instr mech eng, Iowa State Univ, 58-60, asst prof, 60-63. *Mem:* AAAS; Am Soc Mech Eng; Am Soc Eng Educ. *Res:* Flow characteristics in converging passages, particularly axially-symmetric annular passages with rotating center bodies. *Mailing Add:* 715 Columbine Ct Columbia MO 65203

LYSER, KATHERINE MAY, NEUROEMBRYOLOGY. *Current Pos:* from asst prof to assoc prof, 65-76, PROF BIOL SCI, HUNTER COL CITY UNIV NEW YORK, 76- *Personal Data:* b Berkeley, Calif, May 11, 33; m 65. *Educ:* Oberlin Col, AB, 55, Radcliffe Col, MA, 57, PhD(biol), 60. *Prof Exp:* Instr zool, Oberlin Col, 57-58; NSF fel exp embryol, Col France, 60-61; res fel, Med Col, Cornell Univ, 61-62, instr anat, 62-64; asst prof, Sch Med & Dent, Georgetown Univ, 64-65. *Concurrent Pos:* Part-time fac mem, Sarah Lawrence Col, 61-62; USPHS res grants, Med Col, Cornell Univ, 63 & Hunter Col, 65-70; United Cerebral Palsy Res & Educ Found grant, Cornell Univ & Georgetown Univ, 64-65; guest investr, P A Weiss Lab, Rockefeller Univ,

67-70; fac res award, City Univ New York, 76-82, 87-89. *Mem:* Int Soc Develop Neurosci; Am Soc Zool; Soc Neurosci; Soc Develop Biol. *Res:* Factors controlling development in the embryonic nervous system, especially cytological differentiation and cellular morphogenesis in retinal and other neurons and in neuronal tumors. *Mailing Add:* Dept Biol Sci City Univ NY Hunter Col 695 Park Ave New York NY 10021

LYSIAK, RICHARD JOHN, physics, for more information see previous edition

LYSMER, JOHN, EARTHQUAKE ENGINEERING, SOIL DYNAMICS. *Current Pos:* PROF SOIL MECH, UNIV CALIF, BERKELEY, 65- *Personal Data:* b Copenhagen, Denmark, Aug 18, 31; US citizen. *Educ:* Tech Univ Denmark, MSc, 54; Univ Mich, PhD(civil eng), 65. *Prof Exp:* Civil engr, Ove Arup & Partners, London, 55-61. *Concurrent Pos:* Eng consult, 65-; Thomas Middlebrooks Award, Am Soc Civil Engrs, 67, Walter Huber Civil Eng Prize, 76. *Mem:* Am Soc Civil Engrs; Seismol Soc Am; Earthquake Eng Res Inst. *Res:* Theoretical soil mechanics and dynamics; developed computer codes for seismic response analysis of earth dams and soil-structure interaction analysis. *Mailing Add:* 1968 Marin Ave Berkeley CA 94707

LYSNE, PETER C, APPLIED PHYSICS. *Current Pos:* Staff mem, Shock Physics Res, 66-77, staff mem, Geothermal Res, 77-89, DISTINGUISHED MEM TECH STAFF, GEOTHERMAL RES, GEOSCI RES DRILLING OFF, SANDIA NAT LABS, 89- *Personal Data:* b Milwaukee, Wis, July 20, 39; m 62; c 2. *Educ:* Grinnell Col, BA, 61; Ariz State Univ, PhD(physics), 66. *Concurrent Pos:* Chmn, Joides Downhole Measurements Panel, 93-; vchmn bd, Dosecc, Inc, 93- *Mem:* Am Geophys Union; Soc Prof Well Log Analysts. *Res:* Thermodynamics and its relation to shock physics; shock propagation in solid, liquid and porous media; shock-wave induced depolarization of ferroelectrics; neutron log analysis. *Mailing Add:* 1000 Upland Ct NE Albuquerque NM 87112

LYSTER, MARK ALLAN, ORGANIC CHEMISTRY. *Current Pos:* RES CHEMIST, UPJOHN CO, 79- *Personal Data:* b Kalamazoo, Mich, Jan 5, 53; m 75; c 4. *Educ:* Albion Col, BA, 75; Univ Calif, Los Angeles, PhD(org chem), 79. *Mem:* Am Chem Soc. *Res:* Developing processes to produce bulk quantities of prospective new drugs. *Mailing Add:* Upjohn Co 1510-91-1 Kalamazoo MI 49001-0199

LYSYJ, IHOR, ENVIRONMENTAL ENGINEERING. *Current Pos:* CONSULT ENGR, I LYSYJ CONSULTS, 91-; SR ENGR, COMPUT SCI CORP, AIR FORCE FLIGHT TEST CTR, 92- *Personal Data:* b Tarnow, Poland, Apr 13, 29; nat US; m 57, Natalie Bilonok; c 2. *Educ:* Ukrainian Tech Inst, Ger, MS, 50. *Prof Exp:* Analytical chemist, Ex-Lax, Inc, NY, 52-54; dir res, Gaston Johnston Corp, 54-56; analytical chemist, Cent Res Lab, Food Mach & Chem Corp, 56-60; res scientist, Ethicon, Inc, 60-61; prin scientist, Rocketdyne Div, Rockwell Int Corp, 61-84; prog mgr, Combustion Eng, 84-89; sr scientist, Furgo-McClelland, 89-91. *Concurrent Pos:* Sr prin engr, Comput Sci Corp, Air Force Flight Test Ctr. *Mem:* Am Chem Soc. *Res:* Waste water and hazardous materials treatment; chemical detection and sensing technology; environmental quality monitoring systems and networks; regulatory analysis and pollution assessments; environmental engineering. *Mailing Add:* 8485 Carla Lane Canoga Park CA 91304

LYSYK, TIMOTHY JAMES, MODELLING PEST POPULATION DYNAMICS & BIOLOGICAL PROCESSES, MEDICAL-VETERINARY ENTOMOLOGY. *Current Pos:* RES SCIENTIST, AGR CAN, 89- *Personal Data:* b Ottawa, Ont, Aug 6, 59; m 92, Sophia Verzosa; c Emily. *Educ:* Univ Alta, BSc(Hons), 80; SDak State Univ, MS, 82; NC State Univ, PhD(entom), 85. *Honors & Awards:* C Gordon Hewitt Award, Entom Soc Can, 96. *Prof Exp:* Res scientist, Forestry Can, 85-89. *Concurrent Pos:* Guest instr livestock pest mgt, Simon Frazer Univ, 89-; adj prof, Univ Lethbridge, 93- *Mem:* Entom Soc Can; Entom Soc Am. *Res:* Biology and ecology of Diptera affecting livestock, development of population dynamics models and developing integrated pest management strategies. *Mailing Add:* Agr Can PO Box 3000 Lethbridge AB T1K 3Y4 Can. *Fax:* 403-382-3156; *E-Mail:* lysyk@abrsle.agr.ca

LYTHCOTT, GEORGE I, pediatrics; deceased, see previous edition for last biography

LYTLE, CARL DAVID, BIOPHYSICS. *Current Pos:* Res biophysicist, Bur Radiol Health, USPHS, 68-70, chief, Path Studies Sect, 70, chief, Path Studies Sect, Environ Protection Agency, 70-71, chief, Multi Environ Stresses Br, 71-74, res biophysicist, 74-85, dir, Div Life Sci, 85-89, BIOPHYSICIST CTR DEVICES & RADIOL HEALTH, FOOD & DRUG ADMIN, USPHS, 89- *Personal Data:* b Millersburg, Ohio, Jan 28, 41; c 2. *Educ:* Kent State Univ, BS, 63; Cornell Univ, MS, 65; Pa State Univ, PhD(biophys), 68. *Concurrent Pos:* Adj prof, George Washington Univ, 71-72; assoc ed, Photochem & Photobiol, 78-83. *Mem:* AAAS; Am Soc Photobiol; Am Soc Microbiol Planetary Soc. *Res:* Radiation virology; photodynamic virus inactivation; virus penetration of barrier materials. *Mailing Add:* Ctr Devices & Radiol Health FDA 5600 Fishers Lane Rockville MD 20857

LYTLE, CHARLES FRANKLIN, INVERTEBRATE ZOOLOGY. *Current Pos:* assoc prof, 69-72, PROF ZOOL, NC STATE UNIV, 72-, COORDR BIOL SCI PROG, 69- *Personal Data:* b Crawfordsville, Ind, May 13, 32; m 55; c 5. *Educ:* Wabash Col, AB, 53; Ind Univ, MA, 58, PhD(zool), 59. *Prof Exp:* Asst zool, Ind Univ, 53-55, 57-58, res assoc, 59-60; asst prof, Tulane Univ, 60-62; res analyst, US Govt, 62-64; from asst prof to assoc prof zool, Pa State Univ, 64-69. *Concurrent Pos:* Fel embryol, Ind Univ, 59; consult, US Dept Army, 62-63, Educ Testing Serv, 69- & Col Bd, 80-; res assoc, NC Mus of Natural Hist, 77-; vis prof, Duke Univ, Univ Ala, Fla Atlantic Univ; exec dir, NC Student Acad Sci, 85-90; pres sci, NC State Univ, 89- *Mem:* Fel AAAS; Am Soc Zool; Am Inst Biol Sci; Sigma Xi; Soc Col Sci Teachers; Nat Asn Sci Teachers; Nat Asn Biol Teachers. *Res:* Invertebrate zoology; cell biology; cellular structure and function in invertebrate development; differentiation and regulation of cellular organelles; systematics and ecology of Hydrozoa; biological education; instructional television; academic computing. *Mailing Add:* 102 Carmel Ct Cary NC 27511-5560

LYTLE, DEAN WINTON, ELECTRICAL ENGINEERING. *Current Pos:* assoc prof, 58-69, PROF ELEC ENG, UNIV WASH, 69- *Personal Data:* b Long Beach, Calif, May 23, 27; m 55; c 4. *Educ:* Univ Calif, BS, 50; Stanford Univ, MS, 54, PhD(elec eng), 57. *Prof Exp:* Electronic scientist, US Navy Electronics Lab, Calif, 50-53; asst elec eng, Stanford Univ, 53-57; asst prof, Robert Col, Turkey, 57-58. *Concurrent Pos:* Consult, Aerospace Div, Boeing Co, 59- & Seattle Develop Lab, Honeywell, Inc, 63- *Mem:* Inst Elec & Electronics Engrs. *Res:* Information and communication theory. *Mailing Add:* Univ Wash Dept Elec Eng Ft-10 Seattle WA 98195

LYTLE, FARREL WAYNE, SOLID STATE PHYSICS, STRUCTURAL CHEMISTRY. *Current Pos:* RETIRED. *Personal Data:* b Cedar City, Utah, Nov 10, 34; m 54, Manetta Bleak; c Nelson W, W Reed, C Mel & Drew B. *Educ:* Univ Nev, BS, 56, MS, 58. *Honors & Awards:* Warren Diffraction Physics Award, Am Crystallog Asn, 79. *Prof Exp:* Chemist, US Bur Mines, 55-58; sr basic res scientist, Boeing Sci Res Labs, Boeing Co, 60-74, prin res scientist, 74-90. *Concurrent Pos:* Grad Study, Univ Wash, 60-63; pres, Exafs Co, 74-90. *Mem:* Fel AAAS; fel Am Phys Soc; Am Chem Soc; Mat Res Soc. *Res:* X-ray physics, x-ray absorbtion fine structure spectroscopy and x-ray diffraction; materials science; structural inorganic chemistry; amorphous structures; structure of catalysts. *Mailing Add:* HC 74 PO Box 236 Pioche NV 89043

LYTLE, FRED EDWARD, CHEMISTRY. *Current Pos:* from asst prof to assoc prof, 68-74, PROF CHEM, PURDUE UNIV, WEST LAFAYETTE, 79- *Personal Data:* b Lewisburg, Pa, Jan 13, 43; m 67, 88, Joyce Koster; c Bradley & Megan. *Educ:* Juniata Col, BS, 64; Mass Inst Technol, PhD(chem), 68. *Honors & Awards:* Merck Co Found Fac Develop Award, 69; Am Chem Instrumentation Award, 86; Analytical Chem Award, Am Chem Soc Award, 88. *Mem:* Am Chem Soc; Soc Appl Spectros. *Res:* Time resolved spectroscopy; trace analysis; use of lasers in applied spectroscopy. *Mailing Add:* Dept Chem Purdue Univ 1393 Brwn Bldg West Lafayette IN 47907-1393. *E-Mail:* lytle@chem.purdue.edu

LYTLE, LOY DENHAM, PSYCHOPHARMACOLOGY, NEUROSCIENCES. *Current Pos:* ASSOC PROF PSYCHOPHARMACOL, UNIV CALIF, SANTA BARBARA, 77- *Personal Data:* b Glendale, Calif, Apr 8, 43; m 74; c 2. *Educ:* Univ Calif, Santa Barbara, BA, 66; Princeton Univ, PhD(psychol), 70. *Prof Exp:* NIMH fel neuropharmacol, Mass Inst Technol, 70-72, asst prof psychopharmacol, 72-77. *Concurrent Pos:* Alfred P Sloan fel neurosci, 75. *Mem:* Am Soc Pharmacol & Exp Therapeut; Nutrit Soc; Int Soc Develop Psychobiol; Neurosci Soc; AAAS; Sigma Xi. *Res:* Effects of drugs on physiological and behavioral development; diet and drug induced changes in behavior; effects of drugs on brain and peripheral neurotransmitters. *Mailing Add:* Dept Psychol Univ Calif Lab Psychopharmacol Santa Barbara CA 93106-0001

LYTLE, MICHAEL ALLEN, TECHNOLOGY TRANSFER, ACADEMIC GOVERNMENT RELATIONS. *Current Pos:* SR LECTR, CRIMINAL JUSTICE, 95- *Personal Data:* b Salina, Kans, Oct 22, 46; c Eric A. *Educ:* Ind Univ, AB, 73; Tex A&M Univ, MEd, 78. *Prof Exp:* Staff assoc, Tex A&M Univ Syst, 80-81, asst to chancellor, 81-83, asst dir govt rels, 83-84, spec asst to chancellor, 84-87; dir res develop, Syracuse Univ, 87, dir fed rels, 87-93; prin & sr counsel, Erik/Alexander Group, 92-93; exec dir inst develop, Univ Tex, Brownsville, 93-95. *Concurrent Pos:* Mem, Tex Technol Ind Legis Task Force, State Tex, 85-87; mem, Mil Critical Technologies Adv Panel, US Dept Com, 85-90; sr res assoc, Technol & Info Policy, Syracuse Univ, 87-92, adj asst prof, Int Bus Trade, 89-92; chair, Nat Security Defense Admin, Am Soc Pub Admin, 89-91; Sci Freedom & Responsibility Award, AAAS, 90-95. *Mem:* AAAS; Sigma Xi; Am Acad Forensic Scis; Am Soc Pub Admin; Forensic Sci Soc. *Res:* Enabler, facilitator and gatekeeper for science, technology and innovation in the policymaking and political arenas. *Mailing Add:* 3500 Avenida Carmen No 1301 Rancho Viejo TX 78575-9568. *Fax:* 956-544-8988; *E-Mail:* malytle@aol.com

LYTLE, RAYMOND ALFRED, MATHEMATICS. *Current Pos:* RETIRED. *Personal Data:* b Spartanburg, SC, Sept 23, 19; m 44; c 4. *Educ:* Wofford Col, BS, 40; Univ Va, MA, 46; Univ Ga, PhD, 55. *Prof Exp:* Instr math, Univ Va, 42-46. *Concurrent Pos:* Researcher, Univ Ga, 52-; emer prof math, Univ SC, 86- *Mem:* Am Math Soc; Math Asn Am; Sigma Xi. *Res:* Topology. *Mailing Add:* 1301 Brentwood Dr Columbia SC 29206-2868

LYTTON, BERNARD, UROLOGY. *Current Pos:* from asst prof to assoc prof, 62-71, PROF UROL, SCH MED, YALE UNIV, 71-, CHIEF SECT UROL, 67- *Personal Data:* b London, Eng, June 28, 26; US citizen; m 63, Norma Mendle; c Sharon, Susan, Timothy & Jennifer. *Educ:* Univ London, MB, BS, 48; FRCS, 55; Yale Univ, MA. *Honors & Awards:* Hugh H Young Award, Am Urol Asn, 85. *Prof Exp:* House officer med & surg, London Hosp, 55-61.

LYTTON, *Concurrent Pos:* Brit Empire Cancer res fel surg, Univ Hosp, King's Col, Univ London, 61-62; USPHS grant; resident surg, Royal Victoria Hosp, McGill Univ, 57-58; attend, Yale-New Haven Hosp, 62-; consult, West Haven Vet Admin Hosp, 62- & Hartford Hosp & Hosp of St Raphael, 68- *Mem:* AAAS; fel Am Col Surg; Soc Pelvic Surg; Am Asn Genito-Urinary Surg; Clin Soc Genito-Urinary Surgeons; Am Urol Asn. *Res:* Immunologic aspects of cancer; delayed hypersensitivity response to autogenous tumor extracts; problems of renal ischemia; renal responses to alterations in bladder pressure; compensatory renal growth in parabiotic animals and effects of hemodialysis; endoscopic treatment of urinary calculi; orthotopic bladder replacement. *Mailing Add:* 70 High St New Haven CT 06511-6643. *Fax:* 203-785-4043

LYTTON, JACK L(ESTER), MATERIALS SCIENCE, METALLURGY. *Current Pos:* prof, 65-92, EMER PROF METALL ENG, VA POLYTECH INST & STATE UNIV, 92- *Personal Data:* b Los Angeles, Calif, Aug 4, 33; m 54; c 4. *Educ:* Univ Calif, Berkeley, BS, 56, MS, 57; Stanford Univ, PhD(mat sci), 62. *Prof Exp:* Res engr, Inst Eng Res, Univ Calif, Berkeley, 56-57; res scientist, Lockheed Missiles & Space Co, 60-65. *Mem:* Am Soc Metals; Am Inst Mining, Metall & Petrol Engrs. *Res:* Mechanical behavior of solids, recovery and creep at high temperatures; plastic flow and fracture; failure analysis; structure-property relationships; electronmicroscopy. *Mailing Add:* 27387 Tobago Lane Summerland Key FL 33042

LYTTON, ROBERT LEONARD, PAVEMENTS, EXPANSIVE SOILS. *Current Pos:* assoc prof, Tex A&M Univ, 71-76, prof soils & pavements, 76, A P & Florence Wiley chair prof, 90-95, head, Infrastruct & Transp Div, Dept Civil Eng, 93-95, F J BENSON CHAIR PROF, TEX A&M UNIV, 95- *Personal Data:* b Port Arthur, Tex, Oct 23, 37; m 61; c 3. *Educ:* Univ Tex, Austin, BS, 60, MS, 61, PhD(civil eng), 67. *Honors & Awards:* John B Hawley Award, Tex Sect, Am Soc Civil Engrs, 66; Everite Bursary Award, Coun Sci & Indust Res, SAfrica, 84-; Zachry Sr Researcher Award, Tex Transp Inst, 96. *Prof Exp:* Civil engr, Naval Civil Eng Lab, Calif, 60; engr officer, 35th Eng Construct Group, US Army, 61-63; assoc, Dannenbaum Eng Corp, 63-65; asst prof mat & soils, Univ Tex, Austin, 67-68; fel NSF, Australian Commonwealth Sci Inst Res Orgn, 63-65; head, Mat, Pavements & Construct Div, Tex Transp Inst, 82-91. *Concurrent Pos:* Mem pub adv bd, Int J Analysis & Numerical Methods Geo Mech, 77-; mem tech adv bd, Post-Tensioning Inst, 78-; vpres & dir, Meyer, Lytton, Allen, Whitaker, Inc, 80- & ERES Consults, Inc, 81-95; bd consult, US Army CEngr, 84-87; consult, Strategic Hwy Res Prog, 85-87; US Rep, Comt TC-6, Int Soc Soil Mech & Found Engrs, 87-; prin investr, Strategic Highway Res Prog, Proj A005; dir MLA Labs, Inc, Geostruct Tool Kit Inc, Lyric Technol Lic, Trans-tec Inc. *Mem:* Am Soc Civil Engrs; Transp Res Bd; Asn Asphalt Paving Technologists; Post-Tensioning Inst; Am Concrete Inst; Int Soc Soil Mech & Foundations Eng. *Res:* Nondestructive testing of pavements; analysis and design of pavement evaluation, foundations and pavements on expansive clays; fracture mechanics; probabilistic design; operations research; pavement network optimization; climatic and environmental effects. *Mailing Add:* 2108 Barak Lane Bryan TX 77802-4628

LYUBSKY, SERGEY, PATHOLOGY. *Current Pos:* ASSOC DIR, ELECTRON MICROS LAB, VET ADMIN MED CTR, NORTHPORT, NY, 85-, STAFF PATHOLOGIST, 85-; ASST PROF PATH, STATE UNIV NY, STONY BROOK, 85- *Personal Data:* b Moscow, USSR, June 2, 45; US citizen; c 1. *Educ:* Moscow Univ, MD, 68; Inst Human Morphol, Moscow, PhD(cell biol), 75; Am Bd Path, dipl, 85. *Prof Exp:* Postdoctoral fel cytogenetics, Soviet Nat Cancer Inst, Moscow, 68-70; prin investr, Lab Cell Biol, Inst Human Morphol, Moscow, 75-78; vis assoc, Lab Path, Nat Cancer Inst, NIH, 79; resident anat & clin path, George Washington Univ, 80-83; chief resident path, Yale-New Haven Hosp, Conn, 84. *Concurrent Pos:* Mem, Res & Develop Comt, Cancer Comt & Tumor Bd, Vet Admin Hosp. *Res:* Author of numerous papers and abstracts. *Mailing Add:* 2 Williamsburg Dr Northport NY 11768